INTERNATIONAL FINANCIAL STATISTICS YEARBOOK

A Selection of Statistical Publications of the International Monetary Fund

International Financial Statistics (IFS)
Acknowledged as a standard source of statistics on all aspects of international and domestic finance, *IFS* publishes, for most countries of the world, current data on exchange rates, international liquidity, international banking, money and banking, interest rates, prices, production, international transactions (including balance of payments and international investment position), government finance, and national accounts. Information is presented in tables for specific countries and in tables for area and world aggregates. *IFS* is published monthly and annually. *Price:* Subscription price is US$289 a year (US$199 to university faculty and students) for twelve monthly issues and the yearbook. Single copy price is US$40 for a monthly issue and US$72 for a yearbook issue.

Balance of Payments Statistics Yearbook (BOPSY)
Issued in three parts, this annual publication contains balance of payments and international investment position data. Part 1 provides detailed tables on balance of payments statistics for approximately 166 countries and international investment position data for 71 countries. Part 2 presents tables of regional and world totals of major balance of payments components. Part 3 contains descriptions of methodologies, compilation practices, and data sources used by reporting countries *Price:* US$78.

Direction of Trade Statistics (DOTS)
Quarterly issues of this publication provide, for about 156 countries, tables with current data (or estimates) on the value of imports from and exports to their most important trading partners. In addition, similar summary tables for the world, industrial countries, and developing countries are included. The yearbook provides, for the most recent seven years, detailed trade data by country for approximately 186 countries, the world, and major areas. *Price:* Subscription price is US$128 a year (US$89 to university faculty and students) for the quarterly issues and the yearbook. Price for a quarterly issue only is US$25, the yearbook only is US$45, and a guide only is US$12.50.

Government Finance Statistics Yearbook (GFSY)
This annual publication provides detailed data on revenue, grants, expenditure, lending minus repayments, financing, and debt of central governments and indicates the amounts represented by social security funds and extrabudgetary operations. Also provided are data for state and local governments, and information on the institutional units of government. *Price:* US$65.

Balance of Payments Manual
Revised in 1993, the fifth edition of the manual addresses significant changes that have occurred in international transactions since the fourth edition was published in 1977 and presents salient revisions in the structure and classification of international accounts. The new edition also reflects a major shift in orientation that accords prominence to stocks of external financial assets and liabilities (the international investment position) as well as to balance of payments transactions. *Price:* US$27.50.

Government Finance Statistics Manual 2001
The manual, which updates the first edition published in 1986, is a major advance in the standards for compilation and presentation of fiscal statistics and part of a worldwide trend toward greater accountability and transparency in government finances, operations, and oversight. It covers concepts, definitions, classifications, and accounting rules, and provides a comprehensive analytic framework within which the statistics can be summarized and presented. To the extent possible, the manual has been harmonized with *System of National Accounts 1993*. Price: US$50.

Monetary and Financial Statistics Manual
Issued in 2000, this manual offers guidelines for the presentation of monetary and financial statistics. It provides a set of tools for identifying, classifying, and recording stocks and flows of financial assets and liabilities, describes a standard framework in which the statistics may be presented, and identifies a set of analytically useful aggregates within the framework. The concepts and principles set out in this manual are harmonized with those of the *System of National Accounts 1993*. *Price:* US$35.50.

CD-ROM Subscriptions

International Financial Statistics (IFS), *Balance of Payments Statistics (BOPS)*, and *Direction of Trade Statistics (DOTS)* are available on CD-ROM by annual subscription. The CD-ROMs incorporate a Windows-based browser facility, as well as a flat file of the database in scientific notation. *Price of each subscription:* US$1,000 a year for single-user PC license (US$350 for university faculty and students). Network and redistribution licenses are negotiated on a case-by-case basis. Please contact Publication Services for information.

Subscription Packages

Combined Subscription Package
The combined subscription package includes all issues of *IFS, DOTS, BOPSY, GFSY,* and *Staff Papers,* the Fund's economic journal. *Combined subscription price:* US$446 a year. Airspeed delivery available at additional cost; please inquire.

Combined Statistical Yearbook Subscription
This subscription comprises *BOPSY, GFSY, IFSY,* and *DOTSY* at a combined rate of US$195. Because of different publication dates of the four yearbooks, it may take up to one year to service an order. Airspeed delivery available at additional cost; please inquire.

IFS on the Internet

Available at this time only to current *IFS* subscribers, *IFS* on the Internet is found at the following address: http://imf.largo.apdi.net.

Address orders to
Publication Services, IMF, Washington, DC 20431, USA
Telephone: (202) 623-7430   Telefax: (202) 623-7201   E-mail: publications@imf.org
Internet: http://www.imf.org

Note: Prices include the cost of delivery by surface mail. Enhanced delivery is available for an additional charge.

INTERNATIONAL

FINANCIAL

STATISTICS

YEARBOOK

2002

INTERNATIONAL MONETARY FUND

INTERNATIONAL FINANCIAL STATISTICS

Vol. LIV, 2002
Prepared by the IMF Statistics Department
Carol S. Carson, Director

For information related to this publication, please:
    fax the Statistics Department at (202) 623-6460,
    or write Statistics Department
           International Monetary Fund
           Washington, D.C. 20431
    or telephone (202) 623-6180.
For copyright inquiries, please fax the Editorial Division at (202) 623-6579.
For purchases only, please contact Publication Services (see information below).

International Financial Statistics (IFS) is a standard source of statistics on all aspects of international and domestic finance. *IFS* publishes, for most countries of the world, current data on exchange rates, international liquidity, international banking, money and banking, interest rates, prices, production, international transactions (including balance of payments and international investment position), government finance, and national accounts. Information is presented in tables for specific countries and in tables for area and world aggregates. *IFS* is published monthly and annually.

Cutoff Date: August 23, 2002

Address orders to:
International Monetary Fund
Attention: Publication Services
Washington, D.C. 20431
U.S.A.
Telephone: (202) 623-7430
Telefax: (202) 623-7201
E-mail: publications@imf.org
Internet: http://www.imf.org

ISSN 0250-7463
ISBN 1-58906-183-7

POSTMASTER: Send address changes to International Financial Statistics, Publication Services, 700 19th St., N.W., Washington, D.C. 20431. Postage for periodicals paid at Washington, D.C. USPS 049-610

Recycled paper

TABLE OF CONTENTS

The term "country," as used in this publication, does not in all cases refer to a territorial entity that is a state as understood by international law and practice; the term also covers some nonsovereign territorial entities, for which statistical data are maintained and provided internationally on a separate and independent basis.

IMF MEMBERS AND GOVERNORS

Member	Governor*	Alternate*
AFGHANISTAN, ISLAMIC STATE OF	Hedayat Amin-Arsala	Abdul Qadeer Fitrat
ALBANIA	Shkelqim Cani	Gramoz Pashko
ALGERIA	Mohammed Laksaci	Vacant
ANGOLA	Júlio Marceline V. Bessa	Aguinaldo Jaime
ANTIGUA AND BARBUDA	Lester B. Bird	Asot A. Michael
ARGENTINA	Roberto Lavagna	Aldo Pignanelli
ARMENIA	Vartan Khachatryan	Tigran Sargysan
AUSTRALIA	Peter Costello	Ken Henry
AUSTRIA	Klaus Liebscher	Gertrude Tumpel-Gugerell
AZERBAIJAN	Avaz Alekperov	Elman Siradjogly Rustamov
BAHAMAS, THE	James H. Smith	Julian W. Francis
BAHRAIN, KINGDOM OF	Adbulla Hassan Saif	Ahmed Bin Mohammed Al Khalifa
BANGLADESH	M. Saifur Rahman	Fakhruddin Ahmed
BARBADOS	Owen S. Arthur	Marion Williams
BELARUS	Petr Petrovich Prokopovich	Nikolay Petrovich Korbut
BELGIUM	Guy Quaden	Gregoire Brouhns
BELIZE	Said Musa	Joseph Waight
BENIN	Grégoire Laourou	Idriss L. Daouda
BHUTAN	Sonam Wangchuk	Vacant
BOLIVIA	Jacques Trigo Loubiere	Juan Antonio Morales
BOSNIA AND HERZEGOVINA	Anto Domazet	Sefika Hafizovc
BOTSWANA	Linah K. Moholho	Freddy Modise
BRAZIL	Pedro Sampaio Malan	Arminio Fraga Neto
BRUNEI DARUSSALAM	Haji Hassanal Bolkiah	Dato Yakub Abu Bakar
BULGARIA	Svetoslav Veleslavov Gavriiski	Krassimir Katev
BURKINA FASO	Jean Baptiste Compaore	Lucien Marie Noel Bembamba
BURUNDI	Grégoire Banyiyezako	Cyprien Sinzobahamvya
CAMBODIA	CHEA Chanto	ENG Thay San
CAMEROON	Michel Meva'a Meboutou	Sadou Hayatou
CANADA	John Manley	David A. Dodge
CAPE VERDE	Carlos Burgo	Olavo Avelino Garcia Correia
CENTRAL AFRICAN REP.	Eric Sorongope	Anzineyo Wakoutou
CHAD	Idriss Ahmed Idriss	Mahamad Amine Ben Barka
CHILE	Carlos A. Massad	Jorge Marshall Rivera
CHINA	Dai Xianglong	LI Ruogu
COLOMBIA	Miguel Urrutia Montoya	Roberto Junguito Bonnet
COMOROS	Assoumany Aboudou	Said Ahmed Said Ali
CONGO, DEM. REP. OF	Jean-Claude Masangu Mulongo	MATUNGULU Mbuyamu Ilankir
CONGO, REPUBLIC OF	Mathias Dzon	Pacifique Essoïbeka
COSTA RICA	Eduardo Lizano Fait	Jorge Walter Bolaños Rojas
CÔTE D'IVOIRE	Bouabré Bohoun	Lanciné Bakary
CROATIA	Zeljko Rohatinski	Boris Vujcic
CYPRUS	Christodoulos Christodoulou	H. G. Akhniotis
CZECH REPUBLIC	Zdeněk Tůma	Tomáš Potměšil
DENMARK	Bodil Nyboe Andersen	Karsten Dybvad
DJIBOUTI	Djama Mahamoud Haid	Houmed Abdou Daoud
DOMINICA	Ambrose George	Ambrose M.J. Sylvester
DOMINICAN REPUBLIC	Francisco M. Guerrero Prats-R.	Luis Manuel Piantini
East Timor	Maria Madalena Brites Boavida	Aicha Bassarewan
ECUADOR	Carlos Julio Emanuel	Mauricio Yépez Najas
EGYPT	Youssef Boutros-Ghali	Mahmoud Abul-Eyoun
EL SALVADOR	Rafael Barraza	Juan José Daboub
EQUATORIAL GUINEA	Baltasar Engonga Edjo	Francisco Garcia Bernico
ERITREA	TEKIE Beyene	Kubrom Dafla
ESTONIA	Vahur Kraft	Aare Järvan
ETHIOPIA	Teklewold Atnafu	Alemseged Assefa
FIJI	Jone Yavala Kubuabola	Savenaca Narube
FINLAND	Matti Vanhala	Matti Louekoski
FRANCE	Francis Mer	Jean-Claude Trichet
GABON	Paul Toungui	Jean-Paul Leyimangoye
GAMBIA, THE	Famara L. Jatta	Momodou Clarke Bajo
GEORGIA	Irakli Managadze	Temur Basilia
GERMANY	Ernst Welteke	Hans Eichel
GHANA	Paul Acquah	G.A. Agambila
GREECE	Nicholas C. Garganas	Panayiotis Thomopoulos
GRENADA	Anthony Boatswain	Timothy Antoine
GUATEMALA	Lizardo Arturo Sosa López	Eduardo Humberto Weymann Fuentes
GUINEA	Cheick Ahmadou Camara	Ibrahima Cherif Bah
GUINEA-BISSAU	Rui Duarte Barros	Anselmo Pinto
GUYANA	Bharrat Jagdeo	Dolly Sursattie Singh
HAITI	Venel Joseph	Faubert Gustave
HONDURAS	María Elena Mondragón de Villar	José Arturo Alvarado Sánchez
HUNGARY	Zsigmond Járai	Álmos Kovács
ICELAND	Birgir Isl. Gunnarsson	Ólafur Davidsson
INDIA	Jaswant Singh	Bimal Jalan
INDONESIA	Syahril Sabirin	Agus Haryanto
IRAN, ISLAMIC REP. OF	Mohsen Nourbakhsh	Mohammad Jafar Mojarrad
IRAQ	Hikmet M. Ibraheem Al-Azawi	Abdul Ahad P. Toma
IRELAND	John Hurley	Maurice O'Connell
ISRAEL	Silvan Shalom	Meir Sokoler
ITALY	Giulio Tremonti	Vincenzo Desario
JAMAICA	Omar Lloyd Davies	Derick Latibeaudiere
JAPAN	Kiichi Miyazawa	Masaru Hayami
JORDAN	Michel Marto	Umayya Toukan
KAZAKHSTAN	Grigori Marchenko	Mazhit Essenbayev
KENYA	Christopher Mogere Obure	Nahashon Ngige Nyagah
KIRIBATI	Beniamina Tinga	Tebwe Ietaake
KOREA	Yun-Churl Jeon	Seung Park
KUWAIT	Yousef Hamad Al-Ebraheem	Salem Abdulaziz Al-Sabah
KYRGYZ REPUBLIC	Ulan Sarbanov	Kubat Abduldaevich Kanimetov
LAO PEOPLE'S DEM. REPUBLIC	Chansy Phosikham	Liane Thykeo
LATVIA	Gundars Bērziņš	Ilmārs Rimšēvičs
LEBANON	Riad Toufic Salameh	Nasser Saidi
LESOTHO	M.C. Mphutlane	Stephen Mustapha Swaray
LIBERIA	Charles R. Bright	Elie E. Saleeby
LIBYA	Ahmed M. Menesi	Abdalla Ali Khalifa
LITHUANIA	Reinoldijus Šarkinas	Asta Ungulaitiene
LUXEMBOURG	Jean-Claude Juncker	Yves Mersch
MACEDONIA, FORMER YUGOSLAV REP. OF	Ljube Trpeski	Vacant
MADAGASCAR	Narisoa Rajaonarivony	Gaston Edouard Ravelojaona
MALAWI	Elias E. Ngalande	R.P. Dzanjalimodzi
MALAYSIA	Mahathir Mohamad	Zeti Akhtar Aziz
MALDIVES	Mohamed Jaleel	Ibrahim Naeem
MALI	Ousmane Issoufi Maiga	Bangaly N'ko Traore
MALTA	Michael C. Bonello	David A. Pullicino
MARSHALL ISLANDS, REP. OF	Michael Konelios	Smith Michael
MAURITANIA	Yahya Attigh	Ahmed Ould Lefghih
MAURITIUS	Paul Raymond Bérenger	Rameswurlall Basant Roi
MEXICO	Francisco Gil Diaz	Guillermo Ortiz Martinez
MICRONESIA, FEDERATED STATES OF	John Ehsa	Lorin S. Robert
MOLDOVA	Leonid Talmaci	Mariana Durlesteanu
MONGOLIA	Chultem Ulaan	Ochirbat Chuluunbat
MOROCCO	Mohamed Seqat	Vacant
MOZAMBIQUE	Luísa Dias Diogo	Adriano Afonso Maleiane
MYANMAR	Khin Maung Thein	Kyaw Kyaw Maung
NAMIBIA	Nangolo Mbumba	Thomas K. Alweendo
NEPAL	Tilak Rawal	Madhav Prasad Ghimire
NETHERLANDS	A.H.E.M. Wellink	Kees van Dijkhuizen
NEW ZEALAND	Michael Cullen	Ron Carr
NICARAGUA	Mario Alonso Icabalceta	Eduardo Montealegre Rivas
NIGER	Ali Badjo Gamatie	Maliki Barhouni
NIGERIA	Mallam Adamu Ciroma	Joseph Sanusi
NORWAY	Svein Ingvar Gjedrem	Tore Eriksen
OMAN	Ali bin Mohammed bin Moosa	Hamood Sangour Al-Zadjali
PAKISTAN	Ishrat Husain	Mueen Afzal
PALAU	Elbuchel Sadang	Ruth Wong
PANAMA	Norberto Delgado Durán	Bolívar Pariente
PAPUA NEW GUINEA	Mekere Morauta	Leonard Wilson Kamit
PARAGUAY	Raúl Vera Bogado	Vacant
PERU	Richard Webb	Pedro Pablo Kuczynski
PHILIPPINES	Rafael B. Buenaventura	Jose Isidro N. Camacho
POLAND	Grzegorz Kolodko	Ryszard Michalski
PORTUGAL	Vitor Manuel Riberio Constâncio	António Manuel Pereira Marta
QATAR	Yousef Hussain Kamal	Abdullah Khalid Al-Attiyah
ROMANIA	Mugur Isarescu	Enache Jiru
RUSSIA	Aleksei Kudrin	Tatyana Paramonova
RWANDA	Donald Kaberuka	François Kanimba
ST. KITTS AND NEVIS	Halva Hendrickson	Wendell Everton Lawrence
ST. LUCIA	Kenny D. Anthony	Calixte Leon
ST. VINCENT AND THE GRENADINES	Ralph E. Gonsalves	Maurice Edwards
SAMOA	Misa Telefoni Retzlaff	Hinauri Petana
SAN MARINO	Fiorenzo Stolfi	Tito Masi
SÃO TOMÉ AND PRÍNCIPE	Maria C. Pires de Carvalho Silveira	Eugénio Lourenço Soares
SAUDI ARABIA	Ibrahim A. Al-Assaf	Hamad Al-Sayyari
SENEGAL	Abdoulaye Diop	Cheikh Hadjibou Soumaré
SEYCHELLES	James Michel	Francis Chang Leng
SIERRA LEONE	Peter J. Kuyembeh	James S. Koroma
SINGAPORE	LEE Hsien Loong	Koh Yong Guan
SLOVAK REPUBLIC	Marián Jusko	František Hajnovič
SLOVENIA	Mitja Gaspari	Samo Nučič
SOLOMON ISLANDS	Rick Nelson Houenipwela	Shadrach Fanega
SOMALIA	Vacant	Vacant
SOUTH AFRICA	Tito Titus Mboweni	Maria Da Conceicao Ramos
SPAIN	Rodrigo de Rato Figaredo	Jaime Caruana Lacorte
SRI LANKA	Kairshasp Nariman Choksy	A.S. Jayawardena
SUDAN	Elzubair Ahmed Elhassan	Sabir Mohamed Hassan
SURINAME	Humphrey S. Hildenberg	Andre Telting
SWAZILAND	Majozi Vincent Sithole	Martin G. Dlamini
SWEDEN	Urban Bäckström	Sven Hegelund
SWITZERLAND	Jean-Pierre Roth	Kaspar Villiger
SYRIAN ARAB REP.	Muhammad Al-Atrash	Mohammad Bachar Kabbarah
TAJIKISTAN	Murotali M. Alimardonov	Gulomzhon D. Babayev
TANZANIA	Basil Pesambili Mramba	Daudi T.S. Ballali
THAILAND	Pridiyathorn Devakula	Pakorn MALAKUL NA AYUDHYA
TOGO	Tankpadja Lalle	Mongo Aharh-Kpessou
TONGA	Siosiua T.T. 'Utoikamanu	Vacant

IMF MEMBERS AND GOVERNORS (CONT.)

Member	Governor*	Alternate*	Member	Governor*	Alternate*
TRINIDAD AND TOBAGO	Patrick Manning	Conrad Enill	UZBEKISTAN	MULLAJANOV Faizulla Makhsudjanovich	Tatyana N. Guskova
TUNISIA	Mohamed Daouas	Laroussi Bayoudh	VANUATU	Joe Bomal Carlo	Andrew Kausiama
TURKEY	Masum Türker	Süreyya Serdengeçti	VENEZUELA, REPÚBLICA BOLIVARIANA DE	Diego L. Castellanos	Tobías Nóbrega Suárez
TURKMENISTAN	Ymamdurdy Gandymov	Guvanchmurat Geoklenov			
UGANDA	Gerald M. Ssendaula	E. Tumusiime-Mutebile	VIETNAM	Le Duc Thuy	Duong Thu Huong
UKRAINE	Volodymyr Semenovych Stelmakh	Ihor Yushko	YEMEN, REPUBLIC OF	Alawi Saleh Al-Salami	Ahmed Abdul Rahman Al-Samawi
UNITED ARAB EMIRATES	Sultan Bin Nasser Al-Suwaidi	Mohammed Khalfan Bin Khirbash	YUGOSLAVIA, FEDERAL REPUBLIC OF	Mladjan Dinkic	Vesna Arsic
UNITED KINGDOM	Gordon Brown	Edward A. J. George	ZAMBIA	Emmanuel G. Kasonde	Caleb Fundanga
UNITED STATES	Paul H. O'Neill	Alan Greenspan	ZIMBABWE	Simba Herbert Stanley Makoni	Leonard Ladislus Tsumba
URUGUAY	César Rodríguez Batlle	Marcelo Brasca			

*According to the latest appointments.

184 member countries

BOARD OF EXECUTIVE DIRECTORS

Executive Director	From	Alternate	From	Casting Votes of
Vacant	United States	Meg Lundsager	United States	United States
Ken Yagi	Japan	Haruyuki Toyama	Japan	Japan
Karlheinz Bischofberger	Germany	Ruediger von Kleist	Germany	Germany
Pierre Duquesne	France	Sébastien Boitreaud	France	France
Tom W. Scholar	United Kingdom	Martin Brooke	United Kingdom	United Kingdom
Willy Kiekens	Belgium	Johann Prader	Austria	Austria, Belarus, Belgium, Czech Republic, Hungary, Kazakhstan, Luxembourg, Slovak Republic, Slovenia, Turkey
J. de Beaufort Wijnholds	Netherlands	Yuriy G. Yakusha	Ukraine	Armenia, Bosnia and Herzegovina, Bulgaria, Croatia, Cyprus, Georgia, Israel, former Yugoslav Republic of Macedonia, Moldova, Netherlands, Romania, Ukraine
Hernán Oyazábal	Venezuela	Fernando Varela	Spain	Costa Rica, El Salvador, Guatemala, Honduras, Mexico, Nicaragua, Spain, República Bolivariana de Venezuela,
Pier Carlo Padoan	Italy	Harilaos Vittas	Greece	Albania, Greece, Italy, Malta, Portugal, San Marino
Ian E. Bennett	Canada	Nioclás A. O'Murchú	Ireland	Antigua and Barbuda, The Bahamas, Barbados, Belize, Canada, Dominica, Grenada, Ireland, Jamaica, St. Kitts and Nevis, St. Lucia, St. Vincent and the Grenadines
Ólafur Ísleifsson	Iceland	Benny Andersen	Denmark	Denmark, Estonia, Finland, Iceland, Latvia, Lithuania, Norway, Sweden
Michael J. Callaghan	Australia	Diwa Guinigundo	Philippines	Australia, Kiribati, Korea, Marshall Islands, Rep. of, Federated States of Micronesia, Mongolia, New Zealand, Palau, Papua New Guinea, Philippines, Samoa, Seychelles, Solomon Islands, Vanuatu
Sulaiman M. Al-Turki	Saudi Arabia	Ahmed Saleh Alosaimi	Saudi Arabia	Saudi Arabia
Cyrus D.R. Rustomjee	South Africa	Ismaila Usman	Nigeria	Angola, Botswana, Burundi, Eritrea, Ethiopia, The Gambia, Kenya, Lesotho, Liberia, Malawi, Mozambique, Namibia, Nigeria, Sierra Leone, South Africa, Swaziland, Tanzania, Uganda, Zambia, Zimbabwe
Dono Iskandar Djojosubroto	Indonesia	Kwok Mun Low	Singapore	Brunei Darussalam, Cambodia, Fiji, Indonesia, Lao People's Democratic Republic, Malaysia, Myanmar, Nepal, Singapore, Thailand, Tonga, Vietnam
A. Shakour Shaalan	Egypt	Mohamad Chatah	Lebanon	Kingdom of Bahrain, Egypt, Iraq, Jordan, Kuwait, Lebanon, Libya, Maldives, Oman, Qatar, Syrian Arab Republic, United Arab Emirates, Republic of Yemen
WEI Benhua	China	WANG Xiaoyi	China	China
Aleksei V. Mozhin	Russia	Andrei Lushin	Russia	Russian Federation
Roberto F. Cippa	Switzerland	Wieslaw Szczuka	Poland	Azerbaijan, Kyrgyz Republic, Poland, Switzerland, Tajikistan, Turkmenistan, Uzbekistan
Murilo Portugal	Brazil	Vacant	Colombia	Brazil, Colombia, Dominican Republic, Ecuador, Guyana, Haiti, Panama, Suriname, Trinidad and Tobago
Yaga V. Reddy	India	R.A. Jayatissa	Sri Lanka	Bangladesh, Bhutan, India, Sri Lanka
Abbas Mirakhor	Islamic Republic of Iran	Mohammed Daïri	Morocco	Algeria, Ghana, Islamic Republic of Iran, Morocco, Pakistan, Tunisia
A. Guillermo Zoccali	Argentina	Guillermo Le Fort	Chile	Argentina, Bolivia, Chile, Paraguay, Peru, Uruguay
Alexandre Barro Chambrier	Gabon	Damian Ondo Mañe	Equatorial Guinea	Benin, Burkina Faso, Cameroon, Cape Verde, Central African Republic, Chad, Comoros, Republic of Congo, Côte d'Ivoire, Djibouti, Equatorial Guinea, Gabon, Guinea, Guinea-Bissau, Madagascar, Mali, Mauritania, Mauritius, Niger, Rwanda, São Tomé and Príncipe, Senegal, Togo

MANAGEMENT AND SENIOR OFFICERS

Managing Director	Horst Köhler	Secretary's Department	Shailendra J. Anjaria, Secretary
First Deputy Managing Director	Anne O. Krueger	Statistics Department	Carol S. Carson, Director
Deputy Managing Director	Eduardo Aninat	Technology and General Services Dept.	Brian C. Stuart, Director
Deputy Managing Director	Shigemitsu Sugisaki	Treasurer's Department	Eduard Brau, Treasurer
Special Advisor to the Managing Director	Jack Boorman*	Western Hemisphere Department	Claudio M. Loser, Director
Counsellor	Gerd Häusler*	Office of Budget and Planning	Barry Potter, Director
Economic Counsellor	Kenneth S. Rogoff*	Office of Internal Audit and Inspection	Rafael Muñoz, Director
African Department	Abdoulaye Bio Tchane, Director	Office of Technical Assistance Management	Claire Liuksila, Director
Asia and Pacific Department	Yusuke Horiguchi, Director		
European I Department	Michael C. Deppler, Director	Regional Office for Asia and the Pacific	Hiroyuki Hino, Director
European II Department	John Odling-Smee, Director	Office in Europe (Paris)	Flemming Larsen, Director
External Relations Department	Thomas C. Dawson, II, Director	Office in Geneva	Vacant
Fiscal Affairs Department	Teresa M. Ter-Minassian, Director	Office at the United Nations	Reinhard Munzberg, Special Representative to the UN (also supervising the Geneva Office in his personal capacity)
Human Resources Department	Margaret Kelly, Director		
IMF Institute	Mohsin S. Khan, Director		
International Capital Markets Dept.	Gerd Häusler, Director		
Legal Department	François P. Gianviti, General Counsel	Independent Evaluation Office	Montek Singh Ahluwalia, Director
Middle Eastern Department	George T. Abed, Director		
Monetary and Exchange Affairs Dept.	Stefan Ingves, Director		
Policy Development and Review Dept.	Timothy F. Geithner, Director		
Research Department	Kenneth S. Rogoff, Director	*Alphabetical listing.	

GUIDE TO THE COUNTRY COVERAGE OF *IFS* WORLD TABLES

Country Codes	Reserves	Money	Consumer Prices	Exports, Imports	Export Unit Values	Import Unit Values	Country Page
001 WORLD							
010 ALL COUNTRIES							
110 Industrial Countries							
111 United States	x	x	x	x	w	w	x
156 Canada	x	x	x	x	x	x	x
193 Australia	x	x	x	x	w	w	x
158 Japan	x	x	x	x	x	x	x
196 New Zealand	x	x	x	x	w	w	x
122 Austria	x	x	x	x	x		x
124 Belgium	x	x	x	x			
126 Belgium-Luxembourg				x	x		x
128 Denmark	x	x	x	x	x	x	x
163 Euro Area	x	x	x	x	x		x
172 Finland	x	x	x	x	w	w	x
132 France	x	x	x	x	x	x	x
134 Germany	x	x	x	x	w	w	x
174 Greece	x	x	x	x	w	w	x
176 Iceland	x	x	x	x	x	x	x
178 Ireland	x	x	x	x	x	x	x
136 Italy	x	x	x	x	x	x	x
137 Luxembourg	x	x	x	x			
138 Netherlands	x	x	x	x	x	x	x
142 Norway	x	x	x	x	x	x	x
182 Portugal	x	x	x	x	w	w	x
135 San Marino							
184 Spain	x	x	x	x	x		x
144 Sweden	x	x	x	x	w	w	x
146 Switzerland	x	x	x	x	x	x	x
112 United Kingdom	x	x	x	x	x	x	x
200 Developing Countries							
605 Africa							
612 Algeria[1]	x	x	x	x			
614 Angola	x	x		x			
638 Benin	x	x	x	x			
616 Botswana	x	x	x	x			
748 Burkina Faso	x	x	x	x	x		
618 Burundi	x	x	x	x			
622 Cameroon	x	x	x	x			
624 Cape Verde	x	x	x	x			
626 C. African Rep.	x	x	x	x			
628 Chad	x	x	x	x			
632 Comoros	x	x	x	x			
636 Congo, Dem. Rep. of	x	x	x	x			
634 Congo, Rep. of	x	x	x	x			
662 Côte d'Ivoire	x	x	x	x	x	x	
611 Djibouti	x		x	x			
642 Equatorial Guinea	x	x	x				
643 Eritrea							
644 Ethiopia	x	x	x	x			
646 Gabon	x	x	x	x			
648 Gambia, The	x	x	x	x			
652 Ghana	x	x	x	x			
656 Guinea	x	x		x			
654 Guinea-Bissau	x	x	x	x			
664 Kenya	x	x	x	x	x	x	
666 Lesotho	x		x	x		x	

Country Codes	Reserves	Money	Consumer Prices	Exports, Imports	Export Unit Values	Import Unit Values	Country Page
668 Liberia	x	x	x	x			
674 Madagascar	x	x	x	x			x
676 Malawi	x	x	x	x	x	x	
678 Mali	x	x	x	x			
682 Mauritania	x	x	x	x			
684 Mauritius	x	x	x	x			
686 Morocco	x	x	x	x		x	x
688 Mozambique	x		x	x			
728 Namibia	x	x	x	x			
692 Niger	x	x	x	x			
694 Nigeria[1]	x	x	x	x	x		
696 Réunion							x
714 Rwanda	x	x	x	x	w		
856 St. Helena							x
716 São Tomé & Príncipe	x		x	x			
722 Senegal	x	x	x	x	x	x	
718 Seychelles	x	x	x	x			
724 Sierra Leone	x	x	x	x			
726 Somalia							
199 South Africa	x	x	x	x	x	x	
732 Sudan	x	x	x	w		x	
734 Swaziland	x	x	x	x			
738 Tanzania	x	x	x	x			
742 Togo	x	x	x	x	w	x	
744 Tunisia	x	x	x	x	x	w	x
746 Uganda	x	x	x	x			
754 Zambia	x	x	x	x			
698 Zimbabwe	x	x	x	x	x	x	
505 Asia							
512 Afghanistan, I.S. of	x	x	x	x			
859 American Samoa			x				
513 Bangladesh	x	x	x	x			
514 Bhutan	x	x	x	x			x
516 Brunei Darussalam			x				
522 Cambodia	x	x	x				
924 China, P.R.: Mainland	x	x	x	x			
532 China, P.R.: Hong Kong	x	x	x	x	x	x	
546 China, P.R.: Macao	x	x	x				
815 Cook Island				x			
537 East Timor							
819 Fiji	x	x	x	x	x		
887 French Polynesia			x				
829 Guam			x				
534 India	x	x	x	x	x	x	
536 Indonesia[1]	x	x	x	x	x		
826 Kiribati			x				
542 Korea	x	x	x	x	x	x	
544 Lao P. D. Rep.	x	x	x	x			
548 Malaysia	x	x	x	x	x		
556 Maldives	x	x	x	x			
867 Marshall Islands, Rep. of							
868 Micronesia, Fed. States of	x		x				x
948 Mongolia	x	x	x				x
518 Myanmar	x	x	x	x			x
836 Nauru			x				
558 Nepal	x	x	x	x			
839 New Caledonia			x				
564 Pakistan	x	x	x	x	x	x	
565 Palau							

Country Codes	Reserves	Money	Consumer Prices	Exports, Imports	Export Unit Values	Import Unit Values	Country Page
853 Papua New Guinea	x	x	x	x	x		x
566 Philippines	x	x	x	x	w	w	x
862 Samoa	x	x	x	x			
576 Singapore	x	x	x	x	w	w	x
813 Solomon Islands	x	x	x	x			
524 Sri Lanka	x	x	x	x	x	x	
578 Thailand	x	x	x	x	w		x
866 Tonga	x	x	x				
846 Vanuatu	x	x	x	x			
582 Vietnam	x	x					
170 Europe							
914 Albania	x	x	x	x			
911 Armenia	x	x	x	x			
912 Azerbaijan	x	x	x				
913 Belarus	x	x	x				
963 Bosnia & Herzegovina	x						
918 Bulgaria	x	x	x				
960 Croatia	x	x	x	x			
423 Cyprus	x	x	x	x	x	x	
935 Czech Republic	x	x	x	x			
934 Czechoslovakia			x	x	x		
939 Estonia	x	x	x	x			x
816 Faeroe Islands				x			
915 Georgia	x		x				
823 Gibraltar			x				
944 Hungary	x	x	x	x	w	w	x
916 Kazakhstan	x		x				
917 Kyrgyz Rep.	x	x					
941 Latvia	x						
946 Lithuania	x	x	x	x			
962 Macedonia, former Yugoslav Rep. of	x	x					
181 Malta	x	x	x	x	x	x	
921 Moldova	x	x	x	x			
964 Poland	x	x	x	x	w	w	x
968 Romania	x	x	x	x			
922 Russia	x	x	x	x			
936 Slovak Republic	x	x	x				
961 Slovenia	x	x	x	x			
923 Tajikistan							
186 Turkey	x	x	x	x	x	x	
925 Turkmenistan							
926 Ukraine	x	x	x	x			
927 Uzbekistan							
965 Yugoslavia, Fed. Rep. of	x	x					
405 Middle East							
419 Bahrain, Kingdom of	x	x	x	x			
469 Egypt	x	x	x	x			
429 Iran, I.R. of[1]	x	x	x	x	w		
433 Iraq[1]	x	x	x	w		x	
436 Israel	x	x	x	x	x	x	
439 Jordan	x	x	x	x	x	x	
443 Kuwait[1]	x	x	x	x	w		
446 Lebanon	x	x	x				
672 Libya[1]	x	x	x	w		x	
449 Oman[1]	x	x		x	w		x
453 Qatar[1]	x	x	x	x	w		x

Country Codes	Reserves	Money	Consumer Prices	Exports, Imports	Export Unit Values	Import Unit Values	Country Page
456 Saudi Arabia[1]	x	x	x	x	x	w	x
463 Syrian Arab Rep.	x	x	x	x			
466 United Arab Emirates[1]	x	x		x	w		x
473 Yemen Arab Rep.	x	x	x	x			
459 Yemen, P. D. Rep.	x	x					
474 Yemen, Republic of	x	x		x			
205 Western Hemisphere							
311 Antigua & Barbuda	x	x	x	x			x
213 Argentina	x	x	x	x			
314 Aruba	x	x					
313 Bahamas, The	x	x	x	x			x
316 Barbados	x	x	x	x			x
339 Belize	x	x	x				x
319 Bermuda			x				
218 Bolivia	x	x	x	x	x	x	
223 Brazil	x	x	x	x	x	x	x
377 Cayman Islands							
228 Chile	x	x	x	x			x
233 Colombia	x	x	x	x	w	w	x
238 Costa Rica	x	x	x	x			x
928 Cuba	x						
321 Dominica	x	x	x	x			x
243 Dominican Rep.	x	x	x	x			x
248 Ecuador	x	x	x	x			x
253 El Salvador	x	x	x	x			x
323 Falkland Islands				x			
326 Greenland				x			
328 Grenada	x	x	x	x			x
329 Guadeloupe				x			
258 Guatemala	x	x	x	x			x
333 Guiana, French				x			
336 Guyana	x	x	x	x			x
263 Haiti	x	x	x	x			x
268 Honduras	x	x	x	x	x	x	
343 Jamaica	x	x	x	x			x
349 Martinique				x			
273 Mexico	x	x	x	x			x
351 Montserrat				x			
353 Netherlands Ant.	x	x	x	x			x
278 Nicaragua	x	x	x	x			x
283 Panama	x	x	x	x			x
288 Paraguay	x	x	x	x			x
293 Peru	x	x	x	x			x
361 St. Kitts & Nevis	x	x	x	x			x
362 St. Lucia	x	x	x	x			x
363 St. Pierre & Miquelon	x		x				
364 St. Vincent & the Grenadines	x	x	x	x			x
366 Suriname	x	x	x	x			x
369 Trinidad & Tobago	x	x	x	x			x
298 Uruguay	x	x	x	x			x
299 Venezuela, República Bolivariana de[1]	x	x	x	x	w	w	x
999 Oil Exporting Countries							
201 Non-Oil Developing Countries							

Country pages for 177 countries

[1]These countries comprise Oil Exporting Countries grouping shown as a memorandum item to the world tables. The memorandum item for Non-Oil Developing Countries shown in the world tables comprises the remaining Developing Countries.

Country indices compiled from specific prices are marked "w."

GUIDE TO THE COMMODITY COVERAGE OF *IFS* COUNTRY PAGES

Commodity Codes (first 2 alphas of lines 66, 70, 72, 74 and 76) and Country Codes

Code	Commodity	Country Codes
dr	Aluminum	156
u	Bananas	248
k	Beef	111 193 213
fl	Butter	196
vr	Coal	193
r	Cocoa beans	223 652
ai	Coconut oil	566
e	Coffee	223 233 386 799
c	Copper	111 112 156 228
ag	Copra	566 813
j	Corn (Maize)	111 578
f	Cotton	111 469
al	Fish	176 556 813
z	Fishmeal	176 293
kr	Gold	112 156 199 233
bf	Groundnuts	694
p	Hides, Skins	111
g	Iron ore	223
x	Jute	513
pf	Lamb	196
v	Lead	111 112
vx	Logs	548
w	Manganese	534
ul	Newsprint	111 172
pt	Nickel	156
df	Palm kernels	694
dg	Palm oil	548
a	Petroleum	001 111 112 124 142
a	Petroleum (cont.)	156 218 233 248 273 299 369 419 429 433 443 449 453 456 466 536 612 634 672 694 744 968
aw	Phosphates	686
wx	Plywood	566
qr	Potash	156
n	Rice	111 518 578
l	Rubber	111 548 578
rm	Sawnwood	548
bl	Shrimp	111
y	Silver	111
ml	Sisal	639
jf	Soybeans	111
jj	Soybean meal	111
ji	Soybean oil	111
rr	Steel	137
i	Sugar	111 112 223 566
as	Superphosphate	111
s	Tea	112 524
q	Tin	112 218 548 578
m	Tobacco	111
ur	Urea	170
d	Wheat	111 193 213
sl	Wood pulp	144
h	Wool	112 193 196
t	Zinc	111 112 156 218

INTRODUCTION

Table of Contents

1. Overview

The Fund's principal statistical publication, *International Financial Statistics (IFS)*, has been published monthly since January 1948. In 1961, the monthly was supplemented by a yearbook, and in 1991 and 2000, respectively, *IFS* was introduced on CD-ROM and the Internet.

IFS contains country tables for most Fund members, as well as for Aruba, the euro area, and the Netherlands Antilles. The country tables normally include data on a country's exchange rates, Fund position, international liquidity, money and banking accounts, interest rates, prices, production, international transactions, government accounts, national accounts, and population. Selected series, including data on Fund accounts, international reserves, and international trade, are drawn from the country tables and published in area and world tables as well.

"Country" in this publication does not always refer to a territorial entity that is a state as understood by international law and practice; the term also covers the euro area and some nonsovereign territorial entities, for which statistical data are provided internationally on a separate basis.

The monthly printed issue of *IFS* reports current monthly, quarterly, and annual data, while the yearbook reports 30 observations of annual data. Most annual data on the CD-ROM and Internet begin in 1948; quarterly and monthly data generally begin in 1957; most balance of payments data begin in 1970.

The following sections describe conceptual and technical aspects of various data published in *IFS*. The reader will find more detailed descriptions—about coverage, deviations from the standard methodologies, and discontinuities in the data—in the footnotes in the individual country and world tables in the monthly and yearbook issues of *IFS*, in the Print_Me file on the CD-ROM, and in the PDF pages on the Internet. (Where references are made in this introduction to notes in monthly issues, they refer to notes files on the CD-ROM and Internet as well.)

2. Exchange Rates and Exchange Rate Arrangements

Exchange rates in *IFS* are classified into three broad categories, reflecting the role of the authorities in determining the rates and/or the multiplicity of the exchange rates in a country. The three categories are the **market rate**, describing an exchange rate determined largely by market forces; the **official rate**, describing an exchange rate determined by the authorities—sometimes in a flexible manner; and the **principal**, **secondary**, or **tertiary rate**, for countries maintaining multiple exchange arrangements.

In *IFS*, exchange rates are expressed in time series of national currency units per SDR (the unit of account for the Fund) and national currency units per U.S. dollar, or vice versa.

The exchange rates in SDRs are classified and coded as follows:

Series **aa** shows the end-of-period national currency value of the SDR, and series **ac** shows the end-of-period SDR value of the national currency unit.

Series **sa, sb, sc**, and **sd**—provided on the country table for the United States—show the SDR value of U.S. dollars. Series **sa** and **sc** refer to end-of-period values of U.S. dollars per SDR and SDRs per U.S. dollar, respectively, while series **sb** and **sd** are geometric averages of values within the period.

The exchange rates in U.S. dollars are classified and coded as follows:

Series **ae** shows end-of-period national currency units per U.S. dollar, and series **ag** shows end-of-period U.S. dollars per unit of national currency.

Series **rf** shows period-average national currency units per U.S. dollar, and series **rh** shows period-average U.S. dollars per unit of national currency. Series **rf** and **rh** data are the monthly average of market rates or official rates of the reporting country. If those are not available, they are the monthly average rates in New York. Or if the latter are not available, they are estimates based on simple averages of the end-of-month market rates quoted in the reporting country.

The country tables contain two of the U.S. dollar series—either **ae** and **rf** or **ag** and **rh**—depending on the form in which the exchange rate is quoted.

Reciprocal relationships are the following:

The end-of-period rates **aa** and **ac, ae** and **ag,** and **sa** and **sc** are reciprocals of each other. The period-average SDR rates in terms of the U.S. dollar (**sb** and **sd**) are also reciprocals of each other, because they are calculated as geometric averages. Other period average rates (**rf** and **rh**) are calculated as arithmetic averages and are not reciprocals.

The relationship between trade figures in *IFS* and exchange rates is the following:

All trade figures in *IFS* are converted from national currency values to U.S. dollars and from U.S. dollar values to national currency, using series **rf**. Conversions are based on the data available for the shortest period, and these data are summed to obtain data for longer periods. Conversion is based on longer period rates of only the difference, if any, between the longer period data and the sum of the shorter period data. The country table notes in the monthly issues identify the exchange rates used.

For members maintaining dual or multiple exchange rate systems, which often reflect wide ranges of exchange rates in effect in a country, lines **w**, **x**, and **y** are presented. Notes on the tables in the monthly issues for these countries describe the current exchange rate systems and identify the exchange rates shown.

European Currency Unit (ECU) and the Euro

For periods before January 1999, the exchange rate sections in tables for members of the European Union (EU)—Austria, Belgium, Denmark, Finland, France, Germany, Greece, Ireland, Italy, Luxembourg, the Netherlands, Portugal, Spain, Sweden, and the United Kingdom—Norway and the United States contain a time series on the value of the European currency unit (ECU).

The ECU was issued by the European Monetary Institute (EMI)—successor to the European Monetary Cooperation Fund on January 1, 1994—against gold and foreign exchange deposits by the central banks of the EU member states. The ECU was defined as a basket of currencies of the EU member countries. The share of each currency in the basket was based on the gross national product and foreign trade of the country issuing that currency. The equivalent of the ECU was calculated—first in U.S. dollars and then in the currencies of the member countries—by using representative market exchange rates for the U.S. dollar, as reported by the member countries. In *IFS,* series **ea** and **ec** refer to end-of-period values of national currency units per ECU and ECUs per unit of national currency, respectively; series **eb** and **ed** are the arithmetic averages of values within the period.

On January 1, 1999, the euro replaced the ECU, at a rate of one euro per one ECU. Irrevocable conversion factors for the euro, adopted for the eleven countries in the euro area, fixed the central rates between the euro and the currencies participating in the exchange rate mechanism. The irrevocable fixed factors, legally mandated to have six significant digits, are the following: Austria (S 13.7603), Belgium (BF 40.3399), Finland (Fmk 5.94573), France (F 6.55957), Germany (DM 1.95583), Ireland (IR£0.787564), Italy (Lit 1936.27), Luxembourg (Lux F 40.3399), the Netherlands (f. 2.20371), Portugal (Esc 200.482), and Spain (Pta 166.386).

An accord established compulsory intervention rates for the Danish krone (± 2.25 percent around the euro central rate) and the Greek drachma (± 15 percent around the euro central rate) from January 1, 1999 onwards. Greece joined the euro area on January 1, 2001, adopting the euro as its currency, with a conversion factor of 340.750 drachmas per euro.

In addition, from January 1, 1999 onwards, the member countries of the Bank of Central African States and the Central Bank of West African States changed the peg of their currencies from the French franc to the euro, at a rate of CFAF 655.957 per euro. A few other countries also have pegged their currencies to the euro.

On January 1, 2002, euro banknotes and coins were issued. National currencies continued to be accepted in trade for a short transition period that ended in all member countries by the end of February 2002. The statistical treatment of euro banknotes and coins and outstanding national currencies is described in the section *European Economic and Monetary Union* in Section 5—Money and Banking.

Effective Exchange Rates

The country tables, euro area tables, and world tables provide measures of effective exchange rates, compiled by the IMF's Research Department, Policy and Review Department, Statistics Department, and area departments.

A **nominal** effective exchange rate index represents the ratio (expressed on the base 1995=100) of an index of a currency's period-average exchange rate to a weighted geometric average of exchange rates for the currencies of selected countries and the euro area. A **real effective** exchange rate index represents a nominal effective exchange rate index adjusted for relative movements in national price or cost indicators of the home country, selected countries, and the euro area.

Line ahx

For ease of comparison between the nominal effective exchange rate index and the real effective exchange rate index, the average exchange rate expressed in terms of U.S. dollars per unit of each of the national currencies (line **ah**) is also given as an index form based on 1995=100 (line **ahx**). In both cases of the indices, an increase in the index reflects an appreciation. Because of certain data-related limits, particularly where Fund estimates have been used, data users need to exercise considerable caution in interpreting movements in nominal and real effective exchange rates.

The Fund publishes calculated effective exchange rates data only for countries that have given their approval. Please note that similar indices that are calculated by country authorities could cause different results.

Lines neu and reu

The nominal effective exchange rate index (line **neu**) and the real effective exchange rate index (line **reu**) are published in the country tables for approximately 18 industrial countries and the euro area, for which data are available for normalized unit labor costs in manufacturing.

For the nominal effective exchange rate index, weights are derived from trade in manufactured goods among industrial countries over the period 1989–91. For the real effective exchange rate index for these countries (excluding Australia and New Zealand) and the euro area (excluding Ireland and Portugal), data are compiled from the nominal effective exchange rate index and from a cost indicator of relative normalized unit labor costs in manufacturing. The **reu** and **neu** indices are discussed more fully in the world table section of this introduction.

A selection of other measures of real effective exchange rates for these countries and the euro area, using alternative measures of costs and prices, is shown in the world table *Real Effective Exchange Rates Indices*.

Lines nec and rec

The country tables for selected other countries include a nominal effective exchange rate index in line **nec**. This index is based on a methodology that takes account of each country's trade in both *manufactured* goods and *primary* products with its partner, or competitor, countries.

For *manufactured* goods, trade by type of good and market is distinguished in the database. So it is possible to allow at a disaggregated level for competition among various exporters in a foreign market (i.e., third-market competition) as well as that arising from bilateral trade links.

For *primary* products, the weights assigned depend principally on a country's role as a global supplier or buyer of the product. Trade in crude petroleum, petroleum, and other energy products is excluded. For some countries that depend heavily on tourism, bilateral exports of tourism services averaged over 1988–90 are also included in calculating the competitiveness weights.

From January 1990 onwards, the line **nec** index is weighted based on disaggregate trade data for manufactured goods and primary products covering the three-year period 1988–90. Before that, the weights are for the three-year span 1980–82. The series based on the old weights and the new weights are linked by splicing at December 1989, and the reference base is shifted to 1995=100.

The real effective exchange rate index in line **rec** is derived from the nominal effective exchange rate index, adjusted for relative changes in consumer prices. Consumer price indices, often available monthly, are used as a measure of domestic costs and prices for these countries. This practice typically reflects the use of consumer prices by the reference and partner, or competitor, countries in compiling these indices.

For countries where multiple exchange rates are in effect, Fund staff estimates of weighted average exchange rates are used in many cases. A weighted average exchange rate is constructed as an average of the various exchange rates, with the weights reflecting the share of trade transacted at each rate. For countries where a weighted average exchange rate cannot be calculated, the principal rate, generally line **ahx**, is used.

The notes to the country tables in the monthly issues provide information about exceptions in the choice of the consumer price index (generally line 64) and the period average exchange rate index (generally line **ahx**). For a relatively small number of countries, notes in the country tables in the monthly issues indicate 1) where alternative price indices, such as the wholesale/producer price index or a weighted average of several price indices, are used; 2) where data constraints have made it necessary to use weighting schemes based on aggregate bilateral non-oil trade data;

and 3) where trade in services (such as tourism) has been taken into account.

The world table section of this introduction provides a description of the effective exchange rates tables. In addition, a Fund working paper entitled "A Primer on the IMF's Information Notice System" (WP/97/71), distributed in May 1997, provides background on the concepts and methodology underlying the effective exchange rates.

SDR Value

Before July 1974, the value of the SDR (unit of account for the Fund) was fixed in terms of U.S. dollars. Over time, the value changed as follows: SDR 1 = U.S. dollar 1 through November 1971; SDR 1 = U.S. dollar 1.08571 from December 1971 through January 1973; and SDR 1 = U.S. dollar 1.20635 from February 1973 through June 1974.

Since July 1974, the Fund has determined the value of the SDR daily on the basis of a basket of currencies, with each currency being assigned a weight in the determination of that value. The currencies in the basket are valued at their market exchange rates for the U.S. dollar. The U.S. dollar equivalents of each currency are summed to yield the rate of the SDR in terms of the U.S. dollar. The rates for the SDR in terms of other currencies are derived from the market exchange rates of these currencies for the U.S. dollar and the U.S. dollar rate for the SDR.

Although the method of calculating the U.S. dollar/SDR exchange rate has remained the same, the currencies' number and weight have changed over time. Their amount in the SDR basket is reviewed every five years.

From July 1974 through June 1978, the currencies in the basket were of the countries that averaged more than 1 percent share in world exports of goods and services from 1968–72. This established a basket of 16 currencies. Each currency's relative weight was broadly proportionate to the country's exports but modified for the U.S. dollar to reflect its real weight in the world economy. To preserve the continuity of valuation, the amount of each of the 16 currencies was such that on June 28, 1974 the value of SDR 1 = U.S. dollar 1.20635.

From July 1978 through December 1980, the composition of the basket was changed on the basis of updated data for 1972–76. The weights of some currencies were also changed. The amount of each of the 16 currencies in the revised basket was such as to ensure that the value of the SDR in terms of any currency on June 30, 1978 was exactly the same in the revised valuation as in the previous valuation.

Since January 1, 1981, the value of the SDR has been determined based on the currencies of the five member countries having the largest exports of goods and services during the five-year period ending one year before the date of the latest revision to the valuation basket. Broadly reflecting the currencies' relative importance in international trade and finance, the weights are based on the value of the exports of goods and services of the members issuing these currencies and the balances of their currencies officially held by members of the Fund.

From January 1981 through December 1985, the currencies and currency weights of the five members having the largest exports of goods and services during 1975–79 were the U.S. dollar, 42 percent; deutsche mark, 19 percent; French franc, Japanese yen, and pound sterling, 13 percent each.

From January 1986 through December 1990, reflecting the period 1980–84, the weights had changed to U.S. dollar, 42 percent; deutsche mark, 19 percent; Japanese yen, 15 percent; French franc and pound sterling, 12 percent each.

From January 1991 through December 1995, reflecting the period 1985–89, the weights were U.S. dollar, 40 percent; deutsche mark, 21 percent; Japanese yen, 17 percent; French franc and pound sterling, 11 percent each.

On January 1, 1996, the weights were U.S. dollar, 39 percent; deutsche mark, 21 percent; Japanese yen, 18 percent; French franc and pound sterling, 11 percent each.

On January 1, 1999, the currency amount of deutsche mark and French francs were replaced with equivalent amounts of euros, based on the fixed conversion rates between those currencies and the euro, announced on December 31, 1998 by the European Council. The weights in the SDR basket were changed to U.S. dollar, 39 percent; euro, 32 percent (in replacement of the 21 percent for the deutsche mark and 11 percent for the French franc), Japanese yen, 18 percent; and pound sterling, 11 percent.

As of January 1, 2001, the SDR valuation basket weights are the sum of the values of the amounts of each currency in the following amounts: U.S. dollar, 45 percent; euro, 29 percent; Japanese yen, 15 percent; and pound sterling, 11 percent.

World Tables on Exchange Rate Arrangements and Exchange Rates

A table on exchange rate arrangements and Tables A, B, C, and D on exchange rates, described below, are presented in *IFS*. Daily exchange rates are not yet provided on the CD-ROM or Internet.

The table on exchange rate arrangements is based mainly on information supplied to the Fund on the exchange rate arrangements applied by individual member countries. Such notification is required under Article IV, Section 2(a) of the amended Articles of Agreement of the Fund, which entered into force on April 1, 1978. The classification in the table reflects judgments by the Fund staff based on that information.

Table A of exchange rates gives the monthly, quarterly, and annual SDR rates in terms of U.S. dollars and reciprocals of these rates.

Table B reports for the latest available month the daily rates and the monthly averages, both in terms of currency units per U.S. dollar (**af**) and U.S. dollars per currency unit (**ah**) of (1) 16 major currencies, other than the U.S. dollar, as quoted in the markets of these countries, (2) the SDR, and (3) the euro.

Table C gives daily rates of currencies in terms of national currency units per SDR for the latest available month.

Table D provides, in terms of national currency units per SDR, end-of-period rates for the currencies of Fund mem-

bers—including Hong Kong (Special Administrative Region as of 1997)—and the Netherlands Antilles.

Method of Deriving *IFS* Exchange Rates

For countries that have introduced new currencies, the rates shown in *IFS* for the period before the introduction of the most recent currency may be used as conversion factors—they may be used to convert national currency data in *IFS* to U.S. dollar or SDR data. In such cases, the factors are constructed by chain linking the exchange rates of the old and the new currencies. The basis used is the value of the new currency relative to the old currency, as established by the issuing agency at the time the new currency was introduced. Footnotes about the introduction of new currencies are to be found on individual country tables in the monthly issues of *IFS*.

For countries that are members of the euro area, the exchange rates shown are expressed in national currency units per SDR or per U.S. dollar through 1998, and in euros per SDR or per U.S. dollar thereafter.

A detailed description of the derivation of the exchange rates in *IFS*, as well as technical issues associated with these rates, is contained in the *IFS Supplement on Exchange Rates*, No. 9 (1985).

3. Fund Accounts

Data on members' Fund accounts are presented in the Fund Position section in the country tables and in 12 world tables. Details about Fund Accounts terms and concepts and the time series in the country and world tables follow:

Terms and Concepts in Fund Accounts

Quota

When a country joins the Fund, it is assigned a quota that fits into the structure of existing quotas. Quotas are considered in the light of the member's economic characteristics relative to those of other members of comparable size. The size of the member's quota determines, among other things, the member's voting power, the size of its potential access to Fund resources, and its share in allocations of SDRs.

Quotas are reviewed at intervals of not more than five years. The reviews take account of changes in the relative economic positions of members and the growth of the world economy. Initial subscriptions, and normally subscriptions associated with increases in quotas, are paid mainly in the member's own currency, and a smaller portion, not exceeding 25 percent, is paid in reserve assets (SDRs or other members' currencies that are acceptable to the Fund).

General Resources Account

The General Resources Account (GRA) resources consist of the currencies of Fund member countries, SDRs, and gold. These resources are received in the form of subscriptions (which are equal to quotas), borrowings, charges on the use of the Fund's resources, income from investments, and interest on the Fund's holdings of SDRs. Subscriptions are the main source of funds.

Borrowing Arrangements

Borrowings are regarded as a temporary source of funds. The Fund has the authority to borrow the currency of any member from any source with the consent of the issuer.

General Arrangements to Borrow

The Fund's first borrowings were made under the General Arrangements to Borrow (GAB). The Arrangements were established in 1962 initially for four years but, through successive extensions, have been continuously in force since then. The original Arrangements permitted the Fund to borrow the currencies of ten industrial country members (those forming the Group of Ten) to finance purchases by any of these ten countries.

The Fund also had an agreement with Switzerland, under which Switzerland undertook to consider making loans to the Fund to finance additional purchases by members that made purchases financed by the GAB.

The revised GAB, that became effective in December 1983, permits the Fund under certain circumstances to extend GAB resources to members that are not GAB participants, authorize participation of the Swiss National Bank, and permit certain borrowing arrangements between the Fund and nonparticipating members to be associated with the GAB. The GAB decision was amended on December 22, 1992 to take account of Switzerland's membership in the Fund.

Temporary Arrangements

The Fund has also entered into borrowing arrangements to finance purchases under its temporary lending facilities.

Oil Facilities: The Fund arranged in 1974 and 1975 to borrow from the principal oil exporting countries and other countries with strong external positions to finance two special facilities—the 1974 and 1975 Oil Facilities. Under these facilities, repayments were completed in May 1983.

Supplementary Financing Facility: In 1977 the Fund initiated bilateral borrowing arrangements with 14 countries or their institutions to finance commitments under the Supplementary Financing Facility. This facility was established in 1979, and its funds were fully committed by March 1981.

Policy on Enlarged Access: The first borrowing agreement under the Policy on Enlarged Access to the Fund's resources was reached in March 1981 between the Fund and the Saudi Arabian Monetary Agency.

Others: Since then, additional agreements have been entered into with central banks and official agencies of a number of countries, and with international agencies. In December 1986 the Fund entered into a borrowing arrangement with the government of Japan, under which resources were made available for use by the Fund in support of members' adjustment programs, including under the Enlarged Access Policy.

All of the above borrowing arrangements were disbursed and used by December 1991, except for the GAB, which remains intact. Meanwhile, in December 1987 the Fund, as "Trustee," was authorized to enter into borrowing arrange-

ments with official lenders from a wide range of countries to finance loans under the Enhanced Structural Adjustment Facility, renamed Poverty Reduction and Growth Facility in November 1999.

New Arrangements to Borrow

The New Arrangements to Borrow (NAB), which became effective on November 17, 1998, is a set of credit arrangements between the Fund and 25 members and institutions to provide supplementary resources to the Fund. These resources are to forestall or cope with an impairment of the international monetary system or to deal with an exceptional situation that poses a threat to the stability of that system. The NAB does not replace the GAB, which remains in force.

The total amount of resources available to the Fund under the NAB and GAB combined will be up to SDR 34 billion, double the amount available under the GAB alone. By strengthening the Fund's ability to support the adjustment efforts of its members and to address their balance of payments difficulties, the NAB is an important element of the Fund's capacity to respond to potential systemic problems. The NAB will be in effect for five years, beginning on November 17, 1998, and may be renewed.

Financing Policies and Facilities

Purchases (.2kk.)

The principal way the Fund makes its resources available to members is to sell to them currencies of other members or SDRs in exchange for their own currencies. Such transactions change the composition, but not the overall size, of the Fund's resources. A member to whom the Fund sells currencies or SDRs is said to make "purchases" (also referred to as "drawings") from the Fund.

The purpose of making the Fund's resources available to members is to meet their balance of payments needs. The Fund's resources are provided through permanent policies for general balance of payments purposes (the tranche policies), permanent facilities for specific purposes (the Buffer Stock Financing Facility, the Extended Fund Facility, the Compensatory and Contingency Financing Facility, and the Supplemental Reserve Facility (SRF)), and temporary facilities (the Oil Facilities, the Supplementary Financing Facility, the Policy on Enlarged Access to the Fund's resources, and the Systemic Transformation Facility (STF)).

Permanent Policies

Reserve Tranche: A member's reserve tranche is the excess of its quota in the Fund over the adjusted Fund holdings of its currency in the GRA. Adjusted Fund holdings of a member's currency are equal to the actual holdings of the currency less holdings arising from outstanding purchases under the Fund's policies and facilities, which are subject to exclusion under Article XXX(c). Reserve tranche purchases, like all other purchases, may be made only to meet a balance of payments need. However, for reserve tranche purchases the Fund does not challenge a member's statement of need. As the reserve tranche is considered a reserve deposit in the

Fund, a member using its reserve tranche is not considered to be using Fund credit.

Credit Tranche Policy: The credit tranche policy is often referred to as the Fund's basic financing policy. Credit under this policy is viewed as being available in tranches, each tranche being equivalent to 25 percent of quota. Credit tranche purchases may be made outright or under a stand-by arrangement. The latter, which is like a line of credit, assures the member that during a given period it will be able to use the Fund's resources up to a specified amount, so long as it is observing the terms of the arrangement.

Permanent Facilities

Buffer Stock Financing Facility: The Buffer Stock Financing Facility, established in June 1969, is to assist members with a balance of payments need related to their participation in arrangements to finance approved international buffer stocks of primary products.

Extended Fund Facility (EFF): The EFF, established in September 1974, is to make resources available for longer periods and in larger amounts than under the credit tranche policies. It is to assist members that are experiencing balance of payments difficulties owing to structural imbalances in production, trade, and prices, or that are unable to pursue active development policies because of their weak balance of payments positions.

Compensatory and Contingency Financing Facility (CCFF): The CCFF superseded the Compensatory Financing Facility (CFF) in August 1988. The CCFF keeps the essential elements of the CFF and adds a mechanism for contingency financing to support adjustment programs approved by the Fund.

The CFF, established in February 1963, was to assist members, particularly primary producing countries, experiencing balance of payments difficulties attributable to shortfalls in earnings from merchandise exports. Such difficulties were also attributable to invisibles both temporary and due largely to factors beyond their control.

In May 1981 the Fund decided to extend financial assistance to members facing balance of payments difficulties produced by an excess in the cost of their cereal imports. This assistance was integrated with support available under the compensatory financing facility for temporary shortfalls in export receipts.

Supplemental Reserve Facility (SRF): The SRF, established in December 1997, is to financially assist a member country experiencing exceptional balance of payments difficulties caused by a large short-term financing need. This need resulted from a sudden and disruptive loss of market confidence reflected in pressure on the capital account and the member's reserves.

Financing under the SRF, available in the form of additional resources under a Stand-By or Extended Arrangement, may be committed for up to one year and be generally available in two or more tranches. Purchases under the SRF are included as part of either the Stand-By or the Extended Fund Facility, as indicated in the footnote to the world table

"Financing Components of Members' Outstanding Obligations to the Fund."

Access

Under the present guidelines on access limits, adopted on October 24, 1994, member access to the Fund's general resources in the credit tranches and the Extended Facility is subject to an annual limit of 100 percent of quota, and a cumulative limit of 300 percent of quota. This is net of scheduled repurchases and excluding purchases under the Compensatory Financing Facility and the Buffer Stock Financing Facility.

Within these limits, the amount of access in individual cases will vary according to the circumstances of the member. In exceptional circumstances, the Fund may approve Stand-By or Extended Arrangements that provide for amounts over these access limits. The guidelines and access limits are intended to be temporary and are reviewed periodically.

Temporary Facilities

Oil Facilities: The oil facilities, set up in June 1974 and April 1975, were to assist members with balance of payments difficulties owing to the rise in oil prices. Purchases under the facilities were completed in May 1976.

Supplementary Financing Facility (SFF): The SFF, established in February 1979, was to assist members facing payments difficulties that were large in relation to their economies and their Fund quotas. Resources under the facility, which were borrowed and therefore not part of the Fund's ordinary resources, were made available only in connection with an upper credit tranche stand-by arrangement and an extended arrangement. The facility was fully committed by March 1981.

Enlarged Access Policy: The Policy on Enlarged Access to the Fund's resources, which continued the policies of the Supplementary Financing Facility following the full commitment of the latter's resources, became operational in May 1981. Under this policy, resources were provided only under stand-by and extended arrangements. The amount of assistance available to a member under the policy was determined according to guidelines adopted by the Fund from time to time. The policy was discontinued in November 1992 because of the effectiveness of the increases in quotas under the Ninth Review, which increased the Fund's ordinary resources by 50 percent.

Systemic Transformation Facility (STF): The STF could be accessed between April 1993 and December 1995. It was to help member countries facing balance of payments difficulties owing to severe disruptions of their traditional trade and payments arrangements. The disruptions had arisen during a shift from significant reliance on trading at nonmarket prices to multilateral, market-based trade. Countries eligible to draw on the STF included most of those belonging to the former Council for Mutual Economic Assistance, the Baltic countries, Russia, and other countries of the former Soviet Union (BRO), and a number of other countries experiencing similar transformation.

Access

Except for access to the credit tranches and the Extended Facility, which are now subject to common ceilings, access to resources under one policy or facility is independent of access under any other policies or facilities.

All requests for purchases other than those in the reserve tranche are subject to examination by the Fund to determine whether the proposed use of purchases would be consistent with the provisions of the Articles of Agreement and Fund policies. These provisions call for adequate safeguards to ensure that the member will adopt the policies, take measures to overcome its balance of payments difficulties, and meet scheduled repurchases, thereby ensuring the revolving nature of the Fund's resources.

Repurchases

Because the Fund's resources revolve to finance temporary balance of payments deficits, members that purchase from the Fund must subsequently repurchase their currencies with the currencies of other members or SDRs. A member is required to repurchase Fund holdings of its currency that are subject to charges. These holdings include those that result from purchases of currencies or SDRs, other than reserve tranche purchases, and all adjusted Fund holdings that are more than 100 percent of the member's quota.

Members may repurchase at any time the Fund's holdings of their currencies that are subject to charges. However, if their balance of payments and reserve positions improve, they are expected to repurchase the Fund's holdings of their currencies from purchases.

In any event, they must make repurchases—irrespective of their balance of payments positions—in installments within limits of 3¼ to 5 years for purchases under the credit tranche policies, the Compensatory Financing Facility, and the Buffer Stock Financing Facility; 4½ to 10 years for purchases under the Extended Facility and Systemic Transformation Facility financed by ordinary resources; and 3½ to 7 years for purchases under the Policy on Enlarged Access to resources.

Positions in the Fund

The Fund normally determines the currencies that are used in transactions and operations with members. Each quarter, the Fund prepares a financial transactions plan, in which it indicates the amounts of particular currencies and SDRs to be used during the relevant period. The Fund selects the currencies of members with strong balance of payments and reserve positions. It also seeks to promote, over time, balanced "**positions in the Fund**."

The effects of Fund transactions and operations are summarized in the Fund's **holdings of members' currencies** and in two other measures, namely, **reserve position in the Fund** and total **Fund credit and loans outstanding**. (See world table in the monthly printed copy of *IFS* and the yearbook, entitled Fund Accounts: Position to Date, and also the Fund Position section in the country tables.)

These measures are defined as follows:

The Fund's **holdings of a member's currency** reflect, among other things, the transactions and operations of the Fund in that currency. This concept is used in calculating the amounts that a member can draw on the Fund under tranche policies and in respect to certain of its obligations to the Fund.

A member's **reserve position in the Fund** (time series .1c.s), which has the characteristics of a reserve asset, comprises the reserve tranche position and creditor position under the various borrowing arrangements. A reserve tranche position arises from (1) the payment of part of a member's subscription in reserve assets and (2) the Fund's net use of the member's currency. Normally, a member's reserve tranche position is equal to its quota less the adjusted Fund holdings of its currency, less subscriptions receivable, less the balances held in the administrative accounts of the Fund to the extent they are not above 0.1 percent of a member's quota, if positive.

Total Fund credit and loans outstanding (.2tl.) represents the sum of (1) the use of Fund credit within the GRA and (2) outstanding loans under the SAF, PRGF, and the Trust Fund.

Use of Fund credit within the General Resources Account (.2egs) is the sum of a member's outstanding purchases and the Fund's net operational receipts and expenditures in that currency that increase the adjusted Fund holdings above quota. It measures the amount that a member is obligated to repurchase.

Outstanding purchases (.2kk.) are equal to purchases other than reserve tranche purchases, less repurchases, less other members' purchases of that member's currency, and less any other use by the Fund of that member's currency (except administrative expenditures) that the member wishes to attribute to specific outstanding purchases.

Use of Fund credit within the Special Disbursement Account (SDA) relates to outstanding loans under the structural adjustment facility (SAF) and that portion of the enhanced structural adjustment facility (ESAF) loans not financed from the ESAF Trust Account. The SDA is the vehicle for receiving and investing profits from the sale of the IMF's gold (i.e., the net proceeds in excess of the book value of SDR 35 a fine ounce), and for making transfers to other accounts for special purposes authorized in the Articles, in particular for financial assistance to low-income members of the IMF.

Structural Adjustment Facility and Poverty Reduction and Growth Facility

The Structural Adjustment Facility (SAF), established in March 1986, provides additional balance of payments assistance in the form of loans on concessional terms. This assistance is for low-income developing countries that were eligible for International Development Association (IDA) resources, that face protracted balance of payments problems, and that are in need of such assistance.

Resources of the SAF comprise Trust Fund reflows, the interest income on SAF loans, investment income from the resources available for the facility, and amounts not used for the Supplementary Financing Facility (SFF) Subsidy Account, which may be transferred back to the SDA.

The Enhanced Structural Adjustment Facility (ESAF) was established in December 1987 and renamed Poverty Reduction and Growth Facility (PRGF), effective November 22, 1999. It provides additional assistance in the form of loans on concessional terms to low-income developing countries that were eligible for assistance from the SAF.

In contrast to the uniform access limit of 70 percent of quota for SAF loans, individual access limits for PRGF loans are determined on the basis of balance of payments need and the strength of adjustment efforts. The maximum access limit is set at 250 percent of quota, with a provision for higher access in exceptional cases. Repayment of each loan must be made in 10 equal semiannual installments starting 5½ years and finishing 10 years after the date of the disbursement. Outstanding SAF and PRGF loans do not affect a member's access to the Fund's general resources, which remain available under the terms of those policies.

Resources available for disbursement under PRGF arrangements include (1) the resources of the PRGF Trust (previously the ESAF Trust, established in December 1987), which comprise special loans and contributions and are held separately from the property and assets of all other accounts of the Fund, including other administered accounts, (2) amounts available from the SDA that have not been used under SAF arrangements, and (3) amounts made available by associated lenders.

Trust Fund and Supplementary Financing Facility Subsidy Account

The Fund is Trustee for two additional accounts, whose resources are legally separate from the resources of the Fund. These are the Trust Fund and the Supplementary Financing Facility (SFF) Subsidy Account.

The Trust Fund, established in May 1976, provides balance of payments assistance on concessional terms to eligible members and also distributes funds directly to developing members. The resources of the Trust Fund are derived from profits from the sale of about 25 million ounces of the Fund's gold holdings during 1976–80, from income on the investment of these profits, from contributions by members, and from low-interest borrowings.

The SFF Subsidy Account, established in December 1980, reduced the cost for low-income developing countries for using the supplementary financing facility. The SFF Subsidy Account consists of transfers from reflows of Trust Fund loans, donations, loans, and the interest income received from investment of resources held pending disbursement.

SDRs

SDRs are unconditional reserve assets created by the Fund to supplement existing reserve assets. SDRs are allocated to Fund members that participate in the Fund's Operations Division for SDRs and Administered Accounts in proportion to their quotas. Six SDR allocations totaling SDR 21.4 billion have been made by the Fund (in January 1970,

January 1971, January 1972, January 1979, January 1980, and January 1981).

The Fund cannot allocate SDRs to itself but receives them from members through various financial transactions and operations. Entities authorized to conduct transactions in SDRs are the Fund itself, participants in the Fund's Operations Division for SDRs and Administered Accounts, and prescribed "other holders."

The SDR can be used for a wide range of transactions and operations, including for acquiring other members' currencies, settling financial obligations, making donations, and extending loans. SDRs may also be used in swap arrangements and as security for the performance of financial obligations. Forward as well as spot transactions may be conducted in SDRs.

World Tables on Fund Accounts

Twelve world tables on Fund Accounts are presented in *IFS*, as described below. The tables on Fund accounts arrangements, position to date, financing components, and borrowing agreements are not yet available on the CD-ROM or Internet.

The world table Fund Accounts: Arrangements reports the current status of stand-by, extended, and poverty reduction and growth (previously, the enhanced structural adjustment) arrangements.

The table Fund Accounts: Position to Date reports latest monthly data on members' Fund positions, including quota, reserve position in the Fund, total Fund credit and loans outstanding, Fund holdings of currencies, and positions in the SDR Department.

The table Financing Components of Members' Outstanding Obligations to the Fund reports latest monthly data on the sources of financing of Fund credit and loans outstanding.

The tables Purchases (.2kk.) and Repurchases (.2lk.) relate to transactions within the General Resources Account (GRA).

The table Fund Accounts: Borrowing Agreements reports the current status of the Fund's borrowing activities.

The tables Loan Disbursements (.2kl.) and Repayments of Loans (.2ll.) relate to the Structural Adjustment Facility (SAF), Poverty Reduction and Growth Facility (PRGF; which was previously named Enhanced Structural Adjustment Facility-ESAF), and Trust Fund loans.

The table Total Fund Credit and Loans Outstanding (.2tl.) relates to the outstanding use of Fund resources under the GRA and to outstanding loans under the SAF, PRGF, and Trust Fund.

The table Use of Fund Credit: GRA (.2egs) relates to the outstanding use of the Fund resources under the GRA.

The table SDRs (.1b.s) shows holdings of SDRs by members and includes a foot table showing SDR holdings by all participants, the IMF, other holders, and the world.

The table Reserve Position in the Fund (.1c.s) relates to members' claims on the Fund.

Pamphlet on Fund Accounts

A more detailed description of the Fund accounts is contained in the IMF's *Financial Organization and Operations of the IMF*, Pamphlet No. 45, sixth edition, 2001.

4. International Liquidity

Data on international liquidity are presented in the country tables and in world tables on reserves. The international liquidity section in the country tables comprises lines for total reserves minus gold, gold holdings, other foreign assets and foreign liabilities of the monetary authorities, and foreign accounts of other financial institutions. The euro area section for international liquidity covers assets of the European Central Bank (ECB) and the national central banks (NCBs) of the countries that have adopted the euro (details below).

Total Reserves (Minus Gold) and Gold Holdings

Total Reserves Minus Gold (line 1 l.d) is the sum of the items Foreign Exchange, Reserve Position in the Fund, and the U.S. dollar value of SDR holdings by monetary authorities. Monetary authorities comprise central banks and, to the extent that they perform monetary authorities' functions, currency boards, exchange stabilization funds, and treasuries.

Official Gold Holdings (lines 1ad and 1and) are expressed in millions of fine troy ounces and valued, according to national practice, in U.S. dollars.

Under Total Reserves Minus Gold, the line for Foreign Exchange (1d.d) includes monetary authorities' claims on nonresidents in the form of foreign banknotes, bank deposits, treasury bills, short- and long-term government securities, ECUs (for periods before January 1999), and other claims usable in the event of balance of payments need.

For *IFS* yearbook users, this background information on foreign exchange is particularly useful: Before December 1971, when the U.S. dollar was at par with the SDR, foreign exchange data were compiled and expressed in terms of U.S. dollars at official par values. Conversions from national currencies to U.S. dollars from December 1971 through January 1973 were calculated at the cross rates reflecting the parities and central rates agreed to in December 1971. From February 1973 through June 1974, foreign exchange was valued at the cross rates of parities or central rates for countries having effective parities or central rates, and at market rates for the Canadian dollar, Irish pound, Italian lira, Japanese yen, and pound sterling. Beginning in July 1974, foreign exchange is valued at end-of-month market rates or, in the absence of market rate quotations, at other prevailing official rates.

Total Reserves for the Euro Area

Until December 31, 1998, member countries of the European Union (Austria, Belgium, Denmark, Finland, France, Germany, Greece, Ireland, Italy, Luxembourg, the Netherlands, Portugal, Spain, Sweden, and the United Kingdom) held ECU deposits with the European Monetary Cooperation Fund (EMCF) and/or its successor, the European Monetary Institute. The reserves data for each country excluded, from gold and foreign exchange holdings, the deposits of gold and foreign exchange with the EMCF, but the data included, in foreign exchange holdings, the equivalent amounts of ECU deposits.

These deposits were transferred from the EMCF to the EMI upon its creation on January 1, 1994, and to the European Central Bank (ECB) when it succeeded the EMI on June 1, 1998. Each national central bank (NCB) deposited gold and foreign exchange with the ECB. On January 1, 1999, the euro replaced the ECU at a rate of one euro per one ECU.

Total reserves for the euro area and individual euro area countries are based on the statistical definition of international reserves adopted by the ECB's Statistics Committee in December 1998. Defined on a euro area-wide residency basis, they include reserve assets denominated only in currencies of non-euro area countries. All positions with residents of other euro area countries and with the ECB are excluded from reserve assets.

For the euro area countries, Total Reserves minus Gold (line 1 l.d) is defined in broad accordance with the fifth edition of the *Balance of Payments Manual*. It includes the monetary authorities' holdings of SDRs, reserve position in the Fund, and foreign exchange, including financial derivative claims on non-euro area countries. It excludes claims among euro area countries and all euro-denominated claims on non-euro area countries. Total reserves of the euro area comprise the reserve holdings of the NCBs and ECB. Definitions of reserves at the national and euro area levels are harmonized.

Other Foreign Assets, Foreign Liabilities

Time series, where significant, are also provided in international liquidity sections on other foreign assets and foreign liabilities of the monetary authorities.

Other Assets (line 3..d) usually comprises claims on nonresidents that are of limited usability in the event of balance of payments need, such as balances under bilateral payments agreements and holdings of inconvertible currencies. (Claims on nonresidents under Other Assets (line 3..d) are included in line 11.)

Other Liabilities (line 4..d) comprises foreign liabilities of the monetary authorities other than use of Fund credit (GRA), SAF, PRGF, and Trust Fund loans outstanding. Positions with the Fund are reported separately, in SDRs, in the Fund position section of the country tables.

Foreign Accounts of Other Financial Institutions

Where significant, foreign accounts of financial institutions other than the monetary authorities are reported. The measures provided are normally U.S. dollar equivalents of time series reported in the appropriate money and banking sections as follows: line 7a.d is derived from line 21; line 7b.d is derived from line 26c plus line 26cl; line 7e.d is derived from line 41; and line 7f.d is derived from line 46c plus line 46cl. Sometimes the measures are reported directly in U.S. dollars and may differ slightly in coverage.

In addition for some countries, summary data are provided on the foreign accounts of special or international license banks that operate locally but are not presently covered in the money and banking section. Their foreign assets are reported as line 7k.d, and their foreign liabilities as line

7m.d, when available (although 7m.d is not shown separately if it is equal to line 7k.d).

World Tables on Reserves

World tables on reserves report all country table time series on reserves, other than gold at national valuation, and present totals for countries, country groups, and the world.

Also provided is a table on total reserves, with gold valued at SDR 35 per ounce. A foot table to that table reports total reserves of all countries, including gold valued both at SDR 35 per ounce and at market prices. And the yearbook includes a world table on the ratio of nongold reserves (line 1 1.d) to imports (line 71..d), expressed in terms of the number of weeks of imports covered by the stock of nongold reserves.

Except for the world table on gold holdings in physical terms, world tables on reserves are expressed in SDRs. Foreign exchange holdings are expressed in SDRs by converting the U.S. dollar values shown in the country tables on the basis of the end-period U.S. dollar/SDR rate.

Similarly, a foot table to the world table on gold indicates gold holdings valued at SDR 35 per ounce and at market prices for all countries, the IMF, the ECB, the Bank for International Settlements (BIS), and the world. A simple addition of the gold held by all of these holders would involve double-counting, because most of the gold deposited with the BIS is also included in countries' official gold reserves. *IFS* therefore reports BIS gold holdings net of gold deposits, and negative figures for BIS gold holdings are balanced by forward operations. This foot table also provides data on the U.S. dollar price of gold on the London market, the U.S. dollar/SDR rate, and the end-period derived market price of gold in terms of SDRs.

5. Money and Banking

Statistics on the accounts of monetary and other financial institutions are given in money and banking sections 10 through 50 in the country tables and in world tables, described in the world table section of this introduction.

Monetary Authorities

Monetary authorities' data (section 10) in *IFS* generally consolidate the accounts of the central bank with the accounts of other institutions that undertake monetary functions. These functions include issuing currency, holding international reserves, and conducting Fund account transactions. Data on monetary authorities measure the stock of reserve money comprising currency in circulation, deposits of the deposit money banks, and deposits of other residents, apart from the central government, with the monetary authorities.

Major aggregates of the accounts on the asset side are foreign assets (line 11) and domestic assets (line 12*). Domestic assets are broken down into Claims on Central Government (line 12a), Claims on Deposit Money Banks (line 12e), and, if sizable, Claims on State and Local Governments (line 12b); Claims on Nonfinancial Public Enterprises (line 12c); Claims on the Private Sector (line 12d); Claims on Other

Banking Institutions (line 12f), and Claims on Nonbank Financial Institutions (line 12g).

In some countries, where insufficient data are available to provide disaggregations of claims on governmental bodies other than the central government, a classification of Claims on Official Entities (line 12bx) is used. In addition, in countries where insufficient data are available to provide disaggregations of claims on other banking institutions and nonbank financial institutions, a classification of Claims on Other Financial Institutions (line 12f) is used.

The principal liabilities of monetary authorities consist of Reserve Money (line 14); Other Liabilities to Deposit Money Banks (line 14n), comprising liabilities of the central bank to deposit money banks that are excluded from Reserve Money; Liabilities of the Central Bank: Securities (line 16ac); Foreign Liabilities (line 16c); Central Government Deposits (line 16d); and Capital Accounts (line 17a).

Deposit Money Banks

Deposit money banks comprise commercial banks and other financial institutions that accept transferable deposits, such as demand deposits. Deposit money banks' data (section 20) measure the stock of deposit money.

Major aggregates of the accounts on the assets side are Reserves (line 20), comprising domestic currency holdings and deposits with the monetary authorities; Claims on Monetary Authorities: Securities (line 20c), comprising holdings of securities issued by the central bank; Other Claims on Monetary Authorities (line 20n), comprising claims on the central bank that are excluded from Reserves; Foreign Assets (line 21); and Claims on Other Resident Sectors (lines 22*), as described in the preceding section on monetary authorities (lines 12*).

The principal liabilities consist of Demand Deposits (line 24); Time, Savings, and Foreign Currency Deposits (line 25); Money Market Instruments (line 26aa); Bonds (line 26ab); Foreign Liabilities (line 26c); Central Government Deposits (line 26d); Credit from Monetary Authorities (line 26g); Liabilities to Other Banking Institutions (line 26i); Liabilities to Nonbank Financial Institutions (line 26j); and Capital Accounts (line 27a).

Monetary Survey

Monetary authorities' and deposit money banks' data are consolidated into a monetary survey (section 30). The survey measures the stock of narrow Money (line 34), comprising transferable deposits and currency outside deposit money banks, and the Quasi-Money (line 35) liabilities of these institutions, comprising time, savings, and foreign currency deposits.

Standard relationships between the monetary survey lines and the component lines in sections 10 and 20 are as follows:

Foreign Assets (Net) (line 31n) equals the sum of foreign asset lines 11 and 21, less the sum of foreign liability lines 16c and 26c.

Claims on Central Government (Net) (line 32an) equals claims on central government (the sum of lines 12a and 22a), less central government deposits (the sum of lines 16d and 26d), plus, where applicable, the counterpart entries of lines 24..i and 24..r (private sector demand deposits with the postal checking system and with the Treasury).

Claims on State and Local Governments (line 32b) equals the sum of lines 12b and 22b. Note that, for some countries, lack of sufficient data to perform the standard classifications of claims on governmental bodies excluding the central government has resulted in the use of the alternative classification "claims on official entities" (line 32bx), which is the sum of lines 12bx and 22bx. These series may therefore include state and local governments, public financial institutions, and nonfinancial public enterprises.

Claims on Nonfinancial Public Enterprises (line 32c) equals the sum of lines 12c and 22c.

Claims on Private Sector (line 32d) equals the sum of lines 12d and 22d.

Claims on Other Banking Institutions (line 32f) equals the sum of lines 12f and 22f.

Claims on Nonbank Financial Institutions (line 32g) equals the sum of lines 12g and 22g.

Domestic Credit (line 32) is the sum of lines 32an, 32b, 32c, 32d, 32f, and 32g even when, owing to their small size, data for lines 32b, 32c, 32f, and 32g are not published separately. Thus, the data for line 32 may be larger than the sum of its published components.

Money (line 34) equals the sum of currency outside deposit money banks (line 14a) and demand deposits other than those of the central government (lines 14d, 14e, 14f, 14g, and 24) plus, where applicable, lines 24..i and 24..r.

Quasi-Money (line 35) equals the sum of lines 15 and 25, comprising time, savings, and foreign currency deposits of resident sectors other than central government.

The data in line 34 are frequently referred to as M1, while the sum of lines 34 and 35 gives a broader measure of money similar to that which is frequently called M2.

Money Market Instruments (line 36aa) equals the sum of lines 16aa and 26aa.

Bonds (line 36ab) equals the sum of lines 16ab and 26ab.

Liabilities of Central Bank: Securities (line 36ac) equals the outstanding stock of securities issued by the monetary authorities (line 16ac) less the holdings of these securities by deposit money banks (line 20c).

Restricted Deposits (line 36b) equals the sum of lines 16b and 26b.

Long-Term Foreign Liabilities (line 36cl) equals the sum of lines 16cl and 26cl.

Counterpart Funds (line 36e) equals the sum of lines 16e and 26e.

Central Government Lending Funds (line 36f) equals the sum of lines 16f and 26f.

Liabilities to Other Banking Institutions (line 36i) is equal to line 26i.

Liabilities to Nonbank Financial Institutions (line 36j) is equal to line 26j.

Capital Accounts (line 37a) equals the sum of lines 17a and 27a.

These monetary survey lines give the full range of *IFS* standard lines. Some of them are not applicable to every

country, whereas others may not be published separately in sections 10 and 20, because the data are small. Unpublished lines are included in Other Items (Net) (lines 17r and 27r) but are classified in the appropriate monetary survey aggregates in section 30.

Exceptions to the standard calculations of monetary survey aggregates are indicated in the notes to the country tables in the monthly issues. Exceptions also exist in the standard presentation of the consolidation of financial institutions, e.g., for Japan, Nicaragua, the United Kingdom, and the United States.

Other Banking Institutions

Section 40 contains data on the accounts of other banking institutions. This subsector comprises institutions that do not accept transferable deposits but that perform financial intermediation by accepting other types of deposits or by issuing securities or other liabilities that are close substitutes for deposits. This subsector covers such institutions as savings and mortgage loan institutions, post-office savings institutions, building and loan associations, finance companies that accept deposits or deposit substitutes, development banks, and offshore banking institutions.

The major aggregates in this section are claims on the various sectors of the economy (lines 42*), as described in the preceding paragraphs, and quasi-monetary liabilities (line 45), largely in the form of time and savings deposits.

Banking Survey

Where reasonably complete data are available for other banking institutions, a banking survey (section 50) is published. It consolidates data for other banking institutions with the monetary survey and thus provides a broader measure of monetary liabilities.

The sectoral classification of assets in the banking survey follows the classification used in the monetary survey, as outlined in the description for that section.

Nonbank Financial Institutions

For a few countries, data are shown on the accounts of nonbank financial institutions, such as insurance companies, pension funds, and superannuation funds. Given the nature of their liabilities, these institutions generally exert minimal impact on the liquidity of a given economy. However, they can play a significant role in distributing credit from the financial sector to the rest of the economy.

European Economic and Monetary Union (Euro Area)

Stage Three of the European Economic and Monetary Union (EMU), beginning in January 1999, created a monetary union among European countries. New definitions of statistics aggregates were created, resulting in a major break in data series for all participating countries. The euro area, an official descriptor of the monetary union, is defined by its membership as of a specified date. The 11 original members were Austria, Belgium, Finland, France, Germany, Ireland, Italy, Luxembourg, Netherlands, Portugal, and Spain.

Greece joined in January 2001. In 2002, euro banknotes and coins were issued, and national currency banknotes and coins withdrawn.

The main features of the euro area monetary statistics are described as follows:

Creation of the Eurosystem

In Stage Three of the EMU, the "Eurosystem"—the European Central Bank (ECB) and the national central banks (NCBs) of the euro area member states—executes a single monetary policy for the euro area. The new common currency unit is the euro. Until 2002, national currency circulated, and various types of transactions were denominated in either euros or national currency.

The monetary statistics standards for the euro area countries underwent comprehensive revisions. The revisions permitted compilation of consolidated monetary accounts for the euro area and provided the data needed to execute the single monetary policy. Statistical standards are based on the *European System of Accounts 1995 (1995 ESA)* and additional standards prescribed by ECB regulation. Statistics are collected under a "layered approach," whereby monetary statistics compiled at the country level are forwarded to the ECB for consolidation into euro area totals. NCBs are required to compile monetary statistics according to a single set of standards and a common format for submission of data to the ECB.

Denomination in Euros

Beginning with data for 1999, monetary data for euro area countries presented in *IFS* are denominated in euros, except for Greece whose data are denominated in euros beginning in January 2001. Data for the consolidated euro area table are in euros for all time periods.

Residency Principles

Statistics are compiled on the basis of both national residency criteria, described in the fifth edition of the *Balance of Payments Manual*, and euro area-wide residency criteria, based on the EU membership as of a specified date.

In the application of the latter criteria, all institutional units located in euro area countries are treated as resident, and all units outside the euro area as nonresident. For example, claims on government under the national criteria include only claims on the government of the country, whereas claims on government under the euro area-wide residency criteria include claims on the governments of all euro area countries. Under the euro area-wide residency criteria, the ECB is a resident unit, whereas under the national residency criteria, it is a foreign unit for all countries. Under ECB statistical reporting requirements—concerning the consolidated balance sheet of the monetary financial institutions sector—the ECB is to be classified as a resident unit of the country where it is physically located (Germany).

The monetary statistics in the tables for each euro area country are presented on both national and euro area-wide residency bases.

Euro Banknotes and Coins

On January 1, 2002, euro banknotes and coins were issued. The existing national currencies continued to be accepted in trade for a short transition period that ended in all member countries by the end of February 2002, at the latest. The national currencies and coins can be redeemed with the national authorities for extended periods, or indefinitely, as set by national policy. The changeover to euro banknotes and coins was smooth, and the stock of outstanding national currencies rapidly decreased by 86 percent between January 1 and February 28, 2002. The national currencies still outstanding at the end of each reporting period will remain part of the euro area monetary aggregates until at least year-end 2002. Euro area monetary aggregates are net of banknotes and coins held by monetary financial institutions (other depository corporations) in the euro area.

The euro banknotes are issued by the Eurosystem as a whole, comprising the ECB and the national central banks of the euro area countries. Banknotes are put into circulation by each NCB as demanded and are physically identical regardless of the issuing NCB. According to the accounting regime chosen by the Eurosystem, although the ECB does not put banknotes into circulation, a share of 8 percent of the total value of euro banknotes put into circulation is allocated to the balance sheet of the ECB each month. The balance of the remaining 92 percent is allocated among the NCBs on a monthly basis, whereby each NCB of the Eurosystem records on its balance sheet as "banknotes issued" a share proportional to its share in the ECB's capital. This allocation procedure is referred to as the capital share mechanism–CSM.

For each NCB, the difference between the value of the euro banknotes allocated according to the CSM and the value of euro banknotes it puts into circulation is classified as an "Intra-Eurosystem claim/liability related to banknote issue." Each NCB will have a single claim/liability vis-à-vis the Eurosystem, calculated monthly. Similarly, the ECB will always have an Intra-Eurosystem claim equal to its 8 percent share of banknotes issued.

On the country pages for the euro area countries, Intra-Eurosystem claims/liabilities related to banknote issue are classified by the IMF as part of monetary authorities' Claims on Banking Institutions (line 12e.u)/Liabilities to Banking Institutions (line 14c.u). Intra-Eurosystem claims/liabilities related to banknote issue are also recorded within the memo item Net Claims on Eurosystem (line 12e.s). In contrast, in the Monetary Authorities (Eurosystem) section on the euro area page, the Intra-Eurosystem claims/liabilities of the Eurosystem members are recorded as part of Other Items (Net) (line 17r), where they effectively net to zero.

Euro coins are issued by national authorities. The ECB approves the volume of coins to be issued by each country. All have a common design on the obverse and a national design on the reverse. All revenues associated with coin issuance are retained by national authorities without application to an accounting allocation mechanism such as is used for banknotes.

The euro also has been adopted officially by several small jurisdictions within Europe—Andorra, Monaco, San Marino, and the Vatican. It is also used as the principal currency in several areas that were formerly part of Yugoslavia.

TARGET

Effective with data beginning end-November 2000, changes in the operating procedures of the TARGET (Trans-European Automated Real-Time Gross Settlement Express Transfer) euro clearing system affect monetary authorities' Foreign Assets (line 11), Foreign Liabilities (line 16c), Claims on Banking Institutions (line 12e.u), and Liabilities to Banking Institutions (line 14c.u). (See Recording of TARGET System Positions in the following section.)

Monetary Authorities—Euro Area

In *IFS* country tables, the term monetary authorities refers to the national central bank and other institutional units that perform monetary authorities' functions and are included in the central bank subsector (currency boards, exchange stabilization funds, etc). For the euro area member countries, upon joining the union, the monetary authority consists of the NCB, as defined by its membership within the Eurosystem. At the Eurosystem level, monetary authority refers to the ECB and the NCBs of the euro area member countries, based on the actual date of membership.

For purposes of comparison with pre-euro area data, "of which" lines show positions with residents of the country.

Beginning in January 1999, Foreign Assets (line 11) and Foreign Liabilities (line 16c) include only positions with non-euro area countries. All positions with residents of other euro area countries, including the ECB, are classified as domestic positions in the data based on euro area residency.

Claims on General Government (line 12a.u) includes claims on the central government and other levels of government, including the social security system. It also includes claims on general government in other euro area countries.

Claims on Banking Institutions (NCBs and Other Monetary Financial Institutions or MFIs) (line 12e.u) and Liabilities to Banking Institutions (NCBs and Other MFIs) (line 14c.u) include all positions with NCBs and Other MFIs in all euro area countries. Before January 1999, positions with NCBs and Other MFIs in other euro area countries were in Foreign Assets and Foreign Liabilities. Other MFIs are monetary institutions other than the NCB and ECB. Other MFIs were previously called deposit money banks (DMBs) and other banking institutions (OBIs). Beginning in January 1999, other MFIs is defined to include money market funds.

Claims on Other Resident Sectors (line 12d) comprises claims on nonbank financial institutions, public nonfinancial corporations, and the private sector.

Net Claims on Eurosystem (line 12e.s) equals gross claims on, less gross liabilities to, the ECB and other NCBs within the Eurosystem. This item comprises euro-denominated claims equivalent to the transfer of foreign currency reserves to the ECB, Intra-Eurosystem claims/liabilities related to banknote issuance, net claims or liabilities within the TARGET clearing system (see description below), and

other positions such as contra-entries to the NCBs' holdings of assets acquired in conjunction with open-market or intervention operations. NCBs' issues of securities other than shares and money market paper held by other NCBs, which are not separately identifiable, are included in Liabilities to Banking Institutions (line 14c.u). Before January 1999, positions with the EMI or ECB and other euro area NCBs are included in Foreign Assets and Foreign Liabilities.

Currency Issued (line14a): Until 2002, this line covers national currency in circulation. Beginning in 2002, this series is redefined to include euro banknotes issued by each NCB, euro coins issued by each euro area country, and national currency not yet withdrawn. The amount of euro banknotes recorded as issued by each NCB is the legal allocation recorded on its balance sheet according to the accounting regime (CSM) described above in **Euro Banknotes and Coins.** That amount does not correspond to either the actual amount of euro banknotes put into circulation by the NCB or the actual circulation of euro banknotes within the domestic territory. The actual amount of euro banknotes put into circulation by the NCB is included within Memo: Currency Put into Circulation (line 14m). In addition, this item includes euro coin issued and the national currency not yet withdrawn.

Capital Accounts (line 17a) includes general provisions.

Recording of TARGET System Positions

Effective November 2000, external positions of members of the TARGET (Trans-European Automated Real-Time Gross Settlement Express Transfer) euro clearing system with each other are affected by changes in TARGET's operating procedures. Previously, from January 1999 to October 2000, TARGET positions are on a gross bilateral basis between all members, which results in large external asset and liability positions between the TARGET members. From November 2000 onward, multilateral netting by novation procedures results in each member recording only a single TARGET position vis-à-vis the ECB, which is generally a much smaller value than recorded under the previous arrangement.

This change affects Monetary Authorities' Foreign Assets (line 11) and Foreign Liabilities (line 16c) of all TARGET members. It also affects Monetary Authorities' Claims on Banking Institutions (line 12e.u) and Liabilities to Banking Institutions (line 14c.u) of the euro area TARGET members. The non-euro area TARGET members are not permitted to hold a net liability position against TARGET as a whole; therefore, after November 2000, they do not have any TARGET-related Foreign Liabilities.

Banking Institutions—Euro Area

For comparison with pre-euro area data, "of which" lines show positions with residents of the country.

Beginning in January 1999, this section covers the accounts of other MFIs (monetary financial institutions)—monetary institutions other than the NCB and ECB. Other MFIs were previously called deposit money banks (DMBs) and other banking institutions (OBIs). Beginning in January 1999, other MFIs is defined to include money market funds.

Claims on Monetary Authorities (line 20) comprises banking institutions' holdings of euro banknotes and coins, holdings of national currency, deposits with the NCB, and loans to the NCB.

Claims on Banking Institutions (including ECB) in Other Euro Area Countries (line 20b.u) and Liabilities to Banking Institutions (including ECB) in Other Euro Area Countries (line 26h.u) comprise all positions with the ECB, NCBs, and Other MFIs in other euro area countries. These positions are classified as domestic under the euro area residency criteria. Before January 1999, these accounts were classified under Foreign Assets and Foreign Liabilities. Claims include holdings of currencies issued in other euro area countries.

Beginning in January 1999, Foreign Assets (line 21) and Foreign Liabilities (line 26c) include only positions with non-euro area countries. All positions with residents of other euro area countries, including the ECB, are classified as domestic positions.

Claims on General Government (line 22a.u) includes claims on central government and other levels of government in all euro area countries.

Claims on Other Resident Sectors (line 22d.u) comprises claims on nonbank financial institutions, public nonfinancial corporations, and the private sectors in all euro area countries.

Demand Deposits (line 24.u) includes demand deposits in all currencies by other resident sectors in all euro area countries.

Other Deposits (line 25.u) includes deposits with fixed maturity, deposits redeemable at notice, securities repurchase agreements, and subordinated debt in the form of deposits by other resident sectors of all euro area countries. Before January 1999, subordinated debt was included in Other Items (Net) (line 27r).

Money Market Instruments (line 26m.u) includes money market fund shares and money market paper.

Bonds (Debt Securities) (line 26n.u) includes subordinated debt in the form of securities.

Credit from Monetary Authorities (line 26g) comprises banking institutions' borrowing from the NCBs.

Other Items (Net) (line 27r) includes holdings of shares issued by other MFIs.

Banking Survey (Based on National Residency)— Euro Area

This section consolidates the accounts of the monetary authorities and banking institutions based on national residency criteria.

Foreign Assets (Net) (line 31n) includes positions with nonresidents of the country. Positions with the ECB for all euro area countries are classified in Foreign Assets under the national residency criteria.

Claims on General Government (Net) (line 32an) includes claims on general government minus deposits of central government. Deposits of other levels of government are included in liabilities to other resident sectors.

Until 2002, Currency Issued (line 34a.n) covers national currency in circulation. Beginning in 2002, this series is redefined to include euro banknotes issued by each NCB, euro coins issued by each euro area country, and the amount of

national currency not yet withdrawn. Under the accounting regime used by the Eurosystem, the allocation of euro bank notes issued by each NCB is the legal allocation recorded on its balance sheet according to the accounting regime (CSM) described above in **Euro Banknotes and Coins.** The allocation does not correspond to either the actual amount of euro banknotes placed in circulation by the NCB or the actual circulation of banknotes within the domestic territory.

Other Items (Net) (line 37r) includes other MFIs' holdings of shares issued by other MFIs.

Banking Survey (Based on Euro Area-Wide Residency)

This section consolidates the accounts of the monetary authorities and banking institutions based on euro area-wide residency criteria.

Foreign Assets (Net) (line 31n.u) includes all positions with nonresidents of the euro area. Positions with residents of all euro area countries, including the ECB, are classified as domestic positions.

Claims on General Government (Net) (line 32anu) includes claims on central government and all other levels of government of all euro area countries minus deposits of central government of all euro area countries. Deposits of other levels of government are included in liabilities to other resident sectors.

Until 2002, Currency Issued (line 34a.u) covers national currency in circulation. Beginning in 2002, this series is redefined to include euro banknotes issued by each NCB, euro coins issued by each euro area country, and the amount of national currency not yet withdrawn. Under the accounting regime used by the Eurosystem, the allocation of euro banknotes issued by each NCB is the legal allocation recorded on its balance sheet according to the accounting regime (CSM) described above in **Euro Banknotes and Coins.** The allocation does not correspond to either the actual amount of euro banknotes placed in circulation by the NCB or the actual circulation of banknotes within the domestic territory.

Other Items (Net) (line 37r.u) includes other MFIs' holdings of shares issued by other MFIs.

6. Interest Rates

Data are presented in the Interest Rates section in the country tables and in the world tables on national and international interest rates.

Discount Rate/Bank Rate (line 60) is the rate at which the central banks lend or discount eligible paper for deposit money banks, typically shown on an end-of-period basis.

The Eurosystem Marginal Lending Facility Rate (line 60) is the rate at which other MFIs obtain overnight liquidity from NCBs, against eligible assets. The terms and conditions of the lending are identical throughout the euro area. The Eurosystem Refinancing Rate (line 60r) and Interbank Rate (Overnight) (line 60a) are also provided on the euro area table.

Money Market Rate (line 60b) is the rate on short-term lending between financial institutions. Interbank Rate (Three-Month) (line 60b) is shown on the euro area table.

Treasury Bill Rate (line 60c) is the rate at which short-term securities are issued or traded in the market.

Deposit Rate (line 60l) usually refers to rates offered to resident customers for demand, time, or savings deposits. Often, rates for time and savings deposits are classified according to maturity and amounts deposited. In addition, deposit money banks and similar deposit-taking institutions may offer short- and medium-term instruments at specified rates for specific amounts and maturities; these are frequently termed "certificates of deposit." For countries where savings deposits are important, a Savings Rate (line 60k) is also published.

Lending Rate (line 60p) is the bank rate that usually meets the short- and medium-term financing needs of the private sector. This rate is normally differentiated according to creditworthiness of borrowers and objectives of financing.

Government Bond Yield (line 61*) refers to one or more series representing yields to maturity of government bonds or other bonds that would indicate longer term rates.

Interest rates for foreign-currency-denominated instruments are also published for countries where such instruments are important.

Quarterly and annual interest rate data are arithmetic averages of monthly interest rates reported by the countries.

The country notes in the monthly issues carry a brief description of the nature and characteristics of the rates reported and of the financial instrument to which they relate.

A typical series from each of these groups is included in the world tables on national interest rates.

World Table on International Interest Rates

The world table on international interest rates reports London interbank offer rates on deposits denominated in SDRs, U.S. dollars, euros, French francs, deutsche mark, Japanese yen, and Swiss francs and Paris interbank offer rates on deposits denominated in pounds sterling. Monthly data are averages of daily rates. The table includes the premium or discount on three-month forward rates of currencies of the major industrial countries against the U.S. dollar.

This table also reports the SDR interest rate and the rate of remuneration. Monthly data are arithmetic averages of daily rates. Interest is paid on holdings of SDRs, and charges are levied on participants' cumulative allocations. Interest and charges accrue daily at the same rate and are settled quarterly in SDRs. As a result, participants who have SDR holdings above their net cumulative allocations receive net interest, and those with holdings below their net cumulative allocations pay net charges. Other official holders of SDRs—including the Fund's General Resources Account—receive interest on their holdings and pay no charges because they receive no allocations.

The Fund also pays quarterly remuneration to members on their creditor positions arising from the use of their currencies in Fund transactions and operations. This is determined by the positive difference between the remuneration norm and the average daily balances of the member's currency in the General Resources Account.

Effective August 1, 1983, the weekly SDR interest rate has been based on the combined market interest rate. That rate is calculated by applying to the specific amounts of the five currencies included in the SDR valuation basket, converted into SDR equivalents, the market rates on specified short-term money market instruments quoted in the five countries.

As of January 1, 1991, the interest rates used in this calculation are market yield for three-month U.S. treasury bills, three-month interbank deposit rate (line 60bs) in Germany, three-month rate for treasury bills (line 60cs) in France, three-month rate on certificates of deposit (line 60bs) in Japan, and market yield for three-month U.K. treasury bills (line 60cs). These series are shown in the table.

The combined market rate is calculated each Friday and enters into effect each Monday. The interest rate on the SDR is 100 percent of the combined market rate, rounded to two nearest decimal places. The rate of remuneration, effective February 2, 1987, is 100 percent of the rate of interest on the SDR.

7. Prices, Production, and Labor

This section (lines 62 through 67) covers domestic prices, production, and labor market indicators. A more detailed discussion of major price indicators is provided in the *IFS Supplement on Price Statistics*, No. 12 (1986).

The index series are compiled from reported versions of national indices and, for some production and labor series, from absolute data.

There is a wide variation between countries and over time in the selection of base years, depending upon the availability of comprehensive benchmark data that permit an adequate review of weighting patterns. The series are linked by using ratio splicing at the first annual overlap, and the linked series are shifted to a common base period 1995=100.

For industrial production, the data are seasonally adjusted if an appropriate adjusted series is available. Seasonally adjusted series are indicated in the descriptor and also described in the country notes in the monthly issues.

Share Prices

Indices shown for Share Prices (line 62) generally relate to common shares of companies traded on national or foreign stock exchanges. Monthly indices are obtained as simple arithmetic averages of the daily or weekly indices, although in some cases mid-month or end-of-month quotations are included.

All reported indices are adjusted for changes in quoted nominal capital of companies. Indices are, in general, base-weighted arithmetic averages with market value of outstanding shares as weights.

Producer Price Index or Wholesale Price Index

Indices shown for Producer or Wholesale Prices (line 63) are designed to monitor changes in prices of items at the first important commercial transaction. Where a choice is available, preference is given to the Producer Price Index (PPI), because the concept, weighting pattern, and coverage are likely to be more consistent with national accounts and industrial production statistics. In principle, the PPI should include service industries, but in practice it is limited to the domestic agricultural and industrial sectors. The prices should be farm-gate prices for the agricultural sector and ex-factory prices for the industrial sector.

The Wholesale Price Index (WPI), when used, covers a mixture of prices of agricultural and industrial goods at various stages of production and distribution, inclusive of imports and import duties. Preference is given to indices that provide broad coverage of the economy. The indices are computed using the Laspeyres formula, unless otherwise indicated in the country notes in the monthly issues.

Subindices are occasionally included for the PPI or the WPI.

Consumer Price Index

Indices shown for Consumer Prices (line 64) are the most frequently used indicators of inflation and reflect changes in the cost of acquiring a fixed basket of goods and services by the average consumer. Preference is given to series having wider geographical coverage and relating to all income groups, provided they are no less current than more narrowly defined series.

Because the weights are usually derived from household expenditure surveys (which may be conducted infrequently), information on the year to which the weights refer is provided in the country table notes in the monthly issues. The notes also provide information on any limitations in the coverage of commodities for pricing, income groups, or their expenditures in the chosen index. The Laspeyres formula is used unless otherwise indicated in the country notes.

For the European Union (EU) countries, a harmonized index of consumer prices (HICP) (line 64h) is shown. It is compiled according to methodological and sampling standards set by the European Commission. Owing to institutional differences among the EU member countries, the HICP excludes expenditure on certain types of goods and services. Examples are medical care and services of owner-occupied dwellings.

Wage Rates or Earnings

Indices shown for Wages Rates or Earnings (line 65) represent wage rates or earnings per worker employed per specified time period. Where establishment surveys are the source, the indices are likely to have the same coverage as the Industrial Production Index (line 66) and the Industrial Employment Index (line 67). Preference is given to data for earnings that include payments in kind and family allowances and that cover salaried employees as well as wage earners. The indices either are computed from absolute wage data or are as reported directly to the Fund.

Industrial Production

Indices shown for Industrial Production (line 66) are included as indicators of current economic activity. For some countries the indices are supplemented by indicators (such as data on tourism) relevant to a particular country.

Generally, the coverage of industrial production indices comprises mining and quarrying, manufacturing and electricity, and gas and water, according to the UN International Standard Industrial Classification (ISIC). The indices are generally compiled using the Laspeyres formula.

For many developing countries the indices refer to the production of a major primary commodity, such as crude petroleum (see commodity codes on page viii of the printed copies of *IFS*).

Labor

Labor market indicators refer to the levels of the Labor Force (line 67d), Employment (line 67e), Unemployment (line 67c), and the Unemployment Rate (line 67r). Data on labor market statistics cover the economically active civilian population. They are provided by the International Labor Organization (ILO), which publishes these data in its *Yearbook of Labour Statistics* and its quarterly *Bulletin of Labour Statistics* and supplements. The concept of employment and unemployment conforms to the recommendations adopted by the ILO: Thirteenth International Conference of Labor Statisticians, Geneva, 1992. In addition, indices of employment in the industrial sector (line 67) are provided for 49 countries. For the euro area, EUROSTAT provides the data.

8. International Transactions

Summary statistics on the international transactions of a country are given in lines 70 through 79. A section on external trade statistics (lines 70 through 76) provides data on the values (lines 70 and 71), volumes (lines 72 and 73), unit values (lines 74 and 75), and prices (line 76) for exports and imports. A section follows on balance of payments statistics (lines 78 through 79).

External Trade

Merchandise Exports f.o.b. (line 70) and Imports c.i.f. (line 71) are, in general, customs statistics reported under the general trade system, in accordance with the recommendations of the UN International Merchandise Trade Statistics: Concepts and Definitions, 1998. For some countries, data relate to the special trade system. The difference between general and special trade lies mainly in the treatment of the recording of the movement of goods through customs-bonded storage areas (warehouses, free areas, etc.).

Many countries use customs data on exports and imports as the primary source for the recording of exports and imports of goods in the balance of payments. However, customs data and the entries for goods in the balance of payments may not be equal, owing to differences in definition. These differences may relate to the following:

- the coverage of transactions (e.g., the goods item in the balance of payments often includes adjustments for certain goods transactions that may not be recorded by customs authorities, e.g., parcel post),

- the time of recording of transactions (e.g., in the balance of payments, transactions are to be recorded when change of ownership occurs, rather than the moment goods cross the customs border, which generally determines when goods are recorded in customs based trade statistics), and

- some classification differences (e.g., in the balance of payments, repair on goods is part of goods transactions).

The data for Merchandise Imports f.o.b. (line 71.v) are obtained directly from statistical authorities.

Details of commodity exports are presented for commodities that are traded in the international markets and have an impact on world market prices.

Data for petroleum exports are presented only for 12 oil exporting countries. For a number of these countries, data estimated by Fund staff are derived from available data for the volume of production. They are also derived from estimates for prices that are, in part, taken from *Petroleum Intelligence Weekly* and other international sources. The country table notes in the monthly issues provide details of these estimates.

For a number of countries where data are uncurrent or unavailable, additional lines show data, converted from U.S. dollars to national currency, from the Fund's *Direction of Trade Statistics* quarterly publication (*DOTS*). Exports and imports data published in *DOTS* include reported data, updated where necessary with estimates for the current periods. The introduction of *DOTS* gives a description of the nature of the estimates.

Indices for Volume of Exports (line 72) and Volume of Imports (line 73) are either Laspeyres or Paasche. For nine countries, as indicated in the country notes in the monthly issues, export volume indices are calculated from reported volume data for individual commodities weighted by reported values.

Indices for Unit Value of Exports (line 74) and Unit Value of Imports (line 75) are Laspeyres, with weights derived from the data for transactions. For about seven countries, also as indicated in the country notes in the monthly issues, export unit values are calculated from reported value and volume data for individual commodities.

Indices for export and import prices are compiled from survey data for wholesale prices or directly from the exporter or importer (called "direct pricing"). They are shown in line 76, where available. In the absence of national sources, data for wholesale prices are taken from world commodity markets and are converted into national currency at period average exchange rates. Indices based on direct pricing are generally considered preferable to unit value indices, because problems of unit value bias are reduced.

A more detailed presentation of trade statistics is presented in the *IFS Supplement on Trade Statistics*, No. 15 (1988).

Balance of Payments Statistics

The balance of payments lines are presented on the basis of the methodology and presentation of the fifth edition of the *Balance of Payments Manual (BPM5)*. Published by the IMF in 1993, the *BPM5* was supplemented and amended by the *Financial Derivatives, a Supplement to the Fifth Edition (1993) of the Balance of Payments Manual*, published in 2000. Before 1995, issues of the *IFS Yearbook* presented balance of payments data based on the fourth edition of the manual (*BPM4*).

Lines for Balance of Payments Statistics

In *IFS*, balance of payments data are shown in an analytical presentation (i.e., the components are classified into five major data categories, which the Fund regards as useful for analyzing balance of payments developments in a uniform manner). In the analytic presentation, the components are arrayed to highlight the financing items (the reserves and related items). The standard presentation, as described in the *BPM5*, provides structural framework within which balance of payments statistics are compiled. Both analytic and standard presentations are published in the *Balance of Payments Statistics Yearbook*.

Current Account, n.i.e. (line 78ald) is the sum of the balance on goods, services and income (line 78aid), plus current transfers, n.i.e.: credit (line 78ajd), plus current transfers: debit (line 78akd) (i.e., line 78aid, plus line 78ajd, plus line 78akd).

Goods: Exports f.o.b. (line 78aad) and Goods: Imports f.o.b. (line 78abd) are both measured on the "free-on-board" (f.o.b.) basis—that is, by the value of the goods at the border of the exporting economy. For imports, this excludes the cost of freight and insurance incurred beyond the border of the exporting economy. The goods item covers general merchandise, goods for processing, repairs on goods, goods procured in ports by carriers, and nonmonetary gold.

Trade Balance (line 78acd) is the balance of exports f.o.b. and imports f.o.b. (line 78aad plus line 78abd). A positive trade balance shows that merchandise exports are larger than merchandise imports, whereas a negative trade balance shows that merchandise imports are larger than merchandise exports.

Services: Credit (line 78add) and Services: Debit (line 78aed) comprise services in transportation, travel, communication, construction, insurance, finance, computer and information, royalties and license fees, other business, personal, cultural and recreational, and government, n.i.e.

Balance on Goods and Services (line 78afd) is the sum of the balance on goods (line 78acd), plus services: credit (line 78add), plus services: debit (line 78aed) (i.e., line 78acd, plus line 78add, plus line 78aed).

Income: Credit (line 78agd) and Income: Debit (line 78ahd) comprise (1) investment income (consisting of direct investment income, portfolio investment income, and other investment income), and (2) compensation of employees.

Balance on Gds., Serv., & Inc. (i.e., Balance on Goods, Services, and Income) (line 78aid) is the sum of the balance on goods and services (line 78afd), plus income: credit (line 78agd), plus income: debit (line 78ahd) (i.e., line 78afd, plus line 78agd, plus line 78ahd).

Current Transfers, n.i.e.: Credit (line 78ajd) comprise all current transfers received by the reporting economy, except those made to the economy to finance its "overall balance" (see line 78cbd description below); therefore, the label "n.i.e." The latter are included in Exceptional Financing (line 79ded) (see below). (Note: Some of the capital and financial account lines shown below are also labeled "n.i.e." This means that Exceptional Financing items have been excluded from specific capital and financial account components.) Current transfers comprise (1) general government transfers and (2) other sector transfers, including workers' remittances.

Current Transfers: Debit (line 78akd) comprise all current transfers paid by the reporting economy.

Capital Account, n.i.e. (line 78bcd) is the balance on the capital account (capital account, n.i.e.: credit, plus capital account: debit). Capital account, n.i.e.: credit (line 78bad) covers (1) transfers linked to the acquisition of a fixed asset and (2) the disposal of nonproduced, nonfinancial assets. It does not include debt forgiveness, which is classified under Exceptional Financing. Capital account: debit (line 78bbd) covers (1) transfers linked to the disposal of fixed assets, and (2) acquisition of nonproduced, nonfinancial assets.

Financial Account, n.i.e. (line 78bjd) is the net sum of direct investment (line 78bdd plus line 78bed), portfolio investment (line 78bfd plus line 78bgd), financial derivatives (line 78bwd plus line 78bxd), and other investment (line 78bhd plus line 78bid).

Direct Investment Abroad (line 78bdd) and Direct Investment in Rep. Econ., n.i.e. (Direct Investment in the Reporting Economy, n.i.e.) (line 78bed) represent the flows of direct investment capital out of the reporting economy and those into the reporting economy, respectively. Direct investment includes equity capital, reinvested earnings, other capital, and financial derivatives associated with various intercompany transactions between affiliated enterprises. Excluded are flows of direct investment capital into the reporting economy for exceptional financing, such as debt-for-equity swaps. Direct investment abroad is usually shown with a negative figure, reflecting an increase in net outward investment by residents, with a corresponding net payment outflow from the reporting economy. Direct investment in the reporting economy is generally shown with a positive figure, reflecting an increase in net inward investment by nonresidents, with a corresponding net payment inflow into the reporting economy.

Portfolio Investment Assets (line 78bfd) and Portfolio Investment Liab., n.i.e. (Portfolio Investment Liabilities) (line 78bgd) include transactions with nonresidents in financial securities of any maturity (such as corporate securities, bonds, notes, and money market instruments) other than those included in direct investment, exceptional financing, and reserve assets.

Equity Securities Assets (line 78bkd) and Equity Securities Liabilities (line 78bmd) include shares, stocks, participation, and similar documents (such as American depository receipts) that usually denote ownership of equity.

Debt Securities Assets (line 78bld) and Debt Securities Liabilities (line 78bnd) cover (1) bonds, debentures, notes, etc., and (2) money market or negotiable debt instruments.

Financial Derivatives Assets (line 78bwd) and Financial Derivatives Liabilities (line 78bxd) cover financial instruments that are linked to other specific financial instruments, indicators, or commodities, and through which specific financial risks (such as interest rate risk, foreign exchange risk, equity and commodity price risks, credit risk, etc.) can, in their own right, be traded in financial markets. The *IFS* presents gross asset and liability information. However, owing to the unique nature of financial derivatives, and the manner in which some institutions record transactions, some countries can provide only net transactions data. While such net data could be included under assets, in the *IFS* it has been decided to include these net transactions, and net positions when reported, under liabilities, because one common source of demand for these instruments is from entities that are hedging cash flows associated with debt liabilities.

Other Investment Assets (line 78bhd) and Other Investment Liabilities, n.i.e. (line 78bid) include all financial transactions not covered in direct investment, portfolio investment, financial derivatives, or reserve assets. Major categories are transactions in currency and deposits, loans, and trade credits.

Net Errors and Omissions (line 78cad) is a residual category needed to ensure that all debit and credit entries in the balance of payments statement sum to zero. It reflects statistical inconsistencies in the recording of the credit and debit entries. In the *IFS* presentation, net errors and omissions is equal to, and opposite in sign to, the total value of the following items: the current account balance (line 78ald), the capital account balance (line 78bcd), the financial account balance (line 78bjd), and reserves and reserve related items (line 79dad). The item is intended as an offset to the overstatement or understatement of the recorded components. Thus, if the balance of those components is a credit, the item for net errors and omissions will be shown as a debit of equal value, and vice versa.

Overall Balance (line 78cbd) is the sum of the balances on the current account (line 78ald), the capital account (line 78bcd), the financial account (line 78bjd), and net errors and omissions (line 78cad) (i.e., line 78ald, plus line 78bcd, plus line 78bjd, plus line 78cad).

Reserves and Related Items (line 79dad) is the sum of transactions in reserve assets (line79dbd), exceptional financing (line 79ded), and use of Fund credit and loans (line 78dcd) (i.e., line 79dbd, plus line 79ded, plus line 79dcd).

Reserve Assets (line 79dbd) consists of external assets readily available to and controlled by monetary authorities primarily for direct financing of payments imbalances and for indirect regulating of the magnitude of such imbalances through exchange market intervention. Reserve assets comprise monetary gold, special drawing rights, reserve position in the Fund, foreign exchange assets (consisting of currency and deposits and securities), and other claims.

Use of Fund Credit and Loans (line 79dcd) includes purchases and repurchases in the credit tranches of the Fund's General Resource Account, and net borrowings under the Structural Adjustment Facility (SAF), the Poverty Reduction and Growth Facility (PRGF), which was previously named the Enhanced Structural Adjustment Facility (ESAF), and the Trust Fund.

Exceptional Financing (line 79ded) includes any other transactions undertaken by the authorities to finance the "overall balance," as an alternative to, or in conjunction with, the use of reserve assets and the use of Fund credit and loans from the Fund.

A more detailed presentation of balance of payments data for use in cross-country comparisons is published in the *Balance of Payments Statistics Yearbook.*

Lines for International Investment Position

The international investment position (IIP) data are presented in lines 79aad through 79ljd. An economy's IIP is a balance sheet of the stock of external financial assets and liabilities. The coverage of the various components of IIP is similar to that of the corresponding components under the balance of payments. The IIP at the end of a specific period reflects not only the sum of balance of payments transactions over time, but also price changes, exchange rate changes, and other adjustments.

9. Government Finance

Section 80 presents summary statistics on government finance. The summary statistics cover operations of the budgetary central government or of the consolidated central government (i.e., operations of budgetary central government, extrabudgetary units, and social security funds). The coverage of consolidated central government may not necessarily include all existing extrabudgetary units and/or social security funds.

Unless otherwise stated in individual country notes in the monthly issues, data are as reported for *IFS.* In some cases, data are derived from unpublished worksheets and are therefore not attributed to a specific source.

Quarterly and monthly data, when available, may not add up to the annual data, owing to differences in coverage and/or methodology. The country notes in the monthly issues will indicate these differences.

More extensive data for use in cross-country comparisons are published in the *Government Finance Statistics Yearbook (GFSY)* and are based on *A Manual on Government Finance Statistics.* When countries do not report data for *IFS* but provide data for the *GFSY,* these data are published in *IFS.*

The data for lines 80 through 87 are flows and are on a cash basis, as follows:

The Deficit or Surplus (line 80) is calculated as the difference between Revenue and, if applicable, Grants Received (lines 81 and 81z) on the one hand and Expenditure and Lending Minus Repayments (lines 82 and 83) on the other. The deficit/surplus is also equal, with the opposite sign, to the sum of the net borrowing by the government plus the net decrease in government cash, deposits, and securities held for liquidity purposes.

Revenue (line 81) comprises all nonrepayable government receipts, whether requited or unrequited, other than grants; revenue is shown net of refunds and other adjustment transactions.

Grants Received (line 81z) comprises all unrequited, nonrepayable, noncompulsory receipts from other governments—domestic or foreign—and international institutions. Grants are grouped with revenue because, like revenue, they provide the means whereby expenditure can be made without incurring a debt for future repayment.

Expenditure (line 82) comprises all nonrepayable payments by government, whether requited or unrequited and whether for current or capital purposes.

Lending Minus Repayments (line 83) comprises government acquisition of claims on others—both loans and equities—for public policy purposes and is net of repayments of lending and sales of equities previously purchased. Line 83 includes both domestic and foreign lending minus repayments. In determining the deficit or surplus, lending minus repayments is grouped with expenditure, because it is presumed to represent a means of pursuing government policy objectives and not to be an action undertaken to manage government liquidity.

The total of the financing items equals the deficit or surplus with a reverse sign. Total Financing is classified according to the residence of the lender. Where this information is not available, the distinction is based on the currency in which the debt instruments are denominated.

For some countries, Total Financing is broken down between Net Borrowing and Use of Cash Balances. Net Borrowing covers the net change in government liabilities to all other sectors. It represents mainly other sectors' direct loans or advances to government or their holding of government securities acquired from the government itself or in transactions with others. Where possible, data for Domestic and Foreign Net Borrowing are classified according to the residence of the lender.

Use of Cash Balances (line 87) is intended to measure changes over a period—resulting from transactions but not revaluations—in government holdings of currency and deposits with the monetary system. It corresponds to changes in *IFS* lines 16d and 26d. All currency issues are regarded as liabilities of the monetary authorities, rather than government debt. And any proceeds reaching the government are regarded as coming from the monetary authorities.

Data for outstanding Debt (lines 88 and 89) relate to the direct and assumed debt of the central government and exclude loans guaranteed by the government. The distinction between Domestic and Foreign Debt (lines 88a and 89a) is based on residence of the lender, where possible, but otherwise on the currency in which the debt instruments are denominated (lines 88b and 89b).

The euro area table and the tables of the individual euro area countries also present Deficit or Surplus (line 80g) and Debt (line 88g) data for the general government, expressed as percent of harmonized Gross Domestic Product. Both indicators are defined according to the convergence criteria on public finance as laid down in the Maastricht Treaty. Deficit or Surplus corresponds to net lending/borrowing. The data are not comparable with central government Deficit or Surplus (line 80) and Debt (line 88), owing to differences in coverage as well as in definition.

10. National Accounts and Population

The summary data for national accounts are compiled according to the *System of National Accounts (SNA)*. Gross Domestic Product (GDP) is presented in *IFS* as the sum of final expenditures, following the presentation of the *1993 SNA*, as well as the *European System of Accounts (1995 ESA)*.

The national accounts lines shown in the country tables are as follows:

Household Consumption Expenditure, including Non-profit Institutions Serving Households (NPISHs) (line 96f), Government Consumption Expenditure (line 91f), Gross Fixed Capital Formation (line 93e), Changes in Inventories (line 93i) (formerly Increase/Decrease(-) in Stocks), Exports of Goods and Services (line 90c), and Imports of Goods and Services (line 98c).

Gross National Income (GNI) (line 99a) is derived by adding Net Primary Income from Abroad (line 98.n) to GDP. Gross National Disposable Income (GNDI) (line 99i) is derived by adding Net Current Transfers from Abroad (line 98t) to GNI, and Gross Saving (line 99s) is derived by deducting final consumption expenditure (lines 96f + 91f) from GNDI. Consumption of Fixed Capital (line 99cf) is shown for countries that provide these data.

The country table notes in the monthly issues provide information on which countries have implemented the *1993 SNA* or the *1995 ESA*.

The national accounts lines generally do not explicitly show the statistical discrepancies between aggregate GDP compiled from expenditure flows as against GDP compiled from the production or income accounts (or from a mixture of these accounts). Hence, in some cases, the components of GDP that are shown in *IFS* may not add up exactly to the total.

For countries that publish quarterly seasonally adjusted data, the data in *IFS* in the monthly issues are also on a seasonally adjusted basis (codes ending with c or r). For the United States, Japan, Australia, South Africa, Argentina, and Mexico, quarterly data are shown at annual rates, which the country authorities provide as such.

Lines 99b.p and 99b.r are measures of GDP volume at reference year value levels. In the past, these series used a common reference year (e.g., 1990) for publication. With the June 1999 issue, these series are published on the same reference year(s) as reported by the national compilers. The code *p* indicates data that are not seasonally adjusted, whereas code *r* indicates data that are seasonally adjusted.

Lines 99bvp and 99bvr are GDP volume indices that are presented on a standard 1995 reference year and are derived from the GDP volume series reported by national compilers. For this calculation the data series provided by national compilers are linked together (if there is more than one series) to form a single time series. The earliest overlapping year from the different reference year series is used to calculate the link factors.

The GDP Deflator (lines 99bip or 99bir) series shown in the *IFS Yearbook* are not direct measurements of prices but are derived implicitly: the GDP series at current prices is divided by constant price GDP series referenced to 1995. The latter series is constructed by multiplying the 1995 current price GDP level by the GDP volume index (1995=100). The deflator is expressed in index form with 1995=100.

The UN provides the data on Population (line 99z). These data represent midyear estimates and are also published in the UN's *Monthly Bulletin of Statistics*.

11. World Tables

Besides the world tables on exchange rates, members' Fund positions and transactions, international reserves, and interest rates—discussed earlier in this introduction—*IFS* also brings together country data on money, consumer prices, values and unit values of countries' exports and imports, and wholesale prices and unit values (expressed in U.S. dollars) of principal world trade commodities. Tables on balance of payments may be found in the *IFS* yearbook and also in the *Balance of Payments Statistics Yearbook, Part 2*.

Tables showing totals or averages of country series may report data for selected countries only. A full listing of countries whose data are included in the calculation of area and world measures is given on page viii in the monthly issues.

Country Groups

Countries whose data are included in **world/all countries'** totals and averages are arrayed into two main groups—industrial countries and developing countries. The **industrial** countries' group also shows separate data for the euro area. The **developing** countries group is further subdivided into area subgroups for Africa, Asia, Europe, the Middle East, and the Western Hemisphere.

The country composition of the world is all countries for which the topic series are available in the *IFS* files. Consequently, the country coverage of some areas, mainly Africa and Asia, differs from topic to topic, and area and world totals or averages may be biased to some extent toward the larger reporting countries.

Data for subgroups oil exporting countries and non-oil developing countries are shown as memorandum items. Oil exporting countries are defined as those countries whose oil exports (net of any imports of crude oil) both represent a minimum of two thirds of their total exports and are at least equivalent to approximately 1 percent of world exports of oil. The calculations presently used to determine which countries meet the above criteria are based on 1976–78 averages.

Area and World Indices

Area and world indices are obtained as weighted averages of country indices. For the area and world indices on unit values of exports and imports—where the country indices are expressed in U.S. dollars—arithmetic means are used. For consumer prices and industrial production, geometric means are used because, unlike arithmetic means, geometric means are not unduly influenced by data for the few countries with extreme growth rates. Geometric means assure that, if all series have constant although different rates of increase, their average will have a constant rate of increase.

The weights are as follows: For the area averages for consumer prices, the country series are weighted by the 1995 purchasing power parity (PPP) value of GDP. (A comparison of PPP-based GDP weights and exchange rate-based GDP weights is presented in *World Economic Outlook*, May 1993, Annex IV.) For the industrial production table, the country series are weighted by value added in industry, as derived from individual countries' national accounts, expressed in U.S. dollars. And for the export unit values and import unit values tables, the country series are weighted by the 1995 value of exports and imports (both in U.S. dollars), respectively.

Weights are normally updated at about five-year intervals—following international practice—to reflect changes in the importance of each country's data with the data of all other countries. The standard weight base years used are 1953, 1958, 1963, 1970, 1975, 1980, 1984–86, 1990, and 1995. The corresponding time spans to which the weights are applied are 1948–55, 1955–60, 1960–68, 1968–73, 1973–78, 1978–83, 1983–88, 1988–93, and 1994 onward.

Separate averages are calculated for each time span, and the index series are linked by the splicing at overlap years and shifted to the reference base 1995=100.

Calculation of Area Totals and Averages

The calculation of area totals and averages in the world tables takes account of the problem that data for some countries do not run through the end of the period for which world and area data should be calculable. If country data are known that contribute at least 60 percent of the area total or index aggregate during recent periods for which data of all countries of an area are available, then area totals and averages for most topics are estimated for current and for earlier periods.

Area totals or averages are estimated by assuming that the rate of change in the unreported country data is the same as the rate of change in the weighted total or average of the reported country data for that area. These estimates are made for the area totals and averages only; separate country estimates are not calculated.

Except for import unit values, the world totals and averages are made from the calculated and estimated data for the two main groups—industrial countries and developing countries. A world total or average will only be calculated when totals or averages are available for both these country groups.

For import unit values, world data are calculated directly from country data. This is because the number of countries for which the series are available and current is insufficient to allow calculation or estimation of the area averages and because the variability of import unit value indices among countries is judged to be less than that for other topics. World estimates are made when data are available for countries whose combined weights represent at least 80 percent of the total country weights.

For the terms of trade index numbers in the yearbook, the world and area data for export unit values are divided by the corresponding series for import unit values, where possible. Thus terms of trade averages are available only for areas with both export and import unit values. The country coverage within the areas for the export and import unit values is not identical, leading to a small degree of asymmetry in the terms of trade calculation.

Calculation of Individual World Tables

International Reserves: Country series on international reserves begin generally with their appropriate dates and are complete monthly time series; therefore, earlier period estimates are not required. When current data of a few countries of an area are not reported, the area total is estimated by carrying forward the last reported country figure.

Money (and Reserve Money and Money plus Quasi-Money, which are available in the yearbook): Percent changes are based on end-of-year data (over a 12-month period for Money). When there is more than one version or definition of money over time, different time series are chained through a ratio splicing technique. When actual stock data needed for the growth rate calculation are missing, no percent change is shown in the world table.

Ratio of Reserve Money to Money plus Quasi-Money (available in the yearbook): The measures of money used in calculating this ratio are end-of-year data.

Income Velocity of Money plus Quasi-Money: The measure of income in this table is *IFS* data on GDP. The data for money plus quasi-money are annual averages of the highest frequency data available. The ratio is then converted into an index number with a base year of 1995.

Real Effective Exchange Rate Indices: This table shows three real effective exchange rate indices for industrial countries. Two of these comprise alternative measures of costs and prices derived from Relative Unit Labor Costs (line 65um) and Relative Normalized Unit Labor Costs (line reu). They have been applied to the weighting scheme, based on aggregated data for trade in manufactured goods, averaged over the period 1989–91. The weights reflect both the relative importance of a country's trading partners in its direct bilateral trade relations and that resulting from competition in third markets. The measure is expressed as an index 1995=100 in accord with all indices published in *IFS*.

One of the two indices—the index Based on Relative Normalized Unit Labor Costs (line reu)—is also shown in the country tables (except for Ireland), with the Nominal Effective Exchange Rate Index (line neu) from which the measures are drawn.

The third real effective exchange rate index—Based on Relative Consumer Prices (line rec)—is provided as a measure of domestic cost and price developments. It covers trade in manufactured goods and primary products for trading partners—and competitors. It uses the same methodology used to compile nominal and real effective exchange rates for nonindustrial countries, as discussed in the exchange rate and exchange rate arrangements section of this introduction.

Beginning with the October 1992 issue of *IFS*, the data published are from a revised database. The database underwent a comprehensive review and update of the underlying data sources and a change in the method of normalization of output per hour. The method uses the Hodrick-Prescott filter, which smoothes a time series by removing short-run fluctuations while retaining changes of a larger amplitude.

The footnotes to this world table in the monthly issues discuss the data sources used to derive the cost and price indicators for the real effective exchange rates.

Producer/Wholesale Prices (world table available in the yearbook): Data are those prices reported in lines 63* in the country tables. The percent changes are calculated from the index number series.

Consumer Prices: Data are those prices reported in lines 64* in the country tables. The percent changes are calculated from the index number series.

Industrial Production: This table presents seasonally adjusted indices on industrial production for 22 industrial countries, together with an aggregate index for the group. The data are those shown in the country tables as either Industrial Production (lines 66..*) or Manufacturing Production (lines 66ey*), the asterisk representing a wildcard.

Wages (world table available in the yearbook): This table presents indices computed either from absolute wage data or from the wage indices reported to the Fund for the industrial sector for 22 industrial countries. The data are those shown in the country tables as Wage Rates or Earnings (line 65).

Employment (world table available in the yearbook): This table presents indices computed from indices of employment or number of persons employed as reported by the countries for the industrial sector for 20 industrial countries. The data are those shown in the country tables as Employment (lines 67 or 67ey).

Exports and *Imports:* Data are published in U.S. dollars, as reported, if available, by the countries. Otherwise, monthly data in national currency, published in the country tables (lines 70... and 71...), are converted to U.S. dollars using the exchange rate rf. For quarterly and annual data, conversions are made using the trade-weighted average of the monthly exchange rates.

Export Unit Values/Export Prices and *Import Unit Values/Import Prices:* Data are the index numbers reported in the country tables expressed in U.S. dollars at rate **rf.** The country indices are typically unit value data (lines 74 and 75). However, for some countries, they are components of wholesale price indices or are derived from specific price quotations (lines 76, 76.x, and 76aa). The exceptions are coded "w" in the tabulation of country coverage on page viii of the printed copies of *IFS*.

Terms of Trade (world table available in the yearbook): Data are index numbers computed from the export and import unit value indices and shown in the appropriate world table. The percent changes are calculated from the index number series.

Balance of Payments (world tables available in the yearbook): For a precise definition of the concepts used in these tables, the reader is referred to the section in this introduction on international transactions. The concepts and definitions are further described in the fifth edition of the *Balance of Payments Manual*, as supplemented and amended by *Financial Derivatives, a Supplement to the Fifth Edition of the Balance of Payments Manual.*

Trade Balance is the series reported in line 78acd of the country tables. Current Account Balance, Excluding Exceptional Financing is the series reported in line 78ald of the country tables. Capital and Financial Account, Including Net Errors and Omissions but Excluding Reserve Assets, Use of Fund Credit, and Exceptional Financing are the sum of the series reported in lines 78bcd, 78bjd, and 78cad of the country tables. Overall Balance Excluding Reserve Assets, Use of Fund Credit, and Exceptional Financing is the series reported in line 78cbd (calculated as the sum of lines 78ald, 78bcd, 78bjd, and 78cad) of the country tables.

GDP Volume Measures (world table available in the yearbook): Data are derived from those series reported in lines 99bvp and 99bvr in the country tables. The percent changes are calculated from index numbers.

GDP Deflator (world table available in the yearbook): Data are derived from those series reported in lines 99bip in the country tables. The percent changes are calculated from index numbers.

Gross Capital Formation as Percentage of GDP (world table available in the yearbook): Data are the percent share of gross capital formation in GDP at current market prices. Gross capital formation comprises Gross Fixed Capital Formation and Increase/Decrease (-) in Stocks (lines 93e and 93i, respectively).

Final Consumption Expenditure as a Percentage of GDP (world table available in the yearbook): Data are the percent share of final consumption expenditure in GDP at current market prices, which comprises Government Consumption and Private Consumption (91f and 96f, respectively).

Commodity Prices: Data are obtained primarily from the Commodities and Special Issues Division of the IMF's Research Department, from *Commodity Price Data* of the World Bank, from *Monthly Commodity Price Bulletin* of the UNCTAD, and from a number of countries that produce commodities that are significantly traded in the international markets. Data derived from the last source are reported in the country tables. The market price series (lines 76) are expressed as U.S. dollars per quantity units and refer to values often used in the respective commodity markets. For comparison purposes, indices of unit values (lines 74) at base 1995=100 are provided. The accompanying notes to the table (located in the back of the printed copies) provide information specific to each commodity series, including data sources, grades, and quotation frequency.

12. Country Codes and IFS Line Numbers

Each *IFS* time series carries a unique identification code. For publication purposes, the code has been truncated to a three-digit country code and to a five-digit subject code, referred to as the *IFS* line number.

Country (and area) codes are listed on page viii of the monthly book and yearbook. They appear also as part of the descriptor stub on most of the world tables.

Line numbers apply uniformly across countries—that is, a given line number measures the same economic variable for each country, subject to data availability. The line numbers take the form of two numerics followed by three alphabetic codes (NNaaa). The two numerics are the section and subsection codes, the first two alphabetic codes are the classification codes, and the last alphabetic code is the qualification code. Any of these positions may be blank: for publication purposes, blanks in the first or final positions are omitted, whereas embedded blanks are represented by a period. The line numbers are part of the descriptor stub in the country tables.

Production data (lines 66), export data (lines 70, 72, 74, and 76), and import data (lines 71) for petroleum carry the commodity codes (listed on page viii of printed copies of *IFS*) in the alpha positions of the subject code.

Data expressed in units of money (values or prices) are ordinarily expressed in national currency and in natural form, that is, without seasonal adjustment. For these data the qualification code is blank.

Transformation of these data is denoted by various qualification codes. For data that are not seasonally adjusted, qualification codes are *d* for U.S. dollar values, *s* for SDR values, and *p* for constant national currency values. For data that are seasonally adjusted for *IFS*, codes are *f* for U.S. dollar values, *u* for SDR values, and *b* for national currency values. For data that are seasonally adjusted by national compilers, codes are *c* for national currency values and *r* for constant national currency values.

The qualification codes are also used to distinguish separate groups of deposit money banks or other financial institutions when data for separate groups are given.

13. Symbols, Conventions, and Abbreviations

The abbreviation "ff.," often used on the title page of the printed copies of *IFS*, means "following."

Entries printed in bold italics on the country pages of the monthly book refer to updates and revisions made since the publication of the preceding issue of *IFS*.

Italic midheadings in the middle of the pages of the monthly book and yearbook identify the units in which data are expressed and whether data are stocks (end of period), flows (transactions during a period), or averages (for a period).

(—) Indicates that a figure is zero or less than half a significant digit or that data do not exist.

(....) Indicates a lack of statistical data that can be reported or calculated from underlying observations.

(†) Marks a break in the comparability of data, as explained in the relevant notes in the monthly and yearbook. In these instances, data after the symbol do not form a consistent series with those for earlier dates. The break symbols

not explained in the country table notes can show a point of splice, where series having different base years are linked. A case would be the series described in the section of this introduction on prices, production, and labor. They can also point out a change in magnitude for high-inflation countries, as described in the section on electronic products.

(e) In superscript position after the figure marks an observation that is an estimate.

(f) In superscript position after the figure marks an observation that is forecast.

(p) In superscript position after the figure marks that data are in whole or in part provisional or preliminary.

The CD-ROM supports text messages to indicate breaks in the data. The time series observations with footnotes are highlighted in bold blue type within the IFS Data Viewer. When the cursor is moved over the footnoted cell, a small window will be displayed with the footnoted text. These footnotes/comments provide meaningful information about the specific observation, e.g., butt splicing, ratio splicing, extrapolation, estimations, etc.

Because of space limits in the phototypesetting of descriptor stubs on the country tables and table headings of world tables, abbreviations are sometimes necessary. While most are self-explanatory, the following abbreviation in the descriptors and table headings should be noted:

n.i.e. = Not included elsewhere.

Of which: Currency Outside DMBs = Of which: Currency Outside Deposit Money Banks.

Househ.Cons.Expend.,incl.NPISHs = Household Consumption Expenditure, including Nonprofit Institutions Serving Households.

Use of Fund Credit (GRA) = Use of Fund Credit (General Resources Account).

Data relating to fiscal years are allocated to calendar years to which most of their months refer. Fiscal years ending June 30 are allocated to that calendar year. For instance, the fiscal year from July 1, 1999 to June 30, 2000 is shown as calendar year 2000.

For countries that have reported semiannual transactions data, the data for the first half of a year may be given in the monthly book in the column for the second quarter of that year. And those for the second half may be given in the column for the fourth quarter. In these instances, no data are shown in the columns for the first and third quarters.

14. CD-ROM and Internet Account Subscriptions

The *IFS* is available on CD-ROM and the Internet. It contains:

(1) all time series appearing on *IFS* country tables;

(2) all series published in the *IFS* world tables, except for the daily exchange rates appearing in the Exchange Rates tables;

(3) the following exchange rate series as available for all Fund members, plus Aruba and the Netherlands Antilles: aa, ac, ae, af, ag, ah, b, c, de, dg, ea, eb, ec, ed, g, rb, rd, rf, rh, sa, sb, sc, sd, wa, wc, we, wf, wg, wh, xe, xf, ye, yf, nec, rec,

aat, aet, rbt, rft, neu, reu, and ahx (for an explanation of series af, ah, de, dg, rb, and rd, see *IFS Supplement on Exchange Rates,* No. 9 (1985));

(4) Fund accounts time series, denominated in SDR terms, for all countries for which data are available, though some series are not published in the *IFS* monthly book (2af, 2al , 2ap, 2aq, 2as, 2at 2ej, 2ek, 2en, 2eo, 2f.s, 1c.s, 2tl, 2egs, 2eb, 2h.s, 1bd, 1b.s, 2dus, 2krs, 2ees, 2kxs, 2eu, 2ey, 2eg, 2ens, 2ehs, 2eqs, 2ers, 2ets, 2kk, 2lk, 2kl, 2ll, 1ch, and 1cj) and in percentages (2tlp, 2fz, and 1bf); and (5) balance of payments series (78aad to 79ded) for all countries for which data are available, though some series are not published in the *IFS* monthly book.

All series in *IFS* contain publication code F except for the euro data lines that contain the code W.

A partner country code may sometimes be included in the control field. When it exists, it usually is shown in the *IFS* printed copy either in the italic midheading (see Real Effective Exchange Rate Indices table) or in the notes (see Commodity Prices table notes). Occasionally, the partner country code attached to a commodity price refers to a market (e.g., the London Metals Exchange) rather than the country of origin.

In the yearbook, data expressed in national currency for countries that have undergone periods of high inflation (e.g., Argentina, Bolivia, Brazil) are presented in different magnitudes on the same printed line. Users may refer to midheaders on country pages for an indication of the magnitude changes. The practice of expressing different magnitudes on the same line was adopted to prevent early-period data from disappearing from the printed tables. On the CD-ROM and the Internet (CSV format), the data are stored in a scientific notation with six significant digits for all time periods. Therefore, historical as well as current data may be viewed when using the display choices available on the CD-ROM and the Internet.

WORLD AND AREA TABLES

Acceptances of Article VIII, Sections 2, 3, and 4

Fund Members That Have Accepted the Obligations of Article VIII, Sections 2, 3, and 4 of the IMF's Articles of Agreement and Effective Date of Acceptance

Article VIII of the Fund's Articles imposes certain obligations on member countries of the Fund. In particular Article VIII, Sections 2 (a) and 3 prohibit members, except with the approval of the Fund, from imposing restrictions on the making of payments and transfers for current international transactions or from engaging in multiple currency practices or discriminatory currency arrangements. Moreover, Article VIII, Section 4 requires Fund members, subject to certain conditions, to purchase balances of their currency from other Fund members, which represent that the balances have been recently acquired as a result of current international transactions or that the conversion is necessary for the purpose of making payments for current transactions.

Article XIV, Section 2 of the Fund's Articles establishes a limited exception to Article VIII, Sections 2, 3, and 4. Thus, member countries that avail themselves of Article XIV, Section 2 may, without seeking Fund approval, maintain and adapt to changing circumstances the restrictions on payments and transfers for current international transactions that were in effect on their date of membership in the Fund; however, if such restrictions are terminated and subsequently reintroduce restrictions are introduced by these members after their date of membership, they are subject to Fund approval under Article VIII. Moreover, members availing themselves of Article XIV are required to consult annually with the Fund with respect to the retention of Article XIV measures.

Members may accept the obligations of Article VIII, Sections 2, 3, and 4 at any time. When a member country accepts these obligations, it may no longer avail itself of the transitional arrangements of Article XIV, Section 2 and may not maintain any exchange measures inconsistent with Article VIII, Sections 2, 3, and 4.

Member	Effective Date of Acceptance	Member	Effective Date of Acceptance	Member	Effective Date of Acceptance
Algeria	September 15, 1997	Grenada	January 24, 1994	Pakistan	July 1, 1994
Antigua and Barbuda	November 22, 1983	Guatemala	January 27, 1947	Palau	December 16, 1997
Argentina	May 14, 1968	Guinea	November 17, 1995	Panama	November 26, 1946
Armenia	May 29, 1997				
Australia	July 1, 1965	Guinea-Bissau	January 1, 1997	Papua New Guinea	December 4, 1975
		Guyana	December 27, 1966	Paraguay	August 22, 1994
Austria	August 1, 1962	Haiti	December 22, 1953	Peru	February 15, 1961
Bahamas, The	December 5, 1973	Honduras	July 1, 1950	Philippines	September 8, 1995
Bahrain, Kingdom of	March 20, 1973	Hungary	January 1, 1996	Poland	June 1, 1995
Bangladesh	April 11, 1994				
Barbados	November 3, 1993	Iceland	September 19, 1983	Portugal	September 12, 1988
		India	August 20, 1994	Qatar	June 4, 1973
Belarus, Rep. of	December 6, 2001	Indonesia	May 7, 1988	Romania	March 25, 1998
Belgium	February 15, 1961	Ireland	February 15, 1961	Russia	June 1, 1996
Belize	June 14, 1983	Israel	September 21, 1993	Rwanda	December 10, 1998
Benin	June 1, 1996				
Bolivia	June 5, 1967	Italy	February 15, 1961	St. Kitts and Nevis	December 3, 1984
		Jamaica	February 22, 1963	St. Lucia	May 30, 1980
Botswana	November 17, 1995	Japan	April 1, 1964	St. Vincent and the	
Brazil	November 30, 1999	Jordan	February 20, 1995	Grenadines	August 24, 1981
Brunei Darussalam	October 10, 1995	Kazakhstan	July 16, 1996	Samoa	October 6, 1994
Bulgaria	September 24, 1998			San Marino	September 23, 1992
Burkina Faso	June 1, 1996	Kenya	June 30, 1994		
		Kiribati	August 22, 1986	Saudia Arabia	March 22, 1961
Cambodia	January 1, 2002	Korea	November 1, 1988	Senegal	June 1, 1996
Cameroon	June 1, 1996	Kuwait	April 5, 1963	Seychelles	January 3, 1978
Canada	March 25, 1952	Kyrgyz Republic	March 29, 1995	Sierra Leone	December 14, 1995
Central African Rep.	June 1, 1996			Singapore	November 9, 1968
Chad	June 1, 1996	Latvia	June 10, 1994		
		Lebanon	July 1, 1993	Slovak Republic	October 1, 1995
Chile	July 27, 1977	Lesotho	March 5, 1997	Slovenia	September 1, 1995
China, People's Rep.	December 1, 1996	Lithuania	May 3, 1994	Solomon Islands	July 24, 1979
Comoros	June 1, 1996	Luxembourg	February 15, 1961	South Africa	September 15, 1973
Congo, Rep. of	June 1, 1996			Spain	July 15, 1986
Costa Rica	February 1, 1965	Macedonia, FYR	June 19, 1998		
		Madagascar	September 18, 1996	Sri Lanka	March 15, 1994
Côte d'Ivoire	June 1, 1996	Malawi	December 7, 1995	Suriname	June 29, 1978
Croatia	May 29, 1995	Malaysia	November 11, 1968	Swaziland	December 11, 1989
Cyprus	January 9, 1991	Mali	June 1, 1996	Sweden	February 15, 1961
Czech Republic	October 1, 1995			Switzerland	May 29, 1992
Denmark	May 1, 1967	Malta	November 30, 1994		
		Marshall Islands,		Tanzania	July 15, 1996
East Timor	July 23, 2002	Rep. of	May 21, 1992	Thailand	May 4, 1990
Djibouti	September 19, 1980	Mauritania	July 19, 1999	Togo	June 1, 1996
Dominica	December 13, 1979	Mauritius	September 29, 1993	Tonga	March 22, 1991
Dominican Republic	August 1, 1953	Mexico	November 12, 1946	Trinidad and Tobago	December 13, 1993
Ecuador	August 31, 1970				
		Micronesia, Fed.		Tunisia	January 6, 1993
El Salvador	November 6, 1946	States of	June 24, 1993	Turkey	March 22, 1990
Equatorial Guinea	June 1, 1996	Moldova	June 30, 1995	Uganda	April 5, 1994
Estonia	August 15, 1994	Mongolia	February 1, 1996	Ukraine	September 24, 1996
Fiji	August 4, 1972	Morocco	January 21, 1993	United Arab Emirates	February 13, 1974
Finland	September 25, 1979	Namibia	September 20, 1996		
				United Kingdom	February 15, 1961
France	February 15, 1961	Nepal	May 30, 1994	United States	December 10, 1946
Gabon	June 1, 1996	Netherlands	February 15, 1961	Uruguay	May 2, 1980
Gambia, The	January 21, 1993	New Zealand	August 5, 1982	Vanuatu	December 1, 1982
Georgia	December 20, 1996	Nicaragua	July 20, 1964	Venezuela, Rep. Bol.	July 1, 1976
Germany	February 15, 1961	Niger	June 1, 1996		
				Yemen, Rep. of	December 10, 1996
Ghana	February 21, 1994	Norway	May 11, 1967	Zimbabwe	February 3, 1995
Greece	July 7, 1992	Oman	June 19, 1974		

Exchange Rate Arrangements

Exchange Rate Regimes and Anchors of Monetary Policy
(As of December 31, 2001)[1]

Exchange Rate Regime (Number of countries)	Monetary Policy Framework						
	Exchange rate anchor				Monetary aggregate target	Inflation targeting framework	Fund-supported or other monetary program	Other

Exchange Rate Regime (Number of countries)	Exchange rate anchor				Monetary aggregate target	Inflation targeting framework	Fund-supported or other monetary program	Other
Exchange arrangements with no separate legal tender (40)	**Another currency as legal tender** Ecuador* El Salvador[14] Kiribati Marshall Islands Rep. of Micronesia, Fed. States of Palau Panama San Marino	**ECCU[3]** Antigua & Barbuda Dominica Grenada St. Kitts & Nevis St. Lucia St. Vincent & the Grenadines	**CFA Franc Zone** **WAEMU** Benin* Burkina Faso* Côte d'Ivoire* Guinea-Bissau* Mali* Niger* Senegal* Togo	**CAEMC** Cameroon* C. African Rep.* Chad* Congo, Rep.of* Equatorial Guinea Gabon*				**Euro Area[4,5]** Austria Belgium Finland France Germany Greece Ireland Italy Luxembourg Netherlands Portugal Spain
Currency board arrangements (8)	Argentina* Bosnia and Herzegovina* Brunei Darussalam Bulgaria* China, P.R. Hong Kong Djibouti* Estonia* Lithuania*							
Other conventional fixed peg arrangements (including de facto peg arrangements under managed floating) (40)	**Against a single currency (30)** Aruba Bahamas, The[6] Bahrain, Kingdom of Bangladesh Barbados Belize Bhutan Cape Verde China, P.R. Mainland†[7] Comoros[9] Iran[6,7] Jordan*[7] Lebanon[7] Lesotho* Macedonia, FYR*[7] Malaysia Maldives[7]	Namibia Nepal Netherlands Antilles Oman Qatar[7,8] Saudi Arabia[7,8] Sudan[7] Suriname[6,7] Swaziland Syrian Arab Republic[6] Turkmenistan[7] United Arab Emirates[7,8] Zimbabwe[7]	**Against a composite (10)** Botswana[6] Fiji Kuwait Latvia* Libyn A.J. Malta Morocco Samoa Seychelles Vanuatu		China, P.R.: Mainland†[7]			
Pegged exchange rates within horizontal bands (5)[10]	**Within a cooperative arrangement ERM II (1)** Denmark	**Other band arrangements (4)** Cyprus Egypt[6] Hungary† Tonga				Hungary†		
Crawling pegs (4)	Bolivia* Costa Rica[7] Nicaragua* Solomon Islands[7]							
Exchange rates within crawling bands (6)[11]	Belarus Honduras* Israel†	Romania*[7] Uruguay* Venezuela, Rep. Bolivariana				Israel†		

** ECCU: Eastern Caribbean Currency Union; WAEMU: West African Economic and Monetary Union; CAEMC: Central African Economic and Monetary Community

Exchange Rate Regimes and Anchors of Monetary Policy

(As of December 31, 2001)[1]

Exchange Rate Regime (Number of countries)	Monetary Policy Framework					
	Exchange rate anchor	Monetary aggregate target	Inflation targeting framework	Fund-supported or other monetary program	Other	
Managed floating with no preannounced path for exchange rate (42)		Ghana* Guinea* Guyana* Indonesia* Jamaica*[7] Mauritius Mongolia* São Tomé and Príncipe* Slovenia Sri Lanka* Tunisia	Thailand*	Azerbaijan Cambodia[6] Croatia Ethiopia Iraq Kazakhstan Kenya Kyrgyz Republic Lao PDR[6] Mauritania Nigeria Pakistan Russian Federation Rwanda Trinidad & Tobago Ukraine Vietnam Yugoslavia, Fed. Rep. of Zambia	Algeria[4] Angola[4] Burundi[4] Dominican Rep.[4,6] Eritrea[4] Guatemala[4] India[4] Myanmar[4,6,7] Paraguay[4] Singapore[4] Slovak Republic[4] Uzbekistan[4,6]	
Independently floating (41)		Gambia, The* Malawi* Peru* Philippines* Sierra Leone* Turkey* Yemen*	Australia Brazil[13] Canada Chile[6] Colombia* Czech Rep. Iceland Korea Mexico New Zealand Norway Poland South Africa Sweden United Kingdom	Albania Armenia Congo, Dem. Rep. Georgia Madagascar Moldova Mozambique Tajikistan Tanzania Uganda	Afghanistan[6,12] Haiti[4] Japan[4] Liberia[4] Papua New Guinea[4] Somalia[6,12] Switzerland[4] United States[4]	

Source: Staff Reports

Exchange Arrangements with No Separate Legal Tender: The currency of another country circulates as the sole legal tender or the member belongs to a monetary or currency union in which the same legal tender is shared by the members of the union.

Currency Board Arrangements: A monetary regime based on an explicit legislative commitment to exchange domestic currency for a specified foreign currency at a fixed exchange rate, combined with restrictions on the issuing authority to ensure the fulfillment of its legal obligation.

Other Conventional Fixed Peg Arrangements: The country pegs its currency (formally or de facto) at a fixed rate to a major currency or a basket of currencies where the exchange rate fluctuates within a narrow margin of less than ±1 percent around a central rate.

Pegged Exchange Rates Within Horizontal Bands: The value of the currency is maintained within margins of fluctuation around a formal or de facto fixed peg that are wider than at least ±1 percent around a central rate.

Crawling Pegs: The currency is adjusted periodically in small amounts at a fixed, preannounced rate or in response to changes in selective quantitative indicators.

Exchange Rates Within Crawling Bands: The currency is maintained within certain fluctuation margins around a central rate that is adjusted periodically at a fixed preannounced rate or in response to changes in selective quantitative indicators.

Managed Floating with No Preannounced Path for the Exchange Rate: The monetary authority influences the movements of the exchange rate through active intervention in the foreign exchange market without specifying, or precommitting to, a preannounced path for the exchange rate.

Independent Floating: The exchange rate is market determined, with any foreign exchange intervention aimed at moderating the rate of change and preventing undue fluctuations in the exchange rate, rather than at establishing a level for it.

Note: "Country" in this publication does not always refer to a territorial entity that is a state as understood by international law and practice; the term also covers the euro area and some nonsovereign territorial entities for which statistical data are provided internationally on a separate basis.

[1]A country with * indicates that the country has a Fund supported or other monetary program.

[2]A country with † indicates that the country has more than one nominal anchor that may guide monetary policy. It should be noted, however, that it would not be possible, for practical purposes, to infer from this table which nominal anchor plays the principal role in conducting monetary policy.

[3]These countries have a currency board arrangement.

[4]The country has no explicitly stated nominal anchor, but rather monitors various indicators in conducting monetary policy.

[5]Until they are withdrawn in February 2002, national currencies will retain their status as legal tender within their home territories.

[6]Member maintained exchange regimes involving more than one market. The regime shown is that maintained in the major market.

[7]The indicated country has a de facto regime which differs from its de jure regime.

[8]Exchange rates are determined on the basis of a fixed relationship to the SDR, within margins of up to ±7.25%. However, because of the maintenance of a relatively stable relationship with the U.S. dollar, these margins are not always observed.

[9]Comoros has the same arrangement with the French Treasury as do the CFA Franc Zone countries.

[10]The band width for these countries is: Cyprus (±2.25%), Denmark (±2.25%), Egypt (±3%), Hungary (±15%), and Tonga (±5%).

[11]The band for these countries is: Belarus (±5%), Honduras (±7%), Israel (±22%), Romania (unannounced), Uruguay (±3%), and República Bolivariana de Venezuela (±7.5%).

[12]There is no relevant information available for the country.

[13]Brazil maintains a Fund-supported program.

[14]For El Salvador, the printing of new colones, the domestic currency, is prohibited, but the existing stock of colones will continue to circulate, along with the U.S. dollar, as legal tender until all notes physically wear out.

Exchange Rates

Market, Official, or Principal Rate

National Currency Units per SDR: End of Period (aa)

	1972	1973	1974	1975	1976	1977	1978	1979	1980	1981	1982	1983	1984	1985	198
Industrial Countries															
US dollar	1.0857	1.2064	1.2244	1.1707	1.1618	1.2147	1.3028	1.3173	1.2754	1.1640	1.1031	1.0470	.9802	1.0984	1.223
Canadian dollar	1.0809	1.2013	1.2136	1.1899	1.1725	1.3294	1.5451	1.5388	1.5237	1.3803	1.3562	1.3028	1.2952	1.5350	1.688
Australian dollar	.8515	.8107	.9226	.9312	1.0694	1.0642	1.1324	1.1916	1.0802	1.0320	1.1249	1.1607	1.1841	1.6132	1.839
Japanese yen	327.88	337.78	368.47	357.23	340.18	291.53	253.52	315.76	258.91	255.95	259.23	243.10	246.13	220.23	194.6
New Zealand dollar	.9084	.8445	.9307	1.1216	1.2230	1.1912	1.2214	1.3358	1.3254	1.4119	1.5060	1.5994	2.0524	2.2035	2.336
Austrian schilling	†25.123	23.946	20.973	21.669	19.481	18.385	17.415	16.376	17.612	18.490	18.408	20.249	21.614	18.981	16.77
Belgian franc	47.839	49.846	44.227	46.273	41.806	40.013	37.520	36.948	40.205	44.766	51.758	58.252	61.832	55.316	49.42
Danish krone	7.434	†7.588	6.918	7.232	6.724	7.018	6.631	7.067	7.672	8.526	9.248	10.339	11.037	9.852	8.98
Finnish markka	4.5383	†4.6384	4.3477	4.5070	4.3766	4.8807	5.1148	4.8886	4.8976	5.0714	5.8366	6.0828	6.4008	5.9501	5.864
French franc	5.5542	5.6801	5.4416	5.2510	5.7740	5.7152	5.4457	5.2957	5.7598	6.6904	7.4184	8.7394	9.4022	8.3052	7.895
Deutsche mark	3.4759	3.2608	2.9501	3.0698	2.7448	2.5570	2.3815	2.2810	2.4985	2.6245	2.6215	2.8517	3.0857	2.7035	2.374
Greek drachma	32.57	35.83	36.73	41.73	43.02	43.13	46.91	50.43	59.35	67.08	77.85	103.30	125.94	162.30	169.7
Icelandic krona	1.063	1.013	†1.451	1.999	2.204	2.589	4.144	5.202	7.957	†9.513	18.339	30.016	39.743	46.200	49.22
Irish pound	.46238	.51926	.52133	.57853	.68247	.63731	.64035	.61414	.67215	.73668	.78991	.92242	.98861	.88333	.8740
Italian lira	632.4	733.4	795.1	800.2	1,016.6	1,058.7	1,081.0	1,059.1	1,186.8	1,396.8	1,511.3	1,737.4	1,897.6	1,843.7	1,661.
Luxembourg franc	47.839	49.846	44.227	46.273	41.806	40.013	37.520	36.948	40.205	44.766	51.758	58.252	61.832	55.316	49.42
Netherlands guilder	3.5030	3.4073	3.0688	3.1473	2.8546	2.7695	2.5652	2.5102	2.7160	2.8732	2.8951	3.2084	3.4793	3.0448	2.681
Norwegian krone	†7.2091	6.9094	6.3727	6.5381	6.0241	6.2430	6.5433	6.4892	6.6066	6.7597	7.7813	8.0847	8.9072	8.3288	9.051
Portuguese escudo	29.31	31.18	30.11	32.16	36.65	48.41	59.94	65.58	67.65	75.95	98.25	137.62	165.93	172.99	178.7
Spanish peseta	69.02	68.70	†68.70	69.98	79.34	98.28	91.34	87.14	101.08	113.43	138.55	164.06	169.97	169.32	161.9
Swedish krona	†5.1495	5.5341	4.9960	5.1339	4.7943	5.6721	5.5961	5.4623	5.5771	6.4844	8.0466	8.3766	8.8116	8.3650	8.340
Swiss franc	4.0975	3.9134	3.1098	3.0671	2.8459	2.4294	2.1105	2.0814	2.2492	2.0934	2.2002	2.2818	2.5338	2.2809	1.985
Pound sterling	†.46238	.51926	.52133	.57853	.68247	.63731	.64035	.59232	.53476	.61004	.68325	.72174	.84757	.76042	.8295
Developing Countries															
Africa															
Algerian dinar	4.9465	5.0486	4.8937	4.8290	5.0644	4.9014	4.9955	4.9472	5.0653	5.0958	5.1135	5.1473	5.0213	5.2425	5.900
Benin,CFA franc	278.00	284.00	272.08	262.55	288.70	285.76	272.28	264.78	287.99	334.52	370.92	436.97	470.11	415.26	394.78
Botswana pula	.8499	.8097	.8444	1.0180	1.0103	1.0060	1.0789	1.0390	.9461	1.0244	1.1704	1.2098	1.5292	2.3076	2.247
Burkina Faso, CFA franc	278.00	284.00	272.08	262.55	288.70	285.76	272.28	264.78	287.99	334.52	370.92	436.97	470.11	415.26	394.78
Burundi franc	95.00	95.00	96.42	92.19	104.56	109.32	117.25	118.56	114.79	104.76	99.28	122.70	122.70	122.70	151.5
Cameroon, CFA franc	278.00	284.00	272.08	262.55	288.70	285.76	272.28	264.78	287.99	334.52	370.92	436.97	470.11	415.26	394.78
Cape Verde escudo	29.31	31.18	30.11	32.16	36.65	41.18	46.82	50.47	54.19	59.20	69.54	83.73	91.17	93.78	93.6
Cent.African Rep.,CFA franc	278.00	284.00	272.08	262.55	288.70	285.76	272.28	264.78	287.99	334.52	370.92	436.97	470.11	415.26	394.78
Chad, CFA franc	278.00	284.00	272.08	262.55	288.70	285.76	272.28	264.78	287.99	334.52	370.92	436.97	470.11	415.26	394.78
Comorian franc	277.99	284.00	272.08	262.55	288.70	285.76	272.28	264.78	287.98	334.52	370.92	436.97	470.10	415.25	394.78
Congo, Dem.Rep., new zaïre	—	—	—	—	—	—	—	—	—	—	—	—	—	—	—
Congo, Rep. of, CFA franc	278.00	284.00	272.08	262.55	288.70	285.76	272.28	264.78	287.99	334.52	370.92	436.97	470.11	415.26	394.78
Côte d'Ivoire,CFA franc	278.00	284.00	272.08	262.55	288.70	285.76	272.28	264.78	287.99	334.52	370.92	436.97	470.11	415.26	394.78
Djibouti franc	214.39	214.39	217.59	208.05	206.48	215.88	231.53	234.12	226.67	206.86	196.05	186.07	174.20	195.21	217.3
Eq. Guinea, CFA franc	278.00	284.00	272.08	262.55	288.70	285.76	272.28	264.78	287.99	334.52	370.92	436.97	470.11	415.26	394.78
Ethiopian birr	2.4971	2.4971	2.5344	2.4233	2.4050	2.5144	2.6968	2.7269	2.6401	2.4094	2.2834	2.1672	2.0290	2.2737	2.532
Gabon, CFA franc	278.00	284.00	272.08	262.55	288.70	285.76	272.28	264.78	287.99	334.52	370.92	436.97	470.11	415.26	394.78
Gambian dalasi	2.312	2.077	2.085	2.314	2.730	2.549	2.561	2.369	2.139	2.440	2.733	2.887	4.238	3.802	9.084
Ghanaian cedi	1.39	1.39	1.41	1.35	1.34	1.40	3.58	3.62	3.51	3.20	3.03	31.41	49.01	65.89	110.1
Guinean franc	24.68	24.91	25.28	24.69	24.69	24.69	24.69	24.69	24.69	24.69	24.69	24.69	24.69	24.69	288.2
Guinea-Bissau, CFA franc	.5	.5	.5	.5	.6	.6	.7	.7	.7	.7	.7	1.4	1.9	3.0	4.
Kenya shilling	7.755	8.324	8.745	9.660	9.660	9.660	9.660	9.660	9.660	11.950	14.060	14.417	15.187	17.738	19.13
Lesotho loti	.8500	.8097	.8444	1.0180	1.0103	1.0563	1.1329	1.0892	.9507	1.1134	1.1873	1.2793	1.9456	2.8093	2.670
Liberian dollar	1.0857	1.2064	1.2244	1.1707	1.1618	1.2147	1.3028	1.3173	1.2754	1.1640	1.1031	1.0470	.9802	1.0984	1.223
Malagasy franc	278.0	284.0	272.1	262.5	288.7	285.8	272.3	264.8	288.0	334.5	405.6	515.3	645.0	698.4	941.
Malawi kwacha	.9280	1.0224	1.0291	1.0541	1.0541	1.0541	1.0541	1.0541	1.0541	1.0541	1.2122	1.3577	1.5339	1.8445	2.388
Mali, CFA franc	278.00	284.00	272.08	262.55	288.70	285.76	272.28	264.78	287.99	334.52	370.92	436.97	470.11	415.26	394.78
Mauritanian ouguiya	55.60	†56.80	53.01	52.86	50.70	55.94	60.13	60.39	58.71	56.96	58.42	59.71	65.96	84.66	90.61
Mauritian rupee	6.165	6.923	6.951	7.714	7.714	7.714	7.714	†10.000	10.000	12.000	12.000	13.321	15.295	15.718	16.069
Moroccan dirham	5.066	5.175	5.087	4.898	5.210	5.256	5.063	4.925	5.528	6.208	6.914	8.439	9.362	10.568	10.656
Mozambique, metical	29.2	31.1	30.0	32.0	36.5	39.4	42.1	42.3	41.6	41.5	42.0	42.9	42.5	45.1	48.0
Namibia dollar	.85000	.80966	.84435	1.01797	1.01029	1.05627	1.13286	1.08924	.95066	1.11341	1.18729	1.27926	1.94563	2.80926	2.67072
Niger, CFA franc	278.00	284.00	272.08	262.55	288.70	285.76	272.28	264.78	287.99	334.52	370.92	436.97	470.11	415.26	394.78
Nigerian naira	.714	.794	.754	.734	.733	.791	.844	.738	.694	.741	.739	.784	.792	1.098	4.057
Rwanda franc	100.00	100.00	113.67	108.68	107.86	112.77	120.95	122.30	118.41	108.06	102.41	102.71	102.71	102.71	102.7
São Tomé & Príncipe dobra	29.31	31.18	30.11	32.16	36.65	45.25	45.25	45.25	45.25	45.25	45.25	45.25	45.25	45.25	45.25
Senegal, CFA franc	278.00	284.00	272.08	262.55	288.70	285.76	272.28	264.78	287.99	334.52	370.92	436.97	470.11	415.26	394.78
Seychelles rupee	†6.1650	6.9235	6.9511	7.7137	9.0995	8.4974	8.5380	8.3197	8.3197	7.2345	7.2345	7.2345	7.2345	7.2345	7.2345
Sierra Leonean leone	.92	1.04	1.04	1.16	1.36	1.27	1.37	1.37	1.37	1.37	1.36	2.63	2.46	5.74	43.53
South African rand	.8500	.8097	.8444	1.0180	1.0103	1.0563	1.1329	1.0892	.9507	1.1134	1.1873	1.2793	1.9456	2.8093	2.6707
Sudanese pound	.0378	.0420	.0426	.0408	.0405	.0423	.0521	.0659	.0638	.1049	.1434	.1361	.1274	.2746	.3058
Swaziland lilangeni	.8500	.8097	.8444	1.0180	1.0103	1.0563	1.1329	1.0892	.9507	1.1134	1.1873	1.2793	1.9456	2.8093	2.6707
Tanzanian shilling	7.76	8.32	8.75	9.66	9.66	9.66	9.66	10.83	10.44	9.69	10.55	13.04	17.75	18.12	63.26
Togo, CFA franc	278.00	284.00	272.08	262.55	288.70	285.76	272.28	264.78	287.99	334.52	370.92	436.97	470.11	415.26	394.78
Tunisian dinar	†.5255	.5369	.4978	.4979	.5007	.5005	.5255	.5215	.5340	.6002	.6792	.7612	.8495	.8314	1.0277
Uganda shilling	.1	.1	.1	.1	.1	.1	.1	.1	.1	1.0	1.2	2.5	5.1	15.4	17.1
Zambian kwacha	.776	.776	.788	.753	.922	.922	†1.024	1.024	1.024	1.024	1.024	1.280	2.157	6.261	15.546
Zimbabwe dollar	.7079	.7311	.6718	.7314	.7192	.7857	.8796	.8882	.8043	.8347	1.0143	1.1574	1.4727	1.8028	2.0527
Asia															
Afghanistan,afghani	48.857	54.286	55.096	52.680	52.282	54.662	58.626	55.657	58.478	58.896	55.817	52.976	49.599	55.580	61.893
Bangladesh taka	8.770	9.849	9.888	17.356	17.373	17.486	19.456	20.607	20.726	23.101	26.556	26.174	25.485	34.051	37.674
Bhutan,ngultrum	8.773	9.896	9.978	10.462	10.318	9.971	10.668	10.416	10.114	10.591	10.627	10.986	12.205	13.363	16.051
Cambodian riel	203.0	331.7	....	....	....	....	....	....	....	....	....	....	....	....	....
Chinese yuan	2.4321	2.4371	2.2524	2.3019	2.1846	2.1014	2.0546	1.9710	1.9518	2.0317	2.1209	2.0739	2.7404	3.5166	4.5528
Fiji dollar	.9155	.9762	.9795	1.0104	1.0939	1.0575	1.0679	1.1077	1.0089	1.0205	1.0450	1.0954	1.1204	1.2307	1.4010
Hong Kong dollar	†6.1820	6.1403	6.0116	5.8919	5.4292	5.6059	6.2573	6.5181	6.5429	6.6055	7.1647	8.1453	7.6682	8.5798	9.5348
Indian rupee	8.773	9.896	†9.978	10.462	10.318	9.971	10.668	10.416	10.114	10.591	10.627	10.986	12.205	13.363	16.051
Indonesian rupiah	450.6	500.6	508.1	485.8	482.2	504.1	814.2	826.0	799.4	749.6	763.9	1,040.7	1,052.7	1,235.7	2,007.3
Kiribati, Aust.dollar	.8515	.8107	.9226	.9312	1.0694	1.0642	1.1324	1.1916	1.0802	1.0320	1.1249	1.1607	1.1841	1.6132	1.8399
Korean won	433.1	479.5	592.6	566.6	562.3	587.9	630.6	637.6	841.6	815.4	826.0	832.8	811.0	977.8	1,053.7
Lao P.D. Rep., kip	651.43	723.81	734.61	†877.99	232.37	242.94	521.12	†13.17	12.75	34.92	38.61	36.64	34.31	104.35	116.20
Malaysian ringgit	3.05845	2.95797	2.83168	3.03002	2.94524	2.87340	2.87395	2.88364	2.83447	2.60995	2.56065	2.44808	2.37701	2.66532	3.18396
Maldivian rufiyaa	4.750	4.741	4.812	7.170	10.021	10.841	11.237	9.946	9.629	8.788	7.777	7.381	6.910	7.830	8.861

† **See country notes in the monthly *IFS***

Exchange Rates

Market, Official, or Principal Rate

National Currency Units per SDR: End of Period (aa)

1987	1988	1989	1990	1991	1992	1993	1994	1995	1996	1997	1998	1999	2000	2001	
															Industrial Countries
1.4187	1.3457	1.3142	1.4227	1.4304	1.3750	1.3736	1.4599	1.4865	1.4380	1.3493	1.4080	1.3725	1.3029	1.2567	US dollar
1.8440	1.6050	1.5215	1.6507	1.6530	1.7478	1.8186	2.0479	2.0294	1.9694	1.9282	2.1550	1.9809	1.9546	2.0015	Canadian dollar
1.9635	1.5730	1.6578	1.8397	1.8826	1.9968	2.0286	1.8793	1.9953	1.8053	2.0672	2.2936	2.0993	2.3518	2.4613	Australian dollar
175.20	169.36	188.52	191.21	179.09	171.53	153.63	145.61	152.86	166.80	175.34	162.77	140.27	149.70	165.64	Japanese yen
2.1577	2.1418	2.2005	2.4203	2.6436	2.6735	2.4581	2.2721	2.2754	2.0368	2.3195	2.6723	2.6364	2.9598	3.0246	New Zealand dollar
15.960	16.909	15.527	15.190	15.290	15.612	16.679	16.013	14.996	15.751	17.045	16.540	....	....	....	Austrian schilling
47.032	50.255	46.994	44.078	44.730	45.623	49.599	46.478	43.725	46.022	49.814	48.682	....	....	....	Belgian franc
8.649	9.250	8.683	8.217	8.459	8.601	9.302	8.880	8.244	8.548	9.210	8.992	10.155	10.450	10.568	Danish krone
5.5980	5.6102	5.3342	5.1699	5.9120	7.2119	7.9454	6.9244	6.4790	6.6777	7.3139	7.1753	....	....	....	Finnish markka
7.5756	8.1536	7.6064	7.2968	7.4096	7.5714	8.0978	7.8044	7.2838	7.5306	8.0794	7.9161	....	....	....	French franc
2.2436	2.3957	2.2312	2.1255	2.1685	2.2193	2.3712	2.2610	2.1309	2.2357	2.4180	2.3556	....	....	....	Deutsche mark
178.64	199.30	207.36	224.25	250.73	295.05	342.32	350.51	352.36	355.20	381.31	397.87	450.79	476.37	....	Greek drachma
50.589	62.198	80.387	78.801	79.561	87.890	99.899	99.708	96.964	96.185	97.389	97.605	99.576	110.356	129.380	Icelandic krona
.84671	.89267	.84441	.80127	.81748	.84387	.97360	.94360	.92587	.85537	.94327	.94670	....	....	....	Irish pound
1,658.8	1,757.2	1,669.6	1,607.8	1,646.5	2,022.4	2,340.5	2,379.2	2,355.7	2,200.9	2,373.6	2,327.6	....	....	....	Italian lira
47.032	50.255	46.994	44.078	44.730	45.623	49.599	46.478	43.725	46.022	49.814	48.682	....	....	....	Luxembourg franc
2.5217	2.6907	2.5173	2.4043	2.4466	2.4944	2.6659	2.5330	2.3849	2.5072	2.7217	2.6595	....	....	....	Netherlands guilder
8.8418	8.8412	8.6932	8.4044	8.5440	9.5212	10.3264	9.8715	9.3931	9.2641	9.8707	10.7010	11.0343	11.5288	11.3251	Norwegian krone
184.23	196.97	196.92	190.07	191.94	201.79	242.86	232.25	222.10	224.88	247.35	241.94	....	....	....	Portuguese escudo
154.63	152.67	144.19	137.87	138.31	157.61	195.34	192.32	180.47	188.77	204.68	200.79	....	....	....	Spanish peseta
8.2963	8.2855	8.1833	8.1063	7.9096	9.6841	11.4054	10.8927	9.8973	9.8802	10.6280	11.3501	11.7006	12.4232	13.4062	Swedish krona
1.8130	2.0239	2.0323	1.8431	1.9389	2.0020	2.0322	1.9146	1.7102	1.9361	1.9636	1.9382	2.1955	2.1322	2.1079	Swiss franc
.75803	.74369	.81854	.73789	.76465	.90939	.92733	.93430	.95903	.84686	.81585	.84643	.84912	.87315	.86647	Pound sterling
															Developing Countries
															Africa
7.0029	9.0576	10.5559	17.3434	30.5996	31.3244	33.1344	62.6166	77.5576	80.7931	78.8150	84.9790	95.1346	98.1649	97.7982	Algerian dinar
378.78	407.68	380.32	364.84	370.48	378.57	404.89	†780.44	728.38	753.06	807.94	791.61	†896.19	918.49	935.39	Benin,CFA franc
2.2212	2.6049	2.4605	2.6622	2.9646	3.1031	3.5229	3.9670	4.1944	5.2404	5.1400	6.2774	6.3572	6.9861	8.7760	Botswana pula
378.78	407.68	380.32	364.84	370.48	378.57	404.89	†780.44	728.38	753.06	807.94	791.61	†896.19	918.49	935.39	Burkina Faso, CFA franc
161.00	201.00	232.14	232.14	273.07	322.90	362.99	360.78	413.37	462.63	551.56	710.64	860.83	1,014.76	1,090.92	Burundi franc
378.78	407.68	380.32	364.84	370.48	378.57	404.89	†780.44	728.38	753.06	807.94	791.61	†896.19	918.49	935.39	Cameroon, CFA franc
93.31	99.13	95.99	94.02	95.08	100.50	118.12	118.45	115.14	122.46	129.85	132.71	147.65	154.73	157.06	Cape Verde escudo
378.78	407.68	380.32	364.84	370.48	378.57	404.89	†780.44	728.38	753.06	807.94	791.61	†896.19	918.49	935.39	Cent.African Rep.,CFA franc
378.78	407.68	380.32	364.84	370.48	378.57	404.89	†780.44	728.38	753.06	807.94	791.61	†896.19	918.49	935.39	Chad, CFA franc
378.78	407.68	380.31	364.84	370.48	378.57	404.89	†585.32	546.28	564.79	605.95	593.70	†672.14	688.87	701.54	Comorian franc
—	—	—	—	—	.00001	.00048	.04745	.22046	1.66228	1.43021	†3.44967	6.17630	65.14550	....	Congo, Dem.Rep., new zaïre
378.78	407.68	380.32	364.84	370.48	378.57	404.89	†780.44	728.38	753.06	807.94	791.61	†896.19	918.49	935.39	Congo, Rep. of, CFA franc
378.78	407.68	380.32	364.84	370.48	378.57	404.89	†780.44	728.38	753.06	807.94	791.61	†896.19	918.49	935.39	Côte d'Ivoire,CFA franc
252.13	239.16	233.55	252.84	254.22	244.37	244.11	259.45	264.18	255.56	239.79	250.24	243.92	231.55	223.35	Djibouti franc
378.78	407.68	380.32	364.84	370.48	378.57	404.89	†780.44	728.38	753.06	807.94	791.61	†896.19	918.49	935.39	Eq. Guinea, CFA franc
2.9366	2.7856	2.7203	2.9449	2.9610	6.8750	6.8678	8.6861	9.3946	9.2403	9.2613	10.5644	11.1640	10.8324	10.7555	Ethiopian birr
378.78	407.68	380.32	364.84	370.48	378.57	404.89	†780.44	728.38	753.06	807.94	791.61	†896.19	918.49	935.39	Gabon, CFA franc
9.134	8.961	10.928	10.662	12.813	12.673	13.096	13.983	14.330	14.225	14.207	15.476	15.849	19.397	21.279	Gambian dalasi
249.76	309.36	398.23	490.57	558.76	716.15 P	1,125.87	1,536.68	2,154.33	2,522.74	3,066.48	3,274.49	4,852.02	9,182.45	9,035.87	Ghanaian cedi
624.21	740.14	814.78	967.41	1,148.56	1,268.31	1,335.67	1,432.15	1,483.49	1,494.23	1,544.82	1,827.67	2,382.68	2,452.43	2,498.79	Guinean franc
18.6	28.2	40.2	54.9	109.1	183.1	242.2	345.2	501.5	772.9	807.9	791.6	†896.2	918.5	935.4	Guinea-Bissau, CFA franc
23.429	25.029	28.387	34.263	40.158	49.797	93.626	65.458	83.153	79.118	84.568	87.165	100.098	101.674	98.779	Kenya shilling
2.7379	3.1997	3.3327	3.6456	3.9237	4.1979	4.6667	5.1730	5.4220	6.7332	6.5675	8.2511	8.4471	9.8611	15.2397	Lesotho loti
1.4187	1.3457	1.3142	1.4227	1.4304	1.3750	1.3736	1.4599	1.4865	1.4380	1.3493	†60.8973	54.2141	55.6994	62.2081	Liberian dollar
1,751.0	2,054.1	2,014.0	2,085.4	2,621.5	2,626.5	2,695.8	5,651.2	5,088.2	6,224.2	7,130.3	7,606.5	8,980.6	8,534.6	8,333.6	Malagasy franc
2.9136	3.4120	3.5204	3.7656	3.8104	6.0442	6.1733	22.3337	22.7479	22.0340	28.6416	61.7894	63.7362	104.3318	84.5705	Malawi kwacha
378.78	407.68	380.32	364.84	370.48	378.57	404.89	†780.44	728.38	753.06	807.94	791.61	†896.19	918.49	935.39	Mali, CFA franc
101.58	101.91	109.80	110.74	111.32	158.26	170.54	187.40	203.81	204.84	227.15	289.74	308.81	328.72	331.99	Mauritanian ouguiya
17.272	18.616	19.707	20.375	21.162	23.372	25.625	26.077	26.258	25.842	30.041	34.896	34.955	36.327	38.197	Mauritian rupee
11.066	11.049	10.673	11.442	11.658	12.442	13.257	13.080	12.589	12.653	13.107	13.031	13.845	13.836	14.528	Moroccan dirham
571.1	839.7	1,073.4	1,471.7	2,630.3	†4,043.8	7,313.2	9,675.1	16,130.5	16,301.7	15,519.2	17,350.0	18,189.7	†22,332.5	29,307.5	Mozambique, metical
2.73793	3.19971	3.33272	3.64557	3.92371	4.19788	4.66667	5.17298	5.42197	6.73325	6.56747	8.25106	8.44711	9.86107	15.23974	Namibia dollar
378.78	407.68	380.32	364.84	370.48	378.57	404.89	†780.44	728.38	753.06	807.94	791.61	†896.19	918.49	935.39	Niger, CFA franc
5.874	7.204	10.055	12.805	14.107	27.014	30.056	32.113	32.534	31.471	29.530	30.816	134.437	142.734	141.948	Nigerian naira
102.71	102.71	102.71	171.18	171.18	201.39	201.39	201.94	445.67	437.37	411.31	450.75	479.24	560.67	572.84	Rwanda franc
103.32	132.12	184.46	200.57	400.55	516.37	709.72	1,730.37	2,611.58	4,074.04	9,403.91	9,694.29	10,019.32	11,218.90	11,335.34	São Tomé & Príncipe dobra
378.78	407.68	380.32	364.84	370.48	378.57	404.89	†780.44	728.38	753.06	807.94	791.61	†896.19	918.49	935.39	Senegal, CFA franc
7.2345	7.2345	7.2345	7.2345	7.2345	7.2345	7.2345	7.2345	7.2345	7.2345	6.9218	7.6699	7.3671	8.1642	7.2226	Seychelles rupee
32.69	52.57	85.89	268.43	621.93	723.68	793.41	894.90	1,402.35	1,307.24	1,799.00	2,239.84	3,123.90	2,171.52	2,716.13	Sierra Leonean leone
2.7379	3.1997	3.3327	3.6456	3.9237	4.1979	4.6667	5.1730	5.4220	6.7332	6.5675	8.2511	8.4471	9.8611	15.2397	South African rand
.6385	.6056	.5914	.6403	2.1446	18.5811	29.8600	58.3940	78.2363	208.4000	232.3409	334.8295	353.6958	335.3039	328.5469	Sudanese pound
2.7379	3.1997	3.3327	3.6456	3.9237	4.1979	4.6667	5.1730	5.4220	6.7332	6.5675	8.2511	8.4471	9.8611	15.2397	Swaziland lilangeni
118.77	168.21	252.71	279.69	334.58	460.63	659.13	764.16	818.10	856.51	842.70	958.87	1,094.34	1,046.58	1,151.54	Tanzanian shilling
378.78	407.68	380.32	364.84	370.48	378.57	404.89	†780.44	728.38	753.06	807.94	791.61	†896.19	918.49	935.39	Togo, CFA franc
1.1035	1.2090	1.1888	1.1904	1.2366	1.3071	1.4376	1.4470	1.4134	1.4358	1.5483	1.5502	1.7191	1.8049	1.8453	Tunisian dinar
†85.1	222.0	486.2	768.2	1,308.8	1,673.6	1,552.3	1,352.9	1,500.5	1,480.5	1,538.3	1,918.7	2,067.1	2,301.8	2,170.9	Uganda shilling
11.349	13.462	28.451	60.823	127.262	494.604	686.780	993.095	1,421.278	1,844.457	1,908.973	3,236.948	3,612.707	5,417.278	4,813.779	Zambian kwacha
2.3593	2.6145	2.9833	3.7508	7.2244	7.5384	9.5256	12.2440	13.8407	15.5860	25.1070	52.6170	52.3459	71.7461	69.1651	Zimbabwe dollar
															Asia
71.784	68.092	66.496	71.987	72.380	69.575	69.502	729.925	1,486.490	†4,313.880	4,047.750	4,224.090	4,117.530	3,908.730	3,770.190	Afghanistan,afghani
44.262	43.426	42.408	50.917	55.186	53.625	54.736	58.759	60.574	61.041	61.323	68.289	69.998	70.357	71.634	Bangladesh taka
18.268	20.117	22.387	25.712	36.953	36.025	43.102	45.810	52.295	51.666	52.999	59.813	59.690	60.911	60.549	Bhutan,ngultrum
....	....	283.9	853.6	743.8	2,750.0	3,166.1	3,759.1	3,754.9	3,901.2	4,657.6	5,308.3	5,174.4	5,087.9	4,895.0	Cambodian riel
5.2804	5.0088	6.2056	7.4293	7.7732	7.9087	7.9666	†12.3302	12.3637	11.9325	11.1715	11.6567	11.3637	10.7847	10.4017	Chinese yuan
2.0436	1.8906	1.9632	2.0760	2.1067	2.1511	2.1164	2.0570	2.1248	1.9900	2.0902	2.7965	2.6981	2.8479	2.9017	Fiji dollar
11.0088	10.5072	10.2596	11.0982	11.1302	10.6466	10.6121	11.2963	11.4935	11.1241	10.4513	10.9066	10.6658	10.1575	9.7987	Hong Kong dollar
18.268	20.117	22.387	25.712	36.953	36.025	43.102	45.810	52.295	51.666	52.999	59.813	59.690	60.911	60.549	Indian rupee
2,340.8	2,329.4	2,361.5	2,704.5	2,849.4	2,835.3	2,898.2	3,211.7	3,430.8	3,426.7	6,274.0	11,299.4	9,724.2	12,501.4	13,070.0	Indonesian rupiah
1.9635	1.5730	1.6578	1.8397	1.8826	1.9968	2.0286	1.8793	1.9953	1.8053	2.0672	2.2936	2.0993	2.3518	2.4613	Kiribati, Aust.dollar
1,124.0	920.6	893.1	1,019.2	1,088.3	1,084.1	1,110.0	1,151.4	1,151.6	1,213.9	2,287.0	1,695.3	1,561.9	1,647.5	1,650.7	Korean won
549.73	608.93	937.65	989.46	1,017.75	985.88	986.22	1,049.63	†1,372.03	1,344.49	3,554.60	6,017.92	10,431.08	10,707.31	11,926.37	Lao P.D. Rep., kip
3.53644	3.65398	3.55257	3.84332	3.89649	3.59150	3.71067	3.73722	3.77866	3.63660	5.25115	5.35051	5.21554	4.95106	4.77557	Malaysian ringgit
13.328	11.472	12.097	13.686	14.762	14.486	15.253	17.182	17.496	16.925	15.881	16.573	16.154	15.335	16.086	Maldivian rufiyaa

† See country notes in the monthly *IFS*

Exchange Rates

Market, Official, or Principal Rate

National Currency Units per SDR: End of Period (aa)

	1972	1973	1974	1975	1976	1977	1978	1979	1980	1981	1982	1983	1984	1985	1986
Asia (cont.)															
Mongolian togrog	....	....	....	....	....	....	....	....	....	....	....	....	....	....	....
Myanmar kyat	5.8650	5.8653	5.8891	7.7429	7.7429	8.5085	8.5085	8.5085	8.5085	8.5085	8.5085	8.5085	8.5085	8.5085	8.5085
Nepalese rupee	10.993	12.739	12.929	14.633	14.523	15.184	15.633	15.808	15.305	15.364	15.774	15.914	17.644	22.737	26.910
Pakistan rupee	11.947	11.913	12.091	11.561	11.473	11.996	12.865	13.009	12.595	11.494	14.129	14.099	15.018	17.509	21.047
Papua New Guinea kina	.8515	.8107	.9226	.9312	.9435	.9202	.8966	.9093	.8212	.7921	.8250	.9166	.9227	1.1121	1.1757
Philippine peso	7.362	8.119	8.650	8.778	8.630	8.952	9.608	9.768	9.693	9.544	10.117	14.659	19.369	20.905	25.112
Samoa tala	.7313	.7317	.7427	.8982	.9295	.9093	.9308	1.2002	1.1851	1.2794	1.3647	1.6964	2.1397	2.5333	2.6883
Singapore dollar	3.0617	†2.9991	2.8307	2.9144	2.8529	2.8406	2.8186	2.8441	2.6701	2.3836	2.3259	2.2269	2.1349	2.3122	2.6604
Solomon Islands dollar	.8515	.8107	.9226	.9312	1.0694	1.0642	1.1324	1.1306	1.0172	1.0346	1.1527	1.2788	1.3170	1.7714	2.4299
Sri Lanka rupee	7.272	8.140	8.195	9.029	10.257	18.901	20.200	20.346	22.957	23.919	23.518	26.174	25.760	30.105	34.885
Thai baht	22.721	24.579	24.946	23.881	23.701	24.780	26.564	26.906	26.312	26.771	25.372	24.080	26.613	29.273	31.962
Tongan pa'anga	.8515	.8110	.9195	.9280	1.0657	1.0605	1.1284	1.1875	1.0765	1.0284	1.1210	1.1567	1.1800	1.6076	1.8336
Vanuatu,vatu	89.86	91.80	87.95	84.86	93.32	92.37	88.01	85.59	93.09	106.19	106.06	106.55	100.55	110.12	142.18
Vietnamese dong	.1	.2	.2	.2	.2	.2	.3	.3	†.3	1.3	1.3	1.3ᴾ	1.3ᴾ	†24.7	27.5
Europe															
Albanian lek	....	....	....	....	....	....	....	....	....	....	....	....	....	....	....
Armenian dram	....	....	....	....	....	....	....	....	....	....	....	....	....	....	....
Azerbaijan manat	....	....	....	....	....	....	....	....	....	....	....	....	....	....	....
Belarussian rubel	....	....	....	....	....	....	....	....	....	....	....	....	....	....	....
Bulgarian lev	.0012	.0012	.0012	....	....	....	....	....	....	....	....	....	....	.0011	.0011
Croatian kuna	....	....	....	....	....	....	....	....	....	....	....	....	....	....	....
Cyprus pound	.41622	.43511	.43782	.46044	.47822	.46443	.45760	.45527	.46522	.50355	.53850	.58245	.63138	.59681	.62583
Czech Republic koruna	....	....	....	....	....	....	....	....	....	....	....	....	....	....	....
Czechoslovak koruna	....	26.56	26.31	25.46	24.84	18.03	18.81	18.32	18.93	15.32	15.49	15.32	16.79	17.57	17.59
Estonian kroon	....	....	....	....	....	....	....	....	....	....	....	....	....	....	....
Hungarian forint	59.996	56.400	57.241	50.934	47.984	49.317	46.351	46.868	41.084	40.075	43.694	47.315	50.186	52.007	56.177
Kazakh tenge	....	....	....	....	....	....	....	....	....	....	....	....	....	....	....
Kyrgyz som	....	....	....	....	....	....	....	....	....	....	....	....	....	....	....
Latvian lats	....	....	....	....	....	....	....	....	....	....	....	....	....	....	....
Lithuanian litas	....	....	....	....	....	....	....	....	....	....	....	....	....	....	....
Macedonian denar	....	....	....	....	....	....	....	....	....	....	....	....	....	....	....
Maltese lira	.43067	.46649	.45968	.47257	.49566	.47929	.47383	.45297	.45168	.45075	.45827	.46641	.48208	.46557	.45153
Moldovan leu	....	....	....	....	....	....	....	....	....	....	....	....	....	....	....
Polish zloty	.0004	.0004	.0004	.0004	.0004	.0004	.0043	.0051	.0059	.0065	.0095	.0103	.0124	.0162	.0242
Romanian leu	6.0	24.1	24.5	23.4	23.2	24.3	23.5	23.7	23.0	17.5	16.5	19.2	17.4	17.3	18.7
Russian ruble	....	....	....	....	....	....	....	....	....	....	....	....	....	....	....
Slovak koruna	....	....	....	....	....	....	....	....	....	....	....	....	....	....	....
Slovenian tolar	....	....	....	....	....	....	....	....	....	....	....	....	....	....	....
Turkish lira	15	17	17	18	19	24	33	47	115	156	206	296	436	634	927
Ukrainian hryvnia	....	....	....	....	....	....	....	....	....	....	....	....	....	....	....
Middle East															
Bahrain dinar	.47619	.47620	.48330	.46300	.45968	.48060	.50007	.49664	.47955	.43764	.41477	.39365	.36856	.41300	.45992
Egyptian pound	.4720	.5245	.4791	.4581	.4546	.4753	.5098	.9221	.8928	.8148	.7722	.7329	.6861	.7689	.8562
Iranian rial	82.93	81.58	82.80	81.10	82.05	85.61	91.81	92.84	92.30	92.30	92.30	92.30	92.30	92.30	92.30
Iraqi dinar	.36443	.35625	.36157	.34572	.34311	.35872	.38474	.38903	.37665	.34374	.34291	.32545	.30471	.34145	.38024
Israeli new sheqel	.0005	.0005	.0007	.0008	.0010	.0019	.0025	.0047	†.0096	.0182	.0371	.1128	.6261	†1.6471	1.8181
Jordan dinar	.38775	.39696	.38567	.38775	.38775	.38775	.38775	.38775	.38775	.38775	.38775	.38775	.38775	.38775	.38775
Kuwaiti dinar	.35584	.35791	.35462	.34435	.33339	.34023	.35410	.35978	.34601	.32755	.31847	.30630	.29844	.31745	.35760
Lebanese pound	3.3	3.0	2.8	2.8	3.4	3.6	3.9	4.3	4.7	5.4	4.2	5.7	8.7	19.9	106.4
Libyan dinar	.35714	.35714	.36247	.34657	.34396	.35962	.38569	.39000	.37759	.34459	.32658	.30995	.29019	.32519	.38393
Rial Omani	.41666	.41667	.42289	.40435	.40130	.41956	.44998	.45501	.44053	.40203	.38101	.36162	.33856	.37939	.47032
Qatar riyal	4.7619	4.7619	4.8330	4.6679	4.5989	4.8100	5.0008	4.8807	4.6425	4.2368	4.0153	3.8109	3.5680	3.9982	4.4524
Saudi Arabian riyal	4.5057	4.2825	4.3464	4.1324	4.1013	4.2576	4.3187	4.4328	4.2407	3.9749	3.7892	3.6591	3.5043	4.0037	4.5808
Syrian pound	4.147	4.584	4.530	4.331	4.560	4.768	5.113	5.171	5.006	4.569	4.330	4.109	3.847	4.311	4.801
U.A.Emirates dirham	4.7619	4.8344	4.8735	4.6791	4.6206	4.7349	5.0001	4.9611	4.6820	4.2729	4.0495	3.8434	3.5984	4.0323	4.4903
Yemen,Rep.,Yemeni rial	....	....	....	....	....	....	....	....	....	....	....	....	....	....	....
Western Hemisphere															
Antigua & Barbuda,E.Car.$	2.2194	2.4925	2.5024	2.7770	3.1369	3.2797	3.5175	3.5568	3.4436	3.1427	2.9784	2.8268	2.6466	2.9657	3.3026
Argentine peso	—	—	—	—	—	—	—	—	—	—	—	—	.00002	.00009	.00015
Bahamian dollar	1.0857	1.2064	1.2244	1.1707	1.1618	1.2147	1.3028	1.3173	1.2754	1.1640	1.1031	1.0470	.9802	1.0984	1.2232
Barbados dollar	2.2194	2.4925	2.5024	2.3458	2.3281	2.4431	2.6203	2.6495	2.5652	2.3411	2.2187	2.1057	1.9715	2.2093	2.4464
Belize dollar	†1.8495	2.0770	2.0853	2.3141	2.7299	2.4294	2.6056	2.6347	2.5508	2.3279	2.2062	2.0939	1.9604	2.1968	2.4464
Bolivia, boliviano	.00002	.00002	.00002	.00002	.00002	.00002	.00003	.00003	.00003	.00003	.00022	.00053	.00861	†1.85853	2.35219
Brazilian real					†										
Chilean peso	.05	.90	2.45	9.95	20.24	33.96	44.23	51.38	49.74	45.39	64.50	76.23	87.26	201.74	250.75
Colombian peso	24.74	29.91	35.05	38.58	42.20	46.11	53.41	57.96	64.94	68.76	77.54	92.94	111.64	189.15	267.88
Costa Rican colon	7.20	8.02	10.49	10.03	9.96	10.41	11.16	11.29	10.93	42.01	44.40	45.44	46.81	58.99	72.02
Dominica, E.Caribbean dollar	2.2194	2.4925	2.5024	2.7770	3.1369	3.2797	3.5175	3.5568	3.4436	3.1427	2.9784	2.8268	2.6466	2.9657	3.3026
Dominican peso	1.086	1.206	1.224	1.171	1.162	1.215	1.303	1.317	1.275	1.164	1.103	1.047	.980	3.229	3.763
Ecuadoran sucre	27.1	30.2	30.6	29.3	29.0	30.4	32.6	32.9	31.9	29.1	36.6	56.6	65.8	105.2	179.2
Salvadoran colon	2.7143	3.0159	3.0609	2.9267	2.9046	3.0368	3.2570	3.2933	3.1885	2.9099	2.7578	2.6174	2.4505	2.7461	6.1160
Grenada, E.Caribbean dollar	2.2194	2.4925	2.5024	2.7770	3.1369	3.2797	3.5175	3.5568	3.4436	3.1427	2.9784	2.8268	2.6466	2.9657	3.3026
Guatemalan quetzal	1.0857	1.2064	1.2244	1.1707	1.1618	1.2147	1.3028	1.3173	1.2754	1.1640	1.1031	1.0470	.9802	1.0984	3.0580
Guyana dollar	2.410	2.706	2.717	2.985	2.963	3.098	3.322	3.359	3.252	3.492	3.309	3.141	4.068	4.558	5.382
Haitian gourde	5.4276	6.0307	6.1207	5.8523	5.8081	6.0725	6.5128	6.5855	6.3759	5.8188	5.5146	5.2338	4.9002	5.4911	6.1149
Honduran lempira	2.1714	2.4127	2.4487	2.3413	2.3237	2.4294	2.6056	2.6347	2.5508	2.3279	2.2062	2.0939	1.9604	2.1968	2.4464
Jamaica dollar	.9248	†1.0967	1.1130	1.0642	1.0562	1.1043	2.2082	2.3467	2.2720	2.0735	1.9651	3.4317	4.8324	6.0193	6.7031
Mexican peso	.0136	.0151	.0153	.0146	.0232	.0276	.0296	.0300	.0297	.0305	.1064	.1507	.1887	.4083	1.1296
Netherlands Antilles guilder	1.9543	2.1714	2.2038	2.1072	2.0913	2.1865	2.3450	2.3712	2.2957	2.0951	1.9856	1.8845	1.7644	1.9772	2.2017
Nicaraguan gold córdoba	—	—	—	—	—	—	—	†	—	—	—	—	—	—	—
Panamanian balboa	1.0857	1.2064	1.2244	1.1707	1.1618	1.2147	1.3028	1.3173	1.2754	1.1640	1.1031	1.0470	.9802	1.0984	1.2232
Paraguayan guarani	136.8	152.0	154.3	147.5	146.4	153.1	164.2	166.0	160.7	146.7	139.0	131.9	235.3	351.5	672.8
Peruvian new sol	—	—	—	—	—	—	—	—	—	—	—	—	.00001	†.00002	.00002
St.Kitts & Nevis, E.C.dollar	2.2194	2.4925	2.5024	2.7770	3.1369	3.2797	3.5175	3.5568	3.4436	3.1427	2.9784	2.8268	2.6466	2.9657	3.3026
St.Lucia, E.Car. dollar	2.2194	2.4925	2.5024	2.7770	3.1369	3.2797	3.5175	3.5568	3.4436	3.1427	2.9784	2.8268	2.6466	2.9657	3.3026
St. Vinc. & Grens.,E.Car.$	2.2194	2.4925	2.5024	2.7770	3.1369	3.2797	3.5175	3.5568	3.4436	3.1427	2.9784	2.8268	2.6466	2.9657	3.3026
Suriname guilder	1.938	2.153	2.185	2.090	2.074	2.168	2.325	2.351	2.277	2.078	1.969	1.869	1.750	1.961	2.183
Trinidad & Tobago dollar	2.2194	2.4924	2.5024	2.7769	2.7884	2.9153	3.1267	3.1616	3.0610	2.7935	2.6475	2.5127	2.3525	3.9543	4.4035
Uruguayan peso	.0008	.0011	.0020	†.0032	.0046	.0066	.0092	.0111	.0128	.0135	.0370	.0450	.0725	.1370	.2202
Venezuelan bolivar	4.723	5.169	5.246	5.016	4.987	5.214	5.592	5.655	5.475	4.996	4.735	4.502	7.352	8.238	17.736

† See country notes in the monthly *IFS*

Market, Official, or Principal Rate

National Currency Units per SDR: End of Period (aa)

1987	1988	1989	1990	1991	1992	1993	1994	1995	1996	1997	1998	1999	2000	2001	
															Asia (cont.)
....	....	....	19.917	56.359	144.467	†544.630	604.509	704.031	997.240	1,097.156	1,270.043	1,471.839	1,429.292	1,384.916	Mongolian togrog
8.5085	8.5085	8.5085	8.5085	8.5085	8.5085	8.5085	8.5085	8.5085	8.5085	8.5085	8.5085	8.5085	8.5085	8.5085	Myanmar kyat
30.643	33.912	37.585	43.249	61.079	59.400	67.634	72.817	83.243	82.007	85.408	95.288	94.326	96.806	96.108	Nepalese rupee
24.694	25.035	28.079	31.079	35.272	35.249	41.268	44.851	50.785	57.547	59.286	64.608	†71.075	75.607	76.489	Pakistan rupee
1.2462	1.1121	1.1297	1.3558	1.3626	1.3578	1.3479	1.7205	1.9846	1.9366	2.3630	2.9518	3.6995	4.0028	4.7281	Papua New Guinea kina
29.508	28.711	29.490	39.834	38.121	34.507	38.046	35.647	38.967	37.801	53.936	54.996	55.330	65.143	64.601	Philippine peso
2.8527	2.8909	3.0093	3.3193	3.5025	3.5166	3.5816	3.5789	3.7566	3.5004	3.7324	4.2385	4.1428	4.3532	4.4628	Samoa tala
2.8352	2.6190	2.4895	2.4818	2.3323	2.2617	2.2087	2.1324	2.1023	2.0129	2.2607	2.3380	2.2866	2.2560	2.3262	Singapore dollar
2.8009	2.8505	3.1500	3.7184	3.9978	4.2622	4.4611	4.8597	5.1668	5.2081	6.4067	6.8417	6.9671	6.6441	....	Solomon Islands dollar
43.642	44.453	52.566	57.248	60.908	63.250	68.076	72.963	80.341	81.540	82.689	96.164	99.054	107.594	117.075	Sri Lanka rupee
35.566	33.965	33.761	35.979	36.161	35.090	35.081	36.628	37.445	36.826	†63.748	51.662	51.428	56.374	55.575	Thai baht
1.9567	1.5748	1.6539	1.8435	1.8984	1.9050	1.8881	1.8308	1.8818	1.7377	1.8313	2.2670	2.2066	2.5754	2.7736	Tongan pa'anga
142.00	141.37	145.48	155.43	158.48	163.63	165.93	163.62	169.07	159.28	167.73	182.73	176.90	186.07	184.41	Vanuatu,vatu
399.0	1,513.9	7,063.6	11,559.1	16,449.9	†14,526.9	14,892.8	16,132.8	16,373.7	16,031.8	16,585.0	19,557.5	19,253.6	18,910.4	18,956.5	Vietnamese dong
															Europe
....	....	....	....	....	141.488	135.570	139.547	140.087	148.211	201.227	197.941	185.454	185.847	171.606	Albanian lek
....	....	....	....	....	2.85	103.02	591.98	597.57	625.61	667.85	735.03	718.88	719.44	706.04	Armenian dram
....	....	....	....	....	.021	.960	15.474	17.095	22.288	41.476	309.767	439.203	1,537.434	1,985.633	Belarussian rubel
.0012	.0011	.0011	.0040	.0312	.0337	.0449	.0964	.1051	.7008	2.3969	2.3586	2.6721	2.7386	2.7891	Bulgarian lev
....	....	....	....	....	1.09753	9.01316	8.21706	7.90233	7.96572	8.50446	8.79667	10.49648	10.62568	10.50129	Croatian kuna
.62263	.62751	.62924	.61828	.62802	.66419	.71398	.69523	.67867	.67567	.70935	.70152	.78862	.80357	.81712	Cyprus pound
....	....	....	....	....	....	41.14499	40.94733	39.54361	39.30232	46.73262	42.03674	49.38154	49.26694	45.56777	Czech Republic koruna
18.44	19.26	18.78	39.83	39.82	39.74	....	....	....	....	....	....	....	....	....	Czechoslovak koruna
....	....	....	....	....	17.754	19.062	18.088	17.038	17.888	19.343	18.882	21.359	21.915	22.234	Estonian kroon
65.807	70.699	82.192	87.421	108.169	115.459	138.317	161.591	207.321	237.163	274.572	308.401	346.586	370.978	350.665	Hungarian forint
....	....	....	....	....	....	8.67	79.21	95.06	105.40	101.94	117.99	189.68	188.27	188.76	Kazakh tenge
....	....	....	....	....	....	11.030	15.547	16.649	24.014	23.443	41.362	62.352	62.936	59.969	Kyrgyz som
....	....	....	....	....	1.14813	.81727	.80000	.79825	.79951	.79606	.80117	.80017	.79868	.80179	Latvian lats
....	....	....	....	....	5.21125	5.35688	5.83940	5.94596	5.75184	5.39700	5.63212	5.49004	5.21164	5.02692	Lithuanian litas
....	....	....	....	....	....	61.062	59.264	56.456	59.547	74.776	72.987	82.816	86.420	86.930	Macedonian denar
.44221	.44697	.44269	.42788	.43712	.51450	.54272	.53738	.52384	.51712	.52717	.53141	.56558	.57038	.56812	Maltese lira
....	....	....	....	.0024	.5698	†4.9998	6.2336	6.6877	6.7215	6.2882	11.7185	15.9077	16.1343	16.4517	Moldovan leu
.0448	.0676	.8542	1.3515	1.5673	2.1680	2.9317	3.5579	3.6687	4.1349	4.7467	4.9337	5.6936	5.3982	5.0097	Polish zloty
19.5	19.3	19.0	49.4	†270.4	632.5	1,752.7	2,579.6	3,832.2	5,802.2	10,825.0	15,419.3	25,055.2	33,779.2	39,708.9	Romanian leu
....	....	....	....	....	.5706	1.7128	5.1825	6.8973	7.9951	8.0415	†29.0758	37.0578	36.6899	37.8778	Russian ruble
....	....	....	....	....	....	45.605	45.660	43.954	45.864	46.930	51.975	58.011	61.744	60.910	Slovak koruna
....	....	....	....	81.095	135.713	181.093	184.609	187.283	203.443	228.266	226.974	270.069	296.252	315.371	Slovenian tolar
1,448	2,442	3,041	4,168	7,266	11,776	19,879	56,534	88,669	154,976	277,413	442,775	743,077	877,360	1,822,418	Turkish lira
....	....	....	....	....	.0088	.1732	1.5212	2.6668	†2.7163	2.5622	4.8253	7.1594	7.0807	6.6588	Ukrainian hryvnia
															Middle East
.53341	.50598	.49412	.53492	.53784	.51700	.51646	.54890	.55892	.54067	.50732	.52942	.51606	.48990	.47253	Bahrain dinar
.9931	.9420	1.4456	2.8453	4.7665	4.5906	4.6314	4.9504	5.0392	4.8718	4.5713	4.7704	4.6734	4.8077	5.6427	Egyptian pound
92.30	92.30	92.30	92.30	92.30	92.30	2,415.49	2,534.26	2,597.64	2,515.19	2,366.94	2,465.36	2,405.04	2,948.39	2,200.47	Iranian rial
.44100	.41832	.40852	.44225	.44466	.42743	.42698	.45381	.46209	.44700	.41942	.43770	.42665	.40502	.39066	Iraqi dinar
2.1828	2.2675	2.5797	2.9136	3.2657	3.8005	4.1015	4.4058	4.6601	4.6748	4.7709	5.8588	5.7000	5.2651	5.5497	Israeli new sheqel
.38775	.64191	.85158	.94604	.96553	.95011	.96699	1.02336	1.05392	1.01951	.95662	.99829	.97311	.92376	.89102	Jordan dinar
.38289	.38031	.38370	....	.40663	.41621	.40990	.43813	.44436	.43123	.41139	.42461	.41749	.39793	.38602	Kuwaiti dinar
645.5	713.2	663.7	1,197.9	1,257.3	2,527.3	2,350.2	2,404.4	2,372.4	2,231.7	2,060.3	2,123.3	2,069.1	1,964.1	1,894.5	Lebanese pound
.38393[p]	.38393[p]	.38393[p]	.38393[p]	.38393[p]	.41428[p]	.44643	.52500	.52500	.52500	.52500	.53292	.74162	.70403	.81699	Libyan dinar
.54547	.51742	.50529	.54701	.55000	.52869	.52813	.56131	.57156	.55290	.51879	.54139	.52773	.50097	.48321	Rial Omani
5.1639	4.8983	4.7835	5.1785	5.2068	5.0050	4.9998	5.3139	5.4108	5.2342	4.9113	5.1252	4.9959	4.7426	4.5745	Qatar riyal
5.3129	5.0396	4.9215	5.3279	5.3570	5.1494	5.1440	5.4671	5.5669	5.3852	5.0529	5.2731	5.1401	4.8794	4.7065	Saudi Arabian riyal
5.568	15.105	14.751	15.969	16.057	15.434	15.418	16.387	16.686	16.141	15.145	15.805	15.406	14.625	14.107	Syrian pound
5.2079	4.9401	4.8243	5.2226	5.2511	5.0476	5.0423	5.3591	5.4569	5.2788	4.9551	5.1710	5.0405	4.7849	4.6153	U.A.Emirates dirham
....	....	....	17.086	17.179	16.514	16.496	17.533	†74.384	†182.492	176.023	199.447	218.366	215.749	217.754	Yemen,Rep.,Yemeni rial
															Western Hemisphere
3.8304	3.6334	3.5482	3.8412	3.8622	3.7125	3.7086	3.9416	4.0135	3.8825	3.6430	3.8017	3.7058	3.5179	3.3932	Antigua & Barbuda,E. Car.$
.00053	.00180	.23589	.79456	1.42828	1.36194	1.37150	1.45912	1.48649	1.43724	1.34858	1.40733	1.37182	1.30226	1.25610	Argentine peso
1.4187	1.3457	1.3142	1.4227	1.4304	1.3750	1.3736	1.4599	1.4865	1.4380	1.3493	1.4080	1.3725	1.3029	1.2567	Bahamian dollar
2.8373	2.6914	2.6283	2.8453	2.8609	2.7500	2.7471	2.9197	2.9730	2.8759	2.6985	2.8161	2.7450	2.6058	2.5135	Barbados dollar
2.8373	2.6914	2.6283	2.8453	2.8609	2.7500	2.7471	2.9197	2.9730	2.8759	2.6985	2.8161	2.7450	2.6058	2.5135	Belize dollar
†3.13524	3.32388	3.91620	4.83704	5.35696	5.63063	6.14668	6.85400	7.33583	7.45582	7.23873	7.94833	8.22133	8.32559	8.57090	Bolivia, boliviano
—	†—	.00001	.00009	.00056	†.00619	.16288	†1.23503	1.44635	1.49462	1.50630	1.70189	2.45542	2.54667	2.91612	Brazilian real
337.80	333.05	389.75	479.24	536.23	525.70	592.06	589.91	605.19	611.09	593.41	667.08	727.53	746.15	824.67	Chilean peso
374.10	451.97	570.24	809.11	1,011.11	1,116.18	1,260.01	1,213.53	1,468.13	1,445.62	1,745.36	2,122.63	2,571.77	2,849.49	2,892.15	Colombian peso
98.24	106.98	110.85	147.32	193.72	188.97	208.01	240.98	289.72	316.51	329.61	382.17	409.27	414.35	429.39	Costa Rican colon
3.8304	3.6334	3.5482	3.8412	3.8622	3.7125	3.7086	3.9416	4.0135	3.8825	3.6430	3.8017	3.7058	3.5179	3.3932	Dominica, E.Caribbean dollar
7.037	8.532	8.332	16.147	18.109	17.291	17.536	19.071	20.015	20.220	19.383	22.230	22.014	21.725	21.551	Dominican peso
314.2	582.0	852.1	1,249.4	1,817.5	2,535.8	2,807.3	3,312.4	4,345.8	5,227.0	5,974.5	9,609.8	27,783.7	32,572.8	31,418.3	Ecuadoran sucre
7.0933	6.7285	6.5708	11.4240	11.5579	12.6088	11.9088	12.7737	13.0142	12.5893	11.8127	12.3273	12.0163	11.4070	10.9964	Salvadoran colon
3.8304	3.6334	3.5482	3.8412	3.8622	3.7125	3.7086	3.9416	4.0135	3.8825	3.6430	3.8017	3.7058	3.5179	3.3932	Grenada, E.Caribbean dollar
3.5467	3.6401	4.4681	7.1341	7.2142	7.2522	7.9876	8.2460	8.9810	8.5782	8.3342	9.6425	10.7342	10.0731	10.0544	Guatemalan quetzal
14.187	13.457	43.367	64.020	174.512	173.250	179.593	208.029	208.852	203.112	194.292	228.453	247.738	240.713	238.150	Guyana dollar
7.0920	6.7273	6.5696	7.1120	†11.7867	15.0604	17.5884	18.9001	24.0215	21.7028	23.3569	23.2390	24.6577	29.3470	33.1009	Haitian gourde
2.8373	2.6914	2.6283	7.6212	7.7243	8.0163	9.9720	13.7227	15.3751	18.5057	17.6673	19.4415	19.9067	19.7270	20.0068	Honduran lempira
7.8026	7.3744	8.5158	11.4348	30.7435	30.5038	44.6057	48.4692	58.8894	50.1351	49.0326	52.1744	56.6719	59.1715	59.4257	Jamaica dollar
3.1348	3.0695	3.4707	4.1903	4.3929	4.2837	4.2661	7.7737	11.3605	11.2893	10.9064	13.8902	13.0585	12.4717	11.4894	Mexican peso
2.5536	2.4223	2.3523	2.5466	2.5605	2.4613	2.4587	2.6131	2.6608	2.5739	2.4152	2.5204	2.4568	2.3322	2.2495	Netherlands Antilles guilder
—	†.00025	.01003	.85360	7.15200	6.87500	8.72169	10.38202	11.83989	12.83236	13.48575	15.76149	16.90658	17.01249	17.39415	Nicaraguan gold córdoba
1.4187	1.3457	1.3142	1.4227	1.4304	1.3750	1.3736	1.4599	1.4865	1.4380	1.3493	1.4080	1.3725	1.3029	1.2567	Panamanian balboa
780.3	740.1	1,600.6	1,789.7	1,974.0	2,241.3	2,582.3	2,809.8	2,942.7	3,033.6	3,184.2	3,999.1	4,568.9	4,595.2	5,884.0	Paraguayan guarani
.00005	.00067	.00691	.73541	1.37321	2.24125	2.96689	3.18247	3.43379	3.73870	3.68345	4.44937	4.81751	4.59536	4.32818	Peruvian new sol
3.8304	3.6334	3.5482	3.8412	3.8622	3.7125	3.7086	3.9416	4.0135	3.8825	3.6430	3.8017	3.7058	3.5179	3.3932	St.Kitts & Nevis, E.C. dollar
3.8304	3.6334	3.5482	3.8412	3.8622	3.7125	3.7086	3.9416	4.0135	3.8825	3.6430	3.8017	3.7058	3.5179	3.3932	St.Lucia, E.Car. dollar
3.8304	3.6334	3.5482	3.8412	3.8622	3.7125	3.7086	3.9416	4.0135	3.8825	3.6430	3.8017	3.7058	3.5179	3.3932	St. Vinc. & Grens.,E. Car.$
2.532	2.402	2.346	2.539	2.553	2.454	2.452	†597.809	605.001	576.622	541.049	564.620	1,355.354	2,838.389	2,737.786	Suriname guilder
5.1072	5.7192	5.5852	6.0463	6.0793	5.8438	7.9860	8.6616	8.9146	8.9074	8.5001	9.2881	8.6467	8.2078	7.9051	Trinidad & Tobago dollar
.3965	.6056	1.0566	2.2663	3.5589	4.7850	†6.0656	8.1766	10.5704	12.5289	13.5465	15.2307	15.9417	16.3059	18.5594	Uruguayan peso
20.571	19.513	56.612	71.673	88.048	109.244	145.102	†248.175	431.082	685.188	680.359	794.833	889.730	911.711	958.885	Venezuelan bolivar

† **See country notes in the monthly *IFS***

Exchange Rates

SDR Rates: *1982-2002*

sa US Dollars per SDR (*End of Period*)

	Jan.	Feb.	Mar.	April	May	June	July	Aug.	Sept.	Oct.	Nov.	Dec.	I	II	III	IV	Year
1982	1.14784	1.12689	1.11309	1.12967	1.12410	1.09224	1.09208	1.08309	1.07234	1.06237	1.07953	1.10311	1.11309	1.09224	1.07234	1.10311	1.10311
1983	1.08645	1.08995	1.07867	1.08163	1.07734	1.06835	1.05563	1.04461	1.05684	1.05928	1.05058	1.04695	1.07867	1.06835	1.05684	1.04695	1.04695
1984	1.03409	1.06013	1.06420	1.04712	1.04140	1.03121	1.01333	1.01663	.99901	.99623	.98935	.98021	1.06420	1.03121	.99901	.98021	.98021
1985	.97499	.95942	.99127	.99117	.99295	.99828	1.03737	1.03536	1.05940	1.07165	1.09319	1.09842	.99127	.99828	1.05940	1.09842	1.09842
1986	1.11115	1.15584	1.13827	1.17596	1.14314	1.17757	1.20371	1.20689	1.21342	1.18661	1.21030	1.22319	1.13827	1.17757	1.21342	1.22319	1.22319
1987	1.26759	1.26419	1.28563	1.30626	1.28658	1.27802	1.26723	1.29313	1.27964	1.32109	1.37379	1.41866	1.28563	1.27802	1.27964	1.41866	1.41866
1988	1.36642	1.36101	1.38729	1.38417	1.36483	1.31061	1.29648	1.28818	1.29039	1.34592	1.36637	1.34570	1.38729	1.31061	1.29039	1.34570	1.34570
1989	1.31093	1.32150	1.29271	1.29566	1.24362	1.24639	1.28749	1.24652	1.27981	1.27782	1.28771	1.31416	1.29271	1.24639	1.27981	1.31416	1.31416
1990	1.32559	1.31681	1.30083	1.30247	1.31200	1.32388	1.36564	1.38595	1.39256	1.43078	1.42677	1.42266	1.30083	1.32388	1.39256	1.42266	1.42266
1991	1.43476	1.42053	1.34632	1.34081	1.34084	1.31452	1.33400	1.33698	1.36800	1.36652	1.38072	1.43043	1.34632	1.31452	1.36800	1.43043	1.43043
1992	1.39733	1.38091	1.37174	1.36976	1.39632	1.43117	1.44416	1.48286	1.47284	1.40595	1.37896	1.37500	1.37174	1.43117	1.47284	1.37500	1.37500
1993	1.38188	1.37610	1.39773	1.42339	1.42847	1.40360	1.39072	1.40758	1.41840	1.39293	1.38389	1.37356	1.39773	1.40360	1.41840	1.37356	1.37356
1994	1.38067	1.39930	1.41260	1.42138	1.41733	1.44837	1.44327	1.44770	1.46738	1.48454	1.45674	1.45985	1.41260	1.44837	1.46738	1.45985	1.45985
1995	1.47670	1.49440	1.56050	1.57303	1.57591	1.56876	1.55954	1.49249	1.50632	1.49455	1.48615	1.48649	1.56050	1.56876	1.50632	1.48649	1.48649
1996	1.45169	1.46868	1.46121	1.45006	1.44219	1.44334	1.46554	1.45766	1.43937	1.44623	1.44462	1.43796	1.46121	1.44334	1.43937	1.43796	1.43796
1997	1.39466	1.38494	1.38689	1.36553	1.39179	1.38814	1.35862	1.36358	1.36521	1.38362	1.36184	1.34925	1.38689	1.38814	1.36521	1.34925	1.34925
1998	1.34536	1.35023	1.33589	1.34666	1.33536	1.33154	1.32949	1.34222	1.37132	1.40835	1.38017	1.40803	1.33589	1.33154	1.37132	1.40803	1.40803
1999	1.38977	1.36556	1.35784	1.35123	1.34196	1.33587	1.36421	1.36986	1.38769	1.38072	1.36963	1.37251	1.35784	1.33587	1.38769	1.37251	1.37251
2000	1.35288	1.33928	1.34687	1.31921	1.32002	1.33728	1.31335	1.30480	1.29789	1.27934	1.28197	1.30291	1.34687	1.33728	1.29789	1.30291	1.30291
2001	1.29779	1.29248	1.26065	1.26579	1.25423	1.24565	1.25874	1.28823	1.28901	1.27808	1.26608	1.25673	1.26065	1.24565	1.28901	1.25673	1.25673
2002	1.24204	1.24163	1.24691	1.26771	1.29066	1.33046	1.32248						1.24691	1.33046			

sb US Dollars per SDR (*Period Average, geometric*)

	Jan.	Feb.	Mar.	April	May	June	July	Aug.	Sept.	Oct.	Nov.	Dec.	I	II	III	IV	Year
1982	1.15329	1.13288	1.12347	1.11507	1.13472	1.10209	1.09149	1.08656	1.07979	1.07131	1.06707	1.09407	1.13648	1.11721	1.08594	1.07742	1.10401
1983	1.10004	1.09004	1.08544	1.08220	1.08262	1.06890	1.06292	1.04994	1.05087	1.06228	1.05178	1.04272	1.09182	1.07789	1.05456	1.05223	1.06900
1984	1.03579	1.04674	1.06398	1.05716	1.04100	1.03967	1.02009	1.01633	1.00006	.99278	1.00259	.98749	1.04877	1.04591	1.01212	.99427	1.02501
1985	.97558	.96174	.96366	.99036	.98956	.99703	1.01993	1.03341	1.02830	1.06516	1.08003	1.08972	.96697	.99231	1.02720	1.07826	1.01534
1986	1.09786	1.12904	1.14834	1.15007	1.16859	1.16461	1.18935	1.20849	1.21051	1.21175	1.19840	1.20746	1.12489	1.16106	1.20275	1.20586	1.17317
1987	1.25112	1.26216	1.26933	1.29153	1.30442	1.28656	1.26932	1.26927	1.29137	1.29530	1.34938	1.38310	1.26085	1.29415	1.27661	1.34210	1.29307
1988	1.37723	1.35556	1.37141	1.38197	1.37595	1.34654	1.30514	1.29206	1.29368	1.31949	1.35659	1.35588	1.36804	1.36807	1.29695	1.34387	1.34392
1989	1.32525	1.31652	1.30486	1.29975	1.26560	1.24062	1.27158	1.26166	1.24703	1.27221	1.27724	1.30191	1.31552	1.26843	1.26005	1.28372	1.28176
1990	1.31850	1.32659	1.30170	1.30135	1.31832	1.31442	1.34402	1.37719	1.39049	1.42846	1.44481	1.42654	1.31556	1.31134	1.37042	1.43325	1.35675
1991	1.42291	1.44058	1.38077	1.35123	1.34351	1.31934	1.32155	1.33571	1.35355	1.36201	1.38487	1.40799	1.41453	1.33796	1.33687	1.38483	1.36816
1992	1.40925	1.39042	1.36599	1.37060	1.38810	1.41173	1.44375	1.45645	1.45767	1.43476	1.38701	1.38883	1.38844	1.39004	1.45261	1.40336	1.40838
1993	1.37705	1.37168	1.38045	1.41266	1.41561	1.40969	1.39025	1.40151	1.41756	1.40746	1.38903	1.38404	1.37639	1.41265	1.40306	1.39347	1.39633
1994	1.37343	1.38750	1.40197	1.40425	1.41500	1.42736	1.45706	1.45439	1.46377	1.47720	1.47121	1.45201	1.38759	1.41550	1.45840	1.46676	1.43170
1995	1.46580	1.47826	1.53602	1.57620	1.55819	1.56369	1.55763	1.51069	1.48396	1.49828	1.49474	1.48532	1.49305	1.56601	1.51712	1.49277	1.51695
1996	1.46779	1.46625	1.46181	1.45086	1.44464	1.44290	1.45003	1.45830	1.44811	1.43968	1.45295	1.43817	1.46528	1.44613	1.45214	1.44359	1.45176
1997	1.41537	1.38421	1.37811	1.37150	1.38518	1.39032	1.37726	1.35396	1.35939	1.36989	1.37399	1.35418	1.39256	1.38231	1.36350	1.36599	1.37602
1998	1.34310	1.35002	1.34421	1.34312	1.34373	1.33354	1.33092	1.32668	1.36482	1.40747	1.39199	1.40211	1.34577	1.34013	1.34070	1.40051	1.35654
1999	1.40441	1.38073	1.36265	1.35485	1.34869	1.34004	1.33924	1.36415	1.37613	1.38943	1.37626	1.37280	1.38249	1.34785	1.35975	1.37948	1.36732
2000	1.37068	1.34485	1.34286	1.33915	1.31082	1.33062	1.32348	1.30836	1.29409	1.28650	1.28276	1.29440	1.35274	1.32681	1.30859	1.28788	1.31879
2001	1.30203	1.29353	1.27989	1.26764	1.26217	1.25028	1.25125	1.27495	1.28593	1.27882	1.26827	1.26279	1.29179	1.26001	1.27062	1.26995	1.27304
2002	1.25276	1.24463	1.25009	1.25669	1.27713	1.30065	1.33033						1.24915	1.27803			

sc SDRs per US Dollar (*End of Period*)

	Jan.	Feb.	Mar.	April	May	June	July	Aug.	Sept.	Oct.	Nov.	Dec.	I	II	III	IV	Year
1982	.87120	.88740	.89840	.88521	.88960	.91555	.91568	.92328	.93254	.94129	.92633	.90653	.89840	.91555	.93254	.90653	.90653
1983	.92043	.91748	.92707	.92453	.92822	.93602	.94730	.95730	.94622	.94404	.95186	.95515	.92707	.93602	.94622	.95515	.95515
1984	.96703	.94328	.93967	.95500	.96025	.96973	.98685	.98364	1.00100	1.00378	1.01077	1.02019	.93967	.96973	1.00100	1.02019	1.02019
1985	1.02565	1.04230	1.00880	1.00891	1.00710	1.00172	.96398	.96584	.94393	.93314	.91476	.91040	1.00880	1.00172	.94393	.91040	.91040
1986	.89997	.86517	.87853	.85037	.87478	.84921	.83077	.82858	.82412	.84273	.82624	.81753	.87853	.84921	.82412	.81753	.81753
1987	.78890	.79102	.77783	.76554	.77725	.78246	.78913	.77332	.78147	.75695	.72791	.70489	.77783	.78246	.78147	.70489	.70489
1988	.73184	.73475	.72083	.72245	.73269	.76300	.77132	.77629	.77496	.74299	.73187	.74311	.72083	.76300	.77496	.74311	.74311
1989	.76282	.75672	.77357	.77181	.80410	.80232	.77670	.80223	.78137	.78258	.77657	.76094	.77357	.80232	.78137	.76094	.76094
1990	.75438	.75941	.76874	.76777	.76219	.75536	.73226	.72153	.71810	.69892	.70089	.70291	.76874	.75536	.71810	.70291	.70291
1991	.69698	.70396	.74277	.74582	.74580	.76074	.74962	.74795	.73100	.73179	.72426	.69909	.74277	.76074	.73100	.69909	.69909
1992	.71565	.72416	.72900	.73006	.71617	.69873	.69244	.67437	.67896	.71127	.72518	.72727	.72900	.69873	.67896	.72727	.72727
1993	.72365	.72669	.71545	.70255	.70005	.71245	.71905	.71044	.70502	.71791	.72260	.72804	.71545	.71245	.70502	.72804	.72804
1994	.72429	.71465	.70792	.70354	.70555	.69043	.69287	.69075	.68149	.67361	.68646	.68500	.70792	.69043	.68149	.68500	.68500
1995	.67719	.66916	.64082	.63572	.63455	.63745	.64121	.67002	.66387	.66910	.67288	.67273	.64082	.63745	.66387	.67273	.67273
1996	.68885	.68088	.68436	.68963	.69339	.69284	.68234	.68603	.69475	.69145	.69222	.69543	.68436	.69284	.69475	.69543	.69543
1997	.71702	.72205	.72104	.73232	.71850	.72039	.73604	.73336	.73249	.72274	.73430	.74115	.72104	.72039	.73249	.74115	.74115
1998	.74330	.74061	.74856	.74258	.74886	.75101	.75217	.74503	.72922	.71005	.72455	.71021	.74856	.75101	.72922	.71021	.71021
1999	.71954	.73230	.73646	.74007	.74518	.74857	.73303	.73000	.72062	.72426	.73013	.72859	.73646	.74857	72062	72859	72859
2000	.73017	.74667	.74246	.75803	.75757	.74779	.76141	.76640	.77048	.78165	.78005	.76751	.74246	.74779	.77048	.76751	.76751
2001	.77054	.77371	.79324	.79002	.79731	.80280	.79445	.77626	.77579	.78243	.78984	.79572	.79324	.80280	.77579	.79572	.79572
2002	.80513	.80403	.80198	.78883	.77480	.75162	.75615						.80198	.75162			

sd SDRs per US Dollar (*Period Average, geometric*)

	Jan.	Feb.	Mar.	April	May	June	July	Aug.	Sept.	Oct.	Nov.	Dec.	I	II	III	IV	Year
1981	.78869	.81152	.81411	.82629	.84839	.86478	.88051	.89099	.87457	.86656	.85767	.85919	.80469	.84634	.88200	.86113	.84806
1982	.86709	.88270	.89010	.89680	.88128	.90736	.91618	.92034	.92610	.93344	.93714	.91402	.87991	.89509	.92086	.92814	.90579
1983	.90906	.91740	.92128	.92404	.92368	.93554	.94081	.95243	.95160	.94138	.95077	.95903	.91590	.92774	.94826	.95036	.93545
1984	.96545	.95535	.93987	.94593	.96061	.96184	.98031	.98394	.99994	1.00727	.99741	1.01267	.95350	.95611	.98803	1.00577	.97560
1985	1.02503	1.03979	1.03771	1.00974	1.01055	1.00298	.98046	.96767	.97248	.93882	.92590	.91767	1.03416	1.00775	.97352	.92743	.98489
1986	.91086	.88571	.87082	.86951	.85574	.85866	.84080	.82748	.82610	.82526	.83445	.82819	.88898	.86128	.83143	.82929	.85239
1987	.79928	.79229	.78781	.77427	.76662	.77727	.78782	.78785	.77437	.77202	.74108	.72301	.79312	.77271	.78332	.74510	.77335
1988	.72609	.73770	.72918	.72361	.72677	.74264	.76620	.77396	.77299	.75787	.73714	.73753	.73098	.73096	.77104	.74412	.74409
1989	.75458	.75958	.76637	.76938	.79014	.80605	.78642	.79261	.80191	.78603	.78294	.76810	.76016	.78838	.79362	.77899	.78018
1990	.75844	.75381	.76823	.76843	.75854	.76079	.74404	.72612	.71917	.70006	.69213	.70100	.76014	.76258	.72970	.69772	.73706
1991	.70279	.69417	.72423	.74007	.74432	.75795	.75669	.74867	.73880	.73421	.72209	.71023	.70694	.74741	.74802	.72211	.73091
1992	.70960	.71921	.73207	.72961	.72041	.70835	.69264	.68660	.68603	.69698	.72098	.72003	.72024	.71940	.68842	.71258	.71004
1993	.72619	.72903	.72440	.70788	.70641	.70938	.71930	.71352	.70544	.71050	.71993	.72252	.72654	.70789	.71273	.71763	.71616
1994	.72810	.72072	.71328	.71213	.70671	.70059	.68631	.68757	.68317	.67696	.67971	.68870	.72068	.70646	.68568	.68177	.69847
1995	.68222	.67647	.65103	.63444	.64177	.63951	.64200	.66195	.67387	.66743	.66901	.67326	.66977	.63857	.65914	.66990	.65922
1996	.68130	.68201	.68408	.68925	.69221	.69305	.68964	.68573	.69056	.69460	.68825	.69533	.68246	.69150	.68864	.69272	.68882
1997	.70653	.72243	.72563	.72913	.72193	.71926	.72608	.73857	.73562	.72999	.72781	.73845	.71810	.72344	.73341	.73207	.72673
1998	.74455	.74073	.74393	.74453	.74420	.74988	.75136	.75376	.73269	.71114	.71840	.71321	.74307	.74620	.74588	.71424	.73722
1999	.71204	.72425	.73387	.73809	.74146	.74624	.74669	.73306	.72668	.71972	.72661	.72844	.72333	.74192	.73543	.72491	.73136
2000	.72957	.74358	.74468	.74674	.76288	.75153	.75559	.76431	.77275	.77730	.77957	.77256	.73924	.75369	.76418	.77647	.75827
2001	.76803	.77308	.78132	.78887	.79229	.79982	.79920	.78435	.77765	.78197	.78847	.79189	.77412	.79364	.78702	.78744	.78552
2002	.79824	.80345	.79994	.79574	.78301	.76885	.75169						.80054	.78245			

Fund Accounts: Arrangements

(As of July 31, 2002 and Amounts Expressed in Millions of SDRs)

Member	Date of Arrangement	Date of Expiration	Amount Agreed	Undrawn Balance
Stand-By Arrangements				
Argentina	March 10, 2000	March 9, 2003	16,725.09	6,968.78
Brazil	September 14, 2001	December 13, 2002	12,144.40	759.03
Bulgaria	February 27, 2002	February 26, 2004	240.00	182.00
Guatemala	April 1, 2002	March 31, 2003	84.00	84.00
Jordan	July 3, 2002	July 2, 2004	85.28	74.62
Latvia	April 20, 2001	December 19, 2002	33.00	33.00
Lithuania	August 30, 2001	March 29, 2003	86.52	86.52
Peru	February 1, 2002	February 29, 2004	255.00	255.00
Romania	October 31, 2001	April 29, 2003	300.00	248.00
Sri Lanka	April 20, 2001	August 19, 2002	200.00	48.32
Turkey	February 4, 2002	December 31, 2004	12,821.00	3,759.60
Uruguay	April 1, 2002	March 31, 2002	1,752.03	1,243.6
Total			44,726.90	13,742.47
Extended Arrangements				
Colombia	December 20, 1999	December 19, 2002	1,957.00	1,957.00
Indonesia	February 4, 2000	December 31, 2003	3,638.00	1,651.48
Ukraine	September 4, 1998	September 03, 2002	1,919.95	726.95
Yugoslavia, Fed. Rep. of	May 14, 2002	May 13, 2005	650.00	600.00
Total			8,164.95	4,935.43
Total (Stand-By and Extended Arrangements)			**52,891.74**	**18,677.90**
Poverty Reduction and Growth Arrangements				
Albania	June 21, 2002	June 20, 2005	28.00	24.00
Armenia	May 23, 2001	May 22, 2004	69.00	59.00
Azerbaijan	July 6, 2001	July 5, 2004	80.45	64.35
Benin	July 17, 2000	March 31 2004	27.00	8.08
Burkina Faso	September 10, 1999	December 9, 2002	39.12	5.58
Cambodia	October 22, 1999	February 28, 2003	58.50	8.36
Cameroon	December 21, 2000	December 20, 2003	111.42	63.66
Cape Verde	April 10, 2002	April 9, 2005	8.64	7.41
Chad	January 7, 2000	January 6, 2003	47.60	15.80
Congo, Dem. Rep. of	June 12, 2002	June 11, 2005	580.00	160.00
Côte d'Ivoire	March 29, 2002	March 28, 2005	292.68	234.14
Djibouti	October 18, 1999	October 17, 2002	19.08	10.00
Ethiopia	March 22, 2001	March 21, 2004	100.28	41.72
Gambia, The	July 18, 2002	July 17, 2005	20.22	17.33
Georgia	January 12, 2001	January 11, 2004	108.00	58.50
Ghana	May 3, 1999	November 30, 2002	228.80	52.58
Guinea	May 2, 2001	May 1, 2004	64.26	38.56
Guinea-Bissau	December 15, 2000	December 14, 2003	14.20	9.12
Honduras	March 26, 1999	December 31, 2002	156.75	48.45
Kenya	August 4, 2000	August 3, 2003	190.00	156.40
Kyrgyz Republic	December 6, 2001	December 5, 2004	73.40	49.96
Lao People's Dem. Republic	April 25, 2001	April 24, 2004	31.71	22.65
Lesotho	March 9, 2001	March 8, 2004	24.50	14.00
Madagascar	March 1, 2001	February 29, 2004	79.43	56.74
Malawi	December 21, 2000	December 20, 2003	45.11	38.67
Mali	August 6, 1999	August 5, 2003	51.32	19.65
Mauritania	July 21, 1999	December 20, 2002	42.49	6.07
Moldova	December 21, 2000	December 20, 2003	110.88	83.16
Mongolia	September 28, 2001	September 27, 2004	28.49	24.42
Mozambique	June 28, 1999	June 27, 2003	87.20	16.80
Niger	December 22, 2000	December 21, 2003	59.20	33.82
Pakistan	December 6, 2001	December 5, 2004	1,033.70	775.26
São Tomé and Principe	April 28, 2000	April 27, 2003	6.66	4.76
Sierra Leone	September 26, 2001	September 25, 2004	130.84	74.67
Tanzania	April 4, 2000	April 3, 2003	135.00	35.00
Vietnam	April 13, 2001	April 12, 2004	290.00	165.80
Zambia	March 25, 1999	March 28, 2003	278.90	124.02
Total			4,752.82	2,628.65
Total (Stand-by, Extended, and Poverty Reduction and Growth Arrangements)			**57,365.66**	**21,182.34**

Fund Accounts: Position to Date

(As of July 31, 2002 and Expressed in Millions of SDRs)

	Quota	Reserve Position in the Fund	Total Fund Credit and Loans Outstanding				Fund Holdings of Currency		SDR Department		
			Total Amount	Percent of Quota	Outstanding Purchases (GRA)	Outstanding Loans	Amount	Percent of Quota	Net Cumulative Allocation	Holdings of SDRs	
										Amount	Percent of Allocation
	(1)	(2)	(3)	(4)	(5)	(6)	(7)	(8)	(9)	(10)	(11)
All Countries	212,666.1	63,219.8	66,512.2	31.3	60,016.6	6,495.6	209,456.4	98.5	21,433.3	19,466.7	90.8
Industrial Countries	130,566.6	51,790.5	—	—	—	—	78,775.9	60.3	14,595.3	15,370.3	105.3
United States	37,149.3	15,019.3	—	—	—	—	22,129.3	59.6	4,899.5	8,752.8	178.6
Canada	6,369.2	2,486.4	—	—	—	—	3,882.9	61.0	779.3	507.4	65.1
Australia	3,236.4	1,249.5	—	—	—	—	1,987.0	61.4	470.5	92.4	19.6
Japan	13,312.8	5,318.7	—	—	—	—	7,994.2	60.0	891.7	1,801.1	202.0
New Zealand	894.6	347.2	—	—	—	—	547.4	61.2	141.3	14.1	10.0
Austria	1,872.3	723.9	—	—	—	—	1,148.4	61.3	179.0	129.1	72.1
Belgium	4,605.2	1,829.7	—	—	—	—	2,775.5	60.3	485.2	390.7	80.5
Denmark	1,642.8	633.9	—	—	—	—	1,008.9	61.4	178.9	52.5	29.4
Finland	1,263.8	446.3	—	—	—	—	817.6	64.7	142.7	142.3	99.7
France	10,738.5	4,369.6	—	—	—	—	6,368.9	59.3	1,079.9	422.0	39.1
Germany	13,008.2	5,181.2	—	—	—	—	7,827.0	60.2	1,210.8	1,400.5	115.7
Greece	823.0	275.3	—	—	—	—	547.7	66.6	103.5	9.2	8.9
Iceland	117.6	18.6	—	—	—	—	99.0	84.2	16.4	.1	.9
Ireland	838.4	319.5	—	—	—	—	518.9	61.9	87.3	45.7	52.4
Italy	7,055.5	2,830.6	—	—	—	—	4,224.9	59.9	702.4	81.6	11.6
Luxembourg	279.1	109.4	—	—	—	—	169.7	60.8	17.0	5.8	33.9
Netherlands	5,162.4	2,002.9	—	—	—	—	3,159.5	61.2	530.3	494.9	93.3
Norway	1,671.7	644.3	—	—	—	—	1,027.4	61.5	167.8	244.2	145.6
Portugal	867.4	339.7	—	—	—	—	527.7	60.8	53.3	52.2	97.9
San Marino	17.0	4.1	—	—	—	—	12.9	75.9	—	.4	....
Spain	3,048.9	1,214.6	—	—	—	—	1,834.3	60.2	298.8	288.9	96.7
Sweden	2,395.5	933.6	—	—	—	—	1,461.9	61.0	246.5	123.8	50.2
Switzerland	3,458.5	1,339.5	—	—	—	—	2,119.1	61.3	—	92.1	
United Kingdom	10,738.5	4,152.8	—	—	—	—	6,585.7	61.3	1,913.1	226.5	11.8
Developing Countries	82,099.5	11,429.3	66,512.2	81.0	60,016.6	6,495.6	130,680.5	159.2	6,838.1	4,096.5	59.9
Africa	11,498.1	291.2	5,862.8	51.0	1,965.1	3,897.7	13,172.4	114.6	1,382.5	539.7	39.0
Algeria	1,254.7	85.1	1,103.6	88.0	1,103.6	—	2,273.2	181.2	128.6	39.1	30.4
Angola	286.3	—	—	—	—	—	286.4	100.1	—	.1	....
Benin	61.9	2.2	58.7	94.9	—	58.7	59.7	96.5	9.4	.2	2.0
Botswana	63.0	23.8	—	—	—	—	39.2	62.2	4.4	32.1	735.4
Burkina Faso	60.2	7.2	93.2	154.8	—	93.2	53.0	88.0	9.4	.4	3.8
Burundi	77.0	.4	.6	.8	—	.6	76.6	99.5	13.7	.1	.9
Cameroon	185.7	.6	209.9	113.0	—	209.9	185.2	99.7	24.5	.1	.6
Cape Verde	9.6	—	1.2	12.8	—	1.2	9.6	100.0	.6	—	1.3
Central African Rep.	55.7	.1	24.5	43.9	—	24.5	55.6	99.8	9.3	.1	.6
Chad	56.0	.3	76.4	136.4	—	76.4	55.7	99.5	9.4	.1	.6
Comoros	8.9	.5	.5	6.1	—	.5	8.4	93.9	.7	—	1.3
Congo, Dem. Rep. of	533.0	—	—	—	—	—	533.0	100.0	86.3	8.5	9.8
Congo, Republic of	84.6	.5	29.0	34.3	15.1	13.9	99.2	117.2	9.7	.2	1.8
Côte d'Ivoire	325.2	.3	394.4	121.3	—	394.4	324.9	99.9	37.8	1.2	3.1
Djibouti	15.9	1.1	11.2	70.6	2.1	9.1	16.9	106.5	1.2	.1	5.1
Equatorial Guinea	32.6	—	1.3	4.0	—	1.3	32.6	100.0	5.8	.4	6.3
Eritrea	15.9	—	—	—	—	—	15.9	100.0	—	—	....
Ethiopia	133.7	7.2	101.4	75.8	—	101.4	126.6	94.7	11.2	.2	2.0
Gabon	154.3	.2	54.6	35.4	54.6	—	208.7	135.3	14.1	.5	3.7
Gambia, The	31.1	1.5	23.5	75.6	—	23.5	29.6	95.2	5.1	.1	1.4
Ghana	369.0	—	270.0	73.2	—	270.0	369.0	100.0	63.0	4.3	6.8
Guinea	107.1	.1	106.0	99.0	—	106.0	107.0	99.9	17.6	.7	4.0
Guinea-Bissau	14.2	—	17.9	126.2	3.6	14.4	17.8	125.0	1.2	.8	63.4
Kenya	271.4	12.6	71.6	26.4	—	71.6	258.8	95.4	37.0	.7	1.8
Lesotho	34.9	3.5	13.7	39.4	—	13.7	31.4	89.9	3.7	.5	12.1
Liberia	71.3	—	223.8	313.9	200.9	22.9	272.2	381.7	21.0	—	—
Madagascar	122.2	—	100.0	81.8	—	100.0	122.2	100.0	19.3	.1	.6
Malawi	69.4	2.3	55.1	79.3	—	55.1	67.1	96.7	11.0	1.8	16.3
Mali	93.3	8.8	126.0	135.1	—	126.0	84.5	90.5	15.9	.2	1.0
Mauritania	64.4	—	80.7	125.2	—	80.7	64.4	100.0	9.7	.1	.6
Mauritius	101.6	14.5	—	—	—	—	87.1	85.8	15.7	16.9	107.5
Morocco	588.2	70.4	—	—	—	—	517.8	88.0	85.7	98.0	114.4
Mozambique	113.6	—	155.5	136.8	—	155.5	113.6	100.0	—	.1	....
Namibia	136.5	—	—	—	—	—	136.5	100.0	—	—	....
Niger	65.8	8.6	70.8	107.6	—	70.8	57.2	87.0	9.4	1.3	14.1
Nigeria	1,753.2	.1	—	—	—	—	1,753.1	100.0	157.2	1.2	.8
Rwanda	80.1	—	62.8	78.5	1.5	61.4	81.6	101.9	13.7	8.1	59.3
São Tomé & Príncipe	7.4	—	—	—	—	—	7.4	100.0	.6	—	1.8
Senegal	161.8	1.4	200.1	123.6	—	200.1	160.4	99.1	24.5	6.5	26.8

(As of July 31, 2002 and Expressed in Millions of SDRs)

Quota	Reserve Position in the Fund	Total Fund Credit and Loans Outstanding				Fund Holdings of Currency		SDR Department		
		Total Amount	Percent of Quota	Outstanding Purchases (GRA)	Outstanding Loans	Amount	Percent of Quota	Net Cumulative Allocation	Holdings of SDRs	
									Amount	Percent of Allocation
(1)	(2)	(3)	(4)	(5)	(6)	(7)	(8)	(9)	(10)	(11)
										Africa (cont.)
8.8	—	—	—	—	—	8.8	100.0	.4	—	3.4	Seychelles
103.7	—	118.3	114.0	—	118.3	103.7	100.0	17.5	8.9	50.9	Sierra Leone
44.2	—	112.0	253.4	96.7	15.3	140.9	318.8	13.7	—	—	Somalia
1,868.5	.4	—	—	—	—	1,868.1	100.0	220.4	222.6	101.0	South Africa
169.7	—	428.8	252.7	369.5	59.2	539.3	317.8	52.2	.3	.6	Sudan
50.7	6.6	—	—	—	—	44.2	87.1	6.4	2.5	38.2	Swaziland
198.9	10.0	271.7	136.6	—	271.7	188.9	95.0	31.4	.4	1.4	Tanzania
73.4	.3	41.3	56.2	—	41.3	73.1	99.6	11.0	.3	2.8	Togo
286.5	20.2	—	—	—	—	266.3	93.0	34.2	1.0	3.1	Tunisia
180.5	—	201.5	111.6	—	201.5	180.5	100.0	29.4	.6	2.2	Uganda
489.1	—	748.1	153.0	—	748.1	489.1	100.0	68.3	78.6	115.1	Zambia
353.4	.3	203.1	57.5	117.5	85.6	470.6	133.2	10.2	—	—	Zimbabwe
21,940.1	**4,390.0**	**11,507.7**	**52.5**	**10,402.9**	**1,104.8**	**27,945.0**	**127.4**	**2,043.7**	**1,167.1**	**57.1**	**Asia**
120.4	4.9	—	—	—	—	115.5	95.9	26.7	—	—	Afghanistan, I.S. of
533.3	.2	82.2	15.4	73.6	8.6	606.7	113.8	47.1	33.3	70.6	Bangladesh
6.3	1.0	—	—	—	—	5.3	83.8	—	.2	....	Bhutan
150.0	35.3	—	—	—	—	114.7	76.5	—	6.6	....	Brunei Darussalam
87.5	—	75.5	86.3	1.6	73.9	89.1	101.8	15.4	.3	2.2	Cambodia
6,369.2	2,292.7	—	—	—	—	4,076.6	64.0	236.8	704.5	297.5	China,P.R.: Mainland
—	—	—	—	—	—	—	.	—	—	....	China,P.R.:Hong Kong
8.2	—	—	—	—	—	—		—	—	....	East Timor
70.3	15.0	—	—	—	—	55.3	78.7	7.0	4.9	70.6	Fiji
4,158.2	488.8	—	—	—	—	3,669.4	88.2	681.2	7.2	1.1	India
2,079.3	145.5	7,068.4	339.9	7,068.4	—	9,002.2	432.9	239.0	66.5	27.8	Indonesia
5.6	—	—	—	—	—	5.6	100.0	—	—	....	Kiribati
1,633.6	323.9	—	—	—	—	1,309.7	80.2	72.9	4.0	5.5	Korea
52.9	—	30.2	57.0	—	30.2	52.9	100.0	9.4	3.0	32.0	Lao People's Dem.Rep
1,486.6	608.2	—	—	—	—	878.4	59.1	139.0	105.1	75.6	Malaysia
8.2	1.6	—	—	—	—	6.6	81.1	.3	.3	93.3	Maldives
3.5	—	—	—	—	—	3.5	100.0	—	—	....	Marshall Islands,Rep
5.1	—	—	—	—	—	5.1	100.0	—	1.2	....	Micronesia, Fed.Sts.
51.1	.1	34.3	67.1	—	34.3	51.0	99.9	—	—	....	Mongolia
258.4	—	—	—	—	—	258.4	100.0	43.5	.6	1.3	Myanmar
71.3	5.7	4.5	6.3	—	4.5	65.6	91.9	8.1	.1	.7	Nepal
1,033.7	.1	1,499.4	145.1	884.7	614.7	1,918.3	185.6	170.0	16.4	9.6	Pakistan
3.1	—	—	—	—	—	3.1	100.0	—	—	....	Palau
131.6	.3	85.5	65.0	85.5	—	216.8	164.8	9.3	5.7	61.8	Papua New Guinea
879.9	87.3	1,380.3	156.9	1,380.3	—	2,173.0	247.0	116.6	24.9	21.3	Philippines
11.6	.7	—	—	—	—	10.9	94.1	1.1	2.4	206.7	Samoa
862.5	326.2	—	—	—	—	536.3	62.2	16.5	124.5	755.9	Singapore
10.4	.5	—	—	—	—	9.9	94.9	.7	—	.8	Solomon Islands
413.4	47.8	190.9	46.2	151.7	39.2	517.3	125.1	70.9	4.1	5.8	Sri Lanka
1,081.9	—	750.0	69.3	750.0	—	1,831.9	169.3	84.7	1.8	2.1	Thailand
6.9	1.7	—	—	—	—	5.2	75.3	—	.2	....	Tonga
17.0	2.5	—	—	—	—	14.5	85.3	—	.8	....	Vanuatu
329.1	—	306.4	93.1	7.0	299.4	336.1	102.1	47.7	48.6	101.9	Vietnam
17,270.1	**1,380.2**	**25,019.9**	**144.9**	**24,253.1**	**766.8**	**40,143.2**	**232.4**	**374.1**	**623.6**	**166.7**	**Europe**
48.7	3.4	64.1	131.6	2.2	61.9	47.6	97.7	—	63.9	....	Albania
92.0	—	129.8	141.0	15.5	114.3	107.5	116.8	—	9.1	....	Armenia
160.9	—	219.5	136.4	123.5	96.0	284.4	176.8	—	1.9	....	Azerbaijan
386.4	—	40.9	10.6	40.9	—	427.3	110.6	—	.5	....	Belarus
169.1	—	82.3	48.7	82.3	—	251.4	148.7	20.5	.5	2.3	Bosnia & Herzegovina
640.2	32.8	809.8	126.5	809.8	—	1,417.3	221.4	—	31.8	....	Bulgaria
365.1	.2	83.9	23.0	83.9	—	448.9	122.9	44.2	71.3	161.2	Croatia
139.6	44.4	—	—	—	—	95.2	68.2	19.4	1.3	6.6	Cyprus
819.3	173.5	—	—	—	—	645.9	78.8	—	1.5	....	Czech Republic
65.2	—	—	—	—	—	65.2	100.0	—	.1	....	Estonia
150.3	—	238.7	158.8	25.4	213.2	175.7	116.9	—	1.3	....	Georgia
1,038.4	395.0	—	—	—	—	643.4	62.0	—	19.4	....	Hungary
365.7	—	—	—	—	—	365.7	100.0	—	.6	....	Kazakhstan
88.8	—	146.1	164.6	6.7	139.4	95.5	107.6	—	4.1	....	Kyrgyz Republic
126.8	.1	13.3	10.5	13.3	—	140.1	110.5	—	.2	....	Latvia
144.2	—	103.1	71.5	103.1	—	247.3	171.5	—	43.6	....	Lithuania
68.9	—	54.3	78.8	25.3	29.0	94.2	136.7	8.4	1.7	20.2	Macedonia, FYR
102.0	40.3	—	—	—	—	61.7	60.5	11.3	27.0	238.8	Malta
123.2	—	117.4	95.3	89.7	27.7	212.9	172.8	—	—	—	Moldova
1,369.0	478.8	—	—	—	—	890.2	65.0	—	23.9	....	Poland
1,030.2	—	262.1	25.4	262.1	—	1,292.3	125.4	76.0	.5	.7	Romania

Fund Accounts: Position to Date

(As of July 31, 2002 and Expressed in Millions of SDRs)

	Quota	Reserve Position in the Fund	Total Fund Credit and Loans Outstanding				Fund Holdings of Currency		SDR Department		
			Total Amount	Percent of Quota	Outstanding Purchases (GRA)	Outstanding Loans	Amount	Percent of Quota	Net Cumulative Allocation	Holdings of SDRs	
										Amount	Percent of Allocation
	(1)	(2)	(3)	(4)	(5)	(6)	(7)	(8)	(9)	(10)	(11)
Europe (cont.)											
Russia	5,945.4	1.1	5,325.6	89.6	5,325.6	—	11,269.9	189.6	—	6.3	....
Slovak Republic	357.5	—	—	—	—	—	357.5	100.0	—	.5	....
Slovenia	231.7	98.0	—	—	—	—	133.8	57.7	25.4	4.4	17.4
Tajikistan	87.0	—	90.0	103.4	4.7	85.3	91.7	105.4	—	.2	....
Turkey	964.0	112.8	15,378.1	1,595.2	15,378.1	—	16,229.3	1,683.5	112.3	200.0	178.1
Turkmenistan	75.2	—	—	—	—	—	75.2	100.0	—	—	....
Ukraine	1,372.0	—	1,444.2	105.3	1,444.2	—	2,816.2	205.3	—	104.9	....
Uzbekistan	275.6	—	49.9	18.1	49.9	—	325.5	118.1	—	.5	....
Yugoslavia, Fed. Rep	467.7	—	366.9	78.5	366.9	—	834.6	178.5	56.7	2.6	4.5
Middle East	**15,478.5**	**4,086.3**	**670.5**	**4.3**	**431.8**	**238.8**	**11,824.2**	**76.4**	**986.5**	**1,154.5**	**117.0**
Bahrain, Kingdom of	135.0	67.9	—	—	—	—	67.1	49.7	6.2	.8	12.6
Egypt	943.7	—	—	—	—	—	943.7	100.0	135.9	28.4	20.9
Iran, I.R. of	1,497.2	—	—	—	—	—	1,497.2	100.0	244.1	267.7	109.7
Iraq	504.0	—	—	—	—	—	504.0	100.0	68.5	—	—
Israel	928.2	286.7	—	—	—	—	641.5	69.1	106.4	1.8	1.7
Jordan	170.5	.1	386.0	226.4	386.0	—	556.5	326.4	16.9	6.3	37.4
Kuwait	1,381.1	462.7	—	—	—	—	918.4	66.5	26.7	91.4	341.7
Lebanon	203.0	18.8	—	—	—	—	184.2	90.7	4.4	19.7	448.8
Libya	1,123.7	395.5	—	—	—	—	728.2	64.8	58.8	449.7	765.2
Oman	194.0	75.7	—	—	—	—	118.4	61.0	6.3	5.7	91.2
Qatar	263.8	107.8	—	—	—	—	156.0	59.1	12.8	18.8	146.9
Saudi Arabia	6,985.5	2,421.4	—	—	—	—	4,564.1	65.3	195.5	216.2	110.6
Syrian Arab Republic	293.6	—	—	—	—	—	293.6	100.0	36.6	.3	.7
United Arab Emirates	611.7	249.7	—	—	—	—	362.0	59.2	38.7	1.3	3.4
Yemen, Republic of	243.5	—	284.5	116.8	45.8	238.8	289.2	118.8	28.7	46.4	161.4
Western Hemisphere	**15,912.7**	**1,281.6**	**23,451.3**	**147.4**	**22,963.7**	**487.6**	**37,595.6**	**236.3**	**2,051.3**	**611.6**	**29.8**
Antigua and Barbuda	13.5	—	—	—	—	—	13.5	100.0	—	—	....
Argentina	2,117.1	—	10,718.9	506.3	10,718.9	—	12,836.0	606.3	318.4	19.6	6.2
Bahamas, The	130.3	6.2	—	—	—	—	124.1	95.2	10.2	.1	.7
Barbados	67.5	4.8	—	—	—	—	62.7	92.9	8.0	.1	1.2
Belize	18.8	4.2	—	—	—	—	14.6	77.5	—	1.4	....
Bolivia	171.5	8.9	153.1	89.3	—	153.1	162.6	94.8	26.7	27.3	102.3
Brazil	3,036.1	—	10,891.1	358.7	10,891.1	—	13,927.8	458.7	358.7	10.4	2.9
Chile	856.1	325.4	—	—	—	—	530.7	62.0	121.9	24.4	20.0
Colombia	774.0	285.8	—	—	—	—	488.2	63.1	114.3	110.4	96.6
Costa Rica	164.1	20.0	—	—	—	—	144.1	87.8	23.7	.1	.6
Dominica	8.2	—	—	—	—	—	8.2	99.9	.6	—	1.3
Dominican Republic	218.9	—	29.8	13.6	29.8	—	248.7	113.6	31.6	.7	2.2
Ecuador	302.3	17.2	226.7	75.0	226.7	—	511.9	169.3	32.9	.8	2.5
El Salvador	171.3	—	—	—	—	—	171.3	100.0	25.0	25.0	100.0
Grenada	11.7	—	—	—	—	—	11.7	100.0	.9	—	1.5
Guatemala	210.2	—	—	—	—	—	210.2	100.0	27.7	6.3	22.7
Guyana	90.9	—	71.4	78.6	—	71.4	90.9	100.0	14.5	.9	5.9
Haiti	60.7	.1	25.0	41.3	11.4	13.7	72.0	118.7	13.7	.6	4.5
Honduras	129.5	8.6	161.7	124.8	35.6	126.0	156.5	120.8	19.1	.6	3.4
Jamaica	273.5	—	24.6	9.0	24.6	—	298.2	109.0	40.6	1.3	3.2
Mexico	2,585.8	126.4	—	—	—	—	2,459.4	95.1	290.0	283.4	97.7
Nicaragua	130.0	—	123.3	94.9	—	123.3	130.0	100.0	19.5	.2	1.2
Panama	206.6	11.9	39.2	19.0	39.2	—	233.9	113.2	26.3	1.0	3.9
Paraguay	99.9	21.5	—	—	—	—	78.4	78.5	13.7	82.3	600.6
Peru	638.4	—	240.9	37.7	240.9	—	879.3	137.7	91.3	.7	.8
St. Kitts and Nevis	8.9	.1	1.2	13.7	1.2	—	10.0	112.8	—	—	....
St. Lucia	15.3	—	—	—	—	—	15.3	100.0	.7	1.5	198.1
St. Vincent & Grens.	8.3	.5	—	—	—	—	7.8	94.0	.4	—	5.6
Suriname	92.1	6.1	—	—	—	—	86.0	93.4	7.8	1.5	19.2
Trinidad and Tobago	335.6	76.4	—	—	—	—	259.2	77.2	46.2	.1	.2
Uruguay	306.5	35.7	744.4	242.9	744.4	—	1,015.2	331.2	50.0	3.8	7.7
Venezuela, Rep. Bol.	2,659.1	321.9	—	—	—	—	2,337.2	87.9	316.9	7.0	2.2
Memorandum Items											
Oil Exporting Ctys	20,307.3	4,265.4	8,172.0	40.2	8,172.0	—	24,214.1	119.2	1,493.0	1,164.6	78.0
Non-Oil Develop.Ctys	61,792.2	7,163.9	58,340.2	94.4	51,844.6	6,495.6	106,466.4	172.3	5,345.1	2,931.9	54.9

Column 6 is comprised of outstanding SAF, PRGF (previously, ESAF), and Trust Fund loans.

Column 10 does not report separately data on the SDR positions of the Fund's General Resources Account and of Other Holders. Data on the SDR Holdings of the Fund's General Resources Account and of Other Holders are reported in the foot-table to the table on SDRs.

Financing Components of Members' Outstanding Obligations to the Fund

(As of July 31, 2002 and Expressed in Millions of SDRs)

Total Fund Credit and Loans Outstanding	Total Amount	Outstanding Purchases (GRA)								Outstanding Loans			Trust Fund	
		Ordinary Resources				Borrowed Resources				SAF Arrangements	PRGF Arrangements			
		CCFF	STF	Stand-by/ Credit Tranche	Extended Fund Facility	SFF	EAR	GAB	NAB	SDA Resources	SDA Resources	PRGF Trust Resources	Administered Accounts	
(1)	(2)	(3)	(4)	(5)	(6)	(7)	(8)	(9)	(10)	(11)	(12)	(13)	(14)	
66,512.2	60,016.6	666.4	1,157.9	42,051.1	14,978.7	114.1	279.9	768.4	—	161.8	12.8	6,232.5	88.6	**All Countries**
—	—	—	—	—	—	—	—	—	—	—	—	—	—	**Industrial Countries**
—	—	—	—	—	—	—	—	—	—	—	—	—	—	United States
—	—	—	—	—	—	—	—	—	—	—	—	—	—	Canada
—	—	—	—	—	—	—	—	—	—	—	—	—	—	Australia
—	—	—	—	—	—	—	—	—	—	—	—	—	—	Japan
—	—	—	—	—	—	—	—	—	—	—	—	—	—	New Zealand
—	—	—	—	—	—	—	—	—	—	—	—	—	—	Austria
—	—	—	—	—	—	—	—	—	—	—	—	—	—	Belgium
—	—	—	—	—	—	—	—	—	—	—	—	—	—	Denmark
—	—	—	—	—	—	—	—	—	—	—	—	—	—	Finland
—	—	—	—	—	—	—	—	—	—	—	—	—	—	France
—	—	—	—	—	—	—	—	—	—	—	—	—	—	Germany
—	—	—	—	—	—	—	—	—	—	—	—	—	—	Greece
—	—	—	—	—	—	—	—	—	—	—	—	—	—	Iceland
—	—	—	—	—	—	—	—	—	—	—	—	—	—	Ireland
—	—	—	—	—	—	—	—	—	—	—	—	—	—	Italy
—	—	—	—	—	—	—	—	—	—	—	—	—	—	Luxembourg
—	—	—	—	—	—	—	—	—	—	—	—	—	—	Netherlands
—	—	—	—	—	—	—	—	—	—	—	—	—	—	Norway
—	—	—	—	—	—	—	—	—	—	—	—	—	—	Portugal
—	—	—	—	—	—	—	—	—	—	—	—	—	—	San Marino
—	—	—	—	—	—	—	—	—	—	—	—	—	—	Spain
—	—	—	—	—	—	—	—	—	—	—	—	—	—	Sweden
—	—	—	—	—	—	—	—	—	—	—	—	—	—	Switzerland
—	—	—	—	—	—	—	—	—	—	—	—	—	—	United Kingdom
66,512.2	60,016.6	666.4	1,157.9	42,051.1	14,978.7	114.1	279.9	768.4	—	161.8	12.8	6,232.5	88.6	**Developing Countries**
5,862.8	1,965.1	316.1	—	201.2	1,053.7	114.1	279.9	—	—	161.9	10.8	3,636.4	88.6	**Africa**
1,103.6	1,103.6	223.5	—	—	880.1	—	—	—	—	—	—	—	—	Algeria
—	—	—	—	—	—	—	—	—	—	—	—	—	—	Angola
58.7	—	—	—	—	—	—	—	—	—	-.4	1.8	57.3	—	Benin
—	—	—	—	—	—	—	—	—	—	—	—	—	—	Botswana
93.2	—	—	—	—	—	—	—	—	—	—	6.3	86.9	—	Burkina Faso
.6	—	—	—	—	—	—	—	—	—	—	—	.6	—	Burundi
209.9	—	—	—	—	—	—	—	—	—	—	—	209.9	—	Cameroon
1.2	—	—	—	—	—	—	—	—	—	—	—	1.2	—	Cape Verde
24.5	—	—	—	—	—	—	—	—	—	—	—	24.5	—	Central African Rep.
76.4	—	—	—	—	—	—	—	—	—	—	—	76.4	—	Chad
.5	—	—	—	—	—	—	—	—	—	.5	—	—	—	Comoros
—	—	—	—	—	—	—	—	—	—	—	—	—	—	Congo, Dem. Rep. of
29.0	15.1	—	—	15.1	—	—	—	—	—	—	—	13.9	—	Congo, Republic of
394.4	—	—	—	—	—	—	—	—	—	—	—	394.4	—	Côte d'Ivoire
11.2	2.1	—	—	2.1	—	—	—	—	—	—	—	9.1	—	Djibouti
1.3	—	—	—	—	—	—	—	—	—	—	.9	.4	—	Equatorial Guinea
—	—	—	—	—	—	—	—	—	—	—	—	—	—	Eritrea
101.4	—	—	—	—	—	—	—	—	—	14.8	—	86.6	—	Ethiopia
54.6	54.6	—	—	13.2	41.4	—	—	—	—	—	—	—	—	Gabon
23.5	—	—	—	—	—	—	—	—	—	—	—	23.5	—	Gambia, The
270.0	—	—	—	—	—	—	—	—	—	—	—	270.0	—	Ghana
106.0	—	—	—	—	—	—	—	—	—	—	—	106.0	—	Guinea
17.9	3.6	—	—	3.6	—	—	—	—	—	—	—	14.4	—	Guinea-Bissau
71.6	—	—	—	—	—	—	—	—	—	—	—	71.6	—	Kenya
13.7	—	—	—	—	—	—	—	—	—	—	—	13.7	—	Lesotho
223.8	200.9	34.7	—	45.6	—	36.3	84.3	—	—	—	—	—	22.9	Liberia
100.0	—	—	—	—	—	—	—	—	—	—	—	100.0	—	Madagascar
55.1	—	—	—	—	—	—	—	—	—	—	—	55.1	—	Malawi
126.0	—	—	—	—	—	—	—	—	—	—	1.5	124.5	—	Mali
80.7	—	—	—	—	—	—	—	—	—	—	.3	80.3	—	Mauritania
—	—	—	—	—	—	—	—	—	—	—	—	—	—	Mauritius
—	—	—	—	—	—	—	—	—	—	—	—	—	—	Morocco
155.5	—	—	—	—	—	—	—	—	—	—	—	155.5	—	Mozambique
—	—	—	—	—	—	—	—	—	—	—	—	—	—	Namibia
70.8	—	—	—	—	—	—	—	—	—	—	—	70.8	—	Niger
—	—	—	—	—	—	—	—	—	—	—	—	—	—	Nigeria
62.8	1.5	—	—	1.5	—	—	—	—	—	—	—	61.4	—	Rwanda
—	—	—	—	—	—	—	—	—	—	—	—	—	—	São Tomé & Príncipe

Financing Components of Members' Outstanding Obligations to the Fund

(As of July 31, 2002 and Expressed in Millions of SDRs)

		Outstanding Purchases (GRA)									Outstanding Loans			
		Ordinary Resources				Borrowed Resources				SAF Arrangements	PRGF Arrangements		Trust Fund
	Total Amount	CCFF	STF	Stand-by/ Credit Tranche	Extended Fund Facility	SFF	EAR	GAB	NAB	SDA Resources	SDA Resources	PRGF Trust Resources	Administered Accounts
Total Fund Credit and Loans Outstanding (1)	(2)	(3)	(4)	(5)	(6)	(7)	(8)	(9)	(10)	(11)	(12)	(13)	(14)
Africa (cont.)													
Senegal	200.1	—	—	—	—	—	—	—	—	—	—	—	200.1	—
Seychelles	—													
Sierra Leone	118.3	—	—	—	—	—	—	—	—	—	10.8	—	107.5	—
Somalia	112.0	96.7	28.5	—	12.6	—	—	55.5	—	—	8.8	—	—	6.5
South Africa	—													
Sudan	428.8	369.5	29.3	—	43.6	78.7	77.8	140.1	—	—	—	—	—	59.2
Swaziland	—													
Tanzania	271.7	—	—	—	—	—	—	—	—	—	—	—	271.7	—
Togo	41.3	—	—	—	—	—	—	—	—	—	—	—	41.3	—
Tunisia	—													
Uganda	201.5	—	—	—	—	—	—	—	—	—	—	—	201.5	—
Zambia	748.1	—	—	—	—	—	—	—	—	—	127.2	—	620.9	—
Zimbabwe	203.1	117.5	—	—	63.9	53.6	—	—	—	—	—	—	85.6	—
Asia	11,507.7	10,402.9	264.5	8.6	3,508.3	6,621.5	—	—	—	—	-.1	—	1,104.9	
Afghanistan, I.S. of	—													
Bangladesh	82.2	73.6	—	—	73.6	—	—	—	—	—	—	—	8.6	
Bhutan	—													
Brunei Darussalam	—													
Cambodia	75.5	1.6	—	1.6	—	—	—	—	—	—	—	—	73.9	
China, People's Rep.	—													
Fiji	—													
India	—													
Indonesia	7,068.4	7,068.4	—	—	1,284.2	5,784.2	—	—	—	—	—	—	—	
Kiribati	—													
Korea	—													
Lao People's Dem.Rep	30.2	—	—	—	—	—	—	—	—	—	—	—	30.2	
Malaysia	—													
Maldives	—													
Marshall Islands,Rep	—													
Micronesia, Fed.Sts.	—													
Mongolia	34.3	—	—	—	—	—	—	—	—	—	—	—	34.3	
Myanmar	—													
Nepal	4.5	—	—	—	—	—	—	—	—	—	—	—	4.5	
Pakistan	1,499.4	884.7	264.5	—	465.0	155.2	—	—	—	—	-.1	—	614.8	
Palau	—													
Papua New Guinea	85.5	85.5	—	—	85.5	—	—	—	—	—	—	—	—	
Philippines	1,380.3	1,380.3	—	—	698.3	682.1	—	—	—	—	—	—	—	
Samoa	—													
Singapore	—													
Solomon Islands	—													
Sri Lanka	190.9	151.7	—	—	151.7	—	—	—	—	—	—	—	39.2	
Thailand	750.0	750.0	—	—	750.0	—	—	—	—	—	—	—	—	
Tonga	—													
Vanuatu	—													
Vietnam	306.4	7.0	—	7.0	—	—	—	—	—	—	—	—	299.4	—
Europe	25,019.9	24,253.1	56.0	1,149.3	16,621.0	5,658.3	—	—	768.4	—	—	—	766.8	
Albania	64.1	2.2	—	—	2.2	—	—	—	—	—	—	—	61.9	
Armenia	129.8	15.5	—	15.5	—	—	—	—	—	—	—	—	114.3	
Azerbaijan	219.5	123.5	42.2	31.7	—	49.6	—	—	—	—	—	—	96.0	
Belarus	40.9	40.9	—	40.9	—	—	—	—	—	—	—	—	—	
Bosnia & Herzegovina	82.3	82.3	—	—	82.3	—	—	—	—	—	—	—	—	
Bulgaria	809.8	809.8	—	38.7	143.5	627.6	—	—	—	—	—	—	—	
Croatia	83.9	83.9	—	60.0	—	24.0	—	—	—	—	—	—	—	
Cyprus	—													
Czech Republic	—													
Estonia	—													
Georgia	238.7	25.4	—	25.4	—	—	—	—	—	—	—	—	213.2	
Hungary	—													
Kazakhstan	—													
Kyrgyz Republic	146.1	6.7	—	6.7	—	—	—	—	—	—	—	—	139.4	
Latvia	13.3	13.3	—	13.3	—	—	—	—	—	—	—	—	—	
Lithuania	103.1	103.1	—	15.1	—	88.0	—	—	—	—	—	—	—	
Macedonia, FYR	54.3	25.3	13.8	10.3	—	1.1	—	—	—	—	—	—	29.0	

Column 5 includes Korea's purchases and column 6 includes Russia's purchases, both, under terms of the Supplemental Reserve Facility (SRF).

Financing Components of Members' Outstanding Obligations to the Fund

(As of July 31, 2002 and Expressed in Millions of SDRs)

Total Fund Credit and Loans Outstanding	Total Amount	Outstanding Purchases (GRA) Ordinary Resources				Borrowed Resources				Outstanding Loans SAF Arrangements	PRGF Arrangements		Trust Fund	
		CCFF	STF	Stand-by/ Credit Tranche	Extended Fund Facility	SFF	EAR	GAB	NAB	SDA Resources	SDA Resources	PRGF Trust Resources	Administered Accounts	
(1)	(2)	(3)	(4)	(5)	(6)	(7)	(8)	(9)	(10)	(11)	(12)	(13)	(14)	
														Europe (cont.)
—	—	—	—	—	—	—	—	—	—	—	—	—	—	Malta
117.4	89.7	—	11.3	—	78.4	—	—	—	—	—	—	27.7	—	Moldova
—	—	—	—	—	—	—	—	—	—	—	—	—	—	Poland
262.1	262.1	—	62.8	199.3	—	—	—	—	—	—	—	—	—	Romania
5,325.6	5,325.6	—	539.1	471.4	3,546.6	—	—	768.4	—	—	—	—	—	Russia
—	—	—	—	—	—	—	—	—	—	—	—	—	—	Slovak Republic
—	—	—	—	—	—	—	—	—	—	—	—	—	—	Slovenia
90.0	4.7	—	—	4.7	—	—	—	—	—	—	—	85.3	—	Tajikistan
15,378.1	15,378.1	—	—	15,378.1	—	—	—	—	—	—	—	—	—	Turkey
—	—	—	—	—	—	—	—	—	—	—	—	—	—	Turkmenistan
1,444.2	1,444.2	—	228.5	22.7	1,193.0	—	—	—	—	—	—	—	—	Ukraine
49.9	49.9	—	49.9	—	—	—	—	—	—	—	—	—	—	Uzbekistan
366.9	366.9	—	—	316.9	50.0	—	—	—	—	—	—	—	—	Yugoslavia, Fed. Rep
670.5	**431.8**	**29.8**	—	**10.7**	**391.3**	—	—	—	—	—	—	**238.8**	—	**Middle East**
—	—	—	—	—	—	—	—	—	—	—	—	—	—	Bahrain, Kingdom of
—	—	—	—	—	—	—	—	—	—	—	—	—	—	Egypt
—	—	—	—	—	—	—	—	—	—	—	—	—	—	Iran, I.R. of
—	—	—	—	—	—	—	—	—	—	—	—	—	—	Iraq
—	—	—	—	—	—	—	—	—	—	—	—	—	—	Israel
386.0	386.0	29.8	—	10.7	345.5	—	—	—	—	—	—	—	—	Jordan
—	—	—	—	—	—	—	—	—	—	—	—	—	—	Kuwait
—	—	—	—	—	—	—	—	—	—	—	—	—	—	Lebanon
—	—	—	—	—	—	—	—	—	—	—	—	—	—	Libya
—	—	—	—	—	—	—	—	—	—	—	—	—	—	Oman
—	—	—	—	—	—	—	—	—	—	—	—	—	—	Qatar
—	—	—	—	—	—	—	—	—	—	—	—	—	—	Saudi Arabia
—	—	—	—	—	—	—	—	—	—	—	—	—	—	Syrian Arab Republic
—	—	—	—	—	—	—	—	—	—	—	—	—	—	United Arab Emirates
284.5	45.8	—	—	—	45.8	—	—	—	—	—	—	238.8	—	Yemen, Republic of
23,451.3	**22,963.7**	—	—	**21,709.9**	**1,253.9**	—	—	—	—	—	**2.0**	**485.6**	—	**Western Hemisphere**
—	—	—	—	—	—	—	—	—	—	—	—	—	—	Antigua and Barbuda
10,718.9	10,718.9	—	—	9,769.7	949.2	—	—	—	—	—	—	—	—	Argentina
—	—	—	—	—	—	—	—	—	—	—	—	—	—	Bahamas, The
—	—	—	—	—	—	—	—	—	—	—	—	—	—	Barbados
—	—	—	—	—	—	—	—	—	—	—	—	—	—	Belize
153.1	—	—	—	—	—	—	—	—	—	—	—	153.1	—	Bolivia
10,891.1	10,891.1	—	—	10,891.1	—	—	—	—	—	—	—	—	—	Brazil
—	—	—	—	—	—	—	—	—	—	—	—	—	—	Chile
—	—	—	—	—	—	—	—	—	—	—	—	—	—	Colombia
—	—	—	—	—	—	—	—	—	—	—	—	—	—	Costa Rica
—	—	—	—	—	—	—	—	—	—	—	—	—	—	Dominica
29.8	29.8	—	—	29.8	—	—	—	—	—	—	—	—	—	Dominican Republic
226.7	226.7	—	—	226.7	—	—	—	—	—	—	—	—	—	Ecuador
—	—	—	—	—	—	—	—	—	—	—	—	—	—	El Salvador
—	—	—	—	—	—	—	—	—	—	—	—	—	—	Grenada
—	—	—	—	—	—	—	—	—	—	—	—	—	—	Guatemala
71.4	—	—	—	—	—	—	—	—	—	—	2.0	69.5	—	Guyana
25.0	11.4	—	—	11.4	—	—	—	—	—	—	—	13.7	—	Haiti
161.7	35.6	—	—	35.6	—	—	—	—	—	—	—	126.0	—	Honduras
24.6	24.6	—	—	—	24.6	—	—	—	—	—	—	—	—	Jamaica
—	—	—	—	—	—	—	—	—	—	—	—	—	—	Mexico
123.3	—	—	—	—	—	—	—	—	—	—	—	123.3	—	Nicaragua
39.2	39.2	—	—	—	39.2	—	—	—	—	—	—	—	—	Panama
—	—	—	—	—	—	—	—	—	—	—	—	—	—	Paraguay
240.9	240.9	—	—	—	240.9	—	—	—	—	—	—	—	—	Peru
1.2	1.2	—	—	1.2	—	—	—	—	—	—	—	—	—	St. Kitts and Nevis
—	—	—	—	—	—	—	—	—	—	—	—	—	—	St. Lucia
—	—	—	—	—	—	—	—	—	—	—	—	—	—	St. Vincent & Grens.
—	—	—	—	—	—	—	—	—	—	—	—	—	—	Suriname
—	—	—	—	—	—	—	—	—	—	—	—	—	—	Trinidad and Tobago
744.4	744.4	—	—	744.4	—	—	—	—	—	—	—	—	—	Uruguay
—	—	—	—	—	—	—	—	—	—	—	—	—	—	Venezuela, Rep. Bol.
														Memorandum Items
8,172.0	8,172.0	223.5	—	1,284.2	6,664.3	—	—	—	—	—	—	—	—	Oil Exporting Ctys
58,340.2	51,844.6	442.9	1,157.9	40,766.9	8,314.4	114.1	279.9	768.4	—	161.8	12.8	6,232.5	88.6	Non-Oil Develop.Ctys

Purchases*

Expressed in Millions of SDRs

	1972	1973	1974	1975	1976	1977	1978	1979	1980	1981	1982	1983	1984	1985	1986
World	649.7	342.0	3,087.6	3,935.5	6,019.1	3,344.5	1,208.8	1,695.7	3,393.5	6,771.3	7,448.0	12,618.8	7,291.2	4,013.9	3,819.1
Industrial Countries	—	—	1,512.5	1,973.6	2,627.8	2,415.7	98.8	23.8	—	—	54.0	354.8	217.2	—	—
United States	—	—	—	—	—	—	—	—	—	—	—	—	—	—	—
Canada	—	—	—	—	—	—	—	—	—	—	—	—	—	—	—
Australia	—	—	—	—	332.5	—	—	23.8	—	—	32.5	—	—	—	—
Japan	—	—	—	—	—	—	—	—	—	—	—	—	—	—	—
New Zealand	—	—	85.7	156.6	147.9	—	—	—	—	—	—	—	—	—	—
Belgium	—	—	—	—	—	—	—	—	—	—	—	—	—	—	—
Denmark	—	—	—	—	—	—	—	—	—	—	—	—	—	—	—
Finland	—	—	—	71.3	115.1	—	—	—	—	—	—	—	—	—	—
France	—	—	—	—	—	—	—	—	—	—	—	—	—	—	—
Germany	—	—	—	—	—	—	—	—	—	—	—	—	—	—	—
Greece	—	—	36.2	153.5	58.0	—	—	—	—	—	—	—	—	—	—
Iceland	—	—	15.5	15.9	25.1	—	—	—	—	—	—	21.5	—	—	—
Ireland	—	—	—	—	—	—	—	—	—	—	—	—	—	—	—
Italy	—	—	1,375.1	1,080.2	—	90.0	—	—	—	—	—	—	—	—	—
Luxembourg	—	—	—	—	—	—	—	—	—	—	—	—	—	—	—
Netherlands	—	—	—	—	—	—	—	—	—	—	—	—	—	—	—
Norway	—	—	—	—	—	—	—	—	—	—	—	—	—	—	—
Portugal	—	—	—	—	173.3	75.7	—	—	—	—	—	—	—	—	—
Spain	—	—	—	496.2	75.9	—	98.8	—	—	—	—	—	—	—	—
United Kingdom	649.7	—	—	—	1,700.0	2,250.0	—	—	—	—	—	—	354.8	217.2	—
Developing Countries	649.7	342.0	1,575.2	1,961.9	3,391.3	928.9	1,110.1	1,671.9	3,393.5	6,771.3	7,394.1	12,264.1	7,074.0	4,013.9	3,819.7
Africa	83.3	29.5	166.4	326.6	881.4	303.9	285.8	517.3	821.7	1,859.7	2,118.1	1,702.2	1,188.6	941.8	749.9
Algeria	—	—	—	—	—	—	—	—	—	—	—	—	—	—	—
Benin	—	—	—	—	—	—	—	—	—	—	—	—	—	—	—
Burkina Faso	—	—	—	—	—	—	—	—	—	—	—	—	—	—	—
Burundi	—	—	.1	1.2	—	—	—	9.5	—	—	—	—	—	—	—
Cameroon	—	—	4.6	7.5	21.8	—	—	—	—	—	—	—	—	—	—
Cape Verde	—	—	—	—	—	—	—	—	—	—	—	—	—	—	—
Central African Rep.	—	—	2.7	2.3	6.1	—	—	—	4.0	17.0	2.4	4.5	5.0	11.0	6.5
Chad	—	—	5.0	—	6.5	—	—	—	—	7.1	—	—	—	7.0	—
Comoros	—	—	—	—	—	—	—	—	—	—	—	—	—	—	—
Congo, Dem. Rep. of	28.3	—	—	45.0	130.0	33.3	—	20.0	78.4	194.6	106.9	114.5	158.0	169.0	80.6
Congo, Republic of	—	—	—	—	—	—	11.2	3.3	2.0	—	—	—	—	—	9.5
Côte d'Ivoire	—	—	11.2	—	36.4	—	—	—	—	319.2	115.4	154.9	41.4	60.4	50.5
Djibouti	—	—	—	—	—	—	—	—	—	—	—	—	—	—	—
Equatorial Guinea	—	—	—	—	—	—	—	—	9.4	7.2	—	—	—	5.4	—
Ethiopia	—	—	—	—	—	—	—	36.0	—	62.0	23.5	—	—	—	35.3
Gabon	—	—	—	—	—	—	7.5	7.5	—	—	—	—	—	—	27.4
Gambia, The	—	—	—	—	—	3.5	7.0	—	1.6	9.0	16.9	—	2.6	—	5.7
Ghana	—	—	—	38.6	—	—	8.7	32.0	—	—	11.5	263.6	213.6	120.0	32.7
Guinea	—	—	9.5	—	—	—	—	3.0	—	1.9	—	—	1.9	—	15.0
Guinea-Bissau	—	—	—	—	—	—	—	1.1	—	—	—	—	—	—	—
Kenya	—	—	32.0	48.5	27.1	—	—	86.3	60.0	30.0	150.4	129.8	46.2	123.1	—
Lesotho	—	—	—	—	—	—	—	—	—	—	—	—	—	—	—
Liberia	—	1.5	—	—	—	—	—	29.8	18.4	46.6	61.7	58.0	35.5	—	—
Madagascar	—	—	3.5	10.9	—	9.4	—	—	39.2	39.0	52.4	10.2	41.4	29.0	44.2
Malawi	—	—	—	2.4	1.4	5.4	—	22.1	24.4	30.0	10.9	34.2	37.8	23.0	—
Mali	2.0	—	4.0	1.0	4.0	—	—	—	5.1	—	25.4	15.0	24.0	13.0	9.8
Mauritania	—	—	—	—	11.8	4.7	—	—	19.4	10.3	15.5	—	—	9.6	11.7
Mauritius	—	—	—	—	—	11.0	—	28.0	35.0	68.0	22.5	28.4	24.8	35.5	21.0
Morocco	—	—	—	—	115.5	—	56.0	—	184.5	192.8	433.3	114.4	180.0	215.1	30.0
Mozambique	—	—	—	—	—	—	—	—	—	—	—	—	—	—	—
Niger	—	—	—	—	—	—	—	—	—	—	—	30.8	14.4	15.5	12.8
Nigeria	1.5	—	—	—	—	—	—	—	—	—	—	—	—	—	—
Rwanda	—	—	—	—	—	—	—	—	—	—	—	—	—	—	—
São Tomé & Príncipe	—	—	—	—	—	—	—	—	—	—	—	—	—	—	—
Senegal	—	—	—	25.4	—	—	21.0	10.5	43.3	57.7	53.2	31.5	31.5	55.6	32.5
Seychelles	—	—	—	—	—	—	—	—	—	—	—	—	—	—	—
Sierra Leone	—	—	4.3	.6	17.5	7.0	—	7.5	9.5	33.5	—	20.7	19.0	—	8.0
Somalia	—	—	—	—	—	—	—	—	6.0	25.9	32.3	45.0	—	34.6	18.1
South Africa	—	—	—	—	390.0	162.0	—	—	—	—	—	795.0	—	—	—
Sudan	32.5	9.0	45.7	48.3	26.7	—	42.3	83.2	142.8	165.6	70.0	183.6	45.5	—	—
Swaziland	—	—	—	—	—	—	—	—	—	—	—	10.0	—	—	—
Tanzania	—	—	38.9	23.8	21.0	4.7	—	34.0	40.0	15.9	—	—	—	—	33.0
Togo	—	—	—	—	—	7.5	—	—	—	13.3	7.3	—	19.4	18.0	12.0
Tunisia	—	—	—	—	—	—	24.0	—	—	—	—	—	—	—	149.7
Uganda	—	—	5.0	14.2	20.0	—	—	5.0	37.5	122.5	85.0	106.5	21.0	—	—
Zambia	19.0	19.0	—	56.9	38.3	19.0	148.8	100.0	50.0	359.3	34.0	173.7	147.5	—	103.8
Zimbabwe	—	—	—	—	—	—	—	—	—	—	37.5	—	153.6	79.6	—
Asia	217.9	144.6	925.2	719.3	752.8	293.8	302.1	355.7	1,344.8	3,121.2	2,395.4	3,206.3	1,275.9	896.6	1,156.2
Afghanistan, I.S. of	—	7.5	2.5	8.5	—	—	—	—	—	—	—	—	—	—	—
Bangladesh	62.5	—	70.3	58.8	97.2	—	—	57.0	142.0	106.0	131.2	68.4	—	91.0	96.0
Cambodia	6.3	6.3	—	—	—	—	—	—	—	—	—	—	—	—	—
China, People's Rep.	—	—	—	—	—	—	—	—	—	450.0	—	—	—	—	597.7
Fiji	—	—	.3	—	—	6.5	—	—	—	—	13.5	—	—	4.8	—
India	—	—	497.0	201.3	—	—	—	—	266.0	300.0	1,500.0	1,500.0	600.0	—	—
Indonesia	2.7	—	—	—	—	—	—	—	—	—	—	425.1	—	—	—
Kiribati	—	—	—	—	—	—	—	—	—	—	—	—	—	—	—
Korea	—	—	110.0	107.3	104.4	—	—	—	480.0	576.0	106.2	192.0	567.6	135.9	120.0
Lao People's Dem.Rep	—	—	—	3.3	3.3	—	4.0	—	8.0	6.0	—	—	—	—	—
Malaysia	—	—	—	—	93.0	—	—	—	—	189.8	58.5	113.0	—	—	—
Maldives	—	—	—	—	—	—	—	—	—	—	—	—	—	—	—
Micronesia, Fed.Sts.	—	—	—	—	—	—	—	—	—	—	—	—	—	—	—

*Excludes reserve
tranche purchases

1987	1988	1989	1990	1991	1992	1993	1994	1995	1996	1997	1998	1999	2000	2001	
							Expressed in Millions of SDRs								
3,298.8	2,668.7	3,477.7	4,270.0	7,386.5	4,791.1	5,042.2	4,979.5	16,967.9	5,271.0	16,112.9	20,586.2	10,010.1	7,178.0	23,761.6	**World**
—	—	—	—	—	—	—	—	—	—	—	—	—	—	—	**Industrial Countries**
—	—	—	—	—	—	—	—	—	—	—	—	—	—	—	United States
—	—	—	—	—	—	—	—	—	—	—	—	—	—	—	Canada
—	—	—	—	—	—	—	—	—	—	—	—	—	—	—	Australia
—	—	—	—	—	—	—	—	—	—	—	—	—	—	—	Japan
—	—	—	—	—	—	—	—	—	—	—	—	—	—	—	New Zealand
—	—	—	—	—	—	—	—	—	—	—	—	—	—	—	Belgium
—	—	—	—	—	—	—	—	—	—	—	—	—	—	—	Denmark
—	—	—	—	—	—	—	—	—	—	—	—	—	—	—	Finland
—	—	—	—	—	—	—	—	—	—	—	—	—	—	—	France
—	—	—	—	—	—	—	—	—	—	—	—	—	—	—	Germany
—	—	—	—	—	—	—	—	—	—	—	—	—	—	—	Greece
—	—	—	—	—	—	—	—	—	—	—	—	—	—	—	Iceland
—	—	—	—	—	—	—	—	—	—	—	—	—	—	—	Ireland
—	—	—	—	—	—	—	—	—	—	—	—	—	—	—	Italy
—	—	—	—	—	—	—	—	—	—	—	—	—	—	—	Luxembourg
—	—	—	—	—	—	—	—	—	—	—	—	—	—	—	Netherlands
—	—	—	—	—	—	—	—	—	—	—	—	—	—	—	Norway
—	—	—	—	—	—	—	—	—	—	—	—	—	—	—	Portugal
—	—	—	—	—	—	—	—	—	—	—	—	—	—	—	Spain
—	—	—	—	—	—	—	—	—	—	—	—	—	—	—	United Kingdom
3,298.8	2,668.7	3,477.7	4,270.0	7,386.5	4,791.1	5,042.2	4,979.5	16,967.9	5,271.0	16,112.9	20,586.2	10,010.1	7,178.0	23,761.6	**Developing Countries**
479.3	589.7	742.4	176.3	425.6	172.7	678.8	761.5	1,038.5	556.9	370.1	313.6	266.9	35.6	—	**Africa**
—	—	470.9	—	225.0	—	—	587.5	312.8	512.2	337.6	253.3	223.5	—	—	Algeria
—	—	—	—	—	—	—	—	—	—	—	—	—	—	—	Benin
—	—	—	—	—	—	—	—	—	—	—	—	—	—	—	Burkina Faso
—	—	—	—	—	—	—	—	—	—	—	—	—	—	—	Burundi
—	69.5	15.5	—	8.0	—	—	21.9	8.5	19.7	—	—	—	—	—	Cameroon
—	—	—	—	—	—	—	—	—	—	—	—	—	—	—	Cape Verde
1.0	—	—	—	—	—	—	10.7	—	—	—	—	—	—	—	Central African Rep.
—	—	—	—	—	—	—	10.3	—	—	—	—	—	—	—	Chad
—	—	—	—	—	—	—	—	—	—	—	—	—	—	—	Comoros
69.8	—	75.0	—	—	—	—	—	—	—	—	—	—	—	—	Congo, Dem. Rep. of
—	—	—	4.0	—	—	—	12.5	—	—	—	7.2	—	10.6	—	Congo, Republic of
—	89.8	29.3	112.7	33.1	—	—	—	—	—	—	—	—	—	—	Côte d'Ivoire
—	—	—	—	—	—	—	—	—	2.9	1.1	2.3	1.0	—	—	Djibouti
—	—	—	—	—	—	—	—	—	—	—	—	—	—	—	Equatorial Guinea
—	—	—	—	—	—	—	—	—	—	—	—	—	—	—	Ethiopia
15.1	56.2	4.0	6.5	4.0	—	—	44.7	37.5	22.1	16.6	—	—	13.2	—	Gabon
4.1	—	—	—	—	—	—	—	—	—	—	—	—	—	—	Gambia, The
71.6	75.0	—	—	—	—	47.0	—	—	—	—	—	—	—	—	Ghana
6.0	—	—	—	—	—	—	—	—	—	—	—	—	—	—	Guinea
—	—	—	—	—	—	—	—	—	—	—	—	2.1	1.4	—	Guinea-Bissau
—	102.6	—	—	—	—	—	—	—	—	—	—	—	—	—	Kenya
—	—	—	—	—	—	—	—	—	—	—	—	—	—	—	Lesotho
—	—	—	—	—	—	—	—	—	—	—	—	—	—	—	Liberia
20.0	7.8	—	—	—	—	—	—	—	—	—	—	—	—	—	Madagascar
—	9.3	—	—	—	—	—	12.7	—	—	—	—	—	—	—	Malawi
—	2.5	5.1	5.1	—	—	—	—	—	—	—	—	—	—	—	Mali
8.7	4.0	—	—	—	—	—	—	—	—	—	—	—	—	—	Mauritania
—	—	—	—	—	—	—	—	—	—	—	—	—	—	—	Mauritius
160.0	110.0	140.0	48.0	—	18.4	—	—	—	—	—	—	—	—	—	Morocco
—	—	—	—	—	—	—	—	—	—	—	—	—	—	—	Mozambique
8.1	—	—	—	—	—	—	11.1	—	—	—	—	—	—	—	Niger
—	—	—	—	—	—	—	—	—	—	—	—	—	—	—	Nigeria
—	—	—	—	—	—	—	—	8.9	—	14.9	—	—	—	—	Rwanda
—	—	—	—	—	—	—	—	—	—	—	—	—	—	—	São Tomé & Príncipe
30.9	12.9	—	—	—	—	—	30.9	—	—	—	—	—	—	—	Senegal
—	—	—	—	—	—	—	—	—	—	—	—	—	—	—	Seychelles
—	—	—	—	—	—	—	—	—	—	—	11.6	15.6	10.4	—	Sierra Leone
5.5	—	—	—	—	—	—	—	—	—	—	—	—	—	—	Somalia
—	—	—	—	—	—	614.4	—	—	—	—	—	—	—	—	South Africa
—	—	—	—	—	—	—	—	—	—	—	—	—	—	—	Sudan
—	—	—	—	—	—	—	—	—	—	—	—	—	—	—	Swaziland
12.5	—	—	—	—	—	—	—	—	—	—	—	—	—	—	Tanzania
—	10.4	2.6	—	—	—	—	—	—	—	—	—	—	—	—	Togo
41.0	15.0	—	—	155.5	51.8	—	—	—	—	—	—	—	—	—	Tunisia
25.0	24.8	—	—	—	—	—	—	651.7	—	—	—	—	—	—	Uganda
—	—	—	—	102.5	17.4	19.1	19.1	—	—	39.2	24.7	—	—	—	Zambia
—	—	—	—	—	—	—	—	—	—	—	—	—	—	—	Zimbabwe
729.1	250.7	430.4	42.8	2,456.3	1,452.0	755.3	220.2	167.3	109.2	12,801.7	11,259.8	2,236.4	1,267.6	784.7	**Asia**
—	—	—	—	—	—	—	—	—	—	—	—	—	—	—	Afghanistan, I.S. of
136.9	71.9	—	—	—	—	—	—	—	—	—	98.1	—	—	—	Bangladesh
—	—	—	—	—	—	6.3	—	—	—	—	—	—	—	—	Cambodia
—	—	—	—	—	—	—	—	—	—	—	—	—	—	—	China, People's Rep.
—	—	—	—	—	—	—	—	—	—	—	—	—	—	—	Fiji
—	—	—	—	1,988.9	1,109.0	462.0	—	—	—	—	—	—	—	—	India
462.9	—	—	—	—	—	—	—	—	—	2,201.5	4,254.3	1,011.0	851.2	309.7	Indonesia
—	—	—	—	—	—	—	—	—	—	—	—	—	—	—	Kiribati
—	—	—	—	—	—	—	—	—	—	8,200.0	5,850.0	362.5	—	—	Korea
—	—	—	—	—	—	—	—	—	—	—	—	—	—	—	Lao People's Dem.Rep
—	—	—	—	—	—	—	—	—	—	—	—	—	—	—	Malaysia
—	—	—	—	—	—	—	—	—	—	—	—	—	—	—	Maldives
—	—	—	—	—	—	—	—	—	—	—	—	—	—	—	Micronesia, Fed.Sts.

*Excludes reserve
tranche purchases

Purchases*

	1972	1973	1974	1975	1976	1977	1978	1979	1980	1981	1982	1983	1984	1985	1986
					Expressed in Millions of SDRs										
Asia (cont.)															
Mongolia	—	—	—	—	—	—	—	—	—	—	—	—	—	—	—
Myanmar	—	13.5	29.5	9.5	—	25.0	25.0	15.0	—	27.0	25.6	29.2	—	—	—
Nepal	—	—	—	—	4.5	—	—	9.5	10.5	—	—	—	—	10.3	2.
Pakistan	84.0	60.0	129.9	161.4	107.2	67.0	40.0	21.2	105.0	482.9	455.2	285.0	—	—	—
Palau	—	—	—	—	—	—	—	—	—	—	—	—	—	—	—
Papua New Guinea	—	—	—	—	24.8	—	—	—	—	45.0	—	—	—	—	—
Philippines	35.0	38.8	38.8	125.9	222.7	108.8	93.1	135.5	303.3	200.0	—	288.6	85.0	318.0	229.
Samoa	—	—	—	1.3	.7	.5	1.3	.7	—	2.8	—	2.8	3.4	1.7	1.
Solomon Islands	—	—	—	—	—	—	—	1.1	—	.8	1.6	1.0	—	—	1.
Sri Lanka	25.3	18.6	46.9	42.1	28.2	55.0	38.0	80.0	30.0	175.6	39.2	35.8	20.0	—	—
Thailand	2.2	—	—	—	67.0	—	68.8	45.3	—	531.0	64.4	265.5	—	335.0	110.
Vietnam	—	—	—	—	—	31.0	22.5	—	—	28.4	—	—	—	—	—
Europe	31.8	47.5	145.4	265.5	499.7	72.5	203.6	328.9	959.9	1,263.5	1,378.5	1,416.7	1,057.4	255.0	135.
Albania	—	—	—	—	—	—	—	—	—	—	—	—	—	—	—
Armenia	—	—	—	—	—	—	—	—	—	—	—	—	—	—	—
Azerbaijan	—	—	—	—	—	—	—	—	—	—	—	—	—	—	—
Belarus	—	—	—	—	—	—	—	—	—	—	—	—	—	—	—
Bosnia & Herzegovina	—	—	—	—	—	—	—	—	—	—	—	—	—	—	—
Bulgaria	—	—	—	—	—	—	—	—	—	—	—	—	—	—	—
Croatia	—	—	—	—	—	—	—	—	—	—	—	—	—	—	—
Cyprus	—	—	6.4	1.7	35.0	—	—	9.9	8.5	—	—	—	—	—	—
Czech Republic	—	—	—	—	—	—	—	—	—	—	—	—	—	—	—
Czechoslovakia	—	—	—	—	—	—	—	—	—	—	—	—	—	—	—
Estonia	—	—	—	—	—	—	—	—	—	—	—	—	—	—	—
Georgia	—	—	—	—	—	—	—	—	—	—	—	—	—	—	—
Hungary	—	—	—	—	—	—	—	—	—	—	214.5	332.5	425.0	—	—
Kazakhstan	—	—	—	—	—	—	—	—	—	—	—	—	—	—	—
Kyrgyz Republic	—	—	—	—	—	—	—	—	—	—	—	—	—	—	—
Latvia	—	—	—	—	—	—	—	—	—	—	—	—	—	—	—
Lithuania	—	—	—	—	—	—	—	—	—	—	—	—	—	—	—
Macedonia, FYR	—	—	—	—	—	—	—	—	—	—	—	—	—	—	—
Moldova	—	—	—	—	—	—	—	—	—	—	—	—	—	—	—
Poland	—	—	—	—	—	—	—	—	—	—	—	—	—	—	—
Romania	—	47.5	—	40.0	150.0	72.5	39.1	41.3	121.3	309.5	310.0	183.9	183.6	—	—
Russia	—	—	—	—	—	—	—	—	—	—	—	—	—	—	—
Slovak Republic	—	—	—	—	—	—	—	—	—	—	—	—	—	—	—
Tajikistan	—	—	—	—	—	—	—	—	—	—	—	—	—	—	—
Turkey	—	—	—	207.6	129.2	—	164.5	70.0	491.6	400.0	300.0	346.3	168.8	—	—
Ukraine	—	—	—	—	—	—	—	—	—	—	—	—	—	—	—
Uzbekistan	—	—	—	—	—	—	—	—	—	—	—	—	—	—	—
Yugoslavia, SFR	31.8	—	139.0	16.2	185.5	—	—	207.8	338.5	554.0	554.0	554.0	280.0	255.0	135.0
Yugoslavia, Fed. Rep	—	—	—	—	—	—	—	—	—	—	—	—	—	—	—
Middle East	25.0	49.9	81.8	190.1	215.9	105.0	147.4	—	—	—	15.4	9.8	—	57.4	—
Bahrain, Kingdom of	—	—	—	—	—	—	—	—	—	—	—	—	—	—	—
Egypt	—	47.0	40.0	—	125.7	105.0	75.0	—	—	—	—	—	—	—	—
Iran, I.R. of	—	—	—	—	—	—	—	—	—	—	—	—	—	—	—
Iraq	—	—	—	—	—	—	—	—	—	—	—	—	—	—	—
Israel	—	—	32.5	175.8	77.0	—	72.4	—	—	—	—	—	—	—	—
Jordan	—	2.9	—	—	—	—	—	—	—	—	—	—	—	57.4	—
Lebanon	—	—	—	—	—	—	—	—	—	—	—	—	—	—	—
Syrian Arab Republic	25.0	—	—	—	—	—	—	—	—	—	—	—	—	—	—
Yemen Arab Rep.	—	—	—	—	—	—	—	—	—	—	—	—	9.8	—	—
Yemen, P.D. Rep.	—	—	9.3	14.3	13.2	—	—	—	—	—	15.4	—	—	—	—
Yemen, Republic of	—	—	—	—	—	—	—	—	—	—	—	—	—	—	—
Western Hemisphere	291.8	70.5	256.3	460.4	1,041.5	153.7	171.1	470.1	267.2	526.9	1,486.7	5,929.2	3,552.2	1,863.2	1,778.
Antigua and Barbuda	—	—	—	—	—	—	—	—	—	—	—	—	—	—	—
Argentina	174.0	—	—	186.1	269.5	—	—	—	—	—	—	1,120.6	—	984.5	473.0
Barbados	—	—	—	—	—	6.5	—	—	—	—	22.2	14.5	7.8	—	—
Belize	—	—	—	—	—	—	—	—	—	—	—	3.6	1.2	4.8	1.2
Bolivia	4.3	18.2	—	4.7	—	—	15.0	—	53.4	—	24.5	17.9	—	—	96.8
Brazil	—	—	—	—	—	—	—	—	—	—	498.3	2,027.0	1,744.2	—	—
Chile	39.5	—	120.5	176.8	124.4	—	—	—	—	—	—	579.0	—	195.6	250.0
Colombia	—	—	—	—	—	—	—	—	—	—	—	—	—	—	—
Costa Rica	—	—	18.8	12.0	6.8	—	—	20.5	15.4	52.6	—	110.9	—	34.0	—
Dominica	—	—	—	—	—	—	—	1.9	—	4.8	2.8	2.4	1.5	—	—
Dominican Republic	—	—	—	—	21.5	15.0	—	68.3	—	—	46.6	179.1	—	76.9	17.1
Ecuador	8.3	8.3	—	—	—	—	—	—	—	—	—	203.5	39.4	84.4	75.9
El Salvador	8.8	—	17.9	—	—	—	—	—	10.8	32.3	59.8	15.5	—	—	—
Grenada	—	—	—	.8	.4	—	—	.7	—	5.0	—	1.1	—	—	—
Guatemala	—	—	—	—	—	—	—	—	—	95.6	—	38.3	19.1	—	—
Guyana	—	3.9	5.0	—	17.3	—	12.9	12.9	41.9	16.1	5.9	—	—	—	—
Haiti	—	—	6.8	4.5	4.9	3.0	—	—	16.6	17.0	12.0	29.5	14.0	—	—
Honduras	—	—	16.8	—	—	—	—	—	16.0	20.7	61.7	45.9	—	—	—
Jamaica	—	13.3	13.3	—	55.7	19.2	57.8	145.8	—	203.6	165.2	112.2	100.6	51.0	26.6
Mexico	—	—	—	—	319.1	100.0	—	—	—	—	200.6	1,003.1	1,203.8	295.8	741.4
Nicaragua	4.0	12.0	3.3	12.2	—	—	—	43.1	—	—	—	—	—	—	—
Panama	—	—	7.4	10.2	25.1	—	—	—	—	75.3	—	108.9	100.0	35.0	44.0
Paraguay	—	—	—	—	—	—	—	—	—	—	—	—	—	—	—
Peru	30.8	—	—	—	158.8	10.0	85.5	177.0	111.0	—	299.9	165.0	104.7	—	—
St. Kitts and Nevis	—	—	—	—	—	—	—	—	—	—	—	—	—	—	—
St. Lucia	—	—	—	—	—	—	—	—	—	—	—	—	—	—	—
St. Vincent & Grens.	—	—	—	—	—	—	—	—	1.8	2.7	—	—	—	—	—
Suriname	—	—	—	—	—	—	—	—	.4	1.3	—	—	—	—	—
Trinidad and Tobago	—	—	—	—	—	—	—	—	—	—	—	—	—	—	—
Uruguay	22.3	15.0	46.6	53.2	38.0	—	—	—	—	—	86.8	151.2	—	101.2	52.7
Venezuela, Rep. Bol.	—	—	—	—	—	—	—	—	—	—	—	—	—	—	—
Memorandum Items															
Oil Exporting Ctys	4.2	—	—	—	—	—	—	—	—	—	—	425.1	—	—	—
Non-Oil Develop.Ctys	645.4	342.0	1,575.2	1,961.9	3,391.3	928.9	1,110.1	1,671.9	3,393.5	6,771.3	7,394.1	11,839.0	7,074.0	4,013.9	3,819.7

*Excludes reserve
tranche purchases

Purchases*

Expressed in Millions of SDRs

1987	1988	1989	1990	1991	1992	1993	1994	1995	1996	1997	1998	1999	2000	2001	
															Asia (cont.)
—	—	—	—	11.2	2.5	—	—	—	—	—	—	—	—	—	Mongolia
—	—	—	—	—	—	—	—	—	—	—	—	—	—	—	Myanmar
6.3	—	—	—	—	—	—	—	—	—	—	—	—	—	—	Nepal
—	—	194.5	—	122.4	189.6	88.0	123.2	134.0	107.2	91.5	19.0	409.6	150.0	315.0	Pakistan
—	—	—	—	—	—	—	—	—	—	—	—	—	—	—	Palau
—	—	—	42.8	—	—	—	—	33.3	2.0	—	—	—	28.9	56.7	Papua New Guinea
123.0	70.0	235.9	—	333.7	151.0	126.6	36.5	—	—	508.8	538.3	253.3	237.6	—	Philippines
—	—	—	—	—	—	—	—	—	—	—	—	—	—	—	Samoa
—	—	—	—	—	—	—	—	—	—	—	—	—	—	—	Solomon Islands
—	—	—	—	—	—	—	—	—	—	—	—	—	—	103.4	Sri Lanka
—	108.8	—	—	—	—	—	—	—	—	—	1,800.0	500.0	200.0	—	Thailand
—	—	—	—	—	—	72.5	60.5	—	—	—	—	—	—	—	Vietnam
—	287.8	50.0	550.6	2,715.9	1,674.6	1,700.0	3,177.1	5,337.2	3,488.2	2,272.3	5,312.9	1,944.9	3,253.3	9,456.6	**Europe**
—	—	—	—	—	9.7	3.4	—	—	—	8.8	—	—	—	—	Albania
—	—	—	—	—	—	—	16.9	30.4	—	—	—	—	—	—	Armenia
—	—	—	—	—	—	—	67.9	53.8	20.5	15.8	68.6	—	—	—	Azerbaijan
—	—	—	—	—	—	70.1	—	120.1	—	—	—	—	—	—	Belarus
—	—	—	—	—	—	—	—	30.3	—	—	24.2	29.0	27.2	14.0	Bosnia & Herzegovina
—	—	—	—	289.2	200.3	31.0	232.5	—	80.0	355.2	228.9	209.2	209.2	104.6	Bulgaria
—	—	—	—	—	—	—	78.5	65.4	—	28.8	—	—	—	—	Croatia
—	—	—	—	—	—	—	—	—	—	—	—	—	—	—	Cyprus
—	—	—	—	—	—	70.0	—	—	—	—	—	—	—	—	Czech Republic
—	—	—	—	917.9	238.6	—	—	—	—	—	—	—	—	—	Czechoslovakia
—	—	—	—	—	7.8	34.1	—	20.9	—	—	—	—	—	—	Estonia
—	—	—	—	—	—	—	27.8	50.0	—	—	—	—	—	—	Georgia
—	165.4	50.0	127.4	703.8	118.4	56.7	—	—	—	—	—	—	—	—	Hungary
—	—	—	—	—	—	61.9	136.1	92.8	92.8	—	154.7	—	—	—	Kazakhstan
—	—	—	—	—	—	43.9	—	—	—	—	—	—	—	—	Kyrgyz Republic
—	—	—	—	—	25.2	52.6	32.0	—	—	—	—	—	—	—	Latvia
—	—	—	—	17.3	70.7	46.6	41.4	31.1	41.4	—	—	—	—	—	Lithuania
—	—	—	—	—	—	12.4	24.8	9.9	—	—	—	13.8	1.1	—	Macedonia, FYR
—	—	—	—	—	—	63.0	49.5	42.4	22.5	15.0	—	50.0	—	—	Moldova
—	—	357.5	239.1	—	—	—	640.3	—	—	—	—	—	—	—	Poland
—	—	—	—	565.8	338.5	—	245.1	37.7	—	120.6	—	53.0	86.8	52.0	Romania
—	—	—	—	—	719.0	1,078.3	1,078.3	3,594.3	2,587.9	1,467.3	4,600.0	471.4	—	—	Russia
—	—	—	—	—	—	64.4	96.5	—	—	—	—	—	—	—	Slovak Republic
—	—	—	—	—	—	—	—	—	15.0	7.5	7.5	—	—	—	Tajikistan
—	—	—	—	—	—	—	235.5	225.0	—	—	583.2	—	2,622.1	8,895.2	Turkey
—	—	—	—	—	—	—	249.3	788.0	536.0	207.3	281.8	466.6	190.1	290.8	Ukraine
—	—	—	—	—	—	—	—	106.0	59.3	—	—	—	—	—	Uzbekistan
—	122.4	—	65.7	—	—	—	—	—	—	—	—	—	—	—	Yugoslavia, SFR
—	—	—	—	—	—	—	—	—	—	—	—	—	116.9	100.0	Yugoslavia, Fed. Rep
116.0	—	66.2	—	60.0	288.0	11.1	65.6	75.8	166.2	154.0	32.7	77.4	15.2	37.0	**Middle East**
—	—	—	—	—	—	—	—	—	—	—	—	—	—	—	Bahrain, Kingdom of
116.0	—	—	—	60.0	87.2	—	—	—	—	—	—	—	—	—	Egypt
—	—	—	—	—	—	—	—	—	—	—	—	—	—	—	Iran, I.R. of
—	—	—	—	—	—	—	—	—	—	—	—	—	—	—	Iraq
—	—	—	—	—	178.6	—	—	—	—	—	—	—	—	—	Israel
—	—	66.2	—	—	22.2	11.1	65.6	75.8	82.2	96.7	23.7	55.4	15.2	30.5	Jordan
—	—	—	—	—	—	—	—	—	—	—	—	—	—	—	Lebanon
—	—	—	—	—	—	—	—	—	—	—	—	—	—	—	Syrian Arab Republic
—	—	—	—	—	—	—	—	—	—	—	—	—	—	—	Yemen Arab Rep.
—	—	—	—	—	—	—	—	—	—	—	—	—	—	—	Yemen, P.D. Rep.
—	—	—	—	—	—	—	—	—	84.0	57.4	9.0	22.0	—	6.5	Yemen, Republic of
1,974.4	1,540.5	2,188.7	3,500.3	1,728.7	1,203.7	1,896.9	755.1	10,349.1	950.6	514.7	3,667.2	5,484.5	2,606.3	13,483.5	**Western Hemisphere**
—	—	—	—	—	—	—	—	—	—	—	—	—	—	—	Antigua and Barbuda
969.8	398.7	184.0	322.0	292.5	584.6	1,154.8	612.0	1,559.0	548.2	321.0	—	—	1,587.8	8,168.5	Argentina
—	—	—	—	—	36.8	—	—	—	—	—	—	—	—	—	Barbados
—	—	—	—	—	—	—	—	—	—	—	—	—	—	—	Belize
—	45.3	—	—	—	—	—	—	—	—	—	—	—	—	—	Bolivia
—	365.3	—	—	—	127.5	—	—	—	—	—	3,419.0	4,450.1	—	5,277.2	Brazil
225.0	150.0	139.0	—	—	—	—	—	—	—	—	—	—	—	—	Chile
—	—	—	—	—	—	—	—	—	—	—	—	—	—	—	Colombia
—	—	—	—	55.3	4.0	—	—	—	—	—	—	—	—	—	Costa Rica
—	—	—	—	—	—	—	—	—	—	—	—	—	—	—	Dominica
—	—	—	—	44.8	37.4	53.3	—	—	—	—	39.7	—	—	—	Dominican Republic
37.7	57.8	15.7	23.6	18.6	—	—	98.9	—	—	—	—	—	113.3	37.8	Ecuador
—	—	—	—	—	—	—	—	—	—	—	—	—	—	—	El Salvador
—	—	—	—	—	—	—	—	—	—	—	—	—	—	—	Grenada
—	44.8	—	—	—	—	—	—	—	—	—	—	—	—	—	Guatemala
—	13.0	2.0	39.7	9.8	—	—	—	16.4	—	—	15.2	—	—	—	Guyana
—	—	21.3	—	2.3	—	—	—	—	—	—	47.5	—	—	—	Haiti
95.9	43.7	63.8	41.1	87.0	41.8	36.4	34.4	7.0	—	—	—	—	—	—	Jamaica
600.0	350.0	943.0	1,608.4	932.4	233.1	—	—	8,758.0	—	—	—	1,034.4	905.1	—	Mexico
—	—	—	—	17.0	—	—	—	—	—	—	—	—	—	—	Nicaragua
11.0	—	—	—	—	71.6	9.9	9.9	8.7	52.4	33.2	30.0	—	—	—	Panama
—	—	—	—	—	—	—	—	—	—	—	—	—	—	—	Paraguay
—	—	—	—	—	—	642.7	—	—	—	160.5	—	—	—	—	Peru
—	—	—	—	—	—	—	—	—	—	—	—	—	—	—	St. Kitts and Nevis
—	—	—	—	—	—	—	—	—	—	—	1.6	—	—	—	St. Lucia
—	—	—	—	—	—	—	—	—	—	—	—	—	—	—	St. Vincent & Grens.
—	—	—	—	—	—	—	—	—	—	—	—	—	—	—	Suriname
—	85.1	70.7	75.8	37.5	—	—	—	—	—	—	—	—	—	—	Trinidad and Tobago
35.1	—	9.0	—	—	—	16.0	—	—	—	—	114.2	—	—	—	Uruguay
—	—	759.5	1,357.5	231.5	—	—	—	—	350.0	—	—	—	—	—	Venezuela, Rep. Bol.
															Memorandum Items
462.9	—	1,230.4	1,357.5	456.5	—	—	587.5	312.8	862.2	2,539.1	4,507.6	1,234.5	851.2	309.7	Oil Exporting Ctys
2,835.9	2,668.7	2,247.3	2,912.5	6,930.0	4,791.0	5,042.2	4,392.0	16,655.1	4,408.7	13,573.8	16,078.6	8,775.6	6,326.9	23,452.0	Non-Oil Develop.Ctys

*Excludes reserve tranche purchases

Repurchases

	1972	1973	1974	1975	1976	1977	1978	1979	1980	1981	1982	1983	1984	1985	1986
						Expressed in Millions of SDRs									
World	656.3	407.5	374.2	238.9	840.6	2,844.9	4,377.2	3,991.5	2,428.8	1,880.6	1,505.6	2,029.5	2,284.6	3,625.0	5,664.6
Industrial Countries	250.2	—	—	—	—	1,651.7	2,591.4	2,521.8	850.1	609.0	522.9	116.7	—	—	10.8
United States	—	—	—	—	—	—	—	—	—	—	—	—	—	—	—
Canada	—	—	—	—	—	—	—	—	—	—	—	—	—	—	—
Australia	—	—	—	—	—	—	85.6	—	208.9	61.7	—	32.5	—	—	—
Japan	—	—	—	—	—	—	—	—	—	—	—	—	—	—	—
New Zealand	—	—	—	—	—	—	38.4	92.7	136.2	98.7	30.8	2.9	—	—	—
Belgium	—	—	—	—	—	—	—	—	—	—	—	—	—	—	—
Denmark	—	—	—	—	—	—	—	—	—	—	—	—	—	—	—
Finland	—	—	—	—	—	—	34.3	85.7	—	14.3	37.7	14.4	—	—	—
France	—	—	—	—	—	—	—	—	—	—	—	—	—	—	—
Greece	—	—	—	—	—	71.3	25.8	37.9	68.8	64.6	13.9	—	—	—	—
Iceland	—	—	—	—	—	—	9.3	12.4	19.0	9.8	5.1	.9	—	—	10.8
Ireland	—	—	—	—	—	—	—	—	—	—	—	—	—	—	—
Italy	—	—	—	—	—	966.4	858.9	880.0	—	—	—	—	—	—	—
Netherlands	—	—	—	—	—	—	—	—	—	—	—	—	—	—	—
Norway	—	—	—	—	—	—	—	—	—	—	—	—	—	—	—
Portugal	—	—	—	—	—	4.0	29.3	31.9	76.9	46.2	37.7	9.8	—	—	—
Spain	—	—	—	—	—	—	55.5	410.0	—	63.7	136.9	4.8	—	—	—
United Kingdom	250.2	—	—	—	—	610.0	1,454.3	971.2	340.3	250.0	261.0	51.6	—	—	—
Developing Countries	406.0	407.5	374.2	238.9	840.6	1,193.2	1,785.8	1,469.8	1,578.5	1,271.6	982.7	1,912.8	2,284.6	3,625.0	5,653.6
Africa	44.7	15.0	7.3	64.4	181.1	190.1	217.8	457.0	413.4	317.3	243.8	424.3	551.5	765.2	1,472.6
Algeria	—	—	—	—	—	—	—	—	—	—	—	—	—	—	—
Burkina Faso	—	—	—	—	—	—	—	—	—	—	—	—	—	—	—
Burundi	5.3	—	—	-.1	—	—	1.2	—	—	—	—	4.8	4.8	—	—
Cameroon	—	—	—	—	—	—	2.9	8.0	12.8	8.5	3.0	.5	—	—	—
Central African Rep.	—	—	—	—	1.3	—	.9	2.1	4.4	3.1	.6	.3	6.3	9.5	5.3
Chad	—	1.0	2.8	—	—	—	1.9	1.2	2.2	5.4	—	—	2.7	3.5	.9
Comoros	—	—	—	—	—	—	—	—	—	—	—	—	—	—	—
Congo, Dem. Rep. of	—	—	—	—	22.6	5.7	9.7	31.5	65.5	80.3	20.8	10.4	54.0	103.8	94.0
Congo, Republic of	—	—	—	—	—	3.3	—	1.1	5.3	4.6	—	—	—	—	—
Côte d'Ivoire	—	—	—	—	24.2	10.0	24.1	—	—	—	—	—	27.7	97.6	107.2
Djibouti	—	—	—	—	—	—	—	—	—	—	—	—	—	—	—
Equatorial Guinea	—	—	—	—	—	—	—	—	—	.6	—	—	6.1	6.9	1.8
Ethiopia	—	—	—	—	—	—	—	—	—	—	2.3	18.0	25.2	31.0	26.1
Gabon	—	—	—	—	—	—	—	—	—	—	2.0	7.5	1.8	—	—
Gambia, The	—	—	—	—	—	—	1.8	3.5	—	—	2.2	2.6	1.9	2.8	13.4
Ghana	15.4	1.0	—	—	—	—	4.8	9.7	9.7	9.7	4.8	15.4	4.0	—	18.7
Guinea	—	1.9	1.0	2.4	—	—	5.8	4.4	1.1	3.6	.2	—	—	—	5.8
Guinea-Bissau	—	—	—	—	—	—	—	—	—	—	.3	.4	.4	.9	.9
Kenya	—	—	—	12.0	10.6	36.0	2.4	30.6	7.0	7.2	15.6	41.7	56.7	68.4	89.8
Lesotho	—	—	—	—	—	—	—	—	—	—	—	—	—	—	—
Liberia	1.4	1.0	—	—	—	—	—	—	2.4	1.2	—	10.3	19.6	6.9	—
Madagascar	—	—	—	—	—	8.1	2.6	3.7	1.5	7.2	.7	3.7	23.5	33.0	40.8
Malawi	—	—	—	—	—	—	3.8	.8	.9	2.6	12.6	10.3	20.4	16.0	20.6
Mali	1.0	1.0	1.0	1.0	2.5	2.0	1.2	1.8	2.2	2.3	1.1	1.8	3.2	4.5	13.9
Mauritania	—	—	—	—	—	—	—	.9	6.7	6.9	1.5	4.4	9.0	12.4	9.8
Mauritius	—	—	—	—	—	—	—	—	—	11.0	—	14.5	31.5	47.8	37.2
Morocco	—	—	—	—	—	—	—	23.2	66.4	53.4	32.5	23.3	47.5	143.2	274.2
Niger	—	—	—	—	—	—	—	—	—	—	—	—	—	—	1.5
Nigeria	—	1.5	—	—	—	—	—	—	—	—	—	—	—	—	—
Rwanda	—	—	—	—	—	—	—	—	—	—	—	—	—	—	—
Senegal	—	—	—	—	—	—	4.7	6.4	6.4	6.4	13.3	10.5	14.5	40.9	50.4
Sierra Leone	—	—	—	—	—	—	1.2	7.3	9.2	8.0	1.3	2.0	8.3	4.4	20.8
Somalia	—	—	—	—	—	—	—	—	—	—	—	—	2.9	8.8	28.8
South Africa	—	—	—	—	75.0	85.0	80.0	240.0	72.0	—	—	50.0	—	—	347.5
Sudan	19.0	7.5	2.5	6.0	21.0	19.6	22.6	33.7	34.7	19.0	30.2	41.6	31.6	4.9	—
Swaziland	—	—	—	—	—	—	—	—	—	—	—	—	—	1.0	3.4
Tanzania	—	—	—	—	—	1.6	28.7	13.0	25.0	26.3	11.1	25.1	24.4	4.8	15.1
Togo	—	—	—	—	—	—	7.5	—	—	—	—	—	5.2	8.4	2.9
Tunisia	2.6	—	—	—	—	—	—	—	24.0	—	—	—	—	—	—
Uganda	—	—	—	5.1	4.9	—	10.0	8.0	10.0	10.3	1.5	11.9	37.7	64.2	69.7
Zambia	—	—	—	38.0	19.0	19.0	—	26.3	44.0	39.8	86.2	113.5	71.3	18.7	122.6
Zimbabwe	—	—	—	—	—	—	—	—	—	—	—	—	9.4	20.9	49.4
Asia	105.0	224.3	117.6	103.1	458.4	555.9	520.8	370.0	407.7	381.2	294.3	865.0	899.8	1,608.6	1,589.5
Afghanistan, I.S. of	4.4	6.0	5.0	4.0	7.5	1.8	—	—	—	—	—	—	—	—	—
Bangladesh	—	—	—	20.5	33.0	41.4	17.7	63.0	69.6	32.6	33.9	21.1	58.0	68.7	104.5
Cambodia	—	—	—	—	—	—	—	—	—	—	—	—	—	—	—
China, People's Rep.	—	—	—	—	—	—	—	—	—	—	—	450.0	—	—	—
Fiji	—	—	—	—	—	—	—	—	6.5	—	—	—	—	5.1	6.8
India	—	—	—	—	292.0	281.2	201.3	—	—	—	—	33.3	133.0	174.8	331.3
Indonesia	20.0	87.0	18.2	—	—	—	—	—	—	—	—	—	3.6	264.9	—
Korea	—	—	—	—	20.0	10.3	89.5	97.4	25.0	40.8	35.2	40.9	261.5	361.8	226.8
Lao People's Dem.Rep	—	—	—	—	—	—	—	1.6	6.5	1.6	—	—	4.7	6.4	1.9
Malaysia	—	7.3	—	—	—	85.7	—	—	—	—	—	46.2	52.2	155.7	107.2
Mongolia	—	—	—	—	—	—	—	—	—	—	—	—	—	—	—
Myanmar	10.0	6.5	8.0	5.5	6.0	7.8	16.7	21.9	15.1	7.4	2.9	16.2	6.1	13.5	26.7
Nepal	—	—	—	—	—	—	4.1	1.0	—	.2	4.8	4.9	5.2	3.9	—
Pakistan	15.0	40.0	20.0	25.0	42.0	68.9	84.3	80.7	107.0	132.6	48.7	24.3	51.6	149.2	269.5
Papua New Guinea	—	—	—	—	—	—	10.0	5.0	5.0	4.8	—	—	28.3	6.6	10.1
Philippines	29.5	57.8	47.2	29.1	38.8	38.8	73.7	71.1	111.6	44.6	67.7	144.6	212.5	147.0	213.1
Samoa	—	—	—	—	—	.8	.6	.1	.4	.9	.7	.9	.8	1.4	1.3
Solomon Islands	—	—	—	—	—	—	—	1.1	—	—	—	—	.2	.4	1.2
Sri Lanka	24.0	19.8	19.2	18.7	19.2	19.3	22.8	27.1	32.7	39.8	44.6	46.2	22.7	35.9	58.5
Thailand	2.1	—	—	—	—	—	—	—	16.8	67.4	34.4	35.2	59.3	213.5	230.8
Vietnam	—	—	—	—	—	—	—	—	11.5	8.5	21.5	1.3	—	—	—

Expressed in Millions of SDRs

	1987	1988	1989	1990	1991	1992	1993	1994	1995	1996	1997	1998	1999	2000	2001
World	7,881.8	6,670.6	5,912.7	5,853.4	4,744.8	4,201.6	3,814.0	4,572.0	6,650.9	5,071.9	5,681.3	6,694.2	19,398.8	15,249.4	13,274.9
Industrial Countries	209.6	373.1	—	—	—	—	—	—	—	—	—	—	—	—	—
United States	—	—	—	—	—	—	—	—	—	—	—	—	—	—	—
Canada	—	—	—	—	—	—	—	—	—	—	—	—	—	—	—
Australia	—	—	—	—	—	—	—	—	—	—	—	—	—	—	—
Japan	—	—	—	—	—	—	—	—	—	—	—	—	—	—	—
New Zealand	—	—	—	—	—	—	—	—	—	—	—	—	—	—	—
Belgium	—	—	—	—	—	—	—	—	—	—	—	—	—	—	—
Denmark	—	—	—	—	—	—	—	—	—	—	—	—	—	—	—
Finland	—	—	—	—	—	—	—	—	—	—	—	—	—	—	—
France	—	—	—	—	—	—	—	—	—	—	—	—	—	—	—
Greece	—	—	—	—	—	—	—	—	—	—	—	—	—	—	—
Iceland	10.8	—	—	—	—	—	—	—	—	—	—	—	—	—	—
Ireland	—	—	—	—	—	—	—	—	—	—	—	—	—	—	—
Italy	—	—	—	—	—	—	—	—	—	—	—	—	—	—	—
Netherlands	—	—	—	—	—	—	—	—	—	—	—	—	—	—	—
Norway	—	—	—	—	—	—	—	—	—	—	—	—	—	—	—
Portugal	198.8	373.1	—	—	—	—	—	—	—	—	—	—	—	—	—
Spain	—	—	—	—	—	—	—	—	—	—	—	—	—	—	—
United Kingdom	—	—	—	—	—	—	—	—	—	—	—	—	—	—	—
Developing Countries	7,672.2	6,297.5	5,912.7	5,853.4	4,744.8	4,201.6	3,814.0	4,572.0	6,650.9	5,071.9	5,681.3	6,694.2	19,398.8	15,249.4	13,274.9
Africa	1,432.1	952.6	1,122.1	912.0	669.3	601.3	626.5	423.3	1,522.4	269.2	730.0	827.9	407.3	198.2	241.1
Algeria	—	—	—	—	—	117.7	235.4	136.5	112.5	93.8	254.6	320.8	262.8	70.2	110.5
Burkina Faso															
Burundi															
Cameroon					8.7	38.6	33.8	3.9	4.0	4.0	8.2	12.0	13.3	14.1	2.5
Central African Rep.	2.1	6.1	9.0	6.4	2.5	1.1	.6	.4	—	—	2.7	5.6	2.4	—	—
Chad	—	.9	3.5	2.6	—	—	—	—	—	—	3.9	5.2	1.3	—	—
Comoros													.6		
Congo, Dem. Rep. of	125.0	78.3	255.6	108.5	35.5	—	—	3.0	.9	22.7	—	.4	.7	—	—
Congo, Republic of	—	1.2	—	4.8	3.6	—	.5	2.0	1.5	—	1.6	7.8	3.1	—	.9
Côte d'Ivoire	102.7	127.6	120.1	87.7	76.3	65.2	36.5	53.5	56.8	32.8	16.1				
Djibouti													.7	1.7	1.6
Equatorial Guinea		.3	3.0	1.8	.4										
Ethiopia	10.1	7.3	14.8	17.6	4.4										
Gabon				10.7	18.1	25.8	25.7	16.1	34.5	3.8	2.6	16.7	17.9	7.4	8.7
Gambia, The	5.3	3.2	3.1	3.7	4.4	1.5									
Ghana	134.1	196.2	134.4	83.1	56.4	45.3	39.3	27.1	13.1	16.8	34.5	24.6			
Guinea	5.8	—	4.1	9.8	6.4	.8									
Guinea-Bissau	.2	.9	.7												
Kenya	83.9	67.4	98.0	75.2	29.1	58.7	41.5								
Lesotho				1.1											
Liberia	—	1.0	2.2	.7					.1					.2	.3
Madagascar	26.5	29.5	38.3	34.7	25.0	11.5	7.4	4.5	.6						
Malawi	23.6	19.9	19.0	13.8	15.2	13.6	4.2	1.2	—	—	—	6.4	6.4		
Mali	16.5	14.0	15.6	12.9	6.7	4.4	6.3	4.8	1.0						
Mauritania	5.0	3.4	7.4	11.2	9.6	4.6	1.0								
Mauritius	23.4	29.0	28.9	32.1	15.5										
Morocco	243.9	169.1	193.3	164.2	125.0	100.8	112.0	106.1	66.2	32.5	2.3				
Niger	16.1	21.9	12.9	10.0	8.3	5.4	3.5	2.0	—	—	4.2	5.6	1.4		
Nigeria															
Rwanda													4.5	6.7	7.4
Senegal	44.4	41.7	43.4	39.7	34.5	28.1	11.0	2.5	—	—	11.6	15.5	3.9		
Sierra Leone	—	.7	.9	1.6	5.4	1.4	5.9	42.6	—	—	—	—	—	—	37.5
Somalia	16.0	.7	8.8	2.1											
South Africa	397.5	—	—	1.0	—	—	—	—	—	—	307.2	307.2			
Sudan								23.0	24.5	25.5	42.2	27.6	41.1	41.1	
Swaziland	3.4	2.3													
Tanzania	4.1	—	2.6	19.6	19.4	3.9									
Togo	10.8	17.6	16.8	11.2	5.8	7.1	5.2	2.4	2.0	.2					
Tunisia				82.0	99.1	20.9	3.8	—	10.2	32.1	36.6	36.6	36.6	30.4	24.7
Uganda	51.1	55.4	54.3	30.3	24.4	18.7	3.1								
Zambia			14.7	24.8	26.0	49.8	14.6	1,196.2							
Zimbabwe	80.8	58.1	30.0	17.4	4.8	—	—	—	—	5.9	18.5	21.6	24.8	26.4	5.9
Asia	2,422.9	1,824.9	1,427.1	1,695.1	1,350.7	734.3	369.7	1,066.0	1,113.8	1,262.8	831.0	2,514.2	8,330.4	375.5	6,943.9
Afghanistan, I.S. of															
Bangladesh	104.1	58.6	81.8	146.4	102.9	56.0	35.9								
Cambodia						6.3	6.3					1.0	1.0	1.0	1.0
China, People's Rep.				298.9	298.9										
Fiji	1.7	1.8	2.4	.6											
India	637.5	787.5	737.5	531.3	362.5	275.0	137.5	821.7	796.5	881.4	495.5	304.9	246.4	38.5	
Indonesia		42.0	—	115.7	231.4	115.7									1,375.9
Korea	896.5	369.8										2,050.0	7,900.0	—	4,462.5
Lao People's Dem.Rep															
Malaysia															
Mongolia									6.3	6.9	.6				
Myanmar	27.4	10.9													
Nepal			5.4	8.5	3.9	.8									
Pakistan	280.3	196.6	143.1	108.1	71.7	116.1	91.4	34.1	61.2	167.0	138.8	39.7	107.6	161.2	80.8
Papua New Guinea							10.7	21.4	10.7			3.0	16.7	14.7	1.0
Philippines	240.2	119.7	137.9	249.7	215.0	109.9	46.0	188.7	239.1	207.5	156.9	58.2	39.5	6.1	6.1
Samoa	2.1	2.6	1.4	.6	.4	.2									
Solomon Islands	1.3	.3	.2	.6	.5										
Sri Lanka	69.4	64.1	46.0	31.9	63.6	54.4	13.6								
Thailand	162.5	171.1	271.4	202.9										150.0	1,012.5
Vietnam							28.4				39.3	57.4	19.2	4.0	4.0

Repurchases

Expressed in Millions of SDRs

	1972	1973	1974	1975	1976	1977	1978	1979	1980	1981	1982	1983	1984	1985	198
Europe															
Albania	—	—	—	—	—	—	—	—	—	—	—	—	—	—	—
Armenia	—	—	—	—	—	—	—	—	—	—	—	—	—	—	—
Azerbaijan	—	—	—	—	—	—	—	—	—	—	—	—	—	—	—
Belarus	—	—	—	—	—	—	—	—	—	—	—	—	—	—	—
Bosnia & Herzegovina	—	—	—	—	—	—	—	—	—	—	—	—	—	—	—
Bulgaria	—	—	—	—	—	—	—	—	—	—	—	—	—	—	—
Croatia	—	—	—	—	—	—	—	—	—	—	—	—	—	—	—
Cyprus	—	—	—	—	—	—	10.1	4.8	11.6	9.0	9.3	6.8	2.3	3.2	—
Czech Republic	—	—	—	—	—	—	—	—	—	—	—	—	—	—	—
Czechoslovakia	—	—	—	—	—	—	—	—	—	—	—	—	—	—	—
Estonia	—	—	—	—	—	—	—	—	—	—	—	—	—	—	—
Georgia	—	—	—	—	—	—	—	—	—	—	—	—	—	—	—
Hungary	—	—	—	—	—	—	—	—	—	—	—	—	—	88.3	41.
Kazakhstan	—	—	—	—	—	—	—	—	—	—	—	—	—	—	—
Kyrgyz Republic	—	—	—	—	—	—	—	—	—	—	—	—	—	—	—
Latvia	—	—	—	—	—	—	—	—	—	—	—	—	—	—	—
Lithuania	—	—	—	—	—	—	—	—	—	—	—	—	—	—	—
Macedonia, FYR	—	—	—	—	—	—	—	—	—	—	—	—	—	—	—
Moldova	—	—	—	—	—	—	—	—	—	—	—	—	—	—	—
Poland	—	—	—	—	—	—	—	—	—	—	—	—	—	—	—
Romania	—	—	—	—	—	40.0	47.5	50.0	80.0	60.3	35.1	60.9	132.5	172.9	199.3
Russia	—	—	—	—	—	—	—	—	—	—	—	—	—	—	—
Slovak Republic	—	—	—	—	—	—	—	—	—	—	—	—	—	—	—
Slovenia	—	—	—	—	—	—	—	—	—	—	—	—	—	—	—
Tajikistan	—	—	—	—	—	—	—	—	—	—	—	—	—	—	—
Turkey	62.1	—	—	—	—	—	24.8	68.5	119.2	91.0	116.4	168.3	210.8	247.5	320.3
Ukraine	—	—	—	—	—	—	—	—	—	—	—	—	—	—	—
Uzbekistan	—	—	—	—	—	—	—	—	—	—	—	—	—	—	—
Yugoslavia, SFR	15.0	61.7	21.8	—	21.8	106.0	75.0	45.8	53.7	74.6	39.2	169.1	269.3	322.1	362.5
Yugoslavia, Fed. Rep	—	—	—	—	—	—	—	—	—	—	—	—	—	—	—
Middle East	**84.6**	**19.5**	**23.1**	**29.9**	**16.0**	**28.0**	**126.4**	**111.5**	**155.2**	**128.8**	**96.4**	**30.8**	**—**	**13.7**	**23.8**
Egypt	45.0	9.0	9.0	24.5	16.0	28.0	35.0	51.2	78.9	53.9	33.1	2.7	—	11.8	12.5
Iran, I.R. of	—	—	—	—	—	—	—	—	—	—	—	—	—	—	—
Iraq	—	—	—	—	—	—	—	—	—	—	—	—	—	—	—
Israel	32.5	—	—	—	—	—	86.4	47.0	67.8	68.9	60.4	27.2	—	—	—
Jordan	—	5.8	1.6	—	—	—	—	—	—	—	—	—	—	—	—
Syrian Arab Republic	7.1	4.8	12.5	5.4	—	—	—	—	—	—	—	—	—	—	—
Yemen Arab Rep.	—	—	—	—	—	—	—	—	—	—	—	—	—	—	3.6
Yemen, P.D. Rep.	—	—	—	—	—	—	—	5.0	13.3	8.4	6.0	2.9	.9	1.9	7.7
Yemen, Republic of	—	—	—	—	—	—	—	—	—	—	—	—	—	—	—
Western Hemisphere	**94.5**	**87.0**	**204.5**	**41.5**	**163.4**	**273.2**	**763.5**	**362.0**	**337.7**	**209.6**	**148.3**	**187.6**	**218.5**	**403.4**	**1,645.0**
Argentina	—	—	110.0	—	64.0	103.1	340.8	—	—	—	—	—	—	—	337.3
Barbados	—	—	—	—	—	—	—	—	4.2	1.5	.8	.9	—	—	11.2
Belize	—	—	—	—	—	—	—	—	—	—	—	—	—	—	1.2
Bolivia	3.0	8.0	3.7	5.1	18.6	—	—	—	—	1.9	7.5	10.7	20.3	18.2	25.3
Brazil	—	—	—	—	—	—	—	—	—	—	—	—	—	64.5	525.5
Chile	—	—	39.5	6.0	53.0	101.6	73.6	130.6	39.6	54.5	36.1	5.7	—	—	152.4
Colombia	53.3	—	—	—	—	—	—	—	—	—	—	—	—	—	—
Costa Rica	—	—	—	.9	4.5	3.0	13.0	1.0	9.4	9.1	4.0	11.7	24.3	21.4	30.7
Dominica	—	—	—	—	—	—	—	—	—	—	—	.7	1.8	1.5	1.3
Dominican Republic	7.0	3.8	—	—	—	—	—	10.8	49.8	18.2	2.3	8.1	9.5	32.2	38.7
Ecuador	5.5	16.5	—	—	—	—	—	—	—	—	—	—	—	—	5.5
El Salvador	10.2	8.8	—	—	—	17.9	—	—	—	—	—	—	5.4	26.6	45.8
Grenada	—	—	—	—	—	—	—	.9	.5	.1	.8	—	.9	2.1	1.3
Guatemala	—	—	—	—	—	—	—	—	—	—	—	—	—	47.8	48.0
Guyana	2.1	—	3.9	5.6	—	—	1.3	2.8	11.9	9.5	2.2	4.1	1.0	1.0	1.0
Haiti	.8	—	—	—	3.7	6.3	1.3	1.9	2.2	2.2	1.0	.3	—	11.8	19.7
Honduras	—	—	—	—	—	12.5	10.5	—	—	—	—	—	1.6	16.7	41.4
Jamaica	—	5.5	13.3	—	—	—	7.7	18.0	14.6	43.6	40.3	41.5	58.3	61.3	103.3
Mexico	—	—	—	—	—	—	192.5	126.3	100.3	—	—	—	—	—	125.4
Nicaragua	6.8	8.0	5.5	6.7	6.8	6.7	6.8	—	.6	17.5	3.6	4.3	4.3	9.0	—
Panama	—	—	—	—	—	.5	1.8	8.9	13.4	12.9	4.3	.9	7.5	28.3	38.7
Paraguay	—	—	—	—	—	—	—	—	—	—	—	—	—	—	—
Peru	3.3	17.1	13.6	—	—	—	—	60.9	91.2	38.7	43.9	87.5	82.7	49.3	43.5
St. Kitts and Nevis	—	—	—	—	—	—	—	—	—	—	—	—	—	—	—
St. Lucia	—	—	—	—	—	—	—	—	—	—	—	1.5	—	1.7	.3
St. Vincent & Grens.	—	—	—	—	—	—	—	—	—	—	—	—	.5	.7	.3
Trinidad and Tobago	—	—	—	—	—	—	—	—	—	—	—	—	—	—	—
Uruguay	2.7	19.5	15.0	17.3	12.9	21.7	115.5	—	—	—	—	11.2	—	9.5	—
Venezuela, Rep. Bol.	—	—	—	—	—	—	—	—	—	—	—	—	—	—	48.2
Memorandum Items															
Oil Exporting Ctys	20.0	88.5	18.2	—	—	—	—	—	—	—	—	—	—	3.6	264.9	—
Non-Oil Develop.Ctys	386.0	319.0	356.0	238.9	840.6	1,193.2	1,785.8	1,469.8	1,578.5	1,271.6	982.7	1,912.8	2,280.9	3,360.1	5,653.8

Expressed in Millions of SDRs

1987	1988	1989	1990	1991	1992	1993	1994	1995	1996	1997	1998	1999	2000	2001	
															Europe
—	—	—	—	—	—	—	—	.8	5.7	5.8	.9	—	—	4.4	Albania
—	—	—	—	—	—	—	—	—	—	—	.4	9.6	12.0	5.6	Armenia
—	—	—	—	—	—	—	—	—	—	—	—	11.7	39.0	30.9	Azerbaijan
—	—	—	—	—	—	—	—	—	—	—	17.9	42.5	42.1	23.4	Belarus
—	—	—	—	—	—	—	18.4	1.4	.7	—	—	15.2	15.2	6.1	Bosnia & Herzegovina
—	—	—	—	—	60.6	—	48.0	162.3	154.9	64.4	134.7	90.7	105.3	236.2	Bulgaria
—	—	—	—	—	—	17.2	6.2	3.9	3.1	1.6	6.5	22.9	21.8	24.2	Croatia
—	—	—	—	—	—	—	—	—	—	—	—	—	—	—	Cyprus
—	—	—	—	—	—	70.0	780.7	—	—	—	—	—	—	—	Czech Republic
—	—	—	—	—	35.0	—	—	—	—	—	—	—	—	—	Czechoslovakia
—	—	—	—	—	—	—	—	1.0	7.7	14.1	18.7	2.9	3.9	3.9	Estonia
—	—	—	—	—	—	—	—	—	—	—	.7	15.7	19.7	9.3	Georgia
272.9	263.9	174.2	242.8	55.3	122.8	36.2	114.7	522.9	140.0	—	118.7	—	—	—	Hungary
—	—	—	—	—	—	—	—	—	—	4.6	70.0	128.5	335.1	—	Kazakhstan
—	—	—	—	—	—	—	—	—	2.7	7.1	8.5	5.4	5.4	5.4	Kyrgyz Republic
—	—	—	—	—	—	—	—	1.9	17.5	26.7	18.3	11.1	7.6	7.6	Latvia
—	—	—	—	—	—	—	—	—	16.9	31.1	20.6	12.1	20.7	26.7	Lithuania
—	—	—	—	—	—	2.2	1.2	.7	.6	.3	1.7	12.4	14.7	6.0	Macedonia, FYR
—	—	—	—	—	—	—	—	—	—	5.1	14.6	47.2	47.9	18.6	11.3	Moldova
—	—	—	—	—	—	98.9	219.4	918.6	—	—	—	—	—	—	Poland
226.0	250.6	106.9	—	—	153.4	—	89.6	245.8	245.4	98.4	92.3	102.0	72.9	91.7	Romania
—	—	—	—	—	—	—	—	—	359.5	359.5	673.9	3,101.1	2,189.5	2,997.9	Russia
—	—	—	—	—	—	—	61.9	132.3	85.6	37.6	49.8	38.1	96.5	—	Slovak Republic
—	—	—	—	—	—	9.9	3.6	2.2	1.8	.9	—	—	—	—	Slovenia
—	—	—	—	—	—	—	—	—	—	—	—	3.8	7.5	9.4	Tajikistan
344.2	320.9	185.8	36.3	—	—	—	—	—	—	20.1	164.6	210.2	65.6	867.6	Turkey
—	—	—	—	—	—	—	—	—	—	—	77.3	407.0	643.5	361.2	Ukraine
—	—	—	—	—	—	—	—	—	—	—	—	18.4	49.4	35.1	Uzbekistan
385.8	454.2	451.5	260.0	113.1	72.4	9.6	—	—	....	....	....	....	....	....	Yugoslavia, SFR
—	—	—	—	—	—	—	—	—	—	—	—	—	—	—	Yugoslavia, Fed. Rep
23.2	**35.2**	**28.7**	**36.2**	**58.0**	**36.3**	**33.1**	**48.4**	**135.2**	**163.2**	**49.4**	**6.8**	**50.7**	**77.9**	**81.7**	**Middle East**
12.5	12.5	—	29.0	58.0	29.0	—	22.5	62.7	58.6	10.9	—	—	—	—	Egypt
—	—	—	—	—	—	—	—	—	—	—	—	—	—	—	Iran, I.R. of
—	—	—	—	—	—	—	—	—	—	—	—	—	—	—	Iraq
—	—	—	—	—	—	—	—	67.0	89.3	22.3	—	—	—	—	Israel
—	21.5	28.7	7.2	—	7.3	33.1	25.9	5.6	15.3	16.2	6.8	26.0	23.8	40.2	Jordan
—	—	—	—	—	—	—	—	—	—	—	—	—	—	—	Syrian Arab Republic
4.9	1.2	—	—	—	—	—	—	—	—	—	—	—	—	—	Yemen Arab Rep.
5.8	—	—	—	—	—	—	—	—	—	—	—	—	—	—	Yemen, P.D. Rep.
—	—	—	—	—	—	—	—	—	—	—	—	24.8	54.1	41.4	Yemen, Republic of
2,565.2	**2,195.1**	**2,416.5**	**2,671.1**	**2,498.3**	**2,385.6**	**2,540.5**	**1,709.2**	**1,868.8**	**2,329.0**	**3,383.4**	**1,822.5**	**6,301.3**	**10,756.2**	**1,244.3**	**Western Hemisphere**
494.4	381.9	558.2	513.6	723.8	637.7	275.1	289.7	319.3	296.5	347.8	484.2	602.5	970.2	927.6	Argentina
16.8	7.8	4.5	2.8	.5	—	—	—	11.9	18.4	6.5	—	—	—	—	Barbados
1.5	2.3	3.3	2.2	.3	—	—	—	—	—	—	—	—	—	—	Belize
19.2	36.3	4.9	31.4	36.9	22.6	17.0	—	—	—	—	—	—	—	—	Bolivia
877.0	691.4	633.5	563.7	414.5	411.3	360.4	93.5	32.3	48.2	23.7	15.5	1,445.9	5,074.2	—	Brazil
280.9	199.8	155.1	153.6	143.5	144.4	178.5	147.0	199.5	—	—	—	—	—	—	Chile
—	—	—	—	—	—	—	—	—	—	—	—	—	—	—	Colombia
47.7	40.2	26.1	19.0	5.2	2.8	—	13.8	29.1	15.8	.5	—	—	—	—	Costa Rica
1.6	2.2	1.9	1.0	.7	.4	.1	—	—	—	—	—	—	—	—	Dominica
49.0	38.2	68.5	42.8	32.9	10.3	7.2	5.6	22.4	41.0	45.3	21.1	—	—	—	Dominican Republic
90.2	102.3	69.2	84.8	77.0	54.9	20.8	14.9	19.0	15.8	2.0	49.5	49.5	—	—	Ecuador
31.2	3.9	—	—	—	—	—	—	—	—	—	—	—	—	—	El Salvador
.3	.3	.3	.3	—	—	—	—	—	—	—	—	—	—	—	Grenada
15.5	21.0	9.9	8.7	2.1	22.4	22.4	—	—	—	—	—	—	—	—	Guatemala
—	—	.8	69.6	1.3	—	2.4	15.3	15.6	8.1	6.7	1.4	—	—	—	Guyana
18.1	14.1	14.3	6.5	1.6	—	—	14.8	.3	—	—	6.0	8.2	2.2	—	Haiti
32.4	24.3	.3	22.0	1.3	—	2.1	11.2	28.8	26.1	6.4	—	—	—	—	Honduras
172.1	163.2	130.8	82.1	64.1	55.7	51.9	60.9	62.9	49.5	25.1	12.5	13.9	14.5	14.5	Jamaica
280.1	419.0	639.6	877.1	807.4	636.1	841.7	841.0	754.1	1,413.6	2,499.2	783.7	3,726.7	4,164.3	—	Mexico
—	—	—	—	—	—	—	2.1	8.5	6.4	—	—	—	—	—	Nicaragua
55.7	.1	.6	51.9	40.6	141.7	7.3	.9	25.6	35.8	18.8	9.9	17.2	39.3	26.2	Panama
—	—	—	—	—	—	—	—	—	—	—	—	—	—	—	Paraguay
.1	—	18.4	46.5	37.1	34.7	458.7	—	—	—	53.6	107.1	107.1	107.1	120.5	Peru
—	—	—	—	—	—	—	—	—	—	—	—	—	—	—	St. Kitts and Nevis
—	—	—	—	—	—	—	—	—	—	—	—	—	—	—	St. Lucia
—	—	—	—	—	—	—	—	—	—	—	—	—	—	—	St. Vincent & Grens.
—	—	—	—	—	63.7	92.5	50.4	28.7	17.3	13.3	3.1	—	—	—	Trinidad and Tobago
81.5	47.0	76.3	91.6	30.3	18.3	10.2	7.4	6.5	8.0	6.0	—	—	—	—	Uruguay
—	—	—	—	—	77.2	128.6	192.0	140.6	304.2	328.5	328.5	330.3	384.4	155.6	Venezuela, Rep. Bol.
															Memorandum Items
—	42.0	—	115.7	308.6	362.0	427.5	277.1	416.7	422.3	583.2	649.3	593.1	454.7	1,642.0	**Oil Exporting Ctys**
7,672.2	6,255.6	5,912.7	5,737.7	4,436.2	3,839.6	3,386.5	4,295.0	6,234.2	4,649.6	5,098.1	6,044.9	18,805.7	14,794.7	11,633.0	**Non-Oil Develop.Ctys**

Loan Disbursements

	1972	1973	1974	1975	1976	1977	1978	1979	1980	1981	1982	1983	1984	1985	198
						Expressed in Millions of SDRs									
World	—	—	—	—	—	152.9	688.1	526.6	1,256.0	367.7	—	—	—	—	81.
Developing Countries	—	—	—	—	—	152.9	688.1	526.6	1,256.0	367.7	—	—	—	—	81.
Africa	—	—	—	—	—	49.9	296.7	264.8	326.6	4.0	—	—	—	—	54.
Benin	—	—	—	—	—	—	5.4	—	7.3	.1	—	—	—	—	—
Burkina Faso	—	—	—	—	—	—	5.4	3.9	3.3	.1	—	—	—	—	—
Burundi	—	—	—	—	—	2.0	5.8	5.8	4.9	.1	—	—	—	—	8.
Cameroon	—	—	—	—	—	—	14.5	10.6	9.0	.1	—	—	—	—	—
Cape Verde	—	—	—	—	—	—	—	—	—	—	—	—	—	—	—
Central African Rep.	—	—	—	—	—	—	5.4	—	7.3	.1	—	—	—	—	—
Chad	—	—	—	—	—	—	5.4	—	—	—	—	—	—	—	—
Comoros	—	—	—	—	—	—	—	—	—	—	—	—	—	—	—
Congo, Dem. Rep. of	—	—	—	—	—	12.1	34.8	34.2	28.9	.4	—	—	—	—	—
Congo, Republic of	—	—	—	—	—	1.4	4.0	3.9	3.3	.1	—	—	—	—	—
Côte d'Ivoire	—	—	—	—	—	—	21.6	—	29.1	.2	—	—	—	—	—
Djibouti	—	—	—	—	—	—	—	—	—	—	—	—	—	—	—
Equatorial Guinea	—	—	—	—	—	—	—	—	4.5	—	—	—	—	—	—
Ethiopia	—	—	—	—	—	—	11.2	8.2	6.9	.1	—	—	—	—	—
Gambia, The	—	—	—	—	—	.8	2.2	2.1	1.8	—	—	—	—	—	3.
Ghana	—	—	—	—	—	—	—	26.4	22.3	.3	—	—	—	—	—
Guinea	—	—	—	—	—	2.6	7.4	7.3	6.1	.1	—	—	—	—	—
Guinea-Bissau	—	—	—	—	—	—	—	—	—	—	—	—	—	—	—
Kenya	—	—	—	—	—	5.1	14.8	14.5	12.3	.2	—	—	—	—	—
Lesotho	—	—	—	—	—	.5	1.5	1.5	1.3	—	—	—	—	—	—
Liberia	—	—	—	—	—	3.1	8.9	8.8	7.4	.1	—	—	—	—	—
Madagascar	—	—	—	—	—	—	10.8	—	14.5	.1	—	—	—	—	—
Malawi	—	—	—	—	—	1.6	4.6	4.5	3.8	.1	—	—	—	—	—
Mali	—	—	—	—	—	—	9.1	6.7	5.6	.1	—	—	—	—	—
Mauritania	—	—	—	—	—	1.4	4.0	3.9	3.3	.1	—	—	—	—	6.
Mauritius	—	—	—	—	—	—	9.1	—	—	—	—	—	—	—	—
Morocco	—	—	—	—	—	12.1	34.8	34.2	28.9	.4	—	—	—	—	—
Mozambique	—	—	—	—	—	—	—	—	—	—	—	—	—	—	—
Niger	—	—	—	—	—	—	5.4	—	7.3	.1	—	—	—	—	6.
Rwanda	—	—	—	—	—	—	—	5.8	4.9	.1	—	—	—	—	—
São Tomé & Príncipe	—	—	—	—	—	—	—	—	—	—	—	—	—	—	—
Senegal	—	—	—	—	—	—	14.1	10.3	8.7	.1	—	—	—	—	17.
Sierra Leone	—	—	—	—	—	2.7	7.7	7.6	6.4	.1	—	—	—	—	11.
Somalia	—	—	—	—	—	—	—	—	10.6	.1	—	—	—	—	—
Sudan	—	—	—	—	—	—	29.8	21.8	18.4	.3	—	—	—	—	—
Swaziland	—	—	—	—	—	—	—	2.4	2.0	—	—	—	—	—	—
Tanzania	—	—	—	—	—	4.5	12.9	12.7	10.8	.2	—	—	—	—	—
Togo	—	—	—	—	—	—	6.2	4.5	3.8	.1	—	—	—	—	—
Uganda	—	—	—	—	—	—	—	—	22.4	.2	—	—	—	—	—
Zambia	—	—	—	—	—	—	—	23.0	19.5	.3	—	—	—	—	—
Zimbabwe	—	—	—	—	—	—	—	—	—	—	—	—	—	—	—
Asia	—	—	—	—	—	77.6	302.9	182.1	821.8	351.2	—	—	—	—	—
Afghanistan, I.S. of	—	—	—	—	—	—	—	—	—	—	—	—	—	—	—
Bangladesh	—	—	—	—	—	13.4	38.4	37.9	32.0	.5	—	—	—	—	—
Cambodia	—	—	—	—	—	—	—	—	—	—	—	—	—	—	—
China, People's Rep.	—	—	—	—	—	—	—	—	—	309.5	—	—	—	—	—
India	—	—	—	—	—	—	—	—	525.5	3.6	—	—	—	—	—
Lao People's Dem.Rep	—	—	—	—	—	—	5.4	3.9	3.3	.1	—	—	—	—	—
Maldives	—	—	—	—	—	—	—	—	—	—	—	—	—	—	—
Mongolia	—	—	—	—	—	—	—	—	—	—	—	—	—	—	—
Myanmar	—	—	—	—	—	6.4	18.5	18.2	15.4	.2	—	—	—	—	—
Nepal	—	—	—	—	—	1.5	4.3	4.2	3.6	.1	—	—	—	—	—
Pakistan	—	—	—	—	—	25.1	72.3	—	131.4	.9	—	—	—	—	—
Papua New Guinea	—	—	—	—	—	—	8.3	—	11.2	.1	—	—	—	—	—
Philippines	—	—	—	—	—	16.6	47.7	47.0	39.7	.6	—	—	—	—	—
Samoa	—	—	—	—	—	.2	.6	.6	.5	—	—	—	—	—	—
Solomon Islands	—	—	—	—	—	—	—	—	—	—	—	—	—	—	—
Sri Lanka	—	—	—	—	—	—	40.6	29.7	25.1	.4	—	—	—	—	—
Thailand	—	—	—	—	—	14.3	41.2	40.6	34.3	.5	—	—	—	—	—
Vietnam	—	—	—	—	—	—	25.7	—	—	34.9	—	—	—	—	—
Europe	—	—	—	—	—	—	—	—	—	—	—	—	—	—	—
Albania	—	—	—	—	—	—	—	—	—	—	—	—	—	—	—
Armenia	—	—	—	—	—	—	—	—	—	—	—	—	—	—	—
Azerbaijan	—	—	—	—	—	—	—	—	—	—	—	—	—	—	—
Georgia	—	—	—	—	—	—	—	—	—	—	—	—	—	—	—
Kyrgyz Republic	—	—	—	—	—	—	—	—	—	—	—	—	—	—	—
Macedonia, FYR	—	—	—	—	—	—	—	—	—	—	—	—	—	—	—
Moldova	—	—	—	—	—	—	—	—	—	—	—	—	—	—	—
Tajikistan	—	—	—	—	—	—	—	—	—	—	—	—	—	—	—
Middle East	—	—	—	—	—	23.2	66.7	65.7	55.6	.8	—	—	—	—	—
Egypt	—	—	—	—	—	20.1	57.8	57.0	48.1	.7	—	—	—	—	—
Yemen Arab Rep.	—	—	—	—	—	—	—	—	—	—	—	—	—	—	—
Yemen, P.D. Rep.	—	—	—	—	—	3.1	8.9	8.8	7.4	.1	—	—	—	—	—
Yemen, Republic of	—	—	—	—	—	—	—	—	—	—	—	—	—	—	—
Western Hemisphere	—	—	—	—	—	2.3	21.8	13.9	52.0	11.7	—	—	—	—	27.8
Bolivia	—	—	—	—	—	—	15.3	—	20.7	.1	—	—	—	—	18.1
Dominica	—	—	—	—	—	—	—	—	—	—	—	—	—	—	.8
El Salvador	—	—	—	—	—	—	—	—	19.6	.1	—	—	—	—	—
Grenada	—	—	—	—	—	.2	.6	.6	.5	—	—	—	—	—	—
Guyana	—	—	—	—	—	—	—	—	—	11.3	—	—	—	—	—
Haiti	—	—	—	—	—	2.0	5.8	5.8	4.9	.1	—	—	—	—	8.8
Honduras	—	—	—	—	—	—	—	7.6	6.4	.1	—	—	—	—	—
Nicaragua	—	—	—	—	—	—	—	—	—	—	—	—	—	—	—
Memorandum Items															
Non-Oil Develop.Ctys	—	—	—	—	—	152.9	688.1	526.6	1,256.0	367.7	—	—	—	—	81.8

Expressed in Millions of SDRs

1987	1988	1989	1990	1991	1992	1993	1994	1995	1996	1997	1998	1999	2000	2001	
403.4	410.2	961.1	507.0	781.9	544.3	271.7	910.4	1,431.4	708.6	730.6	896.0	736.8	505.8	872.6	**World**
403.4	410.2	961.1	507.0	781.9	544.3	271.7	910.4	1,431.4	708.6	730.6	896.0	736.8	505.8	872.6	**Developing Countries**
251.0	292.4	543.4	359.3	380.6	273.8	142.1	467.1	1,247.8	404.3	348.3	532.6	334.8	364.8	463.2	**Africa**
—	—	6.3	—	9.4	—	15.7	18.1	9.1	13.6	4.5	—	7.2	6.8	8.1	Benin
—	—	—	—	6.3	—	8.8	17.7	17.7	6.6	13.3	13.3	12.2	5.6	16.8	Burkina Faso
—	12.8	8.5	—	4.3	14.9	—	—	—	—	—	—	—	—	—	Burundi
—	—	—	—	—	—	—	—	—	—	27.0	54.0	45.0	52.0	15.9	Cameroon
—	—	—	—	—	—	—	—	—	—	—	—	—	—	—	Cape Verde
6.1	9.1	—	6.1	—	—	—	—	—	—	—	8.2	8.2	—	8.0	Central African Rep.
6.1	—	9.2	6.1	—	—	—	—	8.3	16.5	8.3	8.3	8.3	10.4	13.4	Chad
—	—	—	—	.9	—	—	1.4	—	—	—	—	—	—	—	Comoros
58.2	—	87.3	—	—	—	—	—	—	—	—	—	—	—	—	Congo, Dem. Rep. of
—	—	—	—	—	—	—	—	—	13.9	—	—	—	—	—	Congo, Republic of
—	—	—	—	—	—	—	119.1	119.1	95.3	—	123.9	—	—	—	Côte d'Ivoire
—	—	—	—	—	—	—	—	—	—	—	—	2.7	2.7	3.6	Djibouti
—	3.7	—	—	5.5	—	2.8	1.8	—	—	—	—	—	—	—	Equatorial Guinea
—	—	—	—	—	14.1	21.2	14.1	—	14.7	—	14.7	—	—	34.8	Ethiopia
5.1	3.4	6.8	6.8	3.4	—	—	—	—	—	—	3.4	3.4	6.9	6.9	Gambia, The
40.9	86.3	137.8	48.0	116.5	—	—	—	27.4	27.4	—	82.2	44.3	26.8	52.6	Ghana
11.6	—	17.4	—	8.7	8.7	—	8.7	20.3	—	23.6	23.6	7.9	—	20.7	Guinea
1.5	—	2.3	—	—	—	—	—	1.6	2.1	4.5	2.4	—	5.1	—	Guinea-Bissau
—	28.4	80.5	100.5	35.2	—	22.6	22.6	—	24.9	—	—	—	33.6	—	Kenya
—	3.0	4.5	3.0	2.3	5.3	6.8	3.8	—	—	—	—	—	—	7.0	Lesotho
—	—	—	—	—	—	—	—	—	—	—	—	—	—	—	Liberia
13.3	—	25.6	12.8	12.8	—	—	—	—	13.6	13.6	—	13.6	38.0	22.7	Madagascar
—	9.3	18.6	18.6	14.9	—	—	5.6	7.6	15.3	7.6	12.8	7.6	6.4	—	Malawi
—	10.2	—	—	15.2	—	10.2	10.2	29.5	29.5	20.7	20.7	10.3	17.1	18.2	Mali
10.2	—	8.5	8.5	—	8.5	8.5	17.0	14.3	14.3	14.3	—	6.1	6.1	18.2	Mauritania
—	—	—	—	—	—	—	—	—	—	—	—	—	—	—	Mauritius
—	—	—	—	—	—	—	—	—	—	—	—	—	—	—	Morocco
12.2	18.3	12.2	9.2	30.5	45.8	15.3	14.7	—	12.6	25.2	25.2	21.0	45.2	8.4	Mozambique
10.1	8.4	8.4	6.7	—	—	—	—	—	9.7	19.3	19.3	—	8.5	8.5	Niger
—	—	—	—	8.8	—	—	—	—	—	—	11.9	21.4	19.0	9.0	Rwanda
—	—	.8	—	—	—	—	—	—	—	—	—	—	1.9	—	São Tomé & Príncipe
25.5	29.8	51.1	21.3	42.6	—	—	16.7	54.7	23.8	35.7	35.7	14.3	14.3	30.4	Senegal
—	—	—	—	—	—	—	95.6	13.1	10.2	5.1	—	—	—	46.8	Sierra Leone
8.8	—	—	—	—	—	—	—	—	—	—	—	—	—	—	Somalia
—	—	—	—	—	—	—	—	—	—	—	—	—	—	—	Sudan
—	—	—	—	—	—	—	—	—	—	—	—	—	—	—	Swaziland
21.4	32.1	—	21.4	21.4	64.2	—	—	—	25.7	61.4	35.7	58.8	40.0	29.5	Tanzania
—	7.7	15.4	15.4	—	7.7	—	10.9	21.7	—	10.9	10.9	—	—	—	Togo
19.9	29.9	42.3	59.8	57.3	39.8	—	36.7	36.8	43.5	43.5	36.8	25.7	8.9	8.9	Uganda
—	—	—	—	—	—	—	—	833.4	—	10.0	—	10.0	20.0	74.8	Zambia
—	—	—	—	—	54.7	30.4	33.4	33.4	—	—	—	—	—	—	Zimbabwe
151.2	94.6	372.1	87.7	360.9	209.8	105.5	358.9	100.1	132.2	125.2	113.7	52.2	14.3	194.3	**Asia**
—	—	—	—	—	—	—	—	—	—	—	—	—	—	—	Afghanistan, I.S. of
143.8	38.8	18.7	43.1	186.9	86.3	28.8	—	—	—	—	—	—	—	—	Bangladesh
—	—	—	—	—	—	—	14.0	28.0	—	—	—	8.4	8.4	16.7	Cambodia
—	—	—	—	—	—	—	—	—	—	—	—	—	—	—	China, People's Rep.
—	—	—	—	—	—	—	—	—	—	—	—	—	—	—	India
—	—	5.9	—	8.8	5.9	5.9	5.9	11.7	5.9	5.9	—	—	—	4.5	Lao People's Dem.Rep
—	—	—	—	—	—	—	—	—	—	—	—	—	—	—	Maldives
—	—	—	—	—	—	9.3	14.8	—	5.6	5.6	—	5.9	5.9	4.1	Mongolia
—	—	—	—	—	—	—	—	—	—	—	—	—	—	—	Myanmar
7.5	11.2	7.5	—	—	5.6	5.6	5.6	—	—	—	—	—	—	—	Nepal
—	—	273.2	—	109.3	—	—	202.2	—	—	113.7	113.7	37.9	—	86.2	Pakistan
—	—	—	—	—	—	—	—	—	—	—	—	—	—	—	Papua New Guinea
—	—	—	—	—	—	—	—	—	—	—	—	—	—	—	Philippines
—	—	—	—	—	—	—	—	—	—	—	—	—	—	—	Samoa
—	—	—	—	—	—	—	—	—	—	—	—	—	—	—	Solomon Islands
—	44.6	66.9	44.6	56.0	112.0	56.0	56.0	—	—	—	—	—	—	—	Sri Lanka
—	—	—	—	—	—	—	—	—	—	—	—	—	—	—	Thailand
—	—	—	—	—	—	—	60.4	60.4	120.8	—	—	—	—	82.8	Vietnam
—	—	—	—	—	8.5	25.0	37.4	105.4	178.4	146.2	107.7	72.2		87.4	**Europe**
—	—	—	—	—	8.5	15.5	7.1	—	—	5.9	15.5	14.3	9.4		Albania
—	—	—	—	—	—	—	—	33.8	16.9	37.8	20.9	—	10.0		Armenia
—	—	—	—	—	—	—	—	—	55.6	14.6	11.7	—	8.1		Azerbaijan
—	—	—	—	—	—	—	—	55.5	55.5	27.8	33.3	—	27.0		Georgia
—	—	—	—	—	—	9.5	30.3	16.1	32.3	10.8	19.6	14.3	11.7		Kyrgyz Republic
—	—	—	—	—	—	—	—	18.2	9.1	—	1.7				Macedonia, FYR
—	—	—	—	—	—	—	—	—	—	—	9.2	9.2			Moldova
—	—	—	—	—	—	—	—	40.3	6.7	32.6	12.0				Tajikistan
—	—	—	—	—	—	—	—	—	—	44.0	44.0	62.0	—	88.8	**Middle East**
—	—	—	—	—	—	—	—	—	—	—	—	—	—	—	Egypt
—	—	—	—	—	—	—	—	—	—	—	—	—	—	—	Yemen Arab Rep.
—	—	—	—	—	—	—	—	—	—	—	—	—	—	—	Yemen, P.D. Rep.
—	—	—	—	—	—	—	—	—	—	44.0	44.0	62.0	—	88.8	Yemen, Republic of
1.2	23.2	45.6	59.9	40.4	60.8	15.6	59.4	46.1	66.8	34.8	59.4	180.1	54.5	39.0	**Western Hemisphere**
—	22.7	45.4	22.7	22.7	36.3	—	30.4	16.8	33.7	16.8	33.6	16.8	11.2	19.0	Bolivia
1.2	.5	.3	—	—	—	—	—	—	—	—	—	—	—	—	Dominica
—	—	—	—	—	—	—	—	—	—	—	—	—	—	—	El Salvador
—	—	—	—	—	—	—	—	—	—	—	—	—	—	—	Grenada
—	—	—	37.2	17.7	17.7	8.9	9.0	9.0	17.9	17.9	9.0	9.0	7.0	—	Guyana
—	—	—	—	—	—	—	—	15.2	—	—	—	—	—	—	Haiti
—	—	—	—	—	6.8	6.8	—	20.3	—	—	—	76.0	16.2	20.0	Honduras
—	—	—	—	—	—	—	20.0	—	—	—	16.8	78.3	20.2	—	Nicaragua
															Memorandum Items
403.4	410.2	961.1	507.0	781.9	544.3	271.7	910.4	1,431.4	708.6	730.6	896.0	736.8	505.8	872.6	Non-Oil Develop.Ctys

Repayments of Loans

Expressed in Millions of SDRs

	1972	1973	1974	1975	1976	1977	1978	1979	1980	1981	1982	1983	1984	1985	1986
World	—	—	—	—	—	—	—	—	—	—	3.2	45.2	173.1	299.6	539.0
Developing Countries	—	—	—	—	—	—	—	—	—	—	3.2	45.2	173.1	299.6	539.0
Africa	—	—	—	—	—	—	—	—	—	—	2.0	16.6	70.7	121.6	175.5
Benin	—	—	—	—	—	—	—	—	—	—	—	.2	1.1	1.1	2.5
Burkina Faso	—	—	—	—	—	—	—	—	—	—	—	.2	1.1	2.1	2.5
Burundi	—	—	—	—	—	—	—	—	—	—	.1	.5	1.6	3.1	3.7
Cameroon	—	—	—	—	—	—	—	—	—	—	—	.6	2.9	5.8	6.8
Central African Rep.	—	—	—	—	—	—	—	—	—	—	—	.2	1.1	1.8	2.5
Chad	—	—	—	—	—	—	—	—	—	—	—	.2	1.1	1.1	1.1
Comoros	—	—	—	—	—	—	—	—	—	—	—	—	—	—	—
Congo, Dem. Rep. of	—	—	—	—	—	—	—	—	—	—	.6	3.2	9.4	18.6	22.0
Congo, Republic of	—	—	—	—	—	—	—	—	—	—	.1	.4	1.2	2.1	2.5
Côte d'Ivoire	—	—	—	—	—	—	—	—	—	—	—	—	4.3	7.0	10.1
Equatorial Guinea	—	—	—	—	—	—	—	—	—	—	—	—	—	—	.9
Ethiopia	—	—	—	—	—	—	—	—	—	—	—	—	2.2	4.4	5.3
Gambia, The	—	—	—	—	—	—	—	—	—	—	—	.2	.6	.5	2.0
Ghana	—	—	—	—	—	—	—	—	—	—	—	—	1.1	7.1	9.7
Guinea	—	—	—	—	—	—	—	—	—	—	—	.7	2.0	3.9	4.7
Guinea-Bissau	—	—	—	—	—	—	—	—	—	—	—	—	—	—	—
Kenya	—	—	—	—	—	—	—	—	—	—	.3	1.3	4.6	8.2	9.0
Lesotho	—	—	—	—	—	—	—	—	—	—	—	.1	.4	.8	1.0
Liberia	—	—	—	—	—	—	—	—	—	—	.2	.8	2.4	—	—
Madagascar	—	—	—	—	—	—	—	—	—	—	—	.5	2.2	2.2	5.1
Malawi	—	—	—	—	—	—	—	—	—	—	—	.4	1.2	2.5	2.9
Mali	—	—	—	—	—	—	—	—	—	—	—	.4	1.8	3.6	4.3
Mauritania	—	—	—	—	—	—	—	—	—	—	—	.4	1.2	2.1	2.5
Mauritius	—	—	—	—	—	—	—	—	—	—	—	.4	1.8	1.8	1.8
Morocco	—	—	—	—	—	—	—	—	—	—	.6	3.2	10.8	18.6	22.0
Mozambique	—	—	—	—	—	—	—	—	—	—	—	—	—	—	—
Niger	—	—	—	—	—	—	—	—	—	—	—	—	1.1	1.1	2.5
Rwanda	—	—	—	—	—	—	—	—	—	—	—	—	—	1.5	2.1
São Tomé & Príncipe	—	—	—	—	—	—	—	—	—	—	—	—	—	—	—
Senegal	—	—	—	—	—	—	—	—	—	—	—	.6	2.8	5.6	6.6
Sierra Leone	—	—	—	—	—	—	—	—	—	—	—	.7	2.1	1.0	8.0
Somalia	—	—	—	—	—	—	—	—	—	—	—	—	—	—	2.1
Sudan	—	—	—	—	—	—	—	—	—	—	—	—	3.0	—	—
Swaziland	—	—	—	—	—	—	—	—	—	—	—	—	—	.7	.9
Tanzania	—	—	—	—	—	—	—	—	—	—	.2	1.2	3.5	2.7	12.3
Togo	—	—	—	—	—	—	—	—	—	—	—	.3	1.2	2.5	2.9
Uganda	—	—	—	—	—	—	—	—	—	—	—	—	—	2.0	4.5
Zambia	—	—	—	—	—	—	—	—	—	—	—	—	1.0	6.2	8.5
Zimbabwe	—	—	—	—	—	—	—	—	—	—	—	—	—	—	—
Asia	—	—	—	—	—	—	—	—	—	—	.9	22.0	76.9	131.9	302.7
Afghanistan, I.S. of	—	—	—	—	—	—	—	—	—	—	—	—	—	—	—
Bangladesh	—	—	—	—	—	—	—	—	—	—	—	3.5	10.4	20.5	24.3
Cambodia	—	—	—	—	—	—	—	—	—	—	—	—	—	—	—
China, People's Rep.	—	—	—	—	—	—	—	—	—	—	—	—	—	—	31.0
India	—	—	—	—	—	—	—	—	—	—	—	—	—	—	105.1
Lao People's Dem.Rep	—	—	—	—	—	—	—	—	—	—	—	—	1.1	2.1	2.5
Mongolia	—	—	—	—	—	—	—	—	—	—	—	—	—	—	—
Myanmar	—	—	—	—	—	—	—	—	—	—	—	1.7	5.8	9.9	11.7
Nepal	—	—	—	—	—	—	—	—	—	—	.1	.4	1.4	2.3	2.7
Pakistan	—	—	—	—	—	—	—	—	—	—	—	6.6	19.5	31.5	45.8
Papua New Guinea	—	—	—	—	—	—	—	—	—	—	—	—	1.7	1.7	3.9
Philippines	—	—	—	—	—	—	—	—	—	—	.8	4.3	14.8	25.5	30.2
Samoa	—	—	—	—	—	—	—	—	—	—	—	.1	.2	.3	.4
Solomon Islands	—	—	—	—	—	—	—	—	—	—	—	—	—	—	—
Sri Lanka	—	—	—	—	—	—	—	—	—	—	—	1.7	9.4	16.1	19.1
Thailand	—	—	—	—	—	—	—	—	—	—	—	3.8	12.8	22.0	26.1
Vietnam	—	—	—	—	—	—	—	—	—	—	—	—	—	—	—
Europe	—	—	—	—	—	—	—	—	—	—	—	—	—	—	—
Albania	—	—	—	—	—	—	—	—	—	—	—	—	—	—	—
Kyrgyz Republic	—	—	—	—	—	—	—	—	—	—	—	—	—	—	—
Tajikistan	—	—	—	—	—	—	—	—	—	—	—	—	—	—	—
Middle East	—	—	—	—	—	—	—	—	—	—	.2	6.1	20.4	35.7	42.2
Egypt	—	—	—	—	—	—	—	—	—	—	—	5.3	18.0	30.9	36.6
Yemen Arab Rep.	—	—	—	—	—	—	—	—	—	—	—	—	—	—	—
Yemen, P.D. Rep.	—	—	—	—	—	—	—	—	—	—	.2	.8	2.4	4.8	5.6
Yemen, Republic of	—	—	—	—	—	—	—	—	—	—	—	—	—	—	—
Western Hemisphere	—	—	—	—	—	—	—	—	—	—	.1	.6	5.1	10.5	18.6
Bolivia	—	—	—	—	—	—	—	—	—	—	—	—	3.1	5.0	7.2
Dominica	—	—	—	—	—	—	—	—	—	—	—	—	—	—	—
El Salvador	—	—	—	—	—	—	—	—	—	—	—	—	—	—	3.9
Grenada	—	—	—	—	—	—	—	—	—	—	—	.1	.2	.3	.4
Guyana	—	—	—	—	—	—	—	—	—	—	—	—	—	—	.6
Haiti	—	—	—	—	—	—	—	—	—	—	.1	.5	1.8	3.1	3.7
Honduras	—	—	—	—	—	—	—	—	—	—	—	—	—	2.0	2.8
Nicaragua	—	—	—	—	—	—	—	—	—	—	—	—	—	—	—
Memorandum Items															
Non-Oil Develop.Ctys	—	—	—	—	—	—	—	—	—	—	3.2	45.2	173.1	299.6	539.0

1987	1988	1989	1990	1991	1992	1993	1994	1995	1996	1997	1998	1999	2000	2001	
						Expressed in Millions of SDRs									
550.2	502.5	400.3	270.0	50.7	23.6	133.4	223.4	373.8	484.5	606.0	620.9	595.2	588.6	792.7	**World**
550.2	502.5	400.3	270.0	50.7	23.6	133.4	223.4	373.8	484.5	606.0	620.9	595.2	588.6	792.7	**Developing Countries**
156.8	137.3	104.5	38.9	3.5	14.0	51.5	145.2	230.6	300.0	338.4	350.0	324.5	303.5	504.5	**Africa**
2.5	2.3	1.5	1.5	.1	—	—	.6	1.3	1.3	3.1	3.9	6.5	9.5	11.4	Benin
2.5	2.3	1.5	.4	.1	—	—	—	—	.6	1.3	2.1	3.9	7.5	10.1	Burkina Faso
3.6	3.2	2.1	.6	.1	1.7	3.0	4.3	6.0	6.0	6.0	6.8	5.6	3.8	3.8	Burundi
6.8	6.2	3.9	1.1	.1	—	—	—	—	—	—	—	—	—	—	Cameroon
2.5	2.3	1.5	.8	.1	—	.7	2.9	4.9	4.3	2.7	3.9	1.2	.6	—	Central African Rep.
1.1	.9	—	—	—	—	1.2	1.2	4.6	4.3	4.3	3.1	2.1	.6	2.5	Chad
										.2	.2	.3	.5	.5	Comoros
21.4	18.8	12.6	3.4	.4	—	—	—	—	2.4	—	.2	—	—	—	Congo, Dem. Rep. of
2.5	2.2	1.5	.4	.1	—	—	—	—	—	—	—	—	—	—	Congo, Republic of
10.1	10.1	5.8	3.2	.2	—	—	—	—	—	—	—	6.0	29.8	52.4	Côte d'Ivoire
.9	.9	.9	.9	—	—	—	.4	.7	.8	2.2	2.1	1.8	2.0	2.0	Equatorial Guinea
5.3	5.3	3.0	.8	.1	—	—	—	—	—	—	2.8	7.1	9.9	9.9	Ethiopia
1.4	1.2	.8	.2	—	.7	1.7	2.7	4.1	5.1	5.1	4.1	3.1	1.7	.7	Gambia, The
9.7	9.7	8.6	2.6	.3	—	8.2	30.5	57.8	69.4	85.9	77.7	55.4	28.1	51.4	Ghana
4.7	4.0	2.7	.7	.1	—	2.3	4.1	5.8	5.8	7.5	6.9	5.2	6.1	9.3	Guinea
						.3	.3	.8	.8	.8	.5	.5	.2	.5	Guinea-Bissau
9.1	8.0	4.8	1.5	.2	—	2.8	9.7	25.8	41.9	48.9	46.1	43.7	32.2	18.6	Kenya
1.0	.8	.6	.2	—	—	—	1.1	1.8	2.3	3.1	3.6	4.3	3.9	3.4	Lesotho
						.7					.4	.4	.3	.2	Liberia
5.1	4.6	2.9	2.9	.1	—	2.7	3.9	9.1	11.6	12.9	10.3	9.0	3.8	1.3	Madagascar
2.9	2.5	1.7	.5	.1	—	—	2.8	6.5	10.2	12.3	12.3	10.0	6.9	5.5	Malawi
4.3	3.9	2.5	.7	.1	—	—	2.0	3.6	5.1	5.1	8.1	8.6	13.0	16.9	Mali
2.5	2.2	1.3	.4	.1	1.4	3.4	4.2	5.9	6.8	5.4	5.1	6.8	8.3	10.3	Mauritania
1.8	1.4	—	—	—	—	—	—	—	—	—	—	—	—	—	Mauritius
21.4	18.8	11.2	3.4	.4	—	—	—	—	—	—	—	—	—	—	Morocco
					1.2	4.3	7.3	9.5	22.5	11.0	18.1	22.8	22.2	21.0	Mozambique
2.5	2.5	1.5	1.5	.1	1.3	3.4	5.1	6.7	8.1	6.7	4.7	3.0	1.3	1.0	Niger
2.1	2.1	2.1	.6	.1	—	—	—	.9	1.8	1.8	1.8	1.8	.9	Rwanda
					—	—	.1	.2	.2	.2	.2	.1		—	São Tomé & Príncipe
6.6	6.0	3.8	1.0	.1	3.4	8.5	17.4	26.8	30.6	34.0	28.9	20.0	17.1	21.1	Senegal
1.3	—	.3	1.8	.1	2.3	—	13.8	2.3	2.3	—	—	9.1	19.1	21.7	Sierra Leone
2.0	—	.1	—	—	—	—	—	—	—	—	—	—	—	—	Somalia
					—	—	—	3.0	—	5.2	—	—	—	—	Sudan
.9	.9	.9	.2	—	—	—	—	—	—	—	—	—	—	—	Swaziland
8.0	7.0	4.7	1.3	.2	—	4.3	10.7	12.8	15.0	22.5	27.8	21.4	2.1	17.1	Tanzania
2.9	2.7	1.7	.5	.1	—	.8	2.3	5.4	7.7	8.4	8.4	6.9	7.1	8.1	Togo
4.5	4.5	4.5	2.4	.2	2.0	4.0	17.1	18.8	34.1	41.8	45.8	37.6	37.1	32.4	Uganda
2.8	—	13.8	3.6	.3	—	—	—	6.6	—	—	—	—	—	166.7	Zambia
					—	—	—	—	—	—	14.0	20.4	27.0	4.1	Zimbabwe
332.8	311.7	263.8	205.2	44.7	5.8	77.8	62.0	123.6	152.1	230.4	224.9	222.7	226.5	223.4	**Asia**
														—	Afghanistan, I.S. of
24.3	20.8	14.0	3.8	.5	5.8	28.8	38.4	40.3	58.9	86.3	77.6	70.9	69.0	50.3	Bangladesh
					—	—	—	—	—	—	—	1.4	4.2	8.4	Cambodia
61.9	61.9	61.9	61.9	31.0	—	—	—	—	—	—	—	—	—	—	China, People's Rep.
105.1	105.1	105.1	105.1	3.6	—	—	—	—	—	—	—	—	—	—	India
2.5	2.5	1.5	.4	.1	—	—	—	1.2	2.1	3.5	4.7	5.9	5.9	7.3	Lao People's Dem.Rep
					—	—	—	—	—	—	.9	2.8	4.8	5.4	Mongolia
11.7	10.0	5.9	1.8	.2	—	—	—	—	—	—	—	—	—	—	Myanmar
2.7	2.3	1.4	.4	.1	—	1.5	3.7	5.2	5.2	5.2	4.8	4.3	3.4	3.4	Nepal
45.8	39.2	26.3	14.3	.9	—	—	10.9	54.6	54.6	87.4	76.5	64.7	62.3	62.4	Pakistan
3.9	3.9	2.2	2.2	.1	—	—	—	—	—	—	—	—	—	—	Papua New Guinea
29.4	25.8	15.3	4.7	.6	—	—	—	—	—	—	—	—	—	—	Philippines
.4	.3	.2	.1	—	—	—	—	—	—	—	—	—	—	—	Samoa
					—	—	—	—	—	—	—	—	—	—	Solomon Islands
19.1	17.4	9.7	3.0	.4	—	4.5	8.9	22.3	31.2	48.0	60.4	72.7	64.9	56.0	Sri Lanka
26.1	22.3	13.3	4.1	.5	—	—	—	—	—	—	—	—	—	—	Thailand
—	—	7.0	3.5	7.0	—	43.1	—	—	—	—	—	—	12.1	30.2	Vietnam
—	**—**	**—**	**—**	**—**	**—**	**—**	**—**	**—**	**—**	**—**	**—**	**2.5**	**8.8**	**18.6**	**Europe**
												2.5	5.5	6.2	Albania
													3.3	8.0	Kyrgyz Republic
													—	—	Tajikistan
42.1	**36.2**	**21.9**	**6.6**	**.8**	**—**	**—**	**—**	**—**	**—**	**—**	**—**	**—**	**—**	**—**	**Middle East**
36.6	31.3	18.6	5.7	.7	—	—	—	—	—	—	—	—	—	—	Egypt
														—	Yemen Arab Rep.
5.5	4.8	3.2	.7	—	—	—	—	—	—	—	—	—	—	—	Yemen, P.D. Rep.
			.1	.1	—	—	—	—	—	—	—	—	—	—	Yemen, Republic of
18.6	17.4	10.2	19.2	1.6	3.8	4.0	16.3	19.6	32.4	37.2	46.0	45.5	49.8	46.2	**Western Hemisphere**
7.2	7.2	4.1	2.3	.1	3.6	3.6	10.4	17.2	21.8	24.9	29.9	24.5	22.4	22.9	Bolivia
					.2	.4	.5	.6	.6	.4	.2	—	—	—	Dominica
3.9	3.9	3.9	3.9	.1	—	—	—	—	—	—	—	—	—	—	El Salvador
.4	.3	.3	.1	—	—	—	—	—	—	—	—	—	—	—	Grenada
.7			8.9	1.1	—	—	—	—	8.3	11.9	14.5	16.3	19.0	12.5	Guyana
3.6	3.2	1.9	.6	.1	—	—	5.3	1.8	1.8	—	—	—	—	—	Haiti
2.8	2.8	—	3.6	.1	—	—	—	—	—	—	1.4	2.7	4.4	6.8	Honduras
					—	—	—	—	—	—	—	2.0	4.0	4.0	Nicaragua
															Memorandum Items
550.2	502.5	400.3	270.0	50.7	23.6	133.4	223.4	373.8	484.5	606.0	620.9	595.2	588.6	792.7	**Non-Oil Develop.Ctys**

Total Fund Credit & Loans Outstdg.*

	1972	1973	1974	1975	1976	1977	1978	1979	1980	1981	1982	1983	1984	1985	198
					Expressed in Millions of SDRs										
World	1,089.2	1,027.4	3,740.1	7,435.0	12,607.7	13,230.6	11,118.4	9,343.6	11,109.3	16,358.7	22,297.8	32,841.9	37,675.3	37,650.1	35,348.
Industrial Countries	—	—	1,514.5	3,488.1	6,115.9	6,877.6	4,495.4	1,978.6	1,216.1	545.8	138.2	376.3	593.4	593.4	582.
United States	—	—	—	—	—	—	—	—	—	—	—	—	—	—	—
Canada	—	—	—	—	—	—	—	—	—	—	—	—	—	—	—
Australia	—	—	—	—	332.5	332.5	246.9	270.6	61.7	—	32.5	—	—	—	—
Japan	—	—	—	—	—	—	—	—	—	—	—	—	—	—	—
New Zealand	—	—	85.7	242.2	390.2	388.1	361.2	270.0	132.3	33.7	2.9	—	—	—	—
Belgium	—	—	—	—	—	—	—	—	—	—	—	—	—	—	—
Denmark	—	—	—	—	—	—	—	—	—	—	—	—	—	—	—
Finland	—	—	—	71.3	186.4	186.4	152.1	66.4	66.4	52.1	14.4	—	—	—	—
France	—	—	—	—	—	—	—	—	—	—	—	—	—	—	—
Germany	—	—	—	—	—	—	—	—	—	—	—	—	—	—	—
Greece	—	—	36.2	189.8	247.8	176.5	185.2	147.3	78.5	13.9	—	—	—	—	—
Iceland	—	—	15.5	31.4	56.4	56.4	47.3	34.7	15.7	5.9	22.4	21.5	21.5	21.5	10.
Ireland	—	—	—	—	—	—	—	—	—	—	—	—	—	—	—
Italy	—	—	1,377.1	2,457.3	2,457.3	1,580.9	880.0	—	—	—	—	—	—	—	—
Luxembourg	—	—	—	—	—	—	—	—	—	—	—	—	—	—	—
Netherlands	—	—	—	—	—	—	—	—	—	—	—	—	—	—	—
Norway	—	—	—	—	—	—	—	—	—	—	—	—	—	—	—
Portugal	—	—	—	—	173.3	244.9	202.8	171.7	93.7	47.5	9.8	354.8	571.9	571.9	571.
Spain	—	—	—	496.2	572.1	572.1	615.3	205.4	205.4	141.6	4.8	—	—	—	—
United Kingdom	—	—	—	—	1,700.0	3,339.9	1,804.7	812.5	562.5	312.5	51.6	—	—	—	—
Developing Countries	1,089.2	1,027.4	2,225.6	3,947.0	6,491.8	6,353.0	6,623.0	7,365.0	9,893.2	15,751.8	22,159.6	32,465.6	37,081.9	37,056.7	34,765.
Africa	119.5	133.7	291.9	553.5	1,247.9	1,410.8	1,818.3	2,149.8	2,728.3	4,274.1	6,146.3	7,407.5	7,973.9	8,028.9	7,185.
Algeria	—	—	—	—	—	—	—	—	—	—	—	—	—	—	—
Angola	—	—	—	—	—	—	—	—	—	—	—	—	—	—	—
Benin	—	—	—	—	—	—	5.4	5.4	12.7	12.7	12.7	12.5	11.4	10.3	7.8
Burkina Faso	—	—	—	—	—	—	5.4	9.3	12.7	12.7	12.7	12.5	11.4	9.3	6.7
Burundi	—	—	—	1.2	1.2	3.3	7.9	23.1	28.0	28.1	28.0	22.7	16.4	13.2	18.1
Cameroon	—	—	4.6	12.1	33.9	33.9	47.3	49.9	46.0	37.7	34.7	33.6	30.7	25.0	18.1
Cape Verde	—	—	—	—	—	—	—	—	—	—	—	—	—	—	—
Central African Rep.	—	—	2.7	4.9	9.6	9.6	15.7	13.6	18.4	32.4	34.2	38.2	35.8	35.5	34.1
Chad	2.2	1.0	3.1	3.0	9.5	9.5	13.5	13.0	10.8	12.5	12.5	12.3	8.5	10.9	8.9
Comoros	—	—	—	—	—	—	—	—	—	—	—	—	—	—	—
Congo, Dem. Rep. of	28.2	28.2	28.2	73.3	180.6	220.3	247.1	271.6	292.8	407.5	492.9	593.9	688.5	735.1	699.7
Congo, Republic of	—	—	—	—	—	9.3	16.7	21.6	17.4	12.7	12.6	12.3	11.1	9.0	16.0
Côte d'Ivoire	—	—	11.2	11.2	23.4	13.4	21.6	21.6	50.6	370.0	485.4	640.3	649.7	605.5	538.7
Djibouti	—	—	—	—	—	—	—	—	—	—	—	—	—	—	—
Equatorial Guinea	—	—	—	—	—	—	—	—	12.6	19.2	19.2	19.2	13.2	11.7	9.0
Ethiopia	—	—	—	—	—	—	11.2	55.8	62.3	124.4	145.6	127.6	100.2	64.8	68.8
Gabon	—	—	—	—	—	—	7.6	15.2	11.4	11.3	9.4	1.9	—	—	27.4
Gambia, The	—	—	—	—	—	4.3	11.7	10.4	12.7	21.7	36.4	33.5	33.7	30.4	24.1
Ghana	1.7	—	—	38.6	38.6	38.6	34.4	82.5	82.5	73.2	68.4	316.6	525.1	638.0	642.3
Guinea	3.0	1.0	9.5	7.1	7.1	18.4	20.0	26.2	27.5	23.7	35.0	34.3	32.3	28.4	32.9
Guinea-Bissau	—	—	—	—	—	—	—	1.1	1.1	3.0	2.7	2.3	3.7	2.8	1.9
Kenya	—	—	32.1	68.6	85.0	52.8	72.2	142.7	199.1	222.2	356.7	443.5	428.3	474.7	375.9
Lesotho	—	—	—	—	—	.5	2.1	3.6	4.9	4.9	4.9	4.8	4.3	3.5	2.5
Liberia	—	.1	—	—	—	3.1	12.0	51.0	69.8	115.3	176.8	223.8	237.3	230.4	230.4
Madagascar	—	—	3.5	14.3	14.3	15.7	24.2	20.7	68.2	100.2	152.0	158.1	173.8	167.6	166.0
Malawi	—	—	—	2.4	3.7	10.8	11.8	37.7	62.5	89.9	88.2	111.8	127.9	132.5	109.0
Mali	8.3	7.3	10.4	10.6	12.7	11.2	19.2	22.1	30.3	28.2	52.5	65.3	84.3	89.2	80.8
Mauritania	—	—	—	—	11.8	17.9	22.0	25.1	39.1	42.5	56.4	51.7	41.4	36.5	42.7
Mauritius	—	—	—	—	—	—	11.0	20.3	48.4	79.9	136.9	159.4	172.8	164.2	150.1	132.1
Morocco	—	—	—	—	115.5	127.6	220.0	231.9	358.4	497.4	897.5	985.5	1,107.2	1,160.6	894.4
Mozambique	—	—	—	—	—	—	—	—	—	—	—	—	—	—	—
Namibia	—	—	—	—	—	—	—	—	—	—	—	—	—	—	—
Niger	—	—	—	—	—	—	5.4	5.4	12.7	12.7	12.7	43.5	56.8	71.3	86.8
Nigeria	—	—	—	—	—	—	—	—	—	—	—	—	—	—	—
Rwanda	—	—	—	—	—	—	—	5.8	10.6	10.7	10.7	10.7	10.7	9.2	7.0
São Tomé & Príncipe	—	—	—	—	—	—	—	—	—	—	—	—	—	—	—
Senegal	—	—	—	25.4	25.4	25.4	57.0	70.5	109.9	160.2	200.0	220.5	234.7	243.7	236.3
Seychelles	—	—	—	—	—	—	—	—	—	—	—	—	—	—	—
Sierra Leone	—	—	4.3	4.9	22.4	32.1	35.6	43.8	46.6	72.2	70.9	88.9	97.5	92.0	82.9
Somalia	—	—	—	—	—	—	—	.1	.1	14.0	40.0	72.2	117.2	114.3	140.1	127.3
South Africa	—	—	—	—	315.0	392.0	314.4	76.8	—	—	795.0	745.0	745.0	745.0	397.5
Sudan	28.1	29.0	71.7	113.4	119.1	99.5	150.6	222.4	338.0	484.8	524.6	666.7	677.6	672.7	672.7
Swaziland	—	—	—	—	—	—	—	2.4	4.5	4.5	4.5	14.5	14.5	12.9	8.6
Tanzania	—	—	38.9	62.6	83.6	91.2	81.5	115.5	134.3	125.7	114.4	88.1	60.2	52.6	58.2
Togo	—	—	—	—	7.5	7.5	6.2	10.8	25.5	32.8	32.8	51.9	63.5	67.6	73.8
Tunisia	—	—	—	—	—	24.0	24.0	24.0	—	—	—	—	—	—	149.7
Uganda	10.0	10.0	15.0	24.1	32.7	32.7	29.2	26.2	70.1	182.5	265.9	360.6	343.8	277.6	203.4
Zambia	38.0	57.0	57.0	75.9	95.2	95.2	245.1	343.0	350.8	670.6	618.3	678.5	753.8	728.9	701.6
Zimbabwe	—	—	—	—	—	—	—	—	—	—	37.5	37.5	191.1	261.3	240.5	191.1
Asia	477.4	396.5	1,202.7	1,817.7	2,112.5	1,909.9	2,088.3	2,258.2	3,827.4	6,909.5	9,009.7	11,329.0	11,628.3	10,669.8	9,933.7
Afghanistan, I.S. of	5.7	7.2	4.7	9.2	1.8	—	—	—	—	—	—	—	—	—	—
Bangladesh	62.5	62.5	133.3	171.6	235.8	207.8	229.4	262.3	332.6	398.9	496.2	540.0	471.6	473.3	440.5
Bhutan	—	—	—	—	—	—	—	—	—	—	—	—	—	—	—
Cambodia	6.3	12.5	12.5	12.5	12.5	12.5	12.5	12.5	12.5	12.5	12.5	12.5	12.5	12.5	12.5
China, People's Rep.	—	—	—	—	—	—	—	—	—	759.5	759.5	309.5	309.5	309.5	876.3
Fiji	—	—	.3	—	—	6.5	6.5	6.5	—	—	13.5	13.5	13.2	6.4
India	—	—	497.0	698.3	406.3	125.1	—	—	791.5	1,095.0	2,595.0	4,061.8	4,528.8	4,354.0	3,917.7
Indonesia	107.1	19.2	—	—	—	—	—	—	—	—	425.1	421.5	42.0	42.0
Kiribati	—	—	—	—	—	—	—	—	—	—	—	—	—	—	—
Korea	—	—	110.0	217.3	301.7	280.4	201.8	104.4	535.4	1,070.6	1,141.7	1,292.8	1,598.9	1,373.0	1,266.3
Lao People's Dem.Rep	—	—	—	3.3	6.5	6.5	15.9	18.3	21.2	25.6	25.6	25.6	19.9	11.4	7.0
Malaysia	7.3	—	—	—	93.0	.4	—	—	—	189.8	248.3	315.1	262.9	107.2	—
Maldives	—	—	—	—	—	—	—	—	—	—	—	—	—	—	—

Total Fund Credit & Loans Outstdg.*

Expressed in Millions of SDRs

1987	1988	1989	1990	1991	1992	1993	1994	1995	1996	1997	1998	1999	2000	2001	
30,618.3	26,524.0	24,649.9	23,303.7	26,681.8	27,791.1	29,159.1	30,260.9	41,636.1	42,058.6	52,614.7	66,781.7	57,534.1	49,378.1	59,944.7	World
373.1	—	—	—	—	—	—	—	—	—	—	—	—	—	—	Industrial Countries
—	—	—	—	—	—	—	—	—	—	—	—	—	—	—	United States
—	—	—	—	—	—	—	—	—	—	—	—	—	—	—	Canada
—	—	—	—	—	—	—	—	—	—	—	—	—	—	—	Australia
—	—	—	—	—	—	—	—	—	—	—	—	—	—	—	Japan
—	—	—	—	—	—	—	—	—	—	—	—	—	—	—	New Zealand
—	—	—	—	—	—	—	—	—	—	—	—	—	—	—	Belgium
—	—	—	—	—	—	—	—	—	—	—	—	—	—	—	Denmark
—	—	—	—	—	—	—	—	—	—	—	—	—	—	—	Finland
—	—	—	—	—	—	—	—	—	—	—	—	—	—	—	France
—	—	—	—	—	—	—	—	—	—	—	—	—	—	—	Germany
—	—	—	—	—	—	—	—	—	—	—	—	—	—	—	Greece
—	—	—	—	—	—	—	—	—	—	—	—	—	—	—	Iceland
—	—	—	—	—	—	—	—	—	—	—	—	—	—	—	Ireland
—	—	—	—	—	—	—	—	—	—	—	—	—	—	—	Italy
—	—	—	—	—	—	—	—	—	—	—	—	—	—	—	Luxembourg
—	—	—	—	—	—	—	—	—	—	—	—	—	—	—	Netherlands
—	—	—	—	—	—	—	—	—	—	—	—	—	—	—	Norway
373.1	—	—	—	—	—	—	—	—	—	—	—	—	—	—	Portugal
—	—	—	—	—	—	—	—	—	—	—	—	—	—	—	Spain
—	—	—	—	—	—	—	—	—	—	—	—	—	—	—	United Kingdom
30,245.2	26,524.0	24,649.9	23,303.7	26,681.8	27,791.1	29,159.1	30,260.9	41,636.1	42,058.6	52,614.7	66,781.7	57,534.1	49,378.1	59,944.7	Developing Countries
6,326.4	6,118.6	6,177.9	5,762.7	5,896.2	5,727.2	5,871.5	6,531.6	7,065.3	7,457.3	7,107.3	6,775.7	6,645.5	6,542.4	6,259.9	Africa
—	—	470.9	470.9	695.9	578.2	342.7	793.8	994.1	1,412.5	1,495.5	1,428.0	1,388.7	1,318.5	1,208.0	Algeria
—	—	—	—	—	—	—	—	—	—	—	—	—	—	—	Angola
5.3	3.0	7.8	6.3	15.7	15.7	31.3	48.8	56.6	68.9	70.3	66.4	67.1	64.4	61.1	Benin
4.2	1.9	.4	.1	6.3	6.3	15.2	32.8	50.5	56.5	68.5	79.6	87.9	86.1	92.7	Burkina Faso
14.5	24.1	30.5	30.0	34.2	47.4	44.4	40.1	34.2	28.2	22.2	15.4	9.8	6.0	2.1	Burundi
11.3	74.6	86.2	85.1	84.3	45.7	11.9	29.9	34.4	50.1	68.9	110.9	142.7	180.5	194.0	Cameroon
—	—	—	—	—	—	—	—	—	—	—	—	—	—	—	Cape Verde
36.6	37.3	26.9	25.7	23.3	22.1	21.0	28.3	23.5	19.2	13.8	12.5	17.1	16.5	24.5	Central African Rep.
14.0	12.2	17.9	21.4	21.4	21.4	20.2	29.3	33.0	45.2	45.3	45.3	50.2	60.0	70.9	Chad
—	—	—	—	.9	.9	.9	2.3	2.3	2.3	2.1	1.9	1.6	1.1	.7	Comoros
681.3	584.1	478.2	366.3	330.3	330.3	330.3	327.3	326.4	301.3	301.3	300.7	300.0	300.0	300.0	Congo, Dem. Rep. of
13.6	11.4	8.8	7.6	4.0	4.0	3.5	14.0	12.5	26.4	24.8	24.3	21.1	31.7	30.8	Congo, Republic of
425.8	377.9	281.3	303.1	259.7	194.5	159.1	224.8	287.1	349.6	333.5	457.3	451.4	421.6	369.2	Côte d'Ivoire
—	—	—	—	—	—	—	—	—	2.9	4.0	6.3	9.3	10.3	12.3	Djibouti
8.1	10.6	6.7	4.1	9.2	9.2	12.0	13.4	12.7	11.9	9.8	7.6	5.8	3.8	1.7	Equatorial Guinea
53.4	40.8	23.0	4.5	—	14.1	35.3	49.4	49.4	64.2	64.2	76.1	69.0	59.1	84.0	Ethiopia
42.5	98.7	102.7	98.5	84.3	58.6	32.9	61.4	65.0	83.3	97.2	80.5	62.6	68.4	59.6	Gabon
26.7	25.7	28.7	31.6	30.6	28.4	26.7	23.9	19.8	14.7	9.6	8.9	9.3	14.4	20.6	Gambia, The
610.9	566.4	561.2	523.4	583.1	537.8	537.3	479.7	436.2	377.3	257.0	236.9	225.8	224.5	225.7	Ghana
40.1	36.1	46.7	36.2	38.4	46.3	44.0	48.6	63.1	57.3	73.4	90.0	92.7	86.6	98.1	Guinea
3.1	2.2	3.8	3.8	3.8	3.8	3.5	3.2	4.0	5.3	9.0	11.0	12.6	19.0	18.4	Guinea-Bissau
282.9	338.4	316.1	338.9	344.8	286.1	264.3	277.3	251.5	234.5	185.6	139.5	95.8	97.2	78.6	Kenya
1.6	3.8	7.7	10.6	12.8	18.1	24.9	27.6	25.8	23.5	20.4	16.8	12.5	8.5	12.1	Lesotho
230.4	229.4	227.2	226.5	226.5	226.5	226.5	225.8	225.7	225.7	225.7	225.3	224.8	224.4	223.9	Liberia
167.7	141.4	125.8	101.0	88.7	77.1	67.0	58.6	48.9	50.8	51.5	41.2	45.8	80.0	101.4	Madagascar
82.4	78.6	76.5	80.8	80.5	66.9	62.6	76.9	78.0	83.1	78.4	72.6	63.8	63.4	57.9	Malawi
60.0	54.9	41.9	48.7	42.0	47.5	51.4	74.1	99.0	114.6	130.2	132.4	140.9	134.7	136.0	Mali
54.1	52.5	52.3	49.2	39.5	42.0	46.1	58.8	67.1	74.6	83.4	78.3	77.6	75.4	83.2	Mauritania
106.9	76.5	47.6	15.5	—	—	—	—	—	—	—	—	—	—	—	Mauritius
789.1	711.1	646.6	526.9	401.5	319.1	207.2	101.1	34.8	2.3	—	—	—	—	—	Morocco
12.2	30.5	42.7	51.9	82.4	126.9	137.9	145.2	135.8	125.9	140.1	147.2	145.4	168.5	155.9	Mozambique
—	—	—	—	—	—	—	—	—	—	—	—	—	—	—	Namibia
86.3	70.3	64.4	59.7	51.3	44.6	37.7	41.8	35.0	36.6	45.0	54.1	49.6	56.8	64.3	Niger
—	—	—	—	—	—	—	—	—	—	—	—	—	—	—	Nigeria
4.9	2.8	.7	.1	8.8	8.8	8.8	8.8	17.7	16.8	29.9	40.1	55.3	65.9	66.6	Rwanda
—	—	.8	.8	.8	.8	.8	.7	.6	.4	.2	.1	—	—	—	São Tomé & Príncipe
241.6	236.5	240.4	221.0	228.9	197.4	177.8	205.4	233.3	226.5	216.5	207.8	198.2	195.4	204.7	Senegal
—	—	—	—	—	—	—	—	—	—	—	—	—	—	—	Seychelles
81.5	80.8	79.5	76.2	70.7	67.0	61.0	100.2	110.9	118.8	123.9	135.4	142.0	133.2	120.8	Sierra Leone
123.7	123.0	114.1	112.0	112.0	112.0	112.0	112.0	112.0	112.0	112.0	112.0	112.0	112.0	112.0	Somalia
—	—	—	—	—	—	614.4	614.4	614.4	614.4	307.2	—	—	—	—	South Africa
672.7	672.7	672.7	671.6	671.6	671.6	671.6	671.6	645.7	621.2	590.5	548.4	520.8	479.7	438.6	Sudan
4.3	1.2	.3	—	—	—	—	—	—	—	—	—	—	—	—	Swaziland
80.0	105.1	97.8	98.4	100.2	160.5	156.2	145.5	132.7	143.4	182.4	190.2	227.6	265.5	277.9	Tanzania
60.1	57.9	57.4	61.1	55.3	55.8	49.9	56.0	70.4	62.5	64.9	67.4	60.4	53.3	45.3	Togo
190.7	205.7	205.7	123.7	180.1	211.1	207.3	207.3	197.1	165.0	128.4	91.8	55.2	24.7	—	Tunisia
192.8	187.6	171.2	198.2	230.9	250.1	243.0	262.6	280.6	290.1	291.7	282.7	270.8	242.6	219.1	Uganda
698.8	698.8	685.0	666.7	641.6	615.6	565.8	551.2	833.4	833.4	843.4	843.4	853.4	873.4	781.6	Zambia
110.3	52.2	22.2	4.8	—	157.2	205.0	257.5	310.0	304.1	285.5	289.2	268.8	215.4	205.4	Zimbabwe
8,058.4	6,267.1	5,378.8	3,609.0	5,030.8	5,952.4	6,365.7	5,816.8	4,846.9	3,673.4	15,538.9	24,173.2	17,908.7	18,588.5	12,400.2	Asia
—	—	—	—	—	—	—	—	—	—	—	—	—	—	—	Afghanistan, I.S. of
592.7	623.9	546.8	439.7	523.2	547.7	511.8	473.4	433.1	374.2	287.9	308.4	237.6	168.6	118.3	Bangladesh
—	—	—	—	—	—	—	—	—	—	—	—	—	—	—	Bhutan
12.5	12.5	12.5	12.5	12.5	6.3	6.3	20.3	48.3	48.3	48.3	47.2	53.1	56.2	63.5	Cambodia
814.4	752.5	690.6	329.8	—	—	—	—	—	—	—	—	—	—	—	China, People's Rep.
4.8	3.0	.6	—	—	—	—	—	—	—	—	—	—	—	—	Fiji
3,175.1	2,282.5	1,439.9	803.6	2,426.4	3,260.4	3,584.9	2,763.2	1,966.6	1,085.3	589.8	284.9	38.5	—	—	India
504.9	462.9	462.9	347.2	115.7	—	—	—	—	—	2,201.5	6,455.8	7,466.8	8,318.0	7,251.7	Indonesia
—	—	—	—	—	—	—	—	—	—	—	—	—	—	—	Kiribati
369.8	—	—	—	—	—	—	—	—	—	8,200.0	12,000.0	4,462.5	4,462.5	—	Korea
4.4	1.9	6.3	5.9	14.7	20.5	26.4	32.2	42.8	46.6	49.0	44.3	38.4	32.5	29.7	Lao People's Dem.Rep
—	—	—	—	—	—	—	—	—	—	—	—	—	—	—	Malaysia
—	—	—	—	—	—	—	—	—	—	—	—	—	—	—	Maldives

Total Fund Credit & Loans Outstdg.*

	1972	1973	1974	1975	1976	1977	1978	1979	1980	1981	1982	1983	1984	1985	198
Asia (cont.)						*Expressed in Millions of SDRs*									
Mongolia	—	—	—	—	—	—	—	—	—	—	—	—	—	—	
Myanmar	8.0	15.0	36.5	40.5	34.5	58.1	85.3	97.0	87.7	107.6	130.3	141.5	129.7	106.4	68
Nepal	—	—	—	—	4.5	6.0	15.3	18.6	32.6	32.5	27.7	22.4	15.8	19.8	19.
Pakistan	110.7	129.8	238.9	374.4	439.6	462.8	492.5	434.8	528.5	879.7	1,286.2	1,540.3	1,469.2	1,288.5	973.
Palau															
Papua New Guinea	—	—	—	—	24.8	24.8	23.1	18.1	24.3	64.6	64.6	64.6	34.6	26.3	12.
Philippines	95.3	76.3	67.8	164.7	348.4	435.0	505.5	618.0	819.7	974.5	905.9	1,045.6	903.2	1,048.8	1,034.
Samoa	—	—	—	1.3	1.9	1.8	3.5	4.8	4.5	6.4	5.7	7.6	10.0	10.0	8.
Solomon Islands	—	—	—	—	—	—	—	—	—	.8	2.4	3.4	3.2	2.8	2.
Sri Lanka	74.6	74.1	101.7	124.7	134.3	169.9	226.5	304.8	306.5	442.6	437.2	425.2	413.0	361.1	283.
Thailand	—	—	—	—	67.0	81.3	191.3	278.1	273.1	737.1	767.2	993.8	921.6	1,021.1	874.
Tonga	—	—	—	—	—	—	—	—	—	—	—	—	—	—	
Vietnam	—	—	—	—	—	31.0	79.2	80.1	57.4	111.8	90.3	89.0	89.0	89.0	89.
Europe	**83.5**	**69.3**	**192.9**	**458.4**	**936.4**	**862.9**	**948.7**	**1,111.1**	**1,710.7**	**2,739.4**	**3,917.9**	**4,929.4**	**5,371.8**	**4,792.8**	**4,004.**
Albania	—	—	—	—	—	—	—	—	—	—	—	—	—	—	
Armenia	—	—	—	—	—	—	—	—	—	—	—	—	—	—	
Azerbaijan	—	—	—	—	—	—	—	—	—	—	—	—	—	—	
Belarus	—	—	—	—	—	—	—	—	—	—	—	—	—	—	
Bosnia & Herzegovina	—	—	—	—	—	—	—	—	—	—	—	—	—	—	
Bulgaria	—	—	—	—	—	—	—	—	—	—	—	—	—	—	
Croatia	—	—	—	—	—	—	—	—	—	—	—	—	—	—	
Cyprus	—	—	6.4	8.1	43.1	43.1	32.9	38.0	30.6	21.6	12.3	5.5	3.2	—	
Czech Republic	—	—	—	—	—	—	—	—	—	—	—	—	—	—	
Czechoslovakia	—	—	—	—	—	—	—	—	—	—	—	—	—	—	
Estonia	—	—	—	—	—	—	—	—	—	—	—	—	—	—	
Georgia	—	—	—	—	—	—	—	—	—	—	—	—	—	—	
Hungary	—	—	—	—	—	—	—	—	—	—	—	214.5	547.0	972.0	883.7	842.
Kazakhstan	—	—	—	—	—	—	—	—	—	—	—	—	—	—	
Kyrgyz Republic	—	—	—	—	—	—	—	—	—	—	—	—	—	—	
Latvia	—	—	—	—	—	—	—	—	—	—	—	—	—	—	
Lithuania	—	—	—	—	—	—	—	—	—	—	—	—	—	—	
Macedonia, FYR	—	—	—	—	—	—	—	—	—	—	—	—	—	—	
Moldova	—	—	—	—	—	—	—	—	—	—	—	—	—	—	
Poland	—	—	—	—	—	—	—	—	—	—	—	—	—	—	
Romania	—	47.5	47.5	87.5	237.5	270.0	255.6	246.8	257.4	506.7	781.6	904.7	955.7	782.9	583.
Russia	—	—	—	—	—	—	—	—	—	—	—	—	—	—	
Slovak Republic	—	—	—	—	—	—	—	—	—	—	—	—	—	—	
Slovenia	—	—	—	—	—	—	—	—	—	—	—	—	—	—	
Tajikistan	—	—	—	—	—	—	—	—	—	—	—	—	—	—	
Turkey	—	—	—	207.6	336.8	336.8	477.7	480.3	826.6	1,135.6	1,319.2	1,497.1	1,455.0	1,207.5	887.
Ukraine	—	—	—	—	—	—	—	—	—	—	—	—	—	—	
Uzbekistan	—	—	—	—	—	—	—	—	—	—	—	—	—	—	
Yugoslavia, SFR	83.5	21.8	139.0	155.2	319.0	213.0	182.5	346.0	596.1	1,075.5	1,590.3	1,975.2	1,985.9	1,918.7	1,691.
Yugoslavia, Fed. Rep	—	—	—	—	—	—	—	—	—	—	—	—	—	—	
Middle East	**51.5**	**81.6**	**140.1**	**300.1**	**500.0**	**600.2**	**689.4**	**645.3**	**516.5**	**388.5**	**307.4**	**280.3**	**259.9**	**267.9**	**201.**
Bahrain, Kingdom of	—	—	—	—	—	—	—	—	—	—	—	—	—	—	
Egypt	24.4	62.2	93.0	68.2	177.9	275.0	374.2	381.4	322.1	268.2	235.7	227.8	209.8	167.1	118.
Iran, I.R. of	—	—	—	—	—	—	—	—	—	—	—	—	—	—	
Iraq	—	—	—	—	—	—	—	—	—	—	—	—	—	—	
Israel	—	—	32.5	208.3	285.3	285.2	271.3	224.2	156.4	87.5	27.2	—	—	—	
Jordan	4.5	1.6	—	—	—	—	—	—	—	—	—	—	—	—	
Syrian Arab Republic	22.6	17.9	5.4	—	—	—	—	.8	—	—	—	—	—	—	
Yemen Arab Rep.	—	—	—	—	—	—	—	—	—	—	—	9.8	9.8	9.8	6.
Yemen, P.D. Rep.	—	—	9.3	23.7	36.8	39.9	43.9	39.0	38.0	32.1	44.5	42.8	40.4	33.7	20.3
Yemen, Republic of	—	—	—	—	—	—	—	—	—	—	—	—	—	—	
Western Hemisphere	**357.3**	**346.3**	**397.9**	**817.2**	**1,695.1**	**1,569.3**	**1,078.3**	**1,200.6**	**1,110.2**	**1,440.2**	**2,778.4**	**8,519.4**	**11,848.0**	**13,297.3**	**13,440.**
Antigua and Barbuda	—	—	—	—	—	—	—	—	—	—	—	—	—	—	
Argentina	174.0	174.0	64.0	250.1	455.6	344.5	—	—	—	—	—	1,120.6	1,120.6	2,105.1	2,240.9
Barbados	—	—	—	—	—	6.5	6.5	6.5	2.3	.8	22.2	35.8	43.6	43.6	32.4
Belize	—	—	—	—	—	—	—	—	—	—	—	3.6	4.8	9.5	9.5
Bolivia	7.9	18.1	14.3	13.9	—	—	30.3	30.3	99.0	97.3	114.3	98.0	74.9	157.3	
Brazil	—	—	—	—	—	—	—	—	—	—	498.8	2,525.7	4,269.9	4,205.4	3,679.9
Chile	79.0	79.0	160.0	330.8	402.2	300.6	266.5	135.9	96.3	41.8	5.7	579.0	795.0	990.6	1,088.3
Colombia	—	—	18.8	30.0	32.3	29.3	24.3	43.8	44.6	88.2	84.2	183.3	159.0	171.6	141.0
Costa Rica	—	—	—	—	—	—	—	1.9	1.7	6.5	9.3	11.0	10.7	9.2	8.
Dominica	—	—	—	—	21.5	36.5	36.5	94.3	38.0	19.8	64.1	235.2	225.7	270.4	248.8
Dominican Republic	3.8	—	—	—											
Ecuador	8.3	—	—	—	—	—	—	—	25.0	57.3	—	203.5	242.9	327.3	397.7
El Salvador	8.8	—	17.9	17.9	12.8	1.4	2.0	2.4	2.2	7.1	117.1	132.6	127.2	100.6	50.9
Grenada	—	—	—	.8	1.2	—	—	—	—	—	6.3	7.3	6.3	3.8	2.1
Guatemala	—	—	—	—	—	—	—	—	—	—	95.6	95.6	133.9	153.0	105.2	57.2
Guyana	—	3.9	5.0	—	17.3	17.3	30.3	40.5	67.4	85.3	89.1	85.0	84.0	83.0	82.5
Haiti	—	—	6.6	11.0	12.4	10.5	15.5	19.3	35.7	50.6	61.4	90.1	102.3	87.4	72.8
Honduras	—	—	16.8	16.8	16.8	4.3	—	7.6	25.7	46.5	108.2	154.1	152.5	133.7	89.5
Jamaica	—	13.3	13.3	13.3	68.9	88.1	138.6	266.8	242.5	403.5	528.4	599.1	641.4	631.1	554.4
Mexico	—	—	—	—	—	319.0	419.1	229.4	103.1	—	200.6	1,203.8	2,407.5	2,703.3	3,319.3
Nicaragua	8.3	12.2	10.1	15.5	8.7	2.0	2.0	43.5	38.7	21.2	17.5	13.3	9.0	—	
Panama	—	—	7.4	17.5	42.6	42.2	40.3	31.5	18.1	80.5	76.1	184.1	276.6	283.4	288.6
Paraguay	—	—	—	—	—	—	—	—	—	—	—	—	—	—	
Peru	30.8	13.6	—	—	158.8	168.8	256.1	373.1	371.6	332.9	588.8	666.3	688.3	639.0	595.5
St. Kitts and Nevis	—	—	—	—	—	—	—	—	—	—	—	—	—	—	
St. Lucia	—	—	—	—	—	—	—	—	1.4	4.1	2.6	2.6	2.0	.3	
St. Vincent & Grens.	—	—	—	—	—	—	—	—	.2	1.5	1.5	1.5	1.0	.3	
Suriname	—	—	—	—	—	—	—	—	—	—	—	—	—	—	
Trinidad and Tobago	—	—	—	—	—	—	—	—	—	—	—	—	—	—	
Uruguay	36.7	32.3	63.8	99.7	124.9	98.2	—	—	—	—	—	86.8	226.8	226.8	318.6	323.1
Venezuela, Rep. Bol.	—	—	—	—	—	—	—	—	—	—	—	—	—	—	
Memorandum Items															
Oil Exporting Ctys	107.1	19.2	—	—	—	—	—	—	—	—	—	425.1	421.5	42.0	42.0
Non-Oil Develop.Ctys	982.0	1,008.2	2,225.6	3,947.0	6,491.8	6,353.0	6,623.0	7,365.0	9,893.2	15,751.8	22,159.6	32,040.5	36,660.5	37,014.7	34,723.5

Total Fund Credit & Loans Outstdg.*

1987	1988	1989	1990	1991	1992	1993	1994	1995	1996	1997	1998	1999	2000	2001	
						Expressed in Millions of SDRs									**Asia (cont.)**
—	—	—	—	11.3	13.8	23.0	37.9	31.6	30.3	35.2	34.3	37.5	38.6	37.3	Mongolia
28.9	8.0	2.0	.2	—	—	—	—	—	—	—	—	—	—	—	Myanmar
30.3	39.2	39.9	30.9	26.9	31.7	35.8	37.7	32.5	27.2	22.0	17.2	12.9	9.5	6.2	Nepal
647.2	411.4	709.7	587.3	746.4	819.9	816.5	1,096.8	1,115.0	1,000.5	979.5	996.0	1,271.2	1,197.7	1,455.7	Pakistan
—	—	—	—	—	—	—	—	—	—	—	—	—	—	—	Palau
8.4	4.6	2.3	42.9	42.8	42.8	32.1	10.7	33.3	35.3	35.3	32.4	15.7	29.9	85.5	Papua New Guinea
888.1	812.6	895.3	640.9	759.0	800.1	880.7	728.6	489.5	281.9	633.8	1,114.0	1,327.7	1,559.2	1,553.1	Philippines
5.8	2.9	1.2	.6	.2	—	—	—	—	—	—	—	—	—	—	Samoa
1.6	1.3	1.1	.5	—	—	—	—	—	—	—	—	—	—	—	Solomon Islands
195.1	267.1	278.3	288.1	280.2	337.8	375.7	422.8	400.5	369.2	321.2	260.8	188.1	123.2	170.6	Sri Lanka
685.6	492.1	207.5	.5	—	—	—	—	—	—	1,800.0	2,300.0	2,500.0	2,350.0	1,337.5	Thailand
—	—	—	—	—	—	—	—	—	—	—	—	—	—	—	Tonga
89.0	89.0	82.0	78.5	71.5	71.5	72.5	193.4	253.8	374.6	335.3	277.9	258.7	242.6	291.2	Vietnam
2,775.9	**1,773.9**	**905.5**	**917.1**	**3,464.6**	**4,695.1**	**6,159.5**	**8,036.4**	**11,400.3**	**13,945.3**	**15,708.5**	**19,644.9**	**17,385.4**	**16,860.6**	**21,622.0**	**Europe**
—	—	—	—	—	9.7	21.6	37.1	43.4	37.7	40.7	45.8	58.7	67.5	66.3	Albania
—	—	—	—	—	—	—	16.9	47.3	81.0	97.9	135.3	146.6	134.7	137.4	Armenia
—	—	—	—	—	—	—	—	67.9	121.7	197.7	228.1	296.7	257.7	234.9	Azerbaijan
—	—	—	—	—	—	70.1	70.1	190.2	190.2	190.2	172.3	129.7	87.6	64.3	Belarus
—	—	—	—	—	—	—	—	32.5	31.0	30.3	54.5	68.4	80.4	88.4	Bosnia & Herzegovina
—	—	—	—	289.2	428.9	459.9	644.4	482.1	407.2	698.0	792.3	910.7	1,014.6	883.0	Bulgaria
—	—	—	—	—	—	14.8	87.1	148.6	145.4	172.7	166.1	143.2	121.4	97.2	Croatia
—	—	—	—	—	—	—	—	—	—	—	—	—	—	—	Cyprus
—	—	—	—	—	—	780.7	—	—	—	—	—	—	—	—	Czech Republic
—	—	—	—	917.9	1,121.5	—	—	—	—	—	—	—	—	—	Czechoslovakia
—	—	—	—	—	7.8	41.9	41.9	61.8	54.2	40.0	21.3	18.4	14.5	10.7	Estonia
—	—	—	—	—	—	—	27.8	77.7	133.2	188.7	215.8	233.3	213.7	228.7	Georgia
569.9	471.3	347.1	231.7	880.2	875.8	896.3	781.6	258.7	118.7	118.7	—	—	—	—	Hungary
—	—	—	—	—	—	—	61.9	198.0	290.8	383.6	379.0	463.7	335.1	—	Kazakhstan
—	—	—	—	—	—	43.9	53.3	83.6	97.1	122.2	124.4	138.7	144.3	142.7	Kyrgyz Republic
—	—	—	—	—	25.2	77.8	109.8	107.9	90.4	63.7	45.4	34.3	26.7	19.1	Latvia
—	—	—	—	—	17.3	88.0	134.6	176.0	190.1	200.5	179.8	167.8	147.1	120.3	Lithuania
—	—	—	—	—	—	2.8	14.0	38.1	47.4	65.3	72.7	74.1	62.3	56.3	Macedonia, FYR
—	—	—	—	—	—	63.0	112.5	154.9	172.3	172.7	125.6	127.7	118.3	116.3	Moldova
—	—	—	357.5	596.6	596.6	497.7	918.6	—	—	—	—	—	—	—	Poland
357.6	106.9	—	—	565.8	750.9	750.9	906.4	698.3	453.0	475.2	382.8	333.8	347.7	308.0	Romania
—	—	—	—	—	719.0	1,797.3	2,875.6	6,469.8	8,698.2	9,805.9	13,732.0	11,102.3	8,912.8	5,914.8	Russia
—	—	—	—	—	—	405.2	439.8	307.5	222.0	184.4	134.6	96.5	—	—	Slovak Republic
—	—	—	—	—	—	8.5	4.9	2.7	.9	—	—	—	—	—	Slovenia
—	—	—	—	—	—	—	—	—	15.0	22.5	70.3	73.2	98.4	101.0	Tajikistan
543.0	222.0	36.3	—	—	—	—	235.5	460.5	460.5	440.4	275.8	648.8	3,205.3	11,232.9	Turkey
—	—	—	—	—	—	—	249.3	1,037.3	1,573.3	1,780.6	1,985.0	2,044.6	1,591.2	1,520.7	Ukraine
—	—	—	—	—	—	—	—	106.0	165.2	165.2	165.2	146.8	97.5	62.3	Uzbekistan
1,305.5	973.7	522.2	327.9	214.8	142.5	77.4	77.4	56.8	56.1	56.1	56.1	56.6	—	—	Yugoslavia, SFR
—	—	—	—	—	—	—	—	—	—	—	—	—	116.9	216.9	Yugoslavia, Fed. Rep
252.6	**181.2**	**196.8**	**154.1**	**155.2**	**407.0**	**385.0**	**409.7**	**350.3**	**353.3**	**502.0**	**571.8**	**660.5**	**597.8**	**641.8**	**Middle East**
—	—	—	—	—	—	—	—	—	—	—	—	—	—	—	Bahrain, Kingdom of
184.9	141.0	122.4	87.7	89.0	147.2	147.2	132.2	69.5	10.9	—	—	—	—	—	Egypt
—	—	—	—	—	—	—	—	—	—	—	—	—	—	—	Iran, I.R. of
—	—	—	—	—	—	—	—	—	—	—	—	—	—	—	Iraq
—	—	—	—	—	178.6	178.6	178.6	111.7	22.3	—	—	—	—	—	Israel
57.4	35.9	73.4	66.2	66.2	81.2	59.2	98.9	169.2	236.1	316.6	333.4	362.9	354.3	344.5	Jordan
—	—	—	—	—	—	—	—	—	—	—	—	—	—	—	Syrian Arab Republic
1.2	—	—	—	—	—	—	—	—	—	—	—	....	....	....	Yemen Arab Rep.
9.1	4.2	1.0	—	—	—	—	—	—	—	—	—	—	—	....	Yemen, P.D. Rep.
—	—	—	.1	—	—	—	—	—	84.0	185.4	238.4	297.6	243.5	297.3	Yemen, Republic of
12,832.0	**12,183.3**	**11,990.9**	**12,860.8**	**12,134.9**	**11,009.4**	**10,377.5**	**9,466.4**	**17,973.3**	**16,629.2**	**13,758.1**	**15,616.2**	**14,934.0**	**6,788.8**	**19,020.8**	**Western Hemisphere**
—	—	—	—	—	—	—	—	—	—	—	—	—	—	—	Antigua and Barbuda
2,716.2	2,733.0	2,358.8	2,167.2	1,735.9	1,682.8	2,562.4	2,884.7	4,124.4	4,376.0	4,349.3	3,865.1	3,262.6	3,880.3	11,121.1	Argentina
15.6	7.8	3.3	.5	—	36.8	36.8	36.8	24.9	6.5	—	—	—	—	—	Barbados
8.0	5.8	2.5	.3	—	—	—	—	—	—	—	—	—	—	—	Belize
130.9	155.3	191.6	180.7	171.1	181.1	160.5	180.5	180.1	192.0	183.9	187.6	180.0	168.8	164.8	Bolivia
2,802.9	2,476.8	1,843.4	1,279.7	865.1	581.4	221.0	127.5	95.2	47.0	23.3	3,426.8	6,431.0	1,356.8	6,633.9	Brazil
1,032.4	982.6	966.5	812.9	669.4	525.0	346.5	199.5	—	—	—	—	—	—	—	Chile
—	—	—	—	—	—	—	—	—	—	—	—	—	—	—	Colombia
93.3	53.0	26.9	7.9	58.0	59.3	59.3	45.5	16.3	.5	—	—	—	—	—	Costa Rica
8.2	6.6	5.0	4.0	3.3	2.8	2.3	1.7	1.1	.6	.2	—	—	—	—	Dominica
199.9	161.8	93.2	50.4	62.4	89.4	135.5	129.9	107.5	66.5	21.1	39.7	—	39.7	39.7	Dominican Republic
345.2	300.7	247.2	186.0	127.5	72.6	51.8	135.7	116.7	100.9	98.9	49.5	—	113.3	151.1	Ecuador
15.8	8.0	4.1	.1	—	—	—	—	—	—	—	—	—	—	—	El Salvador
1.5	.9	.4	—	—	—	—	—	—	—	—	—	—	—	—	Grenada
41.7	65.4	55.5	46.8	44.8	22.4	—	—	—	—	—	—	—	—	—	Guatemala
81.7	81.7	80.9	79.4	104.5	122.2	128.6	122.3	115.6	117.1	116.4	109.5	102.2	90.1	77.7	Guyana
51.1	33.8	30.6	25.5	23.8	23.8	23.8	3.8	18.2	31.6	31.6	40.8	32.6	30.4	30.4	Haiti
54.4	27.3	27.0	22.7	23.6	81.4	86.0	74.8	66.4	40.3	33.9	80.0	153.3	165.1	178.3	Honduras
478.2	358.8	291.8	250.7	273.6	259.7	244.2	217.6	161.7	112.2	87.1	74.7	60.8	46.3	31.9	Jamaica
3,639.3	3,570.3	3,873.6	4,604.9	4,729.9	4,327.0	3,485.2	2,644.2	10,648.1	9,234.5	6,735.2	5,951.5	3,259.2	—	—	Mexico
—	—	—	—	17.0	17.0	17.0	34.9	26.4	20.0	20.0	36.8	113.2	129.3	125.3	Nicaragua
243.9	243.8	243.2	191.3	150.7	79.8	82.3	91.3	74.4	91.0	105.4	125.5	108.3	69.1	42.9	Panama
—	—	—	—	—	—	—	—	—	—	—	—	—	—	—	Paraguay
595.4	595.4	577.0	530.5	493.4	458.7	642.7	642.7	642.7	642.7	749.6	642.5	535.4	428.3	307.8	Peru
—	—	—	—	—	—	—	—	—	—	—	1.6	1.6	1.6	1.6	St. Kitts and Nevis
—	—	—	—	—	—	—	—	—	—	—	—	—	—	—	St. Lucia
—	—	—	—	—	—	—	—	—	—	—	—	—	—	—	St. Vincent & Grens.
—	—	—	—	—	—	—	—	—	—	—	—	—	—	—	Suriname
—	85.1	155.8	231.6	269.1	205.3	112.8	62.4	33.8	16.5	3.1	—	—	—	—	Trinidad and Tobago
276.6	229.7	153.4	70.8	40.4	38.1	27.9	20.5	14.0	6.0	—	114.2	114.2	114.2	114.2	Uruguay
—	—	759.5	2,117.0	2,271.3	2,142.8	1,950.7	1,810.2	1,506.0	1,527.4	1,198.9	870.4	540.0	155.6	—	Venezuela, Rep. Bol.
															Memorandum Items
504.9	462.9	1,693.3	2,935.1	3,083.0	2,720.9	2,293.5	2,603.9	2,500.0	2,940.0	4,895.9	8,754.2	9,395.6	9,792.1	8,459.7	Oil Exporting Ctys
29,740.3	26,061.1	22,956.7	20,368.7	23,598.8	25,070.2	26,865.6	27,657.0	39,136.1	39,118.6	47,718.8	58,027.5	48,138.5	39,586.0	51,485.0	Non-Oil Develop.Ctys

(See notes in the back of the book.)

Use of Fund Credit (GRA)

	1972	1973	1974	1975	1976	1977	1978	1979	1980	1981	1982	1983	1984	1985	198
					Expressed in Millions of SDRs										
World	1,089.2	1,027.4	3,740.1	7,435.0	12,607.7	13,077.6	10,277.3	7,976.0	8,485.7	13,367.6	19,309.6	29,898.9	34,905.5	35,179.8	33,334.
Industrial Countries	—	—	1,514.5	3,488.1	6,115.9	6,877.6	4,495.4	1,978.6	1,216.1	607.2	138.2	376.3	593.4	593.4	582.
United States	—	—	—	—	—	—	—	—	—	—	—	—	—	—	—
Canada	—	—	—	—	—	—	—	—	—	—	—	—	—	—	—
Australia	—	—	—	—	332.5	332.5	246.9	270.6	61.7	—	32.5	—	—	—	—
Japan	—	—	—	—	—	—	—	—	—	—	—	—	—	—	—
New Zealand	—	—	85.7	242.2	390.2	388.1	361.2	270.0	132.3	33.7	2.9	—	—	—	—
Belgium	—	—	—	—	—	—	—	—	—	—	—	—	—	—	—
Denmark	—	—	—	—	—	—	—	—	—	—	—	—	—	—	—
Finland	—	—	—	71.3	186.4	186.4	152.1	66.4	66.4	52.1	14.4	—	—	—	—
France	—	—	—	—	—	—	—	—	—	—	—	—	—	—	—
Greece	—	—	36.2	189.8	247.8	176.5	185.2	147.3	78.5	13.9	—	—	—	—	—
Iceland	—	—	15.5	31.4	56.4	56.4	47.3	34.7	15.7	5.9	22.4	21.5	21.5	21.5	10.
Ireland	—	—	—	—	—	—	—	—	—	—	—	—	—	—	—
Italy	—	—	1,377.1	2,457.3	2,457.3	1,580.9	880.0	—	—	—	—	—	—	—	—
Netherlands	—	—	—	—	—	—	—	—	—	—	—	—	—	—	—
Norway	—	—	—	—	—	—	—	—	—	—	—	—	—	—	—
Portugal	—	—	—	—	173.3	244.9	202.8	171.7	93.7	47.5	9.8	354.8	571.9	571.9	571.
Spain	—	—	—	496.2	572.1	572.1	615.3	205.4	205.4	141.6	4.8	—	—	—	—
United Kingdom	—	—	—	—	1,700.0	3,339.9	1,804.7	812.5	562.5	312.5	51.6	—	—	—	—
Developing Countries	1,089.2	1,027.4	2,225.6	3,947.0	6,491.8	6,200.0	5,782.0	5,997.4	7,269.6	12,760.5	19,171.4	29,522.7	34,312.1	34,586.4	32,752.
Africa	119.5	133.7	291.9	553.5	1,247.9	1,360.9	1,471.7	1,538.5	1,790.4	3,332.2	5,206.4	6,484.2	7,121.4	7,298.0	6,575.
Algeria	—	—	—	—	—	—	—	—	—	—	—	—	—	—	—
Burkina Faso	—	—	—	—	—	—	—	—	—	—	—	—	—	—	—
Burundi	—	—	—	1.2	1.2	1.2	—	9.5	9.5	9.5	9.5	4.8	—	—	—
Cameroon	—	—	4.6	12.1	33.9	33.9	32.8	24.8	12.0	3.5	.5	—	—	—	—
Central African Rep.	—	—	2.7	4.9	9.6	9.6	10.3	8.2	5.8	19.7	21.5	25.7	24.4	25.9	27.
Chad	2.2	1.0	3.1	3.0	9.5	9.5	8.2	7.6	5.4	7.1	7.1	7.1	4.4	7.9	7.
Comoros	—	—	—	—	—	—	—	—	—	—	—	—	—	—	—
Congo, Dem. Rep. of	28.2	28.2	28.2	73.3	180.6	208.2	200.3	190.5	182.8	297.0	383.1	487.2	591.2	656.4	642.
Congo, Republic of	—	—	—	—	—	8.0	11.3	12.3	4.8	—	—	—	—	—	9.
Côte d'Ivoire	—	—	11.2	11.2	23.4	13.4	—	—	—	319.2	434.6	589.5	603.2	566.0	509.
Djibouti	—	—	—	—	—	—	—	—	—	—	—	—	—	—	—
Equatorial Guinea	—	—	—	—	—	—	—	—	8.2	14.7	14.7	14.7	8.7	7.2	5.
Ethiopia	—	—	—	—	—	—	—	36.4	36.0	98.0	119.3	101.3	76.1	45.1	54.
Gabon	—	—	—	—	—	—	7.6	15.2	11.4	11.3	9.4	1.9	—	—	27.
Gambia, The	—	—	—	—	—	3.5	8.8	5.3	5.9	14.9	29.5	26.9	27.6	24.8	17.
Ghana	1.7	—	—	38.6	38.6	38.6	34.4	56.1	33.9	24.2	19.4	267.6	477.2	597.2	611.
Guinea	3.0	1.0	9.5	7.1	7.1	15.8	10.0	8.9	4.1	.2	11.5	11.5	11.5	11.5	20.
Guinea-Bissau	—	—	—	—	—	—	—	1.1	1.1	3.0	2.7	2.3	3.7	2.8	1.
Kenya	—	—	32.1	68.6	85.0	47.7	52.3	108.3	152.3	175.3	310.1	398.2	387.6	442.2	352.
Lesotho	—	—	—	—	—	—	—	—	—	—	—	—	—	—	—
Liberia	—	.1	—	—	—	—	—	30.2	41.6	86.9	148.6	196.4	212.3	205.4	205.
Madagascar	—	—	3.5	14.3	14.3	15.7	13.4	9.9	42.9	74.8	126.5	133.1	151.0	147.0	150.
Malawi	—	—	—	2.4	3.7	9.2	5.5	26.9	47.9	75.3	73.6	97.5	114.9	121.9	101.
Mali	8.3	7.3	10.4	10.6	12.7	11.2	10.1	6.3	8.9	6.7	31.0	44.2	65.0	73.5	69.
Mauritania	—	—	—	—	11.8	16.5	16.6	15.8	26.4	29.8	43.7	39.3	30.3	27.6	29.
Mauritius	—	—	—	—	—	11.0	11.2	39.3	70.7	127.7	150.2	164.1	157.3	145.0	128.
Morocco	—	—	—	—	115.5	115.5	173.2	150.8	248.4	386.9	787.7	878.8	1,011.3	1,083.3	839.
Niger	—	—	—	—	—	—	—	—	—	—	—	30.8	45.2	60.7	72.
Nigeria	—	—	—	—	—	—	—	—	—	—	—	—	—	—	—
Rwanda	—	—	—	—	—	—	—	—	—	—	—	—	—	—	—
Senegal	—	—	—	25.4	25.4	25.4	42.9	46.1	76.8	127.0	166.8	187.8	204.9	219.5	201.
Sierra Leone	—	—	4.3	4.9	22.4	29.4	25.2	25.8	22.2	47.7	46.4	65.1	75.8	71.4	58.
Somalia	—	—	—	—	—	—	—	.1	.1	3.4	29.3	61.5	106.5	103.7	118.
South Africa	—	—	—	—	315.0	392.0	314.4	76.8	—	—	795.0	745.0	745.0	745.0	397.
Sudan	28.1	29.0	71.7	113.4	119.1	99.5	120.8	170.8	267.9	414.4	454.3	596.3	610.2	605.3	605.
Swaziland	—	—	—	—	—	—	—	—	—	—	—	10.0	10.0	9.0	5.
Tanzania	—	—	38.9	62.6	83.6	86.7	64.1	85.4	93.4	84.7	73.6	48.5	24.0	19.2	37.
Togo	—	—	—	—	—	7.5	7.5	—	10.9	18.1	18.1	37.5	50.3	56.9	66.
Tunisia	—	—	—	—	—	24.0	24.0	24.0	—	—	—	—	—	—	149.
Uganda	10.0	10.0	15.0	24.1	32.7	32.7	29.2	26.2	47.8	159.9	243.4	338.0	321.3	257.1	187.
Zambia	38.0	57.0	57.0	75.9	95.2	95.2	245.1	320.0	308.3	627.8	575.6	635.7	712.0	693.3	674.
Zimbabwe	—	—	—	—	—	—	—	—	—	—	37.5	37.5	191.1	261.3	191.
Asia	477.4	396.5	1,202.7	1,817.7	2,112.5	1,832.3	1,707.8	1,695.6	2,443.0	5,173.9	7,274.9	9,616.3	9,992.4	9,165.8	8,732.
Afghanistan, I.S. of	5.7	7.2	4.7	9.2	1.8	—	—	—	—	—	—	—	—	—	—
Bangladesh	62.5	62.5	133.3	171.6	235.8	194.4	177.6	172.6	210.9	276.8	374.1	421.3	363.3	385.5	377.
Bhutan	—	—	—	—	—	—	—	—	—	—	—	—	—	—	—
Cambodia	6.3	12.5	12.5	12.5	12.5	12.5	12.5	12.5	12.5	12.5	12.5	12.5	12.5	12.5	12.
China, People's Rep.	—	—	—	—	—	—	—	—	—	450.0	450.0	—	—	—	597.
Fiji	—	—	.3	—	—	6.5	6.5	6.5	—	—	—	13.5	13.5	13.2	6.
India	—	—	497.0	698.3	406.3	125.1	—	—	266.0	566.0	2,066.0	3,532.8	3,999.8	3,825.0	3,493.
Indonesia	107.1	19.2	—	—	—	—	—	—	—	—	425.1	421.5	42.0	42.
Korea	—	—	110.0	217.3	301.7	280.4	201.8	104.4	535.4	1,070.6	1,141.7	1,292.8	1,598.9	1,373.0	1,266.
Lao People's Dem.Rep	—	—	—	3.3	6.5	6.5	10.5	9.0	8.6	12.9	12.9	12.9	8.3	1.9	—
Malaysia	7.3	—	—	—	93.0	.4	—	—	—	189.8	248.3	315.1	262.9	107.2	—
Mongolia	—	—	—	—	—	—	—	—	—	—	—	—	—	—	—
Myanmar	8.0	15.0	36.5	40.5	34.5	51.7	60.4	54.0	29.3	48.9	71.6	84.6	78.5	65.0	38.
Nepal	—	—	—	—	—	4.5	4.5	9.5	8.5	19.0	18.8	14.1	9.2	3.9	12.
Pakistan	110.7	129.8	238.9	374.4	439.6	437.6	395.1	337.4	299.7	650.0	1,056.5	1,317.2	1,265.6	1,116.4	846.
Palau	—	—	—	—	—	—	—	—	—	—	—	—	—	—	—
Papua New Guinea	—	—	—	—	24.8	24.8	14.8	9.8	4.8	45.0	45.0	45.0	16.7	10.1	—
Philippines	95.3	76.3	67.8	164.7	348.4	418.4	441.3	506.8	668.8	823.0	755.3	899.2	771.8	942.7	958.
Samoa	—	—	—	1.3	1.9	1.6	2.7	3.3	2.6	4.5	3.8	5.7	8.3	8.6	7.
Solomon Islands	—	—	—	—	—	—	—	—	—	.8	2.4	3.4	3.2	2.8	2.
Sri Lanka	74.6	74.1	101.7	124.7	134.3	169.9	185.9	234.5	211.1	346.9	341.5	331.1	328.3	292.5	234.
Thailand	—	—	—	—	—	67.0	67.0	135.8	182.0	142.6	606.2	636.2	866.6	807.2	807.
Vietnam	—	—	—	—	—	31.0	53.5	54.4	31.7	51.2	29.7	28.4	28.4	28.4	28.

1987	1988	1989	1990	1991	1992	1993	1994	1995	1996	1997	1998	1999	2000	2001	
							Expressed in Millions of SDRs								
28,752.0	24,750.1	22,315.1	20,731.9	23,378.6	23,967.2	25,196.8	25,611.7	35,929.2	36,127.5	46,559.0	60,451.0	51,061.9	42,990.5	53,477.2	**World**
373.1	—	—	—	—	—	—	—	—	—	—	—	—	—	—	**Industrial Countries**
—	—	—	—	—	—	—	—	—	—	—	—	—	—	—	United States
—	—	—	—	—	—	—	—	—	—	—	—	—	—	—	Canada
—	—	—	—	—	—	—	—	—	—	—	—	—	—	—	Australia
—	—	—	—	—	—	—	—	—	—	—	—	—	—	—	Japan
—	—	—	—	—	—	—	—	—	—	—	—	—	—	—	New Zealand
—	—	—	—	—	—	—	—	—	—	—	—	—	—	—	Belgium
—	—	—	—	—	—	—	—	—	—	—	—	—	—	—	Denmark
—	—	—	—	—	—	—	—	—	—	—	—	—	—	—	Finland
—	—	—	—	—	—	—	—	—	—	—	—	—	—	—	France
—	—	—	—	—	—	—	—	—	—	—	—	—	—	—	Greece
—	—	—	—	—	—	—	—	—	—	—	—	—	—	—	Iceland
—	—	—	—	—	—	—	—	—	—	—	—	—	—	—	Ireland
—	—	—	—	—	—	—	—	—	—	—	—	—	—	—	Italy
—	—	—	—	—	—	—	—	—	—	—	—	—	—	—	Netherlands
—	—	—	—	—	—	—	—	—	—	—	—	—	—	—	Norway
373.1	—	—	—	—	—	—	—	—	—	—	—	—	—	—	Portugal
—	—	—	—	—	—	—	—	—	—	—	—	—	—	—	Spain
—	—	—	—	—	—	—	—	—	—	—	—	—	—	—	United Kingdom
28,379.0	24,750.1	22,315.1	20,731.9	23,378.6	23,967.2	25,196.8	25,611.7	35,929.2	36,127.5	46,559.0	60,451.0	51,061.9	42,990.5	53,477.2	**Developing Countries**
5,622.6	5,259.8	4,880.1	4,144.5	3,900.9	3,472.0	3,525.7	3,863.9	3,380.4	3,668.1	3,308.2	2,793.9	2,653.5	2,490.9	2,249.7	**Africa**
—	—	470.9	470.9	695.9	578.2	342.7	793.8	994.1	1,412.5	1,495.5	1,428.0	1,388.7	1,318.5	1,208.0	Algeria
—	—	—	—	—	—	—	—	—	—	—	—	—	—	—	Burkina Faso
—	—	—	—	—	—	—	—	—	—	—	—	—	—	—	Burundi
—	69.5	85.0	85.0	84.3	45.7	11.9	29.9	34.4	50.1	41.9	29.9	16.6	2.5	—	Cameroon
25.9	19.9	10.8	4.4	2.0	.8	.4	10.7	10.7	10.7	8.0	2.4	—	—	—	Central African Rep.
7.0	6.1	2.6	—	—	—	—	10.3	10.3	10.3	6.5	1.3	—	—	—	Chad
—	—	—	—	—	—	—	—	—	—	—	—	—	—	—	Comoros
587.7	509.4	328.8	220.4	184.8	184.8	184.8	181.8	180.9	158.2	158.2	157.8	157.1	157.1	157.1	Congo, Dem. Rep. of
9.5	9.5	8.3	7.6	4.0	4.0	3.5	14.0	12.5	12.5	10.9	10.4	7.2	17.8	16.9	Congo, Republic of
406.5	368.7	277.9	302.9	259.7	194.5	159.1	105.7	48.9	16.1	—	—	—	—	—	Côte d'Ivoire
—	—	—	—	—	—	—	—	—	2.9	4.0	6.3	6.6	4.8	3.2	Djibouti
5.4	5.1	2.1	.4	—	—	—	—	—	—	—	—	—	—	—	Equatorial Guinea
44.2	36.9	22.1	4.4	—	—	—	—	—	—	—	—	—	—	—	Ethiopia
42.5	98.7	102.7	98.5	84.3	58.6	32.9	61.4	65.0	83.3	97.2	80.5	62.6	68.4	59.6	Gabon
15.9	12.7	9.6	5.9	1.5	—	—	—	—	—	—	—	—	—	—	Gambia, The
548.7	427.6	293.2	210.1	153.7	108.4	116.0	89.0	75.9	59.0	24.6	—	—	—	—	Ghana
21.0	21.0	16.9	7.1	.8	—	—	—	—	—	—	—	—	—	—	Guinea
1.6	.7	—	—	—	—	—	—	—	—	—	—	2.1	3.6	3.6	Guinea-Bissau
268.5	303.7	205.6	129.4	100.3	41.5	—	—	—	—	—	—	—	—	—	Kenya
—	—	—	—	—	—	—	—	—	—	—	—	—	—	—	Lesotho
205.4	204.4	202.2	201.6	201.6	201.6	201.6	201.6	201.5	201.5	201.5	201.5	201.5	201.3	201.0	Liberia
143.9	122.2	83.9	49.2	24.1	12.6	5.2	.6	—	—	—	—	—	—	—	Madagascar
77.7	67.1	48.0	34.3	19.1	5.5	1.2	12.7	12.7	12.7	12.7	6.4	—	—	—	Malawi
52.9	41.5	31.0	23.2	16.6	12.0	5.7	1.0	—	—	—	—	—	—	—	Mali
33.3	33.9	26.4	15.2	5.6	1.0	—	—	—	—	—	—	—	—	—	Mauritania
105.5	76.5	47.6	15.5	—	—	—	—	—	—	—	—	—	—	—	Mauritius
755.2	696.1	642.7	526.5	401.5	319.1	207.2	101.1	34.8	2.3	—	—	—	—	—	Morocco
64.0	42.1	29.2	19.2	10.9	5.5	2.0	11.1	11.1	11.1	6.9	1.4	—	—	—	Niger
—	—	—	—	—	—	—	—	—	—	—	—	—	—	—	Nigeria
—	—	—	—	—	—	—	—	8.9	8.9	23.8	23.8	19.3	12.6	5.2	Rwanda
188.1	159.3	115.9	76.2	41.7	13.5	2.5	30.9	30.9	30.9	19.3	3.9	—	—	—	Senegal
58.6	57.9	56.9	55.4	50.0	48.6	42.6	—	—	—	—	11.6	27.1	37.5	—	Sierra Leone
108.3	107.6	98.8	96.7	96.7	96.7	96.7	96.7	96.7	96.7	96.7	96.7	96.7	96.7	96.7	Somalia
—	—	—	—	—	—	—	614.4	614.4	614.4	307.2	—	—	—	—	South Africa
605.3	605.3	605.3	604.3	604.3	604.3	604.3	604.2	581.3	556.8	531.3	489.1	461.5	420.4	379.4	Sudan
2.3	—	—	—	—	—	—	—	—	—	—	—	—	—	—	Swaziland
45.5	45.5	42.9	23.3	3.9	—	—	—	—	—	—	—	—	—	—	Tanzania
55.3	48.0	33.8	22.7	16.9	9.7	4.6	2.2	.2	—	—	—	—	—	—	Togo
190.7	205.7	205.7	123.7	180.1	211.1	207.3	207.3	197.1	165.0	128.4	91.8	55.2	24.7	—	Tunisia
161.3	130.7	76.5	46.2	21.8	3.1	—	—	—	—	—	—	—	—	—	Uganda
674.5	674.5	674.5	659.8	635.0	609.0	559.2	544.6	—	—	—	—	—	—	—	Zambia
110.3	52.2	22.2	4.8	—	102.5	119.9	139.0	158.1	152.2	133.6	151.3	151.2	124.9	119.0	Zimbabwe
7,038.7	5,464.4	4,467.7	2,815.5	3,921.1	4,638.8	5,024.4	4,178.6	3,232.1	2,078.5	14,049.2	22,794.7	16,700.7	17,592.7	11,433.5	**Asia**
—	—	—	—	—	—	—	—	—	—	—	—	—	—	—	Afghanistan, I.S. of
409.8	423.1	341.3	194.9	92.0	35.9	—	—	—	—	—	98.1	98.1	98.1	98.1	Bangladesh
—	—	—	—	—	—	—	—	—	—	—	—	—	—	—	Bhutan
12.5	12.5	12.5	12.5	12.5	6.3	6.3	6.3	6.3	6.3	6.3	5.2	4.2	3.1	2.1	Cambodia
597.7	597.7	597.7	298.9	—	—	—	—	—	—	—	—	—	—	—	China, People's Rep.
4.8	3.0	.6	—	—	—	—	—	—	—	—	—	—	—	—	Fiji
2,856.3	2,068.8	1,331.3	800.0	2,426.4	3,260.4	3,584.9	2,763.2	1,966.6	1,085.3	589.8	284.9	38.5	—	—	India
504.9	462.9	462.9	347.2	115.7	—	—	—	—	—	2,201.5	6,455.8	7,466.8	8,318.0	7,251.7	Indonesia
369.8	—	—	—	—	—	—	—	—	—	8,200.0	12,000.0	4,462.5	4,462.5	—	Korea
—	—	—	—	—	—	—	—	—	—	—	—	—	—	—	Lao People's Dem.Rep
—	—	—	—	—	—	—	—	—	—	—	—	—	—	—	Malaysia
—	—	—	11.3	13.8	13.8	13.8	7.5	.6	—	—	—	—	—	—	Mongolia
10.9	—	—	—	.8	—	—	—	—	—	—	—	—	—	—	Myanmar
18.7	18.7	13.3	4.7	.8	—	—	—	—	—	—	—	—	—	—	Nepal
566.6	370.0	421.4	313.2	364.0	437.5	434.1	523.2	595.9	536.1	488.8	468.0	770.0	758.8	993.0	Pakistan
—	—	—	—	—	—	—	—	—	—	—	—	—	—	—	Palau
—	—	—	42.8	42.8	42.8	32.1	10.7	33.3	35.3	35.3	32.4	15.7	29.9	85.5	Papua New Guinea
841.6	791.9	890.0	640.3	759.0	800.1	880.7	728.6	489.5	281.9	633.8	1,114.0	1,327.7	1,559.2	1,553.1	Philippines
5.2	2.6	1.2	.6	.2	—	—	—	—	—	—	—	—	—	—	Samoa
1.6	1.3	1.1	.5	—	—	—	—	—	—	—	—	—	—	—	Solomon Islands
164.7	209.4	163.4	131.6	68.0	13.6	—	—	—	—	—	—	—	—	103.4	Sri Lanka
645.4	474.3	202.9	—	—	—	—	—	—	—	1,800.0	2,300.0	2,500.0	2,350.0	1,337.5	Thailand
28.4	28.4	28.4	28.4	28.4	28.4	72.5	133.0	133.0	133.0	93.7	36.3	17.1	13.1	9.1	Vietnam

Use of Fund Credit (GRA)

	1972	1973	1974	1975	1976	1977	1978	1979	1980	1981	1982	1983	1984	1985	198
					Expressed in Millions of SDRs										
Europe	83.5	69.3	192.9	458.4	936.4	862.9	948.7	1,111.1	1,710.7	2,739.4	3,917.9	4,929.4	5,371.8	4,792.8	4,004.
Albania	—	—	—	—	—	—	—	—	—	—	—	—	—	—	—
Armenia	—	—	—	—	—	—	—	—	—	—	—	—	—	—	—
Azerbaijan	—	—	—	—	—	—	—	—	—	—	—	—	—	—	—
Belarus	—	—	—	—	—	—	—	—	—	—	—	—	—	—	—
Bosnia & Herzegovina	—	—	—	—	—	—	—	—	—	—	—	—	—	—	—
Bulgaria	—	—	—	—	—	—	—	—	—	—	—	—	—	—	—
Croatia	—	—	—	—	—	—	—	—	—	—	—	—	—	—	—
Cyprus	—	—	6.4	8.1	43.1	43.1	32.9	38.0	30.6	21.6	12.3	5.5	3.2	—	—
Czech Republic	—	—	—	—	—	—	—	—	—	—	—	—	—	—	—
Czechoslovakia	—	—	—	—	—	—	—	—	—	—	—	—	—	—	—
Estonia	—	—	—	—	—	—	—	—	—	—	—	—	—	—	—
Georgia	—	—	—	—	—	—	—	—	—	—	—	—	—	—	—
Hungary	—	—	—	—	—	—	—	—	—	—	214.5	547.0	972.0	883.7	842.
Kazakhstan	—	—	—	—	—	—	—	—	—	—	—	—	—	—	—
Kyrgyz Republic	—	—	—	—	—	—	—	—	—	—	—	—	—	—	—
Latvia	—	—	—	—	—	—	—	—	—	—	—	—	—	—	—
Lithuania	—	—	—	—	—	—	—	—	—	—	—	—	—	—	—
Macedonia, FYR	—	—	—	—	—	—	—	—	—	—	—	—	—	—	—
Moldova	—	—	—	—	—	—	—	—	—	—	—	—	—	—	—
Poland	—	—	—	—	—	—	—	—	—	—	—	—	—	—	—
Romania	—	47.5	47.5	87.5	237.5	270.0	255.6	246.8	257.4	506.7	781.6	904.7	955.7	782.9	583.
Russia	—	—	—	—	—	—	—	—	—	—	—	—	—	—	—
Slovak Republic	—	—	—	—	—	—	—	—	—	—	—	—	—	—	—
Slovenia	—	—	—	—	—	—	—	—	—	—	—	—	—	—	—
Tajikistan	—	—	—	—	—	—	—	—	—	—	—	—	—	—	—
Turkey	—	—	—	207.6	336.8	336.8	477.7	480.3	826.6	1,135.6	1,319.2	1,497.1	1,455.0	1,207.5	887.
Ukraine	—	—	—	—	—	—	—	—	—	—	—	—	—	—	—
Uzbekistan	—	—	—	—	—	—	—	—	—	—	—	—	—	—	—
Yugoslavia, SFR	83.5	21.8	139.0	155.2	319.0	213.0	182.5	346.0	596.1	1,075.5	1,590.3	1,975.2	1,985.9	1,918.7	1,691.
Yugoslavia, Fed. Rep															
Middle East	51.5	81.6	140.1	300.1	500.0	577.0	599.4	489.6	305.2	176.5	95.5	74.5	74.4	118.1	94.
Egypt	24.4	62.2	93.0	68.2	177.9	254.9	296.3	246.5	139.1	85.1	52.0	49.3	49.3	37.5	25.
Iran, I.R. of	—	—	—	—	—	—	—	—	—	—	—	—	—	—	—
Iraq	—	—	—	—	—	—	—	—	—	—	—	—	—	—	—
Israel	—	—	32.5	208.3	285.3	285.2	271.3	224.2	156.4	87.5	27.2		—	—	—
Jordan	4.5	1.6	—	—	—	—	—	—	—	—	—	—	—	57.4	57.
Syrian Arab Republic	22.6	17.9	5.4	—	—	—	—	.8	—	—	—	—	—	—	—
Yemen Arab Rep.	—	—	—	—	—	—	—	—	—	—	—	9.8	9.8	9.8	6.
Yemen, P.D. Rep.	—	—	9.3	23.7	36.8	36.8	31.9	18.2	9.8	3.8	16.3	15.4	15.4	13.5	5.
Yemen, Republic of	—	—	—	—	—	—	—	—	—	—	—	—	—	—	—
Western Hemisphere	357.3	346.3	397.9	817.2	1,695.1	1,567.0	1,054.3	1,162.6	1,020.2	1,338.5	2,676.8	8,418.4	11,752.1	13,211.8	13,345.
Argentina	174.0	174.0	64.0	250.1	455.6	344.5	—	—	—	—	—	1,120.6	1,120.6	2,105.1	2,240.
Barbados	—	—	—	—	—	6.5	6.5	6.5	2.3	.8	22.2	35.8	43.6	43.6	32.
Belize	—	—	—	—	—	—	—	—	—	—	—	3.6	4.8	9.5	9.
Bolivia	7.9	18.1	14.3	13.9	—	—	15.0	15.0	63.0	61.2	78.1	85.2	64.9	46.7	118.
Brazil	—	—	—	—	—	—	—	—	—	—	498.8	2,525.7	4,269.9	4,205.4	3,679.
Chile	79.0	79.0	160.0	330.8	402.2	300.6	266.5	135.9	96.3	41.8	5.7	579.0	795.0	990.6	1,088.
Colombia	—	—	—	—	—	—	—	—	—	—	—	—	—	—	—
Costa Rica	—	—	18.8	30.0	32.3	29.3	24.3	43.8	44.6	88.2	84.2	183.3	159.0	171.6	141.
Dominica	—	—	—	—	—	—	—	1.9	1.7	6.5	9.3	11.0	10.7	9.2	7.
Dominican Republic	3.8	—	—	—	21.5	36.5	36.5	94.3	38.0	19.8	64.1	235.2	225.7	270.4	248.
Ecuador	8.3	—	—	—	—	—	—	—	—	—	—	203.5	242.9	327.3	397.
El Salvador	8.8	—	17.9	17.9	12.8	—	—	—	5.4	37.6	97.4	112.9	107.5	80.9	35.
Grenada	—	—	—	.8	1.2	1.2	1.2	1.0	.3	5.2	4.3	5.4	2.4	1.
Guatemala	—	—	—	—	—	—	—	—	95.6	95.6	133.9	153.0	105.2	57.
Guyana	—	3.9	5.0	—	17.3	17.3	30.3	40.5	67.4	74.1	77.8	73.8	72.8	71.8	71.
Haiti	—	—	6.6	11.0	12.4	8.4	7.6	5.7	17.2	32.0	43.0	72.2	86.2	74.4	54.
Honduras	—	—	16.8	16.8	16.8	4.3	—	—	11.8	32.4	94.1	140.0	138.4	121.7	80.
Jamaica	—	13.3	13.3	13.3	68.9	88.1	138.6	266.8	242.5	403.5	528.4	599.1	641.4	631.1	554.
Mexico	—	—	—	—	—	—	319.1	419.1	229.4	103.1	—	200.6	1,203.8	2,407.5	3,319.
Nicaragua	8.3	12.2	10.1	15.5	8.7	2.0	2.0	43.5	38.7	21.2	17.5	13.3	9.0	—	—
Panama	—	—	7.4	17.5	42.6	42.2	40.3	31.5	18.1	80.5	76.1	184.1	276.6	283.4	288.
Paraguay	—	—	—	—	—	—	—	—	—	—	—	—	—	—	—
Peru	30.8	13.6	—	—	158.8	168.8	256.1	373.1	371.6	332.9	588.8	666.3	688.3	639.0	595.
St. Kitts and Nevis	—	—	—	—	—	—	—	—	—	—	—	—	—	—	—
St. Lucia	—	—	—	—	—	—	—	—	1.4	4.1	2.6	2.6	2.0	.3	—
St. Vincent & Grens.	—	—	—	—	—	—	—	—	.2	1.5	1.5	1.5	1.0	.3	—
Trinidad and Tobago	—	—	—	—	—	—	—	—	—	—	—	—	—	—	—
Uruguay	36.7	32.3	63.8	99.7	124.9	98.2	—	—	—	—	86.8	226.8	226.8	318.6	323.
Venezuela, Rep. Bol.	—	—	—	—	—	—	—	—	—	—	—	—	—	—	—
Memorandum Items															
Oil Exporting Ctys	107.1	19.2	—	—	—	—	—	—	—	—	—	425.1	421.5	42.0	42.
Non-Oil Develop.Ctys	982.0	1,008.2	2,225.6	3,947.0	6,491.8	6,200.0	5,782.0	5,997.4	7,269.6	12,760.5	19,171.4	29,097.6	33,890.6	34,544.5	32,710.

1987	1988	1989	1990	1991	1992	1993	1994	1995	1996	1997	1998	1999	2000	2001	
						Expressed in Millions of SDRs									
2,775.9	1,773.9	905.5	917.1	3,464.6	4,695.1	6,151.0	8,002.9	11,329.4	13,769.1	15,353.9	19,144.1	16,779.5	16,191.3	20,883.9	**Europe**
—	—	—	—	—	9.7	13.1	13.1	12.3	6.6	9.7	8.8	8.8	8.8	4.4	Albania
—	—	—	—	—	—	—	16.9	47.3	47.3	47.3	46.8	37.3	25.3	19.7	Armenia
—	—	—	—	—	—	—	—	67.9	121.7	142.2	157.9	214.8	175.8	144.9	Azerbaijan
—	—	—	—	—	—	70.1	70.1	190.2	190.2	190.2	172.3	129.7	87.6	64.3	Belarus
—	—	—	—	—	—	—	—	32.5	31.0	30.3	54.5	68.4	80.4	88.4	Bosnia & Herzegovina
—	—	—	—	289.2	428.9	459.9	644.4	482.1	407.2	698.0	792.3	910.7	1,014.6	883.0	Bulgaria
—	—	—	—	—	—	—	14.8	87.1	148.6	145.4	172.7	166.1	143.2	121.4	97.2	Croatia
—	—	—	—	—	—	—	—	—	—	—	—	—	—	—	Cyprus
—	—	—	—	—	—	780.7	—	—	—	—	—	—	—	—	Czech Republic
—	—	—	—	917.9	1,121.5	....	—	—	—	—	—	....	....	....	Czechoslovakia
—	—	—	—	—	7.8	41.9	41.9	61.8	54.2	40.0	21.3	18.4	14.5	10.7	Estonia
—	—	—	—	—	—	—	27.8	77.7	77.7	77.7	77.0	61.3	41.6	32.4	Georgia
569.9	471.3	347.1	231.7	880.2	875.8	896.3	781.6	258.7	118.7	118.7	—	—	—	—	Hungary
—	—	—	—	—	—	61.9	198.0	290.8	383.6	379.0	463.7	335.1	—	—	Kazakhstan
—	—	—	—	—	—	43.9	43.9	41.2	34.1	25.5	20.2	14.8	9.4	Kyrgyz Republic
—	—	—	—	—	25.2	77.8	109.8	107.9	90.4	63.7	45.4	34.3	26.7	19.1	Latvia
—	—	—	—	—	17.3	88.0	134.6	176.0	190.1	200.5	179.8	167.8	147.1	120.3	Lithuania
—	—	—	—	—	—	2.8	14.0	38.1	47.4	47.1	45.4	46.8	33.3	27.3	Macedonia, FYR
—	—	—	—	—	—	63.0	112.5	154.9	172.3	172.7	125.6	127.7	109.1	97.8	Moldova
—	—	—	357.5	596.6	596.6	497.7	918.6	—	—	—	—	—	—	—	Poland
357.6	106.9	—	—	565.8	750.9	750.9	906.4	698.3	453.0	475.2	382.8	333.8	347.7	308.0	Romania
—	—	—	—	—	719.0	1,797.3	2,875.6	6,469.8	8,698.2	9,805.9	13,732.0	11,102.3	8,912.8	5,914.8	Russia
—	—	—	—	—	—	405.2	439.8	307.5	222.0	184.4	134.6	96.5	—	—	Slovak Republic
—	—	—	—	—	—	8.5	4.9	2.7	.9	—	—	—	—	—	Slovenia
—	—	—	—	—	—	—	—	—	15.0	22.5	30.0	26.3	18.8	9.4	Tajikistan
543.0	222.0	36.3	—	—	—	—	235.5	460.5	460.5	440.4	275.8	648.8	3,205.3	11,232.9	Turkey
—	—	—	—	—	—	—	249.3	1,037.3	1,573.3	1,780.6	1,985.0	2,044.6	1,591.2	1,520.7	Ukraine
—	—	—	—	—	—	—	—	106.0	165.2	165.2	165.2	146.8	97.5	62.3	Uzbekistan
1,305.5	973.7	522.2	327.9	214.8	142.5	77.4	77.4	56.8	56.1	56.1	56.1	55.6	—	—	Yugoslavia, SFR
—	—	—	—	—	—	—	—	—	—	—	—	—	116.9	216.9	Yugoslavia, Fed. Rep
187.1	**151.9**	**189.4**	**153.2**	**155.2**	**407.0**	**385.0**	**409.7**	**350.3**	**353.3**	**458.0**	**483.8**	**510.5**	**447.8**	**403.1**	**Middle East**
128.5	116.0	116.0	87.0	89.0	147.2	147.2	132.2	69.5	10.9	—	—	—	—	—	Egypt
—	—	—	—	—	—	—	—	—	—	—	—	—	—	—	Iran, I.R. of
—	—	—	—	—	—	—	—	—	—	—	—	—	—	—	Iraq
—	—	—	—	—	178.6	178.6	178.6	111.7	22.3	—	—	—	—	—	Israel
57.4	35.9	73.4	66.2	66.2	81.2	59.2	98.9	169.2	236.1	316.6	333.4	362.9	354.3	344.5	Jordan
—	—	—	—	—	—	—	—	—	—	—	—	—	—	—	Syrian Arab Republic
1.2	—	....	....	....	....	....	....	....	....	—	—	—	—	—	Yemen Arab Rep.
—	—	....	....	....	....	....	....	....	....	—	—	—	—	....	Yemen, P.D. Rep.
—	—	—	—	—	—	—	—	—	84.0	141.4	150.4	147.6	93.5	58.6	Yemen, Republic of
12,754.7	**12,100.1**	**11,872.3**	**12,701.6**	**11,936.8**	**10,754.3**	**10,110.8**	**9,156.6**	**17,636.9**	**16,258.5**	**13,389.8**	**15,234.5**	**14,417.7**	**6,267.8**	**18,506.9**	**Western Hemisphere**
2,716.2	2,733.0	2,358.8	2,167.2	1,735.9	1,682.8	2,562.4	2,884.7	4,124.4	4,376.0	4,349.3	3,865.1	3,262.6	3,880.3	11,121.1	Argentina
15.6	7.8	3.3	.5	—	36.8	36.8	36.8	24.9	6.5	—	—	—	—	—	Barbados
8.0	5.8	2.5	.3	—	—	—	—	—	—	—	—	—	—	—	Belize
99.0	108.0	103.1	71.7	39.6	17.0	—	—	—	—	—	—	—	—	—	Bolivia
2,802.9	2,476.8	1,843.4	1,279.7	865.1	581.4	221.0	127.5	95.2	47.0	23.3	3,426.8	6,431.0	1,356.8	6,633.9	Brazil
1,032.4	982.6	966.5	812.9	669.4	525.0	346.5	199.5	—	—	—	—	—	—	—	Chile
—	—	—	—	—	—	—	—	—	—	—	—	—	—	—	Colombia
93.3	53.0	26.9	7.9	58.0	59.3	59.3	45.5	16.3	.5	—	—	—	—	—	Costa Rica
6.2	4.0	2.2	1.2	.5	.1	—	—	—	—	—	—	—	—	—	Dominica
199.9	161.8	93.2	50.4	62.4	89.4	135.5	129.9	107.5	66.5	21.1	39.7	39.7	39.7	39.7	Dominican Republic
345.2	300.7	247.2	186.0	127.5	72.6	51.8	135.7	116.7	100.9	98.9	49.5	—	113.3	151.1	Ecuador
3.9	—	.3	—	—	—	—	—	—	—	—	—	—	—	—	El Salvador
.8	.6	.3	—	—	—	—	—	—	—	—	—	—	—	—	Grenada
41.7	65.4	55.5	46.8	44.8	22.4	—	—	—	—	—	—	—	—	—	Guatemala
71.8	71.8	70.9	41.0	49.5	49.5	47.1	31.8	16.2	8.1	1.4	—	—	—	—	Guyana
36.5	22.4	21.1	16.6	15.0	15.0	15.0	.3	16.4	16.4	16.4	25.6	17.4	15.2	15.2	Haiti
47.9	23.6	23.3	22.6	23.6	74.6	72.5	61.3	32.5	6.4	—	47.5	47.5	47.5	47.5	Honduras
478.2	358.8	291.8	250.7	273.6	259.7	244.2	217.6	161.7	112.2	87.1	74.7	60.8	46.3	31.9	Jamaica
3,639.3	3,570.3	3,873.6	4,604.9	4,729.9	4,327.0	3,485.2	2,644.2	10,648.1	9,234.5	6,735.2	5,951.5	3,259.2	—	—	Mexico
—	—	—	—	17.0	17.0	17.0	14.9	6.4	—	—	—	—	—	—	Nicaragua
243.9	243.8	243.2	191.3	150.7	79.8	82.3	91.3	74.4	91.0	105.4	125.5	108.3	69.1	42.9	Panama
—	—	—	—	—	—	—	—	—	—	—	—	—	—	—	Paraguay
595.4	595.4	577.0	530.5	493.4	458.7	642.7	642.7	642.7	642.7	749.6	642.5	535.4	428.3	307.8	Peru
—	—	—	—	—	—	—	—	—	—	—	1.6	1.6	1.6	1.6	St. Kitts and Nevis
—	—	—	—	—	—	—	—	—	—	—	—	—	—	—	St. Lucia
—	—	—	—	—	—	—	—	—	—	—	—	—	—	—	St. Vincent & Grens.
—	85.1	155.8	231.6	269.1	205.3	112.8	62.4	33.8	16.5	3.1	—	—	—	—	Trinidad and Tobago
276.6	229.7	153.4	70.8	40.4	38.1	27.9	20.5	14.0	6.0	—	114.2	114.2	114.2	114.2	Uruguay
—	—	759.5	2,117.0	2,271.3	2,142.8	1,950.7	1,810.2	1,506.0	1,527.4	1,198.9	870.4	540.0	155.6	—	Venezuela, Rep. Bol.
															Memorandum Items
504.9	462.9	1,693.3	2,935.1	3,083.0	2,720.9	2,293.5	2,603.9	2,500.0	2,940.0	4,895.9	8,754.2	9,395.6	9,792.1	8,459.7	**Oil Exporting Ctys**
27,874.1	24,287.2	20,621.8	17,796.8	20,295.6	21,246.2	22,903.4	23,007.7	33,429.1	33,187.5	41,663.2	51,696.8	41,666.3	33,198.5	45,017.5	**Non-Oil Develop.Ctys**

Total Reserves minus Gold

11 s		1972	1973	1974	1975	1976	1977	1978	1979	1980	1981	1982	1983	1984	1985	1986
															Millions of SDRs:	
All Countries	010	110,904	116,836	144,001	158,697	186,626	228,470	245,485	272,867	321,266	329,663	327,911	362,304	407,107	404,860	418,643
Industrial Countries	110	81,699	79,948	79,841	84,762	93,575	120,053	144,811	154,907	186,037	186,502	185,560	206,185	226,023	229,440	251,303
United States	111	2,453	2,260	3,456	3,952	6,153	6,250	5,357	5,909	12,228	16,258	20,677	21,612	24,319	29,220	30,619
Canada	156	4,804	4,013	3,990	3,781	4,273	3,023	2,730	2,174	2,425	3,039	2,730	3,311	2,542	2,278	2,658
Australia	193	5,397	4,465	3,229	2,524	2,470	1,694	1,582	1,081	1,325	1,436	5,776	8,560	7,592	5,251	5,924
Japan	158	16,177	9,412	10,303	10,208	13,553	18,392	24,875	14,819	19,316	24,235	21,153	23,498	26,963	24,325	34,546
New Zealand	196	766	866	522	365	422	364	346	342	276	579	576	743	1,823	1,453	3,083
Euro Area (incl. ECB)	163															
Austria	122	1,775	1,652	2,070	3,060	3,065	2,758	3,874	3,094	4,140	4,540	4,805	4,313	4,330	4,340	5,038
Belgium	124	2,056	2,751	2,890	3,476	3,004	3,257	3,044	4,132	6,133	4,254	3,560	4,502	4,656	4,414	4,527
Finland	172	615	476	487	370	398	437	939	1,169	1,466	1,275	1,376	1,182	2,810	3,414	1,461
France	132	5,700	3,538	3,697	7,224	4,837	4,834	7,122	13,345	21,436	19,126	14,985	18,961	21,362	24,206	25,715
Germany	134	17,800	23,381	22,346	22,394	25,838	28,573	37,208	39,891	38,099	37,560	40,578	40,760	40,951	40,403	42,294
Greece	174	828	745	638	†823	758	863	1,002	1,019	1,055	878	781	860	973	790	†1,242
Ireland	178	1,022	835	1,019	1,292	1,565	1,936	2,048	1,679	2,243	2,278	2,377	2,521	2,400	2,676	2,646
Italy	136	2,721	2,448	2,782	1,116	2,774	6,672	8,527	13,814	18,132	17,298	12,774	19,203	21,214	14,198	16,340
Luxembourg	137	....	....	....	....	....	....	....	....	....	....	....	....	29	30	30
Netherlands	138	2,511	3,525	3,782	4,172	4,457	4,727	3,905	5,762	9,131	8,024	9,185	9,715	9,423	9,816	9,149
Portugal	182	1,189	1,390	948	340	151	301	669	707	624	459	405	368	527	1,270	1,191
Spain	184	4,120	5,114	4,798	4,703	4,049	4,920	7,762	10,039	9,302	9,283	6,939	7,070	12,197	10,174	12,062
Denmark	128	724	1,034	700	686	724	1,308	2,402	2,456	2,655	2,189	2,054	3,458	3,070	4,942	4,059
Iceland	176	76	82	39	39	68	81	104	123	136	197	132	143	130	187	253
Norway	142	1,186	1,271	1,541	1,876	1,884	1,808	2,196	3,200	4,742	5,372	6,231	6,332	9,554	12,670	10,239
Sweden	144	1,251	1,894	1,215	2,425	1,941	2,811	3,165	2,667	2,680	3,094	3,184	3,853	3,923	5,274	5,355
Switzerland	146	4,052	4,151	4,448	5,996	8,268	8,471	13,634	12,476	12,276	12,010	14,015	14,360	15,605	16,402	17,811
United Kingdom	112	4,463	4,633	4,931	3,928	2,905	16,557	12,301	14,986	16,192	13,091	11,238	10,831	9,631	11,707	15,061
Developing Countries	200	29,205	36,889	64,159	73,934	93,053	108,420	100,674	117,962	135,229	143,161	142,351	156,119	181,084	175,421	167,340
Africa	605	3,006	3,776	8,491	8,545	9,057	8,367	6,473	10,128	14,956	10,349	7,151	6,842	6,689	8,295	7,022
Algeria	612	263	756	1,188	964	1,519	1,386	1,520	2,018	2,958	3,175	2,196	1,796	1,494	2,566	1,357
Benin	638	26	27	28	13	17	17	12	11	6	50	4	4	3	4	3
Botswana	616	....	....	....	....	62	80	113	198	262	203	250	359	463	690	950
Burkina Faso	748	44	52	68	65	61	46	28	47	53	61	56	81	108	127	191
Burundi	618	17	18	12	26	42	78	62	68	74	53	27	26	20	27	56
Cameroon	622	40	42	64	25	38	35	40	95	148	73	61	152	55	121	48
Cape Verde	624	....	....	....	....	28	35	30	32	33	33	39	44	42	50	46
Central African Rep.	626	2	1	1	3	16	21	19	33	43	60	42	45	54	45	53
Chad	628	9	1	12	3	20	15	9	9	4	6	11	27	45	30	13
Comoros	632	....	....	....	....	....	....	....	....	5	7	13	14	5	14	19
Congo, Dem. Rep. of	636	113	143	97	41	43	110	97	157	160	130	35	97	140	173	220
Congo, Rep. of	634	10	7	20	12	10	11	7	32	67	106	34	7	4	4	6
Côte d'Ivoire	662	80	73	54	88	66	152	344	112	15	15	2	19	5	4	16
Djibouti	611													46	46	44
Equatorial Guinea	642	....	....	....	....	....	....	....	....	....	....	3	1	1	3	2
Ethiopia	644	77	138	215	236	254	176	117	131	63	229	165	120	45	135	205
Gabon	646	21	40	84	125	100	8	17	15	84	171	283	179	203	175	103
Gambia, The	648	10	13	23	24	18	20	20	1	4	3	8	3	2	2	11
Ghana	652	86	146	58	107	79	122	213	219	141	125	126	138	308	436	419
Guinea	656	....	....	....	....	....	....	....	....	....	....	....	....	....	....	....
Guinea-Bissau	654	....	....	....	....	....	....	....	....	....	....	....	....	....	....	25
Kenya	664	186	193	158	148	237	430	271	477	386	199	192	359	398	356	338
Lesotho	666									39	37	43	64	50	40	49
Liberia	668	....	....	15	16	15	23	14	42	4	7	6	19	4	1	49
Madagascar	674	48	56	40	30	36	57	45	4	7	23	18	28	60	44	94
Malawi	676	33	55	67	52	23	72	57	53	54	42	21	15	58	41	20
Mali	678	3	4	5	4	6	4	6	5	11	15	15	16	27	20	19
Mauritania	682	12	35	85	41	71	41	61	86	110	139	126	101	79	54	39
Mauritius	684	65	55	107	142	77	55	35	22	71	30	34	17	24	27	111
Morocco	686	197	199	319	301	402	416	475	423	313	197	197	102	50	105	173
Mozambique	688	....	....	....	....	....	....	....	....	....	....	....	....	57	42	46
Namibia	728															
Niger	692	38	42	37	43	71	83	99	100	99	91	27	51	90	124	155
Nigeria	694	327	463	4,576	4,771	4,458	3,484	1,448	4,211	8,025	3,347	1,462	946	1,492	1,518	884
Rwanda	714	6	13	11	22	55	68	67	116	146	149	116	106	109	103	133
São Tomé & Príncipe	716	....	....	....	....	....	....	....	....	....	....	....	....	....	....	....
Senegal	722	35	10	5	27	22	28	14	15	6	7	10	12	4	5	8
Seychelles	718	....	4	4	5	6	9	7	9	14	12	12	10	6	8	6
Sierra Leone	724	43	43	45	24	22	27	27	35	24	14	8	15	8	10	11
Somalia	726	29	29	35	58	73	99	97	33	11	26	6	9	1	2	10
South Africa	199	561	372	308	418	366	342	325	330	569	572	440	786	247	286	303
Sudan	732	33	51	102	31	20	19	22	51	38	15	19	16	18	11	48
Swaziland	734	....	....	11	39	63	78	87	86	124	83	69	88	82	76	79
Tanzania	738	110	120	41	56	97	232	77	52	16	16	4	19	27	15	50
Togo	742	34	31	44	35	57	38	54	50	61	130	152	165	207	270	280
Tunisia	744	201	250	337	325	315	289	340	440	463	461	550	542	415	212	250
Uganda	746	33	24	14	27	38	39	40	17	2	26	71	102	†69	25	19
Zambia	754	146	154	134	121	80	55	39	61	61	48	53	52	55	182	57
Zimbabwe	698	56	103	58	68	66	60	114	227	167	146	127	72	46	85	87

	1987	1988	1989	1990	1991	1992	1993	1994	1995	1996	1997	1998	1999	2000	2001		

End of Period

	1987	1988	1989	1990	1991	1992	1993	1994	1995	1996	1997	1998	1999	2000	2001	Country	Code
	507,611	542,816	591,102	655,407	692,661	720,048	797,740	858,324	988,396	1,142,211	1,261,637	1,244,481	1,366,037	1,545,195	1,694,734	All Countries	010
	324,321	353,065	382,214	414,092	400,659	396,746	413,444	433,819	487,693	548,794	577,696	545,591	586,284	649,677	681,359	Industrial Countries	110
	24,474	27,305	48,358	50,791	46,602	43,831	45,395	43,350	50,307	44,536	43,659	50,223	44,080	43,442	45,860	United States	111
	5,130	11,437	12,217	12,544	11,362	8,314	9,087	8,416	10,124	14,202	13,209	16,553	20,493	24,502	27,024	Canada	156
	6,163	10,105	10,486	11,432	11,559	8,152	8,083	7,730	8,003	10,073	12,485	10,398	15,455	13,906	14,287	Australia	193
	57,077	71,879	63,887	55,179	50,376	52,089	71,729	86,214	123,277	150,663	162,793	153,030	209,045	272,392	314,431	Japan	158
	2,298	2,107	2,303	2,902	2,062	2,239	2,430	2,540	2,967	4,140	3,299	2,986	3,246	2,555	2,394	New Zealand	196
												187,335	186,166	186,421		Euro Area (incl. ECB)	163
	5,309	5,475	6,543	6,591	7,223	9,005	10,637	11,523	12,600	15,901	14,628	22,324	†11,017	10,989	9,954	Austria	122
	6,781	6,935	8,192	8,541	8,515	10,037	8,310	9,505	10,883	11,789	11,999	12,977	†7,969	7,671	8,964	Belgium	124
	4,524	4,733	3,889	6,779	5,319	3,792	3,939	7,303	6,753	4,810	6,238	6,885	†5,980	6,497	6,352	Finland	172
	23,296	18,849	18,728	25,851	21,870	19,657	16,489	17,986	18,065	18,635	22,922	31,471	†28,926	28,428	25,263	France	132
	55,515	43,492	46,196	47,729	44,043	66,158	56,525	52,994	57,185	57,844	57,504	52,573	†44,472	43,664	40,827	Germany	134
	1,890	2,690	2,453	2,398	3,628	3,486	5,672	9,924	9,943	12,171	9,335	12,399	13,204	10,303	†4,101	Greece	174
	3,381	3,780	3,087	3,672	4,013	2,502	4,314	4,189	5,806	5,706	4,837	6,674	†3,848	4,114	4,446	Ireland	178
	21,297	25,797	35,551	44,232	34,031	20,104	20,054	22,102	23,482	31,954	41,311	21,227	†16,336	19,622	19,431	Italy	136
	30	31	57	57	56	54	49	52	50	51	47		†56	59	84	Luxembourg	137
	11,280	11,945	12,562	12,289	12,442	15,954	22,820	23,655	22,680	18,614	18,429	15,211	†7,357	7,401	7,189	Netherlands	138
	2,345	3,810	7,573	10,182	14,421	13,912	11,532	10,627	10,663	11,070	11,606	11,239	†6,447	6,837	7,692	Portugal	182
	21,618	27,550	31,554	36,008	46,016	33,094	29,882	28,459	23,199	40,284	50,694	39,245	†24,127	23,784	23,539	Spain	184
	7,096	8,000	4,868	7,445	5,176	8,032	7,499	6,203	7,411	9,834	14,174	10,841	16,238	11,596	13,615	Denmark	128
	219	216	257	307	314	362	310	201	207	316	284	303	349	298	269	Iceland	176
	10,063	9,859	10,489	10,777	9,250	8,684	14,286	13,033	15,148	18,441	17,343	13,215	14,864	15,476	12,324	Norway	142
	5,762	6,310	7,274	12,644	12,815	16,454	13,869	15,929	16,180	13,288	8,023	10,013	10,943	11,407	11,122	Sweden	144
	19,368	17,985	19,234	20,541	20,277	24,185	23,760	23,790	24,496	26,727	28,926	29,254	26,463	24,769	25,462	Switzerland	146
	29,405	32,773	26,457	25,202	29,286	26,648	26,775	28,094	28,265	27,745	23,952	22,877	†26,134	33,687	29,667	United Kingdom	112
	183,290	189,751	208,888	241,314	292,003	323,303	384,296	424,505	500,702	593,417	683,941	698,889	779,753	895,518	1,013,376	Developing Countries	200
	7,099	7,517	9,165	11,768	14,251	12,535	13,657	16,200	17,122	21,221	31,334	28,761	29,886	40,239	48,757	Africa	605
	1,156	669	645	509	1,039	1,060	1,074	1,832	1,349	2,945	5,964	4,862	3,297	9,228	14,388	Algeria	612
	3	3	3	46	134	178	178	177	133	182	188	186	291	352	460	Benin	638
	1,419	1,648	2,124	2,342	2,600	2,759	2,983	3,015	3,159	3,496	4,206	4,219	4,589	4,849	4,693	Botswana	616
	227	238	202	211	242	248	278	163	234	235	256	265	215	187	207	Burkina Faso	748
	43	52	76	74	99	127	119	140	141	97	84	47	35	25	14	Burundi	618
	45	131	61	18	30	15	2	2	3	2	1	1	3	163	264	Cameroon	622
	57	60	57	54	46	55	42	29	25	19	14	6	32	22	36	Cape Verde	624
	68	81	86	83	72	73	82	144	157	162	132	103	99	102	94	Central African Rep.	626
	37	47	85	90	84	59	28	52	96	114	101	85	69	85	97	Chad	628
	22	17	23	21	20	20	28	30	30	35	30	28	27	33	50	Comoros	632
	127	139	148	154	128	114	34	83	99	57	....	....				Congo, Dem. Rep. of	636
	2	3	5	4	3	3	1	34	40	63	44	1	29	170	55	Congo, Rep. of	634
	6	8	11	3	9	5	2	140	356	421	458	608	459	513	811	Côte d'Ivoire	662
	45	48	45	66	70	61	55	51	49	54	49	47	51	52	56	Djibouti	611
	—	4	5	—	7	10	—	—	—	4	1	2	18	56		Equatorial Guinea	642
	86	48	35	14	38	169	332	373	519	509	371	363	334	235	345	Ethiopia	644
	8	50	26	192	229	52	1	120	100	173	209	11	13	146	8	Gabon	646
	18	14	16	39	47	68	77	67	71	71	71	76	81	84	84	Gambia, The	648
	138	164	264	154	385	233	298	400	469	576	399	268	331	178	237	Ghana	652
	....	....	....	....	56	63	96	60	58	61	90	168	145	114	159	Guinea	656
	7	12	16	13	10	13	10	13	14	8	25	25	26	51	55	Guinea-Bissau	654
	180	196	217	144	82	39e	295	382	238	519	584	556	577	689	847	Kenya	664
	48	42	37	51	80	115	184	255	307	320	424	408	364	321	308	Lesotho	666
	—	—	6	....	1	1	2	3	19	—	—	—	—	—	—	Liberia	668
	131	166	187	65	62	61	59	49	73	168	209	122	166	219	317	Madagascar	674
	37	108	76	96	107	29	41	29	74	157	120	192	183	190	165	Malawi	676
	11	27	88	134	223	224	242	152	217	300	308	286	255	293	278	Mali	678
	51	41	63	38	47	44	32	27	57	98	149	144	163	....	....	Mauritania	682
	242	328	394	518	624	596	551	512	581	623	514	397	533	689	665	Mauritius	684
	290	407	372	1,453	2,167	2,607	2,661	2,981	2,423	2,638	2,959	3,150	4,145	3,702	6,743	Morocco	686
	83	129	155	163	†168	170	136	122	131	239	383	432	475	557	569	Mozambique	688
	....	....	....	....	....	36	97	139	149	135	186	185	223	200	186	Namibia	728
	175	172	162	156	142	164	140	76	64	55	39	38	29	62	85	Niger	692
	821	484	1,344	2,716	3,101	703	999	949	971	2,834	5,619	5,043	3,971	7,607	8,321	Nigeria	694
	116	88	54	31	77	57	35	35	67	74	114	120	127	146	169	Rwanda	714
								3	3	9	7	8	9	9	12	São Tomé & Príncipe	716
	6	8	14	8	9	9	2	123	183	200	286	306	294	294	355	Senegal	722
	10	6	9	12	19	23	26	21	18	15	20	15	22	34	30	Seychelles	718
	4	6	3	4	7	14	21	28	23	18	29	31	29	39	41	Sierra Leone	724
	5	11	12	....												Somalia	726
	452	580	730	709	628	721	742	1,154	1,897	655	3,557	3,094	4,629	4,669	4,810	South Africa	199
	8	9	12	8	5	20	27	54	110	74	60	64	138	....	....	Sudan	732
	90	104	137	152	120	225	192	203	201	177	219	255	274	270	216	Swaziland	734
	22	58	41	136	143	238	148	227	182	306	461	426	565	748	920	Tanzania	738
	250	172	217	248	255	198	114	65	88	62	88	84	89	117	100	Togo	742
	370	668	732	559	552	620	622	1,001	1,080	1,320	1,466	1,314	1,648	1,390	1,583	Tunisia	744
	38	37	11	31	41	69	107	220	309	367	470	515	556	620	782	Uganda	746
	77	100	88	136	129	....	140	184	150	155	177	49	33	188	146	Zambia	754
	117	133	72	105	105	162	315	278	401	416	119	93	195	148	51	Zimbabwe	698

Total Reserves minus Gold

		1972	1973	1974	1975	1976	1977	1978	1979	1980	1981	1982	1983	1984	1985	1986
															Millions of SDRs:	
Asia *	505	**7,270**	**8,585**	**10,291**	**10,442**	**15,960**	**21,459**	**22,600**	**26,216**	**29,702**	**36,628**	**43,117**	**54,593**	**67,374**	**66,273**	**79,811**
Afghanistan, Islamic State of	512	19	18	23	74	113	227	300	335	291	236	234	205	233	269	211
Bangladesh	513	249	119	113	127	249	192	242	293	235	119	166	501	398	306	334
Bhutan	514	....	....	....	....	....	....	....	....	....	....	27	32	38	46	46	50
Cambodia	522	....	....	....	....	....	....	....	....	....	....	....	....	....	....	....
China, P.R.: Mainland †	924	....	....	....	....	....	1,931	1,195	1,635	1,996	4,346	10,288	14,315	†17,717	11,588	9,363
China, P.R.: Hong Kong	532	....	....	....	....	....	....	....	....	....	....	....	....	....	....	....
Fiji	819	64	61	89	127	100	121	103	104	131	116	115	111	120	119	140
India	534	844	704	839	930	2,403	4,011	4,933	5,642	5,444	4,032	3,912	4,716	5,960	5,845	5,229
Indonesia	536	527	667	1,217	499	1,288	2,065	2,016	3,083	4,227	4,308	2,851	3,552	4,869	4,529	3,312
Korea	542	482	733	226	667	1,696	2,443	2,122	2,246	2,293	2,304	2,545	2,241	2,809	2,612	2,714
Lao P. D. Rep.	544															
Malaysia	548	836	1,057	1,264	1,244	2,069	2,292	2,490	2,972	3,440	3,521	3,416	3,614	3,798	4,472	4,928
Maldives	556	....	....	....	....	—		1	1	1	8	4	5	4	6
Micronesia, Fed. States of	868	....	....	....	....	....	....	....	....	....	....	....	....	....	....
Mongolia	948	....	....	....	....	....	....	....	....	....	....	....	....	....	....
Myanmar	518	37	76	149	113	102	85	74	154	204	197	95	85	63	31	27
Nepal	558	91	97	99	82	†110	115	111	121	143	173	181	127	84	51	71
Pakistan	564	203	342	320	291	401	370	313	162	389	620	878	1,884	1,056	735	580
Papua New Guinea	853	....	26	27	153	221	351	311	382	332	340	411	420	444	403	348
Philippines	566	442	823	1,192	1,123	1,374	1,218	1,353	1,708	2,232	1,775	805	713	614	560	1,413
Samoa	862	4	4	5	5	5	8	4	4	2	3	3	7	11	13	19
Singapore †	576	1,610	1,895	2,297	2,568	2,895	3,176	4,070	4,417	5,149	6,486	7,687	8,849	10,626	11,695	10,578
Solomon Islands	813	....	....	....	....	....	2	22	28	23	19	34	45	46[e]	32[e]	24
Sri Lanka	524	55	72	63	49	79	241	305	392	192	281	319	284	521	411	288
Thailand	578	887	1,000	1,436	1,434	1,547	1,492	1,542	1,399	1,223	1,488	1,394	1,535	1,959	1,994	2,293
Tonga	866	....	....	....	....	....	7	8	10	11	12	14	20	27	25	18
Vanuatu	846	....	....	....	....	....	....	....	....	....	7	5	6	8	10	18
Vietnam	582	....	....	....	....	....	....	....	....	....	....	....	....	....	....	
of which:																
Taiwan Province of China	528	877	850	892	917	1,305	1,107	1,079	1,114	1,729	6,216	7,734	11,327	15,980	20,535	37,860
Europe	170	**2,352**	**3,379**	**2,878**	**2,544**	**3,808**	**3,270**	**3,712**	**3,318**	**4,790**	**4,865**	**4,839**	**6,897**	**8,469**	**7,110**	**7,739**
Albania	914	....	....	....	....	....	....	....	....	....	....	....	....	....	....	....
Armenia	911	....	....	....	....	....	....	....	....	....	....	....	....	....	....	....
Azerbaijan	912	....	....	....	....	....	....	....	....	....	....	....	....	....	....	....
Belarus	913	....	....	....	....	....	....	....	....	....	....	....	....	....	....	....
Bosnia & Herzegovina	963	....	....	....	....	....	....	....	....	....	....	....	....	....	....	....
Bulgaria	918	....	....	....	....	....	....	....	....	....	....	....	....	....	....	....
Croatia	960	....	....	....	....	....	....	....	....	....	....	....	....	....	....	....
Cyprus	423	279	239	204	169	236	258	265	268	289	366	474	496	551	542	615
Czech Republic	935	....	....	....	....	....	....	....	....	....	....	....	....	....	....	....
Czechoslovakia †	934									1,442	821	703	767	986	778	912
Estonia	939	....	....	....	....	....	....	....	....	....	....	....	....	....	....	....
Georgia	915	....	....	....	....	....	....	....	....	....	....	....	....	....	....	....
Hungary	944	....	....	....	....	....	....	....	....	....	....	....	1,176	1,592	1,960	1,882
Kazakhstan	916	....	....	....	....	....	....	....	....	....	....	....	....	....	....	....
Kyrgyz Republic	917	....	....	....	....	....	....	....	....	....	....	....	....	....	....	....
Latvia	941	....	....	....	....	....	....	....	....	....	....	....	....	....	....	....
Lithuania	946	....	....	....	....	....	....	....	....	....	....	....	....	....	....	....
Macedonia, FYR	962	....	....	....	....	....	....	....	....	....	....	....	....	....	....	....
Malta	181	241	257	316	415	523	592	710	769	776	923	982	1,062	1,010	899	936
Moldova	921	....	....	....	....	....	....	....	....	....	....	....	....	....	....	....
Poland	964	....	....	....	....	....	....	....	429	100	239	586	731	1,128	792	570
Romania	968	....	178	196	461	483	211	289	398	253	347	408	502	724	181	476
Russia	922	....	....	....	....	....	....	....	....	....	....	....	....	....	....	....
Slovak Republic	936	....	....	....	....	....	....	....	....	....	....	....	....	....	....	....
Slovenia	961	....	....	....	....	....	....	....	....	....	....	....	....	....	....	....
Turkey	186	1,162	1,646	1,276	806	853	525	615	500	844	797	979	1,230	1,296	961	1,154
Ukraine	926	....	....	....	....	....	....	....	....	....	....	....	....	....	....	....
Yugoslavia, SFR	188	622	1,058	886	693	1,713	1,683	1,833	954	1,085	1,372	703	933	1,181	997	1,193
Middle East	405	**8,362**	**10,140**	**28,344**	**37,332**	**44,716**	**52,886**	**41,648**	**46,967**	**55,317**	**58,506**	**62,777**	**60,933**	**58,394**	**57,307**	**46,597**
Bahrain, Kingdom of	419	77	53	107	247	376	415	379	466	748	1,327	1,391	1,362	1,329	1,511	1,218
Egypt	469	47	215	206	166	206	355	377	402	820	615	633	737	751	721	678
Iran, I.R. of	429	754	894	6,716	7,469	7,472	9,966	9,194	11,546	8,015	1,379	5,168	....	....	....	....
Iraq	433	576	1,144	2,530	2,186	3,816	5,614									
Israel	436	1,086	1,466	942	971	1,143	1,253	2,015	2,326	2,628	3,004	3,480	3,487	3,122	3,350	3,809
Jordan	439	222	224	255	392	406	529	680	885	896	934	801	787	525	385	357
Kuwait	443	248	316	1,020	1,274	1,465	2,374	1,919	2,179	3,080	3,495	5,360	4,959	4,683	4,981	4,497
Lebanon	446	299	392	1,044	1,026	1,121	1,291	1,408	1,163	1,245	1,303	2,364	1,817	685	978	399
Libya	672	2,609	1,678	2,868	1,790	2,674	3,940	3,151	4,816	10,264	7,735	6,400	4,985	3,708	5,375	4,867
Oman	449	34	39	76	138	189	238	195	315	456	639	791	728	918	993	791
Qatar	453	49	56	52	83	111	133	162	219	269	314	350	367	388	406	468
Saudi Arabia	456	2,195	3,106	11,559	19,812	23,153	24,617	†14,737	14,631	18,376	27,695	26,787	26,064	25,248	22,764	14,980
Syrian Arab Rep.	463	97	314	381	600	253	398	293	441	264	250	180	50	274	76	118
United Arab Emirates	466	....	76	370	844	1,641	659	623	1,087	1,580	2,751	2,008	1,979	2,333	2,917	2,755
Yemen Arab Rep.	473	....	105	162	288	620	1,021	1,120	1,084	1,006	826	502	350	325	270	353
Yemen, P.D. Rep.	459	61	62	55	46	70	82	144	159	183	219	259	269	254	170	113
Yemen, Republic of	474	....	....	....	....	....	....	....	....	....	....	....	....	....	....	....

† See country notes
in the monthly *IFS*

1987	1988	1989	1990	1991	1992	1993	1994	1995	1996	1997	1998	1999	2000	2001		
End of Period																
98,145	110,392	119,928	144,275	175,841	188,185	220,263	261,282	289,589	342,245	382,403	411,690	480,391	545,619	628,916	Asia *	505
197	194	185	187	164	....	....	....	....	....	....	....	....	....	....	Afghanistan, Islamic State of	512
594	777	382	442	894	1,327	1,755	2,150	1,574	1,276	1,172	1,353	1,168	1,140	1,015	Bangladesh	513
53	70	75	60	69	57	....	79	84	128	134	177	200	227	226	Bhutan	514
						18	81	129	185	221	230	286	385	467	Cambodia	522
11,493	13,778	13,666	20,796	30,532	†14,997	16,298	36,246	50,708	74,438	105,809	105,955	114,919	129,155	171,560	China, P.R.: Mainland †	924
			17,269	20,139	25,581	31,295	33,737	37,268	44,374	68,782	63,671	70,117	82,540	88,448	China, P.R.: Hong Kong	532
93	173	161	183	190	230	196	187	235	297	267	274	312	314	292	Fiji	819
4,549	3,641	2,936	1,069	2,535	4,187	7,425	13,493	12,056	14,027	18,298	19,418	23,801	29,090	36,500	India	534
3,942	3,751	4,150	5,243	6,472	7,599	8,200	8,311	9,222	12,692	12,293	16,131	19,268	21,876	21,680	Indonesia	536
2,526	9,175	11,577	10,398	9,578	12,451	14,727	17,563	21,983	23,670	15,096	36,913	53,907	73,781	81,762	Korea	542
—	—	1	1	20ᵉ	29ᵉ	46ᵉ	42ᵉ	62	118	83	80	74	107	104	Lao P. D. Rep.	544
5,241	4,850	5,922	6,856	7,610	12,529	19,838	17,415	15,994	18,783	15,407	18,153	22,286	22,659	24,249	Malaysia	548
6	16	19	17	16	21	19	21	32	53	73	84	93	94	74	Maldives	556
								47	62	64	72	68	87	78	Micronesia, Fed. States of	868
					12	43	56	79	75	130	67	99	137	164	Mongolia	948
19	58	200	220	181	204	221	289	377	159	185	224	193	171	319	Myanmar	518
126	164	161	208	278	340	466	475	395	397	464	537	616	726	826	Nepal	558
354	293	396	208	368	618	871	2,007	1,166	381	886	730	1,101	1,162	2,896	Pakistan	564
308	292	292	283	226	174	103	66	176	406	269	137	149	237	349	Papua New Guinea	853
683	746	1,078	650	2,269	3,202	3,404	4,122	4,287	6,975	5,385	6,552	9,639	10,017	10,696	Philippines	566
26	37	42	49	47	46	37	35	37	42	44	44	50	49	45	Samoa	862
10,733	12,687	15,481	19,505	23,862	29,007	35,208	39,851	46,213	53,442	52,836	53,215	55,987	61,502	59,977	Singapore †	576
26	29	20	12	6	17	15	12	11	23	27	35	37	25	....	Solomon Islands	813
197	165	186	297	479	674	1,186	1,401	1,404	1,364	1,500	1,406	1,192	797	1,024	Sri Lanka	524
2,825	4,530	7,241	9,352	12,246	14,806	17,817	20,093	24,206	26,239	19,403	20,472	24,818	24,573	25,745	Thailand	578
20	23	19	22	23	23	27	24	19	21	20	20	20	21	21	Tonga	866
28	30	27	26	28	31	33	30	32	31	28	32	30	30	30	Vanuatu	846
....	....	....	....	....	....	....	....	890	1,207	1,472	1,422	2,423	2,622	2,924	Vietnam	582
															of which:	
54,099	54,913	55,719	50,919	57,609	59,859	60,844	63,331	60,754	61,224	61,888	64,161	77,376	81,926	97,245	Taiwan Province of China	528
7,524	9,527	14,436	15,217	15,676	15,583	25,334	30,528	57,515	61,537	71,756	72,539	79,261	97,759	111,282	Europe	170
....	....	....	....	....	....	107	140	162	195	229	248	269	270	288	Albania	914
....	....	....	....	....	1	10	22	67	108	170	224	232	244	255	Armenia	911
....	....	....	....	....	—	—	1	81	147	345	318	490	522	714	Azerbaijan	912
....	....	....	....	....	....	69	254	326	292	499	214	269	311	Belarus	913
....	....	....	....	....	....	....	....	....	....	60	124	330	381	972	Bosnia & Herzegovina ...	963
....	....	....	....	217	656	477	686	832	336	1,666	2,010	2,247	2,565	2,698	Bulgaria	918
....	....	....	....	....	121	449	962	1,275	1,609	1,882	2,000	2,204	2,705	3,742	Croatia	960
616	690	855	1,059	972	748	798	1,003	751	1,072	1,031	980	1,335	1,336	1,804	Cyprus	423
....	....	....	....	....	2,759	4,209	9,312	8,590	7,214	8,908	9,330	9,992	11,412	Czech Republic	935
974	1,176	1,641	775	2,230	†815	....	....	....	....	....	....	....	....	....	Czechoslovakia †	934
....	....	....	....	....	124	281	304	390	443	562	576	622	707	653	Estonia	939
....	....	....	....	....	....	....	....	131	131	148	87	96	84	128	Georgia	915
1,152	1,090	948	751	2,750	3,218	4,878	4,614	8,055	6,760	6,232	6,618	7,981	8,588	8,536	Hungary	944
....	....	....	....	....	....	332	574	764	900	1,258	1,038	1,078	1,224	1,589	Kazakhstan	916
....	....	....	....	....	....	35	18	54	66	126	116	167	183	210	Kyrgyz Republic	917
....	....	....	....	....	....	314	373	340	455	522	517	612	653	914	Latvia	941
....	....	....	....	....	33	255	360	509	537	749	1,001	871	1,007	1,287	Lithuania	946
....	....	....	....	....	....	76	102	173	167	190	217	313	330	593	Macedonia, FYR	962
997	1,014	1,031	1,006	932	922	992	1,267	1,079	1,126	1,103	1,181	1,303	1,128	1,326	Malta	181
....	....	....	....	....	2	56	123	173	217	271	102	135	177	182	Moldova	921
1,054	1,527	1,761	3,158	2,540	2,981	2,979	4,002	9,939	12,409	15,125	19,407	19,202	20,387	20,409	Poland	964
988	580	1,414	368	486	601	725	1,429	1,062	1,462	2,819	2,036	1,958	3,010	4,330	Romania	968
....	....	....	....	....	....	4,248	2,727	9,676	7,842	9,557	5,541	6,162	18,623	25,895	Russia	922
....	....	....	....	....	78	303	1,158	2,263	2,378	2,394	2,037	2,456	3,087	3,295	Slovak Republic	936
....	....	....	....	....	520	574	1,027	1,225	1,598	2,457	2,584	2,308	2,453	3,445	Slovenia	961
1,252	1,742	3,638	4,252	3,596	4,480	4,566	4,911	8,370	11,430	13,829	13,841	17,010	17,260	15,022	Turkey	186
....	....	....	....	....	341	118	446	707	1,363	1,735	541	762	1,038	2,352	Ukraine	926
492	1,708	3,147	3,848	1,875	....	....	....	....	....	....	....	....	....	....	Yugoslavia, SFR	188
44,586	40,341	40,983	36,715	40,549	42,936	46,105	45,129	49,592	60,153	72,918	71,819	78,426	92,099	98,269	Middle East	405
810	930	799	868	1,059	1,017	948	801	861	917	956	766	997	1,200	1,340	Bahrain, Kingdom of	419
972	939	1,157	1,886	3,723	7,862	9,395	9,234	10,886	12,099	13,833	12,872	10,553	10,068	10,285	Egypt	469
....	....	....	....	....	....	....	....	....	....	....	....	....	....	....	Iran, I.R. of	429
....	....	....	....	....	....	....	....	....	....	....	....	....	....	....	Iraq	433
4,142	2,984	4,015	4,411	4,390	3,729	4,647	4,653	5,462	7,938	15,069	16,104	16,470	17,869	18,603	Israel	436
299	81	358	597	577	558	1,192	1,159	1,327	1,223	1,631	1,243	1,916	2,557	2,437	Jordan	439
2,919	1,429	2,360	1,372	2,383	3,743	3,068	2,398	2,395	2,444	2,558	2,803	3,515	5,436	7,875	Kuwait	443
259	727	714	464	892	1,088	1,646	2,661	3,050	4,125	4,429	4,656	5,665	4,562	3,990	Lebanon	446
4,115	3,211	3,297	4,104	3,981	4,496	....	....	....	....	....	5,153	5,304	9,564	11,777	Libya	672
988	783	1,031	1,176	1,163	1,443	661	671	766	966	1,148	756	2,016	1,827	1,882	Oman	449
436	353	406	444	467	497	505	451	500	477	608	741	950	889	1,045	Qatar	453
15,990	15,273	12,744	8,201	8,161	4,316	5,408	5,054	5,800	†10,415	11,391	10,536	12,793	15,392	14,573	Saudi Arabia	456
157	143	....	....	....	....	....	....	....	....	....	....	....	....	....	Syrian Arab Rep.	463
3,331	3,295	3,391	3,222	3,751	4,154	4,444	4,561	5,026	5,602	6,205	6,447	7,778	10,379	11,256	United Arab Emirates.......	466
380	212	212	....	....	....	....	....	....	....	....	....	....	....	....	Yemen Arab Rep.	473
68	59	58	....	....	....	....	....	....	....	....	....	....	....	....	Yemen, P.D. Rep.	459
....	....	....	297	475	233	106	175	416	707	892	707	1,072	2,226	2,911	Yemen, Republic of	474

† See country notes
in the monthly *IFS*

Total Reserves minus Gold

ll s

Millions of SDRs: (columns 1985, 1986)

	Code	1972	1973	1974	1975	1976	1977	1978	1979	1980	1981	1982	1983	1984	1985	1986
Western Hemisphere	205	8,021	10,903	14,011	15,071	19,510	22,436	26,241	31,333	30,482	32,825	24,475	26,868	40,102	36,409	26,155
Antigua and Barbuda	311	...	...	...	6	8	4	5	9	6	6	8	9	16	15	23
Argentina	213	289	952	935	246	1,244	2,596	3,812	7,127	5,268	2,808	2,272	1,120	1,268	†2,980	2,222
Aruba	314	...	...	...	...	...	...	...	...	...	...	...	...	...	...	60
Bahamas, The	313	34	36	41	46	41	†55	45	59	72	86	103	117	164	166	189
Barbados	316	26	27	32	34	24	30	46	50	62	86	110	118	135	127	124
Belize	339	...	...	...	...	5	7	11	8	10	9	9	9	6	13	22
Bolivia	218	41	46	144	119	130	174	130	135	83	86	141	153	257	182	134
Brazil	223	3,806	5,272	4,260	3,400	5,584	5,921	9,078	6,806	4,524	5,673	3,561	4,160	11,740	9,654	†4,744
Chile	228	89	101	34	48	349	351	837	1,471	2,449	2,761	1,645	1,945	2,350	2,230	1,922
Colombia	233	285	428	352	405	947	1,438	1,816	2,918	3,788	4,073	3,500	1,816	1,392	1,452	2,204
Costa Rica	238	37	40	34	42	82	157	149	90	114	113	205	297	413	461	428
Dominica	321	...	...	...	—	1	2	1	7	4	3	4	1	5	3	8
Dominican Republic	243	51	70	71	96	106	148	118	181	158	193	117	164	259	310	308
Ecuador	248	112	174	260	216	411	513	488	548	794	543	276	616	624	654	527
El Salvador	253	59	34	63	91	160	174	206	108	61	62	98	153	169	164	139
Grenada	328	5	4	4	†4	7	6	7	9	10	14	8	14	15	19	17
Guatemala	258	107	159	148	242	423	551	569	529	349	129	102	201	280	274	296
Guyana	336	34	12	51	86	23	19	45	13	10	6	10	6	6	6	7
Haiti	263	16	14	16	11	24	28	30	42	13	21	4	9	13	6	13
Honduras	268	32	35	36	83	113	148	142	159	117	87	102	109	131	96	91
Jamaica	343	147	106	156	107	28	39	45	48	82	73	99	60	99	147	80
Mexico	273	899	962	1,011	1,182	1,023	1,357	1,414	1,573	2,321	3,500	756	3,737	7,419	4,467	4,635
Netherlands Antilles	353	46	41	50	61	80	83	51	55	74	116	170	157	120	160	195
Nicaragua	278	74	96	85	104	126	122	39	111	51	96	155	167	...	...	...
Panama	283	40	35	32	29	68	58	115	90	92	103	92	197	220	89	139
Paraguay	288	29	47	71	98	136	221	344	462	597	692	670	650	680	486	365
Peru	293	408	436	756	363	249	294	299	1,154	1,552	1,031	1,223	1,304	1,663	1,677	1,150
St. Kitts and Nevis	361	...	...	...	...	...	...	...	...	...	...	3	3	3	6	7
St. Lucia	362	...	...	...	3	4	5	5	6	6	7	7	8	13	12	21
St. Vincent & Grens.	364	...	...	...	...	4	4	4	7	6	8	4	5	13	13	21
Suriname	366	35	47	55	78	95	77	102	129	148	178	159	56	25	21	17
Trinidad and Tobago	369	54	39	319	641	872	1,220	1,385	1,625	2,180	2,876	2,793	2,010	1,384	1,027	388
Uruguay	298	64	83	66	50	152	265	271	†245	301	369	105	198	137	159	394
Venezuela, Rep. Bol.	299	1,204	1,608	4,928	7,178	6,992	6,368	4,632	5,557	5,178	7,014	5,964	7,300	9,081	9,332	5,263

Memorandum Items

	Code	1972	1973	1974	1975	1976	1977	1978	1979	1980	1981	1982	1983	1984	1985	1986
Oil Exporting Countries	999	8,789	10,803	37,100	47,007	54,779	60,845	44,847	54,913	67,915	67,872	65,637	65,667	68,065	67,791	50,368
Non-Oil Developing Countries	201	20,416	26,085	27,059	26,927	38,274	47,575	55,827	63,049	67,314	75,289	76,713	90,452	113,019	107,629	116,972

1987	1988	1989	1990	1991	1992	1993	1994	1995	1996	1997	1998	1999	2000	2001		
End of Period																
25,883	21,974	24,376	33,339	45,685	64,064	78,936	71,366	86,883	108,261	125,530	114,080	111,788	119,802	126,152	Western Hemisphere	205
18	21	21	19	23	37	28	31	40	33	38	42	51	49	63	Antigua and Barbuda	311
1,140	2,499	1,113	3,228	4,198	7,265	10,040	9,814	9,612	12,590	16,542	17,579	19,127	19,301	11,580	Argentina	213
55	68	66	69	84	103	132	122	146	130	128	158	160	160	234	Aruba	314
120	128	112	111	127	113	125	121	121	119	168	246	299	268	254	Bahamas, The	313
102	101	83	83	61	102	110	134	147	201	196	260	220	363	549	Barbados	316
26	38	46	49	37	39	28	24	25	41	44	31	52	94	89	Belize	339
69	79	156	117	74	132	163	309	444	664	805	602	641	599	610	Bolivia	218
4,440	5,181	5,734	5,230	5,616	16,379	22,281	25,393	33,440	40,560	37,670	30,241	25,352	24,935	28,439	Brazil	223
1,765	2,349	2,761	4,266	4,922	6,667	7,018	8,965	9,512	10,315	12,826	11,124	10,497	11,305	11,315	Chile	228
2,175	2,413	2,752	3,253	4,567	5,634	5,774	5,474	5,616	6,846	7,265	6,144	5,834	6,843	8,079	Colombia	233
345	496	565	366	643	741	746	612	704	696	935	755	1,064	1,011	1,058	Costa Rica	238
13	10	9	10	12	15	14	11	15	16	18	20	23	23	25	Dominica	321
	128	189	125	43	309	363	474	173	246	290	356	506	481	875	Dominican Republic	243
346	295	411	589	646	631	1,005	1,263	1,095	1,292	1,551	1,150	1,197	727	668	Ecuador	248
131	120	202	292	201	307	390	445	510	652	969	1,146	1,460	1,475	1,385	El Salvador	253
16	13	12	12	12	19	20	21	25	25	32	33	37	44	51	Grenada	328
203	149	233	198	564	557	632	591	472	605	824	948	866	1,340	1,824	Guatemala	258
6	3	10	20	87	137	180	169	181	229	234	196	195	234	229	Guyana	336
12	10	10	2	25	20	23	35	129	150	158	188	193	141	113	Haiti	263
75	37	16	28	73	144	71	117	176	173	430	581	916	1,008	1,126	Honduras	268
123	109	82	118^e	74	236	304	504	458	612	506	504	404	809	1,513	Jamaica	343
8,786	3,923	4,816	6,933	12,392	13,776	18,281	4,301	11,333	13,514	21,343	22,584	23,156	27,253	35,601	Mexico	273
153	195	158	151	124	160	170	123	137	131	159	176	193	200	240	Netherlands Antilles	353
12	28	88	75	94	95	40	97	92	137	280	249	371	375	302	Nicaragua	278
55	54	91	241	349	367	435	482	526	603	851	....	....	555	....	Panama	283
350	241	329	465	673	408	460	706	735	730	619	614	713	584	568	Paraguay	288
455	380	615	731	1,708	2,072	2,481	4,790	5,531	7,356	8,140	6,794	6,361	6,427	6,900	Peru	293
7	8	12	11	12	19	21	22	23	23	27	33	36	35	45	St. Kitts and Nevis	361
22	24	29	31	34	40	44	40	42	39	45	50	54	61	71	St. Lucia	362
14	16	17	19	16	24	23	21	20	21	23	28	31	42	49	St. Vincent & Grens	364
11	9	7	15	1	13	13	27	89	67	81	75	28	48	95	Suriname	366
132	94	188	346	237	125	150	241	241	378	524	556	689	1,064	1,517	Trinidad and Tobago	369
374	395	381	368	235	370	552	663	774	870	1,154	1,472	1,516	1,903	2,464	Uruguay	298
4,203	2,297	3,125	5,849	7,457	6,954	6,709	5,526	4,227	8,198	10,656	8,466	8,945	10,046	7,352	Venezuela, Rep. Bol.	299

Memorandum Items

1987	1988	1989	1990	1991	1992	1993	1994	1995	1996	1997	1998	1999	2000	2001		
47,621	41,467	42,837	42,421	47,414	44,674	45,062	42,977	43,274	59,724	70,547	69,883	77,143	102,277	110,344	Oil Exporting Countries	999
135,669	148,284	166,051	198,893	244,589	278,629	339,234	381,528	457,428	533,692	613,394	629,006	702,610	793,241	903,032	Non-Oil Developing Countries	201

Nongold Reserves/Imports

lrl s

Weeks of Imports

		1972	1973	1974	1975	1976	1977	1978	1979	1980	1981	1982	1983	1984	1985	1986
World	001	**15.4**	**13.1**	**11.1**	**11.1**	**11.5**	**12.9**	**12.9**	**11.4**	**10.8**	**10.1**	**10.1**	**11.1**	**10.8**	**11.9**	**12.5**
Industrial Countries	110	**15.0**	**11.9**	**8.4**	**8.5**	**8.1**	**9.6**	**10.8**	**9.1**	**8.8**	**8.5**	**8.5**	**9.2**	**8.6**	**9.5**	**10.3**
United States	111	2.4	1.9	2.0	2.3	2.8	2.5	2.0	1.8	3.2	3.6	4.7	4.4	3.6	4.7	5.1
Canada	156	13.5	10.2	7.4	6.4	6.4	4.5	4.0	2.6	2.6	2.6	2.7	2.8	1.7	1.6	2.0
Australia	193	60.6	37.9	17.2	14.4	12.2	7.9	6.9	4.1	3.9	3.3	12.4	21.7	14.9	11.6	14.4
Japan	158	38.3	15.4	10.6	10.7	12.6	16.3	21.1	9.2	9.1	10.3	9.2	10.1	10.1	10.6	17.2
New Zealand	196	28.4	25.0	9.1	7.0	7.8	6.8	6.7	5.1	3.3	6.1	5.7	7.6	15.0	13.8	32.3
Euro Area																
Austria	122	19.2	14.6	14.6	19.8	16.1	12.2	16.4	10.5	11.2	13.1	14.1	12.1	11.2	11.8	11.9
Belgium	124	....	....	....	....	....	....	....	....	....	....	....	....	....	....	....
Finland	172	11.0	6.9	4.5	3.0	3.3	3.6	8.1	7.0	6.2	5.4	5.9	5.0	11.5	14.7	6.1
France	132	11.9	5.9	4.4	8.2	4.6	4.3	5.9	8.5	10.5	9.6	7.4	9.7	10.4	12.8	12.6
Germany	134	24.9	26.7	20.4	18.2	17.7	17.8	20.7	17.1	13.4	13.9	15.0	14.5	13.6	14.6	14.1
Greece	174	19.9	13.4	9.3	9.4	7.6	8.0	8.7	7.3	6.6	6.0	4.5	4.9	5.3	4.5	7.0
Ireland	178	27.4	18.8	17.0	20.8	22.5	22.7	19.5	11.6	13.3	13.0	14.0	15.0	12.6	15.3	14.5
Italy	136	8.0	5.5	4.3	1.8	3.8	8.8	10.2	12.1	11.9	11.1	8.4	13.1	12.7	9.2	10.3
Luxembourg	137	....	....	....	....	....	....	....	....	....	....	....	....	.5	.5	.4
Netherlands	138	6.9	7.7	6.2	6.2	5.8	5.6	4.3	5.1	6.8	6.4	7.3	7.8	6.9	7.7	7.7
Portugal	182	30.5	28.9	13.4	5.4	2.2	4.0	8.6	7.4	4.4	2.8	2.4	2.4	3.4	9.5	7.8
Spain	184	34.1	33.2	19.8	17.6	14.0	17.4	28.1	27.0	18.1	17.5	12.7	13.2	21.6	19.4	21.9
Denmark	128	8.0	8.3	4.5	4.0	3.5	6.2	11.0	9.1	9.1	7.5	7.1	11.6	9.4	15.5	11.3
Iceland	176	18.7	14.3	4.7	4.9	8.8	8.4	10.5	10.3	9.0	11.7	8.0	9.5	7.9	11.8	14.4
Norway	142	15.3	12.7	11.7	11.8	10.2	8.9	12.9	16.0	18.6	20.8	23.1	25.5	35.1	46.5	32.1
Sweden	144	8.7	10.9	4.6	8.5	6.0	8.8	10.4	6.4	5.3	6.5	6.6	8.0	7.6	10.6	10.4
Switzerland	146	27.0	22.4	19.6	27.4	33.8	29.8	38.8	29.1	22.4	23.7	28.0	26.8	26.9	30.5	27.6
United Kingdom	112	9.1	7.5	5.8	4.5	3.1	16.6	11.0	10.3	9.3	7.7	6.5	5.9	4.7	6.1	7.6
Developing Countries	200	**16.5**	**16.5**	**18.2**	**16.6**	**19.7**	**20.4**	**17.7**	**17.2**	**14.6**	**13.0**	**13.0**	**14.3**	**15.4**	**17.0**	**17.8**
Africa	605	**11.5**	**12.3**	**18.4**	**14.0**	**14.4**	**11.7**	**8.3**	**12.7**	**12.4**	**7.2**	**5.4**	**5.6**	**5.5**	**8.4**	**8.1**
Algeria	612	9.9	21.2	18.7	10.7	18.1	12.3	12.0	16.5	18.6	17.0	11.7	9.4	7.4	14.9	9.4
Benin	638	16.1	15.4	12.2	4.2	4.6	4.0	2.6	2.3	1.3	5.5	.6	.6	.4	.6	.5
Botswana	616	....	....	....	....	18.0	17.6	20.6	25.2	25.1	14.9	19.9	26.1	33.1	58.7	70.4
Burkina Faso	748	36.0	33.2	30.1	26.3	25.8	14.0	8.3	10.6	9.9	10.9	9.3	15.2	21.9	21.9	30.0
Burundi	618	30.4	35.7	17.1	25.9	44.0	66.2	43.0	30.7	29.3	19.8	7.2	7.7	5.5	8.2	17.8
Cameroon	622	7.5	8.0	9.4	2.5	3.7	3.0	2.6	5.1	6.1	3.1	2.9	6.8	2.5	6.0	1.8
Cape Verde	624	....	....	....	....	56.5	58.0	38.3	41.5	32.5	27.8	25.3	25.2	21.9	33.4	20.5
Central African Rep.	626	2.6	1.8	2.0	2.9	17.8	20.8	22.2	32.9	35.2	38.0	19.5	36.0	31.5	22.9	20.3
Chad	628	8.4	.9	9.1	1.2	10.5	5.2	2.8	6.9	3.6	3.5	5.9	9.3	12.7	10.5	3.9
Comoros	632	....	....	....	....	....	....	....	....	11.4	13.5	17.3	16.3	4.2	16.8	24.6
Congo, Dem. Rep. of	636	30.7	35.7	17.7	8.3	11.6	34.3	33.3	54.0	38.1	35.4	12.6	33.7	10.4	12.5	16.0
Congo, Rep. of	634	5.2	3.2	10.0	4.3	3.8	3.4	1.9	7.2	7.7	14.4	2.5	.6	.3	.3	.6
Côte d'Ivoire	662	10.0	6.5	3.5	4.7	3.1	5.5	10.0	3.1	.3	.4	.1	.6	.2	.1	.6
Djibouti	611	....	....	....	....	....	....	....	....	....	....	....	....	10.5	13.2	15.1
Equatorial Guinea	642	....	....	....	....	....	....	....	....	....	....	4.7	3.6	4.1	9.1	6.3
Ethiopia	644	22.8	40.3	48.4	46.0	43.5	31.5	17.5	15.8	5.8	18.8	12.0	7.5	2.5	7.7	6.3
Gabon	646	8.7	13.1	16.2	16.2	12.0	.7	1.9	2.0	8.3	12.3	18.7	14.2	14.3	11.7	7.6
Gambia, The	648	23.9	27.1	31.4	24.9	14.5	16.3	13.5	.7	1.8	1.6	4.2	1.3	1.2	1.0	6.8
Ghana	652	16.7	20.3	4.5	8.2	5.5	7.4	14.3	17.6	8.3	6.8	10.2	3.0	25.8	28.7	25.5
Guinea-Bissau	654	....	....	....	....	....	....	....	....	....	....	....	....	....	....	....
Kenya	664	19.6	19.6	9.8	9.5	14.8	21.1	10.7	19.9	12.0	6.2	6.7	14.7	13.8	14.1	-.5
Lesotho	666	....	....	....	....	....	....	....	....	6.1	4.9	5.4	7.2	5.8	6.7	13.3
Liberia	668	....	....	3.4	3.0	2.2	3.1	1.9	5.6	.5	1.0	.8	2.6	.5	.3	.5
Madagascar	674	13.2	17.4	9.1	5.1	7.7	10.3	6.9	.4	.8	2.5	2.5	3.9	8.4	6.3	16.9
Malawi	676	14.6	24.7	22.7	12.6	6.6	19.4	11.5	9.1	8.1	7.1	3.9	2.6	10.9	7.9	5.0
Mali	678	2.5	1.7	1.8	1.2	2.3	1.8	1.5	.9	1.7	2.4	2.6	2.4	5.0	3.9	1.4
Mauritania	682	10.1	17.2	44.9	15.4	23.9	12.6	22.8	22.9	25.5	31.8	26.2	24.3	19.4	13.2	11.3
Mauritius	684	30.6	20.6	22.0	26.0	12.9	7.7	4.8	2.6	7.7	3.2	4.2	2.1	2.6	2.9	10.3
Morocco	686	14.3	10.9	10.7	7.1	9.3	8.2	10.8	7.9	4.9	2.7	2.6	1.5	.6	1.6	2.9
Namibia	728	....	....	....	....	....	....	....	....	....	....	....	....	....	....	....
Niger	692	32.7	30.8	24.5	25.9	34.0	26.7	21.9	14.9	11.0	10.7	3.3	8.5	16.0	19.2	26.7
Nigeria	694	12.3	15.6	105.1	48.1	32.8	19.8	7.7	28.2	31.9	9.7	5.2	4.2	8.1	9.8	13.9
Rwanda	714	9.6	23.5	11.6	13.5	31.5	35.1	24.2	41.2	39.9	35.1	24.2	21.4	20.0	19.7	24.2
Senegal	722	7.2	1.7	.7	2.8	2.1	2.3	1.3	1.1	.4	.4	.6	.6	.2	.3	.5
Seychelles	718	....	8.9	9.3	10.4	8.6	13.1	8.3	7.4	9.7	7.7	6.9	5.9	3.2	4.5	3.8
Sierra Leone	724	20.3	17.3	12.8	8.0	8.6	9.6	6.5	7.7	3.7	2.5	1.5	5.3	2.6	3.7	5.4
South Africa	199	8.0	4.5	2.5	3.1	3.0	3.5	2.9	2.5	1.9	1.5	1.4	2.7	.8	1.4	1.5
Sudan	732	5.8	7.3	10.1	2.1	1.3	1.1	1.2	3.2	1.6	.6	.8	.8	.8	.8	3.2
Swaziland	734	....	....	5.1	13.3	19.1	27.0	19.0	13.6	13.2	8.5	7.6	8.7	9.4	13.7	14.2
Tanzania	738	15.4	15.1	3.5	4.4	9.1	19.7	4.5	3.2	.8	.8	.2	1.3	2.1	1.0	3.4
Togo	742	22.3	19.6	23.7	12.3	18.7	8.4	8.1	6.6	7.3	18.2	22.2	31.9	39.0	53.5	57.0
Tunisia	744	24.3	23.0	19.0	13.9	12.4	10.0	10.8	10.6	8.7	7.4	9.2	9.5	6.6	4.4	5.5
Uganda	746	11.5	9.3	4.1	7.8	13.4	10.2	10.8	6.0	.5	4.5	10.8	14.7	10.3	4.3	4.9
Zambia	754	14.6	18.1	10.9	7.9	7.2	5.1	4.3	5.6	3.7	2.7	3.0	5.2	4.7	14.4	6.1
Zimbabwe	698	6.7	10.7	4.3	4.5	5.7	5.3	11.2	16.7	7.7	5.2	4.4	3.2	2.1	5.4	5.6
Asia	505	**15.2**	**13.1**	**10.4**	**9.8**	**13.7**	**16.7**	**14.7**	**13.2**	**11.0**	**11.2**	**12.9**	**15.0**	**16.0**	**17.2**	**22.1**
Afghanistan, Islamic State of	512	6.6	6.5	5.9	12.9	26.1	43.7	51.4	53.9	23.0	16.1	13.9	10.5	8.6	12.9	9.6
Bangladesh	513	20.6	7.5	6.7	5.8	15.8	10.4	10.8	10.5	6.0	2.7	3.9	12.6	7.2	6.9	8.4
China, P.R.: Mainland	924	....	....	....	....	....	17.1	7.3	7.2	6.6	11.9	30.6	36.4	32.9	15.7	13.9
China, P.R.: Hong Kong	532	....	....	....	....	....	....	....	....	....	....	....	....	....	....	....
Fiji	819	22.6	17.3	20.8	28.8	22.9	24.9	19.7	15.1	15.5	11.1	13.0	12.4	13.6	14.9	20.5
India	534	21.4	13.7	10.4	8.9	25.6	38.1	42.5	39.3	24.3	15.8	15.2	18.3	19.9	21.0	21.6
Indonesia	536	19.1	15.3	20.2	6.4	13.7	20.9	20.4	29.3	25.9	19.6	9.7	11.8	17.9	25.2	19.7
Korea	542	10.8	10.9	2.1	5.6	11.7	14.3	9.6	7.6	6.8	5.3	6.0	4.7	4.7	4.8	5.5
Lao People's Democratic Rep.	544	....	....	....	....	....	....	....	....	....	....	....	....	....	....	....
Malaysia	548	29.3	27.1	19.6	21.2	32.7	31.9	28.5	25.9	21.2	18.4	15.8	14.8	13.8	20.8	29.0
Maldives	556	....	....	....	....	.1	.4	2.1	1.7	1.7	1.9	10.1	4.2	5.0	4.5	8.0
Mongolia	948	....	....	....	....	....	....	....	....	....	....	....	....	....	....	....
Myanmar	518	15.8	45.1	53.8	35.1	34.7	22.3	16.3	33.2	38.3	31.9	13.3	17.4	13.5	6.2	5.7

Nongold Reserves/Imports

1rl s

Weeks of Imports

1987	1988	1989	1990	1991	1992	1993	1994	1995	1996	1997	1998	1999	2000	2001	Country	Code
14.9	13.2	13.0	13.8	14.2	13.5	15.0	15.1	14.7	15.7	15.7	16.4	16.9	16.1	17.6	World	001
13.1	11.9	11.7	11.9	11.5	10.5	11.5	11.3	11.0	11.5	11.2	10.7	10.6	10.2	10.7	Industrial Countries	110
4.3	4.2	6.7	7.3	6.8	5.7	5.4	4.8	5.0	4.1	3.4	3.9	3.0	2.3	2.5	United States	111
4.1	7.1	7.0	7.5	6.8	4.6	4.7	4.1	4.7	6.1	4.6	5.9	6.6	6.8	7.8	Canada	156
15.5	19.6	15.9	20.1	20.6	13.3	12.7	11.0	10.1	11.5	13.3	11.8	15.9	13.2	14.6	Australia	193
27.9	26.8	20.8	17.3	15.8	16.0	21.2	23.8	28.4	32.3	33.7	39.9	47.9	48.6	58.9	Japan	158
23.3	20.1	17.9	22.6	18.3	17.4	18.0	16.2	16.4	21.0	15.9	17.5	16.2	12.4	11.7	New Zealand	196
															Euro Area	
12.0	10.5	11.5	9.9	10.6	11.9	15.6	15.8	14.7	17.7	15.8	17.1	11.3	10.8	9.2	Austria	122
						5.2	5.5	5.3	5.4	5.4	5.9	3.5	2.9	3.3	Belgium	124
17.0	15.7	10.9	18.6	18.1	12.8	15.6	23.9	18.6	12.3	14.7	15.6	13.5	13.0	12.9	Finland	172
10.8	7.4	6.6	8.2	7.0	5.9	5.8	5.8	5.0	4.9	5.9	8.0	7.0	6.2	5.6	France	132
17.9	12.2	11.7	10.2	8.4	11.8	11.7	10.4	9.5	9.4	9.1	8.2	6.7	5.9	5.5	Germany	134
10.6	15.3	10.4	9.0	12.5	10.9	20.1	35.2	28.7	30.7	23.5	30.9	32.8	23.9	9.0	Greece	174
18.3	17.0	12.1	13.1	14.4	8.0	14.4	12.5	13.8	11.9	8.6	10.8	5.8	5.4	5.7	Ireland	178
12.5	13.0	15.9	18.0	13.9	7.6	9.7	9.9	8.8	11.5	13.8	7.1	5.3	5.6	5.5	Italy	136
.4	.4	.6	.6	.5	.5	.5	.5	.4	.4	.4		.4	.4	.5	Luxembourg	137
9.1	8.4	8.2	7.2	7.3	8.5	13.1	12.7	9.9	7.7	7.3	5.9	2.8	2.5	2.4	Netherlands	138
12.4	14.9	27.1	29.8	40.6	32.8	33.9	29.5	24.7	23.5	23.2	21.4	11.6	12.1		Portugal	182
32.5	31.9	30.4	30.4	36.8	23.7	26.8	23.4	15.8	24.7	29.0	21.6	11.9	10.5	10.0	Spain	184
20.5	21.6	12.5	17.1	11.9	16.3	17.5	13.5	12.7	16.5	22.6	17.5	26.3	18.0	20.5	Denmark	128
10.2	9.5	12.5	13.5	13.3	15.4	16.5	10.3	9.1	11.6	10.0	8.9	9.9	7.8	7.8	Iceland	176
32.8	29.7	30.3	29.3	26.9	24.0	42.6	36.2	35.5	38.7	34.1	26.7	31.2	32.1	25.0	Norway	142
10.4	9.7	10.1	17.2	19.1	23.5	23.2	23.4	19.3	14.8	8.6	10.7	11.4	10.6	11.6	Sweden	144
28.2	22.3	22.6	21.8	22.7	28.0	29.9	28.2	24.6	26.8	28.6	29.0	25.0	22.1	21.6	Switzerland	146
14.1	12.1	9.1	8.3	10.4	8.6	9.3	9.4	8.2	7.2	5.5	5.3	5.9	6.8	6.0	United Kingdom	112
19.8	16.4	16.3	18.7	20.7	19.9	21.8	22.4	22.0	23.5	24.1	28.1	30.1	27.7	30.6	Developing Countries	200
9.1	8.1	9.2	11.6	14.2	11.3	12.9	14.9	13.0	15.8	20.6	20.0	21.0	25.3	28.3	Africa	605
12.1	6.1	4.7	3.9	9.9	8.9	9.9	14.8	10.2	24.9	48.1	37.9	25.7	59.2	78.2	Algeria	612
.5	.7	.9	12.7	41.3	22.1	22.2	31.1	13.8	20.8	19.3	20.2	27.8	38.9	46.2	Benin	638
94.6	79.3	75.2	89.0	99.6	104.5	120.7	139.5	127.8	151.7	130.7	129.4	147.9	133.1	539.0	Botswana	616
38.6	36.8	35.3	29.2	33.8	38.1	39.1	35.4	39.7	27.2	30.5	26.5	26.5	23.0	20.7	Burkina Faso	748
14.9	17.7	27.7	23.7	28.8	40.9	43.2	47.4	46.5	57.1	48.4	21.6	21.1	11.6	6.6	Burundi	618
1.9	7.2	3.3	.9	1.9	.9	.1	.2	.2	.1	—	—	.2			Cameroon	622
41.8	39.8	34.8	29.5	23.1	21.9	19.5	10.5	7.6		4.3	1.9	8.6	6.2	9.5	Cape Verde	624
24.6	40.0	39.1	39.9	57.7	35.8	46.4	78.4	69.8	85.4	64.2	47.6	50.7	266.7		Central African Rep.	626
12.0	14.4	24.7	23.3	24.9	17.2	10.1	22.3	20.3	25.8	21.2	17.5	15.6	17.5	10.1	Chad	628
30.8	23.3	37.6	29.9	26.1	20.6	33.8	43.5	37.0							Comoros	632
12.4	12.7	11.9	12.8	13.4	19.4	6.5	16.4	19.2	10.1						Congo, Dem. Rep. of	636
.2	.2	.3	.5	.4	.5	.1	4.1	4.6	3.1	3.4	.1	4.4	17.6		Congo, Rep. of	634
.2	.3	.4	.1	.3	.2	.1	5.5	9.4	10.9	11.6	14.9	10.1	13.7	20.8	Côte d'Ivoire	662
16.1	16.6	15.7	22.7	24.3	19.8	18.5	19.5	21.2	22.4	23.4	21.8	24.1			Djibouti	611
.6	4.7	5.7	.6	7.3	12.4	.4	.5	—	.1	.8	.1	.4	2.7		Equatorial Guinea	642
6.0	3.0	2.5	1.0	6.0	14.4	30.1	27.4	35.0	27.2			18.1			Ethiopia	644
.9	4.4	2.3	15.5	20.4	5.3	—	12.0	8.7	13.5	13.3	.7	1.1	9.9		Gabon	646
10.5	7.2	6.6	15.3	17.4	22.4	21.1	24.0	30.3	20.6	28.7	22.6	30.1			Gambia, The	648
8.8	12.7	14.2		27.1	7.7	5.4	14.4	19.0	20.4	12.0	7.6	6.8	4.1		Ghana	652
	12.5	14.0	11.1	10.0	9.6	12.0	5.9	7.9	6.9	19.7	27.2	26.7	55.8		Guinea-Bissau	654
7.7	6.9	6.8	4.8	3.1	1.5	11.9	13.9	6.1	13.2	12.5	12.7	14.5	15.0	17.3	Kenya	664
7.5	5.0	4.3	5.6	7.4	9.1	15.1	22.8	24.1	24.0	29.0	34.6	33.2	29.9	29.5	Lesotho	666
.1	.1														Liberia	668
31.9	30.7	34.3	7.4	10.6	9.8	9.0	8.5	10.4	24.7	31.2	17.3	31.3			Madagascar	674
9.1	18.0	10.3	12.4	11.3	2.8	5.4	4.5	12.1	18.8	10.8	24.2	18.7	22.6		Malawi	676
2.2	3.7	17.7	16.4	36.1	26.4	27.3	19.5	21.7	29.0	29.2	27.7	22.2	33.5	27.6	Mali	678
15.9	12.1	19.3	12.8	5.9		5.1									Mauritania	682
17.6	17.8	20.3	23.7	29.8	26.3	22.9	20.1	22.7	20.4	16.5	14.0	16.9			Mauritius	684
5.1	6.0	4.6	15.5	23.5	25.4	28.2	27.4	18.7	20.3	21.8	22.4	29.8	21.7	40.2	Morocco	686
					2.0	5.9	8.8								Namibia	728
41.6	31.2	30.4	29.7	29.7	24.4	26.6	17.5	13.2	9.1	7.1	7.3	5.0	11.2		Niger	692
15.5	7.2	21.9	35.7	25.7	6.1	12.9	10.9	9.1	32.9	41.5	40.1	33.0	59.1	48.9	Nigeria	694
24.3	16.6	11.0	8.0	18.7	14.2	7.4	33.9	21.7	21.6	26.8	30.8	35.8	46.5	44.2	Rwanda	714
.5	.5	.8	.5	.6	.6	.2	9.1	10.0	10.4	13.9	15.9	14.2	13.1		Senegal	722
6.3	2.8	3.8	4.6	8.3	8.5	7.8	7.6	6.1	3.0	4.0	2.9	3.6			Seychelles	718
2.4	2.5	1.1	1.9	3.1	6.8	10.2	14.0	13.5	6.6	21.6	24.2	25.4	17.7	14.8	Sierra Leone	724
2.2	2.2	2.7	2.8	2.5	2.6	2.7	3.8	4.8	1.6	7.6	7.7	12.4	10.7	11.1	South Africa	199
.7	.6		1.0	.4	1.7	2.1	3.5	7.2	3.7	2.7	2.4	6.9	8.3		Sudan	732
15.1	14.3	16.1	17.0	12.5	18.6	15.8	16.7	14.1	11.2	12.9					Swaziland	734
1.8	4.9	2.8	7.4	6.9	11.3	7.1	11.5	8.4	16.5	24.2	21.4	25.9	33.3	35.1	Tanzania	738
43.6	24.8	31.4	31.6	42.7	35.9	45.3	22.1	11.4	6.9	9.6	10.4	10.6	14.0	18.5	Togo	742
9.0	12.7	11.4	7.5	7.9	6.9	7.1	11.5	10.6	12.8	13.0	11.5	13.9	11.0	10.8	Tunisia	744
3.3	2.9	1.7	8.0	15.6	9.7	12.4	19.1	22.6	23.1	25.0	26.6	29.6	27.3	32.1	Uganda	746
7.7	8.3	6.7	8.2	11.7		12.4	23.5	16.5	13.9	15.2					Zambia	754
8.2	8.2	3.0	4.2	3.8	5.2	12.4	9.4	11.6	11.1						Zimbabwe	698
25.8	21.3	19.8	22.9	24.5	22.3	23.2	25.0	23.0	25.0	25.7	34.8	36.3	31.9	37.2	Asia	505
14.6	15.1	15.4	14.8	19.3											Afghanistan, Islamic State of	512
16.1	17.9	7.1	9.0	19.5	25.4	31.4	35.5	18.7	14.4	11.9	14.2	10.8	9.2	7.9	Bangladesh	513
19.6	17.4	15.8	28.8	35.6	13.3	11.3	23.8	30.4	40.1	52.2	55.3	49.5	42.5	46.0	China, P.R.: Mainland	924
			15.5	14.9	14.8	16.1	15.8	14.9	16.7	23.1	25.3	27.9	26.3	28.7	China, P.R.: Hong Kong	532
18.1	26.3	19.0	18.0	21.7	26.1	19.5	16.9	20.4	22.5	19.4	27.8				Fiji	819
20.1	13.3	9.8	3.4	9.2	12.7	23.3	38.2	26.9	27.6	31.0	33.1	36.2	38.4	48.1	India	534
23.5	19.8	17.3	17.8	18.6	19.9	20.7	19.7	17.5	22.1	20.7	43.2	57.3	44.2	38.2	Indonesia	536
4.5	12.4	12.9	11.0	8.7	10.9	12.6	13.0	12.6	11.8	7.3	29.0	32.1	31.1	37.9	Korea	542
—	.2	.4	.5	8.8	7.8	7.6	5.6	8.1	12.8	8.3	10.6	10.0	13.5	12.4	Lao People's Democratic Rep.	544
30.5	20.6	18.0	17.3	15.4	22.5	31.0	22.2	15.9	17.9	13.7	22.8	24.5	18.7	15.3	Malaysia	548
5.3	12.5	11.4	9.2	7.6	7.7	7.1	7.3	9.3	13.1	14.7	17.4	16.4	16.4	12.2	Maldives	556
					2.0	8.2	16.4	14.7	12.4	19.5	9.7	16.7			Mongolia	948
5.3	16.5	71.7	60.2	20.8	22.4	19.4	24.8	21.9	8.8	6.4	6.1	6.0	4.9	7.5	Myanmar	518

Nongold Reserves/Imports

1rl s		1972	1973	1974	1975	1976	1977	1978	1979	1980	1981	1982	1983	1984	1985	1986
															Weeks of Imports	
Asia (cont.)																
Nepal	558	60.1	59.0	47.0	29.0	40.7	43.1	34.1	32.5	27.8	28.4	26.2	14.9	10.2	6.4	9.8
Pakistan	564	16.8	22.0	11.7	8.2	11.1	9.5	6.4	2.7	4.8	6.6	9.2	19.2	9.2	7.1	6.8
Papua New Guinea	853	...	4.6	3.3	15.8	26.6	34.5	27.3	29.0	18.7	16.3	20.1	20.4	20.4	22.8	20.5
Philippines	566	17.6	28.7	21.9	18.2	21.1	18.0	17.8	17.7	17.8	12.7	5.6	4.9	4.9	5.9	17.1
Samoa	862	12.2	11.2	11.8	9.0	9.2	11.5	4.7	3.5	2.3	3.0	3.6	7.8	10.9	14.2	26.3
Singapore	576	26.8	23.2	17.4	19.2	19.3	19.2	21.1	17.1	14.2	14.2	15.7	17.1	18.9	25.4	26.4
Solomon Islands	813	...	...	...	...	...	4.5	35.8	27.5	17.2	12.4	27.3	33.5	29.6	22.3	21.3
Sri Lanka	524	8.4	10.5	5.6	3.9	8.2	21.7	21.4	18.5	6.2	8.9	9.1	8.0	14.2	11.8	9.4
Thailand	578	33.7	30.6	29.1	26.6	26.2	20.4	19.5	13.4	8.8	9.0	9.4	8.1	9.6	12.3	15.9
Tonga	866						23.8	20.6	22.3	19.0	18.1	19.5	29.0	33.4	34.7	28.8
Vanuatu	846	...	...	...	...	...	...	...	...	...	...	7.6	4.9	5.4	6.1	7.9	19.5
Europe	170	...	...	...	...	...	...	...	...	...	...	...	...	...	...	...
Albania	914															
Cyprus	423	49.8	33.3	32.0	33.4	33.0	26.2	23.7	18.2	15.9	19.0	22.4	22.1	20.6	24.8	30.8
Czech Republic	935															
Czechoslovakia	934										7.5	4.2	3.3	3.4	4.2	3.7	4.0
Estonia	939															
Hungary	944													7.5	10.0	13.6	12.5
Kazakhstan	916															
Malta	181	77.4	67.5	55.7	67.3	74.7	72.6	83.6	69.3	54.9	64.9	71.4	79.0	71.8	67.6	67.1
Moldova	921															
Poland	964	...	...	...	...	...	...	...	...	1.8	.4	1.1	3.2	3.6	5.2	3.8	3.1
Romania	968	...	3.0	2.3	4.9	4.4	1.8	2.0	2.3	1.2	1.6	2.2	2.6	3.3	.9	2.6
Russia	922															
Slovak Republic	936															
Turkey	186	42.0	49.5	21.5	10.4	10.0	5.7	9.1	6.8	7.1	5.4	6.4	7.3	6.1	4.8	6.6
Ukraine	926															
Yugoslavia, SFR	188	10.9	14.7	7.5	5.5	14.0	11.0	12.4	5.1	4.8	5.3	3.0	4.2	5.0	4.7	6.5
Middle East	405	37.2	34.0	57.4	50.0	50.3	47.8	35.2	37.0	33.8	27.9	25.4	24.6	24.2	31.4	31.2
Bahrain	419	11.5	6.5	6.1	12.7	13.6	12.9	12.5	12.9	14.2	19.5	22.1	22.7	19.5	27.8	32.2
Egypt	469	3.0	14.8	5.6	2.6	3.3	4.7	3.8	7.2	11.2	4.2	4.0	3.9	3.6	3.7	3.7
Iran, I.R. of	429	17.7	16.5	78.7	44.0	35.0	44.7	46.0	81.2	43.4	5.7	24.8	...	...	...	...
Iraq	433	46.1	80.2	67.9	31.6	59.2	79.1									
Israel	436	24.8	21.7	11.0	9.9	12.2	13.7	18.4	18.6	17.8	17.8	20.7	19.8	16.2	19.4	22.4
Jordan	439	45.8	42.7	33.3	32.6	24.4	24.2	30.6	30.9	24.7	17.9	14.2	14.1	9.6	8.0	9.3
Kuwait	443	17.5	18.9	41.8	32.5	26.6	30.9	28.3	28.7	31.3	30.3	37.1	36.6	34.6	47.4	50.0
Lebanon	446	18.3	19.1	28.2	30.5	110.6	53.0	49.6	29.5	22.6	22.5	40.0	27.0	11.8	25.3	11.5
Libya	672	141.2	58.3	66.1	30.8	50.3	66.0	46.4	62.1	100.5	55.9	51.2	45.0	30.4	74.9	69.6
Oman	449	38.8	21.1	12.3	11.0	15.7	17.2	13.9	17.3	17.5	16.9	16.9	15.9	17.0	18.0	21.0
Qatar	453	19.8	18.0	12.2	12.2	8.2	6.9	9.2	10.5	12.5	12.5	10.3	13.7	17.0	20.4	27.1
Saudi Arabia	456	109.1	98.8	257.3	286.3	160.9	106.1	48.9	41.0	40.4	47.6	37.8	36.2	38.2	55.0	49.9
Syrian Arab Rep.	463	10.1	32.1	19.7	21.7	6.4	9.3	8.1	9.1	4.2	2.9	2.6	.6	3.4	1.1	2.7
United Arab Emirates	466	...	5.8	13.8	19.1	29.7	8.2	7.9	10.7	12.0	17.3	12.2	13.0	17.1	25.4	27.3
Yemen Arab Rep.	473	...	53.7	54.3	59.7	90.8	62.0	59.1	49.8	36.0	28.4	18.9	11.8	10.6	11.8	19.4
Yemen, P.D. Rep.	459	23.2	22.9	8.3	8.7	10.3	9.5	17.0	11.8	8.0	9.3	9.3	9.9	8.4	6.7	14.9
Yemen, Republic of	474	...	...	...	...	...	...	...	...	...	...	...	...	...	...	...
Western Hemisphere	205	20.8	23.9	17.8	17.2	21.1	23.0	25.6	24.9	16.9	15.4	13.5	18.3	24.9	26.7	20.7
Antigua and Barbuda	311	...	...	...	5.7	14.3	7.7	7.6	9.3	4.6	3.4	3.2	4.7	6.1	5.2	7.1
Argentina	213	8.6	26.8	16.4	3.8	24.8	39.4	67.4	72.9	33.1	18.0	24.4	13.5	14.1	44.6	29.9
Aruba	314															20.0
Bahamas, The	313	4.0	2.9	1.4	1.0	.8	1.0	1.0	1.1	.6	.7	.9	1.4	2.0	3.1	3.7
Barbados	316	10.3	10.0	10.0	9.5	6.1	7.1	9.9	8.1	7.8	9.1	11.4	10.3	10.4	11.9	13.4
Belize	339					3.9	4.6	6.8	4.1	4.4	3.3	4.0	4.3	2.4	6.0	11.5
Bolivia	218	12.4	12.4	23.5	13.0	14.2	17.8	10.9	10.4	8.3	5.7	14.6	14.4	26.8	15.1	12.6
Brazil	223	44.9	47.3	19.1	15.2	24.6	28.2	40.9	23.5	12.0	14.3	9.7	13.5	39.3	38.5	19.4
Chile	228	4.6	4.9	1.0	1.9	11.3	8.7	16.6	21.0	28.0	23.3	23.7	34.3	33.5	41.5	35.6
Colombia	233	18.7	25.3	14.0	16.5	34.4	48.3	41.4	59.4	53.0	47.4	36.6	19.9	15.8	20.0	36.3
Costa Rica	238	5.7	5.5	3.0	3.7	6.4	9.7	8.6	4.4	4.9	5.7	13.2	16.4	19.3	24.0	23.7
Dominica	321				.9	3.2	5.3	3.5	23.0	5.5	3.2	4.7	1.7	4.7	3.1	8.9
Dominican Republic	243	7.4	9.0	5.6	6.6	7.3	9.6	8.1	10.2	6.4	7.0	4.6	6.1	9.1	11.9	13.7
Ecuador	248	19.8	27.5	24.4	13.3	25.9	27.3	22.0	23.5	23.4	14.6	7.3	22.5	19.7	21.1	18.5
El Salvador	253	12.2	5.7	7.2	9.1	13.1	11.8	13.6	7.1	4.2	3.8	6.6	9.3	8.8	9.7	9.4
Grenada	328	13.1	12.0	15.3	10.9	16.7	12.3	14.1	14.5	13.4	15.4	8.5	12.9	13.2	15.6	13.2
Guatemala	258	18.7	23.1	13.5	20.1	30.4	33.0	30.0	24.1	14.5	4.6	4.2	9.7	11.2	13.3	19.6
Guyana	336	13.4	4.1	12.8	15.2	3.9	3.8	10.9	2.9	1.7	.8	2.0	1.4	1.4	1.5	1.9
Haiti	263	13.5	10.6	8.2	4.3	7.0	8.3	8.6	10.5	2.2	2.7	.6	1.1	1.5	.8	2.3
Honduras	268	9.4	8.3	6.0	12.6	14.9	16.3	13.8	13.2	7.7	5.5	8.3	7.4	7.5	6.2	6.6
Jamaica	343	13.0	9.8	10.6	5.8	1.8	2.9	3.4	3.3	4.7	3.0	4.1	2.2	4.4	7.5	5.3
Mexico	273	18.7	15.8	10.6	10.9	10.2	15.6	11.8	8.9	7.0	7.4	2.4	16.3	22.7	13.3	16.8
Netherlands Antilles	353	3.0	1.6	.9	1.3	1.3	1.7	1.0	.9	.9	1.2	1.9	1.9	1.5	6.6	11.2
Nicaragua	278	19.1	18.5	9.7	12.2	14.3	10.1	4.4	21.2	3.8	5.8	11.5	11.0	...	...	...
Panama	283	5.1	4.3	2.5	2.0	4.8	4.3	8.3	5.2	4.2	4.0	3.3	7.6	7.9	3.7	7.2
Paraguay	288	19.8	24.2	22.8	29.1	37.2	45.2	62.9	60.8	64.4	69.9	57.2	64.8	59.1	55.3	40.2
Peru	293	28.9	26.9	31.4	8.7	7.4	9.7	17.3	43.4	41.2	17.9	19.5	27.9	38.3	52.2	25.2
St. Kitts and Nevis	361	...	...	...	...	...	...	...	...	...	4.4	4.0	3.2	5.7	7.5	8.5
St. Lucia	362	...	...	...	3.6	5.6	5.0	4.2	4.2	3.5	3.1	3.6	3.2	5.4	5.3	8.4
St. Vincent & Grenadines	364	...	...	...	...	10.2	8.2	7.6	9.9	6.6	8.0	3.8	4.2	8.7	9.1	15.4
Suriname	366	13.5	18.7	15.3	18.9	19.5	12.3	17.0	21.5	19.5	19.0	17.9	6.8	3.7	4.1	3.3
Trinidad and Tobago	369	4.0	3.1	11.0	26.6	26.2	42.4	47.7	52.9	45.5	55.7	43.3	42.4	36.8	38.2	18.3
Uruguay	298	17.0	18.4	8.6	5.5	15.6	23.0	24.2	13.9	11.9	13.6	5.4	13.7	9.0	12.8	28.8
Venezuela, Rep. Bol.	299	27.6	35.9	75.6	72.8	55.1	36.8	26.7	35.7	29.0	32.4	26.4	61.9	59.5	65.8	39.4
Memorandum Items																
Oil Exporting Countries	999	36.0	34.1	73.5	56.2	52.1	45.6	32.1	38.9	36.0	28.3	23.5	25.4	27.7	37.3	34.7
Non-Oil Developing Countries	201	13.4	13.6	8.9	7.5	10.6	12.2	13.2	11.7	9.2	8.8	9.6	11.1	12.3	12.7	14.8

Weeks of Imports

1987	1988	1989	1990	1991	1992	1993	1994	1995	1996	1997	1998	1999	2000	2001	Country	Code
															Asia (cont.)	**170**
16.2	16.9	18.9	22.8	28.0	31.3	37.4	31.2	22.9	21.2	19.2	31.6	30.9	31.2	36.6	Nepal	558
4.5	3.1	3.8	2.1	3.2	4.7	6.5	17.1	7.8	2.3	5.3	5.7	7.6	7.0	18.6	Pakistan	564
19.5	14.7	13.1	17.6	10.4	8.4	5.7	3.3	9.4	17.4	11.0	8.1	8.7	13.9	21.3	Papua New Guinea	853
7.0	6.0	6.6	3.7	13.1	14.8	13.0	13.8	11.7	15.3	9.8	15.2	21.1	20.1	22.3	Philippines	566
31.2	33.8	38.0	44.5	37.5	28.9	25.2	32.4	30.3	31.5	34.5	33.0	30.7	31.3	22.6	Samoa	862
24.3	20.2	21.3	23.7	26.9	28.7	29.5	29.5	28.7	30.4	28.0	37.2	36.0	31.0	33.8	Singapore	576
23.6	21.1	12.0	10.0	4.0	10.9	7.6	6.5	5.4	11.2	....	....	....	....	....	Solomon Islands	813
7.1	5.2	5.7	8.2	11.7	13.8	21.2	22.3	20.5	18.7	17.9	17.4	14.3	7.5	11.3	Sri Lanka	524
16.0	15.6	19.2	20.9	24.2	26.0	27.6	28.0	26.4	27.1	21.7	34.9	35.2	26.9	27.1	Thailand	578
31.2	28.6	24.0	26.3	28.3	26.4	31.4	26.7	19.3	21.4	19.7	21.7	21.9	19.1	....	Tonga	866
30.0	30.0	25.8	20.4	25.1	27.0	30.1	25.3	26.4	23.4	20.7	26.4	22.5	....	....	Vanuatu	846
															Europe	**170**
....	....	....	....	....	6.4	9.7	10.6	15.2	13.6	14.1	15.1	18.1	18.4	....	Albania	914
....	....	....	....	....	....	13.4	17.6	17.6	17.4	24.9	21.9	16.8	16.8	14.2	Cyprus	423
30.6	26.0	25.6	30.5	27.6	16.1	12.7	17.5	27.3	21.9	17.6	21.5	22.6	20.0	....	Czech Republic	935
4.4	5.4	7.5	4.2	15.8	4.4	....	....	....	....	....	....	....	....	....	Czechoslovakia	934
....	....	....	....	....	....	22.5	13.8	11.8	10.3	8.9	9.1	10.8	11.3	10.0	Estonia	939
8.6	8.2	7.4	6.4	17.9	20.7	27.7	24.6	40.5	28.0	20.7	18.9	20.4	18.2	16.5	Hungary	944
....	....	....	....	....	....	6.1	12.2	15.5	15.9	20.5	17.5	20.9	16.4	16.3	Kazakhstan	916
64.6	52.5	47.6	38.0	32.8	28.1	32.6	39.4	28.3	30.1	30.3	32.4	32.7	22.4	33.4	Malta	181
....	....	....	....	....	....	....	.2	6.3	13.3	15.9	15.0	15.9	7.3	....	Moldova	921
6.9	8.4	11.3	27.8	12.0	13.6	11.3	14.2	26.4	25.0	25.1	30.6	29.9	28.2	26.5	Poland	964
8.1	4.9	10.6	2.8	6.2	6.9	7.9	15.3	8.0	9.6	17.5	12.6	13.4	15.6	18.2	Romania	968
....	....	....	....	....	....	9.2	3.7	10.9	7.8	8.5	6.4	10.1	25.7	28.7	Russia	922
....	....	....	....	....	....	....	3.3	12.9	19.0	15.6	15.6	10.9	14.7	15.6	Slovak Republic	936
6.5	8.5	15.7	14.1	12.7	14.0	11.1	16.0	18.1	19.6	20.0	22.1	29.8	21.9	....	Turkey	186
....	....	....	....	....	....	....	3.4	.9	3.1	3.4	5.5	7.1	2.7	4.6	Ukraine	926
2.9	9.1	14.5	15.1	9.5	....	....	....	....	....	....	....	....	....	....	Yugoslavia, SFR	188
31.4	**24.1**	**24.3**	**22.2**	**23.5**	**22.4**	**24.3**	**26.5**	**26.4**	**28.6**	**31.6**	**32.9**	**34.5**	**33.9**	**32.4**	**Middle East**	**405**
22.0	25.1	17.4	17.3	19.1	17.1	17.6	16.2	17.9	16.0	16.7	15.7	19.3	17.6	20.5	Bahrain	419
4.4	2.8	4.2	8.3	34.4	67.5	81.7	68.6	71.6	69.4	73.5	58.3	47.0	48.7	52.7	Egypt	469
....	....	....	....	....	....	....	....	....	....	....	....	....	....	....	Iran, I.R. of	429
....	....	....	....	....	....	....	....	....	....	....	....	....	....	....	Iraq	433
21.3	13.9	19.1	19.4	17.5	17.2	14.7	14.0	14.3	18.8	34.3	40.2	35.4	38.5	34.3	Israel	436
8.2	2.1	11.5	17.0	17.1	12.3	24.1	26.0	27.7	21.3	27.9	23.8	36.8	38.2	32.9	Jordan	439
39.2	16.3	25.6	25.6	37.2	36.9	31.1	27.2	23.8	21.8	21.8	23.8	32.9	51.5	66.5	Kuwait	443
10.2	20.7	21.8	13.6	17.7	18.5	53.1	77.7	43.0	40.9	41.6	48.2	65.1	49.6	35.7	Lebanon	446
70.1	38.3	45.8	56.9	55.2	62.2	56.8	55.9	58.1	53.3	50.9	69.2	98.0	172.7	174.1	Libya	672
40.0	24.9	31.2	32.4	27.1	27.4	11.5	13.0	15.8	16.0	16.0	9.7	30.8	24.6	21.2	Oman	449
28.4	19.5	20.9	19.4	20.2	17.6	19.1	17.7	11.4	12.4	12.8	15.9	27.1	18.5	16.9	Qatar	453
58.7	49.1	41.2	25.2	20.9	9.3	13.7	16.4	16.0	26.8	26.9	24.6	31.6	33.7	29.3	Saudi Arabia	456
1.6	4.5	....	....	....	....	....	....	....	....	....	....	....	....	....	Syrian Arab Rep.	463
34.0	27.1	23.2	21.3	20.3	17.1	16.3	16.5	18.5	18.5	14.5	19.1	16.7	18.4	17.3	United Arab Emirates	466
31.8	10.7	....	....	....	....	....	....	....	....	....	....	....	....	....	Yemen Arab Rep.	473
....	....	....	....	....	....	....	....	....	....	....	....	....	....	....	Yemen, P.D. Rep.	459
....	....	....	....	17.4	6.4	2.7	6.3	20.4	26.0	31.1	23.9	38.1	64.9	82.3	Yemen, Republic of	474
21.0	**14.9**	**14.8**	**19.7**	**23.5**	**26.4**	**29.8**	**24.4**	**26.8**	**29.0**	**26.5**	**23.9**	**23.7**	**20.8**	**....**	**Western Hemisphere**	**205**
5.4	5.8	7.6	5.6	5.7	8.4	6.1	7.0	8.9	6.8	7.1	8.0	8.8	....	....	Antigua and Barbuda	311
14.5	32.9	18.1	58.6	37.7	34.9	42.7	34.6	36.9	39.6	38.1	41.0	53.5	51.8	37.3	Argentina	213
17.3	14.1	11.7	9.5	12.9	....	....	19.9	16.9	14.6	14.2	14.6	....	....	....	Aruba	314
2.9	3.9	2.4	7.4	8.6	7.8	9.4	8.7	7.5	6.5	7.1	9.6	11.2	12.8	8.8	Bahamas, The	313
14.6	12.1	8.4	8.7	6.5	13.9	13.6	16.6	14.8	18.1	13.8	18.8	14.2	21.3	33.0	Barbados	316
13.2	14.8	14.4	17.2	10.8	10.0	7.2	6.9	7.6	11.9	10.8	7.1	10.1	14.2	14.3	Belize	339
6.6	9.3	17.4	12.6	5.7	8.7	9.6	19.4	24.1	30.4	30.5	22.2	26.1	22.2	23.1	Bolivia	218
19.8	22.6	19.7	17.2	18.2	50.8	57.4	53.5	48.1	53.3	40.7	36.5	35.0	28.9	....	Brazil	223
29.6	31.1	26.1	40.8	44.6	46.8	45.0	57.6	46.2	40.3	43.2	41.0	46.9	41.4	41.5	Chile	228
37.1	33.8	37.6	43.1	69.2	61.8	41.9	35.0	31.3	37.4	33.1	30.7	39.1	40.2	41.1	Colombia	233
18.4	24.6	22.5	13.6	25.5	21.7	15.1	12.3	13.5	12.1	13.3	8.9	12.0	10.8	10.5	Costa Rica	238
14.4	8.4	5.7	6.4	8.4	10.1	11.1	8.3	9.8	9.2	10.0	10.6	11.7	10.4	....	Dominica	321
5.2	7.1	3.8	1.6	11.6	10.4	13.9	3.8	5.2	4.4	4.2	4.6	6.0	4.4	....	Dominican Republic	243
11.3	12.1	15.2	23.4	20.0	18.6	28.0	26.5	20.4	24.6	22.0	15.1	28.3	13.2	8.1	Ecuador	248
9.7	8.3	11.9	17.1	10.6	12.9	14.6	15.0	13.8	18.2	22.8	26.9	33.2	26.3	23.4	El Salvador	253
13.3	9.5	8.1	8.6	7.3	12.6	11.8	13.7	15.5	12.2	12.8	12.2	....	....	....	Grenada	328
10.3	6.7	9.6	8.9	22.7	15.7	17.4	16.1	11.1	14.4	15.0	14.9	14.1	19.0	21.3	Guatemala	258
1.7	1.0	2.7	4.8	21.1	22.1	26.6	25.4	26.5	28.7	26.0	....	....	....	25.6	Guyana	336
2.2	2.0	2.3	.5	4.6	5.1	4.7	10.6	15.3	16.9	17.1	17.3	13.4	9.2	7.3	Haiti	263
6.7	2.8	1.1	2.2	5.7	9.9	4.5	8.4	8.3	7.0	14.0	16.8	24.4	23.9	25.2	Honduras	268
7.3	5.3	3.0	4.5	3.0	10.1	10.2	17.2	12.6	15.4	11.3	12.2	9.9	17.0	29.7	Jamaica	343
32.9	9.3	9.0	11.8	17.6	15.1	19.1	3.9	11.5	10.8	13.0	12.6	11.1	10.1	....	Mexico	273
7.5	9.7	6.7	5.2	4.3	6.1	6.2	5.3	....	....	....	....	....	....	....	Netherlands Antilles	353
1.1	2.5	9.8	8.7	9.3	7.9	3.8	8.4	7.1	8.9	13.6	12.2	14.2	14.4	11.1	Nicaragua	278
3.1	5.0	6.3	11.6	15.3	13.0	14.2	15.2	16.2	16.2	19.9	14.6	12.2	11.1	19.2	Panama	283
43.4	29.3	29.6	25.4	34.3	20.5	19.4	25.0	20.4	19.1	14.0	18.2	29.5	....	....	Paraguay	288
9.4	7.9	15.3	15.6	30.3	30.5	36.5	54.3	46.3	58.1	55.6	50.4	56.2	49.5	....	Peru	293
6.9	5.8	8.3	7.7	7.9	14.3	13.0	13.0	13.1	11.4	....	....	....	....	....	St. Kitts and Nevis	361
8.9	7.7	7.3	8.6	8.6	9.2	10.4	10.0	10.7	9.6	9.5	11.0	....	....	....	St. Lucia	362
10.7	9.3	9.3	10.1	8.4	13.1	12.2	12.5	11.4	11.9	8.6	10.5	11.0	17.6	17.2	St. Vincent & Grenadines	364
2.7	1.9	1.1	2.3	.1	1.7	.9	4.9	11.8	10.0	8.6	10.0	6.7	13.3	....	Suriname	366
8.0	5.9	10.5	23.1	10.6	8.1	7.3	16.2	10.9	13.2	12.3	13.6	17.9	21.8	....	Trinidad and Tobago	369
24.1	23.9	21.7	20.3	10.7	13.0	17.0	18.1	20.9	19.6	21.7	28.3	32.2	37.2	52.6	Uruguay	298
32.1	12.6	27.4	59.0	49.8	35.4	38.3	45.7	25.8	62.0	51.2	39.2	45.4	42.0	26.7	Venezuela, Rep. Bol.	299
															Memorandum Items	
39.0	27.9	27.0	26.1	25.2	20.8	22.6	24.4	21.4	28.4	29.0	32.9	36.8	40.0	37.5	Oil Exporting Countries	999
16.9	14.7	14.8	17.6	20.0	19.7	21.6	22.1	22.1	23.0	23.6	27.7	29.5	26.6	29.9	Non-Oil Developing Countries	201

SDRs

1b *s*

		1972	1973	1974	1975	1976	1977	1978	1979	1980	1981	1982	1983	1984	1985	1986
															Millions of SDRs:	
All Countries	010	8,686.1	8,807.1	8,857.9	8,763.8	8,655.4	8,132.7	8,110.0	12,478.9	11,808.5	16,411.2	17,744.6	14,418.2	16,469.5	18,212.8	19,494.1
Industrial Countries	110	7,135.0	7,161.3	7,178.3	7,250.3	7,231.4	6,687.0	6,405.1	9,324.7	8,888.8	11,940.3	14,093.5	11,521.6	13,374.8	14,902.3	16,135.0
United States	111	1,803.1	1,795.6	1,939.3	1,994.6	2,061.2	2,163.9	1,196.3	2,068.1	2,046.0	3,518.5	4,759.1	4,800.0	5,754.6	6,639.4	6,862.9
Canada	156	465.3	467.3	469.1	474.4	480.1	416.0	401.0	444.8	355.4	149.5	64.2	20.1	73.7	198.4	202.2
Australia	193	234.6	234.7	99.9	95.7	36.3	21.8	98.7	31.9	—	44.8	77.7	77.0	213.4	282.5	271.0
Japan	158	424.5	425.1	431.8	443.9	460.2	494.2	1,053.5	1,281.3	1,362.7	1,661.7	1,895.4	1,848.2	1,966.0	1,926.2	1,813.0
New Zealand	196	58.3	58.1	.5	.8	8.4	34.2	46.1	8.9	—	19.6	1.7	2.7	6.8	6.0	9.0
Euro Area																
Austria	122	85.8	85.9	87.0	87.4	95.9	96.6	104.6	155.8	173.4	185.7	226.5	154.0	224.4	191.2	151.8
Belgium	124	523.1	626.4	584.2	615.5	397.4	407.1	414.1	475.8	496.7	627.9	672.0	399.0	454.2	328.4	279.8
Finland	172	67.5	67.8	68.1	66.2	56.1	41.8	61.8	88.1	81.3	124.2	104.3	37.0	145.7	156.4	167.3
France	132	580.6	72.8	202.2	244.4	226.7	233.5	286.3	644.4	733.4	1,080.1	887.3	421.9	583.7	819.4	1,054.4
Germany	134	822.4	1,387.5	1,439.8	1,450.9	1,747.3	1,176.5	1,378.9	1,576.2	1,442.9	1,382.5	1,862.1	1,540.9	1,389.7	1,408.0	1,651.2
Greece	174	25.6	25.2	26.7	17.6	16.9	13.4	13.4	.8	—	—	—	.6	1.1	—	—
Ireland	178	39.3	39.4	40.6	40.9	45.3	45.6	48.1	70.9	71.1	90.9	96.4	65.4	89.4	99.0	113.3
Italy	136	341.5	342.9	180.8	83.0	78.4	118.8	225.7	449.3	521.0	672.8	711.4	564.9	645.3	296.9	480.2
Luxembourg	137	7.3	7.3	7.3	7.3	7.3	7.4	7.6	7.6	11.3	14.9	15.4	16.0	16.6	17.1	17.5
Netherlands	138	649.6	475.4	485.8	520.5	531.4	564.1	243.9	393.9	439.5	591.7	771.7	501.8	525.0	569.3	597.8
Portugal	182				7.0	8.4	3.8	—	.6	—	8.7	2.3	.9	12.5	15.5	54.0
Spain	184	128.7	128.8	133.9	121.4	90.8	48.2	102.7	206.3	230.6	318.6	185.8	65.4	154.5	254.5	353.2
Denmark	128	72.2	119.3	91.5	81.9	81.9	97.1	97.9	137.6	137.6	172.6	176.4	118.7	158.1	178.7	207.2
Iceland	176	6.4	6.3	6.3	4.8	1.8	2.7	1.8	.2	1.8	3.4	2.0	.2	.4	.4	.2
Norway	142	87.9	88.0	88.2	89.0	89.5	92.8	96.3	139.7	157.6	195.3	284.3	257.3	262.2	258.0	318.2
San Marino	135															
Sweden	144	107.1	107.0	107.0	107.0	107.0	107.1	112.0	173.0	174.2	224.5	233.3	123.0	181.4	224.3	261.3
Switzerland	146									5.1	.1	3.7	12.9	9.3	3.0	
United Kingdom	112	604.4	600.4	688.2	696.3	603.3	500.6	414.5	965.5	447.2	852.0	1,060.7	494.0	506.9	1,029.8	1,269.6
Developing Countries	200	1,551.2	1,645.8	1,679.6	1,513.5	1,424.0	1,445.7	1,704.8	3,097.0	2,919.7	4,470.9	3,651.1	2,896.7	3,094.8	3,310.5	3,359.2
Africa	605	320.8	291.0	311.8	322.4	316.5	298.0	312.8	463.1	328.3	627.5	410.8	268.2	191.3	206.7	263.2
Algeria	612	41.8	41.9	42.9	43.0	43.1	46.2	46.4	76.3	75.9	118.9	140.0	102.1	113.2	125.6	136.6
Angola	614	....	....	....	....	....	....	....	....							
Benin	638	4.5	4.5	4.5	4.5	4.5	4.4	4.4	6.1	1.7	2.9	2.0	1.1	.2	—	
Botswana	616	1.6	1.6	1.6	1.6	1.6	1.6	1.6	2.5	2.5	5.3	6.2	7.3	8.5	9.7	14.0
Burkina Faso	748	4.4	4.4	4.4	4.4	4.4	4.4	4.4	6.1	5.8	7.5	7.5	7.5	5.6	5.6	5.6
Burundi	618	3.7	3.6	3.6	3.2	3.0	2.8	2.8	5.3	4.1	5.5	4.2	1.0	.1	.1	.5
Cameroon	622	10.5	10.5	10.5	10.1	8.8	6.8	3.2	—	—	.2	1.6	.6	6.2	4.2	2.8
Cape Verde	624								—	—	.2	.2	.1	.1	.1	.1
Central African Rep.	626	1.2	1.0	.8	2.3	1.6	1.6	1.3	1.4	—	—	.2	.1	.1	.1	.1
Chad	628	1.1	.4	2.4	2.3	1.9	1.7	1.5	1.6	—	—	.3	1.5	2.6	1.5	.4
Comoros	632	....	....	....	....	....	....	....	.2	—	—	—	—	.2	.2	1.7
Congo, Dem. Rep. of	636	7.4	6.9	6.4	20.0	27.1	—	4.4	.1	—	.6	—	21.0	—	.2	.2
Congo, Rep. of	634	2.6	2.5	2.3	2.2	2.1	1.5	1.3	1.2	—	.9	1.0	.2	2.1	1.5	3.8
Côte d'Ivoire	662	15.3	15.3	15.2	14.5	11.8	8.6	7.4	17.9	2.7	10.6	.1	15.5	.2	.1	7.0
Djibouti	611								.1	.1	.5	.5	.4	.4	.4	.4
Equatorial Guinea	642	1.9	1.9	1.9	1.8	1.8	1.7	1.7	.7	—	.1	—	—	—	3.1	—
Ethiopia	644	—	—	—	—	—	—	.4	—	—	10.4	3.2	2.3	3.0	.2	—
Gabon	646	4.7	4.7	4.7	4.6	4.6	4.6	4.6	7.2	5.6	7.0	.7	.4	5.8	2.1	10.1
Gambia, The	648	2.2	2.1	2.0	2.0	2.0	.9	1.1	.7	—	.1	.1	.1	—	—	.6
Ghana	652	10.0	9.7	9.6	7.5	6.7	10.1	9.5	13.7	—	.6	.2	2.1	.1	17.2	1.6
Guinea	656	2.9	1.4	3.4	3.1	2.9	2.2	—	.1	—	.1	.2		.1	—	.3
Guinea-Bissau	654							—	—	—	—	—	—	—	—	—
Kenya	664	17.1	17.1	1.9	3.8	2.8	14.4	11.0	82.1	20.2	9.4	14.0	16.6	2.2	.8	9.9
Lesotho	666	.9	.7	.6	.5	.5	.5	.4	1.1	.9	1.4	1.1	1.0	1.0	1.0	.8
Liberia	668	1.6	3.3	3.2	2.9	3.5	3.3	3.3	6.5	—	1.1	—	—	—	—	—
Madagascar	674	8.7	8.7	.2	.9	1.9	6.9	8.7	—	—	.3	1.1	.1	1.5	—	—
Malawi	676	4.6	4.6	4.6	4.6	4.3	3.9	3.3	3.1	—	5.7	3.6	.8	2.9	—	.4
Mali	678	2.4	2.3	3.0	2.7	2.8	2.7	2.6	1.3	—	.2	.5	.1	1.7	1.7	—
Mauritania	682	2.2	2.1	2.0	1.7	1.2	.6	.7	1.3	—	1.1	—	.7	—	3.9	2.6
Mauritius	684	7.3	7.3	2.8	2.6	2.7	2.3	1.6	.6	—	5.6	1.7	.1	.1	—	.5
Morocco	686	16.6	16.2	15.8	14.8	10.4	8.5	12.6	15.2	.5	1.4	.5	.6	.7	.1	15.8
Mozambique	688	....	....	....	....	....	....	....	....							
Namibia	728															
Niger	692	4.4	4.4	4.4	4.4	4.4	4.4	4.4	6.0	5.8	7.5	7.5	4.6	2.2	—	1.0
Nigeria	694	45.5	45.5	47.5	57.4	61.2	65.8	66.8	107.8	132.5	239.0	40.4	25.7	10.5	1.0	.2
Rwanda	714	.4	2.4	2.5	2.4	2.4	2.4	2.4	4.6	7.7	9.8	10.8	8.4	8.3	8.2	8.1
São Tomé & Príncipe	716						—	—	—	.2	.2	.4	.4	.4	.1	—
Senegal	722	5.7	5.3	4.6	3.3	1.2	1.7	9.7	11.5	—	3.7	4.9	3.8	.1	—	2.5
Seychelles	718								.1	—	.2	.2	.1	—	—	—
Sierra Leone	724	5.7	5.7	4.4	3.9	2.9	1.4	.2	—	—	.1	.5	.1	—	—	.3
Somalia	726	4.6	4.5	4.4	4.4	4.3	4.2	4.1	6.4	5.5	4.2	.7	.4	.1	—	—
South Africa	199	38.2	1.4	39.6	43.4	41.5	39.5	39.3	25.4	37.1	115.5	99.1	27.3	2.3	.5	—
Sudan	732	4.9	13.6	21.5	7.3	—	—	6.0	10.0	—	.5	—	.1	—	—	—
Swaziland	734	.8	.8	.9	1.0	.9	.9	1.0	2.2	1.8	5.9	5.0	1.5	2.3	.3	2.2
Tanzania	738	6.7	6.6	1.7	1.2	5.1	5.6	6.1	2.8	—	.3	—	.1	.1	.3	—
Togo	742	5.1	5.1	5.1	5.1	5.0	4.8	4.4	6.3	5.8	6.5	3.9	1.2	2.1	.1	4.6
Tunisia	744	7.9	7.6	8.5	8.2	10.0	9.6	8.5	14.6	11.8	17.4	16.0	3.6	1.9	.1	.5
Uganda	746	13.7	13.4	5.0	3.2	.9	4.5	8.1	8.4	—	2.6	10.1	.9	.2	.5	22.6
Zambia	754	.2	—	11.7	15.7	19.2	11.4	12.1	4.2	—	7.7	14.5	—	—	—	—
Zimbabwe	698	....	....	....	....	....	....	....	....	—	8.8	6.3	6.1	2.3	13.2	5.0

1987	1988	1989	1990	1991	1992	1993	1994	1995	1996	1997	1998	1999	2000	2001		
End of Period																
20,212.5	20,172.9	20,484.8	20,354.4	20,551.3	12,867.2	14,614.3	15,761.5	19,773.2	18,521.4	20,532.2	20,379.7	18,456.7	18,489.0	19,556.8	All Countries	010
16,476.0	17,559.2	17,663.4	17,615.4	17,455.3	10,468.2	11,454.4	12,485.9	14,998.5	14,521.1	15,511.5	15,844.0	14,726.0	14,411.1	15,967.8	Industrial Countries	110
7,248.3	7,161.0	7,572.0	7,724.3	7,857.6	6,184.2	6,569.4	6,876.4	7,424.8	7,171.5	7,431.5	7,530.2	7,539.0	8,088.5	8,580.4	United States	111
281.2	1,017.4	1,048.1	1,072.5	1,105.7	755.5	773.5	786.4	791.8	812.4	834.3	779.5	383.7	440.6	489.0	Canada	156
260.1	248.3	234.0	218.3	202.4	69.6	59.7	49.9	36.8	25.4	13.8	12.6	52.6	71.8	86.8	Australia	193
1,736.3	2,182.0	1,862.3	2,138.4	1,803.0	795.5	1,123.4	1,427.0	1,821.1	1,837.3	1,955.1	1,891.0	1,935.5	1,870.2	1,891.7	Japan	158
1.0	.7	.4	.4	.3	—	—	.2	.6	.3	.2	1.2	5.0	10.0	12.8	New Zealand	196
															Euro Area	
205.8	199.5	227.1	195.7	197.5	247.6	160.5	193.8	121.7	135.7	124.8	105.9	105.9	102.7	185.3	Austria	122
493.7	418.0	423.2	398.0	411.0	124.1	124.7	123.4	331.1	346.5	362.7	433.3	197.1	235.8	375.7	Belgium	124
160.5	199.8	182.0	152.5	157.7	78.4	83.8	222.7	241.6	201.6	241.7	247.5	211.3	106.5	186.3	Finland	172
1,058.6	1,032.9	1,011.1	901.8	926.8	118.3	240.8	248.3	642.8	682.1	719.9	786.2	252.7	308.9	391.7	France	132
1,384.2	1,380.3	1,372.7	1,321.2	1,340.0	611.4	700.1	763.3	1,346.2	1,326.2	1,324.9	1,326.6	1,427.3	1,352.9	1,426.4	Germany	134
—	.2	.3	.2	.3	—	.1	.2	—	.4	.2	.3	3.8	9.2	7.7	Greece	174
126.5	134.3	145.4	158.3	170.0	90.4	96.6	101.3	107.2	114.9	123.1	137.1	29.2	37.0	43.5	Ireland	178
668.2	705.1	759.5	729.2	650.0	173.2	175.4	85.8	—	20.4	49.6	78.7	122.5	182.4	236.5	Italy	136
18.0	18.4	19.1	19.9	20.6	6.6	7.0	7.2	7.5	7.7	8.0	8.7	1.8	3.2	5.0	Luxembourg	137
636.8	576.5	590.4	504.4	529.9	402.6	424.4	441.9	616.4	566.2	586.5	643.8	742.4	501.1	598.3	Netherlands	138
56.1	2.8	1.4	40.3	68.3	33.5	41.9	48.3	57.0	68.2	79.4	95.9	32.1	41.2	49.4	Portugal	182
420.4	456.8	523.0	489.4	319.0	134.0	157.4	174.5	276.8	313.9	351.3	408.1	189.8	222.6	279.2	Spain	184
214.5	167.0	213.1	151.6	169.0	66.7	62.4	124.6	106.8	116.7	248.7	246.0	249.9	50.5	223.5	Denmark	128
1.9	1.0	—	.3	.1	—	—	.1	—	—	—	—	—	—	.1	Iceland	176
311.2	362.3	345.2	315.5	315.9	139.1	288.4	266.7	311.5	247.2	257.9	294.1	298.0	235.4	282.1	Norway	142
—	—	—	—	—	—	—	.1	.2	.3	.3	.4	.1	.2	.3	San Marino	135
208.5	299.1	259.5	204.0	289.6	32.6	42.2	46.4	296.8	198.9	276.7	292.4	227.8	165.2	157.1	Sweden	144
10.1	15.2	3.6	1.3	1.6	11.7	112.8	162.0	181.3	87.8	170.5	192.3	344.7	124.7	225.0	Switzerland	146
974.3	980.5	870.1	878.0	919.2	393.2	209.9	335.2	278.7	239.5	350.4	332.2	373.9	250.4	234.1	United Kingdom	112
3,736.5	2,613.7	2,821.4	2,739.0	3,095.9	2,398.9	3,159.9	3,275.6	4,774.7	4,000.4	5,020.7	4,535.7	3,730.7	4,077.9	3,589.0	Developing Countries	200
300.4	88.7	100.7	83.6	239.3	148.6	116.3	119.0	134.0	117.1	122.2	280.2	394.4	404.6	463.5	Africa	605
142.7	1.6	3.0	1.9	1.3	.8	4.9	15.7	.8	3.5	.5	1.1	1.4	2.3	9.1	Algeria	612
....	....	—	.1	.1	.1	.1	.1	.1	.1	.1	.1	.1	.1	.1	Angola	614
.1	.1	—	.1	.2	—	.1	—	—	.2	—	—	.2	—	.3	Benin	638
15.4	16.8	18.9	21.7	24.1	22.5	24.0	25.4	27.1	28.7	30.4	32.4	28.1	29.9	31.5	Botswana	616
5.7	5.6	5.6	5.7	5.6	5.6	5.6	5.6	5.5	1.8	1.6	.5	.5	.3	.4	Burkina Faso	748
—	.1	—	—	2.6	1.1	.5	.1	—	.1	—	.1	—	—	—	Burundi	618
.2	—	.2	.5	3.9	.2	.1	—	—	.1	—	—	1.9	5.9	—	Cameroon	622
.1	—	—	—	.1	—	—	—	—	—	—	—	—	—	—	Cape Verde	624
4.9	9.2	—	3.4	.5	—	—	—	—	.2	—	—	—	—	—	Central African Rep.	626
6.4	5.7	1.3	.1	.1	—	—	—	—	—	—	—	—	—	—	Chad	628
.1	.1	.1	.1	—	—	—	.1	—	—	.1	—	—	.1	.1	Comoros	632
.1	—	3.7	—	—	—	—	—	—	—	—	—	—	—	—	Congo, Dem. Rep. of	636
1.9	.8	1.2	1.2	—	—	—	—	—	—	—	.1	—	—	.2	Congo, Rep. of	634
.2	.5	3.9	.8	1.4	.2	.8	.1	1.2	.8	—	.1	2.5	1.0	.6	Côte d'Ivoire	662
.3	.3	.3	.2	.2	.2	.2	.1	.1	.1	.6	.3	.1	.3	.1	Djibouti	611
.2	—	.1	.1	5.6	5.5	.3	—	—	—	—	—	—	—	.8	Equatorial Guinea	642
1.2	—	—	.2	.1	.1	.2	.3	.2	—	.1	.1	—	—	.1	Ethiopia	644
8.2	6.5	—	.2	4.4	.1	—	.2	—	—	—	—	.1	—	—	Gabon	646
3.2	1.0	1.0	1.2	.5	.5	.2	.2	.1	.2	.1	.3	.5	.2	—	Gambia, The	648
11.2	.2	22.8	3.1	8.8	3.2	.4	2.9	1.6	1.6	2.5	42.4	13.3	.4	3.2	Ghana	652
.2	.2	—	.2	9.4	7.9	8.5	3.8	5.0	.5	2.0	1.0	.9	.2	.6	Guinea	656
.1	—	—	—	—	—	—	—	—	—	—	—	.1	—	.2	Guinea-Bissau	654
11.4	.4	8.7	2.8	1.0	.6	.8	.5	.2	.5	.5	.4	1.7	.2	.8	Kenya	664
.6	1.0	.7	.5	.2	.5	.4	.3	.2	.9	.9	.9	.9	.5	.5	Lesotho	666
—	—	—	—	—	—	—	—	—	—	—	—	—	—	—	Liberia	668
.1	.1	.1	.1	—	.2	.1	—	—	—	—	—	.1	—	.1	Madagascar	674
—	2.4	.3	2.2	.2	.1	.2	4.2	.6	.9	.1	4.8	.3	.4	.7	Malawi	676
.2	.2	.1	.3	.3	.1	.1	.1	.3	.2	—	.1	.4	.1	.3	Mali	678
12.1	.1	.1	.6	.1	.1	.1	—	—	—	1.0	—	—	—	.2	Mauritania	682
4.1	3.7	5.0	10.3	18.0	17.6	21.0	21.3	21.7	22.2	22.5	22.8	16.1	16.5	16.8	Mauritius	684
2.9	.3	.4	1.0	102.9	56.3	25.1	18.0	17.3	5.2	.9	2.3	62.1	91.6	98.1	Morocco	686
—	—	—	—	—	—	—	—	—	—	—	—	—	—	.1	Mozambique	688
....	....	....	—	—	—	—	—	—	—	—	—	—	—	—	Namibia	728
.2	.1	.9	—	.3	—	—	.4	.3	.2	1.3	.1	.1	1.0	.3	Niger	692
.1	—	.4	.8	—	—	—	.2	.4	.4	.4	.5	.2	.2	.5	Nigeria	694
8.0	7.9	7.5	7.2	6.7	2.4	2.1	1.7	13.7	12.7	19.6	17.4	10.5	.9	9.8	Rwanda	714
—	—	—	—	—	—	—	—	—	—	—	—	—	—	—	São Tomé & Príncipe	716
—	—	3.6	.2	.3	—	.3	.7	2.6	1.2	.3	.4	1.8	.7	6.0	Senegal	722
—	—	—	—	—	—	—	—	—	—	—	—	—	—	—	Seychelles	718
—	—	—	—	1.2	2.8	6.2	11.5	5.3	8.3	7.4	15.2	4.0	.3	—	Sierra Leone	724
—	—	—	—	—	—	—	—	—	—	—	—	—	—	—	Somalia	726
1.2	.8	1.3	1.6	1.2	.1	8.8	.8	3.3	.8	6.8	131.7	209.6	222.4	222.6	South Africa	199
—	—	—	—	—	—	—	—	—	—	—	—	—	—	—	Sudan	732
2.8	1.2	.8	8.5	8.7	5.8	5.9	5.9	5.9	5.9	5.9	6.0	2.4	2.4	2.5	Swaziland	734
.1	—	—	—	—	—	—	.1	.1	.1	.3	.2	.2	.1	.4	Tanzania	738
.1	.1	1.3	.1	.3	.2	.1	—	.3	.2	—	.1	.2	—	.2	Togo	742
38.1	21.0	6.4	1.7	23.0	8.8	1.3	1.8	4.7	11.1	12.1	2.1	19.3	3.0	1.3	Tunisia	744
—	—	—	4.8	7.2	6.6	—	2.1	.3	.7	4.0	3.5	1.7	2.7	1.5	Uganda	746
—	—	—	—	—	—	—	—	8.2	1.4	.8	.6	.1	17.1	53.3	Zambia	754
16.3	.5	.5	.2	.1	.3	.6	—	.5	6.8	.2	.3	.8	.2	—	Zimbabwe	698

SDRs

1b s

Millions of SDRs

	Code	1972	1973	1974	1975	1976	1977	1978	1979	1980	1981	1982	1983	1984	1985	1986
Asia	505	489.8	507.0	490.0	426.6	388.5	331.7	448.3	785.6	763.3	1,325.0	1,174.8	713.5	1,026.7	1,101.8	1,063.
Afghanistan, Islamic State of	512	1.2	4.3	4.5	5.3	5.1	5.7	5.4	13.4	12.1	16.3	15.6	10.0	13.5	12.4	11.
Bangladesh	513	—	—	—	15.4	16.1	3.9	.1	9.2	.4	.1	.8	12.9	.3	11.9	8.
Bhutan	514	...	...	...	...	...	...	...	—	—	—	—	.1		.1	
Brunei Darussalam	516	...	...	...	—	...	...	...	...							
Cambodia	522	4.2	.5	1.1	.6	.3		—	1.9	3.8	4.5	3.1	1.6			
China, P.R.: Mainland	924	...	...	...	...	...	...	...	72.0	236.3	193.9	320.0		413.8	439.5	465.
Fiji	819	1.4	1.4	1.4	1.3	1.3	1.3	1.3	3.1	2.7	4.5	3.7	.3	6.3	5.1	5.
India	534	246.5	245.3	239.9	212.0	189.1	149.0	225.8	371.0	376.7	468.3	339.4	104.6	337.6	306.2	290.
Indonesia	536	35.8	43.3	55.7	6.3	4.1	21.7	57.4	129.2	137.2	227.2	281.9	3.9	.5	51.2	35.
Kiribati	826	...	...	...	...	...	...	...	...	...	...	...	...	...	...	...
Korea	542	26.1	26.1	1.4	3.4	6.8	10.0	11.4	18.9	9.9	54.1	57.8	60.2	30.9	36.2	14.
Lao P. D. Rep.	544	1.3	1.3	1.3	1.6	1.5	1.5	1.0	.8	.8	.6	.1				
Malaysia	548	63.1	60.6	61.6	61.7	65.1	26.6	38.8	87.3	97.8	125.8	118.1	103.1	99.0	105.4	110.
Maldives	556	...	...	...	...	...	—	.1	.1	.2	.2	—	—	—		
Marshall Islands, Rep. of	867	...	...	...	...	...	...		—	—	—					
Micronesia, Fed. States of	868	...	...	...	...	...	...	...	...	...	...	...	...	...	...	...
Mongolia	948	...	...	...	...	...	...	...	...	...	...	...	...	...	...	...
Myanmar	518	5.6	9.7	9.5	8.0	7.6	7.5	2.9	4.7	5.4	2.4	1.1	.2	.1	—	
Nepal	558	2.2	2.2	2.2	2.2	2.1	1.9	1.2	1.7	.1	—	.8	.2	.1	.1	.1
Pakistan	564	19.1	26.6	19.9	25.0	32.0	28.7	30.5	34.2	22.6	48.5	45.9	.8	37.4	24.1	10.7
Palau	565															
Papua New Guinea	853					1.7	.2	.4	.8	—	33.1	31.0	17.0	5.0	5.9	2.6
Philippines	566	21.9	23.9	27.7	23.5	13.6	19.2	13.1	25.6	.1	1.7	2.5	.9	19.8	35.3	4.7
Samoa	862	.2	.2	.2									.4	.2		.8
Singapore	576	—	—	—	—	—	—	—	12.2	15.1	27.5	49.4	59.7	58.0	66.0	73.8
Solomon Islands	813									1.0	1.2	1.2	1.7	1.3	.8	1.3
Sri Lanka	524	12.8	13.4	14.5	10.8	12.4	19.8	26.3	22.2	—	19.9	6.3	.8	.2	.1	
Thailand	578	28.5	28.5	29.5	29.6	28.9	30.5	26.6	37.1	6.4	52.3	22.2	15.2	2.4	1.3	27.1
Tonga	866	...	...	...	...	...	...	...	...	...	...	...	...	...	...	...
Vanuatu	846													.1	.2	.2
Vietnam	582	19.8	19.8	19.8	19.8	.7	4.2	6.2	12.2	—	.5	—	—	—	.2	.2
Europe	170	60.5	88.1	95.7	79.9	52.4	28.5	22.9	60.7	28.0	90.5	35.5	77.0	36.2	40.5	43.5
Albania	914	...	...	...	...	...	...	...	...	...	...	...	...	...	...	...
Armenia	911	...	...	...	...	...	...	...	...	...	...	...	...	...	...	...
Azerbaijan	912	...	...	...	...	...	...	...	...	...	...	...	...	...	...	...
Belarus	913	...	...	...	...	...	...	...	...	...	...	...	...	...	...	...
Bosnia and Herzegovina	963	...	...	...	...	...	...	...	...	...	...	...	...	...	...	...
Bulgaria	918	...	...	...	...	...	...	...	...	...	...	...	...	...	...	...
Croatia	960	...	...	...	...	...	...	...	...	...	...	...	...	...	...	...
Cyprus	423	10.4	10.5	10.4	10.0	7.9	5.1	1.7	9.9	6.5	3.4	.2	.2	.1	.1	
Czech Republic	935	...	...	...	...	...	...	...	...	...	...	...	...	...	...	...
Czechoslovakia	934	—	—	—	—	—	—	—	—	—	—	—	—	—		
Estonia	939	...	...	...	...	...	...	...	...	...	...	...	...	...	...	...
Georgia	915	...	...	...	...	...	...	...	...	...	...	...	...	...	...	...
Hungary	944	...	...	...	...	...	...	...	...	...	...	2.3	44.4	—	.1	
Kazakhstan	916	...	...	...	...	...	...	...	...	...	...	...	...	...	...	...
Kyrgyz Republic	917	...	...	...	...	...	...	...	...	...	...	...	...	...	...	...
Latvia	941	...	...	...	...	...	...	...	...	...	...	...	...	...	...	...
Lithuania	946	...	...	...	...	...	...	...	...	...	...	...	...	...	...	...
Macedonia, FYR	962	...	...	...	...	...	...	...	...	...	...	...	...	...	...	...
Malta	181	5.1	5.1	5.1	5.1	5.2	5.5	5.8	9.4	11.3	14.6	21.2	31.0	35.7	39.6	43.1
Moldova	921	...	...	...	...	...	...	...	...	...	...	...	...	...	...	...
Poland	964	...	...	...	...	...	...	...	...	...	...	...	...	...	...	...
Romania	968	—	6.0	5.4	8.1	12.6	6.9	—	.6	—	.4	11.8	.2	.3	—	.1
Russia	922	...	...	...	...	...	...	...	...	...	...	...	...	...	...	...
Slovak Republic	936	...	...	...	...	...	...	...	...	...	...	...	...	...	...	...
Slovenia	961	...	...	...	...	...	...	...	...	...	...	...	...	...	...	...
Tajikistan	923	...	...	...	...	...	...	...	...	...	...	...	...	...	...	...
Turkey	186	38.3	28.5	34.7	27.2	18.5	—	.2	.2	—	.2	.1	1.3	.1	.4	.1
Turkmenistan	925	...	...	...	...	...	...	...	...	...	...	...	...	...	...	...
Ukraine	926	...	...	...	...	...	...	...	...	...	...	...	...	...	...	...
Uzbekistan	927	...	...	...	...	...	...	...	...	...	...	...	...	...	...	...
Yugoslavia, Fed. Rep.	965	—	—	—	—	—	—	—	—	—	—	—	—	—	—	—
Yugoslavia, SFR	188	6.7	38.1	40.2	29.5	8.3	11.0	15.2	40.7	10.1	71.9	—		.1	.2	
Middle East	405	114.1	142.3	123.2	115.9	141.3	169.8	191.3	494.2	644.9	855.3	1,288.8	1,144.9	1,270.5	1,281.2	1,149.2
Bahrain, Kingdom of	419							.1	2.2	1.8	5.2	14.0	12.2	13.1	13.6	14.1
Egypt	469	5.1	31.2	30.9	14.5	20.3	23.7	8.2	.4	—	.2	.1	.3	.2	.1	
Iran, I.R. of	429	34.4	36.9	44.5	55.7	64.3	69.6	96.3	167.3	240.5	291.2	299.8	309.2	320.3	328.2	335.7
Iraq	433	23.2	20.1	23.0	23.0	28.0	34.2	45.5	82.2	87.2	113.7	74.2	8.6	.1	—	—
Israel	436	29.2	27.9	2.5	2.0	8.7	22.2	21.0	4.8	8.8	.6	.5	1.6	.1	.1	—
Jordan	439	7.6	7.5	7.4	7.4	7.4	7.4	7.4	11.0	11.7	15.5	16.5	17.4	15.8	21.9	19.6
Kuwait	443										35.4	62.3	35.6	76.0	104.3	128.4
Lebanon	446	—	—	—	—	—	—	—	1.3	—	1.9	2.0	—	.8	1.8	2.6
Libya	672								30.7	46.6	104.1	129.4	157.7	132.6	156.2	177.6
Oman	449	.7	.7	.7	.7	.7	.7	.7	2.8	5.1	5.2	7.9	11.1	9.4	10.9	11.4
Qatar	453	—	—	—	—	—	—	—	4.2	2.7	8.6	14.0	8.7	16.2	18.9	21.1
Saudi Arabia	456	—	—	—	—	—	—	—	149.1	212.6	212.7	578.7	486.8	586.0	528.7	335.8
Syrian Arab Rep.	463	4.0	8.0	8.3	7.3	6.8	6.4	6.0	12.0	9.8	14.7	11.9	8.8	5.3	2.8	.2
United Arab Emirates	466							—	15.4	8.0	29.5	50.3	61.5	66.0	68.3	76.5
Yemen Arab Rep.	473	2.1	2.1	2.1	2.1	2.1	2.1	3.2	7.5	10.3	12.9	14.1	8.6	8.8	23.2	23.1
Yemen, P.D. Rep.	459	7.8	7.8	3.7	3.2	3.0	3.6	3.0	3.5	—	4.0	13.1	17.0	19.8	2.4	3.4
Yemen, Republic of	474	—	—	—	—	—	—	—								

SDRs

End of Period

1987	1988	1989	1990	1991	1992	1993	1994	1995	1996	1997	1998	1999	2000	2001		Code
892.7	832.7	761.3	903.6	768.6	523.0	683.4	647.5	875.4	925.4	1,530.8	1,298.9	906.1	927.8	973.6	**Asia**	505
10.5	9.5	8.1	6.3	4.7	3.2	2.0	1.0								Afghanistan, Islamic State of	512
37.6	40.1	2.3	18.1	49.9	30.1	16.6	24.6	107.3	76.2	21.6	9.1	.7	.3	.9	Bangladesh	513
.1	.2	.2	.3	.3	.3	.4	.4	.4	.5	.5	.5	.1	.2	.2	Bhutan	514
									.5	1.6	2.7	3.8	5.0	6.2	Brunei Darussalam	516
						11.4	10.9	10.2	9.5	8.8	6.9	3.8	.1	.4	Cambodia	522
450.9	435.6	411.1	394.8	403.7	305.1	352.0	369.1	391.6	427.1	446.5	480.1	539.6	612.7	676.8	China, P.R.: Mainland	924
9.9	15.1	15.9	16.5	9.3	6.0	6.3	7.4	7.7	8.0	8.3	8.6	4.1	4.5	4.8	Fiji	819
112.4	71.1	86.2	222.1	32.3	2.8	72.9	1.4	93.3	85.1	57.4	59.0	3.0	3.2	4.1	India	534
4.4	2.0	.7	2.3	2.6	.1	.3	.3	.9	1.5	370.0	221.5	.3	24.5	12.6	Indonesia	536
															Kiribati	826
11.6	4.2	1.2	10.1	20.9	30.6	42.3	52.3	65.7	82.3	43.6	8.1	.5	2.7	2.7	Korea	542
				.3	.6	1.9	7.5	9.5	7.2	9.3	4.3	.1	.1	2.7	Lao P. D. Rep.	544
115.1	119.7	127.1	136.3	145.0	82.3	87.8	92.7	101.6	115.3	129.9	145.8	60.8	80.8	99.6	Malaysia	548
									.1	.1	.1	.1	.2	.2	Maldives	556
															Marshall Islands, Rep. of	867
						.8	.9	.9	.9	1.0	1.0	1.1	1.1	1.1	Micronesia, Fed. States of	868
								2.0	1.7	.3	.5	.3	.1	—	Mongolia	948
.1	.1	.4	.6	.1	—	.2	.1	.1	.1	.1	.2	.1	.1	.4	Myanmar	518
.1	.1	.1	.1	.1	.1					.2				.1	Nepal	558
11.1	4.9	1.1	.6	5.2	.1	.5	.2	9.9	9.2	8.0	.6	.2	10.9	3.1	Pakistan	564
															Palau	565
3.3	3.0	2.7	—	—									9.3	6.9	Papua New Guinea	853
.1		.7	.8	3.1	.4	7.3	16.7	5.4	1.7	1.3	1.4	5.1	1.5	11.2	Philippines	566
1.3	2.4	.7	2.9	2.6	1.9	2.0	2.0	2.0	2.1	2.1	2.2	2.2	2.3	2.3	Samoa	862
81.2	79.0	79.4	81.4	81.3	49.4	56.9	24.1	33.1	42.5	52.2	64.9	89.2	105.3	119.6	Singapore	576
.2	—	.1	.3	.1	—										Solomon Islands	813
.1	.1	10.3	.3	.2	.1	.3	.2	.6	1.3	.3	.9	.7	.3	.7	Sri Lanka	524
42.5	45.2	12.5	9.0	5.7	8.8	15.9	21.8	30.5	41.5	357.6	277.9	188.1	63.4	4.2	Thailand	578
.1	.1	.1	.2	.7	.4	.4	.5	—	.1	.1	.2	—	.1	.2	Tonga	866
.3	.3	.4	.5	.6	.7	.2	.2	.3	.4	.4	.5	.6	.7	.8	Vanuatu	846
						4.9	11.0	2.2	11.9	9.4	1.8	1.1	.3	11.6	Vietnam	582
47.2	50.6	129.7	70.2	214.7	103.4	270.1	373.6	636.8	511.5	784.2	730.0	568.0	558.1	480.8	**Europe**	170
						—	.2	.1	.5	.5	43.4	56.1	58.3	64.9	Albania	914
						—	.2	29.8	28.9	27.6	19.9	29.6	16.5	8.1	Armenia	911
							—	.8	14.5	4.1	.1	5.2	5.1	2.0	Azerbaijan	912
					3.2		3.1	.1	—	.3	.3	.1	.3		Belarus	913
								5.0	1.8	—	3.7	5.6	8.2	4.9	Bosnia and Herzegovina	963
		—	5.9	.3	.8	10.4	20.1	8.3	8.4	21.4	59.5	65.0	1.8		Bulgaria	918
						.8	3.1	94.4	87.3	109.0	164.2	138.1	113.0	85.5	Croatia	960
.3	.1	.1	.1	.1	.1	.1	—		.2	.2	.4		.2	.7	Cyprus	423
						6.0		.1							Czech Republic	935
	—	—	—	97.6	30.8										Czechoslovakia	934
					7.7	41.6	1.1	.2	.1	—		1.0	—	—	Estonia	939
							1.6	1.1	—	.1	3.7	6.1	2.5	3.1	Georgia	915
.2	.2	—	.7		.9	1.9	2.1	1.1	.3	.1	3.7	3.2	9.0	16.4	Hungary	944
							14.0	69.5	154.9	240.2	327.2	275.1	164.2	—	Kazakhstan	916
					—	9.4	.7	9.6	5.1	.7	.2	3.7	.5	1.1	Kyrgyz Republic	917
					19.3	71.1	.2	1.5	1.6	1.5	2.2	2.2	—	.1	Latvia	941
					.9	54.7	10.4	12.2	7.1	8.0	11.5	3.2	1.0	14.7	Lithuania	946
									.2	.3	.8	.9	.5	1.8	Macedonia, FYR	962
46.6	50.1	53.6	59.1	64.2	33.1	35.3	35.6	37.6	39.7	41.9	44.4	22.5	24.5	26.4	Malta	181
						25.1	14.6	8.8	5.5	.9	.5	.2	.3	.6	Moldova	921
.1	.1	.1	.6	5.4	.8	.5	1.0	1.5	3.1	4.0	5.0	8.1	13.6	20.5	Poland	964
	—	76.0	.1	40.3	7.9	1.4	38.1	37.7	2.8	76.9	.8	7.3	.8	5.4	Romania	968
					.6	3.7	2.1	78.5	3.1	90.7	.1	.4	.4	2.3	Russia	922
						.3	58.9	39.0	11.2	19.6	1.2	.6	.4	.5	Slovak Republic	936
									.1	.1	.2	1.2	2.8	4.0	Slovenia	961
									2.2	9.1	2.1	—	6.0	3.9	Tajikistan	923
—	—	.4	—		.1	.8	1.9	1.0	.6	1.0	.1		21.9	3.6	Turkey	186
															Turkmenistan	925
							123.7	97.1	46.7	52.7	129.5	47.9	191.2	199.8	Ukraine	926
									.8	.1	.2	.4	.3	.6	Uzbekistan	927
													15.2	6.8	Yugoslavia, Fed. Rep.	965
—	.1	—	9.2	.2											Yugoslavia, SFR	188
1,224.2	1,072.9	1,292.2	951.5	913.4	765.4	1,014.4	1,090.4	1,165.0	1,397.5	1,556.0	1,424.9	829.9	1,041.5	1,076.7	**Middle East**	405
14.6	15.1	15.9	16.9	17.8	18.7	10.8	11.0	11.3	11.7	11.9	12.1	—	1.0	.8	Bahrain, Kingdom of	419
.2	.3	.1	.4	.9	42.8	50.4	59.2	69.5	85.6	83.9	113.8	30.1	36.9	27.7	Egypt	469
342.3	115.7	304.7	310.4	215.8	7.4	104.8	97.9	89.9	239.8	244.6	1.1	101.3	267.5	267.4	Iran, I.R. of	429
5.1															Iraq	433
.1	.1	.1	.2	.3	.2	.4	.2	.4	1.0	—	.2	.1	.8	1.4	Israel	436
8.5		8.4	.7	.8	.4	4.0	.5	.8	.6	.1	.6	.2	.5	.9	Jordan	439
148.8	166.8	97.8	113.9	128.3	130.4	49.1	55.0	61.3	68.2	74.1	82.5	53.7	69.8	85.9	Kuwait	443
3.4	4.2	5.4	6.9	8.3	9.5	10.5	11.4	12.3	13.3	14.3	15.4	16.4	18.2	19.4	Lebanon	446
197.7	218.8	249.4	287.3	322.6	278.3	303.5	324.7	349.7	373.9	398.5	425.8	372.6	412.8	441.2	Libya	672
7.2	8.7	10.9	13.4	15.5	3.4	5.0	6.2	7.5	8.8	10.1	11.5	1.3	3.1	5.0	Oman	449
24.7	26.4	28.7	31.3	33.8	17.1	18.7	19.9	21.2	22.5	23.8	25.1	10.7	15.8	17.9	Qatar	453
370.8	395.5	467.2	69.9	62.0	202.0	402.7	416.0	448.2	481.3	512.1	545.9	110.5	146.6	192.3	Saudi Arabia	456
						.1						.1		.3	Syrian Arab Rep.	463
79.8	82.3	85.9	90.8	95.5	52.4	54.1	55.0	55.9	57.6	58.4	59.2	4.5	3.1	1.8	United Arab Emirates	466
19.0	23.9	15.9													Yemen Arab Rep.	473
2.1	14.9	1.8													Yemen, P.D. Rep.	459
			9.4	11.7	2.9	.5	33.5	37.0	33.3	124.1	131.6	128.5	65.0	14.7	Yemen, Republic of	474

SDRs

1b s

		1972	1973	1974	1975	1976	1977	1978	1979	1980	1981	1982	1983	1984	1985	1986
																Millions of SDRs
Western Hemisphere	205	566.0	617.4	658.8	568.8	525.3	617.7	729.6	1,293.3	1,155.2	1,572.7	741.2	693.1	570.0	680.4	839.5
Antigua and Barbuda	311	....	....	....	....	....	....	....	....							
Argentina	213	17.8	66.9	83.8	34.8	78.2	73.9	161.6	247.9	256.6	347.1	—	—	.3	.6	—
Bahamas, The	313	—	—	—	—	—	—	—	3.4	2.7	6.1	5.8	1.1	.7	.4	—
Barbados	316	2.8	2.8	2.8	2.8	2.8	2.7	2.5	3.9	1.6	1.4	.8	.3			
Belize	339	....	....	....	....	....	....	....	....							
Bolivia	218	3.0	2.2	2.6	7.0	6.9	5.7	14.1	—	—	.1	—	.1	—	—	2.0
Brazil	223	157.0	157.2	162.8	163.3	171.0	173.2	183.8	290.7	300.7	388.1	.3	.1	.9	.5	—
Chile	228	2.0	.3	13.8	20.9	48.3	54.7	20.7	22.0	3.0	16.4	17.7	5.2	11.7	.3	.2
Colombia	233	17.5	23.1	24.5	20.3	24.3	25.6	37.8	71.9	85.3	119.4	162.4	188.7	.1	—	114.3
Costa Rica	238	4.0	3.9	2.0	3.8	1.2	5.5	3.0	4.5	—		.1	2.9	.1	—	
Dominica	321	....	....	....	....	....	....	....			.7	.3	.4	—	—	.8
Dominican Republic	243	6.9	6.8	7.2	6.5	6.0	5.2	4.7	7.2	—	1.6	.5	.2	.4	28.8	—
Ecuador	248	6.7	5.6	6.5	6.3	6.3	8.2	10.6	19.2	19.0	28.9	—	.1	.5	26.2	45.7
El Salvador	253	3.7	3.8	3.6	3.9	4.0	7.8	7.6	13.2	—	.1	1.7	.1	—	—	—
Grenada	328	....	....	....	.1	.1	....	....	—	—	—	—	.1	—	—	—
Guatemala	258	7.6	11.5	11.5	11.5	11.4	11.5	11.6	18.4	17.7	2.2	—	.6	2.0	—	—
Guyana	336	4.1	4.0	3.9	3.8	3.5	2.7	2.8	2.8	—	1.0	2.6	—	—	—	—
Haiti	263	3.1	1.7	2.5	2.0	1.2	1.6	3.8	5.5	—	—	1.0	1.0	—	—	5.4
Honduras	268	5.5	5.4	5.3	4.0	2.7	3.6	3.0	7.7	—	1.4	1.6	2.1	.2	—	—
Jamaica	343	6.9	6.4	5.1	4.3	.8	14.3	4.5	.4	—	1.1	.1	—	—	—	.3
Mexico	273	127.7	127.8	129.0	86.3	.9	46.8	42.6	152.4	112.9	152.9	5.3	21.9	3.1	.4	7.2
Nicaragua	278	6.2	5.7	5.8	4.6	3.5	3.8	4.3	—	—	.1	.9	—	—	—	—
Panama	283	2.7	2.6	2.3	6.4	5.2	4.5	4.0	3.9	1.1	2.8	3.8	.4	—	11.7	1.4
Paraguay	288	6.6	6.6	6.6	6.6	6.6	6.6	6.6	9.4	11.1	15.1	23.7	30.4	35.0	38.8	42.1
Peru	293	41.0	37.3	37.2	37.1	3.3	2.7	4.8	81.3	9.7	9.8	29.9	.6	22.9	—	—
St. Kitts and Nevis	361	....	....	....	....	....	....	....								
St. Lucia	362	....	....	....	....	....	....	....	—	.1	.2	—	—	—	—	—
St. Vincent & Grens.	364	....	....	....	....	....	....	....	—	.1	.2	—	—	—	—	—
Suriname	366	....	....	....	....	....	....	....	2.6	2.1	5.4	8.5	1.7	1.3	.8	.3
Trinidad and Tobago	369	7.3	7.1	7.9	7.6	7.6	12.2	16.9	31.2	35.8	51.3	73.5	94.4	103.1	107.8	112.0
Uruguay	298	7.8	10.8	12.1	1.6	3.7	8.5	11.4	26.2	26.0	37.2	1.7	3.7	5.1	13.3	9.7
Venezuela, Rep. Bol	299	118.1	118.2	120.3	123.6	126.0	136.5	167.0	267.7	269.9	382.1	399.3	336.8	382.1	451.4	498.0
Memorandum Items																
Oil Exporting Countries....................	999	299.7	306.6	334.6	309.7	327.3	374.5	480.1	1,032.6	1,218.0	1,767.5	2,078.1	1,547.5	1,712.9	1,844.8	1,756.6
Non-Oil Developing Countries...........	201	1,251.5	1,339.2	1,345.0	1,203.9	1,096.7	1,071.2	1,224.8	2,064.4	1,701.7	2,703.5	1,573.0	1,349.2	1,381.8	1,465.8	1,602.6

SDR Holdings

Millions of SDRs: End of Period

		1972	1973	1974	1975	1976	1977	1978	1979	1980	1981	1982	1983	1984	1985	1986
World	001	9,314.9	9,314.9	9,314.9	9,314.8	9,314.9	9,314.8	9,315.1	13,348.0	17,385.9	21,433.5	21,437.0	21,446.5	21,450.2	21,451.9	21,448.1
All Participants	969	8,686.1	8,807.1	8,857.9	8,763.8	8,655.4	8,132.7	8,110.0	12,478.9	11,808.5	16,411.2	17,744.6	14,418.2	16,469.5	18,212.8	19,494.1
IMF	992	628.7	507.7	457.0	551.0	659.5	1,182.1	1,205.1	868.7	5,571.9	5,018.9	3,686.2	6,998.8	4,957.5	3,068.4	1,937.0
Other Holders	970	—	—	—	—	—	—	—	5.6	3.3	6.2	29.4	23.3	170.6	17.1	

End of Period

1987	1988	1989	1990	1991	1992	1993	1994	1995	1996	1997	1998	1999	2000	2001		
1,272.0	568.9	537.5	730.2	960.0	858.6	1,075.7	1,045.1	1,963.5	1,049.0	1,027.6	801.7	1,032.3	1,146.4	594.5	Western Hemisphere	205
															Antigua and Barbuda	311
—	.3	.2	209.0	134.9	272.8	329.5	385.7	362.7	277.4	123.6	187.7	100.3	562.2	8.5	Argentina	213
.3	.4	.1	.4	—	.1	—	—	—	—	—	—	—	.1	.1	Bahamas, The	313
.6	.5	—	—	.5	.1	.1	—	—	—	—	—	—	—	—	Barbados	316
.1	—	—	.1	.1	.2	.3	.4	.5	.6	.7	.8	1.0	1.2	1.4	Belize	339
—	—	—	.7	.1	.1	10.2	17.0	26.9	26.8	26.8	26.8	27.3	27.3	27.3	Bolivia	218
.1	—	.3	.7	8.9	.5	1.7	.3	.7	.7	.4	1.2	7.3	.3	8.4	Brazil	223
28.8	32.9	18.5	—	.7	.5	.8	.9	—	2.1	1.3	1.0	5.9	13.5	18.9	Chile	228
114.3	114.3	114.3	114.2	114.2	42.5	114.9	116.4	118.8	122.8	127.6	139.3	95.2	103.3	107.8	Colombia	233
—	—	—	1.1	.2	.2	.1	.1	—	—	—	—	.6	.3	.1	Costa Rica	238
.7	.6	.3	.2	—	.1	—	—	—	—	—	—	—	—	—	Dominica	321
—	—	—	—	—	.1	10.3	2.5	.3	.3	.2	.2	.2	.3	.3	Dominican Republic	243
.7	1.0	.7	10.3	28.9	.1	3.2	3.0	2.1	1.9	.4	.2	1.7	.2	1.8	Ecuador	248
—	—	—	—	—	—	—	.1	25.0	25.0	25.0	25.0	25.0	25.0	25.0	El Salvador	253
—	—	—	—	—	—	—	—	—	—	—	—	—	—	—	Grenada	328
1.2	.1	.6	—	—	11.4	11.4	11.4	10.6	10.2	9.4	8.7	8.4	7.5	6.7	Guatemala	258
—	—	—	1.5	1.0	.2	—	.1	.1	.1	.1	.9	.1	7.0	2.0	Guyana	336
—	—	.1	—	—	—	—	.4	—	.1	.4	.6	.1	—	.4	Haiti	263
—	—	—	—	—	.1	—	.1	.1	.1	.1	.1	.7	.1	.3	Honduras	268
1.0	—	—	.3	—	9.0	9.1	—	.3	—	—	.2	.5	.5	1.2	Jamaica	343
497.7	292.6	291.5	293.0	409.3	398.8	162.6	121.1	1,074.1	178.7	490.1	239.6	575.5	281.2	283.5	Mexico	273
—	—	—	—	—	—	.1	—	—	—	—	.1	.2	—	.3	Nicaragua	278
—	—	—	19.4	8.1	.1	.1	—	.6	—	.4	.1	1.2	.3	1.1	Panama	283
44.8	47.4	50.8	54.9	58.8	62.1	65.1	67.6	70.6	73.3	76.1	79.1	74.8	78.5	81.3	Paraguay	288
—	—	—	—	—	—	.7	.3	.5	.2	.2	1.5	.3	1.1	1.4	Peru	293
—	—	—	—	—	—	—	—	—	—	—	—	—	—	—	St. Kitts and Nevis	361
—	—	—	1.2	1.3	1.3	1.3	1.4	1.4	1.4	1.4	1.5	1.5	1.4	1.5	St. Lucia	362
—	—	—	—	—	.1	.1	.1	.1	.1	.1	.1	.1	—	—	St. Vincent & Grens.	364
—	—	—	—	—	—	—	—	7.8	8.2	8.2	8.3	2.0	1.8	1.6	Suriname	366
—	—	6.9	.8	1.5	.2	.2	.1	.1	—	—	.1	.1	—	.2	Trinidad and Tobago	369
48.1	22.1	17.5	7.9	3.3	—	.3	—	2.4	2.7	—	.5	.7	.4	1.5	Uruguay	298
533.6	56.4	36.0	6.7	188.3	54.6	353.6	316.9	255.4	317.0	135.3	73.7	92.9	27.7	7.9	Venezuela, Rep. Bol	299

Memorandum Items

1987	1988	1989	1990	1991	1992	1993	1994	1995	1996	1997	1998	1999	2000	2001		
1,857.1	1,074.4	1,284.8	928.7	1,065.6	746.3	1,296.7	1,307.6	1,291.2	1,574.4	1,827.8	1,448.0	749.3	973.4	1,041.7	Oil Exporting Countries	999
1,879.4	1,539.3	1,536.7	1,810.3	2,030.3	1,652.6	1,863.1	1,968.0	3,483.5	2,426.0	3,192.9	3,087.7	2,981.4	3,104.5	2,547.4	Non-Oil Developing Countries	201

SDR Holdings

1987	1988	1989	1990	1991	1992	1993	1994	1995	1996	1997	1998	1999	2000	2001		
21,466.5	21,484.2	21,480.9	21,479.4	21,474.2	21,480.1	21,480.9	21,476.9	21,484.5	21,495.2	21,508.2	21,522.1	21,534.8	21,527.5	21,539.5	World	001
20,212.5	20,172.9	20,484.8	20,354.4	20,551.3	12,867.2	14,614.3	15,761.5	19,773.2	18,521.4	20,532.2	20,379.7	18,456.7	18,489.0	19,556.8	All Participants	969
1,207.1	769.5	947.1	995.3	819.6	8,561.2	6,687.3	5,510.1	652.5	1,726.3	634.8	687.3	2,459.3	2,413.9	1,543.2	IMF	992
46.8	541.7	49.0	129.6	103.3	51.7	179.4	205.3	1,058.9	1,247.4	341.3	455.1	618.9	624.6	439.5	Other Holders	970

Fund Accounts

(As of July 31, 2002 and Amounts Expressed in Millions of SDRs)

Amounts Agreed	Amounts Borrowed *	Amounts Repaid	Outstanding Borrowings	Amounts Expired	Amounts Available for Borrowings	
		Borrowing Agreements				
						General Department
52,500.0	**4,319.8**	**4,319.8**	—	—	**52,500.0**	General Arrangements to Borrow (GAB)
17,000.0	**1,443.5**	**1,443.5**	—	—	**17,000.0**	Belgium
595.0	50.5	50.5	—	—	595.0	Canada
892.5	75.8	75.8	—	—	892.5	France
1,700.0	144.3	144.3	—	—	1,700.0	Germany
2,380.0	202.1	202.1	—	—	2,380.0	Italy
1,105.0	93.8	93.8	—	—	1,105.0	Japan
2,125.0	180.4	180.4	—	—	2,125.0	Netherlands
850.0	72.2	72.2	—	—	850.0	Sweden
382.5	32.5	32.5	—	—	382.5	Switzerland
1,020.0	86.6	86.6	—	—	1,020.0	United Kingdom
1,700.0	144.3	144.3	—	—	1,700.0	United States
4,250.0	360.9	360.9	—	—	4,250.0	Associated Agreement
1,500.0	—	—	—	—	**1,500.0**	Saudi Arabia
1,500.0					1,500.0	New Arrangements to Borrow (NAB)
34,000.0	**2,876.3**	**2,876.3**	—	—	**34,000.0**	Australia
810.0	74.7	74.7	—	—	810.0	Austria
412.0	38.0	38.0	—	—	412.0	Belgium
967.0	89.1	89.1	—	—	967.0	Canada
1,396.0	128.7	128.7	—	—	1,396.0	China, P.R.: Hong Kong
340.0	31.3	31.3	—	—	340.0	Denmark
371.0	34.2	34.2	—	—	371.0	Finland
340.0	31.3	31.3	—	—	340.0	France
2,577.0	237.6	237.6	—	—	2,577.0	Germany
3,557.0	327.9	327.9	—	—	3,557.0	Italy
1,772.0	163.4	163.4	—	—	1,772.0	Japan
3,557.0	327.9	327.9	—	—	3,557.0	Korea
340.0	—	—	—	—	340.0	Kuwait
345.0	31.8	31.8	—	—	345.0	Luxembourg
340.0	31.3	31.3	—	—	340.0	Malaysia
340.0	—	—	—	—	340.0	Netherlands
1,316.0	121.3	121.3	—	—	1,316.0	Norway
383.0	35.3	35.3	—	—	383.0	Saudi Arabia
1,780.0	—	—	—	—	1,780.0	Singapore
340.0	31.3	31.3	—	—	340.0	Spain
672.0	62.0	62.0	—	—	672.0	Sweden
859.0	79.2	79.2	—	—	859.0	Switzerland
1,557.0	143.5	143.5	—	—	1,557.0	Thailand
340.0	—	—	—	—	340.0	United Kingdom
2,577.0	237.6	237.6	—	—	2,577.0	United States
6,712.0	618.8	618.8	—	—	6,712.0	

* The maximum combined amount drawn under the GAB and the NAB cannot exceed SDR 34 billion.

Amounts Agreed	Amounts Borrowed *	Amounts Repaid	Outstanding Borrowings	Amounts Expired	Amounts Available for Borrowings	
		Administered Accounts				
						PRGF Trust:
15,691.1	9,379.5	2,843.3	6,680.2	3.6	6,308.1	
15,447.6	9,280.0	2,703.3	6,576.7	3.6	6,164.0	Loan Account
243.5	99.5	140.0	103.5	—	144.0	Subsidy Account

Reserve Position in the Fund

		1972	1973	1974	1975	1976	1977	1978	1979	1980	1981	1982	1983	1984	1985	1986
															Millions of SDRs.	
All Countries	010	6,324.7	6,168.2	8,844.4	12,624.0	17,736.1	18,088.6	14,838.5	11,759.8	16,835.5	21,322.8	25,455.2	39,112.6	41,569.6	38,730.8	35,339.3
Industrial Countries	110	5,288.0	4,963.1	6,225.4	7,712.6	11,846.8	12,245.8	9,612.6	7,763.9	10,798.2	13,651.8	17,160.8	25,669.7	27,357.0	25,301.1	23,087.8
United States	111	428.0	457.5	1,513.0	1,889.5	3,816.6	4,071.7	803.5	950.9	2,236.5	4,342.2	6,660.8	10,805.0	11,774.1	10,876.2	9,589.5
Canada	156	315.9	280.4	432.6	553.6	812.9	701.5	427.4	296.5	454.0	345.7	331.1	671.9	692.1	647.1	561.1
Australia	193	167.4	166.8	175.8	166.8	166.8	166.3	161.3	156.4	255.2	252.5	.1	108.6	186.7	188.7	188.8
Japan	158	570.8	529.4	603.3	686.4	1,143.5	1,329.3	1,641.7	1,120.9	1,043.9	1,338.8	1,877.5	2,199.3	2,263.8	2,071.1	1,947.3
New Zealand	196	50.5	50.6	—	—	—	—	23.0	—	27.5	27.6	—	28.5	—	.1	.1
Euro Area																
Austria	122	132.5	125.8	130.7	177.2	343.5	324.5	254.3	231.5	228.5	224.0	258.8	447.1	447.2	405.2	361.5
Belgium	124	516.1	492.4	511.1	591.3	814.2	779.3	605.7	524.0	489.4	390.2	328.1	496.5	521.3	472.4	462.3
Finland	172	63.8	63.8	63.8				46.1	44.7	77.4	77.4	77.5	123.0	133.7	130.3	135.0
France	132	459.8	377.0	429.0	622.7	843.0	736.4	460.6	478.5	836.5	883.6	868.3	1,291.6	1,290.9	1,246.8	1,419.3
Germany	134	1,140.2	1,207.0	1,290.4	1,581.4	2,132.7	2,184.8	3,301.9	2,372.2	1,796.0	2,117.4	2,798.9	3,579.9	3,826.1	3,467.0	3,146.1
Greece	174	34.5	34.5					33.5	32.4	55.6	55.6	55.6	86.2	81.4	75.0	70.1
Ireland	178	40.3	40.3	42.1	39.1	68.7	65.7	59.7	60.7	76.6	75.1	75.2	115.7	124.4	120.8	130.7
Italy	136	330.4	297.2	—	5.0	5.0	—	242.5	236.5	645.6	630.6	630.6	945.3	1,095.8	1,056.1	1,036.6
Luxembourg	137	5.0	5.0	5.0	9.0	9.0	8.7	9.6	9.4	12.2	12.2	12.2	12.2	12.2	12.2	12.2
Netherlands	138	553.6	309.4	441.6	746.7	899.8	953.5	631.8	457.7	510.3	497.8	561.3	901.0	963.2	898.2	717.0
Portugal	182	29.3	29.3	29.3						34.8	48.8	48.8	29.7	29.7	29.7	29.7
Spain	184	103.8	103.8	121.1				136.3	133.4	205.6	205.6	205.6	321.5	363.0	369.0	423.1
Denmark	128	65.0	119.1	72.9	61.1	67.0	72.8	68.7	76.8	110.9	105.3	99.8	205.0	214.4	207.5	127.2
Iceland	176	5.8	5.8						5.4	9.0	9.0		4.0	4.0	4.0	4.0
Norway	142	69.0	63.4	68.9	111.8	247.4	234.7	205.7	188.1	201.4	213.8	246.4	411.0	470.4	463.7	481.8
San Marino	135	—	—	—	—	—	—	—	—	—	—	—	—	—	—	—
Sweden	144	89.9	88.0	89.0	95.1	231.7	225.4	191.0	180.7	193.9	165.6	148.9	240.7	258.3	249.6	253.4
Switzerland	146	....	....	....	81.3	250.0	391.2	308.5	207.2	252.4	397.1	467.3	635.8	592.8	500.7	369.8
United Kingdom	112	116.5	116.6	205.9	303.7					1,045.2	1,236.1	1,408.1	2,010.2	2,011.8	1,809.7	1,621.0
Developing Countries	200	1,036.7	1,205.1	2,589.0	4,911.4	5,889.2	5,842.9	5,226.0	3,995.9	6,037.3	7,671.0	8,294.5	13,443.0	14,212.4	13,429.7	12,251.5
Africa	605	270.6	309.2	258.8	322.1	419.4	414.1	460.8	392.2	699.2	800.2	227.0	376.6	347.3	263.1	231.9
Algeria	612	32.5	32.5	32.5	32.5	33.5	32.5	31.6	30.6	101.8	116.8	125.6	172.4	165.5	152.9	148.0
Angola	614	....	....	....	....	....	....	....	....	....	....	....	....	....	....	....
Benin	638	2.1	2.1	2.1	2.1	2.1	2.1	2.0	1.9	2.0	2.0	2.0	2.0	2.0	2.0	2.0
Botswana	616	.6	.6	.6	.6	.6	1.2	1.2	2.2	5.1	9.1	9.2	11.3	12.3	12.9	15.6
Burkina Faso	748	3.1	3.3	3.3	3.3	3.3	4.6	4.6	4.6	5.6	5.6	5.6	5.6	7.5	7.5	7.5
Burundi	618	.3	.4	—	—	—	—	4.8	4.5	7.3	7.3	7.4	9.4	9.4	9.2	9.2
Cameroon	622	6.9	6.9	—	—	—	—	3.5	6.4	12.0	12.0	13.9	7.2	.2	.2	.2
Cape Verde	624	....	....	....	....	....	....	—	.3	.6	.6	.6	1.0	1.0	1.0	.2
Central African Rep.	626	.3	.4	—	—	—	—	1.7	1.9	—	1.2	1.6	.1	.1	.1	.1
Chad	628	....	....	....	....	....	....	1.2	1.8	3.8	3.8	5.1	3.5	.3	.3	.3
Comoros	632								.3							
Congo, Dem. Rep. of	636	28.3	28.3	28.3	—	—	—	—	—	—	23.5					
Congo, Rep. of	634	1.8	1.8	1.9	2.0	2.0	—	—	—	—	2.1	3.3	3.0	.5	.5	.5
Côte d'Ivoire	662	10.8	10.8	—	—	—	—	10.4	12.2	9.5	—	—	—	—	—	—
Djibouti	611	....	....	....	....	....	....	—	.8	1.2	1.2	1.2	1.2	1.2	1.2	1.2
Equatorial Guinea	642	—	—	—	—	1.8	—	—	.2	—	.2	.5	—	—	—	—
Ethiopia	644	6.8	6.8	6.8	6.8	6.8	7.3	—	—	4.1	—	—	4.2	—	—	—
Gabon	646	2.4	2.5	2.5	2.5	2.5	2.5	—	—	—	—	—	7.0	—	—	—
Gambia, The	648	.4	.5	.6	1.8	1.7	—	—	—	—	—	—	—	—	—	.1
Ghana	652	—	5.9	10.6	—	—	—	—	—	—	—	—	—	—	—	—
Guinea	656	—	—	—	—	—	—	—	—	—	—	—	—	—	—	—
Guinea-Bissau	654	....	....	....	....	....	.8	—	—	.5	—	.6	1.5	—	—	—
Kenya	664	12.0	12.3	—	—	—	—	—	—	—	.2	1.5	9.6	10.9	12.2	12.2
Lesotho	666	.2	.4	.6	1.3	1.3	1.3	1.1	1.1	2.0	2.0	.1	1.2	1.3	1.3	1.3
Liberia	668	.3	—	1.4	1.8	—	—	—	—	—	—	—	—	—	—	—
Madagascar	674	5.0	5.0	—	—	—	—	—	—	—	—	.3	1.2	—	—	—
Malawi	676	1.9	3.8	3.8	—	—	—	—	—	—	—	3.8	—	2.2	2.2	2.2
Mali	678	—	—	—	—	—	—	—	—	5.4	7.6	8.7	8.7	8.7	8.7	8.7
Mauritania	682	.8	.9	—	—	—	—	—	—	—	—	—	—	—	—	—
Mauritius	684	2.5	2.5	—	5.5	5.5	—	—	—	—	—	—	—	—	—	—
Morocco	686	28.3	28.2	28.2	28.2	—	—	—	—	—	—	—	—	—	—	—
Mozambique	688	....	....	....	....	....	....	....	....	....	....	....	....	....	....	—
Namibia	728															
Niger	692	2.1	2.1	2.1	2.1	2.1	3.1	5.0	5.0	6.0	6.0	6.1	8.6	8.6	8.6	8.6
Nigeria	694	12.9	33.0	33.8	212.2	333.8	340.3	365.9	295.2	370.7	446.1	—	—	—	.1	.1
Rwanda	714	—	—	—	—	2.1	2.1	2.9	5.5	8.4	7.3	7.3	9.6	9.7	9.3	9.3
São Tomé & Príncipe	716	....	....	....	....	....	....	.4	.4	.7	.7	.7	.7	—	—	—
Senegal	722	3.9	4.2	—	—	—	—	2.1	—	—	—	.9	.9	1.0	1.0	1.0
Seychelles	718	....	....	....	....	.1	.1	.3	.4	.4	.4	—	—	—	—	
Sierra Leone	724	4.9	4.9	—	—	—	—	—	—	—	1.1	—	—	—	—	—
Somalia	726	3.9	3.9	3.9	4.2	4.2	—	—	—	—	—	—	—	—	—	—
South Africa	199	80.5	80.5	81.4	—	—	—	—	—	128.2	107.2	—	70.0	70.0	—	—
Sudan	732	—	.2	—	—	—	—	—	—	—	—	—	—	—	—	—
Swaziland	734	.3	.2	.4	1.1	2.0	2.0	2.8	2.7	4.3	4.3	—	1.7	1.7	1.8	—
Tanzania	738	6.9	10.5	—	—	—	—	—	—	—	—	1.7	—	—	—	—
Togo	742	2.1	2.1	2.1	2.1	2.1	2.1	2.0	3.3	—	—	.2	.2	.2	.2	.2
Tunisia	744	5.9	12.0	12.0	12.0	12.0	12.0	11.7	11.3	19.2	19.2	19.2	30.1	29.4	26.4	—
Uganda	746	—	—	—	—	—	—	5.9	—	—	—	3.5	3.5	3.5	3.5	3.5
Zambia	754	—	—	—	—	—	—	—	—	—	7.5	—	—	—	—	—
Zimbabwe	698	....	....	....	....	....	....	....	....							

1987	1988	1989	1990	1991	1992	1993	1994	1995	1996	1997	1998	1999	2000	2001		
End of Period																
31,467.1	28,272.9	25,471.0	23,748.9	25,887.7	33,902.8	32,802.2	31,725.6	36,673.2	38,005.3	47,078.0	60,630.9	54,785.6	47,377.7	56,861.3	All Countries	010
20,462.9	19,572.2	19,553.6	19,976.5	22,774.1	29,510.6	28,308.8	27,417.0	31,643.8	32,609.8	41,336.5	53,919.2	46,775.8	39,699.5	46,960.1	Industrial Countries	110
8,000.1	7,241.7	6,884.8	6,379.7	6,632.8	8,552.3	8,589.0	8,240.8	9,854.7	10,733.8	13,393.4	17,124.1	13,092.9	11,377.3	14,219.0	United States	111
465.7	375.2	401.6	363.7	414.1	734.9	689.9	629.2	836.2	852.8	1,167.3	1,632.7	2,308.0	1,925.9	2,278.4	Canada	156
188.8	204.6	245.1	245.2	245.3	419.7	400.5	346.9	337.6	334.9	539.0	892.3	1,189.4	953.9	1,123.6	Australia	193
2,010.8	2,435.8	2,677.0	4,197.3	5,398.2	6,284.3	6,014.5	5,912.3	5,449.0	4,639.3	6,777.4	6,813.1	4,773.5	4,032.1	4,018.9	Japan	158
.2	8.2	39.8	40.2	54.0	109.1	103.6	100.8	110.3	126.6	131.9	252.8	308.6	245.7	308.2	New Zealand	196
															Euro Area	
330.0	288.9	274.4	241.8	275.8	389.8	381.5	363.9	458.9	562.4	713.7	969.7	698.7	531.5	662.5	Austria	122
392.4	344.8	341.9	326.3	366.6	586.0	560.2	556.3	675.8	747.3	875.8	1,348.4	1,668.4	1,303.8	1,631.7	Belgium	124
141.6	167.6	178.9	151.0	192.3	241.0	220.4	196.1	259.5	292.8	414.2	595.0	464.3	381.8	439.0	Finland	172
1,348.9	1,200.5	1,076.2	1,003.6	1,164.9	1,804.9	1,681.8	1,626.7	1,853.9	1,874.5	2,119.2	3,161.8	3,949.9	3,471.0	3,893.9	France	132
2,748.8	2,486.6	2,315.3	2,147.8	2,493.7	3,083.2	2,876.6	2,760.5	3,505.0	3,802.5	4,406.9	5,698.3	4,676.6	4,191.0	4,695.8	Germany	134
70.1	71.1	89.2	74.7	74.7	116.9	113.7	113.7	113.7	113.7	113.7	191.5	285.0	227.8	284.3	Greece	174
130.9	134.3	125.4	104.6	123.9	171.3	155.1	151.9	197.5	226.1	252.1	413.6	302.9	252.4	267.7	Ireland	178
1,019.7	941.1	1,095.5	1,204.6	1,576.2	1,774.1	1,575.4	1,392.8	1,320.6	1,289.9	1,660.7	3,075.3	2,583.6	2,230.1	2,559.7	Italy	136
12.2	12.2	12.3	12.3	12.3	25.9	23.6	23.6	22.9	23.6	21.8	59.4	54.4	55.5	78.9	Luxembourg	137
652.5	562.6	536.9	518.8	559.0	834.0	795.3	802.2	1,169.1	1,275.3	1,625.5	2,112.8	1,879.8	1,524.1	1,871.7	Netherlands	138
29.7	29.7	94.9	123.7	188.9	228.3	219.4	230.8	303.0	320.3	313.4	442.1	275.0	242.4	299.4	Portugal	182
553.6	786.0	929.7	796.8	748.8	831.7	750.6	759.5	1,064.9	1,110.3	1,409.5	1,557.8	1,111.2	907.5	1,055.1	Spain	184
123.2	234.7	254.9	219.8	248.6	345.7	309.1	294.6	400.0	421.8	467.9	827.5	582.1	440.1	566.8	Denmark	128
4.0	4.0	4.0	4.0	4.0	10.5	10.5	10.5	10.5	10.5	10.5	10.5	18.6	18.6	18.6	Iceland	176
498.1	451.3	441.9	407.8	399.0	471.4	425.3	440.9	636.2	643.8	725.5	899.1	621.2	448.1	577.3	Norway	142
						2.4	2.4	2.4	2.4	2.4	2.4	4.1	4.1	4.1	San Marino	135
277.4	250.8	253.6	233.9	308.4	451.4	451.4	451.4	451.4	451.4	589.1	899.9	862.9	683.3	827.1	Sweden	144
211.5	102.0	31.6			580.9	604.5	643.2	981.2	1,064.9	1,407.5	1,828.0	1,218.1	963.7	1,258.7	Switzerland	146
1,252.6	1,238.6	1,245.7	1,179.0	1,292.7	1,463.6	1,354.4	1,366.1	1,629.5	1,689.1	2,198.2	3,111.3	3,846.7	3,287.9	4,019.5	United Kingdom	112
11,004.2	8,700.7	5,917.4	3,772.4	3,113.6	4,392.1	4,493.4	4,308.6	5,029.4	5,395.4	5,741.5	6,711.7	8,009.8	7,678.1	9,901.1	Developing Countries	200
188.5	76.3	82.0	76.4	74.7	157.0	157.6	157.6	151.0	152.0	150.5	159.4	335.5	290.0	289.5	Africa	605
107.9												85.1	85.1	85.1	Algeria	612
....	....														Angola	614
2.0	2.0	2.0	2.0	2.0	2.1	2.1	2.1	2.1	2.2	2.2	2.2	2.2	2.2	2.2	Benin	638
15.7	13.6	19.2	16.2	13.5	14.8	16.6	16.3	19.3	19.9	18.1	27.6	22.6	17.7	22.3	Botswana	616
7.5	7.5	7.5	7.2	7.2	7.2	7.2	7.2	7.2	7.2	7.2	7.2	7.2	7.2	7.2	Burkina Faso	748
9.2	9.2	9.2	7.6	7.2	5.9	5.9	5.9	5.9	5.9	5.9	5.9	5.9	5.9	.4	Burundi	618
.2	.2	.2	.2	.2	.3	.3	.3	.4	.4	.4	.4	.5	.5	.5	Cameroon	622
												—	—	—	Cape Verde	624
.1	.1	.1	.1	.1	.1	.1	.1	.1	.1	.1	.1	.1	.1	.1	Central African Rep.	626
.3	.3	.3	.3	.3	.3	.3	.3	.3	.3	.3	.3	.3	.3	.5	Chad	628
					.5	.5	.5	.5	.5	.5	.5	.5	.5	.5	Comoros	632
												—	—	—	Congo, Dem. Rep. of	636
.5	.5	.5	.5	.5	.5	.5	.5	.5	.5	.5	.5	.5	.5	.5	Congo, Rep. of	634
						.1	.1	.1	.1	.2	.2	.2	.3	.3	Côte d'Ivoire	662
1.2	1.2	1.2	1.2	1.2	2.1	—	—	—	—	—	—	1.1	1.1	1.1	Djibouti	611
															Equatorial Guinea	642
—	—	—	—	—	6.9	7.0	7.0	7.0	7.1	7.1	7.1	7.1	7.1	7.1	Ethiopia	644
				.1	.1	.1	.1	.1	.1	.1	.1	.1	.1	.2	Gabon	646
.1	.1	.1	—	—	1.5	1.5	1.5	1.5	1.5	1.5	1.5	1.5	1.5	1.5	Gambia, The	648
—	—	—	—	—	17.4	17.4	17.4	17.4	17.4	17.4	17.4	41.1	—	—	Ghana	652
						.1	.1	.1	.1	.1	.1	.1	.1	.1	Guinea	656
															Guinea-Bissau	654
12.2	12.2	12.2	12.2	12.2	12.2	12.2	12.3	12.3	12.3	12.4	12.4	12.4	12.5	12.5	Kenya	664
1.3	1.3	1.3	1.3	1.3	3.5	3.5	3.5	3.5	3.5	3.5	3.5	3.5	3.5	3.5	Lesotho	666
												—	—	—	Liberia	668
												—	—	—	Madagascar	674
2.2	2.2	2.2	2.2	2.2	2.2	2.2	2.2	2.2	2.2	2.2	2.2	2.2	2.2	2.3	Malawi	676
8.7	8.7	8.7	8.7	8.7	8.7	8.7	8.7	8.7	8.8	8.8	8.8	8.8	8.8	8.8	Mali	678
												—	—	—	Mauritania	682
—	—	—	.1	1.3	6.2	7.3	7.3	7.3	7.4	7.4	7.4	14.5	14.5	14.5	Mauritius	684
					30.3	30.3	30.3	30.3	30.3	30.3	30.3	70.4	70.4	70.4	Morocco	686
												—	—	—	Mozambique	688
												—	—	—	Namibia	728
....	8.6	8.6	8.6	8.6	8.6	8.6	8.6	8.6	8.6	8.6	8.6	8.6	8.6	8.6	Niger	692
8.6	.1	.1	.1	.1	.1	.1	.1	.1	.1	.1	.1	.1	.1	.1	Nigeria	694
9.3	7.1	7.1	6.4	6.5	10.4	9.8	9.8	—	—	—	—	—	—	—	Rwanda	714
												—	—	—	São Tomé & Príncipe	716
1.0	1.0	1.0	1.0	1.0	1.1	1.1	1.1	1.2	1.3	1.3	1.4	1.4	1.4	1.4	Senegal	722
—	—	.1	.1	.1	.8	.8	.8	.8	.8	.8	—	—	—	—	Seychelles	718
												—	—	—	Sierra Leone	724
												—	—	—	Somalia	726
—	—	—	—	—	.1	—	.1	.1	.1	.1	.1	.1	.3	.3	South Africa	199
												—	—	—	Sudan	732
—	—	—	—	—	3.0	3.0	3.0	3.0	3.0	3.0	3.0	6.6	6.6	6.6	Swaziland	734
					10.0	10.0	10.0	10.0	10.0	10.0	10.0	10.0	10.0	10.0	Tanzania	738
.2	.2	.2	.2	.3	.3	.2	.3	.3	.3	.3	.3	.3	.3	.3	Togo	742
												—	20.2	20.2	20.2	Tunisia	744
												—	—	—	Uganda	746
												—	—	—	Zambia	754
—	—	—	—	.1	.1	.1	.1	.1	.1	.1	.2	.3	.3	.3	Zimbabwe	698

Reserve Position in the Fund

1c s

		1972	1973	1974	1975	1976	1977	1978	1979	1980	1981	1982	1983	1984	1985	1986
															Millions of SDRs	
Asia	**505**	**196.6**	**210.8**	**143.2**	**118.5**	**99.9**	**174.7**	**230.1**	**360.7**	**831.6**	**742.0**	**880.1**	**1,196.8**	**1,236.2**	**1,210.9**	**1,220.0**
Afghanistan, Islamic State of	512	—	—	—	—	—	8.3	9.0	9.4	15.1	15.1	15.1	4.8	4.8	4.8	4.8
Bangladesh	513	2.0	1.2	—	—	—	—	—	—	—	—	7.5	22.4	22.4	22.4	22.4
Bhutan	514											.4	.4	.6	.6	.6
Brunei Darussalam	516							…	…		—	—	—	—	—	—
Cambodia	522	—	—	—	—	—	—	—	—	—	—	—	—	—	—	—
China, P.R.: Mainland	924	—	—	—	—	—	—	—	—	150.0	—	—	167.7	260.6	302.6	302.6
China, P.R.: Hong Kong	532	…	…	…	…	…	…	…	…	…	…	…	…	…	…	…
Fiji	819	2.3	2.3	—	3.3	3.3	3.3	3.2	3.1	5.3	5.4	5.4	7.8	7.8	7.8	7.9
India	534	76.2	76.2	—	—	—	—	69.2	161.5	329.7	329.7	364.3	486.9	487.0	487.1	487.2
Indonesia	536	—	—	28.6	—	—	68.0	69.1	73.7	160.8	196.3	218.4	72.4	72.4	72.4	72.4
Kiribati	826															.6
Korea	542	12.5	20.0	3.3	—	—	—	10.4	18.8	—	—	—	51.7	—	.7	.7
Lao P. D. Rep.	544	2.8	2.8	3.3	—	—	—	—	—	—	—	—	—	—	—	—
Malaysia	548	39.3	46.5	49.5	53.8	53.8	52.3	53.6	67.5	116.5	116.5	116.5	159.3	159.4	159.4	159.4
Maldives	556	…	…	…	—	—	—	.2	.2	.3	.3	.3	.5	—	—	—
Marshall Islands, Rep. of	867	…	…	…	…	…	…	…	…	…	…	…	…	…	…	…
Micronesia, Fed. States of	868	…	…	…	…	…	…	…	…	…	…	…	…	…	…	…
Mongolia	948	…	…	…	…	…	…	…	…	…	…	…	…	…	…	…
Myanmar	518	—	—	—	—	—	—	—	—	—	9.0	13.0	6.9	6.9	—	—
Nepal	558	2.9	3.1	3.1	3.1	—	—	2.4	2.3	5.2	5.7	5.7	5.7	5.7	5.7	5.7
Pakistan	564	—	—	—	—	—	—	—	—	—	—	58.8	88.5	88.6	—	—
Palau	565	…	…	…	…	…	…	…	…	…	…	…	…	…	…	…
Papua New Guinea	853	—	—	—	—	—	—	—	2.4	3.8	—	.1	5.3	5.4	5.4	5.4
Philippines	566	—	—	—	—	—	—	—	—	—	—	—	—	8.8	23.8	38.8
Samoa	862	.4	.4	.4	—	—	—	—	—	—	—	—	—	—	—	—
Singapore	576	9.3	9.3	9.3	9.3	9.4	—	9.4	13.1	21.5	44.3	63.4	67.7	68.5	69.1	80.6	79.9
Solomon Islands	813	…	…	…	…	…	…	—	.4	.7	—	—	.5	.5	.5	.5
Sri Lanka	524	—	—	—	—	—	—	—	—	—	—	.5	5.9	17.1	6.0	6.0
Thailand	578	33.5	33.5	33.5	33.5	33.5	33.5	—	—	—	—	—	28.8	28.8	28.8	28.8
Tonga	866	…	…	…	…	…	…	…	…	…	…	…	…	…	.7	.7
Vanuatu	846	…	…	…	…	…	…	…	…	—	—	1.0	1.6	1.6	1.6	1.6
Vietnam	582	15.5	15.5	15.5	15.5	…	…	…	…	…	…	…	…	…	…	…
Europe	**170**	**86.2**	**48.3**	**41.8**	**7.8**	**13.8**	**12.2**	**81.7**	**19.4**	**15.8**	**23.7**	**29.1**	**157.4**	**67.8**	**66.6**	**69.3**
Albania	914	…	…	…	…	…	…	…	…	…	…	…	…	…	…	…
Armenia	911	…	…	…	…	…	…	…	…	…	…	…	…	…	…	…
Azerbaijan	912	…	…	…	…	…	…	…	…	…	…	…	…	…	…	…
Belarus	913	…	…	…	…	…	…	…	…	…	…	…	…	…	…	…
Bosnia and Herzegovina	963	…	…	…	…	…	…	…	…	…	…	…	…	…	…	…
Bulgaria	918	…	…	…	…	…	…	…	…	…	…	…	…	…	…	…
Croatia	960	…	…	…	…	…	…	…	…	…	…	…	…	…	…	…
Cyprus	423	6.5	6.5	—	—	—	—	6.5	6.1	—	—	—	4.7	4.7	4.7	4.7
Czech Republic	935	…	…	…	…	…	…	…	…	…	…	…	…	…	…	…
Czechoslovakia	934	—	—	—	—	—	—	—	—	—	—	—	—	—	—	—
Estonia	939	…	…	…	…	…	…	…	…	…	…	…	…	…	…	…
Georgia	915	…	…	…	…	…	…	…	…	…	…	…	…	…	…	…
Hungary	944	…	…	…	…	…	…	…	…	…	…	—	38.9	—	—	—
Kazakhstan	916	…	…	…	…	…	…	…	…	…	…	…	…	…	…	…
Kyrgyz Republic	917	…	…	…	…	…	…	…	…	…	…	…	…	…	…	…
Latvia	941	…	…	…	…	…	…	…	…	…	…	…	…	…	…	…
Lithuania	946	…	…	…	…	…	…	…	…	…	…	…	…	…	…	…
Macedonia, FYR	962	…	…	…	…	…	…	…	…	…	…	…	…	…	…	…
Malta	181	4.0	4.0	4.0	7.8	13.8	12.2	13.2	13.3	15.8	23.7	25.8	28.8	30.9	29.7	32.4
Moldova	921	…	…	…	…	…	…	…	…	…	…	…	…	…	…	…
Poland	964	…	…	…	…	…	…	…	…	…	…	…	…	…	…	…
Romania	968	47.5	—	—	—	—	—	—	—	—	—	—	—	—	—	—
Russia	922	…	…	…	…	…	…	…	…	…	…	…	…	…	…	…
Slovak Republic	936	…	…	…	…	…	…	…	…	…	…	…	…	…	…	…
Slovenia	961	…	…	…	…	…	…	…	…	…	…	…	…	…	…	…
Tajikistan	923	…	…	…	…	…	…	…	…	…	…	…	…	…	…	…
Turkey	186	28.1	37.8	37.8	—	—	—	—	—	—	—	—	32.3	32.3	32.3	32.3
Turkmenistan	925	…	…	…	…	…	…	…	…	…	…	…	…	…	…	…
Ukraine	926	…	…	…	…	…	…	…	…	…	…	…	…	…	…	…
Uzbekistan	927	…	…	…	…	…	…	…	…	…	…	…	…	…	…	…
Yugoslavia, Fed. Rep.	965	—	—	—	—	—	—	—	—	—	—	—	—	—	—	—
Yugoslavia, SFR	188	—	—	—	—	—	—	62.1	—	—	—	3.3	52.7	—	—	—
Middle East	**405**	**124.0**	**194.3**	**1,412.4**	**3,315.4**	**4,162.9**	**4,105.0**	**3,363.2**	**2,240.2**	**3,011.7**	**4,527.2**	**5,735.9**	**10,264.1**	**11,560.0**	**10,973.4**	**9,957.2**
Bahrain, Kingdom of	419	2.5	2.5	5.5	9.6	4.7	4.8	5.8	5.8	8.5	8.9	12.5	21.4	23.1	24.6	26.0
Egypt	469	—	—	—	—	—	—	—	—	—	—	24.0	30.4	—	—	—
Iran, I.R. of	429	19.3	48.0	422.0	958.8	998.0	985.6	725.2	325.1	234.6	141.4	75.7	70.8	70.8	70.8	70.8
Iraq	433	17.3	27.3	27.3	27.3	27.3	27.5	27.7	47.8	111.9	111.9	111.9	—	—	—	—
Israel	436	—	32.5	—	—	—	—	—	31.6	25.6	—	—	34.8	—	—	—
Jordan	439	5.8	5.8	5.8	5.8	5.8	5.8	5.6	10.3	16.6	16.6	16.6	7.2	—	—	—
Kuwait	443	20.7	19.7	255.8	573.6	742.7	722.2	588.4	389.7	410.5	409.7	461.0	696.7	716.4	639.4	515.8
Lebanon	446	2.3	2.3	2.3	2.3	2.3	2.3	2.3	2.1	6.1	6.1	6.1	18.8	18.8	18.8	18.8
Libya	672	6.0	6.0	6.0	6.0	6.0	6.0	5.9	42.4	148.1	189.2	189.2	189.2	243.5	243.5	243.5
Oman	449	1.8	1.8	15.3	24.4	25.0	19.4	13.9	12.8	14.9	16.5	20.8	30.5	33.2	32.1	32.1
Qatar	453	5.0	5.0	5.0	13.1	16.2	14.5	14.7	13.6	18.1	18.1	18.1	19.4	37.2	35.8	30.7
Saudi Arabia	456	33.5	33.5	595.3	1,570.2	2,205.8	2,215.2	1,895.7	1,289.6	1,896.2	3,428.2	4,621.3	8,902.7	10,187.6	9,706.8	8,838.4
Syrian Arab Rep.	463	—	—	—	7.1	12.5	—	—	—	—	7.1	7.1	—	—	—	—
United Arab Emirates	466	3.8	3.8	69.6	114.8	114.1	96.5	71.7	62.1	93.1	147.9	201.4	214.6	222.3	201.7	181.0
Yemen Arab Rep.	473	2.5	2.5	2.5	2.5	2.5	5.4	6.3	7.3	10.8	—	—	6.0	6.0	—	—
Yemen, P.D. Rep.	459	3.8	3.8	—	—	—	—	—	—	9.4	1.6	—	3.9	—	—	—
Yemen, Republic of	474	—	—	—	—	—	—	—	—	—	—	—	—	—	—	—

1987	1988	1989	1990	1991	1992	1993	1994	1995	1996	1997	1998	1999	2000	2001		
End of Period																1c s
1,213.8	1,231.7	1,409.3	924.3	1,085.5	2,009.0	2,056.7	2,173.8	2,848.4	3,142.2	3,201.8	3,680.0	3,643.0	3,355.3	4,013.9	**Asia**	505
4.8	4.9	4.9	4.9	4.9	4.9	4.9	4.9	4.9	4.9	4.9	4.9	4.9	4.9	4.9	Afghanistan, Islamic State of	512
22.4	22.4	22.4	—	—	.6	.1	.1	.1	.1	.1	.2	.2	.2	.2	Bangladesh	513
.6	.6	.6	.6	.6	.6	.6	.6	.6	.6	.6	.6	1.0	1.0	1.0	Bhutan	514
									35.3	35.3	35.3	35.3	35.3	35.3	Brunei Darussalam...................	516
					.9										Cambodia	522
302.6	302.6	302.6	302.6	302.6	551.2	512.8	517.3	817.8	971.0	1,682.4	2,523.3	1,684.7	1,462.3	2,060.5	China, P.R.: Mainland	924
											31.3				China, P.R.: Hong Kong	532
7.9	7.9	7.9	7.1	6.8	10.4	10.0	10.0	10.0	10.0	10.1	10.1	14.9	15.0	15.0	Fiji	819
487.2	487.2	487.2	—	.2	212.6	212.6	212.6	212.6	212.6	212.6	212.8	488.6	488.6	488.8	India	534
72.4	72.4	72.4	72.4	72.4	194.4	199.7	214.0	270.0	298.0	—	—	145.5	145.5	145.5	Indonesia	536
															Kiribati	826
.7	.7	178.2	224.5	255.4	319.1	339.2	363.6	438.5	474.3	443.7	.1	208.6	208.6	208.8	Korea	542
														—	Lao P. D. Rep.	544
153.0	172.0	169.7	163.9	179.8	240.3	229.1	273.7	456.3	478.2	444.7	444.7	608.2	608.2	608.2	Malaysia	548
—	—	—	—	.9	.9	.9	.9	.9	.9	.9	.9	1.6	1.6	1.6	Maldives	556
														—	Marshall Islands, Rep. of	867
														—	Micronesia, Fed. States of	868
....	....	....	....								—	—	—	.1	Mongolia	948
....	....	....	....									—	—	—	Myanmar	518
5.7	5.7	5.7	5.7	5.7	5.7	5.7	5.7	5.7	5.7	5.7	5.7	5.7	5.7	5.7	Nepal	558
.1	.1	.1	.1	.1	.1	.1	.1	.1	.1	.1	.1	.1	.1	.1	Pakistan	564
														—	Palau	565
6.9	7.0	7.0	—	—	—	.1	.1	.1	.1	.1	.1	.1	.2	.3	Papua New Guinea	853
38.8	38.8	38.8	38.8	38.8	87.1	87.1	87.1	87.1	87.1	87.1	87.1	87.1	87.1	87.2	Philippines	566
					.7	.7	.7	.7	.7	.7	.7	.7	.7	.7	Samoa	862
79.1	77.9	80.1	68.9	60.1	113.4	157.4	172.8	199.8	204.7	248.4	297.6	303.4	237.7	297.5	Singapore	576
.5	.5	.5	.5	.5	.5	.5	.5	.5	.5	.5	.5	.5	.5	.5	Solomon Islands	813
			.1	.1	20.2	20.2	20.2	20.2	20.2	20.2	20.2	47.7	47.7	47.8	Sri Lanka	524
28.8	28.8	28.8	31.8	155.2	243.3	271.5	285.2	318.7	333.5	—	—	—	—	—	Thailand	578
.7	.7	.7	.7	.7	1.2	1.2	1.2	1.2	1.2	1.2	1.2	1.7	1.7	1.7	Tonga	866
1.6	1.6	1.6	1.6	1.6	1.6	2.5	2.5	2.5	2.5	2.5	2.5	2.5	2.5	2.5	Vanuatu	846
															Vietnam	582
68.2	71.3	73.9	67.0	71.0	255.7	262.9	262.8	264.6	268.2	269.2	302.8	653.1	665.3	1,099.4	**Europe**	170
....	....	....	....	—	—	—	—	—	—	—	—	3.4	3.4	3.4	Albania	914
....	....	....	....	—	—	—	—	—	—	—	—	—	—	—	Armenia	911
....	....	....	....	—	—	—	—	—	—	—	—	—	—	—	Azerbaijan	912
....	....	....	....	—	—	—	—	—	—	—	—	—	—	—	Belarus	913
														—	Bosnia and Herzegovina	963
....	....	....	....	—	38.7	32.6	32.6	32.6	32.6	32.6	32.6	32.7	32.7	32.8	Bulgaria	918
										.1	.1	.1	.2	.2	Croatia	960
4.7	11.7	18.1	15.1	17.9	25.5	25.5	25.5	25.5	25.5	25.5	25.5	35.4	35.4	35.4	Cyprus	423
					—	—	—	—	—	—	—	—	2.4	120.5	Czech Republic	935
....	....	....	....	—								....	....	....	Czechoslovakia	934
												—	—	—	Estonia	939
....	....	....	....	—	—	—	—	—	—	—	—	—	—	—	Georgia	915
....	....	....	....	—	56.1	56.1	56.1	56.1	56.1	56.1	56.1	176.8	201.8	322.0	Hungary	944
														—	Kazakhstan	916
														—	Kyrgyz Republic	917
													.1	.1	Latvia	941
														—	Lithuania	946
														—	Macedonia, FYR	962
31.2	27.3	23.5	19.6	20.8	25.3	25.3	25.4	27.3	30.7	31.6	31.6	40.3	40.3	40.3	Malta	181
														—	Moldova	921
—	—	—	—	—	77.1	77.1	77.1	77.1	77.1	77.1	77.1	172.3	172.3	366.8	Poland	964
														—	Romania	968
....	....	....	....	.5	1.0	.8	.8	.9	.9	.9	.9	.9	.9	1.1	Russia	922
					....									—	Slovak Republic	936
					—	12.9	12.9	12.9	12.9	12.9	46.5	78.4	63.2	64.2	Slovenia	961
														—	Tajikistan	923
32.3	32.3	32.3	32.3	32.3	32.3	32.3	32.3	32.3	32.3	32.3	32.3	112.8	112.8	112.8	Turkey	186
					—	—	—	—	—	—	—	—	—	—	Turkmenistan	925
					—	—	—	—	—	—	—	—	—	—	Ukraine	926
—	—	—	—	—	—	—	—	—	—	—	—	—	—	—	Uzbekistan	927
—	—	—	—	—	....										Yugoslavia, Fed. Rep.	965
—	—	—	—	—											Yugoslavia, SFR	188
8,973.5	7,263.0	4,323.8	2,681.7	1,862.3	1,667.2	1,703.3	1,396.5	1,399.0	1,401.7	1,393.2	1,500.1	2,325.2	2,365.1	3,474.4	**Middle East**	405
27.3	27.7	29.6	28.0	29.6	31.1	40.9	42.2	43.7	45.1	46.7	48.5	62.4	64.9	67.2	Bahrain, Kingdom of	419
—	—	—	—	—	53.8	53.8	53.8	53.8	53.8	53.8	53.8	120.1	120.1	—	Egypt	469
70.8	—	—	—	104.6	—	—	—	—	—	—	—	—	—	—	Iran, I.R. of	429
															Iraq	433
												65.5	89.9	157.4	Israel	436
					12.0	—	—	—	—	—	—	—	.1	.1	Jordan	439
378.0	247.3	158.2	123.5	111.1	96.7	167.8	142.6	139.0	136.5	167.5	244.8	368.3	373.8	476.1	Kuwait	443
18.8	18.8	18.8	18.8	18.8	18.8	18.8	18.8	18.8	18.8	18.8	18.8	18.8	18.8	18.8	Lebanon	446
243.5	243.5	243.5	243.5	243.5	319.0	319.0	319.0	319.0	319.0	319.0	319.0	395.5	395.5	395.5	Libya	672
32.1	28.7	27.7	25.2	22.7	39.4	37.8	36.0	34.5	34.0	31.1	31.1	49.8	49.8	65.0	Oman	449
27.8	21.1	19.5	17.3	18.7	36.4	33.8	30.7	29.7	29.2	26.4	26.4	44.7	44.7	79.1	Qatar	453
8,016.2	6,540.4	3,688.0	2,099.1	1,291.6	797.3	868.6	604.3	574.7	560.9	532.5	523.8	987.5	1,042.7	2,035.5	Saudi Arabia	456
															Syrian Arab Rep.	463
159.1	135.3	138.4	126.3	126.1	158.3	162.8	149.1	185.8	204.4	197.4	233.9	212.6	164.8	179.8	United Arab Emirates...............	466
—	—	—	....	....	....	....	....	....	....	....	....	....	....	....	Yemen Arab Rep.	473
—	—	—	—	—	—	—	—	—	—	—	—	—	—	—	Yemen, P.D. Rep.	459
—	—	—	—	—	—	—	—	—	—	—	—	—	—	—	Yemen, Republic of	474

Reserve Position in the Fund

1c *s*

		1972	1973	1974	1975	1976	1977	1978	1979	1980	1981	1982	1983	1984	1985	1986
															Millions of SDRs:	
Western Hemisphere	205	359.3	442.4	732.9	1,147.7	1,193.3	1,136.8	1,090.1	983.5	1,479.0	1,577.9	1,422.4	1,448.2	1,001.0	915.6	773.0
Antigua and Barbuda	311	....	....	....	....	....	....		—				—			
Argentina	213	—	—	11.3	....	....	....	130.5	154.4	262.8	239.2	91.0	—	—	—	—
Bahamas, The	313	—	—	5.0	5.0	5.0	5.0	4.9	4.7	8.8	6.6	6.7	10.9	10.9	10.9	10.9
Barbados	316	2.0	2.0	2.0	3.3	3.3	3.3	3.0	2.9	5.0	5.0	—	2.2	2.2	2.2	2.2
Belize	339	....	....	....	....	....	....	....	....	....	....	1.3	1.9	1.9	1.9	1.9
Bolivia	218	—	—	—	—	6.4	7.4	9.0	—				—	—	—	—
Brazil	223	116.3	116.3	116.3	116.3	162.2	160.2	138.9	183.2	269.5	226.6	259.8	—	—	—	—
Chile	228							38.3	37.1	64.3	64.3	70.5	—	—	—	—
Colombia	233	—	39.3	39.3	39.3	45.3	76.7	70.1	73.6	114.5	151.7	175.2	262.1	—	—	—
Costa Rica	238	.3	.3	—	—	—	—	7.8	7.5	—	—	—	—	—	—	—
Dominica	321	....	....	....	....	....	....	—	—	—	—	—	—	—	—	—
Dominican Republic	243	—	10.8	—	....	....	....	—	—	—	—	—	7.4	—	—	—
Ecuador	248	—	5.6	9.2	13.2	—	—	8.0	9.4	21.8	24.8	—	11.4	—	—	—
El Salvador	253	—	—	—	—	—	5.1	8.8	8.5	—	—	—	—	—	—	—
Grenada	328	....	....	—	—	—	—	—	—	—	—	—	—	—	—	—
Guatemala	258	9.0	9.0	9.0	9.0	12.0	12.4	12.9	14.1	21.7	8.4	—	7.9	—	—	—
Guyana	336	.6	....	1.8	5.0	—	—	—	—	—	—	—	—	—	—	—
Haiti	263	2.9	.2	—	—	—	—	2.4	4.4	—	—	.1	.1	.1	.1	.1
Honduras	268	—	6.3	—	—	—	—	6.3	6.1	—	—	—	4.2	—	—	—
Jamaica	343	—	—	—	—	—	—	—	—	—	2.4	3.8	—	—	—	—
Mexico	273	97.8	97.8	97.8	97.8	—	—	—	—	100.3	161.0	—	90.8	—	—	—
Nicaragua	278	—	—	—	—	—	—	—	—	—	—	—	—	—	—	—
Panama	283	8.0	8.0	—	—	—	—	3.7	2.5	8.1	—	—	8.7	—	—	—
Paraguay	288	4.8	4.8	4.8	4.8	5.8	6.6	6.5	8.2	14.9	25.2	27.6	32.3	32.3	31.6	24.9
Peru	293	—	30.8	30.8	30.8	—	—	—	—	—	—	—	—	—	—	—
St. Kitts and Nevis	361	....	....	....	....	....	....	....	....	....	....	....	....	—	—	—
St. Lucia	362	....	....	....	....	....	....	....	....	....	....	....	—	—	—	—
St. Vincent & Grens.	364	....	....	....	....	....	....	....	....	....	—	—	.4	—	—	—
Suriname	366	....	....	....	....	....	....	4.8	4.8	7.9	7.9	7.9	3.0	—	—	—
Trinidad and Tobago	369	6.6	—	4.8	18.7	27.8	27.6	29.8	37.8	63.0	78.3	96.7	118.6	126.8	124.4	77.2
Uruguay	298							16.7	16.2	26.7	28.0	—	9.5	—	—	—
Venezuela, Rep. Bol	299	111.1	111.5	401.0	804.6	925.6	832.7	588.0	408.1	489.9	548.6	681.8	877.1	827.0	744.6	655.9

Memorandum Items

		1972	1973	1974	1975	1976	1977	1978	1979	1980	1981	1982	1983	1984	1985	1986
Oil Exporting Countries	999	263.8	322.0	1,892.2	4,337.5	5,428.0	5,360.4	4,397.8	2,990.7	4,050.6	5,770.7	6,726.4	11,263.5	12,577.0	11,900.0	10,788.8
Non-Oil Developing Countries	201	773.0	883.1	696.8	573.9	461.2	482.5	828.2	1,005.2	1,986.7	1,900.3	1,568.1	2,179.4	1,635.4	1,529.7	1,462.8

1987	1988	1989	1990	1991	1992	1993	1994	1995	1996	1997	1998	1999	2000	2001		
End of Period																
560.2	58.4	28.4	23.1	20.2	303.3	313.0	318.0	366.5	431.4	726.8	1,069.3	1,053.0	1,002.5	1,024.0	Western Hemisphere	205
—	—	—	—	—	—	—	—	—	—	—	—	—	—	—	Antigua and Barbuda	311
—	—	—	—	—	—	—	—	—	—	—	—	—	—	—	Argentina	213
10.7	9.0	8.6	7.9	7.2	6.8	6.2	6.2	6.2	6.2	6.2	6.2	6.2	6.2	6.2	Bahamas, The	313
2.2	2.2	2.2	2.2	—	—	—	—	—	—	—	—	4.7	4.7	4.7	Barbados	316
1.9	1.9	1.9	1.9	1.9	2.9	2.9	2.9	2.9	2.9	2.9	2.9	4.2	4.2	4.2	Belize	339
—	—	—	—	—	8.9	8.9	8.9	8.9	8.9	8.9	8.9	8.9	8.9	8.9	Bolivia	218
—	—	—	—	—	—	—	—	—	35.0	232.0	429.6	299.4	248.8	245.7	Brazil	223
—	—	—	—	—	69.0	79.8	86.7	135.3	165.1	263.4	408.3	285.8	285.8	285.8	Chile	228
—	—	—	—	—	8.7	8.7	8.7	8.7	8.7	8.7	8.7	20.0	20.0	20.0	Colombia	233
—	—	—	—	—	—	—	—	—	—	—	—	—	—	—	Costa Rica	238
—	—	—	—	—	—	—	—	—	—	—	—	—	—	—	Dominica	321
—	—	—	—	—	—	—	—	—	—	—	—	—	—	—	Dominican Republic	243
—	—	—	—	—	17.1	17.1	17.1	17.2	17.2	17.2	17.2	17.2	17.2	17.2	Ecuador	248
—	—	—	—	—	—	—	—	—	—	—	—	—	—	—	El Salvador	253
—	—	—	—	—	—	—	—	—	—	—	—	—	—	—	Grenada	328
—	—	—	—	—	—	—	—	—	—	—	—	—	—	—	Guatemala	258
—	—	—	—	—	—	—	—	—	—	—	—	—	—	—	Guyana	336
.1	.1	.1	.1	.1	.1	—	—	—	—	—	—	—	—	—	Haiti	263
—	—	—	—	—	—	—	—	—	—	—	—	8.6	8.6	8.6	Honduras	268
—	—	—	—	—	—	—	—	—	—	—	—	—	—	—	Jamaica	343
—	—	—	—	—	—	—	—	.1	.1	.2	—	.3	.3	.4	Mexico	273
—	—	—	—	—	—	—	—	—	—	—	—	—	—	—	Nicaragua	278
—	—	—	—	—	11.9	11.9	11.9	11.9	11.9	11.9	11.9	11.9	11.9	11.9	Panama	283
19.6	15.0	12.5	11.0	11.0	16.9	16.5	14.5	14.5	14.5	14.5	14.5	21.5	21.5	21.5	Paraguay	288
—	—	—	—	—	—	—	—	—	—	—	—	—	—	—	Peru	293
—	—	—	—	—	—	—	—	—	—	—	—	.1	.1	.1	St. Kitts and Nevis	361
—	—	—	—	—	—	—	—	—	—	—	—	—	—	—	St. Lucia	362
—	—	—	—	—	.5	.5	.5	.5	.5	.5	.5	.5	.5	.5	St. Vincent & Grens.	364
—	—	—	—	—	—	—	—	—	—	—	—	6.1	6.1	6.1	Suriname	366
53.0	—	—	—	—	—	—	—	—	—	—	—	—	—	24.6	Trinidad and Tobago	369
—	—	—	—	—	15.4	15.4	15.4	15.4	15.4	15.4	15.4	35.7	35.7	35.7	Uruguay	298
472.8	30.2	3.1	—	—	145.0	145.0	145.0	145.0	145.0	145.0	145.0	321.9	321.9	321.9	Venezuela, Rep. Bol	299
															Memorandum Items	
9,580.5	7,319.1	4,351.0	2,707.3	1,886.3	1,891.0	1,934.5	1,640.7	1,697.7	1,727.0	1,418.9	1,524.0	2,610.9	2,623.9	3,783.6	Oil Exporting Countries	999
1,423.7	1,381.6	1,566.5	1,065.0	1,227.3	2,501.1	2,558.9	2,667.9	3,331.8	3,668.4	4,322.6	5,187.6	5,398.9	5,054.2	6,117.6	Non-Oil Developing Countries	201

Foreign Exchange

1d s		1972	1973	1974	1975	1976	1977	1978	1979	1980	1981	1982	1983	1984	1985	1986
																Millions of SDRs:
All Countries	**010**	**95,700**	**101,755**	**126,154**	**137,309**	**160,234**	**202,249**	**222,536**	**248,628**	**292,622**	**291,929**	**284,711**	**308,773**	**349,068**	**347,916**	**363,809**
Industrial Countries	**110**	**69,276**	**67,823**	**66,437**	**69,800**	**74,497**	**101,121**	**128,793**	**137,817**	**166,350**	**160,909**	**154,306**	**168,994**	**185,291**	**189,236**	**212,080**
United States	**111**	222	7	4	68	275	15	3,357	2,890	7,946	8,397	9,257	6,007	6,790	11,704	14,166
Canada	**156**	4,023	3,266	3,088	2,753	2,980	1,905	1,902	1,433	1,616	2,544	2,334	2,619	1,776	1,433	1,895
Australia	**193**	4,995	4,063	2,953	2,262	2,267	1,506	1,322	893	1,070	1,138	5,698	8,375	7,192	4,780	5,464
Japan	**158**	15,182	8,458	9,268	9,078	11,949	16,569	22,180	12,417	16,910	21,234	17,380	19,451	22,733	20,327	30,786
New Zealand	**196**	658	758	521	364	414	330	277	333	249	532	575	712	1,816	1,447	3,074
Euro Area (incl. ECB)	**163**	....	....	....	....	....	....	....	....	....	....	....	....	....	....	....
Austria	**122**	1,557	1,440	1,852	2,796	2,625	2,337	3,515	2,706	3,738	4,131	4,320	3,712	3,658	3,744	4,524
Belgium	**124**	1,017	1,632	1,794	2,269	1,793	2,070	2,024	3,132	5,147	3,236	2,560	3,607	3,681	3,613	3,785
Finland	**172**	484	345	355	304	342	395	831	1,036	1,308	1,073	1,194	1,022	2,530	3,127	1,159
France	**132**	4,660	3,088	3,065	6,357	3,767	3,864	6,375	12,222	19,867	17,162	13,230	17,247	19,488	22,140	23,241
Germany	**134**	15,838	20,787	19,615	19,362	21,958	25,212	32,527	35,942	34,860	34,060	35,917	35,640	35,735	35,528	37,497
Greece	**174**	768	685	612	†806	741	850	955	986	1,000	822	725	773	891	715	†1,171
Ireland	**178**	942	755	936	1,212	1,451	1,824	1,940	1,548	2,095	2,112	2,205	2,340	2,186	2,456	2,402
Italy	**136**	2,049	1,808	2,601	1,033	2,696	6,553	8,059	13,128	16,966	15,995	11,432	17,693	19,473	12,845	14,824
Luxembourg	**137**	....	....	....	....	....	....	....	....	....	....	....	....	—	—	—
Netherlands	**138**	1,308	2,740	2,855	2,905	3,025	3,210	3,030	4,911	8,181	6,934	7,852	8,312	7,935	8,348	7,834
Portugal	**182**	1,160	1,360	919	333	143	297	669	706	589	401	354	337	485	1,224	1,107
Spain	**184**	3,888	4,882	4,543	4,582	3,958	4,872	7,523	9,699	8,865	8,759	6,548	6,683	11,679	9,550	11,286
Denmark	**128**	587	796	536	543	575	1,138	2,235	2,242	2,407	1,911	1,778	3,135	2,697	4,556	3,724
Iceland	**176**	64	69	32	34	67	78	102	117	125	185	130	138	126	183	249
Norway	**142**	1,029	1,120	1,384	1,675	1,548	1,480	1,894	2,872	4,383	4,963	5,700	5,664	8,822	11,948	9,439
Sweden	**144**	1,054	1,699	1,018	2,223	1,603	2,479	2,862	2,314	2,312	2,704	2,802	3,489	3,483	4,801	4,841
Switzerland	**146**	4,052	4,151	4,448	5,915	8,018	8,079	13,326	12,269	12,018	11,613	13,544	13,711	15,003	15,898	17,441
United Kingdom	**112**	3,742	3,916	4,037	2,928	2,302	16,057	11,887	14,021	14,700	11,003	8,770	8,327	7,112	8,867	12,171
Developing Countries	**200**	**26,424**	**33,932**	**59,717**	**67,509**	**85,737**	**101,128**	**93,744**	**110,812**	**126,272**	**131,019**	**130,405**	**139,779**	**163,777**	**158,680**	**151,729**
Africa	**605**	**2,415**	**3,176**	**7,921**	**7,901**	**8,321**	**7,655**	**5,699**	**9,273**	**13,921**	**8,907**	**6,495**	**6,175**	**6,185**	**7,841**	**6,530**
Algeria	**612**	188	682	1,112	888	1,443	1,307	1,442	1,911	2,780	2,939	1,930	1,522	1,215	2,288	1,073
Benin	**638**	20	21	22	6	10	10	5	3	3	45	—	—	—	2	1
Botswana	**616**	....	....	....	....	60	77	110	194	254	189	235	341	442	668	920
Burkina Faso	**748**	36	44	61	58	54	37	19	36	42	48	43	68	95	114	178
Burundi	**618**	13	14	8	23	39	75	55	59	63	40	15	15	11	18	47
Cameroon	**622**	23	25	54	15	29	28	33	89	136	61	45	144	49	116	45
Cape Verde	**624**	....	....	....	....	28	35	30	32	33	32	38	43	41	49	46
Central African Rep.	**626**	—	—	1	1	15	19	16	30	43	59	41	42	51	44	53
Chad	**628**	8	1	10	—	18	14	6	5	—	2	6	22	44	27	11
Comoros	**632**	....	....	....	....	....	....	....	....	5	7	10	10	3	10	14
Congo, Dem. Rep. of	**636**	78	108	62	21	16	110	92	157	160	106	35	76	140	173	220
Congo, Rep. of	**634**	5	2	15	8	6	10	6	31	67	103	29	4	2	2	1
Côte d'Ivoire	**662**	54	47	38	73	54	144	326	81	3	5	2	3	5	4	9
Djibouti	**611**	....	....	....	....	....	....	....	....	....	....	....	....	44	45	42
Equatorial Guinea	**642**	....	....	....	....	....	....	....	....	....	....	2	1	1	—	2
Ethiopia	**644**	70	131	208	230	247	168	117	131	59	219	162	114	42	135	205
Gabon	**646**	14	33	77	118	93	1	13	8	79	164	282	171	198	173	93
Gambia, The	**648**	8	11	20	21	14	19	19	1	4	3	7	3	2	2	10
Ghana	**652**	76	130	38	99	72	112	203	206	141	124	126	136	308	418	418
Guinea	**656**	....	....	....	....	....	....	....	....	....	....	....	....	....	....	....
Guinea-Bissau	**654**	....	....	....	....	....	....	....	....	....	....	....	....	....	....	–1
Kenya	**664**	157	164	156	144	234	416	260	394	365	189	176	333	385	343	316
Lesotho	**666**	....	....	....	....	....	....	....	....	37	34	42	61	47	37	47
Liberia	**668**	....	....	11	12	11	19	10	35	4	6	6	19	4	1	2
Madagascar	**674**	34	43	40	29	34	50	37	4	7	22	16	28	59	44	94
Malawi	**676**	27	47	58	48	18	68	54	50	54	33	17	12	53	39	18
Mali	**678**	1	1	2	1	3	2	4	3	6	7	6	7	17	10	1
Mauritania	**682**	9	32	83	39	69	41	60	85	110	138	126	100	79	50	37
Mauritius	**684**	55	46	104	134	69	52	34	22	71	25	33	17	24	27	111
Morocco	**686**	152	155	275	258	392	408	462	408	312	196	197	101	49	105	157
Mozambique	**688**	....	....	....	....	....	....	....	....	....	....	....	....	57	42	47
Namibia	**728**	....	....	....	....	....	....	....	....	....	....	....	....	....	....	....
Niger	**692**	32	36	31	36	64	76	89	89	87	77	13	38	80	116	145
Nigeria	**694**	269	385	4,495	4,502	4,063	3,078	1,016	3,808	7,522	2,662	1,421	920	1,481	1,517	884
Rwanda	**714**	5	10	8	19	51	64	62	106	130	132	98	88	91	86	115
São Tomé & Príncipe	**716**	....	....	....	....	....	....	....	....	....	....	....	....	....	....	....
Senegal	**722**	26	1	1	23	21	26	3	3	6	4	4	7	3	4	4
Seychelles	**718**	....	4	4	5	6	9	7	9	14	11	11	9	5	8	6
Sierra Leone	**724**	32	32	40	20	19	26	26	35	24	13	7	15	8	10	11
Somalia	**726**	20	21	26	50	65	95	93	27	6	22	5	8	1	2	10
South Africa	**199**	442	290	187	374	324	303	286	304	404	350	341	689	174	286	302
Sudan	**732**	28	37	80	24	20	19	16	41	38	14	19	16	18	11	48
Swaziland	**734**	....	....	10	37	60	75	83	81	118	73	64	85	78	74	77
Tanzania	**738**	97	103	39	55	92	226	71	49	16	14	4	18	27	15	45
Togo	**742**	26	24	37	28	50	31	47	40	55	124	148	164	205	270	279
Tunisia	**744**	187	231	317	304	293	268	320	414	432	424	515	508	383	185	227
Uganda	**746**	19	11	9	23	37	34	26	9	2	23	57	97	†66	21	20
Zambia	**754**	146	154	123	106	61	43	27	56	61	33	38	52	55	182	57
Zimbabwe	**698**	56	103	58	68	66	60	114	227	167	137	121	66	44	72	82

1987	1988	1989	1990	1991	1992	1993	1994	1995	1996	1997	1998	1999	2000	2001		
End of Period																
455,932	494,370	545,146	611,304	646,222	673,279	750,326	810,841	931,959	1,085,727	1,194,076	1,163,552	1,292,850	1,479,405	1,618,362	All Countries	010
287,383	315,933	344,997	376,501	360,429	356,767	373,683	393,918	441,054	501,666	520,851	475,831	524,786	595,571	618,435	Industrial Countries	110
9,226	12,903	33,901	36,687	32,112	29,095	30,237	28,233	33,028	26,631	22,834	25,568	23,448	23,976	23,061	United States	111
4,383	10,044	10,767	11,108	9,842	6,823	7,623	7,000	8,496	12,537	11,208	14,141	17,801	22,136	24,257	Canada	156
5,714	9,652	10,007	10,969	11,112	7,662	7,623	7,334	7,628	9,713	11,932	9,493	14,213	12,880	13,077	Australia	193
53,330	67,262	59,347	48,843	43,174	45,009	64,591	78,875	116,007	144,187	154,060	144,326	202,336	266,490	308,521	Japan	158
2,297	2,099	2,263	2,862	2,008	2,130	2,326	2,439	2,856	4,013	3,167	2,731	2,933	2,299	2,073	New Zealand	196
....	....	....	....	....	....	....	....	....	....	....	....	164,844	167,158	163,380	Euro Area (incl. ECB)	163
4,774	4,987	6,041	6,153	6,750	8,368	10,095	10,966	12,020	15,203	13,789	14,856	10,212	10,355	9,106	Austria	122
5,895	6,172	7,427	7,817	7,738	9,327	7,625	8,826	9,876	10,696	10,761	11,195	6,103	6,131	6,957	Belgium	124
4,222	4,366	3,528	6,475	4,969	3,472	3,635	6,885	6,252	4,315	5,582	6,043	4,916	5,626	5,723	Finland	172
20,889	16,615	16,640	23,946	19,779	17,734	14,567	16,111	15,568	16,078	20,083	27,523	24,723	24,648	20,977	France	132
51,382	39,625	42,508	44,260	40,210	62,463	52,948	49,470	52,334	52,716	51,772	45,548	†38,368	38,120	34,705	Germany	134
1,820	2,618	2,363	2,323	3,552	3,369	5,558	9,810	9,829	12,057	9,221	12,207	12,915	10,066	†3,809	Greece	174
3,123	3,511	2,817	3,409	3,719	2,240	4,062	3,935	5,501	5,365	4,462	6,123	3,516	3,825	4,135	Ireland	178
19,609	24,151	33,693	42,298	31,805	18,157	18,303	20,623	22,161	30,643	39,601	18,073	†13,569	17,210	16,634	Italy	136
		26	24	23	21	18	21	20	20	18	....	....	....	....	Luxembourg	137
9,991	10,806	11,435	11,266	11,353	14,718	21,600	22,411	20,895	16,773	16,217	12,454	4,735	5,376	4,719	Netherlands	138
2,259	3,777	7,477	10,018	14,164	13,650	11,271	10,348	10,303	10,681	11,214	10,701	5,833	6,554	7,343	Portugal	182
20,644	26,307	30,101	34,722	44,948	32,128	28,974	27,525	21,857	38,860	48,933	37,279	22,826	22,654	22,204	Spain	184
6,758	7,598	4,400	7,073	4,759	7,619	7,128	5,784	6,904	9,295	13,457	9,767	15,406	11,105	12,825	Denmark	128
214	211	253	302	310	352	300	190	197	305	274	292	330	280	250	Iceland	176
9,254	9,046	9,702	10,054	8,535	8,073	13,572	12,325	14,201	17,550	16,360	12,022	13,944	14,793	11,465	Norway	142
5,276	5,761	6,761	12,206	12,217	15,970	13,375	15,431	15,432	12,637	7,157	8,820	9,852	10,559	10,137	Sweden	144
19,146	17,868	19,199	20,540	20,275	23,593	23,042	22,985	23,333	25,574	27,348	27,234	24,900	23,681	23,978	Switzerland	146
27,178	30,554	24,341	23,145	27,074	24,791	25,210	26,392	26,357	25,816	21,403	19,434	†21,914	30,149	25,414	United Kingdom	112
168,549	178,436	200,149	234,803	285,793	316,512	376,643	416,922	490,905	584,061	673,225	687,721	768,064	883,835	999,927	Developing Countries	200
6,662	7,352	8,982	11,608	13,937	12,229	13,384	15,924	16,837	20,952	31,061	28,322	29,156	39,545	48,004	Africa	605
906	667	641	508	1,037	1,059	1,069	1,816	1,348	2,942	5,963	4,861	3,211	9,141	14,293	Algeria	612
—	1	1	44	132	176	175	175	131	180	185	183	289	349	457	Benin	638
1,388	1,617	2,086	2,304	2,562	2,722	2,942	2,973	3,112	3,448	4,158	4,159	4,539	4,802	4,639	Botswana	616
214	225	189	198	229	235	266	150	221	226	247	257	207	179	200	Burkina Faso	748
34	42	67	66	89	120	112	134	135	91	78	41	29	19	14	Burundi	618
45	130	60	17	26	14	1	1	2	1	—	—	1	156	263	Cameroon	622
57	60	57	54	45	55	42	29	25	19	14	6	32	22	36	Cape Verde	624
63	71	86	80	71	73	81	144	157	161	132	103	99	102	94	Central African Rep.	626
30	41	83	89	83	58	28	52	96	114	100	85	69	85	97	Chad	628
21	17	23	21	20	19	28	30	29	35	29	27	26	32	49	Comoros	632
127	139	145	154	128	114	34	83	99	57	....	....	....	....	....	Congo, Dem. Rep. of	636
—	2	3	3	3	2	—	34	39	63	44	—	28	170	54	Congo, Rep. of	634
6	7	7	2	8	5	1	140	355	420	458	607	457	511	810	Côte d'Ivoire	662
43	46	44	64	68	58	55	50	48	53	49	47	50	51	55	Djibouti	611
—	4	4	—	1	4	—	—	—	—	4	1	2	18	56	Equatorial Guinea	642
85	48	35	14	38	162	325	366	512	502	364	356	327	228	337	Ethiopia	644
—	44	26	192	224	52	—	120	100	173	209	11	13	146	8	Gabon	646
15	13	15	38	47	66	75	65	70	69	70	74	79	82	83	Gambia, The	648
126	164	242	151	376	212	280	380	450	557	379	208	276	178	234	Ghana	652
....	....	....	....	47	55	88	56	53	60	88	167	144	113	159	Guinea	656
7	12	16	13	10	13	10	13	14	8	25	25	26	51	55	Guinea-Bissau	654
157	183	196	129	69	26[e]	282	369	225	506	571	543	563	676	834	Kenya	664
46	40	35	49	79	111	180	251	304	316	419	404	360	317	304	Lesotho	666
—	—	6	....	1	1	2	3	19	—	—	—	—	—	—	Liberia	668
130	166	187	65	62	61	59	49	73	167	209	122	165	219	317	Madagascar	674
34	104	74	92	105	27	39	23	71	154	118	184	180	187	162	Malawi	676
2	18	79	125	214	215	233	143	208	291	299	277	246	284	268	Mali	678
38	41	63	37	47	44	32	27	57	97	149	144	163	....	....	Mauritania	682
238	325	389	508	605	573	523	483	552	594	484	367	502	658	634	Mauritius	684
287	406	371	1,452	2,064	2,520	2,605	2,933	2,375	2,603	2,928	3,117	4,013	3,540	6,574	Morocco	686
83	129	155	163	†168	170	136	122	131	239	383	432	475	556	569	Mozambique	688
					36	97	139	149	135	186	185	223	200	186	Namibia	728
166	164	152	148	133	155	131	67	55	45	31	29	19	53	76	Niger	692
821	484	1,343	2,715	3,100	703	999	949	971	2,834	5,619	5,043	3,971	7,606	8,320	Nigeria	694
98	73	39	18	64	44	23	24	53	62	94	102	116	145	159	Rwanda	714
....	....	....	....	....	....	....	....	3	1	9	7	8	9	12	São Tomé & Príncipe	716
5	7	10	7	8	8	1	121	179	198	285	304	290	292	348	Senegal	722
10	6	9	12	19	22	25	20	17	14	19	15	22	34	30	Seychelles	718
4	5	3	4	7	13	18	22	12	13	20	24	14	35	41	Sierra Leone	724
5	11	12	....	....	....	....	....	....	....	....	....	....	....	....	Somalia	726
450	579	729	707	627	721	734	1,153	1,894	654	3,550	2,963	4,419	4,446	4,587	South Africa	199
8	9	12	8	5	20	27	54	110	74	60	64	138	....	....	Sudan	732
87	103	137	144	112	216	184	195	192	168	210	246	265	261	207	Swaziland	734
22	58	41	136	143	228	138	217	172	296	451	415	555	738	910	Tanzania	738
250	172	216	248	255	198	113	64	87	61	88	83	88	117	100	Togo	742
332	647	725	557	529	611	620	999	1,075	1,309	1,454	1,312	1,608	1,367	1,561	Tunisia	744
38	37	11	26	34	62	107	218	308	367	466	512	554	617	781	Uganda	746
77	100	88	136	129	....	140	184	142	153	176	49	33	171	93	Zambia	754
101	132	71	105	104	161	314	277	400	410	118	92	194	148	51	Zimbabwe	698

Foreign Exchange

1d s

Millions of SDRs: (1985, 1986)

		1972	1973	1974	1975	1976	1977	1978	1979	1980	1981	1982	1983	1984	1985	1986
Asia	505	6,584	7,867	9,627	9,897	15,471	20,952	21,922	25,013	28,097	34,564	41,072	52,691	65,133	63,971	77,540
Afghanistan, Islamic State of	512	18	14	18	69	108	213	285	312	264	204	203	190	215	252	195
Bangladesh	513	247	117	113	111	233	188	242	284	235	119	157	465	375	272	304
Bhutan	514										27	32	38	45	45	49
Cambodia	522															
China, P.R.: Mainland †	924						1,931	1,195	1,635	1,774	4,109	10,094	13,827	†17,042	10,846	8,596
China, P.R.: Hong Kong	532															
Fiji	819	60	58	88	122	96	117	99	97	123	106	106	103	106	106	126
India	534	521	382	600	718	2,214	3,862	4,638	5,110	4,738	3,234	3,208	4,124	5,136	5,052	4,451
Indonesia	536	491	624	1,132	493	1,284	1,976	1,889	2,881	3,929	3,884	2,350	3,475	4,796	4,405	3,204
Korea	542	443	687	225	664	1,689	2,433	2,100	2,209	2,283	2,250	2,487	2,130	2,778	2,575	2,699
Lao P. D. Rep.	544															
Malaysia	548	733	950	1,152	1,128	1,950	2,213	2,397	2,817	3,226	3,278	3,181	3,352	3,540	4,207	4,657
Maldives	556							—	—	—	1	7	4	5	4	6
Micronesia, Fed. States of	868															
Mongolia	948															
Myanmar	518	31	66	139	105	94	78	71	150	199	185	80	78	56	31	27
Nepal	558	85	92	94	76	†108	113	108	117	138	168	174	121	78	45	65
Pakistan	564	184	315	301	266	369	341	282	128	366	571	773	1,795	930	711	569
Papua New Guinea	853		26	27	153	220	351	310	379	328	307	379	398	434	392	340
Philippines	566	420	799	1,164	1,099	1,361	1,199	1,340	1,682	2,231	1,773	802	713	586	501	1,369
Samoa	862	4	4	4	5	5	7	4	4	2	3	3	6	11	13	19
Singapore †	576	1,601	1,885	2,287	2,559	2,886	3,166	4,057	4,383	5,089	6,395	7,570	8,721	10,499	11,549	10,424
Solomon Islands	813						2	22	28	22	17	32	43	44e	31e	22
Sri Lanka	524	42	58	49	38	67	221	279	370	192	261	306	266	515	405	288
Thailand	578	825	938	1,373	1,371	1,485	1,428	1,515	1,362	1,217	1,436	1,372	1,491	1,928	1,964	2,237
Tonga	866						7	8	10	11	12	14	20	27	24	18
Vanuatu	846										7	4	5	7	8	16
Vietnam	582															
Europe	170	2,206	3,242	2,741	2,456	3,742	3,229	3,608	3,238	4,746	4,751	4,774	6,662	8,365	7,003	7,626
Albania	914															
Armenia	911															
Azerbaijan	912															
Belarus	913															
Bosnia & Herzegovina	963															
Bulgaria	918															
Croatia	960															
Cyprus	423	262	222	194	159	228	253	257	252	282	363	474	491	547	537	611
Czech Republic	935															
Czechoslovakia †	934									1,442	821	703	767	986	778	912
Estonia	939															
Georgia	915															
Hungary	944												1,093	1,591	1,960	1,882
Kazakhstan	916															
Kyrgyz Republic	917															
Latvia	941															
Lithuania	946															
Macedonia, FYR	962															
Malta	181	232	248	307	402	504	575	691	746	749	884	935	1,003	944	829	861
Moldova	921															
Poland	964								429	100	239	586	731	1,128	792	570
Romania	968		172	191	453	471	204	289	398	253	346	396	501	723	181	476
Russia	922															
Slovak Republic	936															
Slovenia	961															
Turkey	186	1,096	1,580	1,203	779	834	525	615	499	844	797	979	1,197	1,264	929	1,122
Ukraine	926															
Yugoslavia, SFR	188	615	1,019	846	664	1,704	1,672	1,756	913	1,075	1,300	699	880	1,181	996	1,193
Middle East	405	8,124	9,804	26,808	33,901	40,411	48,611	38,093	44,233	51,660	53,124	55,753	49,524	45,564	45,052	35,490
Bahrain, Kingdom of	419	74	51	102	238	371	410	373	458	737	1,313	1,365	1,329	1,293	1,473	1,177
Egypt	469	42	184	175	151	186	331	369	402	820	591	633	706	751	721	678
Iran, I.R. of	429	700	809	6,250	6,454	6,410	8,911	8,372	11,053	7,540	947	4,793				
Iraq	433	536	1,097	2,480	2,136	3,761	5,553									
Israel	436	1,057	1,405	940	969	1,135	1,230	1,994	2,289	2,593	3,004	3,480	3,451	3,122	3,350	3,809
Jordan	439	209	211	242	379	393	516	667	864	868	902	768	763	510	363	338
Kuwait	443	227	296	764	700	722	1,651	1,331	1,789	2,670	3,049	4,837	4,227	3,890	4,237	3,853
Lebanon	446	297	389	1,042	1,024	1,119	1,289	1,406	1,159	1,239	1,295	2,356	1,798	665	957	378
Libya	672	2,603	1,672	2,862	1,784	2,668	3,934	3,145	4,743	10,069	7,441	6,081	4,638	3,331	4,975	4,446
Oman	449	31	37	60	113	163	218	180	300	436	618	762	687	876	950	748
Qatar	453	44	51	47	70	95	119	147	201	248	288	317	321	333	352	416
Saudi Arabia	456	2,162	3,073	10,964	18,242	20,947	22,402	†12,842	13,192	16,267	24,054	21,587	16,674	14,474	12,528	5,806
Syrian Arab Rep.	463	93	306	372	585	233	392	287	429	247	229	168	41	268	73	118
United Arab Emirates	466		72	300	729	1,527	562	551	1,010	1,479	2,574	1,757	1,703	2,045	2,647	2,497
Yemen Arab Rep.	473		101	158	284	615	1,013	1,111	1,069	985	813	488	335	310	247	330
Yemen, P.D. Rep.	459	50	51	51	43	67	78	141	156	174	213	246	248	234	168	109
Yemen, Republic of	474															

† See country notes
in the monthly *IFS*

1987	1988	1989	1990	1991	1992	1993	1994	1995	1996	1997	1998	1999	2000	2001		
End of Period																
96,038	108,328	117,757	142,447	173,987	185,653	217,523	258,461	285,865	338,213	377,707	406,780	475,881	541,376	623,970	Asia	505
182	180	172	176	155	....	....	....	....	....	....	....	....	....	....	Afghanistan, Islamic State of	512
534	715	357	424	844	1,297	1,738	2,125	1,467	1,200	1,150	1,344	1,168	1,140	1,013	Bangladesh	513
52	69	74	60	68	56	....	78	83	127	133	176	199	225	225	Bhutan	514
						6	70	119	175	212	223	283	385	467	Cambodia	522
10,740	13,040	12,953	20,099	29,826	†14,140	15,434	35,360	49,498	73,040	103,680	102,952	112,695	127,080	168,823	China, P.R.: Mainland †	924
....	....	....	17,269	20,139	25,581	31,295	33,737	37,268	44,374	68,782	63,639	70,117	82,540	88,448	China, P.R.: Hong Kong	532
75	150	137	160	174	214	180	170	217	279	249	255	293	295	272	Fiji	819
3,950	3,082	2,363	847	2,503	3,972	7,140	13,279	11,750	13,729	18,028	19,146	23,309	28,601	36,007	India	534
3,865	3,677	4,077	5,168	6,397	7,405	8,000	8,097	8,951	12,393	11,923	15,910	19,122	21,706	21,522	Indonesia	536
2,514	9,170	11,397	10,163	9,302	12,102	14,345	17,147	21,479	23,114	14,608	36,905	53,697	73,570	81,551	Korea	542
—	—	1	1	20e	29e	44e	34e	52	111	74	75	74	107	101	Lao P. D. Rep.	544
4,973	4,558	5,626	6,556	7,285	12,207	19,522	17,048	15,436	18,190	14,833	17,562	21,617	21,970	23,541	Malaysia	548
6	16	19	17	16	20	18	20	31	52	72	83	91	92	72	Maldives	556
....	....	....	....	....	....	....	....	46	61	63	71	66	86	77	Micronesia, Fed. States of	868
....	....	....	....	....	12	43	54	77	74	130	66	99	137	164	Mongolia	948
19	57	200	219	181	204	220	289	377	159	185	223	193	171	318	Myanmar	518
120	158	155	202	272	334	460	469	389	392	458	531	610	720	820	Nepal	558
343	288	395	207	363	618	871	2,006	1,156	372	878	729	1,101	1,151	2,893	Pakistan	564
298	282	283	283	226	173	103	66	175	406	269	137	149	227	342	Papua New Guinea	853
644	707	1,039	610	2,227	3,115	3,310	4,018	4,194	6,886	5,297	6,464	9,547	9,929	10,598	Philippines	566
25	34	41	46	45	42	34	32	34	40	45	41	47	46	42	Samoa	862
10,573	12,530	15,322	19,354	23,721	28,845	34,994	39,654	45,980	53,194	52,535	52,852	55,595	61,159	59,560	Singapore †	576
25	29	19	12	5	17	14	11	10	22	26	34	37	24	....	Solomon Islands	813
197	165	176	297	479	654	1,166	1,381	1,384	1,343	1,480	1,385	1,143	749	975	Sri Lanka	524
2,753	4,456	7,199	9,311	12,085	14,554	17,530	19,786	23,857	25,864	19,045	20,194	24,630	24,509	25,741	Thailand	578
20	22	18	21	21	22	25	23	18	20	19	19	18	19	19	Tonga	866
26	28	25	24	26	29	31	27	30	28	25	29	27	27	27	Vanuatu	846
....	....	....	....	....	....	....	....	888	1,195	1,462	1,420	2,422	2,622	2,912	Vietnam	582
7,409	9,405	14,232	15,080	15,391	15,224	24,801	29,893	56,621	60,761	70,712	71,516	78,052	96,568	109,702	Europe	170
....	....	....	....	....	....	107	140	162	195	228	204	209	209	220	Albania	914
....	....	....	....	....	1	10	22	37	79	142	204	202	228	247	Armenia	911
....	....	....	....	....	—	—	1	80	132	341	318	485	517	712	Azerbaijan	912
....	....	....	....	....	....	....	69	251	326	292	499	214	269	311	Belarus	913
....	....	....	....	....	....	....	....	....	....	60	120	324	373	967	Bosnia & Herzegovina	963
....	....	....	....	211	617	444	643	779	295	1,625	1,956	2,154	2,468	2,663	Bulgaria	918
....	....	....	....	....	121	448	959	1,181	1,522	1,773	1,835	2,066	2,592	3,657	Croatia	960
611	678	837	1,044	954	722	773	978	726	1,047	1,006	954	1,300	1,300	1,768	Cyprus	423
....	....	....	....	....	....	2,753	4,209	9,312	8,590	7,214	8,908	9,330	9,990	11,291	Czech Republic	935
974	1,176	1,641	775	2,132	†784	....	....	....	....	....	....	....	....	....	Czechoslovakia †	934
....	....	....	....	....	116	240	303	390	443	562	576	621	707	653	Estonia	939
....	....	....	....	....	....	....	129	131	148	84	90	81	124		Georgia	915
1,152	1,090	948	751	2,750	3,160	4,820	4,557	7,999	6,703	6,175	6,562	7,801	8,377	8,197	Hungary	944
....	....	....	....	....	....	318	504	609	660	931	763	914	1,223	1,589	Kazakhstan	916
....	....	....	....	....	....	26	17	45	61	125	116	164	183	209	Kyrgyz Republic	917
....	....	....	....	....	....	243	373	339	453	520	517	610	653	914	Latvia	941
....	....	....	....	....	32	200	350	497	530	741	989	867	1,006	1,273	Lithuania	946
....	....	....	....	....	....	76	102	173	167	190	217	312	329	591	Macedonia, FYR	962
919	937	954	928	847	864	931	1,206	1,014	1,056	1,029	1,105	1,240	1,064	1,259	Malta	181
....	....	....	....	—	2	31	109	164	211	270	101	135	176	182	Moldova	921
1,054	1,527	1,761	3,157	2,534	2,903	2,901	3,923	9,860	12,329	15,044	19,325	19,021	20,201	20,021	Poland	964
988	580	1,338	368	445	593	723	1,391	1,024	1,459	2,742	2,036	1,950	3,010	4,325	Romania	968
....	....	....	....	....	....	4,243	2,724	9,596	7,838	9,465	5,540	6,161	18,622	25,891	Russia	922
....	....	....	....	....	....	302	1,100	2,224	2,366	2,375	2,036	2,455	3,087	3,295	Slovak Republic	936
....	....	....	....	78	520	561	1,014	1,212	1,585	2,444	2,537	2,229	2,387	3,377	Slovenia	961
1,219	1,710	3,605	4,220	3,564	4,447	4,533	4,878	8,336	11,397	13,796	13,808	16,897	17,126	14,906	Turkey	186
....	....	....	....	....	....	341	118	322	610	1,316	1,682	411	715	847	2,152	Ukraine	926
492	1,708	3,147	3,838	1,875	....	....	....	....	....	....	....	....	....	....	Yugoslavia, SFR	188
34,389	32,005	35,368	33,082	37,774	40,504	43,388	42,642	47,028	57,354	69,969	68,894	75,271	88,693	93,718	Middle East	405
768	887	754	823	1,011	967	896	748	806	860	898	706	935	1,135	1,272	Bahrain, Kingdom of	419
971	939	1,157	1,886	3,722	7,765	9,290	9,121	10,762	11,960	13,696	12,704	10,403	9,911	10,258	Egypt	469
....	....	....	....	....	....	....	....	....	....	....	....	....	....	....	Iran, I.R. of	429
....	....	....	....	....	....	....	....	....	....	....	....	....	....	....	Iraq	433
4,142	2,984	4,015	4,411	4,389	3,729	4,646	4,653	5,462	7,937	15,069	16,103	16,404	17,778	18,444	Israel	436
	291	81	350	596	577	1,188	1,159	1,326	1,223	1,631	1,243	1,915	2,556	2,436	Jordan	439
2,393	1,015	2,104	1,134	2,144	3,516	2,851	2,200	2,195	2,240	2,317	2,476	3,092	4,992	7,314	Kuwait	443
237	704	690	438	865	1,060	1,616	2,630	3,019	4,093	4,396	4,622	5,630	4,525	3,951	Lebanon	446
3,674	2,749	2,804	3,574	3,415	3,899	....	....	....	....	....	4,418	4,536	8,756	10,940	Libya	672
949	746	992	1,137	1,125	1,400	618	629	724	923	1,107	713	1,965	1,774	1,812	Oman	449
383	305	358	395	414	443	453	400	449	425	558	689	895	828	948	Qatar	453
7,603	8,337	8,589	6,032	6,807	3,317	4,137	4,033	4,777	†8,917	9,981	9,030	11,286	13,843	11,773	Saudi Arabia	456
157	143	....	....	....	....	....	....	....	....	....	....	....	....	....	Syrian Arab Rep.	463
3,092	3,077	3,167	3,005	3,529	3,943	4,227	4,357	4,784	5,340	5,949	6,154	7,561	10,211	11,075	United Arab Emirates	466
361	188	197	....	....	....	....	....	....	....	....	....	....	....	....	Yemen Arab Rep.	473
66	45	57	....	....	....	....	....	....	....	....	....	....	....	....	Yemen, P.D. Rep.	459
....	....	....	287	463	230	105	141	379	674	768	575	944	2,161	2,896	Yemen, Republic of	474

† See country notes
in the monthly *IFS*

Foreign Exchange

1d *s*

		1972	1973	1974	1975	1976	1977	1978	1979	1980	1981	1982	1983	1984	1985	1986
															Millions of SDRs.	
Western Hemisphere	205	7,095	9,843	12,619	13,354	17,792	20,682	24,421	29,056	27,847	29,674	22,312	24,727	38,531	34,813	24,542
Antigua and Barbuda	311	...	...	...	6	8	4	5	9	6	6	8	8	9	16	15	23
Argentina	213	271	885	840	211	1,165	2,522	3,520	6,724	4,749	2,222	2,181	1,119	1,267	†2,980	2,222
Aruba	314															60
Bahamas, The	313	34	36	36	41	36	†50	40	51	61	73	90	104	153	155	178
Barbados	316	21	22	27	28	18	24	40	43	55	80	109	115	133	125	122
Belize	339	...	...	...	...	5	7	11	8	10	9	8	7	4	12	20
Bolivia	218	38	43	141	112	117	161	107	135	83	86	141	153	257	182	132
Brazil	223	3,533	4,999	3,981	3,120	5,251	5,587	8,755	6,333	3,953	5,059	3,301	4,160	11,739	9,654	†4,744
Chile	228	87	100	20	27	300	296	778	1,412	2,382	2,680	1,557	1,940	2,338	2,230	1,922
Colombia	233	267	366	288	346	878	1,336	1,709	2,772	3,588	3,802	3,163	1,365	1,392	1,452	2,090
Costa Rica	238	33	36	32	38	81	151	138	78	114	113	205	294	413	461	428
Dominica	321	...	...	...	—	1	2	1	7	4	2	4	1	5	3	7
Dominican Republic	243	44	52	64	90	100	143	114	174	158	192	116	156	258	281	308
Ecuador	248	105	163	245	197	405	505	469	520	753	490	276	604	623	628	481
El Salvador	253	55	30	60	87	156	161	189	87	61	62	97	153	169	164	139
Grenada	328	5	4	4	†4	7	6	7	9	10	14	8	13	15	19	17
Guatemala	258	90	138	128	222	399	527	545	496	309	118	102	192	278	274	296
Guyana	336	29	8	45	77	20	16	42	10	10	5	7	6	6	6	7
Haiti	263	11	12	14	9	23	26	23	32	13	21	3	8	13	6	8
Honduras	268	27	23	31	79	110	144	132	145	117	85	100	102	131	96	91
Jamaica	343	140	99	150	103	27	25	41	48	82	70	95	60	99	147	80
Mexico	273	673	736	784	998	1,022	1,311	1,371	1,420	2,108	3,187	751	3,625	7,416	4,466	4,628
Netherlands Antilles	353	46	41	50	61	80	83	51	55	74	116	170	157	120	160	195
Nicaragua	278	68	91	80	99	122	118	35	111	51	96	154	167	...	...	...
Panama	283	29	24	30	23	63	54	108	84	83	100	88	188	220	77	138
Paraguay	288	18	36	60	87	123	207	331	445	571	652	619	587	612	415	298
Peru	293	367	368	688	296	246	291	294	1,073	1,543	1,021	1,194	1,304	1,641	1,677	1,150
St. Kitts and Nevis	361	...	...	...	...	...	...	...	...	...	3	3	3	6	7	8
St. Lucia	362	...	...	...	3	4	5	5	6	6	6	7	8	13	12	21
St. Vincent & Grens.	364	...	...	...	...	4	4	4	7	6	8	4	5	13	13	21
Suriname	366	35	47	55	78	95	77	77	97	121	138	165	143	52	24	17
Trinidad and Tobago	369	40	32	306	615	837	1,180	1,339	1,556	2,082	2,746	2,622	1,797	1,154	795	198
Uruguay	298	56	73	54	48	148	257	242	†203	248	304	104	185	132	145	384
Venezuela, Rep. Bol.	299	974	1,379	4,407	6,249	5,941	5,399	3,877	4,881	4,418	6,084	4,883	6,086	7,872	8,136	4,109

Memorandum Items

		1972	1973	1974	1975	1976	1977	1978	1979	1980	1981	1982	1983	1984	1985	1986
Oil Exporting Countries	999	8,225	10,175	34,874	42,360	49,023	55,110	39,969	50,889	62,647	60,334	56,833	52,856	53,776	54,046	37,823
Non-Oil Developing Countries	201	18,199	23,757	24,843	25,149	36,714	46,018	53,774	59,923	63,625	70,685	73,572	86,923	110,002	104,634	113,906

1987	1988	1989	1990	1991	1992	1993	1994	1995	1996	1997	1998	1999	2000	2001		
End of Period																
24,051	21,346	23,810	32,586	44,705	62,903	77,548	70,003	84,553	106,781	123,776	112,209	109,703	117,653	124,533	Western Hemisphere	205
18	21	21	19	23	37	28	31	40	33	38	42	51	49	63	Antigua and Barbuda	311
1,140	2,499	1,113	3,019	4,063	6,992	9,711	9,428	9,249	12,313	16,419	17,392	19,027	18,738	11,572	Argentina	213
55	68	66	69	84	103	132	122	146	130	128	158	160	160	234	Aruba	314
109	118	103	103	119	106	119	115	114	113	162	240	293	262	248	Bahamas, The	313
100	98	81	80	60	102	109	134	147	201	196	260	215	358	545	Barbados	316
24	36	44	47	35	35	25	20	22	37	40	28	47	89	84	Belize	339
69	79	156	117	74	123	144	283	408	628	770	566	605	562	574	Bolivia	218
4,440	5,181	5,734	5,222	5,607	16,378	22,279	25,392	33,439	40,559	37,670	30,239	25,345	24,935	28,430	Brazil	223
1,736	2,316	2,743	4,265	4,922	6,667	7,018	8,965	9,510	10,279	12,593	10,688	10,184	11,037	11,046	Chile	228
2,061	2,299	2,637	3,138	4,453	5,522	5,579	5,270	5,362	6,559	6,874	5,596	5,454	6,454	7,686	Colombia	233
345	496	565	365	643	732	737	603	695	687	926	746	1,043	991	1,038	Costa Rica	238
12	10	9	10	12	15	14	11	15	16	18	20	23	23	25	Dominica	321
128	189	125	43	309	363	464	170	246	243	290	356	505	481	875	Dominican Republic	243
346	294	411	579	617	614	984	1,243	1,076	1,273	1,534	1,133	1,178	709	649	Ecuador	248
131	120	202	292	201	307	390	445	485	627	944	1,121	1,435	1,450	1,360	El Salvador	253
16	13	12	12	12	19	20	21	25	25	32	33	37	44	51	Grenada	328
202	149	232	198	564	545	620	580	462	595	814	940	858	1,333	1,817	Guatemala	258
6	3	10	19	86	137	180	169	181	229	234	196	195	227	227	Guyana	336
12	10	9	2	24	20	23	35	128	150	158	187	192	140	112	Haiti	263
75	37	16	28	73	143	71	117	176	173	430	581	907	999	1,118	Honduras	268
122	109	82	118e	74	227	295	504	458	612	505	503	403	809	1,511	Jamaica	343
8,288	3,630	4,525	6,640	11,982	13,377	18,118	4,179	10,259	13,335	20,853	22,344	22,581	26,972	35,317	Mexico	273
153	195	158	151	124	160	170	123	137	131	159	176	193	200	240	Netherlands Antilles	353
12	28	88	75	94	95	40	97	92	137	280	249	371	375	302	Nicaragua	278
55	54	91	222	341	352	423	471	513	591	838	666	587	542	856	Panama	283
286	178	266	399	603	329	378	624	650	642	529	520	616	484	465	Paraguay	288
455	380	615	731	1,708	2,072	2,480	4,790	5,530	7,356	8,139	6,792	6,361	6,426	6,899	Peru	293
7	8	12	11	12	19	21	22	23	23	27	33	36	35	45	St. Kitts and Nevis	361
22	24	29	30	33	39	42	38	41	38	44	49	53	59	69	St. Lucia	362
14	16	17	19	16	24	22	21	19	20	23	27	30	42	48	St. Vincent & Grens.	364
11	9	7	15	1	13	13	27	82	59	73	67	20	40	87	Suriname	366
79	94	181	345	235	125	150	241	241	378	523	556	689	1,064	1,493	Trinidad and Tobago	369
326	373	364	360	231	355	536	648	756	852	1,138	1,457	1,480	1,867	2,427	Uruguay	298
3,197	2,211	3,086	5,842	7,268	6,755	6,211	5,064	3,826	7,736	10,376	8,247	8,530	9,696	7,022	Venezuela, Rep. Bol.	299

Memorandum Items

1987	1988	1989	1990	1991	1992	1993	1994	1995	1996	1997	1998	1999	2000	2001		
36,184	33,073	37,201	38,785	44,462	42,037	41,831	40,029	40,285	56,423	67,300	66,911	73,782	98,679	105,518	Oil Exporting Countries	999
132,365	145,363	162,948	196,018	241,331	274,475	334,812	376,893	450,620	527,638	605,925	620,810	694,281	785,155	894,409	Non-Oil Developing Countries	201

Gold (Million Ounces)

		1972	1973	1974	1975	1976	1977	1978	1979	1980	1981	1982	1983	1984	1985	1986
																Millions of Ounces:
All Countries	010	1,021.52	1,024.09	1,022.08	1,019.90	1,015.41	1,030.38	1,038.06	946.97	955.69	955.31	951.37	950.20	948.99	951.61	951.69
Industrial Countries	110	904.66	904.62	905.11	903.74	903.51	908.40	910.07	815.00	813.88	813.62	813.29	810.92	810.40	810.84	809.12
United States	111	275.97	275.97	275.97	274.71	274.68	277.55	276.41	264.60	264.32	264.11	264.03	263.39	262.79	262.65	262.04
Canada	156	21.95	21.95	21.95	21.95	21.62	22.01	22.13	22.18	20.98	20.46	20.26	20.17	20.14	20.11	19.72
Australia	193	7.40	7.37	7.38	7.38	7.36	7.65	7.79	7.93	7.93	7.93	7.93	7.93	7.93	7.93	7.93
Japan	158	21.10	21.11	21.11	21.11	21.11	21.62	23.97	24.23	24.23	24.23	24.23	24.23	24.23	24.23	24.23
New Zealand	196	.02	.02	.02	.02	.02	.04	.07	.05	.02	.02	.02	.02	.02	.02	.02
Euro Area (incl. ECB)	163	....	....													
Austria	122	20.85	20.88	20.88	20.88	20.88	21.00	21.05	21.11	21.11	21.11	21.12	21.13	21.13	21.14	21.14
Belgium	124	43.08	42.17	42.17	42.17	42.17	42.45	42.59	34.21	34.18	34.18	34.18	34.18	34.18	34.18	34.18
Finland	172	1.40	.82	.82	.82	.82	.90	.95	.99	.99	1.27	1.27	1.27	1.27	1.91	1.91
France	132	100.69	100.91	100.93	100.93	101.02	101.67	101.99	81.92	81.85	81.85	81.85	81.85	81.85	81.85	81.85
Germany	134	117.36	117.61	117.61	117.61	117.61	118.30	118.64	95.25	95.18	95.18	95.18	95.18	95.18	95.18	95.18
Greece	174	3.50	3.50	3.61	3.63	3.65	3.73	3.77	3.81	3.84	3.85	3.87	3.88	4.11	4.12	3.31
Ireland	178	.46	.43	.45	.45	.45	.47	.45	.38	.36	.36	.36	.36	.36	.36	.36
Italy	136	82.37	82.48	82.48	82.48	82.48	82.91	83.12	66.71	66.67	66.67	66.67	66.67	66.67	66.67	66.67
Luxembourg	137	.44	.44	.44	.44	.44	.45	.46	.46	.46	.46	.46	.46	.43	.43	.43
Netherlands	138	54.17	54.33	54.33	54.33	54.33	54.63	54.78	43.97	43.94	43.94	43.94	43.94	43.94	43.94	43.94
Portugal	182	26.88	27.54	27.84	27.72	27.67	24.11	22.13	22.13	22.17	22.17	22.09	20.43	20.30	20.23	20.16
Spain	184	14.23	14.27	14.27	14.27	14.27	14.44	14.52	14.61	14.61	14.61	14.61	14.61	14.63	14.65	14.82
Denmark	128	1.81	1.81	1.81	1.81	1.81	1.93	1.98	1.64	1.63	1.63	1.63	1.63	1.63	1.63	1.63
Iceland	176	.03	.03	.03	.03	.03	.04	.04	.05	.05	.05	.05	.05	.05	.05	.05
Norway	142	.98	.98	.98	.98	.98	1.08	1.13	1.18	1.18	1.18	1.18	1.18	1.18	1.18	1.18
Sweden	144	5.78	5.79	5.79	5.79	5.79	5.93	6.00	6.07	6.07	6.07	6.07	6.07	6.07	6.07	6.07
Switzerland	146	83.11	83.20	83.20	83.20	83.28	83.28	83.28	83.28	83.28	83.28	83.28	83.28	83.28	83.28	83.28
United Kingdom	112	21.08	21.01	21.03	21.03	21.03	22.23	22.83	18.25	18.84	19.03	19.01	19.01	19.03	19.03	19.01
Developing Countries	200	116.86	119.47	116.97	116.15	111.90	121.98	127.98	131.98	141.81	141.69	138.08	139.27	138.60	140.76	142.56
Africa	605	27.29	28.60	26.64	25.75	20.58	17.87	18.27	18.79	21.13	18.45	16.74	17.18	16.73	14.05	13.87
Algeria	612	5.47	5.47	5.47	5.47	5.47	5.50	5.53	5.58	5.58	5.58	5.58	5.58	5.58	5.58	5.58
Benin	638	....	....	....	—	—	.01	.01	.01	.01	.01	.01	.01	.01	.01	.01
Botswana	616	....	....	....	....	....	....	....	....	....	....	....	....	....	....	....
Burkina Faso	748	....	....	....	....	—	.01	.01	.01	.01	.01	.01	.01	.01	.01	.01
Burundi	618	—	—	—	—	—	.01	.01	.01	.02	.02	.02	.02	.02	.02	.02
Cameroon	622	....	....	....	—	—	.02	.02	.03	.03	.03	.03	.03	.03	.03	.03
Cape Verde	629	....	....	....	....	....	....	....	....	....	....	....	....	....	....	....
Central African Rep.	626	....	....	....	—	—	.01	.01	.01	.01	.01	.01	.01	.01	.01	.01
Chad	628	....	....	....	—	—	.01	.01	.01	.01	.01	.01	.01	.01	.01	.01
Comoros	632	....	....	....	....	....	....	....	....	....	....	....	....	....	....	....
Congo, Dem. Rep. of	636	1.45	1.46	.50	.26	.26	.26	.31	.25	.30	.36	.41	.44	.47	.45	.47
Congo, Rep. of	634	....	....	....	—	—	.01	.01	.01	.01	.01	.01	.01	.01	.01	.01
Côte d'Ivoire	662	....	....	....	....	—	.02	.03	.04	.04	.04	.04	.04	.04	.04	.04
Djibouti	611	....	....	....	....	....	....	....	....	....	....	....	....	....	....	....
Equatorial Guinea	642	....	....	....	....	....	....	....	....	....	....	....	....	....	....	....
Ethiopia	644	.25	.26	.28	.28	.28	.29	.29	.29	.31	.26	.21	.21	.21	.21	.21
Gabon	646	....	....	....	—	—	.01	.01	.01	.01	.01	.01	.01	.01	.01	.01
Gambia, The	648	....	....	....	....	....	....	....	....	....	....	....	....	....	....	....
Ghana	652	.16	.16	.16	.16	.16	.20	.22	.22	.25	.31	.38	.38	.44	.23	.28
Guinea	656	....	....	....	....	....	....	....	....	....	....	....	....	....	....	....
Guinea-Bissau	654	....	....	....	....	....	....	....	....	....	....	....	....	....	....	....
Kenya	664	....	—	—	—	—	.02	.07	.08	.08	.08	.08	.08	.08	.08	.08
Lesotho	666	....	....	....	....	....	....	....	....	....	....	....	....	....	....	....
Liberia	668	....	....	....	....	....	....	....	....	....	....	....	....	....	....	....
Madagascar	674	....	....	....	....	....	....	....	....	....	....	....	....	....	....	....
Malawi	676	—	—	—	—	—	.01	.01	.01	.01	.01	.01	.01	.01	.01	.01
Mali	678	....	....	....	....	....	.01	.01	.02	.02	.02	.02	.02	.02	.02	.02
Mauritania	682	....	....	....	....	....	.01	.01	.01	.01	.01	.01	.01	.01	.01	.01
Mauritius	684	....	....	....	....	—	.01	.03	.04	.04	.04	.04	.04	.04	.04	.04
Morocco	686	.60	.60	.61	.61	.61	.63	.68	.70	.70	.70	.70	.70	.70	.70	.70
Mozambique	688	....	....	....	....	....	....	....	....	....	....	....	....	....	....	....
Namibia	728	....	....	....	....	....	....	....	....	....	....	....	....	....	....	....
Niger	692	....	....	....	....	—	.01	.01	.01	.01	.01	.01	.01	.01	.01	.01
Nigeria	694	.54	.57	.57	.57	.57	.63	.63	.69	.69	.69	.69	.69	.69	.69	.69
Rwanda	714	....	....	....	....	....	—	—	—	—	—	—	—	—	—	—
São Tomé & Príncipe	716	....	....	....	....	....	....	....	....	....	....	....	....	....	....	....
Senegal	722	....	....	....	....	—	.01	.02	.03	.03	.03	.03	.03	.03	.03	.03
Seychelles	718	....	....	....	....	....	....	....	....	....	....	....	....	....	....	....
Sierra Leone	724	....	....	....	....	....	....	....	....	....	....	....	....	....	....	....
Somalia	726	—	—	—	—	—	.01	.01	.01	.02	.02	.02	.02	.02	.02	.02
South Africa	199	17.93	18.99	18.25	17.75	12.67	9.72	9.79	10.03	12.15	9.29	7.57	7.79	7.36	4.84	4.82
Sudan	732	....	....	....	....	....	....	....	....	....	....	....	....	....	....	....
Swaziland	734	....	....	....	....	....	....	....	....	....	....	....	....	....	....	....
Tanzania	738	....	....	....	....	....	....	....	....	....	....	....	....	....	....	....
Togo	742	....	....	....	....	—	.01	.01	.01	.01	.01	.01	.01	.01	.01	.01
Tunisia	744	.13	.13	.13	.13	.13	.15	.16	.17	.19	.19	.19	.19	.19	.19	.19
Uganda	746	....	....	....	....	....	....	....	....	....	....	....	....	....	....	....
Zambia	754	.20	.20	.17	.17	.17	.17	.20	.22	.22	.22	.22	.22	—	—	—
Zimbabwe	698	.55	.75	.50	.35	.27	.15	.16	.26	.35	.47	.39	.59	.70	.77	.54

1987	1988	1989	1990	1991	1992	1993	1994	1995	1996	1997	1998	1999	2000	2001		1ad
End of Period																
946.32	946.98	941.32	939.59	939.61	929.12	919.80	915.80	907.06	904.87	887.36	966.54	964.98	950.64	941.43	All Countries..........	010
804.79	801.12	797.80	795.81	793.68	785.24	770.83	768.05	754.97	748.16	732.47	808.67	810.42	796.51	783.56	Industrial Countries..........	110
262.38	261.87	261.93	261.91	261.91	261.84	261.79	261.73	261.70	261.66	261.64	261.61	261.67	261.61	262.00	United States	111
18.52	17.14	16.10	14.76	12.96	9.94	6.05	3.89	3.41	3.09	3.09	2.49	1.81	1.18	1.05	Canada..........	156
7.93	7.93	7.93	7.93	7.93	7.93	7.90	7.90	7.90	7.90	2.56	2.56	2.56	2.56	2.56	Australia	193
24.23	24.23	24.23	24.23	24.23	24.23	24.23	24.23	24.23	24.23	24.23	24.23	24.23	24.55	24.60	Japan	158
.02	.02	—	—	—	—	—	—	—	—	—	—	—	—	—	New Zealand	196
											402.76	399.54	401.87		Euro Area (incl. ECB)...........	163
21.15	21.15	20.66	20.39	20.03	19.93	18.60	18.34	11.99	10.75	7.87	9.64	13.10	12.14	11.17	Austria	122
33.63	33.67	30.23	30.23	30.23	25.04	25.04	25.04	20.54	15.32	15.32	9.52	8.30	8.30	8.30	Belgium	124
1.96	1.96	2.00	2.00	2.00	2.00	2.00	2.00	1.60	1.60	1.60	2.00	1.58	1.58	1.58	Finland	172
81.85	81.85	81.85	81.85	81.85	81.85	81.85	81.85	81.85	81.85	81.89	102.37	97.24	97.25	97.25	France	132
95.18	95.18	95.18	95.18	95.18	95.18	95.18	95.18	95.18	95.18	95.18	118.98	111.52	111.52	111.13	Germany	134
3.34	3.40	3.40	3.40	3.43	3.43	3.44	3.45	3.46	3.47	3.64	3.62	4.24	4.26	3.94	Greece	174
.36	.36	.36	.36	.36	.36	.36	.36	.36	.36	.36	.45	.18	.18	.18	Ireland	178
66.67	66.67	66.67	66.67	66.67	66.67	66.67	66.67	66.67	66.67	66.67	83.36	78.83	78.83	78.83	Italy	136
.43	.43	†.34	.34	.34	.31	.31	.31	.31	.31	.31	.08	.08	.08	.08	Luxembourg	137
43.94	43.94	43.94	43.94	43.94	43.94	35.05	34.77	34.77	34.77	27.07	33.83	31.57	29.32	28.44	Netherlands	138
20.06	16.07	16.05	15.83	15.87	16.06	16.06	16.07	16.07	16.07	16.07	20.09	19.51	19.51	19.51	Portugal	182
11.92	14.04	15.72	15.61	15.62	15.62	15.62	15.62	15.63	15.63	15.63	19.54	16.83	16.83	16.83	Spain	184
1.63	1.63	1.64	1.65	1.66	1.66	1.64	1.63	1.65	1.66	1.69	2.14	2.14	2.14	2.14	Denmark	128
.05	.05	.05	.05	.05	.05	.05	.05	.05	.05	.05	.06	.06	.06	.06	Iceland	176
1.18	1.18	1.18	1.18	1.18	1.18	1.18	1.18	1.18	1.18	1.18	1.18	1.18	1.18	1.18	Norway	142
6.07	6.07	6.07	6.07	6.07	6.07	6.07	6.07	4.70	4.70	4.72	4.72	5.96	5.96	5.96	Sweden	144
83.28	83.28	83.28	83.28	83.28	83.28	83.28	83.28	83.28	83.28	83.28	83.28	83.28	77.79	70.68	Switzerland	146
19.01	19.00	18.99	18.94	18.89	18.61	18.45	18.44	18.43	18.43	18.42	23.00	20.55	15.67	11.42	United Kingdom	112
141.53	145.86	143.52	143.78	145.93	143.88	148.97	147.75	152.09	156.72	154.89	157.86	154.55	154.13	157.88	Developing Countries	200
14.79	12.32	11.75	12.06	14.95	15.22	13.28	12.69	13.03	12.31	12.70	12.51	12.57	14.25	13.97	Africa	605
5.58	5.58	5.58	5.14	5.58	5.58	5.58	5.58	5.58	5.58	5.58	5.58	5.58	5.58	5.58	Algeria	612
.01	.01	.01	.01	.01	.01	.01	.01	.01	.01	.01	.01	.01	....	....	Benin..........	638
															Botswana	616
.01	.01	.01	.01	.01	.01	.01	.01	.01	.01	.01	.01	.01			Burkina Faso	748
.02	.02	.02	.02	.02	.02	.02	.02	.02	.02	.02	.02	.02	.02	—	Burundi	618
.03	.03	.03	.03	.03	.03	.03	.03	.03	.03	.03	.03	.03	.03	.03	Cameroon	622
															Cape Verde	629
.01	.01	.01	.01	.01	.01	.01	.01	.01	.01	.01	.01	.01	.01	.01	Central African Rep.	626
.01	.01	.01	.01	.01	.01	.01	.01	.01	.01	.01	.01	.01	.01	.01	Chad	628
—	—	—	—	—	—	—	—	—	—						Comoros	632
.49	.45	.22	.11	.03	.03	.02	.03	.03	....	.05	....	....	....	....	Congo, Dem. Rep. of	636
.01	.01	.01	.01	.01	.01	.01	.01	....	.01	.01	.01	.01	.01	.01	Congo, Rep. of	634
.04	.04	.04	.04	.04	.04	.04	.04	.04	.04	.04	.04	.04	....	—	Côte d'Ivoire	662
															Djibouti	611
															Equatorial Guinea	642
.21	.21	.19	.09	.15	.11	.11	.11	.11	—	—	.03	.03	.02	.20	Ethiopia	644
.01	.01	.01	.01	.01	.01	.01	.01	.01	.01	.01	.01	.01	.01	.01	Gabon	646
															Gambia, The	648
.28	.22	.22	.24	.27	.28	.27	.28	.28	.28	.28	.28	.28	.28	.28	Ghana	652
															Guinea	656
															Guinea-Bissau	654
.08	.08	.08	.08	.08	.08	.08	.08	.08	.08	.08	—	—	—	—	Kenya	664
															Lesotho	666
															Liberia	668
															Madagascar	674
.01	.01	.01	.01	.01	.01	.01	.01	.01	.01	.01	.01	.01	.01	.01	Malawi	676
.02	.02	.02	.02	.02	.02	.02	.02	.02	.02	.02	.02	.02	....	....	Mali	678
.01	.01	.01	.01	.01	.01	.01	.01	.01	.01	.01	.01	.01	.01	....	Mauritania	682
.04	.05	.06	.06	.06	.06	.06	.06	.06	.06	.06	.06	.06	.06	.06	Mauritius	684
.70	.70	.70	.70	.70	.70	.70	.70	.70	.70	.70	.70	.70	.71	.71	Morocco	686
										.07	.07	.06	.07	.05	Mozambique	688
															Namibia	728
.01	.01	.01	.01	.01	.01	.01	.01	.01	.01	.01	.01	.01			Niger	692
.69	.69	.69	.69	.69	.69	.69	.69	.69	.69	.69	.69	.69	.69	.69	Nigeria	694
—	—	—	—	—	—	—	—	—	—	—	—	—			Rwanda	714
															São Tomé & Príncipe	716
.03	.03	.03	.03	.03	.03	.03	.03	.03	.03	.03	.03	.03			Senegal	722
															Seychelles	718
															Sierra Leone	724
.02	.02	.02													Somalia	726
5.83	3.47	3.08	4.09	6.47	6.65	4.76	4.20	4.25	3.79	3.99	4.00	3.94	5.90	5.72	South Africa	199
															Sudan	732
															Swaziland	734
															Tanzania	738
.01	.01	.01	.01	.01	.01	.01	.01	.01	.01	.01	.01	.01			Togo	742
.19	.19	.19	.19	.22	.22	.22	.22	.22	.22	.22	.22	.22	.22	.22	Tunisia	744
															Uganda	746
—	.01	.02	.02	.02	....	....	....	—	—	—	—	—	—	—	Zambia	754
.42	.40	.45	.38	.41	.55	.50	.47	.76	.64	.77	.62	.73	.47	.20	Zimbabwe	698

Gold (Million Ounces)

		1972	1973	1974	1975	1976	1977	1978	1979	1980	1981	1982	1983	1984	1985	1986
															Millions of Ounces:	
Asia	505	**19.00**	**18.01**	**18.02**	**17.33**	**17.29**	**31.08**	**33.07**	**34.00**	**37.37**	**38.57**	**39.27**	**38.07**	**39.07**	**41.04**	**43.46**
Afghanistan, Islamic State of	512	.93	.93	.93	.93	.93	.94	.95	.96	.97	.97	.97	.97	.97	.97	.97
Bangladesh	513	—	—	—	—	—	.05	.03	.05	.05	.05	.06	.06	.06	.06	.07
Bhutan	514	....	....	....	....	....										
China, P.R.: Mainland †	924	....	....	....	....	....	12.80	12.80	12.80	12.80	12.70	12.70	12.70	12.70	12.70	12.70
China, P.R.: Hong Kong	532	....	....	....	....	....										
Fiji	819	—	—	—	—	—	.01	.01	.01	.01	.01	.01	.01	.01	.01	.01
India	534	6.95	6.95	6.95	6.95	6.95	7.36	8.36	8.56	8.59	8.59	8.59	8.59	8.74	9.40	10.45
Indonesia	536	.12	.06	.06	.06	.06	.17	.22	.28	2.39	3.10	3.10	3.10	3.10	3.10	3.10
Korea	542	.11	.11	.11	.11	.11	.15	.27	.30	.30	.30	.30	.30	.31	.31	.32
Lao People's Democratic Rep.	544															
Malaysia	548	1.66	1.66	1.66	1.66	1.66	1.74	1.89	2.13	2.32	2.33	2.33	2.33	2.33	2.34	2.34
Maldives	556	....	....	....	....	....	....	....	....	....	—	—	—	—	—	—
Micronesia, Fed. States of	868															
Mongolia	948									.04	.05	.04	.04	.04	.05	.03
Myanmar	518	.32	.20	.20	.20	.20	.23	.24	.25	.25	.25	.25	.25	.25	.25	.25
Nepal	558	.14	.13	.13	.13	.13	.13	.15	.15	.15	.15	.15	.15	.15	.15	.15
Pakistan	564	1.59	1.59	1.59	1.59	1.62	1.62	1.72	1.82	1.82	1.85	1.85	1.86	1.86	1.90	1.93
Papua New Guinea	853	....	....	....	....	....	.03	.04	.05	.06	.06	.06	.06	.06	.06	.06
Philippines	566	1.86	1.06	1.06	1.06	1.06	1.06	1.51	1.70	1.92	1.66	1.87	.29	.79	1.48	2.26
Samoa	862	....	....	....	....	....	....	....	....	....	....	....	....	....	....	....
Singapore	576	....	....	....	....	....	....	....	....	....	....	....	....	....	....	....
Solomon Islands	813	....	....	....	....	....										
Sri Lanka	524	....	....	....	....	....		.04	.06	.06	.06	.06	.06	.06	.06	.06
Thailand	578	2.34	2.34	2.34	2.34	2.34	2.40	2.43	2.46	2.49	2.49	2.49	2.49	2.49	2.49	2.49
Tonga	866	....	....	....	....	....										
Vanuatu	846	....	....	....												
Vietnam	582	.69	.69	.69	....	....	....	....	....	....	.69ᵉ	.69ᵉ	.69ᵉ	.69ᵉ	.69ᵉ	.69ᵉ
Europe	170	**9.36**	**11.75**	**11.44**	**11.21**	**11.73**	**12.13**	**13.27**	**14.76**	**16.11**	**15.43**	**14.87**	**16.05**	**16.76**	**17.07**	**16.47**
Albania	914	....	....	....	....	....	....	....	....	....	....	....	....	....	....	....
Armenia	911	....	....	....	....	....	....	....	....	....	....	....	....	....	....	....
Azerbaijan	912	....	....	....	....	....	....	....	....	....	....	....	....	....	....	....
Bulgaria	918	....	....	....	....	....	....	....	....	....	....	....	....	....	....	....
Croatia	960	....	....	....	....	....	....	....	....	....	....	....	....	....	....	....
Cyprus	423	.43	.43	.43	.43	.43	.44	.44	.46	.46	.46	.46	.46	.46	.46	.46
Czech Republic	935	....	....	....	....	....	....	....	....	....	....	....	....	....	....	....
Czechoslovakia	934	1.85	1.85	1.85	1.85	1.85	1.85	1.85	1.85	3.05	3.14	3.65	3.85	3.91	3.81	3.77
Estonia	939	....	....	....	....	....	....	....	....	....	....	....	....	....	....	....
Georgia	915	....	....	....	....	....	....	....	....	....	....	....	....	....	....	....
Hungary	944	1.67	1.82	1.33	.95	1.32	1.28	1.98	1.78	2.07	1.69	.65	1.53	2.06	2.33	2.35
Kazakhstan	916	....	....	....	....	....	....	....	....	....	....	....	....	....	....	....
Kyrgyz Republic	917	....	....	....	....	....	....	....	....	....	....	....	....	....	....	....
Latvia	941	....	....	....	....	....	....	....	....	....	....	....	....	....	....	....
Lithuania	946	....	....	....	....	....	....	....	....	....	....	....	....	....	....	....
Macedonia, FYR	962	....	....	....	....	....	....	....	....	....	....	....	....	....	....	....
Malta	181	.35	.35	.35	.35	.35	.36	.36	.37	.43	.46	.46	.47	.47	.47	.47
Moldova	921	....	....	....	....	....	....	....	....	....	....	....	....	....	....	....
Poland	964	....	....	....	....	....	....	....	1.29	.76	.47	.47	.47	.47	.47	.47
Romania	968	....	2.28	2.45	2.60	2.75	3.06	3.35	3.54	3.71	3.59	3.55	3.62	3.73	3.82	3.25
Russia	922	....	....	....	....	....	....	....	....	....	....	....	....	....	....	....
Slovak Republic	936	....	....	....	....	....	....	....	....	....	....	....	....	....	....	....
Slovenia	961	....	....	....	....	....	....	....	....	....	....	....	....	....	....	....
Turkey	186	3.57	3.57	3.57	3.57	3.57	3.63	3.67	3.77	3.77	3.77	3.77	3.78	3.80	3.86	3.84
Ukraine	926	....	....	....	....	....	....	....	....	....	....	....	....	....	....	....
Yugoslavia, SFR	188	1.49	1.46	1.47	1.47	1.47	1.51	1.63	1.72	1.86	1.86	1.86	1.86	1.86	1.86	1.87
Middle East	405	**30.68**	**31.01**	**31.66**	**32.10**	**34.25**	**31.47**	**33.24**	**33.51**	**34.96**	**35.89**	**36.13**	**36.21**	**36.31**	**36.27**	**36.27**
Bahrain, Kingdom of	419	.24	.24	.24	.15	.15	.15	.15	.15	.15	.15	.15	.15	.15	.15	.15
Egypt	469	2.43	2.43	2.43	2.43	2.43	2.43	2.47	2.47	2.43	2.43	2.43	2.43	2.43	2.43	2.43
Iran, I.R. of	429	3.74	3.74	3.74	3.74	3.74	3.78	3.82	3.90	4.34	4.34	4.34	4.34	4.34	4.34	4.34
Iraq	433	4.10	4.10	4.10	4.10	4.10	4.14	....	....	....	....	....	....	....	....	....
Israel	436	1.14	1.10	1.10	1.10	1.10	1.16	1.17	1.23	1.19	1.19	1.08	1.02	1.02	1.02	1.02
Jordan	439	.80	.80	.80	.80	.80	.81	.81	.82	1.02	1.07	1.08	1.09	1.06	1.06	1.06
Kuwait	443	2.48	2.85	3.50	3.99	5.58	2.51	2.53	2.54	2.54	2.54	2.54	2.54	2.54	2.54	2.54
Lebanon	446	9.21	9.22	9.22	9.22	9.22	9.22	9.22	9.22	9.22	9.22	9.22	9.22	9.22	9.22	9.22
Libya	672	2.44	2.44	2.44	2.44	2.44	2.45	2.45	2.46	3.08	3.58	3.58	3.58	3.65	3.60	3.60
Oman	449	.01	.01	.03	.03	.05	.10	.19	.19	.21	.27	.28	.29	.29	.29	.29
Qatar	453	.19	.19	.19	.22	.22	.22	.33	.35	.61	.83	.99	1.12	1.18	1.18	1.18
Saudi Arabia	456	3.09	3.09	3.08	3.08	3.08	3.08	4.54	4.57	4.57	4.57	4.60	4.60	4.60	4.60	4.60
Syrian Arab Rep.	463	.80	.80	.79	.79	.79	.81	.81	.83	.83	.83	.83	.83	.83	.83	.83
United Arab Emirates	466	....	—	—	—	.55	.57	.58	.58	.58	.68	.82	.82	.82	.82	.82
Yemen Arab Rep.	473	....	—	—	—	—	—	.01	.01	—	—	—	—	—	—	—
Yemen, P.D. Rep.	459	.02	.02	.02	.02	.02	.03	.03	.04	.04	.04	.04	.04	.04	.04	.04
Yemen, Republic of	474	....	....	....	....	....	....	....	....	....	....	....	....	....	....	....

Gold (Million Ounces)

1987	1988	1989	1990	1991	1992	1993	1994	1995	1996	1997	1998	1999	2000	2001		1ad
End of Period																
46.06	51.96	51.66	52.57	53.81	53.33	53.65	53.70	55.38	56.53	56.76	56.01	55.71	57.17	61.59	**Asia**	505
.97	.97	.97	.97	.97	...	...	...	...	...	...	...	...	...	...	Afghanistan, Islamic State of	512
.07	.07	.08	.08	.08	.09	.09	.09	.09	.09	.10	.11	.11	.11	.11	Bangladesh	513
															Bhutan	514
12.70	12.70	12.70	12.70	12.70	12.70	12.70	12.70	12.70	12.70	12.70	12.70	12.70	12.70	16.10	China, P.R.: Mainland †	924
...	...	...	.23	.23	.23	.07	.07	.07	.07	.07	.07	.07	.07	.07	China, P.R.: Hong Kong	532
—	—	—	—	—	—	—	—	—	—	—	—	—	—	—	Fiji	819
10.45	10.45	10.45	10.69	11.28	11.35	11.46	11.80	12.78	12.78	12.74	11.49	11.50	11.50	11.50	India	534
3.10	3.10	3.11	3.11	3.11	3.10	3.10	3.10	3.10	3.10	3.10	3.10	3.10	3.10	3.10	Indonesia	536
.32	.32	.32	.32	.32	.32	.32	.33	.33	.33	.33	.43	.44	.44	.44	Korea	542
...	...	.02	.02	.02	.02	.02	.02	.02	.02	.02	.02	.12	.02	.07	Lao People's Democratic Rep.	544
2.35	2.35	2.37	2.35	2.35	2.39	2.39	2.39	2.39	2.39	2.35	2.35	1.18	1.17	1.17	Malaysia	548
—	—	—	—	—	—	—	—	—	—	—	—	—	—	—	Maldives	556
—	—	—	—	—	—	—	—	—	—	—	—	—	—	—	Micronesia, Fed. States of	868
.03	.03	.03	.04	.14	.02	.02	.03	.10	.15	.08	.03	—	.08	.18	Mongolia	948
.25	.25	.25	.25	.25	.25	.25	.25	.23	.23	.23	.23	.23	.23	.23	Myanmar	518
.15	.15	.15	.15	.15	.15	.15	.15	.15	.15	.15	.15	.15	.15	.15	Nepal	558
1.94	1.95	1.95	1.95	1.96	2.02	2.04	2.05	2.05	2.06	2.07	2.08	2.09	2.09	2.09	Pakistan	564
.06	.06	.06	.06	.06	.06	.06	.06	.01	.06	.06	.06	.06	.06	.06	Papua New Guinea	853
2.78	2.84	2.45	2.89	3.37	2.80	3.22	2.89	3.58	4.65	4.99	5.43	6.20	7.23	7.98	Philippines	566
...	...	...	...	...	...	...	...	...	...	...	...	...	...	...	Samoa	862
...	...	...	...	...	...	...	...	...	...	...	...	...	...	...	Singapore	576
...	...	...	...	...	...	...	...	...	...	...	...	...	...	...	Solomon Islands	813
.06	.06	.06	.06	.11	.16	.06	.06	.06	.06	.06	.06	.06	.63	.63	Sri Lanka	524
2.48	2.48	2.48	2.48	2.48	2.47	2.47	2.47	2.47	2.47	2.47	2.47	2.47	2.37	2.48	Thailand	578
...	...	...	...	...	...	...	...	...	...	...	...	...	...	...	Tonga	866
...	...	...	...	...	...	...	...	...	...	...	...	...	...	...	Vanuatu	846
...	...	...	...	...	...	...	...	...	...	...	...	...	...	...	Vietnam	582
13.76	13.88	14.14	12.09	13.44	12.11	22.95	21.75	23.00	27.67	30.20	30.59	29.54	28.95	30.39	**Europe**	170
...	...	...	...	...	...	.05	.05	.06	.12	.12	.12	.12	.11	.11	Albania	914
...	...	...	...	...	—	...	.01	.03	.03	.04	.04	.04	.04	.04	Armenia	911
...	...	...	...	...	...	...	...	...	...	...	...	...	...	—	Azerbaijan	912
...	...	...	...	1.02	1.02	1.02	1.03	1.03	1.03	1.03	1.03	1.03	1.03	1.03	Bulgaria	918
...	...	...	...	...	...	...	...	...	...	...	...	...	...	—	Croatia	960
.46	.46	.46	.46	.46	.46	.46	.46	.46	.44	.46	.46	.46	.46	.46	Cyprus	423
...	...	...	...	...	...	1.95	2.10	1.99	1.99	1.04	.29	.45	.45	.44	Czech Republic	935
3.66	3.73	3.62	2.49	2.79	3.29	...	...	...	...	...	...	...	...	...	Czechoslovakia	934
...	...	...	...	...	.08	.01	.01	.01	.01	.01	.01	.01	.01	.01	Estonia	939
...	...	...	...	...	...	...	...	...	...	...	...	...	...	—	Georgia	915
1.64	1.59	1.50	.30	.26	.10	.11	.11	.11	.10	.10	.10	.10	.10	.10	Hungary	944
...	...	...	...	...	...	.65	.99	1.36	1.80	1.81	1.75	1.80	1.84	1.84	Kazakhstan	916
...	...	...	...	...	...	...	...	...	...	...	.08	.08	.08	.08	Kyrgyz Republic	917
...	...	...	...	...	.07	.24	.25	.25	.25	.25	.25	.25	.25	.25	Latvia	941
...	...	...	...	...	.19	.19	.19	.19	.19	.19	.19	.19	.19	.19	Lithuania	946
...	...	...	...	...	.02	.04	.05	.05	.08	.08	.10	.10	.11	.19	Macedonia, FYR	962
.47	.47	.23	.16	.12	.12	.10	.11	.04	.04	.01	.01	.01	—	.01	Malta	181
...	...	...	...	...	...	...	...	...	...	...	...	...	...	...	Moldova	921
.47	.47	.47	.47	.47	.47	.47	.47	.47	.47	.90	3.31	3.31	3.31	3.31	Poland	964
1.36	1.45	2.17	2.21	2.25	2.31	2.37	2.63	2.70	2.82	3.02	3.22	3.32	3.37	3.38	Romania	968
...	...	...	...	...	...	10.20	8.42	9.41	13.49	16.30	14.74	13.33	12.36	13.60	Russia	922
...	...	...	...	...	...	1.29	1.29	1.29	1.29	1.29	1.29	1.29	1.29	1.13	Slovak Republic	936
...	...	...	...	...	...	...	...	...	...	...	...	...	...	.24	Slovenia	961
3.83	3.82	3.78	4.09	4.16	4.05	4.03	3.82	3.75	3.75	3.75	3.75	3.74	3.74	3.73	Turkey	186
...	...	...	...	...	...	.01	.04	.05	.03	.06	.11	.16	.45	.48	Ukraine	926
1.87	1.89	1.90	1.91	1.92	...	...	...	...	...	...	...	...	...	...	Yugoslavia, SFR	188
36.21	35.95	35.90	35.77	35.39	34.98	31.80	31.78	31.88	32.47	31.74	36.36	35.34	35.25	35.26	**Middle East**	405
.15	.15	.15	.15	.15	.15	.15	.15	.15	.15	.15	.15	.15	.15	.15	Bahrain, Kingdom of	419
2.43	2.43	2.43	2.43	2.43	2.43	2.43	2.43	2.43	2.43	2.43	2.43	2.43	2.43	2.43	Egypt	469
4.34	4.34	4.34	4.34	4.34	4.34	4.76	4.74	4.84	...	...	...	...	...	...	Iran, I.R. of	429
...	...	...	...	...	...	...	...	...	...	...	...	...	...	...	Iraq	433
1.02	1.02	1.02	.84	.42	.01	.01	.01	.01	.01	.01	—	—	—	—	Israel	436
1.00	.74	.75	.75	.79	.79	.79	.79	.79	.80	.81	.83	.49	.40	.41	Jordan	439
2.54	2.54	2.54	2.54	2.54	2.54	2.54	2.54	2.54	2.54	2.54	2.54	2.54	2.54	2.54	Kuwait	443
9.22	9.22	9.22	9.22	9.22	9.22	9.22	9.22	9.22	9.22	9.22	9.22	9.22	9.22	9.22	Lebanon	446
3.60	3.60	3.60	3.60	3.60	3.60	...	...	...	...	...	4.62	4.62	4.62	4.62	Libya	672
.29	.29	.29	.29	.29	.29	.29	.29	.29	.29	.29	.29	.29	.29	.29	Oman	449
1.18	1.18	1.18	1.18	1.18	1.18	1.18	1.19	1.19	1.19	.45	.44	.16	.15	.15	Qatar	453
4.60	4.60	4.60	4.60	4.60	4.60	4.60	4.60	4.60	4.60	4.60	4.60	4.60	4.60	4.60	Saudi Arabia	456
.83	.83	.83	.83	.83	.83	.83	.83	.83	.83	.83	.83	.83	.83	.83	Syrian Arab Rep.	463
.82	.82	.80	.80	.80	.80	.80	.80	.80	.80	.80	.80	.40	.40	.40	United Arab Emirates	466
—	—	...	...	...	...	...	...	...	...	...	...	...	...	...	Yemen Arab Rep.	473
.04	.04	...	...	...	...	...	...	...	...	...	...	...	...	...	Yemen, P.D. Rep.	459
...	...	...	.05	.05	.05	.05	.05	.05	.05	.05	.05	.05	.05	.05	Yemen, Republic of	474

Gold (Million Ounces)

		1972	1973	1974	1975	1976	1977	1978	1979	1980	1981	1982	1983	1984	1985	1986
															Millions of Ounces	
Western Hemisphere	205	30.54	30.10	29.21	29.77	28.04	29.43	30.13	30.93	32.26	33.35	31.07	31.77	29.73	32.34	32.50
Antigua and Barbuda	311	....	....	....	....	....	....	....	....	....	....	....	....	....	....	....
Argentina	213	3.99	4.00	4.00	4.00	4.00	4.18	4.28	4.37	4.37	4.37	4.37	4.37	4.37	4.37	4.37
Aruba	314															—
Bahamas, The	313	....	....	....	....	....	.01	.01	.02	—						
Barbados	316	....	....	....	....	....	....	....	....		.01	.01	.01	.01	.01	.01
Belize	339															
Bolivia	218	.41	.41	.41	.41	.41	.60	.64	.68	.76	.83	.89	.91	.91	.89	.89
Brazil	223	1.33	1.33	1.33	1.33	1.33	1.52	1.61	1.70	1.88	2.20	.15	.54	1.47	3.10	2.43
Chile	228	1.36	1.38	1.44	1.30	1.34	1.36	1.39	1.52	1.70	1.70	1.71	....	....	....	1.80
Colombia	233	.43	.43	.43	1.13	1.41	1.73	1.96	2.32	2.79	3.37	3.82	4.22	1.37	1.84	2.01
Costa Rica	238	.06	.06	.06	.06	.06	.07	.08	.09	.09	.03	.05	.09	.02	.06	.07
Dominica	321	....	....	....	....	....	....	....	....	....	....	....	....	....	....	....
Dominican Republic	243	.09	.09	.09	.09	.09	.10	.10	.11	.13	.14	.09	.08	.02	.02	.02
Ecuador	248	.36	.39	.39	.39	.39	.40	.41	.41	.41	.41	.41	.41	.41	.41	.41
El Salvador	253	.49	.49	.49	.49	.49	.50	.50	.51	.52	.52	.52	.47	.47	.47	.47
Grenada	328	....	....	....	....	....	....	....	....	....	....	....	....	....	....	....
Guatemala	258	.49	.49	.49	.49	.49	.51	.51	.52	.52	.52	.52	.52	.52	.52	.52
Guyana	336	....	....	....	....	....	....	....	....	....	....	....	....	....	....	....
Haiti	263	....	—	—	—	—	.01	.01	.02	.02	.02	.02	.02	.02	.02	.02
Honduras	268	—	—	—	—	—	.01	.01	.01	.02	.02	.02	.02	.02	.02	.02
Jamaica	343	....	....	....	....	....	.01	—	.01	—	—	—	—	—	—	—
Mexico	273	4.94	4.63	3.66	3.66	1.60	1.75	1.89	1.98	2.06	2.26	2.07	2.31	2.42	2.36	2.57
Netherlands Antilles	353	.55	.55	.55	.55	.55	.55	.55	.55	.55	.55	.55	.55	.55	.55	.55
Nicaragua	278	.01	.02	.02	.02	.02	.03	.03	.02	.02	.02	.02	.12			
Panama	283	....	....	....	....	....	....	....	....	....	....	....	....	....	....	....
Paraguay	288	—	—	—	—	—	.01	.01	.04	.04	.04	.04	.04	.04	.04	.04
Peru	293	1.09	1.00	1.00	1.00	1.00	1.00	1.00	1.16	1.40	1.40	1.40	1.40	1.40	1.95	2.14
St. Kitts and Nevis	361	....	....	....	....	....	....	....	....	....	....	....	....	....	....	....
St. Lucia	362	....	....	....	....	....	....	....	....	....	....	....	....	....	....	....
St. Vincent & Grens.	364	....	....	....	....	....	....	....	....	....	....	....	....	....	....	....
Suriname	366	.25	.15	.15	.15	.15	.15	.05	.05	.05	.05	.05	.05	.05	.05	.05
Trinidad and Tobago	369	....	....	....	....	....	.03	.04	.05	.05	.05	.05	.05	.05	.05	.05
Uruguay	298	3.54	3.54	3.54	3.54	3.54	3.58	3.64	†3.31	3.42	3.39	2.86	2.60	2.62	2.62	2.61
Venezuela, Rep. Bol.	299	11.17	11.17	11.18	11.18	11.18	11.32	11.39	11.46	11.46	11.46	11.46	11.46	11.46	11.46	11.46

Memorandum Items

		1972	1973	1974	1975	1976	1977	1978	1979	1980	1981	1982	1983	1984	1985	1986
Oil Exporting Countries	999	33.35	33.68	34.36	34.87	37.03	34.47	36.34	36.74	40.18	41.79	42.12	42.25	42.39	42.34	42.34
Non-Oil Developing Countries	201	83.51	85.79	82.62	81.28	74.88	87.51	91.65	95.23	101.63	99.91	95.96	97.02	96.21	98.42	100.22

Gold Holdings at SDR 35 per oz.

Millions of SDRs

		1972	1973	1974	1975	1976	1977	1978	1979	1980	1981	1982	1983	1984	1985	1986
World	001	41,365	41,408	41,349	41,270	40,933	41,067	40,814	40,169	40,331	40,323	40,173	40,107	40,065	40,161	40,183
All Countries	010	35,753	35,843	35,773	35,696	35,539	36,063	36,332	33,144	33,449	33,436	33,298	33,257	33,215	33,306	33,309
of which: ECB	168	....	....	....	....	....	....	....	....	....	....	....	....	....	....	....
IMF	992	5,370	5,370	5,369	5,370	5,233	4,605	4,137	3,739	3,620	3,620	3,620	3,620	3,620	3,620	3,620
EPU / EF	994	41	—	—	—	—	—	—	—	—	—	—	—	—	—	—
EMI	977	—	—	—	—	—	—	—e	2,985	2,997	2,999	3,000	3,000	3,000	3,000	3,029
BIS	993	201	195	207	204	160	399	345	301	264	267	255	230	230	234	225

Gold Holdings at Market Prices

Millions of SDRs

		1972	1973	1974	1975	1976	1977	1978	1979	1980	1981	1982	1983	1984	1985	1986
World	001	70,648	110,085	179,959	141,266	135,640	159,333	202,290	446,065	532,600	393,445	475,408	417,560	360,042	341,598	366,897
All Countries	010	61,063	95,290	155,689	122,188	117,769	139,920	180,076	368,055	441,724	326,245	394,050	346,244	298,482	283,294	304,135
of which: ECB	168	....	....	....	....	....	....	....	....	....	....	....	....	....	....	....
IMF	992	9,171	14,276	23,367	18,381	17,341	17,867	20,505	41,521	47,810	35,325	42,844	37,693	32,534	30,794	33,057
EPU / EF	994	70	—	—	—	—	—	—	—	—	—	—	—	—	—	—
EMI	977	—	—	—	—	—	—	—e	33,147	39,583	29,265	35,500	31,232	26,959	25,517	27,656
BIS	993	343	518	903	697	531	1,547	1,710	3,342	3,483	2,610	3,014	2,390	2,066	1,993	2,050

Gold Prices and SDR Rates

		1972	1973	1974	1975	1976	1977	1978	1979	1980	1981	1982	1983	1984	1985	1986
US Dollars per Oz.(London)	112	64.90	112.25	186.50	140.25	134.75	164.95	226.00	512.00	589.50	397.50	456.90	381.50	308.30	327.00	390.90
US Dollars per SDR	111	1.0857	1.2064	1.2244	1.1707	1.1618	1.2147	1.3028	1.3173	1.2754	1.1640	1.1031	1.0470	.9802	1.0984	1.2232
SDRs per Ounce (g..)	112	59.78	93.05	152.33	119.80	115.98	135.79	173.47	388.66	462.20	341.51	414.19	364.39	314.52	297.70	319.57

Gold (Million Ounces)

End of Period

1987	1988	1989	1990	1991	1992	1993	1994	1995	1996	1997	1998	1999	2000	2001		1ad
30.71	31.74	30.07	31.29	28.34	28.24	27.30	27.83	28.81	27.72	23.49	22.39	21.40	18.51	16.67	Western Hemisphere	205
															Antigua and Barbuda	311
4.37	4.37	4.37	4.23	4.12	4.37	4.37	4.37	4.37	4.37	.36	.36	.34	.02	.01	Argentina	213
		.10	.10	.10	.10	.10	.10	.10	.10	.10	.10	.10	.10	.10	Aruba	314
—	—	—	—	—	—	—	—	—	—	—	—	—	—	—	Bahamas, The	313
.01	.01	.01													Barbados	316
															Belize	339
.89	.89	.89	.89	.89	.89	.89	.89	.89	.94	.94	.94	.94	.94	.94	Bolivia	218
2.43	2.73	2.98	4.57	2.02	2.23	2.93	3.71	4.58	3.69	3.03	4.60	3.17	1.89	.46	Brazil	223
1.81	1.82	1.75	1.86	1.86	1.87	1.87	1.86	1.86	1.86	1.86	1.22	1.22	.07	.07	Chile	228
.68	1.10	.61	.63	.86	.48	.30	.29	.27	.25	.36	.36	.33	.33	.33	Colombia	233
.06	.02	.01	.01	.03	.04	.03	.03	.03	—	—	—	—	—	—	Costa Rica	238
															Dominica	321
.02	.02	.02	.02	.02	.02	.02	.02	.02	.02	.02	.02	.02	.02	.02	Dominican Republic	243
.41	.41	.41	.44	.44	.44	.41	.41	.41	.41	.41	.41	†.85	.85	.85	Ecuador	248
.47	.47	.47	.47	.47	.47	.47	.47	.47	.47	.47	.47	.47	.47	.47	El Salvador	253
															Grenada	328
.52	.52	.54	.21	.21	.12	.21	.21	.21	.21	.21	.22	.22	.22	.22	Guatemala	258
															Guyana	336
.02	.02	.02	.02	.02	.02	.02	.02	.02	.02	.02	.02	—	.02	—	Haiti	263
.02	.02	.02	.02	.02	.02	.02	.02	.02	.02	.02	.02	.02	.02	.02	Honduras	268
															Jamaica	343
2.54	2.55	1.03	.92	.92	.69	.48	.43	.51	.26	.19	.22	.16	.25	.23	Mexico	273
.55	.55	.55	.55	.55	.55	.55	.55	.55	.55	.55	.55	.55			Netherlands Antilles	353
.20	.31	.12	.15	.10	.48	.01	.01	.02	.02	.02	.02	.02	.02	—	Nicaragua	278
															Panama	283
.04	.03	.03	.03	.03	.03	.03	.03	.03	.03	.35	.03	.03	.03	.03	Paraguay	288
1.50	1.71	1.97	2.21	1.83	1.82	1.30	1.12	1.12	1.11	1.11	1.10	1.10	1.10	1.10	Peru	293
															St. Kitts and Nevis	361
															St. Lucia	362
															St. Vincent & Grens	364
.05	.05	.05	.05	.05	.05	.05	.05	.09	.13	.19	.13	.25	.26	.27	Suriname	366
.05	.05	.05	.05	.05	.05	.06	.05	.05	.05	.06	.06	.06	.06	.06	Trinidad and Tobago	369
2.61	2.61	2.61	2.40	2.26	2.03	1.70	1.70	1.72	1.74	1.76	1.78	1.80	1.08	.01	Uruguay	298
11.46	11.46	11.46	11.46	11.46	11.46	11.46	11.46	11.46	11.46	11.46	9.76	9.76	10.24	10.94	Venezuela, Rep. Bol.	299

Memorandum Items

1987	1988	1989	1990	1991	1992	1993	1994	1995	1996	1997	1998	1999	2000	2001		1ad
42.34	42.35	42.33	41.89	42.33	42.32	39.15	39.12	39.23	39.81	39.06	41.98	41.30	41.77	42.47	Oil Exporting Countries	999
99.19	103.52	101.19	101.89	103.60	101.56	109.83	108.63	112.87	116.91	115.83	115.89	113.25	112.36	115.40	Non-Oil Developing Countries	201

End of Period

Gold Holdings at SDR 35 per oz.

1987	1988	1989	1990	1991	1992	1993	1994	1995	1996	1997	1998	1999	2000	2001		1ad
40,086	40,285	40,076	40,053	40,010	39,604	39,251	39,063	38,901	38,740	38,027	37,673	37,619	37,117	36,792	World	001
33,121	33,144	32,946	32,886	32,886	32,519	32,193	32,053	31,747	31,671	31,058	33,829	33,774	33,272	32,950	All Countries	010
												841	841	863	*of which: ECB*	168
3,620	3,620	3,620	3,620	3,620	3,620	3,620	3,620	3,620	3,620	3,620	3,620	3,620	3,620	3,620	IMF	992
—															EPU / EF	994
3,130	3,289	3,277	3,274	3,273	3,228	3,135	3,146	3,278	3,219	3,131					EMI	977
214	231	232	273	230	237	302	244	255	230	218	224	224	224	222	BIS	993

End of Period

Gold Holdings at Market Prices

1987	1988	1989	1990	1991	1992	1993	1994	1995	1996	1997	1998	1999	2000	2001		1ad
390,823	350,892	349,390	309,686	282,586	274,247	318,946	293,003	289,175	284,227	233,686	220,011	227,296	223,385	227,058	World	001
322,919	288,696	287,232	254,272	232,271	225,184	261,597	240,422	235,997	232,360	190,856	197,559	204,068	200,246	203,347	All Countries	010
												5,082	5,062	5,326	*of which: ECB*	168
35,298	31,535	31,563	27,993	25,570	25,070	29,419	27,156	26,913	26,562	22,248	21,143	21,875	21,789	22,343	IMF	992
															EPU / EF	994
30,520	28,646	28,572	25,314	23,118	22,351	25,478	23,594	24,369	23,618	19,240					EMI	977
2,087	2,015	2,023	2,107	1,627	1,643	2,453	1,831	1,896	1,687	1,343	1,309	1,353	1,349	1,368	BIS	993

Gold Prices and SDR Rates

1987	1988	1989	1990	1991	1992	1993	1994	1995	1996	1997	1998	1999	2000	2001		1ad
484.10	410.25	401.00	385.00	353.60	333.25	390.65	383.25	386.75	369.25	290.20	287.80	290.25	274.45	271.45	US Dollars per Oz.(London)	112
1.4187	1.3457	1.3142	1.4227	1.4304	1.3750	1.3736	1.4599	1.4865	1.4380	1.3493	1.4080	1.3725	1.3029	1.2567	US Dollars per SDR	111
341.24	304.86	305.14	270.62	247.20	242.36	284.41	262.53	260.18	256.79	215.08	204.40	211.47	210.64	216.00	SDRs per Ounce (g..)	112

Total Reserves

(with Gold at SDR 35 per ounce)		1972	1973	1974	1975	1976	1977	1978	1979	1980	1981	1982	1983	1984	1985	1986
															Millions of SDRs:	
All Countries	010	146,658	152,679	179,773	194,394	222,165	264,534	281,817	306,011	354,715	363,099	361,208	395,561	440,322	438,166	451,952
Industrial Countries	110	113,362	111,609	111,520	116,393	125,198	151,848	176,663	183,431	214,523	214,978	214,025	234,567	254,387	257,819	279,622
United States	111	12,112	11,919	13,115	13,567	15,767	15,965	15,032	15,170	21,479	25,502	29,918	30,831	33,517	38,412	39,790
Canada	156	5,572	4,782	4,758	4,549	5,029	3,793	3,505	2,951	3,159	3,755	3,439	4,017	3,246	2,982	3,348
Australia	193	5,656	4,723	3,487	2,782	2,728	1,962	1,855	1,359	1,603	1,713	6,053	8,838	7,869	5,528	6,202
Japan	158	16,916	10,151	11,042	10,947	14,292	19,149	25,714	15,667	20,164	25,083	22,001	24,346	27,811	25,173	35,394
New Zealand	196	767	867	522	365	423	366	348	344	277	580	577	744	1,824	1,454	3,084
Euro Area																
Austria	122	2,505	2,382	2,801	3,791	3,795	3,493	4,610	3,832	4,879	5,279	5,544	5,052	5,070	5,080	5,778
Belgium	124	3,564	4,227	4,366	4,952	4,480	4,743	4,535	5,329	7,330	5,451	4,757	5,699	5,853	5,611	5,724
Finland	172	664	505	515	399	427	469	972	1,204	1,501	1,319	1,420	1,227	2,854	3,481	1,528
France	132	9,224	7,070	7,230	10,757	8,373	8,393	10,691	16,212	24,301	21,991	17,850	21,826	24,227	27,071	28,579
Germany	134	21,908	27,497	26,462	26,510	29,954	32,713	41,360	43,225	41,430	40,892	43,909	44,092	44,282	43,735	45,626
Greece	174	950	868	765	†950	886	994	1,134	1,153	1,189	1,013	916	996	1,117	935	†1,357
Ireland	178	1,038	850	1,034	1,308	1,581	1,952	2,064	1,693	2,255	2,290	2,390	2,534	2,412	2,689	2,658
Italy	136	5,605	5,335	5,669	4,003	5,661	9,574	11,436	16,149	20,466	19,631	15,108	21,537	23,548	16,531	18,674
Luxembourg	137	....	....	....	....	....	....	....	....	....	....	....	....	....	....	....
Netherlands	138	4,407	5,427	5,683	6,074	6,358	6,639	5,823	7,301	10,669	9,562	10,723	11,253	10,961	11,354	10,687
Portugal	182	2,130	2,353	1,923	1,310	1,120	1,145	1,443	1,481	1,399	1,234	1,179	1,083	1,237	1,978	1,896
Spain	184	4,618	5,614	5,297	5,203	4,549	5,425	8,270	10,550	9,813	9,794	7,450	7,581	12,709	10,686	12,581
Denmark	128	787	1,097	764	749	788	1,375	2,471	2,514	2,712	2,246	2,111	3,515	3,127	4,999	4,116
Iceland	176	77	83	40	40	69	82	106	125	138	199	133	144	132	189	255
Norway	142	1,220	1,305	1,575	1,911	1,919	1,845	2,235	3,241	4,783	5,414	6,272	6,373	9,596	12,711	10,281
Sweden	144	1,453	2,097	1,417	2,627	2,144	3,019	3,375	2,880	2,893	3,306	3,397	4,065	4,135	5,487	5,568
Switzerland	146	6,961	7,063	7,360	8,908	11,183	11,385	16,549	15,391	15,190	14,925	16,930	17,275	18,520	19,317	20,726
United Kingdom	112	5,201	5,368	5,667	4,664	3,641	17,335	13,100	15,625	16,851	13,757	11,904	11,497	10,297	12,373	15,727
Developing Countries	200	33,295	41,070	68,253	77,998	96,968	112,688	105,154	122,581	140,192	148,120	147,183	160,994	185,935	180,347	172,329
Africa	605	3,962	4,777	9,424	9,446	9,777	8,992	7,112	10,786	15,696	10,995	7,737	7,443	7,275	8,787	7,508
Algeria	612	454	948	1,379	1,155	1,711	1,578	1,714	2,214	3,153	3,370	2,391	1,991	1,689	2,762	1,553
Benin	638	26	27	28	13	17	17	12	11	7	50	5	4	3	4	4
Botswana	616	....	....	....	....	62	80	113	198	262	203	250	359	463	690	950
Burkina Faso	748	44	52	68	65	62	46	28	47	54	61	56	82	109	127	191
Burundi	618	17	18	12	26	42	78	63	69	75	53	27	26	21	27	57
Cameroon	622	40	42	64	25	38	35	41	96	149	74	62	153	56	122	49
Central African Rep.	626	2	1	1	3	16	21	19	34	44	60	42	45	54	46	54
Chad	628	9	1	12	3	20	16	9	9	4	7	12	27	45	31	13
Comoros	632	....	....	....	....	....	....	....	....	....	....	10	14	5	14	19
Congo, Dem. Rep. of	636	164	194	115	50	52	119	107	166	170	143	50	112	156	188	236
Congo, Rep. of	634	10	7	20	12	10	11	8	32	68	106	34	7	5	4	6
Côte d'Ivoire	662	80	73	54	88	66	153	345	113	17	17	4	20	7	6	18
Djibouti	611	....	....	....	....	....	....	....	....	....	....	....	....	46	46	44
Equatorial Guinea	642	....	....	....	....	....	....	....	....	....	3	1	1	1	3	2
Ethiopia	644	85	147	225	246	263	186	127	141	74	238	172	128	53	142	212
Gabon	646	21	40	84	125	100	8	18	16	85	171	283	179	204	176	104
Gambia, The	648	10	13	23	24	18	20	20	1	4	3	8	3	2	2	11
Ghana	652	92	152	64	112	85	129	220	227	150	136	139	152	323	444	429
Guinea-Bissau	654	....	....	....	....	....	....	....	....	....	....	....	....	....	....	25
Kenya	664	186	193	158	148	237	431	273	479	388	201	195	362	400	358	341
Lesotho	666	....	....	....	....	....	....	....	....	39	37	43	64	50	40	49
Liberia	668	....	....	15	16	15	23	14	42	4	7	6	19	4	1	2
Madagascar	674	48	56	40	30	36	57	45	4	7	23	18	28	60	44	94
Malawi	676	33	55	67	52	23	72	58	53	54	43	21	15	58	41	21
Mali	678	4	4	5	4	6	5	7	5	12	16	16	16	28	21	20
Mauritania	682	12	35	85	41	71	41	61	87	110	139	126	102	79	54	40
Mauritius	684	65	55	107	142	77	55	36	23	72	31	36	18	25	29	113
Morocco	686	218	220	340	322	423	438	498	447	337	222	222	127	74	129	197
Mozambique	688	....	....	....	....	....	....	....	....	....	....	....	....	....	....	....
Namibia	728	....	....	....	....	....	....	....	....	....	....	....	....	....	....	....
Niger	692	38	42	37	43	71	83	99	100	99	91	27	51	91	125	155
Nigeria	694	346	483	4,596	4,791	4,478	3,506	1,470	4,236	8,049	3,371	1,486	970	1,516	1,542	908
Rwanda	714	6	13	11	22	55	68	67	116	146	149	116	106	109	103	133
São Tomé & Príncipe	716	....	....	....	....	....	....	....	....	....	....	....	....	....	....	....
Senegal	722	36	10	5	27	22	28	15	16	7	8	11	13	5	6	9
Seychelles	718	....	4	4	5	6	9	7	9	14	12	12	10	6	8	6
Sierra Leone	724	43	43	45	24	22	27	27	35	24	14	8	15	8	10	11
Somalia	726	29	29	35	58	73	99	97	34	12	27	7	9	2	3	11
South Africa	199	1,188	1,037	947	1,039	809	683	667	681	994	898	705	1,059	504	456	471
Sudan	732	33	51	102	31	20	19	22	51	38	15	19	16	18	11	48
Swaziland	734	....	....	11	39	63	78	87	86	124	83	69	88	82	76	79
Tanzania	738	110	120	41	56	97	232	77	52	16	16	4	19	27	15	50
Togo	742	34	31	44	35	57	38	54	50	61	131	152	166	208	270	280
Tunisia	744	205	255	342	329	319	294	346	446	469	467	556	548	421	218	256
Uganda	746	33	24	14	27	38	39	40	17	2	26	71	102	†69	25	24
Zambia	754	153	161	140	127	86	60	46	68	69	56	60	60	55	182	58
Zimbabwe	698	76	130	75	81	75	65	119	236	180	162	141	93	71	112	106

1987	1988	1989	1990	1991	1992	1993	1994	1995	1996	1997	1998	1999	2000	2001	(with Gold at SDR 35 per ounce)	
End of Period																
540,733	575,960	624,048	688,293	725,548	752,567	829,933	890,377	1,020,143	1,173,881	1,292,695	1,278,310	1,399,811	1,578,467	1,727,684	All Countries........................	010
352,489	381,104	410,136	441,946	428,438	424,229	440,423	460,700	514,117	574,980	603,333	573,895	614,649	677,555	708,783	Industrial Countries..............	110
33,657	36,471	57,525	59,958	55,769	52,995	54,558	52,510	59,467	53,694	52,817	59,379	53,238	52,598	55,030	United States	111
5,778	12,037	12,781	13,060	11,816	8,662	9,299	8,552	10,243	14,310	13,317	16,640	20,556	24,544	27,061	Canada	156
6,441	10,383	10,764	11,837	11,710	8,429	8,359	8,007	8,279	10,350	12,575	10,487	15,545	13,996	14,377	Australia	193
57,925	72,727	64,735	56,027	51,224	52,937	72,577	87,062	124,125	151,511	163,641	153,878	209,893	273,251	315,292	Japan	158
2,298	2,108	2,303	2,902	2,062	2,239	2,430	2,540	2,967	4,140	3,299	2,986	3,246	2,555	2,394	New Zealand	196
															Euro Area	
6,049	6,215	7,266	7,305	7,924	9,703	11,288	12,165	13,020	16,277	14,903	22,661	†11,475	11,414	10,345	Austria	122
7,958	8,113	9,250	9,599	9,573	10,914	9,187	10,382	11,601	12,326	12,535	13,310	†8,259	7,961	9,255	Belgium	124
4,592	4,801	3,959	6,849	5,389	3,862	4,009	7,374	6,809	4,866	6,294	6,955	†6,035	6,552	6,407	Finland	172
26,161	21,713	21,592	28,716	24,735	22,522	19,354	20,851	20,930	21,500	25,788	35,054	†32,329	31,831	28,667	France	132
58,846	46,824	49,527	51,060	47,375	69,489	59,856	56,325	60,517	61,176	60,835	56,737	†48,375	47,567	44,717	Germany	134
2,007	2,808	2,572	2,517	3,747	3,606	5,792	10,045	10,064	12,292	9,462	12,526	13,352	10,452	†4,239	Greece	174
3,393	3,793	3,100	3,684	4,026	2,514	4,326	4,201	5,818	5,719	4,849	6,690	†3,855	4,120	4,452	Ireland	178
23,631	28,131	37,884	46,565	36,365	22,438	22,387	24,435	25,815	34,287	43,644	24,144	†19,095	22,382	22,190	Italy	136
....	....	69	69	68	66	60	63	61	62	58	....	†59	61	87	Luxembourg	137
12,818	13,483	14,100	13,827	13,980	17,492	24,046	24,872	23,897	19,832	19,376	16,395	8,462	8,427	8,184	Netherlands	138
3,047	4,372	8,135	10,736	14,977	14,474	12,094	11,189	11,225	11,632	12,169	11,942	†7,130	7,520	8,375	Portugal	182
22,035	28,041	32,104	36,555	46,562	33,640	30,429	29,006	23,746	40,831	51,241	39,929	†24,716	24,373	24,128	Spain	184
7,153	8,057	4,925	7,502	5,234	8,090	7,557	6,260	7,468	9,892	14,233	10,916	16,313	11,671	13,690	Denmark	128
221	218	258	308	316	364	312	202	209	317	286	305	351	301	271	Iceland	176
10,105	9,901	10,531	10,819	9,292	8,725	14,327	13,074	15,190	18,482	17,385	13,256	14,905	15,518	12,366	Norway	142
5,974	6,523	7,487	12,856	13,028	16,667	14,081	16,141	16,344	13,452	8,188	10,178	11,151	11,616	11,331	Sweden	144
22,283	20,900	22,148	23,456	23,191	27,100	26,674	26,704	27,411	29,642	31,840	32,169	29,378	27,492	27,936	Switzerland	146
30,070	33,439	27,121	25,865	29,948	27,300	27,420	28,739	28,910	28,390	24,596	23,682	26,854	34,236	30,067	United Kingdom	112
188,244	194,856	213,911	246,347	297,110	328,338	389,510	429,676	506,025	598,902	689,362	704,415	785,162	900,912	1,018,901	Developing Countries	200
7,616	7,948	9,576	12,190	14,774	13,067	14,122	16,644	17,578	21,652	31,778	29,199	30,326	40,738	49,246	Africa	605
1,352	864	840	689	1,234	1,255	1,269	2,027	1,544	3,141	6,159	5,057	3,493	9,424	14,583	Algeria	612
3	4	3	46	134	179	178	177	134	182	188	186	292	....	....	Benin	638
1,419	1,648	2,124	2,342	2,600	2,759	2,983	3,015	3,159	3,496	4,206	4,219	4,589	4,849	4,693	Botswana	616
228	239	202	212	242	249	279	163	234	236	256	266	215	....	....	Burkina Faso	748
43	52	76	74	99	127	119	141	142	98	84	47	36	26	14	Burundi	618
46	132	62	19	31	16	3	3	4	3	2	2	4	164	265	Cameroon	622
69	81	86	84	72	73	82	144	158	162	133	104	100	103	95	Central African Rep.	626
37	47	85	90	84	59	29	52	96	115	101	86	70	85	98	Chad	628
22	18	23	21	20	20	28	30	30	35	....	....	....	....	....	Comoros	632
145	155	156	158	129	115	34	84	100	....	....	....	29	171	55	Congo, Dem. Rep. of	636
3	4	5	5	4	3	1	35	40	64	45	1	....	....	....	Congo, Rep. of	634
8	9	13	4	11	7	3	141	357	423	460	609	461	....	....	Côte d'Ivoire	662
45	48	45	66	70	61	55	51	49	54	49	47	51	52	56	Djibouti	611
—	4	5	—	7	10	—	—	—	—	4	1	2	18	56	Equatorial Guinea	642
94	55	42	17	43	173	336	377	523	509	371	364	335	236	352	Ethiopia	644
9	51	27	193	229	52	1	120	100	173	210	11	14	146	8	Gabon	646
18	14	16	39	47	68	77	67	71	71	71	76	81	84	84	Gambia, The	648
147	172	272	162	394	242	308	410	479	586	408	277	340	188	247	Ghana	652
7	12	16	13	10	13	10	13	14	8	25	25	26	51	55	Guinea-Bissau	654
183	199	219	147	85	41e	298	385	241	522	587	556	577	689	847	Kenya	664
48	42	37	51	80	115	184	255	307	320	424	408	364	321	308	Lesotho	666
—	—	6	....	1	1	2	3	19	—	—	—	—	—	—	Liberia	668
131	166	187	65	62	61	59	49	73	168	209	122	166	219	317	Madagascar	674
37	109	77	97	108	30	42	30	74	157	121	192	183	190	165	Malawi	676
12	27	89	135	224	225	243	152	218	301	308	287	255	....	....	Mali	678
51	42	63	38	48	45	33	28	58	99	149	144	164	....	....	Mauritania	682
243	330	396	521	627	599	553	514	583	625	516	399	535	691	667	Mauritius	684
314	431	396	1,477	2,192	2,631	2,686	3,006	2,447	2,663	2,984	3,174	4,170	3,727	6,768	Morocco	686
....	....	....	....	....	....	....	....	....	....	386	435	477	559	571	Mozambique	688
....	....	....	....	36	97	139	149	135	....	....	....	....	....	....	Namibia	728
176	173	162	157	142	164	140	76	64	55	40	38	29	....	....	Niger	692
845	508	1,368	2,740	3,125	727	1,023	973	995	2,858	5,643	5,067	3,995	7,631	8,345	Nigeria	694
116	88	54	31	77	57	35	....	....	74	114	120	127	146	169	Rwanda	714
....	....	....	....	....	....	....	3	3	9	7	8	9	12	São Tomé & Príncipe	716
8	9	15	9	10	10	4	124	184	202	287	307	295	....	....	Senegal	722
10	6	9	12	19	23	26	21	18	15	20	15	22	34	30	Seychelles	718
4	6	3	4	7	14	21	28	23	18	29	31	29	39	41	Sierra Leone	724
6	12	12	....	....	....	....	....	....	....	....	....	....	....	....	Somalia	726
656	701	838	852	855	954	909	1,301	2,046	787	3,697	3,234	4,767	4,875	5,011	South Africa	199
8	9	12	8	5	20	27	54	110	74	60	64	138	....	....	Sudan	732
90	104	137	152	120	225	192	203	201	177	219	255	274	270	216	Swaziland	734
22	58	41	136	143	238	148	227	182	306	461	426	565	748	920	Tanzania	738
251	173	218	249	256	199	114	65	88	62	88	84	89	....	....	Togo	742
377	675	738	565	560	627	629	1,009	1,087	1,327	1,474	1,322	1,655	1,398	1,590	Tunisia	744
38	37	11	31	41	69	107	220	309	367	470	515	556	620	782	Uganda	746
77	100	89	136	130	....	....	150	155	177	49	33	188	146	Zambia	754
132	147	88	118	119	181	332	294	427	439	146	115	221	165	58	Zimbabwe	698

Total Reserves

(with Gold at SDR 35 per ounce)

Millions of SDRs:

		1972	1973	1974	1975	1976	1977	1978	1979	1980	1981	1982	1983	1984	1985	1986
Asia *	505	7,935	9,215	10,921	11,049	16,565	22,546	23,758	27,406	31,009	37,977	44,490	55,924	68,740	67,708	81,331
Afghanistan, Islamic State of	512	52	51	55	107	145	260	333	369	325	269	267	238	267	303	245
Bangladesh	513	249	119	113	127	249	193	243	295	237	121	168	503	400	308	337
Bhutan	514	....	....	....	....	....	....	....	....	....	27	32	38	46	46	50
China, P.R.: Mainland †	924	....	....	....	....	....	2,379	1,643	2,083	2,444	4,790	10,733	14,759	†18,161	12,032	9,808
China, P.R.: Hong Kong	532	....	....	....	....	....	....	....	....	....	....	....	....	....	....	....
Fiji	819	64	61	89	127	100	121	104	104	132	116	115	111	120	120	140
India	534	1,087	947	1,083	1,174	2,646	4,268	5,225	5,942	5,745	4,333	4,213	5,017	6,266	6,174	5,594
Indonesia	536	531	669	1,219	501	1,290	2,071	2,024	3,093	4,311	4,416	2,959	3,660	4,978	4,637	3,421
Korea	542	485	737	230	671	1,700	2,448	2,131	2,257	2,304	2,315	2,556	2,252	2,820	2,623	2,725
Lao People's Democratic Rep.	544	....	....	....	....	....	....	....	....	....	....	....	....	....	....	....
Malaysia	548	894	1,115	1,322	1,302	2,127	2,353	2,556	3,046	3,521	3,602	3,497	3,696	3,880	4,554	5,009
Maldives	556	....	....	....	....	—	—	—	1	1	1	8	4	5	4	6
Micronesia, Fed. States of	868	....	....	....	....	....	....	....	....	....	....	....	....	....	....	....
Mongolia	948	....	....	....	....	....	....	....	....	....	....	....	....	....	....	....
Myanmar	518	48	83	156	120	109	93	82	163	213	206	103	94	72	40	36
Nepal	558	95	102	104	86	†114	119	116	126	149	179	186	133	89	56	76
Pakistan	564	259	397	376	346	458	426	373	225	452	684	943	1,949	1,122	802	647
Papua New Guinea	853	....	26	27	153	221	352	312	384	334	343	413	423	446	405	350
Philippines	566	507	860	1,229	1,160	1,411	1,255	1,406	1,767	2,299	1,833	870	724	642	612	1,492
Samoa	862	4	4	5	5	5	8	4	4	2	3	3	7	11	13	19
Singapore	576	1,610	1,895	2,297	2,568	2,895	3,176	4,070	4,417	5,149	6,486	7,687	8,849	10,626	11,695	10,578
Solomon Islands	813	....	....	....	....	....	2	22	28	23	19	34	45	46^e	32^e	24
Sri Lanka	524	55	72	64	50	79	241	307	395	195	283	321	286	523	413	290
Thailand	578	969	1,082	1,518	1,516	1,629	1,576	1,627	1,485	1,310	1,575	1,481	1,622	2,046	2,081	2,380
Tonga	866	....	....	....	....	....	7	8	10	11	12	14	20	27	25	18
Vanuatu	846	....	....	....	....	....	....	....	....	....	7	5	6	8	10	18
*of which:																
Taiwan Province of China	528	957	931	972	998	1,383	1,192	1,164	1,198	1,839	6,330	7,866	11,471	16,136	20,710	38,055
Europe	170	2,680	3,790	3,279	2,936	4,219	3,694	4,177	3,834	5,354	5,405	5,359	7,458	9,055	7,707	8,316
Albania	914	....	....	....	....	....	....	....	....	....	....	....	....	....	....	....
Armenia	911	....	....	....	....	....	....	....	....	....	....	....	....	....	....	....
Azerbaijan	912	....	....	....	....	....	....	....	....	....	....	....	....	....	....	....
Croatia	960	....	....	....	....	....	....	....	....	....	....	....	....	....	....	....
Cyprus	423	294	254	219	184	251	273	281	284	305	382	490	512	568	558	631
Czech Republic	935	....	....	....	....	....	....	....	....	....	....	....	....	....	....	....
Czechoslovakia	934	....	....	....	....	....	....	....	....	1,549	931	831	902	1,123	911	1,044
Estonia	939	....	....	....	....	....	....	....	....	....	....	....	....	....	....	....
Georgia	915	....	....	....	....	....	....	....	....	....	....	....	....	....	....	....
Hungary	944	....	....	....	....	....	....	....	....	....	....	....	1,230	1,664	2,042	1,964
Kazakhstan	916	....	....	....	....	....	....	....	....	....	....	....	....	....	....	....
Kyrgyz Republic	917	....	....	....	....	....	....	....	....	....	....	....	....	....	....	....
Latvia	941	....	....	....	....	....	....	....	....	....	....	....	....	....	....	....
Lithuania	946	....	....	....	....	....	....	....	....	....	....	....	....	....	....	....
Macedonia, FYR	962	....	....	....	....	....	....	....	....	....	....	....	....	....	....	....
Malta	181	253	270	328	427	535	605	723	782	791	939	999	1,079	1,027	915	953
Moldova	921	....	....	....	....	....	....	....	....	....	....	....	....	....	....	....
Poland	964	....	....	....	....	....	....	....	474	127	255	603	747	1,145	809	587
Romania	968	....	258	282	552	580	318	406	522	383	472	532	628	854	315	590
Russia	922	....	....	....	....	....	....	....	....	....	....	....	....	....	....	....
Slovak Republic	936	....	....	....	....	....	....	....	....	....	....	....	....	....	....	....
Slovenia	961	....	....	....	....	....	....	....	....	....	....	....	....	....	....	....
Turkey	186	1,287	1,771	1,400	931	977	652	743	631	976	929	1,111	1,362	1,429	1,096	1,288
Ukraine	926	....	....	....	....	....	....	....	....	....	....	....	....	....	....	....
Yugoslavia, SFR	188	674	1,109	937	744	1,764	1,736	1,890	1,014	1,150	1,437	768	998	1,247	1,062	1,259
Middle East	405	9,436	11,226	29,452	38,455	45,914	53,987	42,811	48,140	56,540	59,762	64,042	62,200	59,665	58,576	47,866
Bahrain, Kingdom of	419	85	61	116	253	381	420	384	471	753	1,332	1,397	1,368	1,334	1,516	1,223
Egypt	469	133	300	291	251	291	440	464	488	905	700	718	822	836	806	763
Iran, I.R. of	429	885	1,025	6,847	7,600	7,603	10,098	9,327	11,682	8,188	1,591	5,376	....	....	....	....
Iraq	433	720	1,287	2,673	2,330	3,960	5,759	....	....	....	....	....	....	....	....	....
Israel	436	1,126	1,504	980	1,010	1,182	1,293	2,056	2,369	2,670	3,046	3,518	3,523	3,158	3,386	3,845
Jordan	439	250	252	283	420	434	558	708	914	932	971	839	825	562	422	395
Kuwait	443	335	415	1,143	1,414	1,660	2,461	2,008	2,268	3,169	3,583	5,449	5,048	4,772	5,069	4,586
Lebanon	446	622	714	1,367	1,349	1,444	1,614	1,731	1,485	1,568	1,626	2,687	2,140	1,008	1,300	722
Libya	672	2,694	1,763	2,953	1,875	2,759	4,026	3,236	4,902	10,372	7,860	6,525	5,110	3,835	5,501	4,993
Oman	449	34	39	77	139	191	242	202	322	463	649	801	738	928	1,003	801
Qatar	453	56	63	59	90	119	141	173	231	290	343	368	395	414	425	480
Saudi Arabia	456	2,303	3,214	11,667	19,920	23,261	24,725	†14,896	14,790	18,536	27,855	26,948	26,224	25,409	22,924	15,141
Syrian Arab Rep.	463	125	342	409	627	280	427	321	470	293	280	209	79	303	105	147
United Arab Emirates	466	....	76	370	844	1,660	679	643	1,107	1,600	2,775	2,037	2,008	2,362	2,946	2,784
Yemen Arab Rep.	473	....	105	162	288	620	1,021	1,120	1,084	1,006	826	502	350	325	270	353
Yemen, P.D. Rep.	459	62	63	55	47	71	83	145	161	185	220	261	270	255	171	114
Yemen, Republic of	474	....	....	....	....	....	....	....	....	....	....	....	....	....	....	....

End of Period — (with Gold at SDR 35 per ounce)

1987	1988	1989	1990	1991	1992	1993	1994	1995	1996	1997	1998	1999	2000	2001		Code
99,757	112,211	121,736	146,115	177,725	190,051	222,141	263,161	291,527	344,224	384,390	413,650	482,341	547,620	631,072	Asia *	505
231	228	219	221	198	...	...	...	...	...	...	...	...	...	...	Afghanistan, Islamic State of	512
597	780	384	445	897	1,330	1,758	2,153	1,577	1,279	1,176	1,357	1,172	1,144	1,018	Bangladesh	513
53	70	75	60	69	57	...	79	84	128	134	177	200	227	226	Bhutan	514
11,938	14,223	14,111	21,241	30,977	†15,441	16,743	36,691	51,152	74,883	106,253	106,400	115,364	129,600	172,124	China, P.R.: Mainland †	924
...	...	...	17,277	20,147	25,589	31,298	33,739	37,270	44,376	68,784	63,673	70,119	82,542	88,450	China, P.R.: Hong Kong	532
93	173	161	183	190	230	196	187	235	297	267	274	312	314	292	Fiji	819
4,915	4,006	3,302	1,443	2,930	4,584	7,826	13,907	12,504	14,474	18,744	19,820	24,203	29,493	36,902	India	534
4,051	3,860	4,259	5,352	6,581	7,708	8,308	8,419	9,330	12,801	12,402	16,240	19,376	21,984	21,789	Indonesia	536
2,537	9,186	11,588	10,409	9,590	12,463	14,738	17,574	21,995	23,682	15,107	36,928	53,922	73,797	81,778	Korea	542
—	—	1	1	20[e]	29[e]	46[e]	42[e]	62	118	83	80	74	107	104	Lao People's Democratic Rep.	544
5,323	4,932	6,005	6,938	7,692	12,613	19,922	17,498	16,077	18,867	15,489	18,235	22,328	22,700	24,290	Malaysia	548
6	16	19	17	16	21	19	21	32	53	73	84	93	94	74	Maldives	556
...	...	...	...	...	...	...	...	...	62	64	...	68	87	...	Micronesia, Fed. States of	868
...	...	...	...	...	13	44	57	82	80	133	68	99	140	170	Mongolia	948
28	66	209	229	189	213	229	298	386	167	193	232	202	179	327	Myanmar	518
131	169	166	213	283	345	471	480	400	403	469	542	621	731	831	Nepal	558
422	361	464	276	437	689	943	2,078	1,238	453	958	803	1,174	1,235	2,970	Pakistan	564
310	295	295	286	228	176	105	68	176	408	271	139	152	239	351	Papua New Guinea	853
780	845	1,164	751	2,387	3,300	3,517	4,223	4,412	7,138	5,560	6,742	9,856	10,270	10,976	Philippines	566
26	37	42	49	47	44	37	35	37	42	48	44	50	49	45	Samoa	862
10,733	12,687	15,481	19,505	23,862	29,007	35,208	39,851	46,213	53,442	52,836	53,215	55,987	61,502	59,977	Singapore	576
26	29	20	12	6	17	15	12	11	23	27	35	37	25	...	Solomon Islands	813
199	167	188	299	483	679	1,188	1,404	1,407	1,366	1,502	1,408	1,194	819	1,046	Sri Lanka	524
2,911	4,617	7,327	9,439	12,333	14,893	17,904	20,179	24,293	26,326	19,490	20,559	24,905	24,655	25,832	Thailand	578
20	23	19	22	23	23	27	24	19	21	20	20	20	21	21	Tonga	866
28	30	27	26	28	31	33	30	32	31	28	32	30	30	30	Vanuatu	846
															*of which:	
54,367	55,385	56,193	51,393	58,082	60,333	61,319	63,806	61,229	61,699	62,362	64,636	77,851	82,400	97,720	Taiwan Province of China	528
8,006	10,013	14,931	15,640	16,147	16,006	26,137	31,289	58,320	62,505	72,813	73,610	80,295	98,772	112,346	Europe	170
...	...	...	...	...	...	109	142	164	199	233	252	273	274	...	Albania	914
...	...	...	...	...	1	10	22	68	109	171	225	234	246	257	Armenia	911
...	...	...	...	...	...	—	1	81	147	345	318	490	522	714	Azerbaijan	912
...	...	...	...	121	—	449	962	1,275	1,609	1,882	2,000	2,204	2,705	3,742	Croatia	960
632	706	871	1,075	988	764	815	1,019	767	1,088	1,048	996	1,352	1,353	1,821	Cyprus	423
...	...	...	...	...	...	2,827	4,282	9,382	8,659	7,251	8,918	9,346	10,008	11,428	Czech Republic	935
1,102	1,307	1,768	862	2,327	†930	...	...	...	...	...	...	...	...	...	Czechoslovakia	934
...	...	...	...	...	127	281	304	390	443	562	576	622	707	653	Estonia	939
...	...	...	...	...	...	...	...	131	131	148	87	96	84	128	Georgia	915
1,209	1,146	1,001	762	2,759	3,222	4,882	4,618	8,059	6,763	6,235	6,622	7,985	8,592	8,539	Hungary	944
...	...	...	...	...	...	355	608	811	963	1,321	1,099	1,141	1,288	1,654	Kazakhstan	916
...	...	...	...	...	...	...	...	...	...	...	119	170	186	213	Kyrgyz Republic	917
...	...	...	...	...	...	323	382	349	...	...	...	621	...	...	Latvia	941
...	...	...	...	...	39	262	366	516	544	755	1,007	877	1,013	1,294	Lithuania	946
...	...	...	...	...	...	78	104	175	169	193	221	317	333	600	Macedonia, FYR	962
1,013	1,030	1,039	1,012	936	927	995	1,271	1,081	1,128	1,103	1,181	1,303	1,129	1,326	Malta	181
...	...	...	...	—	2	56	123	173	217	271	102	135	177	182	Moldova	921
1,070	1,544	1,778	3,174	2,556	2,998	2,996	4,018	9,955	12,426	15,156	19,522	19,318	20,502	20,525	Poland	964
1,036	630	1,491	446	564	681	808	1,521	1,157	1,561	2,925	2,149	2,074	3,128	4,449	Romania	968
...	...	...	...	...	...	4,605	3,021	10,005	8,314	10,127	6,056	6,628	19,056	26,370	Russia	922
...	...	...	...	...	...	348	1,204	2,308	2,423	2,439	2,083	2,501	3,132	3,335	Slovak Republic	936
...	...	...	...	78	520	574	1,027	1,225	1,598	2,457	2,584	2,308	2,453	3,454	Slovenia	961
1,386	1,876	3,770	4,396	3,742	4,621	4,707	5,045	8,501	11,561	13,960	13,972	17,141	17,391	15,153	Turkey	186
...	...	...	...	...	341	118	447	708	1,364	1,737	545	768	1,054	2,369	Ukraine	926
557	1,774	3,214	3,914	1,942	...	...	...	...	...	...	...	...	...	...	Yugoslavia, SFR	188
45,854	41,599	42,240	37,967	41,788	44,160	47,218	46,241	50,708	61,289	74,029	73,092	79,663	93,333	99,503	Middle East	405
815	935	804	873	1,064	1,022	953	806	866	922	962	772	1,003	1,206	1,345	Bahrain, Kingdom of	419
1,057	1,024	1,242	1,971	3,808	7,947	9,480	9,319	10,971	12,184	13,919	12,957	10,638	10,153	10,370	Egypt	469
...	...	...	...	...	...	...	...	...	...	...	...	...	...	...	Iran, I.R. of	429
...	...	...	...	...	...	...	...	...	...	...	...	...	...	...	Iraq	433
4,178	3,020	4,050	4,440	4,404	3,729	4,647	4,653	5,462	7,938	15,069	16,104	16,470	17,869	18,603	Israel	436
334	107	384	623	605	586	1,220	1,187	1,355	1,251	1,659	1,272	1,933	2,571	2,451	Jordan	439
3,008	1,518	2,449	1,461	2,472	3,832	3,157	2,487	2,484	2,533	2,647	2,892	3,603	5,525	7,964	Kuwait	443
582	1,049	1,037	787	1,214	1,411	1,968	2,983	3,372	4,448	4,752	4,979	5,988	4,885	4,312	Lebanon	446
4,241	3,337	3,423	4,230	4,107	4,622	...	...	...	...	...	5,325	5,466	9,726	11,939	Libya	672
998	793	1,041	1,186	1,173	1,453	671	681	776	976	1,158	766	2,027	1,837	1,892	Oman	449
440	394	447	485	508	538	547	492	542	519	624	757	956	894	1,050	Qatar	453
16,151	15,434	12,905	8,362	8,322	4,477	5,569	5,214	5,961	†10,120	11,187	10,260	12,545	15,193	14,162	Saudi Arabia	456
186	173	...	...	...	...	...	...	...	...	...	...	...	...	...	Syrian Arab Rep.	463
3,359	3,323	3,419	3,250	3,779	4,182	4,472	4,589	5,054	5,630	6,233	6,474	7,792	10,393	11,270	United Arab Emirates	466
380	212	212	...	...	...	...	...	...	...	...	...	...	...	...	Yemen Arab Rep.	473
70	61	...	...	...	...	...	...	...	...	...	...	...	...	...	Yemen, P.D. Rep.	459
...	...	...	299	477	235	108	176	418	709	893	709	1,074	2,228	2,913	Yemen, Republic of	474

Total Reserves

(with Gold at SDR 35 per ounce)		1972	1973	1974	1975	1976	1977	1978	1979	1980	1981	1982	1983	1984	1985	198
															Millions of SDRs	
Western Hemisphere	205	9,089	11,957	15,033	16,113	20,492	23,466	27,296	32,415	31,611	33,992	25,563	27,980	41,142	37,541	27,29
Antigua and Barbuda	311	....	....	....	6	8	4	5	9	6	6	8	9	16	15	1
Argentina	213	428	1,092	1,074	386	1,383	2,743	3,962	7,280	5,421	2,961	2,425	1,273	1,421	†3,133	2,37
Aruba	314	....	....	....	....	....			....						....	6
Bahamas, The	313	34	36	41	46	41	†56	45	59	72	86	103	117	164	166	18
Barbados	316	26	27	32	34	24	30	46	50	62	87	110	118	135	127	12
Belize	339	....	....	....	....	5	7	11	8	10	9	9	9	6	13	2
Bolivia	218	55	60	158	134	145	195	153	159	110	115	172	185	289	213	16
Brazil	223	3,853	5,318	4,306	3,447	5,631	5,974	9,134	6,866	4,589	5,750	3,566	4,179	11,792	9,763	†4,82
Chile	228	137	149	84	93	395	399	885	1,525	2,508	2,820	1,705	1,999	2,403	2,284	1,98
Colombia	233	300	443	367	445	997	1,499	1,885	2,999	3,885	4,191	3,634	1,963	1,439	1,517	2,274
Costa Rica	238	39	42	36	44	84	159	152	93	117	114	207	300	414	463	43
Dominica	321	....	....	....	—	1	2	1	7	4	3	4	1	5	3	8
Dominican Republic	243	54	73	74	99	109	152	122	185	163	198	120	166	259	310	308
Ecuador	248	124	188	274	230	424	527	502	563	809	558	290	630	638	668	541
El Salvador	253	76	51	80	108	177	191	223	126	79	80	116	169	186	180	155
Grenada	328	5	4	4	†4	7	6	7	9	10	14	8	14	15	19	17
Guatemala	258	124	176	165	260	440	568	587	547	367	147	120	219	298	292	314
Guyana	336	34	12	51	86	23	19	45	13	10	6	10	6	6	6	7
Haiti	263	17	14	16	11	24	28	30	42	13	21	4	9	14	6	14
Honduras	268	32	35	36	83	113	148	142	159	118	87	102	109	131	97	92
Jamaica	343	147	106	156	107	28	40	45	49	82	73	99	60	99	147	80
Mexico	273	1,072	1,124	1,139	1,310	1,079	1,419	1,480	1,642	2,393	3,579	828	3,818	7,504	4,549	4,725
Netherlands Antilles	353	65	61	69	80	99	102	71	75	93	135	189	176	140	179	215
Nicaragua	278	74	97	86	104	126	123	40	112	51	96	156	171	....	....	
Panama	283	40	35	32	29	68	58	115	93	95	103	92	197	220	89	139
Paraguay	288	29	47	71	98	136	221	345	464	599	693	671	651	681	487	366
Peru	293	446	471	791	399	284	329	334	1,195	1,601	1,079	1,272	1,353	1,712	1,745	1,225
St. Kitts and Nevis	361	....	....	....	....						3	3	3	6	7	8
St. Lucia	362	....	....	....	3	4	5	5	6	6	7	7	8	13	12	21
St. Vincent & Grens.	364	....	....	....		4	4	4	7	6	7	8	5	13	13	21
Suriname	366	43	52	60	83	100	83	104	131	150	180	161	58	27	23	19
Trinidad and Tobago	369	54	39	319	642	872	1,221	1,387	1,626	2,182	2,878	2,794	2,012	1,386	1,029	390
Uruguay	298	187	207	190	174	276	391	398	†361	421	488	205	289	229	250	485
Venezuela, Rep. Bol.	299	1,595	1,999	5,320	7,569	7,384	6,764	5,031	5,958	5,579	7,415	6,365	7,701	9,482	9,733	5,664

Memorandum Items

		1972	1973	1974	1975	1976	1977	1978	1979	1980	1981	1982	1983	1984	1985	198
Oil Exporting Countries	999	9,956	11,982	38,303	48,228	56,075	62,052	46,119	56,199	69,322	69,335	67,111	67,146	69,549	69,273	51,850
Non-Oil Developing Countries	201	23,339	29,088	29,950	29,772	40,895	50,638	59,035	66,383	70,871	78,786	80,072	93,848	116,386	111,074	120,479

(with Gold at SDR 35 per ounce)															*Millions of SDRs:*	
All Countries	010	147	153	180	194	222	265	282	306	355	363	361	396	440	438	452

(with Gold at market prices)															*Millions of SDRs:*	
All Countries	010	171,967	212,127	299,690	280,844	304,358	368,372	425,540	640,888	763,159	656,411	722,552	709,101	706,500	688,974	723,480

End of Period

1987	1988	1989	1990	1991	1992	1993	1994	1995	1996	1997	1998	1999	2000	2001	(with Gold at SDR 35 per ounce)	
26,958	23,085	25,428	34,434	46,677	65,053	79,892	72,340	87,892	109,232	126,352	114,863	112,537	120,450	126,735	Western Hemisphere	205
18	21	21	19	23	37	28	31	40	33	38	42	51	49	63	Antigua and Barbuda	311
1,293	2,652	1,267	3,376	4,342	7,418	10,193	9,967	9,765	12,743	16,555	17,592	19,139	19,301	11,580	Argentina	213
59	71	70	72	87	107	135	125	149	134	131	161	164	163	237	Aruba	314
120	128	112	111	127	113	125	121	121	119	168	246	299	268	254	Bahamas, The	313
103	101	84	83	61	102	110	134	147	201	196	260	220	363	549	Barbados	316
26	38	46	49	37	39	28	24	25	41	44	31	52	94	89	Belize	339
100	110	187	149	106	163	194	340	475	697	838	635	674	631	643	Bolivia	218
4,525	5,276	5,838	5,390	5,687	16,457	22,383	25,523	33,600	40,689	37,776	30,401	25,463	25,001	28,455	Brazil	223
1,829	2,412	2,822	4,331	4,988	6,733	7,084	9,030	9,577	10,381	12,891	11,167	10,539	11,307	11,317	Chile	228
2,199	2,452	2,773	3,275	4,598	5,651	5,784	5,484	5,626	6,855	7,278	6,157	5,846	6,855	8,091	Colombia	233
347	497	565	366	644	742	747	613	705	696	935	755	1,064	1,011	1,058	Costa Rica	238
13	10	9	10	12	15	14	11	15	16	18	20	23	23	25	Dominica	321
129	189	125	44	310	364	475	173	247	244	290	357	506	482	876	Dominican Republic	243
361	310	426	605	662	647	1,019	1,278	1,109	1,307	1,566	1,165	1,476	756	....	Ecuador	248
148	137	219	308	217	323	407	461	527	668	986	1,162	1,476	1,492	1,402	El Salvador	253
16	13	12	12	12	19	20	21	25	25	32	33	37	44	51	Grenada	328
221	168	252	205	572	561	639	599	480	612	831	956	874	1,348	1,832	Guatemala	258
6	3	10	20	87	137	180	169	181	229	234	196	195	234	229	Guyana	336
13	10	10	3	25	20	24	36	130	151	159	189	193	141	113	Haiti	263
75	38	17	29	74	144	71	118	177	174	431	582	917	1,009	1,127	Honduras	268
123	109	82	118^e	74	236	304	504	458	612	506	504	404	809	1,513	Jamaica	343
8,875	4,012	4,852	6,965	12,424	13,800	18,298	4,316	11,351	13,523	21,350	22,592	23,162	27,262	35,609	Mexico	273
172	215	177	170	143	179	190	142	156	151	178	195	212	....	....	Netherlands Antilles	353
....	....	....	....	....	....	40	97	92	138	281	249	372	375	302	Nicaragua	278
55	54	91	241	349	367	435	482	526	603	851	678	600	555	869	Panama	283
352	242	330	466	674	410	461	707	736	731	632	615	714	585	569	Paraguay	288
508	440	684	808	1,772	2,136	2,527	4,829	5,570	7,395	8,179	6,832	6,399	6,466	6,939	Peru	293
7	8	12	11	12	19	21	22	23	23	27	33	36	35	45	St. Kitts and Nevis	361
22	24	29	31	34	40	44	40	42	39	45	50	54	61	71	St. Lucia	362
14	16	17	19	16	24	23	21	20	21	23	28	31	42	49	St. Vincent & Grens.	364
13	11	9	17	3	14	15	29	93	72	88	80	37	57	104	Suriname	366
134	96	189	348	239	127	152	243	243	380	526	558	691	1,066	1,520	Trinidad and Tobago	369
465	487	473	452	314	441	612	723	834	931	1,215	1,535	1,579	1,940	2,465	Uruguay	298
4,604	2,698	3,526	6,250	7,858	7,356	7,111	5,927	4,628	8,599	11,057	8,807	9,287	10,404	7,735	Venezuela, Rep. Bol.	299

Memorandum Items

1987	1988	1989	1990	1991	1992	1993	1994	1995	1996	1997	1998	1999	2000	2001		
49,103	42,949	44,318	43,887	48,896	46,155	46,432	44,346	44,647	61,118	71,914	71,352	78,588	103,739	111,830	Oil Exporting Countries	999
139,140	151,907	169,593	202,459	248,215	282,183	343,078	385,330	461,378	537,784	617,448	633,062	706,574	797,174	907,071	Non-Oil Developing Countries	201

End of Period

1987	1988	1989	1990	1991	1992	1993	1994	1995	1996	1997	1998	1999	2000	2001	(with Gold at SDR 35 per ounce)	
541	576	624	688	726	753	830	890	1,020	1,174	1,293	1,278	1,400	1,578	1,728	All Countries	010

End of Period

1987	1988	1989	1990	1991	1992	1993	1994	1995	1996	1997	1998	1999	2000	2001	(with Gold at market prices)	
831,014	831,852	878,792	890,382	....	....	....	....	....	....	....	....	....	....	....	All Countries	010

		1972	1973	1974	1975	1976	1977	1978	1979	1980	1981	1982	1983	1984	1985	1986
													Percent Change over Previous Year			
Industrial Countries																
United States	111	3.8	8.0	6.1	6.6	5.6	9.8	11.4	6.6	6.0	3.5	6.7	5.5	7.4	10.0	15.0
Canada	156	15.5	16.1	14.1	15.4	9.3	12.1	11.8	8.6	10.1	2.3	4.4	1.4	1.9	5.7	7.8
Australia	193	19.9	26.2	−12.2	28.9	12.0	5.1	−1.1	8.9	9.8	11.0	8.8	12.7	10.9	12.3	8.6
Japan	158	29.0	34.3	16.1	4.0	8.6	8.4	14.9	7.5	6.4	2.7	6.2	5.4	8.5	3.8	8.1
New Zealand	196	64.8	47.2	4.9	−18.9	5.0	9.0	20.7	8.6	−10.9	14.1	7.8	11.8	7.8	11.6	−12.9
Euro Area																
Austria	122	14.9	2.0	10.1	16.9	4.5	4.4	15.4	1.9	7.2	6.4	3.8	6.5	2.2	1.4	7.2
Belgium	124	14.1	12.5	4.3	6.6	6.6	8.8	7.4	3.2	†1.1	1.8	—	3.4	.6	−1.2	5.0
Finland	172	15.5	11.1	17.3	15.8	1.0	9.8	20.8	60.4	34.6	−2.2	13.8	26.2	40.7	12.3	−2.0
France	132	31.7	7.3	13.2	−21.6	7.5	8.9	†12.2	7.1	14.9	4.7	18.1	5.7	10.9	15.9	2.1
Germany	134	26.3	7.4	−1.2	2.9	10.2	7.9	13.1	5.2	−3.7	−1.6	5.3	5.6	3.8	3.3	6.3
Greece	174	19.8	19.2	21.3	21.9	20.5	21.4	20.7	11.3	27.8	44.9	27.9	9.6	30.5	6.2	18.6
Ireland	178	12.4	24.7	24.6	16.4	17.1	13.8	25.4	10.2	15.9	−3.2	9.0	11.0	7.8	7.8	3.4
Italy	136	12.1	15.6	17.7	40.3	20.4	19.3	24.7	14.1	12.8	12.3	15.2	16.4	14.4	17.2	8.0
Luxembourg	137															10.6
Netherlands	138	9.1	4.8	7.9	12.8	9.1	9.0	7.9	7.8	8.3	1.7	7.6	11.9	5.9	3.9	3.6
Portugal	182	19.2	12.9	34.4	37.8	†7.9	5.5	15.1	†31.6	20.8	36.5	29.5	13.4	4.5	5.5	14.2
Denmark	128	5.2	2.2	5.2	38.9	4.2	−12.7	7.7	13.5	4.4	8.8	2.5	7.2	10.1	150.7	−33.7
Iceland	176	20.7	46.6	27.6	34.6	36.3	51.7	50.5	52.2	68.0	65.6	55.4	78.4	38.2	23.5	25.1
Norway	142	4.7	6.6	13.8	17.4	†12.0	12.0	13.0	9.0	8.6	−.6	6.6	4.1	15.8	7.1	−1.2
Sweden	144	9.8	9.6	34.9	−.7	10.7	10.0	13.7	37.3	−9.6	11.7	6.7	2.1	6.5	3.0	25.4
Switzerland	146	7.9	3.8	3.4	2.3	7.7	3.6	17.4	−7.8	1.4	−4.2	6.7	.8	3.9	−1.6	4.9
United Kingdom	112	21.2	31.5	4.1	10.1	19.9	5.3	9.8	9.8	−2.9	3.8	4.3	2.8	−10.9	6.4	†9.8
Developing Countries																
Africa																
Algeria	612	20.5	29.8	13.8	28.5	37.0	17.6	31.0	24.7	20.6	12.3	4.1	20.6	14.7	12.5	15.7
Angola	614															
Benin	638	17.8	2.8	2.6	30.4	17.7	1.8	−4.4	43.6	24.9	61.8	2.7	−20.2	23.1	−18.2	18.6
Botswana	616						11.0	−2.1	60.4	9.4	−15.3	−12.0	4.5	17.0	5.3	43.9
Burkina Faso	748	7.5	21.5	18.4	31.1	13.4	17.7	−3.1	30.8	8.9	21.8	8.7	46.8	36.4	−9.7	41.6
Burundi	618	5.4	7.5	19.9	−2.4	68.2	38.7	17.3	−4.8	10.7	37.7	−14.1	27.4	7.8	24.5	1.7
Cameroon	622	2.5	17.6	22.0	4.0	18.4	30.3	16.4	18.7	15.7	33.4	5.6	28.8	−1.8	14.7	17.8
Cape Verde	624						41.1	14.4	12.9	26.3	10.9	26.4	22.6	6.2	15.3	16.1
Central African Rep.	626	12.4	3.6	26.4	3.9	17.9	23.8	19.5	32.3	36.6	30.7	−2.0	11.5	7.1	.9	12.4
Chad	628	11.8	−1.4	32.2	28.2	18.9	9.5	14.7	35.9	−13.0	9.4	7.9	22.5	53.6	3.1	−.9
Comoros	632													−12.6	41.3	34.1
Congo, Dem. Rep. of	636	26.0	17.4	22.2	40.5	82.5	29.0	56.1	−18.2	114.1	59.3	91.5	1,500.1	−84.2	27.7	60.6
Congo, Rep. of	634	17.2	12.9	30.9	23.9	7.3	5.3	1.4	21.2	30.4	19.1	39.2	4.1	−1.1	11.7	1.8
Côte d'Ivoire	662	13.0	10.2	40.0	13.5	21.5	38.8	32.0	4.1	1.1	9.7	−6.1	7.5	20.0	25.9	6.4
Djibouti	611														−3.1	10.5
Equatorial Guinea	642															57.2
Ethiopia	644	11.2	20.1	27.6	38.6	20.2	−.4	9.6	10.2	12.1	14.7	8.8	—	19.9	4.4	24.7
Gabon	646	14.1	29.4	84.6	29.0	64.8	1.7	−12.7	6.1	18.8	7.1	9.0	9.4	18.2	−7.8	−11.4
Gambia, The	648	9.4	71.9	−1.2	8.1	19.1	−21.0	†52.2	18.0	10.7	36.6	17.6	34.8	†−2.3	80.6	−1.9
Ghana	652	48.0	24.2	35.8	48.0	41.8	61.9	84.5	18.1	30.7	55.4	14.4	43.4	49.1	35.5	59.8
Guinea	656															
Guinea-Bissau	654															
Kenya	664	10.6	10.4	28.2	−9.8	24.0	61.6	7.2	24.8	2.2	4.1	25.7	−2.2	11.4	15.1	39.6
Lesotho	666										5.9	8.2	57.5	17.6	29.6	23.9
Liberia	668				5.9	17.8	19.7	71.6	−4.0	†35.6	−3.6	39.6	25.1	20.9	40.0	39.1
Madagascar	674	15.2	5.6	18.2	6.8	14.1	12.1	33.1	†−2.7	35.1	34.2	−1.2	−4.8	9.2	4.2	70.4
Malawi	676	15.9	109.5	30.2	−11.3	−34.1	84.0	−34.5	−7.5	38.3	34.7	18.1	5.7	76.3	5.0	72.6
Mali	678	9.8	7.3	32.7	†25.6	20.3	21.8	12.0	24.3	6.4	.7	10.0	11.4	†26.8	12.8	12.5
Mauritania	682	37.9	19.1	132.6	−9.8	8.7	13.5	8.4	34.1	6.7	32.1	−1.0	−2.8	.5	39.3	−4.4
Mauritius	684	49.2	18.9	84.1	37.4	18.5	18.5	17.5	−3.4	10.9	4.2	10.9	6.2	6.7	18.2	20.5
Morocco	686	18.7	14.7	20.8	15.0	21.7	15.5	15.4	16.5	5.2	13.5	6.9	13.3	11.5	7.5	23.7
Mozambique	688														17.5	19.3
Namibia	728															
Niger	692	2.0	15.5	41.5	−4.5	40.6	21.4	53.9	13.2	16.1	18.1	1.4	−8.2	27.2	19.7	9.3
Nigeria	694	7.3	23.5	151.2	53.9	27.8	23.7	−3.4	16.2	68.8	−3.3	8.3	3.7	3.1	6.5	6.5
Rwanda	714	11.7	29.4	31.5	1.6	30.8	13.6	2.2	43.9	−6.5	−12.7	3.9	11.4	6.1	12.0	13.5
São Tomé and Príncipe	716															
Senegal	722	4.8	21.0	49.9	7.5	12.1	15.2	25.1	−8.5	21.4	38.3	24.3	−3.3	−1.0	5.9	16.3
Seychelles	718	36.9	12.9	5.0	18.0	33.3	27.4	15.1	32.0	69.1	−9.6	−5.2	6.9	−3.5	12.1	−1.5
Sierra Leone	724	15.4	23.5	12.2	8.3	16.2	16.4	62.5	53.4	−7.5	.8	88.4	25.1	42.2	53.6	105.7
Somalia	726	40.0	16.0	23.1	27.7	19.5	33.2	40.2	24.3	31.6	27.2	−14.9	2.4	61.6	54.4	65.8
South Africa	199	7.9	19.2	16.4	14.8	5.7	7.2	11.9	14.8	62.7	16.9	−11.4	14.0	15.6	11.6	6.9
Sudan	732	9.8	27.8	37.0	18.7	21.6	62.0	32.0	32.9	12.6	61.3	30.6	†10.4	40.4	61.6	42.2
Swaziland	734				113.1	148.7	38.5	−4.6	4.1	23.9	−13.6	11.2	44.7	33.4	11.5	59.7
Tanzania	738	21.9	.7	25.5	15.9	18.7	16.8	21.2	39.0	26.8	28.3	20.9	3.1	30.1	21.3	40.6
Togo	742	−2.7	12.7	40.4	28.1	62.6	5.1	29.9	4.3	17.8	82.5	22.5	10.5	26.4	17.4	2.1
Tunisia	744	13.6	18.4	30.0	14.6	6.8	4.7	17.4	9.7	12.2	26.3	23.1	17.6	10.3	8.8	1.0
Uganda	746	12.5	27.2	33.0	57.4	43.3	14.4	48.7	65.0	36.8	28.3	19.1	60.2	116.1	186.9	163.7
Zambia	754	18.5	31.2	−7.6	42.9	26.6	−1.4	5.2	4.8	13.9	16.5	15.6	14.0	17.7	22.4	170.9
Zimbabwe	698						23.4	11.6	−5.3	16.4	34.9	32.8	19.4	4.8	10.3	15.6
Asia																
Afghanistan, Islamic State of	512	8.7	5.3	14.0	17.2	22.1	33.5	16.0	†21.6	17.6	14.5	†16.4	16.0	9.1	10.6	13.7
Bangladesh	513			25.9	−2.4	2.5	29.5	27.9	16.1	18.7	9.7	†10.6	34.1	35.2	13.8	7.1
Bhutan	514													117.3	139.1	27.2
Cambodia	522															
China, P.R.: Mainland	924															
China, P.R.: Hong Kong	532															23.4
Fiji	819	22.0	51.1	29.0	30.6	−14.1	3.6	13.5	12.4	−8.0	15.3	6.9	6.5	15.7	2.5	13.2
India	534	8.7	22.5	3.5	5.4	16.9	21.1	20.5	21.0	15.2	10.5	18.0	13.0	16.8	23.5	16.3
Indonesia	536					21.8	24.7	9.6	31.4	36.2	16.2	4.8	25.1	10.9	17.9	21.6
Korea	542	48.3	46.0	24.2	39.0	33.5	44.1	35.3	23.8	−6.5	−13.6	36.5	7.1	3.7	1.7	16.2
Lao People's Democratic Rep.	544															
Malaysia	548	30.7	35.6	13.5	2.5	18.7	15.7	15.3	15.6	18.1	10.3	16.7	4.3	3.7	7.6	4.2
Maldives	556							−6.5	−29.8	67.3	58.3	†6.9	−9.2	21.5	32.6	35.0	14.2
Mongolia	948															
Myanmar	518	23.9	26.9	22.8	25.3	31.8	−4.5	12.1	19.8	11.6	20.2	−5.2	11.0	14.2	−10.7	41.5
Nepal	558	13.7	28.9	4.2	9.3	28.9	8.7	17.5	12.7	10.3	14.4	24.7	15.7	16.0	13.1	27.1
Pakistan	564	17.4	12.0	.7	9.8	19.8	22.7	17.6	26.7	16.7	8.2	17.7	13.8	16.4	8.6	19.8

Percent Change over Previous Year

Industrial Countries

1987	1988	1989	1990	1991	1992	1993	1994	1995	1996	1997	1998	1999	2000	2001		
4.6	5.5	4.1	9.0	3.5	8.8	9.1	8.6	4.4	4.7	8.0	6.0	20.0	–6.1	7.8	United States	111
8.8	5.0	4.0	2.3	6.4	2.3	5.5	2.3	1.4	4.3	3.3	6.6	24.3	–7.4	4.2	Canada	156
11.8	11.4	†.2	7.7	3.0	6.0	6.5	8.1	5.0	61.2	–20.3	5.3	–5.4	....	18.9	Australia	193
8.7	13.0	12.9	7.4	–1.4	–3.8	5.8	2.9	7.8	8.5	7.3	3.6	39.3	–18.2	17.3	Japan	158
21.3	†25.2	–2.1	–.5	–2.0	2.2	2.9	11.6	7.1	–2.7	4.9	6.3	76.1	–24.4	9.2	New Zealand	196

Euro Area

1987	1988	1989	1990	1991	1992	1993	1994	1995	1996	1997	1998	1999	2000	2001		
–2.7	1.2	14.1	.1	1.9	10.3	8.1	4.5	–1.0	6.9	–.7	....	....	....	....	Austria	122
2.5	1.2	2.9	–2.8	1.6	–.5	2.9	–6.7	9.2	3.7	2.3	56.2	....	....	....	Belgium	124
48.4	18.9	23.5	–17.3	11.0	5.1	.6	51.1	1.6	–32.8	–7.7	–1.8	....	....	....	Finland	172
11.6	–.8	.3	–3.2	–2.6	–12.7	–3.9	.1	8.7	2.2	3.0	22.4	....	....	....	France	132
9.2	10.7	6.1	12.1	5.3	14.5	–1.3	–1.6	2.0	4.8	–.9	1.1	....	....	....	Germany	134
†23.1	6.9	10.1	22.4	11.1	9.6	8.5	35.6	3.2	12.1	11.3	34.8	25.1	–16.1	....	Greece	174
10.6	3.1	4.8	10.7	–8.7	–8.2	20.5	4.3	26.6	1.1	18.9	....	....	....	....	Ireland	178
9.3	8.9	12.0	6.5	6.7	4.0	–8.9	–5.0	–6.3	2.4	7.4	–29.0	....	....	....	Italy	136
11.2	6.8	—	18.2	–2.8	–5.3	70.0	—	–11.5	17.1	–.2	5.4	....	....	....	Luxembourg	137
9.9	11.3	15.5	3.2	–13.8	30.1	7.4	6.0	–12.3	–4.4	10.2	5.4	....	....	....	Netherlands	138
25.8	13.1	91.4	8.3	22.5	10.6	9.0	–58.8	–2.5	11.2	–1.3	.6	....	....	....	Portugal	182
†–24.2	4.3	–4.1	22.3	–2.8	–12.3	64.2	.7	13.5	33.3	31.1	–22.6	98.8	–22.7	33.4	Denmark	128
6.6	15.8	23.4	–10.4	2.6	3.2	–8.9	3.0	–18.1	26.4	11.4	2.2	....	....	....	Iceland	176
7.5	–2.5	5.8	–1.0	7.7	4.9	10.7	3.3	5.2	53.0	–11.5	–11.0	50.2	–16.3	–.8	Norway	142
4.7	18.3	10.7	8.2	–7.7	24.2	47.7	22.4	–14.9	–33.1	–25.8	3.8	17.0	–5.0	9.6	Sweden	144
5.8	–18.8	–3.9	2.7	–2.6	10.1	–1.3	.6	–2.4	5.1	–2.3	7.7	17.0	–10.6	12.5	Switzerland	146
7.2	9.8	8.5	1.2	1.0	6.0	6.8	5.3	7.0	3.5	7.1	†4.5	18.6	–.3	.6	United Kingdom	112

Developing Countries

Africa

1987	1988	1989	1990	1991	1992	1993	1994	1995	1996	1997	1998	1999	2000	2001		
12.4	8.9	12.1	10.4	16.2	†22.5	27.6	–5.3	7.6	19.9	16.6	13.1	11.4	22.4	41.4	Algeria	612
								....	3,397.1	92.0	49.8	†419.9	217.7	146.6	Angola	614
–17.5	20.1	79.6	59.7	24.6	22.6	–12.9	1.4	–26.1	9.2	19.9	–4.4	75.7	40.7	23.2	Benin	638
20.2	33.4	38.6	33.5	100.3	–17.2	–6.7	–.9	3.5	11.8	26.2	23.6	14.2	6.1	13.1	Botswana	616
18.1	9.6	–14.7	1.3	20.9	6.1	15.4	–.8	24.0	4.7	23.5	–3.6	–14.1	.1	.2	Burkina Faso	748
.1	–3.4	6.1	4.7	15.7	11.1	4.9	26.5	–.8	19.1	1.9	2.7	35.6	–2.6	11.1	Burundi	618
–7.1	†–2.6	6.6	–8.8	–.7	–15.3	–23.0	39.3	–21.0	28.3	40.2	10.2	8.2	34.2	22.3	Cameroon	622
1.6	5.7	6.2	8.0	8.8	31.4	43.4	–38.9	†22.7	–6.3	.5	9.3	6.7	15.8	7.6	Cape Verde	624
–.3	†–1.1	9.8	.7	—	1.5	19.8	84.2	4.5	7.7	–12.4	–20.2	7.7	9.3	–6.2	Central African Rep.	626
10.2	†–10.0	14.4	–7.8	2.9	–5.0	–20.2	23.5	58.2	31.5	–4.2	–10.2	–6.3	16.3	17.4	Chad	628
41.4	–21.6	35.2	–16.6	–8.5	2.2	40.3	14.3	–10.2	36.3	–12.4	†–10.8	19.1	25.9	70.6	Comoros	632
100.8	116.9	79.1	186.5	2,331.5	4,342.5	2,608.4	3,264.3	650.3	....	....	....	....	....	....	Congo, Dem. Rep. of	636
10.4	†–6.8	–1.9	34.8	–19.3	15.8	–4.3	35.4	8.3	8.6	11.6	–20.7	34.2	103.1	–23.4	Congo, Rep. of	634
1.7	–13.8	–21.8	6.3	2.9	–11.2	9.1	56.3	11.6	6.7	11.8	19.1	–7.7	2.0	34.3	Côte d'Ivoire	662
17.2	–.7	–3.7	10.2	.2	23.1	–7.7	5.5	–12.6	–3.7	–2.1	–2.1	4.6	–.8	5.4	Djibouti	611
–22.9	†–44.9	70.6	–68.8	10.4	60.7	–20.4	78.0	99.1	14.6	9.8	–19.9	95.3	48.9	85.6	Equatorial Guinea	642
–1.6	18.8	13.9	14.6	27.5	19.1	4.9	10.3	12.6	–16.6	8.8	–12.3	–10.6	37.1	–8.2	Ethiopia	644
5.6	†8.4	15.8	9.1	28.1	–28.1	–8.2	129.4	–4.2	28.8	1.7	–8.5	–7.9	36.2	–4.2	Gabon	646
19.3	24.2	27.8	6.4	36.0	3.3	11.2	–3.9	25.4	.5	26.8	7.2	14.5	16.8	21.0	Gambia, The	648
41.7	53.8	22.9	2.6	†.4	88.4	4.9	78.9	35.1	44.8	33.4	16.7	12.9	35.8	....	Ghana	652
					11.8	18.9	–10.0	12.3	–1.4	27.2	†4.9	....	....	14.9	Guinea	656
94.2	83.9	36.2	22.7	130.6	65.5	32.2	32.3	32.3	38.7	125.8	–13.3	34.5	87.5	15.9	Guinea-Bissau	654
19.4	2.1	17.0	21.8	15.7	53.5	52.5	22.8	31.0	8.2	2.1	–.4	6.0	–.7	–1.0	Kenya	664
17.5	46.8	–6.0	–6.1	17.8	–22.0	21.9	6.6	32.4	5.0	12.3	38.9	32.8	–6.6	–25.4	Lesotho	666
28.4	19.4	30.2	....		1.2	27.2	5.4	31.3	17.9	8.0	1.9	4.4	†41.3	11.8	Liberia	668
20.7	3.7	37.8	–9.4	55.3	20.8	–6.6	71.9	29.7	48.7	1.1	6.5	26.1	11.8	29.5	Madagascar	674
55.5	11.3	–9.7	–16.3	23.4	17.2	62.6	41.3	89.6	38.5	.2	38.6	32.1	5.8	33.8	Malawi	676
–3.2	10.6	14.5	1.4	31.6	–.2	–9.1	–19.4	10.3	18.3	7.7	–5.6	12.7	26.5	11.9	Mali	678
22.8	13.9	†21.7	–4.2	35.1	21.5	55.1	–3.7	–5.7	–49.5	–13.1	–7.5	4.5	4.9	5.4	Mauritania	682
26.8	24.1	19.7	18.8	133.8	–9.3	–6.8	–7.1	14.5	12.3	–19.8	7.1	7.8	11.8	10.4	Mauritius	684
5.4	15.7	17.7	†21.7	24.8	–8.0	8.6	6.2	5.2	7.6	†7.9	7.1	13.3	3.2	16.3	Morocco	686
59.0	54.5	†30.2	22.7	†34.8	73.3	75.8	66.4	31.7	26.6	16.1	–3.7	17.5	25.7	53.0	Mozambique	688
....	....	....	....	7.9	128.4	5.2	60.2	11.2	22.3	19.9	3.6	43.6	–6.3	8.3	Namibia	728
2.3	21.9	1.2	3.0	–1.8	2.3	–4.3	–24.0	13.0	–5.9	–21.3	–35.7	32.0	3.9	48.6	Niger	692
18.8	41.9	37.3	28.0	42.0	†90.3	49.4	31.3	20.5	6.1	4.5	16.7	21.7	48.2	34.1	Nigeria	694
10.8	–10.2	–14.4	9.4	44.0	–3.4	27.9	9.3	38.7	22.6	11.4	–8.8	14.8	–8.3	22.2	Rwanda	714
									81.1	144.9	10.1	–15.2	29.3	74.7	São Tomé and Príncipe	716
5.4	–.6	24.7	–3.6	7.0	7.2	–30.3	49.2	4.1	–14.2	3.3	6.8	15.9	5.8	34.3	Senegal	722
–.5	26.9	4.5	17.1	25.8	51.1	23.1	47.7	20.8	13.7	18.7	–49.3	9.4	3.1	7.2	Seychelles	718
69.0	77.8	74.3	66.4	63.4	18.9	3.7	25.4	12.1	†23.9	109.0	–20.4	39.0	9.2	29.4	Sierra Leone	724
83.0	68.1	192.7	....												Somalia	726
17.6	37.8	28.5	†13.0	22.8	.2	–8.5	17.8	29.7	13.7	11.4	5.3	21.0	5.8	15.6	South Africa	199
27.5	31.9	85.4	33.2	48.3	†153.6	64.6	39.9	76.7	81.8	34.3	29.4	35.1	†46.7	4.5	Sudan	732
.3	–17.0	30.1	–1.9	–9.4	58.2	–11.3	17.6	2.5	–7.4	5.4	–8.4	11.6	–4.5	–6.4	Swaziland	734
41.4	31.5	19.4	42.3	13.0	60.3	†35.1	48.7	39.1	6.6	8.7	14.7	21.5	9.4	5.0	Tanzania	738
–3.0	–25.3	9.1	11.1	5.5	–17.9	–32.1	2.4	28.8	–12.6	.8	10.9	14.3	21.1	–6.4	Togo	742
7.9	6.4	15.6	13.9	12.0	7.2	4.8	7.2	9.4	35.8	8.1	–11.8	30.5	–11.4	17.8	Tunisia	744
						23.4	48.1	13.7	11.6	9.1	20.0	15.1	21.8	13.4	Uganda	746
40.7	†58.7	65.0	78.3	101.4	....		48.0	–14.6	35.4	48.2	16.8	28.5	53.4	45.7	Zambia	754
6.9	26.0	21.7	25.6	32.2	13.3	52.0	23.6	2.5	65.9	37.8	29.9	60.9	16.0	164.9	Zimbabwe	698

Asia

1987	1988	1989	1990	1991	1992	1993	1994	1995	1996	1997	1998	1999	2000	2001		
57.1	35.1	39.8	41.1	50.6	....	....	....	....	....	....	....	....	....	....	Afghanistan, Islamic State of	512
45.8	10.9	11.5	4.5	–1.5	21.2	24.0	29.6	–9.3	8.7	9.4	13.4	12.7	14.5	24.1	Bangladesh	513
66.9	–11.2	79.9	82.2	26.4	–21.1	†53.7	–33.4	67.1	8.3	9.3	55.4	25.7	21.1	2.3	Bhutan	514
							25.4	10.0	43.0	21.2	47.2	15.9	24.9	17.1	Cambodia	522
12.9	25.2	23.3	30.1	24.2	16.3	†36.2	31.0	20.6	29.5	17.0	2.8	7.6	9.0	....	China, P.R.: Mainland	924
					13.7	26.3	17.1	9.7	3.9	5.0	6.4	2.2	†19.6	6.7	China, P.R.: Hong Kong	532
–4.4	78.6	–23.7	11.3	11.7	19.7	–2.9	1.7	8.8	1.9	5.0	6.3	56.8	–18.9	19.3	Fiji	819
18.2	16.3	18.7	13.7	18.7	8.4	21.7	21.7	12.6	9.5	11.2	12.4	11.4	7.7	10.2	India	534
10.5	–7.2	28.7	16.3	3.3	†19.7	8.3	25.2	17.8	35.8	38.3	59.7	25.3	29.6	–2.3	Indonesia	536
48.9	30.2	31.8	7.7	18.2	10.9	27.5	9.2	16.3	–12.2	–12.5	–8.1	37.6	–.9	16.2	Korea	542
				8.4	18.8	40.6	64.5	22.3	13.4	24.0	43.8	87.7	71.0	59.1	7.3	Lao People's Democratic Rep.	544
5.2	11.5	24.3	22.7	14.5	†21.8	–30.6	36.2	24.7	†35.2	27.4	–38.6	66.4	–7.6	–7.3	Malaysia	548
2.5	22.3	19.1	24.4	22.0	34.5	19.0	14.2	1.6	17.7	15.4	10.9	6.9	4.4	9.7	Maldives	556
					142.6	184.5	103.8	29.0	36.4	23.1	18.3	50.4	20.2	6.8	Mongolia	948
–44.2	75.7	176.0	21.5	†–2.0	30.5	20.7	23.1	27.8	32.0	29.5	26.8	18.7	34.5	51.6	Myanmar	518
18.3	15.1	22.4	22.5	28.2	15.6	30.1	11.7	8.6	9.9	14.9	27.2	10.3	19.3	12.0	Nepal	558
19.5	10.8	17.1	15.9	27.3	8.8	14.2	15.7	17.9	–3.6	14.3	13.0	13.0	–2.1	28.3	Pakistan	564

Percent Change over Previous Year

		1972	1973	1974	1975	1976	1977	1978	1979	1980	1981	1982	1983	1984	1985	1986
Asia (cont.)																
Papua New Guinea	853	....	....	27.3	74.2	18.2	21.0	–4.6	21.4	–57.8	–10.7	1.8	52.6	–7.1	1.8	–3.8
Philippines	566	25.1	12.7	24.6	13.6	12.5	23.6	24.2	22.6	12.4	10.0	5.5	†4.1	58.7	15.1	4.9
Samoa	862	11.3	20.3	14.3	118.2	26.0	35.3	2.6	24.7	549.2	35.1	14.4	11.8	16.3	129.4	40.1
Singapore	576	30.1	37.3	4.0	18.8	16.7	13.3	16.0	13.9	13.1	10.8	18.3	9.3	7.0	4.3	5.4
Solomon Islands	813	....	....	....	....	....	....	....	11.2	–35.5	–44.2	60.8	33.1	38.9	–22.2	2.6
Sri Lanka	524	17.8	17.5	8.2	–6.6	25.7	45.5	12.6	22.1	19.7	18.0	23.7	26.5	16.8	26.5	3.4
Thailand	578	17.8	17.9	13.1	11.1	12.7	9.2	17.3	17.1	14.0	6.6	12.0	10.5	5.6	8.5	10.2
Tonga	866	....	....	....	....	....	....	....	....	....	....	....	32.8	19.8	5.5	23.8
Vanuatu	846	....	....	....	....	....	18.2	15.8	24.4	–12.0	–24.4	5.6	17.5	23.2	25.1	11.7
Vietnam	582	....	....	....	....	....	....	....	....	....	....	....	....	....	....	....
Europe																
Albania	914	....	....	....	....	....	....	....	....	....	....	....	....	....	....	....
Armenia	911	....	....	....	....	....	....	....	....	....	....	....	....	....	....	....
Azerbaijan	912	....	....	....	....	....	....	....	....	....	....	....	....	....	....	....
Belarus	913	....	....	....	....	....	....	....	....	....	....	....	....	....	....	....
Bosnia and Herzegovina	963	....	....	....	....	....	....	....	....	....	....	....	....	....	....	....
Bulgaria	918	....	....	....	....	....	....	....	....	....	....	....	....	....	....	....
Croatia	960	....	....	....	....	....	....	....	....	....	....	....	....	....	....	....
Cyprus	423	19.4	4.9	15.0	1.5	23.3	12.8	16.1	19.7	27.7	22.8	24.0	15.8	17.5	†3.5	8.2
Czech Republic	935	....	....	....	....	....	....	....	....	....	....	....	....	....	....	....
Czechoslovakia	934	....	....	....	....	....	....	....	....	....	–2.1	–4.7	.5	4.8	3.4	2.4
Estonia	939	....	....	....	....	....	....	....	....	....	....	....	....	....	....	....
Georgia	915	....	....	....	....	....	....	....	....	....	....	....	....	....	....	....
Hungary	944	....	....	....	....	....	....	....	....	....	....	....	–10.2	–10.8	14.2	6.7
Kazakhstan	916	....	....	....	....	....	....	....	....	....	....	....	....	....	....	....
Kyrgyz Republic	917	....	....	....	....	....	....	....	....	....	....	....	....	....	....	....
Latvia	941	....	....	....	....	....	....	....	....	....	....	....	....	....	....	....
Lithuania	946	....	....	....	....	....	....	....	....	....	....	....	....	....	....	....
Macedonia, FYR	962	....	....	....	....	....	....	....	....	....	....	....	....	....	....	....
Malta	181	34.6	–3.6	16.0	43.3	27.1	10.5	20.5	11.1	1.8	11.9	2.5	6.5	10.8	.9	.9
Moldova	921	....	....	....	....	....	....	....	....	....	....	....	....	....	....	....
Poland	964	....	....	....	....	....	....	....	....	30.4	†18.4	13.4	8.7	5.7	6.4	4.8
Romania	968	....	....	49.9	29.6	4.5	–.7	24.1	26.5	37.6	9.6	2.7	–5.2	–11.0	†–2.3	14.2
Russia	922	....	....	....	....	....	....	....	....	....	....	....	....	....	....	....
Slovak Republic	936	....	....	....	....	....	....	....	....	....	....	....	....	....	....	....
Slovenia	961	....	....	....	....	....	....	....	....	....	....	....	....	....	....	....
Turkey	186	36.4	26.4	28.8	31.7	21.0	46.9	45.5	55.6	47.9	56.7	41.0	38.2	50.3	38.1	†26.9
Ukraine	926	....	....	....	....	....	....	....	....	....	....	....	....	....	....	....
Yugoslavia, SFR	188	48.5	26.8	6.5	20.8	46.9	†9.9	83.9	20.5	33.3	34.8	41.5	62.9	56.9	62.1	92.4
Middle East																
Bahrain	419	10.7	–36.2	19.5	154.9	48.0	–4.3	9.0	23.2	–2.6	15.1	19.8	–1.1	–6.1	16.5	–5.5
Egypt	469	14.1	24.6	27.0	13.9	19.7	20.4	27.5	28.1	†39.4	25.8	31.5	27.9	14.1	16.8	11.6
Iran, I.R. of	429	36.7	37.2	34.0	24.8	39.2	27.8	....	....	27.0	32.0	40.8	12.2	....	....	....
Iraq	433	18.3	33.9	29.0	28.6	27.1	....	....	....	....	....	....	....	....	....	....
Israel	436	108.8	25.9	20.9	19.1	46.7	221.2	72.4	94.3	115.4	106.4	131.8	271.4	452.4	147.3	4.9
Jordan	439	1.2	16.4	19.9	23.5	24.7	17.9	17.5	26.8	22.9	14.3	11.7	11.3	1.9	3.8	6.5
Kuwait	443	20.3	34.9	34.9	31.0	32.9	91.9	–26.1	19.0	33.5	34.2	61.6	–23.4	–11.5	–1.9	–8.5
Lebanon	446	12.4	14.2	66.8	1.3	33.3	12.4	13.3	–3.3	19.0	15.5	41.8	14.2	13.7	41.6	34.8
Libya	672	16.9	9.3	46.8	14.1	23.2	26.8	28.9	32.3	28.1	–5.7	4.3	–20.4	–4.5	29.3	–4.9
Oman	449	47.3	17.3	95.6	53.6	31.3	24.4	10.6	24.0	32.1	53.1	24.8	–23.9	20.8	3.8	6.3
Qatar	453	32.9	38.5	46.0	58.7	43.8	36.1	32.9	27.6	17.3	3.0	11.0	.8	1.1	–3.2	30.0
Saudi Arabia	456	30.9	51.3	35.0	102.3	61.6	62.8	39.4	–10.8	–11.0	13.7	13.9	–2.1	–1.7	–2.0	8.8
Syrian Arab Rep.	463	18.5	23.0	30.2	19.6	25.1	24.8	30.4	13.8	33.5	8.5	49.0	26.6	32.4	35.8	7.2
United Arab Emirates	466	....	....	155.8	45.1	82.0	36.7	12.2	28.6	–18.7	19.6	13.6	–.9	9.0	15.8	2.6
Yemen Arab Rep.	473	....	....	33.0	77.8	125.0	66.3	27.1	23.3	7.6	15.6	25.4	28.0	27.8	18.9	20.8
Yemen, P.D. Rep.	459	20.7	21.1	1.6	10.3	71.2	28.7	29.4	27.6	19.0	14.3	34.6	25.4	17.7	15.2	13.4
Yemen, Republic of	474	....	....	....	....	....	....	....	....	....	....	....	....	....	....	....
Western Hemisphere																
Antigua and Barbuda	311	....	....	....	....	62.9	–38.4	14.5	63.4	–16.6	–3.6	18.0	14.7	80.0	16.1	38.7
Argentina	213	34.8	584.2	53.1	175.9	357.9	43.2	97.5	85.5	78.9	117.5	744.0	356.2	435.5	386.9	34.7
Aruba	314	....	....	....	....	....	....	....	....	....	....	....	....	....	....	....
Bahamas, The	313	38.0	–4.8	17.1	7.2	12.5	—	13.7	15.6	16.5	–.3	13.8	13.3	19.1	14.3	8.5
Barbados	316	14.7	32.5	33.1	35.8	–4.6	21.6	18.1	33.3	12.0	10.2	4.9	19.3	3.5	9.5	1.7
Belize	339	....	....	....	....	....	36.1	37.0	–9.9	13.9	20.9	17.6	–5.8	34.7	14.7	18.2
Bolivia	218	17.6	40.2	32.5	18.5	45.2	24.8	12.1	11.3	39.8	17.9	293.5	205.7	1,616.6	5,909.7	89.1
Brazil	223	13.6	48.0	37.8	41.2	51.4	50.5	†45.1	85.2	57.9	70.1	86.9	105.8	228.0	250.9	†196.9
Chile	228	179.8	418.2	222.8	255.6	†255.6	93.2	71.9	44.3	62.6	–9.9	113.4	129.6	76.6	108.8	21.4
Colombia	233	23.1	31.1	21.3	25.4	41.5	40.1	†40.1	29.3	29.4	24.3	17.6	18.6	23.5	17.4	20.2
Costa Rica	238	20.9	16.8	14.4	33.1	34.1	46.4	–.4	54.4	18.8	121.6	9.0	33.2	21.1	43.0	29.3
Dominica	321	....	....	....	....	57.0	50.4	–8.5	247.0	–36.8	–36.6	39.7	–38.8	226.0	–14.5	54.1
Dominican Republic	243	8.7	25.6	46.5	–7.8	.2	28.2	8.4	8.4	–3.6	26.0	2.5	16.3	29.1	–1.1	94.6
Ecuador	248	29.5	41.1	41.5	–.5	21.3	21.4	17.0	28.3	13.1	8.0	–18.2	–26.2	12.1	–9.0	–12.1
El Salvador	253	26.1	14.5	15.6	27.6	34.8	5.8	–23.4	–7.6	28.1	17.6	169.3	4.0	11.5	22.6	.9
Grenada	328	–3.5	8.1	7.7	†31.7	73.9	–3.9	24.3	24.5	7.1	25.7	–14.9	5.2	36.3	28.8	–1.0
Guatemala	258	27.3	18.0	15.7	18.0	53.3	12.8	9.6	4.5	–.2	5.8	16.4	–7.7	4.1	61.6	20.6
Guyana	336	30.3	3.8	14.3	47.9	12.8	28.5	41.2	3.6	9.3	28.6	55.7	27.4	28.2	9.6	23.3
Haiti	263	21.8	18.9	4.6	24.3	38.3	18.3	10.5	12.1	23.6	16.4	1.1	–1.4	21.2	12.3	15.2
Honduras	268	2.5	21.3	–3.4	14.5	41.1	15.7	21.2	13.5	2.0	6.6	8.0	7.1	–1.6	–.9	7.2
Jamaica	343	13.1	28.5	21.1	19.0	16.0	16.5	10.7	19.9	41.0	–4.2	–11.4	71.6	92.0	34.9	18.7
Mexico	273	72.2	30.6	40.0	33.7	–7.0	†140.9	28.5	34.7	40.7	44.7	97.9	55.9	51.3	17.0	48.0
Netherlands Antilles	353	15.1	7.4	8.1	27.5	7.7	14.8	–.7	14.2	8.5	1.7	7.2	–8.4	–10.7	74.6	21.7
Nicaragua	278	16.3	41.1	10.6	2.9	26.9	6.1	–9.8	127.5	–6.7	57.1	31.7	†56.5	87.5	183.4	238.3
Panama	283	84.6	–8.9	–8.2	35.1	39.3	9.9	–19.5	98.0	6.9	32.5	–2.3	–1.2	1.5	–3.5	12.5
Paraguay	288	21.9	27.0	17.7	22.9	20.7	31.4	33.1	22.4	27.5	17.7	.6	31.0	17.1	18.9	35.3
Peru	293	31.4	6.6	41.2	5.8	48.4	24.4	55.2	127.2	111.5	55.1	57.0	115.1	142.6	214.9	39.5
St. Kitts and Nevis	361	....	....	....	....	....	....	....	....	–45.3	405.0	–28.4	23.2	45.8	19.4	20.6
St. Lucia	362	....	....	....	....	54.8	7.0	26.0	28.8	8.0	–3.9	8.2	5.5	58.7	25.3	41.9
St. Vincent & Grenadines	364	....	....	....	....	74.3	10.0	7.1	53.8	–14.5	18.7	–10.3	–5.8	86.5	29.7	46.2
Suriname	366	3.8	42.5	–.5	26.0	28.2	23.5	.9	21.5	.2	23.1	9.9	29.2	48.3	52.6	36.1
Trinidad and Tobago	369	9.8	15.5	99.7	57.9	33.5	3.9	4.7	76.2	9.0	22.6	60.7	–5.5	–7.9	7.0	–15.6
Uruguay	298	49.6	76.2	61.8	†68.2	93.5	45.6	84.1	41.8	56.2	16.8	†30.1	73.9	91.1	85.8	77.2
Venezuela, Rep. Bol.	299	12.3	24.0	42.1	40.7	19.1	22.4	10.6	12.9	6.8	17.0	17.1	28.2	25.6	2.9	–18.1

Percent Change over Previous Year

Asia (cont.)

1987	1988	1989	1990	1991	1992	1993	1994	1995	1996	1997	1998	1999	2000	2001	Country	
6.8	5.8	7.3	15.6	-6.5	2.6	17.9	11.3	15.3	91.3	-34.3	20.7	73.3	-16.4	5.5	Papua New Guinea	853
-9.3	12.3	26.1	19.4	19.8	3.9	†18.0	7.9	12.4	32.5	-6.1	2.0	36.7	-10.6	-11.1	Philippines	566
14.9	3.6	38.7	52.3	-9.7	-20.7	-8.0	3.2	4.4	20.5	19.1	-45.7	21.4	8.8	-4.8	Samoa	862
8.1	12.9	15.5	7.2	10.6	10.6	8.4	6.2	9.4	6.7	5.6	-13.3	28.6	-13.7	8.5	Singapore	576
3.7	35.2	-16.2	14.9	35.7	-.1	11.7	30.9	23.0	30.4	-6.2	46.0	-.3	...	...	Solomon Islands	813
10.3	25.8	†5.9	20.6	27.9	8.5	25.2	19.1	16.1	7.9	-2.1	10.5	5.1	4.3	10.4	Sri Lanka	524
22.4	14.9	16.9	18.6	13.3	17.9	16.1	14.5	22.6	13.5	15.8	-4.5	54.8	-12.9	-10.1	Thailand	578
15.5	-10.1	-26.2	65.6	2.9	6.8	-62.8	-4.5	-17.7	43.0	12.3	10.3	7.5	12.6	29.7	Tonga	866
-10.0	11.9	32.1	-13.9	27.9	-2.6	53.6	-6.8	30.4	-4.2	-.2	5.2	22.3	1.9	-.4	Vanuatu	846
...	...	...	...	...	...	27.8	...	...	20.1	12.5	8.7	50.5	25.0	16.7	Vietnam	582

Europe

1987	1988	1989	1990	1991	1992	1993	1994	1995	1996	1997	1998	1999	2000	2001	Country	
...	...	...	...	...	...	...	...	28.1	14.0	48.1	1.5	19.2	21.7	13.5	Albania	914
...	...	...	...	...	...	1,375.5	842.0	92.0	42.8	24.8	4.9	—	34.4	11.1	Armenia	911
...	...	...	...	...	...	1,375.6	642.9	179.8	17.6	41.4	†-24.3	15.9	29.1	†1.5	Azerbaijan	912
...	...	...	...	...	...	...	...	287.9	78.1	107.6	162.9	178.5	124.4	103.9	Belarus	913
...	...	...	...	...	...	...	...	...	...	...	40.7	239.8	16.1	169.2	Bosnia and Herzegovina	963
...	...	...	...	...	50.7	22.0	55.9	†81.6	108.3	751.6	10.3	17.5	11.1	26.7	Bulgaria	918
...	...	...	...	...	502.8	994.1	109.6	43.1	30.0	18.0	-3.8	3.6	13.6	51.9	Croatia	960
10.6	14.7	-10.9	37.4	2.5	6.9	1.6	12.5	-4.3	-8.8	-.8	16.2	14.8	10.8	7.5	Cyprus	423
...	...	...	...	...	...	...	34.4	53.6	.5	†30.9	22.5	8.9	6.9	4.9	Czech Republic	935
-.3	—	6.0	109.9	-58.6	...	...	...	...	...	...	...	...	...	...	Czechoslovakia	934
...	...	...	...	...	166.1	†108.5	11.6	19.9	22.2	37.7	6.4	26.7	14.9	-9.8	Estonia	939
...	...	...	...	...	...	...	...	...	36.3	32.6	-6.3	18.8	27.0	†10.4	Georgia	915
-11.0	-4.5	19.6	-6.0	48.6	21.3	3.0	-1.7	17.8	-8.7	29.9	20.6	26.2	17.3	1.8	Hungary	944
...	...	...	...	...	...	...	623.4	113.5	26.8	†36.8	-29.4	55.7	6.0	30.6	Kazakhstan	916
...	...	...	...	...	...	...	...	...	23.9	21.1	7.6	30.7	11.7	11.5	Kyrgyz Republic	917
...	...	...	...	...	...	...	19.5	1.6	23.0	31.2	6.7	11.6	7.7	13.3	Latvia	941
...	...	...	...	...	...	...	44.2	35.0	2.2	32.4	28.8	-4.0	-3.3	8.3	Lithuania	946
...	...	...	...	...	...	...	71.7	†30.6	-3.2	22.7	5.6	29.6	46.6	8.1	Macedonia, FYR	962
2.8	.2	-4.0	-5.6	6.8	6.3	.2	31.7	-12.2	-4.2	1.5	3.0	6.9	3.5	3.7	Malta	181
...	...	...	...	...	534.0	391.7	128.9	41.3	†9.5	33.3	-6.6	41.7	32.0	25.9	Moldova	921
.9	131.5	474.5	160.6	†27.3	35.8	7.6	22.6	45.0	20.5	34.6	16.9	-1.3	-7.8	30.5	Poland	964
6.2	16.5	39.2	†-41.7	22.5	116.3	†191.5	87.5	56.2	51.4	136.5	20.8	92.4	54.7	59.9	Romania	968
...	...	...	...	...	...	...	203.5	107.8	27.3	27.6	25.3	66.8	68.2	28.6	Russia	922
...	...	...	...	...	...	...	23.9	30.8	28.7	18.2	-5.6	20.0	4.0	.6	Slovak Republic	936
...	...	...	...	...	133.1	38.2	56.9	25.2	15.6	23.0	19.7	21.3	1.9	35.5	Slovenia	961
47.3	78.8	72.0	38.3	49.9	78.2	67.9	119.5	79.5	91.5	99.9	80.4	97.5	46.2	78.6	Turkey	186
...	...	...	...	...	...	1,560.0	407.4	132.8	39.9	49.0	†16.6	41.3	43.8	42.5	Ukraine	926
192.7	255.7	2,273.3	26.7	...	...	...	...	...	...	...	...	...	...	...	Yugoslavia, SFR	188

Middle East

1987	1988	1989	1990	1991	1992	1993	1994	1995	1996	1997	1998	1999	2000	2001	Country	
10.7	-6.2	8.3	9.4	†-4.4	-9.0	-20.1	-4.1	34.5	-11.1	12.6	-21.7	45.5	-.6	14.4	Bahrain	419
6.0	4.1	8.2	28.7	19.2	10.4	19.2	12.5	9.3	4.2	11.1	19.3	1.6	18.7	17.0	Egypt	469
24.9	25.2	13.1	3.2	16.2	13.1	18.8	34.2	48.0	27.1	23.0	18.0	17.1	16.7	6.4	Iran, I.R. of	429
...	...	...	...	...	...	...	...	...	...	...	...	...	...	...	Iraq	433
18.5	6.6	9.8	13.8	8.9	6.9	28.1	-6.7	-26.8	34.9	119.3	14.4	23.8	.6	.7	Israel	436
4.4	23.0	18.4	12.7	30.2	6.3	†5.2	5.1	6.4	-13.4	-2.8	-4.7	12.1	.8	-5.7	Jordan	439
-18.0	-28.0	-1.1	...	-5.8	-6.3	.1	-6.6	.8	-10.1	5.0	30.0	-8.3	-2.5		Kuwait	443
129.6	239.6	69.4	53.3	57.2	90.2	41.9	76.7	21.2	21.2	50.0	-5.5	5.5	6.6	37.2	Lebanon	446
6.5	-15.0	24.0	34.4	—	28.5	-2.4	15.9	7.7	9.0	†6.6	-1.0	-5.3	-.9	10.0	Libya	672
-14.6	1.0	22.0	1.8	3.1	-3.5	-4.8	4.1	3.6	6.4	8.5	7.1	-1.1	8.8	8.8	Oman	449
-.4	-8.9	14.2	8.9	.9	7.9	4.5	-6.9	5.0	6.1	9.7	3.1	12.2	6.7	11.6	Qatar	453
1.1	-6.3	-3.7	25.5	3.9	-1.2	-.2	4.5	-2.3	-1.4	7.6	-1.2	23.5	-4.0	-4.1	Saudi Arabia	456
9.3	-5.3	20.7	28.5	7.5	22.3	14.6	8.6	4.7	7.6	4.8	5.0	7.3	15.2	24.0	Syrian Arab Rep.	463
53.0	-8.1	-11.9	.7	15.8	21.3	-3.3	25.7	13.1	8.1	.5	.2	30.5	36.5	6.0	United Arab Emirates	466
24.1	5.1	4.6	...	...	...	...	...	...	...	...	...	...	...	...	Yemen Arab Rep.	473
7.4	11.3	4.8	...	...	...	...	...	...	...	...	...	...	...	...	Yemen, P.D. Rep.	459
...	...	...	...	9.2	21.4	29.8	35.5	19.8	6.9	-12.5	11.2	20.8	14.0	14.0	Yemen, Republic of	474

Western Hemisphere

1987	1988	1989	1990	1991	1992	1993	1994	1995	1996	1997	1998	1999	2000	2001	Country	
-5.2	11.1	-4.2	3.6	10.1	30.0	-17.2	14.9	17.3	-17.4	4.5	12.9	13.9	-2.7	20.1	Antigua and Barbuda	311
94.7	417.8	7,445.6	†588.7	116.3	40.7	36.1	†8.5	-15.4	2.1	13.6	2.6	.8	-8.8	17.9	Argentina	213
19.3	14.8	-3.6	18.6	25.0	18.3	10.7	-6.4	18.0	-14.3	-4.2	40.5	6.3	-11.5	32.4	Aruba	314
3.3	12.4	4.1	6.3	12.8	-2.7	-.4	12.0	2.8	-2.6	14.5	19.7	20.8	-2.2	10.4	Bahamas, The	313
20.4	4.5	-3.2	19.4	-14.4	13.3	-11.7	-1.9	15.7	34.2	-9.6	9.0	4.2	11.9	13.0	Barbados	316
11.7	-4.4	24.7	-1.7	3.7	21.4	-.7	-2.0	13.4	2.9	5.2	7.8	21.9	22.7	27.1	Belize	339
†25.0	63.8	27.3	27.3	29.3	5.4	32.8	4.3	23.3	†15.7	20.1	-20.8	11.3	10.4	12.1	Bolivia	218
453.7	†306.2	2,549.5	1,849.0	496.6	1,148.2	2,424.4	2,241.7	11.9	22.8	34.2	-11.1	7.8	4.8	19.0	Brazil	223
8.0	2.1	-1.8	54.4	23.7	21.7	13.6	20.7	13.9	15.9	16.0	-3.6	9.4	13.5	7.8	Chile	228
46.0	19.9	†66.5	23.0	27.7	37.6	25.6	28.2	6.8	17.7	16.5	-17.1	39.8	9.1	9.9	Colombia	233
14.6	44.7	16.5	21.0	62.3	17.8	9.5	29.6	16.2	21.9	†16.9	11.2	7.4	-4.7	-25.9	Costa Rica	238
47.6	-18.0	-8.6	31.5	9.3	.6	-4.0	-9.4	18.6	-.6	2.7	11.5	12.2	-2.7	-.7	Dominica	321
-6.1	101.8	29.2	31.5	51.1	12.9	28.3	.5	16.4	10.9	18.9	22.4	15.0	10.3	28.9	Dominican Republic	243
-7.7	-13.9	-2.5	†24.0	-5.0	12.9	47.0	2.5	-9.5	7.0	7.2	†-3.9	†-19.6	-35.5	6.3	Ecuador	248
25.0	16.0	10.7	29.6	22.5	15.1	43.4	23.3	12.4	10.0	13.3	8.3	10.2	-9.7	...	El Salvador	253
8.9	-14.2	3.6	6.6	.8	22.4	-3.9	6.4	8.5	.4	12.4	6.4	6.0	10.4	11.0	Grenada	328
.6	22.4	19.1	33.8	28.1	8.0	23.3	4.5	3.5	12.8	†22.9	-3.9	2.8	19.3	16.2	Guatemala	258
139.7	18.8	-8.0	18.1	156.9	51.7	†-23.1	31.4	19.1	5.9	17.1	11.8	-3.9	14.0	10.9	Guyana	336
20.2	-26.6	64.8	17.2	8.9	29.5	29.2	23.8	14.7	-4.1	†11.1	.3	29.0	25.9	16.9	Haiti	263
24.9	14.7	24.9	24.9	7.8	44.5	6.8	47.0	23.9	43.5	†91.9	16.1	11.6	9.3	10.0	Honduras	268
19.7	37.1	22.7	15.6	28.2	88.6	44.6	34.3	29.7	4.0	15.2	22.1	-4.2	7.8	-6.4	Jamaica	343
70.6	44.9	10.2	35.3	27.8	14.4	10.4	21.2	33.4	23.1	†48.4	27.6	43.5	-6.9	26.3	Mexico	273
-9.1	2.0	-30.5	17.7	-17.2	29.2	5.5	-6.5	19.9	-14.3	15.6	9.9	-5.9	8.2	36.3	Netherlands Antilles	353
593.9	11,540.2	2,481.9	10,348.1	1,298.3	5.7	7.8	52.5	23.6	†34.6	32.5	19.7	5.7	4.7	41.7	Nicaragua	278
-34.9	-20.0	-2.3	53.1	35.8	-19.5	4.1	-1.8	2.8	39.8	2.8	3.3	-1.5	4.9	.4	Panama	283
40.3	†22.7	29.8	22.3	27.8	27.6	13.5	27.3	†26.2	-1.9	7.3	6.5	9.1	-1.0	6.1	Paraguay	288
110.5	568.3	1,436.7	7,782.5	162.2	95.9	59.4	31.0	31.2	37.8	38.7	5.7	15.6	2.0	4.6	Peru	293
5.7	-4.1	24.0	6.6	.8	33.2	11.7	7.3	-1.6	-3.2	6.5	19.7	12.9	8.7	10.3	St. Kitts and Nevis	361
14.4	1.4	12.7	11.0	7.6	-1.1	4.8	-4.7	11.4	-4.4	1.6	13.8	3.2	3.8	16.5	St. Lucia	362
-15.4	-3.6	6.9	14.2	-10.0	30.1	-4.6	-3.2	-5.4	-2.5	9.1	20.8	16.8	20.6	9.5	St. Vincent & Grenadines	364
20.1	21.6	15.3	5.8	26.9	12.6	70.0	207.8	227.0	-10.3	-.4	†65.0	47.4	155.0	14.5	Suriname	366
-21.8	1.9	13.3	10.6	17.1	-9.7	-4.7	56.9	-.7	†8.9	16.1	20.9	3.7	3.1	10.7	Trinidad and Tobago	369
77.4	78.3	93.6	140.5	77.4	45.0	42.6	32.4	30.5	32.5	25.0	†14.4	21.2	9.4	26.2	Uruguay	298
†27.8	24.1	46.7	111.2	75.6	11.5	10.4	64.0	31.7	†96.9	73.9	18.2	33.0	14.8	12.0	Venezuela, Rep. Bol.	299

Money

		1972	1973	1974	1975	1976	1977	1978	1979	1980	1981	1982	1983	1984	1985	1986
														Percent Change over Previous Year		
Industrial Countries																
United States	111	9.4	6.1	2.4	4.5	6.2	9.8	9.5	9.4	4.9	4.9	7.4	7.7	8.8	13.1	17.4
Canada	156	12.4	9.2	1.6	18.9	1.0	10.5	6.8	1.9	10.1	†−.5	8.5	10.3	19.6	33.0	14.7
Australia	193	20.0	16.7	−.7	22.7	8.9	6.6	11.6	15.4	17.5	4.9	−.2	15.3	8.2	3.6	11.4
Japan	158	24.7	16.8	11.5	11.1	12.5	8.2	13.4	3.0	−2.0	10.0	5.7	−.1	6.9	3.0	10.4
New Zealand	196	28.5	26.7	3.6	9.3	9.2	1.9	22.3	3.4	3.1	15.4	3.5	13.1	9.8	9.1	13.7
Euro Area	163	....		....						....	6.2	15.5	9.7	8.0	6.5	8.0
Austria	122	20.7	8.3	5.8	14.1	8.1	1.3	8.6	−7.9	15.1	−2.5	8.1	10.6	4.2	3.1	6.2
Belgium	124	15.2	7.5	6.2	15.7	7.0	8.3	5.9	2.5	†.2	2.2	3.8	8.5	.3	3.0	7.8
Finland	172	23.2	23.3	18.9	34.5	−1.7	2.8	16.5	22.5	6.3	14.7	15.9	7.6	16.4	11.0	.5
Germany	134	14.2	1.7	10.7	14.3	3.3	12.0	14.5	2.9	3.9	−1.5	7.2	8.4	5.9	†5.2	8.1
Greece	174	19.2	23.4	19.8	16.4	22.2	16.9	22.3	16.3	16.3	22.2	21.7	14.5	20.0	17.8	20.5
Ireland	178	21.2	26.1	17.1	18.0	15.8	16.8	33.8	18.8	20.0	20.6	†−1.3	12.2	15.6	1.2	3.7
Italy	136	18.2	19.7	†5.6	15.4	20.8	21.5	27.8	23.7	13.1	11.1	17.2	12.5	12.3	10.4	11.3
Luxembourg	137				12.3	6.8	13.8	6.2	6.5	5.0	5.5	2.2	11.4	3.7	−5.5	9.6
Netherlands	138	17.6	.3	12.2	19.3	8.1	13.0	4.3	3.0	5.7	−2.4	†13.8	10.0	6.9	6.9	6.9
Portugal	182	16.6	35.4	10.2	24.5	†9.8	11.9	13.9	†26.8	20.5	9.6	16.5	8.1	15.8	26.7	37.4
Spain	184	24.1	23.5	17.3	18.7	21.9	18.5	17.3	8.5	13.5	13.0	11.4	†10.0	8.9	14.7	†15.0
Denmark	128	13.6	11.7	4.7	26.7	5.0	7.1	16.0	10.5	7.8	13.6	4.1	23.6	13.0	22.2	7.3
Iceland	176	21.8	38.9	30.1	33.6	24.7	46.9	40.8	46.5	60.4	61.2	27.5	78.2	†42.8	27.4	43.9
Norway	142	16.5	15.3	11.9	16.5	†12.3	14.1	8.6	7.6	5.3	15.0	12.3	12.1	24.4	20.3	3.2
Sweden	144	10.4	8.7	12.6	16.3	10.1	10.1	12.9	12.3	8.5	7.4	6.5	†11.4	11.6	3.7	8.3
Switzerland	146	9.4	3.4	†−1.4	4.2	11.4	.9	23.6	−1.9	−.1	−.4	†10.7	6.6	†.2	−2.5	2.2
United Kingdom	112	14.2	5.1	10.8	†13.2	11.3	20.8	16.3	9.1	4.0	†11.0	17.5	4.4	13.2	18.0	22.2
Developing Countries																
Africa																
Algeria	612	29.3	13.0	28.1	31.9	28.5	18.2	28.1	16.1	16.9	16.0	28.0	21.9	18.1	12.1	1.3
Angola	614	....		....												
Benin	638	10.3	−3.0	27.6	70.8	−4.6	14.4	5.8	†8.8	32.4	35.3	38.1	−1.7	10.5	−3.9	−9.4
Botswana	616					33.7	4.7	34.8	10.3	26.7	11.0	7.8	9.7	25.0	29.3
Burkina Faso	748	4.4	36.5	21.3	37.4	22.5	11.7	11.8	†1.0	19.9	17.2	11.3	11.0	10.2	4.6	22.8
Burundi	618	5.5	15.7	22.4	−6.4	56.4	24.2	28.5	9.5	3.0	24.0	−7.6	21.7	8.1	24.3	9.0
Cameroon	622	7.3	17.4	32.6	4.8	24.6	†33.5	15.7	25.4	13.3	24.4	15.1	26.1	9.7	4.0	4.0
Cape Verde	624						41.1	14.4	12.9	26.3	10.9	26.4	22.6	6.2	15.3	16.1
Central African Rep.	626	17.5	1.1	33.5	−1.5	39.5	†7.5	13.1	27.0	32.3	22.3	−3.8	11.5	6.5	8.5	.2
Chad	628	3.2	−.1	50.2	9.8	26.9	13.8	22.5	14.5	−16.1	19.6	4.7	22.9	59.8	4.9	1.2
Comoros	632	....											41.5	−15.3	16.7	−.8
Congo, Dem. Rep. of	636	25	24	35	18	44	56	57	−2	73	55	76	1,273	−83	29	60
Congo, Rep. of	634	5.7	15.2	39.7	13.2	15.4	†−1.4	7.4	20.0	37.0	38.7	30.3	−6.8	11.7	10.9	−12.9
Côte d'Ivoire	662	12.0	14.3	38.0	10.5	44.6	47.3	8.5	†8.0	1.1	5.8	−.9	6.0	17.7	7.9	2.8
Djibouti	611	....		....											3.0	13.4
Equatorial Guinea	642													....		23.3
Ethiopia	644	12.4	26.0	21.9	25.0	1.2	23.7	16.9	14.1	−.2	9.7	10.0	†14.7	7.8	17.0	21.1
Gabon	646	26.3	23.8	65.3	54.7	76.5	†−8.8	−8.9	−5.3	10.5	21.8	9.9	13.7	17.3	5.2	−13.5
Gambia, The	648	38.9	40.0	3.8	13.0	32.3	−19.5	†−.1	—	6.1	25.6	13.3	15.0	−.7	62.8	2.7
Ghana	652	44.1	21.9	23.7	44.6	41.4	67.9	72.4	13.4	30.1	54.7	19.0	49.2	60.6	42.7	44.0
Guinea	656	....		....											....	
Guinea-Bissau	654	....		....												
Kenya	664	18.2	23.0	8.9	10.3	23.6	43.2	7.4	16.5	−8.1	11.6	13.0	7.9	14.1	−1.3	35.6
Lesotho	666	....		....							21.0	31.6	9.7	22.0	28.9	16.2
Liberia	668				−13.2	52.1	−10.3	36.3	.1	†−10.1	−22.5	22.4	15.0	20.0	26.1	30.6
Madagascar	674	13.6	7.5	18.5	2.1	14.9	25.5	12.9	†22.5	21.8	28.1	7.3	−7.4	24.5	−.6	21.4
Malawi	676	4.6	35.7	33.2	.3	−1.1	37.4	−6.3	−3.4	7.3	18.1	14.0	−2.3	20.7	8.2	32.3
Mali	678	10.7	9.7	53.9	18.3	11.5	14.2	19.3	17.1	4.8	1.2	13.4	18.9	†31.8	6.2	3.3
Mauritania	682	26.1	4.6	64.1	19.4	25.8	11.2	1.0	22.9	11.7	34.8	−6.8	13.4	19.2	26.3	−6.4
Mauritius	684	43.8	24.0	68.0	26.7	10.6	11.0	18.9	−1.6	20.6	−10.9	13.5	13.7	−.6	19.3
Morocco	686	18.5	16.8	26.8	18.1	17.6	19.2	15.5	12.3	8.4	14.6	†10.1	13.7	7.6	9.5	18.3
Mozambique	688	....		....											14.6	18.3
Namibia	728	....		....												
Niger	692	7.6	19.7	29.5	14.2	23.1	30.5	43.5	23.4	12.8	15.7	−5.1	−6.2	17.8	2.8	3.0
Nigeria	694	11.5	†23.9	105.5	52.1	51.4	45.4	−5.9	20.5	50.1	5.6	3.1	12.3	8.2	8.4	−4.3
Rwanda	714	1.9	41.5	20.3	13.1	34.3	23.3	11.5	25.6	6.9	†4.0	−2.4	7.4	8.4	9.3	18.1
São Tomé and Príncipe	716	....		....												
Senegal	722	11.1	13.0	53.3	10.9	26.2	15.0	16.0	†−2.0	13.8	18.3	15.8	.1	1.3	1.0	17.3
Seychelles	718	48.4	6.9	4.0	14.1	41.4	24.0	13.4	20.7	38.4	−.5	−9.2	−8.4	2.6	15.3	−.2
Sierra Leone	724	19.8	24.1	13.6	9.9	19.6	17.1	27.2	18.7	19.6	−.4	66.7	41.9	35.3	85.1	105.8
Somalia	726	33.8	15.1	24.0	31.4	20.5	33.2	30.4	35.1	19.2	32.0	9.8	6.9	23.8	83.2	24.3
South Africa	199	14.8	20.4	18.6	6.8	3.5	4.7	10.4	20.7	35.5	34.2	16.4	26.4	41.2	−8.9	8.8
Sudan	732	16.7	21.6	35.0	18.6	24.5	41.9	27.5	32.0	31.2	39.5	36.6	11.7	18.3	†62.7	41.1
Swaziland	734				38.3	22.9	18.6	9.0	9.9	21.9	2.5	13.7	4.7	11.5	13.4	49.7
Tanzania	738	13.0	19.2	24.6	23.9	24.5	19.7	7.0	52.9	27.9	15.4	19.0	12.2	.2	23.6	40.6
Togo	742	−.5	−2.2	117.0	−14.0	52.8	10.7	31.9	†11.4	5.1	44.5	12.6	−7.8	9.2	−8.8	8.4
Tunisia	744	15.4	16.2	25.1	17.6	8.1	12.1	19.5	14.2	21.0	22.5	24.9	16.8	6.8	13.5	2.5
Uganda	746	35.8	38.0	42.3	8.1	37.3	29.9	20.9	51.1	31.7	101.2	5.9	44.6	123.2	131.1	172.1
Zambia	754	1.4	28.6	2.6	24.4	21.1	−1.9	1.0	30.2	.5	8.6	22.3	15.3	9.4	41.6	87.1
Zimbabwe	698	....		....		8.6	6.4	10.8	11.6	36.6	7.3	21.8	−9.1	16.3	16.8	10.4

Percent Change over Previous Year

1987	1988	1989	1990	1991	1992	1993	1994	1995	1996	1997	1998	1999	2000	2001		
															Industrial Countries	
.3	4.8	1.0	5.0	8.6	11.7	9.7	.1	-.9	1.4	3.5	3.5	10.4	-1.7	11.1	United States	111
6.2	5.9	5.8	1.2	4.4	7.1	8.3	6.6	10.2	12.7	9.2	5.7	10.9	13.0	12.7	Canada	156
20.3	29.6	†7.5	7.3	7.6	20.0	17.8	10.9	6.5	14.0	13.3	5.9	9.7	9.3	21.3	Australia	193
4.8	8.6	2.4	4.5	9.5	3.9	7.0	4.2	13.1	9.7	8.6	5.0	11.7	3.5	13.7	Japan	158
42.8	†23.5	15.0	1.5	2.0	.8	8.0	4.6	5.0	-4.5	6.5	5.1	18.3	6.3	14.0	New Zealand	196
6.8	9.3	9.4	13.6	2.3	5.2	5.3	4.2	37.1	10.6	12.0	10.2	10.7	5.8	6.4	Euro Area	163
9.6	8.3	3.4	6.1	7.7	6.1	9.2	8.6	14.8	4.7	4.7	....	....	....	....	Austria	122
4.6	5.5	5.4	.9	1.6	†-1.1	7.5	1.5	4.9	4.2	3.1	....	....	....	....	Belgium	124
9.0	18.4	15.4	7.2	†192.1	3.2	5.1	8.9	14.0	16.4	5.5	4.8	....	....	....	Finland	172
7.3	11.4	6.0	28.5	4.3	11.7	8.5	4.5	7.0	12.2	2.0	10.0	....	....	....	Germany	134
†15.1	15.1	25.3	23.8	13.2	12.4	11.5	23.5	13.6	10.9	14.4	11.9	34.3	-4.0	....	Greece	174
7.0	8.4	8.5	12.9	-1.7	.5	12.9	12.5	64.1	8.8	-17.4	25.2	....	....	....	Ireland	178
8.1	7.7	†12.6	7.5	11.1	1.4	6.3	3.9	.4	4.9	6.5	11.1	....	....	....	Italy	136
10.4	7.9	13.8	9.1	10.4	1.7	....	....	....	....	3.2	....	....	....	....	Luxembourg	137
7.0	6.9	7.1	4.3	4.2	4.3	10.5	1.7	13.5	12.1	7.8	....	....	....	....	Netherlands	138
20.4	21.5	13.7	5.3	15.3	18.5	10.7	6.6	10.9	12.1	12.9	17.0	....	....	....	Portugal	182
16.2	19.5	14.9	20.1	12.3	-2.0	3.5	7.1	2.9	7.1	14.0	15.8	....	....	....	Spain	184
†40.1	19.5	.4	8.1	†9.2	-.9	10.5	-1.4	4.6	11.5	5.7	4.8	5.8	....	....	Denmark	128
31.3	16.6	33.6	24.5	19.9	1.3	5.4	10.7	9.6	8.5	16.4	20.3	....	....	....	Iceland	176
50.0	22.6	16.6	8.9	7.6	26.4	5.2	4.4	1.1	9.5	6.2	19.3	5.6	7.6	16.7	Norway	142
2.3	.9	12.1	....	....	....	....	....	....	....	....	....	....	....	....	Sweden	144
13.8	2.3	-2.7	-1.6	-1.7	4.0	5.8	4.0	6.1	†27.4	9.0	6.8	9.5	-2.1	8.5	Switzerland	146
†32.7	10.7	14.4	10.1	6.6	†4.3	9.9	.8	16.7	9.3	25.7	†9.4	11.1	14.1	9.6	United Kingdom	112
															Developing Countries	
															Africa	
9.3	12.6	-.9	8.2	20.0	†16.2	19.4	7.8	7.1	13.4	14.6	20.9	8.9	17.3	18.5	Algeria	612
....	....	....	....	....	....	....	....	....	3,392.6	107.5	39.8	†326.2	342.0	168.1	Angola	614
-21.6	16.3	17.3	23.9	11.6	9.9	-13.2	67.3	-13.2	17.2	2.0	-4.7	46.9	35.0	10.0	Benin	638
28.2	30.2	24.6	15.7	4.7	-1.1	14.7	11.1	7.2	14.7	9.1	45.8	17.3	6.9	23.9	Botswana	616
6.7	10.6	4.5	-1.7	5.5	.5	11.6	38.9	25.5	7.0	17.5	-2.6	-1.9	5.3	-3.0	Burkina Faso	748
-.5	4.8	3.6	9.5	11.3	10.3	12.0	28.3	-3.3	12.5	10.5	1.3	41.9	-1.0	16.8	Burundi	618
-13.4	†.4	7.2	-7.5	2.7	-27.6	-14.1	35.1	-11.6	-1.6	34.9	14.5	10.8	17.4	12.8	Cameroon	622
1.6	5.7	6.2	8.0	8.8	31.4	7.0	8.2	†16.6	10.6	21.6	-2.0	17.3	11.4	2.6	Cape Verde	624
3.5	†-2.7	13.9	-3.7	-2.8	-3.7	16.4	74.0	7.6	4.9	-8.1	-18.3	12.6	3.2	-2.6	Central African Rep.	626
2.1	†-12.8	7.9	-.2	3.8	-8.7	-27.7	31.5	42.7	33.5	-4.7	-8.0	-3.1	17.7	21.8	Chad	628
9.3	14.9	13.1	6.0	-7.3	9.4	4.6	9.8	-5.3	8.1	-18.6	†-5.5	16.4	21.0	62.5	Comoros	632
91	119	75	176	2,387	4,114	2,461	5,635	407	....	....	....	....	....	....	Congo, Dem. Rep. of	636
4.8	†-6.7	-1.0	25.3	-7.3	6.4	-19.7	40.4	.3	13.6	8.7	-13.6	27.8	68.2	-23.1	Congo, Rep. of	634
-6.0	-3.5	-11.5	3.0	-3.1	-4.0	.9	61.7	18.2	2.3	11.7	12.9	-1.7	-3.7	14.8	Côte d'Ivoire	662
8.8	6.8	-7.0	8.6	15.7	10.5	4.1	3.3	-1.6	-2.9	-9.6	-10.0	3.5	-7.8	2.6	Djibouti	611
-9.2	†-37.5	38.8	-57.0	-15.5	35.4	-28.6	135.5	58.4	50.1	-4.3	9.7	89.8	34.8	26.0	Equatorial Guinea	642
2.1	11.4	16.1	22.0	17.6	15.2	4.3	21.2	2.8	-1.8	8.4	-7.5	12.3	11.1	4.3	Ethiopia	644
-12.2	†9.9	5.0	5.7	8.0	-27.2	-3.4	41.9	12.3	26.0	8.1	-5.1	-5.1	19.3	3.7	Gabon	646
18.8	7.9	21.9	13.8	32.9	10.6	6.0	-11.7	15.7	-3.8	38.8	-.5	14.3	37.4	15.4	Gambia, The	648
52.6	45.0	52.7	10.8	†7.7	53.0	27.9	50.3	33.4	31.4	45.4	17.3	2.7	22.5	....	Ghana	652
....	....	....	....	....	19.7	19.4	-3.2	8.5	-.2	21.3	†8.7	....	....	12.0	Guinea	656
99.1	84.5	30.5	729.2	-74.8	83.1	27.3	58.1	46.9	51.0	236.3	-12.1	22.4	63.7	7.8	Guinea-Bissau	654
8.0	1.3	13.0	27.2	15.0	47.1	27.4	12.6	3.8	13.9	15.2	3.4	16.4	8.6	6.2	Kenya	664
1.4	40.2	11.5	7.8	18.4	12.3	23.4	12.3	10.5	19.3	22.7	24.9	-2.6	8.2	24.7	Lesotho	666
18.0	7.3	24.4	....	....	-5.6	59.8	7.6	42.4	6.7	-1.4	128.8	14.9	†-11.5	6.7	Liberia	668
28.4	22.4	31.5	-4.0	31.0	21.6	11.9	56.5	15.2	17.3	22.9	10.9	20.2	13.2	30.3	Madagascar	674
35.0	46.3	3.9	6.5	31.5	19.4	34.8	50.5	44.0	24.0	16.7	56.2	33.0	36.8	8.0	Malawi	676
-7.0	4.9	-3.6	-10.8	9.0	.9	8.8	47.9	13.8	21.3	6.5	4.5	-.6	9.4	29.6	Mali	678
17.6	4.7	†7.3	3.5	10.0	4.3	3.6	-5.4	-8.1	-10.9	8.3	5.3	6.3	22.7	14.8	Mauritania	682
35.8	15.6	18.1	23.7	19.7	8.0	3.0	19.4	8.0	2.7	7.9	9.2	3.6	10.8	16.2	Mauritius	684
9.1	14.5	10.9	†17.1	14.4	6.1	4.9	11.1	6.0	5.8	†7.2	7.8	11.6	7.9	15.3	Morocco	686
39.4	60.0	†36.8	35.8	†33.2	45.3	52.0	50.5	35.0	20.0	25.1	14.5	24.6	22.3	17.6	Mozambique	688
....	....	....	....	33.8	22.0	46.3	14.7	8.3	53.6	3.5	27.0	22.2	28.2	9.5	Namibia	728
-11.9	12.3	7.4	-11.7	2.6	-10.5	11.1	15.4	9.2	-9.5	-19.4	-18.5	15.4	11.8	35.3	Niger	692
17.7	43.9	24.3	29.5	41.0	†73.2	57.0	43.4	16.3	13.5	16.8	19.0	22.5	62.1	25.7	Nigeria	694
2.7	3.1	-12.5	5.0	7.8	24.9	10.7	15.6	41.1	11.7	22.7	-.8	7.0	6.7	.8	Rwanda	714
....	....	....	....	....	....	....	....	....	66.5	107.8	-3.3	5.3	23.5	54.3	São Tomé and Príncipe	716
-5.5	.2	7.4	-11.5	4.4	2.0	-9.0	54.4	3.7	8.5	-.1	15.7	10.8	5.5	14.9	Senegal	722
.1	21.0	16.9	-1.3	22.8	10.2	14.5	-2.7	2.6	34.4	44.2	20.3	37.2	6.2	13.5	Seychelles	718
56.0	60.5	87.1	64.3	76.1	25.1	11.7	10.0	29.5	†6.6	57.1	7.3	49.4	4.4	35.4	Sierra Leone	724
147.4	51.2	207.7	....	....	....	....	....	....	....	....	....	....	....	....	Somalia	726
38.0	24.7	8.5	†15.0	....	....	6.7	25.1	18.3	32.0	17.4	23.2	21.7	2.4	17.3	South Africa	199
32.8	44.4	68.5	46.4	60.2	†101.3	76.1	54.6	66.7	86.2	32.5	29.3	27.8	†42.2	15.7	Sudan	732
8.9	13.8	18.4	14.0	9.8	20.2	14.2	7.3	16.6	16.5	16.2	1.9	32.3	-.3	14.2	Swaziland	734
31.6	37.1	†29.6	35.0	22.8	34.1	†32.9	33.3	29.9	4.9	9.9	10.5	16.0	9.9	10.2	Tanzania	738
1.5	-29.3	-1.9	19.2	4.3	-27.2	-18.5	104.6	37.7	-7.8	1.9	6.9	9.9	22.2	-8.7	Togo	742
.7	17.3	1.2	6.1	.7	7.3	3.6	10.7	9.6	13.0	13.0	7.5	16.0	9.9	8.7	Tunisia	744
....	....	....	....	....	....	25.9	36.5	15.4	10.3	13.7	19.5	12.6	16.8	12.8	Uganda	746
40.0	†62.7	51.5	60.6	77.5	....	....	44.8	61.1	19.4	31.0	†16.8	23.6	51.2	34.2	Zambia	754
11.7	28.5	19.5	27.6	23.0	5.8	94.9	18.2	52.4	23.1	53.7	23.5	34.7	53.3	142.8	Zimbabwe	698

Money

		1972	1973	1974	1975	1976	1977	1978	1979	1980	1981	1982	1983	1984	1985	1986
																*Percent Change over Previous Year*

Asia

		1972	1973	1974	1975	1976	1977	1978	1979	1980	1981	1982	1983	1984	1985	1986
Afghanistan, Islamic State of	512	11.9	†.4	10.6	19.6	22.4	29.6	20.5	19.4	16.4	14.8	16.0	....	....	11.2	11.5
Bangladesh	513	...	...	...	−1.3	11.3	26.6	25.4	25.4	9.9	12.6	†8.6	35.6	33.6	8.7	8.8
Bhutan	514	...	...	...	...	...	...	...	...	...	...	...	...	18.4	24.7	5.8
Cambodia	522	...	...	...	...	...	...	...	...	...	...	...	...	...	...	...
China, P.R.: Mainland	924	...	...	...	...	...	...	.1	58.8	24.7	17.1	10.6	17.5	40.1	†14.7	27.9
China, P.R.: Hong Kong	532	...	...	...	...	...	...	...	...	...	...	...	...	...	...	...
China, P.R.: Macao	546	...	...	...	...	...	...	...	...	...	...	...	...	...	...	...
Fiji	819	22.4	8.1	22.1	21.7	1.6	−1.6	17.1	14.1	−10.4	17.6	4.3	9.1	.9	1.3	24.9
India	534	12.6	17.3	10.1	9.9	24.9	16.8	†73.9	12.2	15.7	13.6	17.7	12.7	18.5	12.8	16.1
Indonesia	536	50.5	42.0	40.5	33.0	28.1	25.3	24.0	35.8	48.3	29.2	10.0	6.4	13.3	18.0	14.9
Korea	542	45.1	40.6	29.5	25.0	30.7	40.7	24.9	20.7	16.3	4.6	45.6	17.0	.6	10.8	16.6
Lao People's Dem. Rep.	544	...	...	...	...	...	...	...	...	...	...	...	...	...	...	...
Malaysia	548	25.0	37.6	8.6	7.2	20.9	16.6	18.2	17.2	15.0	12.9	13.3	7.7	−.6	5.8	2.8
Maldives	556	...	...	...	...	...	−14.1	−18.8	42.4	51.2	†28.8	−15.2	−4.2	28.3	43.7	15.3
Micronesia, Fed.Sts.	868	...	...	...	...	...	...	...	...	...	...	...	...	...	...	...
Mongolia	948	...	...	...	...	...	...	...	...	...	...	...	...	...	...	...
Myanmar	518	22.8	26.0	27.2	21.6	11.1	3.6	12.6	11.2	12.8	15.3	7.6	12.9	15.5	−9.6	41.4
Nepal	558	7.3	29.5	18.3	3.4	22.7	18.1	13.9	15.2	13.0	11.9	15.6	17.8	13.2	13.6	23.8
Pakistan	564	20.9	11.3	1.5	13.8	32.9	17.4	18.1	20.4	17.3	8.4	20.8	15.1	5.2	16.3	18.0
Papua New Guinea	853	...	...	41.3	7.4	−10.5	25.4	5.7	9.2	3.1	−3.6	−2.9	9.2	20.9	−1.9	5.1
Philippines	566	29.1	12.3	24.0	14.5	17.1	23.7	13.4	11.2	19.6	4.4	—	†38.8	2.7	6.7	17.4
Samoa	862	19.4	19.5	16.0	8.5	16.3	17.6	9.9	10.4	58.4	54.4	23.5	−2.8	14.4	3.1	8.4
Singapore	576	35.5	10.4	8.6	21.5	15.2	10.3	11.7	15.8	7.5	18.0	12.6	5.5	3.0	−.9	11.8
Solomon Islands	813	...	...	...	...	...	...	...	40.6	37.7	−6.0	10.9	16.9	53.6	—	7.2
Sri Lanka	524	15.7	11.9	6.1	4.8	34.9	29.0	10.6	29.7	22.1	6.6	17.3	25.0	14.1	12.1	12.8
Thailand	578	16.4	20.6	9.3	6.1	†16.8	9.8	20.0	16.6	12.4	3.4	6.8	5.2	6.9	−3.3	19.3
Tonga	866	...	...	...	16.1	4.6	53.9	19.2	2.0	18.3	9.5	111.6	29.7	4.5	8.7	21.6
Vanuatu	846	...	...	...	...	...	...	8.7	6.7	10.9	−10.1	−22.9	20.3	30.3	33.1	−12.7	6.4
Vietnam	582	...	...	...	...	...	...	...	...	...	...	...	...	...	...	...

Europe

		1972	1973	1974	1975	1976	1977	1978	1979	1980	1981	1982	1983	1984	1985	1986
Albania	914	...	...	...	...	...	...	...	...	...	...	...	...	...	...	...
Armenia	911	...	...	...	...	...	...	...	...	...	...	...	...	...	...	...
Azerbaijan	912	...	...	...	...	...	...	...	...	...	...	...	...	...	...	...
Belarus	913	...	...	...	...	...	...	...	...	...	...	...	...	...	...	...
Bosnia & Herzegovina	963	...	...	...	...	...	...	...	...	...	...	...	...	...	...	...
Bulgaria	918	...	...	...	...	...	...	...	...	...	...	...	...	...	...	...
Croatia	960	...	...	...	...	...	...	...	...	...	...	...	...	...	...	...
Cyprus	423	22.9	5.9	10.1	−7.4	28.9	7.4	17.3	28.5	18.4	22.8	16.0	13.7	4.4	10.0	−1.0
Czech Republic	935	...	...	...	...	...	...	...	...	...	...	...	...	...	...	...
Czechoslovakia	934	...	...	...	...	...	...	...	...	...	...	6.7	7.1	3.9	4.8	1.1	.4
Estonia	939	...	...	...	...	...	...	...	...	...	...	...	...	...	...	...
Georgia	915	...	...	...	...	...	...	...	...	...	...	...	...	...	...	...
Hungary	944	...	...	...	...	...	...	...	...	...	...	...	2.5	4.5	19.3	11.2
Kazakhstan	916	...	...	...	...	...	...	...	...	...	...	...	...	...	...	...
Kyrgyz Republic	917	...	...	...	...	...	...	...	...	...	...	...	...	...	...	...
Latvia	941	...	...	...	...	...	...	...	...	...	...	...	...	...	...	...
Lithuania	946	...	...	...	...	...	...	...	...	...	...	...	...	...	...	...
Macedonia, FYR	962	...	...	...	...	...	...	...	...	...	...	...	...	...	...	...
Malta	181	17.9	8.9	13.6	25.0	19.9	11.7	17.5	19.1	11.7	13.5	4.3	6.0	.4	−1.4	.6
Moldova	921	...	...	...	...	...	...	...	...	...	...	...	...	...	...	...
Poland	964	...	...	...	...	...	...	...	...	12.7	†21.1	40.4	9.7	15.5	20.4	21.9
Romania	968	...	...	35.8	8.3	15.6	10.9	12.2	7.7	†12.5	18.4	23.2	−6.4	3.9	†7.5	7.6
Russia	922	...	...	...	...	...	...	...	...	...	...	...	...	...	...	...
Slovak Republic	936	...	...	...	...	...	...	...	...	...	...	...	...	...	...	...
Slovenia	961	...	...	...	...	...	...	...	...	...	...	...	...	...	...	...
Turkey	186	22.1	32.3	27.6	31.2	27.6	38.6	37.4	58.0	66.1	35.1	38.0	47.9	19.0	39.4	†56.6
Ukraine	926	...	...	...	...	...	...	...	...	...	...	...	...	...	...	...
Yugoslavia, SFR	188	41.7	38.4	25.2	32.8	60.2	†16.8	17.6	17.3	32.5	25.8	27.9	20.2	43.2	45.4	110.4

Middle East

		1972	1973	1974	1975	1976	1977	1978	1979	1980	1981	1982	1983	1984	1985	1986
Bahrain, Kingdom of	419	13.7	7.5	3.3	26.8	64.5	19.2	12.4	8.6	3.3	29.4	−10.4	−7.0	.5	5.2	−3.4
Egypt	469	16.9	21.8	24.7	23.9	20.2	31.4	20.7	22.6	†11.6	12.9	24.9	14.5	13.8	18.1	8.7
Iran, I.R. of	429	38.3	29.7	37.2	20.1	45.8	23.0	31.2e	56.7	33.7	16.8	24.9	19.1	....	....	....
Iraq	433	14.4	24.2	43.3	35.3	20.7	...	...	...	...	...	...	...	...	...	...
Israel	436	†28.0	33.2	17.5	22.0	26.9	38.8	44.0	31.6	96.7	91.3	109.2	140.8	352.3	245.7	112.8
Jordan	439	6.5	21.1	23.5	30.6	23.2	18.9	12.6	25.7	24.7	20.8	12.2	10.4	1.0	−3.4	5.8
Kuwait	443	31.8	21.4	13.5	48.4	35.6	24.6	29.7	5.2	7.7	78.5	−.3	−5.3	−18.3	3.1	.2
Lebanon	446	13.6	15.1	14.5	27.9	27.9	3.2	21.5	8.7	14.7	17.5	22.9	16.9	6.5	46.2	50.5
Libya	672	13.3	24.5	46.7	15.1	31.3	26.7	16.9	33.2	29.0	21.2	−8.0	−10.8	−6.0	28.8	−12.9
Oman	449	...	31.6	94.0	48.0	42.5	8.9	2.8	7.7	25.7	37.4	17.0	20.2	−5.1	15.7	−4.8
Qatar	453	45.7	19.5	36.6	78.3	56.8	32.4	10.5	8.0	−8.7	49.6	11.5	−4.5	14.1	−2.8	11.7
Saudi Arabia	456	42.5	39.9	38.7	93.4	71.1	58.3	28.1	11.2	7.8	23.8	14.8	†1.4	−2.3	−1.4	5.4
Syrian Arab Republic	463	25.9	20.5	45.9	25.7	22.9	27.6	26.9	16.3	35.6	13.6	18.9	25.3	23.3	20.5	11.3
United Arab Emirates	466	...	...	58.4	69.4	81.5	10.4	10.8	8.5	17.3	22.0	8.6	−6.3	−2.6	6.9	−3.2
Yemen Arab Rep.	473	...	...	31.7	81.1	116.0	60.7	27.6	23.1	7.6	10.1	28.1	23.2	24.7	14.8	25.8
Yemen, P.D. Rep.	459	8.5	16.4	15.0	20.1	47.2	41.4	24.6	28.7	26.9	10.3	14.8	11.7	11.2	9.3	4.2
Yemen, Republic of	474	...	...	...	...	...	...	...	...	...	...	...	...	...	...	...

Percent Change over Previous Year

1987	1988	1989	1990	1991	1992	1993	1994	1995	1996	1997	1998	1999	2000	2001		
															Asia	
54.4	36.5	39.9	39.8	....										....	Afghanistan, Islamic State of	512
†2.0	4.2	12.9	9.6	7.7	13.6	16.0	24.3	16.7	4.7	7.7	7.4	12.8	18.4	10.7	Bangladesh	513
14.4	30.1	32.6	-1.2	39.0	12.2	†12.1	27.1	26.6	56.8	4.5	21.2	41.7	5.8	28.4	Bhutan	514
							-1.1	38.1	18.1	17.0	41.2	-2.1	1.4	13.0	Cambodia	522
18.5	20.0	6.3	20.1	28.2	30.3	†21.8	27.2	17.3	19.4	26.3	11.2	21.4	16.1	....	China, P.R.: Mainland	924
					24.9	20.9	.1	.3	15.3	-3.8	-4.6	15.4	—	14.3	China, P.R.: Hong Kong	532
												-2.6	-7.4	20.7	China, P.R.: Macao	546
-2.2	62.1	-3.4	.7	3.4	14.4	15.8	-5.3	12.0	18.2	-2.4	10.9	40.6	-14.5	4.6	Fiji	819
13.5	16.5	18.0	14.3	22.6	7.1	18.7	27.4	11.1	14.1	12.6	11.7	16.9	10.6	10.2	India	534
9.2	13.3	42.9	15.9	12.1	†7.9	22.8	22.9	13.7	9.6	33.2	26.9	31.2	36.9	8.8	Indonesia	536
14.7	20.2	17.9	11.0	36.8	13.0	18.1	11.9	19.6	1.7	-11.4	1.6	24.7	5.9	13.8	Korea	542
			-.2	12.5	24.5	48.6	17.4	9.5	12.5	5.8	111.4	29.6	57.3	8.0	Lao People's Dem. Rep.	544
12.8	14.4	17.3	15.6	9.9	†27.3	35.3	16.8	13.2	†23.7	11.7	-29.4	29.2	6.7	4.0	Malaysia	548
5.1	11.7	18.7	18.9	28.5	15.4	49.7	22.5	5.7	17.8	12.9	15.8	14.5	11.1	-5.9	Maldives	556
									-1.1	10.2	-1.1	-6.5	-5.5	13.0	Micronesia, Fed.Sts.	868
					4.5	142.8	78.2	29.0	42.7	25.1	8.5	39.0	13.9	19.4	Mongolia	948
-42.0	65.4	36.1	43.5	†42.2	34.9	25.2	33.8	28.2	33.4	31.0	28.2	22.6	34.5	50.8	Myanmar	518
24.9	13.2	19.3	21.2	24.0	16.0	23.9	20.6	9.9	5.9	8.6	17.9	21.1	14.4	....	Nepal	558
19.1	9.7	14.3	17.3	20.2	21.5	1.7	15.1	12.8	7.5	32.5	4.6	8.6	10.1	10.1	Pakistan	564
9.6	14.5	6.9	-.2	21.3	4.9	35.9	3.4	14.0	52.0	-5.5	10.3	21.0	2.2	3.2	Papua New Guinea	853
24.6	13.7	32.8	14.3	15.9	9.1	†22.3	11.3	21.7	19.8	14.2	7.4	38.3	-1.3	.4	Philippines	566
32.6	5.2	9.8	42.6	-9.2	-11.4	14.7	8.1	29.1	-.2	22.5	-10.7	20.7	16.1	-6.9	Samoa	862
12.3	8.4	14.9	11.0	7.7	12.7	23.6	2.3	8.3	6.7	1.7	-1.0	14.2	6.9	8.5	Singapore	576
22.6	31.7	3.8	26.6	23.4	31.9	18.1	31.4	5.0	15.7	7.4	-.2	25.7	....		Solomon Islands	813
18.3	29.1	†8.9	12.8	17.7	7.4	18.6	18.7	6.7	4.0	9.8	12.1	12.8	9.1	3.2	Sri Lanka	524
29.3	12.2	17.7	11.9	13.8	12.3	18.6	17.0	12.1	9.1	1.5	4.9	64.0	-7.5	-6.5	Thailand	578
14.3	9.5	29.8	15.2	-12.7	20.5	-5.5	-13.9	3.8	2.6	4.7	22.1	10.6	26.2		Tonga	866
50.1	-16.7	24.3	-10.9	12.4	15.5	12.3	.9	10.1	3.5	1.8	14.4	.2	6.1	-.5	Vanuatu	846
						28.9			25.1	19.5	13.1	51.2	33.1	23.5	Vietnam	582
															Europe	
								52.8	52.6	1.4	-8.7	23.0	20.4	15.3	Albania	914
						1,060.1	907.3	124.3	32.4	12.0	19.6	-.9	36.7	10.1	Armenia	911
						980.1	468.3	130.5	30.4	36.1	†-25.6	17.5	†12.9	†7.6	Azerbaijan	912
								273.2	†56.7	115.5	139.1	188.4	117.8	75.0	Belarus	913
										11.9	199.4	27.4	90.6		Bosnia & Herzegovina	963
									115.7	†908.5	21.6	8.7	21.2	28.4	Bulgaria	918
						112.2	24.6	37.9	21.0	-1.4	1.7	30.1	31.5		Croatia	960
11.1	14.3	7.3	11.4	7.8	9.5	8.5	4.9	6.2	6.8	7.8	3.7	42.2	5.3	-1.1	Cyprus	423
							50.2	6.7	4.7	†-7.3	-3.4	10.8	11.4	17.0	Czech Republic	935
3.6	14.3	2.7	-8.4	27.6	15.9										Czechoslovakia	934
					309.9	†75.2	20.9	29.8	37.6	24.0	-6.3	32.1	20.5	19.5	Estonia	939
								37.3	31.1	-10.0	9.9	33.7	†7.2		Georgia	915
15.1	-1.5	25.8	36.2	18.2	32.1	11.7	8.0	3.8	22.3	23.5	17.2	19.2	11.4	16.7	Hungary	944
							576.0	108.2	20.9	†8.2	-21.3	73.4	14.7	14.3	Kazakhstan	916
								16.6	7.8	2.9	31.0	9.6	20.7		Kyrgyz Republic	917
							31.1	.8	20.3	33.3	6.0	6.3	19.6	13.0	Latvia	941
							41.8	40.9	3.5	41.5	9.0	-5.3	7.5	18.9	Lithuania	946
							78.3	†22.7	-3.6	16.2	9.1	32.4	13.1	-50.1	Macedonia, FYR	962
9.7	2.6	1.3	4.3	5.7	.5	4.0	9.1	†7.6	-1.9	—	7.2	10.6	2.6	6.7	Malta	181
					561.3	304.9	116.5	68.8	†12.4	30.6	†-18.0	38.9	36.7	23.6	Moldova	921
25.9	51.3	253.7	401.1	†28.1	38.8	31.3	39.7	36.4	39.8	17.9	16.2	23.1	-6.4	14.0	Poland	964
1.7	16.4	2.5	†8.8	214.3	41.6	95.0	107.8	57.7	58.7	66.9	17.7	34.6	55.9	39.0	Romania	968
						187.0	120.7	27.2	55.0	14.9	53.7	66.9	35.6		Russia	922
						6.2	20.9	15.8	-4.4	-11.4	4.2	21.5	21.3		Slovak Republic	936
					133.7	41.5	35.1	24.8	18.4	18.1	25.2	26.6	6.1	19.9	Slovenia	961
66.7	30.6	73.2	58.4	46.4	72.5	64.8	81.5	68.3	129.5	69.1	63.1	77.0	53.5	60.4	Turkey	186
					1,552.5	444.0	151.7	34.9	43.3	†14.1	36.4	47.1	43.1		Ukraine	926
99.6	214.9	2,020.1	147.5												Yugoslavia, SFR	188
															Middle East	
3.5	-1.0	-2.3	22.2	†1.7	15.4	3.7	-5.5	-3.6	.8	3.7	5.1	16.6	4.6	23.8	Bahrain, Kingdom of	419
14.2	12.8	9.2	16.6	8.1	8.8	12.1	10.7	8.5	7.2	9.4	20.3	.8	5.3	7.9	Egypt	469
17.3	10.2	15.7	18.1	26.1	14.8	30.0	41.6	32.5	33.6	19.9	22.7	21.5	24.7	23.0	Iran, I.R. of	429
															Iraq	433
49.5	11.3	44.4	30.6	13.7	†33.7	27.9	7.7	15.1	20.4	11.3	12.3	20.4	2.5	21.8	Israel	436
9.2	19.1	11.6	9.4	15.5	4.2	†7.1	1.3	-.2	-11.8	6.1	-.8	9.5	14.2	3.8	Jordan	439
5.9	-7.3	-3.6			-7.7	.5	1.1	5.2	4.9	.4	-8.3	19.9	7.0	11.8	Kuwait	443
127.2	165.4	57.1	56.7	53.2	74.0	-4.7	25.7	8.6	12.4	10.0	6.3	10.2	5.7	-1.0	Lebanon	446
13.1	-12.4	16.9	26.4	-3.6	16.2	4.5	13.0	6.2	1.2	5.2	.4	4.7	4.5	1.2	Libya	672
7.2	-5.9	9.6	13.1	3.8	6.7	4.3	4.7	-.3	6.8	9.2	-8.0	1.1	7.5	27.7	Oman	449
6.5	-28.9	.1	19.2	-10.5	10.0	†4.2	-8.1	-4.9	4.4	6.3	2.1	-.9	6.5	17.3	Qatar	453
4.9	3.2	-2.2	11.6	17.7	†6.4	-1.6	3.4	-.2	6.1	6.1	-.6	11.7	5.7	8.4	Saudi Arabia	456
10.8	17.7	19.1	24.9	12.4	17.6	22.0	8.2	8.7	8.6	6.7	8.0	11.1	17.7	13.9	Syrian Arab Republic	463
9.7	6.5	2.8	-2.7	20.9	15.1	21.3	5.6	8.6	6.9	13.9	9.5	8.9	12.6	15.8	United Arab Emirates	466
12.5	2.6	6.4													Yemen Arab Rep.	473
7.7	4.3	25.3													Yemen, P.D. Rep.	459
				11.5	24.3	31.9	35.1	17.5	-4.5	6.3	8.1	15.2	19.3	14.3	Yemen, Republic of	474

		1972	1973	1974	1975	1976	1977	1978	1979	1980	1981	1982	1983	1984	1985	1986
															Percent Change over Previous Year	

Western Hemisphere

		1972	1973	1974	1975	1976	1977	1978	1979	1980	1981	1982	1983	1984	1985	1986
Antigua and Barbuda	311	....	....	....	....	27.9	27.4	−5.0	18.5	10.8	11.9	−3.4	22.5	14.3	17.2	27.6
Argentina	213	65.0	112.1	57.1	218.2	288.6	134.6	146.4	135.5	95.4	76.6	154.2	362.0	582.3	584.3	89.7
Aruba	314	....	....	....	....					....	....	....	....			
Bahamas, The	313	23.4	−11.4	.4	−3.4	12.5	11.3	16.3	25.7	1.0	6.4	10.1	11.7	12.5	9.4	11.5
Barbados	316	8.5	9.4	19.4	20.3	6.8	19.3	18.5	38.3	10.2	1.9	.8	24.4	−2.3	15.6	11.8
Belize	339						15.9	45.9	2.4	12.9	−5.0	−.4	7.6	17.9	17.2	21.2
Bolivia	218	25.2	34.3	43.4	11.8	36.5	20.9	12.4	16.7	42.6	19.7	228.8	207.0	1,798.3	5,784.6	86.1
Brazil	223	37.2	45.8	37.2	42.4	37.5	37.7	†42.5	74.9	69.7	82.6	68.5	102.7	204.1	334.3	†330.1
Chile	228	154.3	322.6	266.0	256.0	†256.0	72.1	99.1	69.4	51.3	9.5	2.8	15.6	22.8	24.2	43.3
Colombia	233	27.1	30.7	17.8	20.1	34.7	30.4	†30.4	24.8	28.0	20.7	25.4	23.4	24.1	10.7	....
Costa Rica	238	13.9	24.9	14.5	29.1	23.0	32.2	24.9	10.7	16.8	49.0	70.3	38.9	17.6	7.7	31.0
Dominica	321	....	....	....	....		9.6	23.2	51.8	72.0	−9.9	−2.5	−3.9		27.5	18.6
Dominican Republic	243	17.5	20.6	38.5	7.2	−1.4	18.6	5.1	27.3	6.3	5.8	10.9	13.7	43.2	19.3	55.1
Ecuador	248	24.6	34.1	48.5	6.7	23.2	30.4	9.7	26.8	23.9	12.1	−14.0	−19.2	12.4	−11.9	−21.5
El Salvador	253	23.5	19.6	19.4	16.5	41.4	7.8	10.0	21.5	8.1	.6	†3.7	−1.3	13.8	27.0	19.7
Grenada	328	20.6	9.2	1.0	22.8	37.8	10.5	28.9	20.0	6.1	10.1	11.7	−2.5	−12.7	6.7	28.1
Guatemala	258	19.8	23.3	15.6	15.8	39.6	20.3	11.8	10.7	2.4	3.1	1.4	6.0	4.3	54.9	19.5
Guyana	336	19.7	12.0	36.7	56.4	4.2	33.0	5.0	−4.3	8.7	25.3	17.4	20.2	20.3	19.4
Haiti	263	26.4	22.7	2.9	17.6	36.5	14.5	14.1	11.8	17.8	23.4	−.2	.9	18.2	14.5	12.7
Honduras	268	13.6	24.1	1.3	9.4	39.2	12.7	17.7	11.6	11.5	4.4	13.5	13.6	2.5	−3.2	8.2
Jamaica	343	7.9	†26.4	18.3	24.9	5.0	40.1	20.1	10.4	13.9	8.1	13.1	21.6	23.7	15.3	40.8
Mexico	273	17.9	22.4	20.7	21.4	29.1	†26.0	27.3	34.3	32.6	33.6	†62.6	40.3	60.0	49.6	67.2
Netherlands Antilles	353	27.9	.1	14.0	12.8	10.9	25.0	20.7	−1.2	4.6	9.4	12.2	3.8	−5.3	13.1	−2.7
Nicaragua	278	21.0	53.1	14.6	−4.4	28.6	5.2	−7.1	96.2	32.4	26.9	25.7	†67.1	83.5	162.8	252.2
Panama	283	45.7	4.9	21.8	−11.8	9.8	12.2	15.4	22.5	11.3	7.3	5.4	−1.8	2.3	7.5	9.8
Paraguay	288	20.0	32.6	21.0	17.9	21.1	32.3	39.3	24.4	25.9	.1	−3.6	25.6	29.4	28.0	26.7
Peru	293	29.4	25.5	39.4	16.9	25.7	19.4	46.2	70.4	58.4	47.3	40.4	96.5	104.3	281.2	87.9
St. Kitts and Nevis	361	....	....	....	....						−13.6	183.0	−3.5	8.2	6.1	51.4
St. Lucia	362	....	....	....	....	40.8	13.6	16.3	17.8	16.5	1.6	7.5	1.4	8.0	12.7	37.4
St. Vincent & Grenadines	364	....	....	....	....	20.4	3.3	36.2	22.6	1.2	18.6	4.8	16.3	17.8	10.0	20.2
Suriname	366	5.2	28.9	5.2	20.5	17.5	10.8	12.0	11.1	7.6	21.7	17.7	8.0	26.9	52.5	39.6
Trinidad and Tobago	369	19.4	.7	27.0	45.4	45.7	26.8	29.1	22.5	16.6	38.7	37.3	−4.4	−5.8	−1.5	−7.6
Uruguay	298	55.9	73.2	59.4	†82.8	65.5	40.4	85.1	71.7	47.4	8.3	†19.8	6.1	50.4	281.2	83.7
Venezuela, Rep. Bol.	299	18.0	19.0	47.6	51.3	12.5	28.8	18.6	5.7	17.1	6.9	4.2	25.7	26.7	8.8	4.4

1987	1988	1989	1990	1991	1992	1993	1994	1995	1996	1997	1998	1999	2000	2001		

Percent Change over Previous Year

Western Hemisphere

1987	1988	1989	1990	1991	1992	1993	1994	1995	1996	1997	1998	1999	2000	2001	Country	Code
26.6	15.9	10.1	11.1	7.0	8.9	1.1	19.3	27.1	-8.7	3.6	24.9	-1.3	-5.0	9.7	Antigua and Barbuda	311
113.5	351.4	4,168.2	†1,023.2	148.6	49.0	33.0	†15.7	1.6	14.6	12.8	—	1.6	-9.1	-20.9	Argentina	213
57.3	20.5	28.2	8.5	18.9	5.5	14.1	16.8	.5	.9	5.7	15.6	7.8	1.1	17.5	Aruba	314
11.5	9.1	1.6	14.3	7.0	3.8	.4	9.1	6.8	.5	15.7	14.7	26.1	6.7	-3.9	Bahamas, The	313
18.1	12.4	-12.5	14.6	-5.9	1.5	-5.1	8.3	-17.0	46.4	-1.1	23.4	20.7	23.5	.2	Barbados	316
18.7	-3.0	22.1	6.1	11.6	6.8	7.9	5.7	7.8	5.5	1.3	12.3	33.0	15.7	32.1	Belize	339
†36.6	35.3	2.3	39.6	45.1	32.9	30.0	29.3	21.1	†21.7	19.0	7.1	-5.8	8.8	18.7	Bolivia	218
215.4	†426.9	1,337.0	2,333.6	429.4	981.8	2,017.8	2,195.4	25.7	29.9	22.3	7.5	13.6	18.9	12.8	Brazil	223
21.0	46.5	17.2	23.3	44.7	26.3	21.2	16.2	22.2	16.2	20.2	-13.3	32.8	5.0	5.2	Chile	228
30.3	25.7	....	†13.0	31.9	45.1	28.1	29.0	20.2	23.4	17.4	-7.8	24.3	25.6	9.6	Colombia	233
.3	53.2	-2.0	3.9	20.0	37.2	7.0	37.9	-6.0	16.9	†54.3	17.1	28.6	19.8	13.2	Costa Rica	238
58.4	-2.5	-1.9	24.7	5.1	17.3	-12.1	-1.8	24.1	5.1	-.3	7.7	24.9	-19.0	.6	Dominica	321
23.2	54.5	26.2	46.8	22.9	17.1	13.9	7.5	17.3	22.3	19.3	6.2	21.8	-1.1	16.4	Dominican Republic	243
-10.9	-21.8	-4.1	†17.4	1.4	2.2	47.7	19.3	-20.3	3.6	6.7	†-13.8	†-29.0	1.3	40.6	Ecuador	248
-.5	7.9	13.4	22.4	18.1	29.5	17.2	5.2	15.8	12.9	-2.1	3.8	8.1	-11.7	....	El Salvador	253
7.2	11.7	6.0	3.5	-1.7	23.0	12.7	12.1	4.7	2.0	5.5	13.9	7.1	7.5	3.6	Grenada	328
9.8	14.4	20.7	33.0	18.6	9.1	20.4	40.1	9.9	13.5	†29.9	13.5	13.6	21.8	11.8	Guatemala	258
51.4	54.8	34.0	54.5	65.5	31.5	†26.6	10.4	16.7	14.5	10.0	-1.6	23.0	10.4	1.2	Guyana	336
17.2	-22.1	61.1	-12.6	7.0	27.8	22.7	31.8	31.6	-13.1	†18.7	.3	26.6	9.5	15.1	Haiti	263
26.6	11.9	20.0	23.6	11.1	22.5	11.9	36.1	21.7	29.4	†41.0	12.7	18.2	8.2	3.6	Honduras	268
5.2	53.0	-8.5	27.4	94.7	71.3	26.2	25.7	38.0	14.4	2.8	6.4	22.8	6.3	13.0	Jamaica	343
118.1	67.8	37.3	63.1	123.9	15.1	17.7	1.1	3.5	36.9	†32.0	15.4	28.3	14.0	17.1	Mexico	273
10.8	1.6	-1.6	13.0	5.5	8.8	6.5	13.8	7.9	-4.3	—	2.6	3.3	2.1	14.3	Netherlands Antilles	353
637.0	11,673.4	2,368.3	6,286.7	1,336.9	11.4	-4.6	36.2	13.2	†25.9	24.7	23.6	23.5	8.3	32.8	Nicaragua	278
-1.6	-31.3	1.0	41.0	28.7	14.8	10.8	13.5	1.3	3.3	18.3	13.0	1.6	2.9	10.3	Panama	283
53.6	†34.8	31.7	28.3	32.4	22.5	16.5	30.0	†28.2	.5	10.4	5.2	9.2	18.2	7.1	Paraguay	288
122.0	515.0	1,648.7	6,724.8	127.2	76.9	52.6	28.9	34.2	19.7	69.1	26.3	16.2	-5.4	1.8	Peru	293
10.9	-12.3	26.3	-2.0	.6	7.9	16.6	-4.1	14.2	6.8	-1.0	22.6	5.9	6.1	-5.1	St. Kitts and Nevis	361
25.6	14.4	12.3	6.3	.4	26.4	6.4	3.5	12.9	-6.9	5.7	6.3	13.5	.5	-1.0	St. Lucia	362
-15.8	17.8	11.5	5.0	-17.5	51.1	-.3	19.2	-.1	6.1	27.2	15.0	22.4	14.3	10.1	St. Vincent & Grenadines	364
27.1	24.5	11.3	4.0	28.2	11.6	87.6	245.6	178.2	-2.0	20.2	†34.6	51.5	104.3	38.2	Suriname	366
3.9	-13.6	13.7	20.8	13.4	-7.7	16.3	19.5	4.7	†6.1	21.1	5.8	12.3	6.6	19.6	Trinidad and Tobago	369
59.9	57.1	79.2	96.2	96.5	71.2	57.9	40.4	32.3	24.8	16.7	†14.1	3.1	-3.5	-4.2	Uruguay	298
†39.7	27.6	7.5	40.1	52.5	11.1	12.0	139.2	38.0	†149.2	77.0	4.7	24.5	25.3	15.5	Venezuela, Rep. Bol.	299

Money plus Quasi-Money

		1972	1973	1974	1975	1976	1977	1978	1979	1980	1981	1982	1983	1984	1985	1986
														Percent Change over Previous Year		
Industrial Countries																
United States	111	12.7	6.8	5.3	12.1	13.4	10.8	8.2	9.3	8.7	10.7	11.1	10.4	11.0	9.1	10.6
Canada	156	15.0	20.8	19.2	15.4	19.0	14.0	16.9	17.8	9.5	†20.4	5.0	−.9	6.1	5.8	7.4
Australia	193	19.7	21.3	9.2	20.6	12.2	5.9	10.5	11.6	14.0	9.9	10.6	13.2	11.7	17.9	9.6
Japan	158	24.7	16.8	11.5	14.5	13.5	11.1	13.1	8.4	6.8	10.7	7.6	6.9	6.9	8.9	9.3
New Zealand	196	36.1	33.8	6.0	10.7	18.3	14.7	24.7	18.6	9.2	16.4	14.1	6.6	20.4	32.6	24.9
Euro Area																
Austria	122	15.7	13.3	12.5	18.3	16.7	9.0	14.3	8.2	12.7	10.1	10.9	5.2	6.5	6.0	8.6
Belgium	124	16.3	14.0	8.7	15.3	12.6	8.4	7.5	6.2	3.3	6.3	7.2	8.3	4.5	5.3	10.5
Finland	172	18.4	12.7	17.5	22.5	9.2	11.6	15.1	18.0	15.1	15.9	13.4	13.4	15.6	18.1	7.9
France	132	18.9	14.6	17.8	15.7	12.3	†14.3	†12.2	13.6	6.9	11.0	9.6	12.8	10.1	−.3	7.2
Germany	134	14.2	9.5	7.5	11.4	7.8	10.0	10.0	5.5	4.7	3.9	6.6	5.5	5.0	†17.8	5.7
Ireland	178	12.9	19.1	19.3	21.7	13.0	20.6	23.5	13.6	20.6	10.8	†16.6	7.1	10.8	5.5	−1.3
Italy	136	18.7	20.2	†12.5	24.8	20.5	21.7	23.8	19.6	12.2	11.3	19.7	13.0	12.0	10.5	8.8
Luxembourg	137	....	....	....	7.5	16.2	12.0	14.4	14.6	19.4	10.7	−.1	9.1	1.0	16.1	11.3
Netherlands	138	14.0	14.9	14.5	13.1	16.1	13.0	11.6	11.0	5.6	7.7	5.6	4.9	6.6	6.8	5.3
Portugal	182	24.2	28.4	13.6	12.6	†17.0	17.1	20.7	†33.5	34.3	28.7	26.8	20.2	27.7	24.5	17.6
Spain	184	23.1	24.3	19.1	19.0	19.3	18.7	20.3	17.9	16.7	15.8	13.9	†−1.1	5.0	11.8	†19.1
Denmark	128	13.4	13.6	8.4	26.9	11.7	9.3	6.4	10.2	11.7	10.8	11.1	27.8	17.2	18.4	9.4
Iceland	176	18.3	32.4	28.6	29.0	32.9	44.1	48.4	57.2	65.3	24.9	70.3	80.1	†34.2	53.5	31.9
Norway	142	12.5	13.5	11.1	15.3	†15.4	17.3	11.9	13.5	10.8	13.3	11.0	10.8	19.2	15.0	2.2
Sweden	144	12.9	13.7	9.7	11.7	5.0	9.1	17.4	17.1	12.2	13.3	8.0	†3.9	8.5	3.3	13.6
Switzerland	146	12.6	7.2	†5.0	7.5	9.0	6.8	11.3	9.5	.5	8.4	†4.8	3.9	†13.8	4.2	3.3
United Kingdom	112	27.9	27.5	12.9	†7.1	11.6	9.5	14.6	12.5	18.5	†25.0	13.7	10.3	11.5	11.2	22.6
Developing Countries																
Africa																
Algeria	612	30.3	12.3	26.6	31.0	29.2	19.1	29.9	18.1	17.4	16.7	26.3	20.3	17.4	15.0	1.4
Angola	614															
Benin	638	13.3	6.4	24.8	72.7	−3.9	14.0	11.7	†4.4	48.9	24.3	30.5	−1.5	15.2	−.1	−2.2
Botswana	616	....	....	....	....	26.0	11.4	64.5	19.0	−4.4	8.5	28.7	16.6	51.1	8.7
Burkina Faso	748	6.7	36.8	21.0	38.7	29.7	12.7	19.5	†8.7	15.1	19.7	12.0	12.2	15.9	.6	22.4
Burundi	618	5.5	21.1	17.3	−4.1	51.7	28.0	29.2	7.8	1.4	30.4	−5.3	30.3	3.0	22.3	.2
Cameroon	622	9.8	22.4	34.9	12.6	25.1	†38.1	15.4	22.5	21.4	28.6	19.0	26.5	20.6	17.4	−4.3
Cape Verde	624						41.0	16.2	17.4	30.6	18.9	26.5	19.3	11.6	20.0	23.6
Central African Rep.	626	16.0	4.3	29.5	.6	42.0	†7.0	10.2	20.1	35.0	23.8	−4.2	11.7	7.5	10.0	2.2
Chad	628	3.4	5.4	41.8	10.4	24.8	13.8	24.1	13.0	−15.3	17.8	4.5	22.3	59.9	6.1	1.1
Comoros	632												34.9	−16.3	15.2	4.3
Congo, Dem. Rep. of	636	21.5	37.8	32.9	10.0	38.1	59.2	54.3	5.0	62.7	52.0	74.9	1,113.0	−81.7	29.6	58.9
Congo, Rep. of	634	6.3	14.8	39.1	13.4	15.8	†2.4	6.7	21.6	36.6	50.4	26.2	−1.5	7.3	21.0	−11.6
Côte d'Ivoire	662	4.4	20.4	50.9	9.6	43.0	50.0	10.9	†6.2	2.8	9.9	3.2	4.8	19.4	13.7	2.7
Djibouti	611	....	....	....	....	....	....	....	....	....	....	....	....	....	18.4	11.3
Equatorial Guinea	642	....	....	....	....	....	....	....	....	....	....	....	....	....	....	17.5
Ethiopia	644	16.1	29.9	15.6	9.6	12.8	17.7	12.7	13.2	4.2	11.0	10.3	†15.0	7.8	15.8	11.9
Gabon	646	27.8	32.1	67.1	61.2	86.7	†−2.9	−14.8	8.1	24.6	15.9	13.5	17.9	15.7	12.1	−10.1
Gambia, The	648	39.0	42.2	9.9	13.4	45.9	−12.1	†16.6	−8.4	10.4	20.9	15.8	26.7	5.5	51.3	7.3
Ghana	652	40.7	18.8	26.7	37.9	37.1	60.3	68.5	15.8	33.8	51.3	23.3	40.2	53.6	46.2	47.9
Guinea	656															
Guinea-Bissau	654	....	....	....	....	....	....	....	....	....	....	....	....	....	....	....
Kenya	664	13.9	24.7	8.6	17.1	24.1	48.2	13.0	13.1	.8	13.3	16.9	14.0	12.8	6.3	32.7
Lesotho	666	....	....	....	....	....	....	....	....	23.6	28.6	17.1	15.3	24.1	13.3
Liberia	668	....	....	−1.5	47.3	12.3	23.5	2.5	†−26.2	−11.5	24.8	10.7	.7	17.7	18.7
Madagascar	674	11.8	3.9	20.8	1.9	16.0	19.9	17.1	†27.6	20.6	23.9	8.9	−9.1	24.0	13.3	25.6
Malawi	676	11.0	34.8	36.6	5.6	−1.1	33.0	4.7	.9	12.6	26.0	14.5	5.9	32.6	−1.0	27.1
Mali	678	11.8	8.8	52.0	19.9	11.5	15.4	23.1	†16.7	4.5	3.0	11.7	20.7	34.5	8.7	6.1
Mauritania	682	26.3	27.5	55.4	26.5	24.8	5.5	1.9	21.1	14.3	29.3	1.6	5.2	11.8	22.2	7.5
Mauritius	684	26.5	30.0	80.1	22.8	7.1	12.8	21.7	8.8	23.2	4.0	23.4	10.1	14.2	31.5	29.1
Morocco	686	18.2	16.6	29.3	20.1	18.1	19.7	17.7	13.9	10.8	16.4	†21.2	17.7	10.2	13.2	16.9
Mozambique	688	....	....	....	....	....	....	....	....	....	....	....	....	....	15.1	19.9
Namibia	728															
Niger	692	6.3	20.2	31.0	9.8	31.1	28.7	44.0	19.0	20.8	20.7	−11.8	−.3	22.2	7.0	12.0
Nigeria	694	15.6	†25.2	89.2	55.7	41.5	34.5	−2.0	31.0	46.1	5.9	9.5	14.0	11.6	9.0	2.0
Rwanda	714	1.8	35.5	32.8	12.1	34.2	26.0	10.3	26.0	8.1	†9.8	1.4	11.8	10.1	17.2	13.6
São Tomé and Príncipe	716															
Senegal	722	12.6	22.3	47.5	11.4	32.0	15.2	21.3	†3.2	10.3	22.1	20.9	4.1	5.2	4.5	11.2
Seychelles	718	43.0	11.1	3.5	29.4	43.5	17.2	13.8	22.3	33.2	−2.2	−7.9	2.8	14.4	14.2	11.5
Sierra Leone	724	17.6	26.1	18.6	8.3	22.2	21.7	31.6	19.7	21.6	2.6	56.8	31.6	28.3	71.1	88.4
Somalia	726	32.4	17.5	28.7	28.4	19.4	28.7	32.5	37.4	20.2	30.8	15.7	7.5	26.0	81.1	34.1
South Africa	199	17.6	22.6	16.6	19.4	8.9	10.1	16.0	16.8	22.8	17.2	13.5	13.8	19.8	14.6	8.8
Sudan	732	18.7	23.6	35.3	18.8	24.9	42.9	27.5	30.2	29.4	42.0	41.2	22.7	19.6	†52.8	27.9
Swaziland	734	....	....	....	51.3	25.4	16.1	28.0	2.6	13.7	5.7	14.2	22.9	11.1
Tanzania	738	17.7	18.2	22.1	24.4	25.1	20.2	12.6	46.9	26.9	18.1	19.5	17.8	20.5	30.3	11.1
Togo	742	−1.5	14.5	91.5	−7.2	45.7	16.7	35.1	†13.4	9.1	38.6	16.5	.5	15.6	5.2	15.6
Tunisia	744	16.7	20.2	28.2	22.2	15.6	13.4	19.8	16.2	18.5	22.7	19.9	16.4	11.7	14.4	4.9
Uganda	746	28.9	35.1	33.9	21.1	32.7	19.4	25.5	47.0	34.8	86.0	11.5	40.0	110.7	127.4	174.4
Zambia	754	7.1	20.4	7.3	12.0	26.3	12.1	−8.5	30.1	9.0	7.9	33.8	11.1	17.2	23.4	93.3
Zimbabwe	698	....	....	....	....	....	....	....	....	29.6	15.4	24.9	−3.3	9.1	17.7	4.2
Asia																
Afghanistan, Islamic State of	512	13.9	7.6	13.5	12.5	24.2	28.0	16.3	18.6	16.9	17.4	18.3	....	....	10.4	12.3
Bangladesh	513	....	....	....	5.3	18.5	23.7	26.3	22.4	20.9	16.8	†14.0	40.0	36.1	13.6	16.2
Bhutan	514	....	....	....	....	....	....	....	....	....	....	....	....	13.1	26.4	7.5
Cambodia	522	....	....	....	....	....	....	....	....	....	....	....	....	....	....	....
China, P.R.: Mainland	924	....	....	....	....	....	3.6	49.2	25.9	18.3	14.6	19.7	32.6	†19.9	30.2
China, P.R.: Hong Kong	532															
Fiji	819	22.4	13.3	39.2	27.1	1.4	18.7	7.6	20.5	12.3	5.2	8.1	13.4	11.1	1.9	17.5
India	534	15.4	19.5	12.2	14.1	24.5	19.2	†71.0	17.7	15.9	17.5	17.2	16.9	18.0	16.9	17.9
Indonesia	536	44.3	49.5	47.3	37.3	31.2	19.5	21.6	37.0	47.8	25.9	14.1	32.5	22.3	29.2	19.1
Korea	542	33.8	36.4	24.0	28.2	33.5	39.7	35.0	24.6	26.9	25.0	27.0	15.2	7.7	15.6	18.4
Lao People's Democratic Rep.	544															
Malaysia	548	23.7	31.2	15.3	14.6	27.7	16.4	17.9	24.1	26.2	17.9	16.3	9.4	11.4	6.7	11.0
Maldives	556	....	....	....	....	....	2.2	5.8	35.4	58.0	†6.7	−10.9	−1.7	32.3	29.2	25.3
Micronesia, Federal States of	868															
Mongolia	948	....	....	....	....	....	....	....	....	....	....	....	....	....	....	....
Myanmar	518	19.3	20.6	22.2	18.7	10.5	4.3	15.7	16.7	17.0	20.4	13.2	15.6	17.7	−1.8	31.3
Nepal	558	16.7	28.6	17.1	11.9	28.9	21.0	19.7	15.8	17.3	19.1	21.4	20.1	13.0	20.0	19.4

Percent Change over Previous Year

1987	1988	1989	1990	1991	1992	1993	1994	1995	1996	1997	1998	1999	2000	2001		
															Industrial Countries	
3.1	6.3	5.8	4.9	3.3	1.7	1.5	—	5.6	6.1	6.6	10.1	8.2	7.0	13.9	United States	111
8.7	10.6	13.4	7.8	4.8	9.4	11.6	8.0	6.2	5.7	8.6	2.3	5.7	13.9	6.6	Canada	156
16.0	21.3	†−23.2	12.8	1.2	7.4	5.7	10.0	8.5	10.6	7.3	8.4	11.7	3.8	13.2	Australia	193
11.2	9.8	11.8	8.2	2.5	−.1	2.2	3.1	2.7	2.3	3.1	4.1	3.4	1.1	2.2	Japan	158
17.6	†14.9	9.8	12.5	.7	2.6	7.0	7.6	9.3	16.1	5.2	1.8	5.0	2.3	6.8	New Zealand	196
															Euro Area	
7.4	5.8	7.4	9.8	7.5	6.8	5.5	5.4	5.0	2.8	2.2	....	....	....		Austria	122
9.1	5.3	10.1	4.1	5.2	†3.3	12.2	2.8	4.9	6.3	7.1	....	....	....		Belgium	124
12.0	23.0	9.5	5.0	†6.4	−1.0	1.5	1.4	6.0	−2.9	2.5	3.7	....	....		Finland	172
4.7	4.0	6.2	4.1	−4.7	−.1	.7	3.3	8.7	—	6.6	....	....	....		France	132
5.1	5.3	4.9	17.7	6.3	7.8	10.9	2.5	4.4	7.4	2.4	5.8	....	....		Germany	134
11.2	6.4	4.5	16.5	4.2	5.4	24.8	10.1	52.8	15.6	19.5	17.8	....	....		Ireland	178
7.5	9.3	†11.7	10.2	9.4	5.4	7.5	1.8	2.3	2.2	−5.8	.6	....	....		Italy	136
15.6	15.8	19.8	16.6	11.4	6.6	....	....	....	....	−4.5	....	....	....		Luxembourg	137
2.0	7.2	10.2	6.9	4.7	4.9	5.7	.3	6.0	5.6	6.7	....	....	....		Netherlands	138
13.7	14.6	12.7	9.2	23.5	17.6	10.7	9.1	8.3	5.6	6.8	5.9	....	....		Portugal	182
8.4	11.5	11.8	15.3	13.3	4.5	9.8	7.1	6.6	2.6	1.4	7.1	....	....		Spain	184
†4.1	5.5	1.3	6.5	†6.1	−.7	19.7	−10.0	6.2	8.1	6.8	3.3	−.9	....		Denmark	128
36.9	30.5	50.6	14.1	15.9	3.9	6.5	2.0	2.5	6.2	9.4	15.2	....	....		Iceland	176
19.2	4.9	8.6	5.6	2.9	8.5	−.7	5.0	3.8	6.9	1.4	15.5	1.7	8.7	8.7	Norway	142
6.0	7.6	11.0	.8	4.2	3.3	4.2	.7	3.1	8.9	1.1	−.4	8.5	1.9	....	Sweden	144
10.6	5.4	6.3	.8	2.3	2.6	8.9	4.2	4.6	†9.6	6.6	5.1	13.3	−16.9	3.9	Switzerland	146
†24.8	16.7	20.1	10.5	1.7	†6.4	4.5	6.8	13.3	10.7	3.8	†7.6	4.5	11.1	7.9	United Kingdom	112
															Developing Countries	
															Africa	
13.6	13.6	5.2	11.4	20.8	†26.1	22.7	13.0	9.2	14.4	18.6	18.9	13.7	13.2	24.8	Algeria	612
									4,105.6	71.9	57.6	†564.8	309.0	160.6	Angola	614
−11.3	1.1	6.5	28.6	10.7	18.7	−3.1	47.9	−1.8	13.0	4.6	−3.6	34.8	26.0	12.2	Benin	638
67.2	21.2	46.3	−14.0	41.6	13.3	−14.4	12.8	12.3	18.8	28.6	39.4	26.3	1.4	31.2	Botswana	616
11.7	16.6	3.7	−.5	4.5	4.0	8.0	29.4	22.3	5.2	17.7	1.0	2.6	6.2	1.6	Burkina Faso	748
2.1	15.5	18.5	9.6	18.4	5.9	8.1	33.3	−11.2	24.3	9.4	−3.7	47.3	4.3	15.7	Burundi	618
−18.3	†2.0	6.1	−1.7	1.8	−21.9	−9.2	26.5	−6.2	−10.1	18.6	7.8	13.3	19.1	15.1	Cameroon	622
8.6	16.9	15.0	14.6	16.2	12.9	18.0	12.2	†18.2	9.7	10.9	2.8	14.9	13.7	9.9	Cape Verde	624
3.6	†−1.1	12.9	−3.7	−4.0	−3.8	12.8	78.5	4.3	4.9	−7.7	−16.1	11.1	2.4	−1.1	Central African Rep.	626
3.7	†−12.6	8.1	−2.4	†5.6	−8.9	−28.3	31.4	48.7	27.9	−4.1	−7.7	−2.6	18.5	22.0	Chad	628
26.2	15.5	17.7	3.9	3.0	5.3	3.4	7.3	−6.1	9.8	−4.2	†−14.2	18.5	14.5	46.7	Comoros	632
95.9	131.2	67.4	195.4	2,388.6	3,794.3	2,853.1	6,968.9	357.6	....						Congo, Dem. Rep. of	636
6.0	†−2.9	3.7	18.5	−4.2	−26.6	28.2	−.1	15.7	9.5	−12.8	19.9	58.5	−22.8		Congo, Rep. of	634
−3.6	1.5	−8.1	−2.6	.1	−1.2	−1.4	46.8	18.1	3.9	8.2	6.0	−1.7	−1.9	12.0	Côte d'Ivoire	662
2.7	7.3	2.4	3.6	4.0	−5.3	.9	3.7	5.3	−7.4	−4.5	−4.1	−3.8	1.1	7.5	Djibouti	611
−10.5	†−34.5	40.7	−52.0	−11.8	31.0	−25.9	139.5	48.9	42.8	9.3	15.6	68.7	36.2	35.1	Equatorial Guinea	642
6.4	11.3	14.3	18.5	17.0	16.2	9.8	25.3	8.7	8.1	15.0	−3.0	6.7	14.2	9.8	Ethiopia	644
−13.0	†4.1	6.0	3.3	7.0	−21.6	−1.7	37.4	10.1	17.2	11.3	−1.8	−3.0	18.3	7.5	Gabon	646
24.6	14.7	20.8	8.4	25.7	13.8	12.8	−3.8	14.2	5.8	23.0	10.2	12.1	34.8	20.0	Gambia, The	648
53.3	46.3	54.7	13.3	†16.7	52.2	26.4	45.7	40.4	32.6	45.5	26.1	16.2	38.4	....	Ghana	652
						23.3	22.8	−3.4	11.3	3.6	18.2	6.4	....	....	Guinea	656
160.9	73.3	37.6	574.6	−67.3	110.9	40.5	48.5	43.0	48.3	119.4	−11.1	21.5	60.8	7.3	Guinea-Bissau	654
11.1	8.0	12.9	20.1	19.6	39.0	28.0	31.5	24.8	25.4	18.7	2.6	6.0	4.5	2.5	Kenya	664
9.9	26.6	13.4	8.4	9.2	9.8	29.4	10.9	9.8	17.1	14.8	15.5	15.5	1.4	17.2	Lesotho	666
15.0	9.7	21.1	....	....	19.6	65.6	11.7	29.5	−11.9	3.5	106.0	11.6	†18.3	12.7	Liberia	668
18.4	22.4	33.7	4.5	31.1	22.3	24.2	52.6	16.2	16.0	20.8	6.2	19.2	17.2	23.8	Madagascar	674
36.8	21.5	6.1	11.1	25.4	15.8	39.9	36.5	56.2	39.6	2.1	60.0	26.5	41.4	14.4	Malawi	676
−4.0	8.3	1.0	−4.9	13.1	3.0	8.4	39.2	7.3	24.5	8.9	4.2	1.0	12.2	19.6	Mali	678
18.5	2.0	†13.7	11.5	9.3	7.2	.7	−.5	−5.1	−5.1	8.0	4.1	2.1	16.1	17.3	Mauritania	682
29.8	28.7	15.4	21.2	21.9	15.9	17.0	12.3	18.7	7.6	16.4	11.2	15.2	9.2	10.9	Mauritius	684
9.9	15.2	12.2	†17.4	16.8	9.3	7.9	10.2	7.0	6.6	†8.0	6.0	10.2	8.4	14.1	Morocco	686
47.2	62.7	†44.3	37.2	†40.9	70.8	67.1	50.4	47.5	19.1	23.9	17.9	31.8	38.4	28.2	Mozambique	688
....	....	....	....	30.3	23.5	25.7	25.9	24.2	29.0	6.7	11.3	18.4	13.0	4.5	Namibia	728
−5.5	15.2	5.8	−4.1	−8.9	−1.0	.1	6.7	3.8	−6.6	−21.3	−18.5	15.4	12.4	31.4	Niger	692
22.4	32.9	12.9	32.7	37.4	†59.1	53.8	34.5	19.4	16.2	16.0	22.3	33.1	48.1	27.0	Nigeria	694
10.3	7.4	−4.2	5.6	5.5	12.4	2.5	−3.7	69.5	8.6	29.1	3.5	7.9	15.6	11.0	Rwanda	714
									84.5	116.4	2.8	7.7	24.9	40.1	São Tomé and Príncipe	716
−.3	.5	10.3	−4.8	5.8	3.6	−12.6	38.7	7.4	11.7	3.7	8.5	13.1	10.7	13.6	Senegal	722
8.8	22.3	17.2	14.5	11.5	13.1	20.9	−.8	10.5	14.8	43.1	20.2	21.7	9.1	12.0	Seychelles	718
64.0	56.9	74.2	74.0	76.3	33.2	21.9	8.8	19.6	†29.7	47.1	11.3	37.8	12.1	33.7	Sierra Leone	724
127.1	57.2	162.8	....												Somalia	726
19.5	27.0	20.6	†11.1			6.3	18.3	16.0	14.3	17.8	13.7	10.9	7.2	16.7	South Africa	199
36.5	32.8	53.3	48.8	67.5	†139.8	104.0	51.2	73.3	65.3	37.7	29.9	23.5	36.9	24.7	Sudan	732
14.1	37.2	25.7	.6	20.1	21.2	13.6	10.9	3.9	16.3	19.4	12.9	15.6	−6.6	10.7	Swaziland	734
32.1	32.8	†32.1	41.9	30.1	40.6	†39.2	35.3	33.0	8.4	12.9	10.8	18.6	14.8	17.1	Tanzania	738
−1.0	−11.9	1.1	9.5	3.1	−18.0	−16.2	44.3	22.3	−6.3	5.3	.1	8.4	15.2	−2.6	Togo	742
14.9	17.5	15.5	7.6	5.8	8.3	6.1	8.1	6.6	13.3	16.5	5.4	18.9	14.1	10.1	Tunisia	744
						57.2	35.8	13.9	19.3	19.4	22.9	13.6	18.1	9.2	Uganda	746
54.3	†61.6	65.2	47.9	97.3	....	....	59.2	55.5	35.0	25.1	†25.6	27.7	73.8	13.6	Zambia	754
27.1	20.8	24.3	15.1	1.4	12.6	71.3	35.1	25.5	33.3	41.2	11.3	35.9	68.9	128.5	Zimbabwe	698
															Asia	
50.6	34.5	37.1	40.6	....											Afghanistan, Islamic State of	512
†18.8	13.6	18.7	10.4	13.7	12.0	10.5	19.3	12.2	10.7	9.8	11.4	15.5	19.3	14.7	Bangladesh	513
10.8	31.0	34.9	10.5	29.6	13.5	†30.0	23.3	35.6	9.0	58.9	13.9	32.0	17.4	7.9	Bhutan	514
							35.6	43.6	40.4	16.6	15.7	17.3	26.9	20.4	Cambodia	522
25.3	20.7	18.7	28.9	26.7	30.8	†23.7	31.5	29.5	25.3	20.7	14.9	14.7	12.3	....	China, P.R.: Mainland	924
					8.5	14.5	11.7	10.6	12.5	8.7	11.1	8.3	9.3	−.3	China, P.R.: Hong Kong	532
4.0	20.6	9.4	25.2	14.3	14.3	6.7	2.7	4.3	.9	−8.7	−.3	14.2	−2.1	−3.1	Fiji	819
16.3	18.3	15.7	15.1	18.3	16.9	17.0	20.3	11.0	18.7	17.7	18.2	17.1	15.2	14.4	India	534
22.8	24.1	39.1	44.6	17.5	†19.8	20.2	20.0	27.2	27.2	25.2	63.5	12.5	15.9	12.8	Indonesia	536
19.1	21.5	19.8	17.2	21.9	14.9	16.6	18.7	15.6	15.8	14.1	27.0	27.4	25.4	13.2	Korea	542
			7.8	15.7	49.0	64.6	31.9	16.4	26.7	65.8	113.3	78.4	46.0	13.7	Lao People's Dem. Rep.	544
3.8	6.7	15.2	10.6	16.9	†29.2	26.6	12.8	20.9	†25.5	17.4	−1.4	16.9	9.9	2.5	Malaysia	548
12.0	14.3	19.8	18.7	24.9	13.0	36.3	24.2	15.6	26.0	23.1	22.8	3.6	4.1	9.0	Maldives	556
									−5.8	3.8	.7	3.4	−1.0	6.0	Micronesia, Federal States of	868
					31.6	227.6	80.0	32.6	17.2	42.2	−1.7	31.6	17.6	27.9	Mongolia	948
−24.7	29.9	32.2	37.7	†35.7	33.7	26.9	35.6	36.5	38.9	28.8	34.2	29.7	42.4	43.9	Myanmar	518
22.4	22.1	21.0	18.5	22.7	20.7	24.8	18.1	15.6	12.2	15.8	24.0	21.6	18.8	....	Nepal	558

Money plus Quasi-Money

351 x

		1972	1973	1974	1975	1976	1977	1978	1979	1980	1981	1982	1983	1984	1985	1986
Asia (cont.)													*Percent Change over Previous Year*			
Pakistan	564	17.5	13.8	−1.2	21.2	32.2	17.9	19.8	19.1	15.7	11.5	21.8	20.9	4.6	14.7	16.1
Papua New Guinea	853	....	....	63.6	−23.3	13.2	54.2	4.8	27.3	−3.2	.3	2.4	14.5	15.1	9.6	13.3
Philippines	566	14.0	23.5	16.3	13.8	28.1	28.5	24.2	12.4	20.6	17.4	18.5	†19.6	17.9	12.5	1.7
Samoa	862	12.2	25.8	18.2	8.9	21.6	21.6	11.3	43.1	32.6	67.2	35.2	−12.2	11.9	20.4	20.5
Singapore	576	25.6	15.5	13.5	17.9	12.7	6.6	10.8	18.8	24.5	22.4	15.9	11.9	6.2	3.8	10.0
Solomon Islands	813	....	....	....	....	....	....	....	44.9	−1.4	−17.6	23.4	20.0	35.0	2.6	9.3
Sri Lanka	524	15.6	2.8	12.0	3.5	32.5	39.6	31.4	42.8	28.7	19.9	25.4	20.9	16.0	12.8	4.2
Thailand	578	23.8	22.3	20.4	16.3	†21.1	20.0	19.4	14.1	22.5	16.3	24.2	23.8	19.4	10.3	13.2
Tonga	866	....	....	....	7.1	31.3	63.6	7.5	12.7	15.8	3.4	39.3	20.2	11.5	25.7	18.9
Vanuatu	846	....	....	....	....	....	7.9	.9	3.0	−12.9	1.2	49.1	8.7	27.0	13.1	26.2
Vietnam	582	....	....	....	....	....	....	....	....	....	....	....	....	....	....	....
Europe																
Albania	914	....	....	....	....	....	....	....	....	....	....	....	....	....	....	....
Armenia	911	....	....	....	....	....	....	....	....	....	....	....	....	....	....	....
Azerbaijan	912	....	....	....	....	....	....	....	....	....	....	....	....	....	....	....
Belarus	913	....	....	....	....	....	....	....	....	....	....	....	....	....	....	....
Bosnia & Herzegovina	963	....	....	....	....	....	....	....	....	....	....	....	....	....	....	....
Bulgaria	918	....	....	....	....	....	....	....	....	....	....	....	....	....	....	....
Croatia	960	....	....	....	....	....	....	....	....	....	....	....	....	....	....	....
Cyprus	423	20.8	12.5	16.0	.5	19.8	14.9	15.0	19.3	15.6	20.0	18.0	11.5	13.7	†10.3	10.3
Czech Republic	935	....	....	....	....	....	....	....	....	....	....	....	....	....	....	....
Czechoslovakia	934	....	....	....	....	....	....	....	....	....	....	7.5	8.3	6.4	6.8	3.8
Estonia	939	....	....	....	....	....	....	....	....	....	....	....	....	....	....	....
Georgia	915	....	....	....	....	....	....	....	....	....	....	....	....	....	....	....
Hungary	944	....	....	....	....	....	....	....	....	....	....	....	2.3	5.1	10.9	8.8
Kazakhstan	916	....	....	....	....	....	....	....	....	....	....	....	....	....	....	....
Kyrgyz Republic	917	....	....	....	....	....	....	....	....	....	....	....	....	....	....	....
Latvia	941	....	....	....	....	....	....	....	....	....	....	....	....	....	....	....
Lithuania	946	....	....	....	....	....	....	....	....	....	....	....	....	....	....	....
Macedonia, FYR	962	....	....	....	....	....	....	....	....	....	....	....	....	....	....	....
Malta	181	11.4	8.5	10.4	19.3	22.7	10.1	13.4	12.0	7.7	10.2	6.1	6.9	−1.2	5.3	5.8
Moldova	921	....	....	....	....	....	....	....	....	....	....	....	....	....	....	....
Poland	964	....	....	....	....	....	....	....	....	....	....	....	....	....	....	....
Romania	968	....	....	26.4	11.5	16.5	13.7	17.2	10.2	13.0	†22.9	37.4	14.3	18.3	21.0	26.5
Russia	922	....	....	....	....	....	....	....	....	†12.8	16.0	14.0	−.7	6.3	†8.7	8.4
Slovak Republic	936	....	....	....	....	....	....	....	....	....	....	....	....	....	....	....
Slovenia	961	....	....	....	....	....	....	....	....	....	....	....	....	....	....	....
Turkey	186	26.0	28.4	25.7	28.0	23.4	33.8	36.5	61.7	74.4	88.2	51.1	29.7	58.7	55.3	†43.8
Ukraine	926	....	....	....	....	....	....	....	....	....	....	....	....	....	....	....
Yugoslavia, SFR	188	23.3	32.3	23.2	32.7	38.3	†19.8	28.2	22.2	37.7	31.5	32.8	38.9	45.9	61.0	82.2
Middle East																
Bahrain	419	20.2	13.4	46.4	26.3	64.9	19.1	19.5	2.6	26.7	35.5	−41.8	93.7	−3.5	9.1	−2.0
Egypt	469	15.7	22.4	30.2	21.5	26.0	34.0	27.0	31.3	†31.7	30.9	31.2	22.6	18.8	18.3	21.0
Iran, I.R. of	429	35.3	30.3	42.8	34.7	43.9	26.1	23.4	35.5	26.3	16.4	25.6	18.7	....	....	....
Iraq	433	13.4	25.4	42.7	39.0	21.2	....	....	....	....	....	....	....	....	....	....
Israel	436	†27.4	22.7	41.6	37.1	40.7	63.2	3.9	57.7	142.6	829.3	141.8	206.9	510.2	168.5	20.8
Jordan	439	8.5	20.4	25.0	32.5	32.6	22.3	28.2	26.3	27.8	20.7	18.9	15.0	8.9	6.6	10.6
Kuwait	443	17.9	8.7	27.7	30.2	36.9	28.6	24.3	16.0	26.3	41.4	12.6	7.6	5.5	−1.5	.4
Lebanon	446	21.0	21.2	23.9	11.2	5.2	28.3	19.9	26.9	31.8	40.1	20.2	27.1	23.6	56.1	171.9
Libya	672	20.3	29.9	56.5	4.9	29.9	25.5	14.9	35.9	26.6	15.7	−7.9	−5.0	.2	27.0	−6.4
Oman	449	....	4.1	82.9	38.4	39.5	25.5	11.6	6.8	32.0	38.7	26.7	23.4	9.9	21.1	−6.8
Qatar	453	43.5	17.0	35.0	66.7	54.7	31.9	15.4	9.6	17.0	41.7	14.6	−.9	22.0	9.2	11.2
Saudi Arabia	456	40.6	35.1	43.5	81.9	66.5	53.9	27.4	13.7	17.4	33.0	20.2	†10.7	6.0	1.1	9.2
Syrian Arab Rep.	463	26.2	20.3	45.8	26.0	23.3	28.8	27.2	16.8	34.4	15.8	20.5	26.0	25.3	20.6	11.8
United Arab Emirates	466	....	....	167.5	46.1	89.9	−7.2	13.1	3.7	29.1	23.7	15.6	8.0	29.0	6.4	4.4
Yemen Arab Rep.	473	....	....	34.0	79.7	124.8	51.3	32.2	19.3	10.6	12.2	25.4	23.6	27.5	20.0	25.5
Yemen, P.D. Rep.	459	9.5	13.2	13.0	28.4	43.7	47.1	†15.5	29.5	31.6	12.3	19.1	16.9	14.1	8.0	4.4
Yemen, Republic of	474	....	....	....	....	....	....	....	....	....	....	....	....	....	....	....
Western Hemisphere																
Antigua and Barbuda	311	....	....	....	....	8.6	−3.7	10.4	15.5	11.2	15.9	13.5	23.8	20.8	11.8	18.2
Argentina	213	110.0	74.6	54.5	152.9	353.5	227.2	172.6	187.4	91.8	100.5	139.1	401.2	655.0	428.2	113.0
Aruba	314	....	....	....	....	....	....	....	....	....	....	....	....	....	....	....
Bahamas, The	313	8.1	1.4	.5	9.6	19.6	2.7	13.4	15.4	14.7	11.0	15.6	13.1	9.3	5.8	9.9
Barbados	316	13.1	−5.4	24.9	14.2	11.9	9.9	22.7	27.8	13.0	13.8	6.4	10.8	7.6	9.1	9.3
Belize	339	....	....	....	....	....	2.6	26.6	3.2	12.8	8.9	6.2	18.5	4.4	8.5	18.7
Bolivia	218	25.9	32.7	44.3	23.2	47.5	29.4	13.0	14.8	39.0	27.2	230.4	172.7	1,428.9	6,987.9	184.4
Brazil	223	25.0	43.1	35.5	42.9	38.9	44.8	†51.1	73.1	61.4	88.1	84.0	135.8	270.1	322.5	†268.7
Chile	228	144.6	334.0	297.3	306.7	†318.7	99.4	94.1	66.3	62.1	28.6	34.8	21.5	22.4	47.3	25.3
Colombia	233	29.2	35.0	25.2	23.2	34.0	33.8	†27.9	22.8	45.0	35.7	20.9	25.4	23.9	20.2	....
Costa Rica	238	19.6	21.9	30.5	42.3	34.4	31.5	27.7	34.4	15.9	87.2	27.0	37.0	17.1	15.6	21.3
Dominica	321	....	....	....	....	12.6	9.5	19.5	43.9	2.4	2.3	18.4	9.8	16.0	4.6	14.9
Dominican Republic	243	25.6	26.9	42.3	16.0	−.2	18.2	1.2	12.4	6.4	8.5	8.9	18.6	28.4	17.8	78.9
Ecuador	248	23.3	30.9	45.1	8.1	41.8	20.8	8.2	30.5	28.6	9.8	−5.5	−18.7	19.0	−15.1	−19.7
El Salvador	253	22.6	18.6	16.6	21.2	30.9	13.2	11.9	9.1	4.8	10.6	†10.2	11.3	15.5	29.2	24.4
Grenada	328	18.7	2.9	−1.8	22.4	18.9	11.1	18.2	18.5	6.1	7.8	3.9	.2	1.0	19.4	28.1
Guatemala	258	24.4	21.6	15.3	21.0	30.1	18.8	14.0	8.0	10.1	12.6	15.0	−1.6	11.3	33.1	21.4
Guyana	336	20.0	17.0	18.4	40.2	7.8	24.7	9.5	8.0	14.8	16.9	26.0	20.3	16.9	21.8	19.3
Haiti	263	31.6	27.7	19.8	25.9	38.2	19.9	17.6	10.0	23.1	12.2	3.3	4.5	13.2	12.9	9.2
Honduras	268	13.9	21.7	3.4	10.4	32.4	18.6	21.0	7.8	8.7	20.1	17.0	10.5	−2.0	9.4
Jamaica	343	12.3	†9.3	18.8	20.6	8.4	16.4	18.2	15.2	20.4	28.3	26.2	27.2	19.0	24.8	27.7
Mexico	273	17.6	26.3	20.9	17.9	48.1	†24.0	33.2	35.8	36.6	49.1	†70.9	61.9	68.5	41.1	72.3
Netherlands Antilles	353	20.8	7.5	23.8	14.0	12.7	13.6	12.3	3.3	12.2	17.9	17.6	5.7	−3.4	2.4	−6.1
Nicaragua	278	29.2	41.5	16.3	.7	33.0	5.8	−7.1	67.1	29.7	37.9	24.8	†53.5	73.3	140.2	234.5
Panama	283	30.0	13.1	19.3	3.3	5.5	16.3	23.8	25.3	26.1	18.6	12.1	−.1	6.6	4.8	20.9
Paraguay	288	23.6	29.0	20.9	26.2	23.4	31.5	30.5	24.2	34.6	19.5	5.7	16.7	16.8	20.8	27.4
Peru	293	24.0	23.1	33.6	15.8	24.0	23.6	61.1	92.0	83.5	68.7	72.0	103.3	127.2	156.5	54.0
St. Kitts and Nevis	361	....	....	....	....	....	....	....	....	13.0	20.9	12.1	15.1	13.4	19.5	13.9
St. Lucia	362	....	....	....	....	22.4	5.9	19.6	17.5	11.8	17.5	9.3	14.5	11.5	19.9	25.4
St. Vincent & Grenadines	364	....	....	....	....	18.4	9.9	27.5	23.3	4.8	18.7	12.6	12.5	12.7	14.5	15.7
Suriname	366	13.0	22.6	7.1	18.8	36.5	18.8	16.1	11.7	7.8	19.5	11.1	10.9	20.3	32.1	25.3
Trinidad and Tobago	369	19.3	13.8	30.4	29.4	34.2	26.6	24.6	29.7	12.6	27.8	34.6	7.3	5.1	1.2	−2.7
Uruguay	298	68.1	66.9	66.7	†106.8	99.1	81.7	91.5	85.5	73.2	48.9	†76.1	11.5	73.2	56.4	94.5
Venezuela, Rep. Bol.	299	19.7	19.7	35.6	53.3	23.3	25.6	15.3	7.5	17.3	13.4	8.5	23.6	18.3	9.7	12.9

Percent Change over Previous Year

1987	1988	1989	1990	1991	1992	1993	1994	1995	1996	1997	1998	1999	2000	2001		
															Asia (cont.)	
16.4	7.7	7.4	11.6	18.9	29.3	18.1	17.4	13.8	20.1	19.9	7.9	4.3	12.1	11.7	Pakistan	564
1.5	4.4	5.3	4.3	17.6	12.5	17.8	-1.3	13.7	30.7	7.7	2.5	9.2	5.0	1.6	Papua New Guinea	853
11.7	23.3	30.2	22.4	17.7	13.1	†28.1	26.7	23.9	23.7	23.1	8.6	16.9	8.1	3.6	Philippines	566
27.7	7.8	16.7	19.3	-1.9	.7	1.4	13.9	24.4	6.3	15.2	2.5	15.7	16.3	6.1	Samoa	862
19.8	13.5	22.5	20.0	12.4	8.9	8.5	14.4	8.5	9.8	10.3	30.2	8.5	-2.0	5.9	Singapore	576
34.7	32.1	-.4	9.8	23.9	24.5	15.6	25.1	9.2	15.3	6.7	2.5	7.0			Solomon Islands	813
15.4	14.9	8.4	19.9	21.9	16.8	23.3	19.7	36.3	11.0	15.6	13.1	12.6	12.8	14.4	Sri Lanka	524
20.4	18.2	26.2	26.7	19.8	15.6	18.4	12.9	17.0	12.6	16.5	9.7	5.4	3.4	2.2	Thailand	578
19.5	-2.4	7.0	20.6	12.0	-4.8	25.0	6.6	.7	5.3	7.8	14.7	11.9	18.8	14.9	Tonga	866
-6.6	5.9	47.6	5.6	-.7	-2.6	5.0	2.9	13.4	10.1	-.4	12.6	-9.2	5.5	5.7	Vanuatu	846
						12.3			25.7	24.3	23.5	66.4	35.4	27.3	Vietnam	582
															Europe	
								51.8	43.8	28.5	20.6	22.3	12.0	19.9	Albania	914
						1,076.8	740.4	64.3	35.1	29.2	36.7	14.0	38.6	13.6	Armenia	911
						825.8	1,116.5	25.4	17.1	41.4	†-17.4	20.1	†73.4	†-10.6	Azerbaijan	912
								158.4	†52.4	111.4	276.0	132.7	219.3	58.9	Belarus	913
											22.0	27.5	10.3	91.7	Bosnia & Herzegovina	963
					231.0	-63.3			117.8	†362.1	11.6	11.9	28.8	26.1	Bulgaria	918
							74.6	40.4	49.2	38.4	13.0	-1.8	29.1	45.7	Croatia	960
13.1	17.5	15.3	16.8	14.9	13.9	16.3	12.5	11.4	10.5	11.0	8.3	15.0	8.0	12.4	Cyprus	423
							20.4	29.3	6.4	†1.7	3.4	2.6	16.0	11.2	Czech Republic	935
6.0	11.5	4.7	-.7	26.7	20.4										Czechoslovakia	934
					76.5	†42.8	30.4	27.5	36.8	37.8	4.2	23.7	25.7	23.0	Estonia	939
									41.4	44.0	-1.1	21.1	39.4	†20.5	Georgia	915
9.6	2.2	16.5	29.2	29.4	41.3	17.7	14.2	20.9	22.1	19.8	15.4	15.8	12.5	16.7	Hungary	944
						576.0	108.2		20.9	†8.2	-14.1	84.4	45.0	20.8	Kazakhstan	916
									14.8	32.2	17.5	33.7	11.7	11.3	Kyrgyz Republic	917
							50.3	-21.4	19.6	37.0	6.7	8.3	27.0	19.8	Latvia	941
							63.0	28.9	-3.5	34.1	14.5	7.7	16.5	21.4	Lithuania	946
							-57.1	†11.7	-1.0	23.5	13.0	32.0	21.4	32.1	Macedonia, FYR	962
9.9	8.7	10.1	11.3	9.0	9.4	10.5	14.9	†11.8	8.6	8.0	8.1	9.8	4.0	8.4	Malta	181
					358.0	318.8	115.7	65.3	†14.8	34.5	†-8.3	42.9	41.7	35.8	Moldova	921
34.2	63.4	527.3	160.1	†47.4	57.5	36.0	38.2	35.0	31.0	29.1	25.2	19.4	11.8	15.0	Poland	964
3.9	10.3	5.3	†18.6	102.2	75.4	143.3	138.1	70.1	67.4	105.0	48.9	44.9	38.0	46.2	Romania	968
							216.5	112.6	29.6	28.0	37.5	56.7	58.4	36.1	Russia	922
							17.4	18.4	16.2	†8.4	14.7	15.0	12.6	7.7	Slovak Republic	936
					123.0	62.2	44.7	29.8	23.3	23.3	19.5	15.1	18.0	30.4	Slovenia	961
50.5	65.3	68.9	53.2	82.7	78.7	64.4	145.3	103.6	117.3	97.5	89.7	98.3	40.0	87.2	Turkey	186
						1,809.2	567.9	115.5	35.1	33.9	†22.2	40.6	44.5	43.0	Ukraine	926
131.5	242.0	2,347.0	39.3												Yugoslavia, SFR	188
															Middle East	
9.4	4.0	4.4	-11.6	†20.5	4.9	5.7	6.0	7.4	3.1	7.8	16.8	4.1	10.2	9.2	Bahrain	419
21.0	21.5	17.5	28.7	19.3	19.4	13.2	11.2	9.9	10.8	10.8	10.8	5.7	11.6	13.2	Egypt	469
19.3	20.1	22.5	18.0	25.6	24.4	30.3	33.3	30.1	32.5	23.7	20.4	21.5	22.4	27.6	Iran, I.R. of	429
															Iraq	433
27.2	22.3	21.1	19.4	17.7	†25.5	22.0	24.6	21.7	25.0	15.0	19.7	15.5	8.0	9.5	Israel	436
15.7	15.5	16.5	8.3	15.8	3.3	†9.3	3.3	5.7	-.9	7.6	6.3	15.5	7.6	8.1	Jordan	439
2.5	6.9	4.8			.7	5.6	5.4	9.4	-.6	3.9	-.8	1.6	6.3	12.8	Kuwait	443
354.3	47.8	13.4	55.1	43.9	114.1	33.1	25.3	16.4	26.4	19.6	16.1	11.7	9.8	7.5	Lebanon	446
3.0	-4.6	11.3	19.0	-1.1	16.5	5.9	14.0	9.6	1.0	-3.7	3.8	7.4	3.1	4.3	Libya	672
5.3	5.9	9.4	10.0	5.5	3.1	3.2	6.7	7.7	8.1	24.5	4.8	6.4	6.0	9.2	Oman	449
8.6	-8.4	13.9	-4.6	2.4	8.0	†5.8	9.1	1.1	5.6	9.9	8.0	11.4	10.7	—	Qatar	453
4.1	6.4	.9	4.6	14.6	†2.6	3.4	3.0	3.4	7.3	5.2	3.6	6.8	4.5	5.1	Saudi Arabia	456
11.6	22.0	19.7	26.4	14.5	19.4	30.3	12.2	9.2	10.2	8.2	10.5	13.4	19.0	23.5	Syrian Arab Rep.	463
5.5	5.9	8.7	-8.2	14.5	4.6	-1.6	7.9	10.2	6.9	9.0	4.2	11.5	15.3	23.2	United Arab Emirates	466
10.1	6.2	4.5													Yemen Arab Rep.	473
7.6	6.1	4.3													Yemen, P.D. Rep.	459
				11.3	20.9	31.1	32.5	50.7	8.1	11.2	11.8	13.8	25.3	20.9	Yemen, Republic of	474
															Western Hemisphere	
18.9	11.2	13.3	4.8	15.2	5.7	8.6	10.9	21.2	-4.0	7.7	15.7	9.9	6.4	5.8	Antigua and Barbuda	311
163.1	442.8	2,235.2	†1,098.6	141.3	62.5	46.5	†17.6	-2.8	25.5	10.5	4.1	1.5	-19.2		Argentina	213
40.3	18.7	20.9	17.2	18.6	12.5	5.7	13.9	4.2	4.3	4.0	13.6	10.2	2.0	6.4	Aruba	314
15.7	8.4	7.9	16.8	6.6	5.5	16.1	8.7	8.5	5.6	23.5	16.2	10.6	9.3	4.9	Bahamas, The	313
14.3	11.1	1.1	13.8	-1.1	5.0	2.9	8.9	4.9	19.3	8.8	7.6	12.1	9.4	2.1	Barbados	316
21.4	4.3	13.9	15.2	10.1	13.0	3.3	8.4	18.2	7.6	11.5	5.9	15.8	12.4	12.3	Belize	339
†45.0	28.6	22.2	52.8	50.5	34.5	33.7	24.2	7.7	†24.2	16.7	12.9	5.7	.4	2.2	Bolivia	218
213.7	†803.7	1,462.7	1,289.2	633.6	1,606.6	2,936.6	1,211.9	31.9	12.2	18.4	10.0	7.4	4.3	12.1	Brazil	223
35.0	27.1	31.2	23.5	28.1	23.3	23.4	11.3	25.8	19.6	16.3	9.6	14.8	6.2	4.5	Chile	228
	21.1		†22.6	20.9	45.6	37.6	39.7	21.7	24.4	41.9	20.9	13.8	14.6	16.0	Colombia	233
16.3	40.2	16.4	27.5	33.7	24.5	15.2	22.0	4.8	47.6	†16.4	26.3	29.0	18.4	10.4	Costa Rica	238
29.6	-3.5	11.9	23.0	15.3	12.1	-2.2	4.4	23.0	6.9	3.6	6.2	9.3	-1.9	6.2	Dominica	321
13.1	50.2	31.2	42.5	35.3	27.0	21.1	12.1	17.8	18.4	24.2	16.6	23.7	17.4	26.9	Dominican Republic	243
-3.7	-20.3	-7.1	†13.8	6.5	4.8	47.1	36.5	6.1	15.6	9.0	†-7.0	†-32.8	11.1	21.5	Ecuador	248
6.2	12.1	12.8	32.4	23.5	30.6	27.4	25.0	10.9	15.5	18.8	10.4	9.1	1.0		El Salvador	253
11.7	18.2	7.5	10.0	5.2	7.5	21.9	12.2	9.6	8.7	10.4	11.8	13.4	15.1	10.5	Grenada	328
7.6	19.8	18.1	25.8	48.9	31.1	15.0	12.0	15.8	13.8	†18.4	19.4	12.5	35.5	18.1	Guatemala	258
46.4	36.6	51.4	52.6	73.4	62.3	†19.7	12.5	24.4	19.4	10.1	6.7	10.8	8.4	8.7	Guyana	336
12.7	-10.3	37.6	2.5	11.9	30.5	29.2	31.4	27.1	1.1	†24.8	9.7	23.0	20.1	14.1	Haiti	263
22.0	14.8	14.5	21.4	17.5	22.4	10.4	30.3	29.2	41.2	†50.5	22.9	24.7	24.4	17.4	Honduras	268
12.6	32.3	6.6	21.5	51.4	75.8	35.9	40.6	31.8	10.9	13.3	7.7	12.2	13.0	8.6	Jamaica	343
141.3	-19.8	124.7	81.9	48.7	24.0	15.2	19.3	31.7	25.3	†34.6	17.2	14.2	-5.7	14.1	Mexico	273
8.9	13.1	-.2	10.1	7.9	8.3	9.4	7.5	-3.5	2.1	4.0	5.6	2.8	14.8		Netherlands Antilles	353
544.2	12,513.1	2,700.2	7,677.8	1,519.6	20.1	25.2	65.9	35.1	†40.6	52.5	32.1	18.8	9.4	41.0	Nicaragua	278
-3.4	-27.6	-2.9	36.6	31.0	25.0	17.2	15.5	7.9	6.1	15.0	13.0	8.5	10.0	9.6	Panama	283
35.0	†20.0	62.9	54.4	49.9	40.1	29.0	23.6	†15.7	14.1	7.7	9.9	18.2	4.8	16.4	Paraguay	288
106.5	621.0	1,917.3	6,384.9	230.6	88.2	71.8	37.2	29.3	37.2	30.8	17.3	14.5	-.4	2.1	Peru	293
-8.7	8.8	21.2	7.7	5.8	15.2	11.0	1.0	14.9	2.2	14.4	11.1	3.8	27.8	1.3	St. Kitts and Nevis	361
16.3	7.5	16.7	12.5	7.8	4.1	1.9	10.2	9.9	4.3	3.9	10.7	9.0	5.5	8.0	St. Lucia	362
7.4	1.1	13.3	14.0	-1.2	8.4	8.5	5.5	5.4	5.9	12.4	15.4	16.5	5.5	8.0	St. Vincent & Grenadines	364
28.0	23.7	18.2	4.3	23.6	19.4	65.7	204.7	181.5	38.5	19.0	†37.8	37.9	80.5	28.2	Suriname	366
3.5	.6	6.4	6.2	2.5	-6.9	15.3	16.7	4.0	†5.8	11.3	14.5	4.2	11.7	6.9	Trinidad and Tobago	369
57.4	83.1	104.0	118.5	79.8	50.0	37.4	42.1	39.0	36.6	28.4	†19.3	13.1	7.2	19.0	Uruguay	298
†30.9	20.4	41.9	64.9	47.6	17.7	25.5	68.9	36.6	†70.2	61.1	15.4	20.7	23.1	15.3	Venezuela, Rep. Bol.	299

Ratio of Reserve Money to Money plus Quasi-Money

39ab i

		1972	1973	1974	1975	1976	1977	1978	1979	1980	1981	1982	1983	1984	1985	1986
																Percent
Industrial Countries																
United States	111	11.0	11.2	11.2	10.7	10.0	9.9	10.1	9.9	9.6	9.0	8.7	8.3	8.0	8.1	8.4
Canada	156	16.2	15.6	14.9	14.9	13.7	13.5	12.9	11.9	12.0	†10.2	10.1	10.3	9.9	9.9	9.9
Australia	193	11.3	11.8	9.5	10.1	10.1	10.0	9.0	8.8	8.4	8.5	8.4	8.4	8.3	7.9	7.8
Japan	158	10.9	12.5	13.0	11.9	11.3	11.1	11.2	11.1	11.1	10.3	10.2	10.0	10.2	9.7	9.6
New Zealand	196	13.3	14.6	14.5	10.6	9.4	8.9	8.6	7.9	6.5	6.3	6.0	6.3	5.6	4.7	3.3
Euro Area																
Austria	122	22.0	19.8	19.4	19.1	17.1	16.4	16.6	15.6	14.8	14.3	13.4	13.6	13.1	12.5	12.3
Belgium	124	19.8	19.5	18.7	17.3	16.4	16.4	16.4	16.0	†15.6	15.0	14.0	13.3	12.8	12.0	11.4
Finland	172	7.3	7.2	7.2	6.8	6.3	6.2	6.5	8.8	10.3	8.7	8.8	9.7	11.9	11.3	10.3
France	132	40.1	37.6	36.1	24.5	23.4	†22.3	†22.3	21.1	22.6	21.3	23.0	21.6	21.7	25.2	24.1
Germany	134	22.2	21.8	20.1	18.5	18.9	18.6	19.1	19.0	17.5	16.6	16.4	16.4	16.2	†14.2	14.3
Ireland	178	24.2	25.3	26.4	25.3	26.2	24.7	25.1	24.3	23.4	20.4	†19.1	19.8	19.3	19.7	20.6
Italy	136	20.6	19.8	†20.7	23.3	23.2	22.8	23.0	21.9	22.0	22.2	21.3	22.0	22.5	23.8	23.6
Luxembourg	137	....	....	....	....	....	....	....	....	....	....	....	....	....	1.1	1.1
Netherlands	138	12.9	11.8	11.1	11.1	10.4	10.1	9.7	9.5	9.7	9.2	9.3	10.0	—	9.9	9.5
Portugal	182	22.8	20.0	23.7	29.0	†26.7	24.1	23.0	†22.6	20.4	21.6	22.1	20.8	17.0	14.4	14.0
Denmark	128	18.9	17.0	16.5	18.1	16.8	13.5	13.6	14.0	13.1	12.9	11.9	10.0	9.4	11.9	12.0
Iceland	176	31.9	35.3	35.0	36.6	37.5	39.5	40.0	38.8	39.4	52.3	47.7	47.3	†48.7	39.2	37.1
Norway	142	17.3	16.2	16.6	16.9	†16.4	15.7	15.8	15.2	14.9	13.0	12.5	11.8	11.4	10.6	10.3
Sweden	144	12.2	11.7	14.4	12.8	13.5	13.6	13.2	15.5	12.5	12.3	12.1	†11.9	11.7	11.7	12.9
Switzerland	146	24.8	24.0	†23.6	22.5	22.2	21.6	22.8	19.2	19.3	17.1	†17.4	16.9	†15.4	14.6	14.8
United Kingdom	112	13.8	14.2	13.1	†13.4	14.4	13.9	13.3	13.0	10.6	†8.8	8.1	7.6	6.0	5.8	†5.2
Developing Countries																
Africa																
Algeria	612	39.2	45.3	40.7	39.9	42.3	41.8	42.2	44.5	45.7	44.0	36.3	36.3	35.5	34.8	39.7
Angola	614	....	....	....	....	....	....	....	....	....	....	....	....	....	....	....
Benin	638	45.7	44.1	36.3	27.4	33.5	30.0	25.6	†35.3	29.6	38.5	30.3	24.5	26.2	21.5	26.0
Botswana	616					38.0	33.5	29.4	28.7	26.4	23.3	18.9	15.4	15.4	10.7	14.2
Burkina Faso	748	58.7	52.2	51.1	48.2	42.2	44.1	35.7	†43.0	40.6	41.3	40.1	52.5	61.8	55.5	64.2
Burundi	618	61.4	54.5	55.7	56.7	62.9	68.1	61.8	54.6	59.6	62.9	57.1	55.8	58.4	59.5	60.4
Cameroon	622	42.8	41.1	37.2	34.4	32.5	†30.7	30.9	30.0	28.6	29.7	26.3	26.8	21.8	21.3	26.2
Cape Verde	624					102.7	102.7	101.1	97.2	94.0	87.7	87.7	90.1	85.8	82.4	77.4
Central African Rep.	626	56.4	56.0	54.7	56.5	46.9	†54.3	58.9	64.9	65.7	69.3	70.9	70.7	70.4	64.6	71.1
Chad	628	69.6	65.2	60.8	70.5	67.2	64.7	59.8	71.9	73.9	68.7	70.9	71.0	68.2	66.3	64.9
Comoros	632	....	....	....	....	....	....	....	....	....	....	56.0	46.1	48.1	46.6	59.9
Congo, Dem. Rep. of	636	57.4	48.9	45.0	57.4	75.9	61.5	62.2	48.5	63.8	66.8	73.2	96.6	83.4	82.2	83.0
Congo, Rep. of	634	49.8	49.0	46.1	50.4	46.7	†48.0	45.6	45.4	43.4	34.4	37.9	40.1	37.0	34.1	39.3
Côte d'Ivoire	662	50.4	46.1	42.8	44.3	37.6	34.8	41.5	†40.6	40.0	39.9	36.3	37.2	37.4	41.4	42.1
Djibouti	611	....	....	....	....	....	....	....	....	....	....	....	....	19.6	16.0	15.9
Equatorial Guinea	642	....	....	....	....	....	....	....	....	....	....	....	....	....	60.2	80.6
Ethiopia	644	50.3	46.5	51.4	64.9	69.2	58.6	57.0	55.4	59.6	61.6	60.8	†52.9	58.8	53.0	59.1
Gabon	646	31.4	30.8	34.0	27.2	24.0	†25.1	25.7	25.3	24.1	22.3	21.4	19.9	20.3	16.7	16.4
Gambia, The	648	23.3	28.2	25.3	24.2	19.7	17.7	†23.1	29.8	29.9	33.8	34.3	36.5	†33.8	40.3	36.9
Ghana	652	48.4	50.6	54.3	58.2	60.2	60.8	66.6	68.0	66.4	68.1	63.2	64.6	62.7	58.1	62.8
Guinea	656	....	....	....	....	....	....	....	....	....	....	....	....	....	....	....
Guinea-Bissau	654	....	....	....	....	....	....	....	....	....	....	....	....	....	....	98.9
Kenya	664	29.4	26.0	30.7	23.7	23.7	25.8	24.5	27.0	27.4	25.2	27.1	25.2	24.9	27.0	28.4
Lesotho	666	....	....	....	....	....	....	....	....	34.5	29.5	24.8	33.4	34.1	35.6	38.9
Liberia	668	....	....	16.4	17.6	14.1	15.0	20.9	19.6	†35.9	39.1	43.8	49.5	59.4	70.6	82.8
Madagascar	674	49.1	49.9	48.8	51.2	50.4	47.1	53.5	†40.8	45.7	49.5	44.9	47.0	41.4	38.1	51.7
Malawi	676	34.4	53.6	51.1	42.9	28.6	39.5	24.7	22.7	27.8	29.7	30.7	30.6	40.7	43.2	58.6
Mali	678	63.7	62.8	54.9	†57.5	62.0	65.5	59.6	†63.5	64.7	63.2	62.2	57.5	†54.2	56.2	59.6
Mauritania	682	41.8	39.0	58.4	41.6	36.3	39.0	41.5	45.9	42.9	43.8	42.7	39.5	35.5	40.5	36.0
Mauritius	684	32.1	29.3	30.0	33.6	37.1	39.0	37.7	33.5	30.1	30.1	27.1	26.1	24.4	21.9	20.5
Morocco	686	42.6	41.9	39.2	37.5	38.6	37.3	36.6	37.4	35.5	34.6	†30.5	29.4	29.7	28.2	29.9
Mozambique	688	....	....	....	....	....	....	....	....	....	....	....	....	40.8	41.6	41.4
Namibia	728															
Niger	692	50.0	48.0	51.9	45.1	48.4	45.7	48.8	46.4	44.6	43.7	50.3	46.3	48.2	53.9	52.6
Nigeria	694	47.1	†46.5	61.7	61.0	55.1	50.7	50.0	44.3	51.2	46.7	46.2	42.1	38.8	38.2	39.9
Rwanda	714	79.6	76.0	75.3	68.3	66.6	60.0	55.6	63.5	54.9	†43.7	44.8	44.7	43.0	41.1	41.1
São Tomé and Príncipe	716															
Senegal	722	42.1	41.7	42.3	40.8	34.7	34.7	35.7	†31.7	34.9	39.6	40.7	37.8	35.6	36.0	37.7
Seychelles	718	27.5	27.9	28.3	25.8	24.0	26.1	26.4	28.5	36.2	33.5	34.5	35.8	30.2	29.6	26.2
Sierra Leone	724	50.3	49.3	46.6	46.6	44.3	42.4	52.3	67.1	51.1	50.2	60.3	57.3	63.5	57.0	62.3
Somalia	726	56.0	55.3	52.9	52.6	52.6	54.5	57.6	52.1	55.5	40.8	38.9	49.8	42.5	52.5
South Africa	199	10.1	9.8	9.8	9.4	9.2	8.9	8.6	8.5	11.2	11.2	8.7	8.7	8.4	8.2	8.1
Sudan	732	52.0	53.8	54.5	54.4	53.0	60.1	62.2	63.5	55.3	62.8	58.1	†52.1	61.1	†64.7	71.9
Swaziland	734			15.6	22.0	43.6	52.0	38.7	39.3	42.8	35.0	34.1	40.1	44.5	40.4	58.0
Tanzania	738	41.5	35.4	36.3	33.8	32.1	31.2	33.6	31.8	31.7	34.5	34.9	30.5	38.3	35.7	39.2
Togo	742	45.8	45.0	33.0	45.6	50.9	45.8	44.1	†40.5	43.7	57.6	60.6	66.6	72.8	81.2	71.8
Tunisia	744	33.4	32.9	33.4	31.3	28.9	26.7	26.1	24.7	23.4	24.0	24.7	24.9	24.6	23.4	22.5
Uganda	746	36.0	33.9	33.7	43.7	47.2	45.3	53.6	60.2	61.1	42.2	45.0	51.5	52.8	66.6	64.0
Zambia	754	31.0	33.8	29.1	37.1	37.2	32.7	37.6	30.3	31.6	34.2	29.5	30.3	30.4	30.2	42.3
Zimbabwe	698	....	....	....	....	....	....	....	19.4	20.2	23.3	22.2	24.1	24.4	24.9	27.6
Asia																
Afghanistan, Islamic State of	512	78.1	76.4	76.8	80.0	78.7	82.1	82.0	†84.1	84.6	82.5	†81.1	....	80.5	80.7	81.7
Bangladesh	513	....	....	37.5	34.8	30.1	31.5	31.9	30.2	29.7	27.9	†27.1	25.9	25.7	25.8	23.8
Bhutan	514	....	....	....	....	....	....	....	....	....	....	....	12.8	24.7	46.6	55.2
Cambodia	522	....	....	....	....	....	....	....	....	....	....	....	....	....	....	....
China, P.R.: Mainland	924	....	....	....	....	....	....	....	....	....	....	....	....	....	†41.4	39.2
China, P.R.: Hong Kong	532															
Fiji	819	26.1	34.8	32.3	33.1	28.1	24.5	25.9	24.1	19.8	21.7	21.4	20.1	20.9	21.1	20.3
India	534	58.0	59.5	54.8	50.7	47.6	48.3	†34.1	35.0	34.6	32.8	33.0	31.9	31.6	33.4	32.9
Indonesia	536	....	....	....	62.2	57.7	60.2	54.3	52.1	48.0	44.3	40.6	38.4	34.8	31.8	32.4
Korea	542	29.4	31.5	31.6	34.2	34.2	35.3	35.3	35.1	25.9	17.9	19.2	17.9	17.2	15.1	14.8
Lao People's Democratic Rep.	544															
Malaysia	548	61.8	63.9	62.9	56.3	52.3	52.0	50.9	47.4	44.3	41.5	41.6	39.7	36.9	37.3	35.0
Maldives	556	....	....	....	....	89.4	81.8	54.3	67.1	67.2	†67.4	68.6	84.9	85.0	88.9	81.0
Mongolia	948															
Myanmar	518	74.4	78.3	78.7	83.1	99.2	90.8	88.0	90.3	86.2	86.0	72.0	69.2	67.1	61.1	65.8
Nepal	558	61.2	61.3	54.6	53.3	53.3	47.9	47.0	45.8	43.1	41.4	42.5	40.9	42.0	39.6	42.1
Pakistan	564	44.6	43.9	44.8	40.5	36.7	38.2	37.5	39.9	40.2	39.0	37.7	35.5	39.4	37.3	38.5

Percent

Industrial Countries

1987	1988	1989	1990	1991	1992	1993	1994	1995	1996	1997	1998	1999	2000	2001	Country	
8.5	8.5	8.3	8.6	8.7	9.3	10.0	10.8	10.7	10.6	10.7	10.3	11.4	10.0	9.5	United States	111
10.0	9.5	8.7	8.2	8.3	7.8	7.4	7.0	6.7	6.6	6.3	6.6	7.7	6.3	6.2	Canada	156
7.6	6.9	†9.1	8.6	8.8	8.7	8.7	8.6	8.3	12.1	9.0	8.8	7.4	7.1	7.5	Australia	193
9.4	9.6	9.7	9.7	9.3	9.0	9.3	9.3	9.7	10.3	10.7	10.7	14.4	11.6	13.4	Japan	158
3.4	†3.7	3.3	2.9	2.8	2.8	2.7	2.8	2.8	2.3	2.3	2.4	4.0	3.0	3.1	New Zealand	196

Euro Area

1987	1988	1989	1990	1991	1992	1993	1994	1995	1996	1997	1998	1999	2000	2001	Country	
11.2	10.7	11.3	10.3	9.8	10.1	10.4	10.3	9.7	10.1	9.8	....	....	....	....	Austria	122
10.8	10.3	9.7	9.0	8.7	†8.4	7.7	7.0	7.3	7.1	6.8	....	....	....	....	Belgium	124
13.6	13.1	14.8	11.7	†12.2	12.9	12.8	19.1	18.3	12.6	11.4	10.8	....	....	....	Finland	172
25.7	24.5	23.1	21.5	22.0	19.2	18.3	17.8	17.8	18.1	17.5	....	....	....	....	France	132
14.8	15.6	15.8	15.0	14.9	15.8	14.1	13.5	13.2	12.9	12.4	11.9	....	....	....	Germany	134
20.5	19.9	19.9	18.9	16.6	14.4	13.9	13.2	10.9	9.6	9.5	....	....	....	....	Ireland	178
24.0	23.9	†24.0	23.2	22.6	22.3	18.9	17.6	16.2	16.2	18.5	13.0	....	....	....	Italy	136
1.1	1.0	.8	.9	.7	.7	1.1	....	1.1	1.1	....	....	....	....	....	Luxembourg	137
10.2	10.6	11.1	10.7	8.8	10.9	11.1	11.7	9.7	8.8	9.1	....	....	....	....	Netherlands	138
15.5	15.1	25.6	25.3	25.1	23.6	8.8	7.9	8.3	7.7	7.3	....	....	....	....	Portugal	182
†8.7	8.6	8.2	9.4	†8.6	7.6	10.4	11.7	12.5	15.4	18.9	14.1	28.4	....	....	Denmark	128
28.9	25.7	21.0	16.5	14.6	14.5	12.4	12.5	10.0	11.9	12.1	10.8	....	....	....	Iceland	176
9.3	8.6	8.4	7.9	8.2	8.0	8.9	8.7	8.9	12.7	11.1	8.5	12.6	9.7	8.9	Norway	142
12.7	14.0	14.0	15.0	13.3	16.0	22.7	27.6	22.7	14.0	10.3	10.7	11.5	10.7	....	Sweden	144
14.1	10.9	9.8	10.0	9.5	10.2	9.3	9.0	8.4	†8.0	7.4	7.5	7.8	8.4	9.1	Switzerland	146
†4.5	4.2	3.8	3.5	3.4	†3.4	3.5	3.5	3.3	3.1	3.1	†3.1	3.5	3.1	2.9	United Kingdom	112

Developing Countries

Africa

1987	1988	1989	1990	1991	1992	1993	1994	1995	1996	1997	1998	1999	2000	2001	Country	
39.2	37.6	40.1	39.7	38.2	†37.1	38.6	32.3	31.9	33.4	32.8	31.2	30.6	33.1	37.5	Algeria	612
								71.9	59.8	66.8	63.5	†49.6	38.6	36.5	Angola	614
24.2	28.8	48.5	60.3	67.8	70.0	63.0	43.2	32.5	31.4	36.0	35.7	46.5	51.9	57.0	Benin	638
10.2	11.2	10.7	16.5	23.4	17.1	18.6	16.4	15.1	14.2	13.9	12.4	11.2	11.7	10.1	Botswana	616
67.9	63.8	52.5	53.5	61.8	63.1	67.5	51.7	52.4	52.2	54.8	52.3	43.8	41.3	40.7	Burkina Faso	748
59.3	49.5	44.4	42.4	41.4	43.5	42.2	40.0	44.7	42.8	39.9	42.6	39.2	36.6	35.1	Burundi	618
29.8	†28.5	28.6	26.5	25.9	28.0	23.8	26.2	22.0	31.4	37.1	38.0	36.2	40.8	43.4	Cameroon	622
72.4	65.5	60.5	57.0	53.4	62.2	75.5	41.2	†42.7	36.5	33.1	35.2	32.7	33.3	32.6	Cape Verde	624
68.3	†68.4	66.5	69.5	72.5	76.5	81.2	83.8	84.0	86.3	82.0	78.0	75.7	80.8	76.6	Central African Rep.	626
69.1	†71.0	75.2	71.0	†69.2	72.1	80.2	75.4	80.2	82.4	82.3	80.1	77.1	75.6	72.8	Chad	628
67.1	45.6	52.3	42.0	37.3	36.2	49.2	52.4	50.1	62.2	56.9	†59.1	59.4	65.3	75.9	Comoros	632
85.1	79.9	85.5	82.9	81.0	92.4	84.7	40.3	66.1	....	55.9	....	....	....	....	Congo, Dem. Rep. of	636
41.0	†39.3	37.2	42.3	35.6	39.2	51.1	54.0	58.5	54.9	55.9	50.8	56.9	72.9	72.4	Congo, Rep. of	634
44.4	37.8	32.1	35.1	36.1	32.4	35.9	38.2	36.1	37.1	38.3	43.0	40.4	42.0	50.4	Côte d'Ivoire	662
18.1	16.8	15.8	16.8	16.2	21.0	19.2	19.6	16.2	16.9	17.3	17.7	19.2	18.9	18.5	Djibouti	611
69.4	†58.5	70.9	46.1	57.7	70.7	75.9	56.4	75.4	60.5	60.8	42.2	48.8	53.4	73.3	Equatorial Guinea	642
54.6	58.3	58.1	56.2	61.2	62.8	60.0	52.8	54.7	42.2	40.0	36.1	30.3	36.3	30.4	Ethiopia	644
20.0	†20.8	22.7	24.0	28.7	26.3	24.6	41.1	35.7	39.3	35.9	33.4	31.7	36.5	32.6	Gabon	646
35.3	38.2	40.4	39.6	42.9	38.9	38.4	38.3	42.1	40.0	41.2	40.1	40.9	35.4	35.8	Gambia, The	648
58.0	61.0	48.5	43.9	†37.8	46.7	38.8	47.6	45.8	50.0	45.9	42.4	41.2	40.4	....	Ghana	652
				71.1	64.4	62.4	58.2	58.7	55.9	60.2	†59.3	....	63.1		Guinea	656
73.6	78.1	77.3	14.1	99.2	77.9	73.3	65.3	60.3	56.4	58.1	56.7	62.7	73.1	79.0	Guinea-Bissau	654
30.5	28.8	29.8	30.3	29.3	32.3	38.5	36.0	37.8	32.6	28.0	27.2	27.2	25.9	25.0	Kenya	664
41.6	48.3	40.0	34.6	37.3	26.5	25.0	24.0	29.0	26.0	25.4	30.5	42.8	39.4	25.1	Lesotho	666
92.4	100.5	108.1	....	114.5	96.9	74.4	70.2	71.2	95.2	99.3	49.1	46.0	†54.9	54.5	Liberia	668
52.7	44.6	46.0	39.9	47.2	46.7	35.1	39.6	44.1	56.6	47.3	47.5	50.2	47.9	50.1	Madagascar	674
66.6	61.0	51.9	39.1	38.5	39.0	45.3	46.9	56.9	56.5	55.4	48.0	50.1	37.5	43.9	Malawi	676
60.1	61.4	69.6	74.2	86.4	83.8	84.4	48.8	50.2	47.7	47.2	42.8	47.7	53.8	50.3	Mali	678
37.3	41.7	†44.6	38.3	47.4	53.7	82.7	80.1	79.6	42.4	34.1	30.3	31.0	28.0	25.2	Mauritania	682
20.0	19.3	20.0	19.6	37.6	29.4	23.4	19.4	18.7	19.5	13.4	12.9	12.1	12.4	12.3	Mauritius	684
28.7	28.8	30.2	†31.3	33.5	28.2	28.3	27.3	26.8	27.1	†27.1	27.4	28.1	26.8	27.3	Morocco	686
44.7	42.5	†38.3	34.3	†32.8	33.3	35.0	38.7	34.6	36.7	34.4	28.1	25.1	22.8	27.2	Mozambique	688
			6.1	5.0	9.3	7.8	9.9	8.9	8.4	9.5	8.8	10.7	8.9	9.2	Namibia	728
56.9	60.2	57.6	61.9	66.7	65.9	46.9	51.1	51.5	51.5	40.6	46.4	42.9	48.5		Niger	692
38.7	41.3	50.2	48.4	50.1	†59.9	58.2	56.8	57.3	52.4	47.2	45.0	41.1	41.2	43.5	Nigeria	694
41.2	34.5	30.8	31.9	43.5	37.4	46.7	53.0	43.4	48.9	42.2	37.2	39.6	31.4	34.6	Rwanda	714
								51.4	50.5	57.1	61.2	48.2	49.9	62.2	São Tomé and Príncipe	716
39.8	39.4	44.6	45.1	45.6	47.2	37.6	40.5	39.2	30.1	30.0	29.5	30.3	28.9	34.2	Senegal	722
23.9	24.8	22.1	22.6	25.5	34.1	34.8	51.7	56.6	56.0	46.5	19.6	17.6	16.7	15.9	Seychelles	718
64.2	72.7	72.8	69.6	64.5	57.6	49.0	56.5	53.0	†50.6	71.9	51.4	51.8	50.5	48.9	Sierra Leone	724
42.3	45.3	50.4	....	....	....	....	....								Somalia	726
8.0	8.6	9.2	†9.4	....	†9.6	8.2	8.2	9.2	9.1	8.6	8.0	8.7	8.6	8.5	South Africa	199
67.1	66.7	80.7	72.2	63.9	†67.6	54.6	50.5	51.5	56.6	55.2	55.0	60.2	†64.5	54.0	Sudan	732
51.0	30.8	31.9	31.1	23.5	30.7	24.0	25.4	25.1	20.0	17.6	14.3	13.8	14.1	11.9	Swaziland	734
42.0	41.5	†37.5	37.7	32.7	37.3	†36.2	39.7	41.6	40.9	39.4	40.8	41.8	39.8	35.7	Tanzania	738
70.3	59.6	64.3	65.3	66.8	66.8	54.1	38.4	40.5	37.8	36.1	40.1	42.3	44.4	42.7	Togo	742
21.1	19.1	19.2	20.3	21.5	21.2	21.0	20.8	21.4	25.6	23.8	19.9	21.8	16.9	18.1	Tunisia	744
					†52.5	41.2	44.9	44.8	41.9	38.3	37.4	37.9	39.1	40.6	Uganda	746
38.6	†37.9	37.8	45.6	46.5	....	49.0	45.6	25.0	25.1	29.8	†27.7	27.8	24.6	31.5	Zambia	754
23.2	24.3	23.8	25.9	33.8	34.0	30.2	27.6	22.5	28.1	27.4	32.0	37.9	26.0	30.1	Zimbabwe	698

Asia

1987	1988	1989	1990	1991	1992	1993	1994	1995	1996	1997	1998	1999	2000	2001	Country	
85.2	85.6	87.3	87.6	....	....	....	....	....	....	....	....	....	....	....	Afghanistan, Islamic State of	512
†29.2	28.5	26.8	25.3	22.0	23.8	26.7	29.0	23.4	23.0	22.9	23.3	22.8	21.9	23.7	Bangladesh	513
83.2	56.4	75.2	124.0	121.0	84.1	†99.4	53.7	66.2	65.8	45.2	61.7	58.7	60.6	57.5	Bhutan	514
								68.4	49.3	51.3	65.2	64.5	63.4	61.7	Cambodia	522
35.3	36.6	38.0	38.4	37.6	33.5	†36.8	36.7	34.2	35.3	34.2	30.6	28.7	27.9	....	China, P.R.: Mainland	924
				8.4	9.8	10.0	9.8	9.2	8.4	8.4	7.7	†8.5	7.2	7.7	China, P.R.: Hong Kong	532
18.7	27.6	19.3	17.1	16.7	17.5	16.0	15.8	16.5	16.7	19.2	20.4	28.1	23.3	28.6	Fiji	819
33.4	32.9	33.7	33.3	33.4	31.0	32.3	32.6	33.1	30.5	28.9	27.4	26.1	24.4	23.5	India	534
29.2	21.8	20.2	16.3	14.3	†14.3	12.9	13.4	12.4	13.3	14.7	14.3	15.9	17.8	15.4	Indonesia	536
18.5	19.9	21.9	20.1	19.5	18.8	20.6	18.9	19.0	14.4	11.1	8.0	8.7	6.8	7.0	Korea	542
		49.6	49.8	51.2	48.3	48.2	44.7	43.6	42.6	37.0	32.5	31.2	34.0	32.1	Lao People's Democratic Rep.	544
35.5	37.1	40.0	44.4	43.4	†41.0	22.5	27.1	28.0	†30.1	32.7	20.4	29.0	24.4	22.1	Malaysia	548
74.2	79.4	78.9	82.7	80.8	96.2	84.0	77.2	67.9	63.2	59.5	53.7	55.5	55.6	56.0	Maldives	556
				20.8	38.4	33.4	37.8	36.8	42.8	37.0	44.5	50.9	52.0	43.4	Mongolia	948
48.7	65.9	137.5	121.4	†87.7	85.5	81.3	73.8	69.1	65.6	66.0	62.3	57.0	53.8	56.8	Myanmar	518
40.7	38.4	38.8	40.2	41.9	40.2	41.9	39.6	37.2	36.5	36.2	37.1	33.6	33.8	....	Nepal	558
39.6	40.7	44.4	46.1	49.3	41.5	40.1	39.6	41.0	32.9	31.4	32.8	35.6	31.1	35.7	Pakistan	564

Ratio of Reserve Money to Money plus Quasi-Money

39ab *i*

		1972	1973	1974	1975	1976	1977	1978	1979	1980	1981	1982	1983	1984	1985	1986
																Percent
Asia (cont.)																
Papua New Guinea	853	....	32.8	25.5	57.9	60.5	47.5	43.2	41.2	18.0	16.0	15.9	21.2	17.1	15.9	13.5
Philippines	566	64.3	58.6	62.8	62.7	55.0	52.9	52.9	57.7	53.8	50.4	44.8	†39.0	52.5	53.8	55.5
Samoa	862	3.3	3.2	3.1	6.1	6.3	7.1	6.5	5.7	27.8	22.4	19.0	24.2	25.1	47.9	55.6
Singapore	576	24.5	29.2	26.7	26.9	27.9	29.6	31.0	29.8	27.0	24.4	25.0	24.4	24.5	24.7	23.6
Solomon Islands	813							88.6	68.0	44.5	30.1	39.3	43.6	44.8	34.0	31.9
Sri Lanka	524	46.4	53.0	51.2	46.2	43.8	45.7	39.1	33.5	31.1	30.6	30.2	31.6	31.8	35.7	35.4
Thailand	578	33.1	31.9	30.0	28.6	†26.7	24.3	23.8	24.5	22.8	20.8	18.8	16.8	14.8	14.6	14.2
Tonga	866	....	....	....	....	....	....	....	....	....	....	109.3	120.7	129.6	108.8	113.3
Vanuatu	846	....	....	....	....	10.5	11.5	13.2	16.0	16.1	12.1	8.5	9.2	9.2	9.9	8.8
Vietnam	582	....	....	....	....	....	....	....	....	....	....	....	....	....	....	....
Europe																
Albania	914	....	....	....	....	....	....	....	....	....	....	....	....	....	....	....
Armenia	911	....	....	....	....	....	....	....	....	....	....	....	....	....	....	....
Azerbaijan	912	....	....	....	....	....	....	....	....	....	....	....	....	....	....	....
Belarus	913	....	....	....	....	....	....	....	....	....	....	....	....	....	....	....
Bosnia & Herzegovina	963	....	....	....	....	....	....	....	....	....	....	....	....	....	....	....
Bulgaria	918	....	....	....	....	....	....	....	....	....	....	....	....	....	....	....
Croatia	960	....	....	....	....	....	....	....	....	....	....	....	....	....	....	....
Cyprus	423	36.3	33.9	33.6	33.9	34.9	34.3	34.6	34.8	38.4	39.3	41.3	42.9	44.3	†41.6	40.8
Czech Republic	935	....	....	....	....	....	....	....	....	....	....	....	....	....	....	....
Czechoslovakia	934	....	....	....	17.1	....	....	....	....	30.6	27.8	24.5	23.1	22.7	22.5	22.2
Estonia	939	....	....	....	....	....	....	....	....	....	....	....	....	....	....	....
Georgia	915	....	....	....	....	....	....	....	....	....	....	....	....	....	....	....
Hungary	944	....	....	....	....	....	....	....	....	....	....	86.4	75.8	64.4	66.2	65.0
Kazakhstan	916	....	....	....	....	....	....	....	....	....	....	....	....	....	....	....
Kyrgyz Republic	917	....	....	....	....	....	....	....	....	....	....	....	....	....	....	....
Latvia	941	....	....	....	....	....	....	....	....	....	....	....	....	....	....	....
Lithuania	946	....	....	....	....	....	....	....	....	....	....	....	....	....	....	....
Macedonia, FYR	962	....	....	....	....	....	....	....	....	....	....	....	....	....	....	....
Malta	181	50.6	44.9	47.2	56.7	58.7	59.0	62.7	62.2	58.8	59.7	57.7	57.5	64.5	61.8	59.0
Moldova	921	....	....	....	....	....	....	....	....	....	....	....	....	....	....	....
Poland	964	....	....	....	....	....	....	....	87.4	100.9	†97.2	80.2	76.3	68.2	60.0	49.7
Romania	968	....	70.1	83.2	96.7	86.8	75.8	80.3	92.2	†112.5	106.3	95.7	91.3	76.4	†68.7	72.3
Russia	922	....	....	....	....	....	....	....	....	....	....	....	....	....	....	....
Slovak Republic	936	....	....	....	....	....	....	....	....	....	....	....	....	....	....	....
Slovenia	961	....	....	....	....	....	....	....	....	....	....	....	....	....	....	....
Turkey	186	52.7	51.9	53.2	54.7	53.6	58.9	62.7	60.3	51.2	42.6	39.8	42.4	40.1	35.7	†31.5
Ukraine	926	....	....	....	....	....	....	....	....	....	....	....	....	....	....	....
Yugoslavia, SFR	188	34.7	33.3	28.8	26.2	27.8	†25.5	36.6	36.1	34.9	35.8	38.2	44.7	48.1	48.5	51.2
Middle East																
Bahrain	419	46.5	26.2	21.4	43.1	38.7	31.1	28.4	34.1	26.2	22.3	45.8	23.4	22.8	24.3	23.4
Egypt	469	65.8	67.0	65.3	61.2	58.2	52.3	52.4	51.2	†54.1	52.0	52.2	54.4	52.2	51.6	47.6
Iran, I.R. of	429	42.9	45.1	42.4	39.2	38.0	38.5	....	45.3	45.6	51.7	57.9	54.7	....	....	58.9
Iraq	433	72.5	77.4	70.0	64.8	67.9	....	....	....	....	....	....	....	....	....	....
Israel	436	†67.7	69.5	59.3	51.5	53.7	105.8	175.4	216.1	191.9	42.6	40.8	49.4	44.8	41.2	35.8
Jordan	439	86.2	83.3	79.9	74.5	70.1	67.6	61.9	62.2	59.8	56.6	53.2	51.5	48.1	46.8	45.1
Kuwait	443	14.4	17.9	18.9	19.0	18.4	27.5	16.3	16.8	17.7	16.8	24.1	17.2	14.4	14.3	13.1
Lebanon	446	25.7	24.3	32.7	29.8	37.7	33.1	31.3	23.8	21.5	17.7	20.9	18.8	17.3	15.7	7.8
Libya	672	71.3	60.0	56.3	61.3	58.2	58.7	65.9	64.2	64.9	52.9	60.0	50.2	47.9	48.7	49.5
Oman	449	31.1	35.0	37.4	41.5	39.1	38.7	38.4	44.6	44.6	49.2	48.5	29.9	32.9	28.2	32.1
Qatar	453	13.2	15.6	16.8	16.0	14.9	15.4	17.7	20.6	20.7	15.0	14.6	14.8	12.3	10.9	12.7
Saudi Arabia	456	57.1	64.0	60.2	66.9	64.9	68.7	75.2	59.0	44.7	38.3	36.2	†32.1	29.7	28.8	28.7
Syrian Arab Rep.	463	79.3	81.0	72.4	68.7	69.7	67.5	69.2	67.4	67.0	62.8	77.6	78.0	82.5	92.9	89.1
United Arab Emirates	466	....	18.2	17.4	17.3	16.6	24.4	24.2	30.0	18.9	18.3	18.0	16.5	13.9	15.2	14.9
Yemen Arab Rep.	473	....	77.3	76.8	76.0	76.0	83.6	80.4	83.1	80.8	83.3	83.3	86.2	86.4	85.6	82.5
Yemen, P.D. Rep.	459	77.5	82.9	74.5	64.0	76.3	66.7	†74.8	73.7	66.7	67.9	76.8	82.4	84.9	90.6	98.4
Yemen, Republic of	474	....	....	....	....	....	....	....	....	....	....	....	....	....	....	....
Western Hemisphere																
Antigua and Barbuda	311	....	....	....	19.9	29.8	19.1	19.8	28.0	21.0	17.4	18.1	16.8	25.0	26.0	30.5
Argentina	213	29.6	116.1	115.0	125.4	126.6	55.4	40.2	25.9	24.2	26.2	92.7	84.3	59.8	55.2	34.9
Aruba	314	....	....	....	....	....	....	....	....	....	....	....	....	....	....	30.9
Bahamas, The	313	18.3	17.2	20.0	19.6	18.4	17.9	18.0	18.0	18.3	16.4	16.2	16.2	17.7	19.1	18.8
Barbados	316	14.2	19.9	21.2	25.2	21.5	23.7	22.9	23.8	23.6	22.9	22.6	24.3	23.3	23.4	21.8
Belize	339	....	....	....	....	19.1	25.3	27.4	23.9	24.1	26.8	29.7	23.6	30.5	32.2	32.1
Bolivia	218	64.0	67.6	62.1	59.7	58.8	56.7	56.3	54.5	54.8	50.8	60.5	67.8	76.1	64.5	42.9
Brazil	223	26.5	27.4	27.9	27.5	30.0	31.2	†30.0	32.1	31.4	28.4	28.8	25.1	22.3	18.5	†14.9
Chile	228	78.4	93.6	76.0	66.5	†56.4	54.7	48.4	42.0	42.2	29.5	46.7	88.4	127.5	180.8	175.2
Colombia	233	50.7	49.3	47.8	48.6	51.4	53.8	†58.9	62.1	55.4	50.7	49.3	46.7	46.5	45.4	....
Costa Rica	238	42.9	41.1	36.0	33.7	33.6	37.4	29.2	33.6	34.4	40.7	34.9	33.9	35.1	43.4	46.3
Dominica	321	....	....	....	11.2	15.7	21.5	16.5	39.8	24.6	15.2	18.0	10.0	28.1	23.0	30.8
Dominican Republic	243	53.5	52.9	54.5	43.3	43.5	47.2	50.5	48.7	44.1	51.2	48.2	47.3	47.5	39.9	43.4
Ecuador	248	46.3	49.9	48.7	44.8	38.3	38.5	41.6	40.9	36.0	35.4	30.7	27.8	26.2	28.1	30.8
El Salvador	253	26.5	25.6	25.4	26.7	27.5	25.8	17.6	14.9	18.3	19.4	†47.5	44.3	42.8	40.7	33.0
Grenada	328	18.4	19.3	21.2	†22.8	33.4	28.9	30.4	31.9	32.2	37.5	30.8	32.3	43.6	47.0	36.4
Guatemala	258	75.4	73.1	73.4	71.6	84.4	80.2	77.1	74.6	67.6	63.6	64.4	60.4	56.5	68.6	68.1
Guyana	336	33.2	29.4	28.4	30.0	31.4	32.4	41.7	40.0	38.1	41.9	51.8	54.9	60.2	54.2	56.0
Haiti	263	62.0	57.7	50.4	49.8	49.9	49.2	46.3	47.2	47.3	49.1	48.0	45.3	48.5	48.3	50.9
Honduras	268	33.2	33.1	30.9	32.1	34.2	33.4	33.4	35.2	33.1	32.4	29.2	26.7	23.8	24.1	23.6
Jamaica	343	20.6	†24.2	24.7	24.4	26.1	26.1	26.1	24.4	25.5	29.8	22.3	15.6	21.1	34.0	34.2
Mexico	273	37.7	39.0	45.1	51.2	32.1	†62.4	60.2	59.8	61.5	59.7	†69.2	66.7	59.9	49.6	42.6
Netherlands Antilles	353	28.3	28.3	24.7	27.6	26.4	26.7	23.6	26.1	25.2	21.8	19.9	17.2	15.9	27.1	35.2
Nicaragua	278	37.7	37.7	35.8	36.6	34.9	35.1	34.0	46.4	33.3	38.0	40.1	†40.8	44.2	52.1	52.7
Panama	283	17.1	13.8	10.6	13.9	18.3	17.3	11.2	17.7	15.0	16.8	14.7	14.5	13.8	12.7	11.8
Paraguay	288	64.9	63.9	62.2	60.5	59.2	59.2	60.4	59.5	56.3	55.5	52.8	59.3	59.4	58.5	62.1
Peru	293	43.5	37.7	39.8	36.3	43.5	43.8	42.2	49.9	57.5	52.9	48.3	51.1	54.6	67.0	60.7
St. Kitts and Nevis	361	....	....	....	....	....	....	....	10.0	4.8	20.2	12.9	13.8	17.8	17.8	18.8
St. Lucia	362	....	....	....	14.1	17.8	18.0	18.9	20.8	20.1	16.4	16.2	15.0	21.3	22.3	25.2
St. Vincent & Grenadines	364	....	....	....	18.9	27.8	27.8	23.4	29.2	23.8	23.8	18.9	15.8	26.2	29.7	37.5
Suriname	366	37.1	43.1	40.1	42.5	39.9	41.5	36.0	39.2	36.4	37.5	37.1	43.2	53.3	61.6	66.9
Trinidad and Tobago	369	15.6	15.9	24.3	29.6	29.5	24.2	20.3	27.6	26.7	25.6	30.6	26.9	23.6	25.0	21.7
Uruguay	298	64.4	67.9	66.0	†53.7	52.1	41.8	40.2	30.7	27.7	21.7	†16.0	25.0	27.6	32.8	29.9
Venezuela, Rep. Bol.	299	34.7	36.0	37.7	34.6	33.4	32.5	31.2	32.7	29.8	30.8	33.2	34.4	36.5	34.3	24.9

Percent

1987	1988	1989	1990	1991	1992	1993	1994	1995	1996	1997	1998	1999	2000	2001		
															Asia (cont.)	
14.2	14.4	14.7	16.3	12.9	11.8	11.8	13.3	13.5	19.8	12.0	14.2	22.5	17.9	18.6	Papua New Guinea	853
45.0	41.1	39.7	38.8	39.5	36.3	†33.4	28.4	25.8	27.7	21.1	19.8	23.2	19.2	16.5	Philippines	566
50.1	48.1	57.2	73.0	67.2	52.9	48.0	43.5	36.5	41.4	42.8	22.7	23.8	22.3	20.0	Samoa	862
21.3	21.2	20.0	17.9	17.6	17.9	17.9	16.6	16.7	16.2	15.6	10.3	12.3	10.8	11.1	Singapore	576
24.6	25.2	21.2	22.1	24.3	19.5	18.8	19.7	22.2	25.0	22.0	31.3	29.2	....	....	Solomon Islands	813
33.8	37.1	†36.2	36.4	38.2	35.5	36.0	35.9	30.5	29.7	25.2	24.6	23.0	21.2	20.5	Sri Lanka	524
14.4	14.0	13.0	12.2	11.5	11.7	11.5	11.7	12.2	12.3	12.2	10.7	15.7	13.2	11.6	Thailand	578
109.5	100.8	69.5	95.4	87.7	98.3	29.2	26.2	21.4	29.1	30.3	29.2	28.0	26.6	30.0	Tonga	866
8.4	8.9	8.0	6.5	8.4	8.4	12.3	11.1	12.8	11.1	11.2	10.4	14.0	13.6	12.8	Vanuatu	846
					56.9	64.8	....	58.2	55.6	50.3	44.3	40.0	36.9	33.9	Vietnam	582
															Europe	
							59.4	50.1	39.7	45.8	38.5	37.6	40.8	38.7	Albania	914
				43.6	54.6	61.2	71.6	75.7	73.1	56.1	49.2	47.7	46.7		Armenia	911
				32.1	51.1	31.2	69.7	69.9	69.9	†64.1	61.8	†46.0	†52.3		Azerbaijan	912
						25.3	38.0	†44.4	43.6	30.5	36.5	25.7	33.0		Belarus	913
										11.4	13.1	35.0	36.8	51.7	Bosnia & Herzegovina	963
				31.6	30.9	24.6	22.5	†23.5	22.4	†41.4	40.9	42.9	37.1	37.2	Bulgaria	918
						22.5	27.0	27.5	23.9	20.4	17.4	18.3	16.1	16.8	Croatia	960
39.9	38.9	30.1	35.4	31.6	29.6	25.9	25.9	22.2	18.4	16.4	17.6	17.6	18.0	17.2	Cyprus	423
						18.2	20.3	24.1	22.8	†29.3	34.8	36.9	34.0	32.1	Czech Republic	935
20.9	18.7	18.9	40.0	13.1											Czechoslovakia	934
				26.3	39.7	†58.0	49.6	46.7	41.7	41.7	42.5	43.6	39.8	29.2	Estonia	939
								85.0	81.9	75.4	71.5	70.1	63.9	†58.5	Georgia	915
52.7	49.3	50.6	36.8	42.3	36.3	31.8	27.3	26.6	19.9	21.6	22.6	24.6	25.7	22.4	Hungary	944
						45.8	49.1	50.3	52.8	†66.7	54.8	46.3	33.9	36.6	Kazakhstan	916
								73.6	79.5	72.8	66.7	65.2	65.2	65.3	Kyrgyz Republic	917
						48.6	38.6	49.9	51.3	49.1	49.2	50.7	43.0	40.6	Latvia	941
						47.0	41.6	43.5	46.1	45.5	51.2	45.6	37.8	33.7	Lithuania	946
						8.6	34.4	†40.2	39.4	39.1	36.5	35.9	43.3	35.5	Macedonia, FYR	962
55.2	50.8	44.3	37.6	36.9	35.8	32.5	37.2	†29.3	25.8	24.3	23.1	22.5	22.4	21.4	Malta	181
				42.5	58.8	69.0	73.3	62.6	†59.7	59.2	†60.3	59.8	55.7	51.6	Moldova	921
37.3	52.9	48.4	48.5	†41.9	36.1	28.6	25.4	27.3	25.1	26.0	24.3	20.1	16.6	18.8	Poland	964
73.9	78.1	103.2	†50.7	30.7	37.9	†45.4	35.8	32.9	29.7	34.3	27.8	36.9	41.4	45.3	Romania	968
						50.1	48.1	47.0	46.2	46.0	41.9	44.6	47.4	44.8	Russia	922
						12.2	12.9	14.2	15.8	†17.2	14.2	14.8	13.6	12.7	Slovak Republic	936
				13.3	13.9	11.9	12.9	12.4	11.6	11.6	11.6	12.3	10.6	11.0	Slovenia	961
30.8	33.3	33.9	30.6	25.1	25.1	25.6	22.9	20.2	17.8	18.0	17.1	17.0	17.8	17.0	Turkey	186
					70.9	61.6	46.8	50.6	52.3	58.2	†55.5	55.8	55.6	55.4	Ukraine	926
64.7	67.3	65.3	59.4												Yugoslavia, SFR	188
															Middle East	
23.7	21.4	22.2	27.4	†21.8	18.9	14.3	12.9	16.2	13.9	14.5	9.7	13.6	12.3	12.9	Bahrain	419
41.7	35.7	32.9	32.9	32.9	30.4	32.0	32.3	32.2	30.2	30.3	32.7	31.4	33.4	34.6	Egypt	469
61.6	64.2	59.3	51.9	48.0	43.6	39.8	40.1	45.6	43.8	43.5	42.7	41.1	39.2	32.7	Iran, I.R. of	429
															Iraq	433
33.3	29.1	26.4	25.1	23.2	†19.8	20.8	15.6	9.4	10.1	19.3	18.4	19.7	18.4	16.9	Israel	436
40.7	43.3	44.0	45.8	51.5	53.0	†51.0	51.9	52.2	45.6	41.2	36.9	35.8	33.5	29.3	Jordan	439
10.4	7.0	6.6	....	9.5	8.9	7.9	7.5	6.4	6.5	5.6	5.9	7.6	6.5	5.7	Kuwait	443
3.9	9.0	13.5	13.3	14.5	12.9	13.8	19.4	20.2	19.4	24.3	19.8	18.7	18.1	23.1	Lebanon	446
51.2	45.6	50.8	57.4	58.0	64.0	58.9	59.9	58.9	63.6	†70.4	67.1	59.2	56.8	60.0	Libya	672
26.1	24.8	27.7	25.6	25.1	23.5	21.6	21.1	20.3	20.0	17.4	17.8	16.6	17.0	16.9	Oman	449
11.7	11.6	11.6	13.3	13.1	13.1	†12.9	11.0	11.4	11.5	11.5	11.0	11.0	10.6	11.9	Qatar	453
27.9	24.5	23.4	28.1	25.5	†24.6	23.7	24.1	22.8	20.9	21.4	20.4	23.6	21.6	19.8	Saudi Arabia	456
87.3	67.8	68.3	69.5	65.2	66.8	58.7	56.9	54.5	53.2	51.6	49.0	46.3	44.9	45.0	Syrian Arab Rep.	463
21.6	18.7	15.2	16.7	16.8	19.5	19.2	22.4	22.9	23.2	21.4	20.6	24.1	28.5	24.5	United Arab Emirates	466
93.0	92.0	92.1	....												Yemen Arab Rep.	473
98.2	103.0	103.5	....												Yemen, P.D. Rep.	459
			90.8	89.2	89.5	88.6	90.6	72.0	71.3	56.1	55.8	59.2	53.9	50.8	Yemen, Republic of	474
															Western Hemisphere	
24.3	24.3	20.6	20.3	19.4	23.9	18.2	18.9	18.3	15.7	15.3	14.9	15.4	14.1	16.0	Antigua and Barbuda	311
25.8	24.6	79.5	†45.7	41.0	35.5	33.0	†30.4	26.5	22.8	20.6	19.1	18.5	16.7	24.3	Argentina	213
26.2	25.4	20.2	20.5	21.6	22.7	23.7	19.5	22.1	18.1	16.7	20.7	19.9	17.3	21.5	Aruba	314
16.8	17.4	16.8	15.3	16.2	14.9	12.8	13.2	12.5	11.5	10.7	11.0	12.0	10.7	11.3	Bahamas, The	313
23.0	21.6	20.7	21.7	18.8	20.3	17.4	15.7	17.3	19.5	16.2	16.4	15.2	15.6	17.2	Barbados	316
29.6	27.1	29.6	25.3	23.8	25.6	24.6	22.3	21.4	20.4	19.3	19.6	20.6	22.5	25.5	Belize	339
†37.0	47.1	49.0	40.8	35.1	27.5	27.3	22.9	26.3	†24.5	25.2	17.7	18.6	20.5	22.4	Bolivia	218
26.3	†11.8	20.1	28.1	22.9	16.7	13.9	24.8	21.1	23.0	26.1	21.1	21.2	21.3	22.6	Brazil	223
140.2	112.6	84.3	105.3	101.6	100.3	92.4	100.2	90.7	87.9	87.7	77.1	73.5	78.5	81.0	Chile	228
43.1	42.7	....	†53.4	56.4	53.3	48.7	44.7	39.2	37.0	30.4	20.9	25.6	24.4	23.1	Colombia	233
45.7	47.1	47.2	44.7	54.3	51.4	48.9	51.9	57.5	47.5	†47.7	42.0	34.9	28.1	18.9	Costa Rica	238
35.1	29.8	24.4	26.1	24.7	22.2	21.8	18.9	18.2	16.9	16.8	17.6	18.1	17.9	16.8	Dominica	321
36.0	48.4	47.7	44.0	49.2	43.7	46.3	41.5	41.0	38.4	36.8	38.6	35.9	33.7	34.3	Dominican Republic	243
29.5	31.9	33.4	†36.4	32.5	35.0	35.0	26.3	22.4	20.7	20.4	†21.1	†25.2	14.6	12.8	Ecuador	248
38.8	40.2	39.4	38.6	38.3	33.7	38.0	37.5	38.0	36.2	34.5	33.9	34.2	30.6	....	El Salvador	253
35.4	25.7	24.8	24.0	23.0	26.2	20.6	19.6	19.4	17.9	18.2	17.3	16.2	15.5	15.6	Grenada	328
63.7	65.1	66.8	71.0	61.1	50.3	53.9	50.3	45.0	44.6	†46.3	37.3	34.1	30.0	29.5	Guatemala	258
91.7	79.8	48.5	37.5	55.6	52.0	†33.4	39.0	37.3	33.1	35.2	36.9	32.0	33.7	34.4	Guyana	336
54.3	44.4	53.2	60.8	59.2	58.8	58.8	55.4	50.0	47.4	†42.2	38.6	40.4	42.3	43.4	Haiti	263
24.1	24.1	26.3	27.1	24.8	29.3	28.4	32.0	30.7	31.2	†39.8	37.6	33.6	29.5	27.7	Honduras	268
36.3	37.7	43.4	41.3	34.9	37.5	39.9	38.1	37.7	35.1	35.7	40.5	34.6	33.0	28.4	Jamaica	343
30.1	54.4	26.7	19.9	17.1	15.8	15.1	15.3	15.5	15.3	†16.8	18.3	23.0	22.7	25.1	Mexico	273
29.3	26.5	18.4	19.7	15.1	18.0	17.4	14.9	16.7	14.8	16.7	17.7	15.8	16.6	19.7	Netherlands Antilles	353
56.8	52.4	48.3	64.9	56.0	49.3	42.5	39.0	35.7	†34.2	29.7	26.9	23.9	22.9	23.0	Nicaragua	278
8.0	8.8	8.9	9.9	10.3	6.6	5.9	5.0	4.8	6.3	5.6	5.1	4.7	4.4	4.1	Panama	283
64.5	†66.0	52.6	41.6	35.5	32.3	28.5	29.3	†32.0	27.5	27.4	26.6	24.5	23.1	21.1	Paraguay	288
61.8	57.3	43.7	53.1	42.1	43.8	40.7	38.8	39.4	39.5	41.9	37.8	38.2	39.1	40.0	Peru	293
21.8	19.2	19.7	19.5	18.5	21.4	21.5	22.9	19.6	18.6	17.3	18.7	20.3	17.3	18.8	St. Kitts and Nevis	361
24.8	23.4	22.6	22.3	22.2	21.1	21.7	18.8	19.1	17.5	17.1	17.6	16.6	16.3	18.1	St. Lucia	362
29.5	28.2	26.6	26.6	24.2	29.1	25.5	23.4	21.0	19.3	18.8	19.6	19.7	22.5	22.9	St. Vincent & Grenadines	364
62.8	61.8	60.3	61.2	62.8	59.2	60.8	61.4	71.3	46.2	38.6	†46.3	49.5	69.9	62.4	Suriname	366
16.4	16.6	17.7	18.4	21.0	20.4	16.8	22.7	21.6	†22.3	23.2	24.5	24.4	22.5	23.3	Trinidad and Tobago	369
33.7	32.8	31.1	34.2	33.8	32.6	33.9	31.6	29.6	28.8	28.0	†26.9	28.8	29.4	31.2	Uruguay	298
†24.3	25.0	25.9	33.2	39.5	37.4	32.9	31.9	30.8	†35.6	38.4	39.4	43.4	40.5	39.3	Venezuela, Rep. Bol.	299

Income Velocity of Money plus Quasi-Money

39ad *i*

		1972	1973	1974	1975	1976	1977	1978	1979	1980	1981	1982	1983	1984	1985	1986
Industrial Countries																
United States	111	88.2	90.1	92.0	91.7	90.7	89.7	93.3	95.8	95.2	97.2	91.8	88.4	90.0	87.3	84.3
Canada	156	149.9	152.7	146.1	143.8	140.0	133.3	130.0	124.8	122.6	126.4	116.6	125.2	134.0	136.3	135.9
Australia	193	84.8	81.0	85.9	86.0	88.8	90.5	91.9	95.2	94.9	97.0	98.1	94.8	95.8	91.1	88.2
Japan	158	134.9	133.6	141.2	138.4	134.9	134.9	132.7	129.5	131.7	130.0	125.1	122.3	122.2	121.1	116.2
New Zealand	196	210.8	173.7	165.9	179.0	184.4	168.1	160.2	156.6	156.9	166.6	167.0	167.0	164.9	148.4	150.6
Euro Area																
Austria	122	158.3	157.3	159.8	146.9	142.1	137.9	130.5	128.2	125.8	120.2	116.3	114.2	115.4	113.9	112.1
Belgium	124	107.0	105.4	110.8	109.5	109.6	108.6	107.8	107.6	113.1	111.6	112.7	113.4	113.4	†115.3	111.8
Finland	172	135.5	146.7	161.3	154.2	153.0	150.1	144.3	144.9	144.2	141.6	138.4	135.5	134.0	124.2	117.0
France	132	71.3	71.2	70.0	68.8	68.2	68.7	92.6	74.8	77.9	78.8	81.4	82.3	80.4	83.1	82.4
Germany	134	130.3	130.2	129.6	123.8	121.6	119.7	117.1	117.1	119.3	118.7	115.9	114.4	115.0	113.4	101.9
Ireland	178	115.8	119.2	109.7	116.1	121.0	128.0	126.7	120.2	126.5	128.5	134.0	133.3	134.8	135.4	147.0
Italy	136	73.2	74.6	80.1	77.1	79.3	80.8	77.7	79.1	87.1	93.3	95.6	94.9	97.0	95.6	97.9
Luxembourg	137	....	....	140.2	121.8	121.3	111.0	106.3	101.0	92.3	88.4	98.4	107.4	108.5	114.9	115.7
Netherlands	138	169.1	167.2	163.4	158.1	155.5	157.4	151.9	146.4	144.1	139.4	133.3	112.6	111.1	109.8	106.9
Portugal	182	90.1	84.6	85.9	84.1	92.4	102.6	108.5	109.7	102.3	90.5	87.6	88.7	87.7	85.9	103.0
Spain	184	94.6	91.4	92.9	91.8	92.9	98.5	100.6	98.6	96.4	93.9	92.7	†106.3	115.0	116.5	108.7
Denmark	128	131.5	132.7	136.4	129.1	124.4	126.6	132.8	134.9	134.8	131.5	136.5	125.7	113.2	106.0	99.7
Iceland	176	111.3	122.6	140.6	158.8	169.7	181.8	196.5	187.6	196.0	192.8	232.5	211.4	195.8	177.9	167.3
Norway	142	122.0	122.8	127.7	128.8	126.3	119.6	†115.8	113.0	119.6	121.0	120.8	121.3	119.7	113.8	107.3
Sweden	144	70.7	69.8	70.1	74.8	77.1	79.2	77.2	75.2	76.8	76.3	73.7	78.5	84.3	88.5	87.3
Switzerland	146	125.7	132.7	135.5	126.0	117.6	111.5	105.9	101.1	108.2	111.6	111.8	110.7	109.3	104.9	107.6
United Kingdom	112	176.9	159.3	150.8	....	182.8	194.8	196.8	207.2	208.9	186.6	172.1	165.9	160.8	156.5	139.5
Developing Countries																
Africa																
Algeria	612	64.2	60.5	89.1	77.2	75.0	67.9	65.6	68.1	71.8	72.1	64.8	59.5	53.1	53.7	50.3
Benin	638	151.6	149.9	151.5	114.0	109.7	106.9	110.3	109.4	97.3	96.1	101.9	103.6	99.0	101.3	102.0
Botswana	616					79.9	76.3	80.0	71.7	74.4	76.4	79.8	90.8	85.1	90.3	89.6
Burkina Faso	748	257.4	208.2	188.1	156.0	126.7	134.2	134.0	131.8	129.8	125.7	124.2	120.9	104.8	178.6	153.0
Burundi	618	167.1	163.8	165.4	193.4	182.0	169.7	146.5	150.8	182.7	151.9	149.0	144.9	147.5	150.5	138.8
Cameroon	622	94.6	93.2	86.6	83.6	78.8	71.0	69.9	70.4	66.5	72.2	68.7	70.5	69.4	65.5	70.3
Central African Rep.	626	132.8	127.8	136.8	156.5	139.5	122.0	124.5	128.9	121.2	118.7	128.7	125.6	126.1	126.2	123.7
Chad	628	87.0	86.4	90.2	86.6	84.8	67.3	76.9	....	....	....	52.1	79.5	64.0	49.2	47.3
Comoros	632												108.7	110.4	128.9	123.4
Congo, Dem. Rep. of	636	*,***.***	*,***.***	*,***.***	*,***.***	*,***.***	*,***.***	*,***.***	*,***.***	*,***.***	*,***.***	*,***.***	—	—	—	—
Congo, Rep. of	634	84.5	85.5	85.7	82.9	79.4	77.7	82.4	93.9	96.5	98.6	97.6	96.4	112.2	99.6	68.8
Côte d'Ivoire	662	118.9	122.7	116.8	103.9	114.1	104.7	94.8	94.3	100.4	102.7	104.4	105.1	112.7	96.3	90.2
Equatorial Guinea	642														70.8	47.7
Ethiopia	644	280.0	238.2	204.3	188.7	172.6	178.8	164.1	162.5	154.6	174.6	†167.1	161.0	136.7	143.2	130.4
Gabon	646	78.3	86.5	135.0	105.8	97.2	71.0	59.8	76.1	88.5	86.8	83.9	81.1	78.2	70.3	70.1
Ghana	652	64.0	66.0	70.4	59.6	53.0	62.4	69.4	71.3	79.8	99.1	89.0	128.5	141.3	124.7	122.4
Guinea-Bissau	654															5,401.5
Kenya	664	129.6	119.7	122.3	126.8	123.5	109.2	99.2	101.6	103.2	109.4	111.7	115.8	114.9	143.6	134.8
Lesotho	666									78.5	78.4	68.2	58.9	59.9	61.0	59.3
Madagascar	674	100.2	102.6	119.4	111.7	110.4	103.6	88.7	87.2	82.0	79.8	82.5	109.3	139.8	133.2	118.9
Malawi	676	101.9	81.6	88.7	78.1	90.5	88.7	86.3	81.0	88.7	83.1	78.9	84.1	83.7	83.9	87.6
Mali	678	119.9	110.7	95.6	92.0	110.9	110.3	98.7	99.8	116.1	142.6	135.5	130.7	111.7	97.2	103.4
Mauritania	682	172.8	143.5	116.2	101.4	100.5	91.8	91.9	87.0	89.3	79.1	74.9	78.9	81.5	79.1	80.1
Mauritius	684	182.1	182.5	239.1	160.8	151.2	182.6	177.7	187.8	187.5	196.3	193.1	179.0	181.3	169.6	153.8
Morocco	686	209.8	199.3	217.8	191.0	178.2	179.5	173.6	165.2	155.7	168.2	156.6	143.4	144.5	147.7	148.7
Mozambique	688													21.6	24.8	22.9
Namibia	728															
Niger	692	171.4	147.5	145.2	133.7	143.6	131.2	128.1	123.1	115.5	106.1	118.3	139.4	110.2	96.0	89.7
Nigeria	694	155.8	144.0	153.1	99.1	81.8	70.6	67.5	67.7	60.6	51.1	48.1	46.7	45.8	47.2	45.0
Rwanda	714	212.9	178.8	162.5	142.0	138.5	125.7	120.5	121.1	119.4	121.0	124.3	127.1	126.8	122.4	106.5
Senegal	722	134.9	127.9	113.8	105.3	90.9	81.3	75.8	74.5	76.0	77.0	77.1	75.4	79.0	86.6	92.4
Seychelles	718	120.0	131.4	146.7	137.3	148.9	149.9	160.0	181.2	167.5	150.9	158.0	161.6	163.7	155.3	152.7
Sierra Leone	724	60.8	53.4	53.7	58.7	55.7	53.5	46.2	44.5	43.4	44.6	43.2	35.9	41.6	42.6	43.1
South Africa	199	77.7	78.1	82.2	77.7	77.7	78.8	79.8	82.3	89.7	87.5	87.5	84.8	86.5	†88.5	92.7
Sudan	732	61.2	66.9	63.0	64.2	65.1	57.3	49.3	45.7	45.5	41.8	33.2	34.2	34.8	29.0	31.2
Swaziland	734	....	....	140.4	113.4	96.2	85.5	76.3	80.5	88.5	95.5	94.0	85.8	77.6	80.1	91.2
Tanzania	738	87.8	86.8	86.3	83.4	84.8	81.8	79.1	65.6	58.7	55.8	58.9	54.7	61.3	70.7	72.7
Togo	742	217.8	213.5	189.5	149.5	147.9	130.8	117.1	106.9	113.8	96.7	77.8	86.3	85.3	79.6	76.9
Tunisia	744	137.0	126.3	136.0	123.4	116.1	115.2	112.4	113.1	117.8	111.3	110.6	111.7	108.3	104.8	98.9
Uganda	746	61.8	54.2	51.0	54.4	49.0	65.4	80.1	88.7	86.6	107.2	116.7	134.9	123.8	143.2	†140.7
Zambia	754	58.2	59.8	57.5	51.6	49.1	40.9	47.5	52.3	50.7	53.7	46.5	44.5	46.2	56.0	†65.1
Zimbabwe	698	....	....	....	....	....	....	....	105.7	74.7	99.1	81.3	90.6	88.2	105.3	108.4
Asia																
Bangladesh	513	....	....	156.2	268.1	200.4	161.2	180.9	173.2	165.9	157.8	160.9	133.0	116.4	109.9	106.1
Bhutan	514												172.3	179.4	161.2	175.7
China, P.R.: Mainland	924	....	....	....	....	....	....	....	3,749.7	3,328.6	3,028.9	2,961.0	2,737.4	2,433.2	176.3	147.2
China, P.R.: Hong Kong	532															
Fiji	819	171.9	189.1	198.6	182.4	173.0	168.2	158.3	165.4	161.7	156.7	155.8	142.9	146.5	139.2	142.0
India	534	242.2	248.1	253.3	242.3	221.1	208.1	139.2	120.5	123.6	122.4	120.3	119.8	113.1	109.0	104.1
Indonesia	536	324.8	328.0	349.2	300.1	274.1	269.6	274.5	298.4	289.5	286.4	246.9	252.2	232.4	202.9	185.7
Korea	542	123.2	113.9	126.9	134.4	142.1	132.6	130.3	131.7	127.3	126.3	112.6	110.3	114.4	114.0	113.2
Lao People's Democratic Rep.	544															
Malaysia	548	221.4	229.4	226.9	193.4	198.0	187.8	192.5	190.8	172.7	157.5	148.2	144.3	148.4	131.9	113.2
Maldives	556						64.3	91.4	83.6	87.1	85.1	92.6	103.2	142.9	127.2	109.6
Mongolia	948															
Myanmar	518	105.3	109.8	†120.2	116.3	120.2	124.1	122.1	115.3	107.1	99.3	94.3	88.4	81.2	76.3	72.5
Nepal	558	303.4	239.4	245.7	†287.8	249.6	195.9	189.1	181.5	161.5	159.6	151.6	137.3	138.8	†139.2	136.6
Pakistan	564	87.7	92.2	119.7	133.9	125.3	117.5	114.0	103.9	105.4	110.9	112.5	102.4	107.1	106.6	101.2

1995=100

1987	1988	1989	1990	1991	1992	1993	1994	1995	1996	1997	1998	1999	2000	2001		
															Industrial Countries	
84.6	85.5	88.0	87.9	86.8	89.8	93.5	97.9	100.0	99.3	99.5	97.2	94.7	93.4	85.8	United States	111
135.3	135.4	130.5	122.2	117.0	111.8	103.9	100.9	100.0	97.3	96.0	94.0	96.9	91.9	89.2	Canada	156
87.8	86.2	122.0	112.4	107.7	106.4	104.7	102.5	100.0	97.1	92.8	91.4	87.5	87.0	84.7	Australia	193
110.0	106.0	103.5	99.6	101.6	103.1	102.7	101.6	100.0	100.1	100.0	95.1	90.4	89.1	85.8	Japan	158
†128.3	132.4	111.4	105.1	98.7	98.0	102.6	102.9	100.0	90.9	87.4	84.7	85.3	87.3	88.0	New Zealand	196
															Euro Area	
107.0	105.1	105.2	105.9	104.8	103.0	99.6	99.0	†100.0	99.3	98.8	....	....	....	....	Austria	122
105.5	105.5	106.4	105.6	104.8	107.9	101.3	98.3	100.0	94.2	94.5	....	....	....	....	Belgium	124
114.8	113.9	107.4	104.3	95.6	91.8	92.8	95.4	100.0	103.9	111.5	117.6	....	....	....	Finland	172
83.2	†88.2	90.1	90.3	95.1	99.0	98.0	99.2	†100.0	97.2	96.5	....	....	....	....	France	132
99.2	99.2	101.0	98.4	†108.1	107.1	101.4	97.7	100.0	95.4	93.2	92.4	....	....	....	Germany	134
147.3	146.4	156.6	†159.3	150.8	158.0	136.4	133.5	100.0	96.1	92.3	89.8	....	....	....	Ireland	178
97.5	99.6	100.0	99.8	100.0	97.4	92.8	93.1	100.0	102.5	109.5	117.9	....	....	....	Italy	136
108.3	105.2	100.0	92.1	88.2	87.1	84.8	91.1	†100.0	104.0	117.5	....	....	....	....	Luxembourg	137
103.7	104.3	101.5	99.3	99.0	98.1	96.1	98.6	100.0	97.9	97.2	....	....	....	....	Netherlands	138
105.1	109.9	112.8	121.0	118.2	110.1	101.9	102.8	100.0	101.7	100.6	101.7	....	....	....	Portugal	182
112.9	113.4	113.5	111.1	106.0	106.2	101.7	99.7	100.0	100.6	105.6	109.1	....	....	....	Spain	184
99.8	99.6	100.9	99.6	95.1	95.2	90.4	91.6	100.0	95.9	93.7	89.9	93.6	....	....	Denmark	128
157.6	148.4	135.1	113.3	108.4	99.7	98.2	99.2	100.0	101.7	102.4	98.4	....	....	....	Iceland	176
97.8	†96.2	97.2	96.2	98.0	96.8	95.9	97.5	100.0	104.3	109.3	105.8	105.3	112.0	108.2	Norway	142
85.7	86.7	88.1	97.1	92.5	93.2	87.8	†92.4	100.0	95.5	95.2	98.5	97.9	96.3	....	Sweden	144
101.6	99.3	101.0	107.5	110.1	110.6	107.2	101.3	100.0	92.3	85.7	83.9	79.3	81.7	95.4	Switzerland	146
123.8	120.0	110.8	103.8	101.1	104.0	104.5	103.5	100.0	93.1	90.9	92.4	92.6	89.1	85.0	United Kingdom	112
															Developing Countries	
															Africa	
49.1	†43.4	52.5	65.4	86.2	84.5	75.6	81.2	100.0	112.7	105.1	89.1	88.6	98.4	....	Algeria	612
108.0	120.7	118.9	99.9	91.2	86.5	84.9	102.9	100.0	109.4	108.2	111.5	110.3	89.0	....	Benin	638
69.1	69.0	82.8	83.7	80.4	75.5	77.9	99.7	100.0	100.0	99.3	85.1	72.3	75.2	....	Botswana	616
127.2	120.9	118.9	116.2	118.8	114.4	110.3	111.3	100.0	94.6	94.0	96.0	91.4	96.8	103.1	Burkina Faso	748
136.7	137.7	133.5	128.6	121.0	122.9	120.2	111.4	100.0	96.4	103.6	118.2	115.0	99.3	101.3	Burundi	618
73.0	139.8	71.1	65.4	64.3	63.3	84.5	91.4	100.0	112.9	123.7	120.9	115.7	108.1	....	Cameroon	622
142.8	139.9	132.0	133.0	142.1	140.0	128.5	110.8	100.0	95.3	104.3	124.0	139.9	133.4	....	Central African Rep.	626
73.1	52.1	59.4	56.6	54.5	61.1	62.9	81.4	100.0	70.2	74.3	87.6	82.3	79.4	83.4	Chad	628
106.8	112.3	102.4	97.4	98.4	95.9	97.5	94.7	100.0	....	....	....	....	....	....	Comoros	632
—	90.8	44.1	45.5	84.0	62.0	52.1		100.0	....	....	....	....	....	....	Congo, Dem. Rep. of	636
72.7	72.3	81.1	72.7	67.2	68.9	83.7	97.1	100.0	112.0	102.7	84.3	106.7	135.5	117.2	Congo, Rep. of	634
88.4	87.4	90.0	94.1	96.5	95.4	100.2	111.6	100.0	104.5	106.3	113.2	....	....	....	Côte d'Ivoire	662
45.7	52.9	65.9	105.8	130.6	153.6	165.0	140.0	100.0	122.8	192.5	148.3	180.5	254.8	....	Equatorial Guinea	642
127.0	121.6	115.5	106.6	101.7	†96.0	107.2	99.5	100.0	103.5	104.5	106.6	....	....	....	Ethiopia	644
61.0	62.6	71.3	75.0	72.2	72.3	89.2	110.0	100.0	105.4	98.0	75.0	91.3	100.2	....	Gabon	646
114.0	111.4	95.8	107.6	115.2	98.9	97.6	98.2	100.0	102.2	95.6	....	....	....	....	Ghana	652
1,512.9	804.7	752.5	80.3	198.8	161.9	109.8	151.9	100.0	66.6	33.5	....	....	....	....	Guinea-Bissau	654
127.3	138.5	136.3	136.3	129.9	120.3	116.0	108.4	100.0	84.4	83.0	84.7	86.1	87.6	....	Kenya	664
70.8	77.7	79.5	84.6	90.8	107.1	98.9	91.6	100.0	103.5	104.7	92.1	101.3	115.0	116.1	Lesotho	666
125.7	133.1	122.7	116.1	105.8	100.1	90.8	91.6	100.0	110.6	99.8	101.3	104.2	101.2	95.1	Madagascar	674
75.8	80.9	83.3	93.3	92.5	85.1	90.8	77.0	100.0	117.0	123.3	123.5	120.4	114.7	....	Malawi	676
99.6	93.6	95.0	104.5	105.9	99.4	94.4	98.1	100.0	91.9	91.4	97.0	95.7	103.9	....	Mali	678
73.5	73.1	77.5	75.6	72.7	69.6	78.6	92.3	100.0	111.7	120.8	....	....	....	....	Mauritania	682
143.0	130.9	127.5	125.5	116.8	109.2	108.7	104.0	100.0	98.0	99.2	99.5	94.8	101.7	94.6	Mauritius	684
137.0	143.5	133.2	128.5	124.3	111.1	105.8	106.5	100.0	106.5	98.2	99.5	92.1	87.3	....	Morocco	686
53.5	57.9	60.2	56.3	117.2	96.2	87.9	92.2	100.0	122.3	121.1	118.8	109.4	....	....	Mozambique	688
....	....	....	†168.6	145.7	137.4	119.1	111.1	100.0	95.6	86.8	91.3	87.5	89.8	....	Namibia	728
86.6	83.7	78.4	81.6	83.0	88.6	88.2	91.1	100.0	111.7	150.1	181.8	....	....	....	Niger	692
62.3	62.5	79.0	75.1	66.2	85.5	88.2	58.1	†100.0	119.3	104.0	85.0	77.2	82.9	64.9	Nigeria	694
93.8	88.0	93.8	104.7	109.4	114.6	110.1	83.5	100.0	100.2	106.2	111.3	101.1	101.5	....	Rwanda	714
88.9	90.6	88.0	89.1	89.8	87.7	92.4	104.2	100.0	95.3	96.6	99.7	....	....	....	Senegal	722
145.5	140.3	130.1	132.0	118.9	121.4	111.7	103.7	100.0	91.3	78.0	64.6	56.1	....	....	Seychelles	718
60.6	63.8	65.0	†67.9	90.0	86.5	86.0	93.2	100.0	102.3	74.8	68.8	64.7	61.4	....	Sierra Leone	724
95.0	90.7	89.0	90.0	86.6	93.1	†103.2	101.4	100.0	97.5	92.1	84.7	85.9	87.6	84.1	South Africa	199
42.5	42.2	49.7	43.9	48.4	44.4	51.0	54.8	†100.0	118.8	127.4	....	....	....	....	Sudan	732
89.5	92.5	81.5	85.2	84.9	85.0	87.1	86.9	100.0	110.0	109.5	107.4	103.2	115.8	....	Swaziland	734
†124.9	147.2	136.3	128.7	128.8	116.4	103.9	102.0	100.0	106.4	116.2	124.8	127.5	122.4	....	Tanzania	738
71.5	87.0	93.9	93.0	87.7	93.6	95.0	120.8	100.0	119.0	141.3	139.3	136.5	130.1	....	Togo	742
101.1	92.9	†87.5	85.9	92.4	96.7	99.8	98.4	100.0	102.8	97.3	96.2	92.2	85.2	79.8	Tunisia	744
169.2	205.7	212.0	180.2	166.4	163.4	117.3	107.2	100.0	93.0	....	....	....	....	....	Uganda	746
57.3	58.3	62.5	83.1	83.6	104.1	123.3	117.1	100.0	89.5	91.8	....	....	....	....	Zambia	754
101.6	109.4	110.2	114.2	132.4	151.7	134.9	116.4	100.0	104.9	98.2	111.2	118.2	....	....	Zimbabwe	698
															Asia	
105.3	101.1	95.4	125.9	124.0	117.6	110.4	103.3	100.0	100.0	98.2	98.7	95.2	86.5	80.0	Bangladesh	513
194.1	176.2	147.1	140.2	127.9	124.0	117.3	109.4	100.0	95.9	81.5	73.1	67.7	62.6	....	Bhutan	514
131.4	130.8	126.0	110.4	99.5	93.7	100.0	104.6	100.0	91.9	82.4	76.2	67.9	64.7	....	China, P.R.: Mainland	924
....	....	....	....	95.3	102.4	103.0	103.8	100.0	99.0	100.1	87.7	78.6	74.5	70.7	China, P.R.: Hong Kong	532
128.6	122.7	121.0	110.9	100.0	97.0	98.2	97.1	100.0	99.8	111.4	123.2	129.8	....	....	Fiji	819
100.9	109.6	106.8	106.0	104.7	100.1	100.1	98.7	100.0	99.5	94.4	91.6	87.0	81.8	....	India	534
179.7	166.3	154.6	123.6	118.0	110.5	†109.2	104.6	100.0	91.7	85.5	80.3	76.2	79.7	....	Indonesia	536
112.2	112.9	107.1	106.2	107.5	102.4	98.2	99.4	100.0	95.3	87.0	71.3	60.7	50.5	45.7	Korea	542
....	....	170.9	183.4	206.6	162.2	120.9	101.8	100.0	98.3	91.7	84.2	87.3	87.2	79.1	Lao People's Democratic Rep.	544
†118.7	130.2	134.9	131.6	132.7	115.4	108.3	100.0	100.0	92.0	85.6	81.0	77.0	77.8	71.8	Malaysia	548
117.9	120.0	123.3	121.3	121.9	121.1	116.8	105.0	100.0	95.0	83.3	71.2	66.7	64.2	57.1	Maldives	556
....	....	....	....	41.3	78.4	94.0	75.7	100.0	100.5	103.3	87.4	81.9	....	....	Mongolia	948
78.6	99.5	120.4	109.5	94.2	95.9	105.2	108.0	100.0	93.5	98.9	110.2	115.8	....	....	Myanmar	518
133.5	131.4	124.2	121.0	117.2	118.5	110.9	106.2	100.0	99.1	99.5	88.5	82.0	75.1	....	Nepal	558
98.0	103.1	111.0	109.7	113.6	108.1	96.1	97.0	100.0	97.2	93.9	90.4	94.8	94.3	93.2	Pakistan	564

Income Velocity of Money plus Quasi-Money

Index Numbers

		1972	1973	1974	1975	1976	1977	1978	1979	1980	1981	1982	1983	1984	1985	1986
Asia (cont.)																
Papua New Guinea	853	....	138.7	112.8	101.3	132.7	†117.8	112.0	103.1	96.9	101.5	102.1	108.2	92.0	86.9	80.6
Philippines	566	176.9	185.8	208.9	214.5	205.5	184.8	167.5	176.6	170.6	169.1	156.7	155.3	184.9	179.3	187.8
Samoa	862											108.8	118.1	154.0	125.7	114.5
Singapore	576	144.1	148.9	160.6	145.8	139.2	141.6	143.3	148.7	142.1	136.4	132.9	128.5	128.1	120.2	112.5
Sri Lanka	524	149.1	167.6	184.7	199.9	186.6	166.4	144.4	134.4	133.8	132.0	113.6	119.8	126.7	116.5	121.6
Thailand	578	227.5	238.1	247.5	226.8	218.9	210.2	214.5	212.0	211.0	203.8	187.9	163.8	147.2	136.0	130.1
Vanuatu	846											139.7	125.0	101.4	91.3	78.3
Vietnam	582	....														....
Europe																
Armenia	911															
Belarus	913															
Bulgaria	918															
Croatia	960															
Cyprus	423	163.2	154.8	125.3	102.0	116.9	126.2	131.9	138.6	144.9	141.1	139.4	136.0	140.8	140.5	137.1
Czech Republic	935															
Estonia	939															
Hungary	944											91.0	94.0	97.7	93.0	90.1
Kazakhstan	916															
Kyrgyz Republic	917															
Latvia	941															
Lithuania	946															
Macedonia, FYR	962															
Malta	181	82.0	84.7	87.1	97.3	96.7	98.9	102.4	107.3	117.3	120.2	117.2	109.1	108.0	108.4	111.0
Moldova	921															
Poland	964									62.5	55.7	81.7	89.2	93.4	†94.0	92.1
Romania	968									67.8	58.3	59.7	59.9	61.7	57.0	55.4
Russia	922															
Slovak Republic	936															
Slovenia	961															
Turkey	186															
Ukraine	926															
Middle East																
Bahrain	419	....	176.3	....	163.7	156.9	142.2	137.0	142.1	143.7	130.3	115.0	106.7	108.2	98.7	79.9
Egypt	469	197.5	176.3	156.5	149.5	149.8	154.5	140.9	136.4	†130.9	111.3	109.9	102.0	101.9	101.8	93.9
Iran, I.R. of	429	106.1	115.8	157.0	118.2	112.4	100.9	76.9	71.3	57.7	57.2	63.7	65.8	64.0	61.5	55.9
Israel	436	206.4	218.3	258.1	229.0	217.4	209.9	324.0	390.3	†470.3	115.2	107.8	111.4	107.3	95.3	100.8
Jordan	439	184.8	165.9	154.7	155.7	149.8	147.4	141.2	131.5	131.6	132.2	132.1	†122.4	119.1	113.5	111.2
Kuwait	443	288.3	286.4	305.8	415.2	327.2	267.9	225.0	304.9	270.5	188.2	127.8	116.2	119.0	116.0	95.3
Libya	672	280.1	283.6	298.9	278.7	288.0	261.9	213.3	238.4	265.6	181.5	190.1	188.8	177.5	150.6	117.7
Oman	449	87.1	102.4	214.0	177.3	171.0	137.4	120.5	150.5	189.7	176.1	139.5	128.8	122.4	111.6	97.8
Qatar	453	231.9	206.0	....	431.3	347.5	262.1	247.0	314.6	332.3	280.5	205.1	171.4	161.1	129.9	93.7
Saudi Arabia	456	481.9	858.0	861.3	625.0	423.3	303.7	233.0	313.9	361.3	294.4	180.8	139.1	123.2	107.5	90.0
Syrian Arab Rep.	463	156.1	135.6	150.4	153.3	148.5	129.1	121.1	120.9	125.9	126.0	114.3	97.5	79.3	74.3	76.7
United Arab Emirates	466	....	322.0	328.4	285.5	218.8	199.6	191.0	244.4	288.4	253.9	192.6	153.3	127.8	111.3	83.1
Yemen, Republic of	474	....														....
Western Hemisphere																
Antigua and Barbuda	311	....	....	....	91.5	84.4	†129.6	132.8	141.7	147.8	149.2	144.6	132.7	120.7	124.7	129.7
Argentina	213	110.7	77.3	61.4	105.2	132.1	100.6	82.1	83.7	99.0	118.2	142.4	184.2	199.5	169.8	137.2
Bahamas, The	313	....	168.4	166.2	197.2	181.4	203.7	219.9	220.4	194.3	197.4	177.3	152.3	147.3	158.9	165.5
Barbados	316	100.1	107.5	151.0	138.6	143.5	131.3	120.5	134.9	147.3	140.1	134.4	132.0	132.6	127.4	127.3
Belize	339					109.1	122.8	125.3	123.9	163.8	130.3	128.3	114.4	120.9	112.7	105.0
Bolivia	218	213.8	242.6	286.8	249.4	214.8	177.0	172.4	184.9	189.3	190.2	210.5	271.2	570.9	977.4	451.7
Brazil	223	85.6	96.0	104.6	109.1	118.4	127.3	123.3	128.5	159.3	189.8	197.3	210.5	219.2	201.9	115.2
Chile	228	154.6	210.2	413.7	350.1	254.6	240.2	209.7	199.7	173.7	137.9	108.2	106.7	103.6	102.0	98.3
Colombia	233	90.9	88.6	88.5	92.2	94.8	91.6	91.6	97.2	100.0	86.9	83.2	86.2	87.3	92.5	93.1
Costa Rica	238	106.5	108.7	110.5	101.9	92.5	86.5	78.2	69.2	67.9	62.0	73.4	66.8	70.6	72.2	75.7
Dominica	321				139.9	143.3	177.4	184.3	125.6	131.2	140.7	148.7	136.7	136.9	139.1	145.6
Dominican Republic	243	131.8	117.3	109.0	102.7	112.7	114.1	107.1	124.4	129.0	139.3	134.1	133.3	141.3	163.1	118.6
Ecuador	248	98.2	100.8	107.8	104.3	102.5	94.8	100.0	101.7	98.6	99.1	98.9	103.6	107.7	110.2	114.0
El Salvador	253	150.1	144.7	140.4	136.1	140.5	134.4	139.8	141.0	137.2	125.4	116.3	120.1	122.0	117.9	125.7
Grenada	328	....	101.2	111.6	122.6	119.1	120.5	128.0	134.1	123.0	120.1	130.7	135.5	154.7	161.3	144.2
Guatemala	258	119.1	116.4	120.9	119.2	111.7	114.6	111.2	113.3	119.8	118.4	101.5	101.2	99.0	102.2	109.7
Guyana	336	153.6	141.6	179.6	173.2	136.1	117.5	104.6	106.7	108.9	99.8	74.9	60.4	59.3	57.9	52.5
Haiti	263	248.0	262.4	†187.8	198.5	181.7	160.0	136.9	136.2	147.6	124.7	123.3	127.4	124.9	129.4	133.1
Honduras	268	126.3	118.1	118.3	122.0	117.7	113.6	111.2	110.0	124.4	126.4	118.5	103.7	95.9	103.1	102.8
Jamaica	343	105.6	†112.6	131.2	128.3	119.1	112.7	125.8	124.0	115.5	104.0	87.4	82.3	90.7	90.9	95.8
Mexico	273	114.1	113.6	120.5	124.1	114.4	115.7	104.5	103.3	110.8	104.6	101.7	116.6	111.6	122.5	134.4
Nicaragua	278	133.2	117.0	132.5	144.4	132.5	129.5	135.0	127.5	103.7	84.4	82.6	81.7	189.2	201.8	227.8
Panama	283	236.4	210.6	218.0	226.7	223.1	214.8	210.1	193.0	206.0	189.3	181.5	181.8	179.3	181.7	165.9
Paraguay	288	159.0	155.8	171.8	159.5	143.4	131.9	124.4	130.8	134.6	136.8	125.6	125.5	137.7	151.0	168.6
Peru	293	79.6	77.9	77.1	75.7	88.4	99.8	110.5	†128.2	113.0	118.4	113.8	108.3	112.0	116.3	121.3
St. Kitts and Nevis	361								93.7	98.2	100.3	88.8	79.5	81.2	79.4	80.0
St. Lucia	362	....	....	....	91.0	92.0	125.0	122.3	126.3	139.9	131.5	130.4	128.3	124.0	118.1	115.0
St. Vincent & Grenadines	364				91.2	91.6	96.9	95.7	90.3	92.0	92.8	97.8	99.6	96.1	94.0	90.6
Suriname	366	79.6	73.0	78.1	78.8	66.4	67.2	65.3	61.7	56.9	56.0	50.4	43.4	37.2	29.3	22.9
Trinidad and Tobago	369	123.3	127.8	179.5	170.4	146.4	142.5	127.8	131.4	146.4	133.2	116.7	96.9	90.3	85.9	83.1
Uruguay	298	177.6	229.0	230.3	225.5	182.2	154.2	132.0	121.4	116.2	93.0	72.0	67.6	66.5	76.9	77.1
Venezuela, Rep. Bol.	299	105.0	105.3	124.0	88.7	76.3	67.5	62.6	70.0	75.7	75.4	67.5	58.8	66.6	65.0	63.0

1995=100

1987	1988	1989	1990	1991	1992	1993	1994	1995	1996	1997	1998	1999	2000	2001		
															Asia (cont.)	
78.1	97.8	91.8	88.0	94.5	93.2	95.6	95.9	100.0	97.9	84.6	87.1	92.7	....	....	Papua New Guinea	853
188.5	183.3	166.3	153.8	147.6	141.9	†130.2	119.2	100.0	93.3	85.5	80.8	80.9	79.6	80.7	Philippines	566
93.4	96.3	86.6	74.9	....	....	....	119.0	100.0	102.3	101.4	....	....	....	....	Samoa	862
104.8	109.7	102.5	96.0	93.6	90.5	99.3	101.8	100.0	98.9	97.7	85.0	69.3	77.8	72.2	Singapore	576
119.5	117.0	121.6	135.5	131.7	124.7	121.6	116.6	100.0	97.0	100.2	96.2	97.7	96.1		Sri Lanka	524
128.4	129.9	125.5	114.2	109.1	104.2	100.3	101.7	100.0	94.5	85.3	73.4	69.2	70.4	70.2	Thailand	578
69.4	77.9	90.1	74.0	84.8	91.5	93.9	98.7	100.0	....	....	....	....	....	....	Vanuatu	846
....	....	....	....	....	81.6	92.2	98.8	100.0	92.5	86.5	80.8	64.0	44.6	37.2	Vietnam	582
															Europe	
....	....	....	....	....	....	....	72.4	100.0	92.2	81.0	73.9	62.7	52.7	47.5	Armenia	911
....	....	....	....	....	....	....	37.9	100.0	95.1	94.6	83.9	94.2	95.1	91.2	Belarus	913
....	....	....	....	†97.4	93.7	91.2	90.1	100.0	81.5	146.9	129.3	125.4	110.4	103.1	Bulgaria	918
....	....	....	....	....	....	104.2	124.8	100.0	74.4	59.0	53.7	54.8	52.6	42.8	Croatia	960
136.4	132.0	128.8	124.0	112.6	113.3	105.4	101.9	100.0	94.0	89.2	86.6	82.8	79.9	....	Cyprus	423
....	....	....	....	....	....	114.5	110.3	100.0	96.6	104.7	108.6	104.4	100.0	97.4	Czech Republic	935
....	....	....	....	21.7	88.1	103.0	97.1	100.0	93.1	82.5	79.5	74.5	65.7	60.5	Estonia	939
92.5	†106.3	114.1	113.8	†107.0	86.7	85.8	91.3	100.0	100.2	104.8	105.2	101.7	102.6	102.4	Hungary	944
....	....	....	....	....	....	41.0	96.3	100.0	90.3	102.2	98.3	109.0	77.8	63.6	Kazakhstan	916
....	....	....	....	....	....	....	....	100.0	116.2	125.6	108.1	124.9	....	....	Kyrgyz Republic	917
....	....	....	....	....	....	110.0	99.8	100.0	138.1	120.6	105.8	112.1	103.5	92.6	Latvia	941
....	....	....	....	....	....	130.0	100.0	100.0	128.1	126.8	116.7	101.4	98.5	88.1	Lithuania	946
....	....	....	....	....	....	16.5	95.5	100.0	98.2	94.7	84.0	69.5	....	....	Macedonia, FYR	962
109.2	110.6	111.1	110.0	111.1	109.1	107.0	103.2	100.0	97.2	96.3	94.3	91.9	92.9	90.4	Malta	181
....	....	....	....	48.5	78.4	139.7	127.6	100.0	83.7	78.9	72.4	81.6	77.6	67.1	Moldova	921
89.8	105.1	124.9	†121.3	104.6	99.3	94.4	100.8	100.0	94.8	88.7	82.7	74.5	72.2	66.3	Poland	964
53.4	49.4	†43.8	39.6	72.2	88.1	128.2	133.8	100.0	89.3	101.4	97.3	93.7	98.0	98.9	Romania	968
....	....	....	....	....	....	88.1	99.1	100.0	91.7	82.0	78.4	83.1	79.2	68.4	Russia	922
....	....	....	....	....	....	98.8	100.0	100.0	92.5	95.6	89.4	81.8	80.3	80.7	Slovak Republic	936
....	....	....	....	131.0	171.1	134.8	117.6	100.0	91.6	85.4	77.6	74.1	70.7	65.6	Slovenia	961
99.3	106.9	107.0	118.4	114.1	105.1	114.3	100.3	100.0	91.6	86.6	77.5	61.3	58.9	....	Turkey	186
....	....	....	....	....	....	47.5	73.2	79.5	100.0	102.2	81.4	73.7	67.8	....	Ukraine	926
															Middle East	
87.8	91.5	88.6	96.2	104.8	96.3	98.4	102.0	100.0	100.4	95.4	82.9	83.3	93.4	....	Bahrain	419
97.2	92.6	98.0	99.9	91.3	98.0	95.6	95.2	100.0	102.0	101.9	102.9	101.5	104.4	....	Egypt	469
57.3	58.1	57.1	67.8	76.9	91.9	85.3	97.1	100.0	102.4	88.9	90.2	102.7	106.2	....	Iran, I.R. of	429
101.3	104.7	103.0	106.8	114.2	136.0	107.3	103.7	†100.0	94.1	89.0	84.5	74.5	73.5	72.6	Israel	436
100.9	90.4	80.5	79.8	80.6	†93.2	90.7	97.2	100.0	102.4	102.2	104.1	96.4	89.5	....	Jordan	439
112.0	98.3	113.0	90.0	47.3	91.4	102.6	103.2	100.0	116.9	110.1	94.6	106.6	127.8	106.5	Kuwait	443
105.7	120.0	128.6	124.5	118.3	123.6	107.2	104.1	100.0	107.6	125.7	114.7	125.4	141.1	....	Libya	672
103.1	96.1	99.1	111.8	†99.2	103.6	99.6	100.1	100.0	102.8	91.6	72.3	77.6	92.9	....	Oman	449
91.5	101.9	109.6	114.9	117.4	117.4	102.1	97.5	100.0	109.9	127.0	105.4	115.5	146.2	....	Qatar	453
85.6	83.4	86.9	106.3	110.5	105.6	94.6	97.4	100.0	118.4	115.5	99.0	105.2	115.7	108.2	Saudi Arabia	456
86.0	107.3	100.5	105.3	95.7	99.6	91.0	100.5	100.0	110.2	111.3	107.4	100.6	92.3	....	Syrian Arab Rep.	463
87.1	82.3	89.2	107.1	105.7	103.2	102.4	101.9	100.0	104.7	106.0	91.9	....	....	....	United Arab Emirates	466
....	....	....	79.4	81.4	89.5	88.7	85.3	100.0	115.0	126.4	109.6	123.9	....	....	Yemen, Republic of	474
															Western Hemisphere	
130.6	135.8	132.9	127.8	119.3	114.6	114.5	111.1	100.0	99.7	106.1	101.2	92.7	87.9	....	Antigua and Barbuda	311
137.5	147.1	175.4	318.8	238.2	167.2	†115.4	97.0	100.0	89.0	78.2	68.6	61.5	59.2	60.4	Argentina	213
162.4	162.9	†172.2	152.8	134.7	125.7	115.0	107.7	100.0	....	....	....	....	....	....	Bahamas, The	313
127.7	121.1	122.8	116.6	109.8	101.0	97.3	98.4	100.0	95.0	92.0	92.4	86.1	....	....	Barbados	316
104.0	108.3	114.4	111.8	104.0	104.8	107.4	104.5	100.0	91.3	84.1	81.0	79.8	77.8	73.9	Belize	339
264.1	253.7	249.3	198.1	161.0	133.9	102.4	98.4	100.0	98.5	91.8	89.4	85.8	89.7	89.2	Bolivia	218
137.8	181.4	171.9	209.8	179.0	125.7	114.8	104.6	100.0	102.1	100.3	89.4	87.9	97.1	96.7	Brazil	223
100.3	101.1	99.5	98.0	102.8	101.1	97.4	97.8	100.0	99.0	94.1	87.3	80.0	82.6	80.0	Chile	228
89.3	97.0	99.5	108.6	115.9	100.2	96.1	108.1	100.0	101.5	91.7	80.0	72.1	72.9	67.9	Colombia	233
74.3	73.9	69.4	66.6	87.2	89.1	90.5	92.4	100.0	89.0	90.4	89.3	87.4	76.7	72.9	Costa Rica	238
128.4	138.8	136.4	125.4	114.6	108.0	110.3	114.4	100.0	98.5	95.3	96.3	92.8	92.3	....	Dominica	321
104.8	119.0	104.8	107.9	133.8	113.6	97.9	96.8	100.0	94.7	94.7	88.2	80.2	78.3	....	Dominican Republic	243
113.4	121.3	145.3	161.3	153.3	164.5	138.5	115.1	100.0	93.8	89.5	89.4	77.0	94.3	....	Ecuador	248
130.1	141.0	149.3	134.1	125.4	116.0	112.5	99.5	100.0	95.7	86.9	79.9	79.3	79.1	....	El Salvador	253
147.0	136.7	142.1	136.6	138.6	132.2	111.1	104.0	100.0	98.0	94.7	94.6	90.4	85.9	....	Grenada	328
107.6	108.0	107.4	128.2	130.8	101.3	107.5	103.3	100.0	105.2	97.0	98.8	93.6	75.7	70.1	Guatemala	258
60.4	54.7	93.2	92.6	142.3	101.7	90.4	101.2	100.0	91.7	85.6	....	....	....	....	Guyana	336
114.7	89.2	98.3	102.3	113.3	91.9	94.3	111.5	100.0	111.8	116.9	118.5	110.4	98.5	94.8	Haiti	263
96.6	89.7	89.8	90.8	98.0	95.6	97.5	104.0	100.0	98.2	85.0	68.7	63.3	55.5	54.2	Honduras	268
93.4	92.9	92.8	105.6	120.7	115.8	110.7	104.4	100.0	100.9	94.5	90.7	87.0	87.2	85.6	Jamaica	343
147.2	171.4	253.9	162.6	116.8	101.6	†102.1	97.8	100.0	106.8	99.3	102.9	104.0	117.7	123.0	Mexico	273
224.5	213.7	201.9	2,009.9	231.1	160.3	161.7	128.5	100.0	83.4	64.9	54.8	49.8	52.4	....	Nicaragua	278
150.0	173.9	195.7	172.5	149.5	132.6	118.0	108.4	100.0	96.9	93.3	88.5	80.4	77.5	....	Panama	283
169.2	173.4	172.7	158.8	128.8	108.9	99.2	99.8	100.0	93.2	90.9	90.7	86.2	83.4	82.8	Paraguay	288
134.6	219.4	243.2	256.0	172.3	140.1	108.7	107.3	100.0	83.3	70.4	63.0	55.8	56.8	57.6	Peru	293
101.3	115.3	105.6	106.1	101.2	99.5	95.9	105.2	100.0	100.7	103.2	94.4	90.9	86.8	....	St. Kitts and Nevis	361
104.9	113.7	108.0	105.4	101.8	105.9	104.1	104.2	100.0	96.3	93.0	94.3	92.5	89.8	....	St. Lucia	362
93.8	111.9	100.3	99.9	102.4	108.1	103.1	96.7	100.0	100.3	97.4	92.4	81.4	78.1	....	St. Vincent & Grenadines	364
20.2	19.0	18.3	20.5	20.3	22.7	35.9	95.1	100.0	76.1	68.5	49.4	....	....	....	Suriname	366
81.8	80.2	82.0	92.0	90.9	97.2	97.8	105.6	100.0	105.0	101.3	91.5	....	....	....	Trinidad and Tobago	369
79.8	83.5	77.6	76.0	79.8	89.4	94.4	101.1	100.0	92.6	87.7	80.8	69.9	65.8	60.6	Uruguay	298
71.6	75.2	96.1	97.9	82.5	88.7	95.3	94.3	100.0	156.2	137.8	123.4	126.3	137.7	....	Venezuela, Rep. Bol.	299

National Interest Rates

	1985	1986	1987	1988	1989	1990	1991	1992	1993	1994	1995	1996	1997	1998	1999	2000	2001
						Central Bank Discount Rates (60)											
						(End of period in percent per annum)											
Industrial Countries																	
United States	7.50	5.50	6.00	6.50	7.00	6.50	3.50	3.00	3.00	4.75	5.25	5.00	5.00	4.50	5.00	6.00	1.25
Canada	9.49	8.49	8.66	11.17	12.47	11.78	7.67	7.36	4.11	7.43	5.79	3.25	4.50	5.25	5.00	6.00	2.50
Japan	5.00	3.00	2.50	2.50	4.25	6.00	4.50	3.25	1.75	1.75	.50	.50	.50	.50	.50	.50	.10
New Zealand	19.80	24.60	18.55	15.10	15.00	13.25	8.30	9.15	5.70	9.75	9.80	8.80	9.70	5.60	5.00	6.50	4.75
Australia	15.98	16.93	14.95	13.20	17.23	15.24	10.99	6.96	5.83	5.75	5.75	....	....	....	....	....	....
Euro Area															4.00	5.75	4.25
Austria	4.00	4.00	3.00	4.00	6.50	6.50	8.00	8.00	5.25	4.50	3.00	2.50	2.50	2.50	....	....	....
Belgium	9.75	8.00	7.00	7.75	10.25	10.50	8.50	7.75	5.25	4.50	3.00	2.50	2.75	2.75	....	....	....
Finland	9.00	7.00	7.00	8.00	8.50	8.50	8.50	9.50	5.50	5.25	4.88	4.00	4.00	3.50	....	....	....
Germany	4.00	3.50	2.50	3.50	6.00	6.00	8.00	8.25	5.75	4.50	3.00	2.50	2.50	2.50	....	....	....
Greece	20.50	20.50	20.50	19.00	19.00	19.00	19.00	19.00	21.50	20.50	18.00	16.50	14.50	....	†11.81	8.10	....
Ireland	10.25	13.25	9.25	8.00	12.00	11.25	10.75	....	7.00	6.25	6.50	6.25	6.75	4.06	....	....	....
Italy	15.00	12.00	12.00	12.50	13.50	12.50	12.00	12.00	8.00	7.50	9.00	7.50	5.50	3.00	....	....	....
Netherlands	5.00	4.50	3.75	4.50	7.00	7.25	8.50	7.75	5.00	....	....	....	....	....	....	....	....
Portugal	19.00	16.00	14.50	13.50	14.50	14.50	†20.00	21.96	11.00	8.88	8.50	6.70	5.31	3.00	....	....	....
Spain	10.50	11.84	13.50	12.40	14.52	14.71	12.50	13.25	9.00	7.38	9.00	6.25	4.75	3.00	....	....	....
Denmark	7.00	7.00	7.00	7.00	7.00	8.50	9.50	9.50	6.25	5.00	4.25	3.25	3.50	3.50	3.00	4.75	3.25
Iceland	30.00	21.00	49.20	24.10	38.40	21.00	21.00	†16.63	....	4.70	5.93	5.70	6.55	†8.50	10.00	12.40	12.00
Norway	10.70	14.80	13.80	12.00	11.00	10.50	10.00	11.00	7.00	6.75	6.75	6.00	5.50	10.00	7.50	9.00	8.50
Sweden	10.50	7.50	7.50	8.50	10.50	11.50	8.00	†10.00	5.00	7.00	7.00	3.50	2.50	2.00	1.50	2.00	2.00
Switzerland	4.00	4.00	2.50	3.50	6.00	6.00	7.00	6.00	4.00	3.50	1.50	1.00	1.00	1.00	.50	†3.20	1.59
Developing Countries																	
Africa																	
Algeria	2.75	5.00	5.00	5.00	7.00	10.50	11.50	11.50	11.50	21.00	†14.00	13.00	11.00	9.50	8.50	6.00	6.00
Angola	....	....	....	....	....	....	....	....	....	....	160.00	2.00	48.00	58.00	120.00	150.00	150.00
Benin	10.50	8.50	8.50	9.50	11.00	11.00	11.00	12.50	10.50	10.00	7.50	6.50	6.00	6.25	5.75	6.50	6.50
Botswana	9.00	9.00	8.50	6.50	6.50	8.50	12.00	14.25	14.25	13.50	13.00	13.00	12.50	12.50	13.25	14.25	14.25
Burkina Faso	10.50	8.50	8.50	9.50	11.00	11.00	11.00	12.50	10.50	10.00	7.50	6.50	6.00	6.25	5.75	6.50	6.50
Burundi	7.00	5.00	7.00	7.00	7.00	8.50	10.00	11.00	10.00	10.00	10.00	10.00	12.00	12.00	12.00	14.00	14.00
Cameroon	9.00	8.00	8.00	9.50	10.00	11.00	10.75	12.00	11.50	†7.75	8.60	7.75	7.50	7.00	7.30	7.00	6.50
Central African Rep.	9.00	8.00	8.00	9.50	10.00	11.00	10.75	12.00	11.50	†7.75	8.60	7.75	7.50	7.00	7.60	7.00	6.50
Chad	9.00	8.00	8.00	9.50	10.00	11.00	10.75	12.00	11.50	†7.75	8.60	7.75	7.50	7.00	7.60	7.00	6.50
Comoros	10.00	10.00	8.50	8.50	....	....	....	....	....	....	....	....	....	....	....	....	....
Congo, Dem. Rep. of	26.00	26.00	29.00	37.00	50.00	45.00	55.00	55.00	95.00	145.00	125.00	238.00	13.00	22.00	120.00	120.00	....
Congo, Republic of	9.00	8.00	8.00	9.50	10.00	11.00	10.75	12.00	11.50	†7.75	8.60	7.75	7.50	7.00	7.60	7.00	6.50
Côte d'Ivoire	10.50	8.50	8.50	9.50	11.00	11.00	11.00	12.50	10.50	10.00	7.50	6.50	6.00	6.25	5.75	6.50	6.50
Equatorial Guinea	9.00	8.00	8.00	9.50	10.00	11.00	10.75	12.00	11.50	†7.75	8.60	7.75	7.50	7.00	7.60	7.00	6.50
Ethiopia	6.00	6.00	3.00	3.00	3.00	3.00	3.00	5.25	12.00	12.00	12.00	....	....	....	....	....	....
Gabon	9.00	8.00	8.00	9.50	10.00	11.00	10.75	12.00	11.50	†7.75	8.60	7.75	7.50	7.00	7.60	7.00	6.50
Gambia, The	15.00	20.00	21.00	19.00	15.00	16.50	15.50	17.50	13.50	13.50	14.00	14.00	14.00	12.00	10.50	10.00	....
Ghana	18.50	20.50	23.50	26.00	26.00	33.00	20.00	30.00	35.00	33.00	45.00	45.00	45.00	37.00	27.00	27.00	27.00
Guinea	....	9.00	10.00	10.00	13.00	15.00	19.00	19.00	17.00	17.00	18.00	18.00	15.00	....	....	11.50	16.25
Guinea-Bissau	....	....	....	....	....	42.00	42.00	45.50	41.00	26.00	39.00	54.00	6.00	6.25	5.75	6.50	6.50
Kenya	12.50	12.50	12.50	16.02	16.50	19.43	20.27	20.46	45.50	21.50	24.50	26.88	32.27	17.07	26.46	19.47	16.81
Lesotho	12.00	9.50	9.00	15.50	17.00	15.75	18.00	15.00	13.50	13.50	15.50	17.00	15.60	19.50	19.00	15.00	13.00
Madagascar	11.50	11.50	11.50	11.50	....	....	....	....	....	....	....	....	....	15.00	....	....	....
Malawi	11.00	11.00	14.00	11.00	11.00	14.00	13.00	20.00	25.00	40.00	50.00	27.00	23.00	43.00	47.00	50.23	46.80
Mali	10.50	8.50	8.50	9.50	11.00	11.00	11.00	12.50	10.50	10.00	7.50	6.50	6.00	6.25	5.75	6.50	6.50
Mauritania	6.50	6.50	6.50	6.50	7.00	7.00	7.00	7.00	....	....	....	....	....	....	....	....	....
Mauritius	11.00	11.00	10.00	10.00	12.00	12.00	11.30	8.30	8.30	13.80	11.40	11.82	10.46	17.19	....	....	....
Morocco	8.13	8.50	8.50	8.50	....	....	....	....	....	7.17	....	....	....	6.04	5.42	5.00	4.71
Mozambique	....	....	....	....	....	....	....	....	....	69.70	57.75	32.00	12.95	9.95	9.95	9.95	9.95
Namibia	....	....	....	....	....	....	20.50	16.50	14.50	15.50	17.50	17.75	16.00	18.75	11.50	11.25	9.25
Niger	10.50	8.50	8.50	8.50	11.00	11.00	11.00	12.50	10.50	10.00	7.50	6.50	6.00	6.25	5.75	6.50	6.50
Nigeria	10.00	10.00	12.75	12.75	18.50	18.50	15.50	17.50	26.00	13.50	13.50	13.50	13.50	13.50	18.00	14.00	20.50
Rwanda	9.00	9.00	9.00	9.00	9.00	14.00	14.00	11.00	11.00	11.00	16.00	16.00	10.75	11.38	11.19	11.69	13.00
São Tomé & Príncipe	....	....	....	....	25.00	25.00	45.00	45.00	30.00	32.00	50.00	35.00	55.00	29.50	17.00	17.00	15.50
Senegal	10.50	8.50	8.50	9.50	11.00	11.00	11.00	12.50	10.50	10.00	7.50	6.50	6.00	6.25	5.75	6.50	6.50
Seychelles	6.00	6.00	6.00	6.00	6.00	†1.00	1.00	1.00	1.00	1.00	1.00	1.00	1.00	1.00	1.00	1.00	1.00
Sierra Leone	14.00	16.00	16.00	16.00	16.00	55.00	55.00	....	....	....	....	....	....	....	....	....	....
Somalia																	
South Africa	13.00	9.50	9.50	14.50	18.00	18.00	17.00	14.00	12.00	13.00	15.00	17.00	16.00	†19.32	12.00	12.00	9.50
Swaziland	12.50	9.50	9.00	11.00	12.00	12.00	13.00	12.00	11.00	12.00	15.00	16.75	15.75	18.00	12.00	11.00	9.50
Tanzania	5.00	8.00	12.50	14.50	15.50	....	....	14.50	14.50	67.50	47.90	19.00	16.20	17.60	20.20	10.70	8.70
Togo	10.50	8.50	8.50	9.50	11.00	11.00	11.00	12.50	10.50	10.00	7.50	6.50	6.00	6.25	5.75	6.50	6.50
Tunisia	9.25	9.25	9.25	9.25	11.37	11.88	11.88	11.38	8.88	8.88	8.88	7.88	....	....	....	....	....
Uganda	24.00	36.00	31.00	45.00	55.00	50.00	46.00	41.00	24.00	15.00	13.30	15.85	14.08	9.10	15.75	18.86	8.88
Zambia	25.00	30.00	15.00	15.00	....	....	....	47.00	72.50	20.50	40.20	47.00	17.70	....	....	....	....
Zimbabwe	9.00	9.00	9.00	9.00	9.00	10.25	20.00	29.50	28.50	29.50	29.50	27.00	31.50	†39.50	74.41	57.84	57.20
Asia																	
Bangladesh	11.25	10.75	10.75	10.75	10.75	9.75	9.25	8.50	6.00	5.50	6.00	7.00	8.00	8.00	7.00	7.00	6.00
China,P.R.: Mainland	....	....	....	....	....	....	7.92	7.20	7.20	10.08	10.08	10.44	9.00	8.55	4.59	3.24	3.24
China,P.R.:Hong Kong	....	....	....	....	....	....	....	4.00	4.00	5.75	6.25	6.00	7.00	6.25	7.00	8.00	3.25
Fiji	11.00	8.00	11.00	11.00	....	8.00	8.00	6.00	6.00	6.00	6.00	6.70	1.88	2.50	2.50	8.00	1.75
India	10.00	10.00	10.00	10.00	10.00	10.00	12.00	12.00	12.00	12.00	12.00	12.00	9.00	9.00	8.00	8.00	6.50
Indonesia	....	....	....	....	....	18.83	18.47	13.50	8.82	12.44	13.99	12.80	20.00	38.44	12.51	14.53	17.62
Korea	5.00	7.00	7.00	8.00	7.00	7.00	7.00	7.00	7.00	5.00	5.00	5.00	5.00	3.00	3.00	3.00	....
Lao People's Dem.Rep	....	....	....	....	....	....	....	23.67	25.00	30.00	32.08	35.00	....	35.00	34.89	35.17	35.00
Malaysia	4.13	3.89	3.20	4.12	4.89	7.23	7.70	7.10	5.24	4.51	6.47	7.28	....	....	....	....	....
Mongolia	....	....	....	....	....	....	....	....	628.80	180.00	150.00	109.00	45.50	23.30	11.40	8.65	8.60
Myanmar	....	....	....	....	....	....	11.00	11.00	11.00	11.00	12.50	15.00	15.00	15.00	12.00	10.00	10.00

Central Bank Discount Rates (60) (cont.)
(End of period in percent per annum)

1985	1986	1987	1988	1989	1990	1991	1992	1993	1994	1995	1996	1997	1998	1999	2000	2001	
																	Asia (cont.)
15.00	11.00	11.00	11.00	11.00	11.00	13.00	13.00	11.00	11.00	11.00	11.00	9.00	9.00	9.00	7.50	6.50	Nepal
10.00	10.00	10.00	10.00	10.00	10.00	10.00	10.00	10.00	†15.00	17.00	20.00	18.00	16.50	13.00	13.00	10.00	Pakistan
9.75	11.40	8.80	10.80	9.55	9.30	9.30	7.12	†6.30	6.55	18.00	10.30	10.20	18.15	12.80	4.41	11.25	Papua New Guinea
†12.75	10.00	10.00	10.00	12.00	14.00	14.00	14.30	9.40	8.30	10.83	11.70	14.64	12.40	7.89	13.81	8.30	Philippines
11.00	11.00	10.00	10.00	14.00	15.00	17.00	17.00	17.00	17.00	17.00	17.00	17.00	17.00	16.00	25.00	....	Sri Lanka
11.00	8.00	8.00	8.00	8.00	12.00	11.00	11.00	9.00	9.50	10.50	10.50	12.50	12.50	4.00	4.00	3.75	Thailand
....	....	....	....	....	....	....	....	....	....	....	....	....	7.00	7.00	7.00	6.50	Vanuatu
....	....	....	....	....	....	....	....	....	....	....	18.90	10.80	12.00	6.00	6.00	4.80	Vietnam
																	Europe
....	....	....	....	....	....	40.00	34.00	25.00	20.50	24.00	32.00	23.44	18.00	10.82	....	....	Albania
....	....	....	....	....	....	....	30.00	210.00	210.00	77.80	26.00	65.10	....	....	....	....	Armenia
....	....	....	....	....	....	....	12.00	100.00	200.00	80.00	20.00	12.00	14.00	10.00	10.00	10.00	Azerbaijan
....	....	....	....	....	....	....	30.00	210.00	480.00	66.00	8.30	8.90	9.60	23.40	†80.00	48.00	Belarus
....	....	....	....	....	....	54.00	41.00	52.00	72.00	34.00	180.00	6.65	5.08	4.46	4.63	....	Bulgaria
....	....	....	....	....	....	....	1,889.39	34.49	8.50	8.50	6.50	5.90	5.90	7.90	5.90	5.90	Croatia
6.00	6.00	6.00	6.00	6.50	6.50	6.50	6.50	6.50	6.50	6.50	†7.50	7.00	7.00	7.00	7.00	5.50	Cyprus
....	....	....	....	....	....	....	....	8.00	8.50	11.30	12.40	14.75	9.50	5.25	5.25	4.75	Czech Republic
11.50	10.50	10.50	14.00	17.00	22.00	22.00	21.00	22.00	25.00	28.00	23.00	20.50	17.00	14.50	11.00	9.75	Hungary
....	....	....	....	....	....	....	....	170.00	230.00	†52.50	35.00	18.50	25.00	18.00	14.00	9.00	Kazakhstan
....	....	....	....	....	....	....	....	....	....	....	....	....	....	....	....	....	Kyrgyz Republic
....	....	....	....	....	....	....	....	27.00	25.00	24.00	9.50	4.00	4.00	4.00	3.50	3.50	Latvia
....	....	....	....	....	....	....	....	295.00	33.00	15.00	9.20	8.90	8.90	8.90	7.90	10.70	Macedonia, FYR
6.00	6.00	5.50	5.50	5.50	5.50	5.50	5.50	5.50	5.50	5.50	5.50	5.50	5.50	4.75	4.75	4.25	Malta
4.00	4.00	4.00	6.00	†104.00	48.00	36.00	32.00	29.00	28.00	25.00	22.00	24.50	18.25	19.00	21.50	14.00	Poland
....	....	....	....	....	....	....	....	....	....	160.00	48.00	28.00	60.00	55.00	25.00	25.00	Russia
....	....	....	....	....	....	....	....	12.00	12.00	9.75	8.80	8.80	8.80	8.80	8.80	....	Slovak Republic
....	....	....	....	....	....	....	....	....	....	....	14.62	11.42	13.78	8.55	8.35	11.85	Slovenia
52.00	48.00	45.00	54.00	54.00	45.00	48.00	48.00	48.00	55.00	50.00	50.00	67.00	67.00	60.00	60.00	60.00	Turkey
....	....	....	....	....	....	....	80.00	240.00	252.00	110.00	40.00	35.00	60.00	45.00	27.00	12.50	Ukraine
....	....	....	....	....	....	....	....	....	....	....	....	....	....	....	....	....	Yugoslavia, SFR
																	Middle East
13.00	13.00	13.00	13.00	14.00	14.00	20.00	18.40	16.50	14.00	13.50	13.00	12.25	12.00	12.00	12.00	11.00	Egypt
79.60	31.40	26.80	30.90	15.00	13.00	14.23	10.39	9.78	17.01	14.19	....	....	....	....	....	....	Israel
6.25	6.25	6.25	6.25	8.00	8.50	8.50	8.50	8.50	8.50	8.50	8.50	7.75	9.00	8.00	6.50	5.00	Jordan
6.00	6.00	6.00	7.50	7.50	....	7.50	7.50	5.75	7.00	7.25	7.25	7.50	7.00	6.75	7.25	4.25	Kuwait
19.70	21.85	21.85	21.84	21.84	21.84	18.04	16.00	20.22	16.49	19.01	25.00	30.00	30.00	25.00	20.00	20.00	Lebanon
5.00	5.00	5.00	5.00	5.00	5.00	5.00	5.00	5.00	....	....	....	....	3.00	5.00	5.00	5.00	Libya
5.00	5.00	5.00	5.00	5.00	5.00	5.00	5.00	5.00	5.00	5.00	5.00	5.00	5.00	5.00	5.00	5.00	Syrian Arab Republic
																	Western Hemisphere
....	9.50	9.50	9.50	9.50	9.50	9.50	9.50	9.50	9.50	9.50	9.50	9.50	9.50	6.50	6.50	6.50	Aruba
8.50	7.50	7.50	9.00	9.00	9.00	9.00	7.50	7.00	6.50	6.50	6.50	6.50	6.50	5.75	5.75	5.75	Bahamas, The
13.00	8.00	8.00	8.00	13.50	13.50	18.00	12.00	8.00	9.50	12.50	12.50	9.00	9.00	10.00	10.00	7.50	Barbados
20.00	12.00	12.00	10.00	12.00	12.00	12.00	12.00	12.00	12.00	12.00	12.00	12.00	12.00	12.00	12.00	12.00	Belize
....	....	....	....	....	....	....	....	....	....	....	16.50	13.25	14.10	12.50	10.00	8.50	Bolivia
....	....	....	....	....	....	....	....	....	....	....	25.34	45.09	39.41	21.37	†18.52	21.43	Brazil
....	....	....	....	....	....	....	....	7.96	13.89	7.96	11.75	7.96	9.12	7.44	8.73	6.50	Chile
27.00	†33.83	34.82	34.25	36.94	†46.45	44.98	34.42	33.49	44.90	40.42	35.05	31.32	42.28	23.05	18.28	16.40	Colombia
28.00	27.50	31.38	31.50	31.61	37.80	42.50	29.00	35.00	37.75	38.50	35.00	31.00	37.00	34.00	31.50	28.75	Costa Rica
23.00	23.00	23.00	23.00	32.00	35.00	49.00	49.00	33.57	44.88	59.41	46.38	37.46	61.84	64.40	†13.16	16.44	Ecuador
9.00	9.00	9.00	9.00	13.00	18.50	16.50	....	....	....	....	....	....	....	....	....	....	Guatemala
14.00	14.00	14.00	14.00	35.00	30.00	32.50	24.30	17.00	20.25	17.25	12.00	11.00	11.25	13.25	11.75	8.75	Guyana
24.00	24.00	24.00	24.00	24.00	28.15	30.09	26.10	....	....	....	....	....	....	....	....	....	Honduras
21.00	21.00	21.00	21.00	21.00	21.00	....	....	....	....	....	....	....	....	....	....	....	Jamaica
8.00	8.00	6.00	6.00	6.00	6.00	6.00	6.00	6.00	5.00	5.00	6.00	6.00	6.00	6.00	6.00	6.00	Netherlands Antilles
....	....	....	12,874.63	310.99	10.00	15.00	15.00	11.75	10.50	....	....	....	....	....	....	....	Nicaragua
....	....	....	10.00	21.00	†33.00	19.75	24.00	27.17	19.15	20.50	15.00	20.00	20.00	20.00	20.00	20.00	Paraguay
42.58	36.07	29.84	748.04	865.61	289.60	67.65	48.50	28.63	16.08	18.44	18.16	15.94	18.72	17.80	14.00	14.00	Peru
7.50	5.97	7.50	9.50	9.50	11.50	13.00	13.00	13.00	13.00	13.00	13.00	13.00	13.00	13.00	13.00	13.00	Trinidad and Tobago
145.10	138.40	143.40	154.50	219.60	251.60	219.00	162.40	164.30	182.30	178.70	160.30	95.50	73.70	66.39	57.26	71.66	Uruguay
8.00	8.00	8.00	8.00	45.00	43.00	43.00	52.20	71.25	48.00	49.00	45.00	45.00	60.00	38.00	38.00	37.00	Venezuela, Rep. Bol.

National Interest Rates

	1985	1986	1987	1988	1989	1990	1991	1992	1993	1994	1995	1996	1997	1998	1999	2000	2001

Money Market Rates (60b)
(Period averages in percent per annum)

Industrial Countries

	1985	1986	1987	1988	1989	1990	1991	1992	1993	1994	1995	1996	1997	1998	1999	2000	2001
United States	8.10	6.81	6.66	7.57	9.22	8.10	5.69	3.52	3.02	4.20	5.84	5.30	5.46	5.35	4.97	6.24	3.89
Canada	9.84	8.16	8.50	10.35	12.06	11.62	7.40	6.79	3.79	5.54	5.71	3.01	4.34	5.11	4.76	5.80	2.24
Australia	14.70	15.75	13.06	11.90	16.75	14.81	10.47	6.44	5.11	5.18	†7.50	7.20	5.50	4.99	†4.78	5.90	5.06
Japan	6.46	4.79	3.51	3.62	4.87	†7.24	7.46	4.58	†3.06	2.20	1.21	.47	.48	.37	.06	.11	.06
New Zealand	24.74	17.70	21.32	15.27	13.40	13.42	9.94	6.63	6.25	6.13	8.91	9.38	7.38	6.86	4.33	6.12	5.76
Euro Area	....	....	....	....	....	....	....	....	....	6.33	6.58	4.92	4.25	3.83	2.97	4.39	4.26
Austria	6.11	5.19	4.35	4.59	7.46	8.53	9.10	9.35	7.22	5.03	4.36	3.19	3.27	3.36	....	....	....
Belgium	8.27	6.64	5.67	5.04	7.00	8.29	†9.38	9.38	8.21	5.72	4.80	3.24	3.46	3.58	....	....	....
Finland	13.46	11.90	10.03	9.97	12.56	14.00	13.08	13.25	7.77	5.35	5.75	3.63	3.23	3.57	2.96	4.39	4.26
France	9.93	7.74	7.98	7.52	9.07	9.85	9.49	10.35	8.75	5.69	6.35	3.73	3.24	3.39	....	....	....
Germany	5.19	4.57	3.72	4.01	6.59	7.92	8.84	9.42	7.49	5.35	4.50	3.27	3.18	3.41	2.73	4.11	4.37
Greece	....	....	....	....	....	....	....	....	....	24.60	16.40	13.80	12.80	13.99	....	....	....
Ireland	11.87	12.28	10.84	7.84	9.55	11.10	10.45	15.12	10.49	†5.75	5.45	5.74	6.43	3.23	3.14	4.84	3.31
Italy	15.25	13.41	11.51	11.29	12.69	12.38	†12.21	14.02	10.20	8.51	10.46	8.82	6.88	4.99	2.95	4.39	4.26
Luxembourg	9.26	7.30	6.71	7.16	10.02	9.67	9.10	8.93	8.09	5.16	4.26	3.29	3.36	3.48	....	....	....
Netherlands	6.30	5.83	5.16	4.48	6.99	8.29	9.01	9.27	7.10	5.14	4.22	2.89	3.07	3.21	....	....	....
Portugal	20.17	†14.52	13.69	12.31	12.68	13.12	15.50	†17.48	13.25	10.62	8.91	7.38	5.78	4.34	2.71	....	....
Spain	11.61	11.49	16.06	11.29	14.39	14.76	13.20	13.01	12.33	7.81	8.98	7.65	5.49	4.34	2.72	4.11	4.36
Denmark	10.33	9.22	10.20	8.52	9.66	10.97	9.78	11.35	†11.49	6.30	6.19	3.98	3.71	4.27	3.37	4.98	4.08
Iceland	....	....	31.52	34.49	21.58	12.73	14.85	12.38	8.61	4.96	6.58	6.96	7.38	8.12	9.24	11.61	14.51
Norway	12.29	14.15	14.66	13.29	11.31	11.45	10.58	13.71	7.64	5.70	5.54	4.97	3.77	6.03	6.87	6.72	7.38
Sweden	13.85	10.15	9.16	10.08	11.52	13.45	11.81	18.42	9.08	7.36	8.54	6.28	4.21	4.24	3.14	3.81	4.08
Switzerland	3.75	3.17	2.51	2.22	6.50	8.33	7.73	7.47	4.94	3.85	2.89	1.78	1.35	1.22	.93	†3.50	1.65
United Kingdom	12.56	10.70	9.50	10.02	13.56	14.73	11.58	9.37	5.91	4.88	6.08	5.96	6.61	7.21	5.20	5.77	5.08

Developing Countries

Africa

	1985	1986	1987	1988	1989	1990	1991	1992	1993	1994	1995	1996	1997	1998	1999	2000	2001
Algeria	....	....	....	....	....	....	....	....	....	19.80	†21.05	18.47	11.80	10.40	10.43	6.77	3.35
Benin	10.66	8.58	8.37	8.72	10.07	10.98	10.94	11.44	....	....	....	....	....	4.81	4.95	4.95	4.95
Burkina Faso	10.67	8.58	8.37	8.72	10.07	10.98	10.94	11.44	....	....	....	....	....	4.81	4.95	4.95	4.95
Côte d'Ivoire	10.66	8.58	8.37	8.72	10.07	10.98	10.94	11.44	....	....	....	....	....	4.81	4.95	4.95	4.95
Guinea-Bissau	10.66	8.58	8.37	8.72	10.07	10.98	10.94	11.45	....	....	....	....	....	4.81	4.95	4.95	4.95
Madagascar	....	....	....	....	....	15.00	15.00	15.00	....	—	29.00	10.00	....	11.24	....	16.00	....
Mali	10.66	8.58	8.37	8.72	10.07	10.98	10.94	11.44	....	....	....	....	....	4.81	4.95	4.95	4.95
Mauritius	11.17	11.05	10.29	10.71	11.98	13.26	12.24	9.05	7.73	10.23	10.35	9.96	9.43	8.99	10.01	7.66	7.25
Morocco	9.41	9.44	....	....	....	....	....	....	....	12.29	10.06	8.42	7.89	6.30	5.64	5.41	4.44
Mozambique	....	....	....	....	....	....	....	....	....	....	....	....	....	....	9.92	16.12	33.64
Niger	10.66	8.58	8.37	8.72	10.07	10.98	10.94	11.44	....	....	....	....	....	4.81	4.95	4.95	4.95
Senegal	10.66	8.58	8.37	8.72	10.07	10.98	10.94	11.44	....	....	....	....	....	4.81	4.95	4.95	4.95
South Africa	18.21	10.92	9.50	13.90	18.77	19.46	17.02	14.11	10.83	10.24	13.07	15.54	15.59	17.11	13.06	9.54	8.84
Swaziland	....	....	....	....	8.39	10.50	10.61	10.25	9.73	7.01	8.52	9.77	10.35	10.63	8.86	5.54	5.06
Togo	10.66	8.58	8.37	8.72	10.07	10.98	10.94	11.44	....	....	....	....	....	4.81	4.95	4.95	4.95
Tunisia	10.28	9.95	10.00	9.15	9.40	11.53	11.79	11.73	10.48	8.81	8.81	8.64	6.88	6.89	5.99	5.88	6.04
Zimbabwe	8.80	9.10	9.30	9.08	8.73	8.68	17.49	34.77	34.18	30.90	29.64	26.18	25.15	37.22	53.13	64.98	21.52

Asia

	1985	1986	1987	1988	1989	1990	1991	1992	1993	1994	1995	1996	1997	1998	1999	2000	2001
China,P.R.:Hong Kong	....	....	....	....	....	11.50	4.63	3.81	4.00	5.44	6.00	5.13	4.50	5.50	5.75	7.13	2.69
China,P.R.:Macao	....	....	....	9.17	8.74	8.17	4.23	4.41	3.79	5.91	6.01	5.60	7.54	5.41	6.11	6.20	1.93
Fiji	6.61	6.55	9.02	1.49	2.34	2.92	4.28	3.06	2.91	4.10	3.95	2.43	1.91	1.27	1.27	2.58	.79
India	10.00	9.97	9.83	9.73	11.39	15.57	19.35	15.23	8.64	7.14	15.57	11.04	5.29	....	....	....	....
Indonesia	10.33	....	14.52	15.00	12.57	13.97	14.91	11.99	8.66	9.74	13.64	13.96	27.82	62.79	23.58	10.32	15.03
Korea	9.35	9.70	8.93	9.62	13.28	14.03	17.03	14.32	12.12	12.45	12.57	12.44	13.24	14.98	5.01	5.16	4.69
Malaysia	6.76	4.19	3.12	4.11	4.72	6.81	7.83	8.01	6.53	4.65	5.78	†6.98	7.61	8.46	3.38	2.66	2.79
Maldives	9.00	9.00	8.67	8.50	7.33	7.00	7.00	7.00	5.00	5.00	6.80	6.80	6.80	6.80	6.80	6.80	6.80
Pakistan	8.13	6.59	6.25	6.32	6.30	7.29	7.64	7.51	11.00	8.36	11.52	11.40	12.10	10.76	9.04	8.57	8.49
Singapore	5.38	4.27	3.89	4.30	5.34	6.61	4.76	2.74	2.50	3.68	2.56	2.93	4.35	5.00	2.04	2.57	1.99
Sri Lanka	14.56	12.95	13.14	18.65	22.19	21.56	25.42	21.63	25.65	18.54	41.87	24.33	18.42	15.74	16.69	17.30	21.24
Thailand	13.48	8.07	5.91	8.66	†10.60	12.87	11.15	6.93	6.54	7.25	10.96	9.23	14.59	13.02	1.77	1.95	2.00
Vanuatu	7.00	6.96	6.50	7.50	7.08	7.00	7.00	5.92	6.00	6.00	6.00	6.00	6.00	8.65	6.99	5.58	5.50

Money Market Rates (60b)(cont.)
(Period averages in percent per annum)

1985	1986	1987	1988	1989	1990	1991	1992	1993	1994	1995	1996	1997	1998	1999	2000	2001	
																	Europe
											48.56	36.41	27.84	23.65	18.63	19.40	Armenia
						48.67	52.39	48.07	66.43	53.09	119.88	66.43	2.48	2.93	3.02	3.74	Bulgaria
							951.20	1,370.50	26.93	21.13	19.26	10.18	14.48	13.72	8.85	3.90	Croatia
											6.85	4.82	4.80	5.15	5.96	4.93	Cyprus
								8.00	12.65	10.93	12.67	17.50	10.08	5.58	5.42	4.69	Czech Republic
									5.67	4.94	3.53	6.45	11.66	5.39	4.57	4.92	Estonia
											43.39	26.58	43.26	34.61	18.17	17.50	Georgia
												43.98	43.71	24.26		11.92	Kyrgyz Republic
									37.18	22.39	13.08	3.76	4.42	4.72	2.97	5.23	Latvia
									69.48	26.73	20.26	9.55	6.12	6.26	3.60	3.37	Lithuania
												28.10	30.91	32.60	20.77	11.04	Moldova
						49.93	†29.49	24.51	23.32	25.82	20.63	22.43	20.59	13.58	18.16	16.23	Poland
										190.43	47.65	20.97	50.56	14.79	7.14	10.10	Russia
															8.08	7.76	Slovak Republic
							67.58	39.15	29.08	12.18	13.98	9.71	7.45	6.87	6.95	6.90	Slovenia
	39.82	60.62	40.66	51.91		72.75	65.35	62.83	136.47	72.30	76.24	70.32	74.60	73.53	56.72	91.95	Turkey
												22.05	40.41	44.98	18.34	16.57	Ukraine
																	Middle East
	7.20	7.07	7.95	9.18	8.54	6.31	3.99	3.53	5.18	6.24	5.69		5.69	5.58	6.89	3.85	Bahrain, Kingdom of
7.59	7.52	6.08	6.12	8.70				7.43	6.31	7.43	6.98	7.05	7.24	6.32	6.82	4.62	Kuwait
4.00	4.00	4.00	4.00	4.00		4.00		4.00					4.00	4.00	4.00	4.00	Libya
																	Western Hemisphere
1,161	135	253	524	1,387,179	9,695,422	71	15	6	8	9	6	7	7	7	8	25	Argentina
										22.42	20.27	13.97	12.57	13.49	7.40	6.99	Bolivia
281.65	105.22	424.38	1,192.87	6,404.97	15,778.57	847.54	1,574.28	3,284.44	4,820.64	53.37	27.45	25.00	29.50	26.26	17.59	17.47	Brazil
															10.09	6.81	Chile
										22.40	28.37	23.83	35.00	18.81	10.87	10.43	Colombia
											14.70	13.01	16.68	15.30	18.28	13.47	Dominican Republic
												10.43	9.43	10.68	6.93	5.28	El Salvador
												7.77	6.62	9.23	9.33	10.58	Guatemala
62.44	88.01	95.59	69.01	†47.43	37.36	23.58	18.87	17.39	16.47	†60.92	33.61	21.91	26.89	24.10	16.96	12.89	Mexico
						12.39	21.59	22.55	18.64	20.18	16.35	12.48	20.74	17.26	10.70	13.45	Paraguay
																	Suriname
									39.82	36.81	28.47	23.43	20.48	13.96	14.82	22.10	Uruguay
											16.70	12.47	18.58	7.48	8.14	13.33	Venezuela, Rep. Bol.

National Interest Rates

	1985	1986	1987	1988	1989	1990	1991	1992	1993	1994	1995	1996	1997	1998	1999	2000	2001
							Treasury Bill Rates (60c) (Period averages in percent per annum)										
Industrial Countries																	
United States	7.49	5.97	5.83	6.67	8.12	7.51	5.41	3.46	3.02	4.27	5.51	5.02	5.07	4.82	4.66	5.84	3.45
Canada	9.43	8.97	8.15	9.48	12.05	12.81	8.73	6.59	4.84	5.54	6.89	4.21	3.26	4.73	4.72	5.49	3.77
Australia	15.42	15.39	12.80	12.14	16.80	14.15	9.96	6.27	5.00	5.69	†7.64	7.02	5.29	4.84	4.76	5.98	4.80
New Zealand	....	19.97	20.50	14.72	13.51	13.78	9.74	6.72	6.21	6.69	8.82	9.09	7.53	7.10	4.58	6.39	5.56
Belgium	9.44	8.09	7.00	6.61	8.45	9.62	9.24	9.36	8.52	5.57	4.67	3.19	3.38	3.51	2.72	4.02	4.16
France	10.08	7.79	8.22	7.88	9.34	†10.18	9.69	10.49	8.41	5.79	6.58	3.84	3.35	3.45	2.72	4.23	4.26
Germany	5.04	3.86	3.28	3.62	6.28	8.13	8.27	8.32	6.22	5.05	4.40	3.30	3.32	3.42	2.88	4.32	3.66
Greece	18.50	18.50	19.50	19.00	20.00	24.00	22.50	22.50	20.25	17.50	14.20	11.20	11.38	10.30	8.30	†6.22	4.08
Iceland	....	....	....	26.39	23.00	12.92	14.25	†11.30	8.35	4.95	7.22	6.97	7.04	7.40	8.61	11.12	11.03
Ireland	11.78	11.85	10.70	7.81	9.70	10.90	10.12	....	†9.06	5.87	6.19	5.36	6.03	5.37	....	....	....
Italy	13.71	11.40	10.73	11.19	12.58	12.38	12.54	14.32	10.58	9.17	10.85	8.46	6.33	4.59	3.01	4.53	4.05
Netherlands	6.23	5.49	5.18	4.34	6.80	....	....	....	....	....	....	....	....	....	....	....	....
Norway																	
Portugal	20.90	†15.56	13.89	12.97	....	13.51	14.20	12.88	....	....	7.75	5.75	4.43	....	....	....	....
Spain	10.90	8.63	†11.38	10.79	13.57	14.17	12.45	12.44	10.53	8.11	9.79	7.23	5.02	3.79	3.01	4.61	3.92
Sweden	14.17	9.83	9.39	10.08	11.50	13.66	11.59	12.85	8.35	7.40	8.75	5.79	4.11	4.19	3.12	3.95	....
Switzerland	4.15	3.54	3.18	3.01	6.60	8.32	7.74	7.76	4.75	3.97	2.78	1.72	1.45	1.32	1.17	2.93	2.68
United Kingdom	11.60	10.34	9.23	9.80	13.28	14.09	10.82	8.94	5.21	5.15	6.33	5.77	6.48	6.82	5.04	5.80	4.77
Developing Countries																	
Africa																	
Algeria	3.25	3.25	3.25	3.25	3.25	3.25	9.50	9.50	9.50	16.50	....	....	....	†9.96	10.05	7.95	5.69
Ethiopia	3.00	3.00	3.00	3.00	3.00	3.00	3.00	5.25	12.00	12.00	12.00	7.22	3.97	3.48	3.65	2.74	3.06
Ghana	17.13	18.47	21.71	19.76	19.84	21.78	29.23	19.38	30.95	27.72	35.38	41.64	42.77	34.33	26.37	36.28	40.96
Kenya	13.90	13.23	12.86	13.48	13.86	14.78	16.59	16.53	49.80	23.32	18.29	22.25	22.87	22.83	13.87	12.05	12.59
Lesotho	17.60	11.21	10.75	11.42	15.75	16.33	15.75	14.20	†10.01	9.44	12.40	13.89	14.83	15.47	12.45	9.06	9.49
Madagascar	....	....	....	....	....	....	....	....	....	....	....	....	....	....	....	....	10.28
Malawi	12.31	12.75	14.25	15.75	15.75	12.92	11.50	15.62	23.54	27.68	46.30	30.83	18.31	32.98	42.85	39.52	42.41
Morocco																	
Mozambique																16.97	24.77
Namibia								13.88	12.16	11.35	13.91	15.25	15.69	17.24	13.28	10.26	9.29
Nigeria								17.89	24.50	12.87	12.50	12.25	12.00	12.26	17.82	15.50	....
Seychelles	12.48	12.90	15.15	13.90	13.41	13.00	13.00	13.00	12.91	12.36	12.15	11.47	10.50	7.96	4.50	4.50	4.50
Sierra Leone	12.00	14.50	16.50	18.00	22.00	47.50	50.67	78.63	28.64	12.19	14.73	29.25	12.71	22.10	32.42	26.22	13.74
South Africa	17.56	10.43	8.71	12.03	16.84	17.80	16.68	13.77	11.31	10.93	13.53	15.04	15.26	16.53	12.85	10.11	9.68
Swaziland	16.47	9.76	5.96	7.28	10.16	11.14	12.67	12.34	8.25	8.35	10.87	13.68	14.37	13.09	11.19	8.30	7.16
Tanzania									34.00	35.09	40.33	15.30	9.59	11.83	10.05	9.78	4.14
Uganda	22.00	30.67	30.50	33.00	42.17	41.00	34.17	....	†21.30	12.52	8.75	11.71	10.59	7.77	7.43	13.19	11.00
Zambia	13.21	24.25	16.50	15.17	18.50	25.92	....	....	124.03	74.21	39.81	52.78	29.48	24.94	36.19	31.37	44.28
Zimbabwe	8.48	8.71	8.73	8.38	8.35	8.39	14.44	26.16	33.04	29.22	27.98	24.53	22.07	32.78	50.48	64.78	17.60
Asia																	
China,P.R.:Hong Kong								3.83	3.17	5.66	5.55	4.45	7.50	5.04	4.94	5.69	1.69
Fiji	7.03	6.36	9.76	1.78	2.75	4.40	5.61	3.65	2.91	2.69	3.15	2.98	2.60	2.00	2.00	3.63	1.51
Lao People's Dem.Rep											20.46	....	....	23.66	30.00	29.94	22.70
Malaysia	4.74	4.12	2.68	3.49	5.29	6.12	7.27	7.66	6.48	3.68	5.50	6.41	6.41	6.86	3.53	2.86	2.79
Nepal	5.00	5.00	5.00	5.00	5.62	7.93	8.80	9.00	4.50	6.50	9.90	11.51	2.52	3.70	4.30	5.30	5.00
Pakistan								12.47	13.03	11.26	12.49	13.61	†15.74	....	....	8.38	10.71
Papua New Guinea	10.40	12.32	10.44	10.12	10.50	11.40	10.33	8.88	6.25	6.85	17.40	14.44	9.94	21.18	22.70	17.00	12.36
Philippines	26.72	16.08	11.51	14.67	18.65	23.67	21.48	16.02	12.45	12.71	11.76	12.34	12.89	15.00	10.00	9.91	9.73
Singapore	2.95	2.03	3.29	4.04	4.68	1.60	1.20	.90	1.35	.65	.71	1.15	1.90	1.15	.40	2.48	.87
Solomon Islands	9.58	12.00	11.33	11.00	11.00	11.00	13.71	13.50	12.15	11.25	12.50	12.75	12.88	6.00	6.00	....	....
Sri Lanka	13.39	10.48	7.30	13.59	14.81	14.08	13.75	16.19	16.52	12.68	16.81	†17.40	....	12.59	12.51	14.02	17.57
Thailand	11.02	6.76	3.63	5.08	....	....	....	....									
Vietnam									26.40	....	....	....	....	....	....	5.42	5.49

Treasury Bill Rates (60c) (cont.)
(Period averages in percent per annum)

1985	1986	1987	1988	1989	1990	1991	1992	1993	1994	1995	1996	1997	1998	1999	2000	2001	
																	Europe
										13.84	17.81	32.59	27.49	17.54	10.80		Albania
										37.81	†43.95	57.54	46.99	55.10	24.40	19.92	Armenia
											12.23	14.10	18.31	16.73		16.51	Azerbaijan
							48.11	45.45	57.72	48.27	114.31	78.35	6.02	5.43	4.21	4.57	Bulgaria
5.50	5.50	5.50	5.50	6.00	6.00	6.00	6.00	6.00	6.00	6.00	6.05	5.38	5.59	5.59	6.01		Cyprus
								6.62	6.98	8.99	11.91	11.21	10.51	5.71	5.37	5.06	Czech Republic
			18.00	20.49	30.13	34.48	22.65	17.22	26.93	32.04	23.96	20.13	17.83	14.68	11.03	10.79	Hungary
									214.34	48.98	28.91	15.15	23.59	15.63	6.59	5.28	Kazakhstan
									143.13	34.90	40.10	35.83	43.67	47.19	32.26	19.08	Kyrgyz Republic
										28.24	16.27	4.73	5.27	6.23	3.83	5.14	Latvia
										26.82	20.95	8.64	10.69	11.14			Lithuania
		4.50	4.24	4.24	4.25	4.46	4.58	4.60	4.29	4.65	4.99	5.08	5.41	5.15	4.89	4.93	Malta
										52.90	39.01	23.63	30.54	28.49	22.20	14.24	Moldova
							44.03	33.16	28.81	25.62	20.32	21.58	19.09	13.14	16.62		Poland
											51.09	85.72	63.99	74.21	51.86	42.18	Romania
										168.04	86.07	23.43			12.12	12.45	Russia
														8.63	10.94	10.88	Slovenia
		41.92	54.56	48.01	43.46	67.01	72.17								33.32	64.61	Turkey
																	Middle East
		6.40	7.39	9.08		5.90	3.78	3.33	4.81	6.07	5.49	5.68	5.53	5.46	6.56	3.78	Bahrain, Kingdom of
											8.80	8.80	9.00	9.10		7.20	Egypt
210.11	19.86	19.97	16.01	12.90	15.08	14.50	11.79	10.54	11.77	14.37	15.54	13.88	12.17				Israel
									6.32	7.35	6.93	6.98					Kuwait
14.96	†18.67	26.91	25.17	18.84	18.84	17.47	22.40	18.27	15.09	19.40	15.19	13.42	12.70	11.57	11.18	11.18	Lebanon
																	Western Hemisphere
7.00	7.00	7.00	7.00	7.00	7.00	7.00	7.00	7.00	7.00	7.00	7.00	7.00	7.00	7.00	7.00	7.00	Antigua and Barbuda
5.90	3.47	2.40	4.46	5.21	5.85	6.49	5.32	3.96	1.88	3.01	4.45	4.35	3.84	1.97	1.03	1.94	Bahamas, The
5.53	4.42	4.84	4.75	4.90	7.07	9.34	10.88	5.44	7.26	8.01	6.85	3.61	5.61	5.83	5.29	3.14	Barbados
12.76	10.81	8.80	8.32	7.36	7.37	6.71	5.38	4.59	4.27	4.10	3.78	3.51	3.83	5.91	5.91	5.91	Belize
									17.89	24.51	19.93	13.65	12.33	14.07	10.99	11.48	Bolivia
										49.93	25.73	24.79	28.57	26.39	18.51	20.06	Brazil
6.50	6.50	6.50	6.50	6.50	6.50	6.50	6.48	6.40	6.40	6.40	6.40	6.40	6.40	6.40	6.40	6.40	Dominica
6.50	6.50	6.50	6.50	6.50	6.50	6.50	6.50	6.50	6.50	6.50	6.50	6.50	6.50	6.50	6.50	6.50	Grenada
12.75	12.75	11.33	11.03	15.19	30.00	30.94	25.75	16.83	17.66	17.51	11.35	8.91	8.33	11.31	9.88	7.78	Guyana
												14.13	16.21	7.71	12.33	13.53	Haiti
19.03	20.88	18.16	18.50	19.10	26.21	25.56	34.36	28.85	42.98	27.65	37.95	21.14	25.65	20.75	18.24	16.71	Jamaica
63.20		103.07	†69.15	44.99	34.76	19.28	15.62	14.99	14.10	48.44	31.39	19.80	24.76	21.41	15.24	11.31	Mexico
7.21	7.34	6.36	5.79	5.96	6.10			4.83	4.48	5.46	5.66	5.77	5.82	6.15	6.15	6.15	Netherlands Antilles
6.50	6.50	6.50	6.50	6.50	6.50		6.50	6.50	6.50	6.50	6.50	6.50	6.50	6.50	6.50	6.17	St. Kitts and Nevis
7.00	7.00	7.00	7.00	7.00	7.00	7.00	7.00	7.00	7.00	7.00	7.00	7.00	7.00	7.00	7.00	7.00	St. Lucia
6.50	6.50	6.50	6.50	6.50	6.50	6.50	6.50	6.50	6.50	6.50	6.50	6.50	6.50	6.50	6.50	6.50	St. Vincent & Grens.
3.47	3.99	4.63	4.88	7.13	7.50	7.67	9.26	9.45	10.00	8.41	10.44	9.83	11.93	10.40	10.56	8.55	Trinidad and Tobago
										44.60	39.40	29.20	23.18				Uruguay

National Interest Rates

	1985	1986	1987	1988	1989	1990	1991	1992	1993	1994	1995	1996	1997	1998	1999	2000	2001
Deposit Rates (60l) except for United States (60lc) (Period averages in percent per annum)																	
Industrial Countries																	
United States	8.05	6.52	6.86	7.73	9.09	8.15	5.84	3.68	3.17	4.63	5.92	5.39	5.62	5.47	5.33	6.46	3.69
Canada	8.40	8.25	7.67	9.54	12.09	12.81	8.62	6.67	4.92	5.59	7.15	4.33	3.59	5.03	4.91	5.70	3.86
Australia	10.46	13.96	13.77	11.92	15.29	13.70	†10.44	6.32	4.76	5.05	7.33	6.86	5.12	4.67	†3.53	4.12	3.25
Japan	3.50	2.32	1.76	1.76	1.97	3.56	†4.14	†3.35	2.14	1.70	.90	.30	.30	.27	.12	.07	.06
New Zealand	14.71	16.32	....	†13.41	10.92	†11.65	8.93	6.58	6.24	6.38	8.49	8.49	7.26	6.78	4.56	6.36	5.35
Euro Area	....	....	....	....	....	....	....	....	....	....	....	4.08	3.41	3.20	2.45	3.45	3.49
Austria	3.94	3.63	3.03	2.73	2.98	3.41	3.75	3.69	2.98	2.31	2.19	1.71	1.50	†2.65	2.21	....	....
Belgium	6.69	5.33	5.00	4.54	5.13	6.13	6.25	6.25	†7.11	4.86	4.04	2.66	2.88	3.01	2.42	3.58	3.40
Finland	8.75	7.33	7.00	7.75	5.75	7.50	7.50	7.50	4.75	3.27	3.19	2.35	2.00	....	1.22	1.63	1.94
France	6.25	5.00	4.50	4.50	4.50	4.50	4.50	4.50	4.50	4.50	4.50	3.67	3.50	3.21	2.69	2.63	3.00
Germany	4.44	3.71	3.20	3.29	5.50	7.07	7.62	8.01	6.27	4.47	3.85	2.83	2.69	2.88	2.43	3.40	3.56
Greece	15.50	15.50	15.33	†17.33	17.14	19.52	20.67	19.92	19.33	18.92	15.75	13.51	10.11	10.70	8.69	6.13	3.32
Ireland	6.98	6.50	6.21	3.63	4.54	6.29	5.21	5.42	2.27	.33	.44	.29	.46	.43	.10	.10	.10
Italy	11.00	8.89	7.01	6.69	6.93	6.80	6.64	7.11	†7.79	6.20	6.45	6.49	4.83	3.16	1.61	1.84	1.96
Luxembourg	6.50	5.50	4.94	4.46	5.04	6.00	6.00	6.00	5.33	5.00	5.00	3.54	3.46	3.31	....	....	....
Netherlands	4.10	3.93	3.55	3.48	3.49	3.31	3.18	3.20	3.11	†4.70	4.40	3.54	3.18	3.10	2.74	2.89	3.10
Portugal	25.08	17.13	14.46	13.21	13.00	13.99	14.80	14.59	11.06	8.37	8.38	6.32	4.56	3.37	2.40	....	....
Spain	10.53	9.05	8.97	9.06	9.55	10.65	10.47	10.43	9.63	6.70	7.68	6.12	3.96	2.92	1.85	2.95	3.08
Denmark	8.21	6.58	7.07	7.75	8.27	†7.93	7.15	7.50	6.52	†3.53	3.85	2.80	2.65	3.08	2.43	3.15	3.30
Iceland	24.69	12.21	15.51	†25.54	23.58	12.31	12.73	5.94	6.63	3.03	3.69	4.25	4.72	4.50	4.82	7.11	....
Norway	10.06	10.97	12.03	11.49	9.63	9.68	9.60	10.69	5.51	5.21	4.95	4.15	3.63	7.24	5.38	6.73	....
Sweden	12.00	9.00	8.75	9.50	†9.16	9.93	7.96	†7.80	5.10	4.91	6.16	2.47	2.50	1.91	1.65	2.15	....
Switzerland	4.36	3.51	3.08	4.50	8.08	8.28	7.63	5.50	3.50	3.63	1.28	1.34	1.00	.69	1.24	†3.00	1.68
United Kingdom	11.79	9.85	8.57	8.55	11.51	12.54	10.28	7.46	3.97	3.66	4.11	3.05	3.63	4.48	....	....	....
Developing Countries																	
Africa																	
Algeria	3.00	4.00	4.00	4.00	8.00	8.00	8.00	8.00	8.00	12.00	†16.00	14.50	9.75	8.50	7.50	7.50	6.25
Angola	....	....	....	....	....	....	....	....	....	....	125.92	147.13	29.25	36.88	36.57	†39.58	47.91
Benin	7.25	6.08	5.25	5.25	6.42	7.00	7.00	7.75	....	....	....	....	....	3.50	3.50	3.50	3.50
Botswana	9.00	8.67	7.50	5.00	5.58	6.11	11.40	12.50	13.49	10.39	9.98	10.43	9.25	8.72	9.46	10.07	10.15
Burkina Faso	7.25	6.08	5.25	5.25	6.42	7.00	7.00	7.75	....	....	....	....	....	3.50	3.50	3.50	3.50
Burundi	4.50	5.96	5.33	4.00	....	....	....	....	....	....	....	....	....	....	....	....	....
Cameroon	7.50	7.35	7.15	7.21	7.50	†7.50	7.50	7.50	7.75	8.08	5.50	5.38	5.04	5.00	5.00	5.00	5.00
Cape Verde	4.00	4.00	4.00	4.00	4.00	4.00	4.00	4.00	4.00	4.00	†5.00	5.00	5.04	5.27	4.76	4.34	4.67
Central African Rep.	7.50	7.35	7.19	7.44	7.50	†7.50	7.50	7.50	7.75	8.08	5.50	5.46	5.00	5.00	5.00	5.00	5.00
Chad	5.50	5.50	5.33	4.31	4.25	†7.50	7.50	7.50	7.75	8.08	5.50	5.46	5.00	5.00	5.00	5.00	5.00
Comoros	7.50	7.50	6.50	6.50	....	....	....	....	....	....	....	....	....	....	....	....	....
Congo, Dem. Rep. of	....	....	....	....	....	....	....	....	....	60.00	60.00	60.00	....	....	....	....	....
Congo, Republic of	8.25	8.10	7.79	7.81	8.00	†7.50	7.50	7.50	7.75	8.08	5.50	5.46	5.00	5.00	5.00	5.00	5.00
Côte d'Ivoire	7.25	6.08	5.25	5.25	6.42	7.00	7.00	7.75	....	....	....	....	....	3.50	3.50	3.50	3.50
Djibouti	....	....	....	....	....	....	....	....	....	....	....	....	....	....	....	....	2.81
Equatorial Guinea	7.50	8.25	7.88	6.33	6.50	†7.50	7.50	7.50	7.75	8.08	5.50	5.46	5.00	5.00	5.00	5.00	5.00
Ethiopia	6.00	6.35	6.70	6.70	6.70	2.43	5.00	3.63	11.50	11.50	11.46	9.42	7.00	6.00	6.32	6.68	6.97
Gabon	7.67	8.00	7.94	8.17	8.75	†7.50	7.50	7.50	7.75	8.08	5.50	5.46	5.00	5.00	5.00	5.00	5.00
Gambia, The	9.75	16.13	15.75	15.00	12.92	11.33	12.71	13.83	13.00	12.58	12.50	12.50	12.50	12.50	12.50	12.50	12.50
Ghana	15.75	17.00	17.58	16.50	....	....	21.32	16.32	23.63	23.15	28.73	34.50	35.76	32.05	23.56	28.60	30.85
Guinea	....	....	15.00	16.83	19.50	21.00	22.00	23.00	19.75	18.00	17.50	....	....	6.38	5.67	7.50	8.03
Guinea-Bissau	....	....	....	23.00	28.00	32.67	36.00	39.33	53.92	28.67	26.50	47.25	4.63	3.50	3.50	3.50	3.50
Kenya	11.25	11.25	10.31	10.33	12.00	13.67	....	....	....	....	13.60	17.59	16.72	18.40	9.55	8.10	6.64
Lesotho	10.42	10.04	7.00	9.58	12.82	13.00	13.00	10.63	8.06	8.43	13.34	12.73	11.81	10.73	7.45	4.92	4.83
Liberia	9.34	7.25	5.88	5.43	6.77	....	....	....	....	6.34	6.37	....	6.43	6.22	6.25	6.18	5.94
Madagascar	....	....	....	....	17.75	20.50	20.50	20.50	19.50	19.50	18.50	19.00	14.38	8.00	15.33	15.00	12.00
Malawi	12.50	12.75	14.25	13.50	12.75	12.10	12.50	16.50	21.75	25.00	37.27	26.33	10.21	19.06	33.21	33.25	34.96
Mali	7.25	6.08	5.25	5.25	6.42	7.00	7.00	7.75	....	....	....	....	....	3.50	3.50	3.50	3.50
Mauritania	7.17	6.58	6.00	6.00	5.00	5.00	5.00	5.00	....	....	....	....	....	....	....	....	....
Mauritius	9.46	9.50	9.38	10.00	11.06	12.56	12.31	10.07	8.40	11.04	12.23	10.77	9.08	9.28	10.92	9.61	9.78
Morocco	8.00	8.50	8.50	8.50	8.50	8.50	8.50	....	....	....	....	....	....	7.26	6.39	5.16	5.04
Mozambique	....	....	....	....	....	....	....	....	....	33.38	38.84	18.14	25.43	8.22	7.86	9.70	15.10
Namibia	....	....	....	....	....	....	12.77	11.36	9.61	9.18	10.84	12.56	12.70	12.94	10.82	7.39	6.79
Niger	7.25	6.08	5.25	5.25	6.42	7.00	7.00	7.75	....	....	....	....	....	3.50	3.50	3.50	3.50
Nigeria	9.12	9.24	13.09	12.95	14.68	19.78	14.92	18.04	23.24	13.09	13.53	13.06	7.17	10.11	12.81	11.69	....
Rwanda	6.25	6.25	6.25	6.25	6.31	6.88	8.75	7.73	5.00	....	....	10.92	9.46	8.50	7.95	8.94	9.22
São Tomé & Príncipe	....	....	....	....	16.00	16.00	35.00	35.00	35.00	35.00	35.00	31.00	36.75	38.29	27.00	†15.00	15.00
Senegal	7.25	6.08	5.25	5.25	6.42	7.00	7.00	7.75	....	....	....	....	....	3.50	3.50	3.50	3.50
Seychelles	9.60	10.00	10.00	10.00	9.59	9.53	9.55	9.60	9.51	8.92	9.22	9.90	9.20	7.53	5.13	4.76	4.92
Sierra Leone	11.33	14.17	12.67	16.33	20.00	40.50	47.80	54.67	27.00	11.63	7.03	13.96	9.91	7.12	9.50	9.25	7.67
Somalia	....	....	....	....	....	....	....	....	....	....	....	....	....	....	....	....	....
South Africa	17.02	10.98	8.70	13.54	18.13	18.86	17.30	13.78	11.50	11.11	13.54	14.91	15.38	16.50	12.24	9.20	9.37
Sudan	....	....	....	....	....	....	....	....	....	....	....	....	....	....	....	....	....
Swaziland	10.19	5.75	4.81	9.23	8.92	8.85	10.85	9.00	7.38	8.00	10.25	12.25	11.25	13.43	7.53	6.53	5.69
Tanzania	4.50	8.50	15.75	17.46	17.00	....	....	....	....	....	24.63	13.59	7.83	7.75	7.75	7.39	4.81
Togo	7.25	6.08	5.25	5.25	6.42	7.00	7.00	7.75	....	....	....	....	....	3.50	3.50	3.50	3.50
Tunisia	5.35	6.75	7.22	7.37	....	....	....	....	....	....	....	....	....	....	....	....	....
Uganda	†20.00	23.33	20.00	21.50	32.17	31.25	31.17	35.83	16.26	9.99	7.61	10.62	11.84	11.36	8.73	9.84	8.47
Zambia	15.33	17.74	13.23	11.44	11.44	25.65	....	48.50	....	46.14	30.24	42.13	34.48	13.08	20.27	20.24	23.41
Zimbabwe	10.04	10.28	9.58	9.68	8.85	8.80	14.20	28.63	29.45	26.75	25.92	21.58	18.60	29.06	38.51	50.17	13.95
Asia																	
Bangladesh	12.00	12.00	12.00	12.00	12.00	12.04	12.05	10.47	8.18	6.40	6.04	7.28	8.11	8.42	8.74	8.56	8.50
Bhutan	6.08	6.50	6.50	6.50	6.50	6.50	6.50	8.00	8.00	8.00	8.00	....	....	....	....	....	....
Cambodia	....	....	....	....	....	....	....	....	....	....	8.71	8.80	8.03	7.80	7.33	6.83	4.36
China,P.R.: Mainland	7.20	7.20	7.20	8.64	11.34	8.64	7.56	7.56	10.98	10.98	10.98	7.47	5.67	3.78	2.25	2.25	2.25
China,P.R.:Hong Kong	....	....	....	....	....	6.67	5.46	3.07	2.25	3.54	5.63	4.64	5.98	6.62	4.50	4.80	2.38
China,P.R.:Macao	3.92	3.50	3.50	4.56	7.04	7.13	5.88	3.50	2.75	4.21	5.93	5.23	6.22	7.00	5.30	5.33	2.59
Fiji	6.00	6.00	6.00	4.88	4.00	4.00	4.06	4.10	3.69	3.15	3.18	3.38	3.08	2.17	1.24	.90	.78
Indonesia	18.00	15.39	16.78	17.72	18.63	†17.53	23.32	19.60	14.55	12.53	16.72	17.26	20.01	39.07	25.74	12.50	15.48
Korea	10.00	10.00	10.00	10.00	10.00	10.00	10.00	10.00	8.58	8.50	8.83	7.50	†10.81	13.29	7.95	7.94	5.79
Lao People's Dem.Rep	....	....	....	....	30.00	30.00	†23.50	15.00	13.33	12.00	14.00	16.00	....	17.79	13.42	12.00	6.50
Malaysia	8.81	7.17	3.00	3.19	4.60	5.90	7.18	7.97	7.04	4.94	5.93	†7.09	7.78	8.51	4.12	3.36	3.37

Deposit Rates (60l) (cont.)
except for United States (60lc)
(Period averages in percent per annum)

1985	1986	1987	1988	1989	1990	1991	1992	1993	1994	1995	1996	1997	1998	1999	2000	2001	
										5.33	4.42	4.26	3.73	4.46	5.01	1.52	**Asia (cont.)** Micronesia, Fed.Sts.
	300.00	300.00	300.00	300.00	300.00	400.00	500.00	125.20	101.10	60.10	36.40	37.90	24.29	19.80	13.80	13.20	Mongolia
1.50	1.50	1.50	1.50	1.50	5.88	9.00	9.00	9.00	9.00	9.75	12.50	12.50	12.50	11.00	9.75	9.50	Myanmar
12.50	12.50	12.50	12.50	12.50	11.92			8.75		9.63	9.79	8.92	7.31		5.96	4.75	Nepal
9.49	11.49	9.60	9.28	8.23	8.67	9.06	7.85	5.03	5.09	12.18	12.19	7.31	13.73	15.46	14.54	8.91	Papua New Guinea
18.91	11.25	8.20	11.32	14.13	19.54	18.80	14.27	9.61	10.54	8.39	9.68	10.19	12.11	8.17	8.31	8.74	Philippines
12.00	13.50	12.00	12.00	12.00	8.25	8.25	6.38	5.50	5.50	5.50	5.50	5.50	6.50	6.50	6.46	5.53	Samoa
4.99	3.91	2.89	2.74	3.21	4.67	4.63	2.86	2.30	3.00	3.50	3.41	3.47	4.60	1.68	1.71	1.54	Singapore
8.73	10.50	10.67	10.23	10.46	10.50	10.50	12.00	9.77	9.00	8.38	6.46	2.42	2.33	2.88			Solomon Islands
17.33	12.21	11.50	13.23	16.43	19.42	†13.83	13.74	13.77	13.10	12.13	12.36	11.25	9.56	9.12	9.17	11.01	Sri Lanka
13.00	9.75	9.50	9.50	9.50	12.25	13.67	8.88	8.63	8.46	11.58	10.33	10.52	10.65	4.73	3.29	2.54	Thailand
6.25	6.25	6.25	6.25	7.25	7.25	7.25	4.25	4.25	4.67	4.75	5.58	5.50	5.50	5.42	5.47	5.47	Tonga
7.34	6.81	5.48	6.94	6.58	7.00	7.00	4.69	5.00	5.06	3.00	4.50	3.73	3.29	1.60	1.27	1.25	Vanuatu
								22.04				8.51	9.23	7.37	3.65	5.30	Vietnam
						18.50	†27.33	19.83	†15.30	16.78	27.28	22.56	12.95	8.30	7.73		**Europe** Albania
										63.18	32.19	26.08	24.94	27.35	18.08	14.90	Armenia
														12.08	12.90	8.46	Azerbaijan
								65.08	89.60	100.82	32.36	15.64	14.33	23.80	37.55	34.18	Belarus
													51.88	9.07	14.67		Bosnia & Herzegovina
					39.49	45.01	42.56	51.14	35.94	74.68	46.83	3.00	3.21	3.10	2.88		Bulgaria
						658.51	379.31	6.52	5.53	5.59	4.30	4.62	4.31	3.74	3.23		Croatia
5.75	5.75	5.75	5.75	5.75	5.75	5.75	5.75	5.75	5.75	5.75	5.75	†6.50	6.50	6.50	6.50	†3.75	Cyprus
								7.03	7.07	6.96	6.79	7.71	8.08	4.48	3.42	2.97	Czech Republic
									11.51	8.74	6.05	6.19	8.07	4.19	3.76	4.03	Estonia
											31.05	13.73	17.00	14.58	10.17	7.75	Georgia
5.00	4.50	4.00	5.25	9.42	†24.68	30.41	24.41	15.65	20.31	26.10	22.21	18.54	16.16	13.27	9.63	9.27	Hungary
											36.73	39.59	35.76	35.58	18.38	12.50	Kyrgyz Republic
								34.78	31.68	14.79	11.71	5.90	5.33	5.04	4.38	5.24	Latvia
								88.29	48.43	20.05	13.95	7.89	5.98	4.94	3.86	3.00	Lithuania
									117.56	24.07	12.75	11.64	11.68	11.40	11.18	9.97	Macedonia, FYR
4.96	4.50	4.50	4.50	4.50	4.50	4.50	4.50	4.50	4.50	4.50	4.50	4.56	4.64	4.86	4.86	4.84	Malta
											25.43	23.47	21.68	27.54	24.87	20.93	Moldova
				100.00	41.67	†53.50	37.75	34.00	†33.40	26.78	20.02	19.36	18.19	11.23	14.17	11.79	Poland
										101.96	55.05	†16.77	17.05	13.68	6.51	4.85	Russia
								8.02	9.32	9.01	9.30	13.44	16.25	14.37	8.45	6.46	Slovak Republic
								33.04	28.10	15.38	15.08	13.19	10.54	7.24	10.05	9.81	Slovenia
49.25	40.58	35.00	49.08	53.45	47.50	62.67	68.74	64.58	87.79	76.02	80.74	79.49	80.11	78.43	47.16	74.70	Turkey
								148.63	208.63	70.29	33.63	18.21	22.25	20.70	13.72	10.99	Ukraine
6.71	5.58	5.00	5.50	7.33	7.50		†3.63	3.03	4.00	5.70	5.18	5.28	4.74	4.80	5.82	2.71	**Middle East** Bahrain, Kingdom of
11.00	11.00	11.00	11.00	11.67	12.00	12.00	12.00	12.00	11.83	10.92	10.54	9.84	9.36	9.22	9.46	9.46	Egypt
178.79	18.59	19.39	14.53	14.10	14.40	13.89	11.29	10.44	12.19	14.08	14.48	13.07	11.00	11.35	8.63	6.18	Israel
					8.15	8.13	7.20	6.88	7.09	7.68	8.50	9.10	8.21	8.30	6.97	5.81	Jordan
7.25	6.80	5.73	5.30	7.40			7.59	7.07	5.70	6.53	6.05	5.93	6.32	5.76	5.89	4.46	Kuwait
13.24	16.42	21.18	21.96	17.54	16.86	16.76	17.09	15.56	14.80	16.30	15.54	13.37	13.61	12.50	11.21	10.85	Lebanon
5.50	5.50	5.50	5.50	5.50	5.50	5.50	5.50	5.50						3.21	3.00	3.00	Libya
9.04	8.33	7.48	7.57	8.66	8.32	7.06	6.29	4.17	4.34	6.53	6.85	7.30	8.46	8.12	7.63	4.50	Oman
6.00	6.00	6.00	6.00	6.00	6.00	6.00	4.75	4.08	4.84	6.19	6.50	6.63	6.56	6.50			Qatar
		6.68	8.03	9.04	8.01	5.83	3.65	3.52	5.10	6.18	5.47	5.79	6.21	6.14	6.67	3.92	Saudi Arabia
4.00	4.00	4.00	4.00	4.00	4.00	4.00	4.00	4.00	4.00	4.00	4.00	4.00	4.00	4.00	4.00	4.00	Syrian Arab Republic
9.88	7.71	6.50	6.50	6.50	8.44	8.21	7.44	6.71	6.50	5.92	5.50	5.50	5.50	5.50	5.50	5.54	**Western Hemisphere** Antigua and Barbuda
630.03	94.69	175.95	371.85	17,235.81	1,517.88	61.68	16.78	11.34	8.08	11.90	7.36	6.97	7.56	8.05	8.34	16.16	Argentina
		6.40	6.70	6.70	6.70	6.30	5.70	4.20	4.40	4.30	4.20	4.40		†6.17	6.20	5.84	Aruba
6.40	5.57	5.50	5.97	6.48	6.57	6.92	6.13	5.19	4.30	4.20	5.14	5.23	5.36	4.57	4.08	4.25	Bahamas, The
5.49	4.28	3.61	4.26	4.78	6.28	6.53	6.68	4.39	4.32	5.11	5.20	4.58	4.20	4.40	4.97	4.04	Barbados
11.63	11.83	9.58	8.42	7.86	8.14	8.42	8.15	8.13	8.55	9.37	9.08	9.19	8.76	8.12	7.69	6.35	Belize
68.75	†33.39	30.35	27.74	23.67	23.83	23.78	23.22	22.18	18.43	18.87	19.16	14.73	12.82	12.26	10.98	9.82	Bolivia
295.42	109.48	401.03	859.43	†5,844.98	9,394.29	913.47	1,560.18	3,293.50	5,175.24	52.25	26.45	24.35	28.00	26.02	17.20	17.86	Brazil
†32.10	19.04	25.28	15.16	27.79	40.35	22.35	18.29	18.24	15.12	13.73	13.48	12.02	14.92	8.56	9.20	6.19	Chile
	31.36	30.79	33.46	33.73	36.44	37.23	26.67	25.84	29.42	32.34	31.15	24.13	32.58	21.33	12.15	12.44	Colombia
16.50	16.67	14.06	15.18	15.62	21.16	27.32	15.80	16.90	17.72	23.88	17.29	13.03	12.76	14.31	13.38	11.77	Costa Rica
5.00	4.92	5.04	5.00	4.54	4.21	4.38	4.08	4.00	4.00	4.00	4.00	4.00	4.00	4.92	5.75	6.00	Dominica
						20.02	16.70	14.04	13.70	14.94	13.91	13.40	17.65	16.07	17.65	15.61	Dominican Republic
21.00	21.39	25.34	34.00	40.24	43.55	41.54	46.81	31.97	33.65	43.31	41.50	28.09	39.39	†10.03	8.46	6.58	Ecuador
12.50	15.00	15.00	15.00	16.25	18.00	16.11	11.51	15.27	13.57	14.37	13.98	11.77	10.32	10.75	9.31		El Salvador
7.04	6.50	6.08	5.50	5.04	6.50	6.17	5.46	5.00	4.17	4.00	4.13	4.50	4.83	5.19	5.71	5.75	Grenada
9.00	10.17	11.00	12.17	13.00	18.21	24.41	10.44	12.63	9.69	7.87	7.65	†5.83	5.44	7.96	10.17	8.75	Guatemala
12.00	12.00	11.08	12.00	15.81	29.18	29.53	22.51	12.26	11.42	12.90	10.49	8.56	8.10	9.08	8.71	7.63	Guyana
												10.74	13.06	7.39	11.85	13.66	Haiti
9.93	9.70	9.62	8.63	8.58	8.78	11.45	12.34	11.60	11.56	11.97	16.70	21.28	18.58	19.97	15.93	14.48	Honduras
19.58	18.76	15.64	15.80	15.95	23.88	24.67	33.63	27.59	36.41	23.21	25.16	13.95	15.61	13.48	11.62	9.64	Jamaica
55.23	75.91	92.44	52.70	30.85	27.88	16.57	14.48	15.06	13.32	38.12	24.70	14.66	13.75	9.61	6.27	4.74	Mexico
5.20	5.19	4.82	4.63	4.71	4.97			4.33	4.05	3.75	3.67	3.66	3.58	3.59	3.63	3.65	Netherlands Antilles
			—	1,585.90	9.50	11.63	12.01	11.61	11.70	11.15	12.35	12.41	10.77	10.28	9.41	9.01	Nicaragua
	6.50	6.59	7.54	8.49	8.40	7.73	†5.67	5.90	6.11	7.18	7.20	7.03	6.76	6.92	7.07	6.83	Panama
					22.92	22.53	20.15	22.10	23.12	21.16	17.16	13.00	15.95	†19.75	15.72	16.22	Paraguay
			161.78	1,135.59	2,439.56	170.54	59.65	44.14	22.35	15.70	14.90	15.01	15.11	16.27	13.29	9.92	Peru
6.33	6.00	5.33	7.00	7.00	7.00	7.00	7.00	5.50	5.50	5.50	5.50	5.46	5.50	5.50	5.50	5.58	St. Kitts and Nevis
9.13	7.50	5.04	5.00	5.00	5.58	6.06	5.52	4.96	4.50	6.25	7.00	6.25	7.08	9.25	9.25	8.10	St. Lucia
5.92	5.96	5.32	4.82	4.29	4.33	4.44	5.00	4.25	4.04	5.00	4.50	5.33	5.50	5.50	5.50	5.67	St. Vincent & Grens.
						4.60	4.50	4.75	7.45	21.00	17.83	17.25	16.00	15.60	15.48	11.86	Suriname
5.31	6.04	6.03		6.01	6.28	5.96	5.79	6.99	7.06	6.91		6.91	7.95	8.51	8.15	7.66	Trinidad and Tobago
81.90	61.70	60.83	67.82	84.70	97.83	75.23	54.47	39.38	36.98	38.24	28.13	19.61	15.09	14.25	12.11	14.32	Uruguay
10.52	8.93	8.94	8.95	28.91	27.82	31.10	35.43	53.75	39.02	24.72	27.58	14.70	34.84	21.28	16.30	15.51	Venezuela, Rep. Bol.

National Interest Rates

Lending Rates (60p)
(Period averages in percent per annum)

	1985	1986	1987	1988	1989	1990	1991	1992	1993	1994	1995	1996	1997	1998	1999	2000	2001
Industrial Countries																	
United States	9.93	8.33	8.20	9.32	10.87	10.01	8.46	6.25	6.00	7.14	8.83	8.27	8.44	8.35	7.99	9.23	6.92
Canada	10.58	10.52	9.52	10.83	13.33	14.06	9.94	7.48	5.94	6.88	8.65	6.06	4.96	6.60	6.44	7.27	5.81
Australia	15.24	18.09	16.56	15.10	19.58	18.17	14.28	11.06	9.72	9.55	11.12	11.00	9.31	8.04	7.51	8.78	8.13
Japan	6.60	6.02	5.21	5.03	5.29	6.95	7.53	6.15	†4.41	4.13	3.51	2.66	2.45	2.32	2.16	2.07	1.97
New Zealand	....	....	†20.84	17.17	15.78	16.01	14.01	11.39	10.34	9.69	12.16	12.27	11.35	11.22	8.49	10.22	9.88
Euro Area	....	....	....	....	....	....	....	....	....	....	....	8.88	7.58	6.73	5.65	6.60	6.83
Austria	....	....	....	....	....	....	....	....	....	....	....	....	....	6.42	5.64	....	....
Belgium	12.54	10.44	9.33	8.92	11.08	13.00	12.88	13.00	11.81	9.42	8.42	7.17	7.06	7.25	6.71	7.98	8.46
Finland	10.41	9.08	8.91	9.72	10.31	11.62	11.80	12.14	9.92	7.91	7.75	6.16	5.29	5.35	4.71	5.61	5.79
France	11.09	9.89	9.60	9.43	10.00	10.57	10.22	10.00	8.90	7.89	8.12	6.77	6.34	6.55	6.36	6.70	6.98
Germany	9.53	8.75	8.36	8.33	9.94	11.59	12.46	13.59	12.85	11.48	10.94	10.02	9.13	9.02	8.81	9.63	10.01
Greece	20.50	20.50	21.82	22.89	23.26	27.62	29.45	28.71	28.56	27.44	23.05	20.96	18.92	18.56	15.00	12.32	8.59
Ireland	12.44	12.23	11.15	8.29	9.42	11.29	10.63	†12.66	9.93	6.13	6.56	5.85	6.57	6.22	3.34	4.77	4.84
Italy	18.06	15.93	13.58	13.57	14.21	†14.09	13.90	15.76	13.87	11.22	12.47	12.06	9.75	7.88	5.58	6.26	6.53
Luxembourg	8.75	7.75	7.19	6.71	7.25	8.23	8.25	8.75	7.65	6.58	6.50	5.50	5.50	5.27	....	....	....
Netherlands	9.25	8.63	8.15	7.77	10.75	11.75	12.40	12.75	10.40	8.29	7.21	5.90	6.13	6.50	†3.46	4.79	5.00
Portugal	27.29	19.63	†18.92	†17.53	19.59	21.78	†25.02	20.43	16.48	15.01	13.80	11.73	9.15	7.24	5.19	....	....
Spain	13.52	12.19	16.36	12.43	15.84	16.01	14.38	14.23	12.78	8.95	10.05	8.50	6.08	5.01	3.95	5.18	5.16
Denmark	14.65	12.98	13.62	12.59	13.44	†14.10	11.38	11.78	10.46	†9.95	10.33	8.70	7.73	7.90	7.13	8.08	8.20
Iceland	32.60	18.78	26.61	30.28	27.97	16.18	17.52	13.05	14.11	10.57	11.58	12.43	12.89	12.78	13.30	16.80	17.95
Norway	13.46	14.37	16.31	16.60	14.88	14.26	14.31	14.16	10.97	8.40	7.78	7.10	5.95	7.91	8.16	8.22	8.87
Sweden	16.89	†12.57	12.65	13.29	14.81	16.69	16.05	†15.20	11.40	10.64	11.11	7.38	7.01	5.94	5.53	5.82	....
Switzerland	5.43	5.46	5.24	5.07	5.85	7.42	7.83	7.80	6.40	5.51	5.48	4.97	4.47	4.07	3.90	4.29	4.30
United Kingdom	12.33	10.83	9.63	10.29	13.92	14.75	11.54	9.42	5.92	5.48	6.69	5.96	6.58	7.21	5.33	5.98	5.08
Developing Countries																	
Africa																	
Algeria	....	....	....	....	....	....	....	....	....	16.00	†19.00	19.00	12.50	11.00	10.00	10.00	9.50
Angola	....	....	....	....	....	....	....	....	....	....	206.25	217.88	37.75	45.00	80.30	†103.16	95.97
Benin	14.50	13.50	13.50	13.58	15.08	16.00	16.00	16.75	....	....	....	....	....	....	....	....	....
Botswana	11.50	11.00	10.00	7.83	7.67	7.88	11.83	14.00	14.92	13.88	14.29	14.50	14.08	13.53	14.63	15.31	15.75
Burkina Faso	14.50	13.50	13.50	13.58	15.13	16.00	16.00	16.75	....	....	....	....	....	....	....	....	....
Burundi	12.00	12.00	12.00	12.00	12.00	12.34	12.78	13.66	13.77	14.20	15.26	....	....	....	15.24	15.77	16.82
Cameroon	14.50	13.50	13.00	13.46	15.00	†18.50	18.15	17.77	17.46	17.50	16.00	22.00	22.00	22.00	22.00	22.00	20.67
Cape Verde	10.00	10.00	10.00	10.00	10.00	10.00	10.00	10.00	10.00	10.67	12.00	12.00	12.06	12.51	12.03	11.94	12.85
Central African Rep.	12.50	12.00	11.42	12.25	13.00	†18.50	18.15	17.77	17.46	17.50	16.00	22.00	22.00	22.00	22.00	22.00	20.67
Chad	11.50	11.00	10.50	10.79	11.50	†18.50	18.15	17.77	17.46	17.50	16.00	22.00	22.00	22.00	22.00	22.00	20.67
Comoros	15.00	15.00	13.00	13.00	....	....	....	....	....	....	....	....	....	....	....	....	....
Congo, Dem. Rep. of	....	....	....	....	....	....	....	....	....	398.25	293.88	247.00	134.58	29.00	124.58	165.00	....
Congo, Republic of	12.00	11.50	11.13	11.79	12.50	†18.50	18.15	17.77	17.46	17.50	16.00	22.00	22.00	22.00	22.00	22.00	20.67
Côte d'Ivoire	14.50	13.50	13.50	13.58	15.08	16.00	16.00	16.75	....	....	....	....	....	....	....	....	....
Djibouti	8.50	8.50	8.50	10.50	10.50	10.50	....	....	....	....	....	....	....	....	....	....	11.46
Equatorial Guinea	15.00	14.50	14.13	14.79	15.50	†18.50	18.15	17.77	17.46	17.50	16.00	22.00	22.00	22.00	22.00	22.00	20.67
Ethiopia	8.50	7.25	6.00	6.00	6.00	6.00	6.00	8.00	14.00	14.33	15.08	13.92	10.50	10.50	10.58	10.89	10.87
Gabon	12.67	11.50	11.13	11.79	12.50	†18.50	18.15	17.77	17.46	17.50	16.00	22.00	22.00	22.00	22.00	22.00	20.67
Gambia, The	14.48	28.00	27.92	29.54	26.83	26.50	26.50	26.75	26.08	25.00	25.04	25.50	25.50	25.38	24.00	24.00	24.00
Ghana	21.17	20.00	25.50	25.58	....	....	....	....	....	....	....	....	....	....	....	....	....
Guinea	....	....	15.00	15.00	17.25	21.17	24.50	27.00	24.50	22.00	21.50	....	....	19.56	19.88	19.38	....
Guinea-Bissau	....	18.00	18.00	30.00	38.33	45.75	47.00	50.33	63.58	36.33	32.92	51.75	....	....	....	....	....
Kenya	14.00	14.00	14.00	15.00	17.25	18.75	19.00	21.07	29.99	36.24	28.80	33.79	30.25	29.49	22.38	22.34	19.67
Lesotho	19.67	13.42	11.13	13.67	18.75	20.42	20.00	18.25	15.83	14.25	16.38	17.71	18.03	20.06	19.06	17.11	16.55
Liberia	19.34	14.45	13.63	13.36	13.82	....	....	....	....	14.53	15.57	....	16.83	†21.74	16.72	20.53	22.14
Madagascar	....	....	....	....	22.25	25.80	24.50	25.00	26.00	30.50	37.50	32.75	30.00	27.00	28.00	26.50	25.25
Malawi	18.38	19.00	19.50	22.25	23.00	21.00	20.00	22.00	29.50	31.00	47.33	45.33	28.25	37.67	53.58	53.13	56.17
Mali	14.50	13.50	13.50	13.58	15.08	16.00	16.00	16.75	....	....	....	....	....	....	....	....	....
Mauritania	12.00	12.00	12.00	12.00	10.00	10.00	10.00	10.00	....	....	....	....	....	....	....	....	....
Mauritius	13.83	14.33	14.13	14.96	16.13	18.00	17.75	17.13	16.58	18.92	20.81	20.81	18.92	19.92	21.63	20.77	21.10
Morocco	7.75	8.75	9.00	9.00	9.00	9.00	9.00	....	....	10.00	....	....	....	13.50	13.50	13.31	13.25
Mozambique	....	....	....	....	....	....	....	....	....	....	....	....	....	24.35	19.63	19.04	22.65
Namibia	....	....	....	....	....	....	23.36	20.21	18.02	17.05	18.51	19.16	20.18	20.72	18.48	15.28	14.53
Niger	14.50	13.50	13.50	13.58	15.13	16.00	16.00	16.75	....	....	....	....	....	....	....	....	....
Nigeria	9.43	9.96	13.96	16.62	20.44	25.30	20.04	24.76	31.65	20.48	20.23	19.84	17.80	18.18	20.29	21.27	....
Rwanda	13.88	14.00	13.00	12.00	12.00	13.17	19.00	16.67	15.00	....	....	....	....	....	....	....	....
São Tomé & Príncipe	....	....	....	....	20.00	20.00	37.00	37.00	37.00	30.00	52.00	38.00	51.50	55.58	40.33	†37.00	37.00
Senegal	14.50	13.50	13.50	13.58	15.13	16.00	16.00	16.75	....	....	....	....	....	....	....	....	....
Seychelles	....	....	....	....	15.52	15.65	15.57	15.58	15.66	15.70	15.76	16.22	14.88	14.39	12.01	11.45	11.14
Sierra Leone	17.00	17.19	28.54	28.00	29.67	52.50	56.25	62.83	50.46	27.33	28.83	32.12	23.87	23.83	26.83	26.25	24.27
Somalia	....	....	....	....	....	....	....	....	....	....	....	....	....	....	....	....	....
South Africa	21.50	14.33	12.50	15.33	19.83	21.00	20.31	18.91	16.16	15.58	17.90	19.52	20.00	21.79	18.00	14.50	13.77
Swaziland	17.00	12.50	11.88	15.00	14.50	14.50	16.25	15.00	14.00	15.00	18.00	19.75	18.75	21.00	15.00	14.00	12.50
Tanzania	12.29	18.50	27.50	29.63	31.00	....	....	....	31.00	39.00	42.83	†33.97	26.27	22.89	21.89	21.58	20.26
Togo	14.50	13.50	13.50	14.50	16.00	16.00	16.00	17.50	....	....	....	....	....	....	....	....	....
Uganda	24.00	33.33	34.67	35.00	40.00	38.67	34.42	....	....	....	20.16	20.29	21.37	20.86	21.55	22.92	22.66
Zambia	18.60	27.40	21.20	18.39	18.39	35.10	....	54.57	113.31	70.56	45.53	53.78	46.69	31.80	40.52	38.80	46.23
Zimbabwe	17.17	13.00	13.00	13.00	13.00	11.71	15.50	19.77	36.33	34.86	34.73	34.23	32.55	42.06	55.39	68.21	38.02
Asia																	
Bangladesh	12.00	14.00	16.00	16.00	16.00	16.00	15.92	15.00	15.00	14.50	14.00	14.00	14.00	14.00	14.13	15.50	15.83
Bhutan	15.00	15.00	15.00	15.00	15.00	15.00	15.00	17.00	17.00	16.58	16.00	....	....	....	....	....	....
Cambodia	....	....	....	....	....	....	....	....	....	....	18.70	18.80	18.40	18.33	17.56	17.34	16.50
China,P.R.: Mainland	7.92	7.92	7.92	9.00	†11.34	9.36	8.64	8.64	10.98	10.98	12.06	10.08	8.64	6.39	5.85	5.85	5.85
China,P.R.:Hong Kong	....	....	....	....	....	10.00	8.50	6.50	6.50	8.50	8.75	8.50	9.50	9.00	8.50	9.50	5.13
China,P.R.:Macao	....	....	6.63	8.06	10.54	10.42	9.42	7.25	6.50	7.95	9.90	9.56	9.73	10.97	9.46	9.89	7.99
Fiji	13.50	13.50	13.50	20.46	11.64	11.86	12.25	12.35	11.74	11.28	11.06	11.33	11.03	9.66	8.77	8.40	8.34
India	16.50	16.50	16.50	16.50	16.50	16.50	17.88	18.92	16.25	14.75	15.46	15.96	13.83	13.54	12.54	12.29	12.08
Indonesia	....	21.49	21.67	22.10	21.70	20.83	25.53	24.03	20.59	17.76	18.85	19.22	21.82	32.15	27.66	18.46	18.55
Korea	10.00	10.00	10.00	10.13	11.25	10.00	10.00	10.00	8.58	8.50	9.00	8.84	†11.88	15.28	9.40	8.55	7.71
Lao People's Dem.Rep	....	....	....	....	....	....	26.00	26.00	†25.33	24.00	†25.67	27.00	....	29.28	32.00	32.00	26.17
Malaysia	11.54	10.69	8.19	7.25	7.00	7.17	8.13	9.31	9.05	7.61	7.63	†8.89	9.53	10.61	7.29	6.77	6.66
Micronesia, Fed.Sts.	....	....	....	....	....	....	....	....	....	....	15.00	15.00	15.00	15.00	15.17	15.33	15.33

Lending Rates (60p) (cont.)
(Period averages in percent per annum)

1985	1986	1987	1988	1989	1990	1991	1992	1993	1994	1995	1996	1997	1998	1999	2000	2001	
																	Asia (cont.)
....	....	....	....	....	....	....	....	300.00	233.56	114.90	91.87	74.83	40.00	37.65	30.25	31.80	Mongolia
8.00	8.00	8.00	8.00	8.00	8.00	....	8.00	....	16.50	16.50	16.50	16.50	16.50	16.13	15.25	15.00	Myanmar
17.00	15.67	15.00	15.00	15.00	14.42	....	....	....	....	....	12.88	14.54	14.00	11.33	9.46	7.67	Nepal
11.54	12.33	11.94	12.68	14.62	15.52	14.17	14.53	11.29	9.16	13.14	13.30	10.45	17.70	18.90	17.54	16.21	Papua New Guinea
28.61	17.53	13.34	15.92	19.27	24.12	23.07	19.48	14.68	15.06	14.68	14.84	16.28	16.78	11.78	10.91	12.40	Philippines
19.00	18.83	17.50	17.50	17.00	13.25	14.75	12.88	12.00	12.00	12.00	12.00	12.00	11.50	11.50	11.00	9.93	Samoa
7.93	6.82	6.10	5.96	6.21	7.36	7.58	5.95	5.39	5.88	6.37	6.26	6.32	7.44	5.80	5.83	5.66	Singapore
12.83	15.13	17.33	18.00	18.00	18.00	19.46	19.75	17.80	15.72	16.59	17.78	15.71	14.84	14.50	....	....	Solomon Islands
13.40	11.57	9.80	12.42	13.17	13.00	†19.39	19.68	20.20	18.13	18.04	18.26	14.69	15.03	14.72	16.16	19.39	Sri Lanka
16.08	13.38	10.71	11.58	12.25	14.42	15.40	12.17	11.17	10.90	13.25	13.40	13.65	14.42	8.98	7.83	7.25	Thailand
10.00	10.00	10.00	10.00	13.50	13.50	13.50	13.50	†9.94	9.39	9.71	10.49	10.10	10.46	10.32	10.69	10.28	Tonga
15.75	16.00	15.42	17.04	17.00	17.33	18.00	16.25	16.00	16.00	10.50	10.50	10.50	10.96	10.29	9.85	9.10	Vanuatu
....	....	....	....	....	....	....	....	32.18	....	....	20.10	14.42	14.40	12.70	10.55	9.42	Vietnam
																	Europe
....	....	....	....	....	....	....	20.58	29.58	23.67	†19.65	23.96	....	....	21.62	22.10	19.65	Albania
....	....	....	....	....	....	....	....	....	....	111.86	66.36	54.23	48.49	38.85	31.57	26.69	Armenia
....	....	....	....	....	....	....	....	....	....	....	....	....	....	19.48	19.66	19.71	Azerbaijan
....	....	....	....	....	....	....	....	71.63	148.50	175.00	62.33	31.80	26.99	51.04	67.67	46.97	Belarus
....	....	....	....	....	....	....	....	....	....	....	....	....	73.50	24.29	30.50	....	Bosnia & Herzegovina
....	....	....	....	....	....	48.37	56.67	58.30	72.58	58.98	123.48	83.96	13.30	12.79	11.52	11.11	Bulgaria
....	....	....	....	....	....	....	1,157.79	1,443.61	22.91	20.24	22.52	15.47	15.75	14.94	12.07	9.55	Croatia
9.00	9.00	9.00	9.00	9.00	9.00	9.00	9.00	9.00	8.83	8.50	8.50	8.08	8.00	8.00	8.00	†7.54	Cyprus
....	....	....	....	....	....	....	....	14.07	13.12	12.80	12.54	13.20	12.81	8.68	7.16	7.06	Czech Republic
....	....	....	....	....	....	....	30.50	27.30	23.08	15.95	13.67	19.82	16.67	8.70	7.62	9.42	Estonia
....	....	....	....	....	....	....	....	....	....	....	58.24	50.64	46.00	33.42	32.75	27.25	Georgia
....	....	....	....	20.33	28.78	35.09	33.05	25.43	27.40	32.61	27.31	21.77	19.28	16.34	12.60	12.12	Hungary
....	....	....	....	....	....	....	....	....	....	....	65.02	49.38	73.44	60.86	51.90	37.33	Kyrgyz Republic
....	....	....	....	....	....	....	....	86.36	55.86	34.56	25.78	15.25	14.29	14.20	11.87	11.17	Latvia
....	....	....	....	....	....	....	....	91.84	62.30	27.08	21.56	14.39	12.21	13.09	12.14	9.63	Lithuania
....	....	....	....	....	....	....	....	....	159.82	45.95	21.58	21.42	21.03	20.45	18.93	19.35	Macedonia, FYR
8.00	8.00	8.00	8.46	8.50	8.50	8.50	8.50	8.50	8.50	†7.38	7.77	7.99	8.09	7.70	7.28	6.90	Malta
....	....	....	....	....	....	....	....	....	....	....	36.67	33.33	30.83	35.54	33.78	28.69	Moldova
12.00	12.00	12.00	16.67	64.00	504.17	54.58	39.00	35.25	32.83	†33.45	26.08	24.96	24.49	16.98	20.01	18.36	Poland
....	....	....	....	....	....	....	....	....	....	320.31	146.81	†32.04	41.79	39.72	24.43	17.91	Russia
....	....	....	....	....	....	....	....	14.41	14.56	16.85	13.92	18.65	21.17	21.07	14.89	11.24	Slovak Republic
....	....	....	....	....	....	824.56	195.11	48.61	38.87	23.36	22.60	20.02	16.09	12.38	15.77	15.05	Slovenia
....	....	....	....	....	....	....	....	184.25	250.28	122.70	79.88	49.12	54.50	54.95	41.53	32.28	Ukraine
																	Middle East
....	8.96	7.50	7.80	†8.50	8.50	9.48	11.85	10.95	10.83	11.83	12.45	12.33	11.92	11.86	11.73	10.81	Bahrain, Kingdom of
15.00	15.00	16.33	17.00	18.33	19.00	....	20.33	18.30	16.51	16.47	15.58	13.79	13.02	12.97	13.22	13.29	Egypt
503.42	60.27	61.43	41.68	31.63	26.45	26.43	19.94	16.44	17.45	20.22	20.68	18.71	16.18	16.36	12.87	10.03	Israel
....	....	....	....	....	10.31	10.37	10.16	10.23	10.45	10.66	11.25	12.25	12.61	12.33	11.80	10.92	Jordan
8.75	8.63	7.86	6.72	8.38	....	....	8.00	7.95	7.61	8.37	8.77	8.80	8.93	8.56	8.87	7.88	Kuwait
17.29	22.21	36.54	44.46	39.86	39.94	38.01	40.21	28.53	23.88	24.69	25.21	20.29	....	19.48	18.15	17.19	Lebanon
7.00	7.00	7.00	7.00	7.00	7.00	7.00	7.00	7.00	....	....	....	....	....	7.00	7.00	7.00	Libya
10.24	9.65	9.10	9.40	10.01	9.68	9.50	9.24	8.49	8.57	9.38	9.23	9.30	10.09	10.32	10.06	9.23	Oman
9.00	9.00	9.00	9.00	9.00	9.00	9.00	9.00	9.00	9.00	9.00	9.00	9.00	9.00	9.00	9.00	9.00	Syrian Arab Republic
9.50	9.50	9.50	9.50	9.50	9.50	9.50	8.13	7.20	8.86	....	....	....	....	....	....	....	Qatar
																	Western Hemisphere
13.00	14.25	12.38	11.50	12.17	12.38	15.50	13.00	13.00	12.50	11.88	11.38	12.00	12.38	12.13	11.42	11.50	Antigua and Barbuda
....	....	....	....	....	....	....	....	....	10.06	17.85	10.51	9.24	10.64	11.04	11.09	27.71	Argentina
....	11.00	10.30	10.30	10.60	10.60	10.60	10.60	10.60	10.60	10.60	10.30	10.00	....	†13.14	12.07	12.10	Aruba
10.33	9.25	9.00	9.00	9.00	9.00	9.00	8.08	7.46	6.88	6.75	6.75	6.75	6.75	6.38	6.00	6.00	Bahamas, The
10.56	9.06	8.75	9.44	9.92	11.42	12.42	13.54	8.92	9.08	10.00	10.00	9.83	9.75	9.40	10.19	9.58	Barbados
....	14.69	14.14	13.56	13.77	14.04	14.24	14.32	14.37	14.78	15.69	16.30	16.29	16.50	16.27	16.01	15.45	Belize
172.15	†65.78	49.41	39.79	37.27	41.81	41.15	45.51	53.88	55.57	51.02	55.97	50.05	39.41	35.37	34.60	20.06	Bolivia
....	....	....	....	....	....	....	....	....	....	....	....	78.19	86.36	80.44	56.83	57.62	Brazil
†39.97	26.36	32.67	21.21	36.01	48.87	28.58	23.97	24.35	20.34	18.16	17.37	15.67	20.17	12.62	14.84	11.89	Chile
....	40.83	41.10	42.69	43.04	45.25	47.13	37.28	35.81	40.47	42.72	41.99	34.22	42.24	†25.77	18.79	20.72	Colombia
20.92	21.80	23.82	28.69	29.17	32.56	38.88	28.46	30.02	33.03	36.70	26.27	22.48	22.47	25.74	24.89	23.83	Costa Rica
10.04	10.25	10.50	10.50	10.50	10.50	10.29	10.00	10.00	9.58	10.33	10.50	10.50	10.50	10.50	10.50	10.50	Dominica
....	....	....	....	....	....	35.26	28.34	29.89	28.68	30.68	23.73	21.01	25.64	25.05	26.80	24.26	Dominican Republic
18.00	18.00	18.42	23.00	30.08	37.50	46.67	60.17	47.83	43.99	55.67	54.50	43.02	49.55	†16.53	16.26	15.46	Ecuador
14.00	17.00	17.00	17.00	18.50	21.17	19.67	16.43	19.42	19.03	19.08	18.57	16.05	14.98	15.46	13.96	....	El Salvador
11.67	11.50	11.42	10.50	10.67	10.50	10.63	10.50	10.50	10.50	10.50	10.50	10.50	10.50	10.50	10.50	10.50	Grenada
12.00	13.17	14.00	15.17	16.00	23.27	34.08	19.49	24.73	22.93	21.16	22.72	†18.64	16.56	19.51	20.88	18.96	Guatemala
15.00	15.00	15.00	15.07	18.94	32.75	33.55	28.69	19.36	18.36	19.22	17.79	17.04	16.77	17.11	17.30	17.01	Guyana
....	....	....	....	....	....	....	....	....	....	....	....	21.00	23.62	22.88	25.09	28.63	Haiti
16.30	16.12	15.54	15.38	15.43	17.05	21.88	21.68	22.06	24.68	26.95	29.74	32.07	30.69	30.15	26.82	23.76	Honduras
24.92	27.34	25.45	25.19	25.22	30.50	31.51	44.81	43.71	49.46	43.58	39.83	32.86	31.59	27.01	23.35	20.61	Jamaica
....	....	....	....	....	....	....	....	22.04	20.38	58.59	36.89	24.55	28.70	25.87	18.23	13.87	Mexico
11.46	11.59	11.37	11.24	11.23	9.25	....	....	12.59	12.73	12.93	13.21	13.29	13.58	13.60	9.98	10.44	Netherlands Antilles
....	....	....	—	558.01	22.00	17.92	19.32	20.23	20.14	19.89	20.72	21.02	21.63	22.15	21.35	22.81	Nicaragua
....	12.36	12.60	12.47	12.92	†11.98	11.79	10.61	10.06	10.15	11.10	10.62	10.63	10.82	10.05	†10.48	10.97	Panama
....	....	....	....	....	31.00	34.94	27.96	30.78	†35.47	33.94	31.88	27.79	30.49	30.21	26.78	28.25	Paraguay
....	40.52	35.74	174.28	1,515.86	4,774.53	751.52	173.80	97.37	53.56	27.16	26.07	29.96	30.80	30.79	27.91	20.43	Peru
10.21	10.21	12.00	12.00	12.00	12.00	12.00	12.67	13.00	13.00	12.58	12.25	13.00	13.00	11.50	11.00	11.38	St. Kitts and Nevis
14.00	14.00	11.58	10.58	10.00	10.54	10.50	10.50	10.17	10.13	10.00	10.33	10.54	10.50	10.50	10.50	10.50	St. Lucia
12.13	12.46	12.46	12.08	12.36	12.50	13.50	11.38	11.21	11.00	11.00	11.00	12.00	12.50	12.50	11.75	11.00	St. Vincent & Grens.
....	....	....	....	....	....	8.90	8.93	9.35	15.38	40.18	35.78	33.13	27.50	27.33	28.95	25.76	Suriname
12.69	12.00	11.50	12.58	13.31	12.87	13.17	15.33	15.50	15.98	15.17	15.79	15.33	17.33	17.04	16.50	15.67	Trinidad and Tobago
94.58	94.73	95.80	101.52	127.58	174.45	152.88	117.77	97.33	95.08	99.10	91.52	71.55	57.93	53.28	49.05	51.71	Uruguay
9.33	8.49	8.47	8.50	22.50	†35.53	37.16	41.33	59.90	54.66	39.74	39.41	23.69	46.35	32.13	25.20	22.45	Venezuela, Rep. Bol.

National Interest Rates

	1985	1986	1987	1988	1989	1990	1991	1992	1993	1994	1995	1996	1997	1998	1999	2000	2001
						Government Bond Yields (61)											
						(Average yields to maturity in percent per annum)											
Industrial Countries																	
United States	10.62	7.68	8.38	8.85	8.50	8.55	7.86	7.01	5.87	7.08	6.58	6.44	6.35	5.26	5.64	6.03	5.02
Canada	11.04	9.52	9.95	10.22	9.92	10.85	9.76	8.77	7.85	8.63	8.28	7.50	6.42	5.47	5.69	5.89	5.78
Australia	13.95	13.42	13.19	12.10	13.41	13.18	10.69	9.22	7.28	9.04	9.17	8.17	6.89	5.50	6.08	6.26	5.64
Japan	6.34	4.94	4.21	4.27	5.05	7.36	6.53	4.94	3.69	3.71	2.53	2.23	1.69	1.10	†1.77	1.75	1.33
New Zealand	17.71	16.52	†16.35	13.45	12.78	12.46	10.00	7.87	6.69	7.48	7.94	8.04	7.21	6.47	6.13	6.85	6.12
Euro Area										8.18	8.73	7.23	5.96	4.70	4.66	5.44	5.03
Austria	7.77	7.33	6.91	6.67	7.14	8.74	8.62	8.27	6.64	6.69	6.47	5.30	4.79	4.29	4.09	....	....
Belgium	10.61	7.93	7.83	7.85	8.64	10.09	9.26	8.64	7.19	7.82	7.45	6.45	5.74	4.72	4.81	5.58	5.13
Finland	....	....	....	....	....	....	....	....	8.84	9.03	8.78	....	....	4.72	4.72	5.48	5.04
France	10.94	8.44	9.43	9.06	8.79	9.94	9.05	8.60	6.91	7.35	7.59	6.39	5.63	4.72	4.69	5.45	5.05
Germany	6.87	5.92	5.84	6.10	7.09	8.88	8.63	7.96	6.28	6.67	6.50	5.63	5.08	4.39	4.26	5.24	4.70
Greece	15.77	15.78	....	16.56	....	....	....	....	....	....	....	....	....	8.48	6.30	6.10	5.30
Ireland	12.64	11.07	11.27	9.49	8.95	10.08	9.17	9.11	7.72	8.19	8.30	7.48	6.49	4.99	....	....	....
Italy	13.00	10.52	9.68	10.16	10.72	11.51	†13.18	13.27	11.31	10.56	12.21	9.40	6.86	4.90	4.73	5.58	5.19
Luxembourg	9.53	8.67	7.96	7.13	7.68	8.51	8.15	7.90	6.93	6.38	6.05	5.21	5.39	5.29	....	....	....
Netherlands	7.34	6.32	6.40	6.42	7.22	8.92	8.74	8.10	6.51	7.20	7.20	6.49	5.81	4.87	4.92	5.51	5.17
Portugal	20.75	15.54	15.02	13.87	15.63	18.55	18.27	15.38	12.45	10.83	10.34	7.25	5.48	4.09	....	....	....
Spain	13.37	11.36	12.81	11.74	13.70	14.68	12.43	12.17	10.16	9.69	11.04	8.18	5.84	4.55	4.30	5.36	4.87
Denmark	11.31	9.91	11.06	9.78	9.75	10.74	9.59	9.47	7.08	7.41	7.58	6.04	5.08	4.59	4.30	5.54	....
Iceland	....	....	....	....	....	....	....	7.75	6.80	5.02	7.18	5.61	5.49	4.73	4.28	5.35	5.33
Norway	12.58	13.47	13.56	12.97	10.84	10.72	9.87	9.78	6.52	7.13	6.82	5.94	5.13	5.35	5.38	6.38	6.31
Sweden	13.09	10.26	†11.68	11.35	11.18	13.08	10.69	10.02	8.54	†9.41	....	....	....	....	....	....	....
Switzerland	4.78	4.29	4.12	4.15	5.20	†6.68	6.35	5.48	4.05	5.23	3.73	3.63	3.08	†2.71	3.62	3.55	3.56
United Kingdom	10.50	9.86	9.47	9.36	9.58	11.08	9.92	9.12	7.87	8.05	8.26	8.10	7.09	5.45	4.70	4.68	4.78
Developing Countries																	
Africa																	
Ethiopia	....	6.00	5.00	5.00	5.00	5.00	5.00	7.00	13.00	13.00	13.00	13.00	....	....	....	....	....
Malawi	11.50	11.50	11.50	11.50	11.50	11.50	11.50	....	....	23.50	38.58	42.67	39.25	....	....	....	....
Namibia	....	....	....	....	....	....	....	15.44	13.94	14.63	16.11	15.48	14.70	15.10	14.90	13.81	11.39
South Africa	16.79	16.37	15.30	16.37	16.90	16.15	16.34	15.44	13.97	14.83	16.11	15.48	14.70	15.12	14.90	13.79	11.41
Uganda	24.00	38.33	40.00	38.50	45.33	44.50	42.00	43.50	....	....	....	....	....	....	....	....	....
Zimbabwe	13.26	13.20	13.87	14.00	14.00	15.24	17.27	17.40	....	....	....	....	....	....	....	....	....
Asia																	
India	8.99	....	....	....	....	....	....	....	....	....	....	....	....	....	....	....	....
Korea	13.58	11.57	12.43	13.04	14.74	15.03	16.46	15.08	12.08	12.30	12.40	10.90	11.70	12.80	8.72	8.50	6.66
Myanmar	....	....	....	....	....	....	....	....	....	10.50	10.50	13.13	14.00	14.00	†11.00	9.00	9.00
Nepal †	13.00	13.00	13.00	13.00	13.17	13.54	10.00	13.33	....	9.00	3.00	9.00	9.00	9.00	8.75	8.50	8.50
Pakistan	9.19	8.77	8.26	8.32	8.18	8.05	7.88	7.67	7.40	7.07	6.63	6.06	5.43	4.79	4.16	....	....
Samoa	15.00	14.17	13.50	13.50	13.50	13.50	13.50	13.50	13.50	13.50	13.50	13.50	13.50	13.50	13.50	13.50	13.50
Solomon Islands	12.00	13.00	12.33	12.00	12.44	12.75	12.92	13.00	13.00	13.00	13.00	11.50	11.75	12.50	12.88	....	....
Sri Lanka	15.33	12.00	12.00	11.49	11.71	12.20	15.68	16.00	16.25	....	....	....	....	....	....	....	....
Thailand	12.11	9.11	7.48	7.50	8.09	10.60	10.75	10.75	10.75	10.75	10.75	10.75	10.75	10.25	6.69	6.95	5.82
Vanuatu	9.50	9.50	9.50	9.50	†8.00	8.00	8.00	8.00	8.00	8.00	8.00	8.00	8.00	8.00	8.00	8.00	8.00
Europe																	
Bulgaria	....	....	....	....	....	....	....	....	....	....	56.86	49.76	....	....	10.10	10.05	7.38	6.70
Cyprus	....	....	....	....	....	....	....	....	....	....	....	....	....	....	....	7.38	6.70
Czech Republic	....	....	....	....	....	....	....	....	....	....	....	....	....	....	....	6.72	4.62
Slovak Republic	....	....	....	....	....	....	....	....	....	....	....	....	....	....	....	8.34	7.75
Western Hemisphere																	
Guatemala	8.00	8.00	8.00	8.00	8.00	8.00	8.00	....	....	....	....	....	....	....	....	....	....
Honduras	10.40	10.40	10.40	10.40	10.40	10.40	10.40	10.40	10.40	23.11	27.24	35.55	29.59	20.34	16.04	14.79	15.28
Jamaica	22.48	22.62	20.83	20.40	20.17	25.46	26.33	30.50	24.82	26.82	26.85	26.87	26.85	....	....	....	....
Mexico	....	....	....	....	....	....	....	....	....	....	51.74	32.81	21.44	....	....	....	....
Netherlands Antilles	9.46	9.29	10.36	10.74	10.63	10.74	....	....	8.14	7.48	8.02	8.25	8.67	8.60	8.75	8.77	9.00
Trinidad and Tobago	9.89	9.62	9.54	9.76	10.77	10.73	10.85	13.30	....	....	....	....	....	....	....	....	....
Venezuela, Rep. Bol.	12.55	12.07	13.49	14.86	17.32	20.06	27.14	31.66	41.03	54.73	53.38	49.09	25.41	47.88	†31.12	21.03	22.12

1987	1988	1989	1990	1991	1992	1993	1994	1995	1996	1997	1998	1999	2000	2001	

London Interbank Offer Rates on SDR Deposits
(99260lsa, 60lsb, 60lsc)
(Period averages in percent per annum)

1987	1988	1989	1990	1991	1992	1993	1994	1995	1996	1997	1998	1999	2000	2001	
6.22	6.56	8.40	9.07	7.70	6.27	4.74	3.86	4.60	3.72	3.91	....	....	....	....	Three-Month
6.31	6.70	8.44	9.17	7.71	6.22	4.64	3.97	4.63	3.79	4.00	....	....	....	....	Six-Month
6.48	6.87	8.46	9.28	7.76	6.34	4.59	4.22	4.72	3.95	4.14	....	....	....	....	One-Year

London Interbank Offer Rates on US Dollar Deposits
(11160lda, 60ldb, 60ldc, 60ldd, 60lde, 60ldf)
(Period averages in percent per annum)

1987	1988	1989	1990	1991	1992	1993	1994	1995	1996	1997	1998	1999	2000	2001	
6.63	7.56	9.21	8.13	5.78	3.60	3.05	4.24	5.90	5.35	5.54	....	....	....	3.98	Overnight
6.82	7.68	9.26	8.20	5.87	3.66	3.08	4.31	5.93	5.40	5.58	5.53	5.16	6.36	3.95	Seven-Day
6.99	7.81	9.24	8.29	5.90	3.72	3.16	4.46	5.97	5.44	5.64	5.60	5.25	6.41	3.88	One-Month
7.18	7.98	9.28	8.31	5.99	3.86	3.29	4.74	6.04	5.51	5.76	5.59	5.41	6.53	3.78	Three-Month
7.30	8.13	9.27	8.35	6.08	3.90	3.41	5.07	6.10	5.59	5.86	5.56	5.53	6.65	3.73	Six-Month
7.61	8.41	9.31	8.45	6.29	4.20	3.64	5.59	6.24	5.78	6.08	5.53	5.71	6.83	3.86	One-Year

London Interbank Offer Rates on Three-Month Deposits (60ea)
(Pound sterling rates relate to Paris market)
(Period averages in percent per annum)

1987	1988	1989	1990	1991	1992	1993	1994	1995	1996	1997	1998	1999	2000	2001	
8.64	8.09	9.35	10.29	9.61	10.37	8.57	5.88	6.68	3.94	3.48	3.64	....	....	....	French Franc
4.06	4.33	7.09	8.51	9.31	9.52	7.30	5.36	4.53	3.31	3.37	3.60	2.96	....	....	Deutsche Mark
4.26	4.51	5.46	7.76	7.38	4.46	3.00	2.31	1.27	.63	.63	.71	.22	.28	.15	Japanese Yen
5.36	4.82	7.40	8.69	9.29	9.37	6.85	5.23	4.47	3.03	3.37	3.55	....	....	....	Netherlands Guilder
3.91	3.20	7.07	8.96	8.25	7.88	4.96	4.16	3.09	2.05	1.71	1.60	1.39	3.10	2.94	Swiss Franc
9.80	10.36	13.94	14.79	11.67	9.70	6.05	5.54	6.73	6.09	6.90	7.39	5.54	6.19	5.04	Pound Sterling
....	....	....	....	....	....	....	....	....	....	....	....	2.96	4.41	4.26	Euro

London Interbank Offer Rates on Six-Month Deposits (60eb)
(Pound sterling rates relate to Paris market)
(Period averages in percent per annum)

1987	1988	1989	1990	1991	1992	1993	1994	1995	1996	1997	1998	1999	2000	2001	
8.79	8.32	9.44	10.43	9.64	10.16	7.92	5.95	6.61	4.02	3.54	3.68	....	....	....	French Franc
4.16	4.47	7.22	8.77	9.40	9.41	6.95	5.35	4.57	3.31	3.42	3.66	3.05	....	....	Deutsche Mark
4.27	4.56	5.50	7.84	7.16	4.32	2.96	2.36	1.26	.71	.65	.71	.24	.31	.15	Japanese Yen
5.40	4.93	7.46	8.86	9.35	9.26	6.57	5.25	4.55	3.08	3.46	3.64	....	....	....	Netherlands Guilder
3.96	3.42	7.06	8.94	8.18	7.81	4.76	4.23	3.16	2.09	1.78	1.68	1.55	3.26	2.87	Swiss Franc
9.76	10.50	13.89	14.72	11.40	9.65	5.93	5.80	6.91	6.13	7.04	7.32	5.62	6.31	5.02	Pound Sterling
....	....	....	....	....	....	....	....	....	....	....	....	3.05	4.54	4.15	Euro

Discounts (-) or Premiums (60f) on Three-Month Forward Exchange Rates
(End of period in percent per annum based on end-of-period quotation of the currencies against the US dollar)

1987	1988	1989	1990	1991	1992	1993	1994	1995	1996	1997	1998	1999	2000	2001	
-1.05	-1.51	-3.90	-3.59	-2.98	-3.37	-3.84	-3.99	-.23	22.78	....	....	....	....	....	Canada
-5.79	-7.92	-9.51	-5.93	-4.74	-3.93	....	....	....	....	....	....	....	-.65	-2.13	Australia
7.97	4.39	1.67	-3.48	-1.50	.03	1.18	3.69	4.86	5.12	5.45	6.25	6.25	5.75	2.78	Japan
2.84	3.34	-.85	-1.61	-5.65	-5.14	-2.21	-1.13	-1.67	2.34	1.99	2.32	....	....	....	Austria
.75	1.77	-1.79	-2.29	-5.50	-4.94	-3.54	1.10	1.43	2.44	2.17	1.90	....	....	....	Belgium
-2.00	1.30	-3.70	-1.70	-5.80	-11.80	-3.30	.20	.80	1.85	1.74	.99	2.36	.97	-1.78	Denmark
-1.60	-1.97	-7.13	-6.71	-7.79	-6.61	-2.61	.43	1.14	2.32	2.12	1.85	....	....	....	Finland
-1.27	.59	.01	1.09 p	-3.32	-6.71	....	....	....	....	....	....	....	....	....	France
3.67	3.89	-.05	-1.87	-5.54	-5.20	-2.66	1.24	1.81	2.26	2.10	1.89	....	....	....	Germany
-4.28	-5.06	-4.34	-5.36	-7.97	-10.37	-7.10	-.87	-4.64	-1.00	-2.62	.51	....	....	....	Italy
2.81	3.50	-14.93	-1.89	-5.52	-4.77	....	....	....	....	....	....	—	—	—	Netherlands
-11.71	-3.07	-3.14	-.51	-7.17	-9.91	-2.47	.09	-1.08	.89	1.98	1.12	.32	-.99	-4.44	Norway
-11.20	-3.46	-16.33	.48	-23.09	-5.51	-.32	-3.67	-7.31	.79	4.81	3.50	....	....	....	Spain
-1.64	.45	-3.91	-2.56	-10.63	-54.41	-1.83	-1.66	-.36	-.37	-.58	.84	2.54	4.07	2.36	Sweden
4.69	2.93	-1.16	-1.39	-3.10	-2.47	-.95	1.98	3.30	2.50	4.21	3.34	4.65	3.30	-.17	Switzerland
-1.36	-3.56	-6.30	-5.99	-6.66	-3.53	-1.91	-.12	-.86	-.89	-1.77	....	....	....	....	United Kingdom

SDR Interest Rate (99260s) and Rate of Remuneration (99260r)
(Period averages in percent per annum)

1987	1988	1989	1990	1991	1992	1993	1994	1995	1996	1997	1998	1999	2000	2001	
5.8679	6.2544	8.2685	9.0912	7.7229	6.2599	4.6394	4.2858	4.5847	3.8998	4.0719	4.1052	3.4759	4.4397	3.4258	**SDR Interest Rate**
5.95	6.88	8.39	7.74	5.53	3.51	3.06	4.35	5.65	5.14	5.20	4.90	4.77	6.00	3.48	United States (3-Mo.T-Bill Rate)
9.54	10.05	13.74	14.64	11.22	9.21	5.35	5.18	6.40	5.89	6.62	7.23	5.14	5.83	4.79	United Kingdom (3-Mo.T-Bill Rate)
8.22	7.88	9.34	†10.18	9.69	10.49	8.41	5.79	6.58	3.84	3.35	3.45	2.72	4.23	4.26	France (3-Mo.T-Bill Rate)
3.99	4.28	7.07	8.43	9.18	9.46	7.24	5.31	4.48	3.27	3.30	3.52	2.94	4.37	4.25	Germany (3-Mo. Interbank Rate)
3.88	4.08	5.37	7.67	†7.31	4.40	2.97	2.24	1.22	.59	.62	.72	.15	.23	....	Japan (3-Mo.Certif. of Deposits)
5.8546	6.2544	8.2685	9.0912	7.7229	6.2599	4.6394	4.2858	4.5847	3.8998	4.0719	4.1052	3.4759	4.4397	3.4258	**Rate of Remuneration**

Real Effective Exchange Rate Indices

65um

Industrial Countries

(1995=100)

Based on Relative Unit Labor Costs (65um.110)

		1987	1988	1989	1990	1991	1992	1993	1994	1995	1996	1997	1998	1999	2000	2001
United States	111	123.0	116.1	121.9	114.2	110.6	105.4	108.4	107.7	100.0	102.6	109.2	112.9	110.9	118.5	132.0
Canada	156	101.0	109.6	116.0	119.1	126.9	119.9	109.4	99.4	100.0	103.9	106.2	102.8	102.1	105.4	98.1
Japan	158	77.4	81.7	76.4	67.3	71.2	76.1	90.8	99.1	100.0	83.8	79.4	76.4	85.9	90.2	81.4
Euro Area	163	93.1	89.9	89.9	97.9	94.7	99.1	96.8	96.2	100.0	99.2	89.9	86.4	82.6	75.5	74.8
Austria	122	126.5	115.3	112.1	112.2	109.7	108.8	107.8	105.4	100.0	95.8	90.6	89.3	87.5	87.0	87.2
Belgium	124	97.5	93.7	91.5	96.4	97.5	98.4	98.8	98.1	100.0	94.2	87.6	88.2	87.2	85.8	86.7
Finland	172	128.7	130.1	134.3	140.3	136.9	106.6	85.3	89.4	100.0	93.8	90.2	89.4	85.5	78.8	80.3
France	132	113.6	105.9	102.0	104.9	100.5	101.1	103.7	100.6	100.0	98.9	93.0	94.6	92.9	90.4	89.9
Germany	134	74.5	77.1	76.8	78.1	75.8	81.4	88.2	91.8	100.0	98.1	91.6	87.0	84.9	79.2	77.8
Ireland	178	149.0	136.5	126.6	130.5	124.9	122.1	115.2	110.5	100.0	99.4	91.7	76.1	67.4	61.0	61.8
Italy	136	128.2	125.7	132.0	138.5	142.0	136.2	116.7	110.2	100.0	114.4	119.0	118.3	118.3	115.4	114.3
Netherlands	138	109.5	104.8	98.5	98.8	97.3	101.5	103.9	99.0	100.0	96.8	94.9	96.4	96.0	95.4	97.4
Spain	184	90.6	95.9	104.3	113.7	116.9	120.3	108.9	101.5	100.0	103.6	102.9	105.3	106.8	106.9	109.6
Denmark	128	105.3	100.6	95.6	102.9	100.3	102.8	108.4	98.5	100.0	104.9	99.3	100.2	101.7	96.2	98.2
Norway	142	94.6	99.3	98.3	97.0	95.9	94.5	92.4	95.2	100.0	101.3	107.6	108.2	114.5	119.2	125.4
Sweden	144	109.8	115.6	120.5	118.9	122.6	123.7	98.1	94.1	100.0	113.3	105.3	105.7	104.2	101.8	91.6
Switzerland	146	85.5	86.1	82.2	88.8	90.3	89.1	90.6	95.4	100.0	97.9	95.3	99.6	99.3	101.7	107.1
United Kingdom	112	106.4	112.4	109.6	111.8	116.1	109.2	97.1	99.9	100.0	106.0	130.4	141.2	141.7	147.6	143.6

Based on Relative Consumer Prices (..rec)

		1987	1988	1989	1990	1991	1992	1993	1994	1995	1996	1997	1998	1999	2000	2001
United States	111	112.4	105.9	109.3	104.7	103.5	101.2	104.7	103.4	100.0	104.3	112.0	120.0	119.3	125.2	134.5
Canada	156	114.7	121.0	129.5	128.0	131.9	121.1	113.6	103.3	100.0	101.7	103.2	98.6	97.6	99.5	98.7
Japan	158	82.5	88.1	80.7	71.6	76.8	79.2	93.6	98.3	100.0	84.5	80.2	78.9	89.3	95.5	85.5
Euro Area	163	99.3	95.2	90.9	99.3	96.1	100.8	95.7	95.2	100.0	99.9	90.8	88.5	88.5	79.1	82.3
Austria	122	92.6	92.1	90.8	92.4	91.6	93.3	95.7	96.4	100.0	98.0	94.6	94.6	92.8	90.3	91.1
Belgium	124	94.8	92.2	90.9	94.8	94.1	95.0	95.0	96.5	100.0	98.2	93.6	93.4	91.8	88.7	89.3
Finland	172	110.3	112.8	119.3	122.4	116.9	101.1	86.2	91.7	100.0	96.0	93.0	93.1	90.7	87.1	89.1
France	132	99.1	96.9	94.8	98.1	95.1	96.6	97.7	97.4	100.0	99.9	95.6	96.0	93.2	88.4	88.4
Germany	134	92.5	90.1	88.1	90.8	87.2	91.5	95.4	95.7	100.0	96.8	92.0	92.5	89.5	84.6	85.6
Ireland	178	108.4	104.7	102.4	107.1	104.1	106.9	99.1	99.4	100.0	101.9	101.6	97.1	94.2	91.2	94.5
Italy	136	124.0	122.9	125.6	131.5	132.5	130.6	110.5	107.2	100.0	111.6	112.3	113.1	110.9	106.3	107.7
Netherlands	138	97.9	95.6	91.8	93.7	92.1	93.7	95.3	96.0	100.0	98.2	93.6	94.4	93.7	89.9	92.7
Spain	184	97.5	102.1	108.1	114.8	116.2	115.7	103.1	98.3	100.0	102.2	97.4	97.4	96.7	94.2	95.9
Denmark	128	96.2	95.7	93.9	98.1	94.9	96.0	96.4	95.9	100.0	99.3	96.5	98.3	97.5	93.5	94.9
Norway	142	105.7	108.3	107.6	106.5	103.2	103.5	99.3	97.2	100.0	99.8	101.1	98.2	97.9	96.1	99.6
Sweden	144	108.2	110.9	113.7	118.2	123.9	123.9	101.7	100.2	100.0	108.4	103.0	100.1	97.0	95.1	87.6
Switzerland	146	90.0	88.5	83.0	89.2	89.3	87.7	89.7	93.9	100.0	97.3	90.0	91.1	89.4	87.3	89.8
United Kingdom	112	104.5	112.8	113.3	117.1	119.8	115.6	103.5	103.7	100.0	102.4	120.5	128.0	127.6	131.9	129.5

1987	1988	1989	1990	1991	1992	1993	1994	1995	1996	1997	1998	1999	2000	2001	Industrial Countries	re u
(1995=100)																
Based on Relative Normalized Unit labor costs (..reu)																
130.9	122.9	124.5	115.8	111.6	109.0	111.1	108.5	100.0	103.6	109.5	116.6	114.8	123.5	135.1	United States	111
94.6	101.4	110.6	113.6	118.8	113.6	107.4	100.8	100.0	100.8	103.5	97.0	95.9	96.0	92.2	Canada	156
74.3	79.1	75.7	68.4	73.3	75.6	89.5	95.1	100.0	85.6	81.7	76.3	86.9	93.3	82.6	Japan	158
92.8	89.9	89.9	98.5	95.6	99.6	97.8	95.7	100.0	100.5	90.5	87.5	83.1	74.1	74.0	Euro Area	163
121.5	116.4	111.7	108.8	104.7	105.6	106.2	103.8	100.0	95.2	90.5	89.2	87.4	85.7	85.4	Austria	122
98.7	94.9	94.3	96.4	97.0	96.6	98.0	97.1	100.0	95.8	92.4	91.9	88.4	85.6	86.5	Belgium	124
126.9	129.7	133.6	134.6	123.7	102.0	86.4	90.6	100.0	92.5	87.2	86.0	82.9	79.0	79.7	Finland	172
108.2	104.5	101.5	102.7	98.4	99.3	100.1	99.0	100.0	96.9	92.9	92.5	91.8	88.2	87.2	France	132
75.6	76.7	76.8	81.9	81.3	84.9	90.5	93.2	100.0	98.7	92.9	90.5	87.8	82.7	82.0	Germany	134
163.5	155.6	145.3	142.8	129.4	126.0	115.2	107.1	100.0	95.0	89.0	80.5	75.2	68.0	67.4	Ireland	178
126.8	125.4	131.4	135.8	138.1	134.7	114.9	108.7	100.0	114.6	117.1	114.8	114.3	110.4	109.7	Italy	136
108.1	102.6	96.5	95.4	92.3	94.6	96.7	97.7	100.0	97.1	92.7	93.9	93.3	91.3	93.1	Netherlands	138
89.7	93.3	100.6	106.4	110.3	115.4	107.5	100.9	100.0	102.6	100.1	102.0	102.3	101.1	103.4	Spain	184
96.3	94.8	93.3	97.7	94.2	95.3	97.9	97.1	100.0	98.2	95.8	97.4	97.2	94.2	95.5	Denmark	128
96.6	98.4	97.6	97.1	96.5	96.8	94.9	94.7	100.0	102.5	106.9	108.1	113.3	115.5	122.0	Norway	142
115.7	120.0	125.7	124.4	122.4	123.8	100.3	99.4	100.0	112.8	110.0	108.2	104.9	104.2	94.7	Sweden	144
88.1	89.6	85.2	89.7	90.8	86.3	86.8	94.1	100.0	100.2	97.2	102.8	102.5	102.2	107.4	Switzerland	146
104.6	109.7	107.2	107.9	113.0	110.1	101.4	103.6	100.0	103.6	123.5	131.3	133.6	141.0	140.6	United Kingdom	112

Industrial Production

		1972	1973	1974	1975	1976	1977	1978	1979	1980	1981	1982	1983	1984	1985	1986

Index Numbers (1995=100):

Country	Code	1972	1973	1974	1975	1976	1977	1978	1979	1980	1981	1982	1983	1984	1985	1986
Industrial Countries	110	60.9	66.6	66.4	60.9	65.9	68.9	71.7	75.1	74.9	74.9	72.8	74.5	79.5	81.7	82.7
United States	111	57.1	61.7	60.8	55.5	60.6	65.5	69.4	71.7	69.7	70.8	67.0	69.5	75.7	77.0	77.8
Canada	156	58.5	64.3	66.5	62.5	65.9	67.4	70.2	†74.3	71.8	73.3	66.1	70.4	78.9	83.3	†83.3
Australia	193	60.0	66.1	68.2	63.0	66.2	†65.2	66.2	69.6	70.0	72.1	71.7	69.6	74.4	80.4	80.2
Japan	158	52.5	60.4	58.1	51.6	57.3	59.7	63.5	68.2	71.4	72.1	72.4	74.5	81.5	84.6	84.4
New Zealand	196	....	....	....	....	....	76.8	75.3	80.1	79.8	83.6	87.5	85.5	97.2	95.5	94.1
Euro Area																
Austria	122	54.6	57.5	60.2	56.4	60.0	62.4	64.0	68.7	70.6	69.8	69.2	69.3	73.4	76.6	77.7
Belgium	124	71.5	75.9	78.7	71.2	77.4	77.4	79.0	82.6	81.6	79.4	79.6	81.1	83.2	84.6	85.4
Finland	172	47.8	51.2	53.5	51.6	52.1	52.4	55.0	60.9	†65.9	67.6	68.2	70.4	73.6	76.4	77.7
France	132	74.3	79.6	81.6	76.3	82.3	83.6	85.6	88.9	†89.6	88.7	88.1	87.5	87.7	87.9	88.7
Germany	134	76.7	80.9	79.1	73.7	79.1	81.0	82.5	86.6	86.8	84.7	82.0	82.4	84.7	88.1	90.0
Greece	174	65.1	75.3	73.8	77.1	85.2	86.5	93.1	98.8	99.7	....	98.3	96.9	98.2	100.7	100.0
Ireland	178	53.2	58.5	60.2	57.8	62.9	67.9	73.3	79.0	†78.0	82.3	81.6	88.2	96.7	100.0	102.2
Italy	136	60.6	66.5	69.5	63.1	70.9	71.7	73.1	77.9	82.2	80.9	78.5	75.9	78.5	79.4	82.2
Luxembourg	137	66.2	74.1	76.6	59.8	61.2	61.5	64.5	66.6	64.4	60.8	61.3	64.6	73.2	78.1	80.3
Netherlands	138	64.0	69.5	72.7	71.9	76.6	76.6	76.6	79.8	†79.0	77.3	74.0	76.7	79.8	83.1	83.1
Portugal	182	59.1	66.0	67.6	64.1	67.2	74.9	80.3	111.7	118.1	64.2	69.1	71.3	73.4	74.2	79.0
Spain	184	61.3	68.2	73.3	†70.0	73.4	77.4	79.2	80.5	80.5	79.9	78.9	81.1	81.8	83.4	86.0
Denmark	128	57.4	59.5	†57.4	54.3	59.8	60.5	62.2	64.6	64.8	64.9	66.3	68.6	76.0	†79.4	85.3
Norway	142	35.7	37.7	39.4	41.5	43.9	43.5	48.1	51.8	†55.1	56.7	56.4	61.6	66.4	68.7	71.1
Sweden	144	70.4	75.5	79.0	77.7	75.7	71.5	70.5	75.4	74.5	73.7	72.4	75.4	80.8	83.2	83.6
Switzerland	146	74.5	78.6	79.4	69.4	69.7	73.8	74.0	75.3	79.7	79.0	76.1	75.6	77.5	82.0	85.0
United Kingdom	112	70.0	76.3	74.8	70.7	73.1	76.8	79.0	82.1	76.7	74.3	75.7	78.5	78.5	82.8	84.8

Wages

Index Numbers (1995=100):

Country	Code	1972	1973	1974	1975	1976	1977	1978	1979	1980	1981	1982	1983	1984	1985	1986
Industrial Countries	110	17.8	19.0	21.4	24.3	26.8	29.5	34.4	37.2	40.9	44.9	48.4	54.8	57.0	59.5	61.4
United States	111	30.9	33.0	35.8	39.0	42.2	45.9	49.9	54.1	58.8	64.6	68.7	71.3	74.3	77.1	78.7
Canada	156	21.3	23.2	26.3	30.4	34.6	38.3	41.1	44.7	49.2	55.1	61.6	†65.9	69.0	71.6	73.7
Australia	193	13.9	15.7	19.2	22.7	25.9	28.7	31.2	33.9	37.9	42.3	†47.3	50.6	55.4	58.2	62.7
Japan	158	24.4	29.0	36.2	42.7	48.0	52.5	56.2	59.4	62.9	66.1	69.4	71.6	74.0	76.4	78.6
New Zealand	196	....	....	....	....	....	....	....	....	....	....	....	....	....	....	....
Euro Area																
Austria	122	22.9	25.8	29.9	33.9	36.9	40.1	42.4	44.8	48.4	51.3	54.5	57.0	59.8	63.4	66.3
Belgium (1990=100)	124	25.1	29.2	35.3	42.4	47.1	51.4	55.0	†59.3	64.8	71.3	75.7	79.0	82.9	85.9	88.3
Finland	172	12.7	14.8	17.7	†21.2	24.7	27.1	29.1	32.2	36.2	40.9	45.3	49.7	54.2	†58.3	61.9
France	132	12.2	†13.8	16.5	19.8	23.1	26.4	30.1	34.7	40.3	46.1	55.4	62.5	67.8	71.9	75.1
Germany (1990=100)	134	30.6	34.6	39.6	44.1	46.7	50.7	54.1	57.9	62.8	67.4	70.9	73.8	76.2	79.3	83.5
Ireland	178	9.0	10.8	12.7	16.6	19.9	23.5	27.0	30.9	36.5	42.6	48.0	53.7	60.2	65.0	69.9
Italy	136	5.7	7.0	8.4	10.8	13.0	16.6	19.4	23.0	28.1	34.8	40.9	47.0	52.3	58.1	60.9
Netherlands	138	†32.9	37.2	43.6	49.5	53.9	57.7	61.0	63.7	66.5	68.7	73.4	75.3	76.2	79.9	81.2
Spain	184	4.4	5.3	6.7	8.6	11.2	14.6	18.4	†22.6	26.8	†30.2	35.1	40.3	45.1	49.6	55.0
Denmark (1990=100)	128	19.5	22.4	26.9	32.0	35.6	39.2	43.2	48.1	53.6	58.3	64.4	68.7	72.0	75.3	79.4
Greece	174	1.5	1.8	2.2	2.8	3.6	4.3	5.4	6.5	8.2	10.5	14.0	16.7	21.1	25.3	28.5
Iceland	176	.4	.5	.7	.9	†1.2	1.6	2.5	3.6	5.6	8.6	13.4	20.3	22.6	29.9	37.5
Norway	142	15.1	16.6	19.5	†23.4	27.0	30.0	32.4	33.4	36.5	40.3	44.3	48.0	52.1	56.4	62.1
Sweden	144	16.4	17.7	19.9	23.4	26.6	28.4	30.9	33.2	36.0	40.4	43.0	45.7	50.3	54.3	57.6
Switzerland (1990=100)	146	†42.5	46.3	†51.1	54.8	55.5	†58.2	59.7	61.8	65.1	69.2	74.2	77.1	79.1	82.1	85.4
United Kingdom	112	10.1	11.5	13.5	17.1	19.9	21.7	24.5	28.3	34.1	38.5	42.1	45.6	48.4	52.4	56.6

Employment

Index Numbers (1995=100):

Country	Code	1972	1973	1974	1975	1976	1977	1978	1979	1980	1981	1982	1983	1984	1985	1986
Industrial Countries	110	91.1	93.3	94.0	91.0	91.3	92.2	93.6	95.5	95.6	95.0	93.0	92.2	93.8	95.3	96.5
United States	111	62.9	65.5	66.8	65.7	67.7	70.4	74.0	76.7	77.2	77.8	76.4	76.9	80.6	83.1	84.8
Canada	156	109.5	114.9	118.4	111.8	113.3	111.8	112.9	116.3	114.1	114.9	104.1	101.2	103.6	105.9	109.6
Australia	193	119.3	124.0	123.2	113.2	114.8	114.5	109.4	109.5	111.8	112.3	108.8	102.5	102.6	101.8	102.1
Japan	158	102.8	103.1	102.7	97.3	95.3	94.5	92.4	91.9	92.9	93.8	94.3	94.0	95.1	96.6	97.2
New Zealand	196	81.9	85.6	89.3	87.9	89.3	90.4	86.7	89.4	89.8	88.0	89.9	85.3	88.0	89.0	106.5
Euro Area																
Austria	122	81.9	85.0	86.6	86.6	87.5	89.2	89.9	90.4	90.9	91.2	90.2	89.1	89.5	89.9	90.6
Finland	172	....	....	....	....	131.8	130.4	126.8	131.7	137.4	139.4	135.3	132.7	131.4	130.7	129.0
France	132	....	....	....	....	....	....	....	....	132.6	128.5	127.3	124.8	121.5	118.2	116.0
Germany (1990=100)	134	116.4	116.9	113.8	106.4	103.9	103.0	102.3	102.6	103.3	101.0	97.5	93.5	92.5	93.7	95.3
Ireland	178	93.3	97.8	99.4	93.3	93.3	95.9	97.8	107.2	107.4	104.3	101.1	95.0	92.2	88.4	87.1
Italy	136	121.6	121.9	125.1	125.1	123.2	124.4	123.0	123.3	123.9	122.6	119.9	116.6	111.6	109.1	107.3
Luxembourg (1990=100)	137	87.7	90.2	93.7	94.1	92.2	90.9	89.7	90.5	91.2	90.6	89.6	87.6	86.5	87.4	89.2
Netherlands	138	139.9	136.0	134.4	130.1	125.9	121.7	118.1	116.1	115.0	111.7	95.5	103.6	102.5	103.6	105.7
Spain	184	104.9	103.9	105.4	103.9	104.2	103.2	101.2	98.8	94.7	91.5	90.4	89.6	88.6	87.8	92.3
Denmark (1990=100)	128	128.6	126.7	123.5	106.7	106.6	106.2	105.1	106.4	103.1	96.1	95.6	97.1	104.0	108.1	111.2
Greece	174	97.5	103.5	104.7	105.6	112.0	117.2	120.9	124.2	125.6	127.0	127.1	125.7	126.1	124.6	124.8
Norway	142	82.9	83.1	83.4	85.1	86.1	87.7	89.2	90.0	92.1	92.9	93.6	94.1	94.7	96.9	100.3
Sweden	144	136.1	138.6	146.1	148.5	142.5	137.3	132.5	133.2	133.3	128.1	123.8	123.3	124.8	127.1	128.4
Switzerland	146	144.2●	142.9	142.5	129.6	120.5	120.2	120.7	120.5	122.6	122.7	118.9	114.7	114.1	115.1	116.6
United Kingdom	112	94.3	96.6	97.2	96.9	96.1	94.3	97.1	104.7	101.0	97.4	95.2	95.5	96.4	96.7	96.6

Sector Coverage

Country		Industrial Sector: Mining	Mfg.	Util.	Other: Constr.	Serv.	Agri.
United States	66..c	x	x	x			
	65ey		x				
	67..c	x	x	x	x	x	
Canada	66..c	x	x	x			
	65ey		x				
	67ey		x				
Australia	66..c	x	x	x			
	65	x	x	x	x	x	x
	67eyc		x				
Japan	66..c	x	x				
	65	x	x	x			
	67eyc		x				
New Zealand	66eyc		x				
	65	x	x	x	x	x	x
	67ey		x				
Austria	66..b	x	x	x			
	65	x	x				
	67	x	x	x	x	x	x

Country		Industrial Sector: Mining	Mfg.	Util.	Other: Constr.	Serv.	Agri.
Belgium	66..b	x	x				
	65	x	x		x		
Denmark	66..c	x	x				
	65		x		x		
	67eyc		x				
Finland	66..c	x	x	x			
	65ey		x				
	67ez	x	x				
France	66..c	x	x				
	65		x	x			
	67..c	x	x				
Germany	66..c	x	x		x	x	x
	65..c	x	x		x	x	x
	67		x				
Greece	66eyb		x				
	65		x				
	67ey	x	x	x			

Industrial Production

1987	1988	1989	1990	1991	1992	1993	1994	1995	1996	1997	1998	1999	2000	2001		
(66..i)																
85.7	**90.4**	**93.6**	**95.0**	94.4	93.8	92.6	96.2	100.0	102.4	106.9	108.0	110.1	115.5	111.4	Industrial Countries..............	110
81.5	85.1	86.7	86.5	84.8	87.4	90.4	95.4	100.0	104.6	111.9	117.6	121.9	127.4	122.7	United States	111
87.3	91.9	91.8	88.8	85.0	†86.0	89.9	95.7	100.0	101.4	†105.8	109.4	115.5	121.9	118.4	Canada.................	156
84.0	88.7	92.7	94.9	†91.5	91.5	94.1	98.8	100.0	103.7	105.7	108.9	112.5	118.6	118.7	Australia	193
87.2	95.6	101.2	105.3	107.2	100.6	96.1	96.7	100.0	102.9	†107.3	99.7	100.1	106.4	98.2	Japan.................	158
93.4	89.0	88.9	85.3	81.7	85.1	90.8	96.4	100.0	100.8	102.4	99.8	101.8	....	....	New Zealand	196
															Euro Area	
77.9	81.5	86.5	93.0	94.4	93.3	91.4	95.0	100.0	100.9	107.9	118.3	124.0	132.9	132.6	Austria	122
87.5	92.7	95.9	99.4	97.4	97.3	92.5	94.1	100.0	100.8	105.1	101.4	110.7	115.5	....	Belgium	124
81.7	84.5	87.3	†87.2	79.6	80.2	84.7	94.3	100.0	102.9	111.7	122.1	128.9	143.8	142.4	Finland	172
90.4	94.7	98.6	†100.4	99.2	98.0	94.3	98.0	100.0	100.3	†104.2	109.6	111.9	115.8	116.6	France	132
90.1	93.3	97.8	103.2	†104.4	103.1	95.9	99.5	100.0	99.8	102.7	106.2	107.7	113.4	113.3	Germany	134
98.0	102.9	105.3	102.3	101.4	100.1	96.6	97.7	100.0	100.3	100.9	106.5	107.1	113.8	115.6	Greece	174
111.4	126.5	141.8	148.2	152.4	69.5	73.2	82.5	100.0	108.4	†129.4	149.2	164.9	218.7	241.4	Ireland	178
85.4	90.5	93.4	93.5	92.6	92.4	90.2	94.9	100.0	99.1	102.4	104.3	104.1	108.2	....	Italy	136
80.7	90.3	97.1	97.5	97.1	96.3	93.7	99.1	100.0	100.7	106.2	114.1	116.4	122.6	126.3	Luxembourg	137
84.0	86.5	89.8	91.5	†94.0	93.8	92.7	†97.2	100.0	103.8	106.6	107.7	107.7	110.5	110.1	Netherlands	138
82.6	85.7	91.0	99.7	101.1	99.2	98.3	96.9	100.0	100.2	102.2	108.4	110.7	116.0	....	Portugal	182
90.0	92.7	96.9	96.9	96.2	93.4	89.0	95.5	100.0	99.3	106.1	111.8	114.8	119.3	118.3	Spain	184
82.8	84.4	86.5	†86.5	86.6	89.1	86.6	95.3	100.0	†101.7	107.4	109.8	112.4	119.7	121.5	Denmark	128
75.7	77.6	85.2	86.5	†88.5	89.6	92.1	97.2	100.0	102.5	106.0	108.8	107.6	110.4	....	Norway	142
85.7	86.8	90.0	†87.8	83.3	82.0	82.9	91.5	†100.0	101.7	108.9	112.9	115.3	125.2	124.4	Sweden	144
86.0	93.0	94.5	97.0	97.0	95.9	93.9	98.0	100.0	100.1	104.7	108.4	112.2	121.1	....	Switzerland	146
88.2	92.5	94.4	94.1	91.0	91.3	93.3	98.3	100.0	102.4	103.4	104.2	105.8	103.7		United Kingdom	112

Wages

1987	1988	1989	1990	1991	1992	1993	1994	1995	1996	1997	1998	1999	2000	2001		
(65, 65ey, 65..c)																
63.3	**70.6**	**75.3**	**78.6**	82.1	85.0	95.2	97.8	100.0	102.6	105.1	105.9	101.4	111.9	114.6	Industrial Countries..............	110
80.1	82.3	84.8	87.5	90.4	92.6	94.9	97.5	100.0	103.2	106.4	109.1	112.4	116.2	120.0	United States	111
76.2	79.1	83.4	87.7	91.8	95.1	97.0	98.6	100.0	103.2	104.1	106.3	106.4	112.3	114.8	Canada.................	156
66.0	70.5	76.2	82.8	86.9	90.4	92.1	95.1	100.0	104.0	108.3	112.7	115.7	121.4	127.4	Australia	193
80.2	83.0	85.6	88.9	91.9	93.9	95.7	97.9	100.0	101.9	103.4	103.1	103.6	104.6	104.7	Japan.................	158
....	....	....	....	....	....	97.5	98.5	100.0	101.9	104.3	106.2	107.8	109.5	111.6	New Zealand	196
															Euro Area	
															Austria	122
68.4	70.9	74.1	79.4	83.5	87.5	92.1	95.8	100.0	....	....	....	....	....	....	Belgium (1990=100)	124
†90.0	90.7	95.8	100.0	105.1	110.1	112.4	114.7								Finland	172
†66.2	71.6	78.1	†85.8		93.0	93.7	95.5	100.0	103.9	....	....	....	....	....	France	132
78.6	81.1	84.9	86.2	90.0	93.4	96.3	99.2	100.0	101.9	104.7	107.6	110.0	115.0	120.2	Germany (1990=100)	134
87.6	91.0	94.9	100.0	107.2	114.8	121.7	123.6	....	....	....	....	....	....	....	Ireland	178
73.4	76.9	80.0	83.1	86.7	90.2	95.1	97.8	100.0	102.5	107.5	111.9	118.4	126.4	136.4	Italy	136
64.8	68.8	72.9	78.2	85.9	94.6	97.0	97.0	100.0	103.2	106.9	109.9	112.4	114.7	116.6	Netherlands	138
82.3	83.4	84.5	87.0	†90.2	94.1	97.1	†98.9	100.0	101.7	104.8	108.1	111.3	115.4	120.2	Spain	184
59.1	62.9	67.5	73.4	79.4	85.5	91.3	95.4	100.0	105.3	109.6	....	115.5	118.3	....	Denmark (1990=100)	128
86.9	92.5	96.2	100.0	104.2	107.2	....	....	....	....	....	....	....			Greece	174
31.2	37.0	44.6	53.2	62.1	70.7	78.1	88.3	100.0	108.6	118.3	123.9	....	....		Iceland	176
62.6	79.4	90.0	†96.9	98.4	98.5	96.3	96.8	100.0	....	104.2	....	....	....	....	Norway	142
72.2	76.0	79.7	84.3	88.7	91.5	93.9	96.6	100.0	107.2	111.4	115.4	118.2	122.1	125.4	Sweden	144
62.5	67.5	74.2	81.1	84.9	88.8	91.7	95.5	100.0	....	....	....	....	....	....	Switzerland (1990=100)	146
87.5	90.7	94.3	100.0	107.5	113.4	116.2	....	....	....	....	....	....	....	....	United Kingdom	112
61.0	66.3	72.4	79.4	85.6	90.8	93.6	97.0	100.0	103.6	108.0	113.4	119.0	124.4	129.8		

Employment

1987	1988	1989	1990	1991	1992	1993	1994	1995	1996	1997	1998	1999	2000	2001		
(67, 67ey, 67..c, 67eyc)																
97.4	**99.0**	**101.0**	**102.4**	101.8	100.8	99.4	99.5	100.0	99.9	100.9	101.8	102.0	102.6	102.0	Industrial Countries..............	110
87.0	89.8	92.1	93.4	92.4	92.7	94.5	97.4	100.0	102.0	104.7	107.4	110.0	112.4	112.6	United States	111
114.6	117.4	119.7	112.6	101.0	95.5	95.3	97.5	100.0	102.4	106.1	110.3	112.8	120.6	120.1	Canada.................	156
103.8	107.0	110.5	107.6	101.1	100.1	95.8	99.1	100.0	100.3	101.8	98.5	96.4	....	....	Australia	193
95.9	96.9	99.1	101.7	104.2	104.9	104.2	101.8	100.0	97.7	96.9	95.6	93.1	90.9	88.5	Japan.................	158
100.9	92.2	86.7	83.7	80.9	86.4	86.4	96.3	100.0	98.7	94.8	97.1	93.3	94.3	96.8	New Zealand	196
															Euro Area	
90.8	91.6	93.3	95.5	97.7	99.6	99.6	100.1	100.0	99.3	99.6	100.2	101.3	102.1	102.6	Austria	122
124.7	121.2	123.0	121.7	110.0	99.2	92.9	93.3	100.0	100.5	101.4	104.0	106.8	108.1	108.8	Finland	172
113.3	112.1	113.0	113.6	111.5	108.5	103.2	101.0	100.0	97.2	96.5	96.9	96.5	97.8	99.1	France	132
95.2	95.0	97.3	100.0	101.4	99.0	91.9	85.9	....	....	....	....	....	....	....	Germany (1990=100)	134
86.2	86.4	88.4	90.7	91.7	90.8	90.9	94.2	100.0	104.8	110.9	114.1	113.1	117.6	118.7	Ireland	178
105.6	106.1	106.1	107.7	108.6	106.8	104.5	102.3	100.0	98.9	98.5	99.5	99.6	99.7	100.7	Italy	136
90.2	93.7	96.2	100.0	95.7	....	....	....	100.0	98.9	100.0	....	....	....	....	Luxembourg (1990=100)	137
106.7	106.7	108.5	110.9	111.1	110.0	106.7	102.2	100.0	98.9	106.0	109.7	114.7	120.2	122.6	Netherlands	138
95.1	97.8	101.8	104.5	104.7	102.7	98.3	97.4	100.0	102.9	106.0	109.7	114.7	120.2	122.6	Spain	184
105.3	102.1	100.9	100.0	96.8	94.7	88.5	....	100.0	99.4	96.2	95.3	....	....	....	Denmark (1990=100)	128
123.1	124.4	124.7	122.8	115.2	109.5	103.0	99.9	100.0	99.4	96.2	95.3	....	....		Greece	174
102.3	101.7	98.5	97.7	96.4	96.5	97.9	97.0	100.0	102.8	....	....	....	....	....	Norway	142
126.3	126.9	127.8	124.7	114.8	104.8	96.3	95.0	100.0	100.9	99.8	100.2	99.4	99.1	97.0	Sweden	144
116.5	116.5	117.7	119.4	117.3	111.3	105.9	101.3	100.0	97.4	95.0	94.4	93.8	94.7	95.7	Switzerland	146
99.1	101.5	103.1	102.5	99.3	97.2	97.8	98.8	100.0	101.3	104.3	105.9	108.0	109.5	109.8	United Kingdom	112

Sector Coverage

Country		Industrial Sector			Other			Country		Industrial Sector			Other		
		Mining	Mfg.	Util.	Constr.	Serv.	Agri.			Mining	Mfg.	Util.	Constr.	Serv.	Agri.
Iceland	65	x	x		x			Portugal	66..b	x	x	x			
Ireland	66..c	x	x	x				Spain	66..c	x	x	x			
	65ey		x						65	x	x	x	x	x	
	67ey		x						67	x	x	x	x	x	
Italy	66..c	x	x	x				Sweden	66..c	x	x				
	65ey	x	x	x	x				65	x	x				
	67	x	x	x					67	x	x	x			
Luxembourg	66..b	x	x	x				Switzerland	66..b	x	x	x			
	67	x	x	x					65	x	x	x	x		x
Netherlands	66..c	x	x	x					67ey	x	x				
	65		x					United Kingdom	66..c	x	x	x			
	67	x	x	x					65..c	x	x		x	x	x
Norway	66..c	x	x	x					67..c	x	x	x	x	x	x
	65		x												
	67	x	x	x											

(For more information please refer to the country notes in the monthly issues of IFS.)

Producer Prices/Wholesale Prices

63 x

		1972	1973	1974	1975	1976	1977	1978	1979	1980	1981	1982	1983	1984	1985	1986
														Percent Change over Previous Year;		
World	001	5.5	14.0	21.5	10.7	9.3	10.9	8.1	13.9	19.1	14.2	11.6	13.2	14.1	11.1	5.8
Industrial Countries	110	4.1	11.7	17.7	8.8	6.5	7.2	6.1	10.3	13.5	8.7	4.7	3.0	4.2	2.0	-2.2
United States	111	4.4	13.1	18.8	9.2	4.6	6.1	7.8	12.5	14.1	9.1	2.0	1.3	2.4	-.5	-2.9
Canada	156	4.5	11.1	19.0	11.4	5.1	7.8	9.2	14.5	13.4	10.2	6.7	3.5	4.5	2.7	.9
Australia	193	4.8	8.6	15.3	15.1	11.3	10.2	8.2	14.8	14.0	8.4	8.9	8.1	5.4	6.6	5.6
Japan	158	1.6	15.7	27.5	2.8	5.5	3.3	-.5	5.0	15.0	1.4	.5	-.6	.1	-.8	-4.7
New Zealand	196	6.9	12.7	8.1	13.3	22.4	16.4	11.5	17.7	22.9	16.9	15.1	5.5	7.1	15.3	5.7
Euro Area	163	…	…	…	…	…	…	…	…	…	…	…	…	…	…	…
Austria	122	3.9	1.2	15.2	6.4	5.8	3.0	1.0	4.2	8.6	8.0	3.2	.6	3.7	2.6	-5.3
Belgium	124	…	…	…	…	…	…	…	…	…	14.1	13.5	6.7	7.6	2.6	-11.5
Finland	172	8.4	17.5	24.3	13.6	8.2	10.1	5.6	9.7	16.4	12.8	7.2	5.6	5.4	4.5	-5.2
France	132	…	…	…	…	…	…	…	…	…	11.7	10.7	8.8	9.2	4.4	-2.8
Germany	134	2.6	6.6	13.4	4.6	3.7	2.8	1.1	4.8	7.6	7.8	5.9	1.5	2.9	2.4	-2.5
Greece	174	6.3	23.5	30.9	8.3	14.1	13.7	10.3	21.0	28.4	25.9	16.0	19.8	21.4	20.6	16.4
Ireland	178	10.4	17.6	13.5	24.5	19.6	17.2	8.9	12.2	10.5	17.3	11.2	6.2	7.7	3.2	-2.2
Italy	136	…	…	…	…	…	…	…	…	…	…	13.1	11.0	10.3	7.7	.2
Luxembourg	137	…	…	…	…	…	…	…	…	…	10.7	17.9	4.9	6.2	3.0	-2.5
Netherlands	138	4.8	6.2	9.0	6.0	6.9	5.5	1.5	2.6	7.4	8.7	5.7	1.3	4.5	1.6	-2.7
Portugal	182	5.5	11.1	28.6	13.2	19.1	29.0	31.4	29.5	6.7	21.4	27.6	16.7	27.5	21.2	9.2
Spain	184	6.9	10.2	18.0	9.1	13.3	20.2	16.4	14.5	17.4	15.7	12.4	14.0	12.2	8.0	.9
Denmark	128	5.8	14.7	21.7	5.7	8.0	7.4	4.3	9.9	17.3	15.7	10.7	5.0	7.5	2.9	-6.8
Norway	142	…	…	…	…	…	…	4.0	7.2	13.4	10.5	8.5	6.5	6.9	4.8	-3.4
Sweden	144	4.5	11.3	24.8	6.6	8.9	9.5	8.0	11.9	14.1	11.2	12.8	11.1	7.7	5.2	-2.8
Switzerland	146	4.1	8.5	14.0	1.2	-1.0	-.1	-1.4	1.9	4.5	5.6	3.7	1.1	2.9	2.0	-1.3
United Kingdom	112	5.2	7.5	1.6	22.9	16.5	18.9	9.0	11.8	16.0	10.7	8.5	6.5	6.0	6.2	1.3
Developing Countries	200	10.3	22.0	32.1	16.6	17.8	21.6	14.1	23.5	34.2	29.3	31.2	43.9	42.3	36.7	28.2
Africa	605	6.3	13.8	19.2	12.1	11.9	12.8	9.3	12.9	13.7	14.2	13.7	9.9	10.9	14.8	16.3
Central African Rep.	626	6.2	2.4	19.8	18.8	4.8	7.8	7.6	13.8	16.1	14.6	14.4	8.8	22.7	6.8	3.7
Congo, Rep. of	634	12.8	5.3	15.3	14.0	13.5	12.3	9.8	8.9	14.0	13.7	15.3	7.0	14.5	6.6	3.8
Morocco	686	2.1	17.3	23.2	3.7	4.5	14.2	8.7	8.7	8.5	17.6	12.1	7.3	13.7	9.6	7.8
Sierra Leone	724	11.1	26.2	26.1	16.8	22.5	18.1	17.0	21.1	22.4	22.0	19.7	43.1	44.9	49.2	…
South Africa	199	8.3	13.3	17.9	16.8	15.8	13.0	9.9	15.2	16.2	13.7	14.0	10.5	8.4	16.8	19.6
Tunisia	744	1.5	5.4	21.2	9.5	1.2	4.9	3.1	7.3	10.8	12.5	16.9	6.6	8.6	11.3	9.9
Zambia	754	5.1	22.0	12.8	-6.7	19.3	22.0	16.4	24.3	13.4	1.4	6.6	24.1	27.9	47.2	115.9
Zimbabwe	698	…	…	…	…	…	…	…	…	…	…	…	…	…	…	…
Asia	505	9.6	19.2	34.2	7.8	5.0	9.1	4.4	19.1	22.5	12.6	4.5	9.1	9.7	3.6	2.1
China, P.R.: Hong Kong	532	…	…	…	…	…	…	…	…	…	…	…	…	…	…	…
India	534	8.8	16.4	28.6	3.9	-2.0	7.6	-.2	11.6	20.1	12.2	2.4	7.9	6.9	4.6	5.6
Indonesia	536	13.5	38.2	48.0	6.3	14.7	14.0	9.6	49.6	26.8	11.1	7.4	17.9	11.0	5.0	2.2
Korea	542	13.8	6.9	42.1	26.6	12.1	9.0	11.6	18.8	38.9	20.4	4.7	.2	.7	.9	-1.5
Malaysia	548	…	…	…	…	…	…	…	…	…	…	…	…	…	-2.1	-6.2
Pakistan	564	10.3	27.2	22.3	22.8	7.4	9.9	6.1	9.7	13.4	11.2	6.7	7.4	9.4	2.9	4.9
Philippines	566	10.1	23.7	47.7	5.4	13.8	7.5	4.8	19.0	18.3	14.6	10.7	16.0	67.3	18.2	.3
Singapore	576	…	…	…	-1.5	6.7	4.5	1.6	14.4	19.6	3.9	-4.2	-3.6	-.6	-2.2	-15.1
Sri Lanka	524	…	…	…	3.4	8.2	21.0	15.8	9.5	33.8	17.0	5.5	25.0	25.6	-15.2	-3.0
Thailand	578	7.8	22.9	28.9	3.7	3.9	7.8	7.5	11.2	20.1	9.5	.9	2.0	-3.1	—	-.4
Europe	170	1.9	2.9	3.3	10.6	4.6	2.0	3.7	2.1	6.7	7.9	72.8	11.2	25.8	22.9	-.4
Armenia	911	…	…	…	…	…	…	…	…	…	…	…	…	…	…	…
Belarus	913	…	…	…	…	…	…	…	…	…	…	…	…	…	…	…
Bulgaria	918	…	…	…	…	…	…	…	…	…	…	…	…	…	…	…
Croatia	960	…	…	…	…	…	…	…	…	…	…	…	…	…	…	.9
Cyprus	423	…	…	…	…	…	…	…	…	…	…	…	…	…	…	…
Czech Republic	935	…	…	…	…	…	…	…	…	…	…	…	…	…	…	…
Czechoslovakia	934	-.1	.1	-.2	-.1	—	4.7	.5	.7	1.7	4.8	7.7	-.3	8.2	1.8	—
Estonia	939	…	…	…	…	…	…	…	…	…	…	…	…	…	…	…
Hungary	944	1.9	2.9	3.3	10.6	4.6	2.0	3.7	2.3	15.3	6.3	4.7	5.6	4.2	5.3	-72.8
Kazakhstan	916	…	…	…	…	…	…	…	…	…	…	…	…	…	…	…
Kyrgyz Republic	917	…	…	…	…	…	…	…	…	…	…	…	…	…	…	…
Latvia	941	…	…	…	…	…	…	…	…	…	…	…	…	…	…	…
Lithuania	946	…	…	…	…	…	…	…	…	…	…	…	…	…	…	…
Poland	964	…	…	…	…	…	…	14.9	2.0	4.2	9.2	122.3	15.3	14.5	14.2	16.7
Romania	968	…	…	…	…	…	…	…	…	…	…	…	…	…	…	…
Russia	922	…	…	…	…	…	…	…	…	…	…	…	…	…	…	…
Slovak Republic	936	…	…	…	…	…	…	…	…	…	4.3	7.5	.9	8.2	1.8	—
Slovenia	961	…	…	…	…	…	…	…	…	…	…	…	…	…	…	…
Turkey	186	…	…	…	…	…	…	…	…	…	…	27.0	30.5	50.3	43.2	29.6
Ukraine	926	…	…	…	…	…	…	…	…	…	…	…	…	…	…	…
Yugoslavia, SFR	188	11.0	13.2	29.9	21.6	6.4	9.6	8.1	12.6	28.7	43.4	24.8	32.7	60.0	84.4	68.5

Calculated from Indices

1987	1988	1989	1990	1991	1992	1993	1994	1995	1996	1997	1998	1999	2000	2001		
11.8	18.4	21.5	26.7	13.6	14.1	16.5	24.5	13.7	6.2	4.7	4.2	4.4	7.8	3.3	**World**	001
1.1	3.1	4.4	2.8	1.1	.6	1.0	1.3	3.3	.8	.5	-1.5	.1	4.5	1.1	**Industrial Countries**	110
2.6	4.0	5.0	3.6	.2	.6	1.5	1.3	3.6	2.3	-.1	-2.5	.8	5.8	1.1	United States	111
2.8	4.3	2.0	.3	-1.0	.5	3.6	6.1	7.4	.4	.9	-.1	1.6	5.1	1.1	Canada	156
7.3	9.1	5.1	6.0	1.5	1.5	2.0	.8	4.2	.3	1.2	-4.0	-.9	7.1	3.1	Australia	193
-3.1	-.6	1.9	1.5	1.0	-.9	-1.6	-1.7	-.8	-1.6	.7	-1.6	-1.5	.1	-.8	Japan	158
7.9	5.2	7.1	4.7	.9	2.1	2.4	1.3	.8	.5	.4	.7	1.0	7.6	6.0	New Zealand	196
....	....	....	....	....	....	....	....	....	.4	1.1	-.8	-.3	5.3	2.4	Euro Area	163
-2.0	-.2	1.8	2.9	.8	-.2	-.4	1.3	.3	—	.4	-.5	-.8	4.0	1.5	Austria	122
-5.0	1.6	6.6	-1.0	-1.0	-1.8	-2.5	1.6	3.3	2.0	3.7	-2.0	.1	10.6	-1.5	Belgium	124
.9	4.1	5.0	3.3	.3	1.1	3.0	1.3	.7	-.9	1.6	-1.4	-.1	8.3	.4	Finland	172
.6	5.2	5.5	-1.2	-1.3	-1.6	-2.8	1.1	6.1	-2.6	-.7	-.9	-1.3	4.4	1.7	France	132
-2.5	1.3	3.2	1.7	2.1	1.4	.2	.6	1.7	-1.2	1.2	-.4	-1.0	3.3	3.0	Germany	134
9.8	10.1	13.4	15.9	16.7	11.3	11.9	8.7	7.8	6.1	3.3	3.9	2.1	7.8	3.5	Greece	174
.6	4.1	5.5	-2.7	1.2	.9	4.7	.9	2.2	.5	-.5	1.5	1.1	6.1	....	Ireland	178
3.0	3.5	5.9	4.1	3.3	1.9	3.8	3.7	7.9	1.9	1.3	.1	-.3	6.0	1.9	Italy	136
-6.5	2.6	7.6	-2.0	-2.6	-2.7	-1.3	1.5	3.9	-3.1	1.5	2.4	-3.1	4.8	1.1	Luxembourg	137
-1.2	.5	3.6	1.0	2.3	1.8	.1	.5	1.5	2.0	1.8	-.2	1.0	4.9	2.8	Netherlands	138
....	....	....	....	....	....	....	....	....	....	....	....	....	....	....	Portugal	182
.8	3.0	4.2	2.1	1.5	1.3	2.5	4.3	6.4	1.7	1.0	-.7	.7	5.4	1.7	Spain	184
-.2	4.1	5.8	1.0	1.0	-1.1	-.6	.9	2.8	1.1	1.9	-.6	.5	5.9	2.0	Denmark	128
3.6	4.6	5.4	4.0	2.4	-.4	-1.0	1.3	2.6	8.5	1.1	-12.7	18.8	38.1	-4.7	Norway	142
2.8	5.3	7.7	4.7	1.4	-1.3	6.3	4.8	7.8	-1.8	1.2	-.6	1.1	5.8	3.3	Sweden	144
-.7	2.1	3.2	2.3	1.3	.7	.4	-.5	-.1	-1.8	-.7	-1.2	-1.0	.9	.5	Switzerland	146
3.5	3.7	4.8	6.2	5.4	3.1	4.0	2.5	4.0	2.6	.9	.6	1.1	2.5	.2	United Kingdom	112
42.8	65.8	76.1	101.7	47.0	50.8	59.5	75.7	33.2	15.8	12.1	14.3	12.0	13.6	7.0	**Developing Countries**	200
10.8	9.5	11.8	10.5	11.4	9.6	8.4	7.7	9.8	6.3	4.2	4.6	5.6	....	....	**Africa**	605
.4	-15.1	4.0	1.6	-1.2	.3	-1.5	....	....	....	—	....	....			Central African Rep.	626
4.6	2.3	2.2	2.0	-3.6	1.7	3.0	....	....	....						Congo, Rep. of	634
1.0	4.3	3.8	4.6	6.4	2.8	4.5	2.3	6.5	4.4	-1.6	3.5	.9			Morocco	686
....	....	....	....	....	....	....	....	....	....	....	....	....			Sierra Leone	724
13.9	13.1	15.2	12.0	11.3	8.2	6.7	8.2	9.5	7.0	7.1	3.6	5.8			South Africa	199
9.2	8.8	5.7	2.8	5.4	3.7	4.7	3.4	5.7	3.7	3.1	2.5	.4	3.3	1.8	Tunisia	744
84.4	11.6	84.2	115.6	91.7	121.3	140.8	70.6	72.0	....	....	....				Zambia	754
....	14.5	18.2	40.7	52.1	20.5	22.3	20.8	17.1	12.9	31.5	57.2				Zimbabwe	698
8.5	7.5	6.5	7.6	9.1	6.2	4.3	7.0	8.3	4.7	5.0	19.6	2.3	6.6	4.1	**Asia**	505
....	....	....	....	3.4	1.8	.7	2.1	2.7	-.1	-.3	-1.8	-1.5	.2	-1.5	China, P.R.: Hong Kong	532
7.0	8.7	6.8	9.0	13.5	11.9	7.5	10.5	9.3	4.5	4.5	5.9	3.5	6.6	4.8	India	534
19.2	4.9	8.6	10.0	5.1	5.2	3.7	5.4	11.4	7.9	9.0	101.8	10.5	12.5	14.2	Indonesia	536
.5	2.7	1.5	4.2	4.7	2.2	1.5	2.7	4.7	3.2	3.9	12.2	-2.1	2.1	1.9	Korea	542
3.7	7.3	3.8	.9	4.0	1.1	1.5	3.9	4.1	2.3	6.6	6.6	....	....	....	Malaysia	548
8.3	9.7	8.4	8.6	12.2	7.1	10.2	19.7	12.8	11.1	11.2	5.8	3.8	4.0	4.6	Pakistan	564
7.9	12.5	10.6	8.5	17.1	3.7	-.1	8.6	5.5	8.9	.5	11.7	5.7	1.9	2.4	Philippines	566
7.5	-1.8	2.6	1.7	-4.1	-4.4	-4.4	-.4	—	.1	-1.2	-3.0	2.1	10.1	-1.6	Singapore	576
13.4	17.8	9.1	22.2	9.2	8.7	7.6	5.0	8.8	20.5	6.9	6.2	-.4	78.9	-36.5	Sri Lanka	524
5.9	8.2	4.6	3.5	6.8	.2	-.4	4.0	8.2	1.8	5.1	12.2	-4.7	3.9	2.5	Thailand	578
21.0	45.2	84.6	141.7	84.4	56.8	45.5	187.7	123.8	43.2	37.1	18.9	39.9	36.2	16.4	**Europe**	170
....	....	....	....	....	....	....	....	....	....	....	14.6	5.9	-.4	1.1	Armenia	911
....	....	....	....	....	....	1,536.3	2,170.8	497.9	35.0	86.5	73.5	355.8	185.6	71.8	Belarus	913
-.3	2.0	.2	11.5	296.3	-60.7	-82.8	1,146.3	55.7	133.9	971.3	16.3	3.1	17.2	4.5	Bulgaria	918
100.0	233.3	1,400.0	400.0	166.7	775.0	1,497.1	77.6	.7	1.4	1.8	-1.0	2.4	8.1	4.8	Croatia	960
....	....	....	....	....	3.0	2.5	3.3	3.6	2.1	2.8	.5	1.2	7.2	1.6	Cyprus	423
....	....	....	....	....	....	9.3	5.3	7.5	4.8	4.9	4.9	1.0	4.9	....	Czech Republic	935
.1	—	-.7	4.4	70.0	....	....									Czechoslovakia	934
....	....	....	....	....	....	....	....	25.6	14.8	8.4	4.2	-1.2	4.9	4.4	Estonia	939
2.9	5.4	15.0	21.5	34.4	10.0	13.9	12.3	28.5	21.8	20.3	11.4	5.0	10.8	5.1	Hungary	944
....	....	....	....	....	....	....	....	....	23.9	15.3	.8	19.0	38.0	.3	Kazakhstan	916
....	....	....	....	....	....	....	215.3	21.8	23.0	26.3	7.9	53.7	30.7	12.0	Kyrgyz Republic	917
....	....	....	....	....	....	117.1	16.8	11.9	13.7	4.1	1.9	-4.0	.6	1.7	Latvia	941
....	....	....	....	....	....	391.9	44.7	28.3	17.3	4.2	-6.7	3.0	19.4	-1.7	Lithuania	946
26.5	59.6	218.2	610.1	50.3	27.7	32.2	30.1	25.5	13.2	12.2	7.2	5.5	7.7	1.7	Poland	964
....	....	....	....	240.7	203.6	165.0	140.5	35.1	49.9	156.9	33.2	44.5	53.4	41.0	Romania	968
....	....	....	....	....	....	943.8	337.0	236.5	50.8	17.2	5.1	58.9	46.5	19.2	Russia	922
.1	-.2	-2.7	4.8	68.9	5.3	17.2	10.0	9.0	4.1	4.5	3.3	3.8	9.8	....	Slovak Republic	936
....	....	....	....	166.0	166.0	21.6	17.7	12.8	6.8	6.1	6.0	2.1	6.0	8.9	Slovenia	961
32.0	70.5	64.0	52.3	55.3	62.1	58.0	121.3	86.0	75.9	81.8	71.8	53.1	51.4	....	Turkey	186
....	....	....	....	....	....	4,619.3	1,143.8	487.9	51.9	7.7	13.2	31.1	....	....	Ukraine	926
94.1	203.0	1,306.3	436.5	113.3	....	....	....	....	....	....	....	....			Yugoslavia, SFR	188

Producer Prices/Wholesale Prices

		1972	1973	1974	1975	1976	1977	1978	1979	1980	1981	1982	1983	1984	1985	1986
													Percent Change over Previous Year;			
Middle East	405	4.1	12.0	18.2	10.3	10.6	15.4	13.4	16.1	31.2	22.9	17.5	20.6	22.6	19.4	17.3
Egypt	469	1.3	6.8	14.3	7.5	7.8	9.3	14.8	9.7	21.7	8.0	9.3	16.0	10.0	13.2	17.3
Iran, I.R. of	429	5.7	11.3	17.0	8.0	9.0	17.2	10.1	14.1	31.3	23.5	12.7	14.7	7.6	5.3	19.0
Israel	436	10.5	19.1	51.5	40.8	30.8	38.5	53.2	79.0	135.1	122.7	125.7	144.5	396.5	266.1	45.1
Jordan	439	....	....	....	....	14.2	6.7	5.4	6.5	14.9	9.0	3.2	4.0	1.7	1.5	-.3
Kuwait	443	....	22.0	10.4	7.6	7.6	7.0	-1.2	6.5	10.5	6.9	1.1	1.9	-.6	-1.3	.6
Saudi Arabia	456															3.8
Syrian Arab Rep.	463	-4.6	32.6	13.8	7.6	12.0	9.0	12.9	8.7	15.0	19.0	10.9	3.0	8.8	10.1	40.5
Western Hemisphere	205	15.4	33.3	38.9	28.2	34.7	38.5	24.7	34.5	53.7	52.5	58.3	101.8	109.1	103.8	86.2
Argentina	213															
Brazil	223	18.6	16.8	29.2	27.2	43.3	42.5	37.6	55.9	106.4	108.2	93.2	167.4	236.3	229.0	140.2
Chile	228	70.0	511.3	1,028.8	481.9	221.1	86.1	43.0	49.4	39.6	9.1	7.2	45.5	24.3	43.4	19.8
Colombia	233	18.3	28.0	36.0	25.4	22.9	26.7	17.6	27.8	24.2	24.1	25.7	21.7	18.3	24.9	22.0
Costa Rica	238	5.5	16.3	39.8	21.6	9.3	7.5	7.8	16.1	23.7	65.3	108.2	26.2	7.7	10.4	9.0
Ecuador	248															
El Salvador	253	5.9	21.1	25.3	1.8	34.7	47.3	-19.8	7.6	15.8	10.0	8.5	6.8	5.9	13.8	32.5
Mexico	273	3.1	15.7	22.3	10.7	22.3	41.2	15.8	18.3	24.5	24.5	56.1	107.4	70.3	53.6	88.4
Panama	283	8.5	10.5	30.2	14.0	7.8	7.2	5.4	14.0	15.3	10.0	8.3	-3.8	1.1	-.4	-16.0
Paraguay	288															
Peru	293	....	....	....	....	....	....	....	....	....	68.2	56.6	113.0	120.1	173.9	60.3
Trinidad and Tobago	369									19.4	16.9	13.8	12.5	5.1	4.7	6.5
Uruguay	298	90.2	114.9	78.6	72.4	50.6	50.3	48.6	80.4	41.8	23.4	12.9	73.5	77.4	76.6	67.2
Venezuela, Rep. Bol.	299	3.4	6.7	16.7	13.7	7.2	10.3	7.4	9.3	20.0	13.8	8.6	6.4	17.5	15.2	17.6
Memorandum Items																
Oil Exporting Countries	999	5.0	9.7	25.3	8.6	10.2	14.1	8.6	25.7	25.2	14.8	8.7	13.1	10.4	6.5	9.2
Non-Oil Developing Countries	201	12.0	25.7	26.8	14.8	15.7	18.7	12.4	23.1	36.0	32.1	35.7	50.2	49.7	43.4	32.8

Indices

Index Numbers:

		1972	1973	1974	1975	1976	1977	1978	1979	1980	1981	1982	1983	1984	1985	1986
World	001	4.4	5.0	6.0	6.7	7.3	8.1	8.8	10.0	11.9	13.6	15.1	17.2	19.6	21.7	23.0
Industrial Countries	110	31.5	35.1	41.4	45.0	47.9	51.4	54.5	60.1	68.2	74.2	77.7	80.0	83.4	85.1	83.2
Developing Countries	200	—	.1	.1	.1	.1	.1	.1	.2	.2	.3	.4	.6	.8	1.1	1.4
Africa	605	7.5	8.5	10.2	11.4	12.7	14.4	15.7	17.7	20.2	23.0	26.2	28.8	31.9	36.6	42.6
Asia	505	11.9	14.2	19.0	20.5	21.5	23.5	24.5	29.2	35.8	40.3	42.1	46.0	50.4	52.3	53.3
Europe	170	.1	.1	.1	.1	.1	.1	.1	.1	.1	.2	.3	.3	.4	.5	.5
Middle East	405	2.5	2.8	3.3	3.7	4.1	4.7	5.3	6.2	8.1	10.0	11.7	14.2	17.3	20.7	24.3
Western Hemisphere (1995=10 mil.)	205	1.7	2.2	3.1	3.9	5.3	7.3	9.1	12.1	18.5	28.0	44.1	87.9	181.6	366.4	677.0
Western Hemisphere	205	....	....	....	....	....	....	....	....	....	....	....	....	....	....	....

1987	1988	1989	1990	1991	1992	1993	1994	1995	1996	1997	1998	1999	2000	2001		
Calculated from Indices																
20.7	21.6	17.5	14.0	16.4	14.6	11.6	14.9	22.3	13.4	5.2	4.1	6.7	7.0	....	Middle East	405
13.7	26.3	27.3	16.8	17.9	12.1	8.6	4.6	6.3	8.3	4.2	1.4	.9	1.8	1.0	Egypt	469
32.3	22.2	20.4	20.6	25.8	33.0	25.6	37.6	60.6	32.9	10.7	11.9	19.2	17.8	....	Iran, I.R. of...........................	429
18.5	17.5	21.1	11.6	16.1	10.2	8.2	7.9	10.7	8.6	6.3	4.2	7.1	3.6	-.1	Israel	436
.9	9.4	33.7	14.4	5.1	4.2	3.4	4.8	-2.4	2.0	1.6	.6	-4.2	-4.1	2.8	Jordan..................................	439
3.3	4.6	8.8	3.8	18.6	.4	1.8	-.2	1.4	5.2	-1.3	-1.6	-1.2	.4	2.0	Kuwait..................................	443
7.2	13.4	1.2	1.7	3.0	1.3	.6	1.8	7.3	-.3	—	-1.9	.4	.4	-.1	Saudi Arabia........................	456
46.7	46.9	13.9	22.0	14.0	2.6	8.5	14.2	6.9	3.2	2.5	-.6	-1.8	....	....	Syrian Arab Rep.	463
124.7	232.6	276.9	462.9	126.2	171.7	245.3	253.9	38.0	20.0	11.9	8.4	13.3	14.3	9.6	Western Hemisphere	205
122.9	412.5	3,432.6	1,606.9	110.5	6.0	1.6	.7	7.8	3.7	-1.1	-3.3	-4.0	3.7	-2.0	Argentina	213
207.1	697.2	1,268.4	2,703.8	401.4	987.8	2,050.1	2,311.6	57.5	6.2	8.1	3.5	16.6	18.1	13.5	Brazil	223
19.2	5.9	15.1	21.8	21.5	11.7	8.6	7.7	7.6	6.2	1.6	1.9	5.2	11.4	7.8	Chile	228
25.1	28.1	28.2	26.6	27.6	20.1	14.2	17.2	18.1	15.0	15.4	17.3	9.8	13.2	9.4	Colombia	233
10.6	17.9	14.6	14.9	28.1	18.4	5.2	13.1	23.9	16.0	11.6	8.8	10.1	....	....	Costa Rica	238
....	....	....	....	....	....	....	....	....	31.2	31.2	31.2	102.7	164.3	....	Ecuador	248
.7	5.5	9.7	18.9	6.9	2.2	7.5	7.9	10.5	4.8	1.0	-6.0	-1.5	3.3	-1.6	El Salvador	253
135.6	107.8	16.1	23.3	20.5	13.4	8.9	6.8	39.1	36.3	18.5	13.9	14.7	8.3	....	Mexico	273
1.5	-6.8	2.4	3.9	.5	1.8	-.2	2.0	3.0	2.1	-2.2	-3.9	2.7	8.8	-23.4	Panama	283
....	....	....	....	....	....	....	....	....	....	1.2	14.9	5.3	14.7	5.8	Paraguay	288
51.5	627.9	2,510.3	6,737.4	306.3	57.2	47.6	17.9	10.5	9.4	7.4	7.3	4.9	4.3	1.4	Peru	293
4.2	5.9	8.9	1.4	.2	.8	5.4	5.4	3.6	2.9	1.9	1.4	1.7	....	....	Trinidad and Tobago	369
63.2	57.4	73.2	107.7	87.6	58.3	33.4	34.2	37.7	25.0	16.4	9.3	-.9	6.8	....	Uruguay	298
44.8	19.3	97.5	27.2	22.3	23.6	35.0	78.2	57.7	103.2	29.8	22.2	16.2	15.2	13.3	Venezuela, Rep. Bol.	299
															Memorandum Items	
23.9	13.0	20.8	13.1	11.9	12.8	11.8	18.4	25.0	20.6	10.1	48.5	11.3	11.9	11.0	Oil Exporting Countries	999
47.4	80.6	91.6	126.5	55.0	59.5	70.9	88.6	34.7	15.0	12.4	9.1	12.1	13.9	6.3	Non-Oil Developing Countries	201

Indices

1987	1988	1989	1990	1991	1992	1993	1994	1995	1996	1997	1998	1999	2000	2001		
1995=100																
25.7	30.4	37.0	46.8	53.2	60.7	70.7	88.0	100.0	106.2	111.2	115.8	120.9	130.4	134.7	World	001
84.2	86.8	90.6	93.0	94.1	94.6	95.5	96.8	100.0	100.8	101.3	99.8	100.0	104.5	105.6	Industrial Countries...........................	110
2.1	3.4	6.0	12.1	17.8	26.8	42.7	75.1	100.0	115.8	129.8	148.4	166.1	188.7	202.0	Developing Countries.........................	200
47.2	51.7	57.8	63.9	71.2	78.0	84.5	91.0	100.0	106.3	110.8	115.9	122.4	....	....	Africa.....................................	605
57.9	62.2	66.3	71.4	77.9	82.7	86.3	92.3	100.0	104.7	110.0	131.6	134.6	143.5	149.4	Asia	505
.6	.8	1.5	3.7	6.8	10.7	15.5	44.7	100.0	143.2	196.3	233.5	326.5	444.7	517.7	Europe	170
29.3	35.7	41.9	47.8	55.6	63.7	71.1	81.8	100.0	113.4	119.3	124.1	132.4	141.7	....	Middle East	405
1,503.9	4,928.2	18,284.5	100,194.4	....	....	....	....	....							Western Hemisphere (1995=10 mil.)	205
....	....	....	1.0	2.2	5.9	20.5	72.5	100.0	120.0	134.3	145.6	165.0	188.6	206.8	Western Hemisphere	205

Consumer Prices

		1972	1973	1974	1975	1976	1977	1978	1979	1980	1981	1982	1983	1984	1985	1986
													Percent Change over Previous Year			
World	001	5.8	10.1	16.4	13.9	11.9	12.3	9.3	12.6	17.2	16.5	15.2	14.8	15.2	15.8	11.7
Industrial Countries	110	4.9	8.0	13.6	11.5	8.7	9.0	7.6	9.6	12.3	10.4	7.7	5.3	5.0	4.4	2.6
United States	111	3.3	6.2	11.0	9.1	5.7	6.5	7.6	11.3	†13.5	10.3	6.2	3.2	4.3	3.6	1.9
Canada	156	4.8	7.6	10.9	10.8	7.5	8.0	8.9	9.1	10.2	†12.5	10.8	5.8	4.3	4.0	4.2
Australia	193	5.9	9.5	15.1	15.1	13.5	12.3	7.9	†9.1	10.1	9.7	11.1	10.1	4.0	6.7	9.1
Japan	158	4.8	11.6	23.2	11.8	9.3	8.2	4.2	3.7	7.8	4.9	2.7	1.9	2.3	2.0	.6
New Zealand	196	6.8	8.2	11.3	14.5	16.8	14.6	11.9	13.7	17.1	15.3	16.2	7.4	6.2	†15.4	13.2
Euro Area	163															
Austria	122	6.4	7.5	9.5	8.4	†7.3	5.5	3.6	3.7	6.3	6.8	5.4	3.3	5.7	3.2	†1.7
Belgium	124	5.4	7.0	12.7	†12.8	9.2	7.1	4.5	4.5	6.7	7.6	8.7	7.7	†6.3	4.9	1.3
Finland	172	†7.1	11.0	16.7	17.8	14.3	†12.7	7.8	7.5	11.6	†12.0	9.6	8.4	7.1	†5.9	2.9
France	132	6.1	7.4	13.6	11.7	9.6	9.5	9.3	10.6	†13.5	13.3	12.0	9.5	7.7	5.8	2.5
Germany	134	5.5	7.0	7.0	5.9	4.3	3.7	2.7	4.1	5.4	6.3	5.3	3.3	2.4	†2.2	-.1
Greece	174	4.3	15.5	26.9	13.4	13.3	12.2	12.5	19.0	24.9	†24.5	20.9	20.2	18.4	19.3	23.0
Ireland	178	8.6	11.4	17.0	20.9	†18.0	13.6	7.6	13.2	†18.2	20.3	17.1	10.5	8.6	†5.4	3.8
Italy	136	5.2	10.7	19.4	16.9	16.6	17.4	12.1	14.6	21.3	17.8	16.4	14.6	10.8	9.2	5.8
Luxembourg	137	5.2	6.1	9.4	10.7	9.8	6.7	3.1	4.5	6.3	8.1	9.4	8.7	†5.6	4.1	.1
Netherlands	138	7.8	8.0	9.6	10.2	9.1	6.5	4.1	4.2	†6.5	6.7	5.9	2.8	3.3	2.2	.1
Portugal	182	8.9	10.4	28.0	20.4	18.2	27.1	22.7	23.6	16.6	20.0	22.7	†25.1	29.3	19.3	11.7
Spain	184	8.3	11.4	15.7	16.9	17.6	24.5	19.8	15.7	15.5	14.6	14.4	12.2	11.3	8.8	8.8
Denmark	128	6.6	9.3	15.3	†9.6	9.0	11.1	10.0	9.6	†12.3	11.8	10.1	6.9	6.3	4.7	3.7
Iceland	176	9.7	21.0	42.7	49.4	†32.8	30.6	44.0	45.4	58.5	50.8	51.0	84.2	29.2	31.7	21.9
Norway	142	7.2	7.4	9.4	11.7	9.2	9.0	8.2	4.8	10.9	13.6	11.4	8.4	6.3	5.7	7.2
Sweden	144	6.0	6.7	9.9	9.8	10.3	11.5	9.9	7.2	†13.7	12.1	8.6	8.9	8.0	7.4	4.2
Switzerland	146	6.7	8.8	9.8	6.7	1.7	1.3	†1.1	3.6	4.0	6.5	†5.7	†3.0	2.9	3.4	.7
United Kingdom	112	7.1	9.2	†15.9	24.2	16.5	15.9	8.2	13.5	18.0	11.9	8.6	4.6	5.0	6.1	3.4
Developing Countries	200	8.5	16.7	23.8	20.3	20.3	21.2	14.5	19.1	27.6	29.8	32.0	36.9	38.5	42.1	32.3
Africa	605	5.7	8.9	13.7	17.9	15.4	18.7	15.4	15.2	14.5	19.4	12.9	17.0	14.9	15.2	13.5
Algeria	612	3.7	6.2	4.7	8.2	9.4	12.0	17.5	11.3	9.5	14.7	†6.5	6.0	8.1	10.5	12.4
Angola	614															
Benin	638															
Botswana	616				12.0	11.7	13.2	9.0	11.7	13.6	†16.4	11.1	10.5	8.6	8.1	10.0
Burkina Faso	748													4.8	6.9	-2.6
Burundi	618	3.8	6.0	15.7	15.7	6.9	6.8	23.9	36.5	†2.5	12.2	5.9	8.2	14.3	3.8	1.7
Cameroon	622	8.1	10.4	17.2	13.6	9.9	14.7	12.5	6.6	†9.6	10.7	13.3	16.6	11.4	8.5	7.8
Cape Verde	624													11.3	5.4	10.9
Central African Rep.	626										—	13.3	14.6	2.5	10.4	2.1
Chad	628													20.3	5.2	†-13.1
Congo, Dem. Rep. of	636	16	16	29	†29	80	69	49	101	47	35	37	77	52	†24	44
Congo, Rep. of	634															4.2
Côte d'Ivoire	662	.3	11.1	17.4	11.4	12.1	27.4	13.2	16.3	14.7	8.8	7.6	5.6	4.3	†1.9	9.7
Djibouti	611									12.1	5.7	-2.4	.9	†1.9	2.1	18.1
Equatorial Guinea	642															-17.8
Ethiopia	644	-6.1	8.9	8.6	6.6	28.5	16.7	14.3	16.0	4.5	6.1	5.9	-.7	8.4	19.1	-9.8
Gabon	646	3.5	6.2	12.1	†28.5	20.2	13.9	10.8	8.0	12.3	8.7	†16.7	10.7	5.9	7.4	6.3
Gambia, The	648	8.7	6.9	†9.2	25.9	17.0	12.4	8.9	6.1	6.8	5.9	10.9	10.6	22.1	18.3	56.6
Ghana	652	10.1	17.7	18.1	29.8	56.1	116.5	73.1	54.4	50.1	116.5	22.3	122.9	39.7	10.3	24.6
Guinea-Bissau	654															
Kenya	664	5.8	9.3	†17.8	19.1	11.4	14.8	16.9	8.0	†13.9	11.6	20.7	11.4	10.3	13.0	2.5
Lesotho	666			13.4	14.2	11.4	16.7	13.5	16.0	16.3	12.4	12.1	17.5	11.0	13.3	18.0
Liberia	668	3.9	19.6	19.0	14.0	5.6	6.2	7.3	11.6	14.7	7.6	6.0	2.7	1.2	-1.0	4.0
Madagascar	674	5.6	6.1	22.1	8.2	5.0	3.1	6.5	14.1	18.2	30.5	31.8	19.3	9.9	10.6	14.5
Malawi	676										11.8	9.8	13.5	20.0	10.5	14.0
Mali	678															
Mauritania	682															7.4
Mauritius	684	5.4	13.5	29.1	†14.7	13.0	9.2	8.5	14.5	42.0	†14.5	11.4	5.6	7.4	†6.7	1.6
Morocco	686	3.8	†4.1	17.6	7.9	8.5	12.6	9.7	8.3	9.4	12.5	10.5	6.2	12.4	7.7	8.7
Mozambique	688															
Namibia	728										14.8	15.5	12.0	9.1	12.0	13.4
Niger	692	9.8	11.8	3.4	9.1	23.5	23.3	10.1	7.3	10.3	22.9	11.6	-2.5	8.4	-.9	-3.2
Nigeria	694	3.5	5.4	12.7	†33.9	24.3	†13.8	21.7	11.7	10.0	20.8	7.7	23.2	†39.6	7.4	5.7
Rwanda	714	3.1	9.4	31.1	†30.2	7.2	13.7	13.3	15.7	7.2	6.5	12.6	6.6	5.4	1.8	-1.1
Senegal	722	6.2	11.3	16.6	31.7	1.1	11.3	3.4	9.7	8.7	5.9	17.4	11.6	11.8	13.0	6.2
Seychelles	718	20.9	18.2	24.4	18.6	14.9	†15.0	11.8	12.5	13.6	†10.6	-.9	6.1	4.1	.8	0.2
Sierra Leone	724	5.5	5.7	14.4	19.9	17.2	8.3	10.9	†21.3	12.9	23.4	26.9	68.5	66.6	76.6	80.9
South Africa	199	6.5	9.5	11.8	†13.4	11.0	11.2	11.1	13.3	13.7	15.3	14.6	12.3	11.5	16.3	18.7
Sudan	732	13.6	15.3	26.2	24.0	1.7	17.1	19.2	31.1	25.4	24.6	25.7	30.6	34.1	†45.4	24.5
Swaziland	734	2.4	11.5	19.3	12.0	6.5	20.8	8.5	†16.5	18.7	20.1	10.8	†11.6	†12.9	20.5	13.7
Tanzania	738	7.6	10.4	19.6	26.1	6.9	†11.6	6.6	12.9	30.2	25.7	28.9	27.1	36.1	33.3	32.4
Togo	742	7.7	†3.6	12.8	18.0	11.6	22.5	.4	7.5	12.3	19.7	11.1	9.4	-3.5	-1.8	4.1
Tunisia	744													8.9	7.3	6.2
Uganda	746										108.7	49.3	24.1	†42.7	157.7	161.0
Zambia	754															55.8
Zimbabwe	698	2.8	3.1	6.6	†10.0	11.0	10.3	5.7	18.2	5.4	13.2	10.6	23.1	20.2	8.5	14.3

Calculated from Indices

1987	1988	1989	1990	1991	1992	1993	1994	1995	1996	1997	1998	1999	2000	2001		
14.1	16.6	12.9	27.6	17.1	16.6	18.3	25.4	14.5	8.4	6.0	5.8	5.2	4.2	4.0	World	001
3.1	3.4	4.6	5.1	4.2	3.2	2.8	2.3	2.4	2.2	2.0	1.4	1.4	2.4	2.2	Industrial Countries	110
3.7	4.0	4.8	5.4	4.2	3.0	3.0	2.6	2.8	2.9	2.3	1.6	2.2	3.4	2.8	United States	111
4.4	4.0	5.0	4.8	5.6	1.5	1.8	.2	†2.2	1.6	1.6	1.0	1.7	2.7	2.5	Canada	156
8.5	7.2	7.6	†7.3	3.2	1.0	1.8	1.9	4.6	2.6	.3	.9	1.5	4.5	4.4	Australia	193
.1	.7	2.3	3.1	3.2	1.7	1.3	.7	-.1	.1	1.7	.7	-.3	-.7	-.7	Japan	158
15.7	6.4	7.5	5.5	1.7	1.0	1.4	†2.4	3.7	2.3	1.2	1.3	-.1	2.6	2.6	New Zealand	196
....	....	....		....		....					1.1	1.1	2.3	2.5	Euro Area	163
1.4	1.9	2.6	3.3	3.3	4.0	3.6	3.0	2.3	†1.8	1.3	.9	.6	2.4	†2.7	Austria	122
1.6	†1.2	3.1	3.5	3.2	2.4	2.8	2.4	1.5	†2.1	1.6	1.0	1.1	2.5	2.5	Belgium	124
4.1	5.1	6.6	6.1	4.1	2.6	2.1	1.1	†1.0	.6	1.2	1.4	1.2	3.4	2.6	Finland	172
3.3	2.7	3.5	†3.4	3.2	2.4	2.1	1.7	1.8	2.0	1.2	†.7	.5	1.7	1.6	France	132
.2	1.3	†2.8	2.7	†1.7	5.1	4.4	2.8	1.7	1.4	1.9	.9	.6	1.9	2.5	Germany	134
16.4	†13.5	13.7	20.4	19.5	15.9	14.4	†10.9	8.9	8.2	5.5	4.8	2.6	†3.2	3.4	Greece	174
3.1	2.2	4.1	3.3	3.2	†3.1	1.4	2.4	2.5	1.7	1.4	2.4	1.6	5.6	4.9	Ireland	178
4.7	5.1	6.2	6.5	6.3	5.1	4.5	4.0	†5.2	4.0	2.0	2.0	1.7	2.5	2.8	Italy	136
-.1	1.5	3.4	†3.7	3.1	3.2	3.6	2.2	1.9	†1.4	1.4	1.0	1.0	3.1	2.7	Luxembourg	137
-.7	.7	1.1	†2.5	3.1	3.2	2.6	2.8	†1.9	2.0	2.2	2.0	2.2	2.5	4.5	Netherlands	138
9.4	9.6	12.6	13.4	†11.4	8.9	6.8	4.9	4.1	3.1	†2.2	2.8	2.3	2.9	4.4	Portugal	182
5.2	4.8	6.8	6.7	5.9	5.9	4.6	4.7	4.7	3.6	2.0	1.8	2.3	3.4	3.6	Spain	184
4.0	4.6	4.8	2.7	2.4	2.1	1.3	2.0	2.1	2.1	2.2	1.9	2.5	2.9	2.4	Denmark	128
17.7	25.8	20.8	15.5	6.8	4.0	4.1	1.6	1.7	2.3	1.7	1.7	3.2	5.2	6.4	Iceland	176
8.7	6.7	4.6	4.1	3.4	2.3	2.3	1.4	2.5	1.3	2.6	†2.3	2.3	3.1	3.0	Norway	142
4.2	5.8	6.4	10.5	9.3	2.3	4.6	2.2	2.5	.5	.5	-.1	.5	1.0	2.4	Sweden	144
1.4	1.9	2.8	5.7	5.9	4.0	3.3	.9	1.8	.8	.5	.1	.7	1.6	1.0	Switzerland	146
4.1	4.9	7.8	9.5	5.9	3.7	1.6	2.5	3.4	2.4	3.1	3.4	1.6	2.9	1.8	United Kingdom	112
40.0	50.3	27.4	71.4	39.5	40.6	47.5	58.4	30.0	16.1	10.7	11.2	9.7	6.5	6.2	Developing Countries	200
13.8	19.4	19.2	15.3	23.5	31.5	25.4	29.6	28.6	20.2	10.0	6.6	5.6	5.3	7.6	Africa	605
7.4	5.9	9.3	†16.6	25.9	31.7	20.5	29.0	29.8	18.7	8.5	2.3	2.6	....	....	Algeria	612
....	....	....	....	83.6	299.1	†1,379.4	948.8	2,671.8	4,145.2	219.2	86.9	†286.2	325.0	152.6	Angola	614
....	....	....	....	....	....	.4	38.5	14.5	4.9	†3.5	5.8	.3	4.2	4.0	Benin	638
9.8	8.4	11.6	11.4	†11.8	16.2	14.3	10.5	10.5	†10.1	8.7	6.7	7.7	8.6	6.6	Botswana	616
-2.7	4.1	-.3	-.8	2.5	-2.0	.6	25.2	7.4	6.2	†2.3	5.1	-1.1	-.3	4.9	Burkina Faso	748
7.1	4.5	11.7	7.0	†9.0	1.8	9.7	14.9	19.3	26.4	31.1	12.5	3.4	24.3	9.2	Burundi	618
13.1	1.7	-1.7	1.1	.1	—	-3.2	†35.1	9.1	3.9	4.8	3.2	1.5	-2.1	4.5	Cameroon	622
3.8	4.1	4.6	10.7	9.6	†3.1	5.8	3.3	8.4	6.0	8.6	4.4	4.4	-2.5	3.7	Cape Verde	624
-6.9	-4.0	.8	-.4	-2.2	-1.4	-2.9	24.6	19.2	3.7	1.6	-1.9	-1.5	....	....	Central African Rep.	626
-6.0	15.5	-3.9	-.2	4.2	-3.1	-7.1	40.4	9.1	12.4	5.6	12.1	-6.8	3.8	12.4	Chad	628
79	†71	104	81	2,154	†4,129	1,987	23,773	542	659	176	....	....	....	....	Congo, Dem. Rep. of	636
.4	1.0	-1.8	2.9	-1.7	-3.7	4.7	42.5	9.4	10.0	....	6.2	5.4	-.9	.1	Congo, Rep. of	634
6.9	6.9	1.0	-.8	1.7	4.2	†2.2	26.1	14.3	†2.5	4.0	4.7	.8	2.5	4.3	Côte d'Ivoire	662
4.1	....	....	....	....	....	....	....	....	....	....	....	....	....	....	Djibouti	611
-12.9	2.3	5.9	1.1	-3.2	†-7.2	†4.0	36.4	....	....	....	....	....	....	....	Equatorial Guinea	642
-2.4	7.1	7.8	5.2	35.7	10.5	3.5	7.6	10.0	†-5.1	2.4	2.6	5.9	—	-11.2	Ethiopia	644
-.9	-8.8	6.7	7.7	-11.7	-9.5	.5	36.1	9.6	.7	4.0	1.4	-1.9	.5	....	Gabon	646
23.5	11.7	8.3	12.2	8.6	9.5	6.5	1.7	7.0	1.1	2.8	1.1	3.8	.8	....	Gambia, The	648
39.8	31.4	25.2	37.3	18.0	10.1	25.0	24.9	59.5	46.6	†27.9	14.6	12.4	25.2	32.9	Ghana	652
....	60.3	80.8	33.0	57.6	69.6	48.1	15.2	45.4	50.7	49.1	6.5	-.7	8.6	3.3	Guinea-Bissau	654
8.6	12.3	13.8	17.8	20.1	27.3	46.0	28.8	1.6	8.9	11.4	6.6	3.5	6.2	.8	Kenya	664
11.8	11.5	14.7	11.6	17.7	17.2	13.1	8.2	9.3	9.3	....	....	8.2	6.1	-9.6	Lesotho	666
5.0	9.6	9.1	....	....	....	....	....	....	....	....	....	....	....	....	Liberia	668
15.0	26.9	9.0	11.8	8.5	14.6	10.0	38.9	49.1	19.8	4.5	6.2	9.9	†12.0	6.9	Madagascar	674
25.2	33.9	12.5	11.8	†12.6	23.8	22.8	34.6	83.3	37.6	9.1	29.7	44.9	29.5	....	Malawi	676
....	....	-.1	.6	1.8	-6.2	-.3	23.2	13.4	6.8	†-4	4.0	-1.2	-.7	5.2	Mali	678
8.2	1.3	12.9	†6.6	5.6	10.1	9.4	4.1	6.5	4.7	4.6	8.0	4.1	3.3	4.7	Mauritania	682
.5	9.2	12.7	13.5	†7.0	4.6	10.5	7.3	6.0	6.6	†6.8	6.8	6.9	4.2	5.4	Mauritius	684
2.7	2.4	3.1	6.9	†8.0	5.7	5.2	5.1	6.1	3.0	1.0	2.8	.7	1.9	.6	Morocco	686
91.0	50.1	40.1	†47.0	32.9	45.5	42.2	63.2	†54.4	46.9	6.4	.6	2.0	....	....	Mozambique	688
12.6	12.9	15.1	12.0	11.9	17.7	8.5	10.8	10.0	8.0	8.8	6.2	8.6	9.0	9.5	Namibia	728
-6.7	-1.4	-2.8	-.8	†-7.8	-4.5	-1.2	36.0	10.6	5.3	†2.9	4.5	-2.3	2.9	4.0	Niger	692
11.3	54.5	50.5	7.4	13.0	44.6	57.2	57.0	72.8	29.3	8.2	10.3	6.6	14.5	16.5	Nigeria	694
4.1	3.0	1.0	4.2	19.6	9.6	12.4	....	41.0	7.4	12.0	6.2	-2.4	3.9	3.3	Rwanda	714
-4.1	-1.8	.4	.3	-1.8	-.1	-.6	32.3	7.9	†2.8	1.6	1.2	.8	.7	3.1	Senegal	722
2.6	1.8	1.6	3.9	2.0	3.2	1.3	1.8	-.3	-1.1	.6	2.6	†6.3	6.3	6.0	Seychelles	718
178.7	34.3	60.8	110.9	102.7	65.5	†22.2	24.2	26.0	23.1	14.9	35.5	34.1	-.8	2.1	Sierra Leone	724
16.2	12.8	14.7	14.3	15.3	13.9	9.7	8.9	8.7	7.4	8.6	6.9	5.2	5.3	5.7	South Africa	199
....	†64.7	66.7	65.2	123.6	117.6	101.4	115.4	68.4	132.8	46.7	17.1	16.0	....	6.4	Sudan	732
13.4	†21.7	7.5	13.1	8.9	7.6	12.0	13.8	12.3	6.4	7.1	8.1	6.1	12.2	5.9	Swaziland	734
29.9	31.2	†25.8	35.8	28.7	21.8	25.3	33.1	28.4	21.0	16.1	12.8	7.9	5.9	5.1	Tanzania	738
.1	-.2	-.8	1.0	.4	1.4	†-1.0	39.2	16.4	4.7	†8.3	1.0	-.1	1.9	5.4	Togo	742
8.2	†7.2	7.7	6.5	8.2	5.8	4.0	4.7	6.2	3.7	3.7	3.1	2.7	2.9	1.9	Tunisia	744
200.0	196.1	61.4	33.1	28.1	52.4	6.1	9.7	8.6	7.2	6.9	—	†6.4	2.8	2.0	Uganda	746
47.0	51.0	123.4	107.0	93.2	169.0	188.1	53.6	34.2	46.3	24.8	....	....	....	....	Zambia	754
12.5	7.4	12.9	†17.4	23.3	42.1	27.6	22.3	22.6	21.4	18.7	31.8	58.5	55.9	76.7	Zimbabwe	698

Consumer Prices

64 x

		1972	1973	1974	1975	1976	1977	1978	1979	1980	1981	1982	1983	1984	1985	1986
															Percent Change over Previous Year	
Asia	505	6.3	17.6	29.7	10.4	2.8	8.6	5.9	10.1	15.3	13.3	7.4	8.2	8.5	5.2	5.5
Afghanistan, Islamic State of	512	....	....	....	....	....	....	....	....	.9	4.9	5.8	-3.0	7.7	112.3	-3.2
Bangladesh	513	....	....	....	....	....	....	....	....	....	....	....	....	....	....	....
Bhutan	514	....	....	....	....	....	....	....	....	....	....	....	....	....	....	....
Cambodia	522	....	....	....	....	....	....	....	....	....	9.9	9.9	18.0	7.0	1.9	10.0
China, P.R.: Mainland	924	....	....	....	....	....	....	....	....	....	....	....	....	....	....	....
China, P.R.: Hong Kong	532	....	....	....	....	....	....	....	....	....	....	....	....	....	....	....
China, P.R.: Macao	546	....	....	....	....	....	....	....	....	....	....	....	....	....	....	....
Fiji	819	22.0	11.1	14.5	13.1	11.4	7.0	6.1	7.8	14.5	11.2	7.0	6.7	5.3	4.4	†1.8
India	534	6.5	16.9	28.6	5.7	-7.6	8.3	2.5	6.3	11.4	13.1	7.9	11.9	8.3	5.6	8.7
Indonesia	536	6.5	31.0	40.6	19.1	19.9	11.0	8.1	†16.3	18.0	12.2	9.5	11.8	10.5	4.7	5.8
Korea	542	11.7	3.2	24.3	25.3	†15.3	10.2	14.5	18.3	28.7	21.3	7.2	†3.4	2.3	2.5	2.8
Lao People's Dem. Rep.	544	....	....	....	....	....	....	....	....	....	....	....	....	....	....	....
Malaysia	548	3.2	10.6	17.3	4.5	2.6	4.8	4.9	3.7	†6.7	9.7	5.8	3.7	3.9	.3	.7
Maldives	556	....	....	....	....	....	....	....	12.7	27.8	23.8	23.7	22.0			
Mongolia	948	....	....	....	....	....	....	....	....	....	....	....	....	....	....	....
Myanmar	518	7.6	25.2	25.2	31.7	22.4	-1.2	-6.0	5.7	.6	†.3	5.3[e]	5.7	†4.8	6.8	9.3
Nepal	558	8.4	11.4	†19.8	7.6	-3.1	9.9	7.3	3.6	14.7	11.1	11.7	12.4	2.8	8.1	19.0
Pakistan	564	5.2	23.1	26.7	20.9	7.2	†10.1	6.1	8.3	11.9	11.9	†5.9	6.4	6.1	5.6	3.5
Papua New Guinea	853	6.1	8.3	23.2	10.5	7.7	†4.5	5.8	5.8	12.1	8.1	5.5	7.9	7.4	3.7	5.5
Philippines	566	8.2	16.6	34.2	6.8	9.2	9.9	7.3	17.5	18.2	†13.1	9.0	5.3	46.7	23.2	-.3
Samoa	862	†7.5	11.8	25.0	8.8	4.9	14.6	2.1	11.1	†33.0	20.5	18.3	16.5	11.9	9.1	5.7
Singapore	576	2.1	19.6	22.4	2.5	-1.8	3.2	4.9	4.1	8.5	8.2	3.9	1.2	2.6	.5	-1.4
Solomon Islands	813	6.9	3.2	18.9	†10.1	4.3	8.6	6.3	8.1	13.1	16.4	13.0	6.2	11.0	9.6	13.6
Sri Lanka	524	6.3	9.6	12.3	6.6	1.3	1.2	12.1	10.7	26.1	18.0	10.8	14.0	16.6	1.5	8.0
Thailand	578	4.8	15.5	24.3	†5.3	4.1	7.6	7.9	9.9	19.7	12.7	5.3	3.7	.9	2.4	†1.8
Tonga	866	....	....	....	....	7.1	17.5	9.6	5.5	22.4	14.9	10.8	9.8	†.1	16.8	21.7
Vanuatu	846	....	....	....	....	....	5.7	6.4	4.2	11.2	26.8	6.7	1.7	5.5	1.1	†4.8
Vietnam	582	....	....	....	....	....	....	....	....	....	....	....	....	....	....	....
Europe	170	5.2	8.3	10.1	9.5	9.9	13.7	22.4	26.2	44.1	23.9	53.7	-2.5	25.3	41.8	21.7
Albania	914	....	....	....	....	....	....	....	....	....	....	....	....	....	....	....
Armenia	911	....	....	....	....	....	....	....	....	....	....	....	....	....	....	....
Azerbaijan	912	....	....	....	....	....	....	....	....	....	....	....	....	....	....	....
Belarus	913	....	....	....	....	....	....	....	....	....	....	....	....	....	....	....
Bulgaria	918	....	....	....	....	....	....	....	....	....	....	....	....	....	....	....
Croatia	960	....	....	....	....	....	....	....	....	....	....	....	....	....	....	2.7
Cyprus	423	4.8	†7.8	6.5	†14.1	3.9	7.3	7.4	9.5	13.5	†10.7	6.4	5.0	6.0	5.0	†1.2
Czech Republic	935	....	....	....	....	....	....	....	....	....	....	....	....	....	....	....
Czechoslovakia	934	-.3	.3	.5	.7	.8	1.3	1.6	3.9	2.9	.8	5.1	.9	.9	2.3	.5
Estonia	939	....	....	....	....	....	....	....	....	....	....	....	....	....	....	....
Georgia	915	....	....	....	....	....	....	....	....	....	....	....	....	....	....	....
Hungary	944	....	3.4	1.8	3.8	5.2	3.9	4.7	9.0	9.3	4.5	7.0	6.4	8.7	†7.0	5.3
Kazakhstan	916	....	....	....	....	....	....	....	....	....	....	....	....	....	....	....
Kyrgyz Republic	917	....	....	....	....	....	....	....	....	....	....	....	....	....	....	....
Latvia	941	....	....	....	....	....	....	....	....	....	....	....	....	....	....	....
Lithuania	946	....	....	....	....	....	....	....	....	....	....	....	....	....	....	....
Macedonia, FYR	962	....	....	....	....	....	....	....	....	....	....	....	....	....	....	....
Malta	181	3.4	7.7	†7.3	8.8	.6	10.0	4.7	7.1	15.7	11.5	5.8	†-.9	-.4	-.2	2.0
Moldova	921	....	....	....	....	....	....	....	....	....	....	....	....	....	....	....
Poland	964	-.1	2.5	7.1	2.3	4.4	†4.9	8.1	7.0	9.7	19.1	103.6	25.5	15.4	11.5	16.5
Romania	968	....	....	....	....	....	....	....	....	....	....	....	....	....	....	....
Russia	922	....	....	....	....	....	....	....	....	....	....	....	....	....	....	....
Slovak Republic	936	....	....	....	....	....	....	....	....	....	....	....	....	....	....	....
Slovenia	961	....	....	....	....	....	....	....	....	....	....	....	....	....	....	....
Turkey	186	11.7	15.4	15.8	19.2	17.4	27.1	45.3	58.7	110.2	36.6	†30.8	31.4	48.4	45.0	34.6
Ukraine	926	....	....	....	....	....	....	....	....	....	....	....	....	....	....	....
Yugoslavia, SFR	188	15.9	19.5	22.0	23.5	11.2	14.7	14.1	20.7	30.9	39.8	31.5	40.2	54.7	72.3	89.8
Middle East	405	4.8	10.3	15.4	16.0	14.3	17.3	14.8	11.8	20.2	18.5	17.1	17.0	20.2	16.6	18.3
Bahrain, Kingdom of	419	5.1	14.3	24.4	16.2	†22.5	17.7	15.8	2.2	3.9	11.3	8.9	3.0	†.3	-2.6	-2.3
Egypt	469	2.1	5.1	10.0	9.7	10.3	12.7	11.1	9.9	†20.7	10.3	14.8	16.1	17.0	12.1	23.9
Iran, I.R. of	429	6.4	9.8	14.2	12.9	11.3	27.3	11.7	10.5	20.6	24.2	18.7	19.7	12.5	†4.4	18.4
Iraq	433	5.2	4.9[e]	7.7[e]	9.5[e]	12.8[e]	9.2[e]	4.6	....	....	....	....	....	....	....	....
Israel	436	12.9	20.0	39.7	†39.3	31.4	34.6	50.6	78.3	†131.0	116.8	120.4	145.6	†373.8	†304.6	†48.1
Jordan	439	7.7	11.1	19.4	†12.0	11.5	14.6	6.9	†14.2	11.1	7.7	7.4	5.0	3.8	†3.0	—
Kuwait	443	....	8.3	13.0	8.4	5.2	9.9	†8.7	7.1	6.9	7.4	7.8	4.7	1.2	1.5	1.0
Lebanon	446	4.9	6.0	11.1	6.1	6.3	6.3	55.2	23.8	10.5	16.0	13.8	7.2	14.6	54.5	95.2
Libya	672	-.3	8.0	7.5	9.1	5.5	6.3	29.4	-6.0	....	....	....	....	....	....	....
Oman	449	....	....	....	....	....	....	....	....	....	....	....	....	....	....	....
Qatar	453	....	....	....	....	....	....	....	....	6.8	†8.5	5.7	2.7	1.1	1.9	†1.6
Saudi Arabia	456	4.3	16.5	21.4	34.6	31.6	11.4	†-1.6	†1.9	†3.8	2.8	1.0	.2	-1.6	-3.1	-3.2
Syrian Arab Republic	463	2.1	20.4	†15.5	11.5	11.4	12.0	4.8	4.6	19.3	18.4	14.3	6.1	9.2	17.3	36.1
Yemen Arab Rep.	473	....	43.0	26.6	24.0	15.4	26.0	12.4	†26.2	5.3	5.0	2.7	5.3	12.8	....	....
Yemen, P.D. Rep.	459	5.2	19.7	20.3	11.9	3.1	5.5	5.8	7.1	13.7	3.8	9.5	11.0	1.1	5.1	....
Yemen, Republic of	474	....	....	....	....	....	....	....	....	....	....	....	....	....	....	....

Calculated from Indices

1987	1988	1989	1990	1991	1992	1993	1994	1995	1996	1997	1998	1999	2000	2001	Country	Code
6.4	7.4	10.8	6.2	8.1	7.6	9.2	14.6	11.8	7.7	4.7	8.5	2.9	1.8	2.7	**Asia**	505
19.5	19.9	75.1	41.9	56.7	...	...	...	...	...	...	...	...	...	...	Afghanistan, Islamic State of	512
9.9	7.4	6.0	6.1	6.4	3.6	3.0	5.3	8.5	4.1	1.7	7.0	8.9	3.9	1.4	Bangladesh	513
6.4	10.1	8.8	10.0	12.3	16.0	11.2	7.0	9.5	8.8	6.5	10.6	6.8	3.9	...	Bhutan	514
...	...	...	...	...	...	...	...	1.1	10.1	3.2	14.8	4.0	−.8	†−.6	Cambodia	522
7.2	18.7	18.3	3.1	3.5	6.3	14.6	24.2	16.9	8.3	2.8	−.8	−1.4	.3	.3	China, P.R.: Mainland	924
...	...	...	...	11.6	9.3	†7.4	8.7	9.1	†6.3	5.8	2.9	−4.0	−3.7	−1.6	China, P.R.: Hong Kong	532
...	...	...	...	...	...	...	...	...	...	...	...	−3.2	−1.6	−2.1	China, P.R.: Macao	546
5.7	11.8	6.2	8.2	6.5	4.9	†5.2	.6	2.2	3.1	3.4	5.7	2.0	1.1	4.3	Fiji	819
8.8	†9.4	6.2	9.0	13.9	11.8	6.4	10.2	10.2	9.0	7.2	13.2	4.7	4.0	3.7	India	534
9.3	8.0	6.4	7.8	9.4	†7.5	9.7	8.5	9.4	†8.0	6.7	57.6	20.5	3.7	11.5	Indonesia	536
3.0	7.1	†5.7	8.6	9.3	†6.2	4.8	6.2	4.5	4.9	4.4	7.5	.8	2.3	†4.3	Korea	542
...	...	61.3	35.6	13.4	9.9	6.3	6.8	19.6	†13.0	27.5	91.0	†128.4	25.1	7.8	Lao People's Dem. Rep.	544
.3	2.6	2.8	†2.6	4.4	4.8	3.5	†3.7	3.5	3.5	2.7	5.3	2.7	†1.5	1.4	Malaysia	548
...	...	†7.2	3.6	14.7	†16.8	20.2	3.4	5.4	6.3	7.6	−1.4	3.0	−1.1	.6	Maldives	556
...	...	...	...	...	...	268.2	87.6	56.8	†49.3	36.6	9.4	7.6	...	...	Mongolia	948
24.8	16.0	27.2	17.6	32.3	21.9	31.8	24.1	25.2	16.3	29.7	51.5	†18.4	−.1	21.1	Myanmar	518
10.8	†9.0	8.8	8.2	15.6	17.1	7.5	8.3	7.6	9.2	4.0	10.0	†8.0	1.5	2.8	Nepal	558
4.7	8.8	7.8	9.1	11.8	†9.5	10.0	12.4	12.3	10.4	11.4	6.2	4.1	4.4	3.1	Pakistan	564
3.3	5.4	4.5	7.0	7.0	4.3	5.0	2.9	17.3	11.6	3.9	13.6	14.9	15.6	9.3	Papua New Guinea	853
3.0	12.2	11.4	13.2	18.5	8.6	6.9	8.4	8.0	9.0	5.8	9.7	6.7	4.3	6.1	Philippines	566
4.6	8.5	6.5	15.2	−1.8	9.0	1.7	12.1	−2.9	5.4	†6.9	2.2	.3	1.0	4.0	Samoa	862
.5	1.5	2.3	3.5	3.4	2.3	2.3	3.1	1.7	1.4	2.0	†−.3	—	1.4	1.0	Singapore	576
11.0	16.7	14.9	†8.7	15.1	10.8	9.2	13.3	9.6	11.8	8.1	12.4	8.3	...	...	Solomon Islands	813
7.7	14.0	11.6	21.5	12.2	11.4	11.7	8.4	7.7	15.9	9.6	9.4	4.7	6.2	14.2	Sri Lanka	524
2.5	3.8	†5.4	5.9	5.7	4.1	3.4	5.0	5.8	5.8	5.6	8.1	.3	†1.5	1.7	Thailand	578
4.7	9.9	4.1	9.7	10.6	7.9	1.0	1.0	†1.4	3.0	2.1	3.3	4.9	5.9	8.3	Tonga	866
16.0	8.8	7.7	4.8	6.5	4.1	3.6	2.3	2.2	.9	2.8	3.3	†2.0	2.5	3.7	Vanuatu	846
...	...	...	...	...	...	...	...	...	5.7	3.2	7.3	4.1	−1.7	−.4	Vietnam	582
26.3	84.8	83.7	167.2	95.5	94.5	77.0	181.8	117.9	45.6	37.1	30.7	48.8	26.3	22.5	**Europe**	170
...	...	...	...	...	226.0	85.0	22.6	7.8	12.7	33.2	20.6	.4	.1	3.1	Albania	914
...	...	...	...	...	...	...	4,962.2	176.0	18.7	†13.9	8.7	.7	−.8	2.9	Armenia	911
...	...	...	...	...	912.3	†1,129.0	1,664.5	411.7	19.8	3.6	−.7	−8.6	1.8	1.5	Azerbaijan	912
...	...	...	...	...	966.5	1,190.2	2,221.0	709.3	52.7	63.9	72.9	293.7	168.6	61.1	Belarus	913
2.7	2.4	†6.4	23.8	†338.4	91.3	72.9	96.1	62.1	121.6	1,058.4	18.7	2.6	10.3	7.4	Bulgaria	918
133.3	185.7	1,400.0	500.0	122.2	625.0	1,500.0	107.3	4.0	4.3	4.2	6.4	3.5	5.3	4.8	Croatia	960
2.8	3.4	3.8	4.5	5.0	†6.5	4.9	4.7	2.6	3.0	3.6	2.2	†1.6	4.1	2.0	Cyprus	423
...	...	...	...	...	...	...	10.0	9.2	8.8	8.5	10.6	2.1	3.9	4.7	Czech Republic	935
.1	.1	1.4	10.0	†57.7	10.8	...	...	...	...	...	...	...	...	...	Czechoslovakia	934
...	...	...	...	...	...	89.8	47.7	28.8	23.1	10.6	8.2	3.3	4.0	5.7	Estonia	939
...	...	...	...	...	...	...	...	162.7	39.4	7.1	3.6	19.2	4.1	4.6	Georgia	915
8.7	15.8	16.9	29.0	34.2	†22.9	22.5	18.9	†28.3	23.4	18.3	14.2	10.0	9.8	9.1	Hungary	944
...	...	...	...	...	...	...	1,876.6	176.2	39.3	17.3	7.1	8.3	13.2	8.4	Kazakhstan	916
...	...	...	...	...	...	...	...	...	31.9	23.4	10.5	35.9	18.7	6.9	Kyrgyz Republic	917
...	...	...	...	...	†243.3	108.8	35.9	25.0	17.6	8.4	4.7	2.4	2.7	2.5	Latvia	941
...	...	...	...	...	...	†410.2	72.2	39.7	24.6	8.9	5.1	.8	1.0	1.2	Lithuania	946
...	...	...	...	...	...	...	126.6	16.4	2.7	1.1	.5	−1.3	2.4	...	Macedonia, FYR	962
.4	.9	.8	3.0	†2.5	†1.6	4.1	4.1	4.0	2.5	3.1	2.4	2.1	2.4	2.9	Malta	181
...	...	...	...	...	...	...	...	12.1	20.9	8.0	6.6	45.9	31.3	9.8	Moldova	921
26.4	58.7	244.6	555.4	†76.7	45.3	36.9	33.3	28.1	19.8	15.1	11.7	7.3	10.1	5.5	Poland	964
...	...	...	...	230.6	211.2	255.2	136.8	32.2	38.8	154.8	59.1	45.8	45.7	34.5	Romania	968
...	...	...	...	...	...	874.6	307.6	197.5	47.7	14.7	27.7	85.7	20.8	21.5	Russia	922
...	...	...	...	...	...	...	13.4	9.9	†5.8	6.1	6.7	10.6	12.0	†7.3	Slovak Republic	936
...	...	...	...	...	156.6	31.9	19.8	12.6	9.7	9.1	8.6	6.6	10.8	9.4	Slovenia	961
†38.8	73.7	63.3	60.3	66.0	70.1	66.1	†106.3	88.1	80.3	85.7	84.6	64.9	54.9	54.4	Turkey	186
...	...	...	...	...	...	4,734.9	891.2	376.7	80.3	15.9	10.6	22.7	...	...	Ukraine	926
120.8	194.1	1,239.9	†583.1	117.4	...	...	...	...	...	...	...	...	...	...	Yugoslavia, SFR	188
22.9	20.6	15.1	10.5	14.5	13.4	12.0	14.2	22.1	13.1	7.4	6.9	7.0	5.1	4.2	**Middle East**	405
−1.7	.3	1.5	.9	.8	−.2	2.5	.8	2.7	−.5	†2.4	−.2	−1.4	−.7	...	Bahrain, Kingdom of	419
19.7	17.7	21.3	16.8	19.7	13.6	12.1	8.2	†15.7	7.2	†4.6	4.2	3.1	2.7	2.3	Egypt	469
28.6	28.7	22.3	7.6	†17.1	25.8	21.2	31.4	49.7	28.9	17.3	17.9	20.1	14.5	11.3	Iran, I.R. of	429
...	...	...	...	...	...	...	...	...	...	...	...	...	...	...	Iraq	433
19.8	16.3	20.2	17.2	19.0	11.9	†10.9	†12.3	10.0	11.3	9.0	5.4	5.2	†1.1	1.1	Israel	436
−.2	6.6	25.7	16.2	8.2	†4.0	3.3	3.5	2.4	6.5	†3.0	3.1	.6	.7	1.8	Jordan	439
.7	1.5	3.3	9.8	9.1	−.5	.4	2.5	2.7	3.6	.7	.2	3.0	1.8	1.7	Kuwait	443
487.6	127.8	48.1	62.7	48.4	80.7	15.7	6.8	...	...	...	...	...	...	...	Lebanon	446
...	...	...	...	...	...	...	...	...	...	...	...	...	...	...	Libya	672
...	...	...	...	4.6	1.0	.9	−.4	−1.3	.1	†.1	−.8	.4	−1.1	−1.1	Oman	449
2.7	4.6	3.3	3.0	4.4	3.1	−.9	1.3	3.0	7.4	2.4	2.9	2.2	1.7	...	Qatar	453
−1.5	.9	1.0	2.1	4.9	−.1	1.1	.6	4.9	1.2	.1	−.4	−1.6	−.8	−.5	Saudi Arabia	456
59.5	34.6	11.4	†19.4	9.0	11.0	13.2	15.3	8.0	8.2	1.9	−.8	−1.9	−.5	...	Syrian Arab Republic	463
...	...	...	...	...	...	...	...	...	...	...	...	...	...	...	Yemen Arab Rep.	473
...	...	...	...	...	...	...	...	...	...	...	...	...	...	...	Yemen, P.D. Rep.	459
...	...	...	...	...	36.0	29.4	34.1	45.8	56.1	30.2	5.4	7.9	...	...	Yemen, Republic of	474

Consumer Prices

		1972	1973	1974	1975	1976	1977	1978	1979	1980	1981	1982	1983	1984	1985	1986
													Percent Change over Previous Year			
Western Hemisphere	205	18.8	34.5	32.2	41.4	55.6	44.2	27.4	34.2	44.7	54.0	65.2	95.1	106.2	124.4	86.5
Antigua and Barbuda	311	....	....	....	....	....	13.8	6.1	16.3	19.0	11.5	4.2	2.3	3.9	1.0	....
Argentina	213	58.4	61.2	†23.5	182.9	444.0	176.0	175.5	159.5	100.8	104.5	164.8	343.8	626.7	672.2	90.1
Aruba	314	....	....	....	....	....	....	....	....	....	....	....	....	....	4.0	1.1
Bahamas, The	313	6.8	5.5	13.1	10.4	4.3	3.2	6.1	9.1	12.1	11.1	†6.0	4.0	4.0	4.6	5.4
Barbados	316	11.9	16.9	38.9	20.3	5.0	8.4	9.5	†13.2	14.4	14.6	10.3	5.2	4.7	3.9	1.3
Belize	339	....	....	....	....	....	....	....	....	....	11.2	6.8	5.0	3.4	4.2	.8
Bolivia	218	6.5	31.5	62.8	8.0	4.5	8.1	10.4	19.7	47.2	32.1	123.5	275.6	1,281.3	11,749.6	276.3
Brazil	223										101.7	100.5	135.0	192.1	226.0	147.1
Chile	228	74.8	361.5	504.7	†374.7	211.8	91.9	40.1	33.4	35.1	19.7	†9.9	27.3	19.9	29.5	20.6
Colombia	233	13.4	20.8	24.3	22.9	20.2	33.1	17.8	24.7	26.5	27.5	24.5	19.8	16.1	24.0	18.9
Costa Rica	238	4.6	15.2	30.1	†17.4	3.5	4.2	6.0	9.2	18.1	37.1	90.1	32.6	12.0	15.1	11.8
Dominica	321	3.7	†12.1	34.4	19.9	10.9	9.5	7.7	....	25.2	13.3	4.4	4.1	2.2	3.7	2.8
Dominican Republic	243	8.6	15.1	13.1	14.5	7.8	12.9	†3.5	9.2	†16.8	7.5	7.6	5.6	20.2	45.3	7.6
Ecuador	248	7.9	†13.0	23.3	15.4	10.7	13.0	11.7	10.3	13.0	†16.4	16.3	48.4	31.2	28.0	23.0
El Salvador	253	1.5	6.4	16.9	19.1	7.0	11.8	13.3	†14.6	17.4	14.8	11.7	13.3	11.5	22.3	31.9
Grenada	328	....	....	....	....	....	18.5	18.1	20.9	21.8	18.8	7.8	6.1	5.7	2.5	.6
Guatemala	258	.5	13.8	16.5	†13.2	†10.7	12.3	8.3	11.3	10.8	11.4	.3	4.5	3.4	18.7	36.9
Guyana	336	....	....	....	....	....	....	....	....	....	....	....	....	....	....	....
Haiti	263	3.2	22.7	15.0	16.8	7.0	6.5	-2.7	13.1	†17.8	10.9	7.4	10.2	6.4	10.6	3.3
Honduras	268	3.6	5.2	12.8	8.4	4.9	8.4	†5.7	12.1	18.1	9.4	9.0	8.3	4.7	3.4	4.4
Jamaica	343	5.4	17.7	27.2	17.4	9.8	11.2	34.9	29.1	27.3	12.7	6.5	11.6	27.8	25.7	15.1
Mexico	273	5.0	12.0	23.8	15.2	15.8	29.0	17.5	18.2	26.4	27.9	58.9	101.8	65.5	57.7	86.2
Netherlands Antilles	353	4.1	8.1	19.5	†15.6	5.3	5.4	8.2	11.4	14.6	12.2	6.1	†2.8	2.1	.5	1.3
Nicaragua	278	....	27.0	13.3	7.5	2.8	11.4	4.6	48.2	†35.3	23.9	24.8	31.1	35.4	†219.5	681.4
Panama	283	5.4	6.9	16.3	†5.9	4.0	4.6	4.2	8.0	13.8	7.3	4.3	2.1	1.6	1.0	-.1
Paraguay	288	9.5	12.5	25.2	6.8	4.6	9.3	10.6	28.3	22.4	14.0	6.8	13.4	20.3	25.2	31.7
Peru	293	7.2	9.5	16.9	23.6	33.5	38.1	57.8	†66.7	59.1	75.4	64.4	111.2	110.2	163.4	†77.9
St. Kitts and Nevis	361	....	....	....	....	....	....	....	....	17.7	10.5	5.9	2.3	2.7	2.6	—
St. Lucia	362	7.9	13.4	34.2	17.7	9.7	8.9	10.9	9.4	19.5	15.1	4.6	1.5	1.2	†1.4	2.0
St. Vincent & Grenadines	364	....	....	....	6.8	11.3	10.2	8.4	15.6	17.2	†12.7	7.2	5.5	2.7	2.1	1.0
Suriname	366	3.2	12.9	16.9	8.4	10.1	9.7	8.8	14.8	†14.1	8.8	7.3	4.4	3.7	10.9	18.7
Trinidad and Tobago	369	9.3	14.8	22.0	†17.0	10.7	11.7	10.3	14.7	17.5	14.3	†11.6	15.2	13.3	7.6	7.7
Uruguay	298	76.5	†97.0	77.2	81.4	50.6	58.2	44.5	66.8	63.5	34.0	19.0	49.2	55.3	†72.2	76.4
Venezuela, Rep. Bol.	299	2.8	4.1	8.3	10.2	7.6	7.8	7.1	12.4	21.5	16.0	9.7	6.3	11.6	11.4	11.5

Memorandum Items

		1972	1973	1974	1975	1976	1977	1978	1979	1980	1981	1982	1983	1984	1985	1986
Oil Exporting Countries	999	4.7	13.1	17.5	17.4	15.0	15.7	10.6	11.1	14.3	14.7	9.2	11.1	11.5	5.2	8.7
Non-Oil Developing Countries	201	11.4	23.5	19.3	16.0	16.6	17.3	11.4	21.4	31.2	33.6	37.9	43.9	46.1	53.0	38.6

Indices

Index Numbers:

World

		1972	1973	1974	1975	1976	1977	1978	1979	1980	1981	1982	1983	1984	1985	1986
Industrial Countries	110	24.4	26.3	29.9	33.3	36.2	39.5	42.5	46.5	52.3	57.7	62.1	65.4	68.7	71.7	73.6
Developing Countries	200	.1	.2	.2	.2	.3	.3	.4	.5	.6	.8	1.0	1.4	1.9	2.8	3.7
Africa	605	2.2	2.4	2.7	3.2	3.7	4.4	5.0	5.8	6.7	8.0	9.0	10.5	12.1	13.9	15.8
Asia	505	11.4	13.4	17.4	19.2	19.7	21.4	22.7	25.0	28.8	32.7	35.1	37.9	41.2	43.3	45.7
Europe (1995=100,000)	170	15.2	16.4	18.1	19.8	21.8	24.8	30.3	38.3	55.1	68.3	105.0	102.4	128.3	181.9	221.4
Europe	170															
Middle East	405	3.2	3.5	4.1	4.7	5.4	6.3	7.2	8.1	9.7	11.5	13.5	15.8	19.0	22.1	26.1
Western Hemisphere(1995=10mil.)	205	4.2	5.7	7.5	10.6	16.5	23.8	30.3	40.7	58.9	90.6	149.8	292.1	602.3	1,351.6	2,520.8
Western Hemisphere	205	....	....	....	....	....	....	....	....	....	....	....	....	....	....	....

Calculated from Indices

1987	1988	1989	1990	1991	1992	1993	1994	1995	1996	1997	1998	1999	2000	2001		Code
119.2	106.6	75.2	461.1	139.8	154.4	222.1	219.0	42.2	22.6	13.8	10.5	9.6	8.7	6.8	Western Hemisphere	205
....	....	....	....	....	....	....	....	....	....	....	....	....	....	....	Antigua and Barbuda	311
131.3	†343.0	3,079.8	2,314.0	171.7	24.9	10.6	4.2	3.4	†.2	.5	.9	-1.2	-.9	-1.1	Argentina	213
3.6	3.1	4.0	5.8	5.6	3.9	5.2	6.3	3.4	3.2	3.0	1.9	†2.3	4.0	2.9	Aruba	314
5.8	4.4	5.4	4.7	7.1	5.7	2.7	1.4	†2.1	1.4	.5	1.3	1.3	1.6	2.0	Bahamas, The	313
3.3	4.9	6.2	3.1	6.3	6.1	1.1	†.1	1.9	2.4	7.7	-1.3	1.6	2.4	2.6	Barbados	316
2.0	5.3	—	†3.0	2.2	2.4	1.5	2.6	2.9	6.4	1.0	-.9	-1.2	.6	1.2	Belize	339
14.6	16.0	15.2	17.1	21.4	†12.1	8.5	7.9	10.2	12.4	4.7	7.7	2.2	4.6	1.6	Bolivia	218
228.3	629.1	1,430.7	†2,947.7	432.8	951.6	†1,928.0	2,075.9	66.0	15.8	6.9	3.2	4.9	7.0	6.9	Brazil	223
19.9	14.7	17.0	26.0	21.8	15.4	12.7	11.4	8.2	7.4	6.1	5.1	3.3	3.8	3.6	Chile	228
23.3	†28.1	25.8	29.1	30.4	27.0	22.6	23.8	21.0	†20.2	18.9	20.4	11.2	9.5	8.7	Colombia	233
16.8	20.8	16.5	19.0	28.7	21.8	9.8	†13.5	23.2	17.5	13.2	11.7	10.0	11.0	11.2	Costa Rica	238
4.0	2.9	6.2	3.2	†5.6	5.5	1.6	—	1.3	1.7	2.4	1.0	1.2	.8	....	Dominica	321
13.6	43.9	40.7	50.5	47.1	4.3	5.3	8.3	12.5	5.4	8.3	†4.8	6.5	7.7	8.9	Dominican Republic	243
29.5	58.2	75.6	†48.5	48.8	54.3	45.0	27.4	†22.9	24.4	30.6	36.1	52.2	96.1	37.7	Ecuador	248
24.9	19.8	17.6	24.0	14.4	†11.2	18.5	10.6	10.0	9.8	4.5	2.5	.5	2.3	3.8	El Salvador	253
†-.9	4.0	5.6	2.7	2.6	3.8	2.8	3.8	1.9	2.0	1.2	1.4	.2	....	....	Grenada	328
12.3	10.8	11.4	41.2	33.2	10.0	11.8	10.9	8.4	11.1	9.2	7.0	4.9	†6.0	7.6	Guatemala	258
								12.2	7.1	3.6	4.6	7.5	6.1	2.6	Guyana	336
-11.4	4.1	6.9	21.3	†15.4	†19.4	29.7	39.3	27.6	20.6	20.6	10.6	8.7	13.7	14.2	Haiti	263
2.5	4.5	9.9	23.3	34.0	8.8	10.7	21.7	29.5	23.8	†20.2	13.7	11.7	11.1	9.7	Honduras	268
6.7	†8.3	14.3	22.0	51.1	77.3	22.1	35.1	19.9	26.4	9.7	8.6	6.0	8.2	7.0	Jamaica	343
131.8	114.2	20.0	26.7	22.7	†15.5	9.8	7.0	35.0	34.4	20.6	15.9	16.6	9.5	6.4	Mexico	273
3.8	2.6	3.9	†3.7	4.0	1.4	2.0	1.8	2.8	†3.6	3.3	1.1	.4	5.8	1.8	Netherlands Antilles	353
911.9	†10205.0	4,770.2	7,485.5	2,945.1	23.7	20.4	†6.7	10.9	11.6	9.2	13.0	11.2	....	....	Nicaragua	278
1.0	†.4	.1	.8	1.3	1.8	.5	1.3	1.0	1.3	1.3	.6	1.2	1.5	.3	Panama	283
21.8	22.6	26.4	†38.2	24.2	15.2	18.2	20.6	13.4	9.8	7.0	11.5	6.8	9.0	7.3	Paraguay	288
85.8	667.0	3,398.7	7,481.7	409.5	73.5	†48.6	23.7	11.1	11.5	8.6	7.2	3.5	3.8	†2.0	Peru	293
1.0	.2	5.2	4.0	4.3	2.9	1.8	1.4	3.0	2.1	8.9	3.4	3.9	....	....	St. Kitts and Nevis	361
7.6	.8	4.1	4.7	5.7	5.1	1.1	2.5	5.7	1.8	.2	2.2	5.4	....	....	St. Lucia	362
3.3	.2	2.8	7.6	5.5	3.5	4.3	1.0	1.7	4.4	.4	2.1	1.0	.2	.8	St. Vincent & Grenadines	364
53.4	7.3	.8	21.7	26.0	43.7	143.5	368.5	235.6	-.7	7.1	19.0	98.9	64.3	....	Suriname	366
10.8	7.8	†11.4	11.1	3.8	6.4	10.8	8.8	5.2	3.4	3.6	5.6	3.4	3.6	....	Trinidad and Tobago	369
63.6	62.2	80.4	112.5	102.0	68.5	54.1	44.7	42.2	28.3	19.8	10.8	5.7	4.8	4.4	Uruguay	298
28.1	29.5	84.5	40.7	34.2	31.4	38.1	60.8	59.9	99.9	50.0	35.8	†23.6	16.2	12.5	Venezuela, Rep. Bol.	299

Memorandum Items

1987	1988	1989	1990	1991	1992	1993	1994	1995	1996	1997	1998	1999	2000	2001		Code
13.7	18.2	18.5	11.2	14.6	17.1	17.8	20.6	25.8	20.3	11.1	29.2	14.9	6.2	9.9	Oil Exporting Countries	999
47.4	60.5	29.1	84.1	44.0	44.9	53.3	64.7	30.6	15.5	10.6	8.8	8.9	6.5	5.7	Non-Oil Developing Countries	201

Indices

1995=100

World

1987	1988	1989	1990	1991	1992	1993	1994	1995	1996	1997	1998	1999	2000	2001		Code
75.9	78.5	82.0	86.2	89.9	92.8	95.4	97.6	100.0	102.2	104.3	105.8	107.2	109.8	112.1	Industrial Countries	110
5.1	7.7	9.8	16.8	23.4	32.9	48.6	76.9	100.0	116.1	128.5	142.8	156.7	166.8	177.1	Developing Countries	200
17.9	21.4	25.5	29.4	36.4	47.8	60.0	77.7	100.0	120.2	132.2	141.0	148.9	156.8	168.6	Africa	605
48.6	52.2	57.9	61.5	66.4	71.5	78.1	89.5	100.0	107.7	112.7	122.3	125.9	128.1	131.6	Asia	505
279.6	522.5	962.0	....	....	....	....	....	....	....	....	....	....	....	....	Europe (1995=100,000)	170
....	....	.9	2.4	4.7	9.2	16.3	45.9	100.0	145.6	199.6	260.9	388.3	490.3	600.5	Europe	170
32.1	38.8	44.6	49.3	56.4	64.0	71.7	81.9	100.0	113.1	121.5	129.9	139.0	146.1	152.2	Middle East	405
5,525.0	11,414.2	19,992.7	....	....	....	....	....	....	....	....	....	....	....	....	Western Hemisphere(1995=10mil.)	205
....	....	.2	1.1	2.7	6.8	22.0	70.3	100.0	122.6	139.5	154.0	168.8	183.5	195.9	Western Hemisphere	205

		1972	1973	1974	1975	1976	1977	1978	1979	1980	1981	1982	1983	1984	1985	1986
															Billions of US Dollars	
World	001	400.4	556.0	817.3	850.7	960.2	1,088.1	1,259.6	1,630.0	1,945.9	1,949.7	1,800.6	1,756.8	1,864.2	1,887.8	2,058.0
Industrial Countries	110	296.7	405.1	541.8	578.0	643.4	729.4	873.1	1,074.2	1,265.1	1,243.9	1,177.2	1,162.7	1,240.5	1,282.0	1,485.0
United States	111	49.199	70.823	99.437	†108.856	116.794	†123.182	145.847	186.363	225.566	238.715	216.442	205.639	223.976	218.815	227.158
Canada	156	21.185	26.437	34.508	34.074	40.598	43.545	48.431	58.294	67.734	72.726	71.234	76.749	90.272	90.950	90.329
Australia	193	6.461	9.559	11.016	11.948	13.193	13.367	14.415	18.663	21.944	21.477	21.360	20.113	23.111	22.604	22.569
Japan	158	29.088	37.017	55.469	55.819	67.304	81.083	98.211	102.299	130.441	151.495	138.385	146.965	169.700	177.164	210.757
New Zealand	196	1.792	2.596	2.435	2.162	2.795	3.196	†3.738	4.706	5.421	5.622	5.571	5.414	5.518	5.720	5.880
Euro Area																
Austria	122	3.883	5.283	7.161	7.519	8.506	9.808	12.175	15.481	17.489	15.841	15.642	15.428	15.739	17.239	22.522
Belgium	124	....	....	....	....	....	....	....	....	....	....	....	....	....	....	....
Belgium-Luxembourg	126	16.152	22.455	28.334	28.804	32.889	37.538	44.947	56.700	64.656	55.694	52.354	51.937	51.891	53.742	68.892
Finland	172	2.913	3.837	5.490	5.502	6.342	7.665	8.570	11.172	14.150	14.004	13.088	12.518	13.471	13.617	16.356
France	132	26.449	36.669	46.259	53.100	56.874	65.130	79.371	100.692	116.030	106.424	96.694	94.943	97.566	101.671	124.831
Germany	134	46.736	67.563	89.368	90.176	102.162	118.072	142.453	171.804	192.860	176.047	176.424	169.417	171.735	183.933	243.326
Greece	174	.870	1.456	2.030	2.294	2.561	2.756	3.368	3.885	5.153	4.246	4.298	4.413	4.811	4.539	5.648
Ireland	178	1.607	2.131	2.658	3.192	3.315	4.404	5.691	7.143	8.398	7.677	8.067	8.599	9.641	10.357	12.639
Italy	136	18.609	22.226	30.465	34.988	37.265	45.305	56.090	72.233	78.104	77.070	73.791	72.877	74.564	76.717	97.204
Luxembourg	137	1.000	1.490	2.130	1.787	1.830	1.913	2.296	2.926	3.005	2.385	2.237	2.180	2.519	2.831	3.721
Netherlands	138	19.154	27.352	37.423	39.888	46.153	50.110	57.590	73.537	84.948	78.597	75.717	73.692	75.055	77.872	†80.255
Portugal	182	1.298	1.842	2.277	1.939	1.811	1.970	2.414	3.479	4.640	4.148	4.164	4.599	5.200	5.685	7.242
Spain	184	3.817	5.198	7.091	7.690	8.730	10.223	13.114	18.208	20.720	20.333	20.498	19.734	23.564	24.247	27.206
Denmark	128	4.432	6.248	7.719	8.712	9.115	10.065	11.883	14.696	16.749	16.095	15.397	16.053	15.980	17.090	21.286
Iceland	176	.189	.290	.331	.306	.401	.512	.641	.782	.918	.894	.685	.740	.739	.815	1.099
Norway	142	3.283	4.725	6.282	7.232	7.951	8.880	10.882	13.546	18.542	18.217	17.593	17.997	18.886	19.985	18.092
Sweden	144	8.769	12.201	15.939	17.383	18.435	†19.082	21.790	27.602	30.906	28.658	26.808	27.446	29.378	30.461	37.263
Switzerland	146	6.842	9.528	11.934	12.953	14.835	17.614	23.560	†26.538	29.632	27.049	26.019	25.591	25.849	27.433	37.471
United Kingdom	112	23.985	29.637	38.197	43.423	45.356	55.860	67.887	86.397	110.137	102.845	97.017	91.868	93.840	101.355	106.956
Developing Countries	200	103.72	150.93	275.49	272.74	316.77	358.74	386.50	555.78	680.79	705.82	623.34	594.10	623.74	605.76	573.06
Africa	605	15.63	22.40	38.51	36.13	40.09	46.94	48.51	70.79	96.02	80.28	67.30	66.80	66.81	65.51	57.13
Algeria	612	1.304	1.887	4.687	4.700	5.259	5.944	6.326	9.551	13.871	14.396	13.170	12.583	12.795	12.841	7.832
Benin	638	.036	.043	.034	.032	.025	.031	.027	.046	.063	.034	.024	.067	.167	.150	.104
Botswana	616	.058	.085	.121	.142	.170	.186	.233	.451	.504	.398	.475	.644	.751	.839	1.043
Burkina Faso	748	.020	.025	.036	.044	.053	.055	.043	.077	.090	.074	.056	.058	.079	.071	.083
Burundi	618	.026	.030	.031	.032	.061	.090	.069	.104	.065	.075	.088	.080	.103	.112	.154
Cameroon	622	.221	.353	.478	.447	.511	.704	.802	1.132	1.384	1.105	1.063	.976	.886	.722	.782
Cape Verde	624	.002	.002	.002	.002	.002	.002	.002	.002	.004	.003	.003	.004	.002	.006	.005
Central African Rep.	626	.039	.037	.048	.047	.061	.082	.072	.080	.116	.079	.107	.074	.085	.092	.066
Chad	628	.036	.038	.037	.048	.063	.107	.099	.088	.071	.083	.058	.105	.131	.062	.099
Comoros	632	.006	.005	.009	.010	.012	.009	.009	.017	.011	.016	.020	.019	.007	.016	.020
Congo, Dem. Rep. of	636	.738	1.013	1.381	.865	.944	.989	.931	1.514	1.627	.544	.399	1.080	1.005	.950	1.100
Congo, Rep. of	634	.060	.089	.229	.178	.221	.267	.308	.496	.911	.811	.993	.640	1.183	1.087	.777
Côte d'Ivoire	662	.553	.857	1.213	1.181	1.632	2.157	2.322	2.514	3.135	2.533	2.298	2.091	2.707	2.969	3.354
Djibouti	611	.008	.019	.021	.015	.016	.019	.018	.011	.012	.009	.013	.011	.013	.014	.020
Equatorial Guinea	642	.019	.019	.034	.026	.010	.014	.017	.029	.014	.011	.012	.013	.015	.017	.024
Ethiopia	644	.167	.239	.269	.240	.280	.333	.306	.418	.425	.389	.404	.403	.417	.333	.455
Gabon	646	.228	.331	.768	.943	1.135	1.343	1.107	1.848	2.173	2.201	2.161	2.000	2.011	1.951	1.271
Gambia, The	648	.019	.025	.043	.044	.035	.047	.039	.058	.031	.027	.044	.048	.049	.043	.035
Ghana	652	.441	.657	.738	.816	.832	1.014	1.093	.995	1.257	1.065	.873	2.624	.528	.617	.863
Guinea-Bissau	654	.003	.004	.004	.007	.006	.013	.012	.013	.011	.014	.012	.009	.017	.012	....
Kenya	664	.359	.477	.603	.606	.790	1.186	1.023	1.090	1.245	1.139	1.025	.869	1.074	.958	1.200
Liberia	668	.244	.324	.400	.394	.460	.447	.504	.537	.600	.529	.477	.428	.452	.436	.408
Lesotho	666	.008	.013	.014	.012	.017	.014	.032	.045	.058	.050	.036	.030	.027	.022	.025
Liberia	668	.244	.324	.400	.394	.460	.447	.504	.537	.600	.529	.477	.428	.452	.436	.408
Madagascar	674	.166	.203	.244	.301	.275	.338	.388	.394	.401	.317	.311	.264	.332	.274	.313
Malawi	676	.080	.098	.120	.140	.166	.200	.185	.233	.295	.283	.239	.229	.314	.246	.246
Mali	678	.042	.053	.064	.053	.084	.125	.112	.148	.205	.155	.146	.165	.133	.124	.212
Mauritania	682	.119	.155	.180	.176	.178	.157	.123	.147	.194	.261	.233	.291	.292	.374	.349
Mauritius	684	.106	.137	.312	.298	.265	.309	.325	.381	.435	.332	.366	.366	.372	.440	.676
Morocco	686	.643	.910	1.708	1.543	1.261	1.302	1.508	1.959	2.441	2.386	2.062	2.006	2.171	2.165	2.433
Mozambique	688	....	....	....	....	....	....	....	....	....	....	....	....	....	....	....
Namibia	728	....	....	....	....	....	....	....	....	....	....	....	....	....	....	....
Niger	692	.054	.062	.053	.091	.134	.161	.282	.448	.566	.455	.332	.299	.259	.259	.317
Nigeria	694	2.180	3.462	9.205	7.834	10.566	11.839	9.938	17.334	25.946	18.231	12.196	10.298	11.843	12.537	5.923
Rwanda	714	.019	.033	.036	.042	.080	.092	.072	.118	.112	.110	.103	.121	.145	.131	.189
São Tomé & Príncipe	716	.007	.013	.017	.007	.008	.023	.021	.027	.017	.009	....	....	.012	.006	.010
Senegal	722	.216	.195	.391	.461	.485	.624	.449	.535	.477	.500	.548	.618	.634	.562	.625
Seychelles	718	.003	.004	.007	.006	.009	.011	.015	.022	.021	.017	.015	.020	.026	.028	.018
Sierra Leone	724	.115	.131	.144	.118	.099	.136	.170	.200	.224	.150	.111	.119	.133	.130	.144
South Africa	199	4.108	†6.064	8.688	8.789	7.850	9.904	12.772	18.258	†25.540	20.775	17.635	18.532	17.334	16.330	18.376
Sudan	732	.357	.434	.350	.438	.554	.661	.518	.535	.543	.657	.498	.624	.629	.374	.333
Swaziland	734	.082	.108	.178	.195	.183	.165	.196	.232	.373	.382	.320	.304	.230	.179	.278
Tanzania	738	.324	.368	.403	.372	.440	.507	.476	.497	.511	.568	.449	.372	.298	.246	.361
Togo	742	.050	.061	.189	.126	.105	.159	.234	.218	.338	.212	.178	.163	.192	.190	.204
Tunisia	744	.315	.422	.921	.856	.788	.929	1.126	1.791	2.231	2.500	1.981	1.850	1.797	1.738	1.760
Uganda	746	.028	.029	.032	.026	.036	.059	.035	.435	.345	.243	.349	.372	.399	....	.436
Zambia	754	.758	1.144	1.407	.810	1.070	.896	.856	1.373	1.305	1.125	1.024	.832	.661	.482	.741
Zimbabwe	698	.515	.688	.863	.932	.891	.877	.888	1.053	1.409	1.266	1.273	1.128	1.147	1.110	1.301

1987	1988	1989	1990	1991	1992	1993	1994	1995	1996	1997	1998	1999	2000	2001		
Billions of US Dollars																
2,431.2	2,779.5	3,024.1	3,438.6	3,530.3	3,757.7	3,761.6	4,281.8	5,123.2	5,343.6	5,530.0	5,436.0	†5,635.8	6,340.5	6,114.8	World	001
1,736.2	1,986.5	2,127.9	2,454.1	2,502.2	2,650.7	2,595.8	2,914.3	3,469.4	3,564.2	3,643.1	3,664.2	†3,741.2	3,993.0	3,862.5	Industrial Countries	110
254.122	322.427	363.812	393.592	421.730	448.164	464.773	512.627	584.743	625.073	688.697	682.138	702.098	781.125	730.803	United States	111
98.168	117.105	121.832	127.629	127.163	134.435	145.178	165.376	192.197	201.633	214.422	214.327	238.446	276.635	259.858	Canada	156
26.621	33.233	37.125	39.752	41.854	42.824	42.723	47.528	53.111	60.300	62.910	55.893	56.079	63.870	63.387	Australia	193
231.286	264.856	273.932	287.581	314.786	339.885	362.244	397.005	443.116	410.901	420.957	387.927	419.367	479.249	403.496	Japan	158
7.195	8.850	8.876	9.394	9.619	9.785	10.542	12.185	13.645	14.360	14.216	12.069	12.454	13.272	13.723	New Zealand	196
															Euro Area	
27.171	31.058	32.492	41.135	41.113	44.411	40.216	45.022	57.642	57.818	58.590	62.742	†64.107	64.155	66.671	Austria	122
....	....	....	....	....	....	125.877	143.658	175.848	175.355	171.881	177.716	†178.961	187.847	189.271	Belgium	124
83.288	92.135	100.075	118.294	118.279	123.524	119.512	137.257	169.671	165.763	165.544	....	....	....	....	Belgium-Luxembourg	126
20.037	21.748	23.298	26.571	23.080	23.981	23.446	29.658	39.573	38.435	39.316	42.963	†41.841	45.473	42.794	Finland	172
148.382	167.790	179.430	216.591	217.096	235.869	210.444	234.021	284.865	287.667	289.952	305.641	†300.757	298.841	294.357	France	132
294.369	323.323	341.231	†410.104	402.843	422.271	382.472	429.722	523.802	524.198	512.427	543.397	†542.869	549.578	570.522	Germany	134
6.533	5.429	7.545	8.105	8.673	9.439	9.093	8.808	10.961	11.948	11.128	10.732	10.475	10.747	9.483	Greece	174
15.994	18.742	20.690	23.746	24.215	28.331	28.611	34.370	44.250	48.671	53.340	58.143	†71.219	77.091	82.976	Ireland	178
116.711	127.859	140.556	170.486	169.473	178.156	169.153	191.421	233.998	252.039	240.404	245.700	†235.175	239.886	241.729	Italy	136
4.375	5.069	5.401	6.305	6.271	6.469	5.892	6.560	7.750	7.210	6.999	7.922	†7.849	7.821	7.918	Luxembourg	137
93.108	103.188	107.854	131.775	133.631	140.335	139.127	155.554	196.276	197.417	194.905	201.374	†200.191	208.812	216.099	Netherlands	138
9.320	10.989	12.799	16.422	16.329	18.374	15.432	18.006	23.206	24.605	23.973	†24.814	†25.227	23.310	23.902	Portugal	182
34.192	40.341	43.451	55.521	58.621	64.840	60.955	72.927	91.046	101.996	104.359	109.228	†109.964	113.325	115.155	Spain	184
25.675	27.653	28.107	35.133	36.001	41.053	37.168	41.417	49.754	50.097	47.715	47.477	48.700	49.471	50.564	Denmark	128
1.375	1.424	1.385	1.592	1.549	1.528	1.399	1.623	1.804	1.639	1.852	2.050	2.005	1.891	2.022	Iceland	176
21.490	22.436	27.107	34.048	34.107	35.178	31.853	34.692	41.992	49.645	48.542	39.645	44.884	57.514	57.960	Norway	142
44.506	49.747	51.547	57.540	55.217	56.118	49.857	61.343	79.801	84.896	82.946	84.994	84.836	86.908	75.139	Sweden	144
45.464	50.704	51.525	63.784	61.517	†61.377	58.687	66.227	78.040	76.196	72.493	75.431	76.122	74.865	78.066	Switzerland	146
131.193	145.457	153.271	185.268	185.264	190.429	181.362	204.004	242.006	262.096	281.061	271.844	268.193	281.564	267.349	United Kingdom	112
694.95	793.04	896.18	984.55	1,028.10	1,107.00	1,165.76	1,367.45	1,653.82	1,779.36	1,886.95	1,771.86	1,894.01	2,347.27	2,252.88	Developing Countries	200
63.14	64.42	69.74	83.95	80.32	79.27	75.26	79.41	93.43	104.49	107.35	91.77	100.48	124.72	123.57	Africa	605
8.225	7.810	9.570	12.930	12.570	11.130	10.230	8.880	10.240	12.620	....	....	....	....	....	Algeria	612
.114	.071	.077	.122	.021	.335	.384	.398	.420	.654	.682	.414	.422	.392	....	Benin	638
1.896	1.798	1.854	1.785	1.843	1.746	1.757	1.848	2.142	2.536	2.842	1.948	....	....	....	Botswana	616
.155	.142	.095	.152	.106	.064	.069	.107	.276	.233	.232	.319	.255	.213	.175	Burkina Faso	748
.090	.133	.078	.075	.091	.073	.062	.121	.106	.040	.087	.065	.054	.050	.039	Burundi	618
.829	.927	1.273	2.002	1.834	1.840	1.429	1.364	1.651	1.769	1.860	1.671	1.601	....	....	Cameroon	622
.008	.003	.007	.006	.006	.005	.004	.005	.009	....	.014	.010	.011	.011	.010	Cape Verde	624
.130	.066	.134	.120	.047	.107	.110	.151	.171	.147	.154	.157	.161	.271	....	Central African Rep.	626
.109	.144	.155	.188	.194	.182	.132	.148	.243	.238	.237	.262	.202	.183	.165	Chad	628
.012	.021	.018	.018	.025	.022	.022	.011	.011	....	....	....	....	....	....	Comoros	632
.974	1.120	1.254	.999	.830	.426	.368	.419	.438	.592	....	....	....	....	....	Congo, Dem. Rep. of	636
.973	.937	1.247	.981	1.030	1.179	1.069	.959	1.173	1.164	1.618	1.174	1.951	3.101	....	Congo, Rep. of	634
3.110	2.770	2.807	3.072	2.686	2.875	2.519	2.742	3.806	4.446	4.451	4.606	4.662	3.888	3.650	Côte d'Ivoire	662
.028	.023	.025	.025	.017	.016	.012	.012	.014	.014	.011	.012	.012	....	....	Djibouti	611
.039	.049	.041	.062	.037	.050	.057	.062	.086	.175	.495	.439	.709	1.097	....	Equatorial Guinea	642
.355	.429	.440	.298	.189	.169	.199	.372	.423	.417	.587	.561	....	....	....	Ethiopia	644
1.288	1.196	1.597	2.204	2.243	2.082	2.295	2.350	2.713	3.184	3.024	....	....	....	....	Gabon	646
.040	.058	.027	.031	.038	.057	.067	.035	.016	.021	.015	.027	.007	....	....	Gambia, The	648
.977	1.009	1.018	....	.617	1.252	.974	1.425	1.724	1.669	1.635	1.795	....	....	....	Ghana	652
....	.016	.014	.019	.020	.006	.028	.086	.044	.028	.048	.027	.051	.062	....	Guinea-Bissau	654
.961	1.067	.951	1.032	1.108	1.339	1.374	1.587	1.879	2.068	2.054	2.008	1.747	1.734	1.944	Kenya	664
.382	.396	.460	....	....	....	....	....	....	....	....	....	....	....	....	Liberia	668
.047	.064	.066	.062	.067	.109	.132	.143	.160	.187	.196	.194	....	....	....	Lesotho	666
.382	.396	.460	....	....	....	....	....	....	....	....	....	....	....	....	Liberia	668
.331	.278	.321	.319	.305	.278	.260	.369	.369	.299	.223	.243	.220	....	....	Madagascar	674
.277	.288	.267	.417	.469	.396	.320	.342	.405	.481	.537	.514	.442	.355	....	Malawi	676
.179	.215	.247	.359	.312	.343	.478	.335	.442	.433	.561	.556	.571	.545	.740	Mali	678
.428	.354	.437	.447	....	....	....	.487	....	....	....	....	....	....	....	Mauritania	682
.880	.997	.986	1.194	1.194	1.302	1.299	1.347	1.538	1.802	1.592	1.645	1.554	....	....	Mauritius	684
2.807	3.626	3.337	4.265	4.284	3.973	3.055	5.556	6.881	6.881	7.032	7.153	7.367	6.961	7.123	Morocco	686
....	....	....	....	....	....	.157	....	.168	.217	.222	.230	.263	.364	....	Mozambique	688
....	1.056	1.122	1.086	1.214	1.342	1.290	1.321	....	....	....	....	....	....	....	Namibia	728
.312	.289	.244	.283	.307	.333	.287	.225	.288	.325	.272	.334	.287	.283	....	Niger	692
7.344	6.916	7.876	13.596	12.264	11.886	9.908	9.415	†12.342	16.154	15.207	9.855	13.856	20.975	....	Nigeria	694
.113	.108	.095	.110	.093	.066	.065	.019	.052	.060	.087	.060	.060	.053	.085	Rwanda	714
.007	.010	.005	.004	.006	.005	.005	.006	.005	.005	.005	....	....	....	....	São Tomé & Príncipe	716
.606	.591	.693	.762	.701	.673	.707	.791	.993	.988	.905	.968	1.027	.920	....	Senegal	722
.022	.032	.034	.057	.049	.048	.051	.052	.053	.140	.113	.122	.145	....	....	Seychelles	718
.130	.106	.138	.138	.145	.149	.118	.116	.042	.047	.017	.007	.006	.013	.028	Sierra Leone	724
21.224	21.814	22.144	23.568	23.279	23.440	24.222	25.308	27.853	29.221	31.027	†26.362	26.707	29.983	29.284	South Africa	199
.504	.509	.672	.374	.305	.319	.417	.524	.556	.620	.594	.596	.780	1.807	1.699	Sudan	732
.425	.461	.500	.557	.591	.639	.680	.781	.956	.893	....	....	....	....	....	Swaziland	734
.289	.275	.365	.331	.342	.416	.450	.519	.682	.784	.753	.589	.543	.663	.776	Tanzania	738
.244	.242	.245	.268	.253	.275	.136	.328	.378	.441	.424	.968	.391	.363	.226	Togo	742
2.139	2.395	2.930	3.527	3.699	4.019	3.802	4.657	5.475	5.517	5.559	5.738	5.872	5.850	6.609	Tunisia	744
.319	.280	.274	.152	.200	.143	.179	.409	.461	.587	.555	.501	.519	.460	.456	Uganda	746
.873	1.178	1.344	1.309	1.083	.756	.826	.927	1.040	1.037	.915	....	....	....	....	Zambia	754
1.425	1.631	1.548	1.722	1.530	1.442	1.565	1.881	2.114	2.406	....	....	....	....	....	Zimbabwe	698

		1972	1973	1974	1975	1976	1977	1978	1979	1980	1981	1982	1983	1984	1985	1986
														Billions of US Dollars		
Asia *	505	24.58	38.20	53.88	53.07	67.18	79.66	95.73	125.95	159.18	175.78	172.27	180.45	208.43	205.96	225.48
Afghanistan, Islamic State of	512	.122	.143	.230	.217	.291	.306	.321	.474	.670	.694	.708	.729	.633	.567	.552
Bangladesh	513	.260	.358	.348	.327	.401	.476	.548	.659	.759	.791	.769	.724	.931	†.999	.880
Bhutan	514	....	....	....	....	....	....	....	....	.017	.020	.017	.016	.018	.022	.031
Cambodia	522	.007	.015	....	....	....	....	....	....	....	....	....	....	....	....	....
China, P.R.: Mainland	924	3.693	5.876	7.108	7.689	6.943	7.520	9.955	13.614	†18.099	22.007	22.321	22.226	26.139	27.350	30.942
China, P.R.: Hong Kong	532	3.436	5.071	5.968	6.026	8.484	9.616	11.453	15.140	19.752	21.827	21.006	21.959	28.323	30.187	35.439
China, P.R.: Macao	546	.072	.100	.110	.133	.188	.219	.258	.389	.538	.697	.726	.760	.912	.901	1.080
Fiji	819	.095	.122	.190	.202	.172	.224	.251	.314	.470	.400	.377	.306	.332	.307	.336
India	534	2.448	2.917	3.926	4.355	5.549	6.378	6.671	7.806	8.586	8.295	9.358	9.148	9.451	9.140	9.399
Indonesia	536	1.777	3.211	7.426	7.102	8.547	10.853	11.643	15.591	21.909	25.165	22.328	21.146	21.888	18.587	14.805
Korea	542	1.625	3.221	4.462	4.945	7.716	10.048	12.722	15.057	17.512	21.268	21.853	24.446	29.245	30.282	34.715
Lao People's Dem. Rep.	544	.042	.054	.095	.012	.012	.004	.003	.019	.028	.023	.040	.041	.044	.054	.055
Malaysia	548	1.722	3.049	4.236	3.843	5.295	6.079	7.404	11.079	12.945	11.770	12.030	14.104	16.484	15.316	13.689
Maldives	556	.003	.004	.004	.003	.003	.003	.004	.005	.008	.009	.010	.013	.018	.023	.025
Mongolia	948	....	....	....	....	....	....	....	....	.403	.469	.562	.610	.674	.689	.716
Myanmar	518	.120	.130	.188	.173	.206	.214	.242	.383	.472	.462	.391	.378	.301	.303	.288
Nepal	558	.058	.063	.066	.100	.098	.081	.091	.109	.080	.141	.088	.093	.127	.160	.142
Pakistan	564	†.694	.959	1.113	1.057	1.172	1.194	1.482	2.066	2.631	2.896	2.408	3.091	2.570	2.753	3.400
Papua New Guinea	853	.222	.515	.654	.441	.551	.683	.714	.964	1.031	.838	.771	.819	.914	.928	1.031
Philippines	566	1.100	1.885	2.725	2.294	2.555	3.127	3.401	4.567	5.741	5.655	4.969	4.890	5.274	4.611	4.806
Samoa	862	.005	.007	.013	.007	.007	.015	.011	.018	.017	.011	.013	.018	.019	.016	.010
Singapore	576	2.189	3.653	5.810	5.376	6.585	8.241	10.134	14.233	19.375	20.967	20.788	21.833	24.070	22.812	22.495
Solomon Islands	813	.011	.014	.026	.016	.024	.033	.038	.070	.074	.066	.058	.061	.093	.070	.065
Sri Lanka	524	.338	.410	.527	.569	.572	.761	.845	.981	1.062	1.088	1.031	1.063	1.467	1.333	1.215
Thailand	578	1.081	1.564	2.444	2.208	2.980	3.490	4.085	5.298	6.505	7.031	6.945	6.368	7.413	7.121	8.876
Tonga	866	.003	.005	.007	.006	.004	.007	.005	.007	.007	.008	.007	.005	.009	.005	.006
Vanuatu	846	.015	.021	.031	.012	.017	.032	.037	.042	.036	.032	.023	.029	.044	.031	.017
* of which:																
Taiwan Province of China	528	2.914	4.383	5.518	5.302	8.155	9.349	12.682	16.081	19.786	22.502	22.075	25.086	30.439	30.696	39.754
Europe	170	....	....	....	....	....	....	....	....	....	....	....	....	....	....	....
Albania	914	....	....	....	....	....	....	....	....	....	....	....	....	....	....	....
Armenia	911	....	....	....	....	....	....	....	....	....	....	....	....	....	....	....
Azerbaijan	912	....	....	....	....	....	....	....	....	....	....	....	....	....	....	....
Belarus	913	....	....	....	....	....	....	....	....	....	....	....	....	....	....	....
Bulgaria	918	2.627	3.269	3.836	....	....	....	....	....	....	....	....	....	....	13.339	14.203
Croatia	960	....	....	....	....	....	....	....	....	....	....	....	....	....	....	....
Cyprus	423	.134	.173	.152	.152	.258	.318	.344	.456	.533	.556	.555	.494	.575	.476	.502
Czech Republic	935	....	....	....	....	....	....	....	....	....	....	....	....	....	....	....
Czechoslovakia	934	....	....	....	6.154	....	....	....	10.926	12.063	11.611	12.059	12.119	11.775	11.900	13.790
Estonia	939	....	....	....	....	....	....	....	....	....	....	....	....	....	....	....
Georgia	915	....	....	....	....	....	....	....	....	....	....	....	....	....	....	....
Hungary	944	2.403	3.354	3.942	4.519	4.927	5.834	6.408	7.930	8.672	8.707	8.773	8.702	8.563	8.538	9.165
Kazakhstan	916	....	....	....	....	....	....	....	....	....	....	....	....	....	....	....
Kyrgyz Republic	917	....	....	....	....	....	....	....	....	....	....	....	....	....	....	....
Latvia	941	....	....	....	....	....	....	....	....	....	....	....	....	....	....	....
Lithuania	946	....	....	....	....	....	....	....	....	....	....	....	....	....	....	....
Macedonia, FYR	962	....	....	....	....	....	....	....	....	....	....	....	....	....	....	....
Malta	181	.068	.098	.134	.166	.228	.289	.342	.424	.483	.449	.411	.363	.394	.400	.497
Moldova	921	....	....	....	....	....	....	....	....	....	....	....	....	....	....	....
Poland	964	4.927	6.432	8.321	10.289	11.024	10.666	12.238	14.082	14.191	10.675	11.213	11.572	11.750	11.489	12.074
Romania	968	2.601	3.691	4.874	5.341	6.138	7.021	8.086	9.724	11.209	12.610	11.559	11.512	12.646	12.167	9.763
Russia	922	....	....	....	....	....	....	....	....	....	....	....	....	....	....	....
Slovak Republic	936	....	....	....	....	....	....	....	....	....	....	....	....	....	....	....
Slovenia	961	....	....	....	....	....	....	....	....	....	....	....	....	....	....	....
Turkey	186	.885	1.317	1.532	1.401	1.960	1.753	2.288	2.261	2.910	4.703	5.746	5.728	7.134	7.958	7.457
Ukraine	926	....	....	....	....	....	....	....	....	....	....	....	....	....	....	....
Yugoslavia, SFR	188	2.237	2.853	3.805	4.072	4.878	5.254	5.671	6.491	8.978	10.940	10.284	9.914	10.254	10.700	10.353
Middle East	405	18.00	27.53	82.44	87.01	105.55	115.17	114.47	180.72	204.32	214.67	167.83	134.39	120.63	102.58	75.32
Bahrain, Kingdom of	419	.347	.481	1.272	1.203	1.516	1.845	1.893	2.488	3.594	4.347	3.789	3.199	3.204	2.897	2.199
Egypt	469	.825	1.121	1.516	1.402	1.522	1.708	1.737	1.840	3.046	3.233	3.120	3.214	3.140	3.714	2.934
Iran, I.R. of	429	1.799	2.669	8.401	7.963	8.935	9.216	8.560	8.310	†7.109	†3.947	12.968	19.378	12.422	13.328	7.171
Iraq	433	1.086	.836	2.392	15.934	18.250	19.012	21.749	42.402	....	....	....	....	....	....	....
Israel	436	1.147	1.449	1.825	1.941	2.415	3.082	3.921	4.546	5.538	5.670	5.255	5.108	5.807	6.260	7.154
Jordan	439	.048	.073	.155	.153	.207	.249	.298	.403	.574	.733	.752	.580	.752	.789	.733
Kuwait	443	2.558	3.815	10.963	9.184	9.846	9.754	10.427	18.404	19.842	16.300	10.961	11.574	12.280	10.597	7.251
Lebanon	446	.377	.921	1.636	1.233	.546	.760	.830	.850	.955	.920	.800	.760	.378	.288	.550
Libya	672	2.938	4.003	8.259	6.834	9.554	11.411	9.895	16.076	21.910	15.571	13.203	12.216	11.148	12.314	8.215
Oman	449	.167	.239	.823	1.044	1.134	1.139	1.096	1.570	2.387	3.212	2.998	3.074	3.068	3.938	1.835
Qatar	453	.397	.628	2.015	1.805	2.210	2.072	2.391	3.753	5.680	5.686	4.341	3.357	....	....	....
Saudi Arabia	456	4.772	8.988	35.555	29.673	38.286	43.466	40.734	63.427	109.116	119.881	79.104	45.827	37.567	27.481	20.185
Syrian Arab Rep.	463	.287	.351	.782	.930	1.074	1.070	1.060	1.644	2.108	2.103	2.026	1.923	1.853	1.637	1.325
United Arab Emirates	466	1.157	1.807	6.414	7.262	9.535	9.636	9.126	13.652	20.676	21.238	16.837	14.672	14.192	14.043	12.387
Yemen Arab Rep.	473	.004	.008	.013	.011	.008	.011	.007	.014	.023	.047	.039	.027	.016	.013	.008
Yemen, P.D. Rep.	459	.008	.007	.016	.017	.007	.181	.192	.466	.777	.607	.795	.674	.645	....	.290
Yemen, Republic of	474	....	....	....	....	....	....	....	....	....	....	....	....	....	....	....

Billions of US Dollars

1987	1988	1989	1990	1991	1992	1993	1994	1995	1996	1997	1998	1999	2000	2001		70 *d*
293.86	**361.31**	**403.81**	**448.91**	**512.68**	**581.59**	**640.81**	**762.90**	**925.86**	**966.09**	**1,029.89**	**976.66**	**1,040.30**	**1,252.12**	**1,177.22**	**Asia ***	**505**
.512	.395	.236	.235	.286	.091	.180	.024	.026	....	....	....	....	....	....	Afghanistan, Islamic State of	512
1.067	1.291	1.305	1.671	1.689	2.098	2.278	2.661	3.173	3.297	3.778	3.831	3.922	4.691	4.958	Bangladesh	513
.055	.075	.070	.070	.063	.066	.065	.066	.103	.100	.118	.108	.116	....	....	Bhutan	514
....	....	....	....	....	....	....	....	....	....	.621	.796	1.323	1.359	....	Cambodia	522
39.437	47.516	52.538	62.091	71.910	84.940	90.970	121.047	148.797	151.197	182.877	183.589	195.150	249.297	266.620	China, P.R.: Mainland	924
48.476	63.163	73.140	82.160	98.577	119.487	135.244	151.399	173.750	180.750	188.059	174.002	173.885	201.860	189.894	China, P.R.: Hong Kong	532
1.404	1.493	1.643	1.701	1.665	1.766	1.787	1.866	1.997	1.996	2.148	2.141	2.200	2.539	2.299	China, P.R.: Macao	546
....	.372	.442	.497	.450	.443	.450	.572	.619	.748	.620	.510	....	....	....	Fiji	819
11.298	13.234	15.872	17.969	17.727	19.628	21.572	25.022	30.630	33.105	35.008	33.437	35.667	42.379	43.611	India	534
17.136	19.219	22.160	25.675	29.142	33.967	36.823	40.055	45.417	49.814	53.443	48.847	48.665	62.124	....	Indonesia	536
47.281	60.696	62.377	65.016	71.870	76.632	82.236	96.013	125.058	129.715	136.164	132.313	143.686	172.268	150.439	Korea	542
.064	.058	.063	.079	.097	.133	.241	.301	.311	.323	.359	.370	.311	.330	.331	Lao People's Dem. Rep.	544
17.958	21.082	25.048	29.451	34.349	40.772	47.131	58.844	73.914	78.327	78.740	73.305	84.455	98.135	88.005	Malaysia	548
.031	.040	.045	.052	.054	.040	.035	.046	.050	.059	.073	.074	.064	.076	.076	Maldives	556
.718	.739	.722	.661	.348	.389	.383	.356	.473	.424	.452	.345	.233	....	....	Mongolia	948
.219	.166	.210	.325	.419	.531	.586	.798	.851	.746	.866	1.065	1.125	1.620	2.271	Myanmar	518
.151	.191	.159	.204	.257	.368	.384	.362	.345	.385	.406	.474	.602	.804	.737	Nepal	558
4.192	4.544	4.731	5.615	6.559	7.351	6.720	7.400	8.029	9.365	8.758	8.514	8.491	9.028	9.238	Pakistan	564
1.241	1.451	1.294	1.177	1.460	1.927	2.585	2.632	2.654	2.529	2.163	1.772	1.924	2.096	1.813	Papua New Guinea	853
5.677	7.022	7.767	8.117	8.801	9.751	11.129	13.304	17.502	20.408	24.882	29.414	36.576	39.783	32.664	Philippines	566
.012	.015	.013	.009	.006	.006	.006	.004	.009	.010	.015	.015	.020	.014	.016	Samoa	862
28.686	39.306	44.661	52.730	58.966	63.472	74.012	96.825	118.268	125.014	124.985	109.895	114.680	137.804	121.751	Singapore	576
.064	.082	.074	.070	.084	.102	.129	.142	.168	.162	.175	.126	....	....	....	Solomon Islands	813
1.393	1.476	1.545	1.912	1.987	2.455	2.859	3.208	3.798	4.095	4.639	4.809	4.594	5.430	4.817	Sri Lanka	524
11.727	15.953	20.078	23.068	28.428	32.472	36.969	45.261	56.439	55.721	57.374	54.456	58.440	69.057	65.113	Thailand	578
.006	.008	.009	.011	.013	.012	.016	.014	.014	.011	.010	.008	.012	....	....	Tonga	866
.018	.020	.022	.019	.018	.024	.023	.025	.028	.030	.035	.034	.026	....	....	Vanuatu	846
															** of which:*	
53.820	60.502	66.195	67.079	76.163	81.387	84.641	92.876	111.563	115.730	121.081	110.518	121.496	147.777	122.505	Taiwan Province of China	528
....	....	....	....	....	**159.56**	**158.50**	**202.71**	**256.88**	**278.05**	**287.87**	**282.19**	**280.24**	**340.14**	**355.54**	**Europe**	**170**
....	....	....	....	....	.076	.122	.140	.202	.207	.139	.205	.264	.261	.305	Albania	914
....	....	....	....	....	.083	.156	.216	.271	.290	.233	.221	.232	.294	.343	Armenia	911
....	....	....	....	....	1.571	.993	.638	.637	.631	.781	.606	.929	....	....	Azerbaijan	912
....	....	....	....	....	3.559	1.970	2.510	4.803	5.652	7.301	7.070	5.909	7.326	7.525	Belarus	913
15.864	17.370	16.278	4.822	3.120	3.914	3.729	3.947	5.359	6.602	5.323	4.195	3.964	4.809	5.109	Bulgaria	918
....	....	....	....	....	....	3.904	4.260	4.633	4.512	4.171	4.541	4.303	4.432	4.659	Croatia	960
.621	.709	.793	.951	.952	.987	.867	.969	1.231	1.391	1.250	1.061	.997	.953	.976	Cyprus	423
....	....	....	....	....	....	†14.466	†16.230	†21.686	21.916	22.746	26.418	26.241	28.996	33.402	Czech Republic	935
15.469	15.322	14.505	11.906	10.939	11.310	....	....	....	....	....	....	....	....	....	Czechoslovakia	934
....	....	....	....	....	....	.803	†1.313	1.838	2.077	2.924	3.131	2.936	3.133	3.274	Estonia	939
....	....	....	....	....	....	....	.156	.151	.199	.240	.192	....	....	....	Georgia	915
9.556	9.949	9.624	9.596	10.199	10.677	8.886	10.434	12.802	15.631	18.989	22.992	24.950	28.016	30.530	Hungary	944
....	....	....	....	....	....	3.277	3.231	5.250	5.911	6.497	5.436	5.598	9.126	8.647	Kazakhstan	916
....	....	....	....	....	....	.340	.340	.409	.505	.604	.514	.454	.504	.476	Kyrgyz Republic	917
....	....	....	....	....	.778	.998	.991	1.305	1.443	1.672	1.811	1.723	1.865	2.001	Latvia	941
....	....	....	....	....	....	2.025	2.029	2.705	3.355	3.860	3.711	3.004	3.810	4.583	Lithuania	946
....	....	....	....	....	....	1.055	1.086	1.204	1.148	1.237	1.311	1.192	1.319	1.155	Macedonia, FYR	962
.605	.714	.844	1.130	1.252	1.543	1.355	1.570	1.914	1.731	1.630	1.834	1.786	2.336	1.917	Malta	181
....	....	....	....	....	.470	.483	.619	.739	.805	.890	.644	....	....	....	Moldova	921
12.205	13.960	13.466	13.627	†14.903	13.324	14.143	17.042	22.895	24.440	25.751	27.191	27.397	31.651	36.092	Poland	964
10.492	11.392	10.487	5.775	4.266	4.363	4.892	6.151	7.910	8.085	8.431	8.300	8.505	10.367	11.391	Romania	968
....	....	....	....	....	42.039	44.297	†67.826	82.913	90.563	89.008	74.884	75.665	105.565	103.139	Russia	922
....	....	....	....	....	....	5.466	6.709	8.595	8.823	8.254	10.721	10.226	11.889	12.627	Slovak Republic	936
....	....	....	....	3.852	†6.681	6.083	6.828	8.316	8.312	8.372	9.048	8.604	8.733	9.251	Slovenia	961
10.190	11.662	11.625	12.959	13.594	14.715	15.345	18.106	21.637	23.224	26.261	26.974	26.588	26.572	....	Turkey	186
....	....	....	....	....	8.045	7.817	10.305	13.317	14.441	14.232	12.637	11.582	....	....	Ukraine	926
11.443	12.663	13.460	14.308	13.953	....	....	....	....	....	....	....	....	....	....	Yugoslavia, SFR	188
91.38	**88.85**	**124.34**	**153.86**	**136.73**	**143.51**	**134.78**	**142.88**	**159.09**	**185.67**	**188.16**	**150.20**	**182.42**	**279.62**	**265.03**	**Middle East**	**405**
2.430	2.411	2.831	3.761	3.513	3.464	3.726	3.617	4.113	4.702	4.384	3.270	4.140	5.703	5.545	Bahrain, Kingdom of	419
4.351	5.706	6.764	4.957	3.705	3.063	2.252	3.476	3.450	3.539	3.921	3.130	3.559	4.689	4.126	Egypt	469
11.916	10.709	13.081	19.305	18.661	19.868	18.080	19.434	18.360	22.391	18.381	13.118	21.030	28.345	....	Iran, I.R. of	429
....	....	....	....	....	....	....	....	....	....	....	....	....	....	....	Iraq	433
8.454	8.198	10.738	11.576	11.921	10.019	14.826	16.884	19.046	20.610	22.503	22.993	25.794	31.404	29.019	Israel	436
.934	1.019	1.107	1.064	1.130	1.219	1.246	1.424	1.769	1.817	1.836	1.802	1.832	1.897	2.293	Jordan	439
8.264	7.758	11.476	7.042	1.088	6.572	10.246	11.260	12.785	14.889	14.224	9.554	12.218	19.439	16.139	Kuwait	443
.650	.780	.485	.494	.539	.560	.452	.470	.656	.736	.643	.662	.677	.715	.870	Lebanon	446
8.043	6.673	8.034	13.225	11.235	....	....	8.954	8.975	9.903	9.656	6.659	7.374	10.247	....	Libya	672
2.491	2.476	4.068	5.508	4.874	5.553	5.370	5.545	6.068	7.346	7.630	5.508	....	....	....	Oman	449
....	....	....	....	....	....	....	3.146	3.481	3.752	3.791	4.880	7.061	....	....	Qatar	453
23.199	24.377	28.382	44.417	47.797	50.286	42.395	42.614	50.040	60.729	60.732	38.822	50.761	77.583	....	Saudi Arabia	456
3.870	1.345	3.006	4.212	3.430	3.093	3.146	3.047	3.563	3.999	3.916	2.890	3.464	†19.260	....	Syrian Arab Rep.	463
14.165	13.934	17.596	23.544	24.436	24.756	....	....	....	....	....	....	....	....	....	United Arab Emirates	466
.048	....	....	....	....	....	....	....	....	....	....	....	....	....	....	Yemen Arab Rep.	473
....	....	....	....	....	....	....	....	....	....	....	....	....	....	....	Yemen, P.D. Rep.	459
....	....	....	....	.659	.619	.611	.934	1.945	2.674	2.504	1.497	2.440	4.079	3.215	Yemen, Republic of	474

Exports, f.o.b.

		1972	1973	1974	1975	1976	1977	1978	1979	1980	1981	1982	1983	1984	1985	1986
															Billions of US Dollars	
Western Hemisphere	205	18.72	25.72	45.13	41.87	48.25	56.09	60.26	79.95	106.19	115.80	102.92	102.09	112.09	103.48	88.43
Antigua and Barbuda	311	.018	.026	.029	.020	.009	†.007	.013	.037	.026	.040	.021	.020	.018	.017	.020
Argentina	213	1.941	3.266	3.931	2.961	3.916	5.652	6.400	7.810	8.021	9.143	7.625	7.836	8.107	8.396	6.852
Aruba	314	....	....	....	....	....	....	....	....	....	....	....	....	....	....	.024
Bahamas, The	313	.343	.530	1.444	2.508	2.992	3.261	3.058	3.786	5.009	6.189	4.534	3.970	3.393	2.728	2.702
Barbados	316	.044	.054	.086	.107	.086	.097	.131	.152	.228	.196	.259	†.323	†.394	.357	.278
Belize	339	.026	.032	.045	.067	.042	.062	.080	.087	.111	.119	.091	.078	.093	.090	.093
Bolivia	218	.201	.261	.557	.444	.568	.632	.629	.760	.942	.912	.828	.755	.725	.623	.638
Brazil	223	3.991	6.199	7.951	8.670	10.128	12.120	12.659	15.244	20.132	23.293	20.175	21.899	27.005	25.639	22.349
Chile	228	.855	1.231	2.481	1.552	2.083	2.190	2.478	3.894	4.705	3.837	3.706	3.831	3.651	3.804	4.191
Colombia	233	.808	1.169	1.509	1.465	1.874	2.403	3.010	3.411	3.924	2.916	3.024	3.001	3.462	3.552	5.102
Costa Rica	238	.281	.345	.440	.493	.593	.828	.865	.934	1.002	1.008	.870	.873	1.006	.976	1.121
Dominica	321	.007	.009	.010	.011	.011	.012	.016	.009	.010	.019	.024	.027	.026	.028	.043
Dominican Republic	243	.348	.442	.637	.894	.716	.780	.676	.869	.962	1.188	.768	.785	.868	.735	.718
Ecuador	248	.326	.532	1.124	.974	1.258	1.436	1.558	2.104	2.481	2.451	2.327	2.348	2.620	2.905	2.172
El Salvador	253	.273	.352	.463	.531	.743	.972	.848	1.223	.967	.797	.699	.735	.717	.679	.755
Grenada	328	.005	.007	.010	.012	.013	.014	.017	.021	.017	.019	.019	.019	.018	.022	.029
Guatemala	258	.327	.436	.572	.624	.760	1.160	1.089	1.241	1.520	1.226	1.120	1.159	1.129	1.057	1.044
Guyana	336	.147	.136	.270	.365	.279	.259	.296	.293	.389	.346	.241	.189	.210	.166	.222
Haiti	263	.044	.053	.072	.080	.124	.149	.155	.185	.226	.152	.178	.166	.179	.168	.184
Honduras	268	.205	.259	.289	.295	.400	.513	.608	.734	.829	.761	.660	.672	.725	.780	.854
Jamaica	343	.391	.390	.604	.759	.630	.768	.833	.818	.963	.974	.767	.718	.705	.566	.589
Mexico	273	1.694	2.250	2.958	2.904	3.417	4.167	6.005	8.982	†18.031	23.307	24.055	25.953	29.101	26.757	21.804
Netherlands Antilles	353	.758	1.369	3.230	2.397	2.524	2.647	2.976	3.966	5.162	5.417	4.891	4.409	3.733	1.031	†.924
Nicaragua	278	.249	.278	.381	.375	.542	.637	.646	.567	.451	.508	.406	.429	.386	.302	.247
Panama	283	.123	.138	.211	.286	.238	.251	.256	.303	.361	.328	.375	.320	.276	.336	.349
Paraguay	288	.085	.124	.167	.176	.181	.279	.257	.305	.310	.296	.330	.269	.335	.304	.234
Peru	293	.944	1.112	1.503	†1.291	1.360	1.726	1.941	3.491	3.898	3.255	3.259	3.015	3.147	2.979	2.531
St. Kitts and Nevis	361	.006	.008	.012	.022	.018	.015	.017	.017	.024	.024	.019	.018	.020	.020	.025
St. Lucia	362	.008	.010	.016	.017	.021	.025	.029	.036	.058	.046	.045	.055	.049	.057	.087
St. Vincent & Grens.	364	.003	.005	.007	.008	.009	.010	.016	.015	.015	.024	.032	.041	.054	.063	.064
Suriname	366	.171	.179	.269	.277	.276	.310	.369	†.444	.514	.474	.429	.367	.356	.329	.335
Trinidad and Tobago	369	.558	.699	2.036	1.771	2.214	2.180	2.040	2.610	4.077	3.761	3.072	2.353	2.173	2.139	1.386
Uruguay	298	.214	.322	.382	.384	.546	.608	.686	.788	1.059	1.215	1.023	1.045	.934	.909	1.088
Venezuela	299	3.166	3.298	11.153	8.800	9.299	9.551	9.187	14.317	19.221	20.980	16.590	13.937	15.997	14.438	8.660

Memorandum Items

		1972	1973	1974	1975	1976	1977	1978	1979	1980	1981	1982	1983	1984	1985	1986
Euro Area	163	....	....	....	....	....	....	....	....	....	....	....	....	....	....	....
Oil Exporting Countries	999	23.30	34.84	107.29	108.14	131.42	143.89	141.07	224.39	267.67	274.74	214.73	176.22	166.77	144.31	96.98
Non-Oil Developing Countries	201	80.68	116.29	160.90	157.05	175.85	204.70	236.22	315.50	394.54	412.15	395.32	408.70	449.57	456.45	476.20

1987	1988	1989	1990	1991	1992	1993	1994	1995	1996	1997	1998	1999	2000	2001		
Billions of US Dollars																
100.46	116.24	129.83	139.83	139.66	147.59	158.28	183.17	223.99	251.43	279.62	276.74	294.95	354.92	342.48	Western Hemisphere	205
.019	.017	.016	.021	.050	.065	.062	.044	.053	.038	.038	.036	.038	....	....	Antigua and Barbuda	311
6.360	9.135	9.579	12.353	11.978	12.235	13.118	15.659	20.967	23.811	26.370	26.441	23.333	26.409	26.655	Argentina....................................	213
.026	.031	.023	.028	.026	....	....	....	.015	.012	.024	.029	.029	....	....	Aruba...	314
2.722	2.153	2.487	†.238	.225	.192	.162	.167	.176	.180	.181	.300	.450	.400	.649	Bahamas, The	313
.161	.177	.188	.215	.207	.190	.187	.182	.239	.281	.283	.252	.264	.272	.259	Barbados.....................................	316
.087	.095	.094	.108	.099	.116	.119	.127	.143	.154	.159	.155	.166	.194	.166	Belize..	339
.570	.600	.822	.926	.849	.710	.728	1.032	1.101	1.137	1.167	1.104	1.051	1.230	1.285	Bolivia.......................................	218
26.224	33.494	34.383	31.414	31.620	35.793	38.555	43.545	46.506	47.747	52.994	51.140	48.011	55.086	58.223	Brazil..	223
5.224	7.052	8.078	8.373	8.942	10.007	9.199	11.604	16.024	15.657	17.902	16.353	17.194	19.246	18.505	Chile...	228
4.642	5.037	5.717	6.766	7.232	6.917	7.116	8.419	10.056	10.587	11.522	10.852	11.576	13.040	12.257	Colombia.....................................	233
1.158	1.246	1.415	1.448	1.598	1.841	2.625	2.869	3.453	3.730	4.268	5.511	6.577	5.865	5.010	Costa Rica...................................	238
.048	.054	.045	.055	.054	.053	.049	.047	.045	.051	.053	.063	.054	.053	....	Dominica.....................................	321
.711	.890	.924	.735	.658	.562	.511	.644	.872	.945	1.017	.880	.805	.966	.805	Dominican Republic	243
1.928	2.192	2.354	2.714	2.852	3.007	2.904	3.820	4.307	4.900	5.264	4.203	4.451	4.927	4.647	Ecuador	248
.591	.609	.498	.582	.588	.598	.732	.844	.998	1.024	1.371	1.256	1.177	1.332	1.214	El Salvador	253
.032	.033	.030	.028	.022	.020	.020	.024	.022	.020	.023	.027				Grenada......................................	328
.987	1.022	1.108	1.163	1.202	1.295	1.340	1.522	2.156	2.031	2.344	2.582	2.398	2.696	2.466	Guatemala	258
.267	.230	.227	.257	.246	.292	.414	.456	.455	.517	.644	.484	.523	.498	.478	Guyana.......................................	336
.214	.179	.144	.160	.167	.073	.080	.082	.110	.090	.212	.320	.334	.318	.274	Haiti..	263
.791	.842	.859	.831	.792	.802	.814	.842	1.220	1.316	1.446	1.533	1.164	1.370	1.318	Honduras	268
.706	.880	.998	1.158	1.105	1.047	1.071	1.212	1.427	1.383	1.383	1.312	1.240	1.296	1.225	Jamaica.......................................	343
27.600	30.691	35.171	40.711	42.688	46.196	51.886	60.882	79.542	96.000	110.431	117.460	136.391	166.368	158.547	Mexico.......................................	273
1.308	1.134	1.454	1.790	1.599	1.559	1.283	1.375	....	....	....	....	....	....	....	Netherlands Antilles	353
.273	.233	.311	.331	.272	.223	.267	.335	.457	.466	.577	.573	.545	.631	.606	Nicaragua....................................	278
.358	.307	.318	.340	.358	.502	.553	.583	.625		.723	.784	.822	.859	.911	Panama.......................................	283
.353	.510	1.006	.959	.737	.657	.725	.817	.919	1.044	1.089	1.014	.741	....	....	Paraguay.....................................	288
2.661	2.701	3.488	3.231	3.329	3.484	3.515	4.555	5.575	5.897	6.841	5.757	6.113	7.028	7.100	Peru..	293
.028	.028	.029	.028	.027	.026	.027	.022	.019	.022	....	....	....	....	....	St. Kitts and Nevis........................	361
.080	.116	.109	.127	.110	.123	.120	.106	.124	.082	.066	....	....	....	....	St. Lucia	362
.052	.085	.075	.083	.067	.078	.058	.050	.043	.046	.046	.050	.049	.047	.041	St. Vincent & Grens.......................	364
.306	.410	.542	.472	.359	.391	1.190	.449	.477	.433	.701	.436	.342	.399	....	Suriname.....................................	366
1.462	1.412	1.578	1.960	1.985	1.691	1.662	1.867	2.455	2.500	2.542	2.258	2.804	4.655	....	Trinidad and Tobago	369
1.189	1.405	1.599	1.693	1.605	1.703	1.645	1.913	2.106	2.397	2.726	2.771	2.237	2.295	2.060	Uruguay......................................	298
10.577	10.244	13.286	17.497	15.155	14.185	14.686	16.089	18.457	23.060	21.624	17.193	20.190	31.802	27.409	Venezuela....................................	299
															Memorandum Items	
....	112.33	150.50	196.58	180.82	192.48	180.02	187.31	210.83	249.03	252.26	886.46	†884.59	922.63	936.32	Euro Area....................................	163
113.40	112.33	150.50	196.58	180.82	192.48	180.02	187.31	210.83	249.03	252.26	199.71	235.77	347.21	335.02	Oil Exporting Countries	999
582.21	683.58	746.02	784.64	846.57	914.00	986.34	1,181.24	1,444.61	1,531.60	1,636.33	1,574.65	1,660.29	2,000.39	1,918.11	Non-Oil Developing Countries	201

Imports, c.i.f.

		1972	1973	1974	1975	1976	1977	1978	1979	1980	1981	1982	1983	1984	1985	1986
														Billions of US Dollars		
World	001	407.9	562.9	827.7	875.2	981.9	1,124.3	1,297.0	1,638.3	2,014.7	1,996.2	1,878.9	1,817.1	1,937.9	1,964.6	2,143.5
Industrial Countries	110	308.0	423.0	603.3	603.7	696.8	788.9	911.2	1,168.0	1,400.4	1,328.8	1,249.4	1,224.8	1,340.2	1,374.7	1,546.8
United States	111	58.862	73.199	110.875	†105.880	132.498	†160.411	186.045	222.228	256.984	273.352	254.884	269.878	346.364	352.463	382.295
Canada	156	20.038	24.713	34.248	36.106	40.243	42.083	46.278	56.642	62.544	70.010	58.128	64.789	77.789	80.640	85.494
Australia	193	5.028	7.393	11.982	10.697	12.232	13.511	15.567	18.191	22.399	26.215	26.667	21.458	25.919	25.889	26.104
Japan	158	23.863	38.389	61.948	57.860	64.894	71.340	79.922	109.831	141.296	142.866	131.499	126.437	136.176	130.488	127.553
New Zealand	196	1.523	2.176	3.648	3.155	3.254	3.361	†3.491	4.553	5.472	5.734	5.782	5.333	6.203	5.992	6.063
Euro Area																
Austria	122	5.216	7.119	9.022	9.394	11.523	14.245	16.019	20.252	24.444	21.043	19.502	19.367	19.629	20.986	26.843
Belgium	124	....														....
Belgium-Luxembourg	126	15.490	22.075	29.880	30.781	35.519	40.406	48.609	60.914	71.864	62.450	58.227	55.313	55.455	56.190	68.656
Finland	172	3.165	4.341	6.813	7.628	7.392	7.608	7.866	11.398	15.635	14.192	13.401	12.826	12.433	13.232	15.339
France	132	26.999	37.738	52.918	53.947	64.082	70.637	81.788	107.009	134.889	120.953	116.509	106.250	104.372	108.337	129.402
Germany	134	40.378	54.891	69.661	74.930	88.421	101.458	121.754	159.646	188.002	163.941	155.323	152.877	153.022	158.488	190.872
Greece	174	2.348	3.477	4.385	5.357	6.059	6.853	7.829	9.614	10.548	8.810	10.026	9.500	9.435	10.134	11.350
Ireland	178	2.102	2.789	3.814	3.778	4.200	5.396	7.121	9.884	11.153	10.608	9.706	9.170	9.674	10.015	11.607
Italy	136	19.319	27.798	41.089	38.526	43.905	48.092	56.496	77.895	100.741	94.261	87.332	79.808	85.162	87.692	100.673
Luxembourg	137	.960	1.340	1.739	1.823	1.861	2.037	2.527	3.111	3.612	2.998	2.732	2.664	2.770	3.144	4.227
Netherlands	138	20.667	28.744	38.949	40.897	46.734	52.903	61.314	77.331	88.419	75.940	72.316	68.237	69.254	73.123	†75.474
Portugal	182	2.204	3.015	4.496	3.839	4.220	4.744	5.237	6.534	9.300	9.800	9.572	8.240	7.961	7.652	9.649
Spain	184	6.829	9.667	15.428	16.265	17.474	17.836	18.712	25.438	34.078	32.150	31.465	29.193	28.831	29.963	35.057
Denmark	128	5.087	7.802	9.927	10.368	12.427	13.265	14.808	18.401	19.340	17.580	16.692	16.266	16.613	18.245	22.878
Iceland	176	.231	.359	.518	.484	.467	.605	.675	.815	.999	1.024	.944	.818	.841	.905	1.119
Norway	142	4.373	6.289	8.420	9.705	11.121	12.883	11.497	13.706	16.926	15.650	15.477	13.497	13.885	15.556	20.301
Sweden	144	8.110	10.907	16.683	17.450	19.628	†20.137	20.589	28.735	33.438	28.840	27.585	26.098	26.426	28.547	32.693
Switzerland	146	8.468	11.626	14.445	13.303	14.775	17.940	23.804	†29.356	36.341	30.682	28.678	29.192	29.521	30.696	41.039
United Kingdom	112	27.661	38.528	54.190	53.341	55.744	63.191	75.813	99.600	115.545	102.708	99.713	100.234	105.214	109.505	126.343
Developing Countries	200	99.90	139.88	224.36	271.50	285.13	335.38	385.78	470.33	614.35	667.39	629.45	592.37	597.72	589.88	596.69
Africa	605	14.72	19.32	29.37	37.15	37.87	45.21	52.84	54.59	80.25	87.33	75.26	66.46	62.57	56.55	55.33
Algeria	612	1.494	2.236	4.035	5.498	5.081	7.125	8.548	8.403	10.559	11.303	10.754	10.399	10.288	9.841	9.228
Benin	638	.092	.112	.147	.188	.219	.268	.311	.320	.331	.543	.464	.318	.288	.331	.387
Botswana	616	.110	.166	.184	.216	.209	.286	.371	.538	.693	.828	.722	.750	.713	.672	.858
Burkina Faso	748	.069	.098	.144	.151	.144	.209	.227	.301	.359	.338	.347	.291	.253	.332	.405
Burundi	618	.032	.031	.043	.062	.058	.074	.098	.152	.168	.161	.213	.182	.187	.186	.202
Cameroon	622	.303	.334	.437	.599	.613	.735	1.056	1.275	1.602	1.427	1.211	1.224	1.112	1.151	1.704
Cape Verde	624	.024	.034	.034	.040	.030	.038	.053	.053	.068	.071	.088	.095	.097	.086	.143
Central African Rep.	626	.034	.052	.046	.069	.055	.063	.057	.070	.081	.095	.123	.068	.087	.113	.167
Chad	628	.062	.082	.087	.133	.116	.189	.217	.085	.074	.108	.109	.157	.181	.166	.212
Comoros	632	.012	.015	.026	.023	.013	.016	.019	.029	.029	.032	.033	.034	.043	.036	.037
Congo, Dem. Rep. of	636	.208	.251	.349	.300	.224	.203	.196	.199	.278	.223	.160	.157	.685	.792	.875
Congo, Rep. of	634	.102	.126	.125	.167	.168	.206	.260	.305	.580	.446	.767	.648	.618	.598	.597
Côte d'Ivoire	662	.454	.710	.969	1.127	1.296	1.756	2.326	2.491	2.991	2.383	2.180	1.839	1.497	1.749	2.055
Djibouti	611	.054	.070	.122	.136	.120	.107	.164	.188	.213	.224	.226	.221	.222	.201	.184
Equatorial Guinea	642	.027	.027	.015	.020	.004	.010	.009	.019	.026	.027	.031	.019	.018	.020	.022
Ethiopia	644	.189	.214	.283	.313	.352	.352	.455	.567	.722	.739	.786	.876	.928	.993	1.102
Gabon	646	.139	.190	.332	.469	.503	.716	.617	.532	.674	.843	.867	.685	.724	.855	.866
Gambia, The	648	.025	.031	.047	.060	.074	.078	.100	.141	.165	.126	.103	.115	.100	.093	.104
Ghana	652	.291	.452	.821	.791	.862	1.038	1.006	.852	1.129	1.106	.705	2.513	.608	.866	1.046
Guinea-Bissau	654	.032	.044	.043	.038	.037	.037	.049	.061	.055	.050	.050	.055	....		
Kenya	664	.535	.619	1.026	.945	.969	1.289	1.711	1.636	2.125	1.939	1.644	1.334	1.469	1.436	1.613
Liberia	668	.179	.193	.288	.331	.399	.464	.481	.507	.535	.447	.428	.412	.363	.284	.259
Lesotho	666	.056	.088	.120	.164	.212	.234	.281	.328	.427	.461	.458	.483	.435	.339	.354
Liberia	668	.179	.193	.288	.331	.399	.464	.481	.507	.535	.447	.428	.412	.363	.284	.259
Madagascar	674	.205	.203	.281	.366	.285	.347	.443	.641	.600	.545	.417	.387	.366	.402	.353
Malawi	676	.129	.140	.188	.253	.206	.235	.338	.399	.439	.359	.304	.311	.271	.294	.258
Mali	678	.079	.128	.180	.176	.155	.159	.286	.361	.439	.380	.332	.353	.278	.299	.444
Mauritania	682	.069	.128	.120	.161	.179	.206	.181	.259	.286	.265	.276	.227	.208	.234	.221
Mauritius	684	.119	.168	.309	.332	.360	.447	.500	.574	.614	.563	.465	.442	.471	.529	.684
Morocco	686	.779	1.144	1.904	2.568	2.618	3.199	2.970	3.678	4.255	4.400	4.315	3.592	3.911	3.850	3.803
Mozambique	688	....	....	....	....	....	....	....	....	....	....	....	....	....	....	....
Namibia	728															
Niger	692	.066	.086	.097	.101	.126	.197	.305	.461	.594	.510	.466	.324	.288	.369	.368
Nigeria	694	1.505	1.862	2.772	6.041	8.213	11.095	12.821	10.218	16.660	20.877	16.061	12.254	9.364	8.877	4.034
Rwanda	714	.035	.034	.058	.099	.106	.123	.188	.192	.243	.256	.276	.269	.278	.298	.349
São Tomé & Príncipe	716	.008	.010	.010	.011	.009	.014	.018	.020	.019	.017	....		.010	.017
Senegal	722	.280	.361	.498	.583	.636	.764	.755	.931	1.052	1.076	.992	1.025	.981	.826	.961
Seychelles	718	.021	.025	.028	.032	.039	.046	.058	.085	.099	.093	.098	.088	.088	.099	.105
Sierra Leone	724	.119	.155	.222	.185	.153	.181	.279	.316	.427	.328	.298	.160	.157	.151	.132
South Africa	199	3.948	†5.163	7.856	8.293	7.285	6.270	7.615	8.989	†19.699	22.918	18.499	15.765	16.243	11.440	12.974
Sudan	732	.320	.436	.642	.887	.980	1.081	1.194	1.109	1.576	1.553	1.282	1.354	1.147	.771	.961
Swaziland	734	.069	.096	.138	.178	.200	.182	.311	.435	.625	.590	.523	.552	.443	.316	.353
Tanzania	738	.404	.497	.753	.778	.638	.744	1.145	1.105	1.258	1.176	1.132	.802	.665	.845	.937
Togo	742	.085	.101	.119	.174	.185	.284	.450	.519	.551	.434	.393	.282	.271	.288	.312
Tunisia	744	.466	.682	1.128	1.424	1.529	1.825	2.138	2.849	3.526	3.791	3.420	3.107	3.221	2.757	2.890
Uganda	746	.162	.163	.213	.207	.172	.241	.254	.197	.293	.345	.377	.377	.344	.327	†.307
Zambia	754	.565	.533	.787	.929	.674	.671	.618	.749	1.088	1.064	1.001	.550	.596	.722	.597
Zimbabwe	698	.478	.606	.865	.932	.703	.710	.685	.930	1.449	1.693	1.644	1.209	1.103	.896	.985

1987	1988	1989	1990	1991	1992	1993	1994	1995	1996	1997	1998	1999	2000	2001		
Billions of US Dollars																
2,512.3	**2,877.4**	**3,113.9**	**3,530.7**	**3,642.0**	**3,870.8**	**3,819.9**	**4,342.4**	**5,187.4**	**5,441.4**	**5,624.7**	**5,545.6**	**†5,776.8**	**6,528.6**	**6,302.5**	**World**	**001**
1,829.9	**2,069.3**	**2,239.7**	**2,575.3**	**2,593.1**	**2,706.9**	**2,559.0**	**2,901.6**	**3,431.6**	**3,553.3**	**3,632.0**	**3,727.6**	**†3,929.3**	**4,335.0**	**4,138.5**	**Industrial Countries**	**110**
424.442	459.542	492.922	516.987	508.363	553.923	603.438	689.215	770.852	822.025	899.020	944.353	1,059.435	1,259.297	1,180.154	United States	111
92.593	112.711	119.792	123.244	124.782	129.262	139.035	155.072	168.041	174.959	200.873	206.066	220.183	244.786	227.291	Canada	156
29.318	36.095	44.933	41.985	41.648	43.807	45.577	53.425	61.283	65.427	65.892	64.630	69.158	71.531	63.886	Australia	193
151.033	187.378	209.715	235.368	236.999	233.246	241.624	275.235	335.882	349.152	338.754	280.484	311.262	379.511	349.089	Japan	158
7.276	7.342	8.784	9.501	8.381	9.201	9.636	11.913	13.957	14.724	14.519	12.495	14.299	13.906	13.347	New Zealand	196
															Euro Area	
32.678	36.570	38.923	49.088	50.788	54.112	48.633	55.335	66.386	67.331	64.776	68.183	†69.533	68.972	70.445	Austria	122
....	....	....	....	....	....	114.398	130.067	159.683	163.604	157.260	162.241	†164.617	176.965	178.468	Belgium	124
83.523	92.439	98.580	120.314	121.059	125.112	112.112	125.639	155.126	152.734	155.435	....	....	....	....	Belgium-Luxembourg	126
19.634	21.130	24.436	27.001	21.809	21.208	18.032	23.214	28.114	29.264	29.784	32.301	†31.616	33.893	32.108	Finland	172
158.477	178.836	192.949	234.447	231.779	239.638	203.202	234.567	281.440	281.750	271.914	288.389	†294.782	309.535	292.526	France	132
228.441	250.467	269.702	†346.153	389.908	402.441	346.027	385.351	464.271	458.783	445.616	471.418	†473.539	497.803	486.294	Germany	134
13.168	12.321	16.151	19.777	21.580	22.818	20.200	21.381	26.795	29.672	27.899	29.388	28.720	29.221	29.928	Greece	174
13.638	15.569	17.420	20.682	20.750	22.477	21.386	25.508	32.638	35.871	39.349	45.087	†47.194	51.472	51.286	Ireland	178
125.661	138.551	153.011	181.968	182.682	188.519	148.273	169.172	206.040	208.092	210.268	218.445	†220.323	238.023	232.983	Italy	136
5.239	5.813	6.210	7.596	8.044	8.221	7.687	8.387	9.748	9.667	9.379	10.237	†10.786	10.612	10.678	Luxembourg	137
91.494	99.444	104.253	126.475	127.213	134.650	124.742	141.317	176.874	180.639	178.130	187.747	†190.281	197.495	194.400	Netherlands	138
13.967	17.940	19.072	25.264	26.421	30.312	24.273	27.303	33.306	35.177	35.064	†38.536	†39.825	38.249	37.922	Portugal	182
49.113	60.502	70.945	87.554	92.965	99.753	79.665	92.191	113.319	121.782	122.711	133.149	†144.436	152.870	153.607	Spain	184
25.499	25.941	26.690	32.228	32.402	35.174	30.542	34.878	45.082	44.432	44.039	45.424	44.068	43.705	43.441	Denmark	128
1.590	1.597	1.401	1.680	1.760	1.684	1.341	1.472	1.756	2.032	1.992	2.489	2.503	2.591	2.253	Iceland	176
22.639	23.220	23.676	27.231	25.572	25.905	23.956	27.308	32.968	35.615	35.709	36.193	34.041	32.655	32.181	Norway	142
40.706	45.627	48.975	54.264	49.990	50.017	42.681	51.725	64.743	66.925	65.702	68.627	68.621	72.632	62.670	Sweden	144
50.591	56.363	58.194	69.681	66.485	†61.737	56.716	64.074	76.985	74.462	71.064	73.877	75.438	76.070	77.070	Switzerland	146
154.387	189.693	199.186	224.412	209.810	221.496	206.101	226.157	265.297	287.426	306.585	314.031	317.959	334.396	320.973	United Kingdom	112
682.44	**808.11**	**874.21**	**955.39**	**1,048.83**	**1,163.93**	**1,260.92**	**1,440.73**	**1,755.76**	**1,888.13**	**1,992.61**	**1,817.97**	**1,847.46**	**2,193.56**	**2,164.01**	**Developing Countries**	**200**
58.05	**65.26**	**68.15**	**74.90**	**74.77**	**79.65**	**75.64**	**82.45**	**101.90**	**100.68**	**106.84**	**105.47**	**101.52**	**107.88**	**112.74**	**Africa**	**605**
7.042	7.690	9.470	9.780	7.770	8.550	7.770	9.370	10.250	8.840	....	....	....	....	....	Algeria	612
.349	.327	.207	.265	.241	.578	.571	.431	.746	.654	.682	.674	.749	.613	.651	Benin	638
1.106	1.453	1.930	1.947	1.941	1.888	1.766	1.640	1.911	1.723	2.258	2.387	2.215	2.469	.569	Botswana	616
.434	.454	.391	.536	.533	.466	.509	.349	.455	.647	.587	.732	.579	.550	.656	Burkina Faso	748
.212	.204	.187	.231	.255	.221	.196	.225	.234	.127	.121	.158	.118	.148	.139	Burundi	618
1.753	1.273	1.261	1.400	1.173	1.163	.885	.717	1.199	1.227	1.359	1.495	1.318	....	....	Cameroon	622
.100	.106	.112	.136	.147	.180	.154	.209	.252	....	.234	.230	.262	.237	.248	Cape Verde	624
.204	.141	.150	.154	.093	.145	.126	.139	.174	.141	.145	.159	.140	.026	....	Central African Rep.	626
.226	.228	.235	.286	.250	.243	.201	.177	.365	.332	.334	.356	.316	.329	.632	Chad	628
.052	.053	.043	.052	.058	.069	.059	.053	.063	....	....	....	....	....	....	Comoros	632
.756	.763	.850	.888	.711	.420	.372	.382	.397	.424	....	....	....	....	....	Congo, Dem. Rep. of	636
.979	1.113	1.030	.621	.594	.451	.582	.631	.670	1.551	.922	.812	.467	.655	....	Congo, Rep. of	634
2.241	2.080	2.111	2.098	2.103	2.352	2.115	1.917	2.931	2.902	2.781	2.991	3.252	2.535	2.545	Côte d'Ivoire	662
.205	.201	.196	.215	.214	.219	.211	.196	.177	.179	.148	.158	.153	....	....	Djibouti	611
.050	.061	.055	.061	.067	.056	.060	.037	.050	.292	.330	.317	.425	.451	....	Equatorial Guinea	642
1.066	1.129	.951	1.081	.472	.839	.787	1.033	1.145	1.401	....	....	1.317	....	....	Ethiopia	644
.732	.791	.767	.918	.834	.700	.845	.756	.882	.957	1.104	1.103	.841	.994	....	Gabon	646
.127	.138	.161	.188	.202	.218	.260	.212	.182	.258	.174	.245	.192	....	....	Gambia, The	648
1.156	.905	1.276	....	1.055	2.169	3.942	2.109	1.907	2.108	2.326	2.563	3.480	2.973	....	Ghana	652
....	.066	.078	.086	.076	.096	.061	.164	.133	.087	.089	.068	.069	.062	....	Guinea-Bissau	654
1.738	1.988	2.174	2.223	1.935	1.841	1.774	2.091	2.991	2.949	3.279	3.197	2.832	3.105	3.192	Kenya	664
.308	.272	....	....	....	....	....	....	....	....	....	....	....	....	....	Liberia	668
.470	.584	.593	.673	.810	.899	.870	.848	.985	.999	1.025	.863	.781	.728	.681	Lesotho	666
.308	.272	....	....	....	....	....	....	....	....	....	....	....	....	....	Liberia	668
.302	.379	.371	.651	.436	.448	.468	.441	.543	.507	.470	.514	.378	....	....	Madagascar	674
.295	.420	.507	.575	.703	.735	.546	.491	.475	.623	.781	.579	.698	.569	....	Malawi	676
.374	.504	.340	.602	.460	.608	.634	.589	.772	.772	.739	.756	.820	.592	.657	Mali	678
.235	.240	.222	.220	....	....	....	.403	....	....	....	....	....	....	....	Mauritania	682
1.013	1.290	1.325	1.618	1.558	1.625	1.715	1.930	1.976	2.289	2.189	2.073	2.247	....	....	Mauritius	684
4.229	4.773	5.492	6.922	6.873	7.348	6.732	8.272	10.023	9.704	9.525	10.290	9.925	11.534	10.962	Morocco	686
....	....	....	....	....	....	....	.524	.704	.759	.739	.790	1.139	1.158	....	Mozambique	688
....	....	....	1.163	1.149	1.283	1.188	1.196	....	....	....	....	....	....	....	Namibia	728
.311	.387	.363	.389	.355	.479	.375	.328	.374	.448	.391	.377	.404	.372	....	Niger	692
3.912	4.717	4.187	5.627	8.986	8.275	5.537	6.613	†8.222	6.438	9.501	9.211	8.588	8.721	....	Nigeria	694
.352	.370	.333	.288	.306	.288	.332	.079	.238	.257	.297	.285	.253	.213	.250	Rwanda	714
.014	.014	.018	.021	.031	.029	.032	.030	.029	.022	.016	....	....	....	....	São Tomé & Príncipe	716
1.024	1.080	1.221	1.220	1.173	1.034	1.087	1.022	1.412	1.436	1.447	1.407	1.471	1.521	....	Senegal	722
.114	.159	.165	.187	.173	.191	.238	.207	.233	.379	.340	.384	.434	....	....	Seychelles	718
.137	.156	.183	.149	.163	.146	.147	.151	.133	.211	.093	.095	.081	.149	.182	Sierra Leone	724
15.295	18.670	18.490	18.399	18.828	19.738	19.991	23.363	30.546	30.182	32.998	†29.242	26.696	29.695	28.405	South Africa	199
.871	1.060	....	.619	.890	.821	.945	1.162	†1.185	1.504	1.580	1.925	1.415	1.553	1.586	Sudan	732
.437	.511	.585	.664	.715	.866	.870	.927	1.103	1.174	1.192	....	....	....	....	Swaziland	734
.929	.823	.990	1.364	1.546	1.510	1.497	1.505	1.675	1.388	1.337	1.453	1.556	1.524	1.712	Tanzania	738
.424	.487	.472	.581	.444	.395	.179	.222	.594	.664	.645	.588	.597	.565	.355	Togo	742
3.039	3.689	4.387	5.513	5.189	6.431	6.214	6.581	7.903	7.700	7.914	8.350	8.474	8.567	9.552	Tunisia	744
.848	.887	.423	.288	.196	.505	.613	.875	1.056	1.191	1.316	1.416	1.342	1.536	1.594	Uganda	746
.736	.839	.906	1.220	.818	.795	.809	.594	.700	.835	.819	....	....	....	....	Zambia	754
1.047	1.132	1.614	1.839	2.037	2.201	1.817	2.241	2.661	2.803	....	....	....	....	....	Zimbabwe	698

Imports, c.i.f.

71 d

		1972	1973	1974	1975	1976	1977	1978	1979	1980	1981	1982	1983	1984	1985	1986
														Billions of US Dollars		
Asia *	505	27.03	40.99	63.08	65.16	70.19	81.30	104.27	136.34	178.79	197.22	191.50	198.11	214.96	220.49	229.83
Afghanistan, Islamic State of	512	.164	.172	.243	.350	.261	.328	.395	.425	.841	.886	.962	1.064	1.390	1.194	1.404
Bangladesh	513	.683	.986	1.078	1.321	.952	1.163	1.513	1.908	2.599	2.699	2.464	2.165	2.825	†2.542	2.546
Bhutan	514	....	....	....	....	....	....	....	....	.050	.068	.068	.072	.073	.084	.093
Cambodia	522	....	.227													
China, P.R.: Mainland	924	2.851	5.208	7.791	7.926	6.660	7.148	11.131	15.621	†19.941	22.015	19.285	21.390	27.410	42.252	42.904
China, P.R.: Hong Kong	532	3.856	5.655	6.778	6.766	8.838	10.446	13.394	17.127	22.447	24.797	23.575	24.017	28.568	29.703	35.367
China, P.R.: Macao	546	.104	.158	.134	.161	.161	.198	.249	.351	.544	.720	.719	.727	.796	.773	.914
Fiji	819	.159	.222	.273	.268	.264	.307	.355	.470	.562	.631	.509	.484	.450	.442	.435
India	534	2.223	3.211	5.136	6.381	5.665	6.647	7.865	9.827	14.864	15.418	14.786	14.061	15.272	15.928	15.421
Indonesia	536	1.562	2.729	3.842	4.770	5.673	6.230	6.690	7.202	10.834	13.272	16.859	16.352	13.882	10.259	10.718
Korea	542	2.522	4.240	6.852	7.274	8.774	10.811	14.972	20.339	22.292	26.131	24.251	26.192	30.631	31.136	31.585
Lao People's Dem. Rep.	544	.063	.057	.150	.045	.045	.014	.016	.070	.092	.110	.132	.150	.162	.193	.186
Malaysia	548	1.611	2.450	4.114	3.566	3.824	4.542	5.909	7.849	10.779	11.550	12.418	13.262	14.051	12.253	10.806
Maldives	556	.005	.007	.007	.007	.006	.010	.014	.021	.029	.031	.043	.057	.053	.053	.045
Mongolia	948	....	....	....	....	....	....	....	....	.548	.704	.791	.928	.975	1.096	1.840
Myanmar	518	.133	.106	.176	.197	.177	.241	.307	.319	.353	.373	.409	.268	.239	.283	.304
Nepal	558	.085	.104	.134	.172	.163	.168	.221	.254	.342	.369	.395	.464	.417	.453	.460
Pakistan	564	†.682	.976	1.737	2.168	2.191	2.458	3.301	4.076	5.376	5.658	5.491	5.354	5.881	5.918	5.399
Papua New Guinea	853	.332	.356	.518	.592	.502	.642	.770	.903	1.176	1.261	1.170	1.120	1.110	1.008	1.080
Philippines	566	1.418	1.800	3.471	3.756	3.942	4.270	5.144	6.613	8.291	8.478	8.272	7.976	6.432	5.455	5.261
Samoa	862	.019	.024	.026	.037	.030	†.041	.052	.073	.063	.057	.050	.048	.050	.051	.047
Singapore	576	3.395	5.127	8.380	8.133	9.071	10.471	13.061	17.643	24.007	27.572	28.167	28.158	28.667	26.285	25.511
Solomon Islands	813	.017	.018	.027	.033	.030	.033	.042	.070	.089	.091	.071	.074	.079	.083	.072
Sri Lanka	524	.368	.430	.720	.756	.582	.701	.967	1.451	2.057	1.905	2.015	1.935	1.869	1.988	1.946
Thailand	578	1.484	2.049	3.143	3.280	3.572	4.616	5.356	7.158	9.214	9.955	8.548	10.287	10.398	9.242	9.178
Tonga	866	.009	.011	.017	.017	.014	.020	.026	.029	.038	.040	.042	.038	.041	.041	.041
Vanuatu	846	.029	.036	.050	.040	.034	.040	.051	.062	.073	.058	.060	.064	.069	.070	.057
* of which:																
Taiwan Province of China	528	2.518	3.801	6.983	5.959	7.609	8.522	11.051	14.793	19.764	21.153	18.827	20.308	22.002	20.124	24.230
Europe	170	....	....	....	....	....	....	....	....	....	....	....	....	....	....	....
Albania	914	....	....	....	....	....	....	....	....	....	....	....	....	....	....	....
Armenia	911	....	....	....	....	....	....	....	....	....	....	....	....	....	....	....
Azerbaijan	912	....	....	....	....	....	....	....	....	....	....	....	....	....	....	....
Belarus	913	....	....	....	....	....	....	....	....	....	....	....	....	....	....	....
Bulgaria	918	2.567	3.239	4.326	5.949	6.228	6.329	....	....	....	....	....	....	....	13.657	15.269
Croatia	960	....	....	....	....	....	....	....	....	....	....	....	....	....	....	....
Cyprus	423	.317	.451	.407	.308	.432	.623	.758	1.010	1.202	1.166	1.215	1.219	1.364	1.247	1.271
Czech Republic	935	....	....	....	....	....	....	....	....	....	....	....	....	....	....	....
Czechoslovakia	934				7.050				11.940	12.774	11.894	12.271	12.250	11.852	12.149	14.666
Estonia	939	....	....	....	....	....	....	....	....	....	....	....	....	....	....	....
Georgia	915	....	....	....	....	....	....	....	....	....	....	....	....	....	....	....
Hungary	944	2.356	3.018	4.453	5.400	5.533	6.531	7.990	8.682	9.245	9.139	8.819	8.509	8.091	8.224	9.599
Kazakhstan	916	....	....	....	....	....	....	....	....	....	....	....	....	....	....	....
Kyrgyz Republic	917	....	....	....	....	....	....	....	....	....	....	....	....	....	....	....
Latvia	941	....	....	....	....	....	....	....	....	....	....	....	....	....	....	....
Lithuania	946	....	....	....	....	....	....	....	....	....	....	....	....	....	....	....
Macedonia, FYR	962	....	....	....	....	....	....	....	....	....	....	....	....	....	....	....
Malta	181	.176	.239	.361	.375	.423	.516	.575	.759	.938	.860	.789	.733	.717	.759	.887
Moldova	921	....	....	....	....	....	....	....	....	....	....	....	....	....	....	....
Poland	964			11.155	12.898	13.420	14.744	16.142	16.690	12.792	10.648	10.927	10.985	11.855	11.535	
Romania	968	2.827	3.738	5.555	5.769	6.583	7.579	9.638	11.789	13.843	13.454	10.525	10.414	11.161	11.267	11.437
Russia	922	....	....	....	....	....	....	....	....	....	....	....	....	....	....	....
Slovak Republic	936	....	....	....	....	....	....	....	....	....	....	....	....	....	....	....
Slovenia	961	....	....	....	....	....	....	....	....	....	....	....	....	....	....	....
Turkey	186	1.563	2.086	3.778	4.739	5.129	5.796	4.599	5.070	7.910	8.933	8.843	9.235	10.757	11.343	11.105
Ukraine	926	....	....	....	....	....	....	....	....	....	....	....	....	....	....	....
Yugoslavia, SFR	188	3.233	4.511	7.542	7.697	7.367	9.634	9.989	12.863	15.076	15.727	13.453	12.154	11.996	12.207	11.751
Middle East	405	12.68	18.73	31.44	45.49	53.72	69.92	80.08	86.91	108.50	126.80	142.03	134.92	123.07	104.16	95.13
Bahrain, Kingdom of	419	.376	.512	1.127	1.189	1.668	2.029	2.045	2.480	3.483	4.124	3.614	3.262	3.480	3.107	2.405
Egypt	469	.899	.915	2.351	3.934	3.807	4.815	6.727	3.837	4.860	8.782	9.078	10.275	10.766	11.104	11.502
Iran, I.R. of	429	2.409	3.393	5.433	10.343	12.894	14.070	13.549	9.738	†12.246	14.693	11.955	18.320	15.370	11.635	10.521
Iraq	433	.705	.894	2.371	4.215	3.897	4.481	4.213	5.888	7.477	7.903	21.534	12.166	11.078	10.556	10.190
Israel	436	2.473	4.240	5.437	5.997	5.669	5.787	7.415	8.576	9.784	10.235	9.655	9.574	9.819	9.875	10.806
Jordan	439	.274	.330	.488	.732	1.006	1.381	1.504	1.963	2.402	3.165	3.240	3.036	2.784	2.733	2.432
Kuwait	443	.797	1.049	1.554	2.388	3.327	4.846	4.598	5.201	6.533	6.969	8.285	7.375	6.896	6.005	5.717
Lebanon	446	.924	1.286	2.355	2.048	.612	1.539	1.922	2.700	3.650	3.499	3.391	3.661	2.948	2.203	2.203
Libya	672	1.043	1.806	2.762	3.542	3.212	3.773	4.603	5.311	6.777	8.382	7.175	6.029	6.222	4.101	4.445
Oman	449	.049	.116	.393	.765	.725	.875	.947	1.246	1.732	2.288	2.682	2.492	2.748	3.153	2.402
Qatar	453	.141	.195	.271	.413	.817	1.225	1.185	1.424	1.423	1.518	1.501	1.456	1.162	1.139	1.099
Saudi Arabia	456	1.136	1.972	2.860	4.213	8.695	14.656	20.422	24.462	30.171	35.244	40.645	39.205	33.696	23.622	19.112
Syrian Arab Rep.	463	.540	.613	1.227	1.685	2.383	2.702	2.459	3.329	4.124	5.172	4.028	4.542	4.116	3.967	2.728
United Arab Emirates	466	.482	.821	1.705	2.685	3.337	5.055	5.371	6.966	8.746	9.646	9.440	8.294	6.936	6.549	6.422
Yemen Arab Rep.	473	.080	.123	.190	.294	.413	1.040	1.284	1.492	1.853	1.758	1.521	1.618	1.556	1.313	1.159
Yemen, P.D. Rep.	459	.149	.171	.419	.323	.412	.544	.575	.925	1.527	1.419	1.599	1.483	1.543	....	.483
Yemen, Republic of	474	....	....	....	....	....	....	....	....	....	....	....	....	....	....	....

1987	1988	1989	1990	1991	1992	1993	1994	1995	1996	1997	1998	1999	2000	2001		71 *d*
Billions of US Dollars																
281.01	**363.28**	**413.54**	**465.40**	**532.98**	**603.79**	**677.87**	**792.99**	**973.15**	**1,023.74**	**1,045.34**	**867.23**	**944.46**	**1,159.76**	**1,103.76**	**Asia ***	**505**
.996	.900	.822	.936	.634	.426	.740	.142	.050	....	....	....	....	....	....	Afghanistan, Islamic State of	512
2.715	3.041	3.650	3.618	3.412	3.732	3.994	4.602	6.502	6.621	6.898	6.974	7.694	8.360	8.397	Bangladesh	513
.087	.127	.090	.081	.083	.125	.090	.092	.112	.128	.137	.134	.182	....	....	Bhutan	514
....	....	....	....	....	....	....	....	....	....	1.112	1.080	1.241	1.419	....	Cambodia	522
43.216	55.268	59.140	53.345	63.791	80.585	103.088	115.681	129.113	138.944	142.189	140.305	165.788	206.132	243.521	China, P.R.: Mainland	924
48.465	63.896	72.155	82.490	100.240	123.407	138.650	161.841	192.751	198.550	208.614	184.518	179.520	212.805	201.076	China, P.R.: Hong Kong	532
1.127	1.291	1.484	1.539	1.852	1.968	2.025	2.001	2.042	2.000	2.082	1.955	2.040	2.255	2.386	China, P.R.: Macao	546
.379	.462	.579	.754	.652	.630	.720	.842	.892	.987	.965	.721	....	....	....	Fiji	819
16.675	19.102	20.549	23.580	20.448	23.579	22.788	26.843	34.707	37.942	41.432	42.980	46.979	51.294	49.618	India	534
12.370	13.249	16.360	21.837	25.869	27.280	28.328	31.983	40.630	42.929	41.694	27.337	24.004	33.515	....	Indonesia	536
41.020	51.811	61.465	69.844	81.525	81.775	83.800	102.348	135.119	150.339	144.616	93.282	119.752	160.481	141.098	Korea	542
.216	.149	.194	.185	.170	.270	.432	.564	.589	.690	.706	.553	.525	.535	.551	Lao People's Dem. Rep.	544
12.681	16.506	22.480	29.258	36.648	39.855	45.650	59.600	77.691	78.418	79.030	58.319	64.966	82.199	73.866	Malaysia	548
.081	.090	.113	.138	.161	.189	.191	.222	.268	.302	.349	.354	.402	.389	.395	Maldives	556
1.105	1.114	.963	.924	.361	.418	.379	.258	.415	.451	.468	.503	.426	....	....	Mongolia	948
.268	.244	.191	.270	.646	.651	.814	.886	1.335	1.358	2.037	2.666	2.300	2.371	2.767	Myanmar	518
.571	.678	.582	.672	.737	.776	.890	1.155	1.333	1.398	1.693	1.246	1.422	1.573	1.473	Nepal	558
5.850	6.622	7.177	7.411	8.479	9.423	9.545	8.931	11.515	12.189	11.650	9.330	10.297	11.293	10.191	Pakistan	564
1.165	1.393	1.530	1.193	1.614	1.485	1.299	1.522	1.452	1.741	1.711	1.240	1.233	1.151	1.073	Papua New Guinea	853
7.187	8.731	11.171	13.004	12.861	15.497	18.688	22.641	28.341	34.126	38.622	31.496	32.568	33.808	31.358	Philippines	566
.062	.076	.075	.081	.094	.110	.105	.081	.095	.100	.097	.097	.115	.106	.130	Samoa	862
32.559	43.864	49.656	60.774	66.095	72.171	85.234	102.670	124.507	131.338	132.437	104.719	111.060	134.545	116.000	Singapore	576
.081	.098	.113	.091	.112	.112	.137	.139	.154	.151	....	....	....	....	....	Solomon Islands	813
2.053	2.237	2.215	2.688	3.055	3.500	4.005	4.767	5.306	5.442	5.864	5.905	5.961	7.177	5.925	Sri Lanka	524
13.000	20.285	25.770	33.045	37.569	40.686	46.077	54.459	70.786	72.332	62.854	42.971	50.342	61.924	62.058	Thailand	578
.048	.056	.054	.062	.059	.063	.061	.069	.077	.075	.073	.069	.073	....	....	Tonga	866
.070	.070	.071	.096	.083	.082	.079	.089	.095	.098	.094	.088	.096	....	....	Vanuatu	846
															* *of which:*	
34.802	49.763	52.507	54.830	63.078	72.181	77.099	85.507	103.698	101.287	113.924	104.946	110.957	139.927	107.274	Taiwan Province of China	528
....	....	....	....	....	**173.76**	**185.64**	**218.15**	**292.68**	**337.66**	**357.80**	**351.72**	**312.17**	**359.91**	....	**Europe**	**170**
....	....	....	....	....	.175	.574	.604	.714	.841	.646	.829	1.140	1.091	1.331	Albania	914
....	....	....	....	....	.206	.254	.394	.674	.856	.892	.902	.800	.882	.874	Armenia	911
....	....	....	....	....	.998	.636	.778	.668	.961	.794	1.077	1.036	....	....	Azerbaijan	912
....	....	....	....	....	3.495	2.539	3.066	5.564	6.939	8.689	8.549	6.674	8.646	8.046	Belarus	913
16.169	16.781	15.233	4.710	2.537	4.460	4.720	4.260	5.661	6.861	5.224	4.949	5.453	6.505	7.242	Bulgaria	918
....	....	....	....	....	....	4.666	5.229	7.510	7.788	9.104	8.383	7.799	7.887	8.044	Croatia	960
1.484	1.857	2.282	2.569	2.620	3.313	2.533	3.019	3.694	3.983	3.655	3.685	3.618	3.846	3.938	Cyprus	423
....	....	....	....	....	....	†15.518	†18.260	†26.385	29.366	28.837	30.338	29.482	33.852	....	Czech Republic	935
16.340	15.298	14.988	13.712	10.473	13.207	....	....	....	....	....	....	....	....	....	Czechoslovakia	934
....	....	....	....	....	....	.893	†1.668	2.545	3.224	4.429	4.613	4.094	4.241	4.280	Estonia	939
....	....	....	....	....	....	....	.338	.392	.687	.944	.887	....	....	....	Georgia	915
9.841	9.345	8.709	8.670	11.417	11.106	12.566	14.266	15.380	18.058	21.116	25.679	27.923	31.955	33.725	Hungary	944
....	....	....	....	....	....	3.887	3.561	3.807	4.241	4.301	4.350	3.687	5.051	6.363	Kazakhstan	916
....	....	....	....	....	.418	.430	.316	.522	.838	.709	.842	.600	.554	.468	Kyrgyz Republic	917
....	....	....	....	....	....	.872	1.251	1.818	2.320	2.721	3.191	2.945	3.184	3.504	Latvia	941
....	....	....	....	....	....	2.279	2.353	3.649	4.559	5.644	5.794	4.835	5.457	6.353	Lithuania	946
....	....	....	....	....	....	1.199	1.484	1.719	1.627	1.779	1.915	1.796	2.085	1.688	Macedonia, FYR	962
1.139	1.352	1.480	1.961	2.114	2.349	2.173	2.441	2.944	2.795	2.552	2.668	2.846	3.416	2.592	Malta	181
....	....	....	....	....	.640	.628	.703	.841	1.079	1.200	1.018	....	....	....	Moldova	921
11.215	12.712	10.659	8.413	†15.757	15.701	18.834	21.383	29.050	37.137	42.308	46.495	45.903	48.940	50.275	Poland	964
8.978	8.254	9.122	9.843	5.793	6.260	6.522	7.109	10.278	11.435	11.280	11.821	10.392	13.055	15.561	Romania	968
....	....	....	....	....	36.984	32.806	†55.497	68.863	74.879	79.076	63.817	43.588	49.125	58.992	Russia	922
....	....	....	....	....	....	6.632	6.839	9.225	11.432	10.774	13.725	11.888	13.423	....	Slovak Republic	936
....	....	....	....	4.147	†6.142	6.499	7.304	9.492	9.423	9.357	10.110	9.952	10.107	10.144	Slovenia	961
14.158	14.335	15.792	22.302	21.047	22.871	29.428	23.270	35.709	43.627	48.559	45.921	40.692	53.499	....	Turkey	186
....	....	....	....	....	7.099	9.533	10.748	16.052	18.639	17.114	14.676	11.846	....	....	Ukraine	926
12.632	13.171	14.829	18.871	14.737	....	....	....	....	....	....	....	....	....	....	Yugoslavia, SFR	188
104.63	**117.07**	**115.20**	**122.55**	**128.08**	**137.01**	**135.52**	**129.46**	**144.96**	**157.10**	**162.10**	**159.62**	**162.23**	**183.93**	**198.44**	**Middle East**	**405**
2.714	2.593	3.134	3.712	4.115	4.263	3.858	3.748	3.716	4.273	4.026	3.566	3.698	4.634	4.263	Bahrain, Kingdom of	419
16.225	23.298	18.774	16.783	8.052	8.325	8.214	10.219	11.760	13.038	13.211	16.166	16.022	14.010	12.756	Egypt	469
9.570	9.454	14.794	20.322	27.927	25.860	21.427	13.774	13.882	16.274	14.196	14.323	12.683	14.296	....	Iran, I.R. of	429
7.415	10.268	....	....	....	....	....	....	....	....	....	....	....	....	....	Iraq	433
14.348	15.018	14.347	16.794	18.658	15.535	22.624	25.237	29.579	31.620	30.781	29.342	33.166	31.404	35.465	Israel	436
2.708	2.732	2.125	2.600	2.508	3.255	3.539	3.382	3.698	4.293	4.102	3.828	3.717	4.539	4.844	Jordan	439
5.495	6.145	6.301	3.972	4.761	7.257	7.038	6.697	7.790	8.373	8.246	8.619	7.617	7.157	7.734	Kuwait	443
1.880	2.457	2.235	2.525	3.743	4.202	†2.215	2.598	5.480	7.540	7.467	7.070	6.207	6.230	7.293	Lebanon	446
4.334	5.869	4.923	5.336	5.361	....	....	5.548	5.392	5.873	6.123	5.466	3.861	3.751	....	Libya	672
1.822	2.202	2.257	2.681	3.194	3.769	4.114	3.915	4.248	4.578	5.026	5.682	4.674	5.040	5.811	Oman	449
1.134	1.267	1.326	1.695	1.720	2.015	1.891	1.927	3.398	2.868	3.322	3.409	2.500	....	....	Qatar	453
20.110	21.784	21.154	24.069	29.079	33.271	28.198	23.338	28.091	27.744	28.732	30.013	28.011	30.238	31.223	Saudi Arabia	456
7.112	2.231	2.097	2.400	2.768	3.490	4.140	5.467	4.709	5.380	4.028	3.895	3.832	†16.706	....	Syrian Arab Rep.	463
7.226	8.522	10.010	11.199	13.746	17.410	19.520	21.024	20.984	22.638	29.952	24.728	33.231	38.139	....	United Arab Emirates	466
.883	1.384	....	....	....	....	....	....	....	....	....	....	....	....	....	Yemen Arab Rep.	473
....	....	....	....	....	....	....	....	....	....	....	....	....	....	....	Yemen, P.D. Rep.	459
....	....	....	....	2.025	2.587	2.821	2.087	1.582	2.038	2.014	2.167	2.008	2.324	2.310	Yemen, Republic of	474

		1972	1973	1974	1975	1976	1977	1978	1979	1980	1981	1982	1983	1984	1985	1986
															Billions of US Dollars	
Western Hemisphere	205	21.74	28.59	50.04	53.35	55.83	61.64	69.41	86.30	119.72	128.61	103.90	79.92	81.97	77.97	80.21
Antigua and Barbuda	311	.047	.048	.070	.067	.035	†.034	.041	.063	.088	.111	.139	.109	.132	.166	.207
Argentina	213	1.905	2.230	3.635	3.947	3.033	4.162	3.834	6.700	10.541	9.430	5.337	4.504	4.585	3.814	4.724
Aruba	314	....	....	....	....	....	....	....	....	....	....	....	....	....	....	.192
Bahamas, The	313	.485	.764	1.908	2.697	3.125	3.568	3.150	3.514	7.546	7.284	6.349	4.616	4.098	3.078	3.289
Barbados	316	.141	.168	.204	.217	.237	.273	.314	.425	.525	.576	.554	†.624	†.662	.611	.591
Belize	339	.043	.044	.064	.088	.073	.090	.106	.132	.150	.162	.128	.112	.130	.128	.122
Bolivia	218	.185	.230	.390	.558	.555	.618	.808	.894	.665	.917	.554	.577	.489	.691	.674
Brazil	223	4.783	6.999	14.168	13.592	13.726	13.257	15.054	19.804	24.961	24.079	21.069	16.801	15.210	14.332	15.557
Chile	228	1.086	1.290	2.148	1.525	†1.864	2.539	3.408	4.808	5.797	7.181	3.989	3.085	3.574	3.072	3.436
Colombia	233	.859	1.062	1.597	1.495	1.662	1.880	2.971	3.364	4.739	5.201	5.480	4.963	4.498	4.141	3.862
Costa Rica	238	.373	.455	.720	.694	.770	1.021	1.166	1.397	1.540	1.209	.889	.988	1.094	1.098	1.148
Dominica	321	.017	.016	.019	.021	.019	.022	.028	.022	.048	.050	.047	.045	.058	.055	.056
Dominican Republic	243	.388	.489	.808	.889	.878	.975	.987	1.213	1.640	1.444	1.471	1.471	1.446	1.487	1.433
Ecuador	248	.319	.397	.678	.987	.958	1.189	1.505	1.600	2.253	†2.246	2.169	1.487	1.616	1.767	1.810
El Salvador	253	.272	.377	.562	.614	.735	.929	1.028	1.037	.966	.986	.857	.891	.977	.961	.935
Grenada	328	.022	.022	.018	.024	.025	.032	.036	.044	.050	.054	.056	.057	.056	.069	.081
Guatemala	258	.324	.431	.700	.733	.839	1.053	1.286	1.504	1.598	1.688	1.388	1.126	1.279	1.175	.959
Guyana	336	.143	.177	.255	.344	.364	.314	.279	.318	.396	.428	.281	.246	.211	.226	.241
Haiti	263	.069	.083	.125	.149	.207	.213	.233	.272	.375	.461	.387	.441	.450	.442	.360
Honduras	268	.193	.262	.382	.400	.456	.575	.693	.826	1.009	.949	.701	.803	.893	.888	.875
Jamaica	343	.638	.677	.936	1.124	.913	.860	.904	.993	1.171	1.473	1.381	1.494	1.146	1.111	.972
Mexico	273	2.718	3.814	6.057	6.580	6.028	5.489	8.109	12.086	†22.144	28.462	17.742	12.476	16.691	19.116	17.573
Netherlands Antilles	353	.870	1.593	3.631	2.827	3.667	3.128	3.491	4.395	5.676	5.862	5.087	4.527	4.032	1.388	†1.112
Nicaragua	278	.218	.327	.562	.517	.532	.762	.596	.360	.887	.999	.776	.826	.848	.964	.857
Panama	283	.440	.502	.822	.892	.848	.861	.942	1.184	1.449	1.540	1.570	1.412	1.423	1.392	1.229
Paraguay	288	.083	.122	.198	.206	.220	.308	.383	.521	.615	.600	.672	.546	.586	.502	.578
Peru	293	.796	1.019	1.531	†2.550	2.037	1.911	1.175	1.820	2.499	3.482	3.601	2.548	2.212	1.835	2.909
St. Kitts and Nevis	361	.016	.018	.019	.024	.022	.022	.024	.032	.045	.048	.044	.051	.052	.051	.063
St. Lucia	362	.036	.038	.044	.046	.048	.059	.083	.101	.124	.129	.118	.144	.119	.125	.155
St. Vincent & Grens.	364	.018	.019	.025	.025	.024	.030	.036	.047	.057	.058	.065	.070	.077	.079	.087
Suriname	366	.145	.157	.230	.252	.294	.398	.406	†.411	.504	.568	.511	.453	.346	.299	.327
Trinidad and Tobago	369	.766	.797	1.846	1.469	2.010	1.819	1.967	2.105	3.178	3.125	3.697	2.582	1.919	1.534	1.350
Uruguay	298	.212	.285	.487	.556	.587	.730	.757	1.206	1.680	1.641	1.110	.788	.777	.708	.870
Venezuela	299	2.463	2.812	4.148	6.000	7.663	10.938	11.767	10.670	11.827	13.106	12.944	6.419	7.774	8.106	8.504

Memorandum Items

Euro Area	163	....	....	....	....	....	....	....	....	....	....	....	....	....	....	....
Oil Exporting Countries	999	13.79	19.89	32.15	50.87	63.53	84.37	94.71	96.73	124.99	145.20	160.28	140.76	125.42	103.84	92.39
Non-Oil Developing Countries	201	86.19	120.02	192.21	218.83	218.60	246.43	286.05	369.55	484.21	515.57	460.41	444.45	466.88	482.85	502.24

1987	1988	1989	1990	1991	1992	1993	1994	1995	1996	1997	1998	1999	2000	2001		
Billions of US Dollars																
90.83	103.08	112.47	125.19	144.87	173.48	189.39	221.86	250.58	279.12	332.71	349.72	337.35	390.50	....	Western Hemisphere	205
.247	.250	.192	.255	.295	.312	.323	.342	.346	.365	.370	.385	.414	....	....	Antigua and Barbuda	311
5.818	5.322	4.203	4.076	8.275	14.872	16.784	21.527	20.122	23.762	30.450	31.404	25.508	25.243	20.311	Argentina................	213
.236	.336	.387	.536	.481	....	....	....	.567	.578	.614	.815	.782	....	....	Aruba..................	314
3.080	2.291	3.137	†1.112	1.091	1.038	.954	1.056	1.243	1.366	1.666	1.873	1.911	1.421	1.891	Bahamas, The...........	313
.518	.582	.677	.704	.699	.524	.577	.614	.771	.834	.996	1.010	1.108	1.156	1.087	Barbados..............	316
.143	.181	.216	.211	.256	.274	.281	.260	.257	.255	.286	.325	.366	.450	.409	Belize................	339
.766	.591	.611	.687	.970	1.090	1.206	1.209	1.424	1.635	1.851	1.983	1.755	1.830	1.724	Bolivia................	218
16.581	16.055	19.875	22.524	22.950	23.068	27.740	35.997	53.783	56.947	64.995	60.631	51.675	58.532	....	Brazil.................	223
4.396	5.292	7.233	7.742	8.207	10.183	11.134	11.820	15.900	19.123	20.825	19.880	15.988	18.507	17.814	Chile.................	228
4.322	5.002	5.004	5.590	4.906	6.516	9.832	11.883	13.853	13.684	15.378	14.635	10.659	11.539	12.834	Colombia.............	233
1.383	1.410	1.717	1.990	1.877	2.441	3.515	3.789	4.036	4.300	4.924	6.230	6.320	6.372	6.564	Costa Rica............	238
.066	.088	.107	.118	.110	.105	.094	.096	.117	.130	.125	.136	.141	.147	....	Dominica..............	321
1.830	1.849	2.258	2.062	1.988	2.501	2.436	3.440	3.639	4.118	4.821	5.631	5.988	7.379	....	Dominican Republic	243
2.252	1.714	1.855	1.865	2.399	2.431	2.562	3.622	4.153	3.935	4.955	5.576	3.017	3.721	5.363	Ecuador	248
.994	1.007	1.161	1.263	1.406	1.699	1.912	2.249	2.853	2.671	2.981	3.121	3.140	3.795	3.866	El Salvador	253
.089	.092	.099	.106	.124	.107	.118	.119	.124	.152	.173	.200	....	....	....	Grenada...............	328
1.447	1.557	1.654	1.649	1.851	2.532	2.599	2.781	3.293	3.146	3.852	4.651	4.382	4.791	5.607	Guatemala	258
.265	.216	.258	.311	.307	.443	.484	.506	.528	.598	.630	....	....	....	.584	Guyana...............	336
.399	.344	.291	.332	.400	.278	.355	.252	.653	.665	.648	.797	1.025	1.036	1.013	Haiti.................	263
.827	.940	.969	.935	.955	1.037	1.130	1.056	1.643	1.840	2.149	2.535	2.676	2.855	2.918	Honduras	268
1.238	1.454	1.852	1.928	1.823	1.676	2.132	2.224	2.818	2.965	3.131	3.035	2.899	3.216	3.331	Jamaica	343
19.696	29.402	36.400	43.548	52.315	65.049	68.439	83.075	75.858	93.674	114.847	130.948	148.648	182.702	....	Mexico...............	273
1.502	1.403	1.610	2.141	2.139	1.868	1.947	1.758	....	....	....	....	....	....	....	Netherlands Antilles	353
.827	.805	.615	.638	.751	.855	.744	.870	.993	1.154	1.450	1.492	1.862	1.759	1.776	Nicaragua	278
1.306	.751	.986	1.539	1.695	2.024	2.188	2.404	2.511	2.780	3.002	3.398	3.516	3.379	2.964	Panama	283
.595	.574	.760	1.352	1.460	1.422	1.689	2.140	2.782	2.850	3.099	2.471	1.725	....	....	Paraguay	288
3.562	3.348	2.749	3.470	4.195	4.861	4.859	6.691	9.224	9.473	10.264	9.867	8.075	8.797	....	Peru	293
.079	.093	.102	.110	.110	.095	.118	.128	.133	.149	....	....	....	....	....	St. Kitts and Nevis	361
.179	.220	.274	.271	.295	.313	.300	.302	.306	.304	.332	.335	....	....	....	St. Lucia	362
.099	.122	.127	.136	.140	.132	.134	.130	.136	.132	.188	.193	.201	.163	.186	St. Vincent & Grens. ...	364
.294	.351	.443	.472	.509	.542	.986	.423	.585	.501	.658	.552	.298	.246	....	Suriname..............	366
1.219	1.127	1.221	1.109	1.667	1.104	1.463	1.131	1.714	2.144	2.990	2.999	2.741	3.308	....	Trinidad and Tobago	369
1.142	1.157	1.203	1.343	1.637	2.045	2.326	2.786	2.867	3.323	3.727	3.811	3.357	3.466	3.061	Uruguay	298
†9.659	12.726	7.803	7.335	11.147	14.066	12.511	9.187	12.650	9.880	14.606	15.818	14.064	16.213	18.022	Venezuela	299
															Memorandum Items	
....	....	....	....	....	....	....	....	....	....	....	794.40	†830.50	911.42	898.96	Euro Area..............	163
90.09	103.89	108.48	120.38	139.98	153.52	142.25	133.88	156.19	157.00	170.97	155.35	149.41	173.10	192.24	Oil Exporting Countries	999
591.90	703.99	765.91	835.02	908.10	1,009.75	1,119.22	1,308.01	1,601.14	1,733.10	1,823.58	1,664.39	1,700.12	2,023.12	1,970.44	Non-Oil Developing Countries	201

Export Unit Values/Export Prices

74 *d*		1972	1973	1974	1975	1976	1977	1978	1979	1980	1981	1982	1983	1984	1985	1986
											Indices of Unit Values (Prices) In Terms of US Dollars:					
World	**001**	**25.3**	**31.0**	**43.2**	**46.4**	**47.0**	**51.6**	**55.9**	**67.2**	**80.0**	**80.4**	**77.0**	**73.7**	**72.2**	**70.8**	**76.2**
Industrial Countries	**110**	**27.5**	**33.3**	**41.9**	**45.9**	**45.8**	**49.5**	**55.9**	**64.6**	**73.0**	**71.5**	**69.1**	**66.9**	**65.1**	**64.8**	**73.5**
United States	111	29.2	34.0	43.4	48.6	50.2	52.0	55.6	63.2	71.8	78.4	79.3	80.1	81.2	80.6	81.4
Canada	156	29.8	34.1	47.6	50.9	54.6	55.2	56.3	68.1	85.2	88.7	86.9	87.0	86.2	82.6	79.6
Australia	193	36.4	55.8	66.1	63.1	64.3	65.5	70.0	82.7	96.5	99.0	91.4	87.3	85.3	76.3	73.9
Japan	158	23.2	27.4	34.3	34.5	34.4	38.0	45.8	48.0	51.7	54.8	51.0	49.9	49.8	49.2	59.0
New Zealand	196	32.6	47.4	47.7	40.6	44.4	49.8	56.5	67.6	74.4	74.9	71.5	67.3	64.8	61.4	63.3
Euro Area																
Belgium	124	....	....	....	....	....	....	....	....	....	....	....	....	....	....	....
Belgium-Luxembourg	126	28.0	34.1	42.5	46.7	47.0	51.6	58.5	69.0	76.2	65.3	60.6	58.2	55.6	55.5	68.2
Finland	172	21.3	31.0	41.7	47.3	47.1	48.6	50.4	59.4	69.0	60.5	61.0	55.5	55.4	54.8	64.0
France	132	....	....	....	....	....	....	....	....	....	....	....	....	....	....	....
Germany	134	25.7	32.2	38.8	44.2	42.1	46.8	54.7	63.1	69.7	59.6	57.9	55.7	51.7	52.0	68.2
Greece	174	28.1	41.7	48.6	46.9	48.7	58.1	61.1	76.2	83.7	80.5	72.2	65.5	66.4	66.2	71.2
Ireland	178	30.5	38.1	42.5	47.7	47.9	53.6	61.7	72.0	80.4	72.2	70.9	67.4	64.1	65.1	76.8
Italy	136	26.1	30.9	39.3	43.5	41.6	46.8	52.2	62.5	73.2	67.9	65.8	63.0	59.6	59.3	72.4
Netherlands	138	25.9	31.8	42.4	47.3	47.9	53.1	59.1	69.3	79.4	73.3	70.8	66.2	63.4	62.5	72.1
Portugal (1990=100)	182	....	....	....	....	....	....	....	....	....	....	....	63.2	62.5	62.0	73.0
Spain	184	32.9	41.2	51.2	55.3	50.2	52.0	57.8	72.3	80.5	69.2	64.9	58.1	58.3	58.9	68.8
Denmark	128	26.5	34.2	40.2	46.8	47.7	51.4	58.1	66.1	70.1	63.3	60.3	57.1	54.2	54.8	69.7
Iceland	176	22.7	31.9	38.5	35.2	39.8	46.6	50.8	56.4	60.9	60.9	56.6	53.2	50.1	50.9	63.2
Norway	142	31.9	40.0	54.6	62.9	61.8	67.5	72.5	88.0	117.5	117.3	111.5	102.0	100.2	98.9	86.3
Sweden	144	26.4	33.1	42.7	49.5	49.8	50.9	53.6	63.1	72.0	65.3	58.9	54.0	54.0	54.1	65.7
Switzerland	146	....	....	....	....	....	....	....	....	....	....	....	....	....	....	....
United Kingdom	112	26.1	28.7	34.8	40.5	39.4	45.3	54.6	66.7	83.5	78.6	72.9	68.5	64.8	65.9	67.8
Developing Countries	**200**	**20.5**	**26.6**	**50.8**	**51.8**	**54.6**	**61.9**	**60.7**	**81.8**	**110.3**	**116.9**	**110.2**	**102.2**	**101.9**	**95.7**	**86.0**
Africa	**605**	**18.3**	**24.6**	**40.4**	**41.3**	**42.7**	**48.7**	**49.3**	**62.0**	**83.9**	**90.6**	**74.4**	**70.8**	**70.0**	**63.2**	**72.2**
Burkina Faso	748	56.4	70.2	95.6	108.3	125.0	136.4	141.4	153.6	168.6	144.6	137.7	135.2	121.3	138.6	126.6
Côte d'Ivoire (1985=100)	662	34.8	50.6	60.2	61.1	73.0	112.4	105.9	120.6	134.3	94.3	82.5	81.1	92.8	100.0	108.9
Ethiopia (1990=100)	644	46.3	58.6	63.2	56.6	100.4	101.8	101.2	110.0	101.2	....	....	107.3	110.4	110.1	146.0
Kenya	664	33.6	39.3	51.0	57.1	67.7	97.3	88.0	97.1	117.6	105.8	96.3	94.8	105.1	90.9	98.5
Liberia (1985=100)	668	42.8	47.5	62.5	81.8	84.2	98.1	88.3	103.9	121.1	100.6	109.1	101.9	100.5	100.0	98.2
Malawi (1985=100)	676	59.7	65.2	80.6	92.0	97.3	129.7	124.9	116.2	120.9	153.5	142.8	131.0	134.7	100.0	103.3
Mauritius	684	19.7	22.6	53.5	66.7	49.3	48.9	51.4	56.7	64.2	59.7	54.3	54.0	51.0	52.0	63.1
Morocco	686	36.3	43.8	85.0	98.7	70.9	65.4	75.2	94.8	117.2	106.9	95.8	86.4	86.4	84.9	92.3
Rwanda	714	33.7	43.8	47.5	42.5	80.2	134.8	98.7	90.4	75.5	95.5	†101.3	123.3	130.4	117.8	144.4
Senegal (1985=100)	722	37.6	50.3	88.6	84.2	73.7	86.1	101.2	114.9	113.2	120.7	96.6	92.8	103.1	100.0	90.9
South Africa	199	29.0	38.5	49.5	51.5	51.0	55.1	59.4	69.8	86.7	85.1	74.6	81.4	69.7	58.3	65.6
Tunisia (1990=100)	744	18.4	26.6	53.7	58.8	48.8	50.5	56.1	79.0	105.1	108.0	98.9	89.2	85.1	79.6	75.0
Asia	**505**	**26.7**	**35.3**	**51.5**	**50.0**	**51.8**	**58.4**	**61.5**	**74.3**	**87.7**	**87.7**	**83.9**	**79.6**	**82.4**	**77.2**	**72.1**
Bangladesh (1990=100)	513	....	....	....	....	....	....	95.8	112.8	131.4	99.2	88.2	89.9	117.3	†130.6	93.8
China, P.R.: Hong Kong	532	34.6	44.9	55.0	55.1	60.1	65.1	69.7	76.1	83.8	81.1	79.9	73.6	77.3	78.0	79.5
Fiji (1985=100)	819	47.3	59.0	96.0	127.4	101.4	107.7	126.0	126.4	173.7	146.3	131.3	127.3	118.3	100.0	136.7
India	534	40.6	44.1	51.3	62.4	62.8	68.2	81.8	82.5	89.5	84.3	87.9	87.6	89.0	91.5	90.8
Indonesia	536	18.6	27.0	59.0	62.4	65.6	73.2	74.2	104.3	152.4	152.6	148.9	132.1	130.6	112.4	74.8
Korea	542	30.8	38.9	49.3	45.7	51.1	55.9	61.9	74.0	77.3	79.7	77.0	†74.1	76.7	73.8	75.3
Malaysia	548	22.9	34.4	62.7	58.7	56.3	69.0	71.6	94.0	111.9	107.8	97.9	93.7	103.9	87.7	55.9
Pakistan	564	26.7	40.5	52.9	46.7	50.9	60.9	69.5	80.5	85.9	89.1	81.7	79.2	82.4	72.5	84.2
Papua New Guinea	853	....	38.2	59.2	39.9	47.2	62.8	62.0	83.5	92.1	71.7	64.6	66.5	68.4	63.3	64.3
Philippines	566	....	....	....	....	....	....	....	....	....	....	....	....	....	....	....
Singapore	576	....	....	....	....	....	....	....	82.0	102.7	107.9	103.3	99.7	94.9	90.2	78.3
Solomon Islands (1990=100)	813	58.0	83.7	157.3	93.5	136.6	181.2	177.2	256.3	288.0	220.2	201.6	174.2	235.1	191.4	114.5
Sri Lanka	524	26.7	29.2	43.6	38.7	37.8	58.0	60.0	65.5	68.9	64.3	58.1	65.9	77.7	64.6	55.8
Thailand	578	26.4	41.8	62.6	55.2	53.7	54.8	59.4	70.7	83.3	80.5	71.0	72.1	69.5	62.1	65.9
Europe	**170**	**186.8**	**226.6**	**279.2**	**294.7**	**291.0**	**335.7**	**250.6**	**280.1**	**310.7**	**317.4**	**312.1**	**306.0**	**273.9**	**258.1**	**281.5**
Cyprus (1985=100)	423	64.7	81.4	89.5	104.5	99.8	101.0	110.5	124.8	136.1	134.1	116.6	110.3	105.9	100.0	110.1
Czechoslovakia (1990=100)	934	....	40.5	46.4	50.9	50.7	74.4	79.1	88.0	97.0	112.1	109.8	107.7	91.6	90.3	103.5
Hungary (1990=100)	944	55.6	67.2	77.5	84.8	85.6	89.9	96.5	107.1	115.6	113.7	107.6	97.3	90.4	89.2	98.7
Latvia	941	....	....	....	....	....	....	....	....	....	....	....	....	....	....	....
Malta (1985=100)	181	55.0	62.8	76.3	81.3	82.0	85.6	102.0	118.5	128.3	122.9	118.8	106.3	101.4	100.0	122.3
Poland	964	....	....	....	1,369.9	1,297.6	1,332.9	109.6	120.2	126.4	118.5	114.4	107.1	97.9	94.2	94.4
Turkey	186	37.2	†46.3	63.0	59.5	61.8	67.7	71.8	84.5	100.0	88.6	82.9	73.2	74.4	....	....
Middle East	**405**	**9.4**	**12.8**	**43.0**	**44.7**	**47.7**	**52.0**	**52.9**	**97.5**	**159.1**	**179.4**	**175.0**	**152.7**	**149.2**	**147.6**	**86.8**
Iran, I.R. of (1985=100)	429	7.4	9.9	36.3	38.9	41.4	45.6	45.6	68.9	121.9	130.0	109.2	101.2	99.3	100.0	48.9
Iraq (1985=100)	433	7.3	9.8	35.6	38.1	40.7	44.7	44.6	65.9	107.2	125.5	118.4	104.4	100.7	100.0	54.0
Israel	436	†24.3	30.3	35.4	37.0	†37.6	44.5	†58.8	†67.6	†76.1	†73.5	69.5	†67.8	†66.6	65.9	68.1
Jordan	439	28.4	31.2	64.7	73.9	66.2	66.7	69.2	70.9	85.0	87.9	90.0	79.9	82.2	77.7	75.4
Kuwait (1985=100)	443	7.0	9.7	38.4	38.8	41.2	45.3	44.8	67.7	109.2	128.4	118.2	101.8	99.9	100.0	73.5
Libya (1985=100)	672	10.2	14.5	43.3	38.8	41.0	46.0	45.5	70.0	119.5	132.8	117.8	102.5	100.0	100.0	....
Oman	449	13.6	18.6	65.2	68.6	71.0	78.5	79.3	121.8	196.5	223.2	210.5	185.0	174.5	164.7	82.0
Qatar (1985=100)	453	7.4	10.1	36.4	38.4	40.3	44.9	44.9	67.2	108.6	127.1	118.7	102.6	100.9	100.0	....
Saudi Arabia	456	....	9.8	34.9	37.5	40.2	43.0	44.1	104.0	173.4	195.6	199.8	173.4	169.1	165.7	118.3
Syrian Arab Rep.	463	68.4	85.5	164.5	141.3	173.0	183.1	196.4	256.4	332.9	369.6	323.0	303.0	309.6	303.0	223.1
United Arab Emirates (1985=100)	466	7.8	10.9	38.7	39.4	42.2	45.6	46.9	70.1	111.7	128.9	123.1	107.6	104.6	100.0	49.3
Western Hemisphere	**205**	**41.6**	**48.2**	**62.1**	**59.5**	**68.9**	**88.1**	**84.3**	**93.4**	**112.8**	**108.6**	**97.0**	**108.2**	**106.3**	**91.1**	**87.7**
Argentina	213	....	....	....	....	....	....	....	....	....	....	....	....	....	....	....
Bolivia	218	17.8	49.5	81.8	82.9	88.9	102.0	110.8	144.4	206.0	196.3	186.3	196.7	193.8	178.5	143.7
Brazil	223	37.7	41.8	43.7	40.3	48.8	63.9	62.4	67.1	79.7	81.1	72.6	79.6	82.3	75.6	72.1
Colombia	233	39.4	49.6	66.5	65.7	96.2	141.4	118.1	116.5	129.9	116.2	115.3	115.6	123.5	115.4	130.7
Costa Rica (1990=100)	238	681.0	766.1	770.5	810.3	916.3	1,171.0	1,092.7	1,144.9	1,292.2	465.5	265.0	238.8	224.3	197.4	200.4
Dominican Republic	243	40.2	48.4	66.6	84.3	78.0	101.6	90.2	97.7	100.2	110.4	78.8	77.4	90.9	82.5	82.4
Ecuador	248	26.5	31.1	67.2	69.2	73.0	82.1	78.1	122.6	170.8	166.6	159.1	139.2	132.7	140.6	88.9
Guatemala (1990=100)	258	....	....	....	....	....	....	....	....	....	....	....	....	....	....	....
Guyana	336	1,658.4	53.0	94.0	117.6	109.9	126.8	114.2	125.1	163.2	5,194.9	4,870.2	4,458.5	136.9	121.5	117.0
Honduras	268	....	....	....	45.4	56.3	81.4	74.1	70.9	84.4	76.5	74.0	74.6	79.0	81.2	97.2
Panama (1990=100)	283	76.8	79.4	88.7	100.2	98.5	91.2	90.2	96.6	104.3	104.5	96.9	104.8	104.5	102.6	94.0
Paraguay (1985=100)	288	109.3	137.0	965.6	1,082.8	534.0	854.1	850.1	1,622.6	2,514.1	1,448.6	1,897.4	978.8	1,056.8	100.0	67.2
Peru	293	28.0	41.9	111.0	†61.7	67.3	74.5	75.3	128.8	174.0	150.7	131.8	130.3	121.2	107.5	74.6
Suriname (1985=100)	366	45.2	44.9	61.3	82.6	89.2	99.3	107.4	118.4	143.7	157.3	152.4	138.7	129.4	100.0	97.9
Trinidad and Tobago (1990=100)	369	14.1	18.1	46.2	50.5	52.0	57.5	57.5	76.0	121.4	133.9	128.2	127.3	126.5	118.3	78.4
Memorandum Items																
Oil Exporting Countries	**999**	**10.0**	**13.9**	**46.4**	**48.6**	**51.7**	**56.6**	**56.9**	**101.8**	**167.3**	**186.8**	**181.1**	**157.5**	**154.0**	**148.3**	**84.1**
Non-Oil Developing Countries	**201**	**39.1**	**48.7**	**64.2**	**63.7**	**66.5**	**78.0**	**74.1**	**85.5**	**98.6**	**99.4**	**91.0**	**91.6**	**91.9**	**85.5**	**85.6**

1987	1988	1989	1990	1991	1992	1993	1994	1995	1996	1997	1998	1999	2000	2001		
1995=100																
84.3	89.1	90.7	97.4	95.5	97.9	89.7	91.2	100.0	98.3	92.1	86.6	85.8	85.8	....	World	001
81.8	87.1	87.5	95.1	94.3	97.0	87.7	90.4	100.0	98.2	91.3	87.8	85.7	83.4	81.6	Industrial Countries	110
82.8	88.6	91.0	91.8	92.6	92.7	93.2	95.2	100.0	100.5	99.2	95.9	94.7	96.2	95.4	United States	111
84.8	91.9	97.8	98.5	96.8	93.9	92.0	93.0	100.0	101.3	99.3	92.3	93.0	100.6	96.5	Canada	156
80.5	100.4	107.2	106.8	97.4	93.7	87.9	91.9	100.0	101.2	97.7	86.7	82.7	81.1	73.8	Australia	193
64.6	70.2	69.7	69.1	74.0	78.7	86.0	92.6	100.0	92.5	86.5	80.5	85.2	89.2	83.6	Japan	158
75.7	89.2	92.1	90.7	84.0	84.6	87.3	91.9	100.0	101.1	94.7	80.3	80.6	81.2	....	New Zealand	196
															Euro Area	
						82.9	86.6	100.0	97.8	89.1	87.9	83.6	79.6	78.8	Belgium	124
77.3	80.7	81.2	92.8	89.1	93.3	85.8	88.1	100.0	97.1	87.7	....				Belgium-Luxembourg	126
75.2	82.8	85.6	95.8	89.2	84.3	70.4	78.1	100.0	95.8	83.1	80.7	73.8	68.9	66.5	Finland	172
			91.0	88.7	93.8	86.1	†87.9	100.0	98.1	87.5	85.9	81.6	71.7		France	132
80.2	82.7	80.8	93.0	90.0	94.9	85.6	86.4	100.0	93.2	81.1	79.5	75.1	67.3	66.6	Germany	134
79.2	86.4	86.2	93.0	89.6	91.2	84.4	86.6	100.0	101.7	92.2	87.8	84.8	81.1	80.7	Greece	174
84.8	93.1	92.4	97.6	94.3	97.0	90.5	91.6	100.0	99.2	95.1	91.7	91.8	83.5	82.0	Ireland	178
84.1	88.1	88.9	103.9	103.3	104.8	91.4	92.4	100.0	110.1	100.3	99.3	94.6	86.3	87.4	Italy	136
79.0	80.9	81.3	93.8	89.9	92.3	84.6	86.7	100.0	95.5	87.6	83.4	77.9	76.9	77.5	Netherlands	138
84.0	90.7	87.9	100.0	98.9	103.6										Portugal (1990=100)	182
80.1	89.4	92.0	104.8	101.9	104.4	88.1	87.4	100.0	99.5	88.8	87.1	82.6	75.8	75.6	Spain	184
80.9	81.9	80.2	93.2	90.3	93.4	85.1	87.7	100.0	98.2	87.8	85.8	83.1	78.4	....	Denmark	128
76.7	78.3	72.8	87.3	99.8	99.3	87.4	88.2	100.0	95.8	90.9	....				Iceland	176
91.5	94.8	100.3	115.5	106.8	102.4	89.7	87.1	100.0	106.1	98.7	81.9	88.4	111.2	106.9	Norway	142
76.6	83.3	85.2	95.5	94.1	95.6	78.3	83.0	100.0	101.1	89.6	85.7	81.6	....		Sweden	144
....	†75.1	71.5	85.0	84.7	86.6	82.4	88.3	100.0	96.6	85.3	84.5	82.7	76.0	77.6	Switzerland	146
78.6	85.9	82.5	92.8	93.2	94.4	90.6	94.2	100.0	99.9	99.2	95.1	92.1	89.2	85.0	United Kingdom	112
92.7	95.3	102.0	104.9	98.2	99.2	96.2	93.7	100.0	98.8	94.7	82.8	86.4	93.5	....	Developing Countries	200
81.5	85.0	81.1	90.7	89.6	90.6	83.9	83.8	100.0	95.6	92.9	87.1	....	....	....	Africa	605
															Burkina Faso	748
151.1	147.8	128.3	165.5	156.1	127.0	114.1	76.3	100.0	95.4	....					Côte d'Ivoire (1985=100)	662
103.2	....														Ethiopia (1990=100)	644
106.9	111.5	107.9	100.0	105.4											Kenya	664
80.5	85.9	79.8	77.6	82.6	79.7	79.4	84.4	100.0	95.6	108.9	107.1	86.1	85.6		Liberia (1985=100)	668
93.6	....														Malawi (1985=100)	676
114.1	118.2	128.5	....												Mauritius	684
73.8	75.2	79.0	84.9	85.8	92.3	88.7	91.2	100.0	107.7	94.8	94.2				Morocco	686
95.9	118.5	93.4	99.8	94.1	91.9	84.4	83.6	100.0	103.5	95.5	92.3	90.9			Rwanda	714
76.5	....	80.5	73.1	66.2	50.0	56.8	36.9	100.0	79.8	122.1	78.3	....			Senegal (1985=100)	722
99.6	....														South Africa	199
76.5	78.8	82.0	87.3	86.3	88.0	84.3	87.3	100.0	93.1	91.3	84.1	....			Tunisia (1990=100)	744
81.9	84.6	87.0	100.0	92.6	94.6	84.2	87.5	....							Asia	505
77.8	84.4	88.2	90.1	90.5	91.5	90.7	93.0	100.0	98.0	94.1	83.0	81.9	82.4	....		
															Bangladesh (1990=100)	513
92.7	105.5	101.9	100.0	98.9	....										China, P.R.: Hong Kong	532
82.5	85.0	89.4	91.9	94.5	95.8	95.5	96.9	100.0	99.8	98.1	94.4	91.6	91.1	88.9	Fiji (1985=100)	819
170.2	141.5	136.5	....												India	534
92.5	111.7	114.4	112.2	109.0	109.1	104.1	105.7	100.0	95.5	108.7	99.4	94.0	93.0	....	Indonesia	536
73.4	69.9	74.2	†90.3	91.0	90.3	88.3	87.6	100.0	105.8	100.5	78.4	....			Korea	542
82.9	†94.2	95.9	94.1	94.7	†93.2	93.6	95.2	100.0	86.8	73.2	61.0	61.5	61.8		Malaysia	548
67.5	71.7	70.6	71.9	72.5	76.9	79.7	85.4	100.0	96.1	91.3	....				Pakistan	564
88.5	86.8	82.2	85.2	80.5	78.4	76.3	82.2	100.0	97.1	97.7	99.3	93.3	86.7	79.4	Papua New Guinea	853
75.1	91.3	77.3	72.6	72.2	72.5	80.0	90.2	100.0	95.7	97.2	77.3	....			Philippines	566
			108.6	98.0	98.8	93.7	96.6	100.0	104.0	96.0	74.8	86.0	71.6	59.3	Singapore	576
83.7	86.4	†88.8	96.0	95.3	94.4	93.0	94.4	100.0	99.6	93.2	†81.1	80.2	83.4	77.2	Solomon Islands (1990=100)	813
107.1	114.0	102.0	100.0	98.6	88.8										Sri Lanka	524
61.6	66.6	69.3	75.7	74.7	88.5	88.1	90.3	100.0	103.5	105.9	111.4	101.4	101.6	94.3	Thailand	578
72.2	79.5	80.5	82.6	85.6	87.4	88.5	91.5	100.0	108.9	104.9	91.2	87.7	85.9	84.7		
294.3	214.1	273.4	223.9	207.1	192.7	170.7	108.2	100.0	86.4	76.7	72.3	67.6	65.0	64.2	Europe	170
121.4	....														Cyprus (1985=100)	423
113.4	110.9	111.9	100.0	57.9	....										Czechoslovakia (1990=100)	934
99.3	98.6	97.2	100.0	110.5	114.1	109.1	114.8	125.8	123.5	115.9	114.0	107.0	98.8	99.5	Hungary (1990=100)	944
						58.4	81.2	100.0	101.7	98.0	96.4	93.6	89.2	88.4	Latvia	941
145.8	168.5	167.4	....												Malta (1985=100)	181
91.1	95.4	92.3	85.9	91.6	90.7	85.7	88.0	100.0	97.1	90.3	91.5	85.8	79.6	81.2	Poland	964
....	....	1,836.0	1,647.1	1,020.6	627.7	381.8	137.4	100.0	53.8	27.5	15.4	8.9	....		Turkey	186
97.2	82.8	93.4	113.6	99.4	100.9	91.1	91.4	100.0	113.0	107.5	78.1	101.9	142.5	125.9	Middle East	405
64.4	55.1	58.4	....												Iran, I.R. of (1985=100)	429
59.8	49.2	....													Iraq (1985=100)	433
72.5	82.7	88.0	†95.3	95.7	96.4	96.8	95.4	100.0	†99.9	99.1	96.1	97.3	97.3	93.9	Israel	436
72.4	76.2	77.5	79.9	86.7	83.6	82.9	86.1	100.0	105.1	102.0	96.3	93.9	89.9	91.0	Jordan	439
60.8	46.7	....													Kuwait (1985=100)	443
															Libya (1985=100)	672
105.3	82.5	....	....		109.8	95.2	92.8	100.0	118.5	113.6	72.7	105.8	163.0	140.3	Oman	449
															Qatar (1985=100)	453
103.9	83.9	96.3	121.9	98.9	103.6	89.9	90.4	100.0	118.1	111.8	72.1	104.6	160.5	138.9	Saudi Arabia	456
206.5	89.5	85.6	111.1	90.0	75.6	74.4	80.0	100.0	105.6	83.3	....				Syrian Arab Rep.	463
62.7	48.7	....													United Arab Emirates (1985=100)	466
89.7	120.2	129.9	127.4	87.1	92.0	87.1	93.2	100.0	105.5	104.7	92.7	109.5	115.2	107.2	Western Hemisphere	205
			89.2	88.5	91.7	91.9	94.6	100.0	106.5	102.5	92.9	....			Argentina	213
135.3	135.6	157.9	143.0	127.7	108.3	89.3	94.8	100.0	98.5	75.2	67.3	66.1	83.3	78.6	Bolivia	218
79.5	85.2	83.8	80.8	81.5	92.4	91.3	96.3	100.0	103.4	109.5	95.9	90.7	97.2	92.2	Brazil	223
100.4	104.9	85.6	89.0	82.7	69.5	69.2	92.2	100.0	93.4	103.0	91.8	85.5	89.6	79.8	Colombia	233
151.0	128.7	116.9	100.0	77.9	71.1	68.7	....								Costa Rica (1990=100)	238
70.6	107.3	116.2	101.3	91.1	89.9	68.8	88.1	100.0	100.7	104.9	82.1	....			Dominican Republic	243
99.6	86.5	101.3	116.2	108.8	108.0	88.9	98.9	100.0	115.0	112.3	84.0	101.5	131.3	113.7	Ecuador	248
168.6	165.0	154.2	100.0	70.6	67.0	67.6	68.7	....							Guatemala (1990=100)	258
122.7	127.4	120.8	128.3	161.0	134.7	103.4	101.7	100.0	168.4	97.5	92.0	....			Guyana	336
88.2	93.7	94.0	94.4	92.4	72.4	74.2	77.4	100.0	92.9	96.8	94.4	....			Honduras	268
103.5	113.5	158.6	100.0	100.9	....										Panama (1990=100)	283
102.2	137.2	153.0	....												Paraguay (1985=100)	288
95.0	93.6	104.2	103.8	84.1	84.9	74.3	84.4	100.0	106.3	102.8	79.9	85.0	113.7	94.2	Peru	293
101.6	137.0	....													Suriname (1985=100)	366
82.2	73.1	83.6	100.0												Trinidad and Tobago (1990=100)	369
															Memorandum Items	
91.4	78.0	86.8	107.0	96.8	98.5	89.5	89.4	100.0	112.6	107.0	75.0	91.8	126.8	114.5	Oil Exporting Countries	999
92.1	97.5	103.9	104.4	98.2	99.1	96.9	94.2	100.0	97.3	93.4	83.7	85.3	88.2	....	Non-Oil Developing Countries	201

75 d		1972	1973	1974	1975	1976	1977	1978	1979	1980	1981	1982	1983	1984	1985	1986
															Indices of Unit Values (Prices) In Terms of US Dollars:	
World	001	27.7	33.9	47.9	52.1	52.7	57.3	61.1	72.9	89.2	90.3	87.1	84.1	82.7	81.1	82.2
Industrial Countries	110	26.2	32.0	45.2	49.2	50.1	54.5	59.0	69.8	85.6	86.2	83.2	79.9	78.7	77.5	79.0
United States	111	23.7	28.2	41.8	45.5	46.9	50.8	54.8	65.4	82.0	86.5	85.1	81.6	83.0	81.0	78.2
Canada	156	30.2	32.5	42.5	47.1	49.8	52.9	56.0	64.4	77.1	85.7	86.9	86.5	86.9	85.3	83.4
Australia	193	21.9	26.1	36.8	42.3	43.3	47.5	52.2	61.7	79.6	81.8	77.1	74.3	74.2	70.1	73.3
Japan	158	24.4	30.1	48.9	52.0	53.3	57.1	59.8	74.7	100.3	103.7	95.8	91.2	88.7	85.2	76.3
New Zealand	196	28.0	33.4	43.5	49.6	50.6	54.3	60.2	66.9	82.6	83.7	80.8	77.9	75.2	72.5	74.8
Euro Area																
Belgium	124	....														
Belgium-Luxembourg	126	26.8	32.3	41.3	46.2	46.9	51.3	58.2	68.3	78.8	70.9	65.9	63.1	60.4	59.7	68.2
Finland	172	24.7	32.2	45.5	48.4	48.7	52.0	57.3	68.3	84.0	72.0	76.0	70.0	68.0	67.5	70.2
France	132	....														
Germany	134	23.5	30.1	39.9	43.2	43.1	48.4	54.4	66.3	78.2	71.6	67.1	63.5	60.4	59.8	68.2
Greece	174	20.0	24.8	33.7	35.2	35.6	39.5	44.7	53.2	59.4	59.8	57.2	52.6	51.0	51.3	61.0
Ireland	178	24.5	27.1	37.8	43.2	41.7	47.5	53.6	62.4	77.9	72.8	69.4	63.4	61.2	61.2	69.2
Italy	136	23.7	30.9	47.4	49.9	49.4	54.0	58.9	71.8	89.7	87.5	82.7	77.2	74.3	73.4	77.4
Netherlands	138	25.1	31.0	43.6	48.5	49.1	54.4	60.6	72.9	84.6	77.6	74.1	70.1	65.7	64.1	71.7
Portugal (1990=100)	182	37.7	47.6	60.2	66.7	67.2	73.6	76.8	83.8	96.0	90.1	82.0	76.8	78.5	72.2	75.2
Spain	184	31.8	40.1	57.6	62.1	58.9	61.5	66.8	78.3	99.8	104.3	98.2	92.1	91.9	88.0	85.1
Denmark	128	24.2	30.8	41.9	46.0	47.3	51.9	56.5	67.5	76.8	71.1	67.0	63.0	60.2	60.1	71.6
Iceland	176	21.8	26.3	35.3	38.4	38.8	41.8	45.5	55.6	62.1	61.0	56.3	55.3	53.7	54.0	61.8
Norway	142	31.8	38.7	50.6	57.1	58.3	64.6	69.0	78.8	90.8	83.6	77.8	72.1	65.7	66.4	77.0
Sweden	144	24.9	31.4	42.9	47.6	48.8	53.5	57.3	71.1	83.5	77.7	71.6	66.2	64.7	64.2	69.5
Switzerland	146	....														
United Kingdom	112	24.5	30.6	42.2	45.6	45.3	50.6	57.2	67.4	80.8	75.5	70.8	67.0	63.8	64.5	70.2
Developing Countries	200	34.3	42.3	60.1	64.9	64.2	69.6	70.3	86.4	104.6	108.0	103.7	102.3	99.8	96.6	95.2
Africa	605															
Burkina Faso	748	32.5	39.3	45.7	59.4	60.5	64.7	68.9	78.8	83.8	78.3	78.7	74.4	67.4	70.5	87.7
Côte d'Ivoire (1985=100)	662	40.3	47.8	59.6	75.2	77.3	80.1	91.8	110.5	126.5	122.8	120.9	114.2	108.2	100.0	113.0
Ethiopia (1990=100)	644	48.0	55.3	61.6	64.9	68.4	73.8	82.0	89.0	100.0	109.5	....				
Kenya	664	21.1	25.5	37.5	46.2	47.1	51.4	58.1	69.6	91.9	96.4	91.8	96.4	91.1	94.6	90.8
Liberia (1985=100)	668	36.7	42.0	61.6	66.9	64.2	78.9	80.9	93.6	109.0	98.3	103.6	98.6	107.9	100.0	105.0
Malawi (1985=100)	676	36.4	41.5	54.6	64.6	69.9	78.6	84.5	99.4	121.9	126.7	116.5	116.7	115.0	100.0	118.7
Mauritius	684	23.8	30.4	47.3	50.7	51.2	56.4	64.2	75.2	90.2	82.9	84.4	76.8	73.2	71.9	66.8
Morocco	686	31.9	40.0	54.7	59.3	53.7	41.3	50.1	70.4	86.6	84.1	75.1	73.0	71.6	69.6	68.8
Senegal (1985=100)	722	42.1	54.3	71.9	85.5	80.7	85.4	91.8	109.4	143.3	124.9	116.7	110.1	105.3	100.0	93.9
South Africa	199	21.8	26.3	34.8	39.9	41.4	46.8	53.8	68.5	89.1	88.9	86.5	90.6	75.9	64.3	73.0
Tunisia (1990=100)	744	58.8	70.6	91.1	109.1	100.4	102.8	108.3	119.1	134.9	130.4	118.1	107.2	100.2	100.0	109.3
Asia	505	27.4	35.7	52.4	54.6	54.7	57.3	62.2	74.0	89.5	91.1	86.1	83.1	84.8	81.0	76.4
Bangladesh (1990=100)	513	....						92.0	92.0	101.9	97.9	91.2	98.3	99.2	†97.9	98.8
China, P.R.: Hong Kong	532	34.0	44.4	58.1	56.4	58.7	64.6	69.2	75.8	82.6	81.7	79.5	74.0	76.7	75.0	78.6
India	534	40.1	40.6	55.9	93.8	102.1	101.5	99.2	113.7	133.9	138.7	130.0	124.4	102.4	121.0	117.2
Korea	542	28.0	37.2	57.9	59.6	58.3	59.6	63.0	77.0	92.6	97.6	90.4	†86.1	87.2	83.5	78.4
Malaysia	548	35.2	47.1	67.7	72.0	69.0	73.0	79.6	90.3	108.9	117.7	115.6	111.4	107.1	100.0	84.8
Pakistan	564	22.5	27.7	47.5	53.9	51.5	53.3	56.3	63.6	79.4	91.1	86.1	78.1	80.0	73.6	67.1
Philippines	566	....														
Singapore	576	....		47.9	48.4	50.6	53.9	60.0	70.8	84.0	86.5	81.7	80.6	79.2	74.8	66.7
Solomon Islands (1990=100)	813	59.0	82.4	119.3	112.8	103.7	102.0	120.0	122.3	145.3	156.3	139.6	124.0	118.1	100.0	98.1
Sri Lanka	524	20.3	25.2	42.5	47.0	35.2	40.9	43.1	65.7	78.5	78.2	75.3	69.5	67.4	68.4	61.3
Thailand	578	17.1	20.2	33.0	36.8	38.8	41.7	45.1	51.9	64.3	71.3	69.4	65.5	64.2	61.2	58.6
Europe	170	176.0	220.1	291.7	314.4	308.2	362.8	296.2	414.4	477.2	496.7	491.5	493.6	460.0	428.6	467.4
Cyprus (1985=100)	423	57.9	69.2	89.1	97.2	88.9	94.1	103.3	121.5	140.5	131.4	117.7	107.9	103.3	100.0	100.9
Czechoslovakia (1990=100)	934	....	34.0	38.8	44.5	45.8	69.7	75.0	84.9	93.4	111.9	111.5	113.8	105.1	102.5	118.3
Hungary (1990=100)	944	42.9	52.5	67.1	77.3	76.3	83.0	89.6	101.3	108.9	108.0	104.7	97.1	92.2	91.8	105.4
Malta (1985=100)	181	41.0	52.9	68.9	73.8	72.5	79.4	92.4	112.1	125.7	124.0	117.6	112.1	103.2	100.0	114.8
Poland	964	....			4,123.7	3,753.9	3,905.9	121.9	360.6	380.4	358.1	348.8	340.2	315.5	296.3	291.2
Turkey	186	21.7	†26.4	39.0	43.5	44.0	48.5	55.3	65.3	100.0	96.9	95.0	85.4	77.4	....	
Middle East	405	25.7	31.5	41.8	45.6	46.5	49.0	57.9	70.4	88.0	94.3	87.4	88.0	87.5	83.5	88.2
Israel	436	†23.9	30.8	41.8	43.7	†42.7	46.5	†57.1	†70.9	†87.1	†84.3	77.1	†73.6	†73.6	72.0	71.6
Jordan	439	40.2	45.8	59.3	82.0	76.9	79.1	82.8	90.2	112.9	123.9	118.0	104.7	109.4	103.8	88.1
Syrian Arab Rep.	463	40.3	49.6	71.4	80.0	96.8	87.5	93.5	116.2	150.9	196.1	184.1	212.7	199.1	167.5	199.1
Western Hemisphere	205	30.3	35.9	57.0	58.2	55.8	58.6	59.2	67.6	85.8	93.5	91.6	85.3	76.2	78.0	73.4
Argentina	213	....														
Brazil	223	23.2	26.2	48.2	47.8	41.6	39.9	40.3	49.1	64.8	70.2	64.8	57.0	52.6	54.7	47.9
Colombia	233	41.9	49.6	63.7	68.0	71.0	75.2	84.2	92.9	101.9	108.1	110.5	108.1	111.5	105.3	97.9
Costa Rica (1990=100)	238	611.9	676.3	777.0	786.5	747.7	787.4	833.6	956.0	1,084.7	456.4	258.1	225.5	205.0	174.4	140.9
Guatemala (1990=100)	258	....														
Trinidad and Tobago (1990=100)	369	13.1	15.0	32.6	35.4	37.2	38.9	40.6	46.0	69.0	78.0	88.3	88.9	89.0	86.4	79.8
Memorandum Items																
Oil Exporting Countries	999	....	....	....	....	....	....	....	....	....	....	....	....	....	....	....
Non-Oil Developing Countries	201	33.8	42.3	61.3	65.3	64.4	70.0	70.3	86.9	105.5	108.5	103.7	101.9	101.2	97.1	95.1

1995=100

1987	1988	1989	1990	1991	1992	1993	1994	1995	1996	1997	1998	1999	2000	2001	Country	Code
88.9	92.1	94.4	101.1	99.3	99.9	90.6	91.4	100.0	98.8	93.4	87.2	85.1	86.2	83.2	World	001
86.5	90.6	91.9	99.9	98.5	99.5	88.7	90.9	100.0	99.0	92.7	87.7	85.6	86.1	83.0	Industrial Countries	110
83.9	88.0	90.6	93.6	93.6	94.3	94.1	95.7	100.0	101.0	98.5	92.6	93.4	99.4	95.9	United States	111
86.3	91.4	95.2	98.4	98.9	97.7	96.5	96.9	100.0	100.3	99.4	96.0	95.7	98.0	93.9	Canada	156
81.4	88.8	88.9	91.3	92.0	90.7	90.7	95.2	100.0	99.9	94.6	86.8	87.2	85.3	72.0	Australia	193
82.0	86.8	90.2	95.0	92.5	91.4	92.1	92.3	100.0	100.7	95.1	83.0	83.8	92.6	86.3	Japan	158
80.6	88.9	87.5	87.9	85.9	85.3	85.3	90.4	100.0	101.9	97.1	81.6	82.4	82.4	....	New Zealand	196
															Euro Area	
						81.3	85.6	100.0	98.5	90.5	87.4	84.5	82.6	82.1	Belgium	124
77.0	80.5	80.5	93.3	90.0	92.5	84.0	86.3	100.0	97.0	88.4	....	....	....	....	Belgium-Luxembourg	126
79.6	83.2	84.5	95.8	91.4	89.0	76.7	83.7	100.0	96.5	86.3	80.9	78.0	76.2	72.0	Finland	172
			93.9	92.7	96.0	87.2	†88.2	100.0	99.2	88.3	86.4	82.4	75.5	....	France	132
77.4	79.8	80.1	90.9	90.0	92.7	82.8	86.0	100.0	93.4	83.2	80.1	75.4	72.4	70.3	Germany	134
70.1	76.3	75.0	86.4	86.1	92.7	86.5	89.3	100.0	97.8	88.0	85.8	83.4	76.5	76.5	Greece	174
76.4	83.4	82.6	91.5	91.1	94.4	86.1	89.5	100.0	98.6	94.0	90.3	88.3	82.9	82.9	Ireland	178
87.7	90.9	92.9	105.6	101.2	101.2	88.6	89.9	100.0	105.6	97.0	92.6	87.6	86.4	85.7	Italy	136
81.5	83.1	85.1	96.1	93.3	97.1	86.3	88.1	100.0	96.1	88.1	84.5	80.9	78.3	78.4	Netherlands	138
84.8	88.8	87.5	100.0	98.9	100.6	....	....	....	....	....	....	....	....	....	Portugal (1990=100)	182
93.7	97.2	97.7	109.5	104.5	104.8	88.6	89.2	100.0	98.8	88.5	84.8	81.0	79.1	76.4	Spain	184
80.5	83.1	82.0	93.6	89.6	91.8	83.5	86.1	100.0	97.3	88.1	86.6	82.8	77.0	....	Denmark	128
70.9	75.7	74.8	87.9	92.0	93.7	87.0	88.9	100.0	99.9	94.3	....	....	....	....	Iceland	176
86.9	92.6	92.6	102.9	97.7	100.0	88.2	88.9	100.0	97.8	88.3	84.0	79.5	73.9	73.7	Norway	142
79.8	85.2	86.0	96.9	95.5	96.9	82.2	86.8	100.0	102.6	91.9	87.4	86.2	....	....	Sweden	144
....	†80.6	78.2	91.4	88.6	92.4	86.0	88.5	100.0	95.6	85.8	82.4	78.0	73.5	74.7	Switzerland	146
80.3	86.7	82.9	92.2	92.6	93.0	86.9	91.5	100.0	98.7	96.9	92.1	88.9	86.5	82.0	United Kingdom	112
97.6	96.2	103.5	103.7	99.5	97.8	96.8	93.0	100.0	98.2	95.8	85.5	83.1	86.5	84.0	Developing Countries	200
....	84.0	82.9	92.8	91.0	91.5	87.7	91.2	100.0	93.4	92.0	84.1	....	....	....	Africa	605
															Burkina Faso	748
90.1	90.9	92.0	115.1	103.0	105.5	100.2	84.1	100.0	101.1	....	....	....	....	....	Côte d'Ivoire (1985=100)	662
129.5	....	....	....	....	....	....	....	....	....	....	....	....	....	....	Ethiopia (1990=100)	644
90.8	92.6	96.5	104.1	96.6	95.5	84.0	79.6	100.0	98.3	102.1	102.0	95.1	97.3	....	Kenya	664
111.5	....	....	....	....	....	....	....	....	....	....	....	....	....	....	Liberia (1985=100)	668
135.7	145.3	154.8	....	....	....	....	....	....	....	....	....	....	....	....	Malawi (1985=100)	676
72.3	75.6	79.3	86.9	86.4	88.7	86.8	91.4	100.0	103.6	90.4	79.8	....	....	....	Mauritius	684
73.3	76.4	82.0	92.8	84.8	82.1	82.8	94.6	100.0	103.7	91.7	79.4	81.2	....	....	Morocco	686
102.9	....	....	....	....	....	....	....	....	....	....	....	....	....	....	Senegal (1985=100)	722
85.6	84.0	82.3	89.3	91.9	93.7	88.3	89.8	100.0	89.0	91.0	83.7	....	....	....	South Africa	199
109.6	....	....	....	....	....	....	....	....	....	....	....	....	....	....	Tunisia (1990=100)	744
78.0	85.0	87.9	90.1	89.5	89.5	89.3	92.3	100.0	100.2	95.6	84.6	83.1	87.6	84.6	Asia	505
															Bangladesh (1990=100)	513
106.7	97.0	97.0	100.0	114.5	....	....	....	....	....	....	....	....	....	....	China, P.R.: Hong Kong	532
81.9	85.2	88.4	90.7	92.7	93.2	92.8	95.3	100.0	98.8	96.4	91.7	89.6	90.0	87.1	India	534
99.1	123.5	129.8	141.5	125.5	118.7	99.1	95.7	100.0	104.3	102.8	91.4	96.6	100.1	....	Korea	542
84.2	†93.1	95.0	96.4	96.4	†94.9	91.3	91.8	100.0	95.9	93.7	76.4	74.5	85.7	....	Malaysia	548
87.9	....	....	....	....	....	....	....	....	....	....	....	....	....	....	Pakistan	564
77.8	83.7	86.2	93.7	91.7	89.2	85.1	91.6	100.0	96.9	43.8	38.7	42.0	46.4	42.3	Philippines	566
....	....	....	....	99.4	84.2	100.9	96.6	100.3	100.0	103.0	93.4	69.2	67.6	57.6	48.1	Singapore	576
74.7	78.5	80.9	86.3	87.7	89.8	88.7	92.9	100.0	99.3	92.9	80.9	81.2	87.0	84.0	Solomon Islands (1990=100)	813
98.5	134.1	....	....	....	....	....	....	....	....	....	....	....	....	....	Sri Lanka	524
65.8	75.5	79.8	91.3	91.8	90.7	86.7	89.7	100.0	102.4	99.6	....	....	....	....	Thailand	578
64.9	72.8	76.7	81.0	84.8	85.7	86.0	88.6	100.0	111.1	106.4	97.9	95.3	100.2	108.7	Europe	170
476.5	290.4	406.4	344.1	261.1	228.2	176.1	107.9	100.0	86.1	74.5	66.8	64.0	63.1	61.0	Cyprus (1985=100)	423
103.6	....	....	....	....	....	....	....	....	....	....	....	....	....	....	Czechoslovakia (1990=100)	934
126.3	120.0	115.1	100.0	82.8	....	....	....	....	....	....	....	....	....	....	Hungary (1990=100)	944
105.0	101.8	97.7	100.0	123.4	128.4	119.7	122.4	134.4	133.8	124.1	120.5	115.0	109.1	110.2	Malta (1985=100)	181
131.4	138.8	136.0	....	....	....	....	....	....	....	....	....	....	....	....	Poland	964
271.1	276.6	229.5	100.5	117.5	106.2	93.1	94.4	100.0	105.4	98.4	97.8	91.3	85.9	88.4	Turkey	186
....	....	1,842.0	1,577.6	955.9	568.9	333.8	132.6	100.0	52.9	25.9	14.5	8.5	....	....	Middle East	405
92.1	85.1	88.2	93.9	90.6	90.7	88.7	91.7	100.0	100.4	95.8	91.3	88.8	91.5	90.6	Israel	436
78.8	85.4	91.1	†98.1	93.4	93.5	90.3	92.2	100.0	†99.3	94.8	89.6	87.0	89.7	88.4	Jordan	439
94.6	90.5	85.5	99.6	95.4	92.1	91.8	88.5	100.0	107.8	105.4	104.5	102.0	104.6	106.9	Syrian Arab Rep.	463
201.2	86.4	83.9	84.7	97.5	83.1	78.8	89.0	100.0	105.9	90.7	....	....	....	....	Western Hemisphere	205
72.6	76.0	80.9	79.9	77.2	72.9	76.4	85.2	100.0	98.5	117.8	107.1	100.2	102.4	100.9	Argentina	213
			101.7	97.8	95.7	93.5	94.9	100.0	98.5	97.1	91.7	....	....	....	Brazil	223
49.9	51.6	64.8	73.5	67.8	63.3	66.6	82.7	100.0	97.9	†132.5	122.5	111.5	116.4	116.1	Colombia	233
97.5	101.3	104.2	99.8	95.5	85.5	84.2	93.5	100.0	101.1	98.5	91.0	84.5	82.5	81.0	Costa Rica (1990=100)	238
129.2	110.4	107.5	100.0	73.0	69.4	65.9	....	....	....	....	....	....	....	....	Guatemala (1990=100)	258
178.8	183.1	177.6	100.0	85.8	106.7	94.4	84.8	....	....	....	....	....	....	....	Trinidad and Tobago (1990=100)	369
91.4	94.7	98.6	100.0	....	....	....	....	....	....	....	....	....	....	....		
															Memorandum Items	
....	95.9	87.3	78.0	74.3	77.1	78.1	84.3	100.0	94.0	95.3	96.1	....	....	....	Oil Exporting Countries	999
97.9	96.0	103.8	104.3	100.1	98.3	97.2	93.2	100.0	98.3	95.8	85.3	82.9	86.4	83.7	Non-Oil Developing Countries	201

Terms of Trade

74tx d

		1972	1973	1974	1975	1976	1977	1978	1979	1980	1981	1982	1983	1984	1985	1986
															Percent Change over Previous Year;	
World	001	1.7	.1	−1.3	−1.3	.1	1.0	1.6	.8	−2.7	−.7	−.6	−1.0	−.3	−.1	6.2
Industrial Countries	110	1.6	−.8	−11.0	.6	−2.1	−.4	4.2	−2.4	−7.8	−2.7	.1	.8	−1.1	1.0	11.3
United States	111	−3.5	−2.1	−13.8	2.6	.2	−4.2	−.9	−4.6	−9.4	3.5	2.8	5.4	−.4	1.8	4.5
Canada	156	1.0	6.3	6.7	−3.6	1.5	−4.7	−3.6	5.0	4.6	−6.3	−3.4	.6	−1.4	−2.4	−1.4
Australia	193	10.0	28.6	−15.9	−17.0	−.5	−7.2	−2.7	−.1	−9.5	−.1	−2.1	−1.0	−2.1	−5.3	−7.4
Japan	158	7.5	−3.9	−23.2	−5.3	−2.9	3.4	15.0	−16.1	−19.8	2.5	.8	2.8	2.7	2.9	33.7
New Zealand	196	15.7	22.0	−22.8	−25.3	7.1	4.5	2.6	7.6	−10.9	−.6	−1.1	−2.5	−.2	−1.8	—
Euro Area																
Belgium	124	....	....	....	....	....	....	....	....	....	....	....	....	....	....	....
Belgium-Luxembourg	126	1.7	1.0	−2.7	−1.6	−.8	.3	−.1	.5	−4.3	−4.6	−.3	.3	−.4	1.1	7.6
Finland	172	−4.2	11.9	−4.8	6.5	−.9	−3.4	−6.0	−1.2	−5.5	2.3	−4.5	−1.1	2.7	−.5	12.4
France	132	....	....	....	....	....	....	....	....	....	....	....	....	....	....	....
Germany	134	2.4	−2.1	−9.2	5.2	−4.5	−1.0	4.0	−5.4	−6.4	−6.6	3.7	1.7	−2.3	1.3	15.1
Greece	174	−.7	19.3	−14.1	−7.8	2.9	7.4	−7.0	4.8	−1.6	−4.5	−6.3	−1.3	4.6	−1.0	−9.5
Ireland	178	9.2	12.9	−20.0	−1.7	3.9	−1.7	1.9	−4.3	−6.3	−3.8	3.0	3.9	−1.5	1.6	4.4
Italy	136	.3	−9.2	−17.3	5.3	−3.3	2.9	2.1	−1.8	−6.2	−4.9	2.5	2.5	−1.6	.6	15.8
Netherlands	138	2.0	−.9	−5.1	.3	—	—	—	−2.6	−1.1	.5	1.2	−1.1	2.3	1.0	3.0
Portugal	182	....	....	....	....	....	....	....	....	....	....	....	....	−3.3	7.9	13.0
Spain	184	3.7	−.7	−13.6	.4	−4.4	−.8	2.3	6.7	−12.6	−17.7	−.4	−4.6	.7	5.4	20.9
Denmark	128	5.0	1.2	−13.4	6.1	−.8	−2.1	3.8	−4.6	−6.8	−2.6	1.0	.8	−.6	1.4	6.6
Iceland	176	−1.0	16.1	−10.0	−16.0	11.9	8.8	.1	−9.1	−3.4	2.0	.6	−4.3	−3.0	1.1	8.5
Norway	142	−1.9	2.9	4.2	2.3	−3.9	−1.3	.5	6.2	15.9	8.4	2.1	−1.2	7.9	−2.4	−24.8
Sweden	144	—	−.5	−5.7	4.7	−1.9	−6.7	−1.8	−5.2	−2.8	−2.5	−2.0	−.9	2.2	1.0	12.2
Switzerland	146	....	....	....	....	....	....	....	....	....	....	....	....	....	....	....
United Kingdom	112	1.7	−11.8	−12.2	7.8	−2.2	3.0	6.5	3.9	4.3	.7	−1.0	−.8	−.6	.5	−5.5
Developing Countries	200	2.6	4.9	34.7	−5.7	6.6	4.6	−3.0	9.7	11.2	2.7	−1.8	−6.0	2.2	−3.0	−8.8
Africa	605															
Burkina Faso	748	−13.3	2.9	17.2	−12.8	13.2	2.1	−2.6	−5.1	3.2	−8.2	−5.3	3.9	−.9	9.2	−26.7
Côte d'Ivoire	662	−14.2	22.7	−4.5	−19.6	16.3	48.6	−17.8	−5.4	−2.8	−27.7	−11.1	4.1	20.7	16.7	−3.6
Ethiopia	644	2.0	9.7	−3.1	−15.0	68.1	−5.9	−10.5	.2	−18.1						
Kenya	664	−7.3	−3.4	−11.6	−8.9	16.2	31.5	−19.9	−7.9	−8.2	−14.3	−4.4	−6.3	17.3	−16.7	12.9
Liberia	668	−10.7	−2.9	−10.4	20.6	7.3	−5.2	−12.2	1.6	.1	−7.8	2.8	−1.8	−9.8	7.3	−6.5
Malawi	676	−8.5	−4.0	−6.1	−3.6	−2.4	18.6	−10.4	−20.9	−15.1	22.2	1.1	−8.3	4.3	−14.6	−12.9
Mauritius	684	12.3	−10.0	52.5	16.3	−26.9	−9.9	−7.6	−5.9	−5.7	1.1	−10.5	9.2	−.9	3.8	30.6
Morocco	686	−7.1	−3.6	41.9	7.0	−20.7	20.0	−5.2	−10.4	.5	−6.0	.3	−7.3	2.1	1.1	10.0
Senegal	722	−5.6	4.0	32.9	−20.2	−7.2	10.4	9.4	−4.8	−24.7	22.2	−14.3	1.8	16.1	2.1	−3.2
Seychelles	718	−7.6	23.8	7.4	−29.0	15.0	25.6	11.2	−7.5	−20.2	−.6	−6.7				
South Africa	199	−6.3	10.1	−2.7	−9.3	−4.4	−4.4	−6.0	−7.7	−4.6	−1.6	−9.8	4.1	2.2	−1.3	−.9
Togo	742	−10.5	4.5	95.0	−9.7	−35.0	23.2	−9.2	.5	−12.4	−7.3	1.4	−5.9	37.9	18.8	....
Tunisia	744	1.6	20.4	56.5	−8.5	−9.9	1.1	5.4	28.1	17.5	6.3	1.1	−.6	2.0	−6.2	−13.8
Asia	505	1.0	1.0	−.5	−6.7	3.3	7.6	−2.9	1.5	−2.5	−1.7	1.2	−1.7	1.4	−1.9	−1.0
Bangladesh	513	....	....	....	....	....	....	....	17.7	5.2	−21.4	−4.6	−5.4	29.3	12.9	−28.8
China, P.R.: Hong Kong	532	2.4	−.4	−6.6	3.2	4.9	−1.6	−.1	−.2	1.0	−2.2	1.3	−1.0	1.3	3.2	−2.8
India	534	6.3	7.6	−15.6	−27.5	−7.5	9.3	22.6	−12.0	−7.9	−9.0	11.2	4.1	23.5	−13.0	2.4
Korea	542	−.4	−5.1	−18.6	−9.7	14.1	7.0	4.8	−2.1	−13.3	−2.1	4.3	.9	2.2	.5	8.8
Malaysia	548	−16.4	12.4	26.8	−12.0	.1	15.7	−4.7	15.7	−1.2	−11.0	−7.4	−.6	15.3	−9.7	−24.8
Pakistan	564	10.3	23.6	−24.1	−22.1	14.0	15.7	8.1	2.4	−14.5	−9.6	−2.9	6.9	1.5	−4.4	27.5
Philippines	566	....	....	....	....	....	....	....	....	....	....	....	....	....	....	....
Singapore	576	....	....	....	....	....	....	....	....	5.6	2.1	1.4	−2.2	−3.2	.7	−2.7
Sri Lanka	524	−5.6	−11.8	−11.4	−19.8	30.6	31.8	−1.8	−28.3	−12.1	−6.3	−6.2	23.0	21.7	−18.1	−3.6
Thailand	578	−1.5	34.5	−8.6	−20.9	−7.8	−5.0	.2	3.3	−4.8	−12.9	−9.3	7.5	−1.7	−6.3	10.8
Europe	170	1.5	−3.0	−7.0	−2.1	.7	−2.0	−8.6	−20.1	−3.7	−1.8	−.6	−2.4	−4.0	1.2	—
Cyprus	423	2.8	5.1	−14.5	6.9	4.4	−4.3	−.4	−4.0	−5.7	5.4	−2.9	3.1	.3	−2.4	9.2
Czechoslovakia	934	....	....	.2	−4.2	−3.2	−3.7	−1.1	−1.8	.3	−3.6	−1.7	−3.9	−7.9	1.1	−.8
Hungary	944	−.2	−1.3	−9.6	−5.1	2.3	−3.4	−.6	−1.8	.3	−.8	−2.3	−2.5	−2.1	−.9	−3.6
Malta	181	2.2	−11.4	−6.8	−.6	2.8	−4.7	2.4	−4.3	−3.4	−3.0	1.9	−6.1	3.7	1.7	6.5
Poland	964	....	....	....	....	4.0	−1.3	163.4	−62.9	−.3	−.4	−.9	−4.0	−1.4	2.4	1.9
Turkey	186	6.4	2.5	−8.0	−15.5	2.7	−.5	−7.0	−.2	−22.8	−8.5	−4.7	−1.7	12.0	....	....
Yugoslavia, SFR	188	.4	−.5	−10.3	3.8	1.5	−1.1	4.1	−2.6	−.9	−1.5	4.4	−1.9			
Middle East	405	1.5	11.4	153.1	−4.8	4.7	3.4	−13.9	51.5	30.5	5.2	5.2	−13.3	−1.8	3.7	−44.3
Israel	436	2.3	−3.3	−13.9	−.1	4.1	8.4	7.7	−7.5	−8.3	−.2	3.4	2.2	−1.8	1.1	3.9
Jordan	439	10.5	−3.7	60.1	−17.4	−4.4	−2.1	−.9	−5.9	−4.3	−5.7	7.5	—	−1.5	−.4	14.3
Syrian Arab Rep.	463	−2.6	1.6	33.7	−23.4	1.2	17.1	.4	5.1	—	−14.6	−6.9	−18.8	9.2	16.4	−38.1
Western Hemisphere	205	13.9	−2.2	−18.8	−6.2	20.8	21.7	−5.2	−3.0	−4.9	−11.6	−8.8	19.8	10.0	−16.3	2.3
Argentina	213	....	....	....	....	....	....	....	....	....	....	....	....	....	....	....
Brazil	223	19.2	−2.1	−42.9	−7.3	39.4	36.7	−3.3	−11.8	−10.2	−5.9	−2.4	24.7	11.9	−11.7	8.9
Chile	228	....	....	....	....	....	....	....	....		−17.1	−24.6	−39.6	−25.8	−39.5	−4.4
Colombia	233	5.1	6.5	4.4	−7.5	40.3	38.7	−25.4	−10.6	1.7	−15.6	−2.9	2.5	3.5	−1.0	21.8
Costa Rica	238	−1.9	1.8	−12.5	3.9	18.9	21.4	−11.9	−8.6	−.5	−14.4	.6	3.1	3.4	3.5	25.6
Guatemala	258	....	....	....	....	....	....	....	....	....	....	....	....	....	....	....
Trinidad and Tobago	369	−6.7	12.2	17.3	.7	−1.9	5.8	−4.3	16.7	6.4	−2.4	−15.4	−1.5	−.7	−3.5	−28.3
Memorandum Items																
Oil Exporting Countries	999	....	....	....	....	....	....	....	....	....	....	....	....	....	....	....
Non-Oil Developing Countries	201	2.4	−.4	−9.0	−6.9	5.8	8.0	−5.5	−6.6	−5.1	−1.9	−4.2	2.4	1.1	−3.1	2.3

Indices

		1972	1973	1974	1975	1976	1977	1978	1979	1980	1981	1982	1983	1984	1985	1986
															Index Numbers:	
World	001	91.3	91.4	90.2	89.1	89.2	90.0	91.5	92.2	89.7	89.0	88.5	87.6	87.3	87.2	92.7
Industrial Countries	110	105.1	104.2	92.8	93.3	91.4	91.0	94.8	92.5	85.3	83.0	83.0	83.7	82.7	83.6	93.0
Developing Countries	200	59.8	62.8	84.6	79.8	85.1	89.0	86.3	94.8	105.4	108.2	106.3	99.9	102.1	99.0	90.3
Africa	605	....	....	....	....	....	....	....	....	....	....	....	....	....	....	....
Asia	505	97.8	98.7	98.2	91.7	94.7	101.9	98.9	100.5	98.0	96.3	97.4	95.8	97.2	95.3	94.4
Europe	170	106.2	102.9	95.7	93.7	94.4	92.5	84.6	67.6	65.1	63.9	63.5	62.0	59.5	60.2	60.2
Middle East	205	137.2	134.2	109.0	102.2	123.5	150.3	142.5	138.1	131.4	116.2	105.9	126.9	139.6	116.8	119.5
Western Hemisphere	405	36.5	40.7	103.0	98.0	102.6	106.1	91.4	138.5	180.8	190.3	200.2	173.6	170.5	176.8	98.5

Calculated from Indices

1987	1988	1989	1990	1991	1992	1993	1994	1995	1996	1997	1998	1999	2000	2001		
2.3	2.1	-.8	.3	-.2	1.9	1.0	.8	.2	-.5	-.9	.8	1.6	-1.3	....	World	001
1.7	1.7	-1.1	.1	.5	1.8	1.3	.6	.6	-.9	-.6	1.6	-.1	-3.1	1.4	**Industrial Countries**	110
-5.1	2.1	-.4	-2.2	.9	-.7	.8	.4	.5	-.5	1.1	2.9	-2.1	-4.6	2.8	United States	111
3.1	2.3	2.1	-2.6	-2.2	-1.8	-.8	.7	4.1	1.0	-1.1	-3.8	1.1	5.6	—	Canada	156
-1.9	14.5	6.5	-2.9	-9.6	-2.3	-6.3	-.4	3.7	1.3	1.9	-3.2	-5.0	.3	7.8	Australia	193
1.8	2.7	-4.4	-5.8	10.0	7.6	8.3	7.6	-.4	-8.1	-1.0	6.6	4.8	-5.1	.6	Japan	158
11.0	6.8	4.9	-1.9	-5.2	1.4	3.2	-.7	-1.6	-.8	-1.7	1.0	-.7	.8	....	New Zealand	196
															Euro Area	
....	....	....	....	....	....	....	-.8	-1.2	-.6	-.8	2.1	-1.7	-2.6	-.3	Belgium	124
.4	-.2	.7	-1.3	-.6	1.9	1.3	-.1	-2.0	.2	-1.0	....	....	....	....	Belgium-Luxembourg	126
3.4	5.5	1.8	-1.3	-2.4	-2.9	-3.2	1.8	7.1	-.7	-3.1	3.6	-5.0	-4.5	2.3	Finland	172
....	....	....	....	-1.3	2.1	.9	1.0	.4	-1.1	.2	.4	-.4	-4.1	....	France	132
3.7	—	-2.7	1.5	-2.3	2.4	.9	-2.8	-.4	-.2	-2.2	1.8	.3	-6.6	1.9	Germany	134
-3.1	.2	1.6	-6.5	-3.3	-5.5	-.7	-.5	3.0	3.9	.8	-2.3	-.6	4.1	-.4	Greece	174
—	.6	.2	-4.6	-2.9	-.7	2.3	-2.6	-2.3	.6	.6	.3	2.4	-3.1	-1.7	Ireland	178
2.5	.9	-1.2	2.9	3.7	1.3	-.3	-.4	-2.7	4.3	-.9	3.7	.7	-7.6	2.2	Italy	136
-3.5	.4	-1.9	2.2	-1.2	-1.4	3.1	.4	1.6	-.6	.1	-.7	-2.5	2.0	.6	Netherlands	138
2.1	3.1	-1.6	-.5	—	3.0	....	....	....	....	....	....	....	....	....	Portugal	182
5.6	7.6	2.5	1.6	1.8	2.3	-.3	-1.4	2.0	.7	-.4	2.4	-.8	-6.0	3.2	Spain	184
3.3	-1.9	-.8	1.9	1.3	.9	.2	-.1	-1.9	1.0	-1.3	-.6	1.2	1.4	....	Denmark	128
5.6	-4.2	-6.0	2.0	9.3	-2.3	-5.2	-1.2	.8	-4.2	.6	....	....	....	....	Iceland	176
-6.0	-2.8	5.7	3.7	-2.7	-6.3	-.7	-3.6	2.0	8.6	3.0	-12.8	13.9	35.3	-3.6	Norway	142
1.6	1.8	1.5	-.5	—	....	-3.4	.4	4.6	-1.4	-1.0	.5	-3.4	....	....	Sweden	144
....	....	-1.9	1.7	2.7	-2.0	2.2	4.3	.2	1.0	-1.6	3.2	3.4	-2.6	.4	Switzerland	146
1.4	1.2	.4	1.2	-.1	.9	2.7	-1.3	-2.8	1.1	.8	.4		-.5	.5	United Kingdom	112
5.1	4.3	-.5	2.6	-2.4	2.7	-1.9	1.3	-.8	.6	-1.8	-2.0	7.2	4.0	....	**Developing Countries**	200
....	....	-3.3	-.1	.7	.7	-3.4	-4.0	8.9	2.3	-1.2	2.4	....	....	....	**Africa**	605
16.3	-3.0	-14.3	3.1	5.4	-20.6	-5.4	-20.3	10.2	-5.7	....	....	....	....	....	Burkina Faso	748
-17.3	....	....	....	....	....	....	....	....	....	....	....	....	....	....	Côte d'Ivoire	662
....	....	....	....	....	....	....	....	....	....	....	....	....	....	....	Ethiopia	644
-18.2	4.6	-10.9	-9.9	14.8	-2.5	13.4	12.2	-5.7	-2.8	9.7	-1.5	-13.8	-2.8	....	Kenya	664
-10.3	....	....	....	....	....	....	....	....	....	....	....	....	....	....	Liberia	668
-3.4	-3.2	2.1	....	....	....	....	....	....	....	....	....	....	....	....	Malawi	676
8.1	-2.7	.2	-1.7	1.6	4.8	-1.8	-2.4	.2	3.9	.9	12.5	....	....	....	Mauritius	684
-2.5	18.5	-26.6	-5.6	3.2	.8	-8.9	-13.3	13.1	-.1	4.3	11.6	-3.7	....	....	Morocco	686
....	....	....	....	....	....	....	....	....	....	....	....	....	....	....	Senegal	722
....	....	....	....	....	....	....	....	....	....	....	....	....	....	....	Seychelles	718
-.5	5.0	6.2	-1.9	-3.9	-.1	1.8	1.7	2.9	4.6	-4.0	.1	....	....	....	South Africa	199
....	....	....	....	....	....	....	....	....	....	-15.5	-13.7	-32.7	3.4	-62.3	Togo	742
9.0	....	....	....	....	....	....	....	....	....	....	....	....	....	....	Tunisia	744
5.7	-.5	1.1	-.4	1.1	1.1	-.6	-.8	-.8	-2.2	.6	-.3	.5	-4.5	....	**Asia**	505
-8.5	25.2	-3.5	-4.8	-13.6	....	....	....	....	....	....	....	....	....	....	Bangladesh	513
-.4	-1.0	1.4	.2	.6	.7	.2	-1.2	-1.7	1.0	.7	1.2	-.7	-1.0	.9	China, P.R.: Hong Kong	532
20.5	-3.1	-2.6	-10.0	9.5	5.8	14.4	5.1	-9.5	-8.4	15.5	2.9	-10.5	-4.5	....	India	534
2.4	2.8	-.3	-3.3	.6	—	4.4	1.2	-3.6	-9.5	-13.6	2.1	3.4	-12.8	....	Korea	542
16.5	....	....	....	....	....	....	....	....	....	....	....	....	....	....	Malaysia	548
-9.4	-8.9	-7.9	-4.7	-3.4	.2	2.0	—	11.5	.2	122.6	14.9	-13.5	-15.8	.5	Pakistan	564
....	....	....	....	6.5	-15.9	-1.0	-.6	3.8	1.0	1.8	5.2	17.6	-2.4	-.8	Philippines	566
-4.5	-1.8	-.4	1.4	-2.3	-3.3	-.2	-3.1	-1.7	.2	—	—	-1.5	-2.9	-4.1	Singapore	576
2.8	-5.8	-1.6	-4.4	-1.9	19.9	4.2	-1.0	-.6	1.0	5.3	....	....	....	....	Sri Lanka	524
-1.1	-1.8	-3.9	-2.9	-1.1	1.1	1.0	.3	-3.2	-2.0	.5	-5.4	-1.2	-6.9	-9.2	Thailand	578
2.6	19.3	-8.7	-3.3	21.9	6.4	14.8	3.5	-.3	.3	2.7	5.0	-2.5	-2.5	2.3	**Europe**	170
7.3	....	....	....	....	....	....	....	....	....	....	....	....	....	....	Cyprus	423
2.6	2.9	5.2	2.8	-30.0	....	....	....	....	....	....	....	....	....	....	Czechoslovakia	934
.9	2.4	2.8	.4	-10.4	-.8	2.5	2.9	-.1	-1.5	1.2	1.3	-1.7	-2.7	-.2	Hungary	944
4.1	9.5	1.4	....	....	....	....	....	....	....	....	....	....	....	....	Malta	181
3.7	2.7	16.6	112.7	-8.8	9.5	7.8	1.2	7.2	-7.8	-.5	2.1	.5	-1.5	-.8	Poland	964
....	....	....	4.7	2.3	3.3	3.6	-9.4	-3.5	1.7	4.3	.1	-1.3	....	....	Turkey	186
....	....	....	....	....	....	....	....	....	....	....	....	....	....	....	Yugoslavia, SFR	188
7.2	-7.8	8.9	14.2	-9.3	1.4	-7.7	-2.9	.3	12.6	-.4	-23.7	34.2	35.7	-10.8	**Middle East**	405
-3.2	5.3	-.3	.6	5.5	.7	3.9	-3.5	-3.3	.7	3.8	2.6	4.2	-2.9	-2.2	Israel	436
-10.6	10.2	7.6	-11.5	11.0	2.0	-.6	7.7	2.8	-2.5	-.7	-4.8	—	-6.7	-.9	Jordan	439
-8.3	-22.4	28.0	28.6	-29.6	-1.5	3.8	-4.8	11.2	-.4	-7.8	....	....	....	....	Syrian Arab Rep.	463
3.5	27.9	1.5	-.7	-29.2	11.7	-9.6	-3.9	-8.6	7.1	-17.0	-2.6	26.3	2.9	-5.5	**Western Hemisphere**	205
....	....	....	....	3.3	5.9	2.5	1.5	.3	8.1	-2.4	-3.9	....	....	....	Argentina	213
5.8	3.7	-21.6	-15.1	9.4	21.4	-6.1	-15.0	-14.1	5.6	-21.7	-5.3	3.9	2.7	-4.9	Brazil	223
3.6	18.2	-5.3	....	....	....	....	....	....	....	....	....	....	....	....	Chile	228
-22.9	.6	-20.6	8.4	-2.9	-6.1	1.2	20.0	1.4	-7.6	13.2	-3.5	.3	7.3	-9.3	Colombia	233
-17.8	-.2	-6.8	-8.0	6.7	-4.0	1.8	....	....	....	....	....	....	....	....	Costa Rica	238
....	-4.4	-3.6	15.2	-17.8	-23.6	14.0	13.1	....	....	....	....	....	....	....	Guatemala	258
-8.4	-14.2	9.8	18.0	....	....	....	....	....	....	....	....	....	....	....	Trinidad and Tobago	369
															Memorandum Items	
....	....	22.3	38.0	-5.1	-2.0	-10.3	-7.4	-5.7	19.9	-6.3	-30.6	....	....	....	Oil Exporting Countries	999
4.4	7.9	-1.5	-.1	-1.9	2.8	-1.0	1.3	-1.0	-1.0	-1.6	.7	4.9	-.8	....	Non-Oil Developing Countries	201

Indices

1995=100

1987	1988	1989	1990	1991	1992	1993	1994	1995	1996	1997	1998	1999	2000	2001		
94.8	96.8	96.0	96.3	96.2	98.0	99.0	99.8	100.0	99.5	98.6	99.3	100.9	99.6	....	World	001
94.6	96.2	95.2	95.2	95.7	97.5	98.8	99.4	100.0	99.1	98.5	100.1	100.0	96.9	98.3	Industrial Countries	110
94.9	99.0	98.5	101.1	98.7	101.4	99.4	100.8	100.0	100.6	98.8	96.8	103.9	108.0	....	Developing Countries	200
....	101.2	97.8	97.7	98.4	99.0	95.6	91.8	100.0	102.3	101.0	103.5	....	....	....	Africa	605
99.7	99.2	100.4	100.0	101.0	102.1	101.6	100.8	100.0	97.8	98.4	98.1	98.6	94.1	....	Asia	505
61.8	73.7	67.3	65.1	79.3	84.4	96.9	100.3	100.0	100.3	103.0	108.2	105.5	102.9	105.3	Europe	170
123.6	158.2	160.5	159.4	112.9	126.1	113.9	109.5	100.0	107.1	88.9	86.6	109.3	112.5	106.3	Middle East	205
105.5	97.3	106.0	121.0	109.7	111.2	102.7	99.7	100.0	112.6	112.2	85.6	114.8	155.8	139.0	Western Hemisphere	405

Trade Balance

Expressed in Millions of US Dollars

1985	1986	1987	1988	1989	1990	1991	1992	1993	1994	1995	1996	1997	1998	1999	2000	2001	
13,941	9,261	31,302	37,409	19,925	23,661	31,213	46,071	70,518	105,657	135,562	110,241	126,228	71,989	38,059	3,128	....	**All Countries**
-43,141	-11,831	-33,640	-10,276	-32,083	-34,641	360	37,118	99,913	94,569	121,806	91,447	94,561	26,765	-111,651	-236,737	....	**Industrial Countries**
-122,180	-144,641	-159,239	-126,609	-117,040	-110,270	-75,700	-95,110	-130,570	-163,760	-172,330	-189,100	-196,180	-244,730	-343,120	-449,570	-423,670	United States
11,867	7,182	9,170	8,849	6,560	9,513	6,126	7,381	10,136	14,834	25,855	31,091	18,565	15,922	27,080	41,763	41,425	Canada
-968	-1,820	492	-677	-3,350	358	3,528	1,643	-29	-3,277	-4,223	-635	1,849	-5,332	-9,730	-4,711	2,023	Australia
55,292	91,188	91,583	92,241	80,122	69,283	96,084	124,764	139,417	144,191	131,787	83,561	101,600	122,389	123,325	116,716	70,214	Japan
-61	103	590	2,173	973	815	2,070	1,627	1,719	1,408	971	524	867	923	-433	636	1,471	New Zealand
																	Euro Area
-3,137	-4,016	-4,809	-4,765	-5,552	-6,969	-8,560	-7,690	-6,476	-7,914	-6,656	-7,315	-4,274	-3,684	-3,629	-2,737	-1,328	Austria
492	2,305	1,294	2,703	2,278	1,671	1,999	3,700	5,780	6,901	9,555	8,690	7,703	6,981	6,496	2,225	3,315	Belgium-Luxembourg
870	1,704	1,507	1,200	-229	701	2,438	4,009	6,449	7,723	12,437	11,314	11,544	12,490	12,168	13,684	12,657	Finland
-4,814	-1,347	-7,775	-7,656	-10,305	-13,253	-9,714	2,371	7,516	7,249	10,998	14,936	26,899	24,940	17,988	1,132	2,853	France
28,421	54,680	68,044	76,348	74,979	68,513	19,441	28,202	41,191	50,915	65,106	69,379	70,119	76,894	70,056	57,292	82,827	Germany
-5,013	-4,375	-5,435	-6,027	-7,327	-10,106	-10,022	-11,561	-10,499	-11,273	-14,425	-15,505	-15,375	....	-17,951	-20,239	-19,087	Greece
631	1,145	2,614	3,822	4,003	3,944	4,294	7,045	8,175	9,366	13,557	15,754	18,625	25,390	24,256	30,003	....	Ireland
-5,367	5,048	83	-924	-1,664	-1,474	-200	28,889	31,568	38,729	54,118	39,878	35,631	23,437	9,549	15,862	....	Italy
....	....	....	....	....	....	....	....	....	....	-1,690	-1,928	-2,003	-2,324	-2,579	-2,350	-2,367	Luxembourg
6,704	7,408	6,252	10,072	9,825	12,058	11,979	12,309	16,904	18,686	23,812	22,767	20,937	21,055	16,034	21,278	23,588	Netherlands
-1,430	-1,611	-3,513	-5,377	-4,742	-6,684	-7,688	-9,387	-8,050	-8,321	-8,910	-9,722	-10,342	-12,211	-13,758	-13,936	-12,979	Portugal
-4,759	-7,197	-13,742	-18,703	-25,406	-29,158	-30,335	-30,420	-14,999	-14,892	-18,415	-16,283	-13,407	-20,758	-30,339	-34,820	-31,500	Spain
-764	-1,050	795	1,883	2,425	4,875	4,748	7,058	7,719	7,441	6,528	7,532	5,369	3,886	6,399	6,754	6,960	Denmark
—	97	-52	-14	134	79	-47	2	181	273	206	19	5	-352	-308	-474	....	Iceland
4,728	-2,115	-759	-209	3,770	7,761	8,696	8,254	6,966	7,496	8,685	12,972	11,648	2,061	10,723	25,942	26,018	Norway
2,385	5,035	4,485	4,880	4,017	3,402	6,357	6,720	7,548	9,558	15,978	18,636	17,999	17,632	15,714	15,215	13,832	Sweden
-2,083	-5,495	-6,017	-5,194	-4,937	-7,154	-4,581	-265	1,592	3,346	3,258	1,868	2,737	933	815	389	....	Switzerland
-3,955	-14,058	-19,209	-38,291	-40,616	-32,549	-18,168	-23,332	-19,648	-16,947	-19,006	-21,228	-20,203	-36,127	-44,295	-45,891	-48,248	United Kingdom
57,082	21,093	64,942	47,685	52,008	58,302	30,854	8,954	-29,395	11,089	13,756	18,794	31,667	45,223	149,710	239,865	....	**Developing Countries**
15,907	7,097	11,724	7,700	9,157	17,053	13,989	4,777	4,363	3,543	2,807	11,366	6,346	-5,991	2,753	16,381	....	**Africa**
4,214	169	2,398	935	1,144	4,179	5,468	....	....	....	....	....	....	....	....	....	....	Algeria
900	260	1,019	1,120	1,676	2,306	2,102	1,845	1,438	1,563	2,255	3,055	2,410	1,464	2,047	....	....	Angola
-28	-94	-97	-141	-63	-86	-300	-215	-168	-54	-203	-32	-153	-158	-214	....	....	Benin
234	244	783	482	635	184	267	187	267	510	555	750	895	77	675	....	....	Botswana
-222	-292	-245	-237	-257	-262	-221	-222	-243	-129	....	....	....	....	....	....	....	Burkina Faso
-36	-36	-61	-42	-58	-116	-103	-105	-99	-92	-63	-60	-9	-59	-42	-59	....	Burundi
490	442	254	620	717	695	850	893	502	402	627	....	....	....	....	....	....	Cameroon
-81	-82	-70	-85	-89	-99	-115	-157	-143	-181	-217	-184	-172	-186	....	....	....	Cape Verde
-37	-72	-69	-45	-38	-91	-53	-73	-26	15	....	....	....	....	....	....	....	Central African Rep.
-104	-113	-116	-83	-85	-29	-56	-61	-63	-77	....	....	....	....	....	....	....	Chad
-13	-8	-33	-23	-18	-27	-29	-37	-28	-34	-42	....	....	....	....	....	....	Comoros
515	160	457	320	629	876	613	740	619	346	516	194	941	....	....	....	....	Congo, Republic of
1,351	1,547	1,086	922	920	1,094	923	995	748	1,289	1,376	1,824	1,793	1,720	1,895	1,797	....	Côte d'Ivoire
....	....	....	....	....	....	....	-218	-184	-181	-171	....	....	....	....	....	....	Djibouti
....	....	-9	-12	-11	-15	-30	-6	10	25	-31	-117	....	....	....	....	....	Equatorial Guinea
-508	-455	-577	-556	-374	-620	-303	-823	-507	-554	-714	-585	-413	-749	-920	-645	....	Ethiopia
1,097	95	555	404	874	1,684	1,367	1,373	1,481	1,589	1,847	2,373	2,002	744	1,588	....	....	Gabon
-12	-20	-20	-23	-25	-30	-42	-31	-57	-57	-40	-98	-87	....	....	....	....	Gambia, The
-36	14	-107	-112	-203	-308	-321	-470	-664	-342	-257	-367	-638	-806	-1,223	-843	....	Ghana
....	....	84	164	1	64	85	-8	-91	-22	-170	-39	111	118	121	94	....	Guinea
-48	-42	-29	-43	-55	-49	-47	-77	-38	-21	-35	-35	-14	....	....	....	....	Guinea-Bissau
-279	-235	-660	-729	-962	-915	-512	-500	-247	-238	-750	-515	-886	-1,012	-983	-1,271	....	Kenya
-302	-316	-405	-496	-526	-613	-736	-823	-734	-667	-825	-812	-828	-673	-607	-516	....	Lesotho
167	149	63	....	....	....	....	....	....	....	....	....	....	....	....	....	....	Liberia
-44	-8	11	-34	1	-249	-111	-144	-180	-96	-122	-120	-178	-154	-158	-174	....	Madagascar
69	94	100	40	64	126	60	-15	-23	-276	....	....	....	....	....	....	....	Malawi
-152	-133	-80	-140	-94	-121	-146	-163	-120	-114	-115	-118	10	....	....	....	....	Mali
38	18	43	89	99	61	37	-55	3	47	184	134	107	40	....	....	....	Mauritania
-12	76	—	-148	-192	-257	-185	-159	-242	-397	-241	-326	-436	-264	-519	-394	....	Mauritius
-1,353	-1,053	-1,066	-760	-1,697	-2,108	-1,764	-2,463	-2,065	-2,107	-2,482	-2,193	-1,864	-2,319	-2,448	-3,235	....	Morocco
-305	-409	-481	-559	-622	-663	-647	-630	-727	-767	-536	-478	-454	-491	-806	-682	....	Mozambique
....	....	....	....	....	-142	-49	-78	-42	-86	-130	-127	-272	-173	....	....	....	Namibia
-86	-28	29	-33	-24	-13	-66	-49	-12	-44	-18	....	....	....	....	....	....	Niger
5,667	1,947	3,478	2,520	4,178	8,653	4,441	4,611	3,248	2,948	3,513	9,679	5,706	-240	4,288	....	....	Nigeria
-93	-75	-146	-161	-149	-125	-132	-172	-200	-335	-162	-157	-185	-169	-187	-153	....	Rwanda
-13	-13	-7	-5	-8	-9	....	....	....	....	....	....	....	....	....	....	....	São Tomé & Príncipe
-248	-189	-248	-243	-200	-226	-266	-331	-350	-203	-250	-276	-271	-313	-346	....	....	Senegal
-80	-85	-88	-118	-120	-109	-114	-132	-165	-136	-161	-185	-188	-228	-232	....	....	Seychelles
-5	20	27	-30	-18	8	11	11	-69	-73	-127	....	....	....	....	....	....	Sierra Leone
-240	-247	-265	-158	-279	....	....	....	....	....	....	....	....	....	....	....	....	Somalia
5,583	6,613	7,547	5,779	5,388	7,056	6,608	6,279	6,232	4,481	2,667	2,695	2,324	2,056	4,073	4,316	4,966	South Africa
-135	-307	-430	-522	-507	-322	-836	-597	-227	-522	-510	-719	-828	-1,137	-476	440	304	Sudan
-96	-18	43	18	-22	-39	-41	-141	-104	-50	-197	-204	-127	-126	-122	-111	....	Swaziland
-541	-577	-713	-646	-655	-779	-867	-929	-857	-790	-657	-449	-449	-776	-825	-674	....	Tanzania
-22	-56	-40	-69	-58	-89	-53	-128	-111	-37	-129	-127	-108	-133	-98	....	....	Togo
-886	-934	-728	-1,097	-1,207	-1,678	-1,199	-2,037	-2,064	-1,567	-1,989	-1,761	-1,955	-2,152	-2,141	-2,252	....	Tunisia
110	46	-142	-257	-311	-313	-204	-271	-278	-251	-367	-348	-450	-656	-596	....	....	Uganda
226	175	267	502	566	-257	420	....	....	....	....	....	54	-153	-98	-221	....	Zambia
201	311	381	501	375	243	48	-255	122	158	....	....	....	....	....	....	....	Zimbabwe
722	325	39	850	489	585	342	308	528	586	603	639	502	405	516	233	237	Africa not specified

Balance of Payments

Trade Balance

Expressed in Millions of US Dollars

	1985	1986	1987	1988	1989	1990	1991	1992	1993	1994	1995	1996	1997	1998	1999	2000	2001
Asia	**-9,508**	**2,814**	**20,607**	**13,626**	**5,988**	**5,235**	**4,791**	**7,278**	**-7,039**	**3,893**	**-266**	**-8,915**	**43,064**	**139,438**	**135,452**	**116,249**	....
Afghanistan, I.S. of	-293	-642	-366	-278	-371												
Bangladesh	-1,287	-1,421	-1,369	-1,443	-1,995	-1,587	-1,386	-1,256	-1,113	-1,416	-2,324	-2,275	-1,711	-1,574	-2,077	-1,654	....
Bhutan																	
Cambodia								-179	-187	-255	-332	-428	-328	-173	-232	-198	
China,P.R.: Mainland	-13,123	-9,140	-1,661	-5,315	-5,620	9,165	8,743	5,183	-10,654	7,290	18,050	19,535	46,222	46,614	35,982	34,474	
China,P.R.:Hong Kong														-7,833	-3,159	-8,193	-8,331
Fiji	-146	-103	3	-16	-112	-226	-187	-189	-282	-229	-242	-168	-283	-186	-116		
India	-5,616	-5,438	-5,777	-6,581	-6,110	-5,151	-2,992	-2,911	-2,093	-4,150	-6,719	-10,052	-10,028	-10,752	-8,679	-12,193	
Indonesia	5,822	2,458	4,674	5,678	6,664	5,352	4,801	7,022	8,231	7,901	6,533	5,948	10,075	18,429	20,644	25,040	
Kiribati	-11	-13	-16	-17	-18	-24	-23	-32	-25	-21							
Korea	-20	4,299	7,529	11,283	4,361	-2,450	-6,803	-1,755	2,319	-2,860	-4,444	-14,965	-3,179	41,627	28,371	16,872	13,392
Lao People's Dem.Rep	-140	-131	-152	-92	-131	-107	-101	-100	-150	-214	-316	-321	-283	-165	-190		
Malaysia	3,573	3,214	5,783	5,427	4,277	2,525	391	3,150	3,037	1,577	-103	3,848	3,510	17,505	22,644	20,854	
Maldives	-33	-32	-27	-33	-48	-43	-66	-103	-125	-120	-151	-186	-214	-216	-263	-233	
Mongolia	-799	-951	-864	-873	-963	-497	-101	-29	21	34	25	-36	115	-62	-56		
Myanmar	-202	-290	-233	-205	-82	-302	-53	-105	-630	-609	-823	-931	-1,132	-1,386	-879	-516	
Nepal	-283	-294	-350	-471	-407	-449	-482	-376	-462	-790	-961	-1,106	-1,278	-757	-882	-793	
Pakistan	-3,245	-2,793	-2,327	-2,705	-2,583	-2,727	-2,272	-2,803	-2,586	-2,239	-2,891	-3,656	-2,399	-1,984	-1,847	-1,159	
Papua New Guinea	51	102	114	91	-23	69	78	625	1,470	1,326	1,408	1,017	677	695	856		
Philippines	-482	-202	-1,017	-1,085	-2,598	-4,020	-3,211	-4,695	-6,222	-7,850	-8,944	-11,342	-11,127	-28	4,958	6,918	2,746
Samoa	-30	-32	-44	-51	-54	-61	-71	-84	-81	-65	-72	-81	-85	-77	-98		
Singapore	-1,518	-940	-1,143	28	-313	-1,633	-110	-1,821	-2,724	1,354	976	2,225	1,118	14,779	11,157	11,400	
Solomon Islands	-1	-4	-6	-23	-20	-7	-9	14	-8	—	14	11	-28	-18	55		
Sri Lanka	-523	-556	-472	-540	-550	-473	-805	-715	-742	-1,085	-985	-800	-640	-505	-769	-1,044	
Thailand	-1,332	388	-424	-2,074	-2,916	-6,751	-5,989	-4,161	-4,297	-3,726	-7,968	-9,488	1,572	16,238	14,013	11,701	8,582
Tonga	-25	-26	-32	-40	-40	-39	-36	-39	-41								
Vanuatu	-34	-38	-43	-43	-44	-66	-59	-49	-47	-50	-51	-51	-44	-42	-51		
Asia not specified	10,277	15,484	18,914	13,117	15,798	14,859	15,660	12,686	10,351	10,090	10,053	14,387	12,535	9,310	16,069	14,314	20,568
Europe	**1,420**	**3,080**	**7,118**	**4,023**	**-10,755**	**-34,095**	**-9,383**	**-8,711**	**-22,480**	**-1,873**	**-15,309**	**-27,487**	**-40,240**	**-44,466**	**-13,320**	**4,992**	....
Albania	-41	-5	-4	-38	-62	-134	-208	-471	-490	-460	-475	-678	-535	-604	-663	-814	-1,027
Armenia									-98	-178	-403	-469	-559	-577	-474		
Azerbaijan											-373	-694	-567	-1,046	-408	319	614
Belarus									-528	-490	-666	-1,149	-1,407	-1,501	-570	-884	-779
Bosnia & Herzegovina														-3,155	-3,333	-2,660	-2,751
Bulgaria	-505	-1,183	-1,011	-606	-692	-1,314	-32	-212	-885	-17	121	188	380	-1,081	-1,176		
Croatia									-709	-1,278	-3,228	-3,488	-5,383	-4,071	-3,299	-3,204	-4,012
Cyprus	-647	-646	-799	-1,068	-1,370	-1,553	-1,602	-2,315	-1,507	-1,736	-2,085	-2,183	-2,071	-2,426	-2,309	-2,606	
Czech Republic									-517	-1,408	-3,685	-5,706	-4,938	-2,647	-1,902	-3,095	-3,091
Czechoslovakia	277	-386	-270	385	143	-1,422	-121	-1,834									
Estonia								-90	-145	-356	-666	-1,019	-1,124	-1,115	-878	-768	-787
Georgia																	
Hungary	448	-465	80	583	1,043	534	358	-11	-4,021	-3,716	-2,433	-2,652	-1,962	-2,354	-2,189	-1,760	-2,018
Kazakhstan											114	-335	-276	-801	344	2,440	896
Kyrgyz Republic									-107	-86	-122	-252	-15	-84	9		
Latvia								-40	3	-301	-580	-798	-848	-1,130	-1,027	-1,058	-1,351
Lithuania									-155	-205	-698	-896	-1,147	-1,518	-1,405	-1,104	-1,108
Macedonia, FYR												-317	-388	-420	-410	-558	
Malta	-237	-252	-372	-442	-436	-571	-582	-513	-568	-603	-724	-763	-657	-593	-571	-618	-490
Moldova										-54	-70	-260	-348	-388	-136	-292	-313
Poland	347	467	790	1,089	47	3,589	-711	-131	-3,505	-575	-1,646	-7,287	-9,822	-12,836	-15,072	-12,308	....
Romania	1,772	1,680	2,178	3,750	2,050	-3,344	-1,106	-1,194	-1,128	-411	-1,577	-2,470	-1,980	-2,625	-1,092	-1,684	....
Russia										17,375	20,310	22,471	17,026	16,869	36,129	60,703	47,839
Slovak Republic									-912	61	-229	-2,283	-2,084	-2,351	-1,109	-895	
Slovenia								789	-154	-336	-953	-825	-776	-789	-1,245	-1,139	-622
Turkey	-2,975	-3,081	-3,229	-1,777	-4,219	-9,555	-7,340	-8,190	-14,160	-4,216	-13,212	-10,582	-15,398	-14,220	-10,443	-22,377	-4,537
Turkmenistan													304	-231			
Ukraine										-2,575	-2,702	-4,296	-4,205	-2,584	244	779	198
Yugoslavia, SFR	-588	-702	82	779	58	-2,676	512										
Europe not specified	-671	-600	-1,941	-2,180	-2,589	-2,371	4,376	-291	-555	91	170	-1,048	-922	-730	-389	-65	-378
Middle East	**16,023**	**-8,634**	**5,222**	**-1,286**	**19,727**	**40,867**	**10,548**	**12,220**	**6,371**	**21,223**	**27,006**	**43,055**	**40,535**	**-3,363**	**36,842**	**102,426**	....
Bahrain, Kingdom of	101	35	-13	77	11	236	-367	-527	107	120	626	665	605	-28	672	1,327	....
Egypt	-5,215	-4,538	-4,980	-6,608	-5,722	-6,379	-5,667	-5,231	-6,378	-5,953	-7,597	-8,390	-8,632	-10,214	-9,928	-8,321	....
Iran, I.R. of	2,169	-3,414	-89	101	-367	975	-6,529	-3,406	-1,207	6,817	5,586	7,402	4,258	-1,168	7,597	13,138	....
Israel	-2,376	-1,841	-3,707	-2,890	-1,905	-2,564	-4,861	-4,769	-5,607	-5,486	-7,227	-7,136	-5,177	-3,267	-4,464	-3,089	-3,264
Jordan	-1,638	-1,426	-1,467	-1,411	-773	-1,237	-1,173	-1,780	-1,899	-1,579	-1,518	-2,001	-1,813	-1,602	-1,460		....
Kuwait	4,655	1,951	3,284	1,709	4,987	3,179	-3,993	-689	3,324	4,669	5,579	6,997	6,533	1,903	5,568	13,027	9,241
Libya	4,599	1,468	437	-109	765	3,777	2,664	2,617	113	1,026	2,781	2,519	2,716	471	2,762		....
Oman	1,943	552	2,036	1,235	1,842	2,885	1,759	1,928	1,336	1,849	2,015	3,142	3,012	307	2,939	6,726	....
Saudi Arabia	7,115	3,119	4,916	4,571	9,154	22,889	21,818	20,039	16,522	21,289	24,390	35,370	34,362	11,287	25,039	49,843	44,387
Syrian Arab Republic	-2,090	-1,326	-869	-639	1,192	2,094	1,084	159	-259	-1,275	-146	-338	454	-178	216	1,423	....
Yemen Arab Rep.	-1,071	-780	-1,141	-862	-677												
Yemen, P.D. Rep.	-581	-417	-386	-514	-440												
Yemen, Republic of						-103	-724	-862	-971	274	149	-31	-133	-785	358	1,609	....
Middle East not spec	8,412	-2,017	7,200	4,053	11,660	15,114	6,535	4,739	1,290	-528	2,369	4,856	4,350	-89	7,544	21,071	13,589

Trade Balance

Expressed in Millions of US Dollars

1985	1986	1987	1988	1989	1990	1991	1992	1993	1994	1995	1996	1997	1998	1999	2000	2001	
33,240	16,736	20,271	23,622	27,891	29,242	10,909	−6,610	−10,610	−15,697	−482	775	−18,038	−40,394	−12,017	−183	....	**Western Hemisphere**
					−28	−28	−33	−33	−37	−46	−51	−53	−60	−78	−79	....	Anguilla
−147	−181	−196	−176	−217	−202	−204	−187	−208	−242	−238	−271	−275	−283	−316	−299	....	Antigua and Barbuda
4,878	2,446	1,017	4,242	5,709	8,628	4,419	−1,396	−2,363	−4,139	2,358	1,760	−2,123	−3,099	−794	2,558	....	Argentina
	−181	−205	−267	−290	−425	−524	−377	−392	−311	−425	−308	−387	−353	−592	−28	....	Aruba
−563	−606	−673	−672	−911	−797	−817	−768	−738	−815	−931	−1,014	−1,116	−1,374	−1,428	−1,306	....	Bahamas, The
−209	−248	−294	−339	−416	−409	−416	−278	−327	−355	−446	−456	−599	−651	−714	−744	....	Barbados
−24	−16	−24	−42	−64	−59	−98	−104	−119	−75	−66	−58	−90	−105	−124	−191	....	Belize
161	−51	−128	−48	−6	55	−44	−432	−396	−30	−182	−236	−477	−655	−488	−381	....	Bolivia
12,466	8,304	11,158	19,168	16,112	10,747	10,578	15,239	14,329	10,861	−3,157	−5,453	−6,652	−6,603	−1,261	−696	2,645	Brazil
884	1,092	1,309	2,210	1,483	1,284	1,485	722	−990	732	1,381	−1,091	−1,558	−2,516	1,664	1,438	....	Chile
−23	1,922	1,868	827	1,474	1,971	2,959	1,234	−1,657	−2,229	−2,545	−2,093	−2,641	−2,452	1,777	2,531	510	Colombia
−62	40	−139	−98	−239	−443	−200	−472	−761	−606	−323	−249	−498	−399	660	....	....	Costa Rica
−24	−5	−10	−20	−48	−48	−40	−37	−43	−47	−53	−48	−51	−44	−69	−79	....	Dominica
−547	−630	−880	−718	−1,039	−1,058	−1,071	−1,612	−1,443	−1,451	−1,391	−1,674	−1,995	−2,617	−2,904	−3,742	....	Dominican Republic
1,294	557	−33	622	662	1,009	643	1,018	214	149	−66	921	492	−1,132	1,588	1,395	....	Ecuador
−216	−124	−349	−356	−663	−666	−705	−962	−962	−1,170	−1,462	−1,242	−1,143	−1,306	−1,345	−1,719	....	El Salvador
−43	−52	−57	−59	−68	−77	−88	−80	−95	−94	−105	−122	−122	−137	−110	−136	....	Grenada
−17	168	−355	−340	−358	−217	−443	−1,044	−1,021	−997	−875	−643	−940	−1,409	−1,445	−1,660	....	Guatemala
5						−61	−68	−41									Guyana
−122	−112	−101	−103	−111	−177	−282	−139	−180	−111	−429	−416	−354	−341	....	....	....	Haiti
−86	23	−41	−34	−45	−12	−72	−151	−204	−250	−141	−287	−294	−323	−740	−658	....	Honduras
−436	−248	−352	−357	−590	−502	−392	−425	−815	−551	−829	−994	−1,132	−1,131	−1,187	−1,354	....	Jamaica
8,399	5,019	8,786	2,611	405	−881	−7,279	−15,934	−13,481	−18,464	7,089	6,533	623	−7,915	−5,583	−8,001	−9,955	Mexico
	−16	−19	−21	−31	−41	−33	−28	−22	−27	−22	5	−20	−18	−18	−18	....	Montserrat
−322	−521	−614	−654	−704	−810	−817	−836	−838	−921	−964	....						Netherlands Antilles
−489	−420	−439	−483	−229	−237	−420	−548	−392	−443	−412	−574	−790	−817	−1,146	−995	....	Nicaragua
−437	−179	−193	157	−124	−158	−400	−376	−334	−250	−589	−644	−685	−1,365	−1,386	−1,190	−826	Panama
−194	−288	−321	−159	164	361	77	9	79	−243	−270	−587	−587	−393	−360	−532	....	Paraguay
1,219	−73	−500	−134	1,246	399	−189	−340	−607	−998	−2,168	−1,986	−1,723	−2,462	−633	−323	....	Peru
−26	−29	−41	−54	−61	−69	−68	−51	−63	−70	−81	−92	−78	−86	−90	−118	....	St. Kitts and Nevis
−62	−52	−75	−72	−125	−108	−148	−142	−139	−166	−155	−181	−222	−225	−251	−253	....	St. Lucia
−8	−11	−32	−20	−35	−35	−53	−38	−61	−67	−57	−76	−105	−120	−127	−91	....	St. Vincent & Grens.
47	59	115	212	390	163	−2	122	84	99	123	−2	36	−27	44	153	....	Suriname
787	169	357	405	506	1,013	564	696	547	741	588	382	−78	−529	−741	....	....	Trinidad and Tobago
178	273	102	292	463	426	61	−122	−387	−706	−563	−687	−704	−772	−897	−937	....	Uruguay
6,977	798	1,694	−1,863	5,694	10,706	4,900	1,322	3,275	7,625	7,013	13,770	10,025	2,471	7,606	17,544	9,774	Venezuela, Rep. Bol.

Memorandum Items

1985	1986	1987	1988	1989	1990	1991	1992	1993	1994	1995	1996	1997	1998	1999	2000	2001	
52,984	8,232	31,228	20,288	47,072	79,509	44,765	41,383	40,356	58,461	65,763	95,891	87,284	39,284	89,073	171,388	....	Oil Exporting Ctys
4,097	12,861	33,714	27,397	4,936	−21,207	−13,911	−32,430	−69,751	−47,373	−52,007	−77,097	−55,618	5,940	60,637	68,478	....	Non-Oil Develop.Ctys

Balance of Payments

Current Account Balance

Excluding Exceptional Financing

	1985	1986	1987	1988	1989	1990	1991	1992	1993	1994	1995	1996	1997	1998	1999	2000	2001
								Expressed in Millions of US Dollars									
All Countries	−85,067	−71,776	−62,374	−73,857	−99,010	−117,056	−125,149	−112,729	−75,633	−53,855	−36,144	−44,394	5,412	−80,872	−138,286	−170,059	....
Industrial Countries	−65,839	−35,496	−70,998	−62,416	−82,904	−99,296	−34,133	−38,841	41,763	15,171	52,824	38,837	74,427	−37,499	−203,492	−306,897	
United States	−124,470	−147,172	−160,653	−121,253	−99,500	−78,960	3,690	−48,480	−82,480	−118,200	−109,890	−120,940	−139,820	−217,411	−324,390	−444,690	−417,440
Canada	−5,734	−11,157	−13,430	−14,818	−21,769	−19,764	−22,345	−21,160	−21,822	−13,024	−4,328	3,378	−8,233	−7,839	1,367	18,596	19,479
Australia	−9,172	−9,807	−7,966	−11,748	−17,866	−15,950	−10,986	−11,124	−9,684	−17,146	−19,323	−15,810	−12,384	−18,014	−23,012	−15,391	−9,194
Japan	51,129	85,877	84,351	79,249	63,215	44,078	68,203	112,574	131,637	130,255	111,044	65,884	94,354	120,696	106,865	116,883	89,280
New Zealand	−2,657	−2,826	−2,910	−1,863	−1,525	−1,453	−1,159	−1,071	−746	−2,384	−3,003	−3,964	−4,366	−2,162	−3,632	−2,734	−1,587
Euro Area																	
Austria	−158	204	−263	−242	248	1,166	61	−753	−1,013	−2,992	−5,448	−4,890	−5,221	−5,258	−6,655	−4,864	−4,103
Belgium-Luxembourg	670	3,059	2,797	3,592	3,600	3,627	4,746	6,650	11,237	12,571	14,232	13,762	13,914	12,168	14,579	11,360	13,037
Finland	−806	−693	−1,731	−2,694	−5,797	−6,962	−6,807	−5,116	−1,135	1,110	5,231	5,003	6,633	7,340	7,657	9,038	8,357
France	−35	2,430	−4,446	−4,619	−4,671	−9,944	−6,518	3,893	8,990	7,415	10,840	20,561	37,801	37,699	35,039	20,428	21,359
Germany	17,578	40,914	46,444	50,354	57,002	48,303	−17,668	−19,145	−13,871	−20,939	−18,932	−7,969	−2,837	−6,640	−17,940	−18,707	3,815
Greece	−3,276	−1,676	−1,223	−958	−2,561	−3,537	−1,574	−2,140	−747	−146	−2,864	−4,554	−4,860	....	−7,295	−9,820	−9,400
Ireland	−736	−847	−76	−25	−581	−361	284	607	1,765	1,577	1,721	2,049	1,866	1,016	354	−593	−1,043
Italy	−4,084	2,462	−2,635	−7,181	−12,812	−16,479	−24,463	−29,217	7,802	13,209	25,076	39,999	32,403	19,998	8,111	−5,781	−163
Luxembourg	....	....	....	....	....	....	....	....	....	....	2,453	2,207	2,005	1,631	1,277	1,617	884
Netherlands	4,248	4,318	4,187	7,132	10,039	8,089	7,466	6,847	13,203	17,294	25,759	21,487	25,060	13,309	14,810	11,156	12,405
Portugal	380	1,166	435	−1,066	153	−181	−716	−184	233	−2,196	−132	−5,216	−6,465	−7,833	−9,764	−10,962	−9,959
Spain	2,785	3,914	−263	−3,795	−10,924	−18,009	−19,798	−21,537	−5,804	−6,389	792	407	2,512	−3,135	−13,761	−19,237	−15,082
Denmark	−2,767	−4,490	−3,002	−1,340	−1,118	1,372	1,983	4,199	4,832	3,189	1,855	3,090	921	−2,008	2,915	2,507	4,142
Iceland	−115	16	−188	−231	−102	−126	−273	−158	42	109	54	−117	−125	−560	−591	−848	....
Norway	3,038	−4,551	−4,102	−3,896	212	3,992	5,032	4,471	3,522	3,760	5,233	10,969	10,036	6	8,378	24,807	25,960
Sweden	−1,010	32	−21	−534	−3,101	−6,339	−4,653	−8,827	−4,159	743	4,940	5,892	7,406	4,639	5,982	6,617	6,696
Switzerland	6,039	4,654	6,288	8,846	8,063	6,955	10,382	14,247	17,926	17,588	21,804	21,051	26,679	26,774	28,159	32,542	....
United Kingdom	3,314	−1,324	−12,590	−35,326	−43,109	−38,811	−19,022	−23,416	−17,966	−10,234	−14,291	−13,440	−2,851	−7,964	−31,944	−28,819	−29,371
Developing Countries	−19,228	−36,281	8,624	−11,441	−16,106	−17,760	−91,016	−73,888	−117,396	−69,026	−88,968	−83,231	−69,015	−43,373	65,205	136,838	....
Africa	1,074	−6,276	−3,190	−8,076	−5,558	−447	−3,511	−5,853	−8,498	−8,661	−11,928	−258	−8,563	−17,914	−9,519	−1,624	....
Algeria	1,015	−2,230	141	−2,040	−1,081	1,420	2,367										
Angola	195	−303	447	−469	−132	−236	−580	−735	−669	−340	−295	3,266	−872	−1,858	−1,702	....	
Benin	−39	−53	−34	−138	−45	−48	−261	−120	−101	−23	−213	−57	−170	−151	−191	....	
Botswana	82	109	628	194	492	−19	303	198	427	212	300	495	721	170	517	....	
Burkina Faso	−63	−18	−50	−47	99	−77	−91	−23	−71	15							
Burundi	−41	−36	−95	−70	−11	−69	−33	−60	−28	−17	10	−40	−1	−54	−27	−49	
Cameroon	−562	−452	−893	−428	−298	−561	−339	−397	−565	−56	90	....	....	....	....	....	
Cape Verde	−9	2	−3	−	−13	−4	−7	−12	−24	−46	−62	−35	−30	−58	....	....	
Central African Rep.	−49	−87	−73	−35	−33	−89	−62	−83	−13	−25	....	....	....	....	....	....	
Chad	−87	−59	−26	26	−56	−46	−66	−86	−117	−38	....	....	....	....	....	....	
Comoros	−14	−16	−21	−7	5	−10	−10	−14	10	−7	−19	....	....	....	....	....	
Congo, Republic of	−161	−601	−223	−445	−85	−251	−462	−317	−553	−793	−650	−1,109	−252	....	....	....	
Côte d'Ivoire	64	−300	−970	−1,241	−967	−1,214	−1,074	−1,013	−892	−14	−492	−162	−155	−290	−121	−13	
Djibouti	....	....	....	....	....	....	....	....	−87	−34	−46	−23	....	....	....	....	
Equatorial Guinea	....	....	−25	−21	−21	−19	−41	−11	3	−	−123	−344	....	....	....	....	
Ethiopia	106	−327	−217	−228	−144	−294	103	−120	−50	−10	125	80	−40	−266	−465	16	
Gabon	−162	−1,057	−449	−616	−192	168	75	−168	−49	317	465	889	531	−596	390	....	
Gambia, The	7	4	6	26	15	22	13	37	−5	8	−8	−48	−24	....	....	....	
Ghana	−134	−85	−98	−67	−94	−223	−252	−377	−560	−255	−145	−325	−550	−443	−933	−413	
Guinea	....	−124	−38	−222	−180	−203	−289	−263	−57	−248	−216	−177	−91	−184	−152	....	
Guinea-Bissau	−76	−63	−57	−68	−93	−60	−79	−104	−65	−48	−51	−60	−30	....	....	....	
Kenya	−118	−47	−503	−472	−591	−527	−213	−180	71	98	−400	−73	−457	−475	−98	−238	
Lesotho	−12	−3	24	−25	10	65	83	38	29	108	−323	−303	−269	−280	−221	−151	
Liberia	55	−18	−145	....	....	....											
Madagascar	−184	−143	−141	−150	−84	−265	−230	−198	−258	−277	−276	−291	−266	−301	−252	−283	
Malawi	−127	−85	−61	−87	−51	−86	−228	−285	−166	−450	....	....	....	....	....	....	
Mali	−210	−254	−219	−243	−155	−221	−173	−241	−189	−163	−284	−273	−178	....	....	....	
Mauritania	−116	−195	−147	−96	−19	−10	−30	−118	−174	−70	22	91	48	77	....	....	
Mauritius	−30	94	65	−56	−104	−119	−17	−	−92	−232	−22	34	−89	3	−131	−33	
Morocco	−891	−209	182	473	−787	−196	−413	−433	−521	−723	−1,296	−58	−169	−146	−171	−501	
Mozambique	−301	−409	−389	−359	−460	−415	−344	−352	−446	−467	−445	−421	−296	−429	−912	−764	
Namibia	....	....	....	....	....	28	105	50	110	85	176	116	90	162	....	....	
Niger	−69	−156	−177	−230	−257	−236	−176	−159	−97	−126	−152	....	....	....	....	....	
Nigeria	2,604	211	−73	−296	1,090	4,988	1,203	2,268	−780	−2,128	−2,578	3,507	552	−4,244	506	....	
Rwanda	−64	−69	−135	−145	−123	−108	−34	−83	−129	−46	57	−8	−62	−83	−72	−7	
São Tomé & Príncipe	−18	−19	−13	−11	−11	−14	....	....	....	....	....	....	....	....	....	....	
Senegal	−361	−370	−430	−405	−348	−363	−372	−401	433	−187	−244	−200	−185	−247	−320	....	
Seychelles	−19	−33	−21	−28	−40	−13	−8	−7	−39	−26	−54	−57	−63	−125	−114	....	
Sierra Leone	3	141	−30	−3	−60	−69	15	−5	−58	−89	−127	....	....	....	....	....	
Somalia	−103	−126	−114	−98	−157	....											
South Africa	2,317	2,828	3,347	1,504	1,343	2,134	2,256	1,967	1,503	112	−2,205	−1,880	−2,273	−2,157	−640	−575	−166
Sudan	149	−26	−232	−358	−150	−372	−955	−506	−202	−602	−500	−827	−828	−957	−465	−557	−618
Swaziland	−38	11	66	95	77	51	47	−41	−64	2	−30	−52	9	−68	6	−40	
Tanzania	−375	−322	−407	−357	−335	−559	−737	−714	−1,048	−711	−646	−511	−630	−956	−746	−480	
Togo	−33	−66	−61	−87	−51	−100	−147	−141	−82	−56	−122	−154	−117	−140	−127	....	
Tunisia	−581	−605	−54	210	−218	−463	−469	−1,104	−1,323	−537	−774	−478	−595	−675	−442	−821	
Uganda	5	−43	−112	−195	−260	−263	−170	−100	−224	−208	−339	−252	−367	−503	−551	....	
Zambia	−395	−348	−245	−293	−219	−594	−306	....	....	....	....	....	−353	−573	−447	−584	
Zimbabwe	−64	17	58	125	17	−140	−457	−604	−116	−425	....	....	....	....	....	....	
Africa not specified	−92	−444	−1,088	−585	−862	−715	−944	−757	−373	−278	15	35	−200	−426	−113	−226	−162

Current Account Balance

Excluding Exceptional Financing

Expressed in Millions of US Dollars

1985	1986	1987	1988	1989	1990	1991	1992	1993	1994	1995	1996	1997	1998	1999	2000	2001	
-15,953	1,375	18,328	9,302	-1,855	-1,327	-3,034	-3,263	-20,887	-4,325	-31,058	-38,364	26,673	117,440	121,191	101,908	....	**Asia**
-243	-537	-167	26	-143												....	Afghanistan, I.S. of
-458	-627	-238	-273	-1,100	-398	65	181	359	200	-824	-991	-286	-35	-364	-306	....	Bangladesh
....	....	....	....	....												....	Bhutan
....	....	....	....	....		-93	-104	-157	-186	-185	-210	-49	-113	-19		....	Cambodia
-11,417	-7,034	300	-3,802	-4,317	11,997	13,272	6,401	-11,609	6,908	1,618	7,243	36,963	31,472	21,115	20,518	....	China,P.R.: Mainland
												3,904	11,479	8,915	11,968		China,P.R.:Hong Kong
19	17	27	71	7	-94	-68	-61	-138	-113	-113	14	-34	-60	13		....	Fiji
-4,177	-4,598	-5,192	-7,172	-6,826	-7,037	-4,292	-4,485	-1,876	-1,676	-5,563	-5,956	-2,965	-6,903	-3,228	-4,198	....	India
-1,923	-3,911	-2,098	-1,397	-1,108	-2,988	-4,260	-2,780	-2,106	-2,792	-6,431	-7,663	-4,889	4,096	5,785	7,985	....	Indonesia
-3	-3	-3	-2	-2	-9	4	-9	-4	1							....	Kiribati
-795	4,709	10,058	14,505	5,361	-2,003	-8,317	-3,944	990	-3,867	-8,507	-23,006	-8,167	40,365	24,477	12,241	8,617	Korea
-164	-142	-165	-103	-137	-111	-115	-111	-139	-284	-346	-347	-306	-150	-121		....	Lao People's Dem.Rep
-600	-101	2,575	1,867	315	-870	-4,183	-2,167	-2,991	-4,520	-8,644	-4,462	-5,935	9,529	12,603	8,409	....	Malaysia
-6	—	8	9	11	10	-9	-20	-54	-11	-18	-7	-34	-23	-82	-53	....	Maldives
-814	-1,061	-991	-1,033	-1,229	-640	-104	-56	31	46	39	-101	55	-129	-112		....	Mongolia
-205	-294	-180	-176	-68	-431	-267	-114	-228	-130	-258	-280	-412	-494	-282	-243	....	Myanmar
-122	-119	-123	-271	-243	-289	-304	-181	-223	-352	-356	-327	-388	-67	-256	-277	....	Nepal
-1,083	-648	-563	-1,430	-1,340	-1,662	-1,403	-1,877	-2,901	-1,812	-3,349	-4,436	-1,712	-2,248	-920	-96	....	Pakistan
-122	-98	-198	-296	-313	-76	-475	-160	474	402	492	189	-192	-29	95		....	Papua New Guinea
-36	952	-444	-390	-1,456	-2,695	-1,034	-1,000	-3,016	-2,950	-1,980	-3,953	-4,351	1,546	7,910	8,459	4,503	Philippines
2	7	7	8	13	7	-29	-52	-39	6	9	12	9	20	-19		....	Samoa
-4	319	-109	1,937	2,964	3,122	4,880	5,915	4,211	11,400	14,900	12,823	17,927	20,334	21,750	21,797	....	Singapore
-28	-12	-17	-38	-33	-28	-36	-1	-8	-3	8	15	-38	8	21		....	Solomon Islands
-418	-417	-326	-394	-414	-298	-595	-451	-382	-757	-770	-683	-395	-228	-561	-1,042	....	Sri Lanka
-1,537	247	-366	-1,654	-2,498	-7,281	-7,571	-6,303	-6,364	-8,085	-13,554	-14,691	-3,021	14,243	12,428	9,313	6,227	Thailand
2	2	2	-13	7	6	—		-6								....	Tonga
-10	-12	-24	-15	-12	-6	-14	-13	-15	-20	-18	-27	-19	15	-3		....	Vanuatu
8,175	14,702	16,529	9,352	10,730	10,482	11,845	8,121	5,249	4,242	2,792	8,455	5,331	2,325	9,576	9,410	19,417	Asia not specified
3,805	5,549	11,298	8,942	-3,034	-24,840	-1,738	-7,483	-16,979	6,054	-4,732	-13,546	-26,790	-26,566	-2,963	15,096	....	**Europe**
-36	-3	5	-27	-39	-118	-168	-51	15	-157	-12	-107	-272	-65	-155	-156	-218	Albania
								-67	-104	-218	-291	-307	-418	-307			Armenia
....	....	....	....	....						-401	-931	-916	-1,365	-600	-168	-52	Azerbaijan
....	....	....	....	....			-435		-444	-458	-516	-859	-1,017	-194	-323	-270	Belarus
													-1,247	-1,561	-1,300	-1,379	Bosnia & Herzegovina
-136	-951	-720	-402	-769	-1,710	-77	-360	-1,099	-32	-26	16	427	-62	-685	-701	....	Bulgaria
								625	553	-1,592	-1,049	-2,825	-1,468	-1,406	-448	-642	Croatia
-180	-19	-8	-108	-249	-154	-420	-638	110	74	-164	-466	-338	-603	-217	-456	....	Cyprus
								466	-820	-1,374	-4,128	-3,622	-1,308	-1,466	-2,690	-2,638	Czech Republic
691	169	371	1,093	936	-1,227	908	-31									....	Czechoslovakia
							36	22	-166	-158	-398	-562	-478	-295	-294	-339	Estonia
....	....	....	....	....													Georgia
-455	-1,365	-676	-572	-588	379	403	352	-4,262	-4,054	-2,530	-1,689	-982	-2,304	-2,106	-1,328	-1,097	Hungary
										-213	-751	-799	-1,225	-171	413	-1,749	Kazakhstan
....	....	....	....	....			-88	-84	-235	-425	-139	-413	-248	-158		Kyrgyz Republic
....	....	....	....	....		191	417	201	-16	-280	-345	-650	-654	-494	-758	Latvia
							-86	-94	-614	-723	-981	-1,298	-1,194	-675	-574	Lithuania
									-288	-275	-312	-109	-107		Macedonia, FYR
-26	7	23	61	-9	-56	-7	30	-84	-132	-361	-404	-201	-222	-122	-469	-172	Malta
								-82	-88	-195	-275	-335	-16	-116		Moldova
-982	-1,106	-379	-107	-1,409	3,067	-2,146	-3,104	-5,788	954	854	-3,264	-5,744	-6,901	-12,487	-9,997	....	Poland
1,381	1,395	2,043	3,922	2,514	-3,254	-1,012	-1,506	-1,231	-455	-1,780	-2,579	-2,137	-2,918	-1,297	-1,359	....	Romania
....	....	....	....	....					8,434	7,488	11,755	2,061	683	24,731	46,405	34,575	Russia
							-580	671	390	-2,090	-1,961	-2,126	-1,155	-694		Slovak Republic
							978	191	573	-99	31	11	-147	-782	-612	-66	Slovenia
-1,013	-1,465	-806	1,596	938	-2,625	250	-974	-6,433	2,631	-2,338	-2,437	-2,679	1,984	-1,360	-9,819	3,396	Turkey
												—	-580			Turkmenistan
....	....	....	....	....					-1,163	-1,152	-1,184	-1,335	-1,296	1,658	1,481	1,402	Ukraine
																	Yugoslavia, SFR
833	1,100	1,248	2,487	2,427	-2,364	-1,161	-287	-629	-45	71	-1,154	-1,155	-487	-399	-149	-594	Europe not specified
-769	-693	-1,800	-2,060	-2,452	-2,435	5,593											
-5,418	-19,473	-7,912	-11,325	2,927	10,755	-64,514	-23,345	-25,719	-10,950	-3,835	8,652	6,430	-25,307	13,132	68,315	....	**Middle East**
39	-69	-201	192	-193	70	-603	-827	-339	-256	237	261	-31	-778	-340	113	....	Bahrain, Kingdom of
-2,166	-1,811	-246	-1,048	-1,309	185	1,903	2,812	2,299	31	-254	-192	-711	-2,566	-1,635	-971	....	Egypt
-476	-5,155	-2,090	-1,869	-191	327	-9,448	-6,504	-4,215	4,956	3,358	5,232	2,213	-2,139	6,589	12,645	....	Iran, I.R. of
988	1,277	-1,407	-838	208	163	-1,278	-875	-2,480	-3,447	-4,972	-5,498	-3,845	-1,325	-3,277	-1,974	-1,852	Israel
-260	-40	-352	-294	385	-227	-394	-835	-629	-398	-259	-222	29	14	405		....	Jordan
4,798	5,616	4,561	4,602	9,136	3,886	-26,478	-450	2,499	3,227	5,016	7,107	7,934	2,215	5,062	14,670	8,566	Kuwait
1,906	-166	-1,043	-1,826	-1,026	2,201	-219	1,392	-1,362	29	1,998	1,477	1,875	-391	1,984		....	Libya
-10	-1,040	784	-309	305	1,106	-251	-598	-1,190	-805	-801	338	-73	-2,993	-369	3,347	....	Oman
-12,932	-11,795	-9,773	-7,340	-9,538	-4,152	-27,546	-17,740	-17,268	-10,487	-5,325	681	305	-13,150	412	14,336	14,502	Saudi Arabia
-958	-504	-298	-151	1,222	1,762	699	55	-203	-791	263	40	461	58	201	1,062	....	Syrian Arab Republic
-287	-125	-452	-694	-579												....	Yemen Arab Rep.
-231	-176	-130	-404	-417												....	Yemen, P.D. Rep.
					393	-862	-1,126	-1,275	178	144	39	-69	-303	577	1,862	....	Yemen, Republic of
4,171	-5,486	2,735	-1,344	4,923	5,040	-37	1,353	-1,555	-3,188	-3,240	-611	-1,660	-3,949	3,524	17,537	8,139	Middle East not spec

Balance of Payments

Current Account Balance

Excluding Exceptional Financing

Expressed in Millions of US Dollars

	1985	1986	1987	1988	1989	1990	1991	1992	1993	1994	1995	1996	1997	1998	1999	2000	2001
Western Hemisphere	-2,736	-17,454	-9,900	-10,283	-8,586	-1,901	-18,219	-33,944	-45,314	-51,145	-37,415	-39,715	-66,766	-91,027	-56,636	-46,858	....
Anguilla	....	....	....	....	....	-9	-7	-16	-13	-11	-9	-20	-19	-20	-51	-56	....
Antigua and Barbuda	-23	-118	-111	-45	-82	-31	-31	-10	15	-6	-1	-60	-47	-63	-77	-79	....
Argentina	-952	-2,859	-4,235	-1,572	-1,305	4,552	-647	-5,653	-8,160	-11,158	-5,210	-6,877	-12,344	-14,626	-12,039	-8,970	....
Aruba	....	-19	-23	-44	-47	-158	-209	44	42	81	—	-69	-196	-19	-333	282	....
Bahamas, The	-3	23	-55	-67	-84	-37	-180	36	49	-42	-146	-263	-472	-995	-672	-402	....
Barbados	51	7	-19	43	25	-11	-27	140	69	134	43	70	-50	-63	-148	-146	....
Belize	9	12	9	-3	-19	15	-26	-29	-49	-40	-17	-7	-32	-60	-78	-139	....
Bolivia	-286	-389	-432	-304	-270	-199	-263	-534	-506	-90	-303	-404	-554	-678	-488	-464	....
Brazil	-280	-5,311	-1,452	4,156	1,002	-3,823	-1,450	6,089	20	-1,153	-18,136	-23,248	-30,491	-33,829	-25,400	-24,632	-23,208
Chile	-1,413	-1,191	-735	-231	-690	-485	-99	-958	-2,554	-1,585	-1,350	-3,510	-3,728	-4,139	-80	-991	....
Colombia	-1,809	383	336	-216	-201	542	2,349	901	-2,102	-3,673	-4,596	-4,757	-5,882	-5,226	361	354	-1,782
Costa Rica	-291	-161	-376	-304	-480	-494	-99	-380	-620	-244	-358	-264	-481	-521	-649	....	....
Dominica	-6	-7	-7	-12	-46	-44	-34	-27	-27	-38	-41	-33	-26	-12	-41	-69	....
Dominican Republic	-108	-183	-364	-19	-327	-280	-157	-708	-533	-283	-183	-213	-163	-338	-429	-1,027	....
Ecuador	76	-582	-1,187	-680	-715	-360	-708	-122	-845	-900	-994	-37	-458	-2,099	942	928	....
El Salvador	-189	-17	-68	-129	-370	-261	-212	-195	-123	-18	-262	-169	-98	-91	-274	-418	....
Grenada	2	-19	-29	-28	-36	-46	-48	-32	-44	-27	-41	-56	-67	-80	-47	-79	....
Guatemala	-246	-18	-443	-414	-367	-233	-184	-706	-702	-625	-572	-452	-634	-1,039	-1,026	-1,049	....
Guyana	-97	....	....	....	....	....	....	-139	-140	-125	-135	....	....	....	....	....	....
Haiti	-95	-45	-31	-40	-63	-22	-92	7	-12	-23	-87	-138	-48	-38	....	....	....
Honduras	-309	-225	-245	-161	-180	-186	-213	-298	-309	-343	-201	-335	-272	-395	-583	-510	....
Jamaica	-273	-18	-126	47	-283	-312	-240	29	-184	82	-99	-143	-332	-328	-211	-275	....
Mexico	800	-1,377	4,247	-2,374	-5,825	-7,451	-14,888	-24,442	-23,400	-29,662	-1,576	-2,529	-7,696	-16,097	-14,017	-17,764	-17,708
Montserrat	....	-5	-7	-16	5	-23	-20	-13	-8	-12	-2	16	-2	2	-1	-9	....
Netherlands Antilles	403	51	-49	75	38	-44	-6	10	1	-98	87	....	....	....	....	....	....
Nicaragua	-771	-691	-690	-715	-362	-385	-534	-834	-644	-714	-578	-629	-673	-504	-697	-505	....
Panama	75	-99	545	721	112	209	-241	-267	-96	16	-471	-201	-507	-1,182	-1,320	-933	-499
Paraguay	-252	-365	-490	-210	256	390	85	-57	59	-274	-92	-353	-650	-160	-90	-137	....
Peru	102	-1,393	-2,065	-1,819	-570	-1,419	-1,504	-2,090	-2,295	-2,560	-4,125	-3,430	-3,057	-3,634	-1,923	-1,628	....
St. Kitts and Nevis	-7	-9	-16	-28	-38	-47	-36	-15	-29	-24	-45	-66	-54	-42	-83	-62	....
St. Lucia	-13	-7	-14	-18	-63	-57	-72	-56	-50	-48	-33	-54	-78	-66	-79	-82	....
St. Vincent & Grens.	4	-10	-20	-17	-30	-24	-46	-24	-44	-57	-41	-36	-84	-94	-72	-26	....
Suriname	-18	-37	136	114	294	67	-133	25	44	59	63	-64	-68	-155	-29	32	....
Trinidad and Tobago	-48	-412	-225	-89	-39	459	-5	139	113	218	294	105	-614	-644	....	....	....
Uruguay	-98	42	-141	22	133	186	42	-9	-244	-438	-213	-233	-287	-476	-508	-593	....
Venezuela, Rep. Bol.	3,327	-2,245	-1,390	-5,809	2,161	8,279	1,736	-3,749	-1,993	2,541	2,014	8,914	3,467	-3,253	3,557	13,111	4,364
Memorandum Items																	
Oil Exporting Ctys	2,971	-25,990	-8,046	-16,921	5,273	21,208	-60,434	-24,010	-24,282	-4,547	-1,335	23,798	14,096	-19,409	30,366	100,129	....
Non-Oil Develop.Ctys	-22,199	-10,291	16,671	5,480	-21,380	-38,968	-30,582	-49,878	-93,114	-64,479	-87,633	-107,029	-83,111	-23,964	34,840	36,709	....

Capital and Financial Account

Including Net Errors and Omissions, but Excluding Reserve Assets,
Use of Fund Credit, and Exceptional Financing

Expressed in Millions of US Dollars

1985	1986	1987	1988	1989	1990	1991	1992	1993	1994	1995	1996	1997	1998	1999	2000	2001	
62,209	70,591	177,613	67,700	112,408	142,407	133,069	113,831	139,215	119,792	163,577	202,927	65,629	57,306	263,922	345,098	....	**All Countries**
62,357	58,268	178,136	100,502	109,788	154,178	20,916	32,491	-13,323	20,264	27,760	40,132	-48,928	31,688	244,617	354,063	....	**Industrial Countries**
128,305	146,862	151,506	125,168	124,788	81,193	-9,449	44,559	83,858	112,853	119,639	114,271	140,837	224,155	315,656	444,989	422,366	United States
2,464	10,738	16,744	22,968	22,462	20,903	20,496	16,375	22,727	12,632	7,039	2,119	5,840	12,836	4,566	-14,876	-17,306	Canada
6,871	510	8,340	17,027	18,467	17,691	10,661	6,397	9,642	16,186	19,719	18,282	15,258	15,974	29,717	14,026	10,290	Australia
-51,629	-70,747	-46,301	-61,689	-76,265	-53,168	-76,593	-111,954	-104,164	-104,990	-52,433	-30,746	-87,787	-126,860	-30,609	-67,928	-48,793	Japan
620	214	662	-1,057	308	1,632	-353	1,202	672	3,117	3,387	5,736	2,924	1,676	3,820	2,590	1,400	New Zealand
																	Euro Area
173	439	595	733	742	-1,181	775	3,341	3,214	3,826	6,839	5,965	2,168	8,740	4,484	4,119	2,215	Austria
-867	-3,030	-363	-2,731	-3,288	-3,223	-4,162	-6,080	-13,359	-12,351	-13,990	-13,169	-12,858	-14,263	-16,446	-12,319	-11,595	Belgium-Luxembourg
1,389	-1,589	5,764	2,952	4,729	10,893	4,921	2,966	1,426	3,603	-5,603	-8,038	-4,329	-7,044	-7,644	-8,679	-7,952	Finland
2,731	-1,249	1,844	-540	3,814	20,891	1,324	-5,469	-13,996	-4,968	-10,128	-20,321	-31,861	-17,884	-36,431	-22,861	-26,825	France
-15,350	-35,488	-24,949	-65,950	-54,143	-41,050	11,484	56,321	-328	18,903	26,156	6,774	-915	10,656	3,825	13,485	-9,281	Germany
2,880	2,326	2,197	1,895	2,213	3,817	3,778	1,766	4,186	6,455	2,841	8,769	345	....	9,730	12,393	3,701	Greece
784	753	962	617	-356	986	179	-2,773	894	-1,752	618	-2,101	-2,974	2,196	-2,327	715	1,438	Ireland
-3,502	-115	8,105	15,598	24,170	28,102	17,745	5,224	-10,938	-11,634	-22,272	-28,092	-19,254	-41,470	-16,162	9,028	-425	Italy
-3,476	-4,649	-1,493	-5,564	-9,532	-7,821	-6,960	-728	-6,562	-16,794	-27,672	-27,177	-27,768	-15,648	-19,421	-10,936	-12,755	Netherlands
327	-1,276	1,341	1,933	4,501	3,723	6,430	28	-3,081	765	-168	5,764	7,438	8,341	9,980	11,333	10,811	Portugal
-5,061	-1,571	12,969	12,212	15,640	25,197	34,105	3,728	600	6,426	-7,206	23,871	9,244	-11,220	-9,090	16,356	13,742	Spain
4,299	3,161	6,733	2,776	-2,720	2,013	-4,887	-124	-5,399	-5,041	643	474	5,611	-2,231	6,522	-8,156	-872	Denmark
179	83	170	232	157	200	282	237	-101	-259	-50	270	81	592	676	780	....	Iceland
414	1,340	3,882	3,758	753	-3,578	-7,782	-5,203	4,731	-3,507	-4,658	-4,499	-11,234	-6,390	-2,394	-21,121	-28,075	Norway
-3,640	145	783	1,472	4,355	13,891	4,590	15,780	6,689	1,639	-6,604	-12,278	-14,118	-1,386	-4,101	-6,446	-7,744	Sweden
-4,811	-3,564	-3,075	-11,228	-6,694	-5,786	-9,390	-9,850	-17,440	-16,579	-21,775	-18,530	-24,525	-25,595	-30,643	-36,546	....	Switzerland
-744	4,973	31,718	39,920	35,686	38,853	23,723	16,749	23,403	11,735	13,438	12,789	-1,051	7,707	30,908	34,117	24,917	United Kingdom
-149	12,323	-523	-32,802	2,620	-11,771	112,153	81,340	152,538	99,528	135,818	162,795	114,556	25,618	19,305	-8,965	....	**Developing Countries**
-4,860	528	-5,590	-3,408	-3,184	-2,473	-2,372	-7,792	-734	3,335	3,686	-1,639	11,461	7,711	4,529	7,062	....	**Africa**
6	732	-493	1,081	307	-1,431	-1,319	....	....	....	....	....	....	....	....	....	....	Algeria
-201	44	-779	-456	-798	-973	-920	-403	-651	-688	-944	-505	307	874	1,418	....	....	Angola
10	-26	-18	-27	-161	-61	-15	53	-56	41	-42	-92	70	65	103	....	....	Benin
172	198	-67	188	85	327	71	208	-30	-76	-93	16	-86	-126	-146	....	....	Botswana
69	42	60	65	-235	84	98	43	74	-22	....	....	....	....	....	....	....	Burkina Faso
57	65	93	77	49	66	66	85	44	52	26	5	11	34	26	53	....	Burundi
621	371	422	265	170	-310	-392	-909	-320	-495	-74	....	....	....	....	....	....	Cameroon
23	-2	6	-1	28	-3	-9	35	39	68	30	57	30	69	....	....	....	Cape Verde
24	83	62	21	17	68	22	46	-1	38	....	....	....	....	....	....	....	Central African Rep.
64	40	26	-60	86	23	46	43	69	43	....	....	....	....	....	....	....	Chad
20	19	30	3	—	6	-16	8	-2	12	9	....	....	....	....	....	....	Comoros
80	202	-265	-22	-318	-113	3	-113	133	639	40	759	-296	....	....	....	....	Congo, Republic of
-233	-92	46	-184	-344	-232	-254	-404	-345	-7	238	-686	-322	-359	-587	-599	....	Côte d'Ivoire
....	....	....	....	....	....	....	72	23	47	-1	....	....	....	....	....	....	Djibouti
....	....	—	3	11	13	27	-17	-13	-18	112	339	....	....	....	....	....	Equatorial Guinea
56	441	109	205	190	95	-459	-144	82	-126	109	-545	-388	-99	459	-56	....	Ethiopia
102	862	314	615	96	-436	-298	-274	-403	-490	-901	-1,140	-729	-71	-788	....	....	Gabon
-13	-36	5	-2	-11	-18	4	-18	17	-2	9	62	31	....	....	....	....	Gambia, The
148	25	238	248	250	329	389	254	613	427	396	304	576	551	843	154	....	Ghana
....	11	-59	100	-5	106	131	88	-40	124	144	117	-40	26	72	....	....	Guinea
84	30	26	27	22	29	4	53	5	-7	10	17	15	....	....	....	....	Guinea-Bissau
66	184	478	428	713	435	169	-77	341	-36	259	460	472	558	64	202	....	Kenya
18	15	-23	18	-18	-48	-41	12	73	13	421	419	410	396	180	169	....	Lesotho
-259	-276	-155	....	....	....	....	....	....	....	....	....	....	....	....	....	....	Liberia
16	26	-22	33	-77	-13	-62	-80	-76	1	-54	197	250	1	148	123	....	Madagascar
101	85	106	147	—	115	243	238	190	415	....	....	....	....	....	....	....	Malawi
183	205	205	261	156	156	202	103	91	98	232	302	169	....	....	....	....	Mali
86	165	16	33	13	-63	46	135	-108	-35	-28	-87	-20	-34	....	....	....	Mauritania
28	28	154	241	249	351	207	43	99	189	131	14	54	-69	321	264	....	Mauritius
859	539	116	-209	808	1,893	1,369	1,223	958	1,206	-599	-615	-820	-494	102	-577	....	Morocco
-65	437	-660	-13	60	17	-114	-171	-200	-99	58	-3	-183	37	586	347	....	Mozambique
....	....	....	....	....	9	-118	-56	-19	-10	-152	-93	-23	-106	....	....	....	Namibia
18	36	99	163	246	146	116	64	73	50	134	....	....	....	....	....	....	Niger
-3,812	-1,270	-4,465	-4,833	-3,756	-3,947	-2,725	-7,906	-1,131	190	-195	-4,268	-536	1,371	-4,043	....	....	Nigeria
65	99	124	95	56	85	99	79	79	50	-5	29	93	21	-74	-132	....	Rwanda
7	8	9	6	6	5	....	....	....	....	....	....	....	....	....	....	....	São Tomé & Príncipe
270	335	334	300	175	226	192	276	292	210	212	-2	90	-1	52	....	....	Senegal
19	32	25	24	39	17	10	3	29	14	40	43	58	90	76	....	....	Seychelles
-77	-237	-23	-69	11	48	-30	22	65	30	81	....	....	....	....	....	....	Sierra Leone
91	29	16	-83	-33	....	....	....	....	....	....	....	....	....	....	....	....	Somalia
-2,923	-2,974	-1,940	-2,219	-816	-1,779	-1,109	-1,464	-2,844	571	3,112	608	6,869	3,077	4,855	975	2,324	South Africa
-570	-175	-111	71	-42	128	682	347	244	621	563	864	846	1,030	580	681	467	Sudan
34	-3	-44	-83	-26	-40	-33	132	—	-14	60	67	16	119	20	33	....	Swaziland
-112	-31	116	-27	8	433	475	510	473	292	288	257	332	447	673	346	....	Tanzania
30	22	-70	39	23	56	99	-20	-107	-41	-72	129	130	123	159	....	....	Togo
355	390	240	207	319	796	451	1,295	1,390	1,063	871	920	981	538	1,180	616	....	Tunisia
29	16	58	158	175	221	138	124	99	145	288	243	326	462	445	....	....	Uganda
215	214	3	61	112	816	126	....	....	....	....	....	-579	-98	-207	64	....	Zambia
146	39	66	-24	-64	226	502	409	342	339	....	....	....	....	....	....	....	Zimbabwe
-726	-519	-494	-405	-1,141	-415	-469	-1,940	-703	-842	-945	-856	-457	-619	-607	-511	-520	Africa not specified

Balance of Payments

Capital and Financial Account

Including Net Errors and Omissions, but Excluding Reserve Assets,
Use of Fund Credit, and Exceptional Financing

Expressed in Millions of US Dollars

	1985	1986	1987	1988	1989	1990	1991	1992	1993	1994	1995	1996	1997	1998	1999	2000	2001
Asia	22,733	22,178	20,366	5,462	13,588	18,582	39,217	28,002	55,634	65,134	70,100	94,928	−21,828	−79,335	−30,506	−34,381	....
Afghanistan, I.S. of	269	518	178	−52	123	....	....	....	....	....	....	....	....	....	....	....	....
Bangladesh	374	711	393	405	751	622	369	454	338	492	312	577	151	324	175	275	....
Bhutan	....	....	....	....	....	....	....	....	....	....	....	....	....	....	....	....	....
Cambodia								106	125	193	212	257	244	80	163	105	....
China,P.R.: Mainland	8,977	4,986	4,483	6,176	3,838	50	1,265	−8,461	13,378	23,545	20,851	24,462	−1,106	−25,224	−12,463	−9,825	....
China,P.R.:Hong Kong													....	−10,693	−1,452	1,128	−7,284
Fiji	−23	13	−74	42	13	159	108	146	125	135	206	65	9	65	−58		....
India	3,780	4,189	5,325	7,157	7,063	5,096	4,057	5,557	6,087	12,067	4,831	9,914	8,286	9,974	9,892	10,285	....
Indonesia	2,433	2,908	2,728	1,284	1,603	5,239	5,788	4,850	2,700	3,576	8,004	12,166	−3,248	−7,789	−3,813	−4,259	....
Kiribati	2	1	−3	−1	−4	2	−15	−8	−1	−7							
Korea	1,006	−4,675	−7,959	−5,178	−1,722	795	7,170	7,667	2,019	8,481	15,546	24,421	−14,812	−14,435	8,784	11,549	4,799
Lao People's Dem.Rep	28	12	13	−1	−27	−15	−10	−11	2	106	196	188	−64	−104	−212		
Malaysia	1,748	1,563	−1,437	−2,325	920	2,821	5,419	8,785	14,341	1,360	6,881	6,975	2,061	489	−7,892	−9,418	
Maldives	7	3	−7	5	−8	−10	8	24	52	17	35	36	56	43	90	49	
Mongolia	838	1,075	1,067	1,034	1,358	538	−26	−27	−17	−40	−7	13	−49	76	93		
Myanmar	190	343	218	256	219	440	221	209	151	175	227	255	443	554	236	220	
Nepal	28	87	187	265	201	309	468	337	288	414	371	358	557	347	34	201	
Pakistan	664	841	643	1,691	1,146	1,347	1,248	2,268	3,328	3,155	2,145	3,656	2,249	−862	−1,596	−2,528	
Papua New Guinea	120	101	200	243	254	97	66	−166	−727	−572	−531	14	15	−192	30		
Philippines	874	182	386	1,064	1,756	2,650	2,789	2,689	3,352	5,277	3,215	8,291	1,257	−267	−4,251	−8,940	−5,183
Samoa	3	—	1	2	−2	4	27	40	29	−10	−7	−5	2	−15	26		
Singapore	1,341	219	1,203	−278	−226	2,309	−683	185	3,367	−6,664	−6,301	−5,427	−9,987	−17,369	−17,556	−14,991	
Solomon Islands	13	−6	10	33	20	14	23	16	6	1	−9	3	47	9	−26		
Sri Lanka	330	325	273	291	465	414	918	652	1,150	1,065	1,009	692	702	451	466	682	
Thailand	1,642	467	1,311	4,250	7,527	10,516	12,190	9,333	10,270	12,254	20,713	16,859	−15,229	−16,938	−11,040	−11,120	−3,752
Tonga	—	−8	5	14	−13	1	1	2	4	....	....	....	....	....	....		
Vanuatu	10	16	23	11	20	11	11	14	18	14	24	22	17	−7	....		
Asia not specified	−1,923	8,308	11,198	−10,931	−11,700	−14,839	−2,208	−6,661	−4,752	100	−6,838	−7,855	−5,986	2,102	9,855	2,931	−1,588
Europe	−11,187	−7,695	−13,642	−14,491	5,830	2,000	−12,559	−9,027	7,133	−19,365	24,110	2,227	29,361	9,091	13,046	3,598	....
Albania	19	2	6	161	364	−120	−56	15	34	164	32	163	312	118	262	276	364
Armenia	....	....	....	....	....	....	....	....	80	101	248	245	357	419	312	....	....
Azerbaijan	—	—	—	—	—	—	—	—	—	—	458	846	1,055	1,305	....	....	....
Belarus	....	....	....	....	....	....	....	....	....	....	....	....	924	697	214	448	186
Bosnia & Herzegovina														718	1,228	1,269	2,035
Bulgaria	434	66	223	1,059	335	−2,744	−197	629	777	−184	470	−754	718	−33	781	838	
Croatia									−436	−277	1,632	2,066	3,216	1,628	1,816	1,059	1,984
Cyprus	151	178	71	178	477	448	355	413	35	173	−199	406	291	520	856	448	
Czech Republic									2,575	4,294	8,827	3,302	1,863	3,199	3,105	3,533	4,425
Czechoslovakia	−802	91	−111	−886	−373	100	−119	−391									
Estonia	....	....	....	....	....	....	....	22	143	184	241	505	778	516	414	422	299
Georgia																	
Hungary	991	1,497	395	730	760	−791	1,392	418	6,807	3,579	7,928	445	807	3,255	4,441	2,380	1,013
Kazakhstan	....	....	....	....	....	....	....	....	....	....	512	910	1,348	782	424	157	2,134
Kyrgyz Republic									58	89	154	405	185	340	198	61	
Latvia	....	....	....	....	....	....	....	−154	−119	−145	−17	491	447	712	819	522	1,072
Lithuania									294	207	783	718	1,206	1,725	1,015	833	672
Macedonia, FYR												193	157	344	228	339	
Malta	−41	−11	−27	−26	24	−41	−71	14	219	514	54	319	208	412	360	247	427
Moldova										95	−88	92	87	−18	−55	142	49
Poland	−1,358	−4,095	−3,227	−10,928	−1,906	−8,569	−4,928	−1,226	2,560	52	8,981	7,088	8,785	12,825	12,643	10,623	
Romania	−1,698	−783	−1,002	−4,207	−1,262	1,760	335	1,368	792	626	1,300	1,997	3,596	2,275	1,536	2,265	....
Russia	....	....	....	....	....	....	....	....	....	−27,404	−15,786	−28,945	−8,553	−22,050	−26,434	−32,482	−23,309
Slovak Republic	....	....	....	....	....	....	....	....	594	535	1,401	2,460	2,060	1,649	1,932	1,614	....
Slovenia								−346	−66	73	339	559	1,277	305	701	790	1,351
Turkey	229	2,005	1,386	−443	1,772	3,568	−1,449	2,458	6,741	−2,428	6,998	6,981	6,022	−1,543	6,564	6,885	−16,284
Turkmenistan												8	978				
Ukraine	....	....	....	....	....	....	....	....	....	−37	−472	581	632	−2,161	−1,842	−908	−409
Yugoslavia, SFR	−674	−264	−1,010	−534	−496	3,732	−1,636										
Europe not specified	1,004	964	2,100	2,376	2,773	2,645	−3,047	960	888	95	397	842	604	417	436	177	629
Middle East	9,578	9,530	10,620	−901	5,002	−25,242	63,772	21,448	21,506	9,174	8,605	2,150	3,920	21,420	−8,348	−51,592	....
Bahrain, Kingdom of	319	−107	−141	−99	5	726	79	736	227	208	−68	−267	134	761	366	87	....
Egypt	1,966	1,780	560	946	775	−10,409	−3,976	548	−2,281	−1,195	−1,573	−1,533	75	1,179	−2,979	−1,059	
Iran, I.R. of	1,030	3,941	1,866	725	2,626	−652	7,357	6,343	4,443	−4,048	−572	−2,791	−5,910	1,148	−6,138	−11,562	....
Israel	−589	−283	2,057	−5,112	471	483	875	−601	2,153	1,337	5,452	6,704	10,922	1,232	3,286	1,846	2,048
Jordan	219	82	493	498	80	648	2,419	698	−232	133	87	34	245	−550	568	....	....
Kuwait	−4,253	−5,699	−6,408	−6,530	−7,861	−4,784	27,754	2,302	−3,976	−3,177	−5,157	−7,132	−7,928	−1,957	−4,144	−12,401	−5,660
Libya	456	389	45	434	1,318	−1,043	474	367	−350	266	49	−10	−6	−123	−1,343		
Oman	132	427	−676	−158	18	−971	793	898	132	144	369	−150	604	2,228	584	−1,085	
Saudi Arabia	12,222	4,176	12,413	5,822	6,030	−1,224	27,595	12,076	18,763	10,341	6,542	5,069	343	12,431	2,403	−11,671	−16,411
Syrian Arab Republic	772	565	377	119	−1,288	−1,726	−627	21	507	1,357	576	947	−12	376	58	−521	
Yemen Arab Rep.	237	194	510	408	569	....	....	....	....	....	....	....	....	....	....		
Yemen, P.D. Rep.	141	118	82	378	401	....	....	....	....	....	....	....	....	....	....		
Yemen, Republic of	....	....	....	....	....	−959	−30	−176	163	−900	−672	−475	4,087	−278	−503	−268	....
Middle East not spec	−3,074	3,946	−557	1,668	1,859	−5,331	1,059	−1,765	1,958	4,707	3,572	1,753	1,368	4,971	−506	−15,953	−7,101

Capital and Financial Account

Including Net Errors and Omissions, but Excluding Reserve Assets,
Use of Fund Credit, and Exceptional Financing

Expressed in Millions of US Dollars

1985	1986	1987	1988	1989	1990	1991	1992	1993	1994	1995	1996	1997	1998	1999	2000	2001	
-16,413	-12,219	-12,276	-19,464	-18,615	-4,638	24,095	48,709	68,999	41,251	29,317	65,131	91,641	66,732	40,583	66,348	....	Western Hemisphere
20	128	109	48	82	30	36	28	-27	14	14	48	50	72	88	73	....	Antigua and Barbuda
106	712	-12	204	-8,332	-5,169	-159	7,547	19,282	10,483	2,899	10,135	15,675	18,716	14,052	7,794	....	Argentina
....	70	35	44	68	170	232	-21	-8	-84	43	43	177	70	336	-298	....	Aruba
21	-54	-5	66	59	48	192	-64	-30	51	143	256	529	1,115	737	341	....	Bahamas, The
-37	7	22	-10	-71	-31	-17	-115	-49	-96	—	17	67	57	185	323	....	Barbados
-7	—	2	24	35	—	9	29	34	36	21	27	33	46	90	96	....	Belize
-101	35	-5	11	-34	38	115	402	472	1	395	672	654	779	515	424	....	Bolivia
-9,199	-8,116	-10,557	-9,961	-12,222	-5,702	-3,974	4,550	6,870	7,751	31,105	31,644	22,240	17,527	8,635	32,612	19,790	Brazil
-1,464	-1,996	-886	-1,025	1,209	2,807	1,356	3,505	2,982	4,736	2,488	6,014	6,912	2,004	-678	1,223	....	Chile
1,963	909	66	409	635	68	-586	374	2,567	3,855	4,591	6,487	6,159	3,829	-673	508	3,007	Colombia
-144	-204	-315	-39	22	-47	262	395	362	141	574	194	288	16	801	....	....	Costa Rica
6	14	15	11	46	49	38	30	28	34	49	35	28	17	52	69	....	Dominica
199	253	221	20	64	-195	414	644	-11	-228	329	173	254	350	581	978	....	Dominican Republic
-954	-1,479	420	-607	-401	706	866	146	172	125	-449	-38	-64	1,315	-1,886	-6,635	....	Ecuador
26	-115	-53	-55	259	288	64	61	181	131	410	334	460	394	473	369	....	El Salvador
4	21	33	23	35	49	51	40	44	32	47	56	74	85	51	86	....	Grenada
-81	-262	115	76	283	-10	815	692	901	632	420	666	863	1,275	901	1,692	....	Guatemala
-42							77	104	119	92						....	Guyana
93	49	37	41	49	-13	104	-14	-11	-26	224	87	77	73	....	....	....	Haiti
136	73	63	-48	-187	-124	54	51	-25	273	160	257	454	239	393	171	....	Honduras
203	-60	426	31	111	442	219	220	294	276	126	414	162	372	75	793	....	Jamaica
-3,529	896	-113	-7,688	5,614	9,669	22,861	26,187	30,632	12,463	-14,735	4,477	28,156	12,596	15,180	29,220	24,584	Mexico
-331	47	20	-42	-82	14	-36	49	43	22	53						....	Netherlands Antilles
175	-378	33	295	-144	-310	-598	-478	-375	-852	-466	-181	358	94	237	51	....	Nicaragua
-204	93	-1,076	-1,726	-944	-345	-87	80	-212	-378	139	467	850	803	1,173	606	201	Panama
112	158	417	-18	-264	-273	148	38	-16	575	137	306	435	177	-211	-205	....	Paraguay
-1,696	-1,352	-1,802	-1,237	-2,040	-722	1,000	1,168	2,076	4,007	3,541	4,292	5,230	2,272	1,057	1,498	....	Peru
9	12	17	27	45	47	36	25	32	24	48	65	57	52	86	58	....	St. Kitts and Nevis
14	18	23	20	69	63	80	54	55	45	39	48	83	81	87	91	....	St. Lucia
3	22	15	19	31	29	42	34	43	58	39	36	85	103	76	38	....	St. Vincent & Grens.
4	-34	-152	-123	-294	-49	55	-47	-31	-24	57	62	87	163	25	-23	....	Suriname
-253	-310	-31	-141	-138	-637	-272	-243	45	-32	-210	133	807	724	....	....	....	Trinidad and Tobago
164	240	189	-46	-74	-54	37	147	437	547	440	386	687	831	398	827	....	Uruguay
-1,628	-1,637	455	1,937	-2,047	-5,803	688	3,087	2,117	-3,485	-3,458	-2,676	-392	322	-2,518	-7,286	-6,426	Venezuela, Rep. Bol.

Memorandum Items

1985	1986	1987	1988	1989	1990	1991	1992	1993	1994	1995	1996	1997	1998	1999	2000	2001	
2,660	8,334	5,307	1,377	-55	-20,647	63,864	17,520	20,841	1,901	3,098	-2,791	-15,837	6,621	-26,531	-63,316	....	Oil Exporting Ctys
-2,809	3,989	-5,830	-34,178	2,675	8,876	48,289	63,820	131,697	97,627	132,720	165,586	130,393	18,997	45,836	54,351	....	Non-Oil Develop.Ctys

Balance of Payments

Expressed in Millions of US Dollars

	1985	1986	1987	1988	1989	1990	1991	1992	1993	1994	1995	1996	1997	1998	1999	2000	2001
All Countries	−22,858	−1,186	115,239	−6,157	13,397	25,351	7,920	1,102	63,582	65,937	124,980	156,327	69,036	−25,197	124,359	173,422	....
Industrial Countries	−3,482	22,772	107,137	38,085	26,884	54,883	−13,217	−6,350	28,440	35,436	78,131	76,763	23,494	−7,442	39,848	45,549	....
United States	3,835	−310	−9,147	3,915	25,288	2,233	−5,759	−3,921	1,378	−5,347	9,749	−6,669	1,017	6,744	−8,734	299	4,926
Canada	−3,270	−419	3,313	8,150	693	1,139	−1,848	−4,786	904	−392	2,711	5,498	−2,393	4,996	5,933	3,720	2,172
Australia	−2,301	703	374	5,279	601	1,740	−324	−4,726	−42	−960	396	2,471	2,873	−2,040	6,705	−1,365	1,096
Japan	−500	15,130	38,050	17,560	−13,050	−9,090	−8,389	620	27,473	25,265	58,611	35,139	6,567	−6,164	76,256	48,955	40,487
New Zealand	−2,037	−2,612	−2,248	−2,921	−1,217	179	−1,511	131	−74	733	384	1,772	−1,442	−486	188	−144	−187
Euro Area																	
Austria	15	643	333	491	990	−15	835	2,588	2,201	834	1,391	1,075	−3,053	3,482	−2,172	−746	−1,888
Belgium-Luxembourg	−197	29	2,434	861	312	404	584	569	−2,122	219	243	593	1,056	−2,095	−1,867	−959	1,442
Finland	583	−2,283	4,033	258	−1,068	3,931	−1,886	−2,150	291	4,714	−372	−3,036	2,304	296	13	359	405
France	2,696	1,181	−2,601	−5,159	−857	10,947	−5,194	−1,576	−5,006	2,448	712	239	5,940	19,815	−1,392	−2,433	−5,466
Germany	2,229	5,426	21,495	−15,596	2,860	7,253	−6,185	37,176	−14,199	−2,036	7,224	−1,195	−3,751	4,016	−14,115	−5,222	−5,466
Greece	−396	650	974	937	−348	280	2,204	−374	3,439	6,309	−23	4,215	−4,515	....	2,435	2,573	−5,699
Ireland	48	−94	886	592	−937	626	463	−2,166	2,660	−176	2,339	−52	−1,109	3,212	−1,973	121	395
Italy	−7,585	2,348	5,470	8,417	11,358	11,623	−6,718	−23,992	−3,135	1,575	2,804	11,907	13,150	−21,472	−8,051	3,247	−588
Netherlands	771	−330	2,693	1,568	507	268	506	6,118	6,641	500	−1,913	−5,691	−2,708	−2,339	−4,611	220	−350
Portugal	707	−111	1,777	867	4,654	3,542	5,713	−156	−2,848	−1,430	−300	547	974	508	216	371	852
Spain	−2,275	2,344	12,706	8,416	4,716	7,188	14,307	−17,809	−5,203	36	−6,414	24,279	11,756	−14,355	−22,850	−2,881	−1,340
Denmark	1,532	−1,329	3,732	1,436	−3,838	3,385	−2,903	4,075	−567	−1,851	2,498	3,563	6,532	−4,239	9,437	−5,649	3,270
Iceland	64	99	−18	1	55	74	9	79	−59	−150	4	153	−44	32	86	−69	....
Norway																	
Sweden	−4,651	177	762	938	1,254	7,552	−63	6,953	2,530	2,381	−1,664	−6,386	−6,712	3,254	1,881	170	−1,048
Switzerland	1,228	1,091	3,213	−2,382	1,369	1,169	992	4,397	486	1,009	29	2,521	2,154	1,179	−2,484	−4,005	....
United Kingdom	2,570	3,650	19,128	4,593	−7,422	42	4,701	−6,667	5,437	1,500	−853	−651	−3,903	−257	−1,036	5,298	−4,454
Developing Countries	−19,376	−23,958	8,101	−44,243	−13,486	−29,531	21,136	7,452	35,142	30,502	46,850	79,564	45,541	−17,755	84,510	127,873	....
Africa	−3,786	−5,748	−8,781	−11,485	−8,742	−2,920	−5,883	−13,645	−9,231	−5,326	−8,242	−1,898	2,898	−10,203	−4,989	5,438	....
Algeria	1,020	−1,498	−352	−959	−774	−10	1,047	....	....	....	....	....	....	....	....	....	....
Angola	−6	−259	−332	−925	−930	−1,209	−1,500	−1,138	−1,320	−1,028	−1,239	2,761	−565	−984	−284	....	....
Benin	−29	−79	−52	−165	−205	−109	−277	−67	−157	18	−255	−149	−100	−87	−89	....	....
Botswana	254	307	562	382	576	307	374	405	397	135	207	511	635	44	371	....	....
Burkina Faso	6	24	10	18	−135	7	8	20	2	−7	....	....	....	....	....	....	....
Burundi	16	29	−3	7	38	−3	33	26	16	35	37	−35	10	−19	−1	4	....
Cameroon	59	−81	−471	−163	−128	−871	−731	−1,305	−885	−551	15	....	....	....	....	....	....
Cape Verde	14	−1	3	−1	15	−7	−16	23	15	22	−32	22	—	11	....	....	....
Central African Rep.	−25	−4	−12	−13	−17	−21	−40	−37	−14	13	....	....	....	....	....	....	....
Chad	−24	−19	....	−34	30	−23	−20	−43	−48	6	....	....	....	....	....	....	....
Comoros	6	3	9	−4	5	−5	−26	−6	8	5	−10	....	....	....	....	....	....
Congo, Republic of	−81	−398	−488	−467	−403	−364	−458	−430	−420	−155	−609	−350	−548	....	....	....	....
Côte d'Ivoire	−169	−392	−924	−1,425	−1,311	−1,447	−1,328	−1,417	−1,237	−20	−254	−848	−477	−650	−708	−612	....
Djibouti	....	....	....	....	....	....	....	−16	−12	1	−24	....	....	....	....	....	....
Equatorial Guinea	....	....	−26	−17	−10	−6	−14	−28	−10	−18	−12	−5	....	....	....	....	....
Ethiopia	162	114	−107	−22	45	−198	−356	−264	32	—	100	−465	−428	−365	−6	−40	....
Gabon	−61	−195	−135	−1	−96	−269	−223	−442	−452	−173	−436	−251	−197	−667	−398	....	....
Gambia, The	−6	−32	11	25	4	4	17	19	11	6	1	14	7	....	....	....	....
Ghana	14	−61	140	181	157	105	137	−123	53	172	251	−20	27	108	−90	−259	....
Guinea	....	−112	−97	−121	−185	−97	−158	−174	−97	−124	−72	−60	−131	−158	−79	....	....
Guinea-Bissau	8	−33	−31	−41	−71	−32	−75	−52	−61	−55	−41	−43	−15	....	....	....	....
Kenya	−52	137	−25	−44	122	−93	−44	−257	412	62	−142	387	15	83	−34	−36	....
Lesotho	6	13	1	−6	−8	17	42	50	102	121	98	117	141	116	−41	18	....
Liberia	−203	−294	−300	....	....	....	....	....	....	....	....	....	....	....	....	....	....
Madagascar	−167	−116	−162	−117	−161	−278	−292	−278	−334	−276	−330	−94	−16	−299	−104	−160	....
Malawi	−26	−1	45	60	−52	29	16	−47	24	−35	....	....	....	....	....	....	....
Mali	−27	−50	−14	18	1	−65	30	−138	−97	−65	−52	29	−9	....	....	....	....
Mauritania	−31	−29	−132	−63	−6	−72	16	17	−282	−105	−6	4	28	43	....	....	....
Mauritius	−3	121	219	185	146	232	191	43	7	−44	109	48	−35	−65	190	231	....
Morocco	−32	331	298	264	21	1,697	956	791	436	483	−1,895	−673	−988	−640	−69	−1,078	....
Mozambique	−366	28	−1,049	−371	−400	−398	−458	−523	−647	−566	−387	−424	−478	−393	−326	−416	....
Namibia	....	....	....	....	....	37	−12	−7	91	75	24	23	68	56	....	....	....
Niger	−50	−120	−78	−67	−11	−90	−60	−95	−24	−76	−18	....	....	....	....	....	....
Nigeria	−1,209	−1,059	−4,539	−5,129	−2,667	1,041	−1,523	−5,638	−1,911	−1,938	−2,774	−761	15	−2,873	−3,538	....	....
Rwanda	2	30	−11	−50	−67	−23	65	−4	−50	4	53	20	31	−62	−146	−139	....
São Tomé & Príncipe	−11	−11	−4	−4	−6	−9	....	....	....	....	....	....	....	....	....	....	....
Senegal	−91	−35	−96	−105	−173	−137	−180	−125	−141	23	−33	−202	−95	−248	−268	....	....
Seychelles	—	−1	4	−4	−1	4	2	−4	−10	−12	−14	−13	−5	−34	−38	....	....
Sierra Leone	−74	−97	−53	−72	−48	−21	−15	16	8	−59	−46	....	....	....	....	....	....
Somalia	−12	−97	−98	−182	−190	....	....	....	....	....	....	....	....	....	....	....	....
South Africa	−606	−146	1,407	−715	528	355	1,147	503	−1,341	683	907	−1,272	4,595	920	4,215	400	2,158
Sudan	−421	−201	−343	−287	−193	−244	−273	−159	42	19	63	38	18	73	115	124	−151
Swaziland	−5	8	21	12	51	11	14	92	−64	−13	30	15	25	50	26	−7	....
Tanzania	−487	−353	−292	−384	−327	−126	−262	−204	−575	−419	−359	−254	−297	−509	−73	−135	....
Togo	−3	−43	−130	−48	−28	−44	−48	−160	−190	−97	−194	−25	13	−17	32	....	....
Tunisia	−226	−215	186	417	101	333	−18	191	67	527	97	442	386	−138	738	−205	....
Uganda	33	−27	−54	−37	−85	−42	−32	24	−125	−62	−51	−9	−41	−41	−106	....	....
Zambia	−181	−134	−242	−232	−106	222	−179	....	....	....	....	....	−932	−671	−654	−520	....
Zimbabwe	82	55	124	102	−47	86	45	−195	226	−86	....	....	....	....	....	....	....
Africa not specified	−818	−962	−1,581	−990	−2,003	−1,130	−1,414	−2,698	−1,076	−1,120	−930	−821	−658	−1,046	−720	−737	−682

Overall Balance

Excluding Reserves Assets, Use of Fund Credit, and Exceptional Financing

Expressed in Millions of US Dollars

1985	1986	1987	1988	1989	1990	1991	1992	1993	1994	1995	1996	1997	1998	1999	2000	2001	
6,780	**23,553**	**38,694**	**14,764**	**11,733**	**17,255**	**36,183**	**24,739**	**34,747**	**60,809**	**39,041**	**56,564**	**4,846**	**38,105**	**90,685**	**67,527**	....	**Asia**
26	−19	11	−26	−20	....	....	....	....	....	....	....	....	....	....	....	....	Afghanistan, I.S. of
−84	84	155	132	−348	224	434	635	698	691	−512	−414	−135	288	−189	−31	....	Bangladesh
....	....	....	....	....	....	....	....	....	....	....	....	....	....	....	....	....	Bhutan
....	....	....	....	....	....	....	13	21	36	26	72	34	31	50	86	....	Cambodia
−2,440	−2,048	4,783	2,374	−479	12,047	14,537	−2,060	1,769	30,453	22,469	31,705	35,857	6,248	8,652	10,693	....	China,P.R.: Mainland
												−6,789	10,028	10,044		4,684	China,P.R.:Hong Kong
−4	29	−46	112	21	65	40	85	−14	23	93	78	−25	5	−45	....	....	Fiji
−397	−409	133	−16	237	−1,941	−235	1,072	4,211	10,391	−733	3,958	5,321	3,071	6,664	6,087	....	India
510	−1,003	630	−113	495	2,251	1,528	2,070	594	784	1,573	4,503	−8,137	−3,693	1,972	3,726	....	Indonesia
—	−2	−7	−3	−5	−7	−11	−17	−5	−6	....	....	....	....	....	....	....	Kiribati
211	34	2,100	9,327	3,639	−1,208	−1,147	3,724	3,009	4,614	7,039	1,416	−22,979	25,930	33,260	23,790	13,416	Korea
−136	−130	−152	−104	−164	−126	−125	−122	−137	−178	−151	−158	−369	−254	−333	....	....	Lao People's Dem.Rep
1,148	1,461	1,139	−458	1,235	1,951	1,236	6,618	11,350	−3,160	−1,763	2,513	−3,875	10,018	4,712	−1,009	....	Malaysia
2	2	1	14	2	—	−1	5	−1	5	17	28	22	20	9	−4	....	Maldives
25	15	76	1	130	−102	−130	−82	15	6	32	−87	7	−53	−19	....	....	Mongolia
−15	49	38	80	151	9	−46	94	−77	45	−32	−25	31	60	−45	−23	....	Myanmar
−93	−33	64	−6	−42	20	163	155	66	63	15	31	169	280	−223	−77	....	Nepal
−419	193	80	261	−194	−314	−155	392	428	1,343	−1,204	−780	538	−3,110	−2,516	−2,624	....	Pakistan
−1	3	2	−53	−59	22	−409	−326	−253	−170	−39	202	−177	−221	125	....	....	Papua New Guinea
838	1,134	−58	674	300	−45	1,755	1,689	336	2,327	1,235	4,338	−3,094	1,279	3,659	−481	−680	Philippines
5	7	9	10	11	11	−2	−13	−9	−4	2	7	11	6	7	....	....	Samoa
1,337	538	1,095	1,659	2,738	5,431	4,197	6,100	7,578	4,736	8,599	7,396	7,940	2,965	4,194	6,806	....	Singapore
−15	−18	−7	−5	−13	−14	−13	14	−2	−2	−1	18	9	17	−5	....	....	Solomon Islands
−88	−92	−53	−104	52	116	324	202	768	308	239	9	307	224	−95	−361	....	Sri Lanka
105	714	945	2,596	5,029	3,235	4,618	3,029	3,907	4,169	7,159	2,167	−18,250	−2,696	1,388	−1,806	2,475	Thailand
1	−5	6	2	−6	6	1	1	−2	....	....	....	....	....	....	....	....	Tonga
—	5	−1	−5	8	5	−3	1	3	−6	−5	−5	−2	8	−3	....	....	Vanuatu
6,252	23,010	27,727	−1,580	−970	−4,357	9,638	1,460	497	4,342	−4,046	601	−655	4,426	19,431	12,341	17,829	Asia not specified
−7,382	**−2,146**	**−2,343**	**−5,549**	**2,796**	**−22,840**	**−14,297**	**−16,510**	**−9,847**	**−13,311**	**19,378**	**−11,319**	**2,571**	**−17,475**	**10,083**	**18,694**	....	**Europe**
−18	−1	12	134	325	−238	−224	−36	49	7	21	56	40	52	107	120	147	Albania
								13	−3	30	−45	50	1	5	....	....	Armenia
								—	—	58	−85	139	−59	....	....	....	Azerbaijan
												65	−319	20	125	−85	Belarus
													−529	−333	−31	655	Bosnia & Herzegovina
298	−885	−497	657	−434	−4,454	−274	269	−322	−216	445	−739	1,145	−94	96	137	....	Bulgaria
								188	276	40	1,017	391	160	410	611	1,342	Croatia
−30	159	64	71	228	294	−66	−225	145	247	−363	−60	−47	−83	639	−8	....	Cyprus
								3,041	3,474	7,453	−825	−1,758	1,890	1,639	844	1,787	Czech Republic
−112	260	260	207	563	−1,127	789	−422	....	....	....	....	....	....	....	....	....	Czechoslovakia
							58	165	17	84	106	216	37	119	128	−40	Estonia
																....	Georgia
536	132	−281	158	172	−413	1,795	770	2,545	−475	5,399	−1,244	−175	951	2,335	1,052	−84	Hungary
										299	159	548	−443	253	570	385	Kazakhstan
								−30	5	−81	−20	46	−73	−50	−97	....	Kyrgyz Republic
						37	298	57	−33	211	102	63	165	28	314	Latvia
								208	113	168	−5	224	427	−179	158	98	Lithuania
											−95	−119	32	119	232	....	Macedonia, FYR
−67	−5	−5	35	14	−96	−79	45	135	383	−307	−85	7	191	238	−222	255	Malta
								13	−175	−103	−188	−353	−120	26	−69	Moldova
−2,340	−5,201	−3,606	−11,035	−3,315	−5,502	−7,074	−4,330	−3,228	1,006	9,835	3,824	3,041	5,924	156	626	....	Poland
−317	612	1,041	−285	1,252	−1,494	−677	−138	−439	171	−480	−582	1,459	−643	239	906	....	Romania
								....	−18,970	−8,298	−17,190	−6,492	−21,367	−1,704	13,923	11,266	Russia
								14	1,205	1,791	370	99	−478	777	920	....	Slovak Republic
							633	125	647	240	590	1,288	158	−81	178	1,285	Slovenia
−784	540	580	1,153	2,710	943	−1,199	1,484	308	203	4,660	4,544	3,343	441	5,204	−2,934	−12,888	Turkey
												8	398			....	Turkmenistan
								....	−1,200	−1,624	−603	−703	−3,457	−184	573	993	Ukraine
159	836	238	1,953	1,931	1,368	−2,797	....	....	....	....	....	....	....	....	....	....	Yugoslavia, SFR
235	271	300	316	321	210	2,546	673	259	49	468	−312	−551	−70	37	28	35	Europe not specified
4,160	**−9,943**	**2,708**	**−12,226**	**7,929**	**−14,487**	**−742**	**−1,897**	**−4,213**	**−1,777**	**4,770**	**10,802**	**10,350**	**−3,888**	**4,784**	**16,723**	....	**Middle East**
357	−176	−343	93	−188	796	−523	−90	−113	−48	169	−6	103	−17	25	200	....	Bahrain, Kingdom of
−200	−31	315	−102	−533	−10,224	−2,073	3,360	18	−1,164	−1,827	−1,725	−635	−1,387	−4,614	−2,030	....	Egypt
554	−1,214	−224	−1,144	2,435	−325	−2,091	−161	228	908	2,786	2,441	−3,697	−991	451	1,083	....	Iran, I.R. of
399	994	650	−5,950	679	646	−404	−1,476	−327	−2,111	480	1,206	7,077	−93	9	−128	196	Israel
−42	43	141	204	465	421	2,025	−137	−861	−265	−171	−188	275	−536	973	....	....	Jordan
545	−83	−1,847	−1,928	1,275	−897	1,276	1,851	−1,478	50	−141	−25	6	258	918	2,268	2,906	Kuwait
2,362	224	−999	−1,392	292	1,158	255	1,759	−1,712	295	2,047	1,467	1,869	−513	641	....	....	Libya
122	−613	108	−467	324	135	543	300	−1,058	−661	−432	189	531	−765	215	2,262	....	Oman
−709	−7,619	2,640	−1,519	−3,508	−5,376	49	−5,664	1,495	−146	1,217	5,749	648	−719	2,815	2,665	−1,909	Saudi Arabia
−186	61	79	−32	−66	36	72	76	304	566	839	987	449	434	259	541	....	Syrian Arab Republic
−50	69	58	−286	−10	....	....	....	....	....	....	....	....	....	....	....	....	Yemen Arab Rep.
−90	−58	−48	−26	−16	....	....	....	....	....	....	....	....	....	....	....	....	Yemen, P.D. Rep.
					−566	−892	−1,302	−1,112	−722	−528	−436	4,018	−581	74	1,594	....	Yemen, Republic of
1,097	−1,540	2,178	324	6,781	−291	1,022	−412	403	1,519	332	1,143	−293	1,022	3,017	1,585	1,038	Middle East not spec

Balance of Payments

Overall Balance

Excluding Reserves Assets, Use of Fund Credit, and Exceptional Financing

Expressed in Millions of US Dollars

	1985	1986	1987	1988	1989	1990	1991	1992	1993	1994	1995	1996	1997	1998	1999	2000	2001
Western Hemisphere	-19,149	-29,673	-22,176	-29,747	-27,202	-6,539	5,876	14,765	23,685	-9,894	-8,098	25,415	24,876	-24,295	-16,053	19,490	....
Anguilla	....	....	....	....	....	3	—	1	1	—	—	1	2	2	2	—	....
Antigua and Barbuda	-3	10	-2	3	—	-1	5	18	-12	8	14	-11	3	9	10	-6	....
Argentina	-846	-2,147	-4,247	-1,368	-9,637	-617	-806	1,894	11,122	-675	-2,311	3,258	3,331	4,090	2,013	-1,176	....
Aruba	....	51	13	—	22	12	23	23	33	-3	43	-26	-18	51	3	-16	....
Bahamas, The	19	-31	-60	-1	-25	12	13	-28	19	9	-3	-8	57	119	65	-61	....
Barbados	14	14	4	34	-46	-41	-44	25	20	38	42	86	17	-6	36	178	....
Belize	2	12	12	22	16	15	-16	—	-14	-4	4	21	1	-14	13	-43	....
Bolivia	-387	-354	-437	-294	-304	-161	-147	-132	-34	-90	92	268	101	101	27	-40	....
Brazil	-9,479	-13,427	-12,009	-5,805	-11,220	-9,525	-5,424	10,639	6,890	6,598	12,969	8,396	-8,251	-16,302	-16,765	7,980	-3,418
Chile	-2,877	-3,187	-1,621	-1,256	519	2,323	1,257	2,547	428	3,151	1,139	2,504	3,184	-2,135	-758	232	....
Colombia	154	1,292	402	193	434	610	1,763	1,274	464	182	-5	1,730	277	-1,397	-312	862	1,225
Costa Rica	-435	-365	-692	-343	-458	-541	163	14	-258	-103	216	-69	-193	-504	151	....	....
Dominica	-1	7	8	-1	—	5	4	3	1	-3	8	2	2	4	11	—	....
Dominican Republic	92	70	-143	1	-263	-474	257	-64	-544	-511	146	-40	91	11	151	-48	....
Ecuador	-878	-2,061	-767	-1,287	-1,116	346	158	24	-674	-776	-1,443	-76	-522	-784	-944	-5,707	....
El Salvador	-163	-132	-122	-184	-111	27	-148	-134	59	113	148	165	363	303	199	-49	....
Grenada	6	2	4	-5	-1	3	2	8	—	5	6	—	7	4	5	7	....
Guatemala	-327	-279	-328	-338	-84	-243	631	-14	200	6	-152	214	230	235	-125	643	....
Guyana	-139	....	....	....	....	....	....	-62	-36	-6	-43	....	....	....	....	....	....
Haiti	-2	4	6	—	-13	-35	13	-6	-23	-50	137	-50	30	34	....	....	....
Honduras	-172	-152	-183	-209	-368	-310	-160	-247	-333	-70	-41	-79	182	-155	-191	-338	....
Jamaica	-71	-78	300	78	-172	130	-21	248	110	358	27	271	-170	44	-136	518	....
Mexico	-2,729	-481	4,134	-10,062	-211	2,218	7,973	1,745	7,232	-17,199	-16,312	1,948	20,460	-3,501	1,163	11,456	6,876
Montserrat	....	1	1	—	....	3	-4	—	—	2	1	—	3	13	-11	-4	....
Netherlands Antilles	72	98	-30	33	-44	-30	-42	59	44	-76	139	....	....	....	....	....	....
Nicaragua	-596	-1,068	-657	-420	-506	-695	-1,133	-1,312	-1,019	-1,566	-1,044	-810	-315	-410	-460	-454	....
Panama	-128	-6	-531	-1,004	-832	-136	-328	-187	-308	-362	-331	267	343	-380	-148	-327	-298
Paraguay	-140	-206	-73	-228	-8	117	233	-19	43	301	45	-47	-216	17	-301	-342	....
Peru	-1,594	-2,746	-3,867	-3,056	-2,610	-2,141	-504	-922	-219	1,447	-584	862	2,173	-1,362	-866	-130	....
St. Kitts and Nevis	2	3	1	—	6	—	3	10	3	-1	2	-1	3	11	3	-4	....
St. Lucia	1	11	9	2	6	6	8	-2	5	-3	6	-6	5	15	8	8	....
St. Vincent & Grens.	6	12	-5	2	1	5	-4	10	-1	—	-1	—	1	9	3	12	....
Suriname	-15	-71	-16	-9	—	18	-78	-22	13	34	120	-2	19	8	-4	10	....
Trinidad and Tobago	-301	-722	-256	-229	-177	-178	-277	-104	159	186	84	238	194	80	....	....	....
Uruguay	66	282	48	-24	60	132	80	138	193	109	228	152	400	355	-110	234	....
Venezuela, Rep. Bol.	1,699	-3,882	-935	-3,872	114	2,476	2,424	-662	124	-944	-1,444	6,238	3,075	-2,931	1,039	5,825	-2,062
Memorandum Items																	
Oil Exporting Ctys	5,631	-17,656	-2,740	-15,544	5,218	561	3,430	-6,490	-3,442	-2,647	1,763	21,007	-1,741	-12,788	3,835	36,813	....
Non-Oil Develop.Ctys	-25,007	-6,302	10,841	-28,698	-18,704	-30,092	17,706	13,942	38,584	33,148	45,087	58,557	47,282	-4,967	80,676	91,060	....

Exports of Goods and Services

As percent of GDP

1985	1986	1987	1988	1989	1990	1991	1992	1993	1994	1995	1996	1997	1998	1999	2000	2001	
																	Industrial Countries
6.9	7.0	7.4	8.4	8.9	9.2	9.7	9.8	9.7	10.0	10.7	10.9	11.2	10.6	10.3	10.8	10.0	United States
28.5	28.0	27.0	26.9	25.8	26.1	24.9	26.8	29.9	33.7	37.1	38.1	39.2	41.2	43.1	45.3	43.2	Canada
16.4	15.9	16.4	16.2	15.7	16.2	17.2	17.8	18.4	18.3	19.3	19.5	20.6	19.9	18.7	21.8	22.3	Australia
14.4	11.4	10.3	9.9	10.5	10.6	10.1	10.0	9.3	9.2	9.3	10.0	11.1	11.1	10.3	11.1	10.8	Japan
31.5	25.9	25.5	25.5	26.2	26.8	28.8	30.6	30.3	30.7	29.7	28.5	28.0	29.7	30.4	35.5	36.0	New Zealand
																	Euro Area
40.2	36.4	35.3	37.6	39.7	39.9	39.6	38.4	36.7	37.4	38.2	39.7	42.9	44.1	....	....	....	Austria
69.2	64.2	64.4	66.2	68.6	66.7	64.9	63.1	61.0	65.3	64.6	65.7	70.4	71.1	....	....	....	Belgium-Luxembourg
28.9	26.5	25.6	24.5	23.6	22.8	22.0	26.5	32.5	35.4	37.1	37.5	39.0	38.8	....	....	....	Finland
25.0	22.1	21.5	22.1	23.6	23.5	23.7	23.7	22.4	22.7	23.3	23.5	26.1	26.7	....	....	....	France
34.4	31.6	30.4	31.0	33.0	31.5	26.5	24.7	22.9	23.8	24.6	25.5	28.1	29.3	....	....	....	Germany
20.8	19.8	21.7	17.2	16.3	15.7	15.9	15.0	14.5	14.7	13.2	12.3	12.2	....	19.9	26.0	....	Greece
60.2	52.7	56.3	60.1	63.5	56.6	57.2	59.9	64.6	69.3	74.5	75.2	76.9	110.5	....	....	....	Ireland
22.6	20.0	19.3	18.8	19.8	20.0	18.6	19.2	22.3	23.9	26.9	25.8	26.3	25.9	....	....	....	Italy
										105.1	109.2	116.6	123.4	....	....	....	Luxembourg
61.5	51.5	49.8	52.1	55.8	53.9	54.2	52.4	50.9	52.2	58.5	59.1	63.5	63.4	....	....	....	Netherlands
37.1	28.6	29.7	29.3	31.3	31.2	27.6	25.2	27.2	28.8	30.8	30.9	32.8	32.2	....	....	....	Portugal
22.7	19.8	19.3	18.9	18.3	17.0	16.9	17.3	19.3	22.3	23.9	25.3	28.4	29.2	....	....	....	Spain
37.8	32.7	31.8	33.4	35.5	36.7	38.1	37.1	35.7	36.5	36.4	36.8	36.8	36.6	40.3	46.9	48.2	Denmark
41.5	39.5	35.5	32.8	35.5	34.0	31.3	30.4	32.8	34.7	35.7	36.5	36.5	35.6	34.7	34.8	....	Iceland
43.4	34.8	32.8	33.4	38.4	40.8	40.4	38.1	38.3	38.4	38.2	41.2	42.0	38.4	40.6	48.8	47.4	Norway
36.0	32.7	32.8	32.9	32.7	30.7	28.9	28.9	33.3	35.7	39.8	38.8	42.3	43.0	44.3	47.0	46.8	Sweden
47.8	44.0	41.1	42.5	45.5	42.4	40.4	41.5	40.9	40.3	40.1	41.1	47.0	46.0	46.0	50.4	....	Switzerland
29.0	25.7	25.5	23.0	23.6	24.2	23.2	23.6	25.5	26.5	28.3	29.3	28.6	26.6	26.2	28.1	27.2	United Kingdom
																	Developing Countries
																	Africa
23.4	13.7	14.9	15.0	18.1	21.8	27.3	....										Algeria
																	Angola
32.1	28.5	29.3	18.7	19.2	19.7	27.7	23.3	25.6	36.1	30.6	29.6	25.2	24.1	25.3	....		Benin
83.6	73.9	111.2	82.5	67.0	57.0	55.6	48.7	50.8	50.1	54.7	55.7	62.4	48.5	65.4	....		Botswana
10.7	9.7	12.2	11.9	9.7	12.2	11.7	9.8	10.0	15.4	....							Burkina Faso
10.8	11.4	9.5	12.5	9.6	7.8	10.5	8.7	9.1	8.9	12.9	5.8	9.9	8.0	7.6	7.8	....	Burundi
24.5	21.3	16.1	10.3	21.2	20.5	20.1	19.5	17.2	26.2	23.3	....						Cameroon
21.7	18.7	18.9	15.0	....													Cape Verde
25.3	19.4	16.4	15.5	17.3	15.2	12.8	11.4	14.2	21.0	....							Central African Rep.
10.9	13.4	9.5	15.9	14.8	16.8	14.0	12.5	13.7	16.1	....							Chad
18.6	18.2	15.2	18.5	17.8	14.3	20.3	18.4	19.7	20.5	20.4	....						Comoros
56.4	42.0	42.4	42.3	52.8	53.2	44.3	42.5	43.8	58.0	58.8	64.8	77.5	....				Congo, Republic of
45.3	39.9	34.5	31.7	32.7	32.4	31.6	32.2	30.7	44.4	43.4	46.2	47.5	44.7				Côte d'Ivoire
																	Djibouti
		36.0	38.5	34.2	31.7	32.8	36.0	43.3	55.4	57.6	64.8	....					Equatorial Guinea
9.9	11.0	9.4	9.3	9.6	7.3	4.7	5.9	8.9	12.9	13.9	13.3	15.8	15.6				Ethiopia
59.6	26.1	36.4	37.0	45.7	50.3	47.2	46.6	48.8	61.7	59.4	62.7	61.3	47.4	60.3			Gabon
39.1	59.8	59.0	59.6	64.8	56.0	74.8	68.7	85.8	71.5								Gambia, The
10.6	14.0	18.7	18.4	16.9	15.8	16.7	17.2	20.3	25.5	24.5	24.9	24.0					Ghana
																	Guinea
	—	.2	.5	.8	1.2	2.7	3.2	6.1	6.0	6.4	9.1	21.5	....				Guinea-Bissau
25.6	25.8	21.3	22.0	23.1	26.1	27.3	26.2	40.4	37.1	32.6	32.7	28.0	24.8	25.2	26.5		Kenya
16.5	16.5	17.1	19.0	18.9	16.3	15.8	18.3	21.0	21.7	21.3	24.3	27.6	27.7	23.7	28.2		Lesotho
43.5	44.2	38.1															Liberia
12.2	12.2	16.5	16.5	18.2	15.3	18.1	16.7	15.5	22.0	23.7	20.1	22.2	22.2	24.4	30.0		Madagascar
24.0	22.7	25.9	24.9	19.7	23.8	23.3	23.8	17.1	32.9								Malawi
18.9	16.0	17.2	16.0	17.1	17.0	18.0	16.2	17.8	22.9	22.3	20.2	26.4					Mali
57.7	52.5	46.7	49.4	49.1	44.8	42.6	38.5	42.4	42.4	47.6	47.3	43.4					Mauritania
53.4	60.4	64.4	64.6	64.1	65.2	62.9	60.0	59.3	57.3	59.1	64.3	60.8	62.1	61.4	53.5		Mauritius
24.4	21.0	22.3	24.3	21.8	24.2	24.1	25.1	26.1	24.9	27.4	26.3	28.5	27.8	30.1	31.3		Morocco
5.7	4.8	13.3	15.9	15.3	16.2	11.5	15.4	15.4	15.7	18.3	16.9	14.7	13.9	14.6			Mozambique
					49.9	51.3	50.5	53.4	48.6	49.5	49.9	47.4	47.2				Namibia
20.4	21.3	24.7	20.8	20.3	21.4	16.8	16.3	14.7	18.1	19.2							Niger
16.6	12.8	28.7	22.6	27.6	44.9	39.7	35.8	24.5	23.6	13.7	13.1	11.9	7.6	38.5			Nigeria
9.4	11.7	7.8	7.2	6.2	5.6	7.3	5.0	5.2	4.3	5.8	6.0	7.7	5.6	6.0	7.5		Rwanda
																	São Tomé & Príncipe
32.0	27.3	23.3	22.3	26.0	25.5	23.6	22.3	21.2	33.8	33.6	29.4	29.1	29.8				Senegal
69.1	61.1	61.4	64.0	58.6	62.1	57.9	55.8	56.4	51.5	53.4	62.4	63.0	68.8	77.2			Seychelles
18.7	31.1	27.7	14.8	19.1	32.3	27.8	29.0	23.0	23.7	14.7	....						Sierra Leone
																	Somalia
31.6	30.6	28.2	27.9	26.5	24.8	22.4	21.4	21.5	22.2	23.0	24.5	24.6	26.0	25.6	28.6	31.2	South Africa
13.6	6.8	3.7	5.7	4.5	2.0	1.4	8.8	7.2	10.3	8.2	8.2	6.2					Sudan
56.7	68.8	81.8	76.9	84.1	76.5	77.9	76.0	78.6	84.7	79.4	77.1	79.8	84.0	75.5	65.9		Swaziland
6.8	9.6	7.7	9.9	12.0	12.6	10.2	12.5	18.0	20.8	24.1	21.1	15.7	13.7	13.5	14.2		Tanzania
49.0	44.2	41.7	39.2	39.9	40.8	39.3	32.8	28.0	40.6	41.9	38.0	34.1	35.0	32.5			Togo
31.8	30.2	34.5	42.1	43.3	42.3	39.2	38.8	39.6	44.2	44.3	41.6	43.2	42.8	42.3	44.2		Tunisia
9.7	9.0	6.4	4.5	5.3	4.8	6.4	5.7	8.7	10.0	10.8	12.4						Uganda
38.4	44.0	43.3	34.4	35.7	36.4	37.2	....	....	....	....	....	31.2	....				Zambia
25.1	24.0	24.0	23.7	23.4	23.0	24.0	27.2	30.2	34.0								Zimbabwe

Balance of Payments

Exports of Goods and Services

	1985	1986	1987	1988	1989	1990	1991	1992	1993	1994	1995	1996	1997	1998	1999	2000	2001
							As percent of GDP										
Asia																	
Afghanistan, I.S. of	....	....	....	....	....	....	....	....	....	....	....	....	....	....	....	....	....
Bangladesh	8.5	7.2	7.6	8.3	8.0	7.1	7.0	8.4	9.7	10.5	11.7	11.6	13.4	13.7	13.9	15.9	....
Cambodia																	
China,P.R.: Mainland	9.4	10.1	12.4	11.6	10.9	15.0	16.5	16.8	14.5	22.0	21.0	20.9	22.9	21.5	22.3	25.9	....
China,P.R.:Hong Kong														130.1	133.6	150.3	144.2
Fiji	44.5	41.8	45.0	55.6	62.8	63.2	56.4	51.7	51.2	56.1	54.4	60.9	56.8	56.4	58.3	....	....
India	6.1	5.8	5.9	5.7	6.8	7.1	8.0	8.6	9.6	9.8	10.4	10.6	10.7	10.8	11.5	13.2	....
Indonesia	21.9	17.7	23.3	23.6	24.5	25.6	25.3	26.7	25.7	25.5	26.2	25.0	29.3	57.5	39.5	46.1	....
Kiribati																	
Korea	32.6	36.6	39.5	37.8	32.1	29.0	27.3	27.6	27.5	27.8	30.1	29.5	34.6	49.7	42.3	44.7	42.9
Lao People's Dem.Rep	4.9	6.1	10.6	13.2	11.8	11.8	13.1	16.5	25.1	25.4	23.1	22.8	24.3	37.9	32.2	....	....
Malaysia	55.0	56.4	62.6	66.2	71.2	74.2	77.5	75.8	78.7	88.9	93.8	91.3	93.1	115.6	121.3	124.6	....
Maldives	71.6	68.1	78.7	75.9	79.2	83.3	75.4	77.0	66.2	76.6	79.4	80.1	80.9	82.8	76.5	81.4	....
Mongolia							18.8	35.1		60.1	41.4	40.6	58.9	55.6	62.0	....	
Myanmar	5.7	4.9	2.8	1.8	1.5	1.3	1.0	1.6	1.5	1.4	1.2	1.0	.8	.7	.5	....	
Nepal	12.5	12.2	13.0	12.6	11.1	12.0	15.9	18.6	20.7	23.5	24.4	26.1	26.5	23.0	25.3	24.3	....
Pakistan	11.8	13.0	14.9	14.0	16.0	17.3	18.5	17.6	17.6	17.3	17.2	17.8	16.8	15.5	15.1	17.1	....
Papua New Guinea	45.0	46.1	51.0	43.7	41.9	42.9	46.2	52.0	58.5	54.2	65.0	56.8	52.1	55.7	63.7	....	....
Philippines	22.3	25.8	24.3	25.0	25.9	25.8	27.5	27.5	29.5	31.6	36.2	40.4	49.0	56.7	51.2	55.2	48.1
Samoa	31.1	26.5	28.3	35.4	40.0	39.8	26.1	27.3	26.5	25.1	33.6	35.3	34.4				
Singapore	157.6	152.8	171.0	191.5	185.5	184.0	175.4	168.7	167.3	173.2	178.2	171.5	165.4	157.7	168.8	179.0	....
Solomon Islands	50.2	55.5	57.6	60.7	60.4	45.9	52.2	52.9	60.7	60.1	....	....	....	....	....	....	....
Sri Lanka	26.1	23.6	25.8	26.0	26.5	28.5	28.3	30.1	33.1	33.8	35.4	35.0	36.5	36.2	35.5	39.1	....
Thailand	23.4	25.8	29.0	33.1	35.0	34.2	36.1	37.1	38.0	38.9	41.8	39.3	48.0	58.9	58.3	66.9	66.4
Tonga	38.0	32.4	33.1	23.4	31.5	30.9	22.7	19.7	22.1	....							
Vanuatu	54.9	38.9	50.8	53.3	38.3	48.3	44.4	46.2	44.1	48.1	46.3	....	....	....	....	....	....
Europe																	
Albania	....	....	....	....	....	....	....	....	....	....	....	....	....	....	....	....	....
Armenia	....	....	....	....	....	....	....	....	.2	35.3	23.3	23.1	20.2	19.0	20.8	....	....
Azerbaijan	....	....	....	....	....	....	....	....	....	....	....	....	....	....	....	....	
Belarus	....	....	....	....	....	....	....	....	....	....	50.0	46.2	55.6	46.6	52.6	73.5	68.1
Bosnia & Herzegovina														22.6	23.1	31.3	....
Bulgaria	35.2	26.8	27.3	22.7	20.1	33.5	54.2	58.4	45.2	53.5	51.7	63.6	61.9	48.8	46.7	58.4	....
Croatia									52.4	48.4	35.8	39.6	39.4	39.4	40.4	45.4	47.5
Cyprus	50.1	46.7	48.8	49.7	52.9	53.0	48.8	50.8	48.5	48.6	47.7	47.8	47.9	44.3	45.4	47.3	....
Czech Republic									54.2	51.4	54.2	52.2	55.6	58.9	60.5	69.7	71.4
Czechoslovakia	35.3	34.9	34.7	34.8	33.9	31.7	40.8										
Estonia									69.4	75.7	72.1	67.0	78.2	79.8	75.8	95.5	91.8
Georgia																	
Hungary	44.6	41.8	41.9	38.6	40.4	36.4	36.5	36.2	28.4	25.9	40.4	44.6	55.5	56.7	57.2	68.7	68.9
Kazakhstan	....	....	....	....	....	....	....	....	....	....	34.7	34.6	36.4	32.1	39.4	54.5	47.1
Kyrgyz Republic	....	....	....	....	....	....	....	....	....	33.6	30.0	32.1	38.2	36.4	42.2	....	....
Latvia	....	....	....	....	....	....	....	79.9	73.1	46.0	46.9	50.9	50.9	51.3	43.7	45.7	45.7
Lithuania									83.3	55.3	53.0	53.4	54.5	47.2	39.7	45.2	50.4
Macedonia, FYR												29.5	35.9	40.6	42.0	....	....
Malta	69.9	69.4	76.1	78.2	79.9	84.4	85.9	90.9	94.4	96.0	92.4	85.3	83.1	85.7	88.6	100.5	85.9
Moldova											61.3	54.9	54.8	46.8	52.5	50.0	50.0
Poland	18.4	18.9	22.3	23.7	19.5	32.3	23.6	22.2	20.7	25.3	28.1	25.9	27.5	27.2	24.8	29.4	....
Romania	22.9	20.1	19.4	20.4	21.1	16.7	17.1	25.7	21.6	23.9	26.5	27.3	28.2	22.6	27.7	32.9	....
Russia	....	....	....	....	....	....	....	....	....	27.4	27.7	24.8	24.1	30.9	43.8	44.5	36.3
Slovak Republic	....	....	....	....	....	....	....	....	58.2	61.6	59.7	55.1	57.9	61.1	61.4	71.6	....
Slovenia									63.1	59.0	60.1	55.4	55.6	56.8	52.4	59.0	60.0
Turkey	....	....	16.3	19.9	17.5	14.0	14.6	15.3	14.6	22.3	21.6	25.1	27.4	27.2	24.7	25.6	....
Turkmenistan	....	....	....	....	....	....	....	....	....	....	....	....	....	....	....	....	....
Ukraine	....	....	....	....	....	....	....	....	....	45.3	46.2	45.7	40.6	42.1	55.4	....	....
Yugoslavia, SFR																	
Middle East																	
Bahrain, Kingdom of	104.3	97.1	97.1	89.5	94.2	97.4	85.0	84.4	84.1	79.7	82.0	88.0	79.1	64.6	73.8	81.9	....
Egypt	12.8	9.5	9.2	8.2	8.3	16.0	30.5	27.2	24.4	23.4	22.0	20.8	19.7	15.2	16.5	17.4	....
Iran, I.R. of	9.1	3.9	4.8	3.4	3.7	3.6	2.5	1.7	26.6	25.4	17.8	16.2	12.1	7.7	8.2	9.0	....
Israel	41.4	37.1	37.0	33.0	34.7	33.0	28.6	29.5	31.7	31.9	30.6	30.0	30.6	31.8	37.8	42.5	34.7
Jordan	38.2	29.0	34.1	40.1	56.9	62.5	58.9	49.7	49.8	47.4	51.0	52.1	48.8	45.5	43.8	....	....
Kuwait	53.7	46.2	41.4	42.9	52.4	44.8	18.8	40.5	48.0	51.1	53.6	53.0	53.7	44.8	47.4	59.4	54.7
Libya	37.5	26.0	28.0	24.3	29.4	39.7	33.8	30.4	28.0	27.1	29.4	28.5	26.7	19.7	24.1	....	....
Oman	48.0	34.9	44.2	40.0	44.0	47.7	43.5	44.7	43.1	43.0	44.0	49.8	50.0	41.2	47.8	58.5	....
Saudi Arabia	35.8	31.1	35.0	35.0	37.2	45.3	43.0	43.6	38.5	38.2	41.9	40.3	39.4	29.8	34.8	43.6	41.9
Syrian Arab Republic	11.8	6.3	6.0	12.2	21.0	21.0	16.2	13.2	13.2	11.5	11.3	9.7	8.5	6.8	7.5	8.6	....
Yemen Arab Rep.	....	....	....	....	....	....	....	....	....	....	....	....	....	....	....	....	....
Yemen, P.D. Rep.	....	....	....	....	....	....	....	....	....	....	....	....	....	....	....	....	....
Yemen, Republic of	....	....	....	....	....	....	10.9	8.1	7.1	8.0	18.1	32.8	37.6	28.6	39.6	....	....

Exports of Goods and Services

1985	1986	1987	1988	1989	1990	1991	1992	1993	1994	1995	1996	1997	1998	1999	2000	2001	
							As percent of GDP										**Western Hemisphere**
....																	Anguilla
88.6	83.7	79.2	78.4	77.9	88.2	90.1	96.1	96.2	87.3	81.4	74.5	76.3	74.7	73.1	69.1	....	Antigua and Barbuda
11.4	8.0	7.5	8.8	15.4	10.5	7.6	6.7	6.9	7.5	9.6	10.4	10.5	10.4	9.8	10.9	....	Argentina
																	Aruba
107.0	75.1	68.8	61.5	57.6	58.5	54.8	56.2	57.9	56.0	57.6	....	....	....	....	....	....	Bahamas, The
66.0	56.8	47.1	50.2	51.9	50.7	48.6	50.9	53.0	57.6	59.5	60.9	56.6	54.4	52.4	....	....	Barbados
61.3	59.4	59.6	61.6	57.9	60.3	57.5	58.4	53.3	50.3	50.6	51.0	53.6	51.9	54.5	49.8	....	Belize
11.1	16.8	15.0	14.6	18.4	20.1	17.2	13.7	15.6	19.7	18.4	17.7	17.8	15.9	15.8	17.4	....	Bolivia
12.4	9.0	9.5	10.9	9.7	7.6	8.6	10.2	9.9	9.0	7.5	6.8	7.3	7.5	10.4	10.9	13.4	Brazil
27.3	29.5	30.7	33.7	34.9	33.7	31.9	29.5	26.3	28.4	29.7	25.2	25.1	23.9	26.6	29.3	....	Chile
12.9	18.4	18.8	17.2	18.5	21.5	22.1	20.9	19.6	13.3	13.3	13.5	13.3	13.6	16.1	18.8	18.1	Colombia
30.9	31.5	31.9	34.9	35.0	34.4	30.6	30.1	30.2	31.4	38.0	40.8	41.7	48.8	51.9	....	....	Costa Rica
39.2	52.8	52.5	54.2	46.5	53.8	51.6	50.9	48.8	46.4	50.9	51.5	56.0	58.4	57.4	51.5	....	Dominica
26.2	23.1	26.8	35.4	29.4	25.9	24.5	21.7	49.4	50.1	48.0	46.5	46.8	47.2	46.0	45.6	....	Dominican Republic
20.7	23.4	23.2	26.4	29.2	30.5	29.0	29.4	26.4	27.8	29.0	29.5	30.6	25.4	39.1	44.0	....	Ecuador
15.8	25.0	19.6	17.1	14.1	18.3	16.9	16.4	19.7	20.2	21.5	21.4	26.2	25.4	25.4	27.8	....	El Salvador
41.3	52.2	47.7	46.7	40.0	42.1	40.4	39.7	44.2	48.3	44.8	44.7	44.1	47.3	58.9	57.4	....	Grenada
10.4	13.8	16.0	16.2	16.9	20.5	18.0	18.2	17.8	17.3	19.3	17.7	17.9	18.0	19.0	20.4	....	Guatemala
56.7	....	....	....	....	....	....	130.4	113.8	107.1	101.2	....	....	....	....	....	....	Guyana
16.8	13.1	14.8	12.3	9.5	12.2	9.5	7.3	7.5	3.3	8.2	6.4	11.7	12.8	....	....	....	Haiti
25.0	26.6	22.9	22.2	20.5	33.9	33.1	30.5	34.9	39.2	43.4	47.1	46.5	46.1	41.9	42.2	....	Honduras
56.1	48.8	47.5	44.0	43.2	48.3	53.0	60.0	49.9	63.3	59.6	52.0	46.6	45.2	46.2	46.4	....	Jamaica
17.2	20.5	23.6	21.2	20.4	19.8	17.7	16.6	15.2	16.9	31.2	32.1	30.3	30.7	30.8	31.0	27.7	Mexico
....	31.0	....	....	....	31.4	38.9	39.8	....	....	....	....	....	....	....	....	....	Montserrat
																	Netherlands Antilles
11.6	6.4	1.2	22.2	33.6	3.6	20.0	17.3	19.2	26.0	33.3	33.4	40.4	40.1	37.8	39.8	....	Nicaragua
61.3	65.0	67.4	73.2	76.2	83.5	92.6	95.3	92.6	96.3	96.3	91.0	96.9	87.6	73.6	76.5	....	Panama
13.6	14.0	17.0	19.3	36.1	47.8	38.9	36.6	48.0	48.2	53.3	45.7	41.4	48.6	42.0	38.4	....	Paraguay
21.7	12.6	8.2	10.6	11.1	14.2	12.3	12.5	12.5	12.6	12.5	13.1	14.2	13.2	14.9	16.1	....	Peru
55.3	61.4	63.9	59.3	55.3	51.7	58.9	62.0	58.2	54.5	51.4	51.4	53.4	52.3	47.4	46.0	....	St. Kitts and Nevis
54.5	61.6	60.9	71.0	66.1	67.7	63.9	65.1	65.9	65.1	68.5	61.8	62.4	62.0	56.7	51.8	....	St. Lucia
73.1	72.5	64.1	75.7	65.1	65.7	53.3	59.2	50.0	46.1	51.6	53.6	50.0	49.6	53.2	52.0	....	St. Vincent & Grens.
69.4	64.9	68.2	52.3	67.3	48.9	31.3	22.7	5.6	76.5	100.4	67.1	54.6	51.5	....	....	....	Suriname
32.6	34.4	33.8	38.7	42.4	45.2	41.1	39.4	40.5	42.5	52.5	49.1	51.2	48.3	....	....	....	Trinidad and Tobago
26.6	25.7	21.6	21.3	24.1	23.2	19.6	20.4	18.4	18.6	18.2	18.8	19.4	18.5	17.0	18.6	....	Uruguay
25.5	15.6	24.4	18.3	32.7	38.7	30.7	25.7	26.8	30.3	26.8	35.8	28.4	19.9	21.4	28.3	....	Venezuela, Rep. Bol.

Balance of Payments

Imports of Goods and Services

	1985	1986	1987	1988	1989	1990	1991	1992	1993	1994	1995	1996	1997	1998	1999	2000	2001
								As percent of GDP									
Industrial Countries																	
United States	9.7	10.1	10.6	10.7	10.6	10.6	10.2	10.3	10.7	11.3	12.0	12.2	12.5	12.5	13.1	14.7	13.4
Canada	26.3	27.1	25.9	26.2	25.8	26.0	25.5	27.3	30.0	32.6	34.0	34.2	37.3	39.3	39.7	40.2	38.1
Australia	19.0	18.6	17.5	17.4	18.3	17.2	16.8	18.1	18.9	19.6	20.7	19.7	20.2	21.7	21.4	23.0	21.9
Japan	11.1	7.5	7.4	7.9	9.0	9.7	8.6	7.9	7.1	7.2	7.9	9.5	10.0	9.2	8.8	9.6	10.2
New Zealand	33.4	27.1	25.2	22.0	25.7	26.8	25.9	28.9	27.9	28.8	28.4	28.1	27.7	29.4	31.7	34.6	33.1
Euro Area																	
Austria	39.9	35.4	34.8	37.1	38.7	38.6	38.6	37.5	36.1	37.7	39.1	40.9	44.4	44.7	....	....	....
Belgium-Luxembourg	67.6	61.1	61.9	63.3	66.9	65.0	63.1	60.5	57.0	60.9	60.6	61.8	66.0	67.2	....	....	....
Finland	28.2	25.1	25.2	24.9	25.7	24.5	23.0	25.5	27.6	29.5	29.2	30.0	30.9	30.0	....	....	....
France	24.1	20.9	21.2	21.7	23.3	23.3	23.1	22.1	20.5	20.9	21.5	21.5	23.0	23.8	....	....	....
Germany	30.3	26.0	25.0	25.7	27.7	28.1	26.6	24.8	22.4	23.2	23.8	24.5	26.7	27.9	....	....	....
Greece	32.2	26.7	27.8	22.0	23.6	23.6	22.6	21.7	20.8	20.6	21.0	20.6	21.1	....	28.4	36.8	....
Ireland	58.1	50.6	51.0	53.2	57.4	52.0	52.4	52.5	54.3	59.7	63.5	64.2	64.8	96.0	....	....	....
Italy	23.1	18.6	18.8	18.8	20.0	19.8	18.6	19.2	19.0	20.3	22.8	20.7	22.3	22.6	....	....	....
Luxembourg											97.4	100.8	105.7	113.6	....	....	....
Netherlands	57.4	48.2	47.6	48.9	52.0	50.0	50.5	48.8	45.7	46.8	52.4	53.1	57.1	57.4	....	....	....
Portugal	40.8	30.9	35.7	38.7	38.4	39.3	36.4	34.4	35.2	36.9	37.8	38.5	41.5	41.9	....	....	....
Spain	20.6	17.7	19.4	20.3	21.6	20.5	20.4	20.4	20.0	22.3	23.8	24.6	27.2	29.0	....	....	....
Denmark	37.9	33.5	30.6	30.7	32.4	31.1	31.7	30.0	28.6	30.5	32.1	31.7	33.4	34.7	35.7	41.2	41.8
Iceland	40.4	35.0	35.8	33.1	32.6	32.7	32.6	30.4	29.7	29.7	32.1	35.9	35.8	40.1	39.3	41.7	....
Norway	36.0	38.2	34.9	34.2	34.4	33.7	32.5	31.2	31.7	32.2	32.0	32.1	33.5	36.5	32.9	31.3	30.0
Sweden	34.2	30.3	31.1	31.4	32.1	30.7	27.4	27.4	29.7	31.6	33.8	32.4	35.5	37.2	38.9	41.8	40.7
Switzerland	45.8	44.0	40.5	41.6	44.6	42.2	38.7	37.8	36.1	35.2	35.4	37.0	41.6	41.2	41.3	45.3	....
United Kingdom	28.1	26.6	26.7	26.6	27.7	26.7	24.2	24.9	26.5	27.2	28.8	29.8	28.5	27.7	27.9	30.0	29.4
Developing Countries																	
Africa																	
Algeria	19.6	15.7	12.5	14.8	17.3	16.3	17.2	....	....	....	....	....	....	....	....	....	....
Angola																	
Benin	41.8	39.0	38.6	28.2	24.6	24.6	46.0	34.7	35.0	42.3	44.5	33.9	35.0	33.1	36.0	....	....
Botswana	65.0	59.3	65.4	64.1	49.1	56.5	53.1	48.3	47.3	41.0	46.3	42.4	48.7	52.5	54.0	....	....
Burkina Faso	32.6	30.7	30.0	29.1	25.7	26.5	25.8	21.7	23.3	27.4	....	....	....	....	....	....	....
Burundi	20.4	21.7	25.1	25.8	21.6	27.7	29.9	29.4	29.5	24.9	25.9	15.8	14.5	19.4	16.1	21.3	....
Cameroon	23.9	21.6	19.1	9.5	19.7	20.2	18.9	16.2	15.8	22.7	18.4	....	....	....	....	....	....
Cape Verde	66.8	52.9	45.6	42.3	....	....	....	....	....	....	....	....	....	....	....	....	....
Central African Rep.	39.2	35.9	29.3	26.1	26.8	28.5	22.9	24.2	22.7	28.7	....	....	....	....	....	....	....
Chad	36.9	35.4	22.3	31.5	33.6	30.2	28.6	28.0	31.0	34.9	....	....	....	....	....	....	....
Comoros	59.9	47.6	50.2	41.8	37.5	36.6	41.0	42.6	37.3	46.9	46.0	....	....	....	....	....	....
Congo, Republic of	53.5	63.3	41.4	48.9	43.2	45.8	47.0	40.1	50.1	90.9	67.5	81.9	58.9	....	....	....	....
Côte d'Ivoire	31.1	32.2	31.9	30.3	30.9	31.9	30.3	30.7	29.8	34.2	38.1	37.5	39.1	37.7	....	....	....
Djibouti	....	....	....	....	....	....	....	....	....	....	....	....	....	....	....	....	....
Equatorial Guinea			71.5	80.1	66.3	66.7	82.4	56.9	55.4	51.5	120.0	171.5	....	....	....	....	....
Ethiopia	17.7	18.4	17.8	17.8	15.0	15.6	8.1	18.3	18.8	23.8	27.2	22.6	22.6	28.3	....	....	....
Gabon	54.5	40.6	38.6	42.0	39.5	33.4	32.3	32.4	34.6	38.3	35.7	33.0	37.2	48.0	38.5	....	....
Gambia, The	42.2	67.8	66.3	63.2	68.7	64.1	86.1	73.8	104.8	82.5	....	....	....	....	....	....	....
Ghana	13.3	17.0	24.7	24.3	24.5	24.2	25.1	28.8	36.4	36.8	32.8	34.6	38.3	....	....	....	....
Guinea	....	....	....	....	....	....	....	....	....	....	....	....	....	....	....	....	....
Guinea-Bissau	....	.3	.9	2.4	3.9	4.2	7.5	19.7	17.7	12.4	19.3	27.4	33.5	....	....	....	....
Kenya	26.6	25.8	26.7	27.4	30.8	31.7	29.0	26.4	36.1	34.4	39.1	37.3	35.6	32.5	31.0	36.4	....
Lesotho	145.4	140.4	118.3	124.9	126.4	122.5	129.7	123.6	115.1	104.7	112.2	111.8	106.6	103.2	91.0	85.7	....
Liberia	32.2	32.3	34.4	....	....	....	....	....	....	....	....	....	....	....	....	....	....
Madagascar	17.6	16.5	21.1	23.3	22.0	26.2	25.4	24.4	24.2	29.4	31.2	25.1	30.5	30.2	32.2	38.3	....
Malawi	28.3	24.1	27.1	33.8	28.7	29.5	35.0	41.9	29.5	74.5	....	....	....	....	....	....	....
Mali	48.0	37.7	33.7	35.4	31.3	33.5	34.7	35.1	33.9	43.5	41.7	36.2	36.8	....	....	....	....
Mauritania	77.6	72.6	61.3	59.1	55.6	49.5	50.2	57.7	61.7	53.1	48.1	53.4	48.8	....	....	....	....
Mauritius	55.4	53.8	62.3	69.6	71.4	72.5	66.6	63.2	65.4	66.1	61.7	65.2	65.6	63.7	66.3	54.9	....
Morocco	33.8	27.3	26.7	24.7	27.3	30.1	29.8	31.8	32.1	30.9	34.1	29.6	31.8	31.9	33.9	37.6	....
Mozambique	19.1	21.7	56.9	72.3	70.7	70.4	38.8	51.6	55.7	57.3	47.0	36.0	29.4	29.7	37.8	....	....
Namibia	....	....	....	....	....	64.8	65.6	64.8	63.9	57.6	59.9	60.5	59.1	56.1	....	....	....
Niger	32.4	27.5	29.8	29.8	29.6	29.3	26.0	24.0	21.8	29.7	27.4	....	....	....	....	....	....
Nigeria	11.2	10.2	18.3	16.1	16.6	21.3	31.0	25.1	20.8	22.9	14.2	8.7	10.6	10.3	33.5	....	....
Rwanda	19.4	21.0	19.3	18.0	15.7	13.9	17.9	17.6	20.7	63.3	29.1	26.5	25.5	21.1	23.5	23.0	....
São Tomé & Príncipe																	
Senegal	45.1	36.4	31.7	29.6	32.8	32.3	31.6	30.6	30.7	41.6	40.7	35.7	35.8	36.8	....	....	....
Seychelles	84.9	78.5	72.7	76.3	72.1	67.0	61.6	59.3	65.9	56.2	62.0	73.7	74.6	85.1	91.0	....	....
Sierra Leone	21.5	29.7	23.8	16.4	22.0	33.1	25.9	29.7	32.3	32.5	29.9	....	....	....	....	....	....
Somalia																	
South Africa	22.7	21.7	20.4	22.6	21.4	18.8	17.5	17.3	17.8	19.8	22.1	23.2	23.5	24.7	23.0	25.8	27.3
Sudan	15.3	10.2	7.6	11.5	7.8	3.6	4.9	24.2	12.3	21.9	14.9	18.9	15.7	....	....	....	....
Swaziland	92.8	79.8	82.1	80.3	86.9	89.3	92.9	101.9	105.7	97.8	99.2	104.9	98.0	104.2	90.9	81.8	....
Tanzania	16.8	25.0	23.9	25.4	30.4	34.6	30.9	36.4	47.5	40.2	40.7	33.4	25.5	28.1	24.7	22.3	....
Togo	57.9	56.0	51.1	51.1	49.2	52.1	53.1	44.8	40.5	49.9	60.5	52.6	46.6	49.6	43.8	....	....
Tunisia	38.1	37.3	36.0	42.1	48.1	49.0	44.1	46.7	49.1	48.4	48.9	43.5	46.0	46.1	44.5	47.8	....
Uganda	9.7	10.5	13.3	12.7	15.6	18.4	20.4	20.6	22.9	21.8	24.1	26.2	....	....	....	....	....
Zambia	36.7	42.6	38.9	26.9	30.5	50.7	33.0	....	....	....	....	....	34.1	....	....	....	....
Zimbabwe	24.5	21.4	21.1	20.2	21.5	22.8	27.8	36.2	31.3	36.5	....	....	....	....	....	....	....

Imports of Goods and Services

As percent of GDP

1985	1986	1987	1988	1989	1990	1991	1992	1993	1994	1995	1996	1997	1998	1999	2000	2001	
																	Asia
....	....	....	....	....	....	....	....	....	....	....	....	....	....	....	....	....	Afghanistan, I.S. of
19.1	18.3	16.9	17.8	19.7	13.6	12.5	13.5	14.5	16.0	20.0	18.7	19.0	18.6	20.0	21.3	....	Bangladesh
....	....	....	....	....	....	....	....	....	....	....	....	....	....	....	....	....	Bhutan
....	....	....	....	....	....	....	....	....	....	....	....	....	....	....	....	....	Cambodia
13.6	12.7	12.3	12.6	12.1	12.2	13.6	15.7	16.4	20.6	19.3	18.8	18.2	17.0	19.2	23.2	....	China,P.R.: Mainland
													129.0	128.2	145.5	138.6	China,P.R.:Hong Kong
44.9	41.6	42.3	51.6	60.5	68.2	59.9	54.2	58.5	59.5	58.3	59.3	57.8	58.5	57.3	....	....	Fiji
9.0	8.5	8.7	8.4	9.4	9.1	9.4	10.3	10.9	11.7	13.2	14.2	13.9	14.1	14.0	16.2	....	India
20.1	18.8	21.7	20.8	21.4	24.0	24.5	25.1	24.2	24.7	26.9	26.1	29.1	46.0	29.8	36.1	....	Indonesia
....	....	....	....	....	....	....	....	....	....	....	....	....	....	....	....	....	Kiribati
32.1	31.4	32.2	30.3	29.9	30.2	30.3	29.1	27.4	28.9	31.7	33.5	36.0	36.3	35.5	41.7	40.5	Korea
15.5	16.8	29.6	30.8	30.1	24.5	23.9	25.8	35.6	43.5	42.4	41.1	40.8	46.9	39.8	....	....	Lao People's Dem.Rep
50.0	50.5	48.7	56.0	65.1	72.2	81.2	74.4	78.8	90.5	97.8	89.9	92.2	93.5	96.3	104.7	....	Malaysia
66.8	60.8	67.1	68.7	73.9	74.0	75.2	76.3	72.8	72.4	78.1	76.7	80.1	79.6	81.4	80.5	....	Maldives
						25.9	40.9		61.9	42.5	48.6	53.0	69.0	76.8	....	....	Mongolia
9.0	8.4	4.8	3.4	1.9	2.5	1.2	1.7	2.4	2.0	1.9	1.6	1.4	1.1	.7	....	....	Myanmar
21.9	21.0	22.0	24.7	21.8	23.7	29.1	27.9	31.5	36.1	38.5	39.6	39.6	31.5	34.0	33.4	....	Nepal
23.8	23.2	22.9	22.4	24.2	25.8	25.6	25.7	25.2	23.2	23.9	26.5	22.6	20.3	19.5	20.5	....	Pakistan
52.9	51.5	57.3	49.8	49.3	46.8	51.4	45.9	39.0	36.3	41.4	43.9	49.0	49.8	52.7	....	....	Papua New Guinea
19.5	19.7	23.8	25.0	28.1	31.5	30.5	31.8	38.0	40.6	45.0	49.9	61.3	60.8	48.3	48.8	47.0	Philippines
67.7	61.4	71.1	71.6	78.4	84.7	78.7	85.9	78.9	52.4	60.1	58.8	60.3	....	....	....	....	Samoa
159.7	152.4	170.8	184.4	177.2	177.1	164.7	158.8	159.4	158.2	162.3	157.8	152.0	137.9	149.2	160.6	....	Singapore
71.9	80.9	81.6	99.8	101.1	75.0	81.8	63.5	77.0	77.6	....	....	....	....	....	....	....	Solomon Islands
38.4	35.3	35.9	36.7	37.5	36.9	39.7	39.6	42.6	45.6	45.9	43.9	43.6	42.3	43.3	49.6	....	Sri Lanka
26.2	23.8	28.5	34.7	37.7	42.0	43.0	41.8	42.5	44.1	48.9	45.9	48.0	43.4	46.0	58.6	60.3	Thailand
82.5	73.6	71.2	67.1	61.1	59.9	48.2	50.0	53.5	....	....	....	....	....	....	....	....	Tonga
70.3	61.8	74.0	72.8	54.6	67.5	55.4	49.3	48.4	50.4	48.3	....	....	....	....	....	....	Vanuatu
																	Europe
....	....	....	....	....	....	....	....	....	....	....	....	....	....	....	....	....	Albania
								.3	67.0	56.4	55.6	58.1	53.6	49.8	....	....	Armenia
....	....	....	....	....	....	....	....	....	....	....	....	....	....	....	....	....	Azerbaijan
										54.6	50.2	61.6	53.3	54.7	77.6	71.2	Belarus
													95.5	93.9	90.9	....	Bosnia & Herzegovina
35.6	29.2	28.5	22.8	20.7	38.7	55.8	62.0	53.9	53.5	49.6	60.5	56.5	48.9	52.9	64.0	....	Bulgaria
								48.8	47.1	48.4	49.7	57.5	48.7	48.8	50.4	52.8	Croatia
58.8	48.7	50.2	53.4	59.7	57.0	57.0	60.6	47.5	47.9	49.9	53.1	52.0	51.0	48.3	53.8	....	Cyprus
								52.7	53.7	57.7	58.8	61.6	60.2	61.8	73.0	74.1	Czech Republic
33.2	34.3	33.9	32.5	32.1	34.4	38.3	....										Czechoslovakia
								73.7	86.6	80.2	78.5	89.7	90.3	81.7	99.6	95.7	Estonia
....	....	....	....	....	....	....	....	....	....	....	....	....	....	....	....	....	Georgia
42.9	43.7	41.0	37.2	38.1	33.3	33.9	34.2	38.2	34.5	42.3	45.0	54.8	57.9	58.9	68.6	68.6	Hungary
										35.5	37.6	39.0	37.1	38.4	47.1	50.2	Kazakhstan
										44.9	48.7	58.8	46.2	56.8	56.1	....	Kyrgyz Republic
							73.1	57.8	44.4	49.3	58.9	59.4	64.9	54.1	54.4	57.2	Latvia
								91.2	61.4	64.8	63.2	65.1	59.1	50.1	51.6	55.8	Lithuania
												40.2	50.3	57.6	56.1	....	Macedonia, FYR
87.8	81.9	87.0	89.2	91.6	98.8	97.8	98.9	104.9	106.8	105.5	98.7	91.1	91.7	94.1	111.2	90.8	Malta
										69.8	73.7	74.3	72.4	66.6	75.4	74.5	Moldova
17.5	18.2	20.8	22.0	19.3	25.6	23.7	21.5	24.1	23.0	26.6	28.6	32.1	32.6	32.6	36.3	....	Poland
18.7	16.4	15.2	13.5	16.6	25.9	21.5	33.2	26.3	25.9	31.9	35.4	35.0	30.4	32.0	38.2	23.6	Romania
								23.6	24.5	20.7	21.5	26.4	27.3	24.1	23.6		Russia
								63.3	56.7	50.8	66.4	67.7	72.0	66.7	73.9	....	Slovak Republic
						55.3	57.2	57.9	57.4	56.6	58.2	58.3	56.8	62.9	60.7		Slovenia
		17.6	17.7	17.8	17.0	16.0	16.8	18.7	20.2	23.7	27.3	29.8	27.6	26.4	31.1	....	Turkey
....	....	....	....	....	....	....	....	....	....	....	....	....	....	....	....	....	Turkmenistan
										49.0	49.4	48.2	43.6	45.0	49.5	....	Ukraine
....	....	....	....	....	....	....	....	....	....	....	....	....	....	....	....	....	Yugoslavia, SFR
																	Middle East
89.9	81.6	87.5	77.3	87.4	94.5	95.6	96.7	80.7	74.0	70.5	76.2	69.5	63.9	62.2	63.4	....	Bahrain, Kingdom of
22.9	16.2	14.7	14.2	13.7	22.7	36.8	32.9	32.6	30.3	28.5	27.0	27.7	25.5	24.3	23.6	....	Egypt
9.6	6.9	5.7	4.1	4.5	4.1	4.0	2.5	34.5	20.2	14.2	12.6	10.8	8.8	5.8	5.3	....	Iran, I.R. of
48.1	42.0	46.2	38.9	38.8	38.5	37.6	36.4	40.8	40.6	39.3	38.3	36.4	35.2	41.6	42.9	38.0	Israel
72.5	53.5	56.7	62.1	71.4	88.8	81.3	80.6	79.3	69.8	71.9	77.1	70.8	65.1	61.8	....	....	Jordan
45.7	51.0	40.3	49.3	43.3	38.8	92.3	59.5	48.1	44.8	47.6	42.0	43.1	52.2	40.7	31.7	37.4	Kuwait
27.1	24.2	32.2	31.1	31.8	31.0	33.6	25.8	31.3	26.1	22.6	23.8	21.8	21.2	17.4	....	....	Libya
36.0	36.4	26.1	31.4	29.8	28.6	35.9	36.6	39.5	35.6	36.5	35.8	38.6	48.6	36.7	30.7	....	Oman
53.3	51.1	50.5	45.6	47.1	42.0	54.9	50.8	42.5	32.6	35.0	31.5	31.7	30.4	27.7	28.1	25.7	Saudi Arabia
23.2	12.0	9.0	15.8	14.0	12.4	12.1	12.2	13.4	13.8	10.9	9.9	7.7	6.8	7.1	6.7	....	Syrian Arab Republic
....	....	....	....	....	....	....	....	....	....	....	....	....	....	....	....	....	Yemen Arab Rep.
....	....	....	....	....	....	....	....	....	....	....	....	....	....	....	....	....	Yemen, P.D. Rep.
						22.2	19.0	16.8	9.1	20.7	38.2	46.7	50.8	42.2	....	....	Yemen, Republic of

Balance of Payments

Imports of Goods and Services

	1985	1986	1987	1988	1989	1990	1991	1992	1993	1994	1995	1996	1997	1998	1999	2000	2001
								As percent of GDP									
Western Hemisphere																	
Anguilla	....	....	....	....	....	....	....	....	....	....	....	....	....	....	....	....	....
Antigua and Barbuda	105.8	119.4	105.8	83.8	90.8	87.0	90.1	91.2	87.3	84.4	88.9	86.5	82.3	79.8	82.3	76.4	....
Argentina	6.5	6.5	7.3	6.0	8.7	4.8	6.1	8.4	9.3	10.6	10.1	11.1	12.8	12.9	11.5	11.5	....
Aruba																	
Bahamas, The	97.5	65.3	63.2	57.2	56.2	54.3	55.2	52.5	52.5	53.7	58.5	....	....	....	....	....	....
Barbados	59.9	54.6	46.3	45.9	49.0	51.0	49.6	42.6	47.6	49.6	56.4	56.7	58.8	56.9	58.1	....	....
Belize	67.6	65.1	64.9	68.1	69.1	61.3	67.5	67.3	64.7	57.9	55.4	53.0	60.7	61.9	64.8	67.7	....
Bolivia	10.9	21.3	21.1	18.4	21.8	22.3	20.9	24.0	25.0	22.6	23.4	23.4	26.0	25.9	24.0	24.9	....
Brazil	7.6	6.8	6.6	6.0	6.2	6.1	6.9	7.2	8.0	8.0	9.0	8.5	9.3	9.4	11.9	12.3	14.5
Chile	24.3	26.0	26.5	27.4	31.2	30.2	27.6	28.2	29.1	27.2	28.1	26.9	26.9	27.2	24.7	28.1	....
Colombia	14.6	14.6	15.1	15.8	15.5	17.0	15.4	18.3	22.4	17.4	17.3	16.9	17.2	17.6	15.5	17.3	19.2
Costa Rica	32.7	30.6	36.1	36.9	39.6	41.1	31.2	34.1	35.7	34.0	40.3	42.7	44.5	50.0	45.5	....	....
Dominica	64.7	59.2	61.3	68.8	78.4	80.5	70.4	65.2	63.7	62.0	67.0	61.5	63.9	62.0	68.2	67.1	....
Dominican Republic	30.9	26.7	33.5	37.3	36.3	31.6	29.1	30.9	57.0	55.7	51.4	51.4	51.6	56.3	53.5	55.2	....
Ecuador	14.1	19.8	25.7	21.9	23.6	23.6	26.5	23.8	28.1	29.5	31.8	26.9	30.9	34.0	30.6	36.7	....
El Salvador	20.7	29.1	26.3	23.9	25.0	30.5	30.4	32.3	34.3	35.2	38.2	34.3	37.8	37.5	37.7	43.0	....
Grenada	67.6	73.5	68.8	65.0	60.4	62.8	62.1	55.2	63.7	61.2	60.9	65.6	67.1	72.0	69.5	74.1	....
Guatemala	11.2	12.4	22.5	22.1	22.1	23.7	21.6	27.3	26.1	24.6	25.4	22.4	23.6	26.0	27.4	29.2	....
Guyana	67.8	....	....	....	....	....	....	155.8	135.4	121.9	113.9	....	....	....	....	....	....
Haiti	27.7	21.2	23.2	21.6	17.9	19.7	22.6	16.2	18.7	11.4	34.3	26.3	27.5	27.2	....	....	....
Honduras	29.9	28.3	25.9	24.7	23.0	37.0	37.1	36.1	42.7	48.4	46.8	55.2	53.3	53.5	55.5	55.3	....
Jamaica	67.6	45.3	46.6	47.6	53.1	52.0	54.7	61.0	57.8	63.8	65.5	60.4	55.8	54.0	53.2	56.3	....
Mexico	13.0	17.1	17.2	19.8	20.5	21.0	21.0	22.2	19.2	21.9	28.7	30.1	30.5	32.9	32.5	33.0	30.0
Montserrat	....	59.7	....	....	....	89.6	91.0	78.4	....	....	....	....	....	....	....	....	....
Netherlands Antilles																	
Nicaragua	31.2	18.7	33.2	69.6	65.7	63.4	48.7	51.3	42.7	53.6	60.1	67.5	81.8	80.5	91.9	82.8	....
Panama	59.7	61.7	63.0	58.8	70.4	78.9	93.1	96.3	92.8	95.2	98.2	92.0	99.9	95.6	81.3	81.5	....
Paraguay	18.5	20.1	25.9	22.1	30.2	41.2	38.1	38.0	49.1	53.4	57.7	52.4	50.4	52.6	45.6	43.1	....
Peru	16.0	14.1	10.3	12.0	8.7	14.1	14.0	15.0	15.9	15.9	18.0	17.9	18.5	18.7	17.5	18.1	....
St. Kitts and Nevis	73.1	77.0	84.5	84.4	83.4	83.1	80.2	68.8	71.0	64.5	74.7	78.5	70.8	67.2	72.4	75.2	....
St. Lucia	68.0	66.4	68.7	75.4	81.8	76.9	76.4	72.4	71.1	71.3	70.9	67.7	71.6	68.5	66.0	60.8	....
St. Vincent & Grens.	79.1	79.9	80.1	82.9	82.6	76.8	72.8	69.3	68.2	69.9	66.1	66.9	77.9	78.5	73.8	59.3	....
Suriname	70.9	68.1	55.6	43.3	49.5	47.3	37.7	23.2	5.1	64.3	87.7	76.1	61.9	70.1	....	....	....
Trinidad and Tobago	28.2	38.0	32.3	33.8	34.4	28.2	32.9	28.6	31.0	29.8	39.6	38.2	55.3	53.7	....	....	....
Uruguay	21.5	20.4	19.5	17.3	18.5	17.8	17.5	19.3	19.1	19.9	18.5	19.4	20.2	20.0	19.1	21.0	....
Venezuela, Rep. Bol.	15.9	16.4	23.7	24.7	21.7	19.4	25.6	28.4	26.7	22.5	21.8	21.0	21.6	21.1	16.4	16.3	....

Current Account Balance

Excluding Exceptional Financing

As percent of GDP

1985	1986	1987	1988	1989	1990	1991	1992	1993	1994	1995	1996	1997	1998	1999	2000	2001	
																	Industrial Countries
-3.0	-3.3	-3.4	-2.4	-1.8	-1.4	.1	-.8	-1.2	-1.7	-1.5	-1.5	-1.7	-2.5	-3.5	-4.5	-4.1	United States
-1.6	-3.1	-3.2	-3.0	-4.0	-3.4	-3.7	-3.6	-3.9	-2.3	-.7	.5	-1.3	-1.3	.2	2.6	2.8	Canada
-5.5	-5.7	-3.9	-4.6	-6.1	-5.2	-3.5	-3.7	-3.3	-5.1	-5.4	-3.9	-3.1	-5.0	-5.9	-4.1	-2.6	Australia
3.7	4.2	3.4	2.7	2.1	1.4	2.0	3.0	3.0	2.7	2.1	1.4	2.2	3.1	2.4	2.5	2.2	Japan
-11.9	-9.7	-7.9	-4.2	-3.5	-3.3	-2.8	-2.6	-1.7	-4.6	-4.9	-6.0	-6.6	-4.0	-6.5	-5.4	-3.1	New Zealand
																	Euro Area
-.2	.2	-.2	-.2	.2	.7	—	-.4	-.6	-1.5	-2.3	-2.1	-2.5	-2.5	...	...	...	Austria
.8	2.5	1.9	2.2	2.2	1.7	2.2	2.8	4.9	5.0	4.8	4.8	5.3	4.5	...	...	...	Belgium-Luxembourg
-1.5	-1.0	-1.9	-2.5	-5.0	-5.1	-5.5	-4.7	-1.3	1.1	4.0	3.9	5.4	5.7	...	...	...	Finland
—	.3	-.5	-.5	-.5	-.8	-.5	.3	.7	.5	.7	1.3	2.7	2.6	...	...	...	France
2.8	4.6	4.2	4.2	4.8	3.2	-1.0	-.9	-.7	-1.0	-.8	-.3	-.1	-.3	...	...	...	Germany
-9.8	-4.3	-2.6	-1.5	-3.8	-4.3	-1.8	-2.2	-.8	-.1	-2.4	-3.7	-4.0	...	-5.8	-8.7	...	Greece
-3.9	-3.2	-.2	-.1	-1.6	-.8	.6	1.1	3.5	2.9	2.6	2.8	2.3	1.2	...	...	...	Ireland
-1.0	.4	-.3	-.9	-1.5	-1.5	-2.1	-2.4	.8	1.3	2.3	3.2	2.8	1.7	...	...	...	Italy
										13.4	12.1	11.5	8.9	...	...	...	Luxembourg
3.2	2.3	1.8	3.0	4.2	2.7	2.5	2.0	4.1	4.9	6.2	5.2	6.7	3.4	...	...	...	Netherlands
1.8	3.4	1.0	-2.2	.3	-.3	-.9	-.2	.3	-2.5	-.1	-4.8	-6.3	-7.3	...	...	...	Portugal
1.7	1.7	-.1	-1.1	-2.9	-3.7	-3.7	-3.7	-1.2	-1.3	.1	.1	.5	-.6	...	...	...	Spain
-4.6	-5.3	-2.8	-1.2	-1.0	1.0	1.5	2.9	3.5	2.1	1.0	1.7	.5	-1.2	1.7	1.6	2.6	Denmark
-3.9	.4	-3.5	-3.9	-1.9	-2.0	-4.0	-2.3	.7	1.7	.8	-1.6	-1.7	-6.9	-6.9	-10.0	...	Iceland
4.8	-6.0	-4.5	-4.0	.2	3.5	4.3	3.5	3.0	3.1	3.6	7.0	6.5	—	5.5	15.6	15.9	Norway
-1.0	—		-.3	-1.6	-2.8	-1.9	-3.6	-2.2	.4	2.1	2.2	3.1	1.9	2.5	2.9	3.2	Sweden
6.3	3.4	3.6	4.7	4.5	3.0	4.5	5.9	7.6	6.7	7.1	7.1	10.4	10.2	10.9	13.6	...	Switzerland
.7	-.2	-1.8	-4.2	-5.1	-3.9	-1.8	-2.2	-1.9	-1.0	-1.3	-1.1	-.2	-.6	-2.2	-2.0	-2.1	United Kingdom
																	Developing Countries
																	Africa
1.7	-3.5	.2	-3.8	-1.9	2.3	5.1	...	...	...	...	...	...	...	...	...	...	Algeria
																	Angola
-3.7	-4.0	-2.2	-8.5	-3.0	-2.6	-13.9	-5.6	-4.8	-1.5	-10.6	-2.6	-7.9	-6.6	-8.1	...	...	Benin
8.5	8.4	40.8	10.1	17.1	-.5	8.1	5.0	11.3	5.1	6.8	11.6	14.8	3.6	11.1	...	...	Botswana
-4.3	-.9	-2.2	-1.9	4.1	-2.7	-3.1	-.7	-2.4	.8	...	...	...	...	...	...	...	Burkina Faso
-3.5	-2.9	-8.2	-6.4	-1.0	-6.0	-2.9	-5.5	-2.9	-1.6	1.0	-4.6	-.1	-6.0	-3.3	-6.9	...	Burundi
-6.5	-3.8	-6.8	-1.9	-2.7	-4.6	-2.9	-3.3	-5.1	-.8	1.0	...	...	...	...	...	...	Cameroon
-6.3	.9	-1.0	-.2														Cape Verde
-6.9	-9.1	-6.1	-2.7	-2.7	-6.2	-4.5	-5.9	-1.0	-2.9	...	...	...	...	...	...	...	Central African Rep.
-10.0	-5.6	-1.3	1.8	-4.2	-2.8	-4.1	-5.1	-8.0	-3.2	...	...	...	...	...	...	...	Chad
-13.3	-10.5	-12.5	-3.1	2.7	-4.3	-4.2	-5.4	3.6	-3.7	-8.4	...	...	...	...	...	...	Comoros
-7.5	-32.5	-9.7	-20.1	-3.6	-9.0	-16.9	-10.8	-20.6	-44.8	-30.7	-43.6	-10.8	...	...	...	...	Congo, Republic of
.9	-3.3	-9.6	-12.1	-9.9	-11.2	-10.2	-9.1	-8.6	-.2	-4.9	-1.5	-1.5	-2.5	...	...	...	Côte d'Ivoire
																	Djibouti
		-20.6	-15.7	-18.6	-14.2	-30.9	-6.6	1.8	-.3	-75.5	-123.8	...	...	...	...	...	Equatorial Guinea
1.7	-5.0	-3.1	-3.1	-1.9	-3.6	1.1	-1.6	-.9	2.4	-.2	1.3	-.7	-4.2	...	...	...	Ethiopia
-4.6	-23.0	-11.7	-16.2	-4.6	3.1	1.4	-3.0	-.9	7.6	9.4	15.6	10.0	-13.3	8.5	...	...	Gabon
3.3	2.7	2.9	10.9	5.9	7.2	4.4	11.2	-1.9	2.7	...	...	...	...	...	...	...	Gambia, The
-2.1	-1.5	-2.0	-1.3	-1.8	-3.6	-3.8	-5.9	-9.4	-4.7	-2.2	-4.7	-8.0	...	...	...	...	Ghana
																	Guinea
...	-.2	-.8	-2.2	-3.8	-2.9	-6.3	-18.5	-15.5	-7.3	-10.9	-19.2	-11.4	...	...	...	...	Guinea-Bissau
-1.9	-.6	-6.3	-5.5	-7.1	-6.2	-2.7	-2.2	1.2	1.4	-4.4	-.8	-4.3	-4.1	-.9	-2.3	...	Kenya
-4.9	-1.0	5.5	-4.9	2.0	10.6	12.2	4.6	3.6	12.9	-34.6	-32.1	-26.3	-31.5	-24.2	-16.8	...	Lesotho
5.2	-1.7	-12.9															Liberia
-6.4	-4.4	-5.5	-6.1	-3.4	-8.6	-8.6	-6.6	-7.7	-9.3	-8.7	-7.3	-7.5	-8.0	-6.8	-7.1	...	Madagascar
-11.2	-7.2	-5.1	-6.5	-3.4	-4.6	-10.3	-15.8	-8.1	-38.4	...	...	...	...	...	...	...	Malawi
-17.0	-14.8	-11.2	-12.3	-7.7	-8.9	-7.0	-8.8	-7.5	-9.2	-11.9	-10.6	-7.3	...	...	...	...	Mali
-16.9	-23.1	-15.7	-10.0	-1.9	-.9	-2.7	-10.7	-18.4	-7.0	2.1	8.4	4.5	...	...	...	...	Mauritania
-2.8	6.4	3.4	-2.6	-4.7	-4.5	-.6	—	-2.9	-6.6	-.6	.8	-2.2	.1	-3.1	-.7	...	Mauritius
-6.9	-1.2	1.0	2.1	-3.4	-.8	-1.5	-1.5	-1.9	-2.4	-3.9	-.2	-.5	-.4	-.5	-1.5	...	Morocco
-11.9	-13.8	-29.3	-30.4	-35.3	-29.3	-12.8	-17.9	-22.0	-21.6	-19.8	-14.8	-8.6	-11.3	-23.0	...	...	Mozambique
					1.1	4.1	1.7	3.9	2.6	5.0	3.3	2.5	4.8	...	...	...	Namibia
-4.7	-8.3	-8.2	-10.3	-12.3	-9.5	-7.4	-6.4	-4.3	-8.9	-9.1	...	...	...	...	...	...	Niger
3.2	.5	-.3	-.9	3.6	15.4	3.6	6.3	-1.7	-5.1	-2.9	2.7	.4	-3.3	1.4	...	...	Nigeria
-3.7	-3.6	-6.3	-6.3	-5.2	-4.2	-1.8	-4.1	-6.6	-6.1	4.5	-.6	-3.3	-4.1	-3.8	-.4	...	Rwanda
																	São Tomé & Príncipe
-14.0	-9.8	-9.4	-8.1	-7.5	-6.4	-6.8	-6.7	-8.0	-5.1	-5.5	-4.3	-4.2	-5.3	...	...	...	Senegal
-11.4	-15.9	-8.5	-10.0	-3.1	-3.5	-2.2	-1.6	-8.3	-5.3	-10.6	-11.2	-11.2	-21.4	-19.3	...	...	Seychelles
.3	28.7	-4.6	-.3	-6.4	-10.7	2.0	-.8	-7.5	-9.8	-14.5	...	...	...	...	...	...	Sierra Leone
																	Somalia
4.0	4.3	3.9	1.6	1.4	1.9	1.9	1.5	1.2	.1	-1.5	-1.3	-1.5	-1.6	-.5	-.4	-.1	South Africa
2.5	-.3	-1.9	-3.4	-.8	-1.5	-3.5	-12.1	-3.9	-10.4	-6.0	-10.1	-8.1	...	...	...	...	Sudan
-10.7	2.4	11.2	13.7	11.1	5.9	5.4	-4.2	-6.4	.2	-2.3	-4.2	.7	-5.4	.5	-3.0	...	Swaziland
-5.8	-7.1	-7.9	-7.0	-7.6	-13.1	-14.9	-15.5	-24.6	-15.8	-12.3	-7.9	-8.2	-11.4	-8.6	-5.3	...	Tanzania
-4.4	-6.2	-4.9	-6.3	-3.8	-6.1	-9.2	-8.4	-6.6	-5.7	-11.0	-10.5	-7.8	-9.9	-9.0	...	...	Togo
-6.9	-6.7	-.6	2.1	-2.2	-3.8	-3.6	-7.1	-9.1	-3.4	-4.3	-2.4	-3.1	-3.4	-2.1	-4.2	...	Tunisia
.1	-.9	-2.1	-3.3	-4.9	-7.0	-5.6	-3.1	-6.7	-3.9	-5.5	-4.0	...	...	...	...	...	Uganda
-17.5	-20.7	-11.8	-8.1	-5.5	-15.9	-9.0	...	...	...	...	...	-9.0	...	...	...	...	Zambia
-1.1	.3	.9	1.6	.2	-1.6	-5.6	-8.9	-1.8	-6.2	...	...	...	...	...	...	...	Zimbabwe

Balance of Payments

Current Account Balance

Excluding Exceptional Financing

As percent of GDP

	1985	1986	1987	1988	1989	1990	1991	1992	1993	1994	1995	1996	1997	1998	1999	2000	2001
Asia																	
Afghanistan, I.S. of	....	....	....	....	....	....	....	....	....	....	....	....	....	....	....	....	....
Bangladesh	-3.2	-4.1	-1.4	-1.5	-5.4	-1.4	.2	.6	1.1	.6	-2.2	-2.5	-.7	-.1	-.8	-.7	....
Bhutan	....	....	....	....	....	....	....	....	....	....	....	....	....	....	....	....	....
Cambodia	....	....	....	....	....	....	....	....	....	....	....	....	....	....	....	....	....
China,P.R.: Mainland	-3.8	-2.4	.1	-1.0	-1.0	3.1	3.3	1.4	-1.9	1.3	.2	.9	4.1	3.3	2.1	1.9	....
China,P.R.:Hong Kong	....	....	....	....	....	....	....	....	....	....	....	....	....	2.4	7.3	5.5	7.4
Fiji	1.6	1.3	2.3	6.4	.6	-7.1	-4.9	-3.9	-8.3	-6.2	-5.7	.6	-1.6	-3.6	.7	....	....
India	-2.0	-2.0	-2.0	-2.4	-2.3	-2.2	-1.5	-1.6	-.7	-.5	-1.5	-1.5	-.7	-1.6	-.7	-.9	....
Indonesia	-2.2	-4.5	-2.7	-1.6	-1.1	-2.6	-3.3	-2.0	-1.3	-1.6	-3.2	-3.4	-2.3	4.3	4.1	5.2	....
Kiribati	....	....	....	....	....	....	....	....	....	....	....	....	....	....	....	....	....
Korea	-.9	4.4	7.4	8.0	2.4	-.8	-2.8	-1.3	.3	-1.0	-1.7	-4.4	-1.7	12.7	6.0	2.7	2.0
Lao People's Dem.Rep	-10.7	-10.8	-19.2	-18.1	-18.7	-12.8	-11.2	-9.4	-10.5	-18.4	-19.6	-18.5	-17.5	-11.7	-8.3	....	....
Malaysia	-1.9	-.4	8.0	5.3	.8	-2.0	-8.5	-3.7	-4.5	-6.1	-9.7	-4.4	-5.9	13.2	15.9	9.3	....
Maldives	-4.3	-.2	5.7	5.3	5.6	4.6	-3.7	-6.9	-16.6	-3.1	-4.6	-1.6	-6.8	-4.5	-14.4	-9.5	....
Mongolia	....	....	....	....	....	....	-5.2	-5.0	....	6.8	3.2	-8.5	5.2	-13.2	-13.1	....	....
Myanmar	-3.1	-3.7	-1.7	-1.5	-.4	-1.8	-.9	-.3	-.4	-.2	-.2	-.2	-.2	-.2	-.1	....	....
Nepal	-4.8	-4.5	-4.2	-8.2	-7.4	-8.2	-9.4	-5.2	-6.3	-8.7	-8.4	-7.4	-8.0	-1.5	-5.1	-5.2	....
Pakistan	-3.6	-2.1	-1.7	-3.8	-3.6	-4.2	-3.3	-3.9	-6.1	-3.5	-5.7	-7.5	-2.9	-3.8	-1.5	-.2	....
Papua New Guinea	-5.5	-4.1	-7.5	-8.1	-8.8	-2.3	-12.5	-3.7	9.5	7.6	10.7	3.6	-3.9	-.8	2.8	....	....
Philippines	-.1	3.2	-1.3	-1.0	-3.4	-6.1	-2.3	-1.9	-5.5	-4.6	-2.7	-4.8	-5.3	2.4	10.4	11.3	6.3
Samoa	2.1	8.0	7.3	6.7	11.7	6.5	-20.1	-33.8	-24.3	3.1	4.9	5.8	3.9	....	....	....	....
Singapore	—	1.8	-.5	7.7	9.9	8.5	11.4	12.1	7.3	16.3	17.9	14.1	19.0	24.7	26.3	23.5	....
Solomon Islands	-17.4	-8.2	-11.5	-22.0	-19.8	-13.3	-16.3	-.6	-2.7	-1.1	....	....	....	....	....	....	....
Sri Lanka	-7.0	-6.5	-4.9	-5.7	-5.9	-3.7	-6.6	-4.6	-3.7	-6.5	-5.9	-4.9	-2.6	-1.4	-3.6	-6.4	....
Thailand	-4.0	.6	-.7	-2.7	-3.5	-8.5	-7.7	-5.7	-5.1	-5.6	-8.1	-8.1	-2.0	12.7	10.1	7.6	5.4
Tonga	2.9	3.7	1.9	-11.5	6.4	4.7	—	-.3	-4.1	....	....	....	....	....	....	....	....
Vanuatu	-10.0	-11.6	-24.8	-14.6	-8.7	-4.0	-7.5	-6.9	-7.6	-9.2	-7.7	....	....	....	....	....	....
Europe																	
Albania	....	....	....	....	....	....	....	....	....	....	....	....	....	....	....	....	....
Armenia	....	....	....	....	....	....	....	-.1	-16.0	-17.0	-18.2	-18.7	-22.1	-16.6	....	....	....
Azerbaijan	....	....	....	....	....	....	....	....	....	....	....	....	....	....	....	....	....
Belarus	....	....	....	....	....	....	....	....	....	....	-4.3	-3.6	-6.1	-6.7	-1.6	-3.1	-2.2
Bosnia & Herzegovina	....	....	....	....	....	....	....	....	....	....	....	....	....	-29.5	-33.3	-29.3	....
Bulgaria	-.4	-2.6	-1.7	-.9	-1.6	-8.3	-1.0	-4.2	-10.1	-.3	-.2	.2	4.2	-.5	-5.5	-5.8	....
Croatia	....	....	....	....	....	....	....	....	5.3	3.8	-8.5	-5.3	-13.9	-6.8	-7.0	-2.4	-3.2
Cyprus	-7.4	-.6	-.2	-2.5	-5.5	-2.8	-7.3	-9.2	1.7	1.0	-1.9	-5.2	-4.0	-6.7	-2.4	-5.2	....
Czech Republic	....	....	....	....	....	....	....	....	1.3	-2.0	-2.6	-7.2	-6.8	-2.3	-2.7	-5.2	-4.6
Czechoslovakia	1.7	.4	.7	2.1	1.9	-2.7	2.7	....	....	....	....	....	....	....	....	....	....
Estonia	....	....	....	....	....	....	....	....	1.3	-7.2	-4.4	-9.1	-12.2	-9.2	-5.7	-5.8	-6.2
Georgia	....	....	....	....	....	....	....	....	....	....	....	....	....	....	....	....	....
Hungary	-2.2	-5.7	-2.6	-2.0	-2.0	1.1	1.2	.9	-11.0	-9.8	-5.7	-3.7	-2.1	-4.9	-4.4	-2.8	-2.1
Kazakhstan	....	....	....	....	....	....	....	....	....	....	-1.2	-3.7	-3.8	-5.8	-1.0	2.2	-7.9
Kyrgyz Republic	....	....	....	....	....	....	....	....	....	....	-7.6	-15.7	-24.2	-7.8	-25.1	-19.8	....
Latvia	....	....	....	....	....	....	....	14.0	19.2	5.5	-.4	-5.4	-6.1	-10.7	-9.8	-6.9	-10.0
Lithuania	....	....	....	....	....	....	....	....	-3.2	-2.2	-10.2	-9.2	-10.2	-12.1	-11.2	-6.0	-4.8
Macedonia, FYR	....	....	....	....	....	....	....	....	....	....	....	-6.5	-7.4	-8.9	-3.2	....	....
Malta	-2.5	.5	1.4	3.3	-.5	-2.4	-.3	1.1	-3.4	-4.8	-11.1	-12.1	-6.0	-6.3	-3.3	-13.1	-4.8
Moldova	....	....	....	....	....	....	....	....	....	....	-6.1	-11.5	-14.3	-19.7	-5.6	-9.0	-8.0
Poland	-1.4	-1.5	-.6	-.2	-1.7	5.2	-2.8	-3.7	-6.7	1.0	.7	-2.3	-4.0	-4.3	-8.1	-6.3	....
Romania	2.9	2.7	3.5	6.5	4.7	-8.5	-3.5	-7.7	-4.7	-1.5	-5.0	-7.3	-6.1	-6.9	-3.6	-3.7	....
Moldova	....	....	....	....	....	....	....	....	....	....	-6.1	-11.5	-14.3	-19.7	-5.6	-9.0	-8.0
Slovak Republic	....	....	....	....	....	....	....	....	....	-4.6	4.6	2.1	-10.6	-9.6	-10.0	-5.9	-3.5
Slovenia	....	....	....	....	....	....	....	7.8	1.5	4.0	-.5	.2	.1	-.8	-3.9	-3.4	-.4
Turkey	....	....	-.9	1.8	.9	-1.7	.2	-.6	-3.6	2.0	-1.4	-1.3	-1.4	1.0	-.7	-4.9	....
Turkmenistan	....	....	....	....	....	....	....	....	....	....	....	....	....	....	....	....	....
Ukraine	....	....	....	....	....	....	....	....	....	-3.2	-3.1	-2.7	-2.7	-3.1	5.4	....	....
Yugoslavia, SFR	....	....	....	....	....	....	....	....	....	....	....	....	....	....	....	....	....
Middle East																	
Bahrain, Kingdom of	1.1	-2.3	-5.9	5.2	-5.0	1.6	-13.1	-17.4	-6.5	-4.6	4.1	4.3	-.5	-12.6	-5.1	1.4	....
Egypt	-4.0	-2.9	-.3	-1.2	-1.5	.3	5.3	6.7	4.9	.1	-.4	-.3	-.9	-3.1	-1.8	-1.0	....
Iran, I.R. of	-.3	-2.7	-.8	-.6	-.1	.1	-1.2	-.6	-5.8	6.3	3.1	3.6	1.4	-1.1	2.4	3.8	....
Israel	4.1	4.3	-4.0	-1.9	.5	.3	-2.2	-1.3	-3.8	-4.6	-5.5	-5.6	-3.8	-1.3	-3.3	-1.8	-1.6
Jordan	-5.1	-.6	-5.4	-4.9	9.3	-5.6	-9.3	-15.6	-11.1	-6.3	-3.8	-3.2	.4	.2	5.0	....	....
Kuwait	22.4	31.4	20.4	22.2	37.6	21.0	-240.4	-2.3	10.4	13.0	18.9	22.9	26.6	8.7	17.3	40.9	26.1
Libya	6.9	-.7	-4.9	-7.7	-4.1	7.6	-.7	4.2	-4.5	.1	6.5	4.4	5.1	-1.2	7.0	....	....
Oman	-.1	-12.6	9.1	-3.7	3.3	9.5	-2.2	-4.8	-9.5	-6.2	-5.8	2.2	-.5	-21.3	-2.4	16.9	....
Saudi Arabia	-14.9	-16.1	-13.3	-9.6	-11.5	-4.0	-23.3	-14.4	-14.6	-8.7	-4.2	.4	.2	-9.0	.3	7.6	7.8
Syrian Arab Republic	-4.5	-2.0	-.9	-.9	6.6	7.4	2.5	.2	-.6	-1.8	.5	.1	.7	.1	.3	1.3	....
Yemen Arab Rep.	....	....	....	....	....	....	....	....	....	....	....	....	....	....	....	....	....
Yemen, P.D. Rep.	....	....	....	....	....	....	....	....	....	....	....	....	....	....	....	....	....
Yemen, Republic of	....	....	....	....	....	....	-7.1	-7.4	-6.7	.7	1.2	.5	-1.0	-5.2	8.6	....	....

Current Account Balance

Excluding Exceptional Financing

As percent of GDP

Western Hemisphere

1985	1986	1987	1988	1989	1990	1991	1992	1993	1994	1995	1996	1997	1998	1999	2000	2001	
....	....	....	....	....	....	....	....	....	....	....	....	....	....	....	....	....	Anguilla
-11.5	-48.1	-38.8	-13.3	-21.9	-7.9	-7.5	-2.3	3.3	-1.3	-.1	-11.0	-8.1	-10.2	-11.9	-12.0	....	Antigua and Barbuda
-1.1	-2.7	-3.9	-1.2	-1.7	3.2	-.3	-2.5	-3.4	-4.3	-2.0	-2.5	-4.2	-4.9	-4.2	-3.2	....	Argentina
....	....	....	....	....	....	....	....	....	....	....	....	....	....	....	....	....	Aruba
-.1	1.1	-2.4	-2.6	-2.9	-1.2	-6.2	1.3	1.7	-1.4	-4.8	....	....	....	....	....	....	Bahamas, The
4.3	.5	-1.3	2.8	1.5	-.6	-1.6	8.8	4.2	7.7	2.3	3.5	-2.3	-2.6	-6.0	....	....	Barbados
4.3	5.2	3.5	-.8	-5.2	3.8	-6.0	-5.9	-9.1	-7.3	-2.9	-1.1	-5.2	-9.5	-11.3	-18.0	....	Belize
-4.4	-9.8	-9.9	-6.6	-5.7	-4.1	-4.9	-9.5	-8.8	-1.5	-4.5	-5.5	-7.0	-8.0	-5.9	-5.6	....	Bolivia
-.1	-2.0	-.5	1.3	.3	-.8	-.4	1.6	—	-.2	-2.6	-3.0	-3.8	-4.3	-4.8	-4.1	-4.6	Brazil
-8.6	-6.7	-3.6	-1.0	-2.5	-1.6	-.3	-2.3	-5.7	-3.1	-2.1	-4.6	-4.5	-5.2	-.1	-1.3	....	Chile
-5.2	1.1	.9	-.6	-.5	1.3	5.7	2.0	-4.1	-4.6	-5.0	-4.9	-5.5	-5.3	.4	.4	-2.2	Colombia
-7.4	-3.6	-8.3	-6.6	-9.2	-8.7	-1.4	-4.4	-6.4	-2.3	-3.1	-2.2	-3.7	-3.7	-4.1	....	....	Costa Rica
-6.5	-6.3	-5.6	-8.6	-29.7	-26.2	-18.9	-14.1	-13.7	-17.4	-18.6	-14.1	-10.7	-4.7	-15.4	-25.7	....	Dominica
-2.1	-3.0	-6.2	-.4	-4.9	-4.0	-2.1	-8.0	-5.5	-2.7	-1.5	-1.6	-1.1	-2.1	-2.5	-5.2	....	Dominican Republic
.5	-5.2	-11.3	-6.8	-7.3	-3.4	-6.0	-1.0	-5.9	-5.4	-5.5	-.2	-2.3	-10.6	6.9	6.8	....	Ecuador
-3.3	-.4	-1.5	-2.4	-5.7	-4.9	-4.0	-3.3	-1.8	-.2	-2.8	-1.6	-.9	-.8	-2.2	-3.2	....	El Salvador
1.7	-13.3	-17.5	-15.1	-17.0	-20.9	-19.9	-12.9	-17.5	-10.3	-14.8	-18.9	-21.3	-22.9	-12.3	-19.3	....	Grenada
-2.2	-.2	-6.2	-5.3	-4.4	-3.0	-2.0	-6.8	-4.8	-3.9	-2.9	-3.6	-5.4	-5.6	-5.5	....	....	Guatemala
-20.9	....	....	....	....	....	....	-37.1	-30.1	-22.9	-21.7	....	....	....	....	....	....	Guyana
-4.7	-2.0	-1.4	-1.8	-2.5	-.8	-3.9	.5	-.8	-1.1	-3.7	-4.6	-1.5	-1.0	....	....	....	Haiti
-8.5	-5.9	-5.9	-3.5	-3.5	-6.1	-7.0	-8.7	-8.8	-10.0	-5.1	-8.2	-5.8	-7.5	-10.8	-8.6	....	Honduras
-13.0	-.6	-3.8	1.2	-6.4	-6.8	-5.8	.8	-3.9	1.7	-1.7	-2.2	-4.6	-4.4	-2.8	-3.6	....	Jamaica
.4	-1.1	3.0	-1.4	-2.8	-3.0	-5.1	-7.3	-5.8	-7.0	-.5	-.8	-1.9	-3.8	-2.9	-3.1	-2.9	Mexico
....	-13.0	....	....	....	-37.6	-39.8	-24.4	....	....	....	....	....	....	....	....	....	Montserrat
....	....	....	....	....	....	....	....	....	....	....	....	....	....	....	....	....	Netherlands Antilles
-26.0	-15.5	-25.6	-58.2	-35.7	-3.6	-31.6	-46.5	-33.7	-40.1	-31.5	-32.8	-34.2	-24.4	-31.5	-21.1	....	Nicaragua
1.4	-1.8	9.7	14.8	2.3	3.9	-4.1	-4.0	-1.3	.2	-6.0	-2.5	-5.9	-12.7	-13.7	-9.3	....	Panama
-5.5	-6.7	-10.8	-3.5	5.9	7.4	1.4	-.9	.9	-3.5	-1.0	-3.7	-6.8	-1.9	-1.2	-1.8	....	Paraguay
.6	-5.4	-4.8	-5.4	-1.4	-4.9	-4.4	-5.8	-6.6	-5.7	-7.7	-6.1	-5.2	-6.4	-3.7	-3.0	....	Peru
-8.6	-9.4	-14.9	-21.7	-26.8	-29.5	-21.6	-8.2	-14.8	-11.0	-19.7	-26.8	-19.6	-14.5	-27.2	-19.0	....	St. Kitts and Nevis
-5.6	-2.5	-4.8	-5.3	-16.6	-13.7	-16.0	-11.3	-10.1	-9.3	-6.0	-9.5	-13.6	-10.6	-11.7	-11.8	....	St. Lucia
3.3	-8.0	-14.2	-10.2	-16.7	-11.9	-21.5	-10.4	-18.4	-23.6	-15.4	-12.8	-28.6	-29.7	-21.9	-7.7	....	St. Vincent & Grens.
-1.9	-3.7	12.4	8.8	19.3	3.8	-6.3	.9	.7	12.2	12.1	-8.5	-7.5	-18.9	....	....	....	Suriname
-.6	-8.6	-4.7	-2.0	-.9	9.1	-.1	2.6	2.5	4.4	5.5	1.8	-10.5	-10.6	....	....	....	Trinidad and Tobago
-2.1	.7	-1.9	.3	1.6	2.0	.4	-.1	-1.6	-2.5	-1.1	-1.1	-1.3	-2.1	-2.4	-3.0	....	Uruguay
5.6	-3.7	-3.0	-9.6	5.0	17.0	3.2	-6.2	-3.3	4.3	2.6	12.6	3.9	-3.4	3.4	10.8	....	Venezuela, Rep. Bol.

GDP Volume Measures

		1972	1973	1974	1975	1976	1977	1978	1979	1980	1981	1982	1983	1984	1985	1986
																Percent Change over Previous Year;
World	001	5.0	6.1	2.2	1.2	5.6	4.3	4.0	4.2	2.5	1.9	.6	2.8	5.1	4.7	3.5
Industrial Countries	110	5.2	6.1	.7	—	4.9	3.8	4.3	3.6	1.1	1.6	−.1	2.8	4.7	3.5	3.1
United States	111	5.4	5.8	−.6	−.4	5.6	4.6	5.5	3.2	−.2	2.5	−2.0	4.3	7.3	3.8	3.4
Canada	156	5.7	7.7	4.4	2.6	6.2	3.6	4.6	3.9	1.5	3.7	−3.2	3.2	6.3	4.8	3.3
Australia	193	2.4	6.4	1.6	1.6	4.2	1.0	3.7	4.3	2.0	3.6	.7	−.6	6.7	5.3	2.1
Japan	158	8.4	7.9	−1.2	2.6	4.8	5.3	5.1	5.2	3.6	3.2	3.1	2.3	3.8	4.3	3.1
New Zealand	196	4.4	7.2	4.0	1.7	.1	−2.7	2.7	2.6	1.1	4.9	−3.3	5.8	5.2	−.2	3.3
Euro Area	163	....	....	....	....	....	....	....	....	....	....	....	....	....	....	....
Austria	122	6.3	5.3	4.3	−1.7	5.8	4.7	−.4	5.5	2.3	−.1	1.9	2.8	.3	2.2	2.3
Belgium	124	5.4	5.9	4.3	−1.5	5.7	.6	2.9	2.2	4.1	−.3	.6	.3	2.5	1.7	1.8
Finland	172	7.6	6.7	3.0	1.1	−.1	.3	2.3	6.8	5.1	2.1	3.1	2.7	3.4	3.1	2.5
France	132	4.4	5.4	3.1	−.3	4.2	3.2	3.3	3.2	1.6	1.2	2.5	.7	1.3	1.9	2.5
Germany	134	4.3	4.8	.3	−1.3	4.9	3.0	3.1	4.3	1.0	.1	−1.0	1.7	2.8	2.3	2.3
Greece	174	8.9	7.3	−3.6	6.1	6.4	3.4	6.7	3.7	1.7	.1	.4	.4	2.7	3.1	1.6
Ireland	178	6.5	6.2	4.1	2.4	1.4	8.2	7.2	3.1	3.1	3.3	2.3	−.2	4.3	3.1	3.7
Italy	136	2.9	6.5	4.7	−2.1	6.5	2.9	3.7	5.7	3.5	.5	.5	1.2	2.8	3.0	2.5
Luxembourg	137	....	....	....	....	....	....	....	....	....	....	....	....	....	....	....
Netherlands	138	2.4	4.8	3.8	.3	4.5	2.9	2.6	−.1	3.2	−1.5	−1.1	1.8	2.9	3.3	3.1
Portugal	182	8.0	11.2	1.1	−4.3	6.9	5.6	2.8	5.6	4.6	1.6	2.1	−.2	−1.9	2.8	4.1
Spain	184	8.1	7.8	5.6	.5	3.3	2.8	1.5	—	1.3	−.2	1.6	2.2	1.5	2.6	3.2
Denmark	128	4.5	3.6	−1.4	−1.7	6.4	1.1	1.8	3.1	−.6	−2.1	2.7	1.7	3.5	3.6	4.0
Iceland	176	5.8	5.8	6.3	.9	6.1	8.9	7.0	5.5	7.0	4.3	2.0	−2.1	4.1	3.3	6.4
Norway	142	5.2	4.1	5.2	4.2	6.8	3.6	4.7	4.3	5.0	1.0	.2	3.5	5.9	5.2	3.6
Sweden	144	2.2	3.9	4.3	2.2	1.2	−2.0	1.3	4.3	2.0	—	1.1	1.8	4.0	2.2	2.2
Switzerland	146	3.5	3.2	1.2	−6.7	−.8	2.4	.6	2.5	4.4	1.6	−1.4	.5	3.0	3.4	1.6
United Kingdom	112	3.6	7.2	−1.6	−.6	2.8	2.3	3.3	2.6	−2.1	−1.5	2.0	3.6	2.5	3.6	3.9
Developing Countries	200	4.3	5.9	6.1	4.3	7.1	5.4	3.1	5.2	5.1	2.5	2.0	2.7	5.7	6.8	4.1
Africa	605	5.0	4.5	7.8	−.8	4.9	4.7	−.7	6.8	4.2	−.5	1.6	−.9	2.0	26.8	2.8
Benin	638	8.9	2.3	−7.5	4.4	4.3	5.7	2.8	5.0	10.9	5.8	10.8	−4.3	7.9	7.5	2.1
Botswana	616	29.8	24.8	24.2	−1.3	19.0	3.5	19.5	9.9	14.3	9.5	7.5	16.0	11.5	7.2	7.5
Burkina Faso	748	....	....	....	....	....	1.7	4.4	2.2	−1.2	1.8	12.9	9.8
Burundi	618	−8.4	7.2	−.8	1.0	7.9	12.4	−1.1	2.0	7.9	10.9	−.4	3.1	−.1	9.5	3.3
Cameroon	622	4.3	1.5	4.5	5.1	1.9	5.7	10.4	11.2	4.2	17.1	7.6	7.0	7.8	8.9	5.2
Chad	628	−6.8	−4.9	13.6	17.3	−1.5	−7.4	−.3	−.3	−.3	11.6	11.6	11.6	−5.0	26.0	−2.7
Congo, Dem. Rep. of	636	.1	8.1	3.1	−5.0	−5.3	.8	−5.3	.4	2.2	2.4	−.5	1.4	5.5	.5	4.7
Congo, Rep. of	634	5.1	6.2	15.1	−3.3	−.1	−5.5	−1.6	9.8	15.8	21.2	23.6	5.6	7.2	−1.2	−6.9
Côte d'Ivoire	662	....	....	....	....	....	....	....	....	....	....	....	....	....	....	....
Gambia, The	648	7.3	4.5	53.9	−4.1	−1.4	−1.4	8.8	1.6	−54.2	119.4	13.5	2.1	1.6	4.0	2.8
Ghana	652	−2.5	15.3	3.4	−12.9	−3.5	2.3	8.5	−3.2	—	−1.8	−7.2	.7	2.6	5.1	5.2
Guinea-Bissau	654	....	....	....	....	....	....	....	....	....	....	....	....	....	....	....
Kenya	664	72.6	6.8	1.5	3.4	7.0	58.2	−25.8	52.6	4.0	6.0	1.8	4.3	.9	23.4	7.1
Lesotho	666	....	....	....	....	....	....	....	....	....	1.0	3.6	−8.6	8.5	3.5	2.0
Liberia	668	3.8	−2.5	7.4	−15.1	4.0	−.8	4.0	4.4	−4.7	2.2	−2.9	−.7	−.9	−1.4	2.0
Madagascar	674	−3.2	−2.0	3.3	3.0	−4.0	3.4	−2.6	9.8	.8	−8.6	−1.8	.8	2.2	1.2	2.0
Malawi	676	....	....	7.4	5.5	6.2	4.3	8.3	3.3	−.4	−5.2	2.8	3.5	4.4	4.5	1.1
Mauritius	684	8.0	11.8	8.0	1.3	16.7	6.6	3.8	3.5	−10.1	5.9	5.5	.4	4.8	6.9	9.7
Morocco	686	2.1	3.8	14.3	−1.2	12.8	7.2	2.2	4.8	3.6	−2.8	9.6	−.6	4.3	6.3	8.3
Mozambique	688	....	....	....	....	....	....	....	....	....	....	....	....	....	1.2	−2.4
Namibia	728	....	....	....	....	....	....	....	....	....	....	....	....	....	....	3.7
Niger	692	....	....	....	....	....	....	....	....	....	....	....	....	....	....	....
Nigeria	694	3.4	5.4	11.2	−5.2	9.0	6.0	−5.8	6.8	4.2	−13.1	−.2	−5.3	−4.8	9.7	2.5
Rwanda	714	.2	3.4	.7	2.0	1.8	5.2	9.8	9.4	−3.6	2.5	4.1	6.0	−4.2	4.4	5.5
Senegal	722	6.4	−5.6	4.2	7.5	8.9	−2.7	−4.0	7.0	−3.3	−1.2	15.3	2.2	−4.0	3.8	4.6
Seychelles	718	....	....	....	....	....	7.9	6.7	15.0	−3.1	−6.6	−1.5	−1.7	8.0	10.3	1.2
Sierra Leone	724	−1.1	3.1	4.0	3.0	−3.0	1.4	.3	7.4	3.0	6.2	1.6	−1.4	1.4	−2.7	−2.4
South Africa	199	1.7	4.6	6.1	1.7	2.2	−.1	3.0	3.8	6.6	5.4	−.4	−1.8	5.1	114.1	−.4
Swaziland	734	....	....	....	....	....	....	....	9.9	14.5	−4.4	6.9	1.2	1.2	6.2	3.8	12.3
Togo	742	3.8	−4.2	4.3	−.6	−.5	5.6	10.1	5.4	1.9	−3.5	−3.8	.7	1.3	.1	3.8
Tunisia	744	17.7	−.6	8.1	7.1	7.9	3.4	6.4	6.6	7.4	5.5	−.5	4.7	6.2	3.2	−2.0
Uganda	746	....	....	....	....	....	....	....	....	....	....	....	....	−4.7	.2	6.0
Zambia	754	9.2	−.9	6.7	−2.4	4.3	−4.8	.6	−3.0	3.0	6.2	−2.8	−2.0	−.4	1.6	.7
Zimbabwe	698	....	1.7	17.3	−3.6	−1.1	−5.1	−2.2	3.8	10.6	12.5	2.6	1.6	−1.9	6.4	2.1
Asia	505	2.6	6.7	4.4	6.2	6.1	7.0	6.8	4.0	6.5	5.9	5.3	7.4	8.3	8.1	6.7
Bangladesh	513	....	....	12.1	3.4	12.3	1.3	6.5	4.6	1.3	6.8	.8	3.6	4.2	3.7	4.7
China, P.R.: Mainland	924	....	....	....	....	....	....	....	7.6	7.8	4.5	8.3	10.4	14.6	16.2	9.8
China, P.R.: Hong Kong	532	11.0	12.7	2.1	.4	17.2	12.0	8.8	11.8	10.4	9.4	2.7	6.3	9.8	.2	11.1
Fiji	819	7.5	11.6	2.5	—	1.8	−3.5	1.8	12.0	−1.7	6.0	−1.1	−4.0	8.4	−5.1	8.1
India	534	−.6	3.0	1.2	9.2	1.8	7.2	5.8	−5.3	6.6	6.5	3.8	7.4	3.7	5.5	4.9
Indonesia	536	9.4	11.3	7.6	5.0	6.9	8.8	7.8	6.3	9.9	7.9	2.2	4.2	7.0	2.5	5.9
Korea	542	4.9	12.3	7.4	6.5	11.2	10.0	9.0	7.1	−2.1	6.5	7.2	10.7	8.2	6.5	11.0
Lao People's Democratic Rep.	544	....	....	....	....	....	....	....	....	....	15.3	4.7	3.0	6.4	9.1	4.8
Malaysia	548	9.4	11.7	8.3	.8	11.6	7.8	6.7	9.3	7.4	6.9	6.0	6.2	7.8	−1.1	1.2
Maldives	556	....	....	....	−2.1	26.2	16.1	15.0	10.3	8.6	−3.0	−3.0	16.3	27.0	15.4	9.4
Mongolia	948	....	....	....	....	....	....	....	....	....	8.3	8.3	5.8	6.0	5.7	9.4
Myanmar	518	....	....	....	....	....	13.0	−1.1	4.7	7.9	6.3	5.4	4.4	4.9	2.9	−1.1
Nepal	558	3.1	−.5	6.3	1.5	4.4	3.0	4.4	2.4	−2.3	8.3	3.8	−3.0	9.7	6.1	4.6
Pakistan	564	.4	6.9	5.5	4.6	4.6	3.8	8.0	4.8	8.7	6.9	6.5	6.8	5.1	7.6	5.5
Papua New Guinea	853	....	....	3.8	.9	−1.6	−4.3	8.6	1.8	−2.3	1.1	.8	3.4	−1.0	3.6	5.7
Philippines	566	5.4	8.9	3.6	5.6	8.8	5.6	5.2	5.6	5.1	3.4	3.6	1.9	−7.3	−7.3	3.4
Samoa	862	1.7	7.3	−10.6	−4.0	9.5	−1.0	6.3	13.3	−6.1	−9.1	−1.0	1.2	1.3	6.0	4.8
Singapore	576	13.4	11.5	6.3	4.1	7.5	7.8	8.6	9.3	9.7	9.6	6.9	8.2	8.3	−1.6	2.3
Solomon Islands	813	....	....	....	....	....	....	....	....	....	6.7	−1.1	3.9	8.3	2.6	−2.2
Sri Lanka	524	3.2	3.6	3.6	2.8	3.1	4.3	8.3	....	....	....	....	....	....	....	....
Thailand	578	4.1	9.9	4.4	4.8	9.4	9.9	10.4	5.3	4.8	5.9	5.4	5.6	5.8	4.6	5.5
Tonga	866	....	....	....	....	.8	4.8	1.9	1.9	15.8	14.0	14.8	5.8	44.1	5.6	8.8
Vanuatu	846	....	....	....	....	....	....	....	....	....	....	....	....	6.9	1.1	−2.0

Calculated from Indices

1987	1988	1989	1990	1991	1992	1993	1994	1995	1996	1997	1998	1999	2000	2001		
4.1	4.7	3.7	3.3	2.6	2.9	2.9	5.0	4.0	4.6	4.2	2.5	3.5	4.3	....	World	001
3.4	4.5	3.7	2.7	1.5	1.8	1.1	3.1	2.4	2.7	3.2	2.8	3.1	3.5	1.2	Industrial Countries	110
3.4	4.2	3.5	1.8	-.5	3.0	2.7	4.0	2.7	3.6	4.4	4.3	4.1	4.1	1.2	United States	111
4.3	4.9	2.4	-.2	-1.8	.8	2.3	4.7	2.8	1.7	4.0	3.6	4.5	4.4	1.5	Canada	156
4.6	4.3	4.5	1.8	-.7	2.1	3.8	4.8	3.5	4.3	3.7	5.2	4.8	3.1	2.6	Australia	193
4.5	6.5	5.4	5.3	3.0	.9	.5	1.0	1.6	3.3	1.9	-1.1	.8	1.5	.1	Japan	158
8.5	1.8	.2	—	-1.1	1.0	6.3	5.1	3.7	3.1	2.6	-.4	4.1	2.0	4.3	New Zealand	196
....	....	....	....	....	....	....	....	1.3	2.2	2.7	2.4	3.5	3.2		Euro Area	163
1.7	3.2	4.2	4.6	3.4	1.3	.5	2.4	1.7	2.0	1.3	3.3	2.8	3.3	1.2	Austria	122
2.3	4.7	3.5	3.1	1.8	1.5	-1.0	3.2	2.4	1.2	3.6	2.2	3.0	4.0	1.0	Belgium	124
4.2	4.7	5.1	—	-6.3	-3.3	-1.1	4.0	3.8	4.0	6.3	5.3	4.0	10.0	.7	Finland	172
2.3	4.5	4.4	2.5	1.1	1.2	-.9	1.8	1.9	1.1	1.9	3.5	3.2	4.2	1.8	France	132
1.4	3.6	3.7	5.7	13.2	2.2	-1.1	2.3	1.7	.8	1.5	1.8	1.9	3.0	.6	Germany	134
-.5	4.5	3.5	-.6	3.5	.4	-.9	1.5	1.9	2.4	3.6	3.4	3.4	4.1	4.1	Greece	174
4.7	4.3	6.1	7.8	1.9	3.3	2.7	5.8	10.0	7.8	10.8	8.6	10.9	11.5	5.9	Ireland	178
3.0	3.9	2.9	2.0	1.4	.8	-.9	2.2	2.9	1.1	2.0	1.8	1.6	2.8	1.8	Italy	136
....	....	....	....	....	....	....	....	....	2.6	9.1	5.9	5.8	7.5		Luxembourg	137
1.4	2.5	4.7	4.0	2.2	2.0	.6	3.2	2.3	3.1	3.6	3.7	8.7	3.6	1.1	Netherlands	138
6.4	7.5	5.4	4.8	2.3	1.9	-1.4	2.4	2.9	3.2	3.5	3.5	7.3	3.3	....	Portugal	182
5.6	5.2	4.7	3.7	2.3	.7	-1.2	2.3	2.7	2.4	3.5	3.8	3.7	5.2	2.8	Spain	184
—	1.2	.2	1.0	1.1	.6	—	5.5	2.8	2.5	3.0	2.5	2.3	3.0	.9	Denmark	128
8.5	-.1	.3	2.3	.7	-3.3	.6	4.5	.1	5.1	4.6	3.8	3.7	5.5	3.0	Iceland	176
2.0	-.1	.9	2.0	3.1	3.3	2.7	5.5	3.8	4.9	4.7	2.0	1.0	2.7	1.6	Norway	142
2.8	2.7	2.4	1.4	-1.7	-1.4	-2.2	3.3	3.7	1.1	2.1	3.6	4.5	3.6	1.2	Sweden	144
.7	3.1	4.3	3.7	-.8	-.1	-.5	.5	.5	.3	1.7	2.4	1.6	3.0	1.3	Switzerland	146
4.5	5.2	2.2	.8	-1.4	.2	2.5	4.7	2.9	2.6	3.4	2.9	2.2	3.3	2.0	United Kingdom	112
5.2	5.1	3.5	4.2	4.1	4.5	5.8	7.4	6.1	7.0	5.4	2.2	4.0	5.3	....	Developing Countries	200
2.3	5.5	3.5	2.6	2.4	-.4	.7	2.7	2.3	6.1	3.2	3.6	....	....	....	Africa	605
-1.5	3.4	-2.8	3.2	4.7	4.0	3.5	4.4	4.6	5.5	5.7	4.5	5.0	5.0	....	Benin	638
8.9	14.7	22.6	6.4	8.8	6.2	-.2	4.0	3.2	5.6	5.6	8.1	4.1	7.7	....	Botswana	616
-1.5	6.2	.2	-1.0	9.5	.4	-3.2	3.9	6.0	6.5	5.8	5.5	6.4	2.4	5.8	Burkina Faso	748
5.5	4.9	1.5	3.5	5.3	1.8	-7.0	-3.1	-7.0	-8.6	.4	4.5	....	....	....	Burundi	618
-2.2	-7.9	-1.8	-6.7	-3.9	-3.0	-3.2	-2.6	3.3	5.0	5.0	....	....	....	....	Cameroon	622
-5.6	....	....	....	....	....	....	....	....	....	....	....	....	....	....	Chad	628
2.7	.5	-1.3	-6.6	-8.4	-10.5	-13.5	-3.9	.7	-.9	-5.7	....	....	....	....	Congo, Dem. Rep. of	636
.2	1.8	1.8	2.2	2.4	1.7	-1.0	-5.5	2.2	4.3	-.5	3.7	-3.2	8.0	....	Congo, Rep. of	634
-.4	1.0	3.0	-1.1	—	-.1	-.4	2.0	7.1	6.9	6.6	6.0	....	....	....	Côte d'Ivoire	662
1.5	4.6	5.6	1.7	5.5	.4	6.6	3.6	-4.1	....	....	....	....	....	....	Gambia, The	648
4.8	5.6	5.1	3.3	5.3	3.9	4.9	3.3	4.0	4.6	4.2	....	....	....	....	Ghana	652
1.5	2.6	4.6	6.1	3.8	1.8	2.5	5.0	3.7	4.8	4.8	....	....	....	....	Guinea-Bissau	654
5.9	6.2	4.7	4.2	1.4	-.8	.4	2.6	4.4	4.1	3.0	.8	....	....	....	Kenya	664
587.7	11.9	7.9	6.2	3.8	4.8	3.8	3.4	4.5	10.0	8.1	-5.3	2.0	2.5	....	Lesotho	666
2.7	—	....	....	....	....	....	....	....	....	....	....	....	....	....	Liberia	668
1.2	3.4	4.1	3.1	-6.3	1.2	2.1	-.1	1.7	2.1	3.7	3.9	4.7	4.8	6.7	Madagascar	674
2.1	3.4	4.0	4.8	7.8	-7.9	10.8	-11.6	13.8	10.4	7.0	2.2	3.6	2.3	....	Malawi	676
10.2	6.8	4.5	7.2	4.3	6.2	5.6	3.9	4.7	5.3	6.3	5.8	3.4	....	....	Mauritius	684
-2.6	10.4	2.4	2.1	8.9	-4.0	-1.0	10.4	-6.6	12.2	-2.3	6.8	.8	.9	6.5	Morocco	686
14.8	8.6	5.0	-.9	1.9	-8.6	8.6	7.0	3.3	6.8	11.3	12.1	9.0	....	....	Mozambique	688
2.3	8.9	2.1	7.9	5.7	7.4	-2.0	7.3	4.1	3.2	4.2	3.3	3.4	3.3	....	Namibia	728
-1.1	6.5	-.7	-.8	1.4	.7	1.0	2.5	1.9	3.9	2.4	8.6	....	....	....	Niger	692
-.7	9.9	7.2	8.2	4.8	2.9	2.2	-.6	2.6	6.4	3.9	....	....	....	....	Nigeria	694
-.6	5.0	.5	2.0	-3.6	6.9	-8.4	-49.7	34.2	14.1	14.2	9.2	6.1	6.0	....	Rwanda	714
4.0	5.1	-1.4	3.9	-.4	2.2	-2.2	2.9	5.2	5.1	5.0	5.7	....	....	....	Senegal	722
4.4	5.3	10.3	7.5	2.7	7.2	6.2	-.8	-.6	4.7	11.7	5.5	2.9	....	....	Seychelles	718
5.4	-7.1	.7	3.4	2.4	-19.0	1.4	-1.9	-8.0	6.1	-17.6	-.9	-8.1	3.8	....	Sierra Leone	724
2.1	4.2	2.4	-.3	-1.0	-2.1	1.2	3.2	3.1	4.2	2.8	.8	2.1	3.4	2.2	South Africa	199
14.6	6.6	9.1	8.9	2.5	1.3	3.3	3.5	3.0	3.6	3.7	4.7	3.5	....	....	Swaziland	734
1.9	6.5	3.9	-.3	-.7	-3.8	-16.6	16.8	6.9	9.7	4.3	-2.2	2.4	3.5	....	Togo	742
4.9	1.6	3.5	7.1	3.9	7.8	2.2	3.2	2.4	7.1	5.4	4.8	6.1	4.7	4.9	Tunisia	744
6.4	7.8	6.9	6.2	5.5	4.6	7.1	10.6	9.6	5.9	....	....	....	....	....	Uganda	746
2.7	6.3	-1.0	-.5	—	-1.7	6.8	-3.5	-2.3	6.5	3.5	....	....	....	....	Zambia	754
1.1	7.6	5.2	7.0	5.5	-9.0	1.3	6.8	-.7	7.6	4.3	....	....	....	....	Zimbabwe	698
7.9	9.3	5.5	5.6	6.3	9.0	8.5	9.6	8.8	9.2	6.1	1.8	6.1	6.6	....	Asia	505
4.2	2.9	2.5	6.6	3.3	5.0	4.6	4.1	4.9	4.6	5.4	5.2	4.9	5.9	5.2	Bangladesh	513
11.6	11.3	4.1	3.8	9.2	14.2	13.5	12.7	10.5	9.6	8.8	7.8	7.1	8.0	....	China, P.R.: Mainland	924
13.0	8.0	2.6	3.4	5.1	6.3	6.1	5.4	3.9	4.5	5.0	-5.3	3.0	10.4	.2	China, P.R.: Hong Kong	532
-6.4	2.2	12.1	4.7	.6	3.1	1.9	....	....	....	....	....	....	....	....	Fiji	819
4.8	9.9	5.7	5.8	.9	5.3	4.9	7.6	7.7	7.2	4.4	6.0	7.1	3.9	....	India	534
4.9	5.8	7.5	7.2	7.0	6.5	6.5	7.5	8.2	7.8	4.7	-13.1	.8	4.8	....	Indonesia	536
11.0	10.5	6.1	9.0	9.2	5.4	5.5	8.3	8.9	6.8	5.0	-6.7	10.9	9.3	3.0	Korea	542
-1.0	-2.1	9.9	6.7	4.0	7.0	4.6	9.5	7.0	6.9	6.9	4.0	7.3	5.7	—	Lao People's Democratic Rep.	544
5.4	9.9	9.1	9.0	9.5	8.9	9.9	9.2	9.8	10.0	7.3	-7.4	5.8	8.5	.6	Malaysia	548
8.8	8.7	9.3	17.0	6.9	6.5	5.4	7.5	7.8	9.1	10.2	8.2	7.4	4.6	2.1	Maldives	556
3.5	5.1	4.2	-2.5	-9.2	-9.5	-3.0	2.3	6.3	2.4	4.0	3.5	....	....	....	Mongolia	948
-4.0	-11.4	3.7	2.8	-.7	9.7	6.0	7.5	6.9	6.4	5.7	5.8	10.9	6.2	....	Myanmar	518
1.7	7.7	4.3	.9	6.4	4.6	3.3	7.9	2.9	5.7	4.8	3.4	4.5	6.4	5.8	Nepal	558
6.5	7.6	5.0	4.5	5.5	7.8	1.9	3.9	5.1	5.0	-.1	2.6	3.7	4.4	3.3	Pakistan	564
2.8	2.9	-1.4	-3.0	9.5	13.8	18.2	5.9	-3.3	-3.9	-1.1	4.6	....	....	....	Papua New Guinea	853
4.3	6.8	6.2	3.0	-.6	.3	2.1	4.4	4.7	5.8	5.2	-.6	3.4	4.0	3.4	Philippines	566
1.0	-.2	1.3	-7.5	-27.9	-2.3	2.4	-3.7	6.8	6.1	1.6	....	....	....	....	Samoa	862
7.4	11.6	9.6	9.0	7.1	6.5	12.7	11.4	8.0	7.7	8.5	-.1	6.9	10.3	-2.0	Singapore	576
-5.1	....	....	....	....	....	....	....	....	....	....	....	....	....	....	Solomon Islands	813
....	....	2.3	6.2	4.6	4.3	6.9	5.6	5.5	314.4	6.3	4.7	4.3	6.0	....	Sri Lanka	524
9.5	13.3	12.2	11.2	8.6	8.1	8.3	9.0	9.2	5.9	-1.4	-10.5	4.4	4.6	1.8	Thailand	578
1.7	-3.5	1.1	4.7	5.9	-3.8	-.1	4.8	....	....	....	....	....	....	....	Tonga	866
.4	.6	4.5	5.2	10.4	-.7	4.5	2.5	3.2	....	....	....	....	....	....	Vanuatu	846

GDP Volume Measures

99bp x		1972	1973	1974	1975	1976	1977	1978	1979	1980	1981	1982	1983	1984	1985	1986
															Percent Change over Previous Year;	
Europe	170	....	....	....	....	....	....	....	....	....	−1.8	.4	4.8	5.7	3.3	4.7
Armenia	911	....	....	....	....	....	....	....	....	....	....	....	....	....	....	....
Belarus	913	....	....	....	....	....	....	....	....	....	....	....	....	....	....	....
Bulgaria	918	....	....	....	....	....	....	....	....	....	....	....	....	....	....	....
Croatia	960	....	....	....	....	....	....	....	....	....	....	....	....	....	....	....
Kazakhstan	916	....	....	....	....	....	....	....	....	....	....	....	....	....	....	....
Cyprus	423	6.8	2.6	−16.9	−19.0	18.0	15.8	7.6	9.9	5.9	3.1	6.3	5.3	8.8	4.7	3.6
Czech Republic	935	....	....	....	....	....	....	....	....	....	....	....	....	....	....	....
Estonia	939	....	....	....	....	....	....	....	....	....	....	....	....	....	....	....
Hungary	944	6.1	6.9	5.9	6.2	3.6	7.6	4.4	2.7	.2	2.9	2.8	.7	2.6	−.3	2.4
Kyrgyz Republic	917	....	....	....	....	....	....	....	....	....	....	....	....	....	....	....
Latvia	941	....	....	....	....	....	....	....	....	....	....	....	....	....	....	....
Lithuania	946	....	....	....	....	....	....	....	....	....	....	....	....	....	....	....
Malta	181	5.8	9.8	10.0	19.6	17.0	12.2	11.2	10.5	7.0	3.3	2.3	−.6	.9	2.6	3.9
Poland	964	....	....	....	....	....	....	....	....	....	−10.0	−4.8	5.6	5.7	5.1	4.2
Romania	968	....	....	....	....	....	....	....	....	....	.1	3.9	6.0	6.0	−.1	2.3
Slovak Republic	936	....	....	....	....	....	....	....	....	....	....	....	....	....	....	....
Slovenia	961	....	....	....	....	....	....	....	....	....	....	....	....	....	....	....
Turkey	186	7.4	3.3	5.6	7.2	10.7	3.2	1.5	−.6	−2.4	4.9	3.6	5.0	6.7	4.2	7.0
Yugoslavia, SFR	188	4.3	4.9	8.6	3.6	3.9	8.0	6.9	7.0	2.3	1.4	.5	−1.0	2.0	.5	3.6
Middle East	405	13.4	8.9	7.4	5.2	15.8	4.1	−6.9	5.2	−1.3	−.6	−.2	5.5	2.7	1.2	−4.4
Bahrain	419	....	....	....	....	23.7	14.7	8.1	−1.1	6.6	4.4	6.0	8.0	3.8	−2.8	1.2
Egypt	469	....	....	....	....	....	....	....	....	....	....	....	5.0	9.8	5.8	4.7
Iran, I.R. of	429	16.3	8.6	8.9	2.8	18.3	7.6	−21.1	−9.3	−13.9	−2.5	13.1	13.2	.9	.2	−15.1
Iraq	433	−2.5	18.7	7.2	15.0	12.1	17.3	12.2	11.7	11.7	−18.0	−1.1	−8.3	.2	—	8.1
Israel	436	—	50.0	—	16.7	3.7	−21.4	13.6	24.0	3.2	4.5	1.3	2.5	2.1	4.0	4.1
Jordan	439	....	....	....	....	....	....	....	....	....	....	....	....	....	....	7.0
Kuwait	443	3.9	−6.5	−12.8	−12.1	12.7	−9.2	7.2	13.7	−20.4	−18.9	−11.8	7.9	5.2	−4.3	8.6
Libya	672	9.1	1.9	22.2	4.0	22.6	8.9	2.6	8.3	.6	....	....	....	....	....	....
Oman	449	9.2	−14.0	28.2	28.6	16.0	17.6	17.7	4.6	5.7	17.0	11.5	16.0	16.7	13.8	2.1
Saudi Arabia	456	19.7	15.1	.3	8.6	15.1	5.9	6.7	10.1	7.9	1.7	−10.7	−.1	−2.2	−4.1	5.6
Syrian Arab Rep.	463	25.0	−8.5	24.1	19.5	11.0	−1.3	8.7	3.6	12.0	9.5	2.1	1.4	−4.1	6.1	−4.9
United Arab Emirates	466	....	....	14.5	6.2	15.0	17.4	−2.3	24.9	26.4	2.9	−8.3	−2.6	4.5	−2.5	−21.2
Yemen Republic	474	....	....	....	....	....	....	....	....	....	....	....	....	....	....	....
Western Hemisphere	205	7.3	8.3	6.7	3.5	5.6	4.8	4.8	6.7	6.2	1.0	−.8	−2.5	3.9	3.2	3.5
Antigua and Barbuda	311	....	....	....	....	....	....	4.2	7.3	8.6	4.1	.2	4.7	9.8	8.0	12.7
Argentina	213	3.7	5.5	6.6	−1.3	−3.9	6.6	−3.4	8.4	−.3	−5.7	−3.1	4.2	2.0	−6.9	7.1
Bahamas, The	313	....	....	....	....	....	....	....	....	....	....	....	....	....	....	....
Barbados	316	1.0	2.0	13.4	−2.0	4.5	3.7	4.9	7.9	4.5	−1.9	−4.9	.4	3.7	1.1	5.1
Belize	339	....	....	....	....	....	....	....	....	5.1	—	−7.6	6.1	11.3	−1.4	7.3
Bolivia	218	5.8	6.7	5.1	6.6	6.1	4.2	3.4	1.8	.6	.3	−3.9	−4.0	−.2	−1.7	−2.6
Brazil	223	12.0	13.9	8.1	5.2	10.2	4.9	5.0	6.8	9.2	−4.2	.8	−2.9	6.4	7.5	7.0
Chile	228	−1.2	−5.6	1.0	−13.3	3.2	8.3	7.8	7.1	7.7	6.7	−13.4	−3.5	6.1	3.5	5.6
Colombia	233	7.7	6.7	5.7	2.3	4.7	4.2	8.5	5.4	4.1	2.3	.9	1.6	3.4	3.1	5.8
Costa Rica	238	8.2	7.7	5.5	2.1	5.5	8.9	6.3	4.9	.8	−2.3	−7.3	2.9	8.0	.7	5.5
Dominica	321	....	....	....	....	....	3.5	11.8	−18.4	12.7	13.6	4.1	2.7	5.4	1.3	7.1
Dominican Republic	243	10.4	12.9	6.0	5.2	6.7	5.0	2.1	4.5	6.1	4.1	1.6	6.9	1.3	−2.1	3.5
Ecuador	248	14.4	25.3	6.4	5.6	9.2	6.5	6.6	5.3	4.9	3.9	1.2	−2.8	4.2	4.3	3.1
El Salvador	253	5.7	5.1	6.4	5.6	4.0	6.1	6.4	−1.7	−8.7	−8.3	−5.6	.8	2.3	2.0	.6
Grenada	328	....	....	....	....	9.0	5.7	8.1	2.4	.2	2.1	5.3	25.2	4.7	8.2	3.9
Guatemala	258	7.3	6.8	6.4	1.9	7.4	7.8	5.0	4.7	3.7	.7	−3.5	−2.6	.5	−.6	....
Guyana	336	−2.0	1.7	7.0	10.4	2.9	−5.2	−1.3	−11.7	1.6	−.3	−10.4	−9.3	−24.5	35.8	−4.7
Haiti	263	.9	4.8	5.8	1.1	8.4	.5	4.9	7.6	7.2	−2.7	−3.4	.8	.3	.3	1.0
Honduras	268	4.0	5.6	−.1	−3.0	10.5	10.4	8.3	6.3	.7	2.5	−1.4	−.9	4.3	4.2	1.7
Jamaica	343	7.8	2.8	−5.9	−.7	−6.3	−2.4	.7	−1.8	−5.7	2.6	1.2	2.3	−.9	−4.6	1.7
Mexico	273	8.5	8.4	6.1	5.6	4.2	3.4	8.3	9.2	8.3	8.5	−.6	−3.5	3.4	2.2	−3.1
Nicaragua	278	2.2	6.4	14.2	−.2	5.2	8.4	−7.8	−26.5	4.6	5.4	−.8	4.6	−1.6	−4.1	−1.0
Panama	283	4.6	5.4	2.4	1.6	1.6	1.1	9.8	20.4	—	9.2	5.3	−4.5	2.7	4.9	3.6
Paraguay	288	6.7	7.5	8.5	7.2	7.3	10.9	11.4	11.4	11.4	8.7	−1.0	−3.0	3.1	4.0	....
Peru	293	2.9	5.4	9.3	3.4	2.0	.4	.3	5.8	4.7	5.5	−2.6	−9.9	5.2	2.8	10.0
St. Kitts and Nevis	361	....	....	....	....	....	....	7.4	9.2	8.2	1.1	−1.6	−1.0	10.4	6.4	11.7
St. Lucia	362	....	....	....	....	....	....	11.3	4.2	−2.1	4.1	2.2	5.4	6.7	7.8	16.7
St. Vincent & Grenadines	364	....	....	2.6	....	10.3	5.8	−5.8	4.7	3.8	6.6	5.8	5.2	5.3	5.4	7.3
Suriname	366	....	....	2.6	−10.0	9.0	10.2	5.5	−5.9	−8.6	7.1	−4.2	−3.9	−1.9	2.0	.8
Trinidad and Tobago	369	5.8	1.7	3.8	1.5	6.4	9.1	10.0	3.6	10.4	4.6	4.0	−9.2	−6.2	−4.1	−3.3
Uruguay	298	−1.6	.4	3.1	5.9	4.0	1.2	5.3	6.2	6.0	1.9	−9.4	−5.9	−1.1	1.5	8.9
Venezuela, Rep. Bol.	299	2.7	6.3	6.1	6.1	8.8	6.7	2.1	1.3	−2.0	−.3	.7	−5.6	−1.4	1.4	6.3

Memorandum Items

	99bp x	1972	1973	1974	1975	1976	1977	1978	1979	1980	1981	1982	1983	1984	1985	1986
Oil Exporting Countries	999	10.1	7.4	7.4	3.0	12.9	7.2	−4.2	4.5	1.3	−1.0	.4	2.1	1.9	1.4	−1.1
Non-Oil Developing Countries	201	7.2	8.6	4.5	3.6	4.5	3.9	4.0	5.3	5.9	3.1	2.3	2.8	6.4	7.8	5.1

Indices

Index Numbers:

	99bp x	1972	1973	1974	1975	1976	1977	1978	1979	1980	1981	1982	1983	1984	1985	1986
World	001	44.7	47.5	48.5	49.1	51.9	54.1	56.2	58.6	60.1	61.3	61.6	63.4	66.6	69.7	72.2
Industrial Countries	110	53.2	56.4	56.8	56.8	59.6	61.8	64.4	66.8	67.5	68.6	68.5	70.5	73.8	76.3	78.7
Developing Countries	200	33.6	35.5	37.7	39.3	42.1	44.4	45.8	48.1	50.6	51.8	52.8	54.3	57.4	61.3	63.8
Africa	605	44.7	46.7	50.3	49.9	52.4	54.9	54.5	58.2	60.6	60.3	61.3	60.8	62.0	78.6	80.9
Asia	505	21.4	22.8	23.8	25.3	26.8	28.7	30.6	31.9	33.9	35.9	37.9	40.7	44.0	47.6	50.8
Europe	170	....	....	....	....	....	....	....	....	83.3	81.9	82.2	86.2	91.1	94.1	98.5
Middle East	405	48.0	52.3	56.1	59.1	68.4	71.2	66.3	69.8	68.9	68.4	68.3	72.0	74.0	74.8	71.5
Western Hemisphere	205	46.0	49.8	53.1	55.0	58.1	60.8	63.7	68.0	72.2	72.9	72.3	70.5	73.3	75.6	78.3

GDP Volume Measures

99bp x

Calculated from Indices

1987	1988	1989	1990	1991	1992	1993	1994	1995	1996	1997	1998	1999	2000	2001		
4.7	2.8	-.6	-2.0	-6.7	-10.6	3.0	7.2	5.2	4.7	4.7	3.0	—	5.1	2.8	Europe	170
								6.9	5.9	3.3	7.3	3.3			Armenia	911
						-7.6	-11.7	-10.4	2.8	11.4	8.4	3.4	5.8	4.1	Belarus	913
			-9.1	-8.4	-7.3	-1.5	1.8	2.9	-10.1	-6.9					Bulgaria	918
			-7.1	-20.6	-11.7	-99.9	5.8	6.8	5.9	6.8	2.5	-.8	3.7	4.1	Croatia	960
								-8.2	.5	1.7	-1.9	2.7	9.8		Kazakhstan	916
7.1	8.3	8.1	7.4	.7	9.4	.7	5.9	6.2	1.9	2.5	5.0	4.5	4.8		Cyprus	423
				-11.6	-.5	.1	2.2	5.9	4.3	-.8	-1.0	.5	3.3	3.3	Czech Republic	935
							-2.0	4.6	4.0	10.4	5.0	-.7	6.9	5.4	Estonia	939
3.8	5.5	.7	-3.5	-11.9	-3.1	-.6	2.9	1.5	1.3	4.6	4.9	4.2	5.2	3.8	Hungary	944
					-13.9	-15.5	-20.1	-5.4	7.1	9.9	2.1	3.6			Kyrgyz Republic	917
				-10.4	-34.9	-14.9	.6	-.8	3.3	8.6	3.9	1.1	6.8		Latvia	941
				-5.7	-21.3	-16.2	-9.8	3.3	4.7	7.3	5.1	-3.9	3.9	5.8	Lithuania	946
4.1	8.4	8.2	6.3	6.3	4.7	4.5	5.7	6.2	4.0	4.9	3.4	4.1	5.5	-.8	Malta	181
2.1	4.0	.3	-11.4	-7.0	-33.9	3.8	44.5	7.0	6.0	6.8	4.8	4.1	4.0	1.0	Poland	964
.8	-.5	-5.8	-5.5	-13.1	-8.7	1.5	3.9	7.1	3.9	-6.1	-4.8	-1.2	1.8	5.3	Romania	968
						1.9	4.9	6.7	6.2	6.2	4.1	1.9	4.8	3.3	Slovak Republic	936
				-8.9	-5.5	2.8	5.3	4.1	3.5	4.6	3.8	5.2	4.6	3.0	Slovenia	961
9.5	2.1	.3	9.3	.9	6.0	8.0	-5.5	7.2	7.0	7.5	3.1	-4.7	7.2		Turkey	186
-1.0	-2.0														Yugoslavia, SFR	188
2.1	—	3.2	8.4	6.0	5.0	2.9	2.8	4.0	4.5	3.7	3.5	2.0	4.7		Middle East	405
10.4	8.6	.4	4.4	11.2	6.7	12.9	-.3	3.9	4.1	3.1	4.8	4.3	5.3		Bahrain	419
3.8	5.5	4.9	5.7	1.1	4.5	2.9	4.0	4.6	5.0	5.5	5.6	6.0	5.1		Egypt	469
1.2	-8.7	3.3	11.7	11.4	5.7	1.6	.7	4.2	6.7	3.7	1.8				Iran, I.R. of	429
															Iraq	433
19.4	3.1	-8.9	—												Israel	436
6.1	3.1	1.3	5.8	6.2	6.6	3.2	6.8	7.1	4.5	2.9	2.7	3.0	6.9		Jordan	439
2.9	-1.9	-13.4	1.0	2.3	17.0	4.6	5.0	6.4	2.1	3.1	2.9				Kuwait	443
8.1	-10.1	25.9	-7.3	-7.3	-7.3	33.8	8.6	1.4	-2.7	1.2	3.2	-1.6	3.9	-1.0	Libya	672
-4.0	5.2	3.0	8.4	6.0	8.5	6.1	3.8	4.8	2.9	6.2	2.7	-.2	5.1		Oman	449
-1.4	7.6	.2	10.7	8.4	2.8	-.6	.5	.5	1.4	2.6	2.8	-.8	4.9	1.2	Saudi Arabia	456
1.9	13.3	-9.0	4.6	7.9	13.5	5.2	7.7	5.8	7.3	2.5	7.6	-2.0	.6		Syrian Arab Rep.	463
3.6	-.2	15.3	17.5	.8	2.7										United Arab Emirates	466
					-2.1	4.8	.4	-3.6	7.9	2.9	8.1	5.3	3.8		Yemen Republic	474
3.1	1.0	1.7	2.3	3.7	2.9	3.8	4.9	1.4	3.5	5.1	2.2	.5	2.5		Western Hemisphere	205
8.3	5.4	5.8	2.5	2.0	.8	5.4	6.3	-4.2	6.6	5.2	3.3	3.7			Antigua and Barbuda	311
2.6	-1.9	-6.9	-1.8	10.6	9.6	5.7	5.8	-2.8	5.5	8.1	3.9	-3.4	-.8	-4.5	Argentina	213
			-3.3	-3.2	-5.8	-2.1	2.0	1.1							Bahamas, The	313
2.6	3.5	3.6	-3.3	-3.9	-7.2	.8	4.3	2.3	2.5	2.9	4.4	2.5			Barbados	316
22.0	10.9	15.5	10.4	7.4	13.4	9.6	3.0	6.2	3.2	2.5	1.1	12.1	8.9	1.2	Belize	339
2.5	2.9	3.8	4.6	5.3	1.6	4.3	4.7	4.7	4.4	5.0	5.0	.4	2.4		Bolivia	218
3.4	-.1	4.0	.4	1.0	-.5	4.9	5.8	4.2	2.7	3.3	.2	.8	.8		Brazil	223
6.6	7.3	10.6	3.7	8.0	12.3	7.0	5.7	10.6	7.4	6.6	3.2	-1.0	4.4	2.8	Chile	228
5.4	4.1	3.4	4.3	2.0	4.0	5.4	5.8	5.2	2.1	3.4	.6	-4.2	2.7	1.4	Colombia	233
4.8	3.4	5.7	3.6	2.3	9.2	7.4	4.7	3.9	.9	5.6	8.4	8.2	2.2	.9	Costa Rica	238
7.5	8.6	-.2	5.3	.6	2.0	1.7	1.4	1.7	2.8	1.9					Dominica	321
10.1	2.2	4.4	-5.5	.9	8.0	3.0	4.3	4.7	7.2	8.3	7.3	8.0	7.7		Dominican Republic	243
-6.0	10.5	.3	3.0	5.0	3.6	2.0	4.3	2.3	2.0	3.4	.4	-7.3	2.3		Ecuador	248
2.7	1.6	1.1	3.4	3.6	7.5	7.4	6.0	6.4	1.7	4.2	3.8	77.3	-40.4	1.8	El Salvador	253
-14.9	5.3	5.7	5.2	2.9	.6										Grenada	328
3.5	3.9	3.9	3.1	3.6	4.8	3.9	4.0	4.9	2.9	4.4	5.0	3.8	3.6	2.3	Guatemala	258
.8	-2.6	-3.3	-4.7	6.0	7.8	8.2									Guyana	336
-.2	-.2	-.4	.2	4.7	-13.2	-2.4	-8.3	4.4	2.7	2.7	2.2	2.7	.9	-1.1	Haiti	263
6.0	4.6	4.3	.1	3.3	5.6	6.2	-1.3	4.1	3.6	5.0	2.9	-1.9	4.9	2.6	Honduras	268
8.0	2.2	7.0	6.3	.8	1.7	2.0	.9	1.0	-1.1	-1.7	-.3	-.4	.7	1.7	Jamaica	343
1.7	1.3	4.2	5.1	4.2	3.6	2.0	4.4	-6.2	5.2	6.8	4.9	3.7	6.6	-.3	Mexico	273
-.7	-12.4	-1.7	-.1	-.2	.4	-.4	3.3	4.3	4.7	5.1	6.1	5.0			Nicaragua	278
-1.8	-13.4	1.6	8.1	9.4	8.2	5.5	2.9	1.8	2.8	4.5	4.4	3.2	2.5	.3	Panama	283
4.3	6.4	5.8	3.1	2.5	1.8	4.1	3.1	4.7	1.3	2.6	-.4	.5	-.4	2.7	Paraguay	288
8.0	-8.7	-11.7	-3.7	2.2	-.4	4.8	12.8	8.6	2.5	6.7	-.5	.9	3.1	.2	Peru	293
8.7	9.1	7.6	2.3	.4	3.3	6.7	5.1	3.7	6.5	6.8	1.1	2.8			St. Kitts and Nevis	361
3.8	14.6	8.1	3.4	-.5	6.5	-.1	2.0	.5	.8	.5					St. Lucia	362
4.6	14.5	2.6	5.1	1.5	5.9	2.4	-2.0	7.6	1.4	3.7	5.2				St. Vincent & Grenadines	364
-6.2	7.8	4.2	—	3.5	5.8	-4.5	-.8								Suriname	366
-4.6	-3.9	-.8	1.5	2.7	-1.6	-1.5	3.6	4.0	3.8	3.1	4.4				Trinidad and Tobago	369
7.9	1.5	1.1	.3	3.5	7.9	2.7	7.3	-1.4	5.6	5.0	4.5	-2.8	-1.4	-3.1	Uruguay	298
4.5	6.2	-7.8	6.9	9.7	6.1	.3	-2.3	4.0	-.2	6.4	.2	-6.1	3.2		Venezuela, Rep. Bol.	299

Memorandum Items

1987	1988	1989	1990	1991	1992	1993	1994	1995	1996	1997	1998	1999	2000	2001		
2.5	2.0	4.2	8.6	7.6	5.0	3.8	3.5	5.3	5.5	4.3	-5.8	-.6	4.5		Oil Exporting Countries	999
5.7	5.6	3.4	3.5	3.6	4.5	6.1	8.0	6.3	7.3	5.6	3.3	4.5	5.4		Non-Oil Developing Countries	201

Indices

1995=100

1987	1988	1989	1990	1991	1992	1993	1994	1995	1996	1997	1998	1999	2000	2001		
75.2	78.7	81.6	84.3	86.5	89.0	91.6	96.1	100.0	104.6	109.0	111.7	115.6	120.6		World	001
81.3	85.0	88.2	90.6	92.0	93.6	94.7	97.6	100.0	102.7	106.0	109.0	112.4	116.4	117.8	Industrial Countries	110
67.2	70.6	73.1	76.2	79.3	82.9	87.7	94.2	100.0	107.0	112.9	115.3	119.9	126.3		Developing Countries	200
82.7	87.2	90.3	92.7	94.9	94.5	95.2	97.7	100.0	106.1	109.5	113.5				Africa	605
54.8	59.9	63.2	66.7	70.9	77.3	83.8	91.9	100.0	109.2	115.9	117.9	125.1	133.3		Asia	505
103.1	106.0	105.4	103.3	96.3	86.1	88.7	95.1	100.0	104.7	109.6	112.9	112.8	118.6	121.9	Europe	170
73.0	73.0	75.3	81.7	86.6	90.9	93.6	96.2	100.0	104.5	108.4	112.2	114.4	119.8		Middle East	405
80.7	81.5	82.9	84.9	88.0	90.6	94.0	98.7	100.0	103.5	108.8	111.2	111.7	114.6		Western Hemisphere	205

GDP Deflators

99bi x

		1972	1973	1974	1975	1976	1977	1978	1979	1980	1981	1982	1983	1984	1985	1986
													Percent Change over Previous Year;			
World	001	7.1	11.0	18.5	13.9	12.9	12.3	11.6	14.7	16.6	14.4	14.3	14.7	14.2	13.4	10.4
Industrial Countries	110	5.8	8.1	12.5	11.2	8.5	8.5	8.2	8.5	10.1	9.2	7.4	5.6	4.9	4.1	3.6
United States	111	4.2	5.6	9.0	9.3	5.7	6.4	7.1	8.3	9.2	9.3	6.2	4.0	3.7	3.2	2.2
Canada	156	5.6	8.9	14.4	9.9	8.7	6.2	6.0	10.0	10.6	10.8	8.7	5.0	3.1	2.6	2.4
Australia	193	7.2	10.8	18.1	15.3	12.8	10.5	6.1	10.5	10.4	10.4	11.0	8.9	6.0	5.7	6.4
Japan	158	5.6	12.9	20.8	7.7	7.2	5.8	4.8	3.0	5.9	4.0	1.8	1.9	2.9	2.5	1.5
New Zealand	196	10.1	8.6	5.5	13.7	20.7	9.2	10.3	13.8	14.9	15.6	16.4	4.9	7.3	15.3	19.4
Euro Area	163	....	....	....	....	....	....	....	....	....	....	....	....	....	....	....
Austria	122	7.5	7.7	9.2	7.9	6.9	5.7	6.0	3.5	5.0	6.6	5.3	3.7	4.6	3.1	2.7
Belgium	124	6.1	7.3	12.5	12.3	7.7	7.5	4.4	4.5	4.8	5.1	7.6	5.6	5.5	4.6	2.8
Finland	172	8.4	14.1	22.5	16.5	13.3	9.7	7.7	8.9	9.7	11.0	9.0	8.4	8.5	5.5	4.3
France	132	7.0	8.5	11.9	13.0	11.1	9.3	13.3	10.1	11.1	11.1	11.6	9.9	7.4	5.0	5.0
Germany	134	5.3	6.4	7.0	5.7	3.6	3.7	4.2	3.8	4.9	4.2	4.4	3.3	2.1	2.1	3.2
Greece	174	5.0	19.4	20.9	12.3	15.4	12.9	13.0	18.6	17.7	19.7	25.1	19.1	20.3	17.7	17.5
Ireland	178	13.4	14.8	5.3	23.9	21.0	13.3	10.5	13.7	14.7	17.4	15.2	11.7	6.4	5.3	5.8
Italy	136	6.2	13.8	20.7	15.9	18.4	19.2	14.0	15.6	20.9	19.1	16.7	15.1	11.5	8.9	7.9
Luxembourg	137	5.8	12.2	17.0	-.8	12.2	1.2	5.1	6.5	7.8	7.2	10.8	6.8	4.4	15.3	3.6
Netherlands	138	10.4	8.8	9.3	9.8	9.6	12.0	5.0	6.6	3.4	6.5	5.3	2.0	1.8	1.6	-.2
Portugal	182	7.8	8.0	18.9	16.2	16.3	26.4	22.4	19.7	20.6	17.6	20.7	24.6	24.7	21.7	37.9
Spain	184	8.5	11.8	16.0	16.8	16.5	23.4	20.6	16.9	13.4	12.6	13.9	11.8	11.6	7.7	11.1
Denmark	128	9.9	10.8	13.6	13.8	9.0	9.9	9.5	7.9	8.6	11.8	11.1	8.4	6.0	4.9	4.0
Iceland	176	18.3	31.6	37.2	41.9	33.0	32.7	46.2	40.8	51.5	50.8	58.2	76.1	25.5	31.3	25.3
Norway	142	5.3	8.9	10.2	10.0	6.8	8.8	4.8	5.7	13.1	12.9	10.4	7.0	6.3	5.2	-.9
Sweden	144	9.4	11.3	13.0	17.4	13.1	8.8	11.5	12.1	14.3	9.6	9.5	12.0	11.9	9.1	9.3
Switzerland	146	9.5	8.0	7.2	6.5	2.1	.3	3.4	2.0	8.8	5.8	6.8	2.7	3.5	2.4	3.1
United Kingdom	112	8.1	7.2	15.0	26.9	15.2	13.7	11.6	14.5	19.4	11.3	7.4	5.4	4.5	5.7	3.3
Developing Countries	200	11.4	19.9	34.9	20.7	24.6	22.5	20.6	27.0	29.9	24.7	28.4	33.8	32.4	31.6	23.5
Africa	605	4.5	10.6	29.5	11.2	9.6	12.1	15.4	12.3	20.0	14.9	10.2	16.4	13.4	-5.2	9.8
Benin	638	3.5	4.7	30.8	.4	13.5	5.3	5.9	14.1	14.4	15.9	24.9	4.7	2.0	-4.9	-3.6
Botswana	616	.7	5.5	12.3	19.0	14.2	12.7	-1.6	25.1	19.1	3.6	-4.3	10.4	8.2	22.7	23.1
Burkina Faso	748	....	....	....	....	....	....	....	....	6.0	14.2	8.5	7.2	.7	50.4	-7.2
Burundi	618	5.8	5.2	12.6	19.0	9.7	14.1	11.8	21.8	16.5	-6.2	6.1	6.1	17.2	7.1	-3.5
Cameroon	622	6.2	10.9	17.7	12.0	11.1	13.7	11.0	5.5	14.6	13.1	12.5	12.6	13.2	11.9	.9
Central African Rep.	626	4.1	.7	18.8	15.9	7.0	7.5									
Congo, Dem. Rep. of	636	11.3	16.2	18.7	12.3	56.8	37.9	46.5	101.3	252.5	34.3	....	....	....	....	....
Côte d'Ivoire	662						35.6	2.0	7.0	2.6	3.0					
Ethiopia	644	-3.9	2.7	9.3	-.6	-49.8	10.5	6.8	3.7	2.0	18.8	14.7	10.3	-3.9	33.9	-5.5
Gambia, The	648	24.5	-3.5	-6.2	45.7	3.5	59.4	-6.6	16.0	111.5	-50.0	1.9	12.4	22.9	11.7	21.4
Ghana	652	15.4	7.9	28.7	30.1	28.0	67.3	73.3	38.9	51.8	72.3	28.4	111.4	43.2	20.6	41.7
Guinea-Bissau	654															
Kenya	664	-37.9	7.3	17.2	8.9	13.0	-19.1	46.7	-27.2	8.6	9.1	10.8	9.1	8.5	12.6	8.7
Lesotho	666										13.3	9.6	14.6	7.5	16.9	12.3
Liberia	668	5.0	4.8	13.9	41.6	-.3	12.7	5.4	9.0	9.3	9.1	12.8	1.6	-5.4	2.5	-4.5
Madagascar	674	5.1	11.2	21.3	2.9	10.7	7.9	6.8	11.4	15.0	25.2	28.6	21.6	35.8	10.4	14.2
Malawi	676	....	....	18.0	8.8	8.8	14.0	1.5	4.5	16.7	16.3	9.3	11.5	13.8	9.0	11.8
Mauritania	682	....	....	11.6	33.4	6.1	7.6	2.1								
Mauritius	684	14.2	15.6	60.8	4.9	3.0	24.5	10.8	17.9	26.6	10.9	8.9	8.4	7.4	8.3	8.0
Morocco	686	3.9	5.8	18.0	9.7	-.1	13.2	8.4	7.3	15.2	9.7	7.2	7.3	8.6	8.4	10.3
Mozambique	688	....	....	....	....	....	....	....	....	....	....	....	....	....	33.7	12.6
Namibia	728	....	....	....	....	....	....	....	....	....	....	....	....	....		12.9
Niger	692															
Nigeria	694	2.9	5.3	43.9	23.5	14.4	10.7	13.9	11.5	12.4	16.2	2.6	16.1	16.9	3.7	-1.5
Rwanda	714	2.0	3.6	17.2	5.2	15.1	10.0	3.2	9.8	15.0	10.7	2.6	2.4	16.9	4.6	-7.1
Senegal	722	4.1	7.7	16.8	11.6	3.8	8.2	6.8	9.7	11.5	8.0	9.3	8.9	12.6	9.3	7.6
Seychelles	718	....	....	....	....	....	25.0	13.1	17.9	20.6	10.5	1.1	4.0	-.1	2.3	5.8
Sierra Leone	724	3.2	7.3	18.6	16.4	10.5	19.6	13.9	12.7	9.0	5.3	22.2	18.6	43.5	64.4	85.2
South Africa	199	11.0	18.3	16.2	10.6	10.2	10.9	11.6	15.3	23.6	11.8	13.7	15.7	11.5	-44.4	17.1
Swaziland	734	....	....	....	....	....	....	2.1	3.2	26.6	11.0	7.9	4.8	7.6	16.8	13.8
Tanzania	738															
Togo	742	3.1	7.7	38.6	-1.2	6.7	17.3	1.7	6.8	10.0	12.1	8.7	9.7	3.9	7.7	4.0
Tunisia	744	2.9	8.6	24.4	5.0	2.9	9.7	6.5	10.4	12.8	11.4	16.0	12.7	6.5	6.1	4.1
Uganda	746	....	....	....	....	....	....	....	....	....	....	....	....	64.1	166.4	141.0
Zambia	754	4.6	19.2	11.2	-14.0	14.8	10.1	12.7	21.9	11.8	7.2	6.1	18.6	18.4	41.1	83.9
Zimbabwe	698	....	5.9	1.5	13.0	9.8	7.0	9.7	15.2	10.3	14.4	14.4	19.5	3.4	33.6	11.5
Asia	505	9.6	18.6	25.1	9.5	6.9	7.6	9.0	13.0	11.2	8.9	6.0	6.3	7.2	6.3	5.1
Bangladesh	513	....	....	40.6	71.1	-23.9	-3.2	30.4	12.9	13.1	10.3	12.7	5.0	16.4	11.7	9.7
Bhutan	514															
China, P.R.: Mainland	924	....	....	....	....	....	....	....	....	3.6	6.2	11.1	8.4	9.8	10.0	6.5
China, P.R.: Hong Kong	532	8.6	13.9	11.9	4.6	8.7	3.5	7.7	17.3	15.0	3.1	3.5	.2	2.9	5.6	5.9
Fiji	819	15.7	15.7	33.1	25.4	7.8	1.6	4.3	8.2	17.6	10.1	8.2	3.9	9.9	5.7	3.6
India	534	10.9	18.1	16.7	-1.5	5.9	5.6	2.5	15.8	11.6	-.1	8.2	5.3	3.0	7.7	4.2
Indonesia	536	13.6	32.9	47.3	12.5	14.5	13.0	10.9	32.5	29.1	10.3	7.4	8.5	7.5	7.5	6.5
Korea	542	17.7	14.8	31.5	26.4	23.1	16.5	23.9	19.6	24.4	18.5	5.1	19.2	8.2	6.8	6.2
Lao People's Democratic Rep.	544	....	....	....	....	....	....	....	....	....	17.8	7.1	6.0	5.6	4.6	5.1
Malaysia	548	.3	17.9	12.7	-3.1	12.7	6.9	9.8	12.1	6.9	1.1	2.5	76.5	36.2	165.4	41.2
Maldives	556	....	....	....	....	....	....	3.8	19.6	31.8	20.8	18.6	5.2	5.5	-1.4	-8.7
Mongolia	948	....	....	....	....	....	....	....	....	....	....	....	-7.1	30.4	1.3	2.8
Myanmar	518	....	....	....	....	....	-4.5	4.5	1.3	4.5	1.5	2.0	1.0	-3.2	-1.5	-9.2
Nepal	558	12.5	-3.4	20.8	27.5	.5	-3.6	9.4	10.0	7.6	3.6	3.6	2.0	2.5	1.6	6.6
Pakistan	564	6.6	15.7	23.0	22.4	12.1	10.7	9.0	5.5	10.5	7.9	9.3	12.3	6.4	11.4	14.4
Papua New Guinea	853	....	....	27.4	-4.3	8.2	37.9	.3	13.5	7.1	11.1	9.4	5.3	9.7	4.5	3.3
Philippines	566	6.1	18.4	32.8	9.2	8.4	8.0	9.5	15.9	6.6	-2.7	3.2	9.2	....		—
Samoa	862	7.7	12.1	24.8	8.8	5.0	14.5	2.2	11.8	22.0	11.7	8.7	14.2	53.3	17.6	3.0
Singapore	576	5.4	12.2	15.6	2.4	1.9	1.6	2.4	5.3	11.5	16.2	-81.9	16.9	8.2	-.4	4.5
Solomon Islands	813	....	....	....	....	....	....	....	....	....	6.7	4.2	3.9	.7	-1.2	-1.4
Sri Lanka	524	4.4	17.5	25.5	7.3	5.8	18.6	7.8	-80.1	18.2	10.7	14.0	-14.1	44.8	4.2	9.0
Thailand	578	6.5	18.9	20.5	3.6	4.5	6.0	9.6	8.7	13.1	20.5	13.6	14.6	17.1	.9	5.8
Vanuatu	846	....	....	....	....	....	....	....	....	....	8.4	5.1	3.6	1.4	2.2	1.7
														-6.4	6.9	

Calculated from Indices

1987	1988	1989	1990	1991	1992	1993	1994	1995	1996	1997	1998	1999	2000	2001		
13.4	19.6	23.6	26.6	16.5	18.0	21.3	19.3	10.2	6.5	5.0	5.0	2.8	3.7	....	World	001
3.1	3.7	4.1	4.3	4.4	2.9	2.4	2.0	2.1	1.7	1.6	1.2	1.2	1.3	1.2	**Industrial Countries**	110
3.0	3.4	3.8	3.9	3.6	2.4	2.4	2.1	2.2	1.9	1.9	1.2	1.5	1.7	1.4	United States	111
4.6	4.7	4.8	3.1	4.5	1.5	1.5	1.1	2.3	1.6	1.5	-.1	1.9	4.6	1.1	Canada	156
7.8	8.6	7.4	4.8	1.9	1.6	1.3	.8	1.8	2.3	1.7	.4	.7	4.0	3.4	Australia	193
-.1	.7	1.9	2.4	3.1	1.7	.5	.1	-.4	-.7	.2	-.1	-1.5	-1.2	-2.1	Japan	158
3.4	6.6	5.4	1.8	.9	2.1	1.8	1.7	2.7	1.5	.6	1.1	—	3.4	4.0	New Zealand	196
									3.1	-.1	3.1	2.0	1.2	2.6	Euro Area	163
2.1	1.6	2.7	3.4	3.7	4.3	2.8	2.8	4.2	1.3	1.2	.7	.6	.8	1.7	Austria	122
1.7	2.2	4.8	2.8	2.9	3.4	4.0	2.1	1.3	1.2	1.3	1.6	1.2	1.4	2.3	Belgium	124
4.2	8.1	6.1	5.4	1.8	.9	2.3	2.0	4.1	-.2	2.1	3.0	-.1	-1.0	2.2	Finland	172
3.1	3.1	3.1	2.9	3.0	2.0	2.4	1.8	1.7	1.4	1.2	.8	.5	.5	1.4	France	132
1.9	1.5	2.4	3.4	6.7	5.0	3.7	2.5	2.0	1.0	.8	1.0	.5	-.4	1.3	Germany	134
14.3	40.0	14.8	21.3	19.4	15.1	13.7	11.8	11.4	7.4	6.8	5.2	3.0	3.4	3.2	Greece	174
2.2	3.4	5.4	4.4	1.8	2.8	5.2	1.7	2.8	2.3	4.3	5.7	4.4	4.3	5.4	Ireland	178
6.2	6.8	6.5	8.2	7.6	4.5	3.9	3.5	5.0	5.3	2.4	2.7	1.7	2.2	2.6	Italy	136
2.2	5.1	7.5	4.1	5.4	5.2	....	....		2.0	1.6	.6	5.4		1.6	Luxembourg	137
-.7	1.2	1.2	2.4	2.8	2.3	2.1	2.4	1.7	1.1	2.1	1.9	-2.4	3.7	4.7	Netherlands	138
10.1	11.2	12.1	12.4	12.2	10.6	7.0	6.1	5.0	3.1	2.7	4.1	3.9	3.2		Portugal	182
5.8	5.7	7.1	7.3	7.1	6.9	4.3	4.0	4.8	3.2	2.0	2.2	9.3	2.8	3.9	Spain	184
5.1	2.5	5.2	3.7	2.8	2.9	1.4	1.7	1.8	2.5	2.2	1.0	2.7	3.7	2.7	Denmark	128
19.5	22.8	19.8	16.9	7.6	3.7	2.3	1.9	2.7	2.0	3.5	5.4	3.4	3.0	9.1	Iceland	176
6.9	5.0	5.7	3.9	2.4	-.4	2.1	-.2	3.1	4.3	3.0	-.8	6.6	14.5	3.2	Norway	142
8.1	8.9	10.6	10.3	6.4	-.4	.3	10.4	7.3	2.5	3.8	4.5	5.2	4.7	3.3	Sweden	144
2.7	2.8	3.1	4.3	6.0	2.7	2.7	1.6	1.2	.3	-.2	—	.6	1.1	1.8	Switzerland	146
5.3	6.1	7.5	7.5	6.6	4.0	2.6	1.4	2.6	3.3	2.9	3.0	2.7	1.4	2.6	United Kingdom	112
33.8	53.6	66.6	71.0	37.9	46.0	57.8	45.8	21.4	12.9	9.5	10.0	4.8	6.8	....	**Developing Countries**	200
20.2	19.3	15.3	13.8	24.5	34.7	27.5	10.0	34.1	14.3	6.5	5.6	....	....		**Africa**	605
3.1	-.3	1.8	1.6	.7	3.4	1.2	33.5	15.4	6.7	4.7	4.2	1.8	4.8	....	Benin	638
-1.9	18.0	35.3	6.0	6.3	4.2	9.1	16.4	7.6	9.7	18.3	5.2	2.5	8.8	....	Botswana	616
1.6	2.6	5.3	1.2	-4.8	-.3	4.5	14.5	6.7	2.8	6.0	3.2	-3.5	.4	3.4	Burkina Faso	748
-3.4	1.5	15.7	5.8	-1.1	8.2	12.7	17.7	-.5	16.2	28.7	11.7	....			Burundi	618
-3.1	83.9	-46.2	1.7	3.6	-1.4	1.7	24.4	11.6	5.5	3.7	....				Cameroon	622
															Central African Rep.	626
...	...	1.3	114.1	2,466.1	4,095.9	1,662.8	3,820.4	3,820.4	....						Congo, Dem. Rep. of	636
															Côte d'Ivoire	662
-7.1	2.9	5.2	3.7	19.7	14.9	13.8	2.6	12.6	.9	3.5	8.9	....			Ethiopia	644
34.9	5.2	12.5	19.8	5.4	11.6	-19.8	10.6	....							Gambia, The	648
39.2	33.4	28.3	38.8	13.5	11.1	31.7	30.2	43.2	39.8	19.5	....				Ghana	652
-28.0	-10.2	23.0	-2.3	-3.4	-16.7	6.5	87.6	-3.8	-5.7	15.8	....				Guinea-Bissau	654
5.4	8.5	8.4	9.4	11.5	20.7	25.5	17.0	11.3	8.9	14.6	10.1	....			Kenya	664
-79.7	15.9	11.5	8.9	14.3	18.3	9.6	7.6	9.2	9.0	7.7	9.3	10.7	8.6		Lesotho	666
3.8	4.8														Liberia	668
23.0	21.2	12.0	11.5	13.9	12.5	13.0	41.6	45.1	17.8	7.3	8.5	9.8	9.4	8.3	Madagascar	674
16.5	26.4	18.1	15.2	13.0	14.0	24.8	29.0	88.5	50.4	8.5	32.6	32.4	20.9		Malawi	676
															Mauritania	682
11.6	10.9	11.0	10.1	8.2	5.5	7.9	7.2	4.7	6.3	5.1	9.3	4.3			Mauritius	684
3.9	5.3	3.9	7.5	4.6	4.4	3.6	1.6	8.0	1.0	2.0	1.1	-.3	1.6		Morocco	686
180.6	47.8	49.6	36.6	188.6	40.2	48.5	55.4	50.3	48.2	11.5	1.6	2.4	....		Mozambique	688
2.9	17.0	14.6	11.8	6.5	9.4	13.6	15.7	5.7	14.5	7.1	8.6	6.5	11.3		Namibia	728
.8	-3.0	.2	2.7	-2.1	-2.8	-2.8	18.6	4.0	4.9	2.4	-1.6				Niger	692
50.1	21.4	44.4	7.2	20.2	83.6	57.3	-7.7	110.7	34.2	.2					Nigeria	694
1.2	-2.3	7.8	10.1	15.3	6.0	14.4	16.8	51.2	11.0	15.8	2.0	-4.9	1.8		Rwanda	714
2.0	2.1	.9	1.2	.4	.6	-1.4	27.8	5.0	1.3	2.2	2.2				Senegal	722
3.7	3.9	2.1	6.4	-2.0	4.6	3.1	2.0	-1.0	-1.3	1.8	2.0	.2			Seychelles	718
170.2	64.3	61.5	70.6	128.8	82.0	26.7	25.1	33.6	24.3	16.8	27.1	25.2	6.0		Sierra Leone	724
14.5	15.2	17.3	15.5	15.7	14.6	13.1	9.6	10.3	8.3	7.6	6.8	6.9	7.0	7.5	South Africa	199
1.1	24.1	6.4	11.7	6.5	12.5	13.2	13.3	19.4	10.0	13.9	7.3	11.2			Swaziland	734
....	47.7	20.6	22.4	28.1	25.4	24.5	31.2	26.9	19.3	20.6	14.2	11.5	6.9		Tanzania	738
—	3.6	1.2	2.8	3.0	1.8	-4.8	32.6	-5.1	23.3	12.0	-2.4	1.8	3.1		Togo	742
7.0	6.1	7.0	5.3	7.0	5.7	4.7	4.5	5.4	4.4	4.0	3.1	3.0	3.3	2.7	Tunisia	744
221.8	162.7	73.7	28.1	31.5	58.6	1.9	16.2	5.4	4.9	....					Uganda	746
47.1	42.8	85.7	106.4	92.7	165.5	143.6	56.7	36.9	24.3	25.5	....				Zambia	754
6.9	17.1	17.9	14.7	30.6	27.6	21.9	23.7	10.4	27.8	15.4	....				Zimbabwe	698
6.7	11.4	8.6	9.4	9.5	7.1	11.4	13.3	10.5	5.5	4.3	8.9	.5	2.7		**Asia**	505
11.2	7.6	7.7	42.7	6.6	3.0	.3	3.8	7.3	4.2	3.1	5.3	4.7	1.9	1.6	Bangladesh	513
8.7	7.9	6.9	5.6	6.7	10.5	6.8	10.7	9.4	12.2	12.0	7.6	9.2	7.9	....	Bhutan	514
4.2	12.1	7.6	7.1	6.4	6.4	17.5	20.1	13.4	6.6	.7	-1.1	-4.1	.9	....	China, P.R.: Mainland	924
8.9	9.6	12.3	7.5	9.2	9.7	8.5	6.9	2.6	5.9	5.8	.4	-5.4	-6.5	-.5	China, P.R.: Hong Kong	532
7.1	5.6	-3.9	8.2	7.6	6.4	4.0	-.3	1.6	3.1	3.4	83.7	-41.3		....	Fiji	819
8.6	15.6	8.6	10.5	13.8	8.8	9.5	9.6	8.9	7.4	6.5	7.9	3.5	4.1		India	534
10.7	9.8	11.9	9.5	10.8	6.1	9.7	7.8	9.9	8.7	12.6	75.3	15.2	11.0		Indonesia	536
5.6	7.6	5.7	10.7	10.9	7.6	7.1	7.7	7.1	3.9	3.1	5.1	-2.0	-1.1	1.3	Korea	542
30.7	45.1	71.7	33.1	13.3	9.3	7.7	6.4	19.7	13.8	19.2	85.3	127.1	25.2	-27.9	Lao People's Democratic Rep.	544
7.5	3.6	4.5	3.8	3.6	2.4	4.0	3.9	3.6	3.7	3.5	8.5	.4	4.8	-2.8	Malaysia	548
18.0	4.5	5.9	2.5	14.1	12.9	11.3	8.6	6.0	5.4	-1.3	-4.8	2.5	-5.5	-9.7	Maldives	556
.8	.9	—	—	99.1	176.4	262.3	66.6	82.7	14.8	23.8	-5.1	....			Mongolia	948
21.2	25.2	57.7	18.5	23.7	21.7	36.2	22.1	19.6	23.0	33.7	35.9	22.7	....		Myanmar	518
12.7	11.8	11.3	14.8	9.4	18.7	11.1	7.7	6.9	7.4	7.6	3.7	8.8	3.8	2.1	Nepal	558
4.5	9.6	8.5	6.3	12.9	9.9	8.5	12.7	13.7	8.2	14.6	7.5	5.9	3.7	5.6	Pakistan	564
—	28.9	-2.5	4.1	7.0	-2.5	4.4	13.2	8.5	6.8	11.5	7.7	....			Papua New Guinea	853
7.5	9.6	9.0	13.0	16.5	7.9	6.8	10.0	7.6	7.7	6.2	10.5	8.0	6.7	6.7	Philippines	566
4.0	16.8	-.5	12.6	83.4	14.6	4.3	19.1	-5.2	3.9	11.8	....				Samoa	862
1.9	5.7	4.7	4.8	4.0	1.4	3.4	2.7	2.2	1.2	.8	-1.8	-4.8	3.5	-2.0	Singapore	576
22.2															Solomon Islands	813
7.0	11.5	9.6	20.0	11.0	10.0	9.5	9.3	8.4	-71.9	8.6	8.4	4.4	6.7		Sri Lanka	524
4.7	5.9	6.1	5.8	5.7	4.5	3.3	5.2	5.6	4.0	4.1	9.2	-4.1	1.2	2.2	Thailand	578
—	—	44.3	3.9	2.9	6.7	5.6	2.4	3.4	....						Vanuatu	846

GDP Deflators

Percent Change over Previous Year;

	99bi x	1972	1973	1974	1975	1976	1977	1978	1979	1980	1981	1982	1983	1984	1985	1986
Europe	170	....	....	....	....	....	....	....	....	....	13.4	59.2	11.0	10.4	9.6	10.6
Armenia	911	....	....	....	....	....	....	....	....	....	....	....	....	....	....	....
Belarus	913	....	....	....	....	....	....	....	....	....	....	....	....	....	....	....
Bulgaria	918	....	....	....	....	....	....	....	....	....	....	....	....	....	....	....
Croatia	960	....	....	....	....	....	....	....	....	....	....	....	....	....	....	....
Cyprus	423	6.3	8.3	11.1	4.2	10.1	9.5	11.2	13.2	14.0	11.8	10.1	5.3	8.1	5.8	4.2
Czech Republic	935	....	....	....	....	....	....	....	....	....	....	....	....	....	....	....
Estonia	939	....	....	....	....	....	....	....	....	....	....	....	....	....	....	....
Hungary	944	2.1	2.7	−1.2	1.2	5.8	2.2	3.6	5.5	5.4	5.1	5.7	4.9	6.4	5.9	2.8
Kazakhstan	916	....	....	....	....	....	....	....	....	....	....	....	....	....	....	....
Kyrgyz Republic	917	....	....	....	....	....	....	....	....	....	....	....	....	....	....	....
Latvia	941	....	....	....	....	....	....	....	....	....	....	....	....	....	....	....
Lithuania	946	....	....	....	....	....	....	....	....	....	....	....	....	....	....	....
Malta	181	−1.4	3.1	3.4	5.4	5.0	4.9	4.1	6.2	12.4	7.8	3.4	−.3	−.2	.6	3.5
Poland	964	....	....	....	....	....	....	....	....	....	21.8	111.5	18.3	17.2	15.9	19.0
Romania	968	....	....	....	....	....	....	....	....	....	1.0	12.2	−.3	.2	.3	.2
Slovak Republic	936	....	....	....	....	....	....	....	....	....	....	....	....	....	....	....
Slovenia	961	....	....	....	....	....	....	....	....	....	....	....	....	....	....	....
Turkey	186	....	....	....	....	....	....	....	....	....	....	....	....	....	....	....
Middle East	405	8.6	34.6	63.2	8.4	10.9	12.7	13.7	30.6	31.4	19.1	9.9	8.1	15.9	12.9	8.6
Bahrain	419	....	....	....	....	12.6	13.1	9.0	13.5	6.7	7.8	−.8	−2.7	−.8	−4.8	−17.4
Egypt	469	....	....	....	....	....	....	....	....	....	....	....	12.0	9.2	11.7	12.5
Iran, I.R. of	429	7.2	35.0	59.8	7.9	13.5	9.8	24.2	29.9	23.4	23.2	16.7	11.5	8.9	6.3	20.1
Israel	436	28.1	−13.8	44.3	19.8	22.0	85.2	45.2	51.1	143.0	127.3	122.0	152.2	384.8	258.1	49.2
Jordan	439	....	....	....	....	....	....	....	....	....	....	....	....	....	....	.1
Kuwait	443	1.9	17.2	172.5	4.0	−2.3	16.3	−1.9	41.5	41.9	12.0	—	−9.3	.4	4.9	−25.7
Libya	672	1.3	22.5	41.5	−6.4	5.8	7.9	−3.8	27.4	37.9	....	....	....	....	....	....
Oman	449	3.0	39.9	161.7	−.9	5.3	−9.0	−15.0	30.2	50.1	4.0	−5.9	−3.3	−5.6	−2.3	−14.3
Saudi Arabia	456	19.9	112.8	40.2	8.5	8.3	3.8	3.8	40.4	25.0	−.8	−11.3	−10.3	−3.4	−6.9	−18.2
Syrian Arab Rep.	463	−7.9	16.8	29.5	8.8	8.2	10.7	10.3	16.1	17.5	17.2	2.4	5.0	7.2	4.1	26.3
United Arab Emirates	466	....	....	138.3	19.6	12.5	5.5	−2.1	5.7	8.7	7.2	1.2	−6.0	−5.4	—	1.3
Yemen Republic	474	....	....	....	....	....	....	....	....	....	....	....	....	....	....	....
Western Hemisphere	205	20.0	35.1	37.5	39.3	52.6	43.9	35.4	43.2	58.9	52.6	67.2	95.0	111.8	123.3	77.2
Antigua and Barbuda	311	....	....	....	....	....	....	8.6	14.8	9.9	8.6	10.7	6.1	3.1	7.6	8.2
Argentina	213	55.8	58.0	31.3	195.8	452.3	158.8	158.9	151.1	170.1	106.5	201.9	381.1	608.2	620.8	75.7
Bahamas, The	313	....	....	....	....	....	....	....	....	....	....	....	....	....	....	....
Barbados	316	9.8	14.9	30.3	12.9	7.1	−1.7	5.4	27.0	22.9	12.2	9.9	5.8	5.1	3.5	4.5
Belize	339	....	....	....	....	....	....	....	....	31.2	−7.8	8.1	−.6	.2	.6	1.5
Bolivia	218	20.4	41.6	58.1	6.5	8.1	10.9	11.6	17.8	35.5	21.7	177.6	262.1	1,406.6	13,850.2	172.5
Brazil	223	19.9	29.6	34.6	33.9	41.2	45.4	38.2	54.4	91.2	104.7	101.9	136.4	204.4	249.5	147.5
Chile	228	86.9	417.9	694.4	344.3	251.7	106.6	57.2	47.9	29.3	11.0	12.4	30.3	14.6	35.4	22.1
Colombia	233	13.0	20.2	25.4	22.8	25.5	29.2	17.1	24.0	27.6	22.8	24.8	20.4	22.2	24.9	29.2
Costa Rica	238	5.7	16.0	23.1	28.1	17.1	13.6	8.6	11.2	16.2	42.3	85.5	28.0	17.0	20.6	18.1
Dominica	321	....	....	....	....	....	....	31.0	11.1	20.2	18.4	−1.4	4.5	8.0	6.6	8.3	6.2
Dominican Republic	243	8.0	4.5	17.9	16.7	2.9	10.6	1.0	11.1	13.7	5.3	7.9	8.3	24.2	38.4	9.4
Ecuador	248	2.3	6.0	40.0	10.0	12.9	17.5	7.9	16.1	19.5	14.4	−1.9	−5.6	−1.8	17.7	−31.5
El Salvador	253	.9	10.0	11.2	7.6	22.6	18.4	.9	13.9	13.4	5.7	9.9	12.3	12.3	20.6	37.0
Grenada	328	....	....	....	....	10.7	9.4	18.7	14.8	−.5	5.1	4.9	−15.6	3.9	16.4	8.1
Guatemala	258	−1.3	14.5	15.7	13.1	11.5	16.4	5.5	8.6	10.0	8.5	5.0	6.5	4.2	18.8	41.5
Guyana	336	8.8	5.9	36.9	13.2	−8.0	5.3	13.2	20.5	11.9	6.2	1.1	10.9	54.8	−14.9	18.6
Haiti	263	1.3	29.2	14.6	19.2	19.0	10.9	−1.5	2.9	15.2	5.2	7.8	9.3	11.5	10.4	10.3
Honduras	268	4.3	6.6	11.7	9.6	8.5	12.2	5.1	9.6	15.2	7.2	4.4	7.0	3.4	5.2	3.9
Jamaica	343	4.1	16.3	33.4	21.3	10.6	12.2	25.6	17.1	17.8	8.4	9.2	16.5	35.0	30.8	27.1
Mexico	273	6.2	12.9	22.7	15.8	19.6	30.4	16.8	20.2	34.5	26.5	60.1	89.6	59.0	57.0	72.4
Nicaragua	278	2.5	17.5	23.0	3.1	9.3	8.0	5.0	38.4	37.0	11.7	16.7	11.0	39.0	167.2	281.5
Panama	283	5.0	8.5	11.6	10.2	4.5	4.9	8.0	−4.9	35.2	3.6	4.9	7.5	1.6	.8	.3
Paraguay	288	8.4	20.4	23.5	5.7	4.8	11.0	9.9	19.9	16.8	16.3	5.0	14.4	26.9	25.2	31.5
Peru	293	8.4	15.7	14.0	18.9	36.3	37.8	58.1	96.6	64.4	66.2	68.6	99.9	109.9	167.4	73.6
St. Kitts and Nevis	361	....	....	....	....	....	....	6.7	6.6	11.3	16.5	7.6	.6	6.3	4.7	8.1
St. Lucia	362	....	....	....	....	....	....	5.2	16.5	19.8	10.0	5.8	2.8	3.4	3.1	3.9
St. Vincent & Grenadines	364	....	....	....	....	7.8	9.9	33.8	11.0	8.0	15.1	9.7	6.6	3.3	4.2	5.9
Suriname	366	....	....	17.5	26.0	1.5	13.0	8.7	13.1	11.4	4.4	7.4	.5	−.3	−.9	1.3
Trinidad and Tobago	369	11.1	21.2	57.5	24.6	8.0	13.3	3.2	24.7	22.7	5.0	12.1	7.5	6.1	1.3	−1.3
Uruguay	298	74.7	105.4	72.1	69.7	48.8	55.8	47.5	75.5	51.0	30.3	16.0	44.8	56.2	74.0	70.9
Venezuela, Rep. Bol.	299	4.3	12.1	44.5	−.8	5.2	8.0	6.3	21.3	24.8	12.5	1.4	5.7	41.6	9.1	3.1
Memorandum Items																
Oil Exporting Countries	999	8.0	30.9	58.2	8.3	10.8	9.5	11.0	26.9	24.6	14.2	3.3	7.8	10.5	4.5	3.4
Non-Oil Developing Countries	201	15.7	31.4	21.3	18.5	21.7	19.9	17.6	27.1	31.0	26.8	33.9	39.5	37.0	37.4	27.6

Indices

Index Numbers:

		1972	1973	1974	1975	1976	1977	1978	1979	1980	1981	1982	1983	1984	1985	1986
World	001	3.5	3.9	4.7	5.3	6.0	6.7	7.5	8.6	10.0	11.5	13.1	15.1	17.2	19.5	21.5
Industrial Countries	110	26.1	28.2	31.7	35.3	38.3	41.5	44.9	48.7	53.6	58.6	62.9	66.4	69.6	72.5	75.0
Developing Countries	200	.1	.1	.2	.2	.3	.3	.4	.5	.7	.8	1.1	1.4	1.9	2.5	3.0
Africa	605	3.2	3.5	4.6	5.1	5.6	6.2	7.2	8.1	9.7	11.1	12.3	14.3	16.2	15.3	16.8
Asia	505	11.5	13.7	17.1	18.7	20.0	21.5	23.5	26.5	29.5	32.1	34.0	36.2	38.8	41.2	43.3
Europe	170	....	....	....	....	....	....	....	....	.2	.2	.4	.4	.5	.5	.6
Middle East	405	2.4	3.2	5.3	5.7	6.3	7.1	8.1	10.6	13.9	16.6	18.2	19.7	22.8	25.8	28.0
Western Hemisphere	205	—	—	—	—	—	—	—	—	—	—	—	—	—	—	—

Calculated from Indices

1987	1988	1989	1990	1991	1992	1993	1994	1995	1996	1997	1998	1999	2000	2001		
16.1	35.8	117.7	110.4	77.2	129.3	157.3	49.6	56.3	40.4	56.1	36.3	33.5	29.3	....	Europe	170
								161.2	19.6	17.7	10.7	.1			Armenia	911
				103.6	1,074.1	1,054.0	1,945.1	661.9	53.7	71.6	76.6	317.0	185.3	78.0	Belarus	913
			26.2	226.4	59.6	51.1	72.7	62.8	121.0	947.6	....				Bulgaria	918
				85.9	629.6	*,***,***	97.5	5.3	3.6	7.4	8.4	4.5	6.5	3.1	Croatia	960
3.9	3.3	4.8	5.5	3.9	6.1	5.1	5.3	3.0	1.9	2.5	2.3	2.1	4.0	....	Cyprus	423
						21.0	13.4	10.2	8.8	8.0	10.6	3.0	1.1	5.3	Czech Republic	935
							39.6	30.9	23.3	10.6	9.3	4.5	4.7	5.8	Estonia	939
8.5	11.3	18.7	25.7	35.7	21.5	21.3	19.5	26.7	21.2	18.5	12.6	8.4	9.7	9.0	Hungary	944
								152.1	28.4	16.6	4.9	23.7	17.8	....	Kazakhstan	916
						830.2	754.9	180.9	42.0	30.0	24.3	9.1	37.7		Kyrgyz Republic	917
				156.2	975.9	71.5	38.3	16.0	16.5	6.6	5.5	7.4	4.1	1.6	Latvia	941
				227.9	943.0	306.2	61.6	38.0	25.1	13.2	6.7	3.2	2.1	.2	Lithuania	946
3.1	1.9	2.1	3.2	3.4	3.6	2.9	3.5	4.8	.8	2.3	2.2	2.7	1.7	4.9	Malta	181
28.1	68.1	298.2	434.7	55.2	114.9	30.6	—	27.9	18.7	14.0	11.8	6.7	7.1	4.4	Poland	964
-.1	1.9	-.9	13.4	195.6	199.7	227.3	139.0	35.3	45.3	147.2	55.3	47.7	44.1	37.0	Romania	968
						16.2	13.8	9.7	4.5	6.6	5.1	6.6	6.3	5.4	Slovak Republic	936
				94.9	208.2	37.1	22.6	15.2	11.1	8.8	7.8	6.6	5.7	9.9	Slovenia	961
	65.5	74.6	63.4	58.8	63.7	67.8	106.5	87.2	77.8	81.5	75.7	55.6	50.7	....	Turkey	186
14.1	16.1	14.5	18.2	14.0	17.8	8.1	18.4	15.9	17.6	5.8	2.3	7.1	9.0	....	Middle East	405
.7	.5	4.0	4.8	-1.9	-3.5	-3.0	7.3	1.1	.2	.9	-7.1	2.6	14.3		Bahrain	419
12.4	13.4	18.8	18.4	15.8	18.3	9.9	7.0	11.4	7.1	5.9	3.5	1.8	5.9		Egypt	469
20.9	32.8	16.4	25.7	25.5	41.4	16.3	48.8	30.5	26.3	9.0	17.6	....	....		Iran, I.R. of	429
20.6	20.3	20.3	17.1	19.9	12.5	11.8	12.9	12.3	10.8	9.4	7.1	1.5	2.3		Israel	436
-.8	4.5	21.0	11.4	5.1	8.7	2.8	6.8	2.0	2.2	1.1	5.6	....	....		Jordan	439
10.8	3.0	-1.7	.8	.8	.8	-7.2	-6.0	5.9	20.6	-3.8	-17.2	16.6	19.1	-7.5	Kuwait	443
														....	Libya	672
9.9	-7.7	8.5	15.0	-8.5	1.2	-5.5	-.4	1.9	7.6	-2.4	-13.4	11.8	20.1		Oman	449
3.0	-3.8	8.8	14.0	4.0	1.5	-3.2	.9	5.9	21.7	1.9	-14.0	11.3	11.7	-2.3	Saudi Arabia	456
25.4	28.6	23.3	22.8	7.6	5.1	5.9	13.6	6.7	12.7	5.3	-1.5	5.7	8.8		Syrian Arab Rep.	463
6.1	.1	-.1	5.0												United Arab Emirates	466
				21.1	21.1	23.3	33.2	54.8	39.6	12.4	-11.2	26.4	....		Yemen Republic	474
116.7	215.1	306.3	425.8	122.8	156.6	224.7	230.4	40.6	22.5	11.9	8.6	7.5	10.9	....	Western Hemisphere	205
7.6	12.1	4.2	2.3	2.7	2.2	2.2	3.0	3.0	2.7	2.2	3.3	1.3			Antigua and Barbuda	311
127.8	385.2	3,038.5	2,064.4	137.3	14.4	-1.4	2.8	3.2	-.1	-.5	-1.7	-1.8	1.0	-1.1	Argentina	213
			7.1	-2.1	5.0	2.0	4.9	-.5	....						Bahamas, The	313
7.4	2.8	6.7	3.8	2.7	.9	3.2	1.0	4.9	4.1	7.5	3.3	2.2	....		Barbados	316
-4.1	6.6	-.1	1.1	-.6	-1.2	-.1	1.1	.2	—	-.5	.9	-2.5	3.2	....	Belize	339
14.6	17.5	13.2	16.3	17.7	13.2	6.6	8.0	11.4	11.6	5.7	7.0	2.4	4.8	.7	Bolivia	218
204.8	648.7	1,121.1	2,774.8	416.7	970.2	1,993.8	2,240.3	77.6	17.4	8.3	4.8	4.6	11.9		Brazil	223
24.6	21.5	12.4	21.2	21.2	11.8	10.6	12.6	9.3	12.4	4.3	1.9	2.7	4.2	1.5	Chile	228
23.4	27.7	24.7	28.2	26.5	23.4	24.3	45.4	18.9	16.9	16.8	14.8	12.6	11.6	7.6	Colombia	233
10.1	22.8	17.7	12.2	64.0	20.4	10.6	15.6	22.2	15.8	14.9	12.1	15.0	6.5	7.1	Costa Rica	238
4.8	4.8	6.9	3.0	7.8	4.1	2.8	6.0	—	4.9	1.7	....				Dominica	321
14.4	43.5	23.6	50.5	58.3	8.3	5.0	8.3	12.7	5.5	8.2	4.9	6.5	7.7	....	Dominican Republic	243
-.6	-13.9	-2.2	5.6	4.7	4.0	10.8	11.3	5.6	4.1	.4	-.6	-25.2	-2.9	....	Ecuador	248
14.0	16.4	16.5	9.5	12.7	8.8	12.8	10.5	10.4	6.8	3.5	3.9	-41.4	76.8	2.7	El Salvador	253
36.4	4.8	9.3	-1.4	6.1	3.3	....									Grenada	328
8.0	11.7	10.9	40.5	33.0	18.8	14.5	11.7	8.7	8.9	8.3	9.5	5.1	5.9	6.3	Guatemala	258
49.9	26.5	158.2	59.1	134.6	11.3	16.9	....								Guyana	336
-3.3	3.3	12.9	4.2	3.7	21.9	35.8	69.6	9.2	28.8	12.7	14.2	7.0	11.1	11.4	Haiti	263
2.8	6.5	7.1	21.2	26.0	9.1	13.6	28.9	24.9	22.9	22.3	11.6	11.6	8.7	9.6	Honduras	268
10.7	14.0	12.5	22.6	50.5	66.8	36.7	32.6	25.0	19.9	10.6	6.3	8.0	11.2	6.9	Jamaica	343
141.0	101.2	25.0	29.0	21.1	13.9	19.1	8.5	37.8	30.7	17.7	15.4	15.2	12.0	5.4	Mexico	273
539.5	13,611.6	4,770.1	47,703.5	377.0	23.7	20.4	7.8	10.9	11.7	9.2	10.8	13.7	....		Nicaragua	278
2.3	-.2	-1.3	.6	.5	5.1	3.6	3.7	.5	.3	1.7	3.4	-.1	1.5	....	Panama	283
30.3	25.1	31.2	36.3	24.8	14.7	19.1	21.0	13.0	10.5	3.0	12.4	2.5	11.9	7.0	Paraguay	288
84.0	562.6	2,638.5	5,281.1	379.9	69.2	47.1	26.2	12.9	10.5	7.6	6.4	3.9	3.6	1.3	Peru	293
5.7	7.4	5.0	8.7	2.9	7.0	2.3	6.4	.3	—	4.8	3.3	3.2	....		St. Kitts and Nevis	361
5.4	-.5	4.7	5.4	8.2	4.3	.2	2.1	6.3	2.3	.1	....				St. Lucia	362
6.0	1.0	5.1	6.3	5.7	3.6	—	4.0	.8	4.0	1.8	2.7	....			St. Vincent & Grenadines	364
17.3	9.9	12.1	16.8	14.5	28.5	125.7	488.4	....							Suriname	366
4.9	4.2	7.2	15.5	2.0	4.2	7.5	15.6	4.0	4.7	2.9	.1	....			Trinidad and Tobago	369
72.9	75.2	75.6	107.1	100.8	59.4	47.9	39.0	41.0	26.4	19.3	9.4	4.2	4.0	5.6	Uruguay	298
32.1	21.4	84.1	43.6	21.4	28.2	31.6	62.9	51.8	115.5	38.4	20.9	27.0	27.6		Venezuela, Rep. Bol.	299

Memorandum Items

1987	1988	1989	1990	1991	1992	1993	1994	1995	1996	1997	1998	1999	2000	2001		
18.2	15.1	22.0	16.3	13.9	20.0	14.9	17.2	23.7	24.8	11.3	35.9	16.1	13.8	....	Oil Exporting Countries	999
36.9	62.0	76.4	81.8	42.1	50.5	65.4	50.5	21.0	11.2	9.3	6.9	3.7	6.1	....	Non-Oil Developing Countries	201

Indices

1995=100

1987	1988	1989	1990	1991	1992	1993	1994	1995	1996	1997	1998	1999	2000	2001		
24.4	29.2	36.1	45.7	53.2	62.7	76.1	90.8	100.0	106.5	111.8	117.4	120.6	125.1	....	World	001
77.4	80.3	83.6	87.2	91.1	93.7	96.0	97.9	100.0	101.7	103.4	104.7	105.9	107.3	108.6	Industrial Countries	110
4.1	6.2	10.4	17.8	24.5	35.8	56.5	82.4	100.0	112.9	123.6	135.9	142.5	152.3	....	Developing Countries	200
20.2	24.1	27.8	31.7	39.5	53.2	67.8	74.6	100.0	114.3	121.8	128.6	....	....	....	Africa	605
46.2	51.5	55.9	61.1	66.9	71.7	79.9	90.5	100.0	105.5	110.0	119.7	120.3	123.5	....	Asia	505
.7	.9	1.9	4.1	7.2	16.6	42.8	64.0	100.0	140.4	219.2	298.8	398.8	515.7	....	Europe	170
31.9	37.1	42.4	50.2	57.2	67.4	72.8	86.3	100.0	117.6	124.4	127.3	136.2	148.5	....	Middle East	405
—	.1	.2	1.2	2.6	6.6	21.5	71.1	100.0	122.5	137.1	148.9	160.1	177.5	....	Western Hemisphere	205

Gross Capital Formation as Percentage of GDP

93e r

		1972	1973	1974	1975	1976	1977	1978	1979	1980	1981	1982	1983	1984	1985	1986
																Percentages
World	001	22.1	24.5	25.0	23.3	24.0	24.2	25.1	25.2	24.8	24.5	23.1	22.7	23.2	23.1	22.7
Industrial Countries	110	24.1	25.5	25.4	22.2	23.3	23.3	23.6	24.4	23.9	23.4	21.8	21.3	22.3	21.9	21.6
United States	111	20.0	20.7	20.1	17.8	19.5	21.0	22.2	22.4	20.6	21.6	19.0	18.9	21.4	20.4	19.9
Canada	156	22.7	24.1	25.9	25.2	24.8	23.9	23.0	24.8	23.4	24.5	19.1	19.3	20.1	20.2	20.6
Australia	193	28.1	28.0	29.2	24.4	25.6	25.5	25.5	26.7	26.6	28.3	26.6	23.6	25.8	26.8	25.7
Japan	158	35.5	38.1	37.3	32.8	31.8	30.8	30.9	32.5	32.4	31.3	30.1	28.2	28.2	28.3	28.0
New Zealand	196	24.5	27.6	37.0	31.8	30.8	24.6	21.4	22.9	20.5	24.2	25.5	25.8	28.2	26.1	23.8
Euro Area	163															
Austria	122	30.6	30.9	31.1	26.0	25.8	26.5	24.9	25.9	27.2	25.3	21.4	20.4	22.0	21.9	21.5
Belgium	124	21.5	22.4	24.6	22.1	21.8	21.6	21.4	21.1	24.5	20.8	19.9	17.3	18.3	17.5	17.1
Finland	172	28.1	30.6	35.4	34.8	29.2	24.8	22.8	26.8	29.8	26.9	26.4	26.3	25.3	25.7	24.8
France	132	26.4	27.2	28.1	23.5	25.4	24.4	23.6	24.2	25.0	22.9	22.8	21.0	20.3	20.0	20.5
Germany	134	25.9	25.2	22.0	19.8	21.6	20.9	21.2	24.8	25.1	23.3	22.0	22.5	22.4	21.8	21.9
Greece	174	29.5	35.8	29.3	27.0	26.3	26.4	27.7	30.2	28.6	25.4	21.1	21.9	20.1	21.3	19.8
Ireland	178	25.1	27.6	29.1	23.3	25.4	27.9	29.0	33.0	27.8	28.4	27.8	23.6	22.6	19.8	18.1
Italy	136	24.0	27.2	30.1	23.9	26.9	24.9	24.1	24.7	27.0	24.7	24.5	22.9	23.8	23.6	22.0
Luxembourg	137	28.5	27.5	21.1	22.9	22.8	20.4	24.9	22.1	25.2	24.5	24.8	24.3	24.7	16.6	19.7
Netherlands	138	24.1	24.5	24.3	20.6	20.6	20.5	20.8	20.4	20.4	17.3	17.0	17.4	18.1	19.2	20.4
Portugal	182	29.3	29.4	28.5	20.3	24.7	29.0	30.9	31.7	34.4	38.6	37.1	29.1	22.2	20.6	23.2
Spain	184	25.8	27.1	30.1	28.5	26.9	24.9	22.9	22.3	23.2	21.9	22.2	21.5	19.7	19.2	20.0
Denmark	128	26.2	27.2	26.3	22.1	25.2	24.2	22.9	23.1	20.1	16.9	18.0	18.1	20.5	21.9	23.7
Iceland	176	26.4	29.7	33.9	33.1	26.6	27.9	23.3	23.9	25.7	25.2	26.9	20.2	21.0	18.5	16.8
Norway	142	30.5	32.6	36.2	37.2	38.7	38.0	29.7	28.5	28.3	27.1	28.2	25.6	26.7	26.4	31.7
Sweden	144	21.7	20.7	23.9	23.3	22.1	20.1	17.2	19.6	21.3	18.2	17.6	17.2	17.8	19.2	17.9
Switzerland	146	31.8	31.3	31.2	23.0	20.7	20.7	21.7	23.9	28.0	26.8	24.5	23.3	25.3	25.2	24.8
United Kingdom	112	19.2	22.6	22.9	19.4	21.1	20.6	20.2	20.5	17.6	16.0	16.7	17.5	18.5	18.4	18.1
Developing Countries	200	17.0	22.2	24.1	25.9	25.8	26.3	27.8	26.5	26.4	26.4	25.5	25.1	24.5	25.3	24.5
Africa	605	20.3	23.7	24.2	27.5	27.1	28.0	29.3	26.6	26.9	27.4	24.9	23.7	22.1	21.0	20.7
Algeria	612	40.2	44.5	39.7	45.2	43.1	46.8	52.1	42.5	39.1	37.0	37.3	37.6	35.1	33.2	33.5
Benin	638	20.5	18.3	20.7	25.5	18.9	18.6	17.8	23.9	23.6	21.7	27.6	16.3	12.8	15.8	14.7
Botswana	616	53.0	52.4	51.7	46.0	38.3	28.1	34.6	34.9	37.7	40.6	43.6	30.1	26.3	30.4	16.2
Burkina Faso	748	17.4	21.2	26.6	25.5	26.4	22.2	20.7	31.6	26.6	23.8	25.5	24.4	24.1	24.1	22.5
Burundi	618	3.2	5.3	4.1	11.1	9.1	11.1	14.1	15.4	13.9	16.1	17.5	17.9	18.1	14.3	15.7
Cameroon	622	19.4	21.0	18.0	20.8	18.5	23.0	24.7	24.0	21.8	27.2	24.8	26.0	25.9	24.5	25.3
Central African Rep.	626	....	....	....	....	....	....	....	....	....	....	....	....	....	18.9	15.0
Congo, Dem. Rep. of	636	—	—	—	....	....	....	....	....	....	....	....	....	....		
Congo, Rep. of	634							27.4	31.3	35.8	48.1	60.3	35.6	30.4	30.3	29.5
Côte d'Ivoire	662	20.6	22.9	22.0	24.3	22.9	26.5	29.8	28.0	26.5	25.9	23.2	18.1	11.6	13.0	12.1
Ethiopia	644	12.7	11.4	9.9	10.5	9.6	8.9	7.5	8.7	10.0	11.3	13.7	12.2	16.8	10.7	16.4
Gabon	646	48.1	37.5	51.8	62.7	73.5	58.1	35.0	32.7	27.5	36.4	35.0	34.5	35.2	38.9	34.2
Ghana	652	7.1	9.0	13.0	12.7	8.9	11.1	6.8	6.5	5.6	4.6	3.4	3.7	6.9	9.6	9.4
Guinea-Bissau	654															.2
Kenya	664	23.2	21.2	30.8	20.5	23.0	27.0	34.3	26.1	35.4	33.3	26.4	25.0	25.5	25.5	21.8
Liberia	668	25.6	17.3	24.0	40.5	38.0	40.5	36.3	36.5	33.3	19.4	21.1	20.4	18.4	12.6	11.7
Madagascar	674	13.9	14.3	13.6	12.8	12.8	12.9	14.5	25.3	23.5	18.1	13.4	13.2	10.8	11.5	....
Malawi	676	24.7	22.4	27.8	34.1	23.9	24.7	38.4	37.9	31.9	23.3	23.6	27.2	12.9	18.6	12.3
Mali	678										24.5	17.6	19.8	15.2	14.5	18.0
Mauritania	682	34.0	27.7	44.9	44.4	50.8	43.7	27.0	26.2	32.1	44.1	48.2	45.8	35.3	....	....
Mauritius	684	16.0	25.9	23.3	33.3	40.5	30.0	30.7	31.2	20.7	25.3	18.2	17.5	22.0	23.5	21.9
Morocco	686	12.6	14.4	20.6	25.2	28.1	34.2	25.7	24.5	24.2	26.1	28.2	24.0	25.3	27.1	22.8
Mozambique	688									19.2	19.5	22.8	20.0	22.0	17.1	18.9
Namibia	728														13.5	12.5
Niger	692	9.0	14.7	13.9	23.8	26.4	28.9	31.6	31.8	31.5	28.0	27.3	15.6	5.2	15.1	13.0
Nigeria	694	12.7	21.3	16.2	24.0	30.0	29.5	27.4	22.4	22.7	22.8	18.7	13.1	6.7	7.1	10.6
Rwanda	714	47.2	47.2	47.8	13.8	13.9	15.1	16.5	11.9	16.1	13.3	17.7	13.5	15.8	17.3	15.9
Senegal	722	14.5	16.1	19.5	15.2	13.6	14.5	14.3	11.4	11.7	12.8	12.2	12.8	12.8	10.5	11.4
Seychelles	718					38.9	40.0	43.3	32.9	38.3	32.6	32.3	21.3	21.7	22.7	24.4
Sierra Leone	724	11.7	11.7	15.8	15.7	11.3	13.1	11.3	13.4	16.2	19.1	13.4	14.3	12.7	10.9	10.6
South Africa	199	25.7	26.0	29.6	32.0	28.5	26.9	25.2	26.8	30.8	33.1	25.2	25.8	24.9	20.5	19.0
Swaziland	734	23.3	23.2	26.8	18.6	22.4	27.0	48.0	42.5	40.7	31.0	32.2	35.0	31.6	26.2	20.0
Tanzania	738	21.8	21.1	22.0	21.1	22.9	26.1	25.2	26.1	23.0	24.7	23.3	16.6	16.5	18.6	19.9
Togo	742	20.1	23.6	17.0	28.5	27.0	38.9	49.3	50.7	34.8	30.7	26.3	21.8	15.0	25.5	29.1
Tunisia	744	21.8	21.1	22.7	31.4	29.9	30.1	30.5	29.7	28.8	32.3	31.6	28.4	31.1	26.1	23.0
Uganda	746	10.5	8.5	10.6	7.6	5.7	4.7	3.9	....	....	....	....	8.5	9.9	8.1	9.0
Zambia	754	35.3	29.2	36.4	40.5	13.8	24.7	23.9	14.1	23.3	19.3	16.8	13.8	14.7	14.9	23.7
Zimbabwe	698	20.7	24.8	27.9	27.1	18.9	19.1	11.9	12.7	18.8	23.2	21.2	15.9	19.0	17.8	18.0
Asia	505	18.3	19.1	20.6	21.5	21.7	21.7	26.9	28.1	27.3	28.2	27.4	28.0	27.8	29.4	28.9
Bangladesh	513	....	8.9	5.6	5.5	8.7	11.7	11.0	9.6	11.3	10.5	10.4	10.3	11.0	10.3	12.3
Bhutan	514	....	....	....	....	....	....	....	....	31.0	38.5	40.5	39.8	36.3	45.3	40.5
China, P.R.: Mainland	924	....	....	....	....	....	....	36.2	34.9	32.3	32.1	33.0	34.5	38.5	38.0
China, P.R.: Hong Kong	532	23.6	23.0	24.4	23.1	25.5	26.7	28.9	32.9	35.1	35.3	31.3	26.9	24.6	21.6	23.7
Fiji	819	24.0	22.2	18.9	20.6	21.5	23.2	25.3	30.1	31.8	34.3	25.6	21.1	18.9	19.1	18.2
India	534	17.1	18.3	19.8	20.8	20.9	19.8	22.1	22.9	20.9	25.0	22.9	21.1	21.2	24.2	23.2
Indonesia	536	18.8	17.9	16.8	20.3	20.7	20.1	20.5	20.9	20.9	29.8	27.9	28.7	26.2	28.1	28.2
Korea	542	21.4	25.6	32.2	28.7	26.9	28.7	33.2	36.3	31.9	28.4	28.7	29.1	30.4	30.0	29.1
Malaysia	548	21.3	23.6	29.6	25.5	22.8	23.8	26.7	28.9	30.4	35.0	37.3	37.8	33.6	27.6	26.0
Myanmar	518	10.8	10.2	10.3	10.0	10.3	13.0	18.2	22.3	21.5	22.9	22.2	18.0	15.1	15.5	12.7
Nepal	558	....	....	....	14.5	15.1	16.0	17.4	15.8	18.3	17.6	17.1	19.6	18.7	21.9	19.0
Pakistan	564	14.2	12.9	13.4	16.4	18.5	19.3	17.9	17.9	18.5	18.8	19.3	18.8	18.3	18.8	18.8
Papua New Guinea	853	38.8	18.6	12.9	22.1	18.1	20.0	19.4	21.7	23.4	25.3	29.8	29.4	27.2	18.8	18.7
Philippines	566	20.6	20.2	25.2	29.5	31.0	28.8	28.9	31.1	29.1	27.5	27.9	29.6	20.3	14.3	15.2
Singapore	576	41.1	39.2	44.6	37.6	40.8	36.2	39.0	43.4	46.3	46.3	47.9	47.9	48.5	42.5	37.5
Solomon Islands	813	....	....	....	....	....	....	....	....	....	....	....	....	23.0	26.2	26.2
Sri Lanka	524	17.3	13.7	15.7	15.6	16.2	14.4	20.0	25.8	33.8	27.8	30.8	28.9	25.8	23.8	23.7
Thailand	578	21.7	27.0	26.6	26.7	24.0	26.9	28.2	27.2	29.1	29.7	26.5	30.0	29.5	25.9	25.9
Vanuatu	846	....	....	....	....	....	....	....	....	....	....		25.7	25.7	29.7	34.8

Percentages

1987	1988	1989	1990	1991	1992	1993	1994	1995	1996	1997	1998	1999	2000	2001		
22.7	23.9	24.6	24.2	23.3	23.0	22.8	23.0	23.4	23.1	23.4	22.8	22.6	23.0	....	World	001
21.7	22.3	22.9	22.4	21.2	20.5	19.9	20.4	20.6	20.6	21.0	21.4	21.5	21.8	20.7	Industrial Countries	110
19.3	18.6	18.6	17.7	16.3	16.5	17.2	18.3	18.3	18.7	19.6	20.3	20.5	21.0	19.4	United States	111
21.7	22.5	23.0	20.7	18.7	17.7	17.8	18.8	18.7	18.1	20.7	20.5	20.3	20.5	19.3	Canada	156
26.0	26.8	28.5	24.5	21.0	20.8	21.8	23.3	22.7	22.3	21.9	23.9	24.5	22.8	21.0	Australia	193
28.8	30.7	31.7	32.8	32.4	30.7	29.2	28.1	28.2	29.1	28.7	26.9	26.1	25.9	25.5	Japan	158
21.5	19.9	22.5	19.5	16.3	17.5	20.2	21.7	22.7	22.6	21.6	19.7	21.1	20.2	20.0	New Zealand	196
			22.4	22.5	21.4	19.4	20.0	20.2	19.3	19.6	21.2	21.4	22.2	21.0	Euro Area	163
22.2	22.1	22.3	22.9	23.8	22.5	21.5	22.4	23.5	23.3	25.1	25.3	....	....	....	Austria	122
18.1	20.2	21.7	22.4	21.1	20.8	20.2	20.3	20.1	19.6	20.3	20.4	20.7	21.5	20.7	Belgium	124
25.6	28.6	31.1	29.7	22.3	18.6	16.2	17.3	17.5	16.6	18.5	19.3	18.9	20.0	20.1	Finland	172
21.1	22.5	23.4	23.4	22.5	20.9	18.1	19.0	19.2	18.3	17.9	19.1	19.6	20.9	20.0	France	132
21.8	22.8	23.6	24.6	24.3	23.8	22.5	23.2	22.7	21.6	21.5	21.8	21.8	22.2	20.0	Germany	134
17.6	22.0	22.2	22.7	23.4	20.9	19.8	18.7	18.9	19.8	20.1	21.3	21.4	22.7	23.0	Greece	174
16.5	15.5	17.9	21.0	19.2	16.3	15.1	16.1	18.1	19.6	21.5	23.4	23.5	23.9	23.4	Ireland	178
22.2	22.6	22.4	22.2	21.7	20.8	18.4	18.5	19.3	18.7	18.9	19.3	19.8	20.4	19.7	Italy	136
22.7	24.3	22.4	24.7	27.3	24.0	25.2	21.9	21.3	20.3	21.8	22.9	24.7	22.9	22.2	Luxembourg	137
19.9	20.5	21.7	21.3	20.5	19.8	18.1	19.0	19.3	18.5	19.5	19.6	22.6	22.6	21.8	Netherlands	138
27.5	30.6	28.9	28.6	26.7	25.9	23.2	23.9	24.4	24.4	25.8	26.5	....	....	....	Portugal	182
21.5	23.7	25.1	25.4	24.6	22.6	19.9	20.1	21.1	20.6	20.7	24.3	24.6	25.6	25.5	Spain	184
21.5	20.6	21.1	20.3	19.1	18.1	16.4	17.6	19.7	18.9	20.8	21.7	20.2	21.7	21.2	Denmark	128
18.6	18.5	16.4	19.6	20.8	19.1	17.7	16.9	17.2	20.0	21.0	24.4	22.0	23.8	21.5	Iceland	176
30.5	29.2	26.3	23.3	21.4	20.7	21.6	22.3	23.7	22.8	25.1	28.3	24.3	21.5	20.6	Norway	142
18.9	19.9	21.9	21.3	17.9	16.5	13.3	15.9	16.6	15.9	15.6	16.8	17.2	18.0	17.6	Sweden	144
25.1	26.9	28.6	28.4	25.3	22.1	20.8	21.2	21.6	20.3	19.8	19.8	19.7	20.9	20.4	Switzerland	146
19.1	21.5	22.2	20.2	17.1	16.2	15.8	16.5	16.9	16.7	17.1	18.1	17.9	17.0	17.2	United Kingdom	112
24.4	26.4	27.3	26.9	26.5	26.8	27.3	27.0	27.8	27.0	27.0	25.0	24.3	24.9	....	Developing Countries	200
19.4	19.3	19.9	20.1	19.6	18.6	18.6	19.9	19.6	18.3	18.1	19.1	18.4	17.6	....	Africa	605
30.0	30.7	30.5	28.9	30.9	29.8	28.3	31.5	31.6	25.1	23.3	26.9	25.7	21.7	....	Algeria	612
14.2	15.6	11.8	14.2	14.6	14.6	14.3	18.5	23.5	17.9	18.4	18.3	19.2	19.8	....	Benin	638
26.6	7.9	30.1	38.4	36.4	30.3	30.5	26.6	25.7	23.7	26.0	30.0	36.8	26.6	26.6	Botswana	616
21.5	21.0	21.9	20.5	23.1	21.3	23.2	16.4	19.1	21.5	25.6	27.6	27.1	26.9	26.6	Burkina Faso	748
17.3	14.2	16.4	15.8	16.7	15.2	15.7	8.7	9.3	11.7	6.8	5.6	9.0	3.9	13.1	Burundi	618
24.7	11.5	17.1	17.9	20.9	13.5	16.7	14.1	13.7	15.1	16.1	....	....	....	....	Cameroon	622
12.6	10.5	11.8	12.7	12.6	12.4	10.6	11.7	14.1	....	....	....	....	....	....	Central African Rep.	626
....	—	....	5.9	6.9	1.8	4.1	9.4	....	....	....	....	....	....	....	Congo, Dem. Rep. of	636
13.9	18.6	16.2	15.9	20.5	21.6	19.1	46.2	36.6	32.8	22.4	26.7	22.3	31.1	38.6	Congo, Rep. of	634
12.3	14.4	8.1	8.5	6.3	5.5	8.3	11.8	15.0	13.6	15.6	....	....	....	....	Côte d'Ivoire	662
15.6	20.4	14.4	12.5	10.4	9.2	14.2	15.2	16.4	19.1	17.0	17.6	....	....	....	Ethiopia	644
23.6	32.4	20.3	23.5	26.9	22.2	22.5	20.8	22.1	22.7	24.5	31.8	....	....	....	Gabon	646
10.4	10.9	13.5	12.3	13.5	13.8	22.2	24.0	20.0	21.5	24.6	....	....	....	....	Ghana	652
.8	1.7	2.8	2.7	5.0	10.4	12.7	....	....	....	....	....	....	....	....	Guinea-Bissau	654
24.3	25.0	24.7	24.3	21.3	16.9	17.6	19.3	21.8	20.4	18.5	17.3	16.1	15.6	....	Kenya	664
11.4	10.1	8.5	....	....	....	....	....	....	....	....	....	....	....	....	Liberia	668
															Madagascar	674
15.4	18.7	21.2	19.1	19.9	19.4	14.5	29.4	16.9	11.8	12.0	12.8	14.6	15.3	....	Malawi	676
21.4	20.3	23.0	20.7	19.0	21.7	17.4	24.4	24.1	20.9	22.8	21.1	20.0	20.0	....	Mali	678
				19.4	25.1	18.6	19.1	20.4	17.8	17.3	....	....	....	....	Mauritania	682
25.6	31.0	31.1	30.9	28.7	29.3	30.6	32.2	25.8	24.8	29.3	25.7	26.0	23.5	22.3	Mauritius	684
21.1	21.0	23.7	25.2	22.6	23.2	22.5	21.3	20.7	19.6	20.7	22.2	23.4	24.4	....	Morocco	686
45.5	57.4	56.2	59.0	19.4	22.8	23.1	22.6	27.8	20.9	18.0	22.4	....	....	....	Mozambique	688
14.8	19.1	15.9	27.4	18.1	21.2	16.5	21.7	21.7	23.1	20.2	25.8	23.3	18.1	....	Namibia	728
10.3	15.9	13.5	15.4	16.1	11.1	8.1	17.1	14.3	17.7	18.0	21.0	....	....	....	Niger	692
8.8	6.5	8.2	11.9	10.9	9.5	8.2	9.3	5.8	6.1	7.0	6.8	5.3	5.4	7.0	Nigeria	694
15.7	15.1	13.6	14.1	12.9	17.0	17.5	10.5	13.1	14.3	13.7	....	....	....	....	Rwanda	714
12.5	12.7	11.9	13.8	12.5	14.4	13.7	17.0	16.7	18.5	....	....	....	....	....	Senegal	722
19.8	25.5	27.5	24.6	22.3	21.2	28.7	27.1	30.3	32.1	34.2	37.8	....	....	....	Seychelles	718
10.2	5.9	8.3	10.0	9.3	12.9	4.1	8.7	5.5	10.0	4.4	5.5	3.5	6.5	....	Sierra Leone	724
17.8	21.0	21.0	17.2	16.7	14.8	15.3	16.8	18.0	17.1	16.7	16.8	15.9	15.9	15.3	South Africa	199
14.9	23.5	23.9	19.6	20.6	26.1	26.6	32.0	33.7	29.7	32.7	....	....	....	....	Swaziland	734
22.1	16.5	18.1	26.1	26.3	27.2	25.1	24.6	19.8	16.6	14.9	16.2	15.5	17.7	....	Tanzania	738
25.2	24.9	24.9	17.2	14.8	14.5	4.3	14.9	18.5	14.7	14.6	15.3	14.7	16.0	....	Togo	742
20.5	19.5	23.9	27.1	26.0	29.2	29.2	24.6	24.7	25.1	26.4	26.9	26.3	27.3	27.5	Tunisia	744
11.9	10.9	10.9	14.2	16.4	14.7	16.2	13.8	16.4	15.1	....	....	....	....	....	Uganda	746
14.4	11.4	10.8	17.3	11.0	11.9	15.0	19.8	30.2	44.9	38.8	....	....	....	....	Zambia	754
14.9	18.7	15.0	17.4	19.1	20.2	22.8	23.5	19.4	23.2	20.2	17.2	....	....	....	Zimbabwe	698
28.9	30.0	30.9	31.4	31.2	32.1	33.4	33.3	34.1	32.4	31.6	27.4	27.4	....	....	Asia	505
12.5	14.5	12.9	17.1	16.9	17.3	17.9	18.4	19.1	20.0	20.7	21.6	22.2	23.0	24.1	Bangladesh	513
30.2	38.6	33.1	32.0	32.0	46.6	46.1	47.4	46.8	44.7	34.1	38.2	43.1	43.8	....	Bhutan	514
36.7	37.4	37.0	35.2	35.3	37.3	43.5	41.3	40.8	39.3	38.0	38.1	38.3	....	....	China, P.R.: Mainland	924
26.4	28.6	26.7	27.4	27.2	28.5	27.6	31.9	34.8	32.1	34.5	29.0	25.0	27.6	25.8	China, P.R.: Hong Kong	532
16.0	14.8	13.4	17.3	14.7	13.3	14.4	13.5	13.6	11.4	11.3	16.0	12.0	....	....	Fiji	819
22.5	22.8	23.7	24.1	21.9	23.8	21.3	23.4	26.5	21.8	22.6	21.4	23.3	22.9	....	India	534
31.3	31.5	35.1	36.1	35.5	35.8	29.5	31.1	31.9	30.7	31.8	16.8	12.2	17.9	....	Indonesia	536
30.2	31.3	33.9	37.7	39.9	37.3	35.5	36.5	37.2	37.9	34.2	21.2	26.7	28.2	26.7	Korea	542
23.1	26.4	29.9	32.4	37.8	35.4	39.2	41.2	43.6	41.5	43.0	26.7	22.4	27.1	23.8	Malaysia	548
11.6	12.8	9.2	13.4	15.3	13.5	12.4	12.4	14.2	12.3	12.5	12.4	13.2	....	....	Myanmar	518
20.2	19.8	21.7	18.4	20.8	21.2	23.1	22.4	24.9	27.3	25.3	24.8	20.5	23.4	23.0	Nepal	558
19.1	18.0	19.0	19.0	19.0	20.2	20.8	19.5	18.5	19.0	17.9	17.7	15.6	15.6	14.7	Pakistan	564
20.0	27.2	23.2	24.4	27.4	23.3	17.6	21.4	22.1	22.7	21.1	17.9	16.4	....	....	Papua New Guinea	853
17.5	18.7	21.6	24.2	20.2	21.3	24.0	24.1	22.5	24.0	24.8	20.3	18.8	17.8	17.6	Philippines	566
37.9	34.2	35.0	36.6	34.8	36.4	37.8	33.5	34.7	37.1	38.6	33.3	31.9	31.6	24.3	Singapore	576
23.1	37.1	....	....	....	....	....	....	....	....	....	....	....	....	....	Solomon Islands	813
23.3	22.8	21.7	22.2	22.9	24.3	25.6	27.0	25.7	24.2	24.4	25.1	27.3	28.0	22.0	Sri Lanka	524
27.9	32.6	35.1	41.4	42.8	40.0	40.0	40.3	42.1	41.8	33.7	20.4	20.5	22.7	24.0	Thailand	578
33.3	29.5	37.1	43.2	28.3	28.6	27.8	28.8	32.7	....	....	....	....	....	....	Vanuatu	846

Gross Capital Formation as Percentage of GDP

93e r

		1972	1973	1974	1975	1976	1977	1978	1979	1980	1981	1982	1983	1984	1985	1986
																Percentages
Europe	170	31.8	35.5	38.9	36.7	36.5	34.1	37.2	33.1	30.8	25.9	30.0	28.3	28.9	28.9	30.6
Armenia	911	....	....	....	....	....	....	....	....	....	....	....	....	....	....	....
Belarus	913	....	....	....	....	....	....	....	....	....	....	....	....	....	....	....
Bulgaria	918	....	....	....	....	....	....	....	....	....	....	....	....	....	....	....
Cyprus	423	23.6	30.2	26.3	22.5	26.6	34.9	37.2	32.1	34.0	35.5	34.1	32.9	33.2	31.6	35.9
Czech Republic	935	....	....	....	....	....	....	....	38.7	37.8	33.8	31.7	30.1	33.6	30.3	25.9
Czechoslovakia	934	24.8	26.3	28.4	28.9	29.0	25.2	24.9	24.6	21.2	19.6	19.7	18.8	19.0	15.1	16.2
Estonia	939	....	....	....	....	....	....	....	....	....	....	....	....	....	....	....
Hungary	944	33.4	33.4	40.6	37.8	35.9	37.2	41.3	34.0	30.7	29.7	28.5	26.5	25.7	25.0	27.0
Kazakhstan	916	....	....	....	....	....	....	....	....	....	....	....	....	....	....	....
Kyrgyz Republic	917	....	....	....	....	....	....	....	....	....	....	....	....	....	....	....
Macedonia, FYR	962	....	....	....	....	....	....	....	....	....	....	....	....	....	....	....
Malta	181	25.0	22.1	27.1	23.5	27.5	26.0	23.5	25.5	24.6	27.1	31.5	30.0	28.9	28.1	25.5
Moldova	921	....	....	....	....	....	....	....	....	....	....	....	....	....	....	....
Poland	964	31.7	36.3	38.7	36.7	36.9	33.3	31.8	29.0	26.4	18.5	28.0	25.0	26.3	27.7	28.9
Romania	968	....	....	....	....	....	....	....	....	39.8	36.3	33.7	34.0	34.2	33.0	34.4
Russia	922	....	....	....	....	....	....	....	....	....	....	....	....	....	....	....
Slovak Republic	936	....	....	....	....	....	....	....	....	....	....	....	....	....	....	....
Slovenia	961	....	....	....	....	....	....	....	....	....	....	....	....	....	....	....
Turkey	186	....	....	....	....	....	....	....	....	....	....	....	....	....	....	....
Ukraine	926	....	....	....	....	....	....	....	....	....	....	....	....	....	....	....
Middle East	405	21.4	20.9	22.1	34.6	36.2	38.7	33.6	26.4	24.9	25.4	27.7	30.0	28.8	23.9	21.7
Egypt	469	13.7	13.7	17.4	27.2	25.2	29.1	31.0	30.4	28.0	30.4	28.9	31.5	29.7	29.3	29.4
Iran, I.R. of	429	29.4	27.8	28.7	50.4	53.1	53.0	47.6	28.5	25.1	26.1	28.2	31.7	29.9	23.7	16.6
Iraq	433	19.0	22.1	28.1	30.3	22.2	24.5	20.1	28.8	30.5	63.0	57.7	14.9	18.1	23.7	19.0
Israel	436	31.3	25.8	35.7	31.3	27.3	24.4	27.0	27.1	22.4	21.1	23.5	23.3	21.7	19.4	19.1
Jordan	439	16.8	14.8	21.8	23.4	29.3	33.1	29.0	30.6	40.3	49.1	38.3	32.3	28.8	20.5	20.5
Kuwait	443	9.3	9.5	6.8	12.7	16.5	23.3	20.2	13.6	13.9	16.5	22.9	24.8	21.0	18.9	22.1
Libya	672	25.1	29.6	26.5	30.6	24.0	25.0	27.3	25.0	26.3	30.8	30.1	29.1	26.3	19.3	21.1
Oman	449	29.8	26.2	30.6	35.6	35.9	30.6	28.9	26.0	22.7	23.4	27.0	24.2	24.9	25.1	26.1
Qatar	453	....	....	....	....	....	....	....	....	17.0	17.7	27.5	21.9	16.6	17.8	18.5
Saudi Arabia	456	13.8	9.3	13.2	20.9	25.4	33.1	27.8	20.7	21.7	19.5	27.2	30.3	33.0	20.9	19.9
Syrian Arab Rep.	463	17.6	18.2	19.6	25.4	31.9	34.1	27.8	26.6	28.0	23.5	24.0	23.9	24.0	24.1	22.5
United Arab Emirates	466	27.3	25.4	15.4	30.6	33.3	39.2	38.8	34.5	28.3	26.3	28.6	31.3	28.9	25.2	30.2
Yemen, Republic of	474	....	....	....	....	....	....	....	....	....	....	....	....	....	....	....
Western Hemisphere	205	21.8	22.8	25.7	24.1	23.1	23.4	23.9	23.8	25.1	24.5	22.1	18.3	17.6	20.0	18.6
Antigua and Barbuda	311						20.6	19.3	24.3	34.8	41.9	39.4	20.4	23.6	27.8	35.7
Argentina	213	19.0	17.1	18.4	26.6	27.1	27.2	23.9	22.6	25.3	22.7	21.8	20.9	20.0	17.6	17.5
Bahamas, The	313	....	....	....	....	....	....	....	....	....	....	....	....	....	....	....
Barbados	316	....	....	24.0	20.0	27.0	21.8	25.8	23.5	22.1	26.0	21.4	19.9	16.2	15.4	16.0
Belize	339	....	24.5	25.0	28.1	31.7	29.7	28.6	28.7	22.6	26.6	22.5	18.9	20.3	17.4	17.4
Bolivia	218	19.8	20.7	16.4	24.4	21.2	20.8	24.7	20.8	14.6	13.3	12.5	12.2	10.6	16.9	13.6
Brazil	223	27.7	28.5	33.7	25.7	23.0	22.0	23.0	22.8	23.2	23.2	21.5	17.2	15.3	21.3	19.1
Chile	228	12.2	7.9	21.2	13.1	12.8	14.4	17.8	17.8	21.0	22.7	11.3	9.8	15.3	21.3	19.1
Colombia	233	18.4	18.1	21.5	17.0	17.6	18.8	18.3	18.2	19.1	20.6	20.5	19.9	13.6	17.2	18.9
Costa Rica	238	22.0	24.0	26.7	21.6	23.7	24.3	23.5	25.3	26.6	29.0	24.7	24.2	19.0	19.0	18.0
Dominica	321	....	....	18.8	22.3	26.5	21.9	23.0	43.5	55.2	33.9	30.9	28.1	22.7	25.9	25.2
Dominican Republic	243	19.7	22.1	23.5	24.5	22.3	21.8	23.9	25.4	25.1	23.6	20.0	19.7	36.9	28.5	22.3
Ecuador	248	20.0	19.5	22.5	26.7	23.8	26.5	28.4	25.3	26.1	23.2	25.2	17.6	19.0	17.8	20.1
El Salvador	253	14.2	18.3	22.6	22.1	19.6	23.4	23.8	18.1	13.3	14.2	13.2	12.1	17.2	18.2	20.9
Grenada	328	....	....	....	6.5	13.2	15.6	8.4	15.8	27.7	44.3	44.7	40.2	12.0	10.8	13.3
Guatemala	258	12.1	13.7	18.6	16.1	21.4	20.0	21.6	18.7	15.9	17.0	14.1	11.1	29.7	26.5	30.0
Guyana	336	21.7	30.4	32.4	36.8	42.0	29.2	20.8	83.2	81.6	92.8	86.9	27.1	11.6	11.5	10.3
Haiti	263	9.5	8.8	15.2	16.3	16.0	15.8	16.9	16.8	17.9	17.7	16.7	16.4	22.9	20.9	26.4
Honduras	268	15.2	18.4	25.6	19.0	19.2	23.1	27.2	26.5	24.8	21.1	14.1	13.8	15.9	16.6	14.5
Jamaica	343	27.3	31.5	24.3	25.8	18.2	12.2	15.0	19.1	15.9	20.3	20.9	12.3	17.3	17.3	13.9
Mexico	273	20.3	21.4	23.2	23.7	22.3	22.8	23.6	26.0	29.6	27.5	22.7	20.8	23.1	24.3	16.9
Nicaragua	278	....	....	....	....	....	....	....	....	....	....	....	....	19.7	20.8	18.1
Panama	283	31.9	33.7	33.8	30.8	31.6	23.6	26.5	27.9	28.1	28.4	26.9	17.9	22.1	23.1	16.8
Paraguay	288	15.1	19.0	21.0	24.1	24.6	24.7	27.2	28.6	28.8	28.8	25.6	21.4	14.8	15.2	17.2
Peru	293	14.2	15.6	18.9	19.8	17.9	15.0	14.2	21.6	28.9	34.3	33.6	24.3	22.9	22.0	25.0
St. Lucia	362	....	....	....	46.1	43.0	40.0	48.6	50.0	49.5	47.5	31.9	23.7	20.2	18.5	20.2
St. Vincent & Grenadines	364	....	....	....	26.5	21.2	37.5	28.0	34.1	39.3	32.7	28.5	24.7	23.3		
Suriname	366	21.7	23.0	29.9	38.0	29.5	37.3	32.4	22.8	26.5	31.2	27.7	15.6	27.9	28.3	30.3
Trinidad and Tobago	369	31.3	26.0	21.8	27.3	24.6	26.7	30.2	29.1	30.6	27.6	28.3	26.5	11.8	14.4	22.0
Uruguay	298	11.8	12.6	11.5	13.5	14.8	15.2	16.0	17.3	17.3	15.4	14.4	14.3	22.1	18.8	21.6
Venezuela, Rep. Bol.	299	31.2	29.3	24.0	30.9	34.4	41.5	42.8	31.6	24.7	22.9	25.9	11.8	12.1	11.4	11.2
														18.1	19.1	20.8
Memorandum Items																
Oil Exporting Countries	999	23.4	24.1	22.2	32.5	34.6	37.0	33.9	26.5	24.6	26.4	27.4	27.2	26.0	23.5	22.8
Non-Oil Developing Countries	201	25.1	17.0	19.3	19.0	18.3	18.3	26.0	26.5	26.8	26.4	25.1	24.7	24.2	25.7	24.8

Gross Capital Formation as Percentage of GDP

Percentages

1987	1988	1989	1990	1991	1992	1993	1994	1995	1996	1997	1998	1999	2000	2001		
29.6	29.2	30.0	26.5	22.9	21.8	22.6	21.0	23.9	24.1	24.5	24.6	24.0	24.7	23.4	**Europe**	170
....	....	....	47.2	39.7	1.6	9.8	23.5	18.4	20.0	19.1	19.1	18.4	19.1	17.8	Armenia	911
....	....	....	....	....	31.8	41.0	32.9	24.8	23.5	26.8	26.7	23.7	25.4	22.2	Belarus	913
32.9	34.4	33.1	30.4	22.6	19.9	15.3	9.4	15.7	8.4	11.4	16.9	19.1	16.6	20.4	Bulgaria	918
25.5	27.5	30.9	27.0	25.8	28.7	24.0	25.4	21.9	21.8	18.8	18.3	17.4	....	....	Cyprus	423
29.3	27.4	26.8	25.2	23.0	26.3	27.4	29.8	34.0	34.2	32.6	30.0	28.1	29.7	30.0	Czech Republic	935
14.9	13.5	12.9	15.7	13.3	....	....	....								Czechoslovakia	934
....	....	....	....	24.4	26.7	26.7	27.4	26.6	27.8	31.0	29.3	24.5	24.6	26.7	Estonia	939
26.7	25.3	26.6	25.4	20.5	16.1	20.0	22.2	23.9	27.2	27.7	29.7	28.5	31.1	27.3	Hungary	944
....	....	....	45.1	26.2	31.8	20.9	26.8	22.5	16.9	16.3	16.6	17.1	17.1	26.2	Kazakhstan	916
....	....	....	....	15.4	19.9	11.7	9.0	18.3	26.2	21.7	15.4	18.0	....	....	Kyrgyz Republic	917
....	....	....	19.0	17.2	15.6	17.9	15.5	20.8	20.1	22.4	23.0	21.0	....	....	Macedonia, FYR	962
27.5	28.8	29.6	33.4	31.6	27.5	29.8	30.7	32.0	28.6	25.6	23.7	24.0	28.3	20.4	Malta	181
....	....	....	....	29.0	59.8	55.8	28.8	24.9	24.2	23.8	25.9	22.9	23.9	20.1	Moldova	921
28.8	32.6	38.5	25.6	19.9	15.2	15.6	17.6	19.7	21.9	24.6	26.2	26.4	26.1	21.7	Poland	964
31.8	28.4	26.8	30.2	28.0	31.4	28.9	24.8	24.3	25.9	20.6	17.7	16.1	19.7	21.9	Romania	968
....	....	....	....	....	34.6	27.0	25.5	25.4	24.6	22.8	15.4	14.7	18.6	22.1	Russia	922
....	....	....	....	33.1	28.3	26.5	22.4	27.3	37.1	36.6	36.1	31.9	27.1	32.0	Slovak Republic	936
....	....	....	....	....	....	....	....	....	....	....	....	28.1	....	....	Slovenia	961
25.8	25.8	24.2	24.3	22.7	23.9	27.6	21.5	25.5	24.6	25.1	24.2	23.4	24.1	....	Turkey	186
....	....	....	....	....	....	34.5	36.3	35.3	26.7	22.7	21.4	20.8	19.8	....	Ukraine	926
17.4	21.0	22.6	27.0	27.5	26.4	24.1	20.3	22.3	23.5	24.4	25.1	24.6	22.3	....	**Middle East**	405
26.1	33.2	31.3	28.8	20.9	18.2	16.2	16.6	17.2	16.6	21.7	25.6	25.5	23.9	....	Egypt	469
9.0	14.9	22.5	38.8	43.4	40.7	31.0	19.4	26.7	33.9	34.6	29.9	31.3	27.9	....	Iran, I.R. of	429
19.7	20.9	19.0	22.5	19.1	14.6	15.5	....								Iraq	433
19.6	18.4	17.3	25.1	25.4	24.9	25.2	24.1	26.8	26.0	24.5	22.2	24.2	22.1	20.1	Israel	436
23.3	23.5	23.7	31.9	25.7	33.1	36.2	33.0	32.6	30.1	25.5	21.7	19.0	20.3	....	Jordan	439
17.6	15.7	12.3	15.9	39.3	19.9	17.2	16.2	15.1	15.3	13.9	20.6	15.0	7.5	8.6	Kuwait	443
17.2	18.7	17.1	18.6	13.1	12.2	16.3	16.3	12.2	15.5	12.4	12.0	11.2	13.3	....	Libya	672
15.6	15.2	14.1	12.3	15.0	16.4	17.5	15.7	15.0	13.7	17.6	24.0	14.9	12.0	....	Oman	449
14.4	16.0	15.3	18.0	19.1	20.6	19.8	24.5	35.1	35.8	31.7	....	....	....	....	Qatar	453
19.0	20.9	21.6	19.5	21.2	22.2	24.2	20.1	20.7	18.1	18.3	22.4	21.1	18.7	18.9	Saudi Arabia	456
18.2	14.0	16.2	16.5	18.0	23.2	26.0	30.0	27.2	23.6	20.9	20.6	18.8	17.4	....	Syrian Arab Rep.	463
24.0	25.0	23.6	20.5	21.9	24.2	29.3	29.4	28.5	26.4	28.1	30.1	....	....	....	United Arab Emirates	466
....	....	....	....	15.0	16.5	23.0	20.8	21.5	21.6	22.2	21.0	29.3	21.0	....	Yemen, Republic of	474
20.9	22.6	23.5	20.0	20.5	20.9	20.9	21.5	21.3	21.3	22.8	22.4	20.4	20.9	19.3	**Western Hemisphere**	205
45.8	39.8	41.2	32.4	37.6	34.8	31.7	32.4	36.9	39.7	41.3	....	....	....	....	Antigua and Barbuda	311
19.6	18.6	15.5	14.0	14.6	16.7	19.7	20.0	18.5	19.6	20.9	21.0	17.9	17.5	15.7	Argentina	213
....	....	25.1	21.8	22.6	23.2	19.6	21.2	23.2	....						Bahamas, The	313
16.0	17.5	19.1	18.8	17.1	9.5	12.7	13.3	14.1	12.7	15.3	....	....	....	....	Barbados	316
22.8	25.4	30.3	26.3	31.5	29.1	30.2	24.1	20.9	23.1	25.0	27.3	32.6	35.6	34.1	Belize	339
13.5	14.0	11.6	12.5	15.6	16.7	16.6	14.4	15.2	16.2	19.6	23.6	18.8	17.2	13.0	Bolivia	218
22.2	22.7	28.6	20.2	19.8	18.9	20.8	22.1	22.3	20.9	21.5	21.1	20.3	21.7	21.0	Brazil	223
22.2	22.8	25.1	25.1	22.6	23.8	26.5	24.1	25.8	27.4	27.7	26.9	21.3	22.5	20.7	Chile	228
20.0	22.0	20.0	18.5	16.0	17.2	21.2	25.5	25.7	22.1	20.8	19.6	12.8	13.2	....	Colombia	233
27.1	24.5	26.6	27.3	17.9	20.2	20.9	20.0	18.2	16.0	18.1	20.5	17.1	16.6	18.2	Costa Rica	238
23.2	31.1	42.8	41.9	32.7	29.5	26.8	26.9	33.1	30.3	32.9	....	....	....	....	Dominica	321
24.3	23.2	25.8	23.3	18.5	20.5	23.9	21.4	19.5	18.9	19.8	23.4	24.2	23.8	....	Dominican Republic	243
22.7	21.5	20.7	17.5	22.2	21.2	21.1	19.0	18.7	17.3	20.2	24.7	12.9	16.8	....	Ecuador	248
12.4	12.8	15.3	13.9	15.4	18.5	18.6	19.7	20.0	15.2	15.1	17.6	16.4	16.9	16.0	El Salvador	253
33.2	33.7	34.1	38.1	41.1	31.2	33.1	37.8	33.7	36.8	38.2	37.8	41.4	....	....	Grenada	328
13.9	13.7	13.5	13.6	14.3	18.3	17.2	15.7	15.1	12.7	13.7	17.4	17.4	17.9	16.9	Guatemala	258
37.2	21.5	34.2	42.3	35.3	53.7	....	....								Guyana	336
14.3	13.5	14.3	14.3	....											Haiti	263
17.4	21.0	19.1	23.0	24.7	26.0	33.6	37.6	31.6	31.1	32.2	30.9	34.6	30.9	30.1	Honduras	268
20.6	23.6	26.6	25.9	24.2	28.5	29.2	27.7	29.3	29.7	29.8	26.7	25.1	27.6	30.1	Jamaica	343
19.2	23.9	24.6	24.6	25.2	25.3	21.0	21.7	19.8	23.1	25.8	24.4	23.5	23.6	20.7	Mexico	273
15.8	26.8	27.2	20.5	20.8	20.9	19.5	22.8	24.9	27.0	31.7	33.8	43.3	34.4	....	Nicaragua	278
18.4	7.5	6.2	16.8	19.2	23.7	24.7	26.8	30.3	30.5	31.1	32.1	33.1	28.7	....	Panama	283
25.1	24.4	23.8	22.9	24.8	22.9	22.9	23.4	23.9	23.4	23.6	22.9	23.0	21.8	18.8	Paraguay	288
21.1	22.1	18.1	16.5	17.3	17.3	19.3	22.2	24.8	22.8	....	23.6	21.5	20.1	18.4	Peru	293
....	....	....	....	....	....	....	....	....	....	....	....	....	....	....	St. Lucia	362
35.2	33.5	31.4	31.0	30.8	26.5	28.4	31.1	33.0	31.2	....	....	....	....	....	St. Vincent & Grenadines	364
26.0	16.7	20.8	20.8	22.1	22.8	23.9	43.2	51.8	38.8	35.0	....	....	....	....	Suriname	366
19.3	13.0	16.6	13.8	16.3	13.8	14.4	20.2	15.9	17.0	26.8	26.4	....	....	....	Trinidad and Tobago	369
14.3	13.6	12.1	12.2	15.1	15.4	15.6	15.9	15.4	15.2	15.2	15.9	15.1	14.0	13.4	Uruguay	298
25.2	27.9	12.9	10.2	18.7	23.7	18.8	14.2	18.1	16.6	21.0	21.9	18.1	17.2	....	Venezuela, Rep. Bol.	299

Memorandum Items

1987	1988	1989	1990	1991	1992	1993	1994	1995	1996	1997	1998	1999	2000	2001		
21.3	23.8	24.9	27.7	29.8	29.6	25.4	23.4	25.0	24.8	25.6	20.8	18.5	18.9	....	Oil Exporting Countries	999
25.1	26.8	27.7	26.7	26.0	26.3	27.6	27.7	28.3	27.4	27.3	25.7	25.4	26.0	....	Non-Oil Developing Countries	201

Final Consumption Expenditure as Percentage of GDP

96f r

		1972	1973	1974	1975	1976	1977	1978	1979	1980	1981	1982	1983	1984	1985	1986
																Percentages
World	001	73.4	74.4	75.1	77.3	76.6	76.5	75.8	75.6	76.2	76.8	77.8	77.8	77.2	77.2	77.7
Industrial Countries	110	75.6	74.5	75.6	77.7	77.2	77.0	76.3	76.3	77.2	77.3	78.6	79.0	78.1	78.4	78.6
United States	111	80.7	79.2	80.1	81.4	80.6	80.1	78.9	78.5	80.0	78.9	81.7	82.5	81.2	82.3	83.1
Canada	156	76.6	74.5	73.4	76.3	75.7	76.6	76.5	74.5	74.8	74.4	77.2	77.9	76.6	77.4	78.6
Australia	193	72.3	71.2	72.5	76.0	76.2	76.9	77.9	75.1	76.2	76.3	78.0	80.1	77.4	77.7	78.9
Japan	158	62.2	61.9	63.4	67.2	67.4	67.5	67.4	68.4	68.5	67.9	69.2	70.1	69.1	68.3	68.1
New Zealand	196	73.2	72.4	75.8	75.7	71.6	76.9	77.9	77.6	79.6	77.5	78.3	76.3	76.0	77.8	75.0
Euro Area	163															
Austria	122	68.8	68.8	69.2	73.4	74.3	74.4	73.3	73.1	73.3	74.6	75.7	77.0	76.4	76.5	76.2
Belgium	124	75.2	75.6	75.1	78.2	78.0	79.3	79.6	81.0	78.9	81.7	82.2	82.4	81.2	81.5	80.5
Finland	172	71.7	70.0	68.3	71.3	73.0	73.7	73.6	71.9	71.3	71.6	72.7	73.2	72.2	73.4	73.9
France	132	72.6	71.9	72.9	75.3	75.3	75.4	75.8	76.2	77.3	79.4	80.3	80.3	80.5	80.7	79.7
Germany	134	72.1	71.8	73.5	77.2	76.4	76.8	76.3	76.0	77.2	78.3	78.3	77.7	77.3	76.8	75.2
Greece	174	77.8	74.9	81.5	82.7	80.8	81.8	81.1	79.7	80.9	85.4	85.7	85.5	84.2	85.9	86.8
Ireland	178	80.3	79.1	85.5	82.7	82.6	81.2	80.9	83.4	85.7	85.8	79.6	79.2	77.7	78.3	79.4
Italy	136	76.3	75.8	75.0	77.2	75.3	75.5	75.3	76.0	77.2	78.5	76.8	76.6	76.6	76.9	76.7
Luxembourg	137	65.3	60.2	57.6	72.7	71.3	75.4	73.6	73.8	75.4	78.3	76.7	75.4	73.5	66.5	64.6
Netherlands	138	73.2	72.3	73.0	76.0	76.0	73.1	74.1	74.9	74.8	74.0	73.9	73.5	71.8	72.2	71.9
Portugal	182	76.7	77.6	86.8	92.1	88.7	86.6	82.8	81.3	82.5	82.8	83.2	85.6	88.4	86.6	82.6
Spain	184	74.0	73.7	74.7	75.4	77.6	77.1	76.4	77.4	79.1	80.2	79.7	79.4	78.2	78.8	77.9
Denmark	128	73.3	74.6	76.5	78.7	79.3	79.3	79.1	79.9	81.0	82.4	81.6	80.1	78.4	77.8	76.9
Iceland	176	75.0	71.9	75.8	75.0	72.4	72.3	73.0	74.2	73.7	75.7	77.8	77.8	79.2	81.4	79.4
Norway	142	68.7	67.7	66.5	68.6	69.7	71.2	69.9	69.1	65.5	65.5	66.5	66.4	64.3	66.1	71.7
Sweden	144	75.7	75.4	76.5	75.4	77.5	80.8	81.5	81.1	80.8	82.2	83.0	80.7	78.7	78.8	78.6
Switzerland	146	69.1	69.8	70.7	74.2	76.0	76.7	75.9	76.6	74.8	74.5	75.4	76.6	74.9	74.5	73.9
United Kingdom	112	80.2	79.8	82.8	83.1	81.8	79.4	79.0	79.3	80.4	81.8	81.7	81.9	81.7	80.8	82.7
Developing Countries	200	67.5	74.1	73.8	76.4	75.2	75.4	75.0	74.3	74.4	75.9	76.3	75.8	75.2	75.2	76.4
Africa	605	74.9	74.2	70.0	75.6	75.0	75.3	77.9	74.8	75.0	77.8	79.1	79.3	79.4	79.2	81.4
Algeria	612	68.0	69.3	57.0	64.0	61.0	64.4	62.5	59.2	56.9	59.3	60.8	60.3	62.6	63.6	70.6
Benin	638	90.7	91.6	83.4	97.0	99.1	103.6	105.7	100.3	98.4	113.4	93.0	99.3	94.6	92.1	96.2
Botswana	616	72.2	72.6	73.0	78.3	79.1	86.3	87.1	77.8	72.3	75.8	84.0	75.0	70.3	67.1	59.2
Burkina Faso	748	99.4	98.3	91.8	99.2	93.8	101.9	101.9	95.6	102.5	104.8	107.8	106.7	98.6	98.1	98.4
Burundi	618	100.2	97.0	101.7	96.9	93.9	88.2	94.0	95.5	98.0	95.9	97.9	95.2	94.3	93.6	91.3
Cameroon	622	86.7	85.1	76.6	82.1	84.6	79.4	76.0	81.4	82.7	76.9	79.6	75.1	72.4	72.2	72.6
Central African Rep.	626	94.4	92.1	91.5	92.7	88.0	87.8			. . . .	80.0	. . . .	. . . .	. . . .	115.8	114.7
Congo, Dem. Rep. of.	636	56.4	55.1	51.7	64.1	73.7	72.0	69.4	60.3	82.5	80.0					
Congo, Rep. of	634	103.4	90.5	83.3	102.6	105.0	101.5	82.4	69.5	58.6	54.2	53.0	54.7	53.6	58.0	84.4
Côte d'Ivoire	662	77.4	77.0	72.6	77.4	71.1	64.2	71.1	75.1	79.6	81.2	79.7	80.7	74.8	72.7	78.6
Ethiopia	644	89.1	86.6	87.0	93.4	91.3	94.2	98.1	96.6	96.3	92.4	94.1	94.5	91.9	97.2	91.4
Gabon	646	51.2	61.3	34.0	35.7	27.0	41.6	50.1	45.1	39.4	41.0	43.0	46.1	51.5	51.2	54.5
Ghana	652	87.1	85.7	89.2	86.4	91.5	90.0	94.6	93.4	95.1	96.1	96.3	96.7	93.4	92.4	92.3
Guinea-Bissau	654															106.5
Kenya	664	84.0	86.4	85.7	97.6	89.9	82.9	92.6	95.7	96.0	94.4	98.9	95.7	99.2	75.4	78.2
Liberia	668	57.1	61.3	61.2	54.3	58.7	68.4	70.0	67.3	66.8	85.8	78.7	81.5	81.5	80.1	75.5
Madagascar	674	89.4	86.6	90.3	91.5	88.5	88.8	90.9	92.0	93.3	93.0	95.2	93.3	96.0	99.7	94.4
Malawi	676	87.8	87.6	83.6	83.0	82.2	79.9	79.5	79.8	82.1	82.5	82.7	80.4	85.2	87.1	89.9
Mali	678					79.5	77.4	83.7	86.6	86.2	92.6	99.1	94.4	96.5	108.3	102.2
Mauritania	682	68.5	74.9	74.3	81.1	86.9	92.0	107.5	102.6	100.2	115.2	104.6	98.4	94.1		
Mauritius	684	80.2	73.3	63.6	67.9	67.4	80.7	81.6	80.5	89.5	85.2	84.6	82.9	81.3	78.4	71.4
Morocco	686	87.5	85.8	78.8	84.4	89.9	84.5	86.6	87.1	87.1	89.1	86.7	86.7	87.8	85.2	86.8
Mozambique	688	. . . .	. . . .	. . . .	. . . .	. . . .	. . . .	. . . .	. . . .	100.0	100.0	102.5	105.3	100.0	95.5	95.9
Namibia	728														74.4	77.6
Niger	692	95.5	93.0	103.8	89.9	83.6	82.3	83.1	79.4	81.3	80.0	85.1	88.8	96.2	92.5	92.5
Nigeria	694	55.0	64.3	62.6	69.4	66.0	68.1	81.4	71.8	73.1	81.1	83.0	85.7	86.3	84.9	87.2
Rwanda	714	57.4	54.2	57.5	94.7	91.0	88.4	92.4	89.8	95.8	98.7	94.8	95.6	91.2	91.7	91.0
Senegal	722	89.0	93.1	85.9	89.4	93.3	93.1	97.9	97.7	105.0	109.1	102.5	101.9	99.3	102.9	95.8
Seychelles	718					77.1	64.0	57.9	73.0	72.9	84.8	96.7	101.0	91.8	92.8	92.9
Sierra Leone	724	89.7	86.8	86.5	94.3	96.7	94.3	93.6	94.8	99.1	97.6	96.8	96.7	89.1	99.6	85.4
South Africa	199	73.6	69.5	67.2	70.8	71.9	72.0	69.6	67.2	64.6	67.5	70.7	71.8	72.4	76.2	77.5
Swaziland	734	74.6	60.5	48.2	65.1	69.5	76.4	75.8	92.9	92.6	98.6	98.0	101.1	104.6	102.0	87.6
Tanzania	738	83.4	85.8	91.6	91.7	79.3	77.2	90.0	86.7	90.2	83.8	85.9	91.1	91.2	91.4	95.5
Togo	742	87.8	86.5	64.0	89.5	82.9	79.8	80.6	76.7	78.4	85.0	87.8	86.2	85.7	82.8	83.1
Tunisia	744	80.4	83.3	75.6	73.6	77.5	80.5	79.2	75.9	75.7	76.1	78.9	76.9	77.6	78.3	82.1
Uganda	746												105.2	103.6	103.1	98.2
Zambia	754	63.1	55.0	54.1	79.0	71.1	77.9	79.5	76.9	80.7	93.2	92.1	87.4	81.5	84.6	77.1
Zimbabwe	698	76.5	75.9	75.7	75.7	77.2	78.5	84.7	87.5	84.2	84.2	84.7	87.2	80.6	81.9	79.4
Asia	505	83.9	79.4	82.7	82.8	80.3	79.8	73.9	74.2	75.0	74.9	75.1	73.7	73.1	73.1	72.8
Bangladesh	513	. . . .	90.1	100.5	100.7	99.8	95.2	85.6	97.4	97.5	98.4	98.3	96.4	95.4	95.5	97.2
Bhutan	514									92.1	93.0	90.7	91.6	92.6	86.4	91.1
China, P.R.: Mainland	924								64.3	65.4	67.5	66.3	66.2	65.5	65.2	64.6
China, P.R.: Hong Kong	532	68.5	70.7	70.9	71.4	63.9	66.9	70.3	66.2	65.9	66.8	68.8	72.0	67.9	68.9	67.8
Fiji	819	83.6	89.8	86.3	80.0	83.2	78.4	81.7	77.9	74.4	78.9	79.8	85.8	81.5	82.8	77.0
India	534	85.1	78.4	85.7	82.7	80.5	81.1	81.5	81.2	82.6	80.8	80.5	80.5	80.3	78.6	79.6
Indonesia	536	83.6	81.5	75.6	79.1	77.9	76.5	72.6	72.6	70.8	66.7	72.3	71.0	70.3	70.2	72.8
Korea	542	83.1	77.1	79.6	81.8	76.8	73.4	71.5	72.5	76.4	76.4	75.2	71.8	69.6	69.4	65.9
Malaysia	548	79.8	70.7	71.3	76.2	67.7	68.6	67.8	62.2	67.1	71.2	71.4	67.9	64.5	67.3	67.9
Maldives	556									95.4	104.8	98.9	98.8	56.3	67.5	67.3
Myanmar	518	89.4	87.2	90.2	91.1	90.4	88.2	86.2	82.0	82.3	82.1	84.9	85.7	88.4	88.5	89.9
Nepal	558				90.0	88.3	86.5	87.1	88.4	88.9	89.1	90.1	91.4	90.1	86.6	89.4
Pakistan	564	87.3	86.5	90.4	92.6	89.2	89.2	91.2	92.9	92.2	90.7	91.7	91.5	92.3	93.7	89.1
Papua New Guinea	853	95.2	83.4	68.8	84.6	89.7	80.0	81.5	78.0	86.4	93.6	91.5	87.8	88.1	90.4	84.4
Philippines	566	80.6	75.3	76.5	76.1	74.1	75.8	76.0	75.8	73.4	73.2	74.7	72.6	76.1	81.2	81.0
Singapore	576	74.3	73.1	71.4	71.4	69.3	68.5	67.9	64.7	61.2	58.3	57.7	55.0	54.7	59.4	60.3
Solomon Islands	813	92.0												78.5	92.3	96.4
Sri Lanka	524	84.3	87.5	91.8	91.9	86.1	81.9	84.7	86.2	88.8	88.3	88.1	86.2	80.1	88.1	88.0
Thailand	578	80.1	76.8	77.4	80.0	79.6	78.0	75.7	77.1	77.7	78.0	76.7	78.0	76.8	75.7	74.1
Tonga	866	. . . .	. . . .	. . . .	101.9	109.9	103.0	108.3	112.7	95.2	112.2	111.1	118.0	. . . .	. . . .	. . . .
Vanuatu	846	. . . .	. . . .	. . . .	. . . .	. . . .	. . . .	. . . .	. . . .	. . . .	. . . .	. . . .	. . . .	89.8	89.8	94.1	95.3

Percentages

1987	1988	1989	1990	1991	1992	1993	1994	1995	1996	1997	1998	1999	2000	2001		96f r
77.3	76.8	76.3	76.5	77.6	77.4	77.5	76.8	76.6	76.6	76.2	76.9	77.3	76.7	....	World	001
78.9	78.1	77.6	77.8	78.7	79.2	79.5	79.0	78.8	78.7	78.1	78.3	78.7	78.9	79.9	Industrial Countries	110
83.7	83.5	82.9	83.6	84.1	83.9	83.8	83.0	82.9	82.4	81.5	81.4	82.1	82.8	84.4	United States	111
77.7	76.6	77.3	79.1	81.9	82.8	82.4	80.2	78.2	77.9	77.4	77.7	76.4	74.2	75.6	Canada	156
76.7	74.8	74.1	74.6	79.4	80.0	79.0	78.0	78.8	77.9	77.8	77.8	78.4	78.2	78.2	Australia	193
68.2	67.1	66.8	66.3	66.0	67.1	68.5	69.9	70.4	70.4	70.2	71.3	72.6	72.6	73.9	Japan	158
76.9	76.7	77.5	80.2	80.6	80.0	76.8	76.4	76.5	76.9	78.1	80.0	80.1	78.1	75.4	New Zealand	196
....	....	....	76.0	77.5	78.2	78.8	78.0	77.5	78.0	77.3	76.3	76.8	77.0	77.4	Euro Area	163
76.1	75.9	75.3	74.5	74.0	75.1	76.4	76.4	76.6	77.5	77.0	76.6	76.8	76.4	76.7	Austria	122
79.9	77.2	75.9	75.7	76.9	76.4	76.2	75.7	75.6	76.4	75.3	75.4	75.0	75.2	76.0	Belgium	124
74.0	71.9	70.9	72.0	78.6	80.4	78.9	76.7	74.6	75.8	73.4	71.9	72.4	70.1	71.2	Finland	172
79.8	78.3	77.0	77.1	77.5	78.1	79.8	79.1	78.7	79.4	78.5	77.7	77.5	77.2	77.7	France	132
75.6	74.8	73.7	72.5	75.9	76.4	77.3	76.4	76.6	77.3	77.1	76.8	77.4	77.4	78.1	Germany	134
89.0	85.2	87.0	88.5	87.4	88.7	89.7	89.1	88.4	88.2	87.3	87.0	85.9	85.2	85.1	Greece	174
77.9	77.0	75.1	75.5	76.9	77.1	75.3	75.0	70.9	69.7	66.7	64.7	62.2	61.3	60.9	Ireland	178
77.4	77.4	77.8	77.7	78.3	79.3	78.4	78.0	76.6	76.4	77.1	77.3	78.2	78.7	78.7	Italy	136
65.9	63.1	59.3	60.1	72.8	70.2	68.3	66.1	65.5	66.8	63.6	61.9	58.7	56.1	58.7	Luxembourg	137
73.6	71.7	70.6	70.3	70.9	71.9	72.1	71.1	70.4	70.7	70.3	70.5	72.9	72.6	72.8	Netherlands	138
82.3	82.4	82.0	83.0	85.5	86.1	87.3	86.5	85.3	85.4	85.2	86.0	83.7	79.4	81.4	Portugal	182
78.3	77.5	78.1	78.0	78.6	80.1	80.7	79.7	78.8	78.5	78.1	80.1	76.7	76.6	76.0	Spain	184
76.7	76.5	75.8	74.6	75.0	75.3	76.8	77.1	76.2	76.1	75.7	76.3	75.1	72.4	72.5	Denmark	128
82.5	82.5	81.3	79.0	80.4	81.0	79.1	77.9	79.1	79.4	78.4	80.2	82.7	83.2	79.0	Iceland	176
71.6	71.3	70.0	70.2	70.5	72.4	71.8	71.4	70.3	68.6	67.4	71.2	69.7	62.7	63.2	Norway	142
78.9	78.2	77.5	78.3	80.5	81.8	83.1	79.4	76.5	77.4	77.1	77.0	76.9	76.7	76.5	Sweden	144
73.9	72.8	71.8	71.2	73.2	74.5	74.4	74.4	74.6	75.6	75.4	75.2	75.0	74.0	74.1	Switzerland	146
82.1	82.2	81.9	82.4	84.0	85.1	85.2	84.2	83.8	83.8	82.9	82.8	83.8	85.1	85.3	United Kingdom	112
74.6	74.8	74.4	74.5	75.9	74.6	74.3	73.5	73.3	73.3	73.2	74.8	75.0	73.3	....	Developing Countries	200
80.3	78.3	81.7	79.7	80.7	82.1	81.0	83.5	84.8	82.2	81.9	86.6	76.6	72.6	....	Africa	605
68.1	68.4	79.7	72.8	63.5	68.2	73.2	74.0	72.6	67.7	68.0	73.3	68.8	55.7	....	Algeria	612
95.9	95.4	94.4	93.6	95.3	96.1	96.9	90.0	88.9	90.5	90.5	89.6	88.1	87.0	....	Benin	638
66.1	62.0	49.4	55.4	59.1	61.4	64.5	62.4	63.7	61.4	56.5	57.5	62.8	60.9	....	Botswana	616
96.1	95.9	94.1	93.7	90.9	90.6	91.1	97.4	97.2	97.5	91.2	89.8	90.8	92.3	89.8	Burkina Faso	748
94.4	95.3	95.8	102.5	101.7	104.1	104.5	107.1	105.1	98.2	97.7	105.7	99.4	111.4	103.5	Burundi	618
78.7	43.6	81.5	81.8	75.1	84.4	82.4	73.9	76.0	75.7	73.5	....	....	....	....	Cameroon	622
98.1	96.8	94.4	96.1	95.9	97.1	94.9	89.9	90.6	....	....	....	....	....	....	Central African Rep.	626
....	—	100.0	100.0	93.6	90.5	96.0	90.8	85.9	....	....	....	....	....	....	Congo, Dem. Rep. of	636
77.1	81.2	72.9	73.0	78.7	80.3	81.2	71.3	61.3	54.9	65.0	91.5	60.5	32.2	36.2	Congo, Rep. of	634
83.9	81.9	82.2	76.9	90.7	91.2	90.3	77.2	79.7	75.8	73.4	....	....	....	....	Côte d'Ivoire	662
92.4	87.5	91.1	92.1	96.6	97.0	94.4	95.0	93.3	93.4	90.1	92.6	....	....	....	Ethiopia	644
63.9	62.4	58.4	58.8	57.7	63.5	63.0	53.2	57.0	50.7	54.5	69.3	....	....	....	Gabon	646
91.8	89.3	94.0	96.4	95.0	97.7	93.4	87.4	88.3	88.1	92.2	....	....	....	....	Ghana	652
102.8	112.6	114.0	105.7	107.1	101.1	101.5	104.7	98.9	112.3	103.1	....	....	....	....	Guinea-Bissau	654
80.8	80.3	82.7	80.9	80.0	83.0	77.6	77.6	84.1	83.7	88.5	90.3	88.6	94.4	....	Kenya	664
78.2	74.6	69.1	....	....	....	....	....	....	....	....	....	....	....	....	Liberia	668
95.8	93.5	90.4	94.5	100.3	97.1	97.8	96.7	96.6	93.7	96.4	95.1	93.1	94.3	90.5	Madagascar	674
87.0	90.8	95.3	90.6	91.9	101.5	101.5	107.3	102.3	107.1	99.5	91.9	101.1	95.7	....	Malawi	676
93.6	95.7	92.4	93.8	95.3	93.8	96.0	95.7	95.4	96.0	85.9	87.1	86.9	90.1	....	Mali	678
....	....	....	....	92.3	97.1	98.4	91.6	80.1	88.3	89.5	....	....	....	....	Mauritania	682
72.4	73.9	76.2	76.4	75.1	73.9	75.5	76.7	76.7	76.0	75.5	75.2	76.9	69.3	73.9	Mauritius	684
87.1	83.4	85.1	80.7	85.3	86.9	86.6	87.7	89.0	88.0	86.5	86.1	85.1	86.7	....	Morocco	686
93.1	94.6	94.6	90.8	113.3	116.6	114.0	110.4	108.7	102.0	99.3	93.9	91.0	....	....	Mozambique	688
95.8	82.3	84.9	82.4	90.8	87.9	90.6	83.3	86.8	88.0	90.9	89.1	89.4	84.8	....	Namibia	728
94.8	92.9	95.6	92.4	92.6	95.9	97.6	93.0	93.5	90.4	90.5	87.5	....	....	....	Niger	692
78.7	84.2	66.2	60.6	71.6	68.5	59.9	85.5	96.0	88.9	86.8	106.9	60.1	54.3	65.2	Nigeria	694
94.1	94.6	92.6	93.8	96.7	95.8	97.2	146.8	109.8	106.2	104.0	100.8	100.1	97.0	....	Rwanda	714
95.1	93.6	93.6	90.7	90.8	91.5	92.3	84.5	91.3	91.0	87.7	85.7	....	....	....	Senegal	722
91.5	86.8	87.0	84.9	84.5	84.7	80.5	75.3	76.4	77.1	77.3	80.1	....	....	....	Seychelles	718
81.0	79.8	85.4	91.8	92.3	90.6	95.4	91.8	95.0	91.7	98.3	94.6	96.0	96.0	....	Sierra Leone	724
79.0	78.6	78.5	82.4	83.1	83.9	82.4	82.1	80.9	81.7	82.4	82.5	81.4	80.9	80.4	South Africa	199
78.4	77.5	76.8	79.6	81.8	81.4	73.5	73.6	70.1	80.2	77.7	78.6	86.5	....	....	Swaziland	734
98.6	98.8	98.6	100.6	100.6	102.4	103.1	101.2	99.2	94.6	93.2	95.9	95.1	90.6	....	Tanzania	738
84.8	77.5	84.6	91.8	94.6	100.5	108.2	94.4	118.2	99.9	97.9	99.3	97.3	97.8	....	Togo	742
80.0	80.5	80.3	80.0	79.0	77.7	78.3	78.3	79.2	76.5	76.0	76.4	75.9	76.2	76.5	Tunisia	744
99.6	99.3	102.4	99.5	99.0	99.3	98.1	93.5	93.3	91.8	....	....	....	....	....	Uganda	746
82.0	81.3	96.2	82.2	85.5	93.6	87.0	84.6	74.7	68.3	73.7	....	....	....	....	Zambia	754
82.3	77.9	83.3	82.6	84.2	89.0	79.0	78.4	83.5	76.6	81.5	....	....	....	....	Zimbabwe	698
70.8	70.7	70.5	69.2	68.9	68.4	67.9	66.9	67.0	67.8	67.3	68.0	70.2	69.0	....	Asia	505
96.8	97.4	97.4	87.1	85.4	86.1	87.7	86.9	86.9	85.1	84.1	82.6	82.3	82.1	82.8	Bangladesh	513
83.0	82.5	77.0	72.0	76.2	77.8	66.4	62.3	57.9	65.0	75.4	77.3	75.0	72.6	....	Bhutan	514
63.2	63.7	64.1	62.0	61.8	61.7	58.5	57.4	57.5	58.5	58.2	58.1	61.0	....	....	China, P.R.: Mainland	924
63.7	62.6	61.8	64.2	66.2	66.2	65.4	66.9	69.5	69.3	68.9	69.9	69.6	67.7	68.9	China, P.R.: Hong Kong	532
82.9	90.0	90.0	90.8	94.0	90.0	88.5	79.8	79.4	78.6	79.0	82.2	75.1	....	....	Fiji	819
79.0	82.6	81.6	79.7	79.7	78.2	78.3	76.3	75.3	76.7	75.3	77.7	78.4	77.4	....	India	534
67.1	66.1	62.5	63.4	64.1	61.8	67.5	67.8	69.4	69.9	68.5	73.5	79.8	74.3	....	Indonesia	536
63.0	59.8	62.6	62.8	62.8	63.7	64.0	64.6	64.4	66.0	66.3	65.6	66.5	67.4	69.9	Korea	542
63.0	63.4	64.1	65.6	65.9	63.3	60.9	60.4	60.3	57.1	56.1	51.3	52.6	52.9	57.8	Malaysia	548
58.2	53.1	56.0	50.8	....	....	....	....	....	....	....	....	....	....	....	Maldives	556
92.0	88.9	91.2	88.3	86.0	87.2	88.6	88.3	86.6	88.5	88.2	88.2	87.0	....	....	Myanmar	518
88.5	90.1	88.6	92.1	90.4	89.2	86.4	85.3	85.2	86.2	86.0	86.2	86.4	85.3	85.8	Nepal	558
86.1	87.6	89.9	86.5	82.6	82.9	85.3	83.2	84.2	85.5	86.8	83.3	86.0	86.0	87.3	Pakistan	564
84.8	81.5	88.9	83.9	82.5	74.5	66.7	60.2	58.8	69.0	77.6	77.4	86.7	....	....	Papua New Guinea	853
79.0	78.9	79.7	81.3	83.4	85.1	86.2	85.1	85.5	85.4	85.8	87.6	85.7	83.5	82.5	Philippines	566
60.5	58.6	57.9	56.6	55.2	54.9	54.7	52.7	50.1	50.8	49.5	49.2	51.2	50.7	54.2	Singapore	576
99.5	105.9	112.7	....	....	....	....	....	....	....	....	....	....	....	....	Solomon Islands	813
87.2	88.0	87.8	85.7	87.2	85.0	84.0	84.8	84.7	84.7	82.7	80.9	80.5	82.5	....	Sri Lanka	524
71.4	66.8	65.0	66.0	64.2	64.7	64.7	63.7	63.1	64.0	64.7	65.2	67.5	67.5	68.6	Thailand	578
....	....	....	....	....	....	....	....	....	....	....	....	....	....	....	Tonga	866
91.4	93.5	94.3	91.2	84.4	81.9	77.7	76.9	73.9	....	....	....	....	....	....	Vanuatu	846

Final Consumption Expenditure as Percentage of GDP

		1972	1973	1974	1975	1976	1977	1978	1979	1980	1981	1982	1983	1984	1985	1986
																Percentages
Europe	170	**68.5**	**68.1**	**69.4**	**71.1**	**69.5**	**71.1**	**68.3**	**70.1**	**72.3**	**77.3**	**69.6**	**70.1**	**69.4**	**68.7**	**68.6**
Armenia	911	....	....	....	....	....	....	....	....	....	....	....	....	....	....	....
Belarus	913	....	....	....	....	....	....	....	....	....	....	....	....	....	....	....
Bulgaria	918	....	....	....	....	....	....	....	....	....	....	....	....	....	68.6	70.3
Cyprus	423	83.7	83.3	93.6	98.7	92.0	89.7	87.4	81.0	80.5	80.1	80.9	82.5	77.8	77.9	75.6
Czech Republic	935															
Czechoslovakia	934	72.1	73.1	72.5	72.1	73.6	76.5	76.2	75.2	60.3	77.6	76.9	77.7	77.0	62.8	63.6
Estonia	939	....	....	....	....	....	....	....	....	....	....	....	....	....	....	....
Hungary	944	67.0	65.8	68.7	69.7	68.2	67.3	67.9	69.3	71.5	71.4	70.7	71.6	71.1	72.9	74.5
Kazakhstan	916	....	....	....	....	....	....	....	....	....	....	....	....	....	....	....
Kyrgyz Republic	917	....	....	....	....	....	....	....	....	....	....	....	....	....	....	....
Macedonia, FYR	962	....	....	....	....	....	....	....	....	....	....	....	....	....	....	....
Malta	181	98.0	97.6	101.7	90.0	84.2	88.4	83.8	79.7	80.8	81.3	84.6	85.0	86.3	87.7	84.6
Moldova	921	....	....	....	....	....	....	....	....	....	....	....	....	....	....	....
Poland	964	68.2	68.3	68.8	70.9	69.4	71.7	71.5	73.7	76.1	83.6	70.9	73.6	72.6	70.8	70.2
Romania	968									63.0	66.0	64.4	60.3	60.5	60.2	59.3
Russia	922	....	....	....	....	....	....	....	....	....	....	....	....	....	....	....
Slovak Republic	936	....	....	....	....	....	....	....	....	....	....	....	....	....	....	....
Slovenia	961	....	....	....	....	....	....	....	....	....	....	....	....	....	....	....
Turkey	186	....	....	....	....	....	....	....	....	....	....	....	....	....	....	....
Ukraine	926	....	....	....	....	....	....	....	....	....	....	....	....	....	....	....
Middle East	405	**69.9**	**60.3**	**57.3**	**65.0**	**61.0**	**63.3**	**69.5**	**65.8**	**65.7**	**72.2**	**74.9**	**77.7**	**79.0**	**80.7**	**83.7**
Egypt	469	92.0	91.7	94.6	92.0	86.6	80.6	83.0	85.6	87.7	81.6	80.4	80.9	80.9	79.4	78.9
Iran, I.R. of	429	75.0	64.7	58.9	71.8	62.3	65.6	76.0	73.0	79.4	85.1	79.9	79.9	81.4	82.9	86.2
Iraq	433	....	....	....	75.1	74.7	81.0	58.3	40.5	38.0	68.2	82.2	93.0	85.8	80.9	90.6
Israel	436	86.5	98.6	97.8	102.6	103.3	96.6	99.4	97.0	92.8	96.3	95.8	94.3	92.7	94.3	93.8
Jordan	439	97.6	99.2	99.0	98.1	94.0	91.2	92.1	106.3	104.3	107.2	113.8	112.2	110.2	115.2	105.6
Kuwait	443	42.8	40.8	22.1	32.8	38.0	48.1	49.1	36.4	41.1	51.5	73.0	65.4	63.5	70.2	79.7
Libya	672	50.2	52.0	46.1	59.2	51.4	50.0	59.0	49.7	48.1	76.8	67.9	66.9	74.1	66.3	71.0
Oman	449	54.5	61.2	43.4	47.5	47.8	54.4	61.5	53.7	52.6	50.1	57.7	61.4	63.1	62.7	75.4
Qatar	453									35.3	43.0	47.5	59.2	59.8	60.3	75.1
Saudi Arabia	456	32.6	19.8	24.3	32.1	36.8	45.1	56.3	46.6	37.8	48.6	67.0	74.9	79.8	87.0	90.9
Syrian Arab Rep.	463	88.0	85.5	90.1	87.1	82.8	86.5	88.5	90.2	89.2	93.8	87.4	88.8	85.7	89.4	88.5
United Arab Emirates	466	27.3	24.6	15.8	24.1	24.1	30.0	34.2	31.0	28.2	38.3	43.4	45.2	44.4	48.2	62.0
Yemen Republic	474	....	....	....	....	....	....	....	....	....	....	....	....	....	....	....
Western Hemisphere	205	**78.8**	**76.0**	**75.1**	**76.7**	**77.6**	**77.2**	**77.6**	**77.5**	**76.8**	**77.4**	**78.2**	**78.4**	**78.7**	**76.2**	**78.8**
Antigua and Barbuda	311	....	....	....	....	....	84.3	77.2	69.4	84.6	80.4	99.9	94.7	86.7	89.8	86.0
Argentina	213	76.2	80.0	79.6	74.1	68.5	69.7	72.2	77.2	76.2	77.8	75.7	75.8	77.2	76.9	80.7
Bahamas, The	313	....	72.6	78.1	73.3	73.8	66.0	63.2	58.9	57.8	56.7	62.1	68.8	69.2	64.2	63.5
Barbados	316	95.6	96.4	90.6	85.9	91.3	102.7	98.8	87.1	77.4	81.7	80.0	78.9	79.0	76.7	81.7
Belize	339	....	83.0	75.0	73.8	86.8	86.7	82.6	84.5	89.1	103.1	101.8	95.7	84.2	91.2	82.2
Bolivia	218	82.9	80.2	77.1	81.2	81.1	82.0	82.7	82.4	79.9	80.0	77.5	77.7	84.4	70.9	91.1
Brazil	223	75.0	69.8	71.7	73.8	79.0	78.5	78.4	80.6	78.5	77.7	81.0	83.2	82.3	75.3	78.2
Chile	228	91.3	93.9	78.2	88.9	82.9	87.4	85.5	85.0	83.2	87.6	90.6	87.5	87.4	80.4	78.1
Colombia	233	81.4	79.5	79.6	81.2	79.3	77.6	78.9	80.1	80.3	82.9	83.8	82.9	81.6	79.7	75.2
Costa Rica	238	84.3	82.1	88.2	86.8	82.3	81.2	84.4	85.0	83.8	75.9	72.4	76.6	76.9	75.9	73.9
Dominica	321	....	....	102.7	97.4	91.9	97.9	99.2	127.8	119.7	110.2	97.4	91.4	95.9	94.9	83.6
Dominican Republic	243	81.9	80.1	82.9	75.5	81.9	82.4	83.0	81.0	84.6	80.6	84.9	86.4	86.4	87.1	83.8
Ecuador	248	83.6	77.3	72.4	79.7	77.6	76.5	77.2	74.1	74.1	75.8	77.1	78.4	76.3	75.9	79.0
El Salvador	253	84.9	84.7	85.6	84.5	81.7	75.9	85.4	82.1	85.8	92.7	92.5	93.4	94.8	96.7	91.1
Grenada	328	....	86.7	89.2	94.1	91.1	94.0	103.4	102.1	100.4	92.1	101.2	94.8	99.1	96.2	76.0
Guatemala	258	87.5	85.6	84.7	85.7	84.6	81.8	84.2	85.8	86.9	89.5	89.8	90.5	90.6	90.1	88.2
Guyana	336	80.3	90.5	73.9	68.7	86.7	89.7	80.6	87.3	95.9	106.8	88.3	93.3	103.5	90.2	84.5
Haiti	263	102.8	96.3	92.1	92.4	93.3	93.8	92.7	93.7	98.8	106.4	97.7	96.5	90.0	94.2	93.6
Honduras	268	84.1	82.7	86.2	90.4	85.8	81.8	77.8	78.3	83.0	85.0	87.3	89.2	88.9	87.4	87.9
Jamaica	343	81.0	78.1	85.9	84.6	90.8	89.4	83.9	82.3	86.2	90.0	90.7	89.8	83.6	85.5	80.1
Mexico	273	80.4	79.7	79.0	79.0	79.1	77.1	77.0	75.3	75.1	75.0	72.3	69.7	72.5	74.1	78.0
Nicaragua	278	81.3	85.8	82.3	88.0	80.3	79.1	83.6	92.1	102.5	96.1	91.5	88.3	90.9	84.0	91.3
Panama	283	73.4	70.6	76.1	76.3	75.3	79.7	77.7	80.2	71.1	69.7	64.6	73.9	81.5	75.7	73.1
Paraguay	288	85.0	80.3	80.7	80.4	78.7	78.3	76.5	76.9	77.5	78.0	82.0	85.6	83.3	82.2	80.5
Peru	293	84.3	85.0	86.0	90.1	87.8	88.6	82.2	66.8	68.2	69.5	69.5	75.5	77.4	75.3	81.1
St. Kitts and Nevis	361	....	119.0	105.4	93.4	85.5	78.3	84.2	89.5	92.0	97.3	96.8	105.4	97.8	92.2	89.4
St. Lucia	362	....	....	....	97.2	88.8	67.2	73.9	76.7	65.7	69.9	74.3	67.0	68.2		
St. Vincent & Grenadines	364	....	....	....	103.7	100.4	109.3	96.4	110.7	111.7	99.3	101.8	99.5	86.0	77.5	76.7
Suriname	366	72.8	73.8	69.1	68.8	70.7	69.5	69.9	77.5	78.9	82.8	87.7	99.1	93.6	88.7	78.2
Trinidad and Tobago	369	75.3	68.3	53.7	54.9	59.7	60.7	65.4	65.2	57.9	62.7	78.9	82.8	77.4	77.1	85.5
Uruguay	298	87.8	86.2	91.1	90.1	86.0	87.7	86.5	87.2	88.3	88.6	88.7	83.7	82.7	83.0	82.9
Venezuela, Rep. Bol.	299	65.5	61.1	51.3	61.2	64.2	66.2	70.3	66.5	67.1	71.2	77.2	77.4	73.8	74.8	79.6
Memorandum Items																
Oil Exporting Countries	999	**65.2**	**59.5**	**53.5**	**62.2**	**59.7**	**62.5**	**67.3**	**62.5**	**62.1**	**67.4**	**71.8**	**72.8**	**73.6**	**74.7**	**79.0**
Non-Oil Developing Countries	201	**94.1**	**61.3**	**62.3**	**63.1**	**62.4**	**62.0**	**76.5**	**76.9**	**77.2**	**77.8**	**77.3**	**76.5**	**76.2**	**75.4**	**75.8**

Final Consumption Expenditure as Percentage of GDP

Percentages

1987	1988	1989	1990	1991	1992	1993	1994	1995	1996	1997	1998	1999	2000	2001		
68.2	76.9	77.4	82.9	86.1	79.1	82.2	81.0	79.8	79.7	80.2	81.0	83.2	82.3	82.4	**Europe**	170
....	....	....	66.9	75.9	112.2	110.6	105.8	117.5	111.7	114.7	111.2	108.3	107.4	104.8	Armenia	911
....	....	....	....	....	66.8	74.7	79.9	79.6	80.6	77.4	77.7	78.1	76.4	84.5	Belarus	913
69.4	68.2	70.7	74.0	73.1	85.9	92.3	91.2	85.9	88.5	83.1	88.0	90.7	89.9	87.2	Bulgaria	918
76.1	77.4	75.5	77.3	84.0	81.5	75.7	74.2	79.8	83.0	84.8	86.8	83.8	....	....	Cyprus	423
68.7	68.4	69.4	72.1	69.9	72.8	71.8	72.9	70.7	72.2	73.4	71.2	73.2	73.7	72.8	Czech Republic	935
64.6	64.9	65.7	67.4	65.9	....	....	....	....	....	....	....	....	....	....	Czechoslovakia	934
....	....	....	....	67.8	71.0	79.1	84.9	84.8	85.5	90.2	81.6	81.6	80.1	77.9	Estonia	939
73.8	72.0	70.1	72.0	80.5	84.2	88.3	84.3	77.3	73.9	72.3	72.4	74.0	72.9	74.9	Hungary	944
....	....	....	76.8	91.6	82.6	88.3	82.6	81.9	83.9	86.4	88.2	80.7	73.8	76.2	Kazakhstan	916
....	....	....	....	85.9	92.1	96.0	97.3	94.5	104.8	86.2	106.1	96.8	....	....	Kyrgyz Republic	917
....	....	....	86.3	95.9	95.8	100.8	94.7	89.0	90.2	90.9	91.4	90.6	....	....	Macedonia, FYR	962
81.8	81.3	81.3	80.3	79.5	79.5	79.8	79.5	81.7	85.3	82.9	81.8	81.6	82.5	84.1	Malta	181
....	....	....	....	72.6	57.5	55.9	75.4	82.9	94.3	97.3	100.9	90.0	103.0	104.4	Moldova	921
68.9	65.3	57.3	67.2	82.0	83.3	83.5	80.2	77.9	79.7	79.8	79.0	80.0	80.8	82.0	Poland	964
61.2	62.1	70.4	79.2	75.9	77.0	76.0	77.3	81.3	82.6	86.4	90.3	88.8	86.0	86.2	Romania	968
....	....	....	....	....	48.3	62.2	69.1	71.1	72.0	76.3	77.2	68.8	61.6	65.2	Russia	922
....	....	....	....	67.6	75.7	78.7	72.8	70.9	74.4	73.2	74.8	73.5	72.0	76.6	Slovak Republic	936
....	....	....	70.6	73.8	75.5	79.6	76.9	78.7	77.6	76.7	75.9	76.0	75.8	74.9	Slovenia	961
76.4	73.0	77.4	79.5	81.3	80.0	82.1	81.6	81.1	78.8	80.3	81.9	87.4	85.2	....	Turkey	186
....	....	....	....	....	63.6	64.0	67.8	76.4	79.9	81.6	81.5	79.1	....	....	Ukraine	926
83.8	85.5	82.0	76.9	83.6	74.8	77.4	74.0	74.6	73.9	74.9	78.4	74.6	70.0	....	**Middle East**	405
83.9	84.7	83.1	83.0	84.2	83.0	83.3	84.9	85.0	87.3	84.5	84.5	83.1	82.7	....	Egypt	469
82.2	85.9	83.6	72.2	65.1	58.9	67.8	60.6	65.3	61.4	67.2	71.3	65.5	59.7	....	Iran, I.R. of	429
83.1	85.3	81.9	76.8	83.5	86.9	86.2	....	....	....	....	....	....	....	....	Iraq	433
98.3	94.7	91.6	91.2	90.1	88.8	90.9	91.2	87.5	87.8	86.4	86.1	89.6	87.8	85.0	Israel	436
102.2	98.5	95.0	99.0	97.4	98.5	94.1	90.1	88.3	94.9	96.6	97.6	99.0	105.9	....	Jordan	439
67.0	79.7	76.7	97.2	294.3	93.9	79.3	75.0	74.2	71.4	72.6	86.8	78.3	64.8	74.0	Kuwait	443
87.8	88.1	85.4	72.8	83.8	82.7	87.0	82.7	81.1	79.7	82.7	89.6	82.2	66.6	....	Libya	672
66.2	76.2	71.1	68.0	76.7	74.5	77.5	76.0	76.5	72.3	70.9	83.5	74.0	60.2	....	Oman	449
76.4	74.7	71.0	60.7	67.0	63.9	68.8	64.4	63.9	60.3	49.4	....	....	....	....	Qatar	453
88.3	83.1	77.7	70.4	75.5	72.1	72.5	67.9	66.1	68.4	68.5	74.4	67.3	62.5	63.6	Saudi Arabia	456
95.1	95.3	83.8	83.1	89.7	88.2	87.1	82.4	79.7	82.7	80.5	79.8	80.9	75.6	....	Syrian Arab Rep.	463
59.3	65.8	61.9	54.1	58.2	62.1	62.2	63.1	64.4	61.4	63.1	69.9	....	....	....	United Arab Emirates	466
....	....	....	91.0	106.2	100.0	109.1	98.7	99.7	80.0	81.5	85.4	87.1	....	....	Yemen Republic	474
76.3	76.8	75.2	79.4	81.6	82.7	80.9	80.2	79.3	78.8	79.1	80.9	80.9	80.0	81.4	**Western Hemisphere**	205
78.0	71.7	68.5	65.6	63.0	62.4	62.8	66.1	71.8	74.8	69.6	66.6	63.0	67.2	....	Antigua and Barbuda	311
80.1	78.0	78.1	80.2	83.7	84.9	82.7	83.1	81.9	81.0	81.4	81.5	83.9	83.1	83.0	Argentina	213
63.6	58.0	83.7	80.1	89.1	83.1	83.9	84.0	83.4	....	....	....	....	....	....	Bahamas, The	313
83.4	82.0	80.9	83.8	85.6	82.4	81.6	77.0	81.7	80.3	83.6	82.9	85.0	....	....	Barbados	316
83.2	80.7	80.7	74.8	79.7	80.1	81.2	82.4	81.1	79.4	83.5	84.9	80.5	87.7	88.1	Belize	339
94.4	90.4	89.1	88.6	89.9	92.3	92.7	91.2	89.4	88.5	88.6	89.3	91.4	91.8	93.2	Bolivia	218
74.2	72.0	66.5	78.6	79.5	78.5	77.7	77.5	79.5	81.0	80.9	81.1	81.3	79.9	80.1	Brazil	223
74.9	70.3	70.2	71.6	73.0	74.8	75.9	74.6	72.4	74.3	74.4	76.4	76.8	76.1	77.3	Chile	228
76.0	75.6	75.8	75.7	76.6	80.9	81.1	80.4	80.6	83.5	85.0	86.2	86.6	86.3	....	Colombia	233
77.0	77.3	77.3	79.6	85.6	84.4	85.6	85.5	84.6	87.5	85.8	82.2	77.2	81.1	84.0	Costa Rica	238
84.9	83.1	90.1	85.2	87.2	85.0	87.0	90.5	84.6	81.3	76.6	76.6	84.0	83.9	....	Dominica	321
83.1	79.2	82.4	81.3	86.3	88.7	83.6	84.1	83.9	85.9	85.0	85.6	83.2	85.7	....	Dominican Republic	243
83.6	80.6	81.1	77.1	76.2	75.0	78.3	78.0	80.3	75.6	78.8	82.0	75.8	71.6	....	Ecuador	248
94.7	93.7	95.1	98.8	97.9	97.8	96.2	95.6	96.1	97.7	96.5	94.7	95.9	98.2	98.0	El Salvador	253
88.8	85.2	87.4	83.7	83.1	86.1	88.4	77.1	84.0	85.7	85.6	89.6	67.7	83.0	....	Grenada	328
92.5	92.1	91.7	90.4	89.7	91.5	90.8	91.6	91.1	92.1	92.0	90.7	91.0	91.0	92.5	Guatemala	258
79.4	83.2	74.4	74.5	67.0	64.0	63.7	63.6	62.3	62.2	65.1	....	....	....	....	Guyana	336
84.8	82.1	76.6	89.2	106.2	111.8	107.3	101.2	121.6	98.8	102.1	99.3	....	....	....	Haiti	263
85.5	81.6	84.2	79.8	78.4	78.1	75.5	72.4	72.8	74.0	73.6	76.7	80.4	83.5	86.3	Honduras	268
79.0	80.5	82.2	77.9	77.0	72.4	79.3	78.7	81.2	82.1	83.3	83.6	83.4	84.1	84.3	Jamaica	343
74.7	80.4	82.6	82.9	86.1	88.9	82.9	82.9	77.4	74.7	74.1	77.8	78.1	78.4	81.6	Mexico	273
86.2	113.5	105.0	99.8	109.9	115.1	108.0	105.4	103.1	109.3	112.7	109.9	114.1	110.0	....	Nicaragua	278
72.8	75.9	85.2	75.1	76.6	72.3	71.2	68.5	66.8	68.3	70.5	72.7	70.9	72.6	....	Panama	283
83.5	78.1	72.5	83.4	83.2	87.6	88.0	95.2	92.5	92.8	92.7	94.0	90.7	92.9	96.5	Paraguay	288
80.5	80.5	79.3	81.6	85.0	85.6	84.6	81.1	80.9	82.1	80.4	81.8	80.8	81.8	83.1	Peru	293
87.9	70.1	70.8	77.7	78.6	68.3	67.4	71.8	77.3	81.4	73.7	72.4	84.3	100.3	....	St. Kitts and Nevis	361
....	....	....	....	....	81.3	76.9	78.5	77.8	81.2	82.2	80.6	82.3	91.1	....	St. Lucia	362
83.5	76.6	88.5	81.2	97.5	84.8	92.2	95.8	84.2	85.1	98.6	97.2	85.3	80.9	....	St. Vincent & Grenadines	364
68.6	78.4	69.3	78.4	81.6	77.6	46.7	38.5	35.8	70.2	72.9	....	....	....	....	Suriname	366
79.3	82.1	75.5	69.9	76.2	77.0	80.3	66.4	69.6	72.6	76.3	78.9	....	....	....	Trinidad and Tobago	369
83.3	82.1	82.1	82.4	82.1	83.8	84.8	84.7	84.7	84.9	84.8	84.9	86.1	87.0	87.8	Uruguay	298
76.7	78.8	75.5	70.5	76.2	78.8	81.5	77.3	76.6	68.3	72.3	79.3	76.6	70.7	....	Venezuela, Rep. Bol.	299

Memorandum Items

1987	1988	1989	1990	1991	1992	1993	1994	1995	1996	1997	1998	1999	2000	2001		
75.1	75.6	72.4	67.9	72.3	66.8	70.3	70.1	71.9	69.5	70.4	77.1	72.3	65.5	....	Oil Exporting Countries	999
74.5	74.7	74.7	75.6	76.5	75.9	75.0	74.1	73.6	74.0	73.8	74.4	75.5	75.0	....	Non-Oil Developing Countries	201

Commodity Prices

Wholesale Prices (lines 76) and Unit Values (lines 74)

		1972	1973	1974	1975	1976	1977	1978	1979	1980	1981	1982	1983	1984	1985	1986
Aluminum (US cents/pound)																
All Origins (London) *	156	26.77	27.18	34.69	39.39	40.37	51.88	60.10	72.70	80.51	57.28	44.98	65.25	56.77	47.21	52.15
Bananas (US cents/pound)																
Latin America (US Ports) *	248	7.34	7.47	8.34	11.15	11.73	12.38	13.00	14.78	17.01	18.21	17.00	19.47	16.76	17.15	17.32
Beef (US cents/pound)																
Australia-NZ (US Ports) *	193	67.14	91.19	71.77	60.20	71.71	68.33	96.99	130.82	125.19	112.12	108.39	110.67	103.11	97.67	94.98
United States (New York)	111	55.82	71.42	59.67	50.49	58.76	57.10	79.98	102.87	97.32	96.91	110.62	107.26	109.02	100.68	86.01
Argentina (frozen)	213	51.84	71.16	76.26	38.87	41.09	52.61	52.54	83.65	97.41	84.12	64.07	66.59	90.89	86.61	111.04
Butter (US cents/pound)																
New Zealand (London)	196	54.19	44.24	53.06	72.10	76.51	84.22	109.64	130.61	151.39	140.88	129.18	111.41	93.93	101.45	115.14
New Zealand	196	50.62	44.15	44.09	50.46	49.32	57.42	68.08	69.34	73.80	96.88	97.16	91.25	76.27	60.22	56.89
Coal (US $/metric ton)																
Australia	193	25.08	29.94	44.51	71.09	83.85	79.44	83.94	81.10	83.83	96.49	104.86	90.87	83.60	73.84	72.65
Cocoa Beans (US cents/pound)																
Brazil	223	26.24	48.51	73.35	56.59	77.02	183.53	153.53	140.73	107.06	87.50	68.29	83.10	105.32	94.97	92.04
New York and London *	652	29.15	51.29	70.77	56.51	92.79	171.96	154.43	149.36	118.09	94.19	79.01	96.10	108.67	102.27	93.82
Coconut Oil (US cents/pound)																
Philippines (New York) *	566	11.23	23.27	45.26	17.85	18.95	26.23	30.99	44.66	30.51	25.86	21.19	33.10	52.39	26.77	13.45
Philippines	566	8.21	15.94	39.91	17.00	15.71	24.19	27.01	41.95	28.06	23.27	19.75	24.15	44.83	24.18	12.10
Coffee (US cents/pound)																
Other Milds (New York) *	386	50.33	62.31	65.84	65.41	142.75	234.67	162.82	173.53	154.20	128.09	139.72	131.69	144.17	145.56	192.74
Brazil (New York) *	223	52.57	69.19	73.34	82.58	149.48	267.14	165.29	178.47	208.79	186.38	143.68	142.75	149.65	148.93	231.19
Brazil	223	42.73	52.68	56.83	49.57	122.37	203.51	142.11	154.72	143.75	83.34	94.88	101.16	112.72	103.97	190.39
Uganda (New York) *	799	45.18	49.89	58.68	61.05	127.62	223.75	147.48	165.47	147.15	102.91	111.04	124.12	138.18	121.24	148.32
Copper (US cents/pound)																
United Kingdom (London) *	112	48.58	80.58	93.23	56.10	63.64	59.41	61.92	89.49	99.12	79.05	67.21	72.23	62.46	64.29	62.13
Copra (US $/metric ton)																
Philippines (Europ. Ports) *	566	142.33	343.92	668.67	256.00	275.08	402.33	470.58	672.67	453.00	378.92	314.00	496.00	710.08	386.42	197.58
Cotton (US cents/pound)																
United States (10 markets) *	111	25.92	42.42	43.79	34.10	51.43	46.58	43.60	46.98	61.50	54.49	45.42	51.77	51.57	44.40	39.89
Liverpool Index *	111	36.26	62.09	65.13	53.09	77.24	71.33	71.95	77.14	93.73	83.97	72.51	84.10	80.94	59.92	47.94
Egypt (Long Staple)	469	64.93	77.79	150.42	138.39	118.46	155.53	119.42	123.40	123.22	121.73	109.69	110.62	142.85	138.35	142.53
Egypt (Long Medium)	469	48.10	62.34	127.61	109.72	84.92	125.75	101.98	109.27	109.17	108.07	80.66	86.85	112.31	133.21	136.23
Fish Meal (US $/metric ton)																
Any Origin (Hamburg) *	293	238.67	542.00	372.00	245.33	376.17	453.92	409.92	394.92	504.42	467.50	353.75	452.50	373.17	280.08	320.58
Iceland	176	166.41	415.35	403.38	222.96	277.64	420.08	415.93	375.80	467.76	470.40	313.51	536.62	330.30	304.59	344.64
Gasoline (US cents/gallon)																
US Gulf Coast *	111	....	....	....	....	....	....	....	84.40	91.93	100.47	91.95	83.48	76.77	76.93	43.62
Gold (US $/fine ounce)																
United Kingdom (London) *	112	58.16	97.33	159.25	161.03	124.82	147.72	193.24	306.67	607.86	459.75	375.80	422.47	360.36	317.18	367.68
Groundnuts (US $/metric ton)																
Nigeria (London) *	694	253.95	391.31	739.06	432.96	422.99	546.86	630.93	562.74	†1236.58	1,257.42	827.50	965.33	836.58	675.75	993.58
Groundnut Meal (US $/metric ton)																
All Origins (Europe) *	694	137.21	299.29	196.33	157.76	198.02	245.23	230.78	237.72	271.41	269.26	208.33	229.00	187.50	146.25	166.00
Groundnut Oil (US $/metric ton)																
Any Origin (Europe) *	694	425.7	544.0	1,058.3	778.2	690.6	845.8	1,079.2	888.7	858.8	1,042.8	585.2	710.9	1,016.7	905.3	569.4
Hides (US cents/pound)																
United States (Chicago) *	111	29.60	34.30	23.60	23.28	33.57	36.95	47.54	73.13	45.92	41.72	38.56	45.13	58.87	51.18	63.96
Iron Ore (US $/metric ton)																
Brazil (North Sea Ports) *	223	12.79	17.13	19.00	22.81	22.72	21.59	19.39	23.44	28.09	28.09	32.50	29.00	26.15	26.56	26.26
Jute (US $/metric ton)																
Bangladesh (Chitta.-Chalna)	513	293.70	284.03	347.67	370.75	295.42	319.00	397.83	384.92	313.50	278.25	283.08	298.25	530.75	582.92	271.75
Lamb (US cents/pound)																
New Zealand (London) *	196	48.66	63.52	65.01	67.79	71.86	78.08	100.65	109.02	131.17	124.98	108.65	87.88	87.70	83.56	92.57
New Zealand	196	27.30	43.51	46.28	39.80	40.90	48.16	55.62	63.94	72.28	78.46	72.04	62.54	57.29	49.50	49.61
Lead (US cents/pound)																
United Kingdom (London) *	112	13.70	19.38	26.80	18.92	20.24	28.02	29.95	54.56	41.07	32.93	24.76	19.29	20.05	17.72	18.40
United States (New York)	111	16.19	17.25	23.46	22.69	24.18	32.34	35.52	55.77	45.81	39.44	28.11	23.73	28.43	20.67	21.38
Linseed Oil (US $/metric ton)																
Any Origin *	001	197.00	544.50	1,094.58	700.75	545.58	461.50	434.17	644.00	697.08	659.92	519.08	484.50	571.50	627.08	419.17
Maize (US $/bushel)																
United States (Chicago)	111	1.21	2.13	2.99	2.68	2.49	2.05	2.15	2.44	2.78	2.93	2.33	2.99	3.02	2.46	1.95
United States (US Gulf Pts) *	111	1.42	2.48	3.36	3.04	2.85	2.42	2.56	2.94	3.19	3.32	2.75	3.45	3.45	2.85	2.23
Thailand	578	1.38	2.64	3.39	3.38	2.92	2.70	2.52	3.49	4.11	3.78	3.25	3.52	3.47	2.59	2.23
Manganese (US $/long ton)																
India (US Ports)	534	64.50	76.17	114.17	140.00	147.33	150.33	144.38	140.00	155.25	167.80	164.12	151.82	143.21	141.01	140.83
Newsprint (US $/short ton)																
United States (New York)	111	120.60	125.94	155.71	189.70	203.95	219.95	233.12	255.11	287.11	316.63	325.67	312.15	333.06	342.45	335.36
Finland	172	125.47	146.55	235.47	315.57	295.04	322.14	332.27	368.04	410.92	405.48	390.37	329.32	317.02	328.07	407.71
Nickel (US cents/pound)																
United Kingdom(N.Europ.Ports)*	156	139.67	153.00	173.92	207.33	225.25	236.00	209.17	271.00	295.68	270.03	219.43	211.96	215.56	222.22	176.39
Palm Kernels (US $/metric ton)																
Malaysia (Rotterdam) *	548	219.08	489.75	1,045.83	408.58	433.25	620.42	763.92	1,049.25	725.50	588.25	458.17	709.00	1,037.17	551.17	288.17
Palm Oil (US $/metric ton)																
Malaysia (N.W.Europe)*	548	217.42	375.92	691.33	420.25	397.33	530.08	600.33	653.83	583.08	570.67	445.08	501.42	728.83	500.92	257.00
Malaysia	548	187.08	239.32	500.45	474.94	359.85	525.18	533.35	594.21	529.53	490.91	416.81	437.54	650.55	493.83	269.89

Country of Origin and, for Wholesale Prices, Pricing Point in Parentheses

1987	1988	1989	1990	1991	1992	1993	1994	1995	1996	1997	1998	1999	2000	2001	Commodity	Code
															Aluminum (US cents/pound)	
70.99	115.51	88.48	74.37	59.15	56.98	51.71	66.93	81.86	68.34	72.54	61.58	61.69	70.39	65.63	All Origins (London) *	156
															Bananas (US cents/pound)	
17.11	21.73	24.80	24.60	25.46	21.69	20.10	19.91	20.02	21.41	22.25	21.61	19.39	....	....	Latin America (US Ports) *	248
															Beef (US cents/pound)	
108.18	114.17	116.46	116.27	120.83	111.34	118.74	105.82	86.50	80.97	84.17	78.30	83.14	87.79	96.54	Australia-NZ (US Ports) *	193
91.34	91.52	97.79	105.80	101.49	101.14	104.87	97.34	94.27	95.17	96.49	....	100.38	....	....	United States (New York)	111
162.19	154.87	148.59	130.90	194.67	253.91	303.09	229.52	210.56	169.00	180.72	235.34	206.91	204.26	165.79	Argentina (frozen)	213
															Butter (US cents/pound)	
113.49	140.56	148.26	147.93	140.85	150.51	141.00	140.54	164.54	....	147.75	144.64	132.51	....	....	New Zealand (London)	196
63.64	69.52	90.97	87.34	78.39	91.57	81.65	84.47	99.25	103.17	86.20	87.60	75.02	67.24	67.77	New Zealand	196
															Coal (US $/metric ton)	
64.70	67.14	76.97	79.02	80.77	76.62	72.85	69.10	74.15	79.81	76.63	69.13	58.25	53.88	61.56	Australia	193
															Cocoa Beans (US cents/pound)	
83.96	72.68	56.85	49.07	47.54	44.99	44.47	55.91	60.46	63.45	72.85	75.09	53.18	41.78	53.86	Brazil	223
90.62	71.84	56.34	57.52	54.10	49.87	50.41	63.31	64.98	66.01	73.43	76.02	51.49	41.00	49.37	New York and London *	652
															Coconut Oil (US cents/pound)	
20.06	25.62	23.44	15.32	19.64	26.22	20.47	27.51	30.37	34.10	29.79	29.95	33.45	20.42	14.48	Philippines (New York) *	566
16.74	23.34	22.39	14.42	16.12	24.74	18.88	25.39	27.96	32.66	28.28	27.15	32.48	20.23	13.36	Philippines	566
															Coffee (US cents/pound)	
112.29	135.10	106.96	89.15	85.03	63.66	69.94	148.53	149.41	120.25	185.02	132.40	101.67	85.05	61.91	Other Milds (New York) *	386
106.37	121.84	98.76	83.80	72.88	56.26	66.58	143.32	145.98	120.29	166.80	121.81	88.92	79.80	50.50	Brazil (New York) *	223
89.98	100.76	74.58	58.80	57.28	43.25	50.08	115.54	123.89	100.21	143.38	106.24	79.56	73.15	43.74	Brazil	223
102.34	95.11	75.69	54.99	49.83	43.63	53.50	119.82	126.83	82.84	80.70	83.93	67.65	42.16	27.32	Uganda (New York) *	799
															Copper (US cents/pound)	
80.79	117.93	129.15	120.72	106.07	103.64	86.86	104.58	133.00	104.03	103.20	75.01	71.33	82.31	71.68	United Kingdom (London) *	112
															Copra (US $/metric ton)	
310.33	395.92	348.02	229.92	295.85	381.85	295.42	416.84	438.50	488.98	433.75	411.03	462.27	308.92	195.55	Philippines (Europ. Ports) *	566
															Cotton (US cents/pound)	
48.01	43.39	48.58	54.34	53.46	41.41	42.26	55.79	71.82	59.77	53.59	51.05	40.18	43.78	30.93	United States (10 markets) *	111
74.77	63.52	75.95	82.56	76.91	57.94	58.02	79.72	98.30	80.54	79.23	65.53	53.13	59.05	48.00	Liverpool Index *	111
173.66	275.29	617.57	516.94	256.14	164.99	130.01	104.92	110.29	188.31	....	....	....	....	....	Egypt (Long Staple)	469
132.11	254.53	555.71	436.98	215.20	110.82	99.20	88.41	97.40	110.94	....	....	....	....	....	Egypt (Long Medium)	469
															Fish Meal (US $/metric ton)	
383.42	544.42	409.08	412.17	477.85	481.52	364.69	376.66	495.00	586.18	606.25	661.55	392.18	412.74	482.72	Any Origin (Hamburg) *	293
386.27	476.67	535.48	480.71	499.53	522.16	405.15	452.21	528.38	611.03	673.15	724.26	493.31	468.77	....	Iceland	176
															Gasoline (US cents/gallon)	
50.53	47.53	55.76	71.13	63.50	57.46	50.86	47.90	50.92	59.65	58.53	41.30	51.84	83.37	73.41	US Gulf Coast *	111
															Gold (US $/fine ounce)	
446.52	437.15	381.28	383.51	362.18	343.42	359.73	384.22	384.16	387.82	331.10	294.20	278.78	279.00	271.09	United Kingdom (London)	112
															Groundnuts (US $/metric ton)	
758.50	935.75	817.50	1,325.50	1,237.83	799.13	1,092.15	954.80	909.92	962.00	988.42	988.75	834.74	843.93	833.16	Nigeria (London) *	694
															Groundnut Meal (US $/metric ton)	
161.92	209.42	200.42	184.75	150.08	152.58	168.08	168.33	168.58	212.75	221.00	116.17	....	....	....	All Origins (Europe) *	694
															Groundnut Oil (US $/metric ton)	
499.8	590.5	774.8	963.7	894.8	609.6	737.9	1,022.6	990.9	897.3	1,010.4	908.6	786.7	712.4	671.8	Any Origin (Europe) *	694
															Hides (US cents/pound)	
79.84	87.65	90.02	92.23	79.45	75.86	80.03	86.81	88.14	87.32	88.25	76.69	72.15	80.22	84.60	United States (Chicago) *	111
															Iron Ore (US cents/pound)	
24.50	23.50	26.50	30.80	33.25	31.60	28.11	25.47	27.00	28.60	28.71	29.69	26.96	....	....	Brazil (North Sea Ports) *	223
															Jute (US $/metric ton)	
320.58	370.00	373.33	408.33	365.42	279.17	271.25	295.67	365.67	454.25	302.00	259.08	275.67	....	....	Bangladesh (Chitta.-Chalna)	513
															Lamb (US cents/pound)	
98.45	109.46	105.31	121.14	104.88	115.42	124.12	125.66	113.26	145.44	150.28	116.00	115.84	112.85	130.25	New Zealand (London) *	196
56.93	†64.07	69.06	88.53	78.99	82.82	100.78	97.94	100.61	120.28	127.06	108.33	112.86	107.66	119.06	New Zealand	196
															Lead (US cents/pound)	
27.05	29.73	30.51	36.72	25.30	24.65	18.48	24.89	28.55	35.11	28.26	23.90	22.76	20.60	21.61	United Kingdom (London) *	112
37.82	38.50	40.39	47.58	34.82	37.05	33.25	39.14	45.21	52.31	50.41	49.37	46.76	46.76	46.76	United States (New York)	111
															Linseed Oil (US $/metric ton)	
317.50	521.50	756.67	709.25	438.88	396.34	448.50	516.74	657.50	565.83	571.24	707.71	512.54	399.39	382.25	Any Origin *	001
															Maize (US $/bushel)	
1.58	2.32	2.45	2.42	2.32	2.30	2.22	2.40	2.61	3.79	2.64	2.20	1.87	1.83	1.89	United States (Chicago)	111
1.92	2.72	2.83	2.78	2.73	2.65	2.59	2.74	3.14	4.18	2.98	2.58	2.29	2.24	2.28	United States (US Gulf Pts) *	111
2.35	3.17	3.42	3.33	3.17	3.68	3.41	4.13	5.13	....	7.12	3.93	3.65	7.96	....	Thailand	578
															Manganese (US $/long ton)	
134.00	149.21	204.75	341.67	391.58	373.75	298.09	212.93	202.79	203.21	203.21	203.21	....	....	....	India (US Ports)	534
															Newsprint (US $/short ton)	
364.47	386.06	375.21	366.15	370.13	336.54	343.48	357.42	495.63	488.48	410.16	439.19	....	390.56	424.71	United States (New York)	111
465.84	550.46	526.07	575.21	556.29	469.86	377.58	401.99	605.05	650.84	470.85	453.66	....	....	....	Finland	172
															Nickel (US cents/pound)	
221.00	624.97	603.87	402.07	370.28	318.22	240.78	287.21	373.02	340.38	314.10	209.72	272.27	391.48	270.70	United Kingdom(N.Europ.Ports)*	156
															Palm Kernels (US $/metric ton)	
426.08	538.75	472.00	333.58	416.33	581.83	437.84	627.75	677.67	727.97	651.83	686.93	695.03	448.72	308.86	Malaysia (Rotterdam) *	548
															Palm Oil (US $/metric ton)	
342.50	437.17	350.42	289.83	339.00	393.69	377.73	529.15	628.58	532.03	545.83	671.30	436.31	309.51	286.45	Malaysia (N.W.Europe)*	548
318.62	416.12	348.83	287.10	329.78	382.41	382.97	482.70	612.41	502.89	504.99	....	....	....	....	Malaysia	548

Commodity Prices

z

Country of Origin and, for Wholesale Prices, Pricing Point in Parentheses

		1972	1973	1974	1975	1976	1977	1978	1979	1980	1981	1982	1983	1984	1985	1986
Pepper, Black (US cents/pound)																
Malaysia (New York)	548	46.24	57.97	84.86	90.95	89.08	113.62	106.43	96.12	90.43	71.84	70.43	†81.40	136.52	183.10	267.57
Singapore	576	....	....	....	....	....						....	†81.40	136.52	183.10	267.57
Petroleum, spot (US$/barrel)																
Average crude price *	001	2.89	3.24	†11.60	10.96	12.23	13.28	13.39	30.21	36.68	35.27	32.45	†29.64	28.55	27.37	14.17
Dubai Fateh *	466	2.48	2.86	†10.98	10.43	11.63	12.57	12.92	29.82	35.85	34.29	31.76	28.47	†27.51	26.51	13.06
U.K. Brent *	112	3.61	4.25	12.93	11.50	13.14	14.31	14.26	32.11	37.89	36.68	33.42	29.78	28.74	27.61	14.43
West Texas Intermediate *	111												30.41	29.39	27.99	15.02
Alaskan North Slope *	111	2.30	2.30	†9.76	9.85	10.71	11.64	11.67	25.74	32.69	31.38	†28.98	26.55	†28.54	27.14	13.89
Phosphate Rock (US $/metric ton)																
Morocco (Casablanca) *	686	11.50	13.75	52.77	68.00	35.83	30.67	29.00	33.00	46.71	49.50	42.38	36.92	38.25	33.92	34.26
Potash (US $/metric ton)																
Canada (Vancouver)	156	33.50	42.50	60.50	81.33	55.50	51.17	56.38	76.48	115.71	112.46	80.75	75.46	83.71	83.96	68.79
Plywood (US cents/sheet)																
Philippines (Tokyo)	566	96.89	189.78	152.74	121.83	147.71	161.53	189.58	262.49	273.84	245.46	234.35	229.87	227.03	210.91	274.15
Pulp (US $/metric ton)																
Sweden (North Sea Ports)	144	186.00	231.60	333.70	441.40	418.20	391.10	344.00	439.20	536.50	542.90	487.90	427.20	509.30	416.30	490.10
Rice (US $/metric ton)																
United States (New Orleans)	111	200.28	367.32	515.26	388.45	285.67	309.87	370.38	353.68	459.36	524.64	340.21	351.12	352.32	354.87	318.07
Thailand (Bangkok) *	578	149.92	296.58	541.50	363.17	254.08	272.42	368.50	334.33	433.67	482.83	293.38	276.83	252.25	217.42	195.67
Thailand	578	101.00	205.32	466.24	301.85	213.70	222.65	319.06	273.02	340.29	398.55	258.63	252.25	237.66	204.16	170.76
Myanmar	518	75.28	117.32	370.31	257.50	168.04	172.11	201.54	223.85	274.95	311.36	211.00	185.41	186.11	164.87	139.78
Rubber (US cents/pound)																
All Origins (New York)	111	16.03	31.10	35.19	26.45	34.98	36.78	44.18	56.82	65.03	50.45	40.08	49.72	43.89	36.99	36.47
Malaysia (Singapore) *	548	15.05	30.75	34.09	25.44	35.10	36.95	44.71	57.25	64.62	50.93	38.90	48.27	43.44	34.42	36.58
Thailand	578	12.78	25.76	30.92	23.28	31.54	34.10	40.50	52.67	60.13	47.73	34.37	41.88	42.16	32.84	34.27
Shrimp (US $/pound)																
United States (U.S. Gulf Ports) *	111	1.88	2.27	2.11	2.67	3.79	3.59	3.64	5.43	4.60	4.41	6.21	6.00	5.24	4.76	5.85
Silver (US cents/troy ounce)																
United States (New York)	111	168.4	255.8	470.8	441.9	435.3	462.3	540.1	1,109.0	2,057.7	1,051.8	794.9	1,144.1	814.1	614.2	546.9
Sisal (US $/metric ton)																
East Africa (Europe)	639	240.00	526.75	1,055.50	580.33	467.50	511.25	474.83	712.92	764.83	645.25	593.17	570.83	583.75	525.67	514.17
Sorghum (US $/metric ton)																
United States (US Gulf Ports)	111	56.20	93.39	120.94	111.87	105.22	89.24	93.84	108.11	128.86	126.36	108.35	128.73	118.19	103.01	82.41
Soybeans (US $/metric ton)																
United States (Rotterdam) *	111	140.00	290.33	276.92	221.67	231.17	280.17	268.33	297.75	296.25	288.42	244.50	281.67	282.08	224.42	208.42
Soybean Meal (US $/metric ton)																
United States (Rotterdam) *	111	129.17	302.58	184.33	155.00	198.33	229.83	213.33	243.00	258.58	252.67	218.00	237.83	197.17	157.17	184.75
Soybean Oil (US $/metric ton)																
All Origins (Dutch Ports) *	111	240.6	436.0	832.2	563.3	438.3	580.3	607.0	662.2	598.3	506.9	447.3	526.9	725.2	576.0	342.4
Sugar (US cents/pound)																
EU Import Price *	112	6.79	6.66	10.65	15.44	13.39	14.01	15.91	19.29	22.09	18.93	18.12	17.57	16.03	16.12	18.60
Caribbean (New York) *	001	7.48	9.62	29.94	20.56	11.56	8.11	7.82	9.66	28.67	16.89	8.41	8.47	5.20	4.05	6.05
U.S. Import Price*	111	8.53	10.29	29.48	22.47	13.31	11.00	13.97	15.53	30.03	19.73	19.92	22.04	21.74	20.35	20.95
Brazil	223	7.22	8.96	25.38	29.18	11.52	8.24	7.70	8.79	21.79	16.92	9.42	9.46	9.17	6.66	7.03
Philippines	566	7.78	9.24	21.03	27.03	13.25	8.71	8.18	7.61	16.22	20.65	15.09	13.44	12.70	14.94	17.59
Superphosphate (US $/metric ton)																
United States (US Gulf Ports)	111	67.50	100.00	308.00	202.50	91.50	97.92	98.04	143.33	180.33	161.00	138.38	134.67	131.25	121.38	121.17
Tea (US cents/pound)																
Average Auction (London) *	112	47.81	47.97	63.29	62.68	69.70	122.02	99.29	97.87	101.06	91.59	87.62	105.44	156.79	89.98	87.48
Sri Lanka	524	46.42	43.41	52.86	58.78	56.62	96.39	96.52	88.88	91.64	82.83	76.35	101.26	137.66	101.24	72.08
Timber (US $/cubic meter)																
Hardwood Logs																
Malaysia, Sarawak *	548	40.57	68.05	81.53	67.51	92.00	92.57	97.36	170.04	141.51	101.60	101.94	91.24	113.34	82.24	97.29
Hardwood Sawnwood																
Malaysia *	548	109.45	156.09	143.08	166.44	168.13	154.09	205.68	339.08	369.65	314.14	226.31	202.56	251.63	182.58	215.98
Softwood Logs																
United States *	111	....	....	....						....	....		89.43	78.22	73.43	75.22
Softwood Sawnwood																
United States *	111	....	....	....						....	....		151.63	141.44	137.10	136.07	149.33
Tin (US cents/pound)																
Any Origin (London) *	112	169.64	217.83	371.23	311.92	344.08	490.08	584.01	700.68	761.03	642.69	581.95	589.11	554.76	523.40	279.48
Malaysia	548	165.89	201.76	335.35	293.23	334.15	471.98	564.11	665.56	751.14	633.55	593.23	587.60	568.07	524.49	282.68
Bolivia	218	169.63	207.74	361.28	312.55	343.90	475.13	566.91	672.37	760.36	633.80	574.63	586.48	554.40	539.32	252.64
Thailand	578	166.18	197.46	332.00	300.19	329.69	471.06	557.11	656.45	740.28	628.38	615.91	585.81	548.99	524.89	283.09
Tobacco (US $/metric ton)																
United States (All Markets) *	111	1,073.64	1,128.02	1,482.07	1,841.99	2,186.72	2,253.93	2,268.02	2,344.43	2,275.86	2,321.69	2,563.96	2,656.55	2,786.32	2,611.82	2,659.16
Urea (US $/metric ton)																
Any Origin (Eastern Europe)	170	....	....	....	....	....	....	....	....	....	....	....	....	....	....	....
Wheat (US $/bushel)																
Australia (Sydney)	193	1.84	3.97	5.32	4.03	3.50	2.91	3.70	4.28	4.77	4.73	4.35	4.34	3.76	3.84	3.26
Australia	193	1.61	2.03	4.73	4.57	3.92	2.90	3.10	3.94	4.91	5.07	4.41	4.67	3.89	3.50	3.14
United States (US Gulf Pts) *	111	1.90	3.81	4.89	4.06	3.62	2.81	3.48	4.36	4.70	4.76	4.36	4.28	4.15	3.70	3.13
Argentina	213	1.81	2.65	5.26	4.68	3.65	2.63	3.20	3.98	5.01	5.27	4.54	3.91	3.60	3.13	2.66
Wool (US cents/kilogram)																
Australia-NZ(UK) 48's *	112	208.48	364.06	285.13	234.39	320.48	338.57	347.34	422.30	429.78	391.43	342.76	320.24	315.54	301.48	325.99
Australia-NZ(UK) 64's *	112	297.59	698.82	492.00	386.50	398.64	429.53	442.92	524.88	597.25	612.58	572.64	539.86	558.93	495.33	465.48
New Zealand	196	106.86	237.50	214.65	147.59	202.92	256.35	249.63	300.35	316.68	274.56	239.68	221.93	230.74	234.94	248.52
Zinc (US cents/pound)																
United Kingdom (London) *	112	17.14	38.16	56.13	33.83	32.32	26.74	26.92	33.61	34.52	38.37	33.78	34.68	41.82	35.53	34.20
United States (New York) *	111	25.31	30.08	51.12	55.53	53.53	49.28	44.96	53.99	54.40	65.26	57.17	61.19	71.38	61.76	57.88
Bolivia	218	17.64	23.76	34.85	36.93	36.08	33.08	27.48	35.90	35.98	41.04	39.10	36.61	45.86	39.41	35.72

Commodity	1987	1988	1989	1990	1991	1992	1993	1994	1995	1996	1997	1998	1999	2000	2001	Code
Pepper,Black (US cents/pound)																
Malaysia (New York)	263.23	208.74	129.33	81.30	64.34	66.70	104.90	139.41	171.86	167.71	286.88	322.29	....	....	....	548
Singapore	263.23	208.74	129.33	81.30	64.34	66.70	104.90	139.41	171.86	167.71	286.88	322.29	309.58	....	....	576
Petroleum,spot (US$/barrel)																
Average crude price *	18.20	14.77	17.91	22.99	19.37	19.04	16.79	15.95	17.20	20.37	19.27	13.07	17.98	28.24	24.28	001
Dubai Fateh *	16.97	13.36	15.78	20.73	16.61	17.14	14.91	14.83	16.13	18.54	18.10	12.09	17.08	26.09	22.71	466
U.K. Brent *	18.44	14.98	18.25	23.71	19.98	19.41	17.00	15.83	17.06	20.45	19.12	12.72	17.70	28.31	24.41	112
West Texas Intermediate *	19.19	15.97	19.69	24.52	21.51	20.56	18.46	17.18	18.43	22.13	20.59	14.42	19.17	30.32	25.87	111
Alaskan North Slope *	18.08	14.26	17.65	22.03	18.35	18.15	16.40	15.76	17.24	....	....	....	....	....	....	111
Phosphate Rock (US $/metric ton)																
Morocco (Casablanca) *	31.00	36.00	40.83	40.50	42.50	41.75	33.00	33.00	35.00	39.00	40.83	43.00	44.00	43.75	41.84	686
Potash (US $/metric ton)																
Canada (Vancouver)	69.04	87.54	98.88	98.13	108.85	112.08	107.42	105.72	117.76	116.93	116.53	.116.89	121.64	122.50	118.00	156
Plywood (US cents/sheet)																
Philippines (Tokyo)	398.72	358.84	350.32	354.87	372.38	380.77	661.42	599.50	584.44	529.52	484.96	374.56	440.56	448.23	409.65	566
Pulp (US $/metric ton)																
Sweden (North Sea Ports)	620.20	739.66	829.70	814.50	596.80	562.95	423.91	552.46	853.45	574.12	554.87	508.77	500.14	664.63	518.71	144
Rice (US $/metric ton)																
United States (New Orleans)	300.16	398.85	379.76	361.48	387.94	372.28	357.05	427.44	389.50	463.97	441.53	446.45	450.65	367.29	306.58	111
Thailand (Bangkok) *	214.42	277.25	299.75	270.67	293.67	267.67	237.25	269.46	320.80	338.06	302.47	305.42	248.97	203.69	172.71	578
Thailand	198.64	269.37	288.07	270.20	287.14	291.03	257.18	484.96	314.85	366.67	216.85	321.01	264.11	265.95	205.37	578
Myanmar	119.92	170.19	211.34	205.49	232.27	211.99	173.25	187.15	209.86	219.04	221.07	327.85	....	....	....	518
Rubber (US cents/pound)																
All Origins (New York)	39.04	43.22	43.13	44.43	42.18	41.30	43.34	43.34	50.17	48.56	47.43	46.61	45.29	47.35	48.86	111
Malaysia (Singapore) *	44.66	53.75	43.99	39.22	37.46	39.09	37.71	51.07	71.68	63.59	46.16	32.73	28.83	31.35	27.25	548
Thailand	40.88	52.00	41.92	35.89	35.20	35.28	35.07	44.08	63.81	59.04	43.30	30.41	23.79	27.02	23.51	578
Shrimp (US $/pound)																
United States (U.S. Gulf Ports)	5.18	5.64	5.09	4.90	5.24	4.97	5.16	5.93	6.13	5.95	6.70	6.45	6.62	....	6.96	111
Silver (US cents/troy ounce)																
United States (New York)	700.9	653.5	549.9	482.0	404.0	393.6	429.8	528.4	519.2	518.3	489.2	553.4	525.0	499.9	438.6	111
Sisal (US $/metric ton)																
East Africa (Europe)	512.08	550.58	653.08	715.00	669.17	505.58	615.42	604.58	710.42	868.25	777.50	821.33	695.75	....	....	639
Sorghum (US $/metric ton)																
United States (US Gulf Ports)	72.76	98.46	105.94	103.94	105.11	102.76	99.03	103.87	118.97	150.03	109.62	98.04	84.39	88.00	95.23	111
Soybeans (US $/metric ton)																
United States (Rotterdam) *	215.75	303.50	275.00	246.75	239.56	235.52	255.25	252.83	259.25	304.50	295.42	245.42	199.58	211.25	195.50	111
Soybean Meal (US $/metric ton)																
United States (Rotterdam) *	203.25	267.50	247.33	200.08	197.08	204.33	208.08	192.50	196.92	267.58	275.75	170.33	152.00	189.58	180.00	111
Soybean Oil (US $/metric ton)																
All Origins (Dutch Ports) *	334.3	463.4	431.5	447.5	453.9	428.7	480.0	616.2	625.2	551.6	564.8	625.9	428.0	338.2	353.6	111
Sugar (US cents/pound)																
EU Import Price *	21.44	23.82	22.75	26.45	27.77	28.48	28.10	28.20	31.21	31.15	28.38	27.13	26.84	25.16	23.88	112
Caribbean (New York) *	6.76	10.19	12.81	12.51	8.98	9.07	10.02	12.11	13.28	11.96	11.40	8.92	6.27	8.08	8.23	001
U.S. Import Price*	21.83	22.12	22.81	23.25	21.55	21.30	21.61	22.03	23.06	22.36	21.93	22.06	21.14	19.40	21.34	111
Brazil	6.80	8.42	12.14	15.94	11.87	11.12	11.61	13.14	13.75	13.10	12.34	10.37	6.74	7.95	8.96	223
Philippines	16.63	19.01	19.02	20.35	18.87	18.91	14.13	15.36	19.72	19.30	17.66	18.62	20.85	17.58	17.69	566
Superphosphate (US $/metric ton)																
United States (US Gulf Ports)	138.00	158.38	144.00	131.82	133.12	120.74	111.95	132.11	149.63	175.83	171.91	173.67	154.50	137.72	126.88	111
Tea (US cents/pound)																
Average Auction (London) *	77.45	81.18	91.25	92.17	83.57	90.60	84.20	83.15	74.46	80.36	107.59	108.21	105.40	112.55	89.87	112
Sri Lanka	81.60	79.79	84.20	103.91	92.23	84.84	85.58	83.81	90.55	114.51	121.78	130.10	104.28	108.61	103.55	524
Timber (US $/cubic meter)																
Hardwood Logs																
Malaysia, Sarawak *	167.46	167.21	167.34	160.28	179.63	196.69	388.98	316.32	257.68	253.74	238.21	162.86	187.02	190.06	160.19	548
Hardwood Sawnwood																
Malaysia *	371.80	371.23	467.71	517.12	524.76	607.21	758.24	821.44	740.19	740.89	662.33	484.16	601.11	599.18	488.26	548
Softwood Logs																
United States *	88.60	103.41	106.21	123.56	125.67	152.47	217.94	201.23	193.84	204.07	185.31	159.10	164.55	180.78	157.73	111
Softwood Sawnwood																
United States *	160.30	162.65	184.18	206.26	216.17	234.64	277.44	299.55	300.62	309.91	294.13	279.81	300.55	284.81	282.83	111
Tin (US cents/pound)																
Any Origin (London) *	303.45	319.86	387.12	276.03	253.83	276.88	234.40	247.66	281.11	279.36	255.85	251.12	244.55	246.57	203.64	112
Malaysia	304.37	322.62	392.91	287.07	266.00	47.64	242.33	238.00	280.51	279.87	242.89	....	....	....	....	548
Bolivia	308.97	320.22	400.71	286.88	253.36	273.91	249.26	247.62	281.70	278.77	174.28	167.50	166.61	167.12	153.38	218
Thailand	301.24	305.53	381.08	280.53	249.24	261.43	232.36	248.56	276.32	....	....	....	....	242.12	....	578
Tobacco (US $/metric ton)																
United States (All Markets) *	2,745.55	2,467.90	3,167.57	3,392.19	3,500.07	3,439.54	2,695.34	2,641.66	2,643.44	3,056.73	3,531.81	3,336.12	3,101.45	2,988.17	2,989.02	111
Urea (US $/metric ton)																
Any Origin (Eastern Europe)	....	....	....	130.74	150.95	123.49	94.40	131.39	193.93	187.48	127.93	103.05	77.71	112.12	....	170
Wheat (US $/bushel)																
Australia (Sydney)	3.11	4.08	4.81	5.29	3.59	5.41	4.20	4.41	5.38	6.19	5.10	4.22	....	....	....	193
Australia	2.43	3.71	4.59	4.25	2.91	4.12	3.72	3.50	5.17	5.83	4.59	3.95	3.52	3.39	3.92	193
United States (US Gulf Pts) *	3.07	3.95	4.61	3.69	3.50	4.11	3.82	4.08	4.82	5.64	4.35	3.43	3.05	3.10	3.45	111
Argentina	2.44	3.18	4.05	3.93	2.44	3.27	3.57	3.57	4.47	5.46	4.30	3.35	3.18	3.13	3.35	213
Wool (US cents/kilogram)																
Australia-NZ(UK) 48's *	407.89	467.57	421.67	343.33	262.69	272.34	255.21	399.59	497.14	428.88	442.79	336.39	276.47	280.98	332.43	112
Australia-NZ(UK) 64's *	713.30	1,164.83	926.58	807.83	556.01	498.37	384.74	745.33	775.31	651.59	759.84	552.81	619.25	733.54	623.44	112
New Zealand	333.01	403.17	386.27	341.47	249.33	242.87	234.25	287.90	356.15	348.34	311.92	236.58	232.31	218.63	200.73	196
Zinc (US cents/pound)																
United Kingdom (London) *	36.20	56.26	75.12	68.85	50.86	56.33	43.73	45.28	46.77	46.49	59.64	46.46	48.80	51.15	40.23	112
United States (New York) *	63.00	82.54	110.73	101.92	75.44	81.40	64.73	66.68	71.32	68.89	86.89	68.21	71.59	75.34	60.18	111
Bolivia	37.43	50.55	74.47	67.09	49.63	55.15	43.78	44.56	46.82	45.92	35.17	27.37	28.63	30.50	24.74	218

Commodity Prices

d

		1972	1973	1974	1975	1976	1977	1978	1979	1980	1981	1982	1983	1984	1985	1986
										Indices of Wholesale Prices (lines 76) and of Unit Values (lines 74)					1995=100	
World (* = non-fuel comm.)	001	34.8	56.2	68.2	57.0	62.8	69.6	70.6	85.6	90.7	81.9	73.8	79.1	79.2	68.8	67.8
Food	001	46.8	84.5	104.6	83.8	78.6	76.3	86.5	100.9	109.6	106.1	90.0	97.1	96.4	80.5	70.7
Beverages	001	39.2	49.7	60.2	56.7	104.9	182.2	136.2	141.9	123.9	98.2	98.6	104.7	121.1	108.4	127.4
Agricultural Raw Materials	001	21.6	34.8	35.5	30.3	39.5	40.1	43.1	59.7	65.3	56.9	54.5	55.9	57.0	49.2	51.9
Metals	001	34.8	47.8	64.4	56.0	58.6	61.7	63.7	81.4	89.6	77.6	70.3	79.8	72.9	66.9	64.6
Fertilizer	001	28.7	34.3	131.7	169.7	89.4	76.5	72.4	82.4	116.6	123.5	105.8	96.9	97.7	88.2	88.6
World Bank LMICs	200	36.5	55.8	75.2	61.7	71.7	89.1	83.3	95.3	103.3	88.8	78.4	84.5	86.0	74.9	75.7
Aluminum (US cents/pound)																
All Origins (London) *	156	32.7	33.2	42.4	48.1	49.3	63.4	73.4	88.8	98.4	70.0	54.9	79.7	69.4	57.7	63.7
Bananas (US cents/pound)																
Latin America (US Ports) *	248	36.6	37.3	41.7	55.7	58.6	61.9	65.0	73.8	85.0	90.9	84.9	97.2	83.7	85.7	86.5
Beef (US cents/pound)																
Australia-NZ (US Ports) *	193	77.6	105.4	83.0	69.6	82.9	79.0	112.1	151.2	144.7	129.6	125.3	127.9	119.2	112.9	109.8
United States (New York)	111	59.2	75.8	63.3	53.6	62.3	60.6	84.8	109.1	103.2	102.8	117.3	113.8	115.7	106.8	91.2
Argentina (frozen)	213	24.6	33.8	36.2	18.5	19.5	25.0	25.0	39.7	46.3	40.0	30.4	31.6	43.2	41.1	52.7
Butter (US cents/pound)																
New Zealand (London)	196	32.9	26.9	32.2	43.8	46.5	51.2	66.5	79.4	92.0	85.6	78.5	67.7	57.1	61.7	70.0
New Zealand	196	51.0	44.5	44.4	50.8	49.7	57.9	68.6	69.9	74.4	97.6	97.9	91.9	76.8	60.7	57.3
Coal (US $/metric ton)																
Australia	193	33.8	40.4	60.0	95.9	113.1	107.1	113.2	109.4	113.0	130.1	141.4	122.5	112.7	99.6	98.0
Cocoa Beans (US cents/pound)																
Brazil	223	43.4	80.2	121.3	93.6	127.4	303.5	253.9	232.7	177.1	144.7	112.9	137.4	174.2	157.1	152.2
New York and London *	652	44.9	78.9	108.9	87.0	142.8	264.6	237.7	229.9	181.7	145.0	121.6	147.9	167.2	157.4	144.4
Coconut Oil (US cents/pound)																
Philippines (New York) *	566	37.0	76.6	149.0	58.8	62.4	86.4	102.0	147.0	100.4	85.1	69.8	109.0	172.5	88.1	44.3
Philippines	566	29.4	57.0	142.8	60.8	56.2	86.5	96.6	150.1	100.4	83.2	70.6	86.4	160.4	86.5	43.3
Coffee (US cents/pound)																
Other Milds (New York) *	386	33.7	41.7	44.1	43.8	95.5	157.1	109.0	116.1	103.2	85.7	93.5	88.1	96.5	97.4	129.0
Brazil (New York) *	223	36.0	47.4	50.2	56.6	102.4	183.0	113.2	122.3	143.0	127.7	98.4	97.8	102.5	102.0	158.4
Brazil	223	34.5	42.5	45.9	40.0	98.8	164.3	114.7	124.9	116.0	67.3	76.6	81.7	91.0	83.9	153.7
Uganda (New York) *	799	35.6	39.3	46.3	48.1	100.6	176.4	116.3	130.5	116.0	81.1	87.6	97.9	109.0	95.6	117.0
Copper (US cents/pound)																
United Kingdom (London) *	112	36.5	60.6	70.1	42.2	47.9	44.7	46.6	67.3	74.5	59.4	50.5	54.3	47.0	48.3	46.7
Copra (US cents/pound)																
Philippines (Europ. Ports) *	566	32.5	78.4	152.5	58.4	62.7	91.8	107.3	153.4	103.3	86.4	71.6	113.1	161.9	88.1	45.1
Cotton (US cents/pound)																
United States (10 markets) *	111	36.1	59.1	61.0	47.5	71.6	64.9	60.7	65.4	85.6	75.9	63.2	72.1	71.8	61.8	55.5
Liverpool Index *	111	36.9	63.2	64.5	54.0	78.6	72.6	73.2	78.5	95.4	85.4	73.8	85.6	82.3	61.0	48.8
Egypt (Long Staple)	469	58.9	70.5	136.4	125.5	107.4	141.0	108.3	111.9	111.7	110.4	99.4	100.3	129.5	125.4	129.2
Egypt (Long Medium)	469	49.4	64.0	131.0	112.7	87.2	129.1	104.7	112.2	112.1	111.0	82.8	89.2	115.3	136.8	139.9
Fish Meal (US $/metric ton)																
Any Origin (Hamburg) *	293	48.2	109.5	75.2	49.6	76.0	91.7	82.8	79.8	101.9	94.4	71.5	91.4	75.4	56.6	64.8
Iceland	176	31.5	78.6	76.3	42.2	52.5	79.5	78.7	71.1	88.5	89.0	59.3	101.6	62.5	57.6	65.2
Gasoline (US cents/gallon)																
US Gulf Coast *	111	. . . .		. . . .	. . . .	. . . .		165.8	180.5	197.3	180.6	163.9	150.8	151.1	85.7
Gold (US $/fine ounce)																
United Kingdom (London)	112	15.1	25.3	41.5	41.9	32.5	38.5	50.3	79.9	158.2	119.7	97.8	110.0	93.8	82.6	95.7
Groundnuts (US $/metric ton)																
Nigeria (London) *	694	27.9	43.0	81.2	47.6	46.5	60.1	69.3	61.8	†135.9	138.2	90.9	106.1	91.9	74.3	109.2
Groundnut Meal (US $/metric ton)																
All Origins (Europe) *	694	81.4	177.5	116.3	93.6	117.5	145.5	136.9	141.0	161.0	159.7	123.6	135.8	111.2	86.8	98.5
Groundnut Oil (US $/metric ton)																
Any Origin (Europe) *	694	43.0	54.9	106.8	78.5	69.7	85.4	108.9	89.7	86.7	105.2	59.1	71.7	102.6	91.4	57.5
Hides (US cents/pound)																
United States (Chicago) *	111	33.6	38.9	26.8	26.4	38.1	41.9	53.9	83.0	52.1	47.3	43.8	51.2	66.8	58.1	72.6
Iron Ore (US $/metric ton)																
Brazil (North Sea Ports) *	223	47.4	63.4	70.4	84.5	84.1	79.9	71.8	86.8	104.0	104.0	120.4	107.4	96.9	98.4	97.3
Jute (US $/metric ton)																
Bangladesh (Chitta.-Chalna)	513	80.3	77.7	95.1	101.4	80.8	87.2	108.8	105.3	85.7	76.1	77.4	81.6	145.1	159.4	74.3
Lamb (US cents/pound)																
New Zealand (London) *	196	43.0	56.1	57.4	59.9	63.4	68.9	88.9	96.3	115.8	110.3	95.9	77.6	77.4	73.8	81.7
New Zealand	196	27.1	43.2	46.0	39.6	40.6	47.9	55.3	63.6	71.8	78.0	71.6	62.2	56.9	49.2	49.3
Lead (US cents/pound)																
United Kingdom (London) *	112	48.0	67.9	93.9	66.3	70.9	98.1	104.9	191.1	143.9	115.3	86.7	67.6	70.2	62.1	64.5
United States (New York)	111	35.8	38.2	51.9	50.2	53.5	71.5	78.6	123.3	101.3	87.2	62.2	52.5	62.9	45.7	47.3
Linseed Oil (US $/metric ton)																
Any Origin *	001	30.0	82.8	166.5	106.6	83.0	70.2	66.0	97.9	106.0	100.4	78.9	73.7	86.9	95.4	63.8
Maize (US $/bushel)																
United States (Chicago)	111	46.5	81.7	114.4	102.8	95.4	78.6	82.2	93.4	106.4	112.4	89.4	114.7	115.8	94.4	74.7
United States (US Gulf Pts) *	111	45.1	79.0	107.2	96.8	90.9	77.3	81.6	93.6	101.8	105.8	87.6	110.2	110.0	91.0	71.1
Thailand	578	26.9	51.4	66.1	65.8	56.9	52.6	49.0	67.9	80.1	73.5	63.3	68.6	67.5	50.4	43.4
Manganese (US $/long ton)																
India (US Ports)	534	31.8	37.6	56.3	69.0	72.7	74.1	71.2	69.0	76.6	82.7	80.9	74.9	70.6	69.5	69.4
Newsprint (US $/short ton)																
United States (New York)	111	24.3	25.4	31.4	38.3	41.2	44.4	47.0	51.5	57.9	63.9	65.7	63.0	67.2	69.1	67.7
Finland	172	20.7	24.2	38.9	52.2	48.8	53.2	54.9	60.8	67.9	67.0	64.5	54.4	52.4	54.2	67.4
Nickel (US cents/pound)																
United Kingdom(N.Europ.Ports)*	156	37.4	41.0	46.6	55.6	60.4	63.3	56.1	72.7	79.3	72.4	58.8	56.8	57.8	59.6	47.3
Palm Kernels (US $/metric ton)																
Malaysia (Rotterdam) *	548	32.3	72.3	154.3	60.3	63.9	91.6	112.7	154.8	107.1	86.8	67.6	104.6	153.0	81.3	42.5
Palm Oil (US $/metric ton)																
Malaysia (N.W.Europe)*	548	34.6	59.8	110.0	66.9	63.2	84.3	95.5	104.0	92.8	90.8	70.8	79.8	115.9	79.7	40.9
Malaysia	548	30.5	39.1	81.7	77.6	58.8	85.8	87.1	97.0	86.5	80.2	68.1	71.4	106.2	80.6	44.1
Pepper,Black (US cents/pound)																
Malaysia (New York)	548	26.9	33.7	49.4	52.9	51.8	66.1	61.9	55.9	52.6	41.8	41.0	†47.4	79.4	106.5	155.7
Singapore	576	. . . .	. . . .	. . . .	. . . .	. . . .				. . . .	. . . .	. . . .	†47.4	79.4	106.5	155.7

Country of Origin and, for Wholesale Prices, Pricing Point in Parentheses
1995=100

1987	1988	1989	1990	1991	1992	1993	1994	1995	1996	1997	1998	1999	2000	2001		
74.1	92.0	90.5	84.7	79.9	80.0	81.4	92.2	100.0	98.7	95.7	81.6	75.9	77.3	73.1	World (* = non-fuel comm.)	001
74.1	95.4	97.1	87.8	87.0	89.0	87.8	92.5	100.0	112.2	100.1	87.5	73.9	73.5	75.8	Food	001
89.1	91.5	75.8	66.2	61.9	53.3	56.6	99.1	100.0	82.6	109.5	92.9	73.1	61.0	49.4	Beverages	001
66.5	71.8	74.1	76.2	73.4	75.4	87.6	95.9	100.0	96.9	91.0	76.2	77.9	79.4	74.0	Agricultural Raw Materials	001
79.4	118.7	111.8	99.9	85.7	83.6	71.8	83.5	100.0	88.1	90.7	75.8	74.8	83.9	75.8	Metals	001
89.7	103.5	105.6	100.9	104.2	98.9	83.7	90.4	100.0	113.7	115.0	118.2	113.4	107.4	101.2	Fertilizer	001
76.0	91.0	88.0	81.8	78.1	75.3	74.9	91.5	100.0	94.1	96.2	81.1	72.2	71.0	64.6	**World Bank LMICs**	200
															Aluminum (US cents/pound)	
86.7	141.1	108.1	90.8	72.3	69.6	63.2	81.8	100.0	83.5	88.6	75.2	75.4	86.0	80.2	All Origins (London) *	156
															Bananas (US cents/pound)	
85.5	108.5	123.9	122.9	127.2	108.4	100.4	99.5	100.0	107.0	111.2	108.0	96.9	....	....	Latin America (US Ports) *	248
															Beef (US cents/pound)	
125.1	132.0	134.6	134.4	139.7	128.7	137.3	122.3	100.0	93.6	97.3	90.5	96.1	101.5	111.6	Australia-NZ (US Ports) *	193
96.9	97.1	†103.7	112.2	107.7	107.3	111.2	103.3	100.0	101.0	102.3	....	106.5	....	....	United States (New York)	111
77.0	73.6	70.6	62.2	92.5	120.6	143.9	109.0	100.0	80.3	85.8	111.8	98.3	97.0	78.7	Argentina (frozen)	213
															Butter (US cents/pound)	
69.0	85.4	90.1	89.9	85.6	91.5	85.7	85.4	100.0	....	89.8	87.9	80.5	....	....	New Zealand (London)	196
64.1	70.0	91.7	88.0	79.0	92.3	82.3	85.1	100.0	104.0	86.9	88.3	75.6	67.7	68.3	New Zealand	196
															Coal (US $/metric ton)	
87.3	90.5	103.8	106.6	108.9	103.3	98.2	93.2	100.0	107.6	103.4	93.2	78.6	72.7	83.0	Australia	193
															Cocoa Beans (US cents/pound)	
138.9	120.2	94.0	81.2	78.6	74.4	73.5	92.5	100.0	104.9	120.5	124.2	88.0	69.1	89.1	Brazil	223
139.5	110.6	86.7	88.5	83.3	76.7	77.6	97.4	100.0	101.6	113.0	117.0	79.2	63.1	76.0	New York and London *	652
															Coconut Oil (US cents/pound)	
66.0	84.4	77.2	50.4	64.7	86.3	67.4	90.6	100.0	112.3	98.1	98.6	110.1	67.2	47.7	Philippines (New York) *	566
59.9	83.5	80.1	51.6	57.7	88.5	67.5	90.8	100.0	116.8	101.2	97.1	116.2	72.3	47.8	Philippines	566
															Coffee (US cents/pound)	
75.2	90.4	71.6	59.7	56.9	42.6	46.8	99.4	100.0	80.5	123.8	88.6	68.1	56.9	41.4	Other Milds (New York) *	386
72.9	83.5	67.7	57.4	49.9	38.5	45.6	98.2	100.0	82.4	114.3	83.4	60.9	54.7	34.6	Brazil (New York) *	223
72.6	81.3	60.2	47.5	46.2	34.9	40.4	93.3	100.0	80.9	115.7	85.8	64.2	59.0	35.3	Brazil	223
80.7	75.0	59.7	43.4	39.3	34.4	42.2	94.5	100.0	65.3	63.6	66.2	53.3	33.2	21.5	Uganda (New York) *	799
															Copper (US cents/pound)	
60.7	88.7	97.1	90.8	79.8	77.9	65.3	78.6	100.0	78.2	77.6	56.4	53.6	61.9	53.9	United Kingdom (London) *	112
															Copra (US $/metric ton)	
70.8	90.3	79.4	52.4	67.5	87.1	67.4	95.1	100.0	111.5	98.9	93.7	105.4	70.5	44.6	Philippines (Europ. Ports) *	566
															Cotton (US cents/pound)	
66.8	60.4	†67.6	75.7	74.4	57.7	58.8	77.7	100.0	83.2	74.6	71.1	55.9	61.0	43.1	United States (10 markets) *	111
76.1	64.6	77.3	84.0	78.2	58.9	59.0	81.1	100.0	81.9	80.6	66.7	54.0	60.1	48.8	Liverpool Index *	111
157.5	249.6	559.9	468.7	232.2	149.6	117.9	95.1	100.0	170.7	....	....	....	....	....	Egypt (Long Staple)	469
135.6	261.3	570.6	448.7	220.9	113.8	101.8	90.8	100.0	113.9	....	....	....	....	....	Egypt (Long Medium)	469
															Fish Meal (US $/metric ton)	
77.5	110.0	82.6	83.3	96.5	97.3	73.7	76.1	100.0	118.4	122.5	133.6	79.2	83.4	97.5	Any Origin (Hamburg) *	293
73.1	90.2	101.3	91.0	94.5	98.8	76.7	85.6	100.0	115.6	127.4	137.1	93.4	88.7	....	Iceland	176
															Gasoline (US cents/gallon)	
99.2	93.3	109.5	139.7	124.7	112.8	99.9	94.1	100.0	117.1	114.9	81.1	101.8	163.7	144.2	US Gulf Coast *	111
															Gold (US $/fine ounce)	
116.2	113.8	99.3	99.8	94.3	89.4	93.6	100.0	100.0	101.0	86.2	76.6	72.6	72.6	70.6	United Kingdom (London)	112
															Groundnuts (US $/metric ton)	
83.4	102.8	89.8	145.7	136.0	87.8	120.0	104.9	100.0	105.7	108.6	108.7	91.7	92.7	91.6	Nigeria (London) *	694
															Groundnut Meal (US $/metric ton)	
96.0	124.2	118.9	109.6	89.0	90.5	99.7	99.9	100.0	126.2	131.1	68.9	....	....	....	All Origins (Europe)	694
															Groundnut Oil (US $/metric ton)	
50.4	59.6	78.2	97.3	90.3	61.5	74.5	103.2	100.0	90.6	102.0	91.7	79.4	71.9	67.8	Any Origin (Europe) *	694
															Hides (US cents/pound)	
90.6	99.4	102.1	104.6	90.1	86.1	90.8	98.5	100.0	99.1	100.1	87.0	81.9	91.0	96.0	United States (Chicago) *	111
															Iron Ore (US $/metric ton)	
90.7	87.0	98.1	114.1	123.1	117.0	104.1	94.3	100.0	105.9	106.3	110.0	99.9	....	....	Brazil (North Sea Ports) *	223
															Jute (US $/metric ton)	
87.7	101.2	102.1	111.7	99.9	76.3	74.2	80.9	100.0	124.2	82.6	70.9	75.4	....	....	Bangladesh (Chitta.-Chalna)	513
															Lamb (US cents/pound)	
86.9	96.6	93.0	107.0	92.6	101.9	109.6	110.9	100.0	128.4	132.7	102.4	102.3	99.6	115.0	New Zealand (London) *	196
56.6	†63.7	68.6	88.0	78.5	82.3	100.2	97.3	100.0	119.5	126.3	107.7	112.2	107.0	118.3	New Zealand	196
															Lead (US cents/pound)	
94.8	104.2	106.9	128.6	88.6	86.4	64.7	87.2	100.0	123.0	99.0	83.7	79.7	72.2	75.7	United Kingdom (London) *	112
83.7	85.2	†89.3	105.2	77.0	82.0	73.5	86.6	100.0	115.7	111.5	109.2	103.4	103.4	103.4	United States (New York)	111
															Linseed Oil (US $/metric ton)	
48.3	79.3	115.1	107.9	66.7	60.3	68.2	78.6	100.0	86.1	86.9	107.6	78.0	60.7	58.1	Any Origin *	001
															Maize (US $/bushel)	
60.6	88.9	†93.9	92.5	89.0	88.0	85.2	91.8	100.0	145.3	101.0	84.1	71.8	70.1	72.3	United States (Chicago)	111
61.2	86.6	90.2	88.5	87.1	84.4	82.7	87.3	100.0	133.3	94.9	82.3	73.1	71.5	72.6	United States (US Gulf Pts) *	111
45.8	61.6	66.7	64.9	61.7	71.6	66.4	80.5	100.0	....	138.6	76.5	71.2	155.0	....	Thailand	578
															Manganese (US $/long ton)	
66.1	73.6	101.0	168.5	193.1	184.3	147.0	105.0	100.0	100.2	100.2	100.2	....	....	....	India (US Ports)	534
															Newsprint (US $/short ton)	
73.5	77.9	†75.7	73.9	74.7	67.9	69.3	72.1	100.0	98.6	82.8	88.6	....	78.8	85.7	United States (New York)	111
77.0	91.0	86.9	95.1	91.9	77.7	62.4	66.4	100.0	107.6	77.8	75.0	....	....	....	Finland	172
															Nickel (US cents/pound)	
59.2	167.5	161.9	107.8	99.3	85.3	64.5	77.0	100.0	91.3	84.2	56.2	73.0	104.9	72.6	United Kingdom(N.Europ.Ports)*	156
															Palm Kernels (US $/metric ton)	
62.9	79.5	69.7	49.2	61.4	85.9	64.6	92.6	100.0	107.4	96.2	101.4	102.6	66.2	45.6	Malaysia (Rotterdam) *	548
															Palm Oil (US $/metric ton)	
54.5	69.5	55.7	46.1	53.9	62.6	60.1	84.2	100.0	84.6	86.8	106.8	69.4	49.2	45.6	Malaysia (N.W.Europe)*	548
52.0	67.9	57.0	46.9	53.8	62.4	62.5	78.8	100.0	82.1	82.5	....	....	....	....	Malaysia	548
															Pepper,Black (US cents/pound)	
153.2	121.5	75.3	47.3	37.4	38.8	61.0	81.1	100.0	97.6	166.9	187.5	....	....	....	Malaysia (New York)	548
153.2	121.5	75.3	47.3	37.4	38.8	61.0	81.1	100.0	97.6	166.9	187.5	180.1	....	....	Singapore	576

Commodity Prices

		1972	1973	1974	1975	1976	1977	1978	1979	1980	1981	1982	1983	1984	1985	1986
Petroleum, spot (US$/barrel)																
Average crude price *	001	16.8	18.9	†67.4	63.7	71.1	77.2	77.8	175.6	213.2	205.0	188.6	†172.3	165.9	159.1	82.4
Dubai Fateh *	466	15.4	17.7	†68.1	64.7	72.1	77.9	80.1	184.9	222.3	212.6	196.9	176.5	†170.6	164.4	81.0
U.K. Brent *	112	21.2	24.9	75.8	67.4	77.0	83.9	83.6	188.3	222.2	215.0	195.9	174.6	168.5	161.9	84.6
West Texas Intermediate *	111	....	....	....	....	....	....	....	....	....	....	....	165.0	159.4	151.9	81.5
Alaskan North Slope *	111	13.3	13.3	†56.6	57.1	62.1	67.5	67.7	149.3	189.6	182.0	†168.1	154.0	†165.6	157.4	80.6
Phosphate Rock (US $/metric ton)																
Morocco (Casablanca) *	686	32.9	39.3	150.8	194.3	102.4	87.6	82.9	94.3	133.5	141.4	121.1	105.5	109.3	96.9	97.9
Potash (US $/metric ton)																
Canada (Vancouver)	156	28.4	36.1	51.4	69.1	47.1	43.5	47.9	64.9	98.3	95.5	68.6	64.1	71.1	71.3	58.4
Plywood (US cents/sheet)																
Philippines (Tokyo)	566	16.6	32.5	26.1	20.8	25.3	27.6	32.4	44.9	46.9	42.0	40.1	39.3	38.8	36.1	46.9
Pulp (US $/metric ton)																
Sweden (North Sea Ports)	144	21.8	27.1	39.1	51.7	49.0	45.8	40.3	51.5	62.9	63.6	57.2	50.1	59.7	48.8	57.4
Rice (US $/metric ton)																
United States (New Orleans)	111	51.4	94.3	132.3	99.7	73.3	79.6	95.1	90.8	117.9	134.7	87.3	90.1	90.5	91.1	81.7
Thailand (Bangkok) *	578	46.7	92.5	168.8	113.2	79.2	84.9	114.9	104.2	135.2	150.5	91.5	86.3	78.6	67.8	61.0
Thailand	578	32.1	65.2	148.1	95.9	67.9	70.7	101.3	86.7	108.1	126.6	82.1	80.1	75.5	64.8	54.2
Myanmar	518	35.9	55.9	176.5	122.7	80.1	82.0	96.0	106.7	131.0	148.4	100.5	88.3	88.7	78.6	66.6
Rubber (US cents/pound)																
All Origins (New York)	111	32.0	62.0	70.1	52.7	69.7	73.3	88.1	113.2	129.6	100.6	79.9	99.1	87.5	73.7	72.7
Malaysia (Singapore) *	548	21.0	42.9	47.6	35.5	49.0	51.6	62.4	79.9	90.1	71.1	54.3	67.3	60.6	48.0	51.0
Thailand	578	20.0	40.4	48.5	36.5	49.4	53.4	63.5	82.5	94.2	74.8	53.9	65.6	66.1	51.5	53.7
Shrimp (US $/pound)																
United States (U.S. Gulf Ports)	111	30.6	37.1	34.4	43.6	61.8	58.6	59.3	88.5	75.0	71.8	101.2	97.9	85.4	77.6	95.5
Silver (US cents/troy ounce)																
United States (New York)	111	32.4	49.3	90.7	85.1	83.9	89.0	104.0	213.6	396.3	202.6	153.1	220.4	156.8	118.3	105.3
Sisal (US $/metric ton)																
East Africa (Europe)	639	33.8	74.1	148.6	81.7	65.8	72.0	66.8	100.4	107.7	90.8	83.5	80.4	82.2	74.0	72.4
Sorghum (US $/metric ton)																
United States (US Gulf Ports)	111	47.2	78.5	101.7	94.0	88.4	75.0	78.9	90.9	108.3	106.2	91.1	108.2	99.3	86.6	69.3
Soybeans (US $/metric ton)																
United States (Rotterdam) *	111	54.0	112.0	106.8	85.5	89.2	108.1	103.5	114.9	114.3	111.3	94.3	108.6	108.8	86.6	80.4
Soybean Meal (US $/metric ton)																
United States (Rotterdam) *	111	65.6	153.7	93.6	78.7	100.7	116.7	108.3	123.4	131.3	128.3	110.7	120.8	100.1	79.8	93.8
Soybean Oil (US $/metric ton)																
All Origins (Dutch Ports) *	111	38.5	69.7	133.1	90.1	70.1	92.8	97.1	105.9	95.7	81.1	71.6	84.3	116.0	92.1	54.8
Sugar (US $/metric ton)																
EU Import Price *	112	21.8	21.3	34.1	49.5	42.9	44.9	51.0	61.8	70.8	60.6	58.1	56.3	51.4	51.7	59.6
Caribbean (New York) *	001	56.4	72.4	225.5	154.8	87.1	61.1	58.9	72.7	215.9	127.2	63.3	63.8	39.2	30.5	45.6
U.S. Import Price*	111	37.0	44.6	127.9	97.5	57.7	47.7	60.6	67.3	130.3	85.6	86.4	95.6	94.3	88.3	90.9
Brazil	223	52.5	65.2	184.6	212.2	83.8	60.0	56.0	63.9	158.5	123.1	68.5	68.8	66.7	48.5	51.2
Philippines	566	39.4	46.8	106.6	137.0	67.2	44.2	41.5	38.6	82.3	104.7	76.5	68.2	64.4	75.7	89.2
Superphosphate (US $/metric ton)																
United States (US Gulf Ports)	111	45.1	66.8	205.8	135.3	61.2	65.4	65.5	95.8	120.5	107.6	92.5	90.0	87.7	81.1	81.0
Tea (US cents/pound)																
Average Auction (London) *	112	64.2	64.4	85.0	84.2	93.6	163.9	133.4	131.4	135.7	123.0	117.7	141.6	210.6	120.8	117.5
Sri Lanka	524	51.3	47.9	58.4	64.9	62.5	106.4	106.6	98.1	101.2	91.5	84.3	111.8	152.0	111.8	79.6
Timber (US $/cubic meter)																
Hardwood Logs																
Malaysia, Sarawak *	548	15.7	26.4	31.6	26.2	35.7	35.9	37.8	66.0	54.9	39.4	39.6	35.4	44.0	31.9	37.8
Hardwood Sawnwood																
Malaysia *	548	14.8	21.1	19.3	22.5	22.7	20.8	27.8	45.8	49.9	42.4	30.6	27.4	34.0	24.7	29.2
Softwood Logs																
United States *	111	....	....	....	....	....	....	....	....	....	....	....	46.1	40.4	37.9	37.3	38.8
Softwood Sawnwood																
United States *	111	....	....	....	....	....	....	....	....	....	....	....	50.4	47.1	45.6	45.3	49.7
Tin (US cents/pound)																
Any Origin (London) *	112	60.3	77.5	132.1	111.0	122.4	174.3	207.8	249.3	270.7	228.6	207.0	209.6	197.3	186.2	99.4
Malaysia	548	59.1	71.9	119.5	104.5	119.1	168.3	201.1	237.3	267.8	225.9	211.5	209.5	202.5	187.0	100.8
Bolivia	218	60.2	74.1	127.7	110.6	121.5	169.9	202.2	238.8	269.7	227.4	204.3	208.3	196.4	185.8	98.7
Thailand	578	60.1	71.5	120.2	108.6	119.3	170.5	201.6	237.6	267.9	227.4	222.9	212.0	198.7	190.0	102.5
Tobacco (US $/metric ton)																
United States (All Markets) *	111	40.6	42.7	56.1	69.7	82.7	85.3	85.8	88.7	86.1	87.8	97.0	100.5	105.4	98.8	100.6
Urea (US $/metric ton)																
Any Origin (Eastern Europe)	170	....	....	....	....	....	....	....	....	....	....	....	....	....	....	....
Wheat (US $/bushel)																
Australia (Sydney)	193	34.2	73.9	99.0	74.9	65.1	54.2	68.7	79.5	88.7	87.9	80.8	80.7	70.0	71.5	60.6
Australia	193	31.1	39.3	91.7	88.6	76.0	56.1	59.9	76.2	95.1	98.2	85.4	90.4	75.3	67.8	60.8
United States (US Gulf Pts) *	111	39.5	79.0	101.6	84.2	75.1	58.3	72.2	90.6	97.6	98.9	90.6	89.0	86.1	76.8	64.9
Argentina	213	40.5	59.3	117.7	104.6	81.6	58.9	71.6	89.0	112.1	117.9	101.5	87.4	80.4	70.1	59.5
Wool (US cents/kilogram)																
Australia-NZ(UK) 48's *	112	41.9	73.2	57.4	47.1	64.5	68.1	69.9	84.9	86.4	78.7	68.9	64.4	63.5	60.6	65.6
Australia-NZ(UK) 64's *	112	38.4	90.1	63.5	49.9	51.4	55.4	57.1	67.7	77.0	79.0	73.9	69.6	72.1	63.9	60.0
New Zealand	196	30.0	66.7	60.3	41.4	57.0	72.0	70.1	84.3	88.9	77.1	67.3	62.3	64.8	66.0	69.8
Zinc (US cents/pound)																
United Kingdom (London) *	112	36.7	81.6	120.0	72.3	69.1	57.2	57.6	71.9	73.8	82.0	72.2	74.1	89.4	76.0	73.1
United States (New York) *	111	35.5	42.2	71.7	77.9	75.1	69.1	63.0	75.7	76.3	91.5	80.2	85.8	100.1	86.6	81.2
Bolivia	218	37.7	50.7	74.4	78.9	77.1	70.7	58.7	76.7	76.9	87.7	83.5	78.2	98.0	84.2	76.3

1987	1988	1989	1990	1991	1992	1993	1994	1995	1996	1997	1998	1999	2000	2001		
															Petroleum, spot (US$/barrel)	
105.8	85.8	104.1	133.6	112.6	110.6	97.6	92.7	100.0	118.4	112.0	76.0	104.5	164.2	141.1	Average crude price *	001
105.2	82.8	97.9	128.5	103.0	103.3	92.4	92.0	100.0	114.9	112.2	75.0	105.9	161.7	140.8	Dubai Fateh *	466
108.1	87.8	107.0	139.0	117.2	113.8	99.7	92.8	100.0	119.9	112.1	74.6	103.8	166.0	143.1	U.K. Brent *	112
104.1	86.7	106.8	133.0	116.7	111.5	100.1	93.2	100.0	120.1	111.7	78.2	104.0	164.5	140.4	West Texas Intermediate *	111
104.9	82.7	102.4	127.8	106.4	105.3	95.1	91.4	100.0	....	....	....	....	....	....	Alaskan North Slope *	111
															Phosphate Rock (US $/metric ton)	
88.6	102.9	116.7	115.7	121.4	119.3	94.3	94.3	100.0	111.4	116.7	122.9	125.7	125.0	119.5	Morocco (Casablanca) *	686
															Potash (US $/metric ton)	
58.6	74.3	84.0	83.3	92.4	95.2	91.2	89.8	100.0	99.3	99.0	99.3	103.3	104.0	100.3	Canada (Vancouver)	156
															Plywood (US cents/sheet)	
68.2	61.4	59.9	60.7	63.7	65.2	113.2	102.6	100.0	90.6	83.0	64.1	75.4	76.7	70.1	Philippines (Tokyo)	566
															Pulp (US $/metric ton)	
72.7	86.7	97.2	95.4	69.9	66.0	49.7	64.7	100.0	67.3	65.0	59.6	58.6	77.9	60.8	Sweden (North Sea Ports)	144
															Rice (US $/metric ton)	
77.1	102.4	†97.5	92.8	99.6	95.6	91.7	109.7	100.0	119.1	113.4	114.6	115.7	94.3	78.7	United States (New Orleans)	111
66.8	86.4	93.4	84.4	91.5	83.4	74.0	84.0	100.0	105.4	94.3	95.2	77.6	63.5	53.8	Thailand (Bangkok) *	578
63.1	85.6	91.5	85.8	91.2	92.4	81.7	154.0	100.0	116.5	68.9	102.0	83.9	84.5	65.2	Thailand	578
57.1	81.1	100.7	97.9	110.7	101.0	82.6	89.2	100.0	104.4	105.3	156.2	....	....	....	Myanmar	518
															Rubber (US cents/pound)	
77.8	86.2	†86.0	88.6	84.1	82.3	83.9	86.4	100.0	96.8	94.5	92.9	90.3	94.4	97.4	All Origins (New York)	111
62.3	75.0	61.4	54.7	52.3	54.5	52.6	71.2	100.0	88.7	64.4	45.7	40.2	43.7	38.0	Malaysia (Singapore) *	548
64.1	81.5	65.7	56.2	55.2	55.3	55.0	69.1	100.0	92.5	67.9	47.7	37.3	42.3	36.8	Thailand	578
															Shrimp (US $/pound)	
84.5	92.0	83.1	79.9	85.4	81.0	84.2	96.8	100.0	97.1	109.2	105.1	108.0	....	113.5	United States (U.S. Gulf Ports)	111
															Silver (US cents/troy ounce)	
135.0	125.9	105.9	92.8	77.8	75.8	82.8	101.8	100.0	99.8	94.2	106.6	101.1	96.3	84.5	United States (New York)	111
															Sisal (US $/metric ton)	
72.1	77.5	91.9	100.6	94.2	71.2	86.6	85.1	100.0	122.2	109.4	115.6	97.9	....	....	East Africa (Europe)	639
															Sorghum (US $/metric ton)	
61.2	82.8	89.0	87.4	88.4	86.4	83.2	87.3	100.0	126.1	92.1	82.4	70.9	74.0	80.0	United States (US Gulf Ports)	111
															Soybeans (US $/metric ton)	
83.2	117.1	106.1	95.2	92.4	90.8	98.5	97.5	100.0	117.5	114.0	94.7	77.0	81.5	75.4	United States (Rotterdam) *	111
															Soybean Meal (US $/metric ton)	
103.2	135.8	125.6	101.6	100.1	103.8	105.7	97.8	100.0	135.9	140.0	86.5	77.2	96.3	91.4	United States (Rotterdam) *	111
															Soybean Oil (US $/metric ton)	
53.5	74.1	69.0	71.6	72.6	68.6	76.8	98.6	100.0	88.2	90.3	100.1	68.5	54.1	56.6	All Origins (Dutch Ports) *	111
															Sugar (US cents/pound)	
68.7	76.3	72.9	84.7	89.0	91.2	90.0	90.3	100.0	99.8	90.9	86.9	86.0	80.6	76.5	EU Import Price *	112
50.9	76.8	96.4	94.2	67.6	68.3	75.5	91.2	100.0	90.0	85.9	67.2	47.2	60.8	62.0	Caribbean (New York) *	001
94.7	95.9	98.9	100.9	93.5	92.4	93.7	95.6	100.0	97.0	95.1	95.7	91.7	84.1	92.5	U.S. Import Price*	111
49.5	68.2	88.3	116.0	86.3	80.9	84.4	95.6	100.0	95.3	89.7	75.5	49.0	57.8	65.2	Brazil	223
84.3	96.4	96.4	103.2	95.7	95.9	71.7	77.9	100.0	97.9	89.5	94.4	105.7	89.1	89.7	Philippines	566
															Superphosphate (US $/metric ton)	
92.2	105.8	96.2	88.1	89.0	80.7	74.8	88.3	100.0	117.5	114.9	116.1	103.3	92.0	84.8	United States (US Gulf Ports)	111
															Tea (US cents/pound)	
104.0	109.0	122.6	123.8	112.2	121.7	113.1	111.7	100.0	107.9	144.5	145.3	141.5	151.1	120.7	Average Auction (London) *	112
90.1	88.1	93.0	114.8	101.9	93.7	94.5	92.6	100.0	126.5	134.5	143.7	115.2	119.9	114.3	Sri Lanka	524
															Timber (US $/cubic meter)	
															Hardwood Logs	
65.0	64.9	64.9	62.2	69.7	76.3	151.0	122.8	100.0	98.5	92.4	63.2	72.6	73.8	62.2	Malaysia, Sarawak *	548
															Hardwood Sawnwood	
50.2	50.2	63.2	69.9	70.9	82.0	102.4	111.0	100.0	100.1	89.5	65.4	81.2	80.9	66.0	Malaysia *	548
															Softwood Logs	
45.7	53.3	54.8	63.7	64.8	78.7	112.4	103.8	100.0	105.3	95.6	82.1	84.9	93.3	81.4	United States *	111
															Softwood Sawnwood	
53.3	54.1	61.3	68.6	71.9	78.1	92.3	99.6	100.0	103.1	97.8	93.1	100.0	94.7	94.1	United States *	111
															Tin (US cents/pound)	
107.9	113.8	137.7	98.2	90.3	98.5	83.4	88.1	100.0	99.4	91.0	89.3	87.0	87.7	72.4	Any Origin (London) *	112
108.5	115.0	140.1	102.3	94.8	17.0	86.4	84.9	100.0	99.8	86.6	....	....	....	....	Malaysia	548
109.5	114.3	139.6	100.9	89.7	97.8	83.6	86.8	100.0	98.0	83.9	84.3	81.6	81.2	77.3	Bolivia	218
109.0	110.6	137.9	101.5	90.2	94.6	84.1	90.0	100.0	....	....	....	....	87.6	....	Thailand	578
															Tobacco (US $/metric ton)	
103.9	93.4	119.8	128.3	132.4	130.1	102.0	99.9	100.0	115.6	133.6	126.2	117.3	113.0	113.1	United States (All Markets) *	111
															Urea (US $/metric ton)	
....	....	....	67.4	77.8	63.7	48.7	67.8	100.0	96.7	66.0	53.1	40.1	57.8	....	Any Origin (Eastern Europe)	170
															Wheat (US $/bushel)	
57.9	76.0	89.4	98.3	66.8	100.5	78.2	82.0	100.0	115.1	94.8	78.4	....	....	....	Australia (Sydney)	193
47.1	71.9	88.8	82.2	56.3	79.7	72.0	67.8	100.0	112.9	88.9	76.4	68.1	65.7	75.9	Australia	193
63.8	82.1	95.6	76.6	72.7	85.4	79.2	84.6	100.0	117.1	90.2	71.3	63.3	64.4	71.7	United States (US Gulf Pts) *	111
54.7	71.2	90.6	87.9	54.6	73.2	79.9	79.8	100.0	122.1	96.1	74.8	71.0	70.1	74.9	Argentina	213
															Wool (US cents/kilogram)	
82.0	94.1	84.8	69.1	52.8	54.8	51.3	80.4	100.0	86.3	89.1	67.7	55.6	56.5	66.9	Australia-NZ(UK) 48's *	112
92.0	150.2	119.5	104.2	71.7	64.3	49.6	96.1	100.0	84.0	98.0	71.3	79.9	94.6	80.4	Australia-NZ(UK) 64's *	112
93.5	113.2	108.5	95.9	70.0	68.2	65.8	80.8	100.0	97.8	87.6	66.4	65.2	61.4	56.4	New Zealand	196
															Zinc (US cents/pound)	
77.4	120.3	160.6	147.2	108.8	120.4	93.5	96.8	100.0	99.4	127.5	99.3	104.3	109.4	86.0	United Kingdom (London) *	112
88.3	115.7	†155.3	142.9	105.8	114.1	90.8	93.5	100.0	96.6	121.8	95.6	100.4	105.6	84.4	United States (New York) *	111
79.9	108.0	159.1	143.3	106.0	117.8	93.5	95.2	100.0	98.1	75.1	58.4	61.1	65.1	52.8	Bolivia	218

COUNTRY
TABLES

Albania

914

		1972	1973	1974	1975	1976	1977	1978	1979	1980	1981	1982	1983	1984	1985	1986
Exchange Rates															*Leks per SDR:*	
Market Rate	aa	...	...	...	...	...	...	...	...	...	...	...	...	...	...	...
Market Rate	ae	...	...	...	...	...	...	...	...	...	...	...	...	...	*Leks per US Dollar:*	
Market Rate	rf	...	...	...	...	...	...	...	...	...	...	...	...	...	...	...
Fund Position															*Millions of SDRs:*	
Quota	2f. s	...	...	...	...	...	...	...	...	...	...	...	...	...	...	...
SDRs	1b. s	...	...	...	...	...	...	...	...	...	...	...	...	...	...	...
Reserve Position in the Fund	1c. s	...	...	...	...	...	...	...	...	...	...	...	...	...	...	...
Total Fund Cred.&Loans Outstg.	2tl	...	...	...	...	...	...	...	...	...	...	...	...	...	...	...
International Liquidity											*Millions of US Dollars Unless Otherwise Indicated:*					
Total Reserves minus Gold	1l. d	...	...	...	...	...	...	...	...	...	...	...	...	...	...	...
SDRs	1b. d	...	...	...	...	...	...	...	...	...	...	...	...	...	...	...
Reserve Position in the Fund	1c. d	...	...	...	...	...	...	...	...	...	...	...	...	...	...	...
Foreign Exchange	1d. d	...	...	...	...	...	...	...	...	...	...	...	...	...	...	...
Gold (Million Fine Troy Ounces)	1ad	...	...	...	...	...	...	...	...	...	...	...	...	...	...	...
Gold (National Valuation)	1an d	...	...	...	...	...	...	...	...	...	...	...	...	...	...	...
Monetary Authorities															*Billions of Leks:*	
Foreign Assets	11	...	...	...	...	...	...	...	...	...	...	...	...	...	...	...
Claims on Central Government	12a	...	...	...	...	...	...	...	...	...	...	...	...	...	...	...
Claims on Banks	12e	...	...	...	...	...	...	...	...	...	...	...	...	...	...	...
Reserve Money	14	...	...	...	...	...	...	...	...	...	...	...	...	...	...	...
of which: Currency Outside Banks	14a	...	...	...	...	...	...	...	...	...	...	...	...	...	...	...
Foreign Liabilities	16c	...	...	...	...	...	...	...	...	...	...	...	...	...	...	...
Central Government Deposits	16d	...	...	...	...	...	...	...	...	...	...	...	...	...	...	...
Capital Accounts	17a	...	...	...	...	...	...	...	...	...	...	...	...	...	...	...
Other Items (Net)	17r	...	...	...	...	...	...	...	...	...	...	...	...	...	...	...
Banking Institutions															*Billions of Leks:*	
Reserves	20	...	...	...	...	...	...	...	...	...	...	...	...	...	...	...
Foreign Assets	21	...	...	...	...	...	...	...	...	...	...	...	...	...	...	...
Claims on Central Government	22a	...	...	...	...	...	...	...	...	...	...	...	...	...	...	...
Claims on Nonfin.Pub.Enterprises	22c	...	...	...	...	...	...	...	...	...	...	...	...	...	...	...
Claims on Private Sector	22d	...	...	...	...	...	...	...	...	...	...	...	...	...	...	...
Demand Deposits	24	...	...	...	...	...	...	...	...	...	...	...	...	...	...	...
Time and Savings Deposits	25a	...	...	...	...	...	...	...	...	...	...	...	...	...	...	...
Foreign Currency Deposits	25b	...	...	...	...	...	...	...	...	...	...	...	...	...	...	...
Foreign Liabilities	26c	...	...	...	...	...	...	...	...	...	...	...	...	...	...	...
Central Government Deposits	26d	...	...	...	...	...	...	...	...	...	...	...	...	...	...	...
Credit from Monetary Authorities	26g	...	...	...	...	...	...	...	...	...	...	...	...	...	...	...
Capital Accounts	27a	...	...	...	...	...	...	...	...	...	...	...	...	...	...	...
Other Items (Net)	27r	...	...	...	...	...	...	...	...	...	...	...	...	...	...	...
Banking Survey															*Billions of Leks:*	
Foreign Assets (Net)	31n	...	...	...	...	...	...	...	...	...	...	...	...	...	...	...
Domestic Credit	32	...	...	...	...	...	...	...	...	...	...	...	...	...	...	...
Claims on Central Govt. (Net)	32an	...	...	...	...	...	...	...	...	...	...	...	...	...	...	...
Claims on Nonfin.Pub.Enterprises	32c	...	...	...	...	...	...	...	...	...	...	...	...	...	...	...
Claims on Private Sector	32d	...	...	...	...	...	...	...	...	...	...	...	...	...	...	...
Money	34	...	...	...	...	...	...	...	...	...	...	...	...	...	...	...
Quasi-Money	35	...	...	...	...	...	...	...	...	...	...	...	...	...	...	...
Capital Accounts	37a	...	...	...	...	...	...	...	...	...	...	...	...	...	...	...
Other Items (Net)	37r	...	...	...	...	...	...	...	...	...	...	...	...	...	...	...
Money plus Quasi-Money	35l	...	...	...	...	...	...	...	...	...	...	...	...	...	...	...
Interest Rates															*Percent Per Annum*	
Bank Rate (End of Period)	60	...	...	...	...	...	...	...	...	...	...	...	...	...	...	...
Treasury Bill Rate	60c	...	...	...	...	...	...	...	...	...	...	...	...	...	...	...
Deposit Rate	60l	...	...	...	...	...	...	...	...	...	...	...	...	...	...	...
Lending Rate	60p	...	...	...	...	...	...	...	...	...	...	...	...	...	...	...
Prices															*Index Numbers (1995=100):*	
Consumer Prices	64	...	...	...	...	...	...	...	...	...	...	...	...	...	...	...
															Number in Thousands:	
Employment	67e	...	...	...	...	...	...	...	...	...	...	...	...	...	776	804
Unemployment	67c	...	...	...	...	...	...	...	...	...	...	...	...	...	...	92
Unemployment Rate (%)	67r	...	...	...	...	...	...	...	...	...	...	...	...	...	...	6.4

1987	1988	1989	1990	1991	1992	1993	1994	1995	1996	1997	1998	1999	2000	2001		
															Exchange Rates	
End of Period																
....	....	....	....	....	141.49	135.57	139.55	140.09	148.21	201.23	197.94	185.45	185.85	171.61	Market Rate	aa
End of Period (ae) Period Average (rf)																
....	....	....	....	....	102.90	98.70	95.59	94.24	103.07	149.14	140.58	135.12	142.64	136.55	Market Rate	ae
....	....	....	....	....	75.03	102.06	94.62	92.70	104.50	148.93	150.63	137.69	143.71	143.48	Market Rate	rf
															Fund Position	
End of Period																
....	....	....	....	25.00	35.30	35.30	35.30	35.30	35.30	35.30	35.30	48.70	48.70	48.70	Quota	2f. s
....	....	....	....	—	.04	.01	.20	.10	.52	.46	43.39	56.06	58.33	64.87	SDRs	1b. s
....	....	....	....	—	.01	.01	.01	.01	.01	.01	.01	3.36	3.36	3.36	Reserve Position in the Fund	1c. s
....	....	....	....	—	9.69	21.60	37.13	43.40	37.70	40.74	45.77	58.69	67.47	66.25	Total Fund Cred.&Loans Outstg.	2tl
															International Liquidity	
End of Period																
....	....	....	....	....	....	147.42	204.80	241.05	280.86	308.93	348.50	369.05	352.22	362.53	Total Reserves minus Gold	1l. d
....	....	....	....	—	.06	.01	.30	.14	.75	.62	61.10	76.95	76.00	81.52	SDRs	1b. d
....	....	....	....	—	.01	.01	.01	.01	.01	.01	.01	4.60	4.37	4.22	Reserve Position in the Fund	1c. d
....	....	....	....	....	....	147.40	204.50	240.90	280.10	308.30	287.40	287.50	271.85	276.80	Foreign Exchange	1d. d
....	....	....	....	....	....	.05	.05	.06	.12	.12	.12	.12	.11	.11	Gold (Million Fine Troy Ounces)	1ad
....	....	....	....	....	....	19.41	20.85	24.30	42.50	33.40	33.70	34.50	30.40	30.70	Gold (National Valuation)	1an d
															Monetary Authorities	
End of Period																
....	....	....	....	....	....	....	22.65	46.76	57.02	85.21	91.04	71.08	92.34	104.90	Foreign Assets	11
....	....	....	....	....	....	....	69.33	45.69	52.90	86.19	78.20	75.30	82.56	74.22	Claims on Central Government	12a
....	....	....	....	....	....	....	3.42	3.31	3.37	7.44	7.00	6.69	6.63	6.73	Claims on Banks	12e
....	....	....	....	....	....	....	42.07	53.88	61.39	90.93	92.32	110.09	134.01	152.14	Reserve Money	14
....	....	....	....	....	....	....	27.63	41.91	47.81	72.73	68.32	81.34	99.24	119.08	*of which: Currency Outside Banks*	14a
....	....	....	....	....	....	....	59.41	33.65	36.81	53.85	55.11	24.15	20.48	18.94	Foreign Liabilities	16c
....	....	....	....	....	....	....	3.75	4.27	3.25	5.62	5.39	5.85	7.62	4.20	Central Government Deposits	16d
....	....	....	....	....	....	....	14.26	10.61	16.83	31.43	38.56	14.82	21.52	20.92	Capital Accounts	17a
....	....	....	....	....	....	....	-24.08	-6.64	-4.99	-3.00	-15.14	-1.85	-2.10	-10.36	Other Items (Net)	17r
															Banking Institutions	
End of Period																
....	....	....	....	....	....	....	11.93	10.30	12.90	16.44	21.57	28.15	30.16	33.75	Reserves	20
....	....	....	....	....	....	....	16.94	23.47	35.44	38.96	49.97	57.97	65.05	83.48	Foreign Assets	21
....	....	....	....	....	....	....	86.55	108.52	142.51	109.70	127.89	148.12	161.30	170.30	Claims on Central Government	22a
....	....	....	....	....	....	....	3.25	3.09	3.41	2.83	2.83	1.67	1.48	1.68	Claims on Nonfin.Pub.Enterprises	22c
....	....	....	....	....	....	....	7.20	8.35	10.89	13.01	14.86	18.22	24.41	34.94	Claims on Private Sector	22d
....	....	....	....	....	....	....	11.14	17.35	42.59	18.94	15.41	21.67	24.81	23.99	Demand Deposits	24
....	....	....	....	....	....	....	18.70	28.12	30.24	70.55	115.53	136.66	140.46	162.25	Time and Savings Deposits	25a
....	....	....	....	....	....	....	13.30	20.08	33.91	36.33	40.26	53.21	63.60	88.23	Foreign Currency Deposits	25b
....	....	....	....	....	....	....	1.82	1.14	1.22	2.02	2.87	4.83	6.83	12.05	Foreign Liabilities	26c
....	....	....	....	....	....	....	68.05	75.92	80.41	25.80	1.05	.80	1.46	2.25	Central Government Deposits	26d
....	....	....	....	....	....	....	.65	—	1.69	3.64	4.73	1.44	5.81	1.05	Credit from Monetary Authorities	26g
....	....	....	....	....	....	....	6.62	9.76	14.21	25.45	26.46	27.00	29.78	33.39	Capital Accounts	27a
....	....	....	....	....	....	....	5.59	1.36	.89	-1.79	10.80	8.52	9.66	.95	Other Items (Net)	27r
															Banking Survey	
End of Period																
....	....	....	....	....	....	....	-21.63	35.44	54.42	68.30	83.03	100.07	130.08	157.39	Foreign Assets (Net)	31n
....	....	....	....	....	....	....	94.52	85.46	126.06	180.31	217.35	236.66	260.67	274.69	Domestic Credit	32
....	....	....	....	....	....	....	84.07	74.02	111.76	164.47	199.65	216.77	234.78	238.07	Claims on Central Govt. (Net)	32an
....	....	....	....	....	....	....	3.25	3.09	3.41	2.83	2.83	1.67	1.48	1.68	Claims on Nonfin.Pub.Enterprises	32c
....	....	....	....	....	....	....	7.20	8.35	10.89	13.01	14.86	18.22	24.41	34.94	Claims on Private Sector	32d
....	....	....	....	....	....	....	38.77	59.25	90.41	91.67	83.73	103.00	124.04	143.07	Money	34
....	....	....	....	....	....	....	32.01	48.20	64.15	106.88	155.80	189.87	204.06	250.48	Quasi-Money	35
....	....	....	....	....	....	....	20.88	20.37	31.04	56.89	65.02	41.83	51.30	54.31	Capital Accounts	37a
....	....	....	....	....	....	....	-18.76	-6.92	-5.11	-6.83	-4.17	2.04	11.35	-15.78	Other Items (Net)	37r
....	....	....	....	....	....	....	70.77	107.45	154.55	198.55	239.53	292.87	328.10	393.55	Money plus Quasi-Money	351
															Interest Rates	
Percent Per Annum																
....	....	....	....	....	40.00	34.00	25.00	20.50	24.00	32.00	23.44	18.00	10.82	....	Bank Rate *(End of Period)*	60
....	....	....	....	....	....	....	13.84	17.81	32.59	27.49	17.54	10.80	....	....	Treasury Bill Rate	60c
....	....	....	....	....	18.50	†27.33	19.83	†15.30	16.78	27.28	22.56	12.95	8.30	7.73	Deposit Rate	60l
....	....	....	....	....	20.58	29.58	23.67	†19.65	23.96	....	....	21.62	22.10	19.65	Lending Rate	60p
															Prices	
Period Averages																
....	....	....	....	12.5	40.9	75.7	92.8	100.0	112.7	150.1	181.1	181.8	181.9	187.6	Consumer Prices	64
Period Averages																
834	856	889	905	851	....	....	....	....	....	....	....	....	....	....	Employment	67e
89	106	113	151	140	....	....	....	....	....	....	....	....	....	....	Unemployment	67c
6.1	7.0	7.3	9.5	9.1	....	....	....	....	....	....	....	....	....	....	Unemployment Rate (%)	67r

Albania

		1972	1973	1974	1975	1976	1977	1978	1979	1980	1981	1982	1983	1984	1985	1986
International Transactions															*Millions of Leks*	
Exports	70	...	...	...	...	...	...	...	...	3,573	3,513	3,156	2,992	2,800	2,665	2,490
Imports, c.i.f.	71	...	...	...	...	...	...	...	...	3,617	3,391	4,026	3,528	3,257	3,176	2,666
Balance of Payments															*Millions of US Dollars:*	
Current Account, n.i.e.	78al d	...	...	...	...	...	...	...	...	16.0	45.0	−66.8	−38.3	−28.1	−36.4	−3.2
Goods: Exports f.o.b.	78aa d	...	...	...	...	...	...	...	...	367.2	418.0	359.9	341.0	319.1	303.5	311.3
Goods: Imports f.o.b.	78ab d	...	...	...	...	...	...	...	...	−353.9	−383.2	−437.7	−382.8	−353.2	−344.1	−316.6
Trade Balance	78ac d	...	...	...	...	...	...	...	...	13.3	34.8	−77.8	−41.8	−34.1	−40.6	−5.3
Services: Credit	78ad d	...	...	...	...	...	...	...	...	10.9	12.0	13.2	13.0	15.4	15.0	16.0
Services: Debit	78ae d	...	...	...	...	...	...	...	...	−17.5	−19.4	−22.1	−22.1	−19.1	−17.9	−19.7
Balance on Goods & Services	78af d	...	...	...	...	...	...	...	...	6.7	27.4	−86.7	−50.9	−37.8	−43.5	−9.0
Income: Credit	78ag d	...	...	...	...	...	...	...	...	7.4	12.0	14.7	7.7	4.3	2.3	.8
Income: Debit	78ah d	...	...	...	...	...	...	...	...	−3.9	−1.5	−1.3	−1.1	−1.1	−.9	−.7
Balance on Gds, Serv. & Inc.	78ai d	...	...	...	...	...	...	...	...	10.2	37.9	−73.3	−44.3	−34.6	−42.1	−8.9
Current Transfers, n.i.e.: Credit	78aj d	...	...	...	...	...	...	...	...	5.8	7.1	6.5	6.0	6.5	5.7	5.7
Current Transfers: Debit	78ak d	...	...	...	...	...	...	...	...	—	—	—	—	—	—	—
Capital Account, n.i.e.	78bc d	...	...	...	...	...	...	...	...	—	—	—	—	—	—	—
Capital Account, n.i.e.: Credit	78ba d	...	...	...	...	...	...	...	...	—	—	—	—	—	—	—
Capital Account: Debit	78bb d	...	...	...	...	...	...	...	...	—	—	—	—	—	—	—
Financial Account, n.i.e.	78bj d	...	...	...	...	...	...	...	...	−2.0	−39.5	55.2	−29.5	8.5	12.8	−1.7
Direct Investment Abroad	78bd d	...	...	...	...	...	...	...	...	—	—	—	—	—	—	—
Dir. Invest. in Rep. Econ., n.i.e.	78be d	...	...	...	...	...	...	...	...	—	—	—	—	—	—	—
Portfolio Investment Assets	78bf d	...	...	...	...	...	...	...	...	—	—	—	—	—	—	—
Equity Securities	78bk d	...	...	...	...	...	...	...	...	—	—	—	—	—	—	—
Debt Securities	78bl d	...	...	...	...	...	...	...	...	—	—	—	—	—	—	—
Portfolio Investment Liab., n.i.e.	78bg d	...	...	...	...	...	...	...	...	—	—	—	—	—	—	—
Equity Securities	78bm d	...	...	...	...	...	...	...	...	—	—	—	—	—	—	—
Debt Securities	78bn d	...	...	...	...	...	...	...	...	—	—	—	—	—	—	—
Financial Derivatives Assets	78bw d	...	...	...	...	...	...	...	...	...	...	...	...	...	...	...
Financial Derivatives Liabilities	78bx d	...	...	...	...	...	...	...	...	...	...	...	...	...	...	...
Other Investment Assets	78bh d	...	...	...	...	...	...	...	...	—	—	—	—	—	—	—
Monetary Authorities	78bo d	...	...	...	...	...	...	...	...	...	...	...	...	...	...	...
General Government	78bp d	...	...	...	...	...	...	...	...	—	—	—	—	—	—	—
Banks	78bq d	...	...	...	...	...	...	...	...	—	—	—	—	—	—	—
Other Sectors	78br d	...	...	...	...	...	...	...	...	—	—	—	—	—	—	—
Other Investment Liab., n.i.e.	78bi d	...	...	...	...	...	...	...	...	−2.0	−39.5	55.2	−29.5	8.5	12.8	−1.7
Monetary Authorities	78bs d	...	...	...	...	...	...	...	...	7.7	−36.0	58.7	−26.7	11.3	15.5	.3
General Government	78bt d	...	...	...	...	...	...	...	...	−9.7	−3.5	−3.5	−2.8	−2.8	−2.7	−2.0
Banks	78bu d	...	...	...	...	...	...	...	...	—	—	—	—	—	—	—
Other Sectors	78bv d	...	...	...	...	...	...	...	...	—	—	—	—	—	—	—
Net Errors and Omissions	78ca d	...	...	...	...	...	...	...	...	−10.6	20.7	−1.9	26.6	7.6	6.0	3.5
Overall Balance	78cb d	...	...	...	...	...	...	...	...	3.4	26.2	−13.5	−41.2	−12.0	−17.6	−1.4
Reserves and Related Items	79da d	...	...	...	...	...	...	...	...	−3.4	−26.2	13.5	41.2	12.0	17.6	1.4
Reserve Assets	79db d	...	...	...	...	...	...	...	...	−3.4	−26.2	13.5	41.2	12.0	17.6	1.4
Use of Fund Credit and Loans	79dc d	...	...	...	...	...	...	...	...	—	—	—	—	—	—	—
Exceptional Financing	79de d	...	...	...	...	...	...	...	...	—	—	—	—	—	—	—
Government Finance															*Millions of Leks:*	
Deficit (-) or Surplus	80	...	...	...	...	...	...	...	...	...	...	...	...	...	...	...
Revenue	81	...	...	...	...	...	...	...	...	...	...	...	...	...	...	...
Grants Received	81z	...	...	...	...	...	...	...	...	...	...	...	...	...	...	...
Expenditure	82	...	...	...	...	...	...	...	...	...	...	...	...	...	...	...
Lending Minus Repayments	83	...	...	...	...	...	...	...	...	...	...	...	...	...	...	...
Financing																
Domestic	84a	...	...	...	...	...	...	...	...	...	...	...	...	...	...	...
Foreign	85a	...	...	...	...	...	...	...	...	...	...	...	...	...	...	...
Debt: Domestic	88a	...	...	...	...	...	...	...	...	...	...	...	...	...	...	...
Foreign	89a	...	...	...	...	...	...	...	...	...	...	...	...	...	...	...
															Millions:	
Population	99z	...	...	...	...	...	...	...	...	...	...	...	...	...	2.96	3.02

	1987	1988	1989	1990	1991	1992	1993	1994	1995	1996	1997	1998	1999	2000	2001		
Millions of Leks																**International Transactions**	
	2,490	2,549	3,203	2,273	1,252	5,707	12,499	13,092	18,712	21,603	21,044	30,656	36,369	37,547	43,771	Exports	70
	2,650	3,217	3,792	3,797	3,026	13,135	58,536	56,732	66,145	87,995	95,021	124,337	157,424	157,219	190,696	Imports, c.i.f.	71
Minus Sign Indicates Debit																**Balance of Payments**	
	5.2	-27.1	-39.3	-118.3	-168.0	-50.7	14.9	-157.3	-11.5	-107.3	-272.2	-65.1	-155.4	-156.3	-217.7	Current Account, n.i.e.	78al d
	311.2	344.6	393.7	322.1	73.0	70.0	111.6	141.3	204.9	243.7	158.6	208.0	275.0	255.7	304.6	Goods: Exports f.o.b.	78aa d
	-315.6	-382.3	-455.8	-455.9	-281.0	-540.5	-601.5	-601.0	-679.7	-922.0	-693.6	-811.7	-938.0	-1,070.0	-1,331.6	Goods: Imports f.o.b.	78ab d
	-4.4	-37.7	-62.1	-133.8	-208.0	-470.5	-489.9	-459.7	-474.8	-678.3	-535.0	-603.6	-663.0	-814.3	-1,027.0	*Trade Balance*	78ac d
	22.3	29.6	40.2	31.5	9.2	20.3	77.6	79.1	98.8	129.2	63.8	86.6	269.4	447.8	533.7	Services: Credit	78ad d
	-20.0	-26.2	-27.9	-29.1	-33.4	-89.1	-161.9	-132.5	-156.5	-189.4	-115.2	-129.3	-163.1	-429.3	-444.0	Services: Debit	78ae d
	-2.1	-34.3	-49.8	-131.4	-232.2	-539.3	-574.2	-513.1	-532.5	-738.5	-586.4	-646.3	-556.7	-795.8	-937.3	*Balance on Goods & Services*	78af d
	1.1	.9	.4	—	.8	2.6	64.9	55.1	72.0	83.7	61.4	86.1	85.5	115.9	162.5	Income: Credit	78ag d
	-.7	-.7	-.5	-1.9	-25.9	-37.7	-31.0	-41.3	-28.4	-11.9	-11.8	-8.7	-10.2	-9.3	-13.5	Income: Debit	78ah d
	-1.7	-34.1	-49.9	-133.3	-257.3	-574.4	-540.3	-499.3	-488.9	-666.7	-536.8	-569.0	-481.4	-689.2	-788.3	*Balance on Gds, Serv. & Inc.*	78ai d
	6.9	7.0	10.6	15.0	89.3	524.0	556.9	347.5	521.2	595.9	299.8	560.8	508.9	629.0	647.5	Current Transfers, n.i.e.: Credit	78aj d
	—	—	—	—	—	-.3	-1.7	-5.5	-43.8	-36.5	-35.2	-56.9	-182.9	-96.1	-76.9	Current Transfers: Debit	78ak d
	—	—	—	—	—	—	—	—	389.4	4.8	2.0	31.0	22.6	78.0	117.7	Capital Account, n.i.e.	78bc d
	—	—	—	—	—	—	—	—	389.4	4.8	2.0	31.0	22.6	78.0	117.7	Capital Account, n.i.e.: Credit	78ba d
																Capital Account: Debit	78bb d
	-5.9	139.3	359.4	-117.7	-181.2	-32.2	44.1	40.2	-411.0	61.5	151.4	15.4	33.7	188.4	116.2	Financial Account, n.i.e.	78bj d
									....	....	....	....				Direct Investment Abroad	78bd d
	—	—	—	—	—	20.0	58.0	53.0	70.0	90.1	47.5	45.0	41.2	143.0	207.3	Dir. Invest. in Rep. Econ., n.i.e.	78be d
	—	—	—	—	—	—	—	—	....	....	....	....	—	-25.0	-23.5	Portfolio Investment Assets	78bf d
	—	—	—	—	—	—	—	—	....	....	....	....	—	—	—	Equity Securities	78bk d
	—	—	—	—	—	—	—	—	....	....	....	....	—	-25.0	-23.5	Debt Securities	78bl d
	—	—	—	—	—	—	—	—	....	....	....	....	—	—	—	Portfolio Investment Liab., n.i.e.	78bg d
									....	....	....	....				Equity Securities	78bm d
									....	....	....	....				Debt Securities	78bn d
																Financial Derivatives Assets	78bw d
																Financial Derivatives Liabilities	78bx d
	—	—	—	—	—	-73.2	-78.6	-97.3	-97.0	-138.6	59.8	-126.9	-130.1	-40.2	-178.3	Other Investment Assets	78bh d
																Monetary Authorities	78bo d
																General Government	78bp d
	—	—	—	—	—	-50.0	-25.5	-22.9	-68.4	-110.5	81.5	-91.2	-96.8	-2.5	-132.3	Banks	78bq d
	—	—	—	—	—	-23.2	-53.1	-74.4	-28.6	-28.1	-21.7	-35.7	-33.3	-37.7	-46.0	Other Sectors	78br d
	-5.9	139.3	359.4	-117.7	-181.2	21.0	64.7	84.5	-384.0	110.0	44.1	97.3	122.6	110.6	110.7	Other Investment Liab., n.i.e.	78bi d
	-3.9	141.3	361.4	-144.8	-202.6	—	—	—	-9.1	10.4	16.0	10.4	8.9	-.2	4.2	Monetary Authorities	78bs d
	-2.0	-2.0	-2.0	27.1	21.4	22.4	50.5	74.6	-404.5	61.3	40.3	81.3	97.9	90.8	86.1	General Government	78bt d
	—	—	—	—	—	-1.4	3.4	2.6	-3.3	4.0	-.6	3.5	16.0	5.2	42.1	Banks	78bu d
	—	—	—	—	—	—	10.8	7.3	32.9	34.3	-11.6	2.0	-.2	14.8	-21.7	Other Sectors	78bv d
	12.3	22.0	4.8	-2.0	125.2	47.4	-10.3	123.9	53.7	96.9	158.4	71.1	206.2	9.8	130.5	Net Errors and Omissions	78ca d
	11.6	134.2	324.9	-238.0	-224.0	-35.5	48.7	6.8	20.6	55.9	39.5	52.4	107.1	119.9	146.7	*Overall Balance*	78cb d
	-11.6	-134.2	-324.9	238.0	224.0	35.5	-48.7	-6.8	-20.6	-55.9	-39.5	-52.4	-107.1	-119.9	-146.7	Reserves and Related Items	79da d
	-11.6	-134.2	-324.9	32.0	28.0	-27.4	-114.9	-55.2	-30.5	-47.6	-43.7	-60.0	-124.7	-132.0	-145.1	Reserve Assets	79db d
	—	—	—	—	—	13.9	16.6	22.3	9.9	-8.3	4.2	6.8	17.5	12.1	-1.6	Use of Fund Credit and Loans	79dc d
	—	—	—	206.0	196.0	49.0	49.5	26.1	....	....	....	.8	.1	—	—	Exceptional Financing	79de d
Year Ending December 31																**Government Finance**	
	....	....	....	....	....	....	....	....	-20,157	-34,689	-41,053	-38,972	....	....	....	Deficit (-) or Surplus	80
	....	....	....	....	....	....	....	....	49,068	47,551	53,205	89,145	....	....	....	Revenue	81
									598	722	2,304	9,005				Grants Received	81z
	....	....	....	....	....	....	....	....	69,687	83,553	97,472	137,254	....	....	....	Expenditure	82
									136	-591	-910	-132				Lending Minus Repayments	83
																Financing	
	....	....	....	....	....	....	....	....	15,919	27,680	36,815	27,464	....	....	....	Domestic	84a
									4,238	7,009	4,238	11,509				Foreign	85a
	....	....	....	....	....	....	....	....	53,876	82,654	120,527	149,439	....	....	....	Debt: Domestic	88a
									25,434	42,668	55,432	64,405				Foreign	89a
Midyear Estimates																	
	3.08	3.14	3.20	3.26	3.26	3.36	3.49	3.55	3.61	3.65	3.73	3.79	3.13	3.13	3.15	**Population**	99z

(See notes in the back of the book.)

Algeria

	1972	1973	1974	1975	1976	1977	1978	1979	1980	1981	1982	1983	1984	1985	1986
Exchange Rates														*Dinars per SDR:*	
Official Rate .... aa	4.946	5.049	4.894	4.829	5.064	4.901	4.996	4.947	5.065	5.096	5.113	5.147	5.021	5.243	5.900
														Dinars per US Dollar:	
Official Rate .... ae	4.556	4.185	3.997	4.125	4.359	4.035	3.835	3.756	3.972	4.378	4.636	4.917	5.123	4.773	4.824
Official Rate .... rf	4.481	3.962	4.181	3.949	4.164	4.147	3.966	3.853	3.837	4.316	4.592	4.789	4.983	5.028	4.702
													Index Numbers (1995=100):		
Nominal Effective Exchange Rate .... ne c	....	....	....	....	....	....	....	815.55	832.69	907.36	988.99	1,069.23	1,167.29	1,224.46	1,052.51
Real Effective Exchange Rate .... re c	....	....	....	....	....	....	....	....	266.30	295.23	308.89	324.02	353.01	380.23	351.18
Fund Position														*Millions of SDRs:*	
Quota ....2f. s	130	130	130	130	130	130	285	285	428	428	428	623	623	623	623
SDRs ....1b. s	42	42	43	43	43	46	46	76	76	119	140	102	113	126	137
Reserve Position in the Fund ....1c. s	33	33	33	33	34	33	32	31	102	117	126	172	165	153	148
Total Fund Cred.&Loans Outstg. 2tl	—	—	—	—	—	—	—	—	—	—	—	—	—	—	—
International Liquidity												*Millions of US Dollars Unless Otherwise Indicated:*			
Total Reserves minus Gold ....1l. d	285	912	1,454	1,128	1,765	1,684	1,981	2,659	3,773	3,695	2,422	1,880	1,464	2,819	1,660
SDRs ....1b. d	45	50	52	50	50	56	60	100	97	138	154	107	111	138	167
Reserve Position in the Fund ....1c. d	35	39	40	38	39	40	41	40	130	136	139	180	162	168	181
Foreign Exchange ....1d. d	204	823	1,362	1,040	1,676	1,588	1,879	2,518	3,546	3,421	2,129	1,593	1,191	2,513	1,312
Gold (Million Fine Troy Ounces) ... 1ad	5.47	5.47	5.47	5.47	5.47	5.50	5.53	5.58	5.58	5.58	5.58	5.58	5.58	5.58	5.58
Gold (National Valuation)....................1an d	208	231	234	224	222	234	252	257	249	227	216	205	192	215	239
Monetary Authorities: Other Assets ... 3.. d	22	16	33	132	64	49	44	5	4	5	4	3	3	3	3
Other Liab.. 4.. d	114	99	152	55	60	52	60	76	108	54	51	49	47	51	53
Deposit Money Banks: Assets ....7a. d	120	172	507	351	497	633	800	656	682	663	649	441	416	382	376
Liabilities ....7b. d	168	800	996	1,353	1,433	1,756	2,609	2,972	2,953	2,423	2,001	2,089	2,983	5,092	7,203
Monetary Authorities														*Billions of Dinars:*	
Foreign Assets 11	2.35	4.76	7.03	6.25	8.95	8.03	8.85	11.05	16.06	17.24	12.03	10.24	8.51	14.54	9.19
Claims on Central Government............... 12a	2.97	.95	.45	.57	2.69	6.43	15.23	14.35	19.74	9.85	16.23	29.24	39.23	42.16	65.86
Claims on Deposit Money Banks........... 12e	3.09	4.75	6.29	7.65	8.78	8.52	7.33	11.54	11.78	22.63	27.04	22.20	26.88	22.05	23.24
Reserve Money 14	7.18	9.33	10.61	13.63	18.68	21.96	28.77	35.88	43.26	48.58	50.58	60.99	69.97	78.72	91.06
of which: Currency Outside DMBs......... 14a	7.05	8.82	10.45	12.74	17.24	20.57	27.37	35.40	42.34	48.06	49.16	60.02	67.46	76.64	89.36
Foreign Liabilities 16c	.52	.41	.61	.23	.26	.21	.23	.29	.43	.24	.24	.24	.24	.25	.25
Central Government Deposits 16d	.49	.33	1.84	.56	.18	.12	.08	.09	.31	.10	.32	.54	.44	.44	.15
Other Items (Net)................................. 17r	.22	.40	.71	.05	1.30	.69	2.34	.68	3.59	.79	4.18	−.08	3.97	−.65	6.82
Deposit Money Banks														*Billions of Dinars:*	
Reserves 20	.14	†.51	.14	.89	.85	.98	1.34	.87	.70	.52	1.22	1.09	2.25	2.32	1.61
Foreign Assets 21	.55	.70	2.03	1.45	2.17	2.55	3.07	2.46	2.71	2.90	3.01	2.17	2.13	1.83	1.81
Claims on Central Government 22a	1.59	3.17	1.97	3.45	3.19	4.11	4.02	5.39	5.22	6.48	7.13	9.17	13.23	16.82	19.71
Claims on Nonfin.Pub.Enterprises 22c															
Claims on Private Sector 22d	13.26	15.56	21.52	28.67	36.92	39.77	51.33	59.66	68.20	88.21	112.48	132.63	155.70	174.53	176.84
Demand Deposits 24	8.43	8.68	10.57	15.11	20.56	23.85	28.84	29.49	33.50	40.08	61.99	76.88	95.28	104.62	95.94
Time Deposits 25	1.39	1.44	1.52	1.77	2.53	3.40	5.25	7.48	9.11	11.23	12.59	13.17	14.28	21.63	22.20
Foreign Liabilities 26c	.17	.46	1.28	.98	1.03	1.29	.65	.86	1.83	1.08	.84	.82	1.08	1.23	1.43
Long-Term Foreign Liabilities 26cl	.60	2.81	2.70	4.60	5.22	5.79	9.35	10.30	9.90	9.53	8.44	9.45	14.21	23.07	33.32
Central Government Deposits 26d	.11	.12	.19	.28	.11	.17	.31	.35	.24	.86	1.05	1.04	1.98	2.87	3.85
Central Govt. Lending Funds 26f	1.54	1.64	2.78	3.13	3.01	2.94	2.55	3.57	3.15	3.66	3.92	6.09	6.62	8.35	9.60
Credit from Monetary Authorities 26g	3.09	4.75	6.29	7.65	8.78	8.52	7.33	11.54	11.78	22.75	27.16	21.95	27.29	23.32	22.43
Other Items (Net) 27r	.20	.04	.33	.94	1.89	1.45	5.47	4.79	7.32	8.91	7.86	15.67	12.57	10.39	11.21
Post Office: Checking Deposits ....24.. i	1.11	1.33	1.96	2.56	2.87	3.46	5.28	6.60	7.83	8.57	12.28	14.07	15.95	18.32	18.31
Treasury: Checking Deposits ....24.. r	.16	.09	1.26	1.56	.40	.67	.72	.73	.77	1.22	1.87	1.80	1.74	2.65	1.21
Monetary Survey														*Billions of Dinars:*	
Foreign Assets (Net) 31n	2.20	4.59	7.17	6.49	9.82	9.08	11.03	12.36	16.51	18.83	13.97	11.35	9.32	14.89	9.32
Domestic Credit 32	18.85	21.00	25.47	36.32	46.12	54.48	76.53	86.61	101.54	113.69	148.97	185.66	223.77	251.25	278.01
Claims on Central Govt. (Net) 32an	5.24	5.10	3.62	7.31	8.86	14.38	24.86	26.62	33.01	25.15	36.15	52.69	67.74	76.63	101.09
Claims on Nonfin.Pub.Enterprises 32c															
Claims on Private Sector..................... 32d	13.61	15.90	21.85	29.01	37.25	40.11	51.66	59.99	68.53	88.54	112.82	132.97	156.03	174.61	176.92
Money 34	16.75	18.93	24.25	31.98	41.08	48.55	62.21	72.21	84.43	97.92	125.30	152.76	180.43	202.23	204.82
Quasi-Money 35	1.39	1.44	1.52	1.77	2.53	3.40	5.25	7.48	9.11	11.23	12.59	13.17	14.28	21.63	22.20
Long-Term Foreign Liabilities 36cl	.60	2.81	2.70	4.60	5.22	5.79	9.35	10.30	9.90	9.53	8.44	9.45	14.21	23.07	33.32
Central Govt. Lending Funds 36f	1.54	1.64	2.78	3.13	3.01	2.94	2.55	3.57	3.15	3.66	3.92	6.09	6.62	8.35	9.60
Other Items (Net) 37r	.78	.77	1.39	1.33	4.11	2.89	8.19	5.41	11.47	10.17	12.69	15.54	17.55	10.86	17.40
Money plus Quasi-Money....................... 35l	18.14	20.36	25.77	33.75	43.60	51.95	67.46	79.69	93.54	109.15	137.89	165.93	194.72	223.86	227.02
Liquid Liabilities 55l	18,999	21,420	27,118	35,440	45,883	55,242	72,071	86,293	103,835	121,235	154,120	185,020	216,633	249,457	257,683
Interest Rates														*Percent Per Annum*	
Discount Rate 60	....	....	2.75	2.75	2.75	2.75	2.75	2.75	2.75	2.75	2.75	2.75	2.75	2.75	5.00
Money Market Rate 60b	....	....	....	....	....	....	....	....	....	....	....	....	....	....	....
Treasury Bill Rate 60c	....	....	....	....	....	....	....	....	3.25	3.25	3.25	3.25	3.25	3.25	3.25
Deposit Rate 60l	....	....	....	....	....	....	....	....	3.00	3.00	3.00	3.00	3.00	3.00	4.00
Lending Rate 60p	....	....	....	....	....	....	....	....	....	....	....	....	....	....	....
Other Banking Institutions														*Billions of Dinars:*	
Deposits... 45	.86	1.06	1.35	1.69	2.28	3.29	4.61	6.60	10.30	12.08	16.23	19.09	21.92	25.60	30.67
Liquid Liabilities 55l	19.00	21.42	27.12	35.44	45.88	55.24	72.07	86.29	103.84	121.24	154.12	185.02	216.63	249.46	257.68
Prices, Production, Labor														*Index Numbers (1995=100):*	
Consumer Prices 64	5.6	6.0	6.2	6.8	7.4	8.3	9.7	10.8	11.9	13.6	†14.5	15.3	16.6	18.3	20.6
Crude Petroleum Production 66aa	137.3	140.4	133.5	123.5	140.7	143.7	155.3	145.9	123.4	105.6	90.6	88.3	83.6	82.5	78.5
														Number in Thousands:	
Employment 67e	....	....	....	....	....	....	....	....	....	....	....	....	....	3,884	....
Unemployment 67c	....	....	....	....	....	....	....	....	....	....	....	....	....	....	....
Unemployment Rate (%)........................ 67r	....	....	....	....	....	....	....	....	....	....	....	....	....	....	....

1987	1988	1989	1990	1991	1992	1993	1994	1995	1996	1997	1998	1999	2000	2001		
															Exchange Rates	
End of Period																
7.003	9.058	10.556	17.343	30.600	31.324	33.134	62.617	77.558	80.793	78.815	84.979	95.135	98.165	97.798	Official Rate	**aa**
End of Period (ae) Period Average (rf)																
4.936	6.731	8.032	12.191	21.392	22.781	24.123	42.893	52.175	56.186	58.414	60.353	69.314	75.343	77.820	Official Rate	**ae**
4.850	5.915	7.609	8.958	18.473	21.836	23.345	35.059	47.663	54.749	57.707	58.739	66.574	75.260	77.215	Official Rate	**rf**
Period Averages																
907.87	754.30	647.09	512.68	255.36	206.72	214.77	151.51	100.00	88.92	94.55	95.33	87.02	86.96	88.11	Nominal Effective Exchange Rate	**ne c**
310.72	256.70	219.94	186.15	110.94	113.25	137.50	120.41	100.00	103.94	114.15	119.64	110.14	107.70	110.46	Real Effective Exchange Rate	**re c**
															Fund Position	
End of Period																
623	623	623	623	623	914	914	914	914	914	914	914	1,255	1,255	1,255	Quota	**2f. s**
143	2	3	2	1	1	5	16	1	3	1	1	1	2	9	SDRs	**1b. s**
108	—	—	—	—	—	—	—	—	—	—	—	85	85	85	Reserve Position in the Fund	**1c. s**
—	—	471	471	696	578	343	794	994	1,413	1,496	1,428	1,389	1,319	1,208	Total Fund Cred.&Loans Outstg.	**2tl**
															International Liquidity	
End of Period																
1,640	900	847	725	1,486	1,457	1,475	2,674	2,005	4,235	8,047	6,846	4,526	12,024	18,081	Total Reserves minus Gold	**1l. d**
202	2	4	3	2	1	7	23	1	5	1	2	2	3	11	SDRs	**1b. d**
153	—	—	—	—	—	—	—	—	—	—	—	117	111	107	Reserve Position in the Fund	**1c. d**
1,285	898	843	722	1,484	1,456	1,468	2,651	2,004	4,230	8,046	6,844	4,407	11,910	17,963	Foreign Exchange	**1d. d**
5.58	5.58	5.58	5.14	5.58	5.58	5.58	5.58	5.58	5.58	5.58	5.58	5.58	5.58	5.58	Gold (Million Fine Troy Ounces)	**1ad**
277	263	257	256	280	269	268	285	290	281	264	275	268	255	246	Gold (National Valuation)	**1and**
3	2	2	1	1	13	12	1	4	3	9	7	19	9	9	Monetary Authorities: Other Assets	**3.. d**
52	38	32	85	152	120	464	466	363	291	414	387	364	208	182	Other Liab.	**4.. d**
253	569	679	741	1,085	914	683	1,046	638	576	396	456	402	376	416	Deposit Money Banks: Assets	**7a. d**
8,305	8,208	7,728	7,941	7,837	7,010	5,201	4,200	2,749	2,088	1,216	1,068	1,015	720	767	Liabilities	**7b. d**
															Monetary Authorities	
End of Period																
9.45	7.17	7.89	10.43	35.52	†36.69	38.66	120.39	111.71	252.88	485.04	423.47	329.89	919.47	1,445.97	Foreign Assets	**11**
82.41	104.35	110.40	98.85	100.57	†162.76	273.80	255.57	243.40	180.87	177.67	174.59	163.48	168.20	144.67	Claims on Central Government	**12a**
18.17	16.90	30.74	65.70	108.40	†78.31	29.39	50.45	188.59	255.13	219.06	226.25	310.80	170.54	—	Claims on Deposit Money Banks	**12e**
102.36	111.49	124.97	137.92	160.28	†196.28	250.41	237.22	255.17	305.91	356.63	403.47	449.46	550.23	777.84	Reserve Money	**14**
96.87	109.76	119.87	135.26	157.20	†184.85	211.31	222.99	249.77	290.88	337.62	390.78	440.26	484.95	577.34	of which: Currency Outside DMBs	**14a**
.26	.26	5.23	9.21	24.54	†20.84	22.55	69.68	96.06	130.45	142.06	144.70	157.34	145.08	132.30	Foreign Liabilities	**16c**
.44	3.89	1.72	5.36	5.97	†2.31	2.94	9.25	9.80	4.41	21.93	75.32	4.46	324.61	420.96	Central Government Deposits	**16d**
6.96	12.78	17.11	22.49	53.71	†58.32	65.96	110.26	182.67	248.11	361.15	200.82	192.89	238.28	259.54	Other Items (Net)	**17r**
															Deposit Money Banks	
End of Period																
5.66	3.54	4.57	4.04	4.97	5.86	37.89	7.32	5.58	12.79	18.77	15.85	13.37	42.74	182.94	Reserves	**20**
1.25	3.83	5.45	9.03	23.22	20.82	16.47	44.88	33.30	32.38	23.11	27.50	27.89	28.32	32.35	Foreign Assets	**21**
20.27	21.12	21.57	44.83	32.14	28.33	300.52	204.63	155.64	141.43	273.15	410.39	459.49	600.38	591.50	Claims on Central Government	**22a**
....	....	....	....	....	332.07	142.04	208.00	461.00	637.71	632.59	601.86	760.48	530.06	549.31	Claims on Nonfin.Pub.Enterprises	**22c**
180.53	191.91	209.30	246.98	325.85	†76.00	77.12	96.75	103.47	137.85	108.56	128.86	173.89	245.31	289.05	Claims on Private Sector	**22d**
103.80	115.53	101.89	105.55	133.11	140.84	188.93	196.45	210.78	234.03	254.83	334.52	352.71	460.27	551.88	Demand Deposits	**24**
33.99	40.76	58.13	72.92	90.28	152.02	198.83	247.68	280.46	325.96	409.95	474.19	578.57	617.87	836.18	Time Deposits	**25**
1.30	1.46	1.59	3.71	9.89	14.00	12.94	35.14	22.58	20.79	15.71	25.48	30.87	26.66	35.18	Foreign Liabilities	**26c**
39.70	53.79	60.48	93.09	157.77	145.70	112.52	145.02	120.88	96.51	55.30	39.00	39.46	27.61	24.50	Long-Term Foreign Liabilities	**26cl**
2.29	1.26	1.29	.87	2.46	5.88	90.19	38.82	44.53	97.53	84.36	55.74	56.66	33.51	26.90	Central Government Deposits	**26d**
10.31	11.25	12.82	13.56	11.64	14.00	13.19	13.61	13.79	12.30	12.90	13.69	13.22	20.95	11.13	Central Govt. Lending Funds	**26f**
13.50	10.49	30.74	66.33	108.56	†78.66	29.39	50.69	190.29	259.13	219.06	226.25	310.80	170.54	—	Credit from Monetary Authorities	**26g**
2.82	-14.14	-26.05	-51.16	-127.53	†-88.01	-71.95	-165.83	-124.31	-84.09	4.07	15.58	52.82	89.39	159.39	Other Items (Net)	**27r**
22.25	25.88	26.96	27.16	31.95	39.83	40.98	48.50	53.74	57.96	71.68	81.05	87.43	89.09	97.00	Post Office: Checking Deposits	**24.. i**
.99	1.04	1.30	2.43	2.21	4.20	5.68	7.89	4.82	6.22	7.43	7.33	9.38	7.07	9.44	Treasury: Checking Deposits	**24.. r**
															Monetary Survey	
End of Period																
9.15	9.28	6.52	6.54	24.31	†22.67	19.65	60.45	26.37	134.02	350.38	280.79	169.57	776.05	1,310.85	Foreign Assets (Net)	**31n**
303.80	339.24	366.59	414.02	484.29	†639.24	748.09	774.38	968.93	1,061.39	1,164.93	1,273.45	1,593.76	1,282.87	1,234.07	Domestic Credit	**32**
123.19	147.25	157.21	167.04	158.44	†226.93	527.84	468.54	403.29	284.55	423.65	542.30	658.66	506.61	394.74	Claims on Central Govt. (Net)	**32an**
....	....	....	....	....	332.07	142.04	208.00	461.00	637.71	632.59	601.86	760.48	530.06	549.31	Claims on Nonfin.Pub.Enterprises	**32c**
180.61	191.99	209.39	246.98	325.85	†76.00	77.16	96.79	103.50	137.88	108.63	129.18	174.48	245.99	289.80	Claims on Private Sector	**32d**
223.91	252.21	250.01	270.40	324.47	†377.24	450.32	485.65	520.29	589.99	675.96	817.26	889.78	1,044.02	1,237.38	Money	**34**
33.99	40.76	58.13	72.92	90.28	152.02	198.83	247.68	280.46	325.96	409.95	474.19	578.57	617.87	836.18	Quasi-Money	**35**
39.70	53.79	60.48	93.09	157.77	145.70	112.52	145.02	120.88	96.51	55.30	39.00	39.46	27.61	24.50	Long-Term Foreign Liabilities	**36cl**
10.31	11.25	12.82	13.56	11.64	14.00	13.19	13.61	13.79	12.30	12.90	13.69	13.22	20.95	11.13	Central Govt. Lending Funds	**36f**
5.04	-9.49	-8.33	-29.42	-75.55	†-27.04	-7.12	-57.13	59.89	170.65	361.21	210.10	242.26	348.47	435.72	Other Items (Net)	**37r**
257.90	292.97	308.15	343.32	414.75	†529.26	649.15	733.33	800.74	915.95	1,085.91	1,291.46	1,468.36	1,661.89	2,073.56	Money plus Quasi-Money	**35l**
295,890	339,145	366,259	408,389	....	....	....	....	....	....	....	....	....	....	....	Liquid Liabilities	**55l**
															Interest Rates	
Percent Per Annum																
5.00	5.00	7.00	10.50	11.50	11.50	11.50	21.00	†14.00	13.00	11.00	9.50	8.50	6.00	6.00	Discount Rate	**60**
....	....	....	....	....	....	....	19.80	†21.05	18.47	11.80	10.40	10.43	6.77	3.35	Money Market Rate	**60b**
3.25	3.25	3.25	3.25	9.50	9.50	9.50	16.50	....	....	....	†9.96	10.05	7.95	5.69	Treasury Bill Rate	**60c**
4.00	4.00	8.00	8.00	8.00	8.00	8.00	12.00	†16.00	14.50	9.75	8.50	7.50	7.50	6.25	Deposit Rate	**60l**
....	....	....	....	....	....	....	16.00	†19.00	19.00	12.50	11.00	10.00	10.00	9.50	Lending Rate	**60p**
															Other Banking Institutions	
End of Period																
37.99	46.18	58.11	65.07	....											Deposits	**45**
295.89	339.15	366.26	408.39	....											Liquid Liabilities	**55l**
															Prices, Production, Labor	
Period Averages																
22.1	23.4	25.6	†29.9	37.6	49.5	59.7	77.1	100.0	118.7	128.7	131.7	135.2	....	....	Consumer Prices	**64**
83.0	83.7	90.8	100.0	104.9	103.1	99.3	96.7	100.0	106.4	110.7	106.6	100.9	....	....	Crude Petroleum Production	**66aa**
Period Averages																
....	....	4,432	4,156	4,538	4,596	....	....	4,928	5,389	5,708	....	....	5,726	....	Employment	**67e**
....	....	946	1,156	1,261	1,482	1,519	1,660	2,105	....	2,049	....	....	2,428	....	Unemployment	**67c**
....	....	17.0	19.7	21.1	23.8	23.1	24.4	27.9	....	26.4	....	....	29.8	....	Unemployment Rate (%)	**67r**

Algeria

		1972	1973	1974	1975	1976	1977	1978	1979	1980	1981	1982	1983	1984	1985	1986
International Transactions															*Millions of Dinars*	
Exports	70	5,854	7,479	19,594	18,563	21,897	24,650	25,088	36,802	52,648	62,837	60,478	60,722	63,758	64,564	36,828
Petroleum	70a	4,614	6,030	17,838	16,963	19,950	23,064	23,224	33,700	48,532	56,041	....	45,334	45,793	....	....
Crude Petroleum	70aa	4,565	5,648	16,953	15,885	18,992	22,457	21,518	30,794	40,980	44,302	26,562	32,281	31,780	....	....
Refined Petroleum	70ab	49	382	885	1,078	958	607	1,706	2,906	7,552	11,739	22,896	13,053	14,013	....	....
Imports, c.i.f.	71	6,694	8,859	16,821	23,755	22,226	29,534	34,439	32,378	40,519	48,780	49,384	49,782	51,257	49,491	43,393
Imports, c.i.f., from DOTS	71y	....	....	....	....	....	....	....	....	....	48,636	49,311	49,782	52,235	49,491	43,393
Volume of Exports															*1995=100*	
Petroleum	72a	162	163	152	150	163	170	181	180	155	145	139	....	....	....	....
Crude Petroleum	72aa	299	289	271	263	290	309	316	315	244	209	138	88	84	83	78
Refined Petroleum	72ab	4	18	17	20	17	10	27	24	53	72	139	....	....	....	....
Export Prices															*1995=100:*	
Crude Petroleum	76aa d	15.9	23.9	68.5	68.0	74.6	81.8	80.4	119.5	211.3	225.2	203.8	179.5	173.5	173.5	
Balance of Payments															*Millions of US Dollars:*	
Current Account, n.i.e.	78al d	....	....	....	....	....	−2,325	−3,540	−1,632	249	90	−183	−85	74	1,015	−2,230
Goods: Exports f.o.b.	78aa d						6,009	6,340	9,484	13,652	14,117	13,509	12,742	12,792	13,034	8,065
Goods: Imports f.o.b.	78ab d						−6,213	−7,316	−7,820	−9,614	−10,105	−9,916	−9,543	−9,245	−8,820	−7,896
Trade Balance	78ac d						−204	−976	1,664	4,037	4,012	3,594	3,199	3,547	4,214	169
Services: Credit	78ad d						288	326	468	476	474	528	679	599	531	549
Services: Debit	78ae d						−1,520	−1,939	−2,379	−2,697	−2,705	−2,644	−2,410	−2,573	−2,565	−2,019
Balance on Goods & Services	78af d						−1,436	−2,589	−247	1,817	1,781	1,477	1,469	1,573	2,180	−1,301
Income: Credit	78ag d						87	69	156	372	481	328	186	179	191	172
Income: Debit	78ah d						−1,258	−1,335	−1,863	−2,241	−2,482	−2,318	−1,978	−1,858	−1,735	−1,865
Balance on Gds, Serv. & Inc.	78ai d						−2,607	−3,855	−1,953	−52	−219	−512	−323	−106	636	−2,994
Current Transfers, n.i.e.: Credit	78aj d						391	451	474	512	513	529	414	350	529	917
Current Transfers: Debit	78ak d						−110	−136	−153	−211	−204	−200	−176	−169	−151	−153
Capital Account, n.i.e.	78bc d						—	—	—	—	—	—	—	—	—	—
Capital Account, n.i.e.: Credit	78ba d						—	—	—	—	—	—	—	—	—	—
Capital Account: Debit	78bb d						—	—	—	—	—	—	—	—	—	—
Financial Account, n.i.e.	78bj d						2,038	3,469	2,523	955	16	−799	−529	−211	−121	590
Direct Investment Abroad	78bd d						−6	—	−16	−34	−15	−11	−15	−15	−2	5
Dir. Invest. in Rep. Econ., n.i.e.	78be d						178	135	26	349	13	−54	—	1	—	5
Portfolio Investment Assets	78bf d						—	—	—	—	—	—	2	—	—	—
Equity Securities	78bk d						—	—	—	—	—	—	2	—	—	—
Debt Securities	78bl d						—	—	—	—	—	—	—	—	—	—
Portfolio Investment Liab., n.i.e.	78bg d						—	—	1	—	—	−3	—	—	—	—
Equity Securities	78bm d						—	—	1	—	—	−3	—	—	—	—
Debt Securities	78bn d						—	—	—	—	—	—	—	—	—	—
Financial Derivatives Assets	78bw d															
Financial Derivatives Liabilities	78bx d															
Other Investment Assets	78bh d						−114	−299	−193	−122	−158	−196	2	49	−285	−23
Monetary Authorities	78bo d						—	—	—	—	—	—	—	—	—	—
General Government	78bp d						−212	−118	−126	−34	−132	−250	−224	−67	−85	−74
Banks	78bq d						98	−161	−79	−88	−26	54	226	116	−199	52
Other Sectors	78br d						—	−20	12	1	—	—	—	—	—	—
Other Investment Liab., n.i.e.	78bi d						1,979	3,633	2,705	762	176	−535	−519	−246	166	602
Monetary Authorities	78bs d						36	13	28	−23	−93	21	8	−10	11	24
General Government	78bt d						68	54	85	−10	−51	−32	−32	−27	20	132
Banks	78bu d						247	822	363	74	142	117	20	11	8	32
Other Sectors	78bv d						1,628	2,744	2,229	721	178	−640	−514	−220	126	413
Net Errors and Omissions	78ca d						−41	143	−407	137	14	−88	193	−197	127	142
Overall Balance	78cb d						−328	73	484	1,341	120	−1,070	−421	−333	1,020	−1,498
Reserves and Related Items	79da d						328	−73	−484	−1,341	−120	1,070	421	333	−1,020	1,498
Reserve Assets	79db d						328	−73	−484	−1,341	−120	1,070	421	333	−1,020	1,498
Use of Fund Credit and Loans	79dc d						—	—	—	—	—	—	—	—	—	—
Exceptional Financing	79de d						—	—	—	—	—	—	—	—	—	—
Government Finance															*Millions of Dinars:*	
Deficit (-) or Surplus	80	−917	−3,133	2,034	....	....	....	....	....	....	....	....	....	....	....	....
Revenue	81	9,358	10,925	23,752	....											
Expenditure	82	7,729	9,913	12,495	....											
Lending Minus Repayments	83	2,545	4,144	9,223	....											
Financing																
Net Borrowing: Domestic	84a	1,001	3,181	−1,597	....											
Foreign	85a	−49	14	30	....											
Use of Cash Balances	87	−35	−63	−466	....											
National Accounts															*Billions of Dinars:*	
Househ.Cons.Expend.,incl.NPISHs	96f	14.1	17.3	25.7	31.5	35.9	44.6	50.9	58.5	70.2	87.2	95.6	106.2	125.8	139.7	156.4
Government Consumption Expend.	91f	4.6	5.0	5.9	8.0	9.2	11.6	14.6	17.5	22.4	26.4	30.7	34.7	39.5	45.8	52.9
Gross Fixed Capital Formation	93e	10.3	13.3	17.0	24.0	31.4	38.4	50.8	50.4	54.9	63.0	71.5	80.3	87.5	92.8	101.3
Changes in Inventories	93i	.8	1.0	5.1	3.9	.6	2.4	3.8	4.1	8.6	7.8	5.9	7.5	5.0	4.0	−2.0
Exports of Goods and Services	90c	6.9	8.1	21.4	20.7	24.4	26.6	26.7	39.9	55.8	66.2	64.2	65.3	67.7	68.6	38.7
Imports of Goods and Services (-)	98c	9.2	12.6	19.6	26.4	27.4	36.3	42.0	42.1	49.3	59.1	60.2	60.3	61.6	59.5	50.8
Gross Domestic Product (GDP)	99b	27.4	32.1	55.6	61.6	74.1	87.2	104.8	128.2	162.5	191.5	207.6	233.8	263.9	291.6	296.6
GDP Volume 1974 Prices	99b.p	....	48.1	48.5	53.5	58.3	62.7	....	....	....	....	....	....	....	....	....
															Millions:	
Population	99z	15.27	15.77	16.28	16.78	17.30	17.91	†17.58	18.19	18.67	19.25	19.86	20.52	21.25	21.85	22.52

	1987	1988	1989	1990	1991	1992	1993	1994	1995	1996	1997	1998	1999	2000	2001		

International Transactions

Millions of Dinars

	1987	1988	1989	1990	1991	1992	1993	1994	1995	1996	1997	1998	1999	2000	2001		
Exports	41,736	45,421	71,937	114,392	233,589	243,087	....	....	....	....	....	....	....	....	....	Exports	70
	....	....	....	....	....	....	....	....	....	....	....	....	....	....	....	Petroleum	70a
	....	....	....	....	....	....	....	....	....	....	....	....	....	....	....	Crude Petroleum	70aa
	....	....	....	....	....	....	....	....	....	....	....	....	....	....	....	Refined Petroleum	70ab
	34,153	43,427	70,072	87,018	139,241	188,406	....	....	....	....	501,580	552,358	610,673	....	....	Imports, c.i.f.	71
	34,153	43,765	69,903	86,708	141,932	188,835	204,533	335,522	513,921	498,523	501,610	552,357	610,673	794,958	923,327	Imports, c.i.f., from DOTS	71y

1995=100

Volume of Exports

	1987	1988	1989	1990	1991	1992	1993	1994	1995	1996	1997	1998	1999	2000	2001		
	....	90	90	97	93	94	97	98	100	104	....	....	....	....	....	Petroleum	72a
	83	71	84	90	90	84	96	99	100	112	....	....	....	....	....	Crude Petroleum	72aa
	....	113	98	105	98	105	98	97	100	95	....	....	....	....	....	Refined Petroleum	72ab

Index of Prices in US Dollars

Export Prices

	1987	1988	1989	1990	1991	1992	1993	1994	1995	1996	1997	1998	1999	2000	2001		
	....	92.1	105.2	138.2	116.3	116.9	98.4	91.8	100.0	121.7						Crude Petroleum	76aa d

Balance of Payments

Minus Sign Indicates Debit

	1987	1988	1989	1990	1991	1992	1993	1994	1995	1996	1997	1998	1999	2000	2001		
	141	−2,040	−1,081	1,420	2,367	....	....	....	....	....						Current Account, n.i.e.	78al d
	9,029	7,620	9,534	12,965	12,330	....	....	....	....	....						Goods: Exports f.o.b.	78aa d
	−6,630	−6,685	−8,390	−8,786	−6,862	....	....	....	....	....						Goods: Imports f.o.b.	78ab d
	2,398	935	1,144	4,179	5,468	....	....	....	....	....						*Trade Balance*	78ac d
	565	470	496	497	393	....	....	....	....	....						Services: Credit	78ad d
	−1,441	−1,337	−1,214	−1,321	−1,163	....	....	....	....	....						Services: Debit	78ae d
	1,523	68	425	3,355	4,698	....	....	....	....	....						*Balance on Goods & Services*	78af d
	110	71	111	73	70	....	....	....	....	....						Income: Credit	78ag d
	−2,009	−2,570	−2,157	−2,341	−2,618	....	....	....	....	....						Income: Debit	78ah d
	−376	−2,430	−1,622	1,087	2,151	....	....	....	....	....						*Balance on Gds, Serv. & Inc.*	78ai d
	628	477	603	400	269	....	....	....	....	....						Current Transfers, n.i.e.: Credit	78aj d
	−111	−86	−62	−67	−53	....	....	....	....	....						Current Transfers: Debit	78ak d
	—	—	—	—	—	....	....	....	....	....						Capital Account, n.i.e.	78bc d
	—	—	—	—	—	....	....	....	....	....						Capital Account, n.i.e.: Credit	78ba d
	—	—	—	—	—	....	....	....	....	....						Capital Account: Debit	78bb d
	309	744	755	−1,094	−1,020	....	....	....	....	....						Financial Account, n.i.e.	78bj d
	−15	−5	−8	−5	−50	....	....	....	....	....						Direct Investment Abroad	78bd d
	4	13	12	—	12	....	....	....	....	....						Dir. Invest. in Rep. Econ., n.i.e.	78be d
	—	—	—	—	—	....	....	....	....	....						Portfolio Investment Assets	78bf d
	—	2	—	—	—	....	....	....	....	....						Equity Securities	78bk d
	—	2	—	—	—	....	....	....	....	....						Debt Securities	78bl d
	—	—	—	—	—	....	....	....	....	....						Portfolio Investment Liab., n.i.e.	78bg d
	—	—	—	—	—	....	....	....	....	....						Equity Securities	78bm d
	—	—	—	—	—	....	....	....	....	....						Debt Securities	78bn d
	—	—	—	—	—	....	....	....	....	....						Financial Derivatives Assets	78bw d
	—	—	—	—	—	....	....	....	....	....						Financial Derivatives Liabilities	78bx d
	73	−131	−97	−229	−145	....	....	....	....	....						Other Investment Assets	78bh d
	—	—	—	—	—	....	....	....	....	....						Monetary Authorities	78bo d
	−122	−45	−14	−4	−37	....	....	....	....	....						General Government	78bp d
	195	−86	−83	−226	−108	....	....	....	....	....						Banks	78bq d
	—	—	—	—	—	....	....	....	....	....						Other Sectors	78br d
	248	865	848	−860	−837	....	....	....	....	....						Other Investment Liab., n.i.e.	78bi d
	8	7	−6	—	−3	....	....	....	....	....						Monetary Authorities	78bs d
	64	240	−51	215	286	....	....	....	....	....						General Government	78bt d
	18	8	138	162	90	....	....	....	....	....						Banks	78bu d
	158	609	767	−1,237	−1,210	....	....	....	....	....						Other Sectors	78bv d
	−802	337	−448	−336	−299	....	....	....	....	....						Net Errors and Omissions	78ca d
	−352	−959	−774	−10	1,047	....	....	....	....	....						*Overall Balance*	78cb d
	352	959	774	10	−1,047	....	....	....	....	....						Reserves and Related Items	79da d
	352	757	121	−138	−1,356	....	....	....	....	....						Reserve Assets	79db d
	—	—	584	—	308	....	....	....	....	....						Use of Fund Credit and Loans	79dc d
	—	201	69	148	—	....	....	....	....	....						Exceptional Financing	79de d

Government Finance

Year Ending December 31

	1987	1988	1989	1990	1991	1992	1993	1994	1995	1996	1997	1998	1999	2000	2001		
	....	....	....	....	....	....	....	†−60,354	−28,243	75,258	....					Deficit (-) or Surplus	80
	....	....	....	....	....	....	....	†439,199	600,847	825,157	....					Revenue	81
	....	....	....	....	....	....	....	†493,626	625,965	749,009	....					Expenditure	82
	....	....	....	....	....	....	....	5,927	3,125	890	....					Lending Minus Repayments	83
																Financing	
	....	....	....	....	....	....	....	−72,763	−105,101	−162,269	....					Net Borrowing: Domestic	84a
	....	....	....	....	....	....	....	141,376	172,158	100,937	....					Foreign	85a
	....	....	....	....	....	....	....	−8,259	−38,814	−13,926	....					Use of Cash Balances	87

National Accounts

Billions of Dinars

	1987	1988	1989	1990	1991	1992	1993	1994	1995	1996	1997	1998	1999	2000	2001		
	154.9	†158.8	265.5	313.6	419.0	548.3	649.1	837.5	1,114.8	1,335.0	1,430.3	1,555.4	1,667.2	1,713.2	....	Househ.Cons.Expend.,incl.NPISHs	96f
	58.0	†60.0	70.8	90.1	128.2	184.8	221.2	263.9	340.2	405.4	459.8	503.6	543.6	560.2	....	Government Consumption Expend.	91f
	92.9	†97.3	115.8	141.9	215.8	278.0	324.1	407.5	541.8	639.4	638.1	728.8	789.8	869.3	....	Gross Fixed Capital Formation	93e
	1.0	†1.0	13.0	18.3	51.0	41.8	12.1	60.4	91.2	5.2	9.3	26.2	35.1	15.2	....	Changes in Inventories	93i
	45.8	†48.9	78.1	129.6	246.5	266.3	252.3	342.6	533.0	781.7	837.2	652.3	918.9	1,749.0	....	Exports of Goods and Services	90c
	40.0	†46.0	121.1	139.1	198.4	244.5	269.1	424.5	616.1	596.7	594.7	656.1	739.5	828.3	....	Imports of Goods and Services (-)	98c
	312.7	†320.0	422.0	554.4	862.1	1,074.7	1,189.7	1,487.4	2,005.0	2,570.0	2,780.2	2,810.1	3,215.1	4,078.7	....	Gross Domestic Product (GDP)	99b
	....	....	....	....	....	....	....	....	....	....	....	....	....	....	....	GDP Volume 1974 Prices	99b. p

Midyear Estimates

	1987	1988	1989	1990	1991	1992	1993	1994	1995	1996	1997	1998	1999	2000	2001		
	23.02	23.73	24.33	25.02	25.64	26.27	26.89	27.50	28.06	28.57	29.05	29.51	29.95	30.99	30.84	**Population**	99z

(See notes in the back of the book.)

Angola

		1972	1973	1974	1975	1976	1977	1978	1979	1980	1981	1982	1983	1984	1985	1986
Exchange Rates												*Kwanzas per Mill. SDRs through 1994; per Thous. SDRs 1995-98;*				
Market Rate	aa	.0293	.0312	.0301	.0322	.0348	.0363	.0390	.0394	.0382	.0348	.0330	.0313	.0293	.0329	.0366
												Kwanzas per Mill. US$ through 1994; per Thous. US$ 1995-98; per US$				
Market Rate	ae	.0270	.0258	.0246	.0275	.0299	.0299	.0299	.0299	.0299	.0299	.0299	.0299	.0299	.0299	.0299
Market Rate	rf	.0271	.0245	.0254	.0256	.0294	.0299	.0299	.0299	.0299	.0299	.0299	.0299	.0299	.0299	.0299
Fund Position															*Millions of SDRs:*	
Quota	2f. s	....	....	....	....	....	....	....	....	....	....	....	....	....	....	....
SDRs	1b. s	....	....	....	....	....	....	....	....	....	....	....	....	....	....	....
Reserve Position in the Fund	1c. s	....	....	....	....	....	....	....	....	....	....	....	....	....	....	....
Total Fund Cred.&Loans Outstg.	2tl	....	....	....	....	....	....	....	....	....	....	....	....	....	....	....
International Liquidity												*Millions of US Dollars Unless Otherwise Indicated:*				
Total Reserves minus Gold	1l. d	....	....	....	....	....	....	....	....	....	....	....	....	....	....	....
SDRs	1b. d	....	....	....	....	....	....	....	....	....	....	....	....	....	....	....
Reserve Position in the Fund	1c. d	....	....	....	....	....	....	....	....	....	....	....	....	....	....	....
Foreign Exchange	1d. d	....	....	....	....	....	....	....	....	....	....	....	....	....	....	....
Monetary Authorities: Other Assets	3.. d	....	....	....	....	....	....	....	....	....	....	....	....	....	....	....
Other Liab.	4.. d	....	....	....	....	....	....	....	....	....	....	....	....	....	....	....
Banking Institutions: Assets	7a. d	....	....	....	....	....	....	....	....	....	....	....	....	....	....	....
Liabilities	7b. d	....	....	....	....	....	....	....	....	....	....	....	....	....	....	....
Monetary Authorities															*Millions of Kwanzas:*	
Foreign Assets	11	....	....	....	....	....	....	....	....	....	....	....	....	....	....	....
Claims on Central Government	12a	....	....	....	....	....	....	....	....	....	....	....	....	....	....	....
Claims on Nonfin.Pub.Enterprises	12c	....	....	....	....	....	....	....	....	....	....	....	....	....	....	....
Claims on Private Sector	12d	....	....	....	....	....	....	....	....	....	....	....	....	....	....	....
Claims on Banking Institutions	12e	....	....	....	....	....	....	....	....	....	....	....	....	....	....	....
Reserve Money	14	....	....	....	....	....	....	....	....	....	....	....	....	....	....	....
of which: Currency Outside Banks	14a	....	....	....	....	....	....	....	....	....	....	....	....	....	....	....
Time & Foreign Currency Deposits	15	....	....	....	....	....	....	....	....	....	....	....	....	....	....	....
Liabs. of Central Bank: Securities	16ac	....	....	....	....	....	....	....	....	....	....	....	....	....	....	....
Foreign Liabilities	16c	....	....	....	....	....	....	....	....	....	....	....	....	....	....	....
Central Government Deposits	16d	....	....	....	....	....	....	....	....	....	....	....	....	....	....	....
Capital Accounts	17a	....	....	....	....	....	....	....	....	....	....	....	....	....	....	....
Other Items (Net)	17r	....	....	....	....	....	....	....	....	....	....	....	....	....	....	....
Banking Institutions															*Millions of Kwanzas:*	
Reserves	20	....	....	....	....	....	....	....	....	....	....	....	....	....	....	....
Claims on Mon.Author.: Securities	20c	....	....	....	....	....	....	....	....	....	....	....	....	....	....	....
Foreign Assets	21	....	....	....	....	....	....	....	....	....	....	....	....	....	....	....
Claims on Central Government	22a	....	....	....	....	....	....	....	....	....	....	....	....	....	....	....
Claims on Local Government	22b	....	....	....	....	....	....	....	....	....	....	....	....	....	....	....
Claims on Nonfin. Pub. Enterprises	22c	....	....	....	....	....	....	....	....	....	....	....	....	....	....	....
Claims on Private Sector	22d	....	....	....	....	....	....	....	....	....	....	....	....	....	....	....
Demand Deposits	24	....	....	....	....	....	....	....	....	....	....	....	....	....	....	....
Time, Savings,& Fgn.Currency Dep.	25	....	....	....	....	....	....	....	....	....	....	....	....	....	....	....
of which: Fgn. Currency Deposits	25b	....	....	....	....	....	....	....	....	....	....	....	....	....	....	....
Money Market Instruments	26aa	....	....	....	....	....	....	....	....	....	....	....	....	....	....	....
Foreign Liabilities	26c	....	....	....	....	....	....	....	....	....	....	....	....	....	....	....
Central Government Deposits	26d	....	....	....	....	....	....	....	....	....	....	....	....	....	....	....
Credit from Monetary Authorities	26g	....	....	....	....	....	....	....	....	....	....	....	....	....	....	....
Capital Accounts	27a	....	....	....	....	....	....	....	....	....	....	....	....	....	....	....
Other Items (Net)	27r	....	....	....	....	....	....	....	....	....	....	....	....	....	....	....
Banking Survey															*Millions of Kwanzas:*	
Foreign Assets (Net)	31n	....	....	....	....	....	....	....	....	....	....	....	....	....	....	....
Domestic Credit	32	....	....	....	....	....	....	....	....	....	....	....	....	....	....	....
Claims on Central Govt.(Net)	32an	....	....	....	....	....	....	....	....	....	....	....	....	....	....	....
Claims on Local Government	32b	....	....	....	....	....	....	....	....	....	....	....	....	....	....	....
Claims on Nonfin.Pub.Enterprises	32c	....	....	....	....	....	....	....	....	....	....	....	....	....	....	....
Claims on Private Sector	32d	....	....	....	....	....	....	....	....	....	....	....	....	....	....	....
Money	34	....	....	....	....	....	....	....	....	....	....	....	....	....	....	....
Quasi-Money	35	....	....	....	....	....	....	....	....	....	....	....	....	....	....	....
Money Market Instruments	36aa	....	....	....	....	....	....	....	....	....	....	....	....	....	....	....
Liabs. of Central Banks: Securities	36ac	....	....	....	....	....	....	....	....	....	....	....	....	....	....	....
Capital Accounts	37a	....	....	....	....	....	....	....	....	....	....	....	....	....	....	....
Other Items (Net)	37r	....	....	....	....	....	....	....	....	....	....	....	....	....	....	....
Money plus Quasi-Money	35l	....	....	....	....	....	....	....	....	....	....	....	....	....	....	....
Interest Rates															*Percent Per Annum*	
Discount Rate (End of Period)	60	....	....	....	....	....	....	....	....	....	....	....	....	....	....	....
Deposit Rate	60l	....	....	....	....	....	....	....	....	....	....	....	....	....	....	....
Lending Rate	60p	....	....	....	....	....	....	....	....	....	....	....	....	....	....	....
Prices															*Index Numbers (1995=100):*	
Consumer Prices	64	....	....	....	....	....	....	....	....	....	....	....	....	....	....	....

Exchange Rates

per SDR Thereafter: End of Period

1987	1988	1989	1990	1991	1992	1993	1994	1995	1996	1997	1998	1999	2000	2001	
.0424	.0403	.0393	.0426	.2575	.7563	8.9281	743.4461	†8.4611	290.4593	354.0108	980.6929	†7.6585	21.9121	40.1517	Market Rate .... aa

Thereafter: End of Period: End of Period (ae) Period Average (rf)

1987	1988	1989	1990	1991	1992	1993	1994	1995	1996	1997	1998	1999	2000	2001	
.0299	.0299	.0299	.0299	.1800	.5500	6.5000	509.2620	†5.6920	201.9940	262.3760	696.5000	†5.5799	16.8178	31.9494	Market Rate .... ae
.0299	.0299	.0299	.0299	.0551	.2514	2.6602	59.5150	†2.7502	128.0292	229.0401	392.8235	†2.7907	10.0405	22.0579	Market Rate .... rf

Fund Position

End of Period

1987	1988	1989	1990	1991	1992	1993	1994	1995	1996	1997	1998	1999	2000	2001	
		145.00	145.00	145.00	207.30	207.30	207.30	207.30	207.30	207.30	207.30	286.30	286.30	286.30	Quota .... 2f. s
		—	.08	.09	.09	.10	.10	.11	.11	.12	.12	.13	.13	.14	SDRs .... 1b. s
		—	—	—	—	—	—	—	—	—	—	—	—	—	Reserve Position in the Fund .... 1c. s
		—	—	—	—	—	—	—	—	—	—	—	—	—	Total Fund Cred.&Loans Outstg. 2tl

International Liquidity

End of Period

1987	1988	1989	1990	1991	1992	1993	1994	1995	1996	1997	1998	1999	2000	2001	
								212.83	551.62	396.43	203.46	496.10	1,198.21	731.87	Total Reserves minus Gold 1l.d
		—	.11	.13	.12	.14	.15	.16	.16	.16	.17	.18	.17	.17	SDRs 1b.d
								—	—	—	—	—	—	—	Reserve Position in the Fund 1c.d
								212.67	551.46	396.27	203.28	495.93	1,198.04	731.69	Foreign Exchange 1d.d
								143.95	6.86	.01					Monetary Authorities: Other Assets .... 3..d
								1,901.59	348.01	329.78	444.98	90.53	212.42	247.35	Other Liab. .... 4..d
								264.62	523.49	833.30	682.25	747.42	878.08	1,170.30	Banking Institutions: Assets 7a.d
								69.68	61.07	137.31	199.46	119.12	49.14	157.42	Liabilities 7b.d

Monetary Authorities

End of Period

1987	1988	1989	1990	1991	1992	1993	1994	1995	1996	1997	1998	1999	2000	2001	
								2.1	112.8	104.0	141.7	†2,768.2	20,151.3	23,382.7	Foreign Assets 11
								4.3	36.2	82.3	330.2	†4,033.1	1,062.1	559.1	Claims on Central Government 12a
								2.9	2.5	3.7	2.5	†32.4	156.4	272.3	Claims on Nonfin.Pub.Enterprises 12c
								—	—	—	—	†9.0	43.2	247.2	Claims on Private Sector 12d
								—	—	48.8	61.5	†76.7	252.6	330.4	Claims on Banking Institutions 12e
								2.6	89.9	172.6	258.6	†1,956.0	6,215.2	15,325.7	Reserve Money 14
								1.2	42.2	101.6	165.7	†665.4	2,968.6	8,215.3	of which: Currency Outside Banks 14a
								2.4	58.5	6.8	7.2	†13.5	41.3	—	Time & Foreign Currency Deposits 15
								—	—	.3	—	†7.0	190.0	3,292.0	Liabs. of Central Bank: Securities 16ac
								10.8	70.3	86.5	309.9	†505.1	3,572.4	7,902.8	Foreign Liabilities 16c
								.3	21.3	—	.2	†2,878.4	14,251.9	1,213.0	Central Government Deposits 16d
								-1.2	18.4	15.1	23.2	†-636.4	-351.9	1,363.0	Capital Accounts 17a
								-5.6	-106.8	-42.4	-63.3	†2,195.7	-2,253.3	-4,304.8	Other Items (Net) 17r

Banking Institutions

End of Period

1987	1988	1989	1990	1991	1992	1993	1994	1995	1996	1997	1998	1999	2000	2001	
								1.1	47.7	82.3	92.4	†1,044.9	2,964.2	7,502.6	Reserves 20
								—	—	—	—	†7.0	175.0	3,292.0	Claims on Mon.Author.: Securities 20c
								1.5	105.7	218.6	475.2	†4,170.6	14,767.4	37,390.5	Foreign Assets 21
								.3	1.0	5.9	55.3	†12.0	3.3	40.4	Claims on Central Government 22a
								—	—	—	—	†.4	10.0	23.1	Claims on Local Government 22b
								—	—	—	.2	†61.1	186.7	608.5	Claims on Nonfin. Pub. Enterprises 22c
								.7	26.5	90.6	90.0	†432.9	1,802.7	7,032.9	Claims on Private Sector 22d
								1.2	51.8	93.3	106.6	†516.0	2,037.0	5,449.5	Demand Deposits 24
								.4	78.0	194.5	344.9	†2,720.5	10,741.5	27,696.7	Time, Savings,& Fgn.Currency Dep. 25
								.4	67.7	170.1	330.7	†2,626.3	10,696.1	26,833.5	of which: Fgn. Currency Deposits 25b
								—	—	—	—	†—	—	321.3	Money Market Instruments 26aa
								.4	12.3	36.0	138.9	†664.7	826.4	5,029.4	Foreign Liabilities 26c
								—	5.2		28.9	†462.8	2,538.1	8,818.7	Central Government Deposits 26d
								—	—	48.0	58.0	†500.6	1,180.8	—	Credit from Monetary Authorities 26g
								.2	16.1	23.9	100.6	†703.7	2,905.2	9,101.0	Capital Accounts 27a
								1.4	17.7	-5.1	-64.9	†160.6	-319.7	-526.6	Other Items (Net) 27r

Banking Survey

End of Period

1987	1988	1989	1990	1991	1992	1993	1994	1995	1996	1997	1998	1999	2000	2001	
								-7.6	135.9	200.1	168.0	†5,768.9	30,520.0	47,841.0	Foreign Assets (Net) 31n
								7.9	39.9	175.7	449.0	†1,239.7	-13,525.7	-1,248.2	Domestic Credit 32
								4.3	10.8	81.4	356.3	†703.9	-15,724.7	-9,432.2	Claims on Central Govt.(Net) 32an
								—	—	—	—	†.4	10.0	23.1	Claims on Local Government 32b
								2.9	2.5	3.7	2.7	†93.5	343.1	880.8	Claims on Nonfin.Pub.Enterprises 32c
								.7	26.5	90.6	90.0	†441.9	1,845.8	7,280.1	Claims on Private Sector 32d
								2.7	93.9	194.9	272.4	†1,206.5	5,332.8	14,298.7	Money 34
								2.8	136.5	201.3	352.1	†2,734.0	10,782.7	27,696.7	Quasi-Money 35
								—	—	—	—	†—	—	321.3	Money Market Instruments 36aa
								—	—	—	.3	†—	15.0	—	Liabs. of Central Banks: Securities 36ac
								-1.0	34.5	38.9	123.8	†67.3	2,553.4	10,464.0	Capital Accounts 37a
								-4.2	-89.1	-59.6	-131.3	†3,000.8	-1,689.6	-6,187.9	Other Items (Net) 37r
								5.5	230.4	396.2	624.6	†3,940.5	16,115.5	41,995.4	Money plus Quasi-Money 35l

Interest Rates

Percent Per Annum

1987	1988	1989	1990	1991	1992	1993	1994	1995	1996	1997	1998	1999	2000	2001	
								160.00	2.00	48.00	58.00	120.00	150.00	150.00	Discount Rate (End of Period) 60
								125.92	147.13	29.25	36.88	36.57	†39.58	47.91	Deposit Rate 60l
								206.25	217.88	37.75	45.00	80.30	†103.16	95.97	Lending Rate 60p

Prices

Period Averages

1987	1988	1989	1990	1991	1992	1993	1994	1995	1996	1997	1998	1999	2000	2001	
			—	—	—	†—	4	100	4,245	13,550	25,327	†97,807	415,684	1,049,855	Consumer Prices 64

Angola

International Transactions		1972	1973	1974	1975	1976	1977	1978	1979	1980	1981	1982	1983	1984	1985	1986
Balance of Payments															*Millions of US Dollars:*	
Current Account, n.i.e.	78al d	…	…	…	…	…	…	…	…	…	…	…	…	…	195.0	−303.0
Goods: Exports f.o.b.	78aa d	…	…	…	…	…	…	…	…	…	…	…	…	…	2,301.0	1,346.0
Goods: Imports f.o.b.	78ab d	…	…	…	…	…	…	…	…	…	…	…	…	…	−1,401.0	−1,086.0
Trade Balance	78ac d	…	…	…	…	…	…	…	…	…	…	…	…	…	900.0	260.0
Services: Credit	78ad d	…	…	…	…	…	…	…	…	…	…	…	…	…	129.0	116.0
Services: Debit	78ae d	…	…	…	…	…	…	…	…	…	…	…	…	…	−641.0	−587.0
Balance on Goods & Services	78af d	…	…	…	…	…	…	…	…	…	…	…	…	…	388.0	−211.0
Income: Credit	78ag d	…	…	…	…	…	…	…	…	…	…	…	…	…	—	—
Income: Debit	78ah d	…	…	…	…	…	…	…	…	…	…	…	…	…	−214.0	−233.0
Balance on Gds, Serv. & Inc.	78ai d	…	…	…	…	…	…	…	…	…	…	…	…	…	174.0	−444.0
Current Transfers, n.i.e.: Credit	78aj d	…	…	…	…	…	…	…	…	…	…	…	…	…	37.0	159.0
Current Transfers: Debit	78ak d	…	…	…	…	…	…	…	…	…	…	…	…	…	−16.0	−18.0
Capital Account, n.i.e.	78bc d	…	…	…	…	…	…	…	…	…	…	…	…	…	—	—
Capital Account, n.i.e.: Credit	78ba d	…	…	…	…	…	…	…	…	…	…	…	…	…	—	—
Capital Account: Debit	78bb d	…	…	…	…	…	…	…	…	…	…	…	…	…	—	—
Financial Account, n.i.e.	78bj d	…	…	…	…	…	…	…	…	…	…	…	…	…	454.0	248.0
Direct Investment Abroad	78bd d	…	…	…	…	…	…	…	…	…	…	…	…	…	—	—
Dir. Invest. in Rep. Econ., n.i.e.	78be d	…	…	…	…	…	…	…	…	…	…	…	…	…	278.0	234.0
Portfolio Investment Assets	78bf d	…	…	…	…	…	…	…	…	…	…	…	…	…	—	—
Equity Securities	78bk d	…	…	…	…	…	…	…	…	…	…	…	…	…	—	—
Debt Securities	78bl d	…	…	…	…	…	…	…	…	…	…	…	…	…	—	—
Portfolio Investment Liab., n.i.e.	78bg d	…	…	…	…	…	…	…	…	…	…	…	…	…	—	—
Equity Securities	78bm d	…	…	…	…	…	…	…	…	…	…	…	…	…	—	—
Debt Securities	78bn d	…	…	…	…	…	…	…	…	…	…	…	…	…	—	—
Financial Derivatives Assets	78bw d	…	…	…	…	…	…	…	…	…	…	…	…	…	…	…
Financial Derivatives Liabilities	78bx d	…	…	…	…	…	…	…	…	…	…	…	…	…	…	…
Other Investment Assets	78bh d	…	…	…	…	…	…	…	…	…	…	…	…	…	…	…
Monetary Authorities	78bo d	…	…	…	…	…	…	…	…	…	…	…	…	…	—	—
General Government	78bp d	…	…	…	…	…	…	…	…	…	…	…	…	…	…	…
Banks	78bq d	…	…	…	…	…	…	…	…	…	…	…	…	…	—	—
Other Sectors	78br d	…	…	…	…	…	…	…	…	…	…	…	…	…	—	—
Other Investment Liab., n.i.e.	78bi d	…	…	…	…	…	…	…	…	…	…	…	…	…	176.0	14.0
Monetary Authorities	78bs d	…	…	…	…	…	…	…	…	…	…	…	…	…	—	—
General Government	78bt d	…	…	…	…	…	…	…	…	…	…	…	…	…	176.0	14.0
Banks	78bu d	…	…	…	…	…	…	…	…	…	…	…	…	…	—	—
Other Sectors	78bv d	…	…	…	…	…	…	…	…	…	…	…	…	…	—	—
Net Errors and Omissions	78ca d	…	…	…	…	…	…	…	…	…	…	…	…	…	−655.0	−204.0
Overall Balance	78cb d	…	…	…	…	…	…	…	…	…	…	…	…	…	−6.0	−259.0
Reserves and Related Items	79da d	…	…	…	…	…	…	…	…	…	…	…	…	…	6.0	259.0
Reserve Assets	79db d	…	…	…	…	…	…	…	…	…	…	…	…	…	−21.0	41.0
Use of Fund Credit and Loans	79dc d	…	…	…	…	…	…	…	…	…	…	…	…	…	—	—
Exceptional Financing	79de d	…	…	…	…	…	…	…	…	…	…	…	…	…	27.0	218.0
															Millions:	
Population	99z	5.80	5.97	6.11	†6.52	6.75	7.00	7.25	7.49	7.72	7.94	8.14	7.57	7.77	7.98	8.19

International Transactions

Balance of Payments

Minus Sign Indicates Debit

Item	1987	1988	1989	1990	1991	1992	1993	1994	1995	1996	1997	1998	1999	2000	2001	Code
Current Account, n.i.e.	447.0	-469.0	-132.0	-235.5	-579.6	-734.8	-668.5	-339.8	-295.0	3,266.4	-872.1	-1,857.6	-1,702.1	....	....	78al d
Goods: Exports f.o.b.	2,322.0	2,492.0	3,014.0	3,883.9	3,449.3	3,832.8	2,900.5	3,016.6	3,722.7	5,095.0	5,006.8	3,542.9	5,156.5	....	....	78aa d
Goods: Imports f.o.b.	-1,303.0	-1,372.0	-1,338.0	-1,578.2	-1,347.2	-1,988.0	-1,462.6	-1,454.1	-1,467.7	-2,040.5	-2,597.0	-2,079.4	-3,109.1	....	....	78ab d
Trade Balance	1,019.0	1,120.0	1,676.0	2,305.7	2,102.1	1,844.8	1,437.9	1,562.5	2,255.0	3,054.5	2,409.8	1,463.5	2,047.4	....	....	78ac d
Services: Credit	93.0	128.0	150.0	108.5	171.3	142.9	105.8	150.2	113.1	267.7	138.8	123.0	154.6	....	....	78ad d
Services: Debit	-423.0	-1,134.0	-1,175.0	-1,807.3	-1,839.1	-2,042.4	-1,561.9	-1,562.9	-2,051.4	-2,423.3	-2,605.4	-2,635.3	-2,594.6	....	....	78ae d
Balance on Goods & Services	689.0	114.0	651.0	606.9	434.3	-54.8	-18.2	149.8	316.7	898.9	-56.8	-1,048.8	-392.6	....	....	78af d
Income: Credit				10.6	15.0	15.7	11.3	13.0	15.9	43.3	112.1	34.5	24.2	....	....	78ag d
Income: Debit	-294.0	-615.0	-779.0	-775.9	-1,057.1	-798.0	-827.4	-747.7	-783.2	-1,516.7	-1,033.2	-1,003.2	-1,396.1	....	....	78ah d
Balance on Gds, Serv. & Inc.	395.0	-501.0	-128.0	-158.4	-607.8	-837.0	-834.3	-584.9	-450.6	-574.4	-977.9	-2,017.5	-1,764.5	....	....	78ai d
Current Transfers, n.i.e.: Credit	60.0	42.0	65.0	65.6	111.1	170.9	253.4	333.2	312.2	3,949.4	187.7	246.6	161.2	....	....	78aj d
Current Transfers: Debit	-8.0	-10.0	-69.0	-142.7	-82.9	-68.7	-87.6	-88.1	-156.7	-108.6	-81.9	-86.7	-98.8	....	....	78ak d
Capital Account, n.i.e.	—	—	—	—	—	—	—	—	—	—	—	—	—	....	....	78bc d
Capital Account, n.i.e.: Credit	—	—	—	—	—	—	—	—	—	—	—	—	—	....	....	78ba d
Capital Account: Debit	—	—	—	—	—	—	—	—	—	—	—	—	—	....	....	78bb d
Financial Account, n.i.e.	55.0	-199.0	-120.0	-954.3	-947.2	-445.9	-274.3	-443.4	-924.8	-654.5	489.5	496.4	1,498.7	....	....	78bj d
Direct Investment Abroad				-.9										....	....	78bd d
Dir. Invest. in Rep. Econ., n.i.e.	119.0	131.0	200.0	-334.8	664.5	288.0	302.1	170.3	472.4	180.6	411.7	1,114.0	2,471.4	....	....	78be d
Portfolio Investment Assets	—	—	—	—	—	—	—	—	—	—	—	—	—	....	....	78bf d
Equity Securities	—	—	—	—	—	—	—	—	—	—	—	—	—	....	....	78bk d
Debt Securities	—	—	—	—	—	—	—	—	—	—	—	—	—	....	....	78bl d
Portfolio Investment Liab., n.i.e.	—	—	—	—	—	—	—	—	—	—	—	—	—	....	....	78bg d
Equity Securities	—	—	—	—	—	—	—	—	—	—	—	—	—	....	....	78bm d
Debt Securities	—	—	—	—	—	—	—	—	—	—	—	—	—	....	....	78bn d
Financial Derivatives Assets														....	....	78bw d
Financial Derivatives Liabilities														....	....	78bx d
Other Investment Assets				-348.8	-190.2	-255.5	-92.9	214.1	-168.4	-327.6	-330.7	-40.8	-186.2	....	....	78bh d
Monetary Authorities														....	....	78bo d
General Government				—	—	-52.6	-156.0	—	-4.4	-48.8	—	—	—	....	....	78bp d
Banks				—	—	—	10.0	—	—	—	—	—	—	....	....	78bq d
Other Sectors				-348.8	-190.2	-202.9	53.1	214.1	-164.1	-278.8	-330.7	-40.8	-186.2	....	....	78br d
Other Investment Liab., n.i.e.	-64.0	-330.0	-320.0	-269.8	-1,421.5	-478.4	-483.5	-827.8	-1,228.8	-507.4	408.5	-576.8	-786.5	....	....	78bi d
Monetary Authorities					14.8	59.8	17.6	-185.9	-114.3	-143.9	39.5	-174.9	-513.3	....	....	78bs d
General Government	-64.0	-330.0	-320.0	-80.6	-1,031.4	-430.8	-583.6	-792.6	-778.1	-202.7	-69.0	-478.7	-180.2	....	....	78bt d
Banks				33.8	-1.3	-9.6	.6	—	—	-1.6	4.8	2.4	3.5	....	....	78bu d
Other Sectors				-223.0	-403.6	-97.8	81.9	150.7	-336.4	-159.2	433.2	74.4	-96.5	....	....	78bv d
Net Errors and Omissions	-834.0	-257.0	-678.0	-19.1	26.9	43.0	-377.1	-244.5	-19.4	149.2	-182.2	377.6	-80.9	....	....	78ca d
Overall Balance	-332.0	-925.0	-930.0	-1,208.9	-1,499.9	-1,137.7	-1,319.9	-1,027.7	-1,239.3	2,761.0	-564.8	-983.6	-284.3	....	....	78cb d
Reserves and Related Items	332.0	925.0	930.0	1,208.9	1,499.9	1,137.7	1,319.9	1,027.7	1,239.3	-2,761.0	564.8	983.6	284.3	....	....	79da d
Reserve Assets	-17.0	-49.0	6.0	-1.5	-48.3	-227.2	192.9	14.2	-30.7	-330.3	162.6	189.6	-288.7	....	....	79db d
Use of Fund Credit and Loans														....	....	79dc d
Exceptional Financing	349.0	974.0	924.0	1,210.4	1,548.2	1,364.9	1,127.0	1,013.5	1,270.0	-2,430.7	402.2	794.0	573.0	....	....	79de d

Midyear Estimates

Item	1987	1988	1989	1990	1991	1992	1993	1994	1995	1996	1997	1998	1999	2000	2001	Code
Population	8.41	8.70	9.74	10.02	9.89	10.61	10.60	10.97	11.34	11.70	12.05	12.40	12.76	13.13	13.53	99z

(See notes in the back of the book.)

Antigua and Barbuda

	1972	1973	1974	1975	1976	1977	1978	1979	1980	1981	1982	1983	1984	1985	1986
Exchange Rates											*E. Caribbean Dollars per SDR: End of Period (aa)*				
Official Rate .... aa	2.2194	2.4925	2.5024	2.7770	3.1369	3.2797	3.5175	3.5568	3.4436	3.1427	2.9784	2.8268	2.6466	2.9657	3.3026
Official Rate .... ae	2.0442	2.0661	2.0439	2.3721	2.7000	2.7000	2.7000	2.7000	2.7000	2.7000	2.7000	2.7000	2.7000	2.7000	2.7000
											Index Numbers (1995=100):				
Official Rate .... ah x	140.7	137.9	131.6	125.0	103.5	100.0	100.0	100.0	100.0	100.0	100.0	100.0	100.0	100.0	100.0
Nominal Effective Exchange Rate .... ne c	....	....	....	....	....	....	....	91.4	89.9	93.4	97.6	100.7	105.6	107.9	103.2
Real Effective Exchange Rate .... re c	....	....	....	....	....	....	....	107.6	110.5	115.7	117.4	118.4	122.6	120.9	112.9
Fund Position														*Millions of SDRs:*	
Quota .... 2f. s	....	....	....	....	....	....	....	....	....	....	3.60	5.00	5.00	5.00	5.00
SDRs .... 1b. s	....	....	....	....	....	....	....	....	....	....	—	—	—	—	—
Reserve Position in the Fund .... 1c. s	....	....	....	....	....	....	....	....	....	....	—	—	—	—	—
Total Fund Cred.&Loans Outstg. 2tl	....	....	....	....	....	....	....	....	....	....	—	—	—	—	—
International Liquidity														*Millions of US Dollars:*	
Total Reserves minus Gold .... 1l. d	....	....	....	7.32	9.67	5.10	5.97	11.23	7.82	7.34	8.52	9.93	15.44	16.58	28.26
SDRs .... 1b. d	....	....	....	....	....	....	....	....	....	—	—	—	—	—	—
Reserve Position in the Fund .... 1c. d	....	....	....	....	....	....	....	....	....	....	—	—	—	—	—
Foreign Exchange .... 1d. d	....	....	....	7.32	9.67	5.10	5.97	11.23	7.82	7.34	8.52	9.93	15.44	16.58	28.26
Deposit Money Banks: Assets .... 7a. d	....	....	....	14.16	3.68	2.31	4.55	5.58	4.45	8.49	11.02	8.39	19.27	27.64	19.09
Liabilities .... 7b. d	....	....	....	15.91	18.28	10.50	14.87	17.20	14.78	18.16	26.10	20.64	30.98	49.21	49.06
Monetary Authorities														*Millions of E. Caribbean Dollars:*	
Foreign Assets 11	....	....	....	17.35	26.10	13.78	16.13	30.33	21.52	20.28	23.67	30.00	37.85	52.07	78.64
Claims on Central Government 12a	....	....	....	2.12	5.62	5.77	6.26	6.26	9.40	9.60	11.56	11.56	32.49	33.95	37.10
Claims on Deposit Money Banks 12e	....	....	....	—	—	—	—	—	—	—	—	—	4.04	.26	1.92
Reserve Money 14	....	....	....	19.47	31.72	19.55	22.39	36.59	30.51	29.41	34.69	39.79	71.60	83.15	115.33
of which: Currency Outside DMBs 14a	....	....	....	10.77	11.92	13.15	15.13	17.09	15.26	16.27	16.32	17.47	23.97	26.50	32.46
Foreign Liabilities 16c	....	....	....	—	—	—	—	—	—	—	—	—	—	—	—
Central Government Deposits 16d	....	....	....	—	—	—	—	—	.41	.48	.54	1.78	2.78	3.14	2.33
Other Items (Net) 17r	....	....	....	—	—	—	—	—	—	—	—	—	—	—	—
Deposit Money Banks														*Millions of E. Caribbean Dollars:*	
Reserves 20	....	....	....	8.70	19.80	6.40	7.26	19.50	15.24	13.14	18.38	22.31	55.24	61.25	85.53
Foreign Assets 21	....	....	....	33.60	9.93	6.24	12.29	15.07	12.02	22.92	29.75	22.67	52.03	74.62	51.54
Claims on Central Government 22a	....	....	....	13.29	32.18	20.04	20.02	31.74	34.91	32.99	39.64	38.33	46.59	48.25	57.57
Claims on Local Government 22b	....	....	....												
Claims on Nonfin.Pub.Enterprises 22c	....	....	....	1.26	2.65	2.33	2.75	6.01	6.24	3.79	8.54	4.56	1.56	5.07	8.17
Claims on Private Sector 22d	....	....	....	65.35	74.32	83.74	90.54	85.88	102.72	131.35	137.75	180.13	211.80	258.34	295.34
Claims on Nonbank Financial Insts 22g	....	....	....	—	—	—	—	1.44	1.82	1.59	1.65	.36	.11	1.11	.66
Demand Deposits 24	....	....	....	8.20	12.35	17.76	14.24	17.72	23.31	26.89	25.38	33.62	34.44	41.95	54.91
Time, Savings,& Fgn.Currency Dep. 25	....	....	....	79.05	82.23	71.61	83.84	95.93	106.79	125.38	149.55	185.71	227.68	251.47	290.76
Foreign Liabilities 26c	....	....	....	37.75	49.36	28.36	40.16	46.45	39.90	49.04	70.47	55.73	83.65	132.87	132.46
Central Government Deposits 26d	....	....	....	—	—	—	—	.63	1.56	1.09	.79	2.73	2.39	1.95	4.76
Credit from Monetary Authorities 26g	....	....	....	—	—	—	—	—	—	—	.09	1.42	1.20	.51	2.20
Capital Accounts 27a	....	....	....	3.00	3.00	3.00	3.00	3.26	4.55	5.72	6.92	5.67	15.18	17.32	21.84
Other Items (Net) 27r	....	....	....	−5.79	−8.05	−2.00	−8.39	−4.36	−3.17	−2.34	−17.49	−16.51	2.79	2.57	−8.12
Monetary Survey														*Millions of E. Caribbean Dollars:*	
Foreign Assets (Net) 31n	....	....	....	13.20	−13.33	−8.34	−11.74	−1.05	−6.36	−5.84	−17.05	−3.06	6.23	−6.18	−2.28
Domestic Credit 32	....	....	....	82.02	114.77	111.87	119.57	130.69	153.11	177.75	197.82	230.44	287.37	341.64	391.76
Claims on Central Govt. (Net) 32an	....	....	....	15.41	37.80	25.81	26.28	37.37	42.34	41.02	49.88	45.39	73.91	77.12	87.59
Claims on Local Government 32b	....	....	....												
Claims on Nonfin.Pub.Enterprises 32c	....	....	....	1.26	2.65	2.33	2.75	6.01	6.24	3.79	8.54	4.56	1.56	5.07	8.17
Claims on Private Sector 32d	....	....	....	65.35	74.32	83.74	90.54	85.88	102.72	131.35	137.75	180.13	211.80	258.34	295.34
Claims on Nonbank Financial Inst 32g	....	....	....	—	—	—	—	1.44	1.82	1.59	1.65	.36	.11	1.11	.66
Money 34	....	....	....	18.97	24.26	30.91	29.37	34.81	38.57	43.16	41.70	51.10	58.40	68.45	87.37
Quasi-Money 35	....	....	....	79.05	82.23	71.61	83.84	95.93	106.79	125.38	149.55	185.71	227.68	251.47	290.76
Capital Accounts 37a	....	....	....	3.00	3.00	3.00	3.00	3.26	4.55	5.72	6.92	5.67	15.18	17.32	21.84
Other Items (Net) 37r	....	....	....	−5.79	−8.05	−2.00	−8.39	−4.36	−3.17	−2.34	−17.41	−15.09	−7.66	−1.78	−10.48
Money plus Quasi-Money 35l	....	....	....	98.02	106.49	102.53	113.21	130.74	145.37	168.54	191.25	236.80	286.08	319.92	378.13
Interest Rates														*Percent Per Annum*	
Treasury Bill Rate 60c	....	....	....	....	....	....	....	....	7.0	7.0	7.0	7.0	7.0	7.0	7.0
Deposit Rate 60l	....	....	....	....	....	....	....	....	6.0	6.3	7.5	11.0	11.0	9.9	7.7
Lending Rate 60p	....	....	....	....	....	....	8.6	8.6	10.0	11.0	13.0	14.0	13.6	13.0	14.3
Prices														*Index Numbers (1985=100):*	
Consumer Prices 64	....	....	....	....	48.0	54.6	57.9	67.4	80.2	89.4	93.1	95.3	99.0	100.0	....

	1987	1988	1989	1990	1991	1992	1993	1994	1995	1996	1997	1998	1999	2000	2001	Code
Exchange Rates																
E. Caribbean Dollars per US Dollar: End of Period (ae)																
Official Rate	3.8304	3.6334	3.5482	3.8412	3.8622	3.7125	3.7086	3.9416	4.0135	3.8825	3.6430	3.8017	3.7058	3.5179	3.3932	aa
Official Rate	2.7000	2.7000	2.7000	2.7000	2.7000	2.7000	2.7000	2.7000	2.7000	2.7000	2.7000	2.7000	2.7000	2.7000	2.7000	ae
Period Averages																
Official Rate	100.0	100.0	100.0	100.0	100.0	100.0	100.0	100.0	100.0	100.0	100.0	100.0	100.0	100.0	100.0	ahx
Nominal Effective Exchange Rate	99.2	96.3	99.2	95.9	97.1	97.1	103.1	103.2	100.0	101.5	104.7	105.7	106.7	111.9	115.1	ne c
Real Effective Exchange Rate	108.3	107.8	108.9	106.1	107.9[e]	106.5[e]	112.7[e]	103.7	100.0	101.6	102.8	105.1	105.5	107.7	111.5[e]	re c
Fund Position																
End of Period																
Quota	5.00	5.00	5.00	5.00	5.00	5.00	8.50	8.50	8.50	8.50	8.50	8.50	13.50	13.50	13.50	2f. s
SDRs	—	—	—	—	—	—	—	—	—	—	—	—	.01	.01	.01	1b. s
Reserve Position in the Fund	—	—	—	—	—	—	—	—	—	—	—	—	—	—	—	1c. s
Total Fund Cred.&Loans Outstg.	—	—	—	—	—	—	—	—	—	—	—	—	—	—	—	2tl
International Liquidity																
End of Period																
Total Reserves minus Gold	25.60	28.03	28.07	27.50	32.54	50.52	37.81	45.81	59.44	47.74	50.70	59.37	69.73	63.56	79.72	1l. d
SDRs	—	—	—	—	—	—	.01	.01	.01	.01	.01	.01	.01	.01	.01	1b. d
Reserve Position in the Fund	—	—	—	—	—	—	—	—	—	—	—	—	—	—	—	1c. d
Foreign Exchange	25.60	28.03	28.07	27.50	32.54	50.52	37.80	45.80	59.43	47.73	50.69	59.36	69.72	63.55	79.71	1d. d
Deposit Money Banks: Assets	30.99	37.31	29.32	30.28	49.41	53.62	56.99	77.30	77.54	72.02	58.79	71.34	160.10	172.16	187.34	7a. d
Liabilities	51.50	56.23	57.00	55.81	50.14	66.79	52.73	60.72	46.57	76.66	101.70	112.56	209.49	262.92	231.74	7b. d
Monetary Authorities																
End of Period																
Foreign Assets	70.50	75.83	76.30	75.07	86.26	134.95	102.00	123.80	160.49	130.16	138.16	161.56	191.56	177.34	222.49	11
Claims on Central Government	36.38	40.55	38.46	45.78	44.71	36.10	39.48	39.11	31.02	28.01	27.35	25.48	21.74	30.40	27.32	12a
Claims on Deposit Money Banks	4.58	7.35	4.15	2.47	1.88	1.60	1.46	1.33	1.18	1.03	.95	.90	.74	.62	.49	12e
Reserve Money	109.33	121.49	116.44	120.61	132.75	172.53	142.83	164.12	192.56	159.14	166.37	187.84	213.93	208.26	250.18	14
of which: Currency Outside DMBs	42.24	51.31	61.47	57.52	57.91	64.31	61.21	65.87	77.22	68.06	66.55	79.78	85.01	84.63	78.13	14a
Foreign Liabilities	—	—	—	—	—	—	—	—	—	—	—	—	—	—	—	16c
Central Government Deposits	2.13	2.25	2.48	2.71	.11	.11	.12	.12	.13	.06	.09	.09	.09	.10	.11	16d
Other Items (Net)	—	—	—	—	—	—	—	—	—	—	—	—	—	—	—	17r
Deposit Money Banks																
End of Period																
Reserves	59.17	65.82	56.66	63.31	77.17	98.34	87.99	96.82	116.90	93.87	99.01	115.73	130.99	117.01	190.80	20
Foreign Assets	83.67	100.75	79.18	81.75	133.42	144.76	153.87	208.72	209.36	194.46	158.72	192.61	432.28	464.85	505.83	21
Claims on Central Government	69.18	85.96	79.98	64.88	80.60	95.19	117.80	124.62	162.83	161.20	192.52	224.83	269.28	283.05	270.51	22a
Claims on Local Government	—	.12	13.53	19.94	—	.72	.81	.23	.72	.72	.52	1.43	—	—	.48	22b
Claims on Nonfin.Pub.Enterprises	12.04	9.58	9.78	7.27	5.70	9.30	9.69	9.53	33.78	33.25	32.44	53.94	77.60	87.36	82.26	22c
Claims on Private Sector	352.05	412.52	468.64	503.09	547.45	586.67	598.33	613.83	706.86	850.34	1,027.00	1,103.30	1,196.01	1,308.64	1,348.71	22d
Claims on Nonbank Financial Insts	2.29	6.30	13.84	22.35	25.23	6.00	5.92	24.50	7.78	6.73	6.75	9.34	16.43	8.24	10.13	22g
Demand Deposits	68.39	76.88	79.63	99.22	109.73	118.20	123.26	154.13	202.47	187.25	197.99	250.64	241.08	225.05	261.66	24
Time, Savings,& Fgn.Currency Dep.	338.82	371.65	425.03	436.34	515.42	539.27	599.16	649.27	773.57	756.28	824.64	929.91	1,058.88	1,163.71	1,219.72	25
Foreign Liabilities	139.04	151.82	153.90	150.68	135.38	180.35	142.36	163.95	125.73	206.99	274.59	303.92	565.62	709.89	625.71	26c
Central Government Deposits	9.43	28.51	27.93	28.18	35.77	49.61	39.82	53.83	65.10	72.77	71.32	69.60	57.57	54.26	55.31	26d
Credit from Monetary Authorities	4.76	8.69	4.83	2.49	1.76	2.12	1.94	1.29	1.17	1.03	4.31	15.63	13.60	10.97	31.50	26g
Capital Accounts	27.90	27.51	30.75	35.85	96.00	81.18	91.18	110.08	126.40	140.19	161.27	178.04	191.83	190.41	221.78	27a
Other Items (Net)	-9.94	15.99	-.46	9.85	-24.51	-29.75	-23.33	-54.32	-56.20	-24.15	-16.96	-46.56	-5.98	-85.13	-6.96	27r
Monetary Survey																
End of Period																
Foreign Assets (Net)	15.13	24.76	1.57	6.13	84.30	99.36	113.51	168.57	244.12	117.62	22.29	50.24	58.22	-67.70	102.61	31n
Domestic Credit	460.37	524.26	593.82	632.43	667.81	684.25	732.08	757.86	877.76	1,007.22	1,215.36	1,348.62	1,523.39	1,663.33	1,683.98	32
Claims on Central Govt. (Net)	93.99	95.75	88.03	79.78	89.43	81.56	117.35	109.78	128.62	116.38	148.45	180.61	233.35	259.09	242.41	32an
Claims on Local Government	—	.12	13.53	19.94	—	.72	.81	.23	.72	.52	.72	1.43	—	—	.48	32b
Claims on Nonfin.Pub.Enterprises	12.04	9.58	9.78	7.27	5.70	9.30	9.69	9.53	33.78	33.25	32.44	53.94	77.60	87.36	82.26	32c
Claims on Private Sector	352.05	412.52	468.64	503.09	547.45	586.67	598.33	613.83	706.86	850.34	1,027.00	1,103.30	1,196.01	1,308.64	1,348.71	32d
Claims on Nonbank Financial Inst	2.29	6.30	13.84	22.35	25.23	6.00	5.92	24.50	7.78	6.73	6.75	9.34	16.43	8.24	10.13	32g
Money	110.62	128.19	141.09	156.74	167.64	182.62	184.61	220.18	279.78	255.39	264.61	330.47	326.13	309.69	339.79	34
Quasi-Money	338.82	371.65	425.03	436.34	515.42	539.27	599.16	649.27	773.57	756.28	824.64	929.91	1,058.88	1,163.71	1,219.72	35
Capital Accounts	27.90	27.51	30.75	35.85	96.00	81.18	91.18	110.08	126.40	140.19	161.27	178.04	191.83	190.41	221.78	37a
Other Items (Net)	-1.84	21.68	-1.48	9.64	-26.95	-19.46	-29.36	-53.10	-57.86	-27.03	-12.87	-39.55	4.78	-68.17	5.30	37r
Money plus Quasi-Money	449.44	499.84	566.12	593.08	683.06	721.89	783.77	869.45	1,053.35	1,011.67	1,089.25	1,260.38	1,385.00	1,473.39	1,559.52	35l
Interest Rates																
Percent Per Annum																
Treasury Bill Rate	7.0	7.0	7.0	7.0	7.0	7.0	7.0	7.0	7.0	7.0	7.0	7.0	7.0	7.0	7.0	60c
Deposit Rate	6.5	6.5	6.5	8.4	8.2	7.4	6.7	6.5	5.9	5.5	5.5	5.5	5.5	5.5	5.5	60l
Lending Rate	12.4	11.5	12.2	12.4	15.5	13.0	13.0	12.5	11.9	11.4	12.0	12.4	12.1	11.4	11.5	60p
Prices																
Period Averages																
Consumer Prices	....	....	....	....	....	....	....	....	....	....	....	....	....	....	....	64

Antigua and Barbuda

		1972	1973	1974	1975	1976	1977	1978	1979	1980	1981	1982	1983	1984	1985	1986
International Transactions														*Millions of US Dollars*		
Exports	70..*d*	18.030	25.715	28.711	19.817	9.030	†6.552	12.537	36.741	26.278	39.815	21.252	19.737	17.589	16.681	19.585
Imports, c.i.f.	71..*d*	47.352	48.236	70.012	66.892	35.123	†34.404	41.007	62.600	87.500	110.856	138.896	108.911	131.893	166.348	207.493
Balance of Payments														*Millions of US Dollars:*		
Current Account, n.i.e.	78al*d*	....	....	....	....	....	−9.60	−2.20	−19.50	−18.80	−32.70	−41.60	−9.10	.60	−23.10	−118.29
Goods: Exports f.o.b.	78aa*d*	....	....	....	....	....	6.60	12.60	12.00	59.50	51.40	49.30	36.50	35.20	28.30	31.53
Goods: Imports f.o.b.	78ab*d*	....	....	....	....	....	−37.00	−42.09	−67.72	−114.71	−125.26	−126.71	−99.72	−150.17	−174.80	−212.49
Trade Balance	78ac*d*	....	....	....	....	....	−30.40	−29.49	−55.72	−55.21	−73.86	−77.41	−63.22	−114.97	−146.50	−180.96
Services: Credit	78ad*d*	....	....	....	....	....	24.70	29.50	38.20	44.60	52.50	51.70	62.80	132.10	150.30	174.36
Services: Debit	78ae*d*	....	....	....	....	....	−6.50	−7.01	−10.28	−17.09	−19.74	−21.59	−18.28	−30.63	−38.40	−81.04
Balance on Goods & Services	78af*d*	....	....	....	....	....	−12.20	−7.00	−27.80	−27.70	−41.10	−47.30	−18.70	−13.50	−34.60	−87.64
Income: Credit	78ag*d*	....	....	....	....	....	.30	.10	.80	2.80	3.20	6.60	5.00	5.10	2.40	1.44
Income: Debit	78ah*d*	....	....	....	....	....	−.50	−.50	−2.60	−4.00	−5.20	−10.30	−6.00	−5.50	−5.10	−37.47
Balance on Gds, Serv. & Inc.	78ai*d*	....	....	....	....	....	−12.40	−7.40	−29.60	−28.90	−43.10	−51.00	−19.70	−13.90	−37.30	−123.68
Current Transfers, n.i.e.: Credit	78aj*d*	....	....	....	....	....	2.90	5.40	11.20	12.40	12.60	11.10	12.60	16.60	16.80	8.94
Current Transfers: Debit	78ak*d*	....	....	....	....	....	−.10	−.20	−1.10	−2.30	−2.20	−1.70	−2.00	−2.10	−2.60	−3.55
Capital Account, n.i.e.	78bc*d*	....	....	....	....	....	—	—	—	—	—	—	—	—	—	6.00
Capital Account, n.i.e.: Credit	78ba*d*	....	....	....	....	....	—	—	—	—	—	—	—	—	—	6.00
Capital Account: Debit	78bb*d*	....	....	....	....	....	—	—	—	—	—	—	—	—	—	—
Financial Account, n.i.e.	78bj*d*	....	....	....	....	....	2.81	5.63	18.86	22.29	36.95	35.41	−3.80	−.90	20.20	122.61
Direct Investment Abroad	78bd*d*	....	....	....	....	....	—	—	—	—	—	—	—	—	—	—
Dir. Invest. in Rep. Econ., n.i.e.	78be*d*	....	....	....	....	....	2.20	−6.90	8.50	19.60	22.40	23.00	5.00	4.40	15.60	22.60
Portfolio Investment Assets	78bf*d*	....	....	....	....	....	—	—	—	—	—	—	—	—	—	—
Equity Securities	78bk*d*	....	....	....	....	....	—	—	—	—	—	—	—	—	—	—
Debt Securities	78bl*d*	....	....	....	....	....	—	—	—	—	—	—	—	—	—	—
Portfolio Investment Liab., n.i.e.	78bg*d*	....	....	....	....	....	—	—	—	—	—	—	—	—	—	—
Equity Securities	78bm*d*	....	....	....	....	....	—	—	—	—	—	—	—	—	—	—
Debt Securities	78bn*d*	....	....	....	....	....	—	—	—	—	—	—	—	—	—	—
Financial Derivatives Assets	78bw*d*	....	....	....	....	....	....	....	....	....	....	....	....	....	....	....
Financial Derivatives Liabilities	78bx*d*	....	....	....	....	....	....	....	....	....	....	....	....	....	....	....
Other Investment Assets	78bh*d*	....	....	....	....	....	1.74	−2.24	−.90	1.15	−19.65	7.61	2.70	10.40	17.80	10.64
Monetary Authorities	78bo*d*	....	....	....	....	....	....	....	....	....	....	....	....	....	....	....
General Government	78bp*d*	....	....	....	....	....	—	—	—	—	−16.50					
Banks	78bq*d*	....	....	....	....	....	—	—	—	—	—	—	—	—	—	—
Other Sectors	78br*d*	....	....	....	....	....	1.74	−2.24	−.90	1.15	−3.15	7.61	2.70	10.40	17.80	10.64
Other Investment Liab., n.i.e.	78bi*d*	....	....	....	....	....	−1.13	14.77	11.26	1.54	34.20	4.80	−11.50	−15.70	−13.20	89.38
Monetary Authorities	78bs*d*	....	....	....	....	....	—	—	—	—	—	—	—	—	—	—
General Government	78bt*d*	....	....	....	....	....	4.85	10.14	8.77	3.77	22.30	6.40	−8.30	−4.80	−4.80	61.64
Banks	78bu*d*	....	....	....	....	....	−7.78	4.37	2.33	−2.43	3.39	−2.60	−5.40	−10.90	−8.40	—
Other Sectors	78bv*d*	....	....	....	....	....	1.80	.26	.17	.20	8.51	1.00	2.20	—	—	27.74
Net Errors and Omissions	78ca*d*	....	....	....	....	....	2.33	−2.66	5.60	−7.30	−6.13	3.00	6.80	−.10	—	−.18
Overall Balance	78cb*d*	....	....	....	....	....	−4.46	.77	4.96	−3.81	−1.88	−3.20	−6.10	−.40	−2.90	10.14
Reserves and Related Items	79da*d*	....	....	....	....	....	4.46	−.77	−4.96	3.81	1.88	3.20	6.10	.40	2.90	−10.14
Reserve Assets	79db*d*	....	....	....	....	....	4.46	−.77	−5.36	3.21	.38	−1.20	−1.40	−7.10	−3.30	−10.14
Use of Fund Credit and Loans	79dc*d*	....	....	....	....	....	—	—	—	—	—	—	—	—	—	—
Exceptional Financing	79de*d*	....	....	....	....	....	—	—	.40	.60	1.50	4.40	7.50	7.50	6.20	—
National Accounts														*Millions of E. Caribbean Dollars*		
Househ.Cons.Expend.,incl.NPISHs	96f	....	....	....	....	....	116.1	121.6	126.9	194.0	206.8	301.2	308.6	319.5	389.9	449.5
Government Consumption Expend.	91f	....	....	....	....	....	34.5	34.3	45.9	57.4	63.4	70.8	83.2	86.5	98.7	121.2
Gross Fixed Capital Formation	93e	....	....	....	....	....	36.9	39.0	60.5	103.5	140.9	146.9	84.6	110.6	151.6	237.0
Exports of Goods and Services	90c	....	....	....	....	....	85.2	124.5	203.7	200.1	246.1	252.6	253.9	350.2	409.5	558.5
Imports of Goods and Services (-)	98c	....	....	....	....	....	94.0	117.3	187.9	257.6	321.2	399.1	316.5	398.2	505.4	702.2
Gross Domestic Product (GDP)	99b	....	99.9	111.6	120.6	120.8	†178.6	202.1	249.1	297.2	336.1	372.5	413.8	468.5	544.3	663.9
Net Primary Income from Abroad	98.n	....	....	....	....	....	2.2	2.2	4.9	−3.2	−5.1	−10.0	−2.7	−1.1	−7.6	−97.3
Gross National Income (GNI)	99a	....	....	....	....	....	180.8	204.3	254.0	294.0	331.0	362.5	411.1	467.4	537.4	566.6
Net Current Transf.from Abroad	98t	....	....	....	....	....	3.2	10.0	22.1	24.3	26.5	30.2	27.0	32.1	33.8	25.6
Gross Nat'l Disposable Inc.(GNDI)	99i	....	....	....	....	....	184.0	214.3	276.1	318.3	357.4	392.7	438.1	499.5	571.2	592.2
Gross Saving	99s	....	....	....	....	....	33.5	58.4	103.3	66.9	87.2	20.7	46.3	93.6	81.8	21.6
GDP Volume 1990 Prices	99b.*p*	....	....	....	....	....	482.3	502.5	539.4	585.7	609.7	610.7	639.3	701.6	757.7	854.0
GDP Volume (1995=100)	99bv *p*	....	....	....	....	....	41.3	43.0	46.2	50.1	52.2	52.3	54.7	60.1	64.9	73.1
GDP Deflator (1995=100)	99bi *p*	....	....	....	....	....	†32.5	35.3	40.5	44.5	48.3	53.5	56.7	58.5	63.0	68.1
Population	99z	.07	.07	.07	.07	.07	.07	.07	.07	.08	.08	.08	.07	.08	.08	*Millions:* .08

	1987	1988	1989	1990	1991	1992	1993	1994	1995	1996	1997	1998	1999	2000	2001	
International Transactions																
Millions of US Dollars																
Exports	19.448	17.004	15.933	20.663	49.500	64.696	62.081	44.448	53.144	37.733	37.874	36.170	37.789	....	....	70..d
Imports, c.i.f.	247.015	250.163	192.433	254.700	295.141	312.211	323.367	341.500	345.711	365.348	370.393	385.241	414.052	....	....	71..d
Balance of Payments																
Minus Sign Indicates Debit																
Current Account, n.i.e.	-111.29	-45.04	-81.65	-30.99	-30.92	-9.87	15.06	-6.34	-.52	-59.60	-47.24	-63.13	-77.48	-79.13	....	78ald
Goods: Exports f.o.b.	26.30	28.19	29.14	33.43	55.20	75.03	62.08	45.23	53.15	38.88	38.80	37.38	36.84	42.28	....	78aad
Goods: Imports f.o.b.	-222.01	-204.50	-246.33	-235.44	-258.79	-261.77	-270.43	-287.50	-291.04	-309.94	-313.86	-320.84	-352.70	-341.33	....	78abd
Trade Balance	-195.71	-176.31	-217.19	-202.01	-203.58	-186.74	-208.35	-242.27	-237.89	-271.06	-275.06	-283.46	-315.87	-299.05	....	78acd
Services: Credit	200.68	237.33	261.79	311.87	314.66	332.34	377.09	391.23	348.46	363.64	404.49	425.86	438.86	414.81	....	78add
Services: Debit	-81.13	-79.30	-92.58	-105.12	-111.10	-124.69	-128.07	-134.42	-147.89	-157.43	-164.43	-173.74	-183.36	-164.34	....	78aed
Balance on Goods & Services	-76.16	-18.27	-47.97	4.74	-.03	20.91	40.67	14.53	-37.32	-64.84	-35.00	-31.33	-60.37	-48.57	....	78afd
Income: Credit	1.41	1.43	1.20	2.49	2.66	3.70	3.11	4.26	5.21	5.79	3.71	4.14	3.60	8.87	....	78agd
Income: Debit	-41.37	-33.06	-46.69	-47.81	-34.86	-33.37	-26.05	-30.81	-32.07	-32.17	-25.73	-33.30	-39.50	-47.75	....	78ahd
Balance on Gds, Serv. & Inc.	-116.12	-49.90	-93.46	-40.59	-32.23	-8.75	17.73	-12.03	-64.18	-91.22	-57.03	-60.48	-96.27	-87.46	....	78aid
Current Transfers, n.i.e.: Credit	9.36	9.81	17.28	14.89	9.16	8.54	9.07	15.15	78.04	35.19	19.90	11.70	22.66	17.24	....	78ajd
Current Transfers: Debit	-4.53	-4.94	-5.47	-5.29	-7.86	-9.66	-11.75	-9.47	-14.38	-3.56	-10.12	-14.34	-3.88	-8.91	....	78akd
Capital Account, n.i.e.	5.24	5.49	6.74	5.21	6.43	5.74	6.81	5.91	6.99	4.36	9.17	13.52	8.44	17.79	....	78bcd
Capital Account, n.i.e.: Credit	5.24	5.49	6.74	5.23	6.43	5.74	6.81	6.53	6.99	4.36	9.17	13.52	8.44	17.79	....	78bad
Capital Account: Debit	—	—	—	-.02	—	—	—	-.62	—	—	—	—	—	—	....	78bbd
Financial Account, n.i.e.	92.73	45.83	76.80	60.57	5.28	8.41	-17.47	-19.88	-10.66	57.61	66.90	57.88	51.17	64.01	....	78bjd
Direct Investment Abroad															....	78bdd
Dir. Invest. in Rep. Econ., n.i.e.	38.60	32.95	43.11	60.61	54.79	19.65	15.24	24.79	31.49	19.35	22.94	27.43	36.53	33.15	....	78bed
Portfolio Investment Assets	—	—	—	....	....	—	—	-1.38	1.19	-.78	—	—	-.09	-.10	....	78bfd
Equity Securities	—	—	—	....	....	—	—	...	...	...	....	....	....	....	....	78bkd
Debt Securities	—	—	—	....	....	—	—	...	...	...	....	....	....	....	....	78bld
Portfolio Investment Liab., n.i.e.	—	—	—	....	....	—	—	-1.28	—	-.81	—	-.29	2.78	2.35	....	78bgd
Equity Securities	...	...	...	....	....	...	...	...	...	...	....	....	....	....	....	78bmd
Debt Securities	...	...	...	....	....	...	...	...	...	...	....	....	....	....	....	78bnd
Financial Derivatives Assets																78bwd
Financial Derivatives Liabilities																78bxd
Other Investment Assets	-7.57	-3.63	8.69	-2.15	-21.65	-6.20	-1.17	-23.89	-31.34	-1.16	10.84	-32.97	-92.28	-.39	....	78bhd
Monetary Authorities																78bod
General Government																78bpd
Banks	-7.57	-3.63	8.69	-2.15												78bqd
Other Sectors																78brd
Other Investment Liab., n.i.e.	61.71	16.51	25.01	2.11	-27.86	-5.04	-31.54	-19.40	-10.71	41.01	33.12	63.71	104.23	29.00	....	78bid
Monetary Authorities																78bsd
General Government	64.23	20.23	28.03	9.27	....	....	...	...	...	...	....	....	....	....	....	78btd
Banks					....	....										78bud
Other Sectors	-2.53	-3.72	-3.02	-7.15	....	....	...	...	...	...	....	....	....	....	....	78bvd
Net Errors and Omissions	10.83	-3.66	-1.85	-35.39	24.47	13.70	-16.25	28.39	17.78	-13.63	-25.87	.40	28.25	-8.85	....	78cad
Overall Balance	-2.49	2.62	.04	-.59	5.26	17.98	-11.84	8.08	13.59	-11.26	2.96	8.67	10.37	-6.18	....	78cbd
Reserves and Related Items	2.49	-2.62	-.04	.59	-5.26	-17.98	11.84	-8.08	-13.59	11.26	-2.96	-8.67	-10.37	6.18	....	79dad
Reserve Assets	2.49	-2.62	-.04	.59	-5.26	-17.98	11.84	-8.08	-13.59	11.26	-2.96	-8.67	-10.37	6.18	....	79dbd
Use of Fund Credit and Loans	—	—	—	—	—	—	—	—	—	—	—	—	—	—	....	79dcd
Exceptional Financing	—	—	—	....	....	—	—	...	...	...	....	....	....	....	....	79ded
National Accounts																
Millions of E. Caribbean Dollars																
Househ.Cons.Expend.,incl.NPISHs	475.4	478.8	499.0	503.5	504.0	504.7	544.1	633.8	672.5	784.0	774.0	750.6	711.3	780.1	....	96f
Government Consumption Expend.	128.1	177.0	191.7	189.8	193.9	209.2	230.2	258.2	284.8	307.7	318.1	364.9	396.4	420.0	....	91f
Gross Fixed Capital Formation	354.3	364.3	415.9	343.0	416.7	398.1	390.6	437.4	491.9	578.8	614.6	720.6	793.8	862.4	....	93e
Exports of Goods and Services	615.7	720.0	816.7	940.4	998.1	1,099.6	1,186.1	1,190.0	1,084.3	1,086.8	1,190.2	1,245.6	1,259.8	1,260.3	....	90c
Imports of Goods and Services (-)	799.9	825.7	915.1	919.1	1,004.7	1,067.5	1,118.2	1,169.2	1,201.0	1,298.3	1,328.1	1,407.5	1,403.3	1,536.2	....	98c
Gross Domestic Product (GDP)	773.5	914.5	1,008.2	1,057.2	1,108.1	1,144.2	1,232.7	1,350.2	1,332.7	1,459.0	1,568.8	1,674.2	1,758.1	1,786.6	....	99b
Net Primary Income from Abroad	-107.9	-80.4	-117.8	-117.4	-87.4	-80.1	-61.9	-71.7	-72.5	-70.8	-72.8	-80.6	-80.8	-84.7	....	98.n
Gross National Income (GNI)	665.6	834.1	890.4	993.9	1,020.7	1,064.1	1,170.7	1,278.6	1,260.2	1,388.2	1,496.0	1,593.6	1,677.3	1,701.9	....	99a
Net Current Transf.from Abroad	24.8	25.3	24.2	21.3	3.5	-3.0	-7.2	2.4	187.3	85.4	33.1	-2.0	55.7	1.7	....	98t
Gross Nat'l Disposable Inc.(GNDI)	690.4	859.4	914.6	961.2	1,024.2	1,061.1	1,163.5	1,281.0	1,447.5	1,473.6	1,529.1	1,591.7	1,733.0	1,703.6	....	99i
Gross Saving	86.9	203.6	223.9	267.8	326.4	347.1	389.3	389.0	490.0	381.9	437.0	476.2	625.4	503.6	....	99s
GDP Volume 1990 Prices	924.6	974.7	1,031.0	1,057.2	1,078.8	1,087.9	1,146.6	1,219.1	1,168.2	1,245.3	1,310.5	1,353.4	1,403.0	....	....	99b.p
GDP Volume (1995=100)	79.1	83.4	88.3	90.5	92.3	93.1	98.1	104.4	100.0	106.6	112.2	115.9	120.1	....	....	99bvp
GDP Deflator (1995=100)	73.3	82.2	85.7	87.6	90.0	92.2	94.2	97.1	100.0	102.7	104.9	108.4	109.8	....	....	99bip
Midyear Estimates																
Population	.06	.06	.06	.06	.06	.06	.07	.07	.07	.07	.07	.07	.07	.07	.08	99z

(See notes in the back of the book.)

		1972	1973	1974	1975	1976	1977	1978	1979	1980	1981	1982	1983	1984	1985	1986
Exchange Rates								*Pesos per Bill. SDRs through 1977, per Mill. SDRs from 1978 to 1983,*								
Official Rate	aa	.05429	.06032	.06122	.71276	3.18922	7.25789	†.01307	.02132	.02541	.08436	.53550	2.43531	†.01752	.08793	.15375
								Pesos per Billion US$ through 1977, per Million US$ from 1978 to 1983,									
Official Rate	ae	.05000	.05000	.05000	.60885	2.74500	5.97500	†.01004	.01619	.01993	.07248	.48545	2.32610	†.01787	.08005	.12570
Official Rate	rf	.05000	.05000	.05000	.36575	1.39983	4.07633	†.00796	.01317	.01837	.04403	.25923	1.05300	†.00676	.06018	.09430
Fund Position														*Millions of SDRs:*		
Quota	2f.s	440.0	440.0	440.0	440.0	440.0	440.0	535.0	535.0	802.5	802.5	802.5	1,113.0	1,113.0	1,113.0	1,113.0
SDRs	1b.s	17.8	66.9	83.8	34.8	78.2	73.9	161.6	247.9	256.6	347.1	—	—	.3	.6	—
Reserve Position in the Fund	1c.s	—	—	11.3	—	—	—	—	—	—	—	—	—	—	—	—
Total Fund Cred.&Loans Outstg.	2tl	174.0	174.0	64.0	250.1	455.6	344.5	130.5	154.4	262.8	239.2	91.0	1,120.6	1,120.6	2,105.1	2,240.9
International Liquidity									*Millions of US Dollars Unless Otherwise Indicated:*							
Total Reserves minus Gold	1l.d	313	1,149	1,144	288	1,445	3,154	4,966	9,388	6,719	3,268	2,506	1,172	1,243	†3,273	2,718
SDRs	1b.d	19	81	103	41	91	90	211	327	327	404	—	—	1	—	—
Reserve Position in the Fund	1c.d	—	—	14	—	—	—	170	203	335	278	100	—	—	—	—
Foreign Exchange	1d.d	294	1,068	1,028	247	1,354	3,064	4,586	8,858	6,057	2,586	2,406	1,172	1,242	†3,273	2,718
Gold (Million Fine Troy Ounces)	1ad	3.993	3.996	3.996	3.996	3.996	4.184	4.278	4.372	4.372	4.372	4.372	4.372	4.372	4.372	4.373
Gold (National Valuation)	1and	152	169	169	169	169	177	181	184	185	185	185	1,421	1,421	1,421	1,421
Monetary Authorities: Other Assets	3..d	121	151	166	389	592	877	1,059	1,069	1,070	1,173	1,247	1,369	1,815	2,100	....
Other Liab.	4..d	176	353	383	457	1,182	871	21	86	194	271	679	1,572	2,155	4,952	6,506
Deposit Money Banks: Assets	7a.d	183	265	254	329	441	420	478	454	2,155	1,008	751	1,217	1,275	1,068	1,063
Liabilities	7b.d	....	....	....	....	....	....	....	....	....	7,196	7,172	7,839	7,206	6,732	6,555
Other Banking Insts.: Assets	7e.d	....	....	....	....	....	....	....	....	....	....	2	2	2	4	3
Liabilities	7f.d	....	....	....	....	....	....	....	....	....	8	5	4	3	1	1
Monetary Authorities							*Thousandths (.000) of Pesos through 1978; Pesos from 1979 to 1984;*									
Foreign Assets	11	29	73	74	515	6,052	25,132	62,161	†172	159	335	1,929	9,270	90,586	†533	888
Claims on Central Government	12a	140	310	540	1,790	4,760	13,570	30,160	†43	127	485	1,438	16,667	84,202	†715	1,247
Claims on Deposit Money Banks	12e	30	800	1,200	3,600	14,700	4,900	5,700	†8	101	367	4,167	12,308	85,568	....	....
Claims on Other Banking Insts	12f	—	100	200	200	1,200	1,300	600	†2	17	52	617	1,631	9,462	....	....
Reserve Money	14	190	1,300	1,990	5,490	25,140	36,000	71,100	†132	236	513	4,332	19,765	105,849	†515	694
of which: Currency Outside DMBs	14a	130	300	400	1,200	4,100	10,700	33,300	†79	164	302	874	4,634	31,340	†202	399
Foreign Liabilities	16c	18	28	23	457	4,699	7,706	215	†1	4	20	329	6,386	58,153	†581	1,162
Central Government Deposits	16d	—	10	10	—	120	210	400	†1	—	3	290	903	653	†26	16
Capital Accounts	17a	8	9	9	209	686	1,507	2,894	†6	9	66	299	1,509	23,878	†149	250
Other Items (Net)	17r	−17	−64	−19	−51	−3,933	−521	24,012	†85	155	637	2,900	11,313	81,286	†455	834
Deposit Money Banks							*Thousandths (.000) of Pesos through 1978; Pesos from 1979 to 1984;*									
Reserves	20	60	1,000	1,590	4,090	19,840	24,000	36,000	†55	75	206	3,190	14,248	71,978	†309	305
Foreign Assets	21	—	—	—	—	—	—	—	†—	—	107	365	2,832	23,140	†86	134
Claims on Central Government	22a	20	210	200	700	2,500	9,600	33,500	†99	168	644	2,314	7,636	55,179	†247	464
Claims on State and Local Govts	22b	....														
Claims on Official Entities	22bx								†—					4,502	†37	107
Claims on Private Sector	22d	460	740	1,170	2,980	12,110	43,350	121,870	†400	835	2,220	6,844	29,079	190,221	†898	1,650
Demand Deposits	24	200	400	700	2,100	8,300	19,400	42,900	†105	196	330	613	2,361	18,191	†146	264
Time, Savings,& Fgn.Currency Dep.	25	300	400	600	800	5,900	31,900	95,300	†315	597	1,283	2,970	15,521	122,633	†568	1,291
Foreign Liabilities	26c	—	—	—	—	—	—	—	†—	—	763	3,484	18,243	128,780	†539	825
Central Government Deposits	26d	—	—	—	100	200	500	1,200	†3	5	23	849	3,666	11,078	†167	216
Credit from Monetary Authorities	26g	100	900	1,300	3,600	14,500	5,100	5,200	†10	80	266	3,627	7,439	34,349	†240	446
Capital Accounts	27a	100	100	100	300	2,200	10,200	27,200	†81	158	482	2,053	9,952	75,135	†344	620
Other Items (Net)	27r	−160	150	260	870	3,350	9,850	19,570	†41	41	29	−884	−3,388	−45,147	†−429	−1,002
Monetary Survey							*Thousandths (.000) of Pesos through 1978; Pesos from 1979 to 1984;*									
Foreign Assets (Net)	31n	11	45	51	58	1,353	17,426	61,946	†171	155	−341	−1,520	−12,527	−73,207	†−502	−966
Domestic Credit	32	620	1,350	2,100	5,570	20,250	67,110	184,530	†540	1,141	3,376	10,073	50,444	331,835	....	....
Claims on Central Govt. (Net)	32an	160	510	730	2,390	6,940	22,460	62,060	†138	289	1,104	2,612	19,733	127,650	†769	1,485
Claims on State and Local Govts	32b	....														
Claims on Official Entities	32bx								†—					4,502	†37	107
Claims on Private Sector	32d	460	740	1,170	2,980	12,110	43,350	121,870	†400	835	2,220	6,844	29,079	190,221	†898	1,650
Claims on Other Banking Insts	32f	—	100	200	200	1,200	1,300	600	†2	17	52	617	1,631	9,462	....	....
Money	34	330	700	1,100	3,500	13,600	31,900	78,600	†185	362	639	1,623	7,500	51,170	†350	664
Quasi-Money	35	300	400	600	800	5,900	31,900	95,300	†315	597	1,283	2,970	15,521	122,633	†568	1,291
Capital Accounts	37a	108	109	109	509	2,886	11,707	30,094	†87	167	549	2,352	11,462	99,013	†494	869
Other Items (Net)	37r	−107	186	341	819	−783	9,029	42,482	†125	171	566	1,608	3,434	−14,188	....	....
Money plus Quasi-Money	35l	630	1,100	1,700	4,300	19,500	63,800	173,900	†500	958	1,921	4,593	23,021	173,803	†918	1,955
Other Banking Institutions							*Thousandths (.000) of Pesos through 1978; Pesos from 1979 to 1984;*									
Reserves	40	—	—	100	200	1,300	200	500	†1	2	13	138	589	1,952	†2	2
Foreign Assets	41	—	—	—	—	—	—	—	†—	—	—	1	4	44	†—	—
Claims on Central Government	42a	—	—	—	—	—	240	400	†1	1	10	30	75	311	†—	1
Claims on Local and State Govts	42b	....														
Claims on Official Entities	42bx	—	—	—	—	100	—	—							†—	—
Claims on Private Sector	42d	20	50	80	210	1,770	8,840	23,800	†64	141	288	566	1,707	7,517	†23	39
Claims on Deposit Money Banks	42e	—	—	—	—	200	3,200	5,900	†9	8	30	29	104	385	†2	3
Time, Savings,& Fgn.Currency Dep.	45	10	20	70	110	1,210	7,910	22,700	†59	120	297	264	1,218	4,513	†16	38
Foreign Liabilities	46c	—	—	—	—	—	—	—	†—	—	1	2	8	59	†—	—
Credit from Monetary Authorities	46g	10	30	110	200	1,200	1,500	1,800	†2	10	32	490	620	2,139	†10	18
Capital Accounts	47a	—	—	—	—	200	800	2,200	†5	11	37	129	510	2,926	†7	8
Other Items (Net)	47r	—	—	—	100	660	2,370	3,900	†9	11	−26	−122	123	573	†−5	−18
Banking Survey							*Thousandths (.000) of Pesos through 1978; Pesos from 1979 to 1984;*									
Foreign Assets (Net)	51n	11	45	51	58	1,353	17,426	61,946	†171	155	−341	−1,521	−12,532	−73,222	†−502	−966
Domestic Credit	52	640	1,300	1,980	5,580	20,820	74,990	208,130	†604	1,266	3,621	10,052	50,595	330,201	†1,728	3,282
Claims on Central Govt. (Net)	52an	160	510	730	2,390	6,940	22,700	62,460	†139	290	1,113	2,642	19,808	127,961	†769	1,486
Claims on State and Local Govts	52b	....														
Claims on Official Entities	52bx	—	—	—	—	100	—	—	†—					4,502	†37	107
Claims on Private Sector	52d	480	790	1,250	3,190	13,880	52,190	145,670	†465	975	2,508	7,409	30,787	197,738	†921	1,688
Liquid Liabilities	55l	640	1,120	1,670	4,210	19,410	71,510	196,100	†558	1,077	2,206	4,720	23,651	176,364	†932	1,991
Capital Accounts	57a	108	109	109	509	3,086	12,507	32,294	†92	178	585	2,481	11,971	101,938	†501	877
Other Items (Net)	57r	−97	116	251	919	−323	8,399	41,682	†126	167	489	1,329	2,441	−21,324	†−207	−552

1987	1988	1989	1990	1991	1992	1993	1994	1995	1996	1997	1998	1999	2000	2001		
															Exchange Rates	
per Thous. SDRs from 1984 to 1988, per SDR thereafter: End of Period																
.53200	1.79920	†.23589	.79456	1.42828	1.36194	1.37150	1.45912	1.48649	1.43724	1.34858	1.40733	1.37182	1.30226	1.25610	Official Rate	**aa**
per Thous.US$ from 1984 to 1988,per US$ after:End Per.(ae) Per.Avg.(rf)																
.37500	1.33700	†.17950	.55850	.99850	.99050	.99850	.99950	1.00000	.99950	.99950	.99950	.99950	.99950	.99950	Official Rate	**ae**
.21443	.87526	†.04233	.48759	.95355	.99064	.99895	.99901	.99975	.99966	.99950	.99950	.99950	.99950	.99950	Official Rate	**rf**
															Fund Position	
End of Period																
1,113.0	1,113.0	1,113.0	1,113.0	1,113.0	1,537.1	1,537.1	1,537.1	1,537.1	1,537.1	1,537.1	1,537.1	2,117.1	2,117.1	2,117.1	Quota	**2f. s**
—	.3	.2	209.0	134.9	272.8	329.5	385.7	362.7	277.4	123.6	187.7	100.3	562.2	8.5	SDRs	**1b. s**
—	—	—	—	—	—	—	—	—	—	—	—	—	—	—	Reserve Position in the Fund	**1c. s**
2,716.2	2,733.0	2,358.8	2,167.2	1,735.9	1,682.8	2,562.4	2,884.7	4,124.4	4,376.0	4,349.3	3,865.1	3,262.6	3,880.3	11,121.1	Total Fund Cred.&Loans Outstg.	**2tl**
															International Liquidity	
End of Period																
1,617	3,363	1,463	4,592	6,005	9,990	13,791	14,327	14,288	18,104	22,320	24,752	26,252	25,147	14,553	Total Reserves minus Gold	**1l. d**
—	—	—	297	193	375	453	563	539	399	167	264	138	733	11	SDRs	**1b. d**
—	—	—	—	—	—	—	—	—	—	—	—	—	—	—	Reserve Position in the Fund	**1c. d**
1,617	3,363	1,463	4,295	5,812	9,615	13,339	13,764	13,749	17,705	22,153	24,488	26,114	24,414	14,542	Foreign Exchange	**1d. d**
4.373	4.373	4.373	4.233	4.123	4.373	4.373	4.374	4.374	4.374	.361	.360	.338	.019	.009	Gold (Million Fine Troy Ounces)	**1ad**
1,421	1,421	1,421	1,421	1,430	1,446	1,672	1,651	1,679	1,611	120	124	121	7	3	Gold (National Valuation)	**1and**
....	....	....	1,154	772	—	—	57	22	30	42	30	13	3	—	Monetary Authorities: Other Assets	**3..d**
6,906	7,826	....	7,394	7,629	558	161	—	—	—	—	—	—	—	5	Other Liab.	**4..d**
1,312	1,270	1,557	2,234	2,812	3,642	5,153	5,587	6,302	10,011	17,732	16,895	15,007	17,911	7,247	Deposit Money Banks: Assets	**7a. d**
7,937	9,338	6,092	7,011	7,869	9,558	9,051	10,995	13,649	15,820	21,048	21,440	22,831	24,170	16,284	Liabilities	**7b. d**
1	1	3	5	10	12	32	26	31	25	24	17	74	42	5	Other Banking Insts.: Assets	**7e. d**
2	—	—	2	49	117	26	39	62	84	148	395	434	405	263	Liabilities	**7f. d**
															Monetary Authorities	
Thousands from 1985 to 1988:Millions Beginning 1989: End of Period																
2,002	10,635	....	†4,114	9,009	11,236	15,448	†16,035	15,989	19,745	22,806	26,249	27,322	26,925	14,922	Foreign Assets	**11**
4,814	17,641	†475	†5,334	10,879	9,272	11,432	†8,361	8,499	8,223	7,867	7,170	6,350	7,468	20,495	Claims on Central Government	**12a**
....	....	....	†14,510	17,922	23,408	22,527	†22,463	24,129	2,106	1,794	2,070	2,160	1,933	6,019	Claims on Deposit Money Banks	**12e**
....	....	....	†6	6	5	5	†4	3	3	—	—	—	—	—	Claims on Other Banking Insts	**12f**
1,352	7,000	†528	†3,617	7,823	11,010	14,989	†16,267	13,769	14,060	15,975	16,392	16,524	15,077	17,768	Reserve Money	**14**
926	4,319	†182	†2,259	5,222	7,686	10,067	†11,229	11,161	11,736	13,331	13,503	13,736	12,571	9,082	*of which: Currency Outside DMBs*	**14a**
4,035	15,381	....	†5,857	10,102	2,843	3,677	†4,211	6,131	6,293	5,868	5,442	4,478	5,056	13,982	Foreign Liabilities	**16c**
204	100	†79	†156	1,097	1,378	1,338	†764	1,677	2,242	325	1,343	935	1,769	4,366	Central Government Deposits	**16d**
1,102	4,074	†446	†5,557	3,786	6,394	7,217	†3,279	3,583	4,053	4,059	4,604	4,415	4,659	3,603	Capital Accounts	**17a**
4,583	24,604	....	†8,777	15,008	22,296	22,191	†22,342	23,461	3,430	6,242	7,708	9,480	9,765	1,717	Other Items (Net)	**17r**
															Deposit Money Banks	
Thousands from 1985 to 1988:Millions Beginning 1989: End of Period																
428	2,550	†189	†1,342	2,900	3,481	5,488	†5,203	2,637	2,358	2,673	2,905	3,101	2,826	8,540	Reserves	**20**
493	1,698	†280	†1,249	2,809	3,606	5,148	†5,587	6,302	10,011	17,732	16,895	15,007	17,911	7,247	Foreign Assets	**21**
1,552	7,247	†948	†6,197	9,830	9,871	11,657	†6,094	10,299	13,013	14,513	17,433	18,982	18,859	20,112	Claims on Central Government	**22a**
....	....	....	....	....	....	....	5,008	5,247	5,273	5,950	5,827	8,924	9,585	9,149	Claims on State and Local Govts	**22b**
310	1,381	†36	†713	795	1,103	1,509	†493	463	565	612	285	276	278	440	Claims on Official Entities	**22bx**
4,882	22,248	†1,279	†10,702	22,550	34,564	42,600	†51,372	50,780	54,093	63,131	70,525	68,431	65,843	54,180	Claims on Private Sector	**22d**
491	2,078	†91	†809	2,404	3,678	5,052	†5,133	5,458	7,305	8,151	7,986	8,099	7,267	6,619	Demand Deposits	**24**
3,727	21,528	†379	†4,845	11,471	19,666	30,334	†37,109	35,352	42,710	56,038	64,162	67,315	70,677	57,444	Time, Savings,& Fgn.Currency Dep.	**25**
2,984	12,485	†1,096	†3,919	7,861	9,462	9,042	†10,995	13,649	15,820	21,048	21,440	22,831	24,170	16,284	Foreign Liabilities	**26c**
345	1,387	†76	†524	1,976	2,958	5,054	†3,014	2,467	3,054	3,990	4,525	3,602	4,474	2,151	Central Government Deposits	**26d**
1,363	5,083	†237	†10,082	18,292	22,967	22,336	†2,184	2,650	1,375	409	393	308	78	4,198	Credit from Monetary Authorities	**26g**
1,728	6,073	†533	†5,966	9,608	10,802	12,503	†13,519	13,771	15,065	15,806	16,674	16,437	16,726	15,920	Capital Accounts	**27a**
–2,972	–13,511	†319	†–5,942	–12,728	–16,908	–17,919	†1,802	2,381	–18	–830	–1,311	–3,868	–8,092	–2,950	Other Items (Net)	**27r**
															Monetary Survey	
Thousands from 1985 to 1988:Millions Beginning 1989: End of Period																
–4,524	–15,532	....	†–4,413	–6,145	2,537	7,877	†6,416	2,510	7,643	13,623	16,262	15,021	15,610	–8,097	Foreign Assets (Net)	**31n**
....	....	....	†22,272	40,987	50,479	60,811	†67,554	71,148	75,874	87,759	95,372	98,427	95,790	97,859	Domestic Credit	**32**
5,818	23,400	†1,267	†10,851	17,636	14,807	16,697	†10,677	14,654	15,940	18,066	18,735	20,795	20,084	34,090	Claims on Central Govt. (Net)	**32an**
....	....	....	....	....	....	....	5,008	5,247	5,273	5,950	5,827	8,924	9,585	9,149	Claims on State and Local Govts	**32b**
310	1,381	†36	†713	795	1,103	1,509	†493	463	565	612	285	276	278	440	Claims on Official Entities	**32bx**
4,882	22,248	†1,279	†10,702	22,550	34,564	42,600	†51,372	50,780	54,093	63,131	70,525	68,431	65,843	54,180	Claims on Private Sector	**32d**
....	....	....	†6	6	5	5	†4	3	3	—	—	—	—	—	Claims on Other Banking Insts	**32f**
1,418	6,402	†273	†3,068	7,626	11,364	15,119	†16,362	16,619	19,042	21,482	21,489	21,836	19,838	15,701	Money	**34**
3,727	21,528	†379	†4,845	11,471	19,666	30,334	†37,109	35,352	42,710	56,038	64,162	67,315	70,677	57,444	Quasi-Money	**35**
2,829	10,147	†979	†11,523	13,394	17,196	19,720	†16,798	17,354	19,118	19,864	21,279	20,852	21,386	19,523	Capital Accounts	**37a**
....	....	....	†–1,577	2,351	4,790	3,515	†3,701	4,333	2,647	3,997	4,704	3,446	–501	–2,907	Other Items (Net)	**37r**
5,145	27,929	†652	†7,913	19,097	31,030	45,453	†53,471	51,971	61,752	77,520	85,651	89,150	90,515	73,145	Money plus Quasi-Money	**35l**
															Other Banking Institutions	
Thousands from 1985 to 1988:Millions Beginning 1989: End of Period																
4	21	†1	†7	12	17	20	†20	14	7	6	7	15	15	89	Reserves	**40**
—	2	†—	†3	10	12	32	†26	31	25	24	17	74	42	5	Foreign Assets	**41**
5	18	†5	†26	37	24	26	†35	37	84	96	114	89	56	16	Claims on Central Government	**42a**
....	....	....	....	....	....	....	2	2	—	2	—	—	—	—	Claims on Local and State Govts	**42b**
1	11	†—	†2	5	6	—	†—	—	—	—	—	—	—	4	Claims on Official Entities	**42bx**
87	337	†9	†51	220	441	644	†838	725	846	1,103	1,681	2,147	2,067	1,826	Claims on Private Sector	**42d**
3	22	†—	†2	5	5	5	†10	13	20	18	22	27	27	22	Claims on Deposit Money Banks	**42e**
98	567	†5	†43	121	272	412	†501	284	348	320	333	295	344	223	Time, Savings,& Fgn.Currency Dep.	**45**
1	—	†—	†1	49	116	26	†39	62	84	148	395	434	405	263	Foreign Liabilities	**46c**
16	35	†1	†6	6	5	5	†4	3	3	—	—	—	—	—	Credit from Monetary Authorities	**46g**
19	178	†8	†76	133	167	202	†236	210	190	233	367	468	557	671	Capital Accounts	**47a**
–33	–368	†1	†–35	–20	–55	82	†151	263	357	547	746	1,155	902	805	Other Items (Net)	**47r**
															Banking Survey	
Thousands from 1985 to 1988:Millions Beginning 1989: End of Period																
–4,524	–15,530	....	†–4,411	–6,184	2,433	7,883	†6,403	2,480	7,585	13,499	15,884	14,661	15,247	–8,355	Foreign Assets (Net)	**51n**
11,103	47,395	†2,597	†22,345	41,243	50,945	61,476	†68,424	71,908	76,802	88,959	97,167	100,663	97,913	99,705	Domestic Credit	**52**
5,823	23,418	†1,272	†10,877	17,673	14,831	16,723	†10,711	14,691	16,024	18,163	18,850	20,884	20,140	34,106	Claims on Central Govt. (Net)	**52an**
....	....	....	....	....	....	....	5,009	5,249	5,273	5,951	5,827	8,924	9,585	9,149	Claims on State and Local Govts	**52b**
311	1,392	†36	†715	800	1,109	1,509	†493	463	565	612	285	276	278	444	Claims on Official Entities	**52bx**
4,969	22,585	†1,288	†10,753	22,770	35,005	43,244	†52,210	51,505	54,939	64,234	72,206	70,578	67,910	56,006	Claims on Private Sector	**52d**
5,239	28,476	†657	†7,949	19,206	31,285	45,845	†53,952	52,241	62,094	77,835	85,977	89,430	90,844	73,280	Liquid Liabilities	**55l**
2,848	10,324	†987	†11,599	13,527	17,363	19,922	†17,034	17,564	19,308	20,098	21,646	21,320	21,942	20,194	Capital Accounts	**57a**
–1,509	–6,935	....	†–1,614	2,326	4,730	3,592	†3,841	4,584	2,984	4,526	5,428	4,573	374	–2,124	Other Items (Net)	**57r**

	1972	1973	1974	1975	1976	1977	1978	1979	1980	1981	1982	1983	1984	1985	1986
Interest Rates														*Percent Per Annum*	
Money Market Rate 60b	...	...	...	...	...	...	...	...	87	185	202	739	1,182	1,161	135
Money Market Rate (Fgn. Cur.) .... 60b. f	...	...	...	...	...	...	...	...	...	...	...	...	...	...	...
Deposit Rate 60l	...	...	...	...	...	115	132	117	80	157	126	281	397	630	95
Deposit Rate (Fgn. Currency) .... 60l. f	...	...	...	...	...	...	...	...	...	...	...	...	...	...	...
Lending Rate 60p	...	...	...	...	...	...	...	...	...	...	...	...	...	...	...
Lending Rate (Fgn. Currency) .... 60p. f	...	...	...	...	...	...	...	...	...	...	...	...	...	...	...
Prices, Production, Labor														*Index Numbers (1995=100):*	
Producer Prices 63	...	...	...	...	...	...	...	...	...	...	...	...	...	...	...
Cons.Prices (1990=100,000) 64.b	...	...	...	...	...	...	...	...	...	...	...	...	.2	1.7	3.1
Consumer Prices 64	—	—	†—	—	—	—	—	—	—	—	—	—	—	—	—
Wages: Monthly Earnings (Mfg) 65ey	—	—	—	...											
Manufacturing Production .... 66ey c	...	...	...	...	...	...	...	...	...	...	...	...	...	...	...
Crude Petroleum Production 66aa	60.4	58.6	57.6	55.3	55.4	59.9	62.9	65.9	68.5	69.1	68.2	68.2	66.7	63.9	60.3
														Number in Thousands:	
Labor Force 67d	...	...	...	...	...	...	...	...	...	...	...	...	...	...	...
Employment 67e	...	...	...	...	...	...	...	...	...	...	...	...	...	...	...
Unemployment 67c	...												152	216	178
Unemployment Rate (%) 67r	...												3.8	5.3	4.4
International Transactions														*Millions of US Dollars*	
Exports .... 70..d	1,941	3,266	3,931	2,961	3,916	5,652	6,400	7,810	8,021	9,143	7,625	7,836	8,107	8,396	6,852
Meat 70k.d	686.3	778.8	437.1	281.5	510.5	622.4	781.0	1,202.5	935.8	907.7	804.9	602.6	404.3	385.7	464.7
Wheat 70d.d	110	274	305	301	432	541	174	606	816	764	676	1,474	966	1,133	395
Imports, c.i.f. .... 71..d	1,905	2,230	3,635	3,947	3,033	4,162	3,834	6,700	10,541	9,430	5,337	4,504	4,585	3,814	4,724
Imports, f.o.b. .... 71.v d	1,686	1,985	3,242	3,512	2,743	3,803	3,492	6,041	9,381	8,430	4,857	4,126	4,201	3,515	4,323
Volume of Exports 72														*1995=100*	
Wheat 72d	23.9	43.5	25.2	25.6	45.9	82.0	23.4	62.3	65.4	54.8	55.3	148.2	105.4	139.4	58.5
Volume of Imports 73	...	...	...	...	...	...	...	...	...	...	...	...	...	...	...
Unit Value of Exports .... 74..d														*1995=100:*	
Frozen Beef .... 74ka d	24.6	33.8	36.2	18.5	19.5	25.0	25.0	39.7	46.3	40.0	30.4	31.6	43.2	41.1	52.7
Corned Beef .... 74kd d	63.9	80.1	110.0	76.8	72.1	72.9	73.9	115.9	139.8	132.5	97.3	88.8	84.9	80.0	88.2
Wheat 74d.d	40.5	59.3	117.7	104.6	81.6	58.9	71.6	89.0	112.1	117.9	101.5	87.4	80.4	70.1	59.5
Unit Value of Imports .... 75..d	...	...	...	...	...	...	...	...	...	...	...	...	...	...	...
Balance of Payments														*Millions of US Dollars:*	
Current Account, n.i.e. .... 78al d					651	1,126	1,856	−513	−4,774	−4,712	−2,353	−2,436	−2,495	−952	−2,859
Goods: Exports f.o.b. .... 78aa d					3,918	5,651	6,401	7,810	8,021	9,143	7,623	7,835	8,100	8,396	6,852
Goods: Imports f.o.b. .... 78ab d					−2,765	−3,799	−3,488	−6,028	−9,394	−8,431	−4,859	−4,119	−4,118	−3,518	−4,406
Trade Balance .... 78ac d					1,153	1,852	2,913	1,782	−1,373	712	2,764	3,716	3,982	4,878	2,446
Services: Credit .... 78ad d					714	951	1,087	1,369	1,876	1,716	1,574	1,455	1,511	1,651	1,597
Services: Debit .... 78ae d					−742	−967	−1,544	−2,814	−3,788	−3,434	−2,018	−2,224	−2,289	−2,187	−2,500
Balance on Goods & Services .... 78af d					1,125	1,836	2,456	337	−3,285	−1,006	2,320	2,947	3,204	4,342	1,543
Income: Credit .... 78ag d					59	136	348	737	1,305	946	558	474	298	282	392
Income: Debit .... 78ah d					−551	−877	−1,016	−1,644	−2,817	−4,630	−5,265	−5,873	−5,999	−5,576	−4,796
Balance on Gds, Serv. & Inc. .... 78ai d					633	1,095	1,788	−570	−4,797	−4,690	−2,387	−2,452	−2,497	−952	−2,861
Current Transfers, n.i.e.: Credit .... 78aj d					30	43	85	88	85	70	51	35	21	18	21
Current Transfers: Debit .... 78ak d					−12	−12	−17	−31	−62	−92	−17	−19	−19	−18	−19
Capital Account, n.i.e. .... 78bc d					—	—	—	—	—	—	—	—	—	—	—
Capital Account, n.i.e.: Credit .... 78ba d					—	—	—	—	—	—	—	—	—	—	—
Capital Account: Debit .... 78bb d					—	—	—	—	—	—	—	—	—	—	—
Financial Account, n.i.e. .... 78bj d					−554	605	−70	4,308	2,305	1,355	−1,972	−2,391	257	638	410
Direct Investment Abroad .... 78bd d					—	1	23	59	110	107	30	−2	—	—	—
Dir. Invest. in Rep. Econ., n.i.e. ... 78be d					—	144	250	206	678	837	227	185	268	919	574
Portfolio Investment Assets .... 78bf d					—	—	—	—	—	—	—	—	—	—	—
Equity Securities .... 78bk d					—	—	—	—	—	—	—	—	—	—	—
Debt Securities .... 78bl d					—	—	—	—	—	—	—	—	—	—	—
Portfolio Investment Liab., n.i.e. ...... 78bg d					−66	−1	101	222	154	1,125	299	649	372	−617	−542
Equity Securities .... 78bm d															
Debt Securities .... 78bn d					−66	−1	101	222	154	1,125	299	649	372	−617	−542
Financial Derivatives Assets .... 78bw d					...	...	...	...	...	...	...	...	...	...	...
Financial Derivatives Liabilities .... 78bx d					...	...	...	...	...	...	...	...	...	...	...
Other Investment Assets .... 78bh d					328	−382	−83	496	−440	−1,605	−552	−374	−241	26	−286
Monetary Authorities .... 78bo d					−203	−286	−105	−61	−29	−155	400	−487	−387	−207	−198
General Government .... 78bp d					6	−10	−1	−10	−11	−14	−17	−12	−20	−29	−36
Banks .... 78bq d					−17	−87	−27	−285	−368	25	−431	−180	−527	−231	5
Other Sectors .... 78br d					542	1	50	852	−32	−1,461	−504	305	693	493	−57
Other Investment Liab., n.i.e. .... 78bi d					−816	843	−361	3,325	1,803	891	−1,976	−2,849	−142	310	664
Monetary Authorities .... 78bs d					−99	−275	−901	74	182	84	−200	−703	−123	−361	−159
General Government .... 78bt d					−48	−10	46	−11	469	977	−15	−841	1,793	2,061	860
Banks .... 78bu d					41	169	102	197	−60	363	1,050	528	−27	898	−28
Other Sectors .... 78bv d					−710	959	392	3,065	1,212	−533	−2,811	−1,833	−1,785	−2,288	−9
Net Errors and Omissions .... 78ca d					−218	134	12	243	−308	−205	−401	−447	−55	−532	302
Overall Balance .... 78cb d					−121	1,865	1,798	4,038	−2,777	−3,562	−4,726	−5,274	−2,293	−846	−2,147
Reserves and Related Items .... 79da d					121	−1,865	−1,798	−4,038	2,777	3,562	4,726	5,274	2,293	846	2,147
Reserve Assets .... 79db d					−1,156	−1,714	−1,716	−4,225	2,598	3,193	669	1,230	−166	−2,016	745
Use of Fund Credit and Loans .... 79dc d					237	−132	−423	—	—	—	—	1,227	—	987	146
Exceptional Financing .... 79de d					1,040	−20	341	187	179	369	4,057	2,817	2,459	1,875	1,256

Percent Per Annum

Interest Rates

	1987	1988	1989	1990	1991	1992	1993	1994	1995	1996	1997	1998	1999	2000	2001	
Money Market Rate	253	524	1,387,179	9,695,422	71	15	6	8	9	6	7	7	7	8	25	60b
Money Market Rate (Fgn. Cur.)	....	....	....	....	....	....	....	....	8	6	6	7	6	8	13	60b. f
Deposit Rate	176	372	17,236	1,518	62	17	11	8	12	7	7	8	8	8	16	60l
Deposit Rate (Fgn. Currency)	....	....	....	....	....	....	....	6	8	6	6	6	6	7	10	60l. f
Lending Rate	....	....	....	....	....	....	....	10	18	11	9	11	11	11	28	60p
Lending Rate (Fgn. Currency)	....	....	....	....	....	....	....	8	14	9	8	9	9	10	18	60p. f

Prices, Production, Labor

Period Averages

	1987	1988	1989	1990	1991	1992	1993	1994	1995	1996	1997	1998	1999	2000	2001	
Producer Prices	—	.1	2.4	40.7	85.6	90.7	92.2	92.8	100.0	†103.7	102.6	99.2	95.2	98.7	96.7	63
Cons.Prices (1990=100,000)	7.3	†32.2	1,024.9	....	....	....	....	....	....	....	....	....	....	....	....	64.b
Consumer Prices	—	†—	1.0	24.7	67.2	83.9	92.9	96.7	100.0	†100.2	100.7	101.6	100.4	99.5	98.4	64
Wages: Monthly Earnings (Mfg)	....	....	....	26.1	65.0	84.6	95.2	101.7	100.0	100.7	....	....	....	....	....	65ey
Manufacturing Production	....	....	....	....	....	....	....	106.7	100.0	102.6	112.2	114.5	105.0	103.6	....	66ey c
Crude Petroleum Production	59.4	62.6	63.8	66.9	67.6	77.4	82.5	92.8	100.0	114.0	116.0	117.7	111.4	107.3	108.1	66aa

Period Averages

	1987	1988	1989	1990	1991	1992	1993	1994	1995	1996	1997	1998	1999	2000	2001	
Labor Force	—	....	....	12,091	....	....	....	....	14,345	....	....	....	....	9,723	....	67d
Employment	....	....	....	4,373	4,333	4,496	4,609	4,386	4,157	7,370	7,858	8,277	8,285	8,262	....	67e
Unemployment	230	251	323	441	†696	827	1,062	1,400	1,959	2,047	....	....	....	....	....	67c
Unemployment Rate (%)	5.3	5.9	7.3	9.2	†6.3	7.2	9.1	11.7	15.9	16.3	....	14.1	15.5	....	....	67r

International Transactions

Millions of US Dollars

	1987	1988	1989	1990	1991	1992	1993	1994	1995	1996	1997	1998	1999	2000	2001	
Exports	6,360	9,135	9,579	12,353	11,978	12,235	13,118	15,659	20,967	23,811	26,370	26,441	23,333	26,409	26,655	70..d
Meat	599.3	607.2	716.3	873.2	....	....	....	....	....	....	....	....	....	....	....	70k. d
Wheat	351	355	658	871	496	716	735	657	1,005	1,066	1,347	1,308	1,002	1,218	1,303	70d. d
Imports, c.i.f.	5,818	5,322	4,203	4,076	8,275	14,872	16,784	21,527	20,122	23,762	30,450	31,404	25,508	25,243	20,311	71..d
Imports, f.o.b.	5,341	4,890	3,864	3,725	7,525	13,623	14,694	19,661	17,962	22,190	28,553	29,558	24,129	22,052	19,148	71.v d

1995=100

	1987	1988	1989	1990	1991	1992	1993	1994	1995	1996	1997	1998	1999	2000	2001	
Volume of Exports	....	....	....	66.0	64.6	63.6	68.1	79.9	100.0	106.6	118.7	132.6	....	....	....	72
Wheat	61.0	39.8	61.3	83.2	79.6	150.4	82.9	75.3	100.0	85.7	126.1	153.0	128.0	160.1	154.6	72d
Volume of Imports	....	....	....	19.9	42.1	77.2	89.1	113.1	100.0	119.8	155.3	170.3	....	....	....	73

Indexes of Unit Values in US Dollars

	1987	1988	1989	1990	1991	1992	1993	1994	1995	1996	1997	1998	1999	2000	2001	
Unit Value of Exports	....	....	....	89.2	88.5	91.7	91.9	94.6	100.0	106.5	102.5	92.9	....	....	....	74..d
Frozen Beef	77.0	73.6	70.6	62.2	92.5	120.6	143.9	109.0	100.0	80.3	85.8	111.8	98.3	97.0	78.7	74ka d
Corned Beef	108.7	80.1	92.7	100.0	116.9	90.9	108.7	116.7	....	....	....	....	....	....	....	74kd d
Wheat	54.7	71.2	90.6	87.9	54.6	73.2	79.9	79.8	100.0	122.1	96.1	74.8	71.0	70.1	74.9	74d. d
Unit Value of Imports	....	....	....	101.7	97.8	95.7	93.5	94.9	100.0	98.5	97.1	91.7	....	....	....	75..d

Balance of Payments

Minus Sign Indicates Debit

	1987	1988	1989	1990	1991	1992	1993	1994	1995	1996	1997	1998	1999	2000	2001	
Current Account, n.i.e.	-4,235	-1,572	-1,305	4,552	-647	-5,653	-8,160	-11,158	-5,210	-6,877	-12,344	-14,626	-12,039	-8,970	....	78al d
Goods: Exports f.o.b.	6,360	9,134	9,573	12,354	11,978	12,399	13,269	16,024	21,162	24,043	26,431	26,433	23,309	26,409	....	78aa d
Goods: Imports f.o.b.	-5,343	-4,892	-3,864	-3,726	-7,559	-13,795	-15,632	-20,163	-18,804	-22,283	-28,554	-29,532	-24,103	-23,851	....	78ab d
Trade Balance	1,017	4,242	5,709	8,628	4,419	-1,396	-2,363	-4,139	2,358	1,760	-2,123	-3,099	-794	2,558	....	78ac d
Services: Credit	1,794	2,015	2,193	2,446	2,408	2,985	3,082	3,348	3,741	4,263	4,407	4,618	4,446	4,536	....	78ad d
Services: Debit	-2,566	-2,702	-2,793	-3,120	-4,007	-5,540	-6,401	-7,134	-7,197	-7,845	-8,857	-9,127	-8,601	-8,871	....	78ae d
Balance on Goods & Services	245	3,555	5,109	7,954	2,820	-3,951	-5,682	-7,925	-1,098	-1,822	-6,573	-7,608	-4,949	-1,777	....	78af d
Income: Credit	252	211	276	1,854	1,746	2,357	2,592	3,464	4,392	4,445	5,489	6,121	6,085	7,397	....	78ag d
Income: Debit	-4,724	-5,338	-6,698	-6,254	-6,006	-4,828	-5,590	-7,159	-9,054	-9,945	-11,713	-13,537	-13,557	-14,879	....	78ah d
Balance on Gds, Serv. & Inc.	-4,227	-1,572	-1,313	3,554	-1,440	-6,422	-8,680	-11,620	-5,760	-7,322	-12,797	-15,024	-12,421	-9,259	....	78ai d
Current Transfers, n.i.e.: Credit	11	2	18	1,015	821	1,032	839	798	821	702	751	711	688	641	....	78aj d
Current Transfers: Debit	-19	-2	-10	-17	-28	-263	-319	-336	-271	-257	-298	-313	-306	-352	....	78ak d
Capital Account, n.i.e.	—	—	—	—	—	15	16	19	14	51	51	73	88	87	....	78bc d
Capital Account, n.i.e.: Credit	—	—	—	—	—	24	25	28	25	72	65	92	99	102	....	78ba d
Capital Account: Debit	—	—	—	—	—	-9	-9	-9	-11	-21	-14	-19	-11	-15	....	78bb d
Financial Account, n.i.e.	100	369	-8,083	-5,884	182	7,627	20,389	11,351	4,915	11,799	16,590	18,971	14,693	8,110	....	78bj d
Direct Investment Abroad	....	....	....	....	....	-1,170	-705	-1,013	-1,498	-1,600	-3,653	-2,326	-1,354	-1,113	....	78bd d
Dir. Invest. in Rep. Econ., n.i.e.	-19	1,147	1,028	1,836	2,439	4,433	2,791	3,635	5,610	6,949	9,161	7,292	23,984	11,665	....	78be d
Portfolio Investment Assets	....	....	....	-241	-8,261	1,613	-1,553	-1,485	-2,882	-2,380	-1,570	-1,905	-2,129	-1,060	....	78bf d
Equity Securities	....	....	....	....	....	-295	-1,363	-762	-402	-593	-837	-838	168	-1,455	....	78bk d
Debt Securities	....	....	....	-241	-8,261	1,908	-190	-723	-2,480	-1,787	-733	-1,067	-2,297	395	....	78bl d
Portfolio Investment Liab., n.i.e.	-572	-718	-1,098	-1,105	8,227	3,154	35,261	9,845	4,733	12,100	11,667	10,693	-4,782	-1,332	....	78bg d
Equity Securities	....	....	....	....	....	1,120	4,979	3,118	1,090	990	1,391	-209	-10,773	-3,227	....	78bm d
Debt Securities	-572	-718	-1,098	-1,105	8,227	2,034	30,282	6,727	3,643	11,110	10,276	10,902	5,991	1,895	....	78bn d
Financial Derivatives Assets	....	....	....	....	....	....	....	....	....	....	....	....	....	....	....	78bw d
Financial Derivatives Liabilities	....	....	....	....	....	....	....	....	....	....	....	....	....	....	....	78bx d
Other Investment Assets	104	879	-399	661	426	-802	-4,658	-3,169	-8,200	-5,188	-7,275	-113	-2,817	-2,182	....	78bh d
Monetary Authorities	—	—	366	-669	273	330	—	—	—	—	—	—	—	—	....	78bo d
General Government	-23	—	-48	-81	83	-880	-1,484	442	-686	62	-89	111	-1,594	921	....	78bp d
Banks	16	—	—	—	—	-696	-1,728	-303	-680	-3,010	-5,505	613	995	-2,348	....	78bq d
Other Sectors	111	879	-717	1,411	70	444	-1,446	-3,308	-6,834	-2,240	-1,681	-837	-2,218	-755	....	78br d
Other Investment Liab., n.i.e.	587	-939	-7,614	-7,035	-2,649	399	-10,747	3,538	7,152	1,918	8,260	5,330	1,791	2,132	....	78bi d
Monetary Authorities	408	426	-1,804	-474	40	-173	-3,996	-16	-94	-214	-11	-10	-12	-17	....	78bs d
General Government	652	5	-438	-420	-3	-515	-8,709	535	1,902	-151	312	1,923	1,204	440	....	78bt d
Banks	-49	23	56	100	-31	773	1,152	1,096	3,254	436	3,847	620	1,134	898	....	78bu d
Other Sectors	-424	-1,393	-5,428	-6,241	-2,655	314	806	1,923	2,090	1,847	4,112	2,797	-535	811	....	78bv d
Net Errors and Omissions	-112	-165	-249	715	-341	-95	-1,123	-887	-2,030	-1,715	-966	-328	-729	-403	....	78ca d
Overall Balance	-4,247	-1,368	-9,637	-617	-806	1,894	11,122	-675	-2,311	3,258	3,331	4,090	2,013	-1,176	....	78cb d
Reserves and Related Items	4,247	1,368	9,637	617	806	-1,894	-11,122	675	2,311	-3,258	-3,331	-4,090	-2,013	1,176	....	79da d
Reserve Assets	1,302	-1,888	1,826	-3,121	-2,040	-3,264	-4,279	-685	82	-3,875	-3,293	-3,436	-1,186	403	....	79db d
Use of Fund Credit and Loans	615	30	-478	-257	-590	-73	1,211	455	1,924	367	-38	-654	-826	773	....	79dc d
Exceptional Financing	2,330	3,226	8,289	3,996	3,436	1,443	-8,054	904	305	250	—	—	—	—	....	79de d

Argentina

		1972	1973	1974	1975	1976	1977	1978	1979	1980	1981	1982	1983	1984	1985	1986
International Investment Position																*Millions of US Dollars*
Assets	79aa *d*	...	...	...	...	...	...	...	...	...	...	...	...	...	...	
Direct Investment Abroad	79ab *d*	...	...	...	...	...	...	...	...	...	...	...	...	...	...	
Portfolio Investment	79ac *d*	...	...	...	...	...	...	...	...	...	...	...	...	...	...	
Equity Securities	79ad *d*	...	...	...	...	...	...	...	...	...	...	...	...	...	...	
Debt Securities	79ae *d*	...	...	...	...	...	...	...	...	...	...	...	...	...	...	
Financial Derivatives	79al *d*	...	...	...	...	...	...	...	...	...	...	...	...	...	...	
Other Investment	79af *d*	...	...	...	...	...	...	...	...	...	...	...	...	...	...	
Monetary Authorities	79ag *d*	...	...	...	...	...	...	...	...	...	...	...	...	...	...	
General Government	79ah *d*	...	...	...	...	...	...	...	...	...	...	...	...	...	...	
Banks	79ai *d*	...	...	...	...	...	...	...	...	...	...	...	...	...	...	
Other Sectors	79aj *d*	...	...	...	...	...	...	...	...	...	...	...	...	...	...	
Reserve Assets	79ak *d*	...	...	...	...	...	...	...	...	...	...	...	...	...	...	
Liabilities	79la *d*	...	...	...	...	...	...	...	...	...	...	...	...	...	...	
Dir. Invest. in Rep. Economy	79lb *d*	...	...	...	...	...	...	...	...	...	...	...	...	...	...	
Portfolio Investment	79lc *d*	...	...	...	...	...	...	...	...	...	...	...	...	...	...	
Equity Securities	79ld *d*	...	...	...	...	...	...	...	...	...	...	...	...	...	...	
Debt Securities	79le *d*	...	...	...	...	...	...	...	...	...	...	...	...	...	...	
Financial Derivatives	79ll *d*	...	...	...	...	...	...	...	...	...	...	...	...	...	...	
Other Investment	79lf *d*	...	...	...	...	...	...	...	...	...	...	...	...	...	...	
Monetary Authorities	79lg *d*	...	...	...	...	...	...	...	...	...	...	...	...	...	...	
General Government	79lh *d*	...	...	...	...	...	...	...	...	...	...	...	...	...	...	
Banks	79li *d*	...	...	...	...	...	...	...	...	...	...	...	...	...	...	
Other Sectors	79lj *d*	...	...	...	...	...	...	...	...	...	...	...	...	...	...	
Government Finance															*Thousandths (.000) of Pesos through 1978; Pesos from 1979 to 1984;*	
Deficit (-) or Surplus	80	...	−100.0	−600.0	−1,700.0	−6,700.0	−8,900.0	−19,800.0	†−43.3	−119.5	−406.1	−923.0	−8,231.6	−29,980.3	†−283.7	−239.4
Revenue	81	...							†94.4	†170.0	336.1	897.1	4,977.2	35,577.2	†271.2	550.1
Exp. & Lending Minus Repay.	82z	...							†137.9	289.5	742.2	1,820.1	13,208.8	65,557.5	†554.9	789.5
Expenditure	82								...							
Lending Minus Repayments	83								...							
Total Financing	84	...								119.7	406.4	923.5	8,230.8	29,980.6	†283.7	239.4
Net Borrowing: Domestic	84a	...							†40.8	117.1	340.9	1,005.8	10,376.7	28,938.5	†275.7	328.2
Foreign	85a	...								2.4	65.4	61.4	−2,145.8	1,042.1	†8.4	−89.2
Use of Cash Balances	87	...							†−.3	.2	.1	−143.7	−.1	—	†−.3	.4
National Accounts															*Thousandths (.000) of Pesos through 1978; Pesos from 1979 to 1984;*	
Househ.Cons.Expend.,incl.NPISHs	96f	1,400	2,400	3,200	8,700	44,600	126,200	317,100	†936	2,925	5,812	16,537	82,990	610,610	†4,082	8,057
Government Consumption Expend.	91f	200	400	700	1,900	7,400	19,700	60,900	†164	—	—	—	—	—	†—	—
Gross Fixed Capital Formation	93e	400	600	900	3,700	20,400	56,900	127,600	†324	970	1,696	4,754	22,870	157,900	†933	1,743
Changes in Inventories	93i	—	—	—	100	200	—	−2,700	†−2	—	—	—	—	—	†—	—
Exports of Goods and Services	90c	200	400	500	1,100	9,400	27,300	61,000	†126	194	517	1,986	10,020	60,030	†623	815
Imports of Goods and Services (-)	98c	200	300	400	1,200	6,100	20,800	40,500	†122	249	551	1,425	6,390	37,620	†333	631
Gross Domestic Product (GDP)	99b	2,100	3,500	4,900	14,300	75,900	209,300	523,400	†1,425	3,840	7,474	21,852	109,500	790,920	†5,305	9,984
Net Primary Income from Abroad	98.n	−29	−40	−30	−200	−1,200	−2,400	−6,200	†−14	−32	−229	−1,266	−6,222	−41,830	†−346	−417
Gross National Income (GNI)	99a	2,000	3,200	4,786	14,100	74,700	206,900	517,200	†1,412	2,801	5,247	13,495	62,044	486,270	†5,000	10,000
GDP Vol. 1960 Prices(Thousandths)	99b.*p*	1	1	1	1	1	1	1	1							
GDP Vol. 1986 Prices(Thousands)	99b.*p*									10,331	9,738	9,431	9,824	10,020	9,324	9,989
GDP Vol. 1993 Prices(Millions)	99b.*p*	...	...	...	...	...	...	...	...							
GDP Volume (1995=100)	99bv *p*	71.9	75.8	80.9	79.8	76.7	81.7	78.9	85.6	†85.4	80.5	77.9	81.2	82.8	77.0	82.5
GDP Deflator (1995=100)	99bi *p*	—	—	—	—	—	—	—	—	—	—	—	—	—	—	—
																Millions:
Population	99z	24.39	24.82	25.22	†26.05	26.48	26.91	27.35	27.79	28.24	28.66	29.09	29.51	29.88	30.32	30.77

| 1987 | 1988 | 1989 | 1990 | 1991 | 1992 | 1993 | 1994 | 1995 | 1996 | 1997 | 1998 | 1999 | 2000 | 2001 | | |

Millions of US Dollars

International Investment Position

1998	1999	2000		
139,950	149,756	152,409	Assets	**79aa** *d*
18,334	19,757	20,859	Direct Investment Abroad	**79ab** *d*
29,955	34,504	34,998	Portfolio Investment	**79ac** *d*
49	28	41	Equity Securities	**79ad** *d*
29,906	34,476	34,957	Debt Securities	**79ae** *d*
—	—	—	Financial Derivatives	**79al** *d*
65,412	68,174	69,627	Other Investment	**79af** *d*
—	—	—	Monetary Authorities	**79ag** *d*
5,930	7,469	6,421	General Government	**79ah** *d*
13,743	12,748	15,095	Banks	**79ai** *d*
45,739	47,957	48,111	Other Sectors	**79aj** *d*
26,249	27,321	26,925	Reserve Assets	**79ak** *d*
206,784	219,587	226,789	Liabilities	**79la** *d*
47,904	62,037	73,088	Dir. Invest. in Rep. Economy	**79lb** *d*
94,552	92,397	86,932	Portfolio Investment	**79lc** *d*
14,297	8,389	3,636	Equity Securities	**79ld** *d*
80,255	84,008	83,296	Debt Securities	**79le** *d*
—	—	—	Financial Derivatives	**79ll** *d*
64,328	65,153	66,769	Other Investment	**79lf** *d*
5,462	4,492	5,066	Monetary Authorities	**79lg** *d*
22,765	23,334	22,819	General Government	**79lh** *d*
16,145	17,279	18,177	Banks	**79li** *d*
19,956	20,048	20,707	Other Sectors	**79lj** *d*

Government Finance

Thousands from 1985 to 1988:Millions Beginning 1989: Yr. Ending Dec. 31

1987	1988	1989	1990	1991	1992	1993	1994	1995	1996	1997	1998	1999	2000	2001		
−628.3	−1,487.1	†−21.5	−226.1	−963.0	−73.0	−1,574.0	−1,885.7	†−1426.0	−5,233.6	−4,357.3	−4,148.3	−8,125.7	−6,817.6	....	Deficit (−) or Surplus	**80**
1,111.4	3,139.6	†153.4	2,741.2	8,028.5	12,889.0	15,555.0	15,591.8	†38060.9	35,501.0	41,944.1	42,921.1	41,132.2	42,437.9	....	Revenue	**81**
1,739.7	4,626.6	†174.8	2,967.3	8,991.5	12,962.0	17,129.0	17,477.5	†39486.9	40,734.6	46,301.4	47,069.4	49,257.9	49,255.5	....	Exp. & Lending Minus Repay.	**82z**
....	....	....	....	....	....	....	....	40,574.5	41,066.1	46,174.3	47,108.3	49,214.2	49,365.9	....	Expenditure	**82**
								−1,087.6	−331.5	127.1	−38.9	43.7	−110.4	....	Lending Minus Repayments	**83**
628.2	1,487.1	†21.5	226.1	963.0	73.0	1,574.0	1,885.7	†1,426.0	5,233.6	4,357.3	4,148.2	8,125.7	6,817.6	....	Total Financing	**84**
181.4	998.9	†−8.6	346.9	869.4	895.0	1,740.0	863.2	....	−1,622.4	2,008.2	−576.8	−2,276.1	−1,924.6	....	Net Borrowing: Domestic	**84a**
446.9	490.6	†30.1	−86.2	310.8	−118.0	1,283.0	1,256.8	....							Foreign	**85a**
−.1	−2.4	†—	−34.6	−217.1	−704.0	−1,449.0	−234.3	†−2371.3	−344.1	1,262.1	−1,585.9	556.5	−533.9	....	Use of Cash Balances	**87**

National Accounts

Thousands from 1985 to 1988; Millions beginning 1989

1987	1988	1989	1990	1991	1992	1993	1994	1995	1996	1997	1998	1999	2000	2001		
18,700	86,673	†2,533	55,268	151,448	192,670	†163,676	180,007	176,909	186,487	203,029	206,434	198,869	197,044	184,954	Househ.Cons.Expend.,incl.NPISHs	**96f**
—	—	†—	—	—	—	†31,953	33,948	34,446	34,023	35,325	37,353	38,908	39,175	38,037	Government Consumption Expend.	**91f**
4,563	20,702	†503	9,647	26,478	37,854	†45,069	51,331	46,285	49,211	56,727	59,595	51,074	46,020	37,916	Gross Fixed Capital Formation	**93e**
—	—	†—	—	—	—	†1,494	78	1,493	4,251	4,350	3,179	−378	3,766	4,353	Changes in Inventories	**93i**
1,837	10,586	†421	7,201	14,046	15,096	†16,342	19,364	24,897	28,301	30,834	31,046	27,751	30,937	30,679	Exports of Goods and Services	**90c**
1,768	6,899	†213	3,194	11,074	18,823	†22,028	27,289	25,998	30,123	37,406	38,659	32,702	32,738	27,302	Imports of Goods and Services (-)	**98c**
23,332	111,062	†3,244	68,922	180,898	226,847	†236,505	257,440	258,032	272,150	292,859	298,948	283,523	284,204	268,638	Gross Domestic Product (GDP)	**99b**
−982	−3,000	†−145	−1,017	−2,301	−2,065	†−2,995	−3,694	−4,662	−5,502	−6,223	−7,414	−7,472	−7,483	−8,095	Net Primary Income from Abroad	**98.n**
22,000	108,000	†3,099	67,906	178,597	224,782	†233,510	253,746	253,370	266,648	286,636	291,531	276,051	276,721	260,543	Gross National Income (GNI)	**99a**
10,248	10,054	9,357	9,185	10,157	11,133	11,770	....	....	....	....	....	....	....	....	GDP Vol. 1960 Prices(Thousandths)	**99b.** *p*
					....	236,505	250,308	243,186	256,626	277,441	288,123	278,369	276,173	263,870	GDP Vol. 1986 Prices(Thousands)	**99b.** *p*
															GDP Vol. 1993 Prices(Millions)	**99b.** *p*
84.7	83.1	77.3	75.9	83.9	92.0	†97.3	102.9	100.0	105.5	114.1	118.5	114.5	113.6	108.5	GDP Volume (1995=100)	**99bv** *p*
—	.1	1.6	35.2	83.5	95.6	†94.2	96.9	100.0	99.9	99.5	97.8	96.0	97.0	95.9	GDP Deflator (1995=100)	**99bi** *p*

Midyear Estimates

1987	1988	1989	1990	1991	1992	1993	1994	1995	1996	1997	1998	1999	2000	2001		
31.22	31.64	32.08	32.53	32.97	33.42	33.87	34.32	34.77	35.22	35.67	36.12	36.58	37.03	36.22	**Population**	**99z**

(See notes in the back of the book.)

Armenia

	1972	1973	1974	1975	1976	1977	1978	1979	1980	1981	1982	1983	1984	1985	1986
Exchange Rates															*Dram per SDR:*
Official Rate .... aa	....	....	....	....	....	....	....	....	....	....	....	....	....	....	....
															Dram per US Dollar:
Official Rate .... ae	....	....	....	....	....	....	....	....	....	....	....	....	....	....	....
Official Rate .... rf	....	....	....	....	....	....	....	....	....	....	....	....	....	....	....
														Index Numbers (1995=100):	
Nominal Effective Exchange Rate .... ne c	....	....	....	....	....	....	....	....	....	....	....	....	....	....	....
Real Effective Exchange Rate .... re c	....	....	....	....	....	....	....	....	....	....	....	....	....	....	....
Fund Position															*Millions of SDRs:*
Quota .... 2f. s	....	....	....	....	....	....	....	....	....	....	....	....	....	....	....
SDRs.................................... 1b. s	....	....	....	....	....	....	....	....	....	....	....	....	....	....	....
Reserve Position in the Fund .... 1c. s	....	....	....	....	....	....	....	....	....	....	....	....	....	....	....
Total Fund Cred.&Loans Outstg. 2tl	....	....	....	....	....	....	....	....	....	....	....	....	....	....	....
International Liquidity								*Millions of US Dollars Unless Otherwise Indicated:*							
Total Reserves minus Gold .... 1l. d	....	....	....	....	....	....	....	....	....	....	....	....	....	....	....
SDRs.................................... 1b. d	....	....	....	....	....	....	....	....	....	....	....	....	....	....	....
Reserve Position in the Fund .... 1c. d	....	....	....	....	....	....	....	....	....	....	....	....	....	....	....
Foreign Exchange......................... 1d. d	....	....	....	....	....	....	....	....	....	....	....	....	....	....	....
Gold (Million Fine Troy Ounces) 1ad	....	....	....	....	....	....	....	....	....	....	....	....	....	....	....
Gold (National Valuation).................... 1an d	....	....	....	....	....	....	....	....	....	....	....	....	....	....	....
Monetary Authorities: Other Assets .... 3.. d	....	....	....	....	....	....	....	....	....	....	....	....	....	....	....
Other Liab. .... 4.. d	....	....	....	....	....	....	....	....	....	....	....	....	....	....	....
Deposit Money Banks: Assets .... 7a. d	....	....	....	....	....	....	....	....	....	....	....	....	....	....	....
Liabilities .... 7b. d	....	....	....	....	....	....	....	....	....	....	....	....	....	....	....
Monetary Authorities															*Millions of Dram:*
Foreign Assets 11	....	....	....	....	....	....	....	....	....	....	....	....	....	....	....
Claims on General Government 12a	....	....	....	....	....	....	....	....	....	....	....	....	....	....	....
Claims on Deposit Money Banks 12e	....	....	....	....	....	....	....	....	....	....	....	....	....	....	....
Reserve Money 14	....	....	....	....	....	....	....	....	....	....	....	....	....	....	....
of which: Currency Outside DMBs.......... 14a	....	....	....	....	....	....	....	....	....	....	....	....	....	....	....
Time,Savings,& Fgn.Currency Dep........ 15	....	....	....	....	....	....	....	....	....	....	....	....	....	....	....
Foreign Liabilities............................ 16c	....	....	....	....	....	....	....	....	....	....	....	....	....	....	....
General Government Deposits 16d	....	....	....	....	....	....	....	....	....	....	....	....	....	....	....
Capital Accounts......................... 17a	....	....	....	....	....	....	....	....	....	....	....	....	....	....	....
Other Items (Net) 17r	....	....	....	....	....	....	....	....	....	....	....	....	....	....	....
Deposit Money Banks															*Millions of Dram:*
Reserves 20	....	....	....	....	....	....	....	....	....	....	....	....	....	....	....
Foreign Assets 21	....	....	....	....	....	....	....	....	....	....	....	....	....	....	....
Claims on General Government 22a	....	....	....	....	....	....	....	....	....	....	....	....	....	....	....
of which: Claims on Local Govts. 22ab	....	....	....	....	....	....	....	....	....	....	....	....	....	....	....
Claims on Other Sectors 22d	....	....	....	....	....	....	....	....	....	....	....	....	....	....	....
Demand Deposits 24	....	....	....	....	....	....	....	....	....	....	....	....	....	....	....
Time,Savings,& Fgn.Currency Dep........... 25	....	....	....	....	....	....	....	....	....	....	....	....	....	....	....
Money Market Instruments 26aa	....	....	....	....	....	....	....	....	....	....	....	....	....	....	....
Foreign Liabilities............................ 26c	....	....	....	....	....	....	....	....	....	....	....	....	....	....	....
General Government Deposits 26d	....	....	....	....	....	....	....	....	....	....	....	....	....	....	....
of which: Local Govt. Deposits........... 26db	....	....	....	....	....	....	....	....	....	....	....	....	....	....	....
Credit from Monetary Authorities 26g	....	....	....	....	....	....	....	....	....	....	....	....	....	....	....
Capital Accounts......................... 27a	....	....	....	....	....	....	....	....	....	....	....	....	....	....	....
Other Items (Net).......................... 27r	....	....	....	....	....	....	....	....	....	....	....	....	....	....	....
Monetary Survey															*Millions of Dram:*
Foreign Assets (Net) 31n	....	....	....	....	....	....	....	....	....	....	....	....	....	....	....
Domestic Credit 32	....	....	....	....	....	....	....	....	....	....	....	....	....	....	....
Claims on General Govt. (Net) 32an	....	....	....	....	....	....	....	....	....	....	....	....	....	....	....
Claims on Other Sectors 32d	....	....	....	....	....	....	....	....	....	....	....	....	....	....	....
Money.................................... 34	....	....	....	....	....	....	....	....	....	....	....	....	....	....	....
Quasi-Money 35	....	....	....	....	....	....	....	....	....	....	....	....	....	....	....
Money Market Instruments 36aa	....	....	....	....	....	....	....	....	....	....	....	....	....	....	....
Capital Accounts........................... 37a	....	....	....	....	....	....	....	....	....	....	....	....	....	....	....
Other Items (Net) 37r	....	....	....	....	....	....	....	....	....	....	....	....	....	....	....
Money plus Quasi-Money....................... 35l	....	....	....	....	....	....	....	....	....	....	....	....	....	....	....
Interest Rates															*Percent Per Annum*
Discount Rate *(End of Period)* 60	....	....	....	....	....	....	....	....	....	....	....	....	....	....	....
Refinancing Rate *(End of Period)*............ 60a	....	....	....	....	....	....	....	....	....	....	....	....	....	....	....
Money Market Rate................................ 60b	....	....	....	....	....	....	....	....	....	....	....	....	....	....	....
Treasury Bill Rate 60c	....	....	....	....	....	....	....	....	....	....	....	....	....	....	....
Deposit Rate 60l	....	....	....	....	....	....	....	....	....	....	....	....	....	....	....
Lending Rate 60p	....	....	....	....	....	....	....	....	....	....	....	....	....	....	....
Prices, Production, Labor														*Index Numbers (1995=100):*	
Producer Prices (1997=100) 63															
Consumer Prices 64	....	....	....	....	....	....	....	....	....	....	....	....	....	....	....
Wages: Avg. Month.Earn.('97=100) 65															
Industrial Production (1997=100) 66										66					
														Number in Thousands:	
Employment 67e	....	....	....	....	....	....	....	....	....	....	....	....	....	....	....
Unemployment 67c	....	....	....	....	....	....	....	....	....	....	....	....	....	....	....
Unemployment Rate (%)......................... 67r	....	....	....	....	....	....	....	....	....	....	....	....	....	....	....

1987	1988	1989	1990	1991	1992	1993	1994	1995	1996	1997	1998	1999	2000	2001		
End of Period															**Exchange Rates**	
....	....	....	....	....	2.85	103.02	591.98	597.57	625.61	667.85	735.03	718.88	719.44	706.04	Official Rate	**aa**
End of Period (ae) Period Average (rf)																
....	....	....	....	....	2.07	75.00	405.51	402.00	435.07	494.98	522.03	523.77	552.18	561.81	Official Rate	**ae**
....	....	....	....	....	....	9.11	288.65	405.91	414.04	490.85	504.92	535.06	539.53	555.08	Official Rate	**rf**
Period Averages																
....	....	....	....	....	....	....	64.99	100.00	217.19	209.90	237.33	324.33	342.55	338.54	Nominal Effective Exchange Rate	**ne c**
....	....	....	....	....	....	....	57.69	100.00	119.76	104.80	111.59	115.53	108.74	98.80	Real Effective Exchange Rate	**re c**
End of Period															**Fund Position**	
....	....	....	....	....	67.50	67.50	67.50	67.50	67.50	67.50	67.50	92.00	92.00	92.00	Quota	**2f.s**
....	....	....	....	....	—	—	.19	29.82	28.86	27.63	19.89	29.64	16.54	8.15	SDRs	**1b.s**
....	....	....	....	....	.01	.01	.01	.01	.01	—	—	—	—	—	Reserve Position in the Fund	**1c.s**
....	....	....	....	....	—	—	16.88	47.25	81.00	97.88	135.25	146.62	134.66	137.35	Total Fund Cred.&Loans Outstg.	**2tl**
End of Period															**International Liquidity**	
....	....	....	....	....	1.29	13.59	32.28	99.58	155.65	228.75	315.29	318.56	318.32	320.53	Total Reserves minus Gold	**1l.d**
....	....	....	....	....	—	—	.28	44.33	41.50	37.28	28.00	40.68	21.55	10.24	SDRs	**1b.d**
....	....	....	....	....	.01	.01	.01	.01	.01	.01	.01	—	—	—	Reserve Position in the Fund	**1c.d**
....	....	....	....	....	1.28	13.58	31.99	55.24	114.14	191.46	287.28	277.88	296.77	310.29	Foreign Exchange	**1d.d**
....	....	....	....	....	—	—	.0100	.0300	.0340	.0361	.0432	.0436	.0446	.0449	Gold (Million Fine Troy Ounces)	**1ad**
....	....	....	....	....	—	—	2.44	10.46	12.82	10.72	12.37	12.69	11.79	12.41	Gold (National Valuation)	**1and**
....	....	....	....	....	99.61	2.93	.20	.10	.52	.25	.10	.05	.11	.01	Monetary Authorities: Other Assets	**3..d**
....	....	....	....	....	5.82	23.96	2.05	1.19	5.09	5.05	2.54	1.59	2.89	6.35	Other Liab.	**4..d**
....	....	....	....	....	14.12	22.68	22.03	24.28	18.14	33.28	33.12	70.34	96.07	101.91	Deposit Money Banks: Assets	**7a.d**
....	....	....	....	....	3.82	3.45	12.98	24.59	50.74	73.39	96.10	111.50	119.90	114.95	Liabilities	**7b.d**
End of Period															**Monetary Authorities**	
....	....	....	....	....	209	1,239	14,162	44,278	73,523	118,657	171,103	173,521	182,342	187,059	Foreign Assets	**11**
....	....	....	....	....	54	1,463	9,536	10,624	27,971	16,491	18,083	18,471	10,296	10,190	Claims on General Government	**12a**
....	....	....	....	....	81	286	3,629	3,781	3,346	3,345	3,253	1,698	3,332	3,905	Claims on Deposit Money Banks	**12e**
....	....	....	....	....	108	1,593	15,002	28,806	41,140	51,333	53,863	53,853	72,389	80,418	Reserve Money	**14**
....	....	....	....	....	60	881	10,056	24,601	34,784	37,596	41,370	42,610	59,486	65,027	*of which: Currency Outside DMBs*	**14a**
....	....	....	....	....	—	—	781	556	116	187	491	346	1	1	Time,Savings,& Fgn.Currency Dep.	**15**
....	....	....	....	....	12	1,797	10,823	28,715	52,890	67,863	100,741	106,234	98,480	100,541	Foreign Liabilities	**16c**
....	....	....	....	....	2	76	1,433	423	8,733	8,165	9,851	10,165	2,004	1,922	General Government Deposits	**16d**
....	....	....	....	....	4	121	596	1,691	7,214	13,733	16,609	12,079	21,202	20,745	Capital Accounts	**17a**
....	....	....	....	....	218	−599	−1,309	−1,509	−5,254	−2,788	10,882	11,013	1,893	−2,474	Other Items (Net)	**17r**
End of Period															**Deposit Money Banks**	
....	....	....	....	....	22	529	3,164	3,987	6,083	13,681	12,033	11,082	12,593	14,747	Reserves	**20**
....	....	....	....	....	29	1,701	8,933	9,759	7,894	16,472	17,287	36,843	53,048	57,253	Foreign Assets	**21**
....	....	....	....	....	9	199	335	354	5,865	9,198	15,436	12,268	16,890	18,477	Claims on General Government	**22a**
....	....	....	....	....	—	—	—	—	—	—	2	5	—	—	*of which:* Claims on Local Govts.	**22ab**
....	....	....	....	....	125	353	20,718	37,946	37,181	48,486	82,159	90,540	109,543	102,950	Claims on Other Sectors	**22d**
....	....	....	....	....	55	443	3,188	5,375	4,968	6,372	11,216	9,553	11,743	13,395	Demand Deposits	**24**
....	....	....	....	....	133	1,584	10,310	9,617	14,424	26,005	42,868	56,881	80,258	93,608	Time,Savings,& Fgn.Currency Dep.	**25**
....	....	....	....	....	—	—	—	—	—	—	24	201	—	90	Money Market Instruments	**26aa**
....	....	....	....	....	8	259	5,262	9,884	22,074	36,328	50,168	58,399	66,207	64,582	Foreign Liabilities	**26c**
....	....	....	....	....	16	217	1,324	1,748	2,533	2,469	3,662	5,205	15,881	18,372	General Government Deposits	**26d**
....	....	....	....	....	11	134	790	857	222	577	349	209	70	58	*of which:* Local Govt. Deposits	**26db**
....	....	....	....	....	1	4	1,367	4,093	3,539	3,710	3,257	1,701	3,342	4,812	Credit from Monetary Authorities	**26g**
....	....	....	....	....	−40	165	3,646	7,579	12,315	17,835	28,685	36,366	38,151	25,346	Capital Accounts	**27a**
....	....	....	....	....	14	112	8,053	13,750	−2,831	−4,882	−12,966	−17,574	−23,507	−26,776	Other Items (Net)	**27r**
End of Period															**Monetary Survey**	
....	....	....	....	....	218	884	7,010	15,438	6,453	30,938	37,481	45,731	70,703	79,190	Foreign Assets (Net)	**31n**
....	....	....	....	....	182	1,728	27,832	46,753	59,753	63,544	102,167	105,941	119,023	111,494	Domestic Credit	**32**
....	....	....	....	....	46	1,370	7,113	8,807	22,570	15,055	20,005	15,368	9,301	8,373	Claims on General Govt. (Net)	**32an**
....	....	....	....	....	125	353	20,718	37,946	37,181	48,486	82,159	90,570	109,722	103,121	Claims on Other Sectors	**32d**
....	....	....	....	....	115	1,331	13,410	30,078	39,830	44,055	52,678	52,227	71,395	78,609	Money	**34**
....	....	....	....	....	133	1,584	11,091	10,173	14,540	26,192	43,360	57,227	80,259	93,609	Quasi-Money	**35**
....	....	....	....	....	—	—	—	—	—	—	24	201	—	90	Money Market Instruments	**36aa**
....	....	....	....	....	−35	286	4,242	9,270	19,530	31,568	45,295	48,445	59,353	46,092	Capital Accounts	**37a**
....	....	....	....	....	188	−590	6,099	12,670	−7,694	−7,333	−1,708	−6,428	−21,280	−27,715	Other Items (Net)	**37r**
....	....	....	....	....	248	2,916	24,501	40,251	54,371	70,247	96,037	109,454	151,653	172,218	Money plus Quasi-Money	**35l**
Percent Per Annum															**Interest Rates**	
....	....	....	....	....	30.00	210.00	210.00	77.80	26.00	65.10	....	....	....	....	Discount Rate *(End of Period)*	**60**
....	....	....	....	....	30.00	210.00	210.00	52.00	60.00	54.00	39.00	†43.00	25.00	15.00	Refinancing Rate *(End of Period)*	**60a**
....	....	....	....	....	....	....	....	....	48.56	36.41	27.84	23.65	18.63	19.40	Money Market Rate	**60b**
....	....	....	....	....	....	....	....	37.81	†43.95	57.54	46.99	55.10	24.40	19.92	Treasury Bill Rate	**60c**
....	....	....	....	....	....	....	....	63.18	32.19	26.08	24.94	27.35	18.08	14.90	Deposit Rate	**60l**
....	....	....	....	....	....	....	....	111.86	66.36	54.23	48.49	38.85	31.57	26.69	Lending Rate	**60p**
Period Averages															**Prices, Production, Labor**	
....	....	....	....	....	....	....	....	....	....	100.0	114.6	121.3	120.8	122.2	Producer Prices (1997=100)	**63**
....	....	....	....	....	....	.7	36.2	100.0	118.7	†135.2	146.9	147.9	146.7	151.3	Consumer Prices	**64**
....	....	....	....	....	....	....	....	....	....	100.0	133.0	158.5	180.7	....	Wages: Avg. Month.Earn.('97=100)	**65**
....	....	....	....	....	....	....	....	....	92.3	100.0	105.3	119.1	127.4	....	Industrial Production (1997=100)	**66**
Period Averages																
....	....	....	....	....	....	....	....	....	....	1,372.2	1,352.5	....	....	....	Employment	**67e**
....	....	....	....	....	....	....	....	....	....	166.1	139.1	....	....	....	Unemployment	**67c**
....	....	....	....	....	....	....	....	....	....	10.8	9.3	....	....	....	Unemployment Rate (%)	**67r**

Armenia

		1972	1973	1974	1975	1976	1977	1978	1979	1980	1981	1982	1983	1984	1985	1986
International Transactions															*Millions of US Dollars*	
Exports	70..d	....	....	....	....	....	....	....	....	....	....	....	....	....	...	...
Imports, c.i.f.	71..d	....	....	....	....	....	....	....	....	....	....	....	....	....	...	...
Imports, f.o.b.	71.v d	....	....	....	....	....	....	....	....	....	....	....	....	....	...	...
Balance of Payments															*Millions of US Dollars:*	
Current Account, n.i.e.	78al d	....	....	....	....	....	....	....	....	....	....	....	....	....	...	...
Goods: Exports f.o.b	78aa d	....	....	....	....	....	....	....	....	....	....	....	....	....	...	...
Goods: Imports f.o.b	78ab d	....	....	....	....	....	....	....	....	....	....	....	....	....	...	...
Trade Balance	78ac d	....	....	....	....	....	....	....	....	....	....	....	....	....	...	...
Services: Credit	78ad d	....	....	....	....	....	....	....	....	....	....	....	....	....	...	...
Services: Debit	78ae d	....	....	....	....	....	....	....	....	....	....	....	....	....	...	...
Balance on Goods & Services	78af d	....	....	....	....	....	....	....	....	....	....	....	....	....	...	...
Income: Credit	78ag d	....	....	....	....	....	....	....	....	....	....	....	....	....	...	...
Income: Debit	78ah d	....	....	....	....	....	....	....	....	....	....	....	....	....	...	...
Balance on Gds, Serv. & Inc.	78ai d	....	....	....	....	....	....	....	....	....	....	....	....	....	...	...
Current Transfers, n.i.e.: Credit	78aj d	....	....	....	....	....	....	....	....	....	....	....	....	....	...	...
Current Transfers: Debit	78ak d	....	....	....	....	....	....	....	....	....	....	....	....	....	...	...
Capital Account, n.i.e.	78bc d	....	....	....	....	....	....	....	....	....	....	....	....	....	...	...
Capital Account, n.i.e.: Credit	78ba d	....	....	....	....	....	....	....	....	....	....	....	....	....	...	...
Capital Account: Debit	78bb d	....	....	....	....	....	....	....	....	....	....	....	....	....	...	...
Financial Account, n.i.e.	78bj d	....	....	....	....	....	....	....	....	....	....	....	....	....	...	...
Direct Investment Abroad	78bd d	....	....	....	....	....	....	....	....	....	....	....	....	....	...	...
Dir. Invest. in Rep. Econ., n.i.e.	78be d	....	....	....	....	....	....	....	....	....	....	....	....	....	...	...
Portfolio Investment Assets	78bf d	....	....	....	....	....	....	....	....	....	....	....	....	....	...	...
Equity Securities	78bk d	....	....	....	....	....	....	....	....	....	....	....	....	....	...	...
Debt Securities	78bl d	....	....	....	....	....	....	....	....	....	....	....	....	....	...	...
Portfolio Investment Liab., n.i.e.	78bg d	....	....	....	....	....	....	....	....	....	....	....	....	....	...	...
Equity Securities	78bm d	....	....	....	....	....	....	....	....	....	....	....	....	....	...	...
Debt Securities	78bn d	....	....	....	....	....	....	....	....	....	....	....	....	....	...	...
Financial Derivatives Assets	78bw d	....	....	....	....	....	....	....	....	....	....	....	....	....	...	...
Financial Derivatives Liabilities	78bx d	....	....	....	....	....	....	....	....	....	....	....	....	....	...	...
Other Investment Assets	78bh d	....	....	....	....	....	....	....	....	....	....	....	....	....	...	...
Monetary Authorities	78bo d	....	....	....	....	....	....	....	....	....	....	....	....	....	...	...
General Government	78bp d	....	....	....	....	....	....	....	....	....	....	....	....	....	...	...
Banks	78bq d	....	....	....	....	....	....	....	....	....	....	....	....	....	...	...
Other Sectors	78br d	....	....	....	....	....	....	....	....	....	....	....	....	....	...	...
Other Investment Liab., n.i.e.	78bi d	....	....	....	....	....	....	....	....	....	....	....	....	....	...	...
Monetary Authorities	78bs d	....	....	....	....	....	....	....	....	....	....	....	....	....	...	...
General Government	78bt d	....	....	....	....	....	....	....	....	....	....	....	....	....	...	...
Banks	78bu d	....	....	....	....	....	....	....	....	....	....	....	....	....	...	...
Other Sectors	78bv d	....	....	....	....	....	....	....	....	....	....	....	....	....	...	...
Net Errors and Omissions	78ca d	....	....	....	....	....	....	....	....	....	....	....	....	....	...	...
Overall Balance	78cb d	....	....	....	....	....	....	....	....	....	....	....	....	....	...	...
Reserves and Related Items	79da d	....	....	....	....	....	....	....	....	....	....	....	....	....	...	...
Reserve Assets	79db d	....	....	....	....	....	....	....	....	....	....	....	....	....	...	...
Use of Fund Credit and Loans	79dc d	....	....	....	....	....	....	....	....	....	....	....	....	....	...	...
Exceptional Financing	79de d	....	....	....	....	....	....	....	....	....	....	....	....	....	...	...
International Investment Position															*Millions of US Dollars*	
Assets	79aa d	....	....	....	....	....	....	....	....	....	....	....	....	....	...	...
Direct Investment Abroad	79ab d	....	....	....	....	....	....	....	....	....	....	....	....	....	...	...
Portfolio Investment	79ac d	....	....	....	....	....	....	....	....	....	....	....	....	....	...	...
Equity Securities	79ad d	....	....	....	....	....	....	....	....	....	....	....	....	....	...	...
Debt Securities	79ae d	....	....	....	....	....	....	....	....	....	....	....	....	....	...	...
Financial Derivatives	79al d	....	....	....	....	....	....	....	....	....	....	....	....	....	...	...
Other Investment	79af d	....	....	....	....	....	....	....	....	....	....	....	....	....	...	...
Monetary Authorities	79ag d	....	....	....	....	....	....	....	....	....	....	....	....	....	...	...
General Government	79ah d	....	....	....	....	....	....	....	....	....	....	....	....	....	...	...
Banks	79ai d	....	....	....	....	....	....	....	....	....	....	....	....	....	...	...
Other Sectors	79aj d	....	....	....	....	....	....	....	....	....	....	....	....	....	...	...
Reserve Assets	79ak d	....	....	....	....	....	....	....	....	....	....	....	....	....	...	...
Liabilities	79la d	....	....	....	....	....	....	....	....	....	....	....	....	....	...	...
Dir. Invest. in Rep. Economy	79lb d	....	....	....	....	....	....	....	....	....	....	....	....	....	...	...
Portfolio Investment	79lc d	....	....	....	....	....	....	....	....	....	....	....	....	....	...	...
Equity Securities	79ld d	....	....	....	....	....	....	....	....	....	....	....	....	....	...	...
Debt Securities	79le d	....	....	....	....	....	....	....	....	....	....	....	....	....	...	...
Financial Derivatives	79ll d	....	....	....	....	....	....	....	....	....	....	....	....	....	...	...
Other Investment	79lf d	....	....	....	....	....	....	....	....	....	....	....	....	....	...	...
Monetary Authorities	79lg d	....	....	....	....	....	....	....	....	....	....	....	....	....	...	...
General Government	79lh d	....	....	....	....	....	....	....	....	....	....	....	....	....	...	...
Banks	79li d	....	....	....	....	....	....	....	....	....	....	....	....	....	...	...
Other Sectors	79lj d	....	....	....	....	....	....	....	....	....	....	....	....	....	...	...
National Accounts															*Millions of Dram*	
Househ.Cons.Expend.,incl.NPISHs	96f	....	....	....	....	....	....	....	....	....	....	....	....	....	...	...
Government Consumption Expend.	91f	....	....	....	....	....	....	....	....	....	....	....	....	....	...	...
Gross Fixed Capital Formation	93e	....	....	....	....	....	....	....	....	....	....	....	....	....	...	...
Changes in Inventories	93i	....	....	....	....	....	....	....	....	....	....	....	....	....	...	...
Exports of Goods and Services	90c	....	....	....	....	....	....	....	....	....	....	....	....	....	...	...
Imports of Goods and Services (-)	98c	....	....	....	....	....	....	....	....	....	....	....	....	....	...	...
Gross Domestic Product (GDP)	99b	....	....	....	....	....	....	....	....	....	....	....	....	....	...	...
Statistical Discrepancy	99bs	....	....	....	....	....	....	....	....	....	....	....	....	....	...	...
GDP Volume (1995=100)	99bv p	....	....	....	....	....	....	....	....	....	....	....	....	....	...	...
GDP Deflator (1995=100)	99bi p	....	....	....	....	....	....	....	....	....	....	....	....	....	...	...
															Millions:	
Population	99z	....	....	....	....	....	....	....	....	....	....	....	....	....	...	...

	1987	1988	1989	1990	1991	1992	1993	1994	1995	1996	1997	1998	1999	2000	2001		
Millions of US Dollars																**International Transactions**	
	....	....	....	....	....	82.90	156.20	215.50	270.90	290.30	232.55	220.50	232.20	294.20	342.80	Exports	70..*d*
	....	....	....	....	....	205.90	254.20	393.80	673.90	855.80	892.30	902.40	799.70	881.90	874.30	Imports, c.i.f.	71..*d*
	....	....	....	....	....	185.30	233.80	343.80	625.40	757.50	779.40	794.10	703.60	776.20	751.90	Imports, f.o.b.	71.v*d*
Minus Sign Indicates Debit																Balance of Payments	
	....	....	....	....	....	....	-66.83	-103.78	-218.37	-290.68	-306.51	-417.96	-307.05	....	....	Current Account, n.i.e.	78al*d*
	....	....	....	....	....	....	156.19	215.35	270.90	290.44	233.64	228.89	247.31	....	....	Goods: Exports f.o.b.	78aa*d*
	....	....	....	....	....	....	-254.18	-393.63	-673.87	-759.63	-793.10	-806.29	-721.35	....	....	Goods: Imports f.o.b	78ab*d*
	....	....	....	....	....	....	-97.99	-178.28	-402.97	-469.19	-559.46	-577.40	-474.04	....	....	*Trade Balance*	78ac*d*
	....	....	....	....	....	....	17.28	13.67	28.60	77.71	96.60	130.34	135.81	....	....	Services: Credit	78ad*d*
	....	....	....	....	....	....	-40.06	-40.70	-52.27	-128.52	-159.38	-208.71	-197.87	....	....	Services: Debit	78ae*d*
	....	....	....	....	....	....	-120.77	-205.31	-426.64	-520.00	-622.24	-655.77	-536.10	....	....	*Balance on Goods & Services*	78af*d*
	....	....	....	....	....	....	....	....	54.63	78.04	138.95	103.91	93.57	....	....	Income: Credit	78ag*d*
	....	....	....	....	....	....	-1.30	-4.02	-14.61	-33.31	-40.44	-43.51	-38.64	....	....	Income: Debit	78ah*d*
	....	....	....	....	....	....	-122.07	-209.33	-386.62	-475.27	-523.73	-595.37	-481.17	....	....	*Balance on Gds, Serv. & Inc.*	78ai*d*
	....	....	....	....	....	....	56.29	106.33	169.95	198.99	252.41	203.02	200.57	....	....	Current Transfers, n.i.e.: Credit	78aj*d*
	....	....	....	....	....	....	-1.05	-.78	-1.70	-14.40	-35.19	-25.61	-26.45	....	....	Current Transfers: Debit	78ak*d*
	....	....	....	....	....	....	5.10	5.74	8.05	13.40	10.88	9.74	12.55	....	....	Capital Account, n.i.e.	78bc*d*
	....	....	....	....	....	....	5.10	5.74	8.05	13.40	10.88	9.74	16.85	....	....	Capital Account, n.i.e.: Credit	78ba*d*
	....	....	....	....	....	....	....	....	....	....	....	—	-4.30	....	....	Capital Account: Debit	78bb*d*
	....	....	....	....	....	....	57.82	89.94	227.48	216.76	334.82	390.43	286.18	....	....	Financial Account, n.i.e.	78bj*d*
	....	....	....	....	....	....	....	....	....	....	....	—	—	....	....	Direct Investment Abroad	78bd*d*
	....	....	....	....	....	....	.80	8.00	25.32	17.57	51.94	220.83	122.04	....	....	Dir. Invest. in Rep. Econ., n.i.e.	78be*d*
	....	....	....	....	....	....		....	....	-.01	-.14	.63	.06	....	....	Portfolio Investment Assets	78bf*d*
	....	....	....	....	....	....		....	....	-.01	-.03	.53	.01	....	....	Equity Securities	78bk*d*
	....	....	....	....	....	....		....	....	....	-.11	.10	.05	....	....	Debt Securities	78bl*d*
	....	....	....	....	....	....		....	....	7.23	15.90	-16.57	1.58	....	....	Portfolio Investment Liab., n.i.e.	78bg*d*
	....	....	....	....	....	....		....	....	1.88	.46	.72	-.32	....	....	Equity Securities	78bm*d*
	....	....	....	....	....	....		....	....	5.35	15.44	-17.29	1.90	....	....	Debt Securities	78bn*d*
	....	....	....	....	....	....	....	....	....	....	....	....	—	....	....	Financial Derivatives Assets	78bw*d*
	....	....	....	....	....	....	....	....	....	....	....	....	—	....	....	Financial Derivatives Liabilities	78bx*d*
	....	....	....	....	....	....	-44.00	35.89	-8.60	35.34	40.76	19.97	2.97	....	....	Other Investment Assets	78bh*d*
	....	....	....	....	....	....	-33.40	....	-8.58	-.08	1.36	.07	.06	....	....	Monetary Authorities	78bo*d*
	....	....	....	....	....	....	-10.60	-6.24	....	....	....	-43.27	15.56	....	....	General Government	78bp*d*
	....	....	....	....	....	....	....	.27	-.02	7.33	-17.57	6.17	-34.42	....	....	Banks	78bq*d*
	....	....	....	....	....	....	....	41.86	....	28.09	56.97	57.00	21.77	....	....	Other Sectors	78br*d*
	....	....	....	....	....	....	101.02	46.05	210.76	156.63	226.36	165.57	159.53	....	....	Other Investment Liab., n.i.e.	78bi*d*
	....	....	....	....	....	....	28.24	-9.18	.53	4.68	-.04	-2.92	-.93	....	....	Monetary Authorities	78bs*d*
	....	....	....	....	....	....	99.05	55.26	151.20	44.21	122.86	35.01	80.16	....	....	General Government	78bt*d*
	....	....	....	....	....	....	-26.27	-.03	.03	26.18	29.04	23.99	11.19	....	....	Banks	78bu*d*
	....	....	....	....	....	....	....	....	59.00	81.56	74.50	109.49	69.11	....	....	Other Sectors	78bv*d*
	....	....	....	....	....	....	17.17	4.83	12.35	15.06	10.83	18.39	13.11	....	....	Net Errors and Omissions	78ca*d*
	....	....	....	....	....	....	13.26	-3.27	29.51	-45.46	50.02	.60	4.79	....	....	*Overall Balance*	78cb*d*
	....	....	....	....	....	....	-13.26	3.27	-29.51	45.46	-50.02	-.60	-4.79	....	....	Reserves and Related Items	79da*d*
	....	....	....	....	....	....	-13.26	-21.24	-76.22	-60.35	-73.48	-52.13	-20.79	....	....	Reserve Assets	79db*d*
	....	....	....	....	....	....	—	24.50	46.71	49.04	23.46	51.53	16.00	....	....	Use of Fund Credit and Loans	79dc*d*
	....	....	....	....	....	....	....	....	....	56.77	....	....	....	....	....	Exceptional Financing	79de*d*
Millions of US Dollars																International Investment Position	
	....	....	....	....	....	....	....	....	....	....	381.90	480.38	488.89	....	....	Assets	79aa*d*
	....	....	....	....	....	....	....	....	....	....	—	—	—	....	....	Direct Investment Abroad	79ab*d*
	....	....	....	....	....	....	....	....	....	....	.61	.18	.12	....	....	Portfolio Investment	79ac*d*
	....	....	....	....	....	....	....	....	....	....	.50	.10	.09	....	....	Equity Securities	79ad*d*
	....	....	....	....	....	....	....	....	....	....	.11	.08	.03	....	....	Debt Securities	79ae*d*
	....	....	....	....	....	....	....	....	....	....	—	—	—	....	....	Financial Derivatives	79al*d*
	....	....	....	....	....	....	....	....	....	....	141.82	187.09	185.77	....	....	Other Investment	79af*d*
	....	....	....	....	....	....	....	....	....	....	.18	.10	.04	....	....	Monetary Authorities	79ag*d*
	....	....	....	....	....	....	....	....	....	....	18.00	61.27	45.71	....	....	General Government	79ah*d*
	....	....	....	....	....	....	....	....	....	....	37.77	33.85	70.12	....	....	Banks	79ai*d*
	....	....	....	....	....	....	....	....	....	....	85.87	91.87	69.90	....	....	Other Sectors	79aj*d*
	....	....	....	....	....	....	....	....	....	....	239.47	293.11	303.00	....	....	Reserve Assets	79ak*d*
	....	....	....	....	....	....	....	....	....	....	949.92	1,332.16	1,607.72	....	....	Liabilities	79la*d*
	....	....	....	....	....	....	....	....	....	....	103.44	312.67	421.36	....	....	Dir. Invest. in Rep. Economy	79lb*d*
	....	....	....	....	....	....	....	....	....	....	21.18	3.44	4.47	....	....	Portfolio Investment	79lc*d*
	....	....	....	....	....	....	....	....	....	....	.44	1.09	.75	....	....	Equity Securities	79ld*d*
	....	....	....	....	....	....	....	....	....	....	20.74	2.35	3.72	....	....	Debt Securities	79le*d*
	....	....	....	....	....	....	....	....	....	....	—	—	—	....	....	Financial Derivatives	79ll*d*
	....	....	....	....	....	....	....	....	....	....	825.30	1,016.05	1,181.89	....	....	Other Investment	79lf*d*
	....	....	....	....	....	....	....	....	....	....	137.49	192.94	202.80	....	....	Monetary Authorities	79lg*d*
	....	....	....	....	....	....	....	....	....	....	496.80	538.29	611.83	....	....	General Government	79lh*d*
	....	....	....	....	....	....	....	....	....	....	112.51	96.73	111.51	....	....	Banks	79li*d*
	....	....	....	....	....	....	....	....	....	....	78.50	188.09	255.75	....	....	Other Sectors	79lj*d*
Millions of Dram																**National Accounts**	
	....	....	....	....	....	....	....	176,885	555,056	664,002	832,638	956,322	951,565	985,821	1,107,598	Househ.Cons.Expend.,incl.NPISHs	96f
	....	....	....	....	....	....	....	21,086	58,336	74,265	90,220	105,589	117,591	123,512	125,777	Government Consumption Expend.	91f
	....	....	....	....	....	....	....	37,855	84,365	118,254	130,336	154,925	162,134	182,394	199,577	Gross Fixed Capital Formation	93e
	....	....	....	....	....	....	....	6,012	11,858	14,029	23,015	27,900	19,085	15,439	10,057	Changes in Inventories	93i
	....	....	....	....	....	....	....	73,569	124,965	153,665	163,065	181,552	204,976	241,856	300,432	Exports of Goods and Services	90c
	....	....	....	....	....	....	....	136,746	324,775	370,208	468,722	504,820	491,769	524,932	539,495	Imports of Goods and Services (-)	98c
	....	....	....	....	....	....	....	187,065	522,256	661,209	804,336	955,385	987,444	1,033,325	1,177,235	Gross Domestic Product (GDP)	99b
	....	....	....	....	....	....	....	8,404	12,451	7,202	33,783	33,917	23,862	9,236	-26,712	Statistical Discrepancy	99bs
	....	....	....	....	....	....	....	93.6	100.0	105.9	109.4	117.4	121.2	....	....	GDP Volume (1995=100)	99bv*p*
	....	....	....	....	....	....	....	38.3	100.0	119.6	140.8	155.8	156.0	....	....	GDP Deflator (1995=100)	99bi*p*
Midyear Estimates																	
	....	....	....	....	....	....	3.73	3.75	3.76	3.77	3.79	3.79	3.80	3.80	3.46	**Population**	99z

(See notes in the back of the book.)

Aruba

		1972	1973	1974	1975	1976	1977	1978	1979	1980	1981	1982	1983	1984	1985	1986
Exchange Rates																*Aruban Florins per SDR:*
Official Rate	aa	....	....	....	....	....	....	....	....	....	....	....	....	....	....	2.1895
																Aruban Florins per US Dollar:
Official Rate	ae	....	....	....	....	....	....	....	....	....	....	....	....	....	....	1.7900
Official Rate	rf	....	....	....	....	....	....	....	....	....	....	....	....	....	....	1.7900
International Liquidity																*Millions of US Dollars:*
Total Reserves minus Gold	1l.d	....	....	....	....	....	....	....	....	....	....	....	....	....	....	73.63
Foreign Exchange	1d.d	....	....	....	....	....	....	....	....	....	....	....	....	....	....	73.63
Gold (Million Fine Troy Ounces)	1ad	....	....	....	....	....	....	....	....	....	....	....	....	....	....	—
Gold (National Valuation)	1and	....	....	....	....	....	....	....	....	....	....	....	....	....	....	5.587
Deposit Money Banks: Assets	7a.d	....	....	....	....	....	....	....	....	....	....	....	....	....	....	37.15
Liabilities	7b.d	....	....	....	....	....	....	....	....	....	....	....	....	....	....	43.52
Monetary Authorities																*Millions of Aruban Florins:*
Foreign Assets	11	....	....	....	....	....	....	....	....	....	....	....	....	....	....	142.11
Reserve Money	14	....	....	....	....	....	....	....	....	....	....	....	....	....	....	97.45
of which: Currency Outside DMBs	14a															32.04
Central Government Deposits	16d	....	....	....	....	....	....	....	....	....	....	....	....	....	....	30.70
Capital Accounts	17a	....	....	....	....	....	....	....	....	....	....	....	....	....	....	10.00
Other Items (Net)	17r															3.96
Deposit Money Banks																*Millions of Aruban Florins:*
Reserves	20	....	....	....	....	....	....	....	....	....	....	....	....	....	....	62.88
Foreign Assets	21	....	....	....	....	....	....	....	....	....	....	....	....	....	....	66.50
Claims on Central Government	22a	....	....	....	....	....	....	....	....	....	....	....	....	....	....	9.27
Claims on Private Sector	22d	....	....	....	....	....	....	....	....	....	....	....	....	....	....	286.51
Demand Deposits	24	....	....	....	....	....	....	....	....	....	....	....	....	....	....	66.27
Time and Savings Deposits	25	....	....	....	....	....	....	....	....	....	....	....	....	....	....	215.55
Bonds	26ab															
Foreign Liabilities	26c	....	....	....	....	....	....	....	....	....	....	....	....	....	....	77.90
Central Government Deposits	26d	....	....	....	....	....	....	....	....	....	....	....	....	....	....	30.14
Capital Accounts	27a	....	....	....	....	....	....	....	....	....	....	....	....	....	....	40.00
Other Items (Net)	27r	....	....	....	....	....	....	....	....	....	....	....	....	....	....	−4.68
Monetary Survey																*Millions of Aruban Florins:*
Foreign Assets (Net)	31n	....	....	....	....	....	....	....	....	....	....	....	....	....	....	130.39
Domestic Credit	32	....	....	....	....	....	....	....	....	....	....	....	....	....	....	234.95
Claims on Central Govt. (Net)	32an	....	....	....	....	....	....	....	....	....	....	....	....	....	....	−51.57
Claims on Private Sector	32d	....	....	....	....	....	....	....	....	....	....	....	....	....	....	286.51
Money	34	....	....	....	....	....	....	....	....	....	....	....	....	....	....	100.18
Quasi-Money	35	....	....	....	....	....	....	....	....	....	....	....	....	....	....	215.55
Bonds	36ab															
Other Items (Net)	37r	....	....	....	....	....	....	....	....	....	....	....	....	....	....	49.61
Money plus Quasi-Money	35l	....	....	....	....	....	....	....	....	....	....	....	....	....	....	315.73
Interest Rates																*Percent Per Annum*
Discount Rate	60	....	....	....	....	....	....	....	....	....	....	....	....	....	....	9.5
Deposit Rate	60l	....	....	....	....	....	....	....	....	....	....	....	....	....	....	6.4
Lending Rate	60p	....	....	....	....	....	....	....	....	....	....	....	....	....	....	11.0
Prices and Tourism																*Index Numbers (1995=100):*
Consumer Prices	64	....	....	....	....	....	....	....	....	....	....	....	....	....	66.3	67.1
Number of Tourists	66ta	....	....	....	....	....	....	....	....	....	....	....	34.0	33.6	29.3
Number of Tourist Nights	66tb	....	....	....	....	....	....	....	....	26.0	....	....	31.0	31.0	28.9
International Transactions																*Millions of US Dollars*
Exports	70..d	....	....	....	....	....	....	....	....	....	....	....	....	....	....	23.7
Imports, c.i.f.	71..d	....	....	....	....	....	....	....	....	....	....	....	....	....	....	191.9

1987	1988	1989	1990	1991	1992	1993	1994	1995	1996	1997	1998	1999	2000	2001		
End of Period															**Exchange Rates**	
2.5394	2.4088	2.3523	2.5466	2.5605	2.4613	2.4587	2.6131	2.6608	2.5739	2.4152	2.5204	2.4568	2.3322	2.2495	Official Rate..................................	aa
End of Period (ae) Period Average (rf)																
1.7900	1.7900	1.7900	1.7900	1.7900	1.7900	1.7900	1.7900	1.7900	1.7900	1.7900	1.7900	1.7900	1.7900	1.7900	Official Rate..................................	ae
1.7900	1.7900	1.7900	1.7900	1.7900	1.7900	1.7900	1.7900	1.7900	1.7900	1.7900	1.7900	1.7900	1.7900	1.7900	Official Rate	rf
End of Period															**International Liquidity**	
78.73	90.92	87.07	97.93	119.59	142.11	181.24	177.59	216.67	187.62	172.33	222.19	219.91	208.01	293.71	Total Reserves minus Gold...................	1l.d
78.73	90.92	87.07	97.93	119.59	142.11	181.24	177.59	216.67	187.62	172.33	222.19	219.91	208.01	293.71	Foreign Exchange	1d.d
—	—	.100	.100	.100	.100	.100	.100	.100	.100	.100	.100	.100	.100	.100	Gold (Million Fine Troy Ounces)...........	1ad
5.587	5.587	26.465	26.465	26.465	25.630	25.630	25.630	26.307	27.978	27.978	22.878	22.900	22.900	30.751	Gold (National Valuation)	1and
64.90	109.14	129.41	160.73	194.37	197.89	213.42	222.37	207.98	233.69	257.38	269.57	280.49	299.19	297.19	Deposit Money Banks: Assets	7a.d
64.48	121.87	112.54	132.85	153.29	143.36	163.04	150.87	161.08	190.85	217.10	190.79	191.93	221.36	228.81	Liabilities...........	7b.d
End of Period															**Monetary Authorities**	
150.94	173.25	203.37	222.78	261.44	300.25	370.30	363.77	434.93	385.91	358.55	438.67	434.74	417.17	580.79	Foreign Assets	11
116.28	133.47	128.67	152.55	190.64	225.48	249.57	233.57	275.54	236.23	226.35	318.08	338.01	299.00	395.80	Reserve Money	14
34.56	41.07	48.32	59.22	66.16	76.23	81.66	87.56	93.70	94.87	101.52	104.91	122.44	121.48	125.96	of which: Currency Outside DMBs	14a
11.57	16.41	13.76	12.54	15.88	23.72	58.57	71.70	99.97	92.55	68.27	65.56	55.64	57.84	96.97	Central Government Deposits	16d
13.87	19.86	57.84	59.37	59.50	59.80	58.60	56.02	66.40	70.48	76.12	71.71	65.95	80.62	90.81	Capital Accounts	17a
9.22	3.51	3.10	-1.67	-4.58	-8.74	3.57	2.48	-6.98	-13.35	-12.19	-16.67	-24.87	-20.28	-2.80	Other Items (Net)............................	17r
End of Period															**Deposit Money Banks**	
71.03	85.52	70.08	82.94	112.89	147.13	168.16	147.44	181.48	154.97	119.11	209.55	224.24	181.36	245.95	Reserves	20
116.16	195.36	231.64	287.71	347.93	354.22	382.02	398.05	372.29	418.30	460.71	482.53	502.08	535.55	531.96	Foreign Assets	21
29.91	15.66	21.65	23.01	34.34	36.23	43.16	67.94	36.88	59.43	59.50	55.91	61.44	43.47	62.37	Claims on Central Government	22a
344.33	467.52	539.79	609.05	690.37	742.74	793.09	946.52	1,017.98	1,121.78	1,185.47	1,248.15	1,376.10	1,502.35	1,581.67	Claims on Private Sector.....................	22d
120.59	145.66	192.43	200.69	242.76	252.72	293.14	350.09	343.90	346.37	366.07	433.80	458.88	471.23	553.43	Demand Deposits	24
274.97	331.13	391.71	478.82	560.40	663.16	673.52	755.64	795.31	853.93	881.59	991.61	1,105.88	1,133.42	1,138.99	Time and Savings Deposits	25
									12.75	—	5.00	5.00	5.00	5.00	Bonds	26ab
115.41	218.15	201.44	237.80	274.40	256.62	291.84	270.06	288.33	341.61	388.62	341.52	343.55	396.23	409.58	Foreign Liabilities	26c
14.91	1.97	1.15	4.06	25.96	10.57	20.90	37.90	22.95	16.33	15.89	11.28	7.93	9.02	6.41	Central Government Deposits	26d
48.71	49.95	55.37	64.53	72.93	62.81	56.56	70.34	85.62	105.49	112.89	105.78	109.64	127.57	146.19	Capital Accounts	27a
-13.16	17.29	21.06	16.81	9.08	34.45	50.48	75.91	72.51	78.00	59.73	107.15	133.00	120.26	162.36	Other Items (Net)............................	27r
End of Period															**Monetary Survey**	
151.15	149.57	231.13	270.16	334.85	396.84	448.02	478.10	517.80	461.50	428.18	578.01	593.16	554.17	700.60	Foreign Assets (Net)	31n
347.76	464.81	546.53	615.47	682.86	744.69	756.79	904.86	931.93	1,072.33	1,160.81	1,227.22	1,373.97	1,478.96	1,540.66	Domestic Credit	32
3.43	-2.72	6.74	6.42	-7.50	1.95	-36.30	-41.66	-86.05	-49.45	-24.66	-20.93	-2.13	-23.39	-41.01	Claims on Central Govt. (Net)	32an
344.33	467.52	539.79	609.05	690.37	742.74	793.09	946.52	1,017.98	1,121.78	1,185.47	1,248.15	1,376.10	1,502.35	1,581.67	Claims on Private Sector	32d
157.56	189.82	243.35	264.13	313.97	331.28	377.89	441.45	443.70	447.47	473.18	547.00	589.73	596.51	701.05	Money..	34
285.50	336.28	392.51	481.08	570.04	663.66	674.03	756.17	804.74	855.08	881.76	991.78	1,106.06	1,133.60	1,139.18	Quasi-Money	35
									12.75	—	5.00	5.00	5.00	5.00	Bonds	36ab
55.85	88.35	141.79	140.42	133.71	146.59	152.88	185.34	201.30	218.52	234.04	261.45	266.35	298.02	396.02	Other Items (Net)............................	37r
443.06	526.10	635.87	745.21	884.01	994.94	1,051.93	1,197.62	1,248.44	1,302.55	1,354.94	1,538.78	1,695.79	1,730.11	1,840.23	Money plus Quasi-Money	35l
Percent Per Annum															**Interest Rates**	
9.5	9.5	9.5	9.5	9.5	9.5	9.5	9.5	9.5	9.5	9.5	9.5	6.5	6.5	6.5	Discount Rate................................	60
6.7	6.7	6.7	6.7	6.3	5.7	4.2	4.4	4.3	4.2	4.4	....	†6.2	6.2	5.8	Deposit Rate.................................	60l
10.3	10.3	10.6	10.6	10.6	10.6	10.6	10.6	10.6	10.3	10.0	....	†13.1	12.1	12.1	Lending Rate.................................	60p
Period Averages															**Prices and Tourism**	
69.5	71.7	74.5	78.9	83.3	86.5	91.0	96.7	100.0	103.2	106.3	108.3	†110.8	115.3	118.6	Consumer Prices.............................	64
37.4	44.9	55.6	69.9	81.0	87.5	90.6	94.1	100.0	103.5	105.0	104.6	110.4	116.5	111.7	Number of Tourists	66ta
36.4	46.5	59.4	75.6	84.2	87.2	90.0	94.6	100.0	104.9	108.3	109.3	115.0	117.3	115.0	Number of Tourist Nights....................	66tb
Millions of US Dollars															**International Transactions**	
26.1	30.5	22.9	27.9	25.7	....	....	....	14.7	12.5	24.1	29.1	29.2	....	....	Exports.......................................	70..d
236.1	336.4	386.6	536.3	481.0	....	....	....	566.5	578.3	614.5	814.7	782.1	....	....	Imports, c.i.f.	71..d

Aruba

		1972	1973	1974	1975	1976	1977	1978	1979	1980	1981	1982	1983	1984	1985	1986
Balance of Payments																*Millions of US Dollars:*
Current Account, n.i.e.	78al *d*	...	...	...	...	...	...	...	...	...	...	...	...	...	...	−18.7
Goods: Exports f.o.b.	78aa *d*	...	...	...	...	...	...	...	...	...	...	...	...	...	...	29.6
Goods: Imports f.o.b.	78ab *d*	...	...	...	...	...	...	...	...	...	...	...	...	...	...	−210.4
Trade Balance	78ac *d*	...	...	...	...	...	...	...	...	...	...	...	...	...	...	−180.9
Services: Credit	78ad *d*	...	...	...	...	...	...	...	...	...	...	...	...	...	...	216.9
Services: Debit	78ae *d*	...	...	...	...	...	...	...	...	...	...	...	...	...	...	−50.6
Balance on Goods & Services	78af *d*	...	...	...	...	...	...	...	...	...	...	...	...	...	...	−14.6
Income: Credit	78ag *d*	...	...	...	...	...	...	...	...	...	...	...	...	...	...	7.3
Income: Debit	78ah *d*	...	...	...	...	...	...	...	...	...	...	...	...	...	...	−13.6
Balance on Gds, Serv. & Inc.	78ai *d*	...	...	...	...	...	...	...	...	...	...	...	...	...	...	−20.9
Current Transfers, n.i.e.: Credit	78aj *d*	...	...	...	...	...	...	...	...	...	...	...	...	...	...	18.4
Current Transfers: Debit	78ak *d*	...	...	...	...	...	...	...	...	...	...	...	...	...	...	−16.1
Capital Account, n.i.e.	78bc *d*	...														—
Capital Account, n.i.e.: Credit	78ba *d*	...														—
Capital Account: Debit	78bb *d*	...														—
Financial Account, n.i.e.	78bj *d*	...														62.8
Direct Investment Abroad	78bd *d*	...														—
Dir. Invest. in Rep. Econ., n.i.e.	78be *d*	...														—
Portfolio Investment Assets	78bf *d*	...	...	...	...	...	...	...	...	...	...	...	...	...	...	—
Equity Securities	78bk *d*	...	...	...	...	...	...	...	...	...	...	...	...	...	...	—
Debt Securities	78bl *d*	...	...	...	...	...	...	...	...	...	...	...	...	...	...	—
Portfolio Investment Liab., n.i.e.	78bg *d*	...	...	...	...	...	...	...	...	...	...	...	...	...	...	—
Equity Securities	78bm *d*	...	...	...	...	...	...	...	...	...	...	...	...	...	...	—
Debt Securities	78bn *d*	...	...	...	...	...	...	...	...	...	...	...	...	...	...	—
Financial Derivatives Assets	78bw *d*	...	...	...	...	...	...	...	...	...	...	...	...	...	...	...
Financial Derivatives Liabilities	78bx *d*	...	...	...	...	...	...	...	...	...	...	...	...	...	...	...
Other Investment Assets	78bh *d*	...	...	...	...	...	...	...	...	...	...	...	...	...	...	1.1
Monetary Authorities	78bo *d*	...	...	...	...	...	...	...	...	...	...	...	...	...	...	...
General Government	78bp *d*	...	...	...	...	...	...	...	...	...	...	...	...	...	...	...
Banks	78bq *d*	...	...	...	...	...	...	...	...	...	...	...	...	...	...	1.1
Other Sectors	78br *d*	...	...	...	...	...	...	...	...	...	...	...	...	...	...	—
Other Investment Liab., n.i.e.	78bi *d*	...	...	...	...	...	...	...	...	...	...	...	...	...	...	61.7
Monetary Authorities	78bs *d*	...	...	...	...	...	...	...	...	...	...	...	...	...	...	—
General Government	78bt *d*	...	...	...	...	...	...	...	...	...	...	...	...	...	...	27.5
Banks	78bu *d*	...	...	...	...	...	...	...	...	...	...	...	...	...	...	−1.2
Other Sectors	78bv *d*	...	...	...	...	...	...	...	...	...	...	...	...	...	...	35.4
Net Errors and Omissions	78ca *d*	...	...	...	...	...	...	...	...	...	...	...	...	...	...	7.1
Overall Balance	78cb *d*	...	...	...	...	...	...	...	...	...	...	...	...	...	...	51.3
Reserves and Related Items	79da *d*	...	...	...	...	...	...	...	...	...	...	...	...	...	...	−51.3
Reserve Assets	79db *d*	...	...	...	...	...	...	...	...	...	...	...	...	...	...	−51.3
Use of Fund Credit and Loans	79dc *d*	...	...	...	...	...	...	...	...	...	...	...	...	...	...	—
Exceptional Financing	79de *d*	...	...	...	...	...	...	...	...	...	...	...	...	...	...	...
																Millions:
Population	99z	...	...	...	...	...	...	...	...	.06	.07	.06	.06	.06	.06	.06

Minus Sign Indicates Debit

1987	1988	1989	1990	1991	1992	1993	1994	1995	1996	1997	1998	1999	2000	2001	Balance of Payments	
−22.6	−44.3	−46.7	−158.2	−209.5	43.8	41.7	81.1	−.3	−69.1	−195.8	−18.8	−333.2	282.3	....	Current Account, n.i.e.	78al *d*
45.1	87.4	107.5	155.5	878.8	1,069.2	1,154.4	1,296.8	1,347.2	1,735.7	1,728.7	1,164.8	1,413.5	2,582.1	....	Goods: Exports f.o.b.	78aa *d*
−249.8	−354.6	−397.4	−580.8	−1,402.8	−1,446.7	−1,546.5	−1,607.3	−1,772.5	−2,043.4	−2,115.9	−1,518.2	−2,005.2	−2,610.4	....	Goods: Imports f.o.b.	78ab *d*
−204.7	−267.3	−289.9	−425.4	−524.1	−377.5	−392.1	−310.6	−425.3	−307.7	−387.2	−353.4	−591.7	−28.3	....	*Trade Balance*	78ac *d*
260.1	326.2	351.3	411.0	472.7	571.2	604.1	624.2	645.1	769.9	815.8	892.1	989.7	1,032.0	....	Services: Credit	78ad *d*
−62.8	−85.3	−100.2	−134.9	−147.8	−159.8	−169.1	−228.7	−245.5	−515.9	−596.1	−553.1	−712.9	−678.7	....	Services: Debit	78ae *d*
−7.4	−26.3	−38.8	−149.3	−199.2	33.9	42.8	85.0	−25.6	−53.6	−167.5	−14.4	−315.0	325.0	....	*Balance on Goods & Services*	78af *d*
8.9	10.9	13.4	14.8	17.9	14.5	13.4	9.6	16.4	19.2	20.7	40.5	37.4	46.8	....	Income: Credit	78ag *d*
−21.2	−27.9	−24.7	−22.6	−25.7	−21.8	−24.6	−22.3	−24.6	−31.0	−37.9	−40.1	−69.0	−53.5	....	Income: Debit	78ah *d*
−19.7	−43.4	−50.1	−157.0	−207.0	26.5	31.6	72.3	−33.8	−65.5	−184.7	−14.0	−346.6	318.3	....	*Balance on Gds, Serv. & Inc.*	78ai *d*
15.4	14.9	18.0	33.8	38.1	45.9	43.4	47.5	71.5	18.4	18.4	29.3	59.3	46.2	....	Current Transfers, n.i.e.: Credit	78aj *d*
−18.3	−15.8	−14.6	−34.9	−40.6	−28.7	−33.3	−38.7	−37.9	−22.0	−29.5	−34.1	−45.9	−82.2	....	Current Transfers: Debit	78ak *d*
—	—	—	—	−3.0	−1.5	−1.8	−4.1	−.5	28.0	21.0	5.2	—	9.9	....	Capital Account, n.i.e.	78bc *d*
—	—	—	—	.8	.9	.9	.3	3.1	28.7	21.6	10.2	.9	10.5	....	Capital Account, n.i.e.: Credit	78ba *d*
—	—	—	—	−3.8	−2.4	−2.8	−4.4	−3.6	−.7	−.6	−5.0	−.9	−.6	....	Capital Account: Debit	78bb *d*
24.6	56.8	47.8	172.2	228.8	−24.1	−8.4	−75.4	41.6	10.7	158.9	64.2	336.4	−314.6	....	Financial Account, n.i.e.	78bj *d*
									−.3	1.7	−1.4	8.9	−11.7	....	Direct Investment Abroad	78bd *d*
—	—	—	130.5	184.7	−37.0	−17.9	−73.2	−5.5	84.5	195.9	83.6	392.1	−227.5	....	Dir. Invest. in Rep. Econ., n.i.e.	78be *d*
			8.7	13.1	11.3	10.8	16.5	−16.6	−7.8	−1.6	−44.1	−65.6	−42.9	....	Portfolio Investment Assets	78bf *d*
															Equity Securities	78bk *d*
			8.7	13.1	11.3	10.8	16.5	−16.6	−7.8	−1.6	−44.1	−65.6	−42.9	....	Debt Securities	78bl *d*
			−15.1	−25.4	−18.2	−14.6	−25.8	....	1.6	−17.4	−3.4	12.2	2.1	....	Portfolio Investment Liab., n.i.e.	78bg *d*
															Equity Securities	78bm *d*
			−15.1	−25.4	−18.2	−14.6	−25.8	....	1.6	−17.4	−3.4	12.2	2.1	....	Debt Securities	78bn *d*
....	....	....	....	....	....	....	....	....	....	....	....	....	....	....	Financial Derivatives Assets	78bw *d*
....	....	....	....	....	....	....	....	....	....	....	....	....	....	....	Financial Derivatives Liabilities	78bx *d*
−27.7	−48.9	−19.4	−10.2	−17.1	13.6	−25.8	5.8	12.5	−11.3	−49.7	29.2	−15.7	−97.7	....	Other Investment Assets	78bh *d*
....	....	....	....	....	....	....	....	....	....	....	....	....	....	....	Monetary Authorities	78bo *d*
							−.8								General Government	78bp *d*
−27.7	−48.9	−19.4	−31.3	−33.6	−3.5	−15.7	−3.7	15.6	−17.0	−30.7	−11.5	−12.2	−21.1	....	Banks	78bq *d*
			21.2	16.5	17.2	−10.1	10.4	−3.1	5.7	−19.0	40.7	−3.5	−76.6	....	Other Sectors	78br *d*
52.3	105.7	67.3	58.3	73.4	6.0	39.2	1.3	51.2	−55.9	30.0	.4	4.5	63.1	....	Other Investment Liab., n.i.e.	78bi *d*
....	....	....	....	....	....	....	....	....	....	....	....	....	....	....	Monetary Authorities	78bs *d*
18.2	13.8	12.3	1.2	1.9	10.0	.6	.4	.6	−10.6	−8.9	22.2	7.5	34.0	....	General Government	78bt *d*
21.0	57.0	−7.4	20.2	19.2	−10.7	18.5	−8.7	10.7	17.0	37.3	−26.4	.5	29.2	....	Banks	78bu *d*
13.1	34.9	62.3	36.9	52.3	6.7	20.1	9.6	39.9	−62.3	1.6	4.6	−3.5		....	Other Sectors	78bv *d*
10.9	−12.8	20.4	−2.4	6.5	4.4	2.0	−4.7	2.0	4.3	−2.5	−.6	−.7	6.5	....	Net Errors and Omissions	78ca *d*
12.9	−.4	21.5	11.7	22.8	22.6	33.4	−3.2	42.7	−26.1	−18.4	51.3	2.5	−15.9		*Overall Balance*	78cb *d*
−12.9	.4	−21.5	−11.7	−22.8	−22.6	−33.4	3.2	−42.7	26.1	18.4	−51.3	−2.5	15.9	....	Reserves and Related Items	79da *d*
−12.9	.4	−21.5	−11.7	−22.8	−22.6	−33.4	3.2	−42.7	26.1	18.4	−51.3	−2.5	15.9		Reserve Assets	79db *d*
—	—	—	—	—	—	—	—	....	....	....	....	....	....	....	Use of Fund Credit and Loans	79dc *d*
....	....	....	....	....	....	....	....	....	....	....	....	....	....	....	Exceptional Financing	79de *d*

Midyear Estimates

1987	1988	1989	1990	1991	1992	1993	1994	1995	1996	1997	1998	1999	2000	2001		
.06	.06	.06	.06	.07	.07	.07	.08	.08	.09	.09	.09	.09	.10	.09	**Population**	99z

(See notes in the back of the book.)

Australia

193	1972	1973	1974	1975	1976	1977	1978	1979	1980	1981	1982	1983	1984	1985	1986
Exchange Rates															*SDRs per Australian Dollar:*
Market Rate ... **ac**	1.1743	1.2335	1.0838	1.0738	.9351	.9396	.8831	.8392	.9257	.9690	.8889	.8616	.8445	.6199	.5435
															US Dollars per Australian Dollar:
Market Rate ... **ag**	1.2750	1.4880	1.3270	1.2571	1.0864	1.1414	1.1505	1.1055	1.1807	1.1279	.9806	.9020	.8278	.6809	.6648
Market Rate ... **rh**	1.1923	1.4215	1.4394	1.3102	1.2252	1.1090	1.1447	1.1179	1.1395	1.1493	1.0174	.9024	.8796	.7008	.6709
															Index Numbers (1995=100):
Market Rate ... **ah x**	160.8	202.8	193.9	176.7	165.2	149.6	154.4	150.8	153.7	155.0	137.2	121.7	118.6	94.5	90.5
Nominal Effective Exchange Rate ... **ne c**	....	....	....	....	....	....	....	106.0	110.0	121.2	118.4	111.9	117.9	99.2	83.1
Real Effective Exchange Rate ... **re c**	....	....	....	....	....	....	....	....	126.0	136.8	137.1	134.4	138.6	116.7	102.1
Fund Position															*Millions of SDRs:*
Quota ... **2f. s**	665	665	665	665	665	665	790	790	1,185	1,185	1,185	1,619	1,619	1,619	1,619
SDRs ... **1b. s**	235	235	100	96	36	22	99	32	—	45	78	77	213	283	271
Reserve Position in the Fund ... **1c. s**	167	167	176	167	167	166	161	156	255	252	—	109	187	189	189
of which: Outstg.Fund Borrowing ... **2c**	—	—	—	—	—	—	—	—	—	—	—	—	—	—	—
Total Fund Cred.&Loans Outstg. ... **2tl**	—	—	—	—	333	333	247	271	62	—	32	—	—	—	—
International Liquidity															*Millions of US Dollars Unless Otherwise Indicated:*
Total Reserves minus Gold ... **1l. d**	5,860	5,386	3,953	2,955	2,870	2,058	2,062	1,424	1,690	1,671	6,371	8,962	7,441	5,768	7,246
SDRs ... **1b. d**	255	283	122	112	42	27	129	42	—	52	86	81	209	310	332
Reserve Position in the Fund ... **1c. d**	182	201	215	195	194	202	210	206	325	294	—	114	183	207	231
Foreign Exchange ... **1d. d**	5,423	4,902	3,616	2,647	2,634	1,829	1,723	1,176	1,365	1,325	6,285	8,768	7,049	5,250	6,684
Gold (Million Fine Troy Ounces) ... **1ad**	7.40	7.37	7.38	7.38	7.36	7.65	7.79	7.93	7.93	7.93	7.93	7.93	7.93	7.93	7.93
Gold (National Valuation) ... **1an d**	280	311	316	299	300	1,228	1,619	3,676	4,722	3,247	3,527	3,080	2,539	2,551	3,100
Monetary Authorities: Other Liab. ... **4.. d**	—	—	—	—	—	—	—	—	—	—	—	—	—	—	—
Deposit Money Banks: Assets ... **7a. d**	209	199	202	275	251	183	272	216	367	396	120	179	†913	1,483	3,631
Liabilities ... **7b. d**	242	315	390	277	304	310	375	429	655	730	727	647	†1,276	2,922	8,967
Monetary Authorities															*Millions of Australian Dollars: Average of Weekly*
Foreign Assets ... **11**	4,794	3,953	3,260	2,907	2,772	3,053	3,334	4,148	5,878	4,263	9,745	13,390	12,003	12,412	15,477
Claims on Central Government ... **12a**	289	584	1,058	2,796	4,741	5,005	5,039	6,562	6,710	7,764	4,102	3,880	5,803	8,640	9,189
Reserve Money ... **14**	3,828	4,830	4,242	5,466	6,123	6,438	6,368	6,932	7,612	8,451	9,199	10,371	11,500	12,914	14,025
of which: Currency Outside DMBs ... **14a**	1,665	1,965	2,355	2,761	3,127	3,550	3,955	4,375	4,975	5,533	6,023	6,882	7,855	8,632	9,538
Foreign Liabilities ... **16c**	—	—	—	—	356	354	280	322	67	—	37	—	—	—	—
Central Government Deposits ... **16d**	....	....	....	....	....	....	....	....	....	....	....	....	....	....	....
Other Items (Net) ... **17r**	1,254	–293	77	237	1,035	1,266	1,726	3,455	4,910	3,576	4,612	6,899	6,305	8,138	10,641
Deposit Money Banks															*Millions of Australian Dollars: Average of Weekly*
Reserves ... **20**	2,200	2,771	1,794	2,589	3,059	2,848	2,350	2,518	2,619	2,910	3,264	3,451	3,648	4,280	4,472
Foreign Assets ... **21**	164	134	152	219	231	160	236	195	311	351	122	198	†1,103	2,178	5,462
Claims on Central Government ... **22a**	5,602	5,799	5,724	7,324	7,386	6,718	7,439	7,957	9,201	9,146	10,599	13,137	12,929	14,100	17,930
Claims on Official Entities ... **22bx**	2,380	2,770	3,118	3,731	4,313	4,764	5,255	5,677	6,116	6,557	6,752	7,761	8,114	7,817	7,016
Claims on Private Sector ... **22d**	10,790	14,011	16,683	19,321	23,091	25,860	29,222	33,822	38,015	43,991	48,833	55,334	64,627	86,991	105,049
Demand Deposits ... **24**	5,227	6,076	5,620	6,998	7,550	7,826	8,740	10,266	12,191	12,488	11,960	13,862	14,615	14,650	16,391
Time, Savings,& Fgn.Currency Dep. ... **25**	13,525	16,726	19,055	22,798	25,911	27,369	30,116	33,136	37,275	41,819	48,194	54,196	61,300	75,505	82,305
Foreign Liabilities ... **26c**	190	212	294	220	280	272	326	388	555	647	741	717	†1,541	4,291	13,488
Central Government Deposits ... **26d**	536	756	604	897	1,562	1,626	1,624	1,748	1,033	1,129	1,393	1,261	1,733	1,131	917
Other Items (Net) ... **27r**	1,658	1,714	1,898	2,269	2,775	3,258	3,696	4,632	5,209	6,873	7,282	9,846	†11,231	19,788	26,828
Monetary Survey															*Millions of Australian Dollars: Average of Weekly*
Foreign Assets (Net) ... **31n**	4,768	3,875	3,118	2,906	2,367	2,587	2,965	3,633	5,567	3,967	9,089	12,871	†11,565	10,299	7,451
Domestic Credit ... **32**	18,724	22,528	26,111	32,433	38,091	41,204	45,575	52,473	59,272	66,685	69,188	79,214	89,890	116,617	138,326
Claims on Central Govt. (Net) ... **32an**	5,355	5,627	6,178	9,222	10,565	10,097	10,853	12,771	14,878	15,781	13,308	15,755	16,999	21,609	26,203
Claims on Official Entities ... **32bx**	2,380	2,770	3,118	3,731	4,313	4,764	5,255	5,677	6,116	6,557	6,752	7,761	8,114	7,817	7,016
Claims on Private Sector ... **32d**	10,990	14,132	16,815	19,480	23,214	26,343	29,466	34,024	38,278	44,347	49,128	55,697	64,778	87,191	105,108
Money ... **34**	6,899	8,050	7,990	9,807	10,681	11,390	12,709	14,661	17,220	18,063	18,032	20,796	22,492	23,298	25,947
Quasi-Money ... **35**	13,525	16,726	19,055	22,798	25,911	27,369	30,116	33,136	37,275	41,819	48,194	54,196	61,300	75,505	82,305
Other Items (Net) ... **37r**	3,068	1,628	2,184	2,734	3,866	5,032	5,715	8,309	10,345	10,770	12,051	17,093	†17,664	28,112	37,525
Money plus Quasi-Money ... **35l**	20,424	24,776	27,045	32,605	36,592	38,759	42,825	47,797	54,495	59,882	66,226	74,992	83,792	98,803	108,252
Money (National Definitions)															*Millions of Australian Dollars: Average of Weekly*
Money Base ... **19ma**	....	....	....	5,394	6,025	6,400	6,343	6,938	7,618	8,452	9,253	10,333	11,520	12,895	13,940
M1 ... **59ma**	....	....	....	10,184	11,115	11,848	13,260	15,280	17,941	18,884	18,897	21,777	23,278	24,875	28,098
M1, Seasonally Adjusted ... **59ma c**	....	....	....	9,810	10,703	11,418	12,766	14,693	17,199	18,078	18,082	20,879	22,340	23,883	26,940
M3 ... **59mb**	....	....	....	32,331	36,395	38,658	42,743	47,669	53,854	59,559	65,968	74,719	83,572	98,146	107,398
M3, Seasonally Adjusted ... **59mb c**	....	....	....	31,772	35,785	38,051	42,099	46,970	53,038	58,735	65,184	73,891	82,716	97,223	106,243
Broad Money ... **59mc**	....	....	....	....	52,471	58,027	65,819	74,708	86,777	98,817	111,059	124,189	138,023	159,150	174,368
Broad Money, Seasonally Adjusted ... **59mc c**	....	....	....	....	51,688	57,206	64,910	73,687	85,564	97,535	109,788	122,851	136,668	157,639	172,545
Interest Rates															*Percent Per Annum*
Discount Rate ... **60**	4.89	6.13	10.22	8.71	8.67	9.91	9.35	9.53	11.11	13.53	15.76	12.14	12.03	15.98	16.93
Money Market Rate ... **60b**	4.65	4.98	7.52	9.49	7.09	8.49	8.72	8.09	9.49	12.07	13.90	9.50	10.84	14.70	15.75
Treasury Bill Rate ... **60c**	4.32	5.21	9.07	7.51	7.51	8.53	8.65	8.88	10.67	13.25	14.64	11.06	10.99	15.42	15.39
Deposit Rate ... **60l**	5.00	5.50	8.00	9.00	8.63	9.00	8.52	8.25	8.58	10.38	12.33	10.81	9.75	10.46	13.96
Lending Rate ... **60p**	....	....	....	11.50	10.50	†10.40	10.35	10.00	10.50	12.74	14.31	13.63	13.58	15.24	18.09
Govt. Bond Yield: Short-Term ... **61a**	4.91	6.30	9.33	8.46	8.69	9.74	8.80	9.62	11.50	13.76	†15.18	12.84	12.25	14.03	13.97
Long-Term ... **61**	5.83	6.93	9.04	9.74	10.03	10.23	9.39	9.75	11.65	13.96	15.38	13.89	13.53	13.95	13.42
Prices, Production, Labor															*Index Numbers (1995=100):*
Share Prices ... **62**	19.2	18.0	13.3	12.5	15.5	14.9	16.9	20.8	†31.0	31.4	24.1	31.2	35.4	44.3	59.8
Prices: Manufacturing Output ... **63**	18.3	19.9	23.0	26.4	29.4	32.4	35.1	40.3	45.9	49.8	54.2	58.6	61.8	65.9	69.5
Consumer Prices ... **64**	16.9	18.5	21.3	24.5	27.8	31.3	33.7	†36.8	40.5	44.4	49.4	54.4	56.5	60.4	65.8
Wages, Weekly Earnings ... **65**	13.9	15.7	19.2	22.7	25.9	28.7	31.2	33.9	37.9	42.3	†47.3	50.6	55.4	58.2	62.7
Industrial Production ... **66.. c**	60.0	66.1	68.2	63.0	66.2	†65.2	66.2	69.6	70.0	72.1	71.7	69.6	74.4	80.4	80.2
Manufacturing Employment ... **67ey c**	119.3	124.0	123.2	113.2	114.8	114.5	109.4	109.5	111.8	112.3	108.8	102.5	102.6	101.8	102.1
															Number in Thousands:
Labor Force ... **67d**	....	....	....	....	....	....	....	....	....	....	....	6,997	7,135	7,300	7,585
Employment ... **67e**	....	....	....	....	....	....	....	....	....	....	....	6,300	6,494	6,697	†6,984
Unemployment ... **67c**	....	....	....	....	....	....	....	....	....	....	....	697	641	603	†601
Unemployment Rate (%) ... **67r**	....	....	....	....	....	....	....	....	....	....	....	10.0	9.0	8.3	†7.9

1987	1988	1989	1990	1991	1992	1993	1994	1995	1996	1997	1998	1999	2000	2001		
															Exchange Rates	
End of Period																
.5093	.6357	.6032	.5436	.5312	.5008	.4930	.5321	.5012	.5539	.4838	.4360	.4764	.4252	.4063	Market Rate	**ac**
End of Period (ag) Period Average (rh)																
.7225	.8555	.7927	.7733	.7598	.6886	.6771	.7768	.7450	.7965	.6527	.6139	.6538	.5540	.5106	Market Rate	**ag**
.7009	.7842	.7925	.7813	.7791	.7353	.6801	.7317	.7415	.7829	.7441	.6294	.6453	.5823	.5176	Market Rate	**rh**
Period Averages																
94.5	105.8	106.9	105.4	105.1	99.2	91.7	98.7	100.0	105.6	100.3	84.9	87.0	78.5	69.8	Market Rate	**ahx**
80.4	88.9	97.4	98.2	100.1	95.4	94.0	103.3	100.0	109.7	111.1	99.0	100.0	93.4	87.6	Nominal Effective Exchange Rate	**ne c**
101.8	112.7	120.8	117.3	115.8	104.9	98.3	102.3	100.0	110.0	109.4	96.9	98.6	94.5	91.1	Real Effective Exchange Rate	**re c**
															Fund Position	
End of Period																
1,619	1,619	1,619	1,619	1,619	2,333	2,333	2,333	2,333	2,333	2,333	2,333	3,236	3,236	3,236	Quota	**2f. s**
260	248	234	218	202	70	60	50	37	25	14	13	53	72	87	SDRs	**1b. s**
189	205	245	245	245	420	400	347	338	335	539	892	1,189	954	1,124	Reserve Position in the Fund	**1c. s**
—	—	—	—	—	—	—	—	—	—	—	75	—	—	—	*of which:* Outstg.Fund Borrowing	**2c**
—	—	—	—	—	—	—	—	—	—	—	—	—	—	—	Total Fund Cred.&Loans Outstg.	**2tl**
															International Liquidity	
End of Period																
8,744	13,598	13,780	16,265	16,535	11,208	11,102	11,285	11,896	14,485	16,845	14,641	21,212	18,118	17,955	Total Reserves minus Gold	**1l. d**
369	334	307	311	290	96	82	73	55	37	19	18	72	94	109	SDRs	**1b. d**
268	275	322	349	351	577	550	506	502	482	727	1,256	1,633	1,243	1,412	Reserve Position in the Fund	**1c. d**
8,107	12,989	13,150	15,605	15,894	10,536	10,470	10,706	11,340	13,967	16,099	13,366	19,507	16,782	16,434	Foreign Exchange	**1d. d**
7.93	7.93	7.93	7.93	7.93	7.93	7.90	7.90	7.90	7.90	2.56	2.56	2.56	2.56	2.56	Gold (Million Fine Troy Ounces)	**1ad**
3,855	3,319	3,248	3,064	2,804	2,639	3,086	3,023	3,055	2,918	740	737	743	699	709	Gold (National Valuation)	**1and**
—	—	6	29	36	37	26	38	67	50	28	66	55	63	47	Monetary Authorities: Other Liab.	**4.. d**
5,399	6,409	7,184	10,602	8,274	8,218	9,062	10,601	12,049	14,830	15,735	13,065	18,752	18,560	21,330	Deposit Money Banks: Assets	**7a. d**
12,070	13,667	22,074	33,997	37,436	37,770	41,840	39,355	49,238	63,521	64,258	73,409	88,291	90,027	98,049	Liabilities	**7b. d**
															Monetary Authorities	
Figures for Last Month of Period																
17,439	19,561	†21,234	24,205	24,506	20,212	21,415	18,344	20,080	22,581	28,325	27,632	38,596	39,820	44,335	Foreign Assets	**11**
8,031	5,257	†4,200	4,280	5,500	14,303	14,265	13,446	17,700	30,608	18,374	23,703	14,684	18,834	20,267	Claims on Central Government	**12a**
15,683	17,478	†17,559	18,917	19,479	20,648	21,987	23,777	24,969	40,261	32,081	33,780	31,943	31,930	37,953	Reserve Money	**14**
10,841	12,267	†13,018	14,342	15,328	16,326	17,279	18,208	19,092	19,628	21,098	22,784	24,604	26,928	28,471	*of which: Currency Outside DMBs*	**14a**
—	—	†8	37	47	54	38	49	90	63	43	108	84	114	92	Foreign Liabilities	**16c**
....	....	1,576	1,350	1,937	2,719	2,634	999	3,131	4,197	2,782	4,431	9,801	12,165	9,906	Central Government Deposits	**16d**
9,787	7,340	†6,291	8,181	8,543	11,094	11,022	6,965	9,590	8,668	11,792	13,016	11,452	14,446	16,652	Other Items (Net)	**17r**
															Deposit Money Banks	
Figures for Last Month of Period																
4,813	5,111	†4,447	4,281	4,084	4,265	4,674	5,498	5,830	13,378	8,789	9,052	5,052	4,228	8,532	Reserves	**20**
7,473	7,491	†9,456	14,827	12,413	14,968	16,281	17,210	22,562	27,893	35,887	37,706	45,742	51,810	60,740	Foreign Assets	**21**
20,156	21,525	†26,618	21,434	24,902	28,405	30,929	28,457	28,072	25,635	19,991	20,182	23,153	13,371	11,756	Claims on Central Government	**22a**
6,513	7,064	†5,477	6,196	5,395	6,195	4,419	3,233	3,591	3,909	4,659	6,550	11,104	10,593	12,131	Claims on Official Entities	**22bx**
122,489	151,623	†225,978	255,618	262,093	273,139	290,232	320,032	355,318	388,126	427,280	477,178	532,435	591,739	639,941	Claims on Private Sector	**22d**
20,352	23,889	†30,478	32,335	34,851	43,929	53,719	60,496	64,771	75,801	86,965	91,864	101,179	110,660	138,456	Demand Deposits	**24**
94,385	111,923	†150,499	172,064	171,102	177,390	180,265	197,542	215,949	236,124	247,668	271,109	305,051	309,634	339,526	Time, Savings,& Fgn.Currency Dep.	**25**
16,706	15,975	†27,847	43,964	49,271	54,850	61,793	50,663	66,091	79,750	98,450	119,579	135,043	162,504	192,028	Foreign Liabilities	**26c**
595	438	†1,759	1,923	2,694	3,566	3,637	2,988	3,523	3,291	3,578	5,721	5,497	5,197	4,399	Central Government Deposits	**26d**
29,406	40,589	†61,393	52,070	50,968	47,238	47,120	62,741	65,038	63,975	59,947	62,395	70,717	83,746	58,690	Other Items (Net)	**27r**
															Monetary Survey	
Figures for Last Month of Period																
8,206	11,077	†2,835	-4,970	-12,399	-19,724	-24,135	-15,158	-23,540	-29,339	-34,282	-54,348	-50,789	-70,988	-87,045	Foreign Assets (Net)	**31n**
156,595	185,031	†258,938	284,255	293,259	315,758	333,575	361,180	398,027	440,790	463,945	517,460	566,078	617,174	669,791	Domestic Credit	**32**
27,592	26,344	†27,483	22,441	25,771	36,423	38,924	37,915	39,118	48,755	32,005	33,732	22,539	14,843	17,718	Claims on Central Govt. (Net)	**32an**
6,513	7,064	†5,477	6,196	5,395	6,195	4,419	3,233	3,591	3,909	4,659	6,550	11,104	10,593	12,131	Claims on Official Entities	**32bx**
122,490	151,623	†225,978	255,618	262,093	273,139	290,232	320,032	355,318	388,126	427,280	477,178	532,435	591,739	639,941	Claims on Private Sector	**32d**
31,218	40,470	†43,518	46,698	50,229	60,294	71,026	78,762	83,899	95,641	108,352	114,794	125,945	137,720	167,035	Money	**34**
94,385	111,923	†150,499	172,064	171,102	177,390	180,265	197,542	215,949	236,124	247,668	271,109	305,051	309,634	339,526	Quasi-Money	**35**
39,199	43,715	†67,756	60,524	59,529	58,350	58,149	69,718	74,640	79,686	73,644	77,210	84,294	98,833	76,185	Other Items (Net)	**37r**
125,603	152,393	†194,017	218,762	221,331	237,683	251,291	276,304	299,848	331,765	356,020	385,903	430,996	447,353	506,560	Money plus Quasi-Money	**35l**
															Money (National Definitions)	
Figures for Last Month of Period																
15,660	17,268	17,487	18,643	19,462	20,637	21,980	23,765	24,958	33,043	29,962	31,926	29,733	31,189	37,017	*Money Base*	**19ma**
33,928	40,088	43,515	46,697	50,228	60,300	71,026	78,762	83,898	95,466	108,137	114,737	125,832	137,621	166,942	*M1*	**59ma**
32,538	38,548	41,879	45,004	48,472	58,121	68,421	75,987	80,916	92,058	104,062	110,454	121,148	133,542	162,637	*M1, Seasonally Adjusted*	**59ma c**
124,605	147,802	182,584	204,489	208,312	224,371	237,660	262,064	286,243	313,435	333,599	358,762	394,886	412,854	473,374	*M3*	**59mb**
123,132	146,114	180,779	201,732	205,625	221,363	234,318	258,598	282,588	309,350	328,895	353,878	389,582	408,087	468,308	*M3, Seasonally Adjusted*	**59mb c**
194,494	225,476	257,009	273,181	272,383	277,190	288,532	313,938	341,113	372,700	400,461	434,029	463,700	493,040	548,566	*Broad Money*	**59mc**
192,439	223,166	254,426	269,935	269,403	274,101	285,220	310,546	337,538	368,702	395,837	429,130	458,271	488,727	543,953	*Broad Money, Seasonally Adjusted*	**59mc c**
															Interest Rates	
Percent Per Annum																
14.95	13.20	17.23	15.24	10.99	6.96	5.83	5.75	5.75	....	....	....	....	....	....	Discount Rate	**60**
13.06	11.90	16.75	14.81	10.47	6.44	5.11	5.18	†7.50	7.20	5.50	4.99	†4.78	5.90	5.06	Money Market Rate	**60b**
12.80	12.14	16.80	14.15	9.96	6.27	5.00	5.69	†7.64	7.02	5.29	4.84	4.76	5.98	4.80	Treasury Bill Rate	**60c**
13.77	11.92	15.29	13.70	†10.44	6.32	4.76	5.05	7.33	6.86	5.12	4.67	†3.53	4.12	3.25	Deposit Rate	**60l**
16.56	15.10	19.58	18.17	14.28	11.06	9.72	9.55	11.12	11.00	9.31	8.04	7.51	8.78	8.13	Lending Rate	**60p**
13.17	12.18	15.14	13.46	9.94	7.25	5.63	†8.19	8.42	7.53	6.00	5.02	5.55	6.18	4.97	Govt. Bond Yield: Short-Term	**61a**
13.19	12.10	13.41	13.18	10.69	9.22	7.28	9.04	9.17	8.17	6.89	5.50	6.08	6.26	5.64	Long-Term	**61**
															Prices, Production, Labor	
Period Averages																
83.3	72.4	77.7	71.8	74.7	76.8	89.7	100.7	100.0	112.1	125.2	131.3	145.1	156.6	161.5	Share Prices	**62**
74.6	81.4	85.5	90.7	92.0	93.4	95.3	96.0	100.0	100.3	101.6	97.5	†96.6	103.5	106.7	Prices: Manufacturing Output	**63**
71.4	76.6	82.4	†88.4	91.2	92.1	93.8	95.6	100.0	102.6	102.9	103.7	105.3	110.0	114.8	Consumer Prices	**64**
66.0	70.5	76.2	82.8	86.9	90.4	92.1	95.1	100.0	104.0	108.3	112.7	115.7	121.4	127.4	Wages, Weekly Earnings	**65**
84.0	88.7	92.7	94.9	†91.5	91.5	94.1	98.8	100.0	103.7	105.7	108.9	112.5	118.6	118.7	Industrial Production	**66.. c**
103.8	107.0	110.5	107.6	101.1	100.1	95.8	99.1	100.0	100.3	101.8	98.5	96.4	....	....	Manufacturing Employment	**67ey c**
Period Averages																
7,754	7,970	8,224	8,440	8,486	8,557	8,613	8,771	8,995	9,115	9,204	9,339	9,466	9,678	9,817	Labor Force	**67d**
7,142	7,413	†7,734	7,877	7,698	7,660	7,699	7,942	8,256	8,364	8,444	8,618	8,808	9,068	9,157	Employment	**67e**
612	†558	†490	563	788	897	914	829	739	751	760	721	658	611	660	Unemployment	**67c**
7.9	7.0	†6.0	6.7	9.3	10.5	10.6	9.5	8.2	8.2	8.3	7.8	7.0	6.3	6.7	Unemployment Rate (%)	**67r**

Australia

193		1972	1973	1974	1975	1976	1977	1978	1979	1980	1981	1982	1983	1984	1985	1986
International Transactions																*Millions of Australian Dollars*
Exports	**70**	5,419	6,719	7,685	9,123	10,774	12,050	12,591	16,711	19,269	18,686	21,032	22,306	26,366	32,408	33,716
Wheat	**70d**	361	201	868	1,062	919	926	765	1,515	1,967	1,471	1,974	1,156	2,454	2,570	2,877
Coal	**70vr**	267	325	489	890	1,185	1,394	1,479	1,608	1,683	2,290	2,533	3,343	3,937	5,061	5,318
Greasy Wool	**70ha**	699	1,212	834	736	1,103	1,068	1,112	1,325	1,300	1,392	1,513	1,525	1,549	2,326	2,374
Imports, c.i.f.	**71**	4,217	5,177	8,358	8,173	9,999	12,186	13,591	16,279	19,632	22,824	26,210	23,839	29,560	37,054	39,033
Imports, f.o.b.	**71.v**	3,876	4,840	7,769	7,636	9,134	11,036	12,329	14,801	17,826	20,592	23,194	21,220	25,877	33,130	35,716
																1995=100
Volume of Exports	**72**	31.8	31.5	30.3	33.1	36.5	36.9	37.6	41.9	41.0	38.9	42.6	40.4	47.8	53.3	55.3
Wheat	**72d**	105.9	55.6	103.9	120.0	112.9	140.0	111.7	169.9	180.1	131.6	179.1	88.0	218.6	202.2	241.7
Coal	**72vr**	17.2	20.9	21.4	22.2	23.5	26.4	27.3	30.0	31.0	37.0	33.3	45.0	56.1	65.1	66.5
Greasy Wool	**72ha**	168.5	134.4	113.5	125.9	162.5	124.2	129.0	135.9	116.6	116.0	119.6	121.7	115.0	150.1	146.1
Volume of Imports	**73**	23.9	29.6	37.8	30.6	34.6	34.9	36.1	37.3	39.6	43.5	45.6	40.1	49.2	51.9	50.7
Export Prices	**76**	22.6	29.1	34.2	†35.7	39.0	43.8	45.4	54.8	62.8	63.9	66.8	71.8	72.1	81.0	81.9
Wheat	**76d**	21.3	38.5	51.1	42.4	39.5	36.2	44.5	52.7	57.8	56.7	59.1	66.4	59.1	75.9	67.2
Coal (Unit Value)	**74vr**	21.0	21.1	30.9	54.3	68.4	71.6	73.3	72.5	73.6	84.0	103.1	100.7	95.0	105.4	108.3
Greasy Wool (Unit Value)	**74ha**	18.5	40.2	32.8	26.1	30.3	38.3	38.4	43.5	49.7	53.6	56.4	55.9	60.1	69.1	72.5
Import Prices	**76.x**	13.6	13.6	19.0	23.9	26.3	31.8	33.8	†40.9	51.8	†52.7	56.3	61.2	62.7	74.4	81.3
Balance of Payments																*Millions of US Dollars:*
Current Account, n.i.e.	**78al*d***	405	358	–2,847	–1,058	–1,941	–3,082	–4,617	–2,738	–4,447	–8,581	–8,512	–6,330	–8,860	–9,172	–9,807
Goods: Exports f.o.b.	**78aa*d***	6,314	9,357	10,907	11,838	13,118	13,351	14,288	18,825	21,892	21,671	21,601	19,766	23,159	22,886	22,639
Goods: Imports f.o.b.	**78ab*d***	–4,301	–6,488	–10,688	–9,575	–11,031	–12,269	–14,139	–16,248	–20,521	–23,906	–23,775	–19,740	–23,901	–23,854	–24,459
Trade Balance	**78ac*d***	2,013	2,868	219	2,262	2,087	1,082	149	2,577	1,371	–2,235	–2,174	26	–742	–968	–1,820
Services: Credit	**78ad*d***	1,109	1,385	1,889	2,021	2,130	2,142	2,749	3,246	3,862	4,284	4,374	4,186	4,543	4,219	4,774
Services: Debit	**78ae*d***	–1,876	–2,684	–3,728	–3,789	–4,211	–4,310	–5,044	–5,611	–6,568	–7,420	–7,546	–6,990	–8,235	–7,677	–7,683
Balance on Goods & Services	**78af*d***	1,247	1,570	–1,620	494	6	–1,086	–2,145	212	–1,334	–5,370	–5,346	–2,778	–4,434	–4,425	–4,728
Income: Credit	**78ag*d***	376	664	777	601	531	540	625	752	957	991	1,028	1,275	1,629	1,431	1,558
Income: Debit	**78ah*d***	–1,051	–1,639	–1,707	–1,846	–2,154	–2,158	–2,543	–3,200	–3,645	–3,827	–3,546	–4,442	–5,740	–5,934	–6,454
Balance on Gds, Serv. & Inc.	**78ai*d***	572	594	–2,550	–750	–1,617	–2,704	–4,063	–2,236	–4,023	–8,206	–7,864	–5,944	–8,545	–8,928	–9,625
Current Transfers, n.i.e.: Credit	**78aj*d***	357	432	542	728	610	611	682	714	904	1,012	980	970	1,012	930	1,096
Current Transfers: Debit	**78ak*d***	–524	–668	–839	–1,036	–933	–990	–1,236	–1,216	–1,328	–1,387	–1,628	–1,356	–1,326	–1,175	–1,278
Capital Account, n.i.e.	**78bc*d***	58	33	8	–49	–9	8	37	72	179	204	203	332	335	538	627
Capital Account, n.i.e.: Credit	**78ba*d***	203	242	252	216	228	246	319	387	504	595	615	757	781	877	954
Capital Account: Debit	**78bb*d***	–144	–209	–244	–265	–237	–237	–283	–315	–325	–391	–412	–425	–446	–339	–327
Financial Account, n.i.e.	**78bj*d***	1,724	–477	841	752	1,860	2,266	3,736	2,127	4,183	7,695	12,656	7,816	6,072	7,535	11,441
Direct Investment Abroad	**78bd*d***	–129	–259	–245	–160	–266	–266	–236	–343	–461	–733	–697	–521	–1,407	–1,879	–3,327
Dir. Invest. in Rep. Econ., n.i.e.	**78be*d***	1,054	147	1,332	455	1,043	1,139	1,678	1,488	1,870	2,347	2,363	2,985	375	2,063	5,336
Portfolio Investment Assets	**78bf*d***	–6	–26	–13	5	–10	–7	–10	–3	–16	–31	–338	–342	–355	–937	–1,848
Equity Securities	**78bk*d***	–6	–26	–13	5	–10	–7	–10	–3	–16	–31	–338	–342	–355	–937	–1,848
Debt Securities	**78bl*d***	—	—	—	—	—	—	—	—	—	—	—	—	—	—	—
Portfolio Investment Liab., n.i.e.	**78bg*d***	721	–681	–685	358	539	913	1,870	983	1,819	1,103	3,254	1,886	2,008	5,149	5,103
Equity Securities	**78bm*d***	717	–516	–549	475	–114	–65	41	360	1,780	520	782	888	–225	964	1,014
Debt Securities	**78bn*d***	5	–165	–136	–117	653	978	1,829	623	39	583	2,473	998	2,233	4,185	4,089
Financial Derivatives Assets	**78bw*d***	....	....	....	....	....	....	....	....	....	—	—	—	—	—	—
Financial Derivatives Liabilities	**78bx*d***	....	....	....	....	....	....	....	....	....	—	—	—	—	—	—
Other Investment Assets	**78bh*d***	–135	165	–534	–46	22	–419	–193	–916	–384	437	–427	–293	–1,820	–1,757	–492
Monetary Authorities	**78bo*d***	....	....	....	....	....	....	....	....	....	—	—	—	—	—	—
General Government	**78bp*d***	–30	162	40	–48	–82	–115	—	–109	–52	16	–101	–235	–197	–199	–45
Banks	**78bq*d***	–42	1	–16	–78	24	67	–77	–58	–113	81	158	146	–66	–258	–611
Other Sectors	**78br*d***	–63	1	–558	81	80	–371	–116	–750	–218	340	–485	–205	–1,557	–1,300	164
Other Investment Liab., n.i.e.	**78bi*d***	218	177	986	139	531	906	628	919	1,355	4,572	8,501	4,102	7,272	4,896	6,669
Monetary Authorities	**78bs*d***	5	18	15	–46	–5	207	–1	–45	–150	207	–171	–1	12	–19	–2
General Government	**78bt*d***	29	16	7	87	–22	–47	204	145	158	–40	353	–67	–173	17	96
Banks	**78bu*d***	185	—	106	–106	75	10	53	68	174	149	292	147	679	1,452	3,719
Other Sectors	**78bv*d***	—	143	858	205	484	735	372	752	1,174	4,257	8,028	4,023	6,754	3,446	2,857
Net Errors and Omissions	**78ca*d***	538	–215	379	–563	–299	–139	756	–208	533	746	385	1,213	1,158	–1,201	–1,559
Overall Balance	**78cb*d***	2,725	–301	–1,618	–919	–389	–947	–89	–746	448	64	4,731	3,030	–1,294	–2,301	703
Reserves and Related Items	**79da*d***	–2,725	301	1,618	919	389	947	89	746	–448	–64	–4,731	–3,030	1,294	2,301	–703
Reserve Assets	**79db*d***	–2,725	301	1,618	919	8	947	194	715	–175	8	–4,766	–2,996	1,294	2,301	–703
Use of Fund Credit and Loans	**79dc*d***	—	—	—	—	381	—	–105	31	–272	–71	35	–34	—	—	—
Exceptional Financing	**79de*d***	....	....	....	....	....	....	....	....	....	....	....	....	....	....	....
International Investment Position																*Millions of US Dollars*
Assets	**79aa*d***	....	....	....	....	....	....	....	....	....	....	....	....	....	....	35,248
Direct Investment Abroad	**79ab*d***	....	....	....	....	....	....	....	....	....	....	....	....	....	....	11,613
Portfolio Investment	**79ac*d***	....	....	....	....	....	....	....	....	....	....	....	....	....	....	5,762
Equity Securities	**79ad*d***	....	....	....	....	....	....	....	....	....	....	....	....	....	....	5,762
Debt Securities	**79ae*d***	....	....	....	....	....	....	....	....	....	....	....	....	....	....	—
Financial Derivatives	**79al*d***	....	....	....	....	....	....	....	....	....	....	....	....	....	....	—
Other Investment	**79af*d***	....	....	....	....	....	....	....	....	....	....	....	....	....	....	7,526
Monetary Authorities	**79ag*d***	....	....	....	....	....	....	....	....	....	....	....	....	....	....	—
General Government	**79ah*d***	....	....	....	....	....	....	....	....	....	....	....	....	....	....	1,759
Banks	**79ai*d***	....	....	....	....	....	....	....	....	....	....	....	....	....	....	1,598
Other Sectors	**79aj*d***	....	....	....	....	....	....	....	....	....	....	....	....	....	....	4,170
Reserve Assets	**79ak*d***	....	....	....	....	....	....	....	....	....	....	....	....	....	....	10,347
Liabilities	**79la*d***	....	....	....	....	....	....	....	....	....	....	....	....	....	....	108,007
Dir. Invest. in Rep. Economy	**79lb*d***	....	....	....	....	....	....	....	....	....	....	....	....	....	....	31,256
Portfolio Investment	**79lc*d***	....	....	....	....	....	....	....	....	....	....	....	....	....	....	18,816
Equity Securities	**79ld*d***	....	....	....	....	....	....	....	....	....	....	....	....	....	....	12,167
Debt Securities	**79le*d***	....	....	....	....	....	....	....	....	....	....	....	....	....	....	6,649
Financial Derivatives	**79ll*d***	....	....	....	....	....	....	....	....	....	....	....	....	....	....	—
Other Investment	**79lf*d***	....	....	....	....	....	....	....	....	....	....	....	....	....	....	57,936
Monetary Authorities	**79lg*d***	....	....	....	....	....	....	....	....	....	....	....	....	....	....	—
General Government	**79lh*d***	....	....	....	....	....	....	....	....	....	....	....	....	....	....	13,166
Banks	**79li*d***	....	....	....	....	....	....	....	....	....	....	....	....	....	....	1,153
Other Sectors	**79lj*d***	....	....	....	....	....	....	....	....	....	....	....	....	....	....	43,618

1987	1988	1989	1990	1991	1992	1993	1994	1995	1996	1997	1998	1999	2000	2001	
Millions of Australian Dollars															**International Transactions**
37,947	42,369	47,005	50,892	53,728	58,363	62,839	64,904	71,657	76,978	84,786	88,977	86,895	110,464	122,664	Exports **70**
2,006	1,409	2,562	2,215	1,582	1,501	2,217	2,283	1,765	3,987	4,407	3,514	3,311	3,813	4,330	Wheat **70d**
5,043	4,612	5,080	6,157	6,757	7,245	7,707	6,700	7,380	7,758	8,784	9,823	8,391	9,340	12,482	Coal **70vr**
3,457	4,657	4,101	2,281	2,447	2,461	1,951	2,394	2,242	2,108	2,446	1,715	1,494	2,103	2,304	Greasy Wool **70ha**
41,816	45,925	56,801	53,785	53,427	59,732	67,027	72,882	82,673	83,543	88,884	102,905	107,154	123,461	123,539	Imports, c.i.f. **71**
38,469	42,416	51,726	49,807	49,678	55,513	62,385	68,087	77,467	78,402	83,364	96,723	101,446	116,840	117,357	Imports, f.o.b. **71.v**
1995=100															
61.7	62.0	64.3	69.4	80.0	84.1	89.4	96.9	100.0	111.6	127.3	126.0	132.5	145.6	149.7	Volume of Exports **72**
227.9	117.1	174.4	160.8	167.4	105.7	160.1	188.0	100.0	211.3	281.1	220.9	239.9	257.3	225.5	Wheat **72d**
74.0	73.0	70.9	82.5	88.3	94.2	97.5	96.1	100.0	103.1	115.6	121.2	126.0	136.8	142.2	Coal **72vr**
168.1	153.3	148.6	95.0	147.6	142.4	131.4	129.0	100.0	120.7	120.7	93.6	97.4	117.9	110.7	Greasy Wool **72ha**
51.5	61.0	73.6	70.3	69.3	75.2	79.4	91.3	100.0	108.5	121.7	131.9	145.6	157.5	150.8	Volume of Imports **73**
85.2	95.3	†100.5	101.4	92.7	94.5	95.8	93.1	100.0	95.9	97.5	102.3	†95.0	103.7	105.8	Export Prices **76**
61.3	72.1	83.8	93.4	63.6	101.5	85.2	83.1	100.0	109.0	94.7	92.6	....	....	....	Wheat **76d**
92.3	85.6	97.1	101.1	103.7	104.2	107.1	94.4	100.0	101.9	103.0	109.8	90.3	92.5	118.9	Coal (Unit Value) **74vr**
91.7	135.5	123.1	107.1	73.9	77.1	66.2	82.7	100.0	77.9	90.4	81.7	68.4	79.6	92.8	Greasy Wool (Unit Value) **74ha**
86.2	84.2	83.4	†86.7	87.6	91.5	98.9	96.6	100.0	94.6	94.5	102.5	†100.2	109.0	103.2	Import Prices **76.x**
Minus Sign Indicates Debit															Balance of Payments
-7,966	-11,748	-17,866	-15,950	-10,986	-11,124	-9,684	-17,146	-19,323	-15,810	-12,384	-18,014	-23,012	-15,391	-9,194	Current Account, n.i.e. **78al*d***
27,377	33,413	37,160	39,642	42,362	42,816	42,637	47,371	53,220	60,397	64,893	55,884	56,096	64,041	63,667	Goods: Exports f.o.b. **78aa*d***
-26,885	-34,090	-40,511	-39,284	-38,833	-41,173	-42,666	-50,648	-57,443	-61,032	-63,044	-61,215	-65,826	-68,752	-61,644	Goods: Imports f.o.b. **78ab*d***
492	-677	-3,350	358	3,528	1,643	-29	-3,277	-4,223	-635	1,849	-5,332	-9,730	-4,711	2,023	*Trade Balance* **78ac*d***
6,118	8,433	8,867	10,201	10,998	11,200	11,942	14,185	16,156	18,531	18,488	16,181	17,354	18,390	16,123	Services: Credit **78ad*d***
-8,771	-10,824	-13,175	-13,772	-13,467	-13,767	-13,412	-15,458	-17,110	-18,606	-18,844	-17,272	-18,304	-18,075	-16,692	Services: Debit **78ae*d***
-2,161	-3,068	-7,659	-3,213	1,059	-924	-1,500	-4,550	-5,177	-710	1,493	-6,422	-10,680	-4,396	1,455	*Balance on Goods & Services* **78af*d***
2,492	2,988	3,510	3,228	3,285	3,774	4,179	4,462	5,258	6,027	7,162	6,532	6,909	8,586	7,720	Income: Credit **78ag*d***
-8,326	-11,551	-13,893	-16,404	-15,456	-13,892	-12,268	-16,829	-19,294	-21,220	-21,000	-17,842	-19,211	-19,533	-18,389	Income: Debit **78ah*d***
-7,995	-11,632	-18,042	-16,389	-11,112	-11,042	-9,589	-16,917	-19,213	-15,903	-12,345	-17,732	-22,983	-15,344	-9,215	*Balance on Gds, Serv. & Inc.* **78ai*d***
1,294	1,576	1,806	2,313	2,145	2,139	2,101	2,206	2,364	2,699	2,765	2,651	3,003	2,622	2,242	Current Transfers, n.i.e.: Credit **78aj*d***
-1,265	-1,692	-1,630	-1,875	-2,019	-2,221	-2,196	-2,434	-2,474	-2,606	-2,805	-2,933	-3,032	-2,669	-2,221	Current Transfers: Debit **78ak*d***
944	1,838	1,682	1,516	1,633	1,050	260	323	558	964	903	670	819	615	590	Capital Account, n.i.e. **78bc*d***
1,287	2,267	2,167	2,114	2,151	1,572	780	908	1,250	1,674	1,606	1,315	1,535	1,406	1,319	Capital Account, n.i.e.: Credit **78ba*d***
-343	-428	-485	-597	-518	-522	-519	-586	-692	-710	-703	-646	-716	-791	-729	Capital Account: Debit **78bb*d***
9,185	15,314	17,101	16,235	9,922	5,023	10,203	15,897	18,632	16,070	16,820	15,117	27,969	14,313	9,131	Financial Account, n.i.e. **78bj*d***
-5,115	-5,823	-2,893	-1,013	-1,211	-5,145	-1,942	-2,817	-3,267	-7,052	-6,368	-3,368	2,989	-5,133	-11,126	Direct Investment Abroad **78bd*d***
5,264	7,377	7,259	8,111	4,312	5,699	4,318	5,001	12,026	6,181	7,631	6,046	5,699	11,512	4,067	Dir. Invest. in Rep. Econ., n.i.e. **78be*d***
-950	-2,381	-2,362	380	-4,969	-4,115	-3,947	1,503	-2,842	-3,307	-79	-3,127	-6,443	-4,714	-6,838	Portfolio Investment Assets **78bf*d***
-950	-2,332	-2,422	584	-2,792	-1,573	-2,358	-543	-1,175	-2,416	-567	-2,882	-3,718	-3,877	-6,329	Equity Securities **78bk*d***
—	-49	60	-204	-2,177	-2,542	-1,589	2,045	-1,668	-892	489	-245	-2,724	-838	-509	Debt Securities **78bl*d***
6,820	12,144	10,285	6,971	14,083	3,301	12,023	14,593	15,200	23,738	13,219	6,917	17,224	14,484	16,828	Portfolio Investment Liab., n.i.e. **78bg*d***
3,204	1,107	1,401	1,275	2,798	798	7,004	8,120	2,585	2,068	8,775	10,776	5,973	-757	8,934	Equity Securities **78bm*d***
3,616	11,037	8,884	5,696	11,286	2,503	5,020	6,473	12,615	21,670	4,444	-3,859	11,251	15,240	7,893	Debt Securities **78bn*d***
—	—	—	—	—	—	—	1,004	2,801	974	-470	-382	247	-966	327	Financial Derivatives Assets **78bw*d***
—	—	—	—	—	—	—	-632	-2,217	-681	1,092	-636	1,054	387	-141	Financial Derivatives Liabilities **78bx*d***
-2,693	-1,296	-2,181	-2,735	-765	1,033	-1,008	-1,597	-3,223	-5,613	-6,735	-243	-2,907	-4,210	314	Other Investment Assets **78bh*d***
—	—	—	—	—	—	—	—	—	-246	-414	-180	-327	133	275	Monetary Authorities **78bo*d***
-105	393	102	-90	-230	222	17	137	-57	-94	-840	-412	-214	-22	-153	General Government **78bp*d***
-357	-1,577	-196	-2,920	-318	873	-47	-2,438	-2,824	-4,618	-4,233	-609	-2,386	-1,177	-3,391	Banks **78bq*d***
-2,231	-112	-2,086	275	-218	-61	-978	704	-342	-656	-1,248	956	20	-3,144	3,584	Other Sectors **78br*d***
5,859	5,292	6,992	4,521	-1,529	4,250	758	-1,158	154	1,829	8,530	9,909	10,105	2,954	5,701	Other Investment Liab., n.i.e. **78bi*d***
4	28	-28	13	-8	11	13	-4	27	-29	-3	9	61	-70	3	Monetary Authorities **78bs*d***
-105	86	7	47	54	25	-9	157	133	103	-91	129	-228	75	-125	General Government **78bt*d***
2,204	2,286	5,385	4,393	-1,732	3,965	2,622	-1,375	2,998	2,717	7,207	7,654	7,833	4,339	4,159	Banks **78bu*d***
3,756	2,892	1,628	68	157	248	-1,868	64	-3,004	-963	1,417	2,116	2,439	-1,390	1,663	Other Sectors **78bv*d***
-1,788	-125	-316	-61	-893	324	-821	-34	529	1,248	-2,466	188	929	-902	569	Net Errors and Omissions **78ca*d***
374	5,279	601	1,740	-324	-4,726	-42	-960	396	2,471	2,873	-2,040	6,705	-1,365	1,096	*Overall Balance* **78cb*d***
-374	-5,279	-601	-1,740	324	4,726	42	960	-396	-2,471	-2,873	2,040	-6,705	1,365	-1,096	Reserves and Related Items **79da*d***
-374	-5,279	-601	-1,740	324	4,726	42	960	-396	-2,471	-2,873	2,040	-6,705	1,365	-1,096	Reserve Assets **79db*d***
—	—	—	—	—	—	—	—	—	—	—	—	—	—	—	Use of Fund Credit and Loans **79dc*d***
....	....	....	....	....	....	....	....	....	....	....	....	....	....	....	Exceptional Financing **79de*d***
Millions of US Dollars															International Investment Position
50,055	72,074	77,063	82,287	88,346	87,569	100,894	119,962	133,885	161,821	173,545	181,748	219,854	208,305	215,156	Assets **79aa*d***
19,953	28,503	28,950	30,507	30,890	34,539	40,510	47,774	53,010	66,816	71,936	77,024	87,186	81,009	88,013	Direct Investment Abroad **79ab*d***
6,500	12,149	15,391	14,856	21,268	24,160	30,247	29,375	35,658	42,023	42,451	47,064	62,612	58,432	58,669	Portfolio Investment **79ac*d***
6,500	10,222	13,651	12,227	16,271	17,092	21,428	22,538	27,029	31,518	32,947	36,908	50,458	46,656	47,408	Equity Securities **79ad*d***
—	1,927	1,740	2,628	4,997	7,067	8,819	6,837	8,629	10,506	9,504	10,156	12,155	11,776	11,262	Debt Securities **79ae*d***
—	—	—	—	—	—	—	8,924	7,679	6,733	8,058	9,282	10,897	11,985	14,224	Financial Derivatives **79al*d***
11,004	14,504	15,693	17,596	16,851	15,022	15,950	19,581	22,589	28,847	34,006	33,001	37,204	38,063	35,585	Other Investment **79af*d***
—	—	—	—	—	—	—	—	—	—	491	766	953	875	536	Monetary Authorities **79ag*d***
2,080	1,530	1,320	1,373	1,569	1,212	1,173	1,201	1,208	1,377	4,044	4,283	4,677	4,223	4,155	General Government **79ah*d***
2,001	5,994	5,962	8,733	8,266	6,994	7,099	9,232	11,905	16,989	18,892	18,470	21,545	20,600	22,333	Banks **79ai*d***
6,924	6,980	8,411	7,489	7,016	6,816	7,678	9,148	9,476	10,481	10,578	9,483	10,029	12,365	8,562	Other Sectors **79aj*d***
12,599	16,918	17,028	19,328	19,338	13,848	14,188	14,308	14,949	17,402	17,094	15,377	21,956	18,817	18,664	Reserve Assets **79ak*d***
138,241	188,012	207,155	224,478	240,021	233,727	264,564	309,880	335,211	388,362	360,313	378,164	441,936	418,430	425,151	Liabilities **79la*d***
42,437	62,072	70,170	73,644	77,057	75,777	82,891	95,519	104,074	116,724	101,043	105,794	122,619	113,320	111,127	Dir. Invest. in Rep. Economy **79lb*d***
24,449	90,165	96,843	106,248	120,068	114,250	137,835	162,325	181,223	218,728	203,158	208,374	241,329	229,772	237,751	Portfolio Investment **79lc*d***
15,386	17,755	17,613	19,647	21,956	18,945	35,916	46,544	51,314	61,123	60,297	72,996	92,817	77,469	84,837	Equity Securities **79ld*d***
9,063	72,410	79,230	86,600	98,112	95,304	101,919	115,780	129,909	157,605	142,861	135,378	148,513	152,303	152,914	Debt Securities **79le*d***
—	—	—	—	—	—	—	7,564	7,250	8,275	9,884	9,862	12,431	12,764	12,048	Financial Derivatives **79ll*d***
71,356	35,775	40,142	44,587	42,895	43,700	43,838	44,472	42,665	44,636	46,227	54,134	65,557	62,574	64,224	Other Investment **79lf*d***
—	50	20	33	24	32	43	46	71	45	33	36	100	18	19	Monetary Authorities **79lg*d***
16,730	13	21	79	204	216	202	397	439	573	237	360	153	210	64	General Government **79lh*d***
1,700	12,012	17,532	21,740	19,942	21,741	24,229	23,637	25,010	27,883	30,851	37,522	46,577	47,255	48,757	Banks **79li*d***
52,925	23,700	22,570	22,735	22,725	21,711	19,363	20,392	17,145	16,134	15,106	16,216	18,727	15,090	15,384	Other Sectors **79lj*d***

		1972	1973	1974	1975	1976	1977	1978	1979	1980	1981	1982	1983	1984	1985	1986
Government Finance																*Millions of Australian Dollars:*
Deficit (-) or Surplus	80	130	−409	−241	−2,479	−3,609	−2,702	−3,290	−3,132	−2,085	−1,078	−590	−4,601	−7,983	−6,810	−5,792
Revenue	81	9,131	9,740	12,296	15,749	18,853	22,126	24,315	26,439	30,623	36,305	41,897	45,936	50,450	59,282	66,660
Expenditure	82	8,284	9,441	11,240	15,679	20,370	23,310	26,269	28,526	31,886	36,419	41,462	49,186	57,315	65,175	71,633
Lending Minus Repayments	83	717	708	1,297	2,549	2,092	1,518	1,336	1,045	822	964	1,025	1,351	1,118	917	819
Financing (by Residence of Lender)																
Domestic	84a	−83	475	371	2,478	3,483	2,345	1,678	1,755	1,837	1,283	222	4,016	7,749	5,889	4,544
Foreign	85a	−47	−66	−130	1	126	357	1,612	1,377	248	−205	585	234	908	1,271
Debt: Domestic	88a	....	....	....	....	....	....	20,321	22,865	23,924	25,537	25,707	30,152	38,353	28,648	32,255
Foreign	89a	....	....	....	....	....	....	3,635	5,246	5,396	4,652	5,352	6,919	7,084	9,857	13,832
Financing (by Currency) Commonwealth and States																
Debt: Australian Dollars	88b	9,964	13,479	14,275	16,587	19,013	21,420	23,287	25,752	27,250	27,820	....	....	....	....	....
Held By: Reserve Bank	88ba	501	611	1,443	1,276	2,739	4,239	4,392	5,197	5,217	4,779	....	....	....	....	....
Deposit Money Banks	88bb	4,168	5,085	5,164	6,571	6,641	6,395	6,382	7,256	7,548	9,027	....	....	....	....	....
Life Insur. Companies	88bc	1,483	1,632	1,786	1,862	2,055	2,226	2,447	2,602	2,798	3,012	....	....	....	....	....
Others	88be	3,812	6,151	5,882	6,878	7,578	8,560	10,066	10,697	11,687	11,002	....	....	....	....	....
Intragovernmental Debt	88bg	2,628	2,610	2,575	3,052	2,490	2,572	3,114	3,180	....	....	....	....	....	....	....
Foreign Currency	89b	1,442	1,265	1,032	1,182	1,325	1,870	....	....	....	....	....	....	....	....	....
Local and Other Governments Total Debt	88.. i	6,060	6,609	....	....	....	....	....	....	....	....					
National Accounts											*Billions of Australian Dollars Quarterly Data Seasonally*					
Househ.Cons.Expend.,incl.NPISHs	96f. c	25.03	29.02	35.08	42.06	49.41	55.88	62.24	69.48	78.98	90.19	103.01	113.92	123.22	137.36	151.25
Government Consumption Expend.	91f. c	6.69	7.84	9.97	13.29	15.78	17.57	19.64	21.54	25.01	28.94	32.94	37.20	42.02	47.08	52.27
Gross Fixed Capital Formation	93e. c	12.49	14.42	16.07	18.30	21.27	23.76	26.79	30.28	35.55	42.96	46.88	46.12	52.30	62.72	67.39
Changes in Inventories	93i. c	−.18	.09	2.05	−.57	.64	.61	−.03	2.03	.74	1.19	−.47	−1.57	2.73	.97	−1.19
Exports of Goods and Services	90c. c	6.24	7.56	8.85	10.62	12.51	14.02	14.86	19.84	22.62	22.60	25.51	26.50	31.57	38.75	40.80
Imports of Goods and Services (-)	98c. c	5.18	6.42	10.04	10.22	12.47	14.97	16.77	19.60	23.82	27.04	30.80	29.63	36.63	45.10	48.04
Gross Domestic Product (GDP)	99b. c	43.87	51.75	62.12	72.80	85.57	95.50	105.07	121.13	136.51	156.07	174.37	188.74	213.40	237.37	257.86
Net Primary Income from Abroad	98.n c	−.57	−.69	−.65	−.98	−1.33	−1.46	−1.68	−2.19	−2.36	−2.47	−2.43	−3.53	−4.68	−6.47	−7.35
Gross National Income (GNI)	99a. c	43.30	51.06	61.47	71.82	84.24	94.04	103.39	118.94	134.15	153.61	171.94	185.21	208.73	230.90	250.51
Net Current Transf.from Abroad	98t. c	.51	.41	.12	−.01	−.06	−.43	−.66	−.60	−.58	−.71	−1.01	.31	2.44	−.02	1.73
Gross Nat'l Disposable Inc.(GNDI)	99i. c	42.98	50.71	60.84	71.62	84.12	93.22	102.61	117.88	133.54	152.61	170.48	184.98	210.84	230.83	251.92
Gross Saving	99s. c	11.26	13.85	15.79	16.28	18.93	19.78	20.74	26.86	29.55	33.48	34.53	33.86	45.60	46.39	48.40
Consumption of Fixed Capital	99cf c	7.50	8.59	9.76	11.16	12.92	14.40	15.92	18.00	20.72	23.67	26.70	29.98	33.11	36.86	42.21
GDP Vol. 1998/99 Ref.,Chained	99b. r	257.58	274.19	278.67	283.12	294.99	297.91	308.79	322.10	328.69	340.36	342.68	340.56	363.40	382.55	390.56
GDP Volume (1995=100)	99bv r	49.8	53.0	53.8	54.7	57.0	57.6	59.7	62.2	63.5	65.8	66.2	65.8	70.2	73.9	75.5
GDP Deflator (1995=100)	99bi r	18.2	20.1	23.8	27.4	31.0	34.2	36.3	40.1	44.3	48.9	54.3	59.2	62.7	66.2	70.5
																Millions:
Population	99z	13.18	13.38	13.70	13.89	14.03	14.19	14.36	14.52	14.70	14.92	15.18	15.39	15.56	15.79	16.02

	1987	1988	1989	1990	1991	1992	1993	1994	1995	1996	1997	1998	1999	2000	2001		
Year Ending June 30																**Government Finance**	
	−2,781	†2,324	6,316	7,877	1,951	−9,514	−14,477	−13,674	−11,641	−4,806	2,028	....	....	....	....	Deficit (-) or Surplus	80
	75,209	†84,092	91,516	98,410	100,944	96,630	98,460	104,775	114,493	125,861	135,271	....	....	....	....	Revenue	81
	77,465	†82,310	85,316	91,754	100,550	108,201	115,441	121,846	127,613	135,843	140,478	....	....	....	....	Expenditure	82
	525	−542	−116	−1,221	−1,557	−2,057	−2,504	−3,397	−1,479	−5,176	−7,235	....	....	....	....	Lending Minus Repayments	83
																Financing (by Residence of Lender)	
	2,055	−893	−3,185	−8,685	1,246	11,422	11,122	10,024	8,349	−3,123	−3,978	−11,213	−5,833	....	....	Domestic	84a
	724	−1,373	−3,150	763	−3,192	−1,911	3,325	3,612	3,292	7,963	1,916	−5,155	−2,845	....	....	Foreign	85a
	34,357	†40,430	38,812	29,886	32,106	43,080	58,025	71,334	79,489	78,892	73,510	60,094	60,089	....	....	Debt: Domestic	88a
	15,064	†22,877	18,576	19,599	17,396	16,794	21,376	22,869	28,012	36,482	42,610	39,355	36,599	....	....	Foreign	89a
																Financing (by Currency) Commonwealth and States	
	....	....	....	....	....	....	....	....	....	....	....	....	....	....	....	Debt: Australian Dollars	88b
	....	....	....	....	....	....	....	....	....	....	....	....	....	....	....	Held By: Reserve Bank	88ba
	....	....	....	....	....	....	....	....	....	....	....	....	....	....	....	Deposit Money Banks	88bb
	....	....	....	....	....	....	....	....	....	....	....	....	....	....	....	Life Insur. Companies	88bc
	....	....	....	....	....	....	....	....	....	....	....	....	....	....	....	Others	88be
	....	....	....	....	....	....	....	....	....	....	....	....	....	....	....	Intragovernmental Debt	88bg
	....	....	....	....	....	....	....	....	....	....	....	....	....	....	....	Foreign Currency	89b
																Local and Other Governments	
	....	....	....	....	....	....	....	....	....	....	....	....	....	....	....	Total Debt	88.. i
Billions of Australian Dollars Not Average to Yearly Data																**National Accounts**	
	167.44	186.82	208.64	221.95	239.28	250.70	260.55	273.28	292.54	307.51	325.09	344.70	365.14	386.81	413.18	Househ.Cons.Expend.,incl.NPISHs	96f. c
	55.70	59.91	65.75	72.44	77.91	80.65	83.57	85.81	89.58	95.54	99.37	103.77	111.67	122.79	127.26	Government Consumption Expend.	91f. c
	75.12	85.95	100.59	95.36	86.73	87.85	93.43	105.45	109.41	113.90	123.57	134.24	143.11	146.45	145.02	Gross Fixed Capital Formation	93e. c
	.59	2.54	4.82	1.41	−3.00	−1.53	1.62	1.77	.83	1.45	−3.97	3.47	6.03	2.17	.08	Changes in Inventories	93i. c
	47.76	53.36	58.21	63.72	68.32	73.48	80.27	84.12	93.72	100.63	111.95	114.86	113.56	142.28	154.43	Exports of Goods and Services	90c. c
	50.78	57.17	67.94	67.91	67.07	74.74	82.42	90.07	100.60	101.66	110.32	124.83	130.17	149.61	151.56	Imports of Goods and Services (-)	98c. c
	290.82	329.65	370.06	394.65	399.37	414.22	435.37	460.19	484.89	517.37	545.62	576.74	608.13	652.04	691.52	Gross Domestic Product (GDP)	99b. c
	−8.36	−10.65	−13.39	−16.79	−15.66	−13.73	−11.75	−16.80	−19.15	−19.33	−18.75	−18.08	−18.91	−18.92	−20.61	Net Primary Income from Abroad	98.n c
	282.46	319.00	356.66	377.86	383.71	400.50	423.62	443.40	465.74	498.04	526.86	558.66	589.23	633.12	670.91	Gross National Income (GNI)	99a. c
	2.07	−70.64	1.11	1.06	−2.41	−2.61	−3.66	−1.41	−.07	.48	−9.45	1.54	−1.48	1.28	.55	Net Current Transf.from Abroad	98t. c
	284.29	248.37	356.45	377.56	380.74	399.56	422.42	446.03	471.30	502.62	529.40	561.92	587.71	634.60	670.79	Gross Nat'l Disposable Inc.(GNDI)	99i. c
	61.16	1.64	82.06	83.18	63.55	68.21	78.30	86.94	89.18	99.56	104.94	113.46	110.91	124.99	130.35	Gross Saving	99s. c
	48.26	55.00	60.04	62.98	65.50	68.10	71.82	75.12	77.49	79.28	83.06	88.70	94.40	100.92	108.06	Consumption of Fixed Capital	99cf c
	408.56	426.31	445.52	453.47	450.29	459.74	477.13	500.19	517.54	539.72	559.56	588.86	616.88	636.19	652.43	GDP Vol. 1998/99 Ref.,Chained	99b. r
	78.9	82.4	86.1	87.6	87.0	88.8	92.2	96.6	100.0	104.3	108.1	113.8	119.2	122.9	126.1	GDP Volume (1995=100)	99bv r
	76.0	82.5	88.7	92.9	94.7	96.2	97.4	98.2	100.0	102.3	104.1	104.5	105.2	109.4	113.1	GDP Deflator (1995=100)	99bi r
Midyear Estimates																	
	16.26	16.53	16.81	17.06	17.28	17.49	17.67	17.85	18.07	18.31	18.52	18.73	18.97	19.16	19.49	Population	99z

(See notes in the back of the book.)

Austria

122		1972	1973	1974	1975	1976	1977	1978	1979	1980	1981	1982	1983	1984	1985	1986
Exchange Rates																*Schillings per SDR through 1998,*
Official Rate	aa	†25.123	23.946	20.973	21.669	19.481	18.385	17.415	16.376	17.612	18.490	18.408	20.249	21.614	18.981	16.770
																Schillings per US Dollar through 1998,
Official Rate	ae	†23.140	19.850	17.130	18.510	16.768	15.135	13.368	12.431	13.809	15.885	16.687	19.341	22.050	17.280	13.710
Official Rate	rf	23.115	19.580	18.693	17.417	17.940	16.527	14.522	13.368	12.938	15.927	17.059	17.963	20.009	20.690	15.267
																Schillings per ECU:
ECU Rate	ea	....	....	....	....	....	....	....	17.9243	18.0843	17.2384	16.1480	16.0027	15.6312	15.3429	14.6752
ECU Rate	eb	....	....	....	....	....	....	18.5005	18.3216	17.9969	17.8004	16.7387	16.0104	15.7870	15.7694	14.9800
																Index Numbers (1995=100):
Official Rate	ahx	43.6	51.8	54.0	57.9	56.2	61.0	69.5	75.4	78.0	63.5	59.1	56.2	50.5	49.1	66.2
Nominal Effective Exchange Rate	neu	64.5	67.2	70.5	72.3	74.7	78.0	78.5	79.7	82.1	81.4	84.0	85.9	85.9	86.3	89.7
Real Effective Exchange Rate	reu	....	....	....	109.3	110.0	110.3	143.6	139.6	†134.9	126.7	125.3	124.3	121.1	118.5	121.3
Fund Position																*Millions of SDRs:*
Quota	2f.s	270	270	270	270	270	270	330	330	495	495	495	776	776	776	776
SDRs	1b.s	86	86	87	87	96	97	105	156	173	186	226	154	224	191	152
Reserve Position in the Fund	1c.s	132	126	131	177	344	325	254	232	228	224	259	447	447	405	361
of which: Outstg.Fund Borrowing	2c	—	—	—	24	100	98	79	66	56	43	42	50	47	41	32
International Liquidity																*Millions of US Dollars Unless Otherwise Indicated:*
Total Res.Min.Gold (Eurosys.Def)	1l.d	1,927	1,992	2,535	3,583	3,560	3,351	5,047	4,075	5,280	5,285	5,300	4,515	4,244	4,767	6,162
SDRs	1b.d	93	104	107	102	111	117	136	205	221	216	250	161	220	210	186
Reserve Position in the Fund	1c.d	144	152	160	207	399	394	331	305	291	261	285	468	438	445	442
Foreign Exchange	1d.d	1,690	1,737	2,268	3,273	3,050	2,839	4,579	3,565	4,768	4,808	4,765	3,886	3,586	4,112	5,534
o/w: Fin.Deriv.Rel.to Reserves	1ddd	....	....	....	....	....	....	....	....	....	....	....	....	....	....	....
Other Reserve Assets	1e.d	....	....	....	....	....	....	....	....	....	....	....	....	....	....	....
Gold (Million Fine Troy Ounces)	1ad	20.85	20.88	20.88	20.88	20.88	21.00	21.05	21.11	21.11	21.11	21.12	21.13	21.13	21.14	21.14
Gold (Eurosystem Valuation)	1and	775	905	1,049	971	1,072	1,195	2,213	3,182	2,863	2,488	2,369	2,044	1,793	2,283	2,888
Memo: Euro Cl. on Non-EA Res.	1dgd	....	....	....	....	....	....	....	....	....	....	....	....	....	....	....
Non-Euro Cl. on EA Res.	1dhd	....	....	....	....	....	....	....	....	....	....	....	....	....	....	....
Mon. Auth.: Other Foreign Assets	3..d	....	....	....	....	....	....	....	....	....	....	....	....	....	....	....
Foreign Liabilities	4..d	26	20	19	24	37	59	202	397	92	31	29	33	52	25	37
Banking Insts.: Foreign Assets	7a.d	2,077	3,341	4,518	5,404	7,669	10,290	13,704	19,329	21,711	22,458	25,039	25,743	26,515	36,754	48,900
Foreign Liab.	7b.d	2,272	3,358	4,591	5,353	7,974	10,983	14,699	20,272	24,955	25,538	26,118	26,355	28,153	38,026	50,891
Monetary Authorities																*Billions of Schillings through 1998;*
Fgn. Assets (Cl.on Non-EA Ctys)	11	62.8	57.7	61.2	84.1	77.5	68.6	96.8	90.0	112.4	123.7	128.3	127.1	133.9	122.4	124.0
Claims on General Government	12a.u	....	....	....	....	....	....	....	....	....	....	....	....	....	....	....
o/w: Claims on Gen.Govt.in Cty	12a	5.0	5.6	5.7	6.1	6.2	6.2	6.2	5.9	5.9	5.8	6.2	6.7	7.3	7.0	6.4
Claims on Banking Institutions	12e.u	....	....	....	....	....	....	....	....	....	....	....	....	....	....	....
o/w: Claims on Bank.Inst.in Cty	12e	8.7	10.4	15.7	7.5	15.9	29.9	28.5	48.6	37.2	42.3	44.2	62.6	66.1	72.1	76.9
Claims on Other Resident Sectors	12d.u	....	....	....	....	....	....	....	....	....	....	....	....	....	....	....
o/w: Cl. on Oth.Res.Sect.in Cty	12d	....	....	....	....	....	....	....	....	....	....	....	....	....	....	....
Currency Issued	14a	46.4	50.7	53.7	57.9	60.9	64.4	69.8	74.6	79.7	80.9	83.9	92.3	93.7	94.5	98.1
Liabilities to Banking Insts	14c.u	....	....	....	....	....	....	....	....	....	....	....	....	....	....	....
o/w: Liabs to Bank.Inst.in Cty	14c	17.2	14.1	17.6	25.5	26.3	26.6	35.3	32.5	35.0	41.2	42.8	42.7	44.3	45.4	51.9
Demand Dep. of Other Res.Sect.	14d.u	....	....	....	....	....	....	....	....	....	....	....	....	....	....	....
o/w: D.Dep.of Oth.Res.Sect.in Cty	14d	....	....	....	....	....	....	....	....	....	....	....	....	....	....	....
Other Dep. of Other Res.Sect.	15..u	....	....	....	....	....	....	....	....	....	....	....	....	....	....	....
o/w: O.Dep.of Oth.Res.Sect.in Cty	15	....	....	....	....	....	....	....	....	....	....	....	....	....	....	....
Money Market Instruments	16m.u	....	....	....	....	....	....	....	....	....	....	....	....	....	....	....
o/w: MMI Held by Resid.of Cty	16m	....	....	....	....	....	....	....	....	....	....	....	....	....	....	....
Bonds (Debt Securities)	16n.u	....	....	....	....	....	....	....	....	....	....	....	....	....	....	....
o/w: Bonds Held by Resid.of Cty	16n	....	....	....	....	....	....	....	....	....	....	....	....	....	....	....
Foreign Liab. (to Non-EA Ctys)	16c	.6	.4	.3	.5	.6	.9	2.7	4.9	1.3	.5	.5	.6	1.1	.4	.5
Central Government Deposits	16d.u	....	....	....	....	....	....	....	....	....	....	....	....	....	....	....
o/w: Cent.Govt.Dep. in Cty	16d	4.5	2.3	2.8	3.2	2.9	3.9	4.0	3.4	2.8	3.8	2.8	3.5	3.4	.8	.6
Other Items (Net)	17r	7.8	6.0	8.1	10.5	8.9	8.9	19.7	29.1	36.7	45.4	48.6	57.2	64.8	60.4	56.2
Memo: Net Claims on Eurosystem	12e.s	....	....	....	....	....	....	....	....	....	....	....	....	....	....	....
Currency Put into Circ.	14m	....	....	....	....	....	....	....	....	....	....	....	....	....	....	....
Banking Institutions																*Billions of Schillings through 1998;*
Claims on Monetary Authorities	20	20.6	18.9	22.8	31.3	32.1	32.2	41.8	40.2	43.4	48.9	50.6	50.6	54.0	55.4	62.0
Claims on Bk.Inst.in Oth.EA Ctys	20b.u	....	....	....	....	....	....	....	....	....	....	....	....	....	....	....
Fgn. Assets (Cl.on Non-EA Ctys)	21	48.4	70.1	†77.4	100.0	128.6	155.7	183.2	240.3	299.8	356.7	417.8	497.9	584.7	635.1	670.4
Claims on General Government	22a.u	....	....	....	....	....	....	....	....	....	....	....	....	....	....	....
o/w: Claims on Gen.Govt.in Cty	22a	44.0	56.3	59.9	86.9	116.4	137.2	158.7	183.2	204.5	220.8	255.5	297.4	†394.2	330.0	475.5
Claims on Other Resident Sectors	22d.u	....	....	....	....	....	....	....	....	....	....	....	....	....	....	....
o/w: Cl. on Oth.Res.Sect.in Cty	22d	254.8	282.6	326.7	360.8	440.5	510.1	577.3	679.3	754.2	840.7	896.0	959.8	†983.1	1,152.0	1,151.3
Demand Deposits	24..u	....	....	....	....	....	....	....	....	....	....	....	....	....	....	....
o/w: D.Dep.of Oth.Res.Sect.in Cty	24	46.4	49.8	52.7	63.5	70.4	68.6	74.7	58.4	73.5	68.5	77.5	86.3	92.5	97.4	105.7
Other Deposits	25..u	....	....	....	....	....	....	....	....	....	....	....	....	....	....	....
o/w: O.Dep.of Oth.Res.Sect.in Cty	25	196.6	227.3	262.3	314.6	377.6	421.6	489.5	552.8	620.0	702.0	782.8	814.3	870.9	928.3	1,012.4
Money Market Instruments	26m.u	....	....	....	....	....	....	....	....	....	....	....	....	....	....	....
o/w: MMI Held by Resid.of Cty	26m	....	....	....	....	....	....	....	....	....	....	....	....	....	....	....
Bonds (Debt Securities)	26n.u	....	....	....	....	....	....	....	....	....	....	....	....	....	....	....
o/w: Bonds Held by Resid.of Cty	26n	26.5	29.9	34.8	43.0	55.2	69.7	87.6	127.9	141.6	147.4	161.2	189.0	203.8	236.5	264.4
Foreign Liab. (to Non-EA Ctys)	26c	52.9	70.4	†78.7	99.1	133.7	166.2	196.5	252.0	344.6	405.7	435.8	509.7	620.8	657.1	697.7
Central Government Deposits	26d.u	....	....	....	....	....	....	....	....	....	....	....	....	....	....	....
o/w: Cent.Govt.Dep. in Cty	26d	11.3	12.9	11.8	17.6	19.3	23.2	25.7	28.0	22.8	26.1	32.3	44.2	49.8	53.6	71.6
Credit from Monetary Authorities	26g	8.7	10.4	15.7	7.5	15.9	29.9	28.5	48.6	37.2	42.3	44.2	62.6	66.1	72.1	76.9
Liab. to Bk.Inst.in Oth. EA Ctys	26h.u	....	....	....	....	....	....	....	....	....	....	....	....	....	....	....
Capital Accounts	27a	20.8	22.7	25.1	28.3	33.3	38.3	44.0	47.1	51.4	54.7	58.9	65.4	72.0	77.8	90.2
Other Items (Net)	27r	4.6	4.6	5.8	5.3	12.1	17.7	14.5	28.1	11.0	20.3	27.2	33.9	39.5	49.7	40.6
Banking Survey (Nat'l Residency)																*Billions of Schillings through 1998;*
Foreign Assets (Net)	31n	57.6	56.9	†59.6	84.6	71.8	57.2	80.8	73.3	66.4	74.3	109.8	114.6	96.7	100.0	96.2
Domestic Credit	32	288.0	329.2	377.6	432.9	540.9	626.4	712.5	837.1	939.1	1,037.3	1,122.6	1,216.1	†1,331.4	1,434.6	1,561.0
Claims on General Govt. (Net)	32an	33.2	46.6	51.0	72.1	100.4	116.3	135.2	157.8	184.9	196.6	226.6	256.3	†348.3	282.6	409.7
Claims on Other Resident Sectors	32d	254.8	282.6	326.7	360.8	440.5	510.1	577.3	679.3	754.2	840.7	896.0	959.8	†983.1	1,152.0	1,151.3
Currency Issued	34a.n	46.4	50.7	53.7	57.9	60.9	64.4	69.8	74.6	79.7	80.9	83.9	92.3	93.7	94.5	98.1
Demand Deposits	34b.n	46.4	49.8	52.7	63.5	70.4	68.6	74.7	58.4	73.5	68.5	77.5	86.3	92.5	97.4	105.7
Other Deposits	35..n	196.6	227.3	262.3	314.6	377.6	421.6	489.5	552.8	620.0	702.0	782.8	814.3	870.9	928.3	1,012.4
Money Market Instruments	36m	....	....	....	....	....	....	....	....	....	....	....	....	....	....	....
Bonds (Debt Securities)	36n	26.5	29.9	34.8	43.0	55.2	69.7	87.6	127.9	141.6	147.4	161.2	189.0	203.8	236.5	264.4
o/w: Bonds Over Two Years	36na	....	....	....	....	....	....	....	....	....	....	....	....	....	....	....
Other Items (Net)	37r	29.8	28.5	33.8	38.4	48.5	59.3	71.8	96.6	90.7	112.8	126.9	148.6	166.6	177.9	176.7

1987	1988	1989	1990	1991	1992	1993	1994	1995	1996	1997	1998	1999	2000	2001		
Euros per SDR Thereafter: End of Period															**Exchange Rates**	
15.960	16.909	15.527	15.190	15.290	15.612	16.679	16.013	14.996	15.751	17.045	16.540	1.3662	1.4002	1.4260	Official Rate	**aa**
Euros per US Dollar Thereafter: End of Period (ae) Period Average (rf)																
11.250	12.565	11.815	10.677	10.689	11.354	12.143	10.969	10.088	10.954	12.633	11.747	.9954	1.0747	1.1347	Official Rate	**ae**
12.643	12.348	13.231	11.370	11.676	10.989	11.632	11.422	10.081	10.587	12.204	12.379	.9386	1.0854	1.1175	Official Rate	**rf**
End of Period (ea) Period Average (eb)																
14.6633	14.7337	14.1426	14.5560	14.3329	13.7486	13.5998	13.4923	13.2581	13.7253	13.9495	13.7058	....	....	....	ECU Rate	**ea**
14.5934	14.6182	14.5856	14.4738	14.4841	14.2511	13.6360	13.5755	13.1880	13.4234	13.8403	13.8648	....	....	....	ECU Rate	**eb**
Period Averages																
79.8	81.7	76.2	88.8	86.6	91.9	86.6	88.4	100.0	95.2	82.6	81.5	....	....	....	Official Rate	**ahx**
92.1	91.9	91.6	93.5	93.1	94.7	97.2	97.3	100.0	98.4	96.2	96.4	95.4	93.4	93.7	Nominal Effective Exchange Rate	**neu**
121.5	116.4	111.7	108.8	104.7	105.6	106.2	103.8	100.0	95.2	90.5	89.2	87.4	85.7	85.4	Real Effective Exchange Rate	**reu**
End of Period															**Fund Position**	
776	776	776	776	776	1,188	1,188	1,188	1,188	1,188	1,188	1,188	1,872	1,872	1,872	Quota	**2f.s**
206	199	227	196	197	248	161	194	122	136	125	106	106	103	185	SDRs	**1b.s**
330	289	274	242	276	390	381	364	459	562	714	970	699	531	662	Reserve Position in the Fund	**1c.s**
19	10	4	—	—	—	—	—	—	—	—	38	—	—	—	*of which:* Outstg.Fund Borrowing	**2c**
End of Period															**International Liquidity**	
7,532	7,368	8,598	9,376	10,332	12,383	14,610	16,822	18,730	22,865	19,736	22,432	†15,120	14,318	12,509	Total Res.Min.Gold (Eurosys.Def)	**1l.d**
292	268	298	278	282	341	220	283	181	195	168	149	145	134	233	SDRs	**1b.d**
468	389	361	344	395	536	524	531	682	809	963	1,365	959	692	833	Reserve Position in the Fund	**1c.d**
6,772	6,711	7,939	8,754	9,655	11,506	13,866	16,008	17,867	21,861	18,605	20,918	14,016	13,492	11,444	Foreign Exchange	**1d.d**
....	....	....	....	....	....	....	....	....	....	....	....	—	—	—	*o/w:* Fin.Deriv.Rel.to Reserves	**1ddd**
....	....	....	....	....	....	....	....	....	....	....	....	—	—	—	Other Reserve Assets	**1e.d**
21.15	21.15	20.66	20.39	20.03	19.93	18.60	18.34	11.99	10.75	7.87	9.64	13.10	12.14	11.17	Gold (Million Fine Troy Ounces)	**1ad**
3,523	3,153	3,277	3,581	3,510	3,291	2,871	3,135	2,223	1,805	1,168	2,795	3,803	3,331	3,089	Gold (Eurosystem Valuation)	**1and**
....	....	....	....	....	....	....	....	....	....	....	....	....	....	....	Memo: Euro Cl. on Non-EA Res.	**1dgd**
....	....	....	....	....	....	....	....	....	....	....	....	2,146	1,453	985	Non-Euro Cl. on EA Res.	**1dhd**
....	....	....	....	....	....	....	....	....	....	....	....	....	....	....	Mon. Auth.: Other Foreign Assets	**3..d**
30	15	20	19	10	15	9	18	19	8	107	....	†1,584	845	925	Foreign Liabilities	**4..d**
58,955	54,604	58,919	65,991	66,189	66,763	68,418	77,885	92,040	89,538	....	....	†62,990	69,678	74,648	Banking Insts.: Foreign Assets	**7a.d**
62,440	59,370	65,954	74,306	76,570	77,427	74,089	84,321	99,148	102,739	....	....	†49,417	49,932	58,514	Foreign Liab.	**7b.d**
Billions of Euros Beginning 1999: End of Period															**Monetary Authorities**	
123.7	131.9	140.9	137.1	147.5	177.5	211.6	217.4	237.0	268.3	263.4	....	21.94	20.48	19.01	Fgn. Assets (Cl.on Non-EA Ctys)	**11**
....	....	....	....	....	....	....	....	....	....	....	....	1.43	1.06	1.45	Claims on General Government	**12a.u**
6.0	6.2	6.7	7.6	8.3	8.8	9.2	9.6	9.6	10.6	11.6	....	.22	.26	.40	*o/w:* Claims on Gen.Govt.in Cty	**12a**
....	....	....	....	....	....	....	....	....	....	....	....	16.20	10.45	6.42	Claims on Banking Institutions	**12e.u**
71.8	70.2	75.4	79.3	77.4	70.8	64.0	62.0	47.6	47.2	74.2	....	5.57	7.08	1.73	*o/w:* Claims on Bank.Inst.in Cty	**12e**
....	....	....	....	....	....	....	....	....	....	....	....	2.33	2.42	2.32	Claims on Other Resident Sectors	**12d.u**
....	....	....	....	....	....	....	....	....	....	....	....	.86	.90	.99	*o/w:* Cl. on Oth.Res.Sect.in Cty	**12d**
102.9	108.4	117.8	124.7	133.4	141.2	149.8	158.3	168.6	176.7	178.8	....	13.96	14.58	10.72	Currency Issued	**14a**
....	....	....	....	....	....	....	....	....	....	....	....	16.21	8.76	6.87	Liabilities to Banking Insts	**14c.u**
43.0	39.2	50.6	43.9	38.5	48.5	55.2	55.9	43.5	50.1	46.3	....	3.28	3.40	6.56	*o/w:* Liabs to Bank.Inst.in Cty	**14c**
....	....	....	....	....	....	....	....	....	....	....	....	.01	.01	.01	Demand Dep. of Other Res.Sect.	**14d.u**
....	....	....	....	....	....	....	....	....	....	....	....	.01	.01	.01	*o/w:* D.Dep.of Oth.Res.Sect.in Cty	**14d**
....	....	....	....	....	....	....	....	....	....	....	....	—	—	—	Other Dep. of Other Res.Sect.	**15..u**
....	....	....	....	....	....	....	....	....	....	....	....	—	—	—	*o/w:* O.Dep.of Oth.Res.Sect.in Cty	**15**
....	....	....	....	....	....	....	....	....	....	....	....	—	—	—	Money Market Instruments	**16m.u**
....	....	....	....	....	....	....	....	....	....	....	....	....	....	....	*o/w:* MMI Held by Resid.of Cty	**16m**
....	....	....	....	....	....	....	....	....	....	....	....	—	—	—	Bonds (Debt Securities)	**16n.u**
....	....	....	....	....	....	....	....	....	....	....	....	....	....	....	*o/w:* Bonds Held by Resid.of Cty	**16n**
.3	.2	.2	.2	.1	.2	.1	.2	.2	.1	1.3	....	1.58	.91	1.05	Foreign Liab. (to Non-EA Ctys)	**16c**
....	....	....	....	....	....	....	....	....	....	....	....	.01	.01	.03	Central Government Deposits	**16d.u**
.2	.2	.3	.2	.2	.2	.3	.3	.2	.3	.2	....	.01	.01	.03	*o/w:* Cent.Govt.Dep. in Cty	**16d**
55.1	60.3	54.1	55.0	61.1	67.0	79.5	74.4	81.6	98.9	122.5	....	10.13	10.15	10.53	Other Items (Net)	**17r**
....	....	....	....	....	....	....	....	....	....	....	....	–5.55	–3.84	3.04	*Memo: Net Claims on Eurosystem*	**12e.s**
....	....	....	....	....	....	....	....	....	....	....	....	....	....	....	*Currency Put into Circ.*	**14m**
Billions of Euros Beginning 1999: End of Period															**Banking Institutions**	
52.7	48.8	65.3	61.8	59.4	69.8	77.4	80.5	74.0	80.1	77.5	....	3.31	3.88	7.98	Claims on Monetary Authorities	**20**
....	....	....	....	....	....	....	....	....	....	....	....	31.09	38.65	44.68	Claims on Bk.Inst.in Oth.EA Ctys	**20b.u**
663.2	686.1	696.1	704.6	707.5	758.0	830.8	854.3	928.5	980.8	....	....	62.70	74.88	84.70	Fgn. Assets (Cl.on Non-EA Ctys)	**21**
....	....	....	....	....	....	....	....	....	....	....	....	52.98	51.74	48.79	Claims on General Government	**22a.u**
556.5	566.6	582.4	598.8	632.6	641.7	676.8	805.6	†833.1	823.9	783.4	....	49.93	48.56	43.70	*o/w:* Claims on Gen.Govt.in Cty	**22a**
....	....	....	....	....	....	....	....	....	....	....	....	208.22	227.10	240.17	Claims on Other Resident Sectors	**22d.u**
1,231.6	1,351.5	1,505.8	1,683.2	1,820.6	1,934.4	2,018.6	2,086.2	†2,228.8	2,376.9	2,595.9	....	197.02	212.99	223.70	*o/w:* Cl. on Oth.Res.Sect.in Cty	**22d**
....	....	....	....	....	....	....	....	....	....	....	....	44.60	45.05	51.04	Demand Deposits	**24..u**
120.5	133.5	132.4	140.6	152.5	162.0	181.2	201.1	244.0	255.2	273.5	....	42.15	42.69	48.41	*o/w:* D.Dep.of Oth.Res.Sect.in Cty	**24**
....	....	....	....	....	....	....	....	....	....	....	....	130.22	132.01	139.88	Other Deposits	**25..u**
1,083.0	1,139.7	1,234.3	1,363.9	1,465.1	1,567.3	1,643.1	1,721.0	1,770.9	1,812.1	1,840.7	....	123.21	124.96	132.13	*o/w:* O.Dep.of Oth.Res.Sect.in Cty	**25**
....	....	....	....	....	....	....	....	....	....	....	....	—	—	—	Money Market Instruments	**26m.u**
....	....	....	....	....	....	....	....	....	....	....	....	....	....	....	*o/w:* MMI Held by Resid.of Cty	**26m**
....	....	....	....	....	....	....	....	....	....	....	....	94.14	114.39	128.42	Bonds (Debt Securities)	**26n.u**
300.7	332.5	357.6	386.6	401.0	419.7	491.9	538.7	596.8	607.9	630.2	....	....	....	....	*o/w:* Bonds Held by Resid.of Cty	**26n**
702.5	746.0	779.2	793.4	818.5	879.1	899.7	924.9	1,000.2	1,125.4	....	....	49.19	53.66	66.40	Foreign Liab. (to Non-EA Ctys)	**26c**
....	....	....	....	....	....	....	....	....	....	....	....	1.61	1.90	3.26	Central Government Deposits	**26d.u**
73.6	59.1	63.8	58.4	77.9	59.6	55.2	74.0	77.4	77.7	69.7	....	1.61	1.90	3.25	*o/w:* Cent.Govt.Dep. in Cty	**26d**
71.8	70.2	75.4	79.3	77.4	70.8	64.0	62.0	47.6	47.2	74.2	....	5.19	7.50	1.98	Credit from Monetary Authorities	**26g**
....	....	....	....	....	....	....	....	....	....	....	....	27.81	31.89	28.08	Liab. to Bk.Inst.in Oth. EA Ctys	**26h.u**
110.6	128.5	147.4	165.7	180.1	194.7	211.4	226.6	238.4	254.7	275.7	....	25.50	27.25	29.28	Capital Accounts	**27a**
41.2	43.3	59.4	60.6	47.5	50.7	57.0	78.3	89.0	81.6	....	....	–19.96	–17.40	–22.02	Other Items (Net)	**27r**
Billions of Euros Beginning 1999: End of Period															**Banking Survey (Nat'l Residency)**	
84.2	71.9	57.5	48.2	36.4	56.3	142.6	146.6	165.1	123.6	....	....	42.55	56.15	71.27	Foreign Assets (Net)	**31n**
1,720.3	1,865.0	2,030.8	2,231.1	2,383.4	2,525.1	2,649.0	2,827.2	†2,993.8	3,133.4	3,321.0	....	246.41	260.79	265.50	Domestic Credit	**32**
488.7	513.5	525.0	547.9	562.8	590.8	630.5	740.9	†765.0	756.5	725.1	....	48.53	46.90	40.81	Claims on General Govt. (Net)	**32an**
1,231.6	1,351.5	1,505.8	1,683.2	1,820.6	1,934.4	2,018.6	2,086.2	†2,228.8	2,376.9	2,595.9	....	197.88	213.89	224.69	Claims on Other Resident Sectors	**32d**
102.9	108.4	117.8	124.7	133.4	141.2	149.8	158.3	168.6	176.7	178.8	....	13.96	14.58	10.72	Currency Issued	**34a.n**
120.5	133.5	132.4	140.6	152.5	162.0	181.2	201.1	244.0	255.2	273.5	....	42.16	42.70	48.42	Demand Deposits	**34b.n**
1,083.0	1,139.7	1,234.3	1,363.9	1,465.1	1,567.3	1,643.1	1,721.0	1,770.9	1,812.1	1,840.7	....	123.21	124.96	132.13	Other Deposits	**35..n**
....	....	....	....	....	....	....	....	....	....	....	....	—	—	—	Money Market Instruments	**36m**
300.7	332.5	357.6	386.6	401.0	419.7	491.9	538.7	596.8	607.9	630.2	....	94.14	114.39	128.42	Bonds (Debt Securities)	**36n**
....	....	....	....	....	....	....	....	....	....	....	....	87.95	104.01	118.54	*o/w:* Bonds Over Two Years	**36na**
197.4	222.7	246.2	263.4	267.8	291.2	325.7	354.7	378.6	405.1	....	....	15.49	20.31	17.08	Other Items (Net)	**37r**

Austria

		1972	1973	1974	1975	1976	1977	1978	1979	1980	1981	1982	1983	1984	1985	1986
Banking Survey (EA-Wide Residency)																*Billions of Euros:*
Foreign Assets (Net)	31n.*u*	...	...	...	...	...	...	...	...	...	...	...	...	...	...	...
Domestic Credit	32..*u*	...	...	...	...	...	...	...	...	...	...	...	...	...	...	...
Claims on General Govt. (Net)	32an*u*	...	...	...	...	...	...	...	...	...	...	...	...	...	...	...
Claims on Other Resident Sect.	32d.*u*	...	...	...	...	...	...	...	...	...	...	...	...	...	...	...
Currency Issued	34a.*u*	...	...	...	...	...	...	...	...	...	...	...	...	...	...	...
Demand Deposits	34b.*u*	...	...	...	...	...	...	...	...	...	...	...	...	...	...	...
Other Deposits	35..*u*	...	...	...	...	...	...	...	...	...	...	...	...	...	...	...
o/w: Other Dep. Over Two Yrs	35ab*u*	...	...	...	...	...	...	...	...	...	...	...	...	...	...	...
Money Market Instruments	36m.*u*	...	...	...	...	...	...	...	...	...	...	...	...	...	...	...
Bonds (Debt Securities)	36n.*u*	...	...	...	...	...	...	...	...	...	...	...	...	...	...	...
o/w: Bonds Over Two Years	36na*u*	...	...	...	...	...	...	...	...	...	...	...	...	...	...	...
Other Items (Net)	37r.*u*	...	...	...	...	...	...	...	...	...	...	...	...	...	...	...
Money (National Definitions)																*Billions of Schillings:*
Central Bank Money	19ma	70.32	69.83	78.85	92.26	98.63	104.05	119.11	†110.42	117.51	125.90	129.53	138.57	141.42	140.71	150.64
Extended Monetary Base	19mb												142.48	140.85	143.04	152.79
Money, M1	39m	102.06	108.29	114.05	134.30	146.98	153.66	165.63	†142.93	157.14	152.86	165.66	185.02	189.71	192.32	201.58
Interest Rates																*Percent Per Annum*
Discount Rate (*End of Period*)	60	5.50	5.50	6.50	6.00	4.00	5.50	4.50	3.75	6.75	6.75	4.75	3.75	4.50	4.00	4.00
Money Market Rate	60b	5.17	6.94	7.26	5.48	4.67	7.49	6.45	5.59	10.38	10.82	8.00	5.36	6.57	6.11	5.19
Deposit Rate	60l							5.00	5.00	5.00	5.00	5.00	4.21	4.00	3.94	3.63
Lending Rate	60p															
Government Bond Yield	61	7.37	8.25	9.74	9.61	8.75	8.74	8.21	7.96	9.24	10.61	9.92	8.17	8.02	7.77	7.33
Prices, Production, Labor																*Index Numbers (1995=100):*
Share Prices	62	31.0	36.5	34.5	34.3	34.8	32.5	30.5	31.0	32.0	28.6	25.5	27.6	28.4	54.3	67.9
Wholesale Prices	63	54.9	55.6	64.0	68.1	†72.0	74.2	74.9	78.1	84.8	91.6	94.5	95.1	98.7	101.2	†95.9
Consumer Prices	64	36.6	39.3	43.1	46.7	†50.1	52.9	54.7	56.8	60.4	64.5	68.0	70.2	74.2	76.6	†77.9
Harmonized CPI	64h															
Wages: Monthly Earnings	65	22.9	25.8	29.9	33.9	36.9	40.1	42.4	44.8	48.4	51.3	54.5	57.0	59.8	63.4	66.3
Wages (1996=100)	65a															
Industrial Production	66	54.5	57.4	60.0	56.3	†59.9	62.3	63.8	68.5	70.4	†69.6	69.1	69.2	73.3	76.5	†77.4
Employment	67	81.9	85.0	86.6	86.6	87.5	89.2	89.9	90.4	90.9	91.2	90.2	89.1	89.5	89.9	90.6
																Number in Thousands:
Labor Force	67d															
Employment	67e														3,235	3,282
Unemployment	67c														130	139	152
Unemployment Rate (%)	67r															5.2
International Transactions																*Billions of Schillings through 1998;*
Exports	70	89.75	101.98	133.36	130.88	152.11	161.78	176.11	206.25	226.17	251.77	266.86	277.14	314.50	353.97	342.48
Imports, c.i.f.	71	120.58	137.87	168.27	163.38	206.08	234.84	231.89	269.86	315.85	334.51	332.55	348.34	392.09	430.97	407.96
																1990=100
Volume of Exports	72	29.9	32.5	36.3	33.7	39.1	40.3	44.3	†50.1	51.5	54.1	54.7	57.1	62.5	68.8	69.3
Volume of Imports	73	36.4	40.2	41.3	38.5	47.4	52.0	51.2	†56.6	59.5	57.0	55.8	59.7	64.9	68.0	71.6
Export Prices	76	64.0	67.6	78.8	81.7	81.7	84.2	84.2	†87.7	92.1	97.7	102.1	101.8	105.4	107.3	104.8
Import Prices	76.x	60.9	63.1	75.2	78.0	79.7	82.7	82.6	†87.2	96.4	106.5	106.9	105.6	105.7	113.8	104.5
Balance of Payments																*Millions of US Dollars:*
Current Account, n.i.e.	78al *d*	−63	−238	−230	−744	−1,429	−2,801	−1,490	−1,954	−3,865	−3,042	703	276	−178	−158	204
Goods: Exports f.o.b.	78aa *d*	3,890	5,291	7,570	7,620	8,472	9,737	12,203	15,474	17,227	15,769	15,552	15,292	15,475	16,876	21,725
Goods: Imports f.o.b.	78ab *d*	−5,018	−6,865	−8,879	−9,587	−11,073	−13,602	−15,504	−19,753	−23,716	−20,713	−18,598	−18,464	−18,717	−20,012	−25,741
Trade Balance	78ac *d*	−1,128	−1,574	−1,309	−1,967	−2,602	−3,865	−3,301	−4,279	−6,489	−4,944	−3,046	−3,172	−3,242	−3,137	−4,016
Services: Credit	78ad *d*	2,207	3,017	3,150	3,729	4,359	5,211	6,632	8,166	9,423	8,198	9,557	9,613	9,240	9,697	12,561
Services: Debit	78ae *d*	−1,026	−1,455	−1,789	−2,223	−2,850	−3,670	−4,330	−5,386	−6,204	−5,752	−5,343	−5,715	−5,768	−6,389	−7,627
Balance on Goods & Services	78af *d*	53	−13	52	−461	−1,094	−2,323	−999	−1,500	−3,271	−2,499	1,169	726	229	171	918
Income: Credit	78ag *d*	169	256	530	598	614	724	974	1,551	2,502	3,168	3,147	2,598	2,876	3,194	3,783
Income: Debit	78ah *d*	−253	−390	−637	−735	−829	−1,062	−1,460	−2,035	−3,030	−3,631	−3,559	−2,966	−3,226	−3,448	−4,459
Balance on Gds, Serv. & Inc.	78ai *d*	−30	−147	−56	−598	−1,309	−2,661	−1,485	−1,984	−3,799	−2,962	757	359	−120	−83	242
Current Transfers, n.i.e.: Credit	78aj *d*	140	197	254	305	356	416	547	726	778	695	673	619	605	630	866
Current Transfers: Debit	78ak *d*	−172	−288	−428	−450	−475	−557	−552	−696	−844	−775	−726	−702	−663	−705	−903
Capital Account, n.i.e.	78bc *d*	−2	4	7	6	6	1	−4	−1	−22	−7	−20	2	−2	−17	−3
Capital Account, n.i.e.: Credit	78ba *d*	9	13	15	14	16	16	18	21	30	26	20	27	23	18	35
Capital Account: Debit	78bb *d*	−11	−9	−7	−8	−10	−15	−22	−22	−52	−33	−40	−25	−25	−35	−38
Financial Account, n.i.e.	78bj *d*	334	−148	667	1,191	766	1,719	1,769	−14	2,891	1,518	−862	−490	188	332	1,670
Direct Investment Abroad	78bd *d*	−38	−39	−20	−26	−56	−86	−90	−85	−101	−211	−139	−189	−70	−73	−317
Dir. Invest. in Rep. Econ., n.i.e.	78be *d*	145	161	177	79	91	97	142	187	239	328	208	216	115	173	187
Portfolio Investment Assets	78bf *d*	−84	−282	−26	−77	−133	−70	−63	−236	−126	−35	−47	−515	−779	−1,022	−491
Equity Securities	78bk *d*	−4	−44	−56	−6	−15	−2	−2	10	3	49	28	−58	−139	−71	−199
Debt Securities	78bl *d*	−79	−239	30	−72	−118	−68	−62	−246	−129	−84	−75	−457	−640	−951	−292
Portfolio Investment Liab., n.i.e.	78bg *d*	191	133	309	963	647	1,249	1,267	414	1,701	1,837	1,552	955	1,266	1,808	2,822
Equity Securities	78bm *d*	6	—	−1	5	2	−3	4	−14	10	−1	5	8	3	107	104
Debt Securities	78bn *d*	185	133	310	958	645	1,252	1,263	428	1,691	1,839	1,547	947	1,264	1,701	2,719
Financial Derivatives Assets	78bw *d*	...	...	...	...	...	...	...	...	...	...	...	...	...	...	...
Financial Derivatives Liabilities	78bx *d*	...	...	...	...	...	...	...	...	...	...	...	...	...	...	...
Other Investment Assets	78bh *d*	−550	−1,022	−512	−1,259	−1,604	−1,655	−2,315	−4,654	−5,090	−3,576	−3,938	−4,759	−4,658	−2,261	−1,695
Monetary Authorities	78bo *d*															
General Government	78bp *d*	−8	−29	−30	−10	−40	17	−43	−12	−286	208	−143	−106	−66	38	−143
Banks	78bq *d*	−547	−981	−474	−1,216	−1,535	−1,681	−1,885	−4,104	−4,399	−3,448	−3,467	−4,093	−3,730	−1,817	−1,475
Other Sectors	78br *d*	4	−12	−8	−32	−29	10	−387	−538	−405	−336	−328	−560	−863	−482	−78
Other Investment Liab., n.i.e.	78bi *d*	670	901	740	1,511	1,821	2,184	2,828	4,360	6,268	3,176	1,503	3,801	4,314	1,708	1,164
Monetary Authorities	78bs *d*	11	−15	−8	9	8	18	126	177	−262	−55	—	7	24	−58	7
General Government	78bt *d*	−69	−23	128	327	80	182	444	−101	58	358	359	95	148	−98	−353
Banks	78bu *d*	665	794	518	1,064	1,753	1,601	1,738	3,840	6,128	2,506	1,225	3,212	3,652	1,386	1,592
Other Sectors	78bv *d*	62	145	102	111	−20	382	520	445	344	366	−81	487	490	478	−82
Net Errors and Omissions	78ca *d*	96	210	−56	719	540	731	1,072	940	2,337	1,909	385	−315	60	−143	−1,228
Overall Balance	78cb *d*	365	−172	388	1,172	−116	−350	1,347	−1,029	1,341	379	207	−528	67	15	643
Reserves and Related Items	79da *d*	−365	172	−388	−1,172	116	350	−1,347	1,029	−1,341	−379	−207	528	−67	−15	−643
Reserve Assets	79db *d*	−365	172	−388	−1,172	116	350	−1,347	1,029	−1,341	−379	−207	528	−67	−15	−643
Use of Fund Credit and Loans	79dc *d*	—	—	—	—	—	—	—	—	—	—	—				
Exceptional Financing	79de *d*	...	...	...	...	...	...	...	...	...	...	...	...	...	...	...

1987	1988	1989	1990	1991	1992	1993	1994	1995	1996	1997	1998	1999	2000	2001	Item	Code
End of Period															**Banking Survey (EA-Wide Residency)**	
....	....	....	....	....	....	....	....	....	....	....	....	33.88	40.79	36.27	Foreign Assets (Net)	31n.*u*
....	....	....	....	....	....	....	....	....	....	....	....	263.33	280.41	289.44	Domestic Credit	32..*u*
....	....	....	....	....	....	....	....	....	....	....	....	52.79	50.89	46.94	Claims on General Govt. (Net)	32an*u*
....	....	....	....	....	....	....	....	....	....	....	....	210.55	229.52	242.49	Claims on Other Resident Sect.	32d.*u*
....	....	....	....	....	....	....	....	....	....	....	....	13.96	14.58	10.72	Currency Issued	34a.*u*
....	....	....	....	....	....	....	....	....	....	....	....	44.61	45.06	51.05	Demand Deposits	34b.*u*
....	....	....	....	....	....	....	....	....	....	....	....	130.22	132.01	139.88	Other Deposits	35..*u*
....	....	....	....	....	....	....	....	....	....	....	....	49.83	50.09	50.65	*o/w:* Other Dep. Over Two Yrs	35ab*u*
....	....	....	....	....	....	....	....	....	....	....	....	—	—	—	Money Market Instruments	36m.*u*
....	....	....	....	....	....	....	....	....	....	....	....	94.14	114.39	128.42	Bonds (Debt Securities)	36n.*u*
....	....	....	....	....	....	....	....	....	....	....	....	87.95	104.01	118.54	*o/w:* Bonds Over Two Years	36na*u*
....	....	....	....	....	....	....	....	....	....	....	....	14.28	15.17	–4.36	Other Items (Net)	37r.*u*
End of Period															**Money (National Definitions)**	
146.12	147.82	168.69	168.80	172.09	189.88	205.24	214.47	212.37	227.13	225.38	....	....	....	....	*Central Bank Money*	19ma
161.11	166.89	182.88	195.58	205.76	216.26	224.39	235.17	250.84	260.35	265.81	....	....	....	....	*Extended Monetary Base*	19mb
222.15	240.93	249.20	262.72	284.19	301.81	334.64	355.58	409.19	431.15	452.30	....	....	....	....	*Money, M1*	39m
Percent Per Annum															**Interest Rates**	
3.00	4.00	6.50	6.50	8.00	8.00	5.25	4.50	3.00	2.50	2.50	2.50	....	....	....	Discount Rate *(End of Period)*	60
4.35	4.59	7.46	8.53	9.10	9.35	7.22	5.03	4.36	3.19	3.27	3.36	....	....	....	Money Market Rate	60b
3.03	2.73	2.98	3.41	3.75	3.69	2.98	2.31	2.19	1.71	1.50	†2.65	2.21	....	....	Deposit Rate	60l
....	....	....	....	....	....	....	....	....	....	....	6.42	5.64	....	....	Lending Rate	60p
6.91	6.67	7.14	8.74	8.62	8.27	6.64	6.69	6.47	5.30	4.79	4.29	4.09	....	....	Government Bond Yield	61
Period Averages															**Prices, Production, Labor**	
57.8	54.8	94.9	154.0	131.2	103.0	100.9	115.3	100.0	105.2	119.9	135.2	....	....	....	Share Prices	62
94.0	93.8	95.4	98.2	99.0	98.8	98.4	99.7	100.0	†100.0	100.4	99.8	99.0	103.0	104.5	Wholesale Prices	63
79.0	80.5	82.6	85.3	88.1	91.7	95.0	97.8	100.0	†101.8	103.2	104.1	104.7	107.2	†110.0	Consumer Prices	64
....	....	....	....	....	....	....	....	100.0	101.8	103.0	103.8	104.3	106.4	108.8	Harmonized CPI	64h
68.4	70.9	74.1	79.4	83.5	87.5	92.1	95.8	100.0	....	....	....	....	....	....	Wages: Monthly Earnings	65
....	....	....	....	....	....	....	....	....	100.0	100.5	104.0	104.6	....	....	Wages (1996=100)	65a
77.8	81.3	86.3	92.8	†94.2	93.2	91.4	95.0	†100.0	100.9	107.8	118.1	123.7	132.6	132.3	Industrial Production	66
90.8	91.6	93.3	95.5	97.7	99.6	99.6	100.1	100.0	99.3	99.6	100.2	101.3	102.1	102.6	Employment	67
Period Averages																
....	....	....	....	3,607	3,679	3,734	3,881	....	3,870	3,884	3,888	....	3,915	....	Labor Force	67d
3,300	3,311	3,346	3,420	3,482	3,547	†3,055	3,742	3,759	3,710	3,719	3,723	3,762	3,777	....	Employment	67e
†164	159	149	166	185	193	222	215	216	231	233	238	222	194	204	Unemployment	67c
†5.6	5.3	5.0	5.4	5.8	5.9	6.8	6.5	6.6	7.0	7.1	7.2	6.7	5.8	6.1	Unemployment Rate (%)	67r
Billions of Euros Beginning 1999															**International Transactions**	
342.43	383.22	429.31	466.07	479.03	487.56	467.66	511.89	580.01	612.19	715.02	774.74	†60.27	69.69	74.45	Exports	70
411.85	451.44	514.69	556.23	591.90	593.92	565.56	629.42	668.03	712.76	790.25	842.13	†65.32	74.94	78.66	Imports, c.i.f.	71
1990=100																
71.1	†79.6	90.3	100.0	105.7	110.8	108.0	....	....	....	....	....	....	....	....	Volume of Exports	72
75.3	†81.5	90.1	100.0	101.3	106.6	105.8	....	....	....	....	....	....	....	....	Volume of Imports	73
102.2	†102.9	100.3	100.0	96.7	94.8	90.6	....	....	....	....	....	....	....	....	Export Prices	76
99.9	†99.9	102.6	100.0	100.2	98.8	95.5	....	....	....	....	....	....	....	....	Import Prices	76.x
Minus Sign Indicates Debit															Balance of Payments	
–263	–242	248	1,166	61	–753	–1,013	–2,992	–5,448	–4,890	–5,221	–5,258	–6,655	–4,864	–4,103	Current Account, n.i.e.	78al*d*
26,626	30,158	31,960	40,414	40,353	44,516	40,271	45,175	57,695	57,937	58,662	63,299	64,422	64,684	66,899	Goods: Exports f.o.b.	78aa*d*
–31,434	–34,922	–37,512	–47,383	–48,913	–52,205	–46,747	–53,089	–64,352	–65,252	–62,936	–66,983	–68,051	–67,421	–68,227	Goods: Imports f.o.b.	78ab*d*
–4,809	–4,765	–5,552	–6,969	–8,560	–7,690	–6,476	–7,914	–6,656	–7,315	–4,274	–3,684	–3,629	–2,737	–1,328	*Trade Balance*	78ac*d*
15,116	17,550	18,377	23,279	25,560	27,326	26,725	28,019	32,211	33,977	29,605	29,759	31,306	31,342	32,896	Services: Credit	78ad*d*
–9,635	–12,077	–11,527	–14,197	–15,333	–17,956	–19,186	–20,743	–27,703	–29,331	–28,569	–27,398	–29,421	–29,653	–31,535	Services: Debit	78ae*d*
672	708	1,298	2,114	1,667	1,680	1,064	–639	–2,149	–2,669	–3,239	–1,323	–1,745	–1,048	33	*Balance on Goods & Services*	78af*d*
4,484	5,324	6,789	9,145	9,544	6,998	7,237	7,074	8,900	9,852	10,393	9,957	12,673	11,992	12,297	Income: Credit	78ag*d*
–5,346	–6,243	–7,723	–10,087	–11,020	–8,414	–8,310	–8,344	–10,498	–10,291	–10,682	–11,958	–15,552	–14,456	–15,292	Income: Debit	78ah*d*
–190	–210	364	1,172	192	264	–9	–1,909	–3,746	–3,107	–3,527	–3,325	–4,624	–3,512	–2,962	*Balance on Gds, Serv. & Inc.*	78ai*d*
1,115	1,258	1,227	1,657	1,699	1,308	1,266	1,370	2,972	3,145	2,912	2,940	2,925	2,914	3,264	Current Transfers, n.i.e.: Credit	78aj*d*
–1,188	–1,289	–1,343	–1,663	–1,830	–2,326	–2,270	–2,453	–4,674	–4,928	–4,605	–4,874	–4,956	–4,267	–4,404	Current Transfers: Debit	78ak*d*
–7	–5	–12	8	55	–50	–448	–68	–62	78	26	–347	–265	–432	–514	Capital Account, n.i.e.	78bc*d*
36	40	50	63	152	247	246	676	540	591	590	483	555	530	485	Capital Account, n.i.e.: Credit	78ba*d*
–43	–44	–62	–55	–97	–297	–694	–744	–602	–513	–564	–831	–820	–962	–999	Capital Account: Debit	78bb*d*
1,035	415	1,367	–19	–12	2,378	3,970	4,311	7,365	5,325	1,666	9,535	4,789	3,407	1,809	Financial Account, n.i.e.	78bj*d*
–313	–310	–867	–1,701	–1,293	–1,693	–1,189	–1,256	–1,134	–1,848	–1,984	–2,794	–3,306	–5,599	–3,046	Direct Investment Abroad	78bd*d*
410	436	587	653	360	1,442	1,129	2,117	1,901	4,485	2,624	4,661	3,008	8,523	5,898	Dir. Invest. in Rep. Econ., n.i.e.	78be*d*
–1,185	–1,598	–1,559	–1,608	–2,272	–2,676	–1,912	–4,475	–2,836	–8,296	–10,157	–11,210	–29,216	–27,145	–11,867	Portfolio Investment Assets	78bf*d*
–274	–572	–524	–430	–60	–178	–618	–842	–545	–1,146	–2,405	–5,280	–5,281	–15,387	–996	Equity Securities	78bk*d*
–911	–1,026	–1,035	–1,178	–2,212	–2,498	–1,294	–3,633	–2,291	–7,150	–7,752	–5,930	–23,935	–11,757	–10,871	Debt Securities	78bl*d*
1,427	3,916	4,193	3,239	2,687	9,164	7,912	4,253	12,292	5,607	10,956	17,942	26,364	30,360	16,583	Portfolio Investment Liab., n.i.e.	78bg*d*
240	389	864	668	186	158	1,182	1,304	1,262	2,652	2,610	1,005	2,131	3,436	–4,441	Equity Securities	78bm*d*
1,188	3,528	3,329	2,571	2,501	9,006	6,729	2,949	11,030	2,955	8,345	16,937	24,232	26,924	21,024	Debt Securities	78bn*d*
....	....	....	....	....	7	–20	–85	–133	215	–191	303	–517	–441	–394	Financial Derivatives Assets	78bw*d*
....	....	....	....	....	....	....	....	....	....	223	–99	100	254	96	Financial Derivatives Liabilities	78bx*d*
–115	–2,522	–1,606	–1,433	–2,207	–7,301	–5,099	–2,545	–9,923	719	–5,208	–690	–11,592	–16,334	–6,172	Other Investment Assets	78bh*d*
....	....	....	....	....	....	....	–17	–131	131	—	–115	–3,561	1,760	539	Monetary Authorities	78bo*d*
92	–106	–24	–244	–331	259	70	–183	–231	324	–647	–512	331	–1,003	–284	General Government	78bp*d*
–270	–1,811	–720	–195	–1,144	–5,955	–5,176	–1,307	–10,848	2,292	–3,873	924	–5,242	–13,593	–5,904	Banks	78bq*d*
63	–604	–862	–994	–732	–1,605	7	–1,039	1,287	–2,027	–687	–988	–3,121	–3,498	–523	Other Sectors	78br*d*
811	493	618	831	2,714	3,434	3,149	6,303	7,199	4,442	5,403	1,423	19,948	13,790	712	Other Investment Liab., n.i.e.	78bi*d*
–12	–12	4	–3	4	—	—	—	—	—	—	–1	6,684	–647	–6,129	Monetary Authorities	78bs*d*
–327	–721	–402	–211	–36	242	–492	1,558	467	–715	–319	526	101	157	491	General Government	78bt*d*
1,271	749	384	721	2,781	1,887	3,088	4,584	6,077	5,142	5,695	1,695	10,740	11,721	6,207	Banks	78bu*d*
–121	478	631	325	–35	1,305	553	160	655	15	27	–797	2,422	2,559	143	Other Sectors	78bv*d*
–433	322	–613	–1,170	731	1,013	–308	–417	–464	562	476	–447	–40	1,143	919	Net Errors and Omissions	78ca*d*
333	491	990	–15	835	2,588	2,201	834	1,391	1,075	–3,053	3,482	–2,172	–746	–1,888	*Overall Balance*	78cb*d*
–333	–491	–990	15	–835	–2,588	–2,201	–834	–1,391	–1,075	3,053	–3,482	2,172	746	1,888	Reserves and Related Items	79da*d*
–333	–491	–990	15	–835	–2,588	–2,201	–834	–1,391	–1,075	3,053	–3,482	2,172	746	1,888	Reserve Assets	79db*d*
—	—	—	—	—	—	—	—	—	—	—	—	—	—	—	Use of Fund Credit and Loans	79dc*d*
....	....	....	....	....	....	....	....	....	....	....	....	....	....	....	Exceptional Financing	79de*d*

Austria

	1972	1973	1974	1975	1976	1977	1978	1979	1980	1981	1982	1983	1984	1985	1986
International Investment Position														*Millions of US Dollars*	
Assets .... 79aa d	....	....	....	....	....	....	....	....	36,355	36,298	38,086	37,553	37,646	57,767	73,093
Direct Investment Abroad .... 79ab d	....	....	....	....	....	....	....	....	530	634	676	756	716	1,343	1,430
Portfolio Investment .... 79ac d	....	....	....	....	....	....	....	....	1,892	1,617	1,618	1,600	2,058	3,889	5,405
Equity Securities .... 79ad d	....	....	....	....	....	....	....	....	477	368	321	327	407	602	985
Debt Securities .... 79ae d	....	....	....	....	....	....	....	....	1,415	1,250	1,297	1,273	1,651	3,287	4,420
Financial Derivatives .... 79al d									—	—	—	—	—	—	—
Other Investment .... 79af d	....	....	....	....	....	....	....	....	25,817	26,297	28,145	28,664	28,834	40,781	51,823
Monetary Authorities .... 79ag d	....	....	....	....	....	....	....	....							
General Government .... 79ah d	....	....	....	....	....	....	....	....	274	186	323	381	397	550	992
Banks .... 79ai d	....	....	....	....	....	....	....	....	21,762	22,509	24,290	24,915	25,415	34,531	45,018
Other Sectors .... 79aj d	....	....	....	....	....	....	....	....	3,781	3,601	3,531	3,368	3,023	5,700	5,813
Reserve Assets .... 79ak d	....	....	....	....	....	....	....	....	8,116	7,750	7,648	6,533	6,037	11,755	14,435
Liabilities .... 79la d	....	....	....	....	....	....	....	....	43,664	45,412	42,617	36,225	41,451	58,513	74,683
Dir. Invest. in Rep. Economy .... 79lb d	....	....	....	....	....	....	....	....	3,163	2,898	2,965	2,755	2,512	3,762	5,222
Portfolio Investment .... 79ld d	....	....	....	....	....	....	....	....	7,645	9,256	10,402	10,031	10,231	14,925	20,737
Equity Securities .... 79ld d	....	....	....	....	....	....	....	....	47	39	43	43	40	174	233
Debt Securities .... 79le d	....	....	....	....	....	....	....	....	7,598	9,216	10,360	9,988	10,191	14,751	20,503
Financial Derivatives .... 79ll d									—	—	—	—	—	—	—
Other Investment .... 79lf d	....	....	....	....	....	....	....	....	32,857	33,258	29,250	23,439	28,708	39,826	48,724
Monetary Authorities .... 79lg d	....	....	....	....	....	....	....	....	92	31	29	33	52		
General Government .... 79lh d	....	....	....	....	....	....	....	....	2,214	1,977	2,262	2,045	1,905	2,517	2,458
Banks .... 79li d	....	....	....	....	....	....	....	....	24,955	25,538	21,532	16,666	22,598	31,105	39,643
Other Sectors .... 79lj d	....	....	....	....	....	....	....	....	5,596	5,713	5,426	4,696	4,154	6,204	6,623
Government Finance															
Federal Government													*Billions of Schillings through 1998;*		
Deficit (-) or Surplus.................... 80	-.85	-8.96	-9.76	-26.34	-34.06	-30.21	-34.92	-35.31	-33.57	-32.52	-54.53	-71.84	-58.22	-63.33	-84.22
Revenue 81	141.63	163.39	189.04	204.75	225.96	253.31	288.56	315.84	221.83	245.76	255.81	270.91	299.83	307.22	321.39
Grants Received 81z	1.47	.58	.68	1.01	1.11	1.25	1.85	2.32	1.53	1.86	1.33	1.31	1.26	1.55	1.67
Expenditure 82	141.00	168.77	192.98	228.37	255.06	280.05	317.46	343.96	218.08	239.68	261.79	277.87	290.38	296.82	319.59
Lending Minus Repayments 83	2.95	4.16	6.50	3.73	6.07	4.72	7.87	9.51	9.36	7.05	9.04	12.47	10.70	9.99	13.29
Financing															
Net Borrowing 84	3.89	6.67	7.17	37.90	35.77	34.78	35.94	37.17	30.66	30.62	51.19	74.96	59.67	66.52	101.57
Domestic 84a	5.49	7.32	2.31	19.80	32.03	21.50	24.13	31.25	22.11	13.99	34.91	63.21	64.32	64.63	95.37
Foreign 85a	-1.60	-.65	4.86	18.10	3.74	13.28	11.81	5.92	8.54	16.63	16.28	11.75	-4.64	1.92	6.20
Use of Cash Balances 87	-3.04	2.29	2.59	-11.56	-1.71	-4.57	-1.02	-1.86	2.91	1.90	3.34	-3.12	-1.45	-3.19	-17.35
Debt: Domestic 88a	40.17	47.44	48.13	68.51	98.85	117.95	139.15	167.73	188.62	201.29	233.24	291.21	351.54	407.94	494.25
Foreign 89a	10.31	9.03	13.55	32.07	34.96	47.42	60.02	63.65	72.64	94.56	108.43	125.59	118.96	118.72	124.61
General Government														*As Percent of*	
Deficit (-) or Surplus.................... 80g	....	....	....	....	....	....	....	....	....	....	....	....	....	....	....
Debt 88g	....	....	....	....	....	....	....	....	....	....	....	....	....	....	....
National Accounts														*Billions of Schillings through 1998;*	
Househ.Cons.Expend.,incl.NPISHs 96f	259.8	291.8	330.6	368.3	418.6	466.8	477.5	519.6	559.8	605.5	657.6	717.0	744.8	783.7	814.0
Government Consumption Expend........ 91f	70.1	81.9	97.4	113.1	132.5	143.9	158.0	171.7	184.8	201.5	221.1	235.5	248.0	264.3	281.9
Gross Fixed Capital Formation 93e	144.9	155.0	175.7	174.9	168.5	193.0	187.2	207.5	230.9	243.1	237.5	246.1	252.1	275.5	288.4
Changes in Inventories 93i	2.0	12.8	16.9	-4.3	22.8	24.8	29.0	37.8	45.6	30.3	10.8	6.2	34.0	23.7	21.4
Exports of Goods and Services 90c	146.4	165.9	204.2	209.0	236.3	256.9	280.8	327.7	366.2	404.5	425.4	444.4	491.4	542.6	516.7
Imports of Goods and Services (-) 98c	143.7	163.9	206.3	204.8	247.3	278.4	280.4	331.6	385.7	418.5	406.9	428.4	489.6	539.9	504.0
Gross Domestic Product (GDP) 99b	479.6	543.5	618.6	656.1	742.1	820.9	866.8	945.9	1,016.1	1,081.7	1,161.2	1,237.4	1,299.0	1,369.1	1,439.0
Net Primary Income from Abroad 98.n	-2.7	-3.4	-3.0	-3.6	-5.0	-6.9	-8.4	-7.8	-8.4	-8.8	-8.4	-8.8	-8.6	-7.1	-11.9
Gross National Income (GNI) 99a	476.9	540.1	615.6	652.5	753.1	842.4	866.5	949.8	1,035.6	1,095.7	1,142.7	1,221.3	1,297.2	1,366.4	1,426.3
Consumption of Fixed Capital 99cf	56.2	62.4	71.5	77.4	555.6	610.6	647.8	709.2	758.6	801.8	861.3	917.9	952.6	1,008.9	1,064.2
GDP Volume 1964 prices 99b.p	338.0	355.8	371.0	364.8	385.8	....	....	....	....	....	....	....	....	....	....
GDP Volume 1983 Prices 99b.p	....	....	....	....	1,050.6	1,099.7	1,095.8	1,155.5	1,182.3	1,181.1	1,203.6	1,237.4	1,241.5	1,269.3	1,299.0
GDP Volume 1995 Prices 99b.p	....	....	....	....	....	....	....	....	....	....	....	....	....	....	....
GDP Volume (1995=100) .... 99bv p	56.5	59.5	62.0	61.0	64.5	67.5	67.3	70.9	72.6	72.5	73.9	76.0	76.2	77.9	79.8
GDP Deflator (1995=100)................... 99bi p	35.8	38.5	42.1	45.4	48.5	51.3	54.3	56.2	59.0	62.9	66.3	68.7	71.9	74.1	76.1
															Millions:
Population............................ 99z	7.49	7.53	7.53	†7.58	7.57	7.57	7.56	7.55	7.55	7.56	7.57	7.55	7.55	7.56	7.59

Millions of US Dollars

1987	1988	1989	1990	1991	1992	1993	1994	1995	1996	1997	1998	1999	2000	2001	International Investment Position	Code
90,627	85,186	94,658	108,096	111,913	117,479	122,090	137,955	160,211	161,785	166,135	194,856	225,924	257,188	....	Assets	79aa d
1,547	1,616	3,267	4,739	6,502	6,817	8,112	9,390	11,707	11,868	15,159	18,726	20,458	22,176	....	Direct Investment Abroad	79ab d
7,911	8,659	10,961	13,862	14,492	16,866	17,096	22,673	27,389	33,303	44,051	58,747	93,299	116,421	....	Portfolio Investment	79ac d
1,502	1,894	2,607	3,362	3,499	3,435	3,722	4,941	5,868	6,454	11,502	17,225	28,936	42,914	....	Equity Securities	79ad d
6,409	6,765	8,354	10,499	10,993	13,431	13,374	17,732	21,521	26,849	32,549	41,522	64,363	73,507	....	Debt Securities	79ae d
						74	109	169	219	201	—	—		....	Financial Derivatives	79al d
63,396	58,798	63,419	72,595	73,038	74,696	75,113	82,040	95,054	89,730	84,853	90,959	93,236	100,964	....	Other Investment	79af d
—	—	—	—	—	—	—	—	—	—	12	189	4,355	2,382	....	Monetary Authorities	79ag d
1,120	1,114	1,253	1,564	3,153	2,686	2,528	1,021	1,209	1,607	2,039	2,828	2,078	2,960	....	General Government	79ah d
55,138	50,879	54,515	61,328	61,821	62,780	62,645	70,380	83,267	77,716	73,651	77,267	74,447	81,310	....	Banks	79ai d
7,138	6,805	7,651	9,703	8,064	9,230	9,940	10,639	10,577	10,407	9,150	10,676	12,357	14,312	....	Other Sectors	79aj d
17,773	16,113	17,011	16,900	17,882	19,099	21,695	23,742	25,893	26,666	21,871	26,423	18,931	17,627	....	Reserve Assets	79ak d
93,867	89,733	98,358	114,967	123,342	127,955	133,600	155,538	189,790	189,264	198,918	236,547	262,994	289,670	....	Liabilities	79la d
6,960	7,107	8,261	10,237	11,058	11,221	11,398	13,246	17,536	18,258	19,694	23,837	23,991	28,928	....	Dir. Invest. in Rep. Economy	79lb d
26,613	28,205	33,322	41,538	48,031	55,813	61,896	69,469	89,473	87,676	97,091	121,674	139,054	155,187	....	Portfolio Investment	79lc d
293	517	1,244	1,976	2,545	2,633	3,591	5,379	6,989	9,056	15,662	15,623	14,745	15,345	....	Equity Securities	79ld d
26,320	27,688	32,078	39,562	45,486	53,179	58,305	64,090	82,484	78,620	81,430	106,052	124,309	139,842	....	Debt Securities	79le d
—	—	—	—	—	—	—	—	129	110	12	—			....	Financial Derivatives	79ll d
60,293	54,421	56,775	63,192	64,253	60,921	60,306	72,705	82,653	83,221	82,121	91,036	99,949	105,555	....	Other Investment	79lf d
—	—	—	—	—	—	—	18	20	9	—		6,141	4,778	....	Monetary Authorities	79lg d
2,640	1,759	999	721	1,413	1,409	1,359	3,045	4,074	3,478	2,955	3,719	3,564	3,509	....	General Government	79lh d
49,120	44,282	47,059	51,990	52,793	50,167	49,543	57,681	65,385	68,267	68,669	76,438	79,628	85,422	....	Banks	79li d
8,533	8,380	8,718	10,480	10,048	9,345	9,405	11,961	13,174	11,466	10,496	10,879	10,616	11,846	....	Other Sectors	79lj d

Government Finance

Millions of Euros Beginning 1999: Year Ending December 31

Federal Government

1987	1988	1989	1990	1991	1992	1993	1994	1995	1996	1997	1998	1999	2000	2001		Code
-81.55	-78.40	-62.84	-80.89	-89.06	-75.48	-107.14	-128.81	....	....	....	....	....	....		Deficit (-) or Surplus	80
333.68	365.43	380.25	626.21	676.73	747.39	777.75	815.10	†859.52	903.03	951.21	979.97	....	....		Revenue	81
1.16	1.50	1.76	3.19	4.36	3.45	3.59	4.03	†23.93	16.36	6.14	8.46	....	....		Grants Received	81z
330.00	344.44	354.01	691.73	749.61	805.16	875.99	917.14	†993.55	1,013.35	978.86	1,058.29	....	....		Expenditure	82
3.40	7.44	-.88	18.56	20.54	21.16	12.49	30.80	....							Lending Minus Repayments	83

Financing

1987	1988	1989	1990	1991	1992	1993	1994	1995	1996	1997	1998	1999	2000	2001		Code
87.33	63.26	70.08	74.60	86.81	68.09	107.42	136.38	....	....	....	....				Net Borrowing	84
89.86	57.61	66.25	65.68	73.36	46.73	82.11	89.13	....							Domestic	84a
-2.53	5.65	3.83	8.92	13.45	21.36	25.31	47.25	....							Foreign	85a
-5.78	15.14	-7.24	6.29	2.25	7.39	-.28	-7.57	....							Use of Cash Balances	87
573.81	617.25	677.00	731.80	797.15	828.70	899.56	975.25	†1053.73	1,120.66	1,190.76	†1384.46	....			Debt: Domestic	88a
124.74	130.80	125.83	135.36	148.46	172.14	212.86	260.94	†296.63	296.47	304.93	†188.43	....			Foreign	89a

Gross Domestic Product

General Government

1987	1988	1989	1990	1991	1992	1993	1994	1995	1996	1997	1998	1999	2000	2001		Code
....	....	....	-2.4	-3.0	-2.0	-4.2	-5.0	-5.1	-3.8	-1.7	-2.4	-2.2	-1.5	.1	Deficit (-) or Surplus	80g
....	....	....	57.9	58.1	58.0	62.7	65.4	69.4	68.3	64.7	63.9	64.9	63.6	61.7	Debt	88g

National Accounts

Billions of Euros Beginning 1999

1987	1988	1989	1990	1991	1992	1993	1994	1995	1996	1997	1998	1999	2000	2001		Code
843.9	886.0	943.3	1,013.0	1,073.0	1,147.7	1,194.1	1,255.1	†1,331.3	1,400.6	1,440.9	1,490.2	†112.3	116.8	121.1	Househ.Cons.Expend.,incl.NPISHs	96f
292.5	302.5	319.6	338.1	367.8	398.3	429.6	455.0	†484.6	497.2	494.5	513.4	†38.7	39.7	40.6	Government Consumption Expend.	91f
306.7	331.3	362.2	397.9	440.3	455.4	455.2	501.6	†552.2	571.2	589.8	615.1	†45.8	48.5	48.1	Gross Fixed Capital Formation	93e
24.4	14.9	11.5	17.0	22.0	8.2	2.7	-1.1	3.8	.5	41.4	47.4	....			Changes in Inventories	93i
522.9	590.8	669.6	728.3	774.7	791.6	786.5	838.8	†903.7	969.9	1,074.3	1,137.7	†89.6	102.7	110.0	Exports of Goods and Services	90c
517.5	582.6	653.4	704.9	758.0	772.0	772.6	843.0	†922.7	997.3	1,113.1	1,153.3	†91.3	104.6	110.8	Imports of Goods and Services (-)	98c
1,494.1	1,565.8	1,676.7	1,813.5	1,945.8	2,057.3	2,125.3	2,237.9	†2,370.7	2,450.0	2,513.5	2,614.7	†196.6	204.8	210.7	Gross Domestic Product (GDP)	99b
-12.9	-8.5	-8.9	-7.3	-13.1	-9.7	-9.4	-8.3	-7.7	-7.6	-3.3	-2.4	....			Net Primary Income from Abroad	98.n
1,488.6	1,557.6	1,660.5	1,790.0	1,929.1	2,037.6	2,111.4	2,242.1	2,338.3	2,428.9	2,528.8	2,617.9	....			Gross National Income (GNI)	99a
1,101.1	194.1	1,239.2	1,351.4	1,452.3	1,532.1	1,573.5	1,641.6	1,716.3	1,763.5	1,828.6	1,897.4	....			Consumption of Fixed Capital	99cf
								....	....	....	....				GDP Volume 1964 prices	99b.p
1,320.9	1,362.7	1,420.3	1,485.0	1,535.8	1,556.4	1,564.4	1,601.7	†1,628.7	....						GDP Volume 1983 Prices	99b.p
....	....	....	....	....	....	....	....	2,370.7	2,418.2	2,450.5	2,530.2	†189.1	195.4	197.6	GDP Volume 1995 Prices	99b.p
81.1	83.7	87.2	91.2	94.3	95.6	96.1	98.3	100.0	102.0	103.4	106.7	†109.7	113.4	114.7	GDP Volume (1995=100)	99bv.p
77.7	78.9	81.1	83.9	87.0	90.8	93.3	96.0	†100.0	101.3	102.6	103.3	†104.0	104.8	106.6	GDP Deflator (1995=100)	99bi.p

Midyear Estimates

1987	1988	1989	1990	1991	1992	1993	1994	1995	1996	1997	1998	1999	2000	2001		Code
7.60	7.62	7.66	7.73	7.81	7.91	7.99	8.03	8.05	8.06	8.07	8.08	8.09	8.11	8.08	Population	99z

(See notes in the back of the book.)

Azerbaijan

912

		1972	1973	1974	1975	1976	1977	1978	1979	1980	1981	1982	1983	1984	1985	1986
Exchange Rates																*Manats per SDR:*
Official Rate	aa	...	...	...	...	...	...	...	...	...	...	...	...	...	...	...
																Manats per US Dollar:
Official Rate	ae	...	...	...	...	...	...	...	...	...	...	...	...	...	...	...
Official Rate	rf	...	...	...	...	...	...	...	...	...	...	...	...	...	...	...
Fund Position																*Millions of SDRs:*
Quota	2f. s	...	...	...	...	...	...	...	...	...	...	...	...	...	...	...
SDRs	1b. s	...	...	...	...	...	...	...	...	...	...	...	...	...	...	...
Reserve Position in the Fund	1c. s	...	...	...	...	...	...	...	...	...	...	...	...	...	...	...
Total Fund Cred.&Loans Outstg.	2tl	...	...	...	...	...	...	...	...	...	...	...	...	...	...	...
International Liquidity														*Millions of US Dollars Unless Otherwise Indicated:*		
Total Reserves minus Gold	1l. d	...	...	...	...	...	...	...	...	...	...	...	...	...	...	...
SDRs	1b. d	...	...	...	...	...	...	...	...	...	...	...	...	...	...	...
Reserve Position in the Fund	1c. d	...	...	...	...	...	...	...	...	...	...	...	...	...	...	...
Foreign Exchange	1d. d	...	...	...	...	...	...	...	...	...	...	...	...	...	...	...
Gold (Million Fine Troy Ounces)	1ad	...	...	...	...	...	...	...	...	...	...	...	...	...	...	...
Gold (National Valuation)	1an d	...	...	...	...	...	...	...	...	...	...	...	...	...	...	...
Monetary Authorities: Other Assets	3.. d	...	...	...	...	...	...	...	...	...	...	...	...	...	...	...
Other Liab.	4.. d	...	...	...	...	...	...	...	...	...	...	...	...	...	...	...
Deposit Money Banks: Assets	7a. d	...	...	...	...	...	...	...	...	...	...	...	...	...	...	...
Liabilities	7b. d	...	...	...	...	...	...	...	...	...	...	...	...	...	...	...
Monetary Authorities																*Billions of Manats:*
Foreign Assets	11	...	...	...	...	...	...	...	...	...	...	...	...	...	...	...
Claims on Central Government	12a	...	...	...	...	...	...	...	...	...	...	...	...	...	...	...
Claims on Nonfin.Pub.Enterprises	12c	...	...	...	...	...	...	...	...	...	...	...	...	...	...	...
Claims on Deposit Money Banks	12e	...	...	...	...	...	...	...	...	...	...	...	...	...	...	...
Reserve Money	14	...	...	...	...	...	...	...	...	...	...	...	...	...	...	...
of which: Currency Outside DMBs	14a	...	...	...	...	...	...	...	...	...	...	...	...	...	...	...
Time, Savings,& Fgn.Currency Dep.	15	...	...	...	...	...	...	...	...	...	...	...	...	...	...	...
Foreign Liabilities	16c	...	...	...	...	...	...	...	...	...	...	...	...	...	...	...
Central Government Deposits	16d	...	...	...	...	...	...	...	...	...	...	...	...	...	...	...
Capital Accounts	17a	...	...	...	...	...	...	...	...	...	...	...	...	...	...	...
Other Items (Net)	17r	...	...	...	...	...	...	...	...	...	...	...	...	...	...	...
Deposit Money Banks																*Billions of Manats:*
Reserves	20	...	...	...	...	...	...	...	...	...	...	...	...	...	...	...
Foreign Assets	21	...	...	...	...	...	...	...	...	...	...	...	...	...	...	...
Claims on Central Government	22a	...	...	...	...	...	...	...	...	...	...	...	...	...	...	...
Claims on Nonfin.Pub.Enterprises	22c	...	...	...	...	...	...	...	...	...	...	...	...	...	...	...
Claims on Private Sector	22d	...	...	...	...	...	...	...	...	...	...	...	...	...	...	...
Claims on Nonbank Financial Insts.	22g	...	...	...	...	...	...	...	...	...	...	...	...	...	...	...
Demand Deposits	24	...	...	...	...	...	...	...	...	...	...	...	...	...	...	...
Time,Savings,& Fgn.Currency Dep.	25	...	...	...	...	...	...	...	...	...	...	...	...	...	...	...
Restricted Deposits	26b	...	...	...	...	...	...	...	...	...	...	...	...	...	...	...
Foreign Liabilities	26c	...	...	...	...	...	...	...	...	...	...	...	...	...	...	...
Central Government Deposits	26d	...	...	...	...	...	...	...	...	...	...	...	...	...	...	...
Credit from Monetary Authorities	26g	...	...	...	...	...	...	...	...	...	...	...	...	...	...	...
Liab. to Nonbank Financial Insts	26j	...	...	...	...	...	...	...	...	...	...	...	...	...	...	...
Capital Accounts	27a	...	...	...	...	...	...	...	...	...	...	...	...	...	...	...
Other Items (Net)	27r	...	...	...	...	...	...	...	...	...	...	...	...	...	...	...
Monetary Survey																*Billions of Manats:*
Foreign Assets (Net)	31n	...	...	...	...	...	...	...	...	...	...	...	...	...	...	...
Domestic Credit	32	...	...	...	...	...	...	...	...	...	...	...	...	...	...	...
Claims on Central Govt. (Net)	32an	...	...	...	...	...	...	...	...	...	...	...	...	...	...	...
Claims on Nonfin.Pub.Enterprises	32c	...	...	...	...	...	...	...	...	...	...	...	...	...	...	...
Claims on Private Sector	32d	...	...	...	...	...	...	...	...	...	...	...	...	...	...	...
Claims on Nonbank Fin. Insts	32g	...	...	...	...	...	...	...	...	...	...	...	...	...	...	...
Money	34	...	...	...	...	...	...	...	...	...	...	...	...	...	...	...
Quasi-Money	35	...	...	...	...	...	...	...	...	...	...	...	...	...	...	...
Restricted Deposits	36b	...	...	...	...	...	...	...	...	...	...	...	...	...	...	...
Liab. to Nonbank Financial Insts	36j	...	...	...	...	...	...	...	...	...	...	...	...	...	...	...
Capital Accounts	37a	...	...	...	...	...	...	...	...	...	...	...	...	...	...	...
Other Items (Net)	37r	...	...	...	...	...	...	...	...	...	...	...	...	...	...	...
Money plus Quasi-Money	35l	...	...	...	...	...	...	...	...	...	...	...	...	...	...	...
Money (National Definitions)																*Billions of Manats:*
Reserve Money	19ma	...	...	...	...	...	...	...	...	...	...	...	...	...	...	...
M1	59ma	...	...	...	...	...	...	...	...	...	...	...	...	...	...	...
M2	59mb	...	...	...	...	...	...	...	...	...	...	...	...	...	...	...
Interest Rates																*Percent Per Annum*
Refinancing Rate	60	...	...	...	...	...	...	...	...	...	...	...	...	...	...	...
Treasury Bill Rate	60c	...	...	...	...	...	...	...	...	...	...	...	...	...	...	...
Deposit Rate	60l	...	...	...	...	...	...	...	...	...	...	...	...	...	...	...
Deposit Rate (Foreign Currency)	60l. f	...	...	...	...	...	...	...	...	...	...	...	...	...	...	...
Lending Rate	60p	...	...	...	...	...	...	...	...	...	...	...	...	...	...	...
Lending Rate (Foreign Currency)	60p. f	...	...	...	...	...	...	...	...	...	...	...	...	...	...	...
Prices and Labor																*Percent Change over*
Consumer Prices	64.xx	...	...	...	...	...	...	...	...	...	...	...	...	...	...	...
																Number in Thousands:
Employment	67e	...	...	...	...	...	...	...	...	...	...	...	...	...	...	...
Unemployment	67c	...	...	...	...	...	...	...	...	...	...	...	...	...	...	...
Unemployment Rate (%)	67r	...	...	...	...	...	...	...	...	...	...	...	...	...	...	...

1987	1988	1989	1990	1991	1992	1993	1994	1995	1996	1997	1998	1999	2000	2001		
															Exchange Rates	
End of Period																
				….	66.83	162.08	6,105.09	6,600.02	5,892.76	5,245.88	5,477.24	6,008.85	5,947.78	6,000.89	Official Rate	**aa**
End of Period (ae) Period Average (rf)																
					48.60	118.00	4,182.00	4,440.00	4,098.00	3,888.00	3,890.00	4,378.00	4,565.00	4,775.00	Official Rate	**ae**
					54.20	99.98	1,570.23	4,413.54	4,301.26	3,985.38	3,869.00	4,120.17	4,474.15	4,656.58	Official Rate	**rf**
End of Period															**Fund Position**	
					78.00	117.00	117.00	117.00	117.00	117.00	117.00	160.90	160.90	160.90	Quota	**2f. s**
					—	—	—	.84	14.48	4.14	.08	5.15	5.07	1.98	SDRs	**1b. s**
					—	.01	.01	.01	.01	.01	.01	.01	.01	.01	Reserve Position in the Fund	**1c. s**
					—	—	—	67.86	121.68	197.73	228.14	296.73	257.73	234.90	Total Fund Cred.&Loans Outstg.	**2tl**
End of Period															**International Liquidity**	
					—	.59	2.03	120.88	211.28	466.09	447.33	672.59	679.61	896.70	Total Reserves minus Gold	**1l. d**
					—	—	—	1.25	20.82	5.59	.11	7.07	6.60	2.49	SDRs	**1b. d**
					—	.01	.01	.01	.01	.01	.01	.01	.01	.01	Reserve Position in the Fund	**1c. d**
					—	.58	2.02	119.62	190.45	460.49	447.20	665.50	672.99	894.20	Foreign Exchange	**1d. d**
					—	—	—	—	—	—	—	—	—	—	Gold (Million Fine Troy Ounces)	**1ad**
					—	—	—	—	2.38	1.38	1.37	—	—	—	Gold (National Valuation)	**1an d**
					80.06	54.28	1.93	1.57	1.91	1.53	1.16	1.03	.05	—	Monetary Authorities: Other Assets	**3.. d**
					124.66	63.09	2.87	1.75	1.33	1.37	13.28	12.34	12.01	.30	Other Liab.	**4.. d**
					66.15	257.48	135.30	167.69	156.17	154.48	97.27	152.11	379.46	193.13	Deposit Money Banks: Assets	**7a. d**
					96.79	152.74	41.05	33.95	75.89	53.16	56.08	69.32	96.54	92.58	Liabilities	**7b. d**
End of Period															**Monetary Authorities**	
					3.89	6.47	16.59	543.70	883.38	1,823.46	†1739.58	2,948.81	3,102.63	†4270.19	Foreign Assets	**11**
					2.42	25.73	428.87	333.46	416.73	360.26	†1903.93	2,563.34	2,518.48	†790.17	Claims on Central Government	**12a**
					.19	.13	1.02	8.48	8.93	8.76	†3.50	3.44	—	†—	Claims on Nonfin.Pub.Enterprises	**12c**
					2.63	23.93	141.69	1,052.40	893.67	865.45	†750.15	746.24	701.25	†101.00	Claims on Deposit Money Banks	**12e**
					2.97	43.84	325.69	911.14	1,071.06	1,514.08	†1181.57	1,369.42	1,767.31	†1797.40	Reserve Money	**14**
					2.72	43.18	276.13	602.40	865.44	1,170.51	†926.05	1,135.84	1,349.81	†1468.99	of which: Currency Outside DMBs	**14a**
					—	—	.88	—	.03	.04	†—	—	—	†2.05	Time, Savings,& Fgn.Currency Dep.	**15**
					6.06	7.44	12.02	455.63	722.52	1,042.60	†1301.25	1,837.03	1,587.77	†1411.05	Foreign Liabilities	**16c**
					.29	5.75	235.86	447.68	334.46	367.65	†1817.21	2,837.37	2,556.29	†1488.12	Central Government Deposits	**16d**
					.09	4.08	44.87	405.19	400.30	1,128.62	†196.15	240.35	333.32	†368.47	Capital Accounts	**17a**
					-.28	-4.85	-31.14	-281.61	-325.66	-995.06	†-99.02	-22.34	77.67	†94.28	Other Items (Net)	**17r**
End of Period															**Deposit Money Banks**	
					.98	6.65	43.89	303.17	242.76	301.94	204.07	177.85	†391.51	†318.49	Reserves	**20**
					3.21	30.38	565.81	744.55	639.97	600.62	378.37	665.95	†1732.24	†922.21	Foreign Assets	**21**
					1.69	.33	51.49	12.49	32.03	52.69	30.04	69.44	†275.99	†324.61	Claims on Central Government	**22a**
					13.95	53.43	623.57	1,403.59	1,719.82	1,635.51	1,658.84	1,722.20	†817.62	†496.61	Claims on Nonfin.Pub.Enterprises	**22c**
					2.61	15.08	62.46	126.52	159.32	386.81	530.06	559.69	†1391.76	†1327.53	Claims on Private Sector	**22d**
					.01	.02	.06	—	—	—	—	—	†3.24	†1.97	Claims on Nonbank Financial Insts.	**22g**
					3.29	22.00	93.70	251.29	250.08	323.80	203.02	215.83	†218.21	†218.73	Demand Deposits	**24**
					3.23	20.59	674.36	455.53	418.73	651.71	662.47	826.07	†2273.28	†1743.55	Time,Savings,& Fgn.Currency Dep.	**25**
					—	—	—	—	—	—	—	†—	†152.01		Restricted Deposits	**26b**
					4.70	18.02	171.66	150.75	311.00	206.69	218.15	303.46	†440.72	†442.07	Foreign Liabilities	**26c**
					4.70	7.19	101.60	98.20	222.31	30.20	82.23	84.95	†185.40	†51.27	Central Government Deposits	**26d**
					3.99	27.06	56.53	893.23	782.36	838.02	615.87	592.89	†654.22	†96.45	Credit from Monetary Authorities	**26g**
					.06	.20	.45	2.84	7.44	6.84	5.55	2.17	†—	†15.87	Liab. to Nonbank Financial Insts	**26j**
					1.16	12.84	121.45	355.30	640.98	831.83	1,020.01	1,152.11	†732.21	†670.34	Capital Accounts	**27a**
					1.32	-2.02	127.51	383.18	160.99	88.51	-5.92	17.67	†108.32	†1.15	Other Items (Net)	**27r**
End of Period															**Monetary Survey**	
					-3.66	11.39	398.73	681.87	489.83	1,174.80	†598.55	1,474.27	†2806.39	†3339.29	Foreign Assets (Net)	**31n**
					15.88	81.77	830.00	1,338.66	1,780.06	2,046.19	†2226.93	1,995.80	†2265.39	†1401.51	Domestic Credit	**32**
					-.88	13.12	142.89	-199.93	-108.00	15.11	†34.53	-289.53	†52.78	†-424.60	Claims on Central Govt. (Net)	**32an**
					14.14	53.56	624.59	1,412.07	1,728.75	1,644.27	†1662.34	1,725.64	†817.62	†496.61	Claims on Nonfin.Pub.Enterprises	**32c**
					2.61	15.08	62.46	126.52	159.32	386.81	†530.06	559.69	†1391.76	†1327.53	Claims on Private Sector	**32d**
					.01	.02	.06	—	—	—	†—	—	†3.24	†1.97	Claims on Nonbank Fin. Insts	**32g**
					6.07	65.52	372.38	858.38	1,119.74	1,524.08	†1183.26	1,390.08	†1569.81	†1693.10	Money	**34**
					3.24	20.59	675.23	455.53	418.76	651.75	†662.47	826.07	†2273.28	†1745.60	Quasi-Money	**35**
					—	—	—	—	—	—	†—	—	†—	†152.01	Restricted Deposits	**36b**
					.06	.20	.45	2.84	7.44	6.84	5.55	2.17	†—	†15.87	Liab. to Nonbank Financial Insts	**36j**
					1.24	16.92	166.33	760.50	1,041.28	1,960.45	†1216.16	1,392.46	†1065.53	†1038.81	Capital Accounts	**37a**
					1.62	-10.07	14.34	-56.72	-317.33	-922.14	†-241.95	-140.72	†163.16	†95.42	Other Items (Net)	**37r**
					9.30	86.11	1,047.62	1,313.92	1,538.50	2,175.83	†1845.73	2,216.15	†3843.09	†3438.71	Money plus Quasi-Money	**35l**
End of Period															**Money (National Definitions)**	
					….	….	….	736.30	985.40	1,339.30	1,057.10	1,256.60	1,541.90	1,680.60	*Reserve Money*	**19ma**
								924.99	1,173.68	1,537.82	1,202.45	1,390.04	1,609.50	1,469.00	*M1*	**59ma**
								957.59	1,204.18	1,556.27	1,218.50	1,404.32	1,661.10	1,687.50	*M2*	**59mb**
Percent Per Annum															**Interest Rates**	
					12.00	100.00	200.00	80.00	20.00	12.00	14.00	10.00	10.00	10.00	Refinancing Rate	**60**
					….	….	….	….	….	12.23	14.10	18.31	16.73	16.51	Treasury Bill Rate	**60c**
												12.08	12.90	8.46	Deposit Rate	**60l**
												10.75	11.12	9.51	Deposit Rate (Foreign Currency)	**60l. f**
												19.48	19.66	19.71	Lending Rate	**60p**
												16.27	17.98	18.67	Lending Rate (Foreign Currency)	**60p. f**
Previous Period															**Prices and Labor**	
					912.3	1,129.0	1,664.5	411.7	19.8	3.6	-.7	-8.6	1.8	1.5	Consumer Prices	**64.xx**
Period Averages																
					2,922.1	2,916.6	2,851.3	2,837.3	2,895.4	2,900.0	….	….	….	….	Employment	**67e**
					….	19.5	23.6	28.3	31.9	38.3	42.3	45.2	43.7	….	Unemployment	**67c**
					….	.5	.7	.8	.9	1.0	1.1	1.2	1.2	….	Unemployment Rate (%)	**67r**

Azerbaijan

912

		1972	1973	1974	1975	1976	1977	1978	1979	1980	1981	1982	1983	1984	1985	1986
International Transactions																*Millions of US Dollars*
Exports	70..d	....	....	....	....	....	....	....	....	....	....	....	....	....	....	....
Imports, cif	71..d	....	....	....	....	....	....	....	....	....	....	....	....	....	....	....
Balance of Payments																*Millions of US Dollars:*
Current Account, n.i.e.	78ald	....	....	....	....	....	....	....	....	....	....	....	....	....	....	....
Goods: Exports f.o.b	78aad	....	....	....	....	....	....	....	....	....	....	....	....	....	....	....
Goods: Imports f.o.b	78abd	....	....	....	....	....	....	....	....	....	....	....	....	....	....	....
Trade Balance	78acd	....	....	....	....	....	....	....	....	....	....	....	....	....	....	....
Services: Credit	78add	....	....	....	....	....	....	....	....	....	....	....	....	....	....	....
Services: Debit	78aed	....	....	....	....	....	....	....	....	....	....	....	....	....	....	....
Balance on Goods & Services	78afd	....	....	....	....	....	....	....	....	....	....	....	....	....	....	....
Income: Credit	78agd	....	....	....	....	....	....	....	....	....	....	....	....	....	....	....
Income: Debit	78ahd	....	....	....	....	....	....	....	....	....	....	....	....	....	....	....
Balance on Gds, Serv., & Inc.	78aid	....	....	....	....	....	....	....	....	....	....	....	....	....	....	....
Current Transfers, n.i.e.: Credit	78ajd	....	....	....	....	....	....	....	....	....	....	....	....	....	....	....
Current Transfers: Debit	78akd	....	....	....	....	....	....	....	....	....	....	....	....	....	....	....
Capital Account, n.i.e.	78bcd	....	....	....	....	....	....	....	....	....	....	....	....	....	....	....
Capital Account, n.i.e.: Credit	78bad	....	....	....	....	....	....	....	....	....	....	....	....	....	....	....
Capital Account: Debit	78bbd	....	....	....	....	....	....	....	....	....	....	....	....	....	....	....
Financial Account, n.i.e.	78bjd	....	....	....	....	....	....	....	....	....	....	....	....	....	....	....
Direct Investment Abroad	78bdd	....	....	....	....	....	....	....	....	....	....	....	....	....	....	....
Dir. Invest. in Rep. Econ., n.i.e.	78bed	....	....	....	....	....	....	....	....	....	....	....	....	....	....	....
Portfolio Investment Assets	78bfd	....	....	....	....	....	....	....	....	....	....	....	....	....	....	....
Equity Securities	78bkd	....	....	....	....	....	....	....	....	....	....	....	....	....	....	....
Debt Securities	78bld	....	....	....	....	....	....	....	....	....	....	....	....	....	....	....
Portfolio Investment Liab., n.i.e.	78bgd	....	....	....	....	....	....	....	....	....	....	....	....	....	....	....
Equity Securities	78bmd	....	....	....	....	....	....	....	....	....	....	....	....	....	....	....
Debt Securities	78bnd	....	....	....	....	....	....	....	....	....	....	....	....	....	....	....
Financial Derivatives Assets	78bwd	....	....	....	....	....	....	....	....	....	....	....	....	....	....	....
Financial Derivatives Liabilities	78bxd	....	....	....	....	....	....	....	....	....	....	....	....	....	....	....
Other Investment Assets	78bhd	....	....	....	....	....	....	....	....	....	....	....	....	....	....	....
Monetary Authorities	78bod	....	....	....	....	....	....	....	....	....	....	....	....	....	....	....
General Government	78bpd	....	....	....	....	....	....	....	....	....	....	....	....	....	....	....
Banks	78bqd	....	....	....	....	....	....	....	....	....	....	....	....	....	....	....
Other Sectors	78brd	....	....	....	....	....	....	....	....	....	....	....	....	....	....	....
Other Investment Liab., n.i.e.	78bid	....	....	....	....	....	....	....	....	....	....	....	....	....	....	....
Monetary Authorities	78bsd	....	....	....	....	....	....	....	....	....	....	....	....	....	....	....
General Government	78btd	....	....	....	....	....	....	....	....	....	....	....	....	....	....	....
Banks	78bud	....	....	....	....	....	....	....	....	....	....	....	....	....	....	....
Other Sectors	78bvd	....	....	....	....	....	....	....	....	....	....	....	....	....	....	....
Net Errors and Omissions	78cad	....	....	....	....	....	....	....	....	....	....	....	....	....	....	....
Overall Balance	78cbd	....	....	....	....	....	....	....	....	....	....	....	....	....	....	....
Reserves and Related Items	79dad	....	....	....	....	....	....	....	....	....	....	....	....	....	....	....
Reserve Assets	79dbd	....	....	....	....	....	....	....	....	....	....	....	....	....	....	....
Use of Fund Credit and Loans	79dcd	....	....	....	....	....	....	....	....	....	....	....	....	....	....	....
Exceptional Financing	79ded	....	....	....	....	....	....	....	....	....	....	....	....	....	....	....
International Investment Position																*Millions of US Dollars*
Assets	79aad	....	....	....	....	....	....	....	....	....	....	....	....	....	....	....
Direct Investment Abroad	79abd	....	....	....	....	....	....	....	....	....	....	....	....	....	....	....
Portfolio Investment	79acd	....	....	....	....	....	....	....	....	....	....	....	....	....	....	....
Equity Securities	79add	....	....	....	....	....	....	....	....	....	....	....	....	....	....	....
Debt Securities	79aed	....	....	....	....	....	....	....	....	....	....	....	....	....	....	....
Financial derivatives	79ald	....	....	....	....	....	....	....	....	....	....	....	....	....	....	....
Other Investment	79afd	....	....	....	....	....	....	....	....	....	....	....	....	....	....	....
Monetary Authorities	79agd	....	....	....	....	....	....	....	....	....	....	....	....	....	....	....
General Government	79ahd	....	....	....	....	....	....	....	....	....	....	....	....	....	....	....
Banks	79aid	....	....	....	....	....	....	....	....	....	....	....	....	....	....	....
Other Sectors	79ajd	....	....	....	....	....	....	....	....	....	....	....	....	....	....	....
Reserve Assets	79akd	....	....	....	....	....	....	....	....	....	....	....	....	....	....	....
Liabilities	79lad	....	....	....	....	....	....	....	....	....	....	....	....	....	....	....
Dir. Invest. in Rep. Economy	79lbd	....	....	....	....	....	....	....	....	....	....	....	....	....	....	....
Portfolio Investment	79lcd	....	....	....	....	....	....	....	....	....	....	....	....	....	....	....
Equity Securities	79ldd	....	....	....	....	....	....	....	....	....	....	....	....	....	....	....
Debt Securities	79led	....	....	....	....	....	....	....	....	....	....	....	....	....	....	....
Financial Derivatives	79lld	....	....	....	....	....	....	....	....	....	....	....	....	....	....	....
Other Investment	79lfd	....	....	....	....	....	....	....	....	....	....	....	....	....	....	....
Monetary Authorities	79lgd	....	....	....	....	....	....	....	....	....	....	....	....	....	....	....
General Government	79lhd	....	....	....	....	....	....	....	....	....	....	....	....	....	....	....
Banks	79lid	....	....	....	....	....	....	....	....	....	....	....	....	....	....	....
Other Sectors	79ljd	....	....	....	....	....	....	....	....	....	....	....	....	....	....	....
Government Finance																*Billions of Manats:*
Deficit(-) / or Surplus	80	....	....	....	....	....	....	....	....	....	....	....	....	....	....	....
Total Revenue and Grants	81y	....	....	....	....	....	....	....	....	....	....	....	....	....	....	....
Revenue	81	....	....	....	....	....	....	....	....	....	....	....	....	....	....	....
Grants	81z	....	....	....	....	....	....	....	....	....	....	....	....	....	....	....
Exp. & Lending Minus Repay.	82z	....	....	....	....	....	....	....	....	....	....	....	....	....	....	....
Expenditure	82	....	....	....	....	....	....	....	....	....	....	....	....	....	....	....
Lending Minus Repayments	83	....	....	....	....	....	....	....	....	....	....	....	....	....	....	....
Total Financing	80h	....	....	....	....	....	....	....	....	....	....	....	....	....	....	....
																Millions:
Population	99z	....	....	....	....	....	....	....	....	....	....	....	....	....	....	....

1987	1988	1989	1990	1991	1992	1993	1994	1995	1996	1997	1998	1999	2000	2001		
Millions of US Dollars															**International Transactions**	
....	....	....	....	....	1,571.2	993.1	637.5	637.2	631.2	781.3	606.2	929.2	....	....	Exports	**70..*d***
....	....	....	....	....	997.9	635.5	777.9	667.6	960.6	794.3	1,077.2	1,035.7	....	....	Imports, cif	**71..*d***
Minus Sign Indicates Debit															Balance of Payments	
....	....	....	....	....	....	....	....	–400.7	–931.2	–915.8	–1,364.5	–599.7	–167.8	–51.8	Current Account, n.i.e.	**78al*d***
....	....	....	....	....	....	....	....	612.3	643.7	808.3	677.8	1,025.2	1,858.3	2,078.9	Goods: Exports f.o.b	**78aa*d***
....	....	....	....	....	....	....	....	–985.4	–1,337.6	–1,375.2	–1,723.9	–1,433.4	–1,539.0	–1,465.1	Goods: Imports f.o.b	**78ab*d***
....	....	....	....	....	....	....	....	–373.1	–693.9	–566.9	–1,046.2	–408.2	319.3	613.9	*Trade Balance*	**78ac*d***
....	....	....	....	....	....	....	....	172.4	149.3	341.8	331.7	256.8	259.8	289.8	Services: Credit	**78ad*d***
....	....	....	....	....	....	....	....	–304.6	–440.9	–726.0	–700.8	–485.1	–484.5	–664.9	Services: Debit	**78ae*d***
....	....	....	....	....	....	....	....	–505.4	–985.6	–951.1	–1,415.2	–636.5	94.6	238.8	*Balance on Goods & Services*	**78af*d***
....	....	....	....	....	....	....	....	9.9	15.1	22.8	38.3	11.0	55.9	41.5	Income: Credit	**78ag*d***
....	....	....	....	....	....	....	....	–16.0	–27.2	–32.3	–51.6	–56.0	–391.4	–408.7	Income: Debit	**78ah*d***
....	....	....	....	....	....	....	....	–511.4	–997.7	–960.6	–1,428.5	–681.5	–240.9	–128.4	*Balance on Gds, Serv., & Inc.*	**78ai*d***
....	....	....	....	....	....	....	....	129.3	107.2	95.7	145.0	134.5	135.0	176.5	Current Transfers, n.i.e.: Credit	**78aj*d***
....	....	....	....	....	....	....	....	–18.5	–40.7	–50.9	–80.9	–52.8	–62.0	–99.9	Current Transfers: Debit	**78ak*d***
....	....	....	....	....	....	....	....	–1.6	—	–10.2	–.7	....	....	....	Capital Account, n.i.e.	**78bc*d***
....	....	....	....	....	....	....	....	....	....	....	....	....	....	....	Capital Account, n.i.e.: Credit	**78ba*d***
....	....	....	....	....	....	....	....	–1.6	—	–10.2	–.7	....	....	....	Capital Account: Debit	**78bb*d***
....	....	....	....	....	....	....	....	400.3	822.5	1,092.1	1,326.0	690.2	493.4	346.6	Financial Account, n.i.e.	**78bj*d***
....	....	....	....	....	....	....	....	—	—	—	—	....	–.8	—	Direct Investment Abroad	**78bd*d***
....	....	....	....	....	....	....	....	330.1	627.3	1,114.8	1,023.0	510.3	129.9	226.5	Dir. Invest. in Rep. Econ., n.i.e.	**78be*d***
....	....	....	....	....	....	....	....	–1.7	—	1.1	—	....	....	....	Portfolio Investment Assets	**78bf*d***
....	....	....	....	....	....	....	....	....	....	....	....	....	....	....	Equity Securities	**78bk*d***
....	....	....	....	....	....	....	....	–1.7	—	1.1	—	....	....	....	Debt Securities	**78bl*d***
....	....	....	....	....	....	....	....	—	—	—	.4	....	....	....	Portfolio Investment Liab., n.i.e.	**78bg*d***
....	....	....	....	....	....	....	....	....	....	....	....	....	....	....	Equity Securities	**78bm*d***
....	....	....	....	....	....	....	....	—	—	—	.4	....	....	....	Debt Securities	**78bn*d***
....	....	....	....	....	....	....	....	....	....	....	....	....	....	....	Financial Derivatives Assets	**78bw*d***
....	....	....	....	....	....	....	....	....	....	....	....	....	....	....	Financial Derivatives Liabilities	**78bx*d***
....	....	....	....	....	....	....	....	–22.1	–216.8	–102.6	22.3	–81.0	–114.2	–173.5	Other Investment Assets	**78bh*d***
....	....	....	....	....	....	....	....	....	....	....	....	....	....	....	Monetary Authorities	**78bo*d***
....	....	....	....	....	....	....	....	....	....	....	....	....	....	....	General Government	**78bp*d***
....	....	....	....	....	....	....	....	–19.6	–136.9	5.3	62.4	–44.2	7.1	–77.7	Banks	**78bq*d***
....	....	....	....	....	....	....	....	–2.5	–79.8	–107.9	–40.1	–36.8	–121.2	–95.8	Other Sectors	**78br*d***
....	....	....	....	....	....	....	....	94.1	412.0	78.8	280.4	260.9	478.4	293.5	Other Investment Liab., n.i.e.	**78bi*d***
....	....	....	....	....	....	....	....	—	—	—	—	—	—	—	Monetary Authorities	**78bs*d***
....	....	....	....	....	....	....	....	30.0	—	70.8	75.6	161.6	246.2	138.6	General Government	**78bt*d***
....	....	....	....	....	....	....	....	–.3	26.5	–18.8	–1.7	–.1	–22.9	3.0	Banks	**78bu*d***
....	....	....	....	....	....	....	....	64.3	385.5	26.8	206.5	99.3	255.0	151.9	Other Sectors	**78bv*d***
....	....	....	....	....	....	....	....	59.7	23.6	–27.0	–20.1	42.4	—	—	Net Errors and Omissions	**78ca*d***
....	....	....	....	....	....	....	....	57.8	–85.0	139.2	–59.2	132.9	325.6	294.8	*Overall Balance*	**78cb*d***
....	....	....	....	....	....	....	....	–57.8	85.0	–139.2	59.2	–132.9	–325.6	–294.8	Reserves and Related Items	**79da*d***
....	....	....	....	....	....	....	....	–161.6	7.1	–244.2	18.7	–228.5	–274.2	–265.6	Reserve Assets	**79db*d***
....	....	....	....	....	....	....	....	103.8	77.9	105.0	40.5	95.6	–51.4	–29.3	Use of Fund Credit and Loans	**79dc*d***
....	....	....	....	....	....	....	....	....	....	....	....	....	....	....	Exceptional Financing	**79de*d***
Millions of US Dollars															International Investment Position	
....	....	....	....	....	....	....	....	....	....	....	....	1,060.9	1,234.0	1,553.2	Assets	**79aa*d***
....	....	....	....	....	....	....	....	....	....	....	....	—	.8	.8	Direct Investment Abroad	**79ab*d***
....	....	....	....	....	....	....	....	....	....	....	....	—	—	—	Portfolio Investment	**79ac*d***
....	....	....	....	....	....	....	....	....	....	....	....	....	....	....	Equity Securities	**79ad*d***
....	....	....	....	....	....	....	....	....	....	....	....	....	....	....	Debt Securities	**79ae*d***
....	....	....	....	....	....	....	....	....	....	....	....	—	—	—	Financial derivatives	**79al*d***
....	....	....	....	....	....	....	....	....	....	....	....	385.1	282.4	336.0	Other Investment	**79af*d***
....	....	....	....	....	....	....	....	....	....	....	....	....	....	....	Monetary Authorities	**79ag*d***
....	....	....	....	....	....	....	....	....	....	....	....	....	....	....	General Government	**79ah*d***
....	....	....	....	....	....	....	....	....	....	....	....	....	....	....	Banks	**79ai*d***
....	....	....	....	....	....	....	....	....	....	....	....	....	....	....	Other Sectors	**79aj*d***
....	....	....	....	....	....	....	....	....	....	....	....	675.8	950.8	1,216.4	Reserve Assets	**79ak*d***
....	....	....	....	....	....	....	....	....	....	....	....	4,715.9	5,232.3	5,643.0	Liabilities	**79la*d***
....	....	....	....	....	....	....	....	....	....	....	....	3,099.5	3,735.2	3,961.7	Dir. Invest. in Rep. Economy	**79lb*d***
....	....	....	....	....	....	....	....	....	....	....	....	—	—	—	Portfolio Investment	**79lc*d***
....	....	....	....	....	....	....	....	....	....	....	....	....	....	....	Equity Securities	**79ld*d***
....	....	....	....	....	....	....	....	....	....	....	....	....	....	....	Debt Securities	**79le*d***
....	....	....	....	....	....	....	....	....	....	....	....	—	—	—	Financial Derivatives	**79ll*d***
....	....	....	....	....	....	....	....	....	....	....	....	1,616.4	1,497.1	1,681.3	Other Investment	**79lf*d***
....	....	....	....	....	....	....	....	....	....	....	....	....	....	....	Monetary Authorities	**79lg*d***
....	....	....	....	....	....	....	....	....	....	....	....	....	....	....	General Government	**79lh*d***
....	....	....	....	....	....	....	....	....	....	....	....	....	....	....	Banks	**79li*d***
....	....	....	....	....	....	....	....	....	....	....	....	....	....	....	Other Sectors	**79lj*d***
Year Ending December 31															**Government Finance**	
....	....	....	....	....	....	....	–209.21	–545.03	–405.89	–341.84	–623.00	–479.46	....	....	Deficit(-) / or Surplus	**80**
....	....	....	....	....	....	....	479.70	1,920.25	1,960.77	2,402.03	3,143.02	3,380.17	....	....	Total Revenue and Grants	**81y**
....	....	....	....	....	....	....	479.70	1,920.25	1,881.02	2,350.03	3,076.02	3,316.97	....	....	Revenue	**81**
....	....	....	....	....	....	....	—	—	79.76	52.00	67.00	63.20	....	....	Grants	**81z**
....	....	....	....	....	....	....	688.91	2,465.27	2,366.67	2,743.88	3,766.02	3,859.64	....	....	Exp. & Lending Minus Repay.	**82z**
....	....	....	....	....	....	....	688.91	2,254.33	2,283.64	3,028.57	3,993.14	4,260.94	....	....	Expenditure	**82**
....	....	....	....	....	....	....	—	210.94	83.03	–284.70	–227.12	–401.31	....	....	Lending Minus Repayments	**83**
....	....	....	....	....	....	....	209.21	545.03	405.90	341.84	623.00	479.46	....	....	Total Financing	**80h**
Midyear Estimates																
....	....	....	....	....	7.38	7.49	7.60	7.68	7.76	7.84	7.91	7.98	8.05	8.11	**Population**	**99z**

(See notes in the back of the book.)

	1972	1973	1974	1975	1976	1977	1978	1979	1980	1981	1982	1983	1984	1985	1986
Exchange Rates													*Bahamian Dollars per SDR:*		
Principal Rate..............aa= ....wa	1.0857	1.2064	1.2244	1.1707	1.1618	1.2147	1.3028	1.3173	1.2754	1.1640	1.1031	1.0470	.9802	1.0984	1.2232
													Bahamian Dollars per US Dollar:		
Principal Rate..............ae= ....we	1.0000	1.0000	1.0000	1.0000	1.0000	1.0000	1.0000	1.0000	1.0000	1.0000	1.0000	1.0000	1.0000	1.0000	1.0000
Secondary Rate ....xe	....	....	....	....	....	....	1.1850	1.1750	1.2250	1.2350	1.2350	1.2350	1.1750	1.1750	1.1750
Secondary Rate ....xf	....	....	....	....	....	....	1.1867	1.1637	1.2135	1.2265	1.2350	1.2350	1.1950	1.1800	1.1750
													Index Numbers (1995=100):		
Principal Rate ....ahx	100.0	100.0	100.0	100.0	100.0	100.0	100.0	100.0	100.0	100.0	100.0	100.0	100.0	100.0	100.0
Nominal Effective Exchange Rate ....nec	....	....	....	....	....	....	....	75.0	75.7	79.9	83.7	87.5	92.2	95.6	91.3
Real Effective Exchange Rate ....rec	....	....	....	....	....	....	....	92.1	96.8	99.4	102.4	105.3	107.6	104.1
Fund Position													*Millions of SDRs:*		
Quota 2f.s	....	20.0	20.0	20.0	20.0	20.0	33.0	33.0	49.5	49.5	49.5	66.4	66.4	66.4	66.4
SDRs 1b.s	....	—	—	—	—	—	—	3.4	2.7	6.1	5.8	1.1	.7	.4	—
Reserve Position in the Fund 1c.s	....	—	5.0	5.0	5.0	5.0	4.9	4.7	8.8	6.6	6.7	10.9	10.9	10.9	10.9
Total Fund Cred.&Loans Outstg. 2tl	....	—	—	—	—	—	—	—	—	—	—	—	—	—	—
International Liquidity												*Millions of US Dollars Unless Otherwise Indicated:*			
Total Reserves minus Gold 1l.d	37.1	43.2	49.8	53.3	47.4	†67.1	58.1	77.5	92.3	100.2	113.5	122.0	161.1	182.5	231.5
SDRs 1b.d	....	—	—	—	—	—	—	4.5	3.5	7.1	6.3	1.2	.7	.4	—
Reserve Position in the Fund 1c.d	....	—	6.1	5.9	5.8	6.1	6.3	6.2	11.3	7.7	7.3	11.4	10.7	12.0	13.4
Foreign Exchange 1d.d	37.1	43.2	43.7	47.4	41.6	†61.0	51.8	66.8	77.5	85.4	99.8	109.4	149.8	170.1	218.1
Deposit Money Banks: Assets 7a.d	5,840	5,138	11,989	16,480	23,583	26,796	31,863	30,040	33,448	43,289	34,691	31,941	32,078	29,385	29,168
Liabilities 7b.d	5,806	5,251	12,127	16,264	23,276	26,622	31,771	29,709	33,246	42,880	34,583	31,775	31,886	29,647	29,770
Other Banking Insts.: Assets 7e.d	....	13	—	—	4	11	5	348	1,675	1,862	2,079	2,204	2,232	2,639	2,476
Liabilities 7f.d	....	—	5	2	—	—	—	359	1,681	1,841	2,012	2,106	2,078	2,459	2,285
Branches of US Banks: Assets 7k.d	12,472	20,235	26,624	37,505	53,778	61,580	71,407	79,712	88,917	103,698	94,778	99,867	94,148	91,390	90,656
Liab. 7m.d	12,479	20,268	26,673	37,333	53,931	61,530	71,898	80,238	89,847	104,531	96,094	101,082	94,979	91,657	92,441
Monetary Authorities													*Millions of Bahamian Dollars:*		
Foreign Assets 11	36	44	50	53	48	67	59	78	92	100	113	123	162	183	232
Claims on Central Government 12a	9	1	10	10	19	12	15	23	42	34	28	36	44	30	32
Claims on Deposit Money Banks 12e	—	1	2	—	—	—	—	2	10	19	20	—	—	—	—
Claims on Nonbank Financial Insts 12g	—	—	—	—	—	—	—	—	—	—	—	—	—	1	2
Reserve Money 14	37	36	42	45	50	50	57	66	77	77	87	99	118	135	146
of which: Currency Outside DMBs 14a	21	20	19	20	21	23	27	30	33	37	41	46	51	58	65
Central Government Deposits 16d	4	3	8	9	4	17	1	13	23	29	22	7	34	21	56
Capital Accounts 17a	3	6	11	11	14	15	13	21	38	35	39	50	55	54	50
Other Items (Net) 17r	1	—	—	-1	-2	-3	2	2	6	13	13	4	—	4	13
Deposit Money Banks													*Millions of Bahamian Dollars:*		
Reserves 20	16	15	21	22	21	20	25	31	36	32	39	42	45	54	62
Foreign Assets 21	5,840	5,138	11,989	16,480	23,583	26,796	31,863	30,040	33,448	43,289	34,691	31,941	32,078	29,385	29,168
Claims on Central Government 22a	19	26	60	69	80	95	91	.89	69	91	101	126	127	123	124
Claims on Official Entities 22bx	—	—	2	—	11	25	22	20	37	22	47	33	25	10	16
Claims on Private Sector 22d	242	370	265	294	265	287	309	348	403	443	483	510	535	592	677
Claims on Other Banking Insts 22f	—	77	199	245	242	64	30	46	12	5	4	8	19	14	13
Demand Deposits 24	64	55	56	53	56	64	77	102	100	104	115	128	135	146	172
Time, Savings,& Fgn.Currency Dep. 25	120	132	133	156	191	189	212	234	286	324	382	434	469	490	534
Bonds 26ab	—	3	—	—	—	—	—	—	—	—	—	—	—	—	—
Foreign Liabilities 26c	5,806	5,251	12,127	16,264	23,276	26,622	31,771	29,709	33,246	42,880	34,583	31,775	31,886	29,647	29,770
Central Government Deposits 26d	—	2	2	7	6	3	5	12	16	6	6	8	10	13	23
Credit from Monetary Authorities 26g	—	3	13	4	—	—	—	2	24	22	12	1	26	24	20
Liabilities to Other Banking Insts 26i	—	164	191	544	415	313	27	47	40	28	81	106	41	19	103
Capital Accounts 27a	43	60	15	23	153	107	265	472	327	525	184	204	274	-160	-568
Other Items (Net) 27r	84	-44	-2	59	105	-12	-18	-3	-35	-4	2	4	-11	-2	5
Monetary Survey													*Millions of Bahamian Dollars:*		
Foreign Assets (Net) 31n	70	-70	-88	269	354	241	150	409	294	510	222	290	355	-80	-371
Domestic Credit 32	265	468	525	602	607	462	461	500	524	562	636	698	707	736	785
Claims on Central Govt. (Net) 32an	24	22	59	62	89	87	100	86	72	91	102	147	128	119	78
Claims on Official Entities 32bx	—	—	2	—	11	25	22	20	37	22	47	33	25	10	16
Claims on Private Sector 32d	242	370	265	294	265	287	309	348	403	443	483	510	535	592	677
Claims on Other Banking Insts 32f	—	77	199	245	242	64	30	46	12	6	4	8	19	14	13
Claims on Nonbank Financial Inst 32g	—	—	—	—	—	—	—	—	—	—	—	—	—	1	2
Money 34	85	75	76	73	82	91	106	134	135	144	158	177	199	217	242
Quasi-Money 35	120	132	133	156	191	189	212	234	286	324	382	434	469	490	534
Bonds 36ab	—	3	—	—	—	—	—	—	—	—	—	—	—	—	—
Liabilities to Other Banking Insts 36i	—	164	191	544	415	313	27	47	40	28	81	106	41	19	103
Capital Accounts 37a	47	66	26	34	168	122	278	493	365	560	223	253	329	-106	-518
Other Items (Net) 37r	85	-42	11	64	105	-13	-13	3	-10	17	14	17	24	36	52
Money plus Quasi-Money 35l	205	207	209	229	273	281	318	367	421	467	540	611	668	707	777
Other Banking Institutions													*Millions of Bahamian Dollars*		
Reserves 40	....	—	2	2	3	3	3	4	5	6	7	8	10	12	15
Foreign Assets 41	....	13	—	—	4	11	5	348	1,675	1,862	2,079	2,204	2,232	2,639	2,476
Claims on Central Government 42a	....	3	4	7	6	9	12	10	8	7	6	8	10	13	14
Claims on Private Sector 42d	....	51	60	65	65	67	75	93	113	126	143	167	202	248	304
Claims on Deposit Money Banks 42e	....	9	6	5	42	7	5	36	57	50	43	25	25	23	48
Demand Deposits 44	....	—	—	—	—	—	—	—	—	—	—	—	—	—	—
Time, Savings,& Fgn.Currency Dep. 45	....	36	42	46	50	58	71	86	100	117	138	168	197	246	294
Foreign Liabilities 46c	....	—	5	2	—	—	—	359	1,681	1,841	2,012	2,106	2,078	2,459	2,285
Central Government Deposits 46d	....	—	—	—	—	—	—	—	—	1	1	2	1	1	2
Credit from Monetary Authorities 46g	....	—	—	—	—	—	—	—	—	—	—	—	3	3	3
Credit from Deposit Money Banks 46h	....	2	1	3	1	2	2	21	6	8	3	4	5	5	9
Capital Accounts 47a	....	23	25	25	32	38	26	27	90	95	124	159	208	251	293
Other Items (Net) 47r	....	15	—	3	37	-3	—	-1	-19	-12	-1	-26	-13	-30	-31
Banking Survey													*Millions of Bahamian Dollars:*		
Foreign Assets (Net) 51n	....	-57	-93	267	358	252	155	399	287	530	288	388	508	100	-180
Domestic Credit 52	....	445	390	429	436	473	517	557	633	688	780	863	899	981	1,087
Claims on Central Govt. (Net) 52an	....	24	63	70	95	96	111	95	81	97	107	153	137	131	89
Claims on Official Entities 52bx	....	—	2	—	11	25	22	20	37	22	47	33	25	10	16
Claims on Private Sector 52d	....	421	325	359	330	353	385	442	516	569	626	677	737	840	981
Claims on Nonbank Financial Inst 52g	....	—	—	—	—	—	—	—	—	—	—	—	—	1	2
Liquid Liabilities 55l	....	244	248	272	321	336	386	449	516	578	672	771	855	941	1,056
Bonds 56ab	....	3	—	—	—	—	—	—	—	—	—	—	—	—	—
Capital Accounts 57a	....	88	51	59	199	160	304	520	455	654	347	412	537	145	-225
Other Items (Net) 57r	....	53	-2	365	273	229	-18	-13	-51	-14	50	68	16	-5	76

1987	1988	1989	1990	1991	1992	1993	1994	1995	1996	1997	1998	1999	2000	2001		
End of Period															**Exchange Rates**	
1.4187	1.3457	1.3142	1.4227	1.4304	1.3750	1.3736	1.4599	1.4865	1.4380	1.3493	1.4080	1.3725	1.3029	1.2567	Principal Rate..........aa=	wa
End of Period (we and xe) Period Average (xf)																
1.0000	1.0000	1.0000	1.0000	1.0000	1.0000	1.0000	1.0000	1.0000	1.0000	1.0000	1.0000	1.0000	1.0000	1.0000	Principal Rate..........ae=	we
1.2250	1.2250	1.2250	1.2250	1.2250	1.2250	1.2250	1.2250	1.2250	1.2250	1.2250	1.2250	1.2250	1.2250	1.2250	Secondary Rate	xe
1.1989	1.2250	1.2250	1.2250	1.2250	1.2250	1.2250	1.2250	1.2250	1.2250	1.2250	1.2250	1.2250	1.2250	1.2250	Secondary Rate	xf
Period Averages																
100.0	100.0	100.0	100.0	100.0	100.0	100.0	100.0	100.0	100.0	100.0	100.0	100.0	100.0	100.0	Principal Rate	ahx
89.3	90.8	96.6	96.9	97.9	98.6	102.2	100.4	100.0	102.2	105.8	107.9	110.6	113.8	117.0	Nominal Effective Exchange Rate	nec
101.9	100.6	102.4	99.4	102.7	105.4	107.8	103.5	100.0	100.5	102.7	104.6	107.5	110.3	113.0	Real Effective Exchange Rate	rec
End of Period															**Fund Position**	
66.4	66.4	66.4	66.4	66.4	94.9	94.9	94.9	94.9	94.9	94.9	94.9	130.3	130.3	130.3	Quota	2f.s
.3	.4	.1	.4	.1	—	—	—	—	—	—	—	—	.1	.1	SDRs	1b.s
10.7	9.0	8.6	7.9	7.2	6.8	6.2	6.2	6.2	6.2	6.2	6.2	6.2	6.2	6.2	Reserve Position in the Fund	1c.s
—	—	—	—	—	—	—	—	—	—	—	—	—	—	—	Total Fund Cred.&Loans Outstg.	2tl
End of Period															**International Liquidity**	
170.1	172.0	146.8	158.2	181.3	155.3	172.3	176.6	179.2	171.4	227.0	346.5	410.5	349.6	319.3	Total Reserves minus Gold	1l.d
.4	.5	.2	.5	.2	—	—	—	—	—	—	—	—	.1	.1	SDRs	1b.d
15.2	12.2	11.4	11.2	10.2	9.4	8.6	9.1	9.3	9.0	8.4	8.8	8.6	8.1	7.8	Reserve Position in the Fund	1c.d
154.5	159.4	135.3	146.4	170.9	145.9	163.7	167.5	169.9	162.4	218.6	337.7	401.9	341.4	311.3	Foreign Exchange	1d.d
39,773	44,475	36,100	33,938	26,707	32,319	35,688	42,817	35,144	41,384	41,310	46,329	58,682	77,649	103,669	Deposit Money Banks: Assets	7a.d
40,868	45,492	37,392	35,820	28,720	33,951	35,958	43,219	35,542	41,796	41,662	47,053	59,127	78,346	104,136	Liabilities	7b.d
2,355	2,414	2,482	2,396	2,355	2,266	1,911	2,232	2,450	2,646	2,836	2,685	2,785	2,907	2,293	Other Banking Insts.: Assets	7e.d
2,156	2,290	2,383	2,230	2,112	1,988	1,541	1,802	1,881	2,084	2,384	2,498	2,626	2,644	2,036	Liabilities	7f.d
104,854	109,722	115,359	103,088	105,310	87,983	87,620	....	....	....	....	....	....	....	....	Branches of US Banks: Assets	7k.d
106,805	112,386	117,579	105,864	108,549	90,049	89,058	....	....	....	....	....	....	....	....	Liab.	7m.d
End of Period															**Monetary Authorities**	
172	172	147	160	172	144	163	170	171	163	219	339	404	343	312	Foreign Assets	11
53	47	90	112	123	137	115	144	149	153	141	62	73	129	190	Claims on Central Government	12a
12	21	13	7	—	1	—	—	—	—	1	—	—	—	—	Claims on Deposit Money Banks	12e
3	3	3	2	2	2	3	3	4	3	4	5	8	9	8	Claims on Nonbank Financial Insts	12g
151	170	177	188	212	206	205	230	236	230	264	315	381	373	411	Reserve Money	14
75	79	80	80	79	84	84	89	93	97	110	126	149	152	154	*of which: Currency Outside DMBs*	14a
18	3	7	16	10	7	3	14	8	8	17	4	14	11	9	Central Government Deposits	16d
58	56	60	68	72	72	74	77	78	80	84	87	90	98	95	Capital Accounts	17a
13	14	9	9	4	–2	–1	–3	2	2	1	—	—	–1	–5	Other Items (Net)	17r
End of Period															**Deposit Money Banks**	
59	72	73	86	113	101	105	123	128	118	146	183	226	208	250	Reserves	20
39,773	44,475	36,100	33,938	26,707	32,319	35,688	42,817	35,144	41,384	41,310	46,329	58,682	77,649	103,669	Foreign Assets	21
120	164	160	187	221	225	330	296	303	313	356	458	489	454	493	Claims on Central Government	22a
28	40	82	106	113	106	89	73	77	82	79	128	158	126	133	Claims on Official Entities	22bx
789	852	927	1,122	1,163	1,215	1,400	1,592	1,777	1,953	2,488	2,767	3,072	3,511	3,782	Claims on Private Sector	22d
25	13	7	7	5	6	11	20	18	16	27	29	25	33	54	Claims on Other Banking Insts	22f
194	214	214	241	267	274	280	309	336	334	398	460	588	630	605	Demand Deposits	24
628	679	751	885	942	1,000	1,221	1,326	1,447	1,551	1,950	2,275	2,423	2,668	2,870	Time, Savings,& Fgn.Currency Dep.	25
—	—	—	9	9	10	18	7	7	5	3	1	4	1	5	Bonds	26ab
40,868	45,492	37,392	35,820	28,720	33,951	35,958	43,219	35,542	41,796	41,662	47,053	59,127	78,346	104,136	Foreign Liabilities	26c
22	18	16	20	35	29	30	36	44	59	65	66	68	71	58	Central Government Deposits	26d
33	33	23	19	—	1	—	—	—	—	1	—	1	1	1	Credit from Monetary Authorities	26g
10	8	24	14	26	30	29	27	40	43	43	42	34	37	48	Liabilities to Other Banking Insts	26i
–942	–816	–1,059	–1,554	–1,667	–1,332	79	–16	13	41	271	–9	432	266	678	Capital Accounts	27a
–20	–13	–13	–7	–10	8	8	14	21	38	13	5	–25	–38	–20	Other Items (Net)	27r
End of Period															**Monetary Survey**	
–923	–845	–1,145	–1,722	–1,841	–1,488	–107	–231	–227	–248	–133	–385	–41	–355	–154	Foreign Assets (Net)	31n
977	1,097	1,246	1,501	1,583	1,654	1,914	2,078	2,277	2,454	3,014	3,379	3,743	4,180	4,594	Domestic Credit	32
133	190	227	263	299	326	412	390	401	399	415	450	481	501	617	Claims on Central Govt. (Net)	32an
28	40	82	106	113	106	89	73	77	82	79	128	158	126	133	Claims on Official Entities	32bx
789	852	927	1,122	1,163	1,215	1,400	1,592	1,777	1,953	2,488	2,767	3,072	3,511	3,782	Claims on Private Sector	32d
25	13	7	7	5	6	11	20	18	16	27	29	25	33	54	Claims on Other Banking Insts	32f
3	3	3	2	2	2	3	3	4	3	4	5	8	9	8	Claims on Nonbank Financial Inst	32g
270	295	299	342	366	380	382	416	445	447	517	593	748	798	767	Money	34
628	679	751	885	942	1,000	1,221	1,326	1,447	1,551	1,950	2,275	2,423	2,668	2,870	Quasi-Money	35
—	—	—	9	9	10	18	7	7	5	3	1	4	1	5	Bonds	36ab
10	8	24	14	26	30	29	27	40	43	43	42	34	37	48	Liabilities to Other Banking Insts	36i
–885	–760	–999	–1,486	–1,595	–1,260	152	60	91	120	355	78	523	364	773	Capital Accounts	37a
30	31	25	15	–7	5	5	9	22	39	13	5	–30	–42	–23	Other Items (Net)	37r
898	974	1,050	1,227	1,309	1,380	1,603	1,743	1,892	1,998	2,467	2,868	3,171	3,466	3,637	Money plus Quasi-Money	35l
End of Period															**Other Banking Institutions**	
17	19	19	16	17	17	13	13	13	13	3	3	4	5	4	Reserves	40
2,355	2,414	2,482	2,396	2,355	2,266	1,911	2,232	2,450	2,646	2,836	2,685	2,785	2,907	2,293	Foreign Assets	41
18	21	22	19	20	34	24	22	22	22	4	3	4	4	3	Claims on Central Government	42a
372	389	405	344	352	364	268	267	283	297	63	69	87	108	120	Claims on Private Sector	42d
22	14	28	14	24	30	25	27	32	43	45	43	59	32	47	Claims on Deposit Money Banks	42e
—	1	3	7	7	9	8	8	11	12	4	5	5	8	8	Demand Deposits	44
353	363	370	313	317	326	245	243	248	260	39	41	66	78	71	Time, Savings,& Fgn.Currency Dep.	45
2,156	2,290	2,383	2,230	2,112	1,988	1,541	1,802	1,881	2,084	2,384	2,498	2,626	2,644	2,036	Foreign Liabilities	46c
3	4	4	5	2	3	—	—	—	—	—	—	—	—	—	Central Government Deposits	46d
3	—	—	—	—	—	—	—	—	—	10	15	—	10	—	Credit from Monetary Authorities	46g
22	11	4	4	2	1	4	13	11	12	23	26	17	25	46	Credit from Deposit Money Banks	46h
338	270	249	232	273	302	316	323	323	292	253	233	255	320	360	Capital Accounts	47a
–91	–82	–59	–3	55	81	126	172	328	362	237	–14	–28	–28	–53	Other Items (Net)	47r
End of Period															**Banking Survey**	
–725	–721	–1,047	–1,556	–1,598	–1,210	262	198	343	314	319	–198	119	–92	103	Foreign Assets (Net)	51n
1,339	1,491	1,662	1,851	1,948	2,044	2,195	2,346	2,564	2,757	3,053	3,423	3,809	4,259	4,663	Domestic Credit	52
149	208	246	277	318	356	435	412	423	421	419	453	485	506	620	Claims on Central Govt. (Net)	52an
28	40	82	106	113	106	89	73	77	82	79	128	158	126	133	Claims on Official Entities	52bx
1,160	1,241	1,332	1,466	1,515	1,580	1,668	1,859	2,060	2,250	2,551	2,837	3,159	3,619	3,902	Claims on Private Sector	52d
3	3	3	2	2	2	3	3	4	3	4	5	8	9	8	Claims on Nonbank Financial Inst	52g
1,234	1,319	1,405	1,531	1,616	1,699	1,844	1,981	2,137	2,256	2,507	2,911	3,238	3,547	3,711	Liquid Liabilities	55l
—	—	—	9	9	10	18	7	7	5	3	1	4	1	5	Bonds	56ab
–547	–490	–749	–1,254	–1,323	–958	468	384	413	413	608	311	778	684	1,133	Capital Accounts	57a
–72	–59	–41	9	48	82	128	174	349	397	254	1	–91	–65	–83	Other Items (Net)	57r

Bahamas, The

313		1972	1973	1974	1975	1976	1977	1978	1979	1980	1981	1982	1983	1984	1985	1986
Interest Rates																*Percent Per Annum*
Bank Rate *(End of Period)*	60	9.50	9.50	9.50	9.50	9.50	9.50	9.50	9.00	11.00	9.00	10.00	9.00	9.50	8.50	7.50
Treasury Bill Rate	60c	7.18	7.02	7.44	6.64	5.32	4.92	3.49	3.07	7.37	8.89	8.76	9.11	6.88	5.90	3.47
Deposit Rate	60l	....	....	....	....	....	....	....	....	6.96	7.48	7.56	7.47	7.44	6.40	5.57
Lending Rate	60p	....	....	....	....	9.50	9.50	9.50	9.13	10.83	11.00	11.00	11.00	11.00	10.33	9.25
Prices and Labor																*Index Numbers (1995=100):*
Consumer Prices	64	26.4	27.9	31.5	34.8	36.3	37.4	39.7	43.3	48.5	53.9	†57.2	59.5	61.8	64.7	68.2
																Number in Thousands:
Labor Force	67d	....	....	....	....	....	....	....	....	....	....	....	....	....	....	....
Employment	67e	....	....	....	....	....	....	....	....	....	....	....	....	....	....	†97
Unemployment	67c	....	....	....	....	....	....	....	....	....	....	....	....	....	....	†14
Unemployment Rate (%)	67r	....	....	....	....	....	....	....	....	....	....	....	....	....	....	12.2
International Transactions																*Millions of Bahamian Dollars*
Exports	70	343	530	1,444	2,508	2,992	3,261	3,058	3,786	5,009	6,189	4,534	3,970	3,393	2,728	2,702
Imports, c.i.f.	71	485	764	1,908	2,697	3,125	3,568	3,150	3,514	7,546	7,284	6,349	4,616	4,098	3,078	3,289
Balance of Payments																*Millions of US Dollars:*
Current Account, n.i.e.	78ald	....	....	....	....	68.1	28.9	2.4	-42.9	-75.3	-139.9	-115.4	-100.6	-100.3	-2.7	23.0
Goods: Exports f.o.b.	78aad	....	....	....	....	2,694.2	2,637.3	2,192.4	3,577.8	5,006.2	3,670.6	2,555.6	2,669.0	2,437.6	862.5	335.3
Goods: Imports f.o.b.	78abd	....	....	....	....	-2,865.5	-2,841.2	-2,455.0	-3,951.5	-5,467.4	-4,171.5	-3,023.4	-3,203.0	-2,983.5	-1,425.8	-940.9
Trade Balance	78acd	....	....	....	....	-171.3	-203.9	-262.6	-373.7	-461.2	-500.9	-467.8	-534.0	-545.9	-563.3	-605.6
Services: Credit	78add	....	....	....	....	440.0	481.9	583.1	657.1	746.0	787.5	794.1	891.1	931.2	1,121.9	1,228.7
Services: Debit	78aed	....	....	....	....	-128.0	-155.1	-177.8	-190.9	-226.2	-274.3	-315.9	-329.0	-324.0	-383.2	-417.7
Balance on Goods & Services	78afd	....	....	....	....	140.7	122.9	142.7	92.5	58.6	12.3	10.4	28.1	61.3	175.4	205.4
Income: Credit	78agd	....	....	....	....	4.5	4.0	6.9	10.9	13.0	17.0	23.8	15.3	18.8	20.4	19.5
Income: Debit	78ahd	....	....	....	....	-80.1	-87.6	-134.7	-144.5	-147.5	-168.9	-155.4	-153.8	-183.9	-201.0	-203.1
Balance on Gds, Serv. & Inc.	78aid	....	....	....	....	65.1	39.3	14.9	-41.1	-75.9	-139.6	-121.2	-110.4	-103.8	-5.2	21.8
Current Transfers, n.i.e.: Credit	78ajd	....	....	....	....	7.2	7.2	9.0	13.8	19.5	13.3	23.6	19.6	17.5	16.8	16.3
Current Transfers: Debit	78akd	....	....	....	....	-4.2	-17.6	-21.5	-15.6	-18.9	-13.6	-17.8	-9.8	-14.0	-14.3	-15.1
Capital Account, n.i.e.	78bcd	....	....	....	....	-14.6	-2.8	-2.2	-2.2	-2.5	-2.5	-2.0	-2.7	-2.7	-2.5	-1.5
Capital Account, n.i.e.: Credit	78bad	....	....	....	....	—	—	—	—	—	—	—	—	—	—	—
Capital Account: Debit	78bbd	....	....	....	....	-14.6	-2.8	-2.2	-2.2	-2.5	-2.5	-2.0	-2.7	-2.7	-2.5	-1.5
Financial Account, n.i.e.	78bjd	....	....	....	....	-2.4	50.4	-24.8	-24.3	16.8	162.7	83.3	—	-33.6	-11.5	26.2
Direct Investment Abroad	78bdd	....	....	....	....	—	—	—	—	—	—	—	—	—	—	—
Dir. Invest. in Rep. Econ., n.i.e.	78bed	....	....	....	....	14.6	31.4	-1.1	9.6	4.1	34.4	2.8	-6.0	-4.9	-30.2	-13.2
Portfolio Investment Assets	78bfd	....	....	....	....	—	—	—	—	—	—	—	—	—	—	—
Equity Securities	78bkd	....	....	....	....	—	—	—	—	—	—	—	—	—	—	—
Debt Securities	78bld	....	....	....	....	—	—	—	—	—	—	—	—	—	—	—
Portfolio Investment Liab., n.i.e.	78bgd	....	....	....	....	-1.5	6.9	-2.3	-3.2	-2.3	-3.0	-3.2	—	—	—	—
Equity Securities	78bmd	....	....	....	....	—	—	—	—	—	—	—	—	—	—	—
Debt Securities	78bnd	....	....	....	....	-1.5	6.9	-2.3	-3.2	-2.3	-3.0	-3.2	—	—	—	—
Financial Derivatives Assets	78bwd	....	....	....	....	....	....	....	....	....	....	....	....	....	....	....
Financial Derivatives Liabilities	78bxd	....	....	....	....	....	....	....	....	....	....	....	....	....	....	....
Other Investment Assets	78bhd	....	....	....	....	-12.0	9.7	.5	-33.1	7.3	17.1	8.5	-19.3	-26.8	24.3	27.0
Monetary Authorities	78bod	....	....	....	....	....	....	....	....	....	....	....	....	....	....	....
General Government	78bpd	....	....	....	....	—	—	—	—	—	—	—	—	—	—	—
Banks	78bqd	....	....	....	....	-12.0	9.7	.5	-33.1	7.3	17.1	8.5	-19.3	-26.8	24.3	27.0
Other Sectors	78brd	....	....	....	....	—	—	—	—	—	—	—	—	—	—	—
Other Investment Liab., n.i.e.	78bid	....	....	....	....	-3.5	2.4	-21.9	2.4	7.7	114.2	75.2	25.3	-1.9	-5.6	12.4
Monetary Authorities	78bsd	....	....	....	....	—	—	—	—	—	—	—	—	—	—	—
General Government	78btd	....	....	....	....	-3.5	1.7	-3.4	-4.5	-5.2	34.3	50.8	19.9	1.7	-7.3	10.1
Banks	78bud	....	....	....	....	—	—	—	—	—	—	—	—	—	—	—
Other Sectors	78bvd	....	....	....	....	—	.7	-18.5	6.9	12.9	79.9	24.4	5.4	-3.6	1.7	2.3
Net Errors and Omissions	78cad	....	....	....	....	-57.0	-57.4	15.6	84.2	71.7	-15.0	48.1	113.9	175.7	35.4	-78.5
Overall Balance	78cbd	....	....	....	....	-5.9	19.1	-9.0	14.8	10.7	5.3	14.0	10.6	39.1	18.7	-30.8
Reserves and Related Items	79dad	....	....	....	....	5.9	-19.1	9.0	-14.8	-10.7	-5.3	-14.0	-10.6	-39.1	-18.7	30.8
Reserve Assets	79dbd	....	....	....	....	5.9	-19.1	9.0	-14.8	-10.7	-5.3	-14.0	-10.6	-39.1	-18.7	30.8
Use of Fund Credit and Loans	79dcd	....	....	....	....	—	—	—	—	—	—	—	—	—	—	—
Exceptional Financing	79ded	....	....	....	....	....	....	....	....	....	....	....	....	....	....	....
Government Finance																*Millions of Bahamian Dollars:*
Deficit (-) or Surplus	80	1.5	2.9	-32.8	-14.1	-23.3	-27.7	-33.0	-8.2	-7.8	-62.2	-78.2	-68.5	-16.4	-28.4	-12.3
Revenue	81	97.8	108.8	114.5	118.3	129.3	136.9	164.0	202.1	244.1	282.2	273.5	298.2	333.5	376.8	398.8
Grants Received	81z	—	—	—	—	—	—	—	—	—	—	—	—	—	—	—
Expenditure	82	97.8	107.8	121.5	127.8	151.5	159.7	185.9	205.1	246.9	289.3	302.3	314.3	343.2	406.0	420.1
Lending Minus Repayments	83	-1.6	-2.0	25.9	4.6	1.2	4.9	11.1	5.2	5.1	55.1	49.5	52.4	6.7	-.9	-9.0
Financing																
Net Borrowing: Domestic	84a	-2.9	-17.1	27.1	23.3	25.5	32.0	24.8	34.7	15.6	18.0	17.5	52.0	37.2	48.5	-15.5
Foreign	85a	-1.8	10.7	2.9	-5.1	-5.0	3.6	-5.8	-7.7	-7.5	31.3	65.9	20.0	1.7	-3.6	55.7
Use of Cash Balances	87	3.1	3.4	2.9	-4.1	2.8	-7.9	14.0	-18.7	-.3	12.9	-5.1	-3.5	-22.5	-16.6	-27.9
Debt: Domestic	88a	46.7	38.5	71.8	95.8	123.4	149.2	173.5	213.5	228.4	235.0	258.1	313.6	328.9	365.7	400.2
Foreign	89a	18.6	33.5	36.4	31.4	26.4	34.8	29.1	21.3	14.7	46.0	93.5	112.9	114.5	112.5	122.5
National Accounts																*Millions of Bahamian Dollars*
Househ.Cons.Expend.,incl.NPISHs	96f	....	345.9	400.2	451.1	482.9	521.0	565.9	617.8	577.7	637.4	713.6	763.1	838.3	897.6	1,015.9
Government Consumption Expend.	91f	....	76.8	85.8	86.9	107.0	109.3	128.4	147.2	173.3	207.3	218.8	250.6	267.6	294.4	306.3
Gross Fixed Capital Formation	93e	....	106.7	99.0	75.4	68.1	89.2	94.4	120.3	172.1	266.2	301.1	311.3	300.8	381.3	419.1
Changes in Inventories	93i	....	....	....	....	....	....	....	....	9.0	40.1	14.1	-49.7	3.7	9.6	16.6
Exports of Goods and Services	90c	....	465.8	601.4	617.3	676.8	643.4	779.0	947.4	1,156.6	1,200.4	1,189.8	1,238.2	1,293.2	1,511.9	1,605.1
Imports of Goods and Services (-)	98c	....	413.0	564.3	497.1	535.9	407.5	469.4	533.8	788.7	860.4	935.7	1,039.7	1,106.3	1,239.4	1,281.2
Statistical Discrepancy	99bs	....	....	....	....	....	....	....	....	....	....	....	....	....	....	....
Gross Domestic Product (GDP)	99b	....	582.2	622.1	733.6	798.9	955.4	1,098.3	1,298.9	1,299.9	1,490.9	1,501.8	1,473.9	1,597.4	1,855.4	2,081.7
Net Primary Income from Abroad	98.n	....	-61.8	-79.3	-61.6	-64.4	-75.4	-114.4	-125.8	-113.6	-136.4	-115.3	-123.3	-148.5	-162.6	-163.8
Gross National Income (GNI)	99a	....	520.4	542.8	672.0	734.5	880.0	983.9	1,173.1	1,186.3	1,354.5	1,386.5	1,350.6	1,448.9	1,692.8	1,917.9
Net Current Transf.from Abroad	98t	....	....	....	....	....	....	....	....	....	....	....	....	....	....	....
Gross Nat'l Disposable Inc.(GNDI)	99i	....	....	....	....	....	....	....	....	....	....	....	....	....	....	....
Gross Saving	99s	....	....	....	....	....	....	....	....	....	....	....	....	....	....	....
GDP Volume 1991 Prices	99b.p	....	....	....	....	....	....	....	....	....	....	....	....	....	....	....
GDP Volume (1995=100)	99bvp	....	....	....	....	....	....	....	....	....	....	....	....	....	....	....
GDP Deflator (1995=100)	99bip	....	....	....	....	....	....	....	....	....	....	....	....	....	....	....
																Millions:
Population	99z	.18	.18	.19	.19	.19	.20	.20	.21	.21	.21	.22	.22	.23	.23	.23

	1987	1988	1989	1990	1991	1992	1993	1994	1995	1996	1997	1998	1999	2000	2001		
Percent Per Annum																**Interest Rates**	
	7.50	9.00	9.00	9.00	9.00	7.50	7.00	6.50	6.50	6.50	6.50	6.50	5.75	5.75	5.75	Bank Rate (*End of Period*)	60
	2.40	4.46	5.21	5.85	6.49	5.32	3.96	1.88	3.01	4.45	4.35	3.84	1.97	1.03	1.94	Treasury Bill Rate	60c
	5.50	5.97	6.48	6.57	6.92	6.13	5.19	4.30	4.20	5.14	5.23	5.36	4.57	4.08	4.25	Deposit Rate	60l
	9.00	9.00	9.00	9.00	9.00	8.08	7.46	6.88	6.75	6.75	6.75	6.75	6.38	6.00	6.00	Lending Rate	60p
Period Averages																**Prices and Labor**	
	72.1	75.3	79.3	83.0	89.0	94.1	96.6	98.0	†100.0	101.4	101.9	103.3	104.6	106.3	108.4	Consumer Prices	64
Period Averages																	
	....	....	....	114	....	135	....	137	....	....	....	296	....	....	....	Labor Force	67d
	....	111	112	....	114	115	119	120	127	130	135	144	....	....	....	Employment	67e
	....	14	15	....	16	20	18	18	16	17	15	12,115	....	....	....	Unemployment	67c
	....	11.0	11.7	....	12.3	14.8	13.1	13.3	10.9	11.5	9.8	7.7	....	....	....	Unemployment Rate (%)	67r
Millions of Bahamian Dollars																**International Transactions**	
	2,722	2,153	2,487	†238	225	192	162	167	176	180	181	300	450	400	649	Exports	70
	3,080	2,291	3,137	†1,112	1,091	1,038	954	1,056	1,243	1,366	1,666	1,873	1,911	1,421	1,891	Imports, c.i.f.	71
Minus Sign Indicates Debit																**Balance of Payments**	
	-54.8	-66.5	-84.2	-36.6	-179.8	35.8	48.7	-42.2	-145.9	-263.5	-472.1	-995.4	-671.9	-401.5	....	Current Account, n.i.e.	78ald
	324.8	310.8	221.0	283.5	229.4	216.6	192.2	198.5	225.4	273.3	295.0	362.9	379.9	690.0	....	Goods: Exports f.o.b.	78aad
	-998.1	-982.9	-1,131.8	-1,080.0	-1,046.3	-984.3	-930.2	-1,013.6	-1,156.7	-1,287.4	-1,410.7	-1,737.1	-1,808.1	-1,996.4	....	Goods: Imports f.o.b.	78abd
	-673.3	-672.1	-910.8	-796.5	-816.9	-767.7	-738.0	-815.3	-931.3	-1,014.1	-1,115.7	-1,374.2	-1,428.2	-1,306.4	....	*Trade Balance*	78acd
	1,265.6	1,275.2	1,474.3	1,500.1	1,354.0	1,389.6	1,459.0	1,510.6	1,542.3	1,578.2	1,592.9	1,533.0	1,811.2	2,022.7	....	Services: Credit	78add
	-461.9	-491.2	-522.0	-573.0	-549.1	-515.5	-567.7	-627.2	-639.1	-715.8	-836.0	-990.9	-953.8	-988.2	....	Services: Debit	78aed
	130.4	111.9	41.5	130.6	-12.0	106.4	153.3	68.1	-28.1	-151.7	-358.8	-832.1	-570.8	-271.9	....	*Balance on Goods & Services*	78afd
	18.1	15.3	236.1	232.1	197.9	103.3	112.2	61.2	75.1	84.6	105.7	147.9	229.6	212.1	....	Income: Credit	78agd
	-201.4	-182.2	-367.7	-404.9	-376.9	-185.9	-240.6	-198.8	-210.8	-233.4	-258.3	-345.4	-367.2	-385.0	....	Income: Debit	78ahd
	-52.9	-55.0	-90.1	-42.2	-191.0	23.8	24.9	-69.5	-163.8	-300.5	-511.4	-1,029.6	-708.4	-444.8	....	*Balance on Gds, Serv. & Inc.*	78aid
	16.7	17.4	9.7	12.1	16.0	19.9	33.1	33.1	25.1	45.9	50.0	45.0	49.0	53.8	....	Current Transfers, n.i.e.: Credit	78ajd
	-18.6	-28.9	-3.8	-6.5	-4.8	-7.9	-9.3	-5.8	-7.2	-8.7	-10.7	-10.8	-12.5	-10.5	....	Current Transfers: Debit	78akd
	-1.7	-3.0	-16.6	-7.7	-5.6	-9.8	-9.4	-11.6	-12.5	-24.4	-12.9	-11.7	-14.5	-16.4	....	Capital Account, n.i.e.	78bcd
																Capital Account, n.i.e.: Credit	78bad
	-1.7	-3.0	-16.6	-7.7	-5.6	-9.8	-9.4	-11.6	-12.5	-24.4	-12.9	-11.7	-14.5	-16.4	....	Capital Account: Debit	78bbd
	-14.9	73.2	88.8	66.8	173.0	-4.4	9.3	66.8	104.6	181.1	412.0	817.7	611.4	429.3	....	Financial Account, n.i.e.	78bjd
	—	—	-.4	.1	1.3	-.3	-.1	.1	-.1	.3	-.4	-1.0	-.2	—	....	Direct Investment Abroad	78bdd
	10.8	36.7	25.4	-17.3	-1.3	.3	27.1	23.4	106.8	87.8	210.0	146.9	144.6	249.6	....	Dir. Invest. in Rep. Econ., n.i.e.	78bed
	—	—	....													Portfolio Investment Assets	78bfd
	—	—	....													Equity Securities	78bkd
	—	—	....													Debt Securities	78bld
	—	—	....													Portfolio Investment Liab., n.i.e.	78bgd
	—	—	....													Equity Securities	78bmd
	—	—	....													Debt Securities	78bnd
			....													Financial Derivatives Assets	78bwd
			....													Financial Derivatives Liabilities	78bxd
	11.9	39.3	8,288.5	2,282.7	7,295.5	-5,520.5	-3,009.4	-7,455.9	7,436.6	-6,428.8	-80.7	-4,872.0	-12,487.1	-19,067.2	....	Other Investment Assets	78bhd
	—	—	—													Monetary Authorities	78bod
	—	—	—													General Government	78bpd
	11.9	39.3	8,288.5	2,282.7	7,295.5	-5,520.5	-3,009.4	-7,455.9	7,436.6	-6,428.8	-80.7	-4,872.0	-12,487.1	-19,067.2	....	Banks	78bqd
	—	—	—													Other Sectors	78brd
	-37.6	-2.8	-8,224.7	-2,198.7	-7,122.5	5,516.1	2,991.7	7,499.2	-7,438.7	6,521.8	283.1	5,543.8	12,954.1	19,246.8	....	Other Investment Liab., n.i.e.	78bid
	—	—	—													Monetary Authorities	78bsd
	-20.7	-8.1	4.9	12.7	4.1	-4.7	-16.4	-5.8	-26.9	-25.2	19.2	-5.9	11.7	-11.1	....	General Government	78btd
	—	—	-8,249.3	-2,240.1	-7,285.7	5,474.1	3,010.7	7,459.6	-7,417.9	6,451.8	141.9	4,901.8	12,578.9	19,039.0	....	Banks	78bud
	-16.9	5.3	19.7	28.7	159.1	46.7	-2.6	45.4	6.1	95.2	122.0	647.9	363.5	218.9	....	Other Sectors	78bvd
	11.5	-4.4	-13.2	-10.8	25.0	-49.6	-30.0	-3.9	50.9	99.0	129.5	308.6	140.2	-72.3	....	Net Errors and Omissions	78cad
	-59.9	-.7	-25.2	11.7	12.6	-28.0	18.6	9.1	-2.9	-7.6	56.5	119.2	65.2	-61.0	....	*Overall Balance*	78cbd
	59.9	.7	25.2	-11.7	-12.6	28.0	-18.6	-9.1	2.9	7.6	-56.5	-119.2	-65.2	61.0	....	Reserves and Related Items	79dad
	59.9	.7	25.2	-11.7	-12.6	28.0	-18.6	-9.1	2.9	7.6	-56.5	-119.2	-65.2	61.0	....	Reserve Assets	79dbd
																Use of Fund Credit and Loans	79dcd
	....	....	....													Exceptional Financing	79ded
Year Ending December 31																**Government Finance**	
	-21.4	†-76.0	-123.5	-75.8	-132.5	-88.1	†-85.1	-20.0	-23.2	-63.5	-136.3	-83.0	-50.9	-12.7	-100.6	Deficit (-) or Surplus	80
	436.1	†432.6	456.7	497.8	490.4	534.6	†537.1	618.2	660.2	685.8	728.1	760.9	868.8	937.2	920.2	Revenue	81
	....	....	....	....	....	....	....	....	....	.5	.5	....	....	....	....	Grants Received	81z
	462.0	†513.8	580.8	554.2	584.6	597.8	†584.0	604.5	657.3	719.7	829.4	808.5	884.4	916.1	961.3	Expenditure	82
	-4.5	†-5.2	-.6	19.4	38.3	24.9	†38.2	33.7	26.1	30.1	35.5	35.4	35.3	33.8	59.5	Lending Minus Repayments	83
																Financing	
	26.4	†82.7	134.0	83.9	157.1	85.0	†93.8	47.3	10.1	94.8	130.4	74.1	36.5	12.1	70.0	Net Borrowing: Domestic	84a
	-18.5	†-18.1	3.2	7.9	4.1	-4.7	†-14.6	-9.6	14.8	-13.7	19.4	-3.0	12.3	8.6	8.6	Foreign	85a
	13.5	†11.4	-13.7	-16.0	-28.7	7.8	†5.9	-17.7	-1.7	-17.5	-14.3	11.5	1.7	-8.0	22.1	Use of Cash Balances	87
	419.4	†474.0	545.8	643.7	738.1	777.1	†954.1	1,032.9	1,074.9	1,158.0	1,281.7	1,342.4	1,407.2	1,403.9	1,483.8	Debt: Domestic	88a
	108.5	†100.4	126.0	129.4	133.5	125.2	†110.6	100.4	90.9	77.0	96.4	93.4	105.7	114.4	123.3	Foreign	89a
Millions of Bahamian Dollars																**National Accounts**	
	1,137.5	1,126.9	†2,040.7	2,027.1	2,122.8	1,938.2	1,986.0	2,054.1	2,077.4	....					....	Househ.Cons.Expend.,incl.NPISHs	96f
	333.8	370.1	†423.1	413.8	450.9	434.7	408.4	511.0	483.9	....					....	Government Consumption Expend.	91f
	512.7	510.7	†726.7	654.2	647.3	650.3	526.4	614.0	698.5	....					....	Gross Fixed Capital Formation	93e
	6.4	27.5	†13.0	9.6	4.2	13.0	32.8	32.4	13.8	....					....	Changes in Inventories	93i
	1,773.0	2,100.8	†1,538.1	1,697.0	1,492.9	1,462.3	1,517.4	1,569.3	1,680.1	....					....	Exports of Goods and Services	90c
	1,451.6	1,557.0	†1,599.1	1,614.1	1,609.4	1,503.8	1,477.4	1,633.3	1,819.6	....					....	Imports of Goods and Services (-)	98c
	....	....	-198.7	-140.6	-220.5	-137.5	-140.1	-94.3	-64.7	....					....	Statistical Discrepancy	99bs
	2,311.7	2,578.9	†2,943.8	3,046.9	2,888.2	2,857.1	2,853.6	3,053.1	3,069.4	....					....	Gross Domestic Product (GDP)	99b
	-162.8	-149.6	†-110.8	-138.3	-132.0	-58.0	-74.5	-89.3	-96.9	....					....	Net Primary Income from Abroad	98.n
	2,148.9	2,429.3	†2,833.0	2,908.6	2,756.2	2,799.1	2,779.1	2,963.8	2,972.5	....					....	Gross National Income (GNI)	99a
	....	....	1.0	10.6	20.3	13.4	14.5	15.7	5.4	....					....	Net Current Transf.from Abroad	98t
	....	....	2,834.0	2,919.2	2,776.5	2,812.5	2,793.6	2,979.5	2,977.9	....					....	Gross Nat'l Disposable Inc.(GNDI)	99i
	....	....	370.2	478.3	202.8	439.7	399.1	423.4	416.6	....					....	Gross Saving	99s
	....	....	3,085.6	2,982.7	2,888.2	2,720.9	2,664.8	2,716.8	2,746.1	....					....	GDP Volume 1991 Prices	99b.p
	....	....	112.4	108.6	105.2	99.1	97.0	98.9	100.0	....					....	GDP Volume (1995=100)	99bv.p
	....	....	†85.4	91.4	89.5	93.9	95.8	100.5	100.0	....					....	GDP Deflator (1995=100)	99bi.p
Midyear Estimates																	
	.24	.25	.25	.26	.26	.26	.27	.27	.28	.28	.29	.30	.30	.30	.31	**Population**	99z

(See notes in the back of the book.)

Bahrain, Kingdom of

		1972	1973	1974	1975	1976	1977	1978	1979	1980	1981	1982	1983	1984	1985	1986
Exchange Rates															*SDRs per Dinar:*	
Official Rate	ac	2.1000	2.1000	2.0691	2.1598	2.1754	2.0807	1.9997	2.0135	2.0853	2.2850	2.4110	2.5403	2.7133	2.4213	2.1743
															US Dollars per Dinar:	
Official Rate	ag	2.2800	2.5333	2.5333	2.5284	2.5275	2.5275	2.6052	2.6525	2.6596	2.6596	2.6596	2.6596	2.6596	2.6596	2.6596
Official Rate	rh	2.2800	2.5046	2.5333	2.5284	2.5278	2.5275	2.5809	2.6206	2.6525	2.6596	2.6596	2.6596	2.6596	2.6596	2.6596
													Index Numbers (1995=100):			
Official Rate	ahx	85.7	94.2	95.3	95.1	95.0	95.0	97.0	98.5	99.7	100.0	100.0	100.0	100.0	100.0	100.0
Nominal Effective Exchange Rate	nec	....	....	....	....	....	....	....	104.3	104.8	114.2	125.2	131.4	139.2	143.8	122.3
Real Effective Exchange Rate	rec	....	....	....	....	....	....	....	....	147.2	162.8	182.4	189.1	193.5	188.0	153.2
Fund Position															*Millions of SDRs:*	
Quota	2f. s	10.0	10.0	10.0	10.0	10.0	10.0	20.0	20.0	30.0	30.0	30.0	48.9	48.9	48.9	48.9
SDRs	1b. s	—	—	—	—	—	—	.1	2.2	1.8	5.2	14.0	12.2	13.1	13.6	14.1
Reserve Position in the Fund	1c. s	2.5	2.5	5.5	9.6	4.7	4.8	5.8	5.8	8.5	8.9	12.5	21.4	23.1	24.6	26.0
International Liquidity													*Millions of US Dollars Unless Otherwise Indicated:*			
Total Reserves minus Gold	1l. d	83.5	64.0	131.3	289.5	436.4	503.9	493.4	613.9	953.4	1,544.1	1,534.8	1,426.4	1,302.4	1,659.7	1,489.4
SDRs	1b. d	—	—	—	—	—	—	.1	2.9	2.2	6.1	15.4	12.8	12.8	15.0	17.3
Reserve Position in the Fund	1c. d	2.7	3.0	6.7	11.2	5.5	5.8	7.5	7.6	10.9	10.4	13.8	22.4	22.6	27.0	31.8
Foreign Exchange	1d. d	80.8	61.0	124.6	278.3	430.9	498.1	485.8	603.4	940.3	1,527.7	1,505.6	1,391.2	1,267.0	1,617.7	1,440.3
Monetary Agency	1da d	54.8	30.0	43.3	148.8	336.4	443.0	434.5	429.3	544.0	812.4	768.2	762.3	619.4	774.0	740.3
Government	1db d	26.0	31.0	81.3	129.5	94.5	55.1	51.3	174.1	396.3	715.3	737.4	628.9	647.6	843.7	700.0
Gold (Million Fine Troy Ounces)	1ad	.237	.237	.238	.150	.150	.150	.150	.150	.150	.150	.150	.150	.150	.150	.150
Gold (National Valuation)	1and	8.2	....	10.1	6.3	6.3	6.3	6.5	6.6	6.6	6.6	6.6	6.6	6.6	6.6	6.6
Monetary Authorities: Other Liab.	4.. d	—	—	—	16.4	122.1	154.4	97.4	8.5	101.1	48.4	21.8	43.1	3.2	27.5	25.4
Deposit Money Banks: Assets	7a. d	106.6	114.4	250.5	406.0	479.8	566.3	635.1	627.8	851.0	912.6	952.3	1,250.2	1,159.1	1,560.6	1,847.4
Liabilities	7b. d	39.4	58.4	154.2	328.0	389.9	499.8	499.7	625.4	627.7	326.7	333.0	398.7	279.2	339.5	403.2
OBU: Foreign Assets	7k. d	....	....	....	1,687	5,568	13,527	20,445	23,074	30,555	41,819	48,890	53,361	53,861	49,148	49,069
Foreign Liabilities	7m. d	....	....	....	1,687	5,617	13,561	20,440	23,076	30,349	41,116	48,275	51,864	53,010	47,939	47,720
Monetary Authorities															*Millions of Dinars:*	
Foreign Assets	11	32.6	23.0	56.0	116.7	174.7	201.5	195.0	236.0	399.3	601.0	589.4	556.0	536.9	649.8	600.2
Reserve Money	14	25.3	16.1	19.3	49.2	72.8	69.7	76.0	93.6	91.2	105.0	125.8	124.4	116.8	136.0	128.5
of which: Currency Outside DMBs	14a	23.8	14.9	16.9	24.0	34.2	43.8	44.1	49.9	58.3	63.3	70.5	73.5	78.2	79.0	80.0
Time and Savings Deposits	15	—	—	—	—	—	6.3	29.9	31.4	37.4	30.2	21.9	14.8	—	—	—
Foreign Liabilities	16c	—	—	—	6.5	48.3	61.1	37.4	3.2	38.0	18.2	8.2	16.2	1.2	10.3	9.5
Central Government Deposits	16d	16.6	13.0	34.9	57.2	44.7	44.9	22.6	80.4	183.3	389.2	334.9	303.0	350.5	386.8	335.7
Capital Accounts	17a	—	—	3.6	9.7	15.0	28.0	41.6	49.9	62.0	66.5	86.2	92.5	100.6	134.4	151.1
Other Items (Net)	17r	–8.8	–5.6	–1.8	–5.9	–6.1	–8.5	–12.5	–22.6	–12.6	–8.1	12.4	5.1	–32.2	–17.8	–24.7
Deposit Money Banks															*Millions of Dinars:*	
Reserves	20	1.5	1.2	2.4	25.3	38.5	25.4	33.9	36.9	37.8	40.8	53.9	36.3	40.0	56.5	47.4
Foreign Assets	21	46.8	45.2	98.9	160.6	189.9	224.1	243.8	236.7	320.0	343.1	358.1	470.1	435.8	586.8	694.6
Claims on Central Government	22a	9.1	2.9	1.1	1.3	3.6	9.2	23.8	26.8	27.2	13.8	26.2	33.7	97.9	89.2	126.6
Claims on Private Sector	22d	53.1	76.4	120.9	160.8	267.9	310.8	325.4	375.8	434.9	487.5	544.6	606.9	640.2	598.4	566.1
Demand Deposits	24	31.4	44.5	44.4	53.8	93.7	108.7	127.2	136.2	133.9	185.4	152.4	133.8	130.1	140.0	131.5
Time and Savings Deposits	25	32.7	40.3	84.5	106.5	175.9	203.0	231.0	225.8	331.8	481.8	198.2	635.8	619.5	684.3	673.7
Foreign Liabilities	26c	17.3	23.1	60.9	129.7	154.2	197.8	191.8	235.8	236.0	122.8	125.2	149.9	105.0	127.6	151.6
Central Government Deposits	26d	13.7	11.3	32.0	50.5	68.7	49.0	66.9	50.8	85.0	59.9	58.9	114.1	240.5	242.6	270.8
Capital Accounts	27a	3.4	6.2	7.6	9.4	14.2	21.5	24.3	34.7	42.6	62.7	122.3	137.6	130.9	167.8	252.7
Other Items (Net)	27r	12.1	.4	–6.2	–1.9	–6.9	–10.7	–14.3	–7.0	–9.5	–27.5	–33.3	–24.3	–12.0	–31.5	–45.7
Monetary Survey															*Millions of Dinars:*	
Foreign Assets (Net)	31n	62.1	45.1	94.0	141.1	162.0	166.7	209.6	233.6	445.3	803.1	814.0	860.0	866.5	1,098.6	1,133.6
Domestic Credit	32	32.0	55.0	55.1	54.4	158.1	226.1	259.7	271.4	193.8	52.1	177.0	223.4	147.1	58.2	86.2
Claims on Central Govt. (Net)	32an	–21.1	–21.4	–65.8	–106.4	–109.8	–84.7	–65.7	–104.4	–241.1	–435.3	–367.6	–383.5	–493.1	–540.3	–479.9
Claims on Private Sector	32d	53.1	76.4	120.9	160.8	267.9	310.8	325.4	375.8	434.9	487.5	544.6	606.9	640.2	598.4	566.1
Money	34	55.2	59.4	61.3	77.8	127.9	152.5	171.3	186.1	192.2	248.8	222.9	207.3	208.3	219.0	211.5
Quasi-Money	35	32.7	40.3	84.5	106.5	175.9	209.3	260.9	257.2	369.2	512.0	220.1	650.6	619.5	684.3	673.7
Other Items (Net)	37r	6.6	1.0	3.3	11.2	16.3	30.9	37.1	61.8	77.6	94.5	189.0	225.5	185.9	253.5	334.6
Money plus Quasi-Money	35l	87.9	99.6	145.8	184.2	303.8	361.8	432.2	443.3	561.5	760.7	443.0	858.0	827.8	903.3	885.2
Other Banking Institutions															*Millions of Dinars*	
Reserves	40	....	....	....	....	....	....	....	....	....	....	....	....	....	....	....
Claims on Mon.Author.: Securities	40c	....	....	....	....	....	....	....	....	....	....	....	....	....	....	....
Foreign Assets	41	....	....	....	....	....	....	....	....	....	....	....	....	....	....	....
Claims on Central Government	42a	....	....	....	....	....	....	....	....	....	....	....	....	....	....	....
Claims on Private Sector	42d	....	....	....	....	....	....	....	....	....	....	....	....	....	....	....
Other Claims on Dep.Money Banks	42e	....	....	....	....	....	....	....	....	....	....	....	....	....	....	....
Time and Saving Deposits	45	....	....	....	....	....	....	....	....	....	....	....	....	....	....	....
Liquid Liabilities	45l	....	....	....	....	....	....	....	....	....	....	....	....	....	....	....
Money Market Instruments	46aa	....	....	....	....	....	....	....	....	....	....	....	....	....	....	....
Foreign Liabilities	46c	....	....	....	....	....	....	....	....	....	....	....	....	....	....	....
Central Government Deposits	46d	....	....	....	....	....	....	....	....	....	....	....	....	....	....	....
Credit from Monetary Authorities	46g	....	....	....	....	....	....	....	....	....	....	....	....	....	....	....
Credit from Deposit Money Banks	46h	....	....	....	....	....	....	....	....	....	....	....	....	....	....	....
Capital Accounts	47a	....	....	....	....	....	....	....	....	....	....	....	....	....	....	....
Other Items (Net)	47r	....	....	....	....	....	....	....	....	....	....	....	....	....	....	....
Banking Survey															*millions of dinars*	
Foreign Assets (Net)	51n	....	....	....	....	....	....	....	....	....	....	....	....	....	....	....
Domestic Credit	52	....	....	....	....	....	....	....	....	....	....	....	....	....	....	....
Claims on Central Govt. (Net)	52an	....	....	....	....	....	....	....	....	....	....	....	....	....	....	....
Claims on Local Government	52	....	....	....	....	....	....	....	....	....	....	....	....	....	....	....
Claims on Private Sector	52d	....	....	....	....	....	....	....	....	....	....	....	....	....	....	....
Liquid Liabilities	55l	....	....	....	....	....	....	....	....	....	....	....	....	....	....	....
Money Market Instruments	56a	....	....	....	....	....	....	....	....	....	....	....	....	....	....	....
Capital Accounts	57a	....	....	....	....	....	....	....	....	....	....	....	....	....	....	....
Other Items (Net)	57r	....	....	....	....	....	....	....	....	....	....	....	....	....	....	....

1987	1988	1989	1990	1991	1992	1993	1994	1995	1996	1997	1998	1999	2000	2001	Item	Code
															Exchange Rates	
End of Period																
1.8747	1.9764	2.0238	1.8695	1.8593	1.9343	1.9363	1.8218	1.7892	1.8495	1.9711	1.8889	1.9377	2.0413	2.1163	Official Rate	ac
End of Period (ag) Period Average (rh)																
2.6596	2.6596	2.6596	2.6596	2.6596	2.6596	2.6596	2.6596	2.6596	2.6596	2.6596	2.6596	2.6596	2.6596	2.6596	Official Rate	ag
2.6596	2.6596	2.6596	2.6596	2.6596	2.6596	2.6596	2.6596	2.6596	2.6596	2.6596	2.6596	2.6596	2.6596	2.6596	Official Rate	rh
Period Averages																
100.0	100.0	100.0	100.0	100.0	100.0	100.0	100.0	100.0	100.0	100.0	100.0	100.0	100.0	100.0	Official Rate	ahx
110.2	104.0	108.3	103.3	103.6	101.8	107.2	105.0	100.0	102.3	108.6	112.6	112.4	118.9	123.9	Nominal Effective Exchange Rate	ne c
132.4	121.6	123.0	112.5	109.0	103.5	108.8	105.0	100.0	99.6	107.7	109.6	106.5	109.4	111.5	Real Effective Exchange Rate	re c
End of Period															**Fund Position**	
48.9	48.9	48.9	48.9	48.9	48.9	82.8	82.8	82.8	82.8	82.8	82.8	135.0	135.0	135.0	Quota	2f. s
14.6	15.1	15.9	16.9	17.8	18.7	10.8	11.0	11.3	11.7	11.9	12.1	—	1.0	.8	SDRs	1b. s
27.3	27.7	29.6	28.0	29.6	31.1	40.9	42.2	43.7	45.1	46.7	48.5	62.4	64.9	67.2	Reserve Position in the Fund	1c. s
End of Period															**International Liquidity**	
1,148.5	1,251.7	1,050.0	1,234.9	1,514.6	1,398.5	1,302.2	1,169.7	1,279.9	1,318.4	1,290.3	1,079.2	1,369.0	1,564.1	1,684.0	Total Reserves minus Gold	1l. d
20.7	20.4	20.9	24.0	25.5	25.7	14.8	16.1	16.8	16.8	16.1	17.1	—	1.3	1.1	SDRs	1b. d
38.7	37.3	38.9	39.8	42.4	42.7	56.2	61.6	65.0	64.8	63.0	68.3	85.6	84.5	84.4	Reserve Position in the Fund	1c. d
1,089.1	1,194.0	990.3	1,171.1	1,446.7	1,330.0	1,231.2	1,092.0	1,198.2	1,236.8	1,211.2	993.8	1,283.4	1,478.3	1,598.5	Foreign Exchange	1d. d
923.5	692.2	693.7	922.2	1,196.3	1,079.6	980.4	841.5	947.3	985.9	960.5	743.0	1,032.9	1,227.4	1,348.5	Monetary Agency	1da d
165.6	501.8	296.6	248.9	250.4	250.4	250.8	250.5	250.9	250.9	250.7	250.8	250.5	250.9	250.0	Government	1db d
.150	.150	.150	.150	.150	.150	.150	.150	.150	.150	.150	.150	.150	.150	.150	Gold (Million Fine Troy Ounces)	1ad
6.6	6.6	6.6	6.6	6.6	6.6	6.6	6.6	6.6	6.6	6.6	6.6	6.6	6.6	6.6	Gold (National Valuation)	1an d
—	—	74.7	116.3	16.4	—										Monetary Authorities: Other Liab.	4.. d
1,846.7	2,276.3	3,113.0	2,505.1	†1,975.0	1,855.1	2,272.9	2,761.7	2,592.0	2,557.2	2,863.0	3,164.1	3,410.6	3,419.9	3,327.9	Deposit Money Banks: Assets	7a. d
390.2	425.9	867.5	762.8	†599.5	675.5	977.1	1,486.2	1,136.4	1,042.3	1,583.2	1,522.1	2,305.3	1,672.9	1,480.6	Liabilities	7b. d
57,879	62,942	67,355	56,806	51,187	67,142	57,673	62,363	61,061	64,435	69,382	....	....	....	....	OBU: Foreign Assets	7k. d
56,828	61,613	66,614	56,888	50,585	66,569	57,180	61,875	60,579	64,068	68,644	....	....	....	....	Foreign Liabilities	7m. d
End of Period															**Monetary Authorities**	
470.5	529.6	547.8	473.8	510.8	498.6	481.9	459.1	496.2	494.7	558.4	549.9	530.9	612.8	676.2	Foreign Assets	11
142.3	133.5	144.6	158.2	†249.4	227.1	181.5	173.9	234.0	208.0	234.1	183.2	266.5	264.9	303.0	Reserve Money	14
84.1	84.4	84.8	105.3	†99.0	99.9	103.8	105.5	103.3	102.9	104.6	93.3	113.0	120.7	122.9	of which: Currency Outside DMBs	14a
—	—	—	—	—	5.0	10.0	10.0	20.0	24.5	23.5	35.9	48.4	26.3	40.3	Time and Savings Deposits	15
—	28.1	43.7	6.2	—											Foreign Liabilities	16c
174.4	249.5	246.6	141.2	118.3	117.7	118.9	120.3	131.4	124.5	122.2	137.5	124.4	133.0	125.1	Central Government Deposits	16d
167.8	166.8	170.4	183.9	184.8	198.4	213.3	206.1	240.3	251.0	270.8	291.5	296.5	313.2	332.9	Capital Accounts	17a
-14.0	-48.3	-57.5	-15.6	†-41.6	-49.6	-41.8	-51.1	-129.3	-113.0	-92.2	-98.2	-204.9	-124.7	-125.1	Other Items (Net)	17r
End of Period															**Deposit Money Banks**	
54.1	48.6	53.5	196.7	†141.5	116.5	73.3	66.3	124.6	99.0	126.6	89.4	153.7	139.1	177.9	Reserves	20
694.3	855.9	1,170.5	941.9	†742.6	697.5	854.6	1,038.4	974.6	961.5	1,076.5	1,189.7	1,282.4	1,285.9	1,251.3	Foreign Assets	21
253.0	114.9	127.8	161.2	†98.0	156.6	132.1	138.5	150.7	166.6	172.1	223.3	323.8	322.3	333.5	Claims on Central Government	22a
498.0	491.6	482.4	474.6	†612.1	676.4	818.5	915.0	947.8	954.7	1,074.3	1,164.2	1,302.5	1,380.5	1,411.3	Claims on Private Sector	22d
134.8	132.2	126.9	153.3	†205.8	252.0	261.1	239.2	229.2	232.4	243.1	272.3	313.2	325.1	429.1	Demand Deposits	24
749.6	791.0	840.8	672.2	†841.9	845.6	896.5	992.7	1,095.0	1,132.6	1,238.3	1,477.7	1,482.1	1,684.6	1,763.7	Time and Savings Deposits	25
146.7	160.1	326.2	286.8	†225.4	254.0	367.4	558.8	427.3	391.9	595.3	572.3	866.8	629.0	556.7	Foreign Liabilities	26c
318.6	334.6	448.1	511.1	†399.6	284.2	337.0	416.7	358.0	433.3	443.1	409.9	431.0	436.7	426.3	Central Government Deposits	26d
201.9	172.3	169.5	132.8	†111.9	155.7	169.1	194.6	185.5	191.5	199.4	254.9	259.6	294.1	312.1	Capital Accounts	27a
-52.2	-79.2	-77.4	18.2	†-190.3	-144.6	-152.8	-243.7	-97.4	-200.0	-269.8	-320.4	-290.2	-241.7	-313.9	Other Items (Net)	27r
															Monetary Survey	
1,018.1	1,197.3	1,348.3	1,122.7	†1,028.0	942.1	969.1	938.7	1,043.5	1,064.3	1,039.6	1,167.3	946.5	1,269.7	1,370.8	Foreign Assets (Net)	31n
258.0	22.5	-84.6	-16.5	†192.2	431.1	494.7	516.5	609.1	563.5	681.1	840.1	1,070.9	1,133.1	1,193.4	Domestic Credit	32
-240.0	-469.2	-566.9	-491.1	†-419.9	-245.3	-323.8	-398.5	-338.7	-391.2	-393.2	-324.1	-231.6	-247.4	-217.9	Claims on Central Govt. (Net)	32an
498.0	491.6	482.4	474.6	†612.1	676.4	818.5	915.0	947.8	954.7	1,074.3	1,164.2	1,302.5	1,380.5	1,411.3	Claims on Private Sector	32d
218.9	216.6	211.6	258.6	†304.8	351.9	364.9	344.7	332.5	335.3	347.7	365.6	426.2	445.8	552.0	Money	34
749.6	791.0	840.8	672.2	†841.9	850.6	906.5	1,002.7	1,115.0	1,157.1	1,261.8	1,513.6	1,530.5	1,710.9	1,804.0	Quasi-Money	35
307.6	212.1	211.3	175.5	†73.7	170.6	192.2	108.0	205.2	135.6	111.1	128.3	60.8	246.0	208.2	Other Items (Net)	37r
968.5	1,007.6	1,052.4	930.7	†1,146.7	1,202.5	1,271.4	1,347.4	1,447.5	1,492.4	1,609.5	1,879.2	1,956.7	2,156.7	2,356.0	Money plus Quasi-Money	35l
End of Period															**Other Banking Institutions**	
....	....	....	....												Reserves	40
....	....	....	....												Claims on Mon.Author.: Securities	40c
....	....	....	....	51,643.2	67,914.9	58,188.8	62,864.3	62,001.2	65,690.8	70,924.9	86,679.9	87,670.6	91,508.8	87,587.6	Foreign Assets	41
....	....	....	....	.5	.5	.5	.4	.5	.7	.7	41.2	65.7	65.0	104.7	Claims on Central Government	42a
....	....	....	....	889.0	1,119.0	973.0	981.4	833.8	739.5	929.5	797.4	793.5	697.8	727.1	Claims on Private Sector	42d
....	....	....	....												Other Claims on Dep.Money Banks	42e
....	....	....	....												Time and Saving Deposits	45
....	....	....	....	631.0	767.0	405.0	474.4	548.3	845.2	1,155.6	1,169.1	1,041.4	750.7	609.5	Liquid Liabilities	45l
....	....	....	....												Money Market Instruments	46aa
....	....	....	....	50,283.7	66,080.4	56,838.3	62,802.5	60,637.1	63,812.3	68,756.8	84,570.2	85,218.2	89,659.3	85,655.9	Foreign Liabilities	46c
....	....	....	....	810.0	714.0	275.0	464.1	982.2	998.3	648.2	505.4	472.0	493.5	606.8	Central Government Deposits	46d
....	....	....	....												Credit from Monetary Authorities	46g
....	....	....	....												Credit from Deposit Money Banks	46h
....	....	....	....												Capital Accounts	47a
....	....	....	....												Other Items (Net)	47r
End of Period															**Banking Survey**	
....	....	....	....												Foreign Assets (Net)	51n
....	....	....	....												Domestic Credit	52
....	....	....	....												Claims on Central Govt. (Net)	52an
....	....	....	....												Claims on Local Government	52
....	....	....	....												Claims on Private Sector	52d
....	....	....	....												Liquid Liabilities	55l
....	....	....	....												Money Market Instruments	56a
....	....	....	....												Capital Accounts	57a
....	....	....	....												Other Items (Net)	57r

Bahrain, Kingdom of

		1972	1973	1974	1975	1976	1977	1978	1979	1980	1981	1982	1983	1984	1985	1986
Interest Rates															*Percent Per Annum*	
Money Market Rate	60b	...	...	...	...									...	...	7.2
Treasury Bill Rate	60c	...	...	...	...											
Deposit Rate	60l	...	...	...	...	6.5	6.5	6.5	6.8	7.9	9.0	8.6	7.0	7.0	6.7	5.6
Lending Rate	60p	...	...	...	...											9.0
Prices, Production, Labor														*Index Numbers (1995=100):*		
Consumer Prices	64	26.6	30.4	37.8	43.9	†53.8	63.3	73.3	75.0	77.9	86.7	94.4	97.2	†97.5	94.9	92.8
Refined Petroleum Production	66ab	90.9	93.4	95.5	83.4	85.1	101.5	96.4	97.3	95.8	102.3	77.3	69.6	80.1	74.0	97.8
															Number in Thousands:	
Labor Force	67d	...	...	...	...	...	...	...	...	...	...	...	...	...	...	...
Employment	67e	...	...	...	...	...	...	...	...	...	...	...	...	...	112	...
Unemployment	67c	...	...	...	...	...	...	...	...	...	...	...	...	...	6	7
International Transactions															*Millions of Dinars*	
Exports	70	152.4	191.5	502.0	438.0	522.2	730.1	733.4	949.5	1,359.6	1,634.6	1,424.8	1,172.9	1,204.7	1,089.2	827.0
Imports, c.i.f.	71	165.1	204.3	445.0	470.4	659.8	802.7	792.2	945.3	1,313.0	1,550.6	1,358.9	1,226.4	1,308.3	1,168.1	904.3
Balance of Payments															*Millions of US Dollars:*	
Current Account, n.i.e.	78ald	...	...	...	-203.0	-360.2	-324.0	-387.7	-222.7	184.4	429.5	425.6	102.7	218.4	38.8	-68.9
Goods: Exports f.o.b.	78aad	...	...	...	1,203.0	1,518.0	1,848.9	1,891.8	2,499.1	3,433.2	4,177.1	3,695.0	3,119.4	3,204.0	2,896.8	2,199.5
Goods: Imports f.o.b.	78abd	...	...	...	-1,090.0	-1,510.1	-1,837.0	-1,873.3	-2,094.8	-2,987.5	-3,559.3	-3,167.8	-2,935.6	-3,131.6	-2,796.0	-2,164.6
Trade Balance	78acd	...	...	...	113.0	7.8	11.9	18.6	404.3	445.6	617.8	527.2	183.8	72.3	100.8	34.8
Services: Credit	78add	...	...	...	156.3	201.5	255.8	364.2	313.7	332.9	360.9	567.6	366.8	813.8	911.4	764.4
Services: Debit	78aed	...	...	...	-179.3	-243.2	-296.2	-342.8	-369.7	-473.7	-610.1	-729.8	-499.5	-555.1	-488.6	-327.1
Balance on Goods & Services	78afd	...	...	...	90.0	-33.9	-28.6	40.0	348.3	304.8	368.6	364.9	51.1	331.1	523.7	472.1
Income: Credit	78agd	...	...	...	45.5	66.7	76.3	106.9	112.2	314.1	517.8	489.9	415.7	335.6	322.6	277.9
Income: Debit	78ahd	...	...	...	-262.2	-309.4	-369.5	-494.0	-687.6	-522.3	-544.7	-501.3	-404.5	-447.3	-692.8	-675.0
Balance on Gds, Serv. & Inc.	78aid	...	...	...	-126.7	-276.5	-321.7	-347.1	-227.2	96.6	341.8	353.5	62.2	219.4	153.5	75.0
Current Transfers, n.i.e.: Credit	78ajd	...	...	...	—	1.3	100.8	94.7	98.0	183.6	194.4	189.6	142.6	124.5	120.2	120.7
Current Transfers: Debit	78akd	...	...	...	-76.4	-84.9	-103.1	-135.2	-93.5	-95.8	-106.6	-117.6	-102.1	-125.5	-234.8	-264.6
Capital Account, n.i.e.	78bcd	...	...	...	—	—	—	—	—	—	—	—	—	—	—	—
Capital Account, n.i.e.: Credit	78bad	...	...	...	—	—	—	—	—	—	—	—	—	—	—	—
Capital Account: Debit	78bbd	...	...	...	—	—	—	—	—	—	—	—	—	—	—	—
Financial Account, n.i.e.	78bjd	...	...	...	149.7	353.6	461.3	-3.1	37.2	-238.7	-502.9	-71.0	-166.0	-35.6	-476.1	-99.7
Direct Investment Abroad	78bdd	...	...	...												
Dir. Invest. in Rep. Econ., n.i.e.	78bed	...	...	...	—	—	—	23.0	145.2	-418.0	—	28.5	64.1	140.7	101.3	-31.9
Portfolio Investment Assets	78bfd	...	...	...	—	—	—	-145.3	-83.6	-8.8	-16.8	-16.0	-47.9	—	-28.5	-26.1
Equity Securities	78bkd	...	...	...	—	—	—	-145.3	-83.6	-8.8	-16.8	-16.0	-47.9	—	-28.5	-26.1
Debt Securities	78bld	...	...	...												
Portfolio Investment Liab., n.i.e.	78bgd	...	...	...	96.1	139.0	195.1	112.0	42.2	121.5	69.9	—	—	—	—	—
Equity Securities	78bmd	...	...	...	96.1	139.0	195.1	112.0	42.2	121.5	69.9	—	—	—	—	—
Debt Securities	78bnd	...	...	...												
Financial Derivatives Assets	78bwd	...	...	...	...	...	...	...	...	...	...	...	...	...	...	...
Financial Derivatives Liabilities	78bxd	...	...	...	...	...	...	...	...	...	...	...	...	...	...	...
Other Investment Assets	78bhd	...	...	...	-164.1	-98.6	-120.8	-76.7	-6.8	-250.4	-88.6	-127.1	-314.6	-17.6	-410.6	-298.9
Monetary Authorities	78bod	...	...	...												
General Government	78bpd	...	...	...	-8.1	-14.7	-22.0	-4.4	-8.9	-1.3	-2.4	-50.5	-8.0	-6.6	-9.0	-5.3
Banks	78bqd	...	...	...	-156.0	-73.8	-85.4	-52.1	18.6	-221.0	-61.7	-39.9	-297.9	91.0	-401.6	-286.7
Other Sectors	78brd	...	...	...	—	-10.1	-13.4	-20.1	-16.5	-28.1	-24.5	-36.7	-8.8	-101.9	—	-6.9
Other Investment Liab., n.i.e.	78bid	...	...	...	217.7	313.2	387.0	83.9	-59.7	317.0	-467.6	43.6	132.4	-158.8	-138.3	257.2
Monetary Authorities	78bsd	...	...	...	16.4	105.7	32.4	-61.2	-89.6	92.3	-52.7	—	—	—	—	—
General Government	78btd	...	...	...	—	25.3	8.1	77.2	26.5	308.8	-126.9	-121.3	-4.3	17.3	-59.3	-16.2
Banks	78bud	...	...	...	174.2	61.9	110.2	-15.5	115.3	.5	-301.1	6.4	65.7	-119.4	60.4	63.8
Other Sectors	78bvd	...	...	...	27.1	120.3	236.3	83.4	-111.9	-84.6	13.0	158.5	71.0	-56.6	-139.4	209.6
Net Errors and Omissions	78cad	...	...	...	222.3	153.2	-70.0	372.8	308.7	396.3	662.7	-358.9	-45.2	-192.8	794.7	-7.1
Overall Balance	78cbd	...	...	...	168.9	146.6	67.3	-18.0	123.2	342.0	589.3	-4.4	-108.5	-10.1	357.4	-175.7
Reserves and Related Items	79dad	...	...	...	-168.9	-146.6	-67.3	18.0	-123.2	-342.0	-589.3	4.4	108.5	10.1	-357.4	175.7
Reserve Assets	79dbd	...	...	...	-168.9	-146.6	-67.3	18.0	-123.2	-342.0	-589.3	4.4	108.5	10.1	-357.4	175.7
Use of Fund Credit and Loans	79dcd	...	...	...	...	...	...	...	...	...	...	...	...	...	...	...
Exceptional Financing	79ded	...	...	...	...	...	...	...	...	...	...	...	...	...	...	...
International Investment Position															*Millions of US Dollars*	
Assets	79aad	...	...	...	...	...	...	...	...	...	...	...	...	...	...	...
Direct Investment Abroad	79abd	...	...	...	...	...	...	...	...	...	...	...	...	...	...	...
Portfolio Investment	79acd	...	...	...	...	...	...	...	...	...	...	...	...	...	...	...
Equity Securities	79add	...	...	...	...	...	...	...	...	...	...	...	...	...	...	...
Debt Securities	79aed	...	...	...	...	...	...	...	...	...	...	...	...	...	...	...
Financial Derivatives	79ald	...	...	...	...	...	...	...	...	...	...	...	...	...	...	...
Other Investment	79afd	...	...	...	...	...	...	...	...	...	...	...	...	...	...	...
Monetary Authorities	79agd	...	...	...	...	...	...	...	...	...	...	...	...	...	...	...
General Government	79ahd	...	...	...	...	...	...	...	...	...	...	...	...	...	...	...
Banks	79aid	...	...	...	...	...	...	...	...	...	...	...	...	...	...	...
Other Sectors	79ajd	...	...	...	...	...	...	...	...	...	...	...	...	...	...	...
Reserve Assets	79akd	...	...	...	...	...	...	...	...	...	...	...	...	...	...	...
Liabilities	79lad	...	...	...	...	...	...	...	...	...	...	...	...	...	...	...
Dir. Invest. in Rep. Economy	79lbd	...	...	...	...	...	...	...	...	...	...	...	...	...	...	...
Portfolio Investment	79lcd	...	...	...	...	...	...	...	...	...	...	...	...	...	...	...
Equity Securities	79ldd	...	...	...	...	...	...	...	...	...	...	...	...	...	...	...
Debt Securities	79led	...	...	...	...	...	...	...	...	...	...	...	...	...	...	...
Financial Derivatives	79lld	...	...	...	...	...	...	...	...	...	...	...	...	...	...	...
Other Investment	79lfd	...	...	...	...	...	...	...	...	...	...	...	...	...	...	...
Monetary Authorities	79lgd	...	...	...	...	...	...	...	...	...	...	...	...	...	...	...
General Government	79lhd	...	...	...	...	...	...	...	...	...	...	...	...	...	...	...
Banks	79lid	...	...	...	...	...	...	...	...	...	...	...	...	...	...	...
Other Sectors	79ljd	...	...	...	...	...	...	...	...	...	...	...	...	...	...	...

	1987	1988	1989	1990	1991	1992	1993	1994	1995	1996	1997	1998	1999	2000	2001			
Percent Per Annum																	**Interest Rates**	
	7.1	8.0	9.2	8.5	6.3	4.0	3.5	5.2	6.2	5.7	....	5.7	5.6	6.9	3.9	Money Market Rate	60b
	6.4	7.4	9.1	....	5.9	3.8	3.3	4.8	6.1	5.5	5.7	5.5	5.5	6.6	3.8	Treasury Bill Rate	60c
	5.0	5.5	7.3	7.5	....	†3.6	3.0	4.0	5.7	5.2	5.3	4.7	4.8	5.8	2.7	Deposit Rate	60l
	7.5	7.8	†8.5	8.5	9.5	11.9	11.0	10.8	11.8	12.5	12.3	11.9	11.9	11.7	10.8	Lending Rate	60p
Period Averages																	**Prices, Production, Labor**	
	91.1	91.4	92.8	93.6	94.3	94.2	96.6	97.4	100.0	99.5	†102.0	101.7	100.3	99.6	....	Consumer Prices	64
	96.9	96.5	97.0	99.3	102.1	102.6	98.1	98.6	100.0	104.0	100.1	99.0	104.8	102.7	95.7	Refined Petroleum Production	66ab
Period Averages																		
	....	....	....	....	226	....	....	....	....	....	....	295	....	....	....	Labor Force	67d
	86	86	92	92	93	103	110	116	....	....	124	....	148	149	....	Employment	67e
	4	4	3	3	3	3	4	4	5	....	6	4	4	6	....	Unemployment	67c
Millions of Dinars																	**International Transactions**	
	913.5	906.7	1,064.5	1,414.0	1,320.0	1,302.6	1,400.0	1,359.9	1,546.4	1,768.0	1,648.2	1,229.6	1,556.8	2,144.5	2,084.8	Exports	70
	1,020.3	975.1	1,178.2	1,395.6	1,547.3	1,602.9	1,450.6	1,409.2	1,397.1	1,606.6	1,513.6	1,340.9	1,390.3	1,742.2	1,602.8	Imports, c.i.f.	71
Minus Sign Indicates Debit																	Balance of Payments	
	-201.3	192.0	-193.1	69.7	-602.7	-826.6	-339.4	-255.6	237.2	260.6	-31.1	-777.7	-340.4	112.8	....	Current Account, n.i.e.	78al d
	2,429.5	2,411.4	2,831.1	3,760.6	3,513.3	3,465.4	3,723.4	3,617.0	4,114.4	4,702.1	4,383.0	3,270.2	4,140.4	5,700.5	....	Goods: Exports f.o.b.	78aa d
	-2,442.3	-2,334.0	-2,820.2	-3,524.2	-3,880.6	-3,992.3	-3,616.2	-3,497.3	-3,488.3	-4,037.0	-3,778.2	-3,298.7	-3,468.4	-4,373.4	....	Goods: Imports f.o.b.	78ab d
	-12.8	77.4	10.9	236.4	-367.3	-526.9	107.2	119.7	626.1	665.2	604.8	-28.5	672.1	1,327.1	....	*Trade Balance*	78ac d
	863.6	901.6	809.6	358.5	411.2	542.8	651.9	818.6	683.2	666.2	637.2	724.7	748.7	830.1	....	Services: Credit	78ad d
	-525.0	-529.3	-556.4	-474.5	-534.3	-604.0	-581.9	-621.8	-634.0	-612.8	-634.8	-651.9	-647.1	-682.7	....	Services: Debit	78ae d
	325.8	449.7	264.1	120.5	-490.4	-588.0	177.1	316.5	675.3	718.6	607.2	44.4	773.7	1,474.5	....	*Balance on Goods & Services*	78af d
	282.2	263.0	377.7	5,496.8	3,517.6	2,525.3	2,283.8	3,112.5	4,087.0	3,815.2	4,270.7	4,763.8	5,094.1	5,902.4	....	Income: Credit	78ag d
	-678.5	-694.1	-738.0	-5,275.3	-3,326.3	-2,493.1	-2,477.7	-3,355.1	-4,146.0	-3,840.2	-4,506.9	-4,926.1	-5,388.8	-6,273.7	....	Income: Debit	78ah d
	-70.5	18.6	-96.3	342.0	-299.2	-555.9	-16.8	73.9	616.2	693.6	371.0	-117.8	479.0	1,103.2	....	*Balance on Gds, Serv. & Inc.*	78ai d
	113.3	368.1	102.1	59.8	65.7	64.9	73.1	101.1	120.7	126.3	232.7	65.2	36.7	22.3	....	Current Transfers, n.i.e.: Credit	78aj d
	-244.1	-194.7	-198.9	-332.2	-369.1	-335.6	-395.7	-430.6	-499.7	-559.3	-634.8	-725.0	-856.1	-1,012.8	....	Current Transfers: Debit	78ak d
	—	—	—	457.4	101.1	101.1	202.1	319.1	156.9	50.0	125.0	100.0	100.0	50.0	....	Capital Account, n.i.e.	78bc d
	—	—	—	457.4	101.1	101.1	202.1	319.1	156.9	50.0	125.0	100.0	100.0	50.0	....	Capital Account, n.i.e.: Credit	78ba d
	—	—	—	....	....	....	....	....	....	....	....	....	....	....	....	Capital Account: Debit	78bb d
	-55.6	-214.4	-264.6	1,156.6	65.4	397.3	593.9	1,301.1	-1,726.6	-510.4	15.4	22.3	287.2	-8.2	....	Financial Account, n.i.e.	78bj d
	—	—	—	-25.0	-50.0	-52.9	-38.8	-198.7	16.0	-305.1	-47.6	-180.9	-163.3	.3	....	Direct Investment Abroad	78bd d
	-35.9	222.1	180.9	-182.7	619.4	868.6	-275.0	208.2	430.6	2,048.1	329.3	179.5	453.7	357.7	....	Dir. Invest. in Rep. Econ., n.i.e.	78be d
	-1.9	—	1.1	697.6	-1,063.0	-1,398.1	-1,335.4	-454.0	-113.3	-779.8	-1,150.8	-1,206.6	-2,048.7	-83.5	....	Portfolio Investment Assets	78bf d
	-1.9	—	1.1	....	....	....	....	....	....	....	....	-75.5	-150.5		....	Equity Securities	78bk d
	—	—	—	697.6	-1,063.0	-1,398.1	-1,335.4	-454.0	-113.3	-779.8	-1,150.8	-1,206.6	-1,973.1	67.0	....	Debt Securities	78bl d
	....	....	....	....	....	....	....	....	....	....	....	194.7	112.8	282.4	....	Portfolio Investment Liab., n.i.e.	78bg d
															....	Equity Securities	78bm d
	....	....	....	....	....	....	....	....	....	....	....	194.7	112.8	282.4	....	Debt Securities	78bn d
															....	Financial Derivatives Assets	78bw d
															....	Financial Derivatives Liabilities	78bx d
	-7.2	-437.0	-916.8	10,768.6	6,531.4	-14,709.8	10,672.3	-4,527.1	1,124.5	-2,579.8	-4,342.0	-14,677.9	967.0	-3,833.8	....	Other Investment Assets	78bh d
															....	Monetary Authorities	78bo d
	-3.7	-7.4	-79.8	-13.3	-16.0	-5.3	-5.3	-8.0	-5.3	-8.0	-8.0	-5.1	-7.7	-5.9	....	General Government	78bp d
	.8	-429.5	-837.0	10,781.9	6,547.3	-14,704.5	10,677.7	-4,519.1	1,129.8	-2,571.8	-4,334.0	-14,672.9	974.7	-3,827.9	....	Banks	78bq d
	-4.3														....	Other Sectors	78br d
	-10.6	.5	470.2	-10,101.9	-5,972.3	15,689.6	-8,429.3	6,272.6	-3,184.3	1,106.1	5,226.6	15,713.6	965.7	3,268.6	....	Other Investment Liab., n.i.e.	78bi d
	12.2	—	17.3												....	Monetary Authorities	78bs d
	-17.6	-10.1	-7.4	-6.4	-10.9	.8	4.5	4.0	11.2	1.3	52.4	44.1	54.8	59.0	....	General Government	78bt d
	-13.0	35.9	441.8	-10,025.5	-6,826.6	15,009.3	-8,660.1	6,268.4	-2,901.9	1,056.4	5,175.5	15,394.4	875.8	3,256.4	....	Banks	78bu d
	7.7	-25.3	18.6	-69.9	865.2	679.5	226.3	.3	-293.6	48.4	-1.3	275.0	35.1	-46.8	....	Other Sectors	78bv d
	-85.8	114.9	269.3	-887.7	-87.3	238.1	-569.2	-1,412.2	1,501.4	193.3	-6.5	638.7	-21.6	45.6	....	Net Errors and Omissions	78ca d
	-342.7	92.5	-188.5	796.0	-523.5	-90.1	-112.5	-47.5	168.9	-6.4	102.8	-16.6	25.3	200.1		*Overall Balance*	78cb d
	342.7	-92.5	188.5	-796.0	523.5	90.1	112.5	47.5	-168.9	6.4	-102.8	16.6	-25.3	-200.1	....	Reserves and Related Items	79da d
	342.7	-92.5	188.5	-796.0	523.5	90.1	112.5	47.5	-168.9	6.4	-102.8	16.6	-25.3	-200.1	....	Reserve Assets	79db d
															....	Use of Fund Credit and Loans	79dc d
	....	....	....	....	....	....	....	....	....	....	....	....	....	....	....	Exceptional Financing	79de d
Millions of US Dollars																	International Investment Position	
	....	....	71,586.5	60,934.0	54,976.7	71,035.4	61,614.0	66,735.3	65,872.8	69,518.5	75,156.1	91,198.8	92,459.2	96,566.3	....	Assets	79aa d
	....	....	694.4	719.4	769.4	822.3	861.2	1,059.8	1,043.9	1,348.7	1,396.3	1,577.1	1,740.4	1,740.2	....	Direct Investment Abroad	79ab d
	....	....	3,109.6	2,413.1	3,476.1	4,870.3	6,201.1	6,647.6	6,760.6	7,538.8	8,696.8	9,899.2	11,947.9	12,031.4	....	Portfolio Investment	79ac d
	....	....	....	....	....	....	....	....	....	....	....	1,064.1	1,139.6	1,289.9	....	Equity Securities	79ad d
	....	....	3,109.6	2,413.1	3,476.1	4,870.3	6,201.1	6,647.6	6,760.6	7,538.8	8,696.8	8,835.1	10,808.2	10,741.5	....	Debt Securities	79ae d
															....	Financial Derivatives	79al d
	....	....	66,701.7	55,920.0	49,372.5	64,076.9	53,398.6	57,917.7	56,787.9	59,359.7	63,694.0	78,366.6	77,391.9	81,220.1	....	Other Investment	79af d
															....	Monetary Authorities	79ag d
															....	General Government	79ah d
	....	....	66,701.7	55,920.0	49,372.5	....	....	....	....	....	....	78,366.6	77,391.9	81,220.1	....	Banks	79ai d
															....	Other Sectors	79aj d
	....	....	1,080.7	1,881.6	1,358.6	1,265.8	1,153.2	1,110.1	1,280.4	1,271.3	1,369.0	1,355.9	1,379.0	1,574.7	....	Reserve Assets	79ak d
	....	....	67,376.7	57,317.3	51,100.0	66,979.9	58,049.1	64,529.7	62,081.8	65,187.7	70,744.6	86,515.3	88,016.3	91,970.9	....	Liabilities	79la d
	....	....	734.6	551.6	1,171.0	2,039.6	1,764.6	1,972.9	2,403.5	4,451.6	4,780.8	4,960.4	5,414.1	5,771.8	....	Dir. Invest. in Rep. Economy	79lb d
	....	....	—	—	—	....	....	....	....	....	....	194.7	307.7	590.2	....	Portfolio Investment	79lc d
															....	Equity Securities	79ld d
	....	....	—	—	—	....	....	....	....	....	....	194.7	307.7	590.2	....	Debt Securities	79le d
															....	Financial Derivatives	79ll d
	....	....	66,642.1	56,765.7	49,928.9	64,940.0	56,284.5	62,556.8	59,678.4	60,736.3	65,963.7	81,360.2	82,294.5	85,608.9	....	Other Investment	79lf d
															....	Monetary Authorities	79lg d
															....	General Government	79lh d
	....	....	66,642.1	56,616.5	49,789.8	....	....	....	....	....	....	81,131.0	82,006.8	85,263.2	....	Banks	79li d
															....	Other Sectors	79lj d

Bahrain, Kingdom of

	1972	1973	1974	1975	1976	1977	1978	1979	1980	1981	1982	1983	1984	1985	1986
Government Finance														*Millions of Dinars:*	
Deficit (-) or Surplus **80**	....	....	39.6	5.5	−36.2	−12.9	−30.6	22.1	68.0	110.8	32.1	−96.2	−23.0	13.7	−51.9
Revenue **81**	....	....	115.3	129.0	186.4	227.4	247.5	277.9	388.9	478.3	497.8	443.5	485.4	503.8	422.2
Grants Received **81z**			2.2	—	.3	27.7	26.4	26.4	56.8	58.3	56.4	47.0	37.6	37.6	37.6
Expenditure **82**	....	....	67.0	112.3	190.9	242.5	285.3	254.5	317.2	380.2	473.7	535.1	538.6	508.5	495.1
Lending Minus Repayments **83**			10.9	11.2	32.0	25.5	19.2	27.7	60.5	45.6	48.4	51.6	7.4	19.2	16.6
Financing															
Total Financing **80h**	....	....	−39.6	−5.5	36.2	12.9	30.6	−22.1	−68.0	−110.8	−32.1	96.2	23.0	−13.7	51.9
Domestic **84a**	....	....	−45.2	−7.9	26.2	10.4	−.7	14.2	3.5	5.6	21.4	52.0	9.5	37.5	−3.6
Foreign **85a**	....	....	5.6	2.4	10.0	2.5	31.3	−36.3	−71.5	−116.4	−53.5	44.2	13.5	−51.2	55.5
Debt: Domestic **88a**	....	—	—	—	—	—	20.0	20.0	20.0	20.0	20.0	30.0	30.0	30.0	74.1
Foreign **89a**	....	4.2	9.7	12.1	22.1	24.6	54.5	64.6	77.1	81.3	91.0	87.3	93.8	71.1	65.2
National Accounts														*Millions of Dinars*	
Househ.Cons.Expend.,incl.NPISHs **96f**	....	....	....	170.8	262.7	336.7	390.6	404.0	370.3	427.7	472.9	481.6	465.6	407.0	370.3
Government Consumption Expend. **91f**	....	....	....	64.6	85.2	111.1	132.3	152.1	150.9	188.6	233.3	254.5	302.2	312.8	312.4
Gross Fixed Capital Formation **93e**	....	....	....	129.1	249.3	349.6	359.5	329.8	356.9	380.5	451.9	536.6	604.1	463.6	370.1
Changes in Inventories **93i**	....	....	....	25.6	17.7	9.3	59.5	92.2	163.7	160.2	57.0	117.7	37.9	25.9	−64.5
Exports of Goods and Services **90c**	....	....	....	531.5	674.0	817.0	826.7	1,050.7	1,421.1	1,714.0	1,621.0	1,344.2	1,455.0	1,397.4	1,132.9
Imports of Goods and Services (-) **98c**	....	....	....	495.7	695.4	853.7	861.0	1,010.6	1,304.8	1,567.3	1,465.5	1,294.4	1,381.3	1,233.6	973.4
Gross Domestic Product (GDP) **99b**	....	....	....	425.9	593.5	770.0	907.6	1,018.2	1,158.1	1,303.9	1,370.8	1,440.4	1,483.5	1,373.1	1,147.7
Net Primary Income from Abroad **98.n**									−46.6	−15.0	−38.0	−69.3	−57.5	−109.7	−117.9
Gross National Income (GNI) **99a**									1,111.5	1,288.9	1,332.8	1,370.9	1,426.0	1,263.4	1,029.8
Consumption of Fixed Capital **99cf**	....	....	....	....	....	....	....	....	....	....	135.5	149.0	167.3	214.9	206.1	208.6
Net National Income **99e**									991.0	1,153.4	1,183.8	1,203.6	1,211.1	1,057.3	821.2
GDP Volume 1977 prices **99b.p**	....	....	....	543.1	672.0	770.8	833.4	824.1	878.2	916.8	971.8	1,049.7	....	....	....
GDP Volume 1989 Prices **99b.p**	....	....	....	....	....	....	....	....	....	....	....	1,182.3	1,227.3	1,193.5	1,207.5
GDP Volume (1995=100) **99bvp**	....	....	....	29.0	35.9	41.2	44.6	44.1	46.9	49.0	51.9	56.1	58.2	56.6	57.3
GDP Deflator (1995=100) **99bip**	....	....	....	66.7	75.1	85.0	92.6	105.1	112.2	121.0	120.0	116.7	115.8	110.2	91.1
															Millions:
Population **99z**	.23	.24	.26	.26	.26	.30	.32	.33	.34	.35	.37	.39	.39	.41	.44

	1987	1988	1989	1990	1991	1992	1993	1994	1995	1996	1997	1998	1999	2000	2001		
Government Finance																	
Year Ending December 31																	
	−122.2	49.1	−115.8	−103.1	−67.6	−115.2	−1.9	−58.3	−126.6	−55.0	−125.3	−116.5	−133.6	66.0	....	Deficit (-) or Surplus	80
	376.4	360.6	403.4	468.8	472.6	464.8	544.8	476.3	526.6	615.5	633.1	516.6	653.5	1,065.9	....	Revenue	81
	37.6	37.6	37.6	26.3	37.6	37.6	18.8	37.6	37.6	18.8	46.9	37.6	37.6	18.8	....	Grants Received	81z
	418.0	445.5	467.5	505.0	502.8	548.8	593.4	623.4	594.1	581.3	620.0	644.6	699.3	777.0	....	Expenditure	82
	118.2	−96.4	89.3	93.2	75.0	68.8	−27.9	−51.2	96.7	108.0	185.3	26.1	125.4	241.7	....	Lending Minus Repayments	83
Financing																	
	122.2	−49.1	115.8	103.1	67.6	115.2	1.9	58.3	126.6	55.0	125.3	116.5	133.6	−66.0	....	Total Financing	80h
	−73.4	80.3	40.3	−35.9	71.7	114.2	-.4	56.6	122.5	54.5	125.1	99.9	113.4	−87.6	....	Domestic	84a
	195.6	−129.4	75.5	139.0	−4.1	1.0	2.3	1.7	4.1	.5	.2	16.6	20.2	21.6	....	Foreign	85a
	102.5	193.8	215.4	84.9	233.5	328.5	323.6	318.8	314.0	297.0	319.5	404.5	482.0	747.9	....	Debt: Domestic	88a
	59.9	60.7	58.1	53.9	50.8	52.0	54.7	55.5	59.6	65.8	85.4	87.6	107.8	129.4	....	Foreign	89a
National Accounts																	
Millions of Dinars																	
	449.6	523.3	578.3	610.8	1,017.7	1,055.8	1,095.3	1,123.4	1,165.4	1,229.3	1,277.4	1,327.6	1,378.4	1,411.8	....	Househ.Cons.Expend.,incl.NPISHs	96f
	310.1	339.2	356.6	385.1	406.0	426.2	435.5	440.0	458.5	464.3	465.1	482.8	518.2	526.2	....	Government Consumption Expend.	91f
	287.3	269.1	287.8	301.0	343.5	386.2	454.2	417.5	381.3	284.1	285.9	326.2	338.4	404.6	....	Gross Fixed Capital Formation	93e
	37.4	12.1	70.1	−39.7	152.9	139.3	−96.3	−6.5	−59.8	46.4	130.6	171.9	−36.1	100.0	....	Changes in Inventories	93i
	1,305.6	1,327.2	1,433.0	1,837.8	1,475.4	1,507.4	1,640.0	1,669.7	1,803.3	2,017.7	1,887.8	1,502.1	1,838.3	2,455.4	....	Exports of Goods and Services	90c
	1,114.7	1,078.8	1,273.0	1,504.6	1,660.0	1,728.2	1,578.5	1,548.8	1,550.0	1,748.3	1,659.3	1,485.4	1,547.5	1,901.1	....	Imports of Goods and Services (-)	98c
	1,275.4	1,392.1	1,452.7	1,590.4	1,735.7	1,786.4	1,955.3	2,093.4	2,199.4	2,294.3	2,387.3	2,325.1	2,489.3	2,996.9	....	Gross Domestic Product (GDP)	99b
	−121.4	−197.8	−196.8	−258.5	71.8	12.0	−72.9	−91.0	−22.2	−9.5	−88.8	−60.9	−100.8	−139.5	....	Net Primary Income from Abroad	98.n
	1,154.0	1,194.3	1,255.9	1,331.9	1,807.5	1,798.3	1,882.5	2,002.4	2,177.2	2,284.8	2,298.5	2,264.3	2,378.5	2,857.4	....	Gross National Income (GNI)	99a
	214.2	227.2	235.1	248.9	261.8	262.8	307.5	326.7	332.6	328.7	332.4	343.5	358.5	364.8	....	Consumption of Fixed Capital	99cf
	939.8	967.1	1,020.8	1,083.0	1,545.7	1,535.5	1,575.0	1,675.7	1,844.6	1,956.2	1,966.2	1,920.8	2,020.0	2,492.6	....	Net National Income	99e
	.....	.....	.....	.....	.....	.....	.....	.....	.....	.....	.....	.....	.....	.....	....	GDP Volume 1977 prices	99b.p
	1,333.0	1,447.5	1,452.7	1,517.2	1,687.8	1,800.6	2,032.5	2,027.4	2,107.0	2,193.5	2,261.5	2,369.7	2,471.9	2,603.3	....	GDP Volume 1989 Prices	99b.p
	63.3	68.7	68.9	72.0	80.1	85.5	96.5	96.2	100.0	104.1	107.3	112.5	117.3	123.6	....	GDP Volume (1995=100)	99bv p
	91.7	92.1	95.8	100.4	98.5	95.0	92.2	98.9	100.0	100.2	101.1	94.0	96.5	110.3	....	GDP Deflator (1995=100)	99bi p
Midyear Estimates																	
	.46	.47	.49	.48	.50	.52	.54	.56	.58	.60	.62	.64	.67	.69	.65	**Population**	99z

(See notes in the back of the book.)

Bangladesh

	1972	1973	1974	1975	1976	1977	1978	1979	1980	1981	1982	1983	1984	1985	1986
Exchange Rates														*Taka per SDR:*	
Official Rate..........aa= ....wa	8.770	9.849	9.888	17.356	17.373	17.486	19.456	20.607	20.726	23.101	26.556	26.174	25.485	34.051	37.674
														Taka per US Dollar:	
Official Rate..........ae= ....we	8.078	8.164	8.077	14.826	14.953	14.396	14.934	15.643	16.251	19.847	24.074	25.000	26.000	31.000	30.800
Official Rate..........rf= ....wf	7.594	7.742	8.113	12.019	15.347	15.375	15.016	15.552	15.454	17.987	22.118	24.615	25.354	†27.995	30.407
Fund Position														*Millions of SDRs:*	
Quota......................................2f. s	125.0	125.0	125.0	125.0	125.0	125.0	152.0	152.0	228.0	228.0	228.0	287.5	287.5	287.5	287.5
SDRs......................................1b. s	—	—	—	15.4	16.1	3.9	.1	9.2	.4	.1	.8	12.9	.3	11.9	8.4
Reserve Position in the Fund ....1c. s	2.0	1.2	—	—	—	—	—	—	—	—	—	—	22.4	22.4	22.4
Total Fund Cred.&Loans Outstg. 2tl	62.5	62.5	133.3	171.6	235.8	207.8	229.4	262.3	332.6	398.9	496.2	540.0	471.6	473.3	440.5
International Liquidity												*Millions of US Dollars Unless Otherwise Indicated:*			
Total Reserves minus Gold ....1l. d	270.5	143.2	138.2	148.3	288.9	232.7	315.2	386.3	299.6	138.4	182.6	524.1	389.9	336.5	409.1
SDRs.......................................1b. d	—	—	—	18.1	18.7	4.8	.1	12.1	.4	.1	.8	13.5	.3	13.1	10.3
Reserve Position in the Fund ....1c. d	2.2	1.5	—	—	—	—	—	—	—	—	8.3	23.5	22.0	24.6	27.4
Foreign Exchange ....1d. d	268.3	141.7	138.2	130.2	270.2	227.9	315.1	374.2	299.2	138.3	173.5	487.1	367.7	298.8	371.4
Gold (Million Fine Troy Ounces) 1ad	—	—	—	—	.054	.027	.054	.054	.054	.054	.057	.057	.059	.060	.066
Gold (National Valuation)................1an d	—	.1	—	—	—	2.3	1.2	15.7	21.5	16.9	24.5	17.5	15.8	12.9	16.8
Monetary Authorities: Other Liab. ....4.. d	....	.1	—	—	21.2	42.2	35.5	80.6	143.1	179.0	197.6	213.6	130.0	95.3	74.6
Deposit Money Banks: Assets ....7a. d	....	....	118.2	121.4	104.2	111.0	127.7	176.1	272.2	228.3	153.0	188.0	221.0	289.0	273.0
Liabilities ...7b. d	....	....	25.2	21.8	26.4	61.2	67.7	77.9	171.0	115.4	94.7	54.0	96.0	127.0	119.0
Monetary Authorities														*Millions of Taka:*	
Foreign Assets 11	....	1,174	1,115	2,084	4,318	3,385	4,728	6,332	5,252	3,052	†5,710	16,444	13,349	13,360	14,414
Claims on Central Government 12a	....	3,353	4,240	5,200	5,544	5,696	5,946	5,320	8,782	13,594	10,350	9,833	9,384	10,658	4,454
Claims on Nonfin.Pub.Enterprises 12c	....	—	160	160	160	160	160	511	460	500	†800	750	580	580	580
Claims on Deposit Money Banks 12e	....	635	1,799	2,220	832	2,625	3,752	5,705	8,554	9,841	15,074	10,596	18,808	22,681	23,117
Claims on Other Financial Insts 12f	....	270	223	156	169	172	305	924	1,675	2,138	2,695	3,605	5,644	7,261	8,810
Reserve Money 14	....	4,095	5,157	5,033	5,158	6,679	8,541	9,914	11,767	12,912	†14,275	19,140	25,870	29,439	31,536
of which: Currency Outside DMBs 14a	....	3,212	4,103	3,618	3,817	4,902	6,329	7,114	8,267	9,143	9,744	13,444	17,250	17,672	19,027
Liabs. of Central Bank: Securities 16ac	....														
Foreign Liabilities..........................16c	....	617	1,318	2,979	4,414	4,240	4,994	6,665	9,218	12,769	19,977	20,872	17,721	21,826	21,116
Central Government Deposits 16d	....	—	—	—	—	—	—	—	—	10	†13	5	411	10	10
Central Govt. Lending Funds 16f	....									5	12	907	1,806	2,418	3,031
Capital Accounts 17a	....	103	133	183	223	263	303	682	1,245	1,862	2,172	2,487	2,867	3,247	3,627
Other Items (Net)..........................17r	....	617	928	1,626	1,227	856	1,053	1,531	2,484	1,576	†−1,820	−2,182	−910	−2,399	−7,946
Deposit Money Banks															
Reserves 20	....	....	1,145	1,276	1,378	1,736	2,051	2,645	3,378	3,798	4,227	5,642	7,867	9,312	10,387
Claims on Mon.Author.: Securities 20c	....	....													
Foreign Assets 21	....	....	955	1,799	1,558	1,077	1,363	1,919	3,498	4,106	5,702	5,939	6,179	8,945	8,415
Claims on Central Government 22a	....	....	2,401	1,942	2,462	3,185	2,961	4,153	5,423	4,616	5,054	10,362	13,004	11,927	17,876
Claims on Nonfin.Pub.Enterprises 22c	....	....	5,194	6,502	6,623	7,622	10,013	12,015	14,774	17,179	22,978	22,567	23,160	26,021	30,385
Claims on Private Sector 22d	....	....	2,603	3,309	4,455	7,450	9,105	12,650	16,205	22,423	26,566	37,799	59,386	75,530	83,242
Claims on Other Financial Insts 22f	....	....	690	137	257	318	645	794	1,225	1,243	†1,336	1,761	1,823	1,844	2,031
Demand Deposits 24	....	....	4,284	4,662	5,399	6,764	8,306	11,240	11,903	13,570	†13,589	18,191	25,016	28,280	30,968
Time Deposits 25	....	....	5,603	6,458	8,255	9,943	12,667	15,049	20,213	24,443	†29,442	42,262	58,315	68,322	82,794
Foreign Liabilities.........................26c	....	....	155	128	181	564	540	612	1,582	2,291	2,279	1,346	2,306	3,949	3,768
Central Government Deposits 26d	....	....									1,682	2,634	3,055	3,800	5,296
Central Govt. Lending Funds 26f	....	....	480	622	411	432	571	701	1,292	1,741	2,284	3,393	4,383	5,615	5,939
Credit from Monetary Authorities 26g	....	....	1,769	1,962	845	2,446	3,385	5,707	8,995	9,971	15,012	9,985	16,432	20,358	21,551
Capital Accounts 27a	....	....	431	423	793	920	959	1,039	1,132	1,255	1,523	2,641	3,223	3,534	3,964
Other Items (Net)..........................27r	....	....	266	712	850	319	−290	−172	−614	92	†51	3,618	−1,311	−279	−1,944
Monetary Survey														*Millions of Taka:*	
Foreign Assets (Net) 31n	....	....	597	776	1,281	−343	557	975	−2,050	−7,902	†−10,844	165	−500	−3,470	−2,056
Domestic Credit 32	....	....	15,511	17,407	19,683	24,602	29,136	36,365	48,533	61,686	†68,083	84,038	109,515	130,011	142,072
Claims on Central Govt. (Net) 32an	....	....	6,641	7,142	8,006	8,881	8,907	9,473	14,195	18,205	†13,709	17,556	18,922	18,775	17,024
Claims on Nonfin.Pub.Enterprises 32c	....	....	5,354	6,662	6,783	7,782	10,173	12,525	15,234	17,679	†23,778	23,317	23,740	26,601	30,965
Claims on Private Sector 32d	....	....	2,603	3,309	4,455	7,450	9,105	12,650	16,205	22,423	26,566	37,799	59,386	75,530	83,242
Claims on Other Financial Insts 32f	....	....	913	293	439	490	950	1,718	2,899	3,380	†4,031	5,366	7,467	9,105	10,841
Money 34	....	....	8,391	8,283	9,216	11,667	14,636	18,356	20,171	22,716	†23,336	31,636	42,269	45,956	49,996
Quasi-Money 35	....	....	5,603	6,458	8,255	9,943	12,667	15,049	20,213	24,443	†29,442	42,262	58,315	68,322	82,794
Central Govt. Lending Funds 36f	....	....	480	622	411	432	571	701	1,292	1,741	†2,296	4,300	6,189	8,033	8,970
Capital Accounts 37a	....	....	563	605	1,016	1,183	1,262	1,721	2,376	3,118	3,695	5,128	6,090	6,781	7,591
Other Items (Net)..........................37r	....	....	1,071	2,215	2,052	1,035	558	1,514	2,431	1,767	†−1,530	878	−3,847	−2,550	−9,353
Money plus Quasi-Money 35l	....	....	13,994	14,741	17,471	21,610	27,302	33,405	40,384	47,159	†52,778	73,898	100,584	114,278	132,790
Interest Rates														*Percent Per Annum*	
Discount Rate *(End of Period)* 60	5.00	5.00	8.00	8.00	8.00	8.00	8.00	8.00	10.50	10.50	10.50	10.50	10.50	11.25	10.75
Deposit Rate 60l	....	....	....	....	6.75	7.00	7.00	7.00	8.25	12.00	12.00	12.00	12.00	12.00	12.00
Lending Rate 60p	....	....	....	....	11.00	11.00	11.00	11.00	11.33	12.00	12.00	12.00	12.00	12.00	14.00
Prices, Production, Labor														*Index Numbers (1995=100):*	
Consumer Prices 64	....	....													58.0
Industrial Production 66	....	....	51.4	54.6	52.8	52.7	49.9	†48.9	51.3	55.5	52.2	53.0	55.7	56.4	55.3
														Number in Thousands:	
Labor Force.................................67d	....	....													
Employment 67e	....	....												30,585	....
Unemployment 67c	....	....													....
Unemployment Rate.......................67r	....	....													
International Transactions														*Millions of Taka*	
Exports 70	1,992	2,764	2,819	3,689	6,150	7,314	8,251	10,242	11,728	14,169	17,049	17,837	23,640	27,997	26,761
Imports, c.i.f. 71	5,207	7,624	8,729	16,251	14,584	17,831	22,832	29,762	40,121	48,736	54,240	53,305	71,673	70,867	77,471
Imports, f.o.b. 71.v	4,640	6,886	7,783	14,452	12,725	16,157	20,603	26,783	36,108	43,861	45,577	47,975	64,522	63,780	69,724
														1995=100	
Unit Value of Exports 74	....	....	....	....	....	....	41.6	50.7	58.7	51.6	56.4	64.0	86.0	105.7	82.5
Unit Value of Imports 75	....	....	....	....	....	....	40.0	41.4	45.6	51.0	58.4	70.0	72.8	79.3	86.9

	1987	1988	1989	1990	1991	1992	1993	1994	1995	1996	1997	1998	1999	2000	2001		
Exchange Rates																	
End of Period																	
	44.262	43.426	42.408	50.917	55.186	53.625	54.736	58.759	60.574	61.041	61.323	68.289	69.998	70.357	71.634	Official Rate..................aa=	wa
End of Period (we) Period Average (wf)																	
	31.200	32.270	32.270	35.790	38.580	39.000	39.850	40.250	40.750	42.450	45.450	48.500	51.000	54.000	57.000	Official Rate..................ae=	we
	30.950	31.733	32.270	34.569	36.596	38.951	39.567	40.212	40.278	41.794	43.892	46.906	49.085	52.142	55.807	Official Rate..................rf=	wf
Fund Position																	
End of Period																	
	287.5	287.5	287.5	287.5	287.5	392.5	392.5	392.5	392.5	392.5	392.5	392.5	533.3	533.3	533.3	Quota	2f.s
	37.6	40.1	2.3	18.1	49.9	30.1	16.6	24.6	107.3	76.2	21.6	9.1	.7	.3	.9	SDRs	1b.s
	22.4	22.4	22.4	—	—	—	.1	.1	.1	.1	.1	.2	.2	.2	.2	Reserve Position in the Fund	1c.s
	592.7	623.9	546.8	439.7	523.2	547.7	511.8	473.4	433.1	374.2	287.9	308.4	237.6	168.6	118.3	Total Fund Cred.&Loans Outstg.	2tl
International Liquidity																	
End of Period																	
	843.1	1,046.1	501.5	628.7	1,278.2	1,824.6	2,410.8	3,138.7	2,339.7	1,834.6	1,581.5	1,905.4	1,603.6	1,486.0	1,275.0	Total Reserves minus Gold	1l.d
	53.3	54.0	3.0	25.8	71.3	41.4	22.8	36.0	159.5	109.6	29.2	12.9	.9	.4	1.2	SDRs	1b.d
	31.8	30.1	29.4	—	—	—	.1	.1	.1	.2	.1	.2	.3	.2	.2	Reserve Position in the Fund	1c.d
	758.1	961.9	469.0	602.9	1,206.9	1,783.2	2,387.9	3,102.6	2,180.1	1,724.9	1,552.1	1,892.3	1,602.5	1,485.3	1,273.6	Foreign Exchange	1d.d
	.068	.074	.076	.080	.084	.087	.092	.094	.094	.094	.101	.105	.106	.109	.111	Gold (Million Fine Troy Ounces)	1ad
	22.8	24.0	21.4	20.8	21.5	22.7	25.9	27.2	26.9	28.0	25.3	22.3	19.6	29.6	30.6	Gold (National Valuation)	1and
	120.7	127.8	83.9	68.4	92.6	38.6	100.2	124.0	171.8	160.9	127.5	257.4	137.6	151.9	289.5	Monetary Authorities: Other Liab.	4..d
	275.8	306.6	391.3	431.7	436.7	356.5	402.5	703.4	730.6	771.6	827.9	794.9	917.0	1,203.4	1,081.0	Deposit Money Banks: Assets	7a.d
	160.7	211.3	212.7	237.6	269.0	242.0	241.7	283.7	327.0	399.7	510.7	437.3	463.7	571.4	673.5	Liabilities	7b.d
Monetary Authorities																	
End of Period																	
	29,137	37,415	19,717	27,580	54,175	76,772	101,190	130,167	97,949	80,687	73,398	93,361	82,779	81,907	74,715	Foreign Assets	11
	13,759	9,999	15,384	16,162	12,469	10,426	5,366	5,697	22,783	38,576	36,371	47,968	72,915	81,529	130,336	Claims on Central Government	12a
	1,046	1,079	874	821	825	649	597	594	591	590	590	2,140	2,140	1,570	1,321	Claims on Nonfin.Pub.Enterprises	12c
	23,371	25,389	36,600	37,122	34,292	27,399	24,409	26,275	29,139	34,551	36,220	40,993	41,282	43,852	45,836	Claims on Deposit Money Banks	12e
	7,918	8,228	8,427	8,475	8,440	8,231	11,721	13,153	11,555	11,521	11,493	11,724	12,617	12,507	11,477	Claims on Other Financial Insts	12f
	45,994	51,021	56,878	59,440	58,531	70,950	87,967	114,017	103,458	112,457	122,988	139,489	157,166	180,023	223,476	Reserve Money	14
	22,490	25,282	27,286	29,950	31,330	37,990	44,987	57,248	64,523	68,195	76,074	80,756	93,870	116,877	127,863	*of which: Currency Outside DMBs*	14a
	—	—	—	62	900	900	1,450	4,000	2,755	7,361	—	—	—	—	—	Liabs. of Central Bank: Securities	16ac
	†29,999	31,215	25,896	24,836	32,450	30,875	32,005	32,807	33,237	29,670	23,454	33,547	23,647	20,063	24,972	Foreign Liabilities	16c
	557	980	977	2,180	2,179	3,670	9,717	4,868	3,986	9	13	14	10	11	10	Central Government Deposits	16d
	3,403	4,865	5,328	9,055	16,100	16,661	13,272	18,977	14,128	11,263	8,452	18,209	22,120	10,516	9,129	Central Govt. Lending Funds	16f
	4,007	4,387	4,650	5,035	5,423	5,966	6,346	6,726	6,665	7,345	8,025	8,705	9,385	12,454	13,041	Capital Accounts	17a
	-8,730	-10,358	-12,726	-10,448	-5,382	-5,545	-7,474	-5,509	-2,212	-2,179	-4,860	-3,778	-595	-1,702	-6,942	Other Items (Net)	17r
Deposit Money Banks																	
End of Period																	
	24,298	27,181	31,140	31,368	29,570	35,787	46,874	56,221	43,333	45,882	48,678	64,661	63,584	65,494	96,995	Reserves	20
	—	—	—	62	900	900	1,450	3,994	2,741	7,358	—	—	—	—	—	Claims on Mon.Author.: Securities	20c
	†8,606	9,894	12,628	15,450	16,848	13,903	16,039	28,313	29,770	32,753	37,628	38,554	46,766	64,985	61,619	Foreign Assets	21
	†17,486	21,156	19,599	19,271	27,904	47,353	54,135	64,899	64,283	63,790	81,206	99,534	117,884	142,606	130,277	Claims on Central Government	22a
	†27,829	29,840	36,273	37,442	40,592	43,412	45,951	33,731	31,717	39,426	42,900	40,712	40,431	46,111	52,784	Claims on Nonfin.Pub.Enterprises	22c
	99,537	119,538	147,546	167,104	175,944	173,881	191,744	220,332	318,484	359,202	411,731	465,130	509,760	577,077	667,883	Claims on Private Sector	22d
	†5,605	6,012	5,839	5,891	5,865	11,543	11,614	14,644	18,114	20,234	19,231	20,312	25,019	26,986	31,434	Claims on Other Financial Insts	22f
	†28,510	27,883	32,718	35,785	39,474	42,452	48,294	58,717	70,819	73,481	76,559	83,214	91,055	102,074	114,572	Demand Deposits	24
	†106,644	125,955	152,535	168,854	195,821	218,159	236,578	277,489	305,996	347,091	383,813	433,586	504,965	603,882	701,196	Time Deposits	25
	†4,724	6,255	6,219	7,893	9,779	8,873	9,122	11,064	12,993	16,782	23,112	21,115	23,554	30,762	38,299	Foreign Liabilities	26c
	†12,419	15,686	12,565	13,355	18,279	23,726	26,845	32,200	34,509	31,250	39,571	50,076	52,881	59,785	54,802	Central Government Deposits	26d
	5,619	4,208	4,040	4,352	4,458	4,952	5,341	5,423	6,443	5,869	7,164	7,174	6,391	6,065	5,431	Central Govt. Lending Funds	26f
	21,852	25,630	38,210	39,408	35,708	30,019	27,192	28,781	30,843	37,623	39,047	43,789	44,463	47,049	48,552	Credit from Monetary Authorities	26g
	4,962	5,973	6,489	7,023	7,491	13,101	18,515	21,068	21,768	24,551	28,660	30,769	36,644	41,889	46,465	Capital Accounts	27a
	†-1,369	2,031	249	-82	-13,387	-14,503	-4,080	-12,608	25,071	31,998	43,448	59,180	43,491	31,753	31,675	Other Items (Net)	27r
Monetary Survey																	
End of Period																	
	†3,019	9,838	231	10,301	28,795	50,927	76,102	114,609	81,489	66,989	64,460	77,253	82,344	96,067	73,064	Foreign Assets (Net)	31n
	160,204	179,186	220,400	239,631	251,581	268,099	284,566	315,982	429,032	502,080	563,938	637,430	735,469	836,297	980,024	Domestic Credit	32
	18,269	14,489	21,441	19,898	19,915	30,383	22,939	33,528	48,571	71,107	77,993	97,412	137,908	164,339	205,801	Claims on Central Govt. (Net)	32an
	28,875	30,919	37,147	38,263	41,417	44,061	46,548	34,325	32,308	40,016	43,490	42,852	42,571	47,681	54,105	Claims on Nonfin.Pub.Enterprises	32c
	99,537	119,538	147,546	167,104	175,944	173,881	191,744	220,332	318,484	359,202	411,731	465,130	517,354	584,784	677,207	Claims on Private Sector	32d
	13,523	14,240	14,266	14,366	14,305	19,774	23,335	27,797	29,669	31,755	30,724	32,036	37,636	39,493	42,911	Claims on Other Financial Insts	32f
	†51,000	53,165	60,004	65,735	70,804	80,442	93,281	115,965	135,342	141,676	152,633	163,970	184,925	218,951	242,437	Money	34
	†106,644	125,955	152,535	168,854	195,821	218,159	236,578	277,489	305,996	347,091	383,813	433,586	504,965	603,882	701,196	Quasi-Money	35
	9,022	9,073	9,368	13,407	20,558	21,613	18,613	24,400	20,571	17,132	15,616	25,383	28,511	16,581	14,560	Central Govt. Lending Funds	36f
	8,969	10,360	11,139	12,058	12,914	19,067	24,861	27,794	28,433	31,896	36,685	39,474	46,029	54,343	59,506	Capital Accounts	37a
	†-12,412	-9,528	-12,415	-10,122	-19,722	-20,255	-12,665	-15,057	20,179	31,274	39,651	52,270	53,383	38,607	35,389	Other Items (Net)	37r
	†157,644	179,120	212,539	234,589	266,625	298,601	329,859	393,454	441,338	488,767	536,446	597,556	689,890	822,833	943,633	Money plus Quasi-Money	35l
Interest Rates																	
Percent Per Annum																	
	10.75	10.75	10.75	9.75	9.25	8.50	6.00	5.50	6.00	7.00	8.00	8.00	7.00	7.00	6.00	Discount Rate *(End of Period)*	60
	12.00	12.00	12.00	12.04	12.05	10.47	8.18	6.40	6.04	7.28	8.11	8.42	8.74	8.56	8.50	Deposit Rate	60l
	16.00	16.00	16.00	16.00	15.92	15.00	15.00	14.50	14.00	14.00	14.00	14.00	14.13	15.50	15.83	Lending Rate	60p
Prices, Production, Labor																	
Period Averages																	
	63.8	68.5	72.6	77.1	82.0	84.9	87.5	92.1	100.0	104.1	105.9	113.2	123.3	128.2	129.9	Consumer Prices	64
	60.6	†60.8	63.6	63.7	68.5	†75.7	86.6	93.7	100.0	106.2	109.8	118.7	125.1	137.8	138.9	Industrial Production	66
Period Averages																	
	....	....	46,494	....	45,397	....	....	....	50,337	....	....	....	....	....	....	Labor Force	67d
	....	....	50,148	50,159	....	....	....	....	....	54,597	....	....	....	....	....	Employment	67e
	....	....	595	997	....	....	....	....	....	1,417	....	....	....	....	....	Unemployment	67c
	....	....	1.2	1.9	....	....	....	....	....	2.5	....	....	....	....	....	Unemployment Rate	67r
International Transactions																	
Millions of Taka																	
	33,030	40,967	42,108	57,885	61,866	81,724	90,183	107,013	127,782	137,944	166,087	179,614	192,571	244,858	276,530	Exports	70
	84,087	96,558	117,797	124,880	124,857	145,328	158,123	185,098	261,878	276,838	302,942	327,575	377,496	436,450	468,239	Imports, c.i.f.	71
	75,678	86,902	106,018	113,435	110,430	137,000	142,055	166,246	235,502	248,932	265,565	298,386	342,064	394,340	421,415	Imports, f.o.b.	71.v
1995=100																	
	83.0	96.9	95.1	100.0	104.7	....	....	....	....	....	....	....	....	....	....	Unit Value of Exports	74
	95.5	89.0	90.6	100.0	121.2	....	....	....	....	....	....	....	....	....	....	Unit Value of Imports	75

Bangladesh

		1972	1973	1974	1975	1976	1977	1978	1979	1980	1981	1982	1983	1984	1985	1986
Balance of Payments															*Millions of US Dollars:*	
Current Account, n.i.e.	78ald	...	...	...	...	−278.7	−283.3	−386.4	−418.5	−704.3	−1,019.5	−505.0	−49.5	−481.0	−457.9	−627.0
Goods: Exports f.o.b.	78aad					400.5	476.4	549.3	655.6	793.2	790.5	768.4	723.9	931.7	999.5	880.0
Goods: Imports f.o.b.	78abd					−820.1	−1,019.1	−1,339.6	−1,725.8	−2,352.8	−2,434.8	−2,221.1	−1,930.7	−2,340.0	−2,286.4	−2,300.7
Trade Balance	78acd					−419.5	−542.6	−790.3	−1,070.2	−1,559.6	−1,644.3	−1,452.6	−1,206.8	−1,408.3	−1,287.0	−1,420.7
Services: Credit	78add					68.3	64.1	101.0	132.6	211.5	211.1	218.2	215.9	207.5	237.9	215.0
Services: Debit	78aed					−131.9	−184.9	−253.1	−372.2	−481.2	−463.5	−439.7	−405.1	−478.0	−477.9	−503.0
Balance on Goods & Services	78afd					−483.2	−663.4	−942.5	−1,309.8	−1,829.3	−1,896.7	−1,674.2	−1,395.9	−1,678.8	−1,527.0	−1,708.7
Income: Credit	78agd					16.4	26.5	34.5	64.4	76.3	41.8	28.9	35.9	68.1	41.6	31.7
Income: Debit	78ahd					−40.2	−58.7	−61.5	−65.9	−69.7	−97.3	−154.2	−117.8	−135.8	−153.7	−167.2
Balance on Gds, Serv. & Inc.	78aid					−507.1	−695.5	−969.5	−1,311.3	−1,822.7	−1,952.2	−1,799.4	−1,477.8	−1,746.4	−1,639.1	−1,844.2
Current Transfers, n.i.e.: Credit	78ajd					229.1	412.8	583.3	893.0	1,118.8	932.9	1,294.6	1,428.6	1,265.6	1,181.6	1,217.5
Current Transfers: Debit	78akd					−.7	−.5	−.3	−.2	−.4	−.2	−.1	−.3	−.2	−.4	−.3
Capital Account, n.i.e.	78bcd					—	—	—	—	—	—	—	—	—	—	—
Capital Account, n.i.e.: Credit	78bad					—	—	—	—	—	—	—	—	—	—	—
Capital Account: Debit	78bbd					—	—	—	—	—	—	—	—	—	—	—
Financial Account, n.i.e.	78bjd					336.0	264.8	406.5	120.3	569.3	703.2	532.0	383.6	544.5	441.8	702.4
Direct Investment Abroad	78bdd					—	—	—	—	—	—	—	—	—	—	—
Dir. Invest. in Rep. Econ., n.i.e.	78bed					—	—	—	—	—	—	—	.4	−.6	—	2.4
Portfolio Investment Assets	78bfd					—	—	—	—	—	—	—	—	—	—	—
Equity Securities	78bkd					—	—	—	—	—	—	—	—	—	—	—
Debt Securities	78bld					—	—	—	—	—	—	—	—	—	—	—
Portfolio Investment Liab., n.i.e.	78bgd					—	—	—	—	—	—	—	1.3	1.6	−7.2	—
Equity Securities	78bmd					—	—	—	—	—	—	—	1.3	1.6	−7.2	—
Debt Securities	78bnd					—	—	—	—	—	—	—	—	—	—	—
Financial Derivatives Assets	78bwd					—	—	—	—	—	—	—	—	—	—	—
Financial Derivatives Liabilities	78bxd					—	—	—	—	—	—	—	—	—	—	—
Other Investment Assets	78bhd					−15.4	−73.5	−60.8	−99.0	−76.8	−115.9	−134.3	−91.5	−60.9	−13.7	−18.0
Monetary Authorities	78bod					—	—	—	—	—	—	—	—	—	—	—
General Government	78bpd					−6.4	−3.5	−10.9	−3.5	52.5	−1.8	−2.3	−2.7	−4.1	−.1	−1.5
Banks	78bqd					−9.0	−70.0	−49.8	−95.5	−129.1	−114.0	−132.0	−88.8	−56.7	−13.6	−16.5
Other Sectors	78brd					—	—	—	—	−.2	—	—	—	—	—	—
Other Investment Liab., n.i.e.	78bid					351.5	338.3	467.2	219.3	646.1	819.0	666.3	473.4	604.3	462.7	717.9
Monetary Authorities	78bsd					21.0	5.1	7.4	21.1	114.5	−4.1	43.2	−50.1	−30.2	.5	−40.6
General Government	78btd					331.3	297.7	412.1	139.9	480.7	537.3	592.4	453.6	543.0	432.1	728.1
Banks	78bud					−.8	39.2	49.3	29.5	50.8	101.3	142.4	78.8	68.7	6.5	−.1
Other Sectors	78bvd					—	−3.6	−1.5	28.8	.1	184.6	−111.7	−8.9	22.8	23.6	30.6
Net Errors and Omissions	78cad					13.8	−14.7	21.6	−4.3	−74.1	93.7	−83.4	−26.4	−95.2	−67.8	8.7
Overall Balance	78cbd					71.2	−33.2	41.6	−302.6	−209.1	−222.6	−56.4	307.7	−31.7	−83.9	84.1
Reserves and Related Items	79dad					−71.2	33.2	−41.6	302.6	209.1	222.6	56.4	−307.7	31.7	83.9	−84.1
Reserve Assets	79dbd					−146.4	63.5	−70.6	−96.0	117.7	140.7	−56.1	−357.6	98.3	79.4	−47.9
Use of Fund Credit and Loans	79dcd					74.5	−32.7	26.5	43.5	89.2	79.1	108.2	46.2	−69.9	1.8	−38.0
Exceptional Financing	79ded					.7	2.3	2.5	355.1	2.2	2.9	4.3	3.7	3.4	2.8	1.8
International Investment Position															*Millions of US Dollars*	
Assets	79aad	...	...	...	...	...	...	...	...	...	...	...	...	...	...	...
Direct Investment Abroad	79abd	...	...	...	...	...	...	...	...	...	...	...	...	...	...	...
Portfolio Investment	79acd	...	...	...	...	...	...	...	...	...	...	...	...	...	...	...
Equity Securities	79add	...	...	...	...	...	...	...	...	...	...	...	...	...	...	...
Debt Securities	79aed	...	...	...	...	...	...	...	...	...	...	...	...	...	...	...
Financial Derivatives	79ald	...	...	...	...	...	...	...	...	...	...	...	...	...	...	...
Other Investment	79afd	...	...	...	...	...	...	...	...	...	...	...	...	...	...	...
Monetary Authorities	79agd	...	...	...	...	...	...	...	...	...	...	...	...	...	...	...
General Government	79ahd	...	...	...	...	...	...	...	...	...	...	...	...	...	...	...
Banks	79aid	...	...	...	...	...	...	...	...	...	...	...	...	...	...	...
Other Sectors	79ajd	...	...	...	...	...	...	...	...	...	...	...	...	...	...	...
Reserve Assets	79akd	...	...	...	...	...	...	...	...	...	...	...	...	...	...	...
Liabilities	79lad	...	...	...	...	...	...	...	...	...	...	...	...	...	...	...
Dir. Invest. in Rep. Economy	79lbd	...	...	...	...	...	...	...	...	...	...	...	...	...	...	...
Portfolio Investment	79lcd	...	...	...	...	...	...	...	...	...	...	...	...	...	...	...
Equity Securities	79ldd	...	...	...	...	...	...	...	...	...	...	...	...	...	...	...
Debt Securities	79led	...	...	...	...	...	...	...	...	...	...	...	...	...	...	...
Financial Derivatives	79lld	...	...	...	...	...	...	...	...	...	...	...	...	...	...	...
Other Investment	79lfd	...	...	...	...	...	...	...	...	...	...	...	...	...	...	...
Monetary Authorities	79lgd	...	...	...	...	...	...	...	...	...	...	...	...	...	...	...
General Government	79lhd	...	...	...	...	...	...	...	...	...	...	...	...	...	...	...
Banks	79lid	...	...	...	...	...	...	...	...	...	...	...	...	...	...	...
Other Sectors	79ljd	...	...	...	...	...	...	...	...	...	...	...	...	...	...	...

	1987	1988	1989	1990	1991	1992	1993	1994	1995	1996	1997	1998	1999	2000	2001	Code
Balance of Payments																
Minus Sign Indicates Debit																
Current Account, n.i.e.	−237.9	−273.2	−1,099.6	−397.9	64.6	180.8	359.3	199.6	−823.9	−991.4	−286.3	−35.2	−364.4	−305.8	....	78ald
Goods: Exports f.o.b.	1,076.9	1,291.0	1,304.8	1,672.4	1,688.7	2,097.9	2,544.7	2,934.4	3,733.3	4,009.3	4,839.9	5,141.4	5,458.3	6,399.2	....	78aad
Goods: Imports f.o.b.	−2,445.6	−2,734.4	−3,300.1	−3,259.4	−3,074.5	−3,353.8	−3,657.3	−4,350.5	−6,057.4	−6,284.6	−6,550.7	−6,715.7	−7,535.5	−8,052.9	....	78abd
Trade Balance	−1,368.8	−1,443.4	−1,995.3	−1,587.0	−1,385.8	−1,255.9	−1,112.6	−1,416.1	−2,324.1	−2,275.3	−1,710.8	−1,574.3	−2,077.2	−1,653.7	....	78acd
Services: Credit	247.9	277.6	334.4	391.6	431.0	483.4	529.4	589.8	698.2	604.8	687.3	723.9	777.7	815.1	....	78add
Services: Debit	−494.2	−613.1	−726.4	−700.5	−695.3	−788.8	−932.2	−1,025.0	−1,531.2	−1,166.0	−1,283.7	−1,237.1	−1,396.7	−1,620.2	....	78aed
Balance on Goods & Services	−1,615.0	−1,778.9	−2,387.3	−1,895.8	−1,650.0	−1,561.4	−1,515.3	−1,851.3	−3,157.1	−2,836.5	−2,307.2	−2,087.4	−2,696.3	−2,458.9	....	78afd
Income: Credit	47.4	54.8	88.7	64.2	70.0	100.1	100.1	150.5	270.1	129.4	86.6	91.5	94.3	78.4	....	78agd
Income: Debit	−172.5	−180.7	−196.9	−179.8	−166.9	−166.0	−175.8	−188.7	−201.8	−193.1	−198.0	−206.1	−258.5	−344.8	....	78ahd
Balance on Gds, Serv. & Inc.	−1,740.1	−1,904.8	−2,495.5	−2,011.4	−1,747.0	−1,627.3	−1,591.0	−1,889.6	−3,088.8	−2,900.2	−2,418.6	−2,202.1	−2,860.4	−2,725.3	....	78aid
Current Transfers, n.i.e.: Credit	1,502.6	1,633.0	1,396.6	1,614.2	1,811.9	1,808.8	1,951.8	2,091.4	2,266.7	1,912.8	2,136.5	2,172.9	2,501.4	2,426.5	....	78ajd
Current Transfers: Debit	−.4	−1.5	−.7	−.7	−.3	−.7	−1.5	−2.2	−1.8	−4.0	−4.3	−5.9	−5.3	−7.0	....	78akd
Capital Account, n.i.e.	—	—	—	—	—	—	—	—	—	371.2	366.8	238.7	364.1	248.7	....	78bcd
Capital Account, n.i.e.: Credit	—	—	—	—	—	—	—	—	—	371.2	366.8	238.7	364.1	248.7	....	78bad
Capital Account: Debit	—	—	—	—	—	—	—	—	—	—	—	—	—	—	....	78bbd
Financial Account, n.i.e.	516.7	398.6	794.5	697.8	467.6	538.4	268.9	748.8	178.8	92.4	−140.2	−116.0	−446.9	−256.0	....	78bjd
Direct Investment Abroad	—	—	—	—	—	—	—	—	—	—	−3.1	−3.0	−.1	—	....	78bdd
Dir. Invest. in Rep. Econ., n.i.e.	3.2	1.8	.2	3.2	1.4	3.7	14.0	11.1	1.9	13.5	139.4	190.1	179.7	280.4	....	78bed
Portfolio Investment Assets	—	—	—	—	—	—	—	—	—	—	—	—	−.2	—	....	78bfd
Equity Securities	—	—	—	—	—	—	—	—	—	—	—	—	−.2	—	....	78bkd
Debt Securities	—	—	—	—	—	—	—	—	—	—	—	—	—	—	....	78bld
Portfolio Investment Liab., n.i.e.	−.1	—	1.7	.3	2.2	8.7	8.4	105.9	−15.2	−117.0	−9.9	−4.1	−1.1	1.3	....	78bgd
Equity Securities	−.1	—	1.7	.3	2.2	8.7	8.4	105.9	−15.2	−117.0	−9.9	−4.2	−1.1	1.2	....	78bmd
Debt Securities	—	—	—	—	—	—	—	—	—	—	—	.1	—	.1	....	78bnd
Financial Derivatives Assets																78bwd
Financial Derivatives Liabilities																78bxd
Other Investment Assets	−21.0	−229.1	−152.0	−207.8	−267.1	−196.0	−178.4	−1.6	−243.9	−426.7	−677.8	−859.7	−1,143.7	−1,246.8	....	78bhd
Monetary Authorities	....	....	....	....	....	....	....	....	....	....	....	....	....	....	....	78bod
General Government	−1.2	−1.6	−.5	−1.6	−.4	—	−.7	−.1	—	—	—	—	—	—	....	78bpd
Banks	−19.8	−227.5	−151.4	−206.1	−266.7	−196.0	−177.7	−1.5	−243.9	−41.1	−70.2	−38.1	−131.4	−315.7	....	78bqd
Other Sectors	—	—	—	—	—	—	—	—	—	−385.6	−607.6	−821.6	−1,012.3	−931.0	....	78brd
Other Investment Liab., n.i.e.	534.6	625.9	944.5	902.0	731.1	722.0	424.8	633.4	436.1	622.6	411.2	560.7	518.4	709.1	....	78bid
Monetary Authorities	−49.2	−7.0	−35.2	−.1	1.3	−.9	−.2	15.0	58.3	−4.3	−25.5	126.6	−118.9	35.2	....	78bsd
General Government	583.4	618.9	878.1	827.0	533.1	667.6	379.3	718.5	374.2	511.3	294.1	404.6	524.7	537.9	....	78btd
Banks	9.1	2.8	91.3	40.9	186.8	14.5	—	−116.3	−34.2	83.0	118.4	2.6	30.7	105.7	....	78bud
Other Sectors	−8.8	11.2	10.3	34.2	9.9	40.8	45.8	16.2	37.9	32.7	24.2	26.9	82.0	30.4	....	78bvd
Net Errors and Omissions	−123.8	6.6	−43.1	−75.7	−98.4	−84.0	69.4	−257.1	133.3	113.5	−75.5	201.0	258.0	282.4	....	78cad
Overall Balance	155.0	132.0	−348.2	224.2	433.8	635.2	697.6	691.3	−511.7	−414.3	−135.1	288.5	−189.2	−30.7	....	78cbd
Reserves and Related Items	−155.0	−132.0	348.2	−224.2	−433.8	−635.2	−697.6	−691.3	511.7	414.3	135.1	−288.5	189.2	30.7	....	79dad
Reserve Assets	−352.3	−176.1	447.8	−78.9	−544.5	−670.1	−647.0	−636.2	572.8	499.9	253.8	−319.1	286.0	121.0	....	79dbd
Use of Fund Credit and Loans	196.5	43.6	−99.6	−145.3	110.7	34.9	−50.6	−55.1	−61.0	−85.6	−118.7	30.6	−96.8	−90.3	....	79dcd
Exceptional Financing	.8	.4							....	....	....	....	....	....	....	79ded
International Investment Position																
Millions of US Dollars																
Assets	....	....	....	....	....	....	....	....	3,067.7	2,614.0	2,386.1	2,715.7	2,534.6	2,714.8	....	79aad
Direct Investment Abroad	....	....	....	....	....	....	....	....	—	—	—	—	—	—	....	79abd
Portfolio Investment	....	....	....	....	....	....	....	....	—	—	—	—	—	—	....	79acd
Equity Securities	....	....	....	....	....	....	....	....	—	—	—	—	—	—	....	79add
Debt Securities	....	....	....	....	....	....	....	....	—	—	—	—	—	—	....	79aed
Financial Derivatives	....	....	....	....	....	....	....	....	—	—	—	—	—	—	....	79ald
Other Investment	....	....	....	....	....	....	....	....	730.6	771.6	827.9	794.9	917.0	1,203.4	....	79afd
Monetary Authorities	....	....	....	....	....	....	....	....	—	—	—	—	—	—	....	79agd
General Government	....	....	....	....	....	....	....	....	—	—	—	—	—	—	....	79ahd
Banks	....	....	....	....	....	....	....	....	730.6	771.6	827.9	794.9	917.0	1,203.4	....	79aid
Other Sectors	....	....	....	....	....	....	....	....	—	—	—	—	—	—	....	79ajd
Reserve Assets	....	....	....	....	....	....	....	....	2,337.2	1,842.4	1,558.2	1,920.8	1,617.6	1,511.4	....	79akd
Liabilities	....	....	....	....	....	....	....	....	17,018.2	15,509.7	15,462.1	14,569.4	15,267.0	....	....	79lad
Dir. Invest. in Rep. Economy	....	....	....	....	....	....	....	....	—	—	—	—	—	—	....	79lbd
Portfolio Investment	....	....	....	....	....	....	....	....	—	—	—	—	—	—	....	79lcd
Equity Securities	....	....	....	....	....	....	....	....	—	—	—	—	—	—	....	79ldd
Debt Securities	....	....	....	....	....	....	....	....	—	—	—	—	—	—	....	79led
Financial Derivatives	....	....	....	....	....	....	....	....	—	—	—	—	—	—	....	79lld
Other Investment	....	....	....	....	....	....	....	....	17,018.2	15,509.7	15,462.1	14,569.4	15,267.0	789.3	....	79lfd
Monetary Authorities	....	....	....	....	....	....	....	....	643.8	538.1	388.5	434.3	326.1	219.6	....	79lgd
General Government	....	....	....	....	....	....	....	....	16,055.5	14,576.3	14,565.1	13,699.8	14,479.1	—	....	79lhd
Banks	....	....	....	....	....	....	....	....	318.8	395.3	508.5	435.4	461.8	569.7	....	79lid
Other Sectors	....	....	....	....	....	....	....	....	—	—	—	—	—	—	....	79ljd

Bangladesh

513

		1972	1973	1974	1975	1976	1977	1978	1979	1980	1981	1982	1983	1984	1985	1986
Government Finance															*Millions of Taka:*	
Deficit (-) or Surplus	80	....	−864	−330	1,444	−3,728	209	4,274	874	4,976	−7,396	3,135 P	9,003 P	2,873 P	−5,924 P	....
Revenue	81	....	3,885	5,295	9,087	9,243	12,371	16,361	18,695	22,628	27,604	32,194 P	31,945 P	32,446 P	39,436 P	....
Grants Received	81z	....	138	675	2,776	1,520	3,541	5,311	5,403	5,440	2,474	9,038 P	12,312 P	11,909 P	8,688 P	....
Expenditure	82	....	4,251	5,299	8,153	11,995	13,167	15,085	21,215	20,026	32,445	34,007 P	32,680 P	38,314 P	50,482 P	....
Lending Minus Repayments	83	....	635	1,001	2,266	2,496	2,536	2,313	2,009	3,066	5,029	4,090 P	2,574 P	3,168 P	3,566 P	....
Financing																
Total Financing	84	....	864	330	−1,444	3,728	−209	−4,274	−874	−4,976	7,396	−3,135 P	−9,003 P	−2,873 P	5,924 P	....
Net Borrowing: Domestic	84a	....	913	1,151	855	3,292	−3,586	−6,685	−4,632	....	1,623	....	....	....	−8,430 P	....
Foreign	85a	....	—	−211	−368	2,812	875	2,411	3,758	....	5,773	....	....	....	14,354 P	....
Use of Cash Balances	87	....	−49	−610	−1,931	−2,376	2,502	....	....	....	....	....	....	....	....	....
National Accounts															*Billions of Taka:*	
Househ.Cons.Expend.,incl.NPISHs	96f	....	38.8	68.3	122.4	102.6	94.6	118.5	157.8	180.7	214.4	245.3	262.3	314.8	366.3	414.3
Government Consumption Expend.	91f	....	1.8	3.2	4.1	4.6	5.7	6.8	10.6	12.3	15.2	15.5	15.9	19.0	20.9	38.1
Gross Fixed Capital Formation	93e	....	4.0	4.0	6.9	9.3	12.4	16.0	16.0	18.8	17.0	22.3	29.7	38.6	41.7	46.2
Changes in Inventories	93i	....	—	—	—	—	—	—	.5	3.5	7.6	5.2	....	—	—	11.1
Exports of Goods and Services	90c	....	2.7	3.0	3.1	5.6	6.7	7.2	9.6	11.0	11.5	12.4	18.0	20.1	23.7	33.9
Imports of Goods and Services (-)	98c	....	2.3	7.3	10.8	14.7	14.0	18.2	21.7	28.3	32.4	35.5	37.5	42.7	54.9	77.3
Gross Domestic Product (GDP)	99b	....	45.1	71.1	125.7	107.5	105.4	146.4	172.8	198.0	233.3	265.1	288.4	349.9	405.4	465.6
Net Primary Income from Abroad	98.n	....	....	....	.3	.3	.4	1.2	1.8	3.5	5.8	5.8	11.6	12.2	8.6	11.9
Gross National Income (GNI)	99a	....	44.4	69.2	124.2	101.7	100.3	140.4	165.8	191.1	225.6	257.1	284.6	343.2	392.2	452.0
Consumption of Fixed Capital	99cf	....	....	....	....	....	....	....	....	....	....	....	....	....	....	....
GDP Volume 1973 prices	99b.p	....	45.1	50.6	52.3	58.7	59.5	63.3	66.2	67.1	71.6	72.2	74.8	78.0	80.9	....
GDP Volume 1984/85 Prices	99b.p	....	....	....	....	....	....	....	....	....	....	....	....	....	405.4	424.6
GDP Volume (1995=100)	99bv p	....	36.7	41.1	42.5	47.7	48.3	51.5	53.8	54.5	58.2	58.7	60.8	63.4	65.7	68.8
GDP Deflator (1995=100)	99bi p	....	8.1	11.3	19.4	14.8	14.3	18.6	21.1	23.8	26.3	29.6	31.1	36.2	40.4	44.3
																Millions:
Population	99z	72.39	74.37	77.03	78.96	80.82	82.72	84.66	86.64	88.68	90.46	92.59	94.65	97.27	99.43	101.67

Bangladesh

1987	1988	1989	1990	1991	1992	1993	1994	1995	1996	1997	1998	1999	2000	2001		
Year Ending June 30															**Government Finance**	
....	....	....	....	....	....	....	....	....	....	....	....	....	....	....	Deficit (-) or Surplus	80
....	....	....	....	....	....	....	....	....	....	....	....	....	....	....	Revenue	81
....	....	....	....	....	....	....	....	....	....	....	....	....	....	....	Grants Received	81z
....	....	....	....	....	....	....	....	....	....	....	....	....	....	....	Expenditure	82
....	....	....	....	....	....	....	....	....	....	....	....	....	....	....	Lending Minus Repayments	83
															Financing	
....	....	....	....	....	....	....	....	....	....	....	....	....	....	....	Total Financing	84
....	....	....	....	....	....	....	....	....	....	....	....	....	....	....	Net Borrowing: Domestic	84a
....	....	....	....	....	....	....	....	....	....	....	....	....	....	....	Foreign	85a
....	....	....	....	....	....	....	....	....	....	....	....	....	....	....	Use of Cash Balances	87
Year Ending June 30															**National Accounts**	
482.0	533.3	551.7	832.1	898.4	976.5	1,037.4	1,110.6	1,254.4	1,342.2	1,440.8	1,558.6	1,707.1	1,838.5	1,979.9	Househ.Cons.Expend.,incl.NPISHs	96f
40.2	48.6	90.5	42.1	45.7	53.2	62.1	66.1	70.6	73.3	78.9	94.7	100.8	108.4	116.5	Government Consumption Expend.	91f
67.5	74.3	85.2	171.1	186.7	206.9	225.0	249.2	291.6	332.5	374.5	433.0	487.6	545.9	609.7	Gross Fixed Capital Formation	93e
.1	12.4	—												—	Changes in Inventories	93i
37.6	45.0	51.2	61.4	73.6	90.7	113.1	121.9	165.7	184.4	216.7	266.8	289.9	331.5	377.4	Exports of Goods and Services	90c
88.1	101.6	119.0	135.8	135.1	147.6	176.8	187.7	263.5	310.9	325.6	365.9	409.9	455.9	518.4	Imports of Goods and Services (-)	98c
539.2	597.1	659.6	1,003.3	1,105.2	1,195.4	1,253.7	1,354.1	1,525.2	1,663.2	1,807.0	2,001.8	2,197.0	2,370.9	2,532.5	Gross Domestic Product (GDP)	99b
15.5	20.5	22.5	20.9	23.6	29.0	34.1	42.3	46.5	49.5	58.5	65.0	75.5	87.1	95.4	Net Primary Income from Abroad	98.n
524.7	584.9	682.1	1,024.2	1,128.8	1,224.4	1,287.8	1,396.5	1,571.7	1,712.8	1,865.5	2,066.7	2,272.5	2,458.0	2,627.9	Gross National Income (GNI)	99a
....	....	....	89.1	97.9	105.3	110.9	120.2	134.1	146.9	158.9	176.0	175.3	187.8	203.9	Consumption of Fixed Capital	99cf
														....	GDP Volume 1973 prices	99b.*p*
442.3	455.1	466.6	497.5	514.4	536.2	560.2	583.8	609.8	642.4	680.2	718.7	756.1	801.7		GDP Volume 1984/85 Prices	99b.*p*
71.7	73.8	75.7	80.7	83.4	87.6	91.6	95.3	100.0	104.6	110.3	116.0	121.7	128.9	135.6	GDP Volume (1995=100)	99bv *p*
49.3	53.1	57.2	81.5	86.9	89.5	89.8	93.2	100.0	104.2	107.5	113.1	118.4	120.6	122.5	GDP Deflator (1995=100)	99bi *p*
Midyear Estimates																
102.56	104.53	106.51	109.47	111.50	115.42	118.15	117.70	119.90	122.10	124.30	131.80	134.58	137.44	140.37	Population	99z

(See notes in the back of the book.)

Barbados

		1972	1973	1974	1975	1976	1977	1978	1979	1980	1981	1982	1983	1984	1985	1986
Exchange Rates													*Barbados Dollars per SDR: End of Period (aa)*			
Official Rate	aa	2.2194	2.4925	2.5024	2.3458	2.3281	2.4431	2.6203	2.6495	2.5652	2.3411	2.2187	2.1057	1.9715	2.2093	2.4464
Official Rate	ae	2.0442	2.0661	2.0439	2.0038	2.0038	2.0113	2.0113	2.0113	2.0113	2.0113	2.0113	2.0113	2.0113	2.0113	2.0000
Fund Position													*Millions of SDRs:*			
Quota	2f. s	13.00	13.00	13.00	13.00	13.00	13.00	17.00	17.00	25.50	25.50	25.50	34.10	34.10	34.10	34.10
SDRs	1b. s	2.77	2.77	2.77	2.77	2.77	2.72	2.49	3.94	1.56	1.44	.79	.29	.02	.01	—
Reserve Position in the Fund	1c. s	2.00	2.00	2.01	3.26	3.27	3.27	2.98	2.89	5.02	5.01	—	2.15	2.16	2.16	2.16
Total Fund Cred.&Loans Outstg.	2tl	—	—	—	—	—	6.50	6.50	6.50	2.27	.77	22.18	35.79	43.59	43.59	32.42
International Liquidity												*Millions of US Dollars Unless Otherwise Indicated:*				
Total Reserves minus Gold	1l. d	27.99	32.37	39.15	39.58	27.98	37.01	59.84	66.12	78.92	100.56	121.60	123.27	132.52	139.77	151.71
SDRs	1b. d	3.01	3.34	3.39	3.24	3.22	3.30	3.24	5.19	1.99	1.68	.87	.30	.02	.01	—
Reserve Position in the Fund	1c. d	2.17	2.41	2.46	3.82	3.80	3.97	3.88	3.81	6.40	5.83	—	2.25	2.12	2.37	2.64
Foreign Exchange	1d. d	22.81	26.62	33.30	32.52	20.96	29.73	52.71	57.12	70.53	93.05	120.73	120.72	130.38	137.39	149.07
Monetary Authorities	1da d	10.50	16.43	19.06	26.12	12.71	22.03	42.51	45.11	56.33	76.62	101.23	101.07	107.91	117.25	131.34
Government	1db d	†12.31	10.19	14.24	6.40	8.25	7.70	10.20	12.01	14.20	16.43	19.50	19.65	22.47	20.15	17.73
Gold (Million Fine Troy Ounces)	1ad	....	....	....	....	....	....	....	....	.0028	.0061	.0061	.0061	.0061	.0061	.0061
Gold (National Valuation)	1an d	....	—	—	—	—	—	.12	.25	1.75	3.36	3.36	3.36	3.36	3.89	3.89
Monetary Authorities: Other Liab.	4.. d						9.94	9.94	7.96	5.97	55.80	60.14	40.85	37.71	27.92	39.96
Deposit Money Banks: Assets	7a. d	19.65	19.39	15.79	16.31	14.48	17.61	15.70	24.26	26.23	25.08	26.28	26.64	46.05	50.12	59.11
Liabilities	7b. d	40.99	51.00	43.36	37.44	41.87	44.66	39.36	42.19	48.36	65.93	65.24	80.84	86.12	88.29	107.10
Monetary Authorities													*Millions of Barbados Dollars:*			
Foreign Assets	11	54.1	69.7	64.4	85.2	58.2	74.7	120.3	135.6	163.9	207.9	251.5	259.9	253.3	287.3	327.4
Claims on Central Government	12a	5.8	11.0	25.8	27.9	38.0	79.5	53.1	89.9	87.4	128.8	126.0	122.8	110.2	134.6	131.3
Claims on Deposit Money Banks	12e	8.8	2.6	2.6	.3	3.0	4.5	—	1.2	1.2	7.5	17.9	22.1	14.9	1.9	.7
Claims on Other Banking Insts	12f	—	—	6.8	12.9	20.1	14.1	24.0	14.4	23.8	50.7	47.8	43.3	70.4	55.7	56.8
Reserve Money	14	33.5	44.4	59.1	80.2	76.5	93.1	109.9	146.5	164.0	180.8	189.6	226.1	233.9	256.1	260.4
of which: Currency Outside DMBs	14a	23.7	26.9	34.1	41.8	47.0	55.7	65.9	80.2	101.6	111.2	110.6	114.1	118.1	123.5	137.4
Foreign Liabilities	16c	—	—	—	—	—	35.9	37.0	33.2	17.8	114.0	170.2	157.5	161.8	152.5	159.2
Central Government Deposits	16d	29.6	31.2	29.8	37.6	35.2	26.7	33.1	38.5	47.3	59.8	48.8	45.9	55.0	113.3	141.2
Capital Accounts	17a	5.5	9.1	12.3	15.2	15.6	17.0	18.6	24.0	28.2	30.8	29.8	28.9	27.9	29.8	31.7
Other Items (Net)	17r	.1	–1.3	–1.7	–6.6	–8.1	.1	–1.2	–1.2	19.1	9.4	4.9	–10.4	–29.6	–72.1	–76.3
Deposit Money Banks													*Millions of Barbados Dollars:*			
Reserves	20	9.8	18.8	14.3	25.8	17.7	33.3	43.6	60.4	58.1	66.1	71.0	78.6	86.9	83.0	103.3
Foreign Assets	21	36.2	40.1	32.3	32.7	29.0	35.4	31.6	48.8	52.8	50.5	52.9	53.6	92.6	100.8	118.2
Claims on Central Government	22a	19.1	9.0	42.5	60.6	82.1	80.0	141.0	138.2	154.8	170.8	201.0	202.9	247.3	263.1	315.7
Claims on Private Sector	22d	214.9	249.9	250.1	271.8	302.9	326.8	362.6	443.9	521.5	618.0	645.0	729.8	741.9	769.4	811.0
Claims on Other Banking Insts	22f	—	3.2	5.1	3.5	5.1	7.8	10.7	14.4	12.5	19.0	22.8	29.6	41.7	55.5	44.6
Demand Deposits	24	44.1	47.2	51.5	62.9	65.6	77.0	93.2	140.4	140.5	135.6	137.4	166.7	159.1	198.9	231.0
Time, Savings,& Fgn.Currency Dep.	25	168.5	149.4	190.5	212.3	243.0	256.3	320.2	392.5	449.7	540.6	589.0	618.3	696.2	739.9	799.6
Foreign Liabilities	26c	75.5	105.4	88.6	75.0	83.9	89.8	79.2	84.9	97.3	132.6	131.2	162.6	173.2	177.6	214.2
Central Government Deposits	26d	19.7	35.5	33.3	57.6	50.9	66.2	86.0	91.5	116.8	103.4	110.3	117.8	137.6	136.0	112.2
Credit from Monetary Authorities	26g	8.8	2.6	2.6	.3	3.0	4.5	—	1.2	1.2	5.4	16.2	26.1	24.3	15.1	13.5
Capital Accounts	27a	—	1.6	3.7	3.9	2.4	5.3	13.2	16.6	19.9	20.7	18.3	13.1	27.2	26.9	37.9
Other Items (Net)	27r	–36.6	–20.6	–26.0	–17.7	–11.9	–15.9	–2.2	–21.2	–25.8	–14.0	–9.8	–10.2	–7.3	–22.6	–15.6
Monetary Survey													*Millions of Barbados Dollars:*			
Foreign Assets (Net)	31n	14.8	4.4	8.0	42.9	3.3	–15.6	35.7	66.3	101.6	11.7	3.0	–6.7	10.9	58.1	72.2
Domestic Credit	32	190.5	206.4	267.0	281.5	362.0	415.1	472.3	570.8	635.9	824.1	883.5	964.7	1,018.9	1,029.0	1,105.9
Claims on Central Govt. (Net)	32an	–24.4	–46.6	5.1	–6.7	33.9	66.5	75.1	98.1	78.1	136.4	168.0	161.9	164.9	148.4	193.5
Claims on Private Sector	32d	214.9	249.9	250.1	271.8	302.9	326.8	362.6	443.9	521.5	618.0	645.0	729.8	741.9	769.4	811.0
Claims on Other Banking Insts	32f	—	3.2	11.9	16.4	25.2	21.9	34.6	28.8	36.3	69.7	70.6	72.9	112.1	111.2	101.4
Money	34	67.8	74.1	86.0	106.5	113.7	135.7	160.7	222.2	244.8	249.6	251.5	312.9	305.7	353.5	395.4
Quasi-Money	35	168.5	149.4	190.5	212.3	243.0	256.3	320.2	392.5	449.7	540.6	589.0	618.3	696.2	739.9	799.6
Capital Accounts	37a	5.5	10.7	15.9	19.0	18.0	22.3	31.8	40.6	48.1	51.6	48.1	42.0	55.1	56.7	69.6
Other Items (Net)	37r	–36.5	–23.3	–20.0	–13.5	–9.4	–14.7	–4.7	–18.2	–5.1	–5.9	–2.1	–15.2	–27.2	–63.0	–86.3
Money plus Quasi-Money	35l	236.3	223.5	279.1	318.8	356.7	391.9	480.9	614.7	694.5	790.1	840.5	931.2	1,002.0	1,093.4	1,194.9
Other Banking Institutions													*Millions of Barbados Dollars:*			
Claims on Central Government	42a	.5	.5	.5	.5	.9	.4	.6	.5	.5	.8	.5	.1	1.0	1.5	3.7
Claims on Private Sector	42d	2.8	4.9	8.2	13.3	20.2	25.9	34.9	51.4	71.5	105.1	127.6	131.1	141.7	149.3	180.1
Claims on Deposit Money Banks	42e	2.0	4.8	3.3	7.1	4.7	2.3	5.8	7.3	1.9	1.4	6.6	11.0	16.7	15.0	9.9
Time Deposits	45	3.9	8.5	10.5	19.8	23.6	26.0	36.3	39.3	50.3	68.3	88.5	98.7	109.0	114.9	120.6
Central Government Deposits	46d	—	—	—	—	—	—	4.2	22.3	19.6	24.6	30.7	27.0	27.5	33.3	54.0
Credit from Deposit Money Banks	46h	—	.1	.1	.1	.6	.8	1.7	.9	1.6	5.0	6.6	5.6	8.4	1.1	2.5
Capital Accounts	47a	1.5	1.5	1.5	1.5	1.5	1.8	2.0	2.5	2.5	3.0	3.6	3.6	3.6	3.6	4.8
Other Items (Net)	47r	–.1	.1	—	–.6	.3		–3.1	–5.8	–.1	6.3	5.4	7.3	10.9	12.9	11.7
Banking Survey													*Millions of Barbados Dollars:*			
Foreign Assets (Net)	51n	14.8	4.4	8.1	42.9	3.3	–15.6	35.7	66.3	101.6	11.7	3.0	–6.7	10.9	58.1	72.2
Domestic Credit	52	193.8	208.6	263.9	278.9	357.9	419.5	468.9	571.6	652.0	835.7	910.4	996.0	1,022.0	1,035.2	1,134.2
Claims on Central Govt. (Net)	52an	–23.9	–46.1	5.6	–6.2	34.8	66.9	71.4	76.4	59.0	112.6	137.8	135.0	138.4	116.6	143.1
Claims on Private Sector	52d	217.7	254.8	258.3	285.1	323.1	352.7	397.5	495.2	593.0	723.1	772.6	860.9	883.6	918.7	991.1
Liquid Liabilities	55l	240.2	232.0	289.1	337.8	379.9	416.2	512.6	645.9	741.3	856.3	926.5	1,029.9	1,111.0	1,208.3	1,315.5
Capital Accounts	57a	7.0	12.2	17.4	20.5	19.5	24.1	33.8	43.1	50.6	54.5	51.7	45.6	58.6	60.3	74.3
Other Items (Net)	57r	–38.5	–31.1	–34.6	–36.5	–38.2	–36.3	–41.8	–51.1	–38.3	–63.4	–64.8	–86.1	–136.7	–175.2	–183.4

1987	1988	1989	1990	1991	1992	1993	1994	1995	1996	1997	1998	1999	2000	2001		
Barbados Dollars per US Dollar: End of Period (ae)															**Exchange Rates**	
2.8373	2.6914	2.6283	2.8453	2.8609	2.7500	2.7471	2.9197	2.9730	2.8759	2.6985	2.8161	2.7450	2.6058	2.5135	Official Rate................	**aa**
2.0000	2.0000	2.0000	2.0000	2.0000	2.0000	2.0000	2.0000	2.0000	2.0000	2.0000	2.0000	2.0000	2.0000	2.0000	Official Rate................	**ae**
End of Period															**Fund Position**	
34.10	34.10	34.10	34.10	34.10	48.90	48.90	48.90	48.90	48.90	48.90	48.90	67.50	67.50	67.50	Quota................	**2f. s**
.63	.46	—	.01	.50	.11	.05	.03	.03	.02	.02	.02	.01	.02	.04	SDRs................	**1b. s**
2.17	2.18	2.18	2.18	—	.03	.03	.03	.03	.03	.03	.03	4.68	4.68	4.71	Reserve Position in the Fund................	**1c. s**
15.60	7.75	3.27	.50	—	36.84	36.84	36.84	24.94	6.52	—	—	—	—	—	Total Fund Cred.&Loans Outstg.	**2tl**
End of Period															**International Liquidity**	
145.21	135.46	109.46	117.54	87.25	139.96	150.45	195.77	219.10	289.69	264.92	365.95	301.94	472.69	690.37	Total Reserves minus Gold................	**1l. d**
.89	.62	—	.01	.72	.15	.07	.04	.04	.03	.03	.03	.01	.02	.05	SDRs................	**1b. d**
3.08	2.93	2.86	3.10	—	.04	.04	.04	.04	.04	.04	.04	6.42	6.09	5.92	Reserve Position in the Fund................	**1c. d**
141.24	131.91	106.60	114.42	86.53	139.77	150.35	195.69	219.02	289.62	264.85	365.88	295.52	466.58	684.40	Foreign Exchange	**1d. d**
125.83	109.10	92.73	104.81	80.06	133.14	143.21	188.28	212.75	280.06	227.62	298.66	226.13	373.25	568.41	Monetary Authorities	**1da d**
15.41	22.81	13.87	9.61	6.47	6.63	7.14	7.41	6.27	9.56	37.23	67.22	69.39	93.33	115.99	Government	**1db d**
.0061	.0061	.0061												—	Gold (Million Fine Troy Ounces)...........	**1ad**
3.89	3.89	3.11												—	Gold (National Valuation)	**1an d**
33.51	36.18	60.14	76.83	86.11	71.79	55.93	38.20	28.12	16.47	8.72	7.72	6.81	—	—	Monetary Authorities: Other Liab.	**4. .d**
120.63	74.85	69.44	77.41	88.48	90.95	95.65	126.53	204.00	341.07	309.48	277.73	338.78	263.09	335.91	Deposit Money Banks: Assets	**7a. d**
169.40	107.67	107.13	126.18	140.60	143.43	152.56	173.11	274.86	402.14	382.40	400.97	450.04	373.02	440.94	Liabilities.........	**7b. d**
End of Period															**Monetary Authorities**	
306.2	290.0	250.5	260.0	207.1	315.2	335.8	442.2	502.6	641.5	592.1	571.8	628.7	967.6	1,396.9	Foreign Assets	**11**
119.0	110.1	160.4	204.9	266.0	239.4	225.3	219.2	117.6	90.3	64.1	50.0	83.1	15.6	.6	Claims on Central Government	**12a**
2.4	3.7	29.8	27.8	33.6	31.2	5.0	—	6.0	—	—	23.5	15.0	—	—	Claims on Deposit Money Banks	**12e**
58.0	52.4	61.4	69.3	61.3	62.3	25.3	10.1	10.1	9.0	9.0	9.0	9.0	9.0	9.0	Claims on Other Banking Insts	**12f**
313.6	327.9	317.4	379.0	324.6	367.6	324.6	318.4	368.5	494.4	446.8	486.9	507.4	567.8	641.5	Reserve Money	**14**
156.6	171.3	182.7	192.9	178.7	176.8	177.0	189.6	200.3	220.1	239.6	268.2	302.7	310.7	312.4	*of which: Currency Outside DMBs*	**14a**
111.3	93.2	128.9	155.1	172.2	244.9	213.1	184.0	130.4	51.7	17.4	15.4	13.6	—	—	Foreign Liabilities	**16c**
121.1	87.7	121.5	80.5	92.3	112.3	110.1	212.0	197.8	255.5	266.7	244.5	261.6	471.5	770.4	Central Government Deposits	**16d**
34.8	33.6	28.6	35.3	35.0	34.1	34.1	35.5	35.9	35.1	33.7	34.6	34.1	32.9	32.2	Capital Accounts	**17a**
−95.2	−86.2	−94.3	−88.0	−56.1	−110.7	−90.5	−78.3	−96.3	−95.9	−99.4	−127.1	−80.9	−80.1	−37.6	Other Items (Net)	**17r**
End of Period															**Deposit Money Banks**	
122.3	140.4	118.4	181.1	127.2	167.4	129.3	114.1	144.9	243.8	166.5	217.2	195.8	255.7	328.1	Reserves	**20**
241.3	149.7	138.9	154.8	177.0	181.9	191.3	253.1	408.0	682.1	619.0	555.5	677.6	526.2	671.8	Foreign Assets	**21**
359.6	394.7	354.3	428.6	441.0	555.1	594.9	603.4	713.5	915.3	981.6	922.9	880.6	1,067.7	1,177.8	Claims on Central Government	**22a**
898.6	965.1	1,102.8	1,104.3	1,144.5	1,121.0	1,128.9	1,268.1	1,470.6	1,536.1	1,839.1	2,138.1	2,445.4	2,508.2	2,523.6	Claims on Private Sector	**22d**
34.4	73.2	79.2	106.9	84.3	66.7	83.7	159.3	39.4	41.2	91.6	108.5	94.1	109.2	83.0	Claims on Other Banking Insts	**22f**
278.5	329.8	260.3	320.6	293.4	305.1	280.8	309.6	208.4	370.0	350.1	493.3	615.6	825.7	837.3	Demand Deposits	**24**
899.1	992.2	1,075.3	1,219.3	1,232.0	1,311.0	1,389.0	1,514.5	1,701.6	1,913.3	2,144.3	2,209.2	2,411.4	2,508.0	2,582.0	Time, Savings,& Fgn.Currency Dep.	**25**
338.8	215.3	214.3	252.4	281.2	286.9	305.1	346.2	549.7	804.3	764.8	801.9	900.1	746.0	881.9	Foreign Liabilities	**26c**
104.6	114.0	125.9	157.2	106.0	125.5	101.3	173.5	215.3	245.8	330.1	287.7	249.8	270.8	391.7	Central Government Deposits	**26d**
20.3	22.4	40.4	42.9	54.1	38.3	19.7	10.1	24.7	28.7	12.2	22.5	38.5	19.6	29.6	Credit from Monetary Authorities	**26g**
37.6	36.9	33.6	34.1	32.6	43.5	46.5	92.2	101.0	105.4	117.1	117.6	137.4	134.0	153.6	Capital Accounts	**27a**
−22.7	12.5	43.8	−50.6	−25.3	−18.2	−14.4	−48.2	−24.6	−48.9	−20.8	10.0	−59.4	−37.1	−91.8	Other Items (Net)	**27r**
End of Period															**Monetary Survey**	
97.4	131.1	46.3	7.3	−69.3	−34.7	8.9	165.0	230.5	467.7	428.9	309.9	392.6	747.8	1,186.8	Foreign Assets (Net)	**31n**
1,243.9	1,393.8	1,510.7	1,676.3	1,798.8	1,806.7	1,846.5	1,874.6	1,938.0	2,090.7	2,388.7	2,696.3	3,000.8	2,967.4	2,632.0	Domestic Credit	**32**
252.8	303.1	267.3	395.9	508.7	556.7	608.7	437.0	417.9	504.4	449.0	440.8	452.3	341.0	16.4	Claims on Central Govt. (Net)	**32an**
898.6	965.1	1,102.8	1,104.3	1,144.5	1,121.0	1,128.9	1,268.1	1,470.6	1,536.1	1,839.1	2,138.1	2,445.4	2,508.2	2,523.6	Claims on Private Sector	**32d**
92.5	125.6	140.6	176.1	145.6	129.0	109.0	169.4	49.5	50.2	100.6	117.5	103.1	118.2	92.0	Claims on Other Banking Insts	**32f**
466.9	524.8	459.0	526.2	495.0	502.3	476.6	516.3	428.5	627.2	620.6	765.7	924.4	1,141.2	1,143.8	Money	**34**
899.1	992.2	1,075.3	1,219.3	1,232.0	1,311.0	1,389.0	1,514.5	1,701.6	1,913.3	2,144.3	2,209.2	2,411.4	2,508.0	2,582.0	Quasi-Money	**35**
72.5	70.6	62.2	69.4	67.6	77.6	80.5	127.7	136.9	140.5	150.8	152.2	171.5	167.0	185.8	Capital Accounts	**37a**
−97.2	−62.6	−39.5	−131.2	−65.2	−118.9	−90.8	−118.9	−98.6	−122.6	−98.1	−120.9	−113.9	−101.0	−92.9	Other Items (Net)	**37r**
1,366.0	1,517.0	1,534.3	1,745.5	1,727.0	1,813.3	1,865.6	2,030.8	2,130.1	2,540.5	2,764.9	2,974.9	3,335.8	3,649.2	3,725.8	Money plus Quasi-Money	**35l**
End of Period															**Other Banking Institutions**	
2.0	1.6	1.4	1.8	1.0	.4	7.1	.5	5.5	4.9	1.3	1.7	1.9	3.2	3.7	Claims on Central Government	**42a**
231.7	283.3	340.1	360.9	384.4	387.1	403.5	417.5	424.7	443.0	381.8	433.4	378.6	423.0	446.4	Claims on Private Sector	**42d**
6.0	19.1	1.6	14.4	13.3	15.9	8.6	2.1	6.3	14.8	19.5	14.0	13.9	53.6	21.3	Claims on Deposit Money Banks	**42e**
201.6	216.2	241.0	269.3	295.4	306.9	339.4	301.8	308.8	326.5	258.8	297.1	241.4	273.2	255.2	Time Deposits	**45**
17.1	45.6	55.4	51.1	50.8	49.8	26.2	34.5	37.7	44.0	31.5	7.5	40.0	50.2	90.7	Central Government Deposits	**46d**
3.7	10.9	8.6	18.4	17.5	4.6	6.3	46.8	49.2	43.8	70.7	92.6	63.4	94.9	54.3	Credit from Deposit Money Banks	**46h**
4.8	4.8	4.8	4.8	4.8	4.8	5.0	5.1	5.1	5.1	7.9	10.9	18.9	18.9	18.9	Capital Accounts	**47a**
12.5	26.5	33.3	33.4	30.2	37.2	42.4	32.0	35.8	43.3	33.7	40.9	30.7	42.6	52.4	Other Items (Net)	**47r**
End of Period															**Banking Survey**	
97.4	131.1	46.3	7.3	−69.3	−34.7	8.9	165.0	230.5	467.7	428.9	310.0	392.7	747.8	1,186.8	Foreign Assets (Net)	**51n**
1,368.0	1,507.5	1,656.3	1,811.7	1,987.8	2,015.3	2,122.0	2,088.7	2,281.0	2,444.5	2,639.6	3,006.4	3,238.1	3,225.1	2,899.4	Domestic Credit	**52**
237.7	259.1	213.3	346.6	458.9	507.3	589.7	403.0	385.7	465.3	418.7	435.0	414.1	294.0	−70.6	Claims on Central Govt. (Net)	**52an**
1,130.3	1,248.4	1,442.9	1,465.1	1,528.9	1,508.0	1,532.3	1,685.7	1,895.2	1,979.1	2,220.9	2,571.4	2,824.0	2,931.1	2,970.0	Claims on Private Sector	**52d**
1,567.6	1,733.1	1,775.3	2,014.7	2,022.4	2,120.1	2,205.0	2,332.5	2,438.9	2,867.0	3,023.6	3,271.9	3,577.0	3,920.1	3,980.5	Liquid Liabilities	**55l**
77.2	75.3	67.0	74.2	72.4	82.4	85.5	132.8	142.0	145.6	158.7	163.1	190.4	185.9	204.8	Capital Accounts	**57a**
−179.5	−169.8	−139.8	−269.9	−176.4	−221.9	−159.6	−211.6	−69.5	−100.4	−113.8	−118.6	−136.6	−133.1	−99.0	Other Items (Net)	**57r**

Barbados

		1972	1973	1974	1975	1976	1977	1978	1979	1980	1981	1982	1983	1984	1985	1986
Interest Rates															*Percent Per Annum*	
Bank Rate *(End of Period)*	60	....	....	....	....	....	6.00	6.00	6.00	7.00	22.00	20.00	16.00	16.00	13.00	8.00
Treasury Bill Rate	60c	5.95	6.57	8.96	5.67	4.43	4.63	4.80	4.88	5.63	9.49	13.25	7.45	6.92	5.53	4.42
Savings Rate	60k	....	....	....	....	....	....	....	....	....	7.33	7.77	5.42	5.50	5.00	3.92
Deposit Rate	60l	....	....	....	....	....	....	....	....	5.30	7.39	8.83	6.73	6.07	5.49	4.28
Lending Rate	60p	....	....	....	....	....	....	....	....	....	11.46	13.38	11.79	11.50	10.56	9.06
Prices, Production, Labor															*Index Numbers (1995=100)*	
Consumer Prices	64	15.7	18.4	25.5	30.7	32.2	34.9	38.2	†43.2	49.5	56.7	62.6	65.8	68.9	71.6	72.6
Industrial Production	66	63.8	67.6	64.2	69.2	80.4	82.6	86.3	86.8	89.3	†86.6	82.9	87.0	86.8	91.0	82.1
															Number in Thousands:	
Labor Force	67d	....	....	....	....	....	....	....	....	....	....	....	....	....		
Employment	67e	....	....	....	....	....	....	....	....	....	....	....	....	....	92	96
Unemployment	67c	....	....	....	....	....	....	....	....	....	....	....	....	....	21	21
Unemployment Rate (%)	67r	....	....	....	....	....	....	....	....	....	....	....	....	....	18.7	17.7
International Transactions															*Millions of Barbados Dollars*	
Exports	70	84.5	103.7	175.0	217.9	172.5	193.0	261.2	303.9	455.4	391.0	517.5	646.0	787.4	713.4	556.7
Imports, c.i.f.	71	270.4	328.6	418.3	437.2	474.1	545.1	628.7	850.8	1,049.1	1,151.1	1,107.5	1,249.0	1,324.7	1,221.6	1,181.1
Balance of Payments															*Millions of US Dollars:*	
Current Account, n.i.e.	78ald	−43.3	−52.3	−47.8	−41.4	−64.3	−51.6	−31.5	−34.4	−21.8	−118.6	−37.1	−43.6	15.7	51.3	7.3
Goods: Exports f.o.b.	78aad	44.2	53.4	85.7	108.9	88.0	104.5	131.7	156.0	228.9	193.0	258.2	322.0	393.5	356.9	283.4
Goods: Imports f.o.b.	78abd	−128.0	−152.6	−185.5	−197.1	−219.5	−251.1	−289.7	−381.3	−483.6	−530.2	−510.0	−574.8	−613.5	−565.7	−531.1
Trade Balance	78acd	−83.9	−99.1	−99.8	−88.3	−131.6	−146.6	−158.0	−225.3	−254.7	−337.2	−251.8	−252.8	−220.0	−208.9	−247.7
Services: Credit	78add	73.2	85.2	91.8	97.1	109.2	143.8	182.1	265.2	345.3	354.2	361.3	359.9	404.3	438.7	468.6
Services: Debit	78aed	−37.1	−44.0	−46.8	−56.1	−59.8	−65.4	−77.9	−98.2	−129.1	−143.3	−155.1	−146.7	−158.1	−155.7	−191.3
Balance on Goods & Services	78afd	−47.8	−57.9	−54.8	−47.3	−82.2	−68.3	−53.8	−58.3	−38.5	−126.3	−45.6	−39.6	26.2	74.2	29.6
Income: Credit	78agd	7.9	10.7	12.3	15.0	13.5	12.7	17.7	22.9	19.9	22.0	21.0	19.8	27.4	26.3	34.6
Income: Debit	78ahd	−9.8	−12.4	−12.3	−16.3	−8.3	−12.0	−12.1	−21.0	−19.6	−28.9	−31.0	−36.0	−44.4	−46.0	−62.2
Balance on Gds, Serv. & Inc.	78aid	−49.8	−59.6	−54.8	−48.6	−77.0	−67.6	−48.2	−56.4	−38.2	−133.2	−55.6	−55.8	9.2	54.6	2.0
Current Transfers, n.i.e.: Credit	78ajd	9.4	11.2	11.0	11.9	18.4	21.5	22.1	30.9	29.0	34.3	26.5	26.3	26.2	24.2	32.7
Current Transfers: Debit	78akd	−2.9	−3.9	−3.9	−4.7	−5.8	−5.5	−5.4	−8.9	−12.6	−19.6	−8.0	−14.0	−19.6	−27.5	−27.4
Capital Account, n.i.e.	78bcd	—	—	—	—	—	—	—	—	—	....	....				
Capital Account, n.i.e.: Credit	78bad	—	—	—	—	—	—	—	—	—	....	....				
Capital Account: Debit	78bbd	—	—	—	—	—	—	—	—	—	....	....				
Financial Account, n.i.e.	78bjd	20.8	34.5	−7.1	21.4	25.2	28.3	16.3	9.3	65.7	162.7	29.4	60.2	−7.4	−.2	79.2
Direct Investment Abroad	78bdd	.1	−.8	−.1	−.8	−1.0	−.4	−.1	−.3	−.6	−1.2	−.5	−1.4	−1.5	−2.3	−2.8
Dir. Invest. in Rep. Econ., n.i.e.	78bed	17.3	5.6	2.4	22.9	6.9	4.9	9.0	5.4	2.8	8.4	4.7	3.7	.1	4.9	7.8
Portfolio Investment Assets	78bfd	—	−.3	.7	−.1	.1	5.0	—	−3.2	.4	−.5	−2.7	−2.0	−4.0	−5.3	−6.7
Equity Securities	78bkd	—	—	—	—	—	—	—	—	.4	−.1	−2.2	−1.6	−4.6	−3.7	−5.9
Debt Securities	78bld	—	−.3	.7	−.1	.1	5.0	—	−3.2	—	−.4	−.5	−.5	.7	−1.6	−.8
Portfolio Investment Liab., n.i.e.	78bgd	.5	.4	−.9	.3	.1	.6	2.0	.3	4.9	.6	−3.2	.2	.2	.2	.3
Equity Securities	78bmd	—	—	—	—	—	—	—	—	4.8	.8	−3.3	−.4	−.3	.1	—
Debt Securities	78bnd	.5	.4	−.9	.3	.1	.6	2.0	.3	.1	−.2	.1	.5	.5	.1	.3
Financial Derivatives Assets	78bwd	....	....	....	....	....	....	....	....	....	....	....				
Financial Derivatives Liabilities	78bxd	....	....	....	....	....	....	....	....	....	....	....				
Other Investment Assets	78bhd	−4.6	−6.2	1.9	1.6	−6.1	−8.2	−22.8	−41.3	−29.8	−32.3	−55.1	−49.3	−75.8	−15.1	8.6
Monetary Authorities	78bod															
General Government	78bpd	−1.9	−1.7	−.4	−.5	−.4	−1.2	−.9	—	−1.4	−1.9	−4.6	−1.3	−1.6	−9.7	−.7
Banks	78bqd	—	—	3.8	−.3	−3.7	−4.0	−5.8	−.5	−2.7	.9	−2.2	−1.6	−21.6	−6.1	−15.8
Other Sectors	78brd	−2.8	−4.5	−1.5	2.4	−2.0	−3.1	−16.1	−40.8	−25.8	−31.3	−48.3	−46.4	−52.6	.7	25.0
Other Investment Liab., n.i.e.	78bid	7.6	35.8	−11.1	−2.4	25.2	26.4	28.0	48.3	88.0	187.6	86.3	109.0	73.6	17.5	72.0
Monetary Authorities	78bsd	.6	−2.9	.5	—	—	—	.1	.1	−2.0	19.0	−1.5	−1.0	−4.0	−3.7	−.7
General Government	78btd	2.9	21.5	−2.9	—	3.5	5.3	5.7	5.5	25.5	49.1	14.8	30.2	9.0	39.4	54.8
Banks	78bud	3.0	13.6	−10.4	−6.7	4.4	3.0	−5.4	−3.8	6.2	17.7	−.7	15.7	5.3	2.2	18.3
Other Sectors	78bvd	1.1	3.6	1.8	4.4	17.4	18.2	27.7	46.5	58.3	101.9	73.7	64.1	63.3	−20.5	−.4
Net Errors and Omissions	78cad	25.5	17.4	48.3	28.6	27.1	15.0	36.3	29.9	−31.3	−54.8	4.3	−16.8	−32.1	−37.0	−72.2
Overall Balance	78cbd	3.1	−.4	−6.7	8.7	−12.0	−8.3	21.2	4.8	12.6	−10.6	−3.4	−.2	−23.8	14.1	14.2
Reserves and Related Items	79dad	−3.1	.4	6.7	−8.7	12.0	8.3	−21.2	−4.8	−12.6	10.6	3.4	.2	23.8	−14.1	−14.2
Reserve Assets	79dbd	−3.1	.4	6.7	−8.7	12.0	−9.2	−21.2	−4.8	−12.0	9.2	−23.8	−22.3	8.5	−22.4	−7.1
Use of Fund Credit and Loans	79dcd	—	—	—	—	—	7.6	—	—	−5.5	−1.7	22.9	14.5	8.1	—	−13.0
Exceptional Financing	79ded	—	—	—	—	—	10.0	—	—	5.0	3.2	4.4	7.9	7.2	8.3	6.0
Government Finance															*Millions of Barbados Dollars:*	
Deficit (−) or Surplus	80	....	....	−48.37	−21.25	−54.40	−85.37	−39.86	−55.34	−50.96	−180.99	−99.88	−87.42	−96.91	−140.38	−168.33
Total Revenue and Grants	81y	....	....	140.60	190.64	202.36	227.22	286.22	340.13	420.89	446.65	486.08	545.92	560.58	622.03	657.92
Revenue	81	....	....	140.60	190.64	202.36	227.22	286.22	340.13	420.89	446.65	486.08	545.92	560.58	622.03	657.92
Grants	81z	....	....	—	—	—	—	—	—	—	—	—	—	—	—	—
Exp. & Lending Minus Repay.	82z	....	....	188.97	211.89	256.76	312.59	326.08	395.47	471.85	627.64	585.96	633.34	657.49	762.41	826.25
Expenditure	82	....	....	190.69	212.58	257.40	306.73	324.98	393.36	474.19	628.44	585.75	607.60	655.53	760.10	818.81
Lending Minus Repayments	83	....	....	−1.72	−.69	−.64	5.86	1.10	2.11	−2.34	−.80	.21	25.74	1.96	2.31	7.44
Statistical Discrepancy	80xx	....	....	....	....	....	....	....	....	....	....	....	....	....	....	....
Total Financing	80h	....	....	....	....	....	....	....	....	....	....	....	....	....	....	....
Domestic	84a	....	....	....	....	....	....	....	....	....	....	....	....	....	....	....
Foreign	85a	....	....	....	....	....	....	....	....	....	....	....	....	....	....	....
Total Debt by Residence	88	....	....	....	....	....	340.0	372.1	426.3	493.2	683.4	760.0	861.3	950.9	1,095.7	1,266.5
Domestic	88a	....	....	....	....	....	274.8	282.9	314.2	329.3	424.0	473.1	514.0	585.6	651.7	713.0
Foreign	89a	....	....	....	....	....	65.2	89.2	112.1	163.9	259.4	286.9	347.3	365.3	444.0	553.5
National Accounts															*Millions of Barbados Dollars*	
Househ.Cons.Expend.,incl.NPISHs	96f	308	349	539	568	646	742	782	965	1,081	1,235	1,263	1,321	1,432	1,392	1,692
Government Consumption Expend.	91f	81	111	100	102	151	172	190	210	258	321	329	346	388	456	469
Gross Capital Formation	93	....	....	169	156	236	194	254	317	383	495	425	421	374	372	424
Exports of Goods and Services	90c	252	298	386	469	406	493	646	882	1,214	1,138	1,270	1,490	1,656	1,633	1,496
Imports of Goods and Services (−)	98c	329	398	472	515	566	607	760	1,027	1,247	1,315	1,323	1,466	1,547	1,448	1,435
Gross Domestic Product (GDP)	99b	407	477	705	780	873	890	984	1,348	1,731	1,905	1,990	2,113	2,303	2,410	2,646
GDP Volume 1965 prices	99b.p	197.0	201.0	228.0	....	....	....	....	....	....	....	....	....	....	....	....
GDP Volume 1974 Prices	99b.p	....	....	640.0	627.0	655.0	679.0	712.0	768.0	802.3	787.0	748.2	751.0	778.5	786.9	827.0
GDP Volume (1995=100)	99bvp	65.5	66.9	75.8	74.3	77.6	80.5	84.4	91.0	95.1	93.3	88.7	89.0	92.3	93.2	98.0
GDP Deflator (1995=100)	99bip	16.6	19.1	24.9	28.1	30.1	29.6	31.2	39.6	48.7	54.6	60.0	63.5	66.8	69.1	72.2
															Millions:	
Population	99z	.24	.24	.24	.25	.25	.25	.26	.25	.25	.25	.25	.25	.25	.25	.25

	1987	1988	1989	1990	1991	1992	1993	1994	1995	1996	1997	1998	1999	2000	2001		
Percent Per Annum																**Interest Rates**	
	8.00	8.00	13.50	13.50	18.00	12.00	8.00	9.50	12.50	12.50	9.00	9.00	10.00	10.00	7.50	Bank Rate *(End of Period)*	**60**
	4.84	4.75	4.90	7.07	9.34	10.88	5.44	7.26	8.01	6.85	3.61	5.61	5.83	5.29	3.14	Treasury Bill Rate	**60c**
	3.00	3.92	4.17	5.71	6.38	6.50	4.17	4.25	5.00	5.00	4.33	4.00	4.17	4.83	4.38	Savings Rate	**60k**
	3.61	4.26	4.78	6.28	6.53	6.68	4.39	4.32	5.11	5.20	4.58	4.20	4.40	4.97	4.04	Deposit Rate	**60l**
	8.75	9.44	9.92	11.42	12.42	13.54	8.92	9.08	10.00	10.00	9.83	9.75	9.40	10.19	9.58	Lending Rate	**60p**
Period Averages																**Prices, Production, Labor**	
	75.0	78.6	83.5	86.0	91.4	97.0	98.1	†98.2	100.0	102.4	110.3	108.9	110.6	113.3	116.2	Consumer Prices	**64**
	84.3	97.6	96.1	102.4	96.7	90.6	95.7	98.3	100.0	101.6	106.3	113.3	111.2	110.3	103.5	Industrial Production	**66**
Period Averages																	
	128	....	....	....	130	132	133	135	137	136	136	136	137	....	....	Labor Force	**67d**
	98	100	107	105	101	96	100	106	110	114	116	120	122	....	....	Employment	**67e**
	21	21	17	19	21	29	31	28	27	21	20	17	14	....	....	Unemployment	**67c**
	17.9	17.4	13.7	15.0	17.1	23.0	24.5	21.9	19.7	15.8	14.5	12.3	10.5	....	....	Unemployment Rate (%)	**67r**
Millions of Barbados Dollars																**International Transactions**	
	322.5	354.2	375.7	430.2	414.7	380.3	374.0	363.0	477.8	561.2	565.9	503.1	527.6	544.7	518.7	Exports	**70**
	1,035.9	1,163.9	1,354.3	1,407.9	1,397.7	1,048.5	1,154.1	1,228.6	1,541.2	1,667.3	1,991.0	2,019.6	2,216.1	2,312.1	2,173.3	Imports, c.i.f.	**71**
Minus Sign Indicates Debit																Balance of Payments	
	-18.9	43.5	25.0	-10.6	-27.1	140.0	68.8	133.6	42.5	69.7	-50.0	-63.0	-148.2	-145.5	....	Current Account, n.i.e.	**78al*d***
	167.1	179.6	187.4	219.0	206.5	189.9	187.8	190.0	245.4	286.7	289.0	270.1	275.3	286.4	....	Goods: Exports f.o.b.	**78aa*d***
	-461.5	-518.4	-603.8	-627.6	-622.8	-467.7	-514.3	-544.7	-691.2	-743.0	-887.7	-920.7	-989.4	-1,030.3	....	Goods: Imports f.o.b.	**78ab*d***
	-294.5	-338.9	-416.4	-408.6	-416.3	-277.8	-326.6	-354.7	-445.9	-456.3	-598.7	-650.6	-714.1	-743.9	....	*Trade Balance*	**78ac*d***
	519.2	598.8	701.4	653.9	617.6	619.1	689.5	813.6	866.6	926.9	959.3	1,023.6	1,029.4	1,090.2	....	Services: Credit	**78ad*d***
	-213.2	-193.0	-235.7	-250.2	-218.7	-209.4	-272.6	-319.0	-363.2	-387.1	-409.5	-432.3	-458.3	-487.4	....	Services: Debit	**78ae*d***
	11.6	67.0	49.3	-4.9	-17.3	131.9	90.4	140.0	57.6	83.6	-48.9	-59.2	-143.0	-141.1	....	*Balance on Goods & Services*	**78af*d***
	32.1	29.1	34.3	30.1	38.0	37.6	40.1	46.1	48.4	54.2	60.5	63.5	66.7	70.2	....	Income: Credit	**78ag*d***
	-65.7	-64.6	-60.2	-75.7	-77.5	-66.5	-81.0	-86.8	-96.1	-106.3	-108.2	-119.4	-138.1	-152.5	....	Income: Debit	**78ah*d***
	-22.1	31.5	23.5	-50.6	-56.8	103.0	49.4	99.3	9.9	31.4	-96.6	-115.2	-214.5	-223.4	....	*Balance on Gds, Serv. & Inc.*	**78ai*d***
	35.5	43.1	48.1	52.0	45.6	51.7	41.8	54.5	56.2	64.8	71.7	78.4	94.0	108.9	....	Current Transfers, n.i.e.: Credit	**78aj*d***
	-32.4	-31.2	-46.5	-12.0	-15.9	-14.7	-22.5	-20.2	-23.6	-26.6	-25.1	-26.2	-27.7	-31.0	....	Current Transfers: Debit	**78ak*d***
	—	—	—	—	—	—	—	—	—	.4	—	.7	.7	-1.8	....	Capital Account, n.i.e.	**78bc*d***
	—	—	—	—	—	—	—	—	—	.4	—	.7	.7	—	....	Capital Account, n.i.e.: Credit	**78ba*d***
	—	—	—	—	—	—	—	—	—	—	—	—	—	-1.8	....	Capital Account: Debit	**78bb*d***
	95.3	37.9	-23.1	42.0	38.1	-80.3	.6	-6.4	-26.4	-22.2	20.0	55.5	118.4	302.9	....	Financial Account, n.i.e.	**78bj*d***
	-2.5	-1.0	-3.0	-1.4	-1.3	-.9	-2.6	-1.1	-3.3	-3.6	-1.2	-1.0	-1.3	-1.1	....	Direct Investment Abroad	**78bd*d***
	7.1	11.6	8.4	11.2	7.4	14.5	9.4	13.0	11.8	13.3	14.8	15.8	17.4	19.4	....	Dir. Invest. in Rep. Econ., n.i.e.	**78be*d***
	-1.4	2.0	-5.0	-3.1	-16.9	-4.1	-9.9	-1.8	-3.1	-17.4	-17.3	-24.8	-18.6	-11.8	....	Portfolio Investment Assets	**78bf*d***
	-1.8	-.6	-5.2	-6.1	-8.3	-4.1	-9.9	-13.3	-7.6	-9.7	-11.3	-14.0	-16.3	-13.9	....	Equity Securities	**78bk*d***
	.5	2.6	.2	3.0	-8.6	—	—	11.5	4.6	-7.8	-6.0	-10.8	-2.3	2.1	....	Debt Securities	**78bl*d***
	—	40.6	.8	-22.2	14.0	-7.8	1.5	48.7	40.4	-1.6	-25.5	-25.6	44.9	100.0	....	Portfolio Investment Liab., n.i.e.	**78bg*d***
	—	.4	.4	—	-.7	—	.9	—	—	—	-.1	-.1	-.1	....	....	Equity Securities	**78bm*d***
	—	40.2	.4	-22.2	14.7	-7.8	.6	48.7	40.4	-1.6	-25.4	-25.6	45.0	100.0	....	Debt Securities	**78bn*d***
	....	....	....	....	....	....	....	....	....	....	....	....	....	....	....	Financial Derivatives Assets	**78bw*d***
	....	....	....	....	....	....	....	....	....	....	....	....	....	....	....	Financial Derivatives Liabilities	**78bx*d***
	40.7	-.3	-21.5	-22.4	7.6	-19.3	-8.2	-88.9	-167.0	-210.9	-12.1	-16.9	-93.9	52.6	....	Other Investment Assets	**78bh*d***
	....	....	....	....	....	....	....	....	—	—	—	—	—	....	....	Monetary Authorities	**78bo*d***
	-.7	-.6	-.6	-.6	-.5	-3.5	-1.4	-7.8	-9.3	-7.1	-14.1	-11.0	-4.4	-4.6	....	General Government	**78bp*d***
	-61.6	40.7	-2.4	-19.0	-11.1	-11.1	-14.9	-32.6	-87.5	-154.1	24.5	21.5	-72.5	66.9	....	Banks	**78bq*d***
	103.0	-40.5	-18.5	-2.8	19.1	-4.8	8.0	-48.6	-70.3	-49.8	-22.5	-27.4	-17.1	-9.7	....	Other Sectors	**78br*d***
	51.3	-15.0	-2.9	79.8	27.3	-62.7	10.4	23.8	94.8	198.0	61.1	107.9	169.9	143.7	....	Other Investment Liab., n.i.e.	**78bi*d***
	-7.6	-1.6	—	.7	12.0	9.5	-1.9	-5.2	-8.5	-6.7	-6.7	—	—	—	....	Monetary Authorities	**78bs*d***
	77.4	.4	17.9	25.4	-26.7	-31.3	-25.2	-41.1	-34.4	10.3	7.9	23.9	4.1	15.7	....	General Government	**78bt*d***
	62.3	-43.4	-16.1	18.4	17.4	13.9	11.2	16.6	101.4	127.3	-19.8	19.0	49.1	-77.0	....	Banks	**78bu*d***
	-80.9	29.6	-4.7	35.4	24.6	-54.8	26.3	53.5	36.3	67.1	79.6	65.1	116.8	204.9	....	Other Sectors	**78bv*d***
	-72.8	-47.8	-48.2	-72.7	-54.6	-34.4	-49.7	-89.4	26.0	38.5	47.4	.7	65.5	22.1	....	Net Errors and Omissions	**78ca*d***
	3.5	33.5	-46.3	-41.3	-43.6	25.3	19.6	37.8	42.1	86.4	17.4	-6.1	36.3	177.6	....	*Overall Balance*	**78cb*d***
	-3.5	-33.5	46.3	41.3	43.6	-25.3	-19.6	-37.8	-42.1	-86.4	-17.4	6.1	-36.3	-177.6	....	Reserves and Related Items	**79da*d***
	15.4	-27.6	48.9	42.3	40.8	-80.3	-21.1	-59.1	-25.0	-61.1	-9.1	5.6	-37.1	-178.1	....	Reserve Assets	**79db*d***
	-21.6	-10.6	-5.8	-3.7	-.7	51.5	—	—	-18.1	-26.8	-9.0	—	—	—	....	Use of Fund Credit and Loans	**79dc*d***
	2.6	4.6	3.2	2.8	3.5	3.4	1.5	21.3	1.0	1.5	.7	.6	.8	.5	....	Exceptional Financing	**79de*d***
Year Ending December 31																**Government Finance**	
	-189.91	-205.85	-74.64	-244.80	-69.27	-32.23	-86.31	-81.17	26.85	-129.65	-39.05	-39.21	-118.39	-77.20	-183.32	Deficit (-) or Surplus	**80**
	700.14	818.92	1,002.44	931.16	1,016.71	985.05	1,022.79	1,017.43	1,140.52	1,194.44	1,424.53	1,526.78	1,545.31	1,694.00	1,731.94	Total Revenue and Grants	**81y**
	700.14	818.92	1,002.44	931.16	1,016.71	985.05	1,022.79	1,017.43	1,140.52	1,194.44	1,424.53	1,526.78	1,545.31	1,694.00	1,731.94	Revenue	**81**
	—	—	—	—	—	—	—	—	—	—	—	—	—	—	—	Grants	**81z**
	890.05	1,024.77	1,077.08	1,175.96	1,085.98	1,017.28	1,109.10	1,098.60	1,113.67	1,324.09	1,463.58	1,565.99	1,663.70	1,771.20	1,915.26	Exp. & Lending Minus Repay.	**82z**
	882.79	931.71	1,046.64	1,178.49	1,079.70	1,003.95	1,103.97	1,070.34	1,125.78	1,324.26	1,458.02	1,573.67	1,660.81	1,767.91	1,895.54	Expenditure	**82**
	7.26	93.06	30.44	-2.53	6.28	13.33	5.13	28.26	-12.10	-.17	5.56	-7.68	2.89	3.29	19.72	Lending Minus Repayments	**83**
	....	....	....	....	....	....	....	-31.79	1.43	-47.47	-10.65	-14.07	28.95	-32.22	295.35	Statistical Discrepancy	**80xx**
	....	....	....	....	....	....	....	112.99	-28.28	177.13	49.70	53.29	89.44	109.43	-112.02	Total Financing	**80h**
	....	....	....	....	....	....	....	69.58	-19.30	162.93	83.98	104.99	6.69	-97.47	-150.50	Domestic	**84a**
	....	....	....	....	....	....	....	43.41	-8.98	14.20	-34.28	-51.70	82.75	206.90	38.48	Foreign	**85a**
	1,461.3	1,611.5	1,695.1	1,857.4	1,901.1	1,991.7	2,322.6	2,492.2	2,479.9	2,721.1	2,737.1	2,796.2	2,897.5	3,225.9	3,668.8	Total Debt by Residence	**88**
	754.4	821.8	878.0	1,020.6	1,113.5	1,236.7	1,618.0	1,777.8	1,762.2	1,967.0	2,036.9	2,121.4	2,108.6	2,204.1	2,334.2	Domestic	**88a**
	706.9	789.7	817.1	836.8	787.6	755.0	704.6	714.4	717.7	754.1	700.2	674.9	788.9	1,021.9	1,334.6	Foreign	**89a**
Millions of Barbados Dollars																**National Accounts**	
	1,934	2,004	2,158	2,189	2,263	1,979	1,966	1,976	2,302	2,355	2,760	2,963	3,206	....	....	Househ.Cons.Expend.,incl.NPISHs	**96f**
	498	537	614	694	642	640	732	707	752	848	927	982	1,027	....	....	Government Consumption Expend.	**91f**
	467	543	656	648	580	301	420	464	527	506	676	....	....	....	....	Gross Capital Formation	**93**
	1,340	1,510	1,724	1,689	1,610	1,588	1,727	1,980	2,177	2,380	2,438	2,471	2,466	....	....	Exports of Goods and Services	**90c**
	1,325	1,495	1,725	1,780	1,701	1,330	1,537	1,684	2,059	2,200	2,530	2,620	2,712	....	....	Imports of Goods and Services (-)	**98c**
	2,914	3,099	3,427	3,440	3,394	3,178	3,308	3,483	3,739	3,988	4,410	4,756	4,980	....	....	Gross Domestic Product (GDP)	**99b**
	....	....	....	....	....	....	....	....	....	....	....	....	....	....	....	GDP Volume 1965 prices	**99b.*p***
	848.1	877.5	909.1	879.1	844.7	784.1	790.6	824.7	843.9	864.8	889.7	928.6	951.9	....	....	GDP Volume 1974 Prices	**99b.*p***
	100.5	104.0	107.7	104.2	100.1	92.9	93.7	97.7	100.0	102.5	105.4	110.0	112.8	....	....	GDP Volume (1995=100)	**99bv*p***
	77.5	79.7	85.1	88.3	90.7	91.5	94.4	95.3	100.0	104.1	111.9	115.6	118.1	....	....	GDP Deflator (1995=100)	**99bi*p***
Midyear Estimates																	
	.25	.25	.26	.26	.26	.26	.26	.26	.26	.26	.26	.27	.27	.27	.27	**Population**	**99z**

(See notes in the back of the book.)

Belarus

		1972	1973	1974	1975	1976	1977	1978	1979	1980	1981	1982	1983	1984	1985	1986
Exchange Rates															*Rubels per SDR:*	
Official Rate	aa	....	....	....	....	....	....	....	....	....	....	....	....	....	....	....
															Rubels per US Dollar:	
Official Rate	ae	....	....	....	....	....	....	....	....	....	....	....	....	....	....	....
Official Rate	rf	....	....	....	....	....	....	....	....	....	....	....	....	....	....	....
Fund Position															*Millions of SDRs:*	
Quota	2f. s	....	....	....	....	....	....	....	....	....	....	....	....	....	....	....
SDRs	1b. s	....	....	....	....	....	....	....	....	....	....	....	....	....	....	....
Reserve Position in the Fund	1c. s	....	....	....	....	....	....	....	....	....	....	....	....	....	....	....
Total Fund Cred.&Loans Outstg.	2tl	....	....	....	....	....	....	....	....	....	....	....	....	....	....	....
International Liquidity												*Millions of US Dollars Unless Otherwise Indicated:*				
Total Reserves minus Gold	1l. d	....	....	....	....	....	....	....	....	....	....	....	....	....	....	....
SDRs	1b. d	....	....	....	....	....	....	....	....	....	....	....	....	....	....	....
Reserve Position in the Fund	1c. d	....	....	....	....	....	....	....	....	....	....	....	....	....	....	....
Foreign Exchange	1d. d	....	....	....	....	....	....	....	....	....	....	....	....	....	....	....
Gold (Million Fine Troy Ounces)	1ad	....	....	....	....	....	....	....	....	....	....	....	....	....	....	....
Gold (National Valuation)	1an d	....	....	....	....	....	....	....	....	....	....	....	....	....	....	....
Monetary Authorities: Other Liab.	4.. d	....	....	....	....	....	....	....	....	....	....	....	....	....	....	....
Dep.Money Banks: Assets Conv.	7ax d	....	....	....	....	....	....	....	....	....	....	....	....	....	....	....
Assets Nonconv.	7ay d	....	....	....	....	....	....	....	....	....	....	....	....	....	....	....
Dep.Money Banks: Liab. Conv.	7bx d	....	....	....	....	....	....	....	....	....	....	....	....	....	....	....
Liab. Nonconv.	7by d	....	....	....	....	....	....	....	....	....	....	....	....	....	....	....
Monetary Authorities															*Millions of Rubels:*	
Foreign Assets	11	....	....	....	....	....	....	....	....	....	....	....	....	....	....	....
Claims on Central Government	12a	....	....	....	....	....	....	....	....	....	....	....	....	....	....	....
Claims on Local Government	12b	....	....	....	....	....	....	....	....	....	....	....	....	....	....	....
Claims on Nonfin.Pub.Enterprises	12c	....	....	....	....	....	....	....	....	....	....	....	....	....	....	....
Claims on Private Sector	12d	....	....	....	....	....	....	....	....	....	....	....	....	....	....	....
Claims on Banks	12e	....	....	....	....	....	....	....	....	....	....	....	....	....	....	....
Reserve Money	14	....	....	....	....	....	....	....	....	....	....	....	....	....	....	....
of which: Currency Outside DMBs	14a	....	....	....	....	....	....	....	....	....	....	....	....	....	....	....
Time, Savings,& Fgn.Currency Dep.	15	....	....	....	....	....	....	....	....	....	....	....	....	....	....	....
Foreign Liabilities	16c	....	....	....	....	....	....	....	....	....	....	....	....	....	....	....
Central Government Deposits	16d	....	....	....	....	....	....	....	....	....	....	....	....	....	....	....
Capital Accounts	17a	....	....	....	....	....	....	....	....	....	....	....	....	....	....	....
Other Items (Net)	17r	....	....	....	....	....	....	....	....	....	....	....	....	....	....	....
Deposit Money Banks															*Millions of Rubels:*	
Reserves	20	....	....	....	....	....	....	....	....	....	....	....	....	....	....	....
Foreign Assets	21	....	....	....	....	....	....	....	....	....	....	....	....	....	....	....
Claims on Central Government	22a	....	....	....	....	....	....	....	....	....	....	....	....	....	....	....
Claims on Local Government	22b	....	....	....	....	....	....	....	....	....	....	....	....	....	....	....
Claims on Nonfin.Pub.Enterprises	22c	....	....	....	....	....	....	....	....	....	....	....	....	....	....	....
Claims on Private Sector	22d	....	....	....	....	....	....	....	....	....	....	....	....	....	....	....
Claims on Nonbank Financial Insts	22g	....	....	....	....	....	....	....	....	....	....	....	....	....	....	....
Demand Deposits	24	....	....	....	....	....	....	....	....	....	....	....	....	....	....	....
Time, Savings,& Fgn. Currency Dep.	25	....	....	....	....	....	....	....	....	....	....	....	....	....	....	....
Foreign Liabilities	26c	....	....	....	....	....	....	....	....	....	....	....	....	....	....	....
Central Government Deposits	26d	....	....	....	....	....	....	....	....	....	....	....	....	....	....	....
Credit from Monetary Authorities	26g	....	....	....	....	....	....	....	....	....	....	....	....	....	....	....
Capital Accounts	27a	....	....	....	....	....	....	....	....	....	....	....	....	....	....	....
Other Items (Net)	27r	....	....	....	....	....	....	....	....	....	....	....	....	....	....	....
Monetary Survey															*Millions of Rubels:*	
Foreign Assets (Net)	31n	....	....	....	....	....	....	....	....	....	....	....	....	....	....	....
Domestic Credit	32	....	....	....	....	....	....	....	....	....	....	....	....	....	....	....
Claims on Central Govt. (Net)	32an	....	....	....	....	....	....	....	....	....	....	....	....	....	....	....
Claims on Local Government	32b	....	....	....	....	....	....	....	....	....	....	....	....	....	....	....
Claims on Nonfin.Pub.Enterprises	32c	....	....	....	....	....	....	....	....	....	....	....	....	....	....	....
Claims on Private Sector	32d	....	....	....	....	....	....	....	....	....	....	....	....	....	....	....
Claims on Nonbank Financ. Insts	32g	....	....	....	....	....	....	....	....	....	....	....	....	....	....	....
Money	34	....	....	....	....	....	....	....	....	....	....	....	....	....	....	....
Quasi-Money	35	....	....	....	....	....	....	....	....	....	....	....	....	....	....	....
Capital Accounts	37a	....	....	....	....	....	....	....	....	....	....	....	....	....	....	....
Other Items (Net)	37r	....	....	....	....	....	....	....	....	....	....	....	....	....	....	....
Money plus Quasi-Money	35l	....	....	....	....	....	....	....	....	....	....	....	....	....	....	....
Interest Rates															*Percent Per Annum*	
Refinancing Rate *(End of Per.)*	60	....	....	....	....	....	....	....	....	....	....	....	....	....	....	....
Deposit Rate	60l	....	....	....	....	....	....	....	....	....	....	....	....	....	....	....
Lending Rate	60p	....	....	....	....	....	....	....	....	....	....	....	....	....	....	....
Prices and Labor															*Percent Change*	
Producer Prices	63.xx	....	....	....	....	....	....	....	....	....	....	....	....	....	....	....
Consumer Prices	64.xx	....	....	....	....	....	....	....	....	....	....	....	....	....	....	....
Wages	65.xx	....	....	....	....	....	....	....	....	....	....	....	....	....	....	....
															Number in Thousands:	
Unemployment	67c	....	....	....	....	....	....	....	....	....	....	....	....	....	....	....
Unemployment Rate (%)	67r	....	....	....	....	....	....	....	....	....	....	....	....	....	....	....
International Transactions															*Millions of US Dollars*	
Exports	70.. d	....	....	....	....	....	....	....	....	....	....	....	....	....	....	....
Imports, c.i.f.	71.. d	....	....	....	....	....	....	....	....	....	....	....	....	....	....	....

1987	1988	1989	1990	1991	1992	1993	1994	1995	1996	1997	1998	1999	2000	2001		
End of Period															**Exchange Rates**	
....	....	....	....	....	.021	.960	15.474	17.095	22.288	41.476	309.767	439.203	1,537.434	1,985.633	Official Rate	**aa**
End of Period (ae) Period Average (rf)																
....	....	....	....	....	.015	.699	10.600	11.500	15.500	30.740	106.000	320.000	1,180.000	1,580.000	Official Rate	**ae**
....	....	....	....	....	....	....	....	11.521	13.230	26.020	46.127	248.795	876.750	1,390.000	Official Rate	**rf**
End of Period															**Fund Position**	
....	....	....	....	....	187.00	280.40	280.40	280.40	280.40	280.40	280.40	386.40	386.40	386.40	Quota	**2f. s**
....	....	....	....	....	—	3.22	.01	3.05	.10	—	.30	.30	.14	.31	SDRs	**1b. s**
....	....	....	....	....	.02	.02	.02	.02	.02	.02	.02	.02	.02	.02	Reserve Position in the Fund	**1c. s**
....	....	....	....	....	—	70.10	70.10	190.20	190.20	190.20	172.27	129.74	87.62	64.26	Total Fund Cred.&Loans Outstg.	**2tl**
End of Period															**International Liquidity**	
....	....	....	....	....	....	....	100.99	377.02	469.15	393.70	702.76	294.27	350.50	390.68	Total Reserves minus Gold	**1l. d**
....	....	....	....	....	—	4.43	.01	4.54	.14	—	.42	.42	.18	.40	SDRs	**1b. d**
....	....	....	....	....	.03	.03	.03	.03	.03	.03	.03	.03	.03	.03	Reserve Position in the Fund	**1c. d**
....	....	....	....	....	....	....	100.95	372.45	468.98	393.67	702.31	293.82	350.29	390.26	Foreign Exchange	**1d. d**
....	....	....	....	....	....	....	....	....	....	....	....	....	....	....	Gold (Million Fine Troy Ounces)	**1ad**
....	....	....	....	....	....	....	....	....	....	....	....	....	....	....	Gold (National Valuation)	**1an d**
....	....	....	....	....	....	....	7.53	11.88	144.97	61.87	78.90	77.31	94.29	137.08	Monetary Authorities: Other Liab.	**4.. d**
....	....	....	....	....	....	....	280.29	261.71	†246.78	276.63	290.03	308.20	280.54	249.61	Dep.Money Banks: Assets Conv.	**7ax d**
....	....	....	....	....	....	....	40.66	27.90	†82.98	93.25	18.54	28.73	49.55	47.20	Assets Nonconv	**7ay d**
....	....	....	....	....	....	....	51.69	88.05	†84.25	89.30	134.49	108.07	99.16	142.17	Dep.Money Banks: Liab. Conv.	**7bx d**
....	....	....	....	....	....	....	36.49	31.68	†58.55	70.10	4.71	7.78	14.90	45.92	Liab. Nonconv	**7by d**
End of Period															**Monetary Authorities**	
....	....	....	....	....	....	....	1,226	4,594	7,411	12,333	76,465	98,355	423,560	706,179	Foreign Assets	**11**
....	....	....	....	....	....	....	1,679	4,876	8,591	14,448	54,930	153,755	302,799	504,345	Claims on Central Government	**12a**
....	....	....	....	....	....	....	—	—	—	—	—	—	—	—	Claims on Local Government	**12b**
....	....	....	....	....	....	....	12	88	112	101	22	44	23	—	Claims on Nonfin.Pub.Enterprises	**12c**
....	....	....	....	....	....	....	7	38	32	343	2,041	7,524	12,577	Claims on Private Sector	**12d**
....	....	....	....	....	....	....	1,435	2,325	6,719	17,046	51,229	60,226	107,082	180,557	Claims on Banks	**12e**
....	....	....	....	....	....	....	1,757	6,817	12,143	25,214	66,300	184,680	414,335	844,955	Reserve Money	**14**
....	....	....	....	....	....	....	736	3,779	6,199	12,300	27,074	86,852	238,796	512,211	of which: Currency Outside DMBs	**14a**
....	....	....	....	....	....	....	15	19	20	23	81	139	306	757	Time, Savings,& Fgn.Currency Dep.	**15**
....	....	....	....	....	....	....	1,263	3,388	6,486	9,791	70,720	81,722	245,979	344,175	Foreign Liabilities	**16c**
....	....	....	....	....	....	....	379	342	1,107	2,010	6,490	15,072	41,741	35,099	Central Government Deposits	**16d**
....	....	....	....	....	....	....	301	637	1,402	3,694	5,968	24,895	129,194	185,695	Capital Accounts	**17a**
....	....	....	....	....	....	....	643	718	1,708	3,266	33,430	7,912	9,433	−7,023	Other Items (Net)	**17r**
End of Period															**Deposit Money Banks**	
....	....	....	....	....	....	....	951	2,842	†5,693	11,889	35,688	92,002	158,118	324,836	Reserves	**20**
....	....	....	....	....	....	....	3,691	3,331	†5,111	11,370	67,886	107,816	389,506	468,964	Foreign Assets	**21**
....	....	....	....	....	....	....	9	640	†2,273	6,084	21,956	53,796	176,938	302,612	Claims on Central Government	**22a**
....	....	....	....	....	....	....	—	—	†4	22	143	358	815	468	Claims on Local Government	**22b**
....	....	....	....	....	....	....	2,866	6,571	†9,232	18,565	84,059	170,553	677,713	1,138,159	Claims on Nonfin.Pub.Enterprises	**22c**
....	....	....	....	....	....	....	3,127	7,360	†12,303	30,292	112,999	279,701	802,505	1,400,762	Claims on Private Sector	**22d**
....	....	....	....	....	....	....	....	....	302	498	480	1,278	1,310	7,938	Claims on Nonbank Financial Insts	**22g**
....	....	....	....	....	....	....	1,877	6,132	†9,240	21,052	52,487	140,714	259,602	376,038	Demand Deposits	**24**
....	....	....	....	....	....	....	4,238	7,889	†11,609	23,904	136,239	271,888	1,104,976	1,673,282	Time, Savings,& Fgn. Currency Dep.	**25**
....	....	....	....	....	....	....	1,014	1,377	†2,213	4,900	30,622	37,073	134,597	297,179	Foreign Liabilities	**26c**
....	....	....	....	....	....	....	238	1,000	†2,848	5,799	20,991	44,722	177,905	443,511	Central Government Deposits	**26d**
....	....	....	....	....	....	....	1,243	2,122	†6,486	15,931	48,371	53,471	84,391	142,487	Credit from Monetary Authorities	**26g**
....	....	....	....	....	....	....	1,107	4,620	†5,277	8,925	25,545	147,109	431,902	567,361	Capital Accounts	**27a**
....	....	....	....	....	....	....	926	−2,396	†−2,753	−1,792	8,955	10,527	13,532	143,882	Other Items (Net)	**27r**
End of Period															**Monetary Survey**	
....	....	....	....	....	....	....	2,640	3,160	†3,823	9,012	43,008	87,376	432,490	533,790	Foreign Assets (Net)	**31n**
....	....	....	....	....	....	....	7,083	18,232	†28,896	62,271	247,452	601,732	1,749,981	2,888,252	Domestic Credit	**32**
....	....	....	....	....	....	....	1,071	4,175	†6,909	12,723	49,405	147,757	260,091	328,347	Claims on Central Govt. (Net)	**32an**
....	....	....	....	....	....	....	—	—	†4	22	143	358	815	468	Claims on Local Government	**32b**
....	....	....	....	....	....	....	2,878	6,659	†9,344	18,665	84,081	170,598	677,736	1,138,159	Claims on Nonfin.Pub.Enterprises	**32c**
....	....	....	....	....	....	....	3,134	7,398	†12,335	30,363	113,343	281,741	810,029	1,413,339	Claims on Private Sector	**32d**
....	....	....	....	....	....	....	....	....	302	498	480	1,278	1,310	7,938	Claims on Nonbank Financ. Insts	**32g**
....	....	....	....	....	....	....	2,687	10,027	†15,708	33,852	80,932	233,415	508,432	889,553	Money	**34**
....	....	....	....	....	....	....	4,253	7,908	†11,629	23,927	136,320	272,027	1,105,282	1,674,039	Quasi-Money	**35**
....	....	....	....	....	....	....	1,407	5,257	†6,678	12,619	31,513	172,005	561,096	753,056	Capital Accounts	**37a**
....	....	....	....	....	....	....	1,375	−1,800	†−1,297	885	41,694	11,661	7,660	105,393	Other Items (Net)	**37r**
....	....	....	....	....	....	....	6,940	17,934	†27,337	57,779	217,252	505,442	1,613,714	2,563,593	Money plus Quasi-Money	**35l**
Percent Per Annum															**Interest Rates**	
....	....	....	....	....	30.0	210.0	480.0	66.0	8.3	8.9	9.6	23.4	†80.0	48.0	Refinancing Rate (End of Per.)	**60**
....	....	....	....	....	....	65.1	89.6	100.8	32.4	15.6	14.3	23.9	37.6	34.2	Deposit Rate	**60l**
....	....	....	....	....	....	71.6	148.5	175.0	62.3	31.8	27.0	51.0	67.7	47.0	Lending Rate	**60p**
over Previous Period															**Prices and Labor**	
....	....	....	....	....	....	1,536.3	2,170.8	†497.9	35.0	86.5	73.5	355.8	185.6	71.8	Producer Prices	**63.xx**
....	....	....	....	....	966.5	1,190.2	2,221.0	709.3	52.7	63.9	72.9	293.7	168.6	61.1	Consumer Prices	**64.xx**
....	....	....	....	....	....	1,106.8	1,504.4	668.9	60.5	87.3	104.2	322.4	200.9	108.8	Wages	**65.xx**
Period Averages																
....	....	....	....	....	24	66	101	131	183	126	106	95	96	....	Unemployment	**67c**
....	....	....	....	....	.5	1.4	2.1	2.7	3.9	2.8	2.3	2.1	2.1	....	Unemployment Rate (%)	**67r**
Millions of US Dollars															**International Transactions**	
....	....	....	....	....	....	3,559	1,970	2,510	4,803	5,652	7,301	7,070	5,909	7,326	7,525	Exports	**70.. d**
....	....	....	....	....	....	3,495	2,539	3,066	5,564	6,939	8,689	8,549	6,674	8,646	8,046	Imports, c.i.f.	**71. d**

Belarus

		1972	1973	1974	1975	1976	1977	1978	1979	1980	1981	1982	1983	1984	1985	1986
Balance of Payments															*Millions of US Dollars:*	
Current Account, n.i.e.	78al *d*	...	...	...	...	...	...	...	...	...	...	...	...	...	...	...
Goods: Exports f.o.b.	78aa *d*	...	...	...	...	...	...	...	...	...	...	...	...	...	...	...
Goods: Imports f.o.b.	78ab *d*	...	...	...	...	...	...	...	...	...	...	...	...	...	...	...
Trade Balance	78ac *d*	...	...	...	...	...	...	...	...	...	...	...	...	...	...	...
Services: Credit	78ad *d*	...	...	...	...	...	...	...	...	...	...	...	...	...	...	...
Services: Debit	78ae *d*	...	...	...	...	...	...	...	...	...	...	...	...	...	...	...
Balance on Goods & Services	78af *d*	...	...	...	...	...	...	...	...	...	...	...	...	...	...	...
Income: Credit	78ag *d*	...	...	...	...	...	...	...	...	...	...	...	...	...	...	...
Income: Debit	78ah *d*	...	...	...	...	...	...	...	...	...	...	...	...	...	...	...
Balance on Gds, Serv. & Inc.	78ai *d*	...	...	...	...	...	...	...	...	...	...	...	...	...	...	...
Current Transfers, n.i.e.: Credit	78aj *d*	...	...	...	...	...	...	...	...	...	...	...	...	...	...	...
Current Transfers: Debit	78ak *d*	...	...	...	...	...	...	...	...	...	...	...	...	...	...	...
Capital Account, n.i.e.	78bc *d*	...	...	...	...	...	...	...	...	...	...	...	...	...	...	...
Capital Account, n.i.e.: Credit	78ba *d*	...	...	...	...	...	...	...	...	...	...	...	...	...	...	...
Capital Account: Debit	78bb *d*	...	...	...	...	...	...	...	...	...	...	...	...	...	...	...
Financial Account, n.i.e.	78bj *d*	...	...	...	...	...	...	...	...	...	...	...	...	...	...	...
Direct Investment Abroad	78bd *d*	...	...	...	...	...	...	...	...	...	...	...	...	...	...	...
Dir. Invest. in Rep. Econ., n.i.e.	78be *d*	...	...	...	...	...	...	...	...	...	...	...	...	...	...	...
Portfolio Investment Assets	78bf *d*	...	...	...	...	...	...	...	...	...	...	...	...	...	...	...
Equity Securities	78bk *d*	...	...	...	...	...	...	...	...	...	...	...	...	...	...	...
Debt Securities	78bl *d*	...	...	...	...	...	...	...	...	...	...	...	...	...	...	...
Portfolio Investment Liab., n.i.e.	78bg *d*	...	...	...	...	...	...	...	...	...	...	...	...	...	...	...
Equity Securities	78bm *d*	...	...	...	...	...	...	...	...	...	...	...	...	...	...	...
Debt Securities	78bn *d*	...	...	...	...	...	...	...	...	...	...	...	...	...	...	...
Financial Derivatives Assets	78bw *d*	...	...	...	...	...	...	...	...	...	...	...	...	...	...	...
Financial Derivatives Liabilities	78bx *d*	...	...	...	...	...	...	...	...	...	...	...	...	...	...	...
Other Investment Assets	78bh *d*	...	...	...	...	...	...	...	...	...	...	...	...	...	...	...
Monetary Authorities	78bo *d*	...	...	...	...	...	...	...	...	...	...	...	...	...	...	...
General Government	78bp *d*	...	...	...	...	...	...	...	...	...	...	...	...	...	...	...
Banks	78bq *d*	...	...	...	...	...	...	...	...	...	...	...	...	...	...	...
Other Sectors	78br *d*	...	...	...	...	...	...	...	...	...	...	...	...	...	...	...
Other Investment Liab., n.i.e.	78bi *d*	...	...	...	...	...	...	...	...	...	...	...	...	...	...	...
Monetary Authorities	78bs *d*	...	...	...	...	...	...	...	...	...	...	...	...	...	...	...
General Government	78bt *d*	...	...	...	...	...	...	...	...	...	...	...	...	...	...	...
Banks	78bu *d*	...	...	...	...	...	...	...	...	...	...	...	...	...	...	...
Other Sectors	78bv *d*	...	...	...	...	...	...	...	...	...	...	...	...	...	...	...
Net Errors and Omissions	78ca *d*	...	...	...	...	...	...	...	...	...	...	...	...	...	...	...
Overall Balance	78cb *d*	...	...	...	...	...	...	...	...	...	...	...	...	...	...	...
Reserves and Related Items	79da *d*	...	...	...	...	...	...	...	...	...	...	...	...	...	...	...
Reserve Assets	79db *d*	...	...	...	...	...	...	...	...	...	...	...	...	...	...	...
Use of Fund Credit and Loans	79dc *d*	...	...	...	...	...	...	...	...	...	...	...	...	...	...	...
Exceptional Financing	79de *d*	...	...	...	...	...	...	...	...	...	...	...	...	...	...	...
International Investment Position															*Millions of US Dollars*	
Assets	79aa *d*	...	...	...	...	...	...	...	...	...	...	...	...	...	...	...
Direct Investment Abroad	79ab *d*	...	...	...	...	...	...	...	...	...	...	...	...	...	...	...
Portfolio Investment	79ac *d*	...	...	...	...	...	...	...	...	...	...	...	...	...	...	...
Equity Securities	79ad *d*	...	...	...	...	...	...	...	...	...	...	...	...	...	...	...
Debt Securities	79ae *d*	...	...	...	...	...	...	...	...	...	...	...	...	...	...	...
Financial Derivatives	79al *d*	...	...	...	...	...	...	...	...	...	...	...	...	...	...	...
Other Investment	79af *d*	...	...	...	...	...	...	...	...	...	...	...	...	...	...	...
Monetary Authorities	79ag *d*	...	...	...	...	...	...	...	...	...	...	...	...	...	...	...
General Government	79ah *d*	...	...	...	...	...	...	...	...	...	...	...	...	...	...	...
Banks	79ai *d*	...	...	...	...	...	...	...	...	...	...	...	...	...	...	...
Other Sectors	79aj *d*	...	...	...	...	...	...	...	...	...	...	...	...	...	...	...
Reserve Assets	79ak *d*	...	...	...	...	...	...	...	...	...	...	...	...	...	...	...
Liabilities	79la *d*	...	...	...	...	...	...	...	...	...	...	...	...	...	...	...
Dir. Invest. in Rep. Economy	79lb *d*	...	...	...	...	...	...	...	...	...	...	...	...	...	...	...
Portfolio Investment	79lc *d*	...	...	...	...	...	...	...	...	...	...	...	...	...	...	...
Equity Securities	79ld *d*	...	...	...	...	...	...	...	...	...	...	...	...	...	...	...
Debt Securities	79le *d*	...	...	...	...	...	...	...	...	...	...	...	...	...	...	...
Financial Derivatives	79ll *d*	...	...	...	...	...	...	...	...	...	...	...	...	...	...	...
Other Investment	79lf *d*	...	...	...	...	...	...	...	...	...	...	...	...	...	...	...
Monetary Authorities	79lg *d*	...	...	...	...	...	...	...	...	...	...	...	...	...	...	...
General Government	79lh *d*	...	...	...	...	...	...	...	...	...	...	...	...	...	...	...
Banks	79li *d*	...	...	...	...	...	...	...	...	...	...	...	...	...	...	...
Other Sectors	79lj *d*	...	...	...	...	...	...	...	...	...	...	...	...	...	...	...

Minus Sign Indicates Debit

1987	1988	1989	1990	1991	1992	1993	1994	1995	1996	1997	1998	1999	2000	2001	Balance of Payments	
....	....	....	....	....	....	−435.0	−443.8	−458.3	−515.9	−859.2	−1,016.5	−193.7	−323.1	−270.3	Current Account, n.i.e.	78al *d*
....	....	....	....	....	....	1,970.1	2,510.0	4,803.0	5,790.1	6,918.7	6,172.3	5,646.4	6,640.5	7,240.1	Goods: Exports f.o.b.	78aa *d*
....	....	....	....	....	....	−2,498.0	−2,999.8	−5,468.7	−6,938.6	−8,325.7	−7,673.4	−6,216.4	−7,524.6	−8,018.8	Goods: Imports f.o.b.	78ab *d*
....	....	....	....	....	....	−527.9	−489.8	−665.7	−1,148.5	−1,407.0	−1,501.1	−570.0	−884.1	−778.7	*Trade Balance*	78ac *d*
....	....	....	....	....	....	184.9	251.4	466.1	908.0	918.8	925.1	753.3	1,015.6	1,043.6	Services: Credit	78ad *d*
....	....	....	....	....	....	−136.8	−199.3	−283.7	−335.9	−364.8	−443.2	−438.8	−562.6	−644.9	Services: Debit	78ae *d*
....	....	....	....	....	....	−479.8	−437.7	−483.3	−576.4	−853.0	−1,019.2	−255.5	−431.1	−380.0	*Balance on Goods & Services*	78af *d*
....	....	....	....	....	....	.1	.5	1.9	74.1	31.2	26.8	20.8	25.7	18.6	Income: Credit	78ag *d*
....	....	....	....	....	....	−7.5	−29.3	−52.9	−104.9	−115.8	−119.7	−62.8	−72.4	−63.0	Income: Debit	78ah *d*
....	....	....	....	....	....	−487.2	−466.5	−534.3	−607.2	−937.6	−1,112.1	−297.5	−477.8	−424.4	*Balance on Gds, Serv. & Inc.*	78ai *d*
....	....	....	....	....	....	64.6	50.9	107.2	135.5	106.1	120.9	137.0	177.1	202.6	Current Transfers, n.i.e.: Credit	78aj *d*
....	....	....	....	....	....	−12.4	−28.2	−31.2	−44.2	−27.7	−25.3	−33.2	−22.4	−48.5	Current Transfers: Debit	78ak *d*
....	....	....	....	....	....	—	23.8	7.3	101.1	133.2	170.1	60.4	69.4	56.3	Capital Account, n.i.e.	78bc *d*
....	....	....	....	....	....	—	23.8	7.3	257.2	248.0	261.3	131.1	125.6	132.3	Capital Account, n.i.e.: Credit	78ba *d*
....	....	....	....	....	....				−156.1	−114.8	−91.2	−70.7	−56.2	−76.0	Capital Account: Debit	78bb *d*
....	....	....	....	....	....	294.1	144.6	204.0	378.7	738.1	354.8	399.5	140.1	248.7	Financial Account, n.i.e.	78bj *d*
....	....	....	....	....	....				....	−2.1	−2.3	−.8	−.2	−.3	Direct Investment Abroad	78bd *d*
....	....	....	....	....	....	17.6	10.5	14.7	104.5	351.6	203.2	444.0	118.8	108.0	Dir. Invest. in Rep. Econ., n.i.e.	78be *d*
....	....	....	....	....	....				−17.7	−61.6	28.0	−15.4	−5.7	10.5	Portfolio Investment Assets	78bf *d*
....	....	....	....	....	....				....	−.6	.3	−7.3	.5	.7	Equity Securities	78bk *d*
....	....	....	....	....	....				−17.7	−61.0	27.7	−8.1	−6.2	9.8	Debt Securities	78bl *d*
....	....	....	....	....	....				3.2	41.8	−13.4	−5.2	50.1	−45.4	Portfolio Investment Liab., n.i.e.	78bg *d*
....	....	....	....	....	....				....	....	2.7	....	.5	2.5	Equity Securities	78bm *d*
....	....	....	....	....	....				3.2	41.8	−16.1	−5.2	49.6	−47.9	Debt Securities	78bn *d*
....	....	....	....	....	....				....	....	....	....	....	....	Financial Derivatives Assets	78bw *d*
....	....	....	....	....	....				....	....	....	....	....	....	Financial Derivatives Liabilities	78bx *d*
....	....	....	....	....	....	−118.1	−232.5	−155.4	−131.5	49.9	199.4	−36.7	41.7	−139.2	Other Investment Assets	78bh *d*
....	....	....	....	....	....				....	1.5	−.9	1.1	−.2	−99.3	Monetary Authorities	78bo *d*
....	....	....	....	....	....	—	—	14.0							General Government	78bp *d*
....	....	....	....	....	....	−60.6	−94.2	58.6	−40.2	−16.4	19.0	−16.4	8.4	17.5	Banks	78bq *d*
....	....	....	....	....	....	−57.5	−138.3	−228.0	−91.3	61.0	181.3	−21.4	33.5	−57.4	Other Sectors	78br *d*
....	....	....	....	....	....	394.6	366.6	344.7	420.2	358.5	−60.1	13.6	−64.6	315.1	Other Investment Liab., n.i.e.	78bi *d*
....	....	....	....	....	....	—	−.3	3.7	133.1	−86.8	6.8	.7	−21.2	17.3	Monetary Authorities	78bs *d*
....	....	....	....	....	....	243.9	239.4	81.7	33.4	62.4	24.7	−28.5	−37.2	27.6	General Government	78bt *d*
....	....	....	....	....	....	−4.8	34.9	24.1	23.1	16.6	−20.3	−24.1	1.9	81.4	Banks	78bu *d*
....	....	....	....	....	....	155.5	92.6	235.2	230.6	366.3	−71.3	65.5	−8.1	188.8	Other Sectors	78bv *d*
....	....	....	....	....	....	3.4	−41.6	168.6	−178.1	53.0	172.3	−246.3	238.9	−119.2	Net Errors and Omissions	78ca *d*
....	....	....	....	....	....	−137.5	−317.0	−78.4	−214.2	65.1	−319.3	19.9	125.3	−84.5	*Overall Balance*	78cb *d*
....	....	....	....	....	....	137.5	317.0	78.4	214.2	−65.1	319.3	−19.9	−125.3	84.5	Reserves and Related Items	79da *d*
....	....	....	....	....	....	12.5	−58.6	−283.7	−78.6	75.3	54.6	34.6	−75.7	5.2	Reserve Assets	79db *d*
....	....	....	....	....	....	98.2		177.8			−24.4	−58.1	−55.8	−29.8	Use of Fund Credit and Loans	79dc *d*
....	....	....	....	....	....	26.8	375.6	184.3	292.8	−140.4	289.1	3.6	6.2	109.1	Exceptional Financing	79de *d*

Millions of US Dollars

1987	1988	1989	1990	1991	1992	1993	1994	1995	1996	1997	1998	1999	2000	2001	International Investment Position	
....	....	....	....	....	....	....	....	....	1,335.4	1,273.7	991.3	1,004.2	996.9	1,107.8	Assets	79aa *d*
....	....	....	....	....	....	....	....	....		2.1	4.4	5.2	5.5	5.8	Direct Investment Abroad	79ab *d*
....	....	....	....	....	....	....	....	....	21.5	83.1	55.1	69.0	57.5	46.6	Portfolio Investment	79ac *d*
....	....	....	....	....	....	....	....	....	2.3	2.9	2.6	9.8	9.3	8.3	Equity Securities	79ad *d*
....	....	....	....	....	....	....	....	....	19.2	80.2	52.5	59.2	48.2	38.3	Debt Securities	79ae *d*
....	....	....	....	....	....	....	....	....	—	—	—	—	—	—	Financial Derivatives	79al *d*
....	....	....	....	....	....	....	....	....	844.8	794.9	592.8	625.4	577.1	709.8	Other Investment	79af *d*
....	....	....	....	....	....	....	....	....	9.0	7.5	8.4	7.4	2.2	98.1	Monetary Authorities	79ag *d*
....	....	....	....	....	....	....	....	....							General Government	79ah *d*
....	....	....	....	....	....	....	....	....	291.7	304.3	285.4	298.2	288.9	268.6	Banks	79ai *d*
....	....	....	....	....	....	....	....	....	544.1	483.1	299.0	319.8	286.0	343.1	Other Sectors	79aj *d*
....	....	....	....	....	....	....	....	....	469.1	393.6	339.0	304.6	356.8	345.6	Reserve Assets	79ak *d*
....	....	....	....	....	....	....	....	....	2,064.7	2,656.7	3,086.9	3,419.6	3,436.8	3,868.9	Liabilities	79la *d*
....	....	....	....	....	....	....	....	....	154.3	505.9	709.1	1,153.1	1,305.5	1,412.8	Dir. Invest. in Rep. Economy	79lb *d*
....	....	....	....	....	....	....	....	....	34.6	76.4	63.0	44.7	78.6	36.1	Portfolio Investment	79lc *d*
....	....	....	....	....	....	....	....	....	5.5	5.5	8.2	8.2	8.8	11.4	Equity Securities	79ld *d*
....	....	....	....	....	....	....	....	....	29.1	70.9	54.8	36.5	69.8	24.7	Debt Securities	79le *d*
....	....	....	....	....	....	....	....	....	—	—	—	—	—	—	Financial Derivatives	79ll *d*
....	....	....	....	....	....	....	....	....	1,875.8	2,074.4	2,314.8	2,221.8	2,052.7	2,420.0	Other Investment	79lf *d*
....	....	....	....	....	....	....	....	....	409.9	303.4	298.6	230.1	142.4	194.9	Monetary Authorities	79lg *d*
....	....	....	....	....	....	....	....	....	639.5	683.0	386.3	375.9	346.0	334.2	General Government	79lh *d*
....	....	....	....	....	....	....	....	....	142.8	159.4	139.1	112.4	114.1	188.1	Banks	79li *d*
....	....	....	....	....	....	....	....	....	683.6	928.6	1,490.8	1,503.4	1,450.2	1,702.8	Other Sectors	79lj *d*

Belarus

	1972	1973	1974	1975	1976	1977	1978	1979	1980	1981	1982	1983	1984	1985	1986
Government Finance															*Billions of Rubels:*
Deficit (-) or Surplus............................ 80	...	...	...	...	...	...	...	...	...	...	...	...	...	...	...
Total Revenue and Grants.................. 81y	...	...	...	...	...	...	...	...	...	...	...	...	...	...	...
Revenue 81	...	...	...	...	...	...	...	...	...	...	...	...	...	...	...
Grants 81z	...	...	...	...	...	...	...	...	...	...	...	...	...	...	...
Exp. & Lending Minus Repay. 82z	...	...	...	...	...	...	...	...	...	...	...	...	...	...	...
Expenditure 82	...	...	...	...	...	...	...	...	...	...	...	...	...	...	...
Lending Minus Repayments 83	...	...	...	...	...	...	...	...	...	...	...	...	...	...	...
Total Financing 80h	...	...	...	...	...	...	...	...	...	...	...	...	...	...	...
Domestic 84a	...	...	...	...	...	...	...	...	...	...	...	...	...	...	...
Foreign 85a	...	...	...	...	...	...	...	...	...	...	...	...	...	...	...
Total Debt by Residence 88	...	...	...	...	...	...	...	...	...	...	...	...	...	...	...
Domestic 88a	...	...	...	...	...	...	...	...	...	...	...	...	...	...	...
Foreign 89a	...	...	...	...	...	...	...	...	...	...	...	...	...	...	...
National Accounts															*Billions of Rubels*
Househ.Cons.Expend.,incl.NPISHs 96f	...	...	...	...	...	...	...	...	...	...	...	...	...	...	...
Government Consumption Expend. 91f	...	...	...	...	...	...	...	...	...	...	...	...	...	...	...
Gross Fixed Capital Formation 93e	...	...	...	...	...	...	...	...	...	...	...	...	...	...	...
Changes in Inventories 93i	...	...	...	...	...	...	...	...	...	...	...	...	...	...	...
Exports of Goods and Services 90c	...	...	...	...	...	...	...	...	...	...	...	...	...	...	...
Imports of Goods and Services (-) 98c	...	...	...	...	...	...	...	...	...	...	...	...	...	...	...
Statistical Discrepancy 99bs	...	...	...	...	...	...	...	...	...	...	...	...	...	...	...
Gross Domestic Product (GDP) 99b	...	...	...	...	...	...	...	...	...	...	...	...	...	...	...
Net Primary Income from Abroad 98.n	...	...	...	...	...	...	...	...	...	...	...	...	...	...	...
Gross National Income (GNI) 99a	...	...	...	...	...	...	...	...	...	...	...	...	...	...	...
Net Current Transf.from Abroad 98t	...	...	...	...	...	...	...	...	...	...	...	...	...	...	...
Gross Nat'l Disposable Inc.(GNDI)........ 99i	...	...	...	...	...	...	...	...	...	...	...	...	...	...	...
Gross Saving 99s	...	...	...	...	...	...	...	...	...	...	...	...	...	...	...
GDP Volume 1995 Ref., Chained 99b.p	...	...	...	...	...	...	...	...	...	...	...	...	...	...	...
GDP Volume 2000 Ref., Chained 99b.p	...	...	...	...	...	...	...	...	...	...	...	...	...	...	...
GDP Volume (1995=100) .... 99bv$p$	...	...	...	...	...	...	...	...	...	...	...	...	...	...	...
GDP Deflator (1995=100)................. 99bi$p$	...	...	...	...	...	...	...	...	...	...	...	...	...	...	...
															Millions:
Population.. 99z	...	...	...	...	...	...	...	...	...	...	...	...	...	...	...

	1987	1988	1989	1990	1991	1992	1993	1994	1995	1996	1997	1998	1999	2000	2001		
Year Ending December 31																**Government Finance**	
Deficit (-) or Surplus	...	...	...	...	...	—	-.04	-.33	-3.22	-3.46	-5.72	-5.99	-60.28	7.30	....	Deficit (-) or Surplus	80
Total Revenue and Grants						.03	.38	6.01	37.10	58.99	117.87	206.59	876.20	2,646.10	....	Total Revenue and Grants	81y
Revenue						.03	.38	6.01	37.10	58.99	117.87	206.59	876.20	2,646.00	....	Revenue	81
Grants														.10	....	Grants	81z
Exp. & Lending Minus Repay.						.03	.42	6.34	40.33	62.46	123.59	212.58	936.48	2,638.80	....	Exp. & Lending Minus Repay.	82z
Expenditure						.03	.42	6.34	40.33	62.51	121.79	213.22	933.90	2,639.80	....	Expenditure	82
Lending Minus Repayments						—				-.06	1.80	-.64	2.58	-1.00	....	Lending Minus Repayments	83
Total Financing						—	.04	.33	3.22	3.46	5.72	5.99	60.22	-7.30	....	Total Financing	80h
Domestic						—	—	-.13	2.79	3.69	4.11	7.97	84.65	42.90	....	Domestic	84a
Foreign						—	.04	.45	.43	-.22	1.61	-1.98	-24.43	-50.20	....	Foreign	85a
Total Debt by Residence						.02	.05	13.51	20.49	22.10	44.65	141.70	....	....	....	Total Debt by Residence	88
Domestic						.01	.05	.51	3.04	7.42	14.63	33.56	....	....	....	Domestic	88a
Foreign						.01	—	13.01	17.46	14.68	30.02	108.14	....	....	....	Foreign	89a
Billions of Rubels																**National Accounts**	
Househ.Cons.Expend.,incl.NPISHs						—	.6	10.6	71.7	115.1	209.3	406.2	1,774.6	5,198.8	9,891.2	Househ.Cons.Expend.,incl.NPISHs	96f
Government Consumption Expend.						—	.2	3.6	24.9	39.4	74.5	139.5	590.2	1,779.1	4,396.6	Government Consumption Expend.	91f
Gross Fixed Capital Formation						—	.3	5.9	30.0	40.4	92.6	182.1	796.7	2,301.9	3,738.5	Gross Fixed Capital Formation	93e
Changes in Inventories						—	.1	-.1	.1	4.7	5.9	5.5	-79.3	18.0	14.2	Changes in Inventories	93i
Exports of Goods and Services						.1	.7	12.7	60.3	88.9	219.6	414.6	1,791.5	6,321.6	11,475.0	Exports of Goods and Services	90c
Imports of Goods and Services (-)						.1	.8	15.0	65.6	96.7	240.8	448.7	1,865.0	6,612.7	12,073.3	Imports of Goods and Services (-)	98c
Statistical Discrepancy											5.8	3.0	17.4	127.8	370.4	Statistical Discrepancy	99bs
Gross Domestic Product (GDP)						.1	1.0	17.8	121.4	191.8	366.8	702.2	3,026.1	9,133.8	16,912.6	Gross Domestic Product (GDP)	99b
Net Primary Income from Abroad							—	—	-.1	.2	-.5	-.4	1.2			Net Primary Income from Abroad	98.n
Gross National Income (GNI)						.1	1.0	17.8	121.4	192.0	366.3	674.8	2,891.6	....		Gross National Income (GNI)	99a
Net Current Transf.from Abroad							—	—	.8	1.2	2.1	4.5	32.6	....		Net Current Transf.from Abroad	98t
Gross Nat'l Disposable Inc.(GNDI)						.1	1.0	17.8	122.2	193.2	368.4	679.3	2,924.2	....		Gross Nat'l Disposable Inc.(GNDI)	99i
Gross Saving							.3	3.6	25.5	38.7	84.5	140.3	656.5	....		Gross Saving	99s
GDP Volume 1995 Ref., Chained				186.1	....	166.2	153.5	135.6	121.4	124.8	139.0	150.7	155.8	164.8	....	GDP Volume 1995 Ref., Chained	99b.p
GDP Volume 2000 Ref., Chained													9,134.0	9,504.0		GDP Volume 2000 Ref., Chained	99b.p
GDP Volume (1995=100)						136.9	126.5	111.7	100.0	102.8	114.5	124.2	128.3	135.8	141.3	GDP Volume (1995=100)	99bv p
GDP Deflator (1995=100)						.1	.6	13.1	100.0	153.7	263.8	465.8	1,942.4	5,541.4	9,861.2	GDP Deflator (1995=100)	99bi p
Midyear Estimates																	
Population					10.27	10.31	10.36	10.31	10.28	10.25	10.22	10.19	10.04	10.00	9.97	**Population**	99z

(See notes in the back of the book.)

Belgium

124		1972	1973	1974	1975	1976	1977	1978	1979	1980	1981	1982	1983	1984	1985	1986
Exchange Rates																*Francs per SDR through 1998,*
Market Rate.....aa=	wa	47.839	49.846	44.227	46.273	41.806	40.013	37.520	36.948	40.205	44.766	51.758	58.252	61.832	55.316	49.429
																Francs per US Dollar through 1998,
Market Rate.....ae=	we	44.063	41.320	36.123	39.528	35.983	32.940	28.800	28.048	31.523	38.460	46.920	55.640	63.080	50.360	40.410
Market Rate.....rf=	wf	44.015	38.977	38.952	36.779	38.605	35.843	31.492	29.319	29.242	37.129	45.691	51.132	57.784	59.378	44.672
Secondary Rate	xe	44.38	41.24	36.10	40.32	35.70	32.99	29.39	28.99	31.65	42.55	48.10	56.55	63.30	50.68	40.82
Secondary Rate	xf	43.96	39.01	39.76	37.80	40.24	35.89	31.95	30.14	29.66	39.31	49.05	52.02	58.65	59.74	45.08
																Francs per ECU:
ECU Rate	ea	....	....	....	....	....	....	....	40.318	41.335	41.747	45.321	46.097	44.717	44.645	43.233
ECU Rate	eb	....	....	....	....	42.921	40.884	40.059	40.166	40.601	41.301	44.680	45.430	45.438	44.913	43.803
																Index Numbers (1995=100):
Market Rate	ahx	66.9	75.8	75.7	80.3	76.4	82.2	93.6	100.5	100.8	79.7	64.8	57.8	51.1	50.0	66.2
Nominal Effective Exchange Rate	neu	82.6	84.0	85.5	86.9	89.8	94.9	97.6	98.4	97.8	93.5	85.2	83.2	82.0	82.7	86.5
Real Effective Exchange Rate	reu	....	....	....	148.5	149.6	153.1	146.5	136.9	†131.5	120.4	101.4	99.7	98.7	96.8	98.0
Fund Position																*Millions of SDRs:*
Quota	2f.s	650	650	650	650	650	650	890	890	1,335	1,335	1,335	2,080	2,080	2,080	2,080
SDRs	1b.s	523	626	584	615	397	407	414	476	497	628	672	399	454	328	280
Reserve Position in the Fund	1c.s	516	492	511	591	814	779	606	524	489	390	328	496	521	472	462
of which: Outstg.Fund Borrowing	2c	—	—	—	50	200	230	207	151	117	75	28	10	7	4	1
International Liquidity																*Millions of US Dollars Unless Otherwise Indicated:*
Total Res.Min.Gold (Eurosys.Def)	1l.d	2,232	3,319	3,538	4,069	3,491	3,956	3,966	5,443	7,823	4,952	3,927	4,714	4,564	4,849	5,538
SDRs	1b.d	568	756	715	720	462	495	540	627	633	731	741	418	445	361	342
Reserve Position in the Fund	1c.d	560	594	626	692	946	947	789	690	624	454	362	520	511	519	565
Foreign Exchange	1d.d	1,104	1,969	2,197	2,656	2,083	2,515	2,637	4,126	6,565	3,767	2,824	3,776	3,608	3,969	4,630
o/w: Fin.Deriv.Rel.to Reserves	1ddd	....	....	....	....	....	....	....	....	....	....	....	....	....	....	....
Other Reserve Assets	1e.d	....	....	....	....	....	....	....	....	....	....	....	....	....	....	....
Gold (Million Fine Troy Ounces)	1ad	43.08	42.17	42.17	42.17	42.17	42.45	42.59	34.21	34.18	34.18	34.18	34.18	34.18	34.18	34.18
Gold (Eurosystem Valuation)	1and	1,682	1,780	1,780	1,780	1,780	1,793	1,797	1,445	†1,443	1,443	1,443	1,443	1,443	1,443	1,443
Memo: Euro Cl. on Non-EA Res.	1dgd	....	....	....	....	....	....	....	....	....	....	....	....	....	....	....
Non-Euro Cl. on EA Res.	1dhd	....	....	....	....	....	....	....	....	....	....	....	....	....	....	....
Mon. Auth.: Other Foreign Assets	3..d	375	409	332	300	386	621	908	789	247	838	701	560	194	335	109
Foreign Liabilities	4..d	38	79	91	91	92	823	1,132	1,191	222	315	524	985	98	133	144
Banking Insts.: Foreign Assets	7a.d	8,207	12,049	16,577	17,777	21,505	28,543	39,438	49,162	60,680	69,943	65,748	66,202	71,607	92,631	117,926
Foreign Liab.	7b.d	9,222	13,708	19,254	20,148	23,914	31,852	44,514	58,635	72,953	83,102	78,374	80,196	86,376	112,925	144,838
Monetary Authorities																*Billions of Francs through 1998;*
Fgn. Assets (Cl.on Non-EA Ctys)	11	194.9	222.5	227.3	253.2	226.9	247.9	243.1	253.9	†324.1	250.4	233.5	298.4	325.5	291.2	270.9
Claims on General Government	12a.u	....	....	....	....	....	....	....	....	....	....	....	....	....	....	....
o/w: Claims on Gen.Govt.in Cty	12a	37.1	42.9	46.1	45.5	61.9	78.7	78.7	79.4	†168.2	242.5	276.0	284.8	298.1	281.3	310.4
Claims on Banking Institutions	12e.u	....	....	....	....	....	....	....	....	....	....	....	....	....	....	....
o/w: Claims on Bank.Inst.in Cty	12e	....	....	....	....	....	....	....	....	57.5	86.1	85.0	97.2	13.0	25.7	2.0
Claims on Other Resident Sectors	12d.u	....	....	....	....	....	....	....	....	....	....	....	....	....	....	....
o/w: Cl. on Oth.Res.Sect.in Cty	12d	....	....	....	....	....	....	....	....	....	....	....	....	....	....	....
Currency Issued	14a	222.6	238.5	256.1	288.4	307.2	335.4	359.9	371.8	†390.7	397.9	397.6	411.4	413.8	409.2	430.2
Liabilities to Banking Insts	14c.u	....	....	....	....	....	....	....	....	....	....	....	....	....	....	....
o/w: Liabs to Bank.Inst.in Cty	14c	8.8	21.9	15.6	.7	.7	.5	.6	.3	†1.2	1.0	1.3	1.1	1.2	1.0	.5
Demand Dep. of Other Res.Sect.	14d.u	....	....	....	....	....	....	....	....	....	....	....	....	....	....	....
o/w: D.Dep.of Oth.Res.Sect.in Cty	14d	....	....	....	....	....	....	....	....	....	....	....	....	....	....	....
Other Dep. of Other Res.Sect.	15..u	....	....	....	....	....	....	....	....	....	....	....	....	....	....	....
o/w: O.Dep.of Oth.Res.Sect.in Cty	15	....	....	....	....	....	....	....	....	....	....	....	....	....	....	....
Money Market Instruments	16m.u	....	....	....	....	....	....	....	....	....	....	....	....	....	....	....
o/w: MMI Held by Resid.of Cty	16m	....	....	....	....	....	....	....	....	....	....	....	....	....	....	....
Bonds (Debt Securities)	16n.u	....	....	....	....	....	....	....	....	....	....	....	....	....	....	....
o/w: Bonds Held by Resid.of Cty	16n	....	....	....	....	....	....	....	....	—	—	—	—	—	—	—
Foreign Liab. (to Non-EA Ctys)	16c	1.7	3.2	3.3	3.6	3.3	27.1	32.6	33.4	†7.1	12.3	24.7	55.1	6.5	7.0	6.1
Central Government Deposits	16d.u	....	....	....	....	....	....	....	....	....	....	....	....	....	....	....
o/w: Cent.Govt.Dep. in Cty	16d	....	....	....	....	....	....	....	....	—	—	—	—	—	—	—
Capital Accounts	17a	....	....	....	....	....	....	....	....	8.4	9.6	11.1	12.3	13.8	15.7	18.7
Other Items (Net)	17r	–1.7	1.3	–1.9	5.1	–23.6	–36.9	–72.1	–72.9	†147.9	162.7	162.0	202.9	202.1	167.9	133.5
Memo: Net Claims on Eurosystem	12e.s	....	....	....	....	....	....	....	....	....	....	....	....	....	....	....
Currency Put into Circ.	14m	....	....	....	....	....	....	....	....	....	....	....	....	....	....	....
Banking Institutions																*Billions of Francs through 1998;*
Claims on Monetary Authorities	20	20.7	30.1	26.7	14.3	14.5	14.8	15.4	19.3	19.5	17.1	17.0	16.9	21.7	20.0	22.9
Claims on Bk.Inst.in Oth.EA Ctys	20b.u	....	....	....	....	....	....	....	....	....	....	....	....	....	....	....
Fgn. Assets (Cl.on Non-EA Ctys)	21	367.8	486.0	598.8	702.7	773.8	940.2	1,135.8	1,378.9	1,912.8	2,690.0	3,084.9	3,683.5	4,517.0	4,664.9	4,765.4
Claims on General Government	22a.u	....	....	....	....	....	....	....	....	....	....	....	....	....	....	....
o/w: Claims on Gen.Govt.in Cty	22a	276.0	323.0	355.1	395.6	445.1	467.5	526.3	609.9	737.1	864.0	1,051.5	1,325.8	1,457.3	1,668.7	1,823.1
Claims on Other Resident Sectors	22d.u	....	....	....	....	....	....	....	....	....	....	....	....	....	....	....
o/w: Cl. on Oth.Res.Sect.in Cty	22d	329.4	386.6	435.5	524.1	599.0	706.6	782.5	921.6	1,014.8	1,060.0	1,090.3	1,144.6	1,244.5	1,272.9	1,388.4
Demand Deposits	24..u	....	....	....	....	....	....	....	....	....	....	....	....	....	....	....
o/w: D.Dep.of Oth.Res.Sect.in Cty	24	273.0	289.6	307.5	362.9	389.8	419.5	439.7	452.0	450.2	458.7	491.0	551.1	556.3	588.3	646.8
Other Deposits	25..u	....	....	....	....	....	....	....	....	....	....	....	....	....	....	....
o/w: O.Dep.of Oth.Res.Sect.in Cty	25	283.9	355.3	399.1	457.5	550.5	596.9	654.0	722.9	771.4	853.8	941.6	1,016.9	1,102.2	1,179.8	1,328.8
Money Market Instruments	26m.u	....	....	....	....	....	....	....	....	....	....	....	....	....	....	....
o/w: MMI Held by Resid.of Cty	26m	35.8	41.8	48.7	58.2	74.3	104.4	125.6	153.0	201.0	245.0	300.2	356.8	393.5	444.5	451.1
Bonds (Debt Securities)	26n.u	....	....	....	....	....	....	....	....	....	....	....	....	....	....	....
o/w: Bonds Held by Resid.of Cty	26n	....	....	....	....	....	....	....	....	....	....	....	....	....	....	....
Foreign Liab. (to Non-EA Ctys)	26c	413.3	552.9	695.5	796.4	860.5	1,049.2	1,282.0	1,644.6	2,299.7	3,196.1	3,677.3	4,462.1	5,448.6	5,686.9	5,852.9
Central Government Deposits	26d.u	....	....	....	....	....	....	....	....	....	....	....	....	....	....	....
o/w: Cent.Govt.Dep. in Cty	26d	....	....	....	....	....	....	....	....	....	....	....	....	....	....	....
Credit from Monetary Authorities	26g	....	....	....	....	....	....	....	....	....	....	....	....	....	....	....
Liab. to Bk.Inst.in Oth. EA Ctys	26h.u	....	....	....	....	....	....	....	....	....	....	....	....	....	....	....
Capital Accounts	27a	....	....	....	....	....	....	....	....	....	....	....	....	....	....	....
Other Items (Net)	27r	–12.3	–14.4	–34.8	–39.2	–42.7	–40.9	–41.3	–42.8	–38.1	–122.5	–166.4	–216.1	–260.1	–273.0	–279.5

1987	1988	1989	1990	1991	1992	1993	1994	1995	1996	1997	1998	1999	2000	2001		
															Exchange Rates	

Euros per SDR Thereafter: End of Period

1987	1988	1989	1990	1991	1992	1993	1994	1995	1996	1997	1998	1999	2000	2001		
47.032	50.255	46.994	44.078	44.730	45.623	49.599	46.478	43.725	46.022	49.814	48.682	1.3662	1.4002	1.4260	Market Rate.................aa=	**wa**

Euros per US Dollar Thereafter: End of Period (we) Period Average (wf)

33.153	37.345	35.760	30.983	31.270	33.180	36.110	31.838	29.415	32.005	36.920	34.575	.9954	1.0747	1.1347	Market Rate.................ae=	**we**
37.334	36.768	39.404	33.418	34.148	32.150	34.597	33.456	29.480	30.962	35.774	36.299	.9386	1.0854	1.1175	Market Rate.................rf=	**wf**
33.22	37.28	35.59	....	....	....	....	....	....	....	....	....	....	....	....	Secondary Rate	**xe**
37.57	37.01	39.51	....	....	....	....	....	....	....	....	....	....	....	....	Secondary Rate	**xf**

End of Period (ea) Period Average (eb)

43.154	43.576	42.592	42.184	41.931	40.178	40.287	39.161	38.698	40.102	40.771	40.340	....	....	....	ECU Rate	**ea**
43.039	43.427	43.378	42.423	42.222	41.604	40.466	39.662	38.537	39.290	40.529	40.623	....	....	....	ECU Rate	**eb**

Period Averages

79.0	80.3	74.8	88.4	86.6	91.8	85.2	88.2	100.0	95.1	82.4	81.2	....	....	....	Market Rate	**ahx**
89.4	88.3	87.7	91.5	91.4	93.3	94.4	96.1	100.0	97.9	94.0	94.0	92.8	90.1	90.5	Nominal Effective Exchange Rate	**neu**
98.7	94.9	94.3	96.4	97.0	96.6	98.0	97.1	100.0	95.8	92.4	91.9	88.4	85.6	86.5	Real Effective Exchange Rate	**reu**

End of Period — **Fund Position**

2,080	2,080	2,080	2,080	2,080	3,102	3,102	3,102	3,102	3,102	3,102	3,102	4,605	4,605	4,605	Quota	**2f. s**
494	418	423	398	411	124	125	123	331	346	363	433	197	236	376	SDRs	**1b. s**
392	345	342	326	367	586	560	556	676	747	876	1,348	1,668	1,304	1,632	Reserve Position in the Fund	**1c. s**
—	—	—	—	—	—	—	—	—	—	—	140	—	—	—	of which: Outstg.Fund Borrowing	**2c**

End of Period — **International Liquidity**

9,620	9,333	10,766	12,151	12,180	13,801	11,415	13,876	16,177	16,953	16,190	18,272	†10,937	9,994	11,266	Total Res.Min.Gold (Eurosys.Def)	**1l. d**
700	563	556	566	588	171	171	180	492	498	489	610	271	307	472	SDRs	**1b. d**
557	464	449	464	524	806	769	812	1,005	1,075	1,182	1,899	2,290	1,699	2,051	Reserve Position in the Fund	**1c. d**
8,363	8,306	9,760	11,121	11,068	12,825	10,474	12,884	14,680	15,380	14,519	15,763	†8,377	7,988	8,743	Foreign Exchange	**1d. d**
....	....	....	....	....	....	....	....	....	....	....	....	....	....	....	o/w: Fin.Deriv.Rel.to Reserves	**1dd d**
....	....	....	....	....	....	....	....	....	....	....	....	....	....	....	Other Reserve Assets	**1e. d**
33.63	33.67	30.23	30.23	30.23	25.04	25.04	25.04	20.54	15.32	15.32	9.52	8.30	8.30	8.30	Gold (Million Fine Troy Ounces)	**1ad**
1,421	1,421	1,277	9,017	10,774	8,321	9,955	8,482	7,306	6,171	5,140	2,565	2,413	2,277	2,294	Gold (Eurosystem Valuation)	**1an d**
												257	....	....	Memo: Euro Cl. on Non-EA Res.	**1dg d**
												139	427	704	Non-Euro Cl. on EA Res.	**1dh d**
82	86	512	609	254	165	140	115	113	100	91	97	†—	—	—	Mon. Auth.: Other Foreign Assets	**3.. d**
151	273	131	274	339	241	341	477	629	144	81	382	†7,341	1,081	1,719	Foreign Liabilities	**4.. d**
149,126	150,374	164,516	192,031	192,024	†197,574	211,230	238,602	273,058	267,758	262,470	....	†112,048	108,165	126,770	Banking Insts.: Foreign Assets	**7a. d**
184,795	186,432	205,526	239,787	229,933	†231,022	228,782	263,337	302,856	293,657	280,033	....	†181,820	163,863	176,323	Foreign Liab.	**7b. d**

Millions of Euros Beginning 1999: End of Period — **Monetary Authorities**

365.2	396.1	435.5	743.6	730.2	716.9	764.7	729.1	692.6	741.4	793.7	712.1	13,303	12,737	15,024	Fgn. Assets (Cl.on Non-EA Ctys)	**11**
												3,683	3,630	3,668	Claims on General Government	**12a.u**
231.5	214.1	176.9	151.5	67.0	71.6	90.3	79.3	86.3	91.0	94.1	47.0	1,123	1,220	1,158	o/w: Claims on Gen.Govt.in Cty	**12a**
												25,795	17,312	9,699	Claims on Banking Institutions	**12e.u**
.4	.7	39.5	33.5	104.9	82.5	155.4	128.3	151.3	151.4	150.5	185.0	20,457	15,481	7,672	o/w: Claims on Bank.Inst.in Cty	**12e**
												92	24	59	Claims on Other Resident Sectors	**12d.u**
												3	3	2	o/w: Cl. on Oth.Res.Sect.in Cty	**12d**
440.3	445.9	458.8	446.3	450.1	448.0	459.3	431.4	465.9	486.2	501.1	505.8	13,535	13,496	9,081	Currency Issued	**14a**
												17,500	13,675	11,116	Liabilities to Banking Insts	**14c.u**
1.3	.8	1.0	.5	3.8	3.8	5.5	2.3	7.6	4.7	1.2	279.0	3,509	7,130	5,945	o/w: Liabs to Bank.Inst.in Cty	**14c**
												19	12	7	Demand Dep. of Other Res.Sect.	**14d.u**
												19	12	7	o/w: D.Dep.of Oth.Res.Sect.in Cty	**14d**
												—	—	—	Other Dep. of Other Res.Sect.	**15.. u**
												—	—	—	o/w: O.Dep.of Oth.Res.Sect.in Cty	**15**
												—	—	—	Money Market Instruments	**16m. u**
												—	—	—	o/w: MMI Held by Resid.of Cty	**16m**
									230.0	230.0		—	—	—	Bonds (Debt Securities)	**16n. u**
												—	—	—	o/w: Bonds Held by Resid.of Cty	**16n**
5.3	10.5	5.1	8.5	10.7	8.4	12.3	15.2	18.5	4.6	3.0	13.2	7,307	1,162	1,950	Foreign Liab. (to Non-EA Ctys)	**16c**
												64	62	118	Central Government Deposits	**16d.u**
						1.3	1.0	.5	.7	.1	.4	64	62	118	o/w: Cent.Govt.Dep. in Cty	**16d**
22.3	25.7	30.1	33.3	36.8	40.0	43.6	46.5	48.6	50.6	53.1	53.6	5,369	5,816	6,108	Capital Accounts	**17a**
131.8	128.0	156.7	439.9	400.6	370.8	488.5	440.2	389.1	206.9	249.8	92.3	−921	−520	72	Other Items (Net)	**17r**
												−8,690	−5,103	−3,736	*Memo: Net Claims on Eurosystem*	**12e. s**
												....	....	....	*Currency Put into Circ.*	**14m**

Millions of Euros Beginning 1999: End of Period — **Banking Institutions**

21.6	20.9	23.2	23.2	17.3	†35.4	34.3	35.1	37.9	245.8	228.6	....	3,509	7,130	5,945	Claims on Monetary Authorities	**20**
												97,105	91,410	90,501	Claims on Bk.Inst.in Oth.EA Ctys	**20b.u**
4,943.9	5,615.7	5,883.1	5,949.6	6,004.6	†6,555.5	7,627.5	7,596.5	8,032.0	8,569.6	9,690.4	....	111,535	116,244	143,844	Fgn. Assets (Cl.on Non-EA Ctys)	**21**
												175,991	160,211	180,771	Claims on General Government	**22a.u**
1,915.1	1,983.5	2,089.4	2,231.6	2,191.4	†5,267.1	5,528.2	6,101.4	6,215.7	6,296.0	6,236.2	....	134,534	119,669	111,139	o/w: Claims on Gen.Govt.in Cty	**22a**
												218,724	225,682	230,985	Claims on Other Resident Sectors	**22d.u**
1,546.4	1,834.1	2,293.6	2,420.0	2,637.2	†5,695.7	5,794.9	5,979.9	6,099.0	6,402.6	6,749.2	....	192,349	196,605	197,749	o/w: Cl. on Oth.Res.Sect.in Cty	**22d**
												53,554	58,499	61,430	Demand Deposits	**24.. u**
682.9	738.0	789.9	813.4	820.1	†966.4	1,060.6	1,111.3	1,152.7	1,200.0	1,237.0	....	50,428	53,682	56,579	o/w: D.Dep.of Oth.Res.Sect.in Cty	**24**
												188,347	182,140	199,529	Other Deposits	**25.. u**
1,495.0	1,573.0	1,787.4	1,900.2	2,047.8	†4,148.9	4,560.7	4,706.0	4,936.3	5,490.4	5,915.4	....	157,750	154,139	167,209	o/w: O.Dep.of Oth.Res.Sect.in Cty	**25**
												1,029	804	1,196	Money Market Instruments	**26m.u**
461.4	468.7	530.0	676.1	809.3	†3,422.9	3,583.8	3,703.8	3,691.3	3,593.6	3,291.5	....	....	....	....	o/w: MMI Held by Resid.of Cty	**26m**
												80,682	85,516	79,747	Bonds (Debt Securities)	**26n.u**
												....	....	....	o/w: Bonds Held by Resid.of Cty	**26n**
6,126.4	6,962.3	7,349.6	7,429.2	7,190.0	†7,665.3	8,261.3	8,384.0	8,908.5	9,398.5	10,338.8	....	180,987	176,102	200,071	Foreign Liab. (to Non-EA Ctys)	**26c**
												1,222	763	1,109	Central Government Deposits	**26d.u**
....	....	....	....	238.1	270.3	217.0	78.8	60.6	245.6		....	863	586	868	o/w: Cent.Govt.Dep. in Cty	**26d**
....	....	....	....	66.1	139.0	123.8	106.7	121.7	75.5		....	20,457	15,481	7,672	Credit from Monetary Authorities	**26g**
												58,685	56,487	73,463	Liab. to Bk.Inst.in Oth. EA Ctys	**26h.u**
....	....	....	....	728.8	787.6	856.8	894.7	1,621.1	2,077.7		....	29,525	33,506	35,047	Capital Accounts	**27a**
−338.8	−288.0	−168.0	−194.5	−18.7	†317.0	321.3	609.7	615.3	27.9	−277.3	....	−7,627	−8,619	−7,217	Other Items (Net)	**27r**

Belgium

	1972	1973	1974	1975	1976	1977	1978	1979	1980	1981	1982	1983	1984	1985	1986
Banking Survey (Nat'l Residency)														*Billions of Francs through 1998;*	
Foreign Assets (Net) **31n**	147.7	152.4	127.3	155.9	136.9	111.8	64.3	−45.2	†−69.9	−268.0	−383.6	−535.3	−612.6	−737.8	−822.7
Domestic Credit **32**	642.5	752.5	836.7	965.3	1,106.0	1,252.8	1,387.5	1,610.9	†1,920.1	2,166.5	2,417.8	2,755.2	2,999.9	3,222.9	3,521.9
Claims on General Govt. (Net) ... **32an**	313.1	365.9	401.2	441.1	507.0	546.2	605.0	689.3	†905.3	1,106.5	1,327.5	1,610.6	1,755.4	1,950.0	2,133.5
Claims on Other Resident Sectors **32d**	329.4	386.6	435.5	524.1	599.0	706.6	782.5	921.6	1,014.8	1,060.0	1,090.3	1,144.6	1,244.5	1,272.9	1,388.4
Currency Issued................. **34a.n**	222.6	238.5	256.1	288.4	307.2	335.4	359.9	371.8	†390.7	397.9	397.6	411.4	413.8	409.2	430.2
Demand Deposits................. **34b.n**	281.8	311.5	323.1	364.5	390.5	420.0	440.2	452.3	451.4	459.7	492.3	552.2	557.5	589.3	647.3
Other Deposits .... **35..n**	283.9	355.3	399.1	457.5	550.5	596.9	654.0	722.9	771.4	853.8	941.6	1,016.9	1,102.2	1,179.8	1,328.8
Money Market Instruments **36m**	35.8	41.8	48.7	58.2	74.3	104.4	125.6	153.0	201.0	245.0	300.2	356.8	393.5	444.5	451.1
Bonds (Debt Securities) **36n**	....	....	....	....	....	....	....	....	—	—	—	....	....	....	....
o/w: Bonds Over Two Years **36na**	....	....	....	....	....	....	....	....				....	....	....	....
Capital Accounts................. **37a**									8.4	9.6	11.1	12.3	13.8	15.7	18.7
Other Items (Net)............... **37r**	−34.7	−43.2	−63.4	−48.4	−80.8	−92.6	−128.8	−135.0	†32.8	−63.0	−106.4	−127.3	−92.7	−150.8	−170.9
Banking Survey (EA-Wide Residency)														*Millions of Euros:*	
Foreign Assets (Net) **31n.u**	....														
Domestic Credit .... **32..u**	....														
Claims on General Govt. (Net) ...... **32an u**	....														
Claims on Other Resident Sect. ... **32d.u**	....														
Currency Issued.................. **34a.u**	....														
Demand Deposits.................. **34b.u**	....														
Other Deposits .... **35..u**	....														
o/w: Other Dep. Over Two Yrs ... **35ab u**	....														
Money Market Instruments **36m.u**	....														
Bonds (Debt Securities) **36n.u**	....														
o/w: Bonds Over Two Years .... **36na u**	....														
Capital Accounts................. **37a**	....														
Other Items (Net)............... **37r.u**	....														
Interest Rates														*Percent Per Annum*	
Discount Rate (*End of Period*) **60**	5.00	7.75	8.75	6.00	9.00	9.00	6.00	10.50	12.00	15.00	11.50	10.00	11.00	9.75	8.00
Money Market Rate................ **60b**	2.51	4.80	9.24	4.68	8.31	5.49	5.23	7.97	11.22	11.47	11.44	8.18	9.47	8.27	6.64
Treasury Bill Rate............... **60c**	6.68	7.17	9.87	6.49	9.53	6.64	6.89	10.51	13.90	14.88	13.96	10.38	11.60	9.44	8.09
Deposit Rate **60l**	2.90	4.27	6.75	5.41	5.62	5.46	4.50	5.50	7.69	7.50	7.46	6.67	7.44	6.69	5.33
Lending Rate **60p**	....	....	....	....	....	....	....	....	....	18.00	15.50	13.75	14.00	12.54	10.44
Government Bond Yield............ **61**	7.04	7.44	8.68	8.54	9.05	8.80	8.45	9.51	12.04	13.71	13.56	11.86	11.98	10.61	7.93
Prices, Production, Labor														*Index Numbers (1995=100):*	
Industrial Share Prices.............. **62**	36	43	35	33	31	28	29	31	31	25	29	37	47	52	75
Producer Prices															
Home and Import Goods.............. **63**	....	....	....	....	....	....	....	....	73.2	83.5	94.7	101.1	108.7	111.6	98.7
Industrial Production Prices **63b**									72.6	81.5	90.6	96.3	102.2	105.0	95.5
Consumer Prices **64**	30.7	32.9	37.0	†41.8	45.6	48.8	51.0	53.3	56.8	61.2	66.5	71.6	†76.1	79.8	80.9
Harmonized CPI **64h**	....	....	....	....	....	....	....	....	....	....	....	....	....	....	....
Wages: Hourly Earnings **65**	25.1	29.2	35.3	42.4	47.1	51.4	55.0	†59.3	64.8	71.3	75.7	79.0	82.9	85.9	88.3
Industrial Production............ **66..b**	71.5	75.9	78.7	71.2	77.4	77.4	79.0	82.6	81.6	79.4	79.6	81.1	83.2	84.6	85.4
														Number in Thousands:	
Labor Force....................... **67d**	....		....	....	....	....	....	....	....	....					
Employment **67e**	....		....	....	....	....	....	....	....	....					
Unemployment **67c**	....		....	....	....	....	....	....	....	....			....	3,514	3,525
Unemployment Rate (%)........... **67r**	....		....	....	....	....	....	....	....	....			596	†558	517
															13.6	12.6
International Transactions															
(For Belgium Only)														*Billions of Francs*	
Exports **70**	....	....												....	....
Imports, c.i.f................... **71**	....	....												....	....
														1995=100	
Volume of Exports................ **72**	....													....	....
Volume of Imports................ **73**	....													....	....
Unit Value of Exports............ **74**	....													....	....
Unit Value of Imports............ **75**	....													....	....
Import Price (1990=100) **76.x**	41	49	61	57	60	60	58	66	†71	83	95	102	111	114	99
(BLEU: Country Code 126)														*Billions of Francs*	
Exports **70**	711.0	870.1	1,099.8	1,056.9	1,266.5	1,344.7	1,410.3	1,661.2	1,890.4	2,062.3	2,393.2	2,651.3	2,992.1	3,167.7	3,070.3
Imports, c.i.f................... **71**	681.8	856.1	1,160.7	1,130.9	1,369.0	1,448.0	1,526.0	1,784.4	2,100.8	2,309.8	2,653.4	2,820.9	3,195.8	3,317.8	3,065.2
														1995=100	
Volume of Exports................ **72**	35	39	40	37	42	†43	45	48	†49	49	50	52	54	56	59
Volume of Imports................ **73**	37	43	45	42	48	†49	51	55	†56	54	54	53	56	57	61
Unit Value of Exports............ **74**	42	45	56	58	62	†63	63	69	†76	82	94	101	109	112	103
Unit Value of Imports............ **75**	40	43	55	58	61	†62	62	68	†78	89	102	109	118	120	103

1987	1988	1989	1990	1991	1992	1993	1994	1995	1996	1997	1998	1999	2000	2001	
Millions of Euros Beginning 1999: End of Period															**Banking Survey (Nat'l Residency)**
−822.6	−961.0	−1,036.1	−744.5	−465.9	†−401.3	118.6	−73.6	−202.4	−92.1	142.3	....	10,450	29,658	49,211	Foreign Assets (Net) **31n**
3,693.0	4,031.7	4,559.9	4,803.1	4,895.6	†10796.3	11,141.2	11,942.6	12,321.7	12,728.3	12,833.8	....	327,082	316,849	309,062	Domestic Credit **32**
2,146.6	2,197.6	2,266.3	2,383.1	2,558.4	†5,100.6	5,346.9	5,962.7	6,222.7	6,325.7	6,084.6	....	134,730	120,241	111,311	Claims on General Govt. (Net).......... **32an**
1,546.4	1,834.1	2,293.6	2,420.0	2,637.2	†5,695.7	5,794.3	5,979.9	6,099.0	6,402.6	6,749.2	....	192,352	196,608	197,751	Claims on Other Resident Sectors **32d**
440.3	445.9	458.8	446.3	450.1	448.0	459.3	431.4	465.9	486.2	501.1	505.8	13,535	13,496	9,081	Currency Issued.......................... **34a.** *n*
684.2	738.8	790.9	813.9	823.9	†966.4	1,060.6	1,111.3	1,152.7	1,200.0	1,237.0	....	50,447	53,694	56,586	Demand Deposits.......................... **34b.** *n*
1,495.0	1,573.0	1,787.4	1,900.2	2,047.8	†4,148.9	4,560.7	4,706.0	4,936.3	5,490.4	5,915.4	....	157,750	154,139	167,209	Other Deposits .... **35..** *n*
461.4	468.7	530.0	676.1	809.3	†3,422.9	3,583.8	3,703.8	3,691.0	3,593.6	3,291.5	....	1,029	804	1,196	Money Market Instruments **36m**
—	—	—	—	—	—	—	—	—	—	230.0	230.0	80,682	85,516	79,747	Bonds (Debt Securities).................. **36n**
												66,704	66,949	64,789	*o/w:* Bonds Over Two Years............ **36na**
22.3	25.7	30.1	33.3	36.8	†768.8	831.2	903.3	943.3	1,671.7	2,130.8	....	34,894	39,322	41,155	Capital Accounts **37a**
−229.0	−181.6	−74.0	188.7	259.7	†639.8	764.6	1,012.6	929.5	−36.0	−329.9	....	−808	−462	3,302	Other Items (Net) **37r**
End of Period															**Banking Survey (EA-Wide Residency)**
....	....	....	....	....	....	....	....	....	....	....	....	−63,456	−48,283	−43,153	Foreign Assets (Net) .... **31n.** *u*
....	....	....	....	....	....	....	....	....	....	....	....	397,204	388,722	414,256	Domestic Credit .... **32..** *u*
....	....	....	....	....	....	....	....	....	....	....	....	178,388	163,016	183,212	Claims on General Govt. (Net) .... **32an** *u*
....	....	....	....	....	....	....	....	....	....	....	....	218,816	225,706	231,044	Claims on Other Resident Sect. .... **32d.** *u*
....	....	....	....	....	....	....	....	....	....	....	....	13,535	13,496	9,081	Currency Issued.......................... **34a.** *u*
....	....	....	....	....	....	....	....	....	....	....	....	53,573	58,511	61,437	Demand Deposits.......................... **34b.** *u*
....	....	....	....	....	....	....	....	....	....	....	....	188,347	182,140	199,529	Other Deposits.......................... **35..** *u*
....	....	....	....	....	....	....	....	....	....	....	....	19,642	21,589	23,861	*o/w:* Other Dep. Over Two Yrs ...... **35ab** *u*
....	....	....	....	....	....	....	....	....	....	....	....	1,029	804	1,196	Money Market Instruments .... **36m.** *u*
....	....	....	....	....	....	....	....	....	....	....	....	80,682	85,516	79,747	Bonds (Debt Securities) .... **36n.** *u*
....	....	....	....	....	....	....	....	....	....	....	....	66,704	66,949	64,789	*o/w:* Bonds Over Two Years............ **36na** *u*
....	....	....	....	....	....	....	....	....	....	....	....	34,894	39,322	41,155	Capital Accounts **37a**
....	....	....	....	....	....	....	....	....	....	....	....	−38,315	−39,348	−21,039	Other Items (Net) .... **37r.** *u*
Percent Per Annum															**Interest Rates**
7.00	7.75	10.25	10.50	8.50	7.75	5.25	4.50	3.00	2.50	2.75	2.75	....	....	....	Discount Rate *(End of Period)*.............. **60**
5.67	5.04	7.00	8.29	†9.38	9.38	8.21	5.72	4.80	3.24	3.46	3.58				Money Market Rate **60b**
7.00	6.61	8.45	9.62	9.24	9.36	8.52	5.57	4.67	3.19	3.38	3.51	2.72	4.02	4.16	Treasury Bill Rate **60c**
5.00	4.54	5.13	6.13	6.25	6.25	†7.11	4.86	4.04	2.66	2.88	3.01	2.42	3.58	3.40	Deposit Rate **60l**
9.33	8.92	11.08	13.00	12.88	13.00	11.81	9.42	8.42	7.17	7.06	7.25	6.71	7.98	8.46	Lending Rate **60p**
7.83	7.85	8.64	10.09	9.26	8.64	7.19	7.82	7.45	6.45	5.74	4.72	4.81	5.58	5.13	Government Bond Yield **61**
Period Averages															**Prices, Production, Labor**
89	88	101	94	91	89	93	106	100	....	....	....	....	....	....	Industrial Share Prices **62**
															Producer Prices
93.8	95.4	101.7	100.6	†99.6	97.8	95.3	96.8	†100.0	102.0	105.7	103.7	103.7	114.7	113.0	Home and Import Goods **63**
91.3	92.4	97.7	98.3	†97.2	97.4	96.5	97.8	†100.0	100.6	102.3	101.0	100.6	109.5	110.3	Industrial Production Prices **63b**
82.1	†83.1	85.7	88.6	91.5	93.7	96.3	98.6	100.0	†102.1	103.7	104.7	105.9	108.6	111.3	Consumer Prices **64**
								100.0	101.8	103.3	104.2	105.4	108.3	110.9	Harmonized CPI **64h**
†90.0	90.7	95.8	100.0	105.1	110.1	112.4	114.7	....	....	....	....	....	....	....	Wages: Hourly Earnings **65**
87.5	92.7	95.9	99.4	97.4	97.3	92.5	94.1	100.0	100.8	105.1	101.4	110.7	115.5	....	Industrial Production .... **66..** *b*
Period Averages															**International Transactions**
		4,144	4,179	4,210	4,237	....	4,160	4,185	4,196	4,214	4,241	4,382	....	....	Labor Force **67d**
3,480	3,496	3,595	3,637	3,731	3,773	3,746	3,755	3,794	3,792	3,839	3,858	†4,007	4,092	....	Employment **67e**
501	459	419	403	430	473	550	589	597	587	568	541	508	474	470	Unemployment **67c**
12.2	11.1	10.1	9.6	10.2	11.2	12.9	13.9	14.1	13.8	13.3	12.6	11.7	10.9	10.8	Unemployment Rate (%) **67r**
Billions of Euros															**International Transactions**
															(For Belgium Only)
....	....	....	....	....	....	4,349.1	4,792.7	5,177.8	5,430.2	6,142.9	6,442.0	†168.09	203.95	211.37	Exports.......................... **70**
....	....	....	....	....	....	3,953.6	4,339.7	4,702.0	5,065.8	5,619.2	5,880.0	†154.63	192.19	199.25	Imports, c.i.f. **71**
1995=100															
....	....	....	....	....	....	86	94	100	102	110	115	119	130	134	Volume of Exports **72**
....	....	....	....	....	....	88	95	100	104	109	117	117	128	133	Volume of Imports **73**
....	....	....	....	....	....	97	98	100	103	108	108	107	118	121	Unit Value of Exports **74**
....	....	....	....	....	....	95	97	100	103	110	108	109	123	125	Unit Value of Imports **75**
93	95	102	100	99	96	....	....	....	....	....	....	....	....	....	Import Price (1990=100) **76.x**
Billions of Francs															(BLEU: Country Code 126)
3,100.1	3,382.3	3,943.1	3,944.5	4,023.4	3,969.8	4,129.0	4,579.0	4,996.1	5,133.1	5,916.2	....	....	....	....	Exports.......................... **70**
3,110.1	3,393.6	3,883.9	4,011.6	4,116.3	4,023.3	3,875.0	4,192.0	4,568.4	4,729.1	5,554.4	....	....	....	....	Imports, c.i.f. **71**
1995=100															
62	66	72	74	77	77	†84	93	100	103	110	....	....	....	....	Volume of Exports **72**
66	70	75	79	82	82	†83	95	100	106	111	....	....	....	....	Volume of Imports **73**
98	101	109	105	103	102	†101	100	100	102	106	....	....	....	....	Unit Value of Exports **74**
98	100	108	106	104	101	†99	98	100	102	107	....	....	....	....	Unit Value of Imports **75**

Belgium

Balance of Payments
(BLEU: Country Code 126)

Millions of US Dollars:

		1972	1973	1974	1975	1976	1977	1978	1979	1980	1981	1982	1983	1984	1985	1986
Current Account, n.i.e.	78al d	...	...	...	181	435	−554	−823	−3,080	−4,931	−4,168	−2,594	−495	−55	670	3,059
Goods: Exports f.o.b.	78aa d	...	...	...	23,797	26,886	32,699	40,055	51,410	57,573	50,719	48,243	47,598	48,001	49,178	62,914
Goods: Imports f.o.b.	78ab d	...	...	...	−24,191	−27,574	−34,537	−41,267	−54,426	−61,432	−54,193	−50,543	−48,264	−48,192	−48,686	−60,608
Trade Balance	78ac d				−394	−687	−1,838	−1,212	−3,016	−3,859	−3,474	−2,300	−666	−191	492	2,305
Services: Credit	78ad d				5,555	6,018	8,277	9,006	11,016	12,925	12,341	10,971	10,770	10,423	10,796	14,618
Services: Debit	78ae d				−4,957	−5,136	−7,071	−8,659	−10,703	−12,827	−11,804	−9,908	−9,392	−9,464	−9,941	−13,163
Balance on Goods & Services	78af d				204	195	−632	−865	−2,703	−3,761	−2,937	−1,237	712	768	1,346	3,760
Income: Credit	78ag d				4,479	4,430	5,263	7,380	11,527	18,427	24,197	22,883	18,333	18,943	20,830	23,665
Income: Debit	78ah d				−3,889	−3,670	−4,563	−6,585	−11,007	−18,366	−24,189	−23,063	−18,441	−18,934	−20,851	−23,420
Balance on Gds, Serv. & Inc.	78ai d				795	955	68	−71	−2,184	−3,700	−2,928	−1,417	604	776	1,325	4,005
Current Transfers, n.i.e.: Credit	78aj d				755	918	1,232	1,588	1,928	1,743	1,403	1,249	1,259	1,300	1,524	1,968
Current Transfers: Debit	78ak d				−1,368	−1,438	−1,854	−2,341	−2,825	−2,973	−2,643	−2,426	−2,358	−2,131	−2,180	−2,913
Capital Account, n.i.e.	78bc d				—	—	—	—	—	—	—	—	—	—	—	—
Capital Account, n.i.e.: Credit	78ba d				—	—	—	—	—	—	—	—	—	—	—	—
Capital Account: Debit	78bb d				—	—	—	—	—	—	—	—	—	—	—	—
Financial Account, n.i.e.	78bj d				−55	−1,183	848	330	2,313	4,083	3,115	2,300	1,187	208	−605	−3,248
Direct Investment Abroad	78bd d				−238	−352	−465	−560	−1,341	−196	−104	69	−355	−293	−296	−1,723
Dir. Invest. in Rep. Econ., n.i.e.	78be d				955	872	1,275	1,436	1,130	1,545	1,386	1,472	1,290	389	1,051	730
Portfolio Investment Assets	78bf d				−1,039	−763	−1,373	−864	−216	−789	−1,583	−2,237	−3,788	−4,141	−6,269	−7,039
Equity Securities	78bk d				−183	97	82	64	146	165	37	173	−11	62	−96	−644
Debt Securities	78bl d				−856	−860	−1,455	−927	−361	−954	−1,620	−2,410	−3,776	−4,203	−6,172	−6,395
Portfolio Investment Liab., n.i.e.	78bg d				−35	213	230	−94	829	1,485	812	246	113	161	267	447
Equity Securities	78bm d				−16	−34	11	−13	74	−1	−27	12	12	−86	185	608
Debt Securities	78bn d				−18	247	219	−82	755	1,486	839	234	101	247	82	−161
Financial Derivatives Assets	78bw d				....	....	....	....	....	....	....	....	....	....	....	....
Financial Derivatives Liabilities	78bx d				....	....	....	....	....	....	....	....	....	....	....	....
Other Investment Assets	78bh d				−8,376	−9,946	−14,827	−18,165	−32,136	−45,092	−17,604	−27,519	−4,785	−31,332	−51,671	−61,223
Monetary Authorities	78bo d															
General Government	78bp d				−87	−54	−47	−131	−152	−101	−116	−122	−139	−114	−98	−143
Banks	78bq d				−8,563	−8,521	−14,164	−16,593	−28,113	−42,259	−14,597	−26,373	−3,929	−30,199	−50,970	−59,184
Other Sectors	78br d				275	−1,370	−615	−1,441	−3,871	−2,731	−2,891	−1,024	−717	−1,019	−604	−1,896
Other Investment Liab., n.i.e.	78bi d				8,678	8,792	16,008	18,577	34,046	47,130	20,208	30,269	8,712	35,424	56,313	65,561
Monetary Authorities	78bs d				29	−20	728	791	318	−703	1,768	1,442	925	−583	−602	1,161
General Government	78bt d				—	−6	27	17	68	905	1,324	1,845	453	1,187	892	346
Banks	78bu d				8,444	8,488	15,112	17,348	30,877	45,519	15,400	26,732	6,730	33,521	55,827	62,395
Other Sectors	78bv d				205	330	141	421	2,782	1,409	1,717	250	603	1,299	196	1,659
Net Errors and Omissions	78ca d				419	113	129	219	−138	981	−1,341	−294	−428	152	−263	218
Overall Balance	78cb d				546	−635	422	−275	−906	133	−2,394	−588	265	305	−197	29
Reserves and Related Items	79da d				−546	635	−422	275	906	−133	2,394	588	−265	−305	197	−29
Reserve Assets	79db d				−546	635	−422	275	906	−133	2,394	588	−265	−305	197	−29
Use of Fund Credit and Loans	79dc d				—	—	—	—	—	—	—	—	—	—	—	—
Exceptional Financing	79de d				....	....	....	....	....	....	....	....	....	....	....	....

International Investment Position
(For Belgium Only)

Millions of US Dollars

		1972	1973	1974	1975	1976	1977	1978	1979	1980	1981	1982	1983	1984	1985	1986
Assets	79aa d	...	...	...	...	...	...	...	...	...	119,152	118,878	118,766	122,580	159,100	212,418
Direct Investment Abroad	79ab d	...	...	...	...	...	...	...	...	...	6,292	5,499	6,111	6,072	9,551	15,194
Portfolio Investment	79ac d	...	...	...	...	...	...	...	...	...	13,651	12,660	16,499	19,103	29,408	44,593
Equity Securities	79ad d	...	...	...	...	...	...	...	...	...	4,290	2,920	4,170	4,090	6,652	11,383
Debt Securities	79ae d	...	...	...	...	...	...	...	...	...	9,360	9,740	12,329	15,013	22,756	33,210
Financial Derivatives	79al d	...	...	...	...	...	...	...	...	...	—	—	—	—	—	—
Other Investment	79af d	...	...	...	...	...	...	...	...	...	79,511	80,413	77,516	81,341	103,296	133,531
Monetary Authorities	79ag d	...	...	...	...	...	...	...	...	...	130	85	90	32	79	198
General Government	79ah d	...	...	...	...	...	...	...	...	...	676	597	557	539	735	965
Banks	79ai d	...	...	...	...	...	...	...	...	...	62,246	61,743	60,694	66,027	83,836	108,018
Other Sectors	79aj d	...	...	...	...	...	...	...	...	...	16,459	17,988	16,175	14,743	18,646	24,350
Reserve Assets	79ak d	...	...	...	...	...	...	...	...	...	19,244	19,944	18,121	15,553	16,326	19,100
Liabilities	79la d	...	...	...	...	...	...	...	...	...	106,344	108,781	111,862	119,673	157,903	211,086
Dir. Invest. in Rep. Economy	79lb d	...	...	...	...	...	...	...	...	...	10,088	11,125	12,311	12,032	18,447	27,394
Portfolio Investment	79lc d	...	...	...	...	...	...	...	...	...	9,984	12,830	13,659	14,822	19,619	28,483
Equity Securities	79ld d	...	...	...	...	...	...	...	...	...	312	405	449	380	814	2,054
Debt Securities	79le d	...	...	...	...	...	...	...	...	...	9,672	12,425	13,210	14,442	18,805	26,429
Financial Derivatives	79ll d	...	...	...	...	...	...	...	...	...	—	—	—	—	—	—
Other Investment	79lf d	...	...	...	...	...	...	...	...	...	86,271	84,825	85,891	92,819	119,837	155,209
Monetary Authorities	79lg d	...	...	...	...	...	...	...	...	...	598	426	359	317	377	445
General Government	79lh d	...	...	...	...	...	...	...	...	...	26	64	72	—	20	49
Banks	79li d	...	...	...	...	...	...	...	...	...	75,689	74,233	76,042	83,291	108,519	142,217
Other Sectors	79lj d	...	...	...	...	...	...	...	...	...	9,958	10,102	9,418	9,211	10,921	12,497

Minus Sign Indicates Debit

Balance of Payments (BLEU: Country Code 126)

	1987	1988	1989	1990	1991	1992	1993	1994	1995	1996	1997	1998	1999	2000	2001	
Current Account, n.i.e.	2,797	3,592	3,600	3,627	4,746	6,650	11,237	12,571	14,232	13,762	13,914	12,168	14,579	11,360	13,037	78al d
Goods: Exports f.o.b.	77,948	87,436	92,123	110,188	107,990	116,841	106,302	122,795	155,219	154,695	149,497	153,558	161,278	164,471	161,428	78aa d
Goods: Imports f.o.b.	-76,653	-84,733	-89,845	-108,517	-105,991	-113,141	-100,522	-115,895	-145,664	-146,004	-141,794	-146,577	-154,782	-162,246	-158,113	78ab d
Trade Balance	1,294	2,703	2,278	1,671	1,999	3,700	5,780	6,901	9,555	8,690	7,703	6,981	6,496	2,225	3,315	78ac d
Services: Credit	18,908	21,045	21,840	28,417	30,583	33,658	33,366	40,440	35,466	34,702	35,503	38,081	41,749	44,008	43,790	78ad d
Services: Debit	-16,464	-18,898	-21,314	-26,581	-28,789	-30,999	-29,995	-36,500	-33,134	-32,069	-31,664	-34,411	-36,839	-38,866	-39,781	78ae d
Balance on Goods & Services	3,739	4,851	2,805	3,507	3,793	6,359	9,151	10,841	11,887	11,322	11,542	10,651	11,406	7,368	7,324	78af d
Income: Credit	27,496	33,127	48,276	65,544	75,452	88,295	83,011	89,403	74,798	62,884	58,237	65,251	71,487	75,740	80,042	78ag d
Income: Debit	-27,011	-32,631	-45,592	-63,228	-72,274	-85,309	-78,138	-84,166	-67,990	-55,838	-51,882	-59,315	-63,485	-67,569	-70,372	78ah d
Balance on Gds, Serv. & Inc.	4,224	5,347	5,489	5,824	6,971	9,345	14,024	16,078	18,695	18,368	17,896	16,588	19,409	15,538	16,994	78ai d
Current Transfers, n.i.e.: Credit	2,500	2,602	2,329	3,825	4,160	4,368	4,198	4,501	7,822	7,474	7,142	7,006	7,041	7,010	7,301	78aj d
Current Transfers: Debit	-3,927	-4,357	-4,217	-6,022	-6,385	-7,063	-6,986	-8,009	-12,285	-12,081	-11,124	-11,426	-11,871	-11,188	-11,258	78ak d
Capital Account, n.i.e.	—	—	—	—	—	—	—	....	378	179	403	-113	-78	-213	23	78bc d
Capital Account: Credit	—	—	—	—	—	—	—	—	734	673	783	323	420	222	485	78ba d
Capital Account: Debit	—	—	—	—	—	—	—	—	-356	-494	-379	-436	-497	-436	-462	78bb d
Financial Account, n.i.e.	-349	-2,793	-2,664	-1,651	-3,155	-7,806	-13,563	-10,182	-12,912	-12,257	-12,091	-16,043	-15,131	-10,860	-12,179	78bj d
Direct Investment Abroad	-2,782	-3,784	-6,486	-6,314	-6,271	-11,407	-4,904	-1,371	-11,603	-8,026	-7,252	-28,845	-121,719	-229,354	-67,545	78bd d
Dir. Invest. in Rep. Econ., n.i.e.	2,355	5,212	7,020	8,047	9,363	11,286	10,750	8,514	10,689	14,064	11,998	22,690	133,059	234,757	51,213	78be d
Portfolio Investment Assets	-4,435	-12,302	-14,324	-9,443	-29,570	-62,887	-58,431	-40,963	-29,472	-48,409	-62,657	-100,234	-161,579	-122,972	-122,505	78bf d
Equity Securities	31	-332	-3,839	1,530	-659	-115	-9,465	-10,649	-3,525	-3,582	-21,006	-29,087	-60,737	-103,445	-55,517	78bk d
Debt Securities	-4,466	-11,970	-10,485	-10,973	-28,911	-62,773	-48,966	-30,314	-25,946	-44,827	-41,651	-71,147	-100,842	-19,528	-66,987	78bl d
Portfolio Investment Liab., n.i.e.	2,006	7,729	11,050	7,946	27,490	59,016	50,472	17,445	4,649	36,666	54,047	59,253	135,259	132,130	147,010	78bg d
Equity Securities	1,433	6,362	10,082	7,014	20,816	56,272	46,838	22,489	6,505	34,243	47,207	58,418	91,794	82,405	95,374	78bm d
Debt Securities	573	1,368	968	932	6,674	2,743	3,634	-5,043	-1,856	2,423	6,840	835	43,466	49,725	51,636	78bn d
Financial Derivatives Assets	....	....	—	—	—	—	—	....	1,213	-970	-330	489	884	-3,653	-7,821	78bw d
Financial Derivatives Liabilities	—	—	—	—	—	—	—	....	630	483	444	302	1,142	1,252	942	78bx d
Other Investment Assets	-122,240	6,361	-55,626	-64,422	-22,023	-49,920	-51,772	11,269	-23,445	-14,977	-48,692	7,467	-58,340	-37,983	-79,161	78bh d
Monetary Authorities												-147	-991	-342	13	78bo d
General Government	-163	-99	-242	-184	-440	-536	-802	-294	-72	-372	-306	371	-1,848	-236	-137	78bp d
Banks	-119,861	8,613	-55,225	-67,666	-25,042	-49,107	-45,916	9,829	-16,926	9,164	-28,220	3,886	-12,806	-22,296	-57,970	78bq d
Other Sectors	-2,216	-2,153	-159	3,429	3,459	-277	-5,054	1,734	-6,447	-23,769	-20,166	3,357	-42,694	-15,109	-21,066	78br d
Other Investment Liab., n.i.e.	124,747	-6,010	55,701	62,536	17,857	46,107	40,321	-5,076	34,426	8,913	40,352	22,836	56,162	14,963	65,686	78bi d
Monetary Authorities	998	2,741	—	—	—	—	—	....	223	-458	-50	193	23,578	-1,386	-3,903	78bs d
General Government	-566	-135	2,167	948	2,417	-2,887	10,758	-5,233	322	-40	-161	203	1,405	-1,231	600	78bt d
Banks	120,145	-10,449	52,731	56,431	7,262	32,419	19,043	64	42,121	6,469	31,211	18,087	6,702	7,139	68,713	78bu d
Other Sectors	4,171	1,833	804	5,156	8,178	16,575	10,520	93	-8,240	2,941	9,352	4,352	24,476	10,441	276	78bv d
Net Errors and Omissions	-14	61	-624	-1,572	-1,007	1,726	204	-2,169	-1,456	-1,091	-1,171	1,893	-1,237	-1,245	561	78ca d
Overall Balance	2,434	861	312	404	584	569	-2,122	219	243	593	1,056	-2,095	-1,867	-959	1,442	78cb d
Reserves and Related Items	-2,434	-861	-312	-404	-584	-569	2,122	-219	-243	-593	-1,056	2,095	1,867	959	-1,442	79da d
Reserve Assets	-2,434	-861	-312	-404	-584	-569	2,122	-219	-243	-593	-1,056	2,095	1,867	959	-1,442	79db d
Use of Fund Credit and Loans	—	—	—	—	—	—	—	—	—	—	—	—	—	—	—	79dc d
Exceptional Financing	....	....	—	—	—	....	....	....	....	....	....	....	....	....	....	79de d

Millions of US Dollars

International Investment Position (For Belgium Only)

	1987	1988	1989	1990	1991	1992	1993	1994	1995	1996	1997	1998	1999	2000	2001	
Assets	276,487	282,260	331,904	401,179	426,203	439,140	468,324	532,665	578,225	580,689	573,702	629,976	655,973	....	....	79aa d
Direct Investment Abroad	19,606	24,903	34,676	40,636	48,385	55,636	62,642	69,541	83,325	87,861	92,308	124,485	139,740	....	....	79ab d
Portfolio Investment	58,155	70,130	86,885	106,350	116,565	124,141	145,694	161,256	186,945	189,033	192,091	200,668	264,712	....	....	79ac d
Equity Securities	13,212	19,708	27,629	33,858	38,727	42,616	59,319	59,804	60,105	58,710	56,717	68,750	83,884	....	....	79ad d
Debt Securities	44,944	50,422	59,256	72,493	77,838	81,525	86,375	101,453	126,840	130,323	135,374	131,918	180,828	....	....	79ae d
Financial Derivatives	—	—	—	—	—	—	—	—	646	1,375	1,869	2,054	2,512	....	....	79al d
Other Investment	172,174	163,610	186,997	229,775	237,544	237,342	238,244	279,199	283,835	279,394	266,143	282,260	235,679	....	....	79af d
Monetary Authorities	211	161	196	258	927	784	775	597	1,632	1,031	135	405	-8,238	....	....	79ag d
General Government	1,418	1,259	1,314	1,775	2,271	2,140	2,049	1,947	2,074	1,906	1,652	1,764	1,507	....	....	79ah d
Banks	138,994	132,253	148,294	181,490	183,019	177,366	178,926	203,816	218,664	206,811	197,671	196,214	182,435	....	....	79ai d
Other Sectors	31,551	29,937	37,192	46,252	51,327	57,052	56,494	72,839	61,465	69,645	66,685	83,877	59,975	....	....	79aj d
Reserve Assets	26,551	23,618	23,347	24,418	23,709	22,021	21,744	22,669	23,474	23,026	21,291	20,509	13,330	....	....	79ak d
Liabilities	270,900	278,538	328,384	391,963	408,826	416,667	437,690	495,611	546,864	539,010	528,738	588,383	594,723	....	....	79la d
Dir. Invest. in Rep. Economy	30,646	39,309	52,824	58,388	70,163	75,678	94,295	105,881	120,211	132,542	140,818	189,880	185,550	....	....	79lb d
Portfolio Investment	39,605	44,183	53,160	64,036	78,286	80,530	93,603	103,808	100,323	92,361	85,861	79,394	104,679	....	....	79lc d
Equity Securities	2,805	3,749	4,754	5,616	5,980	5,937	8,253	9,737	10,539	12,061	13,787	20,391	15,772	....	....	79ld d
Debt Securities	36,800	40,434	48,406	58,420	72,306	74,593	85,350	94,071	89,784	80,300	72,075	59,003	88,907	....	....	79le d
Financial Derivatives	—	—	—	—	—	—	—	—	578	937	1,273	1,764	2,712	....	....	79ll d
Other Investment	200,649	195,046	222,399	269,539	260,377	260,458	249,792	285,921	325,752	313,170	300,785	317,345	301,782	....	....	79lf d
Monetary Authorities	513	616	503	678	768	663	665	848	1,122	531	460	839	8,539	....	....	79lg d
General Government	181	80	419	355	416	573	305	942	850	687	379	406	301	....	....	79lh d
Banks	185,114	179,328	203,160	240,813	229,645	227,818	219,247	251,590	302,193	289,455	276,165	285,818	262,100	....	....	79li d
Other Sectors	14,841	15,022	18,317	27,693	29,549	31,404	29,576	32,540	21,588	22,496	23,781	30,282	30,841	....	....	79lj d

Belgium

		1972	1973	1974	1975	1976	1977	1978	1979	1980	1981	1982	1983	1984	1985	1986
Government Finance																
Central Government															*Billions of Francs through 1998;*	
Deficit (-) or Surplus	80	−67.9	−61.8	−46.6	−109.0	−147.5	−168.3	−209.2	−247.7	−282.0	−446.9	−431.6	−515.9	−596.1	−537.6	−497.3
Revenue	81	553.6	646.9	779.0	924.8	1,056.1	1,180.1	1,296.8	1,393.4	1,508.6	1,595.5	1,781.9	1,857.3	2,040.0	2,201.6	2,271.4
Grants Received	81z	2.4	3.2	2.6	3.1	3.9	3.4	3.9	4.7	2.4	3.0	2.9	2.8	3.1	2.5	2.6
Expenditure	82	619.9	706.8	820.2	1,025.9	1,194.0	1,340.2	1,482.3	1,625.6	1,758.3	2,016.1	2,185.0	2,346.9	2,493.6	2,624.5	2,727.4
Lending Minus Repayments	83	4.0	5.1	8.0	11.0	13.5	11.6	27.6	20.2	34.7	29.3	31.4	29.1	145.6	117.2	43.9
Financing																
Net Borrowing: National Currency	84a	82.3	68.4	40.6	109.1	150.7	167.4	172.7	207.1	211.5	234.6	220.4	394.0	405.8	504.4	423.2
Foreign Currency	85a	−15.0	−3.5	−1.4	.2	−.4	−.3	13.4	43.0	83.5	214.1	189.4	127.0	181.1	26.8	74.1
Use of Cash Balances	87	.6	−3.1	7.4	−.3	−2.8	1.2	23.1	−2.4	−13.0	−1.8	21.8	−5.1	9.2	6.4	—
Debt: National Currency	88a	693.7	749.1	807.9	917.0	1,050.4	1,218.2	1,387.5	1,556.3	1,761.0	2,000.3	2,299.2	2,706.0	3,077.3	3,694.2	4,632.5
Foreign Currency	89a	11.8	8.3	6.9	7.1	6.7	6.4	19.9	62.9	154.9	374.4	591.0	724.8	882.0	919.8	1,020.4
General Government															*As Percent of*	
Deficit (-) or Surplus	80g	....	....	....	....	....	....	....	....	....	....	....	....	....		
Debt	88g	....	....	....	....	....	....	....	....	....	....	....	....	....		
National Accounts															*Billions of Francs through 1998;*	
Househ.Cons.Expend.,incl.NPISHs	96f	948	1,084	1,256	1,421	1,613	1,769	1,890	2,057	1,991	2,147	2,357	2,520	2,670	†2,879	2,968
Government Consumption Expend.	91f	232	264	314	388	441	489	544	588	818	904	964	1,008	1,085	†1,128	1,174
Gross Fixed Capital Formation	93e	328	374	467	512	565	606	646	668	828	754	768	751	796	†867	900
Changes in Inventories	93i	10	25	46	−13	10	8	8	20	44	23	37	−10	49	†−6	−19
Exports of Goods and Services	90c	683	846	1,116	1,065	1,266	1,474	1,540	1,798	2,051	2,320	2,698	2,971	3,423	†3,530	3,389
Imports of Goods and Services (-)	98c	633	811	1,109	1,061	1,261	1,499	1,570	1,866	2,171	2,414	2,783	2,957	3,398	†3,479	3,263
Gross Domestic Product (GDP)	99b	1,569	1,782	2,091	2,313	2,633	2,847	3,058	3,265	3,562	3,733	4,041	4,281	4,626	†4,919	5,148
Net Primary Income from Abroad	98.n	12	9	12	13	17	12	10	−4	−3	—	−19	−22	−14	†−15	−11
Gross National Income (GNI)	99a	1,581	1,792	2,103	2,326	2,650	2,859	3,068	3,261	3,553	3,720	4,005	4,244	4,593	4,881	5,123
Net Current Transf.from Abroad	98t	....	....	....	....	....	....	....	....	....	....	....	....	....	−20	−21
Gross Nat'l Disposable Inc.(GNDI)	99i	....	....	....	....	....	....	....	....	....	....	....	....	....	2,994	3,136
Gross Saving	99s	....	....	....	....	....	....	....	....	....	....	....	....	....	532	591
Consumption of Fixed Capital	99cf	149	162	193	213	231	262	281	303	425	454	495	544	577	†622	653
GDP Volume 1990 prices	99b.p	2,788	2,952	3,078	3,031	3,204	3,222	3,314	3,386	3,526						
GDP Volume 1995 Prices	99b.p	....	....	....	....	....	....	....	....	6,178	6,161	6,198	6,217	6,370	6,476	6,594
GDP Volume (1995=100)	99bvp	59.8	63.4	66.1	65.1	68.8	69.2	71.1	72.7	75.7	75.5	75.9	76.2	78.0	79.3	80.8
GDP Deflator (1995=100)	99bip	32.1	34.5	38.8	43.6	46.9	50.4	52.7	55.0	57.7	60.6	65.2	68.9	72.6	†76.0	78.1
Population	99z	9.71	9.74	9.77	9.79	9.81	9.82	9.83	9.84	9.85	9.85	9.86	9.86	9.86	*Millions:* 9.86	9.86

	1987	1988	1989	1990	1991	1992	1993	1994	1995	1996	1997	1998	1999	2000	2001	Code
Millions of Euros Beginning 1999: Year Ending December 31																
Government Finance — *Central Government* — Deficit (-) or Surplus	-404.0	-364.0	-397.0	-364.6	-416.2	-486.1	-450.2	-324.9	-259.1	†-210.2	-165.1	-162.1	....	....	....	80
Revenue	2,369.9	2,459.7	2,603.4	2,818.9	2,949.4	3,094.5	3,263.4	3,476.4	3,567.5	†3,685.2	3,820.1	3,986.1	....	....	....	81
Grants Received	2.7	2.2	2.8	2.0	2.4	5.8	4.6	5.7	11.1	†5.0	20.3	6.8	....	....	....	81z
Expenditure	2,735.4	2,798.4	2,973.0	3,154.7	3,353.9	3,575.3	3,699.5	3,821.3	3,885.6	†3,909.5	4,032.3	4,152.3	....	....	....	82
Lending Minus Repayments	41.2	27.5	30.2	30.8	14.1	11.1	18.7	-14.3	-47.9	†-9.1	-26.8	2.7	....	....	....	83
Financing — Net Borrowing: National Currency	372.2	341.1	328.2	384.2	548.6	619.5	112.3	360.1	380.1	†612.9	104.7	273.1	....	....	....	84a
Foreign Currency	31.8	22.9	68.8	-19.6	-8.0	-107.6	454.9	-152.4	-262.0	†-334.1	-1.0	-79.6	....	....	....	85a
Use of Cash Balances	—	—	—	—	-124.4	-25.8	-117.0	117.2	141.0	†-68.6	61.4	-31.4	....	....	....	87
Debt: National Currency	5,237.4	5,693.5	6,064.2	6,581.4	7,248.0	7,899.7	8,075.9	8,623.7	9,063.4	†9,576.7	9,702.8	9,717.7	....	....	....	88a
Foreign Currency	1,045.9	1,087.4	1,131.0	1,111.8	1,107.0	1,010.5	1,519.9	1,349.5	1,085.3	†734.0	784.4	701.7	....	....	....	89a
Gross Domestic Product — **General Government** — Deficit (-) or Surplus	....	....	....	-5.5	-6.3	-6.9	-7.1	-4.9	-4.0	-3.7	-1.9	-.8	-.6	.1	.2	80g
Debt	....	....	....	125.7	127.5	129.0	135.2	133.2	132.2	128.3	125.3	119.3	115.0	109.3	107.5	88g
Billions of Euros beginning 1999 — **National Accounts** — Househ.Cons.Expend.,incl.NPISHs	3,070	3,208	3,441	3,648	3,864	4,010	4,093	4,286	4,428	4,575	4,750	4,949	†127	134	140	96f
Government Consumption Expend.	1,212	1,218	1,276	1,338	1,447	1,527	1,597	1,668	1,744	1,809	1,857	1,925	†50	53	55	91f
Gross Fixed Capital Formation	959	1,131	1,329	1,480	1,448	1,500	1,491	1,533	1,621	1,661	1,789	1,875	†49	52	54	93e
Changes in Inventories	11	24	19	-1	6	10	19	64	17	-27	-10	-14	†—	1	—	93i
Exports of Goods and Services	3,438	3,912	4,539	4,665	4,777	4,898	4,813	5,282	5,633	5,897	6,545	6,844	†178	214	217	90c
Imports of Goods and Services (-)	3,333	3,762	4,391	4,541	4,638	4,695	4,548	4,965	5,282	5,556	6,159	6,467	†168	206	208	98c
Gross Domestic Product (GDP)	5,356	5,730	6,213	6,589	6,902	7,248	7,465	7,867	8,161	8,357	8,772	9,112	†236	248	257	99b
Net Primary Income from Abroad	6	5	-16	-10	15	14	87	155	141	141	148	178	†5	6	6	98.n
Gross National Income (GNI)	5,377	5,704	6,166	6,591	6,917	7,301	7,566	7,950	8,302	8,498	8,919	9,290	†240	254	263	99a
Net Current Transf.from Abroad	-20	-24	-20	-24	-24	-29	-32	-38	-34	-51	-51	-59	†-1	-1	....	98t
Gross Nat'l Disposable Inc.(GNDI)	3,275	3,501	3,788	4,019	4,228	4,434	4,609	4,892	5,067	5,171	5,430	5,650	†146	155	....	99i
Gross Saving	644	782	889	955	964	1,032	1,112	1,233	1,274	1,248	1,369	1,426	†38	40	....	99s
Consumption of Fixed Capital	693	770	822	897	929	999	1,008	1,049	1,102	1,184	1,252	1,322	†34	40	....	99cf
GDP Volume 1990 prices	....	....	....	....	....	....	....	....	....	....	....	....	....	....	....	99b.p
GDP Volume 1995 Prices	6,746	7,065	7,310	7,539	7,677	7,794	7,718	7,967	8,162	8,259	8,554	8,746	†223	232	235	99b.p
GDP Volume (1995=100)	82.7	86.6	89.6	92.4	94.1	95.5	94.6	97.6	100.0	101.2	104.8	107.2	†110.4	114.8	116.0	99bv p
GDP Deflator (1995=100)	79.4	81.1	85.0	87.4	89.9	93.0	96.7	98.8	100.0	101.2	102.6	104.2	†105.5	106.9	109.4	99bi p
Midyear Estimates — Population	9.87	9.90	9.94	9.97	9.98	10.06	10.08	10.12	10.14	10.16	10.18	10.21	10.23	10.25	10.26	99z

(See notes in the back of the book.)

		1972	1973	1974	1975	1976	1977	1978	1979	1980	1981	1982	1983	1984	1985	1986
Exchange Rates														*Belize Dollars per SDR: End of Period (aa)*			
Official Rate	aa	†1.8495	2.0770	2.0853	2.3141	2.7299	2.4294	2.6056	2.6347	2.5508	2.3279	2.2062	2.0939	1.9604	2.1968	2.4464
Official Rate	ae	†1.7035	1.7218	1.7032	1.9768	2.3496	2.0000	2.0000	2.0000	2.0000	2.0000	2.0000	2.0000	2.0000	2.0000	2.0000
														Index Numbers (1995=100):			
Official Rate	ahx	125.1	122.6	117.0	111.1	90.3	100.0	100.0	100.0	100.0	100.0	100.0	100.0	100.0	100.0	100.0
Nominal Effective Exchange Rate	nec	...	...	...	...	...	...	...	52.9	52.9	57.2	61.4	65.6	70.6	77.1	73.7
Real Effective Exchange Rate	rec	...	...	...	...	...	...	...	...	102.7	111.4	118.6	125.2	130.3	138.3	123.7
Fund Position														*Millions of SDRs:*			
Quota	2f.s	...	...	...	...	...	...	...	...	...	...	7.20	9.50	9.50	9.50	9.50
SDRs	1b.s	...	...	...	...	...	...	...	...	...	...	...	.02	.01	—	—
Reserve Position in the Fund	1c.s	...	...	...	...	...	...	...	...	...	...	...	...	...	—	—
Total Fund Cred.&Loans Outstg.	2tl	...	...	...	...	...	...	...	...	...	...	1.32	1.90	1.90	1.90	1.90
													3.60	4.80	9.54	9.54
International Liquidity												*Millions of US Dollars Unless Otherwise Indicated:*				
Total Reserves minus Gold	1l.d	...	...	...	...	5.49	8.02	13.98	10.46	12.68	10.33	9.84	9.31	6.07	14.81	26.90
SDRs	1b.d	...	...	...	...	...	...	...	...	...	...	...	.02	.01	—	—
Reserve Position in the Fund	1c.d	...	...	...	...	...	...	...	...	...	...	1.46	1.99	1.86	2.09	2.32
Foreign Exchange	1d.d	...	...	...	...	5.49	8.02	13.98	10.46	12.68	10.33	8.38	7.30	4.20	12.73	24.57
Monetary Authorities: Other Liab.	4..d	...	...	...	...	—	.26	1.08	.45	.45	.19	.19	.45	1.77	.68	.58
Deposit Money Banks: Assets	7a.d	...	...	...	...	1.31	4.79	7.68	12.71	13.51	14.05	7.79	9.36	9.77	10.17	8.48
Liabilities	7b.d	...	...	...	...	4.59	6.31	6.41	14.81	17.29	19.04	23.68	23.04	26.11	21.74	13.17
Other Banking Insts.: Assets	7e.d	...	...	...	...	...	...	...	.01	.01	.01	.01	.01	1.59	1.35	.59
Liabilities	7f.d	...	...	...	...	...	...	6.04	6.61	8.51	10.77	12.00	12.98	16.06	11.81	17.93
Monetary Authorities														*Millions of Belize Dollars:*			
Foreign Assets	11	...	...	...	...	12.90	16.04	27.96	20.93	25.35	20.67	19.67	18.63	12.34	29.63	53.55
Claims on Central Government	12a	...	...	...	...	1.90	4.67	4.73	10.77	11.91	28.08	33.70	39.52	56.70	65.57	61.47
Claims on Deposit Money Banks	12e	...	...	...	...	...	...	...	...	.81	...	...	...	...	...	...
Reserve Money	14	...	...	...	...	13.64	18.58	25.45	22.92	26.11	31.58	37.15	34.99	47.14	54.09	63.94
of which: Currency Outside DMBs	14a	...	...	...	...	11.27	12.55	16.72	16.68	17.51	19.01	20.61	21.53	22.77	22.64	25.90
Foreign Liabilities	16c	...	...	...	...	—	.52	2.16	.91	.90	.39	.38	8.45	12.94	22.31	24.50
Central Government Deposits	16d	...	...	...	...	...	...	.49	...	1.52	5.34	...	...	...	3.77	6.41
Capital Accounts	17a	...	...	...	...	.64	2.00	4.74	7.99	9.55	10.46	10.46	11.14	11.73	15.24	15.36
Other Items (Net)	17r	...	...	...	...	.52	−.39	−.15	−.11	−.02	.99	5.38	3.57	−2.78	−.22	4.81
Deposit Money Banks														*Millions of Belize Dollars:*			
Reserves	20	...	...	...	...	2.37	5.79	8.38	6.22	8.49	12.54	16.52	13.70	19.81	21.07	22.74
Foreign Assets	21	...	...	...	...	3.09	9.59	15.36	25.41	27.02	28.11	15.58	18.71	19.55	20.34	16.95
Claims on Central Government	22a	...	...	...	...	1.57	3.50	7.01	2.59	9.82	6.68	16.17	32.07	30.10	33.58	47.98
Claims on Local Government	22b	...	...	...	...	...	.01	—	...	...	...	.14	.22	.14	...	.29
Claims on Official Entities	22bx	...	...	...	...	4.04	4.38	6.25	8.13	7.00	8.66	9.58	7.00	13.05	3.16	2.74
Claims on Private Sector	22d	...	...	...	...	57.66	52.68	55.32	70.73	77.32	90.79	107.66	117.16	116.14	120.47	119.77
Demand Deposits	24	...	...	...	...	10.03	12.14	19.26	20.19	24.03	20.52	18.76	20.84	22.67	24.44	29.60
Time, Savings,& Fgn.Currency Dep.	25	...	...	...	...	50.28	48.74	56.92	59.04	66.55	78.25	85.67	105.75	104.62	109.13	128.06
Foreign Liabilities	26c	...	...	...	...	10.79	12.62	12.82	29.62	34.59	38.08	47.35	46.09	52.22	43.48	26.34
Central Government Deposits	26d	...	...	...	...	.76	.75	1.09	1.41	.57	2.38	6.18	8.37	10.96	12.20	15.43
Credit from Monetary Authorities	26g	...	...	...	...	...	...	...	...	.40	—	—	—	6.80	.61	1.35
Capital Accounts	27a	...	...	...	...	.70	5.40	5.21	7.25	7.63	8.23	8.35	10.30	10.61	11.29	12.13
Other Items (Net)	27r	...	...	...	...	−3.82	−3.70	−2.97	−4.43	−4.12	−.55	−.60	−2.57	−9.04	−2.28	−2.43
Monetary Survey														*Millions of Belize Dollars:*			
Foreign Assets (Net)	31n	...	...	...	...	5.19	12.49	28.34	15.82	16.88	10.31	−12.48	−17.19	−33.28	−15.82	19.67
Domestic Credit	32	...	...	...	...	64.42	64.48	71.73	90.81	103.95	126.63	161.15	187.53	205.23	207.05	210.41
Claims on Central Govt. (Net)	32an	...	...	...	...	2.71	7.42	10.16	11.95	19.64	27.04	43.69	63.22	75.84	83.18	87.61
Claims on Local Government	32b	...	...	...	...	—	.01	—	...	...	...	.14	.22	.14	...	.29
Claims on Official Entities	32bx	...	...	...	...	4.04	4.38	6.25	8.13	7.00	8.66	9.58	7.00	13.05	3.16	2.74
Claims on Private Sector	32d	...	...	...	...	57.66	52.68	55.32	70.73	77.32	90.79	107.66	117.16	116.14	120.47	119.77
Money	34	...	...	...	...	21.30	24.69	36.01	36.89	41.65	39.56	39.40	42.41	50.01	58.61	71.03
Quasi-Money	35	...	...	...	...	50.28	48.74	56.92	59.04	66.55	78.25	85.67	105.75	104.62	109.13	128.06
Capital Accounts	37a	...	...	...	...	1.34	7.40	9.94	15.23	17.18	18.69	18.81	21.44	22.34	26.53	27.49
Other Items (Net)	37r	...	...	...	...	−3.31	−3.85	−2.80	−4.55	−4.54	.44	4.78	.73	−5.02	−3.04	3.49
Money plus Quasi-Money	35l	...	...	...	...	71.58	73.43	92.93	95.94	108.20	117.81	125.07	148.16	154.63	167.73	199.10
Other Banking Institutions														*Millions of Belize Dollars:*			
Reserves	40	...	...	...	...	...	...	1.01	.83	.91	.53	.89	2.31	.95	.11	1.34
Foreign Assets	41	...	...	...	...	...	...	.01	.03	.02	.02	.02	.02	3.19	2.70	1.17
Claims on Central Government	42a	...	...	...	...	...	...	1.66	1.41	1.09	.64	.24	.77	.64	—	1.09
Claims on Official Entities	42bx	...	...	...	...	...	...	1.67	1.67	1.60	1.38	1.39	1.49	1.29	—	1.03
Claims on Private Sector	42d	...	...	...	...	...	...	12.00	12.74	17.12	22.04	24.20	27.35	30.01	32.26	36.84
Foreign Liabilities	46c	...	...	...	...	...	...	12.07	13.23	17.02	21.55	23.99	25.96	32.13	23.62	35.86
Central Government Deposits	46d	...	...	...	...	...	...	—	—	—	—	—	—	—	—	—
Credit from Monetary Authorities	46g	...	...	...	...	...	...	—	—	.41	—	.75	—	—	—	—
Capital Accounts	47a	...	...	...	...	...	...	2.41	3.61	4.47	3.90	4.72	4.98	4.70	5.39	5.41
Other Items (Net)	47r	...	...	...	...	...	...	1.86	−.16	−1.15	−.82	−1.98	.25	−.75	6.05	.21
Banking Survey														*Millions of Belize Dollars:*			
Foreign Assets (Net)	51n	...	...	...	...	...	...	16.28	2.62	−.11	−11.22	−36.45	−43.13	−62.22	−36.74	−15.02
Domestic Credit	52	...	...	...	...	...	...	87.06	106.62	123.76	150.70	186.97	217.14	237.17	239.30	249.37
Claims on Central Govt. (Net)	52an	...	...	...	...	...	...	11.82	13.36	20.73	27.68	43.94	63.99	76.48	83.18	88.70
Claims on Local Government	52b	...	...	...	...	...	...	—	...	...	...	.14	.22	.14	.20	.24	.29
Claims on Official Entities	52bx	...	...	...	...	...	...	7.92	9.79	8.60	10.05	10.97	8.49	14.34	3.16	3.77
Claims on Private Sector	52d	...	...	...	...	...	...	67.32	83.47	94.43	112.84	131.86	144.51	146.15	152.73	156.61
Liquid Liabilities	55l	...	...	...	...	...	...	91.92	95.11	107.29	117.28	124.18	145.85	153.68	167.63	197.76
Capital Accounts	57a	...	...	...	...	...	...	12.36	18.84	21.65	22.58	23.54	26.42	27.04	31.92	32.89
Other Items (Net)	57r	...	...	...	...	...	...	−.94	−4.70	−5.29	−.38	2.80	1.73	−5.76	3.01	3.70
Interest Rates														*Percent Per Annum*			
Discount Rate (End of Period)	60	...	...	...	...	...	7.00	7.50	10.00	14.00	14.50	13.50	11.50	12.00	20.00	12.00
Treasury Bill Rate	60c	...	...	...	...	...	5.91	6.40	6.40	10.29	11.68	12.00	10.51	9.55	12.76	10.81
Savings Rate	60k	...	...	...	...	4.30	4.50	4.50	4.60	7.50	7.53	7.70	5.70	5.05	...	7.74
Deposit Rate	60l	...	...	...	...	7.10	6.70	6.80	6.80	11.18	14.68	14.87	11.30	9.08	11.63	11.83
Lending Rate	60p	...	...	...	...	11.50	11.30	11.30	11.60	16.50	19.28	...	...	...	...	14.69

1987	1988	1989	1990	1991	1992	1993	1994	1995	1996	1997	1998	1999	2000	2001		
Belize Dollars per US Dollar: End of Period (ae)															**Exchange Rates**	
2.8373	2.6914	2.6283	2.8453	2.8609	2.7500	2.7471	2.9197	2.9730	2.8759	2.6985	2.8161	2.7450	2.6058	2.5135	Official Rate	**aa**
2.0000	2.0000	2.0000	2.0000	2.0000	2.0000	2.0000	2.0000	2.0000	2.0000	2.0000	2.0000	2.0000	2.0000	2.0000	Official Rate	**ae**
Period Averages																
100.0	100.0	100.0	100.0	100.0	100.0	100.0	100.0	100.0	100.0	100.0	100.0	100.0	100.0	100.0	Official Rate	**ahx**
71.3	72.7	79.3	82.7	85.7	87.6	95.1	99.6	100.0	103.1	107.8	110.9	111.9	116.2	120.0	Nominal Effective Exchange Rate	**nec**
114.7	113.5	111.7	104.8	103.3	100.7	106.6	102.3	100.0	105.3	108.5	108.2	105.6	107.1	109.2	Real Effective Exchange Rate	**rec**
End of Period															**Fund Position**	
9.50	9.50	9.50	9.50	9.50	13.50	13.50	13.50	13.50	13.50	13.50	13.50	18.80	18.80	18.80	Quota	**2f.s**
.06	.02	—	.01	.08	.15	.29	.37	.47	.61	.71	.82	1.01	1.20	1.37	SDRs	**1b.s**
1.91	1.91	1.91	1.91	1.91	2.91	2.91	2.91	2.91	2.91	2.91	2.91	4.24	4.24	4.24	Reserve Position in the Fund	**1c.s**
8.03	5.79	2.52	.30	—	—	—	—	—	—	—	—	—	—	—	Total Fund Cred.&Loans Outstg.	**2tl**
End of Period															**International Liquidity**	
36.41	51.66	59.88	69.78	53.02	52.94	38.75	34.52	37.61	58.40	59.42	44.09	71.31	122.90	112.04	Total Reserves minus Gold	**1l.d**
.09	.03	—	.01	.11	.21	.39	.54	.70	.88	.96	1.16	1.39	1.56	1.72	SDRs	**1b.d**
2.71	2.57	2.51	2.72	2.73	4.00	4.00	4.25	4.33	4.19	3.93	4.10	5.82	5.52	5.33	Reserve Position in the Fund	**1c.d**
33.62	49.06	57.37	67.05	50.17	48.74	34.35	29.72	32.58	53.34	54.53	38.82	64.10	115.82	104.99	Foreign Exchange	**1d.d**
.86	.56	1.65	4.14	7.51	8.79	6.81	6.21	5.31	1.77	3.64	1.61	1.04	.84	1.47	Monetary Authorities: Other Liab.	**4..d**
8.04	6.95	12.38	19.39	16.31	12.31	23.64	24.27	26.21	38.45	35.84	37.94	45.64	71.64	69.17	Deposit Money Banks: Assets	**7a.d**
11.14	10.51	8.53	4.58	12.54	23.60	49.15	51.68	39.59	41.40	43.71	50.69	43.06	59.83	71.64	Liabilities	**7b.d**
.36	.12	.25	—	—	.01	—	—	—	—	—	—	—	—	—	Other Banking Insts.: Assets	**7e.d**
19.37	19.42	17.67	16.79	16.05	15.53	14.11	14.20	14.33	13.64	17.88	17.97	21.11	64.25	108.18	Liabilities	**7f.d**
End of Period															**Monetary Authorities**	
73.15	103.51	120.22	139.84	105.88	105.86	77.27	68.94	75.24	116.85	118.89	88.23	142.90	245.85	224.15	Foreign Assets	**11**
50.45	33.64	27.00	5.19	21.95	31.40	61.47	67.54	81.72	110.78	89.86	94.89	67.38	62.49	78.03	Claims on Central Government	**12a**
—	—	—	—	—	10.00	8.50	7.84	7.06	6.39	4.18	2.25	1.00	84.19	84.00	Claims on Deposit Money Banks	**12e**
71.45	68.31	85.16	83.72	86.79	105.38	104.63	102.50	116.21	119.64	125.81	135.57	165.22	202.80	257.79	Reserve Money	**14**
29.56	34.11	40.44	43.46	47.91	50.98	54.19	56.74	61.42	63.61	66.45	70.38	84.15	95.96	105.17	*of which: Currency Outside DMBs*	**14a**
24.50	16.70	9.93	9.13	15.01	17.58	13.62	12.41	10.62	3.54	7.29	3.22	2.08	1.67	2.94	Foreign Liabilities	**16c**
7.63	39.41	33.28	35.28	10.08	13.30	15.06	17.88	19.42	65.93	47.31	21.48	25.87	91.92	31.48	Central Government Deposits	**16d**
14.84	15.49	15.99	16.91	17.36	19.85	17.18	17.78	18.50	19.30	20.19	20.82	21.30	21.52	21.72	Capital Accounts	**17a**
5.18	–2.76	2.86	–.01	–1.41	–8.85	–3.25	–6.24	–.73	25.62	12.35	4.29	–3.19	74.62	72.25	Other Items (Net)	**17r**
End of Period															**Deposit Money Banks**	
25.43	29.43	42.32	37.91	37.30	53.40	49.95	45.13	53.77	54.71	58.68	64.85	59.02	101.45	103.28	Reserves	**20**
16.08	13.90	24.76	38.78	32.62	24.62	47.28	48.53	52.42	76.90	71.68	75.89	91.27	143.27	138.34	Foreign Assets	**21**
48.32	39.87	37.24	51.20	45.44	60.75	48.93	52.99	63.88	39.77	61.92	58.39	80.11	87.12	87.87	Claims on Central Government	**22a**
.35	—	—	—	—	.02	.01	.11	—	.05	.01	.23	1.38	1.16	2.17	Claims on Local Government	**22b**
9.04	7.96	5.45	7.25	4.88	1.16	.31	.27	2.73	2.81	5.18	9.36	4.99	9.03	10.72	Claims on Official Entities	**22bx**
146.60	197.95	231.08	268.35	331.10	372.01	385.99	405.27	436.44	478.03	540.03	610.72	641.14	679.71	771.03	Claims on Private Sector	**22d**
36.80	42.92	56.58	59.45	68.97	74.45	81.65	86.81	93.32	99.12	99.03	115.85	141.86	185.99	225.05	Demand Deposits	**24**
157.35	170.33	187.40	224.80	245.90	285.11	288.57	316.35	388.84	421.56	486.98	504.93	552.39	612.72	631.29	Time, Savings,& Fgn.Currency Dep.	**25**
22.28	21.03	17.07	9.17	25.07	47.21	98.30	103.36	79.18	82.79	87.42	101.39	86.12	119.67	143.27	Foreign Liabilities	**26c**
16.44	31.64	58.30	75.19	86.80	74.24	49.30	43.86	23.59	27.78	26.89	40.68	21.56	24.31	20.93	Central Government Deposits	**26d**
5.84	4.76	3.60	2.86	2.20	7.98	5.32	1.66	1.48	1.28	1.09	.88	.63	.41	.16	Credit from Monetary Authorities	**26g**
13.36	17.08	19.00	21.25	25.06	28.41	31.00	31.04	39.40	43.54	49.77	51.73	69.71	71.33	89.16	Capital Accounts	**27a**
–6.24	1.34	–1.10	10.78	–2.66	–5.45	–21.66	–30.78	–16.57	–23.81	–13.69	4.00	5.64	7.31	3.55	Other Items (Net)	**27r**
End of Period															**Monetary Survey**	
42.45	79.68	117.98	160.33	98.42	65.70	12.64	1.70	37.85	107.43	95.86	59.51	145.97	267.79	216.28	Foreign Assets (Net)	**31n**
230.69	208.37	209.19	221.53	306.49	377.78	432.35	464.44	541.76	537.72	622.80	711.44	747.57	723.29	897.41	Domestic Credit	**32**
74.70	2.46	–27.34	–54.08	–29.49	4.60	46.03	58.80	102.59	56.83	77.58	91.13	100.07	33.38	113.50	Claims on Central Govt. (Net)	**32an**
.35	—	—	—	—	.02	.01	.11	—	.05	.01	.23	1.38	1.16	2.17	Claims on Local Government	**32b**
9.04	7.96	5.45	7.25	4.88	1.16	.31	.27	2.73	2.81	5.18	9.36	4.99	9.03	10.72	Claims on Official Entities	**32bx**
146.60	197.95	231.08	268.35	331.10	372.01	385.99	405.27	436.44	478.03	540.03	610.72	641.14	679.71	771.03	Claims on Private Sector	**32d**
84.30	81.78	99.87	105.99	118.30	126.33	136.35	144.18	155.47	164.02	166.17	186.65	248.24	287.32	379.65	Money	**34**
157.35	170.33	187.40	224.80	245.90	285.11	288.57	316.35	388.84	421.56	486.98	504.93	552.39	612.72	631.29	Quasi-Money	**35**
28.20	32.57	34.99	38.16	42.42	48.26	48.18	48.82	57.90	62.84	69.95	72.55	91.00	92.85	110.88	Capital Accounts	**37a**
3.28	3.36	4.91	12.90	–1.70	–16.23	–28.11	–43.20	–22.59	–3.28	–4.45	6.83	1.92	–1.82	–8.12	Other Items (Net)	**37r**
241.65	252.11	287.27	330.80	364.20	411.45	424.92	460.53	544.31	585.58	653.15	691.58	800.62	900.04	1,010.93	Money plus Quasi-Money	**35l**
End of Period															**Other Banking Institutions**	
1.09	2.49	.83	3.44	4.91	2.38	1.28	1.41	2.47	.93	3.17	1.58	11.35	10.17	20.68	Reserves	**40**
.71	.23	.50	—	—	.02	—	—	—	—	—	—	—	—	—	Foreign Assets	**41**
1.11		—	—	—	—	—	—	—	—	—	—	—	—	—	Claims on Central Government	**42a**
.94	.55	.50	.52	.17	.17	.17	—	—	—	—	—	—	—	—	Claims on Official Entities	**42bx**
34.65	34.64	35.55	33.71	32.87	36.59	40.66	45.70	47.03	53.75	60.78	65.96	61.92	199.33	266.63	Claims on Private Sector	**42d**
38.74	38.84	35.34	33.57	32.10	31.05	28.22	28.41	28.66	27.29	35.77	35.93	42.22	128.50	216.35	Foreign Liabilities	**46c**
—	—	—	.40	.26	.26	.80	1.23	1.40	1.07	1.20	2.71	27.06	6.10	3.35	Central Government Deposits	**46d**
—	—	—	—	—	—	3.08	3.35	4.07	6.30	6.02	5.77	5.36	4.45	85.27	Credit from Monetary Authorities	**46g**
5.72	5.61	4.14	–3.85	–6.36	–1.52	–.26	1.21	3.48	8.69	10.68	11.88	13.80	15.84	23.90	Capital Accounts	**47a**
–5.96	–6.54	–2.10	7.55	11.95	9.36	10.29	12.90	11.89	11.34	10.29	11.25	–15.17	54.61	–41.57	Other Items (Net)	**47r**
End of Period															**Banking Survey**	
4.42	41.07	83.14	126.76	66.32	34.66	–15.58	–26.70	9.20	80.14	60.09	23.58	103.75	139.29	–.07	Foreign Assets (Net)	**51n**
267.38	243.56	245.24	255.36	339.26	414.29	472.39	508.91	587.39	590.40	682.38	774.70	782.43	916.52	1,160.69	Domestic Credit	**52**
75.81	2.46	–27.34	–54.47	–29.75	4.35	45.24	57.57	101.20	55.76	76.38	88.42	73.01	27.29	110.15	Claims on Central Govt. (Net)	**52an**
.35	—	—	—	—	.02	.01	.11	—	.05	.01	.23	1.38	1.16	2.17	Claims on Local Government	**52b**
9.98	8.51	5.95	7.77	5.05	1.33	.48	.27	2.73	2.81	5.18	9.36	4.99	9.03	10.72	Claims on Official Entities	**52bx**
181.25	232.59	266.63	302.06	363.97	408.60	426.66	450.97	483.47	531.79	600.81	676.69	703.06	879.03	1,037.66	Claims on Private Sector	**52d**
240.56	249.62	286.44	327.36	359.28	409.07	423.64	459.12	541.85	584.65	649.98	690.00	789.27	889.87	990.25	Liquid Liabilities	**55l**
33.92	38.18	39.13	34.31	36.06	46.75	47.92	50.04	61.38	71.53	80.63	84.43	104.80	108.69	134.78	Capital Accounts	**57a**
–2.68	–3.18	2.81	20.45	10.25	–6.87	–14.74	–26.95	–6.63	14.36	11.86	23.86	–7.89	57.24	35.58	Other Items (Net)	**57r**
Percent Per Annum															**Interest Rates**	
12.00	10.00	12.00	12.00	12.00	12.00	12.00	12.00	12.00	12.00	12.00	12.00	12.00	12.00	12.00	Discount Rate *(End of Period)*	**60**
8.80	8.32	7.36	7.37	6.71	5.38	4.59	4.27	4.10	3.78	3.51	3.83	5.91	5.91	5.91	Treasury Bill Rate	**60c**
6.25	5.69	5.28	5.36	5.40	5.40	5.40	5.32	5.30	5.30	5.35	5.43	5.42	5.43	5.44	Savings Rate	**60k**
9.58	8.42	7.86	8.14	8.42	8.15	8.13	8.55	9.37	9.08	9.19	8.76	8.12	7.69	6.35	Deposit Rate	**60l**
14.14	13.56	13.77	14.04	14.24	14.32	14.37	14.78	15.69	16.30	16.29	16.50	16.27	16.01	15.45	Lending Rate	**60p**

Belize

		1972	1973	1974	1975	1976	1977	1978	1979	1980	1981	1982	1983	1984	1985	1986
Prices and Labor														*Index Numbers (1995=100):*		
Consumer Prices	64	...	...	...	...	...	...	...	...	59.5	66.2	70.7	74.2	76.7	79.9	80.5
														Number in Thousands:		
Labor Force	67d	...	...	...	...	...	...	...	...	...	...	...	...	...	...	...
Employment	67e	...	...	...	...	...	...	...	...	...	...	...	...	...	...	...
Unemployment	67c	...	...	...	...	...	...	...	...	...	...	...	...	...	...	...
Unemployment Rate (%)	67r	...	...	...	...	...	...	...	...	...	...	...	...	...	...	...
International Transactions														*Millions of Belize Dollars*		
Exports	70	40.89	52.69	76.86	120.40	94.04	124.16	159.57	173.46	221.30	238.01	182.03	155.46	186.40	179.39	185.21
Imports, c.i.f.	71	69.26	72.32	109.18	159.23	161.51	180.15	212.99	263.68	299.51	323.93	256.00	223.58	260.27	256.26	243.93
Balance of Payments														*Millions of US Dollars:*		
Current Account, n.i.e.	78al d	...	...	...	...	...	...	...	...	...	...	...	...	−5.3	9.1	12.0
Goods: Exports f.o.b.	78aa d													93.2	90.2	92.6
Goods: Imports f.o.b.	78ab d													−116.3	−113.8	−108.3
Trade Balance	78ac d													−23.1	−23.7	−15.7
Services: Credit	78ad d													35.4	38.1	42.8
Services: Debit	78ae d													−29.4	−27.6	−40.2
Balance on Goods & Services	78af d													−17.1	−13.1	−13.1
Income: Credit	78ag d													1.3	2.9	9.2
Income: Debit	78ah d													−14.8	−13.2	−11.6
Balance on Gds, Serv. & Inc.	78ai d													−30.6	−23.4	−15.5
Current Transfers, n.i.e.: Credit	78aj d													27.9	34.5	31.3
Current Transfers: Debit	78ak d													−2.6	−2.1	−3.9
Capital Account, n.i.e.	78bc d	...	...			...	...		...			...	...	—	—	—
Capital Account, n.i.e.: Credit	78ba d													—	—	—
Capital Account: Debit	78bb d													—	—	—
Financial Account, n.i.e.	78bj d	...	...			...	...		...			...	...			
Direct Investment Abroad	78bd d													−3.6	9.4	.7
Dir. Invest. in Rep. Econ., n.i.e.	78be d															
Portfolio Investment Assets	78bf d													−3.7	3.7	4.6
Equity Securities	78bk d													—	—	—
Debt Securities	78bl d													—	—	—
Portfolio Investment Liab., n.i.e.	78bg d													.7	.7	
Equity Securities	78bm d													—	—	
Debt Securities	78bn d													.7	.7	
Financial Derivatives Assets	78bw d															
Financial Derivatives Liabilities	78bx d															
Other Investment Assets	78bh d													—	—	—
Monetary Authorities	78bo d															
General Government	78bp d													—	—	—
Banks	78bq d													—	—	—
Other Sectors	78br d													—	—	—
Other Investment Liab., n.i.e.	78bi d													−.6	5.0	−3.9
Monetary Authorities	78bs d													—	—	—
General Government	78bt d													4.3	12.4	3.7
Banks	78bu d													−1.8	−.9	−5.0
Other Sectors	78bv d													−3.0	−6.5	−2.6
Net Errors and Omissions	78ca d	...				...	...		...	...		...	...	3.6	−16.1	−.9
Overall Balance	78cb d													−5.3	2.3	11.8
Reserves and Related Items	79da d	...				...	...		...	...		...	...	5.3	−2.3	−11.8
Reserve Assets	79db d													2.9	−7.2	−11.8
Use of Fund Credit and Loans	79dc d													1.2	4.9	—
Exceptional Financing	79de d													1.2	—	—
Government Finance														*Thousands of Belize Dollars:*		
Deficit (−) or Surplus	80	...	...			...	−12,112	−2,613	†−5,018	†−5,916	...	...	...	−5,214	−14,208	....
Revenue	81						41,913	54,914	†63,326	†80,565	83,621	79,514	78,908	92,795	96,896	
Grants Received	81z						8,167	7,577	†8,359	†4,688	5,461	18,426	16,954	5,600	1,400	
Expenditure	82						61,296	62,568	†73,914	†89,072	102,989	107,655	105,856	105,026	111,895	
Lending Minus Repayments	83						896	2,536	†2,789	†2,097	...	...	...	−1,417	609	....
Financing																
Domestic	84a						8,237	2,513	†6,223	†4,857	...	....	....	....	....	....
Foreign	85a						3,875	100	†−1,205	†1,059	...	....	....	....	....	
Debt: Domestic	88a															
Foreign	89a									...	....	....		....		
National Accounts														*Millions of Belize Dollars*		
Househ.Cons.Expend.,incl.NPISHs	96f	...	75.0	93.6	116.6	131.9	154.0	165.7	185.5	280.2	299.4	290.4	282.8	271.5	293.2	281.5
Government Consumption Expend.	91f	...	16.5	22.0	22.8	27.1	29.5	33.9	53.0	66.8	70.6	74.7	79.0	83.5	88.3	93.4
Gross Fixed Capital Formation	93e	...	21.3	34.4	45.0	46.8	57.1	65.8	66.3	82.5	90.7	87.2	66.6	72.1	55.0	66.2
Changes in Inventories	93i	...	5.7	4.2	8.0	11.2	5.8	3.3	14.7	5.7	4.9	−6.4	4.9	13.6	17.7	13.3
Exports of Goods and Services	90c	...	63.1	111.4	150.1	113.9	155.7	205.9	173.8	215.7	206.0	172.0	185.5	263.4	202.8	253.0
Imports of Goods and Services (-)	98c	...	77.1	115.6	161.7	159.0	196.3	236.5	225.6	267.1	290.7	253.0	245.7	295.9	256.4	264.9
Gross Domestic Product (GDP)	99b	...	110.3	154.2	188.8	183.2	211.6	241.7	282.4	389.5	358.8	358.5	378.0	421.8	418.4	455.8
Net Primary Income from Abroad	98.n						...	...	−2.2	−3.8	−3.8	−9.8	−11.0	−18.6	−19.8	−8.8
Gross National Income (GNI)	99a	...	110.9	145.1	176.4	180.9	....	....	280.2	385.6	382.0	348.7	367.0	403.2	398.6	447.0
Consumption of Fixed Capital	99cf	...							24.2	21.6	23.6	25.4	27.2	29.3	29.3	30.4
GDP Vol.,Fact.Cost,1984 Prices	99ba p								323.8	340.4	340.2	314.5	333.7	371.5	366.2	392.8
GDP Volume (1995=100)	99bv p								32.8	34.5	34.5	31.9	33.8	37.6	37.1	39.8
GDP Deflator (1995=100)	99bi p								73.3	96.2	88.7	95.8	95.3	95.5	96.1	97.6
																Millions:
Population	99z	.13	.13	.13	.13	.14	.14	.14	.14	.14	.15	.15	.16	.16	.17	.17

1987	1988	1989	1990	1991	1992	1993	1994	1995	1996	1997	1998	1999	2000	2001	Item	Code
															Prices and Labor	
															Period Averages	
82.2	86.5	86.5	†89.2	91.2	93.4	94.7	97.2	100.0	106.4	107.5	106.6	105.3	105.9	107.2	Consumer Prices	64
															Period Averages	
...	...	...	...	55	...	...	70	...	...	...	...	...	...	...	Labor Force	67d
...	...	...	...	...	...	62	62	63	...	...	...	...	...	...	Employment	67e
...	...	...	...	...	...	7	8	...	...	...	...	...	...	...	Unemployment	67c
...	...	...	...	...	...	9.8	11.1	...	...	...	...	...	...	...	Unemployment Rate (%)	67r
															International Transactions	
															Millions of Belize Dollars	
205.66	232.51	249.07	265.92	243.44	281.01	272.97	301.98	323.25	335.27	352.16	381.48	338.33	420.77	355.45	Exports	70
285.89	361.95	431.39	422.59	512.49	548.06	561.92	519.86	514.43	510.97	572.43	649.88	749.01	960.79	140.51	Imports, c.i.f.	71
															Balance of Payments	
															Minus Sign Indicates Debit	
9.4	-2.6	-19.1	15.4	-25.8	-28.6	-48.5	-40.1	-17.2	-6.6	-31.9	-59.8	-77.5	-139.5	...	Current Account, n.i.e.	78ald
102.9	119.4	124.4	129.2	126.1	140.6	132.0	156.5	164.6	171.3	193.4	186.2	213.2	212.3		Goods: Exports f.o.b.	78aad
-127.0	-161.3	-188.5	-188.4	-223.6	-244.5	-250.5	-231.9	-230.6	-229.5	-282.9	-290.9	-337.5	-403.7		Goods: Imports f.o.b.	78abd
-24.1	-41.9	-64.1	-59.2	-97.5	-103.9	-118.5	-75.4	-66.1	-58.2	-89.5	-104.7	-124.3	-191.4		*Trade Balance*	78acd
56.0	74.5	85.9	115.4	122.7	142.6	150.5	121.1	132.8	137.9	137.8	140.5	161.6	172.4		Services: Credit	78add
-46.0	-53.4	-62.5	-60.0	-68.2	-81.6	-92.5	-88.0	-94.9	-91.3	-91.7	-99.0	-108.2	-119.8		Services: Debit	78aed
-14.1	-20.8	-40.8	-3.9	-43.0	-42.9	-60.5	-42.2	-28.1	-11.7	-43.3	-63.3	-70.8	-138.8		*Balance on Goods & Services*	78afd
5.9	8.0	9.7	10.6	8.3	6.7	5.9	2.9	2.8	6.3	7.5	7.2	2.7	4.8		Income: Credit	78agd
-13.4	-15.7	-19.1	-20.8	-19.1	-22.8	-23.4	-28.2	-25.1	-32.4	-30.8	-39.3	-46.6	-58.9		Income: Debit	78ahd
-21.6	-28.5	-50.2	-14.1	-53.8	-59.0	-78.0	-67.5	-50.4	-37.8	-66.7	-95.4	-114.7	-192.9		*Balance on Gds, Serv. & Inc.*	78aid
35.1	29.4	34.5	33.6	32.3	35.4	33.8	34.4	38.3	34.2	38.2	38.4	40.6	56.6		Current Transfers, n.i.e.: Credit	78ajd
-4.1	-3.6	-3.4	-4.2	-4.3	-5.0	-4.3	-6.9	-5.2	-3.1	-3.4	-2.8	-3.5	-3.2		Current Transfers: Debit	78akd
—	—	—	—	—	—	—	—	—	-2.2	-3.4	-1.9	-2.0	.5		Capital Account, n.i.e.	78bcd
—	—	—	—	—	—	—	—	—	—	—	—	.5	.9		Capital Account, n.i.e.: Credit	78bad
—	—	—	—	—	—	—	—	—	-2.2	-3.4	-1.9	-2.4	-.5		Capital Account: Debit	78bbd
2.7	27.3	25.5	25.1	22.2	22.4	32.8	3.6	-1.0	11.0	27.6	23.5	91.5	88.4		Financial Account, n.i.e.	78bjd
									-5.7	-3.9	-4.5	...	...		Direct Investment Abroad	78bdd
6.9	14.0	18.7	17.2	13.6	15.6	9.2	15.4	21.1	16.6	12.0	17.7	47.4	17.7		Dir. Invest. in Rep. Econ., n.i.e.	78bed
...	...	...	...	...	...	...	...	...	...	...					Portfolio Investment Assets	78bfd
															Equity Securities	78bkd
															Debt Securities	78bld
					.2	7.0	6.1	3.5	10.1	10.2	12.5	32.9	26.9		Portfolio Investment Liab., n.i.e.	78bgd
															Equity Securities	78bmd
					.2	7.0	6.1	3.5	10.1	10.2	12.5	32.9	26.9		Debt Securities	78bnd
															Financial Derivatives Assets	78bwd
															Financial Derivatives Liabilities	78bxd
—	1.8	—	—	3.0	3.7	-11.6	-17.1	-14.1	-12.2	2.8	—	-8.9	-39.4		Other Investment Assets	78bhd
															Monetary Authorities	78bod
—	.2	—											-11.1		General Government	78bpd
—	1.6	—	—	3.0	3.7	-11.6	-3.3	-1.7	-12.2	2.8	—	-6.3	-26.3		Banks	78bqd
							-13.8	-12.4				-2.7	-2.1		Other Sectors	78brd
-4.2	11.6	6.9	7.9	5.6	3.0	28.2	-.8	-11.5	2.2	6.5	-2.2	20.2	83.3		Other Investment Liab., n.i.e.	78bid
												-.6	41.8		Monetary Authorities	78bsd
.6	9.5	11.3	7.9	10.2	6.1	16.3	8.9	-2.6	19.7	11.5	8.8	14.9	46.1		General Government	78btd
-.2	—	-9.0	-2.0	2.9	9.1	18.7	-9.3	-12.1	-6.3	4.8	7.2	-8.9	15.5		Banks	78bud
-4.6	2.1	4.6	2.1	-7.5	-12.2	-6.8	-.3	3.2	-11.2	-9.8	-18.2	14.8	-20.2		Other Sectors	78bvd
-.2	-2.9	9.1	-25.0	-12.8	6.3	1.5	32.8	22.4	18.4	9.1	24.5	.9	7.3		Net Errors and Omissions	78cad
11.9	21.8	15.5	15.4	-16.4	.1	-14.2	-3.6	4.1	20.6	1.4	-13.7	12.9	-43.3		*Overall Balance*	78cbd
-11.9	-21.8	-15.5	-15.4	16.4	-.1	14.2	3.6	-4.1	-20.6	-1.4	13.7	-12.9	43.3		Reserves and Related Items	79dad
-9.9	-18.7	-11.3	-12.5	16.8	-.1	14.2	3.6	-4.1	-20.6	-1.4	13.7	-27.5	-51.8		Reserve Assets	79dbd
-2.0	-3.0	-4.2	-3.0	-.4	—	—	—	—	—	—	—	—	—		Use of Fund Credit and Loans	79dcd
												14.6	95.2		Exceptional Financing	79ded
															Government Finance	
															Year Beginning April 1	
...	44,922	-5,733	5,633	-27,701	-44,411	-82,365	-70,802	-39,698	-15,671	-32,588[f]	...	...	...	...	Deficit (-) or Surplus	80
...	161,443	190,169	210,747	216,191	245,281	247,864	258,978	261,658	288,256	283,357[f]	...	...	...	...	Revenue	81
...	1,868	5,600	13,000	12,836	9,848	6,953	13,264	1,079	4,076	41,191[f]	...	...	...	...	Grants Received	81z
...	152,670	202,550	228,824	278,901	332,438	342,935	348,953	306,090	317,781	362,261[f]	...	...	...	...	Expenditure	82
...	-34,281	-1,048	-10,710	-22,173	-32,898	-5,753	-5,909	-3,655	-9,778	-5,125[f]	...	...	...	...	Lending Minus Repayments	83
															Financing	
...	-54,966	-1,651	-25,951	8,318	5,348	42,583	45,433	41,604	-33,262	...	...	...	...		Domestic	84a
...	10,044	7,384	20,318	19,383	39,063	39,782	25,369	-1,906	48,933	...	...	...	...		Foreign	85a
...	77,270	75,272	73,808	77,626	113,070	136,104	145,985	167,747	168,330	...	...	...	...		Debt: Domestic	88a
...	123,962	140,002	145,516	177,141	228,555	259,453	285,800	282,610	329,798	...	...	...	...		Foreign	89a
															National Accounts	
															Millions of Belize Dollars	
344.8	403.9	475.6	489.7	567.7	630.3	690.2	723.7	765.5	765.3	822.3	850.0	883.7	1,109.9	1,155.7	Househ.Cons.Expend.,incl.NPISHs	96f
98.8	104.4	110.4	116.8	122.1	146.4	171.4	186.8	186.9	196.5	209.5	219.1	224.5	246.2	263.0	Government Consumption Expend.	91f
118.8	161.6	198.8	211.9	263.0	276.0	318.9	254.3	257.8	273.7	289.8	305.5	407.4	501.5	497.1	Gross Fixed Capital Formation	93e
2.5	-1.8	21.2	1.2	9.8	6.2	1.9	11.7	-12.9	5.8	19.1	38.5	41.8	48.3	52.7	Changes in Inventories	93i
334.4	390.5	419.2	489.2	495.3	568.3	565.9	579.2	601.6	618.2	662.6	666.2	834.5	896.5	887.3	Exports of Goods and Services	90c
346.2	428.8	498.9	496.8	583.0	651.6	685.5	639.4	637.4	642.2	749.2	781.6	974.0	1,208.1	1,193.2	Imports of Goods and Services (-)	98c
533.0	629.8	726.3	810.8	865.2	969.3	1,061.0	1,104.5	1,174.4	1,211.4	1,235.0	1,259.2	1,376.0	1,546.0	1,609.9	Gross Domestic Product (GDP)	99b
-14.2	-17.8	-13.4	-20.4	-20.7	-33.5	-37.4	-43.8	-45.2	-52.8	-46.8	-58.2	-83.4	-109.0	130.2	Net Primary Income from Abroad	98.n
538.9	612.0	712.9	790.4	844.5	935.8	1,023.5	1,060.7	1,129.2	1,158.6	1,188.2	1,201.0	1,292.6	1,437.0	1,479.7	Gross National Income (GNI)	99a
36.7	41.1	44.8	49.6	55.0	59.4	70.4	53.9	60.1	59.5	60.1	996.1	1,098.3	1,183.7	...	Consumption of Fixed Capital	99cf
479.2	531.3	613.5	677.2	727.2	824.3	903.1	930.2	987.5	1,018.7	1,044.0	1,055.4	1,183.2	1,288.4	...	GDP Vol.,Fact.Cost,1984 Prices	99bap
48.5	53.8	62.1	68.6	73.6	83.5	91.5	94.2	100.0	103.2	105.7	106.9	119.8	130.5	...	GDP Volume (1995=100)	99bvp
93.5	99.7	99.5	100.7	100.0	98.9	98.8	99.8	100.0	100.0	99.5	100.3	97.7	100.9	...	GDP Deflator (1995=100)	99bip
															Population	
															Midyear Estimates	
.17	.18	.18	.19	.19	.20	.21	.21	.22	.22	.23	.24	.24	.25	.23	Population	99z

(See notes in the back of the book.)

Benin

		1972	1973	1974	1975	1976	1977	1978	1979	1980	1981	1982	1983	1984	1985	1986
Exchange Rates															*Francs per SDR:*	
Official Rate	aa	278.00	284.00	272.08	262.55	288.70	285.76	272.28	264.78	287.99	334.52	370.92	436.97	470.11	415.26	394.78
															Francs per US Dollar:	
Official Rate	ae	256.05	235.42	222.22	224.27	248.49	235.25	209.00	201.00	225.80	287.40	336.25	417.37	479.60	378.05	322.75
Official Rate	rf	252.03	222.89	240.70	214.31	238.95	245.68	225.66	212.72	211.28	271.73	328.61	381.07	436.96	449.26	346.31
Fund Position															*Millions of SDRs:*	
Quota	2f. s	13.0	13.0	13.0	13.0	13.0	13.0	16.0	16.0	24.0	24.0	24.0	31.3	31.3	31.3	31.3
SDRs	1b. s	4.5	4.5	4.5	4.5	4.5	4.4	4.4	6.1	1.7	2.9	2.0	1.1	.2	—	—
Reserve Position in the Fund	1c. s	2.1	2.1	2.1	2.1	2.1	2.1	2.0	1.9	2.0	2.0	2.0	2.0	2.0	2.0	2.0
Total Fund Cred.&Loans Outstg.	2tl	—	—	—	—	—	—	5.4	5.4	12.7	12.7	12.7	12.5	11.4	10.3	7.8
International Liquidity													*Millions of US Dollars Unless Otherwise Indicated:*			
Total Reserves minus Gold	1l. d	28.4	33.1	34.6	15.0	19.2	20.4	15.5	14.2	8.1	57.6	4.9	3.7	2.5	4.1	3.9
SDRs	1b. s	4.8	5.4	5.4	5.2	5.2	5.4	5.8	8.0	2.2	3.4	2.2	1.2	.1	—	—
Reserve Position in the Fund	1c. d	2.3	2.6	2.6	2.5	2.5	2.6	2.6	2.6	2.6	2.4	2.2	2.1	2.0	2.2	2.5
Foreign Exchange	1d. d	21.3	25.2	26.6	7.3	11.6	12.4	7.1	3.6	3.4	51.9	.5	.4	.3	1.9	1.4
Gold (Million Fine Troy Ounces)	1ad	....	....	....	—	—	.006	.008	.011	.011	.011	.011	.011	.011	.011	.011
Gold (National Valuation)	1and	....	....	....	—	—	.2	.4	.5	.5	4.7	4.7	4.3	3.7	3.6	4.5
Monetary Authorities: Other Liab.	4. d	.3	.2	.1	.9	1.0	1.8	10.6	22.8	8.7	4.1	12.2	47.9	41.6	63.7	74.9
Deposit Money Banks: Assets	7a. d	3.6	5.1	13.6	60.4	7.2	8.2	6.6	5.5	3.6	6.1	2.9	16.8	14.5	13.3	23.2
Liabilities	7b. d	10.8	21.5	19.8	52.0	65.6	70.6	75.6	80.6	85.6	90.6	95.6	100.6	37.2	48.5	56.4
Monetary Authorities															*Billions of Francs:*	
Foreign Assets	11	7.3	7.6	7.7	3.4	4.8	4.8	3.2	2.9	1.8	16.6	1.7	1.5	1.2	1.6	1.3
Claims on Central Government	12a	.9	1.3	1.3	.8	.4	—	2.3	5.6	6.5	8.0	10.0	13.8	15.2	13.7	16.1
Claims on Deposit Money Banks	12e	1.4	1.1	2.3	7.9	7.7	9.3	11.3	15.0	22.8	19.9	34.9	39.3	40.0	42.4	44.5
Reserve Money	14	6.4	6.5	6.7	8.7	10.3	10.5	10.0	14.4	17.9	29.0	29.8	23.8	29.3	24.0	28.4
of which: Currency Outside DMBs	14a	5.8	6.0	6.1	8.4	9.4	9.9	8.0	13.3	16.3	28.1	28.8	22.5	28.1	20.3	26.2
Foreign Liabilities	16c	.1	—	—	.2	.2	.4	5.2	7.5	9.1	9.0	12.3	28.9	28.5	31.2	30.5
Central Government Deposits	16d	1.9	2.2	3.3	1.9	1.0	2.0	1.9	1.4	5.5	7.6	5.8	3.7	.9	4.6	3.7
Other Items (Net)	17r	1.2	1.2	1.3	1.2	1.3	1.3	–.3	.2	–1.5	–1.1	–1.4	–1.7	–2.3	–2.0	–.6
Deposit Money Banks															*Billions of Francs:*	
Reserves	20	.6	.3	.6	.4	.5	.6	3.6	1.4	1.4	1.7	1.8	1.3	1.2	3.4	2.1
Foreign Assets	21	.9	1.2	3.0	13.6	1.8	1.9	1.4	1.1	.8	1.7	1.0	7.0	7.0	5.0	7.5
Claims on Central Government	22a	.4	—	.1	—	.1	.1	.3	†.8	.6	2.7	3.0	3.4	3.7	3.8	3.7
Claims on Private Sector	22d	10.4	12.7	16.5	32.4	32.1	37.6	45.1	†63.5	85.0	87.0	125.9	132.9	116.9	145.4	132.6
Claims on Other Financial Insts	22f	....	....	....	....	....	....	....								
Demand Deposits	24	6.1	5.4	8.7	17.3	14.7	17.6	20.6	†18.1	26.0	30.0	52.0	56.6	59.6	63.6	49.9
Time Deposits	25	1.2	2.5	2.7	5.0	5.0	5.6	8.0	†7.0	16.0	15.0	15.0	15.0	21.1	24.5	30.2
Foreign Liabilities	26c	2.0	4.3	3.6	11.2	15.6	15.7	14.2	†14.1	16.7	22.2	27.0	42.0	17.8	18.3	14.2
Long-Term Foreign Liabilities	26cl	.7	.7	.8	.7	.7	.9	1.6	2.1	2.6	3.8	5.2	—	—	—	4.0
Central Government Deposits	26d	.7	1.3	1.4	3.0	3.3	6.0	8.0	†24.1	19.2	24.0	20.0	17.0	6.4	10.3	10.9
Credit from Monetary Authorities	26g	1.4	1.1	2.3	7.9	7.7	9.3	11.3	†15.0	22.8	19.9	34.9	39.3	40.0	40.7	45.0
Other Items (Net)	27r	.1	–.9	.6	1.4	–12.6	–15.0	–13.4	†–13.5	–15.4	–21.0	–22.4	–25.3	–16.1	.1	–8.3
Treasury Claims: Private Sector	22d. i	—	—	—	—	—	—	—	—	—	—	—	—	—	—	—
Post Office: Checking Deposits	24.. i	.8	.9	1.0	1.2	1.6	1.8	2.5	2.4	2.4	2.3	2.6	2.9	3.0	2.9	2.7
Monetary Survey															*Billions of Francs:*	
Foreign Assets (Net)	31n	6.1	4.5	7.0	5.5	6.3	6.3	.9	†–17.7	–23.2	–12.9	–36.7	–62.4	–38.1	–43.0	–35.9
Domestic Credit	32	9.9	11.6	14.0	29.5	29.8	31.5	40.2	†46.9	69.8	68.4	115.7	132.3	131.5	150.9	140.5
Claims on Central Govt. (Net)	32an	–.5	–1.2	–2.4	–3.0	–2.3	–6.1	–4.9	†–16.6	–15.2	–18.6	–10.2	–.6	14.6	5.5	7.9
Claims on Private Sector	32d	10.4	12.7	16.5	32.4	32.1	37.6	45.1	†63.5	85.0	87.0	125.9	132.9	116.9	145.4	132.6
Claims on Other Financial Insts	32f	....	....	....	....	....	....	....								
Money	34	12.7	12.3	15.7	26.9	25.6	29.3	31.0	†33.7	44.7	60.4	83.4	82.0	90.6	87.1	78.9
Quasi-Money	35	1.2	2.5	2.7	5.0	5.0	5.6	8.0	†7.0	16.0	15.0	15.0	15.0	21.1	24.5	30.2
Long-Term Foreign Liabilities	36cl	.7	.7	.8	.7	.7	.9	1.6	2.1	2.6	3.8	5.2	—	—	—	4.0
Other Items (Net)	37r	1.4	.6	1.8	2.4	4.8	1.9	.5	†–13.6	–16.7	–23.7	–24.6	–27.0	–18.4	–3.6	–8.5
Money plus Quasi-Money	35l	13.9	14.8	18.4	31.9	30.6	34.9	39.0	†40.7	60.7	75.4	98.4	97.0	111.7	111.6	109.1
Other Banking Institutions															*Billions of Francs:*	
Savings Deposits	45	.6	.6	.7	.8	.9	.9	1.0	1.0	1.1	1.5	1.6	1.7	1.7	2.1	2.4
Liquid Liabilities	55l	14.5	15.4	19.1	32.7	31.5	35.8	40.0	†41.7	61.8	76.9	100.0	98.7	113.4	113.7	111.5
Interest Rates															*Percent Per Annum*	
Discount Rate (End of Period)	60	3.50	5.50	5.50	8.00	8.00	8.00	8.00	8.00	10.50	10.50	12.50	10.50	10.50	10.50	8.50
Money Market Rate	60b	....	....	....	....	....	7.28	7.38	7.40	7.72	10.13	13.68	14.66	11.84	10.66	8.58
Deposit Rate	60l	3.00	5.75	5.75	5.88	6.00	6.00	6.00	6.00	6.19	6.25	7.75	7.50	7.25	7.25	6.08
Lending Rate	60p	....	....	....	....	....	12.00	12.00	12.00	14.50	14.50	16.00	14.50	14.50	14.50	13.50
Prices															*Index Numbers (1995=100):*	
Consumer Prices	64	....	....	....	....	....	....	....	....	....	....	....	....	....	....	....
															Number in Thousands:	
Labor Force	67d	....	....	....	....	....	....	....	....	....	....	....	....	....	....	....
Employment	67e	....	....	....	....	....	....	....	....	....	....	....	....	....	81	77
International Transactions															*Billions of Francs:*	
Exports	70	9.19	9.79	8.31	6.79	5.96	7.64	6.14	9.77	13.27	9.14	7.84	25.35	72.82	67.35	36.01
Imports, c.i.f.	71	23.09	24.86	35.30	40.28	52.30	65.79	70.20	68.10	69.97	147.50	152.55	121.02	125.88	148.78	133.85

1987	1988	1989	1990	1991	1992	1993	1994	1995	1996	1997	1998	1999	2000	2001		
															Exchange Rates	
End of Period																
378.78	407.68	380.32	364.84	370.48	378.57	404.89	†780.44	728.38	753.06	807.94	791.61	†896.19	918.49	935.39	Official Rate	aa
End of Period (ae) Period Average (rf)																
267.00	302.95	289.40	256.45	259.00	275.32	294.77	†534.60	490.00	523.70	598.81	562.21	†652.95	704.95	744.31	Official Rate	ae
300.54	297.85	319.01	272.26	282.11	264.69	283.16	†555.20	499.15	511.55	583.67	589.95	†615.70	711.98	733.04	Official Rate	rf
															Fund Position	
End of Period																
31.3	31.3	31.3	31.3	31.3	45.3	45.3	45.3	45.3	45.3	45.3	45.3	61.9	61.9	61.9	Quota	2f. s
.1	.1	—	.1	.2		.1		.1	.2		—	.2	.1	.3	SDRs	1b. s
2.0	2.0	2.0	2.0	2.0	2.1	2.1	2.1	2.1	2.2	2.2	2.2	2.2	2.2	2.2	Reserve Position in the Fund	1c. s
5.3	3.0	7.8	6.3	15.7	15.7	31.3	48.8	56.6	68.9	70.3	66.4	67.1	64.4	61.1	Total Fund Cred.&Loans Outstg.	2tl
															International Liquidity	
End of Period																
3.6	4.2	3.4	64.9	191.6	245.2	244.0	258.2	197.9	261.8	253.1	261.5	400.0	458.1	578.0	Total Reserves minus Gold	1l. d
.1	.1	—	.1	.2	—	.1	—	.1	.3	.1	.1	.2	.1	.4	SDRs	1b. d
2.9	2.7	2.7	2.9	2.9	2.8	2.9	3.1	3.2	3.1	2.9	3.1	3.0	2.9	2.7	Reserve Position in the Fund	1c. d
.6	1.4	.7	61.9	188.5	242.4	241.0	255.1	194.7	258.4	250.1	258.4	396.8	455.2	574.9	Foreign Exchange	1d. d
.011	.011	.011	.011	.011	.011	.011	.011	.011	.011	.011	.011	.011	....	....	Gold (Million Fine Troy Ounces)	1ad
5.2	4.6	4.3	4.2	3.9	3.8	4.1	4.1	4.3	4.2	3.4	3.3	3.3	....	....	Gold (National Valuation)	1and
128.7	143.9	26.4	5.7	8.1	4.7	13.6	3.8	6.1	10.9	12.8	2.6	2.0	1.7	-2.5	Monetary Authorities: Other Liab.	4.. d
20.6	18.5	8.9	25.9	52.9	72.7	96.2	143.9	239.3	278.8	265.0	288.9	253.9	214.2	239.7	Deposit Money Banks: Assets	7a. d
111.7	67.4	72.3	81.1	71.2	56.2	50.7	30.4	50.2	102.0	53.1	89.5	107.3	88.2	99.0	Liabilities	7b. d
															Monetary Authorities	
End of Period																
1.0	1.3	1.0	16.6	49.6	67.5	71.9	138.1	97.0	137.1	151.5	147.0	261.2	322.9	430.3	Foreign Assets	11
15.5	16.9	21.0	30.6	29.5	28.7	23.2	28.3	41.9	42.6	55.1	52.0	52.7	52.8	51.1	Claims on Central Government	12a
48.9	63.4	51.8	50.8	50.3	50.3	50.3	—	—	2.0	1.0					Claims on Deposit Money Banks	12e
23.4	28.2	50.6	80.8	100.6	123.3	107.4	108.9	80.5	87.9	105.4	100.7	177.0	249.1	306.8	Reserve Money	14
19.6	23.7	36.4	41.1	46.5	51.7	25.5	77.3	50.6	68.9	80.8	70.4	160.3	211.8	222.3	*of which: Currency Outside DMBs*	14a
38.4	45.9	11.2	3.8	7.9	7.2	16.7	40.1	44.2	57.6	64.5	54.1	61.4	60.4	55.3	Foreign Liabilities	16c
2.1	4.4	9.0	9.5	16.7	11.6	17.4	18.7	15.1	37.0	31.1	36.7	71.1	63.4	112.8	Central Government Deposits	16d
1.4	3.0	3.0	3.9	4.3	4.4	3.9	-1.4	-.9	-.8	6.6	7.5	4.4	2.9	6.5	Other Items (Net)	17r
															Deposit Money Banks	
End of Period																
3.6	1.5	7.7	36.1	52.6	71.0	93.2	30.9	32.4	17.1	31.9	31.5	16.5	37.1	77.0	Reserves	20
5.5	5.6	2.6	6.6	13.7	20.0	28.4	76.9	117.3	146.0	158.7	162.4	165.8	151.0	178.4	Foreign Assets	21
7.0	12.5	13.6	14.6	7.2	6.4	7.1	44.4	40.6	44.2	32.9	30.7	25.9	25.8	23.1	Claims on Central Government	22a
124.8	137.8	103.4	102.1	86.2	69.4	67.7	75.0	80.4	102.4	71.7	100.1	161.7	194.0	192.8	Claims on Private Sector	22d
—	—	—	—	—	—	—	1.0	1.0							Claims on Other Financial Insts	22f
38.9	42.3	39.9	58.5	67.4	72.9	84.6	106.3	107.8	114.8	107.5	108.4	104.2	146.7	167.2	Demand Deposits	24
35.0	25.9	19.8	29.5	31.7	47.9	59.3	66.1	86.0	90.5	99.6	98.3	110.2	114.6	136.8	Time Deposits	25
24.7	16.5	16.1	15.9	14.8	14.9	14.0	14.9	24.1	52.8	31.0	49.6	67.6	59.8	72.9	Foreign Liabilities	26c
5.1	3.9	4.8	4.9	3.7	.6	.9	1.3	.5	.6	.8	.7	2.4	2.3	.9	Long-Term Foreign Liabilities	26cl
11.4	22.2	31.6	26.9	29.5	19.7	25.6	35.0	34.0	35.1	39.8	56.1	74.4	79.4	84.5	Central Government Deposits	26d
48.9	64.2	51.8	57.0	50.8	50.3	50.3	—	—	4.0	1.0	—	—	—	—	Credit from Monetary Authorities	26g
-23.1	-17.6	-36.7	-33.3	-38.0	-39.4	-38.4	4.5	19.3	12.0	15.5	11.6	10.9	5.2	9.2	Other Items (Net)	27r
—							—	—	—	—	—	—	—	—	Treasury Claims: Private Sector	22d. i
3.0	3.4	3.5	1.6	1.5	1.9	.6	2.0	2.8	5.3	4.4	4.7	5.1	5.8	9.6	Post Office: Checking Deposits	24.. i
															Monetary Survey	
End of Period																
-56.6	-55.6	-23.8	3.6	40.7	65.4	69.5	159.9	146.0	172.7	214.7	205.7	298.0	353.8	480.5	Foreign Assets (Net)	31n
136.7	144.0	100.9	112.4	78.2	75.2	55.7	97.0	117.7	122.4	93.2	94.7	99.9	135.7	79.3	Domestic Credit	32
11.9	6.2	-2.5	10.4	-8.1	5.8	-12.1	21.0	36.3	20.0	21.5	-5.4	-61.7	-58.3	-113.5	Claims on Central Govt. (Net)	32an
124.8	137.8	103.4	102.1	86.2	69.4	67.7	75.0	80.4	102.4	71.7	100.1	161.7	194.0	192.8	Claims on Private Sector	32d
—	—	—	—	—	—	—	1.0	1.0							Claims on Other Financial Insts	32f
61.8	72.0	84.4	104.6	116.7	128.2	111.3	186.2	161.7	189.5	193.4	184.2	270.6	365.4	401.8	Money	34
35.0	25.9	19.8	29.5	31.7	47.9	59.3	66.1	86.0	90.5	99.6	98.3	110.2	114.6	136.8	Quasi-Money	35
5.1	3.9	4.8	4.9	3.7	.6	.9	1.3	.5	.6	.8	.7	2.4	2.3	.9	Long-Term Foreign Liabilities	36cl
-21.8	-13.3	-31.8	-22.9	-33.2	-36.1	-46.3	3.3	15.4	14.5	14.2	17.2	14.6	7.2	20.5	Other Items (Net)	37r
96.8	97.9	104.2	134.0	148.3	176.1	170.6	252.3	247.7	280.0	293.0	282.5	380.8	480.0	538.5	Money plus Quasi-Money	35l
															Other Banking Institutions	
End of Period																
3.3	3.1	3.1	....	....	....	....	....	....	....	....	....	....	....	....	Savings Deposits	45
100.1	101.0	107.3	134.0	....	....	....	....	....	280.0	293.0	282.5	380.8	480.0	....	Liquid Liabilities	55l
															Interest Rates	
Percent Per Annum																
8.50	9.50	11.00	11.00	11.00	12.50	10.50	10.00	7.50	6.50	6.00	6.25	5.75	6.50	6.50	Discount Rate (*End of Period*)	60
8.37	8.72	10.07	10.98	10.94	11.44	....	....	....	....	....	4.81	4.95	4.95	4.95	Money Market Rate	60b
5.25	5.25	6.42	7.00	7.00	7.75	....	....	....	....	....	3.50	3.50	3.50	3.50	Deposit Rate	60l
13.50	13.58	15.08	16.00	16.00	16.75	....	....	....	....	....	....	....	....	....	Lending Rate	60p
															Prices	
Period Averages																
....	....	....	....	....	62.8	63.1	87.4	100.0	104.9	†108.6	114.8	115.2	120.0	124.7	Consumer Prices	64
Period Averages																
....	....	....	....	....	2,085	....	....	....	3,211	....	....	....	....	....	Labor Force	67d
78	78	47	51	52	56	....	....	....	....	....	....	....	....	....	Employment	67e
															International Transactions	
Billions of Francs																
34.27	21.00	24.58	33.25	5.98	88.80	108.60	220.90	209.60	334.70	397.90	244.40	259.50	279.20	....	Exports	70
104.98	97.26	66.13	72.19	68.05	153.02	161.78	239.35	372.20	334.70	397.90	397.90	464.58	433.30	476.90	Imports, c.i.f.	71

Benin

638

		1972	1973	1974	1975	1976	1977	1978	1979	1980	1981	1982	1983	1984	1985	1986
Balance of Payments																*Millions of US Dollars:*
Current Account, n.i.e.	**78al *d***	....	....	–29.3	–53.4	–72.8	–60.7	–96.4	–51.9	–35.7	–93.4	–377.2	–134.8	–57.1	–39.0	–52.8
Goods: Exports f.o.b.	**78aa *d***	....	....	93.0	116.1	85.9	129.1	125.6	132.9	164.0	388.0	135.4	132.3	223.8	297.8	308.7
Goods: Imports f.o.b.	**78ab *d***	....	....	–148.3	–205.6	–208.6	–255.5	–284.8	–289.0	–312.2	–526.8	–514.5	–286.3	–290.9	–326.3	–402.2
Trade Balance	**78ac *d***	....	....	–55.3	–89.5	–122.7	–126.4	–159.2	–156.1	–148.3	–138.8	–379.1	–154.0	–67.1	–28.5	–93.6
Services: Credit	**78ad *d***	....	....	22.0	28.1	30.8	32.5	38.7	43.4	62.3	66.8	48.0	50.2	58.3	37.6	71.6
Services: Debit	**78ae *d***	....	....	–40.6	–57.9	–61.0	–71.3	–85.5	–94.9	–108.6	–142.7	–133.7	–92.4	–93.8	–111.3	–119.3
Balance on Goods & Services	**78af *d***	....	....	–73.9	–119.3	–152.9	–165.2	–206.0	–207.6	–194.6	–214.6	–464.8	–196.3	–102.6	–102.2	–141.2
Income: Credit	**78ag *d***	....	....	4.1	3.5	3.2	3.4	3.9	6.0	15.1	10.6	10.7	4.9	7.4	6.7	2.9
Income: Debit	**78ah *d***	....	....	–1.8	–4.8	–3.2	–3.6	–3.7	–4.8	–6.9	–10.0	–29.6	–51.8	–55.4	–34.7	–28.9
Balance on Gds, Serv. & Inc.	**78ai *d***	....	....	–71.6	–120.6	–152.8	–165.4	–205.8	–206.3	–186.5	–214.1	–483.7	–243.2	–150.7	–130.2	–167.2
Current Transfers, n.i.e.: Credit	**78aj *d***	....	....	46.9	72.3	83.2	108.6	114.4	160.7	157.5	127.2	111.1	113.2	100.2	95.7	120.1
Current Transfers: Debit	**78ak *d***	....	....	–4.6	–5.1	–3.2	–3.9	–5.0	–6.2	–6.8	–6.5	–4.5	–4.8	–6.6	–4.5	–5.8
Capital Account, n.i.e.	**78bc *d***	....	....	—	—	—	—	—	—	—	—	—	—	—	—	—
Capital Account, n.i.e.: Credit	**78ba *d***	....	....	—	—	—	—	—	—	—	—	—	—	—	—	—
Capital Account: Debit	**78bb *d***	....	....	—	—	—	—	—	—	—	—	—	—	—	—	—
Financial Account, n.i.e.	**78bj *d***	....	....	19.1	10.6	45.1	36.7	63.6	36.1	37.9	127.5	318.2	87.4	–1.9	–6.7	–26.9
Direct Investment Abroad	**78bd *d***	....	....	—	—	—	—	—	–.2	—	—	–.5	–.5	–.5	—	—
Dir. Invest. in Rep. Econ., n.i.e.	**78be *d***	....	....	–2.3	1.9	2.5	3.1	.8	3.6	4.3	2.1	—	—	—	—	—
Portfolio Investment Assets	**78bf *d***	....	....	—	—	—	—	—	—	—	—	—	—	—	—	—
Equity Securities	**78bk *d***	....	....	—	—	—	—	—	—	—	—	—	—	—	—	—
Debt Securities	**78bl *d***	....	....	—	—	—	—	—	—	—	—	—	—	—	—	—
Portfolio Investment Liab., n.i.e.	**78bg *d***	....	....	—	—	—	—	—	—	—	—	—	—	—	—	—
Equity Securities	**78bm *d***	....	....	—	—	—	—	—	—	—	—	—	—	—	—	—
Debt Securities	**78bn *d***	....	....	—	—	—	—	—	—	—	—	—	—	—	—	—
Financial Derivatives Assets	**78bw *d***	....	....	....	....	....	....	....	....	....	....	....	....	....	....	....
Financial Derivatives Liabilities	**78bx *d***	....	....	....	....	....	....	....	....	....	....	....	....	....	....	....
Other Investment Assets	**78bh *d***	....	....	–15.0	–71.6	–26.0	–38.0	–30.5	–41.8	16.8	–98.4	106.5	–29.6	–9.1	5.6	–5.2
Monetary Authorities	**78bo *d***	....	....	....	....	....	....	....	....	....	....	....	....	....	....	....
General Government	**78bp *d***	....	....	–.5	–1.0	–.4	–1.0	–.2	–1.0	–1.5	–.3	–1.2	–1.3	–.6	—	—
Banks	**78bq *d***	....	....	–10.5	–71.0	–28.8	–28.5	–26.8	–37.8	96.8	20.0	3.8	4.0	–10.2	5.6	–5.2
Other Sectors	**78br *d***	....	....	–4.0	.5	3.2	–8.5	–3.5	–3.1	–78.5	–118.1	103.9	–32.2	1.8	—	—
Other Investment Liab., n.i.e.	**78bi *d***	....	....	36.4	80.3	68.6	71.5	93.3	74.6	16.8	223.9	212.2	117.5	7.7	–12.2	–21.7
Monetary Authorities	**78bs *d***	....	....	.1	.8	–.1	.7	14.8	10.8	–12.5	–2.5	8.2	40.9	–.1	—	—
General Government	**78bt *d***	....	....	6.2	9.7	16.2	13.6	23.0	25.4	10.5	35.4	145.8	54.0	1.0	–12.9	–22.8
Banks	**78bu *d***	....	....	–2.7	40.3	19.8	14.8	14.7	43.0	3.9	–19.8	–13.6	–13.9	1.5	—	—
Other Sectors	**78bv *d***	....	....	32.8	29.5	32.7	42.4	40.8	–4.5	14.9	210.8	71.8	36.5	5.2	.7	1.2
Net Errors and Omissions	**78ca *d***	....	....	10.7	23.0	24.9	20.1	13.6	12.1	–24.7	–3.0	10.9	10.0	35.6	16.2	.4
Overall Balance	**78cb *d***	....	....	.5	–19.9	–2.8	–3.9	–19.2	–3.6	–22.6	31.2	–48.1	–37.4	–23.3	–29.5	–79.2
Reserves and Related Items	**79da *d***	....	....	–.5	19.9	2.8	3.9	19.2	3.6	22.6	–31.2	48.1	37.4	23.3	29.5	79.2
Reserve Assets	**79db *d***	....	....	–.5	19.9	–5.2	–.1	6.5	3.6	7.5	–51.6	45.9	1.4	1.3	–1.1	.7
Use of Fund Credit and Loans	**79dc *d***	....	....	—	—	—	—	6.7	—	9.6	.1	—	–.2	–1.1	–1.1	–2.9
Exceptional Financing	**79de *d***	....	....	—	—	8.0	4.0	6.1	—	5.4	20.3	2.2	36.2	23.1	31.6	81.4
International Investment Position																*Millions of US Dollars*
Assets	**79aa *d***	....	....	....	....	....	....	....	....	....	....	....	....	....	....	....
Direct Investment Abroad	**79ab *d***	....	....	....	....	....	....	....	....	....	....	....	....	....	....	....
Portfolio Investment	**79ac *d***	....	....	....	....	....	....	....	....	....	....	....	....	....	....	....
Equity Securities	**79ad *d***	....	....	....	....	....	....	....	....	....	....	....	....	....	....	....
Debt Securities	**79ae *d***	....	....	....	....	....	....	....	....	....	....	....	....	....	....	....
Financial Derivatives	**79al *d***	....	....	....	....	....	....	....	....	....	....	....	....	....	....	....
Other Investment	**79af *d***	....	....	....	....	....	....	....	....	....	....	....	....	....	....	....
Monetary Authorities	**79ag *d***	....	....	....	....	....	....	....	....	....	....	....	....	....	....	....
General Government	**79ah *d***	....	....	....	....	....	....	....	....	....	....	....	....	....	....	....
Banks	**79ai *d***	....	....	....	....	....	....	....	....	....	....	....	....	....	....	....
Other Sectors	**79aj *d***	....	....	....	....	....	....	....	....	....	....	....	....	....	....	....
Reserve Assets	**79ak *d***	....	....	....	....	....	....	....	....	....	....	....	....	....	....	....
Liabilities	**79la *d***	....	....	....	....	....	....	....	....	....	....	....	....	....	....	....
Dir. Invest. in Rep. Economy	**79lb *d***	....	....	....	....	....	....	....	....	....	....	....	....	....	....	....
Portfolio Investment	**79lc *d***	....	....	....	....	....	....	....	....	....	....	....	....	....	....	....
Equity Securities	**79ld *d***	....	....	....	....	....	....	....	....	....	....	....	....	....	....	....
Debt Securities	**79le *d***	....	....	....	....	....	....	....	....	....	....	....	....	....	....	....
Financial Derivatives	**79ll *d***	....	....	....	....	....	....	....	....	....	....	....	....	....	....	....
Other Investment	**79lf *d***	....	....	....	....	....	....	....	....	....	....	....	....	....	....	....
Monetary Authorities	**79lg *d***	....	....	....	....	....	....	....	....	....	....	....	....	....	....	....
General Government	**79lh *d***	....	....	....	....	....	....	....	....	....	....	....	....	....	....	....
Banks	**79li *d***	....	....	....	....	....	....	....	....	....	....	....	....	....	....	....
Other Sectors	**79lj *d***	....	....	....	....	....	....	....	....	....	....	....	....	....	....	....
Government Finance																*Millions of Francs:*
Deficit (-) or Surplus	**80**	....	....	....	....	....	1,434	5,052	–1,010	....	....	....	....	....	....	....
Revenue	**81**	....	....	....	....	24,781	27,518	31,611	34,200	....	....	....	....	....	....	....
Grants Received	**81z**	....	....	....	....	....	14,477	9,096	11,705	....	....	....	....	....	....	....
Expenditure	**82**	....	....	....	....	....	37,006	34,304	42,065	....	....	....	....	....	....	....
Lending Minus Repayments	**83**	....	....	....	....	....	3,555	1,351	4,850	....	....	....	....	....	....	....
Financing																
Net Borrowing: Domestic	**84a**	....	....	....	....	....	–430	2,071	147	....	....	....	....	....	....	....
Foreign	**85a**	....	....	....	....	....	887	1,802	2,457	....	....	....	....	....	....	....
Use of Cash Balances	**87**	....	....	....	....	....	–1,891	–8,925	–1,594	....	....	....	....	....	....	....
National Accounts																*Billions of Francs*
Househ.Cons.Expend.,incl.NPISHs	**96f**	64.8	70.4	77.9	96.0	119.5	139.1	156.3	176.7	220.0	276.1	343.8	354.1	372.0	374.1	381.1
Government Consumption Expend.	**91f**	10.5	11.2	11.8	13.4	12.8	14.7	14.4	17.4	21.7	65.2	43.7	60.2	62.6	58.8	63.8
Gross Fixed Capital Formation	**93e**	14.9	14.1	20.2	22.8	22.0	22.9	23.2	38.8	48.2	52.3	112.7	69.4	57.3	63.0	68.2
Changes in Inventories	**93i**	2.2	2.2	2.1	6.0	3.3	4.8	5.5	7.5	9.7	13.1	2.3	2.9	1.5	11.2	–.2
Exports of Goods and Services	**90c**	21.6	25.4	27.8	30.6	31.6	43.3	50.0	50.3	59.5	65.1	107.6	83.5	130.7	156.5	129.5
Imports of Goods and Services (-)	**98c**	30.9	33.2	35.4	55.7	54.8	73.7	80.9	97.2	113.5	130.7	193.6	152.8	164.7	194.0	179.9
Gross Domestic Product (GDP)	**99b**	83.1	89.0	107.6	112.8	133.5	148.5	161.6	193.5	245.6	301.0	416.6	417.4	459.3	469.9	462.5
Net Primary Income from Abroad	**98.n**	....	....	–.3	–.1	.2	.1	.2	.2	.2	–.2	....	....	–11.7	–10.7	–10.4
Gross National Income (GNI)	**99a**	....	....	....	....	134.5	151.3	168.8	193.7	245.8	300.8	....	....	447.6	459.1	452.1
Net National Income	**99e**	....	....	103.5	107.7	126.0	142.4	157.9	181.3	226.0	277.8	....	....	....	....	....
GDP Volume 1985 Prices	**99b.*p***	....	....	....	....	....	....	....	....	....	....	423.2	404.8	436.9	469.8	479.9
GDP Deflator (1995=100)	**99bi *p***	18.0	18.9	24.7	24.8	28.1	29.6	31.4	35.8	40.9	47.4	59.2	62.1	63.3	60.2	58.0
																Millions:
Population	**99z**	2.87	2.95	3.03	3.11	3.20	3.29	3.38	†3.38	3.46	3.58	3.69	3.81	3.93	4.06	4.19

	1987	1988	1989	1990	1991	1992	1993	1994	1995	1996	1997	1998	1999	2000	2001	
Minus Sign Indicates Debit																
Balance of Payments																
Current Account, n.i.e.	-34.3	-137.7	-44.5	-47.7	-261.5	-120.1	-101.0	-23.2	-213.1	-57.4	-169.9	-151.5	-191.4	....	....	78al d
Goods: Exports f.o.b.	366.3	190.2	187.9	237.5	373.5	345.1	393.5	397.9	419.9	527.7	424.0	414.3	421.5	....	....	78aa d
Goods: Imports f.o.b.	-463.2	-331.4	-250.6	-323.4	-673.4	-560.5	-561.4	-451.5	-622.5	-559.7	-576.9	-572.6	-635.2	....	....	78ab d
Trade Balance	-96.8	-141.2	-62.7	-85.9	-299.8	-215.5	-167.9	-53.6	-202.5	-32.0	-152.9	-158.3	-213.7	....	....	78ac d
Services: Credit	90.8	114.4	100.5	126.4	146.0	156.0	146.6	142.2	194.3	126.1	116.0	142.3	176.9	....	....	78ad d
Services: Debit	-139.4	-126.6	-119.1	-130.6	-189.6	-186.2	-175.1	-181.4	-272.2	-188.8	-172.3	-191.4	-215.3	....	....	78ae d
Balance on Goods & Services	-145.4	-153.4	-81.2	-90.1	-343.4	-245.6	-196.4	-92.8	-280.4	-94.7	-209.2	-207.4	-252.2	....	....	78af d
Income: Credit	3.3	4.7	5.6	12.2	24.1	34.1	37.8	18.8	23.5	36.5	25.4	31.1	29.1	....	....	78ag d
Income: Debit	-32.0	-37.0	-36.1	-37.7	-39.5	-27.1	-32.8	-21.7	-31.1	-57.5	-45.4	-44.5	-40.5	....	....	78ah d
Balance on Gds, Serv. & Inc.	-174.0	-185.6	-111.8	-115.6	-358.8	-238.6	-191.4	-95.7	-288.0	-115.6	-229.2	-220.8	-263.6	....	....	78ai d
Current Transfers, n.i.e.: Credit	146.4	72.2	89.3	97.8	127.1	146.5	118.5	98.5	105.4	92.4	77.8	102.0	87.1	....	....	78aj d
Current Transfers: Debit	-6.7	-24.2	-22.0	-29.9	-29.7	-28.1	-28.1	-25.9	-30.5	-34.2	-18.5	-32.7	-14.9	....	....	78ak d
Capital Account, n.i.e.	—	87.3	55.4	49.4	78.7	79.3	75.5	75.2	85.6	6.4	84.5	66.6	69.9	....	....	78bc d
Capital Account, n.i.e.: Credit	—	87.3	55.4	49.4	78.7	79.3	75.5	75.2	85.6	6.4	84.5	66.6	69.9	....	....	78ba d
Capital Account: Debit	—	—	—	—	—	—	—	—	—	—	—	—	....	....	....	78bb d
Financial Account, n.i.e.	34.6	-114.9	-229.9	-121.3	-96.1	-35.7	-123.3	-17.6	-126.3	-104.2	-21.3	-8.9	25.4	....	....	78bj d
Direct Investment Abroad	—	—	—	—	—	—	—	—	—	-21.9	-13.1	-5.2	-2.9	....	....	78bd d
Dir. Invest. in Rep. Econ., n.i.e.	—	—	62.1	62.4	120.8	77.6	1.4	13.6	13.3	35.5	27.0	38.0	40.7	....	....	78be d
Portfolio Investment Assets	—	.3	-.7	-4.6	3.7	-5.6	-9.1	-26.4	-64.2	-7.7	-7.8	1.2	-1.4	....	....	78bf d
Equity Securities	—	—	—	—	—	—	—	—	—	1.4	—	.1	-.9	....	....	78bk d
Debt Securities	—	.3	-.7	-4.6	3.7	-5.6	-9.1	-26.4	-64.2	-9.1	-7.7	1.1	-.5	....	....	78bl d
Portfolio Investment Liab., n.i.e.	—	—	—	—	.1	—	—	—	.3	2.5	2.0	1.2	2.0	....	....	78bg d
Equity Securities	—	—	—	—	.1	—	—	—	.3	2.5	2.0	1.2	2.0	....	....	78bm d
Debt Securities	—	—	—	—	—	—	—	—	—	—	—	—	—	....	....	78bn d
Financial Derivatives Assets	....	....	....	....	....	....	....	....	....	....	—	....	-.1	....	....	78bw d
Financial Derivatives Liabilities	....	....	....	....	....	....	—	—	—	—	—	....	8.6	....	....	78bx d
Other Investment Assets	41.6	21.5	-2.9	-6.2	-1.9	-83.6	-73.9	-52.2	-62.1	-4.0	-12.4	-9.6	-58.3	....	....	78bh d
Monetary Authorities	....	—	—	—	—	—	—	—	—	—	—	—	....	....	....	78bo d
General Government	—	-.2	-.4	-.7	-.2	-.4	-2.2	11.9	-6.9	—	-.1	—	—	....	....	78bp d
Banks	41.6	5.3	11.8	-3.8	-26.8	-23.5	-48.9	-50.8	-44.2	11.8	-41.1	12.4	-26.7	....	....	78bq d
Other Sectors	—	16.4	-14.3	-1.7	25.0	-59.7	-22.9	-13.3	-10.9	-15.8	28.8	-22.0	-31.6	....	....	78br d
Other Investment Liab., n.i.e.	-7.0	-136.7	-288.3	-172.9	-218.8	-24.1	-41.7	47.4	-13.7	-108.6	-17.0	-34.4	36.8	....	....	78bi d
Monetary Authorities	—	31.0	-112.6	-22.3	2.0	-2.2	8.6	.6	-2.7	5.2	4.7	-5.4	.3	....	....	78bs d
General Government	-8.3	-46.9	-227.7	-104.1	-304.8	-23.8	-68.0	-28.1	-36.0	-129.4	-26.8	-29.7	-33.6	....	....	78bt d
Banks	—	-32.8	3.3	-30.7	-17.9	2.3	35.0	9.8	-.5	4.5	-11.6	21.1	33.3	....	....	78bu d
Other Sectors	1.3	-88.0	48.7	-15.8	101.9	-.3	-17.2	65.1	25.4	11.1	16.7	-20.4	36.8	....	....	78bv d
Net Errors and Omissions	-52.6	.4	13.6	11.1	2.1	9.1	-8.1	-16.3	-1.0	6.3	6.7	7.1	7.3	....	....	78ca d
Overall Balance	-52.3	-164.8	-205.3	-108.6	-276.7	-67.4	-156.9	18.1	-254.9	-149.0	-100.0	-86.7	-88.7	....	....	78cb d
Reserves and Related Items	52.3	164.8	205.3	108.6	276.7	67.4	156.9	-18.1	254.9	149.0	100.0	86.7	88.7	....	....	79da d
Reserve Assets	.9	-.9	.8	-57.7	-117.0	-67.3	-15.4	-117.7	81.9	-78.3	-24.5	7.0	-40.2	....	....	79db d
Use of Fund Credit and Loans	-3.2	-3.1	5.9	-1.9	12.5	—	21.9	24.9	12.2	18.0	1.9	-5.3	1.1	....	....	79dc d
Exceptional Financing	54.6	168.8	198.6	168.2	381.2	134.7	150.4	74.6	160.7	209.3	122.6	85.0	127.8	....	....	79de d
International Investment Position																
Assets	....	....	....	....	....	....	....	....	....	613.1	664.5	598.7	726.4	....	....	79aa d
Direct Investment Abroad	....	....	....	....	....	....	....	....	....	13.7	-2.3	5.3	5.6	....	....	79ab d
Portfolio Investment	....	....	....	....	....	....	....	....	....	76.0	75.2	94.4	81.4	....	....	79ac d
Equity Securities	....	....	....	....	....	....	....	....	....	.2	—	2.5	1.7	....	....	79ad d
Debt Securities	....	....	....	....	....	....	....	....	....	75.8	75.2	91.9	79.7	....	....	79ae d
Financial Derivatives	....	....	....	....	....	....	....	....	....	.1	—	—	.1	....	....	79al d
Other Investment	....	....	....	....	....	....	....	....	....	261.6	338.4	236.9	239.2	....	....	79af d
Monetary Authorities	....	....	....	....	....	....	....	....	....	—	—	—	—	....	....	79ag d
General Government	....	....	....	....	....	....	....	....	....	.1	.1	.1	.1	....	....	79ah d
Banks	....	....	....	....	....	....	....	....	....	166.9	186.2	185.1	170.0	....	....	79ai d
Other Sectors	....	....	....	....	....	....	....	....	....	94.6	152.2	51.7	69.2	....	....	79aj d
Reserve Assets	....	....	....	....	....	....	....	....	....	261.8	253.1	262.2	400.1	....	....	79ak d
Liabilities	....	....	....	....	....	....	....	....	....	1,802.5	1,628.9	1,776.1	1,748.1	....	....	79la d
Dir. Invest. in Rep. Economy	....	....	....	....	....	....	....	....	....	62.3	46.9	67.0	73.5	....	....	79lb d
Portfolio Investment	....	....	....	....	....	....	....	....	....	81.7	62.2	91.2	95.1	....	....	79lc d
Equity Securities	....	....	....	....	....	....	....	....	....	2.5	3.5	6.3	6.5	....	....	79ld d
Debt Securities	....	....	....	....	....	....	....	....	....	79.2	58.7	84.9	88.6	....	....	79le d
Financial Derivatives	....	....	....	....	....	....	....	....	....	.8	—	—	8.1	....	....	79ll d
Other Investment	....	....	....	....	....	....	....	....	....	1,657.8	1,519.7	1,618.0	1,571.4	....	....	79lf d
Monetary Authorities	....	....	....	....	....	....	....	....	....	115.1	109.1	102.1	99.6	....	....	79lg d
General Government	....	....	....	....	....	....	....	....	....	1,368.5	1,165.8	1,288.4	1,204.2	....	....	79lh d
Banks	....	....	....	....	....	....	....	....	....	3.2	34.6	59.0	83.7	....	....	79li d
Other Sectors	....	....	....	....	....	....	....	....	....	171.0	210.2	168.4	183.9	....	....	79lj d
Year Ending December 31																
Government Finance																
Deficit (-) or Surplus	....	....	....	....	....	....	....	....	....	....	....	....	....	....	....	80
Revenue	....	....	....	....	....	....	....	....	....	....	....	....	....	....	....	81
Grants Received	....	....	....	....	....	....	....	....	....	....	....	....	....	....	....	81z
Expenditure	....	....	....	....	....	....	....	....	....	....	....	....	....	....	....	82
Lending Minus Repayments	....	....	....	....	....	....	....	....	....	....	....	....	....	....	....	83
Financing																
Net Borrowing: Domestic	....	....	....	....	....	....	....	....	....	....	....	....	....	....	....	84a
Foreign	....	....	....	....	....	....	....	....	....	....	....	....	....	....	....	85a
Use of Cash Balances	....	....	....	....	....	....	....	....	....	....	....	....	....	....	....	87
Billions of Francs																
National Accounts																
Househ.Cons.Expend.,incl.NPISHs	384.5	398.7	390.1	404.1	440.9	481.1	508.9	657.8	791.2	913.9	1,017.2	1,099.4	1,155.2	1,259.2	....	96f
Government Consumption Expend.	65.7	63.7	62.3	66.2	64.0	65.9	69.4	90.1	100.1	108.3	113.8	119.6	125.6	133.3	....	91f
Gross Fixed Capital Formation	66.7	72.8	59.7	67.4	72.6	79.8	89.4	144.1	190.0	196.7	223.1	242.0	271.5	308.3	....	93e
Changes in Inventories	-.1	2.6	-3.1	4.0	4.6	3.6	-3.9	10.0	45.8	5.6	6.2	6.8	7.2	8.0	....	93i
Exports of Goods and Services	128.7	93.4	87.6	102.4	117.7	138.1	144.7	248.9	269.9	300.2	337.2	367.8	398.3	444.5	....	90c
Imports of Goods and Services (-)	179.0	146.8	117.4	141.6	170.0	199.0	212.0	319.9	394.0	395.1	447.7	474.8	504.7	546.5	....	98c
Gross Domestic Product (GDP)	469.7	484.4	479.2	502.3	529.7	569.5	596.4	831.1	1,002.9	1,129.5	1,249.8	1,360.6	1,453.2	1,600.1	....	99b
Net Primary Income from Abroad	-8.6	-7.4	-12.2	-9.4	-4.9	-6.9	-1.8	-14.5	-22.1	....	....	....	....	....	....	98.n
Gross National Income (GNI)	461.0	477.0	467.0	492.9	524.9	562.6	594.6	816.6	980.8	....	....	....	....	....	....	99a
Net National Income	....	....	....	....	....	....	....	....	....	....	....	....	....	....	....	99e
GDP Volume 1985 Prices	472.7	488.9	474.9	490.1	513.4	533.9	552.7	576.9	603.5	636.9	673.3	703.7	738.6	775.8	....	99b.p
GDP Deflator (1995=100)	59.8	59.6	60.7	61.7	62.1	64.2	64.9	86.7	100.0	106.7	111.7	116.3	118.4	124.1	....	99bi p
Midyear Estimates																
Population	4.32	4.46	4.61	4.74	4.89	4.92	5.08	5.24	5.41	5.59	5.64	5.82	5.99	6.17	6.42	99z

(See notes in the back of the book.)

Bhutan

		1972	1973	1974	1975	1976	1977	1978	1979	1980	1981	1982	1983	1984	1985	1986
Exchange Rates																*Ngultrum per SDR:*
Official Rate	aa	8.773	9.896	9.978	10.462	10.318	9.971	10.668	10.416	10.114	10.591	10.627	10.986	12.205	13.363	16.051
																Ngultrum per US Dollar:
Official Rate	ae	8.080	8.203	8.150	8.937	8.881	8.209	8.188	7.907	7.930	9.099	9.634	10.493	12.451	12.166	13.122
Official Rate	rf	7.594	7.742	8.102	8.376	8.960	8.739	8.193	8.126	7.863	8.659	9.455	10.099	11.363	12.369	12.611
Fund Position																*Millions of SDRs:*
Quota	2f. s	....	....	....	....	....	....	....	....	....	1.700	1.700	1.700	2.500	2.500	2.500
SDRs	1b. s	....	....	....	....	....	....	....	....	....	—	—	.020	.050	.080	.110
Reserve Position in the Fund	1c. s	....	....	....	....	....	....	....	....	....	—	.370	.370	.570	.570	.570
Total Fund Cred.&Loans Outstg.	2tl	....	....	....	....	....	....	....	....	....						
International Liquidity															*Millions of US Dollars Unless Otherwise Indicated:*	
Total Reserves minus Gold	1l. d	....	....	....	....	....	....	....	....	....	31.11	35.51	40.22	44.81	50.30	61.00
SDRs	1b. d	....	....	....	....	....	....	....	....	....	—	—	.02	.05	.09	.13
Reserve Position in the Fund	1c. d	....	....	....	....	....	....	....	....	....	—	.41	.39	.56	.63	.70
Foreign Exchange	1d. d	....	....	....	....	....	....	....	....	....	31.11	35.10	39.81	44.21	49.59	60.17
of which: Convertible Currency	1dx d												4.22	7.12	17.42	21.59
Deposit Money Banks: Assets	7a. d	....	....	....	....	....	....	....	....	....	....	....	30.58	34.78	34.60	33.06
Liabilities	7b. d												2.53	3.68	4.38	2.84
Monetary Authorities															*Millions of Ngultrum*	
Foreign Assets	11	....	....	....	....	....	....	....	....	....	....	....	51	103	228	304
Claims on Central Government	12a	....	....	....	....	....	....	....	....	....	....	....				....
Claims on Deposit Money Banks	12e	....	....	....	....	....	....	....	....	....	....	....				....
Claims on Other Financial Insts	12f	....	....	....	....	....	....	....	....	....	....	....		14	16	17
Reserve Money	14	....	....	....	....	....	....	....	....	....	....	....	39	85	204	259
of which: Currency Outside DMBs	14a	....	....	....	....	....	....	....	....	....	....	....	22	46	70	91
Bonds	16ab	....	....	....	....	....	....	....	....	....	....	....				
Foreign Liabilities	16c	....	....	....	....	....	....	....	....	....	....	....				....
Central Government Deposits	16d	....	....	....	....	....	....	....	....	....	....	....	13	24	22	19
Other Items (Net)	17r	....	....	....	....	....	....	....	....	....	....	....	−1	8	18	42
of which: Valuation Adjustment	17rv															
Deposit Money Banks															*Millions of Ngultrum*	
Reserves	20	....	....	....	....	....	....	....	....	....	....	....	9	13	119	143
Foreign Assets	21	....	....	....	....	....	....	....	....	....	....	....	321	433	421	434
Claims on Central Government	22a	....	....	....	....	....	....	....	....	....	....	....	23	59	120	104
Claims on Nonfin.Pub.Enterprises	22c	....	....	....	....	....	....	....	....	....	....	....	57	41	27	20
Claims on Private Sector	22d	....	....	....	....	....	....	....	....	....	....	....	43	58	55	67
Demand Deposits	24	....	....	....	....	....	....	....	....	....	....	....	155	164	191	186
Time & Foreign Currency Deposits	25	....	....	....	....	....	....	....	....	....	....	....	147	157	202	222
Foreign Liabilities	26c	....	....	....	....	....	....	....	....	....	....	....	27	46	53	37
Central Government Deposits	26d	....	....	....	....	....	....	....	....	....	....	....	—	89	78	118
Capital Accounts	27a	....	....	....	....	....	....	....	....	....	....	....	121	111	133	150
Other Items (Net)	27r	....	....	....	....	....	....	....	....	....	....	....	4	38	85	55
Monetary Survey															*Millions of Ngultrum:*	
Foreign Assets (Net)	31n	....	....	....	....	....	....	....	....	....	....	....	346	490	595	700
Domestic Credit	32	....	....	....	....	....	....	....	....	....	....	....	110	59	118	71
Claims on Central Govt. (Net)	32an	....	....	....	....	....	....	....	....	....	....	....	10	−54	20	−33
Claims on Nonfin.Pub.Enterprises	32c	....	....	....	....	....	....	....	....	....	....	....	57	41	27	20
Claims on Private Sector	32d	....	....	....	....	....	....	....	....	....	....	....	43	58	55	67
Claims on Other Financial Insts	32f	....	....	....	....	....	....	....	....	....	....	....	—	14	16	17
Money	34	....	....	....	....	....	....	....	....	....	....	....	177	210	262	277
Quasi-Money	35	....	....	....	....	....	....	....	....	....	....	....	147	157	202	222
Other Items (Net)	37r	....	....	....	....	....	....	....	....	....	....	....	132	182	249	272
Money plus Quasi-Money	35l	....	....	....	....	....	....	....	....	....	....	....	325	367	464	499
Interest Rates															*Percent Per Annum*	
Deposit Rate	60l	....	....	....	....	....	....	....	....	....	....	....	5.5	5.5	6.1	6.5
Lending Rate	60p	....	....	....	....	....	....	....	....	....	....	....	15.0	15.0	15.0	15.0

1987	1988	1989	1990	1991	1992	1993	1994	1995	1996	1997	1998	1999	2000	2001		
End of Period															**Exchange Rates**	
18.268	20.117	22.387	25.712	36.953	36.025	43.102	45.810	52.295	51.666	52.999	59.813	59.690	60.911	60.549	Official Rate	**aa**
End of Period (ae) Period Average (rf)																
12.877	14.949	17.035	18.073	25.834	26.200	31.380	31.380	35.180	35.930	39.280	42.480	43.490	46.750	48.180	Official Rate	**ae**
12.962	13.917	16.226	17.505	22.742	25.918	30.493	31.374	32.427	35.433	36.313	41.259	43.055	44.942	47.186	Official Rate	**rf**
End of Period															**Fund Position**	
2.500	2.500	2.500	2.500	2.500	4.500	4.500	4.500	4.500	4.500	4.500	4.500	6.300	6.300	6.300	Quota	**2f. s**
.140	.160	.200	.250	.300	.340	.376	.405	.438	.471	.504	.541	.134	.174	.211	SDRs	**1b. s**
.570	.570	.570	.570	.570	.570	.570	.570	.570	.570	.570	.570	1.020	1.020	1.020	Reserve Position in the Fund	**1c. s**
—	—	—	—	—	—	—	—	—	—	—	—	—	—	—	Total Fund Cred.&Loans Outstg.	**2tl**
End of Period															**International Liquidity**	
74.94	94.12	98.51	86.01	98.92	77.87	....	115.20	124.29	183.99	181.18	249.63	274.41	295.35	284.60	Total Reserves minus Gold	**1l. d**
.20	.22	.26	.36	.43	.47	.52	.59	.65	.68	.68	.76	.18	.23	.27	SDRs	**1b. d**
.81	.77	.75	.81	.82	.78	.78	.83	.85	.82	.77	.80	1.40	1.33	1.28	Reserve Position in the Fund	**1c. d**
83.54	91.69	85.31	84.85	97.68	76.62	....	113.78	†122.79	182.49	179.73	248.07	272.82	293.79	283.05	Foreign Exchange	**1d. d**
35.26	44.57	46.39	61.29	85.44	75.29	....	110.39	†121.00	144.86	147.73	182.38	195.56	213.32	215.04	of which: Convertible Currency	**1dx d**
49.46	49.09	40.67	25.50	13.50	8.11	13.84	8.88	7.17	43.01	38.86	72.22	93.24	100.88	105.45	Deposit Money Banks: Assets	**7a. d**
3.32	3.08	5.13	6.53	5.30	13.63	18.09	—	—	—	—	—	—	—	20.20	Liabilities	**7b. d**
End of Period															**Monetary Authorities**	
483	697	841	1,145	2,268	2,027	†2,945	3,533	4,337	5,284	6,065	8,022	8,841	10,357	10,716	Foreign Assets	**11**
						74	—	50		51	—	—	—	—	Claims on Central Government	**12a**
....	....	....	....	....	....	108	7	3	308	3	1,193	1,188	893	293	Claims on Deposit Money Banks	**12e**
24	24	30	39	48	44	†	55	5	5	5	—	—	—	—	Claims on Other Financial Insts	**12f**
433	384	691	1,260	1,593	1,257	†1,931	1,287	2,149	2,328	2,545	3,954	4,971	6,022	6,161	Reserve Money	**14**
104	149	188	194	246	345	†335	348	433	423	721	769	969	1,270	1,610	of which: Currency Outside DMBs	**14a**
....	....	....	....	....	....	—	600	550	1,000	681	560	487	410	410	Bonds	**16ab**
....	....	....	....	....	....	—	617	161	250	250	250	—	—	—	Foreign Liabilities	**16c**
9	180	78	65	116	20	†25	30	29	334	28	1,207	1,234	918	338	Central Government Deposits	**16d**
65	156	102	–141	607	794	†1,170	1,062	1,506	1,685	2,619	3,244	3,335	3,901	4,101	Other Items (Net)	**17r**
						....	1,451	1,653	2,013	1,905	1,610	1,780	1,705		of which: Valuation Adjustment	**17rv**
End of Period															**Deposit Money Banks**	
310	244	502	1,009	1,253	828	†1,001	1,416	2,382	2,085	3,009	2,901	3,675	4,669	4,924	Reserves	**20**
637	734	693	461	349	213	†434	279	252	1,545	1,526	3,068	4,055	4,716	5,081	Foreign Assets	**21**
12	3	3	3	3	3	†2	5	2	100	201	50	50	50	370	Claims on Central Government	**22a**
14	32	28	53	65	770	†796	561	535	484	449	411	372	333	315	Claims on Nonfin.Pub.Enterprises	**22c**
82	116	192	216	306	426	†489	724	751	748	1,472	1,472	1,490	1,748	2,424	Claims on Private Sector	**22d**
213	263	358	345	504	496	†487	697	890	1,652	1,447	1,860	2,755	2,669	3,448	Demand Deposits	**24**
236	312	430	539	648	746	†1,120	1,351	1,926	1,465	3,458	3,782	4,741	5,996	5,658	Time & Foreign Currency Deposits	**25**
43	46	87	118	137	357	†568	—	—	—	—	—	—	—	973	Foreign Liabilities	**26c**
307	221	202	299	315	200	†311	140	344	459	209	322	914	631	1,288	Central Government Deposits	**26d**
176	177	229	240	236	534	†330	324	371	371	539	561	633	756	990	Capital Accounts	**27a**
80	110	110	200	136	–95	†–90	473	390	1,016	1,007	1,365	599	1,463	757	Other Items (Net)	**27r**
End of Period															**Monetary Survey**	
1,077	1,384	1,446	1,488	2,480	1,883	†2,811	3,195	4,429	6,579	7,341	10,840	12,896	15,074	14,823	Foreign Assets (Net)	**31n**
–185	–227	–27	–54	–10	1,022	†1,024	1,175	969	545	1,941	404	–236	581	1,484	Domestic Credit	**32**
–305	–399	–277	–361	–428	–218	†–261	–165	–321	–692	15	–1,480	–2,098	–1,499	–1,256	Claims on Central Govt. (Net)	**32an**
14	32	28	53	65	770	†796	561	535	484	449	411	372	333	315	Claims on Nonfin.Pub.Enterprises	**32c**
82	116	192	216	306	426	†489	724	751	748	1,472	1,472	1,490	1,748	2,424	Claims on Private Sector	**32d**
24	24	30	39	48	44	†	55	5	5	5	—	—	—	—	Claims on Other Financial Insts	**32f**
317	412	546	540	750	841	†822	1,044	1,322	2,074	2,168	2,629	3,724	3,939	5,058	Money	**34**
236	312	430	539	648	746	†1,120	1,351	1,926	1,465	3,458	3,782	4,741	5,996	5,658	Quasi-Money	**35**
339	434	442	355	1,072	1,317	†1,897	1,975	2,149	3,585	3,658	4,823	4,193	5,719	5,591	Other Items (Net)	**37r**
553	724	977	1,079	1,398	1,587	†1,942	2,395	3,249	3,540	5,626	6,410	8,465	9,935	10,716	Money plus Quasi-Money	**35l**
Percent Per Annum															**Interest Rates**	
6.5	6.5	6.5	6.5	6.5	8.0	8.0	8.0	8.0	....	....	....	....	....	....	Deposit Rate	**60l**
15.0	15.0	15.0	15.0	15.0	17.0	17.0	16.6	16.0	....	....	....	....	....	....	Lending Rate	**60p**

Bhutan

	1972	1973	1974	1975	1976	1977	1978	1979	1980	1981	1982	1983	1984	1985	1986
Prices and Tourism													*Index Numbers (1995=100):*		
Consumer Prices **64**	...	...	...	...	...	...	...	...	24.6	27.1	29.7	35.1	37.6	38.3	42.1
Electricity Production **66ae**	...	...	...	...	...	...	...	...	...	...	...	...	1.5	1.3	23.7
Tourist Arrivals **66ta**	...	...	...	...	...	...	...	...	29.5	25.8	33.7	40.0	39.9	39.8	50.5
International Transactions													*Millions of Ngultrum:*		
Exports **70**	...	...	...	...	...	...	...	...	131.5	171.7	159.4	160.7	206.4	272.0	387.4
Imports, c.i.f. **71**	...	...	...	...	...	...	...	...	394.6	585.9	646.5	730.0	825.2	1,041.6	1,168.0
Government Finance													*Millions of Ngultrum:*		
Deficit (-) or Surplus **80**	...	...	...	...	...	...	...	...	...	...	10.3	−23.4	31.8	−207.2	−98.3
Revenue **81**	...	...	...	...	...	...	...	...	...	...	137.8	197.3	278.1	268.3	345.0
Grants Received **81z**	...	...	...	...	...	...	...	...	...	...	360.3	478.4	512.1	701.7	777.4
Expenditure **82**	...	...	...	...	...	...	...	...	...	...	487.8	697.5	753.4	1,098.1	1,064.3
Lending Minus Repayments **83**	...	...	...	...	...	...	...	...	...	...	—	1.6	5.0	79.1	156.4
Financing															
Total Financing **84**	...	...	...	...	...	...	...	...	...	...	−10.3	23.4	−31.8	207.2	98.3
Domestic **84a**	...	...	...	...	...	...	...	...	...	...	−18.9	14.4	−49.8	115.9	−73.6
Foreign **85a**	...	...	...	...	...	...	...	...	...	...	8.6	9.0	18.0	91.3	171.9
Debt: Domestic **88a**	...	...	...	...	...	...	...	...	...	...	12.6	37.2	14.1	126.3	77.8
Foreign **89a**	...	...	...	...	...	...	...	...	...	...	12.2	22.4	45.8	135.5	316.2
National Accounts													*Millions of Ngultrum:*		
Househ.Cons.Expend.,incl.NPISHs **96f**	...	...	...	...	...	...	...	...	749	922	1,054	1,195	1,436	1,507	1,974
Government Consumption Expend. **91f**	...	...	...	...	...	...	...	...	276	287	327	443	513	561	576
Gross Fixed Capital Formation **93e**	...	...	...	...	...	...	...	...	330	426	556	691	755	1,003	1,103
Changes in Inventories **93i**	...	...	...	...	...	...	...	...	15	75	60	21	10	82	32
Exports of Goods and Services **90c**	...	...	...	...	...	...	...	...	145	207	213	228	290	368	448
Imports of Goods and Services (-) **98c**	...	...	...	...	...	...	...	...	402	616	688	789	899	1,128	1,332
Gross Domestic Product (GDP) **99b**	...	...	...	...	...	...	...	...	1,113	1,301	1,522	1,789	2,106	2,392	2,801
Net Primary Income from Abroad **98.n**	...	...	...	...	...	...	...	...	−200	−270	−322	−457	−388	−428	−467
Gross National Income (GNI) **99a**	...	...	...	...	...	...	...	...	913	1,032	1,200	1,332	1,718	1,964	2,334
GDP at Factor Cost **99ba**	...	...	...	...	...	...	...	...	1,095	1,280	1,498	1,754	2,060	2,350	2,759
GDP at Fac.Cost,Vol.1980 Prices .... **99ba** *p*	...	...	...	...	...	...	...	...	1,095	1,205	1,269	1,370	1,466	1,520	1,675
GDP Volume (1995=100) .... **99bv** *p*	...	...	...	...	...	...	...	...	37.5	41.3	43.4	46.9	50.2	52.0	57.3
GDP Deflator (1995=100) .... **99bi** *p*	...	...	...	...	...	...	...	...	30.1	32.0	35.5	38.5	42.3	46.5	49.6
													Millions:		
Population **99z**	...	...	...	...	...	...	...	...	1.24	1.27	1.29	1.32	1.35	1.38	1.41

1987	1988	1989	1990	1991	1992	1993	1994	1995	1996	1997	1998	1999	2000	2001		
Period Averages															**Prices and Tourism**	
44.7	49.3	53.6	58.9	66.2	76.8	85.4	91.3	100.0	108.8	115.9	128.1	136.8	....	....	Consumer Prices	64
95.9	80.9	99.7	100.0	100.2	....	....	....	....	....	....	....	....	....	....	Electricity Production	66ae
53.0	46.1	31.1	32.3	43.1	59.9	62.9	83.3	100.0	107.7	113.6	129.4	150.3	158.5	....	Tourist Arrivals	66ta
Year Ending June 30															**International Transactions**	
715.0	1,042.0	1,132.3	1,221.5	1,437.2	1,715.2	1,991.7	2,082.7	3,350.1	3,553.8	4,274.2	4,455.6	4,988.0	....	....	Exports	70
1,124.2	1,772.7	1,464.7	1,424.5	1,889.7	3,238.8	2,745.3	2,876.4	3,641.9	4,525.2	4,977.9	5,516.4	7,834.9	....	....	Imports, c.i.f.	71
Year Ending June 30															**Government Finance**	
....	†31.9	†−470.6	−390.0	−47.0	−247.3	312.2	−45.1	7.8	238.6	−300.9	143.4	−304.9	−764.6	−766.1 P	Deficit (-) or Surplus	80
....	†841.7	†829.0	945.7	996.6	1,207.5	1,650.9	1,666.3	1,877.4	2,127.7	2,424.2	3,133.1	3,656.9	4,585.4	4,777.0 P	Revenue	81
....	†929.9	†791.0	523.0	752.7	785.9	1,230.1	1,456.2	1,773.2	2,363.6	2,232.1	1,816.3	3,262.6	3,274.1	3,565.2 P	Grants Received	81z
....	†1,621.3	†1,538.2	1,774.8	1,752.2	2,138.9	2,397.3	2,891.0	3,655.6	4,152.6	4,630.6	4,588.4	7,284.0	8,334.2	9,081.2 P	Expenditure	82
....	†118.4	†552.4	83.9	44.1	101.8	171.5	276.6	−12.8	100.1	326.6	217.6	−59.6	289.9	27.1 P	Lending Minus Repayments	83
															Financing	
....	†−31.9	†470.6	390.0	47.0	247.4	−312.2	45.1	−7.8	−238.6	300.9	−143.3	304.9	764.6	766.1 P	Total Financing	84
....	†−242.2	†−20.7	332.7	−6.2	157.0	−334.7	21.0	−1.1	−211.8	176.6	−479.5	−248.8	158.0	163.5 P	Domestic	84a
....	†210.3	†491.3	57.3	53.2	90.4	22.5	24.1	−6.7	−26.8	124.3	336.2	553.7	606.6	602.6 P	Foreign	85a
....	†8.9	†4.3	231.3	104.8	226.3	19.3	....	....	....	....	....	....	....	....	Debt: Domestic	88a
....	†560.8	†2,357.6	2,455.7	2,594.1	2,730.2	2,801.8	....	....	....	....	....	....	....	....	Foreign	89a
Calendar Year															**National Accounts**	
2,363	2,605	2,495	2,806	3,176	3,730	3,537	3,770	3,428	5,171	7,138	9,322	10,067	11,329	....	Househ.Cons.Expend.,incl.NPISHs	96f
634	641	879	783	1,015	1,215	1,241	1,585	2,400	2,502	3,651	3,308	4,271	4,422	....	Government Consumption Expend.	91f
1,250	1,508	1,574	1,626	1,838	2,624	3,374	3,945	4,487	5,094	5,514	6,200	8,127	9,447	....	Gross Fixed Capital Formation	93e
−162	10	−121	−31	−75	340	−60	129	228	182	−632	45	108	49	....	Changes in Inventories	93i
773	1,109	1,256	1,408	1,829	2,079	2,264	2,508	3,712	3,979	4,771	5,148	5,714	6,456	....	Exports of Goods and Services	90c
1,249	1,940	1,701	1,609	2,281	3,634	3,163	3,349	4,190	5,120	6,128	7,686	9,164	10,004	....	Imports of Goods and Services (-)	98c
3,609	3,934	4,382	4,983	5,502	6,354	7,193	8,589	10,064	11,808	14,314	16,337	19,122	21,698	....	Gross Domestic Product (GDP)	99b
−350	−344	−172	−326	−491	−734	−734	−634	−1,208	−1,247	−1,141	−2,323	−3,083	−3,458	....	Net Primary Income from Abroad	98.n
3,259	3,589	4,210	4,657	5,010	5,619	6,458	7,954	8,856	10,562	13,173	14,013	16,040	18,240	....	Gross National Income (GNI)	99a
3,531	3,851	4,308	4,848	5,342	6,178	7,008	8,238	9,707	11,449	13,808	15,791	18,514	21,127	....	GDP at Factor Cost	99ba
1,973	1,994	2,087	2,225	2,297	2,405	2,555	2,713	2,921	3,070	3,306	3,514	3,773	3,989	....	GDP at Fac.Cost,Vol.1980 Prices	99ba p
67.5	68.3	71.4	76.2	78.6	82.3	87.5	92.9	100.0	105.1	113.2	120.3	129.2	136.6	....	GDP Volume (1995=100)	99bv p
53.9	58.1	62.1	65.6	70.0	77.3	82.5	91.4	100.0	112.2	125.7	135.2	147.7	159.4	....	GDP Deflator (1995=100)	99bi p
Midyear Estimates																
1.45	1.48	1.52	1.54	1.73	1.75	1.77	1.80	1.83	1.87	1.92	1.97	2.02	2.09	....	Population	99z

(See notes in the back of the book.)

Bolivia

		1972	1973	1974	1975	1976	1977	1978	1979	1980	1981	1982	1983	1984	1985	1986
Exchange Rates													*Bolivianos per Million SDRs through 1983; per Thousand SDRs in 1984*			
Market Rate	aa	21.7	24.1	24.5	23.4	23.2	24.3	26.1	32.3	31.3	28.5	216.2	523.5	8,821.9	†1.8585	2.3522
												Bolivianos per Million US$ through 1983; per Thousand US$ in 1984				
Market Rate	ae	20.0	20.0	20.0	20.0	20.0	20.0	20.0	24.5	24.5	24.5	197.9	504.9	8,783.0	†1.6920	1.9230
Market Rate	rf	13.3	20.0	20.0	20.0	20.0	20.0	20.0	20.4	24.5	24.5	64.1	231.6	3,135.9	†.4400	1.9220
														Index Numbers (1995=100):		
Market Rate	ahx	....	....	....	....	....	....	....	....	....	....	....	....	....	9,881.33	249.92
Nominal Effective Exchange Rate	ne c	....	....	....	....	....	....	....	39,102.03	37,965.97	47,707.78	34,072.44	11,064.62	2,438.85	110.74	3.36
Real Effective Exchange Rate	re c	....	....	....	....	....	....	....	....	174.01	220.92	238.52	222.48	293.49	495.07	147.50
Fund Position														*Millions of SDRs:*		
Quota	2f. s	37.0	37.0	37.0	37.0	37.0	37.0	45.0	45.0	67.5	67.5	67.5	90.7	90.7	90.7	90.7
SDRs	1b. s	3.0	2.2	2.6	7.0	6.9	5.7	14.1	—	—	.1	—	.1	—	—	2.0
Reserve Position in the Fund	1c. s	—	—	—	—	6.4	7.4	9.0	—	—	—	—	—	—	—	—
Total Fund Cred.&Loans Outstg.	2tl	7.9	18.1	14.3	13.9	—	—	—	30.3	30.3	99.0	97.3	114.3	121.4	98.0	74.9	157.3
International Liquidity													*Millions of US Dollars Unless Otherwise Indicated:*			
Total Reserves minus Gold	1l. d	44.3	54.9	176.2	139.5	151.1	211.1	169.8	178.2	106.1	99.8	155.9	160.1	251.6	200.0	163.7
SDRs	1b. d	3.3	2.6	3.2	8.2	8.0	6.9	18.4	—	—	.1	—	.1	—	—	2.5
Reserve Position in the Fund	1c. d	—	—	—	—	7.5	9.0	11.7	—	—	—	—	—	—	—	—
Foreign Exchange	1d. d	41.0	52.3	173.0	131.3	135.6	195.2	139.7	178.2	106.1	99.7	155.9	160.0	251.6	200.0	161.2
Gold (Million Fine Troy Ounces)	1ad	.407	.407	.408	.410	.414	.602	.645	.683	.759	.829	.890	.914	.913	.894	.894
Gold (National Valuation)	1an d	15.4	15.5	17.2	17.3	17.6	25.4	27.2	28.8	31.2	34.2	36.1	37.0	37.9	37.8	37.8
Monetary Authorities: Other Liab.	4..d	13.6	28.7	30.4	33.0	29.0	33.1	28.6	218.5	190.7	443.4	557.7	693.2	618.6	260.0	362.3
Deposit Money Banks: Assets	7a. d	6.4	5.1	7.2	14.9	21.0	22.9	23.9	32.8	43.2	36.8	18.0	34.0	25.0	15.0	41.6
Liabilities	7b. d	8.1	15.0	36.0	41.0	41.0	90.0	173.0	203.0	161.0	191.0	182.0	314.0	282.0	156.6	157.0
Other Banking Insts.: Assets	7e. d	.3	.9	—	.6	.3	.4	1.6	—	—	—	—	—	4.9	7.7	7.3
Liabilities	7f. d	12.3	16.8	25.0	37.7	51.9	56.9	65.0	63.8	68.1	69.4	61.6	49.6	47.6	53.7	50.4
Monetary Authorities													*Bolivianos through 1982; Thousands from 1983 to 1984;*			
Foreign Assets	11	1,196	1,384	3,868	3,142	3,853	4,726	4,004	5,534	3,482	3,989	41,972	†120	2,814	†463	963
Claims on Central Government	12a	2,805	3,330	3,666	5,681	8,941	12,173	13,842	21,593	32,163	43,298	241,541	†726	13,115	†2,444	2,673
Claims on State and Local Govts	12b	—	—	—	—	—	—	—	—	—	—	—	†—	—	†—	—
Claims on Nonfin.Pub.Enterprises	12c	—	—	—	—	—	—	—	—	—	—	—	†—	—	†—	—
Claims on Private Sector	12d	—	—	—	—	—	—	—	—	—	—	—	†—	—	†—	—
Claims on Deposit Money Banks	12e	262	601	621	935	765	791	1,212	1,775	2,618	3,230	13,334	†27	542	†80	227
Claims on Other Banking Insts	12f	218	459	648	661	973	1,454	1,461	1,151	1,363	1,540	7,704	†27	428	†50	133
Claims on Nonbank Financial Insts	12g	—	—	—	—	—	—	—	—	—	—	—	†—	—	†—	—
Reserve Money	14	1,974	2,768	3,668	4,348	6,315	7,884	8,836	9,832	13,741	16,195	63,726	†195	3,345	†201	380
of which: Currency Outside DMBs	14a	1,598	2,073	2,746	3,054	3,968	4,864	5,810	7,211	9,461	10,852	39,093	†125	2,888	†174	294
Time, Savings,& Fgn.Currency Dep.	15	—	—	—	—	—	—	—	—	—	—	—	†—	—	†—	—
of which: Fgn. Currency Deposits	15b	—	—	—	—	—	—	—	—	—	—	—	†—	—	†—	—
Foreign Liabilities	16c	222	613	546	569	330	439	587	5,476	5,851	9,970	105,586	†144	1,974	†304	367
Long-Term Foreign Liabilities	16cl	222	396	413	417	250	224	776	860	1,918	3,673	29,729	†270	4,303	†391	700
Central Government Deposits	16d	1,004	1,452	3,258	4,410	6,875	9,861	9,972	13,711	19,005	26,586	154,752	†450	10,189	†2,649	3,211
Central Govt. Lending Funds	16f	—	—	—	—	—	—	—	—	—	—	—	†—	—	†—	—
Capital Accounts	17a	—	—	—	—	—	—	—	—	—	—	—	†—	—	†—	—
Other Items (Net)	17r	1,060	545	918	676	762	737	348	174	−888	−4,368	−49,243	†−159	−2,911	†−509	−662
Deposit Money Banks													*Bolivianos through 1982; Thousands from 1983 to 1984;*			
Reserves	20	357	677	929	1,269	2,314	2,918	2,947	2,800	4,010	5,332	25,717	†73	674	†111	183
Foreign Assets	21	129	101	145	298	419	459	479	803	1,058	902	3,553	†17	226	†25	80
Claims on Central Government	22a	—	—	—	—	—	—	—	—	—	—	—	†—	—	†—	—
Claims on State and Local Govts	22b	—	—	—	—	—	—	—	—	—	—	—	†—	—	†—	—
Claims on Nonfin.Pub.Enterprises	22c	—	—	—	—	—	—	—	—	—	—	—	†—	—	†—	—
Claims on Private Sector	22d	1,143	1,830	3,005	3,713	5,136	7,365	9,746	12,241	14,350	18,546	69,281	†141	1,526	†291	732
Claims on Other Banking Insts	22f	—	—	—	—	—	—	—	—	—	—	—	†—	—	†—	—
Claims on Nonbank Financial Insts	22g	—	—	—	—	—	—	—	—	—	—	—	†—	—	†—	—
Demand Deposits	24	576	849	1,461	1,607	2,430	2,882	2,856	2,924	4,820	6,299	17,699	†50	432	†24	69
Time, Savings,& Fgn.Currency Dep.	25	631	804	1,189	1,952	3,401	4,957	5,643	6,317	8,419	11,820	39,206	†88	684	†89	448
of which: Fgn. Currency Deposits	25b	50	143	244	454	830	1,455	1,972	2,731	2,712	3,195	849	†1	9	†36	282
Money Market Instruments	26aa	—	—	—	—	—	—	—	—	—	—	—	†—	—	†—	—
Foreign Liabilities	26c	162	252	552	794	807	1,610	2,666	2,561	1,970	2,197	17,889	†112	1,859	†117	150
Long-Term Foreign Liabilities	26cl	—	56	169	32	5	184	802	2,422	1,974	2,484	17,676	†45	678	†148	152
Central Government Deposits	26d	—	—	—	—	—	—	—	—	—	—	—	†—	—	†—	—
Credit from Monetary Authorities	26g	166	491	531	654	719	792	966	1,592	2,405	3,229	9,818	†14	297	†53	144
Liabilities to Other Banking Insts	26i	—	—	—	—	—	—	—	—	—	—	—	†—	—	†—	—
Liab. to Nonbank Financial Insts	26j	—	—	—	—	—	—	—	—	—	—	—	†—	—	†—	—
Capital Accounts	27a	238	290	377	573	793	1,243	1,347	1,458	1,936	1,993	11,347	†26	698	†165	206
Other Items (Net)	27r	−145	−133	−200	−332	−286	−927	−1,108	−1,429	−2,105	−3,243	−15,083	†−104	−2,220	†−170	−174
Monetary Survey													*Bolivianos through 1982; Thousands from 1983 to 1984;*			
Foreign Assets (Net)	31n	940	620	2,914	2,078	3,135	3,136	1,229	−1,699	−3,280	−7,276	−77,950	†−119	−792	†67	526
Domestic Credit	32	3,219	4,223	4,118	5,702	8,232	11,188	15,135	21,274	28,871	36,796	163,773	†445	4,881	†136	327
Claims on Central Govt. (Net)	32an	1,858	1,935	465	1,328	2,123	2,369	3,927	7,882	13,159	16,711	86,789	†276	2,927	†−205	−538
Claims on State and Local Govts	32b	—	—	—	—	—	—	—	—	—	—	—	†—	—	†—	—
Claims on Nonfin.Pub.Enterprises	32c	—	—	—	—	—	—	—	—	—	—	—	†—	—	†—	—
Claims on Private Sector	32d	1,143	1,830	3,005	3,713	5,136	7,365	9,746	12,241	14,350	18,546	69,281	†141	1,526	†291	732
Claims on Other Banking Insts	32f	218	459	648	661	973	1,454	1,461	1,151	1,363	1,540	7,704	†27	428	†50	133
Claims on Nonbank Financial Inst	32g	—	—	—	—	—	—	—	—	—	—	—	†—	—	†—	—
Money	34	2,210	2,969	4,257	4,759	6,497	7,855	8,831	10,304	14,694	17,587	57,827	†178	3,370	†198	369
Quasi-Money	35	634	807	1,192	1,956	3,405	4,960	5,650	6,328	8,430	11,831	39,375	†88	684	†89	448
Money Market Instruments	36aa	—	—	—	—	—	—	—	—	—	—	—	†—	—	†—	—
Long-Term Foreign Liabilities	36cl	222	453	582	449	255	408	1,578	3,282	3,893	6,157	47,404	†315	4,981	†539	852
Central Govt. Lending Funds	36f	—	—	—	—	—	—	—	—	—	—	—	†—	—	†—	—
Liabilities to Other Banking Insts	36i	—	—	—	—	—	—	—	—	—	—	—	†—	—	†—	—
Liab. to Nonbank Financial Insts	36j	—	—	—	—	—	—	—	—	—	—	—	†—	—	†—	—
Capital Accounts	37a	238	290	377	573	793	1,243	1,347	1,458	1,936	1,993	11,347	†26	698	†165	206
Other Items (Net)	37r	855	326	624	43	417	−141	−1,041	−1,797	−3,361	−8,048	−70,130	†−281	−5,644	†−788	−1,022
Money plus Quasi-Money	35l	2,844	3,776	5,449	6,715	9,903	12,815	14,481	16,631	23,124	29,418	97,201	†265	4,053	†287	817

1987	1988	1989	1990	1991	1992	1993	1994	1995	1996	1997	1998	1999	2000	2001		
															Exchange Rates	
and per SDR thereafter: End of Period																
3.1352	3.3239	3.9162	4.8370	5.3570	5.6306	6.1467	6.8540	7.3358	7.4558	7.2387	7.9483	8.2213	8.3256	8.5709	Market Rate	aa
and per US$ thereafter: End of Period (ae) Period Average (rf)																
2.2100	2.4700	2.9800	3.4000	3.7450	4.0950	4.4750	4.6950	4.9350	5.1850	5.3650	5.6450	5.9900	6.3900	6.8200	Market Rate	ae
2.0549	2.3502	2.6917	3.1727	3.5806	3.9005	4.2651	4.6205	4.8003	5.0746	5.2543	5.5101	5.8124	6.1835	6.6069	Market Rate	rf
Period Averages																
233.92	204.44	178.98	151.48	134.08	123.15	112.61	103.91	100.00	94.56	91.36	87.14	82.61	77.65	72.68	Market Rate	ahx
3.78	5.36	10.71	21.33	28.74	39.27	61.34	97.87	100.00	98.22	100.89	100.52	103.42	101.34	102.58	Nominal Effective Exchange Rate	nec
140.05	133.61	128.47	106.22	110.47	108.85	108.17	102.67	100.00	105.02	109.41	114.92	118.44	117.86	117.81	Real Effective Exchange Rate	rec
															Fund Position	
End of Period																
90.7	90.7	90.7	90.7	90.7	126.2	126.2	126.2	126.2	126.2	126.2	126.2	171.5	171.5	171.5	Quota	2f.s
—	—	—	.7	.1	.1	10.2	17.0	26.9	26.8	26.8	26.8	27.3	27.3	27.3	SDRs	1b.s
—	—	—	—	—	8.9	8.9	8.9	8.9	8.9	8.9	8.9	8.9	8.9	8.9	Reserve Position in the Fund	1c.s
130.9	155.3	191.6	180.7	171.1	181.1	160.5	180.5	180.1	192.0	183.9	187.6	180.0	168.8	164.8	Total Fund Cred.&Loans Outstg.	2tl
															International Liquidity	
End of Period																
97.3	105.8	204.9	166.8	106.4	181.8	223.4	451.0	660.0	955.0	1,086.6	847.2	879.6	779.9	767.0	Total Reserves minus Gold	1l.d
—	—	—	1.0	.1	.1	14.0	24.8	40.0	38.5	36.2	37.7	37.4	35.6	34.3	SDRs	1b.d
—	—	—	—	—	12.2	12.2	13.0	13.2	12.8	12.0	12.5	12.2	11.6	11.2	Reserve Position in the Fund	1c.d
97.3	105.8	204.9	165.8	106.3	169.5	197.2	413.2	606.8	903.7	1,038.5	797.0	830.0	732.8	721.5	Foreign Exchange	1d.d
.894	.894	.894	.894	.894	.894	.894	.893	.893	.939	.939	.939	.943	.939	.939	Gold (Million Fine Troy Ounces)	1ad
37.8	37.8	37.8	37.8	37.8	37.8	39.6	37.7	37.7	39.6	39.6	234.9	235.7	244.8	259.6	Gold (National Valuation)	1and
371.5	407.5	520.4	435.4	414.0	486.9	432.1	503.9	545.9	659.8	597.1	578.8	542.0	503.3	444.8	Monetary Authorities: Other Liab.	4..d
50.1	52.1	66.0	61.3	62.4	79.3	72.2	84.5	103.6	124.4	137.9	409.8	471.8	552.8	693.9	Deposit Money Banks: Assets	7a.d
89.5	67.0	50.1	60.0	101.0	189.0	318.1	476.8	544.0	540.9	721.4	879.7	744.6	461.3	214.7	Liabilities	7b.d
6.3	4.5	.8	1.8	.2	—	—	—	—	3.8	6.6	46.9	55.9	63.4	74.3	Other Banking Insts.: Assets	7e.d
31.2	37.2	6.2	7.1	5.6	4.1	4.1	4.1	—	2.5	2.4	8.1	13.3	16.5	15.0	Liabilities	7f.d
															Monetary Authorities	
Millions of Bolivianos Beginning 1985: End of Period																
†1,138	1,288	1,475	1,714	1,969	2,343	2,917	3,702	4,538	†7,032	7,735	8,217	8,906	9,161	9,651	Foreign Assets	11
†2,375	2,797	3,208	4,189	5,108	5,906	4,700	5,009	4,328	†3,889	3,475	3,598	4,123	4,731	5,436	Claims on Central Government	12a
†76	89	111	125	129	150	20	18	—	†—	—	—	—	—	—	Claims on State and Local Govts	12b
†570	621	846	1,086	1,240	1,461	814	891	113	†119	—	—	—	—	—	Claims on Nonfin.Pub.Enterprises	12c
†—	—	—	—	—	—	—	—	—	†2	2	2	2	3	4	Claims on Private Sector	12d
†361	631	942	1,039	1,538	1,789	1,392	2,405	3,032	†3,394	3,427	3,444	3,506	2,873	3,028	Claims on Deposit Money Banks	12e
†179	223	327	404	—	—	—	—	—	†107	66	72	42	52	64	Claims on Other Banking Insts	12f
†1	18	27	54	73	84	91	108	119	†—	—	—	206	220	235	Claims on Nonbank Financial Insts	12g
†533	873	1,110	1,413	1,827	1,925	2,557	2,668	3,291	†4,194	5,036	3,989	4,441	4,905	5,497	Reserve Money	14
†398	529	502	642	754	886	1,034	1,406	1,694	†1,802	2,061	2,193	2,173	2,189	2,422	*of which: Currency Outside DMBs*	14a
†417	351	226	438	526	570	568	1,682	897	†547	452	451	994	542	624	Time, Savings,& Fgn.Currency Dep.	15
†280	227	145	304	257	284	244	1,235	522	†573	442	446	990	530	597	*of which: Fgn. Currency Deposits*	15b
†539	600	1,011	882	705	786	606	800	753	†1,432	1,331	1,491	1,480	1,405	1,417	Foreign Liabilities	16c
†692	893	1,166	1,253	1,398	1,641	1,674	1,898	2,217	†2,175	1,987	1,830	1,782	1,811	1,617	Long-Term Foreign Liabilities	16cl
†2,998	3,340	3,621	4,415	5,390	6,220	2,524	2,589	3,565	†4,460	3,591	3,489	3,642	3,679	3,750	Central Government Deposits	16d
†81	263	637	1,033	1,369	1,741	2,238	2,684	1,240	†1,081	919	989	999	972	936	Central Govt. Lending Funds	16f
†435	412	392	599	341	205	1,075	1,673	2,516	†1,057	1,442	3,287	3,857	4,381	5,247	Capital Accounts	17a
†-997	-1,066	-1,226	-1,422	-1,499	-1,355	-1,307	-1,861	-2,347	†-405	-53	-193	-410	-655	-669	Other Items (Net)	17r
															Deposit Money Banks	
Millions of Bolivianos Beginning 1985: End of Period																
†111	251	563	664	974	1,030	1,539	1,133	1,450	†2,788	3,588	1,426	1,459	1,797	1,827	Reserves	20
†111	129	197	209	234	325	323	397	511	†645	740	2,313	2,826	3,532	4,732	Foreign Assets	21
†—	—	7	4	8	114	29	103	572	†1,522	1,590	1,322	924	1,053	1,530	Claims on Central Government	22a
†—	—	—	—	—	—	—	—	—	†—	—	—	—	—	—	Claims on State and Local Govts	22b
†—	—	—	—	—	—	—	—	—	†—	5	1	2	2	39	Claims on Nonfin.Pub.Enterprises	22c
†1,086	1,543	2,311	3,320	5,093	7,599	10,740	13,452	15,152	†17,568	21,017	26,103	27,331	26,403	24,152	Claims on Private Sector	22d
†—	—	—	—	—	—	—	—	—	†—	—	11	10	—	6	Claims on Other Banking Insts	22f
†—	—	—	—	—	—	—	—	—	†153	131	309	291	263	407	Claims on Nonbank Financial Insts	22g
†110	159	206	350	693	1,037	1,466	1,826	2,219	†867	1,036	1,124	1,031	1,150	1,353	Demand Deposits	24
†643	978	1,537	2,349	3,723	5,167	7,175	7,809	8,887	†13,542	15,916	18,237	19,203	19,424	19,130	Time, Savings,& Fgn.Currency Dep.	25
†510	841	1,418	2,203	3,564	5,039	7,036	7,568	8,700	†13,201	15,546	17,799	18,737	18,947	18,601	*of which: Fgn. Currency Deposits*	25b
†—	—	—	—	—	—	—	—	—	†—	—	70	68	891	1,576	Money Market Instruments	26aa
†144	129	39	84	164	402	1,028	1,570	1,955	†2,088	2,717	3,364	2,868	1,869	527	Foreign Liabilities	26c
†54	36	111	120	215	372	396	669	730	†717	1,153	1,602	1,592	1,079	937	Long-Term Foreign Liabilities	26cl
†10	13	14	18	20	38	49	74	179	†935	1,319	260	97	117	139	Central Government Deposits	26d
†235	472	829	929	1,014	1,297	1,334	2,260	2,984	†3,830	3,721	3,499	3,920	3,914	3,802	Credit from Monetary Authorities	26g
†—	—	—	—	—	—	—	—	—	†—	—	95	93	103	103	Liabilities to Other Banking Insts	26i
†—	—	—	—	—	—	—	—	—	†—	310	520	894	927	2,069	Liab. to Nonbank Financial Insts	26j
†421	500	668	766	976	1,283	1,577	1,899	2,043	†2,352	2,821	3,822	4,626	5,252	5,732	Capital Accounts	27a
†-309	-364	-325	-417	-495	-527	-393	-1,023	-1,312	†-1,655	-1,921	-1,108	-1,550	-1,676	-2,676	Other Items (Net)	27r
															Monetary Survey	
Millions of Bolivianos Beginning 1985: End of Period																
†565	688	622	957	1,335	1,480	1,607	1,730	2,341	†4,157	4,427	5,675	7,384	9,420	12,440	Foreign Assets (Net)	31n
†1,279	1,937	3,202	4,749	6,242	9,056	13,821	16,917	16,541	†17,964	21,377	27,669	29,192	28,931	27,984	Domestic Credit	32
†-632	-556	-420	-240	-294	-238	2,156	2,449	1,156	†16	155	1,171	1,308	1,988	3,078	Claims on Central Govt. (Net)	32an
†76	89	111	125	129	150	20	18	—	†—	—	—	—	—	—	Claims on State and Local Govts	32b
†570	621	846	1,086	1,240	1,461	814	891	113	†119	5	1	2	2	39	Claims on Nonfin.Pub.Enterprises	32c
†1,086	1,543	2,311	3,320	5,093	7,599	10,740	13,452	15,152	†17,570	21,019	26,105	27,333	26,406	24,156	Claims on Private Sector	32d
†179	223	327	404	—	—	—	—	—	†107	66	83	52	52	70	Claims on Other Banking Insts	32f
†1	18	27	54	73	84	91	108	119	†153	131	309	497	483	642	Claims on Nonbank Financial Inst	32g
†516	698	715	997	1,447	1,923	2,499	3,232	3,913	†3,055	3,636	3,895	3,670	3,995	4,743	Money	34
†1,060	1,329	1,762	2,787	4,249	5,737	7,743	9,490	9,784	†14,089	16,368	18,688	20,197	19,966	19,754	Quasi-Money	35
†—	—	—	—	—	—	—	—	—	†—	—	70	68	891	1,576	Money Market Instruments	36aa
†746	929	1,277	1,373	1,613	2,013	2,069	2,567	2,947	†2,892	3,140	3,432	3,374	2,890	2,554	Long-Term Foreign Liabilities	36cl
†140	356	760	1,172	1,502	1,901	2,238	2,684	1,240	†1,081	919	989	999	972	936	Central Govt. Lending Funds	36f
†—	—	—	—	—	—	—	—	—	†—	—	95	93	103	103	Liabilities to Other Banking Insts	36i
†—	—	—	—	—	—	—	—	—	†—	310	520	894	927	2,069	Liab. to Nonbank Financial Insts	36j
†857	912	1,060	1,365	1,317	1,488	2,652	3,573	4,559	†3,409	4,263	7,109	8,483	9,633	10,978	Capital Accounts	37a
†-1,474	-1,599	-1,748	-1,988	-2,552	-2,525	-1,773	-2,899	-3,560	†-2,406	-2,832	-1,454	-1,203	-1,027	-2,290	Other Items (Net)	37r
†1,576	2,027	2,477	3,784	5,696	7,660	10,242	12,722	13,697	†17,145	20,004	22,583	23,867	23,961	24,497	Money plus Quasi-Money	35l

		1972	1973	1974	1975	1976	1977	1978	1979	1980	1981	1982	1983	1984	1985	1986
Other Banking Institutions										*Bolivianos through 1982; Thousands from 1983 to 1984;*						
Reserves	40	33	39	59	94	102	124	172	178	283	283	1,100	†5	70	†2	6
Foreign Assets	41	5	17	—	11	5	8	32	—	—	—	—	†—	43	†13	14
Claims on Central Government	42a	—	—	—	—	—	—	—	—	—	—	—	†—	†—	†—	—
Claims on State and Local Govts	42b	—	—	—	—	—	—	—	—	—	—	—	†—	†—	†—	—
Claims on Nonfin.Pub.Enterprises	42c	—	—	—	—	—	—	—	—	—	—	—	†—	†—	†—	—
Claims on Private Sector	42d	551	949	1,421	1,905	2,335	2,887	3,275	3,889	4,664	5,529	27,800	†74	1,240	†160	244
Claims on Deposit Money Banks	42e	—	—	—	—	—	—	—	—	—	—	—	†—	†—	†—	—
Claims on Nonbank Financial Insts	42g	—	—	—	—	—	—	—	—	—	—	—	†—	†—	†—	—
Demand Deposits	44	—	—	—	—	—	—	—	—	—	—	—	†—	†—	†—	—
Time, Savings,& Fgn.Currency Dep.	45	28	157	47	187	217	270	330	236	376	629	2,100	†6	102	†18	12
of which: Fgn. Currency Deposits	45b															
Money Market Instruments	46aa															
Foreign Liabilities	46c	—	—	17	—	—	—	—	31	13	32	300	†—	†—	†—	—
Long-Term Foreign Liabilities	46cl	245	336	483	754	1,038	1,137	1,301	1,532	1,655	1,670	11,900	†25	418	†91	97
Central Government Deposits	46d	22	64	83	116	115	45	72	80	129	119	800	†3	80	†10	3
Credit from Monetary Authorities	46g	207	340	614	823	916	1,289	1,477	1,127	1,541	1,876	4,000	†19	409	†56	120
Credit from Deposit Money Banks	46h	—	—	—	—	—	—	—	—	—	—	—	†—	†—	†—	—
Liabs. to Nonbank Financial Insts	46j	—	—	—	—	—	—	—	—	—	—	—	†—	†—	†—	—
Capital Accounts	47a	105	118	89	292	455	700	952	1,811	1,973	1,792	2,900	†8	684	†100	135
Other Items (Net)	47r	–18	–9	147	–162	–300	–423	–653	–750	–741	–306	6,900	†17	–340	†–100	–103
Banking Survey											*Bolivianos through 1982; Thousands from 1983 to 1984;*					
Foreign Assets (Net)	51n	946	637	2,897	2,089	3,140	3,144	1,261	–1,730	–3,294	–7,308	–78,250	†–119	–749	†80	540
Domestic Credit	52	3,530	4,650	4,808	6,830	9,478	12,576	16,876	23,933	32,043	40,667	183,070	†488	5,612	†235	435
Claims on Central Govt. (Net)	52an	1,836	1,871	382	1,212	2,008	2,324	3,855	7,803	13,030	16,592	85,989	†272	2,847	†–215	–541
Claims on State and Local Govts	52b	—	—	—	—	—	—	—	—	—	—	—	†—	†—	†—	—
Claims on Nonfin.Pub.Enterprises	52c	—	—	—	—	—	—	—	—	—	—	—	†—	†—	†—	—
Claims on Private Sector	52d	1,694	2,779	4,426	5,618	7,471	10,252	13,021	16,131	19,014	24,075	97,081	†215	2,766	†451	976
Claims on Nonbank Financial Inst	52g	—	—	—	—	—	—	—	—	—	—	—	†—	†—	†—	—
Liquid Liabilities	55l	2,840	3,894	5,437	6,807	10,018	12,961	14,639	16,689	23,217	29,764	98,201	†266	4,086	†303	823
Money Market Instruments	56aa															
Long-Term Foreign Liabilities	56cl	467	789	1,064	1,203	1,293	1,545	2,878	4,814	5,548	7,827	59,304	†340	5,399	†630	949
Central Govt. Lending Funds	56f	—	—	—	—	—	—	—	—	—	—	—	†—	†—	†—	—
Liab. to Nonbank Financial Insts	56j	—	—	—	—	—	—	—	—	—	—	—	†—	†—	†—	—
Capital Accounts	57a	343	407	467	866	1,248	1,942	2,299	3,270	3,909	3,785	14,247	†34	1,382	†265	341
Other Items (Net)	57r	827	197	738	44	59	–728	–1,679	–2,571	–3,924	–8,017	–66,932	†–272	–6,003	†–882	–1,138
Money (National Definitions)											*Bolivianos through 1982; Thousands from 1983 to 1984;*					
Reserve Money	19ma	. . . .	. . . .	. . . .	. . . .	. . . .	7,883	8,836	9,841	13,741	16,195	63,726	†195	3,345	†201	384
M1	59ma	. . . .	. . . .	. . . .	. . . .	. . . .	7,730	8,633	10,085	14,238	17,153	56,555	†175	3,296	†199	363
M'1	59mb	. . . .	. . . .	. . . .	. . . .	. . . .	7,730	8,633	10,085	14,238	17,153	56,555	†175	3,296	†199	363
M2	59mc	. . . .	. . . .	. . . .	. . . .	. . . .	10,117	11,172	12,676	18,556	23,895	75,246	†227	3,603	†233	452
M'2	59md	. . . .	. . . .	. . . .	. . . .	. . . .	10,117	11,172	12,676	18,556	23,895	75,246	†227	3,603	†233	452
M3	59me	. . . .	. . . .	. . . .	. . . .	. . . .	11,394	12,447	13,694	20,249	26,346	97,101	†265	3,975	†256	532
M'3	59mf	. . . .	. . . .	. . . .	. . . .	. . . .	12,933	14,537	16,684	23,092	29,574	98,534	†266	3,986	†290	822
M4	59mg															
M'4	59mh															
Interest Rates															*Percent Per Annum*	
Discount Rate (End of Period)	60	11.00	11.00	13.00	13.00	13.00	13.00	13.00	18.00	19.90	26.00	37.00	61.00	149.00	. . . .	. . . .
Discount Rate (Fgn.Cur.)(End per)	60.. f														. . . .	. . . .
Money Market Rate	60b														. . . .	. . . .
Money Market Rate (Fgn. Cur.)	60b. f														. . . .	. . . .
Treasury Bill Rate	60c														. . . .	. . . .
Treasury Bill Rate (Fgn.Currency)	60c. f														. . . .	. . . .
Savings Rate	60k												43.00	110.00	99.60	29.57
Savings Rate (Fgn.Currency)	60k. f														. . . .	. . . .
Deposit Rate	60l								16.00	18.00	28.42	30.33	39.83	108.33	68.75	†33.39
Deposit Rate (Fgn.Currency)	60l. f													11.20	14.97
Lending Rate	60p								27.00	28.00	42.50	45.00	56.83	120.67	172.15	†65.78
Lending Rate (Fgn.Currency)	60p. f														17.80	23.01
Prices, Production, Labor														*Index Numbers (1995=100):*		
Consumer Prices	64	—	—	—	—	—	—	—	—	—	—	—	—	.1	8.4	31.8
Crude Petroleum Production	66aa	154.3	166.8	160.4	141.9	143.6	122.5	114.5	98.4	84.1	78.2	86.3	78.1	73.7	70.0	62.0
															Number in Thousands:	
Labor Force	67d	. . . .	. . . .	. . . .	. . . .	. . . .	. . . .	. . . .	. . . .	. . . .	. . . .	. . . .	. . . .	. . . .	. . . .	. . . .
Employment	67e	. . . .	. . . .	. . . .	. . . .	. . . .	. . . .	. . . .	. . . .	. . . .	. . . .	. . . .	. . . .	. . . .	1,686	1,661
Unemployment	67c	. . . .	. . . .	. . . .	. . . .	. . . .	. . . .	. . . .	. . . .	. . . .	. . . .	. . . .	. . . .	. . . .	58	46
Unemployment Rate (%)	67r	. . . .	. . . .	. . . .	. . . .	. . . .	. . . .	. . . .	. . . .	. . . .	. . . .	. . . .	. . . .	. . . .	. . . .	. . . .
International Transactions														*Millions of US Dollars*		
Exports	70..d	201.2	260.5	556.5	444.1	568.2	631.7	628.8	759.8	942.2	912.4	827.7	755.2	724.5	623.4	637.8
Tin	70q.d	113.5	131.0	230.1	171.4	216.3	328.8	374.2	395.6	378.2	343.1	278.4	207.9	247.8	186.7	103.3
Zinc	70t.d	15.4	26.0	37.7	40.3	39.1	44.7	31.5	42.7	36.6	40.4	38.4	33.4	37.3	29.5	28.0
Imports, c.i.f.	71..d	185.4	230.2	390.0	557.9	554.6	617.9	807.8	894.3	665.4	917.1	554.1	576.7	488.5	690.9	674.0
Imports, f.o.b.	71.v d	142.8	194.0	364.0	531.5	562.3	644.0	689.8	673.6	574.4	827.7	496.0	496.0	412.3	565.1	564.0
															1995=100	
Volume of Exports	72	161.3	95.9	95.5	89.6	99.1	105.1	97.3	97.8	91.1	99.3	90.1	80.1	80.4	68.8	75.0
Tin	72q	213.0	199.5	203.4	175.0	200.9	218.4	208.9	186.9	158.2	170.3	153.8	112.7	142.4	113.4	118.2
Zinc	72t	27.1	33.8	33.4	33.8	33.6	41.8	35.5	36.8	31.5	30.5	30.4	28.2	25.1	23.1	24.3
															1995=100:	
Unit Value of Exports	74..d	17.8	49.5	81.8	82.9	88.9	102.0	110.8	144.4	206.0	196.3	186.3	196.7	193.8	178.5	143.7
Tin	74q.d	60.2	74.1	127.7	110.6	121.5	169.9	202.2	238.8	269.7	227.4	204.3	208.3	196.4	178.5	98.7
Zinc	74t.d	37.7	50.7	74.4	78.9	77.1	70.7	58.7	76.7	76.9	87.7	83.5	78.2	98.0	84.2	76.3

1987	1988	1989	1990	1991	1992	1993	1994	1995	1996	1997	1998	1999	2000	2001		

Millions of Bolivianos Beginning 1985; End of Period — **Other Banking Institutions**

1987	1988	1989	1990	1991	1992	1993	1994	1995	1996	1997	1998	1999	2000	2001		
†4	15	8	7	3	—	—	1	—	†160	192	80	84	135	178	Reserves	40
†14	10	3	6	1	—	—	—	—	†20	35	265	335	405	507	Foreign Assets	41
†—	—	—	1	1	2	3	3	3	†106	91	118	14	150	529	Claims on Central Government	42a
†—	—	—	—	—	—	—	—	—	†—	—	—	—	—	—	Claims on State and Local Govts	42b
†—	—	—	—	—	—	—	—	—	†—	—	—	—	—	—	Claims on Nonfin.Pub.Enterprises	42c
†290	309	318	390	390	393	389	349	386	†2,226	3,249	3,885	3,703	4,087	4,552	Claims on Private Sector	42d
†—	—	—	—	—	—	—	—	—	†—	—	140	86	346	414	Claims on Deposit Money Banks	42e
†—	—	—	—	—	—	—	—	—	†4	4	26	57	88	164	Claims on Nonbank Financial Insts	42g
†1	—	—	—	—	—	—	—	—	†—	1	1	1	11	4	Demand Deposits	44
†24	20	2	1	2	1	1	1	—	†2,305	3,185	3,693	3,480	4,132	5,132	Time, Savings,& Fgn.Currency Dep.	45
†23	20	2	1	2	1	1	1	—	†2,251	3,114	3,619	3,429	4,075	5,073	of which: Fgn. Currency Deposits	45b
†—	—	—	—	—	—	—	—	—	†—	—	—	—	—	208	Money Market Instruments	46aa
†10	12	—	5	—	—	—	—	—	†2	6	12	6	—	1	Foreign Liabilities	46c
†58	66	19	19	21	17	18	19	—	†11	7	34	74	106	101	Long-Term Foreign Liabilities	46cl
†6	7	6	2	1	1	1	1	—	†6	14	16	8	21	13	Central Government Deposits	46d
†26	33	61	92	112	307	292	272	548	†4	6	8	11	21	80	Credit from Monetary Authorities	46g
†—	—	—	—	—	—	—	—	—	†86	100	72	55	39	47	Credit from Deposit Money Banks	46h
†—	—	—	—	—	—	—	—	—	†245	303	294	301	299	325	Liabs. to Nonbank Financial Insts	46j
†328	366	325	434	257	73	34	21	−289	†447	579	775	819	986	1,188	Capital Accounts	47a
†−144	−169	−82	−149	2	−5	46	40	130	†−592	−630	−391	−476	−470	−756	Other Items (Net)	47r

Millions of Bolivianos Beginning 1985: End of Period — **Banking Survey**

1987	1988	1989	1990	1991	1992	1993	1994	1995	1996	1997	1998	1999	2000	2001		
†568	685	625	958	1,336	1,480	1,607	1,730	2,341	†4,175	4,456	5,928	7,713	9,825	12,945	Foreign Assets (Net)	51n
†1,384	2,017	3,188	4,734	6,631	9,450	14,211	17,269	16,930	†20,187	24,641	31,599	32,907	33,184	33,145	Domestic Credit	52
†−638	−563	−426	−241	−295	−237	2,158	2,452	1,160	†116	232	1,273	1,314	2,117	3,593	Claims on Central Govt. (Net)	52an
†76	89	111	125	129	150	20	18	—	†—	—	—	—	—	—	Claims on State and Local Govts	52b
†570	621	846	1,086	1,240	1,461	814	891	113	†119	5	1	2	2	39	Claims on Nonfin.Pub.Enterprises	52c
†1,376	1,852	2,629	3,710	5,483	7,992	11,128	13,801	15,538	†19,796	24,268	29,991	31,037	30,493	28,708	Claims on Private Sector	52d
†1	18	27	54	73	84	91	108	119	†157	135	335	554	572	806	Claims on Nonbank Financial Inst	52g
†1,596	2,032	2,471	3,778	5,694	7,661	10,243	12,723	13,697	†19,291	22,998	26,198	27,265	27,969	29,456	Liquid Liabilities	55l
†—	—	—	—	—	—	—	—	—	†—	—	70	68	959	1,784	Money Market Instruments	56aa
†803	996	1,295	1,392	1,634	2,029	2,087	2,587	2,947	†2,903	3,147	3,465	3,448	2,996	2,655	Long-Term Foreign Liabilities	56cl
†149	356	771	1,187	1,512	2,023	2,238	2,684	1,240	†1,081	919	989	999	972	936	Central Govt. Lending Funds	56f
†—	—	—	—	—	—	—	—	—	†245	613	813	1,195	1,227	2,394	Liab. to Nonbank Financial Insts	56j
†1,184	1,278	1,384	1,799	1,574	1,561	2,686	3,593	4,270	†3,856	4,842	7,885	9,303	10,619	12,166	Capital Accounts	57a
†−1,780	−1,959	−2,108	−2,464	−2,448	−2,344	−1,435	−2,588	−2,882	†−3,015	−3,422	−1,893	−1,658	−1,733	−3,301	Other Items (Net)	57r

Millions of Bolivianos Beginning 1985: End of Period — **Money (National Definitions)**

1987	1988	1989	1990	1991	1992	1993	1994	1995	1996	1997	1998	1999	2000	2001		
519	693	816	1,073	1,411	1,776	2,352	2,760	3,105	3,963	4,731	3,560	3,685	4,104	4,455	Reserve Money	19ma
506	663	647	830	1,039	1,236	1,417	1,890	2,333	2,580	3,006	3,276	3,153	3,356	3,815	M1	59ma
508	685	706	988	1,447	1,924	2,499	3,232	3,913	4,768	5,682	6,342	5,893	6,524	7,639	M'1	59mb
616	784	744	947	1,134	1,312	1,499	1,997	2,425	2,791	3,300	3,589	3,480	3,690	4,253	M2	59mc
619	826	904	1,358	1,956	2,646	3,544	4,534	5,460	8,028	10,163	11,533	11,212	12,719	15,381	M'2	59md
639	800	765	976	1,198	1,364	1,555	2,132	2,520	2,983	3,470	3,766	3,646	3,848	4,397	M3	59me
1,175	1,683	2,245	3,339	5,171	7,092	9,675	11,767	12,880	18,430	21,983	25,118	25,777	27,334	29,176	M'3	59mf
....	800	765	976	1,198	1,364	1,555	2,136	2,523	3,106	3,476	3,766	3,646	3,848	4,397	M4	59mg
....	1,683	2,245	3,339	5,171	7,092	9,675	12,036	13,330	18,948	22,353	25,552	26,162	27,974	31,342	M'4	59mh

Percent Per Annum — **Interest Rates**

1987	1988	1989	1990	1991	1992	1993	1994	1995	1996	1997	1998	1999	2000	2001		
....	....	....	....	....	....	....	....	....	....	16.50	13.25	14.10	12.50	10.00	8.50	Discount Rate (End of Period)	60
....	....	....	....	....	....	....	....	....	....	9.89	8.58	9.30	9.04	7.41	5.69	Discount Rate (Fgn.Cur.)(End per)	60.. f
....	....	....	....	....	....	....	....	22.42	20.27	13.97	12.57	13.49	7.40	6.99	Money Market Rate	60b
....	....	....	....	....	....	....	....	14.16	9.54	7.85	9.26	8.29	5.68	3.57	Money Market Rate (Fgn. Cur.)	60b. f
....	....	....	....	....	....	....	17.89	24.51	19.93	13.65	12.33	14.07	10.99	11.48	Treasury Bill Rate	60c
....	....	....	....	....	....	....	8.22	13.20	9.89	7.15	7.48	7.84	7.02	4.19	Treasury Bill Rate (Fgn.Currency)	60c. f
24.69	22.76	19.04	18.67	18.65	20.28	20.92	17.46	16.52	16.43	14.30	12.08	10.79	9.39	6.57	Savings Rate	60k
....	7.23	7.42	8.48	8.35	8.14	7.97	7.16	7.03	7.20	6.60	5.93	5.50	4.76	2.68	Savings Rate (Fgn.Currency)	60k. f
30.35	27.74	23.67	23.83	23.78	23.22	22.18	18.43	18.87	19.16	14.73	12.82	12.26	10.98	9.82	Deposit Rate	60l
16.33	16.70	15.69	14.70	12.40	11.40	11.19	9.89	10.36	10.13	8.32	7.96	8.78	7.84	5.21	Deposit Rate (Fgn.Currency)	60l. f
49.41	39.79	37.27	41.81	41.15	45.51	53.88	55.57	51.02	55.97	50.05	39.41	35.37	34.60	20.06	Lending Rate	60p
26.75	25.67	24.34	23.03	21.51	19.13	18.46	16.46	16.86	17.64	16.48	15.66	16.03	15.68	14.46	Lending Rate (Fgn.Currency)	60p. f

Period Averages — **Prices, Production, Labor**

1987	1988	1989	1990	1991	1992	1993	1994	1995	1996	1997	1998	1999	2000	2001		
36.4	42.2	48.6	57.0	69.2	†77.5	84.1	90.8	100.0	112.4	117.7	126.8	129.5	135.5	137.6	Consumer Prices	64
66.6	67.8	70.3	73.8	78.2	74.9	78.4	90.7	100.0	103.2	107.5	133.0	114.5	111.1	126.3	Crude Petroleum Production	66aa

Period Averages

1987	1988	1989	1990	1991	1992	1993	1994	1995	1996	1997	1998	1999	2000	2001		
....	....	....	....	....	2,365	....	....	....	1,369	3,645	....	....	3,824	....	Labor Force	67d
1,670	1,769	1,662	1,843	†988	1,016	1,091	1,195	1,257	†1,849	1,878	....	2,017	2,096	....	Employment	67e
78	....	†95	72	62	59	70	39	47	†74	71	....	157	168	....	Unemployment	67c
....	....	10.0	7.3	5.9	5.5	6.0	3.1	3.6	†3.8	3.7	....	7.2	7.4	....	Unemployment Rate (%)	67r

Millions of US Dollars — **International Transactions**

1987	1988	1989	1990	1991	1992	1993	1994	1995	1996	1997	1998	1999	2000	2001		
569.5	600.2	821.8	926.1	848.6	710.1	727.5	1,032.4	1,100.7	1,137.1	1,166.5	1,103.9	1,051.2	1,229.5	1,284.8	Exports	70..d
68.9	76.9	126.5	106.5	99.7	107.3	83.3	91.1	88.6	85.5	75.1	59.9	65.3	70.5	52.6	Tin	70q.d
32.7	60.2	132.2	146.0	139.7	173.0	119.5	105.3	151.3	153.4	119.3	92.3	91.4	101.3	71.6	Zinc	70t.d
766.3	590.5	610.9	687.2	969.5	1,090.3	1,205.9	1,209.0	1,423.8	1,635.0	1,850.9	1,983.0	1,755.1	1,829.7	1,724.3	Imports, c.i.f.	71..d
646.3	495.1	563.1	633.5	893.7	1,005.0	1,111.6	1,121.7	1,263.2	1,450.5	1,698.1	1,824.4	1,539.1	1,604.5	1,512.1	Imports, f.o.b.	71.v d

1995=100

1987	1988	1989	1990	1991	1992	1993	1994	1995	1996	1997	1998	1999	2000	2001		
66.6	72.3	90.7	99.2	106.8	107.7	95.1	93.2	100.0	102.4	107.2	102.1	93.4	106.1	112.7	Volume of Exports	72
71.0	75.9	102.3	119.1	125.4	123.9	112.4	118.5	100.0	98.5	101.0	80.2	90.3	98.0	76.8	Tin	72q
27.0	36.8	54.9	67.3	87.1	97.1	84.4	73.1	100.0	103.3	104.9	104.4	98.8	102.7	89.5	Zinc	72t

Indices of Unit Values in US Dollars

1987	1988	1989	1990	1991	1992	1993	1994	1995	1996	1997	1998	1999	2000	2001		
135.3	135.6	157.9	143.0	127.7	108.3	89.1	94.8	100.0	98.5	75.2	67.3	66.1	83.3	78.6	Unit Value of Exports	74..d
109.5	114.3	139.6	100.9	89.7	97.8	83.6	86.8	100.0	98.0	83.9	84.3	81.6	81.2	77.3	Tin	74q.d
79.9	108.0	159.1	143.3	106.0	117.8	93.5	95.2	100.0	98.1	75.1	58.4	61.1	65.1	52.8	Zinc	74t.d

Bolivia

	1972	1973	1974	1975	1976	1977	1978	1979	1980	1981	1982	1983	1984	1985	1986
Balance of Payments														*Millions of US Dollars:*	
Current Account, n.i.e. .... 78al *d*	....	....	....	....	−53.5	−117.9	−331.5	−397.0	−6.4	−468.5	−174.4	−141.6	−178.5	−285.8	−388.9
Goods: Exports f.o.b. .... 78aa *d*					563.0	634.3	627.3	759.8	942.2	912.4	827.7	755.1	724.5	623.4	545.5
Goods: Imports f.o.b. .... 78ab *d*					−512.3	−579.0	−723.9	−738.4	−574.4	−827.7	−496.0	−496.0	−412.3	−462.8	−596.5
Trade Balance .... 78ac *d*					50.7	55.3	−96.6	21.4	367.8	84.7	331.7	259.1	312.2	160.6	−51.0
Services: Credit .... 78ad *d*					60.4	60.8	76.2	105.2	87.9	93.0	82.3	103.0	93.5	96.5	121.1
Services: Debit .... 78ae *d*					−147.1	−181.9	−224.2	−392.5	−258.5	−319.8	−221.7	−244.6	−253.5	−246.1	−245.8
Balance on Goods & Services ... 78af *d*					−36.0	−65.8	−244.6	−265.9	197.2	−142.1	192.3	117.5	152.2	11.0	−175.7
Income: Credit .... 78ag *d*					12.8	5.6	2.5	8.4	15.6	16.2	8.4	40.9	30.0	17.5	17.6
Income: Debit .... 78ah *d*					−44.3	−72.7	−116.4	−190.7	−278.7	−378.4	−419.1	−402.7	−444.9	−390.4	−326.1
Balance on Gds, Serv. & Inc. ... 78ai *d*					−67.5	−132.9	−358.5	−448.2	−65.9	−504.3	−218.4	−244.3	−262.7	−361.9	−484.2
Current Transfers, n.i.e.: Credit .... 78aj *d*					16.0	18.0	30.0	53.0	62.0	38.0	46.2	106.8	87.0	80.3	97.0
Current Transfers: Debit .... 78ak *d*					−2.0	−3.0	−3.0	−1.8	−2.5	−2.2	−2.2	−4.1	−2.8	−4.2	−1.7
Capital Account, n.i.e. .... 78bc *d*					—	—	—	—	—	2.8	.7	2.7	3.6	3.4	4.7
Capital Account, n.i.e.: Credit .... 78ba *d*					—	—	—	—	—	3.0	1.0	3.0	3.8	4.2	5.0
Capital Account: Debit .... 78bb *d*					—	—	—	—	—	−.2	−.3	−.3	−.2	−.8	−.3
Financial Account, n.i.e. .... 78bj *d*	....	....	....	....	168.1	227.3	350.4	301.9	27.2	438.5	−49.4	−554.0	29.0	−285.7	−95.7
Direct Investment Abroad .... 78bd *d*					—	—	—	—	−.5	−.1	−.1	−.1	—	—	—
Dir. Invest. in Rep. Econ., n.i.e. ...... 78be *d*					−8.1	−1.2	11.5	67.0	91.0	148.9	61.2	13.0	13.0	19.0	20.0
Portfolio Investment Assets .... 78bf *d*					—	—	—	2.5	−2.6	—	—	—	—	—	—
Equity Securities..................... 78bk *d*					—	—	—	2.5	−2.6	—	—	—	—	—	—
Debt Securities .... 78bl *d*					—	—	—	—	—	—	—	—	—	—	—
Portfolio Investment Liab., n.i.e. .. 78bg *d*					—	—	—	−1.1	−.9	−.9	−15.0	−1.8	−.9	−.9	—
Equity Securities..................... 78bm *d*					—	—	—	—	—	—	—	—	—	—	—
Debt Securities .... 78bn *d*					—	—	—	−1.1	−.9	−.9	−15.0	−1.8	−.9	−.9	—
Financial Derivatives Assets .... 78bw *d*															
Financial Derivatives Liabilities ...... 78bx *d*	....	....		....		....		....	....		....		....		....
Other Investment Assets .... 78bh *d*	....	....			−20.1	−135.1	−63.7	−8.8	−15.3	−4.0	−156.4	−101.5	178.6	15.2	112.2
Monetary Authorities.................. 78bo *d*															
General Government .... 78bp *d*					−2.1	−10.0	−9.1	−3.1	−1.6	−10.6	−28.4	−4.1	−6.6	−5.5	−12.6
Banks .... 78bq *d*					−6.0	−2.1	−4.6	−5.7	−13.7	6.6	19.3	.9	−3.3	−2.5	—
Other Sectors .... 78br *d*					−12.0	−123.0	−50.0	—	—	—	−147.3	−98.3	188.5	23.2	124.8
Other Investment Liab., n.i.e. .... 78bi *d*					196.3	363.6	402.6	242.3	−44.5	294.6	60.9	−463.6	−161.7	−319.0	−227.9
Monetary Authorities.................. 78bs *d*					−11.0	3.5	−15.3	67.6	−2.5	214.0	153.3	−239.1	−16.2	−108.8	−31.5
General Government .... 78bt *d*					148.5	180.5	103.4	81.7	66.9	78.5	−43.0	−118.1	−119.9	−141.6	−170.7
Banks .... 78bu *d*					1.0	40.1	55.2	59.7	−59.7	7.8	−25.1	−32.1	5.0	−32.8	−25.7
Other Sectors .... 78bv *d*					57.8	139.5	259.3	33.3	−49.2	−5.7	−24.3	−74.3	−30.6	−35.8	—
Net Errors and Omissions.................. 78ca *d*					−63.4	−79.0	−84.9	−36.1	−456.0	−260.3	4.1	65.5	−18.1	181.0	126.3
Overall Balance .... 78cb *d*					51.2	30.4	−66.0	−131.2	−435.2	−287.5	−219.0	−627.4	−164.0	−387.1	−353.6
Reserves and Related Items .... 79da *d*					−51.2	−30.4	66.0	131.2	435.2	287.5	219.0	627.4	164.0	387.1	353.6
Reserve Assets .... 79db *d*					−35.1	−67.4	64.8	−18.5	96.1	—	−46.5	−49.3	−95.0	58.0	−214.5
Use of Fund Credit and Loans .... 79dc *d*					−16.1	—	38.2	—	89.5	−2.0	18.6	8.3	−24.0	−23.5	99.8
Exceptional Financing .... 79de *d*					—	37.0	−37.0	149.7	249.7	289.6	246.9	668.4	282.9	352.6	468.3
International Investment Position														*Millions of US Dollars*	
Assets .... 79aa *d*															
Direct Investment Abroad .... 79ab *d*															
Portfolio Investment .... 79ac *d*															
Equity Securities..................... 79ad *d*															
Debt Securities .... 79ae *d*															
Financial Derivatives .... 79al *d*															
Other Investment .... 79af *d*															
Monetary Authorities.................. 79ag *d*															
General Government .... 79ah *d*															
Banks .... 79ai *d*															
Other Sectors .... 79aj *d*															
Reserve Assets .... 79ak *d*															
Liabilities .... 79la *d*															
Dir. Invest. in Rep. Economy........... 79lb *d*															
Portfolio Investment .... 79lc *d*															
Equity Securities..................... 79ld *d*															
Debt Securities .... 79le *d*															
Financial Derivatives .... 79ll *d*															
Other Investment .... 79lf *d*															
Monetary Authorities.................. 79lg *d*															
General Government .... 79lh *d*															
Banks .... 79li *d*															
Other Sectors .... 79lj *d*															
Government Finance										*Bolivianos through 1982; Thousands from 1983 to 1984;*					
Deficit (-) or Surplus..................... 80	−595	−873	−455	−707	−1,399	−3,313	−3,002	−6,651	−9,729	−10,217	−110,959	†−309	−7,661	†−1,182	−126
Revenue 81	1,389	2,479	5,070	5,689	6,841	7,641	8,540	8,384	11,793	14,069	19,316	†47	560	†202	841
Grants Received 81z	34	18													
Expenditure 82	2,019	3,370	5,525	6,395	8,240	10,954	11,542	15,035	21,522	24,286	130,275	†356	8,221	†1,384	967
Financing															
Domestic 84a	434	357													
Foreign.................................. 85a	161	516													
National Accounts										*Bolivianos through 1982; Thousands from 1983 to 1984;*					
Househ.Cons.Expend.,incl.NPISHs 96f	12,376	18,081	28,928	34,244	39,056	44,940	52,700	60,700	82,300	100,000	270,000	†970	12,930	†1,793	6,214
Government Consumption Expend......... 91f	1,920	2,814	4,461	5,699	6,700	8,559	9,500	13,600	15,900	20,000	40,000	†110	4,700	†238	719
Gross Fixed Capital Formation 93e	2,623	4,519	6,550	9,055	10,685	12,414	16,400	17,400	17,500	20,000	50,000	†160	2,260	†336	1,018
Changes in Inventories 93i	797	878	558	2,971	1,264	1,149	2,200	1,400	500	—	—	†10	−50	†148	13
Exports of Goods and Services 90c	2,963	5,878	12,448	10,474	12,698	14,512	17,000	21,800	31,500	40,000	140,000	†430	2,910	†830	1,623
Imports of Goods and Services (-) 98c	3,430	6,114	9,620	13,242	13,956	16,354	22,600	24,700	24,800	30,000	100,000	†300	1,860	†479	1,956
Gross Domestic Product (GDP) 99b	17,249	26,056	43,325	49,201	56,447	65,220	75,200	90,200	122,900	150,000	400,000	†1,390	20,900	†2,867	7,610
Net Primary Income from Abroad 98.n	−309	−488	−822	−792	−896	−1,684	−2,334	−3,572							
Gross National Income (GNI) 99a	16,940	25,568	42,503	48,409	55,551	63,536	72,900	86,600							
GDP Volume 1970 prices(Bolivianos) . 99b. *p*	13,729	14,646	15,400	16,417	17,418	18,151	18,760	19,104	19,212						
GDP Volume 1990 Prices(millions) ..... 99b. *p*	....	....	....	....	....	....	....	....	15,261	15,303	14,701	14,106	14,078	13,842	13,486
GDP Volume (1995=100) .... 99bv *p*	57.8	61.6	64.8	69.1	73.3	76.4	78.9	80.4	80.8	81.1	77.9	74.7	74.6	73.3	71.4
GDP Deflator (1995=10 Billions) .... 99bi *p*	9,262	13,116	20,740	22,094	23,891	26,490	29,552	34,808	47,160	57,401	159,346	577,054	....	....	....
GDP Deflator (1995=100) .... 99bi *p*	—	—	—	—	—	—	—	—	—	—	—	.01	.09	12.13	33.05
Population............................ 99z	4.64	4.67	4.75	†4.89	5.03	5.16	5.30	5.45	5.60	5.76	5.92	6.08	†5.78	5.90	*Millions:* 6.02

Item	1987	1988	1989	1990	1991	1992	1993	1994	1995	1996	1997	1998	1999	2000	2001	Code
Minus Sign Indicates Debit — Balance of Payments																
Current Account, n.i.e.	-432.3	-304.4	-270.1	-198.9	-262.6	-533.9	-505.5	-90.2	-302.5	-404.3	-553.5	-678.1	-488.0	-464.2	....	**78al *d***
Goods: Exports f.o.b.	518.7	542.5	723.5	830.8	760.3	608.4	715.5	985.1	1,041.4	1,132.0	1,166.6	1,104.0	1,051.2	1,229.6	....	**78aa *d***
Goods: Imports f.o.b.	-646.3	-590.9	-729.5	-775.6	-804.2	-1,040.8	-1,111.7	-1,015.3	-1,223.7	-1,368.0	-1,643.6	-1,759.4	-1,539.0	-1,610.1	....	**78ab *d***
Trade Balance	-127.6	-48.4	-6.0	55.2	-43.9	-432.4	-396.2	-30.2	-182.3	-236.0	-477.0	-655.4	-487.8	-380.5	....	**78ac *d***
Services: Credit	131.5	128.3	143.3	145.9	157.0	164.6	181.4	196.0	192.4	180.9	247.2	251.0	259.4	224.1	....	**78ad *d***
Services: Debit	-270.2	-254.8	-298.2	-310.6	-311.2	-311.0	-321.7	-337.5	-350.2	-363.4	-418.7	-441.3	-449.7	-468.1	....	**78ae *d***
Balance on Goods & Services	-266.3	-174.9	-160.9	-109.5	-198.1	-578.8	-536.5	-171.7	-340.1	-418.5	-648.5	-845.7	-678.1	-624.5	....	**78af *d***
Income: Credit	16.2	18.2	23.9	18.8	24.6	17.7	9.2	18.7	28.3	28.6	98.2	127.0	157.3	139.4	....	**78ag *d***
Income: Debit	-293.9	-283.0	-283.0	-267.4	-271.6	-215.4	-215.1	-201.2	-234.9	-236.8	-294.7	-289.3	-353.3	-364.0	....	**78ah *d***
Balance on Gds, Serv. & Inc.	-544.0	-439.7	-420.0	-358.1	-445.1	-776.5	-742.4	-354.2	-546.7	-626.7	-845.0	-1,008.0	-874.1	-849.1	....	**78ai *d***
Current Transfers, n.i.e.: Credit	113.9	140.0	152.5	161.2	185.8	246.3	241.0	269.2	248.0	226.2	300.3	341.6	414.7	418.1	....	**78aj *d***
Current Transfers: Debit	-2.2	-4.7	-2.6	-2.0	-3.3	-3.7	-4.1	-5.2	-3.8	-3.8	-8.8	-11.7	-28.6	-33.2	....	**78ak *d***
Capital Account, n.i.e.	5.5	1.3	5.9	.8	.5	.6	1.0	1.2	2.0	2.8	25.3	9.9	—	—	....	**78bc *d***
Capital Account, n.i.e.: Credit	5.5	1.3	5.9	.8	.5	.6	1.0	1.2	2.0	2.8	25.3	9.9	—	—	....	**78ba *d***
Capital Account: Debit	—	—	—	—	—	—	—	—	—	—	—	—	—	—	....	**78bb *d***
Financial Account, n.i.e.	-155.5	-37.1	-7.7	48.1	61.7	367.4	347.1	315.3	505.2	701.0	889.8	1,083.3	751.8	508.4	....	**78bj *d***
Direct Investment Abroad	-1.7	-1.9	-1.0	-1.1	-2.0	-2.0	-2.0	-2.2	-2.0	-2.1	-2.5	-2.5	-2.4	-2.4	....	**78bd *d***
Dir. Invest. in Rep. Econ., n.i.e.	67.8	-10.1	-24.4	27.2	52.0	93.1	123.8	130.2	392.7	474.1	730.6	957.3	1,016.5	733.2	....	**78be *d***
Portfolio Investment Assets	—	—	—	—	—	—	—	—	—	.3	-53.2	-74.5	-44.4	55.4	....	**78bf *d***
Equity Securities	—	—	—	—	—	—	—	—	—	—	—	—	—	—	....	**78bk *d***
Debt Securities	—	—	—	—	—	—	—	—	—	.3	-53.2	-74.5	-44.4	55.4	....	**78bl *d***
Portfolio Investment Liab., n.i.e.	—	—	—	—	—	—	—	—	—	—	—	—	-16.9	—	....	**78bg *d***
Equity Securities	—	—	—	—	—	—	—	—	—	—	—	—	—	—	....	**78bm *d***
Debt Securities	—	—	—	—	—	—	—	—	—	—	—	—	-16.9	—	....	**78bn *d***
Financial Derivatives Assets	....	....	....	....	....	....	....	....	....	....	—	—	....	....	....	**78bw *d***
Financial Derivatives Liabilities	....	....	....	....	....	....	....	....	....	....	—	—	....	....	....	**78bx *d***
Other Investment Assets	-98.7	-85.5	-161.8	-32.1	-16.3	-13.0	17.1	-104.0	-38.4	12.2	-19.9	-111.4	-168.3	-90.3	....	**78bh *d***
Monetary Authorities	....	....	....	....	....	....	....	....	....	....	—	—	—	—	....	**78bo *d***
General Government	-8.8	-2.4	-23.0	-7.4	-9.3	-6.4	-6.1	—	—	-.2	—	—	—	—	....	**78bp *d***
Banks	6.4	-2.2	-10.9	3.0	-3.4	-14.3	-6.4	-104.0	-38.4	12.4	-19.9	66.1	-24.1	-85.3	....	**78bq *d***
Other Sectors	-96.3	-80.9	-127.9	-27.7	-3.6	7.7	29.6	—	—	—	—	-177.5	-144.2	-5.0	....	**78br *d***
Other Investment Liab., n.i.e.	-122.9	60.4	179.5	54.1	28.0	289.3	208.2	291.3	152.9	216.5	234.8	314.4	-32.7	-187.5	....	**78bi *d***
Monetary Authorities	7.5	81.4	216.3	28.8	8.6	75.2	42.5	40.8	78.0	11.7	1.5	-46.0	-14.2	-21.6	....	**78bs *d***
General Government	-132.1	2.2	-3.3	-60.2	-77.6	-42.6	-23.7	-16.9	-41.0	206.9	199.7	138.6	123.1	131.4	....	**78bt *d***
Banks	-11.4	-44.7	-42.7	30.2	32.9	86.5	124.4	206.3	78.8	2.8	169.7	142.7	-134.5	-283.0	....	**78bu *d***
Other Sectors	13.1	21.5	9.2	55.3	64.1	170.2	65.0	61.1	37.1	-4.9	-136.1	79.1	-7.1	-14.3	....	**78bv *d***
Net Errors and Omissions	144.9	46.6	-32.1	-11.4	53.2	34.3	123.6	-315.8	-112.3	-31.6	-260.6	-314.2	-236.8	-84.3	....	**78ca *d***
Overall Balance	-437.4	-293.6	-304.0	-161.4	-147.2	-131.6	-33.7	-89.5	92.4	268.0	101.0	100.9	26.9	-40.1	....	**78cb *d***
Reserves and Related Items	437.4	293.6	304.0	161.4	147.2	131.6	33.7	89.5	-92.4	-268.0	-101.0	-100.9	-26.9	40.1	....	**79da *d***
Reserve Assets	82.0	12.8	57.3	-5.0	-8.4	-41.2	-81.7	-26.4	-147.4	-310.1	-89.6	-133.2	-31.9	38.8	....	**79db *d***
Use of Fund Credit and Loans	-33.6	30.5	47.5	-13.2	-13.9	14.7	-28.7	28.7	-1.1	17.1	-11.4	5.7	-10.9	-14.5	....	**79dc *d***
Exceptional Financing	389.0	250.2	199.2	179.5	169.5	158.1	144.2	87.3	56.1	25.1	—	26.7	15.9	15.8	....	**79de *d***
Millions of US Dollars — International Investment Position																
Assets	....	....	....	....	....	....	....	....	....	....	1,996.1	2,516.2	2,680.6	2,618.1	....	**79aa *d***
Direct Investment Abroad	....	....	....	....	....	....	....	....	....	....	21.9	25.0	27.0	30.0	....	**79ab *d***
Portfolio Investment	....	....	....	....	....	....	....	....	....	....	60.0	689.0	734.0	678.0	....	**79ac *d***
Equity Securities	....	....	....	....	....	....	....	....	....	....	60.0	—	—	—	....	**79ad *d***
Debt Securities	....	....	....	....	....	....	....	....	....	....	—	689.0	734.0	678.0	....	**79ae *d***
Financial Derivatives	....	....	....	....	....	....	....	....	....	....	—	—	—	—	....	**79al *d***
Other Investment	....	....	....	....	....	....	....	....	....	....	599.9	475.0	558.0	605.0	....	**79af *d***
Monetary Authorities	....	....	....	....	....	....	....	....	....	....	121.2	121.0	123.0	124.0	....	**79ag *d***
General Government	....	....	....	....	....	....	....	....	....	....	—	—	—	—	....	**79ah *d***
Banks	....	....	....	....	....	....	....	....	....	....	128.7	142.0	166.0	250.0	....	**79ai *d***
Other Sectors	....	....	....	....	....	....	....	....	....	....	350.0	212.0	269.0	231.0	....	**79aj *d***
Reserve Assets	....	....	....	....	....	....	....	....	....	....	1,314.3	1,327.2	1,361.6	1,305.1	....	**79ak *d***
Liabilities	....	....	....	....	....	....	....	....	....	....	7,739.4	9,174.2	9,950.0	10,200.9	....	**79la *d***
Dir. Invest. in Rep. Economy	....	....	....	....	....	....	....	....	....	....	2,414.7	3,372.0	4,389.0	5,052.0	....	**79lb *d***
Portfolio Investment	....	....	....	....	....	....	....	....	....	....	15.1	37.0	20.0	20.0	....	**79lc *d***
Equity Securities	....	....	....	....	....	....	....	....	....	....	—	—	—	—	....	**79ld *d***
Debt Securities	....	....	....	....	....	....	....	....	....	....	15.1	37.0	20.0	20.0	....	**79le *d***
Financial Derivatives	....	....	....	....	....	....	....	....	....	....	—	—	—	—	....	**79ll *d***
Other Investment	....	....	....	....	....	....	....	....	....	....	5,309.6	5,765.2	5,541.0	5,128.9	....	**79lf *d***
Monetary Authorities	....	....	....	....	....	....	....	....	....	....	733.4	707.2	668.0	597.9	....	**79lg *d***
General Government	....	....	....	....	....	....	....	....	....	....	3,118.4	3,366.0	3,403.0	3,381.0	....	**79lh *d***
Banks	....	....	....	....	....	....	....	....	....	....	845.4	880.0	743.0	459.0	....	**79li *d***
Other Sectors	....	....	....	....	....	....	....	....	....	....	612.4	812.0	727.0	691.0	....	**79lj *d***
Millions of Bolivianos Beginning 1985: Year Ending December 31 — **Government Finance**																
Deficit (-) or Surplus	-32	-45	....	....	....	....	†-1,161	-902	-697	-869	-1,783	-1,917	-1,969	-2,317	-3,915	**80**
Revenue	1,027	1,247	....	....	....	....	†5,273	6,532	7,687	9,014	9,884	11,699	12,131	13,048	12,906	**81**
Grants Received	....	....	....	....	....	....	....	....	....	....	....	....	....	....	....	**81z**
Expenditure	1,058	1,293	....	....	....	....	†6,434	7,434	8,384	9,883	11,667	13,615	14,100	15,365	16,821	**82**
Financing																
Domestic	....	....	....	....	....	....	†259	165	-327	-355	602	646	860	1,314	2,373	**84a**
Foreign	....	....	....	....	....	....	†903	737	1,024	1,224	1,181	1,271	1,109	1,003	1,543	**85a**
Millions of Bolivianos Beginning 1985 — **National Accounts**																
Househ.Cons.Expend.,incl.NPISHs	7,440	8,537	9,791	11,870	14,891	17,489	19,413	21,444	24,440	28,201	31,113	35,144	37,002	40,009 p	41,292 p	**96f**
Government Consumption Expend.	994	1,230	1,516	1,815	2,310	2,833	3,270	3,750	4,375	5,003	5,790	6,658	7,026	7,412 p	7,769 p	**91f**
Gross Fixed Capital Formation	1,080	1,372	1,522	1,939	2,771	3,592	4,076	4,104	5,007	6,072	7,899	10,841	9,197	9,112 p	7,427 p	**93e**
Changes in Inventories	127	138	-51	-4	209	86	-25	-133	-93	23	276	212	-157	-219 p	-599 p	**93i**
Exports of Goods and Services	1,754	2,028	2,856	3,517	4,109	4,413	4,667	5,987	7,270	8,476	8,791	9,223	8,129	9,174 p	9,658 p	**90c**
Imports of Goods and Services (-)	2,144	2,500	2,939	3,695	5,159	6,398	6,943	7,516	8,764	10,238	12,226	15,256	13,141	13,820 p	12,895 p	**98c**
Gross Domestic Product (GDP)	8,934	10,806	12,694	15,443	19,132	22,014	24,459	27,636	32,235	37,537	41,644	46,822	48,156	51,668 p	52,652 p	**99b**
Net Primary Income from Abroad	....	....	....	....	....	....	....	....	....	....	....	....	....	....	....	**98.n**
Gross National Income (GNI)	....	....	....	....	....	....	....	....	....	....	....	....	....	....	....	**99a**
GDP Volume 1970 prices(Bolivianos)	....	....	....	....	....	....	....	....	....	....	....	....	....	....	....	**99b.*p***
GDP Volume 1990 Prices(millions)	13,818	14,220	14,759	15,443	16,257	16,524	17,230	18,034	18,877	19,701	20,677	21,717	21,809	22,325 p	22,599 p	**99b.*p***
GDP Volume (1995=100)	73.2	75.3	78.2	81.8	86.1	87.5	91.3	95.5	100.0	104.4	109.5	115.0	115.5	118.3 p	119.7 p	**99bv *p***
GDP Deflator (1995=10 Billions)	....	....	....	....	....	....	....	....	....	....	....	....	....	....	....	**99bi *p***
GDP Deflator (1995=100)	37.86	44.50	50.37	58.56	68.92	78.02	83.13	89.74	100.00	111.58	117.94	126.26	129.31	135.53 p	136.44 p	**99bi *p***
Midyear Estimates																
Population	6.16	6.29	6.43	6.57	6.73	6.90	7.07	7.24	7.41	7.59	7.77	7.95	8.14	8.33	8.27	**99z**

(See notes in the back of the book.)

Bosnia & Herzegovina

		1972	1973	1974	1975	1976	1977	1978	1979	1980	1981	1982	1983	1984	1985	1986
Exchange Rates															*Convertible Marka per SDR:*	
Official Rate	aa	....	....	....	....	....	....	....	....	....	....	....	....	....	....	....
															Convertible Marka per US Dollar:	
Official Rate	ae	....	....	....	....	....	....	....	....	....	....	....	....	....	....	....
Official Rate	rf	....	....	....	....	....	....	....	....	....	....	....	....	....	....	....
Fund Position															*Millions of SDRs:*	
Quota	2f. *s*	....	....	....	....	....	....	....	....	....	....	....	....	....	....	....
SDRs	1b. *s*	....	....	....	....	....	....	....	....	....	....	....	....	....	....	....
Reserve Position in the Fund	1c. *s*	....	....	....	....	....	....	....	....	....	....	....	....	....	....	....
Total Fund Cred.&Loans Outstg.	2tl	....	....	....	....	....	....	....	....	....	....	....	....	....	....	....
International Liquidity													*Millions of US Dollars Unless Otherwise Indicated:*			
Total Reserves minus Gold	1l. *d*	....	....	....	....	....	....	....	....	....	....	....	....	....	....	....
SDRs	1b. *d*	....	....	....	....	....	....	....	....	....	....	....	....	....	....	....
Reserve Position in the Fund	1c. *d*	....	....	....	....	....	....	....	....	....	....	....	....	....	....	....
Foreign Exchange	1d. *d*	....	....	....	....	....	....	....	....	....	....	....	....	....	....	....
Monetary Authorities															*Millions of Convertible Marka*	
Foreign Assets	11	....	....	....	....	....	....	....	....	....	....	....	....	....	....	....
Reserve Money	14	....	....	....	....	....	....	....	....	....	....	....	....	....	....	....
of which: Currency Outside Banks	14a	....	....	....	....	....	....	....	....	....	....	....	....	....	....	....
Foreign Liabilities	16c	....	....	....	....	....	....	....	....	....	....	....	....	....	....	....
Central Government Deposits	16d	....	....	....	....	....	....	....	....	....	....	....	....	....	....	....
Capital Accounts	17a	....	....	....	....	....	....	....	....	....	....	....	....	....	....	....
Other Items (Net)	17r	....	....	....	....	....	....	....	....	....	....	....	....	....	....	....
Deposit Money Banks															*Millions of Convertible Marka*	
Reserves	20	....	....	....	....	....	....	....	....	....	....	....	....	....	....	....
Foreign Assets	21	....	....	....	....	....	....	....	....	....	....	....	....	....	....	....
Claims on Central Government	22a	....	....	....	....	....	....	....	....	....	....	....	....	....	....	....
Claims on State Government	22ab	....	....	....	....	....	....	....	....	....	....	....	....	....	....	....
Claims on Local Government	22b	....	....	....	....	....	....	....	....	....	....	....	....	....	....	....
Claims on Other Resident Sectors	22d	....	....	....	....	....	....	....	....	....	....	....	....	....	....	....
Demand Deposits	24	....	....	....	....	....	....	....	....	....	....	....	....	....	....	....
Time & Savings Deposits	25a	....	....	....	....	....	....	....	....	....	....	....	....	....	....	....
Foreign Currency Deposits	25b	....	....	....	....	....	....	....	....	....	....	....	....	....	....	....
Bonds	26ab	....	....	....	....	....	....	....	....	....	....	....	....	....	....	....
Foreign Liabilities	26c	....	....	....	....	....	....	....	....	....	....	....	....	....	....	....
Long-Term Foreign Liabilities	26cl	....	....	....	....	....	....	....	....	....	....	....	....	....	....	....
Central Government Deposits	26d	....	....	....	....	....	....	....	....	....	....	....	....	....	....	....
State Government Deposits	26da	....	....	....	....	....	....	....	....	....	....	....	....	....	....	....
Capital Accounts	27a	....	....	....	....	....	....	....	....	....	....	....	....	....	....	....
Other Items (Net)	27r	....	....	....	....	....	....	....	....	....	....	....	....	....	....	....
Monetary Survey															*Millions of Convertible Marka*	
Foreign Assets (Net)	31n	....	....	....	....	....	....	....	....	....	....	....	....	....	....	....
Domestic Credit	32	....	....	....	....	....	....	....	....	....	....	....	....	....	....	....
Claims on Central Govt. (Net)	32an	....	....	....	....	....	....	....	....	....	....	....	....	....	....	....
Claims on State Government	32ab	....	....	....	....	....	....	....	....	....	....	....	....	....	....	....
Claims on Local Government	32b	....	....	....	....	....	....	....	....	....	....	....	....	....	....	....
Claims on Other Resident Sectors	32d	....	....	....	....	....	....	....	....	....	....	....	....	....	....	....
Money	34	....	....	....	....	....	....	....	....	....	....	....	....	....	....	....
Quasi-Money	35	....	....	....	....	....	....	....	....	....	....	....	....	....	....	....
Bonds	36ab	....	....	....	....	....	....	....	....	....	....	....	....	....	....	....
Capital Accounts	37a	....	....	....	....	....	....	....	....	....	....	....	....	....	....	....
Other Items (Net)	37r	....	....	....	....	....	....	....	....	....	....	....	....	....	....	....
Money plus Quasi-Money	35l	....	....	....	....	....	....	....	....	....	....	....	....	....	....	....
Interest Rates															*Percent Per Annum*	
Deposit Rate	60l	....	....	....	....	....	....	....	....	....	....	....	....	....	....	....
Lending Rate	60p	....	....	....	....	....	....	....	....	....	....	....	....	....	....	....

1987	1988	1989	1990	1991	1992	1993	1994	1995	1996	1997	1998	1999	2000	2001		
End of Period															**Exchange Rates**	
End of Period (ae) Period Average (rf)			....	....	....	....	....	....	....	2.418	2.356	2.672	2.739	2.789	Official Rate..	**aa**
....	....	....	....	....	....	....	....	....	....	1.792	1.673	1.947	2.102	2.219	Official Rate	**ae**
....	....	....	....	....	....	....	....	....	....	1.734	1.760	1.837	2.124	2.187	Official Rate	**rf**
End of Period															**Fund Position**	
....	....	....	....	....	....	....	....	121.2	121.2	121.2	121.2	169.1	169.1	169.1	Quota..	**2f. s**
....	....	....	....	....	....	....	....	5.0	1.8	—	3.7	5.6	8.2	4.9	SDRs..	**1b. s**
....	....	....	....	....	....	....	....	—	—	—	—	—	—	—	Reserve Position in the Fund	**1c. s**
....	....	....	....	....	....	....	....	32.5	31.0	30.3	54.5	68.4	80.4	88.4	Total Fund Cred.&Loans Outstg.	**2tl**
End of Period															**International Liquidity**	
....	....	....	....	....	....	....	....	8	3	80	175	452	497	1,221	Total Reserves minus Gold.....................	**1l. d**
....	....	....	....	....	....	....	....			—	5	8	11	6	SDRs..	**1b. d**
....	....	....	....	....	....	....	....			—	—	—	—	—	Reserve Position in the Fund	**1c. d**
....	....	....	....	....	....	....	....			80	169	445	486	1,215	Foreign Exchange	**1d. d**
End of Period															**Monetary Authorities**	
....	....	....	....	....	....	....	....			144	292	880	1,068	2,737	Foreign Assets	**11**
....	....	....	....	....	....	....	....			170	239	814	945	2,544	Reserve Money	**14**
....	....	....	....	....	....	....	....			113	162	515	652	1,674	*of which: Currency Outside Banks*	**14a**
....	....	....	....	....	....	....	....			71	130	171	230	276	Foreign Liabilities.................................	**16c**
....	....	....	....	....	....	....	....			—	7	9	10	49	Central Government Deposits	**16d**
....	....	....	....	....	....	....	....			1	30	34	59	121	Capital Accounts	**17a**
....	....	....	....	....	....	....	....			−99	−114	−147	−176	−253	Other Items (Net)	**17r**
End of Period															**Deposit Money Banks**	
....	....	....	....	....	....	....	....			71	90	275	284	872	Reserves	**20**
....	....	....	....	....	....	....	....			1,299	1,172	1,134	1,273	1,649	Foreign Assets	**21**
....	....	....	....	....	....	....	....			—	—	—	1	....	Claims on Central Government	**22a**
....	....	....	....	....	....	....	....			129	106	26	24	11	Claims on State Government	**22ab**
....	....	....	....	....	....	....	....			4	7	11	9	22	Claims on Local Government	**22b**
....	....	....	....	....	....	....	....			3,835	4,193	4,129	4,305	4,494	Claims on Other Resident Sectors	**22d**
....	....	....	....	....	....	....	....			134	147	566	723	957	Demand Deposits	**24**
....	....	....	....	....	....	....	....			10	8	22	73	140	Time & Savings Deposits	**25a**
....	....	....	....	....	....	....	....			907	1,219	1,039	958	1,827	*Foreign Currency Deposits*	**25b**
....	....	....	....	....	....	....	....			14	11	9	4	....	Bonds	**26ab**
....	....	....	....	....	....	....	....			3,428	3,375	3,289	3,329	3,096	Foreign Liabilities.................................	**26c**
....	....	....	....	....	....	....	....			3,142	3,116	3,089	1,324	....	Long-Term Foreign Liabilities...............	**26cl**
....	....	....	....	....	....	....	....			—	1	9	18	28	Central Government Deposits	**26d**
....	....	....	....	....	....	....	....			331	288	183	158	318	State Government Deposits....................	**26da**
....	....	....	....	....	....	....	....			1,043	1,305	1,257	1,098	1,113	Capital Accounts	**27a**
....	....	....	....	....	....	....	....			−514	−775	−791	−464	−432	Other Items (Net)	**27r**
End of Period															**Monetary Survey**	
....	....	....	311	....	....	....	....			−2,056	−2,041	−1,446	−1,218	1,014	Foreign Assets (Net)	**31n**
....	....	....	311	....	....	....	....			3,969	4,297	4,148	4,308	4,450	Domestic Credit	**32**
....	....	....	....	....	....	....	....			—	−8	−18	−30	−77	Claims on Central Govt. (Net)	**32an**
....	....	....	....	....	....	....	....			129	106	26	24	11	Claims on State Government	**32ab**
....	....	....	....	....	....	....	....			4	7	11	9	22	Claims on Local Government	**32b**
....	....	....	....	....	....	....	....			3,835	4,193	4,129	4,305	4,494	Claims on Other Resident Sectors	**32d**
....	....	....	....	....	....	....	....			343	384	1,149	1,463	2,790	Money..	**34**
....	....	....	....	....	....	....	....			1,152	1,440	1,177	1,101	2,126	Quasi-Money...	**35**
....	....	....	....	....	....	....	....			14	11	9	4	....	Bonds	**36ab**
....	....	....	....	....	....	....	....			1,045	1,335	1,291	1,157	1,234	Capital Accounts	**37a**
....	....	....	....	....	....	....	....			−627	−902	−915	−632	−686	Other Items (Net)	**37r**
....	....	....	....	....	....	....	....			1,495	1,824	2,326	2,565	4,916	Money plus Quasi-Money......................	**35l**
Percent Per Annum															**Interest Rates**	
....	....	....	....	....	....	....	....			....	51.88	9.07	14.67	....	Deposit Rate..	**60l**
....	....	....	....	....	....	....	....			....	73.50	24.29	30.50	....	Lending Rate	**60p**

Bosnia & Herzegovina

		1972	1973	1974	1975	1976	1977	1978	1979	1980	1981	1982	1983	1984	1985	1986
International Transactions														*Millions of Convertible Marka*		
Exports	70	....	....	....	....	....	....	....	....	....	....	....	....	....	....	....
Imports, f.o.b.	71	....	....	....	....	....	....	....	....	....	....	....	....	....	....	....
Balance of Payments															*Millions of US Dollars:*	
Current Account, n.i.e.	78al *d*	....	....	....	....	....	....	....	....	....	....	....	....	....	....	....
Goods: Exports f.o.b.	78aa *d*	....	....	....	....	....	....	....	....	....	....	....	....	....	....	....
Goods: Imports f.o.b.	78ab *d*	....	....	....	....	....	....	....	....	....	....	....	....	....	....	....
Trade Balance	78ac *d*	....	....	....	....	....	....	....	....	....	....	....	....	....	....	....
Services: Credit	78ad *d*	....	....	....	....	....	....	....	....	....	....	....	....	....	....	....
Services: Debit	78ae *d*	....	....	....	....	....	....	....	....	....	....	....	....	....	....	....
Balance on Goods & Services	78af *d*	....	....	....	....	....	....	....	....	....	....	....	....	....	....	....
Income: Credit	78ag *d*	....	....	....	....	....	....	....	....	....	....	....	....	....	....	....
Income: Debit	78ah *d*	....	....	....	....	....	....	....	....	....	....	....	....	....	....	....
Balance on Gds, Serv. & Inc.	78ai *d*	....	....	....	....	....	....	....	....	....	....	....	....	....	....	....
Current Transfers, n.i.e.: Credit	78aj *d*	....	....	....	....	....	....	....	....	....	....	....	....	....	....	....
Current Transfers: Debit	78ak *d*	....	....	....	....	....	....	....	....	....	....	....	....	....	....	....
Capital Account, n.i.e.	78bc *d*	....	....	....	....	....	....	....	....	....	....	....	....	....	....	....
Capital Account, n.i.e.: Credit	78ba *d*	....	....	....	....	....	....	....	....	....	....	....	....	....	....	....
Capital Account: Debit	78bb *d*	....	....	....	....	....	....	....	....	....	....	....	....	....	....	....
Financial Account, n.i.e.	78bj *d*	....	....	....	....	....	....	....	....	....	....	....	....	....	....	....
Direct Investment Abroad	78bd *d*	....	....	....	....	....	....	....	....	....	....	....	....	....	....	....
Dir. Invest. in Rep. Econ., n.i.e.	78be *d*	....	....	....	....	....	....	....	....	....	....	....	....	....	....	....
Portfolio Investment Assets	78bf *d*	....	....	....	....	....	....	....	....	....	....	....	....	....	....	....
Equity Securities	78bk *d*	....	....	....	....	....	....	....	....	....	....	....	....	....	....	....
Debt Securities	78bl *d*	....	....	....	....	....	....	....	....	....	....	....	....	....	....	....
Portfolio Investment Liab., n.i.e.	78bg *d*	....	....	....	....	....	....	....	....	....	....	....	....	....	....	....
Equity Securities	78bm *d*	....	....	....	....	....	....	....	....	....	....	....	....	....	....	....
Debt Securities	78bn *d*	....	....	....	....	....	....	....	....	....	....	....	....	....	....	....
Financial Derivatives Assets	78bw *d*	....	....	....	....	....	....	....	....	....	....	....	....	....	....	....
Financial Derivatives Liabilities	78bx *d*	....	....	....	....	....	....	....	....	....	....	....	....	....	....	....
Other Investment Assets	78bh *d*	....	....	....	....	....	....	....	....	....	....	....	....	....	....	....
Monetary Authorities	78bo *d*	....	....	....	....	....	....	....	....	....	....	....	....	....	....	....
General Government	78bp *d*	....	....	....	....	....	....	....	....	....	....	....	....	....	....	....
Banks	78bq *d*	....	....	....	....	....	....	....	....	....	....	....	....	....	....	....
Other Sectors	78br *d*	....	....	....	....	....	....	....	....	....	....	....	....	....	....	....
Other Investment Liab., n.i.e.	78bi *d*	....	....	....	....	....	....	....	....	....	....	....	....	....	....	....
Monetary Authorities	78bs *d*	....	....	....	....	....	....	....	....	....	....	....	....	....	....	....
General Government	78bt *d*	....	....	....	....	....	....	....	....	....	....	....	....	....	....	....
Banks	78bu *d*	....	....	....	....	....	....	....	....	....	....	....	....	....	....	....
Other Sectors	78bv *d*	....	....	....	....	....	....	....	....	....	....	....	....	....	....	....
Net Errors and Omissions	78ca *d*	....	....	....	....	....	....	....	....	....	....	....	....	....	....	....
Overall Balance	78cb *d*	....	....	....	....	....	....	....	....	....	....	....	....	....	....	....
Reserves and Related Items	79da *d*	....	....	....	....	....	....	....	....	....	....	....	....	....	....	....
Reserve Assets	79db *d*	....	....	....	....	....	....	....	....	....	....	....	....	....	....	....
Use of Fund Credit and Loans	79dc *d*	....	....	....	....	....	....	....	....	....	....	....	....	....	....	....
Exceptional Financing	79de *d*	....	....	....	....	....	....	....	....	....	....	....	....	....	....	....
National Accounts														*Millions of Convertible Marka*		
Gross Domestic Product (GDP)	99b	....	....	....	....	....	....	....	....	....	....	....	....	....	....	....
															Millions:	
Population	99z	....	....	....	....	....	....	....	....	....	....	....	....	....	....	....

	1987	1988	1989	1990	1991	1992	1993	1994	1995	1996	1997	1998	1999	2000	2001		
Millions of Convertible Marka																**International Transactions**	
	....	....	....	....	....	....	....	....	....	....	....	1,043.0	1,375.0	2,265.0	2,370.0	Exports...	70
	....	....	....	....	....	....	....	....	....	....	....	5,120.0	6,048.0	6,582.0	7,062.0	Imports, f.o.b.	71
Minus Sign Indicates Debit																Balance of Payments	
	....	....	....	....	....	....	....	....	....	....	....	−1,247.0	−1,561.2	−1,300.1	−1,379.2	Current Account, n.i.e.	**78al** *d*
	....	....	....	....	....	....	....	....	....	....	....	652.0	816.2	1,151.5	1,166.4	Goods: Exports f.o.b.	**78aa** *d*
	....	....	....	....	....	....	....	....	....	....	....	−3,807.0	−4,149.2	−3,811.3	−3,917.9	Goods: Imports f.o.b.	**78ab** *d*
	....	....	....	....	....	....	....	....	....	....	....	−3,155.0	−3,333.1	−2,659.9	−2,751.5	*Trade Balance*	**78ac** *d*
	....	....	....	....	....	....	....	....	....	....	....	304.8	266.8	239.6	266.9	Services: Credit	**78ad** *d*
	....	....	....	....	....	....	....	....	....	....	....	−230.7	−249.9	−224.1	−228.4	Services: Debit	**78ae** *d*
	....	....	....	....	....	....	....	....	....	....	....	−3,081.0	−3,316.1	−2,644.4	−2,712.9	*Balance on Goods & Services*	**78af** *d*
	....	....	....	....	....	....	....	....	....	....	....	481.2	454.7	391.8	401.3	Income: Credit	**78ag** *d*
	....	....	....	....	....	....	....	....	....	....	....	−52.1	−61.2	−68.4	−65.2	Income: Debit	**78ah** *d*
	....	....	....	....	....	....	....	....	....	....	....	−2,651.9	−2,922.7	−2,320.9	−2,376.8	*Balance on Gds, Serv. & Inc.*	**78ai** *d*
	....	....	....	....	....	....	....	....	....	....	....	1,404.9	1,361.5	1,020.9	997.6	Current Transfers, n.i.e.: Credit	**78aj** *d*
	....	....	....	....	....	....	....	....	....	....	....	—	—	—	—	Current Transfers: Debit	**78ak** *d*
	....	....	....	....	....	....	....	....	....	....	....	435.2	531.5	406.0	390.6	Capital Account, n.i.e.	**78bc** *d*
	....	....	....	....	....	....	....	....	....	....	....	435.2	531.5	406.0	390.6	Capital Account, n.i.e.: Credit	**78ba** *d*
	....	....	....	....	....	....	....	....	....	....	....					Capital Account: Debit	**78bb** *d*
	....	....	....	....	....	....	....	....	....	....	....	58.0	433.8	677.6	1,452.4	Financial Account, n.i.e.	**78bj** *d*
	....	....	....	....	....	....	....	....	....	....	....				—	Direct Investment Abroad	**78bd** *d*
	....	....	....	....	....	....	....	....	....	....	....	66.7	176.6	146.0	221.9	Dir. Invest. in Rep. Econ., n.i.e.	**78be** *d*
	....	....	....	....	....	....	....	....	....	....	....	—	—	—	—	Portfolio Investment Assets	**78bf** *d*
	....	....	....	....	....	....	....	....	....	....	....	—	—	—	—	Equity Securities..........................	**78bk** *d*
	....	....	....	....	....	....	....	....	....	....	....	—	—	—	....	Debt Securities............................	**78bl** *d*
	....	....	....	....	....	....	....	....	....	....	....	....	....	....	—	Portfolio Investment Liab., n.i.e.	**78bg** *d*
	....	....	....	....	....	....	....	....	....	....	....	—	—	—	—	Equity Securities..........................	**78bm** *d*
	....	....	....	....	....	....	....	....	....	....	....	....	....	....	—	Debt Securities............................	**78bn** *d*
	....	....	....	....	....	....	....	....	....	....	....	—	—	—	—	Financial Derivatives Assets	**78bw** *d*
	....	....	....	....	....	....	....	....	....	....	....	—	—	—	—	Financial Derivatives Liabilities........	**78bx** *d*
	....	....	....	....	....	....	....	....	....	....	....	34.8	297.4	493.3	1,304.0	Other Investment Assets	**78bh** *d*
	....	....	....	....	....	....	....	....	....	....	....	....	....	....	....	Monetary Authorities	**78bo** *d*
	....	....	....	....	....	....	....	....	....	....	....	....	....	....	....	General Government	**78bp** *d*
	....	....	....	....	....	....	....	....	....	....	....	71.9	21.1	−52.9	−190.7	Banks...	**78bq** *d*
	....	....	....	....	....	....	....	....	....	....	....	−37.1	276.3	546.2	1,494.7	Other Sectors	**78br** *d*
	....	....	....	....	....	....	....	....	....	....	....	−43.5	−40.2	38.3	−73.4	Other Investment Liab., n.i.e.	**78bi** *d*
	....	....	....	....	....	....	....	....	....	....	....	—	—	.7	13.6	Monetary Authorities	**78bs** *d*
	....	....	....	....	....	....	....	....	....	....	....	−44.8	−31.3	−29.9	−22.2	General Government	**78bt** *d*
	....	....	....	....	....	....	....	....	....	....	....	−29.8	−47.1	27.2	−115.7	Banks...	**78bu** *d*
	....	....	....	....	....	....	....	....	....	....	....	31.2	38.2	40.4	50.9	Other Sectors	**78bv** *d*
	....	....	....	....	....	....	....	....	....	....	....	225.1	262.5	185.1	191.5	Net Errors and Omissions	**78ca** *d*
	....	....	....	....	....	....	....	....	....	....	....	−528.7	−333.3	−31.4	655.3	*Overall Balance*..............................	**78cb** *d*
	....	....	....	....	....	....	....	....	....	....	....	528.7	333.3	31.4	−655.3	Reserves and Related Items	**79da** *d*
	....	....	....	....	....	....	....	....	....	....	....	−84.0	−319.2	−76.4	−761.1	Reserve Assets	**79db** *d*
	....	....	....	....	....	....	....	....	....	....	....	32.3	18.2	15.5	9.9	Use of Fund Credit and Loans..........	**79dc** *d*
	....	....	....	....	....	....	....	....	....	....	....	580.4	634.3	92.3	95.8	Exceptional Financing	**79de** *d*
Millions of Convertible Marka																**National Accounts**	
	....	....	....	....	....	....	....	....	....	4,192	6,562	7,439	8,604	9,433	....	Gross Domestic Product (GDP)	**99b**
Midyear Estimates																	
	....	....	....	4.38	4.41	4.28	4.22	4.18	4.17	†3.44	3.65	3.85	3.98	4.07	**Population**...	**99z**

(See notes in the back of the book.)

Botswana

		1972	1973	1974	1975	1976	1977	1978	1979	1980	1981	1982	1983	1984	1985	1986
Exchange Rates															*Pula per SDR:*	
Official Rate	aa	.8499	.8097	.8444	1.0180	1.0103	1.0060	1.0789	1.0390	.9461	1.0244	1.1704	1.2098	1.5292	2.3076	2.2477
															Pula per US Dollar:	
Official Rate	ae	.7828	.6712	.6896	.8696	.8696	.8282	.8282	.7887	.7418	.8801	1.0610	1.1555	1.5601	2.1008	1.8376
Official Rate	rf	.7687	.6940	.6795	.7395	.8696	.8420	.8282	.8150	.7772	.8367	1.0297	1.0969	1.2984	1.9026	1.8791
Fund Position															*Millions of SDRs:*	
Quota	2f. *s*	5.00	5.00	5.00	5.00	5.00	5.00	9.00	9.00	13.50	13.50	13.50	22.10	22.10	22.10	22.10
SDRs	1b. *s*	1.57	1.57	1.57	1.57	1.57	1.57	1.57	2.50	2.45	5.25	6.19	7.26	8.53	9.70	14.01
Reserve Position in the Fund	1c. *s*	.61	.62	.62	.62	.61	1.24	1.22	2.18	5.12	9.13	9.15	11.31	12.34	12.93	15.58
Total Fund Cred.&Loans Outstg.	2tl	—	—	—	—	—	—	—	—	—	—	—	—	—	—	—
International Liquidity											*Millions of US Dollars Unless Otherwise Indicated:*					
Total Reserves minus Gold	1l. *d*	...	...	...	...	72.32	96.69	146.93	261.12	334.03	236.70	276.05	376.23	453.83	758.35	1,161.48
SDRs	1b. *d*	1.70	1.89	1.92	1.84	1.82	1.91	2.05	3.29	3.12	6.11	6.83	7.60	8.36	10.65	17.14
Reserve Position in the Fund	1c. *d*	.66	.75	.76	.73	.71	1.51	1.59	2.87	6.53	10.63	10.09	11.84	12.10	14.20	19.06
Foreign Exchange	1d. *d*	...	...	...	...	69.79	93.28	143.30	254.95	324.38	219.96	259.13	356.79	433.37	733.49	1,125.29
Deposit Money Banks: Assets	7a. *d*	26.31	37.64	50.13	69.11	.68	3.37	3.23	4.97	3.29	1.64	4.65	6.34	20.01	17.49	22.77
Liabilities	7b. *d*	7.58	5.17	19.82	33.99	1.13	3.08	3.31	2.84	3.97	7.67	3.06	10.78	11.01	10.33	19.30
Monetary Authorities															*Millions of Pula:*	
Foreign Assets	11	...	...	...	...	65	83	125	211	255	223	311	457	711	1,645	2,201
Reserve Money	14	...	...	...	...	33	36	36	57	62	53	47	49	57	60	86
of which: Currency Outside DMBs	14a	...	...	...	...	10	12	16	18	24	30	29	30	35	43	59
Time Deposits	15	...	...	...	...	—	1	8	50	91	30	15	65	12	183	188
Liabs. of Central Bank: Securities	16ac	...	...	...	...	—	—	—	—	—	—	50	58	71	102	80
Central Government Deposits	16d	...	...	...	...	29	39	63	84	91	76	105	185	368	642	1,270
Capital Accounts	17a	...	...	...	...	5	8	17	15	18	38	61	65	65	465	385
Other Items (Net)	17r	...	...	...	...	-2	-1	1	4	-8	26	33	36	138	194	193
Deposit Money Banks															*Millions of Pula:*	
Reserves	20	1	2	2	3	22	24	20	38	36	22	18	22	17	16	23
Claims on Mon.Author.: Securities	20c	—	—	—	—	—	—	—	—	—	—	50	58	71	102	80
Foreign Assets	21	21	27	35	60	1	3	3	4	2	1	5	7	31	37	42
Claims on Central Government	22a	2	1	1	3	12	13	9	7	5	9	—	—	—	—	—
Claims on Local Government	22b	—	—	—	—	—	—	—	1	1	—	—	—	—	—	—
Claims on Nonfin.Pub.Enterprises	22c	1	—	1	2	1	4	4	—	2	5	8	15	18	25	34
Claims on Private Sector	22d	12	21	36	51	66	68	69	84	93	136	135	155	204	182	217
Claims on Other Financial Insts	22f	—	—	—	—	—	1	1	2	3	4	6	8	16	17	21
Demand Deposits	24	13	17	20	21	33	46	45	64	66	85	98	107	115	145	185
Time and Savings Deposits	25	12	17	21	26	43	50	52	67	55	81	103	114	206	186	175
Foreign Liabilities	26c	6	4	14	30	1	3	3	2	3	7	3	12	17	22	35
Central Government Deposits	26d	7	12	21	42	22	13	4	1	13	1	—	—	—	—	—
Capital Accounts	27a	—	—	—	—	4	6	7	9	9	14	21	25	30	40	41
Other Items (Net)	27r	-2	1	-2	-1	—	-5	-5	-7	-5	-10	-4	6	-10	-15	-19
Monetary Survey															*Millions of Pula:*	
Foreign Assets (Net)	31n	...	...	...	...	65	83	125	212	254	218	313	452	725	1,660	2,207
Domestic Credit	32	...	...	...	...	27	32	17	8	6	77	43	-8	-130	-419	-997
Claims on Central Govt. (Net)	32an	...	...	...	...	-40	-40	-57	-79	-92	-67	-106	-185	-368	-643	-1,270
Claims on Local Government	32b	...	...	...	...	—	—	—	1	1	—	—	—	—	—	—
Claims on Nonfin.Pub.Enterprises	32c	...	...	...	...	1	4	4	—	2	5	8	15	18	25	34
Claims on Private Sector	32d	...	...	...	...	66	68	69	84	93	136	135	155	204	182	217
Claims on Other Financial Insts	32f	...	...	...	...	—	1	1	2	3	4	6	8	16	17	21
Money	34	...	...	...	...	44	58	61	82	91	115	127	137	151	188	243
Quasi-Money	35	...	...	...	...	43	50	60	117	146	112	118	179	218	369	363
Liabs. of Central Bank: Securities	36ac	—	—	—	—	—	—	—	—	—	—	—	—	—	—	—
Capital Accounts	37a	...	...	...	...	8	14	25	24	27	52	82	90	94	505	426
Other Items (Net)	37r	...	...	...	...	-2	-7	-4	-2	-4	16	28	39	132	179	178
Money plus Quasi-Money	35l	...	...	...	...	86	109	121	199	237	226	246	316	369	557	606
Interest Rates															*Percent Per Annum*	
Bank Rate (End of Period)	60	...	...	...	...	8.25	7.75	6.75	5.75	5.75	8.50	12.00	10.50	9.00	9.00	9.00
Deposit Rate	60l	...	...	...	...	...	...	...	...	5.00	8.67	10.75	11.88	10.00	9.00	8.67
Lending Rate	60p	...	...	...	...	...	...	...	...	8.48	9.63	24.21	13.38	12.00	11.50	11.00
Prices, Production, Labor															*Index Numbers (1995=100):*	
Consumer Prices	64	...	...	10.3	11.5	12.9	14.6	15.9	17.8	20.2	†23.5	26.1	28.9	31.4	33.9	37.3
Mining Production	66zx	7.8	8.0	11.5	14.1	20.1	20.9	24.9	29.5	32.4	†34.0	48.3	67.2	79.1	77.5	79.8
															Number in Thousands:	
Labor Force	67d	...	...	...	...	...	...	...	...	...	...	...	...	...	...	...
Employment	67e	...	...	...	...	...	...	...	...	...	...	...	...	...	117	130
International Transactions															*Millions of Pula:*	
Exports	70	44.8	59.2	82.0	105.0	153.2	156.7	192.7	367.3	391.3	347.8	494.3	707.5	857.1	1,384.3	1,619.3
Imports, c.i.f.	71	84.2	115.0	125.4	159.3	181.4	239.6	307.1	438.3	537.6	695.1	742.7	818.3	895.2	1,095.2	1,331.4

1987	1988	1989	1990	1991	1992	1993	1994	1995	1996	1997	1998	1999	2000	2001		
End of Period															**Exchange Rates**	
2.2212	2.6049	2.4605	2.6622	2.9646	3.1031	3.5229	3.9670	4.1944	5.2404	5.1400	6.2774	6.3572	6.9861	8.7760	Official Rate	**aa**
End of Period (ae)	*Period Average (rf)*															
1.5657	1.9357	1.8723	1.8713	2.0725	2.2568	2.5648	2.7174	2.8217	3.6443	3.8095	4.4583	4.6318	5.3619	6.9832	Official Rate	**ae**
1.6789	1.8286	2.0149	1.8605	2.0216	2.1097	2.4231	2.6846	2.7722	3.3242	3.6508	4.2259	4.6244	5.1018	5.8412	Official Rate	**rf**
End of Period															**Fund Position**	
22.10	22.10	22.10	22.10	22.10	36.60	36.60	36.60	36.60	36.60	36.60	36.60	63.00	63.00	63.00	Quota	**2f. s**
15.38	16.79	18.91	21.70	24.10	22.46	24.03	25.39	27.06	28.71	30.36	32.41	28.05	29.89	31.53	SDRs	**1b. s**
15.73	13.64	19.22	16.17	13.45	14.79	16.60	16.34	19.28	19.91	18.13	27.61	22.59	17.74	22.28	Reserve Position in the Fund	**1c. s**
—	—	—	—	—	—	—	—	—	—	—	—	—	—	—	Total Fund Cred.&Loans Outstg.	**2tl**
End of Period															**International Liquidity**	
2,012.95	2,217.14	2,791.00	3,331.46	3,718.66	3,793.42	4,097.34	4,401.47	4,695.48	5,027.66	5,675.00	5,940.67	6,298.72	6,318.21	5,897.25	Total Reserves minus Gold	**1l. d**
21.82	22.59	24.85	30.87	34.47	30.88	33.00	37.07	40.22	41.28	40.96	45.63	38.50	38.94	39.62	SDRs	**1b. d**
22.32	18.36	25.26	23.00	19.24	20.34	22.79	23.86	28.66	28.63	24.46	38.87	31.00	23.11	28.00	Reserve Position in the Fund	**1c. d**
1,968.82	2,176.19	2,740.89	3,277.58	3,664.95	3,742.20	4,041.54	4,340.54	4,626.60	4,957.75	5,609.58	5,856.17	6,229.21	6,256.16	5,829.63	Foreign Exchange	**1d. d**
31.27	33.78	24.06	80.39	74.31	64.91	61.17	63.42	69.60	124.51	211.33	317.73	290.52	267.62	319.47	Deposit Money Banks: Assets	**7a. d**
25.91	23.86	19.72	34.14	23.80	19.40	54.32	24.22	35.05	41.61	31.61	38.49	34.79	41.93	52.65	Liabilities	**7b. d**
End of Period															**Monetary Authorities**	
3,152	4,371	5,225	6,257	7,708	8,561	10,506	10,567	12,115	18,356	21,637	26,502	28,867	33,900	41,211	Foreign Assets	**11**
104	138	191	256	512	424	395	392	405	453	572	707	808	857	970	Reserve Money	**14**
69	96	118	144	158	163	180	195	223	247	276	353	404	427	481	*of which: Currency Outside DMBs*	**14a**
480	482	832	359	491	605	38	46	48	47	63	26	172	183	184	Time Deposits	**15**
175	261	311	192	207	344	1,201	1,451	1,964	2,816	3,308	3,246	4,230	3,712	5,148	Liabs. of Central Bank: Securities	**16ac**
1,817	2,348	3,059	4,001	4,287	5,100	5,630	6,734	6,507	7,267	15,407	19,122	20,256	24,205	27,972	Central Government Deposits	**16d**
374	829	847	866	1,464	1,365	2,167	2,935	2,942	6,107	1,888	3,229	3,415	4,384	6,668	Capital Accounts	**17a**
203	313	−16	585	747	725	1,075	−990	250	1,666	399	172	−14	558	271	Other Items (Net)	**17r**
End of Period															**Deposit Money Banks**	
23	52	66	99	220	124	194	160	166	177	271	331	353	229	263	Reserves	**20**
175	261	311	192	207	344	361	493	832	1,192	1,572	1,322	1,718	1,197	1,874	Claims on Mon.Author.: Securities	**20c**
49	65	45	150	154	146	157	172	196	454	805	1,417	1,346	1,435	2,231	Foreign Assets	**21**
—	—	—	—	—	—	—	2	—	—	—	—	—	—	—	Claims on Central Government	**22a**
—	1	—	1	2	2	3	2	3	2	2	14	15	2	1	Claims on Local Government	**22b**
22	26	55	57	60	76	94	148	95	70	61	267	528	458	480	Claims on Nonfin.Pub.Enterprises	**22c**
261	321	435	662	945	1,285	1,434	1,600	1,560	1,626	1,775	2,461	3,518	4,344	4,915	Claims on Private Sector	**22d**
1	21	39	37	33	35	32	95	122	100	61	231	130	123	64	Claims on Other Financial Insts	**22f**
244	311	389	442	456	444	516	579	607	704	762	1,160	1,371	1,470	1,869	Demand Deposits	**24**
221	340	458	601	1,084	1,267	1,386	1,573	1,809	2,192	3,003	4,183	5,282	5,248	7,082	Time and Savings Deposits	**25**
41	46	37	64	49	44	139	66	99	152	120	172	161	225	368	Foreign Liabilities	**26c**
—	2	3	5	14	9	31	16	19	40	36	29	66	107	61	Central Government Deposits	**26d**
56	63	99	119	160	221	244	308	337	402	464	568	732	843	1,042	Capital Accounts	**27a**
−29	−13	−34	−33	−140	27	−43	131	103	131	162	−70	−5	−103	−594	Other Items (Net)	**27r**
End of Period															**Monetary Survey**	
3,161	4,390	5,234	6,344	7,813	8,664	10,524	10,673	12,213	18,658	22,321	27,747	30,051	35,110	43,075	Foreign Assets (Net)	**31n**
−1,532	−1,981	−2,533	−3,250	−3,260	−3,711	−4,099	−4,904	−4,747	−5,509	−13,543	−16,179	−16,131	−19,384	−22,573	Domestic Credit	**32**
−1,817	−2,350	−3,062	−4,006	−4,301	−5,108	−5,662	−6,748	−6,526	−7,307	−15,442	−19,151	−20,322	−24,312	−28,033	Claims on Central Govt. (Net)	**32an**
—	1	—	1	2	2	3	2	3	2	2	14	15	2	1	Claims on Local Government	**32b**
22	26	55	57	60	76	94	148	95	70	61	267	528	458	480	Claims on Nonfin.Pub.Enterprises	**32c**
261	321	435	662	945	1,285	1,434	1,600	1,560	1,626	1,775	2,461	3,518	4,344	4,915	Claims on Private Sector	**32d**
1	21	39	37	33	35	32	95	122	100	61	231	130	123	64	Claims on Other Financial Insts	**32f**
312	406	506	586	614	607	696	774	829	951	1,038	1,513	1,775	1,897	2,351	Money	**34**
701	822	1,291	960	1,575	1,871	1,424	1,619	1,856	2,239	3,066	4,209	5,454	5,432	7,266	Quasi-Money	**35**
—	—	—	—	—	—	840	958	1,132	1,623	1,736	1,924	2,513	2,515	3,274	Liabs. of Central Bank: Securities	**36ac**
430	892	946	984	1,624	1,585	2,412	3,243	3,279	6,509	2,352	3,797	4,147	5,227	7,710	Capital Accounts	**37a**
186	289	−42	564	740	889	1,053	−823	369	1,827	587	126	32	656	−98	Other Items (Net)	**37r**
1,013	1,228	1,797	1,546	2,188	2,478	2,121	2,392	2,686	3,190	4,104	5,722	7,228	7,328	9,617	Money plus Quasi-Money	**35l**
Percent Per Annum															**Interest Rates**	
8.50	6.50	6.50	8.50	12.00	14.25	14.25	13.50	13.00	13.00	12.50	12.50	13.25	14.25	14.25	Bank Rate *(End of Period)*	**60**
7.50	5.00	5.58	6.11	11.40	12.50	13.49	10.39	9.98	10.43	9.25	8.72	9.46	10.07	10.15	Deposit Rate	**60l**
10.00	7.83	7.67	7.88	11.83	14.00	14.92	13.88	14.29	14.50	14.08	13.53	14.63	15.31	15.75	Lending Rate	**60p**
Period Averages															**Prices, Production, Labor**	
40.9	44.4	49.5	55.1	†61.6	71.6	81.9	90.5	100.0	†110.1	119.7	127.7	137.5	149.4	159.2	Consumer Prices	**64**
80.3	93.2	91.6	103.4	99.0	96.4	89.3	94.0	100.0	....	....	....	....	....	....	Mining Production	**66zx**
Period Averages																
....	....	....	....	432	....	....	....	437	439	....	....	....	....	....	Labor Force	**67d**
150	170	190	209	226	226	227	231	232	230	233	240	....	....	....	Employment	**67e**
Millions of Pula															**International Transactions**	
2,664.7	2,678.3	3,742.6	3,319.1	3,738.0	3,675.0	4,270.9	4,965.0	5,941.5	8,133.4	13,471.7	11,665.4	16,691.2	19,361.0	6,057.8	Exports	**70**
1,572.5	2,172.2	3,019.6	3,619.3	3,927.7	3,970.1	4,285.0	4,407.3	5,305.1	5,742.9	10,422.7	12,432.4	13,456.4	14,423.5	3,323.2	Imports, c.i.f.	**71**

Botswana

		1972	1973	1974	1975	1976	1977	1978	1979	1980	1981	1982	1983	1984	1985	1986
Balance of Payments															*Millions of US Dollars:*	
Current Account, n.i.e.	78al d	....	....	....	-35.6	-20.4	-27.0	-115.6	-60.6	-151.1	-303.7	-144.6	-78.9	-58.8	81.9	108.7
Goods: Exports f.o.b.	78aa d				142.0	169.7	191.6	223.4	442.2	544.5	401.3	460.6	640.3	677.7	727.6	852.5
Goods: Imports f.o.b.	78ab d				-181.2	-180.2	-226.4	-295.0	-442.1	-602.5	-687.1	-579.8	-615.3	-583.4	-493.8	-608.4
Trade Balance	78ac d				-39.2	-10.5	-34.8	-71.6	.1	-58.0	-285.8	-119.2	25.1	94.3	233.8	244.0
Services: Credit	78ad d				30.8	46.8	51.4	50.5	61.1	100.9	97.0	102.5	113.0	107.2	76.3	100.0
Services: Debit	78ae d				-76.0	-78.4	-89.9	-101.9	-155.1	-215.9	-211.8	-181.6	-209.4	-190.2	-130.5	-155.0
Balance on Goods & Services	78af d				-84.4	-42.1	-73.3	-123.0	-93.9	-173.1	-400.5	-198.3	-71.4	11.2	179.7	189.1
Income: Credit	78ag d				47.1	59.3	68.3	58.9	72.3	102.2	106.0	82.4	82.7	92.7	84.9	116.5
Income: Debit	78ah d				6.9	-51.9	-54.4	-68.5	-69.4	-135.1	-49.7	-45.1	-129.9	-190.6	-216.3	-245.7
Balance on Gds, Serv. & Inc.	78ai d				-30.4	-34.6	-59.4	-132.6	-91.0	-206.0	-344.2	-161.0	-118.6	-86.7	48.2	60.0
Current Transfers, n.i.e.: Credit	78aj d				30.6	57.7	95.0	80.7	109.1	144.4	141.6	115.0	145.7	124.8	102.7	133.5
Current Transfers: Debit	78ak d				-35.7	-43.5	-62.6	-63.6	-78.6	-89.4	-101.1	-98.6	-106.0	-96.9	-68.9	-84.8
Capital Account, n.i.e.	78bc d	....	....	....	—	5.6	6.1	4.1	6.6	8.2	8.7	6.7	7.3	7.3	5.2	2.5
Capital Account, n.i.e.: Credit	78ba d				—	5.6	6.1	6.4	7.4	9.1	9.6	7.8	8.4	7.9	5.6	3.2
Capital Account: Debit	78bb d				—	—	—	-2.3	-.7	-.9	-.8	-1.1	-1.1	-.5	-.4	-.7
Financial Account, n.i.e.	78bj d	....	....	....	43.5	73.6	15.9	90.4	87.5	144.0	110.9	90.8	94.7	112.5	123.1	105.6
Direct Investment Abroad	78bd d				—	-.1	-.2	—	—	-2.3	.1	—	1.3	.2	-1.5	—
Dir. Invest. in Rep. Econ., n.i.e.	78be d				-38.3	11.3	12.2	40.8	127.9	111.6	88.4	21.1	23.8	62.2	53.6	70.4
Portfolio Investment Assets	78bf d				—	—	—	—	—	—	—	—	—	—	—	—
Equity Securities	78bk d				—	—	—	—	—	—	—	—	—	—	—	—
Debt Securities	78bl d				—	—	—	—	—	—	—	—	—	—	—	—
Portfolio Investment Liab., n.i.e.	78bg d				—	—	—	4.2	—	—	—	—	—	—	—	—
Equity Securities	78bm d				—	—	—	4.2	—	—	—	—	—	—	—	—
Debt Securities	78bn d				—	—	—	—	—	—	—	—	—	—	—	—
Financial Derivatives Assets	78bw d	....	....	....	....	....	....	....	....	....	....	....	....	....	....	....
Financial Derivatives Liabilities	78bx d	....	....	....	....	....	....	....	....	....	....	....	....	....	....	....
Other Investment Assets	78bh d				-50.4	72.6	10.2	5.6	-28.0	-12.7	-25.3	-17.5	6.6	-16.7	-16.7	-28.7
Monetary Authorities	78bo d															
General Government	78bp d				-5.1	-7.2	-.7	-9.2	-20.0	-2.4	-15.2	-13.0	2.5	1.5	-10.1	-35.8
Banks	78bq d				-34.5	68.1	-2.3	.1	-1.6	1.9	-3.1	-8.8	5.3	-18.4	-2.9	-2.7
Other Sectors	78br d				-10.8	11.7	13.2	14.6	-6.4	-12.2	-7.1	4.4	-1.2	.2	-3.7	9.7
Other Investment Liab., n.i.e.	78bi d				132.3	-10.1	-6.3	39.8	-12.4	47.5	47.7	87.2	63.1	66.9	87.7	63.9
Monetary Authorities	78bs d				—	—	.4	-.2	-.2	2.8	.4	-2.0	1.5	-1.8		
General Government	78bt d				22.3	5.4	-25.2	15.3	-5.3	13.4	15.7	55.4	14.1	17.6	9.4	40.3
Banks	78bu d				21.5	-32.9	1.9	.2	.6	-1.8	7.3	-5.7	-3.5	3.7	30.5	-21.3
Other Sectors	78bv d				88.4	17.4	16.6	24.5	-7.5	33.1	24.4	39.6	50.9	47.3	47.7	44.9
Net Errors and Omissions	78ca d				-8.0	13.0	23.1	60.1	82.5	89.3	110.3	102.0	100.6	63.2	44.0	90.2
Overall Balance	78cb d				—	71.9	18.1	39.1	116.0	90.4	-73.8	54.9	123.6	124.3	254.3	306.9
Reserves and Related Items	79da d				—	-71.9	-18.1	-39.1	-116.0	-90.4	73.8	-54.9	-123.6	-124.3	-254.3	-306.9
Reserve Assets	79db d				—	-71.9	-18.1	-39.1	-116.0	-90.4	73.8	-54.9	-123.6	-124.3	-254.3	-306.9
Use of Fund Credit and Loans	79dc d				—	—	—	—	—	—	—	—	—	—	—	—
Exceptional Financing	79de d	....	....	....	....	....	....	....	....	....	....	....	....	....	....	....
International Investment Position															*Millions of US Dollars*	
Assets	79aa d	....	....	....	....	....	....	....	....	....	....	....	....	....	....	....
Direct Investment Abroad	79ab d	....	....	....	....	....	....	....	....	....	....	....	....	....	....	....
Portfolio Investment	79ac d	....	....	....	....	....	....	....	....	....	....	....	....	....	....	....
Equity Securities	79ad d	....	....	....	....	....	....	....	....	....	....	....	....	....	....	....
Debt Securities	79ae d	....	....	....	....	....	....	....	....	....	....	....	....	....	....	....
Financial Derivatives	79al d	....	....	....	....	....	....	....	....	....	....	....	....	....	....	....
Other Investment	79af d	....	....	....	....	....	....	....	....	....	....	....	....	....	....	....
Monetary Authorities	79ag d	....	....	....	....	....	....	....	....	....	....	....	....	....	....	....
General Government	79ah d	....	....	....	....	....	....	....	....	....	....	....	....	....	....	....
Banks	79ai d	....	....	....	....	....	....	....	....	....	....	....	....	....	....	....
Other Sectors	79aj d	....	....	....	....	....	....	....	....	....	....	....	....	....	....	....
Reserve Assets	79ak d	....	....	....	....	....	....	....	....	....	....	....	....	....	....	....
Liabilities	79la d	....	....	....	....	....	....	....	....	....	....	....	....	....	....	....
Dir. Invest. in Rep. Economy	79lb d	....	....	....	....	....	....	....	....	....	....	....	....	....	....	....
Portfolio Investment	79lc d	....	....	....	....	....	....	....	....	....	....	....	....	....	....	....
Equity Securities	79ld d	....	....	....	....	....	....	....	....	....	....	....	....	....	....	....
Debt Securities	79le d	....	....	....	....	....	....	....	....	....	....	....	....	....	....	....
Financial Derivatives	79ll d	....	....	....	....	....	....	....	....	....	....	....	....	....	....	....
Other Investment	79lf d	....	....	....	....	....	....	....	....	....	....	....	....	....	....	....
Monetary Authorities	79lg d	....	....	....	....	....	....	....	....	....	....	....	....	....	....	....
General Government	79lh d	....	....	....	....	....	....	....	....	....	....	....	....	....	....	....
Banks	79li d	....	....	....	....	....	....	....	....	....	....	....	....	....	....	....
Other Sectors	79lj d	....	....	....	....	....	....	....	....	....	....	....	....	....	....	....

Balance of Payments

Minus Sign Indicates Debit

1987	1988	1989	1990	1991	1992	1993	1994	1995	1996	1997	1998	1999	2000	2001		
628.5	193.9	491.9	−19.3	302.9	197.7	426.9	211.6	299.7	495.0	721.5	170.1	516.8	....	....	Current Account, n.i.e.	78al d
1,586.6	1,468.9	1,819.7	1,795.4	1,871.1	1,743.9	1,722.2	1,874.3	2,160.2	2,217.5	2,819.8	2,060.6	2,671.0			Goods: Exports f.o.b.	78aa d
−803.9	−986.9	−1,185.1	−1,610.9	−1,604.0	−1,556.6	−1,455.4	−1,364.3	−1,605.4	−1,467.7	−1,924.4	−1,983.1	−1,996.5			Goods: Imports f.o.b.	78ab d
782.7	482.0	634.6	184.4	267.2	187.3	266.8	510.0	554.8	749.8	895.4	77.5	674.5			*Trade Balance*	78ac d
125.1	110.3	110.5	209.5	209.9	189.2	191.3	186.1	260.4	163.0	210.2	255.3	372.6			Services: Credit	78ad d
−203.4	−238.8	−228.0	−375.9	−382.5	−360.1	−325.6	−322.0	−444.2	−343.6	−440.7	−522.4	−515.9			Services: Debit	78ae d
704.4	353.6	517.1	18.0	94.5	16.4	132.5	374.2	370.9	569.2	664.9	−189.6	531.2			*Balance on Goods & Services*	78af d
171.8	220.1	244.8	416.2	483.1	542.1	554.5	230.8	483.2	501.7	622.1	622.7	429.8			Income: Credit	78ag d
−415.3	−546.8	−483.6	−522.1	−420.2	−429.7	−260.9	−455.1	−515.6	−754.8	−766.9	−503.1	−696.0			Income: Debit	78ah d
460.9	26.9	278.3	−87.9	157.4	128.8	426.1	149.9	338.5	316.1	520.1	−70.0	265.1			*Balance on Gds, Serv. & Inc.*	78ai d
280.8	301.8	266.8	330.7	421.6	344.5	275.9	356.8	330.7	355.4	456.8	460.9	474.4			Current Transfers, n.i.e.: Credit	78aj d
−113.2	−134.7	−53.2	−262.1	−276.0	−275.6	−275.1	−295.1	−369.5	−176.6	−255.5	−220.8	−222.6			Current Transfers: Debit	78ak d
5.8	—	6.3	64.7	37.5	53.2	84.9	19.2	14.4	6.2	16.9	31.8	20.6	....	....	Capital Account, n.i.e.	78bc d
7.0	—	7.0	65.6	38.5	53.8	86.1	19.6	15.4	18.0	29.4	44.2	33.5			Capital Account, n.i.e.: Credit	78ba d
−1.1	—	−.7	−.9	−1.0	−.5	−1.3	−.4	−.9	−11.9	−12.5	−12.4	−12.9			Capital Account: Debit	78bb d
−89.8	−25.3	113.0	82.6	123.3	275.8	−40.3	41.1	−33.9	42.4	5.6	−202.4	−175.2	....	....	Financial Account, n.i.e.	78bj d
—	—	—	−7.4	−8.5	−9.9	−9.5	−9.5	−40.9	1.1	−4.1	−3.5	−1.5			Direct Investment Abroad	78bd d
113.6	39.9	42.2	95.9	−8.2	−1.6	−286.9	−14.2	70.4	71.2	100.1	95.3	36.7			Dir. Invest. in Rep. Econ., n.i.e.	78be d
								−36.2	−35.5	−28.5	−42.8	−22.8			Portfolio Investment Assets	78bf d
								−30.8	−26.7	−33.1	−16.9	6.5			Equity Securities	78bk d
								−5.4	−8.9	4.7	−25.9	−29.3			Debt Securities	78bl d
			1.3	−1.2	.1	.2	−.1	5.5	28.9	10.8	−14.1	−7.5			Portfolio Investment Liab., n.i.e.	78bg d
								5.5	28.7	10.8	−14.1	−7.5			Equity Securities	78bm d
			1.3	−1.2	.1	.2	−.1	—	.2	—	—	—			Debt Securities	78bn d
								−.2		−15.4	5.2	−4.6			Financial Derivatives Assets	78bw d
								.3	2.1						Financial Derivatives Liabilities	78bx d
−251.6	−68.3	−34.6	−136.9	−53.0	148.9	63.4	15.8	−88.7	−95.6	−166.5	−310.8	−206.1			Other Investment Assets	78bh d
															Monetary Authorities	78bo d
11.4	−41.4	−45.0	−91.8	11.7	139.9	56.1	19.7	−46.1	−28.7	−78.0	−101.1	−17.8			General Government	78bp d
−4.2	−8.9	10.4	−33.5	−23.4	−7.0	14.3	.4	−8.7	−35.1	−76.9	−139.7	−154.7			Banks	78bq d
−258.8	−18.0	—	−11.7	−41.3	16.1	−6.9	−4.3	−34.0	−31.8	−11.6	−70.0	−33.7			Other Sectors	78br d
48.3	3.1	105.4	129.7	194.2	138.2	192.5	49.0	55.9	70.3	109.3	68.2	30.7			Other Investment Liab., n.i.e.	78bi d
															Monetary Authorities	78bs d
38.5	—	28.2	12.3	77.9	54.4	67.0	6.5	−12.3	−19.6	51.3	22.2	−16.1			General Government	78bt d
3.0	3.1	−4.6	9.5	−3.6	−5.6	23.1	−2.8	−2.5	17.8	−3.4	−3.5	1.4			Banks	78bu d
6.7	—	81.8	108.0	119.9	89.4	102.4	45.3	70.7	72.1	61.4	49.5	45.4			Other Sectors	78bv d
16.9	213.7	−34.7	179.2	−89.7	−121.4	−74.5	−136.7	−73.6	−32.9	−108.9	44.6	8.7			Net Errors and Omissions	78ca d
561.5	382.3	576.5	307.2	374.1	405.3	397.0	135.2	206.6	510.7	635.1	44.2	371.0			*Overall Balance*	78cb d
−561.5	−382.3	−576.5	−307.2	−374.1	−405.3	−397.0	−135.2	−206.6	−510.7	−635.1	−44.2	−371.0			Reserves and Related Items	79da d
−561.5	−382.3	−576.5	−307.2	−374.1	−405.3	−397.0	−135.2	−206.6	−510.7	−635.1	−44.2	−371.0			Reserve Assets	79db d
—	—	—	—	—	—	—	—	—	—	—	—	—			Use of Fund Credit and Loans	79dc d
															Exceptional Financing	79de d

International Investment Position

Millions of US Dollars

1987	1988	1989	1990	1991	1992	1993	1994	1995	1996	1997	1998	1999	2000	2001		
....	....	....	....	....	....	....	5,084.0	5,643.9	6,001.0	6,510.5	6,855.1	7,356.3	....	....	Assets	79aa d
							484.5	650.1	576.7	404.5	257.5	596.9			Direct Investment Abroad	79ab d
							26.9	61.5	139.1	132.2	214.6	148.2			Portfolio Investment	79ac d
							16.1	45.8	105.8	81.7	73.6	120.2			Equity Securities	79ad d
							10.9	15.8	33.3	50.5	141.0	28.0			Debt Securities	79ae d
							—	.2		17.1	9.6				Financial Derivatives	79al d
							171.3	239.1	253.1	280.3	433.0	382.4			Other Investment	79af d
							—	—	—	—	—	—			Monetary Authorities	79ag d
															General Government	79ah d
							63.3	69.5	99.9	186.2	291.5	289.9			Banks	79ai d
							107.9	169.6	153.3	94.2	141.5	92.5			Other Sectors	79aj d
							4,401.3	4,693.0	5,032.1	5,676.5	5,940.3	6,228.8			Reserve Assets	79ak d
							2,005.3	1,995.1	1,941.9	2,151.9	2,248.7	2,514.8			Liabilities	79la d
							998.5	1,126.4	1,058.1	1,172.9	1,294.8	1,387.3			Dir. Invest. in Rep. Economy	79lb d
							10.9	15.9	50.4	60.5	34.2	24.0			Portfolio Investment	79lc d
							10.9	15.9	50.4	60.0	33.4	22.7			Equity Securities	79ld d
							—	.2	1.9	.5	.8	1.3			Debt Securities	79le d
															Financial Derivatives	79ll d
							996.0	852.6	831.5	918.5	919.7	1,103.5			Other Investment	79lf d
							—	—	—	—	—	—			Monetary Authorities	79lg d
							496.9	495.8	387.9	483.1	482.6	523.6			General Government	79lh d
							38.9	35.1	27.4	23.7	16.8	15.3			Banks	79li d
							460.1	321.7	416.2	411.7	420.3	564.6			Other Sectors	79lj d

Botswana

	1972	1973	1974	1975	1976	1977	1978	1979	1980	1981	1982	1983	1984	1985	1986
Government Finance														*Millions of Pula:*	
Deficit (-) or Surplus............... 80	−21.00	−14.05	−5.67	1.24	−20.75	−4.58	−6.91	21.38	−1.27	−18.34	−20.09	103.22	188.32	413.83	†539.30
Total Revenue and Grants 81y	28.85	45.63	65.89	89.28	84.87	115.48	160.82	243.17	301.69	315.06	387.60	556.17	791.15	1,120.68	†1547.50
Revenue 81	27.12	39.36	60.60	77.92	68.39	97.39	132.24	206.09	263.88	275.27	340.39	507.97	750.82	1,079.45	†1479.90
Grants 81z	1.73	6.27	5.29	11.36	16.48	18.09	28.58	37.08	37.81	39.79	47.21	48.20	40.33	41.23	†67.60
Exp. & Lending Minus Repay. 82z	49.85	59.68	71.56	88.04	105.62	120.06	167.73	221.79	302.96	333.40	407.69	452.95	602.83	706.85	†1008.20
Expenditure 82	29.74	42.38	62.11	77.61	98.24	112.71	156.34	200.43	261.91	300.13	372.61	401.16	526.23	642.83	†986.40
Lending Minus Repayments 83	20.11	17.30	9.45	10.43	7.38	7.35	11.39	21.36	41.05	33.27	35.08	51.79	76.60	64.02	†21.80
Total Financing 80h	21.00	14.05	5.67	−1.24	20.75	4.58	6.91	−21.38	1.27	18.34	20.09	−103.22	−188.32	−413.83	†−539.30
Total Net Borrowing................. 84	27.00	21.95	19.07	16.16	16.15	9.07	11.06	12.55	7.55	.20	60.33	17.97	35.49	13.71	†80.20
Net Domestic 84a	2.43	.26	1.04	2.51	5.41	2.92	−3.48	.53	−3.31	−11.65	1.47	−2.16	1.82	.49	†14.10
Net Foreign 85a	24.57	21.69	18.03	13.65	10.74	6.15	14.54	12.02	10.86	11.85	58.86	20.13	33.67	13.22	†66.10
Use of Cash Balances 87	−6.00	−7.90	−13.40	−17.40	4.60	−4.49	−4.15	−33.93	−6.28	18.14	−40.24	−121.19	−223.81	−427.54	†−619.50
Total Debt by Currency.............. 88	....	....	....	....	....	117.01	123.99	101.89	113.40	133.80	199.80	232.95	381.12	411.46	†483.20
Domestic 88b	....	....	....	....	....	15.35	14.49	14.28	14.67	1.35	.57	.58	.50	.50	†.30
Foreign 89b	....	....	....	....	....	101.66	109.50	87.61	98.73	132.45	199.23	232.37	380.62	410.96	†482.90
National Accounts														*Millions of Pula:*	
Househ.Cons.Expend.,incl.NPISHs ... 96f	58.1	....	105.7	131.8	179.6	222.6	262.9	330.4	408.9	460.3	513.2	563.2	615.1	784.8	901.8
Government Consumption Expend. 91f	16.0	....	31.7	41.5	58.2	80.2	95.9	110.7	148.7	203.2	242.6	301.9	362.8	443.1	531.8
Gross Fixed Capital Formation 93e	53.1	....	79.6	57.3	79.1	77.8	110.1	162.9	248.8	306.6	304.6	320.3	337.6	484.0	457.9
Changes in Inventories 93i	1.3	....	17.8	44.4	35.9	20.9	32.4	34.7	42.1	49.2	87.9	26.8	28.7	71.6	−64.6
Exports of Goods and Services 90c	39.8	....	76.4	93.8	135.2	190.8	196.3	312.8	410.5	464.5	428.7	711.7	884.9	1,074.5	1,737.5
Imports of Goods and Services (-) ... 98c	65.7	....	121.8	147.6	187.5	241.6	285.5	384.6	487.4	608.3	677.1	770.8	838.2	1,029.4	1,143.8
Gross Domestic Product (GDP) 99b	102.6	135.0	188.3	221.2	300.5	350.7	412.1	566.9	771.6	875.5	899.9	1,153.1	1,390.9	1,828.6	2,420.6
Net Primary Income from Abroad 98.n	—	....	9.3	15.1	18.5	−24.4	−31.9	−44.7	....	64.9	125.1	104.9	195.2	322.8	
Gross National Income (GNI) 99a	....	....	....	....	....	....	....	....	725.1	764.4	835.0	1,028.0	1,286.0	1,633.4	2,097.8
Consumption of Fixed Capital 99cf	5.2	....	23.0	26.2	47.1	56.9	64.5	81.1	104.8	135.5	161.0	214.3	243.7	278.4	349.8
GDP Volume 1993/94 Prices 99b.p	....	....	....	....	....	....	....	....	....	....	....	....	....	....	
GDP Volume (1995=100) .... 99bv p	10.0	12.5	15.5	15.3	18.2	18.8	22.5	24.7	28.3	30.9	33.3	38.6	43.0	46.1	49.6
GDP Deflator (1995=100)........... 99bi p	8.4	8.8	9.9	11.8	13.5	15.2	14.9	18.7	22.3	23.1	22.1	24.4	26.4	32.3	39.8
															Millions:
Population............................... 99z	.63	.65	.66	.69	.69	.71	.73	.79	.89	.94	.97	1.01	1.05	1.09	1.13

1987	1988	1989	1990	1991	1992	1993	1994	1995	1996	1997	1998	1999	2000	2001		
Year Beginning April 1															**Government Finance**	
513.00	768.50	536.40	798.00	697.20	881.40	878.30	195.60	269.90	1,302.40	875.10	-1,387.80	1,535.60	2,838.00	....	Deficit (-) or Surplus	80
1,825.00	2,556.10	2,750.90	3,740.70	4,069.40	4,652.30	5,359.50	4,472.50	5,464.40	7,394.80	8,281.30	7,677.60	11,963.10	14,030.30	....	Total Revenue and Grants	81y
1,719.10	2,446.40	2,710.90	3,622.90	3,999.60	4,552.20	5,172.90	4,396.80	5,427.30	7,311.80	8,169.20	7,539.90	11,837.00	13,975.10	....	Revenue	81
105.90	109.70	40.00	117.80	69.80	100.10	186.60	75.70	37.10	83.00	112.10	137.70	126.10	55.20	....	Grants	81z
1,312.00	1,787.60	2,214.50	2,942.70	3,372.20	3,770.90	4,481.20	4,276.90	5,194.50	6,092.40	7,406.20	9,065.40	10,427.50	11,192.30	....	Exp. & Lending Minus Repay.	82z
1,253.80	1,704.30	1,982.50	2,528.70	2,913.70	3,422.30	4,291.90	4,389.10	5,181.60	6,283.50	7,624.20	9,199.80	10,608.90	11,281.80	....	Expenditure	82
58.20	83.30	232.00	414.00	458.50	348.60	189.30	-112.20	12.90	-191.10	-218.00	-134.40	-181.40	-89.50	....	Lending Minus Repayments	83
-513.00	-768.60	-536.40	-798.00	-697.30	-881.30	-878.30	-195.70	-269.80	-1,302.30	-875.50	1,387.80	-1,535.60	-2,837.90	....	Total Financing	80h
79.00	105.00	101.00	-17.90	225.30	-62.20	90.90	69.50	89.80	-8,148.70	13,466.90	1,098.20	-216.50	401.50	....	Total Net Borrowing	84
10.30	5.20	47.40	-20.80	191.10	-142.50	46.00	91.20	135.80	-8,233.80	13,380.70	1,118.40	-151.90	581.90	....	Net Domestic	84a
68.70	99.80	53.60	2.90	34.20	80.30	44.90	-21.70	-46.00	85.10	86.20	-20.20	-64.60	-180.40	....	Net Foreign	85a
-592.00	-873.60	-637.40	-780.10	-922.60	-819.10	-969.20	-265.20	-359.60	6,846.40	*,***,***	289.60	-1,319.10	-3,239.40	....	Use of Cash Balances	87
557.80	737.90	751.90	787.80	965.80	1,096.20	1,267.80	1,377.70	1,439.90	1,791.20	1,996.90	2,422.70	2,425.30	3,067.50	....	Total Debt by Currency	88
—	—	—	—	—	—	—	—	—	—	—	—	—	—		Domestic	88b
557.80	737.90	751.90	787.80	965.80	1,096.20	1,267.80	1,377.70	1,439.90	1,791.20	1,996.90	2,422.70	2,425.30	3,067.50		Foreign	89b
Year Ending June 30															**National Accounts**	
987.4	1,116.0	1,682.8	2,062.7	2,624.8	3,123.9	3,282.2	3,843.0	4,258.5	4,714.7	5,314.7	6,136.1	6,936.8	7,824.5	....	Househ.Cons.Expend.,incl.NPISHs	96f
722.6	1,052.3	1,182.9	1,558.3	1,846.1	2,016.4	2,595.2	3,048.1	3,546.7	4,006.7	4,711.0	5,452.9	6,578.8	7,524.5	....	Government Consumption Expend.	91f
669.9	1,081.8	1,692.9	2,129.9	2,433.8	2,551.3	2,618.7	2,729.2	3,135.2	3,632.4	4,275.9	5,170.1	6,263.3	6,619.4	....	Gross Fixed Capital Formation	93e
18.6	-804.3	56.1	384.4	322.4	-13.3	165.3	204.3	13.7	-261.4	328.0	885.9	1,653.9	94.4	....	Changes in Inventories	93i
1,838.8	3,119.0	3,701.6	3,658.3	4,107.1	4,346.6	4,082.8	5,421.8	6,071.4	7,411.6	9,881.6	11,392.8	10,051.6	14,108.1	....	Exports of Goods and Services	90c
1,427.5	1,769.2	2,479.5	3,253.9	3,769.1	3,648.3	3,625.0	4,260.3	4,772.5	5,300.1	6,711.1	8,875.3	9,960.6	10,963.1	....	Imports of Goods and Services (-)	98c
2,585.3	3,498.7	5,803.5	6,539.7	7,565.0	8,376.5	9,119.2	11,041.4	12,261.7	14,203.9	17,740.1	20,162.5	21,523.8	25,207.8	....	Gross Domestic Product (GDP)	99b
251.7	465.1	....	....	....	....	....	....	....	....	....	....	....	....	....	Net Primary Income from Abroad	98.n
2,558.2	3,316.1	....	....	....	....	....	....	....	....	....	....	....	....	....	Gross National Income (GNI)	99a
432.4	575.6	765.3	654.3	828.8	1,156.8	1,195.1	1,496.4	1,652.7	1,944.3	....	....	....	....	....	Consumption of Fixed Capital	99cf
6,153.3	7,056.0	8,651.8	9,201.4	10,009.9	10,634.3	10,612.1	11,041.4	11,396.8	12,029.5	12,703.7	13,728.7	14,295.6	15,394.2	....	GDP Volume 1993/94 Prices	99b.p
54.0	61.9	75.9	80.7	87.8	93.3	93.1	96.9	100.0	105.6	111.5	120.5	125.4	135.1	....	GDP Volume (1995=100)	99bvp
39.1	46.1	62.3	66.1	70.2	73.2	79.9	92.9	100.0	109.7	129.8	136.5	139.9	152.2	....	GDP Deflator (1995=100)	99bip
Midyear Estimates																
1.17	1.21	1.24	1.30	1.35	1.36	1.39	1.42	1.46	1.50	1.53	1.57	1.61	1.65	1.55	**Population**	99z

(See notes in the back of the book.)

Brazil

		1972	1973	1974	1975	1976	1977	1978	1979	1980	1981	1982	1983	1984	1985	1986
Exchange Rates													*Reais per Trillion SDRs through 1983, per Bill. 1984-88, per Mill.*			
Principal Rate	aa	2.459	2.735	3.318	3.861	5.216	7.089	9.911	20.373	30.378	54.092	101.354	374.618	†1.135	4.190	6.625
											Reais per Trillion US$ through 1983, per Bill.US$ 1984-88, per Mill.US$					
Principal Rate	ae	2.265	2.267	2.710	3.298	4.489	5.836	7.607	15.465	23.818	46.473	91.880	357.818	†1.158	3.815	5.416
Principal Rate	rf	2.157	2.227	2.468	2.954	3.879	5.141	6.568	9.794	19.159	33.847	65.246	209.731	†.672	2.254	4.963
Fund Position														*Millions of SDRs:*		
Quota	2f. s	440	440	440	440	440	440	665	665	998	998	998	1,461	1,461	1,461	1,461
SDRs	1b. s	157	157	163	163	171	173	184	291	301	388	—	—	1	1	—
Reserve Position in the Fund	1c. s	116	116	116	116	162	160	139	183	270	227	260	—	—	—	—
Total Fund Cred.&Loans Outstg.	2tl	—	—	—	—	—	—	—	—	—	—	499	2,526	4,270	4,205	3,680
International Liquidity												*Millions of US Dollars Unless Otherwise Indicated:*				
Total Reserves minus Gold	1l. d	4,133	6,360	5,216	3,980	6,488	7,192	11,826	8,966	5,769	6,604	3,928	4,355	11,508	10,605	†5,803
SDRs	1b. d	170	190	199	191	199	210	239	383	384	452	—	—	1	1	—
Reserve Position in the Fund	1c. d	126	140	142	136	188	195	181	241	344	264	287	—	—	—	—
Foreign Exchange	1d. d	3,836	6,030	4,874	3,653	6,101	6,787	11,406	8,342	5,042	5,888	3,641	4,355	11,507	10,604	†5,803
Other Liquid Foreign Assets	1e. d															
Gold (Million Fine Troy Ounces)	1ad	1.33	1.33	1.33	1.33	1.33	1.52	1.61	1.70	1.88	2.20	.15	.54	1.47	3.10	2.43
Gold (National Valuation)	1and	50	56	56	56	56	64	68	75	1,143	905	65	207	488	1,004	958
Monetary Authorities: Other Assets	3.. d	476	665	896	1,195	1,473	1,599	1,513	1,613	4,333	3,050	2,804	3,818	4,463	4,965	2,445
Other Liab.	4.. d	618	574	940	1,162	1,765	1,956	3,286	4,504	6,810	6,846	8,557	14,928	18,888	19,198	29,939
Deposit Money Banks: Assets	7a. d	436	895	1,161	929	1,175	1,214	2,043	1,817	1,489	2,088	2,099	1,924	2,274	1,983	3,379
Liabilities	7b. d	1,452	2,258	2,973	2,778	4,797	5,849	8,365	8,109	11,292	15,764	18,150	16,997	17,325	14,053	14,128
Other Banking Insts.: Assets	7e. d	—	—	—	—	—	—	—	—	—	24	99	401	136	8	7
Liabilities	7f. d	1,290	1,613	1,757	2,111	2,276	2,704	4,183	4,823	5,337	6,336	6,794	7,032	6,564	6,539	6,287
Monetary Authorities											*Millionths of Reais through 1974; Thousandths 1975-85; Reais 1986-89;*					
Foreign Assets	11	10,182	15,636	16,000	†16	34	48	†102	165	267	488	621	2,984	18,960	62,094	†47
Claims on Central Government	12a	−727	−2,545	−9,455	†−17	−20	−18	†35	43	157	330	618	1,235	3,144	12,698	†224
Claims on State and Local Govts	12b	—	—	—	† —	—	1	†6	8	9	19	30	67	92	257	† —
Claims on Nonfin.Pub.Enterprises	12c	—	—	—	† —	—	1	†9	21	27	62	79	1,031	4,644	30,605	† —
Claims on Private Sector	12d	12,727	18,182	32,000	†54	86	125	†154	253	435	720	1,253	2,504	5,876	23,337	† —
Claims on Deposit Money Banks	12e	2,182	3,273	6,545	†12	17	24	†26	35	57	129	244	486	1,769	4,977	†114
Claims on Other Banking Insts	12f	1,091	1,455	5,091	†9	16	28	†25	27	37	66	89	132	191	756	†2
Claims on Nonbank Financial Insts	12g															† —
Reserve Money	14	9,091	13,455	18,545	†26	40	60	†86	160	252	429	801	1,649	5,409	18,981	†75
of which: Currency Outside DMBs	14a	4,364	5,818	8,000	†11	17	24	†34	61	105	190	367	684	2,272	8,671	†31
Money Market Instruments	16aa															
Liabs. of Central Bank: Securities	16ac															†74
Restricted Deposits	16b				†3	15	16	†23	30	12	5	3	1	35	134	†33
Foreign Liabilities	16c	1,091	1,091	1,091	†1	4	6	†3	4	41	84	629	2,535	8,086	21,143	†30
Long-Term Foreign Liabilities	16cl	364	364	1,455	†3	4	5	†22	65	120	233	204	3,720	18,495	69,276	†156
Central Government Deposits	16d							88	79	171	478	636	808	7,861	31,981	†36
Capital Accounts	17a	6,182	8,727	15,636	†24	36	55	†64	88	76	−17	−424	−3,272	−12,809	−38,888	† —
Other Items (Net)	17r	8,727	12,364	13,455	†18	35	68	†71	127	316	603	1,086	2,995	7,601	32,095	†−52
Deposit Money Banks											*Millionths of Reais through 1974; Thousandths 1975-85; Reais 1986-89;*					
Reserves	20	2,545	3,636	4,000	†4	9	19	†29	51	84	132	276	552	1,906	5,900	†41
Claims on Mon.Author.: Securities	20c															
Blocked Financial Assets	20d															
Foreign Assets	21	1,091	2,182	3,273	†3	5	7	†15	28	35	97	192	685	2,620	7,528	†18
Claims on Central Government	22a	2,909	4,364	5,818	†9	15	19	†26	37	90	269	524	1,091	4,616	17,369	†28
Claims on State and Local Govts	22b	1,455	1,818	1,818	†3	6	10	†19	38	73	219	498	1,521	4,874	17,612	†36
Claims on Nonfin.Pub.Enterprises	22c							23	49	98	251	583	2,037	6,415	21,781	†105
Claims on Private Sector	22d	19,273	27,636	41,455	†63	95	143	†205	337	572	1,170	2,377	5,731	19,269	67,785	†286
Claims on Other Banking Insts	22f	—	364	364	† —	—	1	†1	4	11	26	98	241	537	3,646	†5
Claims on Nonbank Financial Insts.	22g															† —
Demand Deposits	24	14,182	21,091	28,364	†41	55	77	†103	176	304	561	900	1,866	5,418	25,740	†125
Time and Savings Deposits	25	2,182	2,545	2,909	†4	7	16	†34	56	67	152	412	1,448	7,287	29,729	†100
Money Market Instruments	26aa															
Restricted Deposits	26b															
Foreign Liabilities	26c	1,091	2,545	3,636	†3	10	15	†30	51	120	309	586	1,966	7,914	22,805	†40
Long-Term Foreign Liabilities	26cl	2,182	2,545	4,364	†6	11	19	†33	73	153	449	1,075	4,085	11,751	30,547	†36
Central Government Deposits	26d	364	364	364	†1	1	1	†47	57	104	247	489	745	2,692	6,707	†15
Credit from Monetary Authorities	26g	2,182	3,273	6,182	†12	17	25	†21	33	60	132	246	555	1,809	1,950	†115
Liabilities to Other Banking Insts	26i															
Liab. to Nonbank Financial Insts	26j															
Capital Accounts	27a	4,000	5,455	7,273	†10	16	26	†47	64	111	289	656	2,007	6,881	24,946	†77
Other Items (Net)	27r	1,091	2,182	3,636	†6	14	19	†3	34	45	26	184	−813	−3,516	−802	†10
Monetary Survey											*Millionths of Reais through 1974; Thousandths 1975-85; Reais 1986-89;*					
Foreign Assets (Net)	31n	9,091	14,182	14,545	†15	25	34	†85	138	141	192	−401	−832	5,579	25,675	†−5
Domestic Credit	32	36,364	50,909	76,727	†121	197	309	†368	683	1,234	2,408	5,024	14,036	39,106	157,157	†609
Claims on Central Govt. (Net)	32an	1,818	1,455	−4,000	†−9	−7	—	†−74	−55	−28	−126	17	773	−2,792	−8,621	†175
Claims on State and Local Govts	32b	1,455	1,818	1,818	†3	6	11	†25	46	83	239	528	1,588	4,966	17,869	†36
Claims on Nonfin.Pub.Enterprises	32c	—	—	—	† —	—	1	†32	70	125	313	662	3,067	11,059	52,386	†105
Claims on Private Sector	32d	32,000	45,818	73,455	†117	181	269	†359	590	1,006	1,890	3,629	8,235	25,145	91,122	†286
Claims on Other Banking Insts	32f	1,091	1,818	5,455	†9	16	29	†26	32	48	92	187	372	728	4,402	†7
Claims on Nonbank Financial Inst	32g															† —
Money	34	21,455	31,273	42,909	†61	84	116	†158	276	468	855	1,441	2,922	8,887	38,600	†166
Quasi-Money	35	2,182	2,545	2,909	†4	7	16	†34	56	67	152	412	1,448	7,287	29,729	†100
Money Market Instruments	36aa															
Liabs. of Central Bank: Securities	36ac															†74
Restricted Deposits	36b	—	—	—	†3	15	16	†23	30	12	5	3	1	35	134	†33
Long-Term Foreign Liabilities	36cl	2,545	2,909	5,818	†8	15	24	†56	139	273	682	1,279	7,806	30,246	99,823	†193
Liabilities to Other Banking Insts	36i															
Liab. to Nonbank Financial Insts	36j															
Capital Accounts	37a	10,182	14,182	22,909	†33	52	81	†111	152	188	271	233	−1,265	−5,928	−13,942	†112
Other Items (Net)	37r	9,091	14,182	16,727	†25	49	91	†73	168	367	635	1,256	2,292	4,159	28,488	†−73
Money plus Quasi-Money	35l	23,636	33,818	45,818	†65	91	132	†192	332	535	1,007	1,853	4,370	16,174	68,329	†266

	1987	1988	1989	1990	1991	1992	1993	1994	1995	1996	1997	1998	1999	2000	2001	
Exchange Rates																
1989-92, per Thous.SDRs thereafter: End of Period																
Principal Rate	37.273	374.496	†5.428	91.599	555.943	6,193.750	†162.882	1,235.033	1,446.355	1,494.616	1,506.303	1,701.886	2,455.420	2,546.668	2,916.116	aa
1989-92, per Thous.US$ thereafter: End of Per.(ae) Per. Average (rf)																
Principal Rate	26.273	278.291	†4.130	64.385	388.655	4,504.545	†118.584	846.000	973.000	1,039.400	1,116.400	1,208.700	1,789.000	1,954.600	2,320.400	ae
Principal Rate	14.258	95.272	†1.031	24.836	147.857	1,641.087	†32.163	639.300	917.667	1,005.100	1,077.992	1,160.517	1,814.733	1,830.142	2,357.708	rf
Fund Position																
End of Period																
Quota	1,461	1,461	1,461	1,461	1,461	2,171	2,171	2,171	2,171	2,171	2,171	2,171	3,036	3,036	3,036	2f.s
SDRs	—	—	—	8	9	1	2	—	1	1	—	1	7	—	8	1b.s
Reserve Position in the Fund	—	—	—	—	—	—	—	—	—	—	—	—	—	—	—	1c.s
Total Fund Cred.&Loans Outstg.	2,803	2,477	1,843	1,280	865	581	221	128	95	47	23	3,427	6,431	1,357	6,634	2tl
International Liquidity																
End of Period																
Total Reserves minus Gold	6,299	6,972	7,535	7,441	8,033	22,521	30,604	37,070	49,708	58,323	50,827	42,580	34,796	32,488	35,740	1l.d
SDRs	—	—	—	11	13	1	2	—	1	1	1	2	10	—	11	1b.d
Reserve Position in the Fund	—	—	—	—	—	—	—	—	—	—	—	—	—	—	—	1c.d
Foreign Exchange	6,299	6,971	7,535	7,430	8,020	22,520	30,602	37,069	49,707	58,322	50,826	42,578	34,786	32,488	35,729	1d.d
Other Liquid Foreign Assets	....	1,024	950	798	643	486	501	319	365	467	503	585	618	—	—	1e.d
Gold (Million Fine Troy Ounces)	2.43	2.73	2.98	4.57	2.02	2.23	2.93	3.71	4.58	3.69	3.03	4.60	3.17	1.89	.46	1ad
Gold (National Valuation)	1,159	1,144	1,194	1,735	731	747	1,107	1,418	1,767	1,381	903	1,358	929	523	127	1and
Monetary Authorities: Other Assets	3,315	2,446	2,751	2,425	2,095	2,331	2,056	1,851	4,077	5,050	4,935	5,456	5,334	6,110	—	3..d
Other Liab.	46,405	46,024	46,728	28,502	56,762	47,253	48,399	6,888	5,614	3,239	2,948	8,284	5,288	2,419	1,255	4..d
Deposit Money Banks: Assets	3,544	5,551	8,186	8,628	9,573	11,763	15,196	20,855	18,682	20,345	19,550	17,621	16,754	15,878	16,525	7a.d
Liabilities	13,138	14,167	15,252	15,696	16,776	21,472	31,054	36,771	42,494	51,432	54,756	50,580	41,890	40,646	39,837	7b.d
Other Banking Insts.: Assets	9	127	77	100	27	141	702	1,504	393	177	143	74	65	207	152	7e.d
Liabilities	6,307	4,183	2,849	2,352	2,013	2,242	2,527	2,224	2,247	3,211	4,398	9,406	6,282	7,975	8,532	7f.d
Monetary Authorities																
Thousands 1990-92; Millions Beginning 1993: End of Period																
Foreign Assets	269	†3,257	49,425	†675	4,028	111,731	†3,968	35,326	55,218	69,829	61,745	55,053	69,273	76,097	82,026	11
Claims on Central Government	901	†18,140	300,863	†5,747	29,354	363,345	†7,941	26,509	31,221	27,713	41,233	136,916	121,463	130,779	189,786	12a
Claims on State and Local Govts	—	†—	—	†194	862	172	†9	—	—	—	—	—	—	—	—	12b
Claims on Nonfin.Pub.Enterprises	—	†—	—	†—	—	—	†—	—	—	—	—	—	—	—	—	12c
Claims on Private Sector	—	†8	49	†—	—	2	†—	3	5	5	5	—	—	—	—	12d
Claims on Deposit Money Banks	445	†66	3,733	†153	662	17,299	†120	20,557	34,576	67,642	68,012	40,368	33,755	38,604	20,679	12e
Claims on Other Banking Insts	9	†2	474	†6	6	163	†1	5	5	3	902	—	—	—	1,764	12f
Claims on Nonbank Financial Insts	1	†20	8	†—	1	5	†—	—	—	6	7	1,926	2,036	1,373	1,456	12g
Reserve Money	413	†1,589	42,113	†821	4,897	61,120	†1,543	36,130	40,430	49,638	66,636	59,213	63,849	66,901	79,639	14
of which: Currency Outside DMBs	92	†760	14,677	†356	1,314	14,564	†340	8,700	12,517	15,316	18,141	21,185	25,978	28,641	32,625	14a
Money Market Instruments	....	—	—	†—	—	—	†—	—	—	—	—	3,290	4,708	6,347	6,297	16aa
Liabs. of Central Bank: Securities	594	†97	299	†11	987	94,933	†867	39,289	52,457	83,106	65,724	104,709	62,468	85,839	126,524	16ac
Restricted Deposits	152	†1,148	16,137	†1,498	4,449	5,014	†75	306	190	125	12	10	13	13	15	16b
Foreign Liabilities	270	†1,096	14,227	†203	7,303	28,125	†807	895	478	143	167	7,723	15,942	3,509	19,405	16c
Long-Term Foreign Liabilities	1,047	†12,571	187,771	†1,656	15,237	188,322	†4,968	5,075	5,116	3,292	3,157	8,111	9,297	4,675	2,844	16cl
Central Government Deposits	134	†780	35,195	†874	3,036	42,889	†1,023	12,094	22,239	25,143	41,135	50,403	75,779	88,380	82,516	16d
Capital Accounts	48	†4,468	42,509	†128	727	70,673	†1,838	998	1,408	4,190	4,198	3,809	–4,496	–8,312	6,814	17a
Other Items (Net)	–1,034	†–257	16,303	†1,585	–1,722	1,642	†918	–12,387	–1,293	–438	–9,125	–3,005	–1,034	–500	–28,342	17r
Deposit Money Banks																
Thousands 1990-92; Millions Beginning 1993: End of Period																
Reserves	351	†1,597	21,710	†387	2,325	30,779	†901	22,956	22,126	22,035	42,494	32,716	38,029	38,341	46,389	20
Claims on Mon.Author.: Securities	....	97	299	†9	119	46,131	†320	5,192	6,578	18,932	11,603	37,545	29,240	52,258	61,524	20c
Blocked Financial Assets	....	—	—	†1,251	3,612	1	†—	—	—	—	—	—	—	—	—	20d
Foreign Assets	93	†1,537	33,645	†529	3,720	52,983	†1,802	17,602	18,159	21,130	21,810	21,284	29,960	31,035	38,331	21
Claims on Central Government	88	†1,596	122,967	†336	1,055	27,547	†1,027	7,850	16,118	29,224	92,061	74,110	118,086	138,772	201,663	22a
Claims on State and Local Govts	220	†2,960	44,977	†669	3,770	57,656	†1,522	27,480	20,284	55,986	39,229	38,246	19,020	4,274	2,752	22b
Claims on Nonfin.Pub.Enterprises	673	†2,931	53,009	†636	3,040	42,715	†1,158	10,243	6,093	18,669	5,620	12,553	15,193	3,703	1,467	22c
Claims on Private Sector	949	†20,041	305,429	†3,595	19,971	348,163	†11,589	158,826	199,138	204,681	225,197	259,983	273,380	315,948	345,315	22d
Claims on Other Banking Insts	59	†10	2,903	†18	135	3,046	†79	873	770	1,078	3,353	3,678	3,122	3,339	3,718	22f
Claims on Nonbank Financial Insts.	—	†—	—	†—	—	—	†—	—	—	—	—	5,910	985	794	3,671	22g
Demand Deposits	265	†1,748	22,619	†550	2,581	24,073	†497	13,979	14,034	14,320	27,912	29,059	36,251	45,060	50,880	24
Time and Savings Deposits	311	†10,816	172,322	†2,000	16,548	312,748	†9,980	119,979	159,901	173,714	203,992	225,619	238,851	240,116	268,522	25
Money Market Instruments	....	5	4,909	†53	328	9,140	†283	3,320	4,744	7,029	10,283	12,684	13,377	22,880	32,788	26aa
Restricted Deposits	....	—	—	†1,645	4,396	18	†—	98	1,806	227	—	—	—	414	249	26b
Foreign Liabilities	210	†809	19,268	†275	1,736	70,000	†2,568	21,212	28,209	37,441	38,539	31,974	49,786	56,007	62,167	26c
Long-Term Foreign Liabilities	134	†3,114	43,416	†688	4,783	26,719	†1,115	9,823	13,095	15,976	22,547	29,122	25,121	23,440	30,239	26cl
Central Government Deposits	35	†6,024	111,428	†654	3,194	44,638	†1,411	18,288	14,670	16,074	17,939	11,776	7,394	9,430	11,201	26d
Credit from Monetary Authorities	784	†133	5,335	†181	646	16,508	†146	20,455	23,407	39,025	30,272	11,623	3,159	8,568	23,975	26g
Liabilities to Other Banking Insts	....	1,083	16,385	†164	1,228	31,305	†1,081	11,914	9,396	22,017	21,973	27,590	30,632	31,344	43,214	26i
Liab. to Nonbank Financial Insts	....	12	696	†2	13	442	†1	92	111	60	234	22,200	25,256	41,412	46,122	26j
Capital Accounts	370	†5,855	121,551	†1,471	10,726	143,861	†4,069	44,094	57,704	74,127	95,976	115,114	132,225	133,957	163,177	27a
Other Items (Net)	325	†1,170	67,008	†–250	–8,435	–70,431	†–2,752	–12,232	–37,811	–28,275	–28,300	–30,736	–35,037	–24,163	–27,703	27r
Monetary Survey																
Thousands 1990-92; Millions Beginning 1993: End of Period																
Foreign Assets (Net)	–118	†2,889	49,575	†726	–1,291	66,589	†2,395	30,821	44,690	53,375	44,849	36,640	33,504	47,615	38,785	31n
Domestic Credit	2,654	†38,905	684,056	†9,674	51,964	755,285	†20,892	201,407	236,725	296,148	348,533	471,143	470,112	501,173	657,875	32
Claims on Central Govt. (Net)	742	†12,932	277,207	†4,555	24,180	303,364	†6,535	3,977	10,430	15,720	74,220	148,847	156,376	171,741	297,732	32an
Claims on State and Local Govts	220	†2,960	44,977	†863	4,632	57,828	†1,531	27,480	20,284	55,986	39,229	38,246	19,020	4,274	2,752	32b
Claims on Nonfin.Pub.Enterprises	674	†2,931	53,009	†636	3,040	42,715	†1,158	10,243	6,093	18,669	5,620	12,553	15,193	3,703	1,467	32c
Claims on Private Sector	949	†20,049	305,478	†3,595	19,971	348,165	†11,589	158,829	199,143	204,686	225,202	259,983	273,380	315,948	345,315	32d
Claims on Other Banking Insts	68	†12	3,377	†24	140	3,209	†79	878	775	1,081	4,255	3,678	3,122	3,339	5,482	32f
Claims on Nonbank Financial Inst	1	†20	8	†—	1	5	†—	—	—	6	7	7,836	3,021	2,167	5,127	32g
Money	524	†2,623	37,697	†917	4,856	52,539	†1,113	25,540	32,094	41,683	50,999	54,819	62,287	74,081	83,550	34
Quasi-Money	311	†10,816	172,322	†2,000	16,548	312,748	†9,980	119,979	159,901	173,714	203,992	225,619	238,851	240,116	268,522	35
Money Market Instruments	....	5	4,909	†53	328	9,140	†283	3,320	4,744	7,029	10,283	15,974	18,085	29,227	39,085	36aa
Liabs. of Central Bank: Securities	594	†—	—	†2	868	48,802	†547	34,097	45,879	64,174	54,121	67,164	33,228	33,581	65,000	36ac
Restricted Deposits	152	†1,148	16,137	†3,143	8,845	5,032	†75	404	1,996	352	12	10	13	427	264	36b
Long-Term Foreign Liabilities	1,181	†15,685	231,187	†2,344	20,020	215,041	†6,083	14,898	18,211	19,268	25,704	37,233	34,418	28,115	33,083	36cl
Liabilities to Other Banking Insts	....	1,083	16,385	†164	1,228	31,305	†1,081	11,914	9,396	22,017	21,973	27,590	30,632	31,344	43,214	36i
Liab. to Nonbank Financial Insts	....	12	696	†2	13	442	†1	92	111	60	234	22,200	25,256	41,412	46,122	36j
Capital Accounts	418	†10,323	164,060	†1,599	11,453	214,533	†5,908	45,092	59,112	78,317	100,174	118,923	127,729	125,645	169,991	37a
Other Items (Net)	–643	†98	90,237	†178	–13,488	–67,706	†–1,783	–23,108	–50,029	–57,090	–74,110	–61,749	–66,883	–55,160	–52,169	37r
Money plus Quasi-Money	834	†13,440	210,019	†2,918	21,404	365,286	†11,092	145,519	191,995	215,397	254,991	280,438	301,138	314,197	352,072	35l

Brazil

223		1972	1973	1974	1975	1976	1977	1978	1979	1980	1981	1982	1983	1984	1985	1986
Other Banking Institutions																*Millionths of Reais through 1974; Thousandths 1975-85; Reais 1986-89;*
Reserves	40	727	727	1,091	†1	2	2	†2	4	4	12	25	49	156	3,488	....
Claims on Mon.Author.: Securities	40c	....	....	....	....	....	....	....	....	....	....	....	....	....	....	....
Blocked Financial Assets	40d	....	....	....	....	....	....	....	....	....	....	....	....	....	....	....
Foreign Assets	41	—	—	—	†—	—	—	†—	—	—	1	9	143	157	31	†—
Claims on Central Government	42a	2,545	3,636	5,818	†11	18	28	†43	81	129	374	909	2,641	7,771	20,817	....
Claims on State and Local Govts	42b	364	364	364	†—	1	2	†7	16	32	60	180	574	1,999	7,328	†13
Claims on Nonfin.Pub.Enterprises	42c	....	....	....	....	....	....	33	59	102	291	686	1,735	4,532	26,232	†40
Claims on Private Sector	42d	20,727	32,000	51,636	†84	143	224	†304	516	907	2,013	4,452	11,843	38,604	119,282	....
Claims on Deposit Money Banks	42e	1,091	1,818	4,000	†7	13	22	†23	50	106	252	530	1,351	4,153	17,997	....
Claims on Nonbank Financial Insts.	42g	....	....	....	....	....	....	....	....	....	....	....	....	....	....	†—
Demand Deposits	44	727	1,091	1,455	†2	4	5	†5	9	18	34	60	128	361	1,487	†7
Time and Savings Deposits	45	6,545	11,636	18,909	†34	59	97	†153	272	499	1,214	2,807	8,482	29,133	98,264	....
Money Market Instruments	46aa	1,818	2,182	2,909	†3	4	4	†4	5	6	10	11	29	49	46	....
Restricted Deposits	46b	....	....	....	....	....	....	....	....	....	....	....	....	....	....	....
Foreign Liabilities	46c	....	....	....	....	....	....	....	....	....	....	....	....	....	....	....
Long-Term Foreign Liabilities	46cl	2,909	3,636	4,727	†7	10	16	†32	75	126	294	621	2,504	7,562	24,823	†34
Central Government Deposits	46d	....	....	....	....	....	....	130	230	419	957	2,159	6,056	20,002	70,455	†81
Credit from Monetary Authorities	46g	727	1,455	3,273	†6	10	17	†25	32	34	62	104	173	404	1,257	†2
Credit from Deposit Money Banks	46h	....	....	....	....	....	....	....	....	....	....	....	....	....	....	....
Liab. to Nonbank Financial Insts.	46j	....	....	....	....	....	....	....	....	....	....	....	....	....	....	....
Capital Accounts	47a	6,545	9,818	15,636	†24	37	51	†71	109	186	422	1,061	2,974	10,040	32,843	....
Other Items (Net)	47r	6,182	8,727	16,000	†27	52	88	†-8	-5	-6	9	-33	-2,010	-10,179	-33,999	....
Banking Survey																*Millionths of Reais through 1974; Thousandths 1975-85; Reais 1986-89;*
Foreign Assets (Net)	51n	9,091	14,182	14,545	†15	25	34	†85	138	141	193	-392	-689	5,736	25,706	†-5
Domestic Credit	52	58,909	85,091	129,091	†207	343	535	†600	1,094	1,938	4,096	8,904	24,400	71,282	255,960	....
Claims on Central Govt. (Net)	52an	4,364	5,091	1,818	†2	11	28	†-161	-203	-317	-709	-1,234	-2,643	-15,023	-58,259	....
Claims on State and Local Govts	52b	1,818	2,182	2,182	†4	7	13	†32	61	115	299	708	2,163	6,965	25,196	†49
Claims on Nonfin.Pub.Enterprises	52c	—	—	—	†—	—	1	†66	129	227	604	1,348	4,802	15,591	78,618	†145
Claims on Private Sector	52d	52,727	77,818	125,091	†201	324	493	†663	1,106	1,913	3,903	8,081	20,078	63,749	210,404	....
Claims on Nonbank Financial Inst	52g	....	....	....	....	....	....	....	....	....	....	....	....	....	....	†—
Liquid Liabilities	55l	30,182	45,818	65,091	†100	152	232	†348	609	1,047	2,243	4,695	12,931	45,511	164,591	....
Money Market Instruments	56aa	1,818	2,182	2,909	†3	4	4	†4	5	6	10	11	29	49	46	....
Liabs. of Central Bank: Securities	56ac	....	....	....	....	....	....	....	....	....	....	....	....	....	....	†74
Restricted Deposits	56b	—	—	—	†3	15	16	†23	30	12	5	3	1	35	134	†33
Long-Term Foreign Liabilities	56cl	5,455	6,545	10,545	†15	25	40	†88	213	399	976	1,900	10,309	37,808	124,646	†227
Liab. to Nonbank Financial Insts	56j	....	....	....	....	....	....	....	....	....	....	....	....	....	....	....
Capital Accounts	57a	16,727	24,000	38,545	†57	89	132	†182	262	374	693	1,293	1,709	4,112	18,901	....
Other Items (Net)	57r	13,818	20,727	26,545	†43	83	145	†41	113	241	362	610	-1,268	-10,496	-26,653	....
Nonbank Financial Institutions																*Reais through 1989; Thousands of Reais from 1990 through 1992;*
Reserves	40..*n*	....	....	....	....	....	....	....	....	....	....	....	....	....	....	....
Claims on Mon.Author.: Securities	40c.*n*	....	....	....	....	....	....	....	....	....	....	....	....	....	....	....
Blocked Financial Assets	40d.*n*	....	....	....	....	....	....	....	....	....	....	....	....	....	....	....
Foreign Assets	41..*n*	....	....	....	....	....	....	....	....	....	....	....	....	....	....	....
Claims on Central Government	42a.*n*	....	....	....	....	....	....	....	....	....	....	....	....	....	....	....
Claims on State and Local Govt.	42b.*n*	....	....	....	....	....	....	....	....	....	....	....	....	....	....	....
Claims on Nonfin.Pub.Enterprises	42c.*n*	....	....	....	....	....	....	....	....	....	....	....	....	....	....	....
Claims on Private Sector	42d.*n*	....	....	....	....	....	....	....	....	....	....	....	....	....	....	....
Claims on Deposit Money Banks	42e.*n*	....	....	....	....	....	....	....	....	....	....	....	....	....	....	....
Claims on Other Banking Insts	42f.*n*	....	....	....	....	....	....	....	....	....	....	....	....	....	....	....
Money Market Instruments	46aa*n*	....	....	....	....	....	....	....	....	....	....	....	....	....	....	....
Restricted Deposits	46b.*n*	....	....	....	....	....	....	....	....	....	....	....	....	....	....	....
Foreign Liabilities	46c.*n*	....	....	....	....	....	....	....	....	....	....	....	....	....	....	....
Long-Term Foreign Liabilities	46cl*n*	....	....	....	....	....	....	....	....	....	....	....	....	....	....	....
Central Government Deposits	46d.*n*	....	....	....	....	....	....	....	....	....	....	....	....	....	....	....
Credit from Monetary Authorities	46g.*n*	....	....	....	....	....	....	....	....	....	....	....	....	....	....	....
Cred. from Deposit Money Banks	46h.*n*	....	....	....	....	....	....	....	....	....	....	....	....	....	....	....
Liabilities to Other Banking Insts	46i.*n*	....	....	....	....	....	....	....	....	....	....	....	....	....	....	....
Capital Accounts	47a.*n*	....	....	....	....	....	....	....	....	....	....	....	....	....	....	....
Other Items (Net)	47r.*n*	....	....	....	....	....	....	....	....	....	....	....	....	....	....	....
Money (National Definitions)																*Millionths of Reais through 1974; Thousandths 1975-85; Reais 1986-89;*
Reserve Money	19ma	7,006	10,261	13,421	†18	29	47	70	133	211	353	707	1,271	4,627	16,534	†65
M1	59ma	23,273	34,182	45,455	†65	91	125	176	305	540	1,014	1,689	3,337	10,072	40,719	†165
M2	59mb	32,727	47,636	64,727	†100	152	210	307	479	821	1,953	3,834	7,772	32,468	146,887	†318
M3	59mc	35,273	52,727	75,273	†120	191	275	412	669	1,179	2,857	5,914	14,374	55,199	226,027	†438
M4	59md	49,091	74,909	102,909	†160	243	353	542	875	1,487	3,533	7,605	19,068	73,092	292,254	†561
BA	19ma *a*	....	....	....	....	....	....	....	....	....	....	....	....	....	....	....
B2	19ma *b*	....	....	....	....	....	....	....	....	....	....	....	....	....	....	....
M2A	59mb *a*	....	....	....	....	....	....	....	....	....	....	....	....	....	....	....
M3A	59mc *a*	....	....	....	....	....	....	....	....	....	....	....	....	....	....	....
M4A	59md *a*	....	....	....	....	....	....	....	....	....	....	....	....	....	....	....
Interest Rates																*Percent Per Annum*
Discount Rate (*End of Period*)	60	....	....	....	....	....	....	....	....	....	....	....	....	....	....	....
Money Market Rate	60b	20.00	18.00	18.00	18.00	25.33	28.33	31.50	33.58	†47.33	89.74	120.66	203.23	257.32	281.65	105.22
Treasury Bill Rate	60c	....	....	....	....	....	....	....	....	....	....	....	....	....	....	....
Treasury Bill Rate (Fgn.Currency)	60c. *f*	....	....	....	....	....	....	....	....	....	....	....	....	....	....	....
Savings Rate	60k	....	....	....	....	....	....	....	....	....	....	....	....	....	254.69	113.75
Deposit Rate	60l	....	....	....	....	....	....	....	....	115.00	108.00	156.10	154.56	267.63	295.42	109.48
Lending Rate	60p	....	....	....	....	....	....	....	....	....	....	....	....	....	....	....
Prices, Production, Labor																*Index Numbers (1995=100):*
Share Prices	62	....	....	....	....	....	....	....	....	—	—	—	—	—	—	—
W'sale Prices (1990=100 millions)	63.a	.5	.6	.7	.9	1.3	1.9	2.6	4.1	8.4	17.4	33.6	89.9	302.4	995.1	2,390.1
W'sale Prices(1990=1 million)	63.b	—	—	—	—	—	—	—	—	—	—	—	—	—	—	—
Wholesale Prices	63	—	—	—	†—	—	—	—	—	—	†—	—	—	—	—	—
Consumer Prices (1990=100 millions)	64.a	....	....	....	....	....	....	....	....	.1	.2	.4	.9	2.7	8.8	21.8
Consumer Prices	64	....	....	....	....	....	....	....	....	—	—	—	—	—	—	—
Industrial Production	66.. *c*	....	....	....	....	....	....	....	....	....	....	....	....	....	....	....
																Number in Thousands:
Labor Force	67d	....	....	....	....	....	....	....	....	....	....	....	....	....	....	....
Employment	67e	....	....	....	....	....	....	....	....	....	....	....	....	....	53,761	55,436
Unemployment	67c	....	....	....	....	....	....	....	....	....	....	....	....	2,234	1,875	1,380
Unemployment Rate (%)	67r	....	....	....	....	....	....	....	....	....	....	....	....	4.3	3.4	2.4

1987	1988	1989	1990	1991	1992	1993	1994	1995	1996	1997	1998	1999	2000	2001		
Thousands 1990-92; Millions Beginning 1993: End of Period															**Other Banking Institutions**	
....	†443	3,260	†15	113	2,064	†53	1,526	611	768	1,174	881	224	546	246	Reserves	40
....	—	—	†—	—	829	†15	113	459	1,195	3,015	734	211	662	1,281	Claims on Mon.Author.: Securities	40c
....	—	—	†74	265	—	†—	—	—	—	—	—	—	—	—	Blocked Financial Assets	40d
—	†35	315	†6	11	634	†83	1,269	382	184	159	89	117	404	353	Foreign Assets	41
....	†229	1,671	†3	17	2,965	†95	525	1,633	1,644	3,800	9,204	2,044	2,335	3,205	Claims on Central Government	42a
86	†701	7,763	†113	434	5,852	†156	918	931	1,160	2,400	2,555	3,112	2,964	2,965	Claims on State and Local Govts	42b
188	†1,845	22,984	†311	1,703	15,257	†355	2,705	3,372	3,547	2,811	3,199	1,869	1,727	1,625	Claims on Nonfin.Pub.Enterprises	42c
....	†6,629	72,398	†898	5,766	82,942	†1,981	25,796	27,332	31,802	41,440	51,742	58,542	65,993	65,361	Claims on Private Sector	42d
....	†663	8,845	†397	2,144	31,115	†1,025	11,506	15,624	19,438	22,749	28,058	39,119	50,190	62,870	Claims on Deposit Money Banks	42e
—	†—	—	†—	—	—	†—	—	—	—	—	265	23	284	175	Claims on Nonbank Financial Insts.	42g
17	†—	—	†—	—	—	†—	—	—	—	—	—	—	—	—	Demand Deposits	44
....	†2,953	20,834	†146	856	25,462	†684	7,865	5,298	6,339	7,281	7,505	4,528	4,160	3,978	Time and Savings Deposits	45
....	†131	603	†7	26	427	†9	179	143	563	497	359	447	836	850	Money Market Instruments	46aa
....	—	—	†98	242	4	†—	—	—	—	—	—	—	—	—	Restricted Deposits	46b
....	10	120	†2	3	1,068	†39	239	43	699	550	398	816	978	879	Foreign Liabilities	46c
165	†1,148	11,589	†142	780	9,032	†261	1,638	2,141	2,636	4,356	10,964	10,417	14,609	18,912	Long-Term Foreign Liabilities	46cl
429	†4,237	62,980	†599	3,170	40,373	†1,086	10,432	12,308	14,607	16,443	20,649	23,841	25,818	24,414	Central Government Deposits	46d
16	†281	3,993	†45	188	2,537	†57	778	1,035	1,065	2,020	354	385	287	1,967	Credit from Monetary Authorities	46g
....	1,107	18,033	†177	672	7,865	†145	958	1,162	1,152	3,804	1,667	1,372	1,151	1,862	Credit from Deposit Money Banks	46h
....	—	—	†—	—	—	†—	—	—	—	—	224	194	529	710	Liab. to Nonbank Financial Insts.	46j
....	†2,624	39,943	†467	3,824	54,101	†1,382	16,756	21,323	18,350	19,931	19,697	20,936	22,515	65,269	Capital Accounts	47a
....	†-1,945	-40,859	†135	693	788	†100	5,513	6,891	14,327	22,666	34,910	42,325	54,221	19,241	Other Items (Net)	47r
Thousands 1990-92; Millions Beginning 1993: End of Period															**Banking Survey**	
-118	†2,914	49,770	†730	-1,283	66,155	†2,440	31,851	45,029	52,860	44,458	36,331	32,805	47,041	38,259	Foreign Assets (Net)	51n
....	†44,060	722,515	†10,376	56,574	818,719	†22,314	220,041	256,910	318,613	378,286	513,781	508,739	545,319	701,310	Domestic Credit	52
....	†8,925	215,898	†3,960	21,027	265,956	†5,545	-5,930	-245	2,757	61,577	137,402	134,579	148,258	276,524	Claims on Central Govt. (Net)	52an
306	†3,661	52,740	†976	5,066	63,679	†1,687	28,398	21,215	57,146	41,629	40,801	22,132	7,238	5,717	Claims on State and Local Govts	52b
862	†4,776	75,992	†947	4,743	57,972	†1,513	12,948	9,465	22,216	8,431	15,752	17,062	5,430	3,092	Claims on Nonfin.Pub.Enterprises	52c
....	†26,678	377,876	†4,493	25,737	431,107	†13,570	184,625	226,475	236,488	266,642	311,725	331,922	381,941	410,676	Claims on Private Sector	52d
1	†20	8	†—	1	5	†—	—	—	6	7	8,101	3,044	2,451	5,302	Claims on Nonbank Financial Inst	52g
....	†15,949	227,593	†3,049	22,147	388,684	†11,724	151,858	196,682	220,968	261,098	287,062	305,442	317,811	355,804	Liquid Liabilities	55l
....	†136	5,512	†59	355	9,567	†292	3,499	4,887	7,592	10,780	16,333	18,532	30,063	39,935	Money Market Instruments	56aa
594	†—	—	†2	868	47,972	†532	33,984	45,420	62,979	51,106	66,430	33,017	32,919	63,718	Liabs. of Central Bank: Securities	56ac
152	†1,148	16,137	†3,241	9,087	5,035	†75	404	1,996	352	12	10	13	427	264	Restricted Deposits	56b
1,346	†16,833	242,777	†2,486	20,800	224,073	†6,344	16,536	20,352	21,904	30,060	48,197	44,835	42,724	51,995	Long-Term Foreign Liabilities	56cl
....	12	696	†2	13	442	†1	92	111	60	234	22,424	25,450	41,942	46,831	Liab. to Nonbank Financial Insts	56j
....	†12,947	204,003	†2,066	15,277	268,634	†7,289	61,848	80,435	96,667	120,105	138,620	148,665	148,160	235,260	Capital Accounts	57a
....	†-52	75,567	†202	-13,256	-59,534	†-1,503	-16,329	-47,944	-39,048	-50,651	-28,964	-34,410	-21,686	-54,237	Other Items (Net)	57r
Millions of Reais Beginning 1993: End of Period															**Nonbank Financial Institutions**	
....	33	456	†7	38	353	†—	3	6	31	14	3	4	4	5	Reserves	40..*n*
....	56	5	†1	4	2,804	†8	405	154	350	364	667	333	1,085	1,523	Claims on Mon.Author.: Securities	40c.*n*
....	—	—	†26	91	1	†—	—	—	—	—	—	—	—	—	Blocked Financial Assets	40d.*n*
....	—	25	†—	1	277	†11	76	87	93	45	44	104	118	18	Foreign Assets	41..*n*
....	163	20,154	†48	57	1,528	†65	17	42	1,090	1,228	1,103	2,275	2,063	2,048	Claims on Central Government	42a.*n*
....	449	11,326	†55	56	547	†26	360	330	408	103	617	23	18	17	Claims on State and Local Govt.	42b.*n*
....	109	2,605	†34	171	1,775	†4	36	8	14	14	13	7	11	47	Claims on Nonfin.Pub.Enterprises	42c.*n*
....	2,196	2,430	†12	309	1,515	†91	2,074	2,458	3,599	3,601	18,825	16,552	16,125	15,179	Claims on Private Sector	42d.*n*
....	223	5,147	†51	135	6,165	†178	1,405	1,709	3,062	2,810	11,144	4,636	4,731	4,820	Claims on Deposit Money Banks	42e.*n*
....	9	67	†—	1	13	†1	14	5	12	35	100	88	74	40	Claims on Other Banking Insts	42f.*n*
....	47	486	†7	208	3,919	†131	1,181	3,901	5,482	8,307	9,247	7,033	7,428	6,253	Money Market Instruments	46aa*n*
....	—	—	†6	15	8	†—	—	—	—	—	—	—	—	—	Restricted Deposits	46b.*n*
....	—	—	†—	—	—	†—	—	—	22	176	182	630	685	811	Foreign Liabilities	46c.*n*
....	130	2,397	†34	315	4,757	†170	1,529	2,293	2,972	3,552	4,041	4,483	4,176	3,262	Long-Term Foreign Liabilities	46cl*n*
....	—	—	†—	—	5	†—	—	—	1	1	3	4	4	4	Central Government Deposits	46d.*n*
....	—	—	†—	—	—	†—	—	—	—	—	—	—	—	98	Credit from Monetary Authorities	46g.*n*
....	—	—	†—	—	—	†—	—	—	—	—	6,488	1,062	830	3,646	Cred. from Deposit Money Banks	46h.*n*
....	149	2,079	†14	125	2,873	†118	1,517	1,619	3,670	4,093	5,440	4,643	2,307	1,065	Liabilities to Other Banking Insts	46i.*n*
....	552	12,104	†131	1,025	15,086	†444	5,767	8,783	10,848	11,187	13,141	16,465	16,750	20,005	Capital Accounts	47a.*n*
....	2,360	25,149	†41	-822	-11,669	†-479	-5,604	-11,797	-14,336	-19,102	-6,026	-10,298	-7,952	-11,446	Other Items (Net)	47r.*n*
Thousands 1990-92; Millions Beginning 1993: End of Period															**Money (National Definitions)**	
183	1,323	24,522	†590	2,306	25,167	†517	17,685	21,682	19,796	31,828	39,184	48,430	47,686	53,256	*Reserve Money*	19ma
377	2,525	37,476	†913	3,931	38,027	†848	22,773	28,493	29,807	47,363	50,707	62,744	74,352	83,707	*M1*	59ma
1,356	†16,871	239,226	†2,823	19,342	332,740	†10,223	132,558	178,755	188,735	239,777	254,965	274,770	283,785	321,612	*M2*	59mb
2,159	†16,871	239,226	†2,823	22,089	389,877	†11,759	154,544	225,008	285,942	340,210	376,015	468,728	556,577	625,057	*M3*	59mc
2,535	†27,260	493,379	†3,786	24,574	447,583	†13,938	176,449	261,176	336,148	405,946	459,308	551,092	652,093	756,181	*M4*	59md
....	....	....	....	....	....	....	80,734	122,291	184,050	280,070	352,345	447,132	538,693	646,672	*BA*	19ma *a*
....	....	....	....	....	....	....	101,902	156,428	231,898	318,599	374,282	458,567	540,894	649,254	*B2*	19ma *b*
....	....	....	....	....	....	....	60,443	72,380	60,084	63,353	63,170	271,790	356,298	....	*M2A*	59mb *a*
....	....	....	....	....	....	....	119,882	143,410	142,159	173,436	185,294	386,382	468,390	....	*M3A*	59mc *a*
....	....	....	....	....	....	....	174,523	259,381	342,305	422,306	480,202	575,666	677,021	....	*M4A*	59md *a*
Percent Per Annum															**Interest Rates**	
....	....	....	....	....	....	....	....	....	25.34	45.09	39.41	21.37	†18.52	21.43	Discount Rate (*End of Period*)	60
424.38	1,192.87	6,404.97	15,778.57	847.54	1,574.28	3,284.44	4,820.64	53.37	27.45	25.00	29.50	26.26	17.59	17.47	Money Market Rate	60b
....	....	....	....	....	....	....	....	49.93	25.73	24.79	28.57	26.39	18.51	20.06	Treasury Bill Rate	60c
....	....	....	....	....	....	....	....	17.78	15.13	11.60	15.04	....	....	11.46	Treasury Bill Rate (Fgn.Currency)	60c. *f*
511.32	1,100.72	3,477.82	21,938.25	689.88	1,254.90	2,743.33	4,206.04	40.26	16.39	16.62	14.48	12.31	8.44	8.66	Savings Rate	60k
401.03	859.43	†5844.98	9,394.29	913.47	1,560.18	3,293.50	5,175.24	52.25	26.45	24.35	28.00	26.02	17.20	17.86	Deposit Rate	60l
....	....	....	....	....	....	....	....	....	....	78.19	86.36	80.44	56.83	57.62	Lending Rate	60p
Period Averages															**Prices, Production, Labor**	
—	—	—	—	.01	.08	2.77	85.11	100.00	151.59	263.62	233.93	291.21	410.06	356.56	Share Prices	62
7,339.1	58,505.3	800,599.4	....	....	....	....	....	....	....	....	....	....	....	....	W'sale Prices (1990=100 millions)	63.a
—	.1	.8	22.4	112.5	1,224.3	26,323.2	634,811.2	....	....	....	....	....	....	....	W'sale Prices(1990=1 million)	63.b
—	†—	—	—	—	.1	2.6	63.5	†100.0	106.2	114.9	119.0	138.7	163.8	185.9	Wholesale Prices	63
71.6	522.2	7,994.2	243,640.8	....	....	....	....	....	....	....	....	....	....	....	Consumer Prices (1990=100 millions)	64.a
—	—	—	†—	—	.1	†2.8	60.2	100.0	115.8	123.8	127.7	133.9	143.4	153.2	Consumer Prices	64
....	....	98.9	90.2	87.7	84.6	91.0	98.0	100.0	†100.9	105.1	102.9	102.1	108.9	111.0	Industrial Production	66..c
Period Averages																
....	....	....	....	....	66,139	67,159	....	70,539	70,182	75,213	76,886	79,315	....	....	Labor Force	67d
57,410	58,729	60,622	62,100	....	†65,395	66,570	....	69,629	67,920	69,332	69,963	71,676	....	....	Employment	67e
2,133	2,319	1,891	2,368	....	†4,574	4,396	....	4,510	5,076	5,882	6,923	7,639	....	....	Unemployment	67c
3.6	3.8	3.0	3.7	....	†6.5	†6.2	5.1	6.1	7.0	7.8	9.0	9.6	....	....	Unemployment Rate (%)	67r

Brazil

		1972	1973	1974	1975	1976	1977	1978	1979	1980	1981	1982	1983	1984	1985	1986
International Transactions																*Millions of US Dollars*
Exports	70..d	3,991	6,199	7,951	8,670	10,128	12,120	12,659	15,244	20,132	23,293	20,175	21,899	27,005	25,639	22,349
Coffee	70e.d	989	1,244	864	855	2,173	2,299	1,947	1,918	2,486	1,517	1,858	2,096	2,564	2,369	2,006
Imports, c.i.f.	71..d	4,783	6,999	14,168	13,592	13,726	13,257	15,054	19,804	24,961	24,079	21,069	16,801	15,210	14,332	15,557
Imports, f.o.b.	71.vd	4,232	6,192	12,642	12,210	12,383	12,023	13,683	18,084	22,955	22,091	19,395	15,429	13,916	13,153	14,044
																1995=100
Volume of Exports	72	23	32	39	46	45	41	44	49	54	62	60	59	71	73	67
Coffee	72e	146	149	96	108	112	71	86	78	109	114	123	130	143	143	66
Volume of Imports	73	38	50	55	53	61	62	70	75	72	64	60	55	54	49	60
																1995=100:
Unit Value of Exports	74..d	38	42	44	40	49	64	62	67	80	81	73	80	82	76	72
Coffee (Unit Value)	74e.d	34	43	46	40	99	164	115	125	116	67	77	82	91	84	154
Coffee (Wholesale Price)	76ebd	36	47	50	57	102	183	113	122	143	128	98	98	103	102	158
Unit Value of Imports	75..d	23	26	48	48	42	40	40	49	65	70	65	57	53	55	48
Balance of Payments																*Millions of US Dollars:*
Current Account, n.i.e.	78ald	....	....	....	−6,968	−6,520	−5,049	−6,996	−10,516	−12,831	−11,764	−16,317	−6,834	33	−280	−5,311
Goods: Exports f.o.b.	78aad	....	....	....	8,492	9,961	11,923	12,473	15,244	20,132	23,276	20,173	21,898	27,002	25,634	22,348
Goods: Imports f.o.b.	78abd	....	....	....	−12,042	−12,347	−12,023	−13,631	−17,961	−22,955	−22,091	−19,395	−15,429	−13,916	−13,168	−14,044
Trade Balance	78acd	....	....	....	−3,550	−2,386	−100	−1,158	−2,717	−2,823	1,185	778	6,469	13,086	12,466	8,304
Services: Credit	78add	....	....	....	1,060	1,018	1,207	1,350	1,475	1,737	2,265	1,809	1,724	1,947	2,086	1,816
Services: Debit	78aed	....	....	....	−2,504	−2,603	−2,793	−3,074	−3,799	−4,871	−5,138	−5,397	−4,131	−3,696	−3,790	−4,389
Balance on Goods & Services	78afd	....	....	....	−4,994	−3,971	−1,686	−2,882	−5,041	−5,957	−1,688	−2,810	4,062	11,337	10,762	5,731
Income: Credit	78agd	....	....	....	387	304	380	666	1,279	1,406	1,382	1,487	719	1,256	1,589	967
Income: Debit	78ahd	....	....	....	−2,404	−2,891	−3,806	−4,892	−6,733	−8,424	−11,644	−14,981	−11,726	−12,722	−12,779	−12,089
Balance on Gds, Serv. & Inc.	78aid	....	....	....	−7,011	−6,558	−5,112	−7,108	−10,495	−12,975	−11,950	−16,304	−6,945	−129	−428	−5,391
Current Transfers, n.i.e.: Credit	78ajd	....	....	....	71	49	85	157	180	308	336	184	145	182	171	134
Current Transfers: Debit	78akd	....	....	....	−28	−11	−22	−45	−201	−164	−150	−197	−34	−20	−23	−54
Capital Account, n.i.e.	78bcd	....	....	....	−40	−34	−63	−40	38	25	13	5	−3	9	7	7
Capital Account, n.i.e.: Credit	78bad	....	....	....	62	62	42	96	50	29	34	11	4	10	8	14
Capital Account: Debit	78bbd	....	....	....	−102	−96	−105	−136	−12	−4	−21	−6	−7	−1	−1	−7
Financial Account, n.i.e.	78bjd	....	....	....	6,381	8,735	6,261	11,363	6,344	9,677	12,791	9,146	−3,828	−5,506	−8,676	−8,189
Direct Investment Abroad	78bdd	....	....	....	−112	−183	−146	−124	−196	−367	−207	−376	−187	−42	−81	−143
Dir. Invest. in Rep. Econ., n.i.e.	78bed	....	....	....	1,302	1,555	1,833	2,006	2,419	1,911	2,520	2,910	1,609	1,594	1,441	345
Portfolio Investment Assets	78bfd	....	....	....	—	—	—	—	3	—	−3	−3	−8	−4	−3	1
Equity Securities	78bkd	....	....	....	—	—	—	—	−2	−2	−4	−4	−8	−4	−4	—
Debt Securities	78bld	....	....	....	—	—	—	—	5	2	1	1	—	—	1	1
Portfolio Investment Liab., n.i.e.	78bgd	....	....	....	—	—	—	—	657	354	1	2	−278	−268	−234	−451
Equity Securities	78bmd	....	....	....	—	—	—	—	−2	−11	14	16	−3	−3	−11	9
Debt Securities	78bnd	....	....	....	—	—	—	—	659	365	−13	−14	−275	−265	−223	−460
Financial Derivatives Assets	78bwd	....	....	....	....	....	....	....	....							....
Financial Derivatives Liabilities	78bxd	....	....	....	....	....	....	....	....							....
Other Investment Assets	78bhd	....	....	....	165	−516	−260	−653	16	−405	−1,397	−553	348	−3,325	190	1,385
Monetary Authorities	78bod	....	....	....	8	−9	−7	41	5	12	4	4	1	—	—	71
General Government	78bpd	....	....	....	−19	−38	−126	159	381	−638	−226	−290	178	−111	−100	−46
Banks	78bqd	....	....	....	248	−213	−38	−481	171	−256	−598	17	176	−353	275	687
Other Sectors	78brd	....	....	....	−72	−256	−89	−372	−541	477	−577	−284	−7	−2,861	15	673
Other Investment Liab., n.i.e.	78bid	....	....	....	5,026	7,879	4,834	10,134	3,445	8,184	11,877	7,166	−5,312	−3,461	−9,989	−9,326
Monetary Authorities	78bsd	....	....	....	−37	400	−234	49	−144	69	−47	1,538	−3,950	−7,555	−6,344	−720
General Government	78btd	....	....	....	1,694	1,612	2,454	4,215	3,402	511	324	2,031	2,297	6,573	3,397	−307
Banks	78bud	....	....	....	82	2,205	727	3,232	−108	2,969	5,691	1,528	−2,404	−50	−3,511	−3,641
Other Sectors	78bvd	....	....	....	3,287	3,662	1,887	2,638	295	4,635	5,909	2,069	−1,255	−2,429	−3,531	−4,658
Net Errors and Omissions	78cad	....	....	....	−438	491	−628	301	1,234	−340	−418	−375	−586	399	−530	66
Overall Balance	78cbd	....	....	....	−1,065	2,672	521	4,628	−2,900	−3,469	622	−7,541	−11,251	−5,065	−9,479	−13,427
Reserves and Related Items	79dad	....	....	....	1,065	−2,672	−521	−4,628	2,900	3,469	−622	7,541	11,251	5,065	9,479	13,427
Reserve Assets	79dbd	....	....	....	1,065	−2,672	−521	−4,628	2,900	3,469	−622	4,655	−269	−7,169	573	3,856
Use of Fund Credit and Loans	79dcd	....	....	....	—	—	—	—	—	—	—	546	2,160	1,801	−62	−625
Exceptional Financing	79ded	....	....	....	—	—	—	—	—	—	—	2,340	9,360	10,434	8,968	10,195
Government Finance										*Millionths of Reais through 1974; Thousandths 1975-85; Reais 1986-89;*						
Deficit (-) or Surplus	80	−524	585	3,171	†−2	−1	−8	−23	−13	−111	−218	−463	−1,762	−6,829	−56,093	†−178
Revenue	81	23,807	34,189	50,149	†71	116	203	301	493	1,009	2,183	4,604	11,267	33,010	132,883	†297
Grants Received	81z	178	211	258	†—	1	2	1	4	7	26	46	116	371	836	†4
Expenditure	82	22,004	29,098	42,447	†67	106	169	260	398	912	1,814	3,840	9,069	28,990	127,735	†371
Lending Minus Repayments	83	2,505	4,716	4,789	†7	12	44	65	111	215	613	1,272	4,076	11,219	62,079	†108
Financing																
Domestic	84a	....	....	....	....	....	....	....	....	....	†221	529	1,545	5,996	57,222	†177
Foreign	85a	....	....	....	....	....	....	....	....	....	−3	−69	218	833	−1,127	†1
Debt: Domestic	88a	....	....	....	....	....	....	....	....	365	909	1,558	3,480	10,139	74,070	†227
Foreign	89a	....	....	....	....	....	....	....	....	153	248	248	455	1,287	169	†1
National Accounts										*Millionths of Reais through 1974; Thousandths 1975-85; Reais 1986-89;*						
Househ.Cons.Expend.,incl.NPISHs	96f	81,091	111,273	168,728	†243	407	626	904	1,532	3,139	6,064	12,785	30,378	98,771	330,572	†902
Government Consumption Expend.	91f	13,455	18,545	25,455	†39	62	85	127	215	414	831	1,839	4,119	11,632	49,455	†142
Gross Fixed Capital Formation	93e	31,638	45,457	72,004	†89	133	193	293	507	1,031	2,046	3,940	7,731	22,182	96,364	†255
Changes in Inventories	93i	3,273	7,636	19,273	†9	4	6	10	−13	20	13	−63	−617	−1,600	11,273	†—
Exports of Goods and Services	90c	9,091	14,544	20,727	†27	42	66	88	157	408	840	1,399	4,870	19,020	61,455	†117
Imports of Goods and Services (-)	98c	11,273	16,727	36,000	†42	56	72	104	202	509	874	1,521	3,841	11,125	35,636	†85
Gross Domestic Product (GDP)	99b	126,036	186,109	270,945	†382	594	907	1,315	2,168	4,527	8,876	18,065	41,455	134,218	504,364	†1,336
Net Primary Income from Abroad	98.n	1,089	1,815	2,178	†5	9	15	30	59	−147	−368	−940	−2,483	−7,964	−26,909	†−59
Gross National Income (GNI)	99a	124,289	174,077	255,120	†362	581	889	1,337	2,235	4,353	8,501	17,112	38,948	126,182	477,455	†1,276
Net National Income	99e	117,818	165,091	241,818	†343	552	845	1,272	2,125	4,409	8,489	15,745	....	....	....	....
GDP Vol.1990 Prices (thousands)	99b.p	5,083	5,792	6,263	6,589	7,264	7,622	8,001	8,542	9,330	8,935	9,008	8,744	9,300	10,000	10,700
GDP Volume (1995=100)	99bvp	37.8	43.1	46.6	49.1	54.1	56.7	59.6	63.6	69.5	66.5	67.1	65.1	69.2	74.4	79.7
GDP Deflator (1995=1 Trillion)	99bip	.5	.7	.9	1.2	1.7	2.5	3.4	5.3	10.1	20.7	41.7	98.5	300.0	....	....
GDP Deflator (1995=10 Billions)	99bip	....	....	....	....	....	....	....	....	....	....	....	....	....	3	10	26
GDP Deflator (1995=100)	99bip	....	....	....	....	....	....	....	....	....	....	....	....	....	....	....	....
																Millions:
Population	99z	97.85	99.92	102.40	104.94	107.54	110.21	112.94	115.74	121.29	124.07	126.90	129.77	132.66	†133.56	134.65

	1987	1988	1989	1990	1991	1992	1993	1994	1995	1996	1997	1998	1999	2000	2001	
International Transactions																
Millions of US Dollars																
Exports	26,224	33,494	34,383	31,414	31,620	35,793	38,555	43,545	46,506	47,747	52,994	51,140	48,011	55,086	58,223	70..*d*
Coffee	1,959	2,009	1,560	1,106	1,382	970	1,065	2,219	1,970	1,719	2,746	2,332	2,230	1,559	1,207	70e.*d*
Imports, c.i.f.	16,581	16,055	19,875	22,524	22,950	23,068	27,740	35,997	53,783	56,947	64,995	60,631	51,675	58,532	....	71..*d*
Imports, f.o.b.	15,052	14,605	18,263	20,661	21,041	20,554	25,256	33,079	49,972	53,346	59,744	57,744	49,214	55,745	55,578	71.v*d*
1995=100																
Volume of Exports	71	85	88	84	83	83	91	97	100	99	104	115	114	122	136	72
Coffee	137	125	132	118	152	141	134	121	100	108	120	138	176	134	174	72e
Volume of Imports	62	58	57	57	63	68	77	81	100	108	91	92	85	92	93	73
Indices of Unit Values in US Dollars																
Unit Value of Exports	80	85	84	81	81	92	91	96	100	103	110	96	91	97	92	74..*d*
Coffee (Unit Value)	73	81	60	47	46	35	40	93	100	81	116	86	64	59	35	74e.*d*
Coffee (Wholesale Price)	73	83	68	57	50	39	46	98	100	82	114	83	61	55	35	76eb*d*
Unit Value of Imports	50	52	65	74	68	63	67	83	100	98	†132	123	111	116	116	75..*d*
Balance of Payments																
Minus Sign Indicates Debit																
Current Account, n.i.e.	-1,452	4,156	1,002	-3,823	-1,450	6,089	20	-1,153	-18,136	-23,248	-30,491	-33,829	-25,400	-24,632	-23,208	78al*d*
Goods: Exports f.o.b.	26,210	33,773	34,375	31,408	31,619	35,793	39,630	44,102	46,506	47,851	53,189	51,136	48,011	55,087	58,224	78aa*d*
Goods: Imports f.o.b.	-15,052	-14,605	-18,263	-20,661	-21,041	-20,554	-25,301	-33,241	-49,663	-53,304	-59,841	-57,739	-49,272	-55,783	-55,579	78ab*d*
Trade Balance	11,158	19,168	16,112	10,747	10,578	15,239	14,329	10,861	-3,157	-5,453	-6,652	-6,603	-1,261	-696	2,645	78ac*d*
Services: Credit	1,952	2,279	3,132	3,762	3,319	4,088	3,965	4,908	6,135	4,655	5,989	7,631	7,189	9,382	9,323	78ad*d*
Services: Debit	-4,316	-5,302	-5,917	-7,523	-7,210	-7,430	-9,555	-10,254	-13,630	-12,714	-15,298	-16,676	-14,172	-16,956	-17,070	78ae*d*
Balance on Goods & Services	8,794	16,145	13,327	6,986	6,687	11,897	8,739	5,515	-10,652	-13,512	-15,961	-15,648	-8,244	-8,270	-5,102	78af*d*
Income: Credit	568	771	1,310	1,157	904	1,118	1,308	2,202	3,457	5,350	5,344	4,914	3,936	3,620	3,279	78ag*d*
Income: Debit	-10,882	-12,851	-13,856	-12,765	-10,555	-9,115	-11,630	-11,293	-14,562	-17,527	-21,688	-24,531	-22,780	-21,504	-23,024	78ah*d*
Balance on Gds, Serv. & Inc.	-1,520	4,065	781	-4,622	-2,964	3,900	-1,583	-3,576	-21,757	-25,689	-32,305	-35,265	-27,088	-26,154	-24,847	78ai*d*
Current Transfers, n.i.e.: Credit	158	127	238	840	1,556	2,260	1,704	2,577	3,861	2,699	2,130	1,795	1,969	1,828	1,934	78aj*d*
Current Transfers: Debit	-90	-36	-17	-41	-42	-71	-101	-154	-240	-258	-316	-359	-281	-306	-295	78ak*d*
Capital Account, n.i.e.	5	3	23	35	42	54	81	173	352	494	482	375	339	272	-36	78bc*d*
Capital Account, n.i.e.: Credit	10	4	27	36	43	54	86	175	363	507	519	488	361	300	329	78ba*d*
Capital Account: Debit	-5	-1	-4	-1	-1	—	-5	-2	-11	-13	-37	-113	-22	-28	-365	78bb*d*
Financial Account, n.i.e.	-9,757	-9,137	-11,426	-5,441	-4,868	5,889	7,604	8,020	29,306	33,142	24,918	20,063	8,056	29,369	20,079	78bj*d*
Direct Investment Abroad	-138	-175	-523	-665	-1,014	-137	-491	-1,037	-1,384	467	-1,042	-2,721	-1,690	-2,280	2,259	78bd*d*
Dir. Invest. in Rep. Econ., n.i.e.	1,169	2,804	1,131	989	1,103	2,061	1,292	3,072	4,859	11,200	19,650	31,913	28,576	32,779	22,636	78be*d*
Portfolio Investment Assets	—	—	-30	-67	—	—	-606	-3,052	-936	-257	-335	-594	258	-1,697	-796	78bf*d*
Equity Securities	—	—	—	—	—	—	-607	—	-168	-49	-306	-553	-865	-1,954	-1,122	78bk*d*
Debt Securities	—	—	-30	-67	—	—	1	-3,052	-768	-208	-29	-41	1,123	257	326	78bl*d*
Portfolio Investment Liab., n.i.e.	-428	-498	-391	579	3,808	7,366	12,928	47,784	10,171	21,089	10,393	19,013	3,542	8,646	873	78bg*d*
Equity Securities	61	189	-57	103	578	1,704	6,570	7,280	2,775	5,785	5,099	-1,768	2,572	3,075	2,482	78bm*d*
Debt Securities	-489	-687	-334	476	3,230	5,662	6,358	40,504	7,396	15,304	5,294	20,781	970	5,571	-1,609	78bn*d*
Financial Derivatives Assets	....	....	....	....	....	....	—	—	....	....	....	....	642	386	567	78bw*d*
Financial Derivatives Liabilities	....	....	....	....	....	....	—	—	....	....	....	....	-729	-583	-1,038	78bx*d*
Other Investment Assets	-401	-1,994	-894	-2,864	-3,140	-99	-2,696	-4,368	-1,783	-3,327	2,251	-5,992	-4,399	-2,992	-6,284	78bh*d*
Monetary Authorities	—	-17	-5	22	8	—	-34	—	....	-44	-67	-84	1,668	88	471	78bo*d*
General Government	-121	-98	-62	-108	-17	-44	29	—	....	....	2,146	60	-880	192	-1,086	78bp*d*
Banks	-47	-328	-591	-2,758	-3,357	-37	-2,980	-4,077	-228	-4,610	5,133	3,383	-121	1,444	-1,300	78bq*d*
Other Sectors	-233	-1,551	-236	-20	226	-18	289	-291	-1,555	1,327	-4,961	-9,351	-5,066	-4,716	-4,369	78br*d*
Other Investment Liab., n.i.e.	-9,959	-9,274	-10,719	-3,413	-5,625	-3,302	-2,823	-34,379	18,379	3,970	-5,999	-21,556	-18,144	-4,890	1,862	78bi*d*
Monetary Authorities	-1,278	3,303	1,366	-637	-1,012	-277	-140	-545	-1,652	-3,773	-1,698	-1,704	-6,671	-200	-138	78bs*d*
General Government	259	-3,729	-6,132	-2,715	-2,876	-1,968	-2,622	-35,609	....	-286	....	....	934	1,539	-61	78bt*d*
Banks	-1,730	-1,786	-2,115	-229	386	1,167	-2,269	-1,439	7,071	6,450	-897	-8,570	-5,059	1,717	-1,569	78bu*d*
Other Sectors	-7,210	-7,062	-3,838	168	-2,123	-2,224	2,208	3,214	12,960	1,579	-3,404	-11,282	-7,348	-7,946	3,630	78bv*d*
Net Errors and Omissions	-805	-827	-819	-296	852	-1,393	-815	-442	1,447	-1,992	-3,160	-2,911	240	2,971	-253	78ca*d*
Overall Balance	-12,009	-5,805	-11,220	-9,525	-5,424	10,639	6,890	6,598	12,969	8,396	-8,251	-16,302	-16,765	7,980	-3,418	78cb*d*
Reserves and Related Items	12,009	5,805	11,220	9,525	5,424	-10,639	-6,890	-6,598	-12,969	-8,396	8,251	16,302	16,765	-7,980	3,418	79da*d*
Reserve Assets	-1,014	-1,250	-893	-474	369	-14,670	-8,709	-7,215	-12,920	-8,326	8,284	6,990	7,783	2,261	-3,311	79db*d*
Use of Fund Credit and Loans	-1,151	-462	-808	-771	-566	-399	-504	-133	-49	-70	-33	4,773	4,059	-6,795	6,729	79dc*d*
Exceptional Financing	14,174	7,516	12,921	10,771	5,621	4,430	2,323	750	—	....	—	4,539	4,924	-3,446	—	79de*d*
Government Finance																
Thousands 1990-92; Millions Beg. 1993: Year Ending December 31																
Deficit (-) or Surplus	-507	-4,777	-74,282	†-672	-257	-24,389	†-1,315	-21,270	....	....	-63,664	....	....	....	....	80
Revenue	1,441	6,318	102,300	†3,628	15,553	173,586	†4,272	108,280	....	....	213,409	....	....	....	....	81
Grants Received	13	38	997	†8	40	115	†2	125	....	....	9	....	....	....	....	81z
Expenditure	1,044	9,852	160,561	†4,027	14,683	187,242	†5,250	117,906	....	....	213,484	....	....	....	....	82
Lending Minus Repayments	917	1,280	17,018	†281	1,167	10,848	†338	11,769	....	....	63,597	....	....	....	....	83
Financing																
Domestic	....	....	....	....	....	....	....	....	....	....	....	....	....	....	....	84a
Foreign	....	....	....	....	....	....	....	....	....	....	....	....	....	....	....	85a
Debt: Domestic	....	....	....	....	....	....	....	....	....	....	....	....	....	....	....	88a
Foreign	....	....	....	....	....	....	....	....	....	....	....	....	....	....	....	89a
National Accounts																
Thousands 1990-92; Millions Beginning 1993																
Househ.Cons.Expend.,incl.NPISHs	2,612	18,727	200,000	†6,849	37,117	394,313	†8,470	208,256	386,910	486,813	545,698	566,192	597,418	658,726	712,300	96f
Government Consumption Expend.	510	3,951	65,948	†2,228	10,791	109,367	†2,490	62,388	126,652	144,001	158,502	174,847	185,858	209,334	236,261	91f
Gross Fixed Capital Formation	936	7,151	114,496	†2,386	10,917	118,086	†2,718	72,453	132,753	150,050	172,939	179,982	184,087	211,225	230,179	93e
Changes in Inventories	—	—	—	†-57	1,001	3,277	†220	4,880	11,274	12,903	14,248	13,074	11,314	24,944	18,308	93i
Exports of Goods and Services	397	3,427	38,004	†947	5,231	69,661	†1,481	33,220	49,917	54,430	65,356	67,862	100,148	117,422	158,276	90c
Imports of Goods and Services (-)	260	1,792	23,243	†804	4,771	53,745	†1,282	31,993	61,314	69,311	86,000	87,769	114,957	134,951	170,555	98c
Gross Domestic Product (GDP)	4,209	31,491	400,000	†11,548	60,286	641,701	†14,097	349,205	646,192	778,887	870,743	914,188	963,869	1,086,700	1,184,769	99b
Net Primary Income from Abroad	-159	-1,200	-13,954	†-300	-1,000	-12,000	†-343	-5,913	-10,154	-12,228	-17,436	-21,241	-34,114	-34,427	-46,433	98.n
Gross National Income (GNI)	4,050	30,230	448,503	†10,700	59,300	629,000	†13,754	343,292	636,038	766,659	853,307	892,947	929,755	1,052,273	1,138,336	99a
Net National Income	....	....	....	....	....	....	....	....	....	....	....	....	....	....	....	99e
GDP Vol.1990 Prices (thousands)	11,062	11,055	11,500	11,549	11,668	11,605	12,176	12,888	13,432	13,789	14,240	14,272	14,384	14,498	....	99b.*p*
GDP Volume (1995=100)	82.4	82.3	85.6	86.0	86.9	86.4	90.6	95.9	100.0	102.7	106.0	106.3	107.1	107.9	....	99bv*p*
GDP Deflator (1995=1 Trillion)	....	....	....	....	....	....	....	....	....	....	....	....	....	....	....	99bi*p*
GDP Deflator (1995=10 Billions)	79	592	7,230	207,864	1,073,987	....	....	....	....	....	....	....	....	....	....	99bi*p*
GDP Deflator (1995=100)	....	....	....	....	.01	.11	2.41	56.32	100.00	117.41	127.10	133.15	139.29	155.80	....	99bi*p*
Midyear Estimates																
Population	137.27	139.82	142.31	144.72	147.07	149.36	151.57	153.73	155.82	157.87	159.64	161.79	165.37	167.72	172.39	99z

(See notes in the back of the book.)

Bulgaria

		1972	1973	1974	1975	1976	1977	1978	1979	1980	1981	1982	1983	1984	1985	1986
Exchange Rates															*Leva per SDR:*	
Official Rate	aa	....	....	....										....	.0011	.0011
															Leva per US Dollar:	
Official Rate	ae	.0011	.0010	.0010											.0010	.0009
Official Rate	rf	.0011	.0010	.0010											.0010	.0009
															Index Numbers (1995=100):	
Nominal Effective Exchange Rate	ne c	....	....	....	....	....	....	....	....	....	....	....	....	....	....	....
Real Effective Exchange Rate	re c	....	....	....	....	....	....	....	....	....	....	....	....	....	....	....
Fund Position															*Millions of SDRs:*	
Quota	2f. s	....	....	....	....	....	....	....	....	....	....	....	....	....	....	....
SDRs	1b. s	....	....	....	....	....	....	....	....	....	....	....	....	....	....	....
Reserve Position in the Fund	1c. s	....	....	....	....	....	....	....	....	....	....	....	....	....	....	....
Total Fund Cred.&Loans Outstg.	2tl	....	....	....	....	....	....	....	....	....	....	....	....	....	....	....
International Liquidity													*Millions of US Dollars Unless Otherwise Indicated:*			
Total Reserves minus Gold	1l. d	....	....	....	....	....	....	....	....	....	....	....	....	....	....	....
SDRs	1b. d	....	....	....	....	....	....	....	....	....	....	....	....	....	....	....
Reserve Position in the Fund	1c. d	....	....	....	....	....	....	....	....	....	....	....	....	....	....	....
Foreign Exchange	1d. d	....	....	....	....	....	....	....	....	....	....	....	....	....	....	....
Gold (Million Fine Troy Ounces)	1ad	....	....	....	....	....	....	....	....	....	....	....	....	....	....	....
Gold (National Valuation)	1an d	....	....	....	....	....	....	....	....	....	....	....	....	....	....	....
Monetary Authorities: Other Liab.	4.. d	....	....	....	....	....	....	....	....	....	....	....	....	....	....	....
Deposit Money Banks: Assets	7a. d	....	....	....	....	....	....	....	....	....	....	....	....	....	....	....
Liabilities	7b. d	....	....	....	....	....	....	....	....	....	....	....	....	....	....	....
Monetary Authorities															*Millions of Leva:*	
Foreign Assets	11	....	....	....	....	....	....	....	....	....	....	....	....	....	....	....
Claims on Central Government	12a	....	....	....	....	....	....	....	....	....	....	....	....	....	....	....
Claims on Nonfin.Pub.Enterprises	12c	....	....	....	....	....	....	....	....	....	....	....	....	....	....	....
Claims on Deposit Money Banks	12e	....	....	....	....	....	....	....	....	....	....	....	....	....	....	....
Reserve Money	14	....	....	....	....	....	....	....	....	....	....	....	....	....	....	....
of which: Currency Outside Banks	14a	....	....	....	....	....	....	....	....	....	....	....	....	....	....	....
Other Liab. to Dep. Money Banks	14n	....	....	....	....	....	....	....	....	....	....	....	....	....	....	....
Time, Savings,& Fgn.Currency Dep.	15	....	....	....	....	....	....	....	....	....	....	....	....	....	....	....
Restricted Deposits	16b	....	....	....	....	....	....	....	....	....	....	....	....	....	....	....
Foreign Liabilities	16c	....	....	....	....	....	....	....	....	....	....	....	....	....	....	....
Central Government Deposits	16d	....	....	....	....	....	....	....	....	....	....	....	....	....	....	....
Capital Accounts	17a	....	....	....	....	....	....	....	....	....	....	....	....	....	....	....
Other Items (Net)	17r	....	....	....	....	....	....	....	....	....	....	....	....	....	....	....
Deposit Money Banks															*Millions of Leva:*	
Reserves	20	....	....	....	....	....	....	....	....	....	....	....	....	....	....	....
Other Claims on Dep. Money Banks	20n	....	....	....	....	....	....	....	....	....	....	....	....	....	....	....
Foreign Assets	21	....	....	....	....	....	....	....	....	....	....	....	....	....	....	....
Claims on Central Government	22a	....	....	....	....	....	....	....	....	....	....	....	....	....	....	....
Claims on Local Government	22b	....	....	....	....	....	....	....	....	....	....	....	....	....	....	....
Claims on Nonfin.Pub.Enterprises	22c	....	....	....	....	....	....	....	....	....	....	....	....	....	....	....
Claims on Private Sector	22d	....	....	....	....	....	....	....	....	....	....	....	....	....	....	....
Claims on Other Financial Insts	22f	....	....	....	....	....	....	....	....	....	....	....	....	....	....	....
Demand Deposits	24	....	....	....	....	....	....	....	....	....	....	....	....	....	....	....
Time, Savings,& Fgn.Currency Dep.	25	....	....	....	....	....	....	....	....	....	....	....	....	....	....	....
Money Market Instruments	26aa	....	....	....	....	....	....	....	....	....	....	....	....	....	....	....
Restricted Deposits	26b	....	....	....	....	....	....	....	....	....	....	....	....	....	....	....
Foreign Liabilities	26c	....	....	....	....	....	....	....	....	....	....	....	....	....	....	....
Central Government Deposits	26d	....	....	....	....	....	....	....	....	....	....	....	....	....	....	....
Credit from Central Bank	26g	....	....	....	....	....	....	....	....	....	....	....	....	....	....	....
Capital Accounts	27a	....	....	....	....	....	....	....	....	....	....	....	....	....	....	....
Other Items (Net)	27r	....	....	....	....	....	....	....	....	....	....	....	....	....	....	....
Monetary Survey															*Millions of Leva:*	
Foreign Assets (Net)	31n	....	....	....	....	....	....	....	....	....	....	....	....	....	....	....
Domestic Credit	32	....	....	....	....	....	....	....	....	....	....	....	....	....	....	....
Claims on Central Govt. (Net)	32an	....	....	....	....	....	....	....	....	....	....	....	....	....	....	....
Claims on Local Government	32b	....	....	....	....	....	....	....	....	....	....	....	....	....	....	....
Claims on Nonfin.Pub.Enterprises	32c	....	....	....	....	....	....	....	....	....	....	....	....	....	....	....
Claims on Private Sector	32d	....	....	....	....	....	....	....	....	....	....	....	....	....	....	....
Claims on Other Financial Insts	32f	....	....	....	....	....	....	....	....	....	....	....	....	....	....	....
Money	34	....	....	....	....	....	....	....	....	....	....	....	....	....	....	....
Quasi-Money	35	....	....	....	....	....	....	....	....	....	....	....	....	....	....	....
Money Market Instruments	36aa	....	....	....	....	....	....	....	....	....	....	....	....	....	....	....
Restricted Deposits	36b	....	....	....	....	....	....	....	....	....	....	....	....	....	....	....
Other Items (Net)	37r	....	....	....	....	....	....	....	....	....	....	....	....	....	....	....
Money plus Quasi-Money	35l	....	....	....	....	....	....	....	....	....	....	....	....	....	....	....
Interest Rates															*Percent Per Annum*	
Bank Rate (End of Period)	60	....	....	....	....	....	....	....	....	....	....	....	....	....	....	....
Money Market Rate	60b	....	....	....	....	....	....	....	....	....	....	....	....	....	....	....
Treasury Bill Yield	60c	....	....	....	....	....	....	....	....	....	....	....	....	....	....	....
Deposit Rate	60l	....	....	....	....	....	....	....	....	....	....	....	....	....	....	....
Lending Rate	60p	....	....	....	....	....	....	....	....	....	....	....	....	....	....	....
Government Bond Yield	61	....	....	....	....	....	....	....	....	....	....	....	....	....	....	....

Bulgaria

	1987	1988	1989	1990	1991	1992	1993	1994	1995	1996	1997	1998	1999	2000	2001		
End of Period																**Exchange Rates**	
	.0012	.0011	.0011	.0040	.0312	.0337	.0449	.0964	.1051	.7008	2.3969	2.3586	2.6721	2.7386	2.7891	Official Rate	aa
End of Period (ae) Period Average (rf)																	
	.0009	.0009	.0008	.0028	.0218	.0245	.0327	.0660	.0707	.4874	1.7765	1.6751	1.9469	2.1019	2.2193	Official Rate	ae
	.0009	.0008	.0008	.0022	.0178	.0233	.0276	.0541	.0672	.1779	1.6819	1.7604	1.8364	2.1233	2.1847	Official Rate	rf
Period Averages																	
	....	....	....	....	115.64	164.54	118.51	100.00	56.87	5.55	5.39	5.82	5.86	6.16		Nominal Effective Exchange Rate	ne c
					63.60	97.75	89.03	100.00	85.77	102.59	116.35	118.68	120.71	126.52		Real Effective Exchange Rate	re c
End of Period																**Fund Position**	
	....	....	....	310.00	310.00	464.90	464.90	464.90	464.90	464.90	464.90	464.90	640.20	640.20	640.20	Quota	2f. s
				—	5.86	.32	.83	10.39	20.08	8.31	8.37	21.38	59.53	64.97	1.80	SDRs	1b. s
				—	.01	38.73	32.63	32.63	32.63	32.63	32.63	32.63	32.69	32.74	32.78	Reserve Position in the Fund	1c. s
				—	289.23	428.90	459.90	644.41	482.12	407.25	698.02	792.27	910.74	1,014.62	883.00	Total Fund Cred.&Loans Outstg.	2tl
End of Period																**International Liquidity**	
	....	....	....		311	902	655	1,002	1,236	484	2,249	2,831	3,083	3,342	3,390	Total Reserves minus Gold	1l. d
				—	8.38	.44	1.14	15.16	29.84	11.95	11.29	30.10	81.70	84.65	2.26	SDRs	1b. d
				—	.01	53.25	44.82	47.63	48.50	46.92	44.03	45.95	44.87	42.66	41.19	Reserve Position in the Fund	1c. d
					302	849	609	939	1,158	425	2,193	2,755	2,957	3,215	3,347	Foreign Exchange	1d. d
					1.017	1.017	1.017	1.031	1.031	1.031	1.031	1.031	1.031	1.031	1.031	Gold (Million Fine Troy Ounces)	1ad
					305	305	305	309	309	309	†290	296	265	245	232	Gold (National Valuation)	1an d
					200.50	350.40	355.42	635.08	657.61	689.55	—	—	—	—	—	Monetary Authorities: Other Liab.	4..d
					....	....	....	....	1,426	1,248	1,525	1,627	1,503	1,953	2,119	Deposit Money Banks: Assets	7a. d
									2,375	1,661	385	293	223	361	444	Liabilities	7b. d
End of Period																**Monetary Authorities**	
	....	....	....	....	14.8	31.9	33.9	124.6	†154.0	710.6	4,884.5	5,441.9	6,432.7	7,445.7	7,950.6	Foreign Assets	11
					9.8	23.5	34.8	54.2	†100.7	410.9	1,632.1	1,665.9	2,203.2	2,560.9	2,314.6	Claims on Central Government	12a
						—	—	—	.3	.5	.6	1.4	2.1	2.3	2.3	Claims on Nonfin.Pub.Enterprises	12c
					25.5	20.7	32.1	54.8	44.0	262.5	334.6	256.5	228.6	124.9	70.8	Claims on Deposit Money Banks	12e
					29.6	44.7	54.5	85.0	†129.1	269.0	2,291.2	2,526.1	2,969.3	3,299.7	4,180.0	Reserve Money	14
					11.9	18.3	25.2	38.5	61.6	126.5	1,316.2	1,743.0	1,958.4	2,374.1	3,081.0	of which: Currency Outside Banks	14a
					—	—	.380	3.786	25.169	82.514	—	—	—	—	—	Other Liab. to Dep. Money Banks	14n
					.3	.8	.3	—	—	3.6	1.5	10.9	.3	962.2	823.4	Time, Savings,& Fgn.Currency Dep.	15
										.1		16.2	17.8		13.4	Restricted Deposits	16b
					13.4	23.0	32.3	104.0	†97.2	621.4	1,673.1	1,868.6	2,433.6	2,778.6	2,462.7	Foreign Liabilities	16c
					5.5	10.5	11.8	42.2	†51.0	192.4	1,593.2	1,808.6	2,445.8	2,029.8	1,779.7	Central Government Deposits	16d
					13.7	17.2	30.5	91.3	102.2	307.3	961.7	916.3	1,019.5	1,190.6	1,229.8	Capital Accounts	17a
					-12.5	-20.1	-28.9	-92.7	†-105.8	-91.9	314.9	217.5	-2.0	-144.8	-150.7	Other Items (Net)	17r
End of Period																**Deposit Money Banks**	
	....	....	....	....	20.4	26.7	24.6	43.5	67.6	118.6	802.1	645.9	747.8	601.1	864.4	Reserves	20
									25.2	82.5						Other Claims on Dep. Money Banks	20n
					32.2	37.1	43.5	109.5	100.8	608.1	2,709.2	2,726.0	2,925.7	4,105.2	4,702.7	Foreign Assets	21
					55.6	82.8	179.6	283.6	271.1	863.3	2,391.1	1,589.3	1,250.5	1,107.2	1,366.3	Claims on Central Government	22a
					—	1.4	2.4	2.8	.4	.4		17.1	31.8	31.8	40.9	Claims on Local Government	22b
					102.6	138.7	187.5	239.1	161.0	462.4	699.0	564.1	398.6	184.3	200.3	Claims on Nonfin.Pub.Enterprises	22c
					9.8	11.6	11.1	19.8	185.4	622.1	968.6	1,800.3	2,473.3	3,175.9	4,234.6	Claims on Private Sector	22d
									4.7	24.2	8.2	11.9	16.7	18.7	29.8	Claims on Other Financial Insts	22f
					15.0	19.6	23.2	36.6	50.0	114.8	992.7	1,079.1	1,096.1	1,323.1	1,655.4	Demand Deposits	24
					72.5	111.1	181.3	334.0	463.5	1,004.7	3,273.9	3,415.9	3,917.8	4,609.9	6,393.5	Time, Savings,& Fgn.Currency Dep.	25
									.1	.3	4.3	7.6	56.4	65.7	60.9	Money Market Instruments	26aa
					3.6	3.4	4.2	8.9	13.0	67.3	256.1	247.0	271.1	249.0	271.5	Restricted Deposits	26b
					240.2	288.0	385.2	236.2	167.9	809.3	683.4	490.7	433.7	759.0	986.3	Foreign Liabilities	26c
					11.4	5.1	5.8	13.6	33.1	173.6	354.9	398.0	237.7	231.2	357.9	Central Government Deposits	26d
					6.8	6.4	9.6	28.7	34.5	106.1	58.0	7.6	.8	1.6	.3	Credit from Central Bank	26g
					15.0	22.0	36.1	79.0	87.1	771.6	795.5	1,134.8	1,281.8	1,493.1	1,637.3	Capital Accounts	27a
					-144.0	-157.3	-196.6	-38.8	-32.9	-266.2	1,159.5	573.8	547.9	491.7	75.8	Other Items (Net)	27r
End of Period																**Monetary Survey**	
	....	....	....	....	-206.7	-242.0	-340.1	-106.1	-10.2	-112.0	5,237.2	5,808.6	6,491.1	8,013.3	9,204.3	Foreign Assets (Net)	31n
					160.8	242.4	397.9	543.7	639.4	2,017.7	3,751.6	3,443.4	3,691.6	4,820.1	6,051.0	Domestic Credit	32
					48.5	90.7	196.9	282.1	287.7	908.1	2,075.1	1,048.7	770.2	1,407.2	1,543.3	Claims on Central Govt. (Net)	32an
					—	1.4	2.4	2.8	.4	.4		17.1	31.8	31.8	40.9	Claims on Local Government	32b
					102.6	138.7	187.5	239.1	161.2	462.9	699.6	565.4	400.6	186.6	202.6	Claims on Nonfin.Pub.Enterprises	32c
					9.8	11.6	11.1	19.8	185.4	622.1	968.6	1,800.3	2,473.3	3,175.9	4,234.6	Claims on Private Sector	32d
									4.7	24.2	8.2	11.9	16.7	18.7	29.8	Claims on Other Financial Insts	32f
					24.8	38.0	50.3	76.0	111.9	241.3	2,433.9	2,960.8	3,302.1	3,976.3	4,883.8	Money	34
					72.7	112.0	181.6	334.0	463.5	1,008.4	3,275.4	3,426.7	3,918.1	5,572.0	7,217.0	Quasi-Money	35
									.1	.3	4.3	7.6	56.4	65.7	60.9	Money Market Instruments	36aa
					3.6	3.4	4.2	8.9	13.0	67.4	272.3	264.8	271.2	266.8	284.8	Restricted Deposits	36b
					-147.0	-153.0	-178.2	18.7	40.8	588.3	3,002.9	2,592.0	2,634.9	2,952.7	2,808.8	Other Items (Net)	37r
					97.5	150.0	231.9	410.0	†575.4	1,249.7	5,709.3	6,387.6	7,220.2	9,548.3	12,100.8	Money plus Quasi-Money	35l
Percent Per Annum																**Interest Rates**	
	....	....	....	....	54.00	41.00	52.00	72.00	34.00	180.00	6.65	5.08	4.46	4.63	....	Bank Rate (*End of Period*)	60
					48.67	52.39	48.07	66.43	53.09	119.88	66.43	2.48	2.93	3.02	3.74	Money Market Rate	60b
						48.11	45.45	57.72	48.27	114.31	78.35	6.02	5.43	4.21	4.57	Treasury Bill Yield	60c
					39.49	45.01	42.56	51.14	35.94	74.68	46.83	3.00	3.21	3.10	2.88	Deposit Rate	60l
					48.37	56.67	58.30	72.58	58.98	123.48	83.96	13.30	12.79	11.52	11.11	Lending Rate	60p
					....	....	....	56.86	49.76	....	....	10.10	10.05	7.38	6.70	Government Bond Yield	61

Bulgaria

918

		1972	1973	1974	1975	1976	1977	1978	1979	1980	1981	1982	1983	1984	1985	1986
Prices and Labor															*Index Numbers (1995=100):*	
Producer Prices	63	...	...	...	...	...	...	...	...	...	...	...	...	...	16.8	17.0
Consumer Prices	64	...	...	...	...	...	...	...	...	...	...	...	...	...	1.5	1.6
															Number in Thousands:	
Employment	67e	...	...	...	...	...	...	...	...	...	...	...	...	...	4,098	4,095	4,077
Unemployment	67c	...	...	...	...	...	...	...	...	...	...	...	...	...	...	...
Unemployment Rate (%)	67r	...	...	...	...	...	...	...	...	...	...	...	...	...	...	...
International Transactions															*Millions of Leva*	
Exports	70	2.8	3.2	3.7	4.5	5.2	6.0	6.7	7.7	8.9	9.8	10.9	11.8	13.0	13.7	13.4
Imports, c.i.f.	71	2.8	3.2	4.2	5.2	5.4	6.1	6.8	7.4	8.3	10.0	11.0	12.0	12.8	14.1	14.4
Balance of Payments															*Millions of US Dollars:*	
Current Account, n.i.e.	78al d	...	...	...	...	...	...	...	...	954.0	122.0	177.0	36.0	535.0	-136.0	-951.0
Goods: Exports f.o.b	78aa d	...	...	...	...	...	...	...	...	8,091.0	8,052.0	7,894.0	8,829.0	9,671.0	10,313.0	8,862.0
Goods: Imports f.o.b	78ab d	...	...	...	...	...	...	...	...	-7,445.0	-8,360.0	-8,184.0	-9,235.0	-9,849.0	-10,818.0	-10,045.0
Trade Balance	78ac d	...	...	...	...	...	...	...	...	646.0	-308.0	-290.0	-406.0	-178.0	-505.0	-1,183.0
Services: Credit	78ad d	...	...	...	...	...	...	...	...	1,211.0	1,284.0	1,207.0	1,059.0	1,273.0	1,047.0	958.0
Services: Debit	78ae d	...	...	...	...	...	...	...	...	-549.0	-683.0	-630.0	-598.0	-581.0	-654.0	-631.0
Balance on Goods & Services	78af d	...	...	...	...	...	...	...	...	1,308.0	293.0	287.0	55.0	514.0	-112.0	-856.0
Income: Credit	78ag d	...	...	...	...	...	...	...	...	141.0	182.0	160.0	161.0	173.0	160.0	138.0
Income: Debit	78ah d	...	...	...	...	...	...	...	...	-553.0	-443.0	-372.0	-289.0	-233.0	-257.0	-300.0
Balance on Gds, Serv. & Inc.	78ai d	...	...	...	...	...	...	...	...	896.0	32.0	75.0	-73.0	454.0	-209.0	-1,018.0
Current Transfers, n.i.e.: Credit	78aj d	...	...	...	...	...	...	...	...	80.0	106.0	123.0	134.0	109.0	98.0	89.0
Current Transfers: Debit	78ak d	...	...	...	...	...	...	...	...	-22.0	-16.0	-21.0	-25.0	-28.0	-25.0	-22.0
Capital Account, n.i.e.	78bc d	...	...	...	...	...	...	...	...	—	—	—	—	—	—	—
Capital Account, n.i.e.: Credit	78ba d	...	...	...	...	...	...	...	...	—	—	—	—	—	—	—
Capital Account: Debit	78bb d	...	...	...	...	...	...	...	...	—	—	—	—	—	—	—
Financial Account, n.i.e.	78bj d	...	...	...	...	...	...	...	...	-870.0	-395.0	-57.0	-347.0	-238.0	-165.0	412.0
Direct Investment Abroad	78bd d	...	...	...	...	...	...	...	...	—	—	—	—	—	—	—
Dir. Invest. in Rep. Econ., n.i.e.	78be d	...	...	...	...	...	...	...	...	—	—	—	—	—	—	—
Portfolio Investment Assets	78bf d	...	...	...	...	...	...	...	...	—	—	—	—	—	—	—
Equity Securities	78bk d	...	...	...	...	...	...	...	...	—	—	—	—	—	—	—
Debt Securities	78bl d	...	...	...	...	...	...	...	...	—	—	—	—	—	—	—
Portfolio Investment Liab., n.i.e.	78bg d	...	...	...	...	...	...	...	...	—	—	—	—	—	—	—
Equity Securities	78bm d	...	...	...	...	...	...	...	...	—	—	—	—	—	—	—
Debt Securities	78bn d	...	...	...	...	...	...	...	...	—	—	—	—	—	—	—
Financial Derivatives Assets	78bw d	...	...	...	...	...	...	...	...	...	...	...	...	...	...	...
Financial Derivatives Liabilities	78bx d	...	...	...	...	...	...	...	...	...	...	...	...	...	...	...
Other Investment Assets	78bh d	...	...	...	...	...	...	...	...	-130.0	-74.0	-57.0	-44.0	-332.0	-349.0	-478.0
Monetary Authorities	78bo d	...	...	...	...	...	...	...	...	...	...	...	...	...	...	...
General Government	78bp d	...	...	...	...	...	...	...	...	—	—	—	—	—	—	—
Banks	78bq d	...	...	...	...	...	...	...	...	-130.0	-74.0	-57.0	-44.0	-332.0	-349.0	-478.0
Other Sectors	78br d	...	...	...	...	...	...	...	...	—	—	—	—	—	—	—
Other Investment Liab., n.i.e.	78bi d	...	...	...	...	...	...	...	...	-740.0	-321.0	—	-303.0	94.0	184.0	890.0
Monetary Authorities	78bs d	...	...	...	...	...	...	...	...	—	—	—	—	—	—	—
General Government	78bt d	...	...	...	...	...	...	...	...	—	—	—	—	—	—	—
Banks	78bu d	...	...	...	...	...	...	...	...	-740.0	-321.0	—	-303.0	94.0	184.0	890.0
Other Sectors	78bv d	...	...	...	...	...	...	...	...	—	—	—	—	—	—	—
Net Errors and Omissions	78ca d	...	...	...	...	...	...	...	...	151.0	-88.0	6.0	523.0	120.0	599.0	-346.0
Overall Balance	78cb d	...	...	...	...	...	...	...	...	235.0	-361.0	126.0	212.0	417.0	298.0	-885.0
Reserves and Related Items	79da d	...	...	...	...	...	...	...	...	-235.0	361.0	-126.0	-212.0	-417.0	-298.0	885.0
Reserve Assets	79db d	...	...	...	...	...	...	...	...	-235.0	361.0	-126.0	-212.0	-417.0	-298.0	885.0
Use of Fund Credit and Loans	79dc d	...	...	...	...	...	...	...	...	—	—	—	—	—	—	—
Exceptional Financing	79de d	...	...	...	...	...	...	...	...	—	—	—	—	—	—	—
International Investment Position															*Millions of US Dollars*	
Assets	79aa d	...	...	...	...	...	...	...	...	...	...	...	...	...	...	...
Direct Investment Abroad	79ab d	...	...	...	...	...	...	...	...	...	...	...	...	...	...	...
Portfolio Investment	79ac d	...	...	...	...	...	...	...	...	...	...	...	...	...	...	...
Equity Securities	79ad d	...	...	...	...	...	...	...	...	...	...	...	...	...	...	...
Debt Securities	79ae d	...	...	...	...	...	...	...	...	...	...	...	...	...	...	...
Financial Derivatives	79al d	...	...	...	...	...	...	...	...	...	...	...	...	...	...	...
Other Investment	79af d	...	...	...	...	...	...	...	...	...	...	...	...	...	...	...
Monetary Authorities	79ag d	...	...	...	...	...	...	...	...	...	...	...	...	...	...	...
General Government	79ah d	...	...	...	...	...	...	...	...	...	...	...	...	...	...	...
Banks	79ai d	...	...	...	...	...	...	...	...	...	...	...	...	...	...	...
Other Sectors	79aj d	...	...	...	...	...	...	...	...	...	...	...	...	...	...	...
Reserve Assets	79ak d	...	...	...	...	...	...	...	...	...	...	...	...	...	...	...
Liabilities	79la d	...	...	...	...	...	...	...	...	...	...	...	...	...	...	...
Dir. Invest. in Rep. Economy	79lb d	...	...	...	...	...	...	...	...	...	...	...	...	...	...	...
Portfolio Investment	79lc d	...	...	...	...	...	...	...	...	...	...	...	...	...	...	...
Equity Securities	79ld d	...	...	...	...	...	...	...	...	...	...	...	...	...	...	...
Debt Securities	79le d	...	...	...	...	...	...	...	...	...	...	...	...	...	...	...
Financial Derivatives	79ll d	...	...	...	...	...	...	...	...	...	...	...	...	...	...	...
Other Investment	79lf d	...	...	...	...	...	...	...	...	...	...	...	...	...	...	...
Monetary Authorities	79lg d	...	...	...	...	...	...	...	...	...	...	...	...	...	...	...
General Government	79lh d	...	...	...	...	...	...	...	...	...	...	...	...	...	...	...
Banks	79li d	...	...	...	...	...	...	...	...	...	...	...	...	...	...	...
Other Sectors	79lj d	...	...	...	...	...	...	...	...	...	...	...	...	...	...	...

	Code	1987	1988	1989	1990	1991	1992	1993	1994	1995	1996	1997	1998	1999	2000	2001
Prices and Labor		*Period Averages*														
Producer Prices	63	16.9	17.3	17.3	19.3	†76.4	†30.0	5.2	64.2	†100.0	233.9	2,505.9	2,913.7	3,004.5	3,520.7	3,678.9
Consumer Prices	64	1.6	1.6	†1.8	2.2	†9.5	18.2	31.5	61.7	100.0	221.6	2,567.0	3,046.4	3,124.8	3,447.1	3,700.8
		Period Averages														
Employment	67e	4,109	4,078	4,085	3,846	3,205	2,663	2,267	2,032	1,910	1,852	1,331	....	....	....	....
Unemployment	67c	....	....	....	65	419	577	626	488	424	479	524	465	611	683	....
Unemployment Rate (%)	67r	....	....	....	1.7	11.1	15.3	16.4	12.4	11.1	12.5	13.7	12.2	16.0	17.9	....
International Transactions		*Millions of Leva*														
Exports	70	13.8	14.4	13.7	10.6	57.4	91.5	102.9	216.2	359.7	859.8	8,281.4	7,391.1	7,302.6	10,247.1	11,162.1
Imports, c.i.f.	71	14.1	13.9	12.8	10.3	45.1	104.3	131.5	227.0	380.0	892.1	8,268.5	8,709.4	10,052.8	13,856.8	15,851.0
Balance of Payments		*Minus Sign Indicates Debit*														
Current Account, n.i.e.	78al*d*	-720.0	-402.0	-769.0	-1,710.0	-76.9	-359.9	-1,098.8	-31.8	-25.8	15.7	426.9	-61.8	-684.7	-701.2	....
Goods: Exports f.o.b	78aa*d*	10,297.0	9,283.0	8,268.0	6,113.0	3,737.0	3,956.4	3,726.5	3,935.1	5,345.0	4,890.2	4,939.6	4,193.5	4,006.4	4,824.6	....
Goods: Imports f.o.b	78ab*d*	-11,308.0	-9,889.0	-8,960.0	-7,427.0	-3,769.0	-4,168.7	-4,611.9	-3,951.9	-5,224.0	-4,702.6	-4,559.3	-4,574.2	-5,087.4	-6,000.1	....
Trade Balance	78ac*d*	-1,011.0	-606.0	-692.0	-1,314.0	-32.0	-212.3	-885.4	-16.8	121.0	187.6	380.3	-380.7	-1,081.0	-1,175.5	....
Services: Credit	78ad*d*	1,158.0	1,186.0	1,223.0	837.0	399.9	1,070.3	1,171.3	1,256.9	1,431.4	1,366.0	1,337.4	1,787.9	1,786.3	2,175.3	....
Services: Debit	78ae*d*	-661.0	-656.0	-785.0	-600.0	-485.8	-1,165.2	-1,229.3	-1,246.1	-1,277.9	-1,245.9	-1,171.0	-1,415.1	-1,471.1	-1,669.4	....
Balance on Goods & Services	78af*d*	-514.0	-76.0	-254.0	-1,077.0	-117.9	-307.2	-943.4	-6.0	274.5	307.7	546.7	-7.9	-765.8	-669.6	....
Income: Credit	78ag*d*	115.0	82.0	127.0	120.0	55.6	125.1	92.6	84.6	149.7	181.0	210.8	306.6	265.5	322.9	....
Income: Debit	78ah*d*	-429.0	-511.0	-719.0	-878.0	-83.7	-220.7	-284.9	-277.1	-581.9	-577.2	-567.4	-590.3	-484.2	-644.2	....
Balance on Gds, Serv. & Inc.	78ai*d*	-828.0	-505.0	-846.0	-1,835.0	-146.0	-402.8	-1,135.7	-198.5	-157.7	-88.5	190.1	-291.6	-984.5	-990.9	....
Current Transfers, n.i.e.: Credit	78aj*d*	161.0	183.0	143.0	232.0	123.4	114.1	285.9	357.1	256.8	231.8	275.5	261.4	328.7	354.1	....
Current Transfers: Debit	78ak*d*	-53.0	-80.0	-66.0	-107.0	-54.3	-71.2	-249.0	-190.4	-124.9	-127.6	-38.7	-31.6	-28.9	-64.4	....
Capital Account, n.i.e.	78bc*d*	—	—	—	—	....	—	—	763.3	—	65.9	—	—	-2.4	25.0	....
Capital Account, n.i.e.: Credit	78ba*d*	—	—	—	—	....	—	—	763.3	—	65.9	—	—	....	25.0	....
Capital Account: Debit	78bb*d*	—	—	—	—	....	—	—	—	—	....	—	—	-2.4	....	....
Financial Account, n.i.e.	78bj*d*	480.0	1,545.0	-40.0	-2,814.0	-428.6	613.9	759.0	-1,018.7	326.6	-715.0	462.0	266.7	777.4	883.3	....
Direct Investment Abroad	78bd*d*	—	—	—	—	....	—	—	—	8.0	28.5	1.7	-.1	-16.8	1.9	....
Dir. Invest. in Rep. Econ., n.i.e.	78be*d*	—	—	—	4.0	55.9	41.5	40.0	105.4	90.4	109.0	504.8	537.2	806.1	1,001.5	....
Portfolio Investment Assets	78bf*d*	—	—	—	—	....	—	—	-222.0	9.7	-7.1	-13.7	-129.5	-207.5	-62.0	....
Equity Securities	78bk*d*	—	—	—	—	....	—	—	—	9.7	-7.1	-8.5	-10.7	—	-8.1	....
Debt Securities	78bl*d*	—	—	—	—	....	—	—	-222.0	—	—	-5.2	-118.8	-207.5	-53.9	....
Portfolio Investment Liab., n.i.e.	78bg*d*	—	—	—	—	....	—	—	-9.8	-75.4	-122.2	146.5	-112.0	8.0	-114.9	....
Equity Securities	78bm*d*	—	—	—	—	....	—	—	—	—	2.0	52.0	19.2	1.9	4.8	....
Debt Securities	78bn*d*	—	—	—	—	....	—	—	-9.8	-75.4	-124.2	94.5	-131.2	6.1	-119.7	....
Financial Derivatives Assets	78bw*d*	....	....	....	....	....	....	....	—	—	—	—	—	—	-1.8	....
Financial Derivatives Liabilities	78bx*d*	....	....	....	....	....	....	....	....	....	....	....	....	....	....	....
Other Investment Assets	78bh*d*	-442.0	-548.0	-488.0	384.0	-191.9	244.3	338.4	-209.2	404.2	-568.1	-53.9	222.2	16.6	-136.6	....
Monetary Authorities	78bo*d*	....	....	....	....	....	....	....	—	—	—	—	—	....	.9	....
General Government	78bp*d*	—	-401.0	-204.0	277.0	92.4	307.7	285.5	90.1	292.6	293.7	106.5	-19.8	-17.5	-9.1	....
Banks	78bq*d*	-442.0	-147.0	-284.0	107.0	-284.3	-63.4	52.9	-299.3	111.6	113.7	-440.6	103.0	25.7	-495.7	....
Other Sectors	78br*d*	—	—	—	—	....	—	—	—	—	-975.5	280.2	139.0	8.4	367.3	....
Other Investment Liab., n.i.e.	78bi*d*	922.0	2,093.0	448.0	-3,202.0	-292.6	328.1	380.6	-683.1	-110.3	-155.1	-123.4	-251.1	171.0	195.2	....
Monetary Authorities	78bs*d*	—	—	—	—	—	89.9	3.0	—	—	—	—	—	—	—	....
General Government	78bt*d*	—	—	—	—	—	—	-59.6	-951.0	-1.9	44.0	-82.1	-213.7	-105.0	-224.0	....
Banks	78bu*d*	922.0	2,093.0	448.0	-3,202.0	-292.6	-279.8	10.2	-39.2	-94.8	-179.7	-52.3	-65.1	10.1	108.4	....
Other Sectors	78bv*d*	—	—	—	—	....	518.0	427.0	307.1	-13.6	-19.4	11.0	27.7	265.9	310.8	....
Net Errors and Omissions	78ca*d*	-257.0	-486.0	375.0	70.0	231.5	14.7	18.1	71.6	143.8	-105.3	256.4	-299.2	6.1	-70.1	....
Overall Balance	78cb*d*	-497.0	657.0	-434.0	-4,454.0	-274.0	268.7	-321.7	-215.6	444.6	-738.7	1,145.3	-94.3	96.4	137.0	....
Reserves and Related Items	79da*d*	497.0	-657.0	434.0	4,454.0	274.0	-268.7	321.7	215.6	-444.6	738.7	-1,145.3	94.3	-96.4	-137.0	....
Reserve Assets	79db*d*	497.0	-657.0	434.0	878.0	-318.4	-637.0	247.0	-341.6	-233.7	750.9	-1,641.3	-461.5	-527.6	-408.9	....
Use of Fund Credit and Loans	79dc*d*	—	—	—	—	399.9	196.1	42.7	262.4	-245.9	-108.7	396.9	129.4	161.9	136.0	....
Exceptional Financing	79de*d*	—	—	—	3,576.0	192.5	172.2	32.0	294.8	35.0	96.5	99.1	426.4	269.4	136.0	....
International Investment Position		*Millions of US Dollars*														
Assets	79aa*d*	....	....	....	....	....	....	....	....	....	....	....	8,602.3	9,060.6	....	....
Direct Investment Abroad	79ab*d*	....	....	....	....	....	....	....	....	....	....	....	74.5	90.0	....	....
Portfolio Investment	79ac*d*	....	....	....	....	....	....	....	....	....	....	....	521.9	677.6	....	....
Equity Securities	79ad*d*	....	....	....	....	....	....	....	....	....	....	....	20.6	20.6	....	....
Debt Securities	79ae*d*	....	....	....	....	....	....	....	....	....	....	....	501.4	657.0	....	....
Financial Derivatives	79al*d*	....	....	....	....	....	....	....	....	....	....	....	—	—	....	....
Other Investment	79af*d*	....	....	....	....	....	....	....	....	....	....	....	4,949.5	5,071.3	....	....
Monetary Authorities	79ag*d*	....	....	....	....	....	....	....	....	....	....	....	3.1	2.5	....	....
General Government	79ah*d*	....	....	....	....	....	....	....	....	....	....	....	2,242.4	2,284.1	....	....
Banks	79ai*d*	....	....	....	....	....	....	....	....	....	....	....	1,524.5	1,397.4	....	....
Other Sectors	79aj*d*	....	....	....	....	....	....	....	....	....	....	....	1,179.5	1,387.3	....	....
Reserve Assets	79ak*d*	....	....	....	....	....	....	....	....	....	....	....	3,056.4	3,221.7	....	....
Liabilities	79la*d*	....	....	....	....	....	....	....	....	....	....	....	11,938.0	12,377.1	....	....
Dir. Invest. in Rep. Economy	79lb*d*	....	....	....	....	....	....	....	....	....	....	....	1,596.6	2,402.7	....	....
Portfolio Investment	79lc*d*	....	....	....	....	....	....	....	....	....	....	....	5,173.1	5,195.3	....	....
Equity Securities	79ld*d*	....	....	....	....	....	....	....	....	....	....	....	113.4	97.9	....	....
Debt Securities	79le*d*	....	....	....	....	....	....	....	....	....	....	....	5,059.7	5,097.5	....	....
Financial Derivatives	79ll*d*	....	....	....	....	....	....	....	....	....	....	....	—	—	....	....
Other Investment	79lf*d*	....	....	....	....	....	....	....	....	....	....	....	5,168.3	4,779.1	....	....
Monetary Authorities	79lg*d*	....	....	....	....	....	....	....	....	....	....	....	1,118.0	1,252.9	....	....
General Government	79lh*d*	....	....	....	....	....	....	....	....	....	....	....	3,473.7	2,853.3	....	....
Banks	79li*d*	....	....	....	....	....	....	....	....	....	....	....	440.8	325.3	....	....
Other Sectors	79lj*d*	....	....	....	....	....	....	....	....	....	....	....	135.8	347.6	....	....

Bulgaria

918

		1972	1973	1974	1975	1976	1977	1978	1979	1980	1981	1982	1983	1984	1985	1986
Government Finance																*Millions of Leva:*
Deficit (-) or Surplus	80	...	...	...	...	...	...	...	...	...	...	...	...	...	...	...
Total Revenue and Grants	81y	...	...	...	...	...	...	...	...	...	...	...	...	...	...	...
Revenue	81	...	...	...	...	...	...	...	...	...	...	...	...	...	...	...
Grants	81z	...	...	...	...	...	...	...	...	...	...	...	...	...	...	...
Exp. & Lending Minus Repay.	82z	...	...	...	...	...	...	...	...	...	...	...	...	...	...	...
Expenditure	82	...	...	...	...	...	...	...	...	...	...	...	...	...	...	...
Lending Minus Repayments	83	...	...	...	...	...	...	...	...	...	...	...	...	...	...	...
Total Financing	80h	...	...	...	...	...	...	...	...	...	...	...	...	...	...	...
Total Net Borrowing	84	...	...	...	...	...	...	...	...	...	...	...	...	...	...	...
Net Domestic	84a	...	...	...	...	...	...	...	...	...	...	...	...	...	...	...
Net Foreign	85a	...	...	...	...	...	...	...	...	...	...	...	...	...	...	...
Use of Cash Balances	87	...	...	...	...	...	...	...	...	...	...	...	...	...	...	...
Total Debt by Residence	88	...	...	...	...	...	...	...	...	...	...	...	...	...	...	...
Domestic	88a	...	...	...	...	...	...	...	...	...	...	...	...	...	...	...
Foreign	89a	...	...	...	...	...	...	...	...	...	...	...	...	...	...	...
National Accounts																*Millions of Leva*
Househ.Cons.Expend.,incl.NPISHs	96f	...	...	...	...	...	...	...	...	...	...	...	...	...	...	...
Government Consumption Expend.	91f	...	...	...	...	...	...	...	...	...	...	...	...	...	...	...
Gross Fixed Capital Formation	93e	...	...	...	...	...	...	...	6	7	8	8	8	8	9	9
Changes in Inventories	93i	...	...	...	...	...	...	...	1	1	2	2	2	2	2	3
Exports of Goods and Services	90c	...	...	...	...	...	...	...	...	...	...	...	...	...	...	...
Imports of Goods and Services (-)	98c	...	...	...	...	...	...	...	...	...	...	...	...	...	...	...
Gross Domestic Product (GDP)	99b	11	12	13	14	15	15	...	22	26	28	29	30	32	33	34
Statistical Discrepancy	99bs	...	...	...	...	...	...	...	190	–483	–1,000	–822	–658	–426	–687	–2,127
Net Primary Income from Abroad	98.n	...	...	...	...	...	...	...	...	...	...	...	...	...	...	...
Gross National Income (GNI)	99a	...	...	...	...	...	...	...	...	...	...	...	...	...	...	...
Net Current Transf.from Abroad	98t	...	...	...	...	...	...	...	...	...	...	...	...	...	...	...
Gross Nat'l Disposable Inc.(GNDI)	99i	...	...	...	...	...	...	...	...	...	...	...	...	...	...	...
Gross Saving	99s	...	...	...	...	...	...	...	...	...	...	...	...	...	...	...
GDP Volume (1995=100)	99bv p	...	...	...	...	...	...	...	...	...	...	...	...	...	...	...
GDP Deflator (1995=100)	99bi p	...	...	...	...	...	...	...	...	...	...	...	...	...	...	...
																Millions:
Population	99z	8.58	8.62	8.68	8.72	8.76	8.80	8.81	8.95	8.86	8.89	8.92	8.94	8.96	8.96	8.96

Government Finance

Year Ending December 31

	1987	1988	1989	1990	1991	1992	1993	1994	1995	1996	1997	1998	1999	2000	2001		
Deficit (-) or Surplus	....	-1.6	-.4	-3.7	-6.1	-9.9	-36.1	†-24.5	-46.2	-332.8	353.3	599.2	348.7	152.4	....	Deficit (-) or Surplus	80
Total Revenue and Grants	....	20.2	21.5	22.8	49.9	71.8	100.0	†209.3	315.5	703.3	5,662.1	7,530.6	8,219.9	9,653.5	....	Total Revenue and Grants	81y
Revenue	....	19.9	21.0	22.3	49.5	71.6	99.9	†209.3	314.6	699.1	5,558.0	7,380.3	8,015.0	9,437.8	....	Revenue	81
Grants	....	.3	.5	.5	.4	.2	.1	†—	.9	4.2	104.1	150.3	204.9	215.7	....	Grants	81z
Exp. & Lending Minus Repay.	....	21.8	21.9	26.5	56.0	81.7	136.1	†233.8	361.7	1,036.1	5,308.8	6,931.4	7,871.1	9,501.1	....	Exp. & Lending Minus Repay.	82z
Expenditure	....	20.2	20.7	25.0	54.5	81.6	133.9	†235.9	360.6	1,040.9	5,733.2	7,227.6	8,122.6	9,759.4	....	Expenditure	82
Lending Minus Repayments	....	1.6	1.2	1.5	1.5	.1	2.2	†-2.1	1.1	-4.8	-424.4	-296.2	-251.5	-258.3	....	Lending Minus Repayments	83
Total Financing	....	1.6	.4	3.7	6.1	9.9	36.1	†24.5	46.2	332.8	-353.3	-599.3	-348.9	-152.6	....	Total Financing	80h
Total Net Borrowing	....	1.7	1.4	3.7	11.3	16.5	35.5	†53.0	58.7	295.5	1,261.0	-213.3	227.3	-431.8	....	Total Net Borrowing	84
Net Domestic	....	2.2	1.9	4.1	7.5	13.6	38.3	†44.6	65.5	331.3	1,204.3	-65.8	49.9	-22.0	....	Net Domestic	84a
Net Foreign	....	-.5	-.5	-.4	3.8	2.9	-2.8	†8.4	-6.8	-35.8	56.7	-147.5	177.4	-409.8	....	Net Foreign	85a
Use of Cash Balances	....	-.1	-1.0	—	-5.2	-6.6	.6	†-28.5	-12.5	37.3	-1,614.3	-386.0	-576.2	279.2	....	Use of Cash Balances	87
Total Debt by Residence	....	....	....	....	....	....	....	....	....	....	....	....	....	....	....	Total Debt by Residence	88
Domestic	....	7.3	9.3	15.7	23.1	39.8	112.0	†275.1	345.4	1,052.8	....	....	....	....	....	Domestic	88a
Foreign	....	....	....	....	....	....	....	....	....	....	....	....	....	....	....	Foreign	89a

National Accounts

Millions of Leva

	1987	1988	1989	1990	1991	1992	1993	1994	1995	1996	1997	1998	1999	2000	2001		
Househ.Cons.Expend.,incl.NPISHs	....	....	....	....	73	132	220	389	622	1,340	11,982	15,734	17,037	18,373	20,614	Househ.Cons.Expend.,incl.NPISHs	96f
Government Consumption Expend.					26	41	56	90	134	208	2,188	3,255	3,612	4,499	5,211	Government Consumption Expend.	91f
Gross Fixed Capital Formation	10	10	10	10	†25	33	39	72	134	238	1,841	2,851	3,632	4,111	5,259	Gross Fixed Capital Formation	93e
Changes in Inventories	2	3	3	4	†6	7	7	-23	4	-92	101	786	707	102	775	Changes in Inventories	93i
Exports of Goods and Services					59	95	114	237	393	1,100	10,556	10,361	10,054	14,884	16,494	Exports of Goods and Services	90c
Imports of Goods and Services (-)					53	106	137	240	407	1,046	9,612	10,991	11,819	16,305	18,712	Imports of Goods and Services (-)	98c
Gross Domestic Product (GDP)	37	38	40	45	†136	201	299	526	880	1,749	17,055	21,577	22,776	25,454	29,618	Gross Domestic Product (GDP)	99b
Statistical Discrepancy	-862	-1,014	-1,523	-1,995	....	....	....	—	-1	....	-260	-418	-123	-210	....	Statistical Discrepancy	99bs
Net Primary Income from Abroad					-14	-3	-5	-11	-29	-69	-589	-499	-402	....		Net Primary Income from Abroad	98.n
Gross National Income (GNI)					122	198	294	515	858	1,680	16,466	21,078	22,374	....		Gross National Income (GNI)	99a
Net Current Transf.from Abroad					2	—	—	1	1	17	399	405	551	....		Net Current Transf.from Abroad	98t
Gross Nat'l Disposable Inc.(GNDI)					124	198	294	516	853	1,697	16,865	21,483	22,925	....		Gross Nat'l Disposable Inc.(GNDI)	99i
Gross Saving					25	25	18	37	96	149	2,695	2,494	2,276	....		Gross Saving	99s
GDP Volume (1995=100)	....	....	125.6	†114.1	†104.5	†96.9	†95.5	†97.2	†100.0	†89.9	83.7	....	....	....	....	GDP Volume (1995=100)	99bv p
GDP Deflator (1995=100)	....	....	3.6	4.5	†14.7	23.5	35.6	61.4	100.0	221.0	2,314.8	....	....	....	....	GDP Deflator (1995=100)	99bi p

Midyear Estimates

	1987	1988	1989	1990	1991	1992	1993	1994	1995	1996	1997	1998	1999	2000	2001		
Population	8.97	8.98	8.99	8.99	8.98	8.54	8.47	8.44	8.41	8.36	8.31	8.26	8.21	†7.95	7.87	Population	99z

(See notes in the back of the book.)

Burkina Faso

	1972	1973	1974	1975	1976	1977	1978	1979	1980	1981	1982	1983	1984	1985	1986
Exchange Rates														*Francs per SDR:*	
Official Rate .... **aa**	278.00	284.00	272.08	262.55	288.70	285.76	272.28	264.78	287.99	334.52	370.92	436.97	470.11	415.26	394.78
														Francs per US Dollar:	
Official Rate .... **ae**	256.05	235.42	222.22	224.27	248.49	235.25	209.00	201.00	225.80	287.40	336.25	417.37	479.60	378.05	322.75
Official Rate .... **rf**	252.03	222.89	240.70	214.31	238.95	245.68	225.66	212.72	211.28	271.73	328.61	381.07	436.96	449.26	346.31
Fund Position														*Millions of SDRs:*	
Quota .... **2f.** *s*	13.0	13.0	13.0	13.0	13.0	13.0	16.0	16.0	24.0	24.0	24.0	24.0	31.6	31.6	31.6
SDRs .... **1b.** *s*	4.4	4.4	4.4	4.4	4.4	4.4	4.4	6.1	5.8	7.5	7.5	7.5	5.6	5.6	5.6
Reserve Position in the Fund .... **1c.** *s*	3.1	3.3	3.3	3.3	3.3	4.6	4.6	4.6	5.6	5.6	5.6	5.6	7.5	7.5	7.5
Total Fund Cred.&Loans Outstg. **2tl**	—	—	—	—	—	—	5.4	9.3	12.7	12.7	12.7	12.5	11.4	9.3	6.7
International Liquidity										*Millions of US Dollars Unless Otherwise Indicated:*					
Total Reserves minus Gold .... **1l.** *d*	47.5	62.6	83.6	76.5	71.4	56.2	36.3	61.6	68.2	70.8	61.8	85.0	106.3	139.5	233.5
SDRs .... **1b.** *d*	4.8	5.3	5.4	5.2	5.1	5.4	5.8	8.0	7.4	8.7	8.3	7.9	5.5	6.2	6.9
Reserve Position in the Fund .... **1c.** *d*	3.4	3.9	4.0	3.8	3.8	5.6	6.0	6.0	7.2	6.6	6.2	5.9	7.4	8.3	9.2
Foreign Exchange .... **1d.** *d*	39.3	53.4	74.2	67.5	62.5	45.2	24.6	47.5	53.6	55.6	47.3	71.2	93.4	125.1	217.4
Gold (Million Fine Troy Ounces) **1ad**	....	....	....	....	—	.006	.008	.011	.011	.011	.011	.011	.011	.011	.011
Gold (National Valuation)................... **1an** *d*	....	....	....	....	—	.2	.4	.5	.5	4.7	4.8	4.3	3.7	3.6	4.5
Monetary Authorities: Other Liab. .... **4..** *d*	.3	—	2.3	5.1	11.1	2.4	5.2	6.4	7.2	5.1	8.6	6.0	12.6	21.4	46.3
Deposit Money Banks: Assets .... **7a.** *d*	.5	6.4	2.7	3.1	1.2	3.8	4.2	1.4	7.0	3.5	2.8	4.7	5.8	9.0	10.3
Liabilities .... **7b.** *d*	8.3	12.5	23.3	22.2	28.6	53.9	58.3	61.9	56.5	55.2	53.0	51.6	32.4	45.4	41.4
Monetary Authorities														*Billions of Francs:*	
Foreign Assets **11**	12.1	14.4	18.6	17.2	17.7	13.2	7.6	12.4	15.4	20.4	20.8	35.5	51.0	52.7	75.4
Claims on Central Government **12a**	—	—	—	—	—	2.0	3.5	4.4	5.1	6.1	10.1	12.4	13.8	11.9	12.2
Claims on Deposit Money Banks **12e**	.3	.4	1.5	2.5	6.1	7.5	13.3	11.5	11.8	8.9	10.5	11.2	9.6	7.0	7.5
Claims on Other Financial Insts **12f**	—	—	—	—	.2	.4	.4	.3	.4	.5	.6	.8	.8	.8	1.1
Reserve Money............................... **14**	6.2	7.6	9.0	11.7	13.3	15.7	15.2	19.9	21.6	26.3	28.6	42.0	57.3	51.8	73.3
of which: Currency Outside DMBs **14a**	5.8	7.1	8.5	10.7	12.8	14.7	13.5	17.4	19.9	24.8	27.0	31.7	31.2	31.0	43.4
Foreign Liabilities......................... **16c**	.1	—	.5	1.1	2.8	.6	4.1	6.3	8.8	9.2	11.1	11.4	14.6	14.5	20.4
Central Government Deposits **16d**	4.8	5.9	9.4	5.7	6.6	5.6	5.4	3.3	3.5	1.3	2.7	7.2	4.8	5.2	2.6
Other Items (Net)........................... **17r**	1.3	1.4	1.3	1.0	1.4	1.3	.2	−.9	−1.2	−.9	−.4	−.8	−1.5	1.4	−.1
Deposit Money Banks														*Billions of Francs:*	
Reserves **20**	.4	.4	.4	1.1	.6	.9	1.5	2.1	1.6	1.4	2.0	10.2	25.8	20.2	29.3
Foreign Assets.................................. **21**	.1	1.5	.6	.7	.3	.9	.9	.3	1.6	1.0	.9	1.9	2.8	3.4	3.3
Claims on Central Government............. **22a**	—	.1	.3	5.3	4.8	1.9	5.9	†6.7	8.6	14.1	13.4	12.5	12.7	6.7	6.8
Claims on Private Sector **22d**	7.1	9.0	15.2	21.4	31.9	45.3	54.8	†56.7	58.7	65.0	73.4	76.1	74.4	91.1	96.2
Claims on Other Financial Insts **22f**	....	....	....	....	....	....	....	.5	.5	.6	1.2	1.5	1.7	1.7	2.0
Demand Deposits **24**	3.6	5.8	7.3	10.7	13.6	14.7	18.8	†15.8	20.3	22.5	26.0	27.3	33.4	36.4	39.7
Time Deposits **25**	.7	1.0	1.2	1.8	4.0	4.8	8.1	†11.5	11.5	14.9	17.0	19.7	26.3	23.8	28.8
Foreign Liabilities.......................... **26c**	.6	.6	1.3	.8	2.6	7.7	7.0	7.2	8.4	11.5	13.5	17.1	12.8	14.5	9.8
Long-Term Foreign Liabilities **26cl**	1.6	2.3	3.8	4.2	4.5	5.0	5.2	5.2	4.4	4.4	4.3	4.4	2.7	2.7	3.5
Central Government Deposits **26d**	.6	.7	.5	5.3	5.8	6.6	8.3	†10.7	13.4	17.1	19.2	24.0	28.0	31.1	39.5
Credit from Monetary Authorities **26g**	.3	.4	1.5	2.5	6.1	7.5	13.3	11.5	11.8	8.9	10.5	11.2	9.6	7.0	7.5
Other Items (Net)......................... **27r**	.4	.1	.8	3.1	1.0	2.8	2.4	4.3	1.1	2.7	.3	−1.4	4.5	7.6	8.8
Treasury Claims: Private Sector .... **22d.** *i*	.2	.2	.2	.3	.5	.8	1.1	1.0	1.6	1.8	2.5	1.9	1.8	1.9	1.9
Post Office: Checking Deposits .... **24..** *i*	.5	.5	.6	1.1	1.1	1.4	2.1	1.6	1.4	1.4	1.4	1.3	1.8	2.0	2.1
Monetary Survey														*Billions of Francs:*	
Foreign Assets (Net) **31n**	11.6	15.3	17.3	15.9	12.6	5.9	−2.6	−.9	−.2	.7	−2.9	8.9	26.3	27.1	48.5
Domestic Credit **32**	2.2	2.9	6.1	16.7	25.6	38.8	53.1	†56.2	57.7	69.3	78.2	73.4	72.4	77.8	78.4
Claims on Central Govt. (Net) **32an**	−5.1	−6.3	−9.3	−4.9	−7.0	−7.7	−3.3	†−2.3	−3.4	1.5	.6	−6.9	−6.2	−17.7	−22.8
Claims on Private Sector **32d**	7.3	9.2	15.4	21.7	32.4	46.1	56.0	†57.7	60.2	66.7	75.9	78.0	76.2	93.1	98.1
Claims on Other Financial Insts **32f**	—	—	—	—	.2	.4	.4	†.9	.9	1.1	1.8	2.3	2.5	2.5	3.1
Money..................................... **34**	9.9	13.5	16.4	22.5	27.6	30.8	34.4	†34.8	41.7	48.8	54.4	60.3	66.5	69.5	85.4
Quasi-Money **35**	.7	1.0	1.2	1.8	4.0	4.8	8.1	†11.5	11.5	14.9	17.0	19.7	26.3	23.8	28.8
Long-Term Foreign Liabilities............... **36cl**	1.6	2.3	3.8	4.2	4.5	5.0	5.2	5.2	4.4	4.4	4.3	4.4	2.7	2.7	3.5
Other Items (Net).......................... **37r**	1.7	1.4	2.1	4.2	2.2	4.1	2.8	3.9	—	1.9	−.4	−2.2	3.3	9.0	9.2
Money plus Quasi-Money....................... **35l**	10.6	14.5	17.5	24.3	31.6	35.6	42.5	†46.2	53.2	63.7	71.4	80.1	92.8	93.3	114.2
Other Banking Institutions														*Billions of Francs:*	
Savings Deposits.................................. **45**	1.12	1.37	1.65	2.04	2.50	2.82	2.94	3.37	3.81	4.27	4.36	4.25	4.08	5.47	6.58
Liquid Liabilities **55l**	11.7	15.9	19.2	26.4	34.1	38.4	45.5	†49.6	57.0	68.0	75.7	84.3	96.9	98.8	120.8
Interest Rates														*Percent Per Annum*	
Discount Rate *(End of Period)* **60**	3.50	5.50	5.50	8.00	8.00	8.00	8.00	8.00	10.50	10.50	12.50	10.50	10.50	10.50	8.50
Money Market Rate............................ **60b**	....	....	....	....	7.28	7.27	7.42	7.72	10.55	13.68	14.66	12.23	11.84	10.67	8.58
Deposit Rate **60l**	3.00	5.75	5.75	5.88	6.00	6.00	6.00	6.00	6.19	6.25	7.75	7.50	7.25	7.25	6.08
Lending Rate **60p**	....	....	....	....	....	12.00	12.00	12.00	14.50	14.50	16.00	14.50	14.50	14.50	13.50
Prices and Labor														*Index Numbers (1995=100):*	
Consumer Prices **64**	....	....	....	....	....	....	....	....	....	....	....	67.4	70.6	75.5	73.5
														Number in Thousands:	
Employment **67e**	....	....	....	....	....	....	....	....	....	....	....	....	....	....	128
Unemployment **67c**	....	....	....	....	....	....	....	....	....	....	....	....	....	33	32

Exchange Rates

	1987	1988	1989	1990	1991	1992	1993	1994	1995	1996	1997	1998	1999	2000	2001	Code
End of Period																
Official Rate	378.78	407.68	380.32	364.84	370.48	378.57	404.89	†780.44	728.38	753.06	807.94	791.61	†896.19	918.49	935.39	aa
End of Period (ae) Period Average (rf)																
Official Rate		267.00	302.95	289.40	256.45	275.32	294.77	†534.60	490.00	523.70	598.81	562.21	†652.95	704.95	744.31	ae
Official Rate	300.54	297.85	319.01	272.26	282.11	264.69	283.16	†555.20	499.15	511.55	583.67	589.95	†615.70	711.98	733.04	rf

Fund Position

	1987	1988	1989	1990	1991	1992	1993	1994	1995	1996	1997	1998	1999	2000	2001	Code
End of Period																
Quota	31.6	31.6	31.6	31.6	31.6	44.2	44.2	44.2	44.2	44.2	44.2	44.2	60.2	60.2	60.2	2f.s
SDRs	5.7	5.6	5.6	5.7	5.6	5.6	5.6	5.6	5.5	1.8	1.6	.5	.5	.3	.4	1b.s
Reserve Position in the Fund	7.5	7.5	7.5	7.2	7.2	7.2	7.2	7.2	7.2	7.2	7.2	7.2	7.2	7.2	7.2	1c.s
Total Fund Cred.&Loans Outstg.	4.2	1.9	.4	.1	6.3	6.3	15.2	32.8	50.5	56.5	68.5	79.6	87.9	86.1	92.7	2tl

International Liquidity

	1987	1988	1989	1990	1991	1992	1993	1994	1995	1996	1997	1998	1999	2000	2001	Code
End of Period																
Total Reserves minus Gold	322.6	320.9	265.5	300.5	346.1	341.3	382.3	237.2	347.4	338.6	344.8	373.3	295.0	243.6	260.5	1l.d
SDRs	8.0	7.6	7.4	8.0	8.0	7.7	7.7	8.1	8.2	2.6	2.2	.8	.7	.4	.5	1b.d
Reserve Position in the Fund	10.7	10.1	9.9	10.2	10.3	9.9	9.9	10.5	10.7	10.4	9.7	10.2	9.9	9.4	9.1	1c.d
Foreign Exchange	303.9	303.1	248.2	282.2	327.7	323.7	364.7	218.6	328.4	325.6	332.9	362.4	284.3	233.8	250.9	1d.d
Gold (Million Fine Troy Ounces)	.011	.011	.011	.011	.011	.011	.011	.011	.011	.011	.011	.011	.011	....	....	1ad
Gold (National Valuation)	5.2	4.6	4.3	4.2	3.9	3.8	4.1	4.1	4.3	4.2	3.4	3.3	3.3	....	....	1and
Monetary Authorities: Other Liab.	59.6	53.7	42.6	41.8	40.4	32.5	29.8	14.9	4.1	5.8	29.0	43.9	29.3	37.8	22.6	4..d
Deposit Money Banks: Assets	34.8	30.9	43.5	54.9	38.7	48.6	53.1	155.5	253.5	212.8	167.5	167.5	232.9	212.6	188.8	7a.d
Liabilities	50.6	45.7	57.8	75.7	66.6	43.1	42.5	39.7	58.7	44.0	54.5	67.0	129.1	105.3	119.5	7b.d

Monetary Authorities

	1987	1988	1989	1990	1991	1992	1993	1994	1995	1996	1997	1998	1999	2000	2001	Code
Foreign Assets	86.1	97.2	76.8	77.1	89.6	94.0	112.7	126.8	170.2	177.3	206.5	209.9	192.6	171.7	193.9	11
Claims on Central Government	16.6	17.2	18.2	19.3	21.6	22.6	26.3	44.8	55.7	59.3	80.1	92.9	103.7	104.4	110.7	12a
Claims on Deposit Money Banks	8.1	4.5	4.3	3.9	9.0	9.0	9.0	—	2.5	4.0	14.6	24.7	3.9	10.3	3.3	12e
Claims on Other Financial Insts	1.2	1.3	1.6	1.6	1.3	1.0	.9	.4	.3	.4	.7	1.1	1.1	1.1	1.1	12f
Reserve Money	86.6	94.9	81.0	82.1	99.2	105.2	121.4	120.4	149.3	156.3	193.1	186.2	160.0	160.2	160.5	14
of which: Currency Outside DMBs	43.7	49.3	53.3	58.7	60.9	65.8	78.5	94.9	123.5	139.6	170.1	165.0	142.5	136.6	120.9	14a
Foreign Liabilities	19.1	17.8	12.7	10.8	12.8	11.3	14.9	33.6	38.8	45.6	72.7	87.7	97.9	105.7	103.6	16c
Central Government Deposits	4.0	4.0	4.1	5.3	5.5	6.0	8.4	19.5	37.4	37.3	29.5	48.4	45.0	22.9	41.4	16d
Other Items (Net)	2.2	3.5	3.2	3.8	4.0	3.9	4.1	-1.4	3.2	1.7	6.6	6.2	-1.6	-1.3	3.5	17r

Deposit Money Banks

	1987	1988	1989	1990	1991	1992	1993	1994	1995	1996	1997	1998	1999	2000	2001	Code
End of Period																
Reserves	41.9	42.4	26.2	22.3	36.4	37.7	41.0	20.9	17.7	9.1	15.7	14.4	19.8	18.1	35.4	20
Foreign Assets	9.3	9.3	12.6	14.1	10.0	13.4	15.7	83.1	124.2	111.5	100.3	94.2	152.1	149.9	140.5	21
Claims on Central Government	5.6	6.9	14.7	19.7	15.2	14.0	13.5	35.3	27.3	26.1	28.1	32.7	26.1	21.4	15.0	22a
Claims on Private Sector	102.1	114.5	136.0	141.4	108.4	94.9	87.6	72.3	79.0	89.9	163.2	180.9	186.5	217.6	247.9	22d
Claims on Other Financial Insts	1.5	1.5	1.6	—	1.6	1.2	.3	.3							—	22f
Demand Deposits	44.1	47.2	48.5	42.1	45.8	41.4	42.0	69.8	81.5	80.2	90.7	89.5	107.7	126.0	135.7	24
Time Deposits	36.3	47.8	48.9	49.9	51.0	56.8	57.4	62.6	71.0	70.7	83.7	94.3	108.5	117.5	131.7	25
Foreign Liabilities	9.5	9.2	10.3	14.5	11.2	6.4	6.9	12.2	19.7	23.1	30.5	33.0	77.2	68.4	82.5	26c
Long-Term Foreign Liabilities	4.0	4.7	6.5	4.9	6.1	5.4	5.6	9.0	9.1	—	2.1	4.7	7.1	5.8	6.4	26cl
Central Government Deposits	53.2	57.9	68.6	75.8	51.4	50.9	47.8	59.0	61.3	54.6	57.5	58.0	60.5	60.1	57.1	26d
Credit from Monetary Authorities	8.1	4.5	4.3	3.9	9.0	9.0	9.0	—	2.5	—	14.6	25.2	4.4	10.3	3.3	26g
Other Items (Net)	5.1	3.3	4.1	6.5	-2.9	-8.8	-10.5	-.7	3.1	7.9	28.3	17.6	19.2	18.8	22.1	27r
Treasury Claims: Private Sector	1.0	1.6	1.3	1.3	1.8	2.2	.9	1.7	1.6	1.6	1.8	1.4	1.1	.4	.5	22d.i
Post Office: Checking Deposits	2.8	1.8	2.3	2.3	1.9	1.7	1.6	2.4	2.7	2.7	2.1	2.3	2.3	2.3	1.9	24..i

Monetary Survey

	1987	1988	1989	1990	1991	1992	1993	1994	1995	1996	1997	1998	1999	2000	2001	Code
End of Period																
Foreign Assets (Net)	66.8	79.6	66.5	65.9	75.7	89.6	106.5	164.2	236.0	220.1	203.5	183.4	169.6	147.5	148.4	31n
Domestic Credit	72.5	81.3	101.7	103.2	93.1	78.4	74.1	77.0	66.3	86.5	187.3	203.5	214.2	263.7	278.0	32
Claims on Central Govt. (Net)	-33.3	-37.7	-38.8	-41.2	-20.0	-20.9	-15.7	2.4	-14.6	-5.4	21.5	20.1	25.4	44.7	28.5	32an
Claims on Private Sector	103.1	116.1	137.3	142.8	110.2	97.1	88.5	73.9	80.6	91.5	165.0	182.3	187.6	217.9	248.4	32d
Claims on Other Financial Insts	2.7	2.8	3.2	1.6	2.8	2.2	1.2	.6	.3	.4	.7	1.1	1.1	1.1	1.1	32f
Money	91.2	100.9	105.4	103.6	109.3	109.9	122.6	170.3	213.7	228.7	268.9	261.9	256.9	270.4	262.3	34
Quasi-Money	36.3	47.8	48.9	49.9	51.0	56.8	57.4	62.6	71.0	70.7	83.7	94.3	108.5	117.5	131.7	35
Long-Term Foreign Liabilities	4.0	4.7	6.5	4.9	6.1	5.4	5.6	9.0	9.1	—	2.1	4.7	7.1	5.8	6.4	36cl
Other Items (Net)	7.7	7.5	7.5	10.7	2.3	-4.2	-5.0	-.8	8.5	7.2	36.2	26.0	11.4	17.5	26.0	37r
Money plus Quasi-Money	127.5	148.7	154.3	153.5	160.4	166.7	180.0	232.9	284.7	299.4	352.5	356.2	365.3	387.9	394.0	35l

Other Banking Institutions

	1987	1988	1989	1990	1991	1992	1993	1994	1995	1996	1997	1998	1999	2000	2001	Code
End of Period																
Savings Deposits	6.69	6.68	6.80	6.56	6.63	10.17	....	....	....	....	....	....	....	....	....	45
Liquid Liabilities	134.2	155.4	161.1	160.1	167.0	176.9	180.0	232.9	284.7	299.4	352.5	356.2	365.3	387.9	394.0	55l

Interest Rates

	1987	1988	1989	1990	1991	1992	1993	1994	1995	1996	1997	1998	1999	2000	2001	Code
Percent Per Annum																
Discount Rate (End of Period)	8.50	9.50	11.00	11.00	11.00	12.50	10.50	10.00	7.50	6.50	6.00	6.25	5.75	6.50	6.50	60
Money Market Rate	8.37	8.72	10.07	10.98	10.94	11.44	....	....	....	....	....	4.81	4.95	4.95	4.95	60b
Deposit Rate	5.25	5.25	6.42	7.00	7.00	7.75	....	....	....	....	....	3.50	3.50	3.50	3.50	60l
Lending Rate	13.50	13.58	15.13	16.00	16.00	16.75	....	....	....	....	....	....	....	....	....	60p

Prices and Labor

	1987	1988	1989	1990	1991	1992	1993	1994	1995	1996	1997	1998	1999	2000	2001	Code
Period Averages																
Consumer Prices	71.6	74.5	74.3	73.6	75.5	74.0	74.4	93.1	100.0	106.2	†108.6	114.1	112.9	112.5	118.0	64
Period Averages																
Employment	134	138	146	152	158	163	....	....	....	....	....	....	....	....	....	67e
Unemployment	35	†35	38	42	35	30	30	27	14	13	9	9	8	7	....	67c

Burkina Faso

	1972	1973	1974	1975	1976	1977	1978	1979	1980	1981	1982	1983	1984	1985	1986
International Transactions														*Billions of Francs*	
Exports 70	5.14	5.60	8.70	9.37	12.69	13.61	9.60	16.24	19.07	19.92	18.11	21.71	34.87	31.16	28.67
Imports, c.i.f. 71	17.27	21.69	34.66	32.39	34.42	51.36	51.08	63.92	75.61	91.44	114.01	109.57	111.26	146.24	139.64
														1995=100	
Unit Value of Exports..................... 74	28.5	31.4	46.1	†46.5	59.8	67.1	63.9	65.5	71.4	78.7	90.6	103.2	106.2	124.8	87.8
Unit Value of Imports 75	16.4	17.6	22.0	†25.5	29.0	31.8	31.1	33.6	35.5	42.6	51.8	56.8	59.0	63.4	60.9
Balance of Payments														*Millions of US Dollars:*	
Current Account, n.i.e. .... 78al d	....	....	−5.3	−54.3	−33.5	−84.3	−59.5	−63.8	−48.7	−42.1	−92.1	−60.1	−3.5	−63.0	−18.0
Goods: Exports f.o.b. .... 78aa d	....	....	66.0	73.5	83.1	94.8	107.8	132.7	160.6	159.4	126.4	112.9	140.9	130.5	148.8
Goods: Imports f.o.b. .... 78ab d	....	....	−147.8	−187.8	−167.4	−220.7	−255.4	−312.1	−368.3	−348.4	−359.9	−308.9	−270.1	−352.4	−441.3
Trade Balance .... 78ac d	....	....	−81.8	−114.3	−84.4	−125.9	−147.6	−179.4	−207.7	−189.1	−233.4	−196.0	−129.2	−221.9	−292.4
Services: Credit .... 78ad d	....	....	9.4	14.3	17.0	17.5	23.7	41.6	49.1	40.9	48.3	37.7	27.1	27.1	39.7
Services: Debit .... 78ae d	....	....	−51.5	−74.2	−77.2	−95.1	−135.2	−178.6	−209.0	−185.4	−174.0	−146.9	−124.3	−129.3	−157.1
Balance on Goods & Services ... 78af d	....	....	−123.9	−174.2	−144.5	−203.5	−259.1	−316.5	−367.6	−333.6	−359.2	−305.2	−226.4	−324.1	−409.8
Income: Credit .... 78ag d	....	....	9.0	7.4	6.4	6.2	4.9	7.1	15.6	8.9	9.0	5.9	7.0	9.8	12.2
Income: Debit .... 78ah d	....	....	−11.3	−19.3	−15.8	−26.2	−15.5	−16.0	−19.1	−18.4	−19.2	−16.0	−14.4	−14.7	−17.7
Balance on Gds, Serv. & Inc. ... 78ai d	....	....	−126.1	−186.1	−153.9	−223.4	−269.7	−325.5	−371.1	−343.1	−369.4	−315.2	−233.8	−329.0	−415.3
Current Transfers, n.i.e.: Credit .... 78aj d	....	....	134.9	157.3	147.9	171.9	255.6	315.3	387.2	354.3	319.9	301.2	270.9	310.2	453.1
Current Transfers: Debit .... 78ak d	....	....	−14.0	−25.4	−27.5	−32.8	−45.4	−53.6	−64.8	−53.2	−42.6	−46.1	−40.5	−44.2	−55.8
Capital Account, n.i.e. .... 78bc d	....	....	—	—	—	—	—	—	—	—	—	—	—	—	—
Capital Account, n.i.e.: Credit .... 78ba d	....	....	—	—	—	—	—	—	—	—	—	—	—	—	—
Capital Account: Debit .... 78bb d	....	....	—	—	—	—	—	—	—	—	—	—	—	—	—
Financial Account, n.i.e. .... 78bj d	....	....	19.9	32.6	32.7	55.3	27.7	67.5	63.3	64.4	76.5	87.2	33.1	51.5	39.6
Direct Investment Abroad .... 78bd d	....	....	−.4	−.7	−.3	−.4	−.8	−.4	—	—	−.2	—	—	—	—
Dir. Invest. in Rep. Econ., n.i.e. ..... 78be d	....	....	2.7	.3	2.1	5.0	1.2	1.5	—	2.4	1.9	2.0	1.7	−1.4	3.1
Portfolio Investment Assets .... 78bf d	....	....	−.6	−.8	−.9	−1.4	.4	—	−1.1	−.2	.9	.4	—	—	—
Equity Securities..................... 78bk d	....	....	—	—	—	—	−1.0	—	—	—	—	—	—	—	—
Debt Securities .... 78bl d	....	....	−.6	−.8	−.9	−1.4	1.3	—	−1.1	−.2	.9	.4	—	—	—
Portfolio Investment Liab., n.i.e. ...... 78bg d	....	....	.2	.2	1.2	.1	.4	—	.5	—	—	—	—	—	—
Equity Securities..................... 78bm d	....	....	.2	.2	1.2	.1	.4	—	.5	—	—	—	—	—	—
Debt Securities .... 78bn d	....	....	—	—	—	—	—	—	—	—	—	—	—	—	—
Financial Derivatives Assets .... 78bw d	....	....	....	....	....	....	....	....	....	....	....	....	....	....	....
Financial Derivatives Liabilities .... 78bx d	....	....	....	....	....	....	....	....	....	....	....	....	....	....	....
Other Investment Assets .... 78bh d	....	....	−4.6	7.1	−7.5	−2.1	−2.0	−3.6	−13.1	−4.4	−7.0	−10.7	−7.5	−3.2	−26.0
Monetary Authorities.................... 78bo d	....	....	....	....	....	....	....	....	....	....	....	....	....	....	....
General Government .... 78bp d	....	....	—	—	−.2	.1	−.1	−.1	−3.2	−6.1	−6.9	−2.8	−1.8	−1.4	−2.8
Banks .... 78bq d	....	....	3.2	−.7	−.1	−3.1	−.3	2.1	−11.6	2.3	−2.4	−2.1	−2.5	−1.3	.2
Other Sectors .... 78br d	....	....	−7.8	7.8	−7.2	.9	−1.5	−5.6	1.7	−.6	2.2	−5.8	−3.2	−.5	−23.4
Other Investment Liab., n.i.e. .... 78bi d	....	....	22.5	26.5	38.1	54.1	28.5	69.9	77.0	66.6	80.9	95.5	38.9	56.1	62.5
Monetary Authorities.................... 78bs d	....	....	....	....	....	....	....	....	....	....	....	....	....	....	....
General Government .... 78bt d	....	....	11.0	23.2	22.4	6.1	19.3	53.0	51.0	35.7	56.2	59.0	40.8	35.8	46.5
Banks .... 78bu d	....	....	13.0	−2.0	8.3	21.6	−1.4	1.4	7.8	21.1	11.3	11.6	−18.0	4.5	−11.8
Other Sectors .... 78bv d	....	....	−1.5	5.3	7.4	26.3	10.5	15.5	18.2	9.8	13.4	24.9	16.1	15.9	27.8
Net Errors and Omissions.................... 78ca d	....	....	1.7	15.5	1.3	9.2	.6	4.6	−7.9	−8.1	15.4	9.5	6.2	17.2	2.9
Overall Balance .... 78cb d	....	....	16.3	−6.3	.5	−19.8	−31.2	8.3	6.6	14.2	−.2	36.6	35.9	5.7	24.5
Reserves and Related Items .... 79da d	....	....	−16.3	6.3	−.5	19.8	31.2	−8.3	−6.6	−14.2	.2	−36.6	−35.9	−5.7	−24.5
Reserve Assets .... 79db d	....	....	−16.3	6.3	−1.5	18.4	24.6	−20.6	−10.9	−14.3	.2	−36.3	−34.8	−5.5	−48.6
Use of Fund Credit and Loans .... 79dc d	....	....	—	—	—	—	6.7	5.1	4.3	.1	—	−.2	−1.1	−2.2	−3.0
Exceptional Financing .... 79de d	....	....	—	—	1.0	1.3	—	7.2	—	—	—	—	—	2.0	27.1
Government Finance														*Millions of Francs:*	
Deficit (-) or Surplus............................ 80		354	2,212	−1,664	−1,272	†4,313	1,495	−5,622	879	−4,674	−6,185	562	−3,350	†6,339	−35,330
Total Revenue and Grants 81y		12,862	15,973	15,785	21,430	†28,765	32,235	35,071	43,139	48,720	54,560	54,540	63,088	†71,588	95,840
Revenue 81		12,111	14,998	15,235	20,630	†27,965	32,235	34,071	42,461	45,809	54,170	53,529	62,278	†70,798	68,460
Grants 81z		751	975	550	800	†800	—	1,000	678	2,911	390	1,011	810	†790	27,380
Exp. & Lending Minus Repay. 82z		12,508	13,761	18,326	23,037	†27,101	31,047	41,173	42,260	53,394	60,745	53,978	66,438	†65,249	133,720
Expenditure 82		11,804	13,181	16,246	20,963	†26,954	30,734	40,319	44,047	50,063	63,037	52,614	64,691	†62,883	131,390
Lending Minus Repayments 83		704	580	2,080	2,074	†147	313	854	−1,787	3,331	−2,292	1,364	1,747	†2,366	2,330
Adjustment to Cash Basis 80x		....	....	....	....	....	....	....							2,550
Total Financing....................................... 80h									−879	4,674	6,185	−562	3,350	....	35,330
National Accounts														*Billions of Francs*	
Househ.Cons.Expend.,incl.NPISHs 96f	99.2	96.9	106.9	113.4	118.9	161.9	196.7	192.1	231.3	278.7	315.1	327.6	308.3	563.9	570.0
Government Consumption Expend......... 91f	9.5	10.9	13.4	23.2	21.2	26.5	30.0	49.2	47.4	60.9	72.5	78.8	76.9	86.3	95.0
Gross Fixed Capital Formation 93e	15.5	20.0	28.8	29.5	33.2	35.9	39.2	74.8	66.0	69.9	84.0	90.3	90.8	133.5	145.0
Changes in Inventories 93i	3.5	3.3	6.0	5.6	6.2	5.1	6.8	5.0	6.4	7.2	7.8	2.6	3.3	26.6	7.0
Exports of Goods and Services 90c	11.6	11.8	18.7	18.4	23.9	27.4	29.0	36.2	43.6	53.6	56.2	55.9	88.1	69.2	63.0
Imports of Goods and Services (-) 98c	29.9	33.2	42.8	52.4	54.0	71.9	79.2	104.8	122.7	146.1	176.0	174.2	176.8	216.4	204.0
Gross Domestic Product (GDP) 99b	109.4	109.7	131.0	137.7	149.4	184.9	222.5	252.5	272.0	324.2	359.6	381.0	390.6	663.1	676.0
Net Primary Income from Abroad 98.n	−2.2	−.2	−.2	.3	.5	−.8	−1.5	−1.3	1.1	−.5	−1.0	−.7	−.8	−15.2	.6
Gross National Income (GNI) 99a	107.2	109.5	130.8	138.0	149.4	184.1	221.1	252.2	273.1	323.7	358.6	380.3	389.8	749.3	676.6
GDP Volume 1979 prices 99b.p	....	....	....	....	....	....	....	252.5	256.7	268.0	274.0	270.7	275.5	311.1	....
GDP Volume 1985 Prices.................... 99b.p	....	....	....	....	....	....	....	....	....	....	....	....	....	663.1	728.4
GDP Volume (1995=100) .... 99bv p	....	....	....	....	....	....	....	60.8	61.8	64.5	66.0	65.2	66.4	74.9	82.3
GDP Deflator (1995=100) .... 99bi p	....	....	....	....	....	....	....	37.5	39.8	45.4	49.3	52.8	53.2	80.0	74.2
															Millions:
Population... 99z	5.61	†5.45	5.54	5.64	5.74	5.84	5.94	6.04	6.91	7.09	7.28	7.48	7.68	7.89	8.10

	1987	1988	1989	1990	1991	1992	1993	1994	1995	1996	1997	1998	1999	2000	2001		
																International Transactions	
Billions of Francs																	
Exports	46.59	41.95	30.27	41.28	29.89	16.83	19.66	59.22	138.00	119.04	133.62	190.44	156.20	148.90	126.24	Exports	70
Imports	130.53	134.94	125.35	145.83	150.26	123.36	144.02	193.70	227.00	330.96	342.35	430.33	357.40	393.90	481.20	Imports, c.i.f.	71
1995=100																	
	†91.0	88.2	82.0	90.3	88.2	67.3	64.7	84.8	100.0	97.8	. . . .	. . . .	. . . .	. . . .	. . . .	Unit Value of Exports	74
	†54.2	54.2	58.8	62.8	58.2	55.9	56.8	93.5	100.0	103.7	. . . .	. . . .	. . . .	. . . .	. . . .	Unit Value of Imports	75
																Balance of Payments	
Minus Sign Indicates Debit																	
	−49.8	−46.5	99.3	−76.9	−90.6	−23.0	−71.1	14.9	. . . .							Current Account, n.i.e.	78al d
	229.8	240.0	184.6	280.5	269.1	237.2	226.1	215.6	. . . .							Goods: Exports f.o.b.	78aa d
	−475.1	−477.4	−441.7	−542.5	−490.5	−458.9	−469.1	−344.3	. . . .							Goods: Imports f.o.b.	78ab d
	−245.3	−237.3	−257.2	−261.9	−221.4	−221.7	−243.0	−128.7	. . . .							*Trade Balance*	78ac d
	45.8	54.7	51.4	68.7	68.4	64.5	64.6	56.3	. . . .							Services: Credit	78ad d
	−200.2	−243.0	−185.6	−215.7	−253.2	−207.7	−209.0	−138.3	. . . .							Services: Debit	78ae d
	−399.6	−425.6	−391.3	−409.0	−406.2	−364.9	−387.4	−210.7	. . . .							*Balance on Goods & Services*	78af d
	12.7	18.1	17.8	17.6	16.5	21.7	21.5	8.7	. . . .							Income: Credit	78ag d
	−21.5	−26.9	−24.2	−17.7	−16.2	−19.1	−28.6	−38.1	. . . .							Income: Debit	78ah d
	−408.4	−434.4	−397.7	−409.2	−406.0	−362.3	−394.5	−240.1	. . . .							*Balance on Gds, Serv. & Inc.*	78ai d
	423.8	452.0	571.6	430.2	413.1	419.2	389.6	308.0	. . . .							Current Transfers, n.i.e.: Credit	78aj d
	−65.1	−64.1	−74.6	−97.9	−97.7	−79.9	−66.3	−53.0	. . . .							Current Transfers: Debit	78ak d
	—	—	—	—	—	—	—	—	. . . .							Capital Account, n.i.e.	78bc d
	—	—	—	—	—	—	—	—	. . . .							Capital Account, n.i.e.: Credit	78ba d
	—	—	—	—	—	—	—	—	. . . .							Capital Account: Debit	78bb d
	55.6	63.5	−228.6	82.4	104.8	34.7	69.1	−13.9	. . . .							Financial Account, n.i.e.	78bj d
																Direct Investment Abroad	78bd d
	1.3	3.7	5.7	—	—	—	—	—	. . . .							Dir. Invest. in Rep. Econ., n.i.e.	78be d
	—	—	—	—	—	—	—	—	. . . .							Portfolio Investment Assets	78bf d
	—	—	—	—	—	—	—	—	. . . .							Equity Securities	78bk d
	—	—	—	—	—	—	—	—	. . . .							Debt Securities	78bl d
	—	—	—	—	—	—	—	—	. . . .							Portfolio Investment Liab., n.i.e.	78bg d
	—	—	—	—	—	—	—	—	. . . .							Equity Securities	78bm d
	—	—	—	—	—	—	—	—	. . . .							Debt Securities	78bn d
	. . . .	. . . .	. . . .	. . . .	. . . .	. . . .	. . . .	. . . .	. . . .							Financial Derivatives Assets	78bw d
	. . . .	. . . .	. . . .	. . . .	. . . .	. . . .	. . . .	. . . .	. . . .							Financial Derivatives Liabilities	78bx d
	−35.7	−2.3	−26.7	−6.6	.5	−45.2	24.2	−139.2	. . . .							Other Investment Assets	78bh d
	. . . .	. . . .	. . . .	. . . .	. . . .	. . . .	. . . .	. . . .	. . . .							Monetary Authorities	78bo d
	−22.4	−.8	−12.8	−3.0	15.9	−21.7	24.2	−135.2	. . . .							General Government	78bp d
	−13.3	−1.5	−13.8	−3.7	−15.4	−23.4	—	−4.0	. . . .							Banks	78bq d
	89.9	62.1	−207.6	89.1	104.3	79.9	44.9	125.3	. . . .							Other Sectors	78br d
	—	—	—	—	—	−6.6	—	—	. . . .							Other Investment Liab., n.i.e.	78bi d
	69.3	48.4	−226.5	64.3	78.4	100.0	84.4	29.3	. . . .							Monetary Authorities	78bs d
	−2.6	1.5	13.0	9.2	−7.0	−12.1	−47.1	41.9	. . . .							General Government	78bt d
	23.2	12.1	6.0	15.6	32.9	−1.3	7.7	54.0	. . . .							Banks	78bu d
	4.0	1.1	−5.9	1.6	−6.6	8.3	4.6	−8.3	. . . .							Other Sectors	78bv d
	9.7	18.1	−135.2	7.1	7.7	20.0	2.5	−7.3	. . . .							Net Errors and Omissions	78ca d
	−9.7	−18.1	135.2	−7.1	−7.7	−20.0	−2.5	7.3	. . . .							*Overall Balance*	78cb d
	−28.8	−29.7	50.0	−6.6	−43.6	−15.9	−53.5	−17.4	. . . .							Reserves and Related Items	79da d
	−3.3	−3.1	−1.9	−.5	8.7	—	12.5	25.5	. . . .							Reserve Assets	79db d
	22.3	14.8	87.1	—	27.3	−4.2	38.5	−.7	. . . .							Use of Fund Credit and Loans	79dc d
																Exceptional Financing	79de d
																Government Finance	
Year Ending December 31																	
	−29,840	−36,870	24,960	−29,213	−37,680	−34,620	−37,540	−46,806	−37,971	−23,579	−50,500	−50,300	−63,800	−67,500	. . . .	Deficit (-) or Surplus	80
	122,130	112,070	162,980	114,340	145,490	128,000	139,800	189,669	225,178	223,280	279,200	303,100	377,600	363,000	. . . .	Total Revenue and Grants	81y
	79,210	79,290	79,850	91,470	108,490	93,000	100,800	114,325	137,183	160,812	181,400	199,400	236,500	219,300	. . . .	Revenue	81
	42,920	32,780	83,130	22,870	37,000	35,000	39,000	75,344	87,995	62,468	97,800	103,700	141,100	143,700	. . . .	Grants	81z
	158,290	154,170	140,610	131,490	164,090	164,400	181,940	225,115	244,859	229,859	323,200	347,900	432,100	431,500	. . . .	Exp. & Lending Minus Repay.	82z
	155,680	153,660	138,910	132,760	163,220	164,400	183,940	227,449	247,053	231,552	325,700	348,500	431,800	428,400	. . . .	Expenditure	82
	2,610	510	1,700	−1,270	870	—	−2,000	−2,334	−2,194	−1,693	−2,500	−600	300	3,100	. . . .	Lending Minus Repayments	83
	6,320	5,230	2,590	−12,063	−19,080	1,780	4,600	−11,360	−18,290	−17,000	−6,500	−5,500	−9,300	1,000	. . . .	Adjustment to Cash Basis	80x
	29,840	36,870	−24,960	29,213	37,680	34,620	37,540	46,806	37,971	23,579	50,500	50,300	63,800	67,500	. . . .	Total Financing	80h
																National Accounts	
Billions of Francs																	
	552.0	602.0	621.7	617.8	618.8	619.0	628.1	776.2	891.1	988.6	1,041.2	1,110.7	1,162.9	1,206.6	1,281.2	Househ.Cons.Expend.,incl.NPISHs	96f
	98.0	105.0	110.0	111.8	119.1	117.2	121.0	176.5	183.8	191.9	198.0	218.4	215.7	234.0	252.0	Government Consumption Expend.	91f
	150.6	152.1	164.0	149.8	176.9	173.2	155.1	225.5	273.3	332.3	384.8	448.0	411.5	419.7	454.2	Gross Fixed Capital Formation	93e
	−5.0	3.0	6.3	9.9	11.0	.1	35.8	−64.7	−61.9	−72.1	−36.7	−40.2	—	—	—	Changes in Inventories	93i
	81.0	86.0	73.0	92.6	92.4	76.6	92.2	135.6	152.6	141.4	155.8	213.3	176.7	168.6	190.8	Exports of Goods and Services	90c
	200.0	211.0	197.3	203.4	206.5	173.5	209.8	270.7	332.6	371.0	385.0	470.5	448.7	468.2	471.3	Imports of Goods and Services (-)	98c
	676.6	737.1	777.7	778.5	811.7	812.6	822.4	978.4	1,106.3	1,211.1	1,358.1	1,479.7	1,518.1	1,560.7	1,706.9	Gross Domestic Product (GDP)	99b
	−.8	1.9	1.5	−.1	−.8	1.1	−3.8	−7.8	−5.7	−4.0	−7.8	−7.0	−11.3	−14.3	−13.9	Net Primary Income from Abroad	98.n
	675.8	739.0	779.2	778.4	810.9	813.7	818.6	970.6	1,100.6	2,679.8	1,350.3	1,472.7	1,506.8	1,546.4	1,693.0	Gross National Income (GNI)	99a
	. . . .	. . . .	. . . .	. . . .	. . . .	. . . .	. . . .	. . . .	. . . .							GDP Volume 1979 prices	99b.p
	717.4	762.0	763.5	755.5	827.4	830.4	803.9	835.0	885.0	942.5	996.7	1,051.8	1,118.6	1,145.1	1,211.4	GDP Volume 1985 Prices	99b.p
	81.1	86.1	86.3	85.4	93.5	93.8	90.8	94.4	100.0	106.5	112.6	118.8	126.4	129.4	136.9	GDP Volume (1995=100)	99bv p
	75.4	77.4	81.5	82.4	78.5	78.3	81.8	93.7	100.0	102.8	109.0	112.5	108.6	109.0	112.7	GDP Deflator (1995=100)	99bi p
Midyear Estimates																	
	8.31	8.54	8.77	9.00	9.19	9.43	9.68	9.89	10.20	10.51	11.09	†10.68	11.25	11.54	11.86	Population	99z

(See notes in the back of the book.)

Burundi

		1972	1973	1974	1975	1976	1977	1978	1979	1980	1981	1982	1983	1984	1985	1986
Exchange Rates																*Francs per SDR:*
Official Rate	aa	95.00	95.00	96.42	92.19	104.56	109.32	117.25	118.56	114.79	104.76	99.28	122.70	122.70	122.70	151.50
																Francs per US Dollar:
Official Rate	ae	87.50	78.75	78.75	78.75	90.00	90.00	90.00	90.00	90.00	90.00	90.00	117.41	124.95	111.97	124.17
Official Rate	rf	87.50	80.03	78.75	78.75	86.25	90.00	90.00	90.00	90.00	90.00	90.00	92.95	119.71	120.69	114.17
																Index Numbers (1995=100):
Official Rate	ahx	284.6	311.6	316.2	316.2	289.9	276.7	276.7	276.7	276.7	276.7	276.7	269.5	208.2	206.6	218.8
Nominal Effective Exchange Rate	ne c	....	....	....	....	....	....	....	108.4	108.6	129.0	147.1	157.2	135.5	141.3	123.8
Real Effective Exchange Rate	re c	....	....	....	....	....	....	....	144.5	133.1	160.5	176.7	190.7	176.7	180.4	155.1
Fund Position																*Millions of SDRs:*
Quota	2f. s	19.00	19.00	19.00	19.00	19.00	19.00	23.00	23.00	34.50	34.50	34.50	42.70	42.70	42.70	42.70
SDRs	1b. s	3.65	3.60	3.56	3.24	3.03	2.82	2.76	5.32	4.14	5.53	4.16	.99	.11	.11	.53
Reserve Position in the Fund	1c. s	.28	.39					4.75	4.47	7.34	7.34	7.37	9.42	9.42	9.16	9.16
Total Fund Cred.&Loans Outstg.	2tl	—	—	—	1.20	1.21	3.25	7.87	23.13	28.00	28.07	27.97	22.69	16.36	13.24	18.08
International Liquidity													*Millions of US Dollars Unless Otherwise Indicated:*			
Total Reserves minus Gold	1l. d	18.49	21.48	14.19	30.71	49.03	94.41	81.30	89.99	94.50	61.30	29.49	26.94	19.73	29.47	69.07
SDRs	1b. d	3.96	4.34	4.36	3.79	3.52	3.43	3.60	7.01	5.28	6.44	4.59	1.04	.11	.12	.65
Reserve Position in the Fund	1c. d	.30	.47	—	—	—	—	6.19	5.89	9.36	8.54	8.13	9.86	9.23	10.06	11.20
Foreign Exchange	1d. d	14.22	16.67	9.83	26.92	45.51	90.98	71.52	77.09	79.86	46.32	16.77	16.04	10.39	19.29	57.22
Gold (Million Fine Troy Ounces)	1ad	.001	.001	.001	.001	.001	.009	.009	.013	.017	.017	.017	.017	.017	.017	.017
Gold (National Valuation)	1an d	....	....	.16	.13	.13	1.50	2.05	8.87	10.15	6.85	7.87	6.60	5.33	5.62	6.93
Monetary Authorities: Other Liab.	4.. d	3.76	2.74	1.91	4.41	5.98	7.04	5.26	22.65	21.33	18.13	19.85	10.56	7.11	4.07	23.72
Deposit Money Banks: Assets	7a. d	2.12	1.96	3.00	1.75	2.99	3.57	5.57	8.07	3.47	3.74	1.63	5.64	6.41	5.24	9.70
Liabilities	7b. d	2.03	1.31	2.27	2.71	4.35	3.85	4.49	3.57	6.22	4.24	5.57	9.25	4.46	6.67	9.42
Other Banking Insts.: Assets	7e. d	....	....	....	....	....	....	....	....	—		.24	.65	2.73	.81	1.72	1.49
Liabilities	7f. d	—	—	—	.65	2.38	4.23	4.65	6.70	5.87	6.15	5.58	6.28	6.77	7.50	6.92
Monetary Authorities																*Millions of Francs:*
Foreign Assets	11	1,621	1,695	1,130	2,429	4,424	8,632	7,502	8,897	9,419	6,134	3,363	3,934	3,134	3,962	9,508
Claims on Central Government	12a	833	1,031	1,192	860	1,509	1,880	2,909	5,170	5,808	7,959	9,299	12,355	14,588	17,119	16,414
Claims on Nonfin.Pub.Enterprises	12c	—	—	—	5	5	5	5	14	1,381	598	482	412	362	324	303
Claims on Private Sector	12d	127	135	†27	26	32	65	93	116	110	110	111	124	134	148	126
Claims on Deposit Money Banks	12e	83	46	959	—	16	—	—	1,166	506	3,075	2,095	640	498	51	215
Claims on Other Financial Insts	12f	10	10	10	70	26	108	306	155	144	161	510	693	335	112	105
Reserve Money	14	1,631	1,753	2,103	2,052	3,452	4,788	5,617	5,346	5,916	8,145	6,999	8,916	9,607	11,962	12,160
of which: Currency Outside DMBs	14a	1,370	1,548	1,873	1,710	2,411	3,225	4,542	4,876	5,001	7,073	6,437	7,293	7,519	7,270	8,059
Nonfin.Pub.Ent. Deps.	14e	112	91	207	117	612	478	514	407	521	646	372	532	1,222	1,966	2,210
Bonds	16ab	147	166	243	233	349	259	364	889	971	992	568	768	1,032	765	660
Restricted Deposits	16b	186	212	238	183	345	546	683	530	549	750	382	804	766	910	1,109
Stabilization Fund	16bb	55	20	128	2	413	1,727	470	1,065	547	21	94	338	510	300	1,190
Foreign Liabilities	16c	329	216	151	347	539	846	1,342	3,607	4,043	3,577	3,625	3,441	2,895	2,080	4,355
Central Government Deposits	16d	251	410	399	332	1,076	2,197	1,718	1,773	2,113	1,592	1,658	1,548	1,550	2,477	3,539
Capital Accounts	17a	1,036	996	934	1,241	992	1,741	2,529	3,989	4,241	3,663	4,052	3,598	3,838	3,644	4,492
Other Items (Net)	17r	−960	−855	−876	−1,003	−1,153	−1,413	−1,239	−1,639	−1,015	−707	−1,504	−1,237	−1,147	−420	−834
Deposit Money Banks																
Commercial Banks																*Millions of Francs:*
Reserves	20	150	109	22	237	448	1,379	457	108	79	65	71	1,095	595	2,075	463
Foreign Assets	21	186	154	237	138	269	321	501	727	312	337	147	662	801	587	1,204
Claims on Central Government	22a	233	311	162	713	680	462	103	203	4	5	13	49	317	778	776
Claims on Nonfin.Pub.Enterprises	22c	....	....	....	....	....	....	....	....	....	....	....	....	2,525	3,576	3,782
Claims on Private Sector	22d	945	1,149	2,459	932	1,454	1,507	3,309	5,106	5,592	8,415	7,422	6,949	†4,559	4,812	5,986
Claims on Other Financial Insts	22f	19	15	15	15	15	15	15	15	32	32	382	1,070	889	607	231
Demand Deposits	24	1,035	1,274	1,485	1,507	2,201	2,779	3,274	3,834	3,840	3,871	3,927	5,183	5,325	8,185	8,729
Savings Deposits	25	131	295	199	274	256	529	725	639	499	1,254	1,453	2,818	2,227	2,432	881
Foreign Liabilities	26c	177	103	179	214	391	346	404	289	492	334	453	1,048	531	717	1,140
Central Government Deposits	26d	30	38	48	8	10	8	3	4	8	4	4				
Credit from Monetary Authorities	26g	83	—	966	3	—	—	—	1,197	906	2,884	1,561	48	415	—	250
Capital Accounts	27a	168	233	252	265	307	313	301	402	512	583	733	845	919	1,068	1,148
Other Items (Net)	27r	80	26	−28	68	109	62	120	197	518	76	115	−86	−76	−191	294
Other Monetary Institutions																*Millions of Francs:*
Reserves	20..h	....	....	....	23	49	63	198	889	†828	373	146	147	294	654	679
Claims on Central Government	22a.h	8	10	10	14	14	43	45	997	†1,615	1,900	†88	148	156	280	262
Claims on Nonfin.Pub.Enterprises	22c.h	....	....	....	....	....	....	....	111	305	675	1,178	1,438	1,493	1,458	1,436
Claims on Private Sector	22d.h	29	37	37	43	68	112	296	†391	711	739	855	1,107	1,110	1,111	1,737
Claims on Other Financial Insts	22f.h	....	....	....	....	....	....	....	101	200	270	20	20	40	680	70
Demand Deposits	24..h	8	9	10	13	12	21	29	38	69	103	65	139	148	247	253
Time and Savings Deposits	25..h	—	—	—	—	—	—	—	—	1	1	1	1	1	1	1
Foreign Liabilities	26c.h	....	....	....	....	....	....	....	33	69	48	48	38	27	29	29
Central Government Deposits	26d.h	11	21	26	50	86	96	154	472	†676	958	890	933	1,360	1,862	1,962
Cred.from Monetary Authorities	26g.h	....	....	....	....	....	....	....	—	—	—	472	535			
Other Items (Net)	27r.h	....	....	....	....	....	....	....	20	†−130	−93	†22	9	7	32	8
Monetary Survey																*Millions of Francs:*
Foreign Assets (Net)	31n	1,300	1,530	1,037	2,007	3,763	7,760	6,257	5,696	5,128	2,512	−616	69	482	1,723	5,188
Domestic Credit	32	1,895	2,213	3,429	2,293	2,664	2,166	6,159	10,960	13,106	18,308	19,907	23,915	†23,848	27,417	25,951
Claims on Central Govt. (Net)	32an	785	896	908	1,232	1,103	137	1,291	3,595	3,691	6,368	7,738	11,005	13,511	15,701	13,912
Claims on Nonfin.Pub.Enterprises	32c	—	—	—	55	21	291	1,101	1,358	1,687	1,273	1,660	1,850	4,379	5,357	5,521
Claims on Private Sector	32d	1,072	1,283	2,486	958	1,487	1,572	3,401	5,613	6,414	9,264	8,388	8,180	†4,693	4,960	6,112
Claims on Other Financial Insts	32f	29	25	25	85	41	123	321	270	376	462	911	1,783	1,265	1,399	406
Money	34	2,526	2,922	3,575	3,347	5,235	6,503	8,358	9,156	9,431	11,693	10,801	13,145	14,214	17,667	19,251
Quasi-Money	35	131	295	199	274	256	529	725	639	500	1,255	1,453	2,819	2,227	2,432	881
Other Items (Net)	37r	710	757	898	981	1,327	2,940	3,333	5,416	7,037	5,548	4,082	4,499	5,793	6,668	9,352
Money plus Quasi-Money	35l	2,657	3,217	3,774	3,621	5,492	7,032	9,083	9,795	9,931	12,947	12,255	15,964	16,441	20,100	20,132

1987	1988	1989	1990	1991	1992	1993	1994	1995	1996	1997	1998	1999	2000	2001		
															Exchange Rates	
End of Period																
161.00	201.00	232.14	232.14	273.07	322.90	362.99	360.78	413.37	462.63	551.56	710.64	860.83	1,014.76	1,090.92	Official Rate	aa
End of Period (ae) Period Average (rf)																
114.47	149.94	175.43	165.35	191.10	236.55	264.38	246.94	277.92	322.35	408.38	505.16	628.58	778.20	864.20	Official Rate	ae
123.56	140.40	158.67	171.26	181.51	208.30	242.78	252.66	249.76	302.75	352.35	447.77	563.56	720.67	830.35	Official Rate	rf
Period Averages																
201.7	179.0	157.2	145.6	138.1	119.9	102.7	98.7	100.0	82.6	70.9	56.0	44.4	34.9	30.1	Official Rate	ahx
102.7	90.2	86.2	80.8	86.6	82.5	90.4	102.6	100.0	86.3	81.4	66.9	55.7	48.2	43.7	Nominal Effective Exchange Rate	nec
132.8	116.7	118.2	103.5	106.3	90.3	90.1	94.6	100.0	105.1	124.9	111.8	90.0	93.1	88.9	Real Effective Exchange Rate	rec
															Fund Position	
End of Period																
42.70	42.70	42.70	42.70	42.70	57.20	57.20	57.20	57.20	57.20	57.20	57.20	77.00	77.00	77.00	Quota	2f.s
.04	.08	.01	.04	2.62	1.08	.51	.14	.05	.08	.05	.07	.07	.03	.04	SDRs	1b.s
9.16	9.16	9.16	7.55	7.24	5.86	5.86	5.86	5.86	5.86	5.86	5.86	5.86	5.86	.36	Reserve Position in the Fund	1c.s
14.48	24.12	30.54	29.96	34.16	47.39	44.40	40.13	34.16	28.18	22.20	15.37	9.82	5.98	2.13	Total Fund Cred.&Loans Outstg.	2tl
															International Liquidity	
End of Period																
60.73	69.38	99.62	105.04	141.38	174.17	162.98	204.70	209.45	139.60	113.04	65.52	47.98	32.92	17.71	Total Reserves minus Gold	1l.d
.06	.11	.01	.06	3.75	1.49	.70	.21	.07	.11	.06	.09	.10	.04	.06	SDRs	1b.d
12.99	12.33	12.04	10.74	10.36	8.06	8.05	8.56	8.71	8.43	7.91	8.25	8.04	7.64	.45	Reserve Position in the Fund	1c.d
47.68	56.95	87.57	94.24	127.28	164.63	154.23	195.94	200.67	131.06	105.07	57.18	39.84	25.24	17.20	Foreign Exchange	1d.d
.017	.017	.017	.017	.017	.017	.017	.017	.017	.017	.017	.017	.017	.017	.001	Gold (Million Fine Troy Ounces)	1ad
8.53	7.14	7.03	6.55	6.44	5.79	6.66	6.59	6.66	6.36	4.99	4.95	5.00	4.74	.27	Gold (National Valuation)	1and
17.50	29.59	41.18	46.92	52.69	54.84	48.45	42.95	32.02	20.54	12.53	9.13	6.15	6.37	5.09	Monetary Authorities: Other Liab.	4..d
6.11	5.32	4.46	5.32	6.64	6.51	9.66	19.33	17.13	24.53	11.99	5.25	13.41	18.44	14.27	Deposit Money Banks: Assets	7a.d
6.32	4.93	3.65	5.50	8.77	8.08	7.70	12.95	10.97	7.68	7.46	7.51	7.71	14.28	19.18	Liabilities	7b.d
1.31	.79	.84	—	—	—	—	—	—	—	—	—	—	—	—	Other Banking Insts.: Assets	7e.d
10.69	11.65	13.23	11.54	12.68	12.24	14.00	18.21	18.41	16.20	13.72	12.25	10.35	9.14	8.41	Liabilities	7f.d
															Monetary Authorities	
End of Period																
7,881	10,621	18,792	18,270	28,244	43,387	46,912	54,230	61,439	48,407	49,620	37,711	33,642	33,702	20,573	Foreign Assets	11
17,161	15,837	15,237	15,040	13,450	11,885	9,170	8,698	10,504	12,443	20,702	27,498	41,685	59,106	69,082	Claims on Central Government	12a
306	312	315	316	25	25	25	25	25	25	25	25	25	25	25	Claims on Nonfin.Pub.Enterprises	12c
140	213	244	265	276	325	421	420	1,486	1,563	1,181	1,220	703	827	1,191	Claims on Private Sector	12d
61	2,683	2,153	4,872	2,827	550	3,355	2,538	2,210	9,239	3,838	15,460	13,983	23,028	15,532	Claims on Deposit Money Banks	12e
105	117	446	272	915	1,616	1,487	634	1,307	761	162	781	117	1,660	4,914	Claims on Other Financial Insts	12f
12,176	11,763	12,478	13,068	15,121	16,797	17,617	22,292	22,114	26,346	26,854	27,566	37,387	36,398	40,431	Reserve Money	14
8,780	9,643	9,930	10,824	11,499	12,933	14,440	19,073	19,495	23,974	23,693	24,180	32,087	31,300	34,058	*of which: Currency Outside DMBs*	14a
1,416	1,315	1,525	1,302	990	990	1,118	649	577	371	749	860	710	1,044	347	*Nonfin.Pub.Ent. Deps.*	14e
886	2,961	1,422	1,481	2,091	2,743	2,174	2,701	2,329	2,531	2,400	1,915	3,924	3,689	1,278	Bonds	16ab
580	954	1,294	979	1,429	1,123	1,019	842	1,164	540	2,230	3,014	1,752	5,035	2,941	Restricted Deposits	16b
527	1,143	590	1	68	452	4	4	74	16	20	—	4	47	51	Stabilization Fund	16bb
2,962	4,995	7,375	7,775	10,070	12,972	12,809	10,607	8,899	6,621	5,117	4,613	3,868	4,959	4,396	Foreign Liabilities	16c
4,334	3,338	6,533	8,967	6,307	6,966	8,299	7,710	10,764	7,290	6,062	7,629	7,108	31,081	21,893	Central Government Deposits	16d
4,981	5,717	8,020	6,918	9,730	11,654	12,490	12,744	15,926	17,531	20,418	20,262	22,482	24,206	22,068	Capital Accounts	17a
−793	−1,089	−524	−154	922	5,081	6,958	9,645	15,703	11,562	12,426	17,694	13,630	12,934	18,260	Other Items (Net)	17r
															Deposit Money Banks	
															Commercial Banks	
End of Period																
1,678	353	812	737	2,525	2,469	1,761	2,171	1,290	1,716	2,852	2,839	4,754	3,625	6,289	Reserves	20
699	798	782	879	1,269	1,539	2,553	4,773	4,760	7,907	4,898	2,650	8,427	14,352	12,334	Foreign Assets	21
1,179	1,597	1,157	1,017	901	460	2,441	5,311	6,799	8,824	10,524	10,879	9,888	220	4,361	Claims on Central Government	22a
3,926	5,398	6,128	7,123	6,338	5,793	1,591	2,749	1,322	1,673	2,213	3,515	4,538	3,230	4,634	Claims on Nonfin.Pub.Enterprises	22c
5,930	8,839	12,137	16,437	22,500	23,862	31,557	34,022	29,162	35,886	39,516	52,948	69,385	101,356	110,418	Claims on Private Sector	22d
346	887	827	1,124	346	127	114	142	284	1,748	104	106	105	265	273	Claims on Other Financial Insts	22f
8,637	8,768	9,025	10,399	12,462	13,525	14,721	19,095	18,730	18,038	22,235	22,180	34,296	34,860	44,244	Demand Deposits	24
1,382	3,664	7,334	8,067	11,147	10,695	10,135	14,951	10,681	16,373	17,038	15,955	26,144	30,976	35,126	Savings Deposits	25
689	672	593	863	1,636	1,872	1,969	3,155	3,048	2,447	3,019	3,796	4,848	11,115	16,579	Foreign Liabilities	26c
—	—	—	—	—	25	526	76	192	14	—	180	150	773	476	Central Government Deposits	26d
59	2,821	2,147	4,269	2,845	1,134	4,044	2,602	806	8,020	1,128	14,518	13,199	22,338	14,663	Credit from Monetary Authorities	26g
1,180	2,131	2,423	3,211	3,924	5,111	7,085	8,281	8,221	11,446	12,625	14,510	17,470	21,297	24,892	Capital Accounts	27a
1,810	−184	322	509	1,866	1,888	1,536	1,008	1,939	1,414	4,064	1,798	989	1,689	2,328	Other Items (Net)	27r
															Other Monetary Institutions	
End of Period																
304	309	219	303	†1	4	169	72	....	7	342	....	....	....	....	Reserves	20..h
345	476	332	261	2,097	1,473	1,089	1,376	....	1,264	1,556	1,602	2,203	1,373	1,437	Claims on Central Government	22a.h
1,589	2,021	2,184	2,092	1,876	1,379	1,286	1,071	....	1,896	1,312	....	....	....	....	Claims on Nonfin.Pub.Enterprises	22c.h
1,936	1,672	1,699	2,533	†388	530	1,404	1,675	....	2,690	2,133	....	....	....	....	Claims on Private Sector	22d.h
—	356	116	6	6	6	6	6	....	6	6	....	....	....	....	Claims on Other Financial Insts	22f.h
329	348	314	242	396	506	1,021	1,329	....	1,259	1,527	1,595	2,200	1,369	1,431	Demand Deposits	24..h
3	2	2	2	2	2	347	598	....	1,484	2,052	2	2	2	2	Time and Savings Deposits	25..h
34	67	47	47	41	41	66	43	....	29	29	....	....	....	....	Foreign Liabilities	26c.h
1,643	2,085	2,442	1,843	†2,172	2,186	1,779	1,811	....	639	500	....	....	....	....	Central Government Deposits	26d.h
11	—	—	476	189	469	749	303	....	1,195	1,172	....	....	....	....	Cred.from Monetary Authorities	26g.h
12	126	16	1,272	706	−157	−7	115	....	1,256	69	4	1	2	3	Other Items (Net)	27r.h
															Monetary Survey	
End of Period																
4,895	5,685	11,558	10,464	17,767	30,042	34,621	45,198	54,252	47,217	46,352	31,952	33,353	31,981	11,932	Foreign Assets (Net)	31n
26,691	32,713	32,591	34,986	40,638	38,304	39,985	46,531	39,933	60,834	72,872	90,764	121,389	136,209	173,966	Domestic Credit	32
14,351	14,571	10,192	7,351	7,969	4,642	2,096	5,788	6,347	14,587	26,220	32,169	46,517	28,846	52,510	Claims on Central Govt. (Net)	32an
5,820	7,730	8,627	9,531	8,239	7,197	2,902	3,844	1,347	3,593	3,550	3,540	4,563	3,255	4,659	Claims on Nonfin.Pub.Enterprises	32c
6,070	9,052	12,382	16,702	23,164	24,717	33,381	36,117	30,648	40,138	42,830	54,168	70,087	102,183	111,609	Claims on Private Sector	32d
450	1,360	1,390	1,403	1,267	1,749	1,607	782	1,591	2,516	273	887	222	1,925	5,188	Claims on Other Financial Insts	32f
19,162	20,074	20,793	22,767	25,347	27,955	31,300	40,146	38,802	43,642	48,203	48,816	69,293	68,573	80,080	Money	34
1,386	3,666	7,336	8,069	11,149	10,697	10,482	15,549	10,681	17,857	19,089	15,957	26,146	30,978	35,128	Quasi-Money	35
9,947	12,769	14,381	13,498	21,046	29,349	32,824	36,034	44,703	46,552	51,932	57,943	59,304	68,639	70,689	Other Items (Net)	37r
20,547	23,740	28,129	30,836	36,496	38,652	41,782	55,695	49,482	61,499	67,292	64,773	95,439	99,551	115,209	Money plus Quasi-Money	35l

Burundi

618

Other Banking Institutions
Millions of Francs:

	1972	1973	1974	1975	1976	1977	1978	1979	1980	1981	1982	1983	1984	1985	1986
Cash ....40.. f	1	—	—	1	—	—	—	—	15	25	67	25	44	250	1,017
Foreign Assets ....41.. f									—	22	59	321	101	193	185
Claims on Central Government ....42a. f	—											187	100	99	98
Claims on Private Sector ....42d. f	131	141	164	294	506	715	1,009	1,209	1,684	2,223	2,929	4,539	4,619	4,950	5,624
Bonds ....46ab. f									49	53	94	169	505	879	1,222
Long-Term Foreign Liabilities ....46cl f	—	—	—	51	214	381	418	603	528	553	503	737	846	839	860
Central Govt. Lending Funds ....46f. f				87	87	87	124	110	62	82	182	221	240	266	2,213
Credit from Monetary Authorities ....46g. f	—	—	—	—	6	86	286	166	105	120	430	617	224	10	—
Credit from Depos. Money Banks ....46h. f						14						350	1,039	789	817
Capital Accounts ....47a. f	133	136	135	182	187	192	217	259	748	998	1,652	2,341	2,060	2,501	2,828
Other Items (Net) ....47r. f									309	490	-141	-9	52	120	-199

Banking Survey
Millions of Francs:

	1972	1973	1974	1975	1976	1977	1978	1979	1980	1981	1982	1983	1984	1985	1986
Foreign Assets (Net) 51n									5,127	2,533	-559	388	579	1,916	5,373
Domestic Credit 52	1,997	2,329	3,568	2,551	3,130	2,758	6,847	11,899	14,414	20,069	21,924	26,858	†27,887	31,193	31,440
Claims on Central Govt. (Net) 52an	794	905	918	1,246	1,116	180	1,336	3,718	4,630	7,309	8,959	12,288	14,197	15,926	14,183
Claims on Nonfin.Pub.Enterprises 52c	—	—	—	55	21	291	1,101	1,358	1,687	1,273	1,660	1,850	4,379	5,357	5,521
Claims on Private Sector 52d	1,203	1,424	2,650	1,251	1,993	2,287	4,410	6,822	8,097	11,486	11,316	12,719	†9,311	9,909	11,736
Liquid Liabilities 55l	2,439	2,988	3,451	3,349	4,713	6,550	8,902	9,477	12,844	15,849	15,238	19,414	20,162	23,933	23,330
Other Items (Net) 57r									8,414	7,329	5,446	5,584	8,305	9,175	13,483

Interest Rates
Percent Per Annum

	1972	1973	1974	1975	1976	1977	1978	1979	1980	1981	1982	1983	1984	1985	1986
Discount Rate (End of Period) 60			5.50	5.50	5.50	5.50	5.50	7.00	7.00	7.00	7.00	7.00	7.00	7.00	5.00
Deposit Rate 60l			2.50	2.50	2.50	2.50	2.50	2.50	2.50	4.50	5.00	4.50	4.50	4.50	5.96
Lending Rate 60p							12.00	12.00	12.00	12.00	12.00	12.00	12.00	12.00	12.00

Prices and Labor

	1972	1973	1974	1975	1976	1977	1978	1979	1980	1981	1982	1983	1984	1985	1986
Consumer Prices 64 *(Index Numbers 1995=100)*	10.3	10.9	12.6	14.6	15.6	16.7	20.7	28.2	†28.9	32.5	34.4	37.2	42.5	44.1	44.9
Employment 67e *(Number in Thousands)*														45	47
Unemployment 67c														2	7

International Transactions
Millions of Francs

	1972	1973	1974	1975	1976	1977	1978	1979	1980	1981	1982	1983	1984	1985	1986
Exports 70	2,276	2,371	2,439	2,515	5,415	8,073	6,244	9,360	5,885	6,742	7,899	7,494	12,318	13,522	17,675
Imports, c.i.f. 71	2,765	2,495	3,394	4,847	5,022	6,677	8,846	13,721	15,119	14,511	19,159	16,863	22,383	22,435	23,080

Balance of Payments
Millions of US Dollars: (data only for 1985 and 1986)

	1985	1986
Current Account, n.i.e. 78ald	-41.3	-36.2
Goods: Exports f.o.b. 78aad	113.6	129.1
Goods: Imports f.o.b. 78abd	-149.7	-165.3
Trade Balance 78acd	-36.1	-36.2
Services: Credit 78add	13.2	11.7
Services: Debit 78aed	-89.3	-102.9
Balance on Goods & Services 78afd	-112.2	-127.3
Income: Credit 78agd	1.6	2.1
Income: Debit 78ahd	-19.9	-22.7
Balance on Gds, Serv. & Inc. 78aid	-130.5	-147.9
Current Transfers, n.i.e.: Credit 78ajd	93.6	115.8
Current Transfers: Debit 78akd	-4.3	-4.0
Capital Account, n.i.e. 78bcd	-.8	-1.4
Capital Account, n.i.e.: Credit 78bad	—	-1.4
Capital Account: Debit 78bbd	-.8	-1.4
Financial Account, n.i.e. 78bjd	66.1	85.0
Direct Investment Abroad 78bdd		
Dir. Invest. in Rep. Econ., n.i.e. 78bed	.5	1.5
Portfolio Investment Assets 78bfd	—	—
Equity Securities 78bkd	—	—
Debt Securities 78bld	—	—
Portfolio Investment Liab., n.i.e. 78bgd	—	—
Equity Securities 78bmd	—	—
Debt Securities 78bnd	—	—
Financial Derivatives Assets 78bwd		
Financial Derivatives Liabilities 78bxd		
Other Investment Assets 78bhd	.3	8.0
Monetary Authorities 78bod		
General Government 78bpd	-1.6	-7.0
Banks 78bqd	1.8	-5.4
Other Sectors 78brd	.2	20.4
Other Investment Liab., n.i.e. 78bid	65.2	75.4
Monetary Authorities 78bsd	—	—
General Government 78btd	56.5	67.2
Banks 78bud	—	3.6
Other Sectors 78bvd	8.7	4.6
Net Errors and Omissions 78cad	-8.1	-18.9
Overall Balance 78cbd	15.9	28.5
Reserves and Related Items 79dad	-15.9	-28.5
Reserve Assets 79dbd	-12.7	-34.5
Use of Fund Credit and Loans 79dcd	-3.2	6.0
Exceptional Financing 79ded		

Other Banking Institutions

End of Period

		1987	1988	1989	1990	1991	1992	1993	1994	1995	1996	1997	1998	1999	2000	2001
Cash	40..f	2,402	24	155	†40	114	49	....	132	123	191	†478	102	291	796	178
Foreign Assets	41..f	151	119	147	—	—	...	....	—	—	—	—	—	—	—	—
Claims on Central Government	42a.f	1,144	1,544	1,284	†969	758	208	73	52	111	87	†405	1,057	1,491	481	1,843
Claims on Private Sector	42d.f	7,627	8,500	9,536	†9,928	10,176	11,610	....	12,577	13,319	14,304	†15,376	16,637	18,068	19,251	21,633
Bonds	46ab f	3,694	4,177	4,397	5,380	4,820	4,129	....	3,347	2,324	3,224	†2,829	2,561	2,980	2,783	2,354
Long-Term Foreign Liabilities	46cl f	1,223	1,747	2,322	1,908	2,423	2,896	....	4,496	5,117	5,222	†6,057	6,641	6,962	7,567	7,722
Central Govt. Lending Funds	46f.f	3,942	974	891	897	1,040	1,213	....	1,151	1,185	1,045	914	1,371	1,340	1,280	1,772
Credit from Monetary Authorities	46g.f	—	98	293	110	777	1,347	....	228	1,043	599	—	623	118	972	3,331
Credit from Depos. Money Banks	46h.f	200	739	766	587	—	...	....	—	4	375	—	1	—	—	—
Capital Accounts	47a.f	2,958	3,299	3,385	2,796	3,065	2,897	....	2,990	3,589	4,357	†7,125	7,834	10,142	9,940	11,215
Other Items (Net)	47r.f	−672	−844	−931	−742	−1,076	−624	....	548	290	−242	†−667	−1,235	−1,692	−2,015	−2,740

Banking Survey

End of Period

		1987	1988	1989	1990	1991	1992	1993	1994	1995	1996	1997	1998	1999	2000	2001
Foreign Assets (Net)	51n	5,045	5,804	11,706	10,464	17,767	30,042	34,621	45,198	54,252	47,217	46,352	31,952	33,353	31,981	11,932
Domestic Credit	52	35,683	41,904	42,189	44,916	50,306	48,373	....	58,377	....	72,709	85,811	104,239	136,724	149,206	187,112
Claims on Central Govt. (Net)	52an	16,166	16,622	11,644	8,756	8,727	4,850	2,168	5,840	....	14,674	26,625	33,226	48,000	29,327	54,353
Claims on Nonfin.Pub.Enterprises	52c	5,820	7,730	8,627	9,531	8,239	7,197	2,902	3,844	1,347	3,593	3,550	3,540	4,563	3,255	4,659
Claims on Private Sector	52d	13,697	17,551	21,918	26,630	33,340	36,326	....	48,693	43,967	54,442	55,637	67,473	84,152	116,624	128,100
Liquid Liabilities	55l	22,452	28,217	31,789	35,341	37,246	38,948	....	55,563	....	61,308	66,815	64,671	95,148	98,756	115,031
Other Items (Net)	57r	18,277	19,491	22,106	20,039	30,828	39,467	....	48,012	54,331	58,618	65,349	71,520	74,929	82,431	84,013

Interest Rates

Percent Per Annum

		1987	1988	1989	1990	1991	1992	1993	1994	1995	1996	1997	1998	1999	2000	2001
Discount Rate (End of Period)	60	7.00	7.00	7.00	8.50	10.00	11.00	10.00	10.00	10.00	10.00	12.00	12.00	12.00	14.00	14.00
Deposit Rate	60l	5.33	4.00	....	....	....	....	....	....	....	....	....	....	....	....	....
Lending Rate	60p	12.00	12.00	12.00	12.34	12.78	13.66	13.77	14.20	15.26	....	....	....	15.24	15.77	16.82

Prices and Labor

Period Averages

		1987	1988	1989	1990	1991	1992	1993	1994	1995	1996	1997	1998	1999	2000	2001
Consumer Prices	64	48.0	50.2	56.0	60.0	†65.4	66.6	†73.0	83.8	100.0	126.4	165.8	186.5	192.8	239.7	261.9

Period Averages

		1987	1988	1989	1990	1991	1992	1993	1994	1995	1996	1997	1998	1999	2000	2001
Employment	67e	50	54	49	47	45	....	....	....	....	....					
Unemployment	67c	8	9	11	15	14	7	....	....							

International Transactions

Millions of Francs

		1987	1988	1989	1990	1991	1992	1993	1994	1995	1996	1997	1998	1999	2000	2001
Exports	70	11,117	18,591	12,305	12,774	16,698	15,355	15,019	30,034	25,982	11,372	30,767	28,635	30,971	35,223	31,978
Imports, c.i.f.	71	26,141	28,632	39,371	46,154	46,106	47,435		56,511	58,186	37,332	43,250	70,274	66,308	106,059	115,249

Balance of Payments

Minus Sign Indicates Debit

		1987	1988	1989	1990	1991	1992	1993	1994	1995	1996	1997	1998	1999	2000	2001
Current Account, n.i.e.	78ald	−95.2	−70.1	−11.5	−69.4	−33.3	−59.6	−28.1	−16.9	10.4	−40.0	−1.0	−53.6	−27.0	−48.8	....
Goods: Exports f.o.b.	78aad	98.3	124.4	93.2	72.8	93.0	77.0	73.9	80.7	112.9	40.4	87.5	64.0	55.0	49.1	....
Goods: Imports f.o.b.	78abd	−159.2	−166.1	−151.4	−189.0	−195.9	−181.8	−172.8	−172.6	−175.6	−100.0	−96.1	−123.5	−97.3	−107.9	....
Trade Balance	78acd	−60.8	−41.7	−58.2	−116.3	−103.0	−104.8	−99.0	−91.9	−62.7	−59.6	−8.6	−59.5	−42.3	−58.8	....
Services: Credit	78add	11.9	11.9	15.3	16.7	25.7	17.5	14.6	14.9	16.4	10.5	8.7	7.6	6.3	6.1	....
Services: Debit	78aed	−132.1	−114.9	−92.6	−129.2	−141.3	−137.3	−114.8	−93.9	−83.3	−38.4	−45.4	−49.5	−32.6	−43.4	....
Balance on Goods & Services	78afd	−181.0	−144.7	−135.5	−228.8	−218.6	−224.7	−199.2	−170.9	−129.6	−87.4	−45.3	−101.3	−68.7	−96.1	....
Income: Credit	78agd	2.9	2.9	8.9	8.2	9.7	14.0	11.2	8.1	10.4	6.4	4.3	3.6	1.9	2.4	....
Income: Debit	78ahd	−31.3	−25.8	−26.5	−23.0	−20.7	−27.6	−22.2	−19.5	−22.9	−20.4	−16.8	−11.9	−11.3	−14.5	....
Balance on Gds, Serv. & Inc.	78aid	−209.4	−167.6	−153.1	−243.6	−229.7	−238.2	−210.2	−182.3	−142.1	−101.4	−57.8	−109.6	−78.1	−108.2	....
Current Transfers, n.i.e.: Credit	78ajd	118.3	103.4	142.7	175.5	198.1	180.6	183.8	167.0	154.7	62.5	61.3	59.3	52.9	61.1	....
Current Transfers: Debit	78akd	−4.1	−5.9	−1.1	−1.3	−1.7	−1.9	−1.8	−1.6	−2.1	−1.1	−4.5	−3.3	−1.8	−1.8	....
Capital Account, n.i.e.	78bcd	−1.2	−.5	−.6	−.5	−.7	−.8	−1.2	−.2	−.8	−.3	−.1	—	—	—	....
Capital Account, n.i.e.: Credit	78bad	—	—	—	—	—	—	—	—	—	—	—	—	—	—	....
Capital Account: Debit	78bbd	−1.2	−.5	−.6	−.5	−.7	−.8	−1.2	−.2	−.8	−.3	−.1	—	—	—	....
Financial Account, n.i.e.	78bjd	131.1	84.3	64.4	78.0	70.4	98.7	52.5	31.1	21.1	14.1	13.7	28.8	17.0	58.9	....
Direct Investment Abroad	78bdd	—	—	−.1	—	—	—	—	−.1	−.6	—	—	—	—	—	....
Dir. Invest. in Rep. Econ., n.i.e.	78bed	1.4	1.2	.6	1.3	.9	.6	.5	—	2.0	—	—	—	.2	11.7	....
Portfolio Investment Assets	78bfd	—	—	—	—	—	—	—	—	—	—	—	—	—	—	....
Equity Securities	78bkd	—	—	—	—	—	—	—	—	—	—	—	—	—	—	....
Debt Securities	78bld	—	—	—	—	—	—	—	—	—	—	—	—	—	—	....
Portfolio Investment Liab., n.i.e.	78bgd	—	—	—	—	—	—	—	—	—	—	—	—	—	—	....
Equity Securities	78bmd	—	—	—	—	—	—	—	—	—	—	—	—	—	—	....
Debt Securities	78bnd	—	—	—	—	—	—	—	—	—	—	—	—	—	—	....
Financial Derivatives Assets	78bwd	....	....	....	....	....	....	....	....	....	....	....	....	....	....	....
Financial Derivatives Liabilities	78bxd	....	....	....	....	....	....	....	....	....	....	....	....	....	....	....
Other Investment Assets	78bhd	1.4	−11.5	−7.6	4.1	−3.5	−1.0	−1.5	−1.6	8.2	6.6	15.3	10.7	13.7	5.1	....
Monetary Authorities	78bod	....	....	....	....	....	....	....	....	....	....	....	....	....	....	....
General Government	78bpd	−10.0	−5.8	−1.9	−1.0	−1.1	−.6	−.3	−.8	−.4	−.3	−.4	−.3	−.3		....
Banks	78bqd	4.1	−.7	.1	−.6	−2.1	−1.3	−4.2	−8.8	.1	−10.4	8.5	5.0	−10.3	−8.2	....
Other Sectors	78brd	7.2	−5.0	−5.7	5.7	−.4	1.0	3.0	7.9	8.6	17.3	7.1	6.0	24.3	13.3	....
Other Investment Liab., n.i.e.	78bid	128.3	94.6	71.5	72.7	73.1	99.1	53.6	32.9	11.5	7.6	−1.6	18.1	3.1	42.2	....
Monetary Authorities	78bsd	....	....	....	....	....	....	....	....	....	....	....	....	....	....	....
General Government	78btd	124.5	83.9	65.4	62.1	57.0	90.8	47.2	25.2	4.9	7.3	−8.0	15.3	.2	32.2	....
Banks	78bud	−3.0	1.3	−.6	1.6	1.4	1.1	.4	4.7	−.4	−2.0	1.6	1.7	1.9	8.7	....
Other Sectors	78bvd	6.8	9.4	6.6	9.0	14.6	7.1	6.0	3.0	7.0	2.2	4.8	1.1	1.1	1.2	....
Net Errors and Omissions	78cad	−37.3	−6.6	−14.3	−11.3	−3.9	−12.7	−7.2	21.1	5.9	−9.2	−2.4	5.4	8.7	−6.2	....
Overall Balance	78cbd	−2.6	7.1	38.0	−3.2	32.6	25.5	16.0	35.2	36.7	−35.3	10.2	−19.5	−1.2	3.9	....
Reserves and Related Items	79dad	2.6	−7.1	−38.0	3.2	−32.6	−25.5	−16.0	−35.2	−36.7	35.3	−10.2	19.5	1.2	−3.9	....
Reserve Assets	79dbd	7.3	−20.5	−46.1	4.0	−38.4	−44.0	−11.9	−29.0	−27.6	44.0	−2.0	28.7	8.8	1.2	....
Use of Fund Credit and Loans	79dcd	−4.6	13.3	8.1	−.8	5.8	18.5	−4.1	−6.1	−9.0	−8.7	−8.3	−9.3	−7.6	−5.0	....
Exceptional Financing	79ded	....	....	....	....	....	....	....	....	....	....	....	....	....	....	....

Burundi

618

		1972	1973	1974	1975	1976	1977	1978	1979	1980	1981	1982	1983	1984	1985	1986
Government Finance															*Millions of Francs:*	
Deficit (-) or Surplus	80	183.2	113.2	219.5	-136.6	162.4	390.7	-19.8	67.1	-1,708.0	-1,873.0	-1,362.1	-917.8	231.4	-148.5	3,475.0
Total Revenue and Grants	81y	2,588.4	2,805.8	3,221.3	3,168.7	5,030.1	7,138.3	9,239.5	11,052.3	11,441.0	12,321.1	14,046.8	12,855.9	16,350.6	19,254.1	23,133.4
Revenue	81	....	....	....	....	....	....	....	....	....	....	....	....	....	....	....
Grants	81z	....	....	....	....	....	....	....	....	....	....	....	....	....	....	....
Exp. & Lending Minus Repay.	82z	2,405.2	2,692.6	3,001.8	3,305.3	4,867.7	6,747.6	9,259.3	10,985.2	13,149.0	14,194.1	15,408.9	13,773.7	16,119.2	19,402.6	19,658.4
Expenditure	82	2,377.0	2,663.4	2,937.9	3,267.8	4,839.9	6,714.3	9,264.1	10,986.9	13,149.8	14,194.2	15,409.0	13,773.7	16,119.2	19,402.6	19,658.4
Lending Minus Repayments	83	28.2	29.2	63.9	37.5	27.8	33.3	-4.8	-1.7	-.8	-.1	-.1				
Statistical Discrepancy	80xx	....	....	....	....	....	....	....	....	....	....	....	....	....	....	....
Total Financing	80h	-183.2	-113.2	-219.5	136.6	-162.4	-390.7	19.8	-67.1	1,708.0	1,873.0	1,362.1	917.8	-231.4	148.5	-3,475.0
Domestic	84a	-136.7	-59.7	-171.5	98.5	50.8	-152.7	218.4	162.1	1,700.7	2,231.1	1,680.7	1,487.9	579.4	1,551.3	-3,151.3
Foreign	85a	-46.5	-53.5	-48.0	38.1	-213.2	-238.0	-198.6	-229.2	7.3	-358.1	-318.6	-570.1	-810.8	-1,402.8	-323.7
Total Debt by Residence	88	1,783	2,037	2,103	3,451	4,599	6,321	9,341	14,797	19,216	23,663	28,795	47,992	59,732	69,066	87,584
Domestic	88a	1,194	1,475	1,474	1,726	2,573	2,872	3,989	6,361	8,186	10,638	12,519	15,624	18,633	21,986	22,169
Foreign	89a	589	562	629	1,726	2,026	3,449	5,353	8,437	11,030	13,025	16,276	32,368	41,099	47,080	65,415
National Accounts															*Millions of Francs*	
Househ.Cons.Expend.,incl.NPISHs	96f	18,839	20,805	24,238	27,029	32,938	38,227	41,932	53,586	70,133	69,823	73,894	77,516	92,484	109,478	104,340
Government Consumption Expend.	91f	2,791	2,821	3,421	4,642	3,368	5,495	9,574	11,436	13,746	15,583	18,183	20,414	21,132	22,793	24,252
Gross Fixed Capital Formation	93e	1,137	1,392	1,768	4,181	3,515	5,517	7,709	10,505	10,955	11,948	17,170	19,541	20,364	20,113	18,860
Changes in Inventories	93i	-450	-98	-666	-556	—	—	—	—	921	2,429	-741	-1,083	1,410	73	3,247
Exports of Goods and Services	90c	2,534	2,683	2,652	2,899	5,309	8,671	6,661	9,985	7,328	6,999	8,697	9,683	11,782	13,937	15,625
Imports of Goods and Services (-)	98c	3,256	3,247	4,224	5,523	6,454	8,332	11,055	17,426	17,476	17,696	23,109	23,179	26,721	25,047	25,482
Gross Domestic Product (GDP)	99b	21,595	24,355	27,190	32,672	38,676	49,578	54,821	68,086	85,607	89,086	94,094	102,892	120,451	141,347	140,842
Net Primary Income from Abroad	98.n	-997	-669	-708	-681	-971	-1,231	-1,301	-914	822	455	68	-382	-980	-1,436	-1,697
Gross National Income (GNI)	99a	20,598	23,686	26,482	32,472	37,705	48,347	53,520	67,172	86,429	89,541	94,162	102,510	119,471	139,911	139,145
GDP Volume 1971 prices	99b.p	20,406	21,871	21,689	21,908	23,633	26,558	26,266	26,784	....	....	....	....	....	....	....
GDP Volume 1980 Prices	99b.p	....	....	....	....	....	....	....	79,321	85,607	94,949	94,540	97,479	97,382	106,671	110,138
GDP Volume (1995=100)	99bv p	52.5	56.3	55.8	56.4	60.9	68.4	67.6	69.0	74.4	82.6	82.2	84.8	84.7	92.7	95.8
GDP Deflator (1995=100)	99bi p	16.4	17.3	19.5	23.2	25.4	29.0	32.4	39.5	46.0	43.2	45.8	48.6	56.9	61.0	58.9
																Millions:
Population	99z	3.74	3.80	3.86	†3.74	3.82	3.90	3.98	4.03	4.12	4.23	4.34	4.46	4.58	4.72	4.86

Government Finance

Year Ending December 31

	1987	1988	1989	1990	1991	1992	1993	1994	1995	1996	1997	1998	1999	2000	2001	
Deficit (-) or Surplus	-1,433.2	1,116.1	4,649.1	1,273.7	4,219.3	1,796.8	3,442.6	6,743.1	2,630.0	-7,890.5	†-16777.4	-15,069.5	-15,534.4	-30,270.5	9,176.0	80
Total Revenue and Grants	20,060.8	25,084.9	38,583.8	37,079.4	42,820.3	45,618.7	49,933.2	48,525.1	49,001.6	39,330.5	†52717.4	74,005.8	78,593.9	107,488.7	147,730.6	81y
Revenue											42,446.9	63,531.5	67,239.3	91,613.9	119,053.9	81
Grants											10,270.5	10,474.3	11,354.6	15,874.8	28,676.7	81z
Exp. & Lending Minus Repay.	21,494.0	23,968.8	33,934.7	35,805.7	38,601.0	43,821.9	46,490.6	41,782.0	46,371.6	47,221.0	†69494.8	89,075.3	94,128.3	137,759.2	138,554.6	82z
Expenditure	21,494.0	23,968.8	33,934.7	35,805.7	38,601.0	43,821.9	46,490.6	41,782.0	46,371.6	47,221.0	†70716.6	90,413.7	95,110.7	141,506.3	143,034.0	82
Lending Minus Repayments	—	—	—	—	—	—	—	—	—	—	†-1221.8	-1,338.4	-982.4	-3,747.1	-4,479.4	83
Statistical Discrepancy											-3,605.9	-10,054.2	-16,271.4	-22,621.2	-6,685.1	80xx
Total Financing	1,433.2	-1,116.1	-4,649.1	-1,273.7	-4,219.3	-1,796.8	-3,442.6	-6,743.1	-2,630.0	7,890.5	†16777.4	15,069.5	15,534.4	30,270.5	-9,219.1	80h
Domestic	217.9	-1,007.9	-4,950.1	-1,420.7	-4,483.0	-4,088.5	-2,787.7	-2,803.1	1,452.1	11,412.2	†7,745.1	264.9	3,359.9	-20,562.3	-16,698.6	84a
Foreign	1,215.3	-108.2	301.0	147.0	263.7	2,291.7	-654.9	-3,940.0	-4,082.1	-3,521.7	†9,032.3	14,804.6	12,174.5	50,832.8	7,479.5	85a
Total Debt by Residence	107,766	142,412	170,205	161,951	188,322	235,307	272,757	278,759	323,954	380,464	†464,228	605,411	740,305	920,481	968,168	88
Domestic	24,455	25,937	22,935	22,662	18,080	15,591	13,784	13,630	17,785	27,384	†39,989	49,659	64,528	67,972	80,194	88a
Foreign	83,311	116,475	147,270	139,289	170,242	219,716	258,973	265,129	306,169	353,080	†424,239	555,752	675,777	852,509	887,974	89a

National Accounts

Millions of Francs

	1987	1988	1989	1990	1991	1992	1993	1994	1995	1996	1997	1998	1999	2000	2001	
Househ.Cons.Expend.,incl.NPISHs	107,015	114,298	135,449	163,216	168,126	190,669	217,092	256,656	228,920	215,243	283,030	362,396	386,157	474,498	473,594	96f
Government Consumption Expend.	28,570	31,491	36,547	38,344	40,227	44,429	30,280	32,459	33,600	45,412	52,068	60,461	66,501	95,608	94,008	91f
Gross Fixed Capital Formation	21,114	25,701	26,115	32,234	34,282	36,425	36,193	23,446	23,419	32,712	21,975	24,000	34,314	38,564	71,770	93e
Changes in Inventories	3,762	-4,029	3,247	-1,177	19	-2,158	1,002	53	-199	-1,789	1,459	-1,477	6,739	-18,672	-142	93i
Exports of Goods and Services	13,015	17,298	15,697	15,641	20,013	15,346	21,370	24,029	32,298	15,290	33,603	31,940	34,452	30,341	37,454	90c
Imports of Goods and Services (-)	29,886	31,852	37,507	51,602	57,716	58,854	69,261	66,592	68,173	41,454	49,318	77,117	72,675	108,550	128,028	98c
Gross Domestic Product (GDP)	143,590	152,907	179,548	196,656	204,951	225,857	236,676	270,051	249,865	265,414	342,818	400,203	455,488	511,789	548,656	99b
Net Primary Income from Abroad	-2,092	-2,457	-2,008	-2,550	-2,041	-2,845	-2,674	-2,876	-3,152	-4,003	-3,744	-3,973	-5,498	-8,698	-7,503	98.n
Gross National Income (GNI)	141,498	150,450	177,540	194,106	202,910	223,012	234,002	267,175	246,713	338,815	346,562	396,230	449,990	503,091	541,153	99a
GDP Volume 1971 prices													….	….	….	99b.*p*
GDP Volume 1980 Prices	116,199	121,884	123,692	128,021	134,849	137,284	127,635	123,698	115,013	105,113	105,512	110,249	….	….	….	99b.*p*
GDP Volume (1995=100)	101.0	106.0	107.5	111.3	117.2	119.4	111.0	107.6	100.0	91.4	91.7	95.9	….	….	….	99bv *p*
GDP Deflator (1995=100)	56.9	57.7	66.8	70.7	70.0	75.7	85.4	100.5	100.0	116.2	149.6	167.1	….	….	….	99bi *p*

Midyear Estimates

	1987	1988	1989	1990	1991	1992	1993	1994	1995	1996	1997	1998	1999	2000	2001	
Population	5.00	5.15	5.30	5.46	5.62	5.78	5.77	5.87	5.98	6.09	6.19	6.30	6.48	6.36	6.50	99z

(See notes in the back of the book.)

Cambodia

		1972	1973	1974	1975	1976	1977	1978	1979	1980	1981	1982	1983	1984	1985	1986
Exchange Rates														*Riels per SDR:*		
Official Rate	aa	....	....	....	....	....	....	....	....	....	....	....	....	....	....	....
														Riels per US Dollar:		
Official Rate	ae	....	....	....	....	....	....	....	....	....	....	....	....	....	....	....
Official Rate	rf	....	....	....	....	....	....	....	....	....	....	....	....	....	....	....
Fund Position														*Millions of SDRs:*		
Quota	2f. s	25.00	25.00	25.00	25.00	25.00	25.00	25.00	25.00	25.00	25.00	25.00	25.00	25.00	25.00	25.00
SDRs	1b. s	4.24	.48	1.08	.64	.33	.01	—	1.90	3.78	4.54	3.12	1.58	—	—	—
Reserve Position in the Fund	1c. s	.01	.01	.01	.01	.01	.01	.01	.01	.01	.01	.01	.01	.01	.01	.01
Total Fund Cred.&Loans Outstg.	2tl	6.25	12.50	12.50	12.50	12.50	12.50	12.50	12.50	12.50	12.50	12.50	12.50	12.50	12.50	12.50
International Liquidity														*Millions of US Dollars Unless Otherwise Indicated:*		
Total Reserves minus Gold	1l. d	....	....	....	....	....	....	....	....	....	....	....	....	....	....	....
SDRs	1b. d	4.60	.58	1.32	.75	.38	.01	—	2.50	4.82	5.28	3.44	1.65	....	....	....
Reserve Position in the Fund	1c. d	.01	.01	.01	.01	.01	.01	.01	.01	.01	.01	.01	.01	.01	.01	.01
Foreign Exchange	1d. d	....	....	....	....	....	....	....	....	....	....	....	....	....	....	....
Deposit Money Banks: Assets	7a. d	....	....	....	....	....	....	....	....	....	....	....	....	....	....	....
Liabilities	7b. d	....	....	....	....	....	....	....	....	....	....	....	....	....	....	....
Monetary Authorities														*Billions of Riels:*		
Foreign Assets	11	....	....	....	....	....	....	....	....	....	....	....	....	....	....	....
Claims on Central Government	12a	....	....	....	....	....	....	....	....	....	....	....	....	....	....	....
Claims on Private Sector	12d	....	....	....	....	....	....	....	....	....	....	....	....	....	....	....
Claims on Deposit Money Banks	12e	....	....	....	....	....	....	....	....	....	....	....	....	....	....	....
Reserve Money	14	....	....	....	....	....	....	....	....	....	....	....	....	....	....	....
of which: Currency Outside DMBs	14a	....	....	....	....	....	....	....	....	....	....	....	....	....	....	....
Restricted Deposits	16b	....	....	....	....	....	....	....	....	....	....	....	....	....	....	....
Foreign Liabilities	16c	....	....	....	....	....	....	....	....	....	....	....	....	....	....	....
Central Government Deposits	16d	....	....	....	....	....	....	....	....	....	....	....	....	....	....	....
Capital Accounts	17a	....	....	....	....	....	....	....	....	....	....	....	....	....	....	....
Other Items (Net)	17r	....	....	....	....	....	....	....	....	....	....	....	....	....	....	....
Deposit Money Banks														*Billions of Riels:*		
Reserves	20	....	....	....	....	....	....	....	....	....	....	....	....	....	....	....
Foreign Assets	21	....	....	....	....	....	....	....	....	....	....	....	....	....	....	....
Claims on Central Government	22a	....	....	....	....	....	....	....	....	....	....	....	....	....	....	....
Claims on Nonfin.Pub.Enterprises	22c	....	....	....	....	....	....	....	....	....	....	....	....	....	....	....
Claims on Private Sector	22d	....	....	....	....	....	....	....	....	....	....	....	....	....	....	....
Demand Deposits	24	....	....	....	....	....	....	....	....	....	....	....	....	....	....	....
Time and Savings Deposits	25a	....	....	....	....	....	....	....	....	....	....	....	....	....	....	....
Foreign Currency Deposits	25b	....	....	....	....	....	....	....	....	....	....	....	....	....	....	....
Restricted Deposits	26b	....	....	....	....	....	....	....	....	....	....	....	....	....	....	....
Foreign Liabilities	26c	....	....	....	....	....	....	....	....	....	....	....	....	....	....	....
Central Government Deposits	26d	....	....	....	....	....	....	....	....	....	....	....	....	....	....	....
Credit from Monetary Authorities	26g	....	....	....	....	....	....	....	....	....	....	....	....	....	....	....
Capital Accounts	27a	....	....	....	....	....	....	....	....	....	....	....	....	....	....	....
Other Items (Net)	27r	....	....	....	....	....	....	....	....	....	....	....	....	....	....	....
Monetary Survey														*Billions of Riels:*		
Foreign Assets (Net)	31n	....	....	....	....	....	....	....	....	....	....	....	....	....	....	....
Domestic Credit	32	....	....	....	....	....	....	....	....	....	....	....	....	....	....	....
Claims on Central Govt. (Net)	32an	....	....	....	....	....	....	....	....	....	....	....	....	....	....	....
Claims on Nonfin.Pub.Enterprises	32c	....	....	....	....	....	....	....	....	....	....	....	....	....	....	....
Claims on Private Sector	32d	....	....	....	....	....	....	....	....	....	....	....	....	....	....	....
Money	34	....	....	....	....	....	....	....	....	....	....	....	....	....	....	....
Quasi-Money	35	....	....	....	....	....	....	....	....	....	....	....	....	....	....	....
Capital Accounts	37a	....	....	....	....	....	....	....	....	....	....	....	....	....	....	....
Other Items (Net)	37r	....	....	....	....	....	....	....	....	....	....	....	....	....	....	....
Money plus Quasi-Money	35l	....	....	....	....	....	....	....	....	....	....	....	....	....	....	....
Interest Rates														*Percent Per Annum:*		
Deposit Rate	60l	....	....	....	....	....	....	....	....	....	....	....	....	....	....	....
Lending Rate	60p	....	....	....	....	....	....	....	....	....	....	....	....	....	....	....
Prices and Labor														*Index Numbers (1995=100):*		
Consumer Prices	64	....	....	....	....	....	....	....	....	....	....	....	....	....	....	....
														Number in Thousands:		
Labor Force	67d	....	....	....	....	....	....	....	....	....	....	....	....	....	....	....

1987	1988	1989	1990	1991	1992	1993	1994	1995	1996	1997	1998	1999	2000	2001		
															Exchange Rates	
End of Period																
....	....	283.9	853.6	743.8	2,750.0	3,166.1	3,759.1	3,754.9	3,901.2	4,657.6	5,308.3	5,174.4	5,087.9	4,895.0	Official Rate	aa
End of Period (ae) Period Average (rf)																
....	....	216.0	600.0	520.0	2,000.0	2,305.0	2,575.0	2,526.0	2,713.0	3,452.0	3,770.0	3,770.0	3,905.0	3,895.0	Official Rate	ae
....	....	....	....	....	1,266.6	2,689.0	2,545.3	2,450.8	2,624.1	2,946.3	3,744.4	3,807.8	3,840.8	3,916.3	Official Rate	rf
															Fund Position	
End of Period																
25.00	25.00	25.00	25.00	25.00	25.00	25.00	65.00	65.00	65.00	65.00	65.00	87.50	87.50	87.50	Quota	2f. s
						11.42	10.89	10.21	9.51	8.77	6.95	3.78	.14	.41	SDRs	1b. s
.01	.01	.01	.01	.01	.93										Reserve Position in the Fund	1c. s
12.50	12.50	12.50	12.50	12.50	6.25	6.25	20.25	48.25	48.25	48.25	47.21	53.12	56.24	63.51	Total Fund Cred.&Loans Outstg.	2tl
															International Liquidity	
End of Period																
....	....	....	....	....	....	24.18	118.50	191.98	265.78	298.53	324.28	393.19	501.68	586.81	Total Reserves minus Gold	1l. d
						15.68	15.90	15.18	13.68	11.83	9.78	5.19	.18	.51	SDRs	1b. d
.01	.01	.01	.01	.01	1.28										Reserve Position in the Fund	1c. d
....	....	....	....	....	....	8.50	102.60	176.80	252.10	286.70	314.50	388.00	501.50	586.30	Foreign Exchange	1d. d
....	....	....	....	....	....	103.69	126.75	161.57	186.57	162.08	139.55	154.43	167.33	216.74	Deposit Money Banks: Assets	7a. d
....	....	....	....	....	....	68.43	63.93	65.78	59.55	58.03	59.51	56.88	44.23	50.27	Liabilities	7b. d
															Monetary Authorities	
End of Period																
....	....	....	....	....	....	56.44	305.09	484.88	720.91	1,033.02	1,675.22	1,923.51	2,388.61	2,740.07	Foreign Assets	11
						206.26	215.02	217.11	213.58	211.28	288.55	283.04	271.83	271.14	Claims on Central Government	12a
						3.93	2.70	—	—	—	—	—	—	—	Claims on Private Sector	12d
						32.49	34.20	10.09	9.48	6.19	8.10	4.94	15.81	53.19	Claims on Deposit Money Banks	12e
						228.09	285.91	314.53	449.83	545.33	802.61	929.87	1,161.01	1,359.61	Reserve Money	14
						189.72	176.30	250.92	299.84	356.06	509.06	489.86	494.60	577.78	*of which: Currency Outside DMBs*	14a
						16.23	26.17	24.55	70.93	42.94	68.67	75.52	84.40	98.21	Restricted Deposits	16b
						19.79	76.12	181.17	188.23	224.73	250.59	274.88	286.14	310.89	Foreign Liabilities	16c
						5.59	70.12	62.36	81.86	153.49	106.11	176.26	268.08	346.16	Central Government Deposits	16d
						57.61	127.42	115.87	200.71	391.54	839.59	870.19	1,000.17	1,035.12	Capital Accounts	17a
						-28.17	-28.74	13.60	-47.61	-107.53	-95.70	-115.22	-123.55	-85.58	Other Items (Net)	17r
															Deposit Money Banks	
End of Period																
....	....	....	....	....	....	11.67	88.75	88.15	178.43	199.61	346.00	503.74	737.13	866.85	Reserves	20
						239.01	326.39	408.14	506.15	559.51	526.10	582.19	653.43	844.19	Foreign Assets	21
						.07	.01	.31	.31	.31	.31	.31	.31	.01	Claims on Central Government	22a
						6.21	6.00	5.11	5.22	5.93	5.86	10.14	2.65	6.55	Claims on Nonfin.Pub.Enterprises	22c
						157.67	234.39	293.40	434.55	636.79	654.60	763.23	898.46	936.11	Claims on Private Sector	22d
						11.77	20.94	27.29	29.09	28.70	34.21	42.09	45.04	31.94	Demand Deposits	24
						8.51	17.80	5.07	7.85	13.21	19.77	31.71	45.89	55.50	Time and Savings Deposits	25a
						121.13	232.57	365.55	574.84	664.90	667.03	878.84	1,244.97	1,538.65	Foreign Currency Deposits	25b
						10.30	3.22	4.04	11.45	4.23	3.97	4.04	1.87	1.48	Restricted Deposits	26b
						157.74	164.61	166.15	161.56	200.32	224.37	214.45	172.73	195.82	Foreign Liabilities	26c
						25.43	1.75	7.14	4.38	4.26	4.20	4.15	.71	.01	Central Government Deposits	26d
						3.03	2.96	4.81	3.51	7.02	5.87	7.52	6.04	8.11	Credit from Monetary Authorities	26g
						121.81	356.49	356.11	454.98	602.77	689.78	767.43	791.25	923.56	Capital Accounts	27a
						-45.08	-144.79	-141.05	-123.00	-123.26	-116.34	-90.62	-16.53	-101.37	Other Items (Net)	27r
															Monetary Survey	
End of Period																
....	....	....	....	....	....	117.93	390.75	545.70	877.28	1,167.48	1,726.36	2,016.37	2,583.18	3,077.55	Foreign Assets (Net)	31n
						343.14	386.25	446.43	567.41	696.55	839.01	876.31	904.45	867.64	Domestic Credit	32
						175.32	143.16	147.92	127.64	53.84	178.55	102.95	3.34	-75.02	Claims on Central Govt. (Net)	32an
						6.21	6.00	5.11	5.22	5.93	5.86	10.14	2.65	6.55	Claims on Nonfin.Pub.Enterprises	32c
						161.61	237.09	293.40	434.55	636.79	654.60	763.23	898.46	936.11	Claims on Private Sector	32d
						203.82	201.68	278.49	328.93	384.76	543.27	531.95	539.64	609.72	Money	34
						129.65	250.37	370.62	582.69	678.11	686.80	910.55	1,290.87	1,594.15	Quasi-Money	35
						179.42	483.91	471.98	655.70	994.31	1,529.37	1,637.62	1,791.41	1,958.69	Capital Accounts	37a
						-51.82	-158.95	-128.96	-122.63	-193.15	-194.07	-187.44	-134.30	-217.36	Other Items (Net)	37r
						333.47	452.05	649.11	911.62	1,062.87	1,230.07	1,442.50	1,830.51	2,203.87	Money plus Quasi-Money	35l
															Interest Rates	
Percent Per Annum																
....	....	....	....	....	....	....	....	8.7	8.8	8.0	7.8	7.3	6.8	4.4	Deposit Rate	60l
....	....	....	....	....	....	....	....	18.7	18.8	18.4	18.3	17.6	17.3	16.5	Lending Rate	60p
															Prices and Labor	
Period Averages																
....	....	....	....	....	....	....	99.0	100.0	110.1	113.6	130.4	135.6	134.5	†133.7	Consumer Prices	64
Period Averages																
....	....	....	....	....	3,964	4,010	....	....	4,680	....	5,119	....	....	....	Labor Force	67d

Cambodia

		1972	1973	1974	1975	1976	1977	1978	1979	1980	1981	1982	1983	1984	1985	1986
International Transactions														*Millions of US Dollars*		
Exports	70..d	7.42	14.70	....	....	....	....	....	....	....	....	....	....	....	....	....
Imports, c.i.f.	71..d	....	227.08	....	....	....	....	....	....	....	....	....	....	....	....	....
Balance of Payments														*Millions of US Dollars:*		
Current Account, n.i.e.	78al d	....	....	....	....	....	....	....	....	....	....	....	....	....	....	....
Goods: Exports f.o.b.	78aa d	....	....	....	....	....	....	....	....	....	....	....	....	....	....	....
Goods: Imports f.o.b.	78ab d	....	....	....	....	....	....	....	....	....	....	....	....	....	....	....
Trade Balance	78ac d	....	....	....	....	....	....	....	....	....	....	....	....	....	....	....
Services: Credit	78ad d	....	....	....	....	....	....	....	....	....	....	....	....	....	....	....
Services: Debit	78ae d	....	....	....	....	....	....	....	....	....	....	....	....	....	....	....
Balance on Goods & Services	78af d	....	....	....	....	....	....	....	....	....	....	....	....	....	....	....
Income: Credit	78ag d	....	....	....	....	....	....	....	....	....	....	....	....	....	....	....
Income: Debit	78ah d	....	....	....	....	....	....	....	....	....	....	....	....	....	....	....
Balance on Gds, Serv. & Inc.	78ai d	....	....	....	....	....	....	....	....	....	....	....	....	....	....	....
Current Transfers, n.i.e.: Credit	78aj d	....	....	....	....	....	....	....	....	....	....	....	....	....	....	....
Current Transfers: Debit	78ak d	....	....	....	....	....	....	....	....	....	....	....	....	....	....	....
Capital Account, n.i.e.	78bc d	....	....	....	....	....	....	....	....	....	....	....	....	....	....	....
Capital Account, n.i.e.: Credit	78ba d	....	....	....	....	....	....	....	....	....	....	....	....	....	....	....
Capital Account: Debit	78bb d	....	....	....	....	....	....	....	....	....	....	....	....	....	....	....
Financial Account, n.i.e.	78bj d	....	....	....	....	....	....	....	....	....	....	....	....	....	....	....
Direct Investment Abroad	78bd d	....	....	....	....	....	....	....	....	....	....	....	....	....	....	....
Dir. Invest. in Rep. Econ., n.i.e.	78be d	....	....	....	....	....	....	....	....	....	....	....	....	....	....	....
Portfolio Investment Assets	78bf d	....	....	....	....	....	....	....	....	....	....	....	....	....	....	....
Equity Securities	78bk d	....	....	....	....	....	....	....	....	....	....	....	....	....	....	....
Debt Securities	78bl d	....	....	....	....	....	....	....	....	....	....	....	....	....	....	....
Portfolio Investment Liab., n.i.e.	78bg d	....	....	....	....	....	....	....	....	....	....	....	....	....	....	....
Equity Securities	78bm d	....	....	....	....	....	....	....	....	....	....	....	....	....	....	....
Debt Securities	78bn d	....	....	....	....	....	....	....	....	....	....	....	....	....	....	....
Financial Derivatives Assets	78bw d	....	....	....	....	....	....	....	....	....	....	....	....	....	....	....
Financial Derivatives Liabilities	78bx d	....	....	....	....	....	....	....	....	....	....	....	....	....	....	....
Other Investment Assets	78bh d	....	....	....	....	....	....	....	....	....	....	....	....	....	....	....
Monetary Authorities	78bo d	....	....	....	....	....	....	....	....	....	....	....	....	....	....	....
General Government	78bp d	....	....	....	....	....	....	....	....	....	....	....	....	....	....	....
Banks	78bq d	....	....	....	....	....	....	....	....	....	....	....	....	....	....	....
Other Sectors	78br d	....	....	....	....	....	....	....	....	....	....	....	....	....	....	....
Other Investment Liab., n.i.e.	78bi d	....	....	....	....	....	....	....	....	....	....	....	....	....	....	....
Monetary Authorities	78bs d	....	....	....	....	....	....	....	....	....	....	....	....	....	....	....
General Government	78bt d	....	....	....	....	....	....	....	....	....	....	....	....	....	....	....
Banks	78bu d	....	....	....	....	....	....	....	....	....	....	....	....	....	....	....
Other Sectors	78bv d	....	....	....	....	....	....	....	....	....	....	....	....	....	....	....
Net Errors and Omissions	78ca d	....	....	....	....	....	....	....	....	....	....	....	....	....	....	....
Overall Balance	78cb d	....	....	....	....	....	....	....	....	....	....	....	....	....	....	....
Reserves and Related Items	79da d	....	....	....	....	....	....	....	....	....	....	....	....	....	....	....
Reserve Assets	79db d	....	....	....	....	....	....	....	....	....	....	....	....	....	....	....
Use of Fund Credit and Loans	79dc d	....	....	....	....	....	....	....	....	....	....	....	....	....	....	....
Exceptional Financing	79de d	....	....	....	....	....	....	....	....	....	....	....	....	....	....	....
International Investment Position														*Millions of US Dollars*		
Assets	79aa d	....	....	....	....	....	....	....	....	....	....	....	....	....	....	....
Direct Investment Abroad	79ab d	....	....	....	....	....	....	....	....	....	....	....	....	....	....	....
Portfolio Investment	79ac d	....	....	....	....	....	....	....	....	....	....	....	....	....	....	....
Equity Securities	79ad d	....	....	....	....	....	....	....	....	....	....	....	....	....	....	....
Debt Securities	79ae d	....	....	....	....	....	....	....	....	....	....	....	....	....	....	....
Financial Derivatives	79al d	....	....	....	....	....	....	....	....	....	....	....	....	....	....	....
Other Investment	79af d	....	....	....	....	....	....	....	....	....	....	....	....	....	....	....
Monetary Authorities	79ag d	....	....	....	....	....	....	....	....	....	....	....	....	....	....	....
General Government	79ah d	....	....	....	....	....	....	....	....	....	....	....	....	....	....	....
Banks	79ai d	....	....	....	....	....	....	....	....	....	....	....	....	....	....	....
Other Sectors	79aj d	....	....	....	....	....	....	....	....	....	....	....	....	....	....	....
Reserve Assets	79ak d	....	....	....	....	....	....	....	....	....	....	....	....	....	....	....
Liabilities	79la d	....	....	....	....	....	....	....	....	....	....	....	....	....	....	....
Dir. Invest. in Rep. Economy	79lb d	....	....	....	....	....	....	....	....	....	....	....	....	....	....	....
Portfolio Investment	79lc d	....	....	....	....	....	....	....	....	....	....	....	....	....	....	....
Equity Securities	79ld d	....	....	....	....	....	....	....	....	....	....	....	....	....	....	....
Debt Securities	79le d	....	....	....	....	....	....	....	....	....	....	....	....	....	....	....
Financial Derivatives	79ll d	....	....	....	....	....	....	....	....	....	....	....	....	....	....	....
Other Investment	79lf d	....	....	....	....	....	....	....	....	....	....	....	....	....	....	....
Monetary Authorities	79lg d	....	....	....	....	....	....	....	....	....	....	....	....	....	....	....
General Government	79lh d	....	....	....	....	....	....	....	....	....	....	....	....	....	....	....
Banks	79li d	....	....	....	....	....	....	....	....	....	....	....	....	....	....	....
Other sectors	79lj d	....	....	....	....	....	....	....	....	....	....	....	....	....	....	....
Government Finance														*Trillions of Riels:*		
Deficit (-) or Surplus	80	....	....	....	....	....	....	....	....	....	....	....	....	....	....	....
Revenue	81	....	....	....	....	....	....	....	....	....	....	....	....	....	....	....
Grants	81z	....	....	....	....	....	....	....	....	....	....	....	....	....	....	....
Expenditure	82	....	....	....	....	....	....	....	....	....	....	....	....	....	....	....
Financing																
Domestic	84a	....	....	....	....	....	....	....	....	....	....	....	....	....	....	....
Foreign	85a	....	....	....	....	....	....	....	....	....	....	....	....	....	....	....
																Millions:
Population	99z	7.46	7.71	7.92	†7.10	6.97	6.78	6.59	6.44	6.40	6.46	6.61	6.89	7.29	7.56	7.82

1987	1988	1989	1990	1991	1992	1993	1994	1995	1996	1997	1998	1999	2000	2001		
Millions of US Dollars															**International Transactions**	
....	....	....	....	....	....	....	....	....	....	621.30	796.12	1,322.83	1,358.63	....	Exports	70..*d*
....	....	....	....	....	....	....	....	....	....	1,111.72	1,080.27	1,240.92	1,418.61	....	Imports, c.i.f.	71..*d*
Minus Sign Indicates Debit															Balance of Payments	
....	....	....	....	....	−93.0	−103.9	−156.6	−185.7	−184.9	−209.9	−49.3	−112.6	−19.3	....	Current Account, n.i.e.	78al *d*
....	....	....	....	....	264.5	283.7	489.9	855.2	643.6	736.0	899.9	979.9	1,327.1	....	Goods: Exports f.o.b.	78aa *d*
....	....	....	....	....	−443.4	−471.1	−744.4	−1,186.8	−1,071.8	−1,064.0	−1,073.2	−1,211.5	−1,525.1	....	Goods: Imports f.o.b.	78ab *d*
....	....	....	....	....	−178.9	−187.4	−254.5	−331.6	−428.2	−328.0	−173.3	−231.6	−198.0	....	*Trade Balance*	78ac *d*
....	....	....	....	....	49.7	63.9	54.5	114.0	162.8	160.4	109.2	130.8	169.9	....	Services: Credit	78ad *d*
....	....	....	....	....	−63.6	−120.5	−139.6	−187.9	−214.8	−188.0	−175.1	−204.7	−243.5	....	Services: Debit	78ae *d*
....	....	....	....	....	−192.8	−244.0	−339.6	−405.5	−480.2	−355.6	−239.2	−305.5	−271.6	....	*Balance on Goods & Services*	78af *d*
....	....	....	....	....	....	.5	2.1	9.7	12.6	16.0	17.8	20.4	31.8	....	Income: Credit	78ag *d*
....	....	....	....	....	−20.6	−16.6	−49.1	−66.9	−98.3	−58.5	−51.3	−61.9	−84.0	....	Income: Debit	78ah *d*
....	....	....	....	....	−213.4	−260.1	−386.6	−462.7	−565.9	−398.1	−272.7	−346.9	−323.8	....	*Balance on Gds, Serv. & Inc.*	78ai *d*
....	....	....	....	....	120.4	156.4	230.0	277.9	383.4	188.5	224.0	235.9	304.8	....	Current Transfers, n.i.e.: Credit	78aj *d*
....	....	....	....	....	....	−.2	—	−.9	−2.4	−.3	−.6	−1.6	−.3	....	Current Transfers: Debit	78ak *d*
....	....	....	....	....	126.3	123.4	73.2	78.0	75.8	65.2	42.0	44.1	38.1	....	Capital Account, n.i.e.	78bc *d*
....	....	....	....	....	126.3	123.4	73.2	78.0	75.8	65.2	42.0	44.1	38.1	....	Capital Account, n.i.e.: Credit	78ba *d*
....	....	....	....	....	....	....								....	Capital Account: Debit	78bb *d*
....	....	....	....	....	13.9	.2	54.0	122.4	259.1	219.8	154.5	126.3	107.2	....	Financial Account, n.i.e.	78bj *d*
....	....	....	....	....	....	....	....	....	....	....	....	....	....	....	Direct Investment Abroad	78bd *d*
....	....	....	....	....	33.0	54.1	68.9	150.8	293.6	203.7	120.7	143.6	125.7	....	Dir. Invest. in Rep. Econ., n.i.e.	78be *d*
....	....	....	....	....	....	....	....	....	....	....	....	....	....	....	Portfolio Investment Assets	78bf *d*
....	....	....	....	....	....	....	....	....	....	....	....	....	....	....	Equity Securities	78bk *d*
....	....	....	....	....	....	....	....	....	....	....	....	....	....	....	Debt Securities	78bl *d*
....	....	....	....	....	....	....	....	....	....	....	....	....	....	....	Portfolio Investment Liab., n.i.e.	78bg *d*
....	....	....	....	....	....	....	....	....	....	....	....	....	....	....	Equity Securities	78bm *d*
....	....	....	....	....	....	....	....	....	....	....	....	....	....	....	Debt Securities	78bn *d*
....	....	....	....	....	....	....	....	....	....	....	....	....	....	....	Financial Derivatives Assets	78bw *d*
....	....	....	....	....	....	....	....	....	....	....	....	....	....	....	Financial Derivatives Liabilities	78bx *d*
....	....	....	....	....	−24.1	−51.1	−46.8	−103.4	−118.0	−23.6	−21.0	−61.0	−80.5	....	Other Investment Assets	78bh *d*
....	....	....	....	....	....	....	....	....	....	....	....	....	....	....	Monetary Authorities	78bo *d*
....	....	....	....	....	....	−.4	....	....	....	....	....	....	....	....	General Government	78bp *d*
....	....	....	....	....	....	−25.6	—	−39.8	−23.6	23.6	23.2	−15.0	−13.6	....	Banks	78bq *d*
....	....	....	....	....	−24.1	−25.1	−46.8	−63.6	−94.4	−47.2	−44.2	−46.0	−67.0	....	Other Sectors	78br *d*
....	....	....	....	....	5.0	−2.8	31.9	75.0	83.5	39.7	54.8	43.7	62.0	....	Other Investment Liab., n.i.e.	78bi *d*
....	....	....	....	....	....	....	....	....	....	....	....	....	....	....	Monetary Authorities	78bs *d*
....	....	....	....	....	−2.1	3.2	51.4	73.1	89.7	41.2	53.3	46.3	74.6	....	General Government	78bt *d*
....	....	....	....	....	7.1	−6.0	−19.5	1.9	−6.2	−1.5	1.5	−2.6	−12.7	....	Banks	78bu *d*
....	....	....	....	....	....	....	....	....	....	....	....	....	....	....	Other Sectors	78bv *d*
....	....	....	....	....	−34.0	1.0	65.6	11.5	−78.0	−41.2	−116.5	−7.9	−40.0	....	Net Errors and Omissions	78ca *d*
....	....	....	....	....	13.2	20.8	36.2	26.2	72.0	33.9	30.7	49.9	85.9	....	*Overall Balance*	78cb *d*
....	....	....	....	....	−13.2	−20.8	−36.2	−26.2	−72.0	−33.9	−30.7	−49.9	−85.9	....	Reserves and Related Items	79da *d*
....	....	....	....	....	−4.5	−23.0	−71.2	−73.2	−68.9	−34.3	−29.3	−65.1	−101.4	....	Reserve Assets	79db *d*
....	....	....	....	....	−8.7	—	19.8	42.3	—	—	−1.4	8.3	4.0	....	Use of Fund Credit and Loans	79dc *d*
....	....	....	....	....	....	2.2	15.2	4.7	−3.1	.4	—	6.9	11.5	....	Exceptional Financing	79de *d*
Millions of US Dollars															International Investment Position	
....	....	....	....	....	....	....	....	374.4	711.0	798.4	953.3	1,109.5	....	....	Assets	79aa *d*
....	....	....	....	....	....	....	....	—	—	—	—	—	....	....	Direct Investment Abroad	79ab *d*
....	....	....	....	....	....	....	....	—	—	—	—	—	....	....	Portfolio Investment	79ac *d*
....	....	....	....	....	....	....	....	—	—	—	—	—	....	....	Equity Securities	79ad *d*
....	....	....	....	....	....	....	....	—	—	—	—	—	....	....	Debt Securities	79ae *d*
....	....	....	....	....	....	....	....	—	—	—	—	—	....	....	Financial Derivatives	79al *d*
....	....	....	....	....	....	....	....	182.3	206.9	223.2	206.1	225.0	....	....	Other Investment	79af *d*
....	....	....	....	....	....	....	....	—	—	—	—	—	....	....	Monetary Authorities	79ag *d*
....	....	....	....	....	....	....	....	—	—	—	—	—	....	....	General Government	79ah *d*
....	....	....	....	....	....	....	....	163.3	186.9	163.2	140.1	155.0	....	....	Banks	79ai *d*
....	....	....	....	....	....	....	....	19.0	20.0	60.0	66.0	70.0	....	....	Other Sectors	79aj *d*
....	....	....	....	....	....	....	....	192.1	504.1	575.2	747.2	884.5	....	....	Reserve Assets	79ak *d*
....	....	....	....	....	....	....	....	1,108.0	1,351.2	1,210.5	1,252.9	1,455.4	....	....	Liabilities	79la *d*
....	....	....	....	....	....	....	....	498.1	677.6	580.4	680.9	724.5	....	....	Dir. Invest. in Rep. Economy	79lb *d*
....	....	....	....	....	....	....	....	—	—	—	—	—	....	....	Portfolio Investment	79lc *d*
....	....	....	....	....	....	....	....	—	—	—	—	—	....	....	Equity Securities	79ld *d*
....	....	....	....	....	....	....	....	—	—	—	—	—	....	....	Debt Securities	79le *d*
....	....	....	....	....	....	....	....	—	—	—	—	—	....	....	Financial Derivatives	79ll *d*
....	....	....	....	....	....	....	....	609.9	673.6	630.1	572.0	730.9	....	....	Other Investment	79lf *d*
....	....	....	....	....	....	....	....	71.7	69.4	65.1	66.5	72.9	....	....	Monetary Authorities	79lg *d*
....	....	....	....	....	....	....	....	472.5	544.7	506.9	446.0	601.1	....	....	General Government	79lh *d*
....	....	....	....	....	....	....	....	65.7	59.6	58.1	59.5	56.9	....	....	Banks	79li *d*
....	....	....	....	....	....	....	....	—	—	—	—	—	....	....	Other sectors	79lj *d*
Year Ending December 31															**Government Finance**	
....	....	....	....	....	....	....	....	....	....	....	....	....	....	....	Deficit (-) or Surplus	80
....	....	....	....	....	....	....	....	....	....	....	....	....	....	....	Revenue	81
....	....	....	....	....	....	....	....	....	....	....	....	....	....	....	Grants	81z
....	....	....	....	....	....	....	....	....	....	....	....	....	....	....	Expenditure	82
															Financing	
....	....	....	....	....	....	....	....	....	....	....	....	....	....	....	Domestic	84a
....	....	....	....	....	....	....	....	....	....	....	....	....	....	....	Foreign	85a
Midyear Estimates																
8.07	8.32	8.33	8.57	8.78	9.06	9.31	9.87	10.20	10.34	10.37	†12.34	12.66	12.99	13.31	**Population**	99z

(See notes in the back of the book.)

Cameroon

		1972	1973	1974	1975	1976	1977	1978	1979	1980	1981	1982	1983	1984	1985	1986
Exchange Rates															*Francs per SDR:*	
Official Rate	aa	278.00	284.00	272.08	262.55	288.70	285.76	272.28	264.78	287.99	334.52	370.92	436.97	470.11	415.26	394.78
															Francs per US Dollar:	
Official Rate	ae	256.05	235.42	222.22	224.27	248.49	235.25	209.00	201.00	225.80	287.40	336.25	417.37	479.60	378.05	322.75
Official Rate	rf	252.03	222.89	240.70	214.31	238.95	245.68	225.66	212.72	211.28	271.73	328.61	381.07	436.96	449.26	346.31
														Index Numbers (1995=100):		
Official Rate	ahx	197.9	224.6	207.2	233.0	209.0	203.0	221.4	234.6	236.4	184.6	152.6	131.5	114.5	111.9	144.3
Nominal Effective Exchange Rate	ne c	....	....	....	....	....	....	....	90.9	93.0	87.2	83.4	81.1	80.5	83.7	90.5
Real Effective Exchange Rate	re c	....	....	....	....	....	....	....	....	131.6	120.9	118.2	122.9	125.0	130.7	144.7
Fund Position															*Millions of SDRs:*	
Quota	2f. s	35.00	35.00	35.00	35.00	35.00	35.00	45.00	45.00	67.50	67.50	67.50	92.70	92.70	92.70	92.70
SDRs	1b. s	10.51	10.51	10.47	10.11	8.79	6.75	3.23	.01	—	.23	1.64	.62	6.23	4.21	2.82
Reserve Position in the Fund	1c. s	6.90	6.90	—	—	—	—	3.47	6.39	12.04	12.04	13.90	7.20	.20	.20	.20
Total Fund Cred.&Loans Outstg.	2tl	—	—	4.62	12.13	33.89	33.89	47.27	49.92	46.04	37.68	34.74	33.60	30.70	24.95	18.13
International Liquidity											*Millions of US Dollars Unless Otherwise Indicated:*					
Total Reserves minus Gold	1l. d	43.64	51.15	78.53	28.83	43.80	42.39	52.28	125.70	188.86	85.19	67.23	159.09	53.85	132.46	59.02
SDRs	1b. d	11.41	12.68	12.82	11.84	10.21	8.20	4.21	.01	—	.27	1.81	.65	6.11	4.62	3.45
Reserve Position in the Fund	1c. d	7.49	8.32	—	—	—	—	4.52	8.42	15.36	14.01	15.33	7.54	.20	.22	.24
Foreign Exchange	1d. d	24.74	30.15	65.71	16.99	33.59	34.19	43.56	117.27	173.50	70.90	50.08	150.90	47.55	127.62	55.32
Gold (Million Fine Troy Ounces)	1ad	....	....	....	—	—	.015	.015	.030	.030	.030	.030	.030	.030	.030	.030
Gold (National Valuation)	1an d	....	....	....	—	—	2.46	2.95	15.59	17.65	11.99	13.45	11.33	9.27	9.70	11.74
Monetary Authorities: Other Liab.	4.. d	.06	.05	8.59	2.80	4.38	2.89	3.78	2.85	2.12	.98	1.20	.92	2.89	.97	1.46
Deposit Money Banks: Assets	7a. d	8.51	16.39	6.73	5.85	14.68	28.57	34.00	32.24	34.31	151.65	71.16	129.92	279.74	431.08	127.71
Liabilities	7b. d	30.95	23.54	26.92	32.41	20.29	51.35	109.22	126.81	326.04	195.46	333.63	228.43	167.14	268.42	394.45
Monetary Authorities															*Billions of Francs:*	
Foreign Assets	11	11.16	11.78	17.45	6.47	10.88	10.55	11.55	28.42	46.65	27.93	27.12	71.17	30.27	53.78	22.83
Claims on Central Government	12a	—	2.00	7.65	15.77	25.35	26.01	34.44	36.34	38.60	42.38	44.83	60.79	77.22	74.24	113.86
Claims on Deposit Money Banks	12e	17.17	20.28	18.77	25.07	24.97	44.32	61.20	61.11	68.99	107.19	132.02	162.67	162.33	129.98	192.56
Claims on Other Banking Insts	12f	....	....	....	....	....	....	....	....	....	....	....	....	....	....	....
Reserve Money	14	24.38	28.66	34.98	36.39	43.09	56.13	65.33	77.58	89.78	119.76	126.50	159.97	183.44	216.13	
of which: Currency Outside DMBs	14a	22.78	26.65	32.20	33.71	38.85	50.72	60.05	70.27	80.84	105.26	111.02	131.24	141.08	155.94	171.52
Foreign Liabilities	16c	.02	.01	3.17	3.81	10.87	10.36	17.61	20.44	23.55	24.33	25.98	29.75	30.25	21.09	14.79
Central Government Deposits	16d	.90	2.21	4.24	3.91	3.45	9.87	19.26	18.11	29.85	19.24	36.17	85.15	61.27	37.64	86.94
Capital Accounts	17a	—	.06	.06	.06	.06	.05	.05	.05	3.78	3.23	4.41	4.67	4.35	3.61	3.97
Other Items (Net)	17r	3.04	3.22	1.42	3.14	3.74	4.46	4.92	9.71	7.29	10.94	10.92	12.11	13.97	12.22	7.42
Deposit Money Banks															*Billions of Francs:*	
Reserves	20	1.60	2.02	2.79	2.67	4.24	5.41	5.29	7.30	8.94	14.51	15.48	31.71	18.89	27.50	44.57
Foreign Assets	21	2.18	3.86	1.50	1.31	3.65	†6.72	7.11	6.48	7.75	43.58	23.93	54.23	134.16	162.97	41.22
Claims on Central Government	22a	5.25	5.73	7.31	8.59	10.96	15.85	21.06	21.47	29.32	35.35	49.81	61.87	69.38	82.40	115.69
Claims on Nonfin.Pub.Enterprises	22c	....	....	....	....	....	....	....	....	....	....	....	....	....	....	....
Claims on Private Sector	22d	57.67	64.90	89.30	114.79	144.09	†204.59	266.82	323.75	416.61	559.68	678.74	808.76	806.13	878.29	986.21
Claims on Other Banking Insts	22f	....	....	....	....	....	....	....	....	....	....	....	....	....	....	....
Claims on Nonbank Financial Insts	22g	....	....	....	....	....	....	....	....	....	....	....	....	....	....	....
Demand Deposits	24	24.57	28.93	41.46	43.49	57.34	†77.70	88.48	116.01	130.15	157.12	190.89	249.43	276.35	278.38	280.31
Time and Savings Deposits	25	10.35	15.06	21.60	30.05	37.96	56.87	65.37	75.84	107.18	146.69	184.92	235.35	325.47	437.84	383.07
Bonds	26ab	....	....	....	....	....	....	....	....	....	....	....	....	....	....	....
Foreign Liabilities	26c	6.49	3.98	4.12	6.04	3.76	11.04	20.77	11.14	45.17	15.50	47.42	50.74	19.22	50.14	83.61
Long-Term Foreign Liabilities	26cl	1.43	1.56	1.86	1.23	1.29	1.04	2.06	14.35	28.45	40.67	64.77	44.60	60.94	51.33	43.70
Central Government Deposits	26d	4.82	5.59	6.84	9.38	29.26	34.19	43.99	66.90	76.16	173.82	158.06	127.47	138.50	143.65	120.76
Credit from Monetary Authorities	26g	17.17	20.28	23.99	27.56	28.75	47.82	65.77	64.38	71.14	110.72	132.02	162.67	162.33	129.98	192.56
Capital Accounts	27a	5.97	7.20	8.31	11.36	12.67	13.53	17.46	24.33	26.84	42.16	49.24	62.36	46.64	64.22	82.43
Other Items (Net)	27r	−4.10	−6.09	−7.30	−1.74	−8.09	†−9.63	−3.62	−13.94	−22.47	−33.56	−59.36	23.94	−.88	−4.38	1.25
Monetary Survey															*Billions of Francs:*	
Foreign Assets (Net)	31n	6.84	11.64	11.66	−2.08	−.09	†−4.13	−19.73	3.32	−14.32	31.68	−22.35	44.90	114.96	145.51	−34.35
Domestic Credit	32	57.21	64.83	93.17	125.86	147.69	†202.38	259.07	296.55	378.52	444.35	579.15	718.80	752.96	853.64	1,008.05
Claims on Central Govt. (Net)	32an	−.47	−.07	3.87	11.07	3.60	−2.21	−7.75	−27.20	−38.09	−115.33	−99.59	−89.96	−53.17	−24.64	21.84
Claims on Nonfin.Pub.Enterprises	32c	....	....	....	....	....	....	....	....	....	....	....	....	....	....	....
Claims on Private Sector	32d	57.67	64.90	89.30	114.79	144.09	†204.59	266.82	323.75	416.61	559.68	678.74	808.76	806.13	878.29	986.21
Claims on Other Banking Insts	32f	....	....	....	....	....	....	....	....	....	....	....	....	....	....	....
Claims on Nonbank Financial Inst	32g	....	....	....	....	....	....	....	....	....	....	....	....	....	....	....
Money	34	47.35	55.57	73.66	77.20	96.19	†128.42	148.53	186.28	210.99	262.37	301.91	380.67	417.43	434.32	451.87
Quasi-Money	35	10.35	15.06	21.60	30.05	37.96	56.87	65.37	75.84	107.18	146.69	184.92	235.35	325.47	437.84	383.07
Bonds	36ab	....	....	....	....	....	....	....	....	....	....	....	....	....	....	....
Other Items (Net)	37r	6.35	5.95	9.56	16.53	13.44	†12.95	25.45	37.75	46.03	66.97	69.97	147.68	125.02	127.00	138.77
Money plus Quasi-Money	35l	60.13	73.61	99.28	111.77	139.81	†193.11	222.91	273.17	331.59	426.31	507.36	642.00	774.23	908.94	870.15
Interest Rates															*Percent Per Annum*	
Discount Rate (End of Period)	60	4.50	4.50	5.50	5.50	6.50	6.50	6.50	8.50	8.50	8.50	8.50	8.50	8.50	9.00	8.00
Deposit Rate	60l	....	....	....	....	....	....	....	6.50	7.50	7.50	7.50	7.50	7.50	7.50	7.35
Lending Rate	60p	....	....	....	....	....	....	....	10.25	13.00	13.00	13.00	14.50	14.50	14.50	13.50
Prices															*Index Numbers (1995=100):*	
Consumer Prices	64	13.2	14.6	17.1	19.4	21.4	24.5	27.5	29.4	†32.2	35.6	40.3	47.0	52.4	56.9	61.3

	1987	1988	1989	1990	1991	1992	1993	1994	1995	1996	1997	1998	1999	2000	2001		
End of Period																**Exchange Rates**	
	378.78	407.68	380.32	364.84	370.48	378.57	404.89	†780.44	728.38	753.06	807.94	791.61	†896.19	918.49	935.39	Official Rate	**aa**
End of Period (ae) Period Average (rf)																	
	267.00	302.95	289.40	256.45	259.00	275.32	294.77	†534.60	490.00	523.70	598.81	562.21	†652.95	704.95	744.31	Official Rate	**ae**
	300.54	297.85	319.01	272.26	282.11	264.69	283.16	†555.20	499.15	511.55	583.67	589.95	†615.70	711.98	733.04	Official Rate	**rf**
Period Averages																	
	166.1	167.8	156.5	183.7	177.4	188.9	176.3	90.0	100.0	97.5	85.6	84.7	81.1	70.3	68.1	Official Rate	**ahx**
	94.9	98.7	103.6	122.9	129.8	148.0	164.6	91.9	100.0	100.7	96.8	99.0	100.9	95.4	97.0	Nominal Effective Exchange Rate	**nec**
	161.8	157.8	145.5	149.5	143.1	144.2	134.5	86.6	100.0	101.5	96.9	102.1	106.7	95.6	98.7	Real Effective Exchange Rate	**rec**
End of Period																**Fund Position**	
	92.70	92.70	92.70	92.70	92.70	135.10	135.10	135.10	135.10	135.10	135.10	135.10	185.70	185.70	185.70	Quota	**2f. s**
	.18	.02	.22	.45	3.89	.20	.06	.03	.03	.11	—	.01	1.90	5.93	.01	SDRs	**1b. s**
	.20	.22	.22	.22	.23	.29	.34	.34	.36	.37	.41	.45	.50	.52	.54	Reserve Position in the Fund	**1c. s**
	11.32	74.64	86.18	85.11	84.28	45.66	11.86	29.91	34.41	50.11	68.91	110.94	142.65	180.50	193.96	Total Fund Cred.&Loans Outstg.	**2tl**
End of Period																**International Liquidity**	
	63.76	175.85	79.86	25.54	43.04	20.37	2.45	2.26	3.79	2.77	.86	1.29	4.43	212.00	331.83	Total Reserves minus Gold	**1l. d**
	.26	.03	.29	.64	5.56	.28	.09	.05	.04	.16	—	.02	2.61	7.73	.02	SDRs	**1b. d**
	.28	.30	.29	.31	.33	.40	.47	.49	.53	.53	.55	.63	.69	.67	.68	Reserve Position in the Fund	**1c. d**
	63.22	175.52	79.28	24.59	37.15	19.70	1.90	1.72	3.22	2.08	.31	.64	1.13	203.60	331.14	Foreign Exchange	**1d. d**
	.030	.030	.030	.030	.030	.030	.030	.030	.030	.030	.030	.030	.030	.030	.030	Gold (Million Fine Troy Ounces)	**1ad**
	14.45	12.17	12.01	11.48	10.58	9.95	11.91	†11.33	11.56	11.04	8.72	8.61	†8.69	8.17	8.33	Gold (National Valuation)	**1an d**
	1.63	†440.82	368.76	471.54	506.92	637.31	762.34	650.63	713.03	537.11	300.24	238.09	188.63	62.45	57.36	Monetary Authorities: Other Liab.	**4.. d**
	279.70	396.82	481.78	142.84	173.78	98.99	88.27	135.55	131.07	90.23	105.23	122.82	163.34	163.10	153.17	Deposit Money Banks: Assets	**7a. d**
	567.80	759.14	791.18	338.28	301.01	90.26	125.49	50.01	81.98	71.50	62.51	85.92	84.52	70.75	67.43	Liabilities	**7b. d**
End of Period																**Monetary Authorities**	
	20.91	†56.99	26.59	9.51	13.89	8.35	4.17	7.37	7.53	7.25	5.70	5.57	8.57	155.21	253.18	Foreign Assets	**11**
	95.29	†117.18	133.24	131.32	†320.40	331.57	319.09	340.51	338.23	340.59	338.61	358.64	403.25	434.19	499.81	Claims on Central Government	**12a**
	341.55	†327.91	294.33	273.36	†77.58	51.63	52.06	27.07	21.41	4.93	4.07	13.51	2.17	1.12	.15	Claims on Deposit Money Banks	**12e**
	....															Claims on Other Banking Insts	**12f**
	200.71	†206.40	219.98	200.59	199.14	168.61	129.79	180.77	142.77	183.17	256.74	282.83	305.91	410.67	502.29	Reserve Money	**14**
	175.28	†166.12	162.85	155.98	170.25	149.02	116.13	136.33	102.29	95.32	180.28	205.76	237.40	264.96	296.14	*of which: Currency Outside DMBs*	**14a**
	9.01	†163.97	139.49	151.98	162.52	192.75	229.52	371.17	374.45	319.02	235.47	221.67	251.01	209.81	224.12	Foreign Liabilities	**16c**
	223.70	†123.32	82.72	52.00	43.38	23.62	14.85	44.83	63.03	59.71	49.52	63.96	57.54	171.12	213.39	Central Government Deposits	**16d**
	4.17	†14.30	13.21	12.19	12.58	12.16	13.59	22.17	20.38	21.00	22.19	21.45	25.24	26.74	27.89	Capital Accounts	**17a**
	20.16	†-5.92	-1.24	-2.57	-5.77	-5.59	-12.43	-243.99	-233.45	-230.12	-215.54	-212.19	-225.72	-227.81	-214.56	Other Items (Net)	**17r**
End of Period																**Deposit Money Banks**	
	25.41	†30.91	48.78	41.25	27.69	17.22	12.39	42.57	37.49	82.48	70.57	68.60	62.66	141.59	201.24	Reserves	**20**
	74.68	†120.22	139.43	36.63	45.01	27.25	26.02	72.46	64.22	47.25	63.01	69.05	106.65	114.98	114.01	Foreign Assets	**21**
	140.92	†125.18	119.49	86.05	108.85	†126.05	154.08	185.76	187.67	159.72	171.59	173.66	173.85	168.57	165.04	Claims on Central Government	**22a**
	....	132.76	191.13	182.57	171.91	77.03	52.68	39.45	42.06	36.26	39.76	53.95	54.35	89.19	82.95	Claims on Nonfin.Pub.Enterprises	**22c**
	1,014.56	†897.65	887.42	894.45	892.95	400.06	368.81	369.54	371.39	385.89	348.14	428.82	481.46	543.95	605.78	Claims on Private Sector	**22d**
	....	.01	.31	—	.01	—	.01	.03	.19	.05	.06	.19	.08	—	.04	Claims on Other Banking Insts	**22f**
	....	2.49	2.60	2.10	2.96	3.06	3.05	4.43	8.83	9.16	11.95	14.57	5.41	4.56	7.20	Claims on Nonbank Financial Insts	**22g**
	215.90	†246.49	281.20	259.29	258.45	159.94	150.06	223.09	213.97	213.45	237.72	271.06	294.49	361.99	410.94	Demand Deposits	**24**
	290.71	†303.19	316.98	337.98	340.37	290.32	278.67	329.79	329.30	268.89	267.45	259.81	306.43	374.62	445.75	Time and Savings Deposits	**25**
	....	16.88	16.50	15.00	15.93	6.22	5.01	3.85	3.85	.90	5.30	.90	.90	—	—	Bonds	**26ab**
	98.90	†132.47	151.48	54.22	†47.17	22.92	32.58	17.44	36.08	34.84	34.74	43.80	47.21	39.18	47.73	Foreign Liabilities	**26c**
	52.71	†97.51	77.49	32.53	†30.80	1.93	4.41	9.30	4.09	2.60	2.69	4.50	7.98	10.70	2.46	Long-Term Foreign Liabilities	**26cl**
	221.57	†177.08	189.77	199.60	189.05	†82.24	77.65	97.04	94.00	109.15	55.43	85.19	101.56	117.74	113.66	Central Government Deposits	**26d**
	341.55	†327.91	294.33	273.37	†77.58	51.63	52.06	27.07	21.41	4.93	4.07	13.51	2.17	1.12	.15	Credit from Monetary Authorities	**26g**
	101.34	†95.05	119.51	131.29	†370.23	77.27	75.87	84.39	62.25	102.79	112.58	129.23	150.84	154.45	175.85	Capital Accounts	**27a**
	-67.11	†-87.37	-58.11	-60.24	-80.20	†-41.80	-59.27	-77.72	-53.09	-16.75	-14.91	.84	-27.10	3.03	-20.28	Other Items (Net)	**27r**
End of Period																**Monetary Survey**	
	-12.31	†-206.28	-194.18	-184.89	†-181.58	-181.99	-236.32	-318.07	-342.86	-301.96	-204.18	-195.36	-190.98	10.49	92.89	Foreign Assets (Net)	**31n**
	805.50	†974.85	1,061.70	1,044.88	1,264.64	†831.91	805.22	797.85	791.34	762.82	806.10	881.16	959.54	952.03	1,033.83	Domestic Credit	**32**
	-209.06	†-58.05	-19.76	-34.24	196.81	†351.76	380.67	384.40	368.88	331.46	405.25	383.15	418.00	313.90	337.80	Claims on Central Govt. (Net)	**32an**
	....	132.76	191.13	182.57	171.91	77.03	52.68	39.45	42.06	36.26	39.76	53.95	54.35	89.19	82.95	Claims on Nonfin.Pub.Enterprises	**32c**
	1,014.56	†897.65	887.42	894.45	892.95	400.06	368.81	369.54	371.39	385.89	348.14	428.82	481.46	543.95	605.78	Claims on Private Sector	**32d**
	....	.01	.31	—	.01	—	.01	.03	.19	.05	.06	.19	.08	—	.04	Claims on Other Banking Insts	**32f**
	....	2.49	2.60	2.10	2.96	3.06	3.05	4.43	8.83	9.16	12.89	15.06	5.64	4.99	7.26	Claims on Nonbank Financial Inst	**32g**
	391.21	†421.98	452.40	418.63	429.90	311.33	267.46	361.29	319.24	314.14	423.90	485.29	537.73	631.06	711.98	Money	**34**
	290.71	†303.19	316.98	337.98	340.37	290.32	278.67	329.79	329.30	268.89	267.45	259.81	306.43	374.62	445.75	Quasi-Money	**35**
	....	16.88	16.50	15.00	15.93	6.22	5.01	3.85	3.85	.90	5.30	.90	.90	—	—	Bonds	**36ab**
	111.27	†26.52	81.64	88.38	†296.85	†42.04	17.77	-215.15	-203.91	-123.08	-94.74	-60.19	-76.51	-43.16	-31.04	Other Items (Net)	**37r**
	710.67	†725.18	769.38	756.61	770.28	601.65	546.13	691.08	648.55	583.03	691.35	745.09	844.17	1,005.69	1,157.74	Money plus Quasi-Money	**35l**
Percent Per Annum																**Interest Rates**	
	8.00	9.50	10.00	11.00	10.75	12.00	11.50	†7.75	8.60	7.75	7.50	7.00	7.30	7.00	6.50	Discount Rate *(End of Period)*	**60**
	7.15	7.21	7.50	†7.50	7.50	7.50	7.75	8.08	5.50	5.38	5.04	5.00	5.00	5.00	5.00	Deposit Rate	**60l**
	13.00	13.46	15.00	†18.50	18.15	17.77	17.46	17.50	16.00	22.00	22.00	22.00	22.00	22.00	20.67	Lending Rate	**60p**
Period Averages																**Prices**	
	69.3	70.5	69.3	70.1	70.1	70.1	67.9	†91.7	100.0	103.9	108.9	112.4	114.1	111.7	116.8	Consumer Prices	**64**

Cameroon

		1972	1973	1974	1975	1976	1977	1978	1979	1980	1981	1982	1983	1984	1985	1986
International Transactions															*Billions of Francs*	
Exports	70	55.70	78.32	114.90	96.13	122.03	172.88	181.70	240.62	290.62	299.72	348.23	372.22	381.33	321.75	271.64
Imports, c.i.f.	71	76.47	74.23	104.84	128.10	146.98	180.68	237.25	271.14	337.61	386.09	394.58	466.98	484.43	508.76	590.44
Balance of Payments															*Millions of US Dollars:*	
Current Account, n.i.e.	78al *d*	...	...	...	...	...	−93.1	−187.1	−126.5	−446.0	−482.1	−386.0	−411.9	−168.9	−561.5	−451.8
Goods: Exports f.o.b.	78aa *d*	...	...	...	...	...	809.1	1,095.8	1,354.1	1,657.5	1,410.6	1,357.9	1,366.7	1,588.6	1,626.3	2,076.9
Goods: Imports f.o.b.	78ab *d*	...	...	...	...	...	−719.2	−951.5	−1,270.8	−1,620.3	−1,368.8	−1,217.6	−1,225.2	−1,064.7	−1,135.9	−1,634.5
Trade Balance	78ac *d*	...	...	...	...	...	89.9	144.3	83.3	37.2	41.8	140.3	141.5	524.2	490.4	442.5
Services: Credit	78ad *d*	...	...	...	...	...	161.8	206.5	351.5	401.0	389.5	427.3	440.8	414.7	498.7	467.2
Services: Debit	78ae *d*	...	...	...	...	...	−335.1	−464.1	−464.7	−716.8	−723.3	−752.1	−717.3	−755.8	−936.2	−944.0
Balance on Goods & Services	78af *d*	...	...	...	...	...	−83.4	−113.3	−29.9	−278.6	−292.0	−184.4	−135.0	183.1	53.0	−34.4
Income: Credit	78ag *d*	...	...	...	...	...	8.1	16.3	12.4	38.3	29.8	14.9	28.2	35.7	38.1	36.9
Income: Debit	78ah *d*	...	...	...	...	...	−49.3	−90.4	−108.3	−214.5	−213.2	−209.1	−307.4	−363.1	−634.0	−354.4
Balance on Gds, Serv. & Inc.	78ai *d*	...	...	...	...	...	−124.6	−187.5	−125.8	−454.8	−475.4	−378.6	−414.3	−144.4	−542.9	−351.9
Current Transfers, n.i.e.: Credit	78aj *d*	...	...	...	...	...	64.2	53.1	71.0	140.2	132.7	118.3	145.9	107.0	147.6	71.8
Current Transfers: Debit	78ak *d*	...	...	...	...	...	−32.7	−52.7	−71.7	−131.4	−139.4	−125.6	−143.5	−131.6	−166.2	−171.8
Capital Account, n.i.e.	78bc *d*	...	...	...	...	...	—	—	—	—	—	—	—	—	—	7.3
Capital Account, n.i.e.: Credit	78ba *d*	...	...	...	...	...	—	—	—	—	—	—	—	—	—	7.7
Capital Account: Debit	78bb *d*	...	...	...	...	...	—	—	—	—	—	—	—	—	—	−.4
Financial Account, n.i.e.	78bj *d*	...	...	...	...	...	90.9	173.9	183.6	530.0	418.1	371.6	523.5	204.6	511.8	392.9
Direct Investment Abroad	78bd *d*	...	...	...	...	...	−4.4	−6.9	2.2	8.2	.4	−4.3	−5.2	−10.1	−10.6	−15.7
Dir. Invest. in Rep. Econ., n.i.e.	78be *d*	...	...	...	...	...	8.7	40.5	62.1	129.8	135.4	111.4	213.8	17.7	316.2	−90.7
Portfolio Investment Assets	78bf *d*	...	...	...	...	...	—	—	—	—	—	—	—	—	—	11.0
Equity Securities	78bk *d*	...	...	...	...	...	—	—	—	—	—	—	—	—	—	82.9
Debt Securities	78bl *d*	...	...	...	...	...	—	—	—	—	—	—	—	—	—	−71.8
Portfolio Investment Liab., n.i.e.	78bg *d*	...	...	...	...	...	—	—	—	—	—	—	—	—	—	—
Equity Securities	78bm *d*	...	...	...	...	...	—	—	—	—	—	—	—	—	—	—
Debt Securities	78bn *d*	...	...	...	...	...	—	—	—	—	—	—	—	—	—	—
Financial Derivatives Assets	78bw *d*	...	...	...	...	...	...	...	...	...	...	...	...	...	...	...
Financial Derivatives Liabilities	78bx *d*	...	...	...	...	...	...	...	...	...	...	...	...	...	...	...
Other Investment Assets	78bh *d*	...	...	...	...	...	−42.7	8.3	−90.5	−213.6	−185.8	−64.9	−271.6	−418.0	−141.3	490.5
Monetary Authorities	78bo *d*	...	...	...	...	...	.3	.4	−.3	−.9	.2	.2	.1	−.7	.1	—
General Government	78bp *d*	...	...	...	...	...	−13.5	16.6	−10.2	27.7	−131.9	59.8	−79.5	−183.2	−64.1	351.6
Banks	78bq *d*	...	...	...	...	...	−29.5	−8.7	−80.0	−240.4	−54.2	−125.0	−192.2	−234.2	−77.4	138.9
Other Sectors	78br *d*	...	...	...	...	...										
Other Investment Liab., n.i.e.	78bi *d*	...	...	...	...	...	129.3	131.9	209.8	605.5	468.2	329.4	586.5	615.0	347.5	−2.2
Monetary Authorities	78bs *d*	...	...	...	...	...	−1.5	.4	−1.5	−.8	.5	.4	−.1	.5	.5	.4
General Government	78bt *d*	...	...	...	...	...	77.9	55.0	120.3	180.0	186.7	74.3	81.5	122.8	94.0	174.3
Banks	78bu *d*	...	...	...	...	...	20.1	21.4	−44.0	161.0	−109.2	97.1	10.9	−65.2	64.3	55.4
Other Sectors	78bv *d*	...	...	...	...	...	32.8	55.0	135.1	265.2	390.2	157.5	494.2	556.9	188.7	−232.3
Net Errors and Omissions	78ca *d*	...	...	...	...	...	−2.1	.6	.9	−6.4	4.3	3.9	5.2	−121.6	108.9	−29.0
Overall Balance	78cb *d*	...	...	...	...	...	−4.3	−12.6	58.0	77.5	−59.7	−10.4	116.7	−85.9	59.3	−80.7
Reserves and Related Items	79da *d*	...	...	...	...	...	4.3	12.6	−58.0	−77.5	59.7	10.4	−116.7	85.9	−59.3	80.7
Reserve Assets	79db *d*	...	...	...	...	...	3.6	−4.7	−62.2	−72.9	69.4	13.5	−115.6	88.9	−53.5	88.6
Use of Fund Credit and Loans	79dc *d*	...	...	...	...	...	—	16.6	3.5	−5.3	−10.2	−3.2	−1.2	−3.0	−5.8	−8.0
Exceptional Financing	79de *d*	...	...	...	...	...	.7	.7	.8	.6	.5	.1	.1			
Government Finance															*Billions of Francs:*	
Deficit (-) or Surplus	80	...	...	...	−12.98	−15.85	−3.02	4.07	31.72	7.24	−58.50	−55.22	33.87	...	...	...
Revenue	81	...	...	...	86.82	104.32	128.16	178.78	222.43	230.64	314.54	390.44	612.27	790.52	...	919.06
Grants Received	81z	...	...	...	4.14	5.29	4.59	—	—	.10	—	—	59.56	4.89	.12	4.80
Expenditure	82	...	...	...	103.12	125.27	133.53	168.45	188.98	221.92	371.63	445.56	546.71	...	813.81	...
Lending Minus Repayments	83	...	...	...	.82	.19	2.24	6.26	1.73	1.58	1.41	.10	91.25	...	41.36	...
Financing																
Domestic	84a	...	...	...	5.20	6.61	−16.50	−4.33	−26.47	−17.17	...	...	−56.47	...	...	...
Foreign	85a	...	...	...	7.78	9.24	19.52	.26	−5.25	9.93	...	...	22.60	...	...	...
Adj. to Total Financing	84x	...	...	...	—	—	—									
Debt: Domestic	88a	...	...	...	...	...	...	...	...	...	...	...	...	112.56	125.88	172.74
Foreign	89a	...	...	...	...	130.70	209.23	...	...	...	291.89	359.54	431.53	...	...	...
National Accounts															*Billions of Francs:*	
Househ.Cons.Expend.,incl.NPISHs	96f	262.6	291.9	320.0	408.1	481.4	545.3	632.9	807.8	985.3	1,222.5	1,538.5	1,716.5	2,008.0	2,466.3	2,642.0
Government Consumption Expend.	91f	46.0	49.0	57.3	68.4	74.8	81.9	102.8	116.3	136.8	159.1	192.0	248.7	306.4	345.3	360.5
Gross Fixed Capital Formation	93e	60.3	74.0	74.7	99.2	118.7	163.5	204.7	251.7	282.4	441.4	507.2	654.5	809.5	939.0	1,018.2
Changes in Inventories	93i	8.6	10.3	14.0	21.3	3.0	18.3	34.1	20.9	13.5	47.0	31.5	25.6	19.4	16.3	29.4
Exports of Goods and Services	90c	73.7	89.7	137.9	145.6	150.4	202.6	249.9	259.4	378.6	388.5	434.8	547.5	646.5	799.9	997.0
Imports of Goods and Services (-)	98c	95.2	114.4	111.3	162.5	171.1	221.7	256.3	310.1	386.5	462.1	531.2	574.7	594.7	727.9	941.0
Gross Domestic Product (GDP)	99b	355.9	400.5	492.6	580.2	657.2	789.9	968.1	1,135.4	1,356.2	1,796.4	2,172.8	2,618.1	3,195.0	3,896.0	4,135.0
Net Primary Income from Abroad	98.n	−52.2	−63.9	−108.8	−109.2	−119.6	−162.0	...	...	...	...	...	...	...	...	−245.8
Gross National Income (GNI)	99a	303.7	336.6	383.8	471.0	537.6	627.9									3,860.4
GDP Volume 1970 prices	99b. *p*	322.8	327.5	342.1	359.7	366.6	387.4	427.7	475.6	495.6	...	...	...	...	...	...
GDP Volume 1980 prices	99b. *p*	...	...	...	...	...	...	...	...	1,356.2	1,650.7	1,775.5	1,900.5	2,049.3	2,232.4	...
GDP Volume 1985 Prices	99b. *p*	...	...	...	...	...	...	...	...	...	...	...	...	...	3,896.0	4,099.6
GDP Volume (1995=100)	99bv *p*	52.1	52.9	55.2	58.1	59.2	62.5	69.0	76.8	80.0	93.7	100.7	107.8	116.3	126.7	133.3
GDP Deflator (1995=100)	99bi *p*	15.6	17.4	20.4	22.9	25.4	28.9	32.1	33.9	38.8	43.9	49.4	55.6	62.9	70.5	71.1
																Millions:
Population	99z	7.06	7.21	7.37	7.53	7.70	7.91	†8.18	8.40	8.50	8.97	9.28	9.57	9.87	10.17	10.46

1987	1988	1989	1990	1991	1992	1993	1994	1995	1996	1997	1998	1999	2000	2001		
															International Transactions	
Billions of Francs																
248.77	275.12	405.99	545.11	517.39	487.13	404.70	757.12	824.28	904.87	1,084.51	985.83	985.49	....	....	Exports	70
526.19	378.73	402.24	381.15	330.96	307.79	250.50	398.33	598.71	627.42	793.93	881.78	811.23	....	....	Imports, c.i.f.	71
															Balance of Payments	
Minus Sign Indicates Debit																
−892.7	−428.3	−298.0	−560.7	−338.8	−396.6	−565.4	−56.1	89.9	....	....	....	....	....	....	Current Account, n.i.e.	78al *d*
1,688.6	1,841.2	1,853.8	2,125.4	1,957.4	1,934.1	1,507.7	1,454.2	1,735.9							Goods: Exports f.o.b.	78aa *d*
−1,434.8	−1,220.8	−1,136.8	−1,430.0	−1,107.2	−1,041.4	−1,005.3	−1,052.3	−1,109.0							Goods: Imports f.o.b.	78ab *d*
253.9	620.5	717.0	695.3	850.2	892.7	502.4	401.9	626.9							*Trade Balance*	78ac *d*
411.4	458.9	475.7	382.2	406.0	407.5	390.9	330.8	304.4							Services: Credit	78ad *d*
−1,052.5	−901.4	−1,032.4	−1,045.1	−1,122.3	−907.3	−741.1	−493.2	−498.6							Services: Debit	78ae *d*
−387.2	178.0	160.3	32.4	133.9	392.8	152.2	239.6	432.6							*Balance on Goods & Services*	78af *d*
12.4	16.9	16.8	8.3	18.3	41.8	17.0	19.9	12.4							Income: Credit	78ag *d*
−419.0	−510.9	−430.8	−566.1	−442.7	−823.9	−669.5	−336.4	−424.6							Income: Debit	78ah *d*
−793.7	−316.0	−253.7	−525.4	−290.4	−389.3	−500.3	−76.9	20.4							*Balance on Gds, Serv. & Inc.*	78ai *d*
61.2	63.8	88.0	82.3	57.0	141.0	65.2	83.8	100.7							Current Transfers, n.i.e.: Credit	78aj *d*
−160.2	−176.0	−132.3	−117.5	−105.4	−148.3	−130.2	−63.0	−31.2							Current Transfers: Debit	78ak *d*
—	6.4	5.0	2.8	7.9	17.0	6.3	14.1	20.4							Capital Account, n.i.e.	78bc *d*
—	6.4	5.0	2.9	8.0	17.1	6.4	14.1	21.1							Capital Account, n.i.e.: Credit	78ba *d*
—	—	−.1	−.1	−.1	−.1	−.1	—	−.7							Capital Account: Debit	78bb *d*
826.0	39.4	325.6	−227.3	−361.1	−342.9	−310.0	−626.4	43.3							Financial Account, n.i.e.	78bj *d*
−11.5	−28.6	−26.1	−15.1	−21.5	−33.1	−22.1	−.4	−.6							Direct Investment Abroad	78bd *d*
115.9	92.4	−85.7	−112.8	−14.5	29.2	5.1	−9.0	7.3							Dir. Invest. in Rep. Econ., n.i.e.	78be *d*
—	−10.9	−1.0	55.6	−2.2	−46.5	−106.3	−74.6	−26.2							Portfolio Investment Assets	78bf *d*
—	3.1	.2	104.1	18.6	53.4	8.0	6.4	—							Equity Securities	78bk *d*
—	−14.0	−1.2	−48.4	−20.8	−99.9	−114.4	−81.1	−26.2							Debt Securities	78bl *d*
—	—	—	—	—	—	—	—	—							Portfolio Investment Liab., n.i.e.	78bg *d*
—	—	—	—	—	—	—	—	—							Equity Securities	78bm *d*
—	—	—	—	—	—	—	—	—							Debt Securities	78bn *d*
....	....	....	....	....	....	....	....	....							Financial Derivatives Assets	78bw *d*
....	....	....	....	....	....	....	....	....							Financial Derivatives Liabilities	78bx *d*
299.7	−93.9	−8.9	481.5	−112.3	16.8	105.5	138.4	−146.8							Other Investment Assets	78bh *d*
....	....	....	....	....	....	....	....	....							Monetary Authorities	78bo *d*
—	−.1	—	.3	—	.1	—	—	—							General Government	78bp *d*
−111.3	−145.2	−67.4	377.6	−29.7	26.0	42.8	−27.9	6.6							Banks	78bq *d*
411.0	51.4	58.5	103.6	−82.6	−9.2	62.6	166.3	−153.4							Other Sectors	78br *d*
421.9	80.5	447.3	−636.5	−210.6	−309.4	−292.2	−680.7	209.6							Other Investment Liab., n.i.e.	78bi *d*
−1.1	.7	6.2	−.4	1.1	3.5	−5.4	−181.3	666.9							Monetary Authorities	78bs *d*
401.7	226.1	352.0	−84.6	64.1	−175.8	−22.5	−272.3	−457.0							General Government	78bt *d*
47.1	−62.4	301.3	−397.0	−31.2	−41.3	−104.1	−76.2	17.0							Banks	78bu *d*
−25.8	−83.9	−212.3	−154.6	−244.6	−95.8	−160.1	−150.9	−17.3							Other Sectors	78bv *d*
−403.9	219.1	−160.7	−85.4	−39.1	−582.6	−16.2	117.0	−138.1							Net Errors and Omissions	78ca *d*
−470.7	−163.4	−128.0	−870.6	−731.1	−1,305.2	−885.3	−551.3	15.4							*Overall Balance*	78cb *d*
470.7	163.4	128.0	870.6	731.1	1,305.2	885.3	551.3	−15.4							Reserves and Related Items	79da *d*
7.3	−94.6	96.8	64.6	−31.6	20.9	14.9	.4	14.5							Reserve Assets	79db *d*
−8.7	81.6	14.5	−1.4	−1.2	−54.6	−47.4	25.3	6.7							Use of Fund Credit and Loans	79dc *d*
472.1	176.4	16.7	807.4	763.9	1,338.9	917.8	525.6	−36.6							Exceptional Financing	79de *d*
															Government Finance	
Year Ending June 30																
....	....	−110.24	†−198.44	−174.88	†−81.16	−54.74	−99.05	†8.25	....	....	83.71	7.16			Deficit (-) or Surplus	80
742.78	633.08	601.65	†517.51	547.90	†498.47	448.41	385.90	†536.54	....	....	862.31	867.46			Revenue	81
—	.12	—	†—	—	†—	—	—	†—							Grants Received	81z
....	....	707.47	†709.71	719.76	†578.43	501.15	483.49	†525.27	....	....	777.60	859.80			Expenditure	82
....	....	4.42	†6.24	3.02	†1.20	2.00	1.46	†3.02	....	....	1.00	.50			Lending Minus Repayments	83
															Financing	
....	....	14.53	†39.68	37.27	†14.27	12.45	−13.09	†−13.17	....	....	−19.40	−14.90			Domestic	84a
....	....	95.71	†176.01	141.09	†106.73	61.16	120.84	†14.42	....	....	−63.10	8.50			Foreign	85a
....	....	—	†−17.25	−3.48	†−39.84	−18.87	−8.70	†−9.50	....	....	−1.21	−.76			Adj. to Total Financing	84x
228.30	153.87	....	†141.50	356.43	†377.90	374.16	1,179.18	†1419.89	....	....	1,391.38	1,224.04			Debt: Domestic	88a
....	....	....	†1054.40	1,275.81	†1496.02	1,852.61	4,084.80	†4343.87	....	....	4,261.53	4,432.12			Foreign	89a
															National Accounts	
Year Ending June 30																
2,658.4	2,482.6	2,428.9	2,298.2	2,079.5	2,292.4	2,233.6	2,538.9	3,018.9	3,354.8	3,537.2	....	....	....		Househ.Cons.Expend.,incl.NPISHs	96f
429.0	412.0	434.0	427.6	412.3	387.1	343.0	257.5	299.9	305.0	332.1					Government Consumption Expend.	91f
962.3	757.6	638.2	581.2	693.2	457.1	492.5	533.0	597.5	729.3	850.5					Gross Fixed Capital Formation	93e
6.4	4.1	−37.6	16.0	.9	−27.3	29.8	—	—							Changes in Inventories	93i
710.7	630.2	726.4	682.3	699.8	649.5	531.3	768.5	1,068.3	1,116.3	1,335.8					Exports of Goods and Services	90c
844.8	642.0	677.0	671.1	566.4	584.4	504.7	681.8	834.5	950.4	1,038.2					Imports of Goods and Services (-)	98c
3,922.0	6,644.5	3,513.0	3,334.2	3,319.2	3,174.3	3,125.6	3,786.0	4,365.5	4,836.5	5,266.5	5,572.0	6,008.4	6,602.5		Gross Domestic Product (GDP)	99b
−141.9	−118.0	−154.1	−162.7	−146.8	−174.6	−198.9	−190.0	−168.5	−284.0	−299.0					Net Primary Income from Abroad	98.n
3,780.0	3,526.5	3,358.9	3,171.5	3,172.4	2,999.7	2,926.6	3,226.0	3,981.7	4,271.0	4,718.4					Gross National Income (GNI)	99a
....	....	....	....	....	....	....	....	....							GDP Volume 1970 prices	99b. *p*
															GDP Volume 1980 prices	99b. *p*
4,011.4	3,695.9	3,630.5	3,388.4	3,256.6	3,158.7	3,058.3	2,977.6	3,075.9	3,229.7	3,391.1					GDP Volume 1985 Prices	99b. *p*
130.4	120.2	118.0	110.2	105.9	102.7	99.4	96.8	100.0	105.0	110.2					GDP Volume (1995=100)	99bv *p*
68.9	126.7	68.2	69.3	71.8	70.8	72.0	89.6	100.0	105.5	109.4					GDP Deflator (1995=100)	99bi *p*
Midyear Estimates																
10.82	10.88	11.54	†11.47	11.85	12.28	12.61	12.95	13.28	13.60	14.30	14.44	14.55	14.88	15.20	Population	99z

(See notes in the back of the book.)

Canada

		1972	1973	1974	1975	1976	1977	1978	1979	1980	1981	1982	1983	1984	1985	1986
Exchange Rates														*Canadian Dollars per SDR:*		
Market Rate	aa	1.0809	1.2013	1.2136	1.1899	1.1725	1.3294	1.5451	1.5388	1.5237	1.3803	1.3562	1.3028	1.2952	1.5350	1.6886
															Canadian Dollars per US Dollar:	
Market Rate	ae	.9956	.9958	.9912	1.0164	1.0092	1.0944	1.1860	1.1681	1.1947	1.1859	1.2294	1.2444	1.3214	1.3975	1.3805
Market Rate	rf	.9899	1.0001	.9780	1.0172	.9860	1.0635	1.1407	1.1714	1.1692	1.1989	1.2337	1.2324	1.2951	1.3655	1.3895
														Index Numbers (1995=100):		
Market Rate	ahx	138.6	137.2	140.3	134.9	139.2	129.1	120.3	117.1	117.4	114.5	111.3	111.3	106.0	100.5	98.7
Nominal Effective Exchange Rate	neu	149.3	145.2	149.5	143.3	149.7	138.0	125.3	121.3	121.5	121.1	120.4	121.8	117.6	112.1	105.0
Real Effective Exchange Rate	reu	....	....	....	95.2	104.2	96.9	101.0	97.9	†97.6	100.3	103.5	108.8	107.2	101.4	92.6
Fund Position														*Millions of SDRs:*		
Quota	2f.s	1,100	1,100	1,100	1,100	1,100	1,100	1,357	1,357	2,036	2,036	2,036	2,941	2,941	2,941	2,941
SDRs	1b.s	465	467	469	474	480	416	401	445	355	150	64	20	74	198	202
Reserve Position in the Fund	1c.s	316	280	433	554	813	701	427	297	454	346	331	672	692	647	561
of which: Outstg.Fund Borrowing	2c	—	—	141	247	247	205	129	26	13	13	13	124	164	161	155
International Liquidity												*Millions of US Dollars Unless Otherwise Indicated:*				
Total Reserves minus Gold	1l.d	5,216	4,841	4,885	4,426	4,964	3,672	3,557	2,864	3,093	3,537	3,011	3,466	2,491	2,503	3,251
SDRs	1b.d	505	564	574	555	558	505	522	586	453	174	71	21	72	218	247
Reserve Position in the Fund	1c.d	343	338	530	648	944	852	557	391	579	402	365	703	678	711	686
Foreign Exchange	1d.d	4,368	3,940	3,781	3,223	3,462	2,315	2,478	1,888	2,061	2,961	2,575	2,742	1,741	1,574	2,318
of which: US Dollars	1dx d	4,355	3,927	3,768	3,207	3,446	2,299	2,463	1,864	2,038	2,865	2,455	2,373	1,692	1,524	2,274
Gold (Million Fine Troy Ounces)	1ad	21.95	21.95	21.95	21.95	21.62	22.01	22.13	22.18	20.98	20.46	20.26	20.17	20.14	20.11	19.72
Gold (National Valuation)	1an d	834	927	941	899	879	936	1,009	1,023	937	834	782	779	691	773	845
Deposit Money Banks: Assets	7a.d	8,203	12,343	13,942	13,852	17,237	18,150	21,657	25,406	35,194	38,160	38,150	40,965	41,212	44,169	50,745
Liabilities	7b.d	8,134	12,632	13,333	14,095	16,475	18,874	24,645	32,042	42,959	61,040	57,738	61,289	61,619	64,637	68,905
Monetary Authorities														*Billions of Canadian Dollars:*		
Foreign Assets	11	6.02	5.74	5.77	5.41	5.90	5.04	5.42	4.54	4.81	5.18	4.66	5.23	4.20	4.58	5.65
Claims on Central Government	12a	5.91	6.88	7.54	8.80	9.47	11.29	13.34	15.17	17.06	18.54	18.61	19.00	19.17	17.55	21.06
Reserve Money	14	7.03	8.16	9.31	10.75	11.76	13.18	14.74	16.01	17.62	18.02	18.82	19.08	19.44	20.56	22.15
of which: Currency Outside DMBs	14a	4.55	5.30	5.99	6.92	7.36	8.13	8.98	9.70	10.45	10.88	11.87	12.92	13.93	15.06	16.02
Central Government Deposits	16d	5.26	4.88	4.70	4.22	4.47	3.68	4.29	3.56	3.82	4.94	4.29	4.50	3.28	3.96	4.50
Other Items (Net)	17r	−.35	−.41	−.70	−.76	−.86	−.53	−.27	.14	.43	.77	.16	.64	.66	−2.39	.06
Deposit Money Banks														*Billions of Canadian Dollars:*		
Reserves	20	2.45	2.94	3.44	4.02	4.48	5.13	5.83	6.63	7.28	7.36	7.15	6.08	5.85	5.68	6.24
Foreign Assets	21	8.17	11.90	13.41	13.61	16.93	19.39	25.24	29.19	41.60	44.19	45.29	49.23	52.17	59.91	68.41
Claims on Central Government	22a	7.13	7.24	8.06	7.73	8.58	9.51	9.75	9.93	9.75	9.85	11.55	16.10	14.72	14.84	17.40
Claims on Local Government	22b	1.86	2.19	2.45	3.04	3.05	2.65	2.64	2.73	2.88	4.32	4.08	3.56	2.96	3.21	2.59
Claims on Private Sector	22d	31.45	38.90	47.92	56.05	67.34	80.03	100.24	120.00	136.54	†189.24	193.70	185.80	199.78	216.85	223.58
Demand Deposits	24	15.18	16.23	15.90	19.12	18.94	20.92	22.02	21.91	24.32	†26.00	28.16	31.11	38.86	54.98	64.31
Savings & Fgn Currency Deposits	25	22.93	29.99	39.53	44.82	58.02	67.09	81.36	100.80	110.18	†140.62	146.34	140.45	143.14	137.07	142.03
Foreign Liabilities	26c	8.10	11.49	11.62	12.27	14.65	18.27	26.73	34.69	48.48	68.85	67.37	73.11	78.04	86.57	90.46
Central Government Deposits	26d	2.41	2.36	4.68	3.66	3.10	4.73	6.47	2.42	4.09	7.14	6.91	6.06	2.80	4.35	2.05
Other Items (Net)	27r	2.44	3.09	3.54	4.59	5.68	5.69	7.13	8.66	10.97	†12.35	12.99	10.05	12.65	17.52	19.39
Monetary Survey														*Billions of Canadian Dollars:*		
Foreign Assets (Net)	31n	6.05	6.12	7.48	6.71	8.08	6.05	3.87	−1.05	−2.13	−19.63	−17.55	−18.75	−21.85	−22.20	−16.48
Domestic Credit	32	39.27	48.70	57.55	68.76	81.73	95.74	115.74	142.19	158.48	†209.88	216.75	213.89	230.55	244.14	258.08
Claims on Central Govt. (Net)	32an	5.37	6.89	6.22	8.64	10.48	12.38	12.34	19.12	18.89	16.32	18.97	24.53	27.82	24.08	31.91
Claims on Local Government	32b	1.86	2.19	2.45	3.04	3.05	2.65	2.64	2.73	2.88	4.32	4.08	3.56	2.96	3.21	2.59
Claims on Private Sector	32d	32.04	39.62	48.88	57.08	68.20	80.72	100.76	120.34	136.71	†189.24	193.70	185.80	199.78	216.85	223.58
Money	34	19.73	21.55	21.91	26.05	26.31	29.06	31.03	31.62	34.80	†36.92	40.08	44.22	52.87	70.30	80.65
Quasi-Money	35	22.93	29.99	39.53	44.82	58.02	67.09	81.36	100.80	110.18	†140.62	146.34	140.45	143.14	137.07	142.03
Other Items (Net)	37r	2.65	3.28	3.59	4.60	5.48	5.64	7.21	8.72	11.37	†12.71	12.80	10.48	12.70	14.58	18.93
Money plus Quasi-Money	35l	42.67	51.54	61.44	70.87	84.34	96.15	112.39	132.42	144.98	†177.54	186.41	184.66	196.00	207.37	222.68
Other Banking Institutions														*Billions of Canadian Dollars:*		
Reserves	40	2.08	2.72	3.11	4.10	4.55	5.52	6.33	6.38	7.49	†8.61	9.91	8.67	9.38	9.38	11.02
Claims on Central Government	42a	.76	.59	.52	.52	.58	.79	1.06	1.24	2.06	†1.61	2.19	3.39	3.28	3.50	5.23
Claims on State and Local Govts	42b	1.33	1.35	1.27	1.30	1.37	1.51	1.53	1.56	2.08	†1.82	2.01	1.89	2.26	1.98	1.98
Claims on Private Sector	42d	15.37	19.52	23.32	27.93	34.42	42.04	50.66	61.43	70.82	†64.97	67.18	75.82	85.38	94.74	107.06
Demand Deposits	44	.71	.74	.66	.79	.81	.94	1.04	1.02	1.56	†1.86	2.47	3.66	5.29	7.77	8.43
Time and Savings Deposits	45	15.93	19.92	23.82	28.69	34.95	42.32	50.55	59.78	70.11	†69.46	74.75	81.48	88.31	95.27	108.63
Money Market Instruments	46aa	.20	.39	.50	.51	.68	.88	1.15	1.79	2.54	†.71	.62	1.42	1.16	2.00	1.97
Capital Accounts	47a	3.08	3.45	3.67	4.25	4.89	5.69	6.53	6.79	7.13	†5.76	5.08	5.58	5.99	6.07	6.34
Other Items (Net)	47r	−.37	−.32	−.43	−.39	−.43	.03	.30	1.23	1.10	†−.77	−1.62	−2.38	−.46	−1.51	−.08
Banking Survey														*Billions of Canadian Dollars:*		
Foreign Assets (Net)	51n	6.05	6.12	7.48	6.71	8.08	6.05	3.87	−1.05	−2.13	−19.63	−17.55	−18.75	−21.85	−22.20	−16.48
Domestic Credit	52	56.88	70.32	82.80	98.60	118.18	140.16	169.03	206.47	233.51	†278.28	288.14	294.99	321.47	344.36	372.35
Claims on Central Govt. (Net)	52an	6.12	7.47	6.71	9.15	11.05	13.16	13.36	20.33	20.94	†17.93	21.16	27.92	31.09	27.58	37.14
Claims on State and Local Govts	52b	3.19	3.54	3.72	4.34	4.41	4.16	4.17	4.28	4.95	†6.15	6.09	5.45	5.22	5.19	4.56
Claims on Private Sector	52d	47.41	59.14	72.20	85.01	102.62	122.75	151.42	181.77	207.53	†254.21	260.89	261.62	285.15	311.59	330.64
Liquid Liabilities	55l	57.23	69.48	82.81	96.25	115.55	133.90	157.65	186.84	209.16	†240.25	253.71	261.14	280.23	301.03	328.72
Money Market Instruments	56aa	.20	.39	.50	.51	.68	.88	1.15	1.79	2.54	†.71	.62	1.42	1.16	2.00	1.97
Other Items (Net)	57r	5.51	6.57	6.98	8.55	10.03	11.44	14.10	16.79	19.68	†17.70	16.25	13.68	18.23	19.13	25.19
Nonbank Financial Institutions														*Millions of Canadian Dollars:*		
Reserves	40..n	....	....	.13	.16	.14	.08	.06	.40	.18	.07	.13	.06	.09	.06	.05
Claims on Central Government	42a.n	....	....	....	....	....	....	....	....	....	....	....	....	....	....	....
Claims on Private Sector	42d.n	....	....	8.90	9.60	10.20	10.97	11.74	12.74	13.32	13.75	11.78	11.57	13.04	16.09	16.75
Claims on Deposit Money Banks	42e.n	....	....	....	....	....	....	....	....	....	....	....	....	....	....	....
Money Market Instruments	46aa n	....	....	3.06	3.03	3.17	3.31	3.78	3.86	3.72	3.99	3.68	4.93	6.34	6.06	7.30
Bonds	46ab n	....	....	3.04	3.53	3.95	4.31	4.63	4.82	4.61	4.61	3.68	3.15	3.34	4.13	5.35
Cred. from Deposit Money Banks	46h.n	....	....	.70	.71	.26	.37	.49	1.17	1.06	.79	.56	.61	.34	.36	.37
Capital Accounts	47a.n	....	....	1.44	1.64	1.80	1.93	2.00	2.09	2.23	2.23	2.05	1.94	1.95	2.04	1.97
Other Items (Net)	47r.n	....	....	.79	.84	1.16	1.12	.89	1.21	1.88	2.20	1.94	1.00	1.16	3.57	1.82

1987	1988	1989	1990	1991	1992	1993	1994	1995	1996	1997	1998	1999	2000	2001		
															Exchange Rates	
End of Period																
1.8440	1.6050	1.5215	1.6507	1.6530	1.7478	1.8186	2.0479	2.0294	1.9694	1.9282	2.1550	1.9809	1.9546	2.0015	Market Rate	**aa**
End of Period (ae) Period Average (rf)																
1.2998	1.1927	1.1578	1.1603	1.1556	1.2711	1.3240	1.4028	1.3652	1.3696	1.4291	1.5305	1.4433	1.5002	1.5926	Market Rate	**ae**
1.3260	1.2307	1.1840	1.1668	1.1457	1.2087	1.2901	1.3656	1.3724	1.3635	1.3846	1.4835	1.4857	1.4851	1.5488	Market Rate	**rf**
Period Averages																
103.5	111.5	115.9	117.6	119.8	113.6	106.4	100.5	100.0	100.6	99.1	92.6	92.4	92.4	88.6	Market Rate	**ahx**
107.2	114.2	120.2	120.5	122.5	115.3	108.7	102.0	100.0	101.7	101.9	95.8	95.2	96.3	93.5	Nominal Effective Exchange Rate	**neu**
94.6	101.4	110.6	113.6	118.8	113.6	107.4	100.8	100.0	100.8	103.5	97.0	95.9	96.0	92.2	Real Effective Exchange Rate	**reu**
															Fund Position	
End of Period																
2,941	2,941	2,941	2,941	2,941	4,320	4,320	4,320	4,320	4,320	4,320	4,320	6,369	6,369	6,369	Quota	**2f.s**
281	1,017	1,048	1,072	1,106	756	773	786	792	812	834	780	384	441	489	SDRs	**1b.s**
466	375	402	364	414	735	690	629	836	853	1,167	1,633	2,308	1,926	2,278	Reserve Position in the Fund	**1c.s**
120	30	—	—	—	—	—	—	—	—	—	204	—	—	—	*of which:* Outstg.Fund Borrowing	**2c**
															International Liquidity	
End of Period																
7,277	15,391	16,055	17,845	16,252	11,431	12,481	12,286	15,049	20,422	17,823	23,308	28,126	31,924	33,962	Total Reserves minus Gold	**1l.d**
399	1,369	1,377	1,526	1,582	1,039	1,062	1,148	1,177	1,168	1,126	1,098	527	574	614	SDRs	**1b.d**
661	505	528	517	592	1,011	948	919	1,243	1,226	1,575	2,299	3,168	2,509	2,863	Reserve Position in the Fund	**1c.d**
6,218	13,517	14,150	15,802	14,079	9,382	10,471	10,219	12,629	18,028	15,122	19,911	24,432	28,841	30,484	Foreign Exchange	**1d.d**
6,163	12,608	11,489	11,476	9,440	7,864	9,950	9,693	12,127	17,521	14,630	15,907	18,838	21,692	19,748	*of which: US Dollars*	**1dxd**
18.52	17.14	16.10	14.76	12.96	9.94	6.05	3.89	3.41	3.09	3.09	2.49	1.81	1.18	1.05	Gold (Million Fine Troy Ounces)	**1ad**
920	807	741	735	649	478	292	198	178	155	146	122	524	323	291	Gold (National Valuation)	**1and**
50,734	46,804	48,819	52,070	46,033	46,851	41,114	54,614	64,061	76,144	84,432	86,453	79,191	91,441	102,502	Deposit Money Banks: Assets	**7a.d**
71,734	69,480	70,807	77,946	76,711	73,613	67,151	80,507	77,143	87,951	108,978	111,723	92,325	94,728	109,319	Liabilities	**7b.d**
															Monetary Authorities	
End of Period																
10.65	19.32	19.45	21.56	19.53	15.14	16.91	17.51	20.79	28.18	25.68	35.86	40.72	47.97	54.16	Foreign Assets	**11**
23.39	24.10	25.04	25.37	26.38	27.83	29.63	30.41	30.09	31.03	31.81	32.41	41.68	36.98	40.08	Claims on Central Government	**12a**
24.11	25.32	26.32	26.92	28.64	29.31	30.93	31.65	32.08	33.46	34.58	36.86	45.83	42.45	44.24	Reserve Money	**14**
17.39	18.79	20.10	20.89	22.07	23.60	25.57	27.30	27.99	28.78	30.15	32.32	38.72	36.34	38.66	*of which: Currency Outside DMBs*	**14a**
9.43	17.57	17.47	19.41	17.14	12.58	14.41	15.01	17.69	25.01	22.09	30.83	35.85	43.95	49.85	Central Government Deposits	**16d**
.50	.53	.70	.61	.14	1.08	1.20	1.26	1.11	.75	.82	.57	.72	-1.45	.15	Other Items (Net)	**17r**
															Deposit Money Banks	
End of Period																
6.77	6.71	6.29	6.58	7.15	5.88	5.92	5.04	4.67	5.24	4.79	4.89	8.56	6.87	6.07	Reserves	**20**
63.92	52.88	53.09	57.13	50.81	57.44	51.74	73.94	83.18	97.07	109.86	122.51	105.26	127.80	149.15	Foreign Assets	**21**
15.18	20.94	20.58	24.47	38.35	50.68	69.59	78.33	84.20	81.50	72.55	71.89	70.75	85.79	100.16	Claims on Central Government	**22a**
3.84	3.99	4.53	4.91	7.78	8.90	9.67	13.15	13.01	12.91	14.80	15.24	15.95	16.37	17.58	Claims on Local Government	**22b**
244.52	272.27	306.67	334.55	348.75	372.22	415.63	450.77	474.89	531.94	607.32	617.22	643.28	714.84	757.20	Claims on Private Sector	**22d**
67.91	71.54	75.47	75.92	79.02	84.73	91.87	97.84	109.89	126.60	139.61	147.04	160.24	188.58	214.93	Demand Deposits	**24**
156.35	177.06	207.78	230.30	241.87	266.81	301.19	326.97	342.32	348.69	377.66	380.37	392.79	449.05	464.64	Savings & Fgn Currency Deposits	**25**
87.33	76.73	74.38	82.41	81.13	87.68	82.23	105.94	97.52	113.51	146.31	160.94	122.40	129.33	157.63	Foreign Liabilities	**26c**
1.82	1.84	2.08	3.23	2.08	1.41	2.44	2.78	6.19	4.22	6.63	5.89	11.59	4.17	4.12	Central Government Deposits	**26d**
20.82	29.62	31.45	35.77	48.74	54.50	74.83	87.70	104.04	135.63	139.12	137.51	156.78	180.54	188.84	Other Items (Net)	**27r**
															Monetary Survey	
End of Period																
-13.11	-4.75	-2.14	-4.01	-11.22	-15.49	-13.94	-14.99	5.98	11.55	-10.91	-2.67	23.31	46.35	45.58	Foreign Assets (Net)	**31n**
275.68	301.89	337.28	366.66	402.05	445.64	507.67	554.86	578.31	628.15	697.75	700.04	724.22	805.85	861.05	Domestic Credit	**32**
27.32	25.63	26.07	27.21	45.52	64.52	82.36	90.94	90.41	83.30	75.64	67.58	64.99	74.64	86.26	Claims on Central Govt. (Net)	**32an**
3.84	3.99	4.53	4.91	7.78	8.90	9.67	13.15	13.01	12.91	14.80	15.24	15.95	16.37	17.58	Claims on Local Government	**32b**
244.52	272.27	306.67	334.55	348.75	372.22	415.63	450.77	474.89	531.94	607.32	617.22	643.28	714.84	757.20	Claims on Private Sector	**32d**
85.66	90.67	95.90	97.06	101.35	108.54	117.58	125.32	138.07	155.56	169.92	179.58	199.24	225.19	253.80	Money	**34**
156.35	177.06	207.78	230.30	241.87	266.81	301.19	326.97	342.32	348.69	377.66	380.37	392.79	449.05	464.64	Quasi-Money	**35**
20.56	29.40	31.45	35.29	47.61	54.80	74.96	87.58	103.90	135.45	139.27	137.42	155.51	177.96	188.18	Other Items (Net)	**37r**
242.01	267.74	303.68	327.36	343.22	375.35	418.77	452.29	480.40	504.25	547.57	559.95	592.03	674.24	718.44	Money plus Quasi-Money	**35l**
															Other Banking Institutions	
End of Period																
11.83	12.59	13.42	14.44	16.04	16.80	14.95	14.94	16.77	16.57	15.45	16.93	19.56	20.98	12.19	Reserves	**40**
3.87	4.84	6.87	8.49	9.25	8.96	7.55	6.74	7.41	7.58	5.18	5.47	6.49	1.35	3.30	Claims on Central Government	**42a**
1.85	2.47	2.02	2.28	2.48	3.04	2.13	1.63	1.48	1.33	1.26	.94	.84	1.02	3.26	Claims on State and Local Govts	**42b**
123.55	142.86	162.09	173.64	177.50	177.59	148.62	141.24	140.10	144.18	132.09	133.94	135.34	103.52	111.39	Claims on Private Sector	**42d**
8.92	9.87	11.51	11.43	11.62	11.45	9.47	8.96	8.37	8.69	7.87	8.07	8.11	.13	.19	Demand Deposits	**44**
121.48	140.20	158.62	173.21	177.00	178.95	148.27	141.95	143.53	145.42	131.64	136.34	141.39	116.16	123.39	Time and Savings Deposits	**45**
1.23	1.04	.94	1.03	1.87	1.00	.80	1.01	1.29	3.07	1.63	2.06	2.57	.03	.04	Money Market Instruments	**46aa**
7.71	8.94	10.12	11.03	11.45	11.22	10.27	9.40	9.54	9.84	9.60	9.91	10.18	9.32	10.13	Capital Accounts	**47a**
1.76	2.71	3.23	2.15	3.34	3.76	4.43	3.22	3.03	2.63	3.23	.91	-.03	1.22	-3.62	Other Items (Net)	**47r**
															Banking Survey	
End of Period																
-13.11	-4.75	-2.14	-4.01	-11.22	-15.49	-13.94	-14.99	5.98	11.55	-10.91	-2.67	23.31	46.35	45.58	Foreign Assets (Net)	**51n**
404.94	452.06	508.26	551.07	591.29	635.23	665.97	704.48	727.30	781.23	836.28	840.38	866.88	911.74	979.00	Domestic Credit	**52**
31.18	30.47	32.94	35.70	54.77	73.47	89.91	97.68	97.82	90.88	80.82	73.05	71.48	75.99	89.56	Claims on Central Govt. (Net)	**52an**
5.69	6.46	6.56	7.19	10.27	11.95	11.80	14.79	14.49	14.23	16.06	16.18	16.79	17.39	20.85	Claims on State and Local Govts	**52b**
368.07	415.13	468.77	508.19	526.25	549.81	564.25	592.01	614.99	676.11	739.40	751.15	778.62	818.35	868.60	Claims on Private Sector	**52d**
360.57	405.22	460.38	497.56	515.79	548.96	561.57	588.27	615.53	641.79	671.64	687.42	721.97	769.56	829.83	Liquid Liabilities	**55l**
1.23	1.04	.94	1.03	1.87	1.00	.80	1.01	1.29	3.07	1.63	2.06	2.57	.03	.04	Money Market Instruments	**56aa**
30.03	41.05	44.81	48.46	62.40	69.78	89.66	100.21	116.47	147.92	152.11	148.24	165.66	188.51	194.70	Other Items (Net)	**57r**
															Nonbank Financial Institutions	
End of Period																
.04	.12	.08	.10	.09	.11	.16	.13	.37	.07	.23	1.25	†1.58	1.93	3.83	Reserves	**40..n**
....	....	....	....	....	....	....	....	....	....	....	....	.04	.02	.02	Claims on Central Government	**42a.n**
18.82	19.58	22.30	22.50	20.33	19.11	17.76	20.40	21.45	24.13	33.01	38.64	†53.41	47.79	49.41	Claims on Private Sector	**42d.n**
....	....	....	....	....	....	....	....	....	....	....	....	.17	.08	.07	Claims on Deposit Money Banks	**42e.n**
8.39	8.13	10.06	9.11	7.31	6.73	6.20	8.50	8.89	10.57	16.71	18.80	†28.87	24.19	16.20	Money Market Instruments	**46aan**
6.89	8.38	8.27	9.25	9.73	8.94	8.83	9.45	11.12	11.41	16.83	23.41	†33.80	32.29	36.04	Bonds	**46abn**
.58	.69	.59	.23	.25	.30	.34	.30	.28	.21	.36	.36	†3.34	4.74	4.00	Cred. from Deposit Money Banks	**46h.n**
2.19	2.48	2.50	2.54	3.24	2.99	2.74	2.92	3.15	3.51	3.28	3.67	†6.31	10.74	11.57	Capital Accounts	**47a.n**
.81	.02	.96	1.47	-.11	.28	-.18	-.64	-1.61	-1.49	-3.94	-6.35	†-17.12	-22.14	-14.49	Other Items (Net)	**47r.n**

Canada

		1972	1973	1974	1975	1976	1977	1978	1979	1980	1981	1982	1983	1984	1985	1986
Interest Rates															*Percent Per Annum*	
Bank Rate (End of Period)	60	4.75	7.25	8.75	9.00	8.50	7.50	10.75	14.00	17.26	14.66	10.26	10.04	10.16	9.49	8.49
Money Market Rate	60b	...	...	...	7.41	9.15	7.23	7.52	11.23	13.28	18.14	14.35	9.62	10.91	9.57	9.30
Corporate Paper Rate	60bc	5.10	7.45	10.51	7.94	9.17	7.48	8.83	12.07	13.15	18.33	14.15	9.45	11.19	9.56	9.16
Treasury Bill Rate	60c	3.56	5.47	7.82	7.40	8.87	7.33	8.68	11.69	12.79	17.72	13.66	9.31	11.06	9.43	8.97
Deposit Rate	60l	5.36	6.87	9.97	7.78	9.31	7.53	8.83	12.05	12.87	18.16	13.74	7.91	10.06	8.40	8.25
Lending Rate	60p	6.00	7.65	10.75	9.42	10.04	8.50	9.69	12.90	14.25	19.29	15.81	11.17	12.06	10.58	10.52
Govt. Bond Yield: Med.-Term	61a	6.26	6.98	8.12	7.72	8.35	7.90	9.00	10.42	12.37	15.68	14.00	10.61	11.91	10.39	9.21
Long-Term	61	7.23	7.56	8.90	9.04	9.18	8.70	9.27	10.21	12.48	15.22	14.26	11.79	12.75	11.04	9.52
Prices, Production, Labor															*Index Numbers (1995=100):*	
Industrial Share Prices	62	25.7	27.4	22.9	22.6	23.3	22.8	26.1	35.6	47.9	48.7	37.0	53.4	52.8	61.2	67.9
Prices: Industry Selling	63	24.9	27.7	32.9	36.6	38.5	41.5	45.4	52.0	58.9	64.9	69.3	71.7	74.9	77.0	77.6
Consumer Prices	64	25.0	26.9	29.8	33.1	35.6	38.4	41.8	45.6	50.3	†56.6	62.7	66.3	69.2	71.9	74.9
Wages: Hourly Earnings (Mfg)	65ey	21.3	23.2	26.3	30.4	34.6	38.3	41.1	44.7	49.2	55.1	61.6	†65.9	69.0	71.6	73.7
Industrial Production	66..c	58.5	64.3	66.5	62.5	65.9	67.4	70.2	†74.3	71.8	73.3	66.1	70.4	78.9	83.3	†83.3
Gold Production	66kr	43.6	41.0	35.7	34.1	35.5	36.4	36.4	34.5	33.1	31.8	43.7	49.6	56.3	59.1	69.5
Manufacturing Employment	67ey	109.5	114.9	118.4	111.8	113.3	111.8	112.9	116.3	114.1	114.9	104.1	†101.2	103.6	105.9	109.6
															Number in Thousands:	
Labor Force	67d	...	...	...	...	...	...	...	...	...	...	...	...	...		
Employment	67e	...	...	...	...	...	...	...	...	...	...	...	...	...	11,742	12,095
Unemployment	67c	...	...	...	...	...	...	...	...	...	...	...	...	...	1,381	1,283
Unemployment Rate (%)	67r	...	...	...	...	...	...	...	...	...	...	...	...	...	10.5	9.6
International Transactions															*Millions of Canadian Dollars*	
Exports	70	20,955	26,438	33,743	34,662	40,015	46,337	55,311	68,269	79,208	87,164	87,911	94,603	116,965	124,249	125,497
Imports, f.o.b.	71.v	19,231	24,027	32,674	35,761	38,619	43,634	51,613	64,756	71,353	81,867	69,892	77,855	98,339	107,477	115,887
															1995=100	
Volume of Exports	72	28.4	31.4	30.2	28.0	31.4	34.2	37.6	38.3	37.8	†38.8	38.6	41.4	49.1	52.3	†54.7
Volume of Imports	73	28.2	32.8	36.1	34.1	36.8	37.0	38.2	42.4	40.0	†41.1	34.4	38.2	45.7	50.4	†54.5
Unit Value of Exports	74	21.5	24.8	33.9	37.7	39.2	42.8	46.8	58.1	72.6	†77.5	78.1	78.1	81.4	82.2	†80.6
Unit Value of Imports	75	21.8	23.7	30.3	34.9	35.8	41.0	46.5	55.0	65.7	†74.9	78.1	77.6	82.0	84.9	†84.4
Balance of Payments															*Millions of US Dollars:*	
Current Account, n.i.e.	78ald	−2,405	−2,056	−4,570	−8,196	−7,639	−7,003	−8,188	−8,385	−6,088	−12,505	1,816	−2,543	−1,368	−5,734	−11,157
Goods: Exports f.o.b.	78aad	21,177	26,500	34,277	33,780	39,696	42,883	47,942	57,300	67,532	71,931	70,259	75,376	89,283	89,913	90,097
Goods: Imports f.o.b.	78abd	−19,041	−23,357	−32,518	−34,371	−38,144	−39,990	−43,876	−53,379	−59,593	−66,466	−55,162	−61,200	−73,672	−78,045	−82,915
Trade Balance	78acd	2,135	3,144	1,759	−591	1,553	2,893	4,066	3,921	7,939	5,464	15,097	14,176	15,611	11,867	7,182
Services: Credit	78add	2,789	3,233	4,163	4,313	5,017	5,002	5,469	6,495	7,445	8,385	8,036	8,750	9,235	9,827	11,806
Services: Debit	78aed	−3,924	−4,578	−5,734	−6,797	−8,086	−8,405	−8,868	−9,232	−10,666	−11,964	−11,628	−12,545	−13,147	−13,912	−15,858
Balance on Goods & Services	78afd	1,000	1,798	189	−3,076	−1,516	−510	667	1,184	4,717	1,886	11,505	10,381	11,699	7,782	3,130
Income: Credit	78agd	1,271	2,723	3,926	3,492	3,266	3,981	4,312	7,679	7,868	9,157	11,283	11,283	10,868	9,837	8,036
Income: Debit	78ahd	−4,559	−6,477	−8,583	−8,357	−9,205	−10,253	−12,862	−17,055	−18,631	−23,522	−20,846	−20,724	−23,278	−22,653	−22,046
Balance on Gds, Serv. & Inc.	78aid	−2,288	−1,956	−4,468	−7,941	−7,455	−6,782	−7,883	−8,191	−6,046	−12,480	1,942	−2,205	−711	−5,033	−10,880
Current Transfers, n.i.e.: Credit	78ajd	465	539	681	709	787	813	844	1,037	1,310	1,389	1,463	1,362	1,296	1,234	1,868
Current Transfers: Debit	78akd	−583	−639	−783	−965	−971	−1,033	−1,149	−1,230	−1,352	−1,414	−1,589	−1,700	−1,954	−1,935	−2,145
Capital Account, n.i.e.	78bcd	284	345	550	486	530	429	111	465	424	527	1,262	1,085	1,058	1,066	1,313
Capital Account: n.i.e.: Credit	78bad	448	520	717	653	737	649	541	682	552	658	1,407	1,241	1,208	1,288	1,551
Capital Account: Debit	78bbd	−164	−176	−167	−167	−207	−220	−429	−218	−129	−131	−145	−155	−149	−223	−238
Financial Account, n.i.e.	78bjd	3,830	1,995	4,934	7,873	10,699	6,621	5,084	9,169	5,008	16,663	−2,786	4,187	4,092	5,650	10,801
Direct Investment Abroad	78bdd	−80	−1,166	−1,357	−1,249	−1,003	−1,631	−2,277	−3,829	−4,093	−5,546	−2,371	−2,629	−3,663	−3,864	−3,504
Dir. Invest. in Rep. Econ., n.i.e.	78bed	2,112	3,185	3,723	3,386	2,451	3,372	3,740	5,308	5,813	664	90	1,999	4,754	1,357	2,849
Portfolio Investment Assets	78bfd	246	71	49	−20	79	207	25	−496	−154	−24	−439	−1,035	−1,600	−1,400	−2,106
Equity Securities	78bkd	275	118	69	40	21	228	67	−522	−97	2	−250	−669	−559	−855	−1,974
Debt Securities	78bld	−29	−48	−20	−60	58	−21	−42	27	−57	−26	−189	−366	−1,040	−545	−132
Portfolio Investment Liab., n.i.e.	78bgd	1,211	742	1,971	4,797	9,823	5,383	2,544	3,370	5,388	10,126	8,511	5,784	7,369	7,681	17,853
Equity Securities	78bmd	−24	13	−142	85	−57	−97	−235	451	1,283	−528	−250	740	117	1,133	1,342
Debt Securities	78bnd	1,235	729	2,112	4,712	9,880	5,481	2,779	2,919	4,106	10,655	8,761	5,044	7,252	6,548	16,512
Financial Derivatives Assets	78bwd	...	...	...	...	...	...	...	...	...	...	...	...	...	...	...
Financial Derivatives Liabilities	78bxd	...	...	...	...	...	...	...	...	...	...	...	...	...	...	...
Other Investment Assets	78bhd	−2,162	−5,359	−1,944	−1,031	−4,899	−4,052	−6,641	−6,859	−13,962	−12,770	−5,498	−3,943	−5,481	−230	−8,196
Monetary Authorities	78bod	...	...	...	...	...	...	...	...	...	...	...	...	...	...	...
General Government	78bpd	−214	−227	−318	−333	−422	−472	−209	−442	−410	−491	−364	−502	−480	−479	−477
Banks	78bqd	−1,273	−3,880	−1,501	116	−3,262	−880	−3,479	−4,010	−10,293	−4,432	−108	−3,525	−1,610	−909	−6,247
Other Sectors	78brd	−675	−1,252	−124	−814	−1,215	−2,700	−2,953	−2,406	−3,260	−7,847	−5,025	84	−3,391	1,158	−1,473
Other Investment Liab., n.i.e.	78bid	2,502	4,523	2,492	1,990	4,248	3,341	7,693	11,674	12,016	24,213	−3,079	4,011	2,713	2,107	3,906
Monetary Authorities	78bsd	—	—	—	—	—	—	—	—	—	—	—	—	—	—	—
General Government	78btd	8	63	98	−49	118	569	1,686	−405	509	−85	−492	−117	−1	1,570	−1,248
Banks	78bud	1,981	3,544	687	947	2,463	2,268	4,727	9,022	10,920	18,739	−2,893	3,590	2,242	1,628	4,865
Other Sectors	78bvd	513	916	1,708	1,091	1,667	504	1,280	3,057	587	5,559	306	538	471	−1,091	289
Net Errors and Omissions	78cad	−1,459	−751	−889	−560	−3,021	−1,403	−2,118	−1,133	121	−3,712	−1,880	−2,737	−5,591	−4,252	−1,376
Overall Balance	78cbd	249	−468	25	−398	569	−1,356	−5,111	116	−536	973	−1,588	−7	−1,809	−3,270	−419
Reserves and Related Items	79dad	−249	468	−25	398	−569	1,356	5,111	−116	536	−973	1,588	7	1,809	3,270	419
Reserve Assets	79dbd	−249	468	−25	398	−569	1,356	183	900	−84	−387	496	−490	854	63	−636
Use of Fund Credit and Loans	79dcd	—	—	—	—	—	—	—	—	—	—	—	—	—	—	—
Exceptional Financing	79ded	...	...	...	...	...	...	4,928	−1,015	620	−586	1,092	497	956	3,207	1,055

	1987	1988	1989	1990	1991	1992	1993	1994	1995	1996	1997	1998	1999	2000	2001		
Percent Per Annum																**Interest Rates**	
	8.66	11.17	12.47	11.78	7.67	7.36	4.11	7.43	5.79	3.25	4.50	5.25	5.00	6.00	2.50	Bank Rate (*End of Period*)	60
	8.03	9.21	11.91	12.90	8.97	6.64	4.63	5.05	6.92	4.33	3.26	4.87	4.74	5.52	4.11	Money Market Rate	60b
	8.38	9.67	12.21	13.03	8.91	6.74	4.97	5.66	7.22	4.35	3.61	5.05	4.94	5.71	3.87	Corporate Paper Rate	60bc
	8.15	9.48	12.05	12.81	8.73	6.59	4.84	5.54	6.89	4.21	3.26	4.73	4.72	5.49	3.77	Treasury Bill Rate	60c
	7.67	9.54	12.09	12.81	8.62	6.67	4.92	5.59	7.15	4.33	3.59	5.03	4.91	5.70	3.86	Deposit Rate	60l
	9.52	10.83	13.33	14.06	9.94	7.48	5.94	6.88	8.65	6.06	4.96	6.60	6.44	7.27	5.81	Lending Rate	60p
	9.42	9.77	10.20	11.19	9.16	7.43	6.46	7.79	7.64	6.21	5.33	5.16	5.50	5.99	4.88	Govt. Bond Yield: Med.-Term	61a
	9.95	10.22	9.92	10.85	9.76	8.77	7.85	8.63	8.28	7.50	6.42	5.47	5.69	5.89	5.78	Long-Term	61
Period Averages																**Prices, Production, Labor**	
	80.5	74.5	85.7	77.2	78.2	76.7	88.1	96.6	100.0	118.8	145.7	152.4	159.2	216.7	174.4	Industrial Share Prices	62
	79.8	83.2	84.9	85.2	84.3	84.7	87.8	93.1	100.0	100.4	101.3	101.2	102.9	108.1	†109.2	Prices: Industry Selling	63
	78.2	81.3	85.4	89.5	94.5	95.9	97.7	97.9	†100.0	101.6	103.2	104.2	106.0	108.9	111.7	Consumer Prices	64
	76.2	79.1	83.4	87.7	91.8	95.1	97.0	98.6	100.0	103.2	104.1	106.3	106.4	112.3	114.8	Wages: Hourly Earnings (Mfg)	65ey
	87.3	91.9	91.8	88.8	85.0	†86.0	89.9	95.7	100.0	101.4	†105.8	109.4	115.5	121.9	118.4	Industrial Production	66..c
	78.2	91.0	106.3	111.0	115.6	105.7	100.9	97.8	100.0	....	....	....	....	....	....	Gold Production	66kr
	114.6	117.4	119.7	112.6	101.0	95.5	95.3	97.5	100.0	102.4	106.1	110.3	112.8	120.6	120.1	Manufacturing Employment	67ey
Period Averages																	
	....	....	....	....	....	....	13,946	14,832	14,928	15,145	15,354	15,632	15,721	15,999	16,246	Labor Force	67d
	12,422	12,819	13,086	13,165	12,916	12,842	13,015	13,292	†13,506	13,676	13,941	14,326	14,531	14,910	15,077	Employment	67e
	1,208	1,082	1,065	1,164	1,492	1,640	1,649	1,541	†1,422	1,469	1,414	1,305	1,216	1,103	1,170	Unemployment	67c
	8.9	7.8	7.5	8.1	10.4	11.3	11.2	10.4	†9.6	9.7	9.2	8.3	†7.6	6.8	7.2	Unemployment Rate (%)	67r
Millions of Canadian Dollars																**International Transactions**	
	130,089	144,038	144,248	148,912	145,658	162,596	187,346	225,908	263,697	274,884	296,928	317,903	354,108	410,994	402,172	Exports	70
	119,725	135,416	138,406	140,329	139,427	152,435	175,049	206,626	224,977	232,672	271,422	298,076	319,008	354,728	343,311	Imports, f.o.b.	71.v
1995=100																	
	56.6	61.9	62.7	65.7	66.4	†72.2	81.1	90.8	100.0	106.1	†114.8	124.5	138.2	150.3	150.3	Volume of Exports	72
	57.9	66.1	69.7	69.8	71.4	†76.4	83.5	92.8	100.0	105.3	†125.0	132.7	144.3	158.0	158.0	Volume of Imports	73
	82.0	82.4	84.4	83.8	80.8	†82.7	86.5	92.6	100.0	100.6	†100.2	99.7	100.7	108.8	108.8	Unit Value of Exports	74
	83.3	81.9	82.2	83.7	82.5	†86.0	90.7	96.4	100.0	99.6	†100.3	103.7	103.6	106.0	106.0	Unit Value of Imports	75
Minus Sign Indicates Debit																**Balance of Payments**	
	-13,430	-14,818	-21,769	-19,764	-22,345	-21,160	-21,822	-13,024	-4,328	3,378	-8,233	-7,839	1,367	18,596	19,479	Current Account, n.i.e.	78al d
	99,187	116,693	124,130	130,328	128,914	135,153	147,418	166,990	193,373	205,443	219,063	220,539	247,240	286,476	267,915	Goods: Exports f.o.b.	78aa d
	-90,017	-107,843	-117,569	-120,815	-122,788	-127,772	-137,281	-152,155	-167,517	-174,352	-200,498	-204,617	-220,159	-244,714	-226,490	Goods: Imports f.o.b.	78ab d
	9,170	8,849	6,560	9,513	6,126	7,381	10,136	14,834	25,855	31,091	18,565	15,922	27,080	41,763	41,425	*Trade Balance*	78ac d
	13,083	15,680	17,550	19,210	20,368	20,785	21,868	23,958	26,128	29,243	31,596	33,836	35,715	38,496	36,576	Services: Credit	78ad d
	-17,646	-21,024	-24,425	-28,303	-30,326	-30,868	-32,446	-32,530	-33,473	-35,906	-38,013	-38,156	-40,517	-43,493	-42,000	Services: Debit	78ae d
	4,607	3,505	-315	419	-3,832	-2,702	-442	6,262	18,510	24,428	12,148	11,602	22,278	36,766	36,001	*Balance on Goods & Services*	78af d
	8,831	13,232	13,432	15,072	12,936	11,413	10,697	15,443	18,888	19,204	23,998	21,830	22,165	26,811	22,633	Income: Credit	78ag d
	-25,982	-30,706	-33,915	-34,460	-30,334	-28,925	-31,499	-34,382	-41,609	-40,755	-44,878	-41,815	-43,759	-45,970	-40,411	Income: Debit	78ah d
	-12,544	-13,968	-20,798	-18,968	-21,230	-20,214	-21,243	-12,676	-4,211	2,877	-8,732	-8,383	685	17,607	18,223	*Balance on Gds, Serv. & Inc.*	78ai d
	1,668	2,219	2,227	2,530	2,537	2,564	2,593	2,625	2,878	3,594	3,634	3,407	3,796	4,109	4,535	Current Transfers, n.i.e.: Credit	78aj d
	-2,554	-3,068	-3,198	-3,326	-3,652	-3,510	-3,172	-2,973	-2,995	-3,092	-3,135	-2,863	-3,114	-3,120	-3,280	Current Transfers: Debit	78ak d
	2,803	3,924	4,629	5,331	5,596	7,105	8,292	7,498	4,950	5,833	5,429	3,336	3,400	3,552	3,673	Capital Account, n.i.e.	78bc d
	3,076	4,324	5,096	6,203	6,069	7,470	8,908	7,876	5,416	6,262	5,862	3,794	3,858	4,044	4,163	Capital Account: Credit	78ba d
	-272	-400	-467	-872	-473	-365	-617	-378	-466	-429	-433	-457	-458	-492	-490	Capital Account: Debit	78bb d
	16,280	18,716	19,395	17,283	15,068	6,244	19,505	5,159	-1,277	-9,277	3,394	4,944	-6,470	-14,295	-15,008	Financial Account, n.i.e.	78bj d
	-7,121	-6,221	-5,270	-5,229	-5,837	-3,547	-5,711	-9,303	-11,490	-13,107	-23,069	-34,112	-15,623	-47,311	-35,567	Direct Investment Abroad	78bd d
	8,115	6,071	6,027	7,581	2,874	4,777	4,749	8,224	9,319	9,635	11,523	22,742	24,488	66,017	27,438	Dir. Invest. in Rep. Econ., n.i.e.	78be d
	-2,222	-3,659	-4,625	-2,239	-10,179	-9,800	-13,784	-6,587	-5,328	-14,183	-8,568	-15,106	-15,556	-41,866	-24,468	Portfolio Investment Assets	78bf d
	-1,561	-3,588	-3,269	-2,177	-8,736	-8,586	-9,886	-6,898	-4,570	-12,661	-3,777	-10,428	-13,888	-39,123	-23,239	Equity Securities	78bk d
	-661	-70	-1,356	-62	-1,442	-1,214	-3,898	311	-759	-1,522	-4,792	-4,678	-1,669	-2,743	-1,230	Debt Securities	78bl d
	12,405	18,671	19,674	15,964	27,527	20,506	41,352	17,155	18,402	13,718	11,692	16,590	2,315	9,875	19,750	Portfolio Investment Liab., n.i.e.	78bg d
	4,974	-1,935	3,287	-1,502	-856	830	9,334	4,718	-3,077	5,900	5,461	9,645	9,534	24,064	3,020	Equity Securities	78bm d
	7,431	20,606	16,386	17,466	28,383	19,676	32,018	12,437	21,479	7,818	6,230	6,945	-7,219	-14,189	16,730	Debt Securities	78bn d
	....	....	....	....	....	....	....	....	....	....	....	....	....	....	....	Financial Derivatives Assets	78bw d
	....	....	....	....	....	....	....	....	....	....	....	....	....	....	....	Financial Derivatives Liabilities	78bx d
	-162	3,668	-6,152	-8,442	934	-3,536	-415	-20,378	-8,328	-21,064	-16,167	9,400	9,395	-2,759	-8,940	Other Investment Assets	78bh d
																Monetary Authorities	78bo d
	-324	-293	-361	193	-359	-403	-230	-436	-336	-119	-515	-579	-305	-235	-127	General Government	78bp d
	1,121	5,599	-2,972	-3,936	5,852	-59	5,848	-12,575	-8,314	-13,847	-5,419	969	13,368	-7,301	-2,096	Banks	78bq d
	-960	-1,638	-2,820	-4,699	-4,559	-3,074	-6,033	-7,366	322	-7,098	-10,233	9,010	-3,668	4,776	-6,718	Other Sectors	78br d
	5,266	185	9,742	9,648	-251	-2,156	-6,686	16,049	-3,852	15,724	27,983	5,430	-11,489	1,749	6,780	Other Investment Liab., n.i.e.	78bi d
																Monetary Authorities	78bs d
	556	-860	-770	-389	-109	-278	-179	586	-484	-508	-321	-270	-318	-350	-237	General Government	78bt d
	1,716	-3,373	1,951	6,603	-2,075	-3,202	-6,649	15,233	-4,579	12,707	24,630	953	-16,200	-697	15,155	Banks	78bu d
	2,994	4,418	8,561	3,434	1,933	1,324	142	230	1,211	3,525	3,673	4,747	5,029	2,796	-8,137	Other Sectors	78bv d
	-2,340	328	-1,562	-1,710	-168	3,025	-5,070	-26	3,366	5,563	-2,983	4,555	7,637	-4,133	-5,972	Net Errors and Omissions	78ca d
	3,313	8,150	693	1,139	-1,848	-4,786	904	-392	2,711	5,498	-2,393	4,996	5,933	3,720	2,172	*Overall Balance*	78cb d
	-3,313	-8,150	-693	-1,139	1,848	4,786	-904	392	-2,711	-5,498	2,393	-4,996	-5,933	-3,720	-2,172	Reserves and Related Items	79da d
	-3,877	-8,150	-693	-1,139	1,848	4,786	-904	392	-2,711	-5,498	2,393	-4,996	-5,933	-3,720	-2,172	Reserve Assets	79db d
	—	—	—	—	—	—	—	—	—	—	—	—	—	—	—	Use of Fund Credit and Loans	79dc d
	564	....	....	....	....	....	....	....	....	....	....	....	....	....	....	Exceptional Financing	79de d

Canada

		1972	1973	1974	1975	1976	1977	1978	1979	1980	1981	1982	1983	1984	1985	1986
International Investment Position															*Millions of US Dollars*	
Assets	79aa d	33,409	40,050	44,068	45,920	52,790	56,111	63,786	72,964	92,330	110,267	114,079	117,462	124,866	129,772	146,175
Direct Investment Abroad	79ab d	7,107	8,290	9,790	10,912	11,997	13,005	14,589	18,487	23,783	30,071	30,474	35,830	39,941	43,143	46,935
Portfolio Investment	79ac d	3,370	3,656	3,879	4,181	4,576	4,854	5,403	7,035	7,943	8,407	8,660	10,231	11,981	13,735	16,143
Equity Securities	79ad d	2,822	3,053	3,254	3,512	3,934	4,176	4,667	6,321	7,163	7,587	7,574	8,627	9,164	10,052	11,911
Debt Securities	79ae d	547	604	626	669	642	678	736	714	780	820	1,085	1,604	2,817	3,682	4,231
Financial Derivatives	79af d	—	—	—	—	—	—	—	—	—	—	—	—	—	—	—
Other Investment	79af d	16,886	22,335	24,576	25,503	30,376	33,646	39,225	43,559	56,577	67,419	71,154	67,197	69,761	69,617	79,001
Monetary Authorities	79ag d	—	—	—	—	—	—	—	—	—	—	—	—	—	—	—
General Government	79ah d	2,829	3,126	3,966	4,474	4,597	4,944	5,413	6,485	7,117	7,913	9,804	9,653	10,492	10,479	10,296
Banks	79ai d	8,545	12,356	13,987	13,885	17,479	18,451	21,889	25,957	35,866	38,766	38,536	42,106	42,958	44,406	51,123
Other Sectors	79aj d	5,511	6,853	6,622	7,144	8,300	10,251	11,924	11,118	13,595	20,740	22,813	15,438	16,312	14,733	17,582
Reserve Assets	79ak d	6,047	5,769	5,823	5,324	5,842	4,606	4,569	3,883	4,027	4,370	3,792	4,205	3,183	3,277	4,096
Liabilities	79la d	68,471	77,874	86,630	95,538	113,537	118,844	138,070	161,272	184,635	224,727	225,190	233,435	241,715	257,023	288,742
Dir. Invest. in Rep. Economy	79lb d	30,698	34,120	37,890	38,103	41,244	41,239	42,234	48,613	54,163	59,303	59,227	64,022	65,070	64,657	69,579
Portfolio Investment	79lc d	18,931	20,255	22,541	28,854	38,616	41,413	50,524	56,504	62,211	71,968	79,132	83,279	88,501	98,995	121,362
Equity Securities	79ld d	4,707	5,191	5,470	6,119	6,331	6,666	6,709	8,820	11,247	11,671	10,704	9,904	9,869	10,829	11,769
Debt Securities	79le d	14,224	15,064	17,071	22,735	32,285	34,747	43,815	47,683	50,964	60,297	68,428	73,374	78,632	88,166	109,593
Financial Derivatives	79ll d															
Other Investment	79lf d	18,842	23,499	26,198	28,581	33,678	36,192	45,312	56,156	68,261	93,456	86,831	86,135	88,144	93,371	97,801
Monetary Authorities	79lg d	—	—	—	—	—	—	—	—	—	—	—	—	—	—	—
General Government	79lh d	169	249	297	282	338	943	1,543	2,957	2,910	3,057	2,441	2,506	3,012	4,354	4,837
Banks	79li d	9,136	12,689	13,429	14,316	16,830	19,073	25,465	33,255	44,286	63,554	59,645	63,199	64,883	67,905	72,531
Other Sectors	79lj d	9,537	10,561	12,472	13,983	16,510	16,176	18,304	19,943	21,066	26,845	24,745	20,431	20,249	21,112	20,433
Government Finance															*Billions of Canadian Dollars:*	
Deficit (-) or Surplus	80	−1.74	−1.70	†−1.97	−5.70	−6.30	−9.41	−11.95	−10.56	−10.73	−8.43	−20.81	−25.16	−28.87	−28.68	−20.11
Revenue	81	22.04	25.85	†31.62	34.89	37.72	38.24	41.64	48.22	57.49	72.28	73.24	77.33	85.30	91.10	99.21
Grants Received	81z	....	....	†—	—	—	—	—	—	—	—	—	—	—	—	.02
Expenditure	82	21.32	24.68	†30.08	36.00	39.69	45.06	50.51	55.54	65.52	76.15	89.36	98.81	111.38	117.20	119.33
Lending Minus Repayments	83	2.45	2.88	†3.51	4.59	4.33	2.59	3.08	3.23	2.70	4.56	4.68	3.67	2.79	2.58	.01
Financing																
Total Net Borrowing	84	2.25	1.37	†3.67	4.79	5.40	9.80	15.64	5.42	12.25	9.35	21.84	25.67	28.48	28.15	25.88
Net Domestic	84a	....	....	†3.73	4.82	5.40	9.80	9.59	6.50	10.50	8.02	20.59	24.50	20.38	22.89	15.62
Net Foreign	85a	....	....	†−.06	−.04	—	.01	6.05	−1.08	1.75	1.33	1.26	1.17	8.10	5.26	10.26
Use of Cash Balances	87	−.51	.33	†−1.70	.91	.89	−.39	−3.68	5.14	−1.51	−.92	−1.03	−.51	.40	.53	−5.78
Total Debt	88z	....	....	†34.73	39.45	44.10	53.54	69.08	74.34	86.14	95.28	117.19	145.97	177.17	205.61	231.28
Domestic	88a	....	....	†34.53	39.28	43.94	51.30	60.79	67.12	77.17	84.99	105.63	133.26	156.36	179.53	194.94
Foreign	89a	....	....	†.20	.16	.16	2.25	8.29	7.22	8.97	10.30	11.55	12.72	20.81	26.08	36.34
Other Finan.Institutions	88ac	2,220	1,971	....	....	....	....	....	....	....	....	....	....	....	....	....
Other Dom. Investors	88ae	13,613	13,102	....	....	....	....	....	....	....	....	....	....	....	....	....
Foreigners	88c	844	741	....	....	....	....	....	....	....	....	....	....	....	....	....
Intragovernmental Debt	88s	611	607	....	....	....	....	....	....	....	....	....	....	....	....	....
National Accounts															*Billions of Canadian dollars*	
Househ.Cons.Expend.,incl.NPISHs	96f. c	63.02	72.07	84.23	97.57	111.50	123.56	137.43	153.39	172.42	196.19	210.51	231.45	251.65	274.50	297.48
Government Consumption Expend.	91f. c	20.14	22.85	27.48	33.27	38.27	43.41	47.39	52.29	59.25	68.79	78.66	84.57	89.09	95.52	100.13
Gross Fixed Capital Formation	93e. c	23.88	28.86	35.78	41.85	46.71	50.23	54.58	63.44	72.29	86.12	81.33	81.23	84.70	94.20	101.56
Changes in Inventories	93i. c	.78	1.86	3.59	1.37	2.33	1.86	1.05	4.99	.34	1.19	−9.75	−2.85	4.76	2.28	2.56
Exports of Goods and Services	90c. c	23.74	29.77	37.81	38.95	44.25	51.18	61.15	75.07	87.58	96.88	96.65	103.44	126.04	134.92	138.12
Imports of Goods and Services (-)	98c. c	22.78	28.02	37.37	41.36	45.28	51.25	60.05	73.28	81.93	93.00	82.60	89.83	110.63	123.39	133.37
Gross Domestic Product (GDP)	99b. c	108.63	127.37	152.11	171.54	197.92	217.88	241.60	276.10	309.89	355.99	374.44	405.72	444.74	477.99	505.67
Net Primary Income from Abroad	98.n c	−1.46	−1.73	−2.24	−2.54	−3.54	−4.57	−5.95	−7.16	−7.83	−11.34	−12.67	−11.60	−13.49	−14.33	−16.40
Gross National Income (GNI)	99a. c	107.17	125.64	149.87	169.00	194.39	213.31	235.65	268.94	302.06	344.66	361.77	394.11	431.25	463.66	489.26
Gross Nat'l Disposable Inc.(GNDI)	99i. c	....	....	....	....	....	....	....	....	....	....	....	....	....	....	....
Gross Saving	99s. c	....	....	....	....	....	....	....	....	....	....	....	....	....	....	....
Consumption of Fixed Capital	99cf c	11.73	13.63	16.45	18.76	21.45	23.80	26.62	30.74	35.53	40.68	44.36	47.06	50.88	55.93	60.60
GDP Volume 1986 Prices	99b. r	303.45	326.85	341.24	350.11	371.69	385.12	402.74	418.33	424.54	440.13	425.97	439.45	467.17	489.44	505.67
GDP Volume 1992 Prices	99b. r	....	....	....	....	....	....	....	....	....	....	....	....	....	....	....
GDP Volume 1997 Ref., Chained	99b. r	....	....	....	....	....	....	....	....	....	....	....	....	....	....	....
GDP Volume (1995=100)	99bv r	49.3	53.1	55.4	56.9	60.4	62.5	65.4	67.9	68.9	71.5	69.2	71.4	75.9	79.5	82.1
GDP Deflator (1995=100)	99bi r	27.1	29.5	33.8	37.1	40.4	42.9	45.5	50.0	55.3	61.3	66.6	70.0	72.2	74.0	75.8
																Millions:
Population	99z	21.83	22.07	22.40	22.73	23.03	23.28	23.49	23.70	24.04	24.34	24.58	24.79	24.98	25.16	25.35

International Investment Position

Millions of US Dollars

1987	1988	1989	1990	1991	1992	1993	1994	1995	1996	1997	1998	1999	2000	2001		
163,760	184,684	205,558	227,461	243,944	234,853	246,426	282,944	324,692	371,736	413,614	442,218	484,282	519,459	....	Assets	79aa d
57,037	66,876	77,605	84,808	94,382	87,870	92,468	104,302	118,105	132,329	149,453	167,035	187,197	200,878	....	Direct Investment Abroad	79ab d
20,600	25,917	31,132	34,641	43,773	45,380	53,200	59,601	66,487	79,054	88,816	100,576	121,911	141,382	....	Portfolio Investment	79ac d
14,744	19,490	22,510	25,870	34,021	35,204	39,982	46,543	52,700	63,529	70,026	78,708	101,080	118,237	....	Equity Securities	79ad d
5,856	6,427	8,622	8,771	9,753	10,175	13,218	13,057	13,787	15,525	18,790	21,868	20,831	23,146	....	Debt Securities	79ae d
														....	Financial Derivatives	79al d
77,929	75,694	80,018	89,438	88,889	89,696	88,007	106,564	124,885	139,761	157,361	151,140	146,442	145,333	....	Other Investment	79af d
														....	Monetary Authorities	79ag d
10,799	11,457	12,121	13,124	14,459	15,341	14,966	15,419	15,656	15,868	16,759	18,716	20,835	21,983	....	General Government	79ah d
50,861	44,628	46,961	50,345	43,931	43,015	37,279	49,976	60,268	73,657	75,960	74,501	61,464	65,042	....	Banks	79ai d
16,269	19,609	20,936	25,968	30,499	31,339	35,762	41,170	48,961	50,236	64,643	57,922	64,143	58,308	....	Other Sectors	79aj d
8,194	16,197	16,803	18,575	16,900	11,908	12,751	12,476	15,216	20,591	17,984	23,467	28,732	31,866	....	Reserve Assets	79ak d
327,309	365,706	406,007	445,099	475,328	469,385	490,942	520,374	562,156	599,081	626,343	649,397	671,838	681,927	....	Liabilities	79la d
81,502	95,728	105,945	112,844	117,025	108,503	106,868	110,204	123,181	132,978	138,717	144,820	170,983	194,320	....	Dir. Invest. in Rep. Economy	79lb d
139,002	162,355	182,392	202,704	228,222	234,585	266,961	281,767	309,774	323,661	323,553	338,170	342,806	331,073	....	Portfolio Investment	79lc d
14,001	15,184	17,791	17,806	15,269	14,083	17,685	22,001	27,170	34,537	35,944	42,208	48,637	57,285	....	Equity Securities	79ld d
125,001	147,171	164,600	184,898	212,953	220,502	249,276	259,766	282,604	289,125	287,609	295,961	294,169	273,788	....	Debt Securities	79le d
														....	Financial Derivatives	79ll d
106,805	107,623	117,671	129,551	130,081	126,297	117,113	128,403	129,201	142,442	164,073	166,407	158,048	156,533	....	Other Investment	79lf d
														....	Monetary Authorities	79lg d
6,475	5,555	4,416	4,177	4,254	3,819	3,889	4,568	4,059	3,334	2,790	2,648	2,544	2,020	....	General Government	79lh d
75,966	72,594	74,889	82,598	80,132	75,630	68,757	83,691	79,735	92,486	115,623	118,008	105,158	102,565	....	Banks	79li d
24,364	29,473	38,366	42,776	45,696	46,849	44,468	40,145	45,407	46,622	45,660	45,751	50,346	51,948	....	Other Sectors	79lj d

Government Finance

Year Beginning April 1

1987	1988	1989	1990	1991	1992	1993	1994	1995	1996	1997	1998	1999	2000	2001		
-14.00	†-23.49	-24.89	-31.77	-37.80	-42.13	-42.63	-36.63	-29.13	-15.55	5.33	2.92	8.98	14.15	....	Deficit (-) or Surplus	80
111.55	†124.89	137.31	144.24	149.37	150.21	148.42	157.67	164.35	174.51	188.91	195.30	209.14	225.14	....	Revenue	81
.11	†.37	.44	.46	.49	.46	.54	.53	.52	.54	.52	.50	.56	.57	....	Grants Received	81z
127.08	†149.55	163.50	175.02	187.28	191.39	191.20	196.04	199.90	190.91	186.95	193.58	201.44	210.96	....	Expenditure	82
-1.41	†-.80	-.86	1.45	.38	1.40	.39	-1.20	-5.91	-.31	-2.85	-.70	-.72	.60	....	Lending Minus Repayments	83
															Financing	
22.14	†28.52	25.66	38.61	38.08	38.49	45.41	34.78	39.50	19.43	-6.42	8.38	3.18	-1.13	....	Total Net Borrowing	84
14.29	†25.58	23.04	37.31	37.00	40.46	50.67	41.03	39.39	25.64	-2.26	17.20	-.20	-.55	....	Net Domestic	84a
7.85	†2.94	2.63	1.30	1.08	-1.97	-5.26	-6.25	.11	-6.21	-4.17	-8.82	3.38	-.58	....	Net Foreign	85a
-8.13	†-5.03	-.78	-6.83	-.28	3.64	-2.79	1.85	-10.37	-3.88	1.10	-11.31	-12.15	-13.02	....	Use of Cash Balances	87
253.36	†380.00	406.61	444.56	476.10	514.36	557.60	595.88	634.94	651.24	646.08	651.89	650.77	644.22	....	Total Debt	88z
209.76	†369.21	398.42	437.39	469.93	506.39	544.61	577.02	616.23	626.43	617.08	614.23	616.78	610.41	....	Domestic	88a
43.60	†10.79	8.19	7.17	6.17	7.97	13.00	18.86	18.71	24.81	29.00	37.65	33.99	33.82	....	Foreign	89a
....	....	....	....	....	....	....	....	....	....	....	....	....	....	....	Other Finan.Institutions	88ac
....	....	....	....	....	....	....	....	....	....	....	....	....	....	....	Other Dom. Investors	88ae
....	....	....	....	....	....	....	....	....	....	....	....	....	....	....	Foreigners	88c
....	....	....	....	....	....	....	....	....	....	....	....	....	....	....	Intragovernmental Debt	88s

National Accounts

Billions of Canadian Dollars Adjusted at Annual Rates

1987	1988	1989	1990	1991	1992	1993	1994	1995	1996	1997	1998	1999	2000	2001		
322.77	349.94	378.94	394.32	399.93	412.94	430.16	447.75	462.87	482.37	512.86	534.39	561.57	594.09	620.78	Househ.Cons.Expend.,incl.NPISHs	96f. c
105.79	114.47	124.11	135.15	162.43	168.93	171.27	171.73	172.65	171.35	171.88	176.84	183.29	196.00	204.49	Government Consumption Expend.	91f. c
116.72	132.79	146.08	141.38	134.41	131.23	131.07	144.96	143.00	149.94	174.84	181.62	193.83	209.94	216.49	Gross Fixed Capital Formation	93e. c
3.07	3.80	3.62	-2.84	-5.88	-6.56	-.95	.45	8.91	2.34	8.18	5.79	3.91	8.05	-6.03	Changes in Inventories	93i. c
145.42	159.31	163.90	168.92	172.16	189.78	219.66	262.13	302.48	321.25	348.60	377.35	418.54	484.33	473.00	Exports of Goods and Services	90c. c
140.50	156.38	166.09	171.13	176.09	192.39	219.67	253.01	276.62	287.55	331.27	360.26	386.03	428.93	416.50	Imports of Goods and Services (-)	98c. c
551.60	605.91	650.75	669.51	686.97	702.39	729.58	772.83	812.46	839.06	885.02	915.87	975.26	1,065.00	1,092.25	Gross Domestic Product (GDP)	99b. c
-16.45	-18.71	-21.50	-23.86	-22.85	-25.40	-25.17	-27.99	-28.55	-28.33	-27.70	-30.04	-29.51	-22.37	-24.37	Net Primary Income from Abroad	98.n c
535.15	587.19	629.25	645.61	664.12	677.00	704.41	744.83	783.91	810.73	857.32	885.83	945.75	1,042.63	1,067.88	Gross National Income (GNI)	99a. c
....	....	....	....	662.85	675.86	703.67	744.36	783.75	811.42	858.02	886.57	946.88	1,044.10	1,069.83	Gross Nat'l Disposable Inc.(GNDI)	99i. c
....	....	....	....	....	....	....	....	....	....	....	187.46	198.21	217.22	211.12	Gross Saving	99s. c
64.12	68.13	72.35	78.59	85.91	89.57	94.04	99.63	105.02	110.82	116.57	122.30	127.72	135.78	144.32	Consumption of Fixed Capital	99cf c
527.23	552.96	566.49	565.16	555.05	559.31	....							....		GDP Volume 1986 Prices	99b. r
					698.54	714.58	748.35	769.08	782.13	813.03	842.00	880.25	....		GDP Volume 1992 Prices	99b. r
											....	966.36	1,009.18	1,024.20	GDP Volume 1997 Ref., Chained	99b. r
85.6	89.8	92.0	91.8	90.1	†90.8	92.9	97.3	100.0	101.7	105.7	109.5	†114.5	119.5	121.3	GDP Volume (1995=100)	99bv r
79.3	83.0	87.1	89.8	93.8	95.2	96.6	97.8	100.0	101.6	103.0	103.0	104.9	109.7	110.8	GDP Deflator (1995=100)	99bi r

Midyear Estimates

1987	1988	1989	1990	1991	1992	1993	1994	1995	1996	1997	1998	1999	2000	2001		
25.62	26.89	27.29	27.70	28.03	28.38	28.70	29.04	29.35	29.67	29.99	30.25	30.50	30.77	31.08	Population	99z

(See notes in the back of the book.)

Cape Verde

		1972	1973	1974	1975	1976	1977	1978	1979	1980	1981	1982	1983	1984	1985	1986
Exchange Rates															*Escudos per SDR:*	
Official Rate	aa	29.314	31.178	30.114	32.160	36.655	41.179	46.822	50.467	54.192	59.199	69.540	83.730	91.174	93.778	93.654
															Escudos per US Dollar:	
Official Rate	ae	27.000	25.845	24.596	27.472	31.549	33.900	35.940	38.310	42.490	50.860	63.040	79.975	93.015	85.375	76.565
Official Rate	rf	27.053	24.515	25.408	25.543	30.229	34.046	35.501	37.433	40.175	48.695	58.293	71.686	84.878	91.632	80.145
Fund Position															*Millions of SDRs:*	
Quota	2f. s	...	...	...	...	...	...	2.00	2.00	3.00	3.00	3.00	4.50	4.50	4.50	4.50
SDRs	1b. s	...	...	...	...	...	...	—	.01	—	.18	.15	.11	.10	.10	.10
Reserve Position in the Fund	1c. s	...	...	...	...	...	...	—	.32	.58	.58	.58	.95	.95	.95	
Total Fund Cred.&Loans Outstg.	2tl	...	...	...	...	...	...									
International Liquidity													*Millions of US Dollars Unless Otherwise Indicated:*			
Total Reserves minus Gold	1l. d					32.70	42.02	39.37	42.32	42.40	37.83	42.74	45.90	40.99	55.36	56.36
SDRs	1b. d							—	.01	—	.21	.17	.12	.10	.11	.12
Reserve Position in the Fund	1c. d							—	.42	.74	.68	.64	.99	.93	1.04	
Foreign Exchange	1d. d					32.70	42.02	39.37	41.89	41.66	36.94	41.93	44.79	39.96	54.20	56.24
Monetary Authorities: Other Liab.	4..d					.47	.11	2.27	1.75	.42	2.14	3.36	7.32	2.87	8.02	.93
Deposit Money Banks: Assets	7a. d															
Liabilities	7b. d															
Monetary Authorities															*Millions of Escudos:*	
Foreign Assets	11					1,031.5	1,424.6	1,414.9	1,621.4	1,801.6	1,924.0	2,694.3	3,671.1	3,812.7	4,726.2	4,315.2
Claims on Central Government	12a					87.9	91.8	91.8	121.8	157.0	548.1	547.7	669.0	727.1	938.0	1,248.8
Claims on Local Government	12b					—	—	.9	.6	3.5	19.6	31.8	32.9	34.9	32.2	34.5
Claims on Nonfin.Pub.Enterprises	12c					—	—	125.3	142.8	587.1	770.6	1,046.1	1,030.0	1,346.1	1,483.4	1,517.3
Claims on Private Sector	12d					316.4	308.3	435.0	591.1	506.3	720.3	802.6	1,222.8	1,437.6	2,110.2	2,565.1
Claims on Deposit Money Banks	12e															
Claims on Other Banking Insts	12f					1.5	1.5	1.5	1.5	1.5	1.5	1.5	1.5	1.5	—	—
Claims on Nonbank Financial Insts	12g															
Reserve Money	14					1,000.4	1,411.3	1,614.8	1,822.6	2,302.0	2,552.7	3,227.8	3,956.2	4,201.6	4,843.2	5,620.6
of which: Currency Outside DMBs	14a					464.8	537.2	638.3	736.4	872.2	1,040.5	1,251.9	1,332.9	1,433.6	1,628.1	1,826.4
Time & Foreign Currency Deposits	15					17.1	23.8	52.3	135.2	254.1	486.1	616.1	628.3	914.7	1,297.1	1,966.0
Foreign Liabilities	16c					14.9	3.8	81.5	67.1	17.9	109.0	211.7	585.4	267.2	685.0	71.1
Central Government Deposits	16d					252.8	214.6	88.2	50.8	130.9	119.4	235.3	188.2	364.9	689.6	640.0
Capital Accounts	17a					186.6	357.1	515.0	723.0	880.9	982.3	1,358.7	1,844.4	1,936.9	2,300.0	2,277.7
Other Items (Net)	17r					−34.5	−184.4	−282.4	−319.5	−528.8	−265.4	−525.6	−575.2	−325.4	−524.9	−894.5
Deposit Money Banks															*Millions of Escudos:*	
Reserves	20	...	...	...	...											
Foreign Assets	21	...	...	...	...											
Claims on Central Government	22a	...	...	...	...											
Claims on Local Government	22b	...	...	...	...											
Claims on Nonfin.Pub.Enterprises	22c	...	...	...	...											
Claims on Private Sector	22d	...	...	...	...											
Demand Deposits	24	...	...	...	...											
Time, Savings,& Fgn.Currency Dep.	25	...	...	...	...											
Restricted Deposits	26b	...	...	...	...											
Foreign Liabilities	26c	...	...	...	...											
Central Government Deposits	26d	...	...	...	...											
Counterpart Funds	26e	...	...	...	...											
Credit from Monetary Authorities	26g	...	...	...	...											
Liab. to Nonbank Financial Insts	26j	...	...	...	...											
Capital Accounts	27a	...	...	...	...											
Other Items (Net)	27r	...	...	...	...											
Monetary Survey															*Millions of Escudos:*	
Foreign Assets (Net)	31n	...	...	...	...	1,016.6	1,420.8	1,333.4	1,554.3	1,783.7	1,815.0	2,482.6	3,085.7	3,545.5	4,041.2	4,244.1
Domestic Credit	32	...	...	...	...	153.0	187.0	566.3	807.0	1,124.5	1,940.7	2,194.4	2,768.0	3,182.3	3,874.2	4,725.7
Claims on Central Govt. (Net)	32an	...	...	...	...	−164.9	−122.8	3.6	71.0	26.1	428.7	312.4	480.8	362.2	248.4	608.8
Claims on Local Government	32b	...	...	...	...	—	—	.9	.6	3.5	19.6	31.8	32.9	34.9	32.2	34.5
Claims on Nonfin.Pub.Enterprises	32c	...	...	...	...	—	—	125.3	142.8	587.1	770.6	1,046.1	1,030.0	1,346.1	1,483.4	1,517.3
Claims on Private Sector	32d	...	...	...	...	316.4	308.3	435.0	591.1	506.3	720.3	802.6	1,222.8	1,437.6	2,110.2	2,565.1
Claims on Other Banking Insts	32f	...	...	...	...	1.5	1.5	1.5	1.5	1.5	1.5	1.5	1.5	1.5	—	—
Claims on Nonbank Financial Inst	32g	...	...	...	...											
Money	34	...	...	...	...	1,000.4	1,411.3	1,614.8	1,822.6	2,302.0	2,552.7	3,227.8	3,956.2	4,201.6	4,843.2	5,620.6
Quasi-Money	35	...	...	...	...	17.1	23.8	52.3	135.2	254.1	486.1	616.1	628.3	914.7	1,297.1	1,966.0
Restricted Deposits	36b	...	...	...	...	4.1	6.2	6.9	7.9	7.1	8.0	10.0	13.5	296.7	379.2	272.0
Counterpart Funds	36e	...	...	...	...											
Liab. to Nonbank Financial Insts	36j	...	...	...	...											
Capital Accounts	37a	...	...	...	...	186.6	357.1	515.0	723.0	880.9	982.3	1,358.7	1,844.4	1,936.9	2,300.0	2,277.7
Other Items (Net)	37r	...	...	...	...	−38.6	−190.6	−289.3	−327.4	−535.9	−273.4	−535.6	−588.7	−622.1	−904.1	−1,166.5
Money plus Quasi-Money	35l	...	...	...	...	1,017.5	1,435.1	1,667.1	1,957.8	2,556.1	3,038.8	3,843.9	4,584.5	5,116.3	6,140.3	7,586.6
Other Banking Institutions															*Millions of Escudos:*	
Cash	40	...	...	...	...	31.5	38.8	46.2	50.7	21.4	16.6	21.8	75.0	6.7	9.5	54.3
Foreign Assets	41	...	...	...	...	.1	.1	.1	.1	.1	.2	.3	.3	.3	.3	.2
Claims on Private Sector	42d	...	...	...	...	84.1	86.6	96.6	121.2	178.2	217.3	230.2	265.6	232.2	274.2	254.2
Time, Savings,& Fgn.Currency Dep.	45	...	...	...	...	57.0	64.6	81.8	99.0	116.7	150.5	167.3	235.4	230.2	257.1	256.5
Credit from Monetary Authorities	46g	...	...	...	...	1.5	1.5	1.5	1.5	1.5	1.5	1.5	1.5	—	—	—
Capital Accounts	47a	...	...	...	...											
Other Items (Net)	47r	...	...	...	...	57.2	59.4	59.6	71.5	81.5	82.1	83.5	104.0	9.0	26.9	52.2
Banking Survey															*Millions of Escudos:*	
Foreign Assets (Net)	51n	...	...	...	...	1,016.7	1,420.9	1,333.5	1,554.4	1,783.8	1,815.2	2,482.9	3,086.0	3,545.8	4,041.5	4,244.3
Domestic Credit	52	...	...	...	...	250.4	286.0	674.0	936.9	1,309.9	2,163.8	2,429.0	3,036.6	3,416.1	4,150.9	4,979.9
Claims on Central Govt. (Net)	52an	...	...	...	...	−164.7	−122.6	3.8	71.2	26.3	428.9	312.6	481.0	362.4	248.6	608.8
Claims on Local Government	52b	...	...	...	...	7.4	7.1	7.5	5.7	8.0	23.5	35.1	35.6	37.0	33.7	34.5
Claims on Nonfin.Pub.Enterprises	52c	...	...	...	...	7.2	6.6	131.1	147.7	591.1	773.8	1,048.5	1,031.6	1,346.9	1,484.2	1,517.3
Claims on Private Sector	52d	...	...	...	...	400.5	394.9	531.6	712.3	684.5	937.6	1,032.8	1,488.4	1,669.8	2,384.4	2,819.3
Liquid Liabilities	55l	...	...	...	...	1,043.0	1,460.9	1,702.7	2,006.1	2,651.4	3,172.7	3,989.4	4,744.9	5,339.8	6,387.9	7,788.8
Restricted Deposits	56b	...	...	...	...	4.1	6.2	6.9	7.9	7.1	8.0	10.0	13.5	296.7	379.2	272.0
Capital Accounts	57a	...	...	...	...	186.6	357.1	515.0	723.0	880.9	982.3	1,358.7	1,844.4	1,936.9	2,300.0	2,277.7
Other Items (Net)	57r	...	...	...	...	33.4	−117.3	−217.1	−245.7	−445.7	−184.0	−446.2	−480.2	−611.5	−874.7	−1,114.3

		1987	1988	1989	1990	1991	1992	1993	1994	1995	1996	1997	1998	1999	2000	2001
Exchange Rates		*End of Period*														
Official Rate	aa	93.312	99.131	95.993	94.016	95.081	100.497	118.115	118.452	115.136	122.464	129.845	132.714	147.648	154.734	157.059
		End of Period (ae) Period Average (rf)														
Official Rate	ae	65.775	73.665	73.045	66.085	66.470	73.089	85.992	81.140	77.455	85.165	96.235	94.255	107.575	118.760	124.975
Official Rate	rf	72.466	72.068	77.978	70.031	71.408	68.018	80.427	81.891	76.853	82.591	93.177	98.158	102.700	115.877	123.213
Fund Position		*End of Period*														
Quota	2f. *s*	4.50	4.50	4.50	4.50	4.50	7.00	7.00	7.00	7.00	7.00	7.00	7.00	9.60	9.60	9.60
SDRs	1b. *s*	.07	.03	.04	.03	.04	.05	.02	.05	.02	.04	.02	.04	.01	.04	.01
Reserve Position in the Fund	1c. *s*	—	—	—	—	—	—	—	—	—	—	—	—	—	—	—
Total Fund Cred.&Loans Outstg.	2tl	—	—	—	—	—	—	—	—	—	—	—	—	—	—	—
International Liquidity		*End of Period*														
Total Reserves minus Gold	1l. *d*	80.73	81.33	74.74	76.97	65.10	75.76	57.69	42.08	36.89	27.57	19.32	8.32	43.48	28.20	45.48
SDRs	1b. *d*	.10	.04	.05	.04	.06	.07	.03	.07	.03	.06	.03	.06	.02	.05	.02
Reserve Position in the Fund	1c. *d*	—	—	—	—	—	—	—	—	—	—	—	—	—	—	—
Foreign Exchange	1d. *d*	80.63	81.29	74.69	76.93	65.04	75.69	57.66	42.01	36.86	27.50	19.29	8.26	43.46	28.14	45.46
Monetary Authorities: Other Liab.	4.. *d*	1.73	1.65	1.23	1.13	2.49	2.90	.80	.60	6.47	3.51	2.60	.94	1.11	1.34	1.36
Deposit Money Banks: Assets	7a. *d*	....	....	....	....	....	....	14.47	31.60	10.62	32.35	23.89	33.41	30.71	42.36	43.00
Liabilities	7b. *d*	....	....	....	....	....	....	2.47	3.38	6.32	5.73	9.95	11.16	15.52	16.38	14.10
Monetary Authorities		*End of Period*														
Foreign Assets	11	5,310.0	5,991.4	5,459.2	5,086.5	4,327.2	5,536.9	4,999.9	3,483.1	†5,154.8	4,838.5	4,521.9	3,584.9	8,203.6	4,221.9	6,561.2
Claims on Central Government	12a	1,441.8	1,653.9	1,902.8	2,217.0	3,101.0	4,118.6	5,068.2	4,446.4	†4,964.4	4,315.8	6,001.6	5,615.2	5,865.2	9,209.4	9,024.0
Claims on Local Government	12b	28.3	48.3	60.0	79.7	70.3	68.8	27.6	—	†—	—	—	—	—	—	—
Claims on Nonfin.Pub.Enterprises	12c	1,422.1	2,724.6	2,986.1	3,151.2	3,602.4	3,694.1	2,136.9	119.7	†118.8	113.9	.1	—	86.8	82.3	82.3
Claims on Private Sector	12d	3,179.0	2,223.3	2,877.3	3,444.5	3,948.0	4,731.8	2,005.7	1,091.2	†1,099.4	2,049.4	1,151.9	1,142.7	1,100.8	1,074.9	1,106.3
Claims on Deposit Money Banks	12e	....	....	....	....	....	....	612.8	592.1	†632.7	630.3	519.8	361.6	331.4	1,098.9	438.4
Claims on Other Banking Insts	12f	32.7	137.2	214.2	258.4	308.0	301.4	—	—	†—	—	—	—	—	—	—
Claims on Nonbank Financial Insts	12g	....	....	....	....	....	....	....	....	—	—	—	5.5	5.5	—	—
Reserve Money	14	5,710.4	6,037.9	6,410.5	6,926.4	7,538.1	9,906.6	14,205.4	8,685.9	†10655.6	9,982.8	10,035.2	10,971.4	11,701.4	13,552.2	14,580.5
of which: Currency Outside DMBs	14a	1,955.9	2,219.2	2,490.3	2,842.4	2,971.9	3,191.3	3,549.4	3,929.7	†4,635.1	4,513.0	4,853.6	5,059.8	6,026.1	6,458.2	6,702.9
Time & Foreign Currency Deposits	15	2,527.1	3,591.6	4,659.4	5,754.3	7,195.0	6,730.7	—	173.9	†101.4	—	—	—	—	—	—
Foreign Liabilities	16c	114.0	121.8	89.5	74.6	165.3	211.8	69.2	48.7	†500.9	298.8	249.8	88.8	119.7	159.6	170.0
Central Government Deposits	16d	722.6	929.6	928.9	968.9	649.0	803.9	—	—	†245.9	230.8	944.7	516.6	2,446.1	607.7	675.1
Capital Accounts	17a	2,434.1	2,213.3	2,459.5	2,970.3	2,725.2	3,002.9	2,190.4	2,069.3	†2,338.7	2,739.2	3,114.5	3,051.5	2,374.7	2,917.7	2,999.6
Other Items (Net)	17r	–94.3	–115.5	–1,048.2	–2,457.2	–2,915.7	–2,204.3	–1,613.9	–1,245.3	†–1872.4	–1,303.7	–2,149.0	–3,918.4	–1,048.6	–1,549.9	–1,213.0
Deposit Money Banks		*End of Period*														
Reserves	20	....	....	....	....	....	....	10,604.3	4,803.9	†5,987.1	5,472.5	5,701.4	5,820.3	5,648.0	7,111.0	7,869.1
Foreign Assets	21	....	....	....	....	....	....	1,244.4	2,563.7	†822.3	2,754.7	2,299.1	3,149.0	3,303.5	5,031.1	5,373.5
Claims on Central Government	22a	....	....	....	....	....	....	—	6,046.7	†7,557.0	8,944.3	10,357.8	10,347.4	10,036.0	14,472.6	14,931.6
Claims on Local Government	22b	....	....	....	....	....	....	48.7	76.2	†97.1	109.1	.2	10.7	238.0	289.3	260.9
Claims on Nonfin.Pub.Enterprises	22c	....	....	....	....	....	....	433.9	432.7	†545.0	378.5	24.2	21.4	425.3	73.3	132.9
Claims on Private Sector	22d	....	....	....	....	....	....	5,495.8	6,473.9	†9,292.1	10,159.8	13,540.5	15,308.7	17,289.2	18,252.2	21,099.2
Demand Deposits	24	....	....	....	....	....	....	7,049.3	7,542.3	†7,232.4	8,609.7	11,106.4	10,573.4	12,216.4	13,966.4	14,247.6
Time, Savings,& Fgn.Currency Dep.	25	....	....	....	....	....	....	9,039.4	10,394.4	†12974.5	14,251.9	14,386.0	15,557.7	17,494.4	20,301.7	23,826.3
Restricted Deposits	26b	....	....	....	....	....	....	300.9	203.8	†257.6	491.7	398.1	710.0	242.6	502.8	210.4
Foreign Liabilities	26c	....	....	....	....	....	....	212.8	274.3	†489.7	488.3	957.1	1,051.5	1,669.6	1,944.8	1,761.9
Central Government Deposits	26d	....	....	....	....	....	....	847.8	1,035.7	†2,401.0	2,539.4	2,038.2	2,100.4	1,165.9	1,324.8	1,621.4
Counterpart Funds	26e	....	....	....	....	....	....	....	....	—	—	2.0	3.4	—	—	—
Credit from Monetary Authorities	26g	....	....	....	....	....	....	612.8	592.1	†573.5	551.4	519.8	361.6	331.4	1,098.9	438.4
Liab. to Nonbank Financial Insts	26j	....	....	....	....	....	....	3.4	20.3	†181.1	298.7	125.6	36.2	306.0	257.0	276.3
Capital Accounts	27a	....	....	....	....	....	....	1,292.9	1,638.8	†2,833.5	3,433.6	4,426.3	5,365.6	5,954.5	7,007.2	7,903.9
Other Items (Net)	27r	....	....	....	....	....	....	–1,532.2	–1,304.6	†–2642.8	–2,845.9	–2,036.3	–1,102.3	–2,440.8	–1,174.1	–619.0
Monetary Survey		*End of Period*														
Foreign Assets (Net)	31n	5,196.0	5,869.6	5,369.7	5,011.9	4,161.9	5,325.1	5,962.3	5,723.8	†4,986.5	6,806.0	5,614.0	5,593.6	9,717.8	7,148.6	10,002.8
Domestic Credit	32	5,381.3	5,857.7	7,111.5	8,181.9	10,380.7	12,110.8	14,369.0	17,651.1	†21026.9	23,300.6	28,093.4	29,834.6	31,434.8	41,521.5	44,347.7
Claims on Central Govt. (Net)	32an	719.2	724.3	973.9	1,248.1	2,452.0	3,314.7	4,220.4	9,457.4	†9,874.5	10,489.9	13,376.5	13,345.6	12,289.2	21,749.5	21,659.1
Claims on Local Government	32b	28.3	48.3	60.0	79.7	70.3	68.8	76.3	76.2	†97.1	109.1	.2	10.7	238.0	289.3	260.9
Claims on Nonfin.Pub.Enterprises	32c	1,422.1	2,724.6	2,986.1	3,151.2	3,602.4	3,694.1	2,570.8	552.4	†663.8	492.4	24.3	21.4	512.1	155.6	215.2
Claims on Private Sector	32d	3,179.0	2,223.3	2,877.3	3,444.5	3,948.0	4,731.8	7,501.5	7,565.1	†10391.5	12,209.2	14,692.4	16,451.4	18,390.0	19,327.1	22,205.5
Claims on Other Banking Insts	32f	32.7	137.2	214.2	258.4	308.0	301.4	—	—	†—	—	—	—	—	—	—
Claims on Nonbank Financial Inst	32g	....	....	....	....	....	....	....	....	—	—	—	5.5	5.5	—	7.0
Money	34	5,710.4	6,037.9	6,410.5	6,926.4	7,538.1	9,906.6	10,598.7	11,472.0	†11867.5	13,122.7	15,960.0	15,633.2	18,332.6	20,425.3	20,951.3
Quasi-Money	35	2,527.1	3,591.6	4,659.4	5,754.3	7,195.0	6,730.7	9,039.4	10,568.3	†13075.9	14,251.9	14,386.0	15,557.7	17,494.4	20,301.7	23,826.3
Restricted Deposits	36b	228.1	321.8	185.2	289.2	141.6	142.5	300.9	203.8	†257.6	491.7	398.1	710.0	242.6	502.8	210.4
Counterpart Funds	36e	....	....	....	....	....	....	....	....	—	—	2.0	3.4	—	—	—
Liab. to Nonbank Financial Insts	36j	....	....	....	....	....	....	3.4	20.3	†181.1	298.7	125.6	36.2	306.0	257.0	276.3
Capital Accounts	37a	2,434.1	2,213.3	2,459.5	2,970.3	2,725.2	3,002.9	3,483.3	3,708.1	†5,172.2	6,172.8	7,540.8	8,417.1	8,329.2	9,924.9	10,903.5
Other Items (Net)	37r	–322.4	–437.3	–1,233.4	–2,746.4	–3,057.3	–2,346.8	–3,094.4	–2,597.6	†–4541.0	–4,231.2	–4,705.1	–4,929.4	–3,552.2	–2,741.7	–1,817.3
Money plus Quasi-Money	35l	8,237.5	9,629.5	11,069.9	12,680.7	14,733.1	16,637.3	19,638.1	22,040.3	†24943.4	27,374.6	30,346.0	31,190.9	35,827.0	40,727.0	44,777.6
Other Banking Institutions		*End of Period*														
Cash	40	33.4	42.6	43.8	47.6	57.0	74.6	....	....	....	....	....	....	....	....	....
Foreign Assets	41	.2	.2	.2	.2	.2	.2	....	....	....	....	....	....	....	....	....
Claims on Private Sector	42d	378.5	548.5	717.5	1,013.3	1,016.1	1,126.4	....	....	....	....	....	....	....	....	....
Time, Savings,& Fgn.Currency Dep.	45	308.5	368.4	432.0	506.7	569.7	623.8	....	....	....	....	....	....	....	....	....
Credit from Monetary Authorities	46g	33.8	137.5	214.2	245.4	327.6	301.4	....	....	....	....	....	....	....	....	....
Capital Accounts	47a	—	—	—	—	—	—	....	....	....	....	....	....	....	....	....
Other Items (Net)	47r	69.8	85.4	115.3	309.0	176.0	276.0	....	....	....	....	....	....	....	....	....
Banking Survey		*End of Period*														
Foreign Assets (Net)	51n	5,196.2	5,869.8	5,369.9	5,012.1	4,162.1	5,325.3	....	....	....	....	....	....	....	....	....
Domestic Credit	52	5,727.1	6,269.1	7,614.8	8,936.8	11,088.8	12,935.8	....	....	....	....	....	....	....	....	....
Claims on Central Govt. (Net)	52an	719.2	724.3	973.9	1,248.1	2,452.0	3,314.7	....	....	....	....	....	....	....	....	....
Claims on Local Government	52b	28.3	48.4	60.0	79.7	70.3	68.8	....	....	....	....	....	....	....	....	....
Claims on Nonfin.Pub.Enterprises	52c	1,422.1	2,724.6	2,986.1	3,151.2	3,602.4	3,694.1	....	....	....	....	....	....	....	....	....
Claims on Private Sector	52d	3,557.5	2,771.8	3,594.8	4,457.8	4,964.1	5,858.2	....	....	....	....	....	....	....	....	....
Liquid Liabilities	55l	8,512.6	9,955.3	11,458.1	13,139.8	15,245.8	17,186.5	....	....	....	....	....	....	....	....	....
Restricted Deposits	56b	228.1	321.8	185.2	289.2	141.6	142.5	....	....	....	....	....	....	....	....	....
Capital Accounts	57a	2,434.1	2,213.3	2,459.5	2,970.3	2,725.2	3,002.9	....	....	....	....	....	....	....	....	....
Other Items (Net)	57r	–251.5	–351.5	–1,118.1	–2,450.4	–2,861.7	–2,070.8	....	....	....	....	....	....	....	....	....

Cape Verde

624

		1972	1973	1974	1975	1976	1977	1978	1979	1980	1981	1982	1983	1984	1985	1986
Interest Rates															*Percent Per Annum*	
Deposit Rate	601	....	....												4.00	4.00
Lending Rate	60p	....	....	6.50	6.50	6.50	6.50	6.50	6.50	6.50	6.50	6.50	6.50	6.50	10.00	10.00
Prices and Labor															*Index Numbers (1995=100):*	
Consumer Prices	64	....	....		....	....		....	....	....	....	....	46	51	54	60
															Number in Thousands:	
Unemployment	67c	....	....		....			....	....		....		....	....		
International Transactions															*Millions of Escudos*	
Exports	70	48	48	53	61	48	75	75	92	170	147	191	246	212	524	355
Imports, c.i.f.	71	657	833	869	1,011	912	1,285	1,908	1,987	2,742	3,452	5,102	6,237	7,036	7,663	8,601
Balance of Payments															*Millions of US Dollars:*	
Current Account, n.i.e.	78ald	....	....		....		5.84	-8.57	-1.02	4.32	-21.61	-14.84	-13.35	-6.42	-8.94	1.73
Goods: Exports f.o.b.	78aad						1.24	3.07	4.12	9.12	6.26	3.97	3.30	6.93	6.12	4.00
Goods: Imports f.o.b.	78abd						-45.08	-58.75	-71.25	-79.97	-85.90	-96.71	-104.59	-82.47	-86.74	-85.93
Trade Balance	78acd						-43.84	-55.67	-67.12	-70.85	-79.64	-92.74	-101.29	-75.54	-80.61	-81.93
Services: Credit	78add						.96	4.68	8.19	10.08	17.39	27.45	33.48	23.73	24.81	32.25
Services: Debit	78aed						-3.66	-4.62	-5.48	-7.47	-17.17	-12.62	-12.20	-10.45	-8.60	-16.78
Balance on Goods & Services	78afd						-46.54	-55.61	-64.41	-68.24	-79.42	-77.90	-80.01	-62.26	-64.40	-66.45
Income: Credit	78agd						1.13	.90	2.12	3.48	2.88	1.66	1.32	1.62	1.90	2.64
Income: Debit	78ahd						-.14	-.26	-.83	-.09	-2.36	-6.13	-8.19	-6.12	-5.98	-5.33
Balance on Gds, Serv. & Inc.	78aid						-45.55	-54.98	-63.12	-64.85	-78.90	-82.37	-86.88	-66.75	-68.47	-69.14
Current Transfers, n.i.e.: Credit	78ajd						52.95	48.69	65.59	73.48	61.39	71.29	77.58	63.99	63.37	72.29
Current Transfers: Debit	78akd						-1.57	-2.29	-3.49	-4.30	-4.11	-3.76	-4.05	-3.65	-3.84	-1.41
Capital Account, n.i.e.	78bcd						—	—	—	—	—	—	—	—	—	—
Capital Account, n.i.e.: Credit	78bad						—	—	—	—	—	—	—	—	—	—
Capital Account: Debit	78bbd						—	—	—	—	—	—	—	—	—	—
Financial Account, n.i.e.	78bjd	....	....		....		2.02	3.75	.42	1.14	20.56	21.66	20.24	6.41	18.24	9.23
Direct Investment Abroad	78bdd	....	....		....		—	—	—	—	—	—	—	—	—	—
Dir. Invest. in Rep. Econ., n.i.e.	78bed	....	....		....		—	—	—	—	—	—	—	—	—	-.01
Portfolio Investment Assets	78bfd	....	....		....		—	—	—	—	—	—	—	—	—	—
Equity Securities	78bkd	....	....		....		—	—	—	—	—	—	—	—	—	—
Debt Securities	78bld	....	....		....		—	—	—	—	—	—	—	—	—	—
Portfolio Investment Liab., n.i.e.	78bgd	....	....		....		—	—	—	—	—	—	—	—	—	—
Equity Securities	78bmd	....	....		....		—	—	—	—	—	—	—	—	—	—
Debt Securities	78bnd	....	....		....		—	—	—	—	—	—	—	—	—	—
Financial Derivatives Assets	78bwd	....	....		....		....	....	....	....	....	....	....	....	....	....
Financial Derivatives Liabilities	78bxd	....	....		....		....	....	....	....	....	....	....	....	....	....
Other Investment Assets	78bhd	....	....		....		....	....	....	....	....	....	....	....	....	....
Monetary Authorities	78bod	....	....		....		....	....	....	....	....	....	....	....	....	....
General Government	78bpd	....	....		....		....	....	....	....	....	....	....	....	....	....
Banks	78bqd	....	....		....		....	....	....	....	....	....	....	....	....	....
Other Sectors	78brd	....	....		....		—	—	—	—	—	—	—	—	—	—
Other Investment Liab., n.i.e.	78bid	....	....		....		2.02	3.75	.42	1.14	20.56	21.66	20.24	6.41	18.24	9.24
Monetary Authorities	78bsd						-.33	2.19	-.38	-1.22	1.87	1.76	5.21	-3.75	4.56	-7.66
General Government	78btd						2.28	1.56	.80	2.33	18.67	18.50	14.74	10.23	14.92	12.09
Banks	78bud						—	—	—	—	—	—	—	—	—	—
Other Sectors	78bvd						.07	—	.01	.03	.02	1.40	.29	-.07	-1.24	4.81
Net Errors and Omissions	78cad	....	....		....		1.47	2.17	3.27	-5.63	-3.69	-1.86	-3.69	-4.84	4.94	-11.57
Overall Balance	78cbd						9.33	-2.66	2.67	-.18	-4.74	4.96	3.20	-4.84	14.24	-.61
Reserves and Related Items	79dad	....	....		....		-9.33	2.66	-2.67	.18	4.74	-4.96	-3.20	4.84	-14.24	.61
Reserve Assets	79dbd						-9.33	2.66	-2.67	.18	4.74	-4.96	-3.20	4.84	-14.24	-.89
Use of Fund Credit and Loans	79dcd						—	—	—	—	—	—	—	—	—	—
Exceptional Financing	79ded						—	—	—	—	—	—	—	—	—	1.50
National Accounts															*Millions of Escudos*	
Househ.Cons.Expend.,incl.NPISHs	96f	....	1,312	....	....	2,574	2,955	3,605	4,282	5,386	6,141	7,113	8,498	10,193	11,471	13,407
Government Consumption Expend.	91f	....	124	....	....	368	498	628	649	807	980	1,495	1,954	2,438	2,748	3,380
Gross Fixed Capital Formation	93e	....	279	....	....	553	847	1,537	1,655	2,214	3,271	4,222	4,840	4,966	5,957	6,440
Changes in Inventories	93i	....	56	....	....	-34	121	11	24	214	-175	149	21	-37	-246	439
Exports of Goods and Services	90c	....	321	....	....	185	325	437	610	1,089	1,588	1,880	2,451	2,562	2,887	2,733
Imports of Goods and Services (-)	98c	....	1,016	....	....	1,199	1,684	2,187	2,711	3,793	4,753	6,420	7,622	8,575	9,736	10,841
Gross Domestic Product (GDP)	99b	....	1,075	....	....	2,424	3,172	4,038	4,569	5,919	7,053	8,438	10,140	11,548	13,081	15,558
GDP Volume 1980 Prices	99b.p									5,919	6,296	6,520	7,121	7,381	7,870	8,096
GDP Volume (1995=100)	99bvp	....	....		....		....	....	....	48.2	51.3	53.1	58.0	60.1	64.1	65.9
GDP Deflator (1995=100)	99bip	....	....		....		....	....	....	60.2	67.4	77.9	85.7	94.1	100.0	115.6
															Millions:	
Population	99z	.29	.29	.29	.29	.30	.29	.29	.30	.30	.29	.30	.32	.33	.33	.34

1987	1988	1989	1990	1991	1992	1993	1994	1995	1996	1997	1998	1999	2000	2001		
Percent Per Annum															**Interest Rates**	
4.00	4.00	4.00	4.00	4.00	4.00	4.00	4.00	†5.00	5.00	5.04	5.27	4.76	4.34	4.67	Deposit Rate	60l
10.00	10.00	10.00	10.00	10.00	10.00	10.00	10.67	12.00	12.00	12.06	12.51	12.03	11.94	12.85	Lending Rate	60p
Period Averages															**Prices and Labor**	
62	65	67	75	82	†84	89	92	100	106	115	120	125	122	127	Consumer Prices	64
Period Averages																
....	1	—	—	—	—	1	1	1	....	....	....	....	....	....	Unemployment	67c
Millions of Escudos															**International Transactions**	
567	237	527	398	438	327	312	407	686	....	1,295	1,016	1,170	1,261	1,202	Exports	70
7,281	7,652	8,706	9,495	10,469	12,234	12,387	17,110	19,394	....	21,764	22,598	26,916	27,519	30,519	Imports, c.i.f.	71
Minus Sign Indicates Debit															**Balance of Payments**	
-2.57	-.49	-12.83	-3.83	-6.96	-12.15	-23.93	-45.73	-61.62	-35.04	-29.72	-58.00	....	....	....	Current Account, n.i.e.	78ald
24.04	17.47	23.18	21.90	14.25	11.39	9.05	14.16	16.58	23.88	43.24	32.69				Goods: Exports f.o.b.	78aad
-93.59	-102.80	-111.71	-121.07	-128.82	-168.50	-151.95	-195.26	-233.63	-207.52	-215.10	-218.33				Goods: Imports f.o.b.	78abd
-69.54	-85.33	-88.53	-99.17	-114.56	-157.12	-142.90	-181.10	-217.05	-183.64	-171.87	-185.64				*Trade Balance*	78acd
22.79	25.63	26.70	34.94	33.89	39.31	40.09	47.01	66.90	77.52	91.31	86.45				Services: Credit	78add
-19.57	-18.38	-26.62	-27.88	-20.54	-25.34	-29.39	-34.52	-60.50	-70.03	-71.90	-90.57				Services: Debit	78aed
-66.32	-78.07	-88.45	-92.11	-101.22	-143.14	-132.20	-168.61	-210.65	-176.15	-152.46	-189.76				*Balance on Goods & Services*	78afd
4.17	5.28	7.60	6.41	5.85	5.68	4.81	4.22	4.00	2.98	4.87	2.51				Income: Credit	78agd
-4.39	-4.53	-3.61	-4.12	-4.65	-4.40	-3.85	-4.56	-6.57	-7.38	-8.46	-8.07				Income: Debit	78ahd
-66.54	-77.32	-84.46	-89.82	-100.02	-141.86	-131.24	-168.95	-213.22	-180.55	-156.05	-195.32				*Balance on Gds, Serv. & Inc.*	78aid
64.72	78.08	72.65	87.11	95.14	133.81	110.41	125.55	155.96	148.38	129.91	142.46				Current Transfers, n.i.e.: Credit	78ajd
-.75	-1.25	-1.03	-1.12	-2.08	-4.09	-3.11	-2.33	-4.36	-2.87	-3.58	-5.15				Current Transfers: Debit	78akd
1.66	2.08	1.92	1.62	7.78	9.17	19.02	20.07	20.88	12.83	6.30	19.01				Capital Account, n.i.e.	78bcd
1.66	2.08	1.92	1.62	7.78	9.17	19.02	20.07	20.88	12.83	6.30	19.01				Capital Account, n.i.e.: Credit	78bad
															Capital Account: Debit	78bbd
9.69	.89	12.93	-19.38	16.84	16.82	17.52	39.60	44.51	46.00	44.06	36.97				Financial Account, n.i.e.	78bjd
—	-.18	-.77	-.32	-.54	-1.20	-.66	-.42	-.57	-.26	-.05					Direct Investment Abroad	78bdd
2.79	.60	.17	.25	1.74	.45	3.64	2.13	26.18	28.53	11.58	9.03				Dir. Invest. in Rep. Econ., n.i.e.	78bed
—	—	—	—	—	....	....	....	....	....	....	....				Portfolio Investment Assets	78bfd
—	—	—	—	—	....	....	....	....	....	....	....				Equity Securities	78bkd
—	—	—	—	—	....	....	....	....	....	....	....				Debt Securities	78bld
—	—	—	—	—	....	....	....	....	....	....	....				Portfolio Investment Liab., n.i.e.	78bgd
—	—	—	—	—	....	....	....	....	....	....	....				Equity Securities	78bmd
—	—	—	—	—	....	....	....	....	....	....	....				Debt Securities	78bnd
....	....	....	....	....	....	....	....	....	....	....	....				Financial Derivatives Assets	78bwd
....	....	....	....	....	....	....	....	....	....	....	....				Financial Derivatives Liabilities	78bxd
-.56	-.56	.42	-28.99	6.99	.57	-6.75	1.61	-1.67	-2.25	-1.79	-22.44				Other Investment Assets	78bhd
-.56	-.56	.42	-28.99	6.99	.57	-6.75	1.61	2.32	-2.34	-1.84	4.02				Monetary Authorities	78bod
								....	....	....	-28.39				General Government	78bpd
—	—	—	—	—	—	—	-3.99	.09	.05	3.02					Banks	78bqd
											-1.09				Other Sectors	78brd
7.47	1.04	13.11	9.67	8.65	17.01	21.29	36.28	20.57	19.99	34.33	50.39				Other Investment Liab., n.i.e.	78bid
—	-.27	-.43	-.21	1.27	.68	.88	-1.21	-.93	-.12	-.12	-.01				Monetary Authorities	78bsd
12.17	4.92	13.82	7.54	8.79	18.16	19.69	22.74	17.57	22.88	19.79	28.49				General Government	78btd
						2.65	1.11	2.38	.02	4.94	8.00				Banks	78bud
-4.70	-3.62	-.27	2.34	-1.41	-1.84	-1.93	13.64	1.55	-2.80	9.72	13.91				Other Sectors	78bvd
-5.78	-3.52	13.40	14.62	-33.94	8.71	2.38	8.31	-35.64	-1.34	-20.40	12.78				Net Errors and Omissions	78cad
3.00	-1.04	15.42	-6.97	-16.28	22.55	14.99	22.24	-31.87	22.46	.24	10.76				*Overall Balance*	78cbd
-3.00	1.04	-15.42	6.97	16.28	-22.55	-14.99	-22.24	31.87	-22.46	-.24	-10.76				Reserves and Related Items	79dad
.04	1.52	-14.02	12.29	19.31	-18.46	-11.50	-20.78	30.93	-19.76	9.84	-8.50				Reserve Assets	79dbd
															Use of Fund Credit and Loans	79dcd
-3.04	-.48	-1.40	-5.32	-3.04	-4.09	-3.49	-1.46	.95	-2.70	-10.08	-2.26				Exceptional Financing	79ded
Millions of Escudos															**National Accounts**	
15,134	17,848	....	....	....	....	....	....	....							Househ.Cons.Expend.,incl.NPISHs	96f
3,673	3,968	....	....	....	....	....	....	....							Government Consumption Expend.	91f
7,053	7,721	....	....	....	....	....	....	....							Gross Fixed Capital Formation	93e
328	-434	....	....	....	....	....	....	....							Changes in Inventories	93i
2,984	3,190	....	....	....	....	....	....	....							Exports of Goods and Services	90c
11,189	11,653	....	....	....	....	....	....	....							Imports of Goods and Services (-)	98c
17,984	20,640	....	....	....	....	....	....	....							Gross Domestic Product (GDP)	99b
8,444	8,951	9,461	9,526	9,660	9,954	10,682	11,422	12,278	....	....	....				GDP Volume 1980 Prices	99b.p
68.8	72.9	77.1	77.6	78.7	81.1	87.0	93.0	100.0	....	....	....				GDP Volume (1995=100)	99bvp
128.1	138.7	....	....	....	....	....	....	....							GDP Deflator (1995=100)	99bip
Midyear Estimates																
.35	.33	.33	.34	.35	.36	.37	.37	.39	.40	.41	.42	.43	.43	.44	Population	99z

(See notes in the back of the book.)

Central African Rep.

		1972	1973	1974	1975	1976	1977	1978	1979	1980	1981	1982	1983	1984	1985	1986
Exchange Rates														*Francs per SDR:*		
Official Rate	aa	278.00	284.00	272.08	262.55	288.70	285.76	272.28	264.78	287.99	334.52	370.92	436.97	470.11	415.26	394.78
														Francs per US Dollar:		
Official Rate	ae	256.05	235.42	222.22	224.27	248.49	235.25	209.00	201.00	225.80	287.40	336.25	417.37	479.60	378.05	322.75
Official Rate	rf	252.03	222.89	240.70	214.31	238.95	245.68	225.66	212.72	211.28	271.73	328.61	381.07	436.96	449.26	346.31
														Index Numbers (1995=100):		
Official Rate	ahx	197.9	224.6	207.2	233.0	209.0	203.0	221.4	234.6	236.4	184.6	152.6	131.5	114.5	111.9	144.3
Nominal Effective Exchange Rate	ne c	....	....	....	....	....	....	....	69.3	71.7	68.6	67.1	66.8	68.9	74.1	80.6
Real Effective Exchange Rate	re c	....	....	....	....	....	....	....	....	187.3	180.7	177.8	182.4	171.9	183.3	192.3
Fund Position														*Millions of SDRs:*		
Quota	2f. s	13.00	13.00	13.00	13.00	13.00	13.00	16.00	16.00	24.00	24.00	24.00	30.40	30.40	30.40	30.40
SDRs	1b. s	1.21	1.02	.81	2.25	1.62	1.56	1.30	1.36	—	.07	.17	.71	2.59	1.54	.43
Reserve Position in the Fund	1c. s	.29	.44	—	—	—	—	1.66	1.85	—	—	1.21	1.61	.11	.11	.11
Total Fund Cred.&Loans Outstg.	2tl	—	—	2.66	4.85	9.59	9.59	15.67	13.57	18.43	32.41	34.19	38.15	35.77	35.49	34.13
International Liquidity												*Millions of US Dollars Unless Otherwise Indicated:*					
Total Reserves minus Gold	1l. d	1.72	1.78	1.74	3.83	18.83	25.35	24.13	44.11	54.98	69.27	46.37	46.79	52.68	49.62	65.35
SDRs	1b. d	1.31	1.23	.99	2.63	1.88	1.89	1.69	1.79	—	.08	.19	.74	2.54	1.69	.53
Reserve Position in the Fund	1c. d	.31	.53	—	—	—	—	2.16	2.44	—	—	1.33	1.69	.11	.12	.13
Foreign Exchange	1d. d	.09	.02	.75	1.19	16.95	23.46	20.28	39.88	54.98	69.19	44.85	44.36	50.03	47.81	64.69
Gold (Million Fine Troy Ounces)	1ad	....	....	....	—	—	.006	.009	.011	.011	.011	.011	.011	.011	.011	.011
Gold (National Valuation)	1an d	....	....	....	....	....	.92	1.94	5.79	6.56	4.45	5.00	4.21	3.44	3.60	4.36
Monetary Authorities: Other Liab.	4.. d	.32	.27	2.40	2.37	1.08	1.85	1.21	2.23	1.59	.70	1.74	2.60	1.47	1.12	.52
Deposit Money Banks: Assets	7a. d	6.96	12.91	.83	.77	8.56	4.10	8.36	12.23	14.61	11.70	5.65	9.11	9.68	21.94	28.04
Liabilities	7b. d	9.46	16.71	23.29	24.14	20.20	24.17	26.57	25.16	23.83	17.87	4.16	1.31	2.46	3.26	12.24
Monetary Authorities														*Billions of Francs:*		
Foreign Assets	11	.44	.41	.39	.86	4.68	6.18	5.45	10.04	13.90	21.19	17.27	21.30	26.91	20.12	22.50
Claims on Central Government	12a	2.27	2.63	3.09	3.88	5.38	5.84	9.13	8.49	12.31	19.44	20.48	27.27	26.73	24.22	24.35
Claims on Deposit Money Banks	12e	5.29	6.66	7.23	6.80	3.37	3.42	7.67	8.47	11.69	11.12	16.40	15.74	12.13	18.13	18.85
Claims on Other Banking Insts	12f	....	....	....	....	....	....	....	....	....	....	....	....	....	....	....
Reserve Money	14	5.78	5.99	7.58	7.87	9.28	11.49	13.73	18.16	24.81	32.43	31.77	35.41	37.91	38.27	43.03
of which: Currency Outside DMBs	14a	5.71	5.85	7.44	7.52	8.99	11.19	13.45	17.98	24.38	31.99	31.39	34.93	37.33	38.03	40.95
Foreign Liabilities	16c	.08	.06	1.26	1.80	3.04	3.18	5.99	5.47	9.31	15.29	17.98	23.21	22.88	19.16	16.44
Central Government Deposits	16d	.19	2.54	.20	1.39	.35	.19	.88	.59	.54	.85	.68	.89	.77	.90	1.19
Capital Accounts	17a	—	.01	.01	.01	.02	.01	.01	.01	1.53	1.30	1.69	1.78	1.65	1.36	1.41
Other Items (Net)	17r	1.94	1.10	1.67	.46	.74	.57	1.63	2.76	1.72	1.87	2.04	3.02	2.55	2.79	3.63
Deposit Money Banks														*Billions of Francs:*		
Reserves	20	.07	.14	.14	.36	.29	.30	.28	.18	.43	.43	.38	.48	.58	.24	2.07
Foreign Assets	21	1.78	2.97	.18	.17	2.13	†.97	1.75	2.46	3.30	3.36	1.90	3.80	4.64	8.29	9.05
Claims on Central Government	22a	1.22	2.63	4.31	5.29	5.06	5.25	5.36	5.22	5.17	5.31	1.44	.51	1.01	.40	3.15
Claims on Nonfin.Pub.Enterprises	22c	....	....	....	....	....	....	....	....	....	....	....	....	....	....	....
Claims on Private Sector	22d	8.98	9.83	14.62	13.33	12.04	†14.73	18.24	15.62	23.47	24.43	30.35	30.84	30.62	35.03	31.97
Claims on Other Banking Insts	22f	....	....	....	....	....	....	....	....	....	....	....	....	....	....	....
Claims on Nonbank Financial Insts	22g	....	....	....	....	....	....	....	....	....	....	....	....	....	....	....
Demand Deposits	24	3.42	3.38	4.88	4.62	7.94	†7.04	7.16	8.19	10.25	10.37	9.34	10.47	11.01	14.39	11.58
Time and Savings Deposits	25	.81	1.13	1.09	1.35	2.22	2.29	1.99	.97	2.01	3.01	2.73	3.15	3.87	5.01	6.17
Foreign Liabilities	26c	1.68	3.24	4.67	4.96	4.57	4.78	4.65	5.06	5.38	5.14	1.40	.55	1.18	1.23	3.95
Long-Term Foreign Liabilities	26cl	.74	.60	.50	.45	.45	.91	.91	—	—	—	—	—	—	—	—
Central Government Deposits	26d	.19	.25	.22	.20	.26	.28	.31	.04	.41	1.53	1.45	3.14	4.94	2.16	1.64
Credit from Monetary Authorities	26g	5.29	6.66	7.23	6.80	3.37	3.42	7.67	8.47	11.69	11.12	16.40	15.74	12.13	18.15	18.85
Capital Accounts	27a	.52	.73	.92	1.09	1.27	3.27	3.60	3.70	3.67	4.78	5.76	6.33	8.60	8.87	10.70
Other Items (Net)	27r	−.58	−.42	−.26	−.33	−.55	†−.74	−.66	−2.95	−1.03	−2.41	−3.02	−3.75	−4.87	−5.84	−6.65
Post Office: Checking Deposits	24.. i	.16	.16	.27	.39	.45	.33	.30	.23	.30	.38	.33	.37	.32	.32	.31
Postal Debt	26c. i	1.03	2.39	3.88	4.74	4.47	4.87	5.03	4.95	4.84	4.81	.95		—	—	2.35
Monetary Survey														*Billions of Francs:*		
Foreign Assets (Net)	31n	.46	.08	−5.36	−5.73	−.80	†−.81	−3.44	1.97	2.51	4.12	−.21	1.35	7.50	8.02	11.16
Domestic Credit	32	12.09	12.31	21.60	20.91	21.87	†25.34	31.53	28.71	40.00	46.79	50.14	54.59	52.64	56.60	56.64
Claims on Central Govt. (Net)	32an	3.11	2.48	6.98	7.58	9.83	10.61	13.29	13.09	16.53	22.36	19.80	23.75	22.03	21.57	24.67
Claims on Nonfin.Pub.Enterprises	32c	....	....	....	....	....	....	....	....	....	....	....	....	....	....	....
Claims on Private Sector	32d	8.98	9.83	14.62	13.33	12.04	†14.73	18.24	15.62	23.47	24.43	30.35	30.84	30.62	35.03	31.97
Claims on Other Banking Insts	32f	....	....	....	....	....	....	....	....	....	....	....	....	....	....	....
Claims on Nonbank Financial Inst	32g	....	....	....	....	....	....	....	....	....	....	....	....	....	....	....
Money	34	9.13	9.23	12.32	12.13	16.93	†18.23	20.61	26.17	34.63	42.36	40.73	45.40	48.33	52.42	52.54
Quasi-Money	35	.81	1.13	1.09	1.35	2.22	2.29	1.99	.97	2.01	3.01	2.73	3.15	3.87	5.01	6.17
Other Items (Net)	37r	2.61	2.03	2.83	1.69	1.93	†4.02	5.50	3.53	5.88	5.55	6.47	7.39	7.94	7.19	9.09
Money plus Quasi-Money	35l	9.94	10.36	13.41	13.49	19.15	†20.51	22.60	27.15	36.63	45.37	43.46	48.55	52.20	57.43	58.71
Interest Rates														*Percent Per Annum*		
Discount Rate (End of Period)	60	4.50	4.50	5.50	5.50	6.50	6.50	6.50	8.50	8.50	8.50	8.50	8.50	8.50	9.00	8.00
Deposit Rate	60l	....	....	....	....	....	....	5.50	4.00	5.50	7.50	7.50	7.50	7.50	7.50	7.35
Lending Rate	60p	....	....	....	....	....	....	9.50	8.50	10.50	12.00	12.00	12.50	12.50	12.50	12.00
Prices and Labor														*Index Numbers (1995=100):*		
Wholesale Prices (1990=100)	63	24.5	25.1	30.0	35.7	37.4	40.3	43.4	49.4	57.3	†65.7	75.1	81.7	100.3	107.1	111.1
Consumer Prices	64	....	....	....	....	....	....	....	....	53.3	53.3	60.4	69.2	71.0	78.4	80.1
														Number in Thousands:		
Employment	67e	....	....	....	....	....	....	....	....	....	....	....	....	....	19	18
Unemployment	67c	....	....	....	....	....	....	....	....	....	....	....	....	....	8	10

1987	1988	1989	1990	1991	1992	1993	1994	1995	1996	1997	1998	1999	2000	2001		
															Exchange Rates	
End of Period																
378.78	407.68	380.32	364.84	370.48	378.57	404.89	†780.44	728.38	753.06	807.94	791.61	†896.19	918.49	935.39	Official Rate	aa
End of Period (ae) Period Average (rf)																
267.00	302.95	289.40	256.45	259.00	275.32	294.77	†534.60	490.00	523.70	598.81	562.21	†652.95	704.95	744.31	Official Rate	ae
300.54	297.85	319.01	272.26	282.11	264.69	283.16	†555.20	499.15	511.55	583.67	589.95	†615.70	711.98	733.04	Official Rate	rf
Period Averages																
166.1	167.8	156.5	183.7	177.4	188.9	176.3	90.0	100.0	97.5	85.6	84.7	81.1	70.3	68.1	Official Rate	ahx
85.2	88.8	93.9	107.5	115.5	133.2	147.3	92.4	100.0	105.0	104.4	105.5	105.2	105.4	110.7	Nominal Effective Exchange Rate	ne c
177.6	164.1	156.9	157.8	146.7	144.2	135.2	84.7	100.0	102.2	99.1	96.5	91.4	89.7	....	Real Effective Exchange Rate	re c
															Fund Position	
End of Period																
30.40	30.40	30.40	30.40	30.40	41.20	41.20	41.20	41.20	41.20	41.20	41.20	55.70	55.70	55.70	Quota	2f. s
4.93	9.15	—	3.42	.49	.04	.03	.01	.02	.01	—	.01	.04	—	.01	SDRs	1b. s
.11	.11	.11	.09	.09	.09	.09	.09	.09	.10	.10	.10	.10	.11	.11	Reserve Position in the Fund	1c. s
36.58	37.33	26.88	25.73	23.28	22.09	20.96	28.34	23.48	19.22	13.80	12.47	17.09	16.48	24.48	Total Fund Cred.&Loans Outstg.	2tl
															International Liquidity	
End of Period																
96.73	108.47	113.06	118.63	102.98	100.12	111.98	210.01	233.64	232.24	178.56	145.70	136.28	133.26	118.75	Total Reserves minus Gold	1l. d
6.99	12.31	—	4.87	.70	.06	.04	.01	.02	.01	—	.01	.05	—	.01	SDRs	1b. d
.16	.15	.14	.13	.13	.12	.13	.14	.14	.14	.13	.13	.13	.15	.14	Reserve Position in the Fund	1c. d
89.58	96.01	112.92	113.63	102.15	99.94	111.81	209.86	233.48	232.09	178.43	145.56	136.10	133.11	118.60	Foreign Exchange	1d. d
.011	.011	.011	.011	.011	.011	.011	.011	.011	.011	.011	.011	.011	.011	.011	Gold (Million Fine Troy Ounces)	1ad
5.37	4.52	3.52	3.98	3.94	3.70	4.42	†4.21	4.29	4.10	3.24	3.20	†3.23	3.03	3.09	Gold (National Valuation)	1and
1.14	†25.44	19.72	17.35	16.77	21.20	12.45	12.57	12.79	12.43	11.87	12.90	17.24	16.36	16.85	Monetary Authorities: Other Liab.	4.. d
29.74	13.02	10.57	12.65	9.43	9.12	6.85	11.45	6.39	4.41	4.99	5.91	10.48	7.96	4.52	Deposit Money Banks: Assets	7a. d
12.67	16.24	14.24	16.18	13.22	14.34	12.04	12.10	7.93	7.35	6.36	7.43	8.81	9.39	8.10	Liabilities	7b. d
															Monetary Authorities	
End of Period																
27.27	†34.25	34.01	31.52	27.69	28.59	34.29	114.56	116.59	123.77	108.86	83.71	91.10	96.08	90.69	Foreign Assets	11
22.65	†22.68	17.94	17.41	†27.66	28.23	28.34	41.99	36.97	37.69	32.76	32.28	37.86	41.62	44.43	Claims on Central Government	12a
13.11	†9.15	7.60	11.67	†2.51	2.18	3.66	—	1.60	1.24	.50	5.00	4.79	3.14	2.25	Claims on Deposit Money Banks	12e
....															Claims on Other Banking Insts	12f
42.89	†39.00	42.82	43.13	43.14	43.80	52.46	96.65	101.04	108.82	95.35	76.11	81.96	89.59	84.01	Reserve Money	14
42.28	†38.71	42.24	41.84	42.26	43.36	52.16	88.53	98.97	104.00	92.96	75.25	81.12	88.62	82.57	*of which: Currency Outside DMBs*	14a
15.89	†22.93	15.93	13.84	12.97	14.20	12.16	28.84	23.37	20.98	18.25	17.13	26.57	26.67	35.44	Foreign Liabilities	16c
1.72	†5.14	1.09	2.05	.59	.63	1.69	1.89	1.58	2.82	1.36	.91	3.45	2.36	6.00	Central Government Deposits	16d
1.44	†1.46	1.34	1.11	1.23	.99	1.27	1.01	.83	.90	.65	.64	.97	1.32	1.72	Capital Accounts	17a
1.09	†-2.45	-1.62	.47	-.07	-.62	-1.28	28.16	28.35	29.18	26.51	26.20	20.81	20.90	10.21	Other Items (Net)	17r
															Deposit Money Banks	
End of Period																
.61	†.29	.58	1.29	.88	.44	.30	8.11	2.07	4.82	2.38	.86	.84	.96	1.44	Reserves	20
7.94	†4.01	3.06	3.24	2.44	2.51	2.02	6.12	3.13	2.31	2.99	3.32	6.84	5.61	3.37	Foreign Assets	21
1.72	†1.96	2.20	2.28	3.76	†4.22	5.21	5.07	4.35	3.33	4.47	3.50	3.96	10.68	11.79	Claims on Central Government	22a
....	4.45	6.32	11.03	9.35	4.25	4.54	5.84	7.65	7.14	6.37	7.97	14.71	7.99	7.95	Claims on Nonfin.Pub.Enterprises	22c
29.46	†27.96	30.21	29.15	26.60	16.85	15.93	18.70	23.16	23.25	24.17	27.95	27.77	30.90	34.52	Claims on Private Sector	22d
....															Claims on Other Banking Insts	22f
													.92	.02	Claims on Nonbank Financial Insts	22g
12.09	†11.03	14.42	12.71	10.77	7.68	7.26	14.86	12.27	12.64	14.22	12.33	17.53	13.21	16.58	Demand Deposits	24
6.48	†7.32	7.75	7.47	6.49	6.20	5.16	11.89	8.98	9.42	9.14	9.97	9.69	9.08	10.54	Time and Savings Deposits	25
3.38	†2.77	2.43	2.66	†1.83	3.53	3.18	5.80	3.45	3.43	3.45	3.52	5.66	6.61	6.03	Foreign Liabilities	26c
....	†2.15	1.69	1.49	†1.60	.42	.37	.66	.44	.42	.36	.66	.10	.01	.01	Long-Term Foreign Liabilities	26cl
1.59	†3.01	3.75	5.59	5.30	†2.41	1.98	3.55	7.22	7.77	7.04	4.73	6.25	10.44	5.82	Central Government Deposits	26d
13.11	†9.15	7.60	11.67	†2.51	2.18	3.66	—	1.60	1.24	.50	5.00	4.79	3.14	2.25	Credit from Monetary Authorities	26g
10.75	†7.19	7.49	7.74	†19.97	8.01	8.10	8.70	9.35	7.78	7.44	8.20	13.35	15.49	18.92	Capital Accounts	27a
-7.66	†-3.95	-2.75	-2.34	-5.43	†-2.15	-1.71	-1.62	-2.94	-1.85	-1.77	-.79	-2.31	-1.82	-1.08	Other Items (Net)	27r
.31	.31	....	....	....	....	....	....	....	....	....	....	....	....	....	Post Office: Checking Deposits	24.. i
1.17	....	....	....	....	....	....	....	....	....	....	....	....	....	....	Postal Debt	26c. i
															Monetary Survey	
End of Period																
15.94	†13.97	19.52	18.94	†13.74	12.95	20.60	85.38	92.47	101.25	89.79	65.73	65.62	68.40	52.58	Foreign Assets (Net)	31n
50.52	†48.90	51.83	52.23	†61.47	†50.52	50.35	66.15	63.33	60.82	59.38	66.06	75.53	78.41	86.88	Domestic Credit	32
21.06	†16.49	15.30	12.05	†25.53	†29.41	29.88	41.61	32.52	30.44	28.84	30.14	32.13	39.51	44.41	Claims on Central Govt. (Net)	32an
....	4.45	6.32	11.03	9.35	4.25	4.54	5.84	7.65	7.14	6.37	7.97	14.71	7.99	7.95	Claims on Nonfin.Pub.Enterprises	32c
29.46	†27.96	30.21	29.15	26.60	16.85	15.93	18.70	23.16	23.25	24.17	27.95	27.77	30.90	34.52	Claims on Private Sector	32d
....															Claims on Other Banking Insts	32f
													.92	.02	Claims on Nonbank Financial Inst	32g
54.37	†49.74	56.66	54.56	53.03	51.05	59.42	103.40	111.24	116.64	107.19	87.58	98.64	101.83	99.15	Money	34
6.48	†7.32	7.75	7.47	6.49	6.20	5.16	11.89	8.98	9.42	9.14	9.97	9.69	9.08	10.54	Quasi-Money	35
5.61	†5.81	6.94	9.14	†17.84	†6.23	6.38	36.25	35.58	36.00	32.84	34.25	32.81	35.90	29.77	Other Items (Net)	37r
60.85	†57.06	64.41	62.03	59.52	57.24	64.58	115.29	120.22	126.07	116.33	97.54	108.34	110.91	109.69	Money plus Quasi-Money	35l
															Interest Rates	
Percent Per Annum																
8.00	9.50	10.00	11.00	10.75	12.00	11.50	†7.75	8.60	7.75	7.50	7.00	7.60	7.00	6.50	Discount Rate (*End of Period*)	60
7.19	7.44	7.50	†7.50	7.50	7.50	7.75	8.08	5.50	5.46	5.00	5.00	5.00	5.00	5.00	Deposit Rate	60l
11.42	12.25	13.00	†18.50	18.15	17.77	17.46	17.50	16.00	22.00	22.00	22.00	22.00	22.00	20.67	Lending Rate	60p
															Prices and Labor	
Period Averages																
111.5	94.7	98.4	100.0	98.8	99.1	97.7	....	....		150.6	150.5	....	....	....	Wholesale Prices (1990=100)	63
74.6	71.6	72.2	71.9	70.4	69.4	67.4	83.9	100.0	103.7	105.4	103.4	101.9	....	....	Consumer Prices	64
Period Averages																
18	17	14	15	12	14	....	....	....	....	....	....	....	....	....	Employment	67e
9	9	8	8	8	6	6	10	8	....	....	....	....	....	....	Unemployment	67c

Central African Rep.

		1972	1973	1974	1975	1976	1977	1978	1979	1980	1981	1982	1983	1984	1985	1986
International Transactions															*Millions of Francs*	
Exports	70	9,930	8,328	11,622	10,120	14,623	20,033	16,182	16,937	24,384	21,323	35,461	28,405	37,022	41,217	22,975
Imports, c.i.f.	71	8,547	11,496	11,090	14,615	13,155	15,540	12,775	14,816	17,009	25,646	41,306	25,951	38,193	50,686	57,841
Balance of Payments															*Millions of US Dollars:*	
Current Account, n.i.e.	78al d	...	...	...	...	...	−19.0	−23.1	−16.1	−43.1	−4.3	−42.6	−29.3	−33.4	−48.6	−86.5
Goods: Exports f.o.b.	78aa d	...	...	...	...	...	104.5	110.3	122.2	147.2	117.7	124.4	123.4	114.4	131.0	129.5
Goods: Imports f.o.b.	78ab d	...	...	...	...	...	−103.9	−117.7	−132.9	−185.1	−144.6	−149.7	−137.5	−140.1	−167.7	−201.0
Trade Balance	78ac d	...	...	...	...	...	.6	−7.4	−10.7	−37.9	−26.9	−25.3	−14.1	−25.6	−36.7	−71.5
Services: Credit	78ad d	...	...	...	...	...	23.4	32.7	35.0	53.8	51.7	41.6	35.7	34.8	46.8	56.0
Services: Debit	78ae d	...	...	...	...	...	−70.2	−87.9	−113.3	−142.3	−92.1	−106.4	−103.7	−86.4	−108.0	−141.6
Balance on Goods & Services	78af d	...	...	...	...	...	−46.3	−62.6	−89.0	−126.4	−67.2	−90.1	−82.1	−77.2	−98.0	−157.2
Income: Credit	78ag d	...	...	...	...	...	2.8	3.7	2.6	4.4	8.0	5.0	3.1	2.7	6.7	2.8
Income: Debit	78ah d	...	...	...	...	...	−3.4	−2.5	−8.0	−1.8	−4.7	−12.2	−13.8	−12.4	−14.0	−15.2
Balance on Gds, Serv. & Inc.	78ai d	...	...	...	...	...	−46.9	−61.5	−94.4	−123.8	−63.9	−97.4	−92.8	−86.9	−105.3	−169.5
Current Transfers, n.i.e.: Credit	78aj d	...	...	...	...	...	43.0	56.7	89.9	107.6	81.6	76.8	86.2	75.7	78.9	111.5
Current Transfers: Debit	78ak d	...	...	...	...	...	−15.1	−18.3	−11.5	−26.8	−22.0	−22.1	−22.7	−22.3	−22.2	−28.5
Capital Account, n.i.e.	78bc d	...	...	...	...	...	—	—	—	—	—	—	—	—	—	—
Capital Account, n.i.e.: Credit	78ba d	...	...	...	...	...	—	—	—	—	—	—	—	—	—	—
Capital Account: Debit	78bb d	...	...	...	...	...	—	—	—	—	—	—	—	—	—	—
Financial Account, n.i.e.	78bj d	...	...	...	...	...	15.7	3.9	43.9	61.5	13.5	−1.7	8.3	26.3	31.5	76.0
Direct Investment Abroad	78bd d	...	...	...	...	...	−.1	1.3	−.3	—	—	−.3	−.4	−.3	−.6	−1.3
Dir. Invest. in Rep. Econ., n.i.e.	78be d	...	...	...	...	...	−2.8	6.1	22.8	5.3	5.8	9.2	4.5	5.1	3.0	8.2
Portfolio Investment Assets	78bf d	...	...	...	...	...	—	—	—	—	—	—	—	—	—	—
Equity Securities	78bk d	...	...	...	...	...	—	—	—	—	—	—	—	—	—	—
Debt Securities	78bl d	...	...	...	...	...	—	—	—	—	—	—	—	—	—	—
Portfolio Investment Liab., n.i.e.	78bg d	...	...	...	...	...	—	—	—	—	—	—	—	—	—	—
Equity Securities	78bm d	...	...	...	...	...	—	—	—	—	—	—	—	—	—	—
Debt Securities	78bn d	...	...	...	...	...	—	—	—	—	—	—	—	—	—	—
Financial Derivatives Assets	78bw d	...	...	...	...	...										
Financial Derivatives Liabilities	78bx d	...	...	...	...	...										
Other Investment Assets	78bh d	...	...	...	...	...	.5	−12.7	−6.0	−4.0	−28.0	.4	−17.7	−8.7	−22.3	−16.8
Monetary Authorities	78bo d	...	...	...	...	...					...				...	
General Government	78bp d	...	...	...	...	...	−.1	−1.0	—	—	−2.9	−2.1	−.9	—	−2.7	—
Banks	78bq d	...	...	...	...	...	3.2	−4.4	−2.4	−4.0	−.2	4.5	−5.0	−1.9	−8.1	−2.2
Other Sectors	78br d	...	...	...	...	...	−2.5	−7.3	−3.6	—	−24.9	−1.9	−11.7	−6.7	−11.5	−14.6
Other Investment Liab., n.i.e.	78bi d	...	...	...	...	...	18.1	9.2	27.5	60.1	35.8	−10.9	21.9	30.1	51.4	85.9
Monetary Authorities	78bs d	...	...	...	...	...	1.1	1.5	1.3	7.1	5.1	−7.8	.7	−1.0	−.1	−.3
General Government	78bt d	...	...	...	...	...	6.3	.3	3.5	40.1	6.5	−15.1	14.8	23.0	46.4	79.8
Banks	78bu d	...	...	...	...	...	4.2	−.6	−.2	1.5	−.9	1.9	−1.2	1.7	.6	2.5
Other Sectors	78bv d	...	...	...	...	...	6.4	7.9	22.9	11.4	25.0	10.1	7.7	6.4	4.5	3.9
Net Errors and Omissions	78ca d	...	...	...	...	...	9.3	8.2	−10.0	−12.1	−11.4	2.1	7.6	6.7	−7.8	7.0
Overall Balance	78cb d	...	...	...	...	...	6.0	−11.0	17.8	6.3	−2.2	−42.2	−13.4	−.4	−24.9	−3.6
Reserves and Related Items	79da d	...	...	...	...	...	−6.0	11.0	−17.8	−6.3	2.2	42.2	13.4	.4	24.9	3.6
Reserve Assets	79db d	...	...	...	...	...	−6.1	3.1	−16.9	−14.5	−25.5	21.4	−3.2	−5.0	18.6	−4.9
Use of Fund Credit and Loans	79dc d	...	...	...	...	...	—	7.5	−2.7	6.3	17.0	2.0	4.3	−2.5	−.5	−1.3
Exceptional Financing	79de d	...	...	...	...	...	.1	.4	1.9	1.9	10.6	18.9	12.3	7.9	6.7	9.7
Government Finance															*Millions of Francs:*	
Deficit (-) or Surplus	80	...	...	...	...	...	...	...	...	...	−6,671	...	...	...	...	...
Revenue	81	...	...	...	...	...	...	...	...	...	30,365	...	...	...	...	...
Grants Received	81z	...	...	...	...	...	...	...	...	...	4,686	...	...	...	...	...
Expenditure	82	...	...	...	...	...	...	...	...	...	41,538	...	...	...	...	...
Lending Minus Repayments	83	...	...	...	...	...	...	...	...	...	618	...	...	...	...	...
Overall Cash Adjustment	80x	...	...	...	...	...	...	...	...	...	434	...	...	...	...	...
Financing																
Net Borrowing: Domestic	84a	...	...	...	...	...	...	...	...	...	4,489	...	...	...	...	...
Foreign	85a	...	...	...	...	...	...	...	...	...	3,925	...	...	...	...	...
Use of Cash Balances	87	...	...	...	...	...	...	...	...	...	−1,743	...	...	...	...	...
National Accounts															*Billions of Francs*	
Househ.Cons.Expend.,incl.NPISHs	96f	42	41	52	62	65	73								307	319
Government Consumption Expend.	91f	11	12	14	16	18	21	...	...	...	...	...	...	...	59	61
Gross Fixed Capital Formation	93e	11	13	17	20	22	24	...	...	...	...	...	...	...	48	50
Changes in Inventories	93i	...	...	...	...	...	...	...	...	...	...	...	...	...	12	—
Exports of Goods and Services	90c	12	14	16	13	18	22	...	...	...	...	...	...	...	86	71
Imports of Goods and Services (-)	98c	20	23	26	30	29	33	...	...	...	...	...	...	...	123	111
Gross Domestic Product (GDP)	99b	56	57	72	84	94	107	121	135	168	218	248	252	279	316	331
															Millions:	
Population	99z	1.91	1.96	2.01	2.05	2.10	2.17	2.22	2.28	2.31	2.38	2.44	2.50	2.56	2.61	2.74

	1987	1988	1989	1990	1991	1992	1993	1994	1995	1996	1997	1998	1999	2000	2001	International Transactions	
Millions of Francs																	
	39,180	19,769	42,866	32,770	13,209	28,328	31,079	83,900	85,300	75,100	89,700	92,400	98,900	193,300	....	Exports	70
	61,370	42,002	47,994	42,050	26,186	38,469	35,559	77,300	86,900	72,300	84,400	93,900	86,000	18,500	....	Imports, c.i.f	71
Minus Sign Indicates Debit																Balance of Payments	
	−73.4	−34.6	−33.4	−89.1	−61.8	−83.1	−13.0	−24.7	....	....	....	....	....	....	....	Current Account, n.i.e.	78al *d*
	128.9	133.7	148.1	150.5	125.6	115.9	132.5	145.9	....	....	....	....	....	....	....	Goods: Exports f.o.b.	78aa *d*
	−197.7	−179.1	−186.0	−241.6	−178.7	−189.0	−158.1	−130.6	....	....	....	....	....	....	....	Goods: Imports f.o.b.	78ab *d*
	−68.8	−45.4	−37.9	−91.1	−53.0	−73.2	−25.7	15.3	....	....	....	....	....	....	....	*Trade Balance*	78ac *d*
	67.8	62.3	65.6	69.1	50.5	45.1	49.3	33.1	....	....	....	....	....	....	....	Services: Credit	78ad *d*
	−154.4	−151.0	−144.4	−168.5	−136.7	−152.7	−131.9	−113.8	....	....	....	....	....	....	....	Services: Debit	78ae *d*
	−155.4	−134.1	−116.8	−190.5	−139.2	−180.7	−108.3	−65.4	....	....	....	....	....	....	....	*Balance on Goods & Services*	78af *d*
	2.8	—	.7	.8	5.5	6.4	4.5	—	....	....	....	....	....	....	....	Income: Credit	78ag *d*
	−21.9	−21.2	−21.4	−22.4	−19.0	−22.2	−23.2	−22.7	....	....	....	....	....	....	....	Income: Debit	78ah *d*
	−174.5	−155.3	−137.5	−212.1	−152.7	−196.5	−127.1	−88.1	....	....	....	....	....	....	....	*Balance on Gds, Serv. & Inc.*	78ai *d*
	136.3	156.7	138.3	164.2	129.7	151.0	152.4	92.6	....	....	....	....	....	....	....	Current Transfers, n.i.e.: Credit	78aj *d*
	−35.2	−36.0	−34.2	−41.2	−38.8	−37.6	−38.3	−29.2	....	....	....	....	....	....	....	Current Transfers: Debit	78ak *d*
	....	....	....	....	....	....	....	....	....	....	....	....	....	....	....	Capital Account, n.i.e.	78bc *d*
	—	—	—	—	—	—	....	....	....	....	....	....	....	....	....	Capital Account, n.i.e.: Credit	78ba *d*
	—	—	—	—	—	—	....	....	....	....	....	....	....	....	....	Capital Account: Debit	78bb *d*
	63.4	9.6	15.4	66.7	24.0	20.3	−7.1	52.8	....	....	....	....	....	....	....	Financial Account, n.i.e.	78bj *d*
	−2.6	−4.8	−3.8	−3.8	−3.5	−5.9	−5.3	−7.2	....	....	....	....	....	....	....	Direct Investment Abroad	78bd *d*
	11.9	−3.8	1.3	.7	−4.9	−10.7	−10.0	3.6	....	....	....	....	....	....	....	Dir. Invest. in Rep. Econ., n.i.e.	78be *d*
	—	—	—	—	—	—	....	....	....	....	....	....	....	....	....	Portfolio Investment Assets	78bf *d*
	—	—	—	—	—	—	....	....	....	....	....	....	....	....	....	Equity Securities	78bk *d*
	—	—	—	—	—	—	....	....	....	....	....	....	....	....	....	Debt Securities	78bl *d*
	—	—	—	—	—	—	....	....	....	....	....	....	....	....	....	Portfolio Investment Liab., n.i.e.	78bg *d*
	—	—	—	—	—	—	....	....	....	....	....	....	....	....	....	Equity Securities	78bm *d*
	—	—	—	—	—	—	....	....	....	....	....	....	....	....	....	Debt Securities	78bn *d*
	....	....	....	....	....	....	....	....	....	....	....	....	....	....	....	Financial Derivatives Assets	78bw *d*
	....	....	....	....	....	....	....	....	....	....	....	....	....	....	....	Financial Derivatives Liabilities	78bx *d*
	−12.7	−9.0	−13.3	−16.3	−11.2	−33.2	−18.2	8.1	....	....	....	....	....	....	....	Other Investment Assets	78bh *d*
	−.2	−.1	−.1	−.2	—	—	....	....	....	....	....	....	....	....	....	Monetary Authorities	78bo *d*
	3.7	11.8	1.1	−.7	2.8	—	2.5	—	....	....	....	....	....	....	....	General Government	78bp *d*
	−16.2	−20.7	−14.3	−15.4	−14.0	−33.2	−20.7	8.1	....	....	....	....	....	....	....	Banks	78bq *d*
	66.8	27.2	31.3	86.0	43.6	70.0	26.4	48.3	....	....	....	....	....	....	....	Other Sectors	78br *d*
	−.1	−1.0	−5.3	−2.9	−.5	1.6	−8.4	—	....	....	....	....	....	....	....	Other Investment Liab., n.i.e.	78bi *d*
	68.8	26.9	30.5	83.9	52.3	57.7	23.2	43.9	....	....	....	....	....	....	....	Monetary Authorities	78bs *d*
	−1.9	—	.6	.1	−2.5	1.2	3.2	5.9	....	....	....	....	....	....	....	General Government	78bt *d*
	—	1.3	5.5	4.9	−5.7	9.4	8.4	−1.6	....	....	....	....	....	....	....	Banks	78bu *d*
																Other Sectors	78bv *d*
	−1.6	11.7	1.4	1.4	−1.9	26.2	6.3	−15.0	....	....	....	....	....	....	....	Net Errors and Omissions	78ca *d*
	−11.6	−13.3	−16.6	−21.1	−39.6	−36.6	−13.7	13.1	....	....	....	....	....	....	....	*Overall Balance*	78cb *d*
	11.6	13.3	16.6	21.1	39.6	36.6	13.7	−13.1	....	....	....	....	....	....	....	Reserves and Related Items	79da *d*
	−14.2	−32.4	.8	9.4	13.8	−2.8	−20.1	−56.0	....	....	....	....	....	....	....	Reserve Assets	79db *d*
	3.1	1.1	−13.4	−1.6	−3.3	−1.7	−1.6	10.3	....	....	....	....	....	....	....	Use of Fund Credit and Loans	79dc *d*
	22.7	44.6	29.3	13.3	29.2	41.0	35.4	32.6	....	....	....	....	....	....	....	Exceptional Financing	79de *d*
Year Ending December 31																Government Finance	
	....	....	....	....	....	....										Deficit (−) or Surplus	80
	....	....	....	....	....	....										Revenue	81
	....	....	....	....	....	....										Grants Received	81z
	....	....	....	....	....	....										Expenditure	82
	....	....	....	....	....	....										Lending Minus Repayments	83
	....	....	....	....	....	....										Overall Cash Adjustment	80x
																Financing	
	....	....	....	....	....	....										Net Borrowing: Domestic	84a
																Foreign	85a
	....	....	....	....	....	....										Use of Cash Balances	87
Billions of Francs																National Accounts	
	291	304	309	317	308	299	289	347	422	....	....	....	....	....	....	Househ.Cons.Expend.,incl.NPISHs	96f
	63	61	62	60	65	64	55	78	83	....	....	....	....	....	....	Government Consumption Expend.	91f
	46	37	41	46	47	45	36	56	73	....	....	....	....	....	....	Gross Fixed Capital Formation	93e
	−1	3	5	4	2	1	3	−1	6	....	....	....	....	....	....	Changes in Inventories	93i
	64	67	80	67	67	68	63	62	111	....	....	....	....	....	....	Exports of Goods and Services	90c
	103	94	104	102	102	99	83	118	146	....	....	....	....	....	....	Imports of Goods and Services (−)	98c
	361	377	394	392	389	374	362	473	557	525	569	615	637	665	....	Gross Domestic Product (GDP)	99b
Midyear Estimates																	
	2.72	2.88	2.99	2.94	3.02	3.10	3.18	3.00	3.35	3.43	†3.25	3.56	3.65	3.72	3.78	**Population**	99z

(See notes in the back of the book.)

Chad

		1972	1973	1974	1975	1976	1977	1978	1979	1980	1981	1982	1983	1984	1985	1986
Exchange Rates															*Francs per SDR:*	
Official Rate	aa	278.00	284.00	272.08	262.55	288.70	285.76	272.28	264.78	287.99	334.52	370.92	436.97	470.11	415.26	394.78
															Francs per US Dollar:	
Official Rate	ae	256.05	235.42	222.22	224.27	248.49	235.25	209.00	201.00	225.80	287.40	336.25	417.37	479.60	378.05	322.75
Official Rate	rf	252.03	222.89	240.70	214.31	238.95	245.68	225.66	212.72	211.28	271.73	328.61	381.07	436.96	449.26	346.31
Fund Position															*Millions of SDRs:*	
Quota	2f. s	13.00	13.00	13.00	13.00	13.00	13.00	16.00	16.00	24.00	24.00	24.00	30.60	30.60	30.60	30.60
SDRs	1b. s	1.12	.38	2.41	2.27	1.91	1.70	1.46	1.55	—	.02	.26	1.47	.37	3.52	1.69
Reserve Position in the Fund	1c. s	—	—	—	—	—	—	1.24	1.84	3.84	3.84	5.06	3.46	.26	.26	.26
Total Fund Cred.&Loans Outstg.	2tl	2.18	1.02	3.11	2.97	9.47	9.47	13.54	12.99	10.81	12.49	12.49	12.26	8.52	10.90	8.93
International Liquidity											*Millions of US Dollars Unless Otherwise Indicated:*					
Total Reserves minus Gold	1l. d	10.07	1.47	15.27	3.06	23.27	18.78	11.79	11.27	5.05	7.31	12.41	28.00	44.16	33.46	15.91
SDRs	1b. d	1.22	.46	2.95	2.66	2.22	2.07	1.90	2.04	—	.02	.29	1.54	.36	3.87	2.07
Reserve Position in the Fund	1c. d	—	—	—	—	—	—	1.62	2.42	4.90	4.47	5.58	3.62	.25	.29	.32
Foreign Exchange	1d. d	8.86	1.01	12.32	.40	21.06	16.72	8.27	6.80	.16	2.82	6.54	22.84	43.54	29.31	13.52
Gold (Million Fine Troy Ounces)	1ad	....	....	....	—	—	.006	.009	.011	.011	.011	.011	.011	.011	.011	.011
Gold (National Valuation)	1and	....	....	....	—	—	.92	1.94	5.79	6.56	4.45	5.00	4.21	3.44	3.60	4.36
Monetary Authorities: Other Liab.	4.. d	−.14	−.16	−.95	−.95	−.72	−.82	−1.03	7.14	6.30	5.64	5.27	1.61	2.07	4.05	3.60
Deposit Money Banks: Assets	7a. d	3.24	6.74	2.69	5.73	8.84	6.32	14.83	16.05	14.29	10.85	9.25	7.27	17.42	26.99	16.86
Liabilities	7b. d	6.19	6.94	9.43	10.52	7.95	10.11	11.00	7.65	6.81	6.48	3.54	2.85	3.50	3.20	4.17
Monetary Authorities															*Billions of Francs:*	
Foreign Assets	11	2.57	.23	3.50	.78	5.87	4.71	3.49	3.46	2.66	4.19	6.04	13.86	23.07	14.36	6.98
Claims on Central Government	12a	2.24	2.99	3.22	3.30	4.79	5.84	6.79	9.57	9.37	10.43	9.74	9.51	10.14	8.48	9.71
Claims on Deposit Money Banks	12e	3.46	4.07	5.10	11.16	7.27	8.55	14.80	23.95	23.23	17.97	17.81	17.81	22.36	36.68	42.93
Claims on Other Banking Insts	12f	....	....	....	....	....	....	....	....	....	....	....	....	....	....	....
Reserve Money	14	7.06	6.97	9.21	11.81	14.04	15.38	17.64	23.97	20.87	22.83	24.64	30.18	46.36	47.79	47.35
of which: Currency Outside DMBs	14a	6.90	6.49	8.53	10.88	13.00	14.37	16.49	22.54	17.45	22.14	23.61	29.20	44.93	47.35	46.67
Foreign Liabilities	16c	.57	.25	.63	.57	2.55	2.51	4.94	6.30	6.09	7.60	8.41	8.28	6.92	7.31	5.45
Central Government Deposits	16d	.33	.31	.17	.61	.67	.55	1.08	.84	.66	.39	.42	1.08	2.97	3.65	2.21
Capital Accounts	17a	—	.02	.02	.02	.03	.03	.03	.02	1.40	1.19	1.62	1.72	1.60	1.34	1.41
Other Items (Net)	17r	.99	1.05	1.48	3.16	1.85	2.02	4.24	7.40	7.98	1.81	.52	1.98	1.78	1.44	5.15
Deposit Money Banks															*Billions of Francs:*	
Reserves	20	.16	.48	.68	.92	1.04	1.01	1.15	1.43	3.42	.69	1.03	.99	1.43	.44	.67
Foreign Assets	21	.83	1.55	.60	1.28	2.20	1.49	3.10	3.23	3.23	3.12	3.11	3.03	8.35	10.20	5.44
Claims on Central Government	22a	.16	.15	.16	.14	.14	.14	.12	.17	.17	.17	.18	.18	.18	.18	.18
Claims on Nonfin.Pub.Enterprises	22c	....	....	....	....	....	....	....	....	....	....	....	....	....	....	....
Claims on Private Sector	22d	9.09	10.89	14.59	22.25	19.28	23.45	31.09	38.17	37.48	31.26	29.99	32.46	45.93	64.95	75.00
Claims on Other Banking Insts	22f	....	....	....	....	....	....	....	....	....	....	....	....	....	....	....
Claims on Nonbank Financial Insts	22g	....	....	....	....	....	....	....	....	....	....	....	....	....	....	....
Demand Deposits	24	2.57	3.16	5.42	4.44	6.33	7.92	10.87	8.83	8.83	9.34	9.35	11.36	20.00	20.79	22.34
Time and Savings Deposits	25	.49	.86	.98	1.18	1.34	1.19	1.85	1.66	1.66	1.48	1.49	1.64	2.63	3.55	3.58
Foreign Liabilities	26c	.65	.77	1.23	1.49	1.64	2.15	1.89	1.16	1.16	1.49	.81	.81	1.30	.83	.97
Long-Term Foreign Liabilities	26cl	.94	.82	.87	.87	.34	.23	.41	.38	.38	.38	.38	.38	.38	.38	.38
Central Government Deposits	26d	.09	.10	.11	.69	1.17	1.06	.73	.69	.69	.89	.89	.90	2.35	6.52	4.16
Credit from Monetary Authorities	26g	4.16	5.29	5.10	12.37	8.58	10.19	16.79	23.95	23.23	18.01	17.81	17.81	22.36	36.68	42.93
Capital Accounts	27a	1.90	2.83	4.16	5.00	4.78	5.09	5.04	5.04	5.04	5.16	5.16	5.16	5.52	7.58	8.74
Other Items (Net)	27r	−.57	−.77	−1.85	−1.49	−1.48	−1.74	−2.12	1.29	3.30	−1.49	−1.58	−1.40	1.35	−.56	−1.80
Post Office: Checking Deposits	24.. i	.16	.15	.19	.19	.17	.22	.20	.20	.20	.20	.20	.20	.20	.20	.13
Postal Debt	26c. i	1.08	1.78	2.09	2.76	3.73	3.28	2.82	2.81	2.81	2.81	2.81	2.81	2.80	2.80	2.80
Monetary Survey															*Billions of Francs:*	
Foreign Assets (Net)	31n	1.11	−1.02	.15	−2.75	.15	−1.75	−3.05	−3.59	−4.17	−4.59	−2.88	4.99	20.40	13.62	3.21
Domestic Credit	32	11.16	13.32	18.33	24.12	23.06	31.34	39.22	49.40	48.68	43.58	41.62	43.18	53.93	66.45	81.46
Claims on Central Govt. (Net)	32an	2.89	4.27	5.11	4.93	6.90	7.75	8.01	11.22	11.20	12.32	11.62	10.73	8.00	1.50	6.46
Claims on Nonfin.Pub.Enterprises	32c	....	....	....	....	....	....	....	....	....	....	....	....	....	....	....
Claims on Private Sector	32d	9.42	11.29	14.84	22.41	19.35	23.60	31.20	38.17	37.48	31.26	29.99	32.46	45.93	64.95	75.00
Claims on Other Banking Insts	32f	....	....	....	....	....	....	....	....	....	....	....	....	....	....	....
Claims on Nonbank Financial Inst	32g	....	....	....	....	....	....	....	....	....	....	....	....	....	....	....
Money	34	9.46	9.45	14.20	15.59	19.77	22.51	27.57	31.57	26.48	31.68	33.16	40.75	65.13	68.34	69.14
Quasi-Money	35	.49	.86	.98	1.18	1.34	1.19	1.85	1.66	1.66	1.48	1.49	1.64	2.63	3.55	3.58
Other Items (Net)	37r	3.02	4.35	3.79	7.93	6.28	7.01	9.18	13.75	17.72	5.51	4.10	5.74	6.48	8.46	12.09
Money plus Quasi-Money	35l	10.12	10.66	15.11	16.69	20.83	23.71	29.42	33.24	28.14	33.16	34.65	42.39	67.76	71.90	72.71
Interest Rates															*Percent Per Annum*	
Discount Rate (End of Period)	60	4.50	4.50	5.50	5.50	6.50	6.50	6.50	8.50	8.50	8.50	8.50	9.00	9.00	9.00	8.00
Deposit Rate	60l	....	....	....	....	....	....	4.75	4.50	5.50	5.50	5.50	5.50	5.50	5.50	5.50
Lending Rate	60p	....	....	....	....	....	....	10.50	8.50	11.00	11.00	11.00	11.50	11.50	11.50	11.00
Prices and Labor															*Index Numbers (1995=100):*	
Consumer Prices	64	....	....	....	....	....	....	....	....	....	....	....	60.8	73.1	76.9	†66.9

1987	1988	1989	1990	1991	1992	1993	1994	1995	1996	1997	1998	1999	2000	2001		
End of Period															**Exchange Rates**	
378.78	407.68	380.32	364.84	370.48	378.57	404.89	†780.44	728.38	753.06	807.94	791.61	†896.19	918.49	935.39	Official Rate..	aa
End of Period (ae) Period Average (rf)																
267.00	302.95	289.40	256.45	259.00	275.32	294.77	†534.60	490.00	523.70	598.81	562.21	†652.95	704.95	744.31	Official Rate..	ae
300.54	297.85	319.01	272.26	282.11	264.69	283.16	†555.20	499.15	511.55	583.67	589.95	†615.70	711.98	733.04	Official Rate..	rf
End of Period															**Fund Position**	
30.60	30.60	30.60	30.60	30.60	41.30	41.30	41.30	41.30	41.30	41.30	41.30	56.00	56.00	56.00	Quota..	2f. s
6.35	5.72	1.34	.10	.11	.02	.01	—	.02	.16	.01	.01	.02	—	—	SDRs...	1b. s
.26	.26	.26	.26	.27	.27	.28	.28	.28	.28	.28	.28	.28	.28	.28	Reserve Position in the Fund.................	1c. s
13.97	12.24	17.92	21.42	21.42	21.42	20.20	29.30	32.97	45.20	45.31	45.34	50.17	59.96	70.88	Total Fund Cred.&Loans Outstg.............	2tl
End of Period															**International Liquidity**	
52.11	63.08	111.73	127.78	119.79	80.48	38.94	76.01	142.52	164.48	135.82	120.09	95.02	110.70	122.37	Total Reserves minus Gold...................	1l. d
9.01	7.70	1.76	.14	.16	.03	.01	—	.03	.24	.01	.01	.03	—	—	SDRs...	1b. d
.37	.35	.34	.37	.39	.37	.38	.41	.42	.40	.38	.40	.39	.37	.35	Reserve Position in the Fund.................	1c. d
42.73	55.04	109.63	127.27	119.25	80.08	38.54	75.60	142.07	163.84	135.44	119.68	94.60	110.33	122.02	Foreign Exchange...............................	1d. d
.011	.011	.011	.011	.011	.011	.011	.011	.011	.011	.011	.011	.011	.011	.011	Gold (Million Fine Troy Ounces)...........	1ad
5.37	4.52	3.52	3.98	3.94	3.70	4.42	†4.21	4.29	4.10	3.24	3.20	†3.23	3.03	3.09	Gold (National Valuation).....................	1an d
4.76	18.95	19.62	21.27	22.49	18.94	.01	.75	.44	1.10	16.61	12.47	18.56	21.07	18.28	Monetary Authorities: Other Liab.........	4.. d
18.58	15.63	18.66	57.22	31.08	31.02	8.55	11.09	9.91	10.55	32.35	24.20	39.72	27.66	42.53	Deposit Money Banks: Assets.............	7a. d
13.61	13.12	22.32	22.99	25.12	28.40	26.43	22.36	17.37	8.83	14.78	8.59	14.56	12.96	15.53	Liabilities...........	7b. d
End of Period															**Monetary Authorities**	
15.56	†20.49	33.63	33.87	32.04	23.18	12.75	42.93	75.53	88.29	83.26	69.31	64.15	80.18	93.39	Foreign Assets..	11
11.34	†10.93	11.60	13.43	†13.32	29.91	33.79	48.48	49.71	61.94	65.56	64.83	73.94	89.78	101.14	Claims on Central Government................	12a
38.64	†28.12	20.46	15.12	19.52	13.18	9.69	.50	1.00	7.66	5.20	10.70	4.05	.50	4.50	Claims on Deposit Money Banks............	12e
....	4.62	4.56	4.44	4.32	—	—	—	—	—	1.50	3.85	3.30	4.00	3.00	Claims on Other Banking Insts..............	12f
52.20	†46.52	53.23	49.06	50.47	47.94	38.25	47.24	74.73	98.29	94.13	84.51	79.22	92.11	108.15	Reserve Money..	14
46.70	40.27	43.06	46.81	49.45	46.95	35.84	39.69	61.98	89.36	78.81	73.62	68.25	81.27	94.77	*of which: Currency Outside DMBs*.........	14a
6.88	†10.73	12.49	13.27	13.76	13.32	8.18	23.27	24.23	34.62	46.55	42.91	57.08	69.92	79.91	Foreign Liabilities..................................	16c
4.15	†5.10	1.67	2.42	.28	.44	.56	3.61	10.78	6.99	3.40	9.87	3.27	6.16	9.86	Central Government Deposits.................	16d
1.51	†5.31	4.95	4.58	4.77	4.58	5.06	8.38	8.44	8.81	9.03	8.94	9.93	10.42	10.78	Capital Accounts....................................	17a
1.12	†−3.49	−.12	1.35	.02	−.02	4.12	9.41	8.06	9.18	2.40	2.46	−4.06	−4.16	−6.66	Other Items (Net)...................................	17r
End of Period															**Deposit Money Banks**	
5.49	†6.19	9.57	2.18	.93	.86	1.98	6.17	10.08	7.39	12.77	10.13	10.35	9.89	12.89	Reserves...	20
4.96	†4.78	5.40	14.68	†8.05	8.54	2.52	5.93	4.86	5.52	19.37	13.61	25.94	19.50	31.65	Foreign Assets..	21
.63	†.87	.98	1.14	4.45	5.71	6.37	7.98	8.19	2.22	2.49	1.88	1.60	3.08	7.40	Claims on Central Government..............	22a
....	34.08	24.05	16.06	23.38	12.95	6.71	7.13	7.25	17.24	20.77	19.95	15.05	19.49	21.97	Claims on Nonfin.Pub.Enterprises........	22c
74.17	†34.65	33.54	34.44	31.54	31.22	20.86	23.75	27.79	29.95	29.16	34.03	33.89	34.31	43.29	Claims on Private Sector........................	22d
....	—	—	—	—	—	—	—	—	—	—	—	—	—	—	Claims on Other Banking Insts..............	22f
....	—	.01	—	—	.03	—	—	—	—	—	.36	.27	.02	.16	Claims on Nonbank Financial Insts........	22g
23.68	†21.25	23.35	19.45	19.32	15.79	9.19	18.73	20.68	22.98	27.11	25.38	27.80	31.60	43.43	Demand Deposits...................................	24
4.79	†3.91	4.31	3.73	†4.12	3.62	2.20	2.86	7.87	5.36	5.87	5.77	6.11	7.95	9.92	Time and Savings Deposits...................	25
1.75	†2.29	2.04	1.49	†2.31	3.14	7.58	11.22	8.42	4.62	8.79	4.83	7.52	6.87	9.70	Foreign Liabilities..................................	26c
1.89	†4.40	4.42	4.40	†4.20	4.67	.21	.73	.09	—	.06	—	1.99	2.27	1.86	Long-Term Foreign Liabilities................	26cl
7.35	†11.11	10.78	14.77	†13.06	8.14	6.53	4.91	10.84	13.27	24.60	21.36	23.71	22.77	20.20	Central Government Deposits.................	26d
38.64	†28.12	20.46	15.12	†16.45	9.83	5.88	.50	1.00	7.66	5.20	10.70	4.05	.50	4.50	Credit from Monetary Authorities..........	26g
8.59	†7.04	7.63	9.08	†9.45	27.43	10.64	11.95	11.57	13.45	15.52	15.83	17.83	27.35	39.23	Capital Accounts....................................	27a
−1.43	†2.23	.10	−1.98	−.54	−13.35	−3.79	.06	−2.30	−5.01	−2.60	−3.90	−1.91	−13.03	−11.47	Other Items (Net)...................................	27r
.22	.21	....	....	....	....	....	....	....	....	....	....	....	....	....	Post Office: Checking Deposits...........	24.. i
2.80	....	....	....	....	....	....	....	....	....	....	....	....	....	....	Postal Debt..	26c. i
End of Period															**Monetary Survey**	
9.09	†10.58	22.46	31.85	19.83	10.58	−.70	13.64	47.64	54.57	47.23	35.18	23.50	20.61	33.57	Foreign Assets (Net).............................	31n
77.67	†71.20	57.18	54.27	†63.66	71.24	60.64	78.82	71.33	91.09	91.48	93.68	101.07	121.75	146.90	Domestic Credit.....................................	32
3.49	†−1.74	3.56	−.67	†4.43	27.03	33.07	47.94	36.28	43.90	40.06	35.48	48.57	63.93	78.49	Claims on Central Govt. (Net)...........	32an
....	34.08	24.05	16.06	23.38	12.95	6.71	7.13	7.25	17.24	20.77	19.95	15.05	19.49	21.97	Claims on Nonfin.Pub.Enterprises......	32c
74.17	†34.65	33.54	34.44	31.54	31.22	20.86	23.75	27.79	29.95	29.16	34.03	33.89	34.31	43.29	Claims on Private Sector....................	32d
....	4.62	4.56	4.44	4.32	—	—	—	—	—	1.50	3.85	3.30	4.00	3.00	Claims on Other Banking Insts...........	32f
....	—	.01	—	—	.03	—	—	—	—	—	.36	.27	.02	.16	Claims on Nonbank Financial Inst......	32g
70.60	†61.57	66.46	66.34	68.86	62.86	45.47	59.79	85.33	113.88	108.47	99.75	96.67	113.82	138.69	Money..	34
4.79	†3.91	4.31	2.75	†4.12	3.62	2.20	2.86	7.87	5.36	5.87	5.77	6.11	7.95	9.92	Quasi-Money...	35
8.29	11.34	13.01	15.46	†10.62	15.30	12.22	29.80	25.76	26.43	24.36	23.33	21.79	20.58	31.86	Other Items (Net)...................................	37r
75.38	†65.48	70.77	69.08	†72.98	66.48	47.67	62.66	93.20	119.23	114.35	105.52	102.78	121.78	148.61	Money plus Quasi-Money........................	35l
Percent Per Annum															**Interest Rates**	
8.00	9.50	10.00	11.00	10.75	12.00	11.50	†7.75	8.60	7.75	7.50	7.00	7.60	7.00	6.50	Discount Rate (*End of Period*)...................	60
5.33	4.31	4.25	†7.50	7.50	7.50	7.75	8.08	5.50	5.46	5.00	5.00	5.00	5.00	5.00	Deposit Rate...	60l
10.50	10.79	11.50	†18.50	18.15	17.77	17.46	17.50	16.00	22.00	22.00	22.00	22.00	22.00	20.67	Lending Rate..	60p
Period Averages															**Prices and Labor**	
62.9	72.6	69.7	69.6	72.5	70.3	65.3	91.7	100.0	112.4	118.7	133.1	124.1	128.8	144.8	Consumer Prices.....................................	64

Chad

628

		1972	1973	1974	1975	1976	1977	1978	1979	1980	1981	1982	1983	1984	1985	1986
International Transactions															*Millions of Francs*	
Exports	70	9,028	8,483	9,056	10,103	14,861	26,177	22,329	18,776	14,999	22,665	18,968	39,824	57,384	27,781	34,145
Imports, c.i.f.	71	15,675	18,213	20,859	28,325	27,593	46,465	49,034	18,132	15,533	29,349	35,701	59,707	79,272	74,708	73,437
Balance of Payments															*Millions of US Dollars:*	
Current Account, n.i.e.	78al d	...	...	...	...	...	−28.5	−46.4	−8.3	8.6	20.4	18.5	38.0	9.0	−87.2	−59.4
Goods: Exports f.o.b.	78aa d	...	...	...	...	...	106.5	99.0	88.3	71.0	83.4	57.7	78.2	109.7	61.8	98.6
Goods: Imports f.o.b.	78ab d	...	...	...	...	...	−142.2	−163.4	−64.1	−55.3	−81.2	−81.7	−99.1	−128.3	−166.3	−212.1
Trade Balance	78ac d	...	...	...	...	...	−35.7	−64.4	24.2	15.7	2.2	−24.0	−20.9	−18.7	−104.5	−113.5
Services: Credit	78ad d	...	...	...	...	...	24.2	20.6	4.6	.4	4.1	2.4	24.2	36.8	32.6	44.5
Services: Debit	78ae d	...	...	...	...	...	−103.4	−104.1	−54.4	−24.2	−25.3	−22.1	−77.6	−90.1	−153.9	−165.7
Balance on Goods & Services	78af d	...	...	...	...	...	−114.9	−148.0	−25.6	−8.1	−19.0	−43.7	−74.3	−71.9	−225.7	−234.7
Income: Credit	78ag d	...	...	...	...	...	1.6					1.9	4.4	1.3	5.0	3.5
Income: Debit	78ah d	...	...	...	...	...	−3.9	−3.7	−8.6	−3.7	−1.1	−1.0	−3.3	−6.3	−7.3	−12.4
Balance on Gds, Serv. & Inc.	78ai d	...	...	...	...	...	−117.2	−151.6	−34.2	−11.8	−20.1	−42.7	−73.3	−76.8	−228.0	−243.5
Current Transfers, n.i.e.: Credit	78aj d	...	...	...	...	...	106.2	118.8	35.9	24.5	41.1	61.9	118.1	94.0	153.5	204.7
Current Transfers: Debit	78ak d	...	...	...	...	...	−17.6	−13.6	−10.0	−4.1	−.6	−.7	−6.9	−8.1	−12.8	−20.6
Capital Account, n.i.e.	78bc d	...	...	...	...	...	—	—	—	—	—	—	—	—	—	—
Capital Account, n.i.e.: Credit	78ba d	...	...	...	...	...	—	—	—	—	—	—	—	—	—	—
Capital Account: Debit	78bb d	...	...	...	...	...	—	—	—	—	—	—	—	—	—	—
Financial Account, n.i.e.	78bj d	...	...	...	...	...	30.9	26.1	−19.0	−11.4	−3.8	−6.3	−21.6	−6.0	69.2	30.8
Direct Investment Abroad	78bd d	...	...	...	...	...	—	1.0	−1.3	−.4	−.1	−.1	−.1		−.3	−.4
Dir. Invest. in Rep. Econ., n.i.e.	78be d	...	...	...	...	...	21.2	34.1	—	—	—	—	—	9.2	53.7	28.2
Portfolio Investment Assets	78bf d	...	...	...	...	...	—	—	—	—	—	—	—	—	—	—
Equity Securities	78bk d	...	...	...	...	...	—	—	—	—	—	—	—	—	—	—
Debt Securities	78bl d	...	...	...	...	...	—	—	—	—	—	—	—	—	—	—
Portfolio Investment Liab., n.i.e.	78bg d	...	...	...	...	...	—	—	—	—	—	—	—	—	—	—
Equity Securities	78bm d	...	...	...	...	...	—	—	—	—	—	—	—	—	—	—
Debt Securities	78bn d	...	...	...	...	...	—	—	—	—	—	—	—	—	—	—
Financial Derivatives Assets	78bw d	...	...	...	...	...	....	....	....							
Financial Derivatives Liabilities	78bx d	...	...	...	...	...	....	....	....							
Other Investment Assets	78bh d	...	...	...	...	...	−3.4	−2.1	−.3	—	—	—	—	−12.0	−4.1	13.1
Monetary Authorities	78bo d	...	...	...	...	...										
General Government	78bp d	...	...	...	...	...		−2.1		—	—	—	—	−.1	—	−.6
Banks	78bq d	...	...	...	...	...	−1.9		−.3	—	—	—	—	−11.9	−4.1	13.7
Other Sectors	78br d	...	...	...	...	...	−1.5	—	—	—	—	—	—	—	—	—
Other Investment Liab., n.i.e.	78bi d	...	...	...	...	...	13.1	−7.0	−17.5	−11.0	−3.7	−6.2	−21.5	−3.1	19.9	−10.1
Monetary Authorities	78bs d	...	...	...	...	...	−.6	.1	.1	−.1	−.2	−.2	.3	−.1	−.4	−1.5
General Government	78bt d	...	...	...	...	...	9.3	.3	−2.7	−3.7	−1.8	−1.0	−18.0	−6.7	17.8	17.6
Banks	78bu d	...	...	...	...	...	1.4	−1.2	—	—	—	1.2	−.2	—	−.2	.4
Other Sectors	78bv d	...	...	...	...	...	3.0	−6.2	−14.9	−7.2	−1.6	−6.2	−3.6	3.7	2.7	−26.6
Net Errors and Omissions	78ca d	...	...	...	...	...	−7.0	−5.4	−2.4	−21.0	−1.9	−7.8	−7.5	13.7	−5.5	9.7
Overall Balance	78cb d	...	...	...	...	...	−4.7	−25.7	−29.8	−23.8	14.7	4.4	8.9	16.7	−23.6	−18.9
Reserves and Related Items	79da d	...	...	...	...	...	4.7	25.7	29.8	23.8	−14.7	−4.4	−8.9	−16.7	23.6	18.9
Reserve Assets	79db d	...	...	...	...	...	4.7	7.6	3.0	8.0	−.9	−2.4	−17.7	−21.6	18.6	17.5
Use of Fund Credit and Loans	79dc d	...	...	...	...	...	—	5.0	−.7	−2.9	2.5	—	−.2	−3.7	2.5	−2.2
Exceptional Financing	79de d	...	...	...	...	...	—	13.0	27.5	18.7	−16.4	−2.0	9.0	8.6	2.4	3.6
Government Finance															*Millions of Francs:*	
Deficit (-) or Surplus	80	−2,783	−3,910	−2,543	−2,130	−2,848	....	....	−996			−1,252	....	....	†−9,029
Total Revenue and Grants	81y	12,852	13,450	16,707	18,191	20,292	....	....	29,544			39,311	....	....	†61,530
Revenue	81	11,295	11,478	13,836	14,290	15,122	....	....	20,774			24,510	....	....	†17,577
Grants	81z	1,557	1,972	2,871	3,901	5,170	....	....	8,770			14,801	....	....	†43,953
Exp. & Lending Minus Repay.	82z	15,635	17,360	19,250	20,321	23,140	....	....	30,540			40,563	....	....	†70,559
Expenditure	82	15,637	17,373	19,245	20,341	23,169	....	....	30,042			39,937	....	....	†70,559
Lending Minus Repayments	83	−2	−13	5	−20	−29	....	....	498			626	....	....	†—
Statistical Discrepancy	80xx	—	—	—	—	—	....	....	8,272			14,175	....	....	†—
Total Financing	80h	2,783	3,910	2,543	2,130	2,848	....	....	9,268			15,427	....	....	†9,029
Domestic	84a	2,128	2,793	1,733	584	1,399	....	....	9,268			15,427	....	....	†1,845
Foreign	85a	655	1,117	810	1,546	1,449	....	....	—			—	....	....	†7,184
Total Debt by Residence	88	....	....	....	....	....	....	....					....	....	....
Domestic	88a	....	....	....	....	....	....	....	673			759	....	....	....
Foreign	89a	....	....	....	....	....	....	....					....	....	....
National Accounts															*Billions of Francs*	
Gross Domestic Product (GDP)	99b	93.6	102.3	119.9	149.4	162.2	161.3	208.6	....	....	....	187.6	311.0	384.0	390.0	370.0
GDP Volume 1983 Prices	99b.p	139.2	132.4	150.4	176.5	173.8	160.9	....	....	159.5	....	....	221.6	210.5	265.1	258.1
GDP Volume (1985=100)	99bv p	52.5	49.9	56.7	66.6	65.6	60.7	....	....	60.1	....	....	83.6	79.4	100.0	97.3
GDP Deflator (1985=100)	99bi p	45.7	52.5	54.2	57.6	63.4	68.2	....	....	....	....	....	95.4	124.0	100.0	97.5
																Millions:
Population	99z	3.79	3.86	3.95	4.03	4.12	4.21	4.31	4.38	4.48	4.58	4.68	4.80	4.91	5.02	5.12

Millions of Francs

	1987	1988	1989	1990	1991	1992	1993	1994	1995	1996	1997	1998	1999	2000	2001	International Transactions	
Exports	32,892	42,900	49,570	51,202	54,600	48,250	37,330	82,160	121,273	121,895	138,130	154,455	124,138	130,200	121,200	Exports	70
Imports, c.i.f.	67,894	68,000	75,100	77,742	70,500	64,320	56,910	98,310	182,400	169,733	194,732	210,207	194,523	234,300	463,000	Imports, c.i.f.	71

Balance of Payments

Minus Sign Indicates Debit

	1987	1988	1989	1990	1991	1992	1993	1994	1995	1996	1997	1998	1999	2000	2001		Code
Current Account, n.i.e.	−25.5	25.5	−55.9	−45.6	−65.6	−85.7	−116.6	−37.7	....	....	....	....	....	....	....	Current Account, n.i.e.	78al d
Goods: Exports f.o.b.	109.4	145.9	155.4	230.3	193.5	182.3	151.8	135.3								Goods: Exports f.o.b.	78aa d
Goods: Imports f.o.b.	−225.9	−228.4	−240.3	−259.5	−249.9	−243.0	−215.2	−212.1								Goods: Imports f.o.b.	78ab d
Trade Balance	−116.5	−82.5	−84.9	−29.2	−56.3	−60.7	−63.5	−76.8								Trade Balance	78ac d
Services: Credit	70.4	78.7	42.3	40.9	30.9	26.7	47.1	54.8								Services: Credit	78ad d
Services: Debit	−198.0	−217.9	−210.0	−228.2	−208.0	−224.1	−235.1	−199.4								Services: Debit	78ae d
Balance on Goods & Services	−244.0	−221.7	−252.6	−216.5	−233.4	−258.1	−251.4	−221.4								Balance on Goods & Services	78af d
Income: Credit	2.9	2.1	1.3	3.0	8.9	17.5	4.3	5.0								Income: Credit	78ag d
Income: Debit	−13.1	−15.5	−10.8	−23.8	−11.2	−14.9	−15.7	−12.4								Income: Debit	78ah d
Balance on Gds, Serv. & Inc.	−254.2	−235.0	−262.0	−237.2	−235.7	−255.5	−262.9	−228.7								Balance on Gds, Serv. & Inc.	78ai d
Current Transfers, n.i.e.: Credit	257.0	301.4	241.4	239.3	215.5	222.3	192.4	209.4								Current Transfers, n.i.e.: Credit	78aj d
Current Transfers: Debit	−28.3	−40.8	−35.2	−47.7	−45.3	−52.5	−46.2	−18.4								Current Transfers: Debit	78ak d
Capital Account, n.i.e.	—	—	—	—	—	—	—	—								Capital Account, n.i.e.	78bc d
Capital Account, n.i.e.: Credit	—	—	—	—	—	—	—	—								Capital Account, n.i.e.: Credit	78ba d
Capital Account: Debit	—	—	—	—	—	—	—	—								Capital Account: Debit	78bb d
Financial Account, n.i.e.	9.1	24.2	74.4	56.1	59.0	33.7	68.8	76.3								Financial Account, n.i.e.	78bj d
Direct Investment Abroad	−8.0	−13.8	−12.5	—	−10.5	−13.8	−10.9	−.6								Direct Investment Abroad	78bd d
Dir. Invest. in Rep. Econ., n.i.e.	8.2	1.3	18.7	—	4.2	2.0	15.2	27.1								Dir. Invest. in Rep. Econ., n.i.e.	78be d
Portfolio Investment Assets	—	—	—	—	—	—	—	—								Portfolio Investment Assets	78bf d
Equity Securities	—	—	—	—	—	—	—	—								Equity Securities	78bk d
Debt Securities	—	—	—	—	—	—	—	—								Debt Securities	78bl d
Portfolio Investment Liab., n.i.e.	—	—	—	—	—	—	—	—								Portfolio Investment Liab., n.i.e.	78bg d
Equity Securities	—	—	—	—	—	—	—	—								Equity Securities	78bm d
Debt Securities	—	—	—	—	—	—	—	—								Debt Securities	78bn d
Financial Derivatives Assets	....															Financial Derivatives Assets	78bw d
Financial Derivatives Liabilities	....															Financial Derivatives Liabilities	78bx d
Other Investment Assets	12.1	10.3	3.5	—	24.2	3.9	42.1	.6								Other Investment Assets	78bh d
Monetary Authorities	....															Monetary Authorities	78bo d
General Government	....															General Government	78bp d
Banks	1.6	.8	−3.1	—	23.5	−1.8	31.0	−4.8								Banks	78bq d
Other Sectors	10.5	9.5	6.6	—	.7	5.7	11.0	5.4								Other Sectors	78br d
Other Investment Liab., n.i.e.	−3.1	26.4	64.7	56.1	41.1	41.6	22.5	49.2								Other Investment Liab., n.i.e.	78bi d
Monetary Authorities	.5	−.2	−.1	—	−.9	−6.3	−5.2	−.1								Monetary Authorities	78bs d
General Government	38.2	46.1	79.0	103.4	81.3	71.3	102.1	49.8								General Government	78bt d
Banks	2.6	1.1	—	−36.7	2.2	5.0	—									Banks	78bu d
Other Sectors	−44.4	−20.6	−14.2	−10.6	−41.5	−28.3	−74.4	−.6								Other Sectors	78bv d
Net Errors and Omissions	16.5	−83.7	11.1	−33.3	−13.0	9.2	−.1	−33.0								Net Errors and Omissions	78ca d
Overall Balance	.1	−34.0	29.6	−22.9	−19.6	−42.8	−47.9	5.5								Overall Balance	78cb d
Reserves and Related Items	−.1	34.0	−29.6	22.9	19.6	42.8	47.9	−5.5								Reserves and Related Items	79da d
Reserve Assets	−25.0	14.8	−41.3	3.6	8.2	32.9	39.4	−30.7								Reserve Assets	79db d
Use of Fund Credit and Loans	6.6	−2.3	6.9	4.6	—	—	−1.7	12.7								Use of Fund Credit and Loans	79dc d
Exceptional Financing	18.3	21.5	4.8	14.7	11.4	9.9	10.2	12.4								Exceptional Financing	79de d

Government Finance

Year Ending December 31

	1987	1988	1989	1990	1991	1992	1993	1994	1995	1996	1997	1998	1999	2000	2001		Code
Deficit (-) or Surplus	−8,365	−11,893	−18,763	−23,609	†−42,301	−63,670	−22,954	−82,198	−45,532	−97,696	−65,653	−65,161	−56,178	−47,612	3,653	Deficit (-) or Surplus	80
Total Revenue and Grants	73,380	73,490	86,577	79,643	†57,101	71,072	79,116	87,592	98,502	110,407	128,747	115,415	107,489	136,732	145,106	Total Revenue and Grants	81y
Revenue	19,471	24,775	29,010	31,567	32,243	31,421	29,150	31,964	44,834	59,790	72,359	77,347	79,289	88,750	96,867	Revenue	81
Grants	53,909	48,715	57,567	48,076	24,858	39,651	49,966	55,628	53,668	50,617	56,388	38,068	28,200	47,982	48,239	Grants	81z
Exp. & Lending Minus Repay.	81,745	85,383	105,340	103,252	†99,402	134,742	102,070	169,790	144,034	208,103	194,400	180,576	163,667	184,344	141,453	Exp. & Lending Minus Repay.	82z
Expenditure	81,745	85,341	105,038	103,252	80,542	124,952	104,840	148,300	130,304	151,794	159,400	153,028	163,667	184,344	141,453	Expenditure	82
Lending Minus Repayments	—	42	302	—	18,860	9,790	−2,770	21,490	13,730	56,309	35,000	27,548	—	—	—	Lending Minus Repayments	83
Statistical Discrepancy	—	—	6,695	−1,158	−2,893	−9,536	−4,428	−1,341	31,313	22,600	46,377	13,208	32,642	−23,310	34,390	Statistical Discrepancy	80xx
Total Financing	8,365	11,893	25,458	22,451	†39,408	54,134	18,526	80,857	76,845	120,296	112,030	78,369	88,820	24,302	30,737	Total Financing	80h
Domestic	660	−1,506	−4,629	−1,185	−281	19,927	9,916	−460	−5,817	14,546	28,432	5,041	32,650	9,658	1,141	Domestic	84a
Foreign	7,705	13,399	30,087	23,636	39,689	34,207	8,610	81,317	82,662	105,750	83,598	73,328	56,170	14,644	29,596	Foreign	85a
Total Debt by Residence	....	....	....	156,475	†154,916	196,019	225,936	423,574	435,728	489,035	546,857	525,691	642,939	800,014	862,293	Total Debt by Residence	88
Domestic	....	....	....	29,975	3,316	3,119	4,236	6,503	5,481	4,236	7,108	7,310	24,000	65,113	66,300	Domestic	88a
Foreign	....	96,923	116,900	126,500	151,600	192,900	221,700	417,071	430,247	484,799	539,749	518,381	618,939	734,901	795,993	Foreign	89a

National Accounts

Billions of Francs

	1987	1988	1989	1990	1991	1992	1993	1994	1995	1996	1997	1998	1999	2000	2001		Code
Gross Domestic Product (GDP)	570.0	422.0	427.0	439.0	451.0	441.0	412.0	655.0	717.8	830.0	889.0	1,005.0	967.0	1,016.0	1,236.0	Gross Domestic Product (GDP)	99b
GDP Volume 1983 Prices	243.7	....		....		....		....		....		....		....		GDP Volume 1983 Prices	99b.p
GDP Volume (1985=100)	91.9	....		....		....		....		....		....		....		GDP Volume (1985=100)	99bv p
GDP Deflator (1985=100)	159.0	....		....		....		....		....		....		....		GDP Deflator (1985=100)	99bi p

Midyear Estimates

	1987	1988	1989	1990	1991	1992	1993	1994	1995	1996	1997	1998	1999	2000	2001		Code
Population	5.22	5.32	5.56	5.69	5.82	5.96	6.10	6.21	6.74	6.95	7.17	7.40	7.64	7.89	8.14	Population	99z

(See notes in the back of the book.)

Chile

228		1972	1973	1974	1975	1976	1977	1978	1979	1980	1981	1982	1983	1984	1985	1986
Exchange Rates																*Pesos per Thousand SDRs through 1973*
Market Rate	**aa**	54.29	904.76	†2.45	9.95	20.24	33.96	44.23	51.38	49.74	45.39	64.50	76.23	87.26	201.74	250.75
																Pesos per Thousand US Dollars through 1973
Market Rate	**ae**	50.00	750.00	†2.00	8.50	17.42	27.96	33.95	39.00	39.00	39.00	58.47	72.81	89.02	183.66	205.00
Market Rate	**rf**	20.84	71.64	†.59	4.91	13.05	21.54	31.66	37.25	39.00	39.00	50.91	78.79	98.48	160.86	192.93
																Index Numbers (1995=100):
Market Rate	**ahx**	....	963,665.1	77,520.0	9,915.9	3,135.7	1,875.5	1,255.7	1,066.6	1,016.1	1,016.1	826.1	504.5	409.1	249.9	205.6
Nominal Effective Exchange Rate	**nec**	....	....	....	....	....	....	....	65.2	67.4	79.6	76.9	58.6	59.4	45.6	37.6
Real Effective Exchange Rate	**rec**	....	....	....	....	....	....	....	....	165.2	195.7	176.5	144.6	143.4	113.6	97.2
Fund Position																*Millions of SDRs:*
Quota	**2f.s**	158.0	158.0	158.0	158.0	158.0	158.0	217.0	217.0	325.5	325.5	325.5	440.5	440.5	440.5	440.5
SDRs	**1b.s**	2.0	.3	13.8	20.9	48.3	54.7	20.7	22.0	3.0	16.4	17.7	5.2	11.7	.3	.2
Reserve Position in the Fund	**1c.s**	—	—	—	—	—	—	38.3	37.1	64.3	64.3	70.5	—	—	—	—
Total Fund Cred.&Loans Outstg.	**2tl**	79.0	79.0	160.0	330.8	402.2	300.6	266.5	135.9	96.3	41.8	5.7	579.0	795.0	990.6	1,088.3
International Liquidity																*Millions of US Dollars Unless Otherwise Indicated:*
Total Reserves minus Gold	**1l.d**	96.8	121.6	41.1	55.9	405.1	426.5	1,090.1	1,938.3	3,123.2	3,213.3	1,815.0	2,036.3	2,303.2	2,449.9	2,351.3
SDRs	**1b.d**	2.2	.4	16.9	24.5	56.1	66.4	27.0	28.9	3.8	19.1	19.5	5.4	11.5	.3	.2
Reserve Position in the Fund	**1c.d**	—	—	—	—	—	—	49.9	48.9	82.0	74.8	77.8	—	—	—	—
Foreign Exchange	**1d.d**	94.6	121.2	24.2	31.4	349.0	360.1	1,013.2	1,860.5	3,037.5	3,119.4	1,717.7	2,030.9	2,291.7	2,449.6	2,351.1
Gold (Million Fine Troy Ounces)	**1ad**	1.355	1.376	1.438	1.297	1.336	1.364	1.390	1.524	1.704	1.702	1.712	....	....	....	1.795
Gold (National Valuation)	**1and**	51.5	58.1	60.7	54.8	56.4	57.6	58.7	439.5	963.4	660.4	655.9	566.7[e]	540.1	518.6	668.1
Monetary Authorities: Other Liab.	**4..d**	274.2	490.8	490.8	603.3	157.2	687.4	595.3	1,260.2	1,184.3	836.0	766.9	2,218.8	3,717.9	4,420.8	4,423.5
Deposit Money Banks: Assets	**7a.d**	40.0	66.7	98.4	96.1	124.2	104.7	143.8	298.8	548.2	881.4	959.2	814.0	722.0	413.0	480.0
Liabilities	**7b.d**	240.0	336.1	368.4	323.6	296.5	410.9	831.0	1,579.4	3,535.3	6,238.2	7,282.2	6,311.0	6,733.0	6,572.0	6,221.0
Monetary Authorities																*Millions of Pesos through 1976;*
Foreign Assets	**11**	3.9	87.9	445.2	1,635.7	†10476.0	†18.9	48.6	109.7	165.6	147.1	185.5	231.3	364.1	534.7	630.0
Claims on Central Government	**12a**	88.1	759.8	3,737.1	18,708.2	†39597.0	†87.8	92.1	116.8	108.6	58.0	53.5	163.2	425.8	1,129.9	1,519.4
Claims on Nonfin.Pub.Enterprises	**12c**	....	....	....	....	1,616.0	†1.9	2.1	.7	1.3	.5	.9	.6	.8	.8	.9
Claims on Private Sector	**12d**	.5	6.8	41.5	120.1	†7,874.0	†2.1	34.0	52.5	54.6	59.7	176.4	228.6	278.6	357.5	412.8
Claims on Deposit Money Banks	**12e**	6.9	8.5	216.2	875.7	†3,176.0	†6.1	18.0	20.8	25.4	39.2	152.3	601.8	876.1	1,695.6	1,886.9
Claims on Other Banking Insts	**12f**	....	....	....	....	253.0	†.6	.9	1.0	3.0	2.5	12.9	26.3	47.9	53.8	43.1
Reserve Money	**14**	60.0	310.9	1,003.5	3,568.2	†15110.0	†29.2	50.2	72.4	117.8	106.1	226.5	520.1	918.7	1,918.4	2,328.9
of which: Currency Outside DMBs	**14a**	28.2	95.7	349.3	1,358.2	†4,480.0	†9.3	16.4	24.9	35.6	44.5	43.0	51.9	64.2	79.5	108.5
Time, Savings,& Fgn.Currency Dep.	**15**	....	....	....	....	5,435.0	†6.3	8.0	8.1	11.0	11.3	72.1	158.4	165.5	285.9	328.9
Foreign Liabilities	**16c**	8.7	211.2	1,283.8	8,424.0	†—	†—	—	—	—	—	15.2	79.3	161.1	254.2	267.5
Long-Term Foreign Liabilities	**16cl**	....	....	....	....	10,879.0	†25.3	26.7	43.5	36.9	20.6	46.8	181.9	412.9	735.3	891.8
Central Government Deposits	**16d**	3.2	49.4	177.8	505.2	†5,701.0	†12.9	25.5	50.6	43.5	33.0	22.9	22.6	29.2	87.7	118.4
Capital Accounts	**17a**	6.4	70.9	475.1	2,384.4	†8,985.0	†22.3	51.7	121.5	143.5	139.4	198.9	230.3	173.7	224.6	263.7
Other Items (Net)	**17r**	21.1	220.6	1,499.8	6,457.9	†16882.0	†21.4	33.6	5.4	5.8	−3.3	−.7	59.4	132.1	266.2	294.0
Deposit Money Banks																*Millions of Pesos through 1976;*
Reserves	**20**	33.5	241.1	764.5	3,281.0	†9,742.0	†20.5	31.1	41.8	55.5	40.0	24.4	39.4	43.0	96.0	102.2
Foreign Assets	**21**	1.3	24.4	183.7	817.3	†2,159.0	†3.4	5.7	12.4	21.6	35.5	70.6	71.3	96.7	63.8	96.6
Claims on Central Government	**22a**	10.9	85.2	343.0	1,359.4	†1,090.0	†2.2	3.4	8.5	1.5	1.9	56.5	75.2	109.7	191.9	187.5
Claims on Local Government	**22b**	....	....	....	....	1.0	†—	—	—	.1	—	—	.2	.1	.1	.2
Claims on Nonfin.Pub.Enterprises	**22c**	....	....	....	....	3,179.0	†3.2	3.4	3.3	5.7	7.8	13.9	15.7	24.9	52.3	74.2
Claims on Private Sector	**22d**	22.3	69.9	541.0	2,952.7	†12844.0	†55.5	107.1	211.4	412.1	590.8	845.5	925.8	1,256.5	1,448.4	1,696.3
Claims on Other Banking Insts	**22f**	....	....	....	....	—	†—	.1	.7	9.0	21.1	1.3	.9	1.4	1.8	1.5
Demand Deposits	**24**	25.9	132.9	487.4	1,620.5	†6,141.0	†8.9	22.0	40.4	63.8	65.5	70.5	78.8	97.1	120.8	178.5
Time, Savings,& Fgn.Currency Dep.	**25**	20.0	93.0	441.0	2,218.0	†9,838.0	†27.3	56.2	97.5	167.4	237.5	298.7	298.8	393.5	574.8	713.4
Bonds	**26ab**	....	....	....	....	—	†—	1.3	8.3	28.3	48.5	82.1	110.5	155.0	199.3	241.9
Foreign Liabilities	**26c**	6.0	121.0	689.0	2,751.2	†5,165.0	†15.1	17.0	27.3	52.2	76.0	147.4	124.4	85.2	92.0	164.1
Long-Term Foreign Liabilities	**26cl**	....	....	....	....	—	†—	11.3	39.7	96.7	193.9	388.2	428.0	775.3	926.4	1,089.1
Central Government Deposits	**26d**	17.7	142.7	476.6	2,069.8	†4,655.0	†15.1	17.5	27.3	72.5	59.5	49.0	52.8	59.5	86.0	105.0
Credit from Monetary Authorities	**26g**	8.9	25.0	237.8	701.2	†2,113.0	†8.9	15.8	21.6	26.3	34.6	48.1	463.5	663.1	1,150.9	1,183.2
Liabilities to Other Financ. Insts	**26i**	....	....	....	....	—	†—	—	.7	1.9	4.9	10.8	3.5	16.0	40.6	86.1
Capital Accounts	**27a**	4.0	45.0	617.0	3,642.9	†10688.0	†20.1	25.7	41.9	66.8	78.3	99.2	93.7	93.4	699.9	859.0
Other Items (Net)	**27r**	−14.5	−139.0	−1,116.6	−4,593.2	†−9585.0	†−10.6	−16.0	−26.7	−70.4	−101.7	−181.8	−525.4	−805.6	−2,036.2	−2,461.7
Monetary Survey																*Millions of Pesos through 1976;*
Foreign Assets (Net)	**31n**	−9.5	−219.9	−1,343.9	−8,722.2	†−3409.0	†−18.1	−.7	11.7	1.4	−107.9	−341.5	−510.9	−973.8	−1,409.4	−1,685.9
Domestic Credit	**32**	100.9	729.6	4,008.2	20,565.4	†56098.0	†125.3	200.0	316.9	479.8	649.8	1,089.2	1,361.2	2,057.1	3,062.9	3,712.5
Claims on Central Govt. (Net)	**32an**	78.1	652.9	3,425.7	17,492.6	†30331.0	†62.0	52.5	47.3	−5.9	−32.7	38.2	163.1	446.8	1,148.1	1,483.5
Claims on Local Government	**32b**	....	....	....	....	1.0	†—	—	—	.1	—	—	.2	.1	.1	.2
Claims on Nonfin.Pub.Enterprises	**32c**	....	....	....	....	4,795.0	†5.1	5.5	4.0	7.0	8.3	14.8	16.3	25.7	53.1	75.1
Claims on Private Sector	**32d**	22.8	76.7	582.5	3,072.8	†20718.0	†57.6	141.1	263.9	466.7	650.5	1,021.9	1,154.4	1,535.2	1,805.9	2,109.1
Claims on Other Banking Insts	**32f**	....	....	....	....	253.0	†.6	1.0	1.7	12.0	23.6	14.3	27.3	49.3	55.6	44.6
Money	**34**	54.1	228.6	836.7	2,978.7	†11502.0	†19.8	39.4	66.8	101.0	110.6	113.7	131.5	161.4	200.5	287.2
Quasi-Money	**35**	20.0	93.0	441.0	2,218.0	†15273.0	†33.6	64.2	105.6	178.4	248.8	370.9	457.2	559.0	860.7	1,042.2
Bonds	**36ab**	....	....	....	....	—	†—	1.3	8.3	28.3	48.5	82.1	110.5	155.0	199.3	241.9
Liabilities to Other Financ. Insts	**36i**	....	....	....	....	—	†—	—	.7	1.9	4.9	10.8	3.5	16.0	40.6	86.1
Capital Accounts	**37a**	10.4	115.9	1,092.1	6,027.3	†19673.0	†42.4	77.3	163.5	210.3	217.6	298.1	323.9	267.1	924.4	1,122.7
Other Items (Net)	**37r**	6.9	72.2	294.5	619.2	†6,241.0	†11.4	17.0	−16.2	−38.7	−88.5	−127.9	−176.3	−75.2	−572.0	−753.5
Money plus Quasi-Money	**35l**	74.1	321.6	1,277.7	5,196.7	†26775.0	†53.4	103.6	172.4	279.5	359.4	484.6	588.6	720.4	1,061.2	1,329.4
Other Banking Institutions																*Billions of Pesos:*
Reserves	**40**	....	....	....	....	....	....	....	.9	4.9	1.7	1.4	4.7	8.0	8.0	4.4
Foreign Assets	**41**	....	....	....	....	....	....	....	—	—	—	—	.1	.1	—	—
Claims on Central Government	**42a**	....	....	....	....	....	....	....	4.5	—	—	.1	.6	.5	1.5	2.3
Claims on Local Government	**42b**	....	....	....	....	....	....	....	—	—	—	—	—	—	—	—
Claims on Nonfin.Pub.Enterprises	**42c**	....	....	....	....	....	....	....	.1	.1	.1	.4	.4	.1	.1	.5
Claims on Private Sector	**42d**	....	....	....	....	....	....	....	16.0	37.1	26.2	20.0	18.5	25.5	32.5	34.7
Claims on Deposit Money Banks	**42e**	....	....	....	....	....	....	....	.9	2.3	1.6	2.8	1.9	2.7	4.1	1.9
Time, Savings,& Fgn.Currency Dep.	**45**	....	....	....	....	....	....	....	16.8	28.3	19.6	15.0	15.9	23.0	27.0	27.6
Bonds	**46ab**	....	....	....	....	....	....	....	—	.1	2.1	1.9	2.3	3.6	4.8	5.4
Foreign Liabilities	**46c**	....	....	....	....	....	....	....	—	—	—	—	—	—	.2	—
Long-Term Foreign Liabilities	**46cl**	....	....	....	....	....	....	....	.8	.9	1.2	.8	.9	.8	.5	.2
Central Government Deposits	**46d**	....	....	....	....	....	....	....	—	.1	—	.1	.5	.2	.3	.7
Credit from Monetary Authorities	**46g**	....	....	....	....	....	....	....	.1	1.5	—	4.1	4.8	4.9	6.5	4.6
Credit from Deposit Money Banks	**46h**	....	....	....	....	....	....	....	1.7	8.8	3.3	1.3	.2	1.0	3.1	3.2
Capital Accounts	**47a**	....	....	....	....	....	....	....	3.1	4.7	3.5	3.2	3.0	3.7	4.7	3.3
Other Items (Net)	**47r**	....	....	....	....	....	....	....	—	—	−.2	−1.6	−1.4	−.4	−.8	−1.2

Chile

1987	1988	1989	1990	1991	1992	1993	1994	1995	1996	1997	1998	1999	2000	2001		228
															Exchange Rates	
and per SDR thereafter: End of Period																
337.80	333.05	389.75	479.24	536.23	525.70	592.06	589.91	605.19	611.09	593.41	667.08	727.53	746.15	824.67	Market Rate	aa
and per US Dollar thereafter: End of Period (ae) Period Average (rf)																
238.11	247.49	296.58	336.86	374.87	382.33	431.04	404.09	407.13	424.97	439.81	473.77	530.07	572.68	656.20	Market Rate	ae
219.41	245.01	266.95	304.90	349.22	362.58	404.17	420.18	396.77	412.27	419.30	460.29	508.78	535.47	634.94	Market Rate	rf
Period Averages																
181.0	161.8	149.0	130.2	113.6	109.4	98.1	94.3	100.0	96.1	94.5	86.1	78.0	74.1	62.8	Market Rate	ahx
34.1	37.3	51.6	62.6	63.6	70.4	79.9	94.7	100.0	99.8	105.5	100.5	93.7	93.1	84.0	Nominal Effective Exchange Rate	nec
89.3	84.1	86.3	82.3	84.5	89.5	91.6	94.3	100.0	103.4	113.1	111.1	105.4	106.0	96.6	Real Effective Exchange Rate	rec
															Fund Position	
End of Period																
440.5	440.5	440.5	440.5	440.5	621.7	621.7	621.7	621.7	621.7	621.7	621.7	856.1	856.1	856.1	Quota	2f.s
28.8	32.9	18.5	.7	.5	.5	.9	.5	2.1	1.3	1.0	5.9	13.5	18.9	23.0	SDRs	1b.s
—	—	—	—	—	—	—	—	—	35.0	232.0	429.6	299.4	248.8	245.7	Reserve Position in the Fund	1c.s
1,032.4	982.6	966.5	812.9	669.4	525.0	346.5	199.5	—	—	—	—	—	—	—	Total Fund Cred.&Loans Outstg.	2tl
															International Liquidity	
End of Period																
2,504.2	3,160.5	3,628.6	6,068.5	7,041.3	9,167.7	9,640.3	13,087.6	14,139.8	14,833.2	17,305.8	15,662.6	14,406.8	14,729.3	14,219.4	Total Reserves minus Gold	1l.d
40.8	44.3	24.4	1.0	.8	.6	1.3	.7	3.1	1.9	1.3	8.3	18.5	24.6	28.9	SDRs	1b.d
—	—	—	—	—	—	—	—	—	50.4	313.1	604.9	411.0	324.2	308.7	Reserve Position in the Fund	1c.d
2,463.4	3,116.2	3,604.2	6,067.5	7,040.5	9,167.0	9,639.0	13,086.9	14,136.7	14,780.9	16,991.4	15,049.4	13,977.3	14,380.5	13,881.7	Foreign Exchange	1d.d
1.811	1.824	1.752	1.858	1.863	1.867	1.865	1.864	1.861	1.859	1.858	1.222	1.220	.074	.074	Gold (Million Fine Troy Ounces)	1ad
757.4	679.4	592.0	641.5	596.9	574.0	612.0	652.0	642.8	637.4	533.0	321.9	316.9	318.3	18.6	Gold (National Valuation)	1and
4,912.1	3,921.8	2,605.2	2,380.4	2,103.0	1,995.2	1,917.0	2,388.1	976.2	3.4	3.1	2.7	2.4	2.1	1.8	Monetary Authorities: Other Liab.	4..d
342.0	395.0	378.0	507.0	526.6	520.0	524.0	547.0	490.0	605.0	1,257.2	2,111.6	4,961.5	4,544.0	3,314.0	Deposit Money Banks: Assets	7a.d
5,071.0	4,197.0	3,331.0	2,972.0	2,354.2	3,505.0	3,793.0	4,258.0	3,962.0	3,634.0	2,116.7	2,203.7	1,419.0	1,166.4	1,682.0	Liabilities	7b.d
															Monetary Authorities	
Billions of Pesos Beginning 1977: End of Period																
783.3	971.9	1,209.2	2,313.6	2,923.2	4,115.5	4,749.6	5,999.0	6,439.5	7,230.9	8,440.9	7,590.6	7,972.6	8,607.2	9,549.4	Foreign Assets	11
1,879.5	2,177.3	2,197.4	2,795.4	3,143.0	3,432.4	3,814.8	3,597.8	3,805.1	3,817.6	3,852.4	3,637.4	3,817.3	4,249.0	4,718.6	Claims on Central Government	12a
—	.6	—	—	—	—	—	—	—	—	—	—	—	—	—	Claims on Nonfin.Pub.Enterprises	12c
465.7	511.7	86.6	106.9	127.1	146.7	167.5	188.0	200.8	224.8	301.6	311.3	321.8	340.2	355.2	Claims on Private Sector	12d
2,039.0	1,826.0	1,879.9	2,168.9	2,378.0	2,393.0	2,484.2	2,397.3	2,453.8	2,256.8	1,146.2	1,161.7	1,099.3	1,552.9	2,254.2	Claims on Deposit Money Banks	12e
45.7	42.3	53.6	56.7	58.1	56.1	51.1	43.4	.8	.3	.9	.2	—	—	—	Claims on Other Banking Insts	12f
2,515.6	2,568.6	2,521.9	3,892.9	4,813.8	5,859.8	6,658.9	8,039.8	9,157.9	10,613.0	12,308.1	11,863.9	12,974.3	14,723.7	15,870.7	Reserve Money	14
135.7	181.6	221.8	285.5	368.4	480.5	582.1	667.3	784.2	859.5	985.3	977.3	1,185.6	1,128.3	1,232.7	*of which: Currency Outside DMBs*	14a
404.7	441.1	545.1	570.4	365.7	303.7	285.7	258.9	110.9	62.7	71.2	62.5	58.4	48.1	115.0	Time, Savings,& Fgn.Currency Dep.	15
392.5	330.1	358.7	407.1	362.3	305.3	222.0	155.4	1.1	1.8	3.1	3.4	101.1	21.4	31.6	Foreign Liabilities	16c
1,096.8	979.3	735.6	770.9	804.3	843.8	888.6	1,002.2	648.8	1.6	1.4	1.3	1.3	1.2	1.2	Long-Term Foreign Liabilities	16cl
188.4	219.7	245.1	473.2	806.3	1,200.6	1,371.0	1,573.3	1,753.7	2,011.3	2,390.9	2,085.4	1,495.2	1,324.9	1,097.6	Central Government Deposits	16d
327.6	378.6	478.8	624.9	402.3	802.5	520.7	–113.3	374.1	268.3	–492.0	–892.2	–767.2	–624.5	350.6	Capital Accounts	17a
287.6	612.4	541.6	702.1	1,074.8	827.8	1,320.4	1,309.1	853.5	571.9	–540.8	–423.1	–651.9	–745.5	–589.2	Other Items (Net)	17r
															Deposit Money Banks	
Billions of Pesos Beginning 1977: End of Period																
127.5	160.3	153.1	178.1	337.0	528.6	575.8	711.9	721.7	746.7	564.1	897.9	896.7	864.4	930.2	Reserves	20
81.0	98.7	107.0	179.4	197.3	207.9	225.7	221.0	199.4	256.5	552.4	999.7	2,617.4	2,601.3	2,174.6	Foreign Assets	21
163.6	23.4	22.2	23.0	26.3	27.8	51.3	56.6	84.0	137.0	306.4	188.7	179.8	147.8	194.7	Claims on Central Government	22a
.2	.4	.3	.4	—	.4	.4	.4	.5	.5	.4	.3	.3	.3	.7	Claims on Local Government	22b
98.1	50.9	81.2	301.6	247.1	174.7	165.8	124.5	95.4	88.7	136.4	672.2	219.2	342.8	468.4	Claims on Nonfin.Pub.Enterprises	22c
2,122.2	2,606.7	3,531.5	4,152.1	5,155.6	6,892.8	8,933.2	10,452.6	13,429.8	16,081.7	18,837.3	20,577.1	22,483.0	25,060.6	27,263.2	Claims on Private Sector	22d
2.0	1.9	2.5	.9	2.5	.4	9.9	5.5	26.9	21.7	47.7	23.7	17.7	35.8	42.4	Claims on Other Banking Insts	22f
211.7	327.2	374.6	449.7	695.7	863.1	1,046.3	1,224.6	1,528.3	1,826.6	2,242.6	1,821.9	2,533.0	2,776.6	2,873.7	Demand Deposits	24
1,042.6	1,331.6	1,851.5	2,391.6	3,305.7	4,192.1	5,290.7	5,871.6	7,672.8	9,322.2	10,741.0	12,525.0	13,883.0	14,799.5	15,378.7	Time, Savings,& Fgn.Currency Dep.	25
284.2	336.1	440.9	610.8	843.3	1,086.3	1,449.9	2,090.4	2,902.4	3,717.6	4,586.4	4,844.9	5,263.9	5,661.2	6,270.4	Bonds	26ab
218.9	309.7	452.6	608.6	564.8	1,173.1	1,316.6	1,359.4	1,155.6	1,020.0	332.2	422.1	140.9	252.1	640.5	Foreign Liabilities	26c
978.2	734.5	489.3	443.2	317.3	316.4	318.4	361.3	457.5	524.4	598.7	621.9	607.9	415.9	463.3	Long-Term Foreign Liabilities	26cl
134.4	192.5	156.4	255.9	301.6	357.7	425.4	488.8	707.6	684.2	894.1	749.1	979.4	867.3	1,127.0	Central Government Deposits	26d
1,167.3	912.1	901.0	841.4	836.7	692.0	538.2	439.9	361.1	326.3	236.4	177.0	120.0	140.3	561.7	Credit from Monetary Authorities	26g
158.9	218.8	230.1	322.0	345.3	270.6	287.2	437.4	425.3	323.1	953.0	1,415.4	2,491.7	3,151.4	3,679.3	Liabilities to Other Financ. Insts	26i
998.4	823.7	1,080.7	1,385.4	1,161.1	1,278.7	1,619.7	2,291.5	3,101.1	3,701.1	5,023.1	4,645.1	6,001.7	8,121.9	9,409.4	Capital Accounts	27a
–2,600.0	–2,243.8	–2,079.4	–2,473.1	–2,405.4	–2,397.6	–2,330.4	–2,992.3	–3,754.0	–4,112.9	–5,163.0	–3,862.7	–5,607.5	–7,133.1	–9,329.8	Other Items (Net)	27r
															Monetary Survey	
Billions of Pesos Beginning 1977: End of Period																
–1,822.1	–1,283.0	–720.0	263.2	1,071.9	1,684.7	2,229.8	3,341.8	4,376.0	5,939.7	8,057.8	7,541.6	9,738.8	10,518.0	10,587.6	Foreign Assets (Net)	31n
4,454.2	5,003.0	5,573.7	6,707.9	7,652.0	9,172.8	11,397.4	12,406.6	15,182.0	17,676.8	20,198.1	22,576.5	24,564.6	27,984.4	30,818.4	Domestic Credit	32
1,720.2	1,788.5	1,818.1	2,089.3	2,061.4	1,901.8	2,069.6	1,592.2	1,427.8	1,259.1	873.8	991.6	1,522.5	2,204.7	2,688.6	Claims on Central Govt. (Net)	32an
.2	.4	.3	.4	—	.4	.4	.4	.5	.5	.4	.3	.3	.3	.7	Claims on Local Government	32b
98.1	51.5	81.2	301.7	247.1	174.7	165.8	124.5	95.4	88.7	136.4	672.2	219.2	342.8	468.4	Claims on Nonfin.Pub.Enterprises	32c
2,587.9	3,118.4	3,618.1	4,258.9	5,282.8	7,039.5	9,100.7	10,640.5	13,630.6	16,306.5	19,139.0	20,888.5	22,804.9	25,400.8	27,618.3	Claims on Private Sector	32d
47.7	44.2	56.0	57.6	60.6	56.4	60.9	48.9	27.6	22.0	48.6	23.9	17.7	35.8	42.4	Claims on Other Banking Insts	32f
347.5	509.1	596.5	735.4	1,064.5	1,344.0	1,628.9	1,892.3	2,312.9	2,686.7	3,228.1	2,799.4	3,718.9	3,905.4	4,106.6	Money	34
1,447.3	1,772.7	2,396.6	2,962.1	3,671.3	4,495.9	5,576.3	6,130.5	7,783.7	9,384.8	10,812.2	12,587.5	13,941.4	14,847.7	15,493.7	Quasi-Money	35
284.2	336.1	440.9	610.8	843.3	1,086.3	1,449.9	2,090.4	2,902.4	3,717.6	4,586.4	4,844.9	5,263.9	5,661.2	6,270.4	Bonds	36ab
158.9	218.8	230.1	322.0	345.3	270.6	287.2	437.4	425.3	323.1	953.0	1,415.4	2,491.7	3,151.4	3,679.3	Liabilities to Other Financ. Insts	36i
1,326.0	1,202.2	1,559.5	2,010.3	1,563.4	2,081.2	2,140.4	2,178.1	3,475.2	3,969.4	4,531.2	3,752.9	5,234.5	7,497.4	9,760.0	Capital Accounts	37a
–931.8	–318.8	–370.0	330.6	1,236.1	1,579.6	2,544.4	3,019.6	2,658.5	3,534.7	4,144.9	4,717.9	3,653.0	3,439.3	2,096.1	Other Items (Net)	37r
1,794.8	2,281.8	2,993.1	3,697.5	4,735.8	5,839.8	7,205.3	8,022.8	10,096.6	12,071.6	14,040.4	15,386.9	17,660.2	18,753.1	19,600.2	Money plus Quasi-Money	35l
															Other Banking Institutions	
End of Period																
4.4	5.0	5.2	8.4	19.3	22.2	12.9	13.0	9.4	11.6	14.7	35.9	33.8	12.0	1.7	Reserves	40
—	—	—	—	—	—	—	—	—	—	—	—	—	—	—	Foreign Assets	41
2.3	.7	.4	.4	—	—	—	—	—	—	—	—	—	—	—	Claims on Central Government	42a
—	—	—	—	—	—	—	—	—	—	—	—	—	—	—	Claims on Local Government	42b
.7	.2	.3	2.3	.1	—	4.7	.1	—	—	—	—	—	—	—	Claims on Nonfin.Pub.Enterprises	42c
44.9	58.9	84.6	100.6	141.4	249.1	390.9	500.6	441.7	593.4	747.8	742.5	355.3	272.0	186.2	Claims on Private Sector	42d
3.8	4.6	6.1	6.4	14.6	16.6	29.7	28.7	26.9	24.8	24.6	39.4	12.2	49.9	39.0	Claims on Deposit Money Banks	42e
37.8	46.9	62.0	75.4	119.9	211.9	313.3	378.8	348.4	466.4	593.0	629.9	298.6	260.8	179.4	Time, Savings,& Fgn.Currency Dep.	45
5.3	5.2	5.8	6.7	7.9	10.4	15.0	24.3	1.6	10.5	21.4	24.2	—	—	—	Bonds	46ab
—	—	—	—	—	—	—	—	—	—	—	—	—	—	—	Foreign Liabilities	46c
—	—	—	—	—	—	—	—	—	—	—	—	—	—	—	Long-Term Foreign Liabilities	46cl
.9	1.9	.5	.3	.3	.8	.6	1.4	1.0	2.0	1.2	1.3	1.2	1.0	.9	Central Government Deposits	46d
4.8	3.1	3.3	2.4	2.6	2.8	3.9	3.4	.6	.3	.9	.2	—	—	—	Credit from Monetary Authorities	46g
2.8	3.1	9.3	4.1	6.4	17.0	35.2	39.3	56.4	73.1	80.1	80.2	40.4	7.0	3.8	Credit from Deposit Money Banks	46h
4.5	5.5	7.5	13.3	16.4	24.1	32.9	43.0	31.9	42.5	56.3	61.2	35.6	61.5	22.4	Capital Accounts	47a
—	3.8	8.1	15.9	21.8	21.0	37.2	52.1	38.1	35.0	34.3	20.8	25.5	3.6	20.3	Other Items (Net)	47r

	1972	1973	1974	1975	1976	1977	1978	1979	1980	1981	1982	1983	1984	1985	1986
Banking Survey															*Billions of Pesos:*
Foreign Assets (Net) 51n	....	....	....	....	....	....	....	11.0	.5	−109.0	−342.3	−511.7	−974.5	−1,410.1	−1,686.2
Domestic Credit 52	....	....	....	....	....	....	....	335.8	504.9	652.4	1,095.4	1,353.0	2,033.6	3,041.1	3,704.7
Claims on Central Govt. (Net) 52an	....	....	....	....	....	....	....	51.9	−6.0	−32.7	38.3	163.2	447.1	1,149.3	1,485.1
Claims on Local Government 52b	....	....	....	....	....	....	....	—	.1	—	—	.2	.1	.1	.2
Claims on Nonfin.Pub.Enterprises........ 52c	....	....	....	....	....	....	....	4.0	7.1	8.3	15.2	16.7	25.8	53.2	75.6
Claims on Private Sector 52d	....	....	....	....	....	....	....	279.9	503.8	676.7	1,042.0	1,172.9	1,560.6	1,838.4	2,143.8
Liquid Liabilities 55l	....	....	....	....	....	....	....	188.3	302.9	377.3	498.1	599.8	735.4	1,080.2	1,352.6
Bonds 56ab	....	....	....	....	....	....	....	8.3	28.3	50.6	84.1	112.9	158.6	204.1	247.3
Capital Accounts 57a	....	....	....	....	....	....	....	166.6	215.0	221.1	301.3	326.9	270.8	929.1	1,126.0
Other Items (Net) 57r	....	....	....	....	....	....	....	−16.3	−40.8	−105.7	−130.3	−198.3	−105.7	−582.3	−707.4
Nonbank Financial Institutions															*Billions of Pesos*
Claims on Mon.Author.: Securities ...... 40c. p	....	....	....	....	....	....	....	....	....	....	....	....	26.8	57.4	112.9
Foreign Assets .... 41.. p	....	....	....	....	....	....	....	....	....	....	....	....	....	....	....
Claims on Central Government .... 42a. p	....	....	....	....	....	....	....	....	....	....	....	....	41.6	62.7	89.7
Claims on Private Sector .... 42d. p	....	....	....	....	....	....	....	....	....	....	....	....	2.9	3.1	19.9
Claims on Deposit Money Banks .... 42e. p	....	....	....	....	....	....	....	....	....	....	....	....	90.5	158.4	211.4
Reserve Funds and Capital .... 47a. p	....	....	....	....	....	....	....	....	....	....	....	....	161.6	281.8	433.4
Other Items (Net) .... 47r. p	....	....	....	....	....	....	....	....	....	....	....	....	.2	−.2	.5
Interest Rates															*Percent Per Annum*
Discount Rate *(End of Period)* 60	....	....	....	....	....	....	....	....	....	....	....	....	....	....	....
Money Market Rate.............................. 60b	....	....	....	....	....	....	....	....	....	....	....	....	....	....	....
Savings Rate... 60k	....	....	....	....	....	....	....	....	....	....	....	....	....	....	....
Deposit Rate 60l	....	....	....	....	....	94.92	63.53	45.19	37.72	40.90	48.68	28.01	27.63	†32.10	19.04
Deposit Rate *(Foreign Currency)*............60l. f	....	....	....	....	....	....	....	....	....	....	....	....	....	....	....
Lending Rate 60p	....	....	....	....	....	163.15	86.13	62.11	47.14	52.02	63.86	42.82	38.33	†39.97	26.36
Lending Rate *(Foreign Currency)* ....60p. f	....	....	....	....	....	....	....	....	....	....	....	....	....	....	....
Prices, Production, Labor															*Index Numbers (1995=100):*
Industrial Share Prices 62	....	....	—	—	—	.1	†.3	.5	†1.5	1.2	1.0	.8	1.1	1.4	3.0
Prices: Home & Import Goods 63	—	—	†.1	.5	1.6	3.1	4.4	6.5	9.1	9.9	10.6	15.5	19.3	27.6	33.1
Home Goods 63a	—	—	†.1	.5	1.5	2.8	4.1	6.2	8.6	9.5	10.1	14.3	17.7	24.8	30.6
Consumer Prices 64	—	—	.1	†.5	1.7	3.3	4.6	6.1	8.2	9.9	†10.8	13.8	16.5	21.4	25.8
Wages, Hourly 65a	....	....	....	....	....	....	....	....	....	....	....	....	....	....	....
Manufacturing Production...................... 66ey	63.6	60.9	58.6	42.1	44.2	48.7	52.3	56.4	59.8	59.7	50.8	53.3	58.6	58.6	63.5
Mining Production 66zx	33.3	33.7	40.6	37.8	43.1	43.8	42.7	45.3	46.9	48.8	55.6	55.4	58.2	60.0	60.4
Copper Production 66c	29.4	30.1	36.6	33.7	41.1	42.7	41.7	43.3	43.1	43.7	50.9	50.9	53.0	55.0	56.6
															Number in Thousands:
Labor Force 67d	....	....	....	....	....	....	....	....	....	....	....	....	....	....	....
Employment 67e	....	....	....	....	....	....	....	....	....	....	....	....	....	3,721	3,896
Unemployment 67c	....	....	....	....	....	....	....	....	....	....	....	....	....	517	374
Unemployment Rate (%) 67r	....	....	....	....	....	....	....	....	....	....	....	....	....	12.1	8.8
International Transactions															*Millions of US Dollars*
Exports .... 70..d	855	1,231	2,481	1,552	2,083	2,190	2,478	3,894	4,705	3,837	3,706	3,831	3,651	3,804	4,191
Imports, c.i.f. .... 71..d	1,086	1,290	2,148	1,525	†1,864	2,539	3,408	4,808	5,797	7,181	3,989	3,085	3,574	3,072	3,436
Imports, f.o.b. 71.vd	941	1,098	1,911	1,338	†1,643	2,259	3,002	4,218	5,469	6,513	3,643	2,845	3,288	2,920	3,099
															1995=100
Import Prices 76.x	—	—	†.1	.7	2.2	4.4	6.0	8.5	11.6	12.2	13.5	21.9	28.1	43.6	46.7
Balance of Payments															*Millions of US Dollars:*
Current Account, n.i.e. 78ald	....	....	....	−490	148	−551	−1,088	−1,189	−1,971	−4,733	−2,304	−1,117	−2,111	−1,413	−1,191
Goods: Exports f.o.b. 78aad	....	....	....	1,590	2,116	2,186	2,460	3,835	4,705	3,836	3,706	3,831	3,650	3,804	4,191
Goods: Imports f.o.b. 78abd	....	....	....	−1,520	−1,473	−2,151	−2,886	−4,190	−5,469	−6,513	−3,643	−2,845	−3,288	−2,920	−3,099
Trade Balance 78acd	....	....	....	70	643	35	−426	−355	−764	−2,677	63	986	362	884	1,092
Services: Credit 78add	....	....	....	248	297	417	481	785	1,263	1,172	936	797	664	692	1,042
Services: Debit 78aed	....	....	....	−535	−515	−734	−751	−1,048	−1,583	−1,780	−1,410	−1,236	−1,207	−1,080	−1,506
Balance on Goods & Services 78afd	....	....	....	−217	425	−282	−696	−618	−1,084	−3,285	−411	547	−181	496	628
Income: Credit 78agd	....	....	....	4	12	18	43	126	308	606	512	203	322	201	228
Income: Debit 78ahd	....	....	....	−289	−337	−383	−532	−802	−1,308	−2,162	−2,514	−1,964	−2,359	−2,256	−2,132
Balance on Gds, Serv. & Inc. 78aid	....	....	....	−502	100	−647	−1,185	−1,294	−2,084	−4,841	−2,413	−1,214	−2,218	−1,560	−1,276
Current Transfers, n.i.e.: Credit 78ajd	....	....	....	16	52	101	127	143	194	193	186	161	165	203	106
Current Transfers: Debit 78akd	....	....	....	−4	−4	−5	−30	−38	−81	−85	−77	−64	−58	−56	−22
Capital Account, n.i.e. 78bcd	....	....	....	—	—	—	—	—	—	—	—	—	—	—	—
Capital Account, n.i.e.: Credit 78bad	....	....	....	—	—	—	—	—	—	—	—	—	—	—	—
Capital Account: Debit 78bbd	....	....	....	—	—	—	—	—	—	—	—	—	—	—	—
Financial Account, n.i.e. 78bjd	....	....	....	−67	247	601	1,960	2,161	3,241	4,768	834	−3,224	−80	−1,394	−2,219
Direct Investment Abroad 78bdd	....	....	....	—	—	−5	−4	−11	—	—	—	—	−11	−2	−3
Dir. Invest. in Rep. Econ., n.i.e. 78bed	....	....	....	50	−1	21	181	244	213	383	401	135	78	144	316
Portfolio Investment Assets 78bfd	....	....	....	—	—	—	—	—	−43	−21	−17	−3	—	—	—
Equity Securities 78bkd	....	....	....	—	—	—	—	—	−43	−21	−17	−3	—	—	—
Debt Securities 78bld	....	....	....	—	—	—	—	—	—	—	—	—	—	—	—
Portfolio Investment Liab., n.i.e. 78bgd	....	....	....	−6	−6	−7	—	50	—	—	—	—	—	—	−78
Equity Securities 78bmd	....	....	....	—	—	—	—	—	—	—	—	—	—	—	—
Debt Securities 78bnd	....	....	....	−6	−6	−7	—	50	—	—	—	—	—	—	−78
Financial Derivatives Assets 78bwd	....	....	....	....	....	....	....	....	....	....	....	....	....	....	—
Financial Derivatives Liabilities 78bxd	....	....	....	....	....	....	....	....	....	....	....	....	....	....	—
Other Investment Assets 78bhd	....	....	....	185	67	50	108	5	128	−484	−720	242	153	435	576
Monetary Authorities 78bod	....	....	....	....	....	....	....	....	....	....	....	....	....	....	....
General Government 78bpd	....	....	....	—	−5	−19	—	—	—	−11	−2	—	−5	−4	−9
Banks 78bqd	....	....	....	11	−28	19	−39	−138	−235	−378	−51	122	99	170	−59
Other Sectors 78brd	....	....	....	174	100	50	147	143	363	−95	−667	120	59	269	644
Other Investment Liab., n.i.e. 78bid	....	....	....	−296	187	542	1,675	1,873	2,943	4,890	1,170	−3,598	−300	−1,972	−3,031
Monetary Authorities 78bsd	....	....	....	−83	145	−4	304	319	−36	−320	−58	12	47	−260	−597
General Government 78btd	....	....	....	−28	−62	−97	−124	−315	−56	−39	10	−57	147	179	53
Banks 78bud	....	....	....	−57	−27	115	388	701	2,141	3,126	446	−2,261	−393	−1,230	−1,478
Other Sectors 78bvd	....	....	....	−128	131	528	1,107	1,168	894	2,123	772	−1,292	−101	−660	−1,008
Net Errors and Omissions.................... 78cad	....	....	....	−109	69	114	−128	−12	51	102	−69	68	190	−70	223
Overall Balance 78cbd	....	....	....	−666	464	164	744	961	1,321	137	−1,539	−4,273	−2,001	−2,877	−3,187
Reserves and Related Items 79dad	....	....	....	666	−464	−164	−744	−961	−1,321	−137	1,539	4,273	2,001	2,877	3,187
Reserve Assets 79dbd	....	....	....	80	−413	−51	−700	−887	−1,269	−73	1,379	−94	−312	−103	137
Use of Fund Credit and Loans 79dcd	....	....	....	207	82	−118	−44	−170	−52	−64	−40	623	220	205	115
Exceptional Financing 79ded	....	....	....	380	−133	5	—	96	—	—	200	3,744	2,094	2,774	2,935

1987	1988	1989	1990	1991	1992	1993	1994	1995	1996	1997	1998	1999	2000	2001		
End of Period															**Banking Survey**	
-1,822.2	-1,283.0	-720.0	263.2	1,071.9	1,684.7	2,229.8	3,341.8	4,376.0	5,939.7	8,057.8	7,541.6	9,738.8	10,518.0	10,587.6	Foreign Assets (Net)	51n
4,453.5	5,016.7	5,602.5	6,753.3	7,732.6	9,364.7	11,731.5	12,856.9	15,595.1	18,246.2	20,896.2	23,293.8	24,901.0	28,219.6	30,961.3	Domestic Credit	52
1,721.6	1,787.3	1,818.1	2,089.4	2,061.1	1,901.0	2,069.1	1,590.8	1,426.8	1,257.1	872.6	990.3	1,521.3	2,203.8	2,687.7	Claims on Central Govt. (Net)	52an
.2	.4	.3	.4	—	.4	.4	.4	.5	.5	.4	.3	.3	.3	.7	Claims on Local Government	52b
98.9	51.7	81.5	304.0	247.2	174.7	170.5	124.6	95.4	88.7	136.4	672.2	219.2	342.8	468.4	Claims on Nonfin.Pub.Enterprises	52c
2,632.9	3,177.3	3,702.7	4,359.5	5,424.2	7,288.6	9,491.6	11,141.1	14,072.3	16,899.9	19,886.8	21,631.0	23,160.2	25,672.8	27,804.5	Claims on Private Sector	52d
1,828.2	2,323.6	3,049.9	3,764.5	4,836.4	6,029.5	7,505.7	8,388.6	10,435.6	12,526.3	14,618.7	15,980.9	17,925.1	19,001.9	19,777.9	Liquid Liabilities	55l
289.5	341.3	446.7	617.4	851.2	1,096.7	1,464.9	2,114.8	2,904.1	3,728.1	4,607.8	4,869.2	5,263.9	5,661.2	6,270.4	Bonds	56ab
1,330.5	1,207.7	1,567.0	2,023.6	1,579.8	2,105.3	2,173.3	2,221.2	3,507.1	4,012.0	4,587.4	3,814.1	5,270.1	7,558.9	9,782.4	Capital Accounts	57a
-816.9	-138.9	-181.1	611.0	1,537.1	1,817.9	2,817.4	3,474.1	3,124.3	3,919.4	5,140.1	6,171.3	6,180.7	6,515.6	5,718.1	Other Items (Net)	57r
End of Period															**Nonbank Financial Institutions**	
192.1	267.4	508.7	956.3	1,412.4	1,904.5	2,656.8	3,462.9	3,883.0	4,538.6	4,937.3	5,521.9	5,670.3	6,566.5	6,958.9	Claims on Mon.Author.: Securities	40c.p
—	—	—	—	—	—	38.7	80.5	21.0	63.1	154.8	828.4	2,423.9	2,217.3	3,073.8	Foreign Assets	41..p
75.3	48.4	46.4	35.9	34.7	35.5	32.8	108.3	195.7	384.5	428.7	505.2	655.9	790.0	1,172.1	Claims on Central Government	42a.p
57.0	129.2	256.2	505.0	1,320.1	1,601.7	2,693.5	3,536.8	3,848.1	3,832.4	3,924.8	3,114.6	3,339.1	3,616.8	4,293.7	Claims on Private Sector	42d.p
319.6	446.4	523.4	751.5	1,006.9	1,195.8	1,415.5	1,807.2	2,391.5	2,872.4	4,083.6	4,715.4	6,163.9	7,333.3	7,680.9	Claims on Deposit Money Banks	42e.p
644.7	885.9	1,329.3	2,244.5	3,769.2	4,736.5	6,831.4	8,983.6	10,231.0	11,555.6	13,405.8	14,552.5	18,093.0	20,343.4	22,956.0	Reserve Funds and Capital	47a.p
-.7	5.5	5.3	4.2	5.0	.9	5.9	12.2	108.3	135.4	123.2	133.0	160.1	180.4	223.5	Other Items (Net)	47r.p
Percent Per Annum															**Interest Rates**	
....	....	....	....	....	....	7.96	13.89	7.96	11.75	7.96	9.12	7.44	8.73	6.50	Discount Rate *(End of Period)*	60
....	....	....	....	....	....	....	....	....	....	....	....	....	10.09	6.81	Money Market Rate	60b
3.52	3.42	3.65	3.90	3.81	3.51	3.52	3.53	3.53	3.51	3.50	3.50	3.50	3.50	2.39	Savings Rate	60k
25.28	15.16	27.79	40.35	22.35	18.29	18.24	15.12	13.73	13.48	12.02	14.92	8.56	9.20	6.19	Deposit Rate	60l
....	....	....	....	....	4.21	3.96	4.05	5.45	5.24	5.02	4.41	4.39	5.48	3.51	Deposit Rate *(Foreign Currency)*	60l.f
32.67	21.21	36.01	48.87	28.58	23.97	24.35	20.34	18.16	17.37	15.67	20.17	12.62	14.84	11.89	Lending Rate	60p
....	....	....	....	....	6.77	6.76	8.42	9.96	9.27	9.49	8.73	7.38	7.76	5.50	Lending Rate *(Foreign Currency)*	60p.f
Period Averages															**Prices, Production, Labor**	
5.4	8.1	13.0	20.0	36.2	49.9	56.4	78.5	100.0	89.2	80.9	60.5	65.7	72.7	77.5	Industrial Share Prices	62
39.4	†41.8	48.1	58.6	71.2	79.5	86.3	93.0	100.0	106.2	108.0	110.0	115.8	129.0	139.0	Prices: Home & Import Goods	63
37.2	†39.1	45.5	56.1	69.2	78.3	84.5	91.5	100.0	106.7	109.4	110.5	115.1	128.5	136.1	Home Goods	63a
30.9	35.5	41.5	52.3	63.7	73.5	82.9	92.4	100.0	107.4	113.9	119.8	123.8	128.5	133.1	Consumer Prices	64
....	....	....	....	....	....	84.4	88.8	100.0	114.8	124.7	134.5	142.4	149.9	157.8	Wages, Hourly	65a
66.1	71.3	76.5	77.2	†81.3	91.0	93.0	95.4	100.0	103.7	108.8	109.0	109.0	112.9	115.0	Manufacturing Production	66ey
60.1	62.1	†68.3	68.9	77.0	81.6	84.9	90.2	100.0	122.8	134.0	142.7	166.0	173.4	177.7	Mining Production	66zx
56.7	58.6	†65.7	64.6	74.1	79.0	84.1	89.0	100.0	124.8	137.3	147.8	176.9	185.7	190.5	Copper Production	66c
Period Averages																
....	....	....	....	....	4,990	5,219	5,300	5,274	5,601	5,684	5,852	5,934	5,871	....	Labor Force	67d
4,011	4,266	4,425	4,460	4,540	4,773	4,986	†4,988	5,026	†5,299	5,380	5,432	5,405	5,382	....	Employment	67e
344	286	250	269	254	217	234	†427	402	350	344	384	572	536	535	Unemployment	67c
7.9	6.3	5.3	5.6	5.3	4.4	4.5	†7.9	7.3	6.4	6.1	6.4	9.8	9.2	....	Unemployment Rate (%)	67r
Millions of US Dollars															**International Transactions**	
5,224	7,052	8,078	8,373	8,942	10,007	9,199	11,604	16,024	15,657	17,902	16,353	17,194	19,246	18,505	Exports	70..d
4,396	5,292	7,233	7,742	8,207	10,183	11,134	11,820	15,900	19,123	20,825	19,880	15,988	18,507	17,814	Imports, c.i.f.	71..d
3,994	4,833	6,595	7,089	7,456	9,285	10,189	10,872	14,643	17,699	19,298	18,363	14,735	17,091	16,412	Imports, f.o.b.	71.vd
1995=100																
51.7	†56.3	61.9	71.3	80.2	82.5	91.7	97.5	100.0	110.2	....	....	....	....	....	Import Prices	76.x
Minus Sign Indicates Debit															Balance of Payments	
-735	-231	-690	-485	-99	-958	-2,554	-1,585	-1,350	-3,510	-3,728	-4,139	-80	-991	....	Current Account, n.i.e.	78ald
5,303	7,054	8,078	8,373	8,942	10,007	9,199	11,604	16,025	15,405	16,663	14,831	15,616	18,159	....	Goods: Exports f.o.b.	78aad
-3,994	-4,844	-6,595	-7,089	-7,456	-9,285	-10,189	-10,872	-14,644	-16,496	-18,221	-17,347	-13,952	-16,721	....	Goods: Imports f.o.b.	78abd
1,309	2,210	1,483	1,284	1,485	722	-990	732	1,381	-1,091	-1,558	-2,516	1,664	1,438	....	*Trade Balance*	78acd
1,045	1,089	1,535	1,849	2,127	2,358	2,512	2,840	3,333	3,661	4,109	4,122	3,790	3,931	....	Services: Credit	78add
-1,499	-1,780	-1,994	-2,077	-2,094	-2,535	-2,740	-2,989	-3,657	-3,921	-4,063	-4,236	-4,106	-4,488	....	Services: Debit	78aed
855	1,519	1,024	1,055	1,518	545	-1,218	583	1,057	-1,351	-1,512	-2,630	1,348	881	....	*Balance on Goods & Services*	78afd
176	185	243	484	576	558	502	556	869	795	1,086	1,135	1,103	1,609	....	Income: Credit	78agd
-1,904	-2,116	-2,182	-2,222	-2,504	-2,438	-2,158	-3,056	-3,582	-3,461	-3,823	-3,107	-2,983	-4,018	....	Income: Debit	78ahd
-873	-412	-916	-682	-410	-1,336	-2,874	-1,916	-1,657	-4,017	-4,249	-4,602	-532	-1,528	....	*Balance on Gds, Serv. & Inc.*	78aid
172	218	385	354	501	536	536	449	482	664	877	815	793	870	....	Current Transfers, n.i.e.: Credit	78ajd
-34	-37	-158	-157	-189	-158	-216	-118	-175	-157	-356	-352	-341	-333	....	Current Transfers: Debit	78akd
—	—	—	—	—	—	—	—	—	—	—	—	....	—	....	Capital Account, n.i.e.	78bcd
—	—	—	—	—	—	—	—	—	—	—	—	....	—	....	Capital Account, n.i.e.: Credit	78bad
—	—	—	—	—	—	—	—	—	—	—	—	....	—	....	Capital Account: Debit	78bbd
-743	-903	1,241	2,857	964	3,132	2,995	5,294	2,357	6,665	7,355	3,181	-829	1,239	....	Financial Account, n.i.e.	78bjd
-6	-16	-7	-8	-125	-398	-434	-911	-752	-1,188	-1,865	-2,798	-4,855	-4,777	....	Direct Investment Abroad	78bdd
891	968	1,284	661	822	935	1,034	2,583	2,957	4,634	5,219	4,638	9,221	3,675	....	Dir. Invest. in Rep. Econ., n.i.e.	78bed
—	—	—	—	—	—	-90	-351	-14	-131	-238	-1,420	-2,366	-148	....	Portfolio Investment Assets	78bfd
—	—	—	—	—	—	-90	-351	-14	-131	-238	-1,420	-2,366	-148	....	Equity Securities	78bkd
—	—	—	—	—	—	—	—	—	—	—	—	....	—	....	Debt Securities	78bld
-8	-8	83	361	189	458	820	1,259	48	1,231	2,603	591	2,496	-112	....	Portfolio Investment Liab., n.i.e.	78bgd
—	—	90	367	24	338	816	1,259	-249	661	1,709	529	442	-412	....	Equity Securities	78bmd
-8	-8	-7	-6	165	120	4	—	297	570	894	62	2,054	300	....	Debt Securities	78bnd
—	—	—	—	—	—	—	—	—	—	—	—	....	....	....	Financial Derivatives Assets	78bwd
—	—	—	—	—	—	—	—	—	—	—	—	....	....	....	Financial Derivatives Liabilities	78bxd
256	370	165	355	1,168	-323	726	-152	-309	-327	-843	-2,546	-6,390	-1,239	....	Other Investment Assets	78bhd
—	—	—	-66	12	-15	-4	-57	10	18	-121	16	-3	-96	....	Monetary Authorities	78bod
-10	-17	-37	37	—	47	—	—	—	—	—	—	....	—	....	General Government	78bpd
13	-56	27	-145	-62	-21	7	-26	57	-117	-654	-855	-3,052	782	....	Banks	78bqd
254	443	175	530	1,218	-334	723	-70	-376	-228	-68	-1,707	-3,335	-1,925	....	Other Sectors	78brd
-1,876	-2,218	-284	1,488	-1,089	2,460	939	2,865	427	2,445	2,479	4,716	1,065	3,840	....	Other Investment Liab., n.i.e.	78bid
-52	-948	-696	-400	-66	10	-240	-99	-402	-178	-25	-74	-65	36	....	Monetary Authorities	78bsd
77	108	127	206	80	157	-119	-99	-1,323	-545	-387	-171	-101	-129	....	General Government	78btd
-1,652	-1,188	-566	-320	-570	1,589	61	407	-322	-444	-1,498	-65	-840	-271	....	Banks	78bud
-249	-190	852	2,002	-533	704	1,237	2,656	2,474	3,612	4,390	5,026	2,071	4,204	....	Other Sectors	78bvd
-142	-122	-33	-50	392	373	-13	-558	132	-651	-443	-1,177	151	-16	....	Net Errors and Omissions	78cad
-1,621	-1,256	519	2,323	1,257	2,547	428	3,151	1,139	2,504	3,184	-2,135	-758	232	....	*Overall Balance*	78cbd
1,621	1,256	-519	-2,323	-1,257	-2,547	-428	-3,151	-1,139	-2,504	-3,184	2,135	758	-232	....	Reserves and Related Items	79dad
-66	-756	-548	-2,121	-1,049	-2,344	-170	-2,918	-740	-1,107	-3,184	2,135	758	-232	....	Reserve Assets	79dbd
-70	-70	-21	-209	-197	-203	-249	-210	-298	—	—	—	—	—	....	Use of Fund Credit and Loans	79dcd
1,756	2,082	50	8	-11	—	-9	-22	-101	-1,397	—	—	....	—	....	Exceptional Financing	79ded

		1972	1973	1974	1975	1976	1977	1978	1979	1980	1981	1982	1983	1984	1985	1986
International Investment Position																*Millions of US Dollars*
Assets	79aa *d*	....	....	....	....	....	....	....	....	....	....	....	....	....	....	....
Direct Investment Abroad	79ab *d*	....	....	....	....	....	....	....	....	....	....	....	....	....	....	....
Portfolio Investment	79ac *d*	....	....	....	....	....	....	....	....	....	....	....	....	....	....	....
Equity Securities	79ad *d*	....	....	....	....	....	....	....	....	....	....	....	....	....	....	....
Debt Securities	79ae *d*	....	....	....	....	....	....	....	....	....	....	....	....	....	....	....
Financial Derivatives	79al *d*	....	....	....	....	....	....	....	....	....	....	....	....	....	....	....
Other Investment	79af *d*	....	....	....	....	....	....	....	....	....	....	....	....	....	....	....
Monetary Authorities	79ag *d*	....	....	....	....	....	....	....	....	....	....	....	....	....	....	....
General Government	79ah *d*	....	....	....	....	....	....	....	....	....	....	....	....	....	....	....
Banks	79ai *d*	....	....	....	....	....	....	....	....	....	....	....	....	....	....	....
Other Sectors	79aj *d*	....	....	....	....	....	....	....	....	....	....	....	....	....	....	....
Reserve Assets	79ak *d*	....	....	....	....	....	....	....	....	....	....	....	....	....	....	....
Liabilities	79la *d*	....	....	....	....	....	....	....	....	....	....	....	....	....	....	....
Dir. Invest. in Rep. Economy	79lb *d*	....	....	....	....	....	....	....	....	....	....	....	....	....	....	....
Portfolio Investment	79lc *d*	....	....	....	....	....	....	....	....	....	....	....	....	....	....	....
Equity Securities	79ld *d*	....	....	....	....	....	....	....	....	....	....	....	....	....	....	....
Debt Securities	79le *d*	....	....	....	....	....	....	....	....	....	....	....	....	....	....	....
Financial Derivatives	79ll *d*	....	....	....	....	....	....	....	....	....	....	....	....	....	....	....
Other Investment	79lf *d*	....	....	....	....	....	....	....	....	....	....	....	....	....	....	....
Monetary Authorities	79lg *d*	....	....	....	....	....	....	....	....	....	....	....	....	....	....	....
General Government	79lh *d*	....	....	....	....	....	....	....	....	....	....	....	....	....	....	....
Banks	79li *d*	....	....	....	....	....	....	....	....	....	....	....	....	....	....	....
Other Sectors	79lj *d*	....	....	....	....	....	....	....	....	....	....	....	....	....	....	....
Government Finance																*Millions of Pesos through 1976;*
Deficit (-) or Surplus	80	†−30.0	−84.0	−495.0	45.0	1,756.0	†−3.2	−.5	37.2	58.2	33.0	−12.2	−40.9	†−56.2	−60.7	−31.4
Total Revenue and Grants	81y	†71.0	326.0	2,607.0	12,459.0	41,047.0	†91.5	157.4	263.5	367.1	419.3	374.4	432.2	†547.4	752.1	921.0
Revenue	81	†71.0	326.0	2,548.0	11,450.0	39,192.0	†87.9	150.7	251.8	352.4	401.1	365.7	432.2	†547.4	752.1	921.0
Grants	81z	†—		59.0	1,009.0	1,855.0	†3.6	6.7	11.7	14.7	18.2	8.7	—	†—	—	—
Exp. & Lending Minus Repay.	82z	†101.0	410.0	3,102.0	12,414.0	39,291.0	†94.7	157.9	226.3	308.9	386.3	386.6	473.0	†603.6	812.8	952.4
Expenditure	82	†98.0	399.0	3,042.0	12,164.0	38,757.0	†92.1	155.0	221.6	301.2	374.9	422.8	497.2	†617.1	806.1	969.3
Lending Minus Repayments	83	†3.0	11.0	60.0	250.0	534.0	†2.6	2.9	4.7	7.7	11.4	−36.2	−24.2	†−13.6	6.7	−16.9
Financing																
Net Borrowing	84	†32.0	146.0	684.0	970.0	1,547.0	†13.4	4.3	−10.7	−50.8	−45.0	−7.1	40.9	†56.2	60.7	31.4
Net Borrowing: Domestic	84a	†32.0	149.0	592.0	1,916.0	4,176.0	†16.8	6.6	−3.3	−42.7	−38.3	−3.4	41.2	†42.0	−5.5	−72.4
Foreign	85a	†—	−3.0	92.0	−946.0	−2,629.0	†−3.4	−2.3	−7.5	−8.1	−6.7	−3.7	−.3	†14.2	66.2	103.8
Use of Cash Balances	87	†−2.0	−62.0	−189.0	−1,016.0	−3,303.0	†−10.2	−3.8	−26.5	−7.4	12.0	19.3	....	....	....	....
Total Debt by Residence	88	....	....	....	....	....	....	....	....	....	....	1,460.0				
Domestic	88a	....	....	....	....	....	....	....	....	....	....	122.0				
Foreign	89a	....	....	....	....	....	....	....	....	....	....	1,338.0				
Intragovernmental Debt	88s	....	....	....	....	....	....	....	....	....	....	26.8				
National Accounts																*Millions of Pesos through 1976;*
Househ.Cons.Expend.,incl.NPISHs	96f	176	927	5,742	25,941	88,669	†210	347	546	760	948	933	1,142	1,382	1,776	2,239
Government Consumption Expend.	91f	38	151	1,448	5,560	17,990	†42	70	110	134	167	190	221	274	356	430
Gross Fixed Capital Formation	93e	31	147	1,559	6,271	17,068	†38	72	115	179	237	181	187	234	447	586
Changes in Inventories	93i	−2	−56	386	−1,626	−621	†3	15	22	47	52	−42	−34	24	9	60
Exports of Goods and Services	90c	23	138	1,880	9,040	32,320	†59	100	180	245	209	240	374	459	746	995
Imports of Goods and Services (-)	98c	392	166	1,815	9,726	26,752	†65	117	202	290	341	263	332	480	682	890
Gross Domestic Product (GDP)	99b	234	1,147	9,199	35,447	128,676	†288	488	772	1,075	1,273	1,239	1,558	1,893	2,652	3,419
Net Primary Income from Abroad	98.n	−1	−12	−144	−1,388	−4,204	†−8	−13	−25	−36	−57	−96	−134	−193	−335	−374
Gross National Income (GNI)	99a	233	1,134	9,055	34,058	124,472	†280	474	747	1,039	1,216	1,107	1,398	1,705	2,317	3,045
Consumption of Fixed Capital	99cf	20	121	1,041	5,200	17,048	†34	56	77	104	120	130	181	226	295	372
Net National Income	99e	214	1,016	8,055	29,106	108,303	†249	423	676	940	1,100	1,016	1,217	1,479	2,339	3,064
GDP Volume 1977 prices	99b.*p*	305	288	291												
GDP Volume 1986 Prices(Billions)	99b.*p*	....	....	2,746	2,381	2,458	2,661	2,867	3,071	3,309	3,530	3,056	2,949	3,129	3,238	3,419
GDP Vol.1996 Prices(Billions)	99b.*p*	....	....													
GDP Volume (1995=100)	99bv *p*	42.3	40.0	40.4	35.0	36.1	39.1	42.2	45.2	48.7	51.9	44.9	43.4	46.0	47.6	50.3
GDP Deflator (1995=100)	99bi *p*	—	—	.1	.4	1.4	2.8	4.5	6.6	8.5	9.5	10.7	13.9	15.9	21.5	26.3
Population	99z	9.70	9.86	10.03	10.20	10.37	10.55	†10.82	10.98	11.14	11.33	11.52	11.72	11.92	12.12	*Millions:* 12.33

Millions of US Dollars — International Investment Position

1987	1988	1989	1990	1991	1992	1993	1994	1995	1996	1997	1998	1999	2000	2001	Item	Code
....	....	....	....	....	....	....	....	....	16,257	19,259	18,014	19,234	18,610	....	Assets	79aa d
....	....	....	....	....	....	....	....	....	—	—	—	—	—	....	Direct Investment Abroad	79ab d
....	....	....	....	....	....	....	....	....	—	—	—	—	—	....	Portfolio Investment	79ac d
....	....	....	....	....	....	....	....	....	—	—	—	—	—	....	Equity Securities	79ad d
....	....	....	....	....	....	....	....	....	—	—	—	—	—	....	Debt Securities	79ae d
....	....	....	....	....	....	....	....	....	—	—	—	—	—	....	Financial Derivatives	79al d
....	....	....	....	....	....	....	....	....	597	1,256	1,930	4,492	3,802	....	Other Investment	79af d
....	....	....	....	....	....	....	....	....	—	—	—	—	—	....	Monetary Authorities	79ag d
....	....	....	....	....	....	....	....	....	—	—	—	—	—	....	General Government	79ah d
....	....	....	....	....	....	....	....	....	597	1,256	1,930	4,492	3,802	....	Banks	79ai d
....	....	....	....	....	....	....	....	....	—	—	—	—	—	....	Other Sectors	79aj d
....	....	....	....	....	....	....	....	....	15,660	18,003	16,084	14,742	14,808	....	Reserve Assets	79ak d
....	....	....	....	....	....	....	....	....	27,785	32,310	34,914	38,005	39,313	....	Liabilities	79la d
....	....	....	....	....	....	....	....	....	6,418	9,037	7,669	10,619	9,131	....	Dir. Invest. in Rep. Economy	79lb d
....	....	....	....	....	....	....	....	....	5,224	6,989	5,586	6,282	4,538	....	Portfolio Investment	79lc d
....	....	....	....	....	....	....	....	....	1,194	2,048	2,083	4,337	4,593	....	Equity Securities	79ld d
....	....	....	....	....	....	....	....	....						....	Debt Securities	79le d
....	....	....	....	....	....	....	....	....						....	Financial Derivatives	79ll d
....	....	....	....	....	....	....	....	....	21,367	23,273	27,245	27,386	30,182	....	Other Investment	79lf d
....	....	....	....	....	....	....	....	....	189	165	92	26	62	....	Monetary Authorities	79lg d
....	....	....	....	....	....	....	....	....	2,653	2,269	2,169	2,583	2,410	....	General Government	79lh d
....	....	....	....	....	....	....	....	....	3,599	2,091	2,041	1,349	1,101	....	Banks	79li d
....	....	....	....	....	....	....	....	....	14,926	18,748	22,943	23,428	26,609	....	Other Sectors	79lj d

Billions of Pesos beginning 1977: Year Ending December 31 — Government Finance

1987	1988	1989	1990	1991	1992	1993	1994	1995	1996	1997	1998	1999	2000	2001	Item	Code
†86.3	61.0	108.4	74.3	186.1	346.3	356.6	361.9	667.7	657.8	623.3	131.8	−502.4	56.4	....	Deficit (-) or Surplus	80
†1,155.7	1,334.3	1,610.3	1,917.3	2,700.7	3,491.0	4,172.7	4,822.8	5,747.7	6,626.3	7,358.9	7,726.9	7,737.8	8,976.1	....	Total Revenue and Grants	81y
†1,155.7	1,334.3	1,610.3	1,917.3	2,700.7	3,491.0	4,172.7	4,822.8	5,747.7	6,626.3	7,358.9	7,726.9	7,737.8	8,976.1		Revenue	81
†—															Grants	81z
†1,069.4	1,273.3	1,501.9	1,843.1	2,514.6	3,144.7	3,816.1	4,460.9	5,080.1	5,968.5	6,735.6	7,595.1	8,240.2	8,919.7		Exp. & Lending Minus Repay.	82z
†1,129.9	1,370.9	1,571.1	1,884.5	2,542.0	3,152.0	3,842.7	4,482.0	5,137.1	5,982.8	6,695.3	7,575.8	8,235.4	8,853.3		Expenditure	82
†−60.5	−97.7	−69.2	−41.4	−27.4	−7.3	−26.6	−21.1	−57.0	−14.3	40.3	19.3	4.8	66.4	....	Lending Minus Repayments	83
															Financing	
....	....	....	....	....	....	....	....	....	....	....	....	....	....	....	Net Borrowing	84
....	....	....	....	....	....	....	....	....	....	....	....	....	....	....	Net Borrowing: Domestic	84a
															Foreign	85a
....	....	....	....	....	....	....	....	....	....	....	....	....	....	....	Use of Cash Balances	87
....	3,288.2	3,580.8	4,365.0	4,978.2	5,162.6	5,684.4	5,477.7	5,056.4	4,719.1	4,588.0	4,657.6	5,159.4	5,606.9	....	Total Debt by Residence	88
....	2,127.0	2,209.9	2,530.5	2,844.4	2,981.6	3,431.6	3,305.6	3,432.1	3,392.0	3,476.5	3,491.6	3,684.3	4,129.2	....	Domestic	88a
....	1,161.2	1,370.9	1,834.5	2,133.8	2,181.0	2,254.8	2,172.1	1,624.3	1,327.1	1,111.5	1,165.9	1,475.1	1,477.7	....	Foreign	89a
															Intragovernmental Debt	88s

Billions of Pesos Beginning 1977 — National Accounts

1987	1988	1989	1990	1991	1992	1993	1994	1995	1996	1997	1998	1999	2000	2001	Item	Code
2,906	3,545	4,422	5,720	7,661	9,894	11,847	13,829	16,187	19,785	21,972	23,704	23,949	25,785	27,233	Househ.Cons.Expend.,incl.NPISHs	96f
494	613	742	902	1,170	1,469	1,804	2,129	2,543	3,426	3,860	4,197	4,587	4,982	5,379	Government Consumption Expend.	91f
882	1,202	1,734	2,140	2,412	3,405	4,480	4,980	6,177	8,241	9,414	9,546	7,832	8,500	9,041	Gross Fixed Capital Formation	93e
128	146	116	182	317	210	285	175	497	313	212	282	99	594	−314	Changes in Inventories	93i
1,374	2,046	2,639	3,201	4,012	4,655	4,943	6,270	7,905	8,521	9,404	9,609	10,897	12,838	14,631	Exports of Goods and Services	90c
1,244	1,634	2,298	2,899	3,471	4,447	5,383	5,988	7,434	9,048	10,140	10,802	10,200	12,262	13,778	Imports of Goods and Services (-)	98c
4,541	5,918	7,354	9,246	12,101	15,185	17,975	21,395	25,876	31,237	34,723	36,535	37,164	40,436	42,192	Gross Domestic Product (GDP)	99b
−384	−485	−532	−536	−684	−696	−690	−1,072	−1,106	−1,133	−1,105	−870	−944	−1,548	−1,618	Net Primary Income from Abroad	98.n
4,156	5,433	6,822	8,709	11,416	14,489	17,285	20,323	24,769	30,204	33,618	35,665	36,170	38,888	40,574	Gross National Income (GNI)	99a
464	568	741	943	1,193	1,433	1,693	1,957	2,270	4,122	4,424	4,645	5,062	5,190	....	Consumption of Fixed Capital	99cf
4,184	5,477	6,880	8,769	11,525	14,634	17,415	20,462	24,893	30,414	33,837	35,880	36,410	39,152	40,861	Net National Income	99e
3,645	3,911	4,324	4,484	4,841	5,436	5,816	6,148	6,801	7,305	....	....	....	....	....	GDP Volume 1977 prices	99b.p
....	....	....	....	....	....	....	....	....							GDP Volume 1986 Prices(Billions)	99b.p
									31,237	33,301	34,377	34,041	35,533	36,533	GDP Vol.1996 Prices(Billions)	99b.p
53.6	57.5	63.6	65.9	71.2	79.9	85.5	90.4	100.0	107.4	114.5	118.2	117.1	122.2	125.6	GDP Volume (1995=100)	99bv p
32.7	39.8	44.7	54.2	65.7	73.4	81.2	91.5	100.0	112.4	117.2	119.4	122.7	127.9	129.8	GDP Deflator (1995=100)	99bi p

Midyear Estimates

1987	1988	1989	1990	1991	1992	1993	1994	1995	1996	1997	1998	1999	2000	2001	Item	Code
12.54	12.75	12.96	13.10	13.32	13.54	13.77	13.99	14.20	14.42	14.62	14.82	15.02	15.21	15.40	Population	99z

(See notes in the back of the book.)

China,P.R.: Mainland

		1972	1973	1974	1975	1976	1977	1978	1979	1980	1981	1982	1983	1984	1985	1986
Exchange Rates															*Yuan per SDR:*	
Market Rate...........aa=	wa	2.4321	2.4371	2.2524	2.3019	2.1846	2.1014	2.0546	1.9710	1.9518	2.0317	2.1209	2.0739	2.7404	3.5166	4.5528
															Yuan per US Dollar:	
Market Rate..........ae=	we	2.2401	2.0202	1.8397	1.9663	1.8803	1.7300	1.5771	1.4962	1.5303	1.7455	1.9227	1.9809	2.7957	3.2015	3.7221
Market Rate..........rf=	wf	2.2451	1.9894	1.9612	1.8598	1.9414	1.8578	1.6836	1.5550	1.4984	1.7045	1.8925	1.9757	2.3200	2.9367	3.4528
															Index Numbers (1995=100):	
Nominal Effective Exchange Rate.......... ne c		....	....	....	....	....	....	....	361.52	387.82	378.79	389.18	408.68	388.51	332.49	242.54
Real Effective Exchange Rate .... re c		....	....	....	....	....	....	....	....	367.01	327.43	312.56	307.28	273.90	232.48	169.31
Fund Position															*Millions of SDRs:*	
Quota .... 2f. s		—	—	—	—	—	—	—	—	1,800	1,800	1,800	2,391	2,391	2,391	2,391
SDRs .... 1b. s		—	—	—	—	—	—	—	—	72	236	194	320	414	440	465
Reserve Position in the Fund .... 1c. s		—	—	—	—	—	—	—	—	150	—	—	168	261	303	303
Total Fund Cred.&Loans Outstg. 2tl		—	—	—	—	—	—	—	—	—	760	760	310	310	310	876
International Liquidity											*Millions of US Dollars Unless Otherwise Indicated:*					
Total Reserves Minus Gold .... 1l. d		....	....	....	....	....	2,345	1,557	2,154	2,545	5,058	11,349	14,987	†17,366	12,728	11,453
SDRs .... 1b. d		—	—	—	—	—	—	—	—	92	275	214	335	406	483	569
Reserve Position in the Fund .... 1c. d		—	—	—	—	—	—	—	—	191	—	—	176	255	332	370
Foreign Exchange .... 1d. d		....	....	....	....	....	2,345	1,557	2,154	2,262	4,783	11,135	14,476	†16,705	11,913	10,514
Gold (Million Fine Troy Ounces) 1ad		....	....	....	....	....	12.8	12.8	12.8	12.8	12.7	12.7	12.7	12.7	12.7	12.7
Gold (National Valuation)..................... 1an d		....	....	....	....	....	544	584	590	571	516	491	464	435	486	541
Monetary Authorities: Other Assets .... 3.. d		....	....	....	....	....	322	701	828	908	798	742	829	897	943	1,108
Banking Institutions: Liabilities .... 7b. d		....	....	....	....	....	1,916	2,542	4,373	5,667	3,874	2,907	3,337	3,646	6,634	8,389
Monetary Authorities															*Billions of Yuan:*	
Foreign Assets 11		....	....	....	....	....	....	....	....	....	....	....	....	....	14.57	14.40
Claims on Central Government............... 12a		....	....	....	....	....	....	....	....	....	....	....	....	....	27.51	37.01
Claims on Other Sectors 12d		....	....	....	....	....	....	....	....	....	....	....	....	....	7.84	12.82
Claims on Deposit Money Banks 12e		....	....	....	....	....	....	....	....	....	....	....	....	....	224.86	268.16
Claims on Other Banking Insts 12f		....	....	....	....	....	....	....	....	....	....	....	....	....	—	1.23
Reserve Money 14		....	....	....	....	....	....	....	....	....	....	....	....	....	228.41	281.86
Currency Outside Banking Insts. 14a		....	....	....	....	....	....	....	....	....	....	....	....	....	98.78	121.84
Reserves of Deposit Money Banks 14c		....	....	....	....	....	....	....	....	....	....	....	....	....	96.37	120.08
Deposits of Other Sectors 14d		....	....	....	....	....	....	....	....	....	....	....	....	....	33.26	39.94
Deposits of Other Banking Insts. 14f		....	....	....	....	....	....	....	....	....	....	....	....	....	....	....
Bonds 16ab		....	....	....	....	....	....	....	....	....	....	....	....	....		
Foreign Liabilities 16c		—	—	—	—	—	—	—	—	1.54	1.61	.64	.85	1.09	3.99	
Central Government Deposits 16d		....	....	....	....	....	....	....	....	....	....	....	....	....	36.84	31.15
Capital Accounts 17a		....	....	....	....	....	....	....	....	....	....	....	....	....	23.36	23.23
Other Items (Net) 17r		....	....	....	....	....	....	....	....	....	....	....	....	....	−14.92	−6.61
Banking Institutions															*Billions of Yuan:*	
Reserves 20		....	....	....	....	....	....	....	....	....	....	....	....	....	96.07	111.56
Foreign Assets 21		....	....	....	....	....	....	....	....	....	....	....	....	....	29.67	31.40
Claims on Central Government............... 22a		....	....	....	....	....	....	....	....	....	....	....	....	....		
Claims on Other Sectors 22d		....	....	....	....	....	....	....	....	....	....	....	....	....	594.44	775.50
Demand Deposits 24		....	....	....	....	....	....	....	....	....	....	....	....	....	169.69	224.12
Savings Deposits 25aa		....	....	....	....	....	....	....	....	....	....	....	....	....	39.69	50.58
Time Deposits............................. 25ab		....	....	....	....	....	....	....	....	....	....	....	....	....	21.61	27.96
Other Deposits 25e		....	....	....	....	....	....	....	....	....	....	....	....	....	....	....
Bonds 26ab		....	....	....	....	....	....	....	....	....	....	....	....	....		
Foreign Liabilities 26c		....	....	....	....	....	3.31	4.01	6.54	8.67	6.76	5.59	6.61	10.19	21.24	31.22
Credit from Monetary Authorities 26g		....	....	....	....	....	....	....	....	....	....	....	....	....	224.86	268.39
Capital Accounts 27a		....	....	....	....	....	....	....	....	....	....	....	....	....	65.34	74.13
Other Items (Net) 27r		....	....	....	....	....	....	....	....	....	....	....	....	....	53.41	72.52
Banking Survey															*Billions of Yuan:*	
Foreign Assets (Net) 31n		....	....	....	....	....	2.41	.54	−1.64	−2.78	2.67	16.14	23.95	27.03	†21.91	10.59
Domestic Credit 32		....	....	....	....	....	126.24	139.31	198.11	242.25	273.99	304.67	343.70	451.45	†592.95	794.18
Claims on Central Govt. (Net) 32an		....	....	....	....	....	−40.09	−45.69	−5.85	.82	−2.48	−.56	.59	9.49	†−9.33	5.86
Claims on Other Sectors 32d		....	....	....	....	....	166.33	185.00	203.96	241.43	276.47	305.23	343.11	441.96	†602.28	788.32
Money 34		....	....	....	....	....	58.01	58.04	92.15	114.88	134.52	148.84	174.89	244.94	†301.73	385.90
Quasi-Money 35		....	....	....	....	....	27.83	30.93	40.63	52.23	63.25	77.73	96.39	114.91	†185.76	248.96
Bonds 36ab		....	....	....	....	....	....	....	....	....	....	....	....	....	88.70	97.36
Capital Accounts 37a		....	....	....	....	....	....	....	....	....	....	....	....	....	88.70	97.36
Other Items (Net) 37r		....	....	....	....	....	42.81	50.88	50.56	55.19	55.97	65.76	66.39	85.29	†38.63	72.58
Money plus Quasi-Money...................... 35l		....	....	....	....	....	85.84	88.97	132.78	167.11	197.77	226.57	271.28	359.85	†487.49	634.86
Interest Rates															*Percent per Annum*	
Bank Rate...................................... 60		....	....	....	....	....	....	....	....							
Deposit Rate 60l		....	....	....	....	....	....	....	....	5.40	5.40	5.76	5.76	5.76	7.20	7.20
Lending Rate 60p		....	....	....	....	....	....	....	....	5.04	5.04	7.20	7.20	7.20	7.92	7.92
Prices, Production, Labor														*Percent Change over Corresponding*		
Consumer Prices .... 64.. x		....	....	....	....	....	....	....	....	....	....	....	....	....	....	....
Industrial Production........................ 66.. x		....	....	....	....	....	....	....	....	....	....	....	....	....	....	....
															Number in Thousands:	
Employment 67e		....	....	....	....	....	....	....	....	....	....	....	....	....	498,730	512,820
Unemployment 67c		....	....	....	....	....	....	....	....	....	....	....	....	....	2,385	2,644
Unemployment Rate (%)........................ 67r		....	....	....	....	....	....	....	....	....	....	....	....	....	1.8	2.0

	1987	1988	1989	1990	1991	1992	1993	1994	1995	1996	1997	1998	1999	2000	2001		Code

Exchange Rates

End of Period

| 5.2804 | 5.0088 | 6.2056 | 7.4293 | 7.7732 | 7.9087 | 7.9666 | 12.3302 | 12.3637 | 11.9325 | 11.1715 | 11.6567 | 11.3637 | 10.7847 | 10.4017 | Market Rate...............aa= .... | wa |

End of Period (we) Period Average (wf)

| 3.7221 | 3.7221 | 4.7221 | 5.2221 | 5.4342 | 5.7518 | 5.8000 | 8.4462 | 8.3174 | 8.2982 | 8.2798 | 8.2787 | 8.2795 | 8.2774 | 8.2768 | Market Rate...............ae= .... | we |
| 3.7221 | 3.7221 | 3.7651 | 4.7832 | 5.3234 | 5.5146 | 5.7620 | 8.6187 | 8.3514 | 8.3142 | 8.2898 | 8.2790 | 8.2783 | 8.2785 | 8.2771 | Market Rate...............rf= .... | wf |

Period Averages

| 207.46 | 159.23 | 179.02 | 173.83 | 157.40 | 139.29 | 111.83 | 101.23 | 100.00 | 104.23 | 111.08 | 116.15 | 113.65 | 116.79 | 122.02 | Nominal Effective Exchange Rate | ne c |
| 146.70 | 122.11 | 140.85 | 125.25 | 110.42 | 98.39 | 85.86 | 91.52 | 100.00 | 107.41 | 112.17 | 112.35 | 106.94 | 107.61 | 110.53 | Real Effective Exchange Rate | re c |

Fund Position

End of Period

2,391	2,391	2,391	2,391	2,391	3,385	3,385	3,385	3,385	3,385	3,385	3,385	4,687	4,687	6,369	Quota	2f. s
451	436	411	395	404	305	352	369	392	427	447	480	540	613	677	SDRs	1b. s
303	303	303	303	303	551	513	517	818	971	1,682	2,523	1,685	1,462	2,061	Reserve Position in the Fund	1c. s
814	752	691	330	—	—	—	—	—	—	—	—	—	—	—	Total Fund Cred.&Loans Outstg.	2tl

International Liquidity

End of Period

16,305	18,541	17,960	29,586	43,674	†20,620	22,387	52,914	75,377	107,039	142,762	149,188	157,728	168,278	215,605	Total Reserves Minus Gold	1l.d
640	586	540	562	577	419	484	539	582	614	602	676	741	798	851	SDRs	1b.d
429	407	398	430	433	758	704	755	1,216	1,396	2,270	3,553	2,312	1,905	2,590	Reserve Position in the Fund	1c.d
15,236	17,548	17,022	28,594	42,664	†19,443	21,199	51,620	73,579	105,029	139,890	144,959	154,675	165,574	212,165	Foreign Exchange	1d.d
12.7	12.7	12.7	12.7	12.7	12.7	12.7	12.7	12.7	12.7	12.7	12.7	12.7	12.7	16.1	Gold (Million Fine Troy Ounces)	1ad
629	594	587	623	634	610	612	646	660	637	601	624	608	578	3,093	Gold (National Valuation)	1and
1,450	1,399	1,127	2,006	1,575	1,786	1,498	....	....	....	....	....	....	....	....	Monetary Authorities: Other Assets	3..d
10,155	11,660	10,582	12,868	19,918	19,398	†39,230	44,890	50,370	55,990	59,035	54,685	47,057	49,536	37,477	Banking Institutions: Liabilities	7b.d

Monetary Authorities

End of Period

25.47	28.22	40.50	82.05	139.96	133.04	†154.95	445.13	666.95	956.22	1,345.21	1,376.17	1,485.75	1,558.28	1,986.04	Foreign Assets	11
51.50	57.65	68.46	80.11	106.78	124.11	158.27	168.77	158.28	158.28	158.28	158.28	158.28	158.28	282.13	Claims on Central Government	12a
22.68	30.56	34.53	40.67	44.91	53.39	†68.23	72.83	68.01	65.87	17.10	10.38	10.15	11.02	19.55	Claims on Other Sectors	12d
275.64	336.44	420.95	509.07	591.81	678.02	†960.95	1,045.10	1,151.03	1,451.84	1,435.79	1,305.75	1,537.39	1,351.92	1,131.16	Claims on Deposit Money Banks	12e
1.74	2.36	3.65	5.70	7.37	20.11	25.17	26.99	18.16	11.77	207.23	296.28	383.31	860.04	854.73	Claims on Other Banking Insts	12f
318.17	398.36	491.12	638.73	793.14	922.80	†1314.70	1,721.78	2,075.98	2,688.85	3,145.45	3,233.94	3,478.81	3,791.38	4,171.30	Reserve Money	14
145.45	213.26	234.21	264.12	317.40	432.94	†577.65	728.44	788.19	879.89	1,017.46	1,120.07	1,345.21	1,464.99	1,568.73	Currency Outside Banking Insts.	14a
127.41	145.38	208.15	312.66	399.98	420.51	†557.85	745.44	932.03	1,383.52	1,599.29	1,489.35	1,581.49	1,667.74	1,803.33	Reserves of Deposit Money Banks	14c
45.31	39.72	48.76	61.95	75.76	69.35	†129.17	186.56	251.33	309.88	435.84	553.06	498.99	595.65	775.51	Deposits of Other Sectors	14d
....	....	....	....	....	....	50.03	61.34	104.43	115.56	92.86	71.46	53.12	63.01	23.73	Deposits of Other Banking Insts.	14f
....	....	....	....	....	....	....	....	19.71	....	11.89	11.89	11.89	—		Bonds	16ab
4.30	3.77	4.29	2.45	—	—	—				22.29	20.14	39.90	39.39	50.91	Foreign Liabilities	16c
30.70	27.11	43.80	38.04	48.58	23.06	†47.34	83.33	97.34	122.54	†66.42	72.20	61.73	167.81	98.93	Central Government Deposits	16d
26.38	26.40	30.62	36.29	52.70	68.27	32.92	29.49	40.04	39.51	39.27	39.44	39.37	38.23	37.98	Capital Accounts	17a
-2.52	-.40	-1.74	2.09	-3.59	-5.47	†-27.39	-75.78	-170.64	-206.92	-121.70	-230.76	-56.82	-97.26	-85.50	Other Items (Net)	17r

Banking Institutions

End of Period

113.99	128.86	178.15	263.81	359.32	367.80	†594.32	768.59	1,006.41	1,387.00	1,645.68	1,511.15	1,610.78	1,619.32	1,817.14	Reserves	20
45.83	52.76	54.17	91.39	113.86	147.05	†294.87	440.47	390.50	428.68	531.95	600.90	646.58	903.57	1,017.54	Foreign Assets	21
						7.45	47.82	105.73	182.30	151.98	498.79	607.94	739.31	1,104.50	Claims on Central Government	22a
927.39	1,092.54	1,290.60	1,586.18	1,899.56	2,295.48	†3388.68	4,104.28	5,097.18	6,358.26	7,689.33	8,947.18	9,982.84	11,125.56	11,434.36	Claims on Other Sectors	22d
266.64	295.76	300.45	374.88	505.62	669.14	†969.29	1,238.99	1,520.16	1,876.49	2,381.03	2,648.57	3,235.62	3,846.88	4,414.01	Demand Deposits	24
70.75	94.80	94.62	115.15	145.07	214.06	†1458.29	2,051.60	2,804.55	3,637.34	4,363.52	5,020.57	5,580.51	5,975.44	6,785.08	Savings Deposits	25aa
41.01	59.72	61.37	76.43	101.70	154.83	218.88	194.31	332.42	504.19	673.85	830.19	947.68	1,126.11	1,418.01	Time Deposits	25ab
						214.80	292.13	377.70	401.74	315.07	383.55	496.20	586.97	679.86	Other Deposits	25e
						24.79	21.30	18.91	29.98	354.18	520.38	635.46	742.89	844.80	Bonds	26ab
37.80	43.40	49.97	67.20	108.24	111.57	†227.53	379.15	418.95	464.61	488.80	452.72	389.61	410.03	310.19	Foreign Liabilities	26c
274.99	336.10	420.15	508.29	590.56	670.99	†971.56	1,034.44	1,119.78	1,423.29	1,403.85	1,206.98	828.92	913.44	964.67	Credit from Monetary Authorities	26g
81.46	91.42	99.32	111.49	131.30	131.30	†283.72	343.25	351.58	411.37	428.59	658.27	626.34	739.67	765.98	Capital Accounts	27a
92.06	103.17	107.73	130.81	107.98	14.31	†-83.62	-194.06	-344.23	-392.77	-389.95	-163.21	107.83	46.34	-809.04	Other Items (Net)	27r

Banking Survey

End of Period

29.20	33.81	40.42	103.79	145.58	168.52	†222.29	506.45	638.50	920.29	1,366.07	1,504.20	1,702.82	2,012.43	2,642.48	Foreign Assets (Net)	31n
970.87	1,153.64	1,349.79	1,668.92	2,002.67	2,449.92	†3575.29	4,310.37	5,331.86	6,642.17	7,950.27	9,542.44	10,697.47	11,866.37	12,741.63	Domestic Credit	32
20.80	30.54	24.66	42.07	58.20	101.05	†118.38	133.26	166.67	218.04	243.84	584.88	704.49	729.79	1,287.71	Claims on Central Govt. (Net)	32an
950.07	1,123.10	1,325.13	1,626.85	1,944.47	2,348.87	†3456.91	4,177.11	5,165.19	6,424.13	7,706.44	8,957.56	9,992.99	11,136.58	11,453.91	Claims on Other Sectors	32d
457.40	548.74	583.42	700.95	898.78	1,171.43	†1546.94	1,967.43	2,308.35	2,756.38	3,480.65	3,869.05	4,697.64	5,454.10	6,168.85	Money	34
338.34	411.47	555.89	767.24	961.11	1,261.30	†2021.64	2,724.60	3,766.00	4,853.15	5,706.13	6,686.96	7,406.57	8,141.93	9,472.34	Quasi-Money	35
						24.79	21.30	38.62	29.98	366.07	532.27	647.35	742.89	844.80	Bonds	36ab
107.84	117.82	129.94	147.78	184.00	199.57	†316.64	372.74	391.62	450.88	467.86	697.71	665.70	777.90	803.96	Capital Accounts	37a
96.50	109.43	120.95	156.75	104.36	-13.87	†-112.01	-269.30	-534.23	-527.93	-704.36	-739.35	-1,016.94	-1,238.01	-1,905.85	Other Items (Net)	37r
795.74	960.21	1,139.31	1,468.19	1,859.89	2,432.73	†3568.08	4,692.03	6,074.35	7,609.53	9,186.78	10,556.01	12,104.21	13,596.02	15,641.19	Money plus Quasi-Money	35l

Interest Rates

Percent per Annum

....	....	....	7.92	7.20	7.20	10.08	10.08	10.44	9.00	8.55	4.59	3.24	3.24	3.24	Bank Rate	60
7.20	8.64	11.34	8.64	7.56	7.56	10.98	10.98	10.98	7.47	5.67	3.78	2.25	2.25	2.25	Deposit Rate	60l
7.92	9.00	†11.34	9.36	8.64	8.64	10.98	10.98	10.98	12.06	10.08	8.64	6.39	5.85	5.85	Lending Rate	60p

Prices, Production, Labor

Period of Previous Year

| 7.2 | 18.7 | 18.3 | 3.1 | 3.5 | 6.3 | 14.6 | 24.2 | 16.9 | 8.3 | 2.8 | -.8 | -1.4 | .3 | .3 | Consumer Prices | 64..x |
| .... | .... | .... | .... | — | 21.2 | .... | 21.4 | 16.1 | 15.1 | 13.2 | 9.6 | 9.8 | 11.2 | .... | Industrial Production | 66..x |

Period Averages

527,830	543,340	553,290	639,090	647,990	655,540	663,730	671,990	679,470	688,500	696,000	699,570	705,860	711,500	....	Employment	67e
2,766	2,960	3,779	3,832	3,522	3,603	4,201	4,764	5,196	5,528	5,768	5,710	5,750	5,950	....	Unemployment	67c
2.0	2.0	2.6	2.5	2.3	2.3	2.6	2.8	2.9	3.0	3.0	3.1	3.1	3.1	....	Unemployment Rate (%)	67r

China,P.R.: Mainland

		1972	1973	1974	1975	1976	1977	1978	1979	1980	1981	1982	1983	1984	1985	1986
International Transactions															*Millions of US Dollars*	
Exports	70..d	3,693	5,876	7,108	7,689	6,943	7,520	9,955	13,614	†18,099	22,007	22,321	22,226	26,139	27,350	30,942
Imports, c.i.f.	71..d	2,851	5,208	7,791	7,926	6,660	7,148	11,131	15,621	†19,941	22,015	19,285	21,390	27,410	42,252	42,904
Balance of Payments															*Millions of US Dollars:*	
Current Account, n.i.e.	78al d	....	....	....	....	....	....	....	....	....	....	5,674	4,240	2,030	−11,417	−7,034
Goods: Exports f.o.b.	78aa d											21,125	20,707	23,905	25,108	25,756
Goods: Imports f.o.b.	78ab d											−16,876	−18,717	−23,891	−38,231	−34,896
Trade Balance	78ac d											4,249	1,990	14	−13,123	−9,140
Services: Credit	78ad d											2,512	2,479	2,811	3,055	3,827
Services: Debit	78ae d											−2,024	−1,994	−2,857	−2,524	−2,276
Balance on Goods & Services	78af d											4,737	2,475	−32	−12,592	−7,589
Income: Credit	78ag d											1,092	1,549	2,008	1,478	1,100
Income: Debit	78ah d											−641	−295	−388	−546	−924
Balance on Gds, Serv. & Inc.	78ai d											5,188	3,729	1,588	−11,660	−7,413
Current Transfers, n.i.e.: Credit	78aj d											672	620	596	439	516
Current Transfers: Debit	78ak d											−186	−109	−154	−196	−137
Capital Account, n.i.e.	78bc d											—	—	—	—	—
Capital Account, n.i.e.: Credit	78ba d											—	—	—	—	—
Capital Account: Debit	78bb d											—	—	—	—	—
Financial Account, n.i.e.	78bj d	....	....	....	....	....	....	....	....	....	....	338	−226	−1,003	8,971	5,944
Direct Investment Abroad	78bd d											−44	−93	−134	−629	−450
Dir. Invest. in Rep. Econ., n.i.e.	78be d											430	636	1,258	1,659	1,875
Portfolio Investment Assets	78bf d											−20	−641	−1,721	2,263	−40
Equity Securities	78bk d											—	—	—	—	—
Debt Securities	78bl d											−20	−641	−1,721	2,263	−40
Portfolio Investment Liab., n.i.e.	78bg d											41	20	83	764	1,608
Equity Securities	78bm d											—	—	—	—	—
Debt Securities	78bn d											41	20	83	764	1,608
Financial Derivatives Assets	78bw d											....	....	....	....	....
Financial Derivatives Liabilities	78bx d											....	....	....	....	....
Other Investment Assets	78bh d											−790	−638	−625	−1,101	−328
Monetary Authorities	78bo d											....	....	....	....	....
General Government	78bp d											−472	−388	−303	−104	145
Banks	78bq d											—	—	—	—	—
Other Sectors	78br d											−318	−250	−322	−997	−473
Other Investment Liab., n.i.e.	78bi d											721	490	136	6,015	3,279
Monetary Authorities	78bs d											−13	27	4	68	509
General Government	78bt d											514	304	937	1,219	3,945
Banks	78bu d											−503	8	38	4,688	−1,685
Other Sectors	78bv d											723	151	−843	40	510
Net Errors and Omissions	78ca d	....	....	....	....	....	....	....	....	....	....	293	128	−889	6	−958
Overall Balance	78cb d											6,305	4,142	138	−2,440	−2,048
Reserves and Related Items	79da d	....	....	....	....	....	....	....	....	....	....	−6,305	−4,142	−138	2,440	2,048
Reserve Assets	79db d											−6,305	−3,658	−138	2,440	1,369
Use of Fund Credit and Loans	79dc d												−483	—	—	679
Exceptional Financing	79de d											....	....	....	....	....
Government Finance															*Billions of Yuan:*	
Deficit (-) or Surplus	80	....	....	....	....	....	3.10	1.01	−17.06	−12.75	−2.55	−2.93	−4.35	−4.45	2.16	−8.29
Total Revenue and Grants	81y						87.45	112.11	110.33	108.52	108.95	112.40	124.90	150.19	186.64	212.20
Exp. & Lending Minus Repay.	82z						84.35	111.10	127.39	121.27	111.50	115.33	129.25	154.64	184.48	220.49
Financing																
Domestic	84a											....	....	....	....	....
Foreign	85a											....	....	....	....	....
Use of Cash Balances	87											....	....	....	....	....
National Accounts															*Billions of Yuan*	
Househ.Cons.Expend.,incl.NPISHs	96f	....	....	....	....	....	....	175.9	200.5	231.7	260.4	286.8	318.3	367.5	458.9	517.5
Government Consumption Expend.	91f							48.0	61.4	65.9	70.5	77.0	83.8	102.0	118.4	136.7
Gross Fixed Capital Formation	93e							107.4	115.1	131.8	125.3	149.3	170.9	212.6	264.1	309.8
Changes in Inventories	93i							30.4	32.3	27.2	32.8	26.7	29.6	34.3	74.5	74.8
Exports (Net)	90n							−1.1	−2.0	−1.5	1.1	9.1	5.1	.1	−36.7	−25.5
Gross Domestic Product (GDP)	99b							....	407.4	455.1	490.1	548.9	607.6	716.4	879.2	1,013.3
Net Primary Income from Abroad	98.n							....	....	—	−.7	1.3	1.9	3.2	2.5	−.1
Gross National Income (GNI)	99a	....	....	....	283.9	....	....	362.4	398.8	455.1	489.4	550.2	609.5	719.6	881.7	1,013.2
GDP Volume 1995 Prices	99b.p	....	....	....	....	....	....	1,178.5	1,268.0	1,367.0	1,428.3	1,546.1	1,707.6	1,956.2	2,273.2	2,474.8
GDP Volume (1995=100)	99bv p	....	....	....	....	....	....	20.1	21.7	23.4	24.4	26.4	29.2	33.4	38.9	42.3
GDP Deflator (1995=100)	99bi p	....	....	....	....	....	....	....	32.1	33.3	34.3	35.5	35.6	36.6	38.7	40.9
															Millions:	
Population	99z	871.8	892.1	908.6	924.2	937.2	949.7	962.6	975.4	996.1	1,008.4	1,020.6	1,039.6	1,054.9	1,070.2	1,086.7

International Transactions

Millions of US Dollars

	1987	1988	1989	1990	1991	1992	1993	1994	1995	1996	1997	1998	1999	2000	2001	
Exports	39,437	47,516	52,538	62,091	71,910	84,940	90,970	121,047	148,797	151,197	182,877	183,589	195,150	249,297	266,620	70..d
Imports, c.i.f.	43,216	55,268	59,140	53,345	63,791	80,585	103,088	115,681	129,113	138,944	142,189	140,305	165,788	206,132	243,521	71..d

Balance of Payments

Minus Sign Indicates Debit

	1987	1988	1989	1990	1991	1992	1993	1994	1995	1996	1997	1998	1999	2000	2001	
Current Account, n.i.e.	300	-3,802	-4,317	11,997	13,272	6,401	-11,609	6,908	1,618	7,243	36,963	31,472	21,115	20,518	....	78al d
Goods: Exports f.o.b.	34,734	41,054	43,220	51,519	58,919	69,568	75,659	102,561	128,110	151,077	182,670	183,529	194,716	249,131	....	78aa d
Goods: Imports f.o.b.	-36,395	-46,369	-48,840	-42,354	-50,176	-64,385	-86,313	-95,271	-110,060	-131,542	-136,448	-136,915	-158,734	-214,657	....	78ab d
Trade Balance	-1,661	-5,315	-5,620	9,165	8,743	5,183	-10,654	7,290	18,050	19,535	46,222	46,614	35,982	34,474	....	78ac d
Services: Credit	4,437	4,858	4,603	5,855	6,979	9,249	11,193	16,620	19,130	20,601	24,569	23,895	26,248	30,430	....	78ae d
Services: Debit	-2,485	-3,603	-3,910	-4,352	-4,121	-9,434	-12,036	-16,299	-25,223	-22,585	-27,967	-26,672	-31,589	-36,031	....	78ae d
Balance on Goods & Services	291	-4,060	-4,927	10,668	11,601	4,998	-11,497	7,611	11,958	17,551	42,824	43,837	30,641	28,874	....	78af d
Income: Credit	976	1,469	1,894	3,017	3,719	5,595	4,390	5,737	5,191	7,318	5,710	5,584	8,330	12,550	....	78ag d
Income: Debit	-1,191	-1,630	-1,665	-1,962	-2,879	-5,347	-5,674	-6,775	-16,965	-19,755	-16,715	-22,228	-22,800	-27,216	....	78ah d
Balance on Gds, Serv. & Inc.	76	-4,221	-4,698	11,723	12,441	5,246	-12,781	6,573	184	5,114	31,819	27,193	16,171	14,207	....	78ai d
Current Transfers, n.i.e.: Credit	389	568	477	376	890	1,206	1,290	1,269	1,827	2,368	5,477	4,661	5,368	6,861	....	78aj d
Current Transfers: Debit	-165	-149	-96	-102	-59	-51	-118	-934	-392	-239	-333	-382	-424	-550	....	78ak d
Capital Account, n.i.e.	—	—	—	—	—	—	—	—	—	—	-21	-47	-26	-35	....	78bc d
Capital Account, n.i.e.: Credit	—	—	—	—	—	—	—	—	—	—	-21	-47	-26	....	....	78ba d
Capital Account: Debit	—	—	—	—	—	—	—	—	—	—	-21	-47	-26	-35	....	78bb d
Financial Account, n.i.e.	6,001	7,133	3,723	3,255	8,032	-250	23,474	32,645	38,674	39,966	21,037	-6,275	5,204	1,958	....	78bj d
Direct Investment Abroad	-645	-850	-780	-830	-913	-4,000	-4,400	-2,000	-2,000	-2,114	-2,563	-2,634	-1,775	-916	....	78bd d
Dir. Invest. in Rep. Econ., n.i.e.	2,314	3,194	3,393	3,487	4,366	11,156	27,515	33,787	35,849	40,180	44,237	43,751	38,753	38,399	....	78be d
Portfolio Investment Assets	-140	-340	-320	-241	-330	-450	-597	-380	79	-628	-899	-3,830	-10,535	-11,307	....	78bf d
Equity Securities																78bk d
Debt Securities	-140	-340	-320	-241	-330	-450	-597	-380	79	-628	-899	-3,830	-10,535	-11,307	....	78bl d
Portfolio Investment Liab., n.i.e.	1,191	1,216	140	—	565	393	3,646	3,923	710	2,372	7,842	98	-699	7,317	....	78bg d
Equity Securities	....	....	....	....	....	....	....	....	....	....	5,657	765	612	6,912	....	78bm d
Debt Securities	1,191	1,216	140	—	565	393	3,646	3,923	710	2,372	2,185	-667	-1,311	405	....	78bn d
Financial Derivatives Assets	....	....	....	....	....	....	....	....	....	....	....	....	....	....	....	78bw d
Financial Derivatives Liabilities	....	....	....	....	....	....	....	....	....	....	....	....	....	....	....	78bx d
Other Investment Assets	82	-781	-229	-231	-156	-3,267	-2,114	-1,189	-1,081	-1,126	-39,608	-35,041	-24,394	-43,864	....	78bh d
Monetary Authorities											-7,977	-2,417	-5,715	-7,261	....	78bo d
General Government	151	-729	-121	-116	-48	-3,351	-1,741	-1,136	-367	-1,102					....	78bp d
Banks											-12,572	2,841	6,075	-21,430	....	78bq d
Other Sectors	-69	-52	-108	-115	-108	84	-373	-53	-714	-24	-19,059	-35,465	-24,754	-15,173	....	78br d
Other Investment Liab., n.i.e.	3,199	4,694	1,519	1,070	4,500	-4,082	-576	-1,496	5,116	1,282	12,028	-8,619	3,854	12,329	....	78bi d
Monetary Authorities	-112	198	50	-115	—	140	175	1,004	1,154	1,256	-2,037	-5,441	-3,936	....	....	78bs d
General Government	1,158	3,895	4,699	3,129	2,284	-18	1,564	5,178	6,021	4,995	—	—	3,233	3,153	....	78bt d
Banks	1,884	1,108	-2,661	-2,315	1,655	-786	-415	-5,222	-4,045	-5,959	6,968	-3,150	-5,021	-8,281	....	78bu d
Other Sectors	269	-507	-569	371	561	-3,418	-1,900	-2,456	1,986	990	7,097	-28	9,578	17,457	....	78bv d
Net Errors and Omissions	-1,518	-957	115	-3,205	-6,767	-8,211	-10,096	-9,100	-17,823	-15,504	-22,122	-18,902	-17,641	-11,748	....	78ca d
Overall Balance	4,783	2,374	-479	12,047	14,537	-2,060	1,769	30,453	22,469	31,705	35,857	6,248	8,652	10,693	....	78cb d
Reserves and Related Items	-4,783	-2,374	479	-12,047	-14,537	2,060	-1,769	-30,453	-22,469	-31,705	-35,857	-6,248	-8,652	-10,693	....	79da d
Reserve Assets	-4,704	-2,291	558	-11,555	-14,083	2,060	-1,769	-30,453	-22,469	-31,705	-35,857	-6,248	-8,652	-10,693	....	79db d
Use of Fund Credit and Loans	-79	-82	-79	-492	-454	—	—	—	—	—	—	—	—	—	....	79dc d
Exceptional Financing	....	....	....	....	....	....	....	....	....	....	....	....	....	....	....	79de d

Government Finance

Year Ending December 31

	1987	1988	1989	1990	1991	1992	1993	1994	1995	1996	1997	1998	1999	2000	2001	
Deficit (-) or Surplus	-6.28	-13.40	-15.89	-14.65	-23.72	-25.89	-29.34	-57.45	-58.15	-52.96	-55.85	-92.23	-174.37	-249.13	-247.25	80
Total Revenue and Grants	219.94	235.72	266.49	351.60	365.97	392.83	476.02	558.43	657.00	774.54	901.96	1,020.94	1,173.42	1,367.40	1,667.04	81y
Exp. & Lending Minus Repay.	226.22	249.12	282.38	366.25	389.69	418.72	505.36	615.88	715.15	827.50	957.81	1,113.17	1,347.79	1,616.53	1,914.29	82z
Financing																
Domestic	....	....	....	21.47	31.73	33.91	33.36	63.64	69.96	55.35	56.44	95.25	188.26	260.49	256.90	84a
Foreign	....	....	....	-6.82	-8.02	-8.03	-4.02	3.06	-3.68	6.53	-.60	.56	-9.10	-.45	3.62	85a
Use of Cash Balances	....	....	....	—	—	—	-9.25	-8.13	-7.93	—	-3.58	-4.80	-10.56	....	....	87

National Accounts

Billions of Yuan

	1987	1988	1989	1990	1991	1992	1993	1994	1995	1996	1997	1998	1999	2000	2001	
Househ.Cons.Expend.,incl.NPISHs	596.1	763.3	852.4	911.3	1,031.6	1,246.0	1,568.2	2,081.0	2,694.5	3,215.2	3,485.5	3,692.1	3,943.2	....	....	96f
Government Consumption Expend.	149.0	172.7	203.3	225.2	283.0	349.2	450.0	598.6	669.1	785.2	872.5	948.5	1,062.3	....	....	91f
Gross Fixed Capital Formation	374.2	462.4	433.9	473.2	594.0	831.7	1,298.0	1,685.6	2,030.1	2,333.6	2,515.4	2,818.1	2,964.6	....	....	93e
Changes in Inventories	58.0	87.1	175.6	171.2	157.7	131.9	201.8	240.4	357.7	353.1	330.3	221.5	177.0	....	....	93i
Exports (Net)	1.1	-15.1	-18.6	51.0	61.8	27.6	-68.0	63.4	99.9	145.9	285.7	305.2	241.8	....	....	90n
Gross Domestic Product (GDP)	1,178.4	1,470.4	1,646.6	1,832.0	2,128.0	2,586.4	3,450.1	4,669.1	5,851.1	6,833.0	7,489.5	7,985.3	8,205.4	8,940.4	....	99b
Net Primary Income from Abroad	-.8	-.6	.9	5.1	4.5	1.4	-7.4	-8.9	-98.3	....	....	....	....	....	....	98.n
Gross National Income (GNI)	1,177.6	1,469.8	1,647.5	1,837.0	2,132.5	2,587.7	3,442.7	4,660.1	5,752.7	....	....	....	....	....	....	99a
GDP Volume 1995 Prices	2,761.1	3,072.2	3,197.2	3,319.7	3,624.9	4,141.1	4,699.7	5,294.8	5,851.1	6,412.0	6,976.5	7,520.9	8,055.9	8,700.4	....	99b.p
GDP Volume (1995=100)	47.2	52.5	54.6	56.7	62.0	70.8	80.3	90.5	100.0	109.6	119.2	128.5	137.7	148.7	....	99bv p
GDP Deflator (1995=100)	42.7	47.9	51.5	55.2	58.7	62.5	73.4	88.2	100.0	106.6	107.4	106.2	101.9	102.8	....	99bi p

Midyear

	1987	1988	1989	1990	1991	1992	1993	1994	1995	1996	1997	1998	1999	2000	2001	
Population	1,104.2	1,121.9	1,139.2	1,155.3	1,170.1	1,183.3	1,195.7	1,207.6	1,236.7	1,246.2	1,242.8	1,253.9	1,264.8	1,275.1	1,285.0	99z

(See notes in the back of the book.)

China,P.R.:Hong Kong

		1972	1973	1974	1975	1976	1977	1978	1979	1980	1981	1982	1983	1984	1985	1986
Exchange Rates														*Hong Kong Dollars per SDR:*		
Market Rate	aa	†6.182	6.140	6.012	5.892	5.429	5.606	6.257	6.518	6.543	6.605	7.165	8.145	7.668	8.580	9.535
													Hong Kong Dollars per US Dollar:			
Market Rate	ae	†5.694	5.090	4.910	5.033	4.673	4.615	4.803	4.948	5.130	5.675	6.495	7.780	7.823	7.811	7.795
Market Rate	rf	5.641	5.147	5.032	4.935	4.905	4.662	4.684	5.003	4.976	5.589	6.070	7.265	7.818	7.791	7.803
													Index Numbers (1995=100)			
Nominal Effective Exchange Rate	ne c	...	...	...	...	...	...	...	136.26	137.95	132.26	132.69	114.31	111.81	117.60	103.45
Fund Position													*Millions of SDRs:*			
Reserve Position in the Fund	1c. s	—	—	—	—	—	—	—	—	—	—	—	—	—	—	—
of which: Outstg.Fund Borrowing	2c	—	—	—	—	—	—	—	—	—	—	—	—	—	—	—
International Liquidity												*Billions of US Dollars Unless Otherwise Indicated:*				
Total Reserves minus Gold	1l. d	...	...	...	...	...	...	...	...	...	...	...	...	...	...	...
Reserve Position in the Fund	1c. d	—	—	—	—	—	—	—	—	—	—	—	—	—	—	—
Foreign Exchange	1d. d	...	...	...	...	...	...	...	...	...	...	...	...	...	...	...
Gold (Million Fine Troy Ounces)	1ad	...	...	...	...	...	...	...	...	...	...	...	...	...	...	...
Gold (National Valuation)	1an d	...	...	...	...	...	...	...	...	...	...	...	...	...	...	...
Banking Institutions: Assets	7a. d	†2.40	2.83	5.15	6.64	9.12	11.82	14.06	24.99	34.52	46.19	58.23	67.56	78.75	101.17	155.23
Liabilities	7b. d	.96	2.55	4.94	6.61	9.20	13.07	16.38	21.12	32.59	45.24	54.12	59.63	65.94	83.33	125.78
Monetary Authorities													*Billions of Hong Kong Dollars:*			
Foreign Assets	11	...	...	...	...	...	...	...	...	...	...	...	...	...	...	...
Reserve Money	14	...	...	...	...	...	...	...	...	...	...	...	...	...	...	...
of which: Currency Outside Banks	14a	...	...	...	...	...	...	...	...	...	...	...	...	...	...	...
Foreign Liabilities	16c	...	...	...	...	...	...	...	...	...	...	...	...	...	...	...
Government Deposits	16d	...	...	...	...	...	...	...	...	...	...	...	...	...	...	...
Capital Accounts	17a	...	...	...	...	...	...	...	...	...	...	...	...	...	...	...
Other Items (Net)	17r	...	...	...	...	...	...	...	...	...	...	...	...	...	...	...
Banking Institutions													*Billions of Hong Kong Dollars:*			
Reserves	20	...	...	...	...	...	...	...	...	...	...	...	...	...	...	...
Foreign Assets	21	...	...	...	...	...	...	...	...	...	...	...	...	...	...	...
Claims on Government	22a	...	...	...	...	...	...	...	...	...	...	...	...	...	...	...
Claims on Other Sectors	22d	...	...	...	...	...	...	...	...	...	...	...	...	...	...	...
Demand Deposits	24	...	...	...	...	...	...	...	...	...	...	...	...	...	...	...
Time, Savings,& Fgn.Currency Dep.	25	...	...	...	...	...	...	...	...	...	...	...	...	...	...	...
Money Market Instruments	26aa	...	...	...	...	...	...	...	...	...	...	...	...	...	...	...
Foreign Liabilities	26c	...	...	...	...	...	...	...	...	...	...	...	...	...	...	...
Government Deposits	26d	...	...	...	...	...	...	...	...	...	...	...	...	...	...	...
Capital Accounts	27a	...	...	...	...	...	...	...	...	...	...	...	...	...	...	...
Other Items (Net)	27r	...	...	...	...	...	...	...	...	...	...	...	...	...	...	...
Banking Survey													*Billions of Hong Kong Dollars:*			
Foreign Assets (Net)	31n	...	...	...	...	...	...	...	...	...	...	...	...	...	...	...
Domestic Credit	32	...	...	...	...	...	...	...	...	...	...	...	...	...	...	...
Claims on Government (net)	32an	...	...	...	...	...	...	...	...	...	...	...	...	...	...	...
Claims on Other Sectors	32d	...	...	...	...	...	...	...	...	...	...	...	...	...	...	...
Money	34	...	...	...	...	...	...	...	...	...	...	...	...	...	...	...
Quasi-Money	35	...	...	...	...	...	...	...	...	...	...	...	...	...	...	...
Money Market Instruments	36aa	...	...	...	...	...	...	...	...	...	...	...	...	...	...	...
Capital Accounts	37a	...	...	...	...	...	...	...	...	...	...	...	...	...	...	...
Other Items (Net)	37r	...	...	...	...	...	...	...	...	...	...	...	...	...	...	...
Money plus Quasi-Money	35l	...	...	...	...	...	...	...	...	...	...	...	...	...	...	...
Interest Rates														*Percent Per Annum*		
Discount Rate (End of Period)	60	...	...	...	...	...	...	...	...	...	...	...	...	...	...	...
Money Market Rate	60b	...	...	...	...	...	...	...	...	...	...	...	...	...	...	...
Treasury Bill Rate	60c	...	...	...	...	...	...	...	...	...	...	...	...	...	...	...
Deposit Rate	60l	...	...	...	...	...	...	...	...	...	...	...	...	...	...	...
Lending Rate	60p	...	...	...	...	...	...	...	...	...	...	...	...	...	...	...
Prices, Production, Labor													*Index Numbers (1995=100):*			
Share Prices	62	...	...	...	...	...	...	...	...	...	...	...	...	...	...	...
Producer Prices	63	...	...	...	...	...	...	...	...	...	...	...	...	...	...	...
Consumer Prices	64	...	...	...	...	...	...	...	...	...	...	...	...	...	...	...
Wages: Avg.Earnings(Mfg)	65	...	...	...	...	...	...	...	...	...	...	...	...	...	...	...
Wage Rates (Manufacturing)	65a	...	...	...	...	...	...	...	...	...	...	...	...	...	...	...
Manufacturing Production	66ey	...	...	...	...	...	...	...	...	...	...	...	54.3	61.8	71.7	68.6	79.5
														Number in Thousands:		
Labor Force	67d	...	...	...	...	...	...	...	...	...	...	...	...	...	...	...
Employment	67e	...	...	...	...	...	...	...	...	...	...	...	...	...	2,543	2,624
Unemployment	67c	...	...	...	...	...	...	...	...	...	...	...	...	...	...	76
Unemployment Rate (%)	67r	...	...	...	...	...	...	...	...	...	...	...	...	...	...	2.8
International Transactions														*Billions of US Dollars*		
Exports	70..d	3.44	5.07	5.97	6.03	8.48	9.62	11.45	15.14	19.75	21.83	21.01	21.96	28.32	30.19	35.44
Imports, c.i.f.	71..d	3.86	5.66	6.78	6.77	8.84	10.45	13.39	17.13	22.45	24.80	23.58	24.02	28.57	29.70	35.37
														1995=100		
Volume of Exports	72	5.7	6.4	6.1	6.1	7.9	8.3	9.3	11.3	13.3	15.3	14.8	17.0	20.8	21.9	25.3
Volume of Imports	73	5.9	6.6	5.9	6.3	7.8	8.3	10.2	11.7	14.1	15.7	15.3	16.8	19.2	20.4	23.2
Unit Value of Exports	74	25.2	29.9	35.7	35.2	38.1	39.3	42.2	49.2	53.9	58.6	62.7	69.1	78.2	78.6	80.2
Unit Value of Imports	75	24.8	29.5	37.8	36.0	37.2	39.0	41.9	49.0	53.1	59.0	62.4	69.5	77.6	75.6	79.3

	1987	1988	1989	1990	1991	1992	1993	1994	1995	1996	1997	1998	1999	2000	2001		
End of Period																**Exchange Rates**	
	11.009	10.507	10.260	11.098	11.130	10.647	10.612	11.296	11.494	11.124	10.451	10.907	10.666	10.157	9.799	Market Rate	**aa**
End of Period (ae) Period Average (rf)																	
	7.760	7.808	7.807	7.801	7.781	7.743	7.726	7.738	7.732	7.736	7.746	7.746	7.771	7.796	7.797	Market Rate	**ae**
	7.798	7.806	7.800	7.790	7.771	7.741	7.736	7.728	7.736	7.734	7.742	7.745	7.758	7.791	7.799	Market Rate	**rf**
Period Averages																	
	94.99	92.80	95.32	95.21	97.03	97.89	104.72	104.88	100.00	103.48	109.06	115.28	112.08	113.27	118.22	Nominal Effective Exchange Rate	**ne c**
End of Period																**Fund Position**	
	—	—	—	—	—	—	—	—	—	—	—	31.34	—	—	—	Reserve Position in the Fund	**1c. s**
												31.34				of which: Outstg.Fund Borrowing	**2c**
End of Period																**International Liquidity**	
	....	....	....	24.57	28.81	35.17	42.99	49.25	55.40	63.81	92.80	89.65	96.24	107.54	111.16	Total Reserves minus Gold	**1l.d**
												.04	—	—	—	Reserve Position in the Fund	**1c.d**
	—	—	....	24.57	28.81	35.17	42.99	49.25	55.40	63.81	†92.80	†89.61	96.24	107.54	111.16	Foreign Exchange	**1d.d**
	....	....	....	.228	.228	.228	.068	.068	.067	.067	.067	.067	.067	.067	.067	Gold (Million Fine Troy Ounces)	**1ad**
				.089	.081	.076	.026	.026	.026	.025	.019	.019	.019	.018	.019	Gold (National Valuation)	**1an d**
	266.05	309.74	355.64	464.09	503.20	507.32	518.78	614.80	655.58	608.62	600.63	501.17	475.78	450.48	405.22	Banking Institutions: Assets	**7a.d**
	229.43	269.58	310.13	402.69	461.89	463.87	477.58	582.33	620.40	579.85	597.32	447.35	371.87	319.15	264.39	Liabilities	**7b.d**
End of Period																**Monetary Authorities**	
	....	....	....	123.50	161.40	199.10	290.52	297.27	376.59	463.89	549.97	672.68	691.27	803.69	822.50	Foreign Assets	**11**
				43.27	49.21	62.17	72.79	79.88	82.96	87.12	92.71	94.77	†234.39	215.40	229.74	Reserve Money	**14**
				37.22	42.14	51.70	62.89	67.31	70.87	76.05	80.34	80.92	99.27	91.51	101.38	of which: Currency Outside Banks	**14a**
				.01	.02	.02	.04	.03	1.54	.03	.32	.04	.27	.04	42.08	Foreign Liabilities	**16c**
				63.23	69.80	96.15	115.68	131.24	125.92	145.90	237.63	424.56	392.21	417.16	380.60	Government Deposits	**16d**
				82.64	98.65	106.64	127.54	125.77	160.13	172.86	190.21	242.22	290.86	307.10	302.59	Capital Accounts	**17a**
				−65.64	−56.27	−65.88	−25.52	−41.17	7.56	57.69	29.38	−89.15	−226.22	−155.79	−132.51	Other Items (Net)	**17r**
End of Period																**Banking Institutions**	
	....	....	....	6.05	7.07	10.47	9.91	12.57	12.09	11.07	12.37	13.85	32.67	14.34	12.53	Reserves	**20**
				3,620.34	3,915.38	3,928.17	4,008.11	4,757.31	5,068.93	4,708.31	4,652.49	3,882.07	3,697.31	3,511.95	3,159.51	Foreign Assets	**21**
				17.78	17.89	29.72	56.77	106.77	57.25	104.74	143.61	140.34	166.64	201.19	212.75	Claims on Government	**22a**
				962.04	948.88	1,045.40	1,256.02	1,506.39	1,671.93	1,935.32	2,324.36	2,181.93	1,964.83	2,010.95	1,968.27	Claims on Other Sectors	**22d**
				....	57.56	72.85	87.71	83.38	80.32	98.33	87.44	79.07	85.35	93.05	109.64	Demand Deposits	**24**
				1,115.20	1,193.40	1,357.87	1,534.82	1,713.81	1,923.57	2,113.05	2,374.65	2,560.47	2,816.59	2,781.95	Time, Savings,& Fgn.Currency Dep.	**25**
				....	45.86	38.51	46.83	71.26	82.62	107.13	118.16	116.51	110.77	103.79	107.79	Money Market Instruments	**26aa**
				3,594.00	3,591.78	3,689.75	4,506.08	4,796.95	4,485.74	4,626.87	3,465.16	2,889.78	2,488.13	2,061.42	Foreign Liabilities	**26c**
				6.13	13.69	11.30	26.60	18.87	14.43	19.09	5.16	6.15	3.78	2.93	1.46	Government Deposits	**26d**
				....	63.55	90.86	104.85	113.03	132.61	153.91	170.34	153.67	154.03	164.10	204.26	Capital Accounts	**27a**
	....	....	−171.19	−23.35	−.64	15.04	17.20	55.58	−10.56	−28.33	11.78	22.98	57.27	69.84	86.53	Other Items (Net)	**27r**
End of Period																**Banking Survey**	
	....	....	....	482.77	535.47	608.86	546.96	648.53	686.14	575.54	1,089.32	1,498.76	1,807.70	1,878.52	Foreign Assets (Net)	**31n**
				910.46	883.27	967.68	1,170.50	1,463.04	1,588.84	1,875.07	2,225.17	1,891.55	1,735.49	1,792.05	1,798.96	Domestic Credit	**32**
				−51.57	−65.60	−77.73	−85.51	−43.34	−83.10	−60.25	−99.18	−290.38	−229.34	−218.90	−169.31	Claims on Government (net)	**32an**
				962.04	948.88	1,045.40	1,256.02	1,506.39	1,671.93	1,935.32	2,324.36	2,181.93	1,964.83	2,010.95	1,968.27	Claims on Other Sectors	**32d**
				99.70	124.55	150.60	150.70	151.19	174.38	167.78	159.99	184.62	184.56	211.02	Money	**34**
				....	1,115.20	1,193.40	1,357.87	1,534.82	1,713.81	1,923.57	2,113.05	2,374.65	2,560.47	2,816.59	2,781.95	Quasi-Money	**35**
				45.86	38.51	46.83	71.26	82.62	107.13	118.16	116.51	110.77	103.79	107.79	Money Market Instruments	**36aa**
				162.20	197.50	232.39	238.81	292.75	326.77	360.55	395.89	444.89	471.20	506.85	Capital Accounts	**37a**
				−88.99	−56.91	−50.83	−8.32	14.40	−3.00	29.36	41.16	−66.17	−66.49	23.61	69.86	Other Items (Net)	**37r**
				....	1,214.89	1,317.95	1,508.46	1,685.52	1,865.00	2,097.95	2,280.84	2,534.64	2,745.08	3,001.15	2,992.97	Money plus Quasi-Money	**35l**
Percent Per Annum																**Interest Rates**	
	....	....	....	....	....	4.00	4.00	5.75	6.25	6.00	7.00	6.25	7.00	8.00	3.25	Discount Rate (End of Period)	**60**
	....	....	....	11.50	4.63	3.81	4.00	5.44	6.00	5.13	4.50	5.50	5.75	7.13	2.69	Money Market Rate	**60b**
	....	....	....	....	....	3.83	3.17	5.66	5.55	4.45	7.50	5.04	4.94	5.69	1.69	Treasury Bill Rate	**60c**
	....	....	....	6.67	5.46	3.07	2.25	3.54	5.63	4.64	5.98	6.62	4.50	4.80	2.38	Deposit Rate	**60l**
	....	....	....	10.00	8.50	6.50	6.50	8.50	8.75	8.50	9.50	9.00	8.50	9.50	5.13	Lending Rate	**60p**
Period Averages																**Prices, Production, Labor**	
	....	....	....	33.7	42.2	60.9	82.9	105.9	100.0	127.5	148.6	104.8	140.8	178.1	139.7	Share Prices	**62**
				89.9	93.0	94.7	95.3	97.3	100.0	99.9	99.6	97.8	96.3	96.5	95.1	Producer Prices	**63**
				64.3	71.8	78.5	†84.3	91.7	100.0	†106.3	112.5	115.7	111.1	106.9	105.2	Consumer Prices	**64**
								90.3	100.0	†107.7	116.5	123.9	122.9	124.7	127.4	Wages: Avg.Earnings(Mfg)	**65**
				65.4	72.2	†79.6	87.6	94.7	100.0	107.5	113.2	114.1	113.5	116.0	119.1	Wage Rates (Manufacturing)	**65a**
	92.1	97.7	98.1	97.3	97.9	99.9	99.3	99.1	100.0	96.3	95.5	87.3	81.7	81.2	77.6	Manufacturing Production	**66ey**
Period Averages																	
						2,873	2,972	3,001	3,094	3,216	3,359	....	3,383	....	Labor Force	**67d**
	2,681	2,725	2,723	†2,712	2,753	2,738	2,800	2,873	2,905	†3,093	3,192	3,150	3,133	3,214	....	Employment	**67e**
	47	38	30	†37	50	55	57	57	98	†86	71	158	217	168	....	Unemployment	**67c**
	1.7	1.4	1.1	†1.3	1.8	2.0	2.0	1.9	3.2	†2.8	2.2	4.7	6.3	5.0	....	Unemployment Rate (%)	**67r**
Billions of US Dollars																**International Transactions**	
	48.48	63.16	73.14	82.16	98.58	119.49	135.24	151.40	173.75	180.75	188.06	174.00	173.89	201.86	189.89	Exports	**70..d**
	48.46	63.90	72.15	82.49	100.24	123.41	138.65	161.84	192.75	198.55	208.61	184.52	179.52	212.81	201.08	Imports, c.i.f.	**71..d**
1995=100																	
	33.3	†42.1	46.3	†50.7	59.4	71.3	80.9	89.3	100.0	104.8	111.2	106.4	110.3	129.2	124.9	Volume of Exports	**72**
	30.6	†38.7	42.2	†47.0	55.9	68.4	77.1	87.9	100.0	104.3	111.8	103.9	104.1	122.9	120.4	Volume of Imports	**73**
	83.2	†85.8	90.1	†92.5	95.0	95.8	95.5	96.8	100.0	99.7	98.1	94.5	91.9	89.6	89.6	Unit Value of Exports	**74**
	82.6	†86.0	89.1	†91.3	93.1	93.3	92.8	95.2	100.0	98.8	96.5	91.8	89.9	90.6	87.8	Unit Value of Imports	**75**

		1972	1973	1974	1975	1976	1977	1978	1979	1980	1981	1982	1983	1984	1985	1986
Balance of Payments																*Millions of US Dollars*
Current Account, n.i.e.	78al *d*	....	....	....	....	....	....	....	....	....	....	....	....	....	....	....
Goods: Exports f.o.b.	78aa *d*	....	....	....	....	....	....	....	....	....	....	....	....	....	....	....
Goods: Imports f.o.b.	78ab *d*	....	....	....	....	....	....	....	....	....	....	....	....	....	....	....
Trade Balance	78ac *d*	....	....	....	....	....	....	....	....	....	....	....	....	....	....	....
Services: Credit	78ad *d*	....	....	....	....	....	....	....	....	....	....	....	....	....	....	....
Services: Debit	78ae *d*	....	....	....	....	....	....	....	....	....	....	....	....	....	....	....
Balance on Goods & Services	78af *d*	....	....	....	....	....	....	....	....	....	....	....	....	....	....	....
Income: Credit	78ag *d*	....	....	....	....	....	....	....	....	....	....	....	....	....	....	....
Income: Debit	78ah *d*	....	....	....	....	....	....	....	....	....	....	....	....	....	....	....
Balance on Gds, Serv. & Inc.	78ai *d*	....	....	....	....	....	....	....	....	....	....	....	....	....	....	....
Current Transfers, n.i.e.: Credit	78aj *d*	....	....	....	....	....	....	....	....	....	....	....	....	....	....	....
Current Transfers: Debit	78ak *d*	....	....	....	....	....	....	....	....	....	....	....	....	....	....	....
Capital Account, n.i.e.	78bc *d*	....	....	....	....	....	....	....	....	....	....	....	....	....	....	....
Capital Account, n.i.e.: Credit	78ba *d*	....	....	....	....	....	....	....	....	....	....	....	....	....	....	....
Capital Account: Debit	78bb *d*	....	....	....	....	....	....	....	....	....	....	....	....	....	....	....
Financial Account, n.i.e.	78bj *d*	....	....	....	....	....	....	....	....	....	....	....	....	....	....	....
Direct Investment Abroad	78bd *d*	....	....	....	....	....	....	....	....	....	....	....	....	....	....	....
Dir. Invest. in Rep. Econ., n.i.e.	78be *d*	....	....	....	....	....	....	....	....	....	....	....	....	....	....	....
Portfolio Investment Assets	78bf *d*	....	....	....	....	....	....	....	....	....	....	....	....	....	....	....
Equity Securities	78bk *d*	....	....	....	....	....	....	....	....	....	....	....	....	....	....	....
Debt Securities	78bl *d*	....	....	....	....	....	....	....	....	....	....	....	....	....	....	....
Portfolio Investment Liab., n.i.e.	78bg *d*	....	....	....	....	....	....	....	....	....	....	....	....	....	....	....
Equity Securities	78bm *d*	....	....	....	....	....	....	....	....	....	....	....	....	....	....	....
Debt Securities	78bn *d*	....	....	....	....	....	....	....	....	....	....	....	....	....	....	....
Financial Derivatives Assets	78bw *d*	....	....	....	....	....	....	....	....	....	....	....	....	....	....	....
Financial Derivatives Liabilities	78bx *d*	....	....	....	....	....	....	....	....	....	....	....	....	....	....	....
Other Investment Assets	78bh *d*	....	....	....	....	....	....	....	....	....	....	....	....	....	....	....
Monetary Authorities	78bo *d*	....	....	....	....	....	....	....	....	....	....	....	....	....	....	....
General Government	78bp *d*	....	....	....	....	....	....	....	....	....	....	....	....	....	....	....
Banks	78bq *d*	....	....	....	....	....	....	....	....	....	....	....	....	....	....	....
Other Sectors	78br *d*	....	....	....	....	....	....	....	....	....	....	....	....	....	....	....
Other Investment Liab., n.i.e.	78bi *d*	....	....	....	....	....	....	....	....	....	....	....	....	....	....	....
Monetary Authorities	78bs *d*	....	....	....	....	....	....	....	....	....	....	....	....	....	....	....
General Government	78bt *d*	....	....	....	....	....	....	....	....	....	....	....	....	....	....	....
Banks	78bu *d*	....	....	....	....	....	....	....	....	....	....	....	....	....	....	....
Other Sectors	78bv *d*	....	....	....	....	....	....	....	....	....	....	....	....	....	....	....
Net Errors and Omissions	78ca *d*	....	....	....	....	....	....	....	....	....	....	....	....	....	....	....
Overall Balance	78cb *d*	....	....	....	....	....	....	....	....	....	....	....	....	....	....	....
Reserves and Related Items	79da *d*	....	....	....	....	....	....	....	....	....	....	....	....	....	....	....
Reserve Assets	79db *d*	....	....	....	....	....	....	....	....	....	....	....	....	....	....	....
Use of Fund Credit and Loans	79dc *d*	....	....	....	....	....	....	....	....	....	....	....	....	....	....	....
Exceptional Financing	79de *d*	....	....	....	....	....	....	....	....	....	....	....	....	....	....	....
International Investment Position																*Millions of US Dollars*
Assets	79aa *d*	....	....	....	....	....	....	....	....	....	....	....	....	....	....	....
Direct Investment Abroad	79ab *d*	....	....	....	....	....	....	....	....	....	....	....	....	....	....	....
Portfolio Investment	79ac *d*	....	....	....	....	....	....	....	....	....	....	....	....	....	....	....
Equity Securities	79ad *d*	....	....	....	....	....	....	....	....	....	....	....	....	....	....	....
Debt Securities	79ae *d*	....	....	....	....	....	....	....	....	....	....	....	....	....	....	....
Financial Derivatives	79al *d*	....	....	....	....	....	....	....	....	....	....	....	....	....	....	....
Other Investment	79af *d*	....	....	....	....	....	....	....	....	....	....	....	....	....	....	....
Monetary Authorities	79ag *d*	....	....	....	....	....	....	....	....	....	....	....	....	....	....	....
General Government	79ah *d*	....	....	....	....	....	....	....	....	....	....	....	....	....	....	....
Banks	79ai *d*	....	....	....	....	....	....	....	....	....	....	....	....	....	....	....
Other Sectors	79aj *d*	....	....	....	....	....	....	....	....	....	....	....	....	....	....	....
Reserve Assets	79ak *d*	....	....	....	....	....	....	....	....	....	....	....	....	....	....	....
Liabilities	79la *d*	....	....	....	....	....	....	....	....	....	....	....	....	....	....	....
Dir. Invest. in Rep. Economy	79lb *d*	....	....	....	....	....	....	....	....	....	....	....	....	....	....	....
Portfolio Investment	79lc *d*	....	....	....	....	....	....	....	....	....	....	....	....	....	....	....
Equity Securities	79ld *d*	....	....	....	....	....	....	....	....	....	....	....	....	....	....	....
Debt Securities	79le *d*	....	....	....	....	....	....	....	....	....	....	....	....	....	....	....
Financial Derivatives	79ll *d*	....	....	....	....	....	....	....	....	....	....	....	....	....	....	....
Other Investment	79lf *d*	....	....	....	....	....	....	....	....	....	....	....	....	....	....	....
Monetary Authorities	79lg *d*	....	....	....	....	....	....	....	....	....	....	....	....	....	....	....
General Government	79lh *d*	....	....	....	....	....	....	....	....	....	....	....	....	....	....	....
Banks	79li *d*	....	....	....	....	....	....	....	....	....	....	....	....	....	....	....
Other Sectors	79lj *d*	....	....	....	....	....	....	....	....	....	....	....	....	....	....	....
National Accounts																*Billions of Hong Kong Dollars*
Househ.Cons.Expend.,incl.NPISHs	96f	20	26	30	32	36	44	54	67	85	102	118	137	156	167	189
Government Consumption Expend.	91f	2	3	3	3	4	5	5	7	9	12	15	16	18	20	23
Gross Fixed Capital Formation	93e	7	9	11	11	13	18	23	34	46	56	59	53	57	57	68
Changes in Inventories	93i	—	—	1	1	3	2	2	3	4	4	1	4	6	1	6
Exports of Goods and Services	90c	27	45	52	54	72	78	94	126	127	157	167	207	278	296	348
Imports of Goods and Services (-)	98c	25	33	39	39	50	57	73	100	129	161	168	205	259	271	322
Gross Domestic Product (GDP)	99b	32	41	47	49	63	73	85	112	142	171	192	213	256	272	313
Net Primary Income from Abroad	98.n	....	....	....	....	....	....	....	....	....	....	....	....	....	....	....
Gross National Income (GNI)	99a	....	....	....	....	....	....	....	....	....	....	....	....	....	....	....
Net Current Transf.from Abroad	98t	....	....	....	....	....	....	....	....	....	....	....	....	....	....	....
Gross Nat'l Disposable Inc.(GNDI)	99i	....	....	....	....	....	....	....	....	....	....	....	....	....	....	....
Gross Saving	99s	....	....	....	....	....	....	....	....	....	....	....	....	....	....	....
GDP Volume 1973 Prices	99b.*p*	29	34	35	35	42	46	51	58	64	71	73	....	....	....	....
GDP Volume 1980 Prices	99b.*p*	....	....	....	....	....	....	....	....	....	....	154	163	179	180	199
GDP Volume 1990 Prices	99b.*p*	....	....	....	....	....	....	....	....	....	....	....	....	....	....	450
GDP Volume (1995=100)	99bv *p*	20.1	22.6	23.1	23.2	27.2	30.4	33.1	37.0	40.9	44.7	45.9	48.8	53.5	53.6	59.6
GDP Deflator (1995=100)	99bi *p*	14.8	16.8	18.9	19.7	21.4	22.2	23.9	28.0	32.2	35.5	39.0	40.5	44.5	47.0	48.7
																Millions:
Population	99z	4.12	4.21	4.32	4.40	4.44	†4.51	4.67	4.93	5.06	5.18	5.26	5.35	5.40	5.46	5.52

	1987	1988	1989	1990	1991	1992	1993	1994	1995	1996	1997	1998	1999	2000	2001		
Minus Sign Indicates Debit																**Balance of Payments**	
	....	....	....	....	....	....	....	....	....	....	....	3,904	11,479	8,915	11,968	Current Account, n.i.e.	**78al** ***d***
	....	....	....	....	....	....	....	....	....	....	....	175,833	174,719	202,698	190,926	Goods: Exports f.o.b.	**78aa** ***d***
	....	....	....	....	....	....	....	....	....	....	....	-183,666	-177,878	-210,891	-199,257	Goods: Imports f.o.b.	**78ab** ***d***
	....	....	....	....	....	....	....	....	....	....	....	-7,833	-3,159	-8,193	-8,331	*Trade Balance*	**78ac** ***d***
	....	....	....	....	....	....	....	....	....	....	....	35,673	36,564	41,548	42,426	Services: Credit	**78ad** ***d***
	....	....	....	....	....	....	....	....	....	....	....	-26,053	-24,869	-25,564	-25,079	Services: Debit	**78ae** ***d***
	....	....	....	....	....	....	....	....	....	....	....	1,787	8,536	7,790	9,015	*Balance on Goods & Services*	**78af** ***d***
	....	....	....	....	....	....	....	....	....	....	....	46,831	47,031	53,494	48,010	Income: Credit	**78ag** ***d***
	....	....	....	....	....	....	....	....	....	....	....	-43,117	-42,548	-50,699	-43,377	Income: Debit	**78ah** ***d***
	....	....	....	....	....	....	....	....	....	....	....	5,500	13,019	10,586	13,649	*Balance on Gds, Serv. & Inc.*	**78ai** ***d***
	....	....	....	....	....	....	....	....	....	....	....	669	570	538	813	Current Transfers, n.i.e.: Credit	**78aj** ***d***
	....	....	....	....	....	....	....	....	....	....	....	-2,265	-2,109	-2,208	-2,495	Current Transfers: Debit	**78ak** ***d***
	....	....	....	....	....	....	....	....	....	....	....	-2,382	-1,780	-1,546	-1,162	Capital Account, n.i.e.	**78bc** ***d***
	....	....	....	....	....	....	....	....	....	....	....	377	103	57	36	Capital Account, n.i.e.: Credit	**78ba** ***d***
	....	....	....	....	....	....	....	....	....	....	....	-2,759	-1,883	-1,602	-1,198	Capital Account: Debit	**78bb** ***d***
	....	....	....	....	....	....	....	....	....	....	....	-8,476	1,061	4,165	-5,146	Financial Account, n.i.e.	**78bj** ***d***
	....	....	....	....	....	....	....	....	....	....	....	-16,973	-19,349	-59,338	-8,981	Direct Investment Abroad	**78bd** ***d***
	....	....	....	....	....	....	....	....	....	....	....	14,776	24,587	61,883	22,834	Dir. Invest. in Rep. Econ., n.i.e.	**78be** ***d***
	....	....	....	....	....	....	....	....	....	....	....	25,492	-25,440	-22,022	-39,131	Portfolio Investment Assets	**78bf** ***d***
	....	....	....	....	....	....	....	....	....	....	....	8,507	-30,337	-17,606	-22,654	Equity Securities	**78bk** ***d***
	....	....	....	....	....	....	....	....	....	....	....	16,985	4,897	-4,416	-16,478	Debt Securities	**78bl** ***d***
	....	....	....	....	....	....	....	....	....	....	....	-3,407	58,525	46,508	-531	Portfolio Investment Liab., n.i.e.	**78bg** ***d***
	....	....	....	....	....	....	....	....	....	....	....	-2,106	60,470	46,976	596	Equity Securities	**78bm** ***d***
	....	....	....	....	....	....	....	....	....	....	....	-1,301	-1,944	-468	-1,127	Debt Securities	**78bn** ***d***
	....	....	....	....	....	....	....	....	....	....	....	10,799	21,297	8,414	17,508	Financial Derivatives Assets	**78bw** ***d***
	....	....	....	....	....	....	....	....	....	....	....	-7,523	-11,113	-8,182	-12,490	Financial Derivatives Liabilities	**78bx** ***d***
	....	....	....	....	....	....	....	....	....	....	....	119,830	42,963	18,279	58,243	Other Investment Assets	**78bh** ***d***
	....	....	....	....	....	....	....	....	....	....	....	....	....	....	....	Monetary Authorities	**78bo** ***d***
	....	....	....	....	....	....	....	....	....	....	....	....	....	....	....	General Government	**78bp** ***d***
	....	....	....	....	....	....	....	....	....	....	....	101,774	34,181	23,857	56,847	Banks	**78bq** ***d***
	....	....	....	....	....	....	....	....	....	....	....	18,057	8,781	-5,578	1,396	Other Sectors	**78br** ***d***
	....	....	....	....	....	....	....	....	....	....	....	-151,470	-90,410	-41,375	-42,599	Other Investment Liab., n.i.e.	**78bi** ***d***
	....	....	....	....	....	....	....	....	....	....	....	....	....	....	....	Monetary Authorities	**78bs** ***d***
	....	....	....	....	....	....	....	....	....	....	....	....	....	....	....	General Government	**78bt** ***d***
	....	....	....	....	....	....	....	....	....	....	....	-148,616	-85,768	-44,259	-42,780	Banks	**78bu** ***d***
	....	....	....	....	....	....	....	....	....	....	....	-2,854	-4,642	2,884	181	Other Sectors	**78bv** ***d***
	....	....	....	....	....	....	....	....	....	....	....	164	-732	-1,491	-977	Net Errors and Omissions	**78ca** ***d***
	....	....	....	....	....	....	....	....	....	....	....	-6,789	10,028	10,044	4,684	*Overall Balance*	**78cb** ***d***
	....	....	....	....	....	....	....	....	....	....	....	6,789	-10,028	-10,044	-4,684	Reserves and Related Items	**79da** ***d***
	....	....	....	....	....	....	....	....	....	....	....	6,789	-10,028	-10,044	-4,684	Reserve Assets	**79db** ***d***
	....	....	....	....	....	....	....	....	....	....	....	....	....	....	....	Use of Fund Credit and Loans	**79dc** ***d***
	....	....	....	....	....	....	....	....	....	....	....	....	....	....	....	Exceptional Financing	**79de** ***d***
Millions of US Dollars																**International Investment Position**	
	....	....	....	....	....	....	....	....	....	....	328,651	313,546	417,980	....	....	Assets	**79aa** ***d***
	....	....	....	....	....	....	....	....	....	....	235,796	223,907	321,692	....	....	Direct Investment Abroad	**79ab** ***d***
	....	....	....	....	....	....	....	....	....	....	—	—	—	....	....	Portfolio Investment	**79ac** ***d***
	....	....	....	....	....	....	....	....	....	....	—	—	—	....	....	Equity Securities	**79ad** ***d***
	....	....	....	....	....	....	....	....	....	....	—	—	—	....	....	Debt Securities	**79ae** ***d***
	....	....	....	....	....	....	....	....	....	....	—	—	—	....	....	Financial Derivatives	**79al** ***d***
	....	....	....	....	....	....	....	....	....	....	—	—	—	....	....	Other Investment	**79af** ***d***
	....	....	....	....	....	....	....	....	....	....	....	....	....	....	....	Monetary Authorities	**79ag** ***d***
	....	....	....	....	....	....	....	....	....	....	....	....	....	....	....	General Government	**79ah** ***d***
	....	....	....	....	....	....	....	....	....	....	....	....	....	....	....	Banks	**79ai** ***d***
	....	....	....	....	....	....	....	....	....	....	....	....	....	....	....	Other Sectors	**79aj** ***d***
	....	....	....	....	....	....	....	....	....	....	92,855	89,639	96,287	....	....	Reserve Assets	**79ak** ***d***
	....	....	....	....	....	....	....	....	....	....	249,393	225,142	405,325	....	....	Liabilities	**79la** ***d***
	....	....	....	....	....	....	....	....	....	....	249,393	225,142	405,325	....	....	Dir. Invest. in Rep. Economy	**79lb** ***d***
	....	....	....	....	....	....	....	....	....	....	—	—	—	....	....	Portfolio Investment	**79lc** ***d***
	....	....	....	....	....	....	....	....	....	....	—	—	—	....	....	Equity Securities	**79ld** ***d***
	....	....	....	....	....	....	....	....	....	....	—	—	—	....	....	Debt Securities	**79le** ***d***
	....	....	....	....	....	....	....	....	....	....	—	—	—	....	....	Financial Derivatives	**79ll** ***d***
	....	....	....	....	....	....	....	....	....	....	—	—	—	....	....	Other Investment	**79lf** ***d***
	....	....	....	....	....	....	....	....	....	....	....	....	....	....	....	Monetary Authorities	**79lg** ***d***
	....	....	....	....	....	....	....	....	....	....	....	....	....	....	....	General Government	**79lh** ***d***
	....	....	....	....	....	....	....	....	....	....	....	....	....	....	....	Banks	**79li** ***d***
	....	....	....	....	....	....	....	....	....	....	....	....	....	....	....	Other Sectors	**79lj** ***d***
Billions of Hong Kong Dollars																**National Accounts**	
	219	255	288	330	391	452	514	593	654	722	798	762	733	735	739	Househ.Cons.Expend.,incl.NPISHs	**96f**
	26	30	36	43	51	64	73	84	94	104	114	118	122	122	131	Government Consumption Expend.	**91f**
	92	116	136	154	178	214	245	301	330	372	445	381	317	333	326	Gross Fixed Capital Formation	**93e**
	10	14	3	6	4	8	2	21	46	10	12	-16	-11	16	—	Changes in Inventories	**93i**
	470	604	698	782	927	1,114	1,262	1,411	1,610	1,694	1,754	1,628	1,638	1,900	1,816	Exports of Goods and Services	**90c**
	432	564	637	733	883	1,073	1,199	1,398	1,657	1,711	1,800	1,615	1,571	1,841	1,750	Imports of Goods and Services (-)	**98c**
	384	455	524	583	669	779	897	1,011	1,077	1,192	1,324	1,259	1,227	1,266	1,262	Gross Domestic Product (GDP)	**99b**
	....	....	....	....	....	....	13	12	21	—	10	29	35	22	36	Net Primary Income from Abroad	**98.n**
	....	....	....	....	....	....	911	1,023	1,098	1,192	1,334	1,288	1,262	1,288	1,298	Gross National Income (GNI)	**99a**
	....	....	....	....	....	....	....	....	....	....	-12	-12	-12	-13	-13	Net Current Transf.from Abroad	**98t**
	....	....	....	....	....	....	....	....	....	....	1,322	1,276	1,250	1,275	1,285	Gross Nat'l Disposable Inc.(GNDI)	**99i**
	....	....	....	....	....	....	....	....	....	....	410	396	395	418	416	Gross Saving	**99s**
	....	....	....	....	....	....	....	....	....	....	....	....	....	....	....	GDP Volume 1973 Prices	**99b.** ***p***
	....	....	....	....	....	....	....	....	....	....	....	....	....	....	....	GDP Volume 1980 Prices	**99b.** ***p***
	509	549	563	583	612	650	690	728	756	790	829	785	809	893	894	GDP Volume 1990 Prices	**99b.** ***p***
	67.3	72.7	74.5	77.1	81.0	86.0	91.3	96.3	100.0	104.5	109.7	103.9	107.0	118.1	118.3	GDP Volume (1995=100)	**99bv** ***p***
	53.0	58.1	65.2	70.2	76.6	84.1	91.2	97.5	100.0	105.9	112.1	112.6	106.5	99.5	99.0	GDP Deflator (1995=100)	**99bi** ***p***
Midyear Estimates																	
	5.58	5.63	5.69	5.70	5.75	5.80	5.90	6.04	6.16	6.44	6.49	6.54	6.61	6.67	6.72	**Population**	**99z**

(See notes in the back of the book.)

		1972	1973	1974	1975	1976	1977	1978	1979	1980	1981	1982	1983	1984	1985	1986
Exchange Rates														*Patacas Per SDR:*		
Market Rate	aa	6.171	6.217	6.005	6.413	7.309	6.013	6.696	6.626	6.785	6.728	7.391	8.365	7.869	8.808	9.797
														Patacas per US Dollar:		
Market Rate	ae	5.684	5.154	4.904	5.478	6.291	4.950	5.140	5.030	5.320	5.780	6.700	7.990	8.028	8.019	8.009
Market Rate	rf	5.715	4.929	5.040	5.126	6.061	5.574	5.029	5.177	5.095	5.752	6.226	7.464	8.035	7.999	8.013
International Liquidity														*Billions of US Dollars Unless Otherwise Indicated:*		
Total Reserves minus Gold	1l.d	...	...	...	...	...	...	...	...	...	...	...	...	.07	.06	.10
Foreign Exchange	1d.d	...	...	...	...	...	...	...	...	...	...	...	...	.07	.06	.10
Gold (Million Fine Troy Ounces)	1ad	...	...	...	...	...	...	...	...	...	...	...	...	—	—	—
Gold (National Valuation)	1an.d	...	...	...	...	...	...	...	...	...	...	...	...	—	—	—
Banking Institutions: Assets	7a.d	...	...	...	...	...	...	...	...	...	...	...	...	1.55	1.47	1.55
Liabilities	7b.d	...	...	...	...	...	...	...	...	...	...	...	...	1.18	1.13	.97
Monetary Authorities														*Millions of Patacas:*		
Foreign Assets	11	...	...	...	...	...	...	...	...	...	...	...	...	545.5	514.8	825.4
Claims on Government	12a	...	...	...	...	...	...	...	...	...	...	...	...	369.9	307.8	110.8
Claims on Deposit Money Banks	12e	...	...	...	...	...	...	...	...	...	...	...	...	537.5	600.4	576.5
Reserve Money	14	...	...	...	...	...	...	...	...	...	...	...	...	512.3	599.6	698.3
of which: Currency Outside Banks	14a	...	...	...	...	...	...	...	...	...	...	...	...	313.5	366.2	419.9
Liab. of Central Bank: Securities	16ac	...	...	...	...	...	...	...	...	...	...	...	...	201.1	173.8	20.1
Foreign Liabilities	16c	...	...	...	...	...	...	...	...	...	...	...	...	90.6	72.5	—
Government Deposits	16d	...	...	...	...	...	...	...	...	...	...	...	...	602.6	418.0	545.7
Capital Accounts	17a	...	...	...	...	...	...	...	...	...	...	...	...	138.3	162.4	207.8
Other Items (Net)	17r	...	...	...	...	...	...	...	...	...	...	...	...	−92.0	−3.2	40.9
Banking Institutions														*Millions of Patacas:*		
Reserves	20	...	...	...	...	...	...	...	...	...	...	...	...	198.8	233.4	278.4
Claims on Mon.Author.: Securities	20c	...	...	...	...	...	...	...	...	...	...	...	...	201.1	173.8	20.1
Foreign Assets	21	...	...	...	...	...	...	...	...	...	...	...	...	12,413.7	11,804.1	12,432.8
Claims on Government	22a	...	...	...	...	...	...	...	...	...	...	...	...	—	—	114.0
Claims on Nonfin.Pub. Enterprises	22c	...	...	...	...	...	...	...	...	...	...	...	...			
Claims on Other Sectors	22d	...	...	...	...	...	...	...	...	...	...	...	...	5,495.0	6,884.4	7,500.2
Demand Deposits	24	...	...	...	...	...	...	...	...	...	...	...	...	630.5	795.6	957.5
Time & Savings Deposits	25	...	...	...	...	...	...	...	...	...	...	...	...	7,009.7	8,087.6	9,696.8
Foreign Liabilities	26c	...	...	...	...	...	...	...	...	...	...	...	...	9,455.6	9,042.8	7,804.9
Government Deposits	26d	...	...	...	...	...	...	...	...	...	...	...	...	30.5	44.5	90.2
Credit from Monetary Authorities	26g	...	...	...	...	...	...	...	...	...	...	...	...	537.5	600.4	576.5
Capital Accounts	27a	...	...	...	...	...	...	...	...	...	...	...	...	1,193.9	1,236.1	1,336.0
Other Items (Net)	27r	...	...	...	...	...	...	...	...	...	...	...	...	−549.0	−711.4	−134.9
Banking Survey														*Millions of Patacas:*		
Foreign Assets (Net)	31n	...	...	...	...	...	...	...	...	...	...	...	...	3,413.0	3,203.6	5,453.3
Domestic Credit	32	...	...	...	...	...	...	...	...	...	...	...	...	5,231.8	6,729.7	7,089.1
Claims on Government (net)	32an	...	...	...	...	...	...	...	...	...	...	...	...	−263.2	−154.7	−411.1
Claims on Nonfin.Pub. Enterprises	32c	...	...	...	...	...	...	...	...	...	...	...	...			
Claims on Other Sectors	32d	...	...	...	...	...	...	...	...	...	...	...	...	5,495.0	6,884.4	7,500.2
Money	34	...	...	...	...	...	...	...	...	...	...	...	...	944.0	1,161.8	1,377.4
Quasi-Money	35	...	...	...	...	...	...	...	...	...	...	...	...	7,009.7	8,087.6	9,696.8
Capital Accounts	37a	...	...	...	...	...	...	...	...	...	...	...	...	1,332.2	1,398.5	1,543.8
Other Items (Net)	37r	...	...	...	...	...	...	...	...	...	...	...	...	−641.0	−714.6	−94.0
Interest Rates														*Percent Per Annum*		
Interbank Rate (End of Period)	60b	...	...	...	...	...	...	...	...	...	...	...	...	...	...	...
Money Market Rate	60b	...	...	...	...	...	...	...	...	...	...	...	...	...	...	...
Deposit Rate	60l	...	...	...	...	...	...	...	...	...	...	...	...	...	...	...
Lending Rate	60p	...	...	...	...	...	...	...	...	...	...	...	...	...	3.92	3.50
Prices and Labor														*Index Numbers (1998=100):*		
Consumer Prices	64	...	...	...	...	...	...	...	...	...	...	...	...	...	...	...
														Number in Thousands:		
Labor Force	67d	...	...	...	...	...	...	...	...	...	...	...	...	...	...	...
Employment	67e	...	...	...	...	...	...	...	...	...	...	...	...	...	...	...
Unemployment	67c	...	...	...	...	...	...	...	...	...	...	...	...	...	...	...
Unemployment Rate (%)	67r	...	...	...	...	...	...	...	...	...	...	...	...	...	...	...
International Transactions														*Millions of US Dollars*		
Exports	70..d	71.8	99.9	109.6	133.4	188.1	219.2	258.4	389.1	538.3	697.0	726.2	760.1	911.6	901.2	1,079.8
Imports, c.i.f.	71..d	103.7	157.7	134.3	160.9	160.9	198.2	248.8	351.4	544.4	719.9	718.8	726.6	796.4	772.5	914.4
Government Finance														*Millions of Patacas:*		
Deficit (-) or Surplus	80	...	...	...	...	...	...	...	...	...	...	...	...	...	...	...
Total Revenue and Grants	81y	...	...	...	...	...	...	...	...	...	...	...	...	...	...	...
Revenue	81	...	...	...	...	...	...	...	...	...	...	...	...	...	...	...
Grants	81z	...	...	...	...	...	...	...	...	...	...	...	...	...	...	...
Exp. & Lending Minus Repay.	82z	...	...	...	...	...	...	...	...	...	...	...	...	...	...	...
Expenditure	82	...	...	...	...	...	...	...	...	...	...	...	...	...	...	...
Lending Minus Repayments	83	...	...	...	...	...	...	...	...	...	...	...	...	...	...	...
National Accounts														*Millions of Patacas*		
Househ.Cons.Expend.,incl.NPISHs	96f	...	...	...	...	...	...	...	...	...	...	3,475.1	3,998.7	4,551.0	4,911.5	5,443.6
Government Consumption Expend.	91f	...	...	...	...	...	...	...	...	...	...	359.5	416.7	563.2	684.7	801.5
Gross Capital Formation	93	...	...	...	...	...	...	...	...	...	...	1,601.5	1,811.7	2,231.2	2,383.8	3,118.2
Changes in Inventories	93i	...	...	...	...	...	...	...	...	...	...	115.2	422.5	312.3	317.2	266.8
Exports of Goods and Services	90c	...	...	...	...	...	...	...	...	...	...	7,798.6	9,436.3	11,892.7	11,451.9	13,222.9
Imports of Goods and Services (-)	98c	...	...	...	...	...	...	...	...	...	...	6,191.1	7,521.0	8,899.1	8,799.0	10,381.6
Gross Domestic Product (GDP)	99b	...	...	...	...	...	...	...	...	...	...	7,158.7	8,565.1	10,651.3	10,950.1	12,471.5
GDP Volume 1996 Prices	99b.p	...	...	...	...	...	...	...	...	...	...	23,289.2	25,623.3	27,791.1	27,994.6	29,868.5
GDP Volume (1996=100)	99bv.p	...	...	...	...	...	...	...	...	...	...	42.1	46.3	50.3	50.6	54.0
GDP Deflator (1996=100)	99bi.p	...	...	...	...	...	...	...	...	...	...	30.7	33.4	38.3	39.1	41.8
															Millions:		
Population	99z	.26	.27	.27	.27	.27	.28	.29	.31	.32	.28	.31	.33	.36	.39	.42

Item	Code	1987	1988	1989	1990	1991	1992	1993	1994	1995	1996	1997	1998	1999	2000	2001
Exchange Rates		*End of Period*														
Market Rate	aa	11.323	10.823	10.567	11.430	11.463	10.961	10.928	11.635	11.839	11.457	10.769	11.236	10.987	10.467	10.093
		End of Period (ae) Period Average (rf)														
Market Rate	ae	7.981	8.043	8.041	8.034	8.014	7.972	7.956	7.970	7.965	7.968	7.982	7.980	8.005	8.034	8.031
Market Rate	rf	8.010	8.041	8.034	8.021	8.004	7.972	7.968	7.960	7.968	7.966	7.975	7.979	7.992	8.026	8.034
International Liquidity		*End of Period*														
Total Reserves minus Gold	1l.d	.17	.22	.35	.52	.65	1.30	1.57	1.97	2.26	2.42	2.53	2.46	2.86	3.32	3.51
Foreign Exchange	1d.d	.17	.22	.35	.52	.65	1.30	1.57	1.97	2.26	2.42	2.53	2.46	2.86	3.32	3.51
Gold (Million Fine Troy Ounces)	1ad	—	—	—	—	—	—	—	—	—	—	—	—	—	—	—
Gold (National Valuation)	1and	—	—	—	—	—	—	—	—	—	—	—	—	—	—	—
Banking Institutions: Assets	7a.d	2.19	2.95	3.06	3.71	4.98	5.20	6.61	6.08	6.77	10.83	10.75	12.63	7.83	8.58	9.30
Liabilities	7b.d	1.39	1.76	1.73	2.00	2.36	2.46	4.62	3.96	4.10	7.82	7.92	8.30	3.30	3.06	2.85
Monetary Authorities		*End of Period*														
Foreign Assets	11	1,389.2	1,780.4	2,851.4	4,182.7	5,214.4	10,377.0	12,483.8	15,672.0	17,972.4	19,298.9	20,215.3	19,651.1	22,873.1	30,646.3	33,431.6
Claims on Government	12a	94.1	79.7	68.2	53.9	59.5	49.8	132.6	67.2	69.2	85.5	115.0	143.3	190.9	211.4	263.1
Claims on Deposit Money Banks	12e	551.1	657.4	57.0	100.8	92.6	59.5	45.1	59.6	42.3	55.7	53.6	37.7	515.4	6,284.9	5,113.8
Reserve Money	14	817.1	965.8	1,162.0	1,333.2	1,681.7	2,015.9	2,138.7	2,405.7	2,735.1	2,909.6	3,047.7	3,239.1	3,958.0	3,688.1	3,953.2
of which: Currency Outside Banks	14a	483.0	530.5	627.3	699.7	822.8	968.8	1,080.9	1,197.8	1,280.1	1,426.7	1,518.2	1,554.6	1,819.5	1,740.0	1,977.4
Liab. of Central Bank: Securities	16ac	134.0	641.0	1,171.5	2,294.0	3,129.5	5,701.0	5,876.5	8,686.0	11,242.0	11,207.0	10,942.5	11,803.5	15,086.0	17,530.0	16,927.5
Foreign Liabilities	16c	—	9.7	1.1	21.1	.1	.1	.1	.9	.1	103.1	.1	.2	—	—	4.9
Government Deposits	16d	737.5	560.7	282.1	101.9	–18.8	2,153.1	3,752.9	4,235.7	3,154.9	3,898.1	5,292.5	3,572.4	3,449.7	14,320.4	15,762.8
Capital Accounts	17a	212.3	232.1	513.6	726.2	714.0	889.0	1,221.8	1,071.2	1,569.6	1,693.1	1,979.1	2,437.9	2,333.9	2,878.0	3,077.5
Other Items (Net)	17r	133.6	108.1	–153.9	–139.1	–140.0	–272.8	–328.6	–600.6	–618.0	–370.9	–878.0	–1,220.8	–1,248.3	–1,274.0	–917.5
Banking Institutions		*End of Period*														
Reserves	20	334.1	435.3	534.7	633.5	858.9	1,047.1	1,057.8	1,207.9	1,455.0	1,482.9	1,529.5	1,684.5	2,138.5	1,948.1	1,975.8
Claims on Mon.Author.: Securities	20c	134.0	641.0	1,171.5	2,294.0	3,129.5	5,701.0	5,876.5	8,686.0	11,242.0	11,207.0	10,942.5	11,803.5	15,086.0	17,530.0	16,927.5
Foreign Assets	21	17,469.4	23,713.7	24,617.9	29,812.1	39,898.0	41,419.1	52,554.5	48,434.0	53,955.6	86,316.3	85,763.6	† 100793.3	62,680.8	68,927.7	74,657.0
Claims on Government	22a	121.0	94.5	63.0	246.5	228.1	279.3	214.5	143.0	71.5	—	.3	2.2	—	—	—
Claims on Nonfin.Pub. Enterprises	22c	....	....	....	....	....	....	....	....	....	....	....	....	....	....	1,438.7
Claims on Other Sectors	22d	8,784.0	10,974.9	13,824.2	16,312.2	19,768.8	25,882.3	35,997.1	39,707.3	41,694.5	44,492.5	48,890.5	† 42808.1	42,111.3	39,127.6	34,897.7
Demand Deposits	24	1,345.9	1,645.1	1,958.2	2,026.4	3,410.0	5,454.8	4,679.7	4,038.6	4,337.6	4,289.2	3,790.7	† 3,954.1	3,543.7	3,228.2	4,020.9
Time & Savings Deposits	25	12,449.1	17,825.5	21,665.9	27,919.4	37,717.9	44,378.6	48,552.9	55,976.9	63,825.8	68,616.8	72,873.9	† 75118.9	80,733.2	79,972.4	85,633.3
Foreign Liabilities	26c	11,106.9	14,157.1	13,909.5	16,055.8	18,942.9	19,644.5	36,786.8	31,533.0	32,685.2	62,316.5	63,178.3	† 66239.9	26,433.7	24,598.4	22,861.4
Government Deposits	26d	78.3	143.0	616.1	1,125.5	1,232.2	1,305.4	1,208.3	1,161.6	1,439.4	1,677.6	2,275.6	4,244.5	2,784.9	4,447.9	3,943.1
Credit from Monetary Authorities	26g	551.1	657.4	57.0	100.8	92.6	59.5	45.1	59.6	42.3	55.7	53.6	37.7	515.4	6,284.9	5,113.8
Capital Accounts	27a	1,641.5	1,855.8	2,117.7	2,284.6	2,607.4	3,215.6	3,938.7	4,812.2	5,005.5	5,561.0	6,222.5	6,330.2	5,707.4	6,593.4	7,000.4
Other Items (Net)	27r	–343.8	–413.6	–126.6	–227.6	–113.6	271.5	490.1	596.3	1,082.6	982.0	–1,268.2	1,166.3	2,298.4	2,408.4	1,323.8
Banking Survey		*End of Period*														
Foreign Assets (Net)	31n	7,751.7	11,327.3	13,558.7	17,917.9	26,169.4	32,151.5	28,251.4	32,572.1	39,242.7	43,195.6	42,800.5	† 54204.3	59,120.2	74,975.6	85,222.3
Domestic Credit	32	8,183.3	10,445.4	13,057.2	15,385.2	18,843.0	22,752.9	31,383.0	34,520.2	37,240.9	39,002.3	41,437.7	† 35136.7	36,067.6	20,570.7	16,893.6
Claims on Government (net)	32an	–600.7	–529.5	–767.0	–927.0	–925.8	–3,129.4	–4,614.1	–5,187.1	–4,453.6	–5,490.2	–7,452.8	–7,671.4	–6,043.7	–18,556.9	–19,442.8
Claims on Nonfin.Pub. Enterprises	32c	....	....	....	....	....	....	....	....	....	....	....	....	....	....	1,438.7
Claims on Other Sectors	32d	8,784.0	10,974.9	13,824.2	16,312.2	19,768.8	25,882.3	35,997.1	39,707.3	41,694.5	44,492.5	48,890.5	† 42808.1	42,111.3	39,127.6	34,897.7
Money	34	1,828.9	2,175.6	2,585.5	2,726.1	4,232.8	6,423.6	5,760.6	5,236.4	5,617.7	5,715.9	5,308.9	† 5,508.7	5,363.2	4,968.2	5,998.3
Quasi-Money	35	12,449.1	17,825.5	21,665.9	27,919.4	37,717.9	44,378.6	48,552.9	55,976.9	63,825.8	68,616.8	72,873.9	† 75118.9	80,733.2	79,972.4	85,633.3
Capital Accounts	37a	1,853.8	2,087.9	2,631.3	3,010.8	3,321.4	4,104.6	5,160.5	5,883.4	6,575.1	7,254.1	8,201.6	8,768.1	8,041.3	9,471.4	10,077.9
Other Items (Net)	37r	–210.2	–305.5	–280.5	–366.7	–253.6	–1.3	161.5	–4.3	464.6	611.1	–2,146.2	–54.5	1,050.1	1,134.4	406.3
Interest Rates		*Percent Per Annum*														
Interbank Rate (End of Period)	60b	....	9.17	8.74	8.17	4.23	4.41	3.79	5.91	6.01	5.60	7.54	5.41	6.11	6.20	1.93
Money Market Rate	60b	....	9.17	8.74	8.17	4.23	4.41	3.79	5.91	6.01	5.60	7.54	5.41	6.11	6.20	1.93
Deposit Rate	60l	3.50	4.56	7.04	7.13	5.88	3.50	2.75	4.21	5.93	5.23	6.22	7.00	5.30	5.33	2.59
Lending Rate	60p	6.63	8.06	10.54	10.42	9.42	7.25	6.50	7.95	9.90	9.56	9.73	10.97	9.46	9.89	7.99
Prices and Labor		*Period Averages*														
Consumer Prices	64	....	....	....	....	....	....	....	....	....	....	....	100.0	96.8	95.2	93.3
		Period Averages														
Labor Force	67d	....	....	....	....	....	....	....	177	187	206	207	211	216	215	217
Employment	67e	....	....	....	163	170	169	171	173	180	197	201	201	202	200	203
Unemployment	67c	....	....	....	6	5	4	4	4	7	9	7	10	14	15	14
Unemployment Rate (%)	67r	....	....	....	3.2	3.0	2.2	2.1	2.5	3.6	4.3	3.2	4.6	6.4	6.8	6.4
International Transactions		*Millions of US Dollars*														
Exports	70..d	1,404.0	1,493.3	1,643.5	1,700.8	1,665.4	1,766.4	1,786.6	1,866.0	1,997.3	1,995.8	2,147.8	2,141.1	2,199.6	2,539.0	2,299.5
Imports, c.i.f.	71..d	1,127.1	1,291.0	1,483.8	1,538.9	1,851.6	1,967.6	2,025.5	2,000.7	2,041.6	1,999.8	2,081.8	1,954.9	2,039.5	2,254.7	2,386.3
Government Finance		*Year Ending December 31*														
Deficit (-) or Surplus	80	....	....	....	....	....	....	....	....	....	25.4	882.2	–457.3	–452.8	777.3	....
Total Revenue and Grants	81y	....	....	....	....	....	....	....	....	....	9,491.9	10,934.6	10,098.8	10,749.4	9,809.6	....
Revenue	81	....	....	....	....	....	....	....	....	....	9,491.6	10,934.3	10,098.7	10,749.4	9,809.6	....
Grants	81z	....	....	....	....	....	....	....	....	....	.3	.3	.1	—	—	....
Exp. & Lending Minus Repay.	82z	....	....	....	....	....	....	....	....	....	9,466.5	10,052.4	10,556.1	11,202.2	9,032.3	....
Expenditure	82	....	....	....	....	....	....	....	....	....	8,817.8	9,530.9	10,071.0	11,033.7	9,004.5	....
Lending Minus Repayments	83	....	....	....	....	....	....	....	....	....	648.7	521.5	485.1	168.5	27.8	....
National Accounts		*Millions of Patacas*														
Househ.Cons.Expend.,incl.NPISHs	96f	6,157.9	7,355.5	8,395.9	9,600.5	11,268.8	13,144.1	14,912.0	16,863.9	18,609.9	20,202.2	20,996.5	20,684.6	20,402.9	20,376.4	20,625.4
Government Consumption Expend.	91f	1,022.7	1,309.5	1,775.6	2,308.9	2,837.2	3,036.7	3,500.4	4,056.4	4,673.1	5,204.1	5,732.1	6,029.4	6,771.8	5,900.7	6,062.7
Gross Capital Formation	93	3,817.4	4,561.8	5,483.5	6,413.7	8,779.3	13,472.9	15,481.5	17,101.4	16,043.7	11,791.3	11,836.5	9,667.2	8,668.3	5,918.7	5,194.6
Changes in Inventories	93i	435.9	494.9	376.0	133.3	374.5	350.6	421.6	585.3	253.6	540.7	112.8	–71.8	83.3	73.7	71.9
Exports of Goods and Services	90c	17,179.1	19,398.2	22,495.9	25,354.6	27,342.2	31,813.6	33,991.0	36,530.6	41,044.0	41,806.8	42,355.7	39,779.9	39,237.0	46,708.6	48,678.5
Imports of Goods and Services (-)	98c	12,584.7	14,402.3	16,465.5	17,635.6	20,275.1	22,298.4	23,113.5	25,023.6	25,291.2	24,251.5	25,139.2	24,187.6	26,142.2	29,236.1	30,831.0
Gross Domestic Product (GDP)	99b	16,028.4	18,717.6	22,061.5	26,175.3	30,326.9	39,519.4	45,193.0	50,114.0	55,333.2	55,293.5	55,894.3	51,901.7	49,021.1	49,742.0	49,802.1
GDP Volume 1996 Prices	99b.p	34,137.8	36,804.4	38,653.7	41,738.1	43,265.5	49,019.4	51,561.6	53,754.6	55,526.3	55,293.5	55,139.1	52,619.0	51,021.0	53,381.0	54,519.0
GDP Volume (1996=100)	99bvp	61.7	66.6	69.9	75.5	78.3	88.7	93.3	97.2	100.4	100.0	99.7	95.1	92.3	96.6	98.6
GDP Deflator (1996=100)	99bip	47.0	50.9	57.1	62.7	70.1	80.6	87.7	93.2	99.7	100.0	101.4	98.7	96.2	93.3	91.3
		Midyear Estimates														
Population	99z	.31	.32	.33	.33	.35	.37	.38	.40	.41	.42	.42	.43	.43	.44	.45

(See notes in the back of the book.)

Colombia

		1972	1973	1974	1975	1976	1977	1978	1979	1980	1981	1982	1983	1984	1985	1986
Exchange Rates															*Pesos per SDR:*	
Principal Rate	aa	24.74	29.91	35.05	38.58	42.20	46.11	53.41	57.96	64.94	68.76	77.54	92.94	111.64	189.15	267.88
															Pesos per US Dollar:	
Principal Rate	ae	22.79	24.79	28.63	32.96	36.32	37.96	41.00	44.00	50.92	59.07	70.29	88.77	113.89	172.20	219.00
Principal Rate	rf	21.87	23.64	26.06	30.93	34.69	36.77	39.09	42.55	47.28	54.49	64.08	78.85	100.82	†142.31	194.26
															Index Numbers (1995=100):	
Principal Rate	ahx	4,178.9	3,865.3	3,508.4	2,957.4	2,633.9	2,484.0	2,337.1	2,146.9	1,933.8	1,678.8	1,428.5	1,164.4	909.2	649.0	470.5
Nominal Effective Exchange Rate	ne c	....	....	....	....	....	....	....	336.5	320.2	314.1	305.0	289.0	264.6	215.4	151.3
Real Effective Exchange Rate	re c	....	....	....	....	....	....	....	....	146.7	158.4	168.5	168.6	155.8	135.9	101.2
Fund Position															*Millions of SDRs:*	
Quota	2f. s	157	157	157	157	157	157	193	193	290	290	290	394	394	394	394
SDRs	1b. s	18	23	25	20	24	26	38	72	85	119	162	189	—	—	114
Reserve Position in the Fund	1c. s	—	39	39	39	45	77	70	74	115	152	175	262	—	—	—
Total Fund Cred.&Loans Outstg.	2tl	—	—	—	—	—	—	—	—	—	—	—	—	—	—	—
International Liquidity														*Millions of US Dollars Unless Otherwise Indicated:*		
Total Reserves minus Gold	1l. d	309	516	431	475	1,101	1,747	2,366	3,844	4,831	4,741	3,861	1,901	1,364	1,595	2,696
SDRs	1b. d	19	28	30	24	28	31	49	95	109	139	179	198	—	—	140
Reserve Position in the Fund	1c. d	—	47	48	46	53	93	91	97	146	177	193	274			
Foreign Exchange	1d. d	290	441	353	405	1,020	1,623	2,226	3,652	4,576	4,425	3,489	1,429	1,364	1,595	2,556
Gold (Million Fine Troy Ounces)	1ad	.429	.429	.429	1.126	1.413	1.731	1.961	2.317	2.787	3.366	3.817	4.223	1.367	1.842	2.009
Gold (National Valuation)	1and	16	16	18	48	60	73	137	215	525	764	933	1,025e	426	597	698
Monetary Authorities: Other Assets	3.. d	24	—	—	28	8	18	—	7	77	57	7	23	6	10	1
Other Liab.	4.. d	112	132	137	135	142	175	229	259	302	321	334	348	345	607	776
Deposit Money Banks: Assets	7a. d	5	21	35	57	62	64	89	145	170	179	177	385	528	272	312
Liabilities	7b. d	325	310	578	533	637	476	486	869	1,093	1,147	1,222	1,151	1,202	1,096	961
Other Banking Insts.: Assets	7e. d	....	....	10	14	15	19	14	10	20	13	35	37	38		
Liabilities	7f. d	....	....	102	152	139	175	229	292	435	466	539	530	508		
Monetary Authorities														*Millions of Pesos through 1973:*		
Foreign Assets	11	7,780.0	12,675.1	†11.6	16.4	40.7	69.4	98.6	175.9	259.3	308.0	314.8	242.6	145.4	360.5	987.9
Claims on Central Government	12a	6,990.0	6,200.0	†8.0	10.9	9.0	8.8	†9.5	9.7	13.1	13.7	46.7	106.8	252.3	310.9	410.6
Claims on Nonfin.Pub.Enterprises	12c	....	334.0	†.3	.3	.2	.2	.2	.1	.1	.1	—	2.2	—	.3	47.9
Claims on Private Sector	12d	3,464.0	3,545.0	†1.8	2.2	3.0	3.6	4.5	6.3	5.3	8.0	10.2	14.1	13.2	43.2	21.3
Claims on Deposit Money Banks	12e	3,394.0	5,790.0	†7.6	8.1	7.4	13.9	†32.1	36.0	38.0	48.6	67.8	104.3	121.1	140.3	132.3
Claims on Other Banking Insts	12f	5,875.0	8,055.0	†11.3	19.2	20.6	35.3	†27.8	25.2	27.3	30.0	34.3	53.3	84.4	94.9	126.1
Claims on Nonbank Financial Insts	12g															
Reserve Money	14	18,919.0	24,808.0	†30.1	37.7	53.4	74.9	†115.0	148.7	192.4	239.1	281.2	333.4	411.9	483.6	581.5
of which: Currency Outside DMBs	14a	10,729.0	12,424.0	†15.9	20.8	28.8	40.5	†53.7	67.3	84.1	101.6	130.3	167.7	211.7	186.7	....
Time, Savings,& Fgn.Currency Dep.	15	....	....													
Money Market Instruments	16aa	....	504.0	†1.0	1.6	5.1	16.3	†27.3	39.9	62.0	65.8	106.7	69.6	69.1	178.7	474.9
Restricted Deposits	16b	2,496.0	3,661.0	†3.8	2.0	.9	5.1	†5.9	10.1	12.8	12.0	10.0	25.6	35.9	54.1	62.0
Foreign Liabilities	16c	297.0	812.0	†1.0	.2	.2	.2	†.4	.3	.2	.1	.1	7.4	8.3	43.2	11.7
Long-Term Foreign Liabilities	16cl	2,264.0	2,464.0	†3.0	4.3	5.0	6.4	†9.0	11.1	15.2	18.8	23.4	23.5	31.0	61.4	158.2
Central Government Deposits	16d	1,536.0	1,594.0	†1.9	1.8	2.8	4.1	†5.8	28.7	30.4	32.5	19.3	42.1	39.3	78.7	270.5
Capital Accounts	17a	....	2,530.0	†2.4	2.5	2.7	2.9	†3.6	5.1	7.4	10.0	11.8	15.5	48.5	61.8	74.9
Other Items (Net)	17r	1,991.0	226.1	†−2.7	7.0	10.8	21.2	†5.5	9.2	22.8	29.9	21.3	6.1	−27.5	−11.6	92.3
Deposit Money Banks														*Millions of Pesos through 1973;*		
Reserves	20	6,758.0	10,690.0	†12.6	17.0	24.8	34.3	†60.5	79.3	106.0	134.5	149.7	169.5	202.2	268.8	....
Foreign Assets	21	109.0	510.0	†1.0	1.9	2.2	2.4	†3.6	6.0	8.4	10.3	12.2	28.3	50.9	44.7	....
Claims on Central Government	22a	2,968.0	4,822.0	†6.9	6.9	9.3	14.6	†15.1	15.6	15.5	22.6	30.2	40.6	62.0	52.5	....
Claims on Local Government	22b	....	....													
Claims on Nonfin.Pub.Enterprises	22c	....	....					1.0	1.4	1.1	2.8	3.4	10.9	13.5	16.8	
Claims on Private Sector	22d	25,095.0	29,976.0	†45.1	55.6	73.5	88.6	†108.0	138.1	220.7	298.1	374.2	479.2	584.8	747.8	
Claims on Other Banking Insts	22f	3,081.0	4,465.0	†7.0	10.5	12.1	14.7	†9.1	12.0	15.0	18.6	22.3	26.3	28.7	34.5	
Demand Deposits	24	20,055.0	28,151.0	†31.7	40.9	54.8	69.4	†76.5	93.6	121.4	147.2	180.8	220.9	267.3	341.2	
Time, Savings,& Fgn.Currency Dep.	25	5,127.0	7,408.0	†13.1	17.0	24.0	34.3	†44.0	51.7	103.2	171.4	196.8	250.6	309.1	417.8	
Money Market Instruments	26aa															
Bonds	26ab															2.1
Restricted Deposits	26b															
Foreign Liabilities	26c	7,068.0	7,363.0	†16.2	17.3	22.9	17.8	†19.3	37.7	55.2	67.4	85.7	102.0	136.8	188.7	
Long-Term Foreign Liabilities	26cl	331.0	334.0	†.3	.3	.2	.2	†.3	.3	.2	.2	.1	.1	—	—	
Central Government Deposits	26d								.7	.9	1.3	1.5	2.5	2.8	3.2	3.8
Credit from Monetary Authorities	26g	2,394.0	4,320.0	†6.2	6.4	5.2	16.0	†31.5	35.5	36.7	47.0	68.4	101.2	119.1	148.2	
Liabilities to Other Banking Insts	26i															
Capital Accounts	27a	5,183.0	6,102.0	†5.6	6.8	9.1	11.6	†22.9	28.8	40.3	52.4	66.3	71.9	75.9	21.9	
Other Items (Net)	27r	−2,147.0	−3,215.0	†−.4	3.1	5.8	5.5	†2.8	3.6	8.3	−.1	−8.7	5.3	30.7	41.4	
Monetary Survey														*Millions of Pesos through 1973;*		
Foreign Assets (Net)	31n	524.0	5,010.1	†−4.5	.8	19.8	53.7	†82.4	143.9	212.3	250.7	241.2	161.5	51.3	173.3	....
Domestic Credit	32	45,937.0	55,469.0	†78.7	104.5	124.4	161.6	†169.3	178.4	266.5	364.6	498.5	686.5	996.5	1,218.3	....
Claims on Central Govt. (Net)	32an	6,413.0	5,800.0	†8.8	10.8	14.9	19.2	†18.1	−4.3	−3.1	2.3	55.1	102.5	271.8	280.8	
Claims on Local Government	32b	....	....													
Claims on Nonfin.Pub.Enterprises	32c	....	334.0	†.3	.3	.2	.2	1.8	1.1	1.1	1.2	2.4	13.1	13.5	17.1	
Claims on Private Sector	32d	28,559.0	33,521.0	†47.4	58.9	76.5	92.3	†112.4	144.4	226.0	306.1	384.4	493.3	598.0	791.0	
Claims on Other Banking Insts	32f	8,956.0	12,520.0	†18.4	29.7	32.7	50.1	†36.9	37.2	42.3	48.6	56.6	79.7	113.1	129.4	
Claims on Nonbank Financial Inst	32g															
Money	34	31,854.0	41,647.0	†49.1	58.9	79.4	103.5	†132.9	165.9	212.4	256.4	321.4	396.7	492.4	545.3	....
Quasi-Money	35	5,856.0	9,250.0	†14.6	19.6	25.8	37.2	†47.1	55.1	108.1	178.4	204.2	262.5	324.4	436.8	....
Money Market Instruments	36aa	....	504.0	†1.1	1.6	5.1	16.3	27.3	39.9	62.0	70.0	106.7	69.6	69.1	180.8	....
Bonds	36ab													—		2.1
Restricted Deposits	36b	2,496.0	3,661.0	†3.8	2.0	.9	5.1	†5.9	10.1	12.8	12.0	10.0	25.6	35.9	54.1	....
Long-Term Foreign Liabilities	36cl	2,595.0	2,798.0	†3.3	4.5	5.2	6.7	†9.3	11.4	15.4	19.0	23.5	23.6	31.0	61.4	....
Liabilities to Other Banking Insts	36i															
Capital Accounts	37a	....	8,632.0	†8.0	9.4	11.8	14.6	†26.5	34.0	47.7	62.4	78.1	87.5	124.5	83.8	....
Other Items (Net)	37r	3,660.0	−6,012.9	†−5.7	9.4	16.1	32.0	†2.7	5.9	20.4	17.1	−4.3	−17.6	−29.6	27.3	....
Money plus Quasi-Money	35l	37,710.0	50,897.0	†63.7	78.5	105.1	140.7	†180.0	221.0	320.5	434.7	525.6	659.2	816.8	982.1	....

1987	1988	1989	1990	1991	1992	1993	1994	1995	1996	1997	1998	1999	2000	2001		
															Exchange Rates	
End of Period																
374.10	451.97	570.24	809.11	1,011.11	1,116.18	1,260.01	1,213.53	1,468.13	1,445.62	1,745.36	2,122.63	2,571.77	2,849.49	2,892.15	Principal Rate	aa
End of Period (ae) Period Average (rf)																
263.70	335.86	433.92	568.73	706.86	811.77	917.33	831.27	987.65	1,005.33	1,293.58	1,507.52	1,873.77	2,187.02	2,301.33	Principal Rate	ae
242.61	299.17	382.57	502.26	633.05	759.28	863.06	844.84	912.83	1,036.69	1,140.96	1,426.04	1,756.23	2,087.90	2,299.63	Principal Rate	rf
Period Averages																
376.0	305.6	239.0	182.2	144.2	119.5	105.5	107.8	100.0	87.8	80.3	64.0	52.2	43.7	39.6	Principal Rate	ahx
125.4	116.4	115.9	105.6	95.2	94.9	98.1	110.0	100.0	93.3	91.4	75.5	63.0	55.3	52.4	Nominal Effective Exchange Rate	nec
89.9	87.3	83.7	73.5	75.6	82.4	87.3	98.4	100.0	107.0	119.0	113.5	102.7	95.6	98.0	Real Effective Exchange Rate	rec
															Fund Position	
End of Period																
394	394	394	394	394	561	561	561	561	561	561	561	774	774	774	Quota	2f.s
114	114	114	114	114	42	115	116	119	123	128	139	95	103	108	SDRs	1b.s
—	—	—	—	—	69	80	87	135	165	263	408	286	286	286	Reserve Position in the Fund	1c.s
—	—	—	—	—	—	—	—	—	—	—	—	—	—	—	Total Fund Cred.&Loans Outstg.	2tl
															International Liquidity	
End of Period																
3,086	3,248	3,616	4,628	6,533	7,746	7,930	7,991	8,349	9,845	9,803	8,651	8,008	8,916	10,154	Total Reserves minus Gold	1l.d
162	154	150	163	163	58	158	170	177	177	172	196	131	135	135	SDRs	1b.d
—	—	—	—	—	95	110	127	201	237	355	575	392	372	359	Reserve Position in the Fund	1c.d
2,924	3,094	3,466	4,465	6,370	7,593	7,663	7,694	7,971	9,431	9,275	7,880	7,485	8,409	9,659	Foreign Exchange	1d.d
.682	1.102	.614	.626	.863	.484	.302	.293	.267	.252	.358	.358	.328	.328	.327	Gold (Million Fine Troy Ounces)	1ad
290	468	249	248	323	172	119	112	119	94	104	103	95	89	91	Gold (National Valuation)	1and
—	—	226	336	368	382	378	425	420	420	419	422	418	448	447	Monetary Authorities: Other Assets	3..d
694	580	829	860	870	800	602	383	473	355	249	238	211	187	200	Other Liab.	4..d
321	492	....	269	420	425	544	506	443	484	1,031	944	552	458	387	Deposit Money Banks: Assets	7a.d
944	1,176	....	984	782	1,019	1,655	1,854	2,136	2,654	3,316	2,868	1,712	1,365	1,217	Liabilities	7b.d
....	....	....	16	108	73	149	169	134	257	199	162	211	133	178	Other Banking Insts.: Assets	7e.d
....	....	....	1,201	1,338	1,785	2,271	3,182	3,476	4,241	3,834	3,352	2,837	1,860	1,399	Liabilities	7f.d
															Monetary Authorities	
Billions of Pesos Beginning 1974: End of Period																
1,182.9	1,212.8	†1,786.3	2,738.3	4,377.1	6,047.5	6,709.4	7,073.1	8,760.5	10,402.8	13,295.7	13,841.5	15,954.0	20,665.9	24,660.9	Foreign Assets	11
466.5	526.2	†513.0	543.7	759.7	777.3	679.6	711.1	565.0	725.0	574.3	951.6	2,397.2	2,767.5	2,034.3	Claims on Central Government	12a
97.7	130.2	†221.3	263.6	9.2	9.7	9.3	—	—	—	—	—	—	—	—	Claims on Nonfin.Pub.Enterprises	12c
41.9	65.6	†10.3	4.8	3.7	4.5	6.2	52.2	81.6	105.8	128.3	538.7	577.4	397.6	203.0	Claims on Private Sector	12d
135.3	158.1	†396.8	445.0	148.8	117.1	75.6	66.3	239.9	62.6	416.3	885.4	2,510.0	1,536.3	919.2	Claims on Deposit Money Banks	12e
130.3	171.3	†297.8	246.9	285.4	290.1	322.6	339.0	436.9	264.9	286.0	392.6	435.5	853.9	374.3	Claims on Other Banking Insts	12f
....	....	—	—	—	—	—	—	—	133.1	408.8	579.5	681.6	802.7	893.2	Claims on Nonbank Financial Insts	12g
848.9	1,017.6	†1,695.6	2,086.2	2,663.6	3,665.9	4,605.8	5,902.5	6,301.1	7,415.6	8,640.7	7,165.0	10,014.0	10,922.4	12,003.0	Reserve Money	14
418.8	530.7	....	†837.0	1,054.9	1,438.6	1,804.4	2,373.3	2,994.3	3,536.0	4,453.0	4,997.3	6,507.4	7,676.6	8,653.6	*of which: Currency Outside DMBs*	14a
....	....	279.5	303.5	21.5	28.5	31.7	49.6	9.9	14.0	.8	120.4	101.3	7.9	2.0	Time, Savings,& Fgn.Currency Dep.	15
504.3	547.1	†173.5	319.8	1,283.5	1,627.2	1,231.7	392.2	214.7	723.0	.5	15.8	—	—	—	Money Market Instruments	16aa
84.5	125.3	†128.5	157.7	.4	.4	.4	.4	.4	.4	.3	.3	.3	.3	—	Restricted Deposits	16b
11.7	14.5	†54.6	51.7	50.4	7.7	22.1	83.8	131.2	43.8	3.9	1.4	2.6	4.3	123.0	Foreign Liabilities	16c
171.4	180.2	†293.6	421.9	499.9	582.4	461.4	234.0	335.1	312.3	316.7	358.1	393.2	403.5	338.0	Long-Term Foreign Liabilities	16cl
247.4	79.3	†282.5	375.6	530.3	589.4	414.3	475.6	128.4	247.3	349.0	251.4	235.4	339.6	402.6	Central Government Deposits	16d
144.7	223.0	†255.4	383.5	408.2	498.2	1,104.3	1,388.1	3,110.2	3,231.1	6,120.0	9,644.1	12,087.7	15,696.9	16,963.9	Capital Accounts	17a
41.5	77.1	†62.3	142.4	126.1	246.5	-69.0	-284.5	-147.1	-293.3	-322.6	-367.4	-278.8	-351.0	-747.5	Other Items (Net)	17r
															Deposit Money Banks	
Billions of Pesos Beginning 1974: End of Period																
483.9	560.8	....	†1,000.6	1,323.1	1,791.6	2,461.1	2,937.1	2,736.3	2,890.2	3,544.7	2,157.1	3,242.9	3,008.2	3,201.2	Reserves	20
83.7	166.7	....	†148.0	265.6	313.6	437.3	419.9	437.0	485.9	1,326.9	1,427.0	1,033.9	1,001.5	893.9	Foreign Assets	21
79.5	101.0	....	†138.2	98.3	158.1	337.8	430.9	463.7	617.1	1,441.0	2,454.1	2,167.1	5,525.5	9,616.7	Claims on Central Government	22a
....	....	....	146.5	240.7	233.0	347.3	1,009.7	1,407.0	1,715.4	3,214.1	3,498.4	3,577.6	3,373.2	3,746.1	Claims on Local Government	22b
38.3	40.3	....	†69.8	59.2	50.0	8.1	68.7	100.0	89.1	136.4	301.4	295.5	450.3	395.3	Claims on Nonfin.Pub.Enterprises	22c
1,229.3	1,680.3	....	†3,142.1	3,481.2	4,902.7	7,701.0	11,266.6	15,162.0	18,547.0	26,167.9	33,048.8	31,334.5	32,452.5	36,215.7	Claims on Private Sector	22d
61.4	68.5	....	†157.0	351.6	581.2	560.7	1,081.2	1,581.3	2,714.1	2,970.9	3,125.2	6,597.7	7,243.4	7,015.5	Claims on Other Banking Insts	22f
577.4	723.0	....	†1,140.8	1,502.7	2,164.1	2,883.8	3,626.1	4,271.9	5,272.8	6,251.6	5,673.3	6,533.1	8,825.6	9,622.9	Demand Deposits	24
739.6	817.7	....	†1,476.8	1,898.3	2,777.6	4,217.7	6,447.3	8,005.4	10,036.5	16,709.5	23,452.4	25,587.6	27,956.5	33,498.9	Time, Savings,& Fgn.Currency Dep.	25
....	....	....	193.8	246.0	191.5	221.5	294.7	247.4	185.1	122.9	103.7	56.9	45.2	48.3	Money Market Instruments	26aa
26.1	28.8	....	†—	—	40.5	69.7	670.5	823.2	1,715.6	2,772.2	2,826.9	1,684.7	1,406.3	1,467.1	Bonds	26ab
....	....	....	147.1	34.6	8.2	5.8	18.5	21.8	25.6	32.6	37.9	29.8	140.8	84.0	Restricted Deposits	26b
249.0	394.9	....	†463.4	444.9	745.3	1,283.3	1,448.5	2,003.0	2,557.8	3,889.9	4,048.0	3,009.3	1,689.0	1,977.5	Foreign Liabilities	26c
—	—	....	†79.0	49.6	6.5	46.6	88.7	104.6	106.4	377.8	285.4	195.7	1,295.3	830.0	Long-Term Foreign Liabilities	26cl
6.8	8.7	....	†230.4	374.4	589.8	816.7	1,015.3	1,319.0	1,666.7	2,333.0	2,457.4	2,243.1	2,615.1	3,526.4	Central Government Deposits	26d
173.3	273.2	....	†416.4	207.5	138.5	119.6	122.9	119.4	104.0	73.3	934.0	2,471.6	1,538.5	904.9	Credit from Monetary Authorities	26g
....	....	....	377.5	740.0	1,026.1	1,484.5	1,878.4	2,474.4	2,708.5	3,011.4	4,250.2	3,586.7	4,308.9	3,970.3	Liabilities to Other Banking Insts	26i
75.4	155.3	....	†508.9	696.1	1,076.4	1,719.5	2,676.0	3,558.6	4,808.3	6,159.0	5,179.0	6,120.2	6,201.0	6,477.8	Capital Accounts	27a
128.6	216.1	....	†-231.9	-374.4	-734.3	-1,015.4	-1,072.8	-1,061.4	-2,128.5	-2,931.3	-3,236.2	-3,269.5	-2,967.8	-1,323.7	Other Items (Net)	27r
															Monetary Survey	
Billions of Pesos Beginning 1974: End of Period																
1,006.0	970.1	....	†2,371.2	4,147.3	5,608.1	5,841.3	5,960.7	7,063.2	8,287.1	10,728.8	11,219.1	13,975.9	19,974.2	23,454.3	Foreign Assets (Net)	31n
1,890.7	2,695.4	....	†4,106.4	4,384.3	5,827.4	8,741.6	13,468.5	18,350.1	22,997.5	32,645.6	42,181.4	45,585.7	50,911.8	56,565.0	Domestic Credit	32
291.8	539.2	....	†75.8	-46.7	-243.8	-213.6	-348.9	-418.7	-571.9	-666.7	696.9	2,085.8	5,338.3	7,722.0	Claims on Central Govt. (Net)	32an
....	....	....	146.5	240.7	233.0	347.3	1,009.7	1,407.0	1,715.4	3,214.1	3,498.4	3,577.6	3,373.2	3,746.1	Claims on Local Government	32b
136.0	170.5	....	†333.4	68.4	59.7	17.4	68.7	100.0	89.1	136.4	301.4	295.5	450.3	395.3	Claims on Nonfin.Pub.Enterprises	32c
1,271.1	1,745.9	....	†3,146.9	3,484.9	4,907.2	7,707.2	11,318.8	15,243.6	18,652.8	26,296.2	33,587.5	31,912.0	32,850.1	36,418.6	Claims on Private Sector	32d
191.7	239.8	....	†403.9	637.0	871.3	883.3	1,420.2	2,018.2	2,979.0	3,256.9	3,517.8	7,033.2	8,097.3	7,389.8	Claims on Other Banking Insts	32f
....	....	....	—	—	—	—	—	—	133.1	408.8	579.5	681.6	802.7	893.2	Claims on Nonbank Financial Inst	32g
1,019.6	1,282.0	....	†2,125.0	2,802.1	4,067.0	5,211.3	6,722.4	8,078.5	9,966.0	11,697.9	10,785.7	13,404.5	16,837.0	18,450.6	Money	34
795.7	916.4	....	†1,780.3	1,919.8	2,806.1	4,249.4	6,496.9	8,015.3	10,050.5	16,710.3	23,572.8	25,688.9	27,964.4	33,500.9	Quasi-Money	35
530.4	575.9	....	†513.6	1,529.5	1,818.7	1,453.2	686.9	462.1	908.1	123.4	119.5	56.9	45.2	48.3	Money Market Instruments	36aa
26.1	28.8	....	†—	—	40.5	69.7	670.5	823.2	1,715.6	2,772.2	2,826.9	1,684.7	1,406.3	1,467.1	Bonds	36ab
84.5	125.3	....	†304.8	35.0	8.6	6.2	18.9	22.2	26.0	32.9	38.2	30.2	141.2	84.0	Restricted Deposits	36b
171.4	180.2	....	†500.9	549.5	588.9	508.0	322.7	439.7	418.7	694.5	643.5	588.9	1,698.9	1,168.0	Long-Term Foreign Liabilities	36cl
....	....	....	377.5	740.0	1,026.1	1,484.5	1,878.4	2,474.4	2,708.5	3,011.4	4,250.2	3,586.7	4,308.9	3,970.3	Liabilities to Other Banking Insts	36i
220.1	378.3	....	†892.4	1,104.3	1,574.6	2,823.8	4,064.1	6,668.8	8,039.4	12,279.0	14,823.1	18,207.9	21,897.9	23,441.7	Capital Accounts	37a
48.7	178.7	....	†-16.8	-148.5	-495.0	-1,223.2	-1,431.6	-1,570.8	-2,548.2	-3,947.3	-3,659.5	-3,686.9	-3,413.8	-2,111.6	Other Items (Net)	37r
1,815.3	2,198.4	....	†3,905.3	4,721.9	6,873.1	9,460.7	13,219.3	16,093.8	20,016.5	28,408.2	34,358.5	39,093.3	44,801.4	51,951.5	Money plus Quasi-Money	35l

Colombia

	1972	1973	1974	1975	1976	1977	1978	1979	1980	1981	1982	1983	1984	1985	1986
Other Banking Institutions														*Millions of Pesos through 1973;*	
Reserves 40	....	....	†13.1	4.5	6.0	8.8	11.6	13.9	19.3	28.1	33.3	29.1	43.0	....	....
Foreign Assets 41	....	....	†.3	.4	.5	.7	.6	.4	1.0	.8	2.4	3.3	4.3	....	....
Claims on Central Government 42a	....	....	†.5	1.2	2.9	2.1	3.6	4.1	7.0	9.0	11.3	28.1	34.2	....	....
Claims on Local Government 42b															
Claims on Nonfin.Pub.Enterprises 42c	....	....	†.3	.4	.5	.5	.5	.5	1.1	1.4	1.9	2.5	3.3	4.9	
Claims on Private Sector 42d	....	....	†48.1	61.8	75.7	103.6	140.5	178.9	255.0	344.8	469.0	628.5	841.3	....	....
Claims on Deposit Money Banks 42e	....	....	†2.8	3.5	5.2	6.8	8.9	12.4	15.4	21.1	25.2	30.3	37.5	....	....
Demand Deposits 44	1,030.0	1,450.0	†1.8	2.4	3.1	4.2	4.7	6.8	8.7	10.6	14.6	20.2	24.4	33.1	41.5
Time, Savings,& Fgn.Currency Dep. 45	....	....	†13.3	21.0	32.9	45.7	66.9	87.7	137.2	198.2	267.0	360.0	445.5	....	....
Money Market Instruments 46aa															
Bonds 46ab	....	....	†11.5	12.0	12.8	8.4	16.6	25.0	32.6	44.9	49.9	58.5	74.0		
Restricted Deposits 46b															
Foreign Liabilities 46c	....	....	†1.6	1.8	1.7	2.6	4.3	5.9	11.1	14.3	19.3	22.7	18.2	....	....
Long-Term Foreign Liabilities 46cl	....	....	†1.3	3.2	3.3	4.0	5.0	7.0	11.0	13.3	18.6	24.3	51.0		
Central Government Deposits 46d	....	....	†.3	.4	.4	.3	.5	.5	.1	—	—	—	—		
Credit from Monetary Authorities 46g	....	....	†11.8	13.6	13.6	21.1	28.5	25.2	23.9	31.5	40.8	63.3	102.4		
Credit from Deposit Money Banks 46h	....	....	†5.7	6.5	7.8	9.6	12.6	10.1	11.3	13.4	23.9	29.1	33.4		
Capital Accounts 47a	....	....	†6.2	6.7	11.0	14.4	19.9	26.1	36.6	47.4	72.4	88.8	112.0		
Other Items (Net) 47r	....	....	†11.9	4.2	4.2	12.2	6.6	16.1	26.0	31.7	36.7	55.0	102.7		
Banking Survey														*Millions of Pesos through 1973;*	
Foreign Assets (Net) 51n	....	....	†-5.6	-.2	19.0	52.3	78.7	138.5	202.1	237.2	224.3	142.0	37.3	....	....
Domestic Credit 52	....	....	†104.6	134.1	164.7	217.7	276.4	324.3	487.1	666.3	924.1	1,285.4	1,762.3	....	....
Claims on Central Govt. (Net) 52an	....	....	†9.0	11.6	10.9	21.1	21.2	-.7	3.7	11.3	66.3	130.6	306.1	....	....
Claims on Local Government 52b															
Claims on Nonfin.Pub.Enterprises 52c	25,095.0	334.0	†.6	.7	.7	.7	2.3	1.7	2.3	4.3	4.3	15.6	16.8	22.0	....
Claims on Private Sector 52d	....	....	†95.5	120.7	152.2	195.9	252.9	323.3	481.1	650.9	853.4	1,121.9	1,439.4	....	....
Claims on Nonbank Financial Inst 52g															
Liquid Liabilities 55l	....	....	†52.8	68.8	103.1	181.8	240.0	301.5	447.2	615.3	773.9	1,010.3	1,243.7		
Money Market Instruments 56aa	....	....	†12.5	13.6	17.9	24.7	43.9	64.9	94.6	114.9	156.6	128.1	143.0		
Bonds 56ab							16.6	25.0	32.6	44.9	49.9	58.5	74.0		
Restricted Deposits 56b	2,500.0	3,661.0	†3.8	2.0	.1	5.1	5.9	10.1	12.8	12.0	10.0	25.6	35.9	54.1	62.0
Long-Term Foreign Liabilities 56cl	....	....	†4.6	7.7	8.5	10.7	14.3	18.3	26.5	32.3	42.1	47.9	82.0		
Capital Accounts 57a	....	....	†14.2	16.0	15.4	29.0	46.3	60.1	84.3	109.8	150.5	176.3	236.5		
Other Items (Net) 57r	....	....	†11.0	25.7	38.7	18.7	-12.1	-17.2	-8.7	-25.7	-34.5	-19.2	-15.6	....	....
Money (National Definitions)														*Millions of Pesos through 1973;*	
Reserve Money 19ma	17,636.0	23,504.0	†28.4	37.0	51.8	72.4	101.3	132.0	179.4	219.6	258.5	289.1	335.3	429.3	549.8
M1 .... 39ma	29,842.0	38,572.0	†46.1	58.9	79.4	103.5	134.9	167.6	216.5	259.2	321.5	405.1	499.7	640.4	784.5
M2 .... 59ma	35,864.0	51,205.0	†66.7	90.1	125.3	164.7	235.5	293.6	446.0	631.9	771.6	1,011.8	1,252.3	1,680.9	2,172.0
M3 .... 59mb	....	....	....	....	....	....	....	....	459.5	674.5	818.2	1,059.0	1,311.0	1,750.0	2,249.8
Interest Rates														*Percent Per Annum*	
Discount Rate (*End of Period*) 60	14.0	14.0	16.0	16.0	20.0	20.0	22.0	30.0	30.0	30.0	27.0	27.0	27.0	27.0	†33.8
Money Market Rate 60b															
Deposit Rate 60l															31.4
Lending Rate 60p															40.8
Prices, Production, Labor														*Index Numbers (1995=100):*	
Share Prices 62	.7	.8	.8	.7	.8	1.2	1.8	2.3	2.0	2.3	3.4	2.6	2.1	1.9	2.9
Producer Prices 63	.7	.9	1.3	1.6	2.0	2.5	2.9	3.7	4.6	5.8	7.2	8.8	10.4	13.0	†15.9
Consumer Prices 64	.7	.9	1.1	1.3	1.6	2.1	2.5	3.1	3.9	5.0	6.2	7.5	8.7	10.8	12.8
Manufacturing Production 66ey									64.2	63.0	60.4	60.1	66.1	67.9	72.6
Vol.of Gold Produced(1990=100) 66kr	19.8	22.7	27.9	32.5	32.0	27.1	25.7	28.8	52.4	54.4	48.4	45.4	77.0	120.4	134.8
Crude Petroleum Production 66aa	33.6	31.5	28.8	26.9	25.1	23.6	22.4	21.3	21.6	22.9	24.3	25.5	28.6	30.2	52.0
														Number in Thousands:	
Labor Force 67d															
Employment 67e														3,100	3,248
Unemployment 67c														500	483
Unemployment Rate (%) 67r															
International Transactions														*Millions of US Dollars*	
Exports .... 70..d	807.5	1,168.6	1,508.6	1,465.0	1,873.8	2,403.4	3,009.8	3,410.6	3,924.3	2,916.3	3,023.6	3,000.6	3,461.6	3,551.6	5,101.6
Coffee 70e.d	430.4	597.9	624.8	674.5	977.4	1,525.7	1,993.9	2,024.3	2,375.2	1,458.8	1,577.4	1,536.6	1,798.1	1,784.0	3,046.0
Imports, c.i.f. .... 71..d	858.9	1,061.5	1,597.2	1,494.8	1,661.9	1,880.0	2,971.0	3,364.1	4,738.6	5,200.8	5,479.8	4,963.4	4,497.5	4,140.9	3,861.5
Imports, f.o.b. 71.vd	756.7	918.3	1,431.2	1,345.5	1,544.4	1,825.7	2,555.2	2,912.8	4,200.5	4,685.4	4,936.8	4,471.6	4,052.1	3,731.5	3,564.0
Volume of Exports														*1995=100*	
Coffee 72e	67	69	71	84	64	54	92	114	114	93	91	94	104	102	116
Export Prices in Pesos 76	1	1	2	2	4	6	5	5	7	7	8	10	14	18	†28
Import Prices in Pesos 76.x	1	1	2	2	3	3	4	4	5	6	8	9	12	16	†21
Export Prices														*1995=100:*	
Coffee 76e.d	34.3	44.8	48.0	50.3	96.5	148.8	114.1	113.0	110.2	78.9	86.1	81.1	88.9	89.7	119.8

Other Banking Institutions

Billions of Pesos Beginning 1974: End of Period

1987	1988	1989	1990	1991	1992	1993	1994	1995	1996	1997	1998	1999	2000	2001		
....	....	....	†237.2	240.7	513.4	548.5	702.0	988.1	1,282.4	1,103.8	334.8	641.8	481.5	269.9	Reserves	40
....	....	....	†8.7	68.3	53.7	120.0	140.2	132.0	258.5	256.7	244.9	394.2	289.8	411.0	Foreign Assets	41
....	....	....	†114.4	105.0	172.7	202.0	273.7	131.1	155.7	265.2	1,306.3	3,607.2	3,519.3	3,519.0	Claims on Central Government	42a
....	....	....	1.6	11.2	13.1	30.8	783.2	1,294.4	1,472.6	1,256.2	870.9	649.1	630.1	465.1	Claims on Local Government	42b
....	....	....	†452.6	945.1	1,191.3	1,329.9	676.7	765.9	974.7	1,329.3	2,244.4	1,759.3	1,853.6	1,777.9	Claims on Nonfin.Pub.Enterprises	42c
....	....	....	†3,079.5	3,803.4	5,122.1	7,623.3	10,207.6	13,978.3	17,955.1	19,457.4	18,014.6	18,975.6	13,836.5	11,240.7	Claims on Private Sector	42d
89.4	124.0	....	†80.7	799.4	1,234.2	1,560.4	2,271.5	2,993.6	3,275.9	3,466.2	4,692.0	4,633.3	5,169.5	5,336.4	Claims on Deposit Money Banks	42e
53.2	64.8	....	†4.7	4.3	6.8	....	....	....	....	....	....	....	....	....	Demand Deposits	44
....	....	....	†2,357.8	3,266.9	4,360.4	6,064.6	9,501.0	12,870.1	15,339.3	15,222.5	13,657.5	15,000.6	11,166.5	8,457.3	Time, Savings,& Fgn.Currency Dep.	45
....	....	....	9.9	20.3	16.3	15.2	89.4	35.0	15.1	13.1	16.9	1.5	1.6	1.4	Money Market Instruments	46aa
135.0	78.0	....	†272.6	652.1	625.3	869.0	578.8	1,052.1	3,379.5	3,577.5	2,976.2	2,534.3	1,447.4	1,194.8	Bonds	46ab
....	....	....	17.5	3.8	28.4	7.6	7.1	6.4	5.9	.7	.7	3.1	3.3	22.3	Restricted Deposits	46b
....	....	....	†175.2	125.9	387.6	741.6	1,380.0	1,456.9	1,709.9	1,951.6	1,942.3	1,710.0	492.7	871.3	Foreign Liabilities	46c
....	....	....	†486.5	720.1	929.4	1,083.3	1,258.9	1,973.4	2,548.4	2,983.2	3,122.8	3,600.9	3,572.7	2,356.1	Long-Term Foreign Liabilities	46cl
—	....	....	†96.1	215.0	215.5	261.5	322.8	390.7	357.4	266.1	420.8	598.8	584.0	378.3	Central Government Deposits	46d
....	....	....	†140.6	203.7	215.5	250.2	280.5	232.4	209.5	96.6	362.7	533.7	976.5	375.5	Credit from Monetary Authorities	46g
....	....	....	†39.6	340.4	437.4	628.0	1,112.2	1,632.2	1,617.5	2,176.8	2,505.6	5,695.9	6,519.5	7,440.2	Credit from Deposit Money Banks	46h
....	....	....	†489.6	1,073.6	1,544.8	1,985.7	2,874.4	4,034.8	5,214.9	6,004.5	7,076.0	7,952.5	7,991.1	7,788.8	Capital Accounts	47a
....	....	....	†-115.4	-653.0	-466.9	-491.8	-2,350.2	-3,400.7	-5,022.6	-5,157.8	-4,373.4	-6,970.7	-6,974.7	-5,866.1	Other Items (Net)	47r

Banking Survey

Billions of Pesos Beginning 1974: End of Period

1987	1988	1989	1990	1991	1992	1993	1994	1995	1996	1997	1998	1999	2000	2001		
....	....	....	†2,204.7	4,089.8	5,274.2	5,219.7	4,720.9	5,738.3	6,835.8	9,033.8	9,521.6	12,660.1	19,771.4	22,993.9	Foreign Assets (Net)	51n
....	....	....	†7,254.6	8,397.0	11,239.8	16,782.8	23,666.7	32,110.9	40,219.2	51,430.7	60,679.1	62,944.9	62,070.2	65,799.6	Domestic Credit	52
....	....	....	†94.1	-156.7	-286.6	-273.1	-398.0	-678.3	-773.6	-667.6	1,582.4	5,094.2	8,273.6	10,862.6	Claims on Central Govt. (Net)	52an
....	....	....	148.1	251.9	246.1	378.1	1,792.9	2,701.4	3,188.0	4,470.3	4,369.3	4,226.8	4,003.3	4,211.3	Claims on Local Government	52b
....	....	....	†786.0	1,013.5	1,251.0	1,347.3	745.4	865.9	1,063.8	1,465.7	2,545.8	2,054.8	2,303.9	2,173.2	Claims on Nonfin.Pub.Enterprises	52c
....	....	....	†6,226.4	7,288.3	10,029.3	15,330.5	21,526.4	29,221.9	36,608.0	45,753.6	51,602.1	50,887.6	46,686.7	47,659.3	Claims on Private Sector	52d
....	....	....	....	....	....	....	....	....	133.1	408.8	579.5	681.6	802.7	893.2	Claims on Nonbank Financial Inst	52g
....	....	....	†6,030.6	7,752.4	10,726.9	14,976.8	22,018.3	27,975.8	34,073.4	42,527.0	47,681.3	53,452.1	55,486.4	60,138.9	Liquid Liabilities	55l
....	....	....	†523.5	1,549.8	1,835.0	1,468.4	776.3	497.1	923.2	136.5	136.4	58.4	46.8	49.7	Money Market Instruments	56aa
161.1	106.7	....	†272.6	652.1	665.8	938.7	1,249.3	1,875.3	5,095.1	6,349.7	5,803.1	4,219.0	2,853.7	2,661.9	Bonds	56ab
84.5	125.3	....	†322.3	38.8	37.0	13.8	26.0	28.6	31.9	33.6	38.9	33.2	144.4	106.4	Restricted Deposits	56b
....	....	....	†987.4	1,269.6	1,518.3	1,591.3	1,581.6	2,413.1	2,967.2	3,677.6	3,766.3	4,189.8	5,271.6	3,524.1	Long-Term Foreign Liabilities	56cl
....	....	....	†1,382.0	2,177.9	3,119.4	4,809.5	6,938.5	10,703.6	13,254.3	18,283.5	21,899.1	26,160.4	29,889.0	31,230.5	Capital Accounts	57a
....	....	....	†-59.0	-953.8	-1,388.4	-1,796.0	-4,202.4	-5,644.3	-9,290.1	-10,543.4	-9,124.3	-12,507.8	-11,850.4	-8,917.9	Other Items (Net)	57r

Money (National Definitions)

Billions of Pesos Beginning 1974: End of Period

1987	1988	1989	1990	1991	1992	1993	1994	1995	1996	1997	1998	1999	2000	2001		
715.8	914.9	1,171.7	1,493.5	2,290.0	3,312.5	4,419.0	5,634.4	6,267.1	6,627.6	8,287.1	6,923.1	9,739.6	10,710.4	11,647.9	*Reserve Money*	19ma
1,044.6	1,314.5	1,694.7	2,122.5	2,795.4	3,941.8	5,124.8	6,419.0	7,717.8	8,992.8	10,948.0	10,526.5	12,814.0	16,720.8	18,737.0	*M1*	39ma
2,795.3	3,455.9	4,582.6	6,034.2	8,061.7	11,179.6	15,817.3	22,569.1	28,961.3	34,815.5	43,794.6	48,558.1	53,670.5	56,178.6	62,158.4	*M2*	59ma
2,923.3	3,641.4	4,892.5	6,411.1	8,579.1	11,956.3	17,222.7	24,623.9	31,900.8	41,299.2	52,528.2	56,638.6	60,574.0	62,276.3	68,572.5	*M3*	59mb

Interest Rates

Percent Per Annum

1987	1988	1989	1990	1991	1992	1993	1994	1995	1996	1997	1998	1999	2000	2001		
34.8	34.3	36.9	†46.5	45.0	34.4	33.5	44.9	40.4	35.1	31.3	42.3	23.1	18.3	16.4	Discount Rate (End of Period)	60
....	....	....	....	....	....	....	....	22.4	28.4	23.8	35.0	18.8	10.9	10.4	Money Market Rate	60b
30.8	33.5	33.7	36.4	37.2	26.7	25.8	29.4	32.3	31.2	24.1	32.6	21.3	12.1	12.4	Deposit Rate	60l
41.1	42.7	43.0	45.2	47.1	37.3	35.8	40.5	42.7	42.0	34.2	42.2	†25.8	18.8	20.7	Lending Rate	60p

Prices, Production, Labor

Period Averages

1987	1988	1989	1990	1991	1992	1993	1994	1995	1996	1997	1998	1999	2000	2001		
5.5	7.5	8.2	10.1	†19.2	58.7	65.9	120.1	100.0	104.7	155.9	135.6	121.0	104.7	111.2	Share Prices	62
19.8	25.4	32.6	41.3	†52.7	63.3	72.3	84.7	100.0	†115.0	132.8	155.8	171.1	193.6	211.8	Producer Prices	63
15.8	†20.2	25.5	32.9	42.9	54.4	66.8	82.7	100.0	†120.2	142.9	172.0	191.3	209.4	227.7	Consumer Prices	64
77.8	80.7	82.0	†86.3	86.0	92.0	94.7	97.9	100.0	97.3	99.7	98.2	....	....	....	Manufacturing Production	66ey
89.9	98.3	100.0	100.0	117.6	108.8	92.8	71.1	....	....	....	....	....	....	....	Vol.of Gold Produced(1990=100)	66kr
66.0	64.4	69.3	75.3	72.9	75.3	77.6	77.7	100.0	107.6	109.1	129.6	141.4	....	....	Crude Petroleum Production	66aa

Period Averages

1987	1988	1989	1990	1991	1992	1993	1994	1995	1996	1997	1998	1999	2000	2001		
....	....	....	....	5,286	....	5,261	....	6,153	6,452	6,653	7,056	7,436	....	....	Labor Force	67d
3,443	3,572	3,668	4,325	†4,843	5,053	5,333	5,408	5,494	5,451	5,702	5,655	5,641	5,910	....	Employment	67e
429	403	357	492	†522	505	447	442	522	735	782	998	1,415	1,526	....	Unemployment	67c
....	....	8.9	10.2	†9.8	9.2	7.8	7.6	8.7	11.9	12.1	15.0	20.1	20.5	....	Unemployment Rate (%)	67r

International Transactions

Millions of US Dollars

1987	1988	1989	1990	1991	1992	1993	1994	1995	1996	1997	1998	1999	2000	2001		
4,642.2	5,037.0	5,716.5	6,765.8	7,232.1	6,916.5	7,115.9	8,418.5	10,056.2	10,587.0	11,522.4	10,852.1	11,576.4	13,040.4	12,257.0	Exports	70..d
1,688.5	1,646.1	1,583.5	1,414.7	1,336.4	1,258.9	1,139.7	1,990.1	1,831.8	1,576.5	2,259.0	1,891.0	1,324.0	1,080.3	764.2	Coffee	70e.d
4,321.9	5,001.8	5,004.1	5,589.5	4,906.1	6,516.4	9,831.5	11,882.9	13,852.9	13,683.6	15,377.7	14,634.5	10,658.6	11,538.8	12,833.6	Imports, c.i.f.	71..d
3,907.2	4,531.6	4,573.3	5,144.8	4,512.9	5,980.2	9,085.7	11,039.3	12,921.2	12,793.7	14,408.9	13,726.2	9,990.1	10,783.6	12,009.8	Imports, f.o.b.	71.vd

Volume of Exports — 1995=100

1987	1988	1989	1990	1991	1992	1993	1994	1995	1996	1997	1998	1999	2000	2001		
115	100	111	143	129	169	139	120	100	108	112	115	102	94	112	Coffee	72e
27	34	36	49	57	58	65	85	100	†106	129	143	164	205	201	Export Prices in Pesos	76
26	33	44	55	66	71	80	87	100	†115	123	142	163	189	204	Import Prices in Pesos	76.x

Export Prices — Indices of Prices in US Dollars

1987	1988	1989	1990	1991	1992	1993	1994	1995	1996	1997	1998	1999	2000	2001		
69.2	83.2	65.9	54.9	52.3	39.2	44.4	81.3	100.0	81.0	123.9	90.1	73.4	63.0	43.8	Coffee	76e.d

Colombia

Balance of Payments		1972	1973	1974	1975	1976	1977	1978	1979	1980	1981	1982	1983	1984	1985	1986
														Millions of US Dollars:		
Current Account, n.i.e.	78ald	−191	−55	−352	−172	163	375	258	438	−206	−1,961	−3,054	−3,003	−1,401	−1,809	383
Goods: Exports f.o.b.	78aad	979	1,263	1,495	1,683	2,202	2,660	3,155	3,441	3,986	3,158	3,114	2,970	4,273	3,650	5,331
Goods: Imports f.o.b.	78abd	−850	−983	−1,511	−1,415	−1,654	−1,970	−2,552	−2,978	−4,283	−4,730	−5,358	−4,464	−4,027	−3,673	−3,409
Trade Balance	78acd	129	280	−17	268	548	690	603	463	−297	−1,572	−2,244	−1,494	246	−23	1,922
Services: Credit	78add	226	281	366	431	568	730	780	1,105	1,342	1,148	1,335	844	927	855	1,108
Services: Debit	78aed	−383	−440	−566	−597	−647	−773	−857	−941	−1,170	−1,295	−1,346	−1,302	−1,298	−1,427	−1,684
Balance on Goods & Services	78afd	−28	121	−217	102	468	647	526	627	−126	−1,719	−2,255	−1,952	−125	−595	1,346
Income: Credit	78agd	24	44	88	66	80	112	164	305	532	708	525	289	128	111	175
Income: Debit	78ahd	−222	−255	−273	−388	−437	−430	−505	−596	−777	−1,192	−1,494	−1,504	−1,703	−1,786	−1,923
Balance on Gds, Serv. & Inc.	78aid	−226	−89	−403	−220	112	329	185	336	−371	−2,203	−3,223	−3,167	−1,700	−2,270	−402
Current Transfers, n.i.e.: Credit	78ajd	46	45	61	80	83	84	109	114	178	257	187	186	316	479	801
Current Transfers: Debit	78akd	−11	−11	−10	−32	−32	−38	−36	−12	−13	−15	−17	−22	−17	−18	−16
Capital Account, n.i.e.	78bcd	—	—	—	—	—	—	—	—	—	—	—	—	—	—	—
Capital Account, n.i.e.: Credit	78bad	—	—	—	—	—	—	—	—	—	—	—	—	—	—	—
Capital Account: Debit	78bbd	—	—	—	—	—	—	—	—	—	—	—	—	—	—	—
Financial Account, n.i.e.	78bjd	251	151	278	112	203	−24	102	977	945	2,039	2,232	1,434	944	2,236	1,160
Direct Investment Abroad	78bdd	−1	−1	−6	−4	−11	−22	−41	−24	−106	−37	−29	−104	−23	−7	−32
Dir. Invest. in Rep. Econ., n.i.e.	78bed	18	24	41	37	25	65	107	127	157	265	366	618	584	1,023	674
Portfolio Investment Assets	78bfd	—	—	—	—	—	—	—	—	—	—	—	—	—	—	—
Equity Securities	78bkd	—	—	—	—	—	—	—	—	—	—	—	—	—	—	—
Debt Securities	78bld	—	—	—	—	—	—	—	—	—	—	—	—	—	—	—
Portfolio Investment Liab., n.i.e.	78bgd	−1	42	−4	−2	−2	−3	−2	−11	−3	−2	−7	−2	−3	−1	30
Equity Securities	78bmd	—	—	—	—	—	—	—	—	—	—	—	—	—	—	—
Debt Securities	78bnd	−1	42	−4	−2	−2	−3	−2	−11	−3	−2	−7	−2	−3	−1	30
Financial Derivatives Assets	78bwd	....	....	....	....	....	....	....	....	....	....	....	....	....	....	....
Financial Derivatives Liabilities	78bxd	....	....	....	....	....	....	....	....	....	....	....	....	....	....	....
Other Investment Assets	78bhd	−52	−57	−238	−7		−9	−244	80	−303	−33	−42	−360	−562	−111	−217
Monetary Authorities	78bod	−1	10	10	−19	−3	7	−34	−19	−58	−11	63	−11	23	4	42
General Government	78bpd	−25	−23	−7	−1	−4	−8	−33	−18	−40	31	−4	—		−6	
Banks	78bqd	−12	−18	−30	−24	−2	−1	19	−34	−11	11	23	−194	−133	256	−65
Other Sectors	78brd	−14	−26	−210	37	9	−7	−196	151	−194	−64	−124	−155	−452	−365	−194
Other Investment Liab., n.i.e.	78bid	286	144	485	88	192	−55	282	805	1,199	1,846	1,944	1,282	948	1,332	705
Monetary Authorities	78bsd	52	30	24	9	39	24	95	50	52	69	−3	97	−14	30	108
General Government	78btd	158	176	85	160	−8	−6	20	371	460	590	310	105	368	283	377
Banks	78bud	−2	−62	291	−12	77	−190	17	448	211	72	96	258	−55	−253	−1,247
Other Sectors	78bvd	78	—	84	−68	83	117	150	−64	477	1,115	1,541	822	649	1,272	1,467
Net Errors and Omissions	78cad	106	70	−14	118	255	298	236	98	168	−99	−52	−270	76	−273	−251
Overall Balance	78cbd	165	166	−88	59	621	649	596	1,513	908	−21	−874	−1,839	−381	154	1,292
Reserves and Related Items	79dad	−165	−166	88	−59	−621	−649	−596	−1,513	−908	21	874	1,839	381	−154	−1,292
Reserve Assets	79dbd	−107	−166	88	−59	−621	−649	−596	−1,513	−908	21	874	1,839	381	−154	−1,292
Use of Fund Credit and Loans	79dcd	−58	—	—	—	—	—	—	—	—	—	—	—	—	—	—
Exceptional Financing	79ded	....	....	....	....	....	....	....	....	....	....	....	....	....		....
International Investment Position														*Millions of US Dollars*		
Assets	79aad	....	....	....	....	....	....	....	....	5,948	6,138	5,373	3,925	2,854	2,899	4,638
Direct Investment Abroad	79abd	....	....	....	....	....	....	....	....	136	140	170	274	295	301	316
Portfolio Investment	79acd	....	....	....	....	....	....	....	....	—	—	—	—	—	—	—
Equity Securities	79add	....	....	....	....	....	....	....	....	—	—	—	—	—	—	—
Debt Securities	79aed	....	....	....	....	....	....	....	....	—	—	—	—	—	—	—
Financial Derivatives	79ald	....	....	....	....	....	....	....	....							
Other Investment	79afd	....	....	....	....	....	....	....	....	449	418	345	546	653	407	739
Monetary Authorities	79agd	....	....	....	....	....	....	....	....	—	—	—	—	—	—	—
General Government	79ahd	....	....	....	....	....	....	....	....	359	339	280	291	269	271	229
Banks	79aid	....	....	....	....	....	....	....	....	90	79	56	250	383	127	176
Other Sectors	79ajd	....	....	....	....	....	....	....	....	—	—	9	5	1	9	334
Reserve Assets	79akd	....	....	....	....	....	....	....	....	5,363	5,581	4,858	3,105	1,906	2,191	3,583
Liabilities	79lad	....	....	....	....	....	....	....	....	8,117	9,865	12,218	13,567	14,786	16,837	18,939
Dir. Invest. in Rep. Economy	79lbd	....	....	....	....	....	....	....	....	1,464	1,607	1,720	1,837	2,163	2,654	3,311
Portfolio Investment	79lcd	....	....	....	....	....	....	....	....	31	29	23	20	17	16	46
Equity Securities	79ldd	....	....	....	....	....	....	....	....	—	—	—	—	—	—	—
Debt Securities	79led	....	....	....	....	....	....	....	....	31	29	23	20	17	16	46
Financial Derivatives	79lld	....	....	....	....	....	....	....	....							
Other Investment	79lfd	....	....	....	....	....	....	....	....	6,622	8,229	10,475	11,710	12,606	14,167	15,582
Monetary Authorities	79lgd	....	....	....	....	....	....	....	....	501	570	565	662	650	668	790
General Government	79lhd	....	....	....	....	....	....	....	....		2,713	2,998	3,074	3,412	3,726	4,199
Banks	79lid	....	....	....	....	....	....	....	....	1,159	1,231	1,327	1,585	1,530	1,277	1,256
Other Sectors	79ljd	....	....	....	....	....	....	....	....	2,824	3,715	5,585	6,389	7,014	8,496	9,337

Balance of Payments

Minus Sign Indicates Debit

	1987	1988	1989	1990	1991	1992	1993	1994	1995	1996	1997	1998	1999	2000	2001	Code
Current Account, n.i.e.	336	-216	-201	542	2,349	901	-2,102	-3,673	-4,596	-4,757	-5,882	-5,226	361	354	-1,782	78al d
Goods: Exports f.o.b.	5,661	5,343	6,031	7,079	7,507	7,263	7,429	9,059	10,594	10,966	12,064	11,480	12,037	13,621	12,775	78aa d
Goods: Imports f.o.b.	-3,793	-4,516	-4,557	-5,108	-4,548	-6,029	-9,086	-11,288	-13,139	-13,059	-14,705	-13,932	-10,260	-11,090	-12,265	78ab d
Trade Balance	1,868	827	1,474	1,971	2,959	1,234	-1,657	-2,229	-2,545	-2,093	-2,641	-2,452	1,777	2,531	510	78ac d
Services: Credit	1,166	1,408	1,291	1,600	1,593	1,983	2,520	1,571	1,700	2,189	2,150	1,952	1,885	2,003	2,157	78ad d
Services: Debit	-1,709	-1,670	-1,565	-1,750	-1,812	-2,028	-2,321	-2,626	-2,880	-3,383	-3,650	-3,419	-3,143	-3,312	-3,568	78ae d
Balance on Goods & Services	1,325	565	1,200	1,821	2,740	1,189	-1,458	-3,283	-3,725	-3,287	-4,141	-3,919	519	1,222	-901	78af d
Income: Credit	202	257	287	347	390	449	561	706	677	707	886	886	795	858	739	78ag d
Income: Debit	-2,192	-2,002	-2,586	-2,652	-2,480	-2,471	-2,344	-2,164	-2,277	-2,774	-3,241	-2,640	-2,386	-3,387	-3,715	78ah d
Balance on Gds, Serv. & Inc.	-665	-1,180	-1,099	-484	651	-833	-3,240	-4,741	-5,325	-5,354	-6,496	-5,673	-1,072	-1,307	-3,877	78ai d
Current Transfers, n.i.e.: Credit	1,022	994	928	1,043	1,743	1,871	1,350	1,262	963	814	831	608	1,682	1,899	2,396	78aj d
Current Transfers: Debit	-21	-30	-30	-17	-45	-137	-212	-193	-234	-217	-217	-161	-249	-238	-301	78ak d
Capital Account, n.i.e.	—	—	—	—	—	—	—	—	—	—	—	—	—	—	—	78bc d
Capital Account, n.i.e.: Credit	—	—	—	—	—	—	—	—	—	—	—	—	—	—	—	78ba d
Capital Account: Debit	—	—	—	—	—	—	—	—	—	—	—	—	—	—	—	78bb d
Financial Account, n.i.e.	-1	939	478	-2	-777	183	2,701	3,530	4,476	6,853	6,729	3,715	-592	490	2,477	78bj d
Direct Investment Abroad	-26	-44	-29	-16	-24	-50	-240	-149	-256	-328	-810	-796	-116	-250	-42	78bd d
Dir. Invest. in Rep. Econ., n.i.e.	319	203	576	500	457	729	959	1,447	968	3,112	5,561	2,829	1,468	2,281	2,329	78be d
Portfolio Investment Assets	—	—	—	...	—	—	—	-1,381	394	-586	-770	606	-1,734	-1,014	-3,478	78bf d
Equity Securities	—	—	—	—	—	—	—	—	—	—	—	—	—	—	—	78bk d
Debt Securities	—	—	—	—	—	—	—	-1,381	394	-586	-770	606	-1,734	-1,014	-3,478	78bl d
Portfolio Investment Liab., n.i.e.	48	—	179	-4	86	126	498	1,502	1,041	2,270	1,712	1,056	690	1,436	3,452	78bg d
Equity Securities	—	—	—	—	...	—	—	478	165	292	278	47	-27	17	-43	78bm d
Debt Securities	48	—	179	-4	86	126	498	1,024	876	1,978	1,434	1,009	717	1,419	3,495	78bn d
Financial Derivatives Assets	...	...	...	...	...	...	...	...	...	...	...	...	...	...	...	78bw d
Financial Derivatives Liabilities	—	—	—	—	—	—	—	—	—	—	295	-39	100	-104	-112	78bx d
Other Investment Assets	-295	-315	-95	-102	-522	-637	160	161	320	-855	-1,408	-537	-437	-549	126	78bh d
Monetary Authorities	-3	-1	24	...	...	...	-40	—	—	—	—	-6	7	-8	7	78bo d
General Government	—	—	—	-82	-100	-346	267	—	—	-20	-19	-15	-23	-40	-35	78bp d
Banks	-45	-117	41	17	-272	-110	-74	-70	58	-42	-232	-178	118	145	100	78bq d
Other Sectors	-247	-197	-160	-37	-150	-182	7	231	262	-793	-1,157	-338	-539	-646	54	78br d
Other Investment Liab., n.i.e.	-47	1,095	-153	-380	-774	15	1,325	1,950	2,009	3,240	2,149	596	-563	-1,310	202	78bi d
Monetary Authorities	23	-4	89	-27	—	-131	-99	-191	52	19	-14	-20	-12	-15	-13	78bs d
General Government	-225	371	69	95	-14	-78	-329	-418	-80	-264	-52	347	909	340	225	78bt d
Banks	-190	318	39	10	-362	785	710	726	579	416	486	-861	-1,207	-1,149	-403	78bu d
Other Sectors	345	410	-350	-458	-397	-561	1,043	1,832	1,458	3,069	1,729	1,130	-253	-486	393	78bv d
Net Errors and Omissions	67	-530	157	70	191	191	-135	325	115	-366	-570	114	-81	18	530	78ca d
Overall Balance	402	193	434	610	1,763	1,274	464	182	-5	1,730	277	-1,397	-312	862	1,225	78cb d
Reserves and Related Items	-402	-193	-434	-610	-1,763	-1,274	-464	-182	5	-1,730	-277	1,397	312	-862	-1,225	79da d
Reserve Assets	-402	-193	-434	-610	-1,763	-1,274	-464	-182	5	-1,730	-277	1,397	312	-862	-1,225	79db d
Use of Fund Credit and Loans	—	—	—	—	—	—	—	—	—	—	—	—	—	—	—	79dc d
Exceptional Financing	—	—	—	...	...	...	—	—	—	—	—	—	—	-1	—	79de d

International Investment Position

Millions of US Dollars

	1987	1988	1989	1990	1991	1992	1993	1994	1995	1996	1997	1998	1999	2000	2001	Code
Assets	4,735	5,157	5,295	5,832	8,041	9,212	12,701	15,149	16,445	17,656	20,640	20,138	21,770	24,461	29,043	79aa d
Direct Investment Abroad	335	371	392	402	422	472	592	744	1,028	1,096	1,893	2,648	2,703	2,914	2,902	79ab d
Portfolio Investment	—	—	—	—	—	—	—	447	1,171	2,453	3,268	2,662	4,426	5,441	8,920	79ac d
Equity Securities	—	—	—	—	—	—	—	447	1,171	—	—	—	—	—	—	79ad d
Debt Securities	—	—	—	—	—	—	—	—	—	2,453	3,268	2,662	4,426	5,441	8,920	79ae d
Financial Derivatives	—	—	—	—	—	—	—	—	—	—	—	—	—	—	—	79al d
Other Investment	817	852	811	699	1,012	927	4,163	5,845	5,786	4,168	5,571	6,096	6,540	7,111	6,979	79af d
Monetary Authorities	—	—	—	—	—	—	40	40	40	482	476	473	473	501	502	79ag d
General Government	235	24	—	—	100	—	561	1,545	1,052	109	128	142	165	205	229	79ah d
Banks	187	215	191	128	528	554	1,109	1,150	1,051	262	493	669	551	406	304	79ai d
Other Sectors	395	613	620	571	384	373	2,452	3,110	3,643	3,315	4,474	4,812	5,351	5,999	5,944	79aj d
Reserve Assets	3,583	3,934	4,092	4,731	6,607	7,813	7,946	8,114	8,462	9,939	9,908	8,732	8,101	8,995	10,242	79ak d
Liabilities	20,374	20,839	21,464	23,145	22,890	23,047	24,937	30,129	35,297	44,023	56,111	54,246	51,278	49,089	56,038	79la d
Dir. Invest. in Rep. Economy	3,624	3,827	4,404	4,904	5,362	6,152	5,779	6,916	8,563	11,773	19,694	16,644	13,929	12,204	15,859	79lb d
Portfolio Investment	105	104	276	275	360	419	741	2,026	2,591	5,945	7,936	8,261	8,533	9,723	13,109	79lc d
Equity Securities	—	—	—	—	—	—	215	693	858	942	1,553	880	586	397	325	79ld d
Debt Securities	105	104	276	275	360	419	525	1,333	1,733	5,003	6,383	7,381	7,947	9,326	12,784	79le d
Financial Derivatives	—	—	—	—	—	—	—	—	—	—	295	256	356	253	141	79ll d
Other Investment	16,645	16,908	16,784	17,966	17,168	16,476	18,417	21,187	24,144	26,305	28,186	29,085	28,460	26,909	26,929	79lf d
Monetary Authorities	853	597	687	761	763	650	452	231	301	315	249	236	211	185	149	79lg d
General Government	4,189	4,548	4,855	5,468	5,405	5,589	5,202	5,102	5,144	4,723	4,515	4,999	5,864	6,580	6,878	79lh d
Banks	1,041	1,130	1,166	1,176	855	1,628	3,741	4,518	5,169	5,460	6,003	5,059	3,885	2,713	2,261	79li d
Other Sectors	10,562	10,633	10,076	10,561	10,145	8,609	9,023	11,336	13,530	15,807	17,419	18,791	18,500	17,431	17,641	79lj d

Colombia

		1972	1973	1974	1975	1976	1977	1978	1979	1980	1981	1982	1983	1984	1985	1986
Government Finance													*Millions of Pesos through 1973;*			
Deficit (-) or Surplus	80	−3,676.0	−2,377.0	†−2.8	−1.1	4.5	5.8	6.0	6.0	−10.8	−10.0	−33.7	−53.8	−130.5	−131.8	−90.0
Total Revenue and Grants	81y	16,084.0	20,074.0	†26.2	38.4	48.8	63.4	84.1	114.6	152.5	205.0	257.5	290.9	299.2	446.5	655.5
Revenue	81	....	....	....	....	....	....	....	....	....	....	....	....	....	....	....
Grants	81z															
Exp. & Lending Minus Repay.	82z	19,760.0	22,451.0	†29.0	39.6	44.3	57.6	78.1	108.6	163.2	215.0	291.1	344.7	429.7	578.3	745.5
Expenditure	82	....	....	....	....	....	....	....	....	....	....	....	....	....	....	....
Lending Minus Repayments	83															
Total Financing	80h	3,678.0	2,380.0	†2.8	1.1	−4.5	−5.8	−6.0	−6.0	10.8	10.0	33.7	53.8	130.5	131.8	90.0
Domestic	84a	395.0	−619.0	†2.5	1.7	−3.3	−4.2	−3.8	−11.2	−5.7	−9.5	18.8	60.0	128.9	84.5	−11.9
Foreign	85a	3,283.0	2,999.0	†.3	−.5	−1.2	−1.6	−2.2	5.2	16.5	19.5	14.9	−6.1	1.6	47.3	101.9
Total Debt by Currency	88z	33,205.0	39,615.0	†42.3	52.7	60.4	65.4	68.0	99.7	134.0	157.7	200.5				
National	88b	12,086.0	13,435.0	†14.6	17.8	20.2	19.5	18.6	23.1	27.7	28.0	37.7	104.2	287.7	455.0	595.1
Foreign	89b	21,119.0	26,180.0	†27.8	34.9	40.2	45.9	49.5	76.6	106.4	129.7	162.9	....	....	....	....
National Accounts													*Millions of Pesos through 1973;*			
Househ.Cons.Expend.,incl.NPISHs	96f	136,230	170,230	†229	293	378	500	640	841	1,109	1,438	1,820	2,197	2,722	3,425	4,436
Government Consumption Expend.	91f	18,140	23,010	†28	36	44	55	78	111	159	207	273	335	426	531	666
Gross Fixed Capital Formation	93e	31,000	38,000	†53	62	85	104	140	183	265	350	436	525	654	870	1,204
Changes in Inventories	93i	3,890	6,010	†16	7	9	30	26	32	36	59	76	83	77	75	18
Exports of Goods and Services	90c	25,130	36,290	†47	64	91	121	151	181	256	235	273	319	458	686	1,279
Imports of Goods and Services (-)	98c	24,270	30,790	†50	57	74	95	126	160	246	306	379	404	481	622	814
Gross Domestic Product (GDP)	99b	189,610	243,160	†322	405	532	716	909	1,189	1,579	1,983	2,497	3,054	3,857	4,966	6,788
Net Primary Income from Abroad	98.n	−3,600	−4,480	†−4	−7	−9	−8	−8	−7	−6	−11	−51	−54	−99	−142	−150
Gross National Income (GNI)	99a	186,010	238,680	†319	399	523	708	902	1,182	1,573	1,972	2,447	3,000	3,758	4,824	6,638
Net Current Transf.from Abroad	98t	....	....	....	....	....	....	....	....	....	....	....	....	....	....	....
Gross Nat'l Disposable Inc.(GNDI)	99i	....	....	....	....	....	....	....	....	....	....	....	....	....	....	....
Gross Saving	99s	....	....	....	....	....	....	....	....	....	....	....	....	....	....	....
GDP Volume 1975 Prices(Billions)	99b.p	351	374	396	405	424	442	479	505	526	538	543	551	570	588	622
GDP Volume 1994 Prices	99b.p	....	....	....	....	....	....	....	....	....	....	....	....	....	....	....
GDP Volume (1995=100)	99bv p	38.3	40.9	43.3	44.3	46.4	48.3	52.4	55.2	57.4	58.8	59.3	60.2	62.3	64.2	67.9
GDP Deflator (1995=100)	99bi p	.6	.7	.9	1.1	1.4	1.8	2.1	2.6	3.3	4.0	5.0	6.0	7.3	9.2	11.8
																Millions:
Population	99z	21.67	22.34	22.98	23.64	24.33	†24.23	24.91	25.38	25.89	26.43	26.97	27.50	28.06	28.62	30.02

	1987	1988	1989	1990	1991	1992	1993	1994	1995	1996	1997	1998	1999	2000	2001	Government Finance	
Billions of Pesos Beginning 1974: Year Ending December 31																	
	−39.4	−159.8	−499.1	−163.7	25.2	−1,117.3	−329.2	−1,027.2	−1,939.8	−3,780.2	−4,504.0	−6,940.6	−8,888.9	−11,945.5	−10,032.0	Deficit (-) or Surplus	80
	912.2	1,207.2	1,271.0	2,070.9	3,221.6	4,113.0	5,715.3	7,656.1	9,521.2	12,007.3	15,282.6	16,880.2	20,144.0	23,285.3	29,034.4	Total Revenue and Grants	81y
	....	....	....	....	....	....	....	7,656.1	9,521.2	12,007.3	15,282.6	16,880.2	20,144.0	23,285.3	29,034.4	Revenue	81
	....	....	....	....	....	....	....	—	—	—	—	—	—	—	—	Grants	81z
	951.6	1,367.0	1,770.1	2,234.6	3,196.4	5,230.2	6,044.6	8,683.3	11,461.0	15,787.5	19,786.6	23,820.8	29,032.9	35,230.8	39,066.4	Exp. & Lending Minus Repay.	82z
	....	....	....	....	....	....	....	8,553.8	11,289.5	15,610.9	19,583.6	23,492.0	28,153.8	34,444.4	38,086.1	Expenditure	82
	....	....	....	....	....	....	....	129.5	171.5	176.6	203.0	328.8	879.1	786.4	980.3	Lending Minus Repayments	83
	39.4	159.8	499.1	163.7	−25.3	1,117.3	329.1	1,027.2	1,939.8	3,780.2	4,504.0	6,940.6	8,888.9	11,945.5	10,032.0	Total Financing	80h
	113.0	61.8	402.1	5.9	−25.2	1,093.2	809.8	907.7	1,717.5	2,516.5	3,140.4	4,522.0	4,569.7	7,137.8	4,276.1	Domestic	84a
	−73.6	98.0	97.1	157.8	−.1	24.1	−480.6	119.5	222.3	1,263.7	1,363.6	2,418.6	4,319.2	4,807.7	5,755.9	Foreign	85a
	700.3	....	....	....	....	....	....	....	....	....	....	....	....	....	....	Total Debt by Currency	88z
	700.3	....	....	....	....	....	....	....	....	....	....	....	....	....	....	National	88b
																Foreign	89b
Billions of Pesos Beginning 1974																National Accounts	
	5,835	7,684	9,876	13,239	17,317	23,133	30,513	44,510	55,462	65,966	79,194	92,501	97,631	112,180	....	Househ.Cons.Expend.,incl.NPISHs	96f
	868	1,183	1,597	2,077	2,685	3,965	5,108	9,774	12,622	18,123	24,246	28,548	33,588	37,791	....	Government Consumption Expend.	91f
	1,537	2,288	2,733	3,365	3,810	5,212	8,251	15,727	18,911	21,749	24,592	26,603	20,079	22,129	....	Gross Fixed Capital Formation	93e
	227	292	288	387	354	552	1,049	1,497	2,806	462	708	941	−725	747	....	Changes in Inventories	93i
	1,496	1,911	2,723	4,160	5,572	5,936	7,212	10,129	12,272	15,308	18,063	21,083	27,807	34,594	35,904	Exports of Goods and Services	90c
	1,140	1,626	2,090	2,998	3,631	5,282	8,235	14,127	17,701	20,993	25,261	29,363	26,983	34,030	39,888	Imports of Goods and Services (-)	98c
	8,824	11,731	15,127	20,228	26,107	33,515	43,898	67,533	84,439	100,711	121,708	140,483	151,565	173,730	189,526	Gross Domestic Product (GDP)	99b
	−187	−196	−423	−560	−154	−104	245	−1,200	−1,442	−2,128	−2,706	−3,372	−2,493	....	....	Net Primary Income from Abroad	98.n
	8,638	11,536	14,704	19,669	25,952	33,411	44,143	66,333	82,997	98,583	119,002	137,111	149,072	....	....	Gross National Income (GNI)	99a
	....	288	344	516	1,074	1,180	1,552	36,921	38,075	40,227	14,764	....	....	....	....	Net Current Transf.from Abroad	98t
	....	11,536	14,704	19,669	25,952	33,411	44,143	69,791	87,534	102,541	123,147	....	....	....	....	Gross Nat'l Disposable Inc.(GNDI)	99i
	....	2,640	3,165	4,322	5,920	6,369	8,582	15,506	19,450	18,453	19,707	....	....	....	....	Gross Saving	99s
	655	682	705	735	750	780	822	870	....	....	....	....	....	....	....	GDP Volume 1975 Prices(Billions)	99b.p
	....	....	....	....	....	....	....	67,533	71,046	72,507	74,994	75,421	72,251	74,228	75,268	GDP Volume 1994 Prices	99b.p
	71.6	74.5	77.0	80.3	81.9	85.3	89.8	95.1	100.0	102.1	105.6	106.2	101.7	104.5	105.9	GDP Volume (1995=100)	99bv p
	14.6	18.7	23.3	29.8	37.7	46.6	57.9	84.1	100.0	116.9	136.5	156.7	176.5	196.9	211.9	GDP Deflator (1995=100)	99bi p
Midyear Estimates																	
	30.58	31.14	34.31	34.97	35.69	36.41	37.13	37.85	38.54	39.30	40.06	40.83	41.59	42.32	42.80	Population	99z

(See notes in the back of the book.)

Comoros

632

		1972	1973	1974	1975	1976	1977	1978	1979	1980	1981	1982	1983	1984	1985	1986
Exchange Rates															*Francs per SDR:*	
Official Rate .... aa		277.99	284.00	272.08	262.55	288.70	285.76	272.28	264.78	287.98	334.52	370.92	436.97	470.10	415.25	394.78
															Francs per US Dollar:	
Official Rate .... ae		256.05	235.42	222.22	224.27	248.49	235.25	209.00	201.00	225.80	287.40	336.25	417.37	479.60	378.05	322.75
Official Rate .... rf		252.03	222.89	240.70	214.31	238.95	245.68	225.65	212.72	211.28	271.73	328.60	381.06	436.95	449.26	346.30
Fund Position															*Millions of SDRs:*	
Quota 2f.s		...	...	...	...	1.90	1.90	2.30	2.30	3.50	3.50	3.50	3.50	4.50	4.50	4.50
SDRs 1b.s		...	...	...	...	—	—	—	.24	—	.01	—	—	.23	.21	.18
Reserve Position in the Fund 1c.s		...	...	...	...	—	—	—	—	.30	—	—	—	—	—	—
Total Fund Cred.&Loans Outstg. 2tl		...	...	...	...	—	—	—	—	—	—	—	—	—	—	—
International Liquidity												*Millions of US Dollars Unless Otherwise Indicated:*				
Total Reserves minus Gold 1l.d		...	...	...	...	...	...	...	...	6.37	8.39	10.83	10.79	3.51	11.75	17.55
SDRs 1b.d		...	...	...	...	—	—	—	.32	—	.01	—	—	.23	.23	.22
Reserve Position in the Fund 1c.d		...	...	...	...	—	—	—	—	.38	—	—	—	—	—	—
Foreign Exchange 1d.d		...	...	...	...	...	...	...	...	5.99	8.38	10.83	10.79	3.28	11.52	17.33
Gold (Million Fine Troy Ounces) 1ad		...	...	...	...	...	...	...	...	...	...	—	.001	.001	.001	.001
Gold (National Valuation) 1an.d		...	...	...	...	...	...	...	...	...	...	—	.22	.19	.20	.24
Deposit Money Banks: Assets 7a.d		...	...	...	...	...	...	...	...	...	...	2.36	1.61	.15	3.76	2.11
Liabilities 7b.d		...	...	...	...	...	...	...	...	...	...	.12	.33	.10	1.21	3.81
Monetary Authorities															*Millions of Francs:*	
Foreign Assets 11		...	...	...	...	...	...	...	...	...	...	3,642	4,597	1,775	4,515	5,740
Claims on Central Government 12a		...	...	...	...	...	...	...	...	...	...	670	786	978	1,202	1,251
Claims on Private Sector 12d		...	...	...	...	...	...	...	...	...	...	...	...	...	...	...
Claims on Other Banking Insts 12f		...	...	...	...	...	...	...	...	...	...	...	...	...	...	...
Reserve Money 14		...	...	...	...	...	...	...	...	...	...	3,583	3,976	3,475	3,881	5,205
of which: Currency Outside DMBs 14a		...	...	...	...	...	...	...	...	...	...	2,434	3,427	3,142	3,448	3,118
Foreign Liabilities 16c		...	...	...	...	...	...	...	...	...	...	171	335	177	172	193
Central Government Deposits 16d		...	...	...	...	...	...	...	...	...	...	92	337	80	189	161
Counterpart Funds 16e		...	...	...	...	...	...	...	...	...	...	...	...	...	...	...
Central Govt. Lending Funds 16f		...	...	...	...	...	...	...	...	...	...	...	...	...	...	...
Capital Accounts 17a		...	...	...	...	...	...	...	...	...	...	1,289	1,469	1,674	1,540	1,724
Other Items (Net) 17r		...	...	...	...	...	...	...	...	...	...	−823	−734	−2,653	−65	−292
Deposit Money Banks															*Millions of Francs:*	
Reserves 20		...	...	...	...	...	...	...	...	...	...	481	266	419	66	1,804
Foreign Assets 21		...	...	...	...	...	...	...	...	...	...	795	671	73	1,420	681
Claims on Central Government 22a		...	...	...	...	...	...	...	...	...	...	457	457	457	458	385
Claims on Private Sector 22d		...	...	...	...	...	...	...	...	...	...	3,485	4,436	6,313	3,428	3,982
Demand Deposits 24		...	...	...	...	...	...	...	...	...	...	1,688	2,783	2,016	2,636	2,904
Time and Savings Deposits 25a		...	...	...	...	...	...	...	...	...	...	1,168	1,229	959	1,015	1,432
Foreign Currency Deposits 25b		...	...	...	...	...	...	...	...	...	...	...	...	...	...	...
Restricted Deposits 26b		...	...	...	...	...	...	...	...	...	...	...	...	...	...	...
Foreign Liabilities 26c		...	...	...	...	...	...	...	...	...	...	42	139	50	457	1,231
Central Government Deposits 26d		...	...	...	...	...	...	...	...	...	...	129	70	206	—	348
Credit From Monetary Authorities 26g		...	...	...	...	...	...	...	...	...	...	—	—	2,516	17	—
Capital Accounts 27a		...	...	...	...	...	...	...	...	...	...	350	514	581	617	566
Other Items (Net) 27r		...	...	...	...	...	...	...	...	...	...	1,841	1,094	934	630	373
Monetary Survey															*Millions of Francs:*	
Foreign Assets (Net) 31n		...	...	...	...	...	...	...	...	...	...	4,224	4,794	1,621	5,306	4,997
Domestic Credit 32		...	...	...	...	...	...	...	...	...	...	4,993	6,120	8,399	5,820	5,984
Claims on Central Govt. (Net) 32an		...	...	...	...	...	...	...	...	...	...	1,447	1,621	2,046	2,392	1,982
Claims on Private Sector 32d		...	...	...	...	...	...	...	...	...	...	3,546	4,499	6,353	3,428	4,002
Money 34		...	...	...	...	...	...	...	...	...	...	5,231	7,404	6,268	7,313	7,256
Quasi-Money 35		...	...	...	...	...	...	...	...	...	...	1,168	1,229	959	1,015	1,432
Restricted Deposits 36b		...	...	...	...	...	...	...	...	...	...	...	...	...	...	...
Counterpart Funds 36e		...	...	...	...	...	...	...	...	...	...	...	...	...	...	...
Central Govt. Lending Funds 36f		...	...	...	...	...	...	...	...	...	...	...	...	...	...	...
Other Items (Net) 37r		...	...	...	...	...	...	...	...	...	...	2,818	2,280	2,793	2,798	2,295
Money plus Quasi-Money 35l		...	...	...	...	...	...	...	...	...	...	6,399	8,633	7,227	8,328	8,688
Other Banking Institutions															*Millions of Francs:*	
Reserves 40		...	...	...	...	...	...	...	...	...	...	245	137	60	143	134
Foreign Assets 41		...	...	...	...	...	...	...	...	...	...	...	...	...	...	...
Claims on Central Government 42a		...	...	...	...	...	...	...	...	...	...	2	5	16	1	1
Claims on Private Sector 42d		...	...	...	...	...	...	...	...	...	...	576	925	1,226	1,498	1,749
Time Deposits 45		...	...	...	...	...	...	...	...	...	...	97	182	277	318	375
Central Government Deposits 46d		...	...	...	...	...	...	...	...	...	...	—	—	38	32	66
Long-Term Foreign Liabilities 46cl		...	...	...	...	...	...	...	...	...	...	—	—	—	—	—
Central Govt. Lending Funds 46f		...	...	...	...	...	...	...	...	...	...	413	514	643	896	1,089
Capital Accounts 47a		...	...	...	...	...	...	...	...	...	...	348	392	433	511	520
Other Items (Net) 47r		...	...	...	...	...	...	...	...	...	...	−35	−21	−89	−106	−96
Banking Survey															*Millions of Francs:*	
Foreign Assets (Net) 51n		...	...	...	...	...	...	...	...	...	...	4,224	4,794	1,621	5,307	4,998
Domestic Credit 52		...	...	...	...	...	...	...	...	...	...	5,571	7,050	9,603	7,298	7,737
Claims on Central Govt. (Net) 52an		...	...	...	...	...	...	...	...	...	...	1,449	1,626	2,024	2,372	1,986
Claims on Private Sector 52d		...	...	...	...	...	...	...	...	...	...	4,122	5,424	7,579	4,926	5,751
Liquid Liabilities 55l		...	...	...	...	...	...	...	...	...	...	6,495	8,814	7,503	8,504	8,933
Money 54		...	...	...	...	...	...	...	...	...	...	5,230	7,403	6,267	7,171	7,126
Quasi-Money 55		...	...	...	...	...	...	...	...	...	...	1,265	1,411	1,236	1,333	1,807
Restricted Deposits 56b		...	...	...	...	...	...	...	...	...	...	...	...	...	...	...
Counterpart Funds 56e		...	...	...	...	...	...	...	...	...	...	...	...	...	...	...
Central Govt. Lending Funds 56f		...	...	...	...	...	...	...	...	...	...	763	864	993	1,246	1,439
Other Items (Net) 57r		...	...	...	...	...	...	...	...	...	...	2,537	2,165	2,728	2,852	2,365

1987	1988	1989	1990	1991	1992	1993	1994	1995	1996	1997	1998	1999	2000	2001		
End of Period (aa)															**Exchange Rates**	
378.78	407.68	380.31	364.84	370.48	378.57	404.89	†585.32	546.28	564.79	605.95	593.70	†672.14	688.87	701.54	Official Rate	aa
End of Period (ae) Period Average (rf)																
267.00	302.95	289.40	256.45	259.00	275.32	294.77	†400.95	367.50	392.77	449.10	421.65	†489.72	528.71	558.23	Official Rate	ae
300.53	297.85	319.01	272.26	282.10	264.69	283.16	†416.40	374.36	383.66	437.75	442.46	†461.77	533.98	549.78	Official Rate	rf
															Fund Position	
End of Period																
4.50	4.50	4.50	4.50	4.50	6.50	6.50	6.50	6.50	6.50	6.50	6.50	8.90	8.90	8.90	Quota	2f. s
.14	.11	.06	.08	.02	.02	.07	.03	.07	.04	.10	—	.12	.13	.02	SDRs	1b. s
—	—	—	—	—	.50	.50	.52	.54	.54	.54	.54	.54	.54	.54	Reserve Position in the Fund	1c. s
—	—	—	—	.90	.90	.90	2.25	2.25	2.25	2.07	1.89	1.58	1.13	.68	Total Fund Cred.&Loans Outstg.	2tl
															International Liquidity	
End of Period																
30.67	23.54	30.77	29.69	29.18	27.09	38.63	44.03	44.48	50.55	40.48	39.14	37.15	43.21	62.32	Total Reserves minus Gold	1l. d
.20	.15	.08	.11	.03	.03	.09	.05	.11	.05	.13	.01	.16	.16	.02	SDRs	1b. d
—	—	—	—	—	.69	.69	.76	.80	.78	.73	.76	.74	.70	.68	Reserve Position in the Fund	1c. d
30.48	23.39	30.69	29.58	29.15	26.38	37.85	43.22	43.58	49.72	39.62	38.37	36.24	42.34	61.62	Foreign Exchange	1d. d
.001	.001	.001	.001	.001	.001	.001	.001	.001	.001	.001	....	....	....	....	Gold (Million Fine Troy Ounces)	1ad
.30	.24	.24	.22	.21	.19	.22	.22	.22	.21	.18	.17	.17	.16	.15	Gold (National Valuation)	1an d
.40	5.50	3.90	3.89	5.84	4.35	2.73	.29	2.42	2.16	4.29	†2.04	8.10	5.69	8.71	Deposit Money Banks: Assets	7a. d
6.26	6.30	5.46	6.28	6.93	4.76	2.66	.01	.25	.02	....	†1.99	2.45	4.35	4.18	Liabilities	7b. d
															Monetary Authorities	
End of Period																
8,275	7,205	8,977	7,654	7,595	7,512	11,475	17,729	16,422	19,950	18,305	†16,581	18,295	23,017	34,879	Foreign Assets	11
1,312	1,624	1,830	1,819	2,475	2,510	2,648	3,483	3,589	3,569	3,646	†3,806	3,814	3,858	3,654	Claims on Central Government	12a
....	....	....	....	....	....	....	....	....	....	....	57	49	64	70	Claims on Private Sector	12d
....	....	....	....	....	....	....	....	....	....	....	50	75	75	75	Claims on Other Banking Insts	12f
7,358	5,772	7,801	6,508	5,954	6,085	8,539	9,756	8,760	11,936	10,454	†9,326	11,104	13,980	23,851	Reserve Money	14
3,151	3,688	3,618	4,274	4,046	4,082	4,402	5,100	5,672	5,639	5,433	†5,418	6,310	7,564	12,355	of which: Currency Outside DMBs	14a
88	115	182	196	575	505	524	1,428	1,421	1,393	1,385	†1,183	1,171	915	1,393	Foreign Liabilities	16c
959	1,638	230	752	756	657	2,287	1,743	1,279	1,723	1,515	†542	518	508	712	Central Government Deposits	16d
....	....	....	....	....	....	....	....	....	....	....	56	49	49	49	Counterpart Funds	16e
....	....	....	....	....	....	....	....	....	....	....	504	314	316	1,374	Central Govt. Lending Funds	16f
1,706	1,809	2,585	2,728	2,802	2,976	2,972	8,492	8,673	8,670	8,770	†9,241	9,277	11,120	11,056	Capital Accounts	17a
-523	-505	8	-711	-18	-200	-198	-206	-121	-203	-173	†-359	-197	125	245	Other Items (Net)	17r
															Deposit Money Banks	
End of Period																
3,774	1,722	3,728	1,637	1,261	1,599	2,972	3,082	1,631	4,719	4,024	†5,195	3,796	5,257	8,806	Reserves	20
106	1,667	1,130	997	1,512	1,198	804	115	889	848	1,927	†859	3,966	3,009	4,864	Foreign Assets	21
328	273	178	51	—	—	—	—	415	94		†358	554	300	301	Claims on Central Government	22a
4,734	6,826	6,277	9,023	9,627	9,998	8,829	8,579	9,452	6,712	8,458	†6,948	8,600	9,480	9,223	Claims on Private Sector	22d
3,024	3,831	4,065	4,244	3,465	3,866	3,710	3,954	4,170	4,487	4,518	†4,250	4,386	5,626	8,955	Demand Deposits	24
3,035	3,559	4,608	4,574	5,829	5,720	5,781	5,910	5,442	6,167	7,771	†5,737	6,974	7,237	8,363	Time and Savings Deposits	25a
....	....	....	....	....	....	....	....	....	....	....	21	62	63	125	Foreign Currency Deposits	25b
....	....	....	....	....	....	....	....	....	....	....	260	618	111	482	Restricted Deposits	26b
1,671	1,908	1,580	1,611	1,795	1,311	783	3	93	8	—	†840	1,200	2,298	2,331	Foreign Liabilities	26c
277	83	127	—	—	—	377	—	167	132	209	†362	240	378	509	Central Government Deposits	26d
—	—	—	84	—	—	87	122	—	—	—	†—	—	—	—	Credit From Monetary Authorities	26g
592	632	835	951	1,174	1,405	1,586	1,850	2,194	2,022	2,235	†2,667	3,368	3,504	3,904	Capital Accounts	27a
343	475	98	244	137	493	281	-63	-94	-123	-230	†-776	70	-1,171	-1,475	Other Items (Net)	27r
															Monetary Survey	
End of Period																
6,622	6,849	8,345	6,844	6,737	6,894	10,972	16,413	15,797	19,397	18,847	†15,417	19,890	22,813	36,019	Foreign Assets (Net)	31n
6,516	8,163	10,067	11,918	13,277	14,403	11,465	12,497	12,449	10,213	10,474	†10,315	12,342	12,891	12,103	Domestic Credit	32
1,763	1,304	3,727	2,829	3,523	4,316	2,566	3,822	2,924	3,422	2,016	†3,260	3,610	3,272	2,733	Claims on Central Govt. (Net)	32an
4,753	6,859	6,340	9,089	9,754	10,087	8,899	8,675	9,525	6,791	8,458	†7,005	8,649	9,544	9,294	Claims on Private Sector	32d
....	....	....	....	....	....	....	....	....	....	....	50	83	75	76	Claims on Other Banking Insts	32f
7,931	9,110	10,302	10,916	10,122	11,069	11,575	12,714	12,040	13,021	10,603	†10,015	11,662	14,115	22,937	Money	34
3,035	3,559	4,608	4,574	5,829	5,720	5,781	5,910	5,442	6,167	7,771	†5,758	7,036	7,300	8,487	Quasi-Money	35
....	....	....	....	....	....	....	....	....	....	....	260	618	111	482	Restricted Deposits	36b
....	....	....	....	....	....	....	....	....	....	....	56	49	49	49	Counterpart Funds	36e
....	....	....	....	....	....	....	....	....	....	....	504	314	316	1,374	Central Govt. Lending Funds	36f
2,173	2,343	3,501	3,272	4,062	4,509	5,082	10,287	10,765	10,421	10,947	†9,140	12,557	13,812	14,793	Other Items (Net)	37r
10,966	12,669	14,910	15,490	15,951	16,789	17,356	18,624	17,482	19,188	18,374	†15,773	18,698	21,415	31,424	Money plus Quasi-Money	35l
															Other Banking Institutions	
End of Period																
148	129	337	267	443	511	697	1,340	1,250	856	88	†475	1,060	947	1,484	Reserves	40
1	2	1	2	—	2	2	4	2	5	—	†89	96	9	10	Foreign Assets	41
163	116	162	166	246	—	526	11	—	—	—	†—	—	—	—	Claims on Central Government	42a
2,052	2,114	1,995	1,922	2,000	1,991	1,916	1,985	2,200	3,029	4,022	†4,038	3,329	3,334	2,928	Claims on Private Sector	42d
397	345	308	376	456	472	473	387	267	694	760	†709	768	837	963	Time Deposits	45
75	3	4	4	4	—	—	—	—	—	—	†263	153	749	146	Central Government Deposits	46d
221	448	713	635	1,042	1,284	1,551	1,838	1,964	1,588	1,633	†845	688	527	364	Long-Term Foreign Liabilities	46cl
1,156	1,008	866	595	445	235	233	230	296	317	306	†883	896	280	809	Central Govt. Lending Funds	46f
562	....	687	807	825	854	887	918	1,018	1,399	1,494	†2,090	1,971	1,988	1,978	Capital Accounts	47a
-47	-50	-83	-60	-83	-341	-2	-34	-93	-108	-84	†-189	7	-92	161	Other Items (Net)	47r
															Banking Survey	
End of Period																
6,402	6,403	7,633	6,211	5,695	5,612	9,423	14,579	13,835	17,814	17,214	†14,661	19,298	22,295	35,666	Foreign Assets (Net)	51n
8,656	10,390	12,220	14,002	15,519	16,394	13,907	14,493	14,649	13,242	14,496	†14,040	15,435	15,401	14,809	Domestic Credit	52
1,851	1,417	3,885	2,991	3,765	4,316	3,092	3,833	2,924	3,422	2,016	†2,997	3,457	2,523	2,587	Claims on Central Govt. (Net)	52an
6,805	8,973	8,335	11,011	11,754	12,078	10,815	10,660	11,725	9,820	12,480	†11,043	11,978	12,878	12,221	Claims on Private Sector	52d
11,213	12,889	14,887	15,617	15,981	16,781	17,172	17,704	16,525	19,002	19,114	†16,166	18,522	21,360	30,812	Liquid Liabilities	55l
7,781	8,985	9,971	10,667	9,696	10,589	10,918	11,407	10,816	12,141	10,583	†9,699	10,718	13,223	21,362	Money	54
3,432	3,904	4,916	4,950	6,285	6,192	6,254	6,297	5,709	6,861	8,531	†6,467	7,804	8,137	9,450	Quasi-Money	55
....	....	....	....	....	....	....	....	....	....	....	260	618	111	482	Restricted Deposits	56b
....	....	....	....	....	....	....	....	....	....	....	56	49	49	49	Counterpart Funds	56e
1,506	1,358	1,216	945	795	585	583	230	296	317	306	†1,387	1,210	596	2,183	Central Govt. Lending Funds	56f
2,340	1,939	3,749	3,651	4,437	4,641	5,577	11,138	11,664	11,736	12,289	†10,829	14,336	15,578	16,949	Other Items (Net)	57r

Comoros

		1972	1973	1974	1975	1976	1977	1978	1979	1980	1981	1982	1983	1984	1985	1986
Interest Rates															*Percent Per Annum*	
Discount Rate (End of Period)	60	...	...	...	...	...	...	...	...	...	...	...	10.00	10.00	10.00	10.00
Deposit Rate	60l	...	...	...	...	...	...	...	...	...	...	...	7.50	7.50	7.50	7.50
Lending Rate	60p	...	...	...	...	...	...	...	...	...	...	...	15.00	15.00	15.00	15.00
International Transactions															*Millions of Francs*	
Exports	70	1,511	1,106	2,138	2,036	2,824	2,203	2,099	3,701	2,364	4,462	6,435	7,419	3,079	7,048	7,053
Imports, c.i.f.	71	2,932	3,369	6,203	4,974	3,119	4,053	4,329	6,135	6,147	8,791	10,725	13,099	18,778	16,481	12,849
Balance of Payments															*Millions of US Dollars:*	
Current Account, n.i.e.	78ald	...	...	...	...	...	...	...	...	-8.91	-8.16	-10.96	-11.05	-32.72	-14.26	-15.69
Goods: Exports f.o.b.	78aad	...	...	...	...	...	...	...	...	11.19	16.42	19.58	19.47	7.05	15.69	20.37
Goods: Imports f.o.b.	78abd	...	...	...	...	...	...	...	...	-22.37	-24.89	-25.10	-28.80	-32.65	-28.22	-28.54
Trade Balance	78acd	...	...	...	...	...	...	...	...	-11.18	-8.47	-5.52	-9.33	-25.60	-12.53	-8.17
Services: Credit	78add	...	...	...	...	...	...	...	...	2.24	1.10	2.56	2.64	2.65	4.22	6.76
Services: Debit	78aed	...	...	...	...	...	...	...	...	-11.92	-25.31	-25.41	-21.85	-37.66	-35.89	-42.27
Balance on Goods & Services	78afd	...	...	...	...	...	...	...	...	-20.86	-32.67	-28.38	-28.54	-60.61	-44.21	-43.68
Income: Credit	78agd	...	...	...	...	...	...	...	...	.63	.81	1.27	1.27	1.04	.57	1.50
Income: Debit	78ahd	...	...	...	...	...	...	...	...	-.04	-.56	-.71	-1.73	-1.61	-1.97	-3.13
Balance on Gds, Serv. & Inc.	78aid	...	...	...	...	...	...	...	...	-20.27	-32.43	-27.82	-29.00	-61.18	-45.60	-45.32
Current Transfers, n.i.e.: Credit	78ajd	...	...	...	...	...	...	...	...	12.88	28.09	21.85	22.09	33.89	36.61	36.97
Current Transfers: Debit	78akd	...	...	...	...	...	...	...	...	-1.52	-3.82	-4.98	-4.14	-5.43	-5.27	-7.34
Capital Account, n.i.e.	78bcd	...	...	...	...	...	...	...	...	—	—	—	—	—	—	—
Capital Account, n.i.e.: Credit	78bad	...	...	...	...	...	...	...	...	—	—	—	—	—	—	—
Capital Account: Debit	78bbd	...	...	...	...	...	...	...	...	—	—	—	—	—	—	—
Financial Account, n.i.e.	78bjd	...	...	...	...	...	...	...	...	20.59	14.86	18.42	15.21	27.36	18.60	21.18
Direct Investment Abroad	78bdd	...	...	...	...	...	...	...	...	—	—	—	—	—	—	—
Dir. Invest. in Rep. Econ., n.i.e.	78bed	...	...	...	...	...	...	...	...	—	—	—	—	—	—	—
Portfolio Investment Assets	78bfd	...	...	...	...	...	...	...	...	-.41	-.31	.40	—	—	.02	—
Equity Securities	78bkd	...	...	...	...	...	...	...	...	-.41	-.31	.40	—	—	.02	—
Debt Securities	78bld	...	...	...	...	...	...	...	...	—	—	—	—	—	—	—
Portfolio Investment Liab., n.i.e.	78bgd	...	...	...	...	...	...	...	...	—	—	—	—	—	-.24	
Equity Securities	78bmd	...	...	...	...	...	...	...	...	—	—	—	—	—	—	
Debt Securities	78bnd	...	...	...	...	...	...	...	...	—	—	—	—	—	-.24	
Financial Derivatives Assets	78bwd	...	...	...	...	...	...	...	...	...	...	...	...	...	...	...
Financial Derivatives Liabilities	78bxd	...	...	...	...	...	...	...	...	...	...	...	...	...	...	...
Other Investment Assets	78bhd	...	...	...	...	...	...	...	...	—	—	—	-.53	—	-3.00	-1.49
Monetary Authorities	78bod	...	...	...	...	...	...	...	...	—	—	—	—	—	—	—
General Government	78bpd	...	...	...	...	...	...	...	...	—	—	—	—	—	—	—
Banks	78bqd	...	...	...	...	...	...	...	...	—	—	—	-.53	—	-3.00	2.13
Other Sectors	78brd	...	...	...	...	...	...	...	...	—	—	—	—	—	—	-3.63
Other Investment Liab., n.i.e.	78bid	...	...	...	...	...	...	...	...	21.00	15.17	18.01	15.74	27.36	21.82	22.68
Monetary Authorities	78bsd	...	...	...	...	...	...	...	...	—	—	—	—	—	—	—
General Government	78btd	...	...	...	...	...	...	...	...	22.14	13.90	14.32	15.50	26.77	20.27	19.79
Banks	78bud	...	...	...	...	...	...	...	...	-1.14	1.27	1.42	.24	1.46	1.55	-.17
Other Sectors	78bvd	...	...	...	...	...	...	...	...	—	—	2.27	—	-.88	—	3.06
Net Errors and Omissions	78cad	...	...	...	...	...	...	...	...	-15.19	-3.19	-3.75	-2.08	-.49	1.77	-2.02
Overall Balance	78cbd	...	...	...	...	...	...	...	...	-3.51	3.51	3.71	2.08	-5.85	6.12	3.48
Reserves and Related Items	79dad	...	...	...	...	...	...	...	...	3.51	-3.51	-3.71	-2.08	5.85	-6.12	-3.48
Reserve Assets	79dbd	...	...	...	...	...	...	...	...	3.51	-3.51	-3.71	-2.08	5.85	-6.12	-3.48
Use of Fund Credit and Loans	79dcd	...	...	...	...	...	...	...	...	—	—	—	—	—	—	—
Exceptional Financing	79ded	...	...	...	...	...	...	...	...	—	—	—	—	—	—	—
Government Finance															*Millions of Francs:*	
Deficit (-) or Surplus	80	...	...	...	...	...	...	...	...	...	...	-4,084	-6,353	-8,587	-8,126	-4,816
Revenue	81	...	...	...	...	...	...	...	...	...	...	5,036	6,844	6,977	6,482	8,979
Grants Received	81z	...	...	...	...	...	...	...	...	...	...	4,750	6,868	9,279	9,532	9,496
Cash Adj.& Unall.Rev. & Grants	81x	...	...	...	...	...	...	...	...	...	...	-235	-211	-145	3	35
Expenditure	82	...	...	...	...	...	...	...	...	...	...	13,706	19,825	24,636	24,142	23,326
Lending Minus Repayments	83	...	...	...	...	...	...	...	...	...	...	-70	28	61	1	
Financing																
Domestic	84a	...	...	...	...	...	...	...	...	...	...	154	238	-391	563	2,357
Foreign	85a	...	...	...	...	...	...	...	...	...	...	3,930	6,115	8,977	7,563	2,460
Debt: Domestic	88a	...	...	...	...	...	...	...	...	...	...	...	...	797	...	...
Foreign	89a	...	...	...	...	...	...	...	...	...	...	...	...	81,626	...	...
National Accounts															*Billions of Francs*	
Gross Domestic Product (gdp)	99b	10.0	11.0	16.8	15.0	14.4	...	...	...	...	...	...	40.4	44.2	48.1	51.5
															Millions:	
Population	99z	.28	.29	.31	.32	.34	.35	.36	.38	.38	.41	.42	.42	.44	.45	.48

	1987	1988	1989	1990	1991	1992	1993	1994	1995	1996	1997	1998	1999	2000	2001		
Percent Per Annum																**Interest Rates**	
	8.50	8.50	....	....	....					....	....	....	....	....	....	Discount Rate *(End of Period)*...............	60
	6.50	6.50	....	....	....					....	....	....	....	....	....	Deposit Rate	60l
	13.00	13.00	....	....	....					....	....	....	....	....	....	Lending Rate	60p
Millions of Francs																**International Transactions**	
	3,485	6,399	5,809	4,883	7,028	5,847	6,189	4,688	4,236	....	....	....	....	....	....	Exports..	70
	15,560	15,647	13,576	14,041	16,399	18,139	16,817	21,929	23,411	....	....	....	....	....	....	Imports, c.i.f.	71
Minus Sign Indicates Debit																**Balance of Payments**	
	−21.37	−6.52	5.41	−10.48	−10.25	−14.19	9.57	−7.22	−18.96	....	....	....	....	....	....	Current Account, n.i.e.	78ald
	11.60	21.48	18.05	17.93	24.36	21.43	21.58	10.79	11.32							Goods: Exports f.o.b.	78aad
	−44.15	−44.29	−35.65	−45.23	−53.60	−58.27	−49.54	−44.94	−53.50							Goods: Imports f.o.b.	78abd
	−32.55	−22.81	−17.60	−27.29	−29.24	−36.84	−27.96	−34.16	−42.18							*Trade Balance*	78acd
	14.44	16.85	17.55	16.86	24.70	26.59	31.06	28.84	34.51							Services: Credit	78add
	−41.80	−42.29	−39.61	−43.92	−45.72	−52.97	−49.87	−45.59	−49.85							Services: Debit	78aed
	−59.91	−48.26	−39.66	−54.36	−50.26	−63.22	−46.77	−50.91	−57.53							*Balance on Goods & Services*	78afd
	1.80	1.76	4.30	3.35	2.81	3.49	3.30	2.62	3.40							Income: Credit	78agd
	−2.92	−3.94	−2.94	−4.21	−3.74	.46	−1.27	−2.69	−2.39							Income: Debit	78ahd
	−61.03	−50.44	−38.31	−55.21	−51.19	−59.27	−44.74	−50.98	−56.52							*Balance on Gds, Serv. & Inc.*	78aid
	45.86	48.40	49.17	49.41	47.44	56.11	59.83	49.95	41.06							Current Transfers, n.i.e.: Credit	78ajd
	−6.19	−4.48	−5.45	−4.67	−6.50	−11.04	−5.52	−6.19	−3.50							Current Transfers: Debit	78akd
	—	—	—	—	—	—	—	—	—							Capital Account, n.i.e.	78bcd
	—	—	—	—	—	—	—	—	—							Capital Account, n.i.e.: Credit	78bad
	—	—	—	—	—	—	—	—	—							Capital Account: Debit	78bbd
	29.51	4.19	7.54	13.72	−.43	13.48	4.05	18.54	10.87							Financial Account, n.i.e.	78bjd
				−1.10				—	—							Direct Investment Abroad	78bdd
	7.55	3.77	3.27	.39	2.51	−1.45	.19	.18	.89							Dir. Invest. in Rep. Econ., n.i.e.	78bed
	—	—	—	—	—	—	—	—	—							Portfolio Investment Assets	78bfd
	—	—	—	—	—	—	—	—	—							Equity Securities	78bkd
	—	—	—	—	—	—	—	—	—							Debt Securities...........................	78bld
	—	—	—	—	—	—	—	—	—							Portfolio Investment Liab., n.i.e.	78bgd
	—	—	—	—	—	—	—	—	—							Equity Securities	78bmd
	—	—	—	—	—	—	—	—	—							Debt Securities...........................	78bnd
	....	....	....	....	....	....	....	....	....							Financial Derivatives Assets	78bwd
	....	....	....	....	....	....	....	....	....							Financial Derivatives Liabilities........	78bxd
	8.83	−13.71	−6.73	.60	−2.23	.24	−1.45	1.66	−1.83							Other Investment Assets	78bhd
	4.58																Monetary Authorities	78bod
	1.91	−5.24	.66	.60	−2.23	.24	−1.45	1.66	−1.83							General Government	78bpd
	2.34	−8.46	−7.39	—	—	—	—	—	—							Banks	78bqd
	13.14	14.13	11.01	13.82	−.71	14.69	5.30	16.70	11.81							Other Sectors	78brd
	6.82	8.46	7.20	8.07	9.23	−.29	2.99	7.93	2.02							Other Investment Liab., n.i.e.	78bid
	5.26	1.31	2.79	.66	−13.02	12.03	2.06	10.63	8.72							Monetary Authorities	78bsd
	.32	.80	—	—	—	—	—	—	—							General Government	78btd
	.74	3.57	1.01	5.09	3.08	2.96	.25	−1.86	1.06							Banks	78bud
																Other Sectors	78bvd
	.65	−1.39	−7.60	−8.08	−15.18	−5.32	−5.84	−6.33	−1.77							Net Errors and Omissions	78cad
	8.79	−3.72	5.35	−4.84	−25.85	−6.03	7.78	4.99	−9.86							*Overall Balance*	78cbd
	−8.79	3.72	−5.35	4.84	25.85	6.03	−7.78	−4.99	9.86							Reserves and Related Items	79dad
	−8.79	3.72	−5.35	4.84	1.78	−.39	−14.00	−14.97	3.37							Reserve Assets	79dbd
	—	—	—	—	1.19			1.89	—							Use of Fund Credit and Loans..........	79dcd
	—	—	—	—	22.89	6.42	6.22	8.09	6.49							Exceptional Financing	79ded
Year Ending December 31																**Government Finance**	
	6,820 P	....	....	....	....	....	....	....	....	....	....	....	....	....	....	Deficit (-) or Surplus	80
	....	....	....	....	....	....	....	....	....	....	....	....	....	....	....	Revenue	81
	....	....	....	....	....	....	....	....	....	....	....	....	....	....	....	Grants Received.......................................	81z
	....	....	....	....	....	....	....	....	....	....	....	....	....	....	....	Cash Adj.& Unall.Rev. & Grants	81x
	21,037 P	....	....	....	....	....	....	....	....	....	....	....	....	....	....	Expenditure	82
	67 P	....	....	....	....	....	....	....	....	....	....	....	....	....	....	Lending Minus Repayments	83
																Financing	
	....	....	....	....	....	....	....	....	....	....	....	....	....	....	....	Domestic	84a
	....	....	....	....	....	....	....	....	....	....	....	....	....	....	....	Foreign	85a
	....	....	....	....	....	....	....	....	....	....	....	....	....	....	....	Debt: Domestic	88a
	....	....	....	....	....	....	....	....	....	....	....	....	....	....	....	Foreign	89a
Billions of Francs																**National Accounts**	
	51.5	61.7	64.0	66.4	68.3	69.1	75.5	80.4	84.1	....	....	....	....	....	....	Gross Domestic Product (gdp)	99b
Midyear Estimates																	
	.49	.51	.51	.52	.54	.56	.58	.59	.61	.63	.65	.67	.69	.71	.73	**Population**..	99z

(See notes in the back of the book.)

	1972	1973	1974	1975	1976	1977	1978	1979	1980	1981	1982	1983	1984	1985	1986

Exchange Rates

Congo Francs Bill. SDRs through 1990; per Mill. SDRs 1991-93;

| Market Rate .... aa | .002 | .002 | .002 | .002 | .003 | .003 | .004 | .009 | .013 | .021 | .021 | .105 | .132 | .204 | .290 |

Congo Francs/Bill. US$ through 1990; per Mill. US$ 1991-93, per Thous.

| Market Rate .... ae | .002 | .002 | .002 | .002 | .003 | .003 | .003 | .007 | .010 | .018 | .019 | .100 | .135 | .186 | .237 |
| Market Rate .... rf | .002 | .002 | .002 | .002 | .003 | .003 | .003 | .006 | .009 | .015 | .019 | .043 | .120 | .166 | .199 |

Index Numbers (1995=100):

Market Rate .... ahx	125,497.3	9,912.8	9,912.8	9,912.8	6,581.5	73,241.1	75,558.8	36,884.2	22,747.5	15,434.9	10,916.9	7,896.2	1,746.0	1,265.7	1,056.7
Nominal Effective Exchange Rate .... ne c	....	....	....	....	....	....	....	14,472.8	9,116.1	7,225.4	6,062.3	5,026.2	1,319.6	1,091.0	808.3
Real Effective Exchange Rate .... re c	....	....	....	....	....	....	....		462.1	428.1	451.0	525.5	182.5	164.0	164.6

Fund Position

Millions of SDRs:

Quota .... 2f. s	113.00	113.00	113.00	113.00	113.00	113.00	152.00	152.00	228.00	228.00	228.00	291.00	291.00	291.00	291.00
SDRs .... 1b. s	7.36	6.88	6.39	19.96	27.10	.03	4.39	.12	—	.56	.02	20.97		.19	—
Reserve Position in the Fund .... 1c. s	28.27	28.27	28.27	—	—	—	—	—	—	23.46	—	—	—	—	—
Total Fund Cred.&Loans Outstg. 2tl	28.23	28.23	28.23	73.25	180.64	220.33	247.11	271.57	292.75	407.45	492.93	593.87	688.45	735.11	699.67

International Liquidity

Millions of US Dollars Unless Otherwise Indicated:

Total Reserves minus Gold .... 1l. d	123.18	172.79	118.80	47.91	50.28	133.87	125.75	206.69	204.11	151.55	38.87	101.56	137.37	189.71	268.62
SDRs .... 1b. d	7.99	8.30	7.82	23.37	31.49	.04	5.72	.16	—	.65	.02	21.95		.21	—
Reserve Position in the Fund .... 1c. d	30.69	34.10	34.61	—	—	—	—	—	—	27.31	—	—	—	—	—
Foreign Exchange .... 1d. d	84.50	130.39	76.36	24.54	18.79	133.83	120.03	206.53	204.11	123.59	38.85	79.61	137.37	189.50	268.62
Gold (Million Fine Troy Ounces) 1ad	1.454	1.464	.500	.260	.260	.260	.308	.252	.298	.358	.410	.440	.466	.445	.467
Gold (National Valuation) 1and	50.89	51.24	17.50	9.10	10.98	10.98	58.52	91.44	153.07	136.12	156.94	154.55	141.13	145.52	182.55
Monetary Authorities: Other Liab. .... 4.. d	.67	.32	20.71	28.39	18.61	56.82	47.68	47.66	133.08	61.26	168.72	6,572.27	301.04	801.01	487.75
Deposit Money Banks: Assets .... 7a. d	37.49	50.43	72.47	104.99	113.37	149.31	162.07	131.94	171.64	146.60	110.68	109.51	74.65	77.49	104.39
Liabilities .... 7b. d	11.55	14.84	17.00	149.35	48.72	57.33	41.87	47.78	43.97	39.58	50.29	24.69	12.63	17.97	43.50

Monetary Authorities

Millionths of Congo Francs through 1979; Thousandths 1980-87;

Foreign Assets 11	291.50	371.45	227.16	96.12	300.88	401.36	618.88	2,016.92	†3.55	5.26	5.42	286.59	25.70	28.44	106.41
Claims on Central Government 12a	484.31	573.22	1,007.34	1,392.43	2,492.91	3,681.44	6,203.05	8,276.51	†9.44	15.54	30.96	234.50	45.47	47.56	82.55
Claims on Nonfin.Pub.Enterprises 12c	—	—	—	—	—	—	—	—	†—				.45	.57	.81
Claims on Private Sector 12d	—	—	—	96.93	106.80	107.89	14.38	†.01	.02	.37		.34	.44	4.02
Claims on Deposit Money Banks 12e	—	16.00	61.00	45.00	7.00	69.67	36.33	59.33	†.43	.17	.11	1.91	3.83	7.27	12.43
Claims on Other Banking Insts 12f	1.48	1.48	1.48	1.73	1.73	1.74	3.58	3.58	†—		.01	.01	.07	.55	1.11
Reserve Money 14	521.88	612.48	748.19	1,051.40	1,918.62	2,474.23	3,863.27	3,160.48	†6.77	10.78	20.65	330.41	52.20	66.66	107.03
of which: Currency Outside DMBs 14a	325.52	400.61	530.29	684.57	955.77	1,552.03	2,665.99	1,361.93	†4.18	6.97	10.94	20.47	29.34	40.98	63.29
Time & Foreign Currency Deposits 15	33.05	160.14	168.91	10.03	30.10	44.56	139.54	320.11	†.20	.46	.97	.17	.36	.98	.72
Restricted Deposits 16b	14.57	20.37	17.50	70.71	139.23	778.78	1,491.18	1,958.36	†1.46	1.39	2.72	601.19	7.51	2.99	10.32
Foreign Liabilities 16c	52.31	57.41	92.31	190.62	655.73	898.75	1,241.90	2,736.53	†5.04	9.76	13.64	722.28	131.58	299.14	318.43
Central Government Deposits 16d	38.91	40.77	68.20	81.10	92.05	119.73	898.41	1,217.79	†1.07	2.47	4.08	178.29	1.40	1.68	3.97
Counterpart Funds 16e	16.35	13.18	7.48	5.82	20.44	46.17	86.55	126.91	†.01	.03	.06	6.21	.36	.51	.38
Capital Accounts 17a	99.42	96.32	96.59	98.26	498.97	433.58	821.14	1,005.99	†1.83	2.22	1.96	899.90	14.28	29.30	51.15
Other Items (Net) 17r	.81	−38.51	−3.35	27.35	−455.69	−534.83	−1,572.26	−155.44	†−2.94	−6.11	−7.22	−2,215.45	−118.97	−300.34	−268.21

Deposit Money Banks

Millionths of Congo Francs through 1979; Thousandths 1980-87;

Reserves 20	158.25	156.92	188.68	265.67	903.21	771.47	1,167.34	1,374.08	†2.37	3.37	8.00	10.37	20.15	22.41	40.26
Foreign Assets 21	62.61	84.22	121.03	175.33	325.38	413.59	544.56	890.63	†1.71	2.67	2.12	10.99	10.06	14.41	24.74
Claims on Central Government 22a	81.14	76.37	128.53	156.13	297.78	300.50	393.20	422.17	†.54	.58	.58	.59	.84	.95	2.13
Claims on Nonfin.Pub.Enterprises 22c	5.82	25.80	42.75	114.99	85.47	94.89	49.10	40.27	†.02	.10	.05	.05	.21	.04	.26
Claims on Private Sector 22d	286.00	430.41	734.38	943.44	1,090.35	1,583.57	1,995.40	2,768.31	†3.67	4.22	5.97	9.39	14.69	18.24	31.90
Claims on Other Banking Insts 22f	—	—	—	.17	.20	.30	.30	.30	†—						
Demand Deposits 24	406.49	501.46	718.13	735.76	1,136.91	1,663.42	2,575.47	3,646.00	†4.53	6.37	12.27	20.79	27.39	31.73	54.16
Time & Foreign Currency Deposits 25	98.86	129.90	200.80	291.63	299.50	559.53	709.69	967.64	†1.38	1.67	2.54	2.97	4.14	5.19	8.51
Restricted Deposits 26b	15.05	21.37	63.05	67.25	206.48	266.40	213.20	183.38	†.32	1.24	.28	.83	.61	4.29	6.04
Foreign Liabilities 26c	19.28	24.78	28.40	249.41	139.83	158.80	140.67	322.54	†.44	.72	.96	2.48	1.70	3.34	10.31
Central Government Deposits 26d	8.37	8.57	9.44	12.62	29.07	28.83	97.81	159.33	†.22	.27	.42	2.68	1.33	1.67	1.45
Counterpart Funds 26e	.01	.05	.03	—	—	.56	.59	.03	†—	—	—	—	—	—	—
Credit from Monetary Authorities 26g	—	16.00	61.00	45.00	7.00	69.67	36.33	59.33	†.43	.17	.11	1.91	3.83	7.27	12.43
Capital Accounts 27a	67.82	74.32	86.33	100.90	151.56	173.55	205.38	348.88	†.56	.86	1.28	2.59	4.69	7.28	15.76
Other Items (Net) 27r	−22.08	−2.72	48.20	153.17	732.05	243.54	170.76	−191.36	†.42	−.34	−1.16	−2.86	2.28	−4.72	−9.38
Post Office: Checking Deposits .... 24.. i	9.59	12.48	16.58	21.51	21.68	21.16	20.06	22.48	†.03	.03	.03	.03	.04	.05	.08

Monetary Survey

Millionths of Congo Francs through 1979; Thousandths 1980-87;

Foreign Assets (Net) 31n	282.51	373.49	227.48	−168.58	−169.31	−242.61	−219.13	−151.53	†−.21	−2.55	−7.07	−427.17	−97.52	−259.63	−197.59
Domestic Credit 32	821.05	1,070.43	1,853.42	2,536.68	3,965.94	5,641.82	7,776.36	10,170.89	†12.41	17.76	33.46	63.59	59.39	65.06	117.45
Claims on Central Govt. (Net) 32an	527.76	612.74	1,074.81	1,476.35	2,691.26	3,854.53	5,620.09	7,344.05	†8.71	13.41	27.07	54.14	43.62	45.22	79.35
Claims on Nonfin.Pub.Enterprises 32c	5.82	25.80	42.75	114.99	85.47	94.89	49.10	40.27	†.02	.10	.05	.05	.67	.61	1.07
Claims on Private Sector 32d	286.00	430.41	734.38	943.44	1,187.28	1,690.37	2,103.29	2,782.69	†3.68	4.24	6.34	9.39	15.03	18.68	35.92
Claims on Other Banking Insts 32f	1.48	1.48	1.48	1.89	1.93	2.04	3.88	3.88	†—		.01	.01	.07	.55	1.11
Money 34	776.59	962.17	1,294.74	1,529.64	2,198.67	3,421.83	5,361.91	5,233.45	†9.03	14.00	24.69	339.03	58.11	74.95	119.66
Quasi-Money 35	131.91	290.04	369.71	301.66	329.59	604.10	849.23	1,287.74	†1.58	2.13	3.51	3.14	4.50	6.17	9.24
of which: Fgn. Currency Deposits 35x											.77	.87	1.18	2.68	3.05
Restricted Deposits 36b	29.62	41.74	181.70	137.95	345.71	1,045.19	1,704.38	2,141.73	†1.78	2.62	3.00	602.02	8.13	7.29	16.36
Counterpart Funds 36e	16.36	13.23	7.51	5.82	20.44	46.74	87.15	126.94	†.01	.03	.06	6.21	.36	.51	.38
Capital Accounts 37a	167.25	170.64	182.92	199.16	650.53	607.14	1,026.52	1,354.88	†2.39	3.08	3.25	902.49	18.97	36.59	66.91
Revaluation Accounts 37ar													−72.08	−100.19	1.69
Other Items (Net) 37r	−18.16	−33.91	44.32	193.86	251.69	−325.77	−1,471.96	−125.38	†−2.60	−6.65	−8.13	−2,216.48	−43.25	−203.79	−277.93
Money plus Quasi-Money 35l	908.50	1,252.21	1,664.45	1,831.30	2,528.27	4,025.93	6,211.14	6,521.20	†10.61	16.13	28.21	342.17	62.61	81.12	128.90

Exchange Rates

per Thous. SDRs 1994-97; per SDR Thereafter: End of Period

	1987	1988	1989	1990	1991	1992	1993	1994	1995	1996	1997	1998	1999	2000	2001		
Market Rate	.622	1.229	1.991	9.484	†.304	9.121	480.746	†47.445	220.461	1,662.282	1,430.205	†3.450	6.176	65.146	....	Market Rate	aa

US$ 1994-97, per US$ thereafter: End of Period(ae) Period Average(rf

	1987	1988	1989	1990	1991	1992	1993	1994	1995	1996	1997	1998	1999	2000	2001		
Market Rate	.438	.913	1.515	6.667	†.212	6.633	350.000	†32.500	148.310	1,156.000	1,060.000	†2.450	4.500	50.000	....	Market Rate	ae
Market Rate	.375	.623	1.271	2.395	†.052	2.151	25.144	†11.941	70.245	501.849	1,313.448	†1.607	4.018	21.818	....	Market Rate	rf

Period Averages

	1987	1988	1989	1990	1991	1992	1993	1994	1995	1996	1997	1998	1999	2000	2001		
Market Rate	573.3	348.0	167.6	100.0	11.5	.3	—	—	100.0	13.8	4.1	3.5	1.4	.4	...	Market Rate	ahx
Nominal Effective Exchange Rate	405.0	263.5	161.2	100.0	11.8	.3	—	—	100.0						—	Nominal Effective Exchange Rate	ne c
Real Effective Exchange Rate	140.3	145.5	145.5	119.3	115.7	112.9	149.7	113.8	100.0	99.5	122.0	126.8	340.8	279.6	253.2	Real Effective Exchange Rate	re c

Fund Position

End of Period

	1987	1988	1989	1990	1991	1992	1993	1994	1995	1996	1997	1998	1999	2000	2001		
Quota	291.00	291.00	291.00	291.00	291.00	291.00	291.00	291.00	291.00	291.00	291.00	291.00	291.00	291.00	291.00	Quota	2f, s
SDRs	.08	—	3.74	—	—	—	—	—	—	—	—	—	—	—	—	SDRs	1b, s
Reserve Position in the Fund	—														—	Reserve Position in the Fund	1c, s
Total Fund Cred.&Loans Outstg.	681.26	584.07	478.19	366.28	330.31	330.31	330.31	327.27	326.37	301.26	301.26	300.71	300.03	300.02	300.02	Total Fund Cred.&Loans Outstg.	2tl

International Liquidity

End of Period

	1987	1988	1989	1990	1991	1992	1993	1994	1995	1996	1997	1998	1999	2000	2001		
Total Reserves minus Gold	180.77	186.94	195.08	219.07	182.85	156.73	46.20	120.69	146.60	82.50	....	....	....	....	....	Total Reserves minus Gold	1l. d
SDRs	.11	—	4.91	—	—	—	—	—	—							SDRs	1b. d
Reserve Position in the Fund	—															Reserve Position in the Fund	1c. d
Foreign Exchange	180.66	186.94	190.17	219.07	182.85	156.73	46.20	120.69	146.60	82.50	....	....	....	....	....	Foreign Exchange	1d. d
Gold (Million Fine Troy Ounces)	.488	.450	.216	.108	.029	.028	.022	.028	.028	....	.054	....	....	....	....	Gold (Million Fine Troy Ounces)	1ad
Gold (National Valuation)	237.41	184.57	86.62	42.23	10.25	9.32	8.59	10.71	10.83	....	15.80	....	....	....	....	Gold (National Valuation)	1an d
Monetary Authorities: Other Liab.	248.26	264.08	198.68	217.99	305.63	290.50	272.40	280.95	331.50	....	....					Monetary Authorities: Other Liab.	4.. d
Deposit Money Banks: Assets	125.48	94.58	174.81	131.61	86.13	68.00	62.37	81.18	69.18	....						Deposit Money Banks: Assets	7a. d
Liabilities	48.33	47.34	67.55	53.13	39.62	27.72	27.31	31.29	16.75	....						Liabilities	7b. d

Monetary Authorities

Congo Fr. 1988-91;Thousands 1992-93; Millions Beg. 1994: End of Period

	1987	1988	1989	1990	1991	1992	1993	1994	1995		
Foreign Assets	169.01	†.26	.53	1.71	46.64	†1.22	66.82	†5.15	25.28	Foreign Assets	11
Claims on Central Government	108.05	†.44	1.15	5.41	79.28	†2.43	41.83	†1.68	1.67	Claims on Central Government	12a
Claims on Nonfin.Pub.Enterprises	1.02	†.01	.01	.08	4.31	†.01	.02	†.01	.32	Claims on Nonfin.Pub.Enterprises	12c
Claims on Private Sector	4.86	†.01	.02	.03	.20	†.03	.80	†.03	.70	Claims on Private Sector	12d
Claims on Deposit Money Banks	50.75	†.05	.13	.16	.06	†—	1.27	†.16	8.23	Claims on Deposit Money Banks	12e
Claims on Other Banking Insts	1.34	†—	—	.01	.03	†—	.07	†.01	.93	Claims on Other Banking Insts	12f
Reserve Money	214.97	†.47	.84	2.39	58.17	†2.58	69.99	†2.35	17.67	Reserve Money	14
of which: Currency Outside DMBs	120.85	†.28	.51	1.42	36.15	†1.21	46.93	†2.77	16.84	of which: Currency Outside DMBs	14a
Time & Foreign Currency Deposits	1.33	†—	.01	.11	5.12	†.03	6.88	†.71	1.52	Time & Foreign Currency Deposits	15
Restricted Deposits	14.39	†.04	.07	.41	11.17	†.20	12.62	†1.00	4.87	Restricted Deposits	16b
Foreign Liabilities	532.45	†.96	1.25	4.93	165.15	†4.94	254.14	†24.66	121.12	Foreign Liabilities	16c
Central Government Deposits	4.06	†.04	.10	.24	1.48	†.03	.34	†.30	.66	Central Government Deposits	16d
Counterpart Funds	.35	†—	—	—	—	†—	—	—	—	Counterpart Funds	16e
Capital Accounts	80.81	†.27	.40	1.17	29.82	†1.07	45.37	†4.12	24.84	Capital Accounts	17a
Other Items (Net)	-491.37	†-1.00	-.83	-1.85	-140.37	†-5.17	-278.53	†-26.11	-133.53	Other Items (Net)	17r

Deposit Money Banks

Congo Fr. 1988-91;Thousands 1992-93; Millions Beg. 1994: End of Period

	1987	1988	1989	1990	1991	1992	1993	1994	1995		
Reserves	90.77	†.15	.29	.64	17.59	†1.31	21.22	†.26	.64	Reserves	20
Foreign Assets	55.00	†.09	.26	.88	18.28	†.45	21.83	†2.64	10.26	Foreign Assets	21
Claims on Central Government	8.39	†.01	.02	.04	.14	†—	.23	†.18	.08	Claims on Central Government	22a
Claims on Nonfin.Pub.Enterprises	—	†	—	.02	.21	†—	.08	†.08	.17	Claims on Nonfin.Pub.Enterprises	22c
Claims on Private Sector	76.44	†.13	.21	.38	3.22	†.14	2.46	†.70	3.51	Claims on Private Sector	22d
Claims on Other Banking Insts	—	†	—	—	—	†—	—	—	—	Claims on Other Banking Insts	22f
Demand Deposits	103.19	†.19	.33	.70	19.61	†1.26	16.18	†.92	1.87	Demand Deposits	24
Time & Foreign Currency Deposits	22.84	†.08	.09	.36	6.52	†.23	10.77	†1.41	6.30	Time & Foreign Currency Deposits	25
Restricted Deposits	12.09	†.01	.06	.18	1.58	†.02	1.94	†.06	.21	Restricted Deposits	26b
Foreign Liabilities	21.18	†.04	.10	.35	8.41	†.18	9.56	†1.02	2.48	Foreign Liabilities	26c
Central Government Deposits	4.35	†.01	.02	.05	.60	†.05	1.00	†—	—	Central Government Deposits	26d
Counterpart Funds	1.44	†—								Counterpart Funds	26e
Credit from Monetary Authorities	50.75	†.05	.13	.16	.06	†—	1.27	†.16	8.23	Credit from Monetary Authorities	26g
Capital Accounts	18.09	†.04	.11	.32	2.13	†.10	1.14	†.20	4.12	Capital Accounts	27a
Other Items (Net)	-3.32	†-.04	-.06	-.17	.52	†.05	3.96	†.09	-8.56	Other Items (Net)	27r
Post Office: Checking Deposits	.40	†—								Post Office: Checking Deposits	24.. i

Monetary Survey

Congo Fr. 1988-91;Thousands 1992-93; Millions Beg. 1994: End of Period

	1987	1988	1989	1990	1991	1992	1993	1994	1995		
Foreign Assets (Net)	-329.62	†-.65	-.56	-2.70	-108.64	†-3.45	-175.05	†-17.89	-88.06	Foreign Assets (Net)	31n
Domestic Credit	192.08	†.55	1.29	5.67	85.31	†2.53	44.15	†2.38	6.73	Domestic Credit	32
Claims on Central Govt. (Net)	108.43	†.41	1.04	5.16	77.34	†2.35	40.72	†1.56	1.09	Claims on Central Govt. (Net)	32an
Claims on Nonfin.Pub.Enterprises	1.02	†.01	.01	.09	4.52	†.01	.10	†.08	.49	Claims on Nonfin.Pub.Enterprises	32c
Claims on Private Sector	81.30	†.13	.23	.41	3.42	†.16	3.26	†.73	4.21	Claims on Private Sector	32d
Claims on Other Banking Insts	1.34	†—	—	.01	.03	†—	.07	†.01	.93	Claims on Other Banking Insts	32f
Money	228.29	†.50	.88	2.42	60.19	†2.54	64.95	†3.73	18.89	Money	34
Quasi-Money	24.17	†.08	.10	.47	11.64	†.26	17.65	†2.11	7.83	Quasi-Money	35
of which: Fgn. Currency Deposits	7.36	†.02	.05	.34	10.88	†.23	16.27	†2.09	7.74	of which: Fgn. Currency Deposits	35x
Restricted Deposits	26.47	†.05	.13	.59	12.75	†.23	14.56	†1.07	5.08	Restricted Deposits	36b
Counterpart Funds	1.79	†—								Counterpart Funds	36e
Capital Accounts	98.90	†.31	.51	1.49	31.95	†1.17	46.51	†4.32	28.97	Capital Accounts	37a
Revaluation Accounts	-55.23	†-.29	1.21	3.01	-78.61	†-2.87	-115.72	†-14.35	-68.58	Revaluation Accounts	37ar
Other Items (Net)	-439.97	†-.74	-2.11	-5.00	-61.25	†-2.25	-158.85	†-12.39	-73.52	Other Items (Net)	37r
Money plus Quasi-Money	252.46	†.58	.98	2.89	71.82	†2.80	82.60	†5.84	26.72	Money plus Quasi-Money	35l

	1972	1973	1974	1975	1976	1977	1978	1979	1980	1981	1982	1983	1984	1985	1986
Other Banking Institutions									*Millionths of Congo Francs through 1979; Thousandths in 1980:*						
Claims on Private Sector **42d**	8.79	12.64	19.32	26.49	35.78	43.56	52.54	70.38	†.10	....	....	....	....	....	....
Sight Deposits **44**	.80	2.44	7.07	10.69	13.65	25.91	30.66	53.54	†.09	....	....	....	....	....	....
Time and Savings Deposits........ **45**	21.38	24.45	31.75	38.04	49.30	57.59	73.56	145.27	†.15	....	....	....	....	....	....
Central Govt. Lending Funds **46f**	10.10	10.28	10.46	5.56	5.56	5.56	5.56	—	†—	....	....	....	....	....	....
Other Items (Net)...................... **47r**	−23.48	−24.52	−29.97	−27.80	−32.73	−45.50	−57.23	−128.44	†−.14	....	....	....	....	....	....
Interest Rates															
Discount Rate *(End of Period)* **60**	....	....	....	....	....	....	12.0	12.0	12.0	12.0	15.0	20.0	20.0	26.0	26.0
Deposit Rate **60l**	....	....	....	....	....	....									
Lending Rate **60p**	....	....	....	....	....	....	....	....	....	....	....	....	....	....	....
Prices													*Index Numbers (1995=100):*		
Consumer Prices **64**	—	—		†	—	—								†—	
Mining Production(1980=100)...... **66zx**	100.3[e]	109.7	113.1	109.9	98.1	103.5	94.6	88.7	100.0	106.6	102.1	106.0	110.5		
International Transactions													*Millions of US Dollars*		
Exports .... **70..d**	738	1,013	1,381	865	944	989	931	1,514	1,627	544	399	1,080	1,005	950	1,100
Imports, c.i.f. .... **71..d**	208	251	349	300	224	203	196	199	278	223	160	157	685	792	875
Balance of Payments													*Millions of US Dollars:*		
Financial Derivatives Assets ...... **78bw d**	....	....	....	....	....										
Financial Derivatives Liabilities ...... **78bx d**	....	....	....	....	....										
Government Finance									*Millionths of Congo Francs through 1979; Thousandths (.000) 1980-87;*						
Deficit (-) or Surplus.................. **80**	−273.33	−470.00	−1,081.00	−720.33	−2,090.00	−1,498.67	−1,984.67	−1,828.67	†−1.11	−7.19	−11.61	....	....		
Revenue **81**	1,021.00	1,284.33	1,780.33	1,450.33	1,635.33	2,293.67	2,463.33	6,601.00	†12.66	15.81	20.60	38.21	89.50	142.40	166.83
Grants Received **81z**	126.67	181.00	180.00	184.67	274.00	471.67	570.33	1,585.67	†2.84	3.87	3.35				
Expenditure **82**	1,415.67	1,927.33	2,854.00	2,359.33	4,020.33	4,261.00	5,020.67	10,002.67	†16.60	26.88	35.49	....	....		
Lending Minus Repayments **83**	5.33	8.00	187.33	−4.00	−21.00	3.00	−2.33	12.67	†.01	—	.07				
Financing															
Domestic **84a**	92.67	106.33	686.00	374.33	1,737.00	974.67	1,752.00	1,616.33	†.69	4.79	10.69	....	....	5.20	33.30
Foreign **85a**	180.67	363.67	395.00	346.00	353.00	524.00	232.67	212.33	†.42	2.41	.92	....	....		
Debt: Domestic **88a**	572.33	653.67	1,140.67	1,541.00	2,774.67	3,816.00	5,689.00	8,129.67	†10.41	16.60	27.31	....	....	49.50	83.13
Foreign **89a**	477.00	889.00	1,272.33	1,595.67	3,041.00	3,581.67	4,777.67	9,513.33	†25.32	43.78	26.93	....	585.80		
National Accounts									*Millions of Congo Francs through 1979; Thousandths (.000) 1980-87;*						
Househ.Cons.Expend.,incl.NPISHs **96f**	2,166	2,683	3,135	4,068	6,964	9,495	12,707	22,288	†110	147	212	386	768	908	1,248
Government Consumption Expend. **91f**	883	1,041	1,426	1,506	1,851	2,574	2,978	6,190	†9	20	25	36	62	92	129
Gross Fixed Capital Formation **93e**	1,238	1,240	1,837	1,825	2,186	4,572	3,167	5,086	†12	16	24	48	100	133	206
Changes in Inventories **93i**	51	233		218	286	506	189	2,177	†3	4	−3	−4	−1	16	6
Exports of Goods and Services **90c**	1,258	1,872	2,724	1,732	3,089	3,723	4,054	9,140	†23	30	37	87	237	323	397
Imports of Goods and Services (-) **98c**	1,739	2,152	3,125	2,951	4,842	7,683	4,828	7,865	†21	30	33	80	220	277	377
Gross Domestic Product (GDP) **99b**	3,858	4,918	5,997	6,393	9,533	13,187	18,267	37,017	†133	183	262	473	946	1,196	1,609
Net Primary Income from Abroad **98.n**	—	—				−500			†−3	−7	−6	−14	−55	9	−88
Gross National Income (GNI) **99a**	3,140	4,220	5,055	5,284	7,779	10,506	14,200	28,274	†130	180	257	463	896	1,111	1,533
Net National Income **99e**	2,793	3,783	4,634	4,872	7,194	8,481	11,868	23,230	†127	173	249	448	867	1,075	1,484
GDP Volume 1987 Prices(Thousands) **99b.p**	248	268	277	263	249	251	237	238	244	249	248	252	266	267	280
GDP Volume (1995=100)................. **99bvp**	135.9	146.9	151.5	144.0	136.3	137.4	130.0	130.6	133.5	136.6	136.0	137.9	145.5	146.2	153.1
GDP Deflator (1995=100)............. **99bip**	—	—	—	—	—	—	—	—	—	—	—	—	—	—	—
															Millions:
Population.................................. **99z**	22.86	23.51	24.17	†22.58	23.29	24.02	24.78	†25.56	26.38	27.23	28.12	29.04	29.92	30.98	31.50

	1987	1988	1989	1990	1991	1992	1993	1994	1995	1996	1997	1998	1999	2000	2001	

End of Period

Other Banking Institutions

| .... | .... | .... | .... | .... | .... | .... | .... | .... | .... | .... | .... | .... | .... | .... | Claims on Private Sector | 42d |

(Other Banking Institutions rows all ....)
- Claims on Private Sector 42d
- Sight Deposits 44
- Time and Savings Deposits 45
- Central Govt. Lending Funds 46f
- Other Items (Net) 47r

Percent Per Annum — **Interest Rates**

	1987	1988	1989	1990	1991	1992	1993	1994	1995	1996	1997	1998	1999	2000	2001	
Discount Rate *(End of Period)*	29.0	37.0	50.0	45.0	55.0	55.0	95.0	145.0	125.0	238.0	13.0	22.0	120.0	120.0	....	60
Deposit Rate	....	....	....	....	....	....	....	60.0	60.0	60.0	13.0					60l
Lending Rate	....	....	....	....	....	....	....	398.3	293.9	247.0	134.6	29.0	124.6	165.0	....	60p

Period Averages — **Prices**

	1987	1988	1989	1990	1991	1992	1993	1994	1995	1996	1997	1998	1999	2000	2001	
Consumer Prices	—	†—	—	—	—	†—	.1	15.6	100.0	758.8	2,090.7	†—	....	....	....	64
Mining Production(1980=100)	....	....	....	....	....	....	....	....	....	....	....	....	....	....	....	66zx

Millions of US Dollars — **International Transactions**

	1987	1988	1989	1990	1991	1992	1993	1994	1995	1996	1997	1998	1999	2000	2001	
Exports	974	1,120	999	830	426	368	419	438	592	....	....	....	....	....	....	70..d
Imports, c.i.f.	756	763	850	888	711	420	372	382	397	424	....	....	....	....	....	71..d

Minus Sign Indicates Debit

Balance of Payments
- Financial Derivatives Assets .... 78bw d
- Financial Derivatives Liabilities .... 78bx d

Government Finance

Congo Fr. 1988-91;Thousands 1992-93; Millions Beg. 1994: Yr.End. Dec 31

	1987	1988	1989	1990	1991	1992	1993	1994	1995	1996	1997	1998	1999	2000	2001	
Deficit (-) or Surplus	....	†-.44	—	-1.46	-67.82	†-2.65	-36.94	†-1.23	.08	-9.34	-62.91					80
Revenue	293.47	†.54	1.31	2.26	23.51	†.59	12.16	†2.08	21.20	156.88	403.64					81
Grants Received	....	†.13	.25	.48	5.29	†.06	.30	†.17	11.77	170.91	322.98					81z
Expenditure	....	†1.11	1.56	4.20	96.62	†3.06	48.31	†3.31	32.89	337.13	789.53					82
Lending Minus Repayments	....	†—				†.24	1.09	†.17								83
Financing																
Domestic	28.33	†.44	-.03	1.46	67.82	†2.54	35.96	†1.06	-.08	9.34	62.91					84a
Foreign	....	†—	.04	—	—	†.11	.99	†.17								85a
Debt: Domestic	111.00	†.45	.30	1.76	77.34	†2.35	40.72	†1.56	1.75	36.54	303.63					88a
Foreign	....	†6.42	10.90	63.14	490.57	†20.38	239.25	†116.45	921.66	7,018.96	11,871.33					89a

National Accounts

Congo Fr. 1988-91;Thousands 1992-93; Millions in 1995

	1987	1988	1989	1990	1991	1992	1993	1994	1995	1996	1997	1998	1999	2000	2001	
Househ.Cons.Expend.,incl.NPISHs	2,261	†4	9	16	377	†12	217	....	324	....	....					96f
Government Consumption Expend.	285	†1	1	3	63	†4	42	....	20	....	....					91f
Gross Fixed Capital Formation	398	†1	2	3	29	†1	6	....	38	....	....					93e
Changes in Inventories	8	†—		-1	-2	†—	-1	....	-1	....	....					93i
Exports of Goods and Services	747	†1	3	6	103	†4	31	....	113	....	....					90c
Imports of Goods and Services (-)	827	†2	3	6	110	†3	25	....	94	....	....					98c
Gross Domestic Product (GDP)	2,870	†6	11	22	472	†18	269	....	400	....	....					99b
Net Primary Income from Abroad	-134	†—	—	-1	-6	†—	—	....	....	....	....					98.n
Gross National Income (GNI)	2,763	†5	11	22	467	†18	269	....	344	....	....					99a
Net National Income	2,677	†5	11	21	453	†17	268	....	332	....	....					99e
GDP Volume 1987 Prices(Thousands)	287	288	285	266	244	218	189	181	183	181	171					99b.p
GDP Volume (1995=100)	157.2	157.9	155.9	145.7	133.4	119.4	103.3	99.3	100.0	99.1	93.4	....	....	....	....	99bv p
GDP Deflator (1995=100)	—	—	—	—	—	—	.1	....	100.0	....	....	....	....	....	....	99bi p

Midyear Estimates

	1987	1988	1989	1990	1991	1992	1993	1994	1995	1996	1997	1998	1999	2000	2001	
Population	32.46	33.46	34.49	35.56	36.67	40.10	41.77	43.37	44.83	46.12	47.28	48.39	49.58	50.95	52.52	99z

(See notes in the back of the book.)

Congo, Republic of

634

		1972	1973	1974	1975	1976	1977	1978	1979	1980	1981	1982	1983	1984	1985	1986
Exchange Rates															*Francs per SDR:*	
Official Rate	aa	278.00	284.00	272.08	262.55	288.70	285.76	272.28	264.78	287.99	334.52	370.92	436.97	470.11	415.26	394.78
															Francs per US Dollar:	
Official Rate	ae	256.05	235.42	222.22	224.27	248.49	235.25	209.00	201.00	225.80	287.40	336.25	417.37	479.60	378.05	322.75
Official Rate	rf	252.03	222.89	240.70	214.31	238.95	245.68	225.66	212.72	211.28	271.73	328.61	381.07	436.96	449.26	346.31
Fund Position															*Millions of SDRs:*	
Quota	2f. s	13.00	13.00	13.00	13.00	13.00	13.00	17.00	17.00	25.50	25.50	25.50	37.30	37.30	37.30	37.30
SDRs	1b. s	2.58	2.46	2.33	2.15	2.06	1.48	1.31	1.20	—	.90	.96	.21	2.13	1.51	3.80
Reserve Position in the Fund	1c. s	1.75	1.84	1.93	2.03	2.03	—	—	—	—	—	2.06	3.30	2.98	.48	.48	.48
Total Fund Cred.&Loans Outstg.	2tl	—	—	—	—	—	9.34	16.68	21.58	17.44	12.70	12.63	12.27	11.12	8.99	16.03
International Liquidity												*Millions of US Dollars Unless Otherwise Indicated:*					
Total Reserves minus Gold	1l. d	10.34	7.86	24.10	13.81	12.17	13.53	9.43	42.23	85.90	123.37	37.01	7.36	4.11	3.96	6.82
SDRs	1b. d	2.80	2.97	2.85	2.52	2.39	1.80	1.71	1.58	—	1.05	1.06	.22	2.09	1.66	4.65
Reserve Position in the Fund	1c. d	1.90	2.22	2.37	2.38	2.36	—	—	—	—	2.40	3.64	3.12	.47	.53	.59
Foreign Exchange	1d. d	5.63	2.67	18.88	8.92	7.41	11.73	7.72	40.65	85.90	119.92	32.32	4.02	1.56	1.78	1.58
Gold (Million Fine Troy Ounces)	1ad	....	....	....	—	—	.006	.009	.011	.011	.011	.011	.011	.011	.011	.011
Gold (National Valuation)	1an d	....	....	....	—	—	.92	1.94	5.79	6.56	4.45	5.00	4.21	3.44	3.60	4.36
Monetary Authorities: Other Liab.	4.. d	.09	.04	.08	.06	3.62	3.96	2.76	2.14	1.65	1.53	.72	.47	1.40	.85	.69
Deposit Money Banks: Assets	7a. d	2.59	3.35	4.99	3.21	5.80	6.84	14.11	15.93	13.89	26.31	19.88	13.84	20.93	32.19	30.89
Liabilities	7b. d	11.78	9.10	12.06	21.07	24.97	57.31	63.37	64.79	56.79	93.93	81.13	95.05	106.82	138.92	169.43
Monetary Authorities															*Billions of Francs:*	
Foreign Assets	11	2.64	1.81	5.36	3.10	3.02	3.40	2.38	9.66	20.89	37.02	14.12	4.84	3.62	2.87	3.60
Claims on Central Government	12a	2.65	3.98	4.20	7.86	9.06	11.47	15.18	16.41	17.65	16.30	36.39	40.96	51.45	45.12	60.81
Claims on Deposit Money Banks	12e	4.74	5.41	4.55	5.91	7.58	8.77	11.24	10.27	4.08	8.82	21.94	30.68	38.27	40.65	46.11
Claims on Other Banking Insts	12f	....	....	....	....	....	....	....	....	....	....	....	....	....	....	....
Reserve Money	14	8.36	9.43	12.35	15.31	16.43	17.30	17.55	21.26	27.73	33.03	46.00	47.90	47.39	52.94	53.91
of which: Currency Outside DMBs	14a	7.99	9.15	11.86	14.34	15.29	16.13	16.53	19.17	23.06	31.21	44.21	44.33	45.03	50.19	51.09
Foreign Liabilities	16c	.02	.01	.02	.01	.90	4.00	6.59	8.61	9.04	8.94	9.61	10.92	11.13	7.79	9.13
Central Government Deposits	16d	.36	.34	.44	.29	.72	.41	1.31	1.62	2.03	16.61	12.48	12.17	29.11	22.33	36.83
Capital Accounts	17a	—	.02	.02	.02	.04	.04	.04	.04	1.42	1.21	1.61	1.70	1.57	1.35	1.47
Other Items (Net)	17r	1.29	1.40	1.28	1.23	1.56	1.89	3.32	4.82	2.40	2.35	2.76	3.79	4.14	4.23	9.18
Deposit Money Banks															*Billions of Francs:*	
Reserves	20	.37	.29	.48	.97	1.14	1.17	1.02	2.09	4.67	1.83	1.78	3.58	2.36	2.75	2.78
Foreign Assets	21	.66	.77	1.11	.72	1.44	†1.61	2.95	3.20	3.14	7.56	6.69	5.78	10.04	12.17	9.97
Claims on Central Government	22a	2.73	2.60	3.92	5.45	6.36	9.14	10.54	9.02	10.15	12.73	17.54	28.15	40.24	38.42	44.01
Claims on Nonfin.Pub.Enterprises	22c	....	....	....	....	....	....	....	....	....	....	....	....	....	....	....
Claims on Private Sector	22d	16.06	18.50	21.26	28.23	35.83	†38.93	39.42	45.59	56.00	94.20	131.15	151.95	180.56	201.24	202.88
Claims on Other Banking Insts	22f	....	....	....	....	....	....	....	....	....	....	....	....	....	....	....
Claims on Nonbank Financial Insts	22g	....	....	....	....	....	....	....	....	....	....	....	....	....	....	....
Demand Deposits	24	6.93	8.03	12.13	12.83	16.06	†14.76	16.65	20.65	31.50	44.47	54.41	47.58	57.66	63.73	48.12
Time and Savings Deposits	25	1.27	1.41	1.86	2.14	2.61	3.87	3.92	5.30	7.06	17.01	18.35	23.33	20.92	35.62	32.99
Foreign Liabilities	26c	2.89	1.23	1.20	2.01	2.25	8.50	7.75	7.52	6.98	13.79	9.46	25.29	19.36	14.89	13.39
Long-Term Foreign Liabilities	26cl	.12	.87	1.48	2.71	3.95	4.98	5.49	5.50	5.84	13.21	17.82	14.39	31.88	37.63	41.30
Central Government Deposits	26d	1.34	1.38	1.54	1.67	1.32	2.28	1.50	.97	1.37	4.86	17.38	33.02	41.95	42.15	53.15
Credit from Monetary Authorities	26g	4.21	4.54	4.27	5.55	6.66	8.77	11.24	10.27	5.08	9.11	21.94	30.74	38.27	40.65	46.11
Capital Accounts	27a	2.86	3.19	3.70	4.33	6.61	6.46	7.04	9.03	12.81	13.17	20.99	23.74	28.70	33.95	39.53
Other Items (Net)	27r	.20	1.52	.61	4.13	5.32	†1.22	.33	.65	3.32	.72	−3.19	−8.63	−5.53	−14.04	−14.93
Post Office: Checking Deposits	24.. i	.31	.28	.43	.55	.60	.53	.53	.53	.53	.53	2.59	3.65	5.07	5.43	5.46
Postal Debt	26c. i	1.61	1.45	2.36	3.03	3.99	6.06	6.78	6.05	6.19	5.56	1.18	3.20	2.57	.35	.83
Monetary Survey															*Billions of Francs:*	
Foreign Assets (Net)	31n	.39	1.35	5.25	1.79	1.31	†−7.49	−9.01	−3.27	8.00	21.85	1.74	−25.59	−16.83	−7.63	−8.94
Domestic Credit	32	19.74	23.37	27.41	39.59	49.20	†56.85	62.33	68.43	80.40	101.76	155.23	175.87	201.19	220.31	217.72
Claims on Central Govt. (Net)	32an	3.68	4.87	6.14	11.35	13.37	17.92	22.91	22.85	24.40	7.56	24.07	23.92	20.63	19.06	14.84
Claims on Nonfin.Pub.Enterprises	32c	....	....	....	....	....	....	....	....	....	....	....	....	....	....	....
Claims on Private Sector	32d	16.06	18.50	21.26	28.23	35.83	†38.93	39.42	45.59	56.00	94.20	131.15	151.95	180.56	201.24	202.88
Claims on Other Banking Insts	32f	....	....	....	....	....	....	....	....	....	....	....	....	....	....	....
Claims on Nonbank Financial Inst	32g	....	....	....	....	....	....	....	....	....	....	....	....	....	....	....
Money	34	14.92	17.18	24.00	27.17	31.34	†30.89	33.18	39.82	54.56	75.67	98.62	91.91	102.69	113.92	99.24
Quasi-Money	35	1.27	1.41	1.86	2.14	2.61	3.87	3.92	5.30	7.06	17.01	18.35	23.33	20.92	35.62	32.99
Other Items (Net)	37r	3.94	6.14	6.80	12.07	16.56	†14.60	16.21	20.04	26.78	30.93	39.99	35.05	60.75	63.13	76.56
Money plus Quasi-Money	35l	16.19	18.58	25.85	29.31	33.95	†34.76	37.10	45.12	61.62	92.68	116.97	115.24	123.61	149.54	132.22
Interest Rates															*Percent Per Annum*	
Discount Rate *(End of Period)*	60	4.50	4.50	5.50	5.50	6.50	6.50	6.50	8.50	8.50	8.50	8.50	8.50	8.50	9.00	8.00
Deposit Rate	60l	....	....	....	....	....	....	5.75	5.50	5.50	6.50	6.50	7.50	7.50	8.25	8.10
Lending Rate	60p	....	....	....	....	....	....	13.00	9.00	11.00	11.00	11.00	12.00	12.00	12.00	11.50
Prices and Production															*Index Numbers (1995=100):*	
Wholesale Prices (1990=100)	63	21.0	22.1	25.5	29.0	32.9	†37.0	40.6	44.3	50.5	57.4	66.2	70.8	81.1	86.4	89.7
Consumer Prices	64	....	....	....	....	....	....	....	....	....	....	....	....	....	60.6	63.1
Crude Petroleum Production	66aa	3.6	22.6	24.7	19.3	22.7	19.9	26.4	29.5	35.4	44.3	49.1	57.9	65.0	64.1	64.2

	1987	1988	1989	1990	1991	1992	1993	1994	1995	1996	1997	1998	1999	2000	2001		
Exchange Rates																	
End of Period																	
Official Rate	378.78	407.68	380.32	364.84	370.48	378.57	404.89	†780.44	728.38	753.06	807.94	791.61	†896.19	918.49	935.39		aa
End of Period (ae) Period Average (rf)																	
Official Rate	267.00	302.95	289.40	256.45	259.00	275.32	294.77	†534.60	490.00	523.70	598.81	562.21	†652.95	704.95	744.31		ae
Official Rate	300.54	297.85	319.01	272.26	282.11	264.69	283.16	†555.20	499.15	511.55	583.67	589.95	†615.70	711.98	733.04		rf
Fund Position																	
End of Period																	
Quota	37.30	37.30	37.30	37.30	37.30	57.90	57.90	57.90	57.90	57.90	57.90	57.90	84.60	84.60	84.60		2f. s
SDRs	1.91	.84	1.21	1.17	.04	.04	.01	.03	.02	.01	.01	—	.08	.03	.15		1b. s
Reserve Position in the Fund	.48	.48	.48	.47	.47	.47	.47	.47	.50	.54	.54	.54	.54	.54	.54		1c. s
Total Fund Cred.&Loans Outstg.	13.56	11.40	8.75	7.61	4.00	4.00	3.50	14.00	12.50	26.40	24.83	24.26	21.14	31.71	30.81		2tl
International Liquidity																	
End of Period																	
Total Reserves minus Gold	3.40	4.70	6.10	5.91	4.76	4.01	1.34	50.36	59.30	90.99	59.92	.84	39.35	222.01	68.91		1l.d
SDRs	2.71	1.13	1.59	1.66	.06	.06	.02	.05	.03	.02	.01	.01	.11	.04	.19		1b.d
Reserve Position in the Fund	.68	.65	.63	.67	.67	.65	.64	.68	.75	.77	.72	.75	.74	.70	.67		1c.d
Foreign Exchange	.01	2.93	3.88	3.58	4.03	3.31	.68	49.63	58.52	90.20	59.19	.08	38.51	221.27	68.05		1d.d
Gold (Million Fine Troy Ounces)	.011	.011	.011	.011	.011	.011	.011	.011	.011	.011	.011	.011	.011	.011	.011		1ad
Gold (National Valuation)	5.37	4.52	3.52	3.98	3.94	3.70	4.42	†4.21	4.29	4.10	3.24	3.21	†3.23	3.03	3.09		1and
Monetary Authorities: Other Liab.	1.50	†130.34	144.14	34.87	66.41	43.48	38.71	17.20	18.62	16.48	13.53	35.97	25.10	24.66	22.97		4..d
Deposit Money Banks: Assets	38.61	47.75	39.22	48.90	50.71	68.00	82.84	41.43	33.16	33.17	27.79	29.01	34.07	140.68	21.84		7a.d
Liabilities	85.21	71.80	60.61	59.31	63.58	96.22	58.86	50.04	28.91	25.81	14.13	41.82	39.17	17.98	17.79		7b.d
Monetary Authorities																	
End of Period																	
Foreign Assets	2.35	†5.81	5.87	6.74	2.25	2.12	1.67	29.21	31.17	49.81	37.81	2.27	27.80	158.64	53.60		11
Claims on Central Government	59.95	†53.37	55.19	†51.63	73.25	72.61	77.25	80.75	92.48	110.27	123.14	120.76	128.71	173.15			12a
Claims on Deposit Money Banks	41.55	†28.66	31.44	28.14	†14.85	6.84	1.51	1.54	4.26	3.70	5.01	7.16	6.20	6.45	2.44		12e
Claims on Other Banking Insts	....	12.39	11.94	13.03	12.26	—									—		12f
Reserve Money	59.53	†53.72	52.70	71.02	57.29	66.33	63.50	85.97	93.09	101.08	112.80	89.44	120.07	243.82	186.79		14
of which: Currency Outside DMBs	56.87	†51.20	49.91	66.20	53.28	59.32	53.71	69.49	81.58	87.35	93.26	73.26	102.34	123.87	142.91		14a
Foreign Liabilities	7.08	†44.13	45.04	11.72	18.68	13.49	12.83	20.12	18.23	28.51	28.17	39.43	35.33	46.51	45.91		16c
Central Government Deposits	28.86	†2.48	4.51	17.40	4.22	4.01	4.95	22.34	15.87	24.01	19.59	11.33	12.77	21.03	12.90		16d
Capital Accounts	1.51	†5.42	5.08	4.74	4.90	5.44	6.10	9.35	8.51	8.68	8.99	8.50	9.82	10.89	11.20		17a
Other Items (Net)	6.87	†-5.53	-4.72	-1.77	-4.09	-7.06	-11.58	-29.78	-19.53	-16.30	-16.46	-16.13	-23.24	-28.45	-27.61		17r
Deposit Money Banks																	
End of Period																	
Reserves	2.63	†2.35	2.46	4.09	3.84	4.42	9.68	12.05	7.41	8.99	15.08	13.85	12.72	105.99	30.07		20
Foreign Assets	10.31	†14.03	11.35	12.54	13.13	18.72	24.42	22.15	16.25	17.37	16.64	16.31	22.25	99.17	16.25		21
Claims on Central Government	30.95	†45.16	41.45	39.81	36.96	†36.78	17.84	30.76	28.91	29.45	25.74	28.74	20.12	26.43	15.07		22a
Claims on Nonfin.Pub.Enterprises	....	38.92	32.17	27.23	27.62	26.78	11.28	10.17	13.75	13.96	13.35	16.16	13.98	10.65	6.98		22c
Claims on Private Sector	186.91	†107.02	112.32	119.58	122.97	122.33	66.02	75.62	85.68	98.09	106.53	112.01	158.00	109.59	101.03		22d
Claims on Other Banking Insts	....	.53	.95	1.09	1.26	.41	.06	.06	.02	.01	.30	.13	.78	.08	—		22f
Claims on Nonbank Financial Insts	....	.78	.29	.69	.62	.26	.40	.60	.84	1.05	1.16	1.33	.63	.05	.98		22g
Demand Deposits	47.08	†46.17	46.35	54.10	58.73	57.40	41.94	60.57	49.16	61.08	68.85	68.39	76.68	171.74	81.36		24
Time and Savings Deposits	36.13	†39.07	45.13	46.84	48.61	49.86	28.48	24.78	24.34	31.00	35.14	31.94	26.84	24.70	19.93		25
Foreign Liabilities	12.70	†13.41	14.60	12.87	†12.81	24.81	17.18	26.75	14.04	13.51	8.45	23.51	25.57	12.67	13.24		26c
Long-Term Foreign Liabilities	10.06	†3.03	2.94	2.34	†3.66	1.68	.17	—	.13	.01	.01	—					26cl
Central Government Deposits	49.93	†52.16	16.95	17.15	19.48	†18.08	2.61	6.10	11.03	12.65	10.95	17.44	25.53	56.16	11.83		26d
Credit from Monetary Authorities	41.55	†28.66	31.44	28.14	†14.85	6.84	1.51	1.54	4.26	3.70	5.01	7.16	6.20	6.45	2.44		26g
Capital Accounts	40.75	†36.59	54.45	57.07	†56.84	57.41	36.24	41.05	54.40	59.64	62.30	45.04	62.95	36.19	48.65		27a
Other Items (Net)	-7.38	†-10.30	-10.86	-13.50	-8.58	†-6.38	1.57	-9.42	-4.51	-12.65	-11.91	-4.96	4.70	44.04	-7.08		27r
Post Office: Checking Deposits	5.26	2.56	....												....		24.. i
Postal Debt	1.17																26c. i
Monetary Survey																	
End of Period																	
Foreign Assets (Net)	-7.11	†-40.73	-45.36	-7.65	†-19.77	-19.13	-4.09	4.49	15.02	25.15	17.82	-44.36	-10.86	198.63	10.70		31n
Domestic Credit	199.02	†203.52	231.04	222.06	†229.61	†237.72	160.65	165.98	183.04	198.39	226.80	252.73	275.96	198.32	272.48		32
Claims on Central Govt. (Net)	12.11	†43.88	73.37	60.45	†64.89	†87.94	82.89	79.58	82.75	85.27	105.46	123.10	102.58	77.94	163.49		32an
Claims on Nonfin.Pub.Enterprises	....	38.92	32.17	27.23	27.62	26.78	11.28	10.17	13.75	13.96	13.35	16.16	13.98	10.65	6.98		32c
Claims on Private Sector	186.91	†107.02	112.32	119.58	122.97	122.33	66.02	75.62	85.68	98.09	106.53	112.01	158.00	109.59	101.03		32d
Claims on Other Banking Insts	....	12.92	12.89	14.12	13.52	.41	.06	.06	.02	.01	.30	.13	.78	.08	—		32f
Claims on Nonbank Financial Inst	....	.78	.29	.69	.62	.26	.40	.60	.84	1.05	1.16	1.33	.63	.05	.98		32g
Money	103.98	†97.54	96.59	121.03	112.17	119.32	95.76	134.49	134.85	153.18	166.56	143.98	184.03	309.58	238.08		34
Quasi-Money	36.13	†39.07	45.13	46.84	48.61	49.86	28.48	24.78	24.34	31.00	35.14	31.94	26.84	24.70	19.93		35
Other Items (Net)	51.81	†26.18	43.96	46.54	†49.06	†49.41	32.32	11.20	38.87	39.37	42.92	32.45	54.23	62.67	25.16		37r
Money plus Quasi-Money	140.10	†136.61	141.72	167.87	160.79	169.17	124.24	159.27	159.19	184.17	201.70	175.92	210.87	334.28	258.01		35l
Interest Rates																	
Percent Per Annum																	
Discount Rate (End of Period)	8.00	9.50	10.00	11.00	10.75	12.00	11.50	†7.75	8.60	7.75	7.50	7.00	7.60	7.00	6.50		60
Deposit Rate	7.79	7.81	8.00	†7.50	7.50	7.50	7.75	8.08	5.50	5.46	5.00	5.00	5.00	5.00	5.00		60l
Lending Rate	11.13	11.79	12.50	†18.50	18.15	17.77	17.46	17.50	16.00	22.00	22.00	22.00	22.00	22.00	20.67		60p
Prices and Production																	
Period Averages																	
Wholesale Prices (1990=100)	93.8	96.0	98.1	100.0	96.4	98.0	101.0	....	....	....	....	....	....	....	....		63
Consumer Prices	63.4	64.1	62.9	64.7	63.6	61.3	64.1	91.4	100.0	110.0	....	124.1	130.8	129.7	129.8		64
Crude Petroleum Production	68.2	75.9	85.9	86.6	86.9	93.2	102.9	97.4	100.0	112.0	125.0	132.3	346.1	239.2	220.3		66aa

Congo, Republic of

		1972	1973	1974	1975	1976	1977	1978	1979	1980	1981	1982	1983	1984	1985	1986
International Transactions															*Billions of Francs*	
Exports	70	15.00	19.62	54.86	38.25	52.95	65.51	69.56	105.43	192.40	220.43	326.15	243.82	516.76	488.52	268.99
Imports, c.i.f.	71	25.80	28.00	29.90	35.59	40.24	50.45	58.35	64.86	122.54	121.31	251.90	246.97	269.95	268.70	206.65
Imports, f.o.b.	71.v	22.63	22.17	24.68	29.42	33.90	42.88	47.76	55.89	100.29	98.92	205.75	200.96	219.60	218.63	168.14
Balance of Payments															*Millions of US Dollars:*	
Current Account, n.i.e.	78ald	...	...	...	...	...	...	−180.6	−99.4	−166.7	−460.7	−331.5	−400.9	210.2	−161.3	−600.7
Goods: Exports f.o.b.	78aa d							308.2	495.7	910.6	1,072.7	1,108.5	1,066.2	1,268.4	1,144.7	672.6
Goods: Imports f.o.b.	78ab d							−282.1	−363.0	−545.2	−803.6	−663.8	−649.5	−617.6	−630.1	−512.4
Trade Balance	78ac d							26.1	132.7	365.4	269.1	444.7	416.7	650.8	514.7	160.2
Services: Credit	78ad d							68.8	69.7	110.6	84.0	77.6	87.8	80.3	74.7	103.1
Services: Debit	78ae d							−259.2	−219.8	−480.1	−713.3	−697.3	−727.4	−391.3	−525.6	−656.8
Balance on Goods & Services	78af d							−164.3	−17.4	−4.0	−360.2	−175.1	−222.9	339.8	63.8	−393.5
Income: Credit	78ag d							3.4	3.3	8.0	16.6	19.6	5.4	6.5	9.1	8.1
Income: Debit	78ah d							−58.0	−96.3	−169.6	−128.8	−158.0	−179.3	−133.5	−237.2	−234.2
Balance on Gds, Serv. & Inc.	78ai d							−218.9	−110.4	−165.6	−472.3	−313.4	−396.8	212.9	−164.2	−619.6
Current Transfers, n.i.e.: Credit	78aj d							67.1	50.5	85.3	71.6	37.2	51.3	55.1	51.0	69.1
Current Transfers: Debit	78ak d							−28.7	−39.4	−86.4	−59.9	−55.3	−55.4	−57.8	−48.0	−50.3
Capital Account, n.i.e.	78bc d							—	—	—	—	—	—	—	—	—
Capital Account, n.i.e.: Credit	78ba d							—	—	—	—	—	—	—	—	—
Capital Account: Debit	78bb d							—	—	—	—	—	—	—	—	—
Financial Account, n.i.e.	78bj d							168.4	91.8	174.9	327.8	202.1	297.9	−291.5	38.6	154.3
Direct Investment Abroad	78bd d							—	—	—	—	—	—	—	—	—
Dir. Invest. in Rep. Econ., n.i.e.	78be d							4.1	16.5	40.0	30.8	35.3	56.1	34.9	12.7	22.4
Portfolio Investment Assets	78bf d							—	—	—	—	—	—	—	—	—
Equity Securities	78bk d							—	—	—	—	—	—	—	—	—
Debt Securities	78bl d							—	—	—	—	—	—	—	—	—
Portfolio Investment Liab., n.i.e.	78bg d							—	—	—	—	—	—	—	—	—
Equity Securities	78bm d							—	—	—	—	—	—	—	—	—
Debt Securities	78bn d							—	—	—	—	—	—	—	—	—
Financial Derivatives Assets	78bw d															
Financial Derivatives Liabilities	78bx d															
Other Investment Assets	78bh d							−17.7	−14.0	−93.8	−183.8	−44.4	33.9	−255.5	8.6	157.8
Monetary Authorities	78bo d															
General Government	78bp d								−1.5	.1	—	.3	1.4	—	—	...
Banks	78bq d							−7.2	−.9	−.3	−16.3	2.3	1.0	−9.8	−4.7	6.3
Other Sectors	78br d							−10.5	−11.6	−93.6	−167.5	−47.0	31.5	−245.8	13.4	151.5
Other Investment Liab., n.i.e.	78bi d							182.0	89.3	228.7	480.8	211.1	208.0	−70.9	17.3	−26.0
Monetary Authorities	78bs d							1.5	−.8	−.3	−.2	−.6	−.1	−.6	−.3	−.1
General Government	78bt d							98.9	35.4	119.6	−4.4	183.3	77.7	31.1	−8.0	−177.3
Banks	78bu d							−3.8	−1.1	2.2	21.4	.2	36.3	−2.6	−12.6	−11.4
Other Sectors	78bv d							85.5	55.8	107.2	463.6	28.2	94.0	−100.1	38.2	162.8
Net Errors and Omissions	78ca d							−1.4	29.9	38.5	174.6	45.0	70.9	20.5	41.7	48.1
Overall Balance	78cb d							−13.6	22.3	46.7	41.8	−84.5	−32.1	−60.8	−81.0	−398.2
Reserves and Related Items	79da d							13.6	−22.3	−46.7	−41.8	84.5	32.1	60.8	81.0	398.2
Reserve Assets	79db d							4.6	−28.5	−49.3	−57.1	82.2	32.4	7.8	1.8	−2.0
Use of Fund Credit and Loans	79dc d							9.0	6.4	−5.3	−5.7	−.1	−.4	−1.2	−2.2	8.7
Exceptional Financing	79de d							—	−.1	7.8	21.0	2.4	—	54.2	81.4	391.6
Government Finance															*Billions of Francs:*	
Deficit (-) or Surplus	80							...	...	†−18.8	.4	−93.4	−26.7	...	...	
Total Revenue and Grants	81y	18.8	20.1	44.1	47.8	48.3		...	...	†160.0	215.1	262.9	284.0			
Revenue	81	18.8	20.1	44.1	47.8	48.3				157.4	214.3	261.7	280.5			
Grants	81z	—	—	—	—	—				†2.6	.8	1.2	3.5			
Exp. & Lending Minus Repay.	82z									†178.8	214.7	356.3	310.7			
Expenditure	82									†177.9	214.3	355.6	310.5			
Lending Minus Repayments	83									†.9	.4	.7	.2			
Total Financing	80h									†18.8	−.4	93.4	26.7			
Domestic	84a									†4.9	−.3	24.2	−15.0			
Foreign	85a									†13.9	−.1	69.2	41.6			
Total Debt by Residence	88									...	...	...	...			
Domestic	88a															
Foreign	89a															
National Accounts															*Billions of Francs*	
Househ.Cons.Expend.,incl.NPISHs	96f	66.5	64.7	76.3	109.5	120.9	123.2	117.9	...	147.9	220.6	281.6	317.0	372.2	403.6	380.5
Government Consumption Expend.	91f	27.6	28.2	37.8	54.3	61.2	61.2	45.5	...	63.4	72.8	95.8	120.0	141.7	159.7	159.8
Gross Fixed Capital Formation	93e	21.2	23.9	31.7	41.2	36.1	32.8	46.4	...	118.7	239.7	404.7	280.2	277.3	276.9	182.9
Changes in Inventories	93i	...	...	...	...	...	...	7.9	...	10.2	21.1	24.0	4.3	14.0	17.1	5.7
Exports of Goods and Services	90c	29.3	38.2	75.0	59.4	71.2	...	78.6	...	203.0	314.3	383.5	454.2	590.7	551.9	255.2
Imports of Goods and Services (-)	98c	53.6	52.4	83.3	104.8	116.0	...	97.9	...	182.8	326.9	478.1	376.3	437.3	438.3	343.7
Gross Domestic Product (GDP)	99b	91.0	102.6	137.0	159.6	173.4	181.7	198.3	254.5	360.4	541.7	711.5	799.4	958.5	970.8	640.1
Net Primary Income from Abroad	98.n	−4.6	−10.5	...	...	...	...	...	...	−32.7	−33.2	−59.6	−62.9	−67.6	−102.4	−41.9
Gross National Income (GNI)	99a	...	...	...	...	...	...	...	...	327.7	508.5	650.4	736.4	890.9	868.4	598.5
GDP Volume 1975 Prices	99b.p	134.9	143.3	165.0	159.6	159.4	150.6	148.2	162.7	188.4	...	...	...	...	...	
GDP Volume 1978 Prices	99b.p	...	...	...	...	...	...	...	...	248.6	301.4	372.4	393.3	421.7	416.8	388.1
GDP Volume (1995=100)	99bv p	43.4	46.1	53.1	51.4	51.3	48.5	47.7	52.4	60.6	73.5	90.8	95.9	102.8	101.6	94.6
GDP Deflator (1995=100)	99bi p	19.8	21.1	24.4	29.4	32.0	35.5	39.4	46.0	56.3	69.8	74.2	78.9	88.3	90.4	64.0
															Millions:	
Population	99z	1.26	1.29	1.32	1.35	1.39	1.44	1.45	1.49	1.53	1.72	1.77	1.81	1.87	1.92	1.98

Congo, Republic of

Billions of Francs — International Transactions

1987	1988	1989	1990	1991	1992	1993	1994	1995	1996	1997	1998	1999	2000	2001		
292.40	279.20	397.70	267.10	290.50	312.00	302.63	532.40	585.30	688.10	958.80	747.60	1,074.10	1,978.20	....	Exports	70
294.37	331.45	328.49	169.02	167.68	119.48	164.79	350.41	334.18	793.31	538.18	478.95	287.58	466.49	....	Imports, c.i.f.	71
239.52	269.69	267.26	137.54	136.44	97.22	134.08	340.20	324.50	770.20	522.50	393.15	244.65	321.30	....	Imports, f.o.b.	71.v

Balance of Payments — *Minus Sign Indicates Debit*

1987	1988	1989	1990	1991	1992	1993	1994	1995	1996	1997	1998	1999	2000	2001		
-222.7	-445.5	-85.0	-251.2	-461.5	-316.6	-552.7	-793.4	-649.7	-1,109.0	-251.9	....	....	....	....	Current Account, n.i.e.	78al d
876.7	843.2	1,160.5	1,388.7	1,107.7	1,178.7	1,119.1	958.9	1,167.0	1,554.5	1,744.1	....	....	....	....	Goods: Exports f.o.b.	78aa d
-419.9	-522.7	-532.0	-512.7	-494.5	-438.2	-500.1	-612.7	-650.7	-1,361.0	-802.9	....	....	....	....	Goods: Imports f.o.b.	78ab d
456.8	320.5	628.5	876.0	613.2	740.5	619.1	346.2	516.3	193.5	941.3	....	....	....	....	*Trade Balance*	78ac d
97.2	92.3	95.3	99.2	99.3	66.1	56.2	67.0	76.3	91.1	55.7	....	....	....	....	Services: Credit	78ad d
-532.1	-560.1	-494.0	-769.1	-786.6	-737.5	-845.5	-995.8	-778.5	-721.1	-565.2	....	....	....	....	Services: Debit	78ae d
21.9	-147.4	229.8	206.0	-74.1	69.1	-170.2	-582.7	-185.9	-436.5	431.8	....	....	....	....	*Balance on Goods & Services*	78af d
30.5	7.5	2.2	14.7	18.8	12.5	11.3	2.0	3.0	11.7	5.1	....	....	....	....	Income: Credit	78ag d
-286.2	-313.3	-363.3	-474.9	-401.6	-379.7	-384.9	-291.1	-459.4	-670.1	-668.9	....	....	....	....	Income: Debit	78ah d
-233.8	-453.2	-131.3	-254.2	-456.9	-298.1	-543.9	-871.8	-642.3	-1,094.9	-232.0	....	....	....	....	*Balance on Gds, Serv. & Inc.*	78ai d
88.8	79.8	119.7	86.3	74.1	54.8	50.5	111.3	30.9	29.9	24.7	....	....	....	....	Current Transfers, n.i.e.: Credit	78aj d
-77.7	-72.0	-73.4	-83.4	-78.7	-73.3	-59.3	-33.0	-38.3	-44.0	-44.5	....	....	....	....	Current Transfers: Debit	78ak d
—	—	—	—	—	—	—	—	—	—	—	....	....	....	....	Capital Account, n.i.e.	78bc d
—	—	—	—	—	—	—	—	—	—	—	....	....	....	....	Capital Account, n.i.e.: Credit	78ba d
—	—	—	—	—	—	—	—	—	—	—	....	....	....	....	Capital Account: Debit	78bb d
-293.1	-62.3	-326.7	-72.0	9.6	-153.8	-111.2	605.4	-80.3	657.2	-173.7	....	....	....	....	Financial Account, n.i.e.	78bj d
															Direct Investment Abroad	78bd d
43.4	9.1	—	—	—	—	—	—	—	—	—	....	....	....	....	Dir. Invest. in Rep. Econ., n.i.e.	78be d
—	—	—	—	—	—	—	—	—	—	—	....	....	....	....	Portfolio Investment Assets	78bf d
															Equity Securities	78bk d
															Debt Securities	78bl d
															Portfolio Investment Liab., n.i.e.	78bg d
															Equity Securities	78bm d
															Debt Securities	78bn d
															Financial Derivatives Assets	78bw d
															Financial Derivatives Liabilities	78bx d
-150.8	-59.0	-7.8	-67.9	35.1	-24.9	-22.6	35.5	-10.4	.4	-3.6	....	....	....	....	Other Investment Assets	78bh d
															Monetary Authorities	78bo d
-1.1	-13.9	—	-56.2	2.5	-18.5	-14.8	33.9	-13.4	-3.5	-7.4	....	....	....	....	General Government	78bp d
-149.6	-45.0	-7.8	-11.8	32.6	-6.4	-7.8	1.6	3.0	3.9	3.8	....	....	....	....	Banks	78bq d
															Other Sectors	78br d
-185.8	-12.4	-318.9	-4.0	-25.5	-128.8	-88.6	569.9	-69.9	656.8	-170.1	....	....	....	....	Other Investment Liab., n.i.e.	78bi d
.3	-.4	-1.4													Monetary Authorities	78bs d
-106.1	-66.5	-233.8	-110.9	-227.6	-257.3	-288.9	88.4	-432.5	-317.3	-386.7	....	....	....	....	General Government	78bt d
-3.4															Banks	78bu d
-76.5	54.4	-83.7	106.9	202.1	128.5	200.2	481.4	362.6	974.1	216.6	....	....	....	....	Other Sectors	78bv d
27.6	40.6	8.5	-40.6	-6.3	40.4	244.0	33.1	120.7	102.1	-122.1	....	....	....	....	Net Errors and Omissions	78ca d
-488.2	-467.2	-403.2	-363.9	-458.2	-429.9	-420.0	-154.9	-609.3	-349.7	-547.7	....	....	....	....	*Overall Balance*	78cb d
488.2	467.2	403.2	363.9	458.2	429.9	420.0	154.9	609.3	349.7	547.7	....	....	....	....	Reserves and Related Items	79da d
4.7	-1.7	—	-112.9	32.1	-26.8	-1.7	-55.5	-6.4	-16.8	21.6	....	....	....	....	Reserve Assets	79db d
-3.1	-2.9	-3.4	-1.5	-4.9	—	-.7	15.0	-2.3	20.1	-2.1	....	....	....	....	Use of Fund Credit and Loans	79dc d
486.6	471.8	406.6	478.2	431.0	456.8	422.4	195.4	618.1	346.4	528.2	....	....	....	....	Exceptional Financing	79de d

Government Finance — *Year Ending December 31*

1987	1988	1989	1990	1991	1992	1993	1994	1995	1996	1997	1998	1999	2000	2001		
....	....	....	....	....	-109.7	-95.9	-129.9	-86.3	-24.5	-109.6	-226.0	-81.4	26.5	117.5 P	Deficit (-) or Surplus	80
....	....	....	208.5	....	174.4	183.2	230.6	260.4	362.1	401.6	266.8	394.1	611.3	642.4 P	Total Revenue and Grants	81y
					174.4	183.1	220.2	249.7	357.8	400.2	263.2	387.8	604.5	637.4 P	Revenue	81
						.1	10.4	10.7	4.3	1.4	3.6	6.3	6.8	5.0 P	Grants	81z
					284.1	279.1	360.5	346.6	386.6	511.2	492.8	475.5	584.8	524.9 P	Exp. & Lending Minus Repay.	82z
					276.3	279.1	360.5	346.6	386.6	511.2	492.8	475.5	584.8	524.9 P	Expenditure	82
					7.8									— P	Lending Minus Repayments	83
						125.9	129.9	86.2	24.5	109.6	226.0	81.5	-26.5	....	Total Financing	80h
						91.4	12.9	15.9	-51.1	-77.3	39.7	-4.0	-71.8	....	Domestic	84a
						34.5	117.0	70.3	75.6	186.9	186.3	85.4	45.3	....	Foreign	85a
												4,112.3	3,681.5	....	Total Debt by Residence	88
												390.0	433.6	....	Domestic	88a
												3,722.4	3,247.9	....	Foreign	89a

National Accounts — *Billions of Francs*

1987	1988	1989	1990	1991	1992	1993	1994	1995	1996	1997	1998	1999	2000	2001		
390.7	396.3	408.5	403.2	418.7	430.1	434.7	499.9	510.5	524.1	611.1	807.2	597.5	437.3	517.3	Househ.Cons.Expend.,incl.NPISHs	96f
142.1	138.7	144.6	153.5	186.3	192.4	182.3	200.8	137.0	189.1	270.7	245.6	228.5	249.9	214.6	Government Consumption Expend.	91f
104.0	129.2	126.7	131.2	151.1	159.8	140.7	439.6	362.3	412.3	294.5	279.9	287.7	658.3	773.8	Gross Fixed Capital Formation	93e
-7.8	-6.5	-3.8	-10.1	6.7	7.9	4.2	13.8	24.0	13.9	8.6	27.0	17.2	5.0	7.3	Changes in Inventories	93i
288.3	267.7	368.1	382.4	314.9	323.1	323.5	557.6	615.0	829.5	974.6	741.7	1,087.6	1,934.7	1,738.2	Exports of Goods and Services	90c
266.7	266.4	270.6	298.2	309.0	336.9	325.3	725.4	592.6	669.3	803.8	951.4	853.2	1,150.7	1,229.4	Imports of Goods and Services (-)	98c
690.6	659.0	758.2	762.1	768.7	775.5	760.2	982.3	1,056.2	1,299.7	1,355.7	1,150.1	1,365.3	2,134.5	2,021.9	Gross Domestic Product (GDP)	99b
-76.7	-90.2	-112.8	-125.3	-108.0	-97.4	-105.8	-160.5	-198.2	-463.1	-445.0	-232.0	-474.4	-546.3	513.0	Net Primary Income from Abroad	98.n
613.8	568.7	645.4	636.8	660.7	684.9	662.6	780.9	858.0	836.6	910.7	918.1	890.9	1,588.2	1,508.9	Gross National Income (GNI)	99a
....	....	....	....	....	....	....	....	....	....	....	....	....	....	....	GDP Volume 1975 Prices	99b.p
388.8	395.7	402.7	411.7	421.4	428.7	424.5	401.3	410.1	....	....	....	....	....		GDP Volume 1978 Prices	99b.p
94.8	96.5	98.2	100.4	102.8	104.5	103.5	97.9	100.0	104.3	103.8	107.7	104.2	112.6	....	GDP Volume (1995=100)	99bv p
69.0	64.7	73.1	71.9	70.8	70.2	69.5	95.0	100.0	118.0	123.7	101.1	124.0	179.5	....	GDP Deflator (1995=100)	99bi p

Midyear Estimates

1987	1988	1989	1990	1991	1992	1993	1994	1995	1996	1997	1998	1999	2000	2001		
2.04	2.10	2.16	2.22	2.30	2.37	2.44	2.52	2.60	2.68	2.76	2.85	2.93	3.02	3.11	**Population**	99z

(See notes in the back of the book.)

Costa Rica

		1972	1973	1974	1975	1976	1977	1978	1979	1980	1981	1982	1983	1984	1985	1986
Exchange Rates															*Colones per SDR:*	
Market Rate	aa	7.20	8.02	10.49	10.03	9.96	10.41	11.16	11.29	10.93	42.01	44.40	45.44	46.81	58.99	72.02
															Colones per US Dollar:	
Market Rate	ae	6.64	6.65	8.57	8.57	8.57	8.57	8.57	8.57	8.57	36.09	40.25	43.40	47.75	53.70	58.88
Market Rate	rf	6.64	6.65	7.93	8.57	8.57	8.57	8.57	8.57	8.57	21.76	37.41[e]	41.09	44.53	50.45	55.99
														Index Numbers (1995=100):		
Market Rate	ahx	2,702.5	2,697.8	2,282.5	2,092.3	2,092.3	2,092.3	2,092.3	2,092.3	2,092.3	909.9	480.8[e]	437.9	403.1	354.8	320.5
Nominal Effective Exchange Rate	nec	....	....	....	....	....	....	....	527.0	542.1	252.8	147.8	150.0	152.9	154.0	143.7
Real Effective Exchange Rate	rec	....	....	....	....	....	....	....	....	159.6	86.9	89.3	108.2	110.9	114.1	105.2
Fund Position															*Millions of SDRs:*	
Quota	2f.s	32.00	32.00	32.00	32.00	32.00	32.00	41.00	41.00	61.50	61.50	61.50	84.10	84.10	84.10	84.10
SDRs	1b.s	3.99	3.88	1.96	3.81	1.24	5.53	3.00	4.46	—	—	.07	2.85	.11	.02	.01
Reserve Position in the Fund	1c.s	.28	.28	—	—	—	—	7.78	7.54	—	—	—	—	—	—	—
Total Fund Cred.&Loans Outstg.	2tl	—	—	18.84	29.96	32.30	29.31	24.32	43.81	44.64	88.16	84.18	183.28	158.98	171.64	140.95
International Liquidity											*Millions of US Dollars Unless Otherwise Indicated:*					
Total Reserves minus Gold	1l.d	40.62	48.49	42.13	48.82	95.41	190.49	193.89	118.63	145.57	131.42	226.12	311.27	405.00	506.37	523.37
SDRs	1b.d	4.33	4.68	2.40	4.46	1.44	6.72	3.91	5.88	—	—	.08	2.98	.11	.02	.01
Reserve Position in the Fund	1c.d	.30	.34	—	—	—	—	10.14	9.93	—	—	—	—	—	—	—
Foreign Exchange	1d.d	35.98	43.47	39.73	44.36	93.97	183.77	179.85	102.82	145.57	131.42	226.04	308.29	404.89	506.35	523.36
Gold (Million Fine Troy Ounces)	1ad	.060	.060	.060	.060	.060	.073	.080	.087	.087	.029	.052	.088	.023	.058	.069
Gold (National Valuation)	1and	2.28	2.54	2.53	2.53	2.53	11.69	15.46	36.00	53.86	7.19	22.60	....	....	19.05	26.10
Monetary Authorities: Other Liab.	4..d	25.98	19.61	50.04	68.26	100.47	149.16	238.47	385.30	832.81	921.77	792.03	1,773.48	1,830.95	1,996.51	2,152.13
Deposit Money Banks: Assets	7a.d	18.20	27.55	22.89	11.74	28.67	40.28	55.15	47.06	30.05	65.47	69.44	60.30	38.91	48.51	74.07
Liabilities	7b.d	24.15	36.80	31.20	45.12	65.99	94.92	87.63	120.04	126.72	131.10	139.95	68.41	88.65	79.44	61.32
Other Banking Insts.: Liabilities	7f.d	16.95	11.98	8.73	7.93	7.41	9.85	8.59	7.27	5.93	71.21	71.73	68.80	59.48	54.69	32.70
Monetary Authorities															*Billions of Colones:*	
Foreign Assets	11	.3	.4	.4	.4	.8	1.7	1.8	1.3	3.4	5.3	9.8	18.4	20.6	28.3	32.4
Claims on Central Government	12a	.4	.4	.5	.8	1.1	1.6	2.3	3.2	4.1	9.6	6.1	9.3	9.8	10.8	17.3
Claims on Nonfin.Pub.Enterprises	12c	—	—	—	—	—	—	1.4	2.2	3.1	3.9	7.2	20.1	23.4	24.3	30.9
Claims on Deposit Money Banks	12e	.3	.3	.8	.9	.8	1.1	1.3	3.9	6.2	1.8	1.7	6.3	5.5	8.8	13.5
Claims on Other Banking Insts	12f	.1	.1	.1	.1	.2	.3	.3	.4	.5	.6	.8	1.1	1.4	1.7	1.4
Reserve Money	14	.9	1.1	1.2	1.6	2.2	3.2	3.2	5.0	5.9	13.1	14.3	19.0	23.0	32.9	42.6
of which: Currency Outside DMBs	14a	.5	.6	.7	.9	1.1	1.4	1.7	2.0	2.3	3.5	5.4	6.9	8.6	9.9	13.2
Time, Savings,& Fgn.Currency Dep.	15	—	—	.1	—	.2	.3	.6	1.7	1.9	6.7	3.2	3.4	2.8	.9	.7
Liabs. of Central Bank: Securities	16ac	—	—	—	—	—	.3	.4	.4	.3	1.5	5.3	5.1	4.9	5.6	6.2
Restricted Deposits	16b	—	—	—	—	—	—	—	—	—	.3	—	—	—	—	—
Foreign Liabilities	16c	.1	—	.4	.3	.4	.4	.8	1.0	3.8	17.9	12.3	15.2	12.3	13.6	14.0
Long-Term Foreign Liabilities	16cl	.1	.1	.2	.6	.8	1.2	1.5	2.8	3.9	19.1	23.3	70.1	82.5	103.7	122.8
Central Government Deposits	16d	.1	.1	.2	.2	.4	.3	.3	.2	.7	1.0	2.4	3.7	3.4	5.9	7.8
Counterpart Funds	16e	—	—	—	—	—	—	—	—	—	—	—	—	—	—	—
Capital Accounts	17a	.1	.1	.2	.2	.1	.1	.2	.2	.3	1.3	1.4	1.8	2.0	3.3	4.6
Other Items (Net)	17r	–.2	–.3	–.5	–.7	–1.2	–1.2	—	–.3	–.8	–39.7	–36.7	–62.9	–70.4	–92.1	–103.3
of which: Valuation Adjustment	17rv	....	....	....	....	....	....	–.8	–.8	–.8	–34.1	–47.6	–59.0	–84.1	–110.5	–125.2
Deposit Money Banks															*Billions of Colones:*	
Reserves	20	.4	.4	.5	.8	1.1	1.6	1.4	3.0	3.3	8.2	8.6	11.5	14.6	23.7	28.7
Claims on Mon.Author.: Securities	20c	—	—	—	—	—	—	—	—	—	—	—	—	—	—	—
Foreign Assets	21	.1	.2	.2	.1	.2	.3	.5	.4	.3	2.4	2.8	2.6	1.9	2.6	4.4
Claims on Central Government	22a	.1	.2	.3	.5	.6	.9	1.2	3.2	5.3	1.4	3.1	4.0	4.2	5.2	5.3
Claims on Nonfin.Pub.Enterprises	22c	—	—	—	—	—	—	.2	.2	.3	.3	.4	.8	1.1	1.0	.8
Claims on Private Sector	22d	1.8	2.0	3.1	4.2	5.1	6.0	7.5	8.9	10.2	11.2	16.1	24.8	29.2	34.1	40.2
Claims on Other Banking Insts	22f	.1	.1	.2	.2	.1	.1	.2	.3	.3	.4	.4	.6	.9	.9	.9
Demand Deposits	24	1.0	1.2	1.4	1.9	2.3	3.1	3.9	4.2	4.9	7.2	12.9	18.4	21.4	22.4	29.0
Time, Savings,& Fgn.Currency Dep.	25	.7	.8	1.2	2.1	3.0	3.8	4.8	6.9	8.1	14.7	19.3	27.2	32.8	42.7	49.0
Bonds	26ab	—	—	—	—	—	—	—	—	—	—	—	—	—	—	—
Restricted Deposits	26b	—	—	—	—	—	—	—	—	—	—	—	—	.1	.1	—
Foreign Liabilities	26c	—	.1	—	—	—	.1	.1	.2	.4	1.9	2.1	1.0	1.6	.5	.8
Long-Term Foreign Liabilities	26cl	.1	.2	.2	.3	.5	.7	.7	.9	.7	2.8	3.5	2.0	2.6	3.7	2.8
Central Government Deposits	26d	.2	.2	.3	.3	.6	.5	.5	.6	.7	1.4	.4	.6	.6	1.2	1.1
Credit from Monetary Authorities	26g	.3	.3	.8	.9	.8	1.1	1.3	3.9	6.2	1.8	1.7	6.2	5.2	9.2	10.0
Capital Accounts	27a	.3	.3	.3	.3	.3	.3	.3	.4	.4	4.2	.6	1.1	3.8	4.5	4.5
Other Items (Net)	27r	—	–.1	–.1	–.1	–.4	–.6	–.7	–1.0	–1.6	–10.2	–9.1	–12.2	–14.3	–16.1	–17.0
Monetary Survey															*Billions of Colones:*	
Foreign Assets (Net)	31n	.3	.5	.1	.2	.7	1.6	1.4	.5	–.5	–12.2	–1.9	4.9	8.5	16.7	22.0
Domestic Credit	32	2.2	2.4	3.6	5.3	6.2	8.2	12.2	17.6	22.4	25.0	31.2	56.4	65.9	71.0	87.9
Claims on Central Govt. (Net)	32an	.3	.2	.3	.7	.8	1.8	2.6	5.5	8.0	8.6	6.4	9.0	10.0	8.9	13.7
Claims on Nonfin.Pub.Enterprises	32c	—	—	—	—	—	—	1.6	2.3	3.4	4.1	7.6	20.8	24.4	25.3	31.6
Claims on Private Sector	32d	1.8	2.0	3.1	4.2	5.2	6.1	7.5	9.0	10.3	11.2	16.1	24.8	29.2	34.1	40.2
Claims on Other Banking Insts	32f	.2	.2	.3	.3	.3	.3	.5	.7	.7	1.0	1.2	1.8	2.3	2.6	2.3
Money	34	1.5	1.9	2.1	2.8	3.4	4.5	5.6	6.2	7.3	10.8	18.4	25.6	30.1	32.4	42.5
Quasi-Money	35	.7	.8	1.3	2.1	3.2	4.2	5.4	8.6	10.0	21.4	22.5	30.5	35.6	43.6	49.7
Bonds	36ab	—	—	—	—	—	—	—	—	—	—	—	—	.1	.1	—
Liabs. of Central Bank: Securities	36ac	—	—	—	—	—	.3	.4	.4	.3	1.5	5.3	5.1	4.9	5.6	6.2
Restricted Deposits	36b	—	—	—	—	—	—	—	—	—	.3	—	—	—	—	—
Long-Term Foreign Liabilities	36cl	.2	.3	.4	.9	1.4	1.9	2.2	3.6	4.5	21.9	26.8	72.1	85.2	107.4	125.7
Counterpart Funds	36e	—	—	—	—	—	—	—	—	—	—	—	—	—	—	—
Capital Accounts	37a	.4	.4	.4	.5	.4	.5	.5	.6	.6	5.5	2.0	2.9	3.9	7.1	9.2
Other Items (Net)	37r	–.2	–.4	–.5	–.8	–1.5	–1.6	–.6	–1.3	–.9	–48.6	–45.7	–74.9	–85.3	–108.5	–123.4
Money plus Quasi-Money	35l	2.2	2.6	3.4	4.9	6.6	8.7	11.1	14.9	17.2	32.3	41.0	56.1	65.8	76.0	92.2

1987	1988	1989	1990	1991	1992	1993	1994	1995	1996	1997	1998	1999	2000	2001		
															Exchange Rates	
End of Period																
98.24	106.98	110.85	147.32	193.72	188.97	208.01	240.98	289.72	316.51	329.61	382.17	409.27	414.35	429.39	Market Rate	aa
End of Period (ae) Period Average (rf)																
69.25	79.50	84.35	103.55	135.43	137.43	151.44	165.07	194.90	220.11	244.29	271.42	298.19	318.02	341.67	Market Rate	ae
62.78	75.80	81.50	91.58	122.43	134.51	142.17	157.07	179.73	207.69	232.60	257.23	285.68	308.19	328.87	Market Rate	rf
Period Averages																
286.2	236.7	220.0	196.5	147.3	133.4	126.2	114.2	100.0	86.5	77.2	69.8	62.8	58.2	54.5	Market Rate	ahx
132.8	120.4	128.3	130.3	105.4	102.9	111.1	113.3	100.0	89.8	84.1	78.5	72.0	68.9	66.8	Nominal Effective Exchange Rate	nec
100.7	94.8	99.8	97.7	90.5	95.8	98.8	98.1	100.0	100.7	103.2	104.9	103.5	106.8	111.9	Real Effective Exchange Rate	rec
															Fund Position	
End of Period																
84.10	84.10	84.10	84.10	84.10	119.00	119.00	119.00	119.00	119.00	119.00	119.00	164.10	164.10	164.10	Quota	2f.s
.01	.01	.04	1.14	.21	.17	.12	.12	.04	.01	.02	.05	.59	.33	.07	SDRs	1b.s
—	—	—	—	—	8.73	8.73	8.73	8.73	8.73	8.73	8.73	20.00	20.00	20.00	Reserve Position in the Fund	1c.s
93.27	53.03	26.94	7.94	58.03	59.28	59.28	45.46	16.32	.50	—	—	—	—	—	Total Fund Cred.&Loans Outstg.	2tl
															International Liquidity	
End of Period																
488.86	667.98	742.57	520.63	919.80	1,018.65	1,024.03	893.20	1,046.64	1,000.23	1,261.82	1,063.39	1,460.40	1,317.76	1,329.82	Total Reserves minus Gold	1l.d
.01	.01	.05	1.62	.30	.23	.16	.18	.06	.01	.03	.07	.81	.43	.09	SDRs	1b.d
—	—	—	—	—	12.00	11.98	12.74	12.97	12.55	11.77	12.29	27.45	26.06	25.13	Reserve Position in the Fund	1c.d
488.85	667.97	742.52	519.01	919.50	1,006.41	1,011.89	880.28	1,033.61	987.67	1,250.02	1,051.04	1,432.14	1,291.27	1,304.59	Foreign Exchange	1d.d
.063	.021	.008	.011	.032	.040	.035	.034	.034	.002	.002	.002	.002	.002	.002	Gold (Million Fine Troy Ounces)	1ad
24.91	9.26	3.37	4.32	12.00	95.97	13.46	....	....	.03	.02	.02	.02	.02	.02	Gold (National Valuation)	1and
2,116.11	2,084.06	1,959.77	1,593.10	1,563.21	1,533.13	1,452.73	1,294.60	1,217.58	1,115.12	1,047.67	1,078.46	1,013.79	917.51	811.13	Monetary Authorities: Other Liab.	4..d
86.89	85.96	100.57	96.51	136.31	200.90	151.99	199.11	203.90	248.10	251.59	324.56	284.38	330.69	362.78	Deposit Money Banks: Assets	7a.d
55.45	50.67	54.80	58.64	51.06	49.73	90.29	102.24	166.96	200.85	293.53	333.73	387.96	529.25	651.69	Liabilities	7b.d
4.62	1.85	5.12	4.70	4.27	4.21	3.81	3.58	....	....	....	....	....	....	....	Other Banking Insts.: Liabilities	7f.d
															Monetary Authorities	
End of Period																
35.5	53.4	62.4	58.1	130.9	148.6	162.3	155.9	196.7	203.7	†364.0	370.6	556.3	536.1	534.6	Foreign Assets	11
18.1	21.9	25.3	31.8	37.9	42.8	52.0	71.5	100.2	283.4	†359.7	416.8	312.1	234.5	82.8	Claims on Central Government	12a
30.6	34.8	32.8	37.5	40.5	34.3	28.8	23.5	23.4	25.4	†8.7	9.3	9.9	10.0	9.9	Claims on Nonfin.Pub.Enterprises	12c
18.4	19.6	20.4	24.3	28.0	28.8	30.9	62.7	38.3	43.4	†22.0	20.8	22.9	18.7	17.6	Claims on Deposit Money Banks	12e
1.3	3.3	3.0	2.9	4.1	3.5	3.5	3.3	3.1	3.3	†1.0	.9	.8	.7	.7	Claims on Other Banking Insts	12f
48.8	70.6	82.2	99.5	161.5	190.3	208.4	270.0	313.7	382.2	†446.8	497.0	533.5	508.5	376.6	Reserve Money	14
14.8	24.7	21.9	27.5	34.7	47.9	54.7	74.9	84.8	91.7	†106.8	124.2	152.6	141.4	156.5	*of which: Currency Outside DMBs*	14a
.4	.7	5.9	10.3	7.6	9.2	8.9	4.8	4.7	8.2	†4.2	4.3	3.7	3.2	3.3	Time, Savings,& Fgn.Currency Dep.	15
11.4	23.4	30.8	28.6	34.0	39.6	45.5	78.9	128.5	46.8	†196.4	184.2	379.4	406.9	496.2	Liabs. of Central Bank: Securities	16ac
—	—	—	—	—	—	—	—	—	—	†.3	.3	.3	.3		Restricted Deposits	16b
14.2	11.5	8.7	16.8	20.9	17.7	14.3	11.6	4.9	.3	†8.5	9.2	14.5	8.4	24.1	Foreign Liabilities	16c
141.5	159.9	159.6	149.3	202.0	204.2	218.0	213.0	237.1	245.3	†247.4	283.5	287.8	283.4	253.0	Long-Term Foreign Liabilities	16cl
2.6	9.3	12.5	16.5	16.9	11.7	14.1	9.3	28.5	111.9	†63.2	60.8	80.4	32.1	77.4	Central Government Deposits	16d
—	—	—	—	—	—	—	—	—	—	†8.6	10.8	2.5	2.3	5.0	Counterpart Funds	16e
5.2	6.0	8.6	9.9	15.8	24.5	25.1	26.8	29.0	126.9	†126.5	105.8	-221.0	-280.4	-559.8	Capital Accounts	17a
-120.3	-148.3	-164.5	-176.4	-217.1	-239.2	-256.8	-297.5	-384.8	-362.4	†-346.5	-337.5	-179.1	-164.7	-30.6	Other Items (Net)	17r
-161.6	-188.3	-213.4	-257.6	-248.8	-274.6	-293.3	-335.0	-415.0	-401.3	†-353.0	-346.5	-196.6	-107.2	-41.9	*of which: Valuation Adjustment*	17rv
															Deposit Money Banks	
End of Period																
34.9	52.5	61.0	79.0	129.2	142.1	155.7	196.2	232.3	289.9	†248.8	282.5	294.0	282.1	275.2	Reserves	20
—	—	.6	.6	.7	2.6	1.5	7.7	36.1	30.3	†109.4	36.7	171.9	203.6	181.6	Claims on Mon.Author.: Securities	20c
6.0	6.8	8.5	10.0	18.5	27.6	23.0	32.9	39.7	54.6	†61.5	88.1	84.8	105.2	124.0	Foreign Assets	21
5.7	10.3	12.9	21.3	14.1	7.8	6.6	34.6	28.4	89.7	†130.1	133.1	134.4	162.0	228.5	Claims on Central Government	22a
.8	1.3	2.3	3.3	3.1	2.6	2.6	2.8	2.4	2.5	†7.3	7.0	9.8	23.4	11.1	Claims on Nonfin.Pub.Enterprises	22c
51.3	59.3	66.2	78.9	93.1	138.7	190.3	222.9	223.0	329.9	†434.3	670.6	914.3	1,180.0	1,493.3	Claims on Private Sector	22d
1.1	1.1	1.8	1.7	1.6	2.8	2.9	2.6	.1	—	†9.6	26.4	9.5	20.5	19.4	Claims on Other Banking Insts	22f
27.6	40.2	41.9	38.8	45.0	61.1	62.4	86.6	67.0	84.9	†243.7	279.6	350.5	479.7	542.3	Demand Deposits	24
64.1	84.3	105.0	146.2	210.7	252.3	301.3	355.1	389.7	620.7	†578.1	763.8	989.1	1,164.7	1,267.6	Time, Savings,& Fgn.Currency Dep.	25
—	—	—	—	—	—	—	—	—	—	†7.0	16.3	37.2	35.5	35.3	Bonds	26ab
—	—	—	—	—	—	—	—	—	—	†.3	.1	—	—	.1	Restricted Deposits	26b
1.4	1.5	1.1	2.3	2.6	3.1	8.6	7.3	13.4	22.2	†64.3	75.7	100.2	148.2	201.0	Foreign Liabilities	26c
2.4	2.6	3.5	3.7	4.3	3.7	5.1	9.6	19.1	22.1	†7.4	14.9	15.5	20.1	21.7	Long-Term Foreign Liabilities	26cl
1.6	1.6	1.7	3.9	3.7	5.0	5.6	41.4	15.0	3.4	†—	—	—	—	—	Central Government Deposits	26d
14.5	17.4	18.0	20.6	19.2	18.7	17.4	45.8	14.5	11.0	†9.2	7.9	7.5	4.9	7.7	Credit from Monetary Authorities	26g
6.5	11.3	14.4	20.4	31.4	35.5	43.0	31.8	63.7	95.5	†185.6	229.1	306.7	370.6	486.8	Capital Accounts	27a
-18.4	-27.6	-32.3	-41.1	-56.6	-55.4	-60.8	-78.0	-20.6	-62.7	†-94.6	-143.0	-187.8	-246.8	-229.3	Other Items (Net)	27r
															Monetary Survey	
End of Period																
25.9	47.3	61.1	49.0	125.9	155.4	162.4	169.8	218.1	235.8	†352.6	373.9	526.4	484.7	433.4	Foreign Assets (Net)	31n
104.7	120.9	130.1	157.0	174.0	215.7	267.0	310.5	336.9	618.9	†887.5	1,203.4	1,310.4	1,599.0	1,768.2	Domestic Credit	32
19.6	21.3	24.0	32.7	31.5	33.8	38.8	55.4	85.0	257.8	†426.6	489.1	366.0	364.3	233.9	Claims on Central Govt. (Net)	32an
31.4	36.0	35.1	40.7	43.6	36.9	31.4	26.3	25.8	27.9	†16.0	16.4	19.7	33.4	21.0	Claims on Nonfin.Pub.Enterprises	32c
51.3	59.3	66.2	78.9	93.1	138.7	190.3	222.9	223.0	329.9	†434.3	670.6	914.3	1,180.0	1,493.3	Claims on Private Sector	32d
2.4	4.4	4.7	4.6	5.8	6.3	6.4	5.9	3.1	3.3	†10.6	27.3	10.3	21.3	20.1	Claims on Other Banking Insts	32f
42.6	65.3	64.0	66.5	79.8	109.5	117.2	161.6	151.9	177.5	†354.6	415.4	534.1	639.7	724.2	Money	34
64.5	85.0	110.9	156.5	218.3	261.5	310.2	359.8	394.4	628.8	†582.3	768.1	992.7	1,167.9	1,270.9	Quasi-Money	35
—	—	—	—	—	—	—	—	—	—	†7.0	16.3	37.2	35.5	35.3	Bonds	36ab
11.4	23.4	30.2	28.0	33.3	37.0	44.0	71.2	92.4	16.5	†87.0	147.5	207.5	203.3	314.6	Liabs. of Central Bank: Securities	36ac
—	—	—	—	—	—	—	—	—	—	†.5	.4	.3	.3		Restricted Deposits	36b
143.9	162.4	163.1	153.1	206.3	207.9	223.1	222.6	256.2	267.3	†254.8	298.5	303.3	303.5	274.7	Long-Term Foreign Liabilities	36cl
—	—	—	—	—	—	—	—	—	—	†8.6	10.8	2.5	2.3	5.0	Counterpart Funds	36e
11.7	17.3	23.1	30.3	47.2	60.0	68.1	58.6	92.7	222.3	†312.1	335.0	85.7	90.2	-73.0	Capital Accounts	37a
-143.6	-185.1	-200.1	-228.3	-285.1	-304.9	-333.2	-393.5	-432.7	-457.7	†-366.9	-414.6	-326.4	-359.1	-350.3	Other Items (Net)	37r
107.1	150.2	174.8	222.9	298.1	371.1	427.4	521.4	546.3	806.3	†936.9	1,183.5	1,526.8	1,807.6	1,995.1	Money plus Quasi-Money	35l

Costa Rica

238		1972	1973	1974	1975	1976	1977	1978	1979	1980	1981	1982	1983	1984	1985	1986
Other Banking Institutions																*Billions of Colones:*
Cash	**40**	—	—	—	—	—	—	—	—	—	.1	.3	.2	.6	.4	.2
Claims on Central Government	**42a**	—	—	—	—	—	—	—	—	—	—	.1	—	—	—	.3
Claims on Official Entities	**42bx**	—	—	—	—	—	—	—	—	—	—	—	—	—	.1	—
Claims on Private Sector	**42d**	.6	.6	.6	.7	.8	.9	1.1	1.3	1.3	2.1	2.2	2.8	3.2	3.5	3.9
Demand Deposits	**44**	—	—	—	—	—	—	—	—	—	—	—	—	—	.1	.2
Time, Savings,& Fgn.Currency Dep.	**45**	—	—	—	—	—	—	—	.1	.1	.2	.4	.8	1.2	.6	.3
Bonds	**46ab**	.1	.1	.1	.1	.2	.2	.3	.2	.2	.4	.3	.3	.3	.5	1.1
Long-Term Foreign Liabilities	**46cl**	.1	.1	.1	.1	.1	.1	.1	.1	.1	2.6	2.9	3.0	2.8	2.9	1.9
Central Government Deposits	**46d**	—	—	—	—	—	—	—	—	—	—	—	—	—	—	—
Credit from Monetary Authorities	**46g**	.1	.1	.1	.1	.2	.2	.3	.3	.3	.6	.8	1.1	1.4	1.9	2.9
Credit from Deposit Money Banks	**46h**	.1	.1	.2	.2	.1	.1	.2	.3	.2	.1	.2	.4	.7	.9	.8
Capital Accounts	**47a**	.1	.1	.1	.1	.1	.1	.1	.1	.1	.2	.3	.3	.3	.4	.4
Other Items (Net)	**47r**	—	.1	.1	.1	.1	.2	.2	.2	.2	−2.0	−2.3	−2.9	−3.1	−3.2	−3.3
Banking Survey																*Billions of Colones:*
Foreign Assets (net)	**51n**	.3	.5	.1	.2	.7	1.6	1.4	.5	−.5	−12.2	−1.9	4.9	8.5	16.7	22.0
Domestic Credit	**52**	2.6	2.8	4.0	5.7	6.8	8.8	12.9	18.1	22.9	26.1	32.3	57.5	66.9	72.0	89.8
Claims on Central Govt. (Net)	**52an**	.3	.2	.3	.8	.8	1.8	2.6	5.5	8.0	8.6	6.4	9.0	10.0	9.0	14.0
Claims on Official Entities	**52bx**	—	—	—	—	—	—	1.6	2.3	3.4	4.2	7.6	20.9	24.4	25.4	31.7
Claims on Private Sector	**52d**	2.4	2.6	3.7	4.9	6.0	7.0	8.7	10.3	11.5	13.3	18.3	27.6	32.5	37.7	44.1
Liquid Liabilities	**55l**	2.2	2.6	3.4	4.9	6.6	8.6	11.1	14.9	17.4	32.4	41.1	56.7	66.4	76.2	92.4
Bonds	**56ab**	.1	.1	.1	.1	.2	.5	.7	.6	.5	1.9	5.6	5.4	5.3	6.2	7.4
Long-Term Foreign Liabilities	**56cl**	.3	.4	.5	1.0	1.4	2.0	2.3	3.7	4.6	24.4	29.7	75.1	88.0	110.4	127.6
Capital Accounts	**57a**	.5	.5	.5	.6	.6	.6	.6	.7	.8	5.7	2.3	3.2	4.2	7.5	9.6
Other Items (Net)	**57r**	−.1	−.3	−.5	−.7	−1.3	−1.4	−.4	−1.2	−.8	−50.6	−48.2	−78.0	−88.6	−111.5	−125.3
Interest Rates																*Percent Per Annum*
Discount Rate *(End of Period)*	**60**	5.00	5.00	7.00	7.00	8.00	8.00	15.40	14.80	23.50	23.50	30.00	30.00	28.00	28.00	27.50
Deposit Rate	**60l**	....	....	....	....	....	....	....	....	....	....	18.29	19.50	14.50	16.50	16.67
Lending Rate	**60p**	....	....	....	....	....	....	....	....	....	....	25.00	23.25	18.00	20.92	21.80
Prices and Labor																*Index Numbers (1995=100):*
Producer Prices	**63**	1.3	1.5	2.1	2.5	2.8	3.0	†3.2	3.7	4.6	7.7	15.9	20.1	21.7	23.9	26.1
Consumer Prices	**64**	1.6	1.9	2.5	†2.9	3.0	3.1	3.3	3.6	4.3	5.8	11.1	14.7	16.5	19.0	21.2
																Number in Thousands:
Labor Force	**67d**	....	....	....	....	....	....	....	....	....	....	....	....	....	....	....
Employment	**67e**	....	....	....	....	....	....	....	....	....	....	....	....	....	827	854
Unemployment	**67c**	....	....	....	....	....	....	....	....	....	....	....	....	....	61	57
Unemployment Rate (%)	**67r**	....	....	....	....	....	....	....	....	....	....	....	....	....	6.8	6.2
International Transactions																*Millions of US Dollars*
Exports	**70..*d***	280.9	344.5	440.3	493.3	592.9	828.2	864.9	934.4	1,001.7	1,008.1	870.4	872.6	1,006.4	976.0	1,120.5
Imports, c.i.f.	**71..*d***	372.8	455.3	719.7	694.0	770.4	1,021.4	1,165.7	1,396.8	1,540.4	1,208.5	889.0	987.8	1,093.7	1,098.2	1,147.5
Balance of Payments																*Millions of US Dollars:*
Current Account, n.i.e.	**78al*d***	....	....	....	....	....	−225.6	−363.2	−558.2	−663.9	−409.1	−271.7	−312.6	−251.1	−291.1	−160.6
Goods: Exports f.o.b.	**78aa*d***	....	....	....	....	....	827.8	863.9	942.1	1,000.9	1,002.6	869.0	852.5	997.5	939.1	1,084.8
Goods: Imports f.o.b.	**78ab*d***	....	....	....	....	....	−925.1	−1,049.4	−1,257.2	−1,375.2	−1,090.6	−804.9	−894.3	−992.9	−1,001.0	−1,045.2
Trade Balance	**78ac*d***	....	....	....	....	....	−97.3	−185.5	−315.1	−374.3	−88.0	64.1	−41.8	4.6	−61.9	39.6
Services: Credit	**78ad*d***	....	....	....	....	....	129.9	141.9	154.8	194.2	170.8	242.2	275.2	272.5	274.7	303.0
Services: Debit	**78ae*d***	....	....	....	....	....	−199.0	−228.7	−266.8	−286.2	−217.0	−240.3	−253.4	−261.3	−281.7	−303.6
Balance on Goods & Services	**78af*d***	....	....	....	....	....	−166.4	−272.3	−427.1	−466.3	−134.2	66.0	−20.0	15.8	−68.9	39.0
Income: Credit	**78ag*d***	....	....	....	....	....	11.4	19.2	14.4	23.5	25.9	32.2	44.9	43.7	56.4	52.4
Income: Debit	**78ah*d***	....	....	....	....	....	−86.4	−126.7	−157.7	−235.6	−327.9	−400.8	−373.8	−351.5	−332.2	−323.3
Balance on Gds, Serv. & Inc.	**78ai*d***	....	....	....	....	....	−241.4	−379.8	−570.4	−678.4	−436.2	−302.6	−348.9	−292.0	−344.7	−231.9
Current Transfers, n.i.e.: Credit	**78aj*d***	....	....	....	....	....	26.4	28.0	30.1	33.5	36.9	38.9	45.6	51.3	64.2	82.1
Current Transfers: Debit	**78ak*d***	....	....	....	....	....	−10.6	−11.4	−17.9	−19.0	−9.8	−8.0	−9.3	−10.4	−10.6	−10.8
Capital Account, n.i.e.	**78bc*d***	....	....	....	....	....	—	—	—	—	—	—	—	—	—	—
Capital Account, n.i.e.: Credit	**78ba*d***	....	....	....	....	....	—	—	—	—	—	—	—	—	—	—
Capital Account: Debit	**78bb*d***	....	....	....	....	....	—	—	—	—	—	—	—	—	—	—
Financial Account, n.i.e.	**78bj*d***	....	....	....	....	....	355.8	423.0	317.0	373.9	−32.2	−226.3	−149.3	−330.4	−286.9	−301.6
Direct Investment Abroad	**78bd*d***	....	....	....	....	....	—	−1.6	−1.1	−4.5	−3.4	−2.4	−5.4	−3.9	−4.7	−3.6
Dir. Invest. in Rep. Econ., n.i.e.	**78be*d***	....	....	....	....	....	62.5	48.6	43.5	52.6	69.6	28.9	60.7	55.9	69.9	61.0
Portfolio Investment Assets	**78bf*d***	....	....	....	....	....	—	—	—	—	−.5	−.3	—	—	.7	—
Equity Securities	**78bk*d***	....	....	....	....	....	—	—	—	—	—	—	—	—	.7	—
Debt Securities	**78bl*d***	....	....	....	....	....	—	—	—	—	−.5	−.3	—	—	—	—
Portfolio Investment Liab., n.i.e.	**78bg*d***	....	....	....	....	....	3.5	20.9	—	122.0	−1.9	−1.6	−2.6	−.2	−14.2	−2.5
Equity Securities	**78bm*d***	....	....	....	....	....	—	—	—	—	—	—	—	—	—	−2.5
Debt Securities	**78bn*d***	....	....	....	....	....	3.5	20.9	—	122.0	−1.9	−1.6	−2.6	−.2	−14.2	—
Financial Derivatives Assets	**78bw*d***	....	....	....	....	....	....	....	....	....	....	....	....	....	....	....
Financial Derivatives Liabilities	**78bx*d***	....	....	....	....	....	....	....	....	....	....	....	....	....	....	....
Other Investment Assets	**78bh*d***	....	....	....	....	....	−22.6	−49.2	−113.7	−163.2	−131.2	−145.7	−25.8	−161.8	−95.8	−42.4
Monetary Authorities	**78bo*d***	....	....	....	....	....	....	....	....	....	....	....	....	....	....	....
General Government	**78bp*d***	....	....	....	....	....	−.1	−6.9	−3.2	−5.4	−3.6	−13.1	−1.2	−14.2	—	−12.9
Banks	**78bq*d***	....	....	....	....	....	—	—	—	—	—	—	—	—	—	—
Other Sectors	**78br*d***	....	....	....	....	....	−22.5	−42.3	−110.5	−157.8	−127.6	−132.6	−24.6	−147.6	−95.8	−29.5
Other Investment Liab., n.i.e.	**78bi*d***	....	....	....	....	....	312.4	404.3	388.3	367.0	35.2	−105.2	−176.2	−220.4	−242.8	−314.1
Monetary Authorities	**78bs*d***	....	....	....	....	....	46.0	89.9	98.3	146.8	56.4	−35.4	−103.3	−173.9	−178.0	−213.9
General Government	**78bt*d***	....	....	....	....	....	31.3	70.6	85.7	60.3	33.5	−9.6	14.7	18.2	−39.5	1.3
Banks	**78bu*d***	....	....	....	....	....	42.4	−9.2	40.8	41.5	−50.9	−15.7	−49.3	−16.6	−16.3	−11.6
Other Sectors	**78bv*d***	....	....	....	....	....	192.7	253.0	163.5	118.4	−3.8	−44.5	−38.3	−48.1	−9.0	−89.9
Net Errors and Omissions	**78ca*d***	....	....	....	....	....	−27.4	−50.5	79.2	−69.5	69.6	163.7	78.4	104.4	142.9	97.5
Overall Balance	**78cb*d***	....	....	....	....	....	102.8	9.3	−162.0	−359.5	−371.7	−334.3	−383.6	−477.2	−435.1	−364.7
Reserves and Related Items	**79da*d***	....	....	....	....	....	−102.8	−9.3	162.0	359.5	371.7	334.3	383.6	477.2	435.1	364.7
Reserve Assets	**79db*d***	....	....	....	....	....	−107.3	−20.8	93.2	−92.9	−1.5	−120.9	−152.7	79.7	−72.1	−58.0
Use of Fund Credit and Loans	**79dc*d***	....	....	....	....	....	−3.5	−6.6	25.3	.8	50.1	−4.4	105.6	−24.5	12.2	−36.4
Exceptional Financing	**79de*d***	....	....	....	....	....	8.0	18.1	43.5	451.7	323.0	459.6	430.6	422.0	495.0	459.2

	1987	1988	1989	1990	1991	1992	1993	1994	1995	1996	1997	1998	1999	2000	2001		
End of Period																**Other Banking Institutions**	
	—	.1	1.0	.7	.9	—	.1	—	....	....	....	....	....		....	Cash	40
	.1	—	.2	.1	.4	.6	.8	.4	....	....	....	....	....		....	Claims on Central Government	42a
									....	....	....	....	....		....	Claims on Official Entities	42bx
	2.6	2.8	3.4	3.9	3.8	4.8	5.0	7.3	....	....	....	....	....		....	Claims on Private Sector	42d
	.2	—	—	—	—	—	—	—	....	....	....	....	....		....	Demand Deposits	44
	.4	.5	.9	.9	1.2	.5	.4	.5	....	....	....	....	....		....	Time, Savings,& Fgn.Currency Dep.	45
	.5	.7	.7	.6	.9	1.4	2.0	2.1	....	....	....	....	....		....	Bonds	46ab
	.3	.1	.4	.5	.6	.6	.6	.6	....	....	....	....	....		....	Long-Term Foreign Liabilities	46cl
									....	....	....	....	....		....	Central Government Deposits	46d
	.5	.4	.8	.8	1.0	.7	.7	2.4	....	....	....	....	....		....	Credit from Monetary Authorities	46g
	.8	1.0	1.8	1.8	1.7	2.1	2.3	2.2	....	....	....	....	....		....	Credit from Deposit Money Banks	46h
	.2	.2	.2	.2	.2	.2	.1	.2	....	....	....	....	....		....	Capital Accounts	47a
	−.2	−.1	−.4	−.2	−.5	−.1	−.3	−.1	....	....	....	....	....		....	Other Items (Net)	47r
End of Period																**Banking Survey**	
	25.9	47.3	61.1	49.0	125.9	155.4	162.4	169.8	....	....	....	....	....		....	Foreign Assets (net)	51n
	105.0	119.4	128.9	156.3	172.5	214.8	266.3	312.3	....	....	....	....	....		....	Domestic Credit	52
	19.7	21.3	24.2	32.8	31.9	34.5	39.6	55.8	....	....	....	....	....		....	Claims on Central Govt. (Net)	52an
	31.4	36.0	35.1	40.7	43.6	36.9	31.4	26.3	....	....	....	....	....		....	Claims on Official Entities	52bx
	53.9	62.1	69.6	82.8	97.0	143.5	195.3	230.2	....	....	....	....	....		....	Claims on Private Sector	52d
	107.8	150.6	174.8	223.2	298.4	371.6	427.8	521.8	....	....	....	....	....		....	Liquid Liabilities	55l
	12.0	24.1	31.0	28.6	34.2	38.4	46.0	73.3	....	....	....	....	....		....	Bonds	56ab
	144.2	162.6	163.5	153.5	206.9	208.5	223.7	223.2	....	....	....	....	....		....	Long-Term Foreign Liabilities	56cl
	11.9	17.5	23.3	30.5	47.4	60.1	68.2	58.8	....	....	....	....	....		....	Capital Accounts	57a
	−144.9	−188.1	−202.6	−230.5	−288.6	−308.4	−336.9	−395.0	....	....	....	....	....		....	Other Items (Net)	57r
Percent Per Annum																**Interest Rates**	
	31.38	31.50	31.61	37.80	42.50	29.00	35.00	37.75	38.50	35.00	31.00	37.00	34.00	31.50	28.75	Discount Rate *(End of Period)*	60
	14.06	15.18	15.62	21.16	27.32	15.80	16.90	17.72	23.88	17.29	13.03	12.76	14.31	13.38	11.77	Deposit Rate	60l
	23.82	28.69	29.17	32.56	38.88	28.46	30.02	33.03	36.70	26.27	22.48	22.47	25.74	24.89	23.83	Lending Rate	60p
Period Averages																**Prices and Labor**	
	28.8	34.0	38.9	44.7	†57.3	67.9	†71.4	80.7	100.0	116.0	129.5	140.9	155.2	....	....	Producer Prices	63
	24.8	30.0	34.9	41.5	53.5	65.1	71.5	†81.2	100.0	117.5	133.1	148.6	163.5	181.5	201.9	Consumer Prices	64
Period Averages																	
	....	....	....	....	1,063	1,119	1,160	....	1,199	1,277	1,377	1,383	1,391			Labor Force	67d
	†923	951	987	1,017	1,007	1,043	1,096	1,138	1,174	1,145	1,227	1,300	1,300	1,319	....	Employment	67e
	†55	55	39	50	59	44	47	49	64	76	74	77	83	72		Unemployment	67c
	†5.6	5.5	3.8	4.6	5.5	4.1	4.1	4.2	5.2	6.2	5.7	5.6	6.0	5.2	....	Unemployment Rate (%)	67r
Millions of US Dollars																**International Transactions**	
	1,158.3	1,245.7	1,414.6	1,448.2	1,597.7	1,840.8	2,624.6	2,869.4	3,453.0	3,730.2	4,267.6	5,511.3	6,577.2	5,864.6	5,009.8	Exports	70..d
	1,382.5	1,409.8	1,717.4	1,989.7	1,876.6	2,440.7	3,514.9	3,789.0	4,036.1	4,299.5	4,924.0	6,230.4	6,320.1	6,372.1	6,564.3	Imports, c.i.f.	71..d
Minus Sign Indicates Debit																**Balance of Payments**	
	−376.4	−303.5	−479.9	−494.0	−99.2	−380.4	−620.2	−244.0	−358.1	−263.7	−480.9	−520.8	−649.5	....		Current Account, n.i.e.	78ald
	1,106.7	1,180.7	1,333.4	1,354.2	1,498.1	1,739.1	1,866.8	2,122.0	3,481.8	3,774.1	4,220.6	5,538.3	6,667.7	....		Goods: Exports f.o.b.	78aad
	−1,245.2	−1,278.6	−1,572.0	−1,796.7	−1,697.6	−2,210.9	−2,627.6	−2,727.8	−3,804.4	−4,023.3	−4,718.2	−5,937.4	−6,008.1	....		Goods: Imports f.o.b.	78abd
	−138.5	−97.9	−238.6	−442.5	−199.5	−471.8	−760.8	−605.8	−322.6	−249.2	−497.6	−399.0	659.6	....		*Trade Balance*	78acd
	337.1	430.3	497.9	609.0	691.4	841.3	1,039.3	1,195.0	969.1	1,053.5	1,128.6	1,343.4	1,525.6	....		Services: Credit	78add
	−391.1	−423.7	−496.0	−549.7	−534.8	−710.6	−816.4	−860.1	−913.0	−1,033.3	−988.4	−1,109.8	−1,173.7	....		Services: Debit	78aed
	−192.5	−91.3	−236.7	−383.2	−42.9	−341.1	−537.9	−270.9	−266.5	−228.9	−357.4	−165.5	1,011.6	....		*Balance on Goods & Services*	78afd
	48.5	47.8	119.9	130.3	111.4	112.8	111.2	154.6	146.4	142.5	185.4	182.7	198.2	....		Income: Credit	78agd
	−338.4	−390.4	−489.5	−363.0	−285.3	−315.4	−336.6	−283.0	−371.9	−326.7	−434.4	−651.2	−1,961.4	....		Income: Debit	78ahd
	−482.4	−433.9	−606.3	−615.9	−216.8	−543.7	−763.3	−399.3	−492.0	−413.2	−606.4	−634.0	−751.6	....		*Balance on Gds, Serv. & Inc.*	78aid
	117.2	141.9	130.5	126.0	121.1	168.9	149.3	164.5	165.2	192.7	191.2	190.5	190.7	....		Current Transfers, n.i.e.: Credit	78ajd
	−11.2	−11.5	−4.1	−4.1	−3.5	−5.6	−6.2	−9.2	−31.3	−43.2	−65.7	−77.3	−88.6	....		Current Transfers: Debit	78akd
									28.2	....	....	....	....			Capital Account, n.i.e.	78bcd
	—	—	—	—	—	—	—	—	28.2	....	....	....	....			Capital Account, n.i.e.: Credit	78bad
	—	—	—	—	—	—	—	—		....	....	....	....			Capital Account: Debit	78bbd
	−446.7	−263.9	−186.7	−90.8	162.1	192.8	62.8	−108.4	517.3	47.5	129.7	199.0	576.6	....		Financial Account, n.i.e.	78bjd
	−4.5	−.9	−6.0	−2.1	−5.6	−4.4	−2.3	−4.7	−5.5	−5.7	−4.4	−4.8	−5.0	....		Direct Investment Abroad	78bdd
	80.3	122.3	101.2	162.5	178.4	226.0	246.7	297.6	336.9	427.0	408.2	613.1	669.3	....		Dir. Invest. in Rep. Econ., n.i.e.	78bed
									−.4	....	−22.5	−33.9	−28.1			Portfolio Investment Assets	78bfd
									−.4	....	−22.5	−33.9	−28.1			Equity Securities	78bkd
																Debt Securities	78bld
	—	−6.0	−13.2	−28.2	−13.0	−16.9	−5.1	−1.2	−24.4	−21.5	−190.8	−296.0	−239.7			Portfolio Investment Liab., n.i.e.	78bgd
	—	—	—	—	—	—	—	—								Equity Securities	78bmd
	—	−6.0	−13.2	−28.2	−13.0	−16.9	−5.1	−1.2	−24.4	−21.5	−190.8	−296.0	−239.7			Debt Securities	78bnd
	....	....	....	....	....	....	....	....								Financial Derivatives Assets	78bwd
																Financial Derivatives Liabilities	78bxd
	−72.4	−77.3	−5.9	−124.7	75.6	84.8	54.5	−76.2	16.8	−159.3	−267.4	−95.6	106.8			Other Investment Assets	78bhd
									.1	−6.3	−.1		−.2			Monetary Authorities	78bod
	−.9	−.1	−4.9	−4.7	1.2	−8.5	34.9	−4.4								General Government	78bpd
									−9.8	−17.8	43.3	−29.8	35.6			Banks	78bqd
	−71.5	−77.2	−1.0	−120.0	74.4	93.3	19.6	−71.8	26.5	−135.2	−310.6	−65.8	71.4			Other Sectors	78brd
	−450.1	−302.0	−262.8	−98.3	−73.3	−96.7	−231.0	−323.9	193.9	−192.9	206.7	16.2	73.3			Other Investment Liab., n.i.e.	78bid
	−404.3	−284.8	−293.3	−141.3	−25.5	−76.6	−256.8	−216.1	−94.4	−104.0	−118.6	−98.5	−91.6			Monetary Authorities	78bsd
	−27.4	−36.1	−17.8	−28.1	−68.3	−47.8	−25.7	−106.2	12.9	−85.2	−64.1	−60.7	−77.9			General Government	78btd
	.1	−13.5	4.4	−1.0	−8.7	7.1	27.7	−18.8	23.0	48.7	73.7	37.3	63.6			Banks	78bud
	−18.5	32.4	43.9	72.1	29.2	20.6	23.8	17.2	252.4	−52.3	315.7	138.1	179.2			Other Sectors	78bvd
	131.2	224.6	208.9	43.4	99.9	201.9	299.0	249.1	57.1	118.7	157.8	−182.6	224.2			Net Errors and Omissions	78cad
	−691.9	−342.8	−457.7	−541.4	162.8	14.3	−258.4	−103.3	216.2	−69.3	−193.3	−504.3	151.3			*Overall Balance*	78cbd
	691.9	342.8	457.7	541.4	−162.8	−14.3	258.4	103.3	−216.2	69.3	193.3	504.3	−151.3			Reserves and Related Items	79dad
	25.0	−188.0	−112.3	197.2	−416.1	−176.8	59.6	65.5	−179.2	77.3	−215.7	149.6	−481.0			Reserve Assets	79dbd
	−62.3	−54.1	−33.4	−25.6	67.7	1.7	—	−20.3	−44.4	−23.1	−.7	—	—			Use of Fund Credit and Loans	79dcd
	729.2	585.0	603.3	369.8	185.6	160.8	198.8	58.1	7.4	15.0	409.7	354.7	329.7			Exceptional Financing	79ded

Costa Rica

		1972	1973	1974	1975	1976	1977	1978	1979	1980	1981	1982	1983	1984	1985	1986
International Investment Position																*Millions of US Dollars*
Assets	79aa d	....	....	....	....	....	....	....	....	....	....	....	....	....	....	....
Direct Investment Abroad	79ab d	....	....	....	....	....	....	....	....	....	....	....	....	....	....	....
Portfolio Investment	79ac d	....	....	....	....	....	....	....	....	....	....	....	....	....	....	....
Equity Securities	79ad d	....	....	....	....	....	....	....	....	....	....	....	....	....	....	....
Debt Securities	79ae d	....	....	....	....	....	....	....	....	....	....	....	....	....	....	....
Financial Derivatives	79al d	....	....	....	....	....	....	....	....	....	....	....	....	....	....	....
Other Investment	79af d	....	....	....	....	....	....	....	....	....	....	....	....	....	....	....
Monetary Authorities	79ag d	....	....	....	....	....	....	....	....	....	....	....	....	....	....	....
General Government	79ah d	....	....	....	....	....	....	....	....	....	....	....	....	....	....	....
Banks	79ai d	....	....	....	....	....	....	....	....	....	....	....	....	....	....	....
Other Sectors	79aj d	....	....	....	....	....	....	....	....	....	....	....	....	....	....	....
Reserve Assets	79ak d	....	....	....	....	....	....	....	....	....	....	....	....	....	....	....
Liabilities	79la d	....	....	....	....	....	....	....	....	....	....	....	....	....	....	....
Dir. Invest. in Rep. Economy	79lb d	....	....	....	....	....	....	....	....	....	....	....	....	....	....	....
Portfolio Investment	79lc d	....	....	....	....	....	....	....	....	....	....	....	....	....	....	....
Equity Securities	79ld d	....	....	....	....	....	....	....	....	....	....	....	....	....	....	....
Debt Securities	79le d	....	....	....	....	....	....	....	....	....	....	....	....	....	....	....
Financial Derivatives	79ll d	....	....	....	....	....	....	....	....	....	....	....	....	....	....	....
Other Investment	79lf d	....	....	....	....	....	....	....	....	....	....	....	....	....	....	....
Monetary Authorities	79lg d	....	....	....	....	....	....	....	....	....	....	....	....	....	....	....
General Government	79lh d	....	....	....	....	....	....	....	....	....	....	....	....	....	....	....
Banks	79li d	....	....	....	....	....	....	....	....	....	....	....	....	....	....	....
Other Sectors	79lj d	....	....	....	....	....	....	....	....	....	....	....	....	....	....	....
Government Finance																*Millions of Colones:*
Deficit (-) or Surplus	80	−267	−339	−176	−386	−974	−746	−1,316	−2,310	−3,356	−1,381	−936	−2,464	−187	1,775	−4,171
Total Revenue and Grants	81y	1,041	1,387	1,936	2,279	2,692	3,487	4,111	4,344	5,258	7,453	12,948	21,057	27,281	29,725	39,922
Revenue	81	1,041	1,387	1,936	2,279	2,692	3,487	4,111	4,344	5,258	7,453	12,948	21,057	27,281	29,725	39,922
Grants	81z	—	—	—	—	—	—	—	—	—	—	—	—	—	—	—
Exp. & Lending Minus Repay.	82z															
Expenditure	82	1,309	1,726	2,112	2,665	3,666	4,233	5,426	6,654	8,614	8,834	13,885	23,521	27,469	27,950	44,093
Lending Minus Repayments	83	—	—	—	—	—	—	—	—	—	—	—	—	—	—	—
Total Financing	80h	267	....	....	386	974	746	1,316	2,310	3,356	1,381	936	2,464	187	−1,774	4,171
Domestic	84a	136	....	....	234	744	443	1,102	1,918	2,931	1,125	454	480	−1,853	−2,320	4,140
Foreign	85a	132	....	....	152	230	304	214	392	425	256	482	1,983	2,040	546	31
Total Debt by Residence	88	2,628	3,351	4,030	4,402	6,127	7,354	12,652	13,728	15,689	18,510	31,179	38,605	41,312	45,452	64,656
Domestic Debt	88a	2,054	2,626	2,961	3,135	4,633	5,471	9,821	10,200	10,931	13,134	17,687	23,409	23,830	26,434	44,072
Foreign Debt	89a	574	725	1,069	1,267	1,493	1,882	2,831	3,528	4,758	5,376	13,492	15,196	17,482	19,018	20,584
National Accounts																*Millions of Colones*
Househ.Cons.Expend.,incl.NPISHs	96f	5,748	6,924	9,772	12,036	13,718	17,171	20,412	23,139	27,140	34,344	56,397	79,481	99,837	118,974	144,381
Government Consumption Expend.	91f	1,182	1,417	1,889	2,558	3,306	4,208	5,069	6,243	7,544	8,987	14,192	19,527	25,503	31,175	37,951
Gross Fixed Capital Formation	93e	1,800	2,252	3,175	3,695	4,846	5,889	6,952	9,050	9,895	13,737	19,808	23,269	32,679	38,240	46,023
Changes in Inventories	93i	10	187	359	−58	46	502	132	−295	1,109	2,837	4,262	8,001	4,324	13,000	16,139
Exports of Goods and Services	90c	2,483	3,130	4,380	5,052	5,977	8,128	8,509	9,311	10,963	24,708	43,959	46,601	56,046	60,807	77,280
Imports of Goods and Services (-)	98c	3,007	3,747	6,360	6,478	7,218	9,567	10,879	12,863	15,245	27,510	41,113	47,565	55,378	64,277	75,195
Gross Domestic Product (GDP)	99b	8,216	10,162	13,216	16,805	20,676	26,331	30,194	34,584	41,405	57,103	97,505	129,314	163,011	197,920	246,579
Net Primary Income from Abroad	98.n	−253	−285	−312	−543	−627	−655	−903	−1,279	−1,987	−6,434	−16,087	−13,673	−13,804	−14,115	−15,099
Gross National Income (GNI)	99a	7,958	9,875	12,910	16,283	20,077	25,705	29,315	33,307	39,417	50,669	81,418	115,641	149,207	183,805	231,481
Consumption of Fixed Capital	99cf	504	567	698	892	1,123	1,352	1,584	1,846	2,181	2,711	3,887	4,210	4,861	5,488	6,130
GDP Volume 1966 Prices	99b. p	6,438	6,934	7,319	7,473	7,885	8,587	9,125	9,576	9,648	9,430	8,743	8,993	9,715	9,784	10,326
GDP Volume 1991 Prices	99b. p	....	....	....	....	....	....	....	....	....	....	....	....	....	....	....
GDP Volume (1995=100)	99bv p	40.3	43.4	45.8	46.8	49.3	53.7	57.1	59.9	60.4	59.0	54.7	56.3	60.8	61.2	64.6
GDP Deflator (1995=100)	99bi p	.9	1.1	1.3	1.7	2.0	2.3	2.5	2.8	3.2	4.6	8.5	10.9	12.7	15.4	18.1
																Millions:
Population	99z	1.84	1.87	1.92	1.96	2.01	2.07	2.12	2.17	2.25	2.27	2.42	2.50	2.57	2.64	2.72

International Investment Position — Millions of US Dollars

Item	1987	1988	1989	1990	1991	1992	1993	1994	1995	1996	1997	1998	1999	2000	2001	Code
Assets	...	...	...	...	...	...	...	...	...	1,421.3	1,584.9	1,490.2	1,918.8	...	...	79aa d
Direct Investment Abroad	...	...	...	...	...	...	...	...	...	—	—	—	—	...	...	79ab d
Portfolio Investment	...	...	...	...	...	...	...	...	...	—	—	—	—	...	...	79ac d
Equity Securities	...	...	...	...	...	...	...	...	...	—	—	—	—	...	...	79ad d
Debt Securities	...	...	...	...	...	...	...	...	...	—	—	—	—	...	...	79ae d
Financial Derivatives	...	...	...	...	...	...	...	...	...	...	...	...	...	...	...	79al d
Other Investment	...	...	...	...	...	...	...	...	...	412.4	361.2	415.3	363.2	...	...	79af d
Monetary Authorities	...	...	...	...	...	...	...	...	...	...	...	...	...	...	...	79ag d
General Government	...	...	...	...	...	...	...	...	...	...	...	...	...	...	...	79ah d
Banks	...	...	...	...	...	...	...	...	...	...	...	...	...	...	...	79ai d
Other Sectors	...	...	...	...	...	...	...	...	...	...	...	...	...	...	...	79aj d
Reserve Assets	...	...	...	...	...	...	...	...	...	1,008.9	1,223.7	1,074.9	1,555.6	...	...	79ak d
Liabilities	...	...	...	...	...	...	...	...	...	3,268.3	3,266.1	3,324.2	3,340.7	...	...	79la d
Dir. Invest. in Rep. Economy	...	...	...	...	...	...	...	...	...	...	...	...	...	...	...	79lb d
Portfolio Investment	...	...	...	...	...	...	...	...	...	728.4	827.3	781.0	841.3	...	...	79lc d
Equity Securities	...	...	...	...	...	...	...	...	...	—	—	—	—	...	...	79ld d
Debt Securities	...	...	...	...	...	...	...	...	...	728.4	827.3	781.0	841.3	...	...	79le d
Financial Derivatives	...	...	...	...	...	...	...	...	...	...	...	...	...	...	...	79ll d
Other Investment	...	...	...	...	...	...	...	...	...	2,539.9	2,438.8	2,543.2	2,499.4	...	...	79lf d
Monetary Authorities	...	...	...	...	...	...	...	...	...	...	...	...	...	...	...	79lg d
General Government	...	...	...	...	...	...	...	...	...	...	...	...	...	...	...	79lh d
Banks	...	...	...	...	...	...	...	...	...	...	...	...	...	...	...	79li d
Other Sectors	...	...	...	...	...	...	...	...	...	...	...	...	...	...	...	79lj d

Government Finance — Year Ending December 31

Item	1987	1988	1989	1990	1991	1992	1993	1994	1995	1996	1997	1998	1999	2000	2001	Code
Deficit (-) or Surplus	†-4,912	-5,429	-14,086	-17,458	-23,308	-16,047	-24,131	-85,361	-84,575	-95,471	-81,769	-89,435	-98,989	-140,173	-144,246	80
Total Revenue and Grants	†44,025	53,436	63,765	74,975	100,875	142,671	166,065	191,247	253,699	302,497	363,540	444,486	547,435	599,101	704,131	81y
Revenue	†44,025	53,436	63,765	74,975	100,875	142,671	166,065	191,247	253,699	302,497	363,540	444,486	547,435	599,101	704,131	81
Grants	—	—	—	—	—	—	—	—	—	—	—	—	—	—	—	81z
Exp. & Lending Minus Repay.	†48,937	58,865	77,851	92,433	124,183	158,718	190,196	276,608	338,274	397,968	445,309	533,921	646,424	739,274	848,377	82z
Expenditure	†48,937	58,865	77,851	92,433	124,183	158,718	190,196	276,608	338,274	397,968	445,309	533,921	646,424	739,274	848,377	82
Lending Minus Repayments	—	—	—	—	—	—	—	—	—	—	—	—	—	—	—	83
Total Financing	†4,912	5,429	14,086	17,459	23,308	16,047	24,131	85,361	84,575	95,472	81,769	89,436	98,991	140,175	144,246	80h
Domestic	†4,841	6,833	11,518	15,949	17,007	13,919	33,742	88,498	101,350	120,983	106,561	39,827	34,517	69,303	89,679	84a
Foreign	†71	-1,404	2,568	1,510	6,301	2,128	-9,611	-3,138	-16,775	-25,511	-24,792	49,609	64,474	70,872	54,567	85a
Total Debt by Residence	†60,654	64,079	82,239	97,405	269,047	338,524	398,135	506,771	671,357	922,811	1,080,891	1,283,354	1,427,974	1,677,084	....	88
Domestic Debt	†40,375	44,029	61,393	77,883	125,013	176,706	228,678	320,272	463,933	697,676	706,375	977,150	1,064,311	1,222,975	....	88a
Foreign Debt	†20,279	20,050	20,846	19,522	144,034	161,818	169,457	186,499	207,424	225,135	374,516	306,204	363,663	454,109	....	89a

National Accounts — Millions of Colones

Item	1987	1988	1989	1990	1991	1992	1993	1994	1995	1996	1997	1998	1999	2000	2001	Code
Househ.Cons.Expend.,incl.NPISHs	176,475	215,794	256,923	321,143	633,691	829,736	992,516	1,189,292	1,496,157	1,822,342	2,168,885	2,510,880	2,916,434	3,333,448	3,695,896	96f
Government Consumption Expend.	42,652	54,630	72,283	94,948	117,174	143,472	180,214	228,887	284,636	330,455	390,087	469,886	565,207	652,509	767,637	91f
Gross Fixed Capital Formation	56,313	66,211	87,224	117,071	156,310	227,467	280,900	324,161	399,983	421,650	538,478	740,341	811,325	855,074	956,925	93e
Changes in Inventories	20,857	19,358	26,009	25,786	966	5,892	5,270	8,282	-15,918	-29,099	1,161	4,137	-38,188	-38,991	10,804	93i
Exports of Goods and Services	90,005	118,998	148,435	178,763	294,297	406,115	490,201	589,686	790,800	967,130	1,215,914	1,716,713	2,330,567	2,363,421	2,269,135	90c
Imports of Goods and Services (-)	101,768	125,247	164,963	214,864	325,527	459,477	578,808	682,071	849,971	1,052,522	1,330,505	1,816,627	2,072,582	2,250,373	2,387,254	98c
Gross Domestic Product (GDP)	284,533	349,743	425,911	522,848	876,911	1,153,205	1,370,292	1,658,237	2,105,687	2,459,957	2,984,020	3,625,330	4,512,763	4,915,089	5,313,143	99b
Net Primary Income from Abroad	-18,616	-25,661	-30,739	-21,480	-22,536	-28,745	-34,039	-21,837	-40,473	-38,353	-57,912	-120,500	-520,932	-385,211	-255,767	98.n
Gross National Income (GNI)	265,917	324,082	395,171	501,368	854,374	1,124,460	1,336,253	1,636,400	2,065,214	2,421,604	2,926,108	3,504,830	3,991,831	4,529,878	5,057,376	99a
Consumption of Fixed Capital	7,114	8,919	10,621	13,217	52,064	66,942	78,649	92,123	115,025	138,579	168,727	201,867	264,890	295,606	314,614	99cf
GDP Volume 1966 Prices	10,818	11,190	11,824	12,244	12,521											99b. p
GDP Volume 1991 Prices	...	...	...	...	†876,911	957,166	1,028,127	1,076,753	1,118,971	1,128,892	1,191,864	1,291,955	1,398,182	1,429,384	1,442,560	99b. p
GDP Volume (1995=100)	67.7	70.0	74.0	76.6	78.4	85.5	91.9	96.2	100.0	100.9	106.5	115.5	125.0	127.7	128.9	99bv p
GDP Deflator (1995=100)	20.0	24.5	28.9	32.4	53.2	64.0	70.8	81.8	100.0	115.8	133.0	149.1	171.5	182.7	195.7	99bi p

Population — Midyear Estimates

Item	1987	1988	1989	1990	1991	1992	1993	1994	1995	1996	1997	1998	1999	2000	2001	Code
Population	2.78	2.85	2.92	2.99	3.06	3.13	3.20	3.27	3.33	3.40	3.46	3.53	3.59	3.83	3.87	99z

(See notes in the back of the book.)

Côte d'Ivoire

	1972	1973	1974	1975	1976	1977	1978	1979	1980	1981	1982	1983	1984	1985	1986
Exchange Rates														*Francs per SDR:*	
Official Rate .... aa	278.00	284.00	272.08	262.55	288.70	285.76	272.28	264.78	287.99	334.52	370.92	436.97	470.11	415.26	394.78
														Francs per US Dollar:	
Official Rate .... ae	256.05	235.42	222.22	224.27	248.49	235.25	209.00	201.00	225.80	287.40	336.25	417.37	479.60	378.05	322.75
Official Rate .... rf	252.03	222.89	240.70	214.31	238.95	245.68	225.66	212.72	211.28	271.73	328.61	381.07	436.96	449.26	346.31
														Index Numbers (1995=100):	
Official Rate .... ahx	197.9	224.6	207.2	233.0	209.0	203.0	221.4	234.6	236.4	184.6	152.6	131.5	114.5	111.9	144.3
Nominal Effective Exchange Rate .... ne c	....	....	....	....	....	....	....	52.9	54.7	50.5	48.2	50.2	52.3	57.2	67.8
Real Effective Exchange Rate .... re c	....	....	....	....	....	....	....		149.2	128.2	116.7	112.6	108.4	108.3	130.2
Fund Position														*Millions of SDRs:*	
Quota .... 2f. s	52.0	52.0	52.0	52.0	52.0	52.0	76.0	76.0	114.0	114.0	114.0	165.5	165.5	165.5	165.5
SDRs .... 1b. s	15.3	15.3	15.2	14.5	11.8	8.6	7.4	17.9	2.7	10.6	.1	15.5	.2	.1	7.0
Reserve Position in the Fund .... 1c. s	10.8	10.8	—	—	—	—	10.4	12.2	9.5						
Total Fund Cred.&Loans Outstg. .. 2tl	—	—	11.2	11.2	23.4	13.4	21.6	21.6	50.6	370.0	485.4	640.3	649.7	605.5	538.7
International Liquidity											*Millions of US Dollars Unless Otherwise Indicated:*				
Total Reserves minus Gold .... 1l. d	87.2	88.4	65.7	102.8	76.4	184.8	448.0	147.0	19.7	17.8	2.2	19.7	5.4	4.7	19.6
SDRs .... 1b. d	16.6	18.5	18.6	16.9	13.7	10.4	9.6	23.6	3.5	12.3	.1	16.2	.2	.1	8.5
Reserve Position in the Fund ..... 1c. d	11.7	13.0	—	—	—	—	13.5	16.1	12.1						
Foreign Exchange .... 1d. d	58.9	56.9	47.1	85.8	62.7	174.4	424.9	107.3	4.1	5.6	2.1	3.5	5.2	4.7	11.0
Gold (Million Fine Troy Ounces) ... 1ad	....	....	....	....	—	.022	.034	.045	.045	.045	.045	.045	.045	.045	.045
Gold (National Valuation) 1and	....	....	....	....	—	1.0	1.5	2.1	2.0	18.7	19.0	17.2	14.8	14.4	18.0
Monetary Authorities: Other Liab. ... 4.. d	1.0	7.3	4.1	11.5	2.8	10.7	31.7	31.5	483.0	590.8	453.7	571.8	380.8	190.7	274.1
Deposit Money Banks: Assets ...... 7a. d	31.6	47.9	165.7	36.9	111.0	147.0	118.6	94.9	95.0	100.9	122.8	99.6	146.5	174.8	167.4
Liabilities .... 7b. d	63.5	85.3	116.1	149.9	215.3	212.3	371.7	495.1	612.0	483.3	433.2	422.8	247.6	388.3	520.7
Monetary Authorities														*Billions of Francs:*	
Foreign Assets 11	22.3	20.3	14.6	23.0	19.0	43.5	93.6	29.6	4.4	5.1	.7	8.2	2.6	1.8	6.3
Claims on Central Government 12a	4.8	.1			9.3			6.0	36.0	91.9	166.0	245.3	316.4	333.5	327.4	327.6
Claims on Deposit Money Banks 12e	35.0	51.5	91.1	90.4	103.0	165.2	173.6	197.7	266.2	366.8	405.7	466.9	433.3	392.2	412.9
Claims on Other Financial Insts 12f	—				2.9	4.4	5.7	6.4	5.7	5.5	6.4	7.8	8.6	9.9	11.1
Reserve Money 14	56.7	62.5	87.5	99.3	120.6	167.4	221.0	230.1	232.6	255.2	239.6	257.6	309.2	389.1	406.4
of which: Currency Outside DMBs ... 14a	51.5	57.0	77.5	89.6	106.7	137.3	164.5	193.7	210.9	229.8	219.1	232.0	278.7	307.1	318.7
Foreign Liabilities 16c	.3	1.7	3.9	5.5	7.4	6.3	18.5	18.0	137.5	307.5	346.5	532.4	500.8	334.4	313.2
Central Government Deposits 16d	1.1	3.8	13.4	6.7	2.4	33.2	40.7	21.0	3.5	2.9	87.0	37.7	19.7	25.0	27.0
Other Items (Net) 17r	4.0	4.0	.8	2.1	3.8	6.2	−1.4	.6	−5.4	−22.1	−14.9	−28.4	−51.7	−17.2	11.3
Deposit Money Banks														*Billions of Francs:*	
Reserves 20	5.0	5.1	9.1	8.2	12.0	30.0	55.5	32.6	31.5	25.0	20.9	26.6	39.2	78.1	90.3
Foreign Assets 21	8.1	11.0	36.8	8.3	27.6	34.6	24.8	19.1	21.4	29.0	41.3	41.6	70.3	66.1	54.0
Claims on Central Government 22a	.2	.2	.3	.3	5.1	2.8	6.4	†24.8	12.6	13.9	17.0	17.4	19.4	52.7	74.5
Claims on Private Sector 22d	128.8	167.4	238.5	286.4	377.3	581.7	673.3	†773.7	861.2	947.7	1,010.3	1,091.1	1,076.5	1,053.8	1,061.8
Claims on Other Financial Insts 22f	....	....	....	....	....	....	....	†11.2	17.5	16.6	13.9	15.9	18.9	21.4	30.7
Demand Deposits 24	50.0	59.5	82.8	87.9	151.7	243.4	248.3	†240.0	227.7	234.5	238.2	253.1	290.6	311.2	317.1
Time Deposits 25	19.7	30.0	60.4	64.7	89.7	141.4	166.1	†132.4	143.1	175.3	200.0	203.9	251.5	319.3	327.5
Foreign Liabilities 26c	10.0	12.6	18.0	23.5	41.7	35.7	61.0	73.5	111.7	110.5	108.7	137.5	70.8	78.7	89.8
Long-Term Foreign Liabilities 26cl	6.2	7.1	7.8	10.1	11.8	14.3	16.7	26.0	26.6	28.4	36.9	39.0	48.0	68.1	78.2
Central Government Deposits 26d	11.5	15.1	25.2	16.8	23.6	28.6	64.4	†141.5	140.6	106.4	89.3	78.0	90.8	121.5	118.6
Credit from Monetary Authorities 26g	35.0	51.5	91.1	90.4	103.4	165.2	173.5	196.6	270.0	365.2	407.0	457.0	449.3	393.5	414.5
Other Items (Net) 27r	9.7	8.0	−.6	9.6	.2	20.6	30.1	51.3	24.7	12.0	23.2	24.2	23.6	−20.2	−34.5
Treasury Claims: Private Sector .... 22d. i	4.2	7.9	5.2	6.2	11.7	19.4	17.3	12.2	15.1	9.3	12.0	10.2	11.8	13.6	12.2
Post Office: Checking Deposits ...... 24.. i	1.6	1.4	2.5	2.3	1.6	2.4	2.6	—	—	—	2.9	2.8	5.0	1.8	1.4
Monetary Survey														*Billions of Francs:*	
Foreign Assets (Net) 31n	20.1	17.1	29.5	2.3	−2.6	36.1	38.9	−42.9	−223.3	−383.9	−413.2	−620.0	−498.7	−345.2	−342.7
Domestic Credit 32	122.7	150.2	205.6	267.2	370.4	529.5	588.8	†689.6	844.9	1,040.5	1,119.6	1,335.7	1,351.6	1,320.5	1,361.4
Claims on Central Govt. (Net) 32an	−10.2	−25.2	−38.1	−25.3	−21.6	−76.0	−107.5	†−114.0	−54.7	61.5	77.0	210.7	235.6	221.8	245.7
Claims on Private Sector 32d	132.9	175.4	243.7	292.5	389.0	601.2	690.7	†785.9	876.3	957.0	1,022.3	1,101.3	1,088.6	1,067.4	1,074.0
Claims on Other Financial Insts 32f	....	....	....	....	2.9	4.4	5.7	†17.7	23.2	22.0	20.3	23.7	27.4	31.2	41.7
Money 34	103.2	117.9	162.8	179.8	260.1	383.1	415.6	†433.8	438.7	464.4	460.3	488.0	574.6	620.2	637.4
Quasi-Money 35	19.7	30.0	60.4	64.7	89.7	141.4	166.1	†132.4	143.1	175.3	200.0	203.9	251.5	319.3	327.5
Long-Term Foreign Liabilities 36cl	6.2	7.1	7.8	10.1	11.8	14.3	16.7	26.0	26.6	28.4	36.9	39.0	48.0	68.1	78.2
Other Items (Net) 37r	13.7	12.3	4.1	14.9	6.2	26.8	29.5	54.5	13.2	−11.5	9.1	−15.2	−21.1	−32.3	−24.3
Money plus Quasi-Money 35l	122.8	147.9	223.2	244.6	349.8	524.5	581.6	†566.2	581.8	639.7	660.3	692.0	826.1	939.4	964.9
Other Banking Institutions														*Billions of Francs:*	
Savings Deposits 45	1.2	1.3	1.5	1.5	1.8	2.1	2.1	....	....	....	....	....	....		
Liquid Liabilities 55l	124.0	149.2	224.7	246.1	351.5	526.6	583.7	†566.2	581.8	639.7	660.3	692.0	826.1	939.4	964.9
Interest Rates														*Percent Per Annum*	
Discount Rate (End of Period) 60	3.50	5.50	5.50	8.00	8.00	8.00	8.00	8.00	10.50	10.50	12.50	10.50	10.50	10.50	8.50
Money Market Rate 60b	....	....	....	....	7.28	7.38	7.40	7.72	10.13	13.68	14.66	12.23	11.84	10.66	8.58
Deposit Rate 60l	3.00	5.75	5.75	5.88	6.00	6.00	6.00	6.00	6.19	6.25	7.75	7.50	7.25	7.25	6.08
Lending Rate 60p	....					12.00	12.00	12.00	14.50	14.50	16.00	14.50	14.50	14.50	13.50
Prices, Production, Labor														*Index Numbers (1995=100):*	
Consumer Prices 64	12.4	13.7	16.1	18.0	20.2	25.7	29.1	33.8	38.8	42.2	45.4	48.0	50.0	†51.0	55.9
Industrial Production 66	32.6	37.6	39.8	48.6	60.7	70.6	81.3	†88.2	101.6	102.6	98.7	84.0	†91.0	93.8	101.4
														Number in Thousands:	
Unemployment 67c	....	....	....	....	....	....	....	....	....	....	....	....	....	86	92
Unemployment Rate 67r	....	....	....	....	....	....	....	....	....	....	....	....	....		

1987	1988	1989	1990	1991	1992	1993	1994	1995	1996	1997	1998	1999	2000	2001		
End of Period															**Exchange Rates**	
378.78	407.68	380.32	364.84	370.48	378.57	404.89	†780.44	728.38	753.06	807.94	791.61	†896.19	918.49	935.39	Official Rate	aa
End of Period (ae) Period Average (rf)																
267.00	302.95	289.40	256.45	259.00	275.32	·294.77	†534.60	490.00	523.70	598.81	562.21	†652.95	704.95	744.31	Official Rate	ae
300.54	297.85	319.01	272.26	282.11	264.69	283.16	†555.20	499.15	511.55	583.67	589.95	†615.70	711.98	733.04	Official Rate	rf
Period Averages																
166.1	167.8	156.5	183.7	177.4	188.9	176.3	90.0	100.0	97.5	85.6	84.7	81.1	70.3	68.1	Official Rate	ah x
77.5	84.8	94.9	119.6	127.0	144.9	162.5	93.9	100.0	100.6	96.9	101.2	100.1	94.4	96.3	Nominal Effective Exchange Rate	ne c
144.5	147.9	139.5	141.3	136.3	142.3	140.3	86.5	100.0	100.5	98.9	105.5	103.5	96.5	99.9	Real Effective Exchange Rate	re c
End of Period															**Fund Position**	
165.5	165.5	165.5	165.5	165.5	238.2	238.2	238.2	238.2	238.2	238.2	238.2	325.2	325.2	325.2	Quota	2f. s
.2	.5	3.9	.8	1.4	.2	.8	.1	1.2	.8	—	.1	2.5	1.0	.6	SDRs	1b. s
					—	.1	.1	.1	.1	.2	.2	.2	.3	.3	Reserve Position in the Fund	1c. s
425.8	377.9	281.3	303.1	259.7	194.5	159.1	224.8	287.1	349.6	333.5	457.3	451.4	421.6	369.2	Total Fund Cred.&Loans Outstg.	2tl
End of Period															**International Liquidity**	
8.9	10.4	15.0	4.0	13.4	6.9	2.3	204.3	529.0	605.8	618.4	855.5	630.4	667.8	1,018.9	Total Reserves minus Gold	1l. d
.2	.7	5.1	1.2	2.0	.3	1.1	.2	1.8	1.2	—	.2	3.4	1.3	.7	SDRs	1b. d
					—	.1	.1	.1	.2	.2	.3	.3	.4	.4	Reserve Position in the Fund	1c. d
8.7	9.7	9.8	2.8	11.4	6.7	1.1	204.0	527.0	604.4	618.1	855.0	626.6	666.2	1,017.8	Foreign Exchange	1d. d
.045	.045	.045	.045	.045	.045	.045	.045	.045	.045	.045	.045	.045	....	....	Gold (Million Fine Troy Ounces)	1ad
21.0	18.5	17.4	16.9	15.8	15.4	16.6	16.6	17.1	16.7	13.6	13.1	13.1	....	....	Gold (National Valuation)	1and
597.8	854.8	1,027.9	1,330.7	1,316.0	1,519.8	1,382.4	1.7	9.6	7.8	10.6	14.4	8.1	.5	6.6	Monetary Authorities: Other Liab.	4..d
191.8	154.6	141.3	189.6	163.6	206.9	176.5	202.1	352.6	268.5	266.8	311.3	351.9	252.5	223.3	Deposit Money Banks: Assets	7a. d
775.3	713.5	687.1	614.6	558.6	449.6	486.4	299.8	400.6	312.0	295.4	363.0	389.7	317.2	345.8	Liabilities	7b. d
End of Period															**Monetary Authorities**	
2.4	6.0	6.7	1.0	3.5	1.9	.7	109.2	259.2	317.2	370.3	481.0	412.0	475.1	766.6	Foreign Assets	11
289.6	279.1	245.6	250.3	245.0	239.1	273.2	433.2	382.6	439.8	449.3	572.3	596.4	538.3	491.1	Claims on Central Government	12a
498.8	497.5	452.0	523.9	521.5	533.6	506.6	130.0	140.8	125.8	104.7	114.6	99.8	75.3	36.8	Claims on Deposit Money Banks	12e
11.7	11.9	10.7	10.1	9.4	9.3	10.6	5.1	12.3	14.4	13.4	14.7	14.2	12.7	9.7	Claims on Other Financial Insts	12f
413.2	356.4	278.8	296.4	305.1	271.1	295.8	462.4	516.0	550.8	615.7	733.1	676.7	690.1	926.9	Reserve Money	14
305.0	298.5	254.1	270.7	258.3	252.1	272.5	392.6	451.4	473.2	571.8	652.1	615.5	620.7	774.7	*of which: Currency Outside DMBs*	14a
328.4	416.6	405.8	451.9	437.1	492.1	471.9	176.3	213.8	267.3	275.8	370.2	409.8	387.6	350.3	Foreign Liabilities	16c
33.0	1.9	3.1	16.7	18.5	8.2	13.1	45.8	43.0	49.5	27.8	51.1	56.7	39.3	40.8	Central Government Deposits	16d
27.9	19.6	27.3	20.3	18.7	12.5	10.3	−6.9	22.0	29.5	18.4	28.2	−20.8	−15.6	−13.9	Other Items (Net)	17r
End of Period															**Deposit Money Banks**	
107.7	61.7	26.9	24.8	38.9	22.1	20.6	66.6	58.1	74.7	45.4	67.2	60.7	64.7	96.1	Reserves	20
51.2	46.8	40.9	48.6	42.4	57.0	52.0	108.0	172.8	140.6	159.8	175.0	229.8	178.0	165.5	Foreign Assets	21
98.4	107.0	81.3	76.6	83.1	226.8	224.7	314.9	371.1	413.4	415.9	412.6	382.8	325.4	302.5	Claims on Central Government	22a
1,142.8	1,143.8	1,091.8	1,062.7	1,053.7	928.9	878.5	828.2	997.1	1,016.0	1,147.4	1,186.7	1,084.5	1,136.2	1,192.3	Claims on Private Sector	22d
37.6	29.9	27.3	20.5	11.7	11.2	6.2	5.8	1.7	—	—	—	—	—	—	Claims on Other Financial Insts	22f
292.3	278.3	255.6	254.4	250.1	234.5	219.2	403.3	490.7	489.0	502.8	562.0	576.7	526.7	507.8	Demand Deposits	24
331.4	366.0	356.5	319.0	336.3	346.9	331.0	412.1	485.3	519.6	527.7	485.1	477.7	489.3	515.3	Time Deposits	25
109.3	124.5	128.6	93.0	82.3	78.1	95.8	112.5	160.1	128.2	153.8	172.3	207.1	192.4	185.3	Foreign Liabilities	26c
97.7	91.7	70.3	64.6	62.4	45.7	47.6	47.8	36.2	35.2	23.1	31.7	47.4	31.3	72.1	Long-Term Foreign Liabilities	26cl
164.2	114.4	80.7	97.7	82.5	74.9	92.5	171.1	183.1	243.3	278.9	325.7	234.4	267.3	287.6	Central Government Deposits	26d
480.7	458.4	444.9	514.7	516.4	524.7	497.3	134.4	152.2	124.3	104.7	116.0	91.0	76.8	37.0	Credit from Monetary Authorities	26g
−37.9	−44.1	−68.3	−110.1	−100.3	−58.9	−101.3	42.3	93.0	105.0	177.6	148.7	123.5	120.5	151.2	Other Items (Net)	27r
7.4	6.4	14.7	10.0	12.3	17.5	17.8	26.7	19.0	22.7	22.0	—	16.0	13.4	21.2	Treasury Claims: Private Sector	22d. i
1.6	1.1	1.2	1.4	2.5	1.7	1.7	2.1	1.5	2.4	3.6	2.0	3.0	3.9	3.6	Post Office: Checking Deposits	24.. i
End of Period															**Monetary Survey**	
−384.2	−488.3	−486.8	−495.3	−473.6	−511.3	−515.0	−71.5	58.1	62.3	100.5	113.5	24.8	73.2	396.4	Foreign Assets (Net)	31n
1,384.5	1,456.5	1,374.3	1,307.1	1,303.3	1,334.6	1,289.3	1,372.4	1,540.1	1,593.1	1,722.9	1,811.5	1,789.8	1,709.8	1,670.6	Domestic Credit	32
185.0	264.5	229.9	203.8	216.3	367.7	376.1	506.5	510.1	540.0	540.1	610.1	675.1	547.6	447.5	Claims on Central Govt. (Net)	32an
1,150.2	1,150.3	1,106.5	1,072.7	1,065.9	946.4	896.3	854.9	1,016.0	1,038.7	1,169.4	1,186.7	1,100.5	1,149.5	1,213.5	Claims on Private Sector	32d
49.3	41.8	38.0	30.6	21.0	20.5	16.9	10.9	13.9	14.4	13.4	14.7	14.2	12.7	9.7	Claims on Other Financial Insts	32f
598.9	578.0	511.2	526.4	510.1	489.4	494.0	798.8	944.5	966.4	1,080.0	1,219.3	1,198.0	1,154.0	1,324.8	Money	34
331.4	366.0	356.5	319.0	336.3	346.9	331.0	412.1	485.3	519.6	527.7	485.1	477.7	489.3	515.3	Quasi-Money	35
97.7	91.7	70.3	64.6	62.4	45.7	47.6	47.8	36.2	35.2	23.1	31.7	47.4	31.3	72.1	Long-Term Foreign Liabilities	36cl
−27.7	−67.4	−50.5	−98.2	−79.1	−58.7	−98.3	42.1	132.0	134.2	192.6	188.9	91.6	108.5	154.9	Other Items (Net)	37r
930.3	944.0	867.7	845.4	846.4	836.4	825.0	1,210.9	1,429.9	1,486.0	1,607.7	1,704.4	1,675.7	1,643.3	1,840.1	Money plus Quasi-Money	35l
End of Period															**Other Banking Institutions**	
....	....	....	....	....	....	....	....	....	....	....	....	....	....	....	Savings Deposits	45
930.3	944.0	867.7	845.4	846.4	836.4	825.0	1,210.9	1,429.9	1,486.0	1,607.7	1,704.4	1,675.7	1,643.3	1,840.1	Liquid Liabilities	55l
Percent Per Annum															**Interest Rates**	
8.50	9.50	11.00	11.00	11.00	12.50	10.50	10.00	7.50	6.50	6.00	6.25	5.75	6.50	6.50	Discount Rate (End of Period)	60
8.37	8.72	10.07	10.98	10.94	11.44	....	....	....	....	....	4.81	4.95	4.95	4.95	Money Market Rate	60b
5.25	5.25	6.42	7.00	7.00	7.75	....	....	....	....	....	3.50	3.50	3.50	3.50	Deposit Rate	60l
13.50	13.58	15.08	16.00	16.00	16.75	....	....	....	....	....	....	....	....	....	Lending Rate	60p
Period Averages															**Prices, Production, Labor**	
59.8	63.9	64.6	64.1	65.2	67.9	†69.4	87.5	100.0	†102.5	106.6	111.6	112.5	115.2	120.2	Consumer Prices	64
101.4	98.6	96.9	91.0	88.6	90.0	89.1	91.9	100.0	113.3	126.8	141.0	145.0	133.6	....	Industrial Production	66
Period Averages																
108	121	129	140	137	172	175	186	216	238	....	....	....	....	....	Unemployment	67c
....	....	....	....	....	26.3	27.7	30.0	35.6	38.8	....	....	....	....	....	Unemployment Rate	67r

Côte d'Ivoire

International Transactions		1972	1973	1974	1975	1976	1977	1978	1979	1980	1981	1982	1983	1984	1985	1986
														Billions of Francs		
Exports	70	139.54	190.86	291.77	254.57	392.50	529.21	524.38	534.85	663.92	689.30	747.45	796.77	1,184.34	1,318.06	1,160.44
Imports, c.i.f.	71	114.32	157.52	232.29	241.39	311.61	429.57	522.50	528.85	636.96	653.32	718.59	704.25	658.57	772.98	709.04
Balance of Payments															*Millions of US Dollars:*	
Current Account, n.i.e.	78al d	....	....	....	−378.9	−249.3	−177.3	−839.2	−1,383.3	−1,826.5	−1,411.4	−1,017.3	−931.1	−76.8	63.7	−300.3
Goods: Exports f.o.b.	78aa d				1,238.8	1,735.1	2,412.1	2,615.9	2,722.8	3,012.6	2,435.1	2,347.2	2,066.3	2,624.7	2,761.0	3,187.4
Goods: Imports f.o.b.	78ab d				−1,012.1	−1,161.3	−1,597.2	−2,042.9	−2,233.4	−2,613.6	−2,067.9	−1,789.7	−1,635.1	−1,487.3	−1,409.9	−1,639.9
Trade Balance	78ac d				226.8	573.8	814.9	573.0	489.4	399.0	367.3	557.5	431.2	1,137.4	1,351.1	1,547.5
Services: Credit	78ad d				225.8	235.2	324.8	410.4	510.5	564.2	434.3	450.7	425.1	370.5	399.1	471.5
Services: Debit	78ae d				−550.1	−642.1	−823.9	−1,097.0	−1,363.8	−1,531.1	−1,225.5	−1,163.4	−990.1	−824.3	−763.5	−1,313.6
Balance on Goods & Services	78af d				−97.5	166.8	315.8	−113.6	−363.9	−568.0	−423.9	−155.2	−133.8	683.6	986.7	705.4
Income: Credit	78ag d				38.7	28.0	42.3	60.3	59.2	62.9	46.0	46.0	46.7	37.5	39.4	67.3
Income: Debit	78ah d				−178.2	−185.0	−235.3	−367.4	−506.8	−615.8	−554.2	−545.3	−548.5	−530.9	−705.4	−714.1
Balance on Gds, Serv. & Inc.	78ai d				−237.0	9.9	122.8	−420.7	−811.4	−1,120.8	−932.2	−654.6	−635.6	190.2	320.7	58.6
Current Transfers, n.i.e.: Credit	78aj d				130.2	128.7	160.3	186.0	199.1	242.3	205.2	189.4	174.2	149.9	130.5	184.2
Current Transfers: Debit	78ak d				−272.0	−387.9	−460.4	−604.5	−771.0	−948.0	−684.5	−552.0	−469.7	−417.0	−387.5	−543.2
Capital Account, n.i.e.	78bc d				—	—	—	—	—	—	—	—	—	—	—	—
Capital Account, n.i.e.: Credit	78ba d				—	—	—	—	—	—	—	—	—	—	—	—
Capital Account: Debit	78bb d				—	—	—	—	—	—	—	—	—	—	—	—
Financial Account, n.i.e.	78bj d				288.8	254.4	351.7	1,023.7	1,132.0	1,215.5	906.0	749.5	384.4	−280.8	−317.2	−36.4
Direct Investment Abroad	78bd d				....	....	....	....	....	....	....	....	....	....	....	....
Dir. Invest. in Rep. Econ., n.i.e.	78be d				69.1	44.8	14.7	83.3	74.7	94.7	32.8	47.5	37.5	21.7	29.2	70.7
Portfolio Investment Assets	78bf d				−.9	−5.0	−9.4	−6.6	1.4	2.8	.7	—	1.3	−.9	−1.1	−.3
Equity Securities	78bk d				−.9	−.8	−9.4	−6.6	−.9	.5	.7	.3	1.6	−.7	−1.1	−.3
Debt Securities	78bl d				—	−4.2	—	—	2.4	2.4	—	−.3	−.3	−.2	—	—
Portfolio Investment Liab., n.i.e.	78bg d				−.5	.8	−2.4	.4	—	—	—	−1.2	−1.0	−.7	−.2	—
Equity Securities	78bm d				1.9	1.7	—	1.8	—	—	—	—	—	—	—	—
Debt Securities	78bn d				−2.3	−.8	−2.4	−1.3	—	—	—	−1.2	−1.0	−.7	−.2	—
Financial Derivatives Assets	78bw d				....	....	....	....	....	....	....	....	....	....	....	....
Financial Derivatives Liabilities	78bx d				....	....	....	....	....	....	....	....	....	....	....	....
Other Investment Assets	78bh d				−14.9	−190.4	−371.2	−24.4	205.0	−30.3	−27.6	−10.7	−64.0	−94.5	−30.3	96.2
Monetary Authorities	78bo d															
General Government	78bp d				−50.4	−27.2	−143.7	56.3	111.4	−34.6	29.8	3.7	17.8	−2.5	−4.7	4.0
Banks	78bq d				30.8	−95.8	−66.8	−96.6	175.8	−33.6	−45.6	−12.5	−12.1	−95.0	−26.7	82.6
Other Sectors	78br d				4.7	−67.4	−160.8	16.0	−82.3	37.9	−11.8	−1.8	−69.8	3.0	1.1	9.5
Other Investment Liab., n.i.e.	78bi d				236.1	404.3	720.0	970.9	850.9	1,148.2	900.2	713.9	410.7	−206.4	−314.7	−203.0
Monetary Authorities	78bs d				7.9	−7.5	8.1	15.1	−.9	−23.7	−.7	4.0	−1.6	1.8	6.9	−12.7
General Government	78bt d				104.5	127.6	352.9	528.7	461.6	751.6	656.5	604.4	139.9	−228.4	−239.1	−262.5
Banks	78bu d				56.9	98.3	14.7	170.6	181.0	227.7	18.4	68.2	157.7	−43.7	−42.5	145.2
Other Sectors	78bv d				66.7	185.8	344.4	256.6	209.2	192.6	226.0	37.4	114.7	63.9	−40.1	−73.1
Net Errors and Omissions	78ca d				5.6	−3.7	−48.2	−32.2	−78.8	−76.9	−98.8	−35.2	−154.1	−119.1	84.2	−55.3
Overall Balance	78cb d				−84.5	1.4	126.3	152.4	−330.1	−687.9	−604.2	−302.9	−700.8	−476.7	−169.2	−392.0
Reserves and Related Items	79da d				84.5	−1.4	−126.3	−152.4	330.1	687.9	604.2	302.9	700.8	476.7	169.2	392.0
Reserve Assets	79db d				84.5	−37.1	−115.2	−164.1	329.9	135.5	6.2	20.3	−19.1	10.0	4.8	−10.7
Use of Fund Credit and Loans	79dc d				—	14.6	−11.6	9.9	—	37.0	372.0	125.6	165.3	9.9	−45.4	−78.4
Exceptional Financing	79de d				—	21.1	.5	1.9	.2	515.4	226.1	157.0	554.6	456.7	209.8	481.1
International Investment Position															*Millions of US Dollars*	
Assets	79aa d	....	....	....	....	....	....	....	....	....	....	....	....	....	....	....
Direct Investment Abroad	79ab d	....	....	....	....	....	....	....	....	....	....	....	....	....	....	....
Portfolio Investment	79ac d	....	....	....	....	....	....	....	....	....	....	....	....	....	....	....
Equity Securities	79ad d	....	....	....	....	....	....	....	....	....	....	....	....	....	....	....
Debt Securities	79ae d	....	....	....	....	....	....	....	....	....	....	....	....	....	....	....
Financial Derivatives	79al d	....	....	....	....	....	....	....	....	....	....	....	....	....	....	....
Other Investment	79af d	....	....	....	....	....	....	....	....	....	....	....	....	....	....	....
Monetary Authorities	79ag d	....	....	....	....	....	....	....	....	....	....	....	....	....	....	....
General Government	79ah d	....	....	....	....	....	....	....	....	....	....	....	....	....	....	....
Banks	79ai d	....	....	....	....	....	....	....	....	....	....	....	....	....	....	....
Other Sectors	79aj d	....	....	....	....	....	....	....	....	....	....	....	....	....	....	....
Reserve Assets	79ak d	....	....	....	....	....	....	....	....	....	....	....	....	....	....	....
Liabilities	79la d	....	....	....	....	....	....	....	....	....	....	....	....	....	....	....
Dir. Invest. in Rep. Economy	79lb d	....	....	....	....	....	....	....	....	....	....	....	....	....	....	....
Portfolio Investment	79lc d	....	....	....	....	....	....	....	....	....	....	....	....	....	....	....
Equity Securities	79ld d	....	....	....	....	....	....	....	....	....	....	....	....	....	....	....
Debt Securities	79le d	....	....	....	....	....	....	....	....	....	....	....	....	....	....	....
Financial Derivatives	79ll d	....	....	....	....	....	....	....	....	....	....	....	....	....	....	....
Other Investment	79lf d	....	....	....	....	....	....	....	....	....	....	....	....	....	....	....
Monetary Authorities	79lg d	....	....	....	....	....	....	....	....	....	....	....	....	....	....	....
General Government	79lh d	....	....	....	....	....	....	....	....	....	....	....	....	....	....	....
Banks	79li d	....	....	....	....	....	....	....	....	....	....	....	....	....	....	....
Other Sectors	79lj d	....	....	....	....	....	....	....	....	....	....	....	....	....	....	....

International Transactions

Billions of Francs

Description	Code	1987	1988	1989	1990	1991	1992	1993	1994	1995	1996	1997	1998	1999	2000	2001
Exports	70	929.14	826.47	895.60	836.43	757.76	751.70	713.20	1,522.50	1,899.70	2,274.40	2,598.10	2,717.60	2,870.10	2,768.20	2,675.60
Imports, c.i.f.	71	673.90	619.92	673.45	571.10	593.37	613.17	599.00	1,064.60	1,463.00	1,484.50	1,623.10	1,764.50	2,002.40	1,804.90	1,865.70

Balance of Payments

Minus Sign Indicates Debit — Billions of Francs

Description	Code	1987	1988	1989	1990	1991	1992	1993	1994	1995	1996	1997	1998	1999	2000	2001
Current Account, n.i.e.	78ald	-970.0	-1,241.2	-967.3	-1,214.3	-1,074.1	-1,012.7	-891.7	-13.8	-492.4	-162.3	-154.7	-290.2	-120.5	-12.9	....
Goods: Exports f.o.b.	78aad	2,949.7	2,691.3	2,696.8	2,912.6	2,705.0	2,946.8	2,518.7	2,895.9	3,805.9	4,446.1	4,451.2	4,606.5	4,661.4	3,972.9	....
Goods: Imports f.o.b.	78abd	-1,863.3	-1,769.4	-1,777.1	-1,818.8	-1,781.6	-1,952.1	-1,770.4	-1,606.8	-2,430.3	-2,622.4	-2,658.4	-2,886.5	-2,766.1	-2,175.5	....
Trade Balance	78acd	1,086.4	921.9	919.7	1,093.8	923.4	994.7	748.3	1,289.1	1,375.5	1,823.7	1,792.8	1,720.0	1,895.2	1,797.4	....
Services: Credit	78add	535.4	555.7	485.9	590.2	614.3	649.2	675.9	507.7	530.9	565.7	579.6	614.3	586.0	435.5	....
Services: Debit	78aed	-1,352.6	-1,342.3	-1,230.4	-1,626.0	-1,393.8	-1,477.2	-1,331.7	-1,011.1	-1,375.7	-1,440.3	-1,478.6	-1,524.0	-1,459.0	-1,215.8	....
Balance on Goods & Services	78afd	269.2	135.3	175.2	58.0	143.9	166.8	92.5	785.7	530.7	949.1	893.8	810.2	1,022.3	1,017.2	....
Income: Credit	78agd	77.9	71.8	55.8	58.0	60.3	18.9	97.8	133.8	189.5	170.7	161.2	169.2	162.6	141.0	....
Income: Debit	78ahd	-957.3	-992.8	-995.9	-1,149.2	-1,171.9	-1,099.8	-887.8	-817.5	-976.1	-939.5	-829.2	-876.0	-919.4	-801.4	....
Balance on Gds, Serv. & Inc.	78aid	-610.2	-785.6	-764.9	-1,033.2	-967.7	-914.1	-697.5	102.0	-255.8	180.2	225.8	103.4	265.4	356.8	....
Current Transfers, n.i.e.: Credit	78ajd	276.1	208.8	316.0	370.2	413.7	404.6	270.9	246.8	277.7	204.1	137.7	148.1	136.8	74.2	....
Current Transfers: Debit	78akd	-635.9	-664.4	-518.5	-551.3	-520.0	-503.2	-465.1	-362.6	-514.3	-546.6	-518.3	-541.7	-522.7	-443.8	....
Capital Account, n.i.e.	78bcd	—	—	—	—	—	—	—	527.6	291.3	47.1	40.6	25.6	13.8	14.6	....
Capital Account, n.i.e.: Credit	78bad	—	—	—	—	—	—	—	527.6	291.3	49.8	50.5	35.9	17.4	16.9	....
Capital Account: Debit	78bbd	—	—	—	—	—	—	—	—	—	-2.7	-9.9	-10.3	-3.6	-2.2	....
Financial Account, n.i.e.	78bjd	33.3	-159.1	-305.3	-122.7	-151.4	-450.7	-356.0	-523.1	-88.6	-717.8	-323.0	-417.0	-577.2	-673.6	....
Direct Investment Abroad	78bdd										-.4					....
Dir. Invest. in Rep. Econ., n.i.e.	78bed	87.5	51.7	18.5	48.1	16.3	-230.8	87.9	78.0	211.5	269.2	415.3	379.9	323.7	105.9	....
Portfolio Investment Assets	78bfd	-5.3	-13.4	1.9	4.4	6.4	—	7.4	-27.4	-8.4	-16.0	-26.9	-29.8	-28.7	-9.8	....
Equity Securities	78bkd	-4.3	-13.4	1.9	4.4	6.4	—	7.4	7.7	1.2	-1.6	.2	-1.7	-1.6	-.6	....
Debt Securities	78bld	-1.0	—	—	—	—	—	—	-35.1	-9.6	-14.5	-27.1	-28.1	-27.1	-9.3	....
Portfolio Investment Liab., n.i.e.	78bgd	-2.7	-.7	-.6	—	—	—	—	-.7	10.0	25.0	19.2	19.5	13.5	10.1	....
Equity Securities	78bmd	—	—	—	—	—	—	—	1.1	1.2	10.2	8.6	8.6	5.7	4.2	....
Debt Securities	78bnd	-2.7	-.7	-.6	—	—	—	—	-1.8	8.8	14.9	10.6	10.8	7.8	5.9	....
Financial Derivatives Assets	78bwd										-3.3	—	—	—	—	....
Financial Derivatives Liabilities	78bxd	....	....	....	....	....			—	—	-3.3	-3.1	-3.2	-3.1	-1.1	....
Other Investment Assets	78bhd	-3.0	50.4	21.6	-91.8	-25.2	169.6	51.9	-39.6	-323.2	-256.5	-304.8	-317.5	-350.5	-190.3	....
Monetary Authorities	78bod															....
General Government	78bpd	-11.3	8.4	-25.1	-1.8	-3.2	—	—	-11.9	-14.2	-22.3	-9.9	-7.6	-5.2	-7.4	....
Banks	78bqd	23.3	49.4	36.0	-66.1	2.8	63.8	72.7	-95.3	-33.1	35.2	-25.7	-16.4	-49.0	-3.2	....
Other Sectors	78brd	-15.0	-7.4	10.7	-23.9	-24.8	105.8	-20.8	67.5	-275.9	-269.4	-269.2	-293.4	-296.2	-179.6	....
Other Investment Liab., n.i.e.	78bid	-43.3	-247.1	-346.7	-83.4	-148.9	-389.5	-503.2	-533.3	21.4	-735.8	-422.7	-465.8	-532.1	-588.4	....
Monetary Authorities	78bsd	9.0	-21.5	-.9	55.1	-10.3	-33.2	-44.1	-726.6	1.8	-1.2	4.3	3.2	-5.0	—	....
General Government	78btd	-139.4	-353.5	-482.4	-75.7	-141.1	-207.4	-444.6	249.8	-105.8	-621.6	-473.6	-597.3	-583.6	-523.3	....
Banks	78bud	159.4	65.5	-29.8	-124.5	-18.8	-134.9	7.8	75.1	77.1	-38.5	64.9	37.3	41.9	-22.6	....
Other Sectors	78bvd	-72.2	62.4	166.5	61.7	21.3	-14.0	-22.2	-131.7	48.3	-74.5	-18.3	91.0	14.6	-42.4	....
Net Errors and Omissions	78cad	12.6	-24.4	-38.8	-109.6	-102.2	46.6	11.1	-11.1	35.6	-15.4	-39.0	32.0	-23.9	59.6	....
Overall Balance	78cbd	-924.2	-1,424.8	-1,311.5	-1,446.6	-1,327.6	-1,416.9	-1,236.6	-20.3	-254.2	-848.4	-476.6	-649.6	-707.8	-612.3	....
Reserves and Related Items	79ad	924.2	1,424.8	1,311.5	1,446.6	1,327.6	1,416.9	1,236.6	20.3	254.2	848.4	476.6	649.6	707.8	612.3	....
Reserve Assets	79dbd	-17.2	-.3	11.3	16.3	-.5	-84.4	4.4	-194.5	-302.5	-113.4	-95.4	-179.8	109.7	-82.5	....
Use of Fund Credit and Loans	79dcd	-145.8	-63.0	-123.9	33.4	-58.5	-91.9	-49.0	94.3	94.9	90.3	-22.3	168.8	-8.2	-38.8	....
Exceptional Financing	79ded	1,087.1	1,488.0	1,424.1	1,396.9	1,386.7	1,593.2	1,281.2	120.5	461.8	871.5	594.3	660.6	606.3	733.6	....

International Investment Position

Millions of US Dollars

Description	Code	1994	1995	1996	1997	1998	1999	2000	2001
Assets	79aad	541.8	909.5	875.3	889.9	2,768.1	2,641.1	2,733.0	....
Direct Investment Abroad	79abd								....
Portfolio Investment	79acd	—	—	—	—	158.8	166.9	165.7	....
Equity Securities	79add					10.5	10.6	10.4	....
Debt Securities	79aed					148.3	156.4	155.3	....
Financial Derivatives	79ald								....
Other Investment	79afd	337.4	378.6	268.3	266.9	1,757.2	1,843.8	1,900.0	....
Monetary Authorities	79agd								....
General Government	79ahd								....
Banks	79aid	230.5	249.8	81.0	100.7				....
Other Sectors	79ajd					1,757.2	1,843.8	1,900.0	....
Reserve Assets	79akd	204.4	531.0	607.0	623.0	852.1	630.4	667.3	....
Liabilities	79lad	15,272.6	17,009.2	16,101.1	14,046.3	18,731.3	16,581.3	15,597.6	....
Dir. Invest. in Rep. Economy	79lbd	—	—	—	—	1,858.2	1,905.2	1,871.6	....
Portfolio Investment	79lcd	—	—	—	—	244.4	223.1	216.9	....
Equity Securities	79ldd								....
Debt Securities	79led	—	—	—	—	244.4	223.1	216.9	....
Financial Derivatives	79lld								....
Other Investment	79lfd	15,272.6	17,009.2	16,101.1	14,046.3	16,628.7	14,453.0	13,509.1	....
Monetary Authorities	79lgd	329.8	436.8	510.7	461.3	644.0	619.5	549.3	....
General Government	79lhd					14,790.0	12,756.0	11,758.3	....
Banks	79lid	743.5	522.9	266.2	295.4	437.9	429.1	660.3	....
Other Sectors	79ljd					756.8	648.3	541.2	....

Côte d'Ivoire

662

		1972	1973	1974	1975	1976	1977	1978	1979	1980	1981	1982	1983	1984	1985	1986
Government Finance																*Billions of Francs:*
Deficit (-) or Surplus	80	...	...	...	...	...	...	...	...	...	...	...	...	...	...	...
Total Revenue and Grants	81y	...	...	...	...	...	...	...	...	...	...	...	...	...	...	...
Revenue	81	...	...	...	...	...	...	...	...	...	...	...	...	...	...	...
Grants	81z	...	...	...	...	...	...	...	...	...	...	...	...	...	...	...
Exp. & Lending Minus Repay.	82z	...	...	...	...	...	...	...	...	...	...	...	...	...	...	...
Expenditure	82	...	...	...	...	...	...	...	...	...	...	...	...	...	...	...
Lending Minus Repayments	83	...	...	...	...	...	...	...	...	...	...	...	...	...	...	...
Total Financing	80h	...	...	...	...	...	...	...	...	...	...	...	...	...	...	...
Domestic	84a	...	...	...	...	...	...	...	...	...	...	...	...	...	...	...
Foreign	85a	...	...	...	...	...	...	...	...	...	...	...	...	...	...	...
Total Debt by Residence	88	...	...	...	...	...	...	...	...	...	...	...	...	...	...	...
Domestic	88a	...	...	...	...	...	...	...	...	...	...	...	...	...	...	...
Foreign	89a	...	...	...	...	...	...	...	...	...	...	...	...	...	...	...
National Accounts																*Billions of Francs*
Househ.Cons.Expend.,incl.NPISHs	96f	287.8	340.1	418.1	504.1	616.4	811.9	978.1	1,106.7	1,349.8	1,456.3	1,549.7	1,663.5	1,783.7	1,836.4	2,007.8
Government Consumption Expend.	91f	77.2	95.6	118.7	141.8	180.3	209.7	290.4	353.8	362.4	403.6	432.5	439.3	453.3	441.6	485.9
Gross Fixed Capital Formation	93e	94.3	122.0	143.6	199.4	247.2	397.7	529.0	526.7	523.6	558.4	538.7	461.8	387.5	369.1	374.8
Changes in Inventories	93i	3.1	7.8	19.1	3.4	8.9	23.1	1.8	16.9	46.9	36.0	37.8	8.9	−39.3	37.0	7.7
Exports of Goods and Services	90c	170.2	215.8	337.6	315.2	465.0	656.1	651.0	673.1	752.5	806.0	905.7	963.1	1,354.6	1,466.3	1,252.7
Imports of Goods and Services (-)	98c	149.6	203.4	286.6	326.0	403.8	559.2	667.3	732.5	885.3	968.9	977.9	930.7	950.4	1,015.6	957.2
Gross Domestic Product (GDP)	99b	471.8	566.2	739.0	834.5	1,120.4	1,590.4	1,783.0	1,944.7	2,149.9	2,291.4	2,486.5	2,605.9	2,989.4	3,134.8	3,174.0
Net Primary Income from Abroad	98.n	−12.7	−12.6	−20.5	−27.2	−41.1	−50.5	−69.4	....	....	....	....	....	....	....	−237.0
Gross National Income (GNI)	99a	459.1	553.6	718.5	807.3	1,072.9	1,488.8	1,713.6	....	....	....	....	....	....	....	2,934.7
Net National Income	99e	437.1	528.6	688.5	767.3	1,017.9	1,406.8	1,591.2	1,702.0	....	....	....	....	....	....	....
GDP Volume (1980=100)	99bv *p*	...	...	...	...	79.2	82.9	91.1	92.8	100.0	103.5	...	...	...	...	...
GDP Deflator (1980=100)	99bi *p*	...	...	...	...	65.8	89.2	91.0	97.4	100.0	103.0	...	...	...	...	...
																Millions:
Population	99z	5.86	6.15	6.43	6.77	7.05	7.34	7.61	7.92	8.33	8.52	8.85	9.30	9.56	9.93	10.32

Government Finance

Year Ending December 31

	1994	1995	1996	1997	1998	1999	2000	2001		
Deficit (-) or Surplus	−280.1	−147.3	−57.7	23.2	−84.0	−11.0	....	....	Deficit (-) or Surplus	80
Total Revenue and Grants	878.7	1,142.2	1,274.5	1,374.2	1,442.7	1,482.1	....	....	Total Revenue and Grants	81y
Revenue	849.0	1,107.2	1,234.0	1,330.2	1,392.2	1,442.1	....	....	Revenue	81
Grants	29.7	35.0	40.5	44.1	50.5	40.0			Grants	81z
Exp. & Lending Minus Repay.	1,158.8	1,289.5	1,332.2	1,351.0	1,526.7	1,493.1			Exp. & Lending Minus Repay.	82z
Expenditure	1,166.0	1,322.6	1,385.2	1,494.5	1,557.3	1,533.1			Expenditure	82
Lending Minus Repayments	−7.2	−33.1	−53.0	−143.5	−30.6	−40.0			Lending Minus Repayments	83
Total Financing	280.1	147.3	57.7	−23.2	84.0	11.0			Total Financing	80h
Domestic	−153.1	−61.6	−107.5	−85.0	36.3	−104.2			Domestic	84a
Foreign	433.2	208.9	165.2	61.8	47.7	115.2			Foreign	85a
Total Debt by Residence	9,148.6	9,392.7	9,606.0	10,056.3	7,620.7	....			Total Debt by Residence	88
Domestic	1,320.4	1,230.7	1,137.8	1,070.6	1,039.5	....			Domestic	88a
Foreign	7,828.2	8,162.0	8,468.2	8,985.7	6,581.2	....			Foreign	89a

National Accounts

Billions of Francs

	1987	1988	1989	1990	1991	1992	1993	1994	1995	1996	1997	1998		
Househ.Cons.Expend.,incl.NPISHs	2,041.0	1,971.1	1,979.3	1,761.8	2,199.5	2,220.5	2,174.3	2,684.3	3,367.0	3,592.6	3,898.8	....	Househ.Cons.Expend.,incl.NPISHs	96f
Government Consumption Expend.	501.8	530.0	576.0	499.0	484.0	473.2	487.0	599.4	606.0	611.5	633.4	....	Government Consumption Expend.	91f
Gross Fixed Capital Formation	356.8	336.6	248.8	218.2	220.7	210.0	231.7	454.9	641.0	688.2	887.7	....	Gross Fixed Capital Formation	93e
Changes in Inventories	16.6	104.7	3.2	31.3	−33.0	−46.6	13.7	46.9	105.0	67.7	76.4	....	Changes in Inventories	93i
Exports of Goods and Services	1,013.5	788.7	885.1	812.7	888.0	857.3	851.3	1,730.5	2,051.0	2,396.2	2,553.1	....	Exports of Goods and Services	90c
Imports of Goods and Services (-)	898.0	663.9	705.1	627.9	799.1	810.5	811.5	1,379.8	1,782.0	1,877.3	2,046.2	....	Imports of Goods and Services (-)	98c
Gross Domestic Product (GDP)	3,031.8	3,054.5	3,109.5	2,939.7	2,958.9	2,953.0	2,946.2	4,256.0	4,987.7	5,548.2	6,176.2	6,893.3	Gross Domestic Product (GDP)	99b
Net Primary Income from Abroad	−285.8	−300.2	−359.4	−374.3	−411.3	....	....	....	....	....	....	....	Net Primary Income from Abroad	98.n
Gross National Income (GNI)	2,745.9	2,754.3	2,753.4	2,565.0	2,548.7	....	....	....	....	....	....	....	Gross National Income (GNI)	99a
Net National Income													Net National Income	99e
GDP Volume (1980=100)	....	....	....	....	....	....	....	....	....	....	....	....	GDP Volume (1980=100)	99bv *p*
GDP Deflator (1980=100)	....	....	....	....	....	....	....	....	....	....	....	....	GDP Deflator (1980=100)	99bi *p*

Midyear Estimates

	1987	1988	1989	1990	1991	1992	1993	1994	1995	1996	1997	1998	1999	2000	2001		
Population	10.72	10.82	11.26	11.72	12.19	12.67	13.18	13.70	14.23	14.78	15.04	15.37	15.69	16.40	16.94	Population	99z

(See notes in the back of the book.)

Croatia

960

		1972	1973	1974	1975	1976	1977	1978	1979	1980	1981	1982	1983	1984	1985	1986
Exchange Rates															*Kuna per SDR:*	
Official Rate	aa	...	...	...	...	...	...	...	...	...	...	...	...	...	...	...
															Kuna per US Dollar:	
Official Rate	ae	...	...	...	...	...	...	...	...	...	...	...	...	...	...	...
Official Rate	rf	...	...	...	...	...	...	...	...	...	...	...	...	...	...	...
														Index Numbers (1995=100):		
Nominal Effective Exchange Rate	ne c	...	...	...	...	...	...	...	...	...	...	...	...	...	...	...
Real Effective Exchange Rate	re c	...	...	...	...	...	...	...	...	...	...	...	...	...	...	...
Fund Position															*Millions of SDRs:*	
Quota	2f. s	...	...	...	...	...	...	...	...	...	...	...	...	...	...	...
SDRs	1b. s	...	...	...	...	...	...	...	...	...	...	...	...	...	...	...
Reserve Position in the Fund	1c. s	...	...	...	...	...	...	...	...	...	...	...	...	...	...	...
Total Fund Cred.&Loans Outstg.	2tl	...	...	...	...	...	...	...	...	...	...	...	...	...	...	...
International Liquidity										*Millions of US Dollars Unless Otherwise Indicated:*						
Total Reserves minus Gold	1l. d	...	...	...	...	...	...	...	...	...	...	...	...	...	...	...
SDRs	1b. d	...	...	...	...	...	...	...	...	...	...	...	...	...	...	...
Reserve Position in the Fund	1c. d	...	...	...	...	...	...	...	...	...	...	...	...	...	...	...
Foreign Exchange	1d. d	...	...	...	...	...	...	...	...	...	...	...	...	...	...	...
Gold (Million Fine Troy Ounces)	1ad	...	...	...	...	...	...	...	...	...	...	...	...	...	...	...
Gold (National Valuation)	1an d	...	...	...	...	...	...	...	...	...	...	...	...	...	...	...
Monetary Authorities: Other Liab.	4..d	...	...	...	...	...	...	...	...	...	...	...	...	...	...	...
Deposit Money Banks: Assets	7a. d	...	...	...	...	...	...	...	...	...	...	...	...	...	...	...
Liabilities	7b. d	...	...	...	...	...	...	...	...	...	...	...	...	...	...	...
Monetary Authorities															*Millions of Kuna:*	
Foreign Assets	11	...	...	...	...	...	...	...	...	...	...	...	...	...	...	...
Claims on Central Government	12a	...	...	...	...	...	...	...	...	...	...	...	...	...	...	...
Claims on Private Sector	12d	...	...	...	...	...	...	...	...	...	...	...	...	...	...	...
Claims on Deposit Money Banks	12e	...	...	...	...	...	...	...	...	...	...	...	...	...	...	...
Reserve Money	14	...	...	...	...	...	...	...	...	...	...	...	...	...	...	...
of which: Currency Outside DMBs	14a	...	...	...	...	...	...	...	...	...	...	...	...	...	...	...
Restricted Deposits	16b	...	...	...	...	...	...	...	...	...	...	...	...	...	...	...
Foreign Liabilities	16c	...	...	...	...	...	...	...	...	...	...	...	...	...	...	...
Central Government Deposits	16d	...	...	...	...	...	...	...	...	...	...	...	...	...	...	...
Capital Accounts	17a	...	...	...	...	...	...	...	...	...	...	...	...	...	...	...
Other Items (Net)	17r	...	...	...	...	...	...	...	...	...	...	...	...	...	...	...
Deposit Money Banks															*Millions of Kuna:*	
Reserves	20	...	...	...	...	...	...	...	...	...	...	...	...	...	...	...
Foreign Assets	21	...	...	...	...	...	...	...	...	...	...	...	...	...	...	...
Claims on Central Government	22a	...	...	...	...	...	...	...	...	...	...	...	...	...	...	...
Claims on Local Government	22b	...	...	...	...	...	...	...	...	...	...	...	...	...	...	...
Claims on Nonfin.Pub.Enterprises	22c	...	...	...	...	...	...	...	...	...	...	...	...	...	...	...
Claims on Private Sector	22d	...	...	...	...	...	...	...	...	...	...	...	...	...	...	...
Claims on Other Banking Insts	22f	...	...	...	...	...	...	...	...	...	...	...	...	...	...	...
Claims on Nonbank Financial Insts	22g	...	...	...	...	...	...	...	...	...	...	...	...	...	...	...
Demand Deposits	24	...	...	...	...	...	...	...	...	...	...	...	...	...	...	...
Time, Savings,& Fgn.Currency Dep.	25	...	...	...	...	...	...	...	...	...	...	...	...	...	...	...
Money Market Instruments	26aa	...	...	...	...	...	...	...	...	...	...	...	...	...	...	...
Bonds	26ab	...	...	...	...	...	...	...	...	...	...	...	...	...	...	...
Restricted Deposits	26b	...	...	...	...	...	...	...	...	...	...	...	...	...	...	...
Foreign Liabilities	26c	...	...	...	...	...	...	...	...	...	...	...	...	...	...	...
Central Government Deposits	26d	...	...	...	...	...	...	...	...	...	...	...	...	...	...	...
Credit from Monetary Authorities	26g	...	...	...	...	...	...	...	...	...	...	...	...	...	...	...
Capital Accounts	27a	...	...	...	...	...	...	...	...	...	...	...	...	...	...	...
Other Items (Net)	27r	...	...	...	...	...	...	...	...	...	...	...	...	...	...	...
Monetary Survey															*Millions of Kuna:*	
Foreign Assets (Net)	31n	...	...	...	...	...	...	...	...	...	...	...	...	...	...	...
Domestic Credit	32	...	...	...	...	...	...	...	...	...	...	...	...	...	...	...
Claims on Central Govt. (Net)	32an	...	...	...	...	...	...	...	...	...	...	...	...	...	...	...
Claims on Local Government	32b	...	...	...	...	...	...	...	...	...	...	...	...	...	...	...
Claims on Nonfin.Pub.Enterprises	32c	...	...	...	...	...	...	...	...	...	...	...	...	...	...	...
Claims on Private Sector	32d	...	...	...	...	...	...	...	...	...	...	...	...	...	...	...
Claims on Other Banking Insts	32f	...	...	...	...	...	...	...	...	...	...	...	...	...	...	...
Claims on Nonbank Financial Inst	32g	...	...	...	...	...	...	...	...	...	...	...	...	...	...	...
Money	34	...	...	...	...	...	...	...	...	...	...	...	...	...	...	...
Quasi-Money	35	...	...	...	...	...	...	...	...	...	...	...	...	...	...	...
Money Market Instruments	36aa	...	...	...	...	...	...	...	...	...	...	...	...	...	...	...
Bonds	36ab	...	...	...	...	...	...	...	...	...	...	...	...	...	...	...
Restricted Deposits	36b	...	...	...	...	...	...	...	...	...	...	...	...	...	...	...
Capital Accounts	37a	...	...	...	...	...	...	...	...	...	...	...	...	...	...	...
Other Items (Net)	37r	...	...	...	...	...	...	...	...	...	...	...	...	...	...	...
Money plus Quasi-Money	35l	...	...	...	...	...	...	...	...	...	...	...	...	...	...	...
Interest Rates															*Percent Per Annum*	
Discount Rate (End of Period)	60	...	...	...	...	...	...	...	...	...	...	...	...	...	...	...
Money Market Rate	60b	...	...	...	...	...	...	...	...	...	...	...	...	...	...	...
Deposit Rate	60l	...	...	...	...	...	...	...	...	...	...	...	...	...	...	...
Lending Rate	60p	...	...	...	...	...	...	...	...	...	...	...	...	...	...	...
Prices, Production, Labor															*Index Numbers (1995=100):*	
Wholesale Prices	63	...	...	...	...	...	...	...	...	...	...	...	...	...	...	...
Consumer Prices	64	...	...	...	...	...	...	...	...	...	...	...	...	...	...	...
Wages	65	...	...	...	...	...	...	...	...	...	...	...	...	...	...	...
Industrial Production	66	...	...	...	...	...	...	...	...	...	...	...	...	...	191.5	200.3
Total Employment	67	...	...	...	...	...	...	...	...	97.3	...	...	102.8	104.4	109.5	112.6
															Number in Thousands:	
Employment	67e	...	...	...	...	...	...	...	...	...	...	...	...	...	...	...
Unemployment	67c	...	...	...	...	...	...	...	...	...	...	...	...	...	...	...
Unemployment Rate (%)	67r	...	...	...	...	...	...	...	...	...	...	...	...	...	...	...
International Transactions															*Millions of US Dollars*	
Exports	70..d	...	...	...	...	...	...	...	...	...	...	...	...	...	...	...
Imports, c.i.f.	71..d	...	...	...	...	...	...	...	...	...	...	...	...	...	...	...

1987	1988	1989	1990	1991	1992	1993	1994	1995	1996	1997	1998	1999	2000	2001		
															Exchange Rates	
End of Period																
				....	1.098	9.013	8.217	7.902	7.966	8.504	8.797	10.496	10.626	10.501	Official Rate	aa
End of Period (ae) Period Average (rf)																
					.798	6.562	5.629	5.316	5.540	6.303	6.248	7.648	8.155	8.356	Official Rate	ae
						3.577	5.996	5.230	5.434	6.101	6.362	7.112	8.277	8.340	Official Rate	rf
Period Averages																
					2,410.64	234.83	93.58	100.00	100.35	102.10	100.27	94.79	94.64	98.06	Nominal Effective Exchange Rate	ne c
					64.95	82.67	97.64	100.00	99.17	100.58	100.99	97.05	98.89	103.12	Real Effective Exchange Rate	re c
															Fund Position	
End of Period																
					—	261.6	261.6	261.6	261.6	261.6	261.6	365.1	365.1	365.1	Quota	2f. s
					—	.8	3.1	94.4	87.3	109.0	164.2	138.1	113.0	85.5	SDRs	1b. s
					—	—	—	—	—	.1	.1	.1	.2	.2	Reserve Position in the Fund	1c. s
					—	14.8	87.1	148.6	145.4	172.7	166.1	143.2	121.4	97.2	Total Fund Cred.&Loans Outstg.	2tl
															International Liquidity	
End of Period																
					166.8	616.2	1,405.0	1,895.7	2,314.0	2,539.1	2,815.7	3,025.0	3,524.4	4,703.2	Total Reserves minus Gold	1l. d
					—	1.1	4.5	140.3	125.6	147.1	231.2	189.5	147.2	107.4	SDRs	1b. d
					—	—	—	—	—	.1	.2	.2	.2	.2	Reserve Position in the Fund	1c. d
					166.8	615.1	1,400.5	1,755.4	2,188.4	2,391.9	2,584.4	2,835.3	3,376.9	4,595.6	Foreign Exchange	1d. d
					—	—	—	—	—	—	—	—	—		Gold (Million Fine Troy Ounces)	1ad
					—	—	—	—	—	—	—	—	—		Gold (National Valuation)	1an d
					—	.1	.1	.2	.3	.5	.7	22.2	41.8	68.5	Monetary Authorities: Other Liab.	4..d
					....	946.7	1,258.3	1,748.8	2,265.4	2,567.9	2,042.9	1,621.4	2,416.9	3,926.2	Deposit Money Banks: Assets	7a. d
						1,838.9	2,333.5	2,849.8	2,250.6	2,190.5	2,589.3	2,245.1	2,183.8	2,615.8	Liabilities	7b. d
															Monetary Authorities	
End of Period																
				—	133.2	4,026.5	7,908.3	10,077.7	12,818.8	16,005.6	17,592.6	23,135.7	28,743.7	39,306.1	Foreign Assets	11
				15.5	52.7	535.1	250.6	390.1	218.8	—	3.8	24.1	—		Claims on Central Government	12a
				.1	.3	.7	.9	1.1	24.4	1.0	276.1	289.5	229.2		Claims on Private Sector	12d
				25.7	107.7	191.6	223.8	220.2	213.9	33.5	1,043.7	1,139.4	329.9	18.5	Claims on Deposit Money Banks	12e
				34.1	205.5	2,248.9	4,714.2	6,744.1	8,770.3	10,346.2	9,954.3	10,309.9	11,717.2	17,803.3	Reserve Money	14
				18.3	130.8	1,367.0	2,658.2	3,365.1	4,366.2	5,319.6	5,730.1	5,958.9	6,636.7	8,507.4	of which: Currency Outside DMBs	14a
					.1	1.4	40.3	212.2	243.2	101.1	119.1	380.6	315.0	325.4	Restricted Deposits	16b
				—	—	133.9	716.2	1,175.2	1,160.4	1,471.4	1,465.4	1,672.9	1,630.8	1,593.1	Foreign Liabilities	16c
						—	793.8	395.5	557.6	1,032.7	434.8	397.2	1,157.4	1,752.1	Central Government Deposits	16d
				1.9	114.4	2,366.0	2,066.0	2,019.4	1,900.1	2,361.8	2,902.1	4,535.5	5,216.6	6,425.2	Capital Accounts	17a
				5.2	-26.4	3.2	52.9	142.5	621.0	750.4	3,765.3	7,279.1	9,326.2	11,654.8	Other Items (Net)	17r
															Deposit Money Banks	
End of Period																
					....	862.1	2,039.7	3,508.3	4,573.9	5,056.7	5,908.1	8,987.9	10,588.9	15,002.7	Reserves	20
						6,212.1	7,082.5	9,296.6	12,549.6	16,185.8	12,763.1	12,400.0	19,710.4	32,807.7	Foreign Assets	21
						19,971.9	17,837.0	17,188.1	16,693.4	15,238.8	14,864.2	16,264.4	19,076.0	20,156.3	Claims on Central Government	22a
						11.4	112.9	147.1	145.4	308.8	654.0	905.6	1,174.9	1,280.0	Claims on Local Government	22b
						1,802.4	2,141.4	1,896.2	1,943.8	2,182.5	2,291.8	1,794.2	2,413.4	3,180.0	Claims on Nonfin.Pub.Enterprises	22c
						18,447.9	25,344.4	30,674.5	31,600.7	46,100.9	56,650.9	52,699.9	56,775.7	69,823.7	Claims on Private Sector	22d
						10.2	—	—	—	—	.4	45.4	48.2	73.8	Claims on Other Banking Insts	22f
						15.7	62.1	100.8	140.2	246.8	193.9	154.0	161.7	281.4	Claims on Nonbank Financial Insts	22g
						1,758.7	3,969.7	4,870.0	7,007.5	8,423.8	7,808.9	7,891.5	11,386.0	15,180.6	Demand Deposits	24
						6,878.3	10,828.8	16,257.4	25,204.1	36,876.9	43,654.7	42,363.6	54,552.7	82,050.0	Time, Savings,& Fgn.Currency Dep.	25
						3.3	1.5	.2	.9	7.0	4.5	1.4	—		Money Market Instruments	26aa
						45.0	207.0	130.5	127.2	126.6	149.7	474.6	478.2	317.8	Bonds	26ab
						14,261.5	12,087.7	10,662.4	8,223.6	5,852.3	4,196.0	3,434.2	2,549.6	1,600.8	Restricted Deposits	26b
						12,066.4	13,134.8	15,150.0	12,467.4	13,807.1	16,176.8	17,169.9	17,809.8	21,857.8	Foreign Liabilities	26c
						1,437.8	1,675.0	2,025.6	1,720.9	6,874.7	7,298.3	5,828.6	6,730.5	5,634.7	Central Government Deposits	26d
						275.2	224.6	182.6	267.7	33.7	1,049.2	1,138.7	328.8	16.6	Credit from Monetary Authorities	26g
						11,203.3	13,883.6	15,392.4	15,441.8	17,023.6	19,786.8	21,975.4	24,953.1	25,455.1	Capital Accounts	27a
						-595.9	-1,392.6	-1,859.2	-2,813.9	-3,705.5	-6,798.4	-7,026.5	-8,839.6	-9,507.9	Other Items (Net)	27r
															Monetary Survey	
End of Period																
						-1,961.7	1,139.8	3,049.2	11,740.6	16,912.9	12,713.5	16,692.9	29,013.5	48,662.9	Foreign Assets (Net)	31n
						39,357.0	43,280.3	47,976.5	48,464.9	56,194.8	66,937.0	65,937.9	72,051.5	87,637.6	Domestic Credit	32
						19,061.1	15,618.7	15,157.1	14,633.7	7,331.4	7,134.9	10,062.7	11,188.1	12,769.5	Claims on Central Govt. (Net)	32an
						11.4	112.9	147.1	145.4	308.8	654.0	905.6	1,174.9	1,280.0	Claims on Local Government	32b
						1,802.4	2,141.4	1,896.2	1,943.8	2,182.5	2,291.8	1,794.2	2,413.4	3,180.0	Claims on Nonfin.Pub.Enterprises	32c
						18,448.2	25,345.1	30,675.3	31,601.8	46,125.3	56,651.9	52,976.0	57,065.2	70,052.9	Claims on Private Sector	32d
						10.2	—	—	—	—	10.5	45.4	48.2	73.8	Claims on Other Banking Insts	32f
						15.7	62.1	100.8	140.2	246.8	193.9	154.0	161.7	281.4	Claims on Nonbank Financial Inst	32g
						3,133.9	6,648.8	8,283.6	11,419.6	13,814.3	13,621.1	13,858.9	18,030.2	23,703.6	Money	34
						6,878.3	10,828.8	16,257.4	25,204.1	36,876.9	43,654.7	42,363.6	54,552.7	82,050.0	Quasi-Money	35
						3.3	1.5	.2	.9	7.0	4.5	1.4	—		Money Market Instruments	36aa
						45.0	207.0	130.5	127.2	126.6	149.7	474.6	478.2	317.8	Bonds	36ab
						14,262.9	12,128.0	10,874.6	8,466.8	5,953.4	4,315.1	3,814.8	2,864.6	1,926.2	Restricted Deposits	36b
						13,569.3	15,949.6	17,411.8	17,341.9	19,385.4	22,688.9	26,510.9	30,169.7	31,880.3	Capital Accounts	37a
						-497.5	-1,343.4	-1,932.0	-2,354.7	-3,055.9	-4,783.5	-4,393.5	-5,030.4	-3,577.4	Other Items (Net)	37r
						10,012.2	17,477.6	24,541.0	36,623.7	50,691.2	57,275.8	56,222.5	72,582.9	105,753.6	Money plus Quasi-Money	35l
															Interest Rates	
Percent Per Annum																
					1,889.39	34.49	8.50	8.50	6.50	5.90	5.90	7.90	5.90	5.90	Discount Rate (End of Period)	60
					951.20	1,370.50	26.93	21.13	19.26	10.18	14.48	13.72	8.85	3.90	Money Market Rate	60b
					658.51	379.31	6.52	5.53	5.59	4.30	4.62	4.31	3.74	3.23	Deposit Rate	60l
					1,157.79	1,443.61	22.91	20.24	22.52	15.47	15.75	14.94	12.07	9.55	Lending Rate	60p
															Prices, Production, Labor	
Period Averages																
—	—	—	.2	.4	3.5	55.9	99.3	100.0	101.4	103.2	102.2	104.6	113.1	118.6	Wholesale Prices	63
—	—	—	.2	.4	2.9	46.4	96.2	100.0	104.3	108.7	115.6	119.6	125.9	131.9	Consumer Prices	64
—	-.1	-.4	-.3	-.4	-1.8	28.9	68.6	100.0	111.8	130.7	147.5	168.1	182.9	195.3	Wages	65
205.1	202.3	201.1	178.3	127.5	108.9	102.5	99.7	100.0	103.1	110.3	114.2	112.6	114.5	121.3	Industrial Production	66
114.8	114.6	114.2	110.9	101.9	104.5	102.1	101.4	100.0	93.9	92.5	97.8	96.3	94.6	95.1	Total Employment	67
Period Averages																
					1,159	1,108	1,061	1,027	1,012	996	1,071	1,058	1,050	....	Employment	67e
					267	251	243	241	261	278	288	322	358	....	Unemployment	67c
				14.9	15.3	14.8	14.5	14.5	16.4	17.5	17.2	19.1	21.1		Unemployment Rate (%)	67r
															International Transactions	
Millions of US Dollars																
					....	3,903.8	4,260.4	4,632.7	4,511.8	4,170.7	4,541.1	4,302.5	4,431.6	4,659.3	Exports	70..d
					....	4,666.4	5,229.3	7,509.9	7,787.9	9,104.0	8,383.1	7,798.6	7,886.5	8,043.1	Imports, c.i.f.	71..d

Croatia

960		1972	1973	1974	1975	1976	1977	1978	1979	1980	1981	1982	1983	1984	1985	1986
Balance of Payments																*Millions of US Dollars:*
Current Account, n.i.e.	78al*d*	....	....	....	....	....	....	....	....	....	....	....	....	....	....	....
Goods: Exports f.o.b.	78aa*d*	....	....	....	....	....	....	....	....	....	....	....	....	....	....	....
Goods: Imports f.o.b.	78ab*d*	....	....	....	....	....	....	....	....	....	....	....	....	....	....	....
Trade Balance	78ac*d*	....	....	....	....	....	....	....	....	....	....	....	....	....	....	....
Services: Credit	78ad*d*	....	....	....	....	....	....	....	....	....	....	....	....	....	....	....
Services: Debit	78ae*d*	....	....	....	....	....	....	....	....	....	....	....	....	....	....	....
Balance on Goods & Services	78af*d*	....	....	....	....	....	....	....	....	....	....	....	....	....	....	....
Income: Credit	78ag*d*	....	....	....	....	....	....	....	....	....	....	....	....	....	....	....
Income: Debit	78ah*d*	....	....	....	....	....	....	....	....	....	....	....	....	....	....	....
Balance on Gds, Serv. & Inc.	78ai*d*	....	....	....	....	....	....	....	....	....	....	....	....	....	....	....
Current Transfers, n.i.e.: Credit	78aj*d*	....	....	....	....	....	....	....	....	....	....	....	....	....	....	....
Current Transfers: Debit	78ak*d*	....	....	....	....	....	....	....	....	....	....	....	....	....	....	....
Capital Account, n.i.e.	78bc*d*	....	....	....	....	....	....	....	....	....	....	....	....	....	....	....
Capital Account, n.i.e.: Credit	78ba*d*	....	....	....	....	....	....	....	....	....	....	....	....	....	....	....
Capital Account: Debit	78bb*d*	....	....	....	....	....	....	....	....	....	....	....	....	....	....	....
Financial Account, n.i.e.	78bj*d*	....	....	....	....	....	....	....	....	....	....	....	....	....	....	....
Direct Investment Abroad	78bd*d*	....	....	....	....	....	....	....	....	....	....	....	....	....	....	....
Dir. Invest. in Rep. Econ., n.i.e.	78be*d*	....	....	....	....	....	....	....	....	....	....	....	....	....	....	....
Portfolio Investment Assets	78bf*d*	....	....	....	....	....	....	....	....	....	....	....	....	....	....	....
Equity Securities	78bk*d*	....	....	....	....	....	....	....	....	....	....	....	....	....	....	....
Debt Securities	78bl*d*	....	....	....	....	....	....	....	....	....	....	....	....	....	....	....
Portfolio Investment Liab., n.i.e.	78bg*d*	....	....	....	....	....	....	....	....	....	....	....	....	....	....	....
Equity Securities	78bm*d*	....	....	....	....	....	....	....	....	....	....	....	....	....	....	....
Debt Securities	78bn*d*	....	....	....	....	....	....	....	....	....	....	....	....	....	....	....
Financial Derivatives Assets	78bw*d*	....	....	....	....	....	....	....	....	....	....	....	....	....	....	....
Financial Derivatives Liabilities	78bx*d*	....	....	....	....	....	....	....	....	....	....	....	....	....	....	....
Other Investment Assets	78bh*d*	....	....	....	....	....	....	....	....	....	....	....	....	....	....	....
Monetary Authorities	78bo*d*	....	....	....	....	....	....	....	....	....	....	....	....	....	....	....
General Government	78bp*d*	....	....	....	....	....	....	....	....	....	....	....	....	....	....	....
Banks	78bq*d*	....	....	....	....	....	....	....	....	....	....	....	....	....	....	....
Other Sectors	78br*d*	....	....	....	....	....	....	....	....	....	....	....	....	....	....	....
Other Investment Liab., n.i.e.	78bi*d*	....	....	....	....	....	....	....	....	....	....	....	....	....	....	....
Monetary Authorities	78bs*d*	....	....	....	....	....	....	....	....	....	....	....	....	....	....	....
General Government	78bt*d*	....	....	....	....	....	....	....	....	....	....	....	....	....	....	....
Banks	78bu*d*	....	....	....	....	....	....	....	....	....	....	....	....	....	....	....
Other Sectors	78bv*d*	....	....	....	....	....	....	....	....	....	....	....	....	....	....	....
Net Errors and Omissions	78ca*d*	....	....	....	....	....	....	....	....	....	....	....	....	....	....	....
Overall Balance	78cb*d*	....	....	....	....	....	....	....	....	....	....	....	....	....	....	....
Reserves and Related Items	79da*d*	....	....	....	....	....	....	....	....	....	....	....	....	....	....	....
Reserve Assets	79db*d*	....	....	....	....	....	....	....	....	....	....	....	....	....	....	....
Use of Fund Credit and Loans	79dc*d*	....	....	....	....	....	....	....	....	....	....	....	....	....	....	....
Exceptional Financing	79de*d*	....	....	....	....	....	....	....	....	....	....	....	....	....	....	....
International Investment Position																*Millions of US Dollars*
Assets	79aa*d*	....	....	....	....	....	....	....	....	....	....	....	....	....	....	....
Direct Investment Abroad	79ab*d*	....	....	....	....	....	....	....	....	....	....	....	....	....	....	....
Portfolio Investment	79ac*d*	....	....	....	....	....	....	....	....	....	....	....	....	....	....	....
Equity Securities	79ad*d*	....	....	....	....	....	....	....	....	....	....	....	....	....	....	....
Debt Securities	79ae*d*	....	....	....	....	....	....	....	....	....	....	....	....	....	....	....
Financial Derivatives	79al*d*	....	....	....	....	....	....	....	....	....	....	....	....	....	....	....
Other Investment	79af*d*	....	....	....	....	....	....	....	....	....	....	....	....	....	....	....
Monetary Authorities	79ag*d*	....	....	....	....	....	....	....	....	....	....	....	....	....	....	....
General Government	79ah*d*	....	....	....	....	....	....	....	....	....	....	....	....	....	....	....
Banks	79ai*d*	....	....	....	....	....	....	....	....	....	....	....	....	....	....	....
Other Sectors	79aj*d*	....	....	....	....	....	....	....	....	....	....	....	....	....	....	....
Reserve Assets	79ak*d*	....	....	....	....	....	....	....	....	....	....	....	....	....	....	....
Liabilities	79la*d*	....	....	....	....	....	....	....	....	....	....	....	....	....	....	....
Dir. Invest. in Rep. Economy	79lb*d*	....	....	....	....	....	....	....	....	....	....	....	....	....	....	....
Portfolio Investment	79lc*d*	....	....	....	....	....	....	....	....	....	....	....	....	....	....	....
Equity Securities	79ld*d*	....	....	....	....	....	....	....	....	....	....	....	....	....	....	....
Debt Securities	79le*d*	....	....	....	....	....	....	....	....	....	....	....	....	....	....	....
Financial Derivatives	79ll*d*	....	....	....	....	....	....	....	....	....	....	....	....	....	....	....
Other Investment	79lf*d*	....	....	....	....	....	....	....	....	....	....	....	....	....	....	....
Monetary Authorities	79lg*d*	....	....	....	....	....	....	....	....	....	....	....	....	....	....	....
General Government	79lh*d*	....	....	....	....	....	....	....	....	....	....	....	....	....	....	....
Banks	79li*d*	....	....	....	....	....	....	....	....	....	....	....	....	....	....	....
Other Sectors	79lj*d*	....	....	....	....	....	....	....	....	....	....	....	....	....	....	....
Government Finance																*Millions of Kuna:*
Deficit (-) or Surplus	80	....	....	....	....	....	....	....	....	....	....	....	....	....	....	....
Total Revenue and Grants	81y	....	....	....	....	....	....	....	....	....	....	....	....	....	....	....
Revenue	81	....	....	....	....	....	....	....	....	....	....	....	....	....	....	....
Grants	81z	....	....	....	....	....	....	....	....	....	....	....	....	....	....	....
Exp. & Lending Minus Repay.	82z	....	....	....	....	....	....	....	....	....	....	....	....	....	....	....
Expenditure	82	....	....	....	....	....	....	....	....	....	....	....	....	....	....	....
Lending Minus Repayments	83	....	....	....	....	....	....	....	....	....	....	....	....	....	....	....
Total Financing	80h	....	....	....	....	....	....	....	....	....	....	....	....	....	....	....
Domestic	84a	....	....	....	....	....	....	....	....	....	....	....	....	....	....	....
Foreign	85a	....	....	....	....	....	....	....	....	....	....	....	....	....	....	....
Total Debt by Residence	88	....	....	....	....	....	....	....	....	....	....	....	....	....	....	....
Domestic	88a	....	....	....	....	....	....	....	....	....	....	....	....	....	....	....
Foreign	89a	....	....	....	....	....	....	....	....	....	....	....	....	....	....	....
National Accounts																*Millions of Kuna:*
Househ.Cons.Expend.,incl.NPISHs	96f	....	....	....	....	....	....	....	....	....	....	....	....	....	....	....
Government Consumption Expend.	91f	....	....	....	....	....	....	....	....	....	....	....	....	....	....	....
Gross Fixed Capital Formation	93e	....	....	....	....	....	....	....	....	....	....	....	....	....	....	....
Changes in Inventories	93i	....	....	....	....	....	....	....	....	....	....	....	....	....	....	....
Exports of Goods and Services	90c	....	....	....	....	....	....	....	....	....	....	....	....	....	....	....
Imports of Goods and Services (-)	98c	....	....	....	....	....	....	....	....	....	....	....	....	....	....	....
Gross Domestic Product (GDP)	99b	....	....	....	....	....	....	....	....	44	....	....	....	....	275	....
GDP Volume 1990 Prices	99b.*p*	....	....	....	....	....	....	....	....	....	....	....	....	....	....	....
GDP Volume (1995=100)	99bv*p*	....	....	....	....	....	....	....	....	....	....	....	....	....	....	....
GDP Deflator (1995=100)	99bi*p*	....	....	....	....	....	....	....	....	....	....	....	....	....	....	....
																Millions:
Population	99z	....	....	....	....	....	....	....	....	....	....	....	....	....	....	....

1987	1988	1989	1990	1991	1992	1993	1994	1995	1996	1997	1998	1999	2000	2001		
Minus Sign Indicates Debit															Balance of Payments	
....	....	....	....	....	....	624.7	553.5	–1,591.6	–1,049.1	–2,825.5	–1,468.0	–1,405.6	–447.9	–642.0	Current Account, n.i.e.	**78al** ***d***
....	....	....	....	....	....	3,910.3	4,402.8	4,517.3	4,677.4	4,020.9	4,580.6	4,394.7	4,567.2	4,752.1	Goods: Exports f.o.b.	**78aa** ***d***
....	....	....	....	....	....	–4,619.6	–5,681.3	–7,744.9	–8,165.5	–9,404.2	–8,652.0	–7,693.3	–7,770.9	–8,763.9	Goods: Imports f.o.b.	**78ab** ***d***
....	....	....	....	....	....	–709.3	–1,278.5	–3,227.6	–3,488.1	–5,383.2	–4,071.5	–3,298.6	–3,203.8	–4,011.9	*Trade Balance*	**78ac** ***d***
....	....	....	....	....	....	2,215.8	2,660.5	2,223.6	3,193.3	3,985.1	3,948.9	3,707.9	4,080.7	4,873.1	Services: Credit	**78ad** ***d***
....	....	....	....	....	....	–1,090.0	–1,190.4	–1,361.0	–1,706.8	–2,274.3	–1,887.4	–2,097.9	–1,828.0	–1,940.5	Services: Debit	**78ae** ***d***
....	....	....	....	....	....	416.6	191.7	–2,365.1	–2,001.6	–3,672.4	–2,010.0	–1,688.6	–951.0	–1,079.2	*Balance on Goods & Services*	**78af** ***d***
....	....	....	....	....	....	128.2	149.0	218.8	269.8	363.8	394.9	252.2	334.1	400.6	Income: Credit	**78ag** ***d***
....	....	....	....	....	....	–247.7	–313.5	–247.6	–339.7	–386.2	–558.9	–601.7	–714.2	–929.1	Income: Debit	**78ah** ***d***
....	....	....	....	....	....	297.0	27.2	–2,393.8	–2,071.5	–3,694.8	–2,174.0	–2,038.1	–1,331.1	–1,607.7	*Balance on Gds, Serv. & Inc.*	**78ai** ***d***
....	....	....	....	....	....	507.5	669.1	971.1	1,173.2	964.0	919.1	967.4	1,101.0	1,174.5	Current Transfers, n.i.e.: Credit	**78aj** ***d***
....	....	....	....	....	....	–179.8	–142.8	–168.8	–150.8	–94.6	–213.1	–334.9	–217.8	–208.8	Current Transfers: Debit	**78ak** ***d***
....	....	....	....	....	....	—	—	—	16.2	21.5	19.1	24.9	20.9	133.0	Capital Account, n.i.e.	**78bc** ***d***
....	....	....	....	....	....	—	—	—	18.0	23.6	24.1	28.2	24.4	137.6	Capital Account, n.i.e.: Credit	**78ba** ***d***
....	....	....	....	....	....	—	—	—	–1.8	–2.1	–5.0	–3.4	–3.6	–4.6	Capital Account: Debit	**78bb** ***d***
....	....	....	....	....	....	–156.3	16.4	1,135.4	2,996.1	3,020.8	1,610.3	2,676.3	1,517.0	2,242.2	Financial Account, n.i.e.	**78bj** ***d***
....	....	....	....	....	....	–18.5	–6.8	–5.5	–24.4	–186.1	–97.5	–34.4	–28.6	–121.3	Direct Investment Abroad	**78bd** ***d***
....	....	....	....	....	....	120.3	117.0	114.2	510.8	532.9	932.4	1,479.0	1,114.9	1,446.7	Dir. Invest. in Rep. Econ., n.i.e.	**78be** ***d***
....	....	....	....	....	....	–.4	1.0	.3	6.2	11.1	–.2	–.3	–.2	–6.3	Portfolio Investment Assets	**78bf** ***d***
....	....	....	....	....	....	–.4	1.0	.3	6.2	.2	–.2	–.3	–.2	.3	Equity Securities	**78bk** ***d***
....	....	....	....	....	....	—	—	—	—	11.0	—	—	—	–6.5	Debt Securities	**78bl** ***d***
....	....	....	....	....	....	.4	10.0	4.6	622.1	565.9	15.1	574.3	722.3	722.3	Portfolio Investment Liab., n.i.e.	**78bg** ***d***
....	....	....	....	....	....	.4	10.0	4.6	–6.7	16.0	1.3	–18.9	–8.2	5.9	Equity Securities	**78bm** ***d***
....	....	....	....	....	....	—	—	—	628.8	549.9	13.8	593.1	730.5	716.4	Debt Securities	**78bn** ***d***
....	....	....	....	....	....	....	....	....	....	....	....	....	....	....	Financial Derivatives Assets	**78bw** ***d***
....	....	....	....	....	....	....	....	....	....	....	....	....	....	....	Financial Derivatives Liabilities	**78bx** ***d***
....	....	....	....	....	....	–165.8	–16.0	419.5	794.4	171.3	348.8	–179.9	–848.4	312.4	Other Investment Assets	**78bh** ***d***
....	....	....	....	....	....	....	....	....	....	—	....	....	....	....	Monetary Authorities	**78bo** ***d***
....	....	....	....	....	....	–5.2	–.2	–15.5	–33.4	30.7	–22.3	13.3	–25.6	–18.3	General Government	**78bp** ***d***
....	....	....	....	....	....	–205.4	–189.3	–451.6	–589.2	–371.8	406.1	100.2	–915.2	–1,622.3	Banks	**78bq** ***d***
....	....	....	....	....	....	44.8	173.5	886.6	1,417.0	512.4	–35.0	–293.4	92.4	1,953.0	Other Sectors	**78br** ***d***
....	....	....	....	....	....	–92.3	–88.8	602.3	1,087.0	1,925.8	411.8	837.6	557.0	–111.7	Other Investment Liab., n.i.e.	**78bi** ***d***
....	....	....	....	....	....	—	—	—	—	—	—	—	—	1.0	Monetary Authorities	**78bs** ***d***
....	....	....	....	....	....	–119.3	–131.5	–47.2	268.6	95.7	–61.4	259.0	267.1	–342.3	General Government	**78bt** ***d***
....	....	....	....	....	....	–20.6	52.6	492.6	226.3	670.3	135.7	–31.3	–270.1	281.5	Banks	**78bu** ***d***
....	....	....	....	....	....	47.6	–9.8	156.9	592.2	1,159.9	337.4	610.0	560.0	–51.9	Other Sectors	**78bv** ***d***
....	....	....	....	....	....	–280.1	–293.4	496.5	–946.1	173.7	–1.0	–885.5	–479.2	–391.1	Net Errors and Omissions	**78ca** ***d***
....	....	....	....	....	....	188.3	276.5	40.3	1,017.2	390.5	160.4	410.1	610.7	1,342.0	*Overall Balance*	**78cb** ***d***
....	....	....	....	....	....	–188.3	–276.5	–40.3	–1,017.2	–390.5	–160.4	–410.1	–610.7	–1,342.0	Reserves and Related Items	**79da** ***d***
....	....	....	....	....	....	–466.5	–742.9	–443.1	–533.3	–428.0	–151.5	–378.6	–582.1	–1,311.2	Reserve Assets	**79db** ***d***
....	....	....	....	....	....	19.8	107.0	97.1	–4.5	37.5	–8.9	–31.5	–28.6	–30.8	Use of Fund Credit and Loans	**79dc** ***d***
....	....	....	....	....	....	258.4	359.5	305.7	–479.4	—	—	—	—	—	Exceptional Financing	**79de** ***d***
Millions of US Dollars															International Investment Position	
....	....	....	....	....	....	....	....	....	....	....	5,179.1	5,919.6	7,060.5	....	Assets	**79aa** ***d***
....	....	....	....	....	....	....	....	....	....	....	—	911.3	734.0	....	Direct Investment Abroad	**79ab** ***d***
....	....	....	....	....	....	....	....	....	....	....	—	26.0	10.6	....	Portfolio Investment	**79ac** ***d***
....	....	....	....	....	....	....	....	....	....	....	—	26.0	10.6	....	Equity Securities	**79ad** ***d***
....	....	....	....	....	....	....	....	....	....	....	—	—	—	....	Debt Securities	**79ae** ***d***
....	....	....	....	....	....	....	....	....	....	....	—	—	—	....	Financial Derivatives	**79al** ***d***
....	....	....	....	....	....	....	....	....	....	....	2,363.3	1,957.3	2,791.5	....	Other Investment	**79af** ***d***
....	....	....	....	....	....	....	....	....	....	....	—	—	—	....	Monetary Authorities	**79ag** ***d***
....	....	....	....	....	....	....	....	....	....	....	5.8	49.7	72.5	....	General Government	**79ah** ***d***
....	....	....	....	....	....	....	....	....	....	....	2,107.6	1,670.6	2,503.1	....	Banks	**79ai** ***d***
....	....	....	....	....	....	....	....	....	....	....	249.9	237.0	215.9	....	Other Sectors	**79aj** ***d***
....	....	....	....	....	....	....	....	....	....	....	2,815.8	3,025.0	3,524.4	....	Reserve Assets	**79ak** ***d***
....	....	....	....	....	....	....	....	....	....	....	9,171.7	12,235.3	12,768.8	....	Liabilities	**79la** ***d***
....	....	....	....	....	....	....	....	....	....	....	—	2,755.0	2,900.2	....	Dir. Invest. in Rep. Economy	**79lb** ***d***
....	....	....	....	....	....	....	....	....	....	....	2,058.0	2,700.1	3,248.8	....	Portfolio Investment	**79lc** ***d***
....	....	....	....	....	....	....	....	....	....	....	—	128.3	69.2	....	Equity Securities	**79ld** ***d***
....	....	....	....	....	....	....	....	....	....	....	2,058.0	2,571.8	3,179.6	....	Debt Securities	**79le** ***d***
....	....	....	....	....	....	....	....	....	....	....	—	—	—	....	Financial Derivatives	**79ll** ***d***
....	....	....	....	....	....	....	....	....	....	....	7,113.7	6,780.2	6,619.8	....	Other Investment	**79lf** ***d***
....	....	....	....	....	....	....	....	....	....	....	233.9	196.6	158.2	....	Monetary Authorities	**79lg** ***d***
....	....	....	....	....	....	....	....	....	....	....	1,351.0	1,452.0	1,608.0	....	General Government	**79lh** ***d***
....	....	....	....	....	....	....	....	....	....	....	2,269.6	1,957.1	1,572.4	....	Banks	**79li** ***d***
....	....	....	....	....	....	....	....	....	....	....	3,259.2	3,174.5	3,281.2	....	Other Sectors	**79lj** ***d***
Year Ending December 31															**Government Finance**	
....	....	....	....	....	....	....	543.9	–715.4	–133.8	–1,160.2	1,256.7	–2,522.0	–6,107.9	–3,758.5	Deficit (-) or Surplus	**80**
....	....	....	....	....	....	....	22,817.3	27,485.1	30,813.1	33,702.4	42,376.2	40,277.9	41,774.7	49,156.8	Total Revenue and Grants	**81y**
....	....	....	....	....	....	....	22,817.3	27,385.1	30,813.1	33,702.4	42,376.2	40,277.9	41,774.7	49,156.8	Revenue	**81**
....	....	....	....	....	....	....	—	100.0	—	—	—	—	—	—	Grants	**81z**
....	....	....	....	....	....	....	22,273.4	28,200.5	30,946.9	34,862.5	41,119.6	42,799.9	47,882.6	52,915.3	Exp. & Lending Minus Repay.	**82z**
....	....	....	....	....	....	....	22,282.8	28,475.6	30,971.2	34,395.2	41,390.4	47,379.6	49,567.5	56,386.7	Expenditure	**82**
....	....	....	....	....	....	....	–9.3	–275.1	–24.3	467.4	–270.8	–4,579.7	–1,684.9	–3,471.4	Lending Minus Repayments	**83**
....	....	....	....	....	....	....	–543.9	715.3	134.0	1,160.2	–1,256.7	2,521.9	6,107.8	3,758.5	Total Financing	**80h**
....	....	....	....	....	....	....	–591.2	29.3	–669.9	–1,825.7	–1,247.6	–2,093.1	–813.6	–353.9	Domestic	**84a**
....	....	....	....	....	....	....	47.3	686.0	804.0	2,985.9	–9.1	4,615.0	6,921.4	4,112.4	Foreign	**85a**
....	....	....	....	....	....	....	....	27,739.7	29,814.0	32,760.0	....	....	....	....	Total Debt by Residence	**88**
....	....	....	....	18,502.1	17,218.4	20,768.6	17,284.7	16,405.4	16,533.7	14,501.6	13,697.5	13,944.0	14,549.8	21,944.3	Domestic	**88a**
....	....	....	....	....	....	....	....	11,334.3	13,280.3	18,258.4	....	....	....	....	Foreign	**89a**
Millions of Kuna:															**National Accounts**	
....	....	....	....	....	....	....	46,575	60,476	65,367	77,028	81,067	81,546	90,026	98,295	Househ.Cons.Expend.,incl.NPISHs	**96f**
....	....	....	....	....	....	....	25,738	30,456	29,154	32,183	36,642	39,637	41,702	40,681	Government Consumption Expend.	**91f**
....	....	....	....	....	....	....	12,210	15,398	22,089	29,952	32,857	33,025	33,091	37,022	Gross Fixed Capital Formation	**93e**
....	....	....	....	....	....	....	2,982	1,916	1,599	4,905	–809	376	1,545	3,191	Changes in Inventories	**93i**
....	....	....	....	....	....	....	40,086	37,951	43,402	50,873	54,547	57,902	70,892	78,946	Exports of Goods and Services	**90c**
....	....	....	....	....	....	....	40,149	48,681	53,630	70,351	67,700	69,731	79,745	89,161	Imports of Goods and Services (-)	**98c**
....	....	....	276	408	2,628	41,833	87,441	98,382	107,981	123,812	137,604	142,700	157,511	168,971	Gross Domestic Product (GDP)	**99b**
....	....	....	....	....	....	180	190	203	215	230	235	234	242	252	GDP Volume 1990 Prices	**99b.** ***p***
....	....	....	....	....	....	88.4	93.6	100.0	105.9	113.1	116.0	115.1	119.3	124.2	GDP Volume (1995=100)	**99bv** ***p***
....	....	....	....	....	....	48.1	95.0	100.0	103.6	111.3	120.6	126.0	134.2	138.3	GDP Deflator (1995=100)	**99bi** ***p***
Midyear Estimates																
....	....	....	....	4.51	4.47	4.64	4.65	4.67	4.49	4.57	4.50	4.55	4.38	4.66	**Population**	**99z**

(See notes in the back of the book.)

Cyrus

		1972	1973	1974	1975	1976	1977	1978	1979	1980	1981	1982	1983	1984	1985	1986
Exchange Rates															*SDRs per Pound:*	
Official Rate	ac	2.4026	2.2983	2.2841	2.1719	2.0911	2.1532	2.1853	2.1965	2.1495	1.9859	1.8570	1.7169	1.5838	1.6756	1.5979
															US Dollars per Pound:	
Official Rate	ag	2.6085	2.7725	2.7965	2.5425	2.4295	2.6155	2.8470	2.8935	2.7415	2.3115	2.0485	1.7975	1.5525	1.8405	1.9545
Official Rate	rh	2.6071	2.8612	2.7426	2.7162	2.4371	2.4510	2.6796	2.8220	2.8338	2.3829	2.1071	1.9015	1.7039	1.6407	1.9353
														Index Numbers (1995=100):		
Official Rate	ahx	117.9	129.4	124.0	122.8	110.2	110.8	121.2	127.6	128.2	107.8	95.3	86.0	77.1	74.2	87.5
Nominal Effective Exchange Rate	nec	....	....	....	....	....	....	....	74.2	76.1	75.3	76.5	77.7	79.6	83.0	83.2
Real Effective Exchange Rate	rec	....	....	....	....	....	....	....	....	119.5	115.1	112.4	110.0	109.0	109.2	105.0
Fund Position															*Millions of SDRs:*	
Quota	2f.s	26.0	26.0	26.0	26.0	26.0	26.0	34.0	34.0	51.0	51.0	51.0	69.7	69.7	69.7	69.7
SDRs	1b.s	10.4	10.5	10.4	10.0	7.9	5.1	1.7	9.9	6.5	3.4	.2	.1	.1	.1	—
Reserve Position in the Fund	1c.s	6.5	6.5	—	—	—	—	6.5	6.1	—	—	—	4.7	4.7	4.7	4.7
Total Fund Cred.&Loans Outstg.	2tl	—	—	6.4	8.1	43.1	43.1	32.9	38.0	30.6	21.6	12.3	5.5	3.2		
International Liquidity											*Millions of US Dollars Unless Otherwise Indicated:*						
Total Reserves minus Gold	11.d	303.3	288.7	250.1	197.7	274.5	313.5	345.7	353.1	368.3	426.4	523.2	519.1	540.5	595.3	752.7
SDRs	1b.d	11.3	12.6	12.8	11.8	9.2	6.2	2.2	13.0	8.3	4.0	.2	.2	.1	.1	—
Reserve Position in the Fund	1c.d	7.1	7.9	—	—	—	—	8.5	8.0	—	—	—	4.9	4.6	5.1	5.7
Foreign Exchange	1d.d	284.9	268.2	237.3	185.9	265.3	307.3	335.0	332.0	360.0	422.4	523.0	514.0	535.9	590.0	747.0
Gold (Million Fine Troy Ounces)	1ad	.428	.428	.428	.428	.428	.440	.443	.459	.459	.459	.459	.459	.459	.459	.459
Gold (National Valuation)	1and	....	18.1	17.5	15.9	15.2	16.8	19.1	20.8	19.7	16.7	14.8	13.0	11.2	13.3	14.1
Monetary Authorities: Other Liab.	4..d	4.9	2.5	4.4	7.7	8.4	7.6	10.2	6.7	1.2	1.3	1.0	1.0	.8	2.7	2.8
Deposit Money Banks: Assets	7a.d	13.7	16.0	19.4	11.7	20.8	21.1	33.4	43.9	45.8	55.5	60.7	66.8	84.6	124.3	178.4
Liabilities	7b.d	47.5	58.2	50.5	37.1	48.3	64.9	83.5	118.1	147.7	174.2	212.3	249.1	286.2	364.5	462.7
Other Banking Insts.: Liabilities	7f.d	12.2	13.5	15.5	11.9	11.2	14.4	19.8	28.0	31.7	36.1	35.5	29.8	24.5	335.6	389.6
Monetary Authorities															*Millions of Pounds:*	
Foreign Assets	11	118.0	110.8	102.0	85.9	122.2	127.7	128.6	129.9	142.0	191.9	262.9	298.4	356.1	331.5	393.3
Claims on Central Government	12a	−.3	—	12.9	12.8	28.3	25.1	31.5	59.9	87.5	92.9	75.3	84.2	89.1	122.1	86.7
Claims on Deposit Money Banks	12e	.8	.1	—	.9	2.3	5.1	5.5	9.8	14.2	14.9	20.7	24.5	31.4	42.6	58.7
Reserve Money	14	64.7	67.8	78.0	79.2	97.6	110.1	127.8	153.1	195.4	240.0	297.5	344.5	404.9	414.6	448.7
of which: Currency Outside DMBs	14a	26.3	29.7	35.8	33.7	39.3	43.2	51.2	64.0	76.0	89.5	101.6	115.9	122.2	127.9	130.7
Foreign Liabilities	16c	1.9	.9	4.4	6.7	24.1	22.9	18.7	19.6	14.7	11.5	7.1	3.7	2.5	1.5	1.4
Central Government Deposits	16d	43.4	32.9	22.9	6.9	23.6	17.7	10.5	12.6	14.5	20.5	20.6	18.3	21.3	21.0	17.4
Other Items (Net)	17r	8.6	9.3	9.6	6.8	7.6	7.2	8.6	14.3	19.1	27.7	33.6	40.5	47.8	59.2	71.3
Deposit Money Banks															*Millions of Pounds:*	
Reserves	20	38.0	37.4	42.3	35.0	47.5	54.9	58.7	66.6	94.0	118.9	154.8	181.0	228.0	230.4	253.7
Foreign Assets	21	5.3	5.5	7.0	4.6	8.6	8.1	11.7	15.2	16.7	24.0	29.6	37.2	54.5	67.6	91.3
Claims on Central Government	22a	18.8	13.9	13.6	15.3	34.1	21.0	20.7	18.1	31.6	47.0	54.7	69.4	90.5	98.0	121.5
Claims on Private Sector	22d	119.2	147.3	172.1	178.4	195.6	247.7	292.2	354.6	402.4	460.0	539.7	605.6	683.9	788.6	874.7
Demand Deposits	24	31.2	31.1	31.3	28.4	40.7	42.8	49.6	65.5	77.2	98.4	116.6	132.5	137.1	157.2	151.4
Time and Savings Deposits	25	114.8	132.4	157.6	164.4	191.5	226.0	257.5	296.9	341.2	406.6	483.8	534.6	631.0	696.4	801.0
Foreign Liabilities	26c	18.2	20.1	18.1	14.6	19.9	24.8	29.3	40.8	53.9	75.4	103.6	138.6	184.3	198.1	236.7
Central Government Deposits	26d	3.8	4.6	4.4	5.0	6.8	7.6	10.7	15.7	28.3	18.9	15.0	20.6	21.3	33.6	31.4
Credit from Monetary Authorities	26g	.8	.1	—	.9	2.3	5.1	5.5	9.8	14.2	14.9	20.7	24.5	31.4	42.6	58.7
Other Items (Net)	27r	12.5	15.9	23.7	20.1	24.6	25.4	30.8	25.7	29.7	35.7	39.1	42.4	51.7	56.7	61.9
Monetary Survey															*Millions of Pounds:*	
Foreign Assets (Net)	31n	103.1	95.4	86.5	69.2	86.8	88.1	92.3	84.7	90.1	129.1	181.8	193.2	223.7	199.5	246.4
Domestic Credit	32	90.7	123.9	171.8	195.3	228.2	269.1	323.9	406.3	481.0	562.9	637.0	724.2	825.6	958.4	1,039.2
Claims on Central Govt. (Net)	32an	−28.6	−23.6	−.8	16.2	32.1	20.7	31.0	49.6	76.2	100.6	94.3	114.7	137.0	165.5	159.4
Claims on Local Government	32b	....	....	....	....	....	....	....	....	....	....	....	....	....	....	....
Claims on Nonfin.Pub.Enterprises	32c	....	....	....	....	....	....	....	....	....	....	....	....	....	....	....
Claims on Private Sector	32d	119.3	147.5	172.6	179.1	196.1	248.4	292.9	356.7	404.7	462.4	542.7	609.5	688.7	792.9	879.8
Money	34	57.4	60.9	67.0	62.1	80.0	85.9	100.8	129.5	153.3	188.3	218.5	248.5	259.4	285.3	282.5
Quasi-Money	35	117.7	136.1	161.4	167.6	195.1	230.1	262.5	304.0	347.9	413.2	491.0	542.7	640.1	711.6	817.3
Other Items (Net)	37r	18.6	22.3	29.9	34.8	39.9	41.2	52.9	57.4	69.9	90.6	109.3	126.3	149.8	165.6	190.2
Money plus Quasi-Money	35l	175.2	197.0	228.5	229.7	275.1	316.0	363.3	433.5	501.2	601.4	709.5	791.1	899.4	996.9	1,099.8
Other Banking Institutions															*Millions of Pounds:*	
Reserves	40	6.5	8.5	5.5	4.6	7.2	7.2	8.6	12.0	14.5	15.9	19.3	21.1	23.1	27.1	29.3
Foreign Assets	41	—	—	—	—	—	—	—	—	—	—	—	—	—	—	.1
Claims on Private Sector	42d	21.2	26.7	29.9	30.9	33.5	43.2	50.9	56.4	65.1	69.1	73.8	74.8	83.5	93.0	106.2
Liquid Liabilities	45l	17.2	23.3	22.0	22.6	26.2	33.7	39.8	42.2	46.6	49.4	55.7	61.2	70.4	81.9	88.5
Foreign Liabilities	46c	4.7	4.7	5.5	4.7	4.6	5.5	7.0	9.7	11.6	15.6	17.3	16.6	15.8	25.3	22.9
Capital Accounts	47a	3.1	3.4	4.0	4.8	5.5	6.7	7.9	9.8	11.4	14.7	15.1	10.9	13.6	16.0	18.2
Other Items (Net)	47r	2.8	3.8	3.9	3.6	4.4	4.4	4.9	6.8	10.0	5.3	4.9	7.1	6.8	−3.1	6.0
Banking Survey															*Millions of Pounds:*	
Foreign Assets (Net)	51n	98.5	90.7	81.0	64.5	82.2	82.6	85.4	75.0	78.6	113.4	164.4	176.7	207.9	174.2	223.6
Domestic Credit	52	111.8	150.3	201.1	225.4	261.4	312.3	375.0	461.5	544.7	630.7	711.1	797.9	909.2	1,060.6	1,147.5
Claims on Central Govt. (Net)	52an	−28.5	−23.7	−.9	16.1	32.3	21.4	31.9	50.5	77.2	101.7	97.7	117.5	141.8	179.1	166.6
Claims on Local Government	52b	....	....	....	....	....	....	....	....	....	....	....	....	....	....	....
Claims on Nonfin.Pub.Enterprises	52c	....	....	....	....	....	....	....	....	....	....	....	....	....	....	....
Claims on Private Sector	52d	140.4	174.0	202.0	209.3	229.1	291.0	343.1	411.0	467.5	529.0	613.4	680.4	767.4	881.6	980.9
Monetary Liabilities	54	53.6	56.0	64.7	63.4	78.8	90.1	103.4	130.3	148.9	182.7	210.5	239.0	249.1	273.0	267.0
Quasi-Monetary Liabilities	55	132.3	155.8	180.2	187.4	218.9	256.6	296.0	340.5	391.1	458.8	542.7	600.3	706.7	784.7	899.8
Other Items (Net)	57r	24.5	29.2	37.1	39.1	46.0	48.2	60.9	65.7	83.2	102.7	122.4	135.2	161.3	177.1	204.4
Liquid Liabilities	55l	185.8	211.9	245.0	247.6	294.1	342.5	394.5	463.7	533.3	634.9	745.9	831.2	946.7	1,047.1	1,154.8
Interest Rates															*Percent Per Annum*	
Discount Rate (*End of Period*)	60	6.00	6.00	6.00	6.00	6.00	6.00	6.00	6.00	6.00	6.00	6.00	6.00	6.00	6.00	6.00
Money Market Rate	60b	....	....	....	....	....	....	....	....	....	....	....	....	....	....	....
Treasury Bill Rate	60c	....	....	....	5.50	5.50	5.50	5.50	5.50	5.50	5.50	5.50	5.50	5.50	5.50	5.50
Deposit Rate	60l	5.00	5.00	5.00	5.06	5.75	5.75	5.75	5.75	5.75	5.75	5.75	5.75	5.75	5.75	5.50
Lending Rate	60p	6.00	6.00	....	9.00	9.00	9.00	9.00	9.00	9.00	9.00	9.00	9.00	9.00	9.00	9.00
Government Bond Yield	61	....	....	....	....	....	....	....	....	....	....	....	....	....	....	....

1987	1988	1989	1990	1991	1992	1993	1994	1995	1996	1997	1998	1999	2000	2001		
End of Period															**Exchange Rates**	
1.6061	1.5936	1.5892	1.6174	1.5923	1.5056	1.4006	1.4384	1.4735	1.4800	1.4097	1.4255	1.2680	1.2444	1.2238	Official Rate	ac
End of Period (ag)		*Period Average (rh)*														
2.2785	2.1445	2.0885	2.3010	2.2777	2.0702	1.9238	2.0998	2.1903	2.1282	1.9021	2.0071	1.7404	1.6214	1.5380	Official Rate	ag
2.0802	2.1447	2.0228	2.1874	2.1585	2.2212	2.0120	2.0347	2.2113	2.1446	1.9476	1.9342	1.8440	1.6107	1.5559	Official Rate	rh
Period Averages																
94.1	97.0	91.5	98.9	97.6	100.4	91.0	92.0	100.0	97.0	88.1	87.5	83.4	72.8	70.4	Official Rate	ah x
80.8	82.1	85.1	87.9	89.9	92.1	93.0	96.3	100.0	102.0	102.8	108.3	106.0	102.2	106.0	Nominal Effective Exchange Rate	ne c
99.6	97.7	95.5	93.5	93.7	96.1	96.6	99.0	100.0	100.3	100.1	103.3	99.7	96.5	98.3	Real Effective Exchange Rate	re c
End of Period															**Fund Position**	
69.7	69.7	69.7	69.7	69.7	100.0	100.0	100.0	100.0	100.0	100.0	100.0	139.6	139.6	139.6	Quota	2f. s
.3	.1	.1	.1	.1	.1	.1	.1	.1			.2	.2	.4	.8	1.1	SDRs	1b. s
4.7	11.7	18.1	15.1	17.9	25.5	25.5	25.5	25.5	25.5	25.5	25.5	35.4	35.4	35.4	Reserve Position in the Fund	1c. s
—	—	—	—	—	—	—	—	—	—	—	—	—	—	—	Total Fund Cred.&Loans Outstg.	2tl
End of Period															**International Liquidity**	
873.5	927.9	1,124.0	1,506.9	1,390.2	1,027.9	1,096.7	1,464.5	1,116.9	1,541.9	1,391.6	1,379.7	1,832.9	1,741.1	2,267.8	Total Reserves minus Gold	1l. d
.4	.1	.1	.1	.1	.1	.1	.1	.2			.3	.3	.5	1.0	1.4	SDRs	1b. d
6.6	15.7	23.7	21.5	25.5	35.0	35.0	37.2	37.8	36.6	34.3	35.8	48.5	46.1	44.4	Reserve Position in the Fund	1c. d
866.5	912.1	1,100.2	1,485.3	1,364.5	992.8	1,061.6	1,427.2	1,079.0	1,505.3	1,356.9	1,343.6	1,783.8	1,694.0	2,221.9	Foreign Exchange	1d. d
.459	.459	.459	.459	.459	.459	.459	.460	.459	.460	.440	.462	.462	.464	.464	Gold (Million Fine Troy Ounces)	1ad
16.4	15.5	15.1	16.6	16.4	15.0	14.2	15.6	16.7	170.2	133.9	132.9	142.6	127.6	127.6	Gold (National Valuation)	1an d
11.0	23.7	29.4	69.1	76.8	77.2	53.9	55.7	89.6	56.4	73.2	57.1	49.7	24.5	40.5	Monetary Authorities: Other Liab.	4. d
232.0	318.7	553.2	701.9	1,093.0	1,396.6	1,554.3	1,915.4	3,083.3	3,255.1	3,612.4	3,519.3	3,901.5	5,335.1	6,155.2	Deposit Money Banks: Assets	7a. d
600.2	714.8	924.8	1,400.0	1,728.0	2,010.5	2,187.8	2,697.5	3,738.3	4,302.8	4,694.4	4,790.3	5,458.9	6,841.2	7,955.0	Liabilities	7b. d
578.6	735.1	1,271.1	1,837.0	1,639.4	1,647.7	1,722.9	2,052.7	2,257.4	3,189.6	13,090.6	8,607.2	8,060.5	10,564.4	10,161.4	Other Banking Insts.: Liabilities	7f. d
End of Period															**Monetary Authorities**	
408.0	440.9	546.0	662.3	618.0	504.3	578.1	705.6	518.2	805.2	802.7	754.4	1,135.8	1,153.3	1,558.2	Foreign Assets	11
119.1	166.5	92.5	186.1	240.8	415.2	407.3	398.5	607.2	570.5	558.4	596.7	534.9	770.7	696.4	Claims on Central Government	12a
69.0	83.7	10.4	24.1	24.6	34.2	13.4	12.4	22.4	6.5	.1	104.6	—	3.1	—	Claims on Deposit Money Banks	12e
496.4	†569.2	506.9	696.7	714.0	763.6	775.6	872.4	834.6	761.5	755.5	878.0	1,008.3	1,117.0	1,200.8	Reserve Money	14
142.6	157.6	169.1	183.5	195.5	215.1	229.4	246.6	257.1	265.8	276.3	290.1	313.8	333.6	356.5	of which: Currency Outside DMBs	14a
4.8	11.0	14.1	30.1	33.7	37.3	28.0	26.6	40.9	26.5	38.5	28.4	28.5	15.1	26.3	Foreign Liabilities	16c
18.2	23.9	94.6	111.0	115.8	131.7	154.8	175.2	227.3	342.9	339.5	325.7	316.4	451.2	558.5	Central Government Deposits	16d
76.5	†87.0	33.3	34.8	19.9	21.1	40.4	42.4	45.1	251.3	227.7	223.6	317.4	343.8	469.0	Other Items (Net)	17r
End of Period															**Deposit Money Banks**	
278.0	327.3	334.8	485.6	504.4	542.0	538.0	612.4	555.1	479.7	452.9	455.4	662.0	742.4	921.9	Reserves	20
101.8	148.6	264.9	305.0	479.9	674.6	807.9	912.2	1,407.7	1,529.5	1,899.1	1,753.6	2,241.7	3,290.4	4,002.1	Foreign Assets	21
181.2	222.8	234.6	285.6	310.2	342.5	519.9	566.5	463.7	722.1	834.5	854.0	965.6	884.7	1,319.8	Claims on Central Government	22a
981.0	†1,147.7	1,345.6	1,611.6	1,839.3	2,158.9	2,436.7	2,754.3	3,225.3	3,667.0	4,109.7	4,635.2	5,189.0	5,970.8	6,712.7	Claims on Private Sector	22d
171.1	201.2	214.4	245.3	265.7	289.3	317.2	326.1	353.9	386.5	427.2	439.2	724.0	759.4	724.2	Demand Deposits	24
911.0	1,084.2	1,289.0	1,529.1	1,793.7	2,064.1	2,440.9	2,785.4	3,131.2	3,487.3	3,890.0	4,243.3	4,680.3	5,081.7	5,862.7	Time and Savings Deposits	25
263.4	333.3	442.8	608.4	759.0	971.2	1,137.3	1,284.6	1,706.8	2,021.8	2,468.0	2,386.7	3,136.6	4,219.3	5,172.3	Foreign Liabilities	26c
35.0	35.3	36.1	34.3	36.4	36.4	38.1	38.4	42.7	40.7	44.8	50.3	59.9	72.5	104.8	Central Government Deposits	26d
69.0	83.7	10.4	24.1	24.6	34.2	13.4	12.4	22.4	6.5	.1	5.6	.1	3.1	—	Credit from Monetary Authorities	26g
92.4	108.7	187.2	246.6	254.3	322.8	355.5	398.5	394.8	455.5	466.2	573.1	457.6	752.3	1,092.4	Other Items (Net)	27r
End of Period															**Monetary Survey**	
241.6	245.2	353.9	328.9	305.2	170.4	220.8	306.6	178.3	286.4	195.2	92.7	212.4	209.2	361.6	Foreign Assets (Net)	31n
1,234.0	†1,496.8	1,558.9	1,969.3	2,279.6	2,797.6	3,225.9	3,579.3	4,108.1	4,670.8	5,229.1	5,847.5	6,463.5	7,269.6	8,280.8	Domestic Credit	32
247.0	330.1	196.4	326.5	398.8	589.6	734.2	751.5	800.9	908.9	1,008.6	1,074.8	1,124.2	1,131.7	1,353.0	Claims on Central Govt. (Net)	32an
....	6.3	9.8	19.3	28.7	34.5	37.5	42.9	46.8	55.6	65.4	79.3	86.5	90.6	122.8	Claims on Local Government	32b
....	7.0	6.0	7.3	10.3	12.0	14.9	28.1	34.8	38.9	45.0	57.9	63.3	75.8	92.4	Claims on Nonfin.Pub.Enterprises	32c
987.0	†1,153.4	1,346.7	1,616.3	1,841.8	2,161.5	2,439.2	2,756.8	3,225.7	3,667.4	4,110.0	4,635.6	5,189.6	5,971.6	6,712.7	Claims on Private Sector	32d
314.0	358.9	385.0	429.1	462.4	506.3	549.1	576.2	612.2	653.5	704.5	730.3	1,038.3	1,093.6	1,081.4	Money	34
929.8	†1,102.7	1,300.8	1,539.7	1,800.2	2,070.2	2,448.0	2,794.3	3,142.2	3,495.6	3,900.4	4,255.6	4,695.8	5,101.9	5,883.1	Quasi-Money	35
237.1	†280.3	227.0	329.4	322.1	391.5	449.5	515.4	532.0	808.1	819.6	954.4	941.9	1,283.4	1,678.0	Other Items (Net)	37r
1,243.8	†1,461.7	1,685.8	1,968.8	2,262.6	2,576.5	2,997.1	3,370.5	3,754.4	4,149.1	4,604.9	4,985.9	5,734.1	6,195.5	6,964.5	Money plus Quasi-Money	35l
End of Period															**Other Banking Institutions**	
27.0	27.6	18.6	24.1	9.7	10.1	18.3	27.0	25.1	20.6	32.3	39.6	35.2	76.3	90.1	Reserves	40
.1	†340.1	606.0	795.7	718.6	795.1	894.9	977.1	1,030.2	1,498.6	6,901.6	4,290.9	4,647.4	6,527.0	6,615.8	Foreign Assets	41
115.2	†635.4	768.3	909.0	1,059.4	1,235.1	1,405.8	1,599.8	1,826.0	2,056.5	2,244.4	2,431.6	2,747.0	2,868.3	2,958.4	Claims on Private Sector	42d
99.6	†712.3	835.1	977.8	1,111.1	1,276.6	1,475.7	1,685.0	1,897.6	2,095.8	2,327.6	2,582.7	2,754.2	3,072.8	3,459.1	Liquid Liabilities	45l
20.8	†342.8	608.6	798.3	719.8	795.9	895.6	977.6	1,030.6	1,498.7	6,882.2	4,288.4	4,631.4	6,515.6	6,606.9	Foreign Liabilities	46c
20.2	23.5	26.6	30.5	33.3	34.9	38.3	41.9	39.9	42.9	43.8	48.6	80.0	90.3	92.5	Capital Accounts	47a
1.7	†−75.5	−77.5	−77.9	−76.5	−67.0	−90.6	−100.6	−86.8	−62.0	−75.2	−157.6	−36.0	−207.0	−495.2	Other Items (Net)	47r
End of Period															**Banking Survey**	
220.9	†242.5	351.3	326.2	304.0	169.6	220.1	306.1	177.8	286.0	214.8	95.2	228.4	220.7	370.5	Foreign Assets (Net)	51n
1,347.3	†2,132.1	2,342.0	2,886.5	3,343.2	4,035.8	4,635.8	5,182.2	5,940.0	6,737.5	7,482.1	8,292.5	9,223.6	10,150.6	11,258.5	Domestic Credit	52
251.2	335.6	212.4	339.4	405.5	595.3	740.9	757.2	807.2	919.5	1,017.5	1,088.5	1,137.9	1,145.1	1,372.3	Claims on Central Govt. (Net)	52an
....	6.3	9.8	19.3	28.7	34.5	37.5	42.9	46.8	55.6	65.4	79.3	86.5	90.6	122.8	Claims on Local Government	52b
....	7.0	6.0	7.3	10.3	12.0	14.9	28.1	34.8	38.9	45.0	57.9	63.3	75.8	92.4	Claims on Nonfin.Pub.Enterprises	52c
1,096.1	†1,783.1	2,113.8	2,520.6	2,898.7	3,394.0	3,842.5	4,354.1	5,051.3	5,723.5	6,354.1	7,066.8	7,936.0	8,839.1	9,671.0	Claims on Private Sector	52d
302.3	346.5	381.0	427.8	460.2	503.8	539.8	560.1	601.7	644.7	685.1	708.3	1,025.0	1,039.2	1,016.0	Monetary Liabilities	54
1,022.1	†1,794.3	2,121.6	2,504.3	2,903.7	3,339.3	3,915.3	4,468.6	5,026.2	5,580.0	6,214.4	6,822.0	7,431.7	8,150.8	9,316.9	Quasi-Monetary Liabilities	55
243.8	†233.8	190.7	280.6	283.3	362.3	400.8	459.6	489.9	798.7	797.4	857.5	995.4	1,181.2	1,296.2	Other Items (Net)	57r
1,311.0	†2,146.3	2,502.3	2,922.5	3,364.0	3,843.0	4,454.6	5,028.4	5,626.9	6,224.4	6,900.2	7,529.1	8,453.1	9,192.0	10,334.3	Liquid Liabilities	55l
Percent Per Annum															**Interest Rates**	
6.00	6.00	6.50	6.50	6.50	6.50	6.50	6.50	6.50	†7.50	7.00	7.00	7.00	7.00	5.50	Discount Rate (End of Period)	60
....	....	....	....	....	....	....	....	....	6.85	4.82	4.80	5.15	5.96	4.93	Money Market Rate	60b
5.50	5.50	6.00	6.00	6.00	6.00	6.00	6.00	6.00	6.05	5.38	5.59	5.59	6.01		Treasury Bill Rate	60c
5.75	5.75	5.75	5.75	5.75	5.75	5.75	5.75	5.75	5.75	†6.50	6.50	6.50	6.50	†3.75	Deposit Rate	60l
9.00	9.00	9.00	9.00	9.00	9.00	9.00	8.83	8.50	8.50	8.08	8.00	8.00	8.00	†7.54	Lending Rate	60p
....	....	....	....	....	....	....	....	....	....	....	....	....	....		Government Bond Yield	61

Cyprus

		1972	1973	1974	1975	1976	1977	1978	1979	1980	1981	1982	1983	1984	1985	1986
Prices, Production, Labor															*Index Numbers (1995=100):*	
Wholesale Prices	63															
Wholesale Prices: Home Goods	63a	†25.4	28.3	35.5	39.5	†41.3	44.1	44.9	51.4	65.9	75.2	79.8	81.1	84.5	87.2	78.5
Consumer Prices	64	25.3	†27.3	29.0	†33.1	34.4	36.9	39.7	43.5	49.3	†54.6	58.1	61.1	64.7	68.0	†68.8
Industrial Production	66	50.4	53.3	40.8	34.8	†42.1	48.7	†53.8	58.2	62.5	64.6	67.9	70.0	73.8	72.9	†75.2
Mining Production	66zx	190.6	196.3	133.4	†108.6	108.6	119.5	†145.6	138.8	139.9	121.0	112.5	105.2	89.9	105.3	95.7
															Number in Thousands:	
Labor Force	67d	....	....	....	....	....	....	....	....	....	....	....	....	....	....	....
Employment	67e	....	....	....	....	....	....	....	....	....	....	....	....	....	....	....
Unemployment	67c	....	....	....	....	....	....	....	....	....	....	....	....	....	8	9
Unemployment Rate (%)	67r	....	....	....	....	....	....	....	....	....	....	....	....	....	3.3	3.7
International Transactions															*Millions of Pounds*	
Exports	70	51.31	60.47	55.29	56.01	106.33	129.75	128.37	161.87	188.04	234.77	263.81	260.53	336.83	290.61	260.16
Imports, c.i.f.	71	121.48	157.44	148.03	113.71	177.76	254.01	282.69	357.60	424.29	489.54	577.55	641.96	796.52	762.31	659.07
															1985=100	
Volume of Exports	72	52	†55	43	38	63	80	76	88	94	105	104	97	113	100	95
Volume of Imports	73	47	†55	39	27	41	56	62	70	73	75	88	96	104	100	108
Unit Value of Exports	74	41	†46	53	63	67	67	67	72	78	92	90	95	102	100	93
Unit Value of Imports	75	36	†40	53	59	60	63	63	70	81	90	91	93	99	100	85
Balance of Payments															*Millions of US Dollars:*	
Current Account, n.i.e.	78ald	....		....		−26.6	−104.6	−185.0	−239.8	−258.3	−171.8	−178.2	−205.1	−221.6	−180.2	−18.9
Goods: Exports f.o.b.	78aad					254.1	312.4	339.2	451.1	527.7	551.5	554.1	495.4	573.1	474.9	502.8
Goods: Imports f.o.b.	78abd					−397.8	−558.9	−683.8	−906.2	−1,079.2	−1,042.6	−1,090.3	−1,093.5	−1,224.9	−1,121.9	−1,148.3
Trade Balance	78acd					−143.7	−246.5	−344.6	−455.1	−551.5	−491.2	−536.2	−598.1	−651.8	−647.0	−645.6
Services: Credit	78add					175.9	206.6	258.6	371.3	481.8	526.5	577.2	627.4	701.6	738.4	938.5
Services: Debit	78aed					−111.6	−143.6	−169.5	−226.8	−267.7	−273.6	−294.5	−287.7	−300.5	−301.7	−354.5
Balance on Goods & Services	78afd					−79.4	−183.5	−255.4	−310.6	−337.3	−238.2	−253.5	−258.4	−250.7	−210.3	−61.6
Income: Credit	78agd					29.5	46.6	60.8	74.2	97.7	102.3	115.3	102.9	110.0	115.6	68.5
Income: Debit	78ahd					−24.1	−25.7	−35.1	−50.2	−63.4	−74.5	−89.4	−103.3	−105.5	−107.3	−128.3
Balance on Gds, Serv. & Inc.	78aid					−74.1	−162.7	−229.7	−286.6	−303.1	−210.5	−227.6	−258.8	−246.3	−201.9	−121.4
Current Transfers, n.i.e.: Credit	78ajd					49.2	59.8	46.6	49.1	46.2	39.9	50.5	54.9	25.8	22.7	105.4
Current Transfers: Debit	78akd					−1.7	−1.7	−1.9	−2.3	−1.4	−1.2	−1.1	−1.1	−1.2	−1.0	−2.9
Capital Account, n.i.e.	78bcd					13.2	14.7	22.8	24.8	28.6	24.0	22.1	20.5	18.9	19.1	....
Capital Account, n.i.e.: Credit	78bad					14.6	16.2	24.1	26.5	31.2	26.1	24.2	22.4	20.7	20.6	....
Capital Account: Debit	78bbd					−1.5	−1.5	−1.3	−1.7	−2.5	−2.1	−2.1	−1.9	−1.9	−1.5	....
Financial Account, n.i.e.	78bjd					51.9	99.7	160.1	171.8	250.7	238.5	275.8	215.5	269.6	112.5	205.0
Direct Investment Abroad	78bdd					—	—	—	—	—	—	—	—	—	−.2	—
Dir. Invest. in Rep. Econ., n.i.e.	78bed					32.4	41.4	57.0	70.5	85.0	78.3	71.5	68.4	52.7	58.0	46.3
Portfolio Investment Assets	78bfd					—	—	—	—	—	—	—	—	—	—	−.2
Equity Securities	78bkd					—	—	—	—	—	—	—	—	—	—	—
Debt Securities	78bld					—	—	—	—	—	—	—	—	—	—	—
Portfolio Investment Liab., n.i.e.	78bgd					—	—	—	—	—	—	—	—	—	—	−.2
Equity Securities	78bmd					—	—	—	—	—	—	—	—	—	—	—
Debt Securities	78bnd					—	—	—	—	—	—	—	—	—	—	—
Financial Derivatives Assets	78bwd					....	....	....	....	....	....	....	....	....	....	....
Financial Derivatives Liabilities	78bxd					....	....	....	....	....	....	....	....	....	....	....
Other Investment Assets	78bhd					−12.2	5.4	−7.5	−9.6	−9.1	−16.6	−16.8	−21.1	−32.8	−68.2	−7.3
Monetary Authorities	78bod					−2.2	3.9	2.9	—	—	—	—	−.4	—	—	—
General Government	78bpd					−.5	.2	−.5	−.3	−.3	1.2	−.2	−.4	—	−8.2	36.5
Banks	78bqd					−9.5	1.2	−9.9	−9.3	−4.2	−16.8	−11.4	−14.6	−29.4	−21.4	−43.8
Other Sectors	78brd					—	—	—	—	−4.5	−.9	−5.3	−5.7	−3.4	−39.0	—
Other Investment Liab., n.i.e.	78bid					31.7	52.9	110.6	110.9	174.8	176.8	221.1	168.2	249.7	122.9	166.2
Monetary Authorities	78bsd					1.2	−6.4	1.9	−3.4	−5.4	.2	−.2	.2	—	−.5	—
General Government	78btd					23.4	38.7	34.5	33.9	88.9	56.9	108.5	48.6	87.0	36.7	124.7
Banks	78bud					13.2	13.0	12.3	32.4	37.1	51.0	59.5	66.3	77.7	20.9	76.0
Other Sectors	78bvd					−6.1	7.6	61.8	48.0	54.1	68.6	53.2	53.2	85.0	65.8	−34.5
Net Errors and Omissions	78cad					6.3	5.8	20.3	31.1	16.1	−2.7	20.5	10.8	29.1	19.0	−26.6
Overall Balance	78cbd					44.8	15.6	18.2	−12.0	37.1	88.0	140.2	41.7	95.9	−29.6	159.5
Reserves and Related Items	79dad					−44.8	−15.6	−18.2	12.0	−37.1	−88.0	−140.2	−41.7	−95.9	29.6	−159.5
Reserve Assets	79dbd					−85.3	−23.2	−5.9	5.4	−27.8	−77.3	−129.9	−34.3	−93.5	32.8	−159.5
Use of Fund Credit and Loans	79dcd					40.5	—	−12.8	6.6	−9.3	−10.6	−10.3	−7.4	−2.3	−3.2	—
Exceptional Financing	79ded					—	7.6	.5	—	—	—	—	—	—	....	....
Government Finance															*Millions of Pounds:*	
Deficit (-) or Surplus	80	−4.81	−12.14	−20.90	−20.38	−24.90	−12.71	−28.84	−41.64	−70.01	−46.75	−48.48	−110.13	−71.03	−78.50	−49.13
Revenue	81	52.28	60.42	54.82	59.48	64.29	83.20	100.00	123.52	161.22	191.25	232.83	275.62	333.39	380.39	418.10
Grants Received	81z	.10	—	6.33	7.41	14.48	23.61	13.50	13.25	12.55	12.09	19.52	13.79	10.96	9.71	8.99
Expenditure	82	54.14	70.26	79.20	84.58	100.39	116.52	136.63	174.11	221.52	255.58	297.03	389.13	406.54	450.54	468.37
Lending Minus Repayments	83	3.05	2.30	2.85	2.69	3.28	3.00	5.71	4.30	22.26	−5.49	3.80	10.41	8.84	18.06	7.85
Financing																
Net Borrowing: Domestic	84a	6.58	−4.49	2.98	5.42	14.43	−6.29	17.82	28.93	40.62	26.72	8.54	38.63	44.11	69.35	1.35
Foreign	85a	.15	1.66	.84	1.98	10.92	16.20	18.42	11.68	29.61	25.45	51.96	63.93	36.49	28.21	65.34
Use of Cash Balances	87	−1.92	14.97	17.08	12.98	−.45	2.80	−7.40	1.03	−.22	−5.42	−12.02	7.57	−9.57	−19.06	−17.56
Debt: Domestic	88a	25.15	27.58	32.73	35.36	49.99	43.98	57.29	87.74	131.95	156.17	164.48	202.90	246.88	316.26	318.34
Foreign	89a	4.27	6.66	8.82	10.69	23.22	39.79	59.26	70.14	95.44	133.95	199.05	308.89	372.43	386.92	490.15
National Accounts															*Millions of Pounds*	
Househ.Cons.Expend.,incl.NPISHs	96f	218.9	238.9	242.1	208.7	252.7	320.4	376.6	429.7	508.4	573.8	678.0	765.8	851.5	945.8	979.2
Government Consumption Expend.	91f	29.6	35.8	43.1	44.9	54.5	59.2	66.3	80.5	103.4	127.5	151.5	171.9	188.7	208.5	229.9
Gross Fixed Capital Formation	93e	67.2	94.3	80.0	50.5	70.3	124.6	170.4	219.5	260.0	275.9	304.7	316.0	412.5	403.0	384.0
Changes in Inventories	93i	2.8	5.4	.1	7.4	18.4	23.0	18.1	24.4	27.5	20.3	20.4	26.3	36.8	46.7	31.0
Exports of Goods and Services	90c	115.3	131.6	115.8	91.2	166.1	202.3	214.4	281.4	344.1	440.2	521.9	573.0	731.0	722.4	721.0
Imports of Goods and Services (-)	98c	136.7	176.1	176.5	145.7	209.1	286.7	318.7	401.6	479.5	554.7	658.4	727.2	897.4	872.0	779.2
Gross Domestic Product (GDP)	99b	296.9	329.9	304.6	257.0	333.9	423.1	506.5	629.8	760.4	876.0	1,024.9	1,136.7	1,337.4	1,482.2	1,599.7
Net Primary Income from Abroad	98.n	9.1	11.1	11.9	14.2	13.9	18.8	20.2	22.1	26.6	27.0	30.5	21.8	24.2	25.8	21.1
Gross National Income (GNI)	99a	306.0	341.0	316.5	271.2	347.8	441.9	526.7	651.9	787.0	903.0	1,055.4	1,158.5	1,361.6	1,508.0	1,620.8
Consumption of Fixed Capital	99cf	13.8	34.1	31.7	27.1	28.2	33.7	42.5	54.3	70.4	88.8	104.1	119.0	140.5	158.3	170.8
GDP Volume 1967 prices	99b.p	242.8	249.0	....	....	....	....	....	....	....	....	....	....	....	....	....
GDP Volume 1973 prices	99b.p	....	329.9	274.1	222.0	261.9	....	....	....	....	....	....	....	....	....	....
GDP Volume 1980 prices	99b.p	....	....	....	....	524.3	607.0	653.4	717.9	760.4	783.6	832.8	877.0	954.5	999.8	....
GDP Volume 1985 prices	99b.p	....	....	....	....	....	....	....	....	....	....	....	....	....	....	....
GDP Volume 1990 Prices	99b.p	....	....	....	....	....	....	....	....	....	....	....	....	1,482.2	1,535.3	
GDP Volume (1995=100)	99bvp	37.0	37.9	31.5	25.5	30.1	34.9	37.5	41.2	43.7	45.0	47.9	50.4	54.8	57.4	59.5
GDP Deflator (1995=100)	99bip	20.0	21.7	24.1	25.1	27.7	30.3	33.7	38.1	43.4	48.6	53.5	56.3	60.9	64.4	67.1
															Millions:	
Population	99z	.61	.62	.63	.62	.61	.61	.62	.62	.63	.63	.64	.65	.66	.67	.65

1987	1988	1989	1990	1991	1992	1993	1994	1995	1996	1997	1998	1999	2000	2001		
Period Averages															**Prices, Production, Labor**	
....	....	....	....	88.5	91.1	93.4	96.5	100.0	102.1	105.0	105.5	106.8	114.5	116.3	Wholesale Prices	63
76.3	78.3	78.9	82.7	....	....	....	....	†100.0	102.8	106.2	108.6	110.2	116.0	118.2	Wholesale Prices: Home Goods	63a
70.7	73.2	75.9	79.3	83.3	†88.8	93.1	97.5	100.0	103.0	106.7	109.1	†110.8	115.4	117.7	Consumer Prices	64
82.5	88.7	92.0	†97.3	97.9	101.6	95.1	98.5	100.0	97.0	96.8	99.5	†101.2	105.7	105.1	Industrial Production	66
101.6	99.4	81.9	†82.1	80.5	82.1	100.4	108.6	100.0	102.4	102.6	121.0	†129.2	134.1	130.7	Mining Production	66zx
Period Averages																
....	....	....	....	280	287	....	....	303	....	....	....	....	303	....	Labor Force	67d
....	....	....	....	256	267	267	271	282	285	285	287	279	289	....	Employment	67e
9	7	6	5	8	5	8	8	8	9	10	10	11	11	10	Unemployment	67c
3.4	2.8	2.3	1.8	3.0	1.8	2.6	2.7	2.6	3.1	3.4	3.3	3.6	....	....	Unemployment Rate (%)	67r
Millions of Pounds															**International Transactions**	
297.99	330.86	393.05	435.60	441.79	443.72	431.40	475.98	555.61	649.03	640.01	551.13	542.90	591.86	628.66	Exports	70
711.42	866.77	1,130.30	1,174.54	1,215.83	1,490.76	1,260.05	1,482.22	1,670.41	1,857.51	1,877.34	1,904.84	1,970.93	2,401.93	2,536.59	Imports, c.i.f.	71
1985=100																
115	....	....	....	....	....	....	....	....	....	....	....	....	....	....	Volume of Exports	72
117	....	....	....	....	....	....	....	....	....	....	....	....	....	....	Volume of Imports	73
95	....	....	....	....	....	....	....	....	....	....	....	....	....	....	Unit Value of Exports	74
81	....	....	....	....	....	....	....	....	....	....	....	....	....	....	Unit Value of Imports	75
Minus Sign Indicates Debit															Balance of Payments	
-7.7	-107.6	-248.7	-154.3	-420.3	-638.2	109.8	74.4	-164.0	-465.6	-338.2	-602.9	-217.3	-456.5	....	Current Account, n.i.e.	78al*d*
619.6	709.1	795.4	951.6	951.7	985.9	867.7	967.5	1,228.7	1,392.4	1,245.8	1,064.6	1,000.3	951.0	....	Goods: Exports f.o.b.	78aa*d*
-1,418.6	-1,777.4	-2,165.5	-2,504.4	-2,553.5	-3,301.1	-2,374.5	-2,703.0	-3,314.2	-3,575.7	-3,317.2	-3,490.4	-3,309.5	-3,556.5	....	Goods: Imports f.o.b.	78ab*d*
-799.0	-1,068.3	-1,370.1	-1,552.8	-1,601.8	-2,315.2	-1,506.8	-1,735.5	-2,085.5	-2,183.3	-2,071.4	-2,425.7	-2,309.2	-2,605.5	....	*Trade Balance*	78ac*d*
1,187.9	1,411.6	1,618.6	2,003.6	1,857.1	2,521.4	2,335.1	2,646.7	2,991.2	2,872.3	2,827.6	2,954.7	3,190.0	3,200.0	....	Services: Credit	78ad*d*
-441.1	-501.7	-559.0	-673.9	-729.1	-884.0	-765.0	-862.1	-1,105.8	-1,160.6	-1,109.4	-1,132.6	-1,147.3	-1,160.0	....	Services: Debit	78ae*d*
-52.2	-158.4	-310.5	-223.1	-473.7	-677.8	63.3	49.2	-200.0	-471.6	-353.2	-603.7	-266.5	-565.5	....	*Balance on Goods & Services*	78af*d*
77.5	87.9	119.1	158.9	175.3	156.8	131.9	121.5	371.1	359.2	382.2	416.7	418.5	505.3	....	Income: Credit	78ag*d*
-140.7	-160.7	-172.3	-216.8	-230.8	-234.9	-198.4	-211.1	-363.8	-386.4	-393.1	-445.3	-456.6	-522.0	....	Income: Debit	78ah*d*
-115.4	-231.2	-363.7	-281.0	-529.3	-755.9	-3.2	-40.4	-192.7	-498.8	-364.1	-632.3	-304.6	-582.3	....	*Balance on Gds, Serv. & Inc.*	78ai*d*
110.4	126.9	118.5	131.0	114.3	123.2	118.4	125.0	46.4	43.1	40.9	49.6	113.6	153.3	....	Current Transfers, n.i.e.: Credit	78aj*d*
-2.7	-3.2	-3.4	-4.4	-5.4	-5.6	-5.4	-10.2	-17.7	-9.9	-15.0	-20.3	-26.3	-27.5	....	Current Transfers: Debit	78ak*d*
....	....	....	....	....	....	....	....	....	....	....	....	....	....	....	Capital Account, n.i.e.	78bc*d*
....	....	....	....	....	....	....	....	....	....	....	....	....	....	....	Capital Account, n.i.e.: Credit	78ba*d*
....	....	....	....	....	....	....	....	....	....	....	....	....	....	....	Capital Account: Debit	78bb*d*
146.5	166.3	451.5	436.0	278.2	323.4	-3.8	185.7	-140.8	419.0	383.7	657.9	1,006.4	301.4	....	Financial Account, n.i.e.	78bj*d*
-2.3	-.6	-.8	-4.6	-14.6	-14.7	-12.3	-6.1	-27.6	-48.3	-32.7	-68.9	-146.2	-178.3	....	Direct Investment Abroad	78bd*d*
52.0	62.1	69.7	126.6	81.8	107.4	83.4	75.2	85.8	54.3	75.9	68.7	121.4	160.0	....	Dir. Invest. in Rep. Econ., n.i.e.	78be*d*
....	....	....	....	....	-5.1	-18.9	-244.6	-44.4	-117.5	-125.9	-106.2	-474.8	-295.1	....	Portfolio Investment Assets	78bf*d*
....	....	....	....	....	....	....	....	—	—	—	—	—	....	....	Equity Securities	78bk*d*
....	....	....	....	....	-5.1	-18.9	-244.6	-44.4	-117.5	-125.9	-106.2	-474.8	-295.1	....	Debt Securities	78bl*d*
....	....	92.6	-38.0	125.7	57.6	-33.4	84.5	-27.4	69.7	268.3	303.0	476.5	121.5	....	Portfolio Investment Liab., n.i.e.	78bg*d*
....	....	....	....	....	....	....	....	2.0	2.8	3.1	-12.0	139.2	209.2	....	Equity Securities	78bm*d*
....	....	92.6	-38.0	125.7	57.6	-33.4	84.5	-29.4	66.9	265.2	315.0	337.2	-87.7	....	Debt Securities	78bn*d*
....	....	....	....	....	....	....	....	....	....	....	....	....	....	....	Financial Derivatives Assets	78bw*d*
....	....	....	....	....	....	....	....	....	....	....	....	....	....	....	Financial Derivatives Liabilities	78bx*d*
-.2	-118.5	-231.7	-114.6	-379.0	-321.2	-231.2	56.3	-1,075.5	-158.0	-700.5	659.1	-389.7	-1,349.1	....	Other Investment Assets	78bh*d*
....	....	....	....	....	....	....	....	....	....	....	....	....	....	....	Monetary Authorities	78bo*d*
49.1	-30.4	-18.6	-29.7	-16.8	57.4	10.1	1.0	-11.9	-7.7	-22.8	32.4	.6	1.1	....	General Government	78bp*d*
-19.3	-82.5	-234.7	-83.0	-362.2	-395.5	-246.1	55.3	-1,063.6	-150.3	-677.8	626.7	-390.3	-1,350.2	....	Banks	78bq*d*
-29.9	-5.6	21.6	-2.0	....	16.9	4.8	....	....	....	....	....	....	....	....	Other Sectors	78br*d*
97.1	223.3	521.6	466.5	464.2	499.4	208.5	220.4	948.5	618.9	898.6	-197.7	1,419.3	1,842.5	....	Other Investment Liab., n.i.e.	78bi*d*
7.1	13.3	6.1	34.9	6.9	9.8	-23.1	.4	29.2	-36.2	20.6	-24.3	-5.7	-20.1	....	Monetary Authorities	78bs*d*
27.4	28.7	110.6	-12.4	60.5	-169.1	-155.0	-228.6	-147.2	-95.4	-112.9	-7.1	-39.6	31.8	....	General Government	78bt*d*
55.3	150.0	221.2	361.5	359.8	463.4	331.3	301.5	964.4	693.3	872.0	-125.7	1,411.0	1,713.2	....	Banks	78bu*d*
7.3	31.3	183.8	82.5	37.0	195.3	55.3	147.1	102.1	57.3	118.9	-40.6	53.6	117.6	....	Other Sectors	78bv*d*
-75.2	12.0	25.3	12.2	76.5	89.9	38.8	-13.1	-58.2	-13.3	-92.5	-137.6	-150.0	147.0	....	Net Errors and Omissions	78ca*d*
63.7	70.7	228.0	293.8	-65.6	-224.9	144.8	246.9	-363.1	-59.8	-47.0	-82.5	639.0	-8.0	....	*Overall Balance*	78cb*d*
-63.7	-70.7	-228.0	-293.8	65.6	224.9	-144.8	-246.9	363.1	59.8	47.0	82.5	-639.0	8.0	....	Reserves and Related Items	79da*d*
-63.7	-70.7	-228.0	-293.8	65.6	224.9	-144.8	-246.9	363.1	59.8	47.0	82.5	-639.0	8.0	....	Reserve Assets	79db*d*
—	—	—	—	—	—	—	—	—	—	—	—	—	—	....	Use of Fund Credit and Loans	79dc*d*
....	....	....	....	....	....	....	....	....	....	....	....	....	....	....	Exceptional Financing	79de*d*
Year Ending December 31															**Government Finance**	
-103.74	-93.42	-65.97	-136.08	-182.39	-147.56	-77.82	-51.85	-39.90	-142.08	-231.22	-257.58	-201.27	-150.46	....	Deficit (-) or Surplus	80
454.73	529.10	627.24	706.42	720.83	873.99	987.93	1,140.55	1,266.90	1,321.30	1,373.39	1,473.17	1,590.06	1,863.05	....	Revenue	81
6.98	6.96	5.37	4.04	3.78	1.14	3.75	3.97	3.90	2.35	1.64	.74	.94	2.51	....	Grants Received	81z
549.47	619.47	691.23	836.34	888.91	1,007.37	1,053.83	1,192.36	1,306.10	1,462.72	1,603.53	1,731.70	1,787.73	2,005.59	....	Expenditure	82
15.98	10.01	7.35	10.20	18.09	15.32	15.67	4.01	4.60	3.01	2.72	-.21	4.54	10.43	....	Lending Minus Repayments	83
															Financing	
102.27	112.49	-2.08	168.55	125.75	249.03	219.76	106.87	117.40	203.91	143.13	109.31	52.57	185.30	....	Net Borrowing: Domestic	84a
13.34	21.11	107.41	-22.37	82.85	-54.63	-91.04	-65.02	-77.50	-61.83	88.08	148.28	148.70	-34.84	....	Foreign	85a
-11.87	-40.18	-39.36	-10.10	-26.21	-46.84	-50.90	10.00	—	—	—	-.01	—	—	....	Use of Cash Balances	87
411.02	533.73	531.71	700.02	826.36	1,075.44	1,295.36	1,402.51	1,583.40	1,837.56	1,987.35	2,130.72	2,165.40	2,467.70	....	Debt: Domestic	88a
506.83	511.02	616.92	595.60	682.79	665.27	627.81	556.65	479.27	402.95	515.33	664.77	850.68	820.82	....	Foreign	89a
Millions of Pounds															**National Accounts**	
1,059.8	1,210.2	1,343.3	1,532.2	1,754.1	1,938.6	1,934.3	2,111.0	2,551.8	2,704.4	2,884.5	3,168.1 p	3,309.7 p	....	....	Househ.Cons.Expend.,incl.NPISHs	96f
295.7	332.5	360.7	443.1	493.3	590.7	552.5	608.1	644.2	748.2	821.0	904.7	889.0	....	....	Government Consumption Expend.	91f
417.9	490.8	621.4	628.5	650.2	795.9	741.2	751.5	769.7	826.9	789.3	808.0	807.3	....	....	Gross Fixed Capital Formation	93e
36.6	57.2	75.8	62.3	41.0	94.6	47.6	180.0	108.6	78.8	31.6	50.0	65.0	....	....	Changes in Inventories	93i
841.8	959.6	1,161.4	1,316.8	1,260.8	1,544.4	1,555.2	1,741.1	1,870.1	1,952.1	2,056.9	2,044.2	2,233.8	2,516.7	....	Exports of Goods and Services	90c
894.9	1,067.9	1,351.3	1,456.3	1,526.9	1,881.6	1,569.4	1,755.5	1,999.7	2,208.8	2,274.8	2,398.2	2,392.2	2,747.1	....	Imports of Goods and Services (-)	98c
1,781.1	1,992.4	2,256.2	2,555.7	2,674.7	3,102.9	3,285.4	3,663.2	4,006.6	4,161.0	4,370.6	4,694.5	5,009.1	5,457.7	....	Gross Domestic Product (GDP)	99b
24.1	23.3	35.0	41.6	44.8	39.6	36.6	28.8	41.0	21.0	33.2	12.8	-51.7	....	....	Net Primary Income from Abroad	98.n
1,805.2	2,015.7	2,291.2	2,597.3	2,719.5	3,142.5	3,322.0	3,692.0	4,050.3	4,185.6	4,408.8	4,722.2 p	5,027.1 p	....	....	Gross National Income (GNI)	99a
189.5	211.9	240.5	272.7	285.5	330.0	348.8	387.7	425.3	439.5	462.9	495.8 p	527.8 p	....	....	Consumption of Fixed Capital	99cf
....	....	....	....	....	....	....	....	....	....	....	....	....	....	....	GDP Volume 1967 prices	99b.*p*
....	....	....	....	....	....	....	....	....	....	....	....	....	....	....	GDP Volume 1973 prices	99b.*p*
....	....	....	....	....	....	....	....	....	....	....	....	....	....	....	GDP Volume 1980 prices	99b.*p*
1,644.9	1,781.7	1,925.8	2,068.4	....	....	....	....	....	....	....	....	....	....	....	GDP Volume 1985 prices	99b.*p*
....	....	....	2,555.7	2,574.6	2,815.7	2,834.7	3,001.1	3,184.2	3,244.8	3,325.9	3,492.2	3,649.6	....	....	GDP Volume 1990 Prices	99b.*p*
63.8	69.1	74.6	80.2	80.8	88.3	88.9	94.2	100.0	101.9	104.4	109.7	114.6	120.1	....	GDP Volume (1995=100)	99bv*p*
69.7	72.0	75.4	79.6	82.7	87.7	92.2	97.1	100.0	101.9	104.4	106.8	109.1	113.4	....	GDP Deflator (1995=100)	99bi*p*
Midyear Estimates																
.66	.66	.67	.68	.69	.71	.72	.73	.73	.74	.74	.75	.75	.76	.79	**Population**	99z

(See notes in the back of the book.)

Czech Republic

		1972	1973	1974	1975	1976	1977	1978	1979	1980	1981	1982	1983	1984	1985	1986
Exchange Rates														*Koruny per SDR:*		
Official Rate	aa	....	....	....	....	....	....	....	....	....	....	....	....	....	....	....
															Koruny per US Dollar:	
Official Rate	ae	....	....	....	....	....	....	....	....	....	....	....	....	....	....	....
Official Rate	rf	....	....	....	....	....	....	....	....	....	....	....	....	....	....	....
														Index Numbers (1995=100):		
Nominal Effective Exchange Rate	ne c	....	....	....	....	....	....	....	....	....	....	....	....	....	....	....
Real Effective Exchange Rate	re c	....	....	....	....	....	....	....	....	....	....	....	....	....	....	....
Fund Position															*Millions of SDRs:*	
Quota	2f. s	....	....	....	....	....	....	....	....	....	....	....	....	....	....	....
SDRs	1b. s	....	....	....	....	....	....	....	....	....	....	....	....	....	....	....
Reserve Position in the Fund	1c. s	....	....	....	....	....	....	....	....	....	....	....	....	....	....	....
Total Fund Cred.&Loans Outstg.	2tl	....	....	....	....	....	....	....	....	....	....	....	....	....	....	....
International Liquidity											*Millions of US Dollars Unless Otherwise Indicated:*					
Total Reserves minus Gold	1l. d															....
SDRs	1b. d															....
Reserve Position in the Fund	1c. d															....
Foreign Exchange	1d. d															....
Gold (Million Fine Troy Ounces)	1ad															....
Gold (National Valuation)	1an d															....
Monetary Authorities: Other Assets	3..d															....
Other Liab.	4..d															....
Deposit Money Banks: Assets	7a. d															....
Liabilities	7b. d															....
Monetary Authorities															*Billions of Koruny:*	
Foreign Assets	11	....														....
Claims on Central Government	12a															....
Claims on Nonfin.Pub.Enterprises	12c															....
Claims on Private Sector	12d															....
Claims on Deposit Money Banks	12e															....
Claims on Nonbank Financial Insts	12g															....
Reserve Money	14															....
of which: Currency Outside DMBs	14a															....
Time Deposits	15															....
Foreign Liabilities	16c															....
Central Government Deposits	16d															....
Capital Accounts	17a															....
Other Items (Net)	17r															....
Deposit Money Banks															*Billions of Koruny:*	
Reserves	20	....														....
Foreign Assets	21															....
Claims on General Government	22a															....
of which: Clms.on Natl.Prop.Fd.	22ae															....
Claims on Nonfin.Pub.Enterprises	22c															....
Claims on Private Sector	22d															....
Claims on Nonbank Financial Insts	22g															....
Demand Deposits	24															....
Time & Foreign Currency Deposits	25															....
of which: Fgn. Currency Deposits	25b															....
Bonds	26ab															....
Foreign Liabilities	26c															....
General Government Deposits	26d															....
of which: Natl.Prop.Fd.Deposits	26de															....
Credit from Monetary Authorities	26g															....
Capital Accounts	27a															....
Other Items (Net)	27r															....
Monetary Survey															*Billions of Koruny:*	
Foreign Assets (Net)	31n	....														....
Domestic Credit	32															....
Claims on General Govt. (Net)	32an															....
Claims on Nonfin.Pub.Enterprises	32c															....
Claims on Private Sector	32d															....
Claims on Nonbank Fin. Insts	32g															....
Money	34															....
Quasi-Money	35															....
Bonds	36ab															....
Capital Accounts	37a															....
Other Items (Net)	37r															....
Money plus Quasi-Money	35l	....														....
Interest Rates															*Percent Per Annum*	
Bank Rate (End of Period)	60	....														....
Money Market Rate	60b															....
Treasury Bill Rate	60c															....
Deposit Rate	60l															....
Lending Rate	60p															....
Government Bond Yield	61	....														....
Prices, Production, Labor															*Index Numbers (1995=100):*	
Producer Prices	63	....														....
Consumer Prices	64															41.5
Wages	65															....
Industrial Production	66															....
Industrial Employment	67															....
															Number in Thousands:	
Labor Force	67d	....														....
Employment	67e															....
Unemployment	67c															....
Unemployment Rate (%)	67r															....

1987	1988	1989	1990	1991	1992	1993	1994	1995	1996	1997	1998	1999	2000	2001		
End of Period															**Exchange Rates**	
....	....	....	....	....	....	41.145	40.947	39.544	39.302	46.733	42.037	49.382	49.267	45.568	Official Rate	aa
End of Period (ae) Period Average (rf)																
....	....	....	....	....	....	29.955	28.049	26.602	27.332	34.636	29.855	35.979	37.813	36.259	Official Rate	ae
....	....	....	....	....	....	29.153	28.785	26.541	27.145	31.698	32.281	34.569	38.598	38.035	Official Rate	rf
Period Averages																
....	....	....	131.27	91.32	92.50	97.67	100.00	100.00	101.90	98.38	99.07	99.19	100.24	105.07	Nominal Effective Exchange Rate	ne c
....	....	....	81.92	75.67	79.17	92.06	96.71	100.00	106.65	107.49	116.32	114.74	114.81	121.26	Real Effective Exchange Rate	re c
End of Period															**Fund Position**	
....	....	....	....	....	....	589.6	589.6	589.6	589.6	589.6	589.6	819.3	819.3	819.3	Quota	2f. s
....	....	....	....	....	....	6.0	—	.1	—	—	—	—	.2	.7	SDRs	1b. s
....	....	....	....	....	....	—	—	—	—	—	—	—	2.4	120.5	Reserve Position in the Fund	1c. s
....	....	....	....	....	....	780.7	—	—	—	—	—	—	—	—	Total Fund Cred.&Loans Outstg.	2tl
End of Period															**International Liquidity**	
....	....	....	....	....	....	3,789	6,145	13,843	12,352	9,734	12,542	12,806	13,019	14,342	Total Reserves minus Gold	1l. d
....	....	....	....	....	....	8	—	—	—	—	—	—	—	1	SDRs	1b. d
....	....	....	....	....	....	—	—	—	—	—	—	—	3	151	Reserve Position in the Fund	1c. d
....	....	....	....	....	....	3,781	6,145	13,843	12,352	9,734	12,542	12,806	13,016	14,190	Foreign Exchange	1d. d
....	....	....	....	....	....	1.950	2.098	1.990	1.985	1.041	.288	.446	.446	.444	Gold (Million Fine Troy Ounces)	1ad
....	....	....	....	....	....	129	140	141	137	57	18	23	22	22	Gold (National Valuation)	1and
....	....	....	....	....	....	2,264	1,043	1,084	1,161	843	946	1,285	378	435	Monetary Authorities: Other Assets	3..d
....	....	....	....	....	....	2,905	1,791	1,802	658	696	381	849	366	407	Other Liab.	4..d
....	....	....	....	....	....	2,802	3,203	3,783	5,767	8,585	11,793	13,302	13,259	15,609	Deposit Money Banks: Assets	7a. d
....	....	....	....	....	....	1,459	2,464	6,428	9,048	9,124	10,799	9,678	8,419	7,714	Liabilities	7b. d
End of Period															**Monetary Authorities**	
....	....	....	....	....	....	185.20	205.53	400.83	373.08	368.28	403.23	507.82	507.43	536.61	Foreign Assets	11
....	....	....	....	....	....	44.98	39.73	12.63	.32	—	—	—	—	11.65	Claims on Central Government	12a
....	....	....	....	....	....	1.99	1.27	.70	.71	†.55	.28	.16	.09	—	Claims on Nonfin.Pub.Enterprises	12c
....	....	....	....	....	....	.17	.48	†.81	4.39	9.47	13.84	27.80	27.18	26.74	Claims on Private Sector	12d
....	....	....	....	....	....	78.40	77.71	74.84	84.88	100.49	74.91	50.47	37.10	20.52	Claims on Deposit Money Banks	12e
....	....	....	....	....	....	.16	.04	—	—	12.12	34.38	33.15	15.16	14.03	Claims on Nonbank Financial Insts	12g
....	....	....	....	....	....	166.12	223.23	342.77	344.40	†344.60	422.24	459.78	491.57	515.76	Reserve Money	14
....	....	....	....	....	....	59.04	83.58	104.27	118.90	118.74	127.16	157.90	171.82	180.38	*of which: Currency Outside DMBs*	14a
....	....	....	....	....	....	.14	9.22	52.68	40.27	†.68	.79	.85	.70	.74	Time Deposits	15
....	....	....	....	....	....	119.15	50.25	47.93	17.98	24.11	11.38	30.55	13.83	14.74	Foreign Liabilities	16c
....	....	....	....	....	....	33.41	51.86	41.15	43.09	†68.46	63.07	62.44	57.97	84.25	Central Government Deposits	16d
....	....	....	....	....	....	9.90	18.00	27.34	29.56	60.56	39.07	82.84	36.83	8.25	Capital Accounts	17a
....	....	....	....	....	....	-17.98	-28.26	-22.05	-11.91	-7.51	-9.92	-17.06	-13.93	-14.19	Other Items (Net)	17r
End of Period															**Deposit Money Banks**	
....	....	....	....	....	....	71.45	80.78	160.93	158.50	214.94	288.85	296.54	310.93	333.32	Reserves	20
....	....	....	....	....	....	83.95	89.84	100.64	157.64	297.34	352.08	478.59	501.35	565.97	Foreign Assets	21
....	....	....	....	....	....	78.18	94.64	130.94	103.86	62.05	73.66	93.76	117.90	270.78	Claims on General Government	22a
....	....	....	....	....	....	10.80	12.20	27.80	18.00	17.00	15.00	15.00	—	—	*of which: Clms.on Natl.Prop.Fd.*	22ae
....	....	....	....	....	....	222.92	221.00	234.82	274.46	†155.57	120.02	99.68	81.10	37.19	Claims on Nonfin.Pub.Enterprises	22c
....	....	....	....	....	....	508.67	683.19	801.73	879.38	†1094.54	1,055.83	997.05	946.45	877.91	Claims on Private Sector	22d
....	....	....	....	....	....	.10	.22	.29	5.52	.28	.40	1.74	2.34	1.27	Claims on Nonbank Financial Insts	22g
....	....	....	....	....	....	201.96	307.64	310.89	317.46	297.24	275.68	288.88	326.53	402.50	Demand Deposits	24
....	....	....	....	....	....	428.21	426.43	601.90	663.78	755.75	809.54	797.54	945.94	1,022.98	Time & Foreign Currency Deposits	25
....	....	....	....	....	....	56.73	59.06	57.66	69.33	133.60	137.80	145.26	167.39	178.17	*of which: Fgn. Currency Deposits*	25b
....	....	....	....	....	....	3.78	21.21	46.68	60.88	81.58	113.38	189.74	93.39	76.74	Bonds	26ab
....	....	....	....	....	....	43.70	69.12	170.99	247.29	316.01	322.40	348.22	318.35	279.70	Foreign Liabilities	26c
....	....	....	....	....	....	78.73	90.33	92.38	88.19	51.87	55.31	54.59	50.83	80.54	General Government Deposits	26d
....	....	....	....	....	....	43.48	29.94	40.91	33.95	1.76	8.77	11.06	11.26	17.12	*of which: Natl.Prop.Fd.Deposits*	26de
....	....	....	....	....	....	76.35	77.71	74.01	79.82	96.93	52.76	33.68	18.27	4.66	Credit from Monetary Authorities	26g
....	....	....	....	....	....	160.75	185.37	195.88	204.28	†348.20	395.15	411.80	405.39	291.53	Capital Accounts	27a
....	....	....	....	....	....	-28.25	-8.29	-63.62	-87.77	-122.85	-133.39	-157.09	-198.63	-72.20	Other Items (Net)	27r
End of Period															**Monetary Survey**	
....	....	....	....	....	....	106.29	176.00	282.55	265.44	325.50	421.52	607.64	676.60	808.14	Foreign Assets (Net)	31n
....	....	....	....	....	....	744.88	897.91	1,047.61	1,133.02	†1214.25	1,180.04	1,136.31	1,081.43	1,074.78	Domestic Credit	32
....	....	....	....	....	....	11.03	-7.82	10.04	-27.10	†-58.28	-44.71	-23.27	9.10	117.65	Claims on General Govt. (Net)	32an
....	....	....	....	....	....	224.91	222.27	235.52	275.17	†156.12	120.30	99.84	81.19	37.19	Claims on Nonfin.Pub.Enterprises	32c
....	....	....	....	....	....	508.68	683.21	801.77	879.43	†1104.02	1,069.67	1,024.85	973.63	904.65	Claims on Private Sector	32d
....	....	....	....	....	....	.26	.25	.29	5.52	12.40	34.78	34.89	17.50	15.29	Claims on Nonbank Fin. Insts	32g
....	....	....	....	....	....	268.98	403.97	431.08	451.55	†418.39	404.00	447.81	498.96	583.55	Money	34
....	....	....	....	....	....	428.35	435.65	654.58	704.05	†756.44	810.33	798.39	946.64	1,023.72	Quasi-Money	35
....	....	....	....	....	....	3.78	21.21	46.68	60.88	81.58	113.38	189.74	93.39	76.74	Bonds	36ab
....	....	....	....	....	....	170.10	202.22	221.26	231.06	†408.76	434.22	494.64	442.22	299.78	Capital Accounts	37a
....	....	....	....	....	....	-20.61	9.57	-24.86	-52.94	-125.41	-160.39	-186.63	-223.18	-100.87	Other Items (Net)	37r
....	....	....	....	....	....	697.33	839.62	1,085.66	1,155.59	†1174.83	1,214.33	1,246.20	1,445.60	1,607.27	Money plus Quasi-Money	35l
Percent Per Annum															**Interest Rates**	
....	....	....	....	....	....	8.00	8.50	11.30	12.40	14.75	9.50	5.25	5.25	4.75	Bank Rate *(End of Period)*	60
....	....	....	....	....	....	8.00	12.65	10.93	12.67	17.50	10.08	5.58	5.42	4.69	Money Market Rate	60b
....	....	....	....	....	....	6.62	6.98	8.99	11.91	11.21	10.51	5.71	5.37	5.06	Treasury Bill Rate	60c
....	....	....	....	....	....	7.03	7.07	6.96	6.79	7.71	8.08	4.48	3.42	2.97	Deposit Rate	60l
....	....	....	....	....	....	14.07	13.12	12.80	12.54	13.20	12.81	8.68	7.16	7.06	Lending Rate	60p
....	....	....	....	....	....	....	....	....	....	....	....	....	6.72	4.62	Government Bond Yield	61
Period Averages															**Prices, Production, Labor**	
....	....	....	....	....	....	88.3	93.0	100.0	104.8	109.9	115.3	116.5	122.2	....	Producer Prices	63
....	....	....	....	....	....	83.3	91.6	100.0	108.8	118.1	130.7	133.5	138.7	145.2	Consumer Prices	64
....	....	....	....	....	....	71.2	84.4	100.0	118.4	130.8	143.1	155.1	165.1	179.2	Wages	65
....	....	....	....	....	....	90.1	92.0	100.0	101.9	106.5	109.7	104.8	110.4	117.9	Industrial Production	66
....	....	....	....	....	....	117.2	111.6	100.0	95.3	107.7	107.3	101.2	96.9	97.6	Industrial Employment	67
Period Averages																
....	....	....	....	....	....	....	....	....	5,199	5,215	5,233	5,236	5,181	....	Labor Force	67d
....	....	....	....	....	....	4,932	4,943	4,995	†4,980	4,927	4,853	4,765	4,751	....	Employment	67e
....	....	....	....	....	....	200	202	181	206	248	317	447	469	....	Unemployment	67c
....	....	....	....	....	....	3.8	3.9	3.5	4.0	4.8	6.1	8.6	9.0	....	Unemployment Rate (%)	67r

Czech Republic

	1972	1973	1974	1975	1976	1977	1978	1979	1980	1981	1982	1983	1984	1985	1986
International Transactions														*Millions of Koruny*	
Exports 70	...	...	...	...	...	...	...	...	...	121,402	130,131	134,740	151,989	147,904	148,579
Imports, f.o.b. 71.v	...	...	...	...	...	...	...	...	...	116,471	125,709	131,443	149,832	154,278	160,131
Balance of Payments															
													Millions of US Dollars:		
Current Account, n.i.e. .... 78al *d*	...	...	...	...	...	...	...	...	...	...	...	...	...	...	...
Goods: Exports f.o.b. .... 78aa *d*	...	...	...	...	...	...	...	...	...	...	...	...	...	...	...
Goods: Imports f.o.b. .... 78ab *d*	...	...	...	...	...	...	...	...	...	...	...	...	...	...	...
Trade Balance .... 78ac *d*	...	...	...	...	...	...	...	...	...	...	...	...	...	...	...
Services: Credit .... 78ad *d*	...	...	...	...	...	...	...	...	...	...	...	...	...	...	...
Services: Debit .... 78ae *d*	...	...	...	...	...	...	...	...	...	...	...	...	...	...	...
Balance on Goods & Services .... 78af *d*	...	...	...	...	...	...	...	...	...	...	...	...	...	...	...
Income: Credit .... 78ag *d*	...	...	...	...	...	...	...	...	...	...	...	...	...	...	...
Income: Debit .... 78ah *d*	...	...	...	...	...	...	...	...	...	...	...	...	...	...	...
Balance on Gds, Serv. & Inc. .... 78ai *d*	...	...	...	...	...	...	...	...	...	...	...	...	...	...	...
Current Transfers, n.i.e.: Credit .... 78aj *d*	...	...	...	...	...	...	...	...	...	...	...	...	...	...	...
Current Transfers: Debit .... 78ak *d*	...	...	...	...	...	...	...	...	...	...	...	...	...	...	...
Capital Account, n.i.e. .... 78bc *d*	...	...	...	...	...	...	...	...	...	...	...	...	...	...	...
Capital Account, n.i.e.: Credit .... 78ba *d*	...	...	...	...	...	...	...	...	...	...	...	...	...	...	...
Capital Account: Debit .... 78bb *d*	...	...	...	...	...	...	...	...	...	...	...	...	...	...	...
Financial Account, n.i.e. .... 78bj *d*	...	...	...	...	...	...	...	...	...	...	...	...	...	...	...
Direct Investment Abroad .... 78bd *d*	...	...	...	...	...	...	...	...	...	...	...	...	...	...	...
Dir. Invest. in Rep. Econ., n.i.e. .... 78be *d*	...	...	...	...	...	...	...	...	...	...	...	...	...	...	...
Portfolio Investment Assets .... 78bf *d*	...	...	...	...	...	...	...	...	...	...	...	...	...	...	...
Equity Securities .... 78bk *d*	...	...	...	...	...	...	...	...	...	...	...	...	...	...	...
Debt Securities .... 78bl *d*	...	...	...	...	...	...	...	...	...	...	...	...	...	...	...
Portfolio Investment Liab., n.i.e. ...... 78bg *d*	...	...	...	...	...	...	...	...	...	...	...	...	...	...	...
Equity Securities .... 78bm *d*	...	...	...	...	...	...	...	...	...	...	...	...	...	...	...
Debt Securities .... 78bn *d*	...	...	...	...	...	...	...	...	...	...	...	...	...	...	...
Financial Derivatives Assets .... 78bw *d*	...	...	...	...	...	...	...	...	...	...	...	...	...	...	...
Financial Derivatives Liabilities .... 78bx *d*	...	...	...	...	...	...	...	...	...	...	...	...	...	...	...
Other Investment Assets .... 78bh *d*	...	...	...	...	...	...	...	...	...	...	...	...	...	...	...
Monetary Authorities .... 78bo *d*	...	...	...	...	...	...	...	...	...	...	...	...	...	...	...
General Government .... 78bp *d*	...	...	...	...	...	...	...	...	...	...	...	...	...	...	...
Banks .... 78bq *d*	...	...	...	...	...	...	...	...	...	...	...	...	...	...	...
Other Sectors .... 78br *d*	...	...	...	...	...	...	...	...	...	...	...	...	...	...	...
Other Investment Liab., n.i.e. .... 78bi *d*	...	...	...	...	...	...	...	...	...	...	...	...	...	...	...
Monetary Authorities .... 78bs *d*	...	...	...	...	...	...	...	...	...	...	...	...	...	...	...
General Government .... 78bt *d*	...	...	...	...	...	...	...	...	...	...	...	...	...	...	...
Banks .... 78bu *d*	...	...	...	...	...	...	...	...	...	...	...	...	...	...	...
Other Sectors .... 78bv *d*	...	...	...	...	...	...	...	...	...	...	...	...	...	...	...
Net Errors and Omissions .... 78ca *d*	...	...	...	...	...	...	...	...	...	...	...	...	...	...	...
Overall Balance .... 78cb *d*	...	...	...	...	...	...	...	...	...	...	...	...	...	...	...
Reserves and Related Items .... 79da *d*	...	...	...	...	...	...	...	...	...	...	...	...	...	...	...
Reserve Assets .... 79db *d*	...	...	...	...	...	...	...	...	...	...	...	...	...	...	...
Use of Fund Credit and Loans .... 79dc *d*	...	...	...	...	...	...	...	...	...	...	...	...	...	...	...
Exceptional Financing .... 79de *d*	...	...	...	...	...	...	...	...	...	...	...	...	...	...	...
International Investment Position														*Millions of US Dollars*	
Assets .... 79aa *d*	...	...	...	...	...	...	...	...	...	...	...	...	...	...	...
Direct Investment Abroad .... 79ab *d*	...	...	...	...	...	...	...	...	...	...	...	...	...	...	...
Portfolio Investment .... 79ac *d*	...	...	...	...	...	...	...	...	...	...	...	...	...	...	...
Equity Securities .... 79ad *d*	...	...	...	...	...	...	...	...	...	...	...	...	...	...	...
Debt Securities .... 79ae *d*	...	...	...	...	...	...	...	...	...	...	...	...	...	...	...
Financial Derivatives .... 79al *d*	...	...	...	...	...	...	...	...	...	...	...	...	...	...	...
Other Investment .... 79af *d*	...	...	...	...	...	...	...	...	...	...	...	...	...	...	...
Monetary Authorities .... 79ag *d*	...	...	...	...	...	...	...	...	...	...	...	...	...	...	...
General Government .... 79ah *d*	...	...	...	...	...	...	...	...	...	...	...	...	...	...	...
Banks .... 79ai *d*	...	...	...	...	...	...	...	...	...	...	...	...	...	...	...
Other Sectors .... 79aj *d*	...	...	...	...	...	...	...	...	...	...	...	...	...	...	...
Reserve Assets .... 79ak *d*	...	...	...	...	...	...	...	...	...	...	...	...	...	...	...
Liabilities .... 79la *d*	...	...	...	...	...	...	...	...	...	...	...	...	...	...	...
Dir. Invest. in Rep. Economy .... 79lb *d*	...	...	...	...	...	...	...	...	...	...	...	...	...	...	...
Portfolio Investment .... 79lc *d*	...	...	...	...	...	...	...	...	...	...	...	...	...	...	...
Equity Securities .... 79ld *d*	...	...	...	...	...	...	...	...	...	...	...	...	...	...	...
Debt Securities .... 79le *d*	...	...	...	...	...	...	...	...	...	...	...	...	...	...	...
Financial Derivatives .... 79ll *d*	...	...	...	...	...	...	...	...	...	...	...	...	...	...	...
Other Investment .... 79lf *d*	...	...	...	...	...	...	...	...	...	...	...	...	...	...	...
Monetary Authorities .... 79lg *d*	...	...	...	...	...	...	...	...	...	...	...	...	...	...	...
General Government .... 79lh *d*	...	...	...	...	...	...	...	...	...	...	...	...	...	...	...
Banks .... 79li *d*	...	...	...	...	...	...	...	...	...	...	...	...	...	...	...
Other Sectors .... 79lj *d*	...	...	...	...	...	...	...	...	...	...	...	...	...	...	...

Millions of Koruny

International Transactions

Item	1987	1988	1989	1990	1991	1992	1993	1994	1995	1996	1997	1998	1999	2000	2001	Code
Exports	151,934	159,262	162,085	162,477	233,594	248,090	†421,601	466,403	574,722	594,630	722,501	850,240	908,756	1,121,099	1,269,749	70
Imports, f.o.b.	161,973	160,658	162,169	176,186	208,781	293,399	†426,084	501,549	670,445	752,343	861,770	926,559	973,169	1,241,924	1,386,938	71.v

Minus Sign Indicates Debit

Balance of Payments

Item	1987	1988	1989	1990	1991	1992	1993	1994	1995	1996	1997	1998	1999	2000	2001	Code
Current Account, n.i.e.	...	...	...	...	...	...	466	−820	−1,374	−4,128	−3,622	−1,308	−1,466	−2,690	−2,638	78ald
Goods: Exports f.o.b.	...	...	...	...	...	...	14,231	15,964	21,477	21,950	22,319	25,886	26,259	29,019	33,407	78aa d
Goods: Imports f.o.b.	...	...	...	...	...	...	−14,748	−17,372	−25,162	−27,656	−27,257	−28,532	−28,161	−32,114	−36,498	78ab d
Trade Balance	...	...	...	...	...	...	−517	−1,408	−3,685	−5,706	−4,938	−2,647	−1,902	−3,095	−3,091	78ac d
Services: Credit	...	...	...	...	...	...	4,721	5,167	6,725	8,181	7,132	7,665	7,048	6,839	7,092	78ad d
Services: Debit	...	...	...	...	...	...	−3,709	−4,685	−4,882	−6,264	−5,389	−5,750	−5,850	−5,436	−5,567	78ae d
Balance on Goods & Services	...	...	...	...	...	...	496	−926	−1,842	−3,789	−3,196	−731	−704	−1,692	−1,567	78af d
Income: Credit	...	...	...	...	...	...	548	791	1,197	1,170	1,405	1,713	1,859	1,952	2,170	78ag d
Income: Debit	...	...	...	...	...	...	−664	−812	−1,301	−1,892	−2,197	−2,806	−3,209	−3,323	−3,710	78ah d
Balance on Gds, Serv. & Inc.	...	...	...	...	...	...	379	−947	−1,945	−4,512	−3,987	−1,825	−2,053	−3,063	−3,108	78ai d
Current Transfers, n.i.e.: Credit	...	...	...	...	...	...	242	298	664	617	866	1,067	1,310	948	959	78aj d
Current Transfers: Debit	...	...	...	...	...	...	−154	−171	−92	−233	−501	−550	−722	−575	−489	78ak d
Capital Account, n.i.e.	...	...	...	...	...	...	−563	—	7	1	11	2	−2	−5	−9	78bc d
Capital Account, n.i.e.: Credit	...	...	...	...	...	...	208	—	12	1	17	14	18	6	2	78ba d
Capital Account: Debit	...	...	...	...	...	...	−771	—	−5	—	−5	−12	−21	−11	−11	78bb d
Financial Account, n.i.e.	...	...	...	...	...	...	3,043	4,504	8,225	4,202	1,122	2,908	3,080	3,835	4,058	78bj d
Direct Investment Abroad	...	...	...	...	...	...	−90	−116	−37	−155	−28	−125	−90	−43	−95	78bd d
Dir. Invest. in Rep. Econ., n.i.e.	...	...	...	...	...	...	654	878	2,568	1,435	1,286	3,700	6,313	4,987	4,924	78be d
Portfolio Investment Assets	...	...	...	...	...	...	−232	−47	−325	−50	−159	−44	−1,882	−2,236	125	78bf d
Equity Securities	...	...	...	...	...	...	−232	−47	−325	−50	3	119	−1,409	−1,167	247	78bk d
Debt Securities	...	...	...	...	...	...	...	...	...	...	−162	−163	−473	−1,069	−121	78bl d
Portfolio Investment Liab., n.i.e.	...	...	...	...	...	...	1,840	893	1,695	771	1,152	1,146	499	482	798	78bg d
Equity Securities	...	...	...	...	...	...	1,125	497	1,236	601	378	1,096	120	619	616	78bm d
Debt Securities	...	...	...	...	...	...	715	396	460	170	774	49	380	−137	181	78bn d
Financial Derivatives Assets	...	...	...	...	...	...	...	...	...	...	...	...	...	−129	−254	78bw d
Financial Derivatives Liabilities	...	...	...	...	...	...	...	...	...	...	...	...	...	89	168	78bx d
Other Investment Assets	...	...	...	...	...	...	−2,867	−2,437	−2,492	−2,370	−4,427	−1,552	−2,688	984	−1,271	78bh d
Monetary Authorities	...	...	...	...	...	...										78bo d
General Government	...	...	...	...	...	...	−3,054	−2,362	−2,138	48	16	20	28	76	180	78bp d
Banks	...	...	...	...	...	...	36	−163	−224	−2,317	−4,161	−1,652	−2,642	1,011	−1,299	78bq d
Other Sectors	...	...	...	...	...	...	151	88	−130	−101	−281	80	−74	−102	−152	78br d
Other Investment Liab., n.i.e.	...	...	...	...	...	...	3,738	5,333	6,816	4,571	3,298	−217	927	−300	−337	78bi d
Monetary Authorities	...	...	...	...	...	...	106	−47	40	−2	−11	−7	−57	—	1	78bs d
General Government	...	...	...	...	...	...	3,037	2,821	1,657	−295	−360	−364	−185	−49	−129	78bt d
Banks	...	...	...	...	...	...	4	888	3,310	2,858	1,638	387	886	−974	−1,152	78bu d
Other Sectors	...	...	...	...	...	...	591	1,671	1,809	2,011	2,030	−234	283	723	943	78bv d
Net Errors and Omissions	...	...	...	...	...	...	95	−210	596	−901	730	288	27	−296	376	78ca d
Overall Balance	...	...	...	...	...	...	3,041	3,474	7,453	−825	−1,758	1,890	1,639	844	1,787	78cb d
Reserves and Related Items	...	...	...	...	...	...	−3,041	−3,474	−7,453	825	1,758	−1,890	−1,639	−844	−1,787	79da d
Reserve Assets	...	...	...	...	...	...	−3,039	−2,357	−7,453	825	1,758	−1,890	−1,639	−844	−1,787	79db d
Use of Fund Credit and Loans	...	...	...	...	...	...	−3	−1,117	—	—	—	—	—	—	—	79dc d
Exceptional Financing	...	...	...	...	...	...	...	...	...	...	...	...	...	...	...	79de d

Millions of US Dollars

International Investment Position

Item	1987	1988	1989	1990	1991	1992	1993	1994	1995	1996	1997	1998	1999	2000	2001	Code
Assets	...	...	...	...	...	...	17,950	20,471	29,396	30,629	29,779	36,426	37,465	38,304	42,381	79aa d
Direct Investment Abroad	...	...	...	...	...	...	181	300	345	498	548	804	698	738	832	79ab d
Portfolio Investment	...	...	...	...	...	...	276	433	755	1,372	1,032	1,202	2,900	4,772	5,106	79ac d
Equity Securities	...	...	...	...	...	...	264	334	693	748	417	449	1,843	2,439	1,894	79ad d
Debt Securities	...	...	...	...	...	...	12	99	62	624	615	752	1,057	2,333	3,212	79ae d
Financial Derivatives	...	...	...	...	...	...	—	—	—	—	—	—	—	168	435	79al d
Other Investment	...	...	...	...	...	...	13,621	13,494	14,273	16,323	18,425	21,804	21,042	19,488	21,543	79af d
Monetary Authorities	...	...	...	...	...	...	820	876	984	956	754	875	—	10	10	79ag d
General Government	...	...	...	...	...	...	6,469	6,278	5,987	5,931	5,923	5,902	5,843	5,839	5,813	79ah d
Banks	...	...	...	...	...	...	2,837	2,944	3,469	5,622	8,308	11,263	11,841	10,305	12,116	79ai d
Other Sectors	...	...	...	...	...	...	3,495	3,396	3,833	3,814	3,440	3,763	3,358	3,335	3,605	79aj d
Reserve Assets	...	...	...	...	...	...	3,872	6,243	14,023	12,435	9,774	12,617	12,825	13,139	14,464	79ak d
Liabilities	...	...	...	...	...	...	14,123	18,088	27,182	33,151	32,863	40,361	40,548	43,378	49,216	79la d
Dir. Invest. in Rep. Economy	...	...	...	...	...	...	3,423	4,547	7,350	8,572	9,234	14,375	17,552	21,644	26,764	79lb d
Portfolio Investment	...	...	...	...	...	...	1,956	2,910	4,696	5,298	4,880	5,564	4,602	4,353	4,974	79lc d
Equity Securities	...	...	...	...	...	...	1,101	1,331	2,642	3,398	3,028	3,793	2,724	3,059	3,551	79ld d
Debt Securities	...	...	...	...	...	...	855	1,579	2,054	1,900	1,853	1,771	1,878	1,294	1,423	79le d
Financial Derivatives	...	...	...	...	...	...	—	—	—	—	—	—	—	140	317	79ll d
Other Investment	...	...	...	...	...	...	8,744	10,631	15,136	19,280	18,749	20,422	18,394	17,242	17,160	79lf d
Monetary Authorities	...	...	...	...	...	...	1,272	62	98	85	64	64	6	5	6	79lg d
General Government	...	...	...	...	...	...	2,748	2,910	2,031	1,619	1,098	801	580	521	261	79lh d
Banks	...	...	...	...	...	...	1,283	2,402	6,007	8,964	9,009	10,640	9,682	8,219	7,286	79li d
Other Sectors	...	...	...	...	...	...	3,442	5,257	6,999	8,612	8,577	8,916	8,126	8,497	9,608	79lj d

Czech Republic

935

Government Finance

Billions of Koruny:

		1972	1973	1974	1975	1976	1977	1978	1979	1980	1981	1982	1983	1984	1985	1986
Deficit (-) or Surplus	80	....	....	....	....	....	....	....	....	....	....	....	....	....	....	....
Total Revenue and Grants	81y	....	....	....	....	....	....	....	....	....	....	....	....	....	....	....
Revenue	81	....	....	....	....	....	....	....	....	....	....	....	....	....	....	....
Grants	81z	....	....	....	....	....	....	....	....	....	....	....	....	....	....	....
Exp. & Lending Minus Repay.	82z	....	....	....	....	....	....	....	....	....	....	....	....	....	....	....
Expenditure	82	....	....	....	....	....	....	....	....	....	....	....	....	....	....	....
Lending Minus Repayments	83	....	....	....	....	....	....	....	....	....	....	....	....	....	....	....
Total Financing	80h	....	....	....	....	....	....	....	....	....	....	....	....	....	....	....
Domestic	84a	....	....	....	....	....	....	....	....	....	....	....	....	....	....	....
Foreign	85a	....	....	....	....	....	....	....	....	....	....	....	....	....	....	....
Total Debt by Residence	88	....	....	....	....	....	....	....	....	....	....	....	....	....	....	....
Domestic	88a	....	....	....	....	....	....	....	....	....	....	....	....	....	....	....
Foreign	89a	....	....	....	....	....	....	....	....	....	....	....	....	....	....	....

National Accounts

Billions of Koruny

		1972	1973	1974	1975	1976	1977	1978	1979	1980	1981	1982	1983	1984	1985	1986
Househ.Cons.Expend.,incl.NPISHs	96f	....	....	....	....	....	....	....	....	....	....	....	....	....	....	....
Government Consumption Expend.	91f	....	....	....	....	....	....	....	....	....	....	....	....	....	....	....
Gross Fixed Capital Formation	93e	....	....	....	....	....	....	....	....	....	....	....	....	....	....	....
Changes in Inventories	93i	....	....	....	....	....	....	....	....	....	....	....	....	....	....	....
Exports of Goods and Services	90c	....	....	....	....	....	....	....	....	....	....	....	....	....	....	....
Imports of Goods and Services (-)	98c	....	....	....	....	....	....	....	....	....	....	....	....	....	....	....
Gross Domestic Product (GDP)	99b	....	....	....	....	....	....	....	....	....	....	....	....	....	....	....
Net Primary Income from Abroad	98.n	....	....	....	....	....	....	....	....	....	....	....	....	....	....	....
Gross National Income (GNI)	99a	....	....	....	....	....	....	....	....	....	....	....	....	....	....	....
Net Current Transf.from Abroad	98t	....	....	....	....	....	....	....	....	....	....	....	....	....	....	....
Gross Nat'l Disposable Inc.(GNDI)	99i	....	....	....	....	....	....	....	....	....	....	....	....	....	....	....
Gross Saving	99s	....	....	....	....	....	....	....	....	....	....	....	....	....	....	....
GDP Volume 1995 Prices	99b.*p*	....	....	....	....	....	....	....	....	....	....	....	....	....	....	....
GDP Volume (1995=100)	99bv *p*	....	....	....	....	....	....	....	....	....	....	....	....	....	....	....
GDP Deflator (1995=100)	99bi *p*	....	....	....	....	....	....	....	....	....	....	....	....	....	....	....

Millions:

		1972	1973	1974	1975	1976	1977	1978	1979	1980	1981	1982	1983	1984	1985	1986
Population	99z	....	....	....	....	....	....	....	....	....	....	....	....	....	....	....

	1987	1988	1989	1990	1991	1992	1993	1994	1995	1996	1997	1998	1999	2000	2001		
																Government Finance	
Year Ending December 31																	
	....	....	....	....	....	....	1.1	10.4	7.2	−1.8	−15.9	−29.2	−29.7	−46.1	−67.9	Deficit (-) or Surplus	80
	....	....	....	....	....	....	349.0	381.3	440.4	476.4	500.8	530.6	563.3	583.1	623.2	Total Revenue and Grants	81y
	....	....	....	....	....	....	349.0	381.3	440.4	476.4	500.8	530.6	563.3	583.1	623.2	Revenue	81
																Grants	81z
	....	....	....	....	....	....	347.9	370.9	433.2	478.2	516.7	559.8	593.0	629.2	691.1	Exp. & Lending Minus Repay.	82z
	....	....	....	....	....	....	351.9	373.1	433.9	480.6	521.2	561.6	593.8	629.5	688.2	Expenditure	82
	....	....	....	....	....	....	−4.0	−2.2	−.7	−2.4	−4.5	−1.8	−.8	−.3	2.9	Lending Minus Repayments	83
	....	....	....	....	....	....	−1.1	−10.4	−7.2	1.7	15.9	29.3	29.6	46.1	67.8	Total Financing	80h
	....	....	....	....	....	....	−1.1	−10.4	−7.2	1.7	15.9	29.3	29.6	46.1	67.8	Domestic	84a
															—	Foreign	85a
	....	....	....	....	....	....	158.9	161.7	154.4	155.2	167.2	194.5	228.3	289.3	345.0	Total Debt by Residence	88
	....	....	....	....	....	....	86.5	90.2	101.3	110.9	128.9	169.9	207.1	259.5	323.7	Domestic	88a
	....	....	....	....	....	....	72.4	71.5	53.1	44.3	38.3	24.6	21.2	29.8	21.3	Foreign	89a
																National Accounts	
Billions of Koruny																	
	....	....	....	....	....	....	509.5	607.0	†701.7	818.2	899.9	966.1	1,019.2	1,074.1	1,157.2	Househ.Cons.Expend.,incl.NPISHs	96f
	....	....	....	....	....	....	223.4	255.5	†275.0	312.5	332.5	342.4	373.3	388.3	413.5	Government Consumption Expend.	91f
	....	....	....	....	....	....	289.6	339.8	†442.5	500.6	514.5	535.5	528.3	561.5	610.9	Gross Fixed Capital Formation	93e
	....	....	....	....	....	....	−10.3	12.2	†27.6	36.0	32.9	17.1	5.8	27.2	35.5	Changes in Inventories	93i
	....	....	....	....	....	....	559.6	597.1	†740.8	823.3	949.7	1,080.9	1,152.6	1,385.9	1,539.4	Exports of Goods and Services	90c
	....	....	....	....	....	....	551.5	628.8	†806.5	923.7	1,049.7	1,103.0	1,176.9	1,452.2	1,598.6	Imports of Goods and Services (-)	98c
	....	....	....	....	....	....	1,020.3	1,182.8	1,381.0	1,567.0	1,679.9	1,839.1	1,902.3	1,984.8	2,157.8	Gross Domestic Product (GDP)	99b
	....	....	....	....	....	....	−4.3	−.8	−7.1	−17.3	−20.2	−35.1	−46.7	−53.0	−58.9	Net Primary Income from Abroad	98.n
	....	....	....	....	....	....	1,016.0	1,181.9	1,373.9	1,549.7	1,659.7	1,804.0	1,855.6	1,931.9	2,098.9	Gross National Income (GNI)	99a
	....	....	....	....	....	....	3.2	3.6	15.2	10.4	11.3	16.7	20.4	14.4	17.8	Net Current Transf.from Abroad	98t
	....	....	....	....	....	....	1,003.0	1,185.6	1,389.1	1,560.1	1,671.0	1,820.7	1,876.0	1,946.2	2,116.7	Gross Nat'l Disposable Inc.(GNDI)	99i
	....	....	....	....	....	....	285.3	323.0	412.4	429.4	438.6	512.1	483.5	483.8	546.0	Gross Saving	99s
	....	....	....	....	....	....	1,275.3	1,303.6	1,381.0	1,440.4	1,429.3	1,414.4	1,421.0	1,467.3	1,515.1	GDP Volume 1995 Prices	99b,p
	....	....	....	....	....	....	92.3	94.4	100.0	104.3	103.5	102.4	102.9	106.2	109.7	GDP Volume (1995=100)	99bv p
	....	....	....	....	....	....	80.0	90.7	100.0	108.8	117.5	130.0	133.9	135.3	142.4	GDP Deflator (1995=100)	99bi p
Midyear Estimates																	
	....	....	....	....	....	....	10.33	10.34	10.33	10.32	10.30	10.29	10.28	10.27	10.29	**Population**	99z

(See notes in the back of the book.)

Denmark

		1972	1973	1974	1975	1976	1977	1978	1979	1980	1981	1982	1983	1984	1985	1986
Exchange Rates															*Kroner per SDR:*	
Market Rate	aa	7.434	†7.588	6.918	7.232	6.724	7.018	6.631	7.067	7.672	8.526	9.248	10.339	11.037	9.852	8.981
															Kroner per US Dollar:	
Market Rate	ae	6.847	†6.290	5.650	6.178	5.788	5.778	5.090	5.365	6.015	7.325	8.384	9.875	11.260	8.969	7.343
Market Rate	rf	6.949	6.050	6.095	5.746	6.045	6.003	5.515	5.261	5.636	7.123	8.332	9.145	10.357	10.596	8.091
							Kroner per ECU through 1998; Kroner per Euro Beginning 1999:										
Euro Rate	ea	....	....	....	....	....	....	....	7.7010	7.8494	7.9408	8.1149	8.1827	7.9881	7.9567	7.8619
Euro Rate	ag	....	....	....	....	....	....	....	....	....	....	....	....	....	....	....
Euro Rate	eb	....	....	....	....	6.7627	6.8529	7.0188	7.2105	7.8283	7.9241	8.1544	8.1300	8.1457	8.0183	7.9360
Euro Rate	rh	....	....	....	....	....	....	....	....	....	....	....	....	....	....	....
															Index Numbers (1995=100):	
Market Rate	ahx	80.5	92.8	92.0	97.6	92.6	93.2	101.6	106.4	99.4	78.9	67.4	61.4	54.2	53.2	69.4
Nominal Effective Exchange Rate	neu	95.4	98.9	98.9	101.0	102.8	101.7	101.5	100.1	92.2	87.2	84.0	84.7	82.6	83.7	87.4
Real Effective Exchange Rate	reu	....	....	....	95.5	96.7	95.0	99.4	100.2	†92.2	87.5	85.0	86.9	85.1	87.3	89.4
Fund Position															*Millions of SDRs:*	
Quota	2f.s	260.0	260.0	260.0	260.0	260.0	260.0	310.0	310.0	465.0	465.0	465.0	711.0	711.0	711.0	711.0
SDRs	1b.s	72.2	119.3	91.5	81.9	81.9	97.1	97.9	137.6	137.6	172.6	176.4	118.7	158.1	178.7	207.2
Reserve Position in the Fund	1c.s	65.0	119.1	72.9	61.1	67.0	72.8	68.7	76.8	110.9	105.3	99.8	205.0	214.4	207.5	127.2
of which: Outstg.Fund Borrowing	2c	—	—	—	—	—	—	—	—	—	—	—	—	—	—	—
International Liquidity										*Millions of US Dollars Unless Otherwise Indicated:*						
Total Reserves minus Gold	1l.d	786	1,247	858	803	841	1,589	3,129	3,236	3,387	2,548	2,266	3,621	3,009	5,429	4,964
SDRs	1b.d	78	144	112	96	95	118	128	181	175	201	195	124	155	196	253
Reserve Position in the Fund	1c.d	71	144	89	72	78	88	89	101	141	123	110	215	210	228	156
Foreign Exchange	1d.d	637	960	656	635	669	1,383	2,912	2,953	3,070	2,224	1,961	3,282	2,644	5,004	4,555
Gold (Million Fine Troy Ounces)	1ad	2	2	2	2	2	2	2	2	2	2	2	2	2	2	2
Gold (National Valuation)	1and	69e	77	85	78	87	100	117	92	†542	784	568	573	545	631	650
Monetary Authorities: Other Liab.	4..d	43	43	41	29	142	66	67	75	80	48	83	60	51	72	803
Deposit Money Banks: Assets	7a.d	449	723	1,289	1,068	1,764	2,734	3,832	4,812	4,833	5,265	5,865	6,654	7,975	14,158	16,033
Liabilities	7b.d	409	766	920	992	1,468	2,238	3,763	4,465	4,877	5,271	5,844	7,104	8,289	14,852	16,405
Monetary Authorities															*Billions of Kroner:*	
Foreign Assets	11	5.87	8.32	5.33	5.44	5.37	9.76	16.53	16.82	22.18	21.31	21.71	37.85	38.29	56.89	42.03
Claims on Central Government	12a	.54	.58	1.07	4.03	8.49	11.33	12.09	24.00	35.87	55.53	74.55	87.25	89.96	.64	.64
Claims on Private Sector	12d	8.74	9.31	10.87	11.93	18.25	14.49	12.61	12.08	13.15	13.79	14.44	14.61	14.98	14.84	26.15
Claims on Deposit Money Banks	12e	3.08	3.95	5.12	1.01	1.61	4.14	4.50	4.51	1.75	1.27	6.18	5.42	9.71	22.63	42.42
Claims on Other Banking Insts	12f	....	....	....	....	....	....	....	....	....	....	....	....	....	....	....
Reserve Money	14	8.25	8.44	8.88	12.33	12.85	11.22	12.08	13.71	14.31	15.58	15.97	17.11	18.84	47.24	31.32
of which: Currency Outside DMBs	14a	5.56	5.99	6.04	7.63	8.44	9.91	10.75	11.57	12.36	13.57	14.18	15.42	16.37	17.57	18.82
Foreign Liabilities	16c	.30	.27	.23	.19	.82	.38	.34	.40	.48	.35	.70	.59	.57	.60	5.90
Central Government Deposits	16d	6.87	10.74	10.03	7.20	16.46	24.41	29.91	37.98	47.17	59.41	81.47	105.39	102.92	18.33	49.92
Other Items (Net)	17r	2.80	2.70	3.24	2.69	3.60	3.70	3.41	5.31	10.99	16.57	18.74	22.03	30.60	28.83	24.11
Deposit Money Banks															*Billions of Kroner:*	
Reserves	20	2.03	1.73	2.15	3.61	3.17	.82	.80	1.52	1.14	1.74	1.59	1.27	2.09	25.80	11.23
Foreign Assets	21	3.14	4.54	7.20	7.38	10.66	15.85	20.16	26.27	31.33	41.53	53.17	72.90	104.60	144.27	137.42
Claims on Central Government	22a	1.72	3.47	4.25	4.82	8.55	9.50	10.65	15.74	20.17	27.91	37.83	61.96	77.07	86.60	83.64
Claims on Private Sector	22d	43.87	50.11	53.62	64.49	71.75	79.14	84.07	87.14	94.04	99.41	111.53	132.85	162.01	190.41	251.92
Claims on Other Banking Insts	22f	....	....	....	....	....	....	....	....	....	....	....	....	....	....	....
Demand Deposits	24	21.92	24.13	26.09	31.46	32.66	34.58	40.64	44.23	47.78	55.15	56.74	72.88	80.10	99.81	106.45
Time and Savings Deposits	25	19.70	23.27	26.45	36.08	43.36	47.46	45.30	49.57	58.60	63.28	77.48	103.78	126.95	146.39	160.95
Foreign Liabilities	26c	2.86	4.81	5.14	6.50	8.67	12.99	19.06	23.81	30.36	40.08	50.79	74.16	103.47	146.35	135.43
Credit from Monetary Authorities	26g	3.55	4.52	5.32	1.41	1.53	3.87	4.21	4.39	1.91	1.72	5.12	4.50	7.34	20.37	31.74
Capital Accounts	27a	5.47	6.58	7.09	7.66	10.67	11.47	12.91	14.48	16.39	19.18	21.62	25.57	35.44	40.86	53.00
Other Items (Net)	27r	−2.73	−3.46	−2.87	−2.80	−2.77	−5.06	−6.45	−5.82	−8.41	−8.81	−7.64	−11.90	−9.36	−6.69	−3.35
Other Monetary Institutions															*Billions of Kroner:*	
Reserves	20..h	.31	.41	.53	1.04	1.25	.54	.56	.71	.78	.74	.66	.59	.80	3.93	2.45
Claims on Central Govt. (Net)	22anh	1.20	1.12	.13	−.06	.28	1.60	4.06	7.44	10.86	13.53	16.56	24.89	37.24	41.22	39.94
Claims on Private Sector	22d.h	22.92	26.68	29.01	34.64	38.41	41.97	45.66	47.97	50.26	52.14	56.52	64.94	72.27	83.76	111.29
Demand Deposits	24..h	9.27	10.39	10.83	14.25	14.89	16.15	18.88	21.34	21.97	23.65	25.88	31.03	39.44	46.96	49.27
Time and Savings Deposits	25..h	13.79	15.42	16.88	19.04	21.60	24.66	26.08	28.93	31.88	34.90	37.68	47.22	54.76	63.78	72.28
Other Items (Net)	27r.h	1.37	2.40	1.98	2.33	3.44	3.31	5.31	5.85	8.03	7.86	10.19	12.17	16.11	18.18	32.09
Monetary Survey															*Billions of Kroner:*	
Foreign Assets (Net)	31n	5.80	7.73	7.11	6.14	6.57	13.14	17.45	19.48	23.20	23.14	23.83	35.34	38.26	53.21	40.13
Domestic Credit	32	72.12	80.52	88.91	112.65	129.27	133.62	139.23	156.40	177.16	202.91	229.96	281.11	350.61	399.15	463.67
Claims on Central Govt. (Net)	32an	−3.40	−5.58	−4.59	1.59	.86	−1.98	−3.11	9.21	19.72	37.57	47.47	68.71	101.34	110.14	74.31
Claims on Local Government	32b	....	....	....	....	....	....	....	....	....	....	....	....	....	....	....
Claims on Private Sector	32d	75.52	86.09	93.49	111.06	128.41	135.60	142.34	147.19	157.44	165.34	182.49	212.40	249.27	289.01	389.37
Claims on Other Banking Insts	32f	....	....	....	....	....	....	....	....	....	....	....	....	....	....	....
Money	34	33.64	37.59	39.36	49.86	52.34	56.08	65.06	71.88	77.51	88.03	91.67	113.30	128.08	156.49	167.97
Quasi-Money	35	33.48	38.68	43.34	55.12	64.96	72.11	71.38	78.50	90.48	98.18	115.16	151.00	181.71	210.18	233.23
Other Items (Net)	37r	10.79	11.98	13.34	13.81	18.53	18.58	20.24	25.49	32.31	39.84	46.96	52.15	77.25	85.69	102.55
Money plus Quasi-Money	35l	67.12	76.27	82.70	104.99	117.30	128.19	136.44	150.38	167.99	186.21	206.83	264.31	309.79	366.67	401.19
Money (National Definitions)															*Billions of Kroner:*	
Broad Money	39m	....	....	....	....	....	....	....	....	....	156.58	172.27	217.41	259.45	306.49	333.74
Interest Rates															*Percent Per Annum*	
Discount Rate (End of Period)	60	7.00	9.00	10.00	7.50	10.00	9.00	8.00	11.00	11.00	11.00	10.00	7.00	7.00	7.00	7.00
Money Market Rate	60b	6.26	8.10	13.34	6.47	10.28	14.48	15.42	12.63	16.93	14.84	†16.92	12.81	11.77	10.33	9.22
Deposit Rate	60l	....	....	....	....	....	....	....	....	10.8	10.8	13.0	12.9	12.0	9.0	6.6
Lending Rate	60p	....	....	....	....	....	....	13.9	15.3	17.2	17.7	18.6	14.5	13.4	14.7	13.0
Government Bond Yield	61	10.37	11.08	14.55	13.10	13.21	13.38e	14.54	15.82	17.66	18.92	20.39	14.46	†13.96	11.31	9.91
Mortgage Bond Yield	61a	10.57	11.83	15.12	12.96	15.03	15.74	16.51	16.91	19.03	†19.64	†21.35	15.34	14.63	12.19	10.50

1987	1988	1989	1990	1991	1992	1993	1994	1995	1996	1997	1998	1999	2000	2001		
End of Period															**Exchange Rates**	
8.649	9.250	8.683	8.217	8.459	8.601	9.302	8.880	8.244	8.548	9.210	8.992	10.155	10.450	10.568	Market Rate	aa
End of Period (ae) Period Average (rf)																
6.097	6.874	6.608	5.776	5.914	6.256	6.773	6.083	5.546	5.945	6.826	6.387	7.399	8.021	8.410	Market Rate	ae
6.840	6.732	7.310	6.189	6.396	6.036	6.484	6.361	5.602	5.799	6.604	6.701	6.976	8.083	8.323	Market Rate	rf
End of Period (ea) Period Average (eb)																
7.9446	8.0298	7.8816	7.8826	7.9295	7.5748	7.5508	7.4823	7.2940	7.4466	7.5312	7.4488	†7.4432	7.4631	7.4357	Euro Rate	ea
												1.0046	.9305	.8813	Euro Rate	ag
7.8829	7.9517	8.0487	7.8561	7.9082	7.8119	7.5916	7.5415	7.3271	7.3598	7.4830	7.4999	†7.4356	7.4529	7.4521	Euro Rate	eb
												1.0668	.9240	.8956	Euro Rate	rh
....	....	....														
Period Averages																
81.9	83.3	76.7	90.6	87.8	92.9	86.4	88.2	100.0	96.5	84.8	83.6	80.3	69.4	67.3	Market Rate	ah x
89.9	88.4	86.5	91.4	90.2	92.3	96.2	96.3	100.0	98.6	95.9	96.5	95.4	91.9	93.3	Nominal Effective Exchange Rate	ne u
96.3	94.8	93.3	97.7	94.2	95.3	97.9	97.1	100.0	98.2	95.8	97.4	97.2	94.2	95.5	Real Effective Exchange Rate	re u
End of Period															**Fund Position**	
711.0	711.0	711.0	711.0	711.0	1,069.9	1,069.9	1,069.9	1,069.9	1,069.9	1,069.9	1,069.9	1,642.8	1,642.8	1,642.8	Quota	2f. s
214.5	167.0	213.1	151.6	169.0	66.7	62.4	124.6	106.8	116.7	248.7	246.0	249.9	50.5	223.5	SDRs	1b. s
123.2	234.7	254.9	219.8	248.6	345.7	309.1	294.6	400.0	421.8	467.9	827.5	582.1	440.1	566.8	Reserve Position in the Fund	1c. s
											34.2	—	—	—	*of which:* Outstg.Fund Borrowing	2c
End of Period															**International Liquidity**	
10,066	10,765	6,397	10,591	7,404	11,044	10,301	9,056	11,016	14,140	19,124	15,264	22,287	15,108	17,110	Total Reserves minus Gold	1l. d
304	225	280	216	242	92	86	182	159	168	336	346	343	66	281	SDRs	1b. d
175	316	335	313	356	475	425	430	595	607	631	1,165	799	573	712	Reserve Position in the Fund	1c. d
9,587	10,224	5,782	10,063	6,807	10,477	9,791	8,444	10,262	13,366	18,157	13,753	21,145	14,469	16,117	Foreign Exchange	1d. d
2	2	2	2	2	2	2	2	2	2	2	2	2	2	2	Gold (Million Fine Troy Ounces)	1ad
767	713	711	780	638	580	478	703	714	590	545	677	531	569	557	Gold (National Valuation)	1an d
131	230	220	235	658	4,609	117	253	397	275	124	196	297	381	421	Monetary Authorities: Other Liab.	4..d
24,155	28,781	34,661	45,546	†49,066	45,629	57,272	50,945	56,593	62,392	65,675	76,754	68,432	....	....	Deposit Money Banks: Assets	7a. d
23,421	27,899	35,228	44,803	†47,379	36,845	27,128	30,141	33,246	40,172	50,347	61,484	63,340	....	....	Liabilities	7b. d
End of Period															**Monetary Authorities**	
†67.07	74.07	49.77	67.64	46.44	72.32	70.88	63.18	69.34	86.25	129.49	101.85	169.06	125.83	148.79	Foreign Assets	11
†6.40	5.93	8.06	10.35	16.48	6.79	10.04	20.05	14.83	15.47	15.19	15.50	14.80	14.96	16.02	Claims on Central Government	12a
†.49	.77	1.27	1.43	.91	1.40	.24	2.86	1.64	6.14	6.13	3.44	1.67	2.50	2.84	Claims on Private Sector	12d
†17.70	1.33	18.41	4.07	1.09	24.86	79.21	57.28	45.33	40.72	31.57	36.96	70.19	64.89	94.18	Claims on Deposit Money Banks	12e
29.72	31.28	34.59	36.44	28.15	28.90	30.95	24.99	19.97	21.26	20.24	22.95	24.56	24.80	24.81	Claims on Other Banking Insts	12f
†36.60	38.17	36.62	44.79	43.55	38.18	62.70	63.15	71.69	95.55	125.31	97.00	192.86	149.13	198.90	Reserve Money	14
†19.82	21.39	22.38	22.58	24.24	24.97	25.72	28.93	30.59	30.94	33.25	34.49	36.86	37.67	39.22	*of which:* Currency Outside DMBs	14a
†.80	1.57	1.45	1.36	3.89	28.78	.79	1.54	2.20	1.63	.88	1.25	2.43	3.14	3.75	Foreign Liabilities	16c
†56.85	45.32	37.08	39.50	11.43	31.27	89.57	56.91	35.44	31.65	30.73	34.03	36.49	34.65	40.24	Central Government Deposits	16d
†27.12	28.30	36.94	34.27	34.20	36.04	38.26	46.77	41.78	41.00	43.00	46.66	49.33	46.28	43.75	Other Items (Net)	17r
End of Period															**Deposit Money Banks**	
†4.70	8.37	9.12	8.70	†19.38	16.31	35.33	32.69	39.57	51.62	70.63	54.20	96.26	....	....	Reserves	20
†147.26	197.84	229.03	263.07	†290.15	285.43	387.88	309.90	313.87	370.89	448.30	490.19	506.32	....	....	Foreign Assets	21
†92.90	104.77	96.39	82.18	†103.85	103.49	70.18	124.60	99.53	85.34	69.80	71.14	65.37	....	....	Claims on Central Government	22a
†370.84	371.77	415.79	429.18	†371.95	361.76	317.67	297.74	312.89	331.06	357.73	405.37	420.62	....	....	Claims on Private Sector	22d
				49.92	46.51	136.53	108.44	125.15	157.66	181.52	218.24	191.46	....	....	Claims on Other Banking Insts	22f
†155.78	195.30	192.53	205.86	†233.09	229.77	255.44	248.31	259.86	287.09	304.47	321.44	336.34	....	....	Demand Deposits	24
†238.86	225.83	230.79	242.24	†247.58	246.11	318.06	262.20	282.89	296.17	320.02	325.42	298.27	....	....	Time and Savings Deposits	25
†142.79	191.78	232.77	258.78	†280.18	230.49	183.73	183.35	184.38	238.80	343.67	392.67	468.64	....	....	Foreign Liabilities	26c
†17.73	3.32	19.79	4.72	†7.07	26.50	80.56	58.66	45.94	35.73	21.46	34.03	34.01	....	....	Credit from Monetary Authorities	26g
†75.38	83.67	92.58	91.81	†78.01	86.11	72.13	79.54	75.37	77.42	82.25	87.64	91.43	....	....	Capital Accounts	27a
†−14.83	−17.14	−18.13	−20.30	†−10.67	−5.48	37.67	41.31	42.58	61.35	56.11	77.93	51.34	....	....	Other Items (Net)	27r
End of Period															Other Monetary Institutions	
....	....	....	....	....	....	....	....	....	....	....	....	....			Reserves	20..h
....	....	....	....	....	....	....	....	....	....	....	....	....			Claims on Central Govt. (Net)	22an h
....	....	....	....	....	....	....	....	....	....	....	....	....			Claims on Private Sector	22d. h
....	....	....	....	....	....	....	....	....	....	....	....	....			Demand Deposits	24..h
....	....	....	....	....	....	....	....	....	....	....	....	....			Time and Savings Deposits	25..h
....	....	....	....	....	....	....	....	....	....	....	....	....			Other Items (Net)	27r. h
End of Period															**Monetary Survey**	
†70.74	78.56	44.58	70.57	†52.52	98.49	274.24	188.19	196.62	216.70	233.24	198.12	204.31	....	....	Foreign Assets (Net)	31n
†443.50	469.19	519.00	520.07	†565.73	523.25	482.44	528.22	545.50	592.83	629.40	714.58	697.55	....	....	Domestic Credit	32
†42.44	65.38	67.36	53.03	†108.90	79.00	−9.36	87.74	78.91	69.16	54.26	52.62	43.68	....	....	Claims on Central Govt. (Net)	32an
				5.90	5.67	6.40	6.44	6.93	7.56	12.22	13.73	14.74	....	....	Claims on Local Government	32b
†371.34	372.54	417.06	430.61	†372.86	363.16	317.91	300.61	314.53	337.19	361.17	407.04	423.12	....	....	Claims on Private Sector	32d
....	....	....		78.07	75.41	167.48	133.43	145.13	178.91	201.75	241.19	216.02	....	....	Claims on Other Banking Insts	32f
†188.45	225.11	226.11	244.48	†258.27	256.00	283.00	279.05	291.98	325.52	344.05	360.74	381.77	....	....	Money	34
†238.86	225.83	230.79	242.24	†247.58	246.11	318.06	262.20	282.89	296.17	320.02	325.42	298.27	....	....	Quasi-Money	35
†86.93	96.81	106.68	103.92	†112.41	119.62	155.62	175.16	167.25	187.84	198.57	226.54	221.82	....	....	Other Items (Net)	37r
†427.31	450.95	456.90	486.72	†505.85	502.11	601.06	541.25	574.87	621.69	664.08	686.16	680.04	....	....	Money plus Quasi-Money	35l
End of Period															**Money (National Definitions)**	
343.57	358.25	368.16	391.73	379.42	373.90	416.42	394.03	410.01	439.74	462.66	476.23	495.94	505.91	546.18	*Broad Money*	39m
Percent Per Annum															**Interest Rates**	
7.00	7.00	7.00	8.50	9.50	9.50	6.25	5.00	4.25	3.25	3.50	3.50	3.00	4.75	3.25	Discount Rate (*End of Period*)	60
10.20	8.52	9.66	10.97	9.78	11.35	†11.49	6.30	6.19	3.98	3.71	4.27	3.37	4.98	....	Money Market Rate	60b
7.1	7.8	8.3	†7.9	7.2	7.5	6.5	†3.5	3.9	2.8	2.7	3.1	2.4	3.2	3.3	Deposit Rate	60l
13.6	12.6	13.4	†14.1	11.4	11.8	10.5	†10.0	10.3	8.7	7.7	7.9	7.1	8.1	8.2	Lending Rate	60p
11.06	9.78	9.75	10.74	9.59	9.47	7.08	7.41	7.58	6.04	5.08	4.59	4.30	5.54	....	Government Bond Yield	61
12.54	11.28	10.16	10.97	10.09	10.14	8.17	8.34	8.97	7.84	7.14	6.04	6.08	7.06	....	Mortgage Bond Yield	61a

Denmark

	1972	1973	1974	1975	1976	1977	1978	1979	1980	1981	1982	1983	1984	1985	1986
Prices, Production, Labor															*Index Numbers (1995=100):*
Share Prices: Industrial ... 62a	10	15	11	12	16	16	15	15	14	23	29	51	55	57	57
Shipping ... 62b	5	9	8	8	10	11	12	11	12	19	20	23	27	28	25
Prices: Home & Import Goods ... 63	27.5	31.5	38.3	†40.5	43.8	47.0	49.0	53.9	63.2	73.1	80.9	85.0	†91.3	94.0	87.6
Home Goods ... 63a	28.1	32.3	37.5	†40.5	43.8	47.0	49.8	53.1	60.8	68.8	76.2	80.5	†86.5	89.1	86.2
Consumer Prices ... 64	22.6	24.7	28.4	†31.2	34.0	37.7	41.5	45.5	†51.1	57.1	62.9	67.2	71.5	74.8	77.6
Harmonized CPI ... 64h	....	....	....	....	....	....	....	....	....	....	....	....	....	....	....
Wages: Hourly Earn. (1990=100) ... 65	19.5	22.4	26.9	32.0	35.6	39.2	43.2	48.1	53.6	58.3	64.4	68.7	72.0	75.3	79.4
Industrial Production ... 66..c	57.4	59.5	†57.4	54.3	59.8	60.5	62.2	64.6	64.8	64.9	66.3	68.6	76.0	†79.4	85.3
Agricultural Production ... 66bx	72.5	73.6	74.5	†74.2	74.4	76.2	79.3	83.4	†85.2	85.3	85.9	89.8	88.7	†89.2	91.9
Manufacturing Employment ... 67ey c	128.6	126.7	123.5	106.7	106.6	106.2	105.1	106.4	103.1	96.1	95.6	97.1	104.0	108.1	111.2
															Number in Thousands:
Labor Force ... 67d	....	....	....	....	....	....	....	....	....	....	....	....	....	....	....
Employment ... 67e	....	....	....	....	....	....	....	....	....	....	....	....	....	2,553	2,663
Unemployment ... 67c	....	....	....	....	....	....	....	....	....	....	....	....	....	252	220
Unemployment Rate (%) ... 67r	....	....	....	....	....	....	....	....	....	....	....	....	....	9.1	7.9
International Transactions															*Millions of Kroner*
Exports ... 70	30,789	37,549	46,920	50,030	55,035	60,436	65,314	77,321	94,359	114,263	128,194	146,761	165,335	179,578	171,720
Imports, c.i.f. ... 71	35,337	46,969	60,479	59,707	75,009	79,638	81,404	96,837	108,894	124,710	138,879	148,916	171,827	191,562	184,737
															1995=100
Volume of Exports ... 72	33	35	†37	36	37	39	41	46	49	51	52	54	58	†61	61
Volume of Imports ... 73	45	55	†52	48	57	56	58	62	57	54	55	58	62	†67	66
Unit Value of Exports ... 74	33	37	†44	48	52	55	57	62	71	80	90	93	100	†104	101
Unit Value of Imports ... 75	30	33	†46	47	51	56	56	63	77	90	100	103	111	†114	103
Import Prices ... 76.x	27	30	39	†41	43	47	48	55	68	81	89	93	†100	103	90
Balance of Payments															*Millions of US Dollars:*
Current Account, n.i.e. ... 78al d	....	....	....	–490	–1,914	–1,722	–1,502	....	....	–1,875	–2,259	–1,382	–1,718	–2,767	–4,490
Goods: Exports f.o.b. ... 78aa d	....	....	....	8,652	9,053	10,011	11,807	....	....	16,136	15,685	16,226	16,090	17,123	21,307
Goods: Imports f.o.b. ... 78ab d	....	....	....	–9,956	–11,931	–12,725	–14,163	....	....	–17,063	–16,479	–15,974	–16,285	–17,887	–22,357
Trade Balance ... 78ac d	....	....	....	–1,304	–2,878	–2,715	–2,356	....	....	–927	–794	252	–195	–764	–1,050
Services: Credit ... 78ad d	....	....	....	3,223	3,586	4,113	4,785	....	....	5,853	5,410	5,131	5,049	5,487	6,372
Services: Debit ... 78ae d	....	....	....	–2,159	–2,480	–2,958	–3,596	....	....	–4,663	–4,538	–4,501	–4,301	–4,794	–6,066
Balance on Goods & Services ... 78af d	....	....	....	–240	–1,771	–1,559	–1,167	....	....	262	78	882	553	–71	–743
Income: Credit ... 78ag d	....	....	....	249	255	363	543	....	....	1,187	1,146	909	1,227	1,409	1,995
Income: Debit ... 78ah d	....	....	....	–574	–616	–911	–1,429	....	....	–3,164	–3,298	–2,984	–3,567	–3,970	–5,464
Balance on Gds, Serv. & Inc. ... 78ai d	....	....	....	–566	–2,132	–2,107	–2,053	....	....	–1,715	–2,074	–1,194	–1,787	–2,632	–4,212
Current Transfers, n.i.e.: Credit ... 78aj d	....	....	....	448	641	944	1,196	....	....	753	654	729	935	825	1,341
Current Transfers: Debit ... 78ak d	....	....	....	–373	–424	–559	–645	....	....	–914	–839	–917	–866	–960	–1,619
Capital Account, n.i.e. ... 78bc d	....	....	....	—	—	—	—	....	....	—	—	—	—	—	—
Capital Account, n.i.e.: Credit ... 78ba d	....	....	....	—	—	—	—	....	....	—	—	—	—	—	—
Capital Account: Debit ... 78bb d	....	....	....	—	—	—	—	....	....	—	—	—	—	—	—
Financial Account, n.i.e. ... 78bj d	....	....	....	552	1,819	2,501	2,899	....	....	1,414	2,491	2,853	1,743	4,603	3,446
Direct Investment Abroad ... 78bd d	....	....	....	–79	–64	–161	–33	....	....	–139	–82	–150	–289	–306	–654
Dir. Invest. in Rep. Econ., n.i.e. ... 78be d	....	....	....	267	–190	76	89	....	....	99	134	60	–15	111	163
Portfolio Investment Assets ... 78bf d	....	....	....	—	—	–18	–63	....	....	–18	–95	–61	–142	–346	–2,223
Equity Securities ... 78bk d	....	....	....	—	—	–5	—	....	....	—	—	—	—	—	—
Debt Securities ... 78bl d	....	....	....	—	—	–13	–63	....	....	–18	–95	–61	–142	–346	–2,223
Portfolio Investment Liab., n.i.e. ... 78bg d	....	....	....	—	—	283	541	....	....	81	–46	363	823	1,579	144
Equity Securities ... 78bm d	....	....	....	—	—	–29	–11	....	....	—	—	—	—	—	—
Debt Securities ... 78bn d	....	....	....	—	—	311	552	....	....	81	–46	363	823	1,579	144
Financial Derivatives Assets ... 78bw d	....	....	....	....	....	....	....	....	....	....	....	....	....	....	....
Financial Derivatives Liabilities ... 78bx d	....	....	....	....	....	....	....	....	....	....	....	....	....	....	....
Other Investment Assets ... 78bh d	....	....	....	–172	–563	–1,420	–1,016	....	....	–1,213	–1,102	–1,727	–2,270	–3,816	1,359
Monetary Authorities ... 78bo d	....	....	....	....	....	....	....	....	....	....	....	....	....	....	....
General Government ... 78bp d	....	....	....	–67	38	–74	–139	....	....	—	—	—	—	—	—
Banks ... 78bq d	....	....	....	116	–497	–938	–614	....	....	–1,213	–1,102	–1,727	–2,270	–3,816	1,359
Other Sectors ... 78br d	....	....	....	–221	–104	–408	–263	....	....	—	—	—	—	—	—
Other Investment Liab., n.i.e. ... 78bi d	....	....	....	535	2,636	3,741	3,380	....	....	2,603	3,682	4,367	3,637	7,380	4,658
Monetary Authorities ... 78bs d	....	....	....	–6	70	–74	2	....	....	–22	40	–18	–4	10	650
General Government ... 78bt d	....	....	....	128	1,597	1,405	1,335	....	....	1,015	2,792	1,818	–629	671	4,473
Banks ... 78bu d	....	....	....	206	369	761	1,147	....	....	1,300	1,155	2,294	2,250	4,071	–1,708
Other Sectors ... 78bv d	....	....	....	208	600	1,650	897	....	....	311	–304	273	2,019	2,629	1,242
Net Errors and Omissions ... 78ca d	....	....	....	–104	114	–62	99	....	....	–273	–489	–114	–396	–304	–285
Overall Balance ... 78cb d	....	....	....	–42	19	717	1,496	....	....	–735	–257	1,357	–371	1,532	–1,329
Reserves and Related Items ... 79da d	....	....	....	42	–19	–717	–1,496	....	....	735	257	–1,357	371	–1,532	1,329
Reserve Assets ... 79db d	....	....	....	42	–19	–717	–1,496	....	....	735	257	–1,357	371	–1,532	1,329
Use of Fund Credit and Loans ... 79dc d	....	....	....	—	—	—	—	....	....	—	—	—	—	—	—
Exceptional Financing ... 79de d	....	....	....	....	....	....	....	....	....	....	....	....	....	....	....
International Investment Position															*Millions of US Dollars*
Assets ... 79aa d	....	....	....	....	....	....	....	....	....	....	....	....	....	....	....
Direct Investment Abroad ... 79ab d	....	....	....	....	....	....	....	....	....	....	....	....	....	....	....
Portfolio Investment ... 79ac d	....	....	....	....	....	....	....	....	....	....	....	....	....	....	....
Equity Securities ... 79ad d	....	....	....	....	....	....	....	....	....	....	....	....	....	....	....
Debt Securities ... 79ae d	....	....	....	....	....	....	....	....	....	....	....	....	....	....	....
Financial Derivatives ... 79al d	....	....	....	....	....	....	....	....	....	....	....	....	....	....	....
Other Investment ... 79af d	....	....	....	....	....	....	....	....	....	....	....	....	....	....	....
Monetary Authorities ... 79ag d	....	....	....	....	....	....	....	....	....	....	....	....	....	....	....
General Government ... 79ah d	....	....	....	....	....	....	....	....	....	....	....	....	....	....	....
Banks ... 79ai d	....	....	....	....	....	....	....	....	....	....	....	....	....	....	....
Other Sectors ... 79aj d	....	....	....	....	....	....	....	....	....	....	....	....	....	....	....
Reserve Assets ... 79ak d	....	....	....	....	....	....	....	....	....	....	....	....	....	....	....
Liabilities ... 79la d	....	....	....	....	....	....	....	....	....	....	....	....	....	....	....
Dir. Invest. in Rep. Economy ... 79lb d	....	....	....	....	....	....	....	....	....	....	....	....	....	....	....
Portfolio Investment ... 79lc d	....	....	....	....	....	....	....	....	....	....	....	....	....	....	....
Equity Securities ... 79ld d	....	....	....	....	....	....	....	....	....	....	....	....	....	....	....
Debt Securities ... 79le d	....	....	....	....	....	....	....	....	....	....	....	....	....	....	....
Financial Derivatives ... 79ll d	....	....	....	....	....	....	....	....	....	....	....	....	....	....	....
Other Investment ... 79lf d	....	....	....	....	....	....	....	....	....	....	....	....	....	....	....
Monetary Authorities ... 79lg d	....	....	....	....	....	....	....	....	....	....	....	....	....	....	....
General Government ... 79lh d	....	....	....	....	....	....	....	....	....	....	....	....	....	....	....
Banks ... 79li d	....	....	....	....	....	....	....	....	....	....	....	....	....	....	....
Other Sectors ... 79lj d	....	....	....	....	....	....	....	....	....	....	....	....	....	....	....

	1987	1988	1989	1990	1991	1992	1993	1994	1995	1996	1997	1998	1999	2000	2001	
Period Averages																**Prices, Production, Labor**
Share Prices: Industrial	48	54	75	83	90	82	84	100	100	122	162	175	155	250	....	62a
Shipping	25	33	80	94	94	86	98	107	100	120	215	223	252	328	....	62b
Prices: Home & Import Goods	87.4	91.0	96.2	97.1	98.1	96.9	†96.4	97.3	100.0	101.1	103.0	102.4	102.9	109.1	111.2	63
Home Goods	87.2	90.6	95.5	96.8	98.0	97.4	†96.9	....	100.0	101.6	103.5	102.9	103.9	109.2	112.2	63a
Consumer Prices	80.7	84.4	88.4	90.7	92.9	94.8	96.0	97.9	100.0	102.1	104.4	106.3	108.9	112.1	114.7	64
Harmonized CPI									100.0	102.1	104.1	105.4	107.6	110.5	113.0	64h
Wages: Hourly Earn. (1990=100)	86.9	92.5	96.2	100.0	104.2	107.2	....	....	....							65
Industrial Production	82.8	84.4	86.5	†86.5	86.6	89.1	86.6	95.3	100.0	†101.7	107.4	109.8	112.4	119.7	121.5	66..c
Agricultural Production	89.2	88.9	88.3	90.0	91.9	96.4	†101.7	101.1	100.0	100.2	101.0	104.6	104.8	....	....	66bx
Manufacturing Employment	†105.3	†102.1	100.9	100.0	96.8	94.7	88.5	....								67ey c
Period Averages																
Labor Force	....	....	....	....	2,912	....	2,893	2,777	....	2,822	2,856	2,848	....	....		67d
Employment	2,679	2,695	2,645	2,670	2,647	2,652	2,584	†2,555	2,607	2,627	2,682	2,692	....	....		67e
Unemployment	222	244	265	272	296	318	349	343	288	246	220	183	158	151	....	67c
Unemployment Rate (%)	7.9	8.7	9.5	9.7	10.6	11.3	12.4	12.2	10.3	8.8	7.9	6.6	5.7	5.4	....	67r
Millions of Kroner																**International Transactions**
Exports	175,187	185,819	205,300	216,444	229,764	247,254	241,034	262,365	278,515	290,543	315,001	317,423	339,896	400,832	420,458	70
Imports, c.i.f.	173,837	174,429	195,117	198,782	206,799	212,088	197,957	220,769	252,344	257,655	290,648	303,705	307,478	353,797	361,296	71
1995=100																
Volume of Exports	63	66	71	73	81	85	82	89	100	103	109	111	117	124	....	72
Volume of Imports	70	69	71	72	77	81	75	85	100	101	111	115	117	124	....	73
Unit Value of Exports	99	98	105	103	103	101	99	100	100	102	104	103	103	113	....	74
Unit Value of Imports	98	100	107	103	102	99	97	98	100	101	104	104	103	111	....	75
Import Prices	88	91	97	98	98	96	†95	98	100	100	102	102	101	109	109	76.x
Minus Sign Indicates Debit																**Balance of Payments**
Current Account, n.i.e.	-3,002	-1,340	-1,118	1,372	1,983	4,199	4,832	3,189	1,855	3,090	921	-2,008	2,915	2,507	4,142	78al d
Goods: Exports f.o.b.	25,695	27,537	28,728	36,072	36,783	40,504	36,948	41,741	50,348	50,735	48,103	47,908	49,932	50,754	50,943	78aa d
Goods: Imports f.o.b.	-24,900	-25,654	-26,304	-31,197	-32,035	-33,446	-29,229	-34,300	-43,821	-43,203	-42,734	-44,021	-43,533	-44,001	-43,983	78ab d
Trade Balance	795	1,883	2,425	4,875	4,748	7,058	7,719	7,441	6,528	7,532	5,369	3,886	6,399	6,754	6,960	78ac d
Services: Credit	7,848	9,623	9,570	12,830	14,264	14,083	12,564	13,661	15,307	16,502	14,044	15,212	20,090	24,385	26,913	78ad d
Services: Debit	-7,302	-8,427	-8,638	-10,218	-10,440	-10,736	-10,467	-12,067	-14,040	-14,771	-13,727	-15,779	-18,517	-22,082	-23,506	78ae d
Balance on Goods & Services	1,342	3,078	3,356	7,487	8,592	10,405	9,816	9,035	7,795	9,263	5,685	3,319	7,972	9,056	10,367	78af d
Income: Credit	2,627	3,677	4,718	6,011	8,855	15,956	23,091	22,743	28,433	37,626	18,774	10,401	9,100	9,168	10,997	78ag d
Income: Debit	-6,750	-7,876	-9,049	-11,719	-14,599	-21,282	-27,480	-27,385	-32,982	-42,235	-22,203	-14,247	-11,426	-15,395	-14,595	78ah d
Balance on Gds, Serv. & Inc.	-2,781	-1,121	-975	1,779	2,848	5,079	5,427	4,394	3,246	4,655	2,256	-527	5,646	5,499	6,769	78ai d
Current Transfers, n.i.e.: Credit	1,546	1,799	1,608	2,007	2,083	2,136	2,442	2,261	2,580	2,398	3,633	3,443	4,156	3,303	3,629	78aj d
Current Transfers: Debit	-1,766	-2,018	-1,750	-2,415	-2,948	-3,016	-3,037	-3,466	-3,970	-3,963	-4,968	-4,924	-6,888	-6,296	-6,256	78ak d
Capital Account, n.i.e.	—	—	—	—	—	—	....	....	....	....	128	50	1,083	-14	-25	78bc d
Capital Account, n.i.e.: Credit	—	—	—	—	—	—	....	....	....	....	128	81	1,331	320	253	78ba d
Capital Account: Debit	—	—	—	—	—	—	....	....	....	....	—	-31	-248	-334	-278	78bb d
Financial Account, n.i.e.	6,648	3,395	-2,373	4,420	-2,703	423	-6,545	-5,647	-432	1,882	8,496	-1,489	6,247	-3,689	-3,837	78bj d
Direct Investment Abroad	-619	-720	-2,066	-1,482	-1,852	-2,236	-1,373	-4,162	-2,969	-2,510	-4,355	-4,215	-17,039	-27,672	-9,631	78bd d
Dir. Invest. in Rep. Econ., n.i.e.	85	503	1,090	1,132	1,553	1,017	1,713	5,006	4,139	773	2,792	6,675	16,076	35,532	7,238	78be d
Portfolio Investment Assets	797	-585	-1,527	-1,168	-4,378	1,420	2	-1,175	-1,171	-2,349	-6,239	-7,563	-9,719	-23,623	-14,355	78bf d
Equity Securities											....					78bk d
Debt Securities	797	-585	-1,527	-1,168	-4,378	1,420	2	-1,175	-1,171	-2,349						78bl d
Portfolio Investment Liab., n.i.e.	2,886	1,815	-1,222	4,068	6,232	8,707	12,659	-10,596	7,487	7,865	11,186	-2,598	7,014	5,783	11,033	78bg d
Equity Securities																78bm d
Debt Securities	2,886	1,815	-1,222	4,068	6,232	8,707	12,659	-10,596	7,487	7,865						78bn d
Financial Derivatives Assets																78bw d
Financial Derivatives Liabilities													325	328	522	78bx d
Other Investment Assets	-4,174	-7,443	-4,242	-5,442	-3,012	432	-14,812	12,136	-1,330	-9,339	-8,033	-1,797	-1,188	-1,677	10,045	78bh d
Monetary Authorities																78bo d
General Government																78bp d
Banks	-4,174	-7,443	-4,242	-5,442	-3,012	432	-14,812	12,136	-1,330	-9,339						78bq d
Other Sectors											-8,033	-1,797				78br d
Other Investment Liab., n.i.e.	7,672	9,825	5,594	7,312	-1,246	-8,918	-4,734	-6,856	-6,589	7,442	13,145	8,009	10,778	7,641	-8,690	78bi d
Monetary Authorities	-712	120	-16	11	399	4,301	-4,419	122	133	-108						78bs d
General Government	2,465	-1,480	-679	443	-5,078	1,309	8,648	-4,058	-3,380	-1,563						78bt d
Banks	3,381	8,249	5,449	3,867	1,648	-9,476	-6,497	414	15	9,343						78bu d
Other Sectors	2,538	2,936	840	2,991	1,785	-5,052	-2,467	-3,333	-3,357	-231	13,145	8,009				78bv d
Net Errors and Omissions	85	-619	-347	-2,407	-2,183	-547	1,146	606	1,075	-1,408	-3,012	-792	-808	-4,453	2,990	78ca d
Overall Balance	3,732	1,436	-3,838	3,385	-2,903	4,075	-567	-1,851	2,498	3,563	6,532	-4,239	9,437	-5,649	3,270	78cb d
Reserves and Related Items	-3,732	-1,436	3,838	-3,385	2,903	-4,075	567	1,851	-2,498	-3,563	-6,532	4,239	-9,437	5,649	-3,270	79da d
Reserve Assets	-3,732	-1,436	3,838	-3,385	2,903	-4,075	567	1,851	-2,498	-3,563	-6,532	4,239	-9,437	5,649	-3,270	79db d
Use of Fund Credit and Loans	—	—	—	—	—	—										79dc d
Exceptional Financing																79de d
Millions of US Dollars																**International Investment Position**
Assets	....	....	....	....	102,567	104,156	111,991	109,111	123,004	145,614	156,402	187,516	213,446	224,140	....	79aa d
Direct Investment Abroad					15,558	16,306	15,799	19,892	24,702	27,589	28,128	34,664	38,374	43,011	....	79ab d
Portfolio Investment					19,954	16,625	17,866	17,261	22,899	29,944	37,064	51,792	70,982	84,322	....	79ac d
Equity Securities					6,426	6,394	7,973	8,877	10,819	16,149	22,414	32,623	50,353	55,187	....	79ad d
Debt Securities					13,528	10,231	9,893	8,384	12,081	13,794	14,650	19,169	20,629	29,135	....	79ae d
Financial Derivatives												2,502	9,231	12,716	....	79al d
Other Investment					58,679	59,628	67,183	62,798	63,469	73,513	71,931	82,423	72,189	69,047	....	79af d
Monetary Authorities																79ag d
General Government					2,706	2,718	2,362	2,795	2,524	2,187	2,051	2,524	2,621	2,948	....	79ah d
Banks					42,276	39,965	51,384	46,359	49,766	55,177	56,255	64,534	55,132	51,580	....	79ai d
Other Sectors					13,697	16,945	13,437	13,645	11,179	16,149	13,624	15,365	14,436	14,519	....	79aj d
Reserve Assets					8,376	11,597	11,142	9,160	11,933	14,569	19,279	16,136	22,670	15,044	....	79ak d
Liabilities					158,451	154,104	155,186	151,734	170,934	187,737	197,480	235,320	237,097	251,462	....	79la d
Dir. Invest. in Rep. Economy					14,712	14,387	14,618	18,083	23,801	22,205	22,268	31,055	36,595	47,137	....	79lb d
Portfolio Investment					59,018	65,063	84,016	72,826	88,713	101,607	106,505	117,215	104,705	103,580	....	79lc d
Equity Securities					2,875	2,398	3,248	6,740	8,294	12,448	20,363	20,556	20,702	26,170	....	79ld d
Debt Securities					56,143	62,665	80,768	66,086	80,418	89,158	86,141	96,658	84,002	77,409	....	79le d
Financial Derivatives												2,159	8,871	12,393	....	79ll d
Other Investment					84,721	74,654	56,552	60,825	58,420	63,925	68,708	84,891	86,926	88,352	....	79lf d
Monetary Authorities					676	4,476	148	329	361	336	146	204	328	392	....	79lg d
General Government					3,044	2,877	2,067	3,123	1,983	1,178	732	1,265	949	479	....	79lh d
Banks					39,570	30,853	22,444	27,289	29,210	35,159	42,631	53,475	53,049	60,334	....	79li d
Other Sectors					41,431	36,448	31,894	30,084	26,866	27,252	25,198	29,948	32,601	27,147	....	79lj d

Denmark

		1972	1973	1974	1975	1976	1977	1978	1979	1980	1981	1982	1983	1984	1985	1986
Government Finance																*Millions of Kroner:*
Deficit (-) or Surplus	80	4,089	6,140	1,335	−4,350	†−519	−2,730	−1,066	−2,584	−10,002	−24,690	−37,522	−35,154	−22,241	−3,726	30,082
Revenue	81	53,380	58,268	66,918	69,810	†80,981	90,422	105,617	120,393	136,398	145,706	163,129	188,365	218,810	246,846	281,324
Grants Received	81z	376	524	557	1,593	†3,189	1,491	1,804	2,307	2,499	2,633	3,349	4,220	4,883	4,664	4,328
Expenditure	82	48,968	51,826	65,085	74,767	†83,604	93,654	107,137	124,520	147,376	171,020	202,363	225,514	243,895	253,940	255,127
Lending Minus Repayments	83	699	826	1,055	986	†1,085	989	1,350	764	1,523	2,009	1,637	2,225	2,039	1,296	443
Debt: Kroner	88b	....	....	....	....	....							....	....	....	....
Debt: Foreign	89a	6,106	6,517	7,243	10,429	†16,456	24,410	29,139	35,744	45,346	57,521	79,142	102,514	98,534	92,930	119,913
National Accounts																*Billions of Kroner:*
Househ.Cons.Expend.,incl.NPISHs	96f	79.6	93.6	104.6	119.3	141.4	157.6	173.3	193.5	207.2	228.3	255.4	277.1	302.7	329.2	358.4
Government Consumption Expend.	91f	34.2	39.3	48.2	56.5	64.1	70.7	80.8	91.8	105.3	119.8	138.3	148.6	155.0	164.2	168.9
Gross Fixed Capital Formation	93e	40.2	46.1	50.0	49.8	62.7	67.5	74.1	80.0	78.1	71.4	85.0	95.7	111.4	132.5	155.7
Changes in Inventories	93i	.4	2.4	2.5	−.4	2.6	2.2	−.5	2.4	−.4	−.1	1.8	.5	7.9	6.5	6.4
Exports of Goods and Services	90c	41.0	49.6	61.8	65.4	72.9	81.0	87.1	102.8	124.3	151.9	172.2	190.1	211.9	230.6	218.9
Imports of Goods and Services (-)	98c	40.2	52.8	67.4	67.3	84.5	91.1	93.7	113.2	128.6	149.0	170.5	180.2	205.4	229.0	222.8
Gross Domestic Product (GDP)	99b	155.3	178.2	199.7	223.4	259.2	288.0	321.1	357.3	385.8	422.4	482.2	531.7	583.5	634.0	685.6
Net Primary Income from Abroad	98.n	−.2	1.0	.3	.3	.9	2.0	2.7	−.3	−3.7	−7.5	−12.1	−12.3	−16.5	−18.7	−18.5
Gross National Income (GNI)	99a	155.1	179.2	200.0	223.7	260.1	290.0	323.8	357.0	382.2	414.9	470.1	519.4	567.0	615.3	667.1
GDP Volume 1995 Prices	99b.p	694.8	719.5	709.6	697.4	742.3	750.5	764.3	788.3	783.8	767.7	788.8	802.5	830.7	860.2	894.7
GDP Volume (1995=100)	99bv p	68.8	71.3	70.3	69.1	73.5	74.3	75.7	78.1	77.6	76.0	78.1	79.5	82.3	85.2	88.6
GDP Deflator (1995=100)	99bi p	22.4	24.8	28.1	32.0	34.9	38.4	42.0	45.3	49.2	55.0	61.1	66.3	70.3	73.7	76.6
																Millions:
Population	99z	4.99	5.02	5.05	5.06	5.07	5.09	5.10	5.12	5.12	5.12	5.12	5.11	5.11	5.11	5.12

	1987	1988	1989	1990	1991	1992	1993	1994	1995	1996	1997	1998	1999	2000	2001	
																Government Finance
Year Ending December 31																
	27,410	16,077	8,164	−5,549	†−15,788	−16,116	−21,935	−26,398	−23,692	−3,081	12,661 P	19,479 P	6,296 P	....	....	Deficit (-) or Surplus 80
	291,516	303,078	312,992	314,135	†316,621	339,246	358,056	385,593	391,286	417,948	434,423 P	449,490 P	462,510 P	....	....	Revenue 81
	4,133	4,380	3,824	4,276	†5,239	4,766	5,973	5,546	3,873	3,771	4,583 P	4,826 P	4,665 P	....	....	Grants Received 81z
	266,843	289,116	307,738	321,978	†332,826	356,044	381,805	412,967	417,654	423,596	425,124 P	434,285 P	443,021 P	....	....	Expenditure 82
	1,396	2,265	914	1,983	†4,825	4,083	4,157	4,570	1,195	1,202	1,222 P	554 P	17,857 P	....	....	Lending Minus Repayments 83
	....	....	....	....	....	....	....	....	....	....	....	....	....	....	....	
	127,637	124,333	116,031	119,101	92,339	104,633	....	....	....	....	....	....	....	....	....	Debt: Kroner 88b
																Debt: Foreign 89a
Billions of Kroner																**National Accounts**
	367.1	375.8	393.3	404.9	423.0	439.3	450.2	493.8	509.6	533.2	560.9	581.3	597.5	613.3	630.4	Househ.Cons.Expend.,incl.NPISHs .. 96f
	186.0	196.6	204.6	210.9	220.5	229.2	240.9	250.3	260.3	274.6	284.5	300.5	313.9	325.8	343.0	Government Consumption Expend. 91f
	159.7	154.9	163.2	166.0	165.6	161.0	155.7	168.4	189.3	198.4	220.5	240.3	248.1	283.0	284.3	Gross Fixed Capital Formation 93e
	−4.6	−.6	3.2	1.6	−1.9	−.2	−7.9	1.6	9.3	2.5	11.2	10.1	−3.2	−1.8	.3	Changes in Inventories 93i
	225.2	248.4	276.7	295.7	319.1	324.2	318.6	342.6	357.5	379.4	406.9	413.4	459.6	567.4	607.4	Exports of Goods and Services 90c
	212.5	227.0	252.2	253.8	268.7	265.6	257.3	291.0	316.1	327.2	367.7	390.1	402.3	491.4	522.3	Imports of Goods and Services (-) 98c
	720.9	748.3	788.6	825.3	857.7	887.9	900.2	965.7	1,009.8	1,060.9	1,116.3	1,155.4	1,213.6	1,296.1	1,343.1	Gross Domestic Product (GDP) 99b
	−16.8	−18.2	−21.7	−24.8	−26.4	−22.3	−16.0	−16.0	−12.7	−14.0	−16.0	−12.1	−9.3	−22.7	−23.2	Net Primary Income from Abroad 98.n
	704.2	730.1	766.9	800.6	831.3	865.5	884.2	949.7	997.1	1,046.9	1,100.3	1,143.3	1,204.3	1,273.5	1,320.0	Gross National Income (GNI) 99a
	894.9	905.8	907.2	915.9	926.1	931.8	931.8	982.7	1,009.8	1,035.2	1,065.9	1,092.2	1,117.5	1,151.2	1,162.1	GDP Volume 1995 Prices 99b.p
	88.6	89.7	89.8	90.7	91.7	92.3	92.3	97.3	100.0	102.5	105.6	108.2	110.7	114.0	115.1	GDP Volume (1995=100) .... 99bv p
	80.6	82.6	86.9	90.1	92.6	95.3	96.6	98.3	100.0	102.5	104.7	105.8	108.6	112.6	115.6	GDP Deflator (1995=100) .... 99bi p
Midyear Estimates																
	5.13	5.13	5.13	5.14	5.15	5.17	5.19	5.20	5.23	5.26	5.28	5.30	5.33	5.34	5.33	Population 99z

(See notes in the back of the book.)

Djibouti

611

		1972	1973	1974	1975	1976	1977	1978	1979	1980	1981	1982	1983	1984	1985	1986
Exchange Rates														*Francs per SDR:*		
Official Rate	aa	214.39	214.39	217.59	208.05	206.48	215.88	231.53	234.12	226.67	206.86	196.05	186.07	174.20	195.21	217.39
														Francs per US Dollar:		
Official Rate	ae	197.47	177.72	177.72	177.72	177.72	177.72	177.72	177.72	177.72	177.72	177.72	177.72	177.72	177.72	177.72
Official Rate	rf	197.47	179.94	177.72	177.72	177.72	177.72	177.72	177.72	177.72	177.72	177.72	177.72	177.72	177.72	177.72
Fund Position														*Millions of SDRs:*		
Quota	2f. s	...	...	...	...	...	...	3.80	3.80	5.70	5.70	5.70	5.70	8.00	8.00	8.00
SDRs	1b. s	...	...	...	...	...	...	—	.08	.13	.50	.46	.43	.40	.37	.35
Reserve Position in the Fund	1c. s	...	...	...	...	...	...	—	.76	1.23	1.23	1.24	1.24	1.24	1.24	1.24
Total Fund Cred.&Loans Outstg.	2tl	...	...	...	...	...	...		—	—	—	—	—	—	—	—
International Liquidity													*Millions of US Dollars Unless Otherwise Indicated:*			
Total Reserves minus Gold	1l. d	...	...	...	...	...	...							44.93	50.94	53.62
SDRs	1b. d	...	...	...	...	...	...	—	.11	.17	.58	.51	.45	.39	.41	.43
Reserve Position in the Fund	1c. d	...	...	...	...	...	...	—	1.00	1.57	1.43	1.37	1.30	1.22	1.36	1.52
Foreign Exchange	1d. d	...	...	...	...	...	...				...	...	...	43.33	49.17	51.67
Deposit Money Banks: Assets	7a. d	...	...	...	...	...	...							170.13	195.86	186.92
Liabilities	7b. d	...	...	...	...	...	...							95.37	102.73	79.08
Other Banking Insts.: Liabilities	7f. d	...	...	...	...	...	...							—	—	.62
Monetary Authorities														*Millions of Francs:*		
Foreign Assets	11	...	...	...	...	...	...							7,986	9,053	9,529
Claims on Central Government	12a	...	...	...	...	...	...							—	—	—
Claims on Deposit Money Banks	12e	...	...	...	...	...	...									
Reserve Money	14	...	...	...	...	...	...							7,471	7,237	7,994
of which: Currency Outside DMBs	14a	...	...	...	...	...	...							6,671	6,686	7,180
Central Government Deposits	16d	...	...	...	...	...	...							225	1,357	992
Capital Accounts	17a	...	...	...	...	...	...							357	470	593
Other Items (Net)	17r	...	...	...	...	...	...							−70	−12	−52
Deposit Money Banks														*Millions of Francs:*		
Reserves	20	...	...	...	...	...	...							800	551	790
Foreign Assets	21	...	...	...	...	...	...							30,236	34,809	33,219
Claims on Central Government	22a	...	...	...	...	...	...									
Claims on Nonfin.Pub.Enterprises	22c	...	...	...	...	...	...							561	563	494
Claims on Private Sector	22d	...	...	...	...	...	...							29,114	32,965	35,701
Demand Deposits	24	...	...	...	...	...	...							12,690	13,418	15,601
Time Deposits	25	...	...	...	...	...	...							18,264	24,694	27,050
Foreign Liabilities	26c	...	...	...	...	...	...							16,949	18,257	14,055
Central Government Deposits	26d	...	...	...	...	...	...							3,458	2,625	1,651
Credit From Monetary Authorities	26g	...	...	...	...	...	...							—	—	—
Capital Accounts	27a	...	...	...	...	...	...							8,220	7,649	8,435
Other Items (Net)	27r	...	...	...	...	...	...							1,129	2,245	3,411
Monetary Survey														*Millions of Francs:*		
Foreign Assets (Net)	31n	...	...	...	...	...	...							21,273	25,605	28,693
Domestic Credit	32	...	...	...	...	...	...							26,565	29,975	34,061
Claims on Central Govt. (Net)	32an	...	...	...	...	...	...							−3,952	−4,490	−2,883
Claims on Nonfin.Pub.Enterprises	32c	...	...	...	...	...	...							561	563	494
Claims on Private Sector	32d	...	...	...	...	...	...							29,956	33,902	36,450
Money	34	...	...	...	...	...	...							19,934	20,533	23,290
Quasi-Money	35	...	...	...	...	...	...							18,264	24,694	27,050
Other Items (Net)	37r	...	...	...	...	...	...							9,636	10,352	12,411
Money plus Quasi-Money	35l	...	...	...	...	...	...							38,198	45,227	50,340
Other Banking Institutions														*Millions of Francs:*		
Reserves	40	...	...	...	...	...	...							195	295	184
Claims on Private Sector	42d	...	...	...	...	...	...							795	468	636
Long-Term Foreign Liabilities	46cl	...	...	...	...	...	...									111
Central Govt. Lending Funds	46f	...	...	...	...	...	...							270	270	240
Capital Accounts	47a	...	...	...	...	...	...							477	483	486
Other Items (Net)	47r	...	...	...	...	...	...							243	10	−16
Interest Rates														*Percent Per Annum*		
Deposit Rate	60l	...	...	...	...	...	...									
Lending Rate	60p	...	...	...	...	...	...							8.50	8.50	8.50

	1987	1988	1989	1990	1991	1992	1993	1994	1995	1996	1997	1998	1999	2000	2001		
																Exchange Rates	
End of Period (aa)																	
	252.13	239.16	233.55	252.84	254.22	244.37	244.11	259.45	264.18	255.56	239.79	250.24	243.92	231.55	223.35	Official Rate	**aa**
End of Period (ae) Period Average (rf)																	
	177.72	177.72	177.72	177.72	177.72	177.72	177.72	177.72	177.72	177.72	177.72	177.72	177.72	177.72	177.72	Official Rate	**ae**
	177.72	177.72	177.72	177.72	177.72	177.72	177.72	177.72	177.72	177.72	177.72	177.72	177.72	177.72	177.72	Official Rate	**rf**
																Fund Position	
End of Period																	
	8.00	8.00	8.00	8.00	8.00	11.50	11.50	11.50	11.50	11.50	11.50	11.50	15.90	15.90	15.90	Quota	**2f. s**
	.33	.30	.27	.23	.19	.15	.15	.11	.06	.10	.55	.27	.06	.28	.10	SDRs	**1b. s**
	1.24	1.24	1.24	1.24	1.24	2.11	—	—	—	—	—	—	1.10	1.10	1.10	Reserve Position in the Fund	**1c. s**
	—	—	—	—	—	—	—	—	—	2.88	3.98	6.30	9.28	10.29	12.32	Total Fund Cred.&Loans Outstg.	**2tl**
																International Liquidity	
End of Period																	
	63.53	64.36	59.15	93.64	100.00	83.40	75.10	73.76	72.16	76.97	66.57	66.45	70.61	67.80	70.31	Total Reserves minus Gold	**1l. d**
	.47	.40	.35	.33	.27	.21	.21	.16	.09	.15	.75	.38	.09	.36	.13	SDRs	**1b. d**
	1.76	1.67	1.63	1.76	1.77	2.90	—	—	—	—	—	—	1.51	1.43	1.38	Reserve Position in the Fund	**1c. d**
	61.30	62.29	57.17	91.55	97.95	80.29	74.89	73.60	72.07	76.82	65.82	66.07	69.01	66.01	68.80	Foreign Exchange	**1d. d**
	198.14	198.39	238.27	209.40	225.35	200.09	219.26	211.53	209.96	173.31	167.22	169.95	178.25	166.03	201.85	Deposit Money Banks: Assets	**7a. d**
	79.01	62.80	95.85	68.92	72.10	84.45	84.81	88.65	91.10	89.01	83.33	88.47	45.30	50.12	38.75	Liabilities	**7b. d**
	1.28	2.56	3.36	1.18	2.97	3.62	4.01	3.43	3.21	3.26	....	....	....	....	....	Other Banking Insts.: Liabilities	**7f. d**
																Monetary Authorities	
End of Period																	
	11,290	11,438	10,513	16,642	17,772	14,822	13,347	13,990	12,688	13,683	12,064	11,518	12,507	12,051	12,498	Foreign Assets	**11**
	—	—	—	—	—	—	307	534	534	1,275	1,542	2,176	2,928	2,832	3,234	*Claims on Central Government*	**12a**
	3,023	2,616	3,117	35	37	39	40	42	40	44	44	44	—	—	—	Claims on Deposit Money Banks	**12e**
	9,366	9,301	8,960	9,875	9,899	12,187	11,250	11,869	10,370	9,989	9,783	9,575	10,011	9,932	10,467	Reserve Money	**14**
	8,013	8,439	8,197	9,035	9,263	11,331	10,401	10,693	9,367	9,686	9,450	9,099	9,289	9,207	9,370	*of which: Currency Outside DMBs*	**14a**
	4,366	3,690	3,545	2,637	2,490	114	716	797	1,074	284	106	676	1,152	514	319	Central Government Deposits	**16d**
	792	861	935	1,037	1,244	1,436	1,425	1,390	1,712	1,729	1,872	2,361	2,537	2,713	2,786	Capital Accounts	**17a**
	−211	201	189	3,125	4,179	1,124	303	511	108	3,000	1,889	1,125	1,735	1,724	2,161	Other Items (Net)	**17r**
																Deposit Money Banks	
End of Period																	
	1,432	929	748	894	647	868	925	1,148	1,065	638	778	575	743	718	1,056	Reserves	**20**
	35,214	35,258	42,346	37,214	40,049	35,561	38,967	37,594	37,314	30,801	29,719	30,204	31,679	29,507	35,873	Foreign Assets	**21**
	—	—	—	—	—	—	446	2,525	2,144	1,569	1,678	724	214	111	74	*Claims on Central Government*	**22a**
	459	609	221	572	489	444	483	419	464	599	778	2,115	2,309	1,540	1,758	Claims on Nonfin.Pub.Enterprises	**22c**
	35,684	36,529	38,062	36,165	35,105	34,712	32,057	33,382	37,783	38,826	38,469	42,098	27,491	31,413	26,898	Claims on Private Sector	**22d**
	16,905	18,142	16,444	17,944	20,761	21,595	22,209	21,814	21,157	18,738	17,506	20,146	20,985	18,704	19,275	Demand Deposits	**24**
	26,346	28,391	31,619	31,462	29,554	22,986	22,094	23,030	26,841	23,185	23,943	24,845	21,747	24,697	27,925	Time Deposits	**25**
	14,041	11,161	17,034	12,249	12,814	15,008	15,073	15,755	16,191	15,819	14,810	15,723	8,051	8,908	6,886	Foreign Liabilities	**26c**
	587	1,448	1,814	1,842	1,095	929	925	2,089	727	568	605	877	233	87	31	Central Government Deposits	**26d**
	3,024	1,970	3,127	47	69	39	40	40	40	52	406	40	—	—	—	Credit From Monetary Authorities	**26g**
	8,300	8,643	8,355	7,833	7,961	7,466	8,082	9,854	10,051	10,053	9,609	9,814	8,730	7,550	7,646	Capital Accounts	**27a**
	3,584	3,569	2,984	3,468	4,035	3,562	4,456	2,485	3,763	4,021	4,544	4,271	2,690	3,342	3,896	Other Items (Net)	**27r**
																Monetary Survey	
End of Period																	
	32,463	35,535	35,825	41,607	45,007	35,358	37,222	35,815	33,794	27,904	25,959	24,336	33,720	29,979	38,410	Foreign Assets (Net)	**31n**
	31,603	32,485	33,467	32,641	33,634	36,168	35,446	39,075	45,598	48,918	47,278	45,560	31,557	35,295	31,614	Domestic Credit	**32**
	−5,251	−5,198	−5,259	−4,463	−2,307	739	2,158	5,180	7,233	9,384	7,928	1,347	1,757	2,342	2,958	Claims on Central Govt. (Net)	**32an**
	459	609	221	572	489	444	483	419	464	599	778	2,115	2,309	1,540	1,758	Claims on Nonfin.Pub.Enterprises	**32c**
	36,395	37,074	38,505	36,532	35,452	34,985	32,805	33,476	37,901	38,935	38,572	42,098	27,491	31,413	26,898	Claims on Private Sector	**32d**
	25,331	27,066	25,184	27,362	31,649	34,981	36,404	37,608	36,998	35,925	32,478	29,245	30,274	27,911	28,645	Money	**34**
	26,346	28,391	31,619	31,462	29,554	22,986	22,094	23,030	26,841	23,185	23,943	24,845	21,747	24,697	27,925	Quasi-Money	**35**
	12,387	12,561	12,488	15,421	17,440	13,559	14,171	14,254	15,553	17,715	16,817	15,805	13,256	12,665	13,455	Other Items (Net)	**37r**
	51,677	55,457	56,803	58,824	61,203	57,967	58,498	60,638	63,839	59,110	56,421	54,090	52,021	52,608	56,570	Money plus Quasi-Money	**35l**
																Other Banking Institutions	
End of Period																	
	310	721	561	656	510	251	261	167	80	30	....	....	....	....	Reserves	**40**
	791	975	1,044	1,790	2,860	4,202	4,472	4,277	4,126	3,537	....	....	....	....	Claims on Private Sector	**42d**
	228	455	597	210	527	644	712	610	570	580	....	....	....	....	Long-Term Foreign Liabilities	**46cl**
	390	740	690	1,607	1,463	1,999	1,788	1,542	1,533	1,180	....	....	....	....	Central Govt. Lending Funds	**46f**
	485	436	364	342	1,133	1,529	1,557	1,557	1,817	1,696	....	....	....	....	Capital Accounts	**47a**
	−2	63	−46	287	247	281	676	735	286	111	....	....	....	....	Other Items (Net)	**47r**
																Interest Rates	
Percent Per Annum																	
	....	....	....	....	....	....	....	....	....	....	....	....	....	....	2.81	Deposit Rate	**60l**
	8.50	10.50	10.50	10.50	....	....	....	....	....	....	....	....	....	....	11.46	Lending Rate	**60p**

Djibouti

		1972	1973	1974	1975	1976	1977	1978	1979	1980	1981	1982	1983	1984	1985	1986
International Transactions															*Millions of Francs*	
Exports	70	1,627	3,499	3,678	2,639	2,835	3,364	3,154	2,023	2,221	1,554	2,232	1,919	2,362	2,488	3,628
Imports	71	10,733	12,675	21,698	24,166	21,284	18,949	29,117	33,454	37,920	39,865	40,197	39,307	39,425	35,670	32,731
															1995=100	
Volume of Imports	73	....	....	....	....	....	....	....	....	....	....	....	....	....	....	103.7
Import Prices	76.x	....	....	....	....	....	....	....	....	....	....	....	....	....	....	102.6
Balance of Payments															*Millions of US Dollars:*	
Current Account, n.i.e.	78al *d*	....	....	....	....	....	....	....	....	....	....	....	....	....	....	....
Goods: Exports f.o.b.	78aa *d*	....	....	....	....	....	....	....	....	....	....	....	....	....	....	....
Goods: Imports f.o.b.	78ab *d*	....	....	....	....	....	....	....	....	....	....	....	....	....	....	....
Trade Balance	78ac *d*	....	....	....	....	....	....	....	....	....	....	....	....	....	....	....
Services: Credit	78ad *d*	....	....	....	....	....	....	....	....	....	....	....	....	....	....	....
Services: Debit	78ae *d*	....	....	....	....	....	....	....	....	....	....	....	....	....	....	....
Balance on Goods & Services	78af *d*	....	....	....	....	....	....	....	....	....	....	....	....	....	....	....
Income: Credit	78ag *d*	....	....	....	....	....	....	....	....	....	....	....	....	....	....	....
Income: Debit	78ah *d*	....	....	....	....	....	....	....	....	....	....	....	....	....	....	....
Balance on Gds, Serv. & Inc.	78ai *d*	....	....	....	....	....	....	....	....	....	....	....	....	....	....	....
Current Transfers, n.i.e.: Credit	78aj *d*	....	....	....	....	....	....	....	....	....	....	....	....	....	....	....
Current Transfers: Debit	78ak *d*	....	....	....	....	....	....	....	....	....	....	....	....	....	....	....
Capital Account, n.i.e.	78bc *d*	....	....	....	....	....	....	....	....	....	....	....	....	....	....	....
Capital Account, n.i.e.: Credit	78ba *d*	....	....	....	....	....	....	....	....	....	....	....	....	....	....	....
Capital Account: Debit	78bb *d*	....	....	....	....	....	....	....	....	....	....	....	....	....	....	....
Financial Account, n.i.e.	78bj *d*	....	....	....	....	....	....	....	....	....	....	....	....	....	....	....
Direct Investment Abroad	78bd *d*	....	....	....	....	....	....	....	....	....	....	....	....	....	....	....
Dir. Invest. in Rep. Econ., n.i.e.	78be *d*	....	....	....	....	....	....	....	....	....	....	....	....	....	....	....
Portfolio Investment Assets	78bf *d*	....	....	....	....	....	....	....	....	....	....	....	....	....	....	....
Equity Securities	78bk *d*	....	....	....	....	....	....	....	....	....	....	....	....	....	....	....
Debt Securities	78bl *d*	....	....	....	....	....	....	....	....	....	....	....	....	....	....	....
Portfolio Investment Liab., n.i.e.	78bg *d*	....	....	....	....	....	....	....	....	....	....	....	....	....	....	....
Equity Securities	78bm *d*	....	....	....	....	....	....	....	....	....	....	....	....	....	....	....
Debt Securities	78bn *d*	....	....	....	....	....	....	....	....	....	....	....	....	....	....	....
Financial Derivatives Assets	78bw *d*	....	....	....	....	....	....	....	....	....	....	....	....	....	....	....
Financial Derivatives Liabilities	78bx *d*	....	....	....	....	....	....	....	....	....	....	....	....	....	....	....
Other Investment Assets	78bh *d*	....	....	....	....	....	....	....	....	....	....	....	....	....	....	....
Monetary Authorities	78bo *d*	....	....	....	....	....	....	....	....	....	....	....	....	....	....	....
General Government	78bp *d*	....	....	....	....	....	....	....	....	....	....	....	....	....	....	....
Banks	78bq *d*	....	....	....	....	....	....	....	....	....	....	....	....	....	....	....
Other Sectors	78br *d*	....	....	....	....	....	....	....	....	....	....	....	....	....	....	....
Other Investment Liab., n.i.e.	78bi *d*	....	....	....	....	....	....	....	....	....	....	....	....	....	....	....
Monetary Authorities	78bs *d*	....	....	....	....	....	....	....	....	....	....	....	....	....	....	....
General Government	78bt *d*	....	....	....	....	....	....	....	....	....	....	....	....	....	....	....
Banks	78bu *d*	....	....	....	....	....	....	....	....	....	....	....	....	....	....	....
Other Sectors	78bv *d*	....	....	....	....	....	....	....	....	....	....	....	....	....	....	....
Net Errors and Omissions	78ca *d*	....	....	....	....	....	....	....	....	....	....	....	....	....	....	....
Overall Balance	78cb *d*	....	....	....	....	....	....	....	....	....	....	....	....	....	....	....
Reserves and Related Items	79da *d*	....	....	....	....	....	....	....	....	....	....	....	....	....	....	....
Reserve Assets	79db *d*	....	....	....	....	....	....	....	....	....	....	....	....	....	....	....
Use of Fund Credit and Loans	79dc *d*	....	....	....	....	....	....	....	....	....	....	....	....	....	....	....
Exceptional Financing	79de *d*	....	....	....	....	....	....	....	....	....	....	....	....	....	....	....
Government Finance																*Millions of Francs:*
Deficit (-) or Surplus	80	....	....	....	....	....	....	....	†1,872	†4,062	†5,268	2,798	4,587	2,729	922	†−1,470
Revenue	81	....	....	....	....	....	....	....	†13,918	†17,922	†23,058	24,904	26,706	23,644	22,485	†21,024
Grants Received	81z	....	....	....	....	....	....	....	†8,433	†13,460	†96	2,896	1,916	1,473	1,445	†2,404
Expenditure	82	....	....	....	....	....	....	....	†20,397	†26,916	†16,396	24,190	24,035	22,182	22,918	†24,383
Lending Minus Repayments	83	....	....	....	....	....	....	....	†82	†404	†1,490	812	—	206	90	†515
Financing																
Domestic	84a	....	....	....	....	....	....	....	†163	†−241		....	....	....	....	†1,693
Foreign	85a	....	....	....	....	....	....	....	†−2,035	†−3,821		....	....	....	....	†−223
National Accounts																*Billions of Francs*
Gross Domestic Product (GDP)	99b	19	22	27	30	36	35	38	46	60	67	70	72	....	....	....
																Millions:
Population	99z	....	....	....	.21	.23	.25	.27	.29	.36	.37	.37	.38	.41	.43	.46

1987	1988	1989	1990	1991	1992	1993	1994	1995	1996	1997	1998	1999	2000	2001		
Millions of Francs															**International Transactions**	
4,976	4,116	4,423	4,420	3,083	2,800	2,151	2,151	2,414	2,439	1,917	2,195	2,168	....	....	Exports	70
36,487	35,771	34,920	38,174	38,103	38,860	37,499	34,908	31,395	31,805	26,322	28,120	27,131	....	....	Imports	71
1995=100																
110.1	102.1	94.8	94.8	93.0	95.5	115.7	107.0	100.0	90.8	75.9	88.2	99.3	....	....	Volume of Imports	73
96.5	100.8	104.4	110.4	120.6	125.5	101.4	100.6	100.0	110.5	102.1	103.8	95.3	....	....	Import Prices	76.x
Minus Sign Indicates Debit															**Balance of Payments**	
....	....	....	....	....	−87.5	−34.3	−46.1	−23.0	....	....	....	....	....	....	Current Account, n.i.e.	78al *d*
....	....	....	....	....	53.2	71.2	56.4	33.5	....	....	....	....	....	....	Goods: Exports f.o.b.	78aa *d*
....	....	....	....	....	−271.0	−255.1	−237.1	−205.0	....	....	....	....	....	....	Goods: Imports f.o.b.	78ab *d*
....	....	....	....	....	−217.8	−183.9	−180.7	−171.5	....	....	....	....	....	....	*Trade Balance*	78ac *d*
....	....	....	....	....	145.1	156.9	152.3	151.4	....	....	....	....	....	....	Services: Credit	78ad *d*
....	....	....	....	....	−109.3	−110.8	−89.7	−87.2	....	....	....	....	....	....	Services: Debit	78ae *d*
....	....	....	....	....	−182.0	−137.8	−118.1	−107.3	....	....	....	....	....	....	*Balance on Goods & Services*	78af *d*
....	....	....	....	....	29.4	30.3	23.7	25.9	....	....	....	....	....	....	Income: Credit	78ag *d*
....	....	....	....	....	−9.4	−7.2	−7.0	−8.7	....	....	....	....	....	....	Income: Debit	78ah *d*
....	....	....	....	....	−162.0	−114.8	−101.4	−90.0	....	....	....	....	....	....	*Balance on Gds, Serv. & Inc.*	78ai *d*
....	....	....	....	....	90.7	96.6	73.7	85.4	....	....	....	....	....	....	Current Transfers, n.i.e.: Credit	78aj *d*
....	....	....	....	....	−16.3	−16.1	−18.3	−18.4	....	....	....	....	....	....	Current Transfers: Debit	78ak *d*
....	....	....	....	....	—	—	—	—	....	....	....	....	....	....	Capital Account, n.i.e.	78bc *d*
....	....	....	....	....	—	—	—	—	....	....	....	....	....	....	Capital Account, n.i.e.: Credit	78ba *d*
....	....	....	....	....	—	—	—	—	....	....	....	....	....	....	Capital Account: Debit	78bb *d*
....	....	....	....	....	74.0	16.6	39.0	−2.1	....	....	....	....	....	....	Financial Account, n.i.e.	78bj *d*
....	....	....	....	....	—				....	....	....	....	....	....	Direct Investment Abroad	78bd *d*
....	....	....	....	....	2.3	1.4	1.4	3.2	....	....	....	....	....	....	Dir. Invest. in Rep. Econ., n.i.e.	78be *d*
....	....	....	....	....	—	—	—	—	....	....	....	....	....	....	Portfolio Investment Assets	78bf *d*
....	....	....	....	....	—	—	—	—	....	....	....	....	....	....	Equity Securities	78bk *d*
....	....	....	....	....	—	—	—	—	....	....	....	....	....	....	Debt Securities	78bl *d*
....	....	....	....	....	—	—	—	—	....	....	....	....	....	....	Portfolio Investment Liab., n.i.e.	78bg *d*
....	....	....	....	....	—	—	—	—	....	....	....	....	....	....	Equity Securities	78bm *d*
....	....	....	....	....	—	—	—	—	....	....	....	....	....	....	Debt Securities	78bn *d*
....	....	....	....	....					....	....	....	....	....	....	Financial Derivatives Assets	78bw *d*
....	....	....	....	....					....	....	....	....	....	....	Financial Derivatives Liabilities	78bx *d*
....	....	....	....	....	—	—	—	—	....	....	....	....	....	....	Other Investment Assets	78bh *d*
....	....	....	....	....					....	....	....	....	....	....	Monetary Authorities	78bo *d*
....	....	....	....	....	—	—	—	—	....	....	....	....	....	....	General Government	78bp *d*
....	....	....	....	....	—	—	—	—	....	....	....	....	....	....	Banks	78bq *d*
....	....	....	....	....	—	—	—	—	....	....	....	....	....	....	Other Sectors	78br *d*
....	....	....	....	....	71.7	15.2	37.6	−5.4	....	....	....	....	....	....	Other Investment Liab., n.i.e.	78bi *d*
....	....	....	....	....	—	—	—	—	....	....	....	....	....	....	Monetary Authorities	78bs *d*
....	....	....	....	....	8.1	15.9	12.0	−9.4	....	....	....	....	....	....	General Government	78bt *d*
....	....	....	....	....	37.6	−18.8	11.6	4.0	....	....	....	....	....	....	Banks	78bu *d*
....	....	....	....	....	26.0	18.1	14.1	.1	....	....	....	....	....	....	Other Sectors	78bv *d*
....	....	....	....	....	−2.0	6.0	7.9	.7	....	....	....	....	....	....	Net Errors and Omissions	78ca *d*
....	....	....	....	....	−15.5	−11.7	.8	−24.5	....	....	....	....	....	....	*Overall Balance*	78cb *d*
....	....	....	....	....	15.5	11.7	−.8	24.5	....	....	....	....	....	....	Reserves and Related Items	79da *d*
....	....	....	....	....	15.5	11.3	−3.4	7.3	....	....	....	....	....	....	Reserve Assets	79db *d*
....	....	....	....	....	—	—	—	—	....	....	....	....	....	....	Use of Fund Credit and Loans	79dc *d*
....	....	....	....	....	—	.4	2.6	17.2	....	....	....	....	....	....	Exceptional Financing	79de *d*
Year Ending December 31															**Government Finance**	
....	†−733														Deficit (-) or Surplus	80
....	†20,101														Revenue	81
....	†1,400														Grants Received	81z
....	†22,234														Expenditure	82
....	† —														Lending Minus Repayments	83
															Financing	
....	....	....	....	....	....	....	....	....	....	....	....	....	....	....	Domestic	84a
....	....	....	....	....	....	....	....	....	....	....	....	....	....	....	Foreign	85a
Billions of Francs															**National Accounts**	
....	....	....	....	....	....	....	....	....	....	....	....	....	....	....	Gross Domestic Product (GDP)	99b
Midyear Estimates																
.44	.47	.49	.52	.53	.55	.53	.54	.55	.56	.56	.60	.62	.63	.64	**Population**	99z

(See notes in the back of the book.)

Dominica

		1972	1973	1974	1975	1976	1977	1978	1979	1980	1981	1982	1983	1984	1985	1986
Exchange Rates															*E.Caribbean Dollars per SDR: End of Period (aa)*	
Official Rate	aa	2.2194	2.4925	2.5024	2.7770	3.1369	3.2797	3.5175	3.5568	3.4436	3.1427	2.9784	2.8268	2.6466	2.9657	3.3026
Official Rate	ae	2.0442	2.0661	2.0439	2.3721	2.7000	2.7000	2.7000	2.7000	2.7000	2.7000	2.7000	2.7000	2.7000	2.7000	2.7000
													Index Numbers (1995=100):			
Nominal Effective Exchange Rate	ne c	....	....	....	....	....	....	....	62.21	60.28	64.10	68.39	73.89	84.39	89.68	84.60
Real Effective Exchange Rate	re c	....	....	....	....	....	....	....	87.96	94.76	102.40	105.80	112.58	121.89	125.27	116.23
Fund Position															*Millions of SDRs:*	
Quota	2f. s							1.90	1.90	2.90	2.90	2.90	4.00	4.00	4.00	4.00
SDRs	1b. s	....	....	....	....	....	....				.70	.26	.40			.81
Reserve Position in the Fund	1c. s	....	....	....	....	....	....		—	—	—	—	—	.01	.01	.01
Total Fund Cred.&Loans Outstg.	2tl	....	....	....	....	....	....	—	1.90	1.65	6.47	9.32	11.00	10.66	9.17	8.63
International Liquidity												*Millions of US Dollars Unless Otherwise Indicated:*				
Total Reserves minus Gold	1l. d	....	....	....	.35	1.17	2.23	1.93	9.84	5.08	3.06	4.33	1.48	5.25	3.27	9.59
SDRs	1b. d	....	....	....	....	....	....				.81	.29	.42			.99
Reserve Position in the Fund	1c. d	....	....	....	....	....	....		—	—	—	—	—	.01	.01	.01
Foreign Exchange	1d. d	....	....	....	.35	1.17	2.23	1.93	9.84	5.08	2.24	4.04	1.06	5.24	3.26	8.59
Deposit Money Banks: Assets	7a. d	....	....	....	1.77	.86	1.43	1.50	6.40	4.41	6.28	6.79	7.77	5.53	6.87	14.88
Liabilities	7b. d	....	....	....	3.96	3.88	5.00	5.44	6.69	7.64	10.18	8.86	7.61	8.21	8.76	13.95
Monetary Authorities													*Millions of E. Caribbean Dollars:*			
Foreign Assets	11	....	....	....	.82	3.17	6.02	5.20	26.56	13.71	8.25	11.69	3.99	19.85	10.63	25.91
Claims on Central Government	12a	....	....	....	3.30	3.30	3.70	3.70	11.08	11.49	24.45	33.36	37.68	42.86	46.05	47.29
Claims on Deposit Money Banks	12e	....	....	....	—	—	—	—	—	—	—	—	—	—	—	.72
Reserve Money	14	....	....	....	4.12	6.47	9.72	8.90	30.88	19.52	12.37	17.29	10.58	34.49	29.48	45.42
of which: Currency Outside DMBs	14a	....	....	....	2.77	3.65	4.81	5.15	7.33	7.48	7.73	6.58	6.39	12.22	9.64	6.64
Foreign Liabilities	16c	....	....	....	—	—	—	—	6.76	5.68	20.33	27.76	31.09	28.21	27.20	28.50
Central Government Deposits	16d	....	....	....	—	—	—	—	—	—	—	—	—	—	—	—
Other Items (Net)	17r	....	....	....	—	—	—	—	—	—	—	—	—	—	—	—
Deposit Money Banks													*Millions of E. Caribbean Dollars:*			
Reserves	20	....	....	....	1.35	2.81	4.91	3.75	23.54	12.04	4.64	10.71	4.19	23.00	25.33	39.31
Foreign Assets	21	....	....	....	4.19	2.31	3.87	4.04	17.28	11.92	16.96	18.32	20.97	14.93	18.55	40.18
Claims on Central Government	22a	....	....	....	9.04	10.95	16.94	12.76	13.50	18.49	18.25	18.72	19.04	13.13	15.60	24.94
Claims on Local Government	22b															
Claims on Nonfin.Pub.Enterprises	22c	....	....	....	1.00	1.00	1.00	1.00	3.76	2.20	8.87	4.82	3.31	9.02	7.36	2.38
Claims on Private Sector	22d	....	....	....	25.53	28.82	25.86	34.27	36.76	49.78	60.50	67.49	79.07	81.32	89.03	86.16
Claims on Nonbank Financial Insts	22g	....	....	....					.01	.17	.13	.13	6.16	5.49	5.35	2.92
Demand Deposits	24	....	....	....	5.77	5.70	6.72	12.34	22.75	19.63	18.71	18.83	19.01	20.18	21.58	30.39
Time, Savings,& Fgn.Currency Dep.	25	....	....	....	28.11	31.89	33.63	36.45	47.52	52.36	54.84	70.86	80.31	90.19	96.98	110.24
Foreign Liabilities	26c	....	....	....	9.39	10.48	13.51	14.69	18.07	20.63	27.49	23.93	20.55	22.16	23.65	37.67
Central Government Deposits	26d	....	....	....	—	—	—	—	—	.22	3.76	2.98	5.50	4.19	2.17	3.35
Credit from Monetary Authorities	26g	....	....	....	—	—	—	—	—	—	—	—	—	—	.47	.91
Capital Accounts	27a	....	....	....	1.00	1.80	1.80	1.80	1.84	1.82	2.80	2.95	4.28	4.78	6.09	7.35
Other Items (Net)	27r	....	....	....	-3.16	-3.99	-3.07	-9.47	4.66	-.06	1.75	.66	3.09	5.39	10.29	5.99
Monetary Survey													*Millions of E. Caribbean Dollars:*			
Foreign Assets (Net)	31n	....	....	....	-4.38	-5.01	-3.62	-5.45	19.00	-.69	-22.61	-21.68	-26.68	-15.59	-21.67	-.08
Domestic Credit	32	....	....	....	38.87	44.07	47.50	51.72	65.10	81.92	108.45	121.55	139.76	147.62	161.22	160.34
Claims on Central Govt. (Net)	32an	....	....	....	12.34	14.25	20.64	16.46	24.57	29.77	38.95	49.10	51.22	51.79	59.48	68.88
Claims on Local Government	32b															
Claims on Nonfin.Pub.Enterprises	32c	....	....	....	1.00	1.00	1.00	1.00	3.76	2.20	8.87	4.82	3.31	9.02	7.36	2.38
Claims on Private Sector	32d	....	....	....	25.53	28.82	25.86	34.27	36.76	49.78	60.50	67.49	79.07	81.32	89.03	86.16
Claims on Nonbank Financial Inst	32g	....	....	....	—	—	—	—	.01	.17	.13	.13	6.16	5.49	5.35	2.92
Money	34	....	....	....	8.54	9.36	11.53	17.49	30.09	27.11	26.44	25.41	25.40	32.40	31.22	37.03
Quasi-Money	35	....	....	....	28.11	31.89	33.63	36.45	47.52	52.36	54.84	70.86	80.31	90.19	96.98	110.24
Capital Accounts	37a	....	....	....	1.00	1.80	1.80	1.80	2.55	3.20	4.66	4.70	5.95	6.34	7.84	9.30
Other Items (Net)	37r	....	....	....	-3.16	-3.99	-3.07	-9.47	3.95	-1.44	-.10	-1.10	1.43	3.10	3.52	3.69
Money plus Quasi-Money	35l	....	....	....	36.65	41.25	45.15	53.94	77.60	79.47	81.29	96.26	105.71	122.59	128.20	147.27
Interest Rates															*Percent Per Annum*	
Treasury Bill Rate	60c	....	....	....	....	....	....	....	....	6.5	6.5	6.5	6.5	6.5	6.5	6.5
Deposit Rate	60l	....	....	....	....	....	....	4.0	4.0	4.0	5.0	5.0	5.0	5.0	5.0	4.9
Lending Rate	60p	....	....	....	....	....	....	8.5	8.5	8.5	9.0	9.5	9.5	10.4	10.0	10.3
Prices															*Index Numbers (1995=100):*	
Consumer Prices	64	15.0	†16.8	22.6	27.0	30.0	32.8	35.4	....	55.4	62.8	65.5	68.2	69.7	72.4	74.4
International Transactions															*Millions of E. Caribbean Dollars*	
Exports	70	13.50	16.74	20.95	24.65	29.05	32.30	42.89	25.39	26.30	51.76	66.01	74.00	69.23	76.77	117.24
Imports, c.i.f.	71	32.88	32.29	38.92	45.04	49.83	59.08	76.77	59.97	128.73	134.10	128.19	121.71	156.10	149.38	150.69

	1987	1988	1989	1990	1991	1992	1993	1994	1995	1996	1997	1998	1999	2000	2001		
Exchange Rates																	
E.Caribbean Dollars per US Dollar: End of Period (ae)																	
Official Rate	3.8304	3.6334	3.5482	3.8412	3.8622	3.7125	3.7086	3.9416	4.0135	3.8825	3.6430	3.8017	3.7058	3.5179	3.3932	**aa**	
Official Rate	2.7000	2.7000	2.7000	2.7000	2.7000	2.7000	2.7000	2.7000	2.7000	2.7000	2.7000	2.7000	2.7000	2.7000	2.7000	**ae**	
Period Averages																	
Nominal Effective Exchange Rate	80.52	77.72	81.30	83.40	86.93	90.20	98.38	103.11	100.00	102.92	108.88	115.49	114.43	118.40	123.87	**ne c**	
Real Effective Exchange Rate	111.80	105.13	109.47	104.25	106.06	106.99	110.04	106.16	100.00	101.40	106.92	112.08	111.16	113.34	118.42	**re c**	
Fund Position																	
End of Period																	
Quota	4.00	4.00	4.00	4.00	4.00	6.00	6.00	6.00	6.00	6.00	6.00	6.00	8.20	8.20	8.20	**2f. s**	
SDRs	.70	.55	.32	.21	.01	.07	—	—	—	—	—	—	.01	—	—	**1b. s**	
Reserve Position in the Fund	.01	.01	.01	.01	.01	.01	.01	.01	.01	.01	.01	.01	.01	.01	.01	**1c. s**	
Total Fund Cred.&Loans Outstg.	8.23	6.57	4.99	4.00	3.32	2.78	2.26	1.71	1.15	.59	.19	.03	—	—	—	**2tl**	
International Liquidity																	
End of Period																	
Total Reserves minus Gold	18.43	14.06	11.68	14.46	17.77	20.41	19.92	15.41	22.12	22.89	23.89	27.67	31.57	29.37	31.22	**1l. d**	
SDRs	.99	.74	.42	.30	.01	.10	—	—	—	—	—	—	.01	—	—	**1b. d**	
Reserve Position in the Fund	.01	.01	.01	.01	.01	.01	.01	.01	.01	.01	.01	.01	.01	.01	.01	**1c. d**	
Foreign Exchange	17.42	13.31	11.25	14.15	17.74	20.30	19.90	15.40	22.11	22.88	23.88	27.65	31.55	29.36	31.21	**1d. d**	
Deposit Money Banks: Assets	28.64	40.19	32.54	23.16	22.88	28.13	24.13	26.62	28.14	38.81	43.08	51.84	60.28	44.68	51.24	**7a. d**	
Liabilities	15.42	16.77	18.63	20.40	23.08	27.73	30.94	39.49	34.45	35.35	43.00	45.73	45.38	49.47	46.04	**7b. d**	
Monetary Authorities																	
End of Period																	
Foreign Assets	47.77	37.96	31.54	39.04	47.93	55.10	53.71	41.71	60.54	62.64	64.63	74.70	85.39	79.31	84.32	**11**	
Claims on Central Government	50.41	39.54	35.68	38.33	37.08	27.85	24.04	26.16	19.74	14.78	13.19	11.30	10.77	11.21	10.55	**12a**	
Claims on Deposit Money Banks	.38	1.30	.72	4.05	.02	.02	.37	2.04	.01	.01	.03	.03	.01	3.92	.01	**12e**	
Reserve Money	67.04	54.94	50.23	66.06	72.21	72.64	69.73	63.18	74.91	74.44	76.42	85.19	95.60	92.98	92.32	**14**	
of which: Currency Outside DMBs	20.77	22.83	20.69	24.96	30.76	31.13	27.86	24.49	29.16	28.53	28.21	29.13	34.09	35.45	34.61	**14a**	
Foreign Liabilities	31.52	23.87	17.71	15.36	12.82	10.32	8.38	6.72	—	—	—	—	—	—	—	**16c**	
Central Government Deposits	—	—	—	—	—	—	—	—	.79	.72	.75	.74	.57	1.46	2.56	**16d**	
Other Items (Net)	—	—	—	—	—	—	—	—	—	—	—	—	—	—	—	**17r**	
Deposit Money Banks																	
Reserves	46.46	29.19	29.98	38.33	41.65	41.68	42.78	33.46	45.86	46.52	44.93	56.16	68.92	56.53	58.48	**20**	
Foreign Assets	77.34	108.51	87.86	62.53	61.78	75.95	65.16	71.88	75.98	104.78	116.31	139.96	162.76	120.63	138.34	**21**	
Claims on Central Government	10.36	9.14	11.45	28.00	37.28	42.17	53.46	66.56	77.86	79.34	87.40	87.73	94.14	93.43	110.22	**22a**	
Claims on Local Government	—	—	—	—	—	.01	.05	.23	.17	.17	.12	.09	.06	9.40	.02	**22b**	
Claims on Nonfin.Pub.Enterprises	1.03	6.01	8.27	18.47	24.65	21.40	26.40	29.07	29.13	19.27	21.77	23.05	24.25	27.82	24.29	**22c**	
Claims on Private Sector	93.59	128.73	171.49	211.13	234.43	263.99	289.57	312.48	344.63	358.48	386.35	409.97	419.77	454.09	439.58	**22d**	
Claims on Nonbank Financial Insts	5.33	1.50	4.12	1.54	1.57	1.62	1.29	.42	.46	1.57	1.48	1.52	1.22	3.11	2.86	**22g**	
Demand Deposits	37.89	34.37	35.39	44.96	42.81	54.96	47.87	49.88	62.25	67.43	67.63	74.09	95.00	69.12	70.58	**24**	
Time, Savings,& Fgn.Currency Dep.	132.18	127.06	150.05	183.65	218.76	241.38	244.57	260.18	319.08	342.74	358.88	379.83	398.90	413.50	444.86	**25**	
Foreign Liabilities	41.63	45.27	50.31	55.09	62.32	74.88	83.54	106.61	93.02	95.45	116.10	123.48	122.54	133.57	124.31	**26c**	
Central Government Deposits	8.07	52.55	43.81	29.63	24.72	29.81	43.14	55.43	56.21	48.45	61.70	70.32	65.29	57.56	38.84	**26d**	
Credit from Monetary Authorities	—	.42	1.90	2.68	1.54	—	9.68	2.00	—	—	—	2.80	.85	5.30	—	**26g**	
Capital Accounts	10.00	15.07	16.88	26.08	41.18	40.18	44.26	49.91	55.09	62.59	68.69	83.51	97.16	106.46	116.44	**27a**	
Other Items (Net)	4.33	8.32	14.85	17.92	10.02	5.61	5.66	-9.90	-11.55	-6.53	-14.63	-15.55	-8.62	-20.50	-21.25	**27r**	
Monetary Survey																	
End of Period																	
Foreign Assets (Net)	51.95	77.33	51.38	31.12	34.56	45.85	26.95	.25	38.90	69.69	64.16	91.07	125.62	66.37	98.35	**31n**	
Domestic Credit	152.65	132.36	187.21	267.84	310.29	327.23	351.67	379.50	415.00	424.45	447.86	462.60	484.34	540.04	546.12	**32**	
Claims on Central Govt. (Net)	52.70	-3.87	3.32	36.70	49.64	40.21	34.36	37.30	40.60	44.95	38.14	27.97	39.04	45.63	79.38	**32an**	
Claims on Local Government	—	—	—	—	—	.01	.05	.23	.17	.17	.12	.09	.06	9.40	.02	**32b**	
Claims on Nonfin.Pub.Enterprises	1.03	6.01	8.27	18.47	24.65	21.40	26.40	29.07	29.13	19.27	21.77	23.05	24.25	27.82	24.29	**32c**	
Claims on Private Sector	93.59	128.73	171.49	211.13	234.43	263.99	289.57	312.48	344.63	358.48	386.35	409.97	419.77	454.09	439.58	**32d**	
Claims on Nonbank Financial Inst	5.33	1.50	4.12	1.54	1.57	1.62	1.29	.42	.46	1.57	1.48	1.52	1.22	3.11	2.86	**32g**	
Money	58.67	57.19	56.08	69.92	73.51	86.21	75.80	74.45	92.36	97.04	96.71	104.21	130.18	105.47	106.08	**34**	
Quasi-Money	132.18	127.06	150.05	183.65	218.76	241.38	244.57	260.18	319.08	342.74	358.88	379.83	398.90	413.50	444.86	**35**	
Capital Accounts	12.26	17.22	18.97	28.35	43.46	42.37	46.44	52.25	57.47	64.89	70.85	85.76	99.36	108.54	118.45	**37a**	
Other Items (Net)	1.49	8.22	13.49	17.04	9.12	3.12	11.80	-7.12	-15.01	-10.53	-14.41	-16.12	-18.48	-21.10	-24.92	**37r**	
Money plus Quasi-Money	190.85	184.26	206.13	253.57	292.27	327.59	320.37	334.63	411.44	439.78	455.59	484.03	529.08	518.97	550.95	**35l**	
Interest Rates																	
Percent Per Annum																	
Treasury Bill Rate	6.5	6.5	6.5	6.5	6.5	6.5	6.4	6.4	6.4	6.4	6.4	6.4	6.4	6.4	6.4	**60c**	
Deposit Rate	5.0	5.0	4.5	4.2	4.4	4.1	4.0	4.0	4.0	4.0	4.0	4.0	4.9	5.8	6.0	**60l**	
Lending Rate	10.5	10.5	10.5	10.5	10.3	10.0	10.0	9.6	10.3	10.5	10.5	10.5	10.5	10.5	10.5	**60p**	
Prices																	
Period Averages																	
Consumer Prices	77.4	79.6	84.6	87.3	†92.1	97.2	98.7	98.7	100.0	101.7	104.2	105.2	106.4	107.3	....	**64**	
International Transactions																	
Millions of E. Caribbean Dollars																	
Exports	129.59	146.41	121.77	148.59	146.62	144.35	131.67	127.30	121.81	138.46	143.01	170.34	146.53	143.14	....	**70**	
Imports, c.i.f.	179.22	236.34	289.09	318.39	295.98	284.69	252.99	260.10	316.66	350.85	336.31	367.18	380.11	396.25	....	**71**	

Dominica

		1972	1973	1974	1975	1976	1977	1978	1979	1980	1981	1982	1983	1984	1985	1986
Balance of Payments														*Millions of US Dollars:*		
Current Account, n.i.e.	78al d	....	....	....	....	−1.10	−1.50	−1.30	6.30	−14.30	−12.81	−8.24	−1.83	−7.23	−6.43	−7.11
Goods: Exports f.o.b.	78aa d	....	....	....	....	11.10	12.00	15.90	9.80	10.10	19.70	25.10	27.80	25.60	28.40	44.58
Goods: Imports f.o.b.	78ab d	....	....	....	....	−17.27	−19.91	−25.91	−35.82	−48.36	−45.18	−43.18	−42.81	−50.72	−52.00	−49.16
Trade Balance	78ac d	....	....	....	....	−6.17	−7.91	−10.01	−26.02	−38.26	−25.48	−18.08	−15.01	−25.12	−23.60	−4.58
Services: Credit	78ad d	....	....	....	....	2.50	3.00	3.10	9.50	5.60	3.70	6.60	8.20	11.80	10.20	14.63
Services: Debit	78ae d	....	....	....	....	−1.83	−2.29	−3.39	−4.48	−6.34	−6.92	−6.92	−6.89	−9.48	−11.80	−17.20
Balance on Goods & Services	78af d	....	....	....	....	−5.50	−7.20	−10.30	−21.00	−39.00	−28.70	−18.40	−13.70	−22.80	−25.20	−7.16
Income: Credit	78ag d	....	....	....	....	.40	.30	.20	.30	.60	1.00	1.00	1.26			1.98
Income: Debit	78ah d	....	....	....	....	−.20	−.30	−.40	−.40	−.30	−.50	−.80	−1.70	−1.90	−1.90	−4.39
Balance on Gds, Serv. & Inc.	78ai d	....	....	....	....	−5.30	−7.20	−10.50	−21.10	−38.70	−28.20	−18.20	−14.14	−24.70	−27.10	−9.57
Current Transfers, n.i.e.: Credit	78aj d	....	....	....	....	4.20	7.20	11.40	29.30	26.70	18.09	12.86	16.71	21.97	25.27	5.54
Current Transfers: Debit	78ak d	....	....	....	....	—	−1.50	−2.20	−1.90	−2.30	−2.70	−2.90	−4.40	−4.50	−4.60	−3.09
Capital Account, n.i.e.	78bc d	....	....	....	....	....	....	....	....	....	....	....	....	....	....	12.48
Capital Account, n.i.e.: Credit	78ba d	....	....	....	....	—	—	—	—	—	—	—	—	—	—	16.52
Capital Account: Debit	78bb d	....	....	....	....	—	—	—	—	—	—	—	—	—	—	−4.04
Financial Account, n.i.e.	78bj d	....	....	....	....	.90	2.74	1.27	−1.89	3.59	3.35	7.03	1.37	11.43	6.51	3.34
Direct Investment Abroad	78bd d	....	....	....	....	—	—	—	—	—	—	—	—	—	—	—
Dir. Invest. in Rep. Econ., n.i.e.	78be d	....	....	....	....	—	—	—	—	—	—	.20	.20	2.30	3.00	5.19
Portfolio Investment Assets	78bf d	....	....	....	....	—	—	—	—	—	—	—	—	—	—	—
Equity Securities	78bk d	....	....	....	....	—	—	—	—	—	—	—	—	—	—	—
Debt Securities	78bl d	....	....	....	....	—	—	—	—	—	—	—	—	—	—	—
Portfolio Investment Liab., n.i.e.	78bg d	....	....	....	....	—	—	—	—	−.20	—	.09	.09	—	—	—
Equity Securities	78bm d	....	....	....	....	—	—	—	—	—	—	—	—	—	—	—
Debt Securities	78bn d	....	....	....	....	—	—	—	—	−.20	—	.09	.09	—	—	—
Financial Derivatives Assets	78bw d	....	....	....	....	....	....	....	....	....	....	....	....	....	....	....
Financial Derivatives Liabilities	78bx d	....	....	....	....	....	....	....	....	....	....	....	....	....	....	....
Other Investment Assets	78bh d	....	....	....	....	−.80	−.58	−.06	−3.84	1.17	−1.87	−.50	−3.38	2.24	−1.31	−2.81
Monetary Authorities	78bo d	....	....	....	....	—	—	—	—	—	—	—	—	—	—	—
General Government	78bp d	....	....	....	....	—	—	—	—	—	—	—	—	—	—	—
Banks	78bq d	....	....	....	....	−.80	−.58	−.06	−3.84	1.17	−1.87	−.50	−.98	2.24	−1.31	−2.81
Other Sectors	78br d	....	....	....	....	—	—	—	—	—	—	—	−2.40	—	—	—
Other Investment Liab., n.i.e.	78bi d	....	....	....	....	1.70	3.32	1.34	1.95	2.61	5.22	7.24	4.46	6.90	4.82	.97
Monetary Authorities	78bs d	....	....	....	....	—	—	—	—	—	—	—	—	—	—	—
General Government	78bt d	....	....	....	....	—	.70	.10	.10	.96	.18	4.49	2.61	4.00	3.20	1.30
Banks	78bu d	....	....	....	....	—	1.12	.44	1.25	.95	2.54	−1.32	−1.25	.60	−.18	—
Other Sectors	78bv d	....	....	....	....	1.70	1.50	.80	.60	.70	2.50	4.07	3.10	2.30	1.80	−.32
Net Errors and Omissions	78ca d	....	....	....	....	.60	−.29	.12	1.14	6.77	.94	−.76	−3.99	1.43	−.69	−2.15
Overall Balance	78cb d	....	....	....	....	.40	.96	.10	5.56	−3.94	−8.52	−1.98	−4.46	5.64	−.61	6.57
Reserves and Related Items	79da d	....	....	....	....	−.40	−.96	−.10	−5.56	3.94	8.52	1.98	4.46	−5.64	.61	−6.57
Reserve Assets	79db d	....	....	....	....	−.40	−.96	−.10	−8.05	4.26	2.72	−1.60	2.56	−5.39	2.00	−6.04
Use of Fund Credit and Loans	79dc d	....	....	....	....	—	—	—	2.49	−.32	5.80	3.14	1.81	−.37	−1.52	−.61
Exceptional Financing	79de d	....	....	....	....	—	—	—	—	—	.01	.44	.08	.12	.13	.09
Government Finance														*Millions of E. Caribbean Dollars:*		
Deficit (-) or Surplus	80	....	....	....	....	−4.49	.20	−2.72	−8.11	....	....	....	....	....	....	....
Revenue	81	....	....	....	....	15.83	23.46	31.46	32.46	....	....	....	....	....	....	....
Grants Received	81z	....	....	....	....	5.85	7.54	11.84	19.67	....	....	....	....	....	....	....
Expenditure	82	....	....	....	....	23.21	27.74	44.20	53.40	....	....	....	....	....	....	....
Lending Minus Repayments	83	....	....	....	....	2.96	3.06	1.82	6.84	....	....	....	....	....	....	....
National Accounts														*Millions of E. Caribbean Dollars*		
Househ.Cons.Expend.,incl.NPISHs	96f	....	....	43.1	43.2	43.2	77.2	95.8	112.3	147.5	151.5	141.8	144.9	172.5	192.8	190.8
Government Consumption Expend.	91f	....	....	14.9	18.1	23.4	18.9	25.1	40.5	43.5	45.5	47.7	52.3	60.2	59.9	62.1
Gross Fixed Capital Formation	93e	....	....	8.7	16.0	19.2	21.5	28.0	42.1	81.2	60.7	60.1	60.6	89.4	75.8	67.5
Exports of Goods and Services	90c	....	....	29.4	30.8	36.6	40.5	52.1	33.5	35.1	61.8	80.2	88.8	86.4	97.3	161.4
Imports of Goods and Services (-)	98c	....	....	41.8	45.2	49.9	59.9	79.1	108.8	147.7	140.7	135.3	130.7	165.9	159.6	179.2
Gross Domestic Product (GDP)	99b	....	....	56.5	62.9	72.5	98.2	122.0	119.6	159.6	178.8	194.5	215.8	242.6	266.2	302.6
Net Primary Income from Abroad	98.n	....	....	....	....	....	....	....	....	.8	1.6	.5	1.1	−2.7	−3.4	−6.5
Gross National Income (GNI)	99a	....	....	....	....	....	....	....	....	160.4	180.4	195.1	216.9	239.9	262.8	296.1
Net Current Transf.from Abroad	98t	....	....	....	....	....	....	....	....	....	....	....	....	....	....	....
Gross Nat'l Disposable Inc.(GNDI)	99i	....	....	....	....	....	....	....	....	....	....	....	....	....	....	....
Gross Saving	99s	....	....	....	....	....	....	....	....	....	....	....	....	....	....	....
GDP Volume 1990 Prices	99b. p	....	....	....	....	....	256.7	286.9	234.0	263.7	299.7	312.1	320.5	337.9	342.2	366.4
GDP Deflator (1995=100)	99bi p	....	....	....	....	23.9	31.3	34.7	41.8	49.4	48.8	50.9	55.0	58.7	63.6	67.5
															Millions:	
Population	99z	.07	.07	.07	.07	.07	.08	.08	.07	.07	.07	.08	.08	.08	.08	.08

1987	1988	1989	1990	1991	1992	1993	1994	1995	1996	1997	1998	1999	2000	2001		
Minus Sign Indicates Debit															**Balance of Payments**	
−7.06	−12.30	−45.54	−43.53	−34.19	−27.12	−27.48	−37.55	−40.73	−33.27	−26.20	−12.20	−41.17	−68.93	....	Current Account, n.i.e.	**78al** *d*
49.29	57.04	46.30	56.07	56.47	55.31	49.29	48.33	50.27	52.75	53.77	63.10	54.61	50.29	....	Goods: Exports f.o.b.	**78aa** *d*
−58.86	−77.24	−94.42	−103.95	−96.47	−92.79	−91.96	−95.76	−103.21	−100.50	−104.31	−106.93	−123.35	−129.60	....	Goods: Imports f.o.b.	**78ab** *d*
−9.57	−20.21	−48.12	−47.88	−40.00	−37.48	−42.68	−47.43	−52.94	−47.75	−50.54	−43.84	−68.74	−79.31	....	*Trade Balance*	**78ac** *d*
17.00	20.89	24.95	33.38	36.63	42.36	48.54	51.59	61.36	68.94	83.39	88.41	98.93	88.03	....	Services: Credit	**78ad** *d*
−18.64	−21.64	−25.84	−30.00	−30.48	−32.21	−35.66	−37.76	−43.72	−44.89	−52.17	−54.03	−59.27	−50.56	....	Services: Debit	**78ae** *d*
−11.21	−20.96	−49.01	−44.50	−33.86	−27.33	−29.80	−33.60	−35.30	−23.70	−19.33	−9.45	−29.08	−41.84	....	*Balance on Goods & Services*	**78af** *d*
2.69	4.33	3.60	4.03	2.60	2.50	2.97	3.08	3.29	2.84	3.60	4.65	4.63	4.67	....	Income: Credit	**78ag** *d*
−5.03	−5.89	−7.59	−8.92	−10.27	−9.78	−9.34	−14.10	−16.59	−22.58	−20.83	−20.14	−30.27	−41.86	....	Income: Debit	**78ah** *d*
−13.55	−22.52	−53.00	−49.39	−41.52	−34.61	−36.18	−44.62	−48.59	−43.44	−36.55	−24.94	−54.73	−79.03	....	*Balance on Gds, Serv. & Inc.*	**78ai** *d*
9.54	13.16	10.24	10.39	11.20	10.87	12.42	14.86	16.26	17.83	17.44	19.92	20.46	17.12	....	Current Transfers, n.i.e.: Credit	**78aj** *d*
−3.05	−2.93	−2.78	−4.53	−3.87	−3.38	−3.72	−7.79	−8.39	−7.66	−7.09	−7.18	−6.90	−7.02	....	Current Transfers: Debit	**78ak** *d*
7.07	11.37	13.58	13.50	13.19	9.80	9.72	6.90	24.54	25.30	22.52	14.75	11.76	14.16	....	Capital Account, n.i.e.	**78bc** *d*
8.70	12.85	15.58	14.96	14.74	11.28	11.20	9.37	24.65	25.42	22.64	14.87	12.06	15.67	....	Capital Account, n.i.e.: Credit	**78ba** *d*
−1.63	−1.48	−2.00	−1.45	−1.56	−1.48	−1.48	−2.47	−.11	−.12	−.12	−.13	−.30	−1.52	....	Capital Account: Debit	**78bb** *d*
8.20	5.11	32.03	29.32	25.11	22.28	19.65	30.00	42.15	5.18	15.48	−3.65	36.23	53.23	....	Financial Account, n.i.e.	**78bj** *d*
—	—	—	—	—	—	—	—	—	—	—	—	—	—	....	Direct Investment Abroad	**78bd** *d*
13.52	11.93	17.20	12.89	15.22	20.41	13.20	22.60	54.09	17.80	21.11	6.53	17.96	10.62	....	Dir. Invest. in Rep. Econ., n.i.e.	**78be** *d*
							.01	−7.96				−1.70	−.40	....	Portfolio Investment Assets	**78bf** *d*
—	—	—	—	....	....	....	—	—	—	—	—	—	—	....	Equity Securities	**78bk** *d*
—	—	—	—	....	....	....	—	—	—	—	—	—	—	....	Debt Securities	**78bl** *d*
—	—	—	−.37	—	—	—	—	—	.46	−.18	1.30	30.44	14.03	....	Portfolio Investment Liab., n.i.e.	**78bg** *d*
—	—	—	−.37	....	....	....	....	....	....	....	....	....	....	....	Equity Securities	**78bm** *d*
—	—	—	—	....	....	....	....	....	....	....	....	....	....	....	Debt Securities	**78bn** *d*
....	....	....	....	....	....	....	....	....	....	....	....	....	....	....	Financial Derivatives Assets	**78bw** *d*
....	....	....	....	....	....	....	....	....	....	....	....	....	....	....	Financial Derivatives Liabilities	**78bx** *d*
−11.41	−8.48	8.18	10.78	−.77	−6.61	2.10	−4.31	−3.60	−16.45	−7.28	−14.13	−12.37	−10.42	....	Other Investment Assets	**78bh** *d*
—	—	—	—	....	....	....	....	....	....	....	....	....	....	....	Monetary Authorities	**78bo** *d*
—	—	—	—	....	....	....	....	....	....	....	....	....	....	....	General Government	**78bp** *d*
−11.41	−8.48	8.18	10.78	....	....	....	....	....	....	....	....	....	....	....	Banks	**78bq** *d*
....	....	....	....	....	....	....	....	....	....	....	....	....	....	....	Other Sectors	**78br** *d*
6.09	1.67	6.66	6.02	10.66	8.48	4.34	11.71	−.38	3.37	1.82	2.65	1.90	39.40	....	Other Investment Liab., n.i.e.	**78bi** *d*
—	—	—	—	....	....	....	....	....	....	....	....	....	....	....	Monetary Authorities	**78bs** *d*
6.06	1.83	6.95	7.14	....	....	....	....	....	....	....	....	....	....	....	General Government	**78bt** *d*
.03	−.16	−.30	−1.11	....	....	....	....	....	....	....	....	....	....	....	Banks	**78bu** *d*
.18	−5.22	.11	5.75	.12	−1.59	−.97	−2.71	−17.62	4.66	−10.20	5.55	4.22	2.01	....	Net Errors and Omissions	**78ca** *d*
8.39	−1.03	.18	5.05	4.23	3.36	.92	−3.35	8.34	1.87	1.60	4.44	11.04	.47	....	*Overall Balance*	**78cb** *d*
−8.39	1.03	−.18	−5.05	−4.23	−3.36	−.92	3.35	−8.34	−1.87	−1.60	−4.44	−11.04	−.47	....	Reserves and Related Items	**79da** *d*
−7.92	3.23	1.83	−3.70	−3.29	−2.60	−.19	4.15	−7.48	−1.06	−1.05	−4.22	−11.00	−.47	....	Reserve Assets	**79db** *d*
−.53	−2.27	−2.03	−1.35	−.94	−.76	−.73	−.80	−.86	−.81	−.55	−.22	−.04	—	....	Use of Fund Credit and Loans	**79dc** *d*
.05	.07	.03	—	....	....	....	....	....	....	....	....	....	....	....	Exceptional Financing	**79de** *d*
Year Ending June 30															**Government Finance**	
....	....	....	....	....	....	....	....	....	....	....	....	....	....	....	Deficit (-) or Surplus	**80**
....	....	....	....	....	....	....	....	....	....	....	....	....	....	....	Revenue	**81**
....	....	....	....	....	....	....	....	....	....	....	....	....	....	....	Grants Received	**81z**
....	....	....	....	....	....	....	....	....	....	....	....	....	....	....	Expenditure	**82**
....	....	....	....	....	....	....	....	....	....	....	....	....	....	....	Lending Minus Repayments	**83**
Millions of E. Caribbean Dollars															**National Accounts**	
221.3	247.5	286.2	290.7	322.5	336.7	358.5	408.9	377.4	389.4	363.7	383.5	448.1	447.2	....	Househ.Cons.Expend.,incl.NPISHs	**96f**
68.2	75.0	86.7	91.9	102.5	103.2	112.2	117.4	123.2	128.9	143.1	153.0	159.3	160.6	....	Government Consumption Expend.	**91f**
79.3	120.6	170.7	183.2	154.0	146.9	137.8	148.4	186.4	183.6	207.4	190.9	200.3	226.7	....	Gross Fixed Capital Formation	**93e**
181.6	212.1	195.2	244.9	249.3	269.1	262.8	272.2	301.4	328.6	370.0	407.8	412.6	369.9	....	Exports of Goods and Services	**90c**
209.3	267.0	324.7	361.7	341.1	338.1	330.2	365.1	396.7	392.6	422.5	434.6	497.4	479.9	....	Imports of Goods and Services (-)	**98c**
341.1	388.2	414.1	449.1	487.2	517.8	541.1	581.7	591.7	637.9	661.6	700.5	722.8	724.5	....	Gross Domestic Product (GDP)	**99b**
−6.3	−4.2	−10.8	−13.3	−20.7	−19.9	−17.2	−29.8	−35.9	−53.3	−46.5	−41.7	−73.3	−95.5	....	Net Primary Income from Abroad	**98.n**
334.8	384.0	403.3	435.7	466.7	497.9	523.9	552.0	555.8	584.6	615.1	658.9	649.5	629.1	....	Gross National Income (GNI)	**99a**
....	....	....	....	....	20.2	23.5	19.1	21.2	27.5	28.3	35.7	47.1	30.7	....	Net Current Transf.from Abroad	**98t**
....	....	....	....	....	518.1	547.4	571.1	577.0	612.1	643.5	694.5	696.6	659.8	....	Gross Nat'l Disposable Inc.(GNDI)	**99i**
....	....	....	....	....	78.3	76.7	44.8	76.4	93.8	136.7	158.1	89.2	52.0	....	Gross Saving	**99s**
394.0	427.7	426.7	449.1	451.8	461.1	468.8	475.5	483.5	496.9	506.6	....	....	....	....	GDP Volume 1990 Prices	**99b.** *p*
70.7	74.2	79.3	81.7	88.1	91.8	94.3	100.0	100.0	104.9	106.7	....	....	....	....	GDP Deflator (1995=100)	**99bi** *p*
Midyear Estimates																
.08	.07	.07	.07	.07	.07	.07	.07	.08	.07	.08	.08	†.07	.07	.07	**Population**	**99z**

(See notes in the back of the book.)

		1972	1973	1974	1975	1976	1977	1978	1979	1980	1981	1982	1983	1984	1985	1986
Exchange Rates															*Pesos per SDR:*	
Market Rate..........aa=	wa	1.086	1.206	1.224	1.171	1.162	1.215	1.303	1.317	1.275	1.164	1.103	1.047	.980	3.229	3.763
															Pesos per US Dollar:	
Market Rate..........ae=	we	1.000	1.000	1.000	1.000	1.000	1.000	1.000	1.000	1.000	1.000	1.000	1.000	1.000	2.940	3.077
Market Rate..........rf=	wf	1.000	1.000	1.000	1.000	1.000	1.000	1.000	1.000	1.000	1.000	1.000	1.000	1.000	3.113	2.904
Secondary Rate	xe	....	....	....	....	....	1.250	1.280	1.236	1.232	1.315	1.536	1.800	3.105	....	....
Secondary Rate	xf	1.112	1.124	1.130	1.170	1.190	1.213	1.245	1.217	1.255	1.278	1.457	....	2.737	....	....
															Index Numbers (1995=100):	
Market Rate	ahx	1,359.6	311.1	1,359.6	1,359.6	1,359.6	1,359.6	1,359.6	1,359.6	1,359.6	1,359.6	1,359.6	1,359.6	1,359.6	437.1	467.3
Nominal Effective Exchange Rate	ne c	....	....	....	....	....	....	....	393.3	403.1	436.9	458.6	458.6	301.6	268.4	247.7
Real Effective Exchange Rate	re c	....	....	....	....	....	....	....	....	149.4	151.8	138.6	136.8	97.2	108.6	103.1
Fund Position															*Millions of SDRs:*	
Quota	2f. s	43.0	43.0	43.0	43.0	43.0	43.0	55.0	55.0	82.5	82.5	82.5	112.1	112.1	112.1	112.1
SDRs	1b. s	6.9	6.8	7.2	6.5	6.0	5.2	4.7	7.2	—	1.6	.5	.2	.4	28.8	—
Reserve Position in the Fund	1c. s	—	10.8	—	—	—	—	—	—	—	—	—	7.4	—	—	—
Total Fund Cred.&Loans Outstg.	2tl	3.8	—	—	—	21.5	36.5	36.5	94.3	38.0	19.8	64.1	235.2	225.7	270.4	248.8
International Liquidity														*Millions of US Dollars Unless Otherwise Indicated:*		
Total Reserves minus Gold	1l. d	55.3	84.3	87.1	112.6	123.5	180.1	154.0	238.6	201.8	225.2	129.0	171.3	253.5	340.1	376.3
SDRs	1b. d	7.5	8.2	8.8	7.6	7.0	6.3	6.1	9.5	—	1.9	.6	.2	.4	31.6	—
Reserve Position in the Fund	1c. d	—	13.0	—	—	—	—	—	—	—	—	—	7.7	—	—	—
Foreign Exchange	1d. d	47.8	63.2	78.3	105.0	116.5	173.8	147.9	229.1	201.8	223.3	128.4	163.3	253.1	308.5	376.3
Gold (Million Fine Troy Ounces)	1ad	.086	.086	.086	.086	.086	.104	.104	.113	.131	.142	.091	.077	.018	.018	.018
Gold (National Valuation)	1and	3.3	3.6	3.6	3.6	3.6	4.4	20.2	48.4	72.8	58.7	43.7	31.3	7.9	5.9	7.1
Monetary Authorities: Other Liab.	4.. d	14.9	10.3	32.5	72.0	106.6	139.0	152.0	252.8	519.2	748.0	990.5	1,138.9	1,243.8	1,395.8	229.0
Deposit Money Banks: Assets	7a. d	9.2	8.1	9.8	17.0	36.1	40.4	25.3	56.9	127.4	272.5	292.0	42.8	58.7	41.9	55.9
Liabilities	7b. d	22.3	37.1	69.1	36.5	47.9	76.1	78.9	73.9	154.8	341.3	314.1	93.7	85.1	13.3	26.2
Other Banking Insts.: Liabilities	7f. d	35.0	34.2	36.2	39.6	48.2	51.1	51.5	46.1	38.9	30.6	26.9	23.3	21.0	24.0	22.4
Monetary Authorities															*Millions of Pesos:*	
Foreign Assets	11	74	107	113	141	154	211	203	312	308	320	212	244	311	1,190	1,327
Claims on Central Government	12a	173	189	249	256	260	270	295	335	364	492	660	867	938	953	941
Claims on Nonfin.Pub.Enterprises	12c	2	2	2	2	2	2	2	2	53	56	137	238	258	209	151
Claims on Private Sector	12d	—	5	2	2	6	6	6	6	76	76	76	76	76	76	76
Claims on Deposit Money Banks	12e	64	77	110	142	153	184	301	346	383	543	683	747	723	724	815
Claims on Other Banking Insts	12f	49	55	75	90	117	117	130	196	266	306	327	360	271	305	324
Reserve Money	14	229	288	422	389	390	500	542	587	566	713	731	850	1,097	1,085	2,112
of which: Currency Outside DMBs	14a	99	116	141	158	172	203	224	274	275	324	358	415	593	677	937
Liabs.of Centl.Bank: Securities	16ac	—	—	—	—	—	—	—	—	6	1	—	—	8	55	101
Foreign Liabilities	16c	19	10	32	72	132	183	200	377	568	771	1,061	1,385	1,465	4,977	1,641
Long-Term Foreign Liabilities	16cl	30	56	42	54	64	34	87	103	126	111	89	59	31	97	3,632
Central Government Deposits	16d	11	18	2	61	62	39	4	6	10	6	8	30	2	68	51
Counterpart Funds	16e	—	—	—	—	—	—	—	—	—	—	—	—	—	—	—
Capital Accounts	17a	49	55	58	62	63	69	73	80	81	66	72	112	131	175	-84
Other Items (Net)	17r	23	8	-5	-6	-19	-37	31	42	93	125	132	95	-158	-2,999	-3,817
of which: Revaluation of Reserves	17rv	—	—	—	—	—	—	—	—	—	—	—	—	—	-385	-3,389
Deposit Money Banks															*Millions of Pesos:*	
Reserves	20	144	187	317	260	255	349	365	375	346	462	444	592	692	770	1,797
Foreign Assets	21	9	8	10	17	36	40	25	57	127	272	292	43	59	123	172
Claims on Central Government	22a	57	58	63	102	95	86	78	102	133	133	154	159	195	190	448
Claims on Local Government	22b	3	3	2	2	3	6	12	13	15	17	16	17	16	17	16
Claims on Nonfin.Pub.Enterprises	22c	26	41	67	65	56	91	131	135	142	300	392	474	486	608	589
Claims on Private Sector	22d	282	386	578	685	789	851	885	990	1,166	1,158	1,262	1,363	1,504	1,852	2,766
Claims on Other Banking Insts	22f	36	41	42	49	55	63	70	63	84	77	76	93	101	111	290
Demand Deposits	24	143	179	266	275	263	314	321	419	459	456	502	562	768	985	1,662
Time, Savings,& Fgn.Currency Dep.	25	181	245	360	454	458	540	527	510	544	610	650	812	897	1,037	2,256
Bonds	26ab	—	—	—	—	—	—	—	—	—	—	—	—	—	—	—
Foreign Liabilities	26c	22	37	69	37	48	76	79	74	155	341	314	94	85	39	81
Central Government Deposits	26d	35	40	54	56	79	84	108	57	54	39	51	96	86	182	423
Credit from Monetary Authorities	26g	64	79	123	138	161	166	223	271	327	447	532	518	569	582	683
Capital Accounts	27a	32	44	64	108	124	136	148	163	183	212	219	252	281	371	504
Other Items (Net)	27r	80	98	143	114	156	170	162	242	291	313	368	408	366	475	469
Monetary Survey															*Millions of Pesos:*	
Foreign Assets (Net)	31n	42	68	21	49	10	-8	-50	-82	-287	-520	-871	-1,192	-1,180	-3,703	-223
Domestic Credit	32	582	720	1,024	1,136	1,241	1,368	1,497	1,780	2,234	2,569	3,040	3,520	3,756	4,072	5,127
Claims on Central Govt. (Net)	32an	184	188	256	241	213	232	261	374	433	580	755	900	1,045	894	916
Claims on Local Government	32b	3	3	2	2	3	6	12	13	15	17	16	17	16	17	16
Claims on Nonfin.Pub.Enterprises	32c	28	43	69	66	58	93	133	137	195	356	529	712	744	817	739
Claims on Private Sector	32d	282	391	580	687	794	857	891	996	1,241	1,234	1,337	1,438	1,579	1,927	2,841
Claims on Other Banking Insts	32f	85	96	117	139	172	179	201	259	350	383	403	453	372	416	614
Money	34	248	299	414	444	438	519	545	695	738	781	866	985	1,411	1,683	2,611
Quasi-Money	35	181	245	360	454	458	540	527	510	544	610	650	812	897	1,037	2,256
Bonds	36ab	—	—	—	—	—	—	—	—	—	—	—	—	—	—	—
Liabs.of Centl.Bank: Securities	36ac	—	—	—	—	—	—	—	—	6	1	—	—	8	55	101
Long-Term Foreign Liabilities	36cl	30	56	42	54	64	34	87	103	126	111	89	59	31	97	3,632
Capital Accounts	37a	81	99	122	170	187	206	221	243	263	278	291	364	412	546	419
Other Items (Net)	37r	83	90	108	63	105	61	67	146	270	268	272	109	-184	-3,048	-4,114
Money plus Quasi-Money	35l	429	544	774	898	896	1,059	1,072	1,205	1,282	1,392	1,516	1,797	2,308	2,720	4,866
Other Banking Institutions															*Millions of Pesos:*	
Reserves	40	—	—	2	1	2	3	4	4	7	8	11	12	20	33	47
Claims on Central Government	42a	43	42	46	69	75	85	94	39	51	94	74	82	145	161	164
Claims on Nonfin.Pub.Enterprises	42c	5	5	2	2	2	2	6	5	6	8	4	4	4	5	5
Claims on Private Sector	42d	137	153	206	259	332	437	538	702	879	1,006	1,412	1,597	1,780	2,255	2,811
Claims on Deposit Money Banks	42e	37	61	51	54	61	37	35	63	88	131	214	261	300	309	653
Time, Savings,& Fgn.Currency Dep.	45	32	55	75	101	124	156	196	242	327	395	470	547	619	837	869
Bonds	46ab	5	5	5	14	23	41	65	112	159	214	513	642	768	944	1,682
Long-Term Foreign Liabilities	46cl	35	34	36	40	48	51	52	46	39	31	27	23	21	71	69
Credit from Monetary Authorities	46g	48	63	48	70	86	105	127	145	206	241	254	279	308	364	414
Credit from Deposit Money Banks	46h	5	8	9	10	10	11	9	16	7	9	15	18	26	20	28
Capital Accounts	47a	116	119	123	129	139	150	180	207	234	300	319	361	431	529	652
Other Items (Net)	47r	-20	-22	11	22	43	51	48	44	58	58	117	87	76	-3	-33

1987	1988	1989	1990	1991	1992	1993	1994	1995	1996	1997	1998	1999	2000	2001		
End of Period															**Exchange Rates**	
7.037	8.532	8.332	16.147	18.109	17.291	17.536	19.071	20.015	20.220	19.383	22.230	22.014	21.725	21.551	Market Rate....................aa=..................	**wa**
End of Period (we) Period Average (wf)																
4.960	6.340	6.340	11.350	12.660	12.575	12.767	13.064	13.465	14.062	14.366	15.788	16.039	16.674	17.149	Market Rate....................ae=..................	**we**
3.845	6.113	6.340	8.525	12.692	12.774	12.676	13.160	13.597	13.775	14.265	15.267	16.033	16.415	16.952	Market Rate....................rf=..................	**wf**
....	....	....	....	....	....	....	....	....	....	....	....	....	....	....	Secondary Rate....................	**xe**
....	....	....	....	....	....	....	....	....	....	....	....	....	....	....	Secondary Rate....................	**xf**
Period Averages																
362.1	226.1	211.2	170.0	106.5	106.4	107.3	103.3	100.0	98.7	95.3	88.9	84.8	82.8	80.2	Market Rate....................	**ahx**
196.9	133.3	139.5	116.3	84.0	88.7	97.3	104.5	100.0	100.3	99.6	96.2	91.2	90.9	90.9	Nominal Effective Exchange Rate..........	**nec**
88.0	73.9	89.0	87.9	88.8	89.3	93.2	97.2	100.0	102.3	107.3	106.6	105.6	110.3	117.1	Real Effective Exchange Rate..................	**rec**
End of Period															**Fund Position**	
112.1	112.1	112.1	112.1	112.1	158.8	158.8	158.8	158.8	158.8	158.8	158.8	218.9	218.9	218.9	Quota....................	**2f.s**
—	—	—	—	—	.1	10.3	2.5	.3	.3	.2	.2	.2	.3	.3	SDRs....................	**1b.s**
—	—	—	—	—	—	—	—	—	—	—	—	—	—	—	Reserve Position in the Fund..................	**1c.s**
199.9	161.8	93.2	50.4	62.4	89.4	135.5	129.9	107.5	66.5	21.1	39.7	39.7	39.7	39.7	Total Fund Cred.&Loans Outstg..............	**2tl**
End of Period															**International Liquidity**	
182.2	254.0	164.0	61.6	441.9	499.8	651.2	252.1	365.6	350.3	391.0	501.9	694.0	627.2	1,099.5	Total Reserves minus Gold..................	**1l.d**
—	—	—	—	.1	.1	14.1	3.7	.5	.4	.3	.3	.3	.4	.4	SDRs....................	**1b.d**
—	—	—	—	—	—	—	—	—	—	—	—	—	—	—	Reserve Position in the Fund..............	**1c.d**
182.2	254.0	164.0	61.6	441.8	499.7	637.1	248.4	365.0	349.8	390.7	501.6	693.7	626.8	1,099.0	Foreign Exchange....................	**1d.d**
.018	.018	.018	.018	.018	.018	.018	.018	.018	.018	.018	.018	.018	.018	.018	Gold (Million Fine Troy Ounces)...........	**1ad**
8.8	7.6	7.5	6.8	6.5	6.1	6.9	6.8	6.8	6.7	5.5	5.3	5.2	5.0	5.1	Gold (National Valuation)..................	**1and**
257.7	139.7	202.6	180.5	150.8	26.0	22.3	90.8	102.4	89.5	88.6	50.8	42.1	74.6	91.2	Monetary Authorities: Other Liab..........	**4..d**
215.8	248.3	233.6	219.6	230.4	232.5	191.8	189.4	183.8	174.5	236.7	307.0	322.5	416.4	527.0	Deposit Money Banks: Assets..............	**7a.d**
210.6	212.9	212.2	220.5	226.1	218.2	184.0	183.3	55.0	97.6	188.6	401.4	458.9	739.3	684.5	Liabilities..........	**7b.d**
60.9	107.8	12.9	28.1	41.8	49.3	62.7	91.2	8.4	10.9	6.3	17.2	22.7	24.3	27.2	Other Banking Insts.: Liabilities............	**7f.d**
End of Period															**Monetary Authorities**	
1,185	1,981	1,411	2,086	6,326	7,128	9,008	4,804	6,577	6,962	7,696	10,071	13,599	13,128	22,364	Foreign Assets....................	**11**
1,046	1,087	1,104	1,146	1,972	1,953	938	558	605	1,236	1,537	1,632	2,416	4,026	4,023	Claims on Central Government..............	**12a**
285	291	323	334	979	585	738	2,959	1,609	1,632	1,665	1,987	2,520	2,631	2,676	Claims on Nonfin.Pub.Enterprises..........	**12c**
76	76	96	103	537	550	550	45	45	45	45	5	5	2	1	Claims on Private Sector..................	**12d**
840	896	1,092	1,103	1,349	1,383	1,343	2,075	2,092	3,108	2,161	2,917	2,992	2,874	3,510	Claims on Deposit Money Banks............	**12e**
349	536	532	353	441	1,087	923	292	307	320	388	384	375	345	347	Claims on Other Banking Insts..............	**12f**
1,983	4,001	5,170	6,801	10,277	11,602	14,889	14,956	17,412	19,306	22,963	28,110	32,328	35,667	45,980	Reserve Money....................	**14**
1,313	1,876	2,683	3,733	4,586	5,913	6,905	7,679	8,892	9,635	11,534	12,568	16,889	15,076	16,628	*of which: Currency Outside DMBs*.........	**14a**
156	211	126	138	646	518	196	743	1,991	4,099	4,357	3,499	5,135	4,369	3,276	Liabs.of Centl.Bank: Securities............	**16ac**
2,685	2,266	2,061	2,863	3,039	1,873	2,661	3,663	3,529	2,602	1,682	1,684	1,549	2,106	2,420	Foreign Liabilities....................	**16c**
5,711	8,078	8,492	16,095	17,585	15,734	15,793	10,780	11,652	12,454	12,205	13,110	13,207	13,418	12,818	Long-Term Foreign Liabilities..............	**16cl**
463	111	262	198	1,496	2,308	2,179	151	344	400	351	424	479	414	1,838	Central Government Deposits..............	**16d**
—	—	—	—	—	—	—	—	—	—	—	—	—	—	—	Counterpart Funds....................	**16e**
-90	-575	-1,068	-1,630	-892	501	-922	-491	-1,483	-2,915	-4,143	-5,523	-6,957	-8,645	-9,502	Capital Accounts....................	**17a**
-7,126	-9,225	-10,486	-19,340	-20,545	-19,849	-21,295	-19,069	-22,210	-22,644	-23,924	-24,307	-23,834	-24,323	-23,910	Other Items (Net)....................	**17r**
-5,423	-7,780	-8,318	-14,570	-17,568	-17,627	-17,883	-16,415	-16,961	-17,326	-17,376	-17,872	-18,169	-18,315	-18,315	*of which:* Revaluation of Reserves.......	**17rv**
End of Period															**Deposit Money Banks**	
1,258	2,909	3,315	4,268	7,302	7,438	8,992	9,214	10,654	10,761	12,964	16,947	17,331	26,692	30,404	Reserves....................	**20**
1,070	1,574	1,481	2,493	2,917	2,924	2,449	2,474	2,475	2,453	3,400	4,846	5,172	6,943	9,037	Foreign Assets....................	**21**
214	423	410	552	470	465	371	540	505	536	1,934	1,998	4,144	4,813	11,678	Claims on Central Government..............	**22a**
17	17	10	7	6	3	5	6	29	4	6	4	14	29	32	Claims on Local Government..............	**22b**
789	990	1,130	1,129	1,446	1,424	1,431	1,470	2,366	4,485	4,426	3,938	4,715	2,735	2,566	Claims on Nonfin.Pub.Enterprises..........	**22c**
3,442	4,455	6,858	8,924	11,126	15,806	19,442	22,166	27,688	34,500	44,404	52,744	66,877	82,120	101,941	Claims on Private Sector..................	**22d**
366	180	256	606	555	965	805	799	554	778	764	957	760	593	928	Claims on Other Banking Insts..............	**22f**
1,895	3,081	3,527	5,160	6,610	7,221	8,104	8,470	10,064	13,540	16,081	16,782	18,884	20,290	24,529	Demand Deposits....................	**24**
2,287	3,301	4,580	6,262	9,610	13,322	17,092	19,854	23,458	27,022	34,725	43,380	54,211	70,282	92,908	Time, Savings,& Fgn.Currency Dep..........	**25**
—	—	—	—	—	—	133	122	80	138	76	17	398	112	2	Bonds....................	**26ab**
1,045	1,350	1,345	2,503	2,863	2,743	2,349	2,394	740	1,372	2,710	6,337	7,361	12,328	11,738	Foreign Liabilities....................	**26c**
324	498	556	733	1,535	2,774	2,568	1,746	2,533	2,594	3,076	2,500	3,578	3,192	6,566	Central Government Deposits..............	**26d**
706	864	1,026	1,437	1,214	1,103	902	1,334	1,310	1,220	1,532	2,222	2,449	2,931	3,226	Credit from Monetary Authorities..........	**26g**
640	1,188	1,575	2,122	2,951	3,028	3,388	4,050	4,581	5,203	6,524	8,220	10,224	12,667	16,707	Capital Accounts....................	**27a**
260	266	851	-239	-962	-1,165	-1,042	-1,301	1,506	2,428	3,175	1,975	1,907	2,124	911	Other Items (Net)....................	**27r**
End of Period															**Monetary Survey**	
-1,474	-61	-514	-787	3,341	5,435	6,447	1,221	4,784	5,441	6,704	6,896	9,862	5,638	17,242	Foreign Assets (Net)....................	**31n**
5,797	7,444	9,900	12,221	14,503	17,757	20,457	26,938	30,832	40,542	51,742	60,726	77,768	93,688	115,788	Domestic Credit....................	**32**
473	901	696	767	-588	-2,665	-3,438	-798	-1,766	-1,221	43	706	2,503	5,233	7,296	Claims on Central Govt. (Net)...........	**32an**
17	17	10	7	6	3	5	6	29	4	6	4	14	29	32	Claims on Local Government..............	**32b**
1,074	1,281	1,453	1,463	2,425	2,010	2,170	4,429	3,975	6,117	6,092	5,925	7,235	5,367	5,242	Claims on Nonfin.Pub.Enterprises........	**32c**
3,518	4,530	6,954	9,026	11,664	16,356	19,992	22,211	27,733	34,545	44,449	52,749	66,881	82,122	101,942	Claims on Private Sector..................	**32d**
715	715	788	958	996	2,053	1,728	1,091	861	1,098	1,152	1,342	1,135	938	1,275	Claims on Other Banking Insts.............	**32f**
3,216	4,967	6,266	9,196	11,297	13,231	15,065	16,198	18,996	23,225	27,703	29,416	35,840	35,445	41,258	Money....................	**34**
2,287	3,301	4,580	6,262	9,610	13,322	17,092	19,854	23,458	27,022	34,725	43,380	54,211	70,282	92,908	Quasi-Money....................	**35**
—	—	—	—	—	—	133	122	80	138	76	17	398	112	2	Bonds....................	**36ab**
156	211	126	138	646	518	196	743	1,991	4,099	4,357	3,499	5,135	4,369	3,276	Liabs.of Centl.Bank: Securities............	**36ac**
5,711	8,078	8,492	16,095	17,585	15,734	15,793	10,780	11,652	12,454	12,205	13,110	13,207	13,418	12,818	Long-Term Foreign Liabilities..............	**36cl**
550	612	507	492	2,059	3,528	2,466	3,558	3,098	2,288	2,381	2,696	3,267	4,022	7,205	Capital Accounts....................	**37a**
-7,597	-9,786	-10,585	-20,748	-23,353	-23,141	-23,842	-23,097	-23,659	-23,243	-23,001	-24,496	-24,428	-28,323	-24,437	Other Items (Net)....................	**37r**
5,503	8,268	10,846	15,458	20,908	26,553	32,157	36,052	42,454	50,247	62,428	72,795	90,051	105,727	134,166	Money plus Quasi-Money....................	**35l**
End of Period															**Other Banking Institutions**	
80	130	210	309	327	415	316	329	332	353	429	483	796	951	1,037	Reserves....................	**40**
173	80	13	200	311	277	474	522	774	569	452	837	971	971	699	Claims on Central Government..............	**42a**
5	5	5	5	8	11	10	12	19	18	18	19	19	19	198	Claims on Nonfin.Pub.Enterprises..........	**42c**
3,708	4,725	6,422	7,535	8,828	10,088	10,365	12,263	12,513	13,797	16,324	19,797	24,375	30,407	34,552	Claims on Private Sector..................	**42d**
687	942	1,059	1,092	1,748	2,589	3,388	2,358	3,097	3,674	4,303	5,368	6,433	7,745	11,955	Claims on Deposit Money Banks............	**42e**
1,167	1,386	1,683	1,957	2,706	3,444	3,647	3,679	3,981	4,499	5,464	6,731	6,778	7,282	8,413	Time, Savings,& Fgn.Currency Dep..........	**45**
2,087	2,499	3,292	3,939	5,018	6,310	6,589	7,290	8,474	9,418	11,295	13,120	17,634	22,433	27,956	Bonds....................	**46ab**
302	684	82	319	529	620	800	1,192	113	153	90	271	364	405	467	Long-Term Foreign Liabilities..............	**46cl**
410	627	872	926	1,067	1,216	1,641	1,623	1,464	1,434	1,360	1,298	1,112	1,118	1,092	Credit from Monetary Authorities..........	**46g**
78	68	177	311	298	354	429	424	460	478	457	539	458	513	495	Credit from Deposit Money Banks..........	**46h**
812	1,115	1,429	1,823	2,122	2,554	2,543	2,667	2,818	2,855	3,390	4,430	5,889	7,572	9,200	Capital Accounts....................	**47a**
-204	-497	174	-135	-517	-1,119	-1,096	-1,390	-576	-428	-530	114	359	772	816	Other Items (Net)....................	**47r**

Dominican Republic

		1972	1973	1974	1975	1976	1977	1978	1979	1980	1981	1982	1983	1984	1985	1986
Banking Survey															Millions of Pesos:	
Foreign Assets (Net)	51n	42	68	21	49	10	−8	−50	−82	−287	−520	−871	−1,192	−1,180	−3,703	−223
Domestic Credit	52	681	824	1,162	1,327	1,479	1,713	1,935	2,266	2,820	3,294	4,126	4,750	5,313	6,076	7,492
Claims on Central Govt. (Net)	52an	227	230	303	310	288	317	356	413	484	674	829	981	1,190	1,055	1,080
Claims on Local Government	52b	3	3	2	2	3	6	12	13	15	17	16	17	16	17	16
Claims on Nonfin.Pub.Enterprises	52c	32	47	71	69	61	95	138	142	201	363	533	716	748	821	744
Claims on Private Sector	52d	419	544	786	946	1,127	1,294	1,429	1,698	2,120	2,239	2,749	3,036	3,359	4,183	5,652
Liquid Liabilities	55l	461	599	848	998	1,018	1,212	1,265	1,442	1,602	1,778	1,975	2,332	2,907	3,524	5,688
Bonds	56ab	5	5	5	14	23	41	65	112	159	214	513	642	768	944	1,682
Liabs.of Centl.Bank: Securities	56ac	—	—	—	—	—	—	—	—	6	1	—	—	8	55	101
Long-Term Foreign Liabilities	56cl	65	90	78	94	112	85	139	149	165	142	116	82	52	168	3,700
Capital Accounts	57a	197	218	245	299	325	355	401	450	498	578	610	724	843	1,075	1,071
Other Items (Net)	57r	−5	−20	7	−29	10	11	15	30	104	62	41	−222	−444	−3,392	−4,973
Interest Rates															Percent Per Annum	
Money Market Rate	60b	...	...	...	...	...	...	...	...	...	...	...	...	...	...	...
Savings Rate	60k	...	...	...	...	...	...	...	...	...	...	...	...	...	...	...
Deposit Rate	60l	...	...	...	...	...	...	...	...	...	...	...	...	...	...	...
Lending Rate	60p	...	...	...	...	...	...	...	...	...	...	...	...	...	...	...
Prices and Labor														Index Numbers (1995=100):		
Consumer Prices	64	2.7	3.1	3.5	4.0	4.3	4.9	†5.0	5.5	†6.4	6.9	7.4	7.8	9.4	13.7	14.7
															Number in Thousands:	
Labor Force	67d	...	...	...	...	...	...	...	...	...	...	...	...	...	...	...
Employment	67e	...	...	...	...	...	...	...	...	...	...	...	...	...	...	...
Unemployment	67c	...	...	...	...	...	...	...	...	...	...	...	...	...	...	...
Unemployment Rate (%)	67r	...	...	...	...	...	...	...	...	...	...	...	...	...	...	...
International Transactions															Millions of US Dollars:	
Exports	70..d	347.6	442.1	636.8	893.8	716.4	780.4	675.5	868.6	961.9	1,188.0	767.7	785.2	868.1	735.2	717.6
Imports, f.o.b.	71.vd	337.7	421.9	673.0	772.7	763.6	847.8	859.7	1,054.6	1,425.7	1,450.2	1,255.8	1,279.0	1,257.1	1,293.0	1,245.8
															1995=100:	
Volume of Exports	72	148	165	166	147	159	168	135	161	119	130	118	142	143	127	101
															1995=100:	
Unit Value of Exports	74..d	40	48	67	84	78	102	90	98	100	110	79	77	91	82	82
Balance of Payments															Millions of US Dollars:	
Current Account, n.i.e.	78ald	−47.0	−96.6	−241.0	−72.8	−129.2	−128.6	−311.9	−331.3	−719.9	−389.4	−442.6	−417.9	−163.4	−107.6	−183.4
Goods: Exports f.o.b.	78aad	347.6	442.1	636.8	893.8	716.4	780.5	675.5	868.6	961.9	1,188.0	767.7	785.2	868.1	738.5	722.1
Goods: Imports f.o.b.	78abd	−337.7	−421.9	−673.0	−772.7	−763.6	−849.3	−862.4	−1,137.5	−1,519.7	−1,451.7	−1,257.3	−1,279.0	−1,257.1	−1,285.9	−1,351.7
Trade Balance	78acd	9.9	20.2	−36.2	121.1	−47.2	−68.8	−186.9	−268.9	−557.8	−263.7	−489.6	−493.8	−389.0	−547.4	−629.6
Services: Credit	78add	63.5	71.5	93.4	116.2	127.8	146.7	152.5	266.3	309.4	324.6	374.1	456.6	501.5	584.3	692.9
Services: Debit	78aed	−104.1	−142.0	−243.4	−236.3	−226.4	−247.7	−291.6	−346.8	−399.0	−366.7	−277.3	−298.6	−299.5	−274.5	−283.1
Balance on Goods & Services	78afd	−30.7	−50.3	−186.2	1.0	−145.8	−169.8	−326.0	−349.4	−647.4	−305.8	−392.8	−335.8	−187.0	−237.6	−219.8
Income: Credit	78agd	1.5	2.8	5.0	5.2	8.9	12.3	20.8	31.9	41.8	11.8	4.4	6.9	5.8	21.6	17.0
Income: Debit	78ahd	−48.4	−79.7	−94.8	−118.0	−118.1	−110.7	−156.5	−219.6	−318.8	−288.4	−259.2	−304.0	−247.2	−247.9	−266.7
Balance on Gds, Serv. & Inc.	78aid	−77.6	−127.2	−276.0	−111.8	−255.0	−268.2	−461.7	−537.1	−924.4	−582.4	−647.6	−632.9	−428.4	−463.9	−469.5
Current Transfers, n.i.e.: Credit	78ajd	34.3	34.0	37.9	41.3	127.5	141.5	150.2	207.5	204.8	193.0	205.0	215.0	265.0	356.3	286.1
Current Transfers: Debit	78akd	−3.7	−3.4	−2.9	−2.3	−1.7	−1.9	−.4	−1.7	−.3	—	—	—	—	—	—
Capital Account, n.i.e.	78bcd	—	—	—	—	—	—	—	—	—	—	—	—	—	—	—
Capital Account, n.i.e.: Credit	78bad	—	—	—	—	—	—	—	—	—	—	—	—	—	—	—
Capital Account: Debit	78bbd	—	—	—	—	—	—	—	—	—	—	—	—	—	—	—
Financial Account, n.i.e.	78bjd	93.6	69.9	239.6	179.2	166.9	194.0	121.6	308.4	626.1	413.0	147.2	−92.7	231.9	43.6	171.1
Direct Investment Abroad	78bdd	—	—	—	—	—	—	—	—	—	—	—	—	—	—	—
Dir. Invest. in Rep. Econ., n.i.e.	78bed	43.5	34.5	53.6	63.9	60.0	71.5	63.6	17.1	92.7	79.7	−1.4	48.2	68.5	36.2	50.0
Portfolio Investment Assets	78bfd	—	—	—	—	—	—	—	—	—	—	—	—	—	—	—
Equity Securities	78bkd	—	—	—	—	—	—	—	—	—	—	—	—	—	—	—
Debt Securities	78bld	—	—	—	—	—	—	—	—	—	—	—	—	—	—	—
Portfolio Investment Liab., n.i.e.	78bgd	—	—	—	—	—	—	—	—	—	—	—	—	—	—	—
Equity Securities	78bmd	—	—	—	—	—	—	—	—	—	—	—	—	—	—	—
Debt Securities	78bnd	—	—	—	—	—	—	—	—	—	—	—	—	—	—	—
Financial Derivatives Assets	78bwd	...	...	...	...	...	...	...	...	...	...	...	...	...	...	...
Financial Derivatives Liabilities	78bxd	...	...	...	...	...	...	...	...	...	...	...	...	...	...	...
Other Investment Assets	78bhd	−1.0	−1.4	−1.7	−7.2	−5.8	8.1	15.2	−17.3	10.7	6.4	−19.1	−4.9	−19.6	−64.2	34.2
Monetary Authorities	78bod	...	...	...	...	...	...	...	...	...	...	...	...	...	...	...
General Government	78bpd	−3.2	−2.5	—	—	3.7	−1.4	.2	−6.7	—	—	—	—	—	—	—
Banks	78bqd	2.2	1.1	−1.7	−7.2	−9.5	9.5	15.0	−10.6	10.7	6.4	−19.1	−4.9	−19.6	−64.2	34.2
Other Sectors	78brd	—	—	—	—	—	—	—	—	—	—	—	—	—	—	—
Other Investment Liab., n.i.e.	78bid	51.1	36.8	187.7	122.5	112.7	114.4	42.8	308.6	522.7	326.9	167.7	−136.0	183.0	71.6	86.9
Monetary Authorities	78bsd	3.4	3.5	4.3	39.7	−7.5	3.6	−39.3	−134.5	33.4	−26.7	−46.8	−153.2	−149.1	−73.3	−177.8
General Government	78btd	31.8	23.5	61.7	49.0	59.1	82.2	129.7	314.1	241.7	241.7	331.8	202.8	273.0	202.7	220.0
Banks	78bud	−3.0	14.7	32.1	−32.6	1.5	−.8	3.6	−19.2	−.2	34.9	−27.6	33.6	−4.4	−45.8	44.7
Other Sectors	78bvd	18.9	−4.9	89.6	66.4	59.6	29.4	−51.2	148.2	247.8	77.0	−89.7	−219.2	63.5	−12.0	—
Net Errors and Omissions	78cad	−32.8	50.4	1.5	−68.8	−70.9	−16.8	69.2	−73.5	48.0	−54.5	−31.1	10.6	29.7	155.7	82.3
Overall Balance	78cbd	13.8	23.7	.1	37.6	−33.2	48.6	−121.1	−96.4	−45.8	−30.9	−326.5	−500.0	98.2	91.7	70.0
Reserves and Related Items	79dad	−13.8	−23.7	−.1	−37.6	33.2	−48.6	121.1	96.4	45.8	30.9	326.5	500.0	−98.2	−91.7	−70.0
Reserve Assets	79dbd	2.4	−28.4	−4.1	−27.5	−10.4	−66.9	39.0	−72.3	39.5	−16.8	96.9	−46.3	−87.3	−91.9	−18.0
Use of Fund Credit and Loans	79dcd	−7.6	−4.5	—	—	24.8	17.4	—	75.4	−72.1	−22.0	49.9	185.3	−9.8	49.2	−26.1
Exceptional Financing	79ded	−8.6	9.2	4.0	−10.1	18.8	.9	82.1	93.2	78.4	69.7	179.7	361.1	−1.1	−49.0	−25.9

End of Period — Banking Survey

1987	1988	1989	1990	1991	1992	1993	1994	1995	1996	1997	1998	1999	2000	2001		Code
-1,474	-61	-514	-787	3,341	5,435	6,447	1,221	4,784	5,441	6,704	6,896	9,862	5,638	17,242	Foreign Assets (Net)	51n
8,967	11,538	15,552	19,003	22,654	26,080	29,577	38,644	43,277	53,828	67,384	80,036	101,998	124,148	149,960	Domestic Credit	52
646	980	709	967	-277	-2,388	-2,964	-276	-992	-652	496	1,543	3,474	6,205	7,995	Claims on Central Govt. (Net)	52an
17	17	10	7	6	3	5	6	29	4	6	4	14	29	32	Claims on Local Government	52b
1,079	1,285	1,458	1,468	2,433	2,020	2,180	4,440	3,994	6,134	6,110	5,944	7,254	5,386	5,439	Claims on Nonfin.Pub.Enterprises	52c
7,225	9,255	13,376	16,561	20,491	26,444	30,356	34,474	40,246	48,342	60,772	72,545	91,256	112,529	136,494	Claims on Private Sector	52d
6,590	9,524	12,319	17,105	23,287	29,582	35,488	39,401	46,103	54,392	67,464	79,043	96,033	112,057	141,543	Liquid Liabilities	55l
2,087	2,499	3,292	3,939	5,018	6,310	6,722	7,412	8,554	9,556	11,371	13,137	18,032	22,545	27,958	Bonds	56ab
156	211	126	138	646	518	196	743	1,991	4,099	4,357	3,499	5,135	4,369	3,276	Liabs.of Centl.Bank: Securities	56ac
6,013	8,762	8,574	16,414	18,113	16,354	16,593	11,972	11,765	12,607	12,295	13,381	13,571	13,823	13,285	Long-Term Foreign Liabilities	56cl
1,362	1,727	1,936	2,315	4,181	6,082	5,009	6,225	5,916	5,144	5,771	7,127	9,156	11,595	16,404	Capital Accounts	57a
-8,714	-11,246	-11,209	-21,695	-25,249	-27,331	-27,984	-25,889	-26,268	-26,529	-27,170	-29,255	-30,067	-34,603	-35,263	Other Items (Net)	57r

Percent Per Annum — Interest Rates

1987	1988	1989	1990	1991	1992	1993	1994	1995	1996	1997	1998	1999	2000	2001		Code
....	....	....	....	....	....	....	....	....	14.70	13.01	16.68	15.30	18.28	13.47	Money Market Rate	60b
....	....	....	....	6.20	5.58	5.00	4.87	4.66	5.00	4.74	4.51	4.54	4.29	4.29	Savings Rate	60k
....	....	....	....	20.02	16.70	14.04	13.70	14.94	13.91	13.40	17.65	16.07	17.65	15.61	Deposit Rate	60l
....	....	....	....	35.26	28.34	29.89	28.68	30.68	23.73	21.01	25.64	25.05	26.80	24.26	Lending Rate	60p

Period Averages — Prices and Labor

1987	1988	1989	1990	1991	1992	1993	1994	1995	1996	1997	1998	1999	2000	2001		Code
16.7	24.0	33.8	50.9	74.8	78.0	82.1	88.9	100.0	105.4	114.1	†119.7	127.4	137.2	149.4	Consumer Prices	64

Period Averages

1987	1988	1989	1990	1991	1992	1993	1994	1995	1996	1997	1998	1999	2000	2001		Code
....	....	....	....	....	....	....	....	3,008	2,920	3,594	....	....	....	....	Labor Force	67d
....	....	....	....	2,252	2,406	2,417	2,401	2,401	2,523	2,652	....	....	....	....	Employment	67e
....	....	....	....	548	612	599	457	452	†506	504	....	....	....	....	Unemployment	67c
....	....	....	....	19.7	20.3	19.9	16.0	15.9	†16.7	15.9	....	....	....	....	Unemployment Rate (%)	67r

Millions of US Dollars — International Transactions

1987	1988	1989	1990	1991	1992	1993	1994	1995	1996	1997	1998	1999	2000	2001		Code
711.3	889.7	924.4	734.5	658.3	562.4	511.0	644.0	872.1	945.5	1,017.4	880.2	805.2	966.2	804.8	Exports	70..d
1,591.5	1,608.0	1,963.8	1,792.8	1,728.8	2,174.6	2,118.4	2,991.7	3,164.2	3,580.7	4,192.0	4,896.6	5,206.8	6,416.1	5,936.9	Imports, f.o.b.	71.vd

1995=100

1987	1988	1989	1990	1991	1992	1993	1994	1995	1996	1997	1998	1999	2000	2001		Code
125	126	131	107	102	95	99	96	100	106	109	103	....	....	....	Volume of Exports	72

Indices of Unit Values in US Dollars

1987	1988	1989	1990	1991	1992	1993	1994	1995	1996	1997	1998	1999	2000	2001		Code
71	107	116	101	91	90	69	88	100	101	105	82	....	....	....	Unit Value of Exports	74..d

Minus Sign Indicates Debit — Balance of Payments

1987	1988	1989	1990	1991	1992	1993	1994	1995	1996	1997	1998	1999	2000	2001		Code
-364.1	-18.9	-327.3	-279.6	-157.3	-707.9	-532.9	-283.0	-182.8	-212.7	-163.0	-338.4	-429.2	-1,026.5	....	Current Account, n.i.e.	78ald
711.3	889.7	924.4	734.5	658.3	562.5	3,211.0	3,452.5	3,779.5	4,052.8	4,613.7	4,980.5	5,136.7	5,736.7	....	Goods: Exports f.o.b.	78aad
-1,591.5	-1,608.0	-1,963.8	-1,792.8	-1,728.8	-2,174.3	-4,654.2	-4,903.2	-5,170.4	-5,727.0	-6,608.7	-7,597.3	-8,041.1	-9,478.5	....	Goods: Imports f.o.b.	78abd
-880.2	-718.3	-1,039.4	-1,058.3	-1,070.5	-1,611.8	-1,443.2	-1,450.7	-1,390.9	-1,674.2	-1,995.0	-2,616.8	-2,904.4	-3,741.8	....	*Trade Balance*	78acd
852.0	1,013.4	1,041.1	1,097.2	1,198.7	1,348.6	1,537.1	1,787.9	1,951.3	2,140.0	2,446.6	2,501.5	2,850.3	3,227.6	....	Services: Credit	78add
-360.4	-397.0	-464.7	-440.4	-479.3	-555.1	-823.8	-921.1	-966.4	-1,121.4	-1,171.3	-1,319.5	-1,248.0	-1,373.3	....	Services: Debit	78aed
-388.6	-101.9	-463.0	-401.5	-351.1	-818.3	-729.9	-583.9	-406.0	-655.6	-719.7	-1,434.8	-1,302.1	-1,887.5	....	*Balance on Goods & Services*	78afd
11.6	8.5	107.1	86.3	87.2	54.7	103.6	101.4	128.1	130.3	140.4	168.2	218.3	299.7	....	Income: Credit	78agd
-317.7	-279.1	-355.8	-335.0	-279.9	-376.1	-800.6	-783.3	-897.1	-855.1	-935.8	-1,058.3	-1,193.2	-1,341.0	....	Income: Debit	78ahd
-694.7	-372.5	-711.7	-650.2	-543.8	-1,139.7	-1,426.9	-1,265.8	-1,175.0	-1,380.4	-1,515.1	-2,324.9	-2,277.0	-2,928.8	....	*Balance on Gds, Serv. & Inc.*	78aid
330.6	353.6	384.4	370.6	386.5	431.8	908.4	996.8	1,007.7	1,187.6	1,373.1	2,016.9	1,997.1	2,095.6	....	Current Transfers, n.i.e.: Credit	78ajd
—	—	—	—	—	—	-14.4	-14.0	-15.5	-19.9	-21.0	-30.4	-149.3	-193.3	....	Current Transfers: Debit	78akd
—	—	—	—	—	—	—	—	—	—	—	—	—	—	....	Capital Account, n.i.e.	78bcd
—	—	—	—	—	—	—	—	—	—	—	—	—	—	....	Capital Account, n.i.e.: Credit	78bad
—	—	—	—	—	—	—	—	—	—	—	—	—	—	....	Capital Account: Debit	78bbd
-27.5	-15.6	137.9	-73.8	-134.1	74.8	-226.6	368.0	253.6	64.1	447.6	688.1	1,061.0	1,596.6	....	Financial Account, n.i.e.	78bjd
....	....	....	....	....	....	....	....	....	....	....	....	....	....	....	Direct Investment Abroad	78bdd
89.0	106.1	110.0	132.8	145.0	179.7	189.3	206.8	414.3	96.5	420.6	699.8	1,337.8	952.9	....	Dir. Invest. in Rep. Econ., n.i.e.	78bed
—	—	—	—	—	—	-38.9	-2.9	-7.3	-5.6	-17.5	-433.0	268.4		....	Portfolio Investment Assets	78bfd
....	....	....	....	....	....	....	....	....	-4.0	-2.1	-13.7	-428.9	270.6	....	Equity Securities	78bkd
....	....	....	....	....	....	....	-38.9	-2.9	-3.3	-3.5	-3.8	-4.1	-2.2	....	Debt Securities	78bld
										-1.9	-3.8	-3.8	-3.9	....	Portfolio Investment Liab., n.i.e.	78bgd
....	....	....	....	....	....	....	....	....	....	....	....	....	....	....	Equity Securities	78bmd
										-1.9	-3.8	-3.8	-3.9	....	Debt Securities	78bnd
....	....	....	....	....	....	....	....	....	....	....	....	....	....	....	Financial Derivatives Assets	78bwd
....	....	....	....	....	....	....	....	....	....	....	....	....	....	....	Financial Derivatives Liabilities	78bxd
-34.7	-83.0	-98.0	89.3	-196.6	128.8	-49.2	176.8	-263.1	42.3	-220.1	-66.4	-53.4	-165.0	....	Other Investment Assets	78bhd
....	....	....	....	....	....	....	....	....	....	....	....	....	....	....	Monetary Authorities	78bod
							-15.2	-.6	-.9	-.9	-1.0	-1.0	-1.2	....	General Government	78bpd
-34.7	-83.0	82.0	-.7	-6.6	-1.2	-26.7	18.0	-39.0	17.0	-40.7	-53.2	-18.8	-64.4	....	Banks	78bqd
—	—	-180.0	90.0	-190.0	130.0	-22.5	174.0	-223.5	26.2	-178.5	-12.2	-33.6	-99.4	....	Other Sectors	78brd
-81.8	-38.7	125.9	-295.9	-82.5	-233.7	-366.7	23.3	105.3	-67.4	254.6	76.0	213.4	544.2	....	Other Investment Liab., n.i.e.	78bid
-244.3	-210.6	68.9	-255.5	-72.1	-131.6	-465.2	31.1	27.1	-22.8	-17.3	-88.7	-24.7	72.0	....	Monetary Authorities	78bsd
153.5	124.8	-4.2	-64.4	-20.0	-66.2	-75.9	-59.5	-18.8	-35.3	-64.2	-38.5	124.2	119.1	....	General Government	78btd
9.0	47.1	-3.8	40.8	-4.7	-12.7	-9.5	45.4	32.1	89.7	172.3	218.5	106.9	234.2	....	Banks	78bud
—	—	65.0	-16.8	14.3	-23.2	183.9	6.3	64.9	-99.0	163.8	-15.3	7.0	118.9	....	Other Sectors	78bvd
248.9	35.6	-73.6	-120.7	548.3	569.0	215.1	-596.0	75.3	108.8	-193.7	-338.6	-480.4	-618.5	....	Net Errors and Omissions	78cad
-142.7	1.1	-263.0	-474.1	256.9	-64.0	-544.4	-511.0	146.1	-39.8	90.9	11.1	151.4	-48.4	....	*Overall Balance*	78cbd
142.7	-1.1	263.0	474.1	-256.9	64.0	544.4	511.0	-146.1	39.8	-90.9	-11.1	-151.4	48.4	....	Reserves and Related Items	79dad
209.7	-58.9	90.0	49.0	-357.4	-63.5	-153.5	384.7	-131.2	15.2	-39.5	-98.2	-193.6	69.9	....	Reserve Assets	79dbd
-62.9	-51.2	-88.0	-56.9	15.9	37.3	63.9	-8.1	-34.0	-59.4	-62.4	26.8	—	—	....	Use of Fund Credit and Loans	79dcd
-4.1	109.0	261.0	482.0	84.6	90.2	634.0	134.4	19.1	84.1	11.0	60.3	42.2	-21.5	....	Exceptional Financing	79ded

Dominican Republic

		1972	1973	1974	1975	1976	1977	1978	1979	1980	1981	1982	1983	1984	1985	1986
Government Finance																*Millions of Pesos:*
Deficit (-) or Surplus	80	−7.3	−15.5	−26.0	12.5	29.5	3.4	−67.4	−268.8	−162.7	−141.8	−232.1	−214.2	−71.1	−205.1	125.8
Total Revenue and Grants	81y	316.8	361.0	474.2	652.4	584.7	629.3	596.2	690.8	890.8	926.0	755.6	925.4	1,173.5	1,638.8	2,352.7
Revenue	81	316.8	361.0	474.2	652.4	584.7	629.3	596.2	690.1	889.4	919.4	752.8	924.0	1,167.8	1,636.4	2,148.2
Grants	81z	—	—	—	—	—	—	—	.7	1.4	6.6	2.8	1.4	5.7	2.4	204.5
Exp. & Lending Minus Repay.	82z	....	....	....	....	....	....	....	959.6	1,053.5	1,067.8	987.7	1,139.6	1,244.6	1,843.9	2,226.9
Expenditure	82	324.1	376.5	500.2	639.9	555.2	625.9	663.6	897.9	1,053.5	1,067.9	988.8	1,136.1	1,236.9	1,829.3	2,222.7
Lending Minus Repayments	83	....	....	....	....	....	....	....	61.7	—	−.1	−1.1	3.5	7.7	14.6	4.2
Total Financing	80h	7.3	15.3	26.0	−12.6	−29.5	−3.5	67.4	268.8	162.7	141.7	232.2	214.2	71.1	205.2	−125.8
Domestic	84a	6.5	5.4	30.9	−6.7	−20.1	6.4	78.7	89.0	70.0	88.0	183.8	175.8	−26.2	−21.7	−264.8
Foreign	85a	.8	9.9	−4.9	−5.9	−9.4	−9.9	−11.3	179.8	92.7	53.7	48.4	38.4	97.3	226.9	139.0
National Accounts																*Millions of Pesos*
Househ.Cons.Expend.,incl.NPISHs	96f	1,449	1,685	2,139	2,496	3,083	3,589	3,659	4,034	5,109	5,163	5,986	7,180	9,145	12,562	13,606
Government Consumption Expend.	91f	178	194	292	222	152	189	271	420	504	693	779	786	871	1,112	1,297
Gross Fixed Capital Formation	93e	427	498	644	803	780	939	1,032	1,335	1,584	1,655	1,491	1,754	2,169	2,747	3,492
Changes in Inventories	93i	−35	20	45	79	101	60	98	60	82	61	99	62	34	52	85
Exports of Goods and Services	90c	411	513	730	1,009	840	918	828	1,135	1,271	1,513	1,142	1,962	3,780	4,088	4,041
Imports of Goods and Services (-)	98c	442	565	917	1,010	1,005	1,109	1,154	1,484	1,919	1,818	1,533	2,524	4,405	4,859	4,741
Gross Domestic Product (GDP)	99b	1,987	2,345	2,931	3,599	3,952	4,587	4,734	5,499	6,631	7,267	7,964	9,220	11,594	15,702	17,780
Net Primary Income from Abroad	98.n	−47	−77	−90	−113	−124	−123	−136	−188	−210	−277	−254	−475	−683	−706	−722
Gross National Income (GNI)	99a	1,941	2,268	2,841	3,486	3,828	4,464	4,599	5,311	6,421	6,990	7,710	8,745	10,911	14,996	17,058
Consumption of Fixed Capital	99cf	119	141	175	216	237	273	276	327	395	432	474	548	670	934	1,058
GDP Volume 1970 Prices	99b.p	1,818	2,053	2,176	2,289	2,443	2,565	2,620	2,738	2,904	3,022	3,069	3,280	3,322	3,251	3,366
GDP Volume (1995=100)	99bv p	39.7	44.8	47.5	50.0	53.4	56.0	57.2	59.8	63.4	66.0	67.0	71.6	72.5	71.0	73.5
GDP Deflator (1995=100)	99bi p	3.1	3.2	3.8	4.4	4.6	5.0	5.1	5.7	6.4	6.8	7.3	7.9	9.8	13.6	14.9
																Millions:
Population	99z	4.34	4.48	4.61	4.75	4.89	5.03	5.17	5.30	5.44	5.54	5.98	6.12	6.27	6.42	6.56

	1987	1988	1989	1990	1991	1992	1993	1994	1995	1996	1997	1998	1999	2000	2001		
																	Government Finance	
Year Ending December 31																		
	−69.5	−73.5	143.7	367.3	1,013.7	3,763.3	288.1	−690.6	1,720.3	540.6	2,038.0	2,109.8	−1,267.2	3,449.5	....	Deficit (-) or Surplus	**80**
	2,941.8	4,557.4	5,846.7	6,917.8	10,180.2	17,842.0	20,188.0	21,499.9	24,890.8	27,133.6	34,729.1	38,867.3	43,947.3	51,651.8	....	Total Revenue and Grants	**81y**
	2,877.0	4,424.1	5,785.7	6,867.8	10,113.3	17,572.0	19,776.1	21,482.3	24,890.8	26,921.3	34,729.1	38,564.8	43,483.6	51,271.3	....	Revenue	**81**
	64.8	133.3	61.0	50.0	66.9	270.0	411.9	17.6	—	212.3	—	302.5	463.7	380.5	....	Grants	**81z**
	3,011.3	4,630.9	5,703.0	6,550.5	9,166.5	14,078.7	19,899.9	22,190.5	23,170.5	26,593.0	32,691.1	36,757.5	45,214.5	48,202.3	....	Exp. & Lending Minus Repay.	**82z**
	3,009.3	4,626.7	5,701.4	6,548.2	9,165.2	14,078.7	19,899.9	22,190.5	23,170.5	26,593.0	32,691.1	36,757.5	45,164.5	48,202.3	....	Expenditure	**82**
	2.0	4.2	1.6	2.3	1.3	—	—	—	—	—	—	—	50.0	—	....	Lending Minus Repayments	**83**
	69.6	73.5	−143.7	−367.3	−1,013.7	−3,763.3	−288.1	690.6	−1,720.3	−540.6	−2,038.0	−2,110.0	1,217.1	−3,449.7	....	Total Financing	**80h**
	−62.4	240.7	−97.8	−294.5	−269.6	−2,225.7	1,708.5	2,522.1	1.8	1,289.3	379.2	−8.4	1,862.4	6.4	....	Domestic	**84a**
	132.0	−167.2	−45.9	−72.8	−744.1	−1,537.6	−1,996.6	−1,831.5	−1,722.1	−1,829.9	−2,417.6	−2,101.6	−645.4	−3,456.1	....	Foreign	**85a**
																	National Accounts	
Millions of Pesos																		
	17,410	24,844	33,674	47,290	80,651	96,532	96,467	109,023	127,819	147,252	166,323	187,557	209,068	250,209	....	Househ.Cons.Expend.,incl.NPISHs	**96f**
	1,205	1,164	1,243	1,765	2,451	3,480	5,398	6,692	8,331	10,413	16,403	19,418	22,463	26,503	....	Government Consumption Expend.	**91f**
	5,319	7,533	10,800	13,907	17,543	22,723	28,771	29,020	31,146	34,230	41,945	56,026	66,593	75,925	....	Gross Fixed Capital Formation	**93e**
	118	95	122	174	278	325	351	396	468	529	620	697	802	931	....	Changes in Inventories	**93i**
	5,847	11,327	13,003	18,460	23,717	24,175	59,703	67,847	77,150	84,621	100,513	113,752	127,887	146,749	....	Exports of Goods and Services	**90c**
	7,495	12,112	16,449	23,270	28,307	34,537	68,883	75,412	82,632	93,513	110,739	135,542	148,647	177,451	....	Imports of Goods and Services (-)	**98c**
	22,404	32,851	42,393	60,305	96,333	112,698	121,808	137,566	162,283	183,532	215,064	241,908	278,164	322,866	....	Gross Domestic Product (GDP)	**99b**
	−1,160	−1,572	−1,946	−716	−1,862	−3,893	−8,761	−8,851	−10,405	−9,966	−11,342	−13,565	−15,616	−17,056	....	Net Primary Income from Abroad	**98.n**
	21,244	31,278	40,447	59,589	94,472	108,804	113,047	128,715	151,878	173,566	203,722	228,343	262,547	305,809	....	Gross National Income (GNI)	**99a**
	1,332	1,971	2,544	3,618	5,780	6,762	7,309	8,254	9,737	11,012	12,904	14,514	16,690	19,372	....	Consumption of Fixed Capital	**99cf**
	3,706	3,786	3,953	3,737	3,772	4,073	4,194	4,375	4,579	4,907	5,315	5,701	6,156	6,633	....	GDP Volume 1970 Prices	**99b.p**
	80.9	82.7	86.3	81.6	82.4	88.9	91.6	95.5	100.0	107.2	116.1	124.5	134.4	144.9	....	GDP Volume (1995=100)	**99bv p**
	17.1	24.5	30.3	45.5	72.1	78.1	81.9	88.7	100.0	105.5	114.2	119.7	127.5	137.3	....	GDP Deflator (1995=100)	**99bi p**
Midyear Estimates																		
	6.71	6.87	7.02	7.11	7.32	7.47	7.62	7.77	7.71	7.83	7.97	8.10	8.32	8.40	8.53	**Population**	**99z**

(See notes in the back of the book.)

Ecuador

		1972	1973	1974	1975	1976	1977	1978	1979	1980	1981	1982	1983	1984	1985	1986
Exchange Rates																*Sucres per SDR:*
Principal Rate	aa	27.1	30.2	30.6	29.3	29.0	30.4	32.6	32.9	31.9	29.1	36.6	56.6	65.8	105.2	179.2
																Sucres per US Dollar:
Principal Rate	ae	25.0	25.0	25.0	25.0	25.0	25.0	25.0	25.0	25.0	25.0	33.2	54.1	67.2	95.8	146.5
Principal Rate	rf	25.0	25.0	25.0	25.0	25.0	25.0	25.0	25.0	25.0	25.0	30.0	44.1	62.5	69.6	122.8
																Index Numbers (1995=100):
Principal Rate	ahx	10,223.6	275.6	10,223.6	10,223.6	10,223.6	10,223.6	10,223.6	10,223.6	10,223.6	10,223.6	8,673.7	5,943.5	4,107.0	3,710.1	2,129.7
Nominal Effective Exchange Rate	ne c	....	....	....	....	....	....	....	1,463.5	1,547.2	1,728.1	1,646.5	1,209.1	855.7	789.7	577.5
Real Effective Exchange Rate	re c	....	....	....	....	....	....	....	175.2	196.4	191.9	183.3	152.2	157.4	127.1
Fund Position																*Millions of SDRs:*
Quota	2f. s	33.0	33.0	33.0	33.0	33.0	33.0	70.0	70.0	105.0	105.0	105.0	150.7	150.7	150.7	150.7
SDRs	1b. s	6.7	5.6	6.5	6.3	6.3	8.2	10.6	19.2	19.0	28.9	—	.1	.5	26.2	45.7
Reserve Position in the Fund	1c. s	—	5.6	9.2	13.2	—	—	8.0	9.4	21.8	24.8	—	11.4			
Total Fund Cred.&Loans Outstg.	2tl	8.3	—	—	—	—	—	—	—	—	—	—	203.5	242.9	327.3	397.7
International Liquidity														*Millions of US Dollars Unless Otherwise Indicated:*		
Total Reserves minus Gold	1l. d	121.1	210.4	318.6	253.4	477.4	623.1	635.8	722.0	1,013.0	632.4	304.2	644.5	611.2	718.2	644.1
SDRs	1b. s	7.3	6.7	7.9	7.4	7.3	10.0	13.8	25.2	24.2	33.6	—	.1	.5	28.8	55.9
Reserve Position in the Fund	1c. d		6.8	11.3	15.5	—	—	10.4	12.4	27.8	28.8	—	12.0			
Foreign Exchange	1d. d	113.8	196.9	299.4	230.5	470.1	613.1	611.5	684.4	961.0	570.0	304.2	632.4	610.7	689.4	588.2
Gold (Million Fine Troy Ounces)	1ad	.355	.386	.386	.386	.386	.400	.407	.414	.414	.414	.414	.414	.414	.414	.414
Gold (National Valuation)	1an d	12.4	16.3	16.3	16.3	16.3	16.9	17.2	17.5	17.5	17.5	124.3	124.3	124.3	124.3	124.3
Monetary Authorities: Other Liab.	4.. d	9.4	13.9	62.9	62.9	80.6	99.7	84.2	153.2	227.5	115.0	245.6	1,286.1	2,043.8	3,532.8	2,501.3
Deposit Money Banks: Assets	7a. d	4.6	9.7	14.3	25.7	43.9	74.2	79.8	96.9	115.4	135.6	127.6	171.7	73.5	63.6	65.6
Liabilities	7b. d	4.4	6.4	10.7	14.2	21.8	31.8	33.2	43.0	40.3	58.1	40.7	42.7	64.3	51.6	53.1
Other Banking Insts.: Assets	7e. d	....	....	....												
Liabilities	7f. d	7.4	8.6	10.0	15.7	18.8	37.7	21.6	24.0	32.5	38.5	47.2	44.6	43.0	46.0	113.4
Monetary Authorities																*Millions of US Dollars:*
Foreign Assets	11	142.3	234.9	349.8	286.2	473.5	643.8	675.0	778.2	1,079.9	678.6	454.9	799.7	747.9	874.2	516.3
Claims on Central Government	12a	169.5	177.4	251.2	240.2	238.3	208.2	166.5	162.8	149.9	140.9	115.3	1,329.7	1,260.3	1,467.4	972.0
Claims on State & Local Govts.	12b	23.0	35.7	81.7	103.2	.7	.4	.3	.8	.4	.2	.2	.2	.1	.1	
Claims on Nonfin.Pub.Enterprises	12c	—	—	—	—	—	—	—	.9	.8	6.8	.5	.3	.2	.1	.1
Claims on Private Sector	12d	42.2	42.3	56.2	87.1	133.2	162.0	234.7	342.6	455.4	693.6	492.7	351.5	357.8	257.3	131.7
Claims on Deposit Money Banks	12e	2.6	4.3	16.1	30.6	52.9	103.1	200.8	267.6	360.8	569.8	653.4	881.7	1,183.4	854.4	608.5
Claims on Other Banking Insts.	12f	20.1	29.9	74.1	140.2	172.7	156.5	160.3	212.4	305.9	457.1	418.7	527.1	789.1	666.2	525.3
Reserve Money	14	258.3	364.5	515.9	513.1	622.2	755.6	883.9	1,134.0	1,282.9	1,385.0	1,133.5	836.3	937.6	852.8	749.8
of which: Currency Outside DMBs	14a	115.6	144.7	191.1	215.4	302.8	365.1	411.0	493.5	611.4	696.5	619.0	469.9	525.7	446.0	372.7
Liabs. of Central Bank: Securities	16ac	.1	14.4	7.3	13.1	19.0	67.2	64.5	60.0	70.9	45.3	59.6	27.8	15.6	58.3	36.1
Foreign Liabilities	16c	18.3	13.9	62.9	62.9	80.6	99.7	84.2	153.2	227.5	115.0	245.6	637.5	577.5	699.9	731.7
Long-Term Foreign Liabilities	16cl										—	—	861.7	1,704.4	3,192.5	2,256.0
Central Government Deposits	16d	61.9	105.7	179.9	230.8	207.4	217.9	314.5	249.5	301.8	454.8	197.5	1,535.2	1,849.5	1,040.3	630.5
Capital Accounts	17a	16.0	20.3	41.4	40.4	48.0	40.8	58.3	71.9	146.7	181.0	83.3	-378.4	-1,127.9	-1,906.8	-1,538.3
Other Items (Net)	17r	45.1	5.6	21.7	27.3	94.1	92.9	32.2	96.8	323.4	366.1	416.2	370.2	382.2	182.8	-112.0
Deposit Money Banks																*Millions of US Dollars:*
Reserves	20	98.5	132.5	185.0	214.7	286.3	339.0	383.2	407.2	507.2	493.0	406.6	312.7	461.1	372.9	320.1
Claims on Mon.Author.: Securities	20c	—	2.1	2.3	2.8	3.7	5.0	6.7	8.6	10.9	14.4	13.1	9.4	9.2	7.5	6.1
Foreign Assets	21	4.6	9.7	14.3	25.7	43.9	74.2	79.8	96.9	115.4	135.6	127.6	171.7	73.5	63.6	65.6
Claims on Central Government	22a	1.6	2.7	5.0	5.1	6.1	5.2	2.2	2.0	1.9	1.2	.7	.4	.2	20.5	25.0
Claims on State & Local Govts.	22b	.3	.2	.5	.5	.6	1.3	1.0	.9	.8	.7	.4	.2	.1	.1	—
Claims on Nonfin.Pub.Enterprises	22c	....														
Claims on Private Sector	22d	248.3	302.0	390.2	485.1	637.1	868.8	1,065.3	1,341.7	1,694.9	2,150.7	2,314.2	2,411.2	2,605.3	2,292.4	1,766.9
Claims on Other Banking Insts.	22f	6.7	10.5	12.2	14.1	16.2	19.9	21.8	24.5	28.1	32.8	32.6	25.2	29.5	33.0	31.6
Demand Deposits	24	165.1	217.1	319.7	373.5	513.5	632.5	724.7	848.0	1,119.0	1,238.3	1,125.3	912.7	1,077.1	958.0	715.6
Time, Savings,& Fgn.Currency Dep.	25	102.2	124.3	157.8	165.9	201.1	221.4	240.1	275.0	334.0	362.5	364.3	305.6	420.1	516.5	478.9
Bonds	26ab	73.5	84.9	101.5	133.6	162.3	185.5	214.8	252.7	350.9	455.1	417.2	317.4	383.4	699.9	613.0
Foreign Liabilities	26c	4.4	6.4	10.7	14.2	21.8	31.8	33.2	43.0	40.3	58.1	40.7	42.7	64.3	51.6	53.1
Long-Term Foreign Liabilities	26cl	....														
Central Government Deposits	26d															
Credit from Monetary Authorities	26g	2.4	4.4	8.6	21.8	36.8	162.3	214.7	270.9	359.4	545.6	625.6	1,086.7	1,143.1	750.4	517.5
Liabilities to Other Banking Insts	26i											3.9	8.5	8.2	9.7	13.2	13.2
Capital Accounts	27a	39.6	46.9	56.5	75.2	93.9	123.4	168.3	220.4	280.7	363.6	323.1	253.6	279.6	267.1	248.0
Other Items (Net)	27r	-27.2	-24.3	-45.2	-36.1	-35.7	-43.4	-35.8	-28.1	-125.1	-198.8	-9.3	3.7	-198.3	-466.7	-424.1
Monetary Survey																*Millions of US Dollars:*
Foreign Assets (Net)	31n	124.1	224.2	290.4	234.9	414.9	586.5	637.5	679.0	927.5	641.2	296.2	291.2	179.7	186.4	-203.0
Domestic Credit	32	449.8	494.9	691.3	844.8	997.5	1,204.4	1,337.6	1,839.1	2,336.3	3,029.2	3,177.9	3,110.5	3,193.2	3,696.8	2,822.1
Claims on Central Govt. (Net)	32an	109.1	74.3	76.3	14.5	37.1	-4.5	-145.7	-84.7	-150.0	-312.7	-81.4	-205.1	-589.0	447.7	366.5
Claims on State and Local Govts	32b	23.3	35.9	82.2	103.7	1.3	1.7	1.4	1.7	1.2	.9	.6	.4	.3	.2	—
Claims on Nonfin.Pub.Enterprises	32c								.9	.8	6.8	.5	.3	.2	.1	.1
Claims on Private Sector	32d	290.5	344.3	446.4	572.2	770.2	1,030.8	1,299.9	1,684.3	2,150.3	2,844.4	2,806.9	2,762.7	2,963.1	2,549.7	1,898.6
Claims on Other Banking Insts	32f	26.8	40.4	86.3	154.3	188.9	176.4	182.1	236.9	334.0	489.9	451.3	552.3	818.6	699.1	556.9
Money	34	334.9	448.9	666.6	711.3	876.5	1,142.5	1,253.7	1,589.6	1,968.9	2,207.9	1,897.7	1,533.3	1,723.9	1,518.6	1,191.6
Quasi-Money	35	103.8	125.3	166.7	189.6	400.9	400.5	415.3	588.8	833.4	869.2	1,009.3	828.8	1,086.6	867.0	725.0
Bonds	36ab	73.5	84.9	101.5	133.6	162.3	185.5	214.8	252.7	350.9	455.1	417.2	317.4	383.4	699.9	613.0
Liabs. of Central Bank: Securities	36ac	.1	12.3	5.0	10.3	15.3	62.2	57.8	51.4	60.0	30.9	46.5	18.4	6.5	50.8	30.1
Long-Term Foreign Liabilities	36cl	—	—	—	—	—	—	—	—	—	—	—	861.7	1,704.4	3,192.5	2,256.0
Liabilities to Other Banking Insts	36i											3.9	8.5	8.2	9.7	13.2	13.2
Capital Accounts	37a	55.6	67.2	97.9	115.5	142.0	164.2	226.6	292.3	427.4	544.7	406.4	-124.8	-848.3	-1,639.7	-1,290.3
Other Items (Net)	37r	6.0	-19.5	-55.9	-80.7	-184.5	-163.9	-193.2	-256.6	-376.7	-441.2	-311.3	-41.3	-693.1	-819.0	-919.4
Money plus Quasi-Money	35l	438.7	574.2	833.3	900.9	1,277.3	1,543.0	1,669.0	2,178.4	2,802.2	3,077.0	2,907.0	2,362.1	2,810.4	2,385.6	1,916.6

Ecuador

	1987	1988	1989	1990	1991	1992	1993	1994	1995	1996	1997	1998	1999	2000	2001		
Exchange Rates																	
End of Period																	
Principal Rate	314.2	582.0	852.1	1,249.4	1,817.5	2,535.8	2,807.3	3,312.4	4,345.8	5,227.0	5,974.5	9,609.8	27,783.7	32,572.8	31,418.3	aa
End of Period (ae) Period Average (rf)																	
Principal Rate	221.5	432.5	648.4	878.2	1,270.6	1,844.3	2,043.8	2,269.0	2,923.5	3,635.0	4,428.0	6,825.0	20,243.0	25,000.0	25,000.0	ae
Principal Rate	170.5	301.6	526.3	767.8	1,046.2	1,534.0	1,919.1	2,196.7	2,564.5	3,189.5	3,998.3	5,446.6	11,786.8	24,988.4	25,000.0	rf
Period Averages																	
Principal Rate	1,528.3	899.5	492.2	335.7	245.5	170.9	132.7	116.5	100.0	81.5	63.9	47.9	23.4	10.2	10.2	ahx
Nominal Effective Exchange Rate	384.1	223.1	192.7	163.4	138.2	109.1	107.6	115.4	100.0	83.2	70.3	53.9	27.5	12.7	13.2	ne c
Real Effective Exchange Rate	97.0	72.9	84.5	76.1	80.6	81.0	94.8	101.6	100.0	99.3	106.7	107.7	80.3	73.2	102.3	re c
Fund Position																	
End of Period																	
Quota	150.7	150.7	150.7	150.7	150.7	219.2	219.2	219.2	219.2	219.2	219.2	219.2	302.3	302.3	302.3	2f. s
SDRs	.7	1.0	.7	10.3	28.9	.1	3.2	3.0	2.1	1.9	.4	.2	1.7	.2	1.8	1b. s
Reserve Position in the Fund						17.1	17.1	17.1	17.2	17.2	17.2	17.2	17.2	17.2	17.2	1c. s
Total Fund Cred.&Loans Outstg.	345.2	300.7	247.2	186.0	127.5	72.6	51.8	135.7	116.7	100.9	98.9	49.5	—	—	113.3	151.1	2tl
International Liquidity																	
End of Period																	
Total Reserves minus Gold	491.1	397.6	540.4	838.5	924.3	868.2	1,379.9	1,844.2	1,627.6	1,858.5	2,092.8	1,619.7	1,642.4	947.0	839.8	1l. d
SDRs	.9	1.3	.9	14.7	41.4	.1	4.3	4.3	3.1	2.7	.5	.1	2.3	2.3	2.3	1b. d
Reserve Position in the Fund						23.6	23.5	25.0	25.5	24.7	23.1	24.2	23.5	22.3	21.6	1c. d
Foreign Exchange	490.2	396.3	539.5	823.8	882.9	844.5	1,352.1	1,814.9	1,599.0	1,831.1	2,069.1	1,595.4	1,616.5	924.3	815.9	1d. d
Gold (Million Fine Troy Ounces)	.414	.414	.414	.443	.443	.443	.414	.414	.414	.414	.414	.414	†.845	.845	.845	1ad
Gold (National Valuation)	165.7	165.7	165.7	165.7	165.7	165.7	165.6	165.6	166.6	166.6	166.7	166.7	245.4	232.7	233.8	1an d
Monetary Authorities: Other Liab.	1,635.0	3,343.1	2,214.8	3,513.6	4,484.7	4,119.3	4,109.6	4,003.3	196.2	178.7	147.1	430.3	673.6	252.9	185.5	4.. d
Deposit Money Banks: Assets	67.2	63.1	66.2	90.5	98.8	138.0	153.5	303.4	373.5	544.2	867.3	901.4	740.8	813.1	1,007.1	7a. d
Liabilities	88.2	55.3	54.5	261.3	263.2	307.4	207.7	572.7	792.5	849.5	1,317.1	1,484.4	853.8	588.9	506.5	7b. d
Other Banking Insts.: Assets	....	....	....	8.5	16.2	24.1	26.9	50.8	24.8	17.0	71.6	30.7	8.0	6.3	6.0	7e. d
Liabilities	178.3	200.8	195.4	109.8	109.9	117.6	183.4	272.0	281.8	380.3	479.3	545.8	8.1	6.3	5.8	7f. d
Monetary Authorities																	
End of Period																	
Foreign Assets	267.9	548.3	452.7	†444.2	353.1	229.7	1,489.3	1,986.6	1,746.7	1,992.2	2,254.8	†1,696.9	†1,458.9	1,516.0	1,539.1	11
Claims on Central Government	832.6	1,491.0	974.3	†706.7	740.2	671.1	3,924.6	4,021.3	194.7	166.1	129.0	†289.5	†1,479.2	1,425.0	1,278.8	12a
Claims on State & Local Govts.	—	—	—	†					—	—	—	†	†	—	—	12b
Claims on Nonfin.Pub.Enterprises	—	—	—	†.3	.2	.2	.1	.1	—	—	—	†	†	—	—	12c
Claims on Private Sector	72.5	55.7	73.4	†56.8	24.0	14.3	14.6	21.2	6.1	8.2	7.2	†17.6	†1.8	3.6	2.9	12d
Claims on Deposit Money Banks	398.9	165.8	99.5	†146.2	108.8	93.3	73.1	13.7	132.6	267.0	44.8	†897.9	†419.3	333.3	341.6	12e
Claims on Other Banking Insts.	357.6	181.9	156.3	†38.3	31.5	10.6	4.9	2.0	53.3	.4		†10.8	†5.1	5.7	32.1	12f
Reserve Money	692.3	596.0	580.9	†765.5	727.4	821.4	1,207.2	1,237.8	1,120.3	1,198.6	1,285.0	†1,007.0	†914.7	589.6	626.9	14
of which: Currency Outside DMBs	337.6	286.6	271.9	†310.6	302.2	323.9	417.8	494.7	470.6	517.8	538.5	†426.6	†576.3	31.7	21.8	14a
Liabs. of Central Bank: Securities	147.5	117.6	95.7	†70.9	70.0	69.0	88.5	36.0	19.8	9.4	.4	†305.6	†341.8	6.2	54.7	16ac
Foreign Liabilities	636.6	766.0	462.2	†324.6	220.1	124.3	245.4	257.3	190.8	165.2	156.0	†86.1	†178.4	82.0	182.5	16c
Long-Term Foreign Liabilities	1,488.1	2,981.7	2,077.4	†1,500.4	1,338.9	846.6	3,905.6	3,993.6	178.8	158.2	124.9	†413.8	†495.2	318.5	193.0	16cl
Central Government Deposits	386.2	421.1	408.8	†561.3	405.3	413.0	627.0	816.1	634.1	699.4	600.5	†373.5	†388.7	887.9	818.0	16d
Capital Accounts	-1,233.5	-2,430.2	-1,763.9	†-1683.0	-1,381.4	57.1	303.1	344.6	331.8	533.1	448.8	†1,169.7	†1,295.6	1,570.7	1,530.2	17a
Other Items (Net)	-188.1	-9.5	-104.9	†-147.1	-122.6	-1,312.2	-870.2	-640.5	-342.3	-330.0	-179.9	†-443.0	†-250.0	-171.4	-210.6	17r
Deposit Money Banks																	
End of Period																	
Reserves	247.8	235.7	229.9	†282.6	299.5	324.0	391.1	360.7	405.4	502.7	536.7	†631.5	†169.9	210.0	235.8	20
Claims on Mon.Author.: Securities	6.5	5.3	4.7	†5.6	20.6	47.0	37.0	36.0	19.8	9.4	.4	†.1	†177.3	6.2	8.3	20c
Foreign Assets	67.2	63.1	66.2	†91.0	99.6	137.9	153.2	304.5	373.5	544.1	866.7	†901.4	†740.8	813.1	1,007.1	21
Claims on Central Government	2.6	2.9	.5	†12.9	8.3	10.6	29.1	52.0	126.7	210.6	382.4	†856.9	†382.2	352.4	517.7	22a
Claims on State & Local Govts.	—	—	—	†					—	—	—	†	†	—	—	22b
Claims on Nonfin.Pub.Enterprises	....	....	....	33.0	20.5	8.7	21.3	—	—	—	—	†	†	—	—	22c
Claims on Private Sector	1,520.3	910.7	832.2	†1,083.2	1,286.0	1,429.4	2,317.5	3,732.9	4,312.3	4,531.6	5,540.8	†5,663.5	†3,998.3	4,304.2	5,514.1	22d
Claims on Other Banking Insts.	31.0	25.5	23.9	†28.4	39.4	37.2	23.7	7.0	188.9	341.8	23.7	†86.4	†59.5	40.0	13.4	22f
Demand Deposits	613.9	465.7	431.2	†529.6	546.1	556.4	804.5	977.4	765.9	819.1	883.3	†729.0	†614.9	996.7	1,552.7	24
Time, Savings,& Fgn.Currency Dep.	522.9	412.2	407.7	†925.7	1,073.0	1,214.1	1,720.5	2,601.2	3,287.2	3,998.8	4,410.6	†3,854.0	†2,286.2	2,669.9	2,987.0	25
Bonds	530.9	321.3	323.7	†60.9	50.5	49.9	51.1	40.5	150.3	411.6	508.3	†329.9	†155.8	113.4	104.0	26ab
Foreign Liabilities	88.2	55.3	54.5	†34.3	35.6	56.6	89.6	428.3	662.1	694.3	1,117.9	†1,360.6	†851.7	587.6	505.2	26c
Long-Term Foreign Liabilities	....	....	....	228.6	229.7	250.7	117.7	146.5	130.7	155.0	198.3	†123.8	†2.2	1.3	1.3	26cl
Central Government Deposits									2.6	4.1	6.5	†73.4	†48.0	128.6	222.8	26d
Credit from Monetary Authorities	331.2	134.4	70.4	†133.8	107.5	91.5	88.0	25.5	135.4	132.9	5.4	†744.5	†310.7	136.2	168.8	26g
Liabilities to Other Banking Insts	17.4	12.5	9.3	†17.7	17.7	19.0	54.0	128.7	209.1	23.3	18.1	†34.5	†89.7	137.7	138.2	26i
Capital Accounts	223.9	193.7	192.6	†262.6	352.1	410.7	657.1	961.7	1,274.5	1,447.5	1,760.1	†1,719.8	†1,132.5	1,136.9	1,236.8	27a
Other Items (Net)	-453.0	-351.9	-332.2	†-656.4	-638.2	-654.0	-609.6	-816.6	-1,191.1	-1,546.4	-1,557.6	†-829.9	†36.5	-182.6	379.8	27r
Monetary Survey																	
End of Period																	
Foreign Assets (Net)	-389.7	-209.9	2.1	†176.3	197.0	186.7	1,307.4	1,605.5	1,267.4	1,676.8	1,847.7	†1,151.6	†1,169.7	1,659.5	1,858.6	31n
Domestic Credit	2,430.0	2,246.7	1,651.7	†1,398.5	1,744.9	1,769.0	5,708.8	7,020.4	4,245.2	4,555.2	5,476.2	†6,477.8	†5,489.3	5,114.3	6,318.3	32
Claims on Central Govt. (Net)	448.6	1,072.8	566.0	†158.4	343.1	268.7	3,326.7	3,257.1	-315.4	-326.7	-95.6	†699.5	†1,424.6	760.9	755.7	32an
Claims on State and Local Govts	—	—	—	†					—	—	—	†.1	†	—	—	32b
Claims on Nonfin.Pub.Enterprises	—	—	—	†33.3	20.7	8.9	21.4	.1	—	—	—	†	†	—	—	32c
Claims on Private Sector	1,592.8	966.5	905.5	†1,140.0	1,310.0	1,443.7	2,332.1	3,754.1	4,318.4	4,539.8	5,548.0	†5,681.1	†4,000.1	4,307.7	5,517.0	32d
Claims on Other Banking Insts	388.6	207.4	180.2	†66.7	70.9	47.8	28.6	9.1	242.2	342.2	23.8	†97.2	†64.6	45.7	45.6	32f
Money	1,061.3	830.0	796.1	†975.3	988.6	1,010.8	1,492.8	1,781.2	1,420.0	1,471.7	1,570.9	†1,330.7	†1,338.0	1,355.7	1,905.5	34
Quasi-Money	784.4	640.7	570.0	†1,058.3	1,177.3	1,259.7	1,847.6	2,779.3	3,419.0	4,121.3	4,523.9	†3,854.0	†2,286.2	2,669.9	2,987.0	35
Bonds	530.9	321.3	323.7	†60.9	50.5	49.9	51.1	40.5	150.3	411.6	508.3	†635.5	†155.8	113.4	104.0	36ab
Liabs. of Central Bank: Securities	141.0	112.3	90.9	†65.4	49.4	22.0	51.4	—	—	—	—	†305.5	†164.4		46.4	36ac
Long-Term Foreign Liabilities	1,488.1	2,981.7	2,077.4	†1,729.0	1,568.5	1,097.4	4,023.3	4,140.1	309.4	313.1	323.3	†537.7	†497.4	319.8	194.3	36cl
Liabilities to Other Banking Insts	17.4	12.5	9.3	†17.7	17.7	19.0	54.0	128.7	209.1	23.3	18.1	†34.5	†104.5	154.1	150.5	36i
Capital Accounts	-1,009.5	-2,236.5	-1,571.3	†-1420.4	-1,029.3	467.8	960.1	1,306.2	1,606.3	1,980.7	2,208.8	†2,889.5	†2,428.1	2,707.6	2,767.0	37a
Other Items (Net)	-973.3	-625.2	-642.4	†-911.2	-880.9	-1,970.6	-1,464.2	-1,550.2	-1,601.4	-2,089.8	-1,829.4	†-1958.0	†-315.4	-546.7	22.3	37r
Money plus Quasi-Money	1,845.8	1,470.7	1,366.2	†2,033.6	2,165.9	2,270.4	3,340.4	4,560.5	4,838.9	5,593.0	6,094.8	†5,184.7	†3,624.2	4,025.6	4,892.4	35l

Ecuador

Other Banking Institutions		1972	1973	1974	1975	1976	1977	1978	1979	1980	1981	1982	1983	1984	1985	1986
														Millions of US Dollars:		
Reserves	40	9.6	10.8	18.1	13.6	25.4	29.8	39.8	41.6	55.1	83.2	30.2	36.0	23.5	26.2	32.7
Claims on Mon.Author.: Securities	40c	....	....	....	....	....	....	....	....	....	....	....	....	....	....	....
Foreign Assets	41	....	....	....	....	....	....	....	....	....	....	....	....	....	....	....
Claims on Central Government	42a	—	—	—	—	—	—	—	—	—	—	—	—	—	—	—
Claims on State & Local Govts.	42b	—	—	—	—	—	—	—	—	—	—	—	—	—	—	—
Claims on Nonfin.Pub.Enterprises	42c	—	—	—	—	—	—	—	—	—	—	—	—	—	—	—
Claims on Private Sector	42d	83.5	115.6	217.0	316.8	389.7	418.3	448.9	468.0	529.2	617.1	445.9	410.9	474.7	484.2	533.1
Claims on Deposit Money Banks	42e	.3	11.7	17.4	25.5	29.9	44.4	50.0	52.4	50.9	59.0	55.5	35.9	35.0	35.2	28.2
Demand Deposits	44	16.9	25.1	53.5	65.3	94.7	111.7	101.7	103.1	139.8	184.8	134.9	112.2	112.8	107.2	94.2
Time, Savings,& Fgn.Currency Dep.	45	12.4	19.8	32.6	33.7	42.6	51.5	51.9	61.8	67.4	79.6	60.1	49.5	69.9	71.9	62.9
Bonds	46ab	.3	.1	.1	—	—	—	—	—	1.9	21.2	34.3	42.6	60.6	57.5	80.8
Foreign Liabilities	46c	....	....	....	....	....	....	....	....	....	....	....	....	....	....	....
Long-Term Foreign Liabilities	46cl	7.4	8.6	10.0	15.7	18.8	37.7	21.6	24.0	32.5	38.5	47.2	44.6	43.0	46.0	113.4
Credit from Monetary Authorities	46g	21.2	34.2	79.3	136.8	178.2	132.2	121.7	151.0	185.2	215.3	167.9	142.3	140.9	152.1	157.8
Credit from Deposit Money Banks	46h	6.7	8.5	12.5	15.2	18.2	23.2	22.7	13.6	25.0	30.4	24.4	17.2	18.2	19.5	12.1
Capital Accounts	47a	29.4	35.7	70.4	88.2	117.0	133.7	217.4	204.1	198.6	217.2	147.3	100.7	136.6	169.1	108.4
Other Items (Net)	47r	-.9	6.2	-6.0	1.1	-24.4	2.7	1.6	4.4	-15.3	-27.8	-84.5	-26.2	-48.8	-77.6	-35.5
Banking Survey														*Millions of US Dollars:*		
Foreign Assets (Net)	51n	124.1	224.2	290.4	234.9	414.9	586.5	637.5	679.0	927.5	641.2	296.2	291.2	179.7	186.4	-203.0
Domestic Credit	52	506.5	570.1	822.0	1,007.3	1,198.3	1,446.4	1,604.4	2,070.2	2,531.5	3,156.4	3,172.5	2,969.1	2,849.3	3,481.9	2,798.4
Claims on Central Govt. (Net)	52an	109.1	74.3	76.3	14.5	37.1	-4.5	-145.7	-84.7	-150.0	-312.7	-81.4	-205.1	-589.0	447.7	366.5
Claims on State and Local Govts	52b	23.3	35.9	82.2	103.7	1.3	1.7	1.4	1.7	1.2	.9	.6	.4	.3	.2	—
Claims on Nonfin.Pub.Enterprises	52c	—	—	—	—	—	—	—	.9	.8	6.8	.5	.3	.2	.1	.1
Claims on Private Sector	52d	374.1	459.9	663.4	889.0	1,159.9	1,449.2	1,748.8	2,152.3	2,679.4	3,461.4	3,252.8	3,173.6	3,437.8	3,034.0	2,431.8
Liquid Liabilities	55l	458.4	608.2	901.3	986.3	1,389.2	1,676.3	1,782.9	2,301.7	2,954.4	3,258.2	3,071.7	2,487.8	2,969.7	2,538.4	2,040.9
Bonds	56ab	73.8	99.5	108.9	146.8	181.3	252.7	279.3	312.7	423.6	521.7	511.0	387.8	459.6	815.8	730.0
Liabs. of Central Bank: Securities	56ac	....	....	....	....	....	....	....	....	....	....	....	....	....	....	....
Long-Term Foreign Liabilities	56cl	7.4	8.6	10.0	15.7	18.8	37.7	21.6	24.0	32.5	38.5	47.2	906.3	1,747.3	3,238.6	2,369.4
Capital Accounts	57a	85.0	102.9	168.4	203.7	259.0	297.9	444.1	496.3	626.0	761.9	553.7	-24.1	-711.8	-1,470.6	-1,181.8
Other Items (Net)	57r	6.0	-24.8	-76.2	-110.3	-235.0	-231.7	-286.0	-385.5	-577.6	-782.7	-715.0	-497.5	-1,435.9	-1,453.8	-1,363.0
Interest Rates														*Percent Per Annum*		
Discount Rate *(End of Period)*	60	8.00	8.00	8.00	8.00	8.00	8.00	8.00	8.00	8.00	15.00	15.00	19.00	23.00	23.00	23.00
Savings Rate	60k	....	....	....	....	....	....	....	....	....	....	....	15.00	17.17	20.00	21.09
Deposit Rate	60l	....	....	....	....	....	....	....	....	....	....	....	16.00	18.17	21.00	21.39
Lending Rate	60p	....	....	....	....	....	....	....	....	9.00	9.00	9.25	12.33	16.17	18.00	18.00
Prices, Production, Labor														*Index Numbers (1995=100):*		
Producer Prices	63	....	....	....	....	....	....	....	....	....	....	....	....	....	....	....
Consumer Prices	64	.3	†.3	.4	.5	.5	.6	.7	.8	.9	†1.0	1.2	1.7	2.3	2.9	3.6
Crude Petroleum Production	66aa	20.4	54.4	46.1	41.9	48.8	47.7	52.5	55.7	53.3	54.9	55.0	61.8	67.0	73.0	75.9
														Number in Thousands:		
Labor Force	67d	....	....	....	....	....	....	....	....	....	....	....	....	....	....	....
Employment	67e	....	....	....	....	....	....	....	....	....	....	....	....	....	....	....
Unemployment	67c	....	....	....	....	....	....	....	....	....	....	....	....	....	....	....
Unemployment Rate (%)	67r	....	....	....	....	....	....	....	....	....	....	....	....	....	....	....
International Transactions														*Millions of US Dollars*		
Exports	70..d	326.3	532.0	1,123.5	973.9	1,257.5	1,436.3	1,557.5	2,104.2	2,480.8	2,451.4	2,327.4	2,347.7	2,620.4	2,904.7	2,171.5
Imports, c.i.f.	71..d	318.6	397.3	678.2	987.0	958.3	1,188.5	1,505.1	1,599.7	2,253.3	†2,246.1	2,168.9	1,487.4	1,616.3	1,766.6	1,810.2
Imports, f.o.b.	71.vd	274.9	344.6	589.8	863.8	850.2	1,041.5	1,324.8	1,416.8	1,989.8	†1,895.2	1,897.7	1,304.6	1,395.5	1,543.9	1,575.0
														1995=100		
Volume of Exports	72	....	....	....	....	....	....	....	....	....	....	....	....	....	....	....
Volume of Imports	73	....	....	....	....	....	....	....	....	....	....	....	....	....	....	....
														1995=100:		
Unit Value of Exports	74..d	26.5	31.1	67.2	69.2	73.0	82.1	78.1	122.6	170.8	166.6	159.1	139.2	132.7	140.6	88.9

	1987	1988	1989	1990	1991	1992	1993	1994	1995	1996	1997	1998	1999	2000	2001		
Other Banking Institutions																	
End of Period																	
Reserves	55.7	13.8	14.8	†8.7	14.7	17.1	32.8	52.6	39.5	36.4	30.0	†23.7	†15.0	19.0	14.9	40
Claims on Mon.Author.: Securities	....	....	....									†	†16.5	—	.5	40c
Foreign Assets	....	....	....	8.5	16.4	24.1	26.8	51.0	24.8	17.0	71.6	†30.7	†8.0	6.3	6.0	41
Claims on Central Government	—	—	—	†.4	—	.7	4.3	12.3	2.7	10.7	5.3	†24.9	†	32.9	35.9	42a
Claims on State & Local Govts.	—	—	—	†	—	—	—	—	—	—	—	†	†	—	—	42b
Claims on Nonfin.Pub.Enterprises	—	—	—	†	—	—	—	—	—	—	—	†	†	—	—	42c
Claims on Private Sector	473.4	382.6	374.3	†271.6	245.8	333.3	553.7	915.1	1,075.3	1,060.0	1,199.7	†1,367.6	†186.6	243.7	363.1	42d
Claims on Deposit Money Banks	24.0	13.5	12.2	†5.8	6.2	6.5	6.1	11.9	10.5	6.3	7.1	†12.7	†7.8	16.8	37.8	42e
Demand Deposits	80.6	40.7	36.8	†	—	—	—	—	—	—	—	†	†	—	—	44
Time, Savings,& Fgn.Currency Dep.	57.8	40.2	33.7	†155.4	148.6	144.5	219.3	388.6	440.5	350.2	375.5	†320.8	†201.4	248.2	299.7	45
Bonds	54.9	27.4	22.6	†31.2	36.2	33.5	8.8	21.1	11.1	96.5	179.5	†233.3	†	—	27.5	46ab
Foreign Liabilities	....	....	....	31.7	46.3	15.4	26.3	57.2	34.8	10.4	58.9	†137.5	†1.3	.8	.6	46c
Long-Term Foreign Liabilities	178.3	200.8	195.4	†78.7	64.4	102.1	156.9	215.8	247.1	369.8	420.1	†408.4	†6.9	5.6	5.2	46cl
Credit from Monetary Authorities	118.9	73.2	92.8	†19.0	4.6	3.7	1.6	.6	27.4	—	1.4	†3.0	†.4	.2	.2	46g
Credit from Deposit Money Banks	7.2	3.7	6.0	†3.0	5.8	8.2	22.6	38.0	59.1	14.9	29.0	†44.5	†13.6	9.6	8.4	46h
Capital Accounts	77.6	40.3	32.9	†111.0	100.8	205.4	323.8	485.4	539.2	553.0	538.3	†514.4	†159.6	184.9	157.9	47a
Other Items (Net)	−22.0	−16.5	−19.1	†−134.9	−123.6	−131.2	−135.5	−163.7	−206.6	−264.5	−288.9	†−202.2	†−115.5	−130.6	−41.4	47r
Banking Survey																	
End of Period																	
Foreign Assets (Net)	−389.7	−209.9	2.1	†153.1	167.0	195.4	1,308.0	1,599.3	1,257.4	1,683.4	1,860.4	†1,044.8	†1,176.5	1,665.1	1,864.0	51n
Domestic Credit	2,514.9	2,421.9	1,845.8	†1,603.8	1,919.8	2,055.3	6,238.3	7,938.7	5,081.0	5,283.7	6,657.5	†7,773.0	†5,645.1	5,345.2	6,671.7	52
Claims on Central Govt. (Net)	448.6	1,072.8	566.0	†158.8	343.2	269.5	3,331.0	3,269.4	−312.7	−316.1	−90.3	†724.3	†1,458.4	793.8	791.6	52an
Claims on State and Local Govts	—	—	—	†	—	—	—	—	—	—	—	†	†.1	—	—	52b
Claims on Nonfin.Pub.Enterprises	—	—	—	†33.3	20.7	8.9	21.4	.1	—	—	—	†	†	—	—	52c
Claims on Private Sector	2,066.2	1,349.1	1,279.9	†1,411.6	1,555.9	1,776.9	2,885.8	4,669.2	5,393.7	5,599.8	6,747.7	†7,048.7	†4,186.7	4,551.4	5,880.1	52d
Liquid Liabilities	1,928.4	1,537.9	1,421.9	†2,180.3	2,299.8	2,397.9	3,526.9	4,896.5	5,240.0	5,906.8	6,440.2	†5,481.8	†3,810.6	4,254.8	5,177.3	55l
Bonds	733.3	466.3	442.0	†92.1	86.6	83.4	59.9	61.7	161.5	508.2	687.8	†868.8	†155.8	113.4	131.5	56ab
Liabs. of Central Bank: Securities	....	....	....	†65.4	49.4	22.0	51.4	—	—	—	—	†305.5	†147.9	—	45.9	56ac
Long-Term Foreign Liabilities	1,666.4	3,182.6	2,272.8	†1,807.7	1,632.9	1,199.5	4,180.2	4,355.9	556.5	683.0	743.4	†946.1	†504.3	325.4	199.5	56cl
Capital Accounts	−932.0	−2,196.2	−1,538.4	†−1309.4	−928.5	673.2	1,283.9	1,791.6	2,145.6	2,533.7	2,747.1	†3,403.9	†2,587.7	2,892.5	2,924.9	57a
Other Items (Net)	−1,270.9	−778.6	−750.4	†−1079.1	−1,053.5	−2,125.2	−1,556.1	−1,567.6	−1,765.1	−2,664.5	−2,100.7	†−2188.1	†−384.7	−575.9	56.7	57r
Interest Rates																	
Percent Per Annum																	
Discount Rate *(End of Period)*	23.00	23.00	32.00	35.00	49.00	49.00	33.57	44.88	59.41	46.38	37.46	61.84	64.40	†13.16	16.44	60
Savings Rate	21.87	22.62	27.62	28.47	29.79	31.12	19.22	16.71	21.64	19.90	16.62	16.25	†4.91	4.47	3.49	60k
Deposit Rate	25.34	34.00	40.24	43.55	41.54	46.81	31.97	33.65	43.31	41.50	28.09	39.39	†10.03	8.46	6.58	60l
Lending Rate	18.42	23.00	30.08	37.50	46.67	60.17	47.83	43.99	55.67	54.50	43.02	49.55	†16.53	16.26	15.46	60p
Prices, Production, Labor																	
Period Averages																	
Producer Prices	....	....	....	....	....	....	....	....	100.0	....	....	225.7	457.6	1,209.5	....	63
Consumer Prices	4.6	7.4	12.9	†19.2	28.5	44.0	63.9	81.4	†100.0	124.4	162.5	221.1	336.7	660.2	908.9	64
Crude Petroleum Production	58.7	80.5	74.4	75.6	77.7	83.4	89.3	98.7	100.0	100.2	101.1	97.7	97.2	104.4	106.0	66aa
Period Averages																	
Labor Force	....	....	....	3,220	....	....	....	....	....	3,169	3,326	3,560	....	....	....	67d
Employment	1,148	2,068	2,192	†2,331	2,562	2,693	2,651	2,698	2,892	2,889	3,062	3,151	....	....	....	67e
Unemployment	90	155	187	†150	158	263	241	207	213	335	312	409	....	....	....	67c
Unemployment Rate (%)	7.2	7.0	7.9	†6.1	5.8	8.9	8.3	7.1	6.9	10.4	9.2	11.5	....	....	....	67r
International Transactions																	
Millions of US Dollars																	
Exports	1,927.8	2,192.4	2,353.8	2,714.3	2,851.5	3,007.4	2,903.7	3,819.9	4,307.2	4,899.9	5,264.4	4,202.9	4,451.0	4,926.5	4,647.4	70..d
Imports, c.i.f.	2,251.5	1,713.5	1,854.8	1,865.1	2,399.0	2,431.0	2,562.2	3,622.0	4,152.6	3,934.5	4,954.9	5,575.7	3,017.3	3,721.1	5,362.9	71..d
Imports, f.o.b.	1,981.7	1,517.4	1,634.1	1,644.5	2,115.5	1,975.5	2,223.0	3,252.5	3,774.8	3,570.9	4,520.1	5,012.7	2,736.9	3,400.9	4,936.0	71.vd
1995=100																	
Volume of Exports	....	....	....	65.0	69.6	75.3	80.5	89.4	100.0	102.4	102.1	96.7	92.9	100.3	101.2	72
Volume of Imports	....	....	....	72.7	70.8	73.4	49.3	74.6	100.0	96.3	132.6	166.1	95.6	99.9	124.4	73
Indices of Unit Values in US Dollars																	
Unit Value of Exports	99.6	86.5	101.3	116.2	108.8	108.0	88.9	98.9	100.0	115.0	112.3	84.0	101.5	131.3	113.7	74..d

Ecuador

		1972	1973	1974	1975	1976	1977	1978	1979	1980	1981	1982	1983	1984	1985	1986
Balance of Payments															*Millions of US Dollars:*	
Current Account, n.i.e.	78al d	....	....	....	....	−10	−343	−703	−630	−642	−998	−1,182	−115	−273	76	−582
Goods: Exports f.o.b.	78aa d	....	....	....	....	1,307	1,401	1,529	2,151	2,520	2,527	2,327	2,348	2,621	2,905	2,200
Goods: Imports f.o.b.	78ab d	....	....	....	....	−1,048	−1,361	−1,704	−2,097	−2,242	−2,353	−2,187	−1,421	−1,567	−1,611	−1,643
Trade Balance	78ac d	....	....	....	....	259	40	−175	54	278	174	140	927	1,054	1,294	557
Services: Credit	78ad d	....	....	....	....	111	202	174	260	367	399	381	315	291	397	441
Services: Debit	78ae d	....	....	....	....	−268	−426	−475	−569	−704	−834	−723	−491	−535	−636	−583
Balance on Goods & Services	78af d	....	....	....	....	103	−183	−475	−256	−59	−262	−202	751	810	1,055	415
Income: Credit	78ag d	....	....	....	....	13	24	35	62	88	69	26	23	59	29	32
Income: Debit	78ah d	....	....	....	....	−153	−220	−304	−467	−701	−831	−1,026	−913	−1,162	−1,088	−1,074
Balance on Gds, Serv. & Inc.	78ai d	....	....	....	....	−37	−380	−744	−660	−672	−1,023	−1,202	−139	−293	−4	−627
Current Transfers, n.i.e.: Credit	78aj d	....	....	....	....	30	42	43	32	36	35	30	38	25	85	51
Current Transfers: Debit	78ak d	....	....	....	....	−2	−6	−2	−2	−6	−10	−10	−14	−5	−5	−6
Capital Account, n.i.e.	78bc d	....	....	....	....	3	—	—	—	—	—	—	—	—	—	—
Capital Account, n.i.e.: Credit	78ba d	....	....	....	....	3	—	—	—	—	—	—	—	—	—	—
Capital Account: Debit	78bb d	....	....	....	....	—	—	—	—	—	—	—	—	—	—	—
Financial Account, n.i.e.	78bj d	....	....	....	....	223	503	663	666	980	717	766	−2,571	−1,407	−1,122	−1,033
Direct Investment Abroad	78bd d															
Dir. Invest. in Rep. Econ., n.i.e.	78be d	....	....	....	....	−20	35	49	63	70	60	40	50	50	62	81
Portfolio Investment Assets	78bf d	....	....	....	....	—	—	—	—	—	—	—	—	—	—	—
Equity Securities	78bk d					—	—	—	—	—	—	—	—	—	—	—
Debt Securities	78bl d					—	—	—	—	—	—	—	—	—	—	—
Portfolio Investment Liab., n.i.e.	78bg d	....	....	....	....	6	52	—	—	—	—	—	—	—	—	—
Equity Securities	78bm d					—	—	—	—	—	—	—	—	—	—	—
Debt Securities	78bn d					6	52	—	—	—	—	—	—	—	—	—
Financial Derivatives Assets	78bw d	....	....	....	....	....	....	....	....	....	....	....	....	....	....	....
Financial Derivatives Liabilities	78bx d	....	....	....	....	....	....	....	....	....	....	....	....	....	....	....
Other Investment Assets	78bh d	....	....	....	....	−102	−41	−104	−34	−231	−449	503	−168	−26	54	−23
Monetary Authorities	78bo d	....	....	....	....	....	....	....	....	....	....	....	....	....	....	....
General Government	78bp d	....	....	....	....	−25	−37	−13	−48	−66	90	−15	−15	−27	−5	−2
Banks	78bq d	....	....	....	....	−15	−31	1	−3	−34	−21	25	−84	11	−28	−15
Other Sectors	78br d	....	....	....	....	−62	26	−92	17	−132	−518	493	−69	−10	87	−6
Other Investment Liab., n.i.e.	78bi d	....	....	....	....	339	458	718	636	1,141	1,106	223	−2,453	−1,431	−1,238	−1,091
Monetary Authorities	78bs d					44	25	−11	70	75	−107	183	96	−107	−63	188
General Government	78bt d					234	352	379	331	570	916	247	−1,699	−164	−649	−1,192
Banks	78bu d					—	5	65	−6	22	17	25	84	−4	−35	8
Other Sectors	78bv d	....	....	....	....	61	77	286	241	475	280	−232	−934	−1,156	−491	−95
Net Errors and Omissions	78ca d	....	....	....	....	−13	−48	46	8	−68	−89	−802	794	97	168	−446
Overall Balance	78cb d	....	....	....	....	203	112	6	44	270	−370	−1,218	−1,892	−1,583	−878	−2,061
Reserves and Related Items	79da d	....	....	....	....	−203	−112	−6	−44	−270	370	1,218	1,892	1,583	878	2,061
Reserve Assets	79db d	....	....	....	....	−203	−112	−6	−44	−270	370	370	−327	60	−97	124
Use of Fund Credit and Loans	79dc d	....	....	....	....	—	—	—	—	—	—	—	214	40	89	83
Exceptional Financing	79de d	....	....	....	....	—	—	—	—	—	—	879	2,005	1,483	886	1,854
Government Finance															*Millions of US Dollars:*	
Deficit (-) or Surplus	80	−35.7	†5.0	−.1	−26.6	−86.4	−215.5	−91.8	−60.8	−164.8	−673.5	−615.5	−318.4	−108.5	315.9	†−253.3
Revenue	81	220.6	318.9	455.6	495.6	586.1	658.1	762.3	923.1	1,502.0	1,571.9	1,531.9	1,364.3	1,597.0	2,724.0	†1,522.2
Expenditure	82	256.3	314.0	455.7	522.3	672.5	873.6	854.1	983.9	1,666.7	2,245.4	2,147.4	1,682.7	1,705.5	2,408.1	†1,775.5
Financing																
Domestic	84a	6.5	−2.9	5.2	36.1	71.0	172.3	130.6	105.2	102.6	367.2	282.8	369.8	173.4	−261.5	†70.0
Foreign	85a	38.2	−2.0	−5.1	−9.4	15.4	43.2	−38.7	−44.4	62.1	306.3	332.6	−51.4	−64.9	−54.4	†183.3
Use of Cash Balances	87	−9.0	....	....	....	....	....	....	....	....	....	....	....	....	....	....
Debt: Sucres	88b	261.9	....	....	....	....	....	....	....	....	....	....	....	....	....	....
National Accounts															*Millions of US Dollars:*	
Househ.Cons.Expend.,incl.NPISHs	96f	1,377	1,668	2,220	2,812	3,381	4,103	4,850	5,732	6,995	8,587	8,733	8,372	8,325	10,289	7,540
Government Consumption Expend.	91f	190	256	466	625	745	986	1,058	1,203	1,702	1,990	1,937	1,588	1,593	1,831	1,358
Gross Fixed Capital Formation	93e	338	435	674	996	1,179	1,571	2,003	2,217	2,773	3,105	3,136	2,109	2,003	2,563	2,118
Changes in Inventories	93i	37	49	160	156	84	194	174	154	292	126	355	123	236	337	232
Exports of Goods and Services	90c	352	620	1,344	1,130	1,367	1,653	1,633	2,425	2,952	3,036	2,916	3,016	3,356	4,269	2,563
Imports of Goods and Services (-)	98c	420	540	1,153	1,409	1,439	1,852	2,064	2,373	2,981	2,898	3,231	2,507	2,517	3,331	2,545
Gross Domestic Product (GDP)	99b	1,874	2,489	3,711	4,310	5,317	6,655	7,654	9,359	11,733	13,946	13,845	12,700	12,995	15,957	11,266
Net Primary Income from Abroad	98.n	−67	−142	−227	−99	−162	−179	−221	−398	−582	−732	−1,029	−947	−1,160	−1,175	−909
Gross National Income (GNI)	99a	1,807	2,347	3,484	4,211	5,154	6,476	7,433	8,961	11,152	13,214	12,817	11,753	11,834	14,782	10,357
Net National Income	99e	1,638	2,132	3,219	3,857	4,711	5,911	6,764	8,064	9,208	11,752	11,334	10,325	10,287	12,833	8,731
GDP Volume 1975 Prices	99b.p	3,060	3,835	4,082	4,310	4,707	5,015	5,345	5,629	5,905	6,138	6,211	6,035	6,289	6,562	6,765
GDP Volume (1995=100)	99bv p	35.6	44.6	47.4	50.1	54.7	58.3	62.1	65.4	68.6	71.3	72.2	70.2	73.1	76.3	78.6
GDP Deflator (1995=100)	99bi p	29.4	31.1	43.6	48.0	54.2	63.6	68.7	79.7	95.3	109.0	106.9	100.9	99.1	116.6	79.9
																Millions:
Population	99z	6.38	6.60	6.82	7.03	7.24	7.45	7.67	7.89	8.12	8.36	8.61	8.64	8.87	9.10	9.33

Balance of Payments

Minus Sign Indicates Debit

Item	1987	1988	1989	1990	1991	1992	1993	1994	1995	1996	1997	1998	1999	2000	2001	Code
Current Account, n.i.e.	-1,187	-680	-715	-360	-708	-122	-845	-900	-994	-37	-458	-2,099	942	928	....	78al d
Goods: Exports f.o.b.	2,021	2,205	2,354	2,724	2,851	3,101	3,136	3,936	4,468	4,929	5,361	4,326	4,616	5,137	....	78aa d
Goods: Imports f.o.b.	-2,054	-1,583	-1,692	-1,715	-2,208	-2,083	-2,922	-3,787	-4,535	-4,008	-4,869	-5,458	-3,028	-3,743	....	78ab d
Trade Balance	-33	622	662	1,009	643	1,018	214	149	-66	921	492	-1,132	1,588	1,395	....	78ac d
Services: Credit	421	440	516	538	556	617	636	676	728	683	686	678	730	849	....	78ad d
Services: Debit	-648	-606	-626	-804	-900	-933	-1,090	-1,108	-1,173	-1,111	-1,230	-1,242	-1,158	-1,256	....	78ae d
Balance on Goods & Services	-260	456	552	743	299	702	-240	-283	-512	494	-52	-1,695	1,159	988	....	78af d
Income: Credit	28	17	20	25	31	35	32	61	98	80	128	119	75	71	....	78ag d
Income: Debit	-1,087	-1,250	-1,384	-1,235	-1,148	-979	-892	-1,001	-1,023	-1,103	-1,155	-1,290	-1,382	-1,482	....	78ah d
Balance on Gds, Serv. & Inc.	-1,319	-777	-812	-467	-818	-242	-1,101	-1,223	-1,436	-529	-1,079	-2,866	-147	-424	....	78ai d
Current Transfers, n.i.e.: Credit	135	104	106	119	123	134	318	391	506	616	738	933	1,188	1,437	....	78aj d
Current Transfers: Debit	-3	-7	-9	-12	-13	-14	-62	-69	-64	-124	-117	-166	-99	-85	....	78ak d
Capital Account, n.i.e.							5	18	17	14	11	14	2	-1	....	78bc d
Capital Account, n.i.e.: Credit							8	21	21	18	17	23	11	8	....	78ba d
Capital Account: Debit							-3	-3	-4	-4	-6	-9	-9	-10	....	78bb d
Financial Account, n.i.e.	-209	-632	-515	580	732	361	-40	177	-32	135	-13	1,445	-1,368	-6,619	....	78bj d
Direct Investment Abroad															....	78bd d
Dir. Invest. in Rep. Econ., n.i.e.	123	155	160	126	160	178	474	576	453	500	724	870	648	720	....	78be d
Portfolio Investment Assets															....	78bf d
Equity Securities															....	78bk d
Debt Securities															....	78bl d
Portfolio Investment Liab., n.i.e.							1	6	3	-4	-242	-34	-46	-5,583	....	78bg d
Equity Securities							1	6	13	6	22	5	1		....	78bm d
Debt Securities									-10	-10	-264	-40	-47	-5,583	....	78bn d
Financial Derivatives Assets															....	78bw d
Financial Derivatives Liabilities															....	78bx d
Other Investment Assets	4	14	-68	—	—	—	-140	-177	-668	-302	-560	-54	-748	-1,288	....	78bh d
Monetary Authorities															....	78bo d
General Government	-4	1	-15	—	—										....	78bp d
Banks	26	3	-32	—	—										....	78bq d
Other Sectors	-18	10	-21	—	—		-140	-177	-668	-302	-560	-54	-748	-1,288	....	78br d
Other Investment Liab., n.i.e.	-336	-801	-607	454	572	183	-375	-230	180	-59	65	663	-1,222	-469	....	78bi d
Monetary Authorities	21	70	-221	-53	-6	-4	-119	-57	-48	-40	-18	229	-84	-135	....	78bs d
General Government	-357	-856	-426	-508	-585	-678	-637	-743	-689	139	-188	-38	125	216	....	78bt d
Banks	—	-15	-3				27	27	31	99	26	-24	-73	-48	....	78bu d
Other Sectors	—	—	43	1,015	1,163	865	354	544	886	-257	244	496	-1,190	-502	....	78bv d
Net Errors and Omissions	629	25	114	126	134	-215	206	-70	-433	-188	-62	-144	-521	-15	....	78ca d
Overall Balance	-767	-1,287	-1,116	346	158	24	-674	-776	-1,443	-76	-522	-784	-944	-5,707	....	78cb d
Reserves and Related Items	767	1,287	1,116	-346	-158	24	674	776	1,443	76	522	784	944	5,707	....	79da d
Reserve Assets	185	26	-118	-261	-79	54	-442	-578	174	-247	-253	460	489	-307	....	79db d
Use of Fund Credit and Loans	-69	-58	-69	-85	-79	-77	-29	122	-29	-23	-3	-67	-68	151	....	79dc d
Exceptional Financing	650	1,319	1,303	—	—		1,145	1,232	1,297	346	778	390	523	5,863	....	79de d

Government Finance

Year Ending December 31

Item	1987	1988	1989	1990	1991	1992	1993	1994	1995	1996	1997	1998	1999	2000	2001	Code
Deficit (-) or Surplus	-245.4	-4.5	184.7	192.2	177.8	300.5	287.0	52.4	-163.8	-88.7	-291.4	68.7	-99.0	90.0	98.9	80
Revenue	1,388.9	1,377.5	1,587.2	1,765.1	1,739.7	1,961.3	2,248.2	2,570.9	3,131.4	3,334.1	3,380.3	3,280.3	2,705.1	3,056.6	3,873.7	81
Expenditure	1,634.3	1,382.0	1,402.4	1,572.9	1,561.9	1,660.8	1,961.3	2,518.5	3,295.2	3,422.7	3,671.7	3,211.6	2,804.1	2,966.6	3,774.8	82
Financing																
Domestic	170.7	121.8	-10.9	6.3	87.8	19.5	-30.9	237.5	365.4	150.2	824.4	-68.8	32.3	-269.4	-22.3	84a
Foreign	74.6	-117.2	-173.9	-198.5	-265.6	-320.0	-256.0	-290.0	-201.6	-61.5	-533.0	.1	66.8	179.4	-76.9	85a
Use of Cash Balances																87
Debt: Sucres																88b

National Accounts

Millions of US Dollars

Item	1987	1988	1989	1990	1991	1992	1993	1994	1995	1996	1997	1998	1999	2000	2001	Code
Househ.Cons.Expend.,incl.NPISHs	7,447	6,919	7,041	7,323	8,059	8,571	10,096	11,392	12,140	12,162	13,294	13,882	8,964	8,446	....	96f
Government Consumption Expend.	1,352	1,150	921	920	895	917	1,103	1,560	2,257	2,240	2,288	2,299	1,419	1,292	....	91f
Gross Fixed Capital Formation	2,385	2,131	2,034	1,970	2,310	2,467	2,844	3,119	3,329	3,386	3,765	4,140	2,030	2,201	....	93e
Changes in Inventories	1	21	-1	-100	295	217	172	37	23	-94	226	723	-260	85	....	93i
Exports of Goods and Services	2,532	2,848	2,888	3,499	3,688	3,989	3,743	4,435	5,326	5,805	5,930	4,988	5,074	5,774	....	90c
Imports of Goods and Services (-)	3,190	3,058	3,060	2,925	3,494	3,506	3,653	3,938	5,136	4,459	5,734	6,311	3,537	4,191	....	98c
Gross Domestic Product (GDP)	10,527	10,012	9,823	10,686	11,752	12,656	14,304	16,606	17,939	19,040	19,769	19,723	13,689	13,607	....	99b
Net Primary Income from Abroad	-717	-686	-730	-819	-704	-607	-572	-1,279	-1,262	-1,304	-1,422	-1,625	....	....	....	98.n
Gross National Income (GNI)	9,810	9,326	9,093	9,867	11,049	12,049	13,732	15,327	16,677	17,736	18,347	18,098	....	....	....	99a
Net National Income	7,960	7,529	7,317	8,022	9,112	10,089	11,456	12,887	14,024	14,214	....	....	....	....	....	99e
GDP Volume 1975 Prices	6,361	7,028	7,048	7,260	7,626	7,897	8,058	8,406	8,603	8,773	9,070	9,107	8,445	8,642	....	99b.p
GDP Volume (1995=100)	73.9	81.7	81.9	84.4	88.6	91.8	93.7	97.7	100.0	102.0	105.4	105.9	98.2	100.5	....	99bv p
GDP Deflator (1995=100)	79.4	68.3	66.8	70.6	73.9	76.9	85.1	94.7	100.0	104.1	104.5	103.9	77.7	75.5	....	99bi p

Midyear Estimates

Item	1987	1988	1989	1990	1991	1992	1993	1994	1995	1996	1997	1998	1999	2000	2001	Code
Population	9.56	9.79	10.03	10.26	10.50	10.74	10.98	11.22	11.46	11.70	11.94	12.17	12.41	12.65	12.88	99z

(See notes in the back of the book.)

Egypt

469		1972	1973	1974	1975	1976	1977	1978	1979	1980	1981	1982	1983	1984	1985	1986
Exchange Rates																*Pounds per SDR:*
Market Rate ..... aa=	wa	.4720	.5245	.4791	.4581	.4546	.4753	.5098	.9221	.8928	.8148	.7722	.7329	.6861	.7689	.8562
																Pounds per US Dollar:
Market Rate ..... ae=	we	.4348	.4348	.3913	.3913	.3913	.3913	.3913	.7000	.7000	.7000	.7000	.7000	.7000	.7000	.7000
Secondary Rate	xe	....	....	....	....	.7000	.7000	.7000	....	....	.8317	.8317	.8317	.8317	1.3300	1.3600
Secondary Rate	xf	....	....	....	....	....	.7000	....	....	....	.7390	.8317	.8317	.8317	1.3010	1.3503
Tertiary Rate	yf	....	....	....	....	....	....	....	....	....	....	....	1.1453	1.2543	1.5488	1.8838
Fund Position																*Millions of SDRs:*
Quota	2f.s	188	188	188	188	188	188	228	228	342	342	342	463	463	463	463
SDRs	1b.s	5	31	31	14	20	24	8	—	—	—	—	—	—	—	—
Reserve Position in the Fund	1c.s	—	—	—	—	—	—	—	—	—	24	—	30	—	—	—
Total Fund Cred.&Loans Outstg.	2tl	24	62	93	68	178	275	374	381	322	269	236	228	210	167	118
International Liquidity																*Millions of US Dollars Unless Otherwise Indicated:*
Total Reserves minus Gold	1l.d	52	260	252	194	240	431	492	529	1,046	716	698	771	736	792	829
SDRs	1b.d	6	38	38	17	24	29	11	—	—	—	—	—	—	—	—
Reserve Position in the Fund	1c.d	—	—	—	—	—	—	—	—	—	28	—	32	—	—	—
Foreign Exchange	1d.d	46	222	214	177	216	402	481	529	1,046	688	698	739	736	792	829
Gold (Million Fine Troy Ounces)	1ad	2.432	2.432	2.432	2.432	2.432	2.432	2.473	2.472	2.432	2.432	2.432	2.432	2.432	2.432	2.432
Gold (National Valuation)	1and	85	85	103	103	103	103	104	104	103	775	578	757	679	578	622
Monetary Authorities: Other Assets	3..d	75	124	265	631	300	347	510	409	529	849	1,106	1,349	1,257	1,290	1,439
Other Liab.	4..d	673	791	978	2,554	2,798	4,041	8,915	5,173	†5,082	4,768	5,126	4,487	4,403	4,133	4,732
Deposit Money Banks: Assets	7a.d	138.7	374.0	1,042.4	1,265.3	1,965.5	3,406.5	4,420.6	2,745.1	†4,633.7	4,711.9	7,444.6	9,063.1	8,377.7	8,774.9	13,208.3
Liabilities	7b.d	211.4	302.2	957.8	1,789.9	1,961.6	1,598.0	1,942.5	1,228.4	†2,598.9	3,702.4	5,099.7	6,283.1	6,252.7	6,239.3	9,392.9
Other Banking Insts.: Assets	7e.d	2.3	2.3	2.6	2.6	2.6	2.6	2.6	5.7	†5.6	11.1	14.3	10.3	8.3	6.9	45.6
Liabilities	7f.d	....	....	....	....	....	20.7	43.4	41.4	†63.1	99.4	149.0	377.1	388.9	501.3	594.9
Monetary Authorities																*Millions of Pounds:*
Foreign Assets	11	92	185	201	265	251	344	590	763	†1,187	1,639	1,667	2,030	1,888	1,888	2,128
Claims on Central Government	12a	668	823	982	1,511	1,594	1,878	4,178	6,211	†6,184	8,093	10,393	12,627	14,377	15,966	17,841
Claims on Nonfin.Pub.Enterprises	12c	—	—	—	—	—	—	—	—	†625	676	329	351	334	425	492
Claims on Deposit Money Banks	12e	383	395	580	775	1,105	1,544	1,633	1,153	†1,757	333	357	643	898	1,075	1,173
Claims on Other Banking Insts	12f	6	6	5	5	5	104	170	121	†213	314	518	551	665	837	1,078
Reserve Money	14	802	1,000	1,270	1,446	1,730	2,083	2,655	3,402	†5,611	7,056	9,281	11,875	13,544	15,814	17,655
of which: Currency Outside DMBs	14a	631	777	948	1,156	1,388	1,750	2,184	2,657	†3,398	4,291	5,503	6,475	7,098	8,285	8,803
Foreign Liabilities	16c	304	376	427	1,031	1,176	1,712	3,679	3,972	†3,845	3,557	3,770	3,308	3,226	3,021	3,413
Central Government Deposits	16d	18	20	34	38	40	47	101	693	†362	406	300	847	1,062	933	1,209
Other Items (Net)	17r	26	13	37	43	9	30	136	181	†148	36	−88	172	330	422	435
Deposit Money Banks																*Millions of Pounds:*
Reserves	20	185	260	382	370	451	495	505	803	†1,325	2,392	3,557	5,039	6,124	7,164	9,262
Foreign Assets	21	60	163	408	495	769	1,333	1,730	1,922	†3,244	3,298	5,211	6,344	5,864	6,142	9,246
Claims on Central Government	22a	704	741	923	1,369	1,646	1,816	2,393	2,546	†2,775	1,335	1,785	1,206	1,973	2,684	3,911
Claims on Nonfin.Pub.Enterprises	22c	....	....	....	....	....	....	....	....	2,685	3,809	3,950	5,576	7,145	8,529	9,683
Claims on Private Sector	22d	425	410	587	881	1,147	1,537	1,790	2,396	†2,174	4,242	5,549	6,876	8,284	10,145	12,888
Claims on Other Banking Insts	22f	122	115	196	207	174	102	67	136	†119	304	272	309	391	686	1,123
Demand Deposits	24	357	425	553	706	849	1,194	1,369	1,697	†2,504	2,886	3,498	3,798	4,554	5,606	6,135
Time, Savings,& Fgn.Currency Dep.	25	266	331	498	567	822	1,160	1,659	2,490	†3,589	5,920	8,240	10,884	13,486	15,978	21,127
Bonds	26ab	....	....	....	....	....	....	....	....	—	—	—	—	—	—	—
Restricted Deposits	26b	....	....	....	....	....	....	....	....	†897	1,279	1,478	1,677	1,753	1,942	3,108
Foreign Liabilities	26c	92	131	375	700	768	625	760	860	†1,819	2,592	3,570	4,398	4,377	4,368	6,575
Central Government Deposits	26d	130	128	184	211	247	366	596	821	†349	494	488	545	555	663	1,059
Credit from Monetary Authorities	26g	383	395	578	771	1,105	1,530	1,589	1,078	†1,780	372	552	858	1,108	1,242	1,550
Other Items (Net)	27r	268	278	308	367	397	409	512	857	†1,384	1,837	2,500	3,189	3,949	5,551	6,558
Monetary Survey																*Millions of Pounds:*
Foreign Assets (Net)	31n	−244	−160	−193	−971	−923	−660	−2,119	−2,148	†−1,234	−1,211	−461	668	150	641	1,386
Domestic Credit	32	1,777	1,947	2,475	3,725	4,279	5,024	7,901	9,897	†14,065	17,871	22,008	26,104	31,553	37,674	44,747
Claims on Central Govt. (Net)	32an	1,224	1,416	1,686	2,632	2,953	3,282	5,874	7,243	†8,248	8,527	11,390	12,441	14,733	17,053	19,484
Claims on Nonfin.Pub.Enterprises	32c	....	....	....	....	....	....	....	....	†3,310	4,485	4,279	5,927	7,479	8,953	10,175
Claims on Private Sector	32d	426	411	587	881	1,147	1,537	1,790	2,396	†2,174	4,242	5,549	6,876	8,284	10,145	12,888
Claims on Other Banking Insts	32f	127	120	201	212	179	206	237	257	†333	617	790	860	1,056	1,523	2,200
Money	34	989	1,205	1,503	1,863	2,239	2,943	3,553	4,354	†6,775	7,646	9,552	10,933	12,443	14,696	15,973
of which: Foreign Currency Deps.	34a	....	....	....	....	....	....	....	....	874	1,030	1,361	1,612	1,913	2,454	2,848
Quasi-Money	35	266	331	498	567	822	1,160	1,659	2,490	†3,589	5,920	8,240	10,885	13,486	15,980	21,129
of which: Fgn. Currency Deposits	35a	....	....	....	....	....	....	....	....	1,493	2,524	3,640	4,301	4,616	5,230	8,645
Bonds	36ab	....	....	....	....	....	....	....	....	—	—	—	—	—	—	—
Restricted Deposits	36b	....	....	....	....	....	....	....	....	†897	1,279	1,478	1,677	1,753	1,942	3,108
Other Items (Net)	37r	278	251	281	325	295	262	570	904	†1,571	1,815	2,277	3,277	4,020	5,697	5,922
Money plus Quasi-Money	35l	1,255	1,536	2,000	2,430	3,061	4,103	5,212	6,844	†10,364	13,566	17,792	21,817	25,929	30,676	37,102
Other Banking Institutions																
Specialized Banks																*Millions of Pounds:*
Cash	40	....	....	....	....	....	....	1	1	†49	49	33	36	25	28	44
Foreign Assets	41	1	1	1	1	1	1	1	4	†4	8	10	7	6	5	32
Claims on Nonfin.Pub.Enterprises	42c	....	....	....	....	....	....	....	....	†130	215	390	492	651	808	1,004
Claims on Private Sector	42d	140	153	154	137	138	185	210	243	†327	511	674	1,182	1,490	1,794	2,472
Demand Deposits	44	23	25	28	29	36	40	54	93	†89	96	155	142	172	221	234
Time and Savings Deposits	45	....	....	....	....	....	....	....	....	†47	85	138	258	296	383	455
Restricted Deposits	46b	....	....	....	....	....	....	....	....	†8	12	16	23	26	2	10
Foreign Liabilities	46c	....	....	....	....	....	8	17	29	†44	70	104	264	272	351	416
Central Government Deposits	46d	12	13	23	23	28	48	58	70	†67	97	111	194	168	89	87
Credit from Monetary Authorities	46g	6	6	6	6	7	106	175	125	†213	309	519	556	665	844	1,076
Credit from Deposit Money Banks	46h	121	115	194	203	175	102	61	118	†119	303	267	375	501	623	1,088
Other Items (Net)	47r	−21	−6	−96	−123	−105	−117	−152	−187	†−78	−189	−203	−94	72	123	186
Post Office: Savings Deposits	45.. i	90	101	119	136	152	163	187	203	216	261	300	353	403	459	531
Banking Survey																*Millions of Pounds:*
Foreign Assets (Net)	51n	....	....	....	....	....	....	....	....	†−1,274	−1,273	−555	411	−117	295	1,001
Domestic Credit	52	....	....	....	....	....	....	....	....	†14,342	18,147	22,475	27,083	32,883	39,134	46,481
Claims on Central Govt. (Net)	52an	....	....	....	....	....	....	....	....	†8,401	8,694	11,583	12,606	14,978	17,434	19,943
Claims on Nonfin.Pub.Enterprises	52c	....	....	....	....	....	....	....	....	†3,440	4,700	4,669	6,419	8,131	9,761	11,179
Claims on Private Sector	52d	....	....	....	....	....	....	....	....	†2,501	4,753	6,223	8,058	9,774	11,940	15,360
Liquid Liabilities	55l	....	....	....	....	....	....	....	....	†10,668	13,959	18,351	22,534	26,776	31,710	38,277
Bonds	56ab	....	....	....	....	....	....	....	....	—	—	—	—	—	—	—
Restricted Deposits	56b	....	....	....	....	....	....	....	....	†905	1,291	1,494	1,700	1,779	1,944	3,118
Other Items (Net)	57r	....	....	....	....	....	....	....	....	†1,496	1,624	2,075	3,260	4,211	5,775	6,087

1987	1988	1989	1990	1991	1992	1993	1994	1995	1996	1997	1998	1999	2000	2001	
															Exchange Rates
End of Period															
.9931	.9420	1.4456	2.8453	4.7665	4.5906	4.6314	4.9504	5.0392	4.8718	4.5713	4.7704	4.6734	4.8077	5.6427	Market Rate....................aa= .... wa
End of Period															
.7000	.7000	1.1000	2.0000	3.3322	3.3386	3.3718	3.3910	3.3900	3.3880	3.3880	3.3880	3.4050	3.6900	4.4900	Market Rate....................ae= .... we
1.8700	2.3529	2.5580	2.8736	....	....	....	....	....	....	....	....	....	....	....	Secondary Rate .... xe
1.5183	2.2233	2.5171	2.7072	....	....	....	....	....	....	....	....	....	....	....	Secondary Rate .... xf
2.1838	2.3731	2.6949	2.7978	....	....	....	....	....	....	....	....	....	....	....	Tertiary Rate .... yf
															Fund Position
End of Period															
463	463	463	463	463	678	678	678	678	678	678	678	944	944	944	Quota .... 2f. s
—	—	—	—	1	43	50	59	70	86	84	114	30	37	28	SDRs .... 1b. s
—	—	—	—	—	54	54	54	54	54	54	54	120	120	—	Reserve Position in the Fund .... 1c. s
185	141	122	88	89	147	147	132	70	11	—	—	—	—	—	Total Fund Cred.&Loans Outstg. 2tl
															International Liquidity
End of Period															
1,378	1,263	1,520	2,684	5,325	10,810	12,904	13,481	16,181	17,398	18,665	18,124	14,484	13,118	12,926	Total Reserves minus Gold..................... 1l. d
—	—	—	1	1	59	69	86	103	123	113	160	41	48	35	SDRs .... 1b. d
—	—	—	—	—	74	74	78	80	77	73	76	165	156	—	Reserve Position in the Fund .... 1c. d
1,378	1,263	1,520	2,683	5,324	10,677	12,761	13,316	15,998	17,198	18,479	17,888	14,278	12,913	12,891	Foreign Exchange .... 1d. d
2.432	2.432	2.432	2.432	2.432	2.432	2.432	2.432	2.432	2.432	2.432	2.432	2.432	2.432	2.432	Gold (Million Fine Troy Ounces)........... 1ad
814	794	679	641	656	616	616	694	704	695	609	541	475	511	488	Gold (National Valuation) 1and
255	618	604	1,078	1,287	1,280	1,274	1,293	1,131	1,003	938	874	811	762	715	Monetary Authorities: Other Assets .... 3..d
9,136	12,620	16,108	15,622	11,852	12,457	11,842	12,551	13,298	12,324	11,384	11,873	11,296	11,091	10,569	Other Liab. .... 4..d
20,829.4	24,290.9	8,481.6	10,365.5	12,606.9	11,326.8	10,786.5	11,432.3	11,070.3	10,736.2	9,153.2	7,815.1	7,441.1	7,297.1	5,915.0	Deposit Money Banks: Assets .... 7a. d
11,673.7	12,171.9	3,485.4	3,714.3	3,423.6	2,343.2	1,782.0	1,465.3	1,500.2	1,844.2	3,555.7	4,995.3	4,318.3	4,232.6	4,268.9	Liabilities........... 7b. d
24.7	32.6	40.0	35.1	33.6	42.9	51.2	29.5	29.8	22.0	16.9	14.8	7.3	7.0	10.3	Other Banking Insts.: Assets .... 7e. d
790.7	1,100.7	770.5	530.7	423.3	436.1	486.5	457.1	275.5	255.4	267.4	219.9	215.1	240.8	161.5	Liabilities .... 7f. d
															Monetary Authorities
End of Period															
2,646	2,704	3,639	11,029	26,086	45,911	55,894	60,529	61,901	65,189	68,799	66,782	52,923	52,478	61,332	Foreign Assets 11
21,058	24,588	34,263	52,238	56,562	56,993	52,849	50,978	51,615	47,015	44,368	61,209	75,447	95,715	116,392	Claims on Central Government 12a
545	559	694	722	725	823	820	799	799	900	849	817	1,029	1,177	1,330	Claims on Nonfin.Pub.Enterprises........... 12c
1,992	2,191	3,309	4,608	6,157	8,279	11,655	12,224	12,892	12,700	12,438	8,359	6,462	6,577	7,094	Claims on Deposit Money Banks 12e
1,155	1,256	1,425	1,624	1,823	1,974	2,134	2,040	2,095	2,147	2,261	2,275	3,336	2,846	2,901	Claims on Other Banking Insts 12f
18,714	19,476	21,082	27,137	32,356	35,712	42,554	47,888	52,357	54,562	60,610	72,336	73,522	87,271	102,094	Reserve Money 14
9,537	10,406	10,934	12,410	13,524	15,241	17,818	20,612	22,750	24,954	28,215	31,502	35,310	37,902	40,548	*of which: Currency Outside DMBs* 14a
6,579	8,967	17,895	31,494	39,917	42,264	40,609	43,215	45,430	41,807	38,570	40,224	38,464	40,926	47,454	Foreign Liabilities.. 16c
1,626	1,289	2,308	9,211	18,634	35,109	38,481	33,617	29,661	28,476	26,738	22,296	23,298	27,676	42,862	Central Government Deposits 16d
477	1,566	2,045	2,379	445	894	1,707	1,851	1,855	3,105	2,797	4,586	3,913	2,920	-3,359	Other Items (Net) 17r
															Deposit Money Banks
End of Period															
10,545	11,054	12,068	14,726	19,330	19,540	23,097	25,402	28,094	28,146	30,241	33,262	34,636	46,432	61,180	Reserves 20
14,581	17,004	21,696	29,786	41,980	37,722	36,370	38,767	37,528	36,374	31,011	26,477	25,337	26,926	26,559	Foreign Assets 21
5,233	7,302	7,360	6,747	17,699	40,681	41,262	42,398	41,882	47,567	54,479	47,244	40,363	47,276	54,991	Claims on Central Government 22a
11,148	13,091	16,615	23,026	28,214	23,928	29,283	29,998	33,180	37,481	38,643	38,801	42,109	38,141	42,062	Claims on Nonfin.Pub.Enterprises........... 22c
14,881	17,330	20,428	24,454	24,816	30,978	36,885	48,831	66,777	83,810	105,545	133,799	159,958	176,693	197,038	Claims on Private Sector 22d
1,284	1,629	1,695	2,095	2,056	1,250	1,432	1,284	1,630	2,424	2,988	4,251	2,958	3,429	4,918	Claims on Other Banking Insts 22f
7,460	8,308	9,742	10,849	12,703	13,985	14,940	15,919	17,282	18,026	18,920	19,335	20,506	21,747	23,515	Demand Deposits 24
26,635	33,969	41,619	56,302	70,126	86,761	98,598	109,810	121,175	135,764	150,966	162,512	174,713	198,421	228,053	Time, Savings,& Fgn.Currency Dep.......... 25
—	—	—	—	—	—	—	—	—	800	1,675	1,675	2,238	2,238	2,238	Bonds 26ab
5,079	5,070	6,023	7,423	8,152	7,076	8,239	9,182	10,858	12,513	14,081	15,771	18,113	17,502	19,658	Restricted Deposits.. 26b
8,172	8,520	8,916	10,673	11,400	7,804	6,009	4,969	5,086	6,248	12,047	16,924	14,704	15,618	19,167	Foreign Liabilities.. 26c
1,201	1,415	1,373	2,070	5,778	10,206	6,907	7,805	11,016	13,638	14,670	18,906	23,889	28,596	34,429	Central Government Deposits 26d
2,401	2,726	4,142	5,930	7,859	9,613	15,598	17,571	20,842	20,648	20,938	11,244	7,256	7,464	7,547	Credit from Monetary Authorities 26g
6,723	7,402	8,048	7,588	18,076	18,654	18,040	21,423	22,832	28,165	29,609	37,468	43,943	47,310	52,141	Other Items (Net) 27r
															Monetary Survey
End of Period															
2,476	2,220	-1,476	-1,353	16,748	33,566	45,646	51,111	48,914	53,508	49,194	36,111	25,092	22,860	21,270	Foreign Assets (Net) 31n
52,476	63,052	78,798	99,625	107,483	111,311	119,278	134,906	157,300	179,230	207,724	247,195	278,013	309,006	342,342	Domestic Credit 32
23,464	29,186	37,941	47,705	49,848	52,358	48,724	51,953	52,820	52,467	57,439	67,252	68,623	86,720	94,091	Claims on Central Govt. (Net) 32an
11,692	13,651	17,309	23,748	28,940	24,751	30,103	30,797	33,979	38,381	39,492	39,618	43,138	39,318	43,393	Claims on Nonfin.Pub.Enterprises........ 32c
14,881	17,330	20,428	24,454	24,816	30,978	36,885	48,831	66,777	83,810	105,545	133,799	159,958	176,693	197,038	Claims on Private Sector 32d
2,439	2,885	3,120	3,720	3,879	3,224	3,566	3,324	3,724	4,571	5,248	6,526	6,294	6,275	7,820	Claims on Other Banking Insts 32f
18,241	20,579	22,471	26,205	28,337	30,832	34,571	38,275	41,540	44,521	48,708	58,577	59,066	62,195	67,078	Money 34
3,878	4,484	5,588	8,249	11,104	10,253	10,918	9,892	10,980	10,260	9,332	10,225	11,148	17,493	31,330	*of which: Foreign Currency Deps.* 34a
26,637	33,970	41,623	56,303	70,127	86,762	98,602	109,834	121,227	135,882	151,129	162,795	174,844	198,804	228,413	Quasi-Money.. 35
12,214	17,124	21,749	29,802	36,093	27,608	25,964	30,851	33,335	32,015	31,792	33,271	37,435	47,102	60,149	*of which: Fgn. Currency Deposits*............ 35a
—	—	—	—	—	—	—	—	—	800	1,675	1,675	2,238	2,238	2,238	Bonds 36ab
5,079	5,070	6,023	7,423	8,152	7,076	8,239	9,182	10,858	12,513	14,081	15,771	18,113	17,502	19,658	Restricted Deposits.. 36b
4,994	5,654	7,206	8,342	17,616	20,207	23,512	28,727	32,590	39,021	41,325	44,489	48,845	51,125	46,226	Other Items (Net) 37r
44,878	54,549	64,094	82,508	98,464	117,594	133,174	148,109	162,766	180,404	199,837	221,372	233,909	260,999	295,491	Money plus Quasi-Money 35l
															Other Banking Institutions
															Specialized Banks
End of Period															
59	69	82	94	180	134	184	169	262	288	300	467	382	583	912	Cash 40
17	23	44	70	112	143	173	100	101	74	57	50	25	26	46	Foreign Assets 41
1,147	1,289	1,435	1,584	1,758	1,881	1,961	2,067	2,130	2,170	2,112	2,073	2,397	2,246	2,262	Claims on Nonfin.Pub.Enterprises........... 42c
2,983	3,596	4,047	4,950	5,442	5,458	6,361	7,425	8,785	11,355	13,814	17,607	20,657	22,884	25,728	Claims on Private Sector 42d
307	351	481	475	458	575	722	912	1,195	1,434	2,010	2,366	652	660	774	Demand Deposits 44
666	775	849	875	1,291	1,330	1,705	2,322	2,751	3,464	4,297	5,703	8,835	9,807	11,304	Time and Savings Deposits 45
27	25	27	21	19	19	32	20	32	36	42	59	53	43	14	Restricted Deposits.. 46b
554	771	848	1,061	1,411	1,456	1,640	1,550	934	865	906	745	732	889	725	Foreign Liabilities.. 46c
153	418	465	573	194	427	592	713	893	1,614	1,980	1,712	1,860	2,058	2,146	Central Government Deposits 46d
1,145	1,256	1,426	1,630	1,830	2,008	2,067	2,043	2,112	2,155	2,279	2,299	3,375	3,372	3,435	Credit from Monetary Authorities 46g
1,150	1,489	1,524	1,888	1,945	1,236	1,410	1,021	1,500	2,292	2,790	3,932	2,442	2,911	4,496	Credit from Deposit Money Banks 46h
205	-109	-12	175	345	565	509	1,180	1,861	2,027	1,980	3,381	5,513	5,999	6,054	Other Items (Net) 47r
589	643	694	773	894	1,046	1,335	1,866	2,591	3,524	4,877	6,680	8,783	11,322	14,584	Post Office: Savings Deposits ....45.. *i*
															Banking Survey
End of Period															
1,940	1,473	-2,280	-2,344	15,450	32,253	44,178	49,661	48,081	52,717	48,346	35,416	24,384	21,997	20,591	Foreign Assets (Net) 51n
54,630	65,297	81,406	102,675	111,585	116,128	124,880	142,295	166,797	190,938	222,041	266,064	301,818	337,171	374,998	Domestic Credit 52
23,927	29,431	38,187	47,940	50,629	53,060	49,570	53,175	55,127	55,223	61,079	72,968	75,668	96,030	106,577	Claims on Central Govt. (Net) 52an
12,839	14,940	18,744	25,331	30,698	26,632	32,064	32,864	36,108	40,551	41,603	41,691	45,535	41,564	45,655	Claims on Nonfin.Pub.Enterprises........ 52c
17,864	20,926	24,475	29,404	30,258	36,436	43,246	56,256	75,562	95,164	119,359	151,406	180,615	199,577	222,766	Claims on Private Sector 52d
46,380	56,249	66,036	84,537	100,927	120,411	136,752	153,040	169,041	188,538	210,721	235,654	251,797	282,205	321,241	Liquid Liabilities 55l
—	—	—	—	—	—	—	—	—	800	1,675	1,675	2,238	2,238	2,238	Bonds 56ab
5,106	5,095	6,050	7,443	8,171	7,095	8,271	9,202	10,890	12,550	14,123	15,830	18,166	17,546	19,672	Restricted Deposits.. 56b
5,083	5,425	7,041	8,352	17,937	20,876	24,035	29,714	34,948	41,768	43,868	48,322	54,003	57,178	52,439	Other Items (Net) 57r

Egypt

		1972	1973	1974	1975	1976	1977	1978	1979	1980	1981	1982	1983	1984	1985	1986
Interest Rates															*Percent Per Annum*	
Discount Rate *(End of Period)*	60	5.00	5.00	5.00	5.00	6.00	7.00	8.00	9.00	11.00	12.00	13.00	13.00	13.00	13.00	13.00
Treasury Bill Rate	60c	....	....	....	....	....	....	....	....	....	....	....	....	....	....	....
Deposit Rate	60l	....	....	....	....	3.0	4.7	5.9	7.0	8.3	10.0	11.0	11.0	11.0	11.0	11.0
Lending Rate	60p	....	....	....	....	8.0	8.8	10.2	12.0	13.3	15.0	15.0	15.0	15.0	15.0	15.0
Prices and Labor															*Index Numbers (1995=100):*	
Industrial Share Price (1992=100)	62	....	....	....	....	....	....	....	....	....	....	....	....	....	....	....
Wholesale Prices	63	6.2	6.6	7.6	8.1	8.8	9.6	11.0	12.1	14.7	15.9	17.3	20.1	22.1	25.0	29.4
Consumer Prices	64	4.7	5.0	5.5	6.0	6.6	7.5	8.3	9.1	†11.0	12.1	13.9	16.2	18.9	21.2	26.3
															Number in Thousands:	
Labor Force	67d	....	....	....	....	....	....	....	....	....	....	....	....	....	....	....
Employment	67e	....	....	....	....	....	....	....	....	....	....	....	....	....	....	....
Unemployment	67c	....	....	....	....	....	....	....	....	....	....	....	....	....	....	....
Unemployment Rate (%)	67r	....	....	....	....	....	....	....	....	....	....	....	....	....	....	....
International Transactions															*Millions of Pounds*	
Exports	70	358.8	444.2	593.3	548.6	595.5	668.5	679.8	1,287.8	2,132.2	2,263.0	2,184.1	2,250.1	2,197.9	2,600.0	2,054.0
Suez Canal Dues	70.s	—	—	—	33.2	121.7	167.4	201.1	412.1	464.3	621.8	657.8	678.8	665.4	654.2	769.0
Imports, c.i.f.	71	390.8	361.1	920.1	1,539.3	1,489.8	1,884.3	2,632.2	2,686.0	3,401.9	6,147.4	6,354.5	7,192.7	7,536.1	7,772.8	8,051.4
Balance of Payments															*Millions of US Dollars:*	
Current Account, n.i.e.	78ald	....	....	....	....	....	−1,200	−1,220	−1,542	−438	−2,136	−1,851	−330	−1,988	−2,166	−1,811
Goods: Exports f.o.b.	78aad						1,974	1,939	2,424	3,854	3,999	4,018	3,693	3,864	3,836	2,632
Goods: Imports f.o.b.	78abd						−4,038	−4,743	−6,002	−6,814	−7,918	−7,733	−8,251	−10,080	−9,050	−7,170
Trade Balance	78acd						−2,064	−2,804	−3,578	−2,960	−3,919	−3,715	−4,558	−6,216	−5,215	−4,538
Services: Credit	78add						1,601	1,633	1,788	2,393	2,537	2,800	3,133	2,990	3,024	3,358
Services: Debit	78aed						−1,448	−1,548	−1,773	−2,343	−2,487	−2,727	−2,767	−3,096	−3,190	−3,012
Balance on Goods & Services	78afd						−1,912	−2,719	−3,563	−2,911	−3,869	−3,642	−4,192	−6,323	−5,381	−4,192
Income: Credit	78agd						39	86	172	270	401	402	437	522	418	406
Income: Debit	78ahd						−315	−412	−420	−589	−897	−1,092	−1,080	−1,092	−1,211	−1,126
Balance on Gds, Serv. & Inc.	78aid						−2,188	−3,044	−3,811	−3,230	−4,366	−4,332	−4,835	−6,892	−6,174	−4,912
Current Transfers, n.i.e.: Credit	78ajd						988	1,824	2,269	2,791	2,230	2,481	4,505	4,904	4,007	3,101
Current Transfers: Debit	78akd						—	—	—	—	—	—	—	—	—	—
Capital Account, n.i.e.	78bcd						—	—	—	—	—	—	—	—	—	—
Capital Account, n.i.e.: Credit	78bad						—	—	—	—	—	—	—	—	—	—
Capital Account: Debit	78bbd						—	—	—	—	—	—	—	—	—	—
Financial Account, n.i.e.	78bjd						−773	143	1,488	956	2,046	1,458	285	1,718	1,381	1,936
Direct Investment Abroad	78bed						−7	−20	−5	−7	−6	−8	−19	−16	−3	−6
Dir. Invest. in Rep. Econ., n.i.e.	78bed						105	318	1,216	548	753	294	490	729	1,178	1,217
Portfolio Investment Assets	78bfd						6	4	3	5	7	—	6	1	20	—
Equity Securities	78bkd												6	1	20	
Debt Securities	78bld						6	4	3	5	7	—	—	—	—	—
Portfolio Investment Liab., n.i.e.	78bgd						—	—	—	—	—	—	—	—	—	—
Equity Securities	78bmd						—	—	—	—	—	—	—	—	—	—
Debt Securities	78bnd						—	—	—	—	—	—	—	—	—	—
Financial Derivatives Assets	78bwd						....	....	....	....	....	....	....	....	....	....
Financial Derivatives Liabilities	78bxd						....	....	....	....	....	....	....	....	....	....
Other Investment Assets	78bhd						−136	−194	−407	−249	379	250	−389	488	−369	479
Monetary Authorities	78bod						−6	−16	−9	−16	−6	−11	−11	−10	−15	−4
General Government	78bpd						−56	−25	−18	−10	−14	−3	−2	−2	−2	—
Banks	78bqd						−74	−153	−380	−223	399	265	−376	500	−352	483
Other Sectors	78brd						—	—	—	—	—	—	—	—	—	—
Other Investment Liab., n.i.e.	78bid						−741	34	680	658	914	922	196	516	555	245
Monetary Authorities	78bsd						−239	−264	−253	−326	−499	−351	−373	−288	−585	−438
General Government	78btd						569	843	734	729	1,853	1,559	1,143	838	890	1,105
Banks	78bud						−930	−341	279	340	−343	−166	−1	−40	16	−316
Other Sectors	78bvd						−141	−204	−80	−85	−97	−121	−573	6	233	−106
Net Errors and Omissions	78cad						66	13	39	92	143	148	131	24	585	−156
Overall Balance	78cbd						−1,906	−1,064	−16	610	53	−245	87	−247	−200	−31
Reserves and Related Items	79dad						1,906	1,064	16	−610	−53	245	−87	247	200	31
Reserve Assets	79dbd						−130	22	−52	−559	−105	−178	−152	55	−107	−282
Use of Fund Credit and Loans	79dcd						114	125	10	−77	−63	−36	−9	−18	−43	−57
Exceptional Financing	79ded						1,922	917	58	26	115	460	74	210	350	370
Government Finance															*Millions of Pounds:*	
Deficit (-) or Surplus	80	....	....	....	−938	−1,557	−1,114	−1,246	−1,964	....	†−1,096	−3,554	−2,364	−3,258	−3,439	−4,655
Revenue	81				2,039	2,306	3,388	3,758	4,666	....	†8,072	9,711	10,977	12,345	13,681	15,508
Grants Received	81z				250	223	60	62	20	....	†9	6	100	1	219	374
Expenditure	82				2,912	3,774	3,911	4,151	5,590	....	†7,892	11,595	11,195	13,361	14,945	17,552
Lending Minus Repayments	83				315	312	651	915	1,060	....	†1,285	1,676	2,246	2,243	2,394	2,985
Financing																
Domestic	84a	....	....	....	461	917	588	945	1,567	....	†731	3,019	2,034	3,001	2,947	4,432
Foreign	85a				477	640	526	301	397	....	†365	535	330	257	492	223
National Accounts															*Millions of Pounds:*	
Househ.Cons.Expend.,incl.NPISHs	96f	2,237	2,339	2,871	3,281	3,863	4,917	6,279	8,623	†11,023	†11,155	14,485	17,208	20,684	24,076	28,338
Government Consumption Expend.	91f	905	1,020	1,101	1,213	1,571	1,697	1,841	2,059	†2,549	†2,841	3,584	4,160	4,957	5,668	6,462
Gross Fixed Capital Formation	93e	405	462	640	1,228	1,385	1,825	2,618	3,346	†4,062	5,108	6,150	8,164	8,921	10,389	12,753
Changes in Inventories	93i	62	40	90	100	195	561	416	450	†266	100	351	150	500	600	240
Exports of Goods and Services	90c	457	531	890	894	1,034	1,470	1,945	3,251	†4,322	5,307	5,913	6,159	6,387	6,597	6,034
Imports of Goods and Services (-)	98c	649	729	1,395	1,831	1,772	2,260	3,316	5,254	†6,410	7,361	8,504	8,981	10,357	10,636	9,837
Gross Domestic Product (GDP)	99b	3,417	3,663	4,197	4,886	6,276	8,210	9,783	12,475	†15,470	17,150	22,465	26,424	31,693	37,451	44,131
Net Primary Income from Abroad	98.n	−14	−29	−112	−148	133	433	983	785	†1,685	742	446	1,217	2,005	1,681	1,176
Gross National Income (GNI)	99a	3,403	3,634	4,085	4,738	6,409	8,643	10,766	13,260	†17,231	17,892	21,327	26,051	30,605	35,892	39,397
GDP Volume 1981/82 Prices	99b.p	....	....	....	....	....	....	....	....	....	....	22,460	23,590	25,900	27,400	28,700
GDP Volume 1986/87 Prices	99b.p	....	....	....	....	....	....	....	....	....	....	....	....	....	....	....
GDP Volume 1991/92 Prices	99b.p	....	....	....	....	....	....	....	....	....	....	....	....	....	....	....
GDP Volume 1996/97 Prices	99b.p	....	....	....	....	....	....	....	....	....	....	....	....	....	....	....
GDP Volume (1995=100)	99bvp												54.5	57.2	62.8	66.5	69.6
GDP Deflator (1995=100)	99bip												20.2	22.6	24.7	27.6	31.1
																Millions:
Population	99z	34.84	35.62	36.42	37.23	37.87	38.79	39.82	40.98	42.13	41.67	42.84	44.02	45.23	46.47	47.81

1987	1988	1989	1990	1991	1992	1993	1994	1995	1996	1997	1998	1999	2000	2001		
Percent Per Annum															**Interest Rates**	
13.00	13.00	14.00	14.00	20.00	18.40	16.50	14.00	13.50	13.00	12.25	12.00	12.00	12.00	11.00	Discount Rate *(End of Period)*	60
....	....	....	....	....	....	....	....	....	....	8.8	8.8	9.0	9.1	7.2	Treasury Bill Rate	60c
11.0	11.0	11.7	12.0	12.0	12.0	12.0	11.8	10.9	10.5	9.8	9.4	9.2	9.5	9.5	Deposit Rate	60l
16.3	17.0	18.3	19.0	....	20.3	18.3	16.5	16.5	15.6	13.8	13.0	13.0	13.2	13.3	Lending Rate	60p
Period Averages															**Prices and Labor**	
....	....	....	....	....	....	....	....	....	....	449.11	474.64	586.65	703.91	770.15	Industrial Share Price (1992=100)	62
33.4	42.1	53.6	62.6	73.9	82.8	†89.9	94.1	100.0	108.3	112.8	114.4	115.4	117.5	118.7	Wholesale Prices	63
31.4	37.0	44.9	52.4	62.7	71.3	79.9	86.4	†100.0	107.2	†112.1	116.8	120.4	123.7	126.5	Consumer Prices	64
Period Averages																
....	....	15,698	15,964	15,599	15,862	16,494	17,174	17,365	....	....	18,027	18,616	....	....	Labor Force	67d
....	....	†14,926	14,361	13,827	14,399	†14,703	15,241	15,344	....	15,830	16,183	16,750	....	....	Employment	67e
....	....	1,108	1,347	1,463	1,416	1,801	1,877	1,917	....	†1,446	1,448	1,481	....	....	Unemployment	67c
....	....	6.9	8.6	9.6	9.0	10.9	11.0	11.3	....	†8.4	8.2	8.1	....	....	Unemployment Rate (%)	67r
Millions of Pounds															**International Transactions**	
3,046.0	3,994.4	5,734.7	6,953.8	11,764.6	10,173.4	7,558.8	11,767.9	11,703.8	12,004.1	13,285.9	10,605.9	12,086.1	16,273.8	16,335.6	Exports	70
844.5	904.6	1,506.8	3,177.6	5,707.9	6,187.9	6,628.4	6,998.1	6,692.9	6,381.4	6,072.5	6,108.9	6,015.3	6,223.1	7,545.6	Suez Canal Dues	70.s
11,357.8	16,308.6	16,623.7	24,823.2	25,216.2	27,656.1	27,553.8	34,598.9	39,892.0	44,218.0	44,769.0	54,771.0	54,399.0	48,645.0	50,660.0	Imports, c.i.f.	71
Minus Sign Indicates Debit															Balance of Payments	
–246	–1,048	–1,309	185	1,903	2,812	2,299	31	–254	–192	–711	–2,566	–1,635	–971	....	Current Account, n.i.e.	78al*d*
3,115	2,770	3,119	3,924	4,164	3,670	3,545	4,044	4,670	4,779	5,525	4,403	5,237	7,061	....	Goods: Exports f.o.b.	78aa*d*
–8,095	–9,378	–8,841	–10,303	–9,831	–8,901	–9,923	–9,997	–12,267	–13,169	–14,157	–14,617	–15,165	–15,382	....	Goods: Imports f.o.b.	78ab*d*
–4,980	–6,608	–5,722	–6,379	–5,667	–5,231	–6,378	–5,953	–7,597	–8,390	–8,632	–10,214	–9,928	–8,321	....	*Trade Balance*	78ac*d*
3,627	4,408	4,203	5,971	6,783	7,716	7,895	8,070	8,590	9,271	9,380	8,141	9,494	9,803	....	Services: Credit	78ad*d*
–2,742	–3,082	–3,283	–3,788	–3,364	–4,867	–5,367	–5,645	–4,873	–5,084	–6,770	–6,492	–6,452	–7,513	....	Services: Debit	78ae*d*
–4,095	–5,283	–4,802	–4,196	–2,248	–2,382	–3,850	–3,528	–3,880	–4,203	–6,021	–8,565	–6,886	–6,031	....	*Balance on Goods & Services*	78af*d*
503	575	709	857	860	915	1,110	1,330	1,578	1,901	2,122	2,030	1,788	1,871	....	Income: Credit	78ag*d*
–983	–776	–1,389	–1,879	–2,143	–2,797	–1,967	–2,114	–1,983	–1,556	–1,185	–1,075	–1,045	–983	....	Income: Debit	78ah*d*
–4,575	–5,484	–5,482	–5,218	–3,531	–4,264	–4,707	–4,312	–4,285	–3,858	–5,085	–7,610	–6,143	–5,143	....	*Balance on Gds, Serv. & Inc.*	78ai*d*
4,329	4,436	4,183	5,417	5,434	7,076	7,006	4,622	4,284	3,888	4,738	5,166	4,564	4,224	....	Current Transfers, n.i.e.: Credit	78aj*d*
—	—	–10	–14	—	—	—	–279	–253	–222	–363	–122	–55	–52	....	Current Transfers: Debit	78ak*d*
—	—	—	—	—	—	—	—	—	—	....	....	....	—	....	Capital Account, n.i.e.	78bc*d*
—	—	—	—	—	—	—	—	—	—	....	....	....	—	....	Capital Account, n.i.e.: Credit	78ba*d*
—	—	—	—	—	—	—	—	—	—	....	....	....	....	....	Capital Account: Debit	78bb*d*
–332	1,308	361	–11,039	–4,706	–168	–762	–1,450	–1,845	–1,459	1,958	1,901	–1,421	–1,646	....	Financial Account, n.i.e.	78bj*d*
–19	–12	–23	–12	–62	–4	—	–43	–93	–5	–129	–45	–38	–51	....	Direct Investment Abroad	78bd*d*
948	1,190	1,250	734	253	459	493	1,256	598	636	891	1,076	1,065	1,235	....	Dir. Invest. in Rep. Econ., n.i.e.	78be*d*
2	—	—	15	21	6	—	—	....	—	....	–63	–22	–3	....	Portfolio Investment Assets	78bf*d*
—	—	—	—	—	—	—	—	....	—	....	–63	–22	–3	....	Equity Securities	78bk*d*
2	—	—	15	21	6	—	—	....	—	....	....	....	....	....	Debt Securities	78bl*d*
—	—	—	—	—	—	4	3	20	545	816	–537	617	269	....	Portfolio Investment Liab., n.i.e.	78bg*d*
—	—	—	—	—	—	—	—	....	—	515	–160	658	269	....	Equity Securities	78bm*d*
—	—	—	—	—	—	4	3	20	545	301	–377	–41	....	....	Debt Securities	78bn*d*
....	....	....	....	....	....	....	—	....	—	....	....	....	....	....	Financial Derivatives Assets	78bw*d*
....	....	....	....	....	....	....	—	....	—	....	....	....	....	....	Financial Derivatives Liabilities	78bx*d*
–909	546	–1,299	–1,921	–2,298	1,183	319	–905	–396	–565	–170	39	–1,805	–2,991	....	Other Investment Assets	78bh*d*
–10	–7	–25	–16	–46	–13	–21	–25	65	65	37	24	–14	–21	....	Monetary Authorities	78bo*d*
–1	–17	–26	–2	–18	–104	–4	—	....	—	....	....	....	....	....	General Government	78bp*d*
–898	571	–1,249	–1,904	–2,234	1,300	523	–634	371	338	1,599	1,357	372	257	....	Banks	78bq*d*
—	—	—	—	—	—	–179	–246	–832	–968	–1,806	–1,342	–2,163	–3,227	....	Other Sectors	78br*d*
–354	–416	432	–9,855	–2,620	–1,812	–1,578	–1,761	–1,974	–2,070	551	1,431	–1,240	–105	....	Other Investment Liab., n.i.e.	78bi*d*
–832	–250	–372	–29	–113	–42	629	–5	–21	–4	–19	–204	–3	–5	....	Monetary Authorities	78bs*d*
754	387	688	–10,032	–2,204	–1,175	–1,761	–1,536	–1,783	–2,578	–1,506	–946	–989	–1,109	....	General Government	78bt*d*
–537	–749	–138	237	–333	–383	–202	–256	–148	324	1,715	1,393	–692	–129	....	Banks	78bu*d*
261	196	254	–31	30	–212	–244	36	–22	188	361	1,188	444	1,138	....	Other Sectors	78bv*d*
892	–362	414	630	730	716	–1,519	255	272	–74	–1,882	–722	–1,558	587	....	Net Errors and Omissions	78ca*d*
315	–102	–533	–10,224	–2,073	3,360	18	–1,164	–1,827	–1,725	–635	–1,387	–4,614	–2,030	....	*Overall Balance*	78cb*d*
–315	102	533	10,224	2,073	–3,360	–18	1,164	1,827	1,725	635	1,387	4,614	2,030	....	Reserves and Related Items	79da*d*
–669	153	435	–2,508	–2,775	–6,330	–2,809	–1,193	–409	–1,010	–1,185	535	4,027	1,306	....	Reserve Assets	79db*d*
89	–59	–24	–48	—	81	—	–22	–95	–85	–15	—	—	—	....	Use of Fund Credit and Loans	79dc*d*
266	7	122	12,781	4,849	2,889	2,791	2,379	2,331	2,820	1,836	852	587	724	....	Exceptional Financing	79de*d*
Year Ending June 30															**Government Finance**	
–2,613	–4,716	–4,126	–5,494	–1,067	–4,831	2,681	589	1,828	†–4,411	–5,178	–2,591	....	....	....	Deficit (-) or Surplus	80
16,764	19,916	22,601	23,435	35,430	49,678	59,443	67,828	73,654	†69,233	72,782	69,091	....	....	....	Revenue	81
1,087	548	1,023	1,428	2,820	3,337	3,269	2,811	2,056	†1,954	1,392	1,689	....	....	....	Grants Received	81z
18,091	22,548	23,913	26,738	35,499	54,649	56,143	65,382	68,689	†74,400	78,503	72,048	....	....	....	Expenditure	82
2,373	2,632	3,837	3,619	3,818	3,197	3,888	4,668	5,193	†1,198	849	1,323	....	....	....	Lending Minus Repayments	83
															Financing	
2,298	5,033	4,551	6,164	2,296	6,708	–1,319	1,454	–60	†5,844	6,785	4,397	....	....	....	Domestic	84a
315	–317	–425	–670	–1,229	–1,877	–1,362	–2,043	–1,768	†–1,433	–1,607	–1,806	....	....	....	Foreign	85a
Year Ending June 30															**National Accounts**	
35,900	43,550	54,100	68,900	82,200	101,000	115,000	130,500	151,900	176,490	190,600	208,620	220,830	245,500	....	Househ.Cons.Expend.,incl.NPISHs	96f
7,350	8,600	9,700	10,900	12,500	14,500	16,000	18,000	21,500	23,800	26,100	28,250	30,420	32,800	....	Government Consumption Expend.	91f
14,100	20,150	23,100	25,900	24,700	26,500	25,500	29,000	33,100	36,760	58,200	66,100	69,170	72,900	....	Gross Fixed Capital Formation	93e
–650	300	900	1,800	–1,200	–1,200	—	—	2,000	1,340	–2,500	5,610	7,950	7,500	....	Changes in Inventories	93i
6,476	10,700	13,800	19,300	30,900	39,500	40,100	39,500	45,990	47,620	50,100	45,540	45,780	54,300	....	Exports of Goods and Services	90c
11,740	21,700	24,800	31,500	39,800	45,000	48,700	50,100	58,290	61,100	66,200	73,900	71,700	76,500	....	Imports of Goods and Services (-)	98c
51,526	61,600	76,800	96,100	112,500	139,100	157,300	175,000	204,000	229,400	256,300	280,200	302,400	336,500	....	Gross Domestic Product (GDP)	99b
2,768	6,730	7,524	....	....	....	....	....	....	....	....	....	....	....	....	Net Primary Income from Abroad	98.n
46,818	....	....	....	....	....	....	....	....	....	....	....	....	....	....	Gross National Income (GNI)	99a
29,800	....	....	....	....	....	....	....	....	....	....	....	....	....	....	GDP Volume 1981/82 Prices	99b.*p*
51,530	54,340	57,010	60,250	60,920	63,650	....	....	....	....	....	....	....	....	....	GDP Volume 1986/87 Prices	99b.*p*
....	....	....	....	....	139,100	143,140	148,820	155,730	163,500	172,480	....	....	....	....	GDP Volume 1991/92 Prices	99b.*p*
....	....	....	....	....	....	....	....	....	....	256,300	270,600	286,900	301,600	....	GDP Volume 1996/97 Prices	99b.*p*
72.3	76.3	80.0	84.5	85.5	89.3	91.9	95.6	100.0	105.0	110.8	116.9	124.0	130.3	....	GDP Volume (1995=100)	99bv*p*
34.9	39.6	47.1	55.7	64.5	76.3	83.9	89.8	100.0	107.1	113.4	117.5	119.6	126.6	....	GDP Deflator (1995=100)	99bi*p*
Midyear Estimates																
49.05	50.27	50.86	51.91	52.99	54.08	55.20	56.34	57.51	58.76	60.08	61.34	62.65	63.98	†67.89	**Population**	99z

(See notes in the back of the book.)

El Salvador

		1972	1973	1974	1975	1976	1977	1978	1979	1980	1981	1982	1983	1984	1985	1986
Exchange Rates														*Colones per SDR: End of Period (aa)*		
Market Rate	aa	2.714	3.016	3.061	2.927	2.905	3.037	3.257	3.293	3.189	2.910	2.758	2.617	2.451	2.746	6.116
Market Rate	ae	2.500	2.500	2.500	2.500	2.500	2.500	2.500	2.500	2.500	2.500	2.500	2.500	2.500	2.500	5.000
Fund Position															*Millions of SDRs:*	
Quota	2f. s	35.0	35.0	35.0	35.0	35.0	35.0	43.0	43.0	64.5	64.5	64.5	89.0	89.0	89.0	89.0
SDRs	1b. s	3.7	3.8	3.6	3.9	4.0	7.8	7.6	13.2	—	.1	1.7	.1	—	—	—
Reserve Position in the Fund	1c. s	—	—	—	—	—	5.1	8.8	8.5	—	—	—	—	—	—	—
Total Fund Cred.&Loans Outstg.	2tl	8.8	—	17.9	17.9	12.8	—	—	—	25.0	57.3	117.1	132.6	127.2	100.6	50.9
International Liquidity												*Millions of US Dollars Unless Otherwise Indicated:*				
Total Reserves minus Gold	1l. d	63.9	41.3	77.6	107.0	185.4	211.2	268.1	142.6	77.7	71.9	108.5	160.2	165.8	179.6	169.7
SDRs	1b. d	4.1	4.6	4.4	4.6	4.7	9.5	9.9	17.4	—	.1	1.8	.1	—	—	—
Reserve Position in the Fund	1c. d	—	—	—	—	—	6.2	11.4	11.2	—	—	—	—	—	—	—
Foreign Exchange	1d. d	59.8	36.7	73.2	102.4	180.7	195.6	246.8	114.0	77.7	71.8	106.7	160.1	165.8	179.6	169.7
Gold (Million Fine Troy Ounces)	1ad	.486	.486	.486	.486	.486	.501	.501	.508	.516	.516	.516	.469	.469	.469	.469
Gold (National Valuation)	1and	18.5	20.5	20.5	20.5	20.5	21.1	21.1	21.5	21.8	21.8	21.8	19.8	19.8	19.8	19.8
Monetary Authorities: Other Liab.	4.. d	28.0	19.1	80.9	83.9	96.4	79.3	165.5	177.4	428.0	559.9	568.6	574.8	572.4	561.3	501.5
Deposit Money Banks: Assets	7a. d	8.0	14.4	21.0	14.6	15.7	10.6	24.3	14.6	43.0	67.5	39.0	87.0	104.7	148.4	94.5
Liabilities	7b. d	7.6	22.2	33.3	9.9	21.5	37.7	55.8	43.9	9.1	22.4	22.5	37.0	47.0	42.2	23.7
Other Banking Insts.: Assets	7e. d	....	....	....	....	....	....	....	....	....	....	....	....	....	....	....
Liabilities	7f. d	....	....	....	....	....	....	....	....	....	....	....	....	....	....	....
Monetary Authorities															*Millions of Colones:*	
Foreign Assets	11	206	154	245	319	515	581	723	404	249	234	286	406	416	446	1,322
Claims on Central Government	12a	152	131	253	281	295	391	401	688	1,158	1,781	1,675	1,601	2,014	2,157	2,105
Claims on Local Government	12b	....	....	....	....	....	....	....	....	....	....	—	2	2	1	1
Claims on Nonfin.Pub.Enterprises	12c	....	....	....	....	....	....	....	....	....	....	264	268	277	305	345
Claims on Private Sector	12d	77	90	128	194	231	275	306	360	878	887	†50	54	118	98	64
Claims on Deposit Money Banks	12e	149	222	287	243	285	336	316	533	606	586	638	788	677	886	817
Claims on Other Banking Insts	12f	....	....	....	....	....	....	....	....	....	....	860	669	803	916	945
Reserve Money	14	209	239	277	353	476	504	386	357	457	537	1,447	1,505	1,678	2,058	2,076
of which: Currency Outside DMBs	14a	175	201	241	253	380	432	500	743	719	703	732	724	836	1,080	1,157
Time, Savings,& Fgn.Currency Dep.	15	....	....	....	....	....	....	....	....	....	....	2	2	—	3	13
Bonds	16ab	—	—	—	—	—	—	—	—	—	—	—	—	—	8	—
Foreign Liabilities	16c	28	6	67	60	45	2	55	15	499	823	928	635	585	531	735
Long-Term Foreign Liabilities	16cl	66	42	190	202	233	196	358	429	651	743	816	1,149	1,158	1,149	2,083
Central Government Deposits	16d	31	47	72	85	131	235	213	195	260	305	158	216	590	610	1,093
Counterpart Funds	16e	....	....	....	....	....	....	....	....	....	....	52	—	—	150	250
Central Govt. Lending Funds	16f	....	....	....	....	....	....	....	....	....	....	97	103	52	52	105
Capital Accounts	17a	99	77	94	103	118	138	181	248	310	343	347	358	380	398	493
Other Items (Net)	17r	151	186	214	234	323	508	553	743	715	736	†−75	−178	−136	−150	−1,248
Deposit Money Banks															*Millions of Colones:*	
Reserves	20	218	256	295	378	484	529	419	393	508	567	†624	693	784	902	833
Foreign Assets	21	20	36	52	36	39	27	61	37	108	169	†97	218	262	371	473
Claims on Central Government	22a	7	9	22	18	31	52	54	91	34	154	†101	150	208	291	418
Claims on Local Government	22b	....	....	....	....	....	....	....	....	—	—	†—	—	—	—	—
Claims on Private Sector	22d	720	909	1,072	1,128	1,350	1,647	1,914	2,128	2,124	2,244	†2,574	2,848	3,081	3,977	4,917
Claims on Other Banking Insts	22f	....	....	....	....	....	....	....	....	....	....	6	2	3	3	2
Demand Deposits	24	208	263	314	392	512	550	579	567	693	693	†755	746	879	1,095	1,451
Time, Savings,& Fgn.Currency Dep.	25	418	492	560	705	854	1,015	1,154	1,125	1,135	1,397	†1,470	1,834	2,144	2,805	3,586
Bonds	26ab	120	121	135	117	123	139	149	162	178	191	†246	263	241	246	226
Foreign Liabilities	26c	16	52	81	22	52	94	139	110	15	48	†49	88	114	103	107
Long-Term Foreign Liabilities	26cl	3	3	3	2	2	—	—	—	8	7	†7	5	4	3	11
Central Government Deposits	26d	13	13	17	21	24	44	50	48	66	60	†54	60	121	190	262
Credit from Monetary Authorities	26g	143	218	287	243	285	336	316	533	606	586	†638	788	677	886	817
Liabilities to Other Banking Insts	26i	....	....	....	....	....	....	....	....	....	....	152	114	183	201	426
Liab. to Nonbank Financial Insts	26j	....	....	....	....	....	....	....	....	....	....	32	68	136	115	199
Capital Accounts	27a	70	83	79	90	107	131	149	164	181	181	†211	211	215	237	273
Other Items (Net)	27r	−26	−35	−33	−32	−55	−54	−90	−60	−108	−30	†−211	−266	−374	−336	−717
Monetary Survey															*Millions of Colones:*	
Foreign Assets (Net)	31n	182	132	150	273	457	511	589	316	−157	−469	†−594	−99	−21	184	952
Domestic Credit	32	912	1,079	1,386	1,516	1,753	2,086	2,413	3,025	3,868	4,700	†5,344	5,341	5,818	6,966	7,457
Claims on Central Govt. (Net)	32an	115	80	186	193	171	164	192	537	866	1,570	†1,565	1,476	1,512	1,648	1,168
Claims on Local Government	32b	3	4	8	7	14	30	37	78	25	47	†—	2	2	1	1
Claims on Nonfin.Pub.Enterprises	32c	....	....	....	....	....	....	....	....	....	....	290	289	299	323	360
Claims on Private Sector	32d	797	998	1,200	1,322	1,582	1,922	2,220	2,488	3,002	3,130	†2,624	2,902	3,199	4,075	4,981
Claims on Other Banking Insts	32f	....	....	....	....	....	....	....	....	....	....	865	672	806	919	947
Money	34	390	466	557	648	917	988	1,087	1,321	1,429	1,437	†1,578	1,557	1,773	2,251	2,694
Quasi-Money	35	418	492	560	705	854	1,015	1,154	1,125	1,135	1,397	†1,471	1,835	2,144	2,808	3,599
Bonds	36ab	120	121	135	117	123	221	230	243	190	250	†246	263	241	254	226
Long-Term Foreign Liabilities	36cl	69	45	193	204	235	196	358	429	659	750	†823	1,154	1,161	1,152	2,095
Counterpart Funds	36e	....	....	....	....	....	....	....	....	....	....	52	—	—	150	250
Central Govt. Lending Funds	36f	....	....	....	....	....	....	....	....	....	....	97	103	52	52	105
Liabilities to Other Banking Insts	36i	....	....	....	....	....	....	....	....	....	....	152	114	183	201	426
Liab. to Nonbank Financial Insts	36j	....	....	....	....	....	....	....	....	....	....	32	68	136	115	199
Capital Accounts	37a	169	160	173	193	225	270	330	412	491	524	†558	569	594	635	766
Other Items (Net)	37r	−72	−73	−81	−78	−144	−93	−158	−189	−193	−127	†−259	−424	−488	−468	−1,949
Money plus Quasi-Money	35l	807	958	1,116	1,353	1,770	2,004	2,241	2,446	2,563	2,834	†3,049	3,393	3,917	5,059	6,293

Exchange Rates

	1987	1988	1989	1990	1991	1992	1993	1994	1995	1996	1997	1998	1999	2000	2001	
Colones per US Dollar: End of Period (ae)																
Market Rate	7.093	6.729	6.571	11.424	11.558	12.609	11.909	12.774	13.014	12.589	11.813	12.327	12.016	11.407	10.996	aa
Market Rate	5.000	5.000	5.000	8.030	8.080	9.170	8.670	8.750	8.755	8.755	8.755	8.755	8.755	8.755	8.750	ae

Fund Position

End of Period

	1987	1988	1989	1990	1991	1992	1993	1994	1995	1996	1997	1998	1999	2000	2001	
Quota	89.0	89.0	89.0	89.0	89.0	125.6	125.6	125.6	125.6	125.6	125.6	125.6	171.3	171.3	171.3	2f. s
SDRs	—	—	—	—	—	—	—	.1	25.0	25.0	25.0	25.0	25.0	25.0	25.0	1b. s
Reserve Position in the Fund	—	—	—	—	—	—	—	—	—	—	—	—	—	—	—	1c. s
Total Fund Cred.&Loans Outstg.	15.8	8.0	4.1	.1	—	—	—	—	—	—	—	—	—	—	—	2tl

International Liquidity

End of Period

	1987	1988	1989	1990	1991	1992	1993	1994	1995	1996	1997	1998	1999	2000	2001	
Total Reserves minus Gold	186.1	161.6	265.9	414.8	287.2	422.1	536.2	649.4	758.3	936.9	1,307.9	1,613.1	2,003.8	1,922.4	1,741.0	1l. d
SDRs	—	—	—	—	—	—	—	.1	37.1	35.9	33.7	35.2	34.3	32.6	31.4	1b. d
Reserve Position in the Fund	—	—	—	—	—	—	—	—	—	—	—	—	—	—	—	1c. d
Foreign Exchange	186.1	161.6	265.9	414.8	287.2	422.1	536.2	649.3	721.2	901.0	1,274.2	1,577.9	1,969.5	1,889.8	1,709.6	1d. d
Gold (Million Fine Troy Ounces)	.469	.469	.469	.469	.469	.469	.469	.469	.469	.469	.469	.469	.469	.469	.469	1ad
Gold (National Valuation)	19.8	19.8	19.8	19.8	19.8	19.8	19.8	19.8	19.8	19.8	19.8	19.8	19.8	19.8	19.8	1and
Monetary Authorities: Other Liab.	395.1	374.0	484.8	546.7	342.1	368.1	293.1	158.6	175.6	217.9	244.4	169.5	166.5	151.4	....	4..d
Deposit Money Banks: Assets	81.8	72.3	93.1	86.9	65.8	81.1	94.0	59.3	67.4	103.2	111.7	118.8	124.3	279.1	....	7a. d
Liabilities	17.0	29.1	51.8	17.1	18.0	31.4	48.5	140.8	348.0	397.2	532.2	512.0	543.5	606.2	....	7b. d
Other Banking Insts.: Assets								.3	2.5	3.0	1.7	2.5	1.0	1.0	....	7e. d
Liabilities								1.5	13.7	7.4	2.7	2.5	6.1	6.1		7f. d

Monetary Authorities

End of Period

	1987	1988	1989	1990	1991	1992	1993	1994	1995	1996	1997	1998	1999	2000	2001	
Foreign Assets	1,398	1,275	1,966	4,391	3,734	5,094	6,385	7,473	8,211	9,721	12,720	15,556	17,258	16,567	....	11
Claims on Central Government	2,214	2,494	3,474	5,170	6,330	6,867	6,825	6,314	6,200	5,813	5,688	5,383	5,579	5,900	....	12a
Claims on Local Government	2	2	5	5	11	12	12	12	11	10	9	8	7	6	....	12b
Claims on Nonfin.Pub.Enterprises	414	382	334	—	—	13	—	—	—	—	—	—	—	—	....	12c
Claims on Private Sector	55	7	—	—	10											12d
Claims on Deposit Money Banks	1,098	1,261	2,094	2,249	1,094	1,243	1,317	—	—	—	172	711	1,160	1,026	....	12e
Claims on Other Banking Insts	1,003	1,307	1,303	556	629	638	657	2,292	2,979	3,510	3,514	3,456	3,381	2,953	....	12f
Reserve Money	2,595	3,011	3,332	4,318	5,289	6,086	8,730	10,762	12,101	13,313	15,084	16,339	18,004	16,265	....	14
of which: Currency Outside DMBs	1,298	1,326	1,727	1,856	2,023	2,433	2,655	2,999	3,161	3,130	3,250	3,531	4,716	3,932	....	14a
Time, Savings,& Fgn.Currency Dep.	23	15	278	546	773	693	853	841	887	327	74	56	26	27	....	15
Bonds	90	8	91	596	1,815	2,935	3,347	2,836	1,844	2,581	3,741	4,192	5,219	5,338	....	16ab
Foreign Liabilities	327	357	683	1,430	356	551	300	63	79	26	25	—	25	25	....	16c
Long-Term Foreign Liabilities	1,760	1,567	1,768	2,962	2,407	2,825	2,242	1,325	1,458	1,882	2,115	1,484	1,433	1,301	....	16cl
Central Government Deposits	907	1,213	1,137	1,521	1,772	1,446	1,496	2,009	1,767	1,214	1,220	4,100	4,623	5,091	....	16d
Counterpart Funds	1,098	1,214	1,727	900	528	716	99	54	18	13	15	11	11	11	....	16e
Central Govt. Lending Funds	105	105	362	105	517	22	20	1	1	1	1					16f
Capital Accounts	528	533	551	1,474	1,573	1,982	2,158	2,235	1,989	1,978	2,022	2,183	2,331	2,188	....	17a
Other Items (Net)	−1,249	−1,292	−752	−1,478	−3,223	−3,389	−4,047	−4,033	−2,744	−2,281	−2,192	−3,251	−4,287	−3,794	....	17r

Deposit Money Banks

End of Period

	1987	1988	1989	1990	1991	1992	1993	1994	1995	1996	1997	1998	1999	2000	2001	
Reserves	1,193	1,577	1,525	2,874	3,175	4,252	6,341	8,383	8,470	9,279	11,426	12,056	15,936	16,127	....	20
Foreign Assets	409	362	465	698	532	744	815	519	591	903	978	1,040	1,088	2,443	....	21
Claims on Central Government	485	446	645	557	774	765	1,009	1,347	1,368	1,346	1,261	791	1,123	3,194	....	22a
Claims on Local Government	—										17	25	70		....	22b
Claims on Private Sector	5,345	6,063	6,604	7,345	8,598	12,267	14,405	19,638	24,636	29,341	37,566	42,891	47,352	47,168	....	22d
Claims on Other Banking Insts	2	3	2	4	4	5	2	27	19	40	26	—	692	1,373	....	22f
Demand Deposits	1,278	1,459	1,474	2,045	2,139	3,059	3,506	3,539	3,934	4,996	4,921	5,268	5,416	5,517	....	24
Time, Savings,& Fgn.Currency Dep.	3,977	4,584	4,887	6,618	8,297	11,206	14,934	20,312	22,185	26,560	33,919	38,131	41,736	43,553	....	25
Bonds	215	223	244	171	158	150	112	100	397	1,040	1,642	1,677	2,113	2,866	....	26ab
Foreign Liabilities	80	143	258	136	144	288	420	1,157	2,787	2,816	3,502	2,613	2,458	3,144	....	26c
Long-Term Foreign Liabilities	6	2	1	1	2	—	—	75	260	662	1,157	1,869	2,301	2,163	....	26cl
Central Government Deposits	338	392	383	462	521	541	562	873	1,432	1,609	2,046	2,827	2,645	2,921	....	26d
Credit from Monetary Authorities	1,098	1,261	2,094	2,249	1,094	1,238	1,317	—	—	—	172	711	1,297	1,026	....	26g
Liabilities to Other Banking Insts	402	372	358	412	330	284	274	2,251	2,579	2,641	2,949	3,398	3,778	3,648	....	26i
Liab. to Nonbank Financial Insts	299	361	330	435	432	574	616	675	695	777	1,208	1,131	707	467	....	26j
Capital Accounts	311	386	416	409	743	809	860	2,102	2,620	3,352	4,310	5,125	5,579	6,119	....	27a
Other Items (Net)	−568	−732	−1,203	−1,461	−776	−117	−29	−1,170	−1,805	−3,543	−4,553	−5,947	−1,769	−1,120	....	27r

Monetary Survey

End of Period

	1987	1988	1989	1990	1991	1992	1993	1994	1995	1996	1997	1998	1999	2000	2001	
Foreign Assets (Net)	1,400	1,137	1,491	3,523	3,765	4,999	6,480	6,772	5,936	7,782	10,171	13,983	15,863	15,841	....	31n
Domestic Credit	8,290	9,110	10,859	11,667	14,065	18,579	20,852	26,749	32,014	37,237	44,816	45,628	50,978	52,582	....	32
Claims on Central Govt. (Net)	1,454	1,335	2,599	3,744	4,812	5,645	5,777	4,779	4,369	4,335	3,683	−753	−566	1,082	....	32an
Claims on Local Government	2	2	5	5	11	12	12	12	11	10	26	33	77	6	....	32b
Claims on Nonfin.Pub.Enterprises	429	393	347	12	1	13	—						41		....	32c
Claims on Private Sector	5,400	6,070	6,604	7,345	8,608	12,267	14,405	19,638	24,636	29,341	37,566	42,891	47,352	47,168	....	32d
Claims on Other Banking Insts	1,005	1,310	1,305	560	633	643	659	2,320	2,997	3,551	3,541	3,456	4,074	4,326	....	32f
Money	2,680	2,892	3,281	4,017	4,745	6,142	7,198	7,569	8,766	9,898	9,693	10,064	10,880	9,608	....	34
Quasi-Money	3,999	4,598	5,165	7,165	9,070	11,900	15,787	21,153	23,072	26,887	33,993	38,187	41,761	43,580	....	35
Bonds	305	230	335	766	1,973	3,085	3,459	2,936	2,241	3,622	5,383	5,869	7,332	8,204	....	36ab
Long-Term Foreign Liabilities	1,766	1,569	1,769	2,963	2,409	2,825	2,242	1,400	1,718	2,543	3,272	3,353	3,734	3,464	....	36cl
Counterpart Funds	1,098	1,214	1,727	900	528	716	99	54	18	13	15	11	11	11	....	36e
Central Govt. Lending Funds	105	105	362	105	517	22	20	1	1	1	1					36f
Liabilities to Other Banking Insts	402	372	358	412	330	284	274	2,251	2,579	2,641	2,949	3,398	3,778	3,648	....	36i
Liab. to Nonbank Financial Insts	299	361	330	435	432	574	616	675	695	777	1,208	1,131	707	467	....	36j
Capital Accounts	839	918	966	1,883	2,316	2,792	3,018	4,337	4,609	5,330	6,331	7,308	7,910	8,308	....	37a
Other Items (Net)	−1,802	−2,012	−1,943	−3,455	−4,490	−4,760	−5,378	−6,854	−5,750	−6,692	−7,859	−9,711	−9,274	−8,867	....	37r
Money plus Quasi-Money	6,680	7,491	8,447	11,181	13,815	18,042	22,984	28,722	31,839	36,784	43,686	48,251	52,641	53,188	....	35l

El Salvador

		1972	1973	1974	1975	1976	1977	1978	1979	1980	1981	1982	1983	1984	1985	1986
Other Banking Institutions																*Millions of Colones:*
Reserves	40	...	...	...	...	...	...	...	...	...	...	...	...	...	...	...
Foreign Assets	41	...	...	...	...	...	...	...	...	...	...	...	...	...	...	...
Claims on Central Government	42a	...	...	...	...	...	...	...	...	...	...	...	...	...	...	...
Claims on Private Sector	42d	...	...	...	...	...	...	...	...	...	...	...	...	...	...	...
Claims on Deposit Money Banks	42e	...	...	...	...	...	...	...	...	...	...	...	...	...	...	...
Time, Savings,& Fgn.Currency Dep.	45	...	...	...	...	...	...	...	...	...	...	...	...	...	...	...
Money Market Instruments	46aa	...	...	...	...	...	...	...	...	...	...	...	...	...	...	...
Foreign Liabilities	46c	...	...	...	...	...	...	...	...	...	...	...	...	...	...	...
Long-Term Foreign Liabilities	46cl	...	...	...	...	...	...	...	...	...	...	...	...	...	...	...
Central Government Deposits	46d	...	...	...	...	...	...	...	...	...	...	...	...	...	...	...
Credit from Monetary Authorities	46g	...	...	...	...	...	...	...	...	...	...	...	...	...	...	...
Credit from Deposit Money Banks	46h	...	...	...	...	...	...	...	...	...	...	...	...	...	...	...
Capital Accounts	47a	...	...	...	...	...	...	...	...	...	...	...	...	...	...	...
Other Items (Net)	47r	...	...	...	...	...	...	...	...	...	...	...	...	...	...	...
Banking Survey																*Millions of Colones:*
Foreign Assets (Net)	51n	...	...	...	...	...	...	...	...	...	...	...	...	...	...	...
Domestic Credit	52	...	...	...	...	...	...	...	...	...	...	...	...	...	...	...
Claims on Central Govt. (Net)	52an	...	...	...	...	...	...	...	...	...	...	...	...	...	...	...
Claims on Local Government	52b	...	...	...	...	...	...	...	...	...	...	...	...	...	...	...
Claims on Nonfin.Pub.Enterprises	52c	...	...	...	...	...	...	...	...	...	...	...	...	...	...	...
Claims on Private Sector	52d	...	...	...	...	...	...	...	...	...	...	...	...	...	...	...
Liquid Liabilities	55l	...	...	...	...	...	...	...	...	...	...	...	...	...	...	...
Money Market Instruments	56aa	...	...	...	...	...	...	...	...	...	...	...	...	...	...	...
Bonds	56ab	...	...	...	...	...	...	...	...	...	...	...	...	...	...	...
Long-Term Foreign Liabilities	56cl	...	...	...	...	...	...	...	...	...	...	...	...	...	...	...
Counterpart Funds	56e	...	...	...	...	...	...	...	...	...	...	...	...	...	...	...
Central Govt. Lending Funds	56f	...	...	...	...	...	...	...	...	...	...	...	...	...	...	...
Liab. to Nonbank Financial Insts	56j	...	...	...	...	...	...	...	...	...	...	...	...	...	...	...
Capital Accounts	57a	...	...	...	...	...	...	...	...	...	...	...	...	...	...	...
Other Items (Net)	57r	...	...	...	...	...	...	...	...	...	...	...	...	...	...	...
Interest Rates																*Percent Per Annum*
Money Market Rate	60b	...	...	...	...	...	...	...	...	...	...	...	...	...	...	...
Deposit Rate	60l	...	...	...	...	...	...	...	...	...	...	...	12.50	12.50	12.50	15.00
Deposit Rate (Fgn. Currency)	60l. *f*	...	...	...	...	...	...	...	...	...	...	...	...	...	...	...
Lending Rate	60p	...	...	...	...	...	...	...	...	...	...	...	15.00	14.00	14.00	17.00
Lending Rate (Fgn. Currency)	60p. *f*	...	...	...	...	...	...	...	...	...	...	...	...	...	...	...
Prices and Labor																*Index Numbers (1995=100):*
Wholesale Prices	63	8.3	10.0	12.6	12.8	17.2	25.4	†20.3	21.9	25.3	27.9	30.2	32.3	34.2	38.9	51.5
Consumer Prices	64	3.5	3.8	4.4	5.2	5.6	6.3	7.1	†8.1	9.6	11.0	12.3	13.9	15.5	18.9	25.0
																Number in Thousands:
Labor Force	67d	...	...	...	...	...	...	...	...	...	...	...	...	...	...	...
Employment	67e	...	...	...	...	...	...	...	...	...	...	...	...	...	1,373	299
Unemployment	67c	...	...	...	...	...	...	...	...	...	...	...	...	...	280	†28
Unemployment Rate (%)	67r	...	...	...	...	...	...	...	...	...	...	...	...	...	16.9	†7.9
International Transactions																*Millions of US Dollars*
Exports	70..d	273.3	352.0	462.6	531.4	743.3	972.4	848.4	1,223.2	966.8	796.6	699.4	735.3	717.3	679.0	754.9
Imports, c.i.f.	71..d	272.4	377.2	562.5	614.0	734.7	929.1	1,028.0	1,037.0	966.1	985.6	856.8	891.5	977.4	961.4	934.9
Balance of Payments																*Millions of US Dollars:*
Current Account, n.i.e.	78ald	...	...	...	...	23.6	37.4	−278.7	32.2	33.9	−250.5	−120.0	−147.8	−188.7	−188.7	−17.1
Goods: Exports f.o.b.	78aad	...	...	...	...	744.6	973.5	801.6	1,132.3	1,075.3	798.0	699.6	758.0	725.9	679.0	777.9
Goods: Imports f.o.b.	78abd	...	...	...	...	−681.0	−861.0	−951.1	−954.7	−897.0	−898.4	−799.8	−832.2	−914.5	−895.0	−902.3
Trade Balance	78acd	...	...	...	...	63.7	112.5	−149.4	177.6	178.4	−100.3	−100.2	−74.3	−188.6	−216.0	−124.4
Services: Credit	78add	...	...	...	...	116.1	113.0	121.0	133.0	138.8	124.7	117.4	135.8	165.4	223.9	241.1
Services: Debit	78aed	...	...	...	...	−171.4	−208.6	−256.8	−300.6	−273.5	−263.4	−253.0	−246.3	−242.0	−290.8	−281.0
Balance on Goods & Services	78afd	...	...	...	...	8.4	16.8	−285.3	10.0	43.7	−239.0	−235.9	−184.7	−265.1	−282.8	−164.4
Income: Credit	78agd	...	...	...	...	38.9	39.9	37.0	90.4	56.6	47.5	50.9	37.0	62.9	48.5	36.9
Income: Debit	78ahd	...	...	...	...	−52.8	−65.5	−88.8	−130.3	−118.6	−119.3	−142.4	−151.6	−159.1	−137.9	−138.9
Balance on Gds, Serv. & Inc.	78aid	...	...	...	...	−5.6	−8.7	−337.2	−30.0	−18.3	−310.9	−327.4	−299.3	−361.3	−372.3	−266.4
Current Transfers, n.i.e.: Credit	78ajd	...	...	...	...	38.1	50.0	61.8	65.6	52.9	75.2	210.5	154.1	176.1	186.7	251.8
Current Transfers: Debit	78akd	...	...	...	...	−8.9	−3.9	−3.4	−3.3	−.6	−14.8	−3.1	−2.6	−3.5	−3.1	−2.5
Capital Account, n.i.e.	78bcd	...	...	...	...	—	−6.5	−7.1	−10.8	−3.3	—	—	—	—	—	—
Capital Account, n.i.e.: Credit	78bad	...	...	...	...	—	—	—	—	—	—	—	—	—	—	—
Capital Account: Debit	78bbd	...	...	...	...	—	−6.5	−7.1	−10.8	−3.3	—	—	—	—	—	—
Financial Account, n.i.e.	78bjd	...	...	...	...	85.6	43.9	340.4	−49.0	30.6	187.6	138.6	87.0	32.7	2.9	26.7
Direct Investment Abroad	78bdd	...	...	...	...	...	...	...	...	...	...	...	...	...	...	...
Dir. Invest. in Rep. Econ., n.i.e.	78bed	...	...	...	...	13.0	18.6	23.4	−10.0	5.9	−5.7	−1.0	28.1	12.4	12.4	24.1
Portfolio Investment Assets	78bfd	...	...	...	...	—	−.8	−1.1	—	—	—	—	—	—	—	—
Equity Securities	78bkd	...	...	...	...	—	—	—	—	—	—	—	—	—	—	—
Debt Securities	78bld	...	...	...	...	—	−.8	−1.1	—	—	—	—	—	—	—	—
Portfolio Investment Liab., n.i.e.	78bgd	...	...	...	...	17.8	1.5	5.1	−5.7	−1.0	—	−1.0	.1	—	—	−3.1
Equity Securities	78bmd	...	...	...	...	3.3	−1.4	2.1	−2.2	—	—	—	—	—	—	—
Debt Securities	78bnd	...	...	...	...	14.5	2.9	3.0	−3.5	−1.0	—	−1.0	.1	—	—	−3.1
Financial Derivatives Assets	78bwd	...	...	...	...	...	...	...	...	...	...	...	...	...	...	...
Financial Derivatives Liabilities	78bxd	...	...	...	...	...	...	...	...	...	...	...	...	...	...	...
Other Investment Assets	78bhd	...	...	...	...	−30.2	−143.4	−33.0	7.3	−24.3	−22.4	−1.2	−45.2	−20.7	−51.6	54.4
Monetary Authorities	78bod	...	...	...	...	...	...	...	...	...	...	...	...	...	...	...
General Government	78bpd	...	...	...	...	−1.1	−2.0	−1.6	−1.0	−4.2	−4.6	−21.1	−1.6	−2.2	−10.4	−1.5
Banks	78bqd	...	...	...	...	−1.2	5.1	−13.7	9.7	−28.4	−24.5	28.6	−48.1	−17.7	−43.8	55.6
Other Sectors	78brd	...	...	...	...	−27.9	−146.5	−17.7	−1.4	8.2	6.7	−8.7	4.5	−.8	2.5	.3
Other Investment Liab., n.i.e.	78bid	...	...	...	...	85.0	167.9	346.0	−40.7	50.0	215.7	141.8	104.0	41.0	42.2	−48.8
Monetary Authorities	78bsd	...	...	...	...	−8.4	5.0	58.6	13.4	73.9	63.7	7.3	−12.4	−74.6	−45.7	−81.0
General Government	78btd	...	...	...	...	25.2	20.6	52.0	55.9	110.5	154.9	119.6	161.0	88.8	104.2	62.5
Banks	78bud	...	...	...	...	12.9	15.2	17.6	−11.9	−35.6	13.3	.2	14.6	10.0	−4.6	−18.0
Other Sectors	78bvd	...	...	...	...	55.2	127.0	217.8	−98.1	−98.8	−16.2	14.7	−59.3	16.8	−11.8	−12.4
Net Errors and Omissions	78cad	...	...	...	...	−24.9	−33.8	−29.1	−106.2	−318.2	−58.6	−61.4	−50.5	−51.9	23.0	−141.8
Overall Balance	78cbd	...	...	...	...	84.3	40.9	25.4	−133.8	−257.0	−121.6	−42.9	−111.3	−207.9	−162.8	−132.2
Reserves and Related Items	79dad	...	...	...	...	−84.3	−40.9	−25.4	133.8	257.0	121.6	42.9	111.3	207.9	162.8	132.2
Reserve Assets	79dbd	...	...	...	...	−78.4	−26.0	−55.4	133.8	68.1	11.3	−36.5	−40.2	−1.4	—	14.1
Use of Fund Credit and Loans	79dcd	...	...	...	...	−5.9	−14.9	—	—	33.4	36.8	65.1	16.5	−5.3	−27.2	−57.9
Exceptional Financing	79ded	...	...	...	...	—	—	30.0	—	155.5	73.5	14.3	135.0	214.6	190.0	176.1

		1987	1988	1989	1990	1991	1992	1993	1994	1995	1996	1997	1998	1999	2000	2001
Other Banking Institutions		*End of Period*														
Reserves	40	....	....	....	....	....	....	....	732	1,203	1,235	488	197	17	28	....
Foreign Assets	41	....	....	....	....	....	....	....	2	22	27	15	22	9	9	....
Claims on Central Government	42a	....	....	....	....	....	....	....	—	—	146	—	—	—	—	....
Claims on Private Sector	42d	....	....	....	....	....	....	....	3,409	4,944	4,179	2,012	1,229	590	616	....
Claims on Deposit Money Banks	42e	....	....	....	....	....	....	....	181	147	283	73	3	4	16	....
Time, Savings,& Fgn.Currency Dep.	45	....	....	....	....	....	....	....	3,701	5,015	4,985	1,886	917	226	280	....
Money Market Instruments	46aa	....	....	....	....	....	....	....	80	173	75	—	—	—	—	....
Foreign Liabilities	46c	....	....	....	....	....	....	....	13	120	57	24	22	54	53	....
Long-Term Foreign Liabilities	46cl	....	....	....	....	....	....	....	—	—	8	—	—	—	—	....
Central Government Deposits	46d	....	....	....	....	....	....	....	149	124	55	1	—	—	—	....
Credit from Monetary Authorities	46g	....	....	....	....	....	....	....	17	—	—	63	—	—	—	....
Credit from Deposit Money Banks	46h	....	....	....	....	....	....	....	60	91	10	26	25	2	—	....
Capital Accounts	47a	....	....	....	....	....	....	....	281	407	548	–27	–130	–248	–235	....
Other Items (Net)	47r	....	....	....	....	....	....	....	23	385	132	614	617	586	570	....
Banking Survey		*End of Period*														
Foreign Assets (Net)	51n	....	....	....	....	....	....	....	6,761	5,837	7,752	10,162	13,983	15,818	15,797	....
Domestic Credit	52	....	....	....	....	....	....	....	27,688	33,837	37,956	43,286	43,400	47,494	48,872	....
Claims on Central Govt. (Net)	52an	....	....	....	....	....	....	....	4,630	4,245	4,426	3,682	–753	–566	1,082	....
Claims on Local Government	52b	....	....	....	....	....	....	....	12	11	10	26	33	77	6	....
Claims on Nonfin.Pub.Enterprises	52c	....	....	....	....	....	....	....	—	—	—	—	—	41	—	....
Claims on Private Sector	52d	....	....	....	....	....	....	....	23,047	29,580	33,520	39,578	44,120	47,942	47,784	....
Liquid Liabilities	55l	....	....	....	....	....	....	....	31,691	35,652	40,534	45,084	48,971	52,850	53,440	....
Money Market Instruments	56aa	....	....	....	....	....	....	....	80	173	75	—	—	—	—	....
Bonds	56ab	....	....	....	....	....	....	....	2,936	2,241	3,622	5,383	5,869	7,332	8,204	....
Long-Term Foreign Liabilities	56cl	....	....	....	....	....	....	....	1,400	1,718	2,551	3,272	3,353	3,734	3,464	....
Counterpart Funds	56e	....	....	....	....	....	....	....	54	18	13	15	11	11	11	....
Central Govt. Lending Funds	56f	....	....	....	....	....	....	....	1	1	1	1	—	—	—	....
Liab. to Nonbank Financial Insts	56j	....	....	....	....	....	....	....	675	695	777	1,208	1,131	707	467	....
Capital Accounts	57a	....	....	....	....	....	....	....	4,618	5,016	5,878	6,304	7,178	7,663	8,073	....
Other Items (Net)	57r	....	....	....	....	....	....	....	–7,004	–5,839	–7,742	–7,820	–9,130	–8,985	–8,990	....
Interest Rates		*Percent Per Annum*														
Money Market Rate	60b	....	....	....	....	....	....	....	....	....	....	10.43	9.43	10.68	6.93	5.28
Deposit Rate	60l	15.00	15.00	16.25	18.00	16.11	11.51	15.27	13.57	14.37	13.98	11.77	10.32	10.75	9.31	....
Deposit Rate (Fgn. Currency)	60l. *f*	....	....	....	....	....	....	....	....	....	8.38	7.68	6.86	6.61	6.50	5.48
Lending Rate	60p	17.00	17.00	18.50	21.17	19.67	16.43	19.42	19.03	19.08	18.57	16.05	14.98	15.46	13.96	....
Lending Rate (Fgn. Currency)	60p. *f*	....	....	....	....	....	....	....	....	....	12.53	10.82	9.93	10.38	10.74	9.60
Prices and Labor		*Period Averages*														
Wholesale Prices	63	51.9	54.8	60.1	71.4	76.4	78.1	83.9	90.5	100.0	104.8	105.9	99.5	98.1	101.3	99.7
Consumer Prices	64	31.2	37.4	44.0	54.5	62.4	†69.4	82.2	90.9	100.0	109.8	114.7	117.6	118.2	120.9	125.5
		Period Averages														
Labor Force	67d	....	....	....	....	939	1,683	....	2,010	2,051	2,140	2,188	2,403	2,445	....	....
Employment	67e	....	†717	790	885	890	†1,782	....	1,951	1,973	2,056	2,076	2,228	2,275	....	....
Unemployment	67c	....	†74	72	98	72	81	†109	162	163	171	180	176	170	....	....
Unemployment Rate (%)	67r	....	†9.4	8.4	10.0	7.5	7.9	†9.9	7.7	7.7	7.7	8.0	7.3	7.0	....	....
International Transactions		*Millions of US Dollars*														
Exports	70..*d*	590.9	608.8	497.5	581.5	588.0	597.5	731.7	843.9	998.0	1,024.4	1,371.1	1,256.4	1,176.6	1,332.3	1,213.5
Imports, c.i.f.	71..*d*	994.1	1,007.0	1,161.3	1,262.5	1,405.9	1,698.5	1,912.2	2,248.7	2,853.3	2,670.9	2,980.5	3,121.4	3,140.0	3,794.7	3,865.8
Balance of Payments		*Minus Sign Indicates Debit*														
Current Account, n.i.e.	78al*d*	–68.2	–129.2	–369.7	–260.8	–212.4	–195.1	–122.8	–18.0	–261.6	–169.0	–97.8	–90.7	–274.2	–417.7	....
Goods: Exports f.o.b.	78aa*d*	589.6	610.6	557.5	643.9	586.8	598.1	1,031.8	1,252.3	1,651.1	1,787.4	2,437.1	2,459.5	2,534.3	2,971.6	....
Goods: Imports f.o.b.	78ab*d*	–938.7	–966.5	–1,220.2	–1,309.5	–1,291.4	–1,560.5	–1,994.0	–2,422.3	–3,113.5	–3,029.7	–3,580.3	–3,765.2	–3,879.4	–4,690.2	....
Trade Balance	78ac*d*	–349.1	–355.9	–662.7	–665.6	–704.6	–962.3	–962.3	–1,170.0	–1,462.3	–1,242.3	–1,143.2	–1,305.7	–1,345.1	–1,718.7	....
Services: Credit	78ad*d*	318.1	328.0	351.0	329.2	310.9	377.1	335.5	387.2	388.6	414.4	475.8	588.5	629.0	673.9	....
Services: Debit	78ae*d*	–280.1	–341.4	–392.1	–314.7	–322.9	–364.7	–386.7	–428.9	–509.8	–504.6	–628.0	–737.3	–821.9	–952.0	....
Balance on Goods & Services	78af*d*	–311.1	–369.3	–703.9	–651.1	–716.6	–949.9	–1,013.4	–1,211.7	–1,583.5	–1,332.5	–1,295.4	–1,454.5	–1,538.0	–1,996.8	....
Income: Credit	78ag*d*	42.9	24.2	26.1	29.5	30.3	31.7	30.8	35.5	54.0	44.1	75.1	111.4	112.8	141.4	....
Income: Debit	78ah*d*	–134.9	–129.6	–127.4	–161.1	–151.1	–128.9	–142.4	–130.1	–120.7	–134.4	–238.3	–274.4	–405.6	–391.3	....
Balance on Gds, Serv. & Inc.	78ai*d*	–403.1	–474.7	–805.2	–782.7	–837.4	–1,047.1	–1,125.0	–1,306.4	–1,650.2	–1,422.8	–1,458.6	–1,617.5	–1,830.7	–2,246.7	....
Current Transfers, n.i.e.: Credit	78aj*d*	336.8	347.6	437.6	524.6	627.5	852.8	1,004.7	1,290.9	1,393.2	1,258.6	1,363.6	1,534.1	1,565.5	1,830.4	....
Current Transfers: Debit	78ak*d*	–1.9	–2.1	–2.1	–2.7	–2.5	–.7	–2.5	–2.5	–4.6	–4.8	–2.7	–7.3	–9.0	–1.4	....
Capital Account, n.i.e.	78bc*d*	—	—	—	—	—	—	—	—	—	—	11.6	28.6	31.9	109.2	....
Capital Account, n.i.e.: Credit	78ba*d*	—	—	—	—	—	—	—	—	—	—	11.6	28.9	32.1	109.7	....
Capital Account: Debit	78bb*d*	—	—	—	—	—	—	—	—	—	....	—	–.3	–.2	–.5	....
Financial Account, n.i.e.	78bj*d*	–60.3	52.3	118.2	–11.4	–61.1	–4.3	73.9	115.8	438.3	358.1	653.2	1,034.3	584.8	330.2	....
Direct Investment Abroad	78bd*d*	—	—	—	—	—	—	—	—	—	–2.4	—	–1.0	–53.8	6.6	....
Dir. Invest. in Rep. Econ., n.i.e.	78be*d*	18.3	17.0	14.4	1.9	25.2	15.3	16.4	—	38.0	–4.8	59.0	1,103.7	231.4	185.4	....
Portfolio Investment Assets	78bf*d*	—	—	—	—	—	—	—	—	—	.5	—	—	–2.1	–9.1	....
Equity Securities	78bk*d*	—	—	—	—	—	—	—	—	—	.5	—	—	—	....	....
Debt Securities	78bl*d*	—	—	—	—	—	—	—	—	—	....	—	—	–2.1	–9.1	....
Portfolio Investment Liab., n.i.e.	78bg*d*	—	—	—	—	—	—	—	—	68.5	150.0	115.9	–226.4	74.8	63.2	....
Equity Securities	78bm*d*	—	—	—	—	—	—	—	—	....	....	—	—	—	....	....
Debt Securities	78bn*d*	—	—	—	—	—	—	—	—	68.5	150.0	115.9	–226.4	74.8	63.2	....
Financial Derivatives Assets	78bw*d*	....	....	....	....	....	....	....	....	....	....	....	....	....	....	....
Financial Derivatives Liabilities	78bx*d*	....	....	....	....	....	....	....	....	....	....	....	....	....	....	....
Other Investment Assets	78bh*d*	9.7	10.6	–1.1	–20.9	15.0	—	18.5	–8.7	24.2	4.7	–19.9	12.2	–124.3	–248.2	....
Monetary Authorities	78bo*d*	....	....	....	....	....	....	14.4	—	35.0	—	—	—	—	....	....
General Government	78bp*d*	–1.2	–.4	–.3	–.6	–.2	—	—	—	—	—	—	—	—	....	....
Banks	78bq*d*	12.6	9.5	.8	–17.2	21.3	—	4.1	–8.7	–10.2	—	2.1	–8.0	–1.8	–149.6	....
Other Sectors	78br*d*	–1.8	1.5	–1.7	–3.1	–6.0	—	—	—	–.6	4.7	–21.9	20.2	–122.4	–98.6	....
Other Investment Liab., n.i.e.	78bi*d*	–88.3	24.7	104.9	7.5	–101.3	–19.6	39.0	124.5	307.5	210.2	498.2	145.7	458.7	332.4	....
Monetary Authorities	78bs*d*	–121.1	–42.1	–17.7	–51.1	–139.4	–92.8	–91.1	–147.2	38.2	51.2	27.9	–72.2	–5.7	–8.8	....
General Government	78bt*d*	52.0	67.1	103.2	84.5	14.3	42.2	115.4	177.0	46.4	162.8	154.6	162.9	51.3	84.4	....
Banks	78bu*d*	–7.2	11.4	12.0	–25.3	.7	—	14.7	94.7	219.9	–3.2	130.8	–20.4	31.8	66.5	....
Other Sectors	78bv*d*	–11.9	–11.7	7.4	–.7	23.0	31.0	—	—	3.1	–.6	184.9	75.5	381.4	190.3	....
Net Errors and Omissions	78ca*d*	6.9	–107.1	140.9	299.4	125.6	65.6	107.6	15.4	–28.4	–24.2	–204.4	–668.9	–143.2	–70.5	....
Overall Balance	78cb*d*	–121.6	–184.1	–110.6	27.1	–147.9	–133.8	58.6	113.3	148.3	164.8	362.7	303.3	199.2	–48.8	....
Reserves and Related Items	79da*d*	121.6	184.1	110.6	–27.1	147.9	133.8	–58.6	–113.3	–148.3	–164.8	–362.7	–303.3	–199.2	48.8	....
Reserve Assets	79db*d*	–36.8	30.1	–110.0	–164.6	70.0	–91.6	–111.9	–113.3	–148.3	–164.8	–362.7	–303.3	–199.2	48.8	....
Use of Fund Credit and Loans	79dc*d*	–45.0	–10.5	–5.0	–5.2	–.2	—	—	—	—	—	—	—	—	—	....
Exceptional Financing	79de*d*	203.5	164.5	225.7	142.7	78.1	225.5	53.3	—	—	—	—	—	—	—	....

El Salvador

	1972	1973	1974	1975	1976	1977	1978	1979	1980	1981	1982	1983	1984	1985	1986
International Investment Position														*Millions of US Dollars*	
Assets .... 79aa d	...	...	....	....	....	....	....	....	....	....	....	....	....	....	...
Direct Investment Abroad .... 79ab d	...	...	....	....	....	....	....	....	....	....	....	....	....	....	...
Portfolio Investment .... 79ac d	...	...	....	....	....	....	....	....	....	....	....	....	....	....	...
Equity Securities .... 79ad d	...	...	....	....	....	....	....	....	....	....	....	....	....	....	...
Debt Securities .... 79ae d	...	...	....	....	....	....	....	....	....	....	....	....	....	....	...
Financial Derivatives .... 79al d	...	...	....	....	....	....	....	....	....	....	....	....	....	....	...
Other Investment .... 79af d	...	...	....	....	....	....	....	....	....	....	....	....	....	....	...
Monetary Authorities .... 79ag d	...	...	....	....	....	....	....	....	....	....	....	....	....	....	...
General Government .... 79ah d	...	...	....	....	....	....	....	....	....	....	....	....	....	....	...
Banks .... 79ai d	...	...	....	....	....	....	....	....	....	....	....	....	....	....	...
Other Sectors .... 79aj d	...	...	....	....	....	....	....	....	....	....	....	....	....	....	...
Reserve Assets .... 79ak d	...	...	....	....	....	....	....	....	....	....	....	....	....	....	...
Liabilities .... 79la d	...	...	....	....	....	....	....	....	....	....	....	....	....	....	...
Dir. Invest. in Rep. Economy....... 79lb d	...	...	....	....	....	....	....	....	....	....	....	....	....	....	...
Portfolio Investment .... 79lc d	...	...	....	....	....	....	....	....	....	....	....	....	....	....	...
Equity Securities .... 79ld d	...	...	....	....	....	....	....	....	....	....	....	....	....	....	...
Debt Securities .... 79le d	...	...	....	....	....	....	....	....	....	....	....	....	....	....	...
Financial Derivatives .... 79ll d	...	...	....	....	....	....	....	....	....	....	....	....	....	....	...
Other Investment .... 79lf d	...	...	....	....	....	....	....	....	....	....	....	....	....	....	...
Monetary Authorities .... 79lg d	...	...	....	....	....	....	....	....	....	....	....	....	....	....	...
General Government .... 79lh d	...	...	....	....	....	....	....	....	....	....	....	....	....	....	...
Banks .... 79li d	...	...	....	....	....	....	....	....	....	....	....	....	....	....	...
Other Sectors .... 79lj d	...	...	....	....	....	....	....	....	....	....	....	....	....	....	...
Government Finance														*Millions of Colones:*	
Deficit (-) or Surplus............. 80	−24.2	11.7	−54.3	−24.7	−21.4	179.7	−122.3	−121.9	−396.7	−549.2	−607.3	−324.4	−382.4	−192.6	42.1
Total Revenue and Grants.......... 81y	326.5	403.1	488.1	580.8	805.2	1,256.6	1,048.4	1,171.1	1,028.9	1,068.2	1,091.3	1,258.2	1,573.9	1,901.9	2,821.9
Revenue 81	....	....	....	....	....	....	....	....	....	....	....	....	....	....	....
Grants 81z	....	....	....	....	....	....	....	....	....	....	....	....	....	....	....
Exp. & Lending Minus Repay. 82z	350.7	391.4	542.4	605.5	826.6	1,076.9	1,170.7	1,293.0	1,425.6	1,617.4	1,698.6	1,582.6	1,956.3	2,094.5	2,779.8
Expenditure 82	350.7	391.4	542.4	605.5	826.6	1,076.9	1,184.2	1,280.1	1,422.4	1,581.5	1,694.6	1,571.4	1,820.7	2,149.6	2,723.1
Lending Minus Repayments 83	—	—	—	—	—	—	−13.5	12.9	3.2	35.9	4.0	11.2	135.6	−55.1	56.7
Total Financing 80h	24.1	−11.6	54.1	24.8	21.6	−179.5	122.4	122.0	396.8	549.2	607.3	324.4	382.4	192.6	−42.1
Domestic 84a	8.7	−46.8	−8.1	9.9	−1.4	−179.1	86.8	93.7	375.1	488.0	483.8	285.9	350.8	191.3	42.0
Foreign 85a	15.4	35.2	62.2	14.9	23.0	−.4	35.6	28.3	21.7	61.2	123.5	38.5	31.6	1.3	−84.1
Use of Cash Balances 87	1.7	−7.0	−12.8	6.7	−26.8	−88.8	32.6	21.0	−54.2	−13.3	47.2	−10.3	9.3	49.3	8.7
Total Debt by Residence 88	405.7	459.4	604.9	817.2	1,002.5	999.9	1,307.7	1,577.4	2,150.5	3,406.3	4,264.6	4,732.0	5,504.5	5,956.7	9,390.6
Domestic 88a	129.5	138.5	160.3	194.2	289.2	299.0	459.9	581.0	962.8	1,774.2	2,225.1	2,245.4	2,790.0	3,021.3	3,120.1
Foreign 89a	276.2	320.9	444.6	623.0	713.3	700.9	847.8	996.4	1,187.7	1,632.1	2,039.5	2,486.6	2,714.5	2,935.4	6,270.5
National Accounts														*Millions of Colones*	
Househ.Cons.Expend.,incl.NPISHs .. 96f	2,138	2,474	2,946	3,283	3,973	4,634	5,574	5,933	6,405	6,644	6,877	7,871	9,184	11,640	15,206
Government Consumption Expend.......... 91f	308	349	429	501	686	805	996	1,133	1,247	1,369	1,415	1,607	1,869	2,220	2,803
Gross Fixed Capital Formation 93e	474	521	719	1,031	1,145	1,521	1,652	1,512	1,210	1,173	1,130	1,180	1,336	1,723	2,594
Changes in Inventories 93i	−66	88	174	−40	−26	158	183	45	−27	58	56	44	59	−169	26
Exports of Goods and Services 90c	839	998	1,279	1,480	2,028	2,735	2,328	3,182	3,046	2,307	2,042	2,486	2,536	3,199	4,875
Imports of Goods and Services (-) 98c	811	1,099	1,610	1,711	2,101	2,686	3,041	3,197	2,964	2,904	2,553	3,036	3,327	4,283	5,740
Gross Domestic Product (GDP) 99b	2,882	3,332	3,944	4,478	5,706	7,167	7,692	8,607	8,917	8,647	8,966	10,152	11,657	14,331	19,763
Net Primary Income from Abroad 98.n	−27	−38	−53	−69	−17	−72	−130	−60	−128	−149	−229	−370	−343	−354	−471
Gross National Income (GNI) 99a	2,855	3,294	3,891	4,409	5,689	7,095	7,562	8,547	8,789	8,498	8,737	9,782	11,314	13,977	19,292
Net National Income 99e	2,718	3,146	3,714	4,210	5,458	6,826	7,244	8,191	8,420	8,140	8,367	9,362	10,832	13,385	18,477
GDP Volume 1962 Prices........... 99b.p	2,646	2,780	2,958	3,123	3,247	3,444	3,665	3,602	3,289	3,017	2,848	2,870	2,936	2,994	3,013
GDP Volume 1990 Prices.................... 99b.p	....	....	....	....	....	....	....	....	....	....	....	....	....	....	....
GDP Volume (1995=100) .... 99bv p	59.7	62.7	66.7	70.4	73.2	77.7	82.7	81.2	74.2	68.1	64.2	64.8	66.2	67.5	68.0
GDP Deflator (1995=100)................. 99bi p	5.8	6.4	7.1	7.6	9.4	11.1	11.2	12.7	14.5	15.3	16.8	18.9	21.2	25.5	35.0
															Millions:
Population............................ 99z	†3.67	3.77	3.89	4.01	4.12	4.26	4.35	4.44	4.51	4.59	4.66	4.72	4.78	4.86	4.95

International Investment Position

Millions of US Dollars

	1987	1988	1989	1990	1991	1992	1993	1994	1995	1996	1997	1998	1999	2000	2001	
Assets	...	...	...	...	...	...	758.7	872.8	1,029.7	1,771.3	2,153.8	2,445.6	2,832.4	3,004.0	...	79aa d
Direct Investment Abroad							—	—	—	55.7	55.7	56.7	110.5	103.9	...	79ab d
Portfolio Investment										—	—	—	2.1	11.0		79ac d
Equity Securities										—	—	—	—	—		79ad d
Debt Securities										—	—	—	2.1	11.0		79ae d
Financial Derivatives																79al d
Other Investment							51.4	59.9	70.1	615.9	635.8	623.5	747.5	995.8		79af d
Monetary Authorities																79ag d
General Government										22.0	22.0	22.0	22.0	22.0		79ah d
Banks										115.8	113.8	121.8	123.5	273.1		79ai d
Other Sectors										478.0	500.0	479.7	602.0	700.7		79aj d
Reserve Assets							707.3	812.9	959.6	1,099.7	1,462.3	1,765.4	1,972.3	1,893.2		79ak d
Liabilities							2,042.7	2,198.1	2,530.1	4,335.6	4,990.5	6,025.5	6,854.7	7,358.3		79la d
Dir. Invest. in Rep. Economy							—	—	—	421.2	480.3	1,583.9	1,815.2	2,000.6		79lb d
Portfolio Investment										241.0	357.0	130.5	205.0	202.8		79lc d
Equity Securities																79ld d
Debt Securities										241.0	357.0	130.5	205.0	202.8		79le d
Financial Derivatives																79ll d
Other Investment							2,042.7	2,198.1	2,530.1	3,673.3	4,153.3	4,311.1	4,834.5	5,154.9		79lf d
Monetary Authorities										220.4	237.5	165.4	202.4	181.9		79lg d
General Government										2,075.8	2,194.9	2,350.1	2,423.2	2,448.3		79lh d
Banks										406.2	531.0	516.5	548.3	673.8		79li d
Other Sectors										970.9	1,189.9	1,279.1	1,660.6	1,850.9		79lj d

Government Finance

Year Ending December 31

	1987	1988	1989	1990	1991	1992	1993	1994	1995	1996	1997	1998	1999	2000	2001	
Deficit (-) or Surplus	85.8	-175.1	-730.5	-27.1	-1,184.9	-1,839.3	-1,284.4	†-521.8	-455.2	-1,841.3	-1,102.1	-1,920.9	-2,456.0	-2,658.6	...	80
Total Revenue and Grants	2,981.0	2,927.6	2,631.2	3,852.7	4,072.1	5,715.6	7,215.7	†9,529.7	11,436.9	12,248.9	12,204.7	13,202.2	12,570.2	13,857.3	...	81y
Revenue												13,104.2	12,471.4	13,030.6	...	81
Grants												98.0	98.8	826.7	...	81z
Exp. & Lending Minus Repay.	2,895.2	3,102.7	3,361.7	3,879.8	5,257.0	7,554.9	8,500.1	†10051.5	11,892.1	14,090.2	13,306.8	15,123.1	15,026.2	16,515.9	...	82z
Expenditure	3,022.8	3,095.8	3,306.7	3,854.7	4,927.9	7,253.7	8,314.0	†9,970.9	11,755.7	14,070.3	13,533.6	15,227.1	15,094.3	16,628.1	...	82
Lending Minus Repayments	-127.6	6.9	55.0	25.1	329.1	301.2	186.1	†80.6	136.4	19.9	-226.8	-104.0	-68.1	-112.2	...	83
Total Financing	-85.8	175.1	730.5	27.1	...	...		†521.9	455.2	1,841.3	1,102.1	1,920.1	2,456.0	2,658.7	...	80h
Domestic	-189.7	-127.3	471.6	117.1	...	...		†-844.2	-542.3	-86.2	-553.4	2,159.8	1,296.7	1,300.6	...	84a
Foreign	103.9	302.4	258.9	-90.0	...	1,305.0		†1,366.1	997.5	1,927.5	1,655.5	-239.7	1,159.3	1,358.1	...	85a
Use of Cash Balances	-172.3	-381.3	-218.5	-74.0	...	...		-527.8	-313.6						...	87
Total Debt by Residence	11,786.2	11,364.7	13,880.2	19,119.2	23,697.4	25,142.3	25,292.0	†21305.8	22,066.6	23,968.0	24,759.7	24,663.7	27,714.1	30,634.4	...	88
Domestic	5,226.2	4,494.7	6,293.7	7,472.5	9,050.3	9,494.8	9,995.6	†8,463.0	8,226.3	7,883.7	7,460.9	7,119.9	8,015.2	10,687.0	...	88a
Foreign	6,560.0	6,870.0	7,586.5	11,646.7	14,647.1	15,647.5	15,296.4	†12842.8	13,840.3	16,084.3	17,298.8	17,543.8	19,698.9	19,947.4	...	89a

National Accounts

Millions of Colones

	1987	1988	1989	1990	1991	1992	1993	1994	1995	1996	1997	1998	1999	2000	2001	
Househ.Cons.Expend.,incl.NPISHs	18,744	22,153	26,729	32,435	37,463	44,082	52,854	61,658	72,683	79,719	85,218	89,305	93,686	101,547	105,702	96f
Government Consumption Expend.	3,181	3,484	3,930	3,618	4,236	4,670	5,196	5,942	7,184	8,438	8,842	10,243	10,928	11,406	12,068	91f
Gross Fixed Capital Formation	3,158	3,456	4,293	5,004	6,456	8,561	10,737	13,067	15,557	14,266	15,663	17,517	17,522	19,460	19,851	93e
Changes in Inventories	-297	45	646	54	107	673	478	865	1,106	-559	-936	927	394	-50	-650	93i
Exports of Goods and Services	4,395	4,327	4,261	6,771	7,332	8,019	11,683	14,126	17,987	19,023	25,228	26,048	27,197	31,420	34,796	90c
Imports of Goods and Services (-)	6,040	6,099	7,636	11,394	13,000	16,166	20,588	24,909	31,388	30,627	36,586	38,966	40,661	46,616	51,552	98c
Gross Domestic Product (GDP)	23,141	27,366	32,224	36,488	42,594	49,839	60,359	70,748	83,130	90,261	97,428	105,074	109,066	114,968	120,215	99b
Net Primary Income from Abroad	-525	-509	-568	-971	-1,145	-901	-979	-804	-839	-1,062	-1,429	-1,426	-2,468	-2,215	-2,325	98.n
Gross National Income (GNI)	22,616	26,857	31,656	35,517	41,449	48,938	59,380	69,944	82,291	89,199	95,999	103,647	106,597	112,753	117,891	99a
Net National Income	21,661	25,728	30,327	35,517	41,449	48,938	59,380	69,944	82,291	89,199	95,999	103,647	106,597	112,753	117,891	99e
GDP Volume 1962 Prices	3,094	3,144	3,177	3,285												99b.p
GDP Volume 1990 Prices				36,487	37,791	40,643	43,638	46,278	49,238	50,078	52,204	54,162	96,020	57,250	58,297	99b.p
GDP Volume (1995=100)	69.8	70.9	71.7	74.1	76.8	82.5	88.6	94.0	100.0	101.7	106.0	110.0	195.0	116.3	118.4	99bv p
GDP Deflator (1995=100)	39.9	46.4	54.1	59.2	66.8	72.6	81.9	90.5	100.0	106.8	110.5	114.9	67.3	118.9	122.1	99bi p

Midyear Estimates

	1987	1988	1989	1990	1991	1992	1993	1994	1995	1996	1997	1998	1999	2000	2001	
Population	5.05	5.09	5.19	5.03	5.35	5.48	5.43	5.55	5.67	5.79	5.91	6.03	6.15	6.28	6.40	99z

(See notes in the back of the book.)

Equatorial Guinea

		1972	1973	1974	1975	1976	1977	1978	1979	1980	1981	1982	1983	1984	1985	1986
Exchange Rates															*Francs per SDR:*	
Official Rate	aa	278.00	284.00	272.08	262.55	288.70	285.76	272.28	264.78	287.99	334.52	370.92	436.97	470.11	415.26	394.78
															Francs per US Dollar:	
Official Rate	ae	256.05	235.42	222.22	224.27	248.49	235.25	209.00	201.00	225.80	287.40	336.25	417.37	479.60	378.05	322.75
Official Rate	rf	252.03	222.89	240.70	214.31	238.95	245.68	225.66	212.72	211.28	271.73	328.61	381.07	436.96	449.26	346.31
															Index Numbers (1995=100):	
Nominal Effective Exchange Rate	ne c	....	....	....	....	....	....	....	1,072.36	787.98	506.02	498.21	480.93	500.28	97.43	108.00
Real Effective Exchange Rate	re c	....	....	....	....	....	....	....	....	....	....	....	....	....	187.13	157.77
Fund Position															*Millions of SDRs:*	
Quota	2f. s	8.00	8.00	8.00	8.00	8.00	8.00	10.00	10.00	15.00	15.00	15.00	18.40	18.40	18.40	18.40
SDRs	1b. s	1.87	1.86	1.85	1.81	1.77	1.74	1.70	.65	.02	.12	.02	—	—	3.09	.61
Reserve Position in the Fund	1c. s	.01	.01	.01	.01	1.76	1.74		.18	—	.24	.50	—	—		
Total Fund Cred.&Loans Outstg.	2tl	—	—	—	—	—	—	—		12.62	19.24	19.24	19.24	13.19	11.70	9.01
International Liquidity													*Millions of US Dollars Unless Otherwise Indicated:*			
Total Reserves minus Gold	1l. d												2.77	1.30	1.38	3.47	2.68
SDRs	1b. d	2.03	2.24	2.27	2.12	2.06	2.11	2.21	.86	.03	.14	.02	1.30	1.38	3.39	.75
Reserve Position in the Fund	1c. d	.01	.01	.01	.01	2.04	—		.24		.28	.55	—	—	—	—
Foreign Exchange	1d. d	....	....	....	....	....	....	....	....	....	....	....	2.20	1.30	1.38	.07	1.93
Monetary Authorities: Other Liab.	4.. d	....	....	....	....	....	....	....	....	....	....	....	....	....	....	5.07	.34
Deposit Money Banks: Assets	7a. d	....	....	....	....	....	....	....	....	....	....	....	....	....	....	5.40	2.04
Liabilities	7b. d	....	....	....	....	....	....	....	....	....	....	....	....	....	....	—	—
Monetary Authorities															*Billions of Francs:*	
Foreign Assets	11	....	....	....	....	....	....	....	....	....	....	....	....	....	....	1.31	.86
Claims on Central Government	12a	....	....	....	....	....	....	....	....	....	....	....	....	....	....	6.46	5.11
Claims on Deposit Money Banks	12e	....	....	....	....	....	....	....	....	....	....	....	....	....	....	3.21	4.26
Claims on Other Banking Insts	12f	....	....	....	....	....	....	....	....	....	....	....	....	....	....	....	....
Reserve Money	14	....	....	....	....	....	....	....	....	....	....	....	....	....	....	5.68	8.93
of which: Currency Outside DMBs	14a	....	....	....	....	....	....	....	....	....	....	....	....	....	....	5.24	7.48
Foreign Liabilities	16c	....	....	....	....	....	....	....	....	....	....	....	....	....	....	6.78	3.67
Central Government Deposits	16d	....	....	....	....	....	....	....	....	....	....	....	....	....	....	1.02	.27
Capital Accounts	17a	....	....	....	....	....	....	....	....	....	....	....	....	....	....		
Other Items (Net)	17r	....	....	....	....	....	....	....	....	....	....	....	....	....	....	-2.49	-2.62
Deposit Money Banks															*Billions of Francs:*	
Reserves	20	....	....	....	....	....	....	....	....	....	....	....	....	....	....	.44	1.45
Foreign Assets	21	....	....	....	....	....	....	....	....	....	....	....	....	....	....	2.04	.66
Claims on Central Government	22a	....	....	....	....	....	....	....	....	....	....	....	....	....	....	—	—
Claims on Nonfin.Pub.Enterprises	22c	....	....	....	....	....	....	....	....	....	....	....	....	....	....		
Claims on Private Sector	22d	....	....	....	....	....	....	....	....	....	....	....	....	....	....	6.53	8.36
Claims on Other Banking Insts	22f	....	....	....	....	....	....	....	....	....	....	....	....	....	....		
Claims on Nonbank Financial Insts	22g	....	....	....	....	....	....	....	....	....	....	....	....	....	....		
Demand Deposits	24	....	....	....	....	....	....	....	....	....	....	....	....	....	....	2.81	2.44
Time and Savings Deposits	25	....	....	....	....	....	....	....	....	....	....	....	....	....	....	.93	.62
Foreign Liabilities	26c	....	....	....	....	....	....	....	....	....	....	....	....	....	....	—	—
Long-Term Foreign Liabilities	26cl	....	....	....	....	....	....	....	....	....	....	....	....	....	....	—	—
Central Government Deposits	26d	....	....	....	....	....	....	....	....	....	....	....	....	....	....	.50	.18
Credit from Monetary Authorities	26g	....	....	....	....	....	....	....	....	....	....	....	....	....	....	3.21	4.26
Capital Accounts	27a	....	....	....	....	....	....	....	....	....	....	....	....	....	....	.67	.71
Other Items (Net)	27r	....	....	....	....	....	....	....	....	....	....	....	....	....	....	.90	2.25
Monetary Survey															*Billions of Francs:*	
Foreign Assets (Net)	31n	....	....	....	....	....	....	....	....	....	....	....	....	....	....	-3.43	-2.14
Domestic Credit	32	....	....	....	....	....	....	....	....	....	....	....	....	....	....	11.47	13.02
Claims on Central Govt. (Net)	32an	....	....	....	....	....	....	....	....	....	....	....	....	....	....	4.94	4.66
Claims on Nonfin.Pub.Enterprises	32c	....	....	....	....	....	....	....	....	....	....	....	....	....	....	....	....
Claims on Private Sector	32d	....	....	....	....	....	....	....	....	....	....	....	....	....	....	6.53	8.36
Claims on Other Banking Insts	32f	....	....	....	....	....	....	....	....	....	....	....	....	....	....	....	....
Claims on Nonbank Financial Inst	32g	....	....	....	....	....	....	....	....	....	....	....	....	....	....	....	....
Money	34	....	....	....	....	....	....	....	....	....	....	....	....	....	....	8.05	9.92
Quasi-Money	35	....	....	....	....	....	....	....	....	....	....	....	....	....	....	.93	.62
Other Items (Net)	37r	....	....	....	....	....	....	....	....	....	....	....	....	....	....	-.93	.34
Money plus Quasi-Money	35l	....	....	....	....	....	....	....	....	....	....	....	....	....	....	8.97	10.54
Interest Rates															*Percent Per Annum*	
Discount Rate *(End of Period)*	60	....	....	....	....	....	....	....	....	....	....	....	....	....	....	9.00	8.00
Deposit Rate	60l	....	....	....	....	....	....	....	....	....	....	....	....	....	....	7.50	8.25
Lending Rate	60p	....	....	....	....	....	....	....	....	....	....	....	....	....	....	15.00	14.50
Prices															*Index Numbers (1990=100):*	
Consumer Prices	64	....	....	....	....	....	....	....	....	....	....	....	....	....	....	127.42	104.76

Equatorial Guinea
642

1987	1988	1989	1990	1991	1992	1993	1994	1995	1996	1997	1998	1999	2000	2001		
															Exchange Rates	
End of Period																
378.78	407.68	380.32	364.84	370.48	378.57	404.89	†780.44	728.38	753.06	807.94	791.61	†896.19	918.49	935.39	Official Rate	aa
End of Period(ae)Period Average(rf)																
267.00	302.95	289.40	256.45	259.00	275.32	294.77	†534.60	490.00	523.70	598.81	562.21	†652.95	704.95	744.31	Official Rate	ae
300.54	297.85	319.01	272.26	282.11	264.69	283.16	†555.20	499.15	511.55	583.67	589.95	†615.70	711.98	733.04	Official Rate	rf
Period Averages																
115.57	117.42	120.69	134.73	136.07	144.72	153.62	95.56	100.00	99.53	96.39	98.07	96.67	92.42	93.08	Nominal Effective Exchange Rate	ne c
136.33	130.14	127.25	127.07	117.16	112.37	118.53	84.75	100.00	100.84	98.65	106.00	102.83	102.42	108.51	Real Effective Exchange Rate	re c
															Fund Position	
End of Period																
18.40	18.40	18.40	18.40	18.40	24.30	24.30	24.30	24.30	24.30	24.30	24.30	32.60	32.60	32.60	Quota	2f. s
.15	.03	.09	.05	5.57	5.52	.28	.01	.01	.01	—	.01	—	.09	.79	SDRs	1b. s
														—	Reserve Position in the Fund	1c. s
8.11	10.61	6.72	4.10	9.20	9.20	11.96	13.43	12.70	11.93	9.75	7.64	5.80	3.77	1.75	Total Fund Cred.&Loans Outstg.	2tl
															International Liquidity	
.57	5.50	5.97	.71	9.47	13.41	.48	.39	.04	.52	4.93	.80	3.35	23.01	70.85	Total Reserves minus Gold	1l. d
.21	.04	.12	.07	7.96	7.59	.38	.02	.01	.01	—	.01	—	.12	.99	SDRs	1b. d
														—	Reserve Position in the Fund	1c. d
.36	5.46	5.85	.64	1.51	5.82	.10	.37	.03	.51	4.93	.79	3.35	22.89	69.86	Foreign Exchange	1d. d
11.01	†17.24	11.66	20.21	20.15	28.89	11.02	9.16	2.97	.12	.11	4.80	7.46	7.52	6.94	Monetary Authorities: Other Liab.	4.. d
7.49	4.15	3.37	5.10	5.68	6.08	4.07	5.78	5.08	4.92	2.38	18.07	39.45	27.51	41.56	Deposit Money Banks: Assets	7a. d
.30	1.17	1.72	3.49	2.34	2.96	2.17	2.67	3.56	1.96	6.18	5.22	19.31	14.82	21.88	Liabilities	7b. d
															Monetary Authorities	
End of Period																
.15	†1.67	1.73	.18	†2.45	3.69	.14	.21	.02	.27	2.95	.45	2.19	16.22	52.74	Foreign Assets	11
4.62	†6.06	4.25	3.09	9.27	9.71	12.18	17.84	17.42	17.33	15.86	14.03	20.90	14.24	3.90	Claims on Central Government	12a
3.82	†3.24	3.24	4.65	† —	—	—	—	—	—	—	—	—	—	—	Claims on Deposit Money Banks	12e
....															Claims on Other Banking Insts	12f
6.88	†3.28	5.59	1.74	1.92	3.09	2.46	4.38	8.72	9.99	10.97	8.79	17.17	25.57	47.45	Reserve Money	14
6.69	†1.96	4.79	.90	1.09	1.62	1.21	3.77	6.78	8.50	6.59	5.79	12.06	15.20	17.63	of which: Currency Outside DMBs	14a
6.01	†9.55	5.93	6.68	8.63	11.44	8.09	15.38	10.70	9.05	7.94	8.74	10.07	8.77	6.80	Foreign Liabilities	16c
.72	†1.74	.26	.07	.25	.35	.17	.06	.07	.08	.48	1.08	1.19	1.92	7.44	Central Government Deposits	16d
....	2.36	2.22	2.12	2.40	2.42	2.55	4.82	4.53	4.63	4.95	4.83	5.56	5.91	6.22	Capital Accounts	17a
-5.02	†-5.96	-4.78	-2.70	†-1.48	-3.87	-.95	-6.58	-6.58	-6.15	-5.54	-8.96	-10.90	-11.71	-11.26	Other Items (Net)	17r
															Deposit Money Banks	
End of Period																
.20	†1.31	.80	.84	.84	1.47	1.25	.62	1.95	1.49	4.38	3.00	5.11	10.37	29.02	Reserves	20
2.00	†1.26	.98	1.31	†1.47	1.67	1.20	3.09	2.49	2.57	1.43	10.16	25.76	19.39	30.93	Foreign Assets	21
—	†.57	.62	.78	†1.08	2.76	.05	.23	.25	.51	1.63	.94	.46	1.89	.30	Claims on Central Government	22a
....	.24	.47	.64	.04	.29	.44	.72	.72	.96	.80	.72	.03	—	.40	Claims on Nonfin.Pub.Enterprises	22c
7.52	†7.37	7.79	7.87	†11.96	7.57	1.99	2.25	3.40	6.20	12.02	14.13	21.29	27.06	36.49	Claims on Private Sector	22d
....	—	—	—	—	—	—	—	—	—	—	—	—	—	—	Claims on Other Banking Insts	22f
														—	Claims on Nonbank Financial Insts	22g
2.32	†3.26	2.46	2.23	†1.55	1.95	1.34	2.24	2.73	5.78	7.07	9.19	16.39	23.14	29.88	Demand Deposits	24
.43	†.38	.63	.67	†.70	.80	.69	1.76	2.05	2.23	4.38	5.86	6.72	9.58	16.42	Time and Savings Deposits	25
—	†.17	.25	.65	†.36	.56	.41	1.24	1.60	.92	3.67	2.94	12.61	9.90	15.97	Foreign Liabilities	26c
.08	†.18	.25	.25	†.25	.25	.23	.19	.14	.11	.03	—	—	.55	.31	Long-Term Foreign Liabilities	26cl
.09	.76	.75	1.07	†1.10	1.05	.53	.46	.88	1.86	3.10	6.12	10.76	6.49	24.82	Central Government Deposits	26d
3.82	†3.24	3.24	4.64	† —	—	—	—	—	—	—	—	—	—	—	Credit from Monetary Authorities	26g
1.16	†2.36	2.54	2.70	†10.49	9.63	1.67	1.36	2.30	1.26	3.02	5.26	6.67	7.69	13.44	Capital Accounts	27a
1.82	†.43	.53	-.77	†1.43	-.13	.07	-.33	-.91	-.43	-1.03	-.42	-.50	1.37	-3.70	Other Items (Net)	27r
															Monetary Survey	
End of Period																
-3.86	†-6.98	-3.73	-6.09	†-5.31	-6.89	-7.39	-13.51	-9.94	-7.23	-7.26	-1.07	5.27	16.40	60.58	Foreign Assets (Net)	31n
11.33	†11.74	12.12	11.24	†21.49	18.93	13.96	20.52	20.83	23.05	26.72	22.66	30.73	34.78	8.84	Domestic Credit	32
3.81	†4.12	3.86	2.73	†9.00	11.07	11.53	17.55	16.72	15.90	13.90	7.78	9.41	7.72	-28.05	Claims on Central Govt. (Net)	32an
....	.24	.47	.64	.04	.29	.44	.72	.72	.96	.80	.72	.03	—	.40	Claims on Nonfin.Pub.Enterprises	32c
7.52	†7.37	7.79	7.87	†11.96	7.57	1.99	2.25	3.40	6.20	12.02	14.13	21.29	27.06	36.49	Claims on Private Sector	32d
....	—	—	—	—	—	—	—	—	—	—	—	—	—	—	Claims on Other Banking Insts	32f
....											.03	—	—	—	Claims on Nonbank Financial Inst	32g
9.00	†5.22	7.25	3.12	2.64	3.57	2.55	6.01	9.51	14.28	13.66	14.99	28.45	38.33	48.31	Money	34
.43	†.38	.63	.67	.70	.80	.69	1.76	2.05	2.23	4.38	5.86	6.72	9.58	16.42	Quasi-Money	35
-2.05	†-.06	.74	1.37	12.84	8.05	3.34	-.73	-.66	-.68	1.59	.75	.84	3.27	4.69	Other Items (Net)	37r
9.43	†5.60	7.88	3.79	3.34	4.37	3.24	7.76	11.56	16.51	18.04	20.85	35.16	47.91	64.73	Money plus Quasi-Money	35l
															Interest Rates	
Percent Per Annum																
8.00	9.50	10.00	11.00	10.75	12.00	11.50	†7.75	8.60	7.75	7.50	7.00	7.60	7.00	6.50	Discount Rate (End of Period)	60
7.88	6.33	6.50	†7.50	7.50	7.50	7.75	8.08	5.50	5.46	5.00	5.00	5.00	5.00	5.00	Deposit Rate	601
14.13	14.79	15.50	†18.50	18.15	17.77	17.46	17.50	16.00	22.00	22.00	22.00	22.00	22.00	20.67	Lending Rate	60p
															Prices	
Period Averages																
91.28	93.40	98.91	100.00	96.84	†89.90	†93.49	127.54	....	....	....	....	....	....	....	Consumer Prices	64

Equatorial Guinea

		1972	1973	1974	1975	1976	1977	1978	1979	1980	1981	1982	1983	1984	1985	1986
International Transactions															*Millions of Francs*	
Exports	70	...	...	...	...	...	...	...	...	...	3,067	3,797	5,074	6,526	7,441	8,446
Imports, c.i.f.	71	...	...	...	...	...	...	...	...	...	7,390	10,029	7,250	7,656	8,947	7,656
Balance of Payments															*Millions of US Dollars:*	
Current Account, n.i.e.	78al *d*	...	...	...	...	...	...	...	...	...	...	...	...	...	...	...
Goods: Exports f.o.b.	78aa *d*	...	...	...	...	...	...	...	...	...	...	...	...	...	...	...
Goods: Imports f.o.b.	78ab *d*	...	...	...	...	...	...	...	...	...	...	...	...	...	...	...
Trade Balance	78ac *d*	...	...	...	...	...	...	...	...	...	...	...	...	...	...	...
Services: Credit	78ad *d*	...	...	...	...	...	...	...	...	...	...	...	...	...	...	...
Services: Debit	78ae *d*	...	...	...	...	...	...	...	...	...	...	...	...	...	...	...
Balance on Goods & Services	78af *d*	...	...	...	...	...	...	...	...	...	...	...	...	...	...	...
Income: Credit	78ag *d*	...	...	...	...	...	...	...	...	...	...	...	...	...	...	...
Income: Debit	78ah *d*	...	...	...	...	...	...	...	...	...	...	...	...	...	...	...
Balance on Gds, Serv. & Inc.	78ai *d*	...	...	...	...	...	...	...	...	...	...	...	...	...	...	...
Current Transfers, n.i.e.: Credit	78aj *d*	...	...	...	...	...	...	...	...	...	...	...	...	...	...	...
Current Transfers: Debit	78ak *d*	...	...	...	...	...	...	...	...	...	...	...	...	...	...	...
Capital Account, n.i.e.	78bc *d*	...	...	...	...	...	...	...	...	...	...	...	...	...	...	...
Capital Account, n.i.e.: Credit	78ba *d*	...	...	...	...	...	...	...	...	...	...	...	...	...	...	...
Capital Account: Debit	78bb *d*	...	...	...	...	...	...	...	...	...	...	...	...	...	...	...
Financial Account, n.i.e.	78bj *d*	...	...	...	...	...	...	...	...	...	...	...	...	...	...	...
Direct Investment Abroad	78bd *d*	...	...	...	...	...	...	...	...	...	...	...	...	...	...	...
Dir. Invest. in Rep. Econ., n.i.e.	78be *d*	...	...	...	...	...	...	...	...	...	...	...	...	...	...	...
Portfolio Investment Assets	78bf *d*	...	...	...	...	...	...	...	...	...	...	...	...	...	...	...
Equity Securities	78bk *d*	...	...	...	...	...	...	...	...	...	...	...	...	...	...	...
Debt Securities	78bl *d*	...	...	...	...	...	...	...	...	...	...	...	...	...	...	...
Portfolio Investment Liab., n.i.e.	78bg *d*	...	...	...	...	...	...	...	...	...	...	...	...	...	...	...
Equity Securities	78bm *d*	...	...	...	...	...	...	...	...	...	...	...	...	...	...	...
Debt Securities	78bn *d*	...	...	...	...	...	...	...	...	...	...	...	...	...	...	...
Financial Derivatives Assets	78bw *d*	...	...	...	...	...	...	...	...	...	...	...	...	...	...	...
Financial Derivatives Liabilities	78bx *d*	...	...	...	...	...	...	...	...	...	...	...	...	...	...	...
Other Investment Assets	78bh *d*	...	...	...	...	...	...	...	...	...	...	...	...	...	...	...
Monetary Authorities	78bo *d*	...	...	...	...	...	...	...	...	...	...	...	...	...	...	...
General Government	78bp *d*	...	...	...	...	...	...	...	...	...	...	...	...	...	...	...
Banks	78bq *d*	...	...	...	...	...	...	...	...	...	...	...	...	...	...	...
Other Sectors	78br *d*	...	...	...	...	...	...	...	...	...	...	...	...	...	...	...
Other Investment Liab., n.i.e.	78bi *d*	...	...	...	...	...	...	...	...	...	...	...	...	...	...	...
Monetary Authorities	78bs *d*	...	...	...	...	...	...	...	...	...	...	...	...	...	...	...
General Government	78bt *d*	...	...	...	...	...	...	...	...	...	...	...	...	...	...	...
Banks	78bu *d*	...	...	...	...	...	...	...	...	...	...	...	...	...	...	...
Other Sectors	78bv *d*	...	...	...	...	...	...	...	...	...	...	...	...	...	...	...
Net Errors and Omissions	78ca *d*	...	...	...	...	...	...	...	...	...	...	...	...	...	...	...
Overall Balance	78cb *d*	...	...	...	...	...	...	...	...	...	...	...	...	...	...	...
Reserves and Related Items	79da *d*	...	...	...	...	...	...	...	...	...	...	...	...	...	...	...
Reserve Assets	79db *d*	...	...	...	...	...	...	...	...	...	...	...	...	...	...	...
Use of Fund Credit and Loans	79dc *d*	...	...	...	...	...	...	...	...	...	...	...	...	...	...	...
Exceptional Financing	79de *d*	...	...	...	...	...	...	...	...	...	...	...	...	...	...	...
National Accounts															*Millions of Francs*	
Househ.Cons.Expend.,incl.NPISHs	96f											...	16,083	17,511	30,566	28,754
Government Consumption Expend.	91f											...	7,080	8,505	5,909	7,240
Gross Fixed Capital Formation	93e											...	3,018	3,224	4,551	7,590
Changes in Inventories	93i											...	−158	418	−1,721	−624
Exports of Goods and Services	90c											...	1,477	1,886	10,388	12,092
Imports of Goods and Services (-)	98c											...	1,851	2,012	11,626	17,847
Gross Domestic Product (GDP)	99b											...	25,649	29,532	38,067	37,205
GDP Volume 1985 Prices	99b. *p*														38,756	37,286
GDP Volume (1985=100)	99bv *p*	...											...	...	62.6	60.2
GDP Deflator (1995=100)	99bi *p*	...												...	74.6	75.8
															Millions:	
Population	99z	.30	.31	.32	.32	.33	.33	.34	.35	.35	.23	.25	.27	.29	.31	.32

	1987	1988	1989	1990	1991	1992	1993	1994	1995	1996	1997	1998	1999	2000	2001		
International Transactions																	
Millions of Francs																	
Exports	11,630	14,719	12,925	16,996	10,536	13,306	16,060	34,420	42,683	89,682	289,204	258,957	436,735	780,819	....	**70**	
Imports, c.i.f.	15,064	18,230	17,473	16,586	18,970	14,824	17,000	20,514	24,897	149,384	192,800	187,167	261,784	320,800	....	**71**	
Balance of Payments																	
Minus Sign Indicates Debit																	
Current Account, n.i.e.	−25.44	−20.57	−21.00	−18.99	−40.72	−10.57	2.84	−.38	−123.40	−344.04	....	....	....	....	....	Current Account, n.i.e.	**78al** *d*
Goods: Exports f.o.b.	38.48	44.65	32.71	37.82	37.35	49.54	61.06	62.00	89.93	175.31	....	....	....	....	....	Goods: Exports f.o.b.	**78aa** *d*
Goods: Imports f.o.b.	−47.87	−56.51	−43.61	−53.17	−67.24	−56.00	−51.03	−36.95	−120.57	−292.04	....	....	....	....	....	Goods: Imports f.o.b.	**78ab** *d*
Trade Balance	−9.38	−11.86	−10.91	−15.36	−29.89	−6.47	10.03	25.05	−30.64	−116.73	....	....	....	....	....	*Trade Balance*	**78ac** *d*
Services: Credit	6.11	5.87	5.84	4.51	5.84	8.15	8.99	3.36	4.18	4.88	....	....	....	....	....	Services: Credit	**78ad** *d*
Services: Debit	−40.68	−48.69	−31.22	−35.76	−41.45	−35.17	−38.53	−23.82	−75.54	−184.58	....	....	....	....	....	Services: Debit	**78ae** *d*
Balance on Goods & Services	−43.96	−54.68	−36.29	−46.61	−65.50	−33.49	−19.51	4.59	−102.00	−296.43	....	....	....	....	....	*Balance on Goods & Services*	**78af** *d*
Income: Credit	—	—	—	—	—	1.32	—	—	.10	.16	....	....	....	....	....	Income: Credit	**78ag** *d*
Income: Debit	−6.51	−7.93	−8.55	−10.25	−9.20	−4.92	−9.30	−8.75	−25.03	−45.18	....	....	....	....	....	Income: Debit	**78ah** *d*
Balance on Gds, Serv. & Inc.	−50.46	−62.61	−44.84	−56.86	−74.70	−37.09	−28.80	−4.16	−126.93	−341.44	....	....	....	....	....	*Balance on Gds, Serv. & Inc.*	**78ai** *d*
Current Transfers, n.i.e.: Credit	28.66	46.90	36.84	54.92	42.40	33.63	37.76	5.67	6.83	4.03	....	....	....	....	....	Current Transfers, n.i.e.: Credit	**78aj** *d*
Current Transfers: Debit	−3.64	−4.87	−12.99	−17.05	−8.42	−7.11	−6.11	−1.89	−3.30	−6.62	....	....	....	....	....	Current Transfers: Debit	**78ak** *d*
Capital Account, n.i.e.	—	—	—	—	—	—	—	—	—	—	....	....	....	....	....	Capital Account, n.i.e.	**78bc** *d*
Capital Account, n.i.e.: Credit	—	—	—	—	—	—	—	—	—	—	....	....	....	....	....	Capital Account, n.i.e.: Credit	**78ba** *d*
Capital Account: Debit	—	—	—	....	....	....	....	—	—	—	....	....	....	....	....	Capital Account: Debit	**78bb** *d*
Financial Account, n.i.e.	−.95	4.90	10.02	11.68	28.51	−16.08	13.95	−15.04	101.56	313.75	....	....	....	....	....	Financial Account, n.i.e.	**78bj** *d*
Direct Investment Abroad	—	—	—	—	—	—	—	—	—	—	....	....	....	....	....	Direct Investment Abroad	**78bd** *d*
Dir. Invest. in Rep. Econ., n.i.e.	—	—	.89	11.07	41.32	6.02	22.30	17.00	126.92	376.18	....	....	....	....	....	Dir. Invest. in Rep. Econ., n.i.e.	**78be** *d*
Portfolio Investment Assets	—	—	—	—	—	—	—	—	—	—	....	....	....	....	....	Portfolio Investment Assets	**78bf** *d*
Equity Securities	—	—	—	—	—	—	—	—	—	—	....	....	....	....	....	Equity Securities	**78bk** *d*
Debt Securities	—	—	—	—	—	—	—	—	—	—	....	....	....	....	....	Debt Securities	**78bl** *d*
Portfolio Investment Liab., n.i.e.	—	—	—	—	—	—	—	—	—	—	....	....	....	....	....	Portfolio Investment Liab., n.i.e.	**78bg** *d*
Equity Securities	—	—	—	—	—	—	—	—	—	—	....	....	....	....	....	Equity Securities	**78bm** *d*
Debt Securities	—	—	—	—	—	—	—	—	—	—	....	....	....	....	....	Debt Securities	**78bn** *d*
Financial Derivatives Assets	....	....	....	....	....	....	....	....	....	....	....	....	....	....	....	Financial Derivatives Assets	**78bw** *d*
Financial Derivatives Liabilities	....	....	....	....	....	....	....	....	....	....	....	....	....	....	....	Financial Derivatives Liabilities	**78bx** *d*
Other Investment Assets	−4.91	−1.12	—	—	—	—	—	—	—	—	....	....	....	....	....	Other Investment Assets	**78bh** *d*
Monetary Authorities	....	....	....	....	....	....	....	....	....	....	....	....	....	....	....	Monetary Authorities	**78bo** *d*
General Government	−1.27	−1.12	....	—	—	—	—	—	—	—	....	....	....	....	....	General Government	**78bp** *d*
Banks	−3.64	—	—	—	—	—	—	—	—	—	....	....	....	....	....	Banks	**78bq** *d*
Other Sectors	—	—	—	—	—	—	—	—	—	—	....	....	....	....	....	Other Sectors	**78br** *d*
Other Investment Liab., n.i.e.	3.95	6.02	9.13	.61	−12.81	−22.09	−8.35	−32.04	−25.36	−62.43	....	....	....	....	....	Other Investment Liab., n.i.e.	**78bi** *d*
Monetary Authorities	—	—	—	—	—	—	—	—	—	—	....	....	....	....	....	Monetary Authorities	**78bs** *d*
General Government	5.98	10.38	11.51	2.94	−9.87	1.17	−3.12	−7.32	−13.95	−3.84	....	....	....	....	....	General Government	**78bt** *d*
Banks	—	2.92	1.60	.38	.01	1.05	−1.98	1.84	−1.57	....	....	....	....	....	Banks	**78bu** *d*
Other Sectors	−2.03	−7.28	−3.97	−2.71	−1.21	−23.28	−6.28	−22.73	−13.25	−57.02	....	....	....	....	....	Other Sectors	**78bv** *d*
Net Errors and Omissions	.82	−1.70	.77	1.61	−1.64	−1.13	−27.17	−2.93	10.33	24.82	....	....	....	....	....	Net Errors and Omissions	**78ca** *d*
Overall Balance	−25.58	−17.37	−10.20	−5.70	−13.85	−27.78	−10.38	−18.36	−11.52	−5.46	....	....	....	....	....	*Overall Balance*	**78cb** *d*
Reserves and Related Items	25.58	17.37	10.20	5.70	13.85	27.78	10.38	18.36	11.52	5.46	....	....	....	....	....	Reserves and Related Items	**79da** *d*
Reserve Assets	3.64	−7.11	.74	−3.27	−11.27	4.36	−1.02	−.92	−8.98	−3.59	....	....	....	....	....	Reserve Assets	**79db** *d*
Use of Fund Credit and Loans	−1.14	3.44	−5.01	−3.53	7.18	—	3.79	2.08	−1.11	−1.11	....	....	....	....	....	Use of Fund Credit and Loans	**79dc** *d*
Exceptional Financing	23.08	21.05	14.47	12.50	17.94	23.42	7.61	17.20	21.61	10.17	....	....	....	....	....	Exceptional Financing	**79de** *d*
National Accounts																	
Millions of Francs																	
Househ.Cons.Expend.,incl.NPISHs	26,630	29,096	22,956	23,593	35,225	31,042	25,150	2,430	18,646	49,826	157,939	....	....	....	....	Househ.Cons.Expend.,incl.NPISHs	**96f**
Government Consumption Expend.	5,210	7,804	9,397	6,765	6,696	5,294	7,996	6,938	10,791	18,274	27,811	....	....	....	....	Government Consumption Expend.	**91f**
Gross Fixed Capital Formation	10,190	11,133	8,285	15,328	8,525	15,885	17,620	55,126	64,528	176,141	197,359	....	....	....	....	Gross Fixed Capital Formation	**93e**
Changes in Inventories	654	−685	−7	−1,365	−1,091	−987	531	−20	−9	−11	−13	....	....	....	....	Changes in Inventories	**93i**
Exports of Goods and Services	18,568	19,187	17,083	26,483	13,174	15,269	19,837	36,308	45,088	105,083	292,158	....	....	....	....	Exports of Goods and Services	**90c**
Imports of Goods and Services (-)	21,930	23,786	15,458	26,455	13,174	24,133	25,361	42,332	59,662	211,429	358,965	....	....	....	....	Imports of Goods and Services (-)	**98c**
Gross Domestic Product (GDP)	37,200	39,100	36,000	36,300	37,200	42,400	45,800	65,500	81,600	142,200	322,700	264,800	467,000	891,900	....	Gross Domestic Product (GDP)	**99b**
GDP Volume 1985 Prices	40,074	42,189	41,025	....	....	42,311	46,323	53,358	61,956	89,995	182,536	....	....	....	....	GDP Volume 1985 Prices	**99b.** *p*
GDP Volume (1985=100)	64.7	68.1	66.2	....	....	68.3	74.8	86.1	100.0	145.3	294.6	....	....	....	....	GDP Volume (1985=100)	**99bv** *p*
GDP Deflator (1995=100)	70.5	70.4	66.6	....	....	76.1	75.1	93.2	100.0	120.0	134.2	....	....	....	....	GDP Deflator (1995=100)	**99bi** *p*
Midyear Estimates																	
Population	.33	.33	.34	.35	.36	.37	.38	.39	.40	.41	.42	.43	.44	.46	.47	Population	**99z**

(See notes in the back of the book.)

Estonia

939		1972	1973	1974	1975	1976	1977	1978	1979	1980	1981	1982	1983	1984	1985	1986
Exchange Rates																*Krooni per SDR:*
Official Rate	aa	....	....	....	....	....	....	....	....	....	....	....	....	....	....	....
																Krooni per US Dollar:
Official Rate	ae	....	....	....	....	....	....	....	....	....	....	....	....	....	....	....
Official Rate	rf	....	....	....	....	....	....	....	....	....	....	....	....	....	....	....
Fund Position																*Millions of SDRs:*
Quota	2f.*s*	....	....	....	....	....	....	....	....	....	....	....	....	....	....	....
SDRs	1b.*s*	....	....	....	....	....	....	....	....	....	....	....	....	....	....	....
Reserve Position in the Fund	1c.*s*	....	....	....	....	....	....	....	....	....	....	....	....	....	....	....
Total Fund Cred.&Loans Outstg.	2tl	....	....	....	....	....	....	....	....	....	....	....	....	....	....	....
International Liquidity																*Millions of US Dollars Unless Otherwise Indicated:*
Total Reserves minus Gold	1l.*d*	....	....	....	....	....	....	....	....	....	....	....	....	....	....	....
SDRs	1b.*d*	....	....	....	....	....	....	....	....	....	....	....	....	....	....	....
Reserve Position in the Fund	1c.*d*	....	....	....	....	....	....	....	....	....	....	....	....	....	....	....
Foreign Exchange	1d.*d*	....	....	....	....	....	....	....	....	....	....	....	....	....	....	....
Gold (Million Fine Troy Ounces)	1ad	....	....	....	....	....	....	....	....	....	....	....	....	....	....	....
Gold (National Valuation)	1an*d*	....	....	....	....	....	....	....	....	....	....	....	....	....	....	....
Monetary Authorities: Other Liab.	4..*d*	....	....	....	....	....	....	....	....	....	....	....	....	....	....	....
Banks: Assets	7a.*d*	....	....	....	....	....	....	....	....	....	....	....	....	....	....	....
Liabilities	7b.*d*	....	....	....	....	....	....	....	....	....	....	....	....	....	....	....
Monetary Authorities																*Millions of Krooni:*
Foreign Assets	11	....	....	....	....	....	....	....	....	....	....	....	....	....	....	....
Claims on Central Government	12a	....	....	....	....	....	....	....	....	....	....	....	....	....	....	....
Claims on Nonfin.Pub.Enterprises	12c	....	....	....	....	....	....	....	....	....	....	....	....	....	....	....
Claims on Private Sector	12d	....	....	....	....	....	....	....	....	....	....	....	....	....	....	....
Claims on Banks	12e	....	....	....	....	....	....	....	....	....	....	....	....	....	....	....
Reserve Money	14	....	....	....	....	....	....	....	....	....	....	....	....	....	....	....
of which: Currency Outside Banks	14a	....	....	....	....	....	....	....	....	....	....	....	....	....	....	....
Foreign Liabilities	16c	....	....	....	....	....	....	....	....	....	....	....	....	....	....	....
Central Government Deposits	16d	....	....	....	....	....	....	....	....	....	....	....	....	....	....	....
Capital Accounts	17a	....	....	....	....	....	....	....	....	....	....	....	....	....	....	....
Other Items (Net)	17r	....	....	....	....	....	....	....	....	....	....	....	....	....	....	....
Banking Institutions																*Millions of Krooni:*
Reserves	20	....	....	....	....	....	....	....	....	....	....	....	....	....	....	....
Foreign Assets	21	....	....	....	....	....	....	....	....	....	....	....	....	....	....	....
Claims on Central Government	22a	....	....	....	....	....	....	....	....	....	....	....	....	....	....	....
Claims on Local Government	22b	....	....	....	....	....	....	....	....	....	....	....	....	....	....	....
Claims on Nonfin.Pub.Enterprises	22c	....	....	....	....	....	....	....	....	....	....	....	....	....	....	....
Claims on Private Sector	22d	....	....	....	....	....	....	....	....	....	....	....	....	....	....	....
Claims on Nonbank Financial Insts	22g	....	....	....	....	....	....	....	....	....	....	....	....	....	....	....
Demand Deposits	24	....	....	....	....	....	....	....	....	....	....	....	....	....	....	....
Time, Savings,& Fgn.Currency Dep.	25	....	....	....	....	....	....	....	....	....	....	....	....	....	....	....
Money Market Instruments	26aa	....	....	....	....	....	....	....	....	....	....	....	....	....	....	....
Bonds	26ab	....	....	....	....	....	....	....	....	....	....	....	....	....	....	....
Foreign Liabilities	26c	....	....	....	....	....	....	....	....	....	....	....	....	....	....	....
Central Government Deposits	26d	....	....	....	....	....	....	....	....	....	....	....	....	....	....	....
Counterpart Funds	26e	....	....	....	....	....	....	....	....	....	....	....	....	....	....	....
Government Lending Funds	26f	....	....	....	....	....	....	....	....	....	....	....	....	....	....	....
Credit from Monetary Authorities	26g	....	....	....	....	....	....	....	....	....	....	....	....	....	....	....
Capital Accounts	27a	....	....	....	....	....	....	....	....	....	....	....	....	....	....	....
Other Items (Net)	27r	....	....	....	....	....	....	....	....	....	....	....	....	....	....	....
Banking Survey																*Millions of Krooni:*
Foreign Assets (Net)	31n	....	....	....	....	....	....	....	....	....	....	....	....	....	....	....
Domestic Credit	32	....	....	....	....	....	....	....	....	....	....	....	....	....	....	....
Claims on Central Govt. (Net)	32an	....	....	....	....	....	....	....	....	....	....	....	....	....	....	....
Claims on Local Government	32b	....	....	....	....	....	....	....	....	....	....	....	....	....	....	....
Claims on Nonfin.Pub.Enterprises	32c	....	....	....	....	....	....	....	....	....	....	....	....	....	....	....
Claims on Private Sector	32d	....	....	....	....	....	....	....	....	....	....	....	....	....	....	....
Claims on Nonbank Financial Inst	32g	....	....	....	....	....	....	....	....	....	....	....	....	....	....	....
Money	34	....	....	....	....	....	....	....	....	....	....	....	....	....	....	....
Quasi-Money	35	....	....	....	....	....	....	....	....	....	....	....	....	....	....	....
Money Market Instruments	36aa	....	....	....	....	....	....	....	....	....	....	....	....	....	....	....
Bonds	36ab	....	....	....	....	....	....	....	....	....	....	....	....	....	....	....
Counterpart Funds	36e	....	....	....	....	....	....	....	....	....	....	....	....	....	....	....
Government Lending Funds	36f	....	....	....	....	....	....	....	....	....	....	....	....	....	....	....
Capital Accounts	37a	....	....	....	....	....	....	....	....	....	....	....	....	....	....	....
Other Items (Net)	37r	....	....	....	....	....	....	....	....	....	....	....	....	....	....	....
Money plus Quasi-Money	35l	....	....	....	....	....	....	....	....	....	....	....	....	....	....	....
Interest Rates																*Percent Per Annum*
Money Market Rate	60b	....	....	....	....	....	....	....	....	....	....	....	....	....	....	....
Deposit Rate	60l	....	....	....	....	....	....	....	....	....	....	....	....	....	....	....
Lending Rate	60p	....	....	....	....	....	....	....	....	....	....	....	....	....	....	....
Prices and Labor																*Index Numbers (1995=100):*
Producer Prices	63	....	....	....	....	....	....	....	....	....	....	....	....	....	....	....
Consumer Prices	64	....	....	....	....	....	....	....	....	....	....	....	....	....	....	....
																Number in Thousands:
Labor Force	67d	....	....	....	....	....	....	....	....	....	....	....	....	....	....	....
Employment	67e	....	....	....	....	....	....	....	....	....	....	....	....	....	....	....
Unemployment	67c	....	....	....	....	....	....	....	....	....	....	....	....	....	....	....
Unemployment Rate (%)	67r	....	....	....	....	....	....	....	....	....	....	....	....	....	....	....
International Transactions																*Millions of Krooni*
Exports	70	....	....	....	....	....	....	....	....	....	....	....	....	....	....	....
Imports, c.i.f.	71	....	....	....	....	....	....	....	....	....	....	....	....	....	....	....
Imports, f.o.b.	71.v	....	....	....	....	....	....	....	....	....	....	....	....	....	....	....

	1987	1988	1989	1990	1991	1992	1993	1994	1995	1996	1997	1998	1999	2000	2001	
Exchange Rates *End of Period*																
Official Rate	....	....	....	....	....	17.754	19.062	18.088	17.038	17.888	19.343	18.882	21.359	21.915	22.234	**aa**
End of Period (ae) Period Average (rf)																
Official Rate	....	....	....	....	....	12.912	13.878	12.390	11.462	12.440	14.336	13.410	15.562	16.820	17.692	**ae**
Official Rate	....	....	....	....	....	....	13.223	12.991	11.465	12.034	13.882	14.075	14.678	16.969	17.564	**rf**
Fund Position *End of Period*																
Quota	....	....	....	....	....	46.50	46.50	46.50	46.50	46.50	46.50	46.50	65.20	65.20	65.20	**2f.s**
SDRs	....	....	....	....	....	7.72	41.56	1.09	.20	.12	.01	.05	.99	.01	.03	**1b.s**
Reserve Position in the Fund	....	....	....	....	....	—	—	.01	.01	.01	.01	.01	.01	.01	.01	**1c.s**
Total Fund Cred.&Loans Outstg.	....	....	....	....	....	7.75	41.85	41.85	61.81	54.15	40.01	21.31	18.41	14.53	10.66	**2tl**
International Liquidity *End of Period*																
Total Reserves minus Gold	....	....	....	....	....	170.18	386.12	443.35	579.91	636.82	757.72	810.60	853.49	920.64	820.24	**1l.d**
SDRs	....	....	....	....	....	10.62	57.08	1.58	.29	.17	.01	.07	1.36	.02	.03	**1b.d**
Reserve Position in the Fund	....	....	....	....	....	—	—	.01	.01	.01	.01	.01	.01	.01	.01	**1c.d**
Foreign Exchange	....	....	....	....	....	159.56	329.04	441.76	579.61	636.64	757.70	810.53	852.12	920.62	820.20	**1d.d**
Gold (Million Fine Troy Ounces)	....	....	....	....	....	.0820	.0080	.0080	.0080	.0080	.0080	.0080	.0080	.0080	.0080	**1ad**
Gold (National Valuation)	....	....	....	....	....	25.36	3.22	3.61	3.19	3.03	2.39	2.37	2.38	2.25	2.29	**1and**
Monetary Authorities: Other Liab.	....	....	....	....	....	42.44	†65.89	60.88	65.84	48.52	24.75	1.02	.63	3.29	1.04	**4..d**
Banks: Assets	....	....	....	....	....	122.81	103.10	243.80	322.58	320.69	563.45	483.29	563.67	615.88	874.72	**7a.d**
Liabilities	....	....	....	....	....	7.95	14.34	55.98	140.83	337.97	913.11	884.58	879.19	976.66	989.70	**7b.d**
Monetary Authorities *End of Period*																
Foreign Assets	....	....	....	....	1,782.8	3,596.7	†5,418.0	5,540.6	6,688.0	7,954.2	10,900.8	10,908.7	13,334.3	15,539.2	14,573.2	**11**
Claims on Central Government	....	....	....	....	—	—	†45.2	—	3.0	48.5	4.1	3.0	3.1	3.4	1.3	**12a**
Claims on Nonfin.Pub.Enterprises	....	....	....	....	651.9	—	†63.5	14.8	.8	—	—	—	—	—	—	**12c**
Claims on Private Sector	....	....	....	....	14.6	—	†4.6	8.2	14.5	44.2	44.1	57.2	66.5	69.5	74.8	**12d**
Claims on Banks	....	....	....	....	275.4	583.7	†473.7	480.9	194.0	168.0	82.4	280.3	267.3	9.8	8.0	**12e**
Reserve Money	....	....	....	....	700.0	1,862.8	†3,786.6	4,225.1	5,066.7	6,190.9	8,526.7	9,070.3	11,496.0	13,207.1	11,910.2	**14**
of which: Currency Outside Banks	....	....	....	....	212.4	1,040.7	†2,380.6	3,071.3	3,803.6	4,268.5	4,588.5	4,538.6	5,711.3	6,201.3	6,951.9	**14a**
Foreign Liabilities	....	....	....	....	444.8	685.6	†1,712.2	1,511.2	1,807.7	1,572.3	1,128.8	416.1	403.0	373.8	255.4	**16c**
Central Government Deposits	....	....	....	....	30.4	.3	†5.1	.2	.1	.3	355.5	6.4	27.1	7.2	7.8	**16d**
Capital Accounts	....	....	....	....	1,094.9	1,672.7	†1,342.2	1,256.1	1,223.2	1,325.9	1,881.1	2,276.5	2,141.3	2,424.1	2,889.7	**17a**
Other Items (Net)	....	....	....	....	454.7	-41.0	†-841.1	-948.0	-1,197.4	-874.7	-860.7	-520.1	-396.2	-390.3	-405.8	**17r**
Banking Institutions *End of Period*																
Reserves	....	....	....	....	598.3	835.0	1,437.7	1,208.4	1,293.1	1,922.5	3,885.3	4,509.5	5,790.9	6,787.1	4,896.6	**20**
Foreign Assets	....	....	....	....	852.9	1,585.7	1,430.8	3,020.7	3,697.4	3,989.4	8,077.7	6,480.9	8,771.9	10,358.9	15,475.5	**21**
Claims on Central Government	....	....	....	....	1.8	1.8	293.2	297.0	345.4	614.0	561.1	303.6	404.5	445.4	445.5	**22a**
Claims on Local Government	....	....	....	....	—	12.7	1.5	108.3	303.9	159.9	547.2	651.5	767.6	822.9	1,296.9	**22b**
Claims on Nonfin.Pub.Enterprises	....	....	....	....	202.4	644.4	416.7	346.0	334.5	304.6	328.6	225.8	372.5	262.7	141.8	**22c**
Claims on Private Sector	....	....	....	....	330.1	986.1	2,409.8	4,176.0	6,041.3	10,088.3	16,908.5	18,532.4	19,810.4	22,134.0	26,246.5	**22d**
Claims on Nonbank Financial Insts	....	....	....	....	—	—	8.7	12.2	628.9	2,036.4	5,127.7	6,336.8	6,489.2	12,370.2	16,106.6	**22g**
Demand Deposits	....	....	....	....	451.4	1,813.8	2,847.4	3,248.6	4,399.6	7,019.6	9,357.2	8,577.3	11,600.5	14,456.8	17,967.9	**24**
Time, Savings,& Fgn.Currency Dep.	....	....	....	....	725.1	1,242.9	1,241.0	2,088.8	2,616.6	3,560.9	6,467.6	8,208.1	9,024.3	12,292.5	15,855.1	**25**
Money Market Instruments	....	....	....	....	—	—	.6	220.2	11.5	—	44.8	85.9	266.3	296.5	508.9	**26aa**
Bonds	....	....	....	....	—	—	—	40.0	82.5	67.5	70.0	65.6	113.0	41.5	14.1	**26ab**
Foreign Liabilities	....	....	....	....	19.4	102.6	199.0	693.5	1,614.2	4,204.4	13,090.4	11,862.2	13,682.0	16,427.2	17,509.9	**26c**
Central Government Deposits	....	....	....	....	31.4	35.1	527.8	1,180.9	1,894.8	1,735.4	2,472.6	1,881.5	1,345.4	2,342.5	2,311.4	**26d**
Counterpart Funds	....	....	....	....	—	51.5	114.3	112.0	102.0	—	—	—	—	—	—	**26e**
Government Lending Funds	....	....	....	....	—	9.8	151.8	487.1	819.5	987.7	739.7	555.2	540.7	450.9	306.4	**26f**
Credit from Monetary Authorities	....	....	....	....	122.6	271.0	337.9	401.7	88.6	47.9	23.2	14.5	11.4	8.4	6.3	**26g**
Capital Accounts	....	....	....	....	228.8	493.9	776.8	994.4	1,834.9	2,519.4	5,372.5	7,845.3	8,459.5	8,340.0	10,432.5	**27a**
Other Items (Net)	....	....	....	....	406.9	45.1	-198.5	-298.6	-819.7	-1,027.6	-2,202.0	-2,055.1	-2,636.0	-1,475.3	-303.2	**27r**
Banking Survey *End of Period*																
Foreign Assets (Net)	....	....	....	....	2,171.5	4,394.2	†4,937.5	6,356.5	6,963.5	6,166.8	4,759.3	5,111.3	8,021.2	9,097.1	12,283.4	**31n**
Domestic Credit	....	....	....	....	1,139.1	1,609.6	†2,813.3	3,781.4	5,777.4	11,663.5	20,796.6	24,222.7	26,541.6	33,758.5	41,994.3	**32**
Claims on Central Govt. (Net)	....	....	....	....	-59.9	-33.6	†-194.5	-884.1	-1,546.6	-1,073.3	-2,262.9	-1,581.4	-964.9	-1,901.0	-1,872.4	**32an**
Claims on Local Government	....	....	....	....	—	12.7	†1.5	108.3	303.9	159.9	547.2	651.5	767.6	822.9	1,296.9	**32b**
Claims on Nonfin.Pub.Enterprises	....	....	....	....	854.4	644.4	†480.1	360.8	335.3	304.6	328.6	225.8	372.5	262.7	141.8	**32c**
Claims on Private Sector	....	....	....	....	344.7	986.1	†2,414.5	4,184.3	6,055.8	10,132.5	16,952.7	18,589.7	19,876.9	22,203.5	26,321.2	**32d**
Claims on Nonbank Financial Inst	....	....	....	....	—	—	†111.7	12.2	628.9	2,139.7	5,231.0	6,337.1	6,489.5	12,370.5	16,106.7	**32g**
Money	....	....	....	....	696.5	2,854.6	†5,228.2	6,319.9	8,203.2	11,289.7	13,998.0	13,119.8	17,335.5	20,884.1	24,948.2	**34**
Quasi-Money	....	....	....	....	1,625.1	1,242.9	†1,301.0	2,191.8	2,650.5	3,562.9	6,467.6	8,208.1	9,054.3	12,292.5	15,855.1	**35**
Money Market Instruments	....	....	....	....	—	—	.6	220.2	11.5	—	44.8	85.9	266.3	296.5	508.9	**36aa**
Bonds	....	....	....	....	—	—	—	40.0	82.5	67.5	70.0	65.6	113.0	41.5	14.1	**36ab**
Counterpart Funds	....	....	....	....	—	51.5	114.3	112.0	102.0	—	—	—	—	—	—	**36e**
Government Lending Funds	....	....	....	....	—	9.8	151.8	487.1	819.5	987.7	739.7	555.2	540.7	450.9	306.4	**36f**
Capital Accounts	....	....	....	....	1,323.8	2,166.6	†2,119.1	2,250.4	3,058.1	3,845.3	7,253.6	10,121.8	10,600.8	10,764.1	13,322.2	**37a**
Other Items (Net)	....	....	....	....	-334.7	-321.6	†-1164.3	-1,483.5	-2,186.4	-1,922.7	-3,017.9	-2,822.4	-3,347.7	-1,873.9	-677.1	**37r**
Money plus Quasi-Money	....	....	....	....	2,321.6	4,097.5	†6,529.2	8,511.7	10,853.7	14,852.6	20,465.6	21,327.9	26,389.9	33,176.6	40,803.2	**35l**
Interest Rates *Percent Per Annum*																
Money Market Rate	....	....	....	....	....	....	....	5.67	4.94	3.53	6.45	11.66	5.39	4.57	4.92	**60b**
Deposit Rate	....	....	....	....	....	....	....	11.51	8.74	6.05	6.19	8.07	4.19	3.76	4.03	**60l**
Lending Rate	....	....	....	....	....	30.50	33.66	24.65	19.01	14.87	11.76	15.06	11.09	7.43	7.78	**60p**
Prices and Labor *Period Averages*																
Producer Prices	....	....	....	....	....	....	....	79.6	100.0	114.8	†124.4	129.7	128.1	134.3	140.2	**63**
Consumer Prices	....	....	....	....	....	27.7	52.6	77.7	100.0	123.1	136.1	147.2	152.1	158.2	167.3	**64**
Period Averages																
Labor Force	....	....	....	....	....	....	....	....	734	....	708	711	....	705	....	**67d**
Employment	....	....	....	826	808	766	708	693	656	646	†648	640	614	609	....	**67e**
Unemployment	....	....	....	5	12	29	50	57	71	72	†69	70	86	96	89	**67c**
Unemployment Rate (%)	....	....	....	....	....	3.7	6.5	7.6	9.7	10.0	†9.7	9.9	12.3	13.7	12.6	**67r**
International Transactions *Millions of Krooni*																
Exports	....	....	....	....	....	5,549	10,642	†16,941	21,040	25,024	40,662	43,952	43,178	53,324	57,528	**70**
Imports, c.i.f.	....	....	....	....	....	5,128	11,848	†21,525	29,101	38,887	61,610	64,897	60,248	72,309	75,163	**71**
Imports, f.o.b.	....	....	....	....	....	4,736	10,944	†19,883	26,881	35,920	56,909	59,945	55,651	66,792	69,428	**71.v**

Estonia

939

		1972	1973	1974	1975	1976	1977	1978	1979	1980	1981	1982	1983	1984	1985	1986
Balance of Payments																*Millions of US Dollars:*
Current Account, n.i.e.	78ald	....	....	....	....	....	....	....	....	....	....	....	....	....	....	....
Goods: Exports f.o.b.	78aad	....	....	....	....	....	....	....	....	....	....	....	....	....	....	....
Goods: Imports f.o.b.	78abd	....	....	....	....	....	....	....	....	....	....	....	....	....	....	....
Trade Balance	78acd	....	....	....	....	....	....	....	....	....	....	....	....	....	....	....
Services: Credit	78add	....	....	....	....	....	....	....	....	....	....	....	....	....	....	....
Services: Debit	78aed	....	....	....	....	....	....	....	....	....	....	....	....	....	....	....
Balance on Goods & Services	78afd	....	....	....	....	....	....	....	....	....	....	....	....	....	....	....
Income: Credit	78agd	....	....	....	....	....	....	....	....	....	....	....	....	....	....	....
Income: Debit	78ahd	....	....	....	....	....	....	....	....	....	....	....	....	....	....	....
Balance on Gds, Serv. & Inc.	78aid	....	....	....	....	....	....	....	....	....	....	....	....	....	....	....
Current Transfers, n.i.e.: Credit	78ajd	....	....	....	....	....	....	....	....	....	....	....	....	....	....	....
Current Transfers: Debit	78akd	....	....	....	....	....	....	....	....	....	....	....	....	....	....	....
Capital Account, n.i.e.	78bcd	....	....	....	....	....	....	....	....	....	....	....	....	....	....	....
Capital Account, n.i.e.: Credit	78bad	....	....	....	....	....	....	....	....	....	....	....	....	....	....	....
Capital Account: Debit	78bbd	....	....	....	....	....	....	....	....	....	....	....	....	....	....	....
Financial Account, n.i.e.	78bjd	....	....	....	....	....	....	....	....	....	....	....	....	....	....	....
Direct Investment Abroad	78bdd	....	....	....	....	....	....	....	....	....	....	....	....	....	....	....
Dir. Invest. in Rep. Econ., n.i.e.	78bed	....	....	....	....	....	....	....	....	....	....	....	....	....	....	....
Portfolio Investment Assets	78bfd	....	....	....	....	....	....	....	....	....	....	....	....	....	....	....
Equity Securities	78bkd	....	....	....	....	....	....	....	....	....	....	....	....	....	....	....
Debt Securities	78bld	....	....	....	....	....	....	....	....	....	....	....	....	....	....	....
Portfolio Investment Liab., n.i.e.	78bgd	....	....	....	....	....	....	....	....	....	....	....	....	....	....	....
Equity Securities	78bmd	....	....	....	....	....	....	....	....	....	....	....	....	....	....	....
Debt Securities	78bnd	....	....	....	....	....	....	....	....	....	....	....	....	....	....	....
Financial Derivatives Assets	78bwd	....	....	....	....	....	....	....	....	....	....	....	....	....	....	....
Financial Derivatives Liabilities	78bxd	....	....	....	....	....	....	....	....	....	....	....	....	....	....	....
Other Investment Assets	78bhd	....	....	....	....	....	....	....	....	....	....	....	....	....	....	....
Monetary Authorities	78bod	....	....	....	....	....	....	....	....	....	....	....	....	....	....	....
General Government	78bpd	....	....	....	....	....	....	....	....	....	....	....	....	....	....	....
Banks	78bqd	....	....	....	....	....	....	....	....	....	....	....	....	....	....	....
Other Sectors	78brd	....	....	....	....	....	....	....	....	....	....	....	....	....	....	....
Other Investment Liab., n.i.e.	78bid	....	....	....	....	....	....	....	....	....	....	....	....	....	....	....
Monetary Authorities	78bsd	....	....	....	....	....	....	....	....	....	....	....	....	....	....	....
General Government	78btd	....	....	....	....	....	....	....	....	....	....	....	....	....	....	....
Banks	78bud	....	....	....	....	....	....	....	....	....	....	....	....	....	....	....
Other Sectors	78bvd	....	....	....	....	....	....	....	....	....	....	....	....	....	....	....
Net Errors and Omissions	78cad	....	....	....	....	....	....	....	....	....	....	....	....	....	....	....
Overall Balance	78cbd	....	....	....	....	....	....	....	....	....	....	....	....	....	....	....
Reserves and Related Items	79dad	....	....	....	....	....	....	....	....	....	....	....	....	....	....	....
Reserve Assets	79dbd	....	....	....	....	....	....	....	....	....	....	....	....	....	....	....
Use of Fund Credit and Loans	79dcd	....	....	....	....	....	....	....	....	....	....	....	....	....	....	....
Exceptional Financing	79ded	....	....	....	....	....	....	....	....	....	....	....	....	....	....	....
International Investment Position																*Millions of US Dollars*
Assets	79aad	....	....	....	....	....	....	....	....	....	....	....	....	....	....	....
Direct Investment Abroad	79abd	....	....	....	....	....	....	....	....	....	....	....	....	....	....	....
Portfolio Investment	79acd	....	....	....	....	....	....	....	....	....	....	....	....	....	....	....
Equity Securities	79add	....	....	....	....	....	....	....	....	....	....	....	....	....	....	....
Debt Securities	79aed	....	....	....	....	....	....	....	....	....	....	....	....	....	....	....
Financial Derivatives	79ald	....	....	....	....	....	....	....	....	....	....	....	....	....	....	....
Other Investment	79afd	....	....	....	....	....	....	....	....	....	....	....	....	....	....	....
Monetary Authorities	79agd	....	....	....	....	....	....	....	....	....	....	....	....	....	....	....
General Government	79ahd	....	....	....	....	....	....	....	....	....	....	....	....	....	....	....
Banks	79aid	....	....	....	....	....	....	....	....	....	....	....	....	....	....	....
Other Sectors	79ajd	....	....	....	....	....	....	....	....	....	....	....	....	....	....	....
Reserve Assets	79akd	....	....	....	....	....	....	....	....	....	....	....	....	....	....	....
Liabilities	79lad	....	....	....	....	....	....	....	....	....	....	....	....	....	....	....
Dir. Invest. in Rep. Economy	79lbd	....	....	....	....	....	....	....	....	....	....	....	....	....	....	....
Portfolio Investment	79lcd	....	....	....	....	....	....	....	....	....	....	....	....	....	....	....
Equity Securities	79ldd	....	....	....	....	....	....	....	....	....	....	....	....	....	....	....
Debt Securities	79led	....	....	....	....	....	....	....	....	....	....	....	....	....	....	....
Financial Derivatives	79lld	....	....	....	....	....	....	....	....	....	....	....	....	....	....	....
Other Investment	79lfd	....	....	....	....	....	....	....	....	....	....	....	....	....	....	....
Monetary Authorities	79lgd	....	....	....	....	....	....	....	....	....	....	....	....	....	....	....
General Government	79lhd	....	....	....	....	....	....	....	....	....	....	....	....	....	....	....
Banks	79lid	....	....	....	....	....	....	....	....	....	....	....	....	....	....	....
Other Sectors	79ljd	....	....	....	....	....	....	....	....	....	....	....	....	....	....	....

Minus Sign Indicates Debit

1987	1988	1989	1990	1991	1992	1993	1994	1995	1996	1997	1998	1999	2000	2001	Balance of Payments	
....	....	....	....	....	36.2	21.6	−166.3	−157.8	−398.3	−561.7	−478.4	−294.6	−294.0	−339.0	Current Account, n.i.e.	78al *d*
....	....	....	....	....	460.7	811.7	1,225.0	1,696.3	1,812.3	2,289.6	2,690.1	2,453.1	3,311.4	3,338.1	Goods: Exports f.o.b.	78aa *d*
....	....	....	....	....	−551.1	−956.6	−1,581.4	−2,362.3	−2,831.5	−3,413.7	−3,805.4	−3,330.6	−4,079.5	−4,125.0	Goods: Imports f.o.b.	78ab *d*
....	....	....	....	....	−90.4	−144.9	−356.5	−666.0	−1,019.2	−1,124.1	−1,115.2	−877.5	−768.1	−786.9	*Trade Balance*	78ac *d*
....	....	....	....	....	203.1	334.6	515.3	876.8	1,108.3	1,318.0	1,479.6	1,489.7	1,499.0	1,642.8	Services: Credit	78ad *d*
....	....	....	....	....	−160.4	−259.4	−410.2	−497.7	−589.8	−726.6	−910.1	−917.6	−936.3	−1,064.9	Services: Debit	78ae *d*
....	....	....	....	....	−47.7	−69.7	−251.3	−286.9	−500.7	−532.7	−545.7	−305.4	−205.4	−209.0	*Balance on Goods & Services*	78af *d*
....	....	....	....	....	.5	26.9	37.3	63.6	112.2	115.1	133.5	133.8	117.6	170.6	Income: Credit	78ag *d*
....	....	....	....	....	−13.6	−40.8	−66.9	−60.8	−110.3	−260.8	−214.5	−235.5	−321.7	−451.8	Income: Debit	78ah *d*
....	....	....	....	....	−60.8	−83.6	−280.9	−284.1	−498.8	−678.4	−626.7	−407.1	−409.6	−490.1	*Balance on Gds, Serv. & Inc.*	78ai *d*
....	....	....	....	....	97.4	108.4	120.3	134.5	116.8	135.3	172.9	153.7	144.7	180.4	Current Transfers, n.i.e.: Credit	78aj *d*
....	....	....	....	....	−.3	−3.2	−5.7	−8.2	−16.3	−18.6	−24.6	−41.3	−29.1	−29.3	Current Transfers: Debit	78ak *d*
....	....	....	....	....	27.4	—	−.6	−.8	−.7	−.2	1.8	1.2	16.5	5.1	Capital Account, n.i.e.	78bc *d*
....	....	....	....	....	27.4	—	.5	1.4	.2	.7	2.1	1.4	16.8	5.5	Capital Account, n.i.e.: Credit	78ba *d*
....	....	....	....	....	—	—	−1.1	−2.2	−.8	−.9	−.3	−.2	−.2	−.4	Capital Account: Debit	78bb *d*
....	....	....	....	....	−1.3	188.9	167.2	233.4	540.9	802.8	508.1	418.2	406.7	306.4	Financial Account, n.i.e.	78bj *d*
....	....	....	....	....	−1.9	−6.2	−2.4	−2.5	−40.1	−136.6	−6.3	−82.9	−63.4	−199.6	Direct Investment Abroad	78bd *d*
....	....	....	....	....	82.3	162.2	214.4	201.5	150.2	266.2	580.5	305.2	387.3	539.4	Dir. Invest. in Rep. Econ., n.i.e.	78be *d*
....	....	....	....	....	—	−.4	−22.5	−33.2	−52.7	−165.0	−10.9	−132.3	39.8	13.0	Portfolio Investment Assets	78bf *d*
....	....	....	....	....	—	−.4	−14.5	5.1	−15.0	−87.8	35.1	12.9	3.5	13.9	Equity Securities	78bk *d*
....	....	....	....	....	—	—	−8.0	−38.2	−37.6	−77.2	−46.0	−145.2	36.4	−.9	Debt Securities	78bl *d*
....	....	....	....	....	—	.2	8.4	11.1	198.1	427.5	1.1	153.3	75.6	83.0	Portfolio Investment Liab., n.i.e.	78bg *d*
....	....	....	....	....	—	.1	8.4	9.9	172.3	127.8	25.7	235.4	−28.5	31.5	Equity Securities	78bm *d*
....	....	....	....	....	—	.1	—	1.2	25.8	299.7	−24.6	−82.1	104.1	51.5	Debt Securities	78bn *d*
....	....	....	....	....	....	....	....	....	....	....	....	....	−4.7	−.1	Financial Derivatives Assets	78bw *d*
....	....	....	....	....	....	....	....	....	....	....	....	....	5.4	−2.0	Financial Derivatives Liabilities	78bx *d*
....	....	....	....	....	−122.4	−144.7	−146.7	−98.9	−7.3	−334.2	−168.5	−110.3	−177.1	−297.7	Other Investment Assets	78bh *d*
....	....	....	....	....	−72.8	5.7	.1	.1	.1	—	—	−18.3	−9.6	−11.1	Monetary Authorities	78bo *d*
....	....	....	....	....	—	−17.1	.4	−.4	−3.3	−24.7	−61.9	−60.8	32.7	−17.3	General Government	78bp *d*
....	....	....	....	....	−48.5	−44.7	−102.8	−41.1	20.8	−195.9	61.3	−53.8	−77.0	−214.4	Banks	78bq *d*
....	....	....	....	....	−1.1	−88.6	−44.4	−57.5	−24.9	−113.5	−167.9	22.5	−123.3	−54.9	Other Sectors	78br *d*
....	....	....	....	....	40.7	177.8	115.9	155.4	292.6	744.8	112.1	285.2	143.8	170.5	Other Investment Liab., n.i.e.	78bi *d*
....	....	....	....	....	8.1	14.9	6.2	−13.5	−6.7	−2.5	−1.1	7.3	1.7	−5.3	Monetary Authorities	78bs *d*
....	....	....	....	....	11.1	77.3	19.8	61.0	31.3	−3.3	4.4	9.8	−17.2	−7.2	General Government	78bt *d*
....	....	....	....	....	7.2	7.2	37.5	82.2	173.7	492.4	−17.3	188.3	76.8	58.2	Banks	78bu *d*
....	....	....	....	....	14.3	78.4	52.3	25.7	94.4	258.2	126.0	79.8	82.5	124.7	Other Sectors	78bv *d*
....	....	....	....	....	−4.4	−45.9	17.2	8.7	−35.6	−25.1	5.9	−5.5	−1.6	−12.8	Net Errors and Omissions	78ca *d*
....	....	....	....	....	57.9	164.6	17.5	83.5	106.3	215.9	37.3	119.3	127.6	−40.3	*Overall Balance*	78cb *d*
....	....	....	....	....	−57.9	−164.6	−17.5	−83.5	−106.3	−215.9	−37.3	−119.3	−127.6	40.3	Reserves and Related Items	79da *d*
....	....	....	....	....	−69.2	−212.4	−17.5	−112.9	−95.3	−196.4	−11.7	−115.3	−122.4	45.2	Reserve Assets	79db *d*
....	....	....	....	....	11.3	47.7	—	29.4	−11.1	−19.4	−25.6	−4.0	−5.2	−4.9	Use of Fund Credit and Loans	79dc *d*
....	....	....	....	....	....	....	....	....	....	....	....	....	....	....	Exceptional Financing	79de *d*

Millions of US Dollars

1987	1988	1989	1990	1991	1992	1993	1994	1995	1996	1997	1998	1999	2000	2001	International Investment Position	
....	....	....	....	....	....	....	....	....	1,344.1	2,045.5	2,300.4	2,415.1	2,614.0	2,920.5	Assets	79aa *d*
....	....	....	....	....	....	....	....	....	107.7	215.3	198.4	281.2	259.1	441.8	Direct Investment Abroad	79ab *d*
....	....	....	....	....	....	....	....	....	121.0	249.3	211.2	305.2	271.8	262.1	Portfolio Investment	79ac *d*
....	....	....	....	....	....	....	....	....	26.1	98.5	31.5	12.4	26.4	22.5	Equity Securities	79ad *d*
....	....	....	....	....	....	....	....	....	94.9	150.9	179.7	292.9	245.4	239.6	Debt Securities	79ae *d*
....	....	....	....	....	....	....	....	....	—	—	—	—	9.1	8.7	Financial Derivatives	79al *d*
....	....	....	....	....	....	....	....	....	475.9	820.4	1,077.4	972.4	1,151.0	1,385.3	Other Investment	79af *d*
....	....	....	....	....	....	....	....	....	—	—	—	—	1.0	6.9	Monetary Authorities	79ag *d*
....	....	....	....	....	....	....	....	....	4.6	26.7	97.7	129.6	87.5	98.0	General Government	79ah *d*
....	....	....	....	....	....	....	....	....	246.9	392.8	360.9	374.4	411.8	601.1	Banks	79ai *d*
....	....	....	....	....	....	....	....	....	224.3	400.8	618.7	468.4	650.8	679.2	Other Sectors	79aj *d*
....	....	....	....	....	....	....	....	....	639.6	760.5	813.5	856.2	922.9	822.5	Reserve Assets	79ak *d*
....	....	....	....	....	....	....	....	....	1,974.9	3,757.8	4,451.9	5,199.6	5,389.5	6,017.7	Liabilities	79la *d*
....	....	....	....	....	....	....	....	....	824.6	1,147.9	1,821.7	2,467.3	2,644.7	3,159.9	Dir. Invest. in Rep. Economy	79lb *d*
....	....	....	....	....	....	....	....	....	117.4	954.2	702.9	771.8	761.4	764.3	Portfolio Investment	79lc *d*
....	....	....	....	....	....	....	....	....	76.3	572.9	301.2	500.7	431.6	403.0	Equity Securities	79ld *d*
....	....	....	....	....	....	....	....	....	41.1	381.3	401.7	271.2	329.8	361.3	Debt Securities	79le *d*
....	....	....	....	....	....	....	....	....	—	—	—	—	10.2	6.3	Financial Derivatives	79ll *d*
....	....	....	....	....	....	....	....	....	1,033.0	1,655.6	1,927.4	1,960.4	1,973.1	2,087.2	Other Investment	79lf *d*
....	....	....	....	....	....	....	....	....	151.4	55.7	30.8	25.8	22.1	14.4	Monetary Authorities	79lg *d*
....	....	....	....	....	....	....	....	....	175.3	161.4	173.6	178.6	153.6	155.6	General Government	79lh *d*
....	....	....	....	....	....	....	....	....	299.1	747.1	692.7	778.2	809.0	827.8	Banks	79li *d*
....	....	....	....	....	....	....	....	....	407.1	691.5	1,030.3	977.8	988.6	1,089.5	Other Sectors	79lj *d*

Estonia

		1972	1973	1974	1975	1976	1977	1978	1979	1980	1981	1982	1983	1984	1985	1986
Government Finance															*Millions of Krooni:*	
Deficit (-) or Surplus	80	....	....	....	....	....	....	....	....	....	....	....	....	....	....	....
Revenue	81	...	...	...	...	...	...	...	...	...	...	...	...	...	...	...
Grants Received	81z	...	...	...	...	...	...	...	...	...	...	...	...	...	...	...
Expenditure	82	...	...	...	...	...	...	...	...	...	...	...	...	...	...	...
Lending Minus Repayments	83	...	...	...	...	...	...	...	...	...	...	...	...	...	...	...
Financing																
Domestic	84a	...	...	...	...	...	...	...	...	...	...	...	...	...	...	...
Foreign	85a	...	...	...	...	...	...	...	...	...	...	...	...	...	...	...
Total Debt																
Domestic	88a	...	...	...	...	...	...	...	...	...	...	...	...	...	...	...
Foreign	89a	...	...	...	...	...	...	...	...	...	...	...	...	...	...	...
National Accounts															*Millions of Krooni*	
Househ.Cons.Expend.,incl.NPISHs	96f	...	...	...	...	...	...	...	...	...	...	...	...	...	...	...
Government Consumption Expend.	91f	...	...	...	...	...	...	...	...	...	...	...	...	...	...	...
Gross Fixed Capital Formation	93e	...	...	...	...	...	...	...	...	...	...	...	...	...	...	...
Changes in Inventories	93i	...	...	...	...	...	...	...	...	...	...	...	...	...	...	...
Exports of Goods and Services	90c	...	...	...	...	...	...	...	...	...	...	...	...	...	...	...
Imports of Goods and Services (-)	98c	...	...	...	...	...	...	...	...	...	...	...	...	...	...	...
Gross Domestic Product (GDP)	99b	...	...	...	...	...	...	...	...	...	...	...	...	...	...	...
Net Primary Income from Abroad	98.n	...	...	...	...	...	...	...	...	...	...	...	...	...	...	...
Gross National Income (GNI)	99a	...	...	...	...	...	...	...	...	...	...	...	...	...	...	...
Net Current Transf.from Abroad	98t	...	...	...	...	...	...	...	...	...	...	...	...	...	...	...
Gross Nat'l Disposable Inc.(GNDI)	99i	...	...	...	...	...	...	...	...	...	...	...	...	...	...	...
Gross Saving	99s	...	...	...	...	...	...	...	...	...	...	...	...	...	...	...
Consumption of Fixed Capital	99cf	...	...	...	...	...	...	...	...	...	...	...	...	...	...	...
GDP Volume 1995 Prices	99b.p	...	...	...	...	...	...	...	...	...	...	...	...	...	...	...
GDP Volume (1995=100)	99bvp	...	...	...	...	...	...	...	...	...	...	...	...	...	...	...
GDP Deflator (1995=100)	99bip	...	...	...	...	...	...	...	...	...	...	...	...	...	...	...
Population	99z	...	...	...	...	...	...	...	...	...	...	...	...	...	*Millions:* ...	...

	1987	1988	1989	1990	1991	1992	1993	1994	1995	1996	1997	1998	1999	2000	2001		
Year Ending December 31																**Government Finance**	
	....	....	....	....	7.2	163.3	−458.5	416.8	−233.6	−433.7	1,632.4	−42.3	−120.9	137.4	....	Deficit (-) or Surplus	80
	....	....	....	....	448.1	2,994.8	6,320.3	10,566.8	14,649.3	17,544.8	22,360.5	24,006.5	23,397.4	26,474.5	....	Revenue	81
	....	....	....	....	14.9	219.9	243.7	—	132.0	—	25.0	124.0	302.5	258.5	....	Grants Received	81z
	....	....	....	....	404.7	3,024.0	6,088.5	9,590.3	14,523.5	17,713.7	20,551.8	24,103.3	26,815.5	27,373.3	....	Expenditure	82
	....	....	....	....	51.1	27.4	934.0	559.7	491.4	264.8	201.3	69.5	−2,994.7	−777.7	....	Lending Minus Repayments	83
																Financing	
	....	....	....	....	−7.2	−172.1	....	....	−150.2	49.3	−974.0	524.0	469.7	−87.4	....	Domestic	84a
	....	....	....	....	—	8.8	....	....	383.8	384.4	−658.4	−481.7	−348.8	−50.0	....	Foreign	85a
																Total Debt	
	....	....	....	....	....	....	....	....	....	682.1	572.5	413.4	338.8	210.0	....	Domestic	88a
	....	....	....	....	....	....	....	....	....	2,584.6	2,770.9	2,715.6	3,175.1	2,505.6	....	Foreign	89a
Millions of Krooni																**National Accounts**	
	....	....	....	....	1,002	7,261	12,705	18,249	23,982	31,815	43,039	43,348	44,424	49,873	54,536	Househ.Cons.Expend.,incl.NPISHs	96f
	....	....	....	....	241	2,084	4,569	7,117	10,681	13,015	14,728	16,651	17,851	18,594	19,720	Government Consumption Expend.	91f
	....	....	....	....	357	2,755	5,280	8,004	10,576	14,015	17,962	21,761	19,023	19,965	24,212	Gross Fixed Capital Formation	93e
	....	....	....	....	91	763	541	181	305	564	1,882	−189	−308	1,072	1,213	Changes in Inventories	93i
	....	....	....	....	584	7,893	15,197	22,486	29,451	35,186	50,213	58,590	58,947	81,499	87,432	Exports of Goods and Services	90c
	....	....	....	....	495	7,121	16,125	25,739	32,736	41,229	57,633	66,267	62,703	85,802	91,403	Imports of Goods and Services (-)	98c
	....	....	....	....	1,832	13,158	21,826	29,867	40,897	52,423	64,045	73,538	76,327	85,436	95,275	Gross Domestic Product (GDP)	99b
	....	....	....	....	....	....	−185	−378	28	26	−2,011	−1,164	−1,506	−3,483	−5,124	Net Primary Income from Abroad	98.n
	....	....	....	....	....	....	21,641	29,489	40,925	52,449	62,034	72,374	74,821	81,953	90,151	Gross National Income (GNI)	99a
	....	....	....	....	....	....	1,392	1,486	1,446	1,210	1,620	2,080	1,654	2,344	2,932	Net Current Transf.from Abroad	98t
	....	....	....	....	....	....	22,817	30,707	42,180	53,682	63,934	74,243	75,508	82,290	93,330	Gross Nat'l Disposable Inc.(GNDI)	99i
	....	....	....	....	....	....	5,759	5,608	7,708	8,830	10,966	14,455	14,199	15,829	18,827	Gross Saving	99s
	....	....	....	....	....	....	2,674	3,334	4,580	5,727	7,511	10,111	11,429	12,397	14,123	Consumption of Fixed Capital	99cf
	....	....	....	....	....	....	39,899	39,104	40,897	42,529	46,969	49,339	48,996	52,369	55,192	GDP Volume 1995 Prices	99b.*p*
	....	....	....	....	....	....	97.6	95.6	100.0	104.0	114.8	120.6	119.8	128.1	135.0	GDP Volume (1995=100)	99bv*p*
	....	....	....	....	....	....	54.7	76.4	100.0	123.3	136.4	149.0	155.8	163.1	172.6	GDP Deflator (1995=100)	99bi*p*
Midyear Estimates																	
	....	....	....	....	1.57	1.54	1.52	1.50	1.48	1.47	1.46	1.43	1.41	1.37	1.38	**Population**	99z

(See notes in the back of the book.)

Ethiopia

		1972	1973	1974	1975	1976	1977	1978	1979	1980	1981	1982	1983	1984	1985	1986
Exchange Rates															*Birr per SDR:*	
Official Rate	aa	2.4971	2.4971	2.5344	2.4233	2.4050	2.5144	2.6968	2.7269	2.6401	2.4094	2.2834	2.1672	2.0290	2.2737	2.5320
															Birr per US Dollar:	
Official Rate	ae	2.3000	2.0700	2.0700	2.0700	2.0700	2.0700	2.0700	2.0700	2.0700	2.0700	2.0700	2.0700	2.0700	2.0700	2.0700
Official Rate	rf	2.3000	2.0988	2.0700	2.0700	2.0700	2.0700	2.0700	2.0700	2.0700	2.0700	2.0700	2.0700	2.0700	2.0700	2.0700
Fund Position															*Millions of SDRs:*	
Quota	2f. s	27.0	27.0	27.0	27.0	27.0	27.0	36.0	36.0	54.0	54.0	54.0	70.6	70.6	70.6	70.6
SDRs	1b. s	—	—	—	—	—	—	—	.4	—	10.4	3.2	2.3	3.0	.2	—
Reserve Position in the Fund	1c. s	6.8	6.8	6.8	6.8	6.8	7.3	—	—	4.1	—	—	4.2	—	—	—
Total Fund Cred.&Loans Outstg.	2tl	—	—	—	—	—	—	11.2	55.8	62.3	124.4	145.6	127.6	100.2	64.8	68.8
International Liquidity											*Millions of US Dollars Unless Otherwise Indicated:*					
Total Reserves minus Gold	1l. d	83.2	166.0	263.6	276.7	294.7	213.3	152.9	172.7	80.1	266.7	181.8	125.9	44.3	148.0	250.5
SDRs	1b. d								.5	—	12.1	3.5	2.4	2.9	.2	—
Reserve Position in the Fund	1c. d	7.4	8.2	8.4	8.0	7.9	8.9	—	—	5.2	—	—	4.4	—	—	—
Foreign Exchange	1d. d	75.8	157.8	255.2	268.7	286.8	204.4	152.9	172.2	74.9	254.6	178.3	119.1	41.4	147.8	250.5
Gold (Million Fine Troy Ounces)	1ad	.249	.257	.275	.275	.275	.286	.286	.286	.309	.260	.209	.209	.209	.209	.209
Gold (National Valuation)	1and	9.5	10.8	11.0	11.0	10.8	11.3	11.3	11.8	24.5	23.3	21.3	21.3	21.3	21.3	21.3
Monetary Authorities: Other Liab.	4..d	1.0	2.3	3.5	4.5	5.1	4.3	6.5	3.4	5.2	9.6	7.4	10.4	6.0	12.9	12.5
Deposit Money Banks: Assets	7a. d	21.1	52.5	48.1	40.3	38.8	57.9	45.4	70.0	50.8	63.8	90.1	71.9	64.9	57.4	72.6
Liabilities	7b. d	24.5	23.6	21.4	23.0	22.4	25.0	22.2	23.8	40.7	60.0	71.6	66.7	62.1	59.2	57.0
Other Banking Insts.: Assets	7e. d	.2	.2	.5	.7	.3	.4	3.6	1.2	1.7	.2	.6	.6	.5	1.4	.9
Liabilities	7f. d	12.4	20.5	24.0	31.4	33.5	37.1	46.4	49.1	73.6	36.4	32.5	29.2	29.1	33.4	43.0
Monetary Authorities															*Millions of Birr:*	
Foreign Assets	11	218	371	567	595	627	498	401	410	214	586	424	306	140	361	569
Claims on Central Government	12a	171	148	126	307	512	605	787	950	1,093	1,033	1,284	1,574	1,892	1,722	2,061
Claims on Other Financial Insts	12f	—	—	—	83	105	167	282	441	692	855	982	845	1,014	1,194	1,333
Reserve Money	14	393	472	603	835	1,004	1,001	1,097	1,209	1,355	1,554	1,690	1,690	2,027	2,117	2,638
of which: Currency Outside DMBs	14a	340	404	533	689	575	769	895	1,012	1,029	1,039	1,150	1,251	1,272	1,418	1,640
Foreign Liabilities	16c	2	5	7	9	11	9	44	159	175	319	348	298	216	174	200
Central Government Deposits	16d	49	65	93	87	123	134	148	144	95	107	118	170	208	339	374
Capital Accounts	17a	49	47	65	77	97	122	151	174	178	187	192	200	210	218	266
Other Items (Net)	17r	−104	−70	−74	−24	10	5	32	116	196	306	342	366	386	430	484
Deposit Money Banks															*Millions of Birr:*	
Reserves	20	56	70	72	155	435	229	201	194	325	514	540	†440	757	703	998
Foreign Assets	21	49	109	100	83	80	120	94	145	105	132	187	†149	134	119	150
Claims on Central Government	22a	14	43	52	65	86	158	198	229	217	292	363	†914	951	1,451	1,449
Claims on Nonfin.Pub.Enterprises	22c	—	—	—	—	—	—	—	468	586	636	677	†601	509	488	568
Claims on Private Sector	22d	444	473	545	464	467	568	732	†411	289	369	386	†387	361	374	375
Claims on Other Financial Insts	22f	26	18	24	30	30	14	16	†51	72	90	89	†—			
Demand Deposits	24	151	215	221	253	378	409	484	559	539	681	742	†892	1,037	1,285	1,633
Time, Savings,& Fgn.Currency Dep.	25	265	363	381	302	450	473	483	536	628	718	797	†1,056	1,140	1,292	1,195
Foreign Liabilities	26c	23	17	15	21	21	29	25	31	68	110	136	†128	121	117	115
Long-Term Foreign Liabilities	26cl	34	32	29	27	25	23	21	18	16	14	12	10	8	5	3
Central Government Deposits	26d	13	14	21	25	31	24	28	39	68	89	98	†117	89	81	123
Capital Accounts	27a	60	61	64	65	74	83	81	89	85	232	223	†318	339	354	399
Other Items (Net)	27r	43	11	63	105	119	48	119	227	188	190	233	†−30	−22		72
Monetary Survey															*Millions of Birr:*	
Foreign Assets (Net)	31n	241	457	645	649	675	580	426	365	76	288	126	†28	−62	188	405
Domestic Credit	32	594	604	635	837	1,047	1,355	1,840	†2,368	2,785	3,079	3,565	†4,034	4,430	4,808	5,288
Claims on Central Govt. (Net)	32an	124	113	65	259	445	606	809	996	1,146	1,129	1,431	†2,201	2,546	2,753	3,012
Claims on Nonfin.Pub.Enterprises	32c	—	—	—	—	—	—	—	468	586	636	677	†601	509	488	568
Claims on Private Sector	32d	444	473	545	464	467	568	732	†411	289	369	386	†387	361	374	375
Claims on Other Financial Insts	32f	26	19	24	113	135	181	299	†492	764	945	1,071	†845	1,014	1,194	1,333
Money	34	491	619	754	942	953	1,179	1,378	1,572	1,568	1,720	1,892	†2,142	2,309	2,702	3,273
Quasi-Money	35	265	363	381	302	450	473	483	536	628	718	797	†1,056	1,140	1,292	1,195
Long-Term Foreign Liabilities	36cl	34	32	29	27	25	23	21	18	16	14	12	10	8	5	3
Capital Accounts	37a	109	108	129	142	171	205	232	262	264	419	415	†519	550	571	665
Other Items (Net)	37r	−63	−60	−14	73	123	55	152	344	385	496	575	†336	361	426	556
Money plus Quasi-Money	35l	756	982	1,135	1,244	1,403	1,652	1,861	2,108	2,196	2,438	2,689	†3,198	3,449	3,994	4,468
Other Banking Institutions															*Millions of Birr:*	
Cash	40	8	15	9	9	31	43	41	30	49	53	34	75	64	38	217
Foreign Assets	41	1	1	1	2	1	1	8	2	4	—	1	1	1	3	2
Claims on Nonfin.Pub.Enterprises	42c	—	—	—	—	—	—	—	—	—	—	—	—	—	—	—
Claims on Private Sector	42d	154	201	245	369	391	459	621	838	1,161	1,149	1,262	1,138	1,347	1,553	1,705
Demand Deposits	44	—	—	—	—	—	—	—	—	—	—	—	—	—	—	—
Time and Savings Deposits	45	28	34	42	58	77	86	124	144	228	179	229	251	267	279	425
Foreign Liabilities	46c	29	42	50	65	69	77	96	102	152	75	67	61	60	69	89
Central Govt. Lending Funds	46f	18	31	32	29	24	24	24	23	22	15	15	14	14	14	14
Credit from Monetary Authorities	46g	—	—	—	83	105	167	282	441	692	855	982	845	1,014	1,194	1,333
Credit from Deposit Money Banks	46h	23	22	29	34	29	31	35	40	53	70	24	23	21	22	24
Capital Accounts	47a	69	88	105	115	115	118	118	115	115	104	91	73	81	95	125
Other Items (Net)	47r	−3	−3	−2	−3	3	1	−8	4	−49	−95	−112	−52	−45	−79	−86
Liquid Liabilities	55l	776	1,001	1,167	1,293	1,449	1,695	1,944	2,222	2,375	2,565	2,884	3,374	3,652	4,235	4,676
Interest Rates															*Percent Per Annum*	
Discount Rate	60	....	....	....	....	....	....	....	....	....	....	....	....	....	6.00	6.00
Treasury Bill Rate	60c	....	....	....	....	....	....	2.03	2.02	2.80	2.80	3.00	3.00	3.00	3.00	3.00
Deposit Rate	60l	....	....	....	....	....	....	....	....	....	....	....	....	....	6.00	6.35
Lending Rate	60p	....	....	....	....	....	....	....	....	....	....	....	....	....	8.50	7.25
Government Bond Yield	61	....	....	....	....	....	....	....	....	....	....	....	....	....		6.00
Prices and Labor															*Index Numbers (1995=100):*	
Consumer Prices	64	13.5	14.7	16.0	17.0	21.9	25.5	29.1	33.8	35.3	37.5	39.7	39.4	42.8	50.9	45.9
															Number in Thousands:	
Labor Force	67d	....	....	....	....	....	....	....	....	....	....	....	....	....	....	....
Employment	67e	....	....	....	....	....	....	....	....	....	....	....	....	....	....	....
Unemployment	67c	....	....	....	....	....	....	....	....	....	....	....	....	....	56	53
Unemployment Rate (%)	67r	....	....	....	....	....	....	....	....	....	....	....	....	54.7	56.4	52.6

	1987	1988	1989	1990	1991	1992	1993	1994	1995	1996	1997	1998	1999	2000	2001		
Exchange Rates																	
End of Period																	
Official Rate	2.9366	2.7856	2.7203	2.9449	2.9610	6.8750	6.8678	8.6861	9.3946	9.2403	9.2613	10.5644	11.1640	10.8324	10.7555		**aa**
End of Period (ae) Period Average (rf)																	
Official Rate	2.0700	2.0700	2.0700	2.0700	2.0700	5.0000	5.0000	5.9500	6.3200	6.4260	6.8640	7.5030	8.1340	8.3140	8.5583		**ae**
Official Rate	2.0700	2.0700	2.0700	2.0700	2.0700	2.8025	5.0000	5.4650	6.1583	6.3517	6.7093	7.1159	7.9423	8.2173	8.4575		**rf**
Fund Position																	
End of Period																	
Quota	70.6	70.6	70.6	70.6	70.6	98.3	98.3	98.3	98.3	98.3	98.3	98.3	133.7	133.7	133.7		**2f. s**
SDRs	1.2	—	—	.2	.1	.1	.2	.3	.2	.3	.1	.1	—	—	.1		**1b. s**
Reserve Position in the Fund						6.9	7.0	7.0	7.0	7.1	7.1	7.1	7.1	7.1	7.1		**1c. s**
Total Fund Cred.&Loans Outstg.	53.4	40.8	23.0	4.5	—	14.1	35.3	49.4	49.4	64.2	64.2	76.1	69.0	59.1	84.0		**2tl**
International Liquidity																	
End of Period																	
Total Reserves minus Gold	122.7	64.2	46.1	20.2	54.5	232.4	455.8	544.2	771.5	732.2	501.1	511.1	458.5	306.3	433.2		**1l. d**
SDRs	1.7	—	.1	.3	.2	.1	.3	.4	.3	.3	.1	.1	—	—	.2		**1b. d**
Reserve Position in the Fund						9.5	9.6	10.2	10.5	10.1	9.5	10.0	9.7	9.2	9.0		**1c. d**
Foreign Exchange	121.0	64.2	46.0	19.9	54.3	222.8	445.9	533.6	760.8	722.0	491.4	501.0	448.7	297.1	424.1		**1d. d**
Gold (Million Fine Troy Ounces)	.209	.209	.192	.091	.147	.113	.113	.113	.113	.002	.002	.030	.030	.020	.205		**1ad**
Gold (National Valuation)	21.3	21.3	17.3	9.4	15.1	11.4	11.4	11.4	11.4	.4	.4	.4	.3	.3	.3		**1an d**
Monetary Authorities: Other Liab.	18.1	37.8	48.8	60.8	18.9	174.0	161.5	146.5	134.8	169.2	90.1	107.2	95.1	77.4	106.0		**4. d**
Deposit Money Banks: Assets	52.3	71.6	64.1	43.6	151.4	192.2	236.2	533.3	454.2	428.6	672.1	647.8	536.1	592.9	619.1		**7a. d**
Liabilities	56.2	62.3	60.9	67.9	77.5	65.9	91.4	134.8	216.0	229.1	249.6	252.6	282.3	257.1	206.1		**7b. d**
Other Banking Insts.: Assets	4.0	.9	1.3	3.1	2.5	2.2	1.0	3.5	2.5	8.6	9.3	9.2	6.8	5.7	.6		**7e. d**
Liabilities	50.4	63.2	73.2	112.7	132.6	55.5	58.9	52.8	45.0	39.0	36.9	27.2	28.1	29.5	28.9		**7f. d**
Monetary Authorities																	
End of Period																	
Foreign Assets	348	188	142	78	154	1,229	2,737	3,481	4,964	4,725	3,459	3,896	3,669	2,521	3,598		**11**
Claims on Central Government	2,047	2,492	2,838	3,553	4,668	5,724	8,244	8,444	8,131	7,656	8,529	9,201	10,301	13,896	12,525		**12a**
Claims on Other Financial Insts	1,588	1,786	1,945	2,064	2,081	2,102	458	464	465	465	465	465	465	394	394		**12f**
Reserve Money	2,596	3,085	3,515	4,028	5,137	6,120	6,421	7,084	7,977	6,653	7,236	6,346	5,673	7,779	7,141		**14**
of which: Currency Outside DMBs	1,744	1,962	2,341	3,081	4,007	4,709	4,776	5,380	5,718	5,401	4,964	3,978	4,507	4,591	4,870		**14a**
Foreign Liabilities	194	192	163	139	39	967	1,050	1,301	1,316	1,544	1,076	1,297	1,215	965	1,120		**16c**
Central Government Deposits	313	387	363	453	661	590	2,038	1,787	1,809	1,750	2,195	2,070	2,522	3,212	4,638		**16d**
Capital Accounts	358	318	330	334	342	518	466	733	880	1,159	1,198	1,272	1,423	1,647	2,101		**17a**
Other Items (Net)	521	483	553	740	725	861	1,464	1,483	1,579	1,739	748	2,577	3,603	3,209	1,517		**17r**
Deposit Money Banks																	
End of Period																	
Reserves	852	1,126	1,169	941	1,130	1,413	1,635	1,666	2,197	1,228	2,173	2,312	1,315	3,197	2,213		**20**
Foreign Assets	108	148	133	90	313	961	1,181	3,173	2,871	2,754	4,613	4,861	4,361	4,929	5,299		**21**
Claims on Central Government	1,476	1,498	1,869	2,639	2,630	2,617	2,617	2,617	2,773	2,613	2,361	2,629	5,234	5,556	7,500		**22a**
Claims on Nonfin.Pub.Enterprises	708	886	863	785	773	825	1,515	1,630	1,630	1,795	1,590	1,612	798	776	852		**22c**
Claims on Private Sector	516	386	389	409	411	624	1,350	1,988	3,706	6,449	8,007	8,694	11,216	11,836	12,187		**22d**
Claims on Other Financial Insts										279	248	217	487	435	390		**22f**
Demand Deposits	—	1,597	1,759	1,981	2,192	2,192	2,433	2,674	3,646	3,562	3,713	4,919	5,168	5,763	6,819	7,027	**24**
Time, Savings,& Fgn.Currency Dep.	1,413	1,570	1,726	1,894	2,188	2,607	3,252	4,378	5,297	6,636	8,224	8,417	8,475	10,002	11,610		**25**
Foreign Liabilities	115	129	126	140	160	329	457	802	1,365	1,472	1,713	1,895	2,296	2,138	1,764		**26c**
Long-Term Foreign Liabilities	1														—		**26cl**
Central Government Deposits	130	150	149	153	178	243	412	619	810	737	974	1,153	1,176	1,004	1,287		**26d**
Capital Accounts	432	438	466	493	538	548	825	979	1,238	2,028	2,566	3,078	3,219	3,737	4,093		**27a**
Other Items (Net)	−28	−1	−26	−9	1	280	678	649	905	531	595	614	2,481	3,030	2,658		**27r**
Monetary Survey																	
End of Period																	
Foreign Assets (Net)	146	15	−15	−112	268	894	2,411	4,551	5,153	4,463	5,282	5,565	4,519	4,348	6,013		**31n**
Domestic Credit	5,892	6,510	7,392	8,843	9,725	11,059	11,734	12,736	14,087	16,769	18,031	19,596	24,803	28,678	27,922		**32**
Claims on Central Govt. (Net)	3,080	3,453	4,195	5,586	6,460	7,508	8,411	8,654	8,286	7,782	7,721	8,608	11,837	15,237	14,099		**32an**
Claims on Nonfin.Pub.Enterprises	708	886	863	785	773	825	1,515	1,630	1,630	1,795	1,590	1,612	798	776	852		**32c**
Claims on Private Sector	516	386	389	409	411	624	1,350	1,988	3,706	6,449	8,007	8,694	11,216	11,836	12,187		**32d**
Claims on Other Financial Insts	1,588	1,786	1,945	2,064	2,081	2,102	458	464	465	744	713	682	952	829	784		**32f**
Money	3,341	3,722	4,322	5,273	6,199	7,142	7,450	9,027	9,280	9,114	9,883	9,146	10,270	11,409	11,898		**34**
Quasi-Money	1,413	1,570	1,726	1,894	2,188	2,607	3,252	4,378	5,297	6,636	8,224	8,417	8,475	10,002	11,610		**35**
Long-Term Foreign Liabilities	1														—		**36cl**
Capital Accounts	790	755	796	827	880	1,066	1,291	1,712	2,118	3,187	3,764	4,351	4,641	5,383	6,194		**37a**
Other Items (Net)	493	479	533	738	726	1,138	2,152	2,171	2,545	2,294	1,441	3,248	5,935	6,230	4,232		**37r**
Money plus Quasi-Money	4,754	5,291	6,048	7,167	8,387	9,749	10,702	13,405	14,577	15,751	18,108	17,563	18,745	21,412	23,508		**35l**
Other Banking Institutions																	
End of Period																	
Cash	211	208	351	331	308	297	369	234	10	8	23	8	12	8	6		**40**
Foreign Assets	8	2	3	7	5	11	5	21	16	55	64	69	55	47	5		**41**
Claims on Nonfin.Pub.Enterprises									492	575	397	300	258	226	201		**42c**
Claims on Private Sector	2,013	2,335	2,479	3,067	3,113	2,701	954	1,206	701	1,173	1,774	2,476	2,917	3,251	2,109		**42d**
Demand Deposits									10	22	31	16	26	11	6		**44**
Time and Savings Deposits	456	557	657	677	641	497	530	538	49	2	234	681	735	717	678		**45**
Foreign Liabilities	104	131	152	233	274	278	295	314	285	250	254	204	228	246	248		**46c**
Central Govt. Lending Funds	23	34	28	28	27	29	100	54	14	14	14	14	14	14	14		**46f**
Credit from Monetary Authorities	1,588	1,786	1,945	2,064	2,081	2,102	458	464	465	465	465	465	465	394	394		**46g**
Credit from Deposit Money Banks	18	27	2	1	1	97	97	116	415	685	958	894	1,416	1,640	450		**46h**
Capital Accounts	142	128	154	87	61	−41	−106	101	177	391	361	381	397	415	429		**47a**
Other Items (Net)	−98	−119	−106	314	339	47	−44	−128	−194	−18	−61	197	−39	95	102		**47r**
Liquid Liabilities	4,999	5,640	6,354	7,514	8,721	9,949	10,862	13,709	14,616	15,745	18,319	18,236	19,468	22,121	24,180		**55l**
Interest Rates																	
Percent Per Annum																	
Discount Rate	3.00	3.00	3.00	3.00	3.00	5.25	12.00	12.00	12.00	....	....	....	....	....	....		**60**
Treasury Bill Rate	3.00	3.00	3.00	3.00	3.00	5.25	12.00	12.00	12.00	7.22	3.97	3.48	3.65	2.74	3.06		**60c**
Deposit Rate	6.70	6.70	6.70	2.43	5.00	3.63	11.50	11.50	11.46	9.42	7.00	6.00	6.32	6.68	6.97		**60l**
Lending Rate	6.00	6.00	6.00	6.00	6.00	8.00	14.00	14.33	15.08	13.92	10.50	10.50	10.58	10.89	10.87		**60p**
Government Bond Yield	5.00	5.00	5.00	5.00	5.00	7.00	13.00	13.00	13.00	13.00	....	....	....	....	....		**61**
Prices and Labor																	
Period Averages																	
Consumer Prices	44.8	48.0	51.7	54.4	73.8	81.6	84.5	90.9	100.0	†94.9	97.2	99.7	105.5	105.5	93.7		**64**
Period Averages																	
Labor Force											26,408	....	27,272	....	....		**67d**
Employment		....	....	....	....	....	683	....	....	....	....	....	....	....	....		**67e**
Unemployment	539																**67c**
Unemployment	58	55	51	44	44	71	63	65	23	28	35	29	26				
Unemployment Rate (%)	58.2	55.3	51.3	44.2	44.3	70.9	62.9	....	....	....	....	....	....				**67r**

Ethiopia

		1972	1973	1974	1975	1976	1977	1978	1979	1980	1981	1982	1983	1984	1985	1986
International Transactions															*Millions of Birr*	
Exports	70	384.1	502.4	556.2	497.8	580.6	689.0	633.6	864.3	878.8	805.1	835.5	833.3	862.7	689.4	941.6
Imports, c.i.f.	71	435.6	448.2	586.0	647.9	729.5	727.8	942.7	1,174.6	1,494.7	1,528.9	1,627.8	1,813.3	1,921.4	2,056.4	2,280.4
Balance of Payments															*Millions of US Dollars:*	
Current Account, n.i.e.	78al d	....	....	....	....	....	−82.6	−111.7	−91.4	−226.1	−249.5	−194.9	−169.9	−130.1	106.3	−327.1
Goods: Exports f.o.b.	78aa d						333.3	306.2	430.3	419.3	374.1	402.8	402.6	416.8	332.9	477.1
Goods: Imports f.o.b.	78ab d						−417.0	−436.5	−522.9	−649.6	−629.8	−675.2	−740.0	−798.4	−840.5	−932.6
Trade Balance	78ac d						−83.7	−130.3	−92.5	−230.3	−255.7	−272.4	−337.3	−381.5	−507.7	−455.4
Services: Credit	78ad d						83.9	79.5	86.3	125.4	132.4	135.1	138.9	186.5	288.8	243.9
Services: Debit	78ae d						−139.5	−151.1	−175.3	−208.3	−206.6	−212.4	−224.8	−252.6	−270.8	−271.7
Balance on Goods & Services	78af d						−139.2	−201.9	−181.4	−313.1	−329.9	−349.7	−423.2	−447.7	−489.6	−483.2
Income: Credit	78ag d						19.3	18.1	20.5	28.1	24.8	41.4	30.7	23.8	24.7	34.0
Income: Debit	78ah d						−19.1	−12.6	−12.5	−13.5	−13.3	−27.4	−28.0	−37.5	−39.9	−61.1
Balance on Gds, Serv. & Inc.	78ai d						−139.1	−196.4	−173.5	−298.6	−318.4	−335.7	−420.6	−461.4	−504.7	−510.3
Current Transfers, n.i.e.: Credit	78aj d						59.3	86.8	85.4	74.3	70.3	143.4	254.3	332.5	612.5	184.2
Current Transfers: Debit	78ak d						−2.8	−2.1	−3.2	−1.8	−1.4	−2.7	−3.6	−1.2	−1.4	−1.0
Capital Account, n.i.e.	78bc d						−1.4	−.9	−.7	−.6	−.4	−.3	−.5	−.3	−.4	−.1
Capital Account, n.i.e.: Credit	78ba d						—	—	—	—	—	—	—	—	—	—
Capital Account: Debit	78bb d						−1.4	−.9	−.7	−.6	−.4	−.3	−.5	−.3	−.4	−.1
Financial Account, n.i.e.	78bj d						17.7	−4.9	53.4	158.2	365.9	109.0	171.6	224.2	225.0	239.6
Direct Investment Abroad	78bd d						—	—	—	—	—	—	—	—	—	—
Dir. Invest. in Rep. Econ., n.i.e.	78be d						5.8	—	—	—	—	—	—	—	—	—
Portfolio Investment Assets	78bf d						—	—	—	—	—	—	—	—	—	—
Equity Securities	78bk d						—	—	—	—	—	—	—	—	—	—
Debt Securities	78bl d						—	—	—	—	—	—	—	—	—	—
Portfolio Investment Liab., n.i.e.	78bg d						—	—	—	—	—	—	—	—	—	—
Equity Securities	78bm d						—	—	—	—	—	—	—	—	—	—
Debt Securities	78bn d						—	—	—	—	—	—	—	—	—	—
Financial Derivatives Assets	78bw d						....	....	....	....	....	....	....	....	....	....
Financial Derivatives Liabilities	78bx d						....	....	....	....	....	....	....	....	....	....
Other Investment Assets	78bh d						−26.7	−35.2	−23.6	63.9	21.1	17.6	−23.9	24.3	12.3	—
Monetary Authorities	78bo d						—	—	—	—	—	—	—	—	—	—
General Government	78bp d						−20.1	−17.0	15.0	11.2	—	—	—	—	—	—
Banks	78bq d						—	—	—	—	—	—	—	—	—	—
Other Sectors	78br d						−6.6	−18.2	−38.6	52.8	21.1	17.6	−23.9	24.3	12.3	—
Other Investment Liab., n.i.e.	78bi d						38.5	30.3	77.0	94.3	344.8	91.4	195.5	200.0	212.7	239.6
Monetary Authorities	78bs d						−.7	2.2	−4.1	18.5	76.5	11.4	2.7	−3.3	6.7	—
General Government	78bt d						39.3	36.7	73.1	46.1	215.7	72.9	221.1	98.2	179.4	194.8
Banks	78bu d						2.7	−2.8	1.5	−.5	19.3	11.7	−14.0	−1.9	−4.5	−1.0
Other Sectors	78bv d						−2.8	−5.7	6.4	30.2	33.3	−4.5	−14.3	107.0	31.1	45.7
Net Errors and Omissions	78ca d						3.3	29.2	19.5	−33.4	−7.5	10.8	−54.1	−150.6	−168.8	201.6
Overall Balance	78cb d						−63.0	−88.4	−19.2	−101.9	108.4	−75.4	−52.9	−56.8	162.2	113.9
Reserves and Related Items	79da d						63.0	88.4	19.2	101.9	−108.4	75.4	52.9	56.8	−162.2	−113.9
Reserve Assets	79db d						63.0	74.4	−39.0	93.4	−180.9	51.7	72.1	83.7	−126.0	−117.4
Use of Fund Credit and Loans	79dc d						—	14.0	58.2	8.5	72.6	23.7	−19.2	−28.0	−36.2	3.5
Exceptional Financing	79de d						—	—	—	.1	−.1			1.2		
Government Finance															*Millions of Birr:*	
Deficit (-) or Surplus	80	†−64.2	−49.2	−43.8	−226.2	−325.1	−232.5	−421.9	−254.5	−380.5	−334.2	†−491.5	−1,350.8	−621.5	−861.8	−805.0
Total Revenue and Grants	81y	†587.0	652.7	717.6	806.5	855.1	1,096.3	1,256.1	1,436.8	1,604.0	1,794.7	†1,878.4	2,188.4	2,303.9	2,345.4	2,781.6
Revenue	81	†494.1	561.0	619.7	710.4	777.9	1,013.7	1,184.3	1,410.1	1,597.1	1,791.7	†1,865.3	2,158.4	2,283.2	2,266.0	2,730.4
Grants	81z	†92.9	91.7	97.9	96.1	77.2	82.6	71.8	26.7	6.9	3.0	†13.1	30.0	20.7	79.4	51.2
Exp. & Lending Minus Repay.	82z	†651.2	701.9	761.4	1,032.7	1,180.2	1,328.8	1,678.0	1,691.3	1,984.5	2,128.9	†2,369.9	3,539.2	2,925.4	3,207.2	3,586.6
Expenditure	82	†647.9	678.6	733.0	985.4	1,144.5	1,320.0	1,664.1	1,690.5	1,994.9	2,136.3	†2,377.4	3,159.2	2,874.6	3,150.3	3,540.5
Lending Minus Repayments	83	†3.3	23.3	28.4	47.3	35.7	8.8	13.9	.8	−10.4	−7.4	†−7.5	380.0	50.8	56.9	46.1
Total Financing	80h	†64.2	49.2	43.8	226.2	325.1	232.5	421.9	254.5	380.5	334.2	†491.5	1,350.8	621.5	861.8	805.0
Domestic	84a	†20.1	9.4	−3.1	127.9	220.9	145.7	348.2	83.7	230.0	203.7	†16.6	929.8	413.0	533.1	334.8
Foreign	85a	†44.1	39.8	46.9	98.3	104.2	86.8	73.7	170.8	150.5	130.5	†474.9	421.0	208.5	328.7	470.2
Financing																
Net Borrowing: Domestic	84a	†20.1	9.4	−3.1	127.9	220.9	145.7	348.2	83.7	230.0	203.7	†16.6	929.8	413.0	533.1	334.8
Foreign	85a	†44.1	39.8	46.9	98.3	104.2	86.8	73.7	170.8	150.5	130.5	†474.9	421.0	208.5	328.7	470.2
Total Debt by Residence	88	†561.3	593.0	647.1	891.5	1,199.5	1,431.7	1,853.6	2,108.1	2,488.6	2,822.8	†3,314.3	4,666.6	5,288.1	6,156.9	6,916.6
Domestic	88a	†225.9	225.1	237.1	383.2	587.0	732.4	1,080.6	1,164.3	1,394.3	1,598.0	†1,614.6	2,544.4	2,957.4	3,490.5	3,825.4
Foreign	89a	†335.4	367.9	410.0	508.3	612.5	699.3	773.0	943.8	1,094.3	1,224.8	†1,699.7	2,122.2	2,330.7	2,666.4	3,091.2
National Accounts															*Millions of Birr:*	
Househ.Cons.Expend.,incl.NPISHs	96f	3,720	3,797	4,244	4,428	4,618	5,461	5,885	6,483	6,881	7,886	†8,375	9,158	8,192	10,661	10,261
Government Consumption Expend.	91f	508	538	586	730	866	967	1,240	1,314	1,346	1,429	†1,630	1,973	1,905	1,997	2,143
Gross Capital Formation	93	603	569	549	579	578	606	545	699	854	1,367	†1,457	1,436	1,851	1,394	2,226
Exports of Goods and Services	90c	491	654	828	682	760	822	866	943	1,210	1,072	†1,007	1,065	1,165	1,057	1,272
Imports of Goods and Services (-)	98c	578	552	655	896	818	1,030	1,271	1,368	1,749	1,676	†1,833	1,856	2,125	2,083	2,326
Gross Domestic Product (GDP)	99b	4,744	5,006	5,552	5,523	6,004	6,826	7,265	8,071	8,541	10,079	†10,636	11,775	10,988	13,027	13,575
Net Primary Income from Abroad	98.n	−29	−47	−36	−35	−3	−6	−9	−8	−14	−14	†−17	−27	−64	−61	−61
Gross National Income (GNI)	99a	4,715	4,958	5,515	5,489	6,001	6,820	7,256	8,063	8,527	10,065	†10,619	11,994	11,299	13,503	14,176
GDP at Factor Cost	99ba	....	....	....	....	5,530	6,146	6,487	7,087	7,625	9,324	†9,812	11,118	10,008	12,102	12,565
GDP Fact.Cost,Vol.'60/61 Prices	99ba p	....	....	....	....	4,031	4,055	4,009	4,222	4,454	4,586	24,807	....	....	....	....
GDP Fact.Cost,Vol.'80/81 Prices	99ba p	....	....	....	....	....	....	....	....	....	....	....	9,979	10,254	9,608	9,536
GDP Volume (1995=100)	99bv p	....	....	....	....	68.4	68.8	68.0	71.6	75.5	77.8	78.9	81.1	76.0	68.6	75.4
GDP Deflator (1995=100)	99bi p	41.5	42.6	46.6	46.3	23.3	25.7	27.4	28.5	29.0	34.5	†39.6	43.6	41.9	56.1	53.0
																Millions:
Population	99z	25.89	26.19	26.78	27.47	28.19	†35.92	36.76	37.63	38.75	39.59	40.41	41.18	42.69	44.25	45.74

1987	1988	1989	1990	1991	1992	1993	1994	1995	1996	1997	1998	1999	2000	2001		
Millions of Birr															**International Transactions**	
735.2	888.6	911.5	615.8	390.5	448.4	994.2	2,062.4	2,602.9	2,650.6	3,941.3	3,966.0	....	....	....	Exports	70
2,205.9	2,336.2	1,967.7	2,238.5	976.8	2,604.3	3,936.7	5,658.0	7,052.5	8,899.2	....	....	10,514.7	....	....	Imports, c.i.f.	71
Minus Sign Indicates Debit															**Balance of Payments**	
–216.9	–227.5	–144.4	–293.8	103.1	–120.0	–50.0	125.4	–9.7	80.3	–40.2	–265.8	–465.2	16.2	....	Current Account, n.i.e.	78al d
355.2	400.0	443.8	292.0	167.6	169.9	198.8	372.0	423.0	417.5	588.3	560.3	467.4	486.0		Goods: Exports f.o.b.	78aa d
–932.7	–956.0	–817.9	–912.1	–470.8	–992.7	–706.0	–925.7	–1,136.7	–1,002.2	–1,001.6	–1,309.8	–1,387.2	–1,131.4		Goods: Imports f.o.b.	78ab d
–577.4	–556.0	–374.1	–620.1	–303.2	–822.9	–507.1	–553.7	–713.7	–584.7	–413.4	–749.4	–919.8	–645.4		*Trade Balance*	78ac d
296.9	271.7	289.2	304.6	268.3	267.6	277.2	294.6	344.5	377.2	390.8	428.8	473.6	506.2		Services: Credit	78ad d
–307.7	–330.1	–323.4	–358.8	–284.3	–368.3	–299.0	–310.4	–357.9	–349.7	–394.2	–482.3	–466.3	–490.7		Services: Debit	78ae d
–588.3	–614.4	–408.3	–674.3	–319.3	–923.5	–528.9	–569.5	–727.1	–557.2	–416.8	–802.9	–912.5	–629.9		*Balance on Goods & Services*	78af d
21.9	17.1	12.7	9.2	14.4	22.3	25.9	42.9	68.3	41.2	24.2	21.0	16.6	16.2		Income: Credit	78ag d
–58.7	–72.8	–85.0	–77.7	–96.7	–104.1	–78.4	–74.6	–87.2	–75.2	–65.5	–58.0	–50.4	–50.4		Income: Debit	78ah d
–625.1	–670.0	–480.6	–742.9	–401.5	–1,005.3	–581.4	–601.1	–745.9	–591.1	–458.1	–839.9	–946.3	–664.1		*Balance on Gds, Serv. & Inc.*	78ai d
412.9	443.2	337.5	451.3	505.9	887.4	532.6	728.5	737.3	679.0	425.5	589.8	500.8	697.9		Current Transfers, n.i.e.: Credit	78aj d
–4.6	–.7	–1.3	–2.2	–1.3	–2.0	–1.2	–2.0	–1.1	–7.5	–7.6	–15.7	–19.7	–17.7		Current Transfers: Debit	78ak d
–.6	–.3	–.1	—	—	—	—	3.7	—	–1.7	–.8	—	—	....		Capital Account, n.i.e.	78bc d
—	—	—	—	—	—	—	3.7	—	—	—	—	—	....		Capital Account, n.i.e.: Credit	78ba d
–.6	–.3	–.1	—	—	—	—	—	—	–1.7	–.8	....	....			Capital Account: Debit	78bb d
292.8	299.6	222.0	230.0	–204.1	–62.9	97.7	–199.0	158.3	–499.6	241.2	–23.5	54.3	156.6		Financial Account, n.i.e.	78bj d
—	—	—	—	—	—	—	....	....	....	....	....	....	....		Direct Investment Abroad	78bd d
—	—	—	—	—	—	—	....	....	....	....	....	....	....		Dir. Invest. in Rep. Econ., n.i.e.	78be d
—	—	—	—	—	—	—	....	....	....	....	....	....	....		Portfolio Investment Assets	78bf d
—	—	—	—	—	—	—	....	....	....	....	....	....	....		Equity Securities	78bk d
—	—	—	—	—	—	—	....	....	....	....	....	....	....		Debt Securities	78bl d
—	—	—	—	—	—	—	....	....	....	....	....	....	....		Portfolio Investment Liab., n.i.e.	78bg d
—	—	—	—	—	—	—	....	....	....	....	....	....	....		Equity Securities	78bm d
—	—	—	—	—	—	—	....	....	....	....	....	....	....		Debt Securities	78bn d
....	....														Financial Derivatives Assets	78bw d
....	....														Financial Derivatives Liabilities	78bx d
....	....	50.0	87.0	–166.7	–87.1	–31.7	–318.5	57.7	–306.8	318.5	45.1	–87.8	103.3		Other Investment Assets	78bh d
....	....	....	....	....	....	....	....	....	....	....	....	....	....		Monetary Authorities	78bo d
....	....	....	....	....	....	....	....	....	....	....	....	....	....		General Government	78bp d
—	—	19.2	28.0	–108.9	–26.7	–40.2	–358.5	44.7	–283.0	350.7	11.7	–69.6	20.2		Banks	78bq d
—	—	30.8	59.0	–57.8	–60.4	8.4	40.0	13.1	–23.7	–32.2	33.5	–18.2	83.1		Other Sectors	78br d
292.8	299.6	171.9	143.0	–37.4	24.2	129.4	119.5	100.5	–192.8	–77.3	–68.6	142.0	53.3		Other Investment Liab., n.i.e.	78bi d
		8.6	12.0	–41.8	37.3	–50.9	25.4	.4	–7.9	–.1	–.4	.4	47.0		Monetary Authorities	78bs d
239.3	290.7	266.2	121.7	–41.7	1.0	209.1	82.4	37.7	–131.5	–91.0	–79.9	109.8	–.9		General Government	78bt d
	6.8	–3.5	–2.6	8.3	1.1	26.5	55.3	91.2	205.6	15.0	14.8	63.5	–28.7		Banks	78bu d
53.5	2.1	–99.4	11.9	37.9	–15.2	–55.2	–43.6	–28.8	–259.0	–1.3	–3.1	–31.6	35.9		Other Sectors	78bv d
–182.8	–94.0	–32.0	–134.6	–254.9	–81.2	–15.2	69.5	–49.0	–44.1	–627.9	–75.6	405.1	–212.3		Net Errors and Omissions	78ca d
–107.4	–22.3	45.5	–198.3	–355.9	–264.0	32.4	–.4	99.6	–465.0	–427.7	–364.9	–5.8	–39.6		*Overall Balance*	78cb d
107.4	22.3	–45.5	198.3	355.9	264.0	–32.4	.4	–99.6	465.0	427.7	364.9	5.8	39.6		Reserves and Related Items	79da d
126.9	39.1	–22.7	34.7	–37.2	–95.9	–296.2	–124.7	–204.8	20.0	192.1	178.9	–49.7	–84.5		Reserve Assets	79db d
–19.9	–16.8	–22.8	–25.2	–6.5	19.9	29.7	20.8	—	21.2	—	16.9	–9.7	–13.0		Use of Fund Credit and Loans	79dc d
.4	—		188.8	399.6	340.0	234.0	104.3	105.2	423.8	235.6	169.1	65.2	137.0		Exceptional Financing	79de d
Year Ending July 7															**Government Finance**	
–689.1	–784.2	–1,028.0	–1,739.1	–1,684.5	†–1454.3	–1,465.3	–2,814.8	–1,379.3	–749.2	–635.8	–1,786.5	–2,524.3	....		Deficit (–) or Surplus	80
2,927.6	3,478.7	4,072.9	3,170.7	2,784.2	†2,751.0	3,733.5	5,060.7	6,874.1	7,824.0	9,381.4	9,673.5	8,265.5	....		Total Revenue and Grants	81y
2,847.8	3,432.3	3,882.0	3,103.9	2,680.0	†2,208.0	3,206.6	3,842.6	5,839.2	6,817.3	7,877.4	8,400.2	7,847.0			Revenue	81
79.8	46.4	190.9	66.8	104.2	543.0	526.9	1,218.1	1,034.9	1,006.7	1,504.0	1,273.3	418.5			Grants	81z
3,616.7	4,262.9	5,100.9	4,909.8	4,468.7	†4,205.3	5,198.8	7,875.5	8,253.4	8,573.2	10,017.2	11,460.0	10,789.8			Exp. & Lending Minus Repay.	82z
3,604.1	4,161.5	4,785.7	4,832.3	4,421.1	....	....	....	....	....	....	....	....			Expenditure	82
12.6	101.4	315.2	77.5	47.6	....	....	....	....	....	....	....	....			Lending Minus Repayments	83
689.1	784.2	1,028.0	1,739.1	1,684.5	1,454.3	1,465.3	2,814.8	1,379.3	749.2	635.8	1,786.5	2,524.5			Total Financing	80h
362.3	382.2	426.4	1,243.2	1,263.7	1,155.1	750.8	709.6	60.0	–652.6	–92.1	1,007.0	1,175.8			Domestic	84a
326.8	402.0	601.6	495.9	420.8	299.2	714.5	2,105.2	1,319.3	1,401.8	727.9	779.5	1,348.7			Foreign	85a
															Financing	
362.3	382.2	426.4	1,243.2	1,263.7	1,155.1	750.8	709.6	60.0	–652.6	–92.1	1,007.0	1,175.8			Net Borrowing: Domestic	84a
326.8	402.0	601.6	495.9	420.8	299.2	714.5	2,105.2	1,319.3	1,401.8	727.9	779.5	1,348.7			Foreign	85a
7,671.5	8,503.6	9,517.1	12,186.2	14,182.0	13,051.0	27,645.6	37,063.1	39,599.8	38,967.1	....	....	....			Total Debt by Residence	88
4,187.7	4,564.3	4,990.6	6,272.5	7,536.2	8,691.4	9,474.5	11,778.3	11,654.8	11,950.8	....	....	....			Domestic	88a
3,483.8	3,939.3	4,526.5	5,913.7	6,645.8	4,359.6	18,171.1	25,284.8	27,945.0	27,016.3	....	....	....			Foreign	89a
Year Ending July 7															**National Accounts**	
11,036	10,396	11,281	12,258	15,369	†18,059	22,359	23,748	27,942	31,291	32,831	35,472	....	....		Househ.Cons.Expend.,incl.NPISHs	96f
2,262	2,707	3,061	3,232	3,166	†2,108	2,819	3,155	3,675	4,158	4,526	6,251	....	....		Government Consumption Expend.	91f
2,245	3,061	2,269	2,101	1,996	†1,911	3,792	4,294	5,569	7,246	7,049	7,927	....	....		Gross Capital Formation	93
1,187	1,205	1,423	1,295	1,062	†937	2,223	3,223	4,852	4,962	6,731	7,251	6,977	8,151		Exports of Goods and Services	90c
2,338	2,398	2,292	2,060	2,398	†2,223	4,521	6,091	8,154	9,719	9,672	11,866	14,506	16,420		Imports of Goods and Services (–)	98c
14,391	14,971	15,742	16,826	19,195	†20,792	26,671	28,329	33,885	37,938	41,465	45,035	....	....		Gross Domestic Product (GDP)	99b
–89	–126	–158	–130	–142	†–179	–414	–460	–378	–275	–224	–178	....	....		Net Primary Income from Abroad	98.n
14,773	14,845	15,585	16,696	19,053	†20,613	26,257	27,869	33,508	37,662	41,241	44,857	....	....		Gross National Income (GNI)	99a
13,313	13,787	14,550	15,699	17,979	†19,897	25,209	26,283	31,434	35,093	38,189	41,358	....	....		GDP at Factor Cost	99ba
....	....	....	....	....	....	....	....	....	....	....	....	....	....		GDP Fact.Cost,Vol.'60/61 Prices	99ba p
10,875	10,948	10,986	11,433	10,938	10,535	11,724	11,910	12,645	13,987	14,708	14,631	....	....		GDP Fact.Cost,Vol.'80/81 Prices	99ba p
86.0	86.6	86.9	90.4	86.5	83.3	92.7	94.2	100.0	110.6	116.3	115.7	....	....		GDP Volume (1995=100)	99bv p
49.2	50.7	53.3	55.2	66.1	†76.0	86.5	88.8	100.0	100.9	104.4	113.7	....	....		GDP Deflator (1995=100)	99bi p
Midyear Estimates																
44.15	45.45	46.93	48.36	49.95	51.57	53.24	53.48	54.65	56.37	58.12	59.88	61.67	63.49	65.37	**Population**	99z

(See notes in the back of the book.)

Euro Area

		1972	1973	1974	1975	1976	1977	1978	1979	1980	1981	1982	1983	1984	1985	1986
Exchange Rates																*Euros per SDR:*
Market Rate	aa	...	...	...	...	...	...	...	...	...	...	...	...	...	...	...
Market Rate	ae	...	...	...	...	...	...	...	...	...	...	...	...	...	...	*Euros per US Dollar:*
Market Rate	rf	...	...	...	...	...	...	...	...	...	...	...	...	...	...	...
														Index Numbers (1995=100):		
Nominal Effective Exchange Rate	neu	94.60	102.07	101.94	106.93	104.43	105.61	104.93	108.33	106.11	91.39	87.79	84.41	79.90	78.69	88.58
Real Effective Exchange Rate	reu							101.14	103.15	98.73	84.56	82.57	81.82	79.11	78.92	87.86
International Liquidity													*Millions of US Dollars Unless Otherwise Indicated:*			
Tot.Res.minus Gold (Eurosyst.Def)	1l.d	...	...	...	...	...	...	...	...	...	...	...	...	...	...	...
SDRs	1b.d	3,524	3,902	3,954	3,798	3,816	3,332	3,744	5,365	5,358	5,934	6,106	3,944	4,157	4,565	6,019
Reserve Position in the Fund	1c.d	3,664	3,681	3,751	4,406	5,938	6,138	7,489	5,992	6,266	6,009	6,470	8,651	8,633	9,016	9,631
Foreign Exchange	1d.d	...	...	...	...	...	...	...	...	...	...	...	...	...	...	...
of which: Fin.Deriv.rel.to Res.	1dd d	...	...	...	...	...	...	...	...	...	...	...	...	...	...	...
Other Reserve Assets	1e.d	...	...	...	...	...	...	...	...	...	...	...	...	...	...	...
Gold (Million Fine Troy Ounces)	1ad	...	...	...	...	...	...	...	...	...	...	...	...	...	...	...
Gold (Eurosystem Valuation)	1an d	...	...	...	...	...	...	...	...	...	...	...	...	...	...	...
Memo: Euro Cl. on Non-EA Res.	1dg d	...	...	...	...	...	...	...	...	...	...	...	...	...	...	...
Non-Euro Cl. on EA Res.	1dh d	...	...	...	...	...	...	...	...	...	...	...	...	...	...	...
Mon. Auth.: Other Foreign Assets	3..d	...	...	...	...	...	...	...	...	...	...	...	...	...	...	...
Foreign Liabilities	4..d	...	...	...	...	...	...	...	...	...	...	...	...	...	...	...
Banking Insts: Foreign Assets	7a.d	...	...	...	...	...	...	...	...	...	...	...	...	...	...	...
Foreign Liabs.	7b.d	...	...	...	...	...	...	...	...	...	...	...	...	...	...	...
Monetary Authorities (Eurosyst.)														*Billions of Euros:*		
Foreign Assets (on Non-EA Ctys)	11	...	...	...	...	...	...	...	...	...	...	...	...	...	...	...
Claims on General Government	12a.u	...	...	...	...	...	...	...	...	...	...	...	...	...	...	...
Claims on EA Banking Sector	12e.u	...	...	...	...	...	...	...	...	...	...	...	...	...	...	...
Claims on Other Resident Sectors	12d.u	...	...	...	...	...	...	...	...	...	...	...	...	...	...	...
Currency in Circulation	14a	...	...	...	...	...	...	...	...	...	...	...	...	...	...	...
Liabilities to EA Banking Sector	14c.u	...	...	...	...	...	...	...	...	...	...	...	...	...	...	...
Deposits of Other Resident Sect.	15..u	...	...	...	...	...	...	...	...	...	...	...	...	...	...	...
Money Market Instruments	16m.u	...	...	...	...	...	...	...	...	...	...	...	...	...	...	...
Bonds (Debt Securities)	16n.u	...	...	...	...	...	...	...	...	...	...	...	...	...	...	...
Foreign Liabs. (to Non-EA Ctys)	16c	...	...	...	...	...	...	...	...	...	...	...	...	...	...	...
Central Government Deposits	16d.u	...	...	...	...	...	...	...	...	...	...	...	...	...	...	...
Capital Accounts	17a	...	...	...	...	...	...	...	...	...	...	...	...	...	...	...
Other Items (Net)	17r	...	...	...	...	...	...	...	...	...	...	...	...	...	...	...
Banking Institutions (Oth.MFIs)														*Billions of Euros:*		
Claims on EA Banking Sector	20..u	...	...	...	...	...	...	...	...	...	...	...	...	...	...	...
Foreign Assets (on Non-EA Ctys)	21	...	...	...	...	...	...	...	...	...	...	...	...	...	...	...
Claims on General Government	22a.u	...	...	...	...	...	...	...	...	...	...	...	...	...	...	...
Claims on Oth. Resident Sectors	22d.u	...	...	...	...	...	...	...	...	...	...	...	...	...	...	...
Demand (Overnight) Deposits	24..u	...	...	...	...	...	...	...	...	206.8	219.7	262.6	288.5	316.2	339.6	368.2
Deposits with Agreed Maturity	25a.u	...	...	...	...	...	...	...	...	...	...	...	...	...	...	...
Deposits Redeemable at Notice	25b.u	...	...	...	...	...	...	...	...	...	...	...	...	...	...	...
Repurchase Agreements	25f.u	...	...	...	...	...	...	...	...	...	...	...	...	...	...	...
Money Market Instruments	26m.u	...	...	...	...	...	...	...	...	...	...	...	...	...	...	...
Bonds (Debt Securities)	26n.u	...	...	...	...	...	...	...	...	...	...	...	...	...	...	...
Foreign Liabs. (to Non-EA Ctys)	26c	...	...	...	...	...	...	...	...	...	...	...	...	...	...	...
Central Government Deposits	26d.u	...	...	...	...	...	...	...	...	...	...	...	...	...	...	...
Credit fr. EA Banking Sector	26g.u	...	...	...	...	...	...	...	...	...	...	...	...	...	...	...
Capital Accounts	27a	...	...	...	...	...	...	...	...	...	...	...	...	...	...	...
Other Items (Net)	27r	...	...	...	...	...	...	...	...	...	...	...	...	...	...	...
Banking Survey														*Billions of Euros:*		
Foreign Assets (Net)	31n.u	...	...	...	...	...	...	...	...	...	...	...	...	...	...	...
Domestic Credit	32..u	...	...	...	...	...	...	...	...	...	...	...	...	...	...	...
Claims on General Govt. (Net)	32an u	...	...	...	...	...	...	...	...	...	...	...	...	...	...	...
Claims on Oth. Resident Sectors	32d.u	...	...	...	...	...	...	...	...	...	...	...	...	...	...	...
Currency in Circulation	34a.u	...	...	...	...	...	...	...	...	111.9	118.5	127.2	138.9	145.7	153.2	163.8
Demand (Overnight) Deposits	34b.u	...	...	...	...	...	...	...	...	208.8	222.0	265.9	292.2	320.0	342.6	371.9
Deposits with Agreed Maturity	35a.u	...	...	...	...	...	...	...	...	...	...	...	...	...	...	...
of which: Over 2-Yr. Maturity	35ab u	...	...	...	...	...	...	...	...	...	...	...	...	...	...	...
Deposits Redeemable at Notice	35b.u	...	...	...	...	...	...	...	...	...	...	...	...	...	...	...
of which: Over 3-Mos Notice	35bb u	...	...	...	...	...	...	...	...	...	...	...	...	...	...	...
Repurchase Agreements	35f.u	...	...	...	...	...	...	...	...	...	...	...	...	...	...	...
Money Market Instruments	36m.u	...	...	...	...	...	...	...	...	...	...	...	...	...	...	...
Bonds	36n.u	...	...	...	...	...	...	...	...	...	...	...	...	...	...	...
of which: Over 2-Yr. Maturity	36na u	...	...	...	...	...	...	...	...	...	...	...	...	...	...	...
Capital Accounts	37a	...	...	...	...	...	...	...	...	...	...	...	...	...	...	...
Other Items (Net)	37r.u	...	...	...	...	...	...	...	...	...	...	...	...	...	...	...
Money (Eurosystem Definition)														*Billions of Euros:*		
M1	39ma u	...	...	...	...	...	...	...	...	492.7	519.1	570.6	628.7	682.4	732.8	796.0
M2	39mb u	...	...	...	...	...	...	...	...	1,198.0	1,308.3	1,449.9	1,579.3	1,710.9	1,833.6	1,955.3
M3	39mc u	...	...	...	...	...	...	...	...	1,230.5	1,356.9	1,511.6	1,647.6	1,788.8	1,927.9	2,058.9
Nonmonetary Liabs. of MFIs	39md u	...	...	...	...	...	...	...	...	...	...	...	...	...	...	...
Interest Rates														*Percent Per Annum*		
Eurosyst.Marg.Lending Fac.Rate	60	...	...	...	...	...	...	...	...	...	...	...	...	...	...	...
Eurosyst. Refinancing Rate	60r	...	...	...	...	...	...	...	...	...	...	...	...	...	...	...
Eurosyst. Deposit Facility Rate	60x	...	...	...	...	...	...	...	...	...	...	...	...	...	...	...
Interbank Rate (Overnight)	60a	...	...	...	...	...	...	...	...	...	...	...	...	...	...	...
Interbank Rate (3-Mos Maturity)	60b	...	...	...	...	...	...	...	...	...	...	...	...	...	...	...
Deposit Rate	60l	...	...	...	...	...	...	...	...	...	...	...	...	...	...	...
Lending Rate	60p	...	...	...	...	...	...	...	...	...	...	...	...	...	...	...
Government Bond Yield	61	...	...	...	...	...	...	...	...	...	...	...	...	...	...	...

1987	1988	1989	1990	1991	1992	1993	1994	1995	1996	1997	1998	1999	2000	2001		Code
															Exchange Rates	
												1.36623	1.40023	1.42600	*End of Period* — Market Rate	aa
												.99542	1.07469	1.13469	*End of Period (ae) Period Average (rf)* — Market Rate	ae
												.93863	1.08540	1.11751	Market Rate	rf
94.60	91.58	91.25	100.47	97.82	101.15	97.48	95.74	100.00	100.13	91.28	91.24	87.13	78.90	80.11	*Period Averages* — Nominal Effective Exchange Rate	ne u
92.80	89.89	89.93	98.46	95.55	99.59	97.75	95.70	100.00	100.50	90.50	87.45	83.11	74.10	73.99	Real Effective Exchange Rate	re u
															International Liquidity	
												257,119	242,557	234,281	*End of Period* — Tot.Res.minus Gold (Eurosyst.Def)	1l.d
7,418	6,896	6,906	6,986	6,853	2,778	3,039	3,519	5,572	5,440	5,359	6,015	4,546	4,032	4,747	SDRs	1b.d
10,442	9,358	9,179	9,434	11,018	13,709	12,691	12,941	16,100	16,572	18,637	27,364	24,245	19,662	21,937	Reserve Position in the Fund	1c.d
												226,250	217,792	205,324	Foreign Exchange	1d.d
															of which: Fin.Deriv.rel.to Res.	1dd d
												2,078	1,071	2,273	Other Reserve Assets	1e.d
												402.76	399.54	401.87	Gold (Million Fine Troy Ounces)	1ad
												116,902	109,653	111,118	Gold (Eurosystem Valuation)	1an d
															Memo: Euro Cl. on Non-EA Res.	1dg d
												14,481	14,700	21,919	Non-Euro Cl. on EA Res.	1dh d
															Mon. Auth.: Other Foreign Assets	3..d
												49,993	27,856	31,417	Foreign Liabilities	4..d
												1,727,480	1,885,360	2,121,090	Banking Insts: Foreign Assets	7a.d
												1,878,989	2,139,669	2,364,903	Foreign Liabs.	7b.d
															Monetary Authorities (Eurosyst.)	
										323.7	322.3	400.6	380.7	399.0	*End of Period* — Foreign Assets (on Non-EA Ctys)	11
										132.9	106.6	105.8	110.7	127.5	Claims on General Government	12a.u
										216.2	205.7	426.3	429.9	390.2	Claims on EA Banking Sector	12e.u
										4.5	4.4	11.5	12.7	11.1	Claims on Other Resident Sectors	12d.u
										355.0	359.1	393.3	390.2	285.9	Currency in Circulation	14a
										92.4	94.2	279.3	270.4	342.4	Liabilities to EA Banking Sector	14c.u
										3.4	3.5	8.8	9.8	14.4	Deposits of Other Resident Sect.	15..u
										13.4	8.5	3.3	—	—	Money Market Instruments	16m.u
										14.8	5.3	4.6	3.8	4.6	Bonds (Debt Securities)	16n.u
										32.8	18.6	49.8	29.9	35.6	Foreign Liabs. (to Non-EA Ctys)	16c
										51.7	54.4	53.4	47.1	35.1	Central Government Deposits	16d.u
										106.0	97.1	174.3	197.5	209.8	Capital Accounts	17a
										7.8	−1.7	−22.8	−14.7	−.1	Other Items (Net)	17r
															Banking Institutions (Oth.MFIs)	
										3,545.7	3,875.3	4,242.9	4,443.7	4,796.1	*End of Period* — Claims on EA Banking Sector	20..u
										1,600.0	1,591.8	1,719.6	2,026.2	2,406.8	Foreign Assets (on Non-EA Ctys)	21
										1,877.2	1,934.1	1,952.1	1,813.8	1,898.6	Claims on General Government	22a.u
										5,131.4	5,652.3	6,203.4	6,866.5	7,412.3	Claims on Oth. Resident Sectors	22d.u
389.3	423.2	466.5	544.9	545.2	568.9	600.1	621.7	949.9	1,072.7	1,231.0	1,387.1	1,537.6	1,648.9	1,882.2	Demand (Overnight) Deposits	24..u
										1,901.9	1,929.1	2,043.2	2,159.8	2,261.3	Deposits with Agreed Maturity	25a.u
										1,329.1	1,393.2	1,331.5	1,276.9	1,405.0	Deposits Redeemable at Notice	25b.u
										205.4	176.5	143.9	174.9	220.4	Repurchase Agreements	25f.u
										391.1	403.0	499.5	528.9	629.1	Money Market Instruments	26m.u
										1,924.7	2,100.0	2,325.0	2,507.4	2,684.7	Bonds (Debt Securities)	26n.u
										1,381.4	1,507.0	1,870.4	2,299.5	2,683.4	Foreign Liabs. (to Non-EA Ctys)	26c
										102.1	95.4	88.6	117.4	103.9	Central Government Deposits	26d.u
										3,009.9	3,305.2	3,590.9	3,679.4	3,823.7	Credit fr. EA Banking Sector	26g.u
										688.4	754.6	849.1	941.5	1,043.2	Capital Accounts	27a
										−10.7	2.5	−161.7	−184.4	−222.9	Other Items (Net)	27r
															Banking Survey	
										509.6	388.5	200.0	77.5	86.7	*End of Period* — Foreign Assets (Net)	31n.u
										6,992.1	7,547.5	8,130.8	8,639.2	9,310.6	Domestic Credit	32..u
										1,856.2	1,890.9	1,915.9	1,760.0	1,887.1	Claims on General Govt. (Net)	32an u
										5,135.9	5,656.7	6,214.9	6,879.2	7,423.5	Claims on Oth. Resident Sectors	32d.u
178.2	196.8	211.8	224.5	242.0	264.7	277.1	292.2	303.8	313.3	320.6	323.4	350.8	348.4	239.7	Currency in Circulation	34a.u
393.6	428.3	471.8	552.0	552.4	570.8	602.9	624.5	952.6	1,075.7	1,234.4	1,390.6	1,546.4	1,658.7	1,896.3	Demand (Overnight) Deposits	34b.u
										1,901.9	1,929.1	2,043.2	2,159.8	2,261.6	Deposits with Agreed Maturity	35a.u
										1,004.1	1,033.0	1,160.9	1,168.3	1,168.9	of which: Over 2-Yr. Maturity	35ab u
										1,329.1	1,393.2	1,331.5	1,276.9	1,405.0	Deposits Redeemable at Notice	35b.u
										219.8	214.8	112.2	125.4	115.8	of which: Over 3-Mos Notice	35bb u
										205.4	176.5	143.9	174.9	220.4	Repurchase Agreements	35f.u
										303.9	304.2	372.9	387.4	475.4	Money Market Instruments	36m.u
										1,302.8	1,383.5	1,498.9	1,575.4	1,677.5	Bonds	36n.u
										1,232.0	1,312.3	1,446.1	1,525.3	1,613.8	of which: Over 2-Yr. Maturity	36na u
										700.2	681.4	807.7	894.6	996.5	Capital Accounts	37a
										203.3	354.2	235.5	240.7	224.9	Other Items (Net)	37r.u
															Money (Eurosystem Definition)	
853.4	925.6	1,015.2	1,128.5	1,171.5	1,215.3	1,287.9	1,343.1	1,423.1	1,528.5	1,624.9	1,781.3	1,965.4	2,077.1	2,206.8	*End of Period* — M1	39ma u
2,080.9	2,233.0	2,419.1	2,658.7	2,808.4	2,939.9	3,150.3	3,243.8	3,397.5	3,562.5	3,685.6	3,916.8	4,136.0	4,290.0	4,667.4	M2	39mb u
2,221.6	2,410.0	2,659.9	2,980.0	3,204.6	3,433.2	3,651.8	3,735.8	3,937.4	4,090.4	4,265.8	4,468.6	4,702.4	4,900.7	5,425.5	M3	39mc u
										3,156.1	3,241.4	3,526.9	3,713.5	3,895.1	Nonmonetary Liabs. of MFIs	39md u
															Interest Rates	
												4.00	5.75	4.25	*Percent Per Annum* — Eurosyst.Marg.Lending Fac.Rate	60
												2.71	....	†4.30	Eurosyst. Refinancing Rate	60r
												1.71	3.06	3.23	Eurosyst. Deposit Facility Rate	60x
							6.18	6.09	4.58	4.02	3.73	2.74	4.12		Interbank Rate (Overnight)	60a
							6.33	6.58	4.92	4.25	3.83	2.97	4.39		Interbank Rate (3-Mos Maturity)	60b
									4.08	3.41	3.20	2.45	3.45	3.49	Deposit Rate	60l
									8.88	7.58	6.73	5.65	6.60	6.83	Lending Rate	60p
							8.18	8.73	7.23	5.96	4.70	4.66	5.44	5.03	Government Bond Yield	61

Euro Area

		1972	1973	1974	1975	1976	1977	1978	1979	1980	1981	1982	1983	1984	1985	1986
Prices, Production, Labor														*Index Numbers (1995=100):*		
Producer Prices	63	...	...	...	...	...	...	...	...	...	...	...	...	...	...	...
Harmonized CPI (hcpi)	64h	...	...	...	...	...	...	...	...	...	...	...	...	...	...	...
Wages/Labor Costs (1996=100)	65.. c	...	...	...	...	...	...	...	...	...	...	...	...	...	...	...
Industrial Production	66.. c	...	...	...	...	...	...	...	...	...	...	...	...	...	...	...
Employment	67.. c	...	...	...	...	...	...	...	...	...	...	...	...	...	...	...
															Number in Thousands:	
Unemployment	67c. c	...	...	...	...	...	...	...	...	...	...	...	...	...	...	...
Unemployment Rate (%)	67r. c	...	...	...	...	...	...	...	...	...	...	...	...	...	...	...
International Transactions														*Billions of Ecus through 1998;*		
Exports	70	...	...	...	...	...	...	...	...	...	...	...	...	...	...	...
Imports, c.i.f.	71	...	...	...	...	...	...	...	...	...	...	...	...	...	...	...
															1995=100	
Volume of Exports	72	...	...	...	...	...	...	...	...	...	...	...	...	...	...	...
Volume of Imports	73	...	...	...	...	...	...	...	...	...	...	...	...	...	...	...
Unit Value of Exports	74	...	...	...	...	...	...	...	...	...	...	...	...	...	...	...
Unit Value of Imports	75	...	...	...	...	...	...	...	...	...	...	...	...	...	...	...
Balance of Payments														*Billions of US Dollars*		
Current Account, n.i.e.	78ald	...	...	...	...	...	...	...	...	...	...	...	...	...	...	...
Goods: Exports f.o.b.	78aad	...	...	...	...	...	...	...	...	...	...	...	...	...	...	...
Goods: Imports f.o.b.	78abd	...	...	...	...	...	...	...	...	...	...	...	...	...	...	...
Trade Balance	78acd	...	...	...	...	...	...	...	...	...	...	...	...	...	...	...
Services: Credit	78add	...	...	...	...	...	...	...	...	...	...	...	...	...	...	...
Services: Debit	78aed	...	...	...	...	...	...	...	...	...	...	...	...	...	...	...
Balance on Goods & Services	78afd	...	...	...	...	...	...	...	...	...	...	...	...	...	...	...
Income: Credit	78agd	...	...	...	...	...	...	...	...	...	...	...	...	...	...	...
Income: Debit	78ahd	...	...	...	...	...	...	...	...	...	...	...	...	...	...	...
Balance on Gds, Serv. & Inc.	78aid	...	...	...	...	...	...	...	...	...	...	...	...	...	...	...
Current Transfers, n.i.e.: Credit	78ajd	...	...	...	...	...	...	...	...	...	...	...	...	...	...	...
Current Transfers: Debit	78akd	...	...	...	...	...	...	...	...	...	...	...	...	...	...	...
Capital Account, n.i.e.	78bcd	...	...	...	...	...	...	...	...	...	...	...	...	...	...	...
Capital Account, n.i.e.: Credit	78bad	...	...	...	...	...	...	...	...	...	...	...	...	...	...	...
Capital Account: Debit	78bbd	...	...	...	...	...	...	...	...	...	...	...	...	...	...	...
Financial Account, n.i.e.	78bjd	...	...	...	...	...	...	...	...	...	...	...	...	...	...	...
Direct Investment Abroad	78bdd	...	...	...	...	...	...	...	...	...	...	...	...	...	...	...
Dir. Invest. in Rep. Econ., n.i.e.	78bed	...	...	...	...	...	...	...	...	...	...	...	...	...	...	...
Portfolio Investment Assets	78bfd	...	...	...	...	...	...	...	...	...	...	...	...	...	...	...
Equity Securities	78bkd	...	...	...	...	...	...	...	...	...	...	...	...	...	...	...
Debt Securities	78bld	...	...	...	...	...	...	...	...	...	...	...	...	...	...	...
Portfolio Investment Liab., n.i.e.	78bgd	...	...	...	...	...	...	...	...	...	...	...	...	...	...	...
Equity Securities	78bmd	...	...	...	...	...	...	...	...	...	...	...	...	...	...	...
Debt Securities	78bnd	...	...	...	...	...	...	...	...	...	...	...	...	...	...	...
Financial Derivatives Assets	78bwd	...	...	...	...	...	...	...	...	...	...	...	...	...	...	...
Financial Derivatives Liabilities	78bxd	...	...	...	...	...	...	...	...	...	...	...	...	...	...	...
Other Investment Assets	78bhd	...	...	...	...	...	...	...	...	...	...	...	...	...	...	...
Monetary Authorities	78bod	...	...	...	...	...	...	...	...	...	...	...	...	...	...	...
General Government	78bpd	...	...	...	...	...	...	...	...	...	...	...	...	...	...	...
Banks	78bqd	...	...	...	...	...	...	...	...	...	...	...	...	...	...	...
Other Sectors	78brd	...	...	...	...	...	...	...	...	...	...	...	...	...	...	...
Other Investment Liab., n.i.e.	78bid	...	...	...	...	...	...	...	...	...	...	...	...	...	...	...
Monetary Authorities	78bsd	...	...	...	...	...	...	...	...	...	...	...	...	...	...	...
General Government	78btd	...	...	...	...	...	...	...	...	...	...	...	...	...	...	...
Banks	78bud	...	...	...	...	...	...	...	...	...	...	...	...	...	...	...
Other Sectors	78bvd	...	...	...	...	...	...	...	...	...	...	...	...	...	...	...
Net Errors and Omissions	78cad	...	...	...	...	...	...	...	...	...	...	...	...	...	...	...
Overall Balance	78cbd	...	...	...	...	...	...	...	...	...	...	...	...	...	...	...
Reserves and Related Items	79dad	...	...	...	...	...	...	...	...	...	...	...	...	...	...	...
Reserve Assets	79dbd	...	...	...	...	...	...	...	...	...	...	...	...	...	...	...
Use of Fund Credit and Loans	79dcd	...	...	...	...	...	...	...	...	...	...	...	...	...	...	...
Exceptional Financing	79ded	...	...	...	...	...	...	...	...	...	...	...	...	...	...	...
Government Finance														*As Percent of*		
Deficit (-) or Surplus	80g	...	...	...	...	...	...	...	...	...	...	...	...	...	...	...
Debt	88g	...	...	...	...	...	...	...	...	...	...	...	...	...	...	...
National Accounts														*Billions of Ecus through 1998;*		
Househ.Cons.Expend.,incl.NPISHs	96f. c	...	...	...	...	...	...	...	...	...	...	...	...	...	...	...
Government Consumption Expend.	91f. c	...	...	...	...	...	...	...	...	...	...	...	...	...	...	...
Gross Fixed Capital Formation	93e. c	...	...	...	...	...	...	...	...	...	...	...	...	...	...	...
Changes in Inventories	93i. c	...	...	...	...	...	...	...	...	...	...	...	...	...	...	...
Exports of Goods and Services	90c. c	...	...	...	...	...	...	...	...	...	...	...	...	...	...	...
Imports of Goods and Services (-)	98c. c	...	...	...	...	...	...	...	...	...	...	...	...	...	...	...
Gross Domestic Product (GDP)	99b. c	...	...	...	...	...	...	...	...	...	...	...	...	...	...	...
Net Primary Income from Abroad	98.n c	...	...	...	...	...	...	...	...	...	...	...	...	...	...	...
Gross National Income (GNI)	99a. c	...	...	...	...	...	...	...	...	...	...	...	...	...	...	...
GDP Volume 1995 Prices	99b. r	...	...	...	...	...	...	...	...	...	...	...	...	...	...	...
GDP Volume (1995=100)	99bv r	...	...	...	...	...	...	...	...	...	...	...	...	...	...	...
GDP Deflator (1995=100)	99bi r	...	...	...	...	...	...	...	...	...	...	...	...	...	...	...

	1987	1988	1989	1990	1991	1992	1993	1994	1995	1996	1997	1998	1999	2000	2001	Prices, Production, Labor	
Period Averages												100.6	100.3	105.6	108.1	Producer Prices	63
	....	....	....	....	....	....	....	....	....	....	....	104.9	106.1	108.5	111.3	Harmonized CPI (hcpi)	64h
	....	....	....	....	....	....	....	....	....	....	....	104.7	....	....	....	Wages/Labor Costs (1996=100)	65..c
	....	....	....	....	....	....	....	....	....	....	....	109.1	110.7	116.0	117.8	Industrial Production	66..c
	....	....	....	....	....	....	....	....	....	....	....	....	104.7	106.9	108.4	Employment	67..c
Period Averages												....	12,253	11,092	11,061	Unemployment	67c.c
	....	....	....	....	....	....	....	....	....	....	....	....	9	8	8	Unemployment Rate (%)	67r.c
																International Transactions	
Billions of Euros beginning 1999												791.5	†831.8	1,003.0	1,046.4	Exports	70
	....	....	....	....	....	....	....	....	....	....	....	709.3	†780.5	990.5	1,003.9	Imports, c.i.f.	71
1995=100												124.5	127.6	142.8	144.6	Volume of Exports	72
	....	....	....	....	....	....	....	....	....	....	....	129.2	137.0	143.7	141.9	Volume of Imports	73
	....	....	....	....	....	....	....	....	....	....	....	106.6	108.9	117.8	123.0	Unit Value of Exports	74
	....	....	....	....	....	....	....	....	....	....	....	102.8	106.2	129.4	130.7	Unit Value of Imports	75
																Balance of Payments	
Minus Sign Indicates Debit												35.85	−19.31	−54.91	†−2.15	Current Account, n.i.e.	78ald
	....	....	....	....	....	....	....	....	....	....	....	878.68	870.74	908.17	†929.28	Goods: Exports f.o.b.	78aad
	....	....	....	....	....	....	....	....	....	....	....	−756.38	−790.31	−875.64	†−858.74	Goods: Imports f.o.b.	78abd
	....	....	....	....	....	....	....	....	....	....	....	122.28	80.43	32.53	†70.53	*Trade Balance*	78acd
	....	....	....	....	....	....	....	....	....	....	....	259.92	260.11	257.10	†284.86	Services: Credit	78add
	....	....	....	....	....	....	....	....	....	....	....	−261.25	−272.90	−272.00	†−282.03	Services: Debit	78aed
	....	....	....	....	....	....	....	....	....	....	....	120.94	67.65	17.63	†73.36	*Balance on Goods & Services*	78afd
	....	....	....	....	....	....	....	....	....	....	....	222.34	220.56	242.91	†255.49	Income: Credit	78agd
	....	....	....	....	....	....	....	....	....	....	....	−254.41	−258.54	−267.52	†−288.28	Income: Debit	78ahd
	....	....	....	....	....	....	....	....	....	....	....	88.86	29.67	−6.99	†40.56	*Balance on Gds, Serv. & Inc.*	78aid
	....	....	....	....	....	....	....	....	....	....	....	70.14	69.67	62.77	†67.32	Current Transfers, n.i.e.: Credit	78ajd
	....	....	....	....	....	....	....	....	....	....	....	−123.15	−118.64	−110.69	†−110.03	Current Transfers: Debit	78akd
	....	....	....	....	....	....	....	....	....	....	....	13.91	13.65	8.90	†7.64	Capital Account, n.i.e.	78bcd
	....	....	....	....	....	....	....	....	....	....	....	19.84	20.32	16.82	†14.71	Capital Account, n.i.e.: Credit	78bad
	....	....	....	....	....	....	....	....	....	....	....	−5.93	−6.67	−7.92	†−7.07	Capital Account: Debit	78bbd
	....	....	....	....	....	....	....	....	....	....	....	−87.32	.49	73.00	†−79.51	Financial Account, n.i.e.	78bjd
	....	....	....	....	....	....	....	....	....	....	....	−195.25	−333.07	−351.28	†−201.65	Direct Investment Abroad	78bdd
	....	....	....	....	....	....	....	....	....	....	....	101.73	208.14	378.55	†109.36	Dir. Invest. in Rep. Econ., n.i.e.	78bed
	....	....	....	....	....	....	....	....	....	....	....	−403.78	−331.22	−385.31	†−242.25	Portfolio Investment Assets	78bfd
	....	....	....	....	....	....	....	....	....	....	....	−129.31	−165.35	−269.88	†−86.68	Equity Securities	78bkd
	....	....	....	....	....	....	....	....	....	....	....	−274.47	−165.86	−115.43	†−155.57	Debt Securities	78bld
	....	....	....	....	....	....	....	....	....	....	....	280.33	279.18	270.00	†272.97	Portfolio Investment Liab., n.i.e.	78bgd
	....	....	....	....	....	....	....	....	....	....	....	117.31	96.36	32.99	†213.83	Equity Securities	78bmd
	....	....	....	....	....	....	....	....	....	....	....	163.02	182.83	237.00	†59.14	Debt Securities	78bnd
	....	....	....	....	....	....	....	....	....	....	....	—	....	....	....	Financial Derivatives Assets	78bwd
	....	....	....	....	....	....	....	....	....	....	....	−9.41	4.72	−.83	†−18.49	Financial Derivatives Liabilities	78bxd
	....	....	....	....	....	....	....	....	....	....	....	−86.63	−35.51	−166.71	†−219.20	Other Investment Assets	78bhd
	....	....	....	....	....	....	....	....	....	....	....	−.84	−2.20	−.98	†.56	Monetary Authorities	78bod
	....	....	....	....	....	....	....	....	....	....	....	−.76	3.56	−2.77	†2.98	General Government	78bpd
	....	....	....	....	....	....	....	....	....	....	....	−21.81	19.67	−119.34	†−202.19	Banks	78bqd
	....	....	....	....	....	....	....	....	....	....	....	−63.19	−56.53	−43.62	†−20.55	Other Sectors	78brd
	....	....	....	....	....	....	....	....	....	....	....	225.70	208.24	328.59	†219.75	Other Investment Liab., n.i.e.	78bid
	....	....	....	....	....	....	....	....	....	....	....	4.02	7.26	.54	†3.82	Monetary Authorities	78bsd
	....	....	....	....	....	....	....	....	....	....	....	−6.82	−14.03	.36	†−1.38	General Government	78btd
	....	....	....	....	....	....	....	....	....	....	....	211.64	174.14	273.44	†213.82	Banks	78bud
	....	....	....	....	....	....	....	....	....	....	....	16.88	40.87	54.24	†3.50	Other Sectors	78bvd
	....	....	....	....	....	....	....	....	....	....	....	27.92	−6.41	−43.14	†57.13	Net Errors and Omissions	78cad
	....	....	....	....	....	....	....	....	....	....	....	−9.64	−11.58	−16.14	†−16.89	*Overall Balance*	78cbd
	....	....	....	....	....	....	....	....	....	....	....	9.64	11.58	16.14	†16.89	Reserves and Related Items	79dad
	....	....	....	....	....	....	....	....	....	....	....	9.64	11.58	16.14	†16.89	Reserve Assets	79dbd
	....	....	....	....	....	....	....	....	....	....	....	—	....	....	....	Use of Fund Credit and Loans	79dcd
	....	....	....	....	....	....	....	....	....	....	....	—	....	....	....	Exceptional Financing	79ded
																Government Finance	
Gross Domestic Product			−4.1	−4.4	−4.6	−5.6	−5.1	−4.8	−4.2	−2.6	−2.1	−1.2	.3	....	Deficit (-) or Surplus	80g
	....	....	58.4	58.3	61.8	68.3	70.7	73.4	74.4	74.2	73.5	72.0	69.7	....	Debt	88g
																National Accounts	
Billions of Euros beginning 1999											3,309.5	†3,482.2	3,664.4	3,905.3	Househ.Cons.Expend.,incl.NPISHs	96f.c
	....	....	....	....	....	....	....	....	....	....	1,168.0	†1,229.8	1,283.2	1,359.3	Government Consumption Expend.	91f.c
	....	....	....	....	....	....	....	....	....	....	1,186.8	†1,291.4	1,387.0	1,434.1	Gross Fixed Capital Formation	93e.c
	....	....	....	....	....	....	....	....	....	....	59.9	†22.3	37.9	−2.4	Changes in Inventories	93i.c
	....	....	....	....	....	....	....	....	....	....	1,925.5	†2,052.7	2,410.3	2,538.1	Exports of Goods and Services	90c.c
	....	....	....	....	....	....	....	....	....	....	1,778.2	†1,951.1	2,342.4	2,423.9	Imports of Goods and Services (-)	98c.c
	....	....	....	....	....	....	....	....	....	....	5,871.3	†6,132.8	6,424.4	6,805.3	Gross Domestic Product (GDP)	99b.c
	....	....	....	....	....	....	....	....	....	....	−35.6	−39.1	....	....	Net Primary Income from Abroad	98.nc
	....	....	....	....	....	....	....	....	....	....	5,835.4	6,093.7	....	....	Gross National Income (GNI)	99a.c
	....	....	....	....	....	....	....	....	....	....	5,647.3	5,819.7	6,023.7	6,219.0	GDP Volume 1995 Prices	99b.r
	....	....	....	....	....	....	....	....	....	....	106.4	109.0	112.8	116.5	GDP Volume (1995=100)	99bv r
	....	....	....	....	....	....	....	....	....	....	106.2	†108.2	109.5	112.4	GDP Deflator (1995=100)	99bi r

(See notes in the back of the book.)

Fiji

	1972	1973	1974	1975	1976	1977	1978	1979	1980	1981	1982	1983	1984	1985	1986
Exchange Rates														*Fiji Dollars per SDR:*	
Official Rate .... aa	.9155	.9762	.9795	1.0104	1.0939	1.0575	1.0679	1.1077	1.0089	1.0205	1.0450	1.0954	1.1204	1.2307	1.4010
														Fiji Dollars per US Dollar:	
Official Rate .... ae	.8432	.8092	.8000	.8631	.9415	.8705	.8197	.8409	.7911	.8767	.9473	1.0462	1.1430	1.1204	1.1453
Official Rate .... rf	.8252	.7942	.8056	.8219	.8977	.9174	.8468	.8357	.8180	.8546	.9324	1.0170	1.0826	1.1536	1.1329
													Index Numbers (1995=100):		
Official Rate .... ahx	170.5	177.2	174.6	171.3	156.8	153.3	166.1	168.3	172.0	164.8	150.9	138.4	130.1	122.0	124.2
Nominal Effective Exchange Rate .... ne c	....	....	....	....	....	....	....	115.5	119.8	123.6	127.6	128.0	131.3	137.9	130.1
Real Effective Exchange Rate .... re c	....	....	....	....	....	....	....		137.9	141.6	142.2	141.5	143.5	145.5	130.8
Fund Position														*Millions of SDRs:*	
Quota .... 2f. s	13.00	13.00	13.00	13.00	13.00	13.00	18.00	18.00	27.00	27.00	27.00	36.50	36.50	36.50	36.50
SDRs .... 1b. s	1.38	1.38	1.37	1.33	1.33	1.27	1.30	3.10	2.71	4.52	3.72	.28	6.31	5.14	5.82
Reserve Position in the Fund .... 1c. s	2.30	2.30	—	3.25	3.25	3.25	3.15	3.06	5.34	5.36	5.40	7.79	7.81	7.83	7.85
Total Fund Cred.&Loans Outstg. .. 2tl			.34	—	—	6.50	6.50	6.50	—	—	13.50	13.50	13.50	13.19	6.44
International Liquidity												*Millions of US Dollars Unless Otherwise Indicated:*			
Total Reserves minus Gold 1l.d	69.42	73.95	109.15	148.59	116.32	147.13	134.70	136.48	167.51	135.08	126.92	115.82	117.42	130.84	171.05
SDRs 1b.d	1.50	1.66	1.68	1.56	1.55	1.54	1.69	4.08	3.46	5.26	4.10	.29	6.19	5.65	7.12
Reserve Position in the Fund 1c.d	2.50	2.77		3.80	3.78	3.95	4.10	4.03	6.81	6.24	5.96	8.16	7.66	8.60	9.60
Foreign Exchange 1d.d	65.42	69.51	107.47	143.23	111.00	141.64	128.90	128.37	157.24	123.58	116.86	107.37	103.58	116.59	154.33
Gold (Million Fine Troy Ounces) 1ad	—	—	—	—	—	.006	.008	.011	.011	.011	.011	.011	.011	.011	.011
Gold (National Valuation) 1and	—	—	—	—	—	.24	.38	.51	.50	.45	.43	.41	.38	.43	.47
Deposit Money Banks: Assets 7a.d	18.31	8.61	9.55	6.37	4.96	4.83	5.16	3.66	8.38	10.02	4.95	7.87	8.42	44.42	111.97
Liabilities 7b.d	7.27	14.47	20.77	18.65	22.25	22.79	13.24	13.62	16.27	19.98	23.53	18.67	14.82	55.56	120.11
Monetary Authorities														*Millions of Fiji Dollars:*	
Foreign Assets 11	54.5	†67.8	91.6	129.1	110.3	128.7	110.3	116.9	132.5	116.0	123.4	122.5	130.0	146.5	195.9
Claims on Central Government 12a	3.6	2.6	2.8	3.0	2.8	1.6	5.1	10.4	6.1	4.6	11.1	8.2	16.7	4.3	1.8
Claims on Official Entities 12bx	—	.4	.1	—	.3	1.3	2.9	9.4	2.9	1.0	2.8	11.4	6.5	6.2	.3
Reserve Money 14	24.9	37.6	48.5	63.4	54.5	56.4	64.1	72.0	66.2	76.4	81.6	86.9	100.5	103.0	116.7
of which: Currency Outside DMBs 14a	14.9	17.2	21.5	27.3	30.7	34.0	38.8	45.2	44.1	48.7	52.8	58.7	61.0	61.8	63.1
Liabs.of Central Bank: Securities 16ac															
Central Government Deposits 16d	12.7	19.7	13.7	24.2	20.6	21.3	15.1	16.1	29.3	16.9	13.1	13.3	10.6	7.4	13.9
Capital Accounts 17a	2.0	9.1	10.8	10.8	20.4	18.2	19.4	24.7	16.2	23.4	28.4	34.0	36.3	47.7	69.9
Other Items (Net) 17r	18.5	†4.4	21.5	33.7	18.0	35.8	19.8	23.9	29.8	4.7	14.2	7.9	5.9	−1.1	−2.5
Deposit Money Banks														*Millions of Fiji Dollars:*	
Reserves 20	12.6	16.7	18.6	25.3	18.1	20.8	19.1	20.4	22.2	23.3	28.2	28.3	39.5	41.4	53.4
Claims on Mon.Author.: Securities .. 20c	—	—	—	—	—	—	—	—	—	—	—	—	—	—	—
Foreign Assets 21	13.9	7.0	7.6	5.5	4.7	4.2	4.2	3.1	6.6	8.8	4.7	8.2	9.6	49.8	128.2
Claims on Central Government 22a	8.8	10.0	16.2	22.2	27.0	31.4	39.6	42.8	53.0	40.3	51.6	52.9	44.8	50.2	77.2
Claims on Official Entities 22bx	6.8	7.1	7.5	10.0	13.7	13.3	17.7	16.7	18.3	25.0	46.4	61.8	52.0	53.4	56.1
Claims on Private Sector 22d	40.4	57.7	75.5	78.2	102.3	119.5	127.2	167.9	188.7	233.2	245.9	275.3	324.8	350.4	367.6
Demand Deposits 24	31.5	35.4	39.4	47.3	47.9	48.4	53.5	61.8	56.6	65.4	70.1	76.0	74.9	76.0	108.8
Time Deposits 25	43.1	50.6	65.9	80.8	96.6	119.1	140.0	174.9	205.4	234.1	257.5	297.5	344.1	351.6	402.9
Foreign Liabilities 26c	5.5	11.7	16.6	16.1	21.0	19.8	10.8	11.5	12.9	17.5	22.3	19.5	16.9	62.2	137.6
Central Government Deposits 26d	3.7	4.0	5.3	2.7	5.0	5.1	5.3	7.1	8.1	7.7	11.1	14.9	21.7	17.3	17.7
Other Items (Net) 27r	−1.3	−3.3	−1.8	−5.7	−4.7	−3.3	−1.9	−4.3	5.7	6.0	15.8	18.7	13.1	38.0	15.5
Monetary Survey														*Millions of Fiji Dollars:*	
Foreign Assets (Net) 31n	62.9	†63.1	82.2	118.4	94.1	106.2	96.8	101.3	126.3	107.3	91.7	96.4	107.6	117.7	177.6
Domestic Credit 32	43.2	54.1	83.1	86.6	120.5	140.7	172.0	224.1	231.5	279.4	333.7	381.5	412.6	439.9	471.3
Claims on Central Govt. (Net) 32an	−4.0	−11.1	—	−1.6	4.2	6.7	24.2	30.0	21.6	20.2	38.6	32.9	29.3	29.8	47.3
Claims on Official Entities 32bx	6.8	7.5	7.6	10.0	14.0	14.6	20.5	26.2	21.2	25.9	49.3	73.3	58.5	59.6	56.4
Claims on Private Sector 32d	40.4	57.7	75.5	78.2	102.3	119.5	127.2	167.9	188.7	233.2	245.9	275.3	324.8	350.4	367.6
Money 34	52.3	56.5	69.1	84.0	85.4	84.1	98.4	112.3	100.7	118.4	123.6	134.8	136.0	137.8	172.1
Quasi-Money 35	43.1	51.6	81.4	107.2	108.5	146.0	149.0	186.0	234.4	234.2	257.6	297.5	344.1	351.6	402.9
Liabs.of Central Bank: Securities 36ac	—	—	—	—	—	—	—	—	—	—	—	—	—	—	—
Capital Accounts 37a	2.0	9.1	10.8	10.8	20.4	18.2	19.4	24.7	16.2	23.4	28.4	34.0	36.3	47.7	69.9
Other Items (Net) 37r	8.7	†−.1	4.1	2.9	.3	−1.3	1.9	2.4	6.5	10.6	15.8	11.7	3.8	20.6	4.0
Money plus Quasi-Money 35l	95.4	108.1	150.5	191.3	193.9	230.1	247.4	298.3	335.1	352.6	381.2	432.2	480.1	489.4	575.0
Nonbank Financial Institutions														*Millions of Fiji Dollars:*	
Claims on Central Government ....42a. l	9.3	9.6	10.9	9.3	9.6	13.7	18.4	23.1	26.8	30.8	34.3	39.2	44.1	46.6	54.7
Claims on Local Government ....42b. l	4.4	5.1	5.1	5.2	5.2	5.5	5.6	6.4	6.3	8.9	8.6	10.6	11.1	12.7	14.1
Claims on Nonfin.Pub.Enterprises ....42c. l	—	.1	.1	.2	.4	.8	1.7	2.4	4.6	5.2	5.5	6.7	7.8	9.3	11.6
Claims on Private Sector ....42d. l	3.3	4.7	5.7	6.7	7.6	8.0	9.4	10.7	12.1	14.2	19.4	21.8	24.2	28.1	32.5
Incr.in Total Assets(Within Per.) ......49z. l	1.9	2.8	2.9	2.3	4.2	8.3	6.1	7.3	7.7	9.5	11.4	12.1	13.5	15.2	16.4
Interest Rates														*Percent Per Annum*	
Bank Rate *(End of Period)* .. 60	....	....	6.38	6.25	5.50	5.50	5.58	6.50	7.50	8.83	9.50	10.17	11.00	11.00	8.00
Money Market Rate 60b	....	....	....	....	....	....	....	....	....	....	5.07	6.20	8.74	6.61	6.55
Treasury Bill Rate 60c	....	....	....	4.34	4.34	4.34	4.50	5.32	5.36	5.72	5.96	6.17	7.09	7.03	6.36
Deposit Rate 60l	....	....	3.96	4.00	4.00	4.00	4.04	4.50	4.50	6.00	6.00	6.00	6.00	6.00	6.00
Lending Rate 60p	10.00	10.00	10.00	10.00	10.00	10.00	10.50	10.50	12.00	13.50	13.50	13.50	13.50	13.50	13.50
Prices, Production, Labor														*Index Numbers (1995=100):*	
Consumer Prices 64	19.1	21.2	24.3	27.5	30.6	32.8	34.8	37.5	42.9	47.7	51.1	54.5	57.4	59.9	†61.0
Wage Rates 65	21.2	27.4	33.7	41.1	46.0	48.9	54.3	58.4	63.9	69.9	75.4	80.4	81.5	82.6	82.6
Industrial Production 66	....	....	....	....	....	....	....	92.0	84.9	93.5	98.1	82.7	98.3	87.4	74.8
Tourist Arrivals 66.t	....	....	....	....	....	....	....	....	61.5	59.6	63.8	60.2	73.9	71.6	80.9
Industrial Employment 67	....	....	....	....	....	....	78.7	80.7	82.7	83.7	80.5	82.3	80.8	83.3	82.1
														Number in Thousands:	
Labor Force 67d	....	....	....	....	....	....	....	....	....	....	....	....	....	....	....
Employment 67e	....	....	....	....	....	....	....	....	....	....	....	....	....	....	....
Unemployment 67c	....	....	....	....	....	....	....	....	....	....	....	....	....	81	80
Unemployment Rate (%) 67r	....	....	....	....	....	....	....	....	....	....	....	....	....	19	18
														8.1	7.5

	1987	1988	1989	1990	1991	1992	1993	1994	1995	1996	1997	1998	1999	2000	2001		
End of Period																**Exchange Rates**	
	2.0436	1.8906	1.9632	2.0760	2.1067	2.1511	2.1164	2.0570	2.1248	1.9900	2.0902	2.7965	2.6981	2.8479	2.9017	Official Rate	aa
End of Period (ae) Period Average (rf)																	
	1.4405	1.4049	1.4939	1.4592	1.4728	1.5645	1.5408	1.4090	1.4294	1.3839	1.5492	1.9861	1.9658	2.1858	2.3089	Official Rate	ae
	1.2439	1.4303	1.4833	1.4809	1.4756	1.5030	1.5418	1.4641	1.4063	1.4033	1.4437	1.9868	1.9696	2.1286	2.2766	Official Rate	rf
Period Averages																	
	114.9	98.4	94.9	95.0	95.3	93.6	91.2	96.1	100.0	100.2	97.5	70.8	71.4	66.5	61.8	Official Rate	ahx
	113.0	93.7	97.8	98.8	99.3	97.8	99.1	100.8	100.0	101.3	104.7	83.5	82.7	82.5	81.1	Nominal Effective Exchange Rate	ne c
	111.2	95.2	95.0	95.3	98.2	98.7	102.4	101.9	100.0	101.9	106.9	88.8	89.1	87.7	88.0	Real Effective Exchange Rate	re c
End of Period																**Fund Position**	
	36.50	36.50	36.50	36.50	36.50	51.10	51.10	51.10	51.10	51.10	51.10	51.10	70.30	70.30	70.30	Quota	2f. s
	9.90	15.08	15.90	16.48	9.26	5.97	6.26	7.39	7.67	7.99	8.29	8.62	4.10	4.47	4.81	SDRs	1b. s
	7.87	7.87	7.89	7.12	6.76	10.43	9.95	9.99	10.00	10.05	10.08	10.12	14.94	14.98	15.00	Reserve Position in the Fund	1c. s
	4.75	2.97	.59	—	—	—	—	—	—	—	—	—	—	—	—	Total Fund Cred.&Loans Outstg.	2tl
End of Period																**International Liquidity**	
	132.17	233.36	211.59	260.79	271.43	316.87	269.46	273.14	349.03	427.24	360.29	385.42	428.69	409.68	366.39	Total Reserves minus Gold	1l. d
	14.04	20.29	20.90	23.45	13.25	8.21	8.59	10.79	11.41	11.49	11.18	12.14	5.63	5.82	6.04	SDRs	1b. d
	11.16	10.59	10.37	10.13	9.67	14.34	13.67	14.58	14.87	14.45	13.60	14.25	20.50	19.52	18.85	Reserve Position in the Fund	1c. d
	106.96	202.48	180.33	227.22	248.51	294.32	247.19	247.77	322.76	401.30	335.51	359.04	402.55	384.34	341.50	Foreign Exchange	1d. d
	.001	.001	.001	.001	.001	.001	.001	.001	.001	.001	.001	.001	.001	.001	.001	Gold (Million Fine Troy Ounces)	1ad
	.41	.41	.30	.32	.29	.28	.33	.32	.32	.31	.24	.24	.24	.23	.23	Gold (National Valuation)	1and
	26.29	38.35	51.99	77.88	49.90	44.47	58.69	62.91	50.13	78.07	89.31	136.34	200.07	81.06	84.21	Deposit Money Banks: Assets	7a. d
	25.05	41.56	54.40	83.02	66.05	67.17	64.30	65.66	73.89	124.33	123.48	108.04	159.49	114.08	120.65	Liabilities	7b. d
End of Period																**Monetary Authorities**	
	190.2	326.8	316.1	380.5	399.7	498.0	414.8	384.9	498.9	591.2	558.1	765.5	842.7	900.1	846.0	Foreign Assets	11
	26.9	1.5	9.0	.1	.1	—	6.7	—	.1	—	—	—	50.7	56.1	66.2	Claims on Central Government	12a
	5.3	—	—	.1	.1	.1	2.2	.1	—	—	—	—	—	—	—	Claims on Official Entities	12bx
	111.6	199.3	152.1	169.3	189.1	226.4	219.9	223.6	243.4	247.9	260.4	276.8	434.2	352.2	420.0	Reserve Money	14
	64.9	67.7	78.0	86.0	91.0	103.1	112.4	115.6	117.8	125.4	134.0	159.8	189.9	163.3	181.7	*of which: Currency Outside DMBs*	14a
	—	—	56.9	96.2	95.4	163.9	108.9	126.6	220.5	253.3	210.7	252.9	255.8	415.7	338.6	Liabs.of Central Bank: Securities	16ac
	.9	49.0	42.9	36.2	31.7	21.8	14.3	14.8	6.8	47.2	40.0	22.3	42.6	22.5	17.3	Central Government Deposits	16d
	110.8	76.1	80.6	83.5	73.0	82.8	62.7	45.8	49.3	42.3	50.5	197.1	169.0	136.5	115.3	Capital Accounts	17a
	-.8	4.0	-7.5	-4.5	10.7	3.3	17.9	-25.8	-21.0	.4	-3.4	16.4	-8.3	29.2	21.0	Other Items (Net)	17r
End of Period																**Deposit Money Banks**	
	46.7	131.5	73.1	83.2	97.8	123.3	107.5	107.9	125.5	120.2	126.4	111.5	237.3	174.2	233.3	Reserves	20
	—	—	20.3	60.7	39.9	60.2	44.6	44.0	104.1	106.0	60.4	44.4	54.5	43.7	17.1	Claims on Mon.Author.: Securities	20c
	37.9	53.9	77.7	113.6	73.5	69.6	90.4	88.6	71.7	108.0	138.4	270.8	393.3	177.2	194.4	Foreign Assets	21
	62.5	83.6	71.6	60.8	82.2	91.6	88.9	80.7	65.4	78.8	87.0	107.0	117.8	95.3	129.9	Claims on Central Government	22a
	60.9	70.4	67.9	75.2	97.5	118.4	141.9	144.4	137.7	145.8	164.5	154.4	137.1	138.7	120.0	Claims on Official Entities	22bx
	393.6	411.5	540.8	676.4	802.9	880.4	994.4	1,080.9	1,112.2	1,165.0	1,013.9	963.8	997.0	1,145.9	1,081.8	Claims on Private Sector	22d
	103.4	205.2	184.5	179.2	183.1	211.0	251.4	229.0	268.3	328.7	311.3	328.6	497.6	415.7	434.2	Demand Deposits	24
	429.9	448.4	525.6	722.9	855.4	977.4	1,013.7	1,069.7	1,089.6	1,032.1	913.2	859.9	851.6	920.1	846.2	Time Deposits	25
	36.1	58.4	81.3	121.1	97.3	105.1	99.1	92.5	105.6	172.1	191.3	214.6	313.5	249.3	278.6	Foreign Liabilities	26c
	7.5	26.4	18.2	13.6	15.1	6.8	21.5	40.5	40.1	21.0	37.8	78.6	122.5	54.6	56.1	Central Government Deposits	26d
	24.8	12.5	41.8	33.0	42.8	43.2	81.9	114.7	112.8	170.1	136.9	170.2	151.8	135.1	161.6	Other Items (Net)	27r
End of Period																**Monetary Survey**	
	182.3	316.7	311.3	373.0	376.0	462.5	406.2	381.0	464.9	527.2	505.2	821.7	922.5	827.9	761.8	Foreign Assets (Net)	31n
	540.9	491.6	628.2	762.7	935.9	1,061.9	1,198.2	1,250.7	1,268.3	1,321.3	1,187.6	1,124.3	1,137.5	1,358.8	1,324.6	Domestic Credit	32
	81.0	9.7	19.4	11.1	35.5	63.0	59.8	25.3	18.4	10.5	9.1	6.1	3.3	74.2	122.8	Claims on Central Govt. (Net)	32an
	66.2	70.4	68.0	75.2	97.6	118.5	144.1	144.5	137.8	145.8	164.5	154.4	137.1	138.7	120.0	Claims on Official Entities	32bx
	393.6	411.5	540.8	676.4	802.9	880.4	994.4	1,080.9	1,112.2	1,165.0	1,013.9	963.8	997.0	1,145.9	1,081.8	Claims on Private Sector	32d
	168.3	272.9	263.6	265.3	274.4	314.1	363.8	344.6	386.2	456.3	445.3	493.9	694.5	593.7	620.9	Money	34
	429.9	448.4	525.6	722.9	855.4	977.4	1,013.7	1,069.7	1,089.6	1,032.1	913.2	859.9	851.6	920.1	846.2	Quasi-Money	35
	—	—	36.6	35.5	55.6	103.7	64.4	82.5	116.4	147.3	150.3	208.4	201.3	372.0	321.4	Liabs.of Central Bank: Securities	36ac
	110.8	76.1	80.6	83.5	73.0	82.8	62.7	45.8	49.3	42.3	50.5	197.1	169.0	136.5	115.3	Capital Accounts	37a
	14.2	10.9	33.1	28.5	53.5	46.4	99.8	89.0	91.8	170.5	133.4	186.6	143.5	164.3	182.5	Other Items (Net)	37r
	598.2	721.3	789.2	988.2	1,129.8	1,291.5	1,377.5	1,414.4	1,475.7	1,488.4	1,358.5	1,353.8	1,546.1	1,513.9	1,467.1	Money plus Quasi-Money	35l
End of Period																**Nonbank Financial Institutions**	
	58.1	63.9	67.2	61.7	54.4	55.6	55.3	58.1	58.2	77.4	127.7	127.0	134.8	146.8	164.2	Claims on Central Government	42a. l
	13.5	12.7	10.7	12.9	14.1	14.1	14.9	20.6	26.8	26.9	—	—	—	—	—	Claims on Local Government	42b. l
	11.4	13.1	13.0	13.7	11.9	14.2	15.2	26.7	36.2	54.4	—	—	—	—	—	Claims on Nonfin.Pub.Enterprises	42c. l
	37.2	32.8	36.1	29.1	33.0	37.6	42.6	59.0	68.3	73.8	93.5	100.5	119.8	126.7	134.5	Claims on Private Sector	42d. l
	10.5	5.0	11.4	12.2	14.0	19.9	22.1	23.2	27.6	15.1	-14.4	14.8	28.7	25.9	35.6	*Incr.in Total Assets(Within Per.)*	49z. l
Percent Per Annum																**Interest Rates**	
	11.00	11.00	8.00	8.00	8.00	6.00	6.00	6.00	6.00	6.00	1.88	2.50	2.50	8.00	1.75	Bank Rate *(End of Period)*	60
	9.02	1.49	2.34	2.92	4.28	3.06	2.91	4.10	3.95	2.43	1.91	1.27	1.27	2.58	.79	Money Market Rate	60b
	9.76	1.78	2.75	4.40	5.61	3.65	2.91	2.69	3.15	2.98	2.60	2.00	2.00	3.63	1.51	Treasury Bill Rate	60c
	6.00	4.88	4.00	4.00	4.06	4.10	3.69	3.15	3.18	3.38	3.08	2.17	1.24	.90	.78	Deposit Rate	60l
	13.50	20.46	11.64	11.86	12.25	12.35	11.74	11.28	11.06	11.33	11.03	9.66	8.77	8.40	8.34	Lending Rate	60p
Period Averages																**Prices, Production, Labor**	
	64.5	72.1	76.5	82.8	88.2	92.5	†97.3	97.9	100.0	103.1	106.5	112.6	114.8	116.1	121.0	Consumer Prices	64
	87.0	89.2	87.0	92.2	82.7	88.4	95.8	98.7	100.0	112.3	104.1	. . . .	. . . .	. . . .	. . . .	Wage Rates	65
	67.7	71.2	78.1	83.7	86.0	87.6	92.7	97.2	100.0	91.9	90.9	. . . .	. . . .	. . . .	. . . .	Industrial Production	66
	59.6	65.4	78.7	87.6	81.4	87.5	90.3	100.1	100.0	106.6	112.8	116.6	128.7	. . . .	. . . .	Tourist Arrivals	66.t
	80.3	79.7	92.4	92.5	94.3	96.1	97.5	98.0	100.0	113.2	118.0	116.4	. . . .	. . . .	. . . .	Industrial Employment	67
Period Averages																	
	. . . .	. . . .	. . . .	250	253	265	269	. . . .	. . . .	. . . .	. . . .	. . . .	. . . .	. . . .	. . . .	Labor Force	67d
	78	78	88	89	92	92	94	95	97	. . . .	. . . .	. . . .	. . . .	. . . .	. . . .	Employment	67e
	23	23	15	16	15	14	16	16	15	. . . .	. . . .	. . . .	. . . .	. . . .	. . . .	Unemployment	67c
	9.3	9.4	6.1	6.4	5.9	5.4	5.9	5.7	5.4	. . . .	. . . .	. . . .	. . . .	. . . .	. . . .	Unemployment Rate (%)	67r

Fiji

		1972	1973	1974	1975	1976	1977	1978	1979	1980	1981	1982	1983	1984	1985	1986
International Transactions															*Millions of Fiji Dollars*	
Exports	70	79.38	96.48	152.11	168.64	155.61	204.15	211.10	262.50	381.45	344.21	353.92	312.04	362.40	352.23	383.02
Imports, c.i.f.	71	131.55	176.34	219.33	220.97	238.04	281.01	300.00	392.87	458.75	539.91	475.58	493.17	486.99	508.00	493.60
Imports, f.o.b.	71.v	115.87	155.50	189.56	190.77	205.40	242.48	256.56	345.63	403.72	475.13	418.51	433.99	428.54	447.18	434.51
															1985=100	
Unit Value of Exports	74	†33.9	40.6	67.1	90.8	78.9	†85.7	92.5	91.6	123.1	108.4	106.2	112.3	111.1	100.0	134.3
Balance of Payments															*Millions of US Dollars:*	
Current Account, n.i.e.	78al d	....	....	....	....	....	....	....	−58.8	−17.5	−161.3	−84.3	−55.4	−18.4	18.7	16.8
Goods: Exports f.o.b.	78aa d	....	....	....	....	....	....	....	270.2	373.6	314.7	286.9	240.9	258.1	235.3	275.8
Goods: Imports f.o.b.	78ab d	....	....	....	....	....	....	....	−412.6	−492.1	−545.1	−441.0	−421.7	−390.7	−381.7	−379.2
Trade Balance	78ac d	....	....	....	....	....	....	....	−142.5	−118.6	−230.3	−154.0	−180.8	−132.6	−146.4	−103.4
Services: Credit	78ad d	....	....	....	....	....	....	....	191.3	200.5	219.7	236.2	251.2	249.0	272.9	263.1
Services: Debit	78ae d	....	....	....	....	....	....	....	−106.7	−124.3	−167.7	−154.7	−130.5	−128.5	−130.9	−157.7
Balance on Goods & Services	78af d	....	....	....	....	....	....	....	−57.9	−42.3	−178.4	−72.5	−60.1	−12.0	−4.4	2.1
Income: Credit	78ag d	....	....	....	....	....	....	....	14.0	23.0	30.9	22.5	20.6	20.9	35.0	41.2
Income: Debit	78ah d	....	....	....	....	....	....	....	−27.5	−40.2	−41.7	−58.7	−48.7	−49.0	−45.8	−49.4
Balance on Gds, Serv. & Inc.	78ai d	....	....	....	....	....	....	....	−71.3	−59.5	−189.2	−108.7	−88.1	−40.1	−15.2	−6.1
Current Transfers, n.i.e.: Credit	78aj d	....	....	....	....	....	....	....	19.3	48.5	44.1	42.4	47.1	36.5	51.4	37.4
Current Transfers: Debit	78ak d	....	....	....	....	....	....	....	−6.7	−6.5	−16.2	−17.9	−14.4	−14.7	−17.5	−14.6
Capital Account, n.i.e.	78bc d	....	....	....	....	....	....	....	−7.9	−9.4	−10.9	−6.9	−8.0	−6.9	−10.4	−13.4
Capital Account, n.i.e.: Credit	78ba d	....	....	....	....	....	....	....	.9	.6	1.4	1.2	.7	1.3	.6	.7
Capital Account: Debit	78bb d	....	....	....	....	....	....	....	−8.8	−9.9	−12.3	−8.2	−8.7	−8.2	−11.0	−14.1
Financial Account, n.i.e.	78bj d	....	....	....	....	....	....	....	57.0	71.7	139.5	85.3	67.9	35.0	−2.0	−1.1
Direct Investment Abroad	78bd d	....	....	....	....	....	....	....	—	−2.2	1.5	−.8	−.1	−.6	−13.0	.7
Dir. Invest. in Rep. Econ., n.i.e.	78be d	....	....	....	....	....	....	....	10.2	36.3	36.2	36.8	31.9	23.3	21.7	8.0
Portfolio Investment Assets	78bf d	....	....	....	....	....	....	....	—	—	—	—	—	—	—	—
Equity Securities	78bk d	....	....	....	....	....	....	....	—	—	—	—	—	—	—	—
Debt Securities	78bl d	....	....	....	....	....	....	....	—	—	—	—	—	—	—	—
Portfolio Investment Liab., n.i.e.	78bg d	....	....	....	....	....	....	....	—	—	—	—	—	—	—	—
Equity Securities	78bm d	....	....	....	....	....	....	....	—	—	—	—	—	—	—	—
Debt Securities	78bn d	....	....	....	....	....	....	....	—	—	—	—	—	—	—	—
Financial Derivatives Assets	78bw d	....	....	....	....	....	....	....	—	—	—	—	—	—	—	—
Financial Derivatives Liabilities	78bx d	....	....	....	....	....	....	....	—	—	—	—	—	—	—	—
Other Investment Assets	78bh d	....	....	....	....	....	....	....	1.4	−18.9	12.7	5.6	2.8	5.0	−47.9	−61.5
Monetary Authorities	78bo d	....	....	....	....	....	....	....	—	−1.1	—	—	—	—	—	—
General Government	78bp d	....	....	....	....	....	....	....	—	—	—	—	—	—	—	—
Banks	78bq d	....	....	....	....	....	....	....	1.4	−4.3	−2.5	4.4	−3.5	−1.2	−34.8	−62.4
Other Sectors	78br d	....	....	....	....	....	....	....	—	−13.4	15.2	1.2	6.2	6.3	−13.1	.9
Other Investment Liab., n.i.e.	78bi d	....	....	....	....	....	....	....	45.5	56.5	89.0	43.7	33.3	7.2	37.2	51.7
Monetary Authorities	78bs d	....	....	....	....	....	....	....	—	—	—	—	—	—	—	—
General Government	78bt d	....	....	....	....	....	....	....	22.9	57.6	78.9	43.4	34.0	6.4	—	.2
Banks	78bu d	....	....	....	....	....	....	....	−.4	1.6	.7	2.5	−.1	1.0	36.3	61.1
Other Sectors	78bv d	....	....	....	....	....	....	....	23.0	−2.7	9.4	−2.3	−.6	−.2	.9	−9.5
Net Errors and Omissions	78ca d	....	....	....	....	....	....	....	15.0	−5.1	10.8	−15.8	−9.9	.8	−10.6	27.2
Overall Balance	78cb d	....	....	....	....	....	....	....	5.4	39.8	−21.9	−21.7	−5.4	10.5	−4.2	29.5
Reserves and Related Items	79da d	....	....	....	....	....	....	....	−5.4	−39.8	21.9	21.7	5.4	−10.5	4.2	−29.5
Reserve Assets	79db d	....	....	....	....	....	....	....	−5.4	−31.2	21.9	6.4	5.4	−10.5	4.8	−21.5
Use of Fund Credit and Loans	79dc d	....	....	....	....	....	....	....	—	−8.6	—	15.3	—	—	−.6	−7.9
Exceptional Financing	79de d	....	....	....	....	....	....	....	....	....	....	....	....	....	....	....
Government Finance															*Millions of Fiji Dollars:*	
Deficit (-) or Surplus	80	−4.0	−11.2	−16.0	−7.7	−23.6	−35.2	−30.6	−24.8	−29.5	−45.3	−70.3	−43.3	−38.7	−35.4	−70.6
Total Revenue and Grants	81y	55.1	68.2	80.0	109.3	124.1	134.1	157.0	194.0	224.4	262.9	264.8	293.7	329.2	339.7	340.1
Revenue	81	53.2	64.9	76.7	107.4	122.7	131.6	152.8	188.7	220.4	255.2	254.7	283.7	319.1	329.2	330.6
Grants	81z	1.9	3.3	3.3	1.9	1.4	2.5	4.3	5.3	3.9	7.7	10.1	10.0	10.1	10.5	9.5
Exp. & Lending Minus Repay.	82z	59.1	79.4	96.1	117.0	147.7	169.3	187.6	218.8	253.9	308.1	335.1	336.9	367.9	375.1	410.6
Expenditure	82	58.2	79.0	94.3	115.1	147.0	168.1	185.9	219.6	255.3	292.2	323.9	329.5	366.1	371.7	383.3
Lending Minus Repayments	83	.9	.4	1.8	1.9	.7	1.2	1.7	−.8	−1.5	15.9	11.3	7.4	1.8	3.4	27.3
Total Financing	80h	4.0	11.2	16.0	7.7	23.6	35.2	30.6	24.8	29.5	45.3	70.3	43.3	38.7	35.4	70.6
Domestic	84a	4.2	5.7	9.8	2.1	13.8	16.0	32.8	16.6	4.8	13.4	52.4	38.1	34.4	33.4	73.7
Foreign	85a	−.1	5.4	6.2	5.5	9.9	19.2	−2.2	8.2	24.8	31.9	18.0	5.2	4.3	2.1	−3.2
Total Debt by Residence	88	46.7	73.6	83.5	99.1	121.7	154.0	168.0	193.7	247.2	292.2	358.1	399.2	446.4	475.9	546.2
Domestic	88a	36.5	47.2	51.5	63.0	75.7	91.5	109.6	125.5	157.1	168.8	216.0	250.8	289.4	319.0	389.3
Foreign	89a	10.2	26.4	32.0	36.1	45.9	62.5	58.4	68.3	90.2	123.4	142.1	148.4	157.0	157.0	156.9
National Accounts															*Millions of Fiji Dollars*	
Househ.Cons.Expend.,incl.NPISHs	96f	180.5	261.3	334.4	382.5	433.7	415.1	458.2	519.6	574.7	660.0	684.7	748.2	794.1	838.1	873.3
Government Consumption Expend.	91f	37.9	42.4	54.0	67.5	85.3	102.3	115.1	143.9	156.7	173.1	203.8	231.6	244.8	252.4	252.6
Gross Fixed Capital Formation	93e	53.1	65.7	74.2	103.4	119.5	128.9	149.8	197.3	249.8	280.5	262.6	239.2	218.0	239.1	215.4
Changes in Inventories	93i	9.5	9.5	10.9	12.6	14.5	24.1	27.8	59.6	63.4	81.7	21.9	2.3	23.3	12.2	51.1
Exports of Goods and Services	90c	119.9	153.2	221.1	241.8	235.1	289.9	299.5	385.8	477.5	454.4	481.3	498.1	546.2	583.6	609.0
Imports of Goods and Services (-)	98c	144.2	198.8	244.6	245.4	264.6	308.1	330.5	432.1	510.8	606.6	552.6	560.1	559.8	588.6	577.0
Gross Domestic Product (GDP)	99b	261.2	338.3	450.0	562.4	623.5	660.0	702.1	852.1	983.7	1,056.1	1,113.4	1,142.2	1,275.3	1,316.5	1,461.7
Net Primary Income from Abroad	98.n	−9.1	−4.6	−1.8	−6.0	−1.0	−8.6	−4.5	−12.5	−14.6	−9.2	−33.8	−28.2	−30.3	−36.3	−34.3
Gross National Income (GNI)	99a	252.2	333.7	448.2	556.4	622.5	651.4	697.6	839.6	969.2	1,046.9	1,079.6	1,114.0	1,245.0	1,280.2	1,427.4
Net National Income	99e	239.4	318.7	431.2	539.7	593.9	616.3	654.2	787.1	903.7	969.4	991.7	1,034.4	1,156.7	1,185.2	1,324.5
GDP at Factor Cost	99ba	230.5	300.6	410.5	515.4	570.6	605.7	642.9	779.4	901.0	953.6	1,020.5	1,031.8	1,151.7	1,177.7	1,326.1
GDP at Fact.Cost,Vol.'68 Prices	99ba p	170.0	191.6	196.6	196.8	202.1	211.1	216.4	....	....	....	....	....	....	....	....
GDP at Fact.Cost,Vol.'77 Prices	99ba p	....	....	....	....	....	....	616.6	690.9	679.3	719.9	712.2	683.9	741.3	703.7	760.5
GDP at Fact.Cost,Vol.'89 Prices	99ba p	....	....	....	....	....	....	....	....	....	....	....	....	....	....	....
GDP Volume (1995=100)	99bv p	50.3	56.7	58.1	58.2	59.8	62.4	63.6	71.2	70.0	74.2	73.4	70.5	76.4	72.5	78.4
GDP Deflator (1995=100)	99bi p	19.1	22.1	29.4	36.9	39.7	40.4	42.1	45.6	53.6	53.5	57.9	60.9	62.7	67.6	70.4
																Millions:
Population	99z	.54	.55	.56	.57	.58	.60	.61	.62	.63	.65	.66	.67	.69	.70	.71

1987	1988	1989	1990	1991	1992	1993	1994	1995	1996	1997	1998	1999	2000	2001		Code
															International Transactions	
Millions of Fiji Dollars																
483.12	531.19	658.62	731.87	664.60	666.98	692.40	833.60	869.94	1,049.81	897.04	1,016.29	....			Exports	70
465.11	658.82	860.44	1,112.90	961.77	947.11	1,109.81	1,229.10	1,253.90	1,384.50	1,392.50	1,433.80	....			Imports, c.i.f.	71
409.43	579.95	638.26	950.20	810.60	809.80	1,006.50	1,053.70	1,070.80	1,178.70	1,182.20	1,221.00	....			Imports, f.o.b.	71.v
1985=100																
183.5	175.4	175.5	....	....	....	....	....	....	....	....	....	....			Unit Value of Exports	74
															Balance of Payments	
Minus Sign Indicates Debit																
27.3	70.5	7.5	−94.0	−68.2	−61.3	−138.1	−112.8	−112.7	13.5	−34.1	−59.9	12.7	....		Current Account, n.i.e.	78al d
328.5	372.9	377.1	415.6	362.6	349.8	370.9	490.2	519.6	672.2	535.6	428.9	537.7			Goods: Exports f.o.b.	78aa d
−325.0	−389.2	−489.0	−641.6	−549.4	−538.8	−652.8	−719.7	−761.4	−839.9	−818.9	−614.6	−653.3			Goods: Imports f.o.b.	78ab d
3.5	−16.3	−111.8	−226.1	−186.8	−189.0	−281.9	−229.5	−241.8	−167.7	−283.2	−185.6	−115.6			*Trade Balance*	78ac d
201.8	244.7	365.1	417.0	427.6	453.2	481.1	534.7	564.1	612.6	667.9	503.2	525.1			Services: Credit	78ad d
−173.1	−183.2	−226.4	−257.4	−289.2	−303.7	−321.1	−366.0	−398.6	−412.9	−405.6	−352.0	−389.8			Services: Debit	78ae d
32.2	45.2	26.8	−66.5	−48.3	−39.5	−121.8	−60.8	−76.3	31.9	−20.9	−34.4	19.7			*Balance on Goods & Services*	78af d
40.0	46.2	51.2	49.1	51.8	52.3	52.1	49.2	55.4	63.6	61.7	54.6	47.3			Income: Credit	78ag d
−49.7	−61.6	−75.7	−75.2	−72.4	−79.8	−80.4	−105.7	−94.6	−91.6	−99.2	−110.6	−82.8			Income: Debit	78ah d
22.4	29.9	2.4	−92.6	−68.9	−66.9	−150.1	−117.3	−115.5	4.0	−58.4	−90.4	−15.8			*Balance on Gds, Serv. & Inc.*	78ai d
28.2	53.6	27.0	24.3	32.4	34.9	40.2	38.1	36.0	44.1	54.6	45.3	42.7			Current Transfers, n.i.e.: Credit	78aj d
−23.3	−12.9	−21.8	−25.7	−31.8	−29.3	−28.2	−33.5	−33.1	−34.6	−30.3	−14.7	−14.2			Current Transfers: Debit	78ak d
−13.6	−12.1	48.4	47.6	71.1	72.5	57.1	43.4	87.0	70.8	48.5	60.6	14.0			Capital Account, n.i.e.	78bc d
.1	.1	70.0	69.6	97.9	96.7	83.7	76.0	120.1	114.5	88.9	100.6	59.3			Capital Account, n.i.e.: Credit	78ba d
−13.7	−12.2	−21.6	−22.0	−26.8	−24.2	−26.7	−32.6	−33.1	−43.8	−40.5	−40.0	−45.3			Capital Account: Debit	78bb d
−72.8	46.6	−26.2	82.2	13.1	84.0	45.1	61.0	88.3	3.6	−15.1	28.7	−104.0			Financial Account, n.i.e.	78bj d
−29.2	−1.5	−28.6	−13.1	6.8	−25.8	−28.9	.3	2.8	−9.8	−30.0	−62.6	−53.0			Direct Investment Abroad	78bd d
16.2	31.6	8.8	91.9	5.2	103.6	91.2	67.5	69.5	2.4	15.6	107.0	−33.2			Dir. Invest. in Rep. Econ., n.i.e.	78be d
—	—	—	—	—	—	—	—	—	—	—	—	....			Portfolio Investment Assets	78bf d
—	—	—	—	—	—	—	—	—	—	—	—				Equity Securities	78bk d
—	—	—	—	—	—	—	—	—	—	—	—				Debt Securities	78bl d
—	—	—	—	—	—	—	—	—	—	—	—				Portfolio Investment Liab., n.i.e.	78bg d
—	—	—	—	—	—	—	—	—	—	—	—				Equity Securities	78bm d
—	—	—	—	—	—	—	—	—	—	—	—				Debt Securities	78bn d
															Financial Derivatives Assets	78bw d
....	....														Financial Derivatives Liabilities	78bx d
45.3	−6.8	−22.3	−18.0	27.2	2.6	−13.5	1.2	12.0	−25.9	−21.1	−66.6	−62.2			Other Investment Assets	78bh d
—	—	—	—	—	—	—	—	—	—	—	—				Monetary Authorities	78bo d
—	—	—	—	—	—	—	—	—	—	—	—				General Government	78bp d
72.6	−11.2	−22.3	−18.0	27.2	2.6	−13.5	1.2	12.0	−25.9	−21.1	−66.6	−62.2			Banks	78bq d
−27.3	4.4	—													Other Sectors	78br d
−105.1	23.3	15.9	21.3	−26.0	3.7	−3.8	−8.1	3.9	36.8	20.4	51.0	44.4			Other Investment Liab., n.i.e.	78bi d
—	—	—	—	—	—	—	—	—	—	—	—				Monetary Authorities	78bs d
−11.2	9.7	—													General Government	78bt d
−80.2	14.3	15.9	21.3	−26.0	3.7	−3.8	−8.1	3.9	36.8	20.4	51.0	44.4			Banks	78bu d
−13.7	−.7	—													Other Sectors	78bv d
12.8	7.1	−9.1	29.2	23.9	−10.6	22.4	30.9	30.4	−9.7	−24.3	−24.6	32.5			Net Errors and Omissions	78ca d
−46.2	112.2	20.6	65.0	39.9	84.6	−13.6	22.5	93.0	78.1	−25.1	4.9	−44.9			*Overall Balance*	78cb d
46.2	−112.2	−20.6	−65.0	−39.9	−84.6	13.6	−22.5	−93.0	−78.1	25.1	−4.9	44.9			Reserves and Related Items	79da d
48.4	−109.8	15.5	−34.1	−8.9	−59.3	45.2	10.7	−76.6	−71.1	29.7	−27.4	−30.5			Reserve Assets	79db d
−2.1	−2.4	−3.1	−.8												Use of Fund Credit and Loans	79dc d
....	....	−33.0	−30.1	−31.0	−25.3	−31.7	−33.2	−16.4	−7.0	−4.6	22.5	75.3			Exceptional Financing	79de d
															Government Finance	
Year Ending December 31																
−73.9	−11.9	−54.8	†−54.7	−103.4	−112.1	−158.7	−114.6	−92.7	−211.4	−281.9	−104.3	....			Deficit (−) or Surplus	80
336.2	389.8	459.8	†551.2	576.4	602.5	654.0	697.9	718.9	743.6	803.4	1,141.2	....			Total Revenue and Grants	81y
324.8	367.6	447.9	†542.5	569.1	595.3	649.9	693.4	712.6	736.3	798.5	1,138.6	....			Revenue	81
11.4	22.2	11.9	†8.7	7.3	7.2	4.1	4.5	6.3	7.3	4.9	2.6	....			Grants	81z
410.1	401.7	514.7	†605.9	679.8	714.6	812.7	812.5	811.6	955.0	1,085.3	1,245.5	....			Exp. & Lending Minus Repay.	82z
398.2	397.2	477.9	†596.9	667.3	708.3	799.1	794.4	803.6	945.2	1,081.8	1,231.5	....			Expenditure	82
11.9	4.5	36.7	†9.0	12.5	6.3	13.6	18.1	8.0	9.8	3.5	14.0	....			Lending Minus Repayments	83
73.9	11.9	54.8	†54.7	103.4	112.1	158.7	114.6	92.7	211.4	281.9	104.3	....			Total Financing	80h
88.8	29.4	83.7	†34.3	80.7	100.7	146.9	83.6	71.5	193.9	273.2	93.5	....			Domestic	84a
−14.9	−17.5	−28.9	†20.4	22.7	11.4	11.8	31.0	21.2	17.5	8.7	10.8	....			Foreign	85a
....	....	....	†775.5	805.0	843.5	923.7	981.8	1,001.8	1,133.5	1,356.3	1,454.9	....			Total Debt by Residence	88
498.3	....	....	†547.1	593.9	638.1	733.3	792.2	807.3	942.8	1,156.1	1,060.6	....			Domestic	88a
....	....	....	†228.4	211.1	205.4	190.4	189.6	194.5	190.7	200.2	394.3	....			Foreign	89a
															National Accounts	
Millions of Fiji Dollars																
959.6	1,166.0	1,273.7	1,442.7	1,581.8	1,683.2	1,802.3	1,694.8	1,776.7	1,855.1	1,909.9	2,123.1	2,105.3			Househ.Cons.Expend.,incl.NPISHs	96f
255.1	263.4	303.9	329.3	360.2	418.3	466.4	437.2	446.4	474.1	507.5	574.1	588.2			Government Consumption Expend.	91f
229.9	223.1	211.2	303.5	278.3	280.8	331.8	320.4	350.0	296.8	306.5	485.6	390.2			Gross Fixed Capital Formation	93e
4.5	12.6	24.5	35.0	26.0	30.0	38.0	40.0	30.0	40.0	40.0	40.0	40.0			Changes in Inventories	93i
663.9	894.8	1,099.4	1,231.5	1,164.5	1,205.2	1,311.6	1,507.8	1,532.2	1,769.1	1,724.9	1,779.8	2,062.8			Exports of Goods and Services	90c
616.3	814.6	1,058.9	1,329.7	1,235.5	1,264.2	1,499.0	1,587.7	1,629.7	1,756.2	1,622.5	1,698.5	1,818.5			Imports of Goods and Services (-)	98c
1,465.2	1,587.6	1,752.8	1,951.9	2,066.3	2,334.8	2,564.9	2,673.1	2,799.9	2,962.3	3,060.2	3,283.2	3,588.4			Gross Domestic Product (GDP)	99b
−47.9	−35.2	−36.3	−41.8	−40.4	−28.3	−32.0	....	....	....	....	....	....			Net Primary Income from Abroad	98.n
1,417.3	1,552.6	1,716.5	1,910.1	2,025.9	2,167.2	2,337.2	3,001.0	....	....	....	....	....			Gross National Income (GNI)	99a
1,306.2	1,433.7	1,576.6	1,756.3	1,858.4	1,983.9	....	....	....	....	....	....	....			Net National Income	99e
1,329.2	1,433.3	1,555.3	1,744.3	1,827.0	2,033.8	2,201.6	2,307.3	2,402.0	2,552.8	2,616.4	2,807.2	3,051.9			GDP at Factor Cost	99ba
....	....	....	....	....	....	....	....	....	....	....	....	....			GDP at Fact.Cost,Vol.'68 Prices	99ba p
711.5	726.8	820.5	....	....	....	....	....	....	....	....	....	....			GDP at Fact.Cost,Vol.'77 Prices	99ba p
....	....	1,555.3	1,611.5	1,568.1	1,640.4	1,707.5	1,794.4	1,838.9	1,895.6	1,878.9	1,097.2	2,032.8			GDP at Fact.Cost,Vol.'89 Prices	99ba p
73.3	74.9	84.6	87.6	85.3	89.2	92.9	97.6	100.0	103.1	102.2	59.7	110.5			GDP Volume (1995=100)	99bv p
75.5	79.6	76.6	82.9	89.2	94.9	98.7	98.4	100.0	103.1	106.6	195.9	114.9			GDP Deflator (1995=100)	99bi p
Midyear Estimates																
.72	.72	†.75	.73	.74	.75	.77	.78	.80	.78	.79	.80	.81	.81	.83	Population	99z

(See notes in the back of the book.)

Finland

		1972	1973	1974	1975	1976	1977	1978	1979	1980	1981	1982	1983	1984	1985	1986
Exchange Rates														*Markkaa per SDR through 1998,*		
Official Rate	aa	4.5383	†4.6384	4.3477	4.5070	4.3766	4.8807	5.1148	4.8886	4.8976	5.0714	5.8366	6.0828	6.4008	5.9501	5.8640
													Markkaa per US Dollar through 1998;			
Official Rate	ae	4.1800	†3.8450	3.5510	3.8500	3.7670	4.0180	3.9260	3.7110	3.8400	4.3570	5.2910	5.8100	6.5300	5.4170	4.7940
Official Rate	rf	4.1463	3.8212	3.7738	3.6787	3.8644	4.0294	4.1173	3.8953	3.7301	4.3153	4.8204	5.5701	6.0100	6.1979	5.0695
														Markkaa per ECU:		
ECU Rate	ea	....	....	....	....	....	....	....	5.3509	5.0289	4.7282	5.1201	4.8072	4.6291	4.8098	5.1315
ECU Rate	eb	....	....	....	....	....	....	5.2453	5.3388	5.1886	4.8229	4.7298	4.9645	....	4.7240	4.9742
														Index Numbers (1995=100):		
Official Rate	ahx	105.2	114.3	115.7	118.8	112.9	108.4	106.0	112.0	117.0	101.3	91.0	78.4	72.7	70.8	86.1
Nominal Effective Exchange Rate	neu	117.5	115.8	118.8	117.7	120.3	114.1	102.7	102.5	106.1	109.1	110.9	106.0	108.3	108.8	106.9
Real Effective Exchange Rate	reu	....	....	....	100.1	106.3	100.6	130.4	128.3	†131.7	137.0	138.2	131.9	134.2	133.2	128.8
Fund Position														*Millions of SDRs:*		
Quota	2f.s	190.0	190.0	190.0	190.0	190.0	190.0	262.0	262.0	393.0	393.0	393.0	574.9	574.9	574.9	574.9
SDRs	1b.s	67.5	67.8	68.1	66.2	56.1	41.8	61.8	88.1	81.3	124.2	104.3	37.0	145.7	156.4	167.3
Reserve Position in the Fund	1c.s	63.8	63.8	63.8	—	—	—	46.1	44.7	77.4	77.4	77.5	123.0	133.7	130.3	135.0
of which: Outstg.Fund Borrowing	2c	—	—	—	—	—	—	—	—	—	—	—	—	—	—	—
Total Fund Cred.&Loans Outstg.	2tl	—	—	—	71.3	186.4	186.4	152.1	66.4	66.4	52.1	14.4	—	—	—	—
International Liquidity													*Millions of US Dollars Unless Otherwise Indicated:*			
Total Res.Min.Gold (Eurosys.Def)	1l.d	667.6	574.3	595.9	433.2	462.1	531.1	1,222.9	1,540.0	1,870.2	1,483.7	1,517.5	1,237.7	2,754.3	3,749.9	1,787.1
SDRs	1b.d	73.2	81.8	83.4	77.5	65.2	50.8	80.4	116.1	103.7	144.6	115.0	38.7	142.8	171.8	204.6
Reserve Position in the Fund	1c.d	69.2	76.9	78.1	—	—	—	60.0	58.8	98.8	90.1	85.5	128.7	131.1	143.1	165.2
Foreign Exchange	1d.d	525.2	415.6	434.4	355.7	396.9	480.3	1,082.4	1,365.1	1,667.7	1,249.0	1,317.0	1,070.3	2,480.4	3,435.0	1,417.4
o/w: Fin.Deriv.Rel.to Reserves	1dd d	....	....	....	....	....	....	....	....	....	....	....	....	....	....	....
Other Reserve Assets	1e.d	....	....	....	....	....	....	....	....	....	....	....	....	....	....	....
Gold (Million Fine Troy Ounces)	1ad	1.397	.823	.823	.823	.823	.905	.945	.986	.986	1.269	1.270	1.270	1.270	1.912	1.912
Gold (Eurosystem Valuation)	1an d	50.0e	31.0	34.1	31.4	32.1	33.1	43.0	289.1	279.4	317.2	261.2	238.0	211.8	384.2	434.1
Memo: Euro Cl. on Non-EA Res.	1dg d	....	....	....	....	....	....	....	....	....	....	....	....	....	....	....
Non-Euro Cl. on EA Res.	1dh d	....	....	....	....	....	....	....	....	....	....	....	....	....	....	....
Mon. Auth.: Other Foreign Assets	3..d	25.5	92.7	4.6	129.0	125.5	143.1	132.4	45.5	58.7	476.0	306.0	101.3	62.5	47.2	716.6
Foreign Liabilities	4..d	29.6	37.6	128.7	44.6	26.9	349.1	15.4	228.0	255.9	21.9	504.9	356.4	123.9	106.3	6.4
Banking Insts.: Foreign Assets	7a.d	418	531	686	593	718	1,136	1,401	2,026	2,762	3,231	4,154	4,777	6,258	7,671	14,310
Foreign Liab.	7b.d	354	490	815	1,209	1,332	1,693	1,778	2,788	4,566	4,909	6,293	7,205	9,441	12,812	20,531
Monetary Authorities													*Millions of Markkaa through 1998;*			
Fgn. Assets (Cl.on Non-EA Ctys)	11	3,047	2,710	2,258	2,290	2,339	2,848	5,501	6,970	8,480	9,920	13,263	11,387	20,126	22,651	14,084
Claims on General Government	12a.u	....														
o/w: Claims on Gen.Govt.in Cty	12a	196	223	300	335	442	391	633	884	1,226	1,236	1,041	2,178	1,951	1,023	1,002
Claims on Banking Institutions	12e.u	....														
o/w: Claims on Bank.Inst.in Cty	12e	946	2,792	3,558	4,260	3,845	4,979	2,220	4,229	6,035	3,769	4,542	8,464	6,727	7,596	13,314
Claims on Other Resident Sectors	12d.u	....														
o/w: Cl. on Oth.Res.Sect.in Cty	12d	328	393	763	1,181	1,586	1,559	1,418	1,698	2,424	3,390	4,386	4,793	5,068	5,143	5,479
Currency Issued	14a	1,895	2,098	2,462	2,855	2,885	3,167	3,822	4,375	4,954	5,595	6,062	6,574	7,442	8,072	8,667
Liabilities to Banking Insts	14c.u	....														
o/w: Liabs to Bank.Inst.in Cty	14c	2	2	8	4	4	5	2	1,768	3,318	2,492	3,138	5,041	8,843	10,222	9,270
Demand Dep. of Other Res.Sect.	14d.u	....														
o/w: D.Dep.of Oth.Res.Sect.in Cty	14d	1	8	1	3	—	—	7	1	1	1	1	2	62	67	56
Other Dep. of Other Res.Sect.	15..u	....														
o/w: O.Dep.of Oth.Res.Sect.in Cty	15	688	25	34	118	80	167	89	137	850	1,455	1,426	1,325	2,146	3,863	4,690
Money Market Instruments	16m.u	....														
o/w: MMI Held by Resid.of Cty	16m	....														
Bonds (Debt Securities)	16n.u	....														
o/w: Bonds Held by Resid.of Cty	16n	....														
Foreign Liab. (to Non-EA Ctys)	16c	122	147	457	493	917	2,312	838	1,171	1,308	359	2,755	2,071	809	576	31
Central Government Deposits	16d.u	....														
o/w: Cent.Govt.Dep. in Cty	16d	189	1,985	1,598	408	62	368	1,153	2,069	2,491	2,178	1,701	3,001	4,277	4,301	2,001
Capital Accounts	17a	932	972	1,021	1,896	1,992	2,136	2,259	2,469	2,408	4,476	4,865	5,237	6,955	7,013	6,723
Other Items (Net)	17r	690	883	1,298	2,291	2,272	1,622	1,602	1,789	2,836	1,757	3,284	3,572	3,338	2,300	2,442
Memo: Currency Put into Circ.	14m	....														
Banking Institutions													*Millions of Markkaa through 1998;*			
Claims on Monetary Authorities	20	366	335	319	351	345	342	342	486	3,971	3,263	4,028	5,985	10,415	12,159	11,592
Claims on Bk.Inst.in Oth.EA Ctys	20b.u	....														
Fgn. Assets (Cl.on Non-EA Ctys)	21	1,714	2,072	2,436	2,282	2,706	4,565	5,502	7,519	10,605	14,077	21,979	27,754	40,865	41,553	68,603
Claims on General Government	22a.u	....														
o/w: Claims on Gen.Govt.in Cty	22a	568	494	242	461	127	148	392	347	1,110	976	1,958	3,485	3,662	2,050	2,624
Claims on Other Resident Sectors	22d.u	....														
o/w: Cl. on Oth.Res.Sect.in Cty	22d	25,299	31,382	39,167	47,208	52,392	59,229	65,222	76,418	90,309	103,913	123,875	146,111	170,515	203,221	231,015
Demand Deposits	24..u	....														
o/w: D.Dep.of Oth.Res.Sect.in Cty	24	3,413	4,325	5,116	7,261	7,057	7,029	8,006	10,178	10,673	12,361	14,746	15,798	19,007	21,483	21,425
Other Deposits	25..u	....														
o/w: O.Dep.of Oth.Res.Sect.in Cty	25	20,712	23,555	27,601	32,854	37,010	42,068	48,388	56,524	65,600	75,758	85,719	98,611	113,168	134,052	146,223
Money Market Instruments	26m.u	....														
o/w: MMI Held by Resid.of Cty	26m	....														
Bonds (Debt Securities)	26n.u	....														
o/w: Bonds Held by Resid.of Cty	26n	....														
Foreign Liab. (to Non-EA Ctys)	26c	1,451	1,909	2,893	4,654	5,017	6,802	6,980	10,345	17,533	21,389	33,295	41,861	61,652	69,401	98,424
Central Government Deposits	26d.u	....														
o/w: Cent.Govt.Dep. in Cty	26d	1,543	2,170	2,633	1,766	2,663	2,618	4,315	3,371	3,420	4,769	6,193	5,959	6,820	7,467	15,510
Credit from Monetary Authorities	26g	941	2,757	3,508	3,911	4,912	4,894	2,256	3,356	6,044	3,722	4,493	8,432	6,670	7,572	13,140
Liab. to Bk.Inst.in Oth. EA Ctys	26h.u	....														
Capital Accounts	27a	1,303	1,786	1,638	1,880	1,934	1,969	2,095	2,428	2,872	3,012	3,936	4,873	6,669	7,488	9,175
Other Items (Net)	27r	−1,417	−2,219	−1,225	−2,026	−3,024	−1,097	−584	−1,432	−148	1,216	3,457	7,801	11,471	11,519	9,936

1987	1988	1989	1990	1991	1992	1993	1994	1995	1996	1997	1998	1999	2000	2001	
															Exchange Rates
Euros per SDR Thereafter: End of Period															
5.5980	5.6102	5.3342	5.1699	5.9120	7.2119	7.9454	6.9244	6.4790	6.6777	7.3139	7.1753	1.3662	1.4002	1.4260	Official Rate................ aa
Euros per US Dollar Thereafter: End of Period (ae) Period Average (rf)															
3.9460	4.1690	4.0590	3.6340	4.1330	5.2450	5.7845	4.7432	4.3586	4.6439	5.4207	5.0960	.9954	1.0747	1.1347	Official Rate................ ae
4.3956	4.1828	4.2912	3.8235	4.0440	4.4794	5.7123	5.2235	4.3667	4.5936	5.1914	5.3441	.9386	1.0854	1.1175	Official Rate................ rf
End of Period (ea) Period Average (eb)															
5.1432	4.8886	4.8586	4.9542	5.5419	6.3512	6.4785	5.8343	5.7282	5.8188	5.9856	5.9458	....	....	....	ECU Rate................ ea
5.0739	4.9520	4.7307	4.8673	5.0166	5.8090	6.6963	6.2084	5.7122	5.8245	5.8874	5.9855	....	....	....	ECU Rate................ eb
Period Averages															
99.4	104.0	101.8	114.3	108.2	97.8	76.4	83.9	100.0	95.0	84.1	81.7	....	....	....	Official Rate................ ahx
107.9	109.2	113.6	114.6	110.3	96.1	84.1	90.8	100.0	96.6	94.2	93.4	91.8	88.0	89.6	Nominal Effective Exchange Rate........ neu
126.9	129.7	133.6	134.6	123.7	102.0	86.4	90.6	100.0	92.5	87.2	86.0	82.9	79.0	79.7	Real Effective Exchange Rate........ reu
															Fund Position
End of Period															
574.9	574.9	574.9	574.9	574.9	861.8	861.8	861.8	861.8	861.8	861.8	861.8	1,263.8	1,263.8	1,263.8	Quota................ 2f.s
160.5	199.8	182.0	152.5	157.7	78.4	83.8	222.7	241.6	201.6	241.7	247.5	211.3	106.5	186.3	SDRs................ 1b.s
141.6	167.6	178.9	151.0	192.3	241.0	220.4	196.1	259.5	292.8	414.2	595.0	464.3	381.8	439.0	Reserve Position in the Fund 1c.s
—	—	—	—	—	—	—	—	—	—	—	31.3	—	—	—	of which: Outstg.Fund Borrowing 2c
—	—	—	—	—	—	—	—	—	—	—	—	—	—	—	Total Fund Cred.&Loans Outstg. 2tl
															International Liquidity
End of Period															
6,417.5	6,369.2	5,111.2	9,644.1	7,608.7	5,213.4	5,410.8	10,662.0	10,038.3	6,916.3	8,416.6	9,694.5	†8,207.3	8,464.7	7,982.8	Total Res.Min.Gold (Eurosys.Def) 1l.d
227.7	268.9	239.2	216.9	225.6	107.8	115.1	325.1	359.2	289.9	326.1	348.5	290.1	138.7	234.1	SDRs 1b.d
200.8	225.6	235.0	214.8	275.1	331.3	302.7	286.3	385.8	421.1	558.8	837.8	637.3	497.5	551.7	Reserve Position in the Fund 1c.d
5,989.0	5,874.7	4,636.9	9,212.4	7,108.0	4,774.3	4,993.0	10,050.6	9,293.4	6,205.3	7,531.7	8,508.2	6,747.0	7,330.5	7,192.0	Foreign Exchange 1d.d
....	....	....	....	....	....	....	....	....	....	....	....	533	498	5	o/w: Fin.Deriv.Rel.to Reserves....... 1dd d
															Other Reserve Assets 1e.d
1.955	1.955	2.002	2.002	2.002	2.002	2.002	2.003	1.600	1.600	1.600	2.002	1.577	1.577	1.577	Gold (Million Fine Troy Ounces)........ 1ad
539.3	510.4	537.1	599.9	527.5	415.6	376.9	459.6	399.7	375.1	321.4	427.8	458.0	433.0	436.0	Gold (Eurosystem Valuation) 1and
....	....	....	....	....	....	....	....	....	....	....	....	2,686	—	—	Memo: Euro Cl. on Non-EA Res. ... 1dgd
												682	799	653	Non-Euro Cl. on EA Res. ... 1dh d
325.4	257.4	22.7	20.6	8.2	...	...	...	...	...	...	...	†—	—	—	Mon. Auth.: Other Foreign Assets .... 3..d
34.1	59.3	171.8	270.6	11.2	452.7	33.4	27.5	278.6	201.2	107.8	143.9	†437.0	458.7	97.8	Foreign Liabilities .... 4..d
18,825	20,542	22,242	27,000	24,272	21,499	21,608	22,295	24,169	26,986	21,364	21,845	†15,715	19,914	35,258	Banking Insts.: Foreign Assets 7a.d
32,917	37,756	42,581	59,906	53,452	40,169	31,854	30,679	29,269	25,884	17,916	19,991	†9,370	15,328	27,775	Foreign Liab. 7b.d
															Monetary Authorities
Millions of Euros Beginning 1999: End of Period															
30,668	31,759	24,216	37,678	34,095	29,928	33,478	52,752	48,916	36,461	51,505	51,999	10,926	8,897	9,419	Fgn. Assets (Cl.on Non-EA Ctys) 11
													91	107	142	Claims on General Government 12a.u
977	1,039	1,137	1,314	1,376	2,447	1,788	1,806	1,882	1,907	2,015	2,074				o/w: Claims on Gen.Govt.in Cty ... 12a
												4,565	1,654	2,327	Claims on Banking Institutions ... 12e.u
3,639	12,095	36,542	13,075	15,648	11,547	7,575	1,718	8,415	13,301	2,837	19	1,513	471	1,294	o/w: Claims on Bank.Inst.in Cty ... 12e
												535	429	361	Claims on Other Resident Sectors 12d.u
5,188	5,204	4,681	3,793	3,054	2,921	4,404	3,951	3,302	2,462	1,877	1,541	234	171	106	o/w: Cl. on Oth.Res.Sect.in Cty ... 12d
9,990	11,550	13,129	14,555	14,528	14,508	14,994	14,315	15,611	16,891	17,817	17,689	3,350	3,336	2,687	Currency Issued 14a
												8,238	2,646	5,007	Liabilities to Banking Insts 14c.u
16,668	20,170	26,037	17,819	21,447	23,295	23,037	43,148	42,766	22,359	18,412	17,888	4,884	2,475	4,111	o/w: Liabs to Bank.Inst.in Cty ... 14c
												—	—	—	Demand Dep. of Other Res.Sect. ... 14d.u
36	31	38	36	—	—	—	—	—	—	—	—	—	—	—	o/w: D.Dep.of Oth.Res.Sect.in Cty 14d
												1	—	—	Other Dep. of Other Res.Sect. .... 15..u
4,831	6,497	10,228	9,925	7,057	3,362	2,087	1,549	994	574	32	6	1	—	—	o/w: O.Dep.of Oth.Res.Sect.in Cty 15
												—	—	—	Money Market Instruments 16m.u
															o/w: MMI Held by Resid.of Cty 16m
												—	—	—	Bonds (Debt Securities) 16n.u
															o/w: Bonds Held by Resid.of Cty 16n
135	247	697	983	46	2,375	193	130	1,214	934	584	733	435	493	111	Foreign Liab. (to Non-EA Ctys) 16c
												—	—	—	Central Government Deposits 16d.u
901	1,903	5,324	1,321	4	90	784	93	75	—	—	—	—	—	—	o/w: Cent.Govt.Dep. in Cty 16d
6,728	6,288	6,594	6,904	6,607	6,790	6,895	6,749	6,691	6,716	6,810	6,785	4,552	5,061	5,332	Capital Accounts 17a
1,183	3,412	4,529	4,317	4,483	-3,577	-745	-5,756	-4,836	6,658	14,579	12,533	-459	-449	-890	Other Items (Net) 17r
															Memo: Currency Put into Circ. 14m
															Banking Institutions
Millions of Euros Beginning 1999: End of Period															
18,642	23,990	29,863	22,400	27,162	29,983	27,638	46,653	45,976	25,604	21,711	20,774	4,884	2,475	4,111	Claims on Monetary Authorities 20
												5,775	7,515	3,951	Claims on Bk.Inst.in Oth.EA Ctys 20b.u
74,283	85,641	90,280	98,117	100,316	112,765	124,993	105,751	105,344	125,320	115,806	111,320	15,643	21,401	40,007	Fgn. Assets (Cl.on Non-EA Ctys) 21
												8,690	9,035	11,596	Claims on General Government 22a.u
2,662	2,487	2,205	1,993	†3,426	7,568	11,117	15,630	37,442	30,796	37,738	41,067	7,792	9,895		o/w: Claims on Gen.Govt.in Cty 22a
												65,481	70,733	78,285	Claims on Other Resident Sectors 22d.u
271,469	348,149	402,750	449,853	467,798	437,016	398,932	360,408	350,038	347,768	337,266	358,798	64,975	70,091	77,784	o/w: Cl. on Oth.Res.Sect.in Cty 22d
												38,335	37,129	39,014	Demand Deposits .... 24..u
23,047	27,472	32,634	34,837	†121,832	125,425	131,365	143,547	163,521	191,188	201,557	211,632	38,277	37,033	38,866	o/w: D.Dep.of Oth.Res.Sect.in Cty 24
												22,246	23,873	25,103	Other Deposits .... 25..u
165,112	204,011	218,087	228,976	†158,200	154,861	153,618	145,670	142,710	104,963	102,154	103,542	22,209	23,823	24,980	o/w: O.Dep.of Oth.Res.Sect.in Cty 25
												19,086	14,728	16,119	Money Market Instruments 26m.u
															o/w: MMI Held by Resid.of Cty 26m
												6,227	10,694	12,670	Bonds (Debt Securities) 26n.u
															o/w: Bonds Held by Resid.of Cty 26n
129,890	157,404	172,837	217,697	220,917	210,685	184,260	145,519	127,572	120,204	97,118	101,876	9,327	16,473	31,516	Foreign Liab. (to Non-EA Ctys) 26c
												2,553	4,368	1,697	Central Government Deposits 26d.u
17,715	17,068	16,884	21,058	11,314	9,843	10,174	11,250	19,057	19,881	27,569	17,951	2,552	4,368	1,696	o/w: Cent.Govt.Dep. in Cty 26d
2,843	10,844	36,011	12,419	†15,648	13,132	7,576	1,718	8,415	13,301	2,837	19	1,514	455	1,293	Credit from Monetary Authorities 26g
												3,153	1,964	2,397	Liab. to Bk.Inst.in Oth. EA Ctys 26h.u
10,618	14,842	20,404	38,623	49,103	38,497	38,496	31,789	31,579	29,799	34,003	34,113	6,763	8,156	16,986	Capital Accounts 27a
17,832	28,626	28,242	18,754	†21,689	34,890	37,190	48,948	45,947	50,152	47,285	62,826	-8,733	-6,683	-8,843	Other Items (Net) 27r

Finland

	1972	1973	1974	1975	1976	1977	1978	1979	1980	1981	1982	1983	1984	1985	1986
Banking Survey (Nat'l Residency)													*Millions of Markkaa through 1998;*		
Foreign Assets (Net) ... **31n**	3,188	2,727	1,345	−575	−889	−1,702	3,184	2,973	244	2,248	−809	−4,790	−1,471	−5,773	−15,768
Domestic Credit ... **32**	24,659	28,337	36,241	47,011	51,821	58,341	62,197	73,906	89,158	102,567	123,365	147,606	170,100	199,670	222,610
Claims on General Govt. (Net) ... **32an**	−969	−3,438	−3,689	−1,378	−2,156	−2,447	−4,443	−4,209	−3,575	−4,736	−4,896	−3,297	−5,483	−8,694	−13,884
Claims on Other Resident Sectors ... **32d**	25,628	31,775	39,930	48,389	53,978	60,788	66,640	78,115	92,733	107,303	128,261	150,903	175,583	208,364	236,494
Currency Issued ... **34a.n**	1,895	2,098	2,462	2,855	2,885	3,167	3,822	4,375	4,954	5,595	6,062	6,574	7,442	8,072	8,667
Demand Deposits ... **34b.n**	3,413	4,333	5,117	7,264	7,057	7,029	8,013	10,179	10,674	12,362	14,747	15,799	19,069	21,550	21,481
Other Deposits ... **35..n**	21,400	23,579	27,635	32,972	37,089	42,235	48,477	56,661	66,451	77,213	87,146	99,936	115,313	137,915	150,913
Money Market Instruments ... **36m**	....	....	....	....	....	....	....	....	....	....	....	....	....	....	....
Bonds (Debt Securities) ... **36n**	....	....	....	....	....	....	....	....	....	....	....	....	....	....	....
o/w: Bonds Over Two Years ... **36na**	....	....	....	....	....	....	....	....	....	....	....	....	....	....	....
Capital Accounts ... **37a**	2,235	2,758	2,659	3,776	3,926	4,105	4,354	4,897	5,279	7,489	8,801	10,111	13,624	14,501	15,898
Other Items (Net) ... **37r**	−1,097	−1,704	−287	−430	−25	102	715	767	2,044	2,156	5,801	10,397	13,181	11,859	9,882
Banking Survey (EA-Wide Residency)													*Millions of Euros:*		
Foreign Assets (Net) ... **31n.u**	....	....	....	....	....	....	....	....	....	....	....	....	....	....	....
Domestic Credit ... **32..u**	....	....	....	....	....	....	....	....	....	....	....	....	....	....	....
Claims on General Govt. (Net) ... **32an u**	....	....	....	....	....	....	....	....	....	....	....	....	....	....	....
Claims on Other Resident Sect. ... **32d.u**	....	....	....	....	....	....	....	....	....	....	....	....	....	....	....
Currency Issued ... **34a.u**	....	....	....	....	....	....	....	....	....	....	....	....	....	....	....
Demand Deposits ... **34b.u**	....	....	....	....	....	....	....	....	....	....	....	....	....	....	....
Other Deposits ... **35..u**	....	....	....	....	....	....	....	....	....	....	....	....	....	....	....
o/w: Other Dep. Over Two Yrs ... **35ab u**	....	....	....	....	....	....	....	....	....	....	....	....	....	....	....
Money Market Instruments ... **36m.u**	....	....	....	....	....	....	....	....	....	....	....	....	....	....	....
Bonds (Debt Securities) ... **36n.u**	....	....	....	....	....	....	....	....	....	....	....	....	....	....	....
o/w: Bonds Over Two Years ... **36na u**	....	....	....	....	....	....	....	....	....	....	....	....	....	....	....
Capital Accounts ... **37a**	....	....	....	....	....	....	....	....	....	....	....	....	....	....	....
Other Items (Net) ... **37r.u**	....	....	....	....	....	....	....	....	....	....	....	....	....	....	....
Liquid Liabilities ... **55l**	27,079	30,499	35,823	43,838	47,955	53,458	61,318	71,849	82,503	95,428	108,096	122,453	141,388	166,752	179,907
Interest Rates													*Percent Per Annum*		
Discount Rate *(End of Period)* ... **60**	7.75	9.25	9.25	9.25	9.25	8.25	7.25	8.50	9.25	9.25	8.50	9.50	9.50	9.00	7.00
Money Market Rate ... **60b**	....	....	....	....	....	....	11.75	9.26	12.35	11.46	11.66	14.67	16.50	13.46	11.90
Deposit Rate ... **60l**	....	....	....	....	....	....	....	....	....	9.00	8.56	8.75	9.25	8.75	7.33
Lending Rate ... **60p**	....	....	....	....	....	8.85	8.22	8.03	9.77	9.84	9.32	9.56	10.49	10.41	9.08
Government Bond Yield ... **61**	....	....	....	....	....	....	....	....	....	....	....	....	....	....	....
Prices, Production, Labor													*Index Numbers (1995=100):*		
Industrial Share Prices ... **62**	6.1	9.5	9.2	8.3	7.4	6.1	5.9	7.2	7.7	7.9	10.6	16.1	22.6	19.4	29.7
Prices: Domestic Supply ... **63**	23.2	27.3	33.9	†38.5	41.7	45.9	48.5	53.2	†61.9	69.8	74.8	79.0	83.2	86.9	82.4
Producer, Manufacturing ... **63ey**	21.9	26.5	33.3	†38.2	40.8	44.6	46.7	51.2	†59.4	64.5	71.2	74.8	79.0	82.3	78.8
Consumer Prices ... **64**	†18.4	20.4	23.8	28.1	32.1	†36.2	39.0	41.9	46.8	†52.4	57.4	62.2	66.6	†70.5	72.6
Harmonized CPI ... **64h**	....	....	....	....	....	....	....	....	....	....	....	....	....	....	....
Wages: Hourly Earnings ... **65ey**	12.7	14.8	17.7	†21.2	24.7	27.1	29.1	32.2	36.2	40.9	45.3	49.7	54.2	†58.3	61.9
Industrial Production ... **66..c**	47.8	51.2	53.5	51.6	52.1	52.4	55.0	60.9	†65.9	67.6	68.2	70.4	73.6	76.4	77.7
Industrial Employment ... **67ey c**	....	....	....	....	131.8	130.4	126.8	131.7	137.4	139.4	135.3	132.7	131.4	130.7	129.0
													Number in Thousands:		
Labor Force ... **67d**	....	....	....	....	....	....	....	....	....	....	....	....	....	....	....
Employment ... **67e**	....	....	....	....	....	....	....	....	....	....	....	....	....	2,466	2,458
Unemployment ... **67c**	....	....	....	....	....	....	....	....	....	....	....	....	....	129	138
Unemployment Rate (%) ... **67r**	....	....	....	....	....	....	....	....	....	....	....	....	....	5.0	5.4
International Transactions													*Millions of Markkaa through 1998*		
Exports ... **70**	12,082	14,609	20,687	20,246	24,506	30,931	35,206	43,430	52,804	60,308	63,026	69,751	80,923	83,976	82,699
Newsprint ... **70ul**	751	816	1,114	993	1,089	1,201	1,679	2,200	2,419	2,972	2,761	2,967	3,519	3,685	3,350
Imports, c.i.f. ... **71**	13,126	16,548	25,676	28,011	28,555	30,707	32,338	44,221	58,247	61,269	64,751	71,519	74,685	81,350	77,631
													1995=100		
Volume of Exports ... **72**	38.2	40.9	40.9	33.8	39.5	†43.6	46.9	51.4	55.9	57.5	56.3	58.2	64.5	64.2	64.8
Newsprint ... **72ul**	119.7	120.8	103.9	70.9	79.2	76.7	101.8	127.2	130.8	140.8	121.6	134.1	153.1	150.2	134.4
Volume of Imports ... **73**	52.2	59.2	63.7	63.7	61.1	†56.0	53.2	63.1	70.9	66.7	67.0	69.1	69.5	73.8	78.0
Unit Value of Exports ... **74**	18.0	20.3	28.8	33.9	34.9	†40.3	43.0	48.4	53.8	59.7	63.6	68.1	72.0	74.1	72.6
Newsprint ... **74ul**	19.7	21.2	33.6	43.9	43.2	49.1	51.8	54.3	58.0	66.2	71.2	69.4	72.1	77.0	78.2
Unit Value of Imports ... **75**	19.6	22.0	31.7	34.4	36.8	†42.7	47.1	54.8	63.7	71.3	74.7	79.9	83.4	86.1	77.1
Export Prices ... **76**	20.2	27.2	36.1	†39.8	41.7	44.9	47.5	53.0	†59.0	59.8	67.4	70.9	76.3	77.8	74.4
Import Prices ... **76.x**	23.5	28.2	39.3	†40.8	43.1	48.0	54.0	60.9	†71.7	71.2	83.9	89.2	93.5	95.9	81.5

	1987	1988	1989	1990	1991	1992	1993	1994	1995	1996	1997	1998	1999	2000	2001	
Millions of Euros Beginning 1999: End of Period																**Banking Survey (Nat'l Residency)**
	-25,074	-40,251	-59,038	-82,886	-86,552	-70,367	-25,982	12,854	25,474	40,643	69,609	60,710	20,914	22,122	21,904	Foreign Assets (Net) **31n**
	261,680	337,909	388,565	434,574	†464,336	440,018	405,283	370,451	373,532	363,052	351,327	385,529	70,449	73,650	86,089	Domestic Credit **32**
	-14,977	-15,445	-18,867	-19,072	†-6,516	81	1,947	6,092	20,192	12,821	12,184	25,190	5,240	3,388	8,199	Claims on General Govt. (Net) **32an**
	276,657	353,353	407,431	453,646	470,852	439,937	403,335	364,359	353,340	350,231	339,143	360,339	65,209	70,262	77,890	Claims on Other Resident Sectors **32d**
	9,990	11,550	13,129	14,555	14,528	14,508	14,994	14,315	15,611	16,891	17,817	17,689	3,350	3,336	2,687	Currency Issued **34a.n**
	23,083	27,503	32,672	34,873	121,832	125,425	131,365	143,547	163,521	191,188	201,557	211,632	38,277	37,033	38,866	Demand Deposits **34b.n**
	169,942	210,508	228,315	238,901	165,257	158,223	155,705	147,218	143,704	105,537	102,186	103,548	22,210	23,823	24,980	Other Deposits .... **35..n**
	....	....	....	....	....	....	....	....	....	....	....	....	19,086	14,728	16,119	Money Market Instruments **36m**
	....	....	....	....	....	....	....	....	....	....	....	....	6,227	10,694	12,670	Bonds (Debt Securities) **36n**
	....	....	....	....	....	....	....	....	....	....	....	....	4,985	8,682	9,419	o/w: Bonds Over Two Years **36na**
	17,345	21,130	26,997	45,527	55,709	45,287	45,391	38,538	38,270	36,514	40,813	40,897	11,315	13,217	22,318	Capital Accounts **37a**
	16,245	26,967	28,413	17,833	20,457	26,209	31,846	39,688	37,901	53,564	58,563	72,473	-9,104	-7,061	-9,647	Other Items (Net) **37r**
End of Period																**Banking Survey (EA-Wide Residency)**
	....	....	....	....	....	....	....	....	....	....	....	....	16,807	13,332	17,799	Foreign Assets (Net) .... **31n. u**
	....	....	....	....	....	....	....	....	....	....	....	....	72,244	75,936	88,687	Domestic Credit .... **32.. u**
	....	....	....	....	....	....	....	....	....	....	....	....	6,228	4,774	10,041	Claims on General Govt. (Net) .... **32an u**
	....	....	....	....	....	....	....	....	....	....	....	....	66,016	71,162	78,646	Claims on Other Resident Sect. .... **32d. u**
	....	....	....	....	....	....	....	....	....	....	....	....	3,350	3,336	2,687	Currency Issued .... **34a. u**
	....	....	....	....	....	....	....	....	....	....	....	....	38,335	37,129	39,014	Demand Deposits .... **34b. u**
	....	....	....	....	....	....	....	....	....	....	....	....	22,247	23,873	25,103	Other Deposits .... **35.. u**
	....	....	....	....	....	....	....	....	....	....	....	....	2,088	2,631	2,230	o/w: Other Dep. Over Two Yrs .... **35ab u**
	....	....	....	....	....	....	....	....	....	....	....	....	19,086	14,728	16,119	Money Market Instruments .... **36m. u**
	....	....	....	....	....	....	....	....	....	....	....	....	6,227	10,694	12,670	Bonds (Debt Securities) .... **36n. u**
	....	....	....	....	....	....	....	....	....	....	....	....	4,985	8,682	9,419	o/w: Bonds Over Two Years .... **36na u**
	....	....	....	....	....	....	....	....	....	....	....	....	11,315	13,217	22,318	Capital Accounts **37a**
	....	....	....	....	....	....	....	....	....	....	....	....	-11,511	-13,711	-11,425	Other Items (Net) .... **37r. u**
	201,436	247,681	271,105	284,690	†297,849	295,786	300,560	303,261	320,845	311,794	319,857	331,750	....	....	....	Liquid Liabilities **551**
Percent Per Annum																**Interest Rates**
	7.00	8.00	8.50	8.50	8.50	9.50	5.50	5.25	4.88	4.00	4.00	3.50	....	....	....	Discount Rate (End of Period) **60**
	10.03	9.97	12.56	14.00	13.08	13.25	7.77	5.35	5.75	3.63	3.23	3.57	2.96	4.39	4.26	Money Market Rate **60b**
	7.00	7.75	5.75	7.50	7.50	7.50	4.75	3.27	3.19	2.35	2.00	....	1.22	1.63	1.94	Deposit Rate **60l**
	8.91	9.72	10.31	11.62	11.80	12.14	9.92	7.91	7.75	6.16	5.29	5.35	4.71	5.61	5.79	Lending Rate **60p**
	....	....	....	....	....	....	8.8	9.0	8.8	....	....	....	4.7	5.5	5.0	Government Bond Yield **61**
Period Averages																**Prices, Production, Labor**
	†46.9	62.3	66.6	50.2	36.7	34.6	58.4	90.2	100.0	88.3	117.2	165.8	285.5	545.6	313.7	Industrial Share Prices **62**
	83.2	86.5	†90.9	93.9	94.2	95.2	†98.0	99.3	100.0	99.1	100.6	99.2	†99.1	107.3	107.7	Prices: Domestic Supply **63**
	79.4	83.0	†87.9	89.8	89.6	91.9	95.2	96.7	100.0	100.1						Producer, Manufacturing **63ey**
	75.5	79.4	84.6	89.8	93.5	95.9	98.0	99.0	†100.0	100.6	101.8	103.2	104.4	108.0	110.7	Consumer Prices **64**
	....	....	....	....	....	....			100.0	101.1	102.3	103.7	105.0	108.1	111.0	Harmonized CPI **64h**
	†66.2	71.6	78.1	†85.8	....	93.0	93.7	95.5	100.0	103.9						Wages: Hourly Earnings **65ey**
	81.7	84.5	87.3	†87.2	79.6	80.2	84.7	94.3	100.0	102.9	111.7	122.1	128.9	143.8	142.4	Industrial Production .... **66.. c**
	124.7	121.2	123.0	121.7	110.0	99.2	92.9	93.3	100.0	100.5	101.4	104.0	106.8	108.1	108.8	Industrial Employment .... **67ey c**
Period Averages																
	....	....	....	2,586	....	....	2,507	....	2,481	2,490	2,484	2,507	2,557	2,580	2,605	Labor Force **67d**
	2,452	2,458	2,531	2,504	2,402	2,233	†2,099	2,080	2,099	2,127	†2,169	2,222	2,296	2,336	2,347	Employment **67e**
	130	116	89	82	193	328	444	456	382	363	†315	285	261	253	238	Unemployment **67c**
	5.0	4.5	3.4	3.4	7.5	13.0	17.9	18.4	17.2	16.3	†12.6	11.4	10.2	9.8	9.1	Unemployment Rate (%) **67r**
Millions of Euros Beginning 1999																**International Transactions**
	87,706	90,901	99,854	101,380	93,088	107,471	133,962	153,690	172,380	176,592	204,202	229,233	†39,306	49,485	47,768	Exports **70**
	3,250	3,053	2,687	2,917	2,875	2,656	2,955	2,915	3,187	3,342	3,169	3,205	†593	594	....	Newsprint **70ul**
	85,799	88,555	104,782	103,066	87,821	94,984	103,162	119,897	122,428	134,422	154,681	172,315	†29,691	36,837	35,845	Imports, c.i.f. **71**
1995=100																
	65.9	67.6	67.3	69.8	63.7	69.3	82.1	93.3	100.0	105.6	118.4	....	....	....	....	Volume of Exports **72**
	131.6	109.9	98.7	109.9	106.0	104.6	113.6	115.1	100.0	92.7	107.5	109.6	111.7	....	....	Newsprint **72ul**
	84.4	92.2	102.1	97.9	81.6	79.4	77.3	92.9	100.0	107.8	117.0	....	....	....	....	Volume of Imports **73**
	74.2	78.0	83.7	82.8	82.8	88.2	92.5	94.1	100.0	100.0	101.6	....	....	....	....	Unit Value of Exports **74**
	77.5	87.1	85.4	83.2	85.1	79.7	81.6	79.5	100.0	113.2	92.5	91.8	....	....	....	Newsprint **74ul**
	75.8	77.7	80.4	81.5	83.4	92.4	103.8	100.6	100.0	101.9	105.1	....	....	....	....	Unit Value of Imports **75**
	75.6	79.3	84.1	†83.9	82.6	86.5	92.0	93.4	100.0	100.8	98.8	98.7	†94.4	101.9	101.3	Export Prices **76**
	80.2	79.7	83.0	†83.9	84.6	91.3	100.3	100.1	100.0	101.5	102.7	99.0	†99.6	112.7	109.5	Import Prices **76.x**

Finland

		1972	1973	1974	1975	1976	1977	1978	1979	1980	1981	1982	1983	1984	1985	1986
Balance of Payments														*Millions of US Dollars:*		
Current Account, n.i.e.	78al d	....	....	....	−2,140	−1,114	−99	680	−163	−1,403	−478	−923	−1,124	−21	−806	−693
Goods: Exports f.o.b.	78aa d				5,508	6,295	7,609	8,504	11,100	14,070	13,662	12,842	12,172	13,087	13,351	16,291
Goods: Imports f.o.b.	78ab d				−7,241	−6,978	−7,182	−7,427	−10,755	−14,752	−13,307	−12,641	−12,025	−11,607	−12,481	−14,587
Trade Balance	78ac d				−1,733	−684	427	1,077	345	−683	354	201	147	1,480	870	1,704
Services: Credit	78ad d				1,100	1,253	1,455	1,861	2,249	2,733	2,915	2,723	2,532	2,438	2,429	2,606
Services: Debit	78ae d				−1,103	−1,208	−1,376	−1,614	−2,009	−2,555	−2,603	−2,523	−2,515	−2,672	−2,920	−3,333
Balance on Goods & Services	78af d				−1,736	−639	506	1,324	584	−505	666	401	164	1,245	379	977
Income: Credit	78ag d				134	132	147	225	368	530	683	571	520	872	999	1,023
Income: Debit	78ah d				−504	−566	−709	−823	−1,011	−1,313	−1,716	−1,766	−1,670	−1,967	−2,014	−2,309
Balance on Gds, Serv. & Inc.	78ai d				−2,107	−1,073	−55	726	−59	−1,288	−367	−794	−986	150	−635	−310
Current Transfers, n.i.e.: Credit	78aj d				28	28	29	37	50	68	90	86	78	84	91	83
Current Transfers: Debit	78ak d				−61	−69	−73	−83	−154	−182	−201	−216	−216	−255	−262	−466
Capital Account, n.i.e.	78bc d				−2	−3	−6	−6	−6	−7	−5	−6	−5	−4	−5	—
Capital Account, n.i.e.: Credit	78ba d				—	—	—	—	—	—	—	—	—	—	—	—
Capital Account: Debit	78bb d				−2	−3	−6	−6	−6	−7	−5	−6	−5	−4	−5	—
Financial Account, n.i.e.	78bj d				2,166	725	498	−54	638	1,515	120	1,130	814	2,344	1,433	−2,079
Direct Investment Abroad	78bd d				−26	−31	−72	−63	−125	−137	−129	−78	−139	−492	−348	−760
Dir. Invest. in Rep. Econ., n.i.e.	78be d				68	58	48	34	28	28	100	1	84	136	113	348
Portfolio Investment Assets	78bf d				—	—	—	—	−13	−120	13	−3	−31	−66	−191	−516
Equity Securities	78bk d				—	—	—	—	—	−2	−1	−1	—	−13	14	−1
Debt Securities	78bl d				—	—	—	—	−13	−119	14	−2	−31	−53	−205	−514
Portfolio Investment Liab., n.i.e.	78bg d				233	174	224	694	162	154	317	517	364	1,339	1,534	1,992
Equity Securities	78bm d				—	—	—	—	—	—	—	—	—	—	—	203
Debt Securities	78bn d				233	174	224	694	162	154	317	517	364	1,339	1,534	1,790
Financial Derivatives Assets	78bw d				....	....	....	....	....	....	....	....	....	....	....	....
Financial Derivatives Liabilities	78bx d				....	....	....	....	....	....	....	....	....	....	....	....
Other Investment Assets	78bh d				−98	−428	−507	−691	−765	−1,480	−1,812	−2,237	−1,332	−1,652	−177	−2,434
Monetary Authorities	78bo d				....	....	....	....	....	....	....	....	....	....	....	−629
General Government	78bp d				−268	15	86	−19	87	−32	−456	−310	108	356	−28	−81
Banks	78bq d				2	−106	−341	−188	−444	−725	−859	−1,786	−1,064	−2,200	−31	−1,666
Other Sectors	78br d				168	−336	−252	−483	−407	−723	−497	−142	−376	193	−118	−59
Other Investment Liab., n.i.e.	78bi d				1,989	951	804	−28	1,351	3,071	1,631	2,931	1,867	3,079	502	−708
Monetary Authorities	78bs d				−76	−19	322	−334	207	38	−220	485	−139	−218	−26	−116
General Government	78bt d				101	119	129	152	282	127	214	300	146	146	−1	−35
Banks	78bu d				466	92	335	18	860	1,890	744	2,038	1,328	2,707	1,069	1,215
Other Sectors	78bv d				1,497	759	19	136	2	1,015	893	108	532	444	−540	−1,772
Net Errors and Omissions	78ca d				−240	281	−348	89	−84	175	143	−5	89	−495	−38	489
Overall Balance	78cb d				−217	−112	45	709	385	280	−220	196	−227	1,824	583	−2,283
Reserves and Related Items	79da d				217	112	−45	−709	−385	−280	220	−196	227	−1,824	−583	2,283
Reserve Assets	79db d				129	−20	−45	−665	−274	−280	237	−155	243	−1,824	−583	2,283
Use of Fund Credit and Loans	79dc d				89	132	—	−44	−110	—	−17	−42	−16	—	—	—
Exceptional Financing	79de d				....	....	....	....	....	....	....	....	....	....	....	....
International Investment Position															*Millions of US Dollars*	
Assets	79aa d				3,746	4,321	4,811	6,425	8,179	10,064	10,473	11,310	11,658	14,365	17,769	20,880
Direct Investment Abroad	79ab d				318	356	397	471	626	737	550	671	754	1,306	1,829	2,342
Portfolio Investment	79ac d				34	—	—	—	13	132	104	90	111	159	438	1,040
Equity Securities	79ad d				—	—	—	—	—	2	3	3	3	15	3	5
Debt Securities	79ae d				34	—	—	—	13	130	101	86	108	144	435	1,036
Financial Derivatives	79al d				—	—	—	—	—	—	—	—	—	—	—	—
Other Investment	79af d				2,929	3,469	3,848	4,685	5,707	7,046	8,018	8,771	9,319	9,879	11,368	15,277
Monetary Authorities	79ag d				337	345	374	412	330	460	845	1,076	960	497	536	1,256
General Government	79ah d				247	279	165	210	227	241	266	266	286	300	415	553
Banks	79ai d				516	593	1,004	1,222	1,765	2,356	2,852	3,815	4,424	5,916	5,926	8,455
Other Sectors	79aj d				1,830	2,252	2,305	2,842	3,385	3,989	4,055	3,615	3,648	3,167	4,491	5,013
Reserve Assets	79ak d				466	495	565	1,268	1,832	2,150	1,801	1,779	1,476	3,020	4,134	2,221
Liabilities	79la d				8,837	10,421	11,645	13,048	14,809	17,536	18,831	20,068	21,249	23,755	27,947	32,880
Dir. Invest. in Rep. Economy	79lb d				292	397	427	480	533	540	1,202	1,044	1,013	1,040	1,339	1,680
Portfolio Investment	79lc d				873	1,118	1,512	2,438	2,582	2,640	2,825	3,220	3,556	4,539	6,851	10,014
Equity Securities	79ld d				—	—	—	—	—	—	—	—	—	—	—	702
Debt Securities	79le d				873	1,118	1,512	2,438	2,582	2,640	2,825	3,220	3,556	4,539	6,851	9,312
Financial Derivatives	79ll d				—	—	—	—	—	—	—	—	—	—	—	—
Other Investment	79lf d				7,672	8,906	9,706	10,130	11,695	14,356	14,805	15,803	16,680	18,177	19,757	21,186
Monetary Authorities	79lg d				339	467	807	495	601	742	451	869	832	558	595	546
General Government	79lh d				232	350	505	719	1,021	1,085	1,252	1,459	1,487	1,460	1,746	2,028
Banks	79li d				1,205	1,325	1,630	1,685	2,659	4,410	4,807	6,146	7,025	8,849	9,798	12,236
Other Sectors	79lj d				5,896	6,765	6,765	7,231	7,413	8,119	8,295	7,328	7,336	7,310	7,619	6,376

	1987	1988	1989	1990	1991	1992	1993	1994	1995	1996	1997	1998	1999	2000	2001		
Minus Sign Indicates Debit																**Balance of Payments**	
	-1,731	-2,694	-5,797	-6,962	-6,807	-5,116	-1,135	1,110	5,231	5,003	6,633	7,340	7,657	9,038	8,357	Current Account, n.i.e.	78al d
	19,526	22,202	23,249	26,531	23,098	24,101	23,587	29,881	40,558	40,725	41,148	43,393	41,983	45,703	42,980	Goods: Exports f.o.b.	78aa d
	-18,019	-21,001	-23,479	-25,829	-20,660	-20,093	-17,138	-22,158	-28,121	-29,411	-29,604	-30,903	-29,815	-32,019	-30,323	Goods: Imports f.o.b.	78ab d
	1,507	1,200	-229	701	2,438	4,009	6,449	7,723	12,437	11,314	11,544	12,490	12,168	13,684	12,657	*Trade Balance*	78ac d
	3,338	3,833	4,057	4,649	4,101	4,656	4,412	5,490	7,415	7,129	6,640	6,698	6,522	6,169	5,796	Services: Credit	78ad d
	-4,521	-5,507	-6,198	-7,627	-7,684	-7,577	-6,637	-7,335	-9,584	-8,817	-8,235	-7,767	-7,952	-8,473	-8,221	Services: Debit	78ae d
	324	-474	-2,371	-2,276	-1,145	1,088	4,225	5,878	10,268	9,627	9,949	11,421	10,738	11,381	10,232	*Balance on Goods & Services*	78af d
	1,496	2,368	2,513	3,505	2,598	1,536	1,154	1,789	2,879	2,868	4,136	4,237	5,664	7,265	8,445	Income: Credit	78ag d
	-3,074	-4,090	-5,192	-7,239	-7,279	-6,946	-6,086	-6,103	-7,318	-6,503	-6,600	-7,320	-7,712	-8,989	-9,637	Income: Debit	78ah d
	-1,253	-2,196	-5,050	-6,010	-5,827	-4,322	-707	1,564	5,828	5,992	7,485	8,338	8,690	9,657	9,041	*Balance on Gds, Serv. & Inc.*	78ai d
	111	367	222	288	345	427	475	410	1,536	1,253	1,210	1,523	1,608	1,715	1,549	Current Transfers, n.i.e.: Credit	78aj d
	-589	-865	-969	-1,240	-1,326	-1,221	-903	-863	-2,133	-2,242	-2,062	-2,521	-2,641	-2,334	-2,233	Current Transfers: Debit	78ak d
	—	—	—	—	-71	—	—	—	66	56	247	91	84	92	65	Capital Account, n.i.e.	78bc d
	—	—	—	—	—	—	—	—	114	130	247	91	149	100	75	Capital Account, n.i.e.: Credit	78ba d
	—	—	—	—	-71	—	—	—	-48	-74	—	—	-65	-7	-10	Capital Account: Debit	78bb d
	7,135	2,101	3,471	12,405	4,196	3,071	374	4,093	-4,284	-7,718	-2,976	-1,722	-6,379	-8,841	-10,973	Financial Account, n.i.e.	78bj d
	-1,141	-2,624	-2,968	-2,782	120	757	-1,401	-4,354	-1,494	-3,583	-5,260	-18,698	-6,739	-23,898	-8,363	Direct Investment Abroad	78bd d
	265	532	490	812	-233	396	864	1,496	1,044	1,118	2,129	12,029	4,649	9,125	3,427	Dir. Invest. in Rep. Econ., n.i.e.	78be d
	-612	-481	-61	-469	-334	-622	-604	775	204	-4,186	-4,600	-3,906	-15,699	-18,920	-11,594	Portfolio Investment Assets	78bf d
	-9	-14	-62	1	87	-10	-151	-78	-209	-736	-1,694	-2,099	-5,527	-7,164	-5,153	Equity Securities	78bk d
	-603	-467	1	-470	-421	-612	-452	853	414	-3,450	-2,906	-1,807	-10,173	-11,756	-6,441	Debt Securities	78bl d
	2,227	3,538	3,752	5,696	8,610	8,243	6,836	6,180	-1,779	1,153	3,843	3,866	13,550	17,116	5,985	Portfolio Investment Liab., n.i.e.	78bg d
	133	111	304	96	20	89	2,216	2,541	2,027	1,915	4,023	7,931	10,279	10,114	3,960	Equity Securities	78bm d
	2,093	3,427	3,448	5,600	8,590	8,154	4,620	3,640	-3,807	-761	-181	-4,065	3,271	7,002	2,025	Debt Securities	78bn d
	....	....	....	....	—	—	—	51	38	38	-72	89	—	—	....	Financial Derivatives Assets	78bw d
	....	....	....	....	—	—	—	5	600	325	114	-725	-419	-630	38	Financial Derivatives Liabilities	78bx d
	1,261	-1,723	-1,717	720	-2,965	-3,285	-1,832	-668	-2,863	-4,683	-2,201	331	-3,288	-5,636	-10,118	Other Investment Assets	78bh d
	52	85	428	151	-1	-416	-29	99	146	27	94	145	-307	-129	77	Monetary Authorities	78bo d
	-75	-97	-97	-82	-83	-275	-344	-445	-366	-719	-609	-126	-224	-171	-967	General Government	78bp d
	1,326	-1,155	-1,208	935	-1,900	-896	-987	-511	-1,926	-3,815	-1,725	41	-1,566	-4,107	-8,197	Banks	78bq d
	-42	-555	-840	-284	-981	-1,698	-472	189	-717	-175	39	270	-1,191	-1,229	-1,032	Other Sectors	78br d
	5,136	2,858	3,974	8,428	-1,003	-2,418	-3,488	607	-35	2,099	3,072	5,292	1,567	14,001	9,652	Other Investment Liab., n.i.e.	78bi d
	-16	-11	59	96	-251	1,244	-298	-107	92	-96	-173	-180	-872	1,433	282	Monetary Authorities	78bs d
	-62	-436	-344	-104	257	255	983	965	-331	764	1,478	394	-420	-1,272	467	General Government	78bt d
	4,635	3,336	1,936	4,764	-414	-5,034	-4,970	-1,088	869	-626	1,876	3,607	-154	4,098	8,703	Banks	78bu d
	579	-31	2,323	3,672	-595	1,117	796	837	-666	2,056	-110	1,471	3,014	9,742	200	Other Sectors	78bv d
	-1,371	851	1,258	-1,512	796	-105	1,053	-489	-1,384	-375	-1,600	-5,412	-1,349	70	2,956	Net Errors and Omissions	78ca d
	4,033	258	-1,068	3,931	-1,886	-2,150	291	4,714	-372	-3,036	2,304	296	13	359	405	*Overall Balance*	78cb d
	-4,033	-258	1,068	-3,931	1,886	2,150	-291	-4,714	372	3,036	-2,304	-296	-13	-359	-405	Reserves and Related Items	79da d
	-4,033	-258	1,068	-3,931	1,886	2,150	-291	-4,714	372	3,036	-2,304	-296	-13	-359	-405	Reserve Assets	79db d
	—	—	—	—	—	—	—	—	—	—	—	—	—	—	—	Use of Fund Credit and Loans	79dc d
	....	....	....	....	....	....	....	....	....	....	....	....	....	....	....	Exceptional Financing	79de d
Millions of US Dollars																**International Investment Position**	
	30,344	32,180	35,473	45,048	44,118	39,957	40,838	51,570	57,970	65,385	71,091	85,854	109,967	148,101	166,438	Assets	79aa d
	4,433	5,708	7,938	11,227	10,845	8,565	9,178	12,534	14,993	17,666	20,297	29,407	33,850	52,109	57,632	Direct Investment Abroad	79ab d
	1,949	2,330	2,280	2,582	2,803	3,257	4,067	3,417	3,572	7,713	11,659	16,825	33,621	51,125	55,905	Portfolio Investment	79ac d
	17	30	96	210	103	89	308	418	738	1,564	3,245	5,271	13,670	20,263	20,157	Equity Securities	79ad d
	1,932	2,300	2,185	2,372	2,700	3,168	3,758	2,999	2,835	6,149	8,414	11,554	19,951	30,862	35,748	Debt Securities	79ae d
	—	—	—	—	—	—	77	103	41	-5	259	151	3,469	2,816	2,073	Financial Derivatives	79al d
	17,005	17,262	19,606	20,994	22,333	22,510	21,729	24,395	28,153	32,173	29,385	29,684	30,348	33,636	42,407	Other Investment	79af d
	1,430	1,276	848	729	659	928	874	969	911	830	617	1,078	821	886	767	Monetary Authorities	79ag d
	755	811	936	1,411	1,415	1,521	1,841	2,481	2,966	3,636	3,497	3,611	3,670	3,460	4,352	General Government	79ah d
	8,830	8,896	10,487	10,997	12,164	11,301	10,933	12,021	14,203	17,872	18,430	18,004	18,169	20,957	31,303	Banks	79ai d
	5,990	6,279	7,335	7,857	8,095	8,759	8,081	8,924	10,073	9,835	6,842	6,992	7,688	8,334	5,986	Other Sectors	79aj d
	6,957	6,880	5,648	10,245	8,137	5,626	5,788	11,122	11,210	7,839	9,490	9,787	8,679	8,415	8,420	Reserve Assets	79ak d
	47,511	51,754	61,646	84,362	86,073	83,423	85,949	107,281	111,245	118,245	119,705	186,126	327,251	330,167	261,225	Liabilities	79la d
	2,620	3,040	3,965	5,132	4,220	3,689	4,217	6,714	8,465	8,797	9,530	16,455	18,320	24,272	25,411	Dir. Invest. in Rep. Economy	79lb d
	14,358	17,193	21,277	34,243	40,475	44,974	53,875	69,508	69,408	75,311	76,436	131,124	267,648	253,376	176,145	Portfolio Investment	79lc d
	1,159	1,279	2,007	1,390	1,004	979	5,251	12,767	14,625	23,457	28,870	79,722	219,531	204,361	128,284	Equity Securities	79ld d
	13,198	15,914	19,270	32,853	39,471	43,995	48,624	56,741	54,782	51,855	47,566	51,403	48,116	49,015	47,861	Debt Securities	79le d
	—	—	—	—	—	—	-1,055	-1,092	354	723	1,153	229	2,965	1,925	1,633	Financial Derivatives	79ll d
	30,533	31,521	36,404	44,987	41,378	34,760	28,913	32,151	33,018	33,414	32,586	38,317	38,319	50,594	58,037	Other Investment	79lf d
	649	610	690	876	558	1,301	908	996	1,176	1,018	713	734	-690	614	887	Monetary Authorities	79lg d
	2,429	1,791	1,403	1,412	1,551	1,689	2,767	4,016	3,886	4,299	5,340	6,133	5,575	4,040	4,273	General Government	79lh d
	19,413	21,525	24,323	27,789	25,905	19,348	12,708	12,620	13,824	12,527	13,003	16,135	14,484	17,825	31,360	Banks	79li d
	8,042	7,595	9,988	14,909	13,363	12,423	12,530	14,519	14,133	15,570	13,530	15,316	18,951	28,115	21,517	Other Sectors	79lj d

Finland

172

		1972	1973	1974	1975	1976	1977	1978	1979	1980	1981	1982	1983	1984	1985	1986
Government Finance																
Central Government													*Millions of Markkaa through 1998;*			
Deficit (-) or Surplus	80	†715	2,044	755	–2,315	–32	–1,938	–2,645	–4,105	–4,154	–1,968	–5,070	–7,965	–3,111	–2,702	394
Total Revenue and Grants	81y	....														
Revenue	81	†15,359	19,212	23,355	28,604	35,865	38,897	40,280	44,938	52,050	61,518	68,775	77,049	87,235	98,617	111,091
Grants	81z	†286	306	346	496	696	734	781	882	910	1,022	1,297	1,498	1,798	1,865	2,305
Exp. & Lending Minus Repay.	82z	†14,930	17,474	22,946	31,415	36,593	41,569	43,706	49,925	57,114	64,508	75,142	86,512	92,144	103,184	113,002
Expenditure	82	†14,073	16,275	21,465	28,920	33,305	37,679	41,275	47,702	53,858	61,878	72,671	84,892	90,321	100,887	110,383
Lending Minus Repayments	83	†857	1,199	1,481	2,495	3,288	3,890	2,431	2,223	3,256	2,630	2,471	1,620	1,823	2,297	2,619
Total Financing	80h	†–715	–2,044	–755	2,315	32	1,938	2,645	4,105	4,154	1,968	5,070	7,965	3,111	2,702	–394
Total Net Borrowing	84															
Net Domestic	84a	†–679	–1,882	–567	1,927	–556	1,210	–358	1,822	2,632	–349	2,297	5,541	414	1,096	–322
Net foreign	85a	†–36	–162	–188	388	588	728	3,003	2,283	1,522	2,317	2,773	2,424	2,697	1,606	–72
Use of Cash Balances	87															
Total Debt by Currency	88	3,842	3,192	2,718	3,630	4,627	6,718	12,227	15,218	17,983	22,109	30,251	37,681	44,064	46,776	51,852
Domestic	88b	....	....	....	....	....	....	....	....	....	....	....	....	....	....	....
Foreign	89b	....	....	....	....	....	....	....	....	....	....	....	....	....	....	....
Financing (By Currency)																
Net Borrowing	84	....	....	....	....	....	....	....	....	....	....	....	....	....	....	....
By Currency																
Debt: Markkaa	88b	....	....	....	....	....	....	....	....	....	....	....	....	....	....	....
Foreign Currency	89b	....	....	....	....	....	....	....	....	....	....	....	....	....	....	....
General Government															*As Percent of*	
Deficit (-) or Surplus	80g	....	....	....	....	....	....	....	....	....	....	....	....	....	....	....
Debt	88g	....	....	....	....	....	....	....	....	....	....	....	....	....	....	....
National Accounts															*Billions of Markkaa through 1998;*	
Househ.Cons.Expend.,incl.NPISHs	96f	33.04	39.27	47.81	56.76	65.09	71.95	79.43	90.47	102.73	116.09	132.88	147.90	163.11	178.66	190.97
Government Consumption Expend.	91f	8.97	10.70	13.70	18.85	22.53	25.46	27.66	31.25	36.43	42.44	48.09	54.84	61.26	69.60	75.88
Gross Fixed Capital Formation	93e	16.37	20.56	26.86	34.67	35.10	37.59	36.97	39.88	52.15	58.62	66.31	74.58	78.69	86.00	90.31
Changes in Inventories	93i	.08	1.29	4.99	2.20	–.09	–4.82	–3.80	5.53	6.06	1.01	–.58	–1.57	–.18	.94	–.87
Exports of Goods and Services	90c	14.95	18.15	24.79	24.31	29.31	36.74	42.76	52.09	62.94	72.79	75.92	83.57	95.25	98.65	95.60
Imports of Goods and Services (-)	98c	14.80	18.60	28.10	30.71	31.86	34.78	37.42	49.91	65.01	69.64	73.83	82.23	87.35	95.81	90.57
Gross Domestic Product (GDP)	99b	58.61	71.37	90.05	106.08	120.08	132.14	145.59	169.30	195.29	221.31	248.77	277.08	310.79	338.04	361.33
Net Primary Income from Abroad	98.n	–.65	–.82	–1.04	–1.36	–1.67	–2.27	–2.46	–2.51	–2.93	–4.45	–5.73	–6.39	–6.60	–6.30	–6.52
Gross National Income (GNI)	99a	57.97	70.56	89.01	104.72	118.35	129.87	143.13	166.78	192.36	216.86	243.05	270.69	304.19	331.74	354.80
Consumption of Fixed Capital	99cf	8	9	12	16	19	22	24	27	32	36	41	46	51	55	60
Net Current Transf.from Abroad	98t	....	....	....	–.13	–.17	–.20	–.21	–.30	–.40	–.50	–.64	–.80	–1.01	–1.10	–1.94
Gross Nat'l Disposable Inc.(GNDI)	99i	....	....	....	104.59	118.17	129.67	142.92	166.48	191.96	216.37	242.41	269.89	303.18	330.64	352.87
Gross Saving	99s	....	....	....	28.97	30.57	32.27	35.83	44.77	52.81	57.84	61.44	67.16	78.82	82.37	86.02
Net National Income	99e	50.44	61.22	76.75	87.17	98.03	106.66	117.77	138.27	159.79	179.61	201.66	224.24	252.92	276.12	295.41
GDP Volume 1980 prices	99b.p	148.12	158.07	162.86	164.73	....	....	....	....	....	....	....	....	....	....	....
GDP Volume 1995 Prices	99b.p	....	....	....	373.57	373.20	374.46	383.19	409.12	430.00	439.27	453.05	465.47	481.38	496.33	508.69
GDP Volume (1995=100)	99bv p	59.5	63.5	65.4	66.2	66.1	66.3	67.9	72.5	76.2	77.8	80.2	82.4	85.3	87.9	90.1
GDP Deflator (1995=100)	99bi p	17.4	19.9	24.4	28.4	32.2	35.3	38.0	41.4	45.4	50.4	54.9	59.5	64.6	68.1	71.0
																Millions:
Population	99z	4.64	4.67	4.69	4.71	4.73	4.74	4.75	4.76	4.78	4.80	4.83	4.86	4.88	4.90	4.92

Government Finance

Central Government

Millions of Euros Beginning 1999; Year Ending December 31

Indicator	Code	1987	1988	1989	1990	1991	1992	1993	1994	1995	1996	1997	1998	1999	2000	2001
Deficit (-) or Surplus	80	-6,690	1,754	8,807	945	-34,096	-70,346	-64,554	-58,781	-53,599	-36,571	-15,523	-1,904	3,235	4,515	1,006
Total Revenue and Grants	81y				164,108	158,314	161,995	165,820	173,827	187,954	199,273	205,870	226,344	35,669	38,937	35,974
Revenue	81	114,733	134,761	151,922	160,241	154,141	156,114	160,235	168,307	178,584	192,955	199,126	221,033	35,669	38,937	35,974
Grants	81z	2,355	2,512	3,633	3,867	4,173	5,881	5,585	5,520	9,370	6,318	6,744	5,311	—	—	—
Exp. & Lending Minus Repay.	82z	123,778	135,519	146,748	163,163	192,410	232,341	230,374	232,608	241,553	235,844	221,394	228,250	32,434	34,421	34,967
Expenditure	82	121,278	132,038	143,593	158,673	184,225	203,201	218,612	223,119	232,883	231,425	219,527	230,509	32,651	34,352	33,967
Lending Minus Repayments	83	2,500	3,481	3,155	4,490	8,185	29,140	11,762	9,489	8,670	4,419	1,867	-2,259	-217	69	1,000
Total Financing	80h	6,690	-1,754	-8,807	-945	34,096	70,346	64,554	58,751	53,599	36,571	15,524	1,906	-3,236	-4,516	-1,004
Total Net Borrowing	84								58,781	53,599	36,571	15,524	1,906	-3,413	-4,505	-1,286
Net Domestic	84a	4,176	-59	-5,920	-4,377	11,301	19,449	15,431	26,024	53,823	36,203	34,420	9,721	-3,413	-4,505	-1,286
Net foreign	85a	2,514	-1,695	-2,887					32,727	-224	368	-18,896	-7,815			
Use of Cash Balances	87													177	-11	282
Total Debt by Currency	88	58,511	58,084	55,394	56,654	87,915	171,930	272,778	314,285	362,202	396,718	419,346	421,390	68,052	63,435	61,760
Domestic	88b								123,434	174,874	196,836	210,088	211,413	57,008	53,844	52,678
Foreign	89b								190,851	187,328	199,882	209,258	209,977	11,044	9,590	9,082

Financing (By Currency)

Indicator	Code	1994	1995	1996	1997	1998
Net Borrowing	84	58,781	53,599	36,571	15,524	1,906

By Currency

Indicator	Code	1994	1995	1996	1997	1998	1999	2000	2001
Debt: Markkaa	88b	123,434	174,874	196,836	210,088	211,413	57,008	53,844	52,678
Foreign Currency	89b	190,851	187,328	199,882	209,258	209,977	11,044	9,590	9,082

General Government

Gross Domestic Product

Indicator	Code	1990	1991	1992	1993	1994	1995	1996	1997	1998	1999	2000	2001
Deficit (-) or Surplus	80g	5.4	-1.5	-5.9	-8.0	-6.4	-4.6	-3.2	-1.5	1.3	1.9	7.0	4.9
Debt	88g	14.5	23.0	41.5	58.0	59.6	58.1	57.1	54.1	48.8	46.8	44.0	43.6

National Accounts

Billions of Euros Beginning in 1999

Indicator	Code	1987	1988	1989	1990	1991	1992	1993	1994	1995	1996	1997	1998	1999	2000	2001
Househ.Cons.Expend.,incl.NPISHs	96f	207.12	228.47	251.53	263.59	268.45	267.38	269.14	278.70	292.12	308.50	323.56	346.02	†61.15	64.90	67.59
Government Consumption Expend.	91f	83.46	90.89	100.05	112.94	124.04	123.89	119.72	122.15	128.91	135.63	142.64	149.43	†26.12	27.07	28.60
Gross Fixed Capital Formation	93e	100.43	119.60	146.28	149.58	121.78	96.92	80.62	80.85	91.97	99.73	114.30	128.91	†22.83	25.29	26.70
Changes in Inventories	93i	.02	7.58	8.16	5.67	-10.52	-6.16	-.99	9.67	6.82	-2.32	3.18	4.34	†-.11	.95	.40
Exports of Goods and Services	90c	100.19	108.73	117.06	119.00	109.89	128.77	159.92	183.33	209.14	219.91	248.31	267.47	†45.57	56.31	54.53
Imports of Goods and Services (-)	98c	98.71	110.79	127.12	127.75	114.28	123.87	135.80	152.39	164.40	175.59	196.46	206.65	†35.45	44.03	42.65
Gross Domestic Product (GDP)	99b	392.52	444.48	495.96	523.03	499.36	486.92	492.61	522.31	564.57	585.87	635.53	689.52	†120.48	131.23	135.06
Net Primary Income from Abroad	98.n	-6.92	-7.17	-11.50	-14.19	-18.86	-24.19	-28.08	-22.76	-20.63	-16.90	-12.70	-16.83	†-1.96	-1.96	-2.23
Gross National Income (GNI)	99a	385.60	437.31	484.46	508.84	480.50	462.73	464.53	499.55	543.93	568.97	622.83	672.69	†118.52	129.27	132.82
Consumption of Fixed Capital	99cf	66	73	83	93	96	96	98	100	102	103	106	112	†19.56	20.96	22.11
Net Current Transf.from Abroad	98t	-2.10	-2.07	-3.21	-3.64	-3.90	-3.51	-2.45	-2.42	-.75	-3.78	-3.61	-5.43	†-.97	-.81	-.94
Gross Nat'l Disposable Inc.(GNDI)	99i	383.50	435.24	481.25	505.21	476.60	459.22	462.08	497.13	543.18	565.18	619.22	668.89	†117.55	129.28	131.88
Gross Saving	99s	92.91	115.89	129.68	128.40	84.12	67.96	73.21	96.29	122.15	121.05	152.93	171.82	†30.28	36.48	35.71
Net National Income	99e	322.09														
GDP Volume 1980 prices	99b.p															
GDP Volume 1995 Prices	99b.p	530.13	555.23	583.77	583.95	547.42	529.24	523.16	543.85	564.57	587.20	624.15	657.45	†119.84	126.53	127.47
GDP Volume (1995=100)	99bv.p	93.9	98.3	103.4	103.4	97.0	93.7	92.7	96.3	100.0	104.0	110.6	116.5	†121.1	133.3	134.2
GDP Deflator (1995=100)	99bi.p	74.0	80.1	85.0	89.6	91.2	92.0	94.2	96.0	100.0	99.8	101.8	104.9	†104.8	103.7	106.0

Midyear Estimates

Indicator	Code	1987	1988	1989	1990	1991	1992	1993	1994	1995	1996	1997	1998	1999	2000	2001
Population	99z	4.93	4.95	4.96	4.99	5.01	5.04	5.07	5.09	5.11	5.12	5.14	5.15	5.17	5.18	5.19

(See notes in the back of the book.)

France

		1972	1973	1974	1975	1976	1977	1978	1979	1980	1981	1982	1983	1984	1985	1986
Exchange Rates													*Francs per SDR through 1998,*			
Market Rate	aa	5.5542	5.6801	5.4416	5.2510	5.7740	5.7152	5.4457	5.2957	5.7598	6.6904	7.4184	8.7394	9.4022	8.3052	7.8957
														Francs per US Dollar through 1998,			
Market Rate	ae	5.1157	4.7085	4.4445	4.4855	4.9698	4.7050	4.1800	4.0200	4.5160	5.7480	6.7250	8.3475	9.5920	7.5610	6.4550
Market Rate	rf	5.0445	4.4528	4.8096	4.2878	4.8029	4.9052	4.5131	4.2544	4.2256	5.4346	6.5721	7.6213	8.7391	8.9852	6.9261
															Francs per ECU:	
ECU Rate	ea	....	....	....	....	....	....	....	5.7931	5.9392	6.2018	6.5221	6.9036	6.8307	6.7047	6.8750
ECU Rate	eb	....	....	....	....	....	5.3446	5.6060	5.7396	5.8288	5.8694	6.0405	6.4255	6.7689	6.8714	6.7951	6.7981
														Index Numbers (1995=100):			
Market Rate	ahx	98.9	112.4	103.8	116.4	104.0	101.7	110.7	117.3	118.2	92.3	76.3	65.8	57.2	56.0	72.1
Nominal Effective Exchange Rate	neu	111.8	115.6	108.1	118.4	115.3	111.0	109.6	109.2	109.7	103.0	95.4	89.9	87.0	88.2	90.6
Real Effective Exchange Rate	reu	....	....	....	109.9	107.9	103.8	114.1	115.2	†118.6	115.2	115.4	111.3	108.6	110.5	111.4
Fund Position															*Millions of SDRs:*	
Quota	2f.s	1,500	1,500	1,500	1,500	1,500	1,500	1,919	1,919	2,879	2,879	2,879	4,483	4,483	4,483	4,483
SDRs	1b.s	581	73	202	244	227	233	286	644	733	1,080	887	422	584	819	1,054
Reserve Position in the Fund	1c.s	460	377	429	623	843	736	461	479	837	884	868	1,292	1,291	1,247	1,419
of which: Outstg.Fund Borrowing	2c	—	—	—	—	—	38	16	—	—	—	—	—	—	—	—
International Liquidity												*Millions of US Dollars Unless Otherwise Indicated:*				
Total Res.Min.Gold (Eurosys.Def)	1l.d	6,189	4,268	4,526	8,457	5,620	5,872	9,278	17,579	27,340	22,262	16,531	19,851	20,940	26,589	31,454
SDRs	1b.d	630	88	248	286	263	284	373	849	935	1,257	979	442	572	900	1,290
Reserve Position in the Fund	1c.d	499	455	525	729	979	895	600	630	1,067	1,029	958	1,352	1,265	1,370	1,736
Foreign Exchange	1d.d	5,059	3,725	3,753	7,442	4,377	4,694	8,305	16,100	25,338	19,976	14,594	18,057	19,102	24,319	28,428
o/w: Fin.Deriv.Rel.to Reserves	1dd d	....	....	....	....	....	....	....	....	....	....	....	....	....	....	....
Other Reserve Assets	1e.d	....	....	....	....	....	....	....	....	....	....	....	....	....	....	....
Gold (Million Fine Troy Ounces)	1ad	100.69	100.91	100.93	100.93	101.02	101.67	101.99	81.92	81.85	81.85	81.85	81.85	81.85	81.85	81.85
Gold (Eurosystem Valuation)	1and	3,826	4,261	4,261	14,133	12,840	16,717	22,340	34,195	49,991	33,877	36,848	30,786	26,832	27,580	33,932
Memo: Euro Cl. on Non-EA Res.	1dg d	....	....	....	....	....	....	....	....	....	....	....	....	....	....	....
Non-Euro Cl. on EA Res.	1dh d	....	....	....	....	....	....	....	....	....	....	....	....	....	....	....
Mon. Auth.: Other Foreign Assets	3..d	....	....	....	....	....	....	....	....	....	....	....	....	....	....	....
Foreign Liabilities	4..d	221	356	605	934	942	†453	849	8,570	13,926	11,188	10,155	12,882	10,897	10,891	11,552
Banking Insts.: Foreign Assets	7a.d	19,806	32,215	33,120	41,173	41,292	†72,689	†108,876	137,587	160,208	158,090	162,959	156,322	158,643	184,380	217,992
Foreign Liab.	7b.d	23,090	33,516	35,691	41,924	51,500	66,835	†95,239	119,652	146,678	153,793	164,669	167,068	174,374	197,183	228,288
Monetary Authorities													*Billions of Francs through 1998;*			
Fgn. Assets (Cl.on Non-EA Ctys)	11	54	44	44	†101	94	110	136	†254	420	377	397	460	488	446	495
Claims on General Government	12a.u	....	....	....	....	....	....	....	....	....	....	....	....	....	....	....
o/w: Claims on Gen.Govt.in Cty	12a	13	11	11	22	22	18	23	24	24	11	25	39	66	59	62
Claims on Banking Institutions	12e.u	....	....	....	....	....	....	....	....	....	....	....	....	....	....	....
o/w: Claims on Bank.Inst.in Cty	12e	66	86	98	51	54	59	89	87	90	116	221	175	154	159	130
Claims on Other Resident Sectors	12d.u	....	....	....	....	....	....	....	....	....	....	....	....	....	....	....
o/w: Cl. on Oth.Res.Sect.in Cty	12d	....	....	....	....	....	1	1	1	1	1	2	1	1	1	1
Currency Issued	14a	87	93	101	111	119	126	136	145	149	167	184	200	209	217	224
Liabilities to Banking Insts	14c.u	....	....	....	....	....	....	....	....	....	....	....	....	....	....	....
o/w: Liabs to Bank.Inst.in Cty	14c	37	40	49	7	7	12	18	21	42	32	52	49	65	104	104
Demand Dep. of Other Res.Sect.	14d.u	....	....	....	....	....	....	....	....	....	....	....	....	....	....	....
o/w: D.Dep.of Oth.Res.Sect.in Cty	14d	1	2	2	2	2	2	2	3	2	2	3	3	4	3	3
Other Dep. of Other Res.Sect.	15..u	....	....	....	....	....	....	....	....	....	....	....	....	....	....	....
o/w: O.Dep.of Oth.Res.Sect.in Cty	15	....	....	....	....	....	....	....	....	....	....	....	....	....	....	....
Money Market Instruments	16m.u	....	....	....	....	....	....	....	....	....	....	....	....	....	....	....
o/w: MMI Held by Resid.of Cty	16m	....	....	....	....	....	....	....	....	....	....	....	....	....	....	....
Bonds (Debt Securities)	16n.u	....	....	....	....	....	....	....	....	....	....	....	....	....	....	....
o/w: Bonds Held by Resid.of Cty	16n	....	....	....	....	....	....	....	....	....	....	....	....	....	....	....
Foreign Liab. (to Non-EA Ctys)	16c	1	2	3	4	5	2	4	34	63	64	68	108	105	82	75
Central Government Deposits	16d.u	....	....	....	....	....	....	....	....	....	....	....	....	....	....	....
o/w: Cent.Govt.Dep. in Cty	16d	....	....	....	....	....	3	27	23	28	24	58	38	58	47	57
Capital Accounts	17a	....	....	....	....	....	65	79	†160	273	235	302	319	318	260	269
Other Items (Net)	17r	6	6	−2	†50	37	−22	−18	†−18	−22	−19	−22	−40	−50	−49	−44
Memo: Currency Put into Circ.	14m	....	....	....	....	....	....	....	....	....	....	....	....	....	....	....
Banking Institutions													*Billions of Francs through 1998;*			
Claims on Monetary Authorities	20	38	40	50	10	11	†16	†22	25	47	38	58	57	74	112	113
Claims on Bk.Inst.in Oth.EA Ctys	20b.u	....	....	....	....	....	....	....	....	....	....	....	....	....	....	....
Fgn. Assets (Cl.on Non-EA Ctys)	21	101	148	147	185	205	†342	†455	553	724	909	1,096	1,305	1,522	1,394	1,407
Claims on General Government	22a.u	....	....	....	....	....	....	....	....	....	....	....	....	....	....	....
o/w: Claims on Gen.Govt.in Cty	22a	13	4	4	33	34	34	†268	297	308	374	478	529	584	670	724
Claims on Other Resident Sectors	22d.u	....	....	....	....	....	....	....	....	....	....	....	....	....	....	....
o/w: Cl. on Oth.Res.Sect.in Cty	22d	396	468	551	629	767	†926	†1,623	1,848	2,107	2,383	2,739	3,065	3,398	3,646	4,056
Demand Deposits	24..u	....	....	....	....	....	....	....	....	....	....	....	....	....	....	....
o/w: D.Dep.of Oth.Res.Sect.in Cty	24	174	192	219	262	279	†313	†532	610	655	737	805	914	1,016	1,102	1,189
Other Deposits	25..u	....	....	....	....	....	....	....	....	....	....	....	....	....	....	....
o/w: O.Dep.of Oth.Res.Sect.in Cty	25	185	226	275	331	392	†465	†1,015	1,171	1,300	1,423	1,593	1,753	1,888	2,006	2,165
Money Market Instruments	26m.u	....	....	....	....	....	....	....	....	....	....	....	....	....	....	....
o/w: MMI Held by Resid.of Cty	26m	....	....	....	....	....	....	1	1	1	1	1	1	1	9	39
Bonds (Debt Securities)	26n.u	....	....	....	....	....	....	....	....	....	....	....	....	....	....	....
o/w: Bonds Held by Resid.of Cty	26n	....	....	....	....	77	†177	200	250	303	363	445	530	629	793
Foreign Liab. (to Non-EA Ctys)	26c	118	154	159	188	256	314	†398	481	662	884	1,107	1,395	1,673	1,491	1,474
Central Government Deposits	26d.u	....	....	....	....	....	....	....	....	....	....	....	....	....	....	....
o/w: Cent.Govt.Dep. in Cty	26d	....	....	....	....	....	....	58	61	71	69	76	81	84	88	102
Credit from Monetary Authorities	26g	66	86	98	51	54	59	89	87	90	116	221	175	154	159	130
Liab. to Bk.Inst.in Oth. EA Ctys	26h.u	....	....	....	....	....	....	....	....	....	....	....	....	....	....	....
Capital Accounts	27a	....	....	....	....	....	72	†112	146	170	193	223	261	300	344	439
Other Items (Net)	27r	6	—	—	26	35	15	†−14	−34	−13	−22	−18	−69	−68	−6	−30

1987	1988	1989	1990	1991	1992	1993	1994	1995	1996	1997	1998	1999	2000	2001	
															Exchange Rates
Euros per SDR Thereafter: End of Period															
7.5756	8.1536	7.6064	7.2968	7.4096	7.5714	8.0978	7.8044	7.2838	7.5306	8.0794	7.9161	1.3662	1.4002	1.4260	Market Rate... aa
Euros per US Dollar Thereafter: End of Period (ae) Period Average (rf)															
5.3400	6.0590	5.7880	5.1290	5.1800	5.5065	5.8955	5.3460	4.9000	5.2370	5.9881	5.6221	.9954	1.0747	1.1347	Market Rate... ae
6.0107	5.9569	6.3801	5.4453	5.6421	5.2938	5.6632	5.5520	4.9915	5.1155	5.8367	5.8995	.9386	1.0854	1.1175	Market Rate... rf
End of Period (ea) Period Average (eb)															
6.9834	7.0982	6.9204	6.9501	6.9534	6.6678	6.5742	6.5758	6.4458	6.5619	6.6135	6.5596	....	....	....	ECU Rate... ea
6.9289	7.0361	7.0237	6.9141	6.9733	6.8496	6.6334	6.5796	6.5250	6.4928	6.6122	6.6015	....	....	....	ECU Rate... eb
Period Averages															
83.1	83.9	78.3	91.8	88.7	94.4	88.2	90.0	100.0	97.5	85.6	84.7				Market Rate... ahx
90.6	88.7	87.8	91.5	90.0	92.9	96.2	97.1	100.0	99.9	96.7	97.2	95.8	92.7	93.0	Nominal Effective Exchange Rate .... neu
108.2	104.5	101.5	102.7	98.4	99.3	100.1	99.0	100.0	96.9	92.9	92.5	91.8	88.2	87.2	Real Effective Exchange Rate .... reu
End of Period															**Fund Position**
4,483	4,483	4,483	4,483	4,483	7,415	7,415	7,415	7,415	7,415	7,415	7,415	10,739	10,739	10,739	Quota .... 2f. s
1,059	1,033	1,011	902	927	118	241	248	643	682	720	786	253	309	392	SDRs .... 1b. s
1,349	1,200	1,076	1,004	1,165	1,805	1,682	1,627	1,854	1,875	2,119	3,162	3,950	3,471	3,894	Reserve Position in the Fund .... 1c. s
—	—	—	—	—	—	—	—	—	—	—	382			—	of which: Outstg.Fund Borrowing 2c
End of Period															**International Liquidity**
33,049	25,364	24,611	36,778	31,284	27,028	22,649	26,257	26,853	26,796	30,927	44,312	†39,701	37,039	31,749	Total Res.Min.Gold (Eurosys.Def)........ 1l. d
1,502	1,390	1,329	1,283	1,326	163	331	362	955	981	971	1,107	347	402	492	SDRs .... 1b. d
1,914	1,615	1,414	1,428	1,666	2,482	2,310	2,375	2,756	2,695	2,859	4,452	5,421	4,522	4,894	Reserve Position in the Fund .... 1c. d
29,634	22,359	21,868	34,067	28,292	24,384	20,008	23,520	23,142	23,120	27,097	38,753	33,933	32,114	26,363	Foreign Exchange .... 1d. d
....	....	....	....	....	....	....	....	....	....	....	....	—	—	—	o/w: Fin.Deriv.Rel.to Reserves ...... 1dd d
....	....	....	....	....	....	....	....	....	....	....	....	—	—	—	Other Reserve Assets .... 1e. d
81.85	81.85	81.85	81.85	81.85	81.85	81.85	81.85	81.85	81.85	81.89	102.37	97.24	97.25	97.25	Gold (Million Fine Troy Ounces)........ 1ad
41,496	33,686	33,982	31,321	31,704	26,313	30,729	30,730	31,658	30,368	25,002	29,871	28,225	26,689	26,888	Gold (Eurosystem Valuation) .... 1an d
....	....	....	....	....	....	....	....	....	....	....	....	—	—	—	Memo: Euro Cl. on Non-EA Res........ 1dg d
....	....	....	....	....	....	....	....	....	....	....	....	3,330	3,870	3,562	Non-Euro Cl. on EA Res. .... 1dh d
															Mon. Auth.: Other Foreign Assets .... 3..d
19,554	13,601	13,022	12,338	12,795	29,541	20,553	11,650	11,649	†796	618	1,014	†7,678	1,007	3,233	Foreign Liabilities................ 4..d
290,077	299,721	358,829	455,781	457,104	512,485	581,393	599,906	705,082	684,056	736,795	....	†427,935	435,469	447,009	Banking Insts.: Foreign Assets .... 7a. d
296,772	315,902	384,692	519,809	523,456	526,214	523,077	592,630	662,469	671,759	694,578	....	†329,796	381,962	396,805	Foreign Liab. .... 7b. d
Millions of Euros Beginning 1999: End of Period															**Monetary Authorities**
474	430	405	407	396	345	351	372	346	309	335	420	68,150	68,300	66,406	Fgn. Assets (Cl.on Non-EA Ctys) 11
....	....	....	....	....	....	....	....	....	....	....	....	4,051	4,044	3,691	Claims on General Government 12a.u
												4,051	4,044	3,691	o/w: Claims on Gen.Govt.in Cty 12a
												65,188	42,512	44,767	Claims on Banking Institutions 12e.u
212	238	271	162	166	294	372	200	147	143	125	167	48,444	29,013	16,413	o/w: Claims on Bank.Inst.in Cty 12e
												380	361	341	Claims on Other Resident Sectors 12d.u
3	2	3	4	4	4	4	4	6	18	19	20	380	361	341	o/w: Cl. on Oth.Res.Sect.in Cty 12d
235	247	259	270	270	271	267	270	275	278	283	287	49,282	49,187	34,575	Currency Issued.............................. 14a
												51,345	28,083	29,467	Liabilities to Banking Insts 14c.u
128	115	103	78	68	22	14	10	30	33	36	129	24,371	28,083	29,467	o/w: Liabs to Bank.Inst.in Cty 14c
												1,573	801	846	Demand Dep. of Other Res.Sect. 14d.u
5	4	4	4	4	3	3	3	4	4	4	4	1,573	801	846	o/w: D.Dep.of Oth.Res.Sect.in Cty 14d
....	....	....	....	....	....	....	....	....	....	....	....	—	—	—	Other Dep. of Other Res.Sect. .... 15..u
....	....	....	....	....	....	....	....	....	....	....	....	—	—	—	o/w: O.Dep.of Oth.Res.Sect.in Cty 15
....	....	....	....	....	....	....	....	....	....	....	....			—	Money Market Instruments 16m.u
....	....	....	....	....	....	....	....	....	....	....	....				o/w: MMI Held by Resid.of Cty 16m
....	....	....	....	....	....	....	....	....	....	....	....	—	—	—	Bonds (Debt Securities)...................... 16n.u
....	....	....	....	....	....	....	....	....	....	....	....			—	o/w: Bonds Held by Resid.of Cty 16n
104	82	75	63	66	163	121	62	57	4	4	6	7,643	1,082	3,669	Foreign Liab. (to Non-EA Ctys) 16c
												1,057	1,982	2,455	Central Government.Deposits 16d.d
120	76	107	104	86	148	198	123	58	20	43	89	1,057	1,982	2,455	o/w: Cent.Govt.Dep. in Cty 16d
276	255	244	201	205	182	225	201	177	191	201	168	35,675	39,750	44,024	Capital Accounts 17a
−116	−45	−56	−67	−59	−51	−26	−23	−44	−3	−39	−25	−8,807	−5,668	169	Other Items (Net) 17r
....	....	....	....	....	....	....	....	....	....	....	....	....	....	....	*Memo: Currency Put into Circ.* 14m
Millions of Euros Beginning 1999: End of Period															**Banking Institutions**
138	125	114	91	80	34	27	26	47	51	48	....	24,371	28,083	29,467	Claims on Monetary Authorities 20
											....	192,393	186,176	211,491	Claims on Bk.Inst.in Oth.EA Ctys 20b.u
1,549	1,816	2,077	2,338	2,368	2,822	3,428	3,207	3,455	3,582	4,412	....	425,976	467,995	507,215	Fgn. Assets (Cl.on Non-EA Ctys)............ 21
											....	386,731	338,623	336,930	Claims on General Government 22a.u
704	695	696	681	630	699	798	1,074	1,275	1,566	1,729	....	312,415	267,985	269,527	o/w: Claims on Gen.Govt.in Cty 22a
											....	1,156,145	1,276,367	1,380,548	Claims on Other Resident Sectors 22d.u
4,545	5,074	5,698	6,358	6,661	6,930	6,712	6,589	6,745	6,653	6,785	....	1,111,777	1,225,372	1,314,276	o/w: Cl. on Oth.Res.Sect.in Cty 22d
											....	246,895	269,174	305,546	Demand Deposits .... 24..u
1,243	1,291	1,375	1,430	1,351	1,349	1,364	1,415	1,557	1,554	1,670	....	242,376	264,944	300,271	o/w: D.Dep.of Oth.Res.Sect.in Cty 24
											....	649,980	654,675	684,583	Other Deposits .... 25..u
2,228	2,350	2,451	2,519	2,565	2,619	2,776	3,012	3,374	3,582	3,855	....	632,781	636,781	666,151	o/w: O.Dep.of Oth.Res.Sect.in Cty 25
											....	314,039	352,424	424,149	Money Market Instruments 26m.u
163	274	426	781	851	1,128	1,174	1,062	973	859	827	....	....	....	....	o/w: MMI Held by Resid.of Cty 26m
											....	346,488	363,052	388,593	Bonds (Debt Securities)...................... 26n.u
900	1,053	1,166	1,230	1,315	1,458	1,500	1,475	1,575	1,407	1,324	....	....	....	....	o/w: Bonds Held by Resid.of Cty 26n
1,585	1,914	2,227	2,666	2,712	2,898	3,084	3,168	3,246	3,518	4,159	....	328,286	410,491	450,250	Foreign Liab. (to Non-EA Ctys) 26c
											....	10,109	5,865	4,937	Central Government Deposits 26d.u
117	116	118	111	95	96	50	55	124	156	152	....	9,844	5,637	4,403	o/w: Cent.Govt.Dep. in Cty 26d
212	238	271	162	166	294	372	200	147	143	125	167	48,448	29,013	16,413	Credit from Monetary Authorities 26g
											....	150,237	139,026	149,425	Liab. to Bk.Inst.in Oth. EA Ctys 26h.u
584	664	774	881	989	1,105	1,240	1,293	1,284	1,288	1,320	....	245,031	249,326	270,482	Capital Accounts 27a
−97	−189	−222	−311	−306	−462	−595	−785	−759	−654	−459	....	−153,897	−175,799	−228,727	Other Items (Net) 27r

France

	1972	1973	1974	1975	1976	1977	1978	1979	1980	1981	1982	1983	1984	1985	1986
Banking Survey (Nat'l Residency)													*Billions of Francs through 1998;*		
Foreign Assets (Net) 31n	36	37	30	†94	39	†135	†189	†291	418	337	317	263	232	267	353
Domestic Credit 32	422	483	566	685	824	†976	†1,831	2,086	2,342	2,677	3,110	3,516	3,907	4,241	4,685
Claims on General Govt. (Net) 32an	26	16	16	55	56	49	†207	237	233	292	369	450	508	594	628
Claims on Other Resident Sectors 32d	396	468	551	629	767	†927	†1,624	1,849	2,109	2,385	2,741	3,067	3,399	3,647	4,057
Currency Issued.................................. 34a.n	87	93	101	111	119	†126	†136	145	149	167	184	200	209	217	224
Demand Deposits............................... 34b.n	175	194	221	263	281	†315	†534	612	657	739	808	917	1,020	1,105	1,193
Other Deposits .... 35..n	185	226	275	331	392	†465	†1,015	1,171	1,300	1,423	1,593	1,753	1,888	2,006	2,165
Money Market Instruments 36m	....	....	....	....	....	....	1	1	1	1	1	1	1	9	39
Bonds (Debt Securities)..................... 36n	....	....	....	....	....	77	†177	200	250	303	363	445	530	629	793
o/w: Bonds Over Two Years 36na	....	....	....	....	....									....	....
Capital Accounts............................... 37a	....	....	....	....	....	137	†192	†306	443	428	525	580	617	604	708
Other Items (Net)............................... 37r	12	7	–3	†72	68	†–8	†–35	†–57	–40	–47	–46	–117	–126	–63	–83
Banking Survey (EA-Wide Residency)													*Millions of Euros:*		
Foreign Assets (Net) 31n.u	....	....	....	....	....	....	....	....	....	....	....	....	....	....	....
Domestic Credit .... 32..u	....	....	....	....	....	....	....	....	....	....	....	....	....	....	....
Claims on General Govt. (Net) .... 32an u	....	....	....	....	....	....	....	....	....	....	....	....	....	....	....
Claims on Other Resident Sect. 32d.u	....	....	....	....	....	....	....	....	....	....	....	....	....	....	....
Currency Issued.................................. 34a.u	....	....	....	....	....	....	....	....	....	....	....	....	....	....	....
Demand Deposits............................... 34b.u	....	....	....	....	....	....	....	....	....	....	....	....	....	....	....
Other Deposits .... 35..u	....	....	....	....	....	....	....	....	....	....	....	....	....	....	....
o/w: Other Dep. Over Two Yrs ...... 35ab u	....	....	....	....	....	....	....	....	....	....	....	....	....	....	....
Money Market Instruments 36m.u	....	....	....	....	....	....	....	....	....	....	....	....	....	....	....
Bonds (Debt Securities)..................... 36n.u	....	....	....	....	....	....	....	....	....	....	....	....	....	....	....
o/w: Bonds Over Two Years .... 36na u	....	....	....	....	....	....	....	....	....	....	....	....	....	....	....
Capital Accounts............................... 37a	....	....	....	....	....	....	....	....	....	....	....	....	....	....	....
Other Items (Net).............................. 37r.u	....	....	....	....	....	....	....	....	....	....	....	....	....	....	....
Money (National Definitions)													*Billions of Francs:*		
M1 .... 39ma	....	....	....	....	....	602	665	750	800	899	983	1,104	1,215	1,294	1,386
M1, Seasonally Adjusted .... 39ma c	....	....	....	....	....	579	603	680	740	824	921	1,007	1,105	1,198	1,298
M2 .... 39mb	....	....	....	....	....	1,069	1,212	1,370	1,481	1,683	1,885	2,136	2,333	2,471	2,585
M2, Seasonally Adjusted .... 39mb c	....	....	....	....	....	1,040	1,105	1,264	1,378	1,540	1,752	1,957	2,162	2,322	2,469
M3 .... 39mc	....	....	....	....	....	1,404	1,583	1,805	1,979	2,196	2,450	2,735	3,005	3,218	3,425
M3, Seasonally Adjusted .... 39mc c	....	....	....	....	....	1,376	1,466	1,664	1,850	2,072	2,313	2,551	2,812	3,058	3,282
M4 .... 39md	....	....	....	....	....	1,404	1,583	1,805	1,979	2,196	2,450	2,735	3,005	3,221	3,448
M4, Seasonally Adjusted .... 39md c	....	....	....	....	....	1,378	1,466	1,664	1,850	2,072	2,313	2,551	2,812	3,058	3,305
Interest Rates													*Percent Per Annum*		
Repurchase of Agreements 60a	....	....	11.23	7.72	7.56	8.92	6.32	8.98	11.90	....	14.53	12.35	11.68	9.85	7.52
Money Market Rate............................ 60b	4.95	8.91	12.91	7.92	8.56	9.07	7.98	9.04	11.85	15.30	14.87	12.53	11.74	9.93	7.74
Treasury Bill Rate............................. 60c	5.51	9.13	13.02	7.84	8.69	9.22	8.16	9.48	12.20	15.26	14.73	12.63	11.88	10.08	7.79
Deposit Rate..................................... 60l	4.25	4.25	6.25	7.50	6.50	6.50	6.50	6.50	7.25	7.75	8.50	8.08	7.08	6.25	5.00
Lending Rate.................................... 60p	6.38	8.57	11.98	10.00	9.08	9.50	9.12	9.81	12.54	14.28	13.63	12.25	12.15	11.09	9.89
Government Bond Yield....................... 61	7.36	8.27	10.48	9.57	9.32	9.87	9.50	9.81	13.03	15.79	15.69	13.63	12.54	10.94	8.44
Prices, Production, Labor													*Index Numbers (1995=100):*		
Share Prices 62	†17.2	19.0	14.2	15.6	15.1	12.1	15.8	20.1	23.3	†20.5	19.9	†26.9	†36.3	†42.4	64.9
Producer Prices															
Indust. Goods,Tax Incl. 63	30.4	34.9	45.1	42.5	45.6	48.2	50.3	57.0	62.0	68.8	76.4	84.9	96.1	100.0	....
Intermediate Indust. Goods 63a									60.0	67.1	74.3	80.8	88.3	92.2	89.6
Imported Raw Materials.................... 63b	27.8	35.0	46.7	38.4	43.4	46.9	†47.6	56.2	65.7	77.4	82.7	93.9	109.7	102.1	77.8
Consumer Prices 64	21.7	23.3	26.4	29.5	32.4	35.4	38.7	42.8	†48.6	55.1	61.7	67.6	72.7	77.0	78.9
Harmonized CPI 64h															
Labor Costs 65	12.2	†13.8	16.5	19.8	23.1	26.4	30.1	34.7	40.3	46.1	55.4	62.5	67.8	71.9	75.1
Industrial Production .... 66..c	74.3	79.6	81.6	76.3	82.3	83.6	85.6	88.9	†89.6	88.7	88.1	87.5	87.7	87.9	88.7
Industrial Employment .... 67..c	....	....	....	....	....	....	....	....	132.6	128.5	127.3	124.8	121.5	118.2	116.0
														Number in Thousands:		
Labor Force....................................... 67d	....	....	....	....	....	....	....	....	....	....	....	....	....		
Employment 67e	....	....	....	....	....	....	....	....	....	....	....	....	....	21,450	21,551
Unemployment 67c	....	....	....	....	....	....	....	....	....	....	....	....	....		2,517
Unemployment Rate (%)..................... 67r	....	....	....	....	....	....	....	....	....	....	....	....	....	10.2	10.4
International Transactions													*Billions of Francs through 1998;*		
Exports 70	133.39	162.46	222.07	227.20	273.24	319.22	357.60	427.95	490.55	576.66	633.07	723.07	850.95	906.89	863.54
Imports, c.i.f. 71	136.19	167.25	254.20	231.18	308.12	346.36	368.59	454.69	569.99	654.85	763.55	806.52	909.60	967.92	895.89
Imports, f.o.b. 71.v	126.95	155.51	239.17	221.47	293.69	331.01	354.99	438.03	550.97	635.77	704.99	757.54	870.72	930.93	863.17
														1995=100	
Volume of Exports.............................. 72	33.9	†37.3	40.9	†39.2	42.8	45.6	48.3	53.2	54.3	55.9	54.2	56.1	59.1	60.7	†61.0
Volume of Imports.............................. 73	34.6	†39.3	41.0	†38.1	46.0	46.4	48.8	54.5	57.9	56.0	57.9	56.8	58.2	60.6	†62.6
Unit Value of Exports......................... 74	....	....	....	....	....	....	....	....	....	....	....	....	....	....	....
Unit Value of Imports 75	....	....	....	....	....	....	....	....	....	....	....	....	....	....	....

Banking Survey (Nat'l Residency)

Millions of Euros Beginning 1999: End of Period

1987	1988	1989	1990	1991	1992	1993	1994	1995	1996	1997	1998	1999	2000	2001		
334	250	180	15	−14	106	573	349	497	369	584	....	295,087	295,431	329,584	Foreign Assets (Net)	31n
5,077	5,643	6,229	6,909	7,188	7,484	7,342	7,560	7,903	8,118	8,390	....	1,417,722	1,490,143	1,580,977	Domestic Credit	32
529	567	529	547	523	550	626	968	1,152	1,447	1,586	....	305,565	264,410	266,360	Claims on General Govt. (Net)	32an
4,548	5,076	5,700	6,362	6,665	6,934	6,716	6,593	6,751	6,671	6,804	....	1,112,157	1,225,733	1,314,617	Claims on Other Resident Sectors	32d
235	247	259	270	270	271	267	270	275	278	283	287	49,282	49,187	34,575	Currency Issued	34a.n
1,248	1,294	1,378	1,434	1,355	1,352	1,368	1,418	1,561	1,557	1,674	....	243,949	265,745	301,117	Demand Deposits	34b.n
2,228	2,350	2,451	2,519	2,565	2,619	2,776	3,012	3,374	3,582	3,855	....	632,781	636,781	666,151	Other Deposits	35..n
163	274	426	781	851	1,128	1,174	1,062	973	859	827	....	314,039	352,424	424,149	Money Market Instruments	36m
900	1,053	1,166	1,230	1,315	1,458	1,500	1,475	1,575	1,407	1,324	....	346,488	363,052	388,593	Bonds (Debt Securities)	36n
												322,255	338,332	357,016	o/w: Bonds Over Two Years	36na
860	918	1,018	1,082	1,195	1,287	1,465	1,494	1,462	1,479	1,521	....	280,706	289,076	314,506	Capital Accounts	37a
−223	−245	−289	−391	−376	−525	−633	−824	−819	−675	−509	....	−154,437	−170,688	−218,530	Other Items (Net)	37r

Banking Survey (EA-Wide Residency)

End of Period

1987	1988	1989	1990	1991	1992	1993	1994	1995	1996	1997	1998	1999	2000	2001		
....	....	....	....	....	....	....	....	....	....	....	....	158,197	124,722	119,702	Foreign Assets (Net)	31n.u
....	....	....	....	....	....	....	....	....	....	....	....	1,536,141	1,611,548	1,714,118	Domestic Credit	32..u
....	....	....	....	....	....	....	....	....	....	....	....	379,616	334,820	333,229	Claims on General Govt. (Net)	32an u
....	....	....	....	....	....	....	....	....	....	....	....	1,156,525	1,276,728	1,380,889	Claims on Other Resident Sect.	32d.u
....	....	....	....	....	....	....	....	....	....	....	....	49,282	49,187	34,575	Currency Issued	34a.u
....	....	....	....	....	....	....	....	....	....	....	....	248,468	269,975	306,392	Demand Deposits	34b.u
....	....	....	....	....	....	....	....	....	....	....	....	649,980	654,675	684,583	Other Deposits	35..u
....	....	....	....	....	....	....	....	....	....	....	....	299,588	281,832	279,539	o/w: Other Dep. Over Two Yrs	35ab u
....	....	....	....	....	....	....	....	....	....	....	....	314,039	352,424	424,149	Money Market Instruments	36m.u
....	....	....	....	....	....	....	....	....	....	....	....	346,488	363,052	388,593	Bonds (Debt Securities)	36n.u
....	....	....	....	....	....	....	....	....	....	....	....	322,255	338,332	357,016	o/w: Bonds Over Two Years	36na u
....	....	....	....	....	....	....	....	....	....	....	....	280,706	289,076	314,506	Capital Accounts	37a
....	....	....	....	....	....	....	....	....	....	....	....	−194,626	−242,116	−318,978	Other Items (Net)	37r.u

Money (National Definitions)

End of Period

1987	1988	1989	1990	1991	1992	1993	1994	1995	1996	1997	1998	1999	2000	2001		
1,446	1,506	1,622	1,685	1,606	1,603	1,626	1,671	1,800	1,815	1,933	1,993	....	....	....	M1	39ma
1,360	1,396	1,475	1,535	1,532	1,521	1,513	1,559	1,581	1,666	1,735	1,884	....	....	....	M1, Seasonally Adjusted	39ma c
2,696	2,796	2,918	2,944	2,845	2,807	2,854	3,003	3,246	3,363	3,624	3,781	....	....	....	M2	39mb
2,556	2,651	2,755	2,786	2,766	2,719	2,696	2,806	2,935	3,143	3,356	3,641	....	....	....	M2, Seasonally Adjusted	39mb c
3,808	4,117	4,523	4,930	5,029	5,287	5,134	5,225	5,463	5,281	5,385	5,532	....	....	....	M3	39mc
3,569	3,919	4,257	4,635	4,920	5,138	5,217	5,083	5,283	5,318	5,263	5,492	....	....	....	M3, Seasonally Adjusted	39mc c
3,848	4,157	4,586	4,979	5,078	5,343	5,184	5,296	5,541	5,364	5,511	5,622	....	....	....	M4	39md
3,610	3,965	4,315	4,688	4,975	5,190	5,273	5,142	5,360	5,409	5,369	5,590	....	....	....	M4, Seasonally Adjusted	39md c

Interest Rates

Percent Per Annum

1987	1988	1989	1990	1991	1992	1993	1994	1995	1996	1997	1998	1999	2000	2001		
7.75	7.16	8.64	9.55	9.07	9.56	7.60	5.44	4.96	3.60	3.15	3.28	....	....	....	Repurchase of Agreements	60a
7.98	7.52	9.07	9.85	9.49	10.35	8.75	5.69	6.35	3.73	3.24	3.39	....	....	....	Money Market Rate	60b
8.22	7.88	9.34	†10.18	9.69	10.49	8.41	5.79	6.58	3.84	3.35	3.45	2.72	4.23	4.26	Treasury Bill Rate	60c
4.50	4.50	4.50	4.50	4.50	4.50	4.50	4.50	4.50	3.67	3.50	3.21	2.69	2.63	3.00	Deposit Rate	60l
9.60	9.43	10.00	10.57	10.22	10.00	8.90	7.89	8.12	6.77	6.34	6.55	6.36	6.70	6.98	Lending Rate	60p
9.43	9.06	8.79	9.94	9.05	8.60	6.91	7.35	7.59	6.39	5.63	4.72	4.69	5.45	5.05	Government Bond Yield	61

Prices, Production, Labor

Period Averages

1987	1988	1989	1990	1991	1992	1993	1994	1995	1996	1997	1998	1999	2000	2001		
75.2	†68.7	95.8	98.0	96.1	100.2	110.3	110.2	100.0	113.7	149.6	201.8	249.7	337.4	270.2	Share Prices	62
															Producer Prices	
															Indust. Goods,Tax Incl.	63
90.2	94.8	100.0	98.8	97.5	95.9	†93.2	94.2	†100.0	97.4	96.7	95.9	94.6	98.8	100.5	Intermediate Indust. Goods	63a
†80.7	103.1	127.9	101.7	91.4	82.2	†74.7	88.3	100.0	†87.1	98.2	83.5	84.8	110.4	102.7	Imported Raw Materials	63b
81.5	83.7	86.7	†89.6	92.5	94.7	96.6	98.3	100.0	102.0	103.2	†103.9	104.5	106.3	108.0	Consumer Prices	64
....	....	....	....	....	....	....	....	100.0	102.1	103.4	104.1	104.7	106.6	108.5	Harmonized CPI	64h
78.6	81.1	84.9	86.2	90.0	93.4	96.3	99.2	100.0	†101.9	104.7	107.6	110.0	115.0	120.2	Labor Costs	65
90.4	94.7	98.6	†100.4	99.2	98.0	94.3	98.0	100.0	100.3	†104.2	109.6	111.9	115.8	116.6	Industrial Production	66..c
113.3	112.1	113.0	113.6	111.5	108.5	103.2	101.0	100.0	97.2	96.5	96.9	96.5	97.8	99.1	Industrial Employment	67..c

Period Averages

1987	1988	1989	1990	1991	1992	1993	1994	1995	1996	1997	1998	1999	2000	2001		
....	....	....	....	....	....	25,756	....	26,803	26,404	26,404	....	....	26,226	....	Labor Force	67d
21,631	21,830	22,154	13,454	22,316	†21,609	†20,705	21,875	20,233	22,311	20,413	22,479	20,864	23,262	....	Employment	67e
2,622	2,563	2,532	2,505	2,709	2,911	3,172	3,329	†2,893	3,063	3,102	2,977	2,772	2,338	....	Unemployment	67c
10.5	10.0	9.4	8.9	9.4	†10.1	11.1	12.4	11.6	12.1	12.3	11.8	11.7	10.0	....	Unemployment Rate (%)	67r

International Transactions

Billions of Euros Beginning 1999

1987	1988	1989	1990	1991	1992	1993	1994	1995	1996	1997	1998	1999	2000	2001		
888.91	997.65	1,143.24	1,177.17	1,221.43	1,248.83	1,190.46	1,294.81	1,420.27	1,471.64	1,692.65	274.98	†282.52	324.41	328.81	Exports	70
949.82	1,063.14	1,229.75	1,273.62	1,302.86	1,268.37	1,149.13	1,298.43	1,403.80	1,441.62	1,585.34	253.21	†276.89	336.20	326.66	Imports, c.i.f.	71
920.52	1,030.47	1,187.18	1,226.74	1,250.98	1,217.81	1,101.03	1,244.07	1,357.60	1,394.18	1,521.75	1,638.34	†269.69	328.48	319.75	Imports, f.o.b.	71.v

1995=100

1987	1988	1989	1990	1991	1992	1993	1994	1995	1996	1997	1998	1999	2000	2001		
63.2	68.7	74.1	77.8	†81.4	†84.4	85.9	93.0	100.0	103.9	†114.5	122.1	129.2	143.9	....	Volume of Exports	72
67.0	71.4	77.6	81.5	†83.4	†84.6	87.0	95.1	100.0	102.4	†110.3	118.9	123.9	137.3	....	Volume of Imports	73
....	....	....	99.3	100.3	99.5	97.6	97.8	100.0	100.6	102.3	101.6	100.6	102.2	....	Unit Value of Exports	74
....	....	....	102.4	104.7	101.8	99.0	98.1	100.0	101.7	103.2	102.1	101.6	107.6	....	Unit Value of Imports	75

France

		1972	1973	1974	1975	1976	1977	1978	1979	1980	1981	1982	1983	1984	1985	1986
Balance of Payments															*Billions of US Dollars:*	
Current Account, n.i.e.	78al d	...	...	...	2.74	−3.36	−.41	7.06	5.14	−4.21	−4.81	−12.08	−5.17	−.88	−.03	2.43
Goods: Exports f.o.b.	78aa d	...	...	...	50.42	54.05	61.99	75.19	95.51	109.69	102.58	93.38	91.32	93.37	97.10	120.53
Goods: Imports f.o.b.	78ab d	...	...	...	−49.39	−59.05	−65.34	−75.22	−99.14	−123.77	−112.72	−108.83	−99.73	−97.87	−101.92	−121.88
Trade Balance	78ac d	...	...	...	1.03	−4.99	−3.35	−.03	−3.63	−14.08	−10.14	−15.45	−8.41	−4.49	−4.81	−1.35
Services: Credit	78ad d	...	...	...	18.18	19.23	22.86	30.13	36.26	43.51	41.24	35.84	34.25	34.33	35.56	43.08
Services: Debit	78ae d	...	...	...	−13.99	−15.39	−17.72	−21.02	−25.70	−32.15	−33.29	−28.04	−25.66	−25.43	−25.89	−33.03
Balance on Goods & Services	78af d	...	...	...	5.22	−1.15	1.79	9.08	6.94	−2.72	−2.19	−7.64	.17	4.41	4.85	8.70
Income: Credit	78ag d	...	...	...	5.14	5.33	6.36	9.29	14.35	20.92	26.16	25.44	20.22	20.42	21.79	24.24
Income: Debit	78ah d	...	...	...	−5.00	−5.10	−5.72	−8.03	−12.12	−18.24	−24.55	−25.25	−21.74	−22.81	−24.05	−25.92
Balance on Gds, Serv. & Inc.	78ai d	...	...	...	5.37	−.91	2.42	10.34	9.17	−.04	−.58	−7.46	−1.35	2.02	2.59	7.02
Current Transfers, n.i.e.: Credit	78aj d	...	...	...	2.58	2.66	3.22	4.08	5.54	6.16	5.33	4.93	5.05	5.01	5.89	9.49
Current Transfers: Debit	78ak d	...	...	...	−5.21	−5.10	−6.04	−7.35	−9.56	−10.33	−9.56	−9.55	−8.87	−7.91	−8.52	−14.08
Capital Account, n.i.e.	78bc d	...	...	...	—	—	—	—	—	—	—	—	—	—	—	—
Capital Account, n.i.e.: Credit	78ba d	...	...	...	—	—	—	—	—	—	—	—	—	—	—	—
Capital Account: Debit	78bb d	...	...	...	—	—	—	—	—	—	—	—	—	—	—	—
Financial Account, n.i.e.	78bj d	...	...	...	−.58	−.48	−.39	−3.71	−3.89	8.49	3.51	9.27	8.41	3.16	2.44	−2.06
Direct Investment Abroad	78bd d	...	...	...	−1.34	−1.64	−1.00	−1.90	−1.99	−3.10	−4.55	−2.85	−1.71	−2.12	−2.24	−5.40
Dir. Invest. in Rep. Econ., n.i.e.	78be d	...	...	...	1.56	.98	1.90	2.47	2.59	3.28	2.47	1.59	1.73	2.40	2.60	3.26
Portfolio Investment Assets	78bf d	...	...	...	−.58	−.68	−.45	−1.02	−1.88	−2.07	−2.17	.19	−1.63	−.47	−2.47	−5.96
Equity Securities	78bk d	...	...	...	...	...	...	...	...	...	...	...	−.31	.15	.68	−1.17
Debt Securities	78bl d	...	...	...	−.58	−.68	−.45	−1.02	−1.88	−2.07	−2.17	.19	−1.32	−.62	−3.15	−4.79
Portfolio Investment Liab., n.i.e.	78bg d	...	...	...	1.69	1.99	1.41	.93	.28	2.37	1.84	7.00	7.40	7.46	8.95	7.83
Equity Securities	78bm d	...	...	...	...	...	...	...	...	...	...	...	.38	.20	2.00	4.19
Debt Securities	78bn d	...	...	...	1.69	1.99	1.41	.93	.28	2.37	1.84	7.00	7.02	7.25	6.95	3.64
Financial Derivatives Assets	78bw d	...	...	...	...	...	...	...	...	...	...	...	...	...	...	...
Financial Derivatives Liabilities	78bx d	...	...	...	...	...	...	...	...	...	...	...	...	...	...	...
Other Investment Assets	78bh d	...	...	...	−9.71	−14.65	−17.99	−20.97	−28.16	−31.46	−17.25	−11.51	−5.98	−13.54	−6.86	−9.87
Monetary Authorities	78bo d	...	...	...	...	...	...	...	...	...	...	...	...	...	...	...
General Government	78bp d	...	...	...	−.33	−.38	−.36	—	−.68	−1.88	−1.37	−1.48	−1.79	−1.66	−1.77	−2.93
Banks	78bq d	...	...	...	−10.02	−11.17	−16.58	−21.23	−22.71	−25.62	−8.79	−9.83	−1.69	−9.28	−6.11	−8.55
Other Sectors	78br d	...	...	...	.63	−3.09	−1.05	.26	−4.78	−3.96	−7.09	−.20	−2.50	−2.61	1.02	1.61
Other Investment Liab., n.i.e.	78bi d	...	...	...	7.80	13.52	15.74	16.78	25.27	39.46	23.17	14.85	8.61	9.43	2.47	8.09
Monetary Authorities	78bs d	...	...	...	.16	.26	−.46	.49	−.04	.67	1.64	1.59	−1.89	−.17	.31	.07
General Government	78bt d	...	...	...	.01	.03	.01	.02	−.06	−.03	.04	1.99	5.10	−.08	−2.04	−3.87
Banks	78bu d	...	...	...	7.35	9.80	12.78	14.26	19.73	29.26	14.44	7.23	2.78	6.92	3.52	12.20
Other Sectors	78bv d	...	...	...	.28	3.42	3.41	2.01	5.64	9.56	7.04	4.05	2.62	2.77	.67	−.30
Net Errors and Omissions	78ca d	...	...	...	1.83	1.00	.92	−.06	.56	2.27	−2.28	−.96	.36	.65	.29	.81
Overall Balance	78cb d	...	...	...	3.99	−2.83	.13	3.30	1.81	6.56	−3.59	−3.77	3.61	2.93	2.70	1.18
Reserves and Related Items	79da d	...	...	...	−3.99	2.83	−.13	−3.30	−1.81	−6.56	3.59	3.77	−3.61	−2.93	−2.70	−1.18
Reserve Assets	79db d	...	...	...	−3.99	2.83	−.13	−3.30	−1.81	−6.56	3.59	3.77	−3.61	−2.93	−2.70	−1.18
Use of Fund Credit and Loans	79dc d	...	...	...	—	—	—	—	—	—	—	—	—	—	—	—
Exceptional Financing	79de d	...	...	...	...	...	...	...	...	...	...	...	...	...	...	...
International Investment Position															*Billions of US Dollars*	
Assets	79aa d	...	...	...	...	...	...	...	...	...	...	...	...	...	...	...
Direct Investment Abroad	79ab d	...	...	...	...	...	...	...	...	...	...	...	...	...	...	...
Portfolio Investment	79ac d	...	...	...	...	...	...	...	...	...	...	...	...	...	...	...
Equity Securities	79ad d	...	...	...	...	...	...	...	...	...	...	...	...	...	...	...
Debt Securities	79ae d	...	...	...	...	...	...	...	...	...	...	...	...	...	...	...
Financial Derivatives	79al d	...	...	...	...	...	...	...	...	...	...	...	...	...	...	...
Other Investment	79af d	...	...	...	...	...	...	...	...	...	...	158.59	152.41	154.38	178.15	206.31
Monetary Authorities	79ag d	...	...	...	...	...	...	...	...	...	...	—	—	—	—	—
General Government	79ah d	...	...	...	...	...	...	...	...	...	...	...	...	...	...	...
Banks	79ai d	...	...	...	...	...	...	...	...	...	...	147.00	141.37	143.44	162.52	184.82
Other Sectors	79aj d	...	...	...	...	...	...	...	...	...	...	...	...	...	...	...
Reserve Assets	79ak d	...	...	...	...	...	...	...	...	79.76	56.23	53.37	51.63	47.83	54.75	65.36
Liabilities	79la d	...	...	...	...	...	...	...	...	134.39	140.76	174.88	178.53	167.77	182.00	183.39
Dir. Invest. in Rep. Economy	79lb d	...	...	...	...	...	...	...	...	...	...	...	...	...	...	...
Portfolio Investment	79lc d	...	...	...	...	...	...	...	...	...	...	...	...	...	...	...
Equity Securities	79ld d	...	...	...	...	...	...	...	...	...	...	...	...	...	...	...
Debt Securities	79le d	...	...	...	...	...	...	...	...	...	...	...	...	...	...	...
Financial Derivatives	79ll d	...	...	...	...	...	...	...	...	...	...	...	...	...	...	...
Other Investment	79lf d	...	...	...	...	...	...	...	...	134.39	140.76	174.88	178.53	167.77	182.00	204.03
Monetary Authorities	79lg d	...	...	...	...	...	...	...	...	...	...	3.76	2.39	1.94	2.91	3.43
General Government	79lh d	...	...	...	...	...	...	...	...	...	...	2.39	7.54	7.38	5.29	1.56
Banks	79li d	...	...	...	...	...	...	...	...	131.82	138.35	141.54	139.41	140.25	153.57	178.40
Other Sectors	79lj d	...	...	...	...	...	...	...	...	—	—	27.19	29.18	18.20	20.22	20.64

Minus Sign Indicates Debit

1987	1988	1989	1990	1991	1992	1993	1994	1995	1996	1997	1998	1999	2000	2001	Balance of Payments	
-4.45	-4.62	-4.67	-9.94	-6.52	3.89	8.99	7.42	10.84	20.56	37.80	37.70	35.04	20.43	21.36	Current Account, n.i.e.	78al d
143.00	161.59	172.19	208.93	209.17	227.44	199.04	230.81	278.63	281.85	286.07	303.02	300.05	295.53	291.41	Goods: Exports f.o.b.	78aa d
-150.78	-169.24	-182.49	-222.19	-218.89	-225.07	-191.53	-223.56	-267.63	-266.91	-259.17	-278.08	-282.06	-294.40	-288.56	Goods: Imports f.o.b.	78ab d
-7.78	-7.66	-10.31	-13.25	-9.71	2.37	7.52	7.25	11.00	14.94	26.90	24.94	17.99	1.13	2.85	Trade Balance	78ac d
50.49	54.52	59.94	76.46	80.10	91.77	86.38	75.52	84.09	83.53	80.79	84.96	82.39	81.74	80.39	Services: Credit	78ad d
-40.11	-43.84	-46.34	-61.05	-63.69	-72.65	-69.54	-57.67	-66.12	-67.28	-64.16	-67.73	-64.45	-62.63	-62.48	Services: Debit	78ae d
2.61	3.03	3.29	2.15	6.70	21.49	24.36	25.10	28.97	31.19	43.52	42.17	35.93	20.24	20.76	Balance on Goods & Services	78af d
27.56	34.02	41.29	55.74	69.77	87.60	98.99	41.56	45.18	47.55	57.13	66.67	64.96	71.36	79.57	Income: Credit	78ag d
-29.20	-34.97	-41.57	-59.63	-75.50	-96.21	-108.16	-48.32	-54.15	-50.25	-50.04	-58.00	-53.03	-57.65	-64.19	Income: Debit	78ah d
.97	2.08	3.01	-1.75	.96	12.87	15.19	18.34	20.01	28.48	50.62	50.83	47.86	33.95	36.15	Balance on Gds, Serv. & Inc.	78ai d
10.87	13.01	11.52	14.79	18.76	20.73	16.74	18.22	22.01	22.76	19.61	19.65	18.88	17.35	17.16	Current Transfers, n.i.e.: Credit	78aj d
-16.28	-19.71	-19.21	-22.99	-26.24	-29.71	-22.94	-29.15	-31.11	-30.68	-32.43	-32.79	-31.70	-30.87	-31.95	Current Transfers: Debit	78ak d
—	-.19	-.21	-4.13	-.03	.66	.03	-4.18	.51	1.23	1.48	1.47	1.57	1.39	-.12	Capital Account, n.i.e.	78bc d
—	.22	.23	.22	.25	.93	.30	.99	1.16	1.88	2.41	2.10	1.89	1.92	1.15	Capital Account, n.i.e.: Credit	78ba d
—	-.40	-.45	-4.35	-.28	-.27	-.28	-5.16	-.66	-.65	-.93	-.63	-.31	-.53	-1.28	Capital Account: Debit	78bb d
.99	-1.31	10.36	24.76	-3.07	-8.04	-16.67	-4.78	-7.33	-22.34	-37.60	-29.29	-36.13	-30.28	-31.57	Financial Account, n.i.e.	78bj d
-9.21	-14.50	-19.50	-34.82	-23.93	-31.27	-20.60	-24.44	-15.82	-30.36	-35.49	-45.70	-119.49	-169.48	-83.19	Direct Investment Abroad	78bd d
5.14	8.49	10.30	13.18	15.15	21.84	20.75	15.80	23.73	21.97	23.05	29.52	46.63	43.17	52.50	Dir. Invest. in Rep. Econ., n.i.e.	78be d
-3.27	-4.15	-6.65	-8.41	-15.33	-19.51	-31.16	-21.96	-7.42	-46.63	-60.79	-105.22	-126.81	-96.80	-83.67	Portfolio Investment Assets	78bf d
-1.98	-1.16	-1.46	.50	-2.98	-1.55	-2.52	....	1.78	-1.08	-9.67	-24.46	-20.73	-31.91	-17.30	Equity Securities	78bk d
-1.29	-2.99	-5.20	-8.91	-12.35	-17.96	-28.64	....	-9.20	-45.55	-51.12	-80.76	-106.08	-64.89	-66.37	Debt Securities	78bl d
8.71	11.95	32.04	43.22	29.54	52.50	34.52	-27.90	13.08	-15.35	35.32	59.75	117.52	132.96	102.24	Portfolio Investment Liab., n.i.e.	78bg d
3.41	1.75	7.00	5.90	7.66	5.41	13.58	....	6.82	12.20	11.97	17.21	49.35	49.36	10.97	Equity Securities	78bm d
5.30	10.20	25.05	37.32	21.87	47.09	20.94	....	6.26	-27.56	23.36	42.54	68.17	83.60	91.28	Debt Securities	78bn d
....	....	....	....	-.39	1.04	-.34	....	....	-6.47	—	—	—	—	—	Financial Derivatives Assets	78bw d
....	....	....	....	....	....	....	....	1.00	7.81	4.10	-.44	-2.23	4.14	.95	Financial Derivatives Liabilities	78bx d
-47.04	-28.18	-62.79	-61.54	.15	-61.09	-13.38	23.06	-40.16	26.31	-53.64	26.11	-26.62	.96	-55.90	Other Investment Assets	78bh d
....	....	....	....	....	....	....	-.24	.50	.13	-.43	-.05	-10.31	-6.00	-12.50	Monetary Authorities	78bo d
-5.67	-5.16	-4.47	-1.57	-5.13	-4.96	-3.91	3.08	-.65	1.11	1.18	.86	.74	.68	-.09	General Government	78bp d
-36.85	-23.52	-52.30	-52.83	8.74	-65.09	-46.69	22.72	-43.19	28.59	-46.82	41.70	-11.66	6.64	-42.28	Banks	78bq d
-4.52	-.50	-6.02	-7.14	-3.46	8.96	37.22	-2.50	3.18	-3.52	-7.57	-16.40	-5.39	-.37	-1.03	Other Sectors	78br d
46.66	25.08	56.96	73.14	-8.26	28.44	-6.46	30.67	18.26	20.38	49.85	6.70	74.88	54.77	35.50	Other Investment Liab., n.i.e.	78bi d
7.09	-4.10	3.54	-.33	.64	22.02	-1.07	-14.41	.45	-.47	.13	.31	28.86	-23.39	1.15	Monetary Authorities	78bs d
-.37	-.23	-.02	-.56	-.13	.11	.23	3.16	1.10	-.01	4.67	.15	2.14	2.18	1.32	General Government	78bt d
33.99	27.36	57.50	80.26	-5.07	10.39	-5.69	32.11	13.12	15.83	39.05	2.26	43.89	56.41	39.11	Banks	78bu d
5.95	2.06	-4.07	-6.24	-3.69	-4.08	.07	9.81	3.59	5.04	6.00	3.98	-.01	19.56	-6.08	Other Sectors	78bv d
.85	.95	-6.34	.26	4.42	1.90	2.65	3.99	-3.31	.79	4.26	9.94	-1.87	6.03	4.86	Net Errors and Omissions	78ca d
-2.60	-5.16	-.86	10.95	-5.19	-1.58	-5.01	2.45	.71	.24	5.94	19.82	-1.39	-2.43	-5.47	Overall Balance	78cb d
2.60	5.16	.86	-10.95	5.19	1.58	5.01	-2.45	-.71	-.24	-5.94	-19.82	1.39	2.43	5.47	Reserves and Related Items	79da d
2.60	5.16	.86	-10.95	5.19	1.58	5.01	-2.45	-.71	-.24	-5.94	-19.82	1.39	2.43	5.47	Reserve Assets	79db d
—	—	—	—	—	—	—	—	—	—	—	—	—	—	—	Use of Fund Credit and Loans	79dc d
....	....	....	....	....	....	....	....	....	....	....	....	....	....	—	Exceptional Financing	79de d

Billions of US Dollars

1987	1988	1989	1990	1991	1992	1993	1994	1995	1996	1997	1998	1999	2000	2001	International Investment Position	
....	....	587.46	736.31	754.91	812.07	905.94	1,182.14	1,365.43	1,470.16	1,664.07	2,005.48	2,114.72	2,407.20	....	Assets	79aa d
51.69	51.46	75.41	110.12	129.90	140.58	141.43	303.44	378.58	467.07	579.81	731.20	910.97	1,006.24	....	Direct Investment Abroad	79ab d
....	....	73.65	81.05	91.51	96.10	130.18	184.91	203.62	260.66	340.35	488.98	559.06	614.32	....	Portfolio Investment	79ac d
....	....	45.23	40.20	44.42	42.51	51.84	53.74	58.37	73.53	99.14	143.04	180.23	197.73	....	Equity Securities	79ad d
....	....	28.42	40.85	47.08	53.59	78.35	131.17	145.25	187.13	241.22	345.94	378.83	416.58	....	Debt Securities	79ae d
—	—	—	—	—	—	—	24.78	31.32	34.70	42.61	76.07	20.29	120.31	....	Financial Derivatives	79al d
278.86	289.40	379.60	476.45	470.24	521.77	581.82	623.32	704.29	659.47	658.79	666.80	556.35	602.78	....	Other Investment	79af d
—	—	—	—	—	—	—	1.23	.94	.75	1.86	2.10	1.00	17.21	....	Monetary Authorities	79ag d
....	....	35.18	40.48	44.79	46.47	54.21	31.29	34.81	33.32	29.80	31.62	25.61	26.98	....	General Government	79ah d
247.79	257.87	313.85	388.96	382.75	431.52	464.58	469.33	530.26	484.61	498.42	487.70	384.26	427.47	....	Banks	79ai d
....	....	30.56	47.01	42.70	43.78	63.02	47.73	55.69	61.75	53.02	54.37	39.08	52.95	....	Other Sectors	79aj d
75.33	59.76	58.80	68.70	63.26	53.62	52.51	45.68	47.62	48.27	42.50	42.43	68.05	63.55	....	Reserve Assets	79ak d
250.22	260.43	561.52	757.99	813.85	848.02	955.81	1,128.84	1,260.91	1,284.36	1,394.70	1,753.62	2,103.83	2,347.00	....	Liabilities	79la d
....	—	60.52	84.93	97.45	100.21	103.20	271.29	303.08	312.89	354.04	485.72	723.51	702.71	....	Dir. Invest. in Rep. Economy	79lb d
....	....	153.44	215.27	260.85	287.42	366.13	366.63	417.67	424.24	477.94	638.09	792.53	869.09	....	Portfolio Investment	79lc d
....	....	50.29	54.83	71.18	71.39	103.60	102.21	120.75	155.31	200.03	300.55	448.86	460.78	....	Equity Securities	79ld d
24.47	27.48	103.14	160.44	189.67	216.04	262.52	264.42	296.92	268.92	277.91	337.54	343.67	408.30	....	Debt Securities	79le d
—	—	—	—	—	—	—	20.25	32.93	38.33	45.24	81.09	16.58	119.85	....	Financial Derivatives	79ll d
272.67	280.13	347.55	457.80	455.54	460.39	486.49	470.68	507.23	508.91	517.48	548.72	571.22	655.35	....	Other Investment	79lf d
6.80	6.73	8.32	8.43	8.21	26.26	18.37	1.72	2.01	2.26	2.30	2.68	1.41	2.33	....	Monetary Authorities	79lg d
5.72	.96	.93	.49	.37	.38	.31	9.45	11.24	10.65	16.32	15.05	7.74	15.91	....	General Government	79lh d
237.69	252.74	318.62	427.18	424.39	413.30	389.41	435.10	466.40	468.95	472.90	501.82	356.23	528.34	....	Banks	79li d
22.45	19.71	19.68	21.70	22.57	20.45	78.40	24.42	27.58	27.06	25.96	29.17	19.99	42.62	....	Other Sectors	79lj d

France

		1972	1973	1974	1975	1976	1977	1978	1979	1980	1981	1982	1983	1984	1985	1986
Government Finance																
Central Government													*Billions of Francs through 1998;*			
Deficit (-) or Surplus	**80**	†6.8	4.7	5.8	−37.8	−17.1	−22.3	−29.6	−37.0	−2.0	−73.2	−121.9	−140.7	−116.3	−127.7	−170.2
Revenue	**81**	†331.3	372.0	455.9	512.6	625.5	695.6	787.1	935.4	1,112.9	1,275.5	1,482.4	1,652.5	1,817.1	1,962.4	2,076.6
Grants Received	**81z**	†3.3	3.5	3.8	5.4	6.1	6.3	7.0	7.7	12.2	13.5	16.6	21.3	19.8	18.9	26.4
Exp. & Lending Minus Repay.	**82z**	†329.1	366.0	453.3	555.5	642.4	719.8	835.4	970.0	1,121.9	1,353.1	1,638.8	1,805.3	1,971.6	2,122.8	2,268.7
Expenditure	**82**	†320.2	356.7	440.4	536.9	620.7	701.2	818.6	945.4	1,110.0	1,328.2	1,570.5	1,774.1	1,943.4	2,099.4	2,228.7
Lending Minus Repayments	**83**	†8.9	9.3	12.9	18.6	21.7	18.6	16.8	24.6	11.9	24.9	68.3	31.2	28.2	23.4	40.0
Overall Adj. to Cash Basis	**80x**	†1.3	−4.8	−.6	−.3	−6.3	−4.4	11.7	−10.1	−5.2	−9.1	17.9	−9.2	17.8	13.8	−4.5
Financing																
Net Borrowing	**84**	†1.8	.1	−4.0	46.3	20.8	35.7	56.0	40.0	31.6	83.8	185.3	119.8	160.4	164.3	135.5
Domestic	**84a**	†1.7	−1.2	−4.9	46.2	19.4	34.0	56.2	38.5	31.5	82.5	185.5	117.7	161.9	163.5	135.3
Foreign	**85a**	†.1	1.3	.9	.1	1.4	1.7	−.2	1.5	.1	1.3	−.2	2.1	−1.5	.8	.2
Finance from Foreign Aid	**86a**	....	....	....	....	....	....	....	....	....	....	....	....	....	....	....
Use of Cash Balances	**87**	†−8.3	−5.6	−.7	−8.6	−3.3	−13.1	−26.4	−3.0	−29.6	−10.6	−63.4	20.9	−44.1	−36.6	34.8
Adj. to Total Financing	**84x**	†−.3	.8	−1.1	.1	−.4	−.3	—	—	—	—	—	—	—	—	—
Debt: Francs	**88b**	78.1	77.7	87.4	123.3	133.9	149.7	188.1	362.5	404.4	485.3	599.4	751.0	883.7	1,030.8	1,162.9
Foreign Currency	**89b**	8.3	8.3	8.2	5.9	4.8	5.7	9.6	10.3	13.9	15.1	17.3	29.4	31.7	40.0	31.9
General Government														*As Percent of*		
Deficit (-) or Surplus	**80g**	....	....	....	....	....	....	....	....	....	....	....	....	....	....	....
Debt	**88g**	....	....	....	....	....	....	....	....	....	....	....	....	....	....	....
National Accounts													*Billions of Francs through 1998;*			
Househ.Cons.Expend.,incl.NPISHs	**96f. c**	567.3	641.6	745.6	857.8	988.4	1,111.4	1,238.5	1,411.9	1,609.4	1,846.7	2,119.2	2,334.0	2,530.3	2,720.8	2,891.1
Government Consumption Expend.	**91f. c**	149.8	171.1	204.2	247.9	292.9	335.2	464.5	531.9	619.7	726.2	856.2	957.2	1,058.9	1,131.6	1,200.7
Gross Fixed Capital Formation	**93e. c**	244.4	285.2	336.1	354.3	407.2	439.4	514.7	586.6	686.4	748.5	833.1	869.3	909.1	968.5	1,046.6
Changes in Inventories	**93i. c**	16.1	22.1	30.1	−10.0	24.5	29.4	16.3	31.6	34.0	−6.4	13.2	−7.6	−2.1	−11.9	4.7
Exports of Goods and Services	**90c. c**	165.1	198.6	269.6	279.8	333.0	392.8	438.1	512.3	587.5	690.8	771.5	879.6	1,027.0	1,094.9	1,043.5
Imports of Goods and Services (-)	**98c. c**	154.9	188.7	282.7	262.3	345.4	390.5	428.9	524.7	657.8	770.2	889.9	936.1	1,067.4	1,138.0	1,056.8
Gross Domestic Product (GDP)	**99b. c**	987.9	1,129.8	1,303.0	1,467.9	1,700.6	1,917.8	2,245.7	2,552.2	2,882.2	3,239.1	3,706.8	4,100.9	4,460.8	4,771.2	5,135.4
Net Primary Income from Abroad	**98.n c**	2.2	2.4	4.1	2.4	2.9	3.9	.1	−1.3	−16.3	−11.2	−1.0	10.7	23.8	18.6	15.9
Gross National Income (GNI)	**99a. c**	990.1	1,132.2	1,307.1	1,470.3	1,703.5	1,921.7	2,245.6	2,553.5	2,898.4	3,250.2	3,707.8	4,090.2	4,436.9	4,752.6	5,119.5
Net Current Transf.from Abroad	**98t. c**	....	....	....	....	....	....	−20.4	−23.4	−25.2	−29.6	−36.0	−37.1	−30.3	−34.2	−30.3
Gross Nat'l Disposable Inc.(GNDI)	**99i. c**	....	....	....	....	....	....	2,225.2	2,530.1	2,873.2	3,220.7	3,671.8	4,053.1	4,406.7	4,718.4	5,089.1
Gross Saving	**99s. c**	....	....	....	....	....	....	522.2	586.2	644.2	647.7	696.4	761.9	817.5	866.0	997.3
Consumption of Fixed Capital	**99cf c**	95.7	111.1	138.3	163.6	192.6	222.1	253.0	292.4	346.2	397.2	456.7	508.5	551.6	589.4	632.0
GDP Volume 1980 Prices	**99b. r**	2,220.2	2,340.9	2,413.7	2,407.0	2,509.1	2,589.9	2,676.6	2,763.4	2,808.3	2,841.3	2,913.7	2,933.9	2,972.5	3,028.4	3,104.6
GDP Vol. 1995 Ref., Chained	**99b. r**	....	....	....	....	....	....	....	....	....	....	....	....	....	....	....
GDP Volume (1995=100)	**99bv r**	59.5	62.7	64.6	64.5	67.2	69.4	71.7	74.0	75.2	76.1	78.0	78.6	79.6	81.1	83.1
GDP Deflator (1995=100)	**99bi r**	21.4	23.2	26.0	29.3	32.6	35.6	40.4	44.4	49.4	54.9	61.2	67.3	72.2	75.8	79.6
																Millions:
Population	**99z**	51.70	52.13	52.49	52.79	52.91	53.15	53.38	53.61	53.88	54.18	54.48	54.73	54.95	55.17	55.55

1987	1988	1989	1990	1991	1992	1993	1994	1995	1996	1997	1998	1999	2000	2001		
															Government Finance	
															Central Government	
Millions of Euros Beginning 1999: Year Ending December 31																
−64.5	−134.2	−118.6	−136.5	−85.6	−274.0	−402.0	−412.0	−502.6	−413.3	−284.4	....	....	....	....	Deficit (−) or Surplus	80
2,206.9	2,342.8	2,495.6	2,638.7	2,766.2	2,845.5	2,871.3	2,983.5	3,116.5	3,271.2	3,438.7	....				Revenue	81
26.3	35.5	33.2	34.6	51.7	47.2	50.2	48.8	53.0	46.6	51.8	....				Grants Received	81z
2,313.8	2,480.3	2,612.8	2,761.6	2,983.3	3,159.0	3,319.0	3,429.8	3,662.0	3,740.9	3,797.3	....				Exp. & Lending Minus Repay.	82z
2,325.8	2,462.9	2,595.3	2,770.0	2,950.5	3,154.7	3,336.9	3,458.2	3,564.7	3,687.2	3,789.2	....				Expenditure	82
−12.0	17.4	17.5	−8.4	32.8	4.3	−17.9	−28.4	97.3	53.7	8.1	....				Lending Minus Repayments	83
16.1	−32.2	−34.6	−48.2	79.8	−7.7	−4.5	−14.5	−10.1	9.8	22.4	....				Overall Adj. to Cash Basis	80x
															Financing	
128.5	84.1	151.9	152.7	84.7	328.8	460.3	326.7	451.5	364.9	....					Net Borrowing	84
121.1	60.3	105.8	81.9	66.1	293.9	420.5	375.9	396.1	350.0	....					Domestic	84a
7.4	23.8	46.1	70.8	18.6	34.9	39.8	−49.2	55.4	14.9	....					Foreign	85a
										....					Finance from Foreign Aid	86a
−64.0	50.1	−33.3	−16.2	.9	−54.8	−58.3	85.3	51.1	48.4	....					Use of Cash Balances	87
										....					Adj. to Total Financing	84x
1,248.5	1,438.3	1,582.0	1,744.1	1,827.1	2,056.9	2,417.1	2,859.2	3,214.2	3,506.8	3,738.2	3,977.9	....			Debt: Francs	88b
33.4	36.7	40.4	38.4	37.8	55.4	57.9	62.6	58.6	57.1	56.4	49.8	....			Foreign Currency	89b
Gross Domestic Product															*General Government*	
....	....	−1.6	−2.1	−3.9	−5.8	−5.8	−4.9	−4.2	−3.0	−2.7	−1.6	−1.3	−1.4		Deficit (−) or Surplus	80g
....	....	35.5	35.8	39.8	45.3	48.5	52.8	57.1	59.3	59.5	58.5	57.4	57.2		Debt	88g
															National Accounts	
Billions of Euros Beginning 1999																
3,071.2	†3,242.7	3,437.7	3,632.9	3,790.2	3,912.7	3,998.6	4,113.2	†4,257.7	4,393.9	4,459.9	4,645.3	†734.4	764.6	796.4	Househ.Cons.Expend.,incl.NPISHs	96f. c
1,250.3	†1,326.0	1,398.5	1,473.9	1,551.6	1,644.3	1,769.4	1,808.9	†1,851.9	1,922.5	1,985.6	2,007.6	†315.7	329.9	340.6	Government Consumption Expend.	91f. c
1,136.2	†1,281.2	1,414.5	1,496.4	1,514.6	1,491.0	1,398.2	1,428.4	†1,458.8	1,470.4	1,472.8	1,578.1	†259.9	285.1	296.3	Gross Fixed Capital Formation	93e. c
6.0	30.5	55.2	50.0	37.9	−3.6	−90.0	−5.2	†34.9	−11.8	−5.2	59.7	†5.6	11.0	−3.7	Changes in Inventories	93i. c
1,069.3	†1,189.2	1,398.5	1,411.6	1,479.4	1,529.0	1,494.8	1,610.2	†1,747.8	1,832.1	2,093.7	2,234.1	†350.3	404.9	413.4	Exports of Goods and Services	90c. c
1,122.6	†1,238.7	1,421.4	1,474.1	1,511.0	1,489.2	1,385.8	1,510.4	†1,637.2	1,699.7	1,849.9	2,012.0	†320.0	386.1	385.4	Imports of Goods and Services (−)	98c. c
5,416.4	†5,837.1	6,277.6	6,621.8	6,895.3	7,119.2	7,227.2	7,488.2	†7,759.9	7,955.2	8,206.9	8,564.4	†1,354.3	1,418.1	1,464.1	Gross Domestic Product (GDP)	99b. c
7.5	14.3	22.8	26.2	37.5	25.8	6.4	−28.9	−18.2	−31.8	−34.3	−40.4	†−6.3	−6.7	....	Net Primary Income from Abroad	98.n c
5,408.9	5,822.8	6,247.5	6,594.6	6,846.7	7,100.2	7,220.1	7,471.0	7,711.5	7,946.8	8,226.1	8,605.7	†1,349.0	1,405.0	....	Gross National Income (GNI)	99a. c
−27.6	−39.5	−12.9	−10.7	−18.7	−18.6	−26.0	−28.9	−18.2	−31.9	−34.3	−40.1	†−6.4	−7.2	−6.6	Net Current Transf.from Abroad	98t. c
5,381.2	5,783.3	6,214.8	6,562.6	6,812.1	7,059.5	7,170.5	7,418.0	7,666.5	7,892.3	8,170.9	8,542.0	†1,359.9	1,415.5	1,459.0	Gross Nat'l Disposable Inc.(GNDI)	99i. c
1,059.7	1,214.6	1,352.0	1,424.4	1,441.8	1,461.5	1,370.8	1,440.5	1,512.2	1,528.7	1,673.8	1,837.3	†301.8	313.5	312.6	Gross Saving	99s. c
673.5	725.0	776.1	828.9	880.1	905.9	925.8	954.6	983.9	1,000.9	1,031.6	....				Consumption of Fixed Capital	99cf c
3,174.5	3,317.3														GDP Volume 1980 Prices	99b. r
....	6,892.7	7,193.3	7,374.5	7,455.6	7,548.2	7,480.8	7,615.4	7,758.9	7,841.5	7,990.3	8,268.1	†1,300.7	1,354.9	1,379.1	GDP Vol. 1995 Ref., Chained	99b. r
85.0	88.8	92.7	95.0	96.1	97.3	96.4	98.2	100.0	101.1	103.0	106.6	†110.0	114.5	116.6	GDP Volume (1995=100)	99bv r
82.1	†84.7	87.3	89.8	92.5	94.3	96.6	98.3	†100.0	101.4	102.7	103.6	†104.1	104.7	106.1	GDP Deflator (1995=100)	99bi r
Midyear Estimates																
55.82	55.12	56.42	56.73	57.05	57.37	57.65	57.90	58.14	58.37	58.61	58.85	59.10	58.89	59.19	**Population**	99z

(See notes in the back of the book.)

Gabon

		1972	1973	1974	1975	1976	1977	1978	1979	1980	1981	1982	1983	1984	1985	1986
Exchange Rates															*Francs per SDR:*	
Official Rate	aa	278.00	284.00	272.08	262.55	288.70	285.76	272.28	264.78	287.99	334.52	370.92	436.97	470.11	415.26	394.78
															Francs per US Dollar:	
Official Rate	ae	256.05	235.42	222.22	224.27	248.49	235.25	209.00	201.00	225.80	287.40	336.25	417.37	479.60	378.05	322.75
Official Rate	rf	252.03	222.89	240.70	214.31	238.95	245.68	225.66	212.72	211.28	271.73	328.61	381.07	436.96	449.26	346.31
															Index Numbers (1995=100):	
Official Rate	ahx	197.9	224.6	207.2	233.0	209.0	203.0	221.4	234.6	236.4	184.6	152.6	131.5	114.5	111.9	144.3
Nominal Effective Exchange Rate	ne c	....	....	....	....	....	....	....	104.2	107.8	100.8	97.6	96.1	96.4	102.0	111.1
Real Effective Exchange Rate	re c	....	....	....	....	....	....	....	....	204.6	182.1	183.7	180.8	173.5	178.9	194.7
Fund Position															*Millions of SDRs:*	
Quota	2f. s	15.00	15.00	15.00	15.00	15.00	15.00	30.00	30.00	45.00	45.00	45.00	73.10	73.10	73.10	73.10
SDRs	1b. s	4.73	4.70	4.66	4.63	4.62	4.61	4.55	7.21	5.64	6.97	.74	.42	5.82	2.08	10.05
Reserve Position in the Fund	1c. s	2.43	2.46	2.49	2.53	2.53	2.53				.03	.04	7.03	.03	.03	.03
Total Fund Cred.&Loans Outstg.	2tl							7.61	15.22	11.36	11.34	9.35	1.85	—	—	27.41
International Liquidity													*Millions of US Dollars Unless Otherwise Indicated:*			
Total Reserves minus Gold	1l. d	23.23	47.86	103.29	146.07	116.16	9.91	22.57	20.13	107.50	198.85	311.88	186.90	199.45	192.55	126.35
SDRs	1b. d	5.14	5.67	5.71	5.42	5.37	5.60	5.93	9.50	7.19	8.11	.82	.44	5.70	2.28	12.29
Reserve Position in the Fund	1c. d	2.64	2.97	3.05	2.97	2.94	3.08	—	—	—	.03	.04	7.36	.03	.03	.04
Foreign Exchange	1d. d	15.45	39.22	94.53	137.68	107.84	1.23	16.65	10.64	100.31	190.71	311.02	179.10	193.72	190.23	114.02
Gold (Million Fine Troy Ounces)	1ad	....	....	....	—	—	.006	.010	.013	.013	.013	.013	.013	.013	.013	.013
Gold (National Valuation)	1and	....	....	....	—	—	1.06	2.24	6.68	7.57	5.14	5.77	4.86	3.97	4.16	5.03
Monetary Authorities: Other Liab.	4..d	.08	.05	.02	.03	.04	.11	.35	.16	.20	.18	.35	.23	1.37	1.35	.65
Deposit Money Banks: Assets	7a. d	6.97	6.48	10.31	11.31	30.26	25.39	18.61	32.81	17.74	30.43	34.60	23.24	15.56	26.49	43.01
Liabilities	7b. d	16.44	21.85	43.42	39.62	54.01	131.16	125.31	108.73	80.92	105.51	83.10	36.35	16.73	94.46	122.00
Monetary Authorities															*Billions of Francs:*	
Foreign Assets	11	5.94	11.06	22.95	32.76	28.86	2.58	5.19	5.40	25.99	58.63	106.81	80.05	97.56	74.38	42.40
Claims on Central Government	12a			1.00	4.10	9.27	27.03	28.57	33.98	23.90	3.79	5.16	.81			28.51
Claims on Deposit Money Banks	12e	4.39	5.37	7.02	6.84	4.81	17.15	11.88	12.07	8.83	7.14	6.21	7.27	8.03	26.98	22.83
Claims on Other Banking Insts	12f	....	....	....	....	....	....	....	....	....	....	....	....	....	....	....
Reserve Money	14	7.93	10.26	18.95	24.44	40.27	40.94	35.72	37.91	45.06	48.26	52.59	57.53	68.00	62.68	55.56
of which: Currency Outside DMBs	14a	7.38	9.56	15.63	22.22	33.65	34.27	31.34	30.34	35.85	37.82	45.45	50.24	54.29	57.39	49.12
Foreign Liabilities	16c	.02	.01	.01	.01	.01	.03	2.15	4.06	3.32	3.84	3.59	1.02	1.52	.51	11.03
Central Government Deposits	16d	1.01	4.50	10.45	17.34	.21	3.21	3.15	2.15	1.79	9.12	55.89	25.19	33.33	35.25	8.34
Capital Accounts	17a	—	.02	.02	.03	.03	.04	.04	.05	1.64	1.39	1.98	2.10	1.93	1.92	1.96
Other Items (Net)	17r	1.37	1.64	1.55	1.89	2.43	2.55	4.57	7.28	6.92	6.94	4.12	2.29	.82	1.00	16.84
Deposit Money Banks															*Billions of Francs:*	
Reserves	20	.55	.70	3.32	2.22	6.62	6.66	4.39	7.58	9.21	10.44	7.15	7.29	13.72	5.29	6.44
Foreign Assets	21	1.78	1.49	2.29	2.54	7.52	†5.97	3.89	6.60	4.01	8.75	11.63	9.70	7.46	10.02	13.88
Claims on Central Government	22a	3.38	4.95	13.22	11.61	34.80	39.63	27.45	27.07	30.56	30.36	49.38	55.49	83.50	109.78	81.37
Claims on Nonfin.Pub.Enterprises	22c															
Claims on Private Sector	22d	24.78	33.13	48.77	66.63	99.75	†124.71	129.98	123.35	142.59	170.99	184.98	229.11	251.83	303.20	336.33
Claims on Other Banking Insts	22f	....	....	....	....	....	....	....	....	....	....	....	....	....	....	....
Claims on Nonbank Financial Insts	22g	....	....	....	....	....	....	....	....	....	....	....	....	....	....	....
Demand Deposits	24	11.41	13.70	22.82	37.26	71.33	†65.26	59.37	55.56	59.03	77.76	81.58	94.20	115.11	120.78	105.00
Time and Savings Deposits	25	1.30	3.27	5.89	11.98	28.43	33.82	22.94	36.94	58.11	61.67	74.08	92.73	105.05	129.41	122.51
Bonds	26ab	....	....	....	....	....	....	....	....	....	....	....	....	....	....	....
Foreign Liabilities	26c	1.80	2.40	6.80	5.43	9.42	26.77	22.45	17.68	10.91	25.06	19.75	7.86	1.56	29.99	33.77
Long-Term Foreign Liabilities	26cl	2.40	2.63	2.85	3.46	4.00	4.09	3.74	4.17	7.37	5.27	8.20	7.31	6.47	5.72	5.60
Central Government Deposits	26d	4.34	6.38	13.93	9.40	17.71	19.31	37.19	22.60	17.62	22.22	26.23	48.52	65.31	62.75	57.60
Credit from Monetary Authorities	26g	4.39	5.37	6.16	6.18	4.33	16.16	11.32	11.63	8.48	6.65	6.21	7.27	8.03	26.98	22.83
Capital Accounts	27a	3.36	4.27	5.20	7.01	10.19	14.40	19.36	23.72	25.68	36.40	36.83	46.75	49.41	58.20	62.56
Other Items (Net)	27r	1.50	2.26	3.95	2.28	3.28	†-2.82	-10.66	-7.70	-.83	-14.47	.26	-3.05	5.57	-5.54	28.15
Monetary Survey															*Billions of Francs:*	
Foreign Assets (Net)	31n	5.90	10.14	18.44	29.86	26.95	†-18.24	-15.52	-9.75	15.77	38.47	95.10	80.87	101.94	53.90	11.48
Domestic Credit	32	22.81	27.20	38.60	55.60	125.90	†168.86	145.66	159.66	177.64	173.81	157.39	211.69	236.69	314.98	380.27
Claims on Central Govt. (Net)	32an	-1.96	-5.93	-10.17	-11.03	26.15	44.15	15.68	36.30	35.05	2.82	-27.58	-17.41	-15.14	11.78	43.94
Claims on Nonfin.Pub.Enterprises	32c															
Claims on Private Sector	32d	24.78	33.13	48.77	66.63	99.75	†124.71	129.98	123.35	142.59	170.99	184.98	229.11	251.83	303.20	336.33
Claims on Other Banking Insts	32f	....	....	....	....	....	....	....	....	....	....	....	....	....	....	....
Claims on Nonbank Financial Inst	32g	....	....	....	....	....	....	....	....	....	....	....	....	....	....	....
Money	34	18.79	23.26	38.44	59.48	104.97	†99.53	90.70	85.90	94.88	115.58	127.02	144.43	169.40	178.16	154.11
Quasi-Money	35	1.30	3.27	5.89	11.98	28.43	33.82	22.94	36.94	58.11	61.67	74.08	92.73	105.05	129.41	122.51
Bonds	36ab	....	....	....	....	....	....	....	....	....	....	....	....	....	....	....
Other Items (Net)	37r	8.63	10.82	12.71	14.01	19.45	†17.27	16.51	27.08	40.42	35.03	51.39	55.40	64.19	61.30	115.12
Money plus Quasi-Money	35l	20.09	26.53	44.33	71.46	133.40	†133.35	113.64	122.83	152.99	177.25	201.11	237.16	274.44	307.58	276.62
Interest Rates															*Percent Per Annum*	
Discount Rate (End of Period)	60	4.50	4.50	5.50	5.50	6.50	6.50	6.50	8.50	8.50	8.50	8.50	8.50	8.50	9.00	8.00
Deposit Rate	60l	....	....	....	....	....	....	7.50	6.50	7.50	7.50	7.50	7.50	7.50	7.67	8.00
Lending Rate	60p	....	....	....	....	....	....	10.50	8.50	12.50	12.50	12.46	13.00	13.00	12.67	11.50
Prices and Production															*Index Numbers (1995=100):*	
Consumer Prices	64	16.9	17.9	20.1	†25.8	31.0	35.3	39.0	42.2	47.4	51.5	†60.1	66.5	70.4	75.5	80.3
Crude Petroleum	66aa	....	....	....	....	....	....	65.9	59.9	51.4	44.0	45.2	45.9	44.8	44.9	47.6

1987	1988	1989	1990	1991	1992	1993	1994	1995	1996	1997	1998	1999	2000	2001		
End of Period															**Exchange Rates**	
378.78	407.68	380.32	364.84	370.48	378.57	404.89	†780.44	728.38	753.06	807.94	791.61	†896.19	918.49	935.39	Official Rate	**aa**
End of Period (ae)	*Period Average (rf)*															
267.00	302.95	289.40	256.45	259.00	275.32	294.77	†534.60	490.00	523.70	598.81	562.21	†652.95	704.95	744.31	Official Rate	**ae**
300.54	297.85	319.01	272.26	282.11	264.69	283.16	†555.20	499.15	511.55	583.67	589.95	†615.70	711.98	733.04	Official Rate	**rf**
Period Averages																
166.1	167.8	156.5	183.7	177.4	188.9	176.3	90.0	100.0	97.5	85.6	84.7	81.1	70.3	68.1	Official Rate	**ah** x
118.9	126.6	138.3	162.1	163.2	173.5	179.0	96.0	100.0	100.5	97.1	99.5	97.0	91.7	92.9	Nominal Effective Exchange Rate	**ne** c
191.3	165.4	167.2	181.4	153.4	138.5	134.3	90.6	100.0	98.9	97.4	100.7	96.3	89.7	91.0	Real Effective Exchange Rate	**re** c
End of Period															**Fund Position**	
73.10	73.10	73.10	73.10	73.10	110.30	110.30	110.30	110.30	110.30	110.30	110.30	154.30	154.30	154.30	Quota	**2f.** s
8.19	6.54	.17	.19	4.44	.08	.03	.17	—	.02	—	.01	—	.05	.04	SDRs	**1b.** s
.03	.03	.04	.04	.05	.05	.05	.05	.05	.07	.07	.07	.11	.15	.18	Reserve Position in the Fund	**1c.** s
42.50	98.68	102.69	98.49	84.34	58.55	32.89	61.42	64.95	83.26	97.20	80.52	62.60	68.38	59.64	Total Fund Cred.&Loans Outstg.	**2tl**
End of Period															**International Liquidity**	
12.00	67.44	34.43	273.76	327.48	71.21	.75	175.19	148.09	248.72	282.60	15.41	17.95	190.09	9.85	Total Reserves minus Gold	**1l.** d
11.62	8.80	.22	.27	6.35	.10	.03	.25	—	.03	—	.01	.01	.07	.06	SDRs	**1b.** d
.04	.04	.05	.06	.07	.07	.07	.08	.08	.09	.09	.09	.15	.19	.23	Reserve Position in the Fund	**1c.** d
.34	58.59	34.15	273.44	321.05	71.04	.64	174.86	148.01	248.59	282.51	15.30	17.79	189.83	9.57	Foreign Exchange	**1d.** d
.013	.013	.013	.013	.013	.013	.013	.013	.013	.013	.013	.013	.013	.013	.013	Gold (Million Fine Troy Ounces)	**1ad**
6.19	5.21	4.07	4.59	4.55	4.28	5.11	†4.85	4.95	4.73	3.74	3.69	†3.73	3.50	3.57	Gold (National Valuation)	**1an** d
64.52	†125.25	73.66	76.97	74.50	45.95	35.48	33.67	34.56	33.52	53.73	34.62	46.34	44.91	41.61	Monetary Authorities: Other Liab.	**4..** d
39.44	40.77	82.79	89.44	88.02	61.55	53.13	82.23	75.69	159.03	64.55	71.56	74.88	239.68	132.33	Deposit Money Banks: Assets	**7a.** d
57.85	33.13	142.16	143.75	154.76	117.45	89.15	41.28	79.93	94.16	50.58	56.73	77.78	91.62	81.39	Liabilities	**7b.** d
End of Period															**Monetary Authorities**	
4.87	†22.02	11.45	71.48	85.99	20.78	1.70	96.30	74.99	132.74	171.45	10.74	14.15	136.47	9.99	Foreign Assets	**11**
81.99	†90.14	101.00	40.26	†42.53	58.00	62.47	95.83	101.92	123.60	87.49	211.13	200.78	157.33	248.21	Claims on Central Government	**12a**
28.82	†19.77	17.39	16.70	†11.77	23.54	19.82	.16	3.74	.75	—	8.11	11.63	.22	3.00	Claims on Deposit Money Banks	**12e**
....	4.48	7.67	7.91	9.00	3.11	—	—	—	—	—	—	—	—	—	Claims on Other Banking Insts	**12f**
58.65	†54.63	63.28	69.02	88.44	63.58	58.38	133.91	128.24	165.20	167.93	153.60	141.52	192.68	184.59	Reserve Money	**14**
51.46	†48.13	57.50	61.88	62.88	56.79	50.47	76.93	100.69	110.88	121.03	124.72	105.26	116.18	128.19	of which: Currency Outside DMBs	**14a**
33.33	†78.17	60.37	55.67	50.54	34.82	23.78	65.94	64.24	80.26	110.71	83.21	86.36	94.46	86.76	Foreign Liabilities	**16c**
12.44	†11.34	31.05	23.87	22.41	7.97	3.11	18.51	10.67	32.35	16.13	12.14	26.10	43.18	24.57	Central Government Deposits	**16d**
2.05	†7.67	7.09	6.90	7.16	6.97	7.59	12.49	11.53	11.89	12.32	11.87	13.76	14.46	15.24	Capital Accounts	**17a**
9.21	†-15.39	-24.28	-19.12	†-19.26	-7.90	-8.87	-38.56	-34.03	-32.61	-48.15	-30.85	-41.17	-50.75	-49.97	Other Items (Net)	**17r**
End of Period															**Deposit Money Banks**	
7.19	†5.81	5.53	7.07	25.49	5.94	7.86	56.87	27.06	48.32	44.10	27.47	34.75	75.73	56.10	Reserves	**20**
10.53	†12.38	23.96	22.94	22.80	16.95	15.66	43.96	37.09	83.28	38.65	40.23	48.89	168.96	98.49	Foreign Assets	**21**
90.40	†102.34	102.20	101.17	95.20	†105.35	99.25	172.94	161.16	152.37	143.46	135.76	137.99	92.91	88.71	Claims on Central Government	**22a**
....	22.49	22.84	19.06	19.90	8.78	9.88	10.17	9.49	13.60	26.91	23.20	22.32	17.11	21.39	Claims on Nonfin.Pub.Enterprises	**22c**
293.33	†192.09	208.58	210.54	224.39	162.01	157.91	157.20	196.08	191.93	269.89	285.12	286.06	313.79	375.04	Claims on Private Sector	**22d**
....	.17	—	.01	—	—	—	.88	.88	.91	1.39	.60	.74	.74	.60	Claims on Other Banking Insts	**22f**
....	2.18	2.64	4.06	4.04	4.65	4.22	7.07	10.22	7.99	7.66	7.55	10.53	25.30	22.05	Claims on Nonbank Financial Insts	**22g**
83.80	†114.24	113.40	118.98	132.48	84.71	86.92	117.96	117.90	159.11	174.41	156.99	161.85	203.51	203.74	Demand Deposits	**24**
105.46	†99.98	107.72	107.01	112.54	99.11	99.87	130.98	139.87	144.78	169.98	176.47	177.21	206.85	234.47	Time and Savings Deposits	**25**
....	.23	.16	.11	1.01	.90	1.20	.30	.30	.23	.15	.08	3.09	5.55	2.65	Bonds	**26ab**
-6.74	†9.43	4.76	12.45	†21.78	19.86	19.37	13.73	36.34	46.79	28.24	22.66	38.99	56.61	58.85	Foreign Liabilities	**26c**
22.19	†34.97	36.44	24.42	†18.31	12.48	6.91	8.34	2.83	2.52	2.05	9.24	11.80	7.98	1.72	Long-Term Foreign Liabilities	**26cl**
51.27	†39.59	35.32	34.31	39.42	†22.88	16.72	32.21	15.35	20.93	20.62	21.82	29.67	112.30	71.32	Central Government Deposits	**26d**
28.82	†19.77	17.39	16.70	†11.77	23.54	19.82	.16	3.74	.75	—	8.11	11.63	.22	3.00	Credit from Monetary Authorities	**26g**
77.28	†19.22	56.45	54.15	†58.91	54.68	54.55	133.44	128.50	123.58	115.89	122.47	120.48	85.73	107.75	Capital Accounts	**27a**
39.37	†.02	-5.90	-3.27	-4.40	†-14.49	-10.58	11.97	-2.78	-.21	20.78	-.92	-15.89	18.68	-20.73	Other Items (Net)	**27r**
End of Period															**Monetary Survey**	
-11.18	†-88.18	-66.16	1.88	†18.16	-29.43	-32.70	52.25	8.68	86.45	69.10	-64.14	-74.10	146.38	-38.86	Foreign Assets (Net)	**31n**
402.00	†362.96	378.57	324.83	†333.22	†311.04	313.90	393.36	453.74	437.12	500.04	629.38	602.65	451.70	660.10	Domestic Credit	**32**
108.68	†141.55	136.83	83.25	†75.90	†132.50	141.89	218.05	237.06	222.68	194.19	312.92	283.00	94.76	241.03	Claims on Central Govt. (Net)	**32an**
....	22.49	22.84	19.06	19.90	8.78	9.88	10.17	9.49	13.60	26.91	23.20	22.32	17.11	21.39	Claims on Nonfin.Pub.Enterprises	**32c**
293.33	†192.09	208.58	210.54	224.39	162.01	157.91	157.20	196.08	191.93	269.89	285.12	286.06	313.79	375.04	Claims on Private Sector	**32d**
....	4.65	7.67	7.92	9.00	3.11	—	.88	.88	.91	1.39	.60	.74	.74	.60	Claims on Other Banking Insts	**32f**
....	2.18	2.64	4.06	4.04	4.65	4.22	7.07	10.22	7.99	7.66	7.55	10.53	25.30	22.05	Claims on Nonbank Financial Inst	**32g**
135.26	†163.06	171.16	180.93	195.43	142.35	137.44	195.01	219.09	276.00	298.25	283.12	268.61	320.46	332.22	Money	**34**
105.46	†99.98	107.72	107.01	112.54	99.11	99.87	130.98	139.87	144.78	169.98	176.47	177.21	206.85	234.47	Quasi-Money	**35**
....	.23	.16	.11	1.01	.90	1.20	.30	.30	.23	.15	.08	3.09	5.55	2.25	Bonds	**36ab**
150.10	†11.52	33.37	38.65	†42.41	†39.26	42.69	119.33	103.23	102.64	100.84	102.57	77.17	68.12	52.30	Other Items (Net)	**37r**
240.72	†263.04	278.87	287.94	307.97	241.46	237.31	325.98	358.96	420.78	468.22	459.59	445.82	527.31	566.69	Money plus Quasi-Money	**35l**
Percent Per Annum															**Interest Rates**	
8.00	9.50	10.00	11.00	10.75	12.00	11.50	†7.75	8.60	7.75	7.50	7.00	7.60	7.00	6.50	Discount Rate (*End of Period*)	**60**
7.94	8.17	8.75	†7.50	7.50	7.50	7.75	8.08	5.50	5.46	5.00	5.00	5.00	5.00	5.00	Deposit Rate	**60l**
11.13	11.79	12.50	†18.50	18.15	17.77	17.46	17.50	16.00	22.00	22.00	22.00	22.00	22.00	20.67	Lending Rate	**60p**
Period Averages															**Prices and Production**	
79.5	72.6	77.4	83.4	73.7	66.6	67.0	91.2	100.0	100.7	104.7	106.2 P	104.2 P	104.7 P	....	Consumer Prices	**64**
45.8	51.4	64.6	81.4	82.5	87.5	86.4	96.7	100.0	105.5	107.6	103.5	99.6	....	....	Crude Petroleum	**66aa**

Gabon

		1972	1973	1974	1975	1976	1977	1978	1979	1980	1981	1982	1983	1984	1985	1986
International Transactions															*Billions of Francs*	
Exports	70	57.50	73.10	184.36	201.92	271.48	329.96	249.85	393.19	459.06	598.00	710.00	762.20	878.90	876.70	440.00
Imports, c.i.f.	71	35.00	42.29	79.89	100.56	120.24	176.00	139.17	113.11	142.31	229.00	285.00	261.10	316.20	384.00	300.00
Imports, c.i.f., from DOTS	71y	....	....	....	....	....	....	....	....	....	228.10	262.39	261.24	345.81	429.96	312.02
Balance of Payments															*Millions of US Dollars:*	
Current Account, n.i.e.	78ald	....	....	....	....	....	....	73.9	247.6	383.9	403.3	309.4	97.9	112.7	-162.5	-1,057.4
Goods: Exports f.o.b.	78aad	....	....	....	....	....	....	1,308.6	1,815.0	2,084.4	2,200.2	2,160.4	2,000.1	2,017.8	1,951.4	1,074.2
Goods: Imports f.o.b.	78abd	....	....	....	....	....	....	-557.9	-554.8	-686.1	-841.2	-722.6	-725.5	-733.2	-854.7	-979.1
Trade Balance	78acd	....	....	....	....	....	....	750.7	1,260.2	1,398.3	1,359.0	1,437.8	1,274.6	1,284.6	1,096.7	95.1
Services: Credit	78add	....	....	....	....	....	....	169.9	208.8	324.6	307.6	170.3	200.8	137.8	138.5	123.6
Services: Debit	78aed	....	....	....	....	....	....	-577.6	-741.9	-789.4	-868.2	-926.1	-1,031.4	-1,018.5	-1,058.3	-882.7
Balance on Goods & Services	78afd	....	....	....	....	....	....	343.0	727.1	933.5	798.4	681.9	444.0	403.9	176.8	-664.0
Income: Credit	78agd	....	....	....	....	....	....	4.4	7.3	24.9	25.2	20.0	43.2	47.7	29.2	18.1
Income: Debit	78ahd	....	....	....	....	....	....	-231.1	-368.8	-450.5	-355.2	-333.3	-299.8	-272.8	-272.8	-264.7
Balance on Gds, Serv. & Inc.	78aid	....	....	....	....	....	....	116.2	365.6	507.9	468.4	368.6	187.4	179.8	-66.8	-910.6
Current Transfers, n.i.e.: Credit	78ajd	....	....	....	....	....	....	57.9	69.8	72.7	61.6	36.8	43.0	50.3	42.0	52.8
Current Transfers: Debit	78akd	....	....	....	....	....	....	-100.2	-187.7	-196.8	-126.7	-96.0	-132.4	-117.4	-137.7	-199.7
Capital Account, n.i.e.	78bcd	....	....	....	....	....	....	—	—	—	—	—	—	—	—	—
Capital Account, n.i.e.: Credit	78bad	....	....	....	....	....	....	—	—	—	—	—	—	—	—	—
Capital Account: Debit	78bbd	....	....	....	....	....	....	—	—	—	—	—	—	—	—	—
Financial Account, n.i.e.	78bjd	....	....	....	....	....	....	-20.2	-234.2	-265.9	-277.6	-111.3	-91.5	-15.8	164.2	910.9
Direct Investment Abroad	78bdd	....	....	....	....	....	....	—	-6.7	-8.0	-7.1	-4.8	-5.7	-3.4	-4.1	-6.6
Dir. Invest. in Rep. Econ., n.i.e.	78bed	....	....	....	....	....	....	56.5	55.0	31.5	54.6	131.7	111.8	8.1	15.1	110.2
Portfolio Investment Assets	78bfd	....	....	....	....	....	....	—	—	—	—	—	—	—	—	—
Equity Securities	78bkd	....	....	....	....	....	....	—	—	—	—	—	—	—	—	—
Debt Securities	78bld	....	....	....	....	....	....	—	—	—	—	—	—	—	—	—
Portfolio Investment Liab., n.i.e.	78bgd	....	....	....	....	....	....	—	—	—	—	—	—	—	—	—
Equity Securities	78bmd	....	....	....	....	....	....	—	—	—	—	—	—	—	—	—
Debt Securities	78bnd	....	....	....	....	....	....	—	—	—	—	—	—	—	—	—
Financial Derivatives Assets	78bwd	....	....	....	....	....	....	....	....	....	....	....	....	....	....	....
Financial Derivatives Liabilities	78bxd	....	....	....	....	....	....	....	....	....	....	....	....	....	....	....
Other Investment Assets	78bhd	....	....	....	....	....	....	-17.8	-177.3	-205.6	-239.1	-263.7	-175.7	-237.9	-184.2	-45.5
Monetary Authorities	78bod	....	....	....	....	....	....	-2.8	1.2	-1.6	-.6	-.5				
General Government	78bpd	....	....	....	....	....	....	14.8	-16.5	17.5	-14.4	-8.8	5.1	5.1	-5.8	-11.1
Banks	78bqd	....	....	....	....	....	....	-29.8	-162.0	-221.5	-224.2	-254.4	-180.8	-243.1	-178.4	-34.3
Other Sectors	78brd	....	....	....	....	....	....	-58.9	-105.3	-83.8	-86.0	25.4	-21.9	217.3	337.3	852.7
Other Investment Liab., n.i.e.	78bid	....	....	....	....	....	....	.2	-.2							
Monetary Authorities	78bsd	....	....	....	....	....	....	48.6	-152.8	-103.5	-161.5	-129.5	-97.8	69.4	86.6	356.0
General Government	78btd	....	....	....	....	....	....	-2.3	-10.2	-22.1	43.4	.3	-39.6	-15.0	58.5	26.4
Banks	78bud	....	....	....	....	....	....	-105.4	57.9	41.7	32.2	154.6	115.5	162.9	192.2	470.3
Other Sectors	78bvd	....	....	....	....	....	....									
Net Errors and Omissions	78cad	....	....	....	....	....	....	-45.3	-29.9	-22.0	-7.8	-51.4	-95.7	-83.8	-62.6	-48.9
Overall Balance	78cbd	....	....	....	....	....	....	8.4	-16.5	96.0	117.9	146.7	-89.3	13.1	-60.9	-195.4
Reserves and Related Items	79dad	....	....	....	....	....	....	-8.4	16.5	-96.0	-117.9	-146.7	89.3	-13.1	60.9	195.4
Reserve Assets	79dbd	....	....	....	....	....	....	-18.2	6.8	-91.1	-117.8	-144.5	97.2	-11.2	60.9	99.3
Use of Fund Credit and Loans	79dcd	....	....	....	....	....	....	9.8	9.7	-4.9	—	-2.2	-8.0	-1.9	—	33.1
Exceptional Financing	79ded	....	....	....	....	....	....	—	—	—	—	—	—	—	—	63.0
Government Finance																*Billions of Francs:*
Deficit (-) or Surplus	80	....	-17.6	-15.5	-37.0	†-158.1	....	....	†-3.5	55.1	8.2	35.1	-16.3	3.1	1.1	....
Revenue	81	....	38.9	89.2	167.4	†189.1	....	....	†275.0	350.6	419.4	488.4	505.0	602.0	643.4	....
Grants Received	81z	....	—	—	—	—	....	....	†—	3.2	3.8	—	4.4	4.8	5.0	....
Expenditure	82	....	54.9	98.9	195.4	†340.5	....	....	†276.9	330.3	415.6	451.0	516.3	594.9	637.2	....
Lending Minus Repayments	83	....	1.6	5.7	9.0	†6.7	....	....	†1.6	-31.6	-.6	2.3	9.4	8.8	10.1	....
Financing																
Domestic	84a	....	1.7	-5.9	2.8	†22.8	....	....	....	-55.1	-8.1	-35.1	16.1	-2.8	-3.8	....
Foreign	85a	....	15.9	21.4	34.2	†135.3	....	....	....	—	-.1	—	.2	-.3	2.7	....
National Accounts																*Billions of Francs*
Househ.Cons.Expend.,incl.NPISHs	96f	†36.3	73.6	91.8	108.7	118.3	162.1	196.6	213.0	236.6	280.7	325.1	385.7	464.7	501.2	562.1
Government Consumption Expend.	91f	†19.2	25.1	34.4	56.5	76.0	124.9	73.8	77.9	119.6	149.5	186.7	222.3	284.4	306.3	303.9
Gross Capital Formation	93	†52.2	60.4	192.4	289.7	528.5	400.8	188.8	211.0	248.9	381.5	416.3	454.8	512.9	613.6	543.5
Exports of Goods and Services	90c	†79.3	94.8	213.9	229.0	327.8	356.1	333.0	376.9	585.2	665.0	732.3	792.5	919.6	935.7	475.8
Imports of Goods and Services (-)	98c	†78.4	92.9	160.8	221.5	331.5	353.9	253.0	234.2	285.9	427.1	471.6	562.7	625.6	711.0	684.2
Gross Domestic Product (GDP)	99b	108.5	161.1	371.7	462.4	719.1	690.2	539.2	644.6	904.5	1,049.0	1,188.9	1,320.0	1,455.6	1,576.0	1,590.0
Net Primary Income from Abroad	98.n	-9.6	-14.5	-27.2	-29.6	-33.8	-38.8	-76.6	-76.9	-50.3	-64.0	-62.3	-82.5	-83.1	-91.9	-63.7
Gross National Income (GNI)	99a	98.9	146.6	344.5	432.8	685.3	651.4	462.6	567.7	854.2	985.6	1,126.6	1,210.1	1,472.9	1,553.9	1,137.4
Consumption of Fixed Capital	99cf	†23.8	22.7	46.0	66.5	88.3	94.1	87.0	....	84.0	93.6	119.0	116.2	176.5	162.7	230.2
																Millions:
Population	99z	.97	.98	.99	1.00	1.02	†1.00	1.02	1.04	†.81	.84	.88	.91	.95	.99	1.02

	1987	1988	1989	1990	1991	1992	1993	1994	1995	1996	1997	1998	1999	2000	2001		
Billions of Francs																**International Transactions**	
	387.00	356.10	509.60	600.00	632.70	551.10	649.80	1,304.90	1,354.40	1,628.70	1,765.20	....	....	....	....	Exports..	70
	220.00	235.70	244.60	250.00	235.40	185.20	239.30	420.00	440.20	489.30	644.30	650.80	518.00	708.00	....	Imports, c.i.f.	71
	236.60	276.48	261.43	230.49	306.39	256.43	259.86	392.82	485.46	468.29	750.33	671.62	972.12	1,016.55	1,079.38	Imports, c.i.f., from DOTS	71y
Minus Sign Indicates Debit																**Balance of Payments**	
	–449.1	–615.5	–192.2	167.7	74.8	–168.1	–49.1	317.4	464.7	888.6	531.4	–595.5	390.4	....	....	Current Account, n.i.e.	78al *d*
	1,286.4	1,195.6	1,626.0	2,488.8	2,227.9	2,259.2	2,326.2	2,365.3	2,727.8	3,334.2	3,032.7	1,907.6	2,498.8	....	....	Goods: Exports f.o.b.	78aa *d*
	–731.8	–791.2	–751.7	–805.1	–861.0	–886.3	–845.1	–776.7	–880.9	–961.6	–1,030.6	–1,163.2	–910.5	....	....	Goods: Imports f.o.b.	78ab *d*
	554.5	404.3	874.3	1,683.7	1,366.9	1,372.9	1,481.1	1,588.6	1,846.9	2,372.5	2,002.1	744.4	1,588.3	....	....	*Trade Balance*	78ac *d*
	114.8	213.0	289.0	241.6	324.0	347.6	311.1	219.6	217.1	233.9	232.9	219.6	280.9	....	....	Services: Credit	78ad *d*
	–752.3	–811.0	–900.8	–1,006.6	–881.6	–924.8	–1,022.7	–826.7	–891.6	–917.8	–952.7	–991.0	–867.0	....	....	Services: Debit	78ae *d*
	–83.0	–193.7	262.5	918.7	809.3	795.6	769.5	981.4	1,172.4	1,688.6	1,282.3	–27.0	1,002.2	....	....	*Balance on Goods & Services*	78af *d*
	16.0	15.1	19.0	20.1	28.0	47.2	32.1	11.9	35.0	42.8	39.0	57.5	84.2	....	....	Income: Credit	78ag *d*
	–258.7	–292.7	–347.8	–636.7	–642.7	–868.9	–658.3	–509.9	–700.5	–805.8	–755.5	–572.5	–653.1	....	....	Income: Debit	78ah *d*
	–325.7	–471.2	–66.2	302.0	194.6	–26.1	143.4	483.4	507.0	925.6	565.8	–542.1	433.3	....	....	*Balance on Gds, Serv. & Inc.*	78ai *d*
	57.1	53.8	42.3	58.9	44.0	51.4	48.0	18.7	58.0	65.2	62.7	36.6	42.6	....	....	Current Transfers, n.i.e.: Credit	78aj *d*
	–180.5	–198.1	–168.3	–193.3	–163.8	–193.4	–240.5	–184.8	–100.3	–102.1	–97.1	–90.0	–85.6	....	....	Current Transfers: Debit	78ak *d*
	—	—	—	—	—	—	—	—	4.8	5.1	5.8	1.8	5.4	....	....	Capital Account, n.i.e.	78bc *d*
	—	—	—	—	—	—	—	—	5.6	9.6	7.5	3.6	5.7	....	....	Capital Account, n.i.e.: Credit	78ba *d*
	—	—	—	—	—	—	—	....	–.8	–4.5	–1.7	–1.8	–.3	....	....	Capital Account: Debit	78bb *d*
	364.9	716.6	61.1	–398.3	–306.7	–218.2	–389.2	–745.0	–724.7	–1,047.6	–626.2	–165.8	–686.8	....	....	Financial Account, n.i.e.	78bj *d*
	–7.7	–9.7	–8.0	–28.8	–14.9	–25.7	–2.5	—	–35.0	–2.3	–21.0	–33.2	–73.9	....	....	Direct Investment Abroad	78bd *d*
	89.8	132.5	–30.5	73.5	–54.6	126.9	–113.7	–99.6	–314.5	–489.1	–311.3	146.6	–156.6	....	....	Dir. Invest. in Rep. Econ., n.i.e.	78be *d*
	—	—	—	—	—	—	—	....	–29.8	–21.1	260.1	19.2	22.4	....	....	Portfolio Investment Assets	78bf *d*
	—	—	—	—	—	—	—	....	–45.0	–16.7	311.3	19.2	44.0	....	....	Equity Securities	78bk *d*
	—	—	—	—	—	—	—	....	15.2	–4.4	–51.2	—	–21.6	....	....	Debt Securities	78bl *d*
	—	—	—	—	—	—	—	....	80.3	4.6	–20.7	–.2	–.7	....	....	Portfolio Investment Liab., n.i.e.	78bg *d*
	—	—	—	—	—	—	—	....	—	–7.5	—	–.2	—	....	....	Equity Securities	78bm *d*
	—	—	—	—	—	—	—	....	80.3	12.1	–20.7	—	–.7	....	....	Debt Securities	78bn *d*
	....	....	....	....	....	....	....	....	....	....	....	....	....	....	....	Financial Derivatives Assets	78bw *d*
	....	....	....	....	....	....	....	....	....	....	....	....	....	....	....	Financial Derivatives Liabilities	78bx *d*
	–113.1	42.1	–278.3	–285.1	–14.2	–27.2	–7.8	–258.6	–39.9	–215.1	18.3	–220.7	–109.0	....	....	Other Investment Assets	78bh *d*
	....	....	....	....	....	....	....	....	–2.1	1.2	25.0	–21.5	17.5	....	....	Monetary Authorities	78bo *d*
	....	....	....	....	....	....	....	....	....	....	....	....	....	....	....	General Government	78bp *d*
	11.1	–6.1	–36.4	10.0	.7	6.8	4.6	–22.9	13.8	–90.3	76.5	–2.7	–14.0	....	....	Banks	78bq *d*
	–124.2	48.2	–241.9	–295.0	–14.9	–34.0	–12.4	–235.8	–51.5	–126.0	–83.2	–196.4	–112.5	....	....	Other Sectors	78br *d*
	395.8	551.7	378.0	–157.8	–223.0	–292.8	–265.2	–386.7	–385.7	–324.7	–551.6	–77.5	–369.1	....	....	Other Investment Liab., n.i.e.	78bi *d*
	—	—	—	–31.8	–2.9	1.9	–6.4	–203.9	—	—	—	—	—	....	....	Monetary Authorities	78bs *d*
	285.2	288.1	223.0	–187.7	–149.2	–236.1	–174.1	–133.1	–280.3	–208.4	–251.7	–276.0	–268.5	....	....	General Government	78bt *d*
	–84.4	–32.6	16.6	29.0	11.3	–2.6	1.8	–54.9	34.3	19.8	–32.6	2.7	30.7	....	....	Banks	78bu *d*
	195.1	296.3	138.4	32.6	–82.2	–55.9	–86.5	5.2	–139.7	–136.1	–267.3	195.8	–131.3	....	....	Other Sectors	78bv *d*
	–51.0	–101.9	35.0	–38.0	8.6	–55.1	–13.6	254.6	–181.1	–97.4	–108.4	92.5	–106.7	....	....	Net Errors and Omissions	78ca *d*
	–135.2	–.8	–96.1	–268.6	–223.3	–442.0	–451.9	–173.0	–436.3	–251.2	–197.4	–667.0	–397.8	....	....	*Overall Balance*	78cb *d*
	135.2	.8	96.1	268.6	223.3	442.0	451.9	173.0	436.3	251.2	197.4	667.0	397.8	....	....	Reserves and Related Items	79da *d*
	115.6	–55.7	29.8	–219.3	–54.0	246.3	67.5	–173.8	42.2	–112.8	–66.8	272.2	–4.9	....	....	Reserve Assets	79db *d*
	19.7	74.6	5.0	–5.9	–19.4	–36.3	–35.9	40.9	5.0	26.4	19.4	–22.7	–24.5	....	....	Use of Fund Credit and Loans.......	79dc *d*
	–.1	–18.1	61.3	493.8	296.7	232.0	420.3	306.0	389.1	337.6	244.8	417.5	427.3	....	....	Exceptional Financing	79de *d*
Year Ending December 31																**Government Finance**	
	....	....	†–64.1	51.0	–25.2	....	....	....	....	....	....	....	....	....	....	Deficit (-) or Surplus	80
	....	....	†282.6	373.4	441.7	....	....	....	....	....	....	....	....	....	....	Revenue	81
	....	....	†6.0	5.0	6.0	....	....	....	....	....	....	....	....	....	....	Grants Received	81z
	....	....	†351.7	326.7	465.5	....	....	....	....	....	....	....	....	....	....	Expenditure	82
	....	....	†1.0	.7	7.4	....	....	....	....	....	....	....	....	....	....	Lending Minus Repayments	83
																Financing	
	....	....	†60.5	–94.0	25.5	....	....	....	....	....	....	....	....	....	....	Domestic	84a
	....	....	†3.6	43.0	–.3	....	....	....	....	....	....	....	....	....	....	Foreign	85a
Billions of Francs																**National Accounts**	
	496.3	487.9	565.2	617.0	661.4	717.3	729.5	959.6	1,119.3	1,169.1	1,348.2	1,408.6	....	....	....	Househ.Cons.Expend.,incl.NPISHs........	96f
	242.2	220.6	215.4	251.3	217.5	223.4	234.3	278.9	291.0	308.8	345.0	425.7	....	....	....	Government Consumption Expend.	91f
	272.5	367.3	271.7	347.6	410.1	329.2	344.7	483.2	546.0	662.4	760.6	842.1	....	....	....	Gross Capital Formation	93
	421.2	377.7	587.0	746.9	722.0	692.4	750.4	1,451.7	1,455.8	1,853.5	1,920.4	1,362.3	....	....	....	Exports of Goods and Services	90c
	411.6	439.9	471.2	652.0	492.2	493.2	521.2	865.2	952.4	1,133.5	1,266.9	1,310.7	....	....	....	Imports of Goods and Services (-)	98c
	1,156.0	1,135.1	1,335.6	1,477.3	1,524.1	1,480.3	1,530.8	2,326.7	2,475.2	2,912.6	3,109.0	2,645.2	2,839.6	3,610.5	....	Gross Domestic Product (GDP)	99b
	–62.8	–75.1	–100.7	–163.3	–141.4	–264.3	–190.6	–308.2	–376.8	–400.7	–395.8	–416.7	....	....	....	Net Primary Income from Abroad	98.n
	957.7	938.5	1,067.4	1,310.3	1,377.4	1,210.8	1,347.1	2,000.0	2,082.9	2,459.4	2,711.5	2,311.3	....	....	....	Gross National Income (GNI)	99a
	195.6	121.8	169.3	180.0	188.6	192.5	216.6	243.7	274.2	308.5	347.1	390.5	....	....	....	Consumption of Fixed Capital	99cf
Midyear Estimates																	
	1.05	.88	.91	.94	.96	.99	1.02	1.05	1.08	1.11	1.14	1.15	1.18	1.21	1.24	**Population**...............................	99z

(See notes in the back of the book.)

Gambia, The

		1972	1973	1974	1975	1976	1977	1978	1979	1980	1981	1982	1983	1984	1985	1986
Exchange Rates															*Dalasis per SDR:*	
Market Rate	aa	2.312	2.077	2.085	2.314	2.730	2.549	2.561	2.369	2.139	2.440	2.733	2.887	4.238	3.802	9.084
															Dalasis per US Dollar:	
Market Rate	ae	2.129	1.722	1.703	1.977	2.350	2.099	1.966	1.799	1.677	2.096	2.478	2.757	4.323	3.461	7.426
Market Rate	rf	2.001	1.702	1.711	1.808	2.226	2.293	2.086	1.888	1.721	1.990	2.290	2.639	3.584	3.894	6.938
														Index Numbers (1995=100):		
Market Rate	ah x	477.76	566.32	558.34	530.35	431.15	416.66	458.19	506.42	555.29	484.07	417.85	362.11	272.31	247.55	139.82
Nominal Effective Exchange Rate	ne c	....	....	....	....	....	....	....	164.78	181.38	185.44	187.54	188.17	164.09	165.92	82.84
Real Effective Exchange Rate	re c	....	....	....	....	....	....	....	....	139.66	133.74	134.38	135.46	128.71	138.00	99.19
Fund Position															*Millions of SDRs:*	
Quota	2f. s	7.00	7.00	7.00	7.00	7.00	7.00	9.00	9.00	13.50	13.50	13.50	17.10	17.10	17.10	17.10
SDRs	1b. s	2.18	2.10	2.02	2.01	2.00	.86	1.13	.69	—	.05	.12	.12	—	—	.59
Reserve Position in the Fund	1c. s	.44	.52	.59	1.75	1.74						.04	.04	.04	.04	.05
Total Fund Cred.&Loans Outstg.	2tl	—	—	—	—	—		4.26	11.70	10.36	12.67	21.70	36.35	33.52	33.65	33.65	30.36	24.13
International Liquidity												*Millions of US Dollars Unless Otherwise Indicated:*				
Total Reserves minus Gold	1l. d	11.38	16.24	28.05	28.55	20.64	24.39	26.07	1.93	5.67	3.95	8.39	2.92	2.26	1.73	13.56
SDRs	1b. d	2.37	2.53	2.47	2.35	2.32	1.04	1.47	.91	—	.06	.13	.13	—	—	.72
Reserve Position in the Fund	1c. d	.48	.63	.72	2.05	2.02						.04	.04	.04	.04	.06
Foreign Exchange	1d. d	8.54	13.08	24.85	24.15	16.29	23.35	24.60	1.02	5.67	3.89	8.21	2.75	2.22	1.69	12.78
Other Official Inst. Assets	3b. d	12.39	2.03	.58	.32	.03	.02	.15	.05	...	...	...	...	...	...	...
Monetary Authorities: Other Liab.	4.. d					.27	.27	.29	5.57	5.41	6.03	7.72	23.90	46.53	69.12	46.72
Deposit Money Banks: Assets	7a. d	.94	1.13	3.05	2.42	1.25	2.21	3.13	6.33	9.96	7.82	3.77	2.07	5.18	5.37	3.66
Liabilities	7b. d		.57	.72	.08	.37	2.13	2.63	6.63	20.87	17.55	12.82	10.47	1.33	3.64	1.77
Monetary Authorities															*Millions of Dalasis:*	
Foreign Assets	11	21.87	27.96	47.77	56.44	48.47	51.18	51.27	12.39	9.53	8.27	23.19	8.04	15.37	10.66	102.57
Claims on Central Government	12a	—	—	.68	—	3.64	20.59	†16.96	41.92	15.02	60.01	33.85	79.96	95.54	142.15	23.79
Claims on Official Entities	12bx	—	—	—	—	—	—	3.09	3.09	9.09	21.34	39.33	76.96	94.12	113.39	109.00
Claims on Private Sector	12d	2.97	—	—	—	—		.30	.44	.58	.87	1.37	1.40	1.48	1.57	1.68
Claims on Deposit Money Banks	12e	7.00	23.56	24.71	29.90	32.55	11.81	33.62	46.95	86.41	110.48	129.61	132.18	131.81	154.64	151.71
Reserve Money	14	16.23	27.90	27.57	29.81	35.51	28.06	†42.72	50.40	55.80	76.20	89.59	120.80	†57.35	103.57	101.63
of which: Currency Outside DMBs	14a	14.94	25.21	24.06	27.15	32.08	19.79	34.53	36.53	36.76	42.62	55.92	57.18	58.38	85.67	91.18
Restricted Deposits	16b	—	20.38	41.82	52.39	33.34	29.34	12.77	.02	.29				†78.61	124.24	110.97
Foreign Liabilities	16c	—	—	—	—	.63	11.42	30.54	34.57	36.18	65.59	118.46	162.68	343.78	354.69	566.12
Central Government Deposits	16d	7.88	2.79	2.05	3.85	8.33	10.72	†3.51	2.26	4.13	28.55	4.86	17.25	†13.67	26.83	112.74
Capital Accounts	17a	6.11	6.11	6.11	6.77	10.88	10.94	12.21	13.73	13.11	16.94	18.90	23.28	30.67	29.40	55.52
Other Items (Net)	17r	1.62	-5.66	-4.39	-6.48	-4.03	-6.90	3.50	3.82	11.12	13.69	-4.47	-25.46	†-185.76	-216.32	-558.23
of which: Valuation Adjustment	17rv	—	-7.18	-7.18	-6.62	-4.90	-7.19	4.15	1.82	9.49	5.48	-4.06	-21.49	-93.30	-72.55	-398.89
Deposit Money Banks															*Millions of Dalasis:*	
Reserves	20	1.30	2.78	2.77	2.66	3.43	8.31	7.16	5.56	21.17	35.16	43.17	61.01	—	14.71	14.04
Foreign Assets	21	1.81	1.95	5.20	4.79	2.93	4.63	6.16	11.39	16.70	16.39	9.34	5.72	22.41	18.59	27.21
Claims on Central Government	22a	.50	—	.75	.75	3.50	5.40	12.18	4.75	14.54	3.75	17.37	26.39	35.61	37.26	57.41
Claims on Official Entities	22bx	3.97	12.20	14.80	25.25	34.55	13.68	13.08	27.77	62.12	73.75	101.53	65.06	60.14	51.74	95.78
Claims on Private Sector	22d	12.50	20.94	24.08	22.96	39.12	53.74	75.40	83.06	98.46	104.44	102.91	137.59	158.17	212.37	192.34
Demand Deposits	24	7.81	6.63	8.98	10.20	17.35	20.01	†22.93	20.06	23.95	33.50	30.34	41.43	40.45	74.98	73.14
Time and Savings Deposits	25	4.29	6.62	9.21	10.56	20.49	21.65	31.90	24.41	29.42	32.69	39.80	60.64	70.20	94.85	109.15
Restricted Deposits	26b	...	...	...	...	...								60.70	55.79	30.11
Foreign Liabilities	26c	—	.98	1.22	.16	.86	4.46	5.18	11.93	35.01	36.79	31.76	28.87	†5.77	12.61	13.11
Central Government Deposits	26d	—	—	—	—	—		.09	.09	.09	.09	.09	.09	3.10	4.09	4.05
Credit from Monetary Authorities	26g	7.00	23.56	23.22	29.90	32.55	17.86	33.12	46.96	86.16	101.28	130.78	131.64	130.59	149.73	140.94
Capital Accounts	27a	1.26	1.41	1.85	4.39	8.41	12.03	16.60	19.26	22.84	25.61	30.34	21.07	20.24	15.10	36.67
Other Items (Net)	27r	-.28	-1.33	3.12	1.20	3.87	9.75	4.16	9.82	15.52	3.53	11.21	12.03	†-54.72	-72.48	-20.39
Monetary Survey															*Millions of Dalasis:*	
Foreign Assets (Net)	31n	23.68	28.93	51.75	61.07	49.91	39.93	21.72	-22.71	-44.96	-77.72	-117.69	-177.79	†-311.77	-338.05	-449.44
Domestic Credit	32	12.06	30.35	38.26	45.11	72.48	82.69	†117.41	158.68	195.59	235.52	291.41	370.02	†428.29	527.56	363.21
Claims on Central Govt. (Net)	32an	-7.38	-2.79	-.62	-3.10	-1.19	15.27	†25.54	44.32	25.34	35.12	46.27	89.01	†114.38	148.49	-35.59
Claims on Official Entities	32bx	3.97	12.20	14.80	25.25	34.55	13.68	16.17	30.86	71.21	95.09	140.86	142.02	154.26	165.13	204.78
Claims on Private Sector	32d	15.47	20.94	24.08	22.96	39.12	53.74	75.70	83.50	99.04	105.31	104.28	138.99	159.65	213.94	194.02
Money	34	22.75	31.84	33.04	37.35	49.43	39.80	†57.78	57.78	61.28	76.97	87.22	100.32	99.58	162.10	166.49
Quasi-Money	35	4.29	6.62	9.21	10.56	20.49	21.65	31.90	24.41	29.42	32.69	39.80	60.64	70.20	94.85	109.15
Restricted Deposits	36b	—	20.38	41.82	52.39	33.34	29.34	12.77	.02	.29				17.91	68.45	80.86
Capital Accounts	37a	7.37	7.52	7.96	11.16	19.29	22.97	28.81	32.99	35.95	42.55	49.24	44.35	50.91	44.50	92.19
Other Items (Net)	37r	1.33	-7.08	-2.02	-5.28	-.16	8.86	7.87	20.77	23.69	5.59	-2.55	-13.07	†-122.08	-180.39	-534.93
Money plus Quasi-Money	35l	27.04	38.46	42.25	47.91	69.92	61.45	†89.68	82.19	90.70	109.66	127.02	160.96	169.78	256.95	275.64
Other Banking Institutions															*Millions of Dalasis:*	
Deposits	45	1.03	.83	.79	.97	1.16	1.34	1.09	1.19	1.11	1.04	1.04 e	.88	.80	.72	1.22
Liquid Liabilities	55l	28.07	39.29	43.04	48.88	71.08	62.79	†90.77	83.38	91.81	110.70	128.06	161.84	170.58	257.67	276.86
Interest Rates															*Percent Per Annum:*	
Discount Rate *(End of Period)*	60	....	....	6.00	6.00	6.00	6.00	6.00	6.00	8.00	9.50	9.50	9.50	9.50	15.00	20.00
Deposit Rate	60l	....	....	....	....	....	....	5.00	5.00	5.00	8.50	8.50	8.50	9.00	9.75	16.13
Lending Rate	60p	....	....	....	....	....		15.00	15.00	15.00	18.00	18.00	18.00	18.00	14.48	28.00
Prices															*Index Numbers (1995=100):*	
Consumer Prices	64	6.2	6.6	†7.2	9.1	10.6	11.9	13.0	13.8	14.7	15.6	17.3	19.1	23.4	27.7	43.3
															Number in Thousands:	
Labor Force	67d	....	....	....	....	....	....	....	....	....	....	....	....	....		
Employment	67e	....	....	....	....	....	....	....	....	....	....	....	....	....	24	21

	1987	1988	1989	1990	1991	1992	1993	1994	1995	1996	1997	1998	1999	2000	2001		
																Exchange Rates	
End of Period																	
	9.134	8.961	10.928	10.662	12.813	12.673	13.096	13.983	14.330	14.225	14.207	15.476	15.849	19.397	21.279	Market Rate	**aa**
End of Period (ae) Period Average (rf)																	
	6.439	6.659	8.315	7.495	8.957	9.217	9.535	9.579	9.640	9.892	10.530	10.991	11.547	14.888	16.932	Market Rate	**ae**
	7.074	6.709	7.585	7.883	8.803	8.888	9.129	9.576	9.546	9.789	10.200	10.643	11.395	12.788	15.653	Market Rate	**rf**
Period Averages																	
	135.14	142.62	126.56	121.49	109.37	107.15	104.67	99.66	100.00	97.55	93.64	89.72	83.83	75.02	56.39	Market Rate	**ahx**
	74.90	82.10	86.24	88.31	85.02	87.49	99.80	104.75	100.00	100.72	104.61	103.47	98.51	94.88	81.50	Nominal Effective Exchange Rate	**ne c**
	104.57	114.21	109.69	104.74	100.20	102.44	110.93	103.10	100.00	99.06	103.57	101.97	99.85	95.04	85.59	Real Effective Exchange Rate	**re c**
																Fund Position	
End of Period																	
	17.10	17.10	17.10	17.10	17.10	17.10	22.90	22.90	22.90	22.90	22.90	22.90	31.10	31.10	31.10	Quota	**2f. s**
	3.24	.96	1.03	1.24	.54	.45	.23	.18	.09	.20	.09	.30	.49	.17	.01	SDRs	**1b. s**
	.05	.05	.05	.03	.03	1.48	1.49	1.48	1.48	1.48	1.48	1.48	1.48	1.48	1.48	Reserve Position in the Fund	**1c. s**
	26.65	25.69	28.67	31.55	30.61	28.39	26.68	23.94	19.84	14.71	9.58	8.91	9.26	14.42	20.61	Total Fund Cred.&Loans Outstg.	**2tl**
																International Liquidity	
End of Period																	
	25.76	19.05	20.59	55.39	67.62	94.03	105.75	98.02	106.15	102.13	96.04	106.36	111.25	109.43	106.01	Total Reserves minus Gold	**1l. d**
	4.60	1.29	1.35	1.76	.77	.62	.31	.26	.13	.29	.11	.42	.67	.23	.02	SDRs	**1b. d**
	.07	.07	.07	.04	.04	2.04	2.04	2.17	2.21	2.14	2.00	2.09	2.04	1.93	1.87	Reserve Position in the Fund	**1c. d**
	21.09	17.69	19.17	53.58	66.80	91.38	103.40	95.59	103.81	99.71	93.92	103.85	108.54	107.27	104.13	Foreign Exchange	**1d. d**
	....	....	....	....	....	....	....	....	....	....	....	....	....	....	....	Other Official Inst. Assets.	**3b. d**
	39.39	33.06	25.64	34.51	39.88	33.69	29.54	26.15	22.03	17.38	11.69	12.22	12.71	18.79	25.90	Monetary Authorities: Other Liab.	**4.. d**
	5.10	4.59	2.86	4.50	4.33	12.47	2.81	3.59	5.64	3.43	10.68	6.54	10.92	9.23	7.56	Deposit Money Banks: Assets	**7a. d**
	1.43	1.30	1.24	.37	.24	1.35	4.05	3.03	2.52	6.28	14.52	12.93	17.01	8.88	....	Liabilities	**7b. d**
																Monetary Authorities	
End of Period																	
	134.66	187.06	233.43	405.09	589.07	869.92	1,020.68	948.01	1,030.19	1,011.63	1,010.13	1,163.67	1,277.17	1,626.32	1,794.94	Foreign Assets	**11**
	21.61	35.16	.89	29.99	21.60	258.76	270.72	297.93	253.65	259.73	240.84	239.90	239.39	223.20	250.52	Claims on Central Government	**12a**
	46.85	43.73	22.73	—	—	—	—	—	—	—	—	—	—	—	—	Claims on Official Entities	**12bx**
	2.64	2.97	6.13	9.18	11.56	13.97	15.02	17.02	20.45	21.54	21.08	20.86	21.91	22.71	24.13	Claims on Private Sector	**12d**
	84.11	86.05	50.20	50.08	51.27	—	—	—	—	—	—	—	—	—	56.98	Claims on Deposit Money Banks	**12e**
	121.21	150.55	192.35	204.62	278.28	287.44	319.64	307.08	385.02	386.85	490.42	525.60	601.65	702.68	850.40	Reserve Money	**14**
	95.02	111.99	134.78	152.17	182.28	207.08	224.49	207.36	247.97	255.03	360.51	347.55	379.72	540.26	600.75	of which: Currency Outside DMBs	**14a**
	97.06	81.81	32.38	14.67	14.67	—	—	—	—	—	—	—	—	—	—	Restricted Deposits	**16b**
	497.07	430.05	451.72	449.15	530.31	453.55	407.04	354.07	284.26	209.19	136.05	137.85	146.82	279.79	438.56	Foreign Liabilities	**16c**
	165.69	189.20	181.63	361.69	475.00	383.29	553.08	597.69	559.54	669.41	718.02	782.05	808.47	984.40	767.72	Central Government Deposits	**16d**
	56.78	56.65	65.96	68.01	65.91	71.12	73.70	75.50	83.59	80.87	81.34	85.33	86.76	91.53	107.09	Capital Accounts	**17a**
	-647.94	-553.29	-610.65	-603.80	-690.67	-52.75	-47.04	-71.38	-8.11	-53.42	-153.78	-106.39	-105.23	-186.16	-37.21	Other Items (Net)	**17r**
	-450.50	-459.31	-532.64	-322.93	-482.57	250.37	199.18	217.07	249.70	231.01	129.79	154.75	390.50	306.25	97.67	of which: Valuation Adjustment	**17rv**
																Deposit Money Banks	
End of Period																	
	23.52	20.87	55.97	38.03	98.21	83.15	98.01	97.09	117.71	128.16	129.91	178.05	221.93	162.43	249.65	Reserves	**20**
	32.86	30.55	23.81	33.73	38.83	114.93	26.80	34.41	54.36	33.94	112.47	71.90	126.06	137.47	128.02	Foreign Assets	**21**
	71.78	83.06	127.39	134.29	132.80	168.52	135.74	100.50	228.00	355.70	447.25	516.62	587.86	819.73	—	Claims on Central Government	**22a**
	48.42	61.44	13.55	11.91	12.45	1.54	3.81	.10	.18	.43	1.11	3.86	9.20	11.86	75.79	Claims on Official Entities	**22bx**
	184.14	208.53	231.31	265.45	300.52	222.85	361.90	385.44	342.35	341.89	425.26	489.76	591.41	652.18	673.31	Claims on Private Sector	**22d**
	100.32	97.86	120.03	137.90	211.30	228.09	236.89	200.17	223.50	198.46	268.90	279.02	336.32	443.27	534.66	Demand Deposits	**24**
	145.70	180.67	215.93	219.90	255.16	303.15	371.17	393.49	443.45	514.30	560.66	685.01	754.26	998.82	1,242.70	Time and Savings Deposits	**25**
	27.58	25.97	—	—	—	—	—	—	—	—	—	—	—	—	—	Restricted Deposits	**26b**
	9.19	8.69	10.33	2.74	2.19	12.47	38.65	28.98	24.25	62.10	152.86	142.17	196.46	132.14	....	Foreign Liabilities	**26c**
	4.05	4.05	4.05	3.99	4.05	3.96	3.96	3.96	3.96	3.96	3.96	3.96	3.96	3.96	—	Central Government Deposits	**26d**
	85.30	84.80	57.78	53.18	53.18	—	—	—	—	—	—	—	—	—	—	Credit from Monetary Authorities	**26g**
	51.75	49.57	55.37	108.42	111.41	49.71	68.77	72.28	77.98	88.13	113.08	126.34	188.41	246.75	315.19	Capital Accounts	**27a**
	-63.17	-47.16	-11.46	-42.72	-54.48	-6.39	-93.18	-81.34	-30.54	-6.83	16.54	23.69	57.05	-41.27	....	Other Items (Net)	**27r**
																Monetary Survey	
End of Period																	
	-338.74	-221.13	-204.80	-13.07	95.40	518.83	601.79	599.37	776.05	774.28	833.70	955.55	1,059.95	1,351.87	....	Foreign Assets (Net)	**31n**
	205.70	241.64	216.32	85.14	-.12	278.39	230.15	199.34	281.13	305.92	413.56	484.99	637.34	741.32	....	Domestic Credit	**32**
	-76.35	-75.03	-57.40	-201.40	-324.65	40.03	-150.58	-203.22	-81.85	-57.94	-33.89	-29.49	14.82	54.57	....	Claims on Central Govt. (Net)	**32an**
	95.27	105.17	36.28	11.91	12.45	1.54	3.81	.10	.18	.43	1.11	3.86	9.20	11.86	75.79	Claims on Official Entities	**32bx**
	186.78	211.50	237.44	274.63	312.08	236.82	376.92	402.46	362.80	363.43	446.34	510.62	613.32	674.89	697.44	Claims on Private Sector	**32d**
	197.83	213.52	260.25	296.19	393.58	435.17	461.38	407.53	471.47	453.49	629.41	626.57	716.04	983.53	1,135.41	Money	**34**
	145.70	180.67	215.93	219.90	255.16	303.15	371.17	393.49	443.45	514.30	560.66	685.01	754.26	998.82	1,242.70	Quasi-Money	**35**
	69.48	55.84	32.38	14.67	14.67	—	—	—	—	—	—	—	—	—	—	Restricted Deposits	**36b**
	108.53	106.22	121.33	176.43	177.32	120.83	142.47	147.78	161.57	169.00	194.42	211.67	275.17	338.28	422.28	Capital Accounts	**37a**
	-654.58	-535.74	-618.37	-635.12	-745.45	-61.93	-143.08	-150.09	-19.31	-56.59	-137.24	-82.70	-48.18	-227.44	....	Other Items (Net)	**37r**
	343.53	394.19	476.18	516.09	648.74	738.32	832.55	801.02	914.92	967.79	1,190.07	1,311.58	1,470.30	1,982.35	2,378.11	Money plus Quasi-Money	**35l**
																Other Banking Institutions	
End of Period																	
	.99	1.22	1.03	.93	....	....	....	....	....	....	....	....	....	....	....	Deposits	**45**
	344.52	395.41	477.21	517.02	....	....	....	....	....	....	....	....	....	....	....	Liquid Liabilities	**55l**
																Interest Rates	
Percent Per Annum																	
	21.00	19.00	15.00	16.50	15.50	17.50	13.50	13.50	14.00	14.00	14.00	12.00	10.50	10.00	....	Discount Rate *(End of Period)*	**60**
	15.75	15.00	12.92	11.33	12.71	13.83	13.00	12.58	12.50	12.50	12.50	12.50	12.50	12.50	12.50	Deposit Rate	**60l**
	27.92	29.54	26.83	26.50	26.50	26.75	26.08	25.00	25.04	25.50	25.50	25.38	24.00	24.00	24.00	Lending Rate	**60p**
																Prices	
Period Averages																	
	53.5	59.8	64.7	72.6	78.8	86.3	91.9	93.5	100.0	101.1	103.9	105.1	109.1	110.0	....	Consumer Prices	**64**
Period Averages																	
	....	....	....	....	....	....	325	....	....	....	....	....	....	....	....	Labor Force	**67d**
	26	30	31	....	....	....	....	....	....	....	....	....	....	....	....	Employment	**67e**

Gambia, The

		1972	1973	1974	1975	1976	1977	1978	1979	1980	1981	1982	1983	1984	1985	1986
International Transactions																*Millions of Dalasis*
Exports	70	37.38	39.98	72.21	77.00	74.67	110.19	82.91	109.82	54.26	51.46	98.53	126.90	162.57	172.92	235.73
Imports, c.i.f.	71	49.53	53.39	79.54	108.12	164.32	177.71	209.78	266.31	285.40	246.76	235.63	304.60	354.16	362.27	733.39
Balance of Payments															*Millions of US Dollars: F.Y. Ending*	
Current Account, n.i.e.	78al d	....	....	....	....	....	....	−44.72	−35.00	−86.93	−49.51	−22.54	−33.53	8.07	7.29	4.29
Goods: Exports f.o.b.	78aa d							40.08	53.75	48.29	45.13	58.56	54.55	90.73	62.79	64.87
Goods: Imports f.o.b.	78ab d							−81.00	−94.74	−137.69	−128.69	−94.41	−89.70	−99.43	−74.84	−84.57
Trade Balance	78ac d							−40.92	−40.99	−89.40	−83.57	−35.85	−35.15	−8.71	−12.05	−19.70
Services: Credit	78ad d							13.27	22.51	17.96	20.16	24.32	27.19	27.73	24.42	28.69
Services: Debit	78ae d							−26.15	−37.27	−41.56	−41.59	−36.17	−29.92	−25.88	−19.30	−21.48
Balance on Goods & Services	78af d							−53.80	−55.75	−113.00	−105.00	−47.70	−37.88	−6.86	−6.92	−12.49
Income: Credit	78ag d							1.93	1.92	—	.96	.22				
Income: Debit	78ah d							−4.68	−4.42	−2.20	−2.72	−11.41	−17.66	−.01	−.05	−.86
Balance on Gds, Serv. & Inc.	78ai d							−56.55	−58.25	−115.21	−107.72	−58.15	−55.32	−6.86	−6.96	−13.35
Current Transfers, n.i.e.: Credit	78aj d							13.40	25.82	29.09	60.79	39.01	24.53	16.12	14.87	18.57
Current Transfers: Debit	78ak d							−1.57	−2.58	−.81	−2.58	−3.40	−2.73	−1.19	−.61	−.93
Capital Account, n.i.e.	78bc d							.08	.23	—	—	.07	.54	—	—	—
Capital Account, n.i.e.: Credit	78ba d							.33	.47	—	—	.20	.75	—	—	—
Capital Account: Debit	78bb d							−.25	−.24	—	—	−.12	−.20	—	—	—
Financial Account, n.i.e.	78bj d							12.10	20.52	−2.03	42.04	10.69	−5.13	−21.47	−3.90	−9.34
Direct Investment Abroad	78bd d							—	—	—	—	—	—	—	—	—
Dir. Invest. in Rep. Econ., n.i.e.	78be d							2.00	11.68	—	2.28	—	—	—	—	—
Portfolio Investment Assets	78bf d							—	—	—	—	—	—	—	—	—
Equity Securities	78bk d							—	—	—	—	—	—	—	—	—
Debt Securities	78bl d							—	—	—	—	—	—	—	—	—
Portfolio Investment Liab., n.i.e.	78bg d							—	—	—	—	—	—	—	—	—
Equity Securities	78bm d							—	—	—	—	—	—	—	—	—
Debt Securities	78bn d							—	—	—	—	—	—	—	—	—
Financial Derivatives Assets	78bw d							....	....	....	....	....	....			
Financial Derivatives Liabilities	78bx d							....	....	....	....	....	....			
Other Investment Assets	78bh d							2.54	.68	−6.19	3.35	−7.63	5.06	2.22	−6.53	4.26
Monetary Authorities	78bo d							—	—	—	—	—	—	—	—	—
General Government	78bp d							−.17	—	—	—	—	—	—	—	—
Banks	78bq d							2.69	−.39	−.54	−1.80	−4.60	2.50	2.22	−6.53	4.26
Other Sectors	78br d							.02	1.07	−5.65	5.15	−3.02	2.56			
Other Investment Liab., n.i.e.	78bi d							7.55	8.16	4.16	36.40	18.31	−10.19	−23.68	2.63	−13.60
Monetary Authorities	78bs d							−.87	1.63	—	—	−.34	−.80	−1.74	−1.60	
General Government	78bt d							8.00	6.51	5.27	11.89	17.76	−5.43	−10.13	1.98	−9.78
Banks	78bu d							1.19	1.66	−1.11	24.51	.55	−4.42	−12.75	2.38	−2.22
Other Sectors	78bv d							−.77	−1.64							
Net Errors and Omissions	78ca d							15.78	−5.33	53.39	2.46	−17.52	15.79	−6.52	−9.15	−26.72
Overall Balance	78cb d							−16.77	−19.58	−35.57	−5.02	−29.30	−22.32	−19.92	−5.76	−31.77
Reserves and Related Items	79da d							16.77	19.58	35.57	5.02	29.30	22.32	19.92	5.76	31.77
Reserve Assets	79db d							12.23	14.47	4.12	−19.11	16.62	1.91	−2.71	3.69	.14
Use of Fund Credit and Loans	79dc d							2.41	3.47	6.79	9.46	7.84	6.84	.36	−5.08	−3.06
Exceptional Financing	79de d							2.13	1.64	24.66	14.67	4.83	13.57	22.27	7.15	34.69
Government Finance															*Millions of Dalasis:*	
Deficit (-) or Surplus	80	†−4.58	.30	−2.79	−6.61	−6.65	−26.49	−35.85	−38.42	−18.32	−50.10	−33.86				
Revenue	81	†22.70	22.80	26.91	32.28	45.61	64.59	83.03	75.40	95.78	76.52	87.05	103.10	122.97	146.04	203.67
Grants Received	81z	†—	.09	.04	2.76	1.89	—	19.74	13.46	13.27	20.90	48.02	....	....	....	14.46
Expenditure	82	†27.12	22.43	28.87	40.81	51.21	85.86	130.68	115.68	131.56	143.68	159.48				
Lending Minus Repayments	83	†.16	.16	.87	.84	2.94	5.22	7.94	11.60	−4.19	3.84	9.45		16.74	1.17	47.08
Financing																
Domestic	84a	†1.17	−3.86	.12	1.35	1.39	20.48	8.47	18.41	13.44	14.09	−1.80				
Foreign	85a	†3.41	3.56	2.67	5.26	5.26	6.01	27.38	20.01	4.88	36.01	35.66				
Debt: Domestic	88a	....	3.46	4.21	10.73	11.21	12.50	33.48	57.01	69.61	78.10	73.69				
Foreign	89a	....	13.19	16.95	21.59	26.54	33.62	69.51	82.04	92.00	111.03	144.80				
National Accounts															*Millions of Dalasis:*	
Gross Domestic Product (GDP)	99b	108.8	109.8	158.4	221.2	278.3	355.1	360.7	425.0	411.6	451.4	522.1	599.4	748.5	869.6	1,085.2
GDP Volume 1970 Prices	99b.p	101.6	106.2	163.4	156.7	167.0	155.0	....	....							
GDP Volume 1976 Prices	99b.p	....	....	....	....	....	336.0	365.4	371.1	169.9	372.8	423.1	432.1	439.0	456.7	469.4
GDP Volume (1995=100)	99bv p	37.3	39.0	60.0	57.5	....	56.0	60.9	61.8	28.3	62.1	70.5	72.0	73.1	76.1	78.2
GDP Deflator (1990=100)	99bi p	11.0	10.6	9.9	14.5	15.0	23.9	22.3	25.9	54.8	27.4	27.9	31.4	38.6	43.1	52.3
																Millions:
Population	99z	.49	.49	.51	.52	.54	.55	.57	.58	.60	.62	.64	.70	.72	.74	.77

	1987	1988	1989	1990	1991	1992	1993	1994	1995	1996	1997	1998	1999	2000	2001	International Transactions	
Millions of Dalasis																	
	281.39	388.72	198.05	244.80	333.45	510.52	604.73	337.80	155.23	209.15	149.82	285.97	80.60	....	....	Exports	70
	897.24	919.36	1,221.01	1,482.11	1,759.38	1,944.94	2,372.27	2,032.75	1,741.26	2,527.62	1,773.80	2,605.39	2,186.82	....	....	Imports, c.i.f.	71
June 30: Minus Sign Indicates Debit																Balance of Payments	
	6.13	26.50	15.02	21.63	13.15	37.16	−5.32	8.17	−8.19	−47.70	−23.56	....	....			Current Account, n.i.e.	78al *d*
	74.51	83.06	100.20	110.62	142.87	146.95	157.03	124.97	122.96	118.75	119.61	....	....			Goods: Exports f.o.b.	78aa *d*
	−94.95	−105.92	−125.35	−140.51	−185.00	−177.76	−214.46	−181.62	−162.53	−217.10	−207.09	....	....			Goods: Imports f.o.b.	78ab *d*
	−20.43	−22.86	−25.16	−29.88	−42.13	−30.81	−57.43	−56.65	−39.57	−98.35	−87.48					*Trade Balance*	78ac *d*
	49.37	62.21	65.73	57.48	80.53	80.86	79.57	90.47	53.71	101.21	109.35					Services: Credit	78ad *d*
	−44.32	−48.17	−50.60	−51.83	−72.23	−66.93	−74.56	−67.04	−69.25	−77.03	−74.67					Services: Debit	78ae *d*
	−15.38	−8.83	−10.03	−24.23	−33.83	−16.89	−52.42	−33.22	−55.11	−74.17	−52.81					*Balance on Goods & Services*	78af *d*
	.81	1.44	2.01	1.59	3.78	4.85	5.82	4.87	4.37	6.01	3.73					Income: Credit	78ag *d*
	−17.60	−13.24	−15.81	−13.04	−11.30	−7.31	−5.11	−5.14	−9.58	−9.28	−11.30					Income: Debit	78ah *d*
	−32.17	−20.62	−23.84	−35.67	−41.35	−19.35	−51.71	−33.50	−60.32	−77.44	−60.38					*Balance on Gds, Serv. & Inc.*	78ai *d*
	42.85	54.45	46.36	59.98	58.58	60.51	49.99	45.85	55.81	35.10	45.04					Current Transfers, n.i.e.: Credit	78aj *d*
	−4.56	−7.33	−7.51	−2.67	−4.08	−4.00	−3.60	−4.18	−3.68	−5.35	−8.22					Current Transfers: Debit	78ak *d*
	—	—	—	—	—	—	—	—	—	8.52	5.74					Capital Account, n.i.e.	78bc *d*
	—	—	—	—	—	—	—	—	—	8.52	5.74					Capital Account, n.i.e.: Credit	78ba *d*
	—	—	—	—	—	—	—	—	—	....	....					Capital Account: Debit	78bb *d*
	−.60	9.63	9.48	−6.09	20.76	18.71	39.39	33.13	24.77	58.59	39.44					Financial Account, n.i.e.	78bj *d*
	—	—	—	—	—	—	—	—	—	....	....					Direct Investment Abroad	78bd *d*
	1.48	1.17	14.79	—	10.20	6.16	11.07	9.81	7.78	10.80	11.98					Dir. Invest. in Rep. Econ., n.i.e.	78be *d*
	—	—	—	—	—	—	—	—	—	—	—					Portfolio Investment Assets	78bf *d*
	—	—	—	—	—	—	—	—	....	....	....					Equity Securities	78bk *d*
	—	—	—	—	—	—	—	—	....	....	....					Debt Securities	78bl *d*
	—	—	—	—	—	—	—	—	—	—	—					Portfolio Investment Liab., n.i.e.	78bg *d*
	—	—	—	—	—	—	—	—	....	....	....					Equity Securities	78bm *d*
	—	—	—	—	—	—	—	—	....	....	....					Debt Securities	78bn *d*
	....	....	....	....	....	....	....	....	....	....	....					Financial Derivatives Assets	78bw *d*
	....	....	....	....	....	....	....	....	....	....	....					Financial Derivatives Liabilities	78bx *d*
	−1.57	1.63	−2.42	−1.04	−.60	−1.52	1.40	3.79	−3.66	5.62	10.28					Other Investment Assets	78bh *d*
	—	—	—	—	—	—	—	—	—	—	—					Monetary Authorities	78bo *d*
	—	—	—	—	—	—	—	—	—	—	—					General Government	78bp *d*
	−1.57	1.63	−2.42	−1.04	−.60	−1.52	1.40	3.79	−3.66	4.71	7.14					Banks	78bq *d*
	—	—	—	—	—	—	—	—	....	.91	3.14					Other Sectors	78br *d*
	−.51	6.83	−2.89	−5.05	11.17	14.07	26.92	19.54	20.65	42.18	17.19					Other Investment Liab., n.i.e.	78bi *d*
	−1.51	—	—	—	—	—	—	—	—	34.01	3.00					Monetary Authorities	78bs *d*
	1.61	6.39	−4.14	−4.85	11.64	13.82	23.12	17.79	22.60	3.11	10.49					General Government	78bt *d*
	−.46	1.02	1.39	.81	−.32	.47	3.80	1.75	−1.95	−.26	.13					Banks	78bu *d*
	−.16	−.57	−.15	−1.01	−.15	−.22	—	—	—	5.32	3.57					Other Sectors	78bv *d*
	5.47	−11.29	−20.84	−11.71	−16.66	−36.65	−22.72	−35.12	−15.63	−4.94	−14.22					Net Errors and Omissions	78ca *d*
	11.00	24.83	3.65	3.83	17.26	19.22	11.35	6.19	.94	14.47	7.40					*Overall Balance*	78cb *d*
	−11.00	−24.83	−3.65	−3.83	−17.26	−19.22	−11.35	−6.19	−.94	−14.47	−7.40					Reserves and Related Items	79da *d*
	−11.61	−30.07	3.91	−2.86	−15.64	−35.24	−8.92	−3.30	4.23	−7.45	−.12					Reserve Assets	79db *d*
	−5.82	2.39	3.52	4.13	−1.76	.28	−2.43	−2.89	−5.17	−7.02	−7.27					Use of Fund Credit and Loans	79dc *d*
	6.43	2.85	−11.08	−5.10	10.14	15.84	—	—								Exceptional Financing	79de *d*
Year Ending June 30																Government Finance	
	....	....	.50	†23.18	†−42.60	140.84 [P]	120.69 [P]	....								Deficit (-) or Surplus	80
			434.60	†486.17	†562.80	644.46 [P]	791.77 [P]	....								Revenue	81
	23.97	....	56.16	†66.07	†75.24	45.81 [P]	8.14 [P]	....								Grants Received	81z
	....	....	496.67	†549.10	†684.71	563.60 [P]	695.14 [P]	....								Expenditure	82
	....	....	−6.41	†−20.04	†−4.07	−14.17 [P]	−15.92 [P]	....								Lending Minus Repayments	83
																Financing	
	....	....	−23.56	....	†−68.82	−280.05 [P]	−219.12 [P]									Domestic	84a
	....	....	23.06	....	†109.42	139.21 [P]	98.43 [P]									Foreign	85a
	....	....	....	....	....											Debt: Domestic	88a
	....	....	....	....	....											Foreign	89a
Year Ending June 30																National Accounts	
	1,486.0	1,635.5	1,942.3	2,366.4	2,629.6	2,947.6	2,518.5	2,886.3	....	....						Gross Domestic Product (GDP)	99b
																GDP Volume 1970 Prices	99b. *p*
	476.6	498.4	526.2	535.1	564.3	566.8	604.0	626.1	600.4	....						GDP Volume 1976 Prices	99b. *p*
	79.4	83.0	87.6	89.1	94.0	94.4	100.6	104.3	100.0	....						GDP Volume (1995=100)	99bv *p*
	70.5	74.2	83.5	100.0	105.4	117.6	94.3	104.3	....	....						GDP Deflator (1990=100)	99bi *p*
Midyear Estimates																	
	.81	.85	.88	.92	.96	.88	1.04	1.08	1.12	1.15	1.19	1.23	1.38	1.39	1.42	Population	99z

(See notes in the back of the book.)

Georgia

	1972	1973	1974	1975	1976	1977	1978	1979	1980	1981	1982	1983	1984	1985	1986

Exchange Rates *Lari per SDR:*
Official Rate .... **aa** ....

Lari per US Dollar:
Official Rate .... **ae** ....
Official Rate .... **rf** ....

Index Numbers (1995=100):
Nominal Effective Exchange Rate .... **ne c** ....
Real Effective Exchange Rate .... **re c** ....

Fund Position *Millions of SDRs:*
Quota .... **2f. s** ....
SDRs .... **1b. s** ....
Reserve Position in the Fund .... **1c. s** ....
Total Fund Cred.& Loans Outstg. **2tl**

International Liquidity *Millions of US Dollars Unless Otherwise Indicated:*
Total Reserves minus Gold .... **1l. d** ....
SDRs .... **1b. d** ....
Reserve Position in the Fund .... **1c. d** ....
Foreign Exchange .... **1d. d** ....
Gold(Millions Fine Troy Ounces) .... **1ad** ....
Gold (National Valuation) .... **1an d** ....
Monetary Authorities: Other Assets .... **3.. d** ....
Other Liab. .... **4.. d** ....
Deposit Money Banks: Assets .... **7a. d** ....
Liabilities .... **7b. d** ....

Monetary Authorities *Millions of Lari:*
Foreign Assets .... **11** ....
Claims on General Government .... **12a** ....
Claims on Nonfin. Pub. Enterprises .... **12c** ....
Claims on Private Sector .... **12d** ....
Claims on Deposit Money Banks .... **12e** ....
Reserve Money .... **14** ....
of which: Currency Outside DMBs .... **14a** ....
Time, Savings,& Fgn. Currency Dep. ...... **15** ....
Foreign Liabilities .... **16c** ....
General Government Deposits .... **16d** ....
Counterpart Funds .... **16e** ....
Capital Accounts .... **17a** ....
Other Items (Net) .... **17r** ....

Deposit Money Banks *Millions of Lari:*
Reserves .... **20** ....
Foreign Assets .... **21** ....
Claims on General Government .... **22a** ....
of which: Claims on Local Govt. .... **22ab** ....
Claims on Nonfin. Pub. Enterprises .... **22c** ....
Claims on Private Sector .... **22d** ....
Claims on Nonbank Fin. Insts. .... **22g** ....
Demand Deposits .... **24** ....
Time,Savings,& Fgn.Currency Dep. .... **25** ....
Money Market Instruments .... **26aa** ....
Foreign Liabilities .... **26c** ....
General Government Deposits .... **26d** ....
of which: Local Govt. Deposits .... **26db** ....
Counterpart Funds .... **26e** ....
Central Govt. Lending Funds .... **26f** ....
Credit from Monetary Authorities .... **26g** ....
Liab. to Nonbank Financial Insts. .... **26j** ....
Capital Accounts .... **27a** ....
Other Items (Net) .... **27r** ....

Monetary Survey *Millions of Lari:*
Foreign Assets (Net) .... **31n** ....
Domestic Credit .... **32** ....
Claims on General Govt. (Net) .... **32an** ....
Claims on Nonfin. Pub. Enterprises ..... **32c** ....
Claims on Private Sector .... **32d** ....
Claims on Nonbank Fin. Insts. .... **32g** ....
Money .... **34** ....
Quasi-Money .... **35** ....
Money Market Instruments .... **36aa** ....
Counterpart Funds .... **36e** ....
Central Govt. Lending Funds .... **36f** ....
Liab. to Nonbank Financial Insts. .... **36j** ....
Capital Accounts .... **37a** ....
Other Items (Net) .... **37r** ....
Money plus Quasi-Money .... **35l** ....

Interest Rates *Percent Per Annum*
Money Market Rate .... **60b** ....
Deposit Rate .... **60l** ....
Deposit Rate (Foreign Currency) .... **60l. f** ....
Lending Rate .... **60p** ....
Lending Rate (Foreign Currency) .... **60p. f** ....

Prices *Index Numbers (1998=100):*
Consumer Prices .... **64** ....

	1987	1988	1989	1990	1991	1992	1993	1994	1995	1996	1997	1998	1999	2000	2001		

End of Period — **Exchange Rates**

1995	1996	1997	1998	1999	2000	2001		
1.8284	1.8348	1.7594	2.5345	2.6489	2.5732	2.5889	Official Rate	aa

End of Period (ae) Period Average (rf)

1995	1996	1997	1998	1999	2000	2001		
1.2300	1.2760	1.3040	1.8000	1.9300	1.9750	2.0600	Official Rate	ae
....	1.2628	1.2975	1.3898	2.0245	1.9762	2.0730	Official Rate	rf

Period Averages

1994	1995	1996	1997	1998	1999	2000	2001		
158.36	100.00	117.88	138.71	159.99	....	....	...	Nominal Effective Exchange Rate	ne c
44.73	100.00	129.37	136.48	135.73	....	....	...	Real Effective Exchange Rate	re c

End of Period — **Fund Position**

1990	1991	1992	1993	1994	1995	1996	1997	1998	1999	2000	2001		
		111.00	111.00	111.00	111.00	111.00	111.00	111.00	150.30	150.30	150.30	Quota	2f. s
		—	—	1.61	1.12	.05	.10	3.69	6.13	2.51	3.15	SDRs	1b. s
	.01	.01	.01	.01	.01	.01	.01	.01	.01	.01	.01	Reserve Position in the Fund	1c. s
		—	—	27.75	77.70	133.20	188.70	215.76	233.33	213.68	228.65	Total Fund Cred.& Loans Outstg.	2tl

End of Period — **International Liquidity**

1992	1993	1994	1995	1996	1997	1998	1999	2000	2001		
		2.35	194.01	188.91	199.80	122.99	132.39	109.41	160.30	Total Reserves minus Gold	1l. d
			1.66	.07	.13	5.20	8.42	3.27	3.96	SDRs	1b. d
.01	.01	.01	.01	.01	.01	.01	.01	.01	.01	Reserve Position in the Fund	1c. d
			192.33	188.83	199.66	117.78	123.96	106.13	156.33	Foreign Exchange	1d. d
		—	—	—	—	—	—	—	—	Gold(Millions Fine Troy Ounces)	1ad
		—	—	—	—	—	—	—	—	Gold (National Valuation)	1an d
			.11	—	—	—	—	—	—	Monetary Authorities: Other Assets	3..d
			.06	.06	27.75	36.68	41.18	38.79	40.27	Other Liab.	4..d
			26.88	33.88	39.10	46.41	48.57	54.11	84.53	Deposit Money Banks: Assets	7a. d
			49.26	4.80	11.95	35.99	46.94	57.64	70.58	Liabilities	7b. d

End of Period — **Monetary Authorities**

1995	1996	1997	1998	1999	2000	2001		
238.75	241.15	260.50	221.53	255.50	216.12	†337.19	Foreign Assets	11
112.45	296.72	437.52	541.78	717.82	802.49	†767.62	Claims on General Government	12a
—	—	—	—	—	—	†79.04	Claims on Nonfin. Pub. Enterprises	12c
—	—	36.67	66.67	80.86	77.88	†1.17	Claims on Private Sector	12d
3.66	14.30	5.26	6.56	1.86	4.49	†1.76	Claims on Deposit Money Banks	12e
153.28	208.96	277.07	259.72	308.47	391.66	†431.78	Reserve Money	14
124.78	176.76	239.87	212.19	244.00	315.18	†348.85	of which: Currency Outside DMBs	14a
—	—	—	—	—	—	†1.82	Time, Savings,& Fgn. Currency Dep.	15
142.14	244.47	368.19	612.84	697.55	626.45	†674.90	Foreign Liabilities	16c
57.17	87.86	52.08	41.94	21.74	20.26	†28.60	General Government Deposits	16d
—	—	—	4.41	.75	—	†—	Counterpart Funds	16e
14.88	18.53	94.02	−14.88	182.32	176.07	†74.20	Capital Accounts	17a
−12.61	−7.65	−51.41	−67.49	−154.79	−113.47	†−24.51	Other Items (Net)	17r

End of Period — **Deposit Money Banks**

1995	1996	1997	1998	1999	2000	2001		
38.00	30.39	39.62	45.01	56.37	76.65	†82.45	Reserves	20
33.06	43.23	50.99	83.55	93.73	106.86	†174.12	Foreign Assets	21
1.47	1.27	4.86	1.12	1.70	5.72	†17.02	Claims on General Government	22a
1.42	1.26	1.09	1.12	—	.30	†2.04	of which: Claims on Local Govt.	22ab
—	—	—	—	—	—	†25.00	Claims on Nonfin. Pub. Enterprises	22c
148.71	127.80	175.06	239.95	339.74	446.96	†496.38	Claims on Private Sector	22d
.31	.06	—	—	—	—	†—	Claims on Nonbank Fin. Insts.	22g
30.02	35.78	38.67	38.38	31.51	53.20	†45.33	Demand Deposits	24
28.51	46.69	94.82	118.63	171.44	254.51	†341.94	Time,Savings,& Fgn.Currency Dep.	25
—	—	—	—	—	—	†.02	Money Market Instruments	26aa
60.59	6.12	15.58	64.79	90.59	113.84	†145.40	Foreign Liabilities	26c
14.27	18.30	9.08	15.61	10.71	11.15	†26.46	General Government Deposits	26d
4.91	4.72	3.50	4.69	3.88	4.54	†6.45	of which: Local Govt. Deposits	26db
—	10.26	10.37	8.10	1.33	.24	†.36	Counterpart Funds	26e
—	—	—	—	3.52	6.29	†6.29	Central Govt. Lending Funds	26f
—	—	—	—	—	—	†1.21	Credit from Monetary Authorities	26g
—	—	—	—	—	—	†.15	Liab. to Nonbank Financial Insts.	26j
61.09	90.82	145.14	200.17	280.27	376.61	†471.60	Capital Accounts	27a
27.08	−5.22	−43.12	−76.05	−97.82	−179.64	†−243.80	Other Items (Net)	27r

End of Period — **Monetary Survey**

1995	1996	1997	1998	1999	2000	2001		
69.09	33.79	−72.29	−372.55	−438.90	−417.31	†−308.98	Foreign Assets (Net)	31n
191.50	319.69	592.96	791.97	1,107.67	1,301.63	†1331.16	Domestic Credit	32
42.48	191.83	381.22	485.35	687.07	776.79	†729.58	Claims on General Govt. (Net)	32an
—	—	—	—	—	—	†104.04	Claims on Nonfin. Pub. Enterprises	32c
148.71	127.80	211.73	306.62	420.60	524.84	†497.55	Claims on Private Sector	32d
.31	.06	—	—	—	—	†—	Claims on Nonbank Fin. Insts.	32g
154.80	212.54	278.54	250.58	275.50	368.37	†394.23	Money	34
28.51	46.69	94.82	118.63	171.44	254.51	†343.76	Quasi-Money	35
—	—	—	—	—	—	†.02	Money Market Instruments	36aa
—	10.26	10.37	12.50	2.08	.24	†.36	Counterpart Funds	36e
—	—	—	—	3.52	6.29	†6.29	Central Govt. Lending Funds	36f
—	—	—	—	—	—	†.15	Liab. to Nonbank Financial Insts.	36j
75.97	109.35	239.16	185.30	462.58	552.68	†545.80	Capital Accounts	37a
1.31	−25.36	−102.21	−147.58	−246.36	−297.77	†−268.44	Other Items (Net)	37r
183.31	259.23	373.36	369.20	446.94	622.88	†737.99	Money plus Quasi-Money	35l

Percent Per Annum — **Interest Rates**

1995	1996	1997	1998	1999	2000	2001		
...	43.39	26.58	43.26	34.61	18.17	17.50	Money Market Rate	60b
...	31.05	13.73	17.00	14.58	10.17	7.75	Deposit Rate	60l
...	24.55	19.11	15.75	14.58	12.00	10.42	Deposit Rate (Foreign Currency)	60l. f
...	58.24	50.64	46.00	33.42	32.75	27.25	Lending Rate	60p
...	51.92	54.16	46.75	42.92	36.58	32.17	Lending Rate (Foreign Currency)	60p. f

Period Averages — **Prices**

1994	1995	1996	1997	1998	1999	2000	2001		
24.6	64.7	90.2	96.6	100.0	119.2	124.0	129.8	Consumer Prices	64

Georgia

		1972	1973	1974	1975	1976	1977	1978	1979	1980	1981	1982	1983	1984	1985	1986
International Transactions																Millions of Lari
Exports	70	....	....	....	....	....	....	....	....	....	....	....	....	....	....	....
Imports, c.i.f.	71	....	....	....	....	....	....	....	....	....	....	....	....	....	....	....
Imports, f.o.b.	71.v	....	....	....	....	....	....	....	....	....	....	....	....	....	....	....
Balance of Payments																Millions of US Dollars:
Current Account, n.i.e.	78al d	....	....	....	....	....	....	....	....	....	....	....	....	....	....	....
Goods: Exports f.o.b	78aa d	....	....	....	....	....	....	....	....	....	....	....	....	....	....	....
Goods: Imports f.o.b	78ab d	....	....	....	....	....	....	....	....	....	....	....	....	....	....	....
Trade Balance	78ac d	....	....	....	....	....	....	....	....	....	....	....	....	....	....	....
Services: Credit	78ad d	....	....	....	....	....	....	....	....	....	....	....	....	....	....	....
Services: Debit	78ae d	....	....	....	....	....	....	....	....	....	....	....	....	....	....	....
Balance on Goods & Services	78af d	....	....	....	....	....	....	....	....	....	....	....	....	....	....	....
Income: Credit	78ag d	....	....	....	....	....	....	....	....	....	....	....	....	....	....	....
Income: Debit	78ah d	....	....	....	....	....	....	....	....	....	....	....	....	....	....	....
Balance on Gds, Serv. & Inc.	78ai d	....	....	....	....	....	....	....	....	....	....	....	....	....	....	....
Current Transfers, n.i.e.: Credit	78aj d	....	....	....	....	....	....	....	....	....	....	....	....	....	....	....
Current Transfers: Debit	78ak d	....	....	....	....	....	....	....	....	....	....	....	....	....	....	....
Capital Account, n.i.e.	78bc d	....	....	....	....	....	....	....	....	....	....	....	....	....	....	....
Capital Account, n.i.e.: Credit	78ba d	....	....	....	....	....	....	....	....	....	....	....	....	....	....	....
Capital Account: Debit	78bb d	....	....	....	....	....	....	....	....	....	....	....	....	....	....	....
Financial Account, n.i.e.	78bj d	....	....	....	....	....	....	....	....	....	....	....	....	....	....	....
Direct Investment Abroad	78bd d	....	....	....	....	....	....	....	....	....	....	....	....	....	....	....
Dir. Invest. in Rep. Econ., n.i.e.	78be d	....	....	....	....	....	....	....	....	....	....	....	....	....	....	....
Portfolio Investment Assets	78bf d	....	....	....	....	....	....	....	....	....	....	....	....	....	....	....
Equity Securities	78bk d	....	....	....	....	....	....	....	....	....	....	....	....	....	....	....
Debt Securities	78bl d	....	....	....	....	....	....	....	....	....	....	....	....	....	....	....
Portfolio Investment Liab., n.i.e.	78bg d	....	....	....	....	....	....	....	....	....	....	....	....	....	....	....
Equity Securities	78bm d	....	....	....	....	....	....	....	....	....	....	....	....	....	....	....
Debt Securities	78bn d	....	....	....	....	....	....	....	....	....	....	....	....	....	....	....
Financial Derivatives Assets	78bw d	....	....	....	....	....	....	....	....	....	....	....	....	....	....	....
Financial Derivatives Liabilities	78bx d	....	....	....	....	....	....	....	....	....	....	....	....	....	....	....
Other Investment Assets	78bh d	....	....	....	....	....	....	....	....	....	....	....	....	....	....	....
Monetary Authorities	78bo d	....	....	....	....	....	....	....	....	....	....	....	....	....	....	....
General Government	78bp d	....	....	....	....	....	....	....	....	....	....	....	....	....	....	....
Banks	78bq d	....	....	....	....	....	....	....	....	....	....	....	....	....	....	....
Other Sectors	78br d	....	....	....	....	....	....	....	....	....	....	....	....	....	....	....
Other Investment Liab., n.i.e.	78bi d	....	....	....	....	....	....	....	....	....	....	....	....	....	....	....
Monetary Authorities	78bs d	....	....	....	....	....	....	....	....	....	....	....	....	....	....	....
General Government	78bt d	....	....	....	....	....	....	....	....	....	....	....	....	....	....	....
Banks	78bu d	....	....	....	....	....	....	....	....	....	....	....	....	....	....	....
Other Sectors	78bv d	....	....	....	....	....	....	....	....	....	....	....	....	....	....	....
Net Errors and Omissions	78ca d	....	....	....	....	....	....	....	....	....	....	....	....	....	....	....
Overall Balance	78cb d	....	....	....	....	....	....	....	....	....	....	....	....	....	....	....
Reserves and Related Items	79da d	....	....	....	....	....	....	....	....	....	....	....	....	....	....	....
Reserve Assets	79db d	....	....	....	....	....	....	....	....	....	....	....	....	....	....	....
Use of Fund Credit and Loans	79dc d	....	....	....	....	....	....	....	....	....	....	....	....	....	....	....
Exceptional Financing	79de d	....	....	....	....	....	....	....	....	....	....	....	....	....	....	....
Government Finance																Millions of Lari:
Deficit (-) or Surplus	80	....	....	....	....	....	....	....	....	....	....	....	....	....	....	....
Total Revenue and Grants	81y	....	....	....	....	....	....	....	....	....	....	....	....	....	....	....
Revenue	81	....	....	....	....	....	....	....	....	....	....	....	....	....	....	....
Grants	81z	....	....	....	....	....	....	....	....	....	....	....	....	....	....	....
Exp.& Lending Minus Repayments	82z	....	....	....	....	....	....	....	....	....	....	....	....	....	....	....
Expenditure	82	....	....	....	....	....	....	....	....	....	....	....	....	....	....	....
Lending Minus Repayments	83	....	....	....	....	....	....	....	....	....	....	....	....	....	....	....
Total Financing	80h	....	....	....	....	....	....	....	....	....	....	....	....	....	....	....
Domestic	84a	....	....	....	....	....	....	....	....	....	....	....	....	....	....	....
Foreign	85a	....	....	....	....	....	....	....	....	....	....	....	....	....	....	....
Total Debt by Residence	88	....	....	....	....	....	....	....	....	....	....	....	....	....	....	....
Domestic	88a	....	....	....	....	....	....	....	....	....	....	....	....	....	....	....
Foreign	89a	....	....	....	....	....	....	....	....	....	....	....	....	....	....	....
																Millions:
Population	99z	....	....	....	....	....	....	....	....	....	....	....	....	....	....	....

	1987	1988	1989	1990	1991	1992	1993	1994	1995	1996	1997	1998	1999	2000	2001		
Millions of Lari																**International Transactions**	
Exports	....	....	....	....	....	....	....	163	194	251	312	269	....	....	....	Exports	70
Imports, c.i.f.	....	....	....	....	....	....	....	288	507	868	1,225	1,230	....	....	....	Imports, c.i.f.	71
Imports, f.o.b.	....	....	....	....	....	....	....	259	456	781	1,103	1,107	....	....	....	Imports, f.o.b.	71.v
Minus Sign Indicates Debit																**Balance of Payments**	
Current Account, n.i.e.	....	....	....	....	....	....	....	....	....	....	-514.2	-275.7	-198.4	-269.0	....	Current Account, n.i.e.	78al d
Goods: Exports f.o.b.	....	....	....	....	....	....	....	....	....	....	376.5	299.9	329.5	459.0	....	Goods: Exports f.o.b.	78aa d
Goods: Imports f.o.b	....	....	....	....	....	....	....	....	....	....	-1,162.9	-994.5	-863.4	-970.5	....	Goods: Imports f.o.b	78ab d
Trade Balance	....	....	....	....	....	....	....	....	....	....	-786.4	-694.6	-533.9	-511.5	....	*Trade Balance*	78ac d
Services: Credit	....	....	....	....	....	....	....	....	....	....	198.0	365.3	216.9	206.4	....	Services: Credit	78ad d
Services: Debit	....	....	....	....	....	....	....	....	....	....	-249.7	-345.2	-224.0	-216.3	....	Services: Debit	78ae d
Balance on Goods & Services	....	....	....	....	....	....	....	....	....	....	-838.1	-674.5	-541.0	-521.4	....	*Balance on Goods & Services*	78af d
Income: Credit	....	....	....	....	....	....	....	....	....	....	186.6	243.4	211.4	178.6	....	Income: Credit	78ag d
Income: Debit	....	....	....	....	....	....	....	....	....	....	-59.2	-52.7	-64.5	-61.1	....	Income: Debit	78ah d
Balance on Gds, Serv. & Inc.	....	....	....	....	....	....	....	....	....	....	-710.7	-483.8	-394.1	-403.9	....	*Balance on Gds, Serv. & Inc.*	78ai d
Current Transfers, n.i.e.: Credit	....	....	....	....	....	....	....	....	....	....	205.5	219.9	228.7	163.2	....	Current Transfers, n.i.e.: Credit	78aj d
Current Transfers: Debit	....	....	....	....	....	....	....	....	....	....	-9.0	-11.8	-33.0	-28.3	....	Current Transfers: Debit	78ak d
Capital Account, n.i.e.	....	....	....	....	....	....	....	....	....	....	-6.5	-6.1	-7.1	-4.8	....	Capital Account, n.i.e.	78bc d
Capital Account, n.i.e.: Credit	....	....	....	....	....	....	....	....	....	....	—	—	—	—	....	Capital Account, n.i.e.: Credit	78ba d
Capital Account: Debit	....	....	....	....	....	....	....	....	....	....	-6.5	-6.1	-7.1	-4.8	....	Capital Account: Debit	78bb d
Financial Account, n.i.e.	....	....	....	....	....	....	....	....	....	....	322.7	348.8	135.5	92.8	....	Financial Account, n.i.e.	78bj d
Direct Investment Abroad	....	....	....	....	....	....	....	....	....	....	—	-1.0	.5		....	Direct Investment Abroad	78bd d
Dir. Invest. in Rep. Econ., n.i.e.	....	....	....	....	....	....	....	....	....	....	242.5	265.3	82.3	131.1	....	Dir. Invest. in Rep. Econ., n.i.e.	78be d
Portfolio Investment Assets	....	....	....	....	....	....	....	....	....	....	....	....	....	2.7	....	Portfolio Investment Assets	78bf d
Equity Securities	....	....	....	....	....	....	....	....	....	....	....	....	....	2.7	....	Equity Securities	78bk d
Debt Securities																Debt Securities	78bl d
Portfolio Investment Liab., n.i.e	....	....	....	....	....	....	....	....	....	....	2.4	—	6.2	—	....	Portfolio Investment Liab., n.i.e	78bg d
Equity Securities	....	....	....	....	....	....	....	....	....	....	2.4	—	6.2	—	....	Equity Securities	78bm d
Debt Securities																Debt Securities	78bn d
Financial Derivatives Assets																Financial Derivatives Assets	78bw d
Financial Derivatives Liabilities																Financial Derivatives Liabilities	78bx d
Other Investment Assets	....	....	....	....	....	....	....	....	....	....	-24.8	-86.9	9.3	-7.7	....	Other Investment Assets	78bh d
Monetary Authorities																Monetary Authorities	78bo d
General Government	....	....	....	....	....	....	....	....	....	....	—	-45.0	—	—	....	General Government	78bp d
Banks	....	....	....	....	....	....	....	....	....	....	-15.0	-23.2	9.3	-7.7	....	Banks	78bq d
Other Sectors	....	....	....	....	....	....	....	....	....	....	-9.8	-18.7	—	—	....	Other Sectors	78br d
Other Investment Liab., n.i.e.	....	....	....	....	....	....	....	....	....	....	102.6	170.4	38.7	-33.8	....	Other Investment Liab., n.i.e.	78bi d
Monetary Authorities	....	....	....	....	....	....	....	....	....	....	—	—	—	—	....	Monetary Authorities	78bs d
General Government	....	....	....	....	....	....	....	....	....	....	90.0	141.5	17.6	-41.1	....	General Government	78bt d
Banks	....	....	....	....	....	....	....	....	....	....	7.4	37.4	26.3	7.3	....	Banks	78bu d
Other Sectors	....	....	....	....	....	....	....	....	....	....	5.2	-8.5	-5.2	—	....	Other Sectors	78bv d
Net Errors and Omissions	....	....	....	....	....	....	....	....	....	....	136.0	-170.5	55.7	187.4	....	Net Errors and Omissions	78ca d
Overall Balance	....	....	....	....	....	....	....	....	....	....	-62.0	-103.5	-14.3	6.4	....	*Overall Balance*	78cb d
Reserves and Related Items	....	....	....	....	....	....	....	....	....	....	62.0	103.5	14.3	-6.4	....	Reserves and Related Items	79da d
Reserve Assets	....	....	....	....	....	....	....	....	....	....	-14.1	67.6	-9.6	19.8	....	Reserve Assets	79db d
Use of Fund Credit and Loans	....	....	....	....	....	....	....	....	....	....	76.1	35.8	23.9	-26.2	....	Use of Fund Credit and Loans	79dc d
Exceptional Financing	....	....	....	....	....	....	....	....	....	....	....	....	....	....	....	Exceptional Financing	79de d
Year Ending December 31																**Government Finance**	
Deficit (-) or Surplus	....	....	....	....	....	....	....	....	....	....	-210.80	-175.40	-251.30	....	....	Deficit (-) or Surplus	80
Total Revenue and Grants	....	....	....	....	....	....	....	....	....	....	593.20	621.80	724.00	....	....	Total Revenue and Grants	81y
Revenue	....	....	....	....	....	....	....	....	....	....	568.80	591.40	674.60	....	....	Revenue	81
Grants	....	....	....	....	....	....	....	....	....	....	24.40	30.40	49.40	....	....	Grants	81z
Exp.& Lending Minus Repayments	....	....	....	....	....	....	....	....	....	....	804.00	797.20	975.30	....	....	Exp.& Lending Minus Repayments	82z
Expenditure	....	....	....	....	....	....	....	....	....	....	788.70	761.50	849.10	....	....	Expenditure	82
Lending Minus Repayments	....	....	....	....	....	....	....	....	....	....	15.30	35.70	126.20	....	....	Lending Minus Repayments	83
Total Financing	....	....	....	....	....	....	....	....	....	....	210.80	175.40	251.30	....	....	Total Financing	80h
Domestic	....	....	....	....	....	....	....	....	....	....	101.30	145.50	106.40	....	....	Domestic	84a
Foreign	....	....	....	....	....	....	....	....	....	....	109.50	29.90	144.90	....	....	Foreign	85a
Total Debt by Residence	....	....	....	....	....	....	....	....	....	....	1,977.10	2,857.80	4,077.90	....	....	Total Debt by Residence	88
Domestic	....	....	....	....	....	....	....	....	....	....	439.10	541.40	1,345.50	....	....	Domestic	88a
Foreign	....	....	....	....	....	....	....	....	....	....	1,538.00	2,316.40	2,734.40	....	....	Foreign	89a
Midyear Estimates					5.46	5.45	5.44	5.43	5.42	5.42	5.31	5.30	5.10	4.95	5.24	**Population**	99z

(See notes in the back of the book.)

Germany

134		1972	1973	1974	1975	1976	1977	1978	1979	1980	1981	1982	1983	1984	1985	1986
Exchange Rates																*Deutsche Mark per SDR through 1998,*
Market Rate	aa	3.4759	3.2608	2.9501	3.0698	2.7448	2.5570	2.3815	2.2810	2.4985	2.6245	2.6215	2.8517	3.0857	2.7035	2.3740
																Deutsche Mark per US Dollar through 1998,
Market Rate	ae	3.2015	2.7030	2.4095	2.6223	2.3625	2.1050	1.8280	1.7315	1.9590	2.2548	2.3765	2.7238	3.1480	2.4613	1.9408
Market Rate	rf	3.1886	2.6726	2.5878	2.4603	2.5180	2.3222	2.0086	1.8329	1.8177	2.2600	2.4266	2.5533	2.8459	2.9440	2.1715
																Deutsche Mark per ECU:
ECU Rate	ea	....	....	....	....	....	....	....	2.4906	2.5656	2.4444	2.3001	2.2575	2.2318	2.1839	2.0761
ECU Rate	eb	....	....	....	....	2.8165	2.6485	2.5557	2.5108	2.5244	2.5147	2.3770	2.2705	2.2380	2.2263	2.1287
																Index Numbers (1995=100):
Market Rate	ahx	44.9	54.0	55.4	58.3	56.9	61.7	71.4	78.2	78.9	63.6	59.1	56.2	50.5	49.0	66.2
Nominal Effective Exchange Rate	neu	46.4	51.4	54.3	55.1	59.1	64.0	67.5	70.4	70.8	68.0	72.0	75.6	75.3	75.7	82.2
Real Effective Exchange Rate	reu	....	....	....	80.1	81.1	85.3	65.2	66.0	†65.0	60.1	61.8	64.1	63.5	64.5	70.6
Fund Position																*Millions of SDRs:*
Quota	2f.s	1,600	1,600	1,600	1,600	1,600	1,600	2,156	2,156	3,234	3,234	3,234	5,404	5,404	5,404	5,404
SDRs	1b.s	822	1,388	1,440	1,451	1,747	1,177	1,379	1,576	1,443	1,383	1,862	1,541	1,390	1,408	1,651
Reserve Position in the Fund	1c.s	1,140	1,207	1,290	1,581	2,133	2,185	3,302	2,372	1,796	2,117	2,799	3,580	3,826	3,467	3,146
of which: Outstg.Fund Borrowing	2c	—	—	—	150	600	1,031	1,278	948	629	929	1,205	878	853	723	424
International Liquidity																*Millions of US Dollars Unless Otherwise Indicated:*
Total Res.Min.Gold (Eurosys.Def)	1l.d	19,326	28,206	27,359	26,216	30,019	34,708	48,474	52,549	48,592	43,719	44,762	42,674	40,141	44,380	51,734
SDRs	1b.d	893	1,674	1,763	1,698	2,030	1,429	1,796	2,076	1,840	1,609	2,054	1,613	1,362	1,547	2,020
Reserve Position in the Fund	1c.d	1,238	1,456	1,580	1,851	2,478	2,654	4,302	3,125	2,291	2,465	3,088	3,748	3,750	3,808	3,848
Foreign Exchange	1d.d	17,195	25,076	24,016	22,666	25,511	30,625	42,376	47,348	44,461	39,645	39,620	37,313	35,028	39,025	45,866
o/w: Fin.Deriv.Rel.to Reserves	1ddd	....	....	....	....	....	....	....	....	....	....	....	....	....	....	....
Other Reserve Assets	1e.d	....	....	....	....	....	....	....	....	....	....	....	....	....	....	....
Gold (Million Fine Troy Ounces)	1ad	117.36	117.61	117.61	117.61	117.61	118.30	118.64	95.25	95.18	95.18	95.18	95.18	95.18	95.18	95.18
Gold (Eurosystem Valuation)	1and	4,364	5,179	5,810	5,339	5,926	6,684	9,344	7,906	6,988	6,071	5,761	5,026	4,349	5,562	7,054
Memo: Euro Cl. on Non-EA Res.	1dgd	....	....	....	....	....	....	....	....	....	....	....	....	....	....	....
Non-Euro Cl. on EA Res.	1dhd	....	....	....	....	....	....	....	....	....	....	....	....	....	....	....
Mon. Auth.: Other Foreign Assets	3..d	772	919	1,511	1,442	1,569	1,683	1,360	1,433	1,274	1,114	1,042	913	794	1,003	1,263
Foreign Liabilities	4..d	917	710	914	713	1,160	939	3,757	2,839	5,214	5,064	6,475	5,177	4,813	7,451	12,137
Banking Insts.: Foreign Assets	7a.d	15,410	21,139	29,433	38,321	48,229	58,271	73,206	82,558	85,171	84,535	81,729	74,756	75,232	112,932	178,483
Foreign Liab.	7b.d	12,093	15,759	18,572	21,912	30,201	38,371	57,927	76,697	72,093	66,795	64,692	57,923	58,224	75,773	101,288
Monetary Authorities																*Billions of Deutsche Mark through 1998;*
Fgn. Assets (Cl.on Non-EA Ctys)	11	77.6	92.5	83.5	86.4	88.5	90.2	107.2	107.0	104.4	103.7	108.0	111.0	111.8	108.7	110.4
Claims on General Government	12a.u	....	....	....	....	....	....	....	....	....	....	....	....	....	....	....
o/w: Claims on Gen.Govt.in Cty	12a	13.9	16.7	15.5	22.4	15.9	16.4	19.6	18.1	22.4	24.9	23.6	25.9	24.3	22.2	26.5
Claims on Banking Institutions	12e.u	....	....	....	....	....	....	....	....	....	....	....	....	....	....	....
o/w: Claims on Bank.Inst.in Cty	12e	20.2	11.2	15.5	8.5	19.5	19.6	24.3	36.2	57.6	68.1	74.9	85.5	96.3	105.3	96.4
Claims on Other Resident Sectors	12d.u	....	....	....	....	....	....	....	....	....	....	....	....	....	....	....
o/w: Cl. on Oth.Res.Sect.in Cty	12d	....	....	....	....	....	....	....	....	....	....	....	....	....	....	....
Currency Issued	14a	48.9	51.0	55.4	60.6	64.7	71.7	81.4	86.4	91.2	91.6	96.7	104.7	109.6	114.7	123.7
Liabilities to Banking Insts	14c.u	....	....	....	....	....	....	....	....	....	....	....	....	....	....	....
o/w: Liabs to Bank.Inst.in Cty	14c	49.1	54.4	48.7	46.6	53.4	55.9	62.9	65.4	55.0	52.1	54.8	55.3	56.3	56.5	58.3
Demand Dep. of Other Res.Sect.	14d.u	....	....	....	....	....	....	....	....	....	....	....	....	....	....	....
o/w: D.Dep.of Oth.Res.Sect.in Cty	14d	.6	.6	.6	.6	.6	.5	.6	.7	.7	.7	.7	.6	.8	.9	.9
Other Dep. of Other Res.Sect.	15..u	....	....	....	....	....	....	....	....	....	....	....	....	....	....	....
o/w: O.Dep.of Oth.Res.Sect.in Cty	15	....	....	....	....	....	....	....	....	....	....	....	....	....	....	....
Money Market Instruments	16m.u	....	....	....	....	....	....	....	....	....	....	....	....	....	....	....
Bonds (Debt Securities)	16n.u	....	....	....	....	....	....	....	....	....	....	....	....	....	....	....
Foreign Liab. (to Non-EA Ctys)	16c	3.0	1.9	2.2	1.9	2.7	2.0	6.9	5.0	14.4	11.4	15.4	14.1	15.2	18.3	23.6
Central Government Deposits	16d.u	....	....	....	....	....	....	....	....	....	....	....	....	....	....	....
o/w: Cent.Govt.Dep. in Cty	16d	2.8	2.8	.9	4.8	2.7	2.1	4.6	2.9	1.0	.7	1.2	2.1	.9	2.2	1.1
Capital Accounts	17a	2.7	2.5	2.7	2.9	3.2	3.3	3.3	3.4	3.4	4.4	8.6	9.3	11.6	14.4	11.6
Other Items (Net)	17r	4.6	7.2	4.0	.1	–3.4	–9.2	–8.5	–2.4	18.8	35.8	29.1	36.3	38.1	29.2	14.1
Memo: Net Claims on Eurosystem	12e.s	....	....	....	....	....	....	....	....	....	....	....	....	....	....	....
Currency Put into Circ.	14m	....	....	....	....	....	....	....	....	....	....	....	....	....	....	....
Banking Institutions																*Billions of Deutsche Mark through 1998;*
Claims on Monetary Authorities	20	53.5	60.5	55.5	54.3	59.4	62.9	72.3	78.8	70.4	66.5	69.0	69.5	75.6	†78.3	80.2
Claims on Bk.Inst.in Oth.EA Ctys	20b.u	....	....	....	....	....	....	....	....	....	....	....	....	....	....	....
Fgn. Assets (Cl.on Non-EA Ctys)	21	49.7	56.4	70.9	100.5	113.9	122.7	133.8	143.0	166.9	190.6	194.2	203.6	236.8	†278.0	346.4
Claims on General Government	22a.u	....	....	....	....	....	....	....	....	....	....	....	....	....	....	....
o/w: Claims on Gen.Govt.in Cty	22a	104.6	114.1	132.6	180.8	211.5	238.7	273.4	301.4	322.2	369.2	409.1	428.5	447.4	†467.6	472.2
Claims on Other Resident Sectors	22d.u	....	....	....	....	....	....	....	....	....	....	....	....	....	....	....
o/w: Cl. on Oth.Res.Sect.in Cty	22d	621.7	694.8	742.1	780.0	854.2	934.1	1,031.1	1,157.4	1,270.9	1,365.6	1,439.5	1,538.6	1,634.1	†1,740.4	1,808.7
Demand Deposits	24..u	....	....	....	....	....	....	....	....	....	....	....	....	....	....	....
o/w: D.Dep.of Oth.Res.Sect.in Cty	24	87.1	87.7	98.2	114.6	116.2	130.6	150.7	153.6	158.8	154.7	167.4	181.1	194.2	†209.7	227.2
Other Deposits	25..u	....	....	....	....	....	....	....	....	....	....	....	....	....	....	....
o/w: O.Dep.of Oth.Res.Sect.in Cty	25	350.0	393.8	418.8	462.3	506.2	553.6	599.9	638.9	671.1	710.4	755.6	789.6	826.1	†885.3	927.7
Money Market Instruments	26m.u	....	....	....	....	....	....	....	....	....	....	....	....	....	....	....
Bonds (Debt Securities)	26n.u	....	....	....	....	....	....	....	....	....	....	....	....	....	....	....
o/w: Bonds Held by Resid.of Cty	26n	169.0	213.8	240.7	277.5	322.1	355.1	397.5	467.4	524.3	600.5	634.1	687.8	739.6	†796.2	843.3
Foreign Liab. (to Non-EA Ctys)	26c	39.0	42.1	44.8	57.5	71.4	80.8	105.9	132.8	141.2	150.6	153.7	157.8	183.3	†186.5	196.6
Central Government Deposits	26d.u	....	....	....	....	....	....	....	....	....	....	....	....	....	....	....
o/w: Cent.Govt.Dep. in Cty	26d	107.1	115.8	119.2	125.8	128.5	131.5	134.7	138.8	149.3	161.3	164.4	171.0	176.9	†188.2	199.5
Credit from Monetary Authorities	26g	20.2	11.2	15.5	8.5	19.5	19.6	24.3	36.2	57.6	68.1	74.9	85.5	96.3	105.3	96.4
Liab. to Bk.Inst.in Oth. EA Ctys	26h.u	....	....	....	....	....	....	....	....	....	....	....	....	....	....	....
Capital Accounts	27a	48.5	54.2	60.0	66.1	73.9	81.2	88.6	96.6	103.3	112.8	121.7	132.6	144.2	†161.2	176.7
Other Items (Net)	27r	8.7	7.3	4.0	3.4	1.4	6.0	9.0	16.3	24.8	33.5	40.0	34.9	33.4	†31.7	40.1

	1987	1988	1989	1990	1991	1992	1993	1994	1995	1996	1997	1998	1999	2000	2001		
																	Exchange Rates	
Euros per SDR Thereafter: End of Period																		
	2.2436	2.3957	2.2312	2.1255	2.1685	2.2193	2.3712	2.2610	2.1309	2.2357	2.4180	2.3556	1.3662	1.4002	1.4260	Market Rate	aa
Euros per US Dollar Thereafter: End of Period (ae) Period Average (rf)																		
	1.5815	1.7803	1.6978	1.4940	1.5160	1.6140	1.7263	1.5488	1.4335	1.5548	1.7921	1.6730	.9954	1.0747	1.1347	Market Rate	ae
	1.7974	1.7562	1.8800	1.6157	1.6595	1.5617	1.6533	1.6228	1.4331	1.5048	1.7341	1.7597	.9386	1.0854	1.1175	Market Rate	rf
End of Period (ea) Period Average (eb)																		
	2.0603	2.0778	2.0241	2.0420	2.0355	1.9556	1.9357	1.9053	1.8840	1.9465	1.9763	1.9558	....	....	...	ECU Rate	ea
	2.0715	2.0744	2.0700	2.0519	2.0507	2.0210	1.9368	1.9248	1.8736	1.9096	1.9642	1.9692	....	....	...	ECU Rate	eb
Period Averages																		
	79.8	81.7	76.2	88.8	86.6	91.9	86.6	88.4	100.0	95.2	82.7	81.5	....	....	...	Market Rate	ah x
	87.0	86.4	85.7	89.5	88.7	91.3	94.9	95.1	100.0	97.4	92.9	93.1	91.3	87.5	88.1	Nominal Effective Exchange Rate	ne u
	75.6	76.7	76.8	81.9	81.3	84.9	90.5	93.2	100.0	98.7	92.9	90.5	87.8	82.7	82.0	Real Effective Exchange Rate	re u
																	Fund Position	
End of Period																		
	5,404	5,404	5,404	5,404	5,404	8,242	8,242	8,242	8,242	8,242	8,242	8,242	13,008	13,008	13,008	Quota	2f. s
	1,384	1,380	1,373	1,321	1,340	611	700	763	1,346	1,326	1,325	1,327	1,427	1,353	1,426	SDRs	1b. s
	2,749	2,487	2,315	2,148	2,494	3,083	2,877	2,760	3,505	3,803	4,407	5,698	4,677	4,191	4,696	Reserve Position in the Fund	1c. s
	173	—	—	—	—	—	—	—	—	—	—	530	—	—	—	*of which: Outstg.Fund Borrowing*	2c
																	International Liquidity	
End of Period																		
	78,756	58,528	60,709	67,902	63,001	90,967	77,640	77,363	85,005	83,178	77,587	74,024	†61,039	56,890	51,309	Total Res.Min.Gold (Eurosys.Def)	1l. d
	1,964	1,857	1,804	1,880	1,917	841	962	1,114	2,001	1,907	1,788	1,868	1,959	1,763	1,793	SDRs	1b. d
	3,900	3,346	3,043	3,056	3,567	4,239	3,951	4,030	5,210	5,468	5,946	8,023	6,419	5,460	5,901	Reserve Position in the Fund	1c. d
	72,893	53,324	55,862	62,967	57,517	85,887	72,727	72,219	77,794	75,803	69,853	64,133	†52,661	49,667	43,615	Foreign Exchange	1d. d
	....	....	....	....	....	....	....	....	....	....	....	....	....	—	—	*o/w: Fin.Deriv.Rel.to Reserves*	1dd d
	....	....	....	....	....	....	....	....	....	....	....	....	....	—	—	Other Reserve Assets	1e. d
	95.18	95.18	95.18	95.18	95.18	95.18	95.18	95.18	95.18	95.18	95.18	118.98	111.52	111.52	111.13	Gold (Million Fine Troy Ounces)	1ad
	8,656	7,690	8,062	9,162	9,029	8,481	7,929	8,838	9,549	8,804	7,638	10,227	32,368	30,606	30,728	Gold (Eurosystem Valuation)	1and
	....	....	....	....	....	....	....	....	....	....	....	....	9,191	279	264	Memo: Euro Cl. on Non-EA Res.	1dg d
	....	....	....	....	....	....	....	....	....	....	....	....	—	—	—	Non-Euro Cl. on EA Res.	1dh d
	1,542	1,372	1,434	1,623	1,715	1,637	1,548	1,539	1,371	944	559	680	†9,204	291	276	Mon. Auth.: Other Foreign Assets	3.. d
	12,794	15,306	30,417	34,979	27,925	16,423	22,909	15,620	11,435	10,035	9,436	9,551	†6,195	6,125	7,670	Foreign Liabilities	4.. d
	232,608	230,090	292,860	395,487	402,020	386,841	461,962	484,892	578,196	606,018	650,287	828,893	†513,967	579,527	641,339	Banking Insts.: Foreign Assets	7a. d
	131,375	131,000	159,529	226,371	231,086	264,432	286,135	378,834	482,236	490,213	561,585	760,827	†490,158	558,159	570,693	Foreign Liab.	7b. d
																	Monetary Authorities	
Billions of Euros Beginning 1999: End of Period																		
	140.7	113.6	114.9	117.5	109.1	152.0	134.5	128.7	132.9	132.2	129.7	135.1	102.2	94.1	93.5	Fgn. Assets (Cl.on Non-EA Ctys)	11
													4.4	4.4	4.4	Claims on General Government	12a. u
	24.2	25.4	25.5	26.3	27.0	33.2	27.7	26.6	24.7	24.0	24.2	24.3	4.4	4.4	4.4	*o/w: Claims on Gen.Govt.in Cty*	12a
													135.9	151.5	135.3	Claims on Banking Institutions	12c. u
	82.4	144.7	175.3	208.5	225.3	188.9	257.5	217.7	213.1	226.2	235.2	216.0	90.6	139.2	123.0	*o/w: Claims on Bank.Inst.in Cty*	12e
	....	....	....	....	....	....	....	....	....	....	....	....	—	—	—	Claims on Other Resident Sectors	12d. u
	....	....	....	....	....	....	....	....	....	....	....	....	—	—	—	*o/w: Cl. on Oth.Res.Sect.in Cty*	12d
	135.9	154.8	162.1	179.7	194.6	227.3	238.6	250.9	263.5	275.7	276.2	271.0	148.2	142.2	82.8	Currency Issued	14a
													48.8	53.9	88.4	Liabilities to Banking Insts	14c. u
	63.0	65.5	71.6	81.9	81.3	88.9	73.4	56.2	49.7	51.9	48.7	57.7	41.9	47.0	57.4	*o/w: Liabs to Bank.Inst.in Cty*	14c
	....	....	....	....	....	....	....	....	....	....	....	....	.5	.4	1.0	Demand Dep. of Other Res.Sect.	14d. u
	.8	.8	.9	1.3	1.0	.8	.8	.7	.7	1.3	1.1	1.0	.5	.4	1.0	*o/w: D.Dep.of Oth.Res.Sect.in Cty*	14d
	....	....	....	....	....	....	....	....	....	....	....	....	—	—	—	Other Dep. of Other Res.Sect.	15.. u
	....	....	....	....	....	....	....	....	....	....	....	....	—	—	—	*o/w: O.Dep.of Oth.Res.Sect.in Cty*	15
	....	....	....	....	....	....	....	....	....	....	....	....	—	—	—	Money Market Instruments	16m. u
	....	....	....	....	....	....	....	....	....	....	....	....	—	—	—	Bonds (Debt Securities)	16n. u
	20.2	27.3	51.6	52.3	42.3	26.5	23.2	19.6	16.4	15.6	16.9	16.0	6.2	6.6	8.7	Foreign Liab. (to Non-EA Ctys)	16c
	....	....	....	....	....	....	....	....	....	....	....	....	—	—	—	Central Government Deposits	16d. u
	4.6	3.5	6.1	19.0	12.7	.4	13.4	.2	.1	.4	.3	.2	—	—	—	*o/w: Cent.Govt.Dep. in Cty*	16d
	11.0	10.6	12.5	13.1	14.4	18.8	21.1	23.1	22.4	23.1	24.6	21.5	41.7	46.0	48.4	Capital Accounts	17a
	11.7	21.3	10.9	5.1	15.2	11.5	49.2	22.2	17.9	14.4	21.3	8.0	-2.8	1.0	3.9	Other Items (Net)	17r
	....	....	....	....	....	....	....	....	....	....	....	....	38.5	5.4	-18.6	*Memo: Net Claims on Eurosystem*	12e. s
	....	....	....	....	....	....	....	....	....	....	....	....	....	....	....	*Currency Put into Circ.*	14m
																	Banking Institutions	
Billions of Euros Beginning 1999: End of Period																		
	83.6	89.0	96.8	117.7	112.8	115.0	102.0	86.5	87.0	88.6	89.5	92.1	45.6	51.0	56.4	Claims on Monetary Authorities	20
													203.1	244.4	286.3	Claims on Bk.Inst.in Oth.EA Ctys	20b. u
	367.9	409.6	497.2	590.9	609.5	624.4	797.5	751.0	828.8	942.2	1,165.4	1,386.7	511.6	622.8	727.7	Fgn. Assets (Cl.on Non-EA Ctys)	21
													735.7	720.4	708.8	Claims on General Government	22a. u
	501.3	543.6	550.7	608.0	635.2	746.2	849.3	937.4	1,078.7	1,161.4	1,223.7	1,251.8	632.1	616.9	587.8	*o/w: Claims on Gen.Govt.in Cty*	22a
													2,391.7	2,529.4	2,608.3	Claims on Other Resident Sectors	22d. u
	1,865.5	1,950.2	2,083.7	2,446.1	2,699.6	2,939.1	3,206.4	3,451.4	3,630.7	3,900.1	4,137.6	4,471.9	2,326.4	2,445.7	2,497.1	*o/w: Cl. on Oth.Res.Sect.in Cty*	22d
													426.0	448.2	532.7	Demand Deposits	24.. u
	240.8	265.0	282.9	392.0	402.3	439.6	484.8	505.3	545.4	631.8	650.0	747.7	419.5	441.4	525.0	*o/w: D.Dep.of Oth.Res.Sect.in Cty*	24
													1,541.7	1,533.6	1,557.2	Other Deposits	25.. u
	967.4	996.2	1,040.8	1,176.5	1,261.9	1,337.9	1,500.9	1,523.6	1,572.2	1,649.6	1,692.4	1,752.4	1,435.6	1,432.3	1,457.8	*o/w: O.Dep.of Oth.Res.Sect.in Cty*	25
													96.1	108.6	82.5	Money Market Instruments	26m. u
													1,274.0	1,367.6	1,439.6	Bonds (Debt Securities)	26n. u
	894.7	917.1	1,003.5	1,130.9	1,266.3	1,370.0	1,467.6	1,612.5	1,786.9	1,948.0	2,075.8	2,196.0				*o/w: Bonds Held by Resid.of Cty*	26n
	207.8	233.2	270.8	338.2	350.3	426.8	494.0	586.7	691.3	762.2	1,006.4	1,272.9	487.9	599.8	647.6	Foreign Liab. (to Non-EA Ctys)	26c
													46.6	69.9	49.1	Central Government Deposits	26d. u
	204.0	208.6	219.0	241.2	251.8	237.5	242.9	249.5	245.4	248.1	248.4	251.3	45.9	67.6	46.9	*o/w: Cent.Govt.Dep. in Cty*	26d
	82.4	144.7	175.3	208.5	225.3	188.9	257.5	217.7	213.1	226.2	235.2	216.0	92.1	139.3	125.0	Credit from Monetary Authorities	26g
													166.3	190.5	215.9	Liab. to Bk.Inst.in Oth. EA Ctys	26h. u
	191.0	198.5	211.0	265.0	312.7	352.1	391.6	410.1	438.1	463.9	507.0	544.9	237.0	258.5	275.7	Capital Accounts	27a
	30.2	29.1	25.0	10.3	-13.5	71.8	116.1	120.7	132.8	162.7	201.0	221.4	-480.0	-547.8	-537.5	Other Items (Net)	27r

134	1972	1973	1974	1975	1976	1977	1978	1979	1980	1981	1982	1983	1984	1985	1986
Banking Survey (Nat'l Residency)												*Billions of Deutsche Mark through 1998;*			
Foreign Assets (Net) **31n**	85.3	104.9	107.4	127.6	128.4	130.1	128.3	112.2	115.6	132.3	133.1	142.7	150.2	†181.8	236.7
Domestic Credit **32**	630.3	707.0	770.1	852.7	950.5	1,055.6	1,184.8	1,335.2	1,465.2	1,597.7	1,706.5	1,819.9	1,928.0	†2,039.9	2,106.8
Claims on General Govt. (Net) **32an**	8.6	12.2	28.0	72.7	96.3	121.5	153.7	177.8	194.3	232.1	267.0	281.3	294.0	†299.5	298.2
Claims on Other Resident Sectors **32d**	621.7	694.8	742.1	780.0	854.2	934.1	1,031.1	1,157.4	1,270.9	1,365.6	1,439.5	1,538.6	1,634.1	†1,740.4	1,808.7
Currency Issued................................ **34a.n**	48.9	51.0	55.4	60.6	64.7	71.7	81.4	86.4	91.2	91.6	96.7	104.7	109.6	114.7	123.7
Demand Deposits........................ **34b.n**	87.7	88.2	98.7	115.2	116.7	131.1	151.3	154.3	159.4	155.4	168.1	181.8	195.0	†210.6	228.1
Other Deposits .... **35..n**	350.0	393.8	418.8	462.3	506.2	553.6	599.9	638.9	671.1	710.4	755.6	789.6	826.1	†885.3	927.7
Money Market Instruments **36m**	....	....	....	....	....	....	....	....	....	....	....	....	....	....	....
Bonds (Debt Securities) **36n**	169.0	213.8	240.7	277.5	322.1	355.1	397.5	467.4	524.3	600.5	634.1	687.8	739.6	†796.2	843.3
o/w: Bonds Over Two Years **36na**	....	....	....	....	....	....	....	....	....	....	....	....	....	....	....
Capital Accounts........................... **37a**	51.1	56.7	62.7	69.0	77.1	84.5	92.0	100.0	106.8	117.2	130.3	141.9	155.8	†175.5	188.4
Other Items (Net)......................... **37r**	8.9	8.4	1.2	−4.3	−8.1	−10.2	−8.9	.5	28.1	54.9	54.8	56.9	52.2	†39.2	32.2
Banking Survey (EA-Wide Residency)														*Billions of Euros:*	
Foreign Assets (Net) **31n.u**	....	....	....	....	....	....	....	....	....	....	....	....	....	....	....
Domestic Credit .... **32..u**	....	....	....	....	....	....	....	....	....	....	....	....	....	....	....
Claims on General Govt. (Net) .... **32an u**	....	....	....	....	....	....	....	....	....	....	....	....	....	....	....
Claims on Other Resident Sect. **32d.u**	....	....	....	....	....	....	....	....	....	....	....	....	....	....	....
Currency Issued............................. **34a.u**	....	....	....	....	....	....	....	....	....	....	....	....	....	....	....
Demand Deposits.......................... **34b.u**	....	....	....	....	....	....	....	....	....	....	....	....	....	....	....
Other Deposits .... **35..u**	....	....	....	....	....	....	....	....	....	....	....	....	....	....	....
o/w: Other Dep. Over Two Yrs .... **35ab u**	....	....	....	....	....	....	....	....	....	....	....	....	....	....	....
Money Market Instruments................. **36m.u**	....	....	....	....	....	....	....	....	....	....	....	....	....	....	....
Bonds (Debt Securities) **36n.u**	....	....	....	....	....	....	....	....	....	....	....	....	....	....	....
o/w: Bonds Over Two Years .... **36na u**	....	....	....	....	....	....	....	....	....	....	....	....	....	....	....
Capital Accounts **37a**	....	....	....	....	....	....	....	....	....	....	....	....	....	....	....
Other Items (Net) **37r.u**	....	....	....	....	....	....	....	....	....	....	....	....	....	....	....
Money (National Definitions)													*Billions of Deutsche Mark:*		
Central Bank Money,Seas. Adj............. **19m. c**	50.0	54.7	58.2	63.5	69.1	75.3	80.7	87.2	91.7	94.2	97.6	105.4	110.9	115.2	122.8
M1, Seasonally Adjusted .... **39ma c**	125.0	132.3	140.1	159.6	176.2	190.6	216.2	232.5	237.9	240.8	249.4	275.0	284.0	296.2	325.9
M2. Seasonally Adjusted .... **39mb c**	206.1	243.1	262.2	260.9	275.1	298.3	333.5	369.2	403.8	446.1	476.1	489.9	506.6	529.3	568.5
M3, Seasonally Adjusted .... **39mc c**	345.2	386.8	420.6	452.1	497.1	543.6	601.5	655.3	689.8	734.1	782.1	833.9	865.8	909.1	†973.3
Extended Money M3,Seas.Adj.......... **39md c**	....	....	429.1	459.7	502.7	549.2	606.6	664.6	708.2	767.3	823.6	877.6	916.5	960.9	1,041.5
Liquid Liabilities **55l**	537.0	591.4	636.8	709.3	766.1	841.3	923.6	977.1	1,025.0	1,066.4	1,133.9	1,193.8	1,247.2	1,336.0	1,403.1
Interest Rates													*Percent Per Annum*		
Discount Rate (End of Period) **60**	4.50	7.00	6.00	3.50	3.50	3.00	3.00	6.00	7.50	7.50	5.00	4.00	4.50	4.00	3.50
Money Market Rate............................ **60b**	4.30	10.18	8.87	4.40	3.89	4.14	3.36	5.87	9.06	11.26	8.67	5.36	5.55	5.19	4.57
Treasury Bill Rate **60c**	....	....	....	5.40	5.19	4.36	3.76	5.48	7.85	10.37	8.31	5.63	5.66	5.04	3.86
Deposit Rate **60l**	....	....	....	....	....	....	3.06	5.14	7.95	9.74	7.54	4.86	4.86	4.44	3.71
Lending Rate **60p**	....	....	....	....	....	....	7.33	8.63	12.04	14.69	13.50	10.05	9.82	9.53	8.75
Government Bond Yield...................... **61**	7.90	9.30	10.40	8.50	7.80	6.20	5.80	7.40	8.50	10.38	8.95	7.89	7.78	6.87	5.92
Prices, Production, Labor													*Index Numbers (1995=100):*		
Share Prices **62**	30.5	28.1	23.6	28.2	29.6	29.8	32.2	30.9	29.7	30.2	31.0	41.8	47.2	65.3	89.1
Producer Prices **63**	49.7	53.0	60.1	62.9	65.2	67.0	67.8	71.1	76.4	82.4	87.2	88.5	91.1	93.3	90.9
Consumer Prices **64**	44.8	47.9	51.3	54.3	56.7	58.8	60.3	62.8	66.2	70.4	74.1	76.6	78.4	†80.1	80.0
Harmonized CPI **64h**	....	....	....	....	....	....	....	....	....	....	....	....	....	....	....
Wages: Hrly Earn.,s.a.(1990=100) .... **65..c**	30.6	34.6	39.6	44.1	46.7	50.7	54.1	57.9	62.8	67.4	70.9	73.8	76.2	79.3	83.5
Industrial Production .... **66..c**	76.7	80.9	79.1	73.7	79.1	81.0	82.5	86.6	86.8	84.7	82.0	82.4	84.7	88.1	90.0
Investment Goods .... **66iy c**	67.0	71.7	69.8	66.5	71.4	74.7	74.7	78.1	80.3	80.1	78.8	78.0	80.2	87.6	91.3
Other Prod. Goods .... **66jy c**	....	....	....	....	....	....	....	....	....	....	....	....	....	....	....
Consumer Goods .... **66hy c**	92.7	94.4	89.9	85.1	91.1	94.0	94.2	97.2	96.0	90.3	85.9	87.3	89.3	90.3	92.0
Labor Force **67d**	....	....	....	....	....	....	....	....	....	....	....	....	*Number in Thousands:*		
Employment **67e**	....	....	....	....	....	....	....	....	....	....	....	....	....	....	....
Unemployment **67c**	....	....	....	....	....	....	....	....	....	....	....	....	....	....	....
Unemployment Rate (%)...................... **67r**	....	....	....	....	....	....	....	....	....	....	....	....	....	....	....
International Transactions													*Billions of Deutsche Mark through 1998;*		
Exports **70**	149.02	178.40	230.58	221.59	256.64	273.61	284.91	314.47	350.33	396.90	427.74	432.28	488.22	537.16	526.36
Imports, c.i.f. **71**	128.74	145.42	179.73	184.31	222.17	235.18	243.71	292.04	341.38	369.18	376.46	390.19	434.26	463.81	413.74
Imports, f.o.b. **71.v**	121.72	137.73	171.88	177.06	214.56	227.69	235.75	282.66	331.41	357.33	365.17	378.51	421.42	451.15	402.94
															1995=100
Volume of Exports **72**	36.4	41.5	46.1	40.9	48.5	50.5	52.1	54.6	55.5	59.2	61.1	61.0	66.5	70.5	71.4
Volume of Imports **73**	39.6	41.8	40.1	40.0	47.1	48.2	51.5	55.3	55.3	52.6	53.3	55.4	58.3	60.7	64.4
Unit Value of Exports....................... **74**	57.3	60.1	70.1	75.8	74.0	75.9	76.6	80.7	88.4	93.9	98.0	99.3	102.8	106.7	103.3
Unit Value of Imports **75**	52.3	56.1	72.0	74.1	75.8	78.5	76.2	84.8	99.2	112.9	113.6	113.2	119.9	122.9	103.4
Export Prices............................... **76**	51.0	54.3	63.5	66.0	68.6	69.8	70.9	74.2	78.8	83.4	87.0	88.5	91.6	94.1	92.4
Import Prices................................ **76.x**	52.4	59.1	76.0	74.7	79.3	80.5	77.5	86.5	99.5	113.1	115.6	115.3	122.2	123.9	104.5

Billions of Euros Beginning 1999: End of Period — Banking Survey (Nat'l Residency)

	1987	1988	1989	1990	1991	1992	1993	1994	1995	1996	1997	1998	1999	2000	2001	
Foreign Assets (Net)	280.6	262.8	289.6	317.9	325.9	323.1	414.9	273.3	254.0	296.6	271.7	233.0	267.3	272.3	363.1	31n
Domestic Credit	2,182.4	2,307.0	2,434.7	2,820.1	3,097.3	3,480.6	3,827.2	4,165.6	4,488.6	4,837.1	5,137.0	5,496.5	2,917.1	2,999.4	3,042.3	32
Claims on General Govt. (Net)	316.9	356.8	351.1	374.1	397.7	541.6	620.7	714.2	857.8	937.0	999.4	1,024.6	590.6	553.8	545.3	32an
Claims on Other Resident Sectors	1,865.5	1,950.2	2,083.7	2,446.1	2,699.6	2,939.1	3,206.4	3,451.4	3,630.7	3,900.1	4,137.6	4,471.9	2,326.4	2,445.7	2,497.1	32d
Currency Issued	135.9	154.8	162.1	179.7	194.6	227.3	238.6	250.9	263.5	275.7	276.2	271.0	148.2	142.2	82.8	34a.n
Demand Deposits	241.6	265.7	283.8	393.3	403.3	440.4	485.6	506.1	546.2	633.0	651.1	748.7	420.0	441.8	526.0	34b.n
Other Deposits	967.4	996.2	1,040.8	1,176.5	1,261.9	1,337.9	1,500.9	1,523.6	1,572.2	1,649.6	1,692.4	1,752.4	1,435.6	1,432.3	1,457.8	35..n
Money Market Instruments													96.1	108.6	82.5	36m
Bonds (Debt Securities)	894.7	917.1	1,003.5	1,130.9	1,266.3	1,370.0	1,467.6	1,612.5	1,786.9	1,948.0	2,075.8	2,196.0	1,274.0	1,367.6	1,439.6	36n
o/w: Bonds Over Two Years													1,226.2	1,303.8	1,316.1	36na
Capital Accounts	202.0	209.1	223.5	278.1	327.1	370.9	412.6	433.2	460.5	487.0	531.6	566.4	278.7	304.5	324.1	37a
Other Items (Net)	21.3	26.9	10.6	−20.4	−29.9	57.2	136.7	112.7	113.3	140.3	181.5	194.9	−468.2	−525.1	−507.3	37r

End of Period — Banking Survey (EA-Wide Residency)

	1999	2000	2001	
Foreign Assets (Net)	119.7	110.5	165.0	31n.u
Domestic Credit	3,085.2	3,184.4	3,272.4	32..u
Claims on General Govt. (Net)	693.5	655.0	664.1	32an u
Claims on Other Resident Sect.	2,391.7	2,529.4	2,608.3	32d.u
Currency Issued	148.2	142.2	82.8	34a.u
Demand Deposits	426.5	448.7	533.7	34b.u
Other Deposits	1,541.7	1,533.6	1,557.2	35..u
o/w: Other Dep. Over Two Yrs	664.4	674.0	672.8	35ab u
Money Market Instruments	96.1	108.6	82.5	36m.u
Bonds (Debt Securities)	1,274.0	1,367.6	1,439.6	36n.u
o/w: Bonds Over Two Years	1,226.2	1,303.8	1,316.1	36na u
Capital Accounts	278.7	304.5	324.1	37a
Other Items (Net)	−560.3	−610.1	−582.4	37r.u

End of Period — Money (National Definitions)

	1987	1988	1989	1990	1991	1992	1993	1994	1995	1996	1997	1998	1999	2000	2001	
Central Bank Money, Seas. Adj.	133.9	148.0	161.3	310.5	188.6	205.7	229.8	249.7	258.8	274.3	282.5	281.8				19m.c
M1, Seasonally Adjusted	355.3	389.9	414.4	473.6	547.4	586.3	641.2	703.0	729.0	805.0	872.9	930.6				39ma c
M2, Seasonally Adjusted	606.5	644.7	703.2	837.2	991.5	1,108.9	1,204.4	1,279.2	1,206.5	1,224.6	1,265.7	1,322.1				39mb c
M3, Seasonally Adjusted	1,047.3	1,114.2	1,177.8	1,321.1	1,476.5	1,596.5	1,720.8	1,875.1	1,885.6	2,026.1	2,151.3	2,245.2				39mc c
Extended Money M3, Seas.Adj.	1,112.8	1,187.9	1,287.5	†1,461.6	1,649.2	1,802.0	1,986.0	2,179.7	2,215.8	2,341.6	2,460.5	2,569.4				39md c
Liquid Liabilities	1,465.1	1,538.2	1,611.1	1,879.2	1,996.2	2,148.8	2,375.4	2,437.6	2,542.5	2,729.1	2,800.4	2,956.9				55l

Interest Rates — Percent Per Annum

	1987	1988	1989	1990	1991	1992	1993	1994	1995	1996	1997	1998	1999	2000	2001	
Discount Rate (End of Period)	2.50	3.50	6.00	6.00	8.00	8.25	5.75	4.50	3.00	2.50	2.50	2.50				60
Money Market Rate	3.72	4.01	6.59	7.92	8.84	9.42	7.49	5.35	4.50	3.27	3.18	3.41	2.73	4.11	4.37	60b
Treasury Bill Rate	3.28	3.62	6.28	8.13	8.27	8.32	6.22	5.05	4.40	3.30	3.32	3.42	2.88	4.32	3.66	60c
Deposit Rate	3.20	3.29	5.50	7.07	7.62	8.01	6.27	4.47	3.85	2.83	2.69	2.88	2.43	3.40	3.56	60l
Lending Rate	8.36	8.33	9.94	11.59	12.46	13.59	12.85	11.48	10.94	10.02	9.13	9.02	8.81	9.63	10.01	60p
Government Bond Yield	5.84	6.10	7.09	8.88	8.63	7.96	6.28	6.67	6.50	5.63	5.08	4.39	4.26	5.24	4.70	61

Prices, Production, Labor — Period Averages

	1987	1988	1989	1990	1991	1992	1993	1994	1995	1996	1997	1998	1999	2000	2001	
Share Prices	76.4	65.3	83.8	96.8	88.6	84.5	90.6	102.7	100.0	114.1	156.3	200.0	207.3	258.7	197.3	62
Producer Prices	88.7	89.8	92.6	94.2	†96.2	97.6	97.7	98.3	†100.0	98.8	99.9	99.5	98.5	101.8	104.9	63
Consumer Prices	80.2	81.2	†83.5	85.7	†87.2	91.6	95.7	98.3	100.0	101.4	103.3	104.3	104.9	107.0	109.6	64
Harmonized CPI									100.0	101.2	102.7	103.4	104.0	106.2	108.7	64h
Wages: Hrly Earn.,s.a.(1990=100)	87.6	91.0	94.9	100.0	107.2	114.8	121.7	123.6								65..c
Industrial Production	90.1	93.3	97.8	103.2	†104.4	103.1	95.9	99.5	100.0	99.8	102.7	106.2	107.7	113.4	113.3	66..c
Investment Goods	91.7	94.8	101.6	107.1	†111.9	108.3	94.0	96.9	100.0	102.0	106.8	116.3	118.0	130.9	134.5	66iy c
Other Prod. Goods					101.3	100.6	93.8	99.9	100.0	99.9	106.1	110.8	113.7	120.8		66jy c
Consumer Goods	92.9	95.7	99.2	106.6	†110.3	107.1	102.2	101.5	100.0	100.0	100.5	101.7	103.3	105.6	105.3	66hy c

Period Averages — Labor

	1990	1991	1992	1993	1994	1995	1996	1997	1998	1999	2000	2001	
Labor Force		39,128	39,044	39,139	39,218	40,083	39,455	39,694	39,709	39,905	39,731		67d
Employment		37,445	36,940	36,380	†36,075	36,048	35,982	35,805	35,860	36,402	36,604		67e
Unemployment		2,207	2,621	3,443	3,693	3,612	3,980	4,400	4,266	4,093	3,887	3,852	67c
Unemployment Rate (%)				9.8	10.6	10.4	11.5	12.7	12.3	11.7	10.7		67r

International Transactions — Billions of Euros Beginning 1999

	1987	1988	1989	1990	1991	1992	1993	1994	1995	1996	1997	1998	1999	2000	2001	
Exports	527.38	567.65	641.04	†660.72	666.17	658.47	632.22	694.69	749.54	788.94	888.64	954.67	†510.01	596.85	637.33	70
Imports, c.i.f.	409.64	439.61	506.47	†556.08	645.41	628.19	571.91	622.92	664.23	690.40	772.33	828.29	†444.80	540.97	543.14	71
Imports, f.o.b.	399.49	428.42	493.40	†542.92	629.14	612.56	556.41	605.96	646.14	671.59	751.29	805.72	†432.68	526.24	528.34	71.v

1995=100

	1987	1988	1989	1990	1991	1992	1993	1994	1995	1996	1997	1998	1999	2000	2001	
Volume of Exports	73.4	78.3	84.7	85.9	85.9	87.8	84.0	96.0	†100.0	107.6	120.7	130.5	136.4			72
Volume of Imports	67.9	72.2	77.5	86.7	97.7	100.0	90.3	98.4	†100.0	106.0	115.5	126.9	132.9			73
Unit Value of Exports	100.6	101.3	106.0	104.8	104.2	103.4	98.7	97.8	†100.0	97.8	98.2	97.6	96.2	†99.8	101.6	74
Unit Value of Imports	97.0	97.8	105.1	102.5	104.2	101.0	95.5	97.4	†100.0	98.1	100.6	98.4	96.6	†107.2	107.2	75
Export Prices	91.5	93.4	96.0	96.1	97.1	97.7	97.8	98.6	100.0	100.0	101.5	101.4	100.9	104.4	105.4	76
Import Prices	98.8	100.0	104.5	102.2	103.0	100.5	98.9	99.8	100.0	100.4	104.0	100.8	100.2	111.5	112.2	76.x

Germany

		1972	1973	1974	1975	1976	1977	1978	1979	1980	1981	1982	1983	1984	1985	1986
Balance of Payments															*Billions of US Dollars:*	
Current Account, n.i.e.	78ald	.34	4.22	9.15	3.09	3.77	3.91	9.36	−5.45	−13.32	−3.50	4.86	4.60	9.57	17.58	40.91
Goods: Exports f.o.b.	78aad	46.19	66.75	89.13	90.06	101.70	117.27	141.15	170.23	191.16	174.15	174.43	167.49	169.98	182.69	241.52
Goods: Imports f.o.b.	78abd	−40.19	−54.26	−70.54	−76.39	−86.41	−98.80	−117.88	−155.13	−183.22	−158.73	−150.29	−148.07	−148.48	−154.27	−186.84
Trade Balance	78acd	5.99	12.49	18.59	13.67	15.29	18.47	23.27	15.10	7.94	15.42	24.14	19.42	21.51	28.42	54.68
Services: Credit	78add	6.74	8.64	10.14	12.59	17.46	19.51	24.82	28.57	33.06	31.37	32.09	30.43	29.53	30.67	39.33
Services: Debit	78aed	−8.56	−11.73	−13.58	−16.91	−21.65	−24.81	−30.67	−37.96	−42.38	−38.27	−38.09	−35.86	−33.30	−33.64	−43.76
Balance on Goods & Services	78afd	4.18	9.40	15.15	9.35	11.10	13.18	17.42	5.70	−1.38	8.52	18.15	13.99	17.73	25.45	50.25
Income: Credit	78agd	3.15	4.39	5.37	5.50	5.98	6.47	9.47	12.07	13.96	13.67	14.00	14.31	15.16	15.55	22.69
Income: Debit	78ahd	−3.53	−4.75	−6.03	−5.47	−5.64	−7.61	−8.06	−11.62	−13.04	−14.02	−15.98	−13.22	−12.15	−12.75	−18.64
Balance on Gds, Serv. & Inc.	78aid	3.80	9.03	14.48	9.38	11.44	12.04	18.84	6.15	−.46	8.17	16.17	15.08	20.75	28.26	54.30
Current Transfers, n.i.e.: Credit	78ajd	1.65	2.54	2.95	2.98	3.50	5.16	7.13	7.65	8.01	6.99	6.68	7.32	7.13	7.02	10.77
Current Transfers: Debit	78akd	−5.11	−7.35	−8.29	−9.27	−11.17	−13.29	−16.61	−19.24	−20.87	−18.66	−17.99	−17.80	−18.30	−17.70	−24.16
Capital Account, n.i.e.	78bcd	−.03	−.03	−.03	−.02	—	.01	−.04	−.25	−.92	−.07	−.07	−.08	−.05	−.18	−.02
Capital Account, n.i.e.: Credit	78bad	.05	.07	.07	.09	.09	.13	.10	.15	.15	.12	.13	.15	.12	.11	.21
Capital Account: Debit	78bbd	−.08	−.10	−.10	−.11	−.09	−.12	−.14	−.40	−1.07	−.19	−.19	−.23	−.16	−.29	−.23
Financial Account, n.i.e.	78bjd	3.67	2.88	−10.82	−3.94	−.18	.75	5.76	4.49	5.65	1.00	.50	−6.35	−12.16	−18.30	−36.97
Direct Investment Abroad	78bdd	−1.81	−1.96	−2.13	−2.18	−2.61	−2.42	−3.94	−5.02	−4.70	−4.48	−3.02	−3.67	−4.66	−5.30	−10.56
Dir. Invest. in Rep. Econ., n.i.e.	78bed	1.90	2.12	2.18	.69	1.32	.95	1.60	1.73	.33	.30	.75	1.72	.53	.49	1.02
Portfolio Investment Assets	78bfd	1.27	.12	−.42	−1.08	−.35	−2.36	−2.07	−1.82	−4.19	−2.67	−4.59	−4.20	−5.42	−11.03	−9.73
Equity Securities	78bkd	−.09	.06	−.16	−.51	.17	−.38	−.31	.41	−.21	.05	−.17	−1.87	−.04	−1.57	−2.21
Debt Securities	78bld	1.35	.06	−.26	−.58	−.52	−1.98	−1.76	−2.23	−3.98	−2.72	−4.42	−2.33	−5.38	−9.46	−7.53
Portfolio Investment Liab., n.i.e.	78bgd	3.37	2.55	−.75	−.57	1.86	1.05	1.62	3.18	.45	.42	1.07	5.11	5.87	12.85	33.15
Equity Securities	78bmd	.94	−.10	.02	.78	.65	.70	1.52	1.00	.32	1.06	.21	1.11	1.29	2.11	6.82
Debt Securities	78bnd	2.43	2.65	−.77	−1.35	1.21	.35	.10	2.17	.13	−.65	.86	4.00	4.59	10.74	26.34
Financial Derivatives Assets	78bwd	—	—	—	—	—	—	—	—	—	—	—	—	—	—	—
Financial Derivatives Liabilities	78bxd	—	—	—	—	—	—	—	—	—	—	—	—	—	—	—
Other Investment Assets	78bhd	−1.18	−3.24	−14.68	−13.06	−11.94	−7.45	−11.43	−12.66	−19.41	−17.34	−4.62	−8.33	−18.83	−22.92	−54.49
Monetary Authorities	78bod															
General Government	78bpd	−.39	−.77	−.82	−.62	−.70	−.53	−1.05	−.66	−.56	−1.77	−1.80	−2.54	−2.14	−1.57	−2.01
Banks	78bqd	.16	−1.71	−5.73	−10.71	−5.19	−3.81	−5.67	−3.84	−8.55	−7.03	.66	−.41	−7.83	−15.73	−34.75
Other Sectors	78brd	−.95	−.76	−8.12	−1.74	−6.06	−3.10	−4.71	−8.15	−10.30	−8.54	−3.49	−5.37	−8.86	−5.62	−17.73
Other Investment Liab., n.i.e.	78bid	.12	3.29	4.97	12.26	11.53	10.96	19.97	19.08	33.17	24.78	10.92	3.02	10.34	7.61	3.64
Monetary Authorities	78bsd	.27	−.83	.04	1.24	.32	−.40	2.48	−1.16	5.40	−1.91	1.66	−.13	.20	1.07	2.35
General Government	78btd	.24	−.09	.51	1.76	1.88	.52	1.18	.50	12.47	10.77	3.85	3.17	1.18	−.60	−2.32
Banks	78bud	.21	.96	1.45	4.97	6.19	5.53	14.19	15.96	3.18	3.51	−.06	−2.62	6.50	6.90	11.54
Other Sectors	78bvd	−.60	3.24	2.97	4.30	3.14	5.32	2.13	3.77	12.12	12.41	5.47	2.59	2.46	.23	−7.93
Net Errors and Omissions	78cad	1.00	1.97	1.27	−.11	.20	−.20	−2.15	−2.23	−1.06	.09	−2.45	−.12	2.28	3.13	1.50
Overall Balance	78cbd	4.98	9.04	−.43	−.98	3.79	4.46	12.92	−3.44	−9.64	−2.48	2.84	−1.95	−.35	2.23	5.43
Reserves and Related Items	79dad	−4.98	−9.04	.43	.98	−3.79	−4.46	−12.92	3.44	9.64	2.48	−2.84	1.95	.35	−2.23	−5.43
Reserve Assets	79dbd	−4.98	−9.04	.43	.98	−3.79	−4.46	−12.92	3.44	9.64	2.48	−2.84	1.95	.35	−2.23	−5.43
Use of Fund Credit and Loans	79dcd	—	—	—	—	—	—	—	—	—	—	—	—	—	....	....
Exceptional Financing	79ded	....	....	....	....	....	....	....	....	....	....	....	....	....	....	....
International Investment Position															*Billions of US Dollars*	
Assets	79aad	....	....	....	....	....	....	....	....	257.40	250.64	254.39	242.91	242.89	341.81	501.72
Direct Investment Abroad	79abd	....	....	....	....	....	....	....	....	31.35	32.20	32.61	31.48	32.09	42.60	58.12
Portfolio Investment	79acd	....	....	....	....	....	....	....	....	20.37	21.26	25.93	29.69	33.56	51.60	71.26
Equity Securities	79add	....	....	....	....	....	....	....	....	5.21	4.65	5.22	8.03	7.74	12.56	18.86
Debt Securities	79aed	....	....	....	....	....	....	....	....	15.16	16.61	20.71	21.66	25.83	39.04	52.40
Financial Derivatives	79ald	....	....	....	....	....	....	....	....							
Other Investment	79afd	....	....	....	....	....	....	....	....	164.58	162.68	160.29	151.80	151.31	213.65	325.15
Monetary Authorities	79agd	....	....	....	....	....	....	....	....	2.06	1.59	1.03	.90	.78	1.00	1.26
General Government	79ahd	....	....	....	....	....	....	....	....	18.61	18.32	19.70	20.09	19.78	26.89	35.85
Banks	79aid	....	....	....	....	....	....	....	....	69.11	68.31	65.57	59.24	60.51	90.61	147.43
Other Sectors	79ajd	....	....	....	....	....	....	....	....	74.80	74.45	73.99	71.57	70.24	95.16	140.62
Reserve Assets	79akd	....	....	....	....	....	....	....	....	41.10	34.51	35.55	29.94	25.93	33.95	47.19
Liabilities	79lad	....	....	....	....	....	....	....	....	224.02	221.48	223.93	210.31	200.99	289.02	405.38
Dir. Invest. in Rep. Economy	79lbd	....	....	....	....	....	....	....	....	25.34	21.61	20.73	19.44	17.43	22.84	32.35
Portfolio Investment	79lcd	....	....	....	....	....	....	....	....	37.56	42.79	46.89	53.77	54.32	98.52	161.35
Equity Securities	79ldd	....	....	....	....	....	....	....	....	10.09	9.69	10.55	13.74	13.93	34.09	51.72
Debt Securities	79led	....	....	....	....	....	....	....	....	27.46	33.10	36.34	40.03	40.39	64.43	109.63
Financial Derivatives	79lld	....	....	....	....	....	....	....	....							
Other Investment	79lfd	....	....	....	....	....	....	....	....	161.13	157.07	156.30	137.09	129.23	167.65	211.68
Monetary Authorities	79lgd	....	....	....	....	....	....	....	....	13.84	10.07	10.78	8.68	7.99	11.32	17.20
General Government	79lhd	....	....	....	....	....	....	....	....	.49	1.80	2.25	1.23	.75	.54	.31
Banks	79lid	....	....	....	....	....	....	....	....	73.50	68.13	65.38	57.12	57.54	74.28	99.76
Other Sectors	79ljd	....	....	....	....	....	....	....	....	73.31	77.07	77.90	70.06	62.95	81.52	94.42

Minus Sign Indicates Debit — Balance of Payments

1987	1988	1989	1990	1991	1992	1993	1994	1995	1996	1997	1998	1999	2000	2001		
46.44	50.35	57.00	48.30	-17.67	-19.14	-13.87	-20.94	-18.93	-7.97	-2.84	-6.64	-17.94	-18.71	3.82	Current Account, n.i.e.	78al d
291.49	322.11	340.10	411.01	403.98	430.48	382.68	430.54	523.58	522.58	510.02	542.60	542.72	549.17	570.59	Goods: Exports f.o.b.	78aa d
-223.45	-245.76	-265.12	-342.50	-384.54	-402.28	-341.49	-379.63	-458.48	-453.20	-439.90	-465.71	-472.67	-491.87	-487.76	Goods: Imports f.o.b.	78ab d
68.04	76.35	74.98	68.51	19.44	28.20	41.19	50.92	65.11	69.38	70.12	76.89	70.06	57.29	82.83	*Trade Balance*	78ac d
45.83	47.60	50.06	63.70	65.06	69.02	64.70	66.25	81.84	85.56	84.42	85.31	86.34	83.89	83.74	Services: Credit	78ad d
-53.70	-60.75	-62.62	-81.00	-86.24	-99.70	-97.76	-105.94	-127.20	-129.82	-125.63	-131.21	-138.17	-134.02	-133.88	Services: Debit	78ae d
60.18	63.19	62.42	51.22	-1.74	-2.47	8.14	11.22	19.75	25.12	28.91	30.99	18.22	7.16	32.68	*Balance on Goods & Services*	78af d
29.66	36.00	45.39	65.60	74.15	80.44	77.13	68.51	84.89	81.36	80.40	83.60	87.21	97.16	108.36	Income: Credit	78ag d
-26.33	-28.97	-31.10	-44.77	-52.46	-62.45	-63.85	-61.68	-84.59	-80.42	-81.77	-90.86	-95.99	-98.15	-113.46	Income: Debit	78ah d
63.51	70.22	76.72	72.05	19.96	15.52	21.42	18.05	20.04	26.06	27.54	23.72	9.45	6.17	27.58	*Balance on Gds, Serv. & Inc.*	78ai d
12.15	11.68	10.48	13.07	13.42	14.90	13.38	13.89	16.87	17.89	16.47	16.45	17.33	15.81	15.08	Current Transfers, n.i.e.: Credit	78aj d
-29.21	-31.55	-30.19	-36.82	-51.04	-49.56	-48.67	-52.88	-55.84	-51.92	-46.85	-46.81	-44.72	-40.69	-38.84	Current Transfers: Debit	78ak d
-.09	-.01	.09	-1.33	-.65	.60	.49	.15	-2.73	-2.18	—	.72	-.16	13.85	-.82	Capital Account, n.i.e.	78bc d
.19	.27	.40	.41	.77	1.12	1.38	1.56	1.68	2.76	2.83	3.31	3.00	17.06	1.86	Capital Account, n.i.e.: Credit	78ba d
-.28	-.28	-.32	-1.73	-1.41	-.52	-.89	-1.42	-4.41	-4.94	-2.82	-2.59	-3.16	-3.21	-2.69	Capital Account: Debit	78bb d
-24.00	-67.56	-59.07	-54.78	5.22	51.80	16.21	30.43	43.98	16.13	1.13	17.63	-40.48	13.20	-55.76	Financial Account, n.i.e.	78bj d
-9.76	-12.07	-15.26	-24.20	-23.72	-19.67	-15.26	-17.26	-39.10	-50.75	-42.73	-89.68	-109.80	-52.05	-42.27	Direct Investment Abroad	78bd d
1.82	1.02	7.15	2.53	4.11	2.64	1.95	1.94	11.99	6.43	12.80	23.30	55.79	189.18	28.70	Dir. Invest. in Rep. Econ., n.i.e.	78be d
-13.52	-40.52	-26.23	-13.99	-17.25	-44.72	-25.33	-41.48	-18.05	-30.89	-90.08	-145.53	-191.07	-197.52	-111.02	Portfolio Investment Assets	78bf d
.12	-10.18	-4.97	1.06	-8.64	-40.45	-16.80	-20.97	.28	-17.52	-42.62	-78.34	-87.43	-131.35	-28.17	Equity Securities	78bk d
-13.64	-30.34	-21.26	-15.05	-8.61	-4.27	-8.53	-20.51	-18.33	-13.37	-47.46	-67.19	-103.64	-66.17	-82.85	Debt Securities	78bl d
18.01	4.18	23.80	12.29	41.19	76.93	145.72	10.64	53.15	93.90	91.04	150.80	174.21	36.46	95.36	Portfolio Investment Liab., n.i.e.	78bg d
-.79	3.02	12.08	-1.90	1.64	-2.80	7.54	3.92	-1.51	12.98	12.87	56.76	28.76	-30.51	81.07	Equity Securities	78bm d
18.81	1.17	11.72	14.19	39.55	79.73	138.18	6.72	54.66	80.92	78.17	94.05	145.46	66.97	14.30	Debt Securities	78bn d
-.24	-.30	-.40	-1.18	-.71	-3.35	-7.33	-10.71							....	Financial Derivatives Assets	78bw d
-.42	-.01	.60	1.15	1.06	3.07	6.67	11.25	-.66	-5.73	-8.70	-7.63	-.99	-3.53	-.51	Financial Derivatives Liabilities	78bx d
-24.01	-34.92	-90.85	-74.67	-24.28	-7.29	-131.42	-.62	-61.28	-39.77	-83.53	-85.02	-79.92	-74.83	-89.74	Other Investment Assets	78bh d
....	....	....	....	....	-.02	-.01	.17	.28	.35	.29	-.11	-51.70	39.37	20.70	Monetary Authorities	78bo d
-2.67	-2.58	-4.58	-7.93	-5.17	-6.36	-7.07	2.46	-6.72	-.34	-2.33	-.63	8.46	-18.13	14.84	General Government	78bp d
-16.13	-15.16	-47.13	-38.20	-2.19	3.63	-88.21	14.98	-55.18	-39.13	-80.40	-79.22	-47.03	-91.99	-118.03	Banks	78bq d
-5.21	-17.18	-39.15	-28.54	-16.92	-4.54	-36.13	-18.23	.35	-.64	-1.09	-5.06	10.35	-4.08	-7.26	Other Sectors	78br d
4.12	15.06	42.12	43.28	24.82	44.18	41.22	76.66	97.94	42.93	122.34	171.39	111.29	115.49	63.72	Other Investment Liab., n.i.e.	78bi d
-2.03	3.62	12.91	.40	-5.81	-9.53	-1.57	-2.04	-2.65	-1.17	-.39	2.16	-2.21	.37	2.35	Monetary Authorities	78bs d
-5.57	-5.80	-2.80	.24	-.55	-1.19	3.73	2.12	3.84	3.45	-7.75	.10	-12.29	.52	.34	General Government	78bt d
11.50	11.24	22.58	26.22	10.51	48.01	35.34	69.19	83.71	36.62	120.20	159.94	103.52	112.55	52.63	Banks	78bu d
.23	6.01	9.43	16.42	20.67	6.88	3.72	7.39	13.04	4.03	10.29	9.19	22.28	2.05	8.40	Other Sectors	78bv d
-.86	1.62	4.84	15.06	6.91	3.92	-17.02	-11.68	-15.09	-7.17	-2.05	-7.70	44.46	-13.56	47.30	Net Errors and Omissions	78ca d
21.49	-15.60	2.86	7.25	-6.18	37.18	-14.20	-2.04	7.22	-1.20	-3.75	4.02	-14.11	-5.22	-5.47	*Overall Balance*	78cb d
-21.49	15.60	-2.86	-7.25	6.18	-37.18	14.20	2.04	-7.22	1.20	3.75	-4.02	14.11	5.22	5.47	Reserves and Related Items	79da d
-21.49	15.60	-2.86	-7.25	6.18	-37.18	14.20	2.04	-7.22	1.20	3.75	-4.02	14.11	5.22	5.47	Reserve Assets	79db d
—	—	—	—	—	—	—	—	—	—	—	—	—	—	—	Use of Fund Credit and Loans	79dc d
....	....	....	....	....	....	....	....	....	....	....	....	....	....	....	Exceptional Financing	79de d

Billions of US Dollars — International Investment Position

1987	1988	1989	1990	1991	1992	1993	1994	1995	1996	1997	1998	1999	2000	2001		
665.68	689.50	863.59	1,086.51	1,141.85	1,172.60	1,285.19	1,431.95	1,663.83	1,699.68	1,750.85	2,211.14	2,392.77	2,530.34	....	Assets	79aa d
75.49	80.20	94.99	124.96	143.57	148.46	156.70	188.32	234.13	250.14	298.23	368.09	411.30	425.15	....	Direct Investment Abroad	79ab d
93.89	135.51	171.29	185.23	213.57	246.49	279.91	320.00	385.42	413.69	502.18	723.34	893.85	1,008.77	....	Portfolio Investment	79ac d
20.06	32.96	43.95	44.96	58.00	94.61	115.20	145.79	165.97	187.49	241.39	370.58	506.95	576.76	....	Equity Securities	79ad d
73.83	102.54	127.33	140.27	155.57	151.88	164.70	174.22	219.45	226.20	260.80	352.77	386.90	432.01	....	Debt Securities	79ae d
															Financial Derivatives	79al d
420.31	420.61	539.87	706.69	722.20	690.08	778.99	850.27	959.66	958.95	879.65	1,039.60	994.15	1,009.12	....	Other Investment	79af d
1.54	1.37	1.43	1.62	1.71	1.62	1.52	1.52	1.36	.93	.54	.64	49.14	6.47	....	Monetary Authorities	79ag d
46.64	44.17	50.16	32.79	39.04	43.37	48.60	52.34	62.62	59.52	55.32	61.63	44.37	61.10	....	General Government	79ah d
193.12	193.07	252.04	370.74	371.11	346.69	413.31	426.96	504.96	516.49	545.60	662.82	625.10	679.04	....	Banks	79ai d
179.00	182.00	236.23	301.54	310.34	298.40	315.56	369.45	390.72	382.01	278.19	314.50	275.53	262.52	....	Other Sectors	79aj d
76.00	53.19	57.44	69.63	62.50	87.58	69.59	73.35	84.62	76.90	70.79	80.11	93.47	87.30	....	Reserve Assets	79ak d
497.26	480.66	595.02	750.52	829.56	909.26	1,079.71	1,236.60	1,534.68	1,610.14	1,675.86	2,211.74	2,302.17	2,461.38	....	Liabilities	79la d
40.37	39.81	44.10	75.45	79.08	75.48	71.17	85.72	101.48	101.73	188.88	250.34	274.36	422.10	....	Dir. Invest. in Rep. Economy	79lb d
188.89	176.16	225.39	207.58	261.02	326.07	486.93	493.72	636.90	705.19	756.01	1,023.12	1,080.07	1,035.47	....	Portfolio Investment	79lc d
39.69	48.32	81.04	80.70	83.38	69.46	93.61	99.51	110.78	140.29	186.98	289.96	375.57	298.60	....	Equity Securities	79ld d
149.19	127.84	144.36	126.88	177.64	256.61	393.32	394.21	526.13	564.90	569.04	733.16	704.51	736.87	....	Debt Securities	79le d
															Financial Derivatives	79ll d
268.01	264.69	325.52	467.49	489.47	507.72	521.62	657.16	796.29	803.22	730.97	938.29	947.73	1,003.82	....	Other Investment	79lf d
19.71	21.89	36.97	43.71	36.79	25.00	22.01	22.13	20.88	18.88	16.02	19.31	14.59	13.90	....	Monetary Authorities	79lg d
.56	.76	1.08	30.76	29.84	26.82	28.17	33.51	46.24	45.54	32.26	35.00	18.43	17.84	....	General Government	79lh d
129.70	129.56	157.59	221.51	229.40	263.47	285.75	380.24	485.00	493.21	564.48	760.02	779.92	844.75	....	Banks	79li d
118.04	112.48	129.88	171.51	193.44	192.43	185.69	221.29	244.18	245.59	118.21	123.96	134.79	127.33	....	Other Sectors	79lj d

Germany

		1972	1973	1974	1975	1976	1977	1978	1979	1980	1981	1982	1983	1984	1985	1986
Government Finance																
Central Government										*Billions of Deutsche Mark through 1998;*						
Deficit (-) or Surplus	80	5.83	12.43	†–6.43	†–37.16	–31.21	–25.57	–26.49	–27.63	–26.91	–36.31	–32.02	–32.96	–32.31	–20.01	–17.56
Revenue	81	208.63	241.96	†258.86	†271.79	303.47	326.52	349.83	377.18	423.94	450.02	478.05	490.83	524.21	551.33	572.59
Grants Received	81z	2.26	1.92	†2.00	†2.23	2.35	3.39	3.78	3.15	2.52	2.18	2.68	3.16	3.00	3.10	3.07
Adj. to Cash-Revenue & Grants	81x	–2.55	–1.49	†–.38	†–.93	–3.27	–.54	–1.09	–2.59	–.63	–.50	—	—	—	—	—
Expenditure	82	199.82	226.13	†263.62	†304.14	330.16	352.68	375.76	400.37	447.54	481.64	506.03	520.05	549.04	564.55	584.66
Lending Minus Repayments	83	2.69	3.83	†3.29	†6.11	3.60	2.26	3.25	5.00	5.20	5.92	5.56	7.04	8.09	7.44	4.58
Overall Cash Adjustment	80x	....	....	....	....	....	—	—	—	—	–.45	–1.16	.14	–2.39	–2.45	–3.98
Financing																
Net Borrowing	84	...	...	...	†36.29	19.98	20.53	26.32	27.17	28.01	40.62	36.63	31.82	28.03	23.50	22.22
Domestic	84a	...	...	...	†34.48	15.20	20.06	24.57	25.05	7.17	19.45	29.15	18.32	18.56	5.42	–6.13
Foreign	85a	...	...	...	†1.81	4.78	.47	1.75	2.12	20.84	21.17	7.48	13.50	9.47	18.08	28.35
Seigniorage	86d	...	...	...	....	....	....	....	....	....	....	....	....	....	....	....
Pending Redemptions	87c	...	...	...	....	....	....	....	....	....	....	....	....	....	....	....
Use of Cash Balances	87	...	...	...	†.87	11.23	5.04	.17	.46	–1.10	–4.31	–4.61	1.14	4.28	–3.49	–4.66
Debt	88	55.30	61.36	†72.14	†103.32	128.88	153.58	179.94	205.60	235.77	277.99	314.44	347.27	373.91	399.15	421.99
Domestic	88a	...	...	...	†97.85	118.62	142.83	164.85	188.39	197.72	218.77	247.73	267.08	284.25	291.41	285.90
Foreign	89a	...	...	...	†5.47	10.26	10.75	15.09	17.21	38.05	59.22	66.71	80.19	89.66	107.74	136.09
Intragovernmental Debt	88s	...	...	...	†11.79	6.23	2.09	2.18	2.19	2.50	2.82	2.80	2.86	2.57	2.25	....
Other Deficits(-)or Surpluses																
Equalization of Burden Fund	80..i	.28	.47	†.53	†.29	.46	.98	.68	.16	....	....	....	....	....	....	....
Social Insurance System	80.r	5.35	5.92	†1.52	†–5.12	–5.97	–6.18	....	....	....	....	....	....	....	....	....
General Government																
Deficit (-) or Surplus	80g	...	...	...	....	....	....	....	....	....	....	....	....	....	*As Percent of*	
Debt	88g	...	...	...	....	....	....	....	....	....	....	....	....	....	....	....
National Accounts											*Billions of Deutsche Mark: through 1998;*					
Househ.Cons.Expend.,incl.NPISHs	96f.c	452.0	495.6	533.6	583.5	631.9	682.1	725.9	781.3	837.0	883.5	916.1	959.3	1,001.2	1,036.5	1,066.4
Government Consumption Expend.	91f.c	141.0	163.1	190.1	210.1	221.9	235.1	253.1	273.5	298.0	318.4	326.4	336.4	350.4	365.7	382.6
Gross Fixed Capital Formation	93e.c	209.2	219.3	212.7	209.4	225.7	242.4	264.9	301.3	332.1	331.3	323.5	340.8	350.7	355.8	373.5
Changes in Inventories	93i.c	4.3	12.4	3.7	–6.4	15.7	7.0	7.2	43.0	37.0	26.3	26.1	34.2	40.6	41.4	48.9
Exports of Goods and Services	90c.c	....	....	....	....	....	....	329.6	349.2	388.9	440.8	472.2	477.9	536.8	596.1	582.8
Imports of Goods and Services (-)	98c.c	....	....	....	....	....	....	359.9	422.2	464.8	477.3	481.6	530.1	569.5	526.3	
Gross Domestic Product (GDP)	99b.c	822.9	917.4	985.1	1,027.7	1,117.5	1,194.2	1,283.0	1,388.4	1,471.0	1,535.5	1,586.9	1,667.1	1,749.5	1,826.0	1,927.9
Net Primary Income from Abroad	98.n c	1.5	1.6	–.2	1.1	3.3	.3	5.9	5.4	6.5	4.1	3.4	8.6	13.7	8.4	8.2
Gross National Income (GNI)	99a.c	824.6	918.8	983.7	1,027.7	1,123.8	1,195.6	1,289.4	1,393.8	1,477.4	1,539.6	1,590.3	1,675.7	1,763.3	1,834.5	1,936.1
Net Current Transf.from Abroad	98t.c	....	....	....	....	....	....	....	....	....	....	....	....	....	....	....
Gross Nat'l Disposable Inc.(GNDI)	99i.c	....	....	....	....	....	....	....	....	....	....	....	....	....	....	....
Gross Saving	99s.c	....	....	....	....	....	....	....	....	....	....	....	....	....	....	....
Net National Income	99e.c	643.5	720.4	769.7	800.6	878.2	933.7	1,007.2	1,084.0	1,139.6	1,179.8	1,214.2	1,278.1	1,347.1	1,406.8	1,497.6
GDP Volume 1991 Prices	99b.r	1,657.4	1,737.2	1,742.7	1,720.6	1,805.2	1,859.7	1,916.7	1,998.2	2,017.9	2,020.7	1,999.6	2,034.4	2,091.8	2,139.4	2,189.2
GDP Volume 1995 Prices	99b.r															
GDP Volume (1995=100)	99bv r	55.2	57.8	58.0	57.3	60.1	61.9	63.8	66.5	67.2	67.3	66.6	67.7	69.6	71.2	72.9
GDP Deflator (1995=100)	99bi r	42.3	45.0	48.2	50.9	52.8	54.8	57.1	59.3	62.2	64.8	67.7	69.9	71.3	72.8	75.1
															Millions:	
Population	99z	61.67	61.97	62.04	61.83	61.51	61.40	61.31	61.44	61.54	61.66	61.60	61.38	61.13	60.97	61.01

1987	1988	1989	1990	1991	1992	1993	1994	1995	1996	1997	1998	1999	2000	2001		
															Government Finance	
															Central Government	
-21.57	-35.54	-3.60	†-39.55	-62.29	†-73.39	-78.79	-44.85	-61.83	-74.19	-48.97[P]	-35.12[P]	....	....	....	Deficit (-) or Surplus	80
588.77	605.00	655.37	†698.99	808.44	†985.18	1,017.55	1,099.41	1,124.66	1,133.06	1,160.25	1,188.14	—			Revenue	81
2.77	2.87	3.14	†2.60	3.45	†4.52	5.11	5.24	6.10	6.70	6.44	6.31	....			Grants Received	81z
—	—	—	†	—	†					[P]	[P]	....			Adj. to Cash-Revenue & Grants	81x
609.79	637.41	654.91	†716.28	860.74	†1045.45	1,084.30	1,142.81	1,188.04	1,213.20	1,214.65	1,233.89	—			Expenditure	82
3.30	3.92	6.73	†9.64	11.98	†13.83	12.10	15.84	3.60	3.02	-3.01	-17.98	—			Lending Minus Repayments	83
-.02	-2.08	-.47	†-15.22	-1.46	†-3.81	-5.05	9.15	-.95	2.27	-4.02	-13.66	....			Overall Cash Adjustment	80x
															Financing	
27.97	34.70	16.39	†65.04	76.45	†56.40	91.49	34.23	46.86	70.19	50.41	35.73	25.10			Net Borrowing	84
11.27	25.24	-2.81	†51.73	31.40	†1.78	-16.45	57.19	-11.61	15.91	-29.50	-44.59	2.16			Domestic	84a
16.70	9.46	19.20	†13.31	45.05	†54.62	107.94	-22.96	58.47	54.28	79.91	80.32	22.94			Foreign	85a
....	....	....	....	....	....	....	....	....	....	....	....	....			Seigniorage	86d
....	....	....	....	....	....	....	....	....	....	....	....	....			Pending Redemptions	87c
-6.40	.84	-12.79	†-25.49	-14.16	†16.99	-12.70	10.62	14.97	4.00	-1.44	-.61	-6.30			Use of Cash Balances	87
446.56	481.26	497.66	†599.14	680.87	†801.86	902.71	1,004.15	1,289.81	1,373.07	1,423.68	1,461.87	772.44			Debt	88
293.77	319.01	316.21	†404.38	437.66	†504.03	496.94	610.53	762.27	791.26	758.67	716.52	368.41			Domestic	88a
152.79	162.25	181.45	†194.76	243.21	†297.83	405.77	393.62	527.54	581.81	665.01	745.35	404.03			Foreign	89a
....	....	....	....	....	....	....	....	....	....	....	....	....			Intragovernmental Debt	88s
															Other Deficits(-)or Surpluses	
....	....	....	....	....	....	....	....	....	....	....	....	....			Equalization of Burden Fund	80.. i
....	....	....	....	....	....	....	....	....	....	....	....	....			Social Insurance System	80.r
															General Government	
			-2.1	-3.1	-2.6	-3.2	-2.4	-3.3	-3.4	-2.7	-2.2	-1.6	1.2	-2.7	Deficit (-) or Surplus	80g
			43.8	41.5	44.1	48.0	50.2	58.3	59.8	60.9	60.9	61.3	60.3	59.8	Debt	88g
															National Accounts	
1,108.0	1,153.7	1,221.0	1,318.7	†1,665.4	1,786.0	1,857.5	1,925.1	2,001.6	2,055.4	2,113.0	2,170.7	†1,149.6	1,182.8	1,218.1	Househ.Cons.Expend.,incl.NPISHs	96f. c
397.3	412.4	418.8	444.1	†563.9	623.6	643.0	669.2	697.8	717.5	712.9	722.8	†378.4	384.5	393.2	Government Consumption Expend.	91f. c
385.8	409.9	448.5	507.8	†698.0	758.5	745.2	785.2	790.6	779.4	788.6	804.9	†426.0	438.1	417.8	Gross Fixed Capital Formation	93e. c
48.9	66.8	77.1	89.1	†15.7	-7.0	-17.3	1.9	8.1	-5.6	1.3	17.2	†3.5	12.1	-5.2	Changes in Inventories	93i. c
576.3	617.6	701.7	783.6	†772.7	774.0	736.5	800.1	862.3	908.8	1,025.2	1,092.1	†586.6	683.3	721.4	Exports of Goods and Services	90c. c
525.0	566.1	643.5	713.8	†777.6	779.8	729.5	787.1	837.4	869.5	974.4	1,037.7	†569.8	675.3	682.3	Imports of Goods and Services (-)	98c. c
1,991.2	2,094.3	2,223.5	2,431.2	†2,938.0	3,155.2	3,235.4	3,394.4	3,523.0	3,586.0	3,666.6	3,769.9	†1,974.3	2,025.5	2,063.0	Gross Domestic Product (GDP)	99b. c
11.8	13.8	25.5	18.8	†102.1	95.0	94.0	60.3	44.8	-15.1	-18.0	-25.6	†-7.9	-7.5	....	Net Primary Income from Abroad	98.n c
2,003.0	2,108.0	2,249.1	2,448.2	†2,955.7	3,170.6	3,248.9	3,380.6	3,504.4	3,570.9	3,648.6	3,758.6	†1,966.4	2,018.0	....	Gross National Income (GNI)	99a. c
				†-42.0	-31.7	-37.5	-39.7	-32.7	-33.7	-36.3	-39.5	†-19.6	-19.7		Net Current Transf.from Abroad	98t. c
				2,914.7	3,139.7	3,212.3	3,341.6	3,471.8	3,537.6	3,612.6	3,719.4	†1,946.7	1,998.3		Gross Nat'l Disposable Inc.(GNDI)	99i. c
				683.4	728.2	710.5	745.1	770.2	764.8	787.1	819.1	†423.5	434.1		Gross Saving	99s. c
1,550.0	1,635.5	1,738.0	1,891.8	†2,544.3	2,719.5	2,766.3	2,878.1	2,983.3	3,038.6	3,104.1	3,200.6	†1,674.8	1,716.5	....	Net National Income	99e. c
2,219.3	2,299.0	2,383.4	2,520.4	2,853.6											GDP Volume 1991 Prices	99b. r
				†3,346.0	3,421.0	3,383.8	3,463.2	3,523.0	3,549.6	3,601.1	3,666.5	†1,911.1	1,968.5	1,979.6	GDP Volume 1995 Prices	99b. r
73.9	76.5	79.3	83.9	95.0	97.1	96.0	98.3	100.0	100.8	102.2	104.1	†106.1	109.3	109.9	GDP Volume (1995=100)	99bv r
76.5	77.7	79.6	82.3	†87.8	92.2	95.6	98.0	100.0	101.0	101.8	102.8	†103.3	102.9	104.2	GDP Deflator (1995=100)	99bi r
61.09	61.42	78.68	79.36	79.98	80.57	81.19	81.42	81.66	81.90	82.06	82.02	82.09	82.18	82.36	**Population**	99z

Millions of Euros Beginning 1999: Year Ending December 31

Gross Domestic Product

Billions of Euros Beginning 1999

Midyear Estimates

(See notes in the back of the book.)

Ghana

		1972	1973	1974	1975	1976	1977	1978	1979	1980	1981	1982	1983	1984	1985	1986
Exchange Rates																*Cedis per SDR:*
Market Rate	aa	1.39	1.39	1.41	1.35	1.34	1.40	3.58	3.62	3.51	3.20	3.03	31.41	49.01	65.89	110.10
																Cedis per US Dollar:
Market Rate	ae	1.28	1.15	1.15	1.15	1.15	1.15	2.75	2.75	2.75	2.75	2.75	30.00	50.00	59.99	90.01
Market Rate	rf	1.33	1.17	1.15	1.15	1.15	1.15	1.76	2.75	2.75	2.75	2.75	8.83	35.99	54.37	89.20
																Index Numbers (1995=100):
Nominal Effective Exchange Rate	ne c	....	....	....	....	....	....	....	14,238.33	14,398.37	16,717.84	18,936.82	7,891.60	1,943.41	1,417.93	711.88
Real Effective Exchange Rate	re c	....	....	....	....	....	....	....	....	651.28	1,452.06	1,813.92	1,221.69	474.17	342.71	197.01
Fund Position																*Millions of SDRs:*
Quota	2f. s	87.0	87.0	87.0	87.0	87.0	87.0	106.0	106.0	159.0	159.0	159.0	204.5	204.5	204.5	204.5
SDRs	1b. s	10.0	9.7	9.6	7.5	6.7	10.1	9.5	13.7	—	.6	.2	2.1	.1	17.2	1.6
Reserve Position in the Fund	1c. s	—	5.9	10.6												
Total Fund Cred.&Loans Outstg.	2tl	1.7	—	—	38.6	38.6	38.6	34.4	82.5	82.5	73.2	68.4	316.6	525.1	638.0	642.3
International Liquidity															*Millions of US Dollars Unless Otherwise Indicated:*	
Total Reserves minus Gold	1l. d	93.7	176.1	71.5	124.7	91.7	148.6	277.2	289.1	180.4	145.6	138.9	144.8	301.6	478.5	513.0
SDRs	1b. d	10.9	11.7	11.8	8.8	7.7	12.3	12.4	18.0	—	.7	.2	2.2	.1	18.9	2.0
Reserve Position in the Fund	1c. d	—	7.2	13.0												
Foreign Exchange	1d. d	82.8	157.2	46.7	115.9	84.0	136.3	264.8	271.1	180.4	144.9	138.7	142.6	301.5	459.6	511.0
Gold (Million Fine Troy Ounces)	1ad	.160	.160	.160	.160	.160	.200	.219	.219	.253	.309	.384	.384	.440	.225	.284
Gold (National Valuation)	1an d	5.6	5.6	5.6	5.6	5.6	7.2	8.1	8.1	19.0	48.2	68.8	72.5	91.7	46.1	76.6
Monetary Authorities: Other Assets	3.. d	7.6	6.1	15.3	18.5	5.9	6.8	2.3	2.5	16.2	2.4	3.5	1.2	11.5	7.4	15.1
Monetary Authorities: Other Liab.	4.. d	5.5	7.7	94.1	8.7	32.1	110.6	129.8	64.3	20.0	134.2	84.8	101.2	233.1	354.4	832.0
Deposit Money Banks: Assets	7a. d	1.4	12.2	.1	.1	8.9	6.3	2.1	.8	.8	3.2	3.7	30.7	9.2	7.5	4.3
Liabilities	7b. d	9.5	2.1	11.9	3.9	15.1	14.5	7.0	11.0	21.3	50.5	60.1	92.9	12.6	38.3	28.5
Monetary Authorities															*Millions of Cedis through 1985;*	
Foreign Assets	11	147.5	229.5	144.9	212.8	129.3	247.2	783.7	816.6	588.0	512.1	580.5	6,519.8	19,661.1	31,921.2	†91.8
Claims on Central Government	12a	304.8	339.5	573.8	881.3	1,513.5	2,527.5	4,286.8	4,413.2	5,723.6	9,494.2	10,165.1	24,342.8	35,053.5	45,017.6	†78.6
Claims on Nonfin.Pub.Enterprises	12c	156.5	76.3	145.9	90.8	108.6	90.0	627.9	1,093.6	1,346.5	2,191.0	4,966.0	154.7	3,482.1	12,543.6	†15.9
Claims on Deposit Money Banks	12e	10.9			3.0	4.5	6.0	6.1	6.0	6.0	6.0	6.0	6.0	6.0	6.0	†—
Claims on Other Financial Insts	12f	18.7	48.8	67.5	72.2	77.2	85.3	79.3	73.6	73.0	99.3	128.6	199.6	997.3	2,789.4	†3.8
Reserve Money	14	352.1	437.2	594.0	878.8	1,246.1	2,017.3	3,721.4	4,396.2	5,743.8	8,925.8	10,212.8	14,641.2	21,827.6	29,569.5	†47.2
of which: Currency Outside DMBs	14a	239.2	245.0	336.0	485.6	706.9	1,157.1	2,121.6	2,458.5	3,521.3	6,049.5	6,957.2	10,389.0	17,631.2	22,557.4	†32.3
Nonfin.Pub.Ent. Deps.	14e	3.4	27.8	41.4	28.5	40.1	118.3	219.4	348.7	475.7	55.7	199.6	853.2	439.9	2,510.3	†5.1
Liabs. of Central Bank: Securities	16ac	....	....													
Restricted Deposits	16b	193.7	147.1	126.6	149.7	154.0	259.7	489.9	648.3	458.4	698.9	1,817.3	3,536.1	5,735.4	8,312.9	†12.9
Foreign Liabilities	16c	9.4	8.8	108.3	62.0	88.5	181.1	480.2	475.7	344.5	603.4	440.4	12,980.9	37,385.6	63,298.6	†145.6
Central Government Deposits	16d	12.9	30.9	40.0	57.8	111.5	84.0	131.9	217.3	276.5	535.0	1,868.7	609.9	1,439.7	1,160.8	†6.9
Counterpart Funds	16e	11.1		.1		.2		1.0	.5	.2	29.2	20.9	1.8			†—
Capital Accounts	17a	96.8	131.7	149.2	168.9	197.3	272.2	416.0	664.0	572.1	1,036.8	1,576.6	3,943.2	4,576.1	6,036.3	†13.6
Other Items (Net)	17r	−37.6	−61.7	−86.1	−57.0	35.5	141.7	543.2	.9	341.8	473.6	−90.5	−4,490.2	−11,764.3	−16,100.3	†−36.1
Deposit Money Banks															*Millions of Cedis through 1985;*	
Reserves	20	114.0	171.1	214.9	375.3	510.5	714.3	1,423.0	1,667.7	1,854.4	2,801.8	3,365.9	4,340.7	8,757.3	10,847.7	†20.2
Claims on Mon.Author.: Securities	20c	....	....													
Foreign Assets	21	1.7	14.0	.2	.2	10.2	7.2	5.8	2.3	2.3	8.9	10.1	921.8	461.8	449.3	†.4
Claims on Central Government	22a	114.6	108.4	124.8	158.8	240.1	434.1	555.1	873.4	1,300.6	1,980.8	3,030.5	4,872.4	4,443.8	5,179.3	†6.2
Claims on Nonfin.Pub.Enterprises	22c	11.1	†154.5	192.0	204.5	284.5	332.8	484.7	540.5	615.9	1,202.6	1,117.0	1,181.9	806.1	3,775.0	†4.3
Claims on Private Sector	22d	283.2	†187.1	264.5	305.6	385.2	560.2	739.0	795.5	939.6	1,341.7	1,558.2	2,838.4	5,977.8	10,663.3	†18.6
Demand Deposits	24	219.9	290.9	320.0	494.6	679.0	1,119.0	1,786.9	1,872.6	2,090.0	3,309.8	4,048.0	5,477.0	8,778.1	13,240.1	†17.7
Time and Savings Deposits	25	205.1	229.8	307.7	377.5	474.0	651.2	1,005.0	1,262.3	1,863.6	2,615.5	3,634.5	4,086.3	5,113.0	8,410.2	†14.0
Foreign Liabilities	26c	12.2	2.4	13.6	4.4	17.4	16.7	19.4	30.2	58.5	138.9	165.2	255.5	632.3	2,298.4	†2.6
Central Government Deposits	26d	48.1	40.8	74.7	57.9	68.7	95.0	187.1	166.5	229.3	291.1	269.6	550.5	598.2	984.4	†1.3
Credit from Monetary Authorities	26g															†—
Capital Accounts	27a	28.6	32.2	35.0	39.9	44.5	55.3	77.2	114.2	144.4	253.5	409.6	852.5	1,297.5	2,337.8	†5.0
Other Items (Net)	27r	10.7	39.1	45.5	70.1	147.0	111.4	131.9	433.6	327.0	726.9	554.7	2,933.7	4,027.7	3,643.7	†9.0
Monetary Survey															*Millions of Cedis through 1985;*	
Foreign Assets (Net)	31n	127.6	232.3	23.1	146.6	33.7	56.6	289.8	313.0	187.3	−221.2	−15.0	−5,794.7	−17,894.9	−33,226.5	†−56.0
Domestic Credit	32	827.9	†842.9	1,253.8	1,597.5	2,428.8	3,851.0	6,453.6	7,405.9	9,493.5	15,483.4	18,826.9	32,429.3	48,722.7	77,823.0	†119.1
Claims on Central Govt. (Net)	32an	358.4	376.2	584.0	924.4	1,573.3	2,782.6	4,522.9	4,902.7	6,518.4	10,648.9	11,057.2	28,054.7	37,459.4	48,051.7	†76.6
Claims on Nonfin.Pub.Enterprises	32c	167.6	†230.8	337.9	295.3	393.1	422.8	1,112.5	1,634.1	1,962.5	3,393.6	6,083.0	1,336.6	4,288.2	16,318.6	†20.2
Claims on Private Sector	32d	283.2	†187.1	264.5	305.6	385.2	560.2	739.0	795.5	939.6	1,341.7	1,558.2	2,838.4	5,977.8	10,663.3	†18.6
Claims on Other Financial Insts	32f	18.7	48.8	67.5	72.2	77.2	85.3	79.3	73.6	73.0	99.3	128.6	199.6	997.3	2,789.4	†3.8
Money	34	462.6	563.8	697.4	1,008.6	1,426.0	2,394.4	4,127.9	4,679.6	6,087.0	9,415.0	11,204.7	16,719.2	26,849.2	38,307.8	†55.2
Quasi-Money	35	205.1	229.8	307.7	377.5	474.0	651.2	1,005.0	1,262.3	1,863.6	2,615.5	3,634.5	4,086.3	5,113.0	8,410.2	†14.0
Liabs. of Central Bank: Securities	36ac															
Restricted Deposits	36b	193.7	147.1	126.6	149.7	154.0	259.7	489.9	648.3	458.4	698.9	1,817.3	3,536.1	5,735.4	8,312.9	†12.9
Counterpart Funds	36e	11.1		.1		.2		1.0	.5	.2	29.2	20.9	1.8			†—
Capital Accounts	37a	125.4	163.8	184.2	208.8	241.8	327.5	493.2	778.2	716.5	1,290.3	1,986.2	4,795.4	5,873.6	8,374.1	†18.5
Other Items (Net)	37r	−42.4	−29.3	−39.0	−.5	166.6	274.7	626.5	349.8	555.3	1,213.2	148.3	−2,504.3	−12,743.4	−18,808.5	†−37.4
Money plus Quasi-Money	35l	667.66	793.51	1,005.03	1,386.11	1,899.93	3,045.65	5,132.83	5,942.11	7,950.55	12,030.57	14,839.23	20,805.48	31,962.20	46,718.00	†69.11
Other Banking Institutions															*Billions of Cedis:*	
Reserves	40	....	....	....	....	....	....	....	....	....	....	....	....	....	....	....
Claims on Mon.Author.: Securities	40c	....	....	....	....	....	....	....	....	....	....	....	....	....	....	....
Claims on Central Government	42a	....	....	....	....	....	....	....	....	....	....	....	....	....	....	....
Claims on Nonfin.Pub.Enterprises	42c	....	....	....	....	....	....	....	....	....	....	....	....	....	....	....
Claims on Deposit Money Banks	42e	....	....	....	....	....	....	....	....	....	....	....	....	....	....	....
Claims on Other Financial Insts	42f	....	....	....	....	....	....	....	....	....	....	....	....	....	....	....
Quasi-Monetary Liabilities	45	....	....	....	....	....	....	....	....	....	....	....	....	....	....	....
Money Market Instruments	46aa	....	....	....	....	....	....	....	....	....	....	....	....	....	....	....
Credit from Monetary Authorities	46g	....	....	....	....	....	....	....	....	....	....	....	....	....	....	....
Capital Accounts	47a	....	....	....	....	....	....	....	....	....	....	....	....	....	....	....
Other Items (Net)	47r	....	....	....	....	....	....	....	....	....	....	....	....	....	....	....

1987	1988	1989	1990	1991	1992	1993	1994	1995	1996	1997	1998	1999	2000	2001		Code
															Exchange Rates	
End of Period																
249.76	309.36	398.23	490.57	558.76	716.15[e]	1,125.87	1,536.68	2,154.33	2,522.74	3,066.48	3,274.49	4,852.02	9,182.45	9,035.87	Market Rate	aa
End of Period (ae) Period Average (rf)																
176.06	229.89	303.03	344.83	390.63	520.83[e]	819.67	1,052.63	1,449.28	1,754.39	2,272.73	2,325.58	3,535.14	7,047.65	7,189.98	Market Rate	ae
153.73	202.35	270.00	326.33	367.83	437.09[e]	649.06	956.71	1,200.43	1,637.23	2,050.17	2,314.15	2,669.30	5,455.06	7,170.76	Market Rate	rf
Period Averages																
424.21	350.00	309.68	269.85	255.47	227.08	178.75	130.72	100.00	75.43	64.10	59.08	53.58	28.75	21.85	Nominal Effective Exchange Rate	ne c
151.61	145.71	136.74	136.12	139.19	122.98	108.02	86.86	100.00	109.03	115.60	125.07	125.72	81.12	81.66	Real Effective Exchange Rate	re c
															Fund Position	
End of Period																
204.5	204.5	204.5	204.5	204.5	274.0	274.0	274.0	274.0	274.0	274.0	274.0	369.0	369.0	369.0	Quota	2f. s
11.2	.2	22.8	3.1	8.8	3.2	.4	2.9	1.6	1.6	2.5	42.4	13.3	.4	3.2	SDRs	1b. s
—	—	—	—	—	17.4	17.4	17.4	17.4	17.4	17.4	17.4	41.1	—	—	Reserve Position in the Fund	1c. s
610.9	566.4	561.2	523.4	583.1	537.8	537.3	479.7	436.2	377.3	257.0	236.9	225.8	224.5	225.7	Total Fund Cred.&Loans Outstg.	2tl
															International Liquidity	
End of Period																
195.1	221.3	347.3	218.8	550.2	319.9	409.7	583.9	697.5	828.7	537.8	377.0	453.8	232.1	298.2	Total Reserves minus Gold	1l. d
15.9	.3	29.9	4.4	12.5	4.4	.5	4.2	2.4	2.2	3.4	59.7	18.2	.5	4.0	SDRs	1b. d
—	—	—	—	—	23.9	23.9	25.4	25.8	25.0	23.4	24.5	56.5	—	—	Reserve Position in the Fund	1c. d
179.2	221.0	317.4	214.4	537.7	291.6	385.3	554.3	669.2	801.5	511.0	292.8	379.1	231.5	294.2	Foreign Exchange	1d. d
.282	.217	.221	.235	.266	.275	.275	.275	.275	.275	.275	.277	.279	.280	.281	Gold (Million Fine Troy Ounces)	1ad
81.5	77.5	78.3	63.3	74.0	78.1	77.2	77.2	77.4	77.2	77.3	78.8	78.9	79.3	78.9	Gold (National Valuation)	1an d
50.5	...	...	...	...	...	...	...	...	...	...	...	...	...	...	Monetary Authorities: Other Assets	3.. d
180.7	283.4	519.8	445.2	59.1	67.6	56.3	96.5	34.8	45.4	126.7	52.0	102.4	168.5	...	Monetary Authorities: Other Liab.	4.. d
27.2	28.0	112.9	289.9	306.3	311.1	313.8	405.4	327.9	396.7	392.3	361.3	339.4	355.2	335.7	Deposit Money Banks: Assets	7a. d
49.2	56.6	105.8	110.1	132.2	115.9	161.4	225.4	265.2	364.9	400.1	432.2	604.6	635.4	533.8	Liabilities	7b. d
															Monetary Authorities	
Billions of Cedis Beginning 1986: End of Period																
57.5	77.1	141.3	113.4	†269.6	192.2	380.0	663.2	1,079.9	1,182.1	1,337.6	1,372.3	1,631.2	2,028.3	...	Foreign Assets	11
161.7	160.2	134.0	166.8	†344.2	482.6	850.6	893.0	1,405.5	1,553.3	2,001.7	2,000.1	2,175.4	3,088.1	...	Claims on Central Government	12a
15.1	1.2	25.1	5.8	†20.3	3.8	44.8	148.8	151.9	135.8	71.9	9.9	10.0	7.5	...	Claims on Nonfin.Pub.Enterprises	12c
—	—	—	1.6	†8.1	4.2	6.8	6.7	8.3	9.4	33.0	11.1	11.1	15.4	...	Claims on Deposit Money Banks	12e
4.8	6.2	9.2	9.0	†—				37.2	10.7	4.6	.9	.9		...	Claims on Other Financial Insts	12f
67.0	103.0	126.5	129.8	†130.5	245.8	257.9	461.3	623.1	902.2	1,203.1	1,403.5	1,583.9	2,150.6	...	Reserve Money	14
49.0	67.9	82.9	80.1	†89.9	183.5	222.2	368.8	546.3	724.0	981.8	1,083.6	1,186.1	1,739.1	...	*of which: Currency Outside DMBs*	14a
10.0	21.7	10.3	15.7	†13.1	2.2	3.3	3.5	6.3	7.9	6.3	3.2	2.8	3.9	...	*Nonfin.Pub.Ent. Deps.*	14e
...	...	...	...	101.9	148.1	334.5	479.5	722.4	518.2	182.6	1.1	—	—	...	Liabs. of Central Bank: Securities	16ac
15.7	5.9	1.3	—	†.9	.9	.9	.9	.9	.9					...	Restricted Deposits	16b
184.4	223.2	324.3	327.0	†348.9	420.4	651.1	838.7	990.3	1,031.5	1,076.0	896.7	1,457.8	3,249.0	...	Foreign Liabilities	16c
8.9	14.1	17.5	33.9	†11.0	5.0	47.4	65.0	106.1	180.6	217.1	431.8	74.0		...	Central Government Deposits	16d
			—	†62.6	99.2	189.8	253.1	388.2	143.9	267.7	408.4	803.6		...	Counterpart Funds	16e
15.3	16.6	15.8	22.3	†47.7	48.4	88.5	127.1	296.7	351.1	626.1	623.6	738.1	1,090.0	...	Capital Accounts	17a
-52.2	-118.0	-175.9	-216.4	†-61.3	-285.0	-287.8	-514.0	-444.9	-237.2	-123.7	-370.8	-829.0	-1,350.2	...	Other Items (Net)	17r
															Deposit Money Banks	
Billions of Cedis Beginning 1986: End of Period																
18.5	23.8	45.1	44.7	†59.3	78.7	41.6	88.7	106.7	194.1	219.2	326.5	448.7	502.2	1,058.3	Reserves	20
...	...	...	...	79.5	56.7	263.1	369.4	564.1	475.3	153.3	.2	—	—	...	Claims on Mon.Author.: Securities	20c
4.8	6.4	34.2	100.0	†119.7	162.0	257.2	426.8	475.3	695.9	891.7	840.2	1,199.9	2,503.2	2,458.0	Foreign Assets	21
5.9	5.1	6.4	3.0	†.9	.3	.3	.3	.4	74.1	737.0	1,417.8	2,270.9	2,825.6	4,009.8	Claims on Central Government	22a
5.0	6.9	16.0	24.1	†34.9	68.5	43.0	29.5	44.5	57.4	144.0	184.2	483.8	1,247.8	1,762.2	Claims on Nonfin.Pub.Enterprises	22c
23.5	33.0	82.8	94.7	†88.8	138.5	187.3	273.3	393.3	680.9	1,156.6	1,639.3	2,466.3	3,835.8	4,471.7	Claims on Private Sector	22d
25.2	32.4	93.2	110.7	†132.0	174.8	235.3	320.9	371.1	482.1	776.5	982.5	939.2	861.7	2,009.1	Demand Deposits	24
21.8	33.0	53.4	65.2	†109.7	165.2	203.3	275.2	434.4	586.9	856.3	1,234.1	1,714.4	2,714.2	4,238.1	Time and Savings Deposits	25
8.7	13.0	32.1	38.0	†51.6	60.4	132.3	237.2	384.3	640.1	909.4	1,005.1	2,137.3	4,478.0	3,908.5	Foreign Liabilities	26c
1.8	3.0	13.0	16.5	†17.7	22.5	63.5	69.2	76.0	105.4	37.9	55.0	52.1	57.3	78.4	Central Government Deposits	26d
—	—	3.4	1.1	†16.6	2.1	5.8	19.8	17.6	29.4	44.4	47.3	32.8	89.6	10.6	Credit from Monetary Authorities	26g
7.4	7.4	-2.4	48.0	†76.0	90.2	131.9	249.9	270.2	359.0	525.0	596.5	863.3	1,410.8	1,902.8	Capital Accounts	27a
-7.0	-13.5	-8.1	-13.1	†-5.6	-10.6	20.4	15.8	30.6	-25.2	152.3	487.5	1,130.3	1,303.0	1,612.6	Other Items (Net)	27r
															Monetary Survey	
Billions of Cedis Beginning 1986: End of Period																
-130.8	-152.6	-180.8	-151.5	†-11.3	-126.5	-146.2	14.0	180.6	206.4	243.9	310.7	-764.1	-3,195.5	...	Foreign Assets (Net)	31n
205.4	195.5	243.0	252.8	†460.3	666.1	1,015.2	1,210.6	1,850.6	2,226.2	3,860.9	4,765.3	7,281.0	10,947.5	...	Domestic Credit	32
156.9	148.2	109.9	119.3	†316.3	455.4	740.1	759.1	1,223.7	1,341.4	2,483.7	2,931.1	4,320.1	5,856.4	...	Claims on Central Govt. (Net)	32an
20.1	8.1	41.1	29.9	†55.3	72.3	87.8	178.3	196.4	193.2	215.9	194.1	493.8	1,255.4	...	Claims on Nonfin.Pub.Enterprises	32c
23.5	33.0	82.8	94.7	†88.8	138.5	187.3	273.3	393.3	680.9	1,156.6	1,639.3	2,466.3	3,835.8	...	Claims on Private Sector	32d
4.8	6.2	9.2	9.0	†—				37.2	10.7	4.6	.9	.9		...	Claims on Other Financial Insts	32f
84.2	122.0	186.4	206.4	†235.7	360.7	461.3	693.5	925.3	1,215.7	1,767.3	2,073.1	2,129.4	2,607.5	...	Money	34
21.8	33.0	53.4	65.2	†109.7	165.2	203.3	275.2	434.4	586.9	856.3	1,234.1	1,714.4	2,714.2	...	Quasi-Money	35
...	...	...	...	22.4	91.5	71.4	110.1	158.4	43.0	29.3	1.0	—	—	...	Liabs. of Central Bank: Securities	36ac
15.7	5.9	1.3	—	†.9	.9	.9	.9	.9	.9					...	Restricted Deposits	36b
			—	†62.6	99.2	189.8	253.1	388.2	143.9	267.7	408.4	803.6		...	Counterpart Funds	36e
22.6	24.0	13.5	70.3	†123.6	138.6	220.3	377.0	566.9	710.1	1,151.1	1,220.1	1,601.4	2,500.8	...	Capital Accounts	37a
-69.7	-141.9	-192.4	-240.7	†-106.0	-316.4	-278.1	-485.2	-442.8	-267.9	33.1	139.3	268.1	-70.5	...	Other Items (Net)	37r
105.97	155.01	239.75	271.64	†345.49	525.93	664.67	968.70	1,359.67	1,802.61	2,623.60	3,307.19	3,843.78	5,321.63	...	Money plus Quasi-Money	35l
															Other Banking Institutions	
End of Period																
...	...	...	...		.2	.5	.6	.3	.5	.5	.9	2.7	2.8	.4	Reserves	40
...	...	...	...		26.0	30.8	41.1	50.7	36.9	29.3	1.0	—	—	5.0	Claims on Mon.Author.: Securities	40c
...	...	...	...							15.3	60.1	87.4	132.0	299.1	Claims on Central Government	42a
...	...	...	...		7.2	1.2					—	—	—	3.0	Claims on Nonfin.Pub.Enterprises	42c
...	...	...	...		.2	2.3	.8	6.9	5.3	8.3	2.1	5.1	14.2	16.5	Claims on Deposit Money Banks	42e
...	...	...	...		.3	.1	.2	1.7	—	—	—	.2	1.6		Claims on Other Financial Insts	42f
...	...	...	...		32.1	30.8	37.7	23.0	35.1	44.5	67.6	60.3	127.5	296.5	Quasi-Monetary Liabilities	45
												11.5	.1	93.6	Money Market Instruments	46aa
...	...	...	...		2.9	—	—	33.4	10.7	3.7	.5	18.8	4.9	15.4	Credit from Monetary Authorities	46g
...	...	...	...		3.6	3.6	7.3	6.0	4.7	9.2	11.8	15.9	12.8	15.7	Capital Accounts	47a
...	...	...	...		-4.7	.4	-2.3	-2.8	-7.8	-4.1	-15.8	-11.0	6.7	-95.5	Other Items (Net)	47r

Ghana

	1972	1973	1974	1975	1976	1977	1978	1979	1980	1981	1982	1983	1984	1985	1986
Banking Survey														*Billions of Cedis:*	
Foreign Assets (Net) **51n**	....	....	....	....	....	....	....	....	....	....	....	....	....	....	....
Domestic Credit **52**	....	....	....	....	....	....	....	....	....	....	....	....	....	....	....
Claims on Central Govt. (Net) ... **52an**	....	....	....	....	....	....	....	....	....	....	....	....	....	....	....
Claims on Nonfin.Pub.Enterprises .. **52c**	....	....	....	....	....	....	....	....	....	....	....	....	....	....	....
Claims on Private Sector **52d**	....	....	....	....	....	....	....	....	....	....	....	....	....	....	....
Claims on Other Financial Insts ... **52f**	....	....	....	....	....	....	....	....	....	....	....	....	....	....	....
Liquid Liabilities **55l**	....	....	....	....	....	....	....	....	....	....	....	....	....	....	....
Money Market Instruments **56aa**	....	....	....	....	....	....	....	....	....	....	....	....	....	....	....
Liabs. of Central Bank: Securities ... **56ac**	....	....	....	....	....	....	....	....	....	....	....	....	....	....	....
Restricted Deposits **56b**	....	....	....	....	....	....	....	....	....	....	....	....	....	....	....
Counterpart Funds **56e**	....	....	....	....	....	....	....	....	....	....	....	....	....	....	....
Capital Accounts **57a**	....	....	....	....	....	....	....	....	....	....	....	....	....	....	....
Other Items (Net) **57r**	....	....	....	....	....	....	....	....	....	....	....	....	....	....	....
Interest Rates														*Percent Per Annum*	
Discount Rate (End of Period) **60**	8.0	6.0	6.0	8.0	8.0	8.0	13.5	13.5	13.5	19.5	10.5	14.5	18.0	18.5	20.5
Treasury Bill Rate **60c**							13.0	13.0	13.0	13.0	13.0	13.0	14.2	17.1	18.5
Deposit Rate **60l**	....	....	....	....	....	....	11.5	11.5	11.5	11.5	11.5	11.5	15.0	15.8	17.0
Lending Rate **60p**							19.00	19.00	19.00	19.00	19.00	19.00	21.17	21.17	20.00
Prices and Labor														*Index Numbers (1995=100):*	
Consumer Prices **64**	—	—	—	.1	.1	.2	.4	.6	.9	1.9	2.3	5.1	7.1	7.9	9.8
														Number in Thousands:	
Employment **67e**	....	....	....	....	....	....	....	....	....	....	....	....	....	464	414
Unemployment **67c**	....	....	....	....	....	....	....	....	....	....	....	....	....	24	26
International Transactions														*Millions of Cedis through 1985;*	
Exports **70**	580	763	849	938	957	1,166	1,645	2,737	3,458	2,928	2,402	10,225	18,942	33,185	†77
Cocoa Beans **70r**	275	397	466	556	516	680	988	1,846	2,564	1,118	1,072	6,343	12,795	18,323	†42
Imports, c.i.f. **71**	393	526	944	909	992	1,193	1,682	2,344	3,104	3,041	1,939	11,022	21,887	47,155	†93
Volume of Exports														*1995=100*	
Cocoa Beans **72r**	171.6	187.3	131.4	134.4	129.7	100.2	84.5	75.0	102.0	71.9	95.0	68.9	60.3	66.2	84.9
Export Prices															
Cocoa Beans (Unit Value) **74r**	—	—	.1	.1	.1	.1	.3	.5	.6	.3	.3	2.0	4.6	6.1	10.7
Balance of Payments														*Millions of US Dollars:*	
Current Account, n.i.e. **78ald**	....	....	....	17.6	−74.0	−79.7	−45.9	123.5	30.2	−419.2	−107.3	−172.2	−38.8	−133.9	−85.3
Goods: Exports f.o.b. **78aad**	....	....	....	801.0	779.0	889.6	892.8	1,065.7	1,103.6	710.7	607.0	439.1	565.9	632.4	749.3
Goods: Imports f.o.b. **78abd**	....	....	....	−650.5	−690.3	−860.2	−780.3	−803.1	−908.3	−954.3	−588.7	−499.7	−533.0	−668.7	−735.1
Trade Balance **78acd**	....	....	....	150.4	88.8	29.4	112.5	262.6	195.3	−243.6	18.3	−60.6	32.9	−36.3	14.2
Services: Credit **78add**	....	....	....	90.0	112.4	128.3	103.3	97.0	106.7	119.1	103.9	38.2	43.8	38.0	54.8
Services: Debit **78aed**	....	....	....	−231.0	−260.3	−261.0	−292.6	−260.9	−269.9	−295.3	−228.2	−134.7	−163.0	−167.7	−240.8
Balance on Goods & Services ... **78afd**	....	....	....	9.4	−59.0	−103.4	−76.8	98.7	32.1	−419.9	−106.0	−157.1	−86.3	−166.0	−171.7
Income: Credit **78agd**	....	....	....	4.4	2.5	2.5	1.3	1.9	2.8	2.0	3.0	.3	2.0	5.6	.6
Income: Debit **78ahd**	....	....	....	−40.8	−44.3	−37.4	−28.7	−57.4	−85.3	−86.0	−88.2	−89.7	−116.8	−115.9	−105.3
Balance on Gds, Serv. & Inc. ... **78aid**	....	....	....	−26.9	−100.8	−138.3	−104.2	43.2	−50.4	−503.8	−191.3	−246.5	−201.1	−276.3	−276.4
Current Transfers, n.i.e.: Credit ... **78ajd**	....	....	....	56.6	40.3	71.4	69.7	89.5	89.3	93.3	90.1	88.0	169.0	147.4	200.1
Current Transfers: Debit **78akd**	....	....	....	−12.1	−13.5	−12.9	−11.5	−9.2	−8.7	−8.7	−6.1	−13.7	−6.7	−5.0	−9.0
Capital Account, n.i.e. **78bcd**	....	....	....	—	—	—	—	−1.5	−1.0	−1.6	−1.5	−1.9	—	−.3	−.5
Capital Account, n.i.e.: Credit **78bad**	....	....	....	—	—	—	—	—	—	—	—	—	—	—	—
Capital Account: Debit **78bbd**	....	....	....	—	—	—	—	−1.5	−1.0	−1.6	−1.5	−1.9	—	−.3	−.5
Financial Account, n.i.e. **78bjd**	....	....	....	82.4	−36.6	58.9	103.0	53.9	69.9	108.5	123.5	119.1	206.9	84.9	61.9
Direct Investment Abroad **78bdd**	....	....	....	—	—	—	—	—	—	—	—	—	—	—	—
Dir. Invest. in Rep. Econ., n.i.e. ... **78bed**	....	....	....	70.9	−18.3	19.2	9.7	−2.8	15.6	16.3	16.3	2.4	2.0	5.6	4.3
Portfolio Investment Assets **78bfd**	....	....	....	—	—	—	—	—	—	—	—	—	—	—	—
Equity Securities **78bkd**	....	....	....	—	—	—	—	—	—	—	—	—	—	—	—
Debt Securities **78bld**	....	....	....	—	—	—	—	—	—	—	—	—	—	—	—
Portfolio Investment Liab., n.i.e. ... **78bgd**	....	....	....	—	—	—	—	—	—	—	—	—	—	—	—
Equity Securities **78bmd**	....	....	....	—	—	—	—	—	—	—	—	—	—	—	—
Debt Securities **78bnd**	....	....	....	—	—	—	—	—	—	—	—	—	—	—	—
Financial Derivatives Assets **78bwd**	....	....	....	....	....	....	....	....	....	....	....	....	....	....	....
Financial Derivatives Liabilities ... **78bxd**	....	....	....	....	....	....	....	....	....	....	....	....	....	....	....
Other Investment Assets **78bhd**	....	....	....	−3.1	3.9	1.7	10.8	20.7	−6.3	14.9	−.3	−25.8	11.1	5.8	−2.2
Monetary Authorities **78bod**	....	....	....												−7.2
General Government **78bpd**	....	....	....	−3.1	12.6	−1.0	4.6	−.3	−6.3	17.3	.2	1.1	−10.3	4.1	—
Banks **78bqd**	....	....	....	—	−8.7	2.6	6.2	1.3	—	−2.4	−.5	−26.9	21.4	1.7	5.0
Other Sectors **78brd**	....	....	....	—	—	—	—	19.7	—	—	—	—	—	—	—
Other Investment Liab., n.i.e. **78bid**	....	....	....	14.7	−22.2	38.1	82.5	36.0	60.6	77.3	107.5	142.5	193.8	73.5	59.8
Monetary Authorities **78bsd**	....	....	....	−8.9	−.9	−1.4	2.7	−5.3	—	−.1	−12.2	−.1	—	11.2	−2.2
General Government **78btd**	....	....	....	23.7	7.6	64.3	90.7	93.8	53.9	90.7	112.8	19.6	212.2	39.3	128.2
Banks **78bud**	....	....	....	−8.0	11.2	−.5	−7.5	4.0	10.3	29.2	9.6	32.8	−80.2	25.6	−21.4
Other Sectors **78bvd**	....	....	....	7.9	−40.2	−24.3	−3.5	−56.5	−3.6	−42.5	−2.7	90.2	61.8	−2.6	−44.8
Net Errors and Omissions **78cad**	....	....	....	6.3	−26.7	12.4	−119.4	−106.1	−100.4	24.0	−32.6	−126.0	−132.5	63.4	−36.9
Overall Balance **78cbd**	....	....	....	106.3	−137.3	−8.4	−62.4	69.8	−1.3	−288.3	−17.9	−180.9	35.6	14.1	−60.8
Reserves and Related Items **79dad**	....	....	....	−106.3	137.3	8.4	62.4	−69.8	1.3	288.3	17.9	180.9	−35.6	−14.1	60.8
Reserve Assets **79dbd**	....	....	....	−45.6	59.3	−109.4	−80.2	3.1	124.1	47.2	6.6	−4.8	−146.7	−183.4	13.0
Use of Fund Credit and Loans **79dcd**	....	....	....	48.1	—	—	−5.3	62.1	.4	−10.9	−5.4	260.5	212.9	115.7	5.9
Exceptional Financing **79ded**	....	....	....	−108.9	78.0	117.8	147.9	−135.0	−123.3	252.0	16.6	−74.7	−101.8	53.5	41.9

	1987	1988	1989	1990	1991	1992	1993	1994	1995	1996	1997	1998	1999	2000	2001		
End of Period																**Banking Survey**	
	....	....	....	....	....	−126.5	−146.2	14.0	180.6	206.4	243.9	310.7	−764.1	−3,195.5	....	Foreign Assets (Net)	**51n**
	....	....	....	....	....	675.8	1,016.4	1,210.8	1,852.2	2,226.2	3,876.1	4,825.5	7,368.6	11,082.5	....	Domestic Credit	**52**
	....	....	....	....	....	455.4	740.1	759.1	1,223.7	1,341.4	2,499.0	2,991.2	4,407.5	5,988.4	....	Claims on Central Govt. (Net)	**52an**
	....	....	....	....	....	79.5	88.9	178.3	196.4	193.2	215.9	194.1	493.8	1,258.3	....	Claims on Nonfin.Pub.Enterprises	**52c**
	....	....	....	....	....	138.5	187.3	273.3	393.3	680.9	1,156.6	1,639.3	2,466.3	3,835.8	....	Claims on Private Sector	**52d**
	....	....	....	....	....	.3	.1	.2	38.9	10.7	4.6	.9	1.1	—	....	Claims on Other Financial Insts.	**52f**
	....	....	....	....	....	557.9	695.0	1,005.8	1,382.4	1,837.2	2,667.6	3,373.9	3,901.4	5,446.3	....	Liquid Liabilities	**55l**
	....	....	....	....	....							—	11.5	.1	....	Money Market Instruments	**56aa**
	....	....	....	....	....	65.5	40.6	69.0	107.6	6.1	—	—	—	—	....	Liabs. of Central Bank: Securities	**56ac**
	....	....	....	....	....	.9	.9	.9	.9	.9	—	—	—	—	....	Restricted Deposits	**56b**
	....	....	....	....	....	99.2	189.8	253.1	388.2	143.9	267.7	408.4	803.6	—	....	Counterpart Funds	**56e**
	....	....	....	....	....	142.2	223.9	384.3	572.9	714.7	1,160.3	1,231.9	1,617.3	2,513.6	....	Capital Accounts	**57a**
	....	....	....	....	....	−316.4	−280.0	−488.3	−419.1	−270.3	24.5	121.9	270.7	−73.0	....	Other Items (Net)	**57r**
Percent Per Annum																**Interest Rates**	
	23.5	26.0	26.0	33.0	20.0	30.0	35.0	33.0	45.0	45.0	45.0	37.0	27.0	27.0	27.0	Discount Rate (End of Period)	**60**
	21.7	19.8	19.8	21.8	29.2	19.4	31.0	27.7	35.4	41.6	42.8	34.3	26.4	36.3	41.0	Treasury Bill Rate	**60c**
	17.6	16.5			21.3	16.3	23.6	23.1	28.7	34.5	35.8	32.0	23.6	28.6	30.9	Deposit Rate	**60l**
	25.50	25.58	....	....	....	....	....	....	....	....	....	....	....	....	....	Lending Rate	**60p**
Period Averages																**Prices and Labor**	
	13.7	18.0	22.5	30.9	36.5	40.2	50.2	62.7	100.0	146.6	†187.4	214.8	241.5	302.3	401.8	Consumer Prices	**64**
Period Averages																	
	394	307	215	230	186	....	....	....	....	....	....	....	....	....	....	Employment	**67e**
		29	27	30	31	31	39	37	41	....	....	....	....	....	....	Unemployment	**67c**
Billions of Cedis Beginning 1986																**International Transactions**	
	147	206	275	....	....	547	632	1,359	2,070	2,733	3,353	4,151			....	Exports	**70**
	80	94	112	121	127	118	162	266	457	791	826	1,437	1,422	2,170	....	Cocoa Beans	**70r**
	175	186	347	....	388	951	2,439	2,029	2,289	3,452	4,769	5,932	9,347	16,171	....	Imports, c.i.f.	**71**
1995=100																Volume of Exports	
	83.4	87.6	107.2	106.2	95.7	88.6	101.6	94.3	100.0	142.3	103.4	138.1	151.3	....	....	Cocoa Beans	**72r**
																Export Prices	
	20.3	23.4	22.9	24.9	28.8	29.2	34.9	61.8	100.0	121.4	1,748.6	242.8	204.6	....	....	Cocoa Beans (Unit Value)	**74r**
Minus Sign Indicates Debit																Balance of Payments	
	−97.9	−67.1	−93.9	−223.2	−252.1	−377.0	−559.8	−254.6	−144.7	−324.7	−549.7	−443.1	−932.5	−412.6	....	Current Account, n.i.e.	**78ald**
	826.8	881.0	808.2	896.8	997.7	986.3	1,063.6	1,237.7	1,431.2	1,570.1	1,489.9	2,090.8	2,005.5	1,898.4	....	Goods: Exports f.o.b.	**78aa d**
	−933.9	−993.4	−1,011.6	−1,205.0	−1,318.7	−1,456.5	−1,728.0	−1,579.9	−1,687.8	−1,937.0	−2,128.2	−2,896.5	−3,228.1	−2,741.3	....	Goods: Imports f.o.b.	**78ab d**
	−107.1	−112.4	−203.4	−308.2	−321.0	−470.2	−664.4	−342.2	−256.6	−366.9	−638.3	−805.7	−1,222.6	−842.9	....	Trade Balance	**78ac d**
	78.7	76.7	80.9	86.4	102.8	118.4	144.7	147.5	150.6	156.8	164.9	438.6	467.8	504.3	....	Services: Credit	**78ad d**
	−266.9	−268.0	−275.9	−300.5	−336.4	−389.3	−445.3	−420.8	−432.7	−456.4	−505.0	−673.6	−665.9	−597.3	....	Services: Debit	**78ae d**
	−295.3	−303.7	−398.4	−522.3	−554.6	−741.1	−965.0	−615.5	−538.7	−666.5	−978.4	−1,040.7	−1,420.7	−935.9	....	Balance on Goods & Services	**78af d**
	.6	1.0	4.9	6.8	7.5	10.5	11.6	11.8	13.7	23.5	26.7	26.7	15.0	15.6	....	Income: Credit	**78ag d**
	−127.0	−131.9	−122.7	−118.2	−126.9	−116.7	−123.9	−122.7	−142.9	−163.4	−158.1	−163.0	−146.8	−123.2	....	Income: Debit	**78ah d**
	−421.7	−434.6	−516.2	−633.7	−674.0	−847.3	−1,077.3	−726.4	−667.9	−806.4	−1,109.8	−1,177.0	−1,552.5	−1,043.5	....	Balance on Gds, Serv. & Inc.	**78ai d**
	333.1	376.8	432.2	421.1	434.1	484.8	532.0	487.3	538.9	497.9	576.5	751.0	637.8	649.3	....	Current Transfers, n.i.e.: Credit	**78aj d**
	−9.3	−9.3	−9.9	−10.6	−12.2	−14.5	−14.5	−15.5	−15.7	−16.2	−16.4	−17.1	−17.8	−18.4	....	Current Transfers: Debit	**78ak d**
	−.6	−.7	−.8	—	−.9	−1.0	−1.0	−1.0	−1.0	−1.0	−1.0	−1.0	−1.0	—	....	Capital Account, n.i.e.	**78bc d**
	....	....	....	....	....	....	....	....	....	....	....	....	....	....	....	Capital Account, n.i.e.: Credit	**78ba d**
	−.6	−.7	−.8	—	−.9	−1.0	−1.0	−1.0	−1.0	−1.0	−1.0	−1.0	−1.0	—	....	Capital Account: Debit	**78bb d**
	218.4	208.2	181.3	250.5	367.8	275.9	642.6	481.7	462.1	285.1	493.8	449.9	554.5	265.8	....	Financial Account, n.i.e.	**78bj d**
	....	....	....	....	....	....	....	....	....	....	....	....	....	....	....	Direct Investment Abroad	**78bd d**
	4.7	5.0	15.0	14.8	20.0	22.5	125.0	233.0	106.5	120.0	82.6	55.7	62.6	110.3	....	Dir. Invest. in Rep. Econ., n.i.e.	**78be d**
	....	....	....	....	....	....	....	....	....	....	....	....	....	....	....	Portfolio Investment Assets	**78bf d**
	....	....	....	....	....	....	....	....	....	....	....	....	....	....	....	Equity Securities	**78bk d**
	....	....	....	....	....	....	....	....	....	....	....	....	....	....	....	Debt Securities	**78bl d**
	....	....	....	....	....	....	....	....	....	....	....	....	....	....	....	Portfolio Investment Liab., n.i.e.	**78bg d**
	....	....	....	....	....	....	....	....	....	....	....	....	....	....	....	Equity Securities	**78bm d**
	....	....	....	....	....	....	....	....	....	....	....	....	....	....	....	Debt Securities	**78bn d**
	....	....	....	....	....	....	....	....	....	....	....	....	....	....	....	Financial Derivatives Assets	**78bw d**
	....	....	....	....	....	....	....	....	....	....	....	....	....	....	....	Financial Derivatives Liabilities	**78bx d**
	−31.5	−.4	−49.8	−94.2	26.2	−49.8	5.8	−119.6	−20.0	−179.4	33.1	88.1	183.1	41.0	....	Other Investment Assets	**78bh d**
	−6.8	.4	4.2	−11.8	−19.6	1.6	12.5	3.2	3.0	−.4	.2	.1	−3.3	.2	....	Monetary Authorities	**78bo d**
	....	....	....	....	....	....	....	....	....	....	....	....	....	....	....	General Government	**78bp d**
	−24.7	−.8	−54.0	−64.7	18.3	−5.1	−1.2	−93.3	77.6	−72.0	34.4	83.7	200.3	26.7	....	Banks	**78bq d**
				−17.7	27.5	−46.3	−5.5	−29.5	−100.6	−107.0	−1.5	4.3	−13.9	14.1	....	Other Sectors	**78br d**
	245.2	203.6	216.1	329.9	321.6	303.2	511.8	368.3	375.6	344.5	378.1	306.1	308.8	114.5	....	Other Investment Liab., n.i.e.	**78bi d**
	.4	7.4	21.6	22.5	−42.3	−33.4	32.2	−19.4	−39.1	—					....	Monetary Authorities	**78bs d**
	218.0	179.9	171.2	290.4	356.6	386.5	370.2	295.3	215.5	341.2	499.4	348.9	144.8	139.7	....	General Government	**78bt d**
	32.3	7.4	19.0	−4.0	−6.1	−16.2	44.8	64.8	−31.2	30.6					....	Banks	**78bu d**
	−5.5	8.9	4.3	21.0	13.4	−33.7	64.6	27.6	230.4	−27.3	−121.3	−42.8	164.0	−25.2	....	Other Sectors	**78bv d**
	20.2	40.7	70.0	78.0	21.9	−20.7	−28.5	−54.0	−65.6	20.2	83.6	102.1	289.4	−111.7	....	Net Errors and Omissions	**78ca d**
	140.1	181.1	156.6	105.3	136.7	−122.8	53.3	172.1	250.8	−20.4	26.7	107.9	−89.6	−258.5	....	Overall Balance	**78cb d**
	−140.1	−181.1	−156.6	−105.3	−136.7	122.8	−53.3	−172.1	−250.8	20.4	−26.7	−107.9	89.6	258.5	....	Reserves and Related Items	**79da d**
	−41.5	−48.9	−52.4	−17.5	−220.5	186.2	−52.2	−89.2	−185.6	105.7	139.0	−81.8	104.6	260.8	....	Reserve Assets	**79db d**
	−36.7	−59.1	−8.8	−53.8	83.8	−63.4	−1.1	−82.9	−65.2	−85.3	−165.8	−26.1	−15.0	−2.3	....	Use of Fund Credit and Loans	**79dc d**
	−61.9	−73.2	−95.4	−34.0	....	....	....	....	....	....	....	....	....	....	....	Exceptional Financing	**79de d**

Ghana

	1972	1973	1974	1975	1976	1977	1978	1979	1980	1981	1982	1983	1984	1985	1986
Government Finance												*Millions of Cedis through 1985; Billions of Cedis Beginning 1986:*			
Deficit (-) or Surplus.............. 80	†−161.2	−186.6	−196.1	−401.3	−736.2	−1,056.8	−1,896.7	−1,800.0	−1,808.0	−4,706.8	−4,848.0	†−4933.3	−4,843.0	−7,579.0	†.3
Revenue 81	†418.7	391.1	578.9	809.0	869.8	1,140.9	1,392.1	2,600.0	2,951.0	3,234.1	4,804.0	†10185.0	21,728.0	38,691.0	†69.8
Grants Received 81z	†3.2	.5	4.7	.9	—	30.3	1.0	—	—	45.0	52.0	†56.6	914.0	1,620.0	†3.9
Expenditure 82	†543.1	548.5	754.1	1,146.2	1,484.0	2,136.6	3,164.8	4,295.7	4,668.0	7,719.3	9,530.0	†14755.3	26,694.0	45,763.0	†70.7
Lending Minus Repayments 83	†40.0	29.7	25.6	65.0	122.0	91.4	125.0	104.3	91.0	266.6	174.0	†419.6	791.0	2,127.0	†2.7
Financing															
Domestic................................ 84a	†79.4	167.8	197.7	399.9	734.4	1,044.1	1,720.0	1,800.0	1,518.0	4,339.5	4,421.0	†3,824.8	3,028.0	4,043.0	†5.3
Foreign................................. 85a	†81.8	18.8	−1.6	1.4	1.8	12.7	67.2	—	290.0	367.3	389.0	†970.1	1,815.0	3,522.0	†−5.6
Use of Cash Balances 87	....	....	....	....	....	....	....	....	....	....	....	....	....	....	....
Unallocable Financing............ 87c	†—	—	—	—	—	—	109.5	—	—	—	38.0	†138.4	—	14.0	†—
Debt: Domestic 88a	†928.1	1,055.9	1,275.5	1,486.0	2,269.5	3,208.2	5,136.0	6,154.0	7,622.0	11,846.2	17,487.7	†29315.5	32,908.0	37,766.0	....
Foreign............................. 89a	†228.3	261.4	263.9	482.2	482.2	....	....	2,741.7	3,104.8	3,588.6	4,083.0	†5,052.5	6,869.0	9,839.0	....
National Accounts													*Millions of Cedis through 1985;*		
Househ.Cons.Expend.,incl.NPISHs 96f	2,096	2,619	3,588	3,873	5,171	8,638	17,473	23,455	35,953	63,333	77,619	167,147	233,023	284,621	†415
Government Consumption Expend..... 91f	355	382	569	689	799	1,409	2,371	2,903	4,784	6,384	5,603	10,787	19,641	32,241	†57
Gross Fixed Capital Formation.............. 93e	244	267	555	614	641	1,049	1,355	1,899	2,613	3,430	3,053	6,922	18,542	32,689	†48
Changes in Inventories 93i	−44	48	53	59	−62	186	66	−54	−203	−109	−132	−21	65	139	†—
Exports of Goods and Services 90c	648	820	956	1,023	1,025	1,171	1,754	3,169	3,629	3,454	2,886	10,225	20,161	33,185	†82
Imports of Goods and Services (-) 98c	484	635	1,061	974	1,047	1,289	2,033	3,150	3,923	3,966	2,578	11,022	20,871	39,826	†90
Gross Domestic Product (GDP) 99b	2,815	3,502	4,660	5,283	6,526	11,163	20,986	28,222	42,853	72,526	86,451	184,038	270,561	343,048	†511
Net Primary Income from Abroad 98.n	−40	−30	−47	−42	−48	−40	−48	−98	−182	−232	−225	−1,640	−3,643	−5,769	†−13
Gross National Income (GNI) 99a	2,775	3,472	4,613	5,241	6,478	11,123	20,938	28,124	42,671	72,294	86,225	182,398	266,918	337,280	†499
Consumption of Fixed Capital 99cf	171	216	256	323	378	525	724	1,052	1,512	2,218	2,628	4,197	11,206	16,339	†29
GDP Volume 1975 Prices(Millions)..... 99b.p	5,088	5,864	6,063	5,283	5,097	5,212	5,654	5,475	5,475	5,377	4,990	5,025	5,158	5,420	5,702
GDP Volume 1993 Prices............... 99b.p	....	....	....	....	....	....	....	....	....	....	....	....	....	....	
GDP Volume (1995=100) .... 99bv p	60.2	69.4	71.7	62.5	60.3	61.7	66.9	64.8	64.8	63.6	59.0	59.5	61.0	64.1	67.5
GDP Deflator (1995=100).................. 99bi p	.1	.1	.1	.1	.1	.2	.4	.6	.9	1.5	1.9	4.0	5.7	6.9	9.8
															Millions:
Population................................. 99z	9.09	9.39	9.61	9.87	10.31	10.41	10.75	†10.48	10.73	11.07	11.47	11.92	12.39	12.72	13.05

INTERNATIONAL FINANCIAL STATISTICS YEARBOOK

Year Ending June 30 through 1982, Year Ending December 31 thereafter

Government Finance

	1987	1988	1989	1990	1991	1992	1993	1994	1995	1996	1997	1998	1999	2000	2001	
Deficit (-) or Surplus	4.1	3.9	10.3	3.3	39.0	−144.4	−97.3	111.7	70.3	−335.5	−297.6	−1,048.8	....	....	....	80
Revenue	105.0	142.2	193.2	239.5	354.4	333.6	657.6	1,221.8	1,691.0	2,191.0	2,549.9	3,276.1	....	....	....	81
Grants Received	6.0	11.6	21.3	27.8	36.3	32.7	66.6	39.5	93.8	77.5	66.6	161.9	....	....	....	81z
Expenditure	102.1	143.9	196.5	254.5	340.3	498.8	813.5	1,141.3	1,698.7	2,515.2	2,908.9	4,513.2	....	....	....	82
Lending Minus Repayments	4.9	6.0	7.7	9.5	11.4	11.9	8.0	8.3	15.8	88.8	5.2	−26.4	....	....	....	83
Financing																
Domestic	−2.9	−6.2	−15.3	−28.0	−51.7	144.1	45.4	−26.7	−27.7	531.1	728.0	672.6	....	....	....	84a
Foreign	−1.2	2.3	4.9	24.6	12.7	.3	51.9	−85.0	−42.6	−195.7	−430.3	376.2	....	....	....	85a
Use of Cash Balances	....	....	....	....	....	....	....	....	....	....	....	....	....	....	....	87
Unallocable Financing	—	—	—	—	—	—	—	—	—	—	—	—	....	....	....	87c
Debt: Domestic	....	....	....	....	....	....	....	....	....	....	....	....	....	....	....	88a
Foreign	....	....	....	....	....	....	....	....	....	....	....	....	....	....	....	89a

National Accounts

Billions of Cedis Beginning 1986

	1987	1988	1989	1990	1991	1992	1993	1994	1995	1996	1997	1998	1999	2000	2001	
Househ.Cons.Expend.,incl.NPISHs	610	834	1,187	1,736	2,012	2,338	3,049	3,835	5,910	8,629	11,267	....	....	....	....	96f
Government Consumption Expend.	75	105	145	222	294	400	568	714	936	1,366	1,744	....	....	....	....	91f
Gross Fixed Capital Formation	77	114	191	248	326	386	921	1,175	1,638	2,332	3,338	....	....	....	....	93e
Changes in Inventories	1	1	1	1	2	2	−61	72	−86	102	127	....	....	....	....	93i
Exports of Goods and Services	158	218	292	313	405	483	693	1,172	1,899	2,827	2,795	....	....	....	....	90c
Imports of Goods and Services (-)	175	221	399	488	611	806	1,298	1,762	2,544	3,917	5,158	....	....	....	....	98c
Gross Domestic Product (GDP)	746	1,051	1,417	2,032	2,428	2,803	3,873	5,205	7,753	11,339	14,113	....	....	....	....	99b
Net Primary Income from Abroad	−21	−27	−28	−37	−44	−46	73	106	155	220	274	....	....	....	....	98.n
Gross National Income (GNI)	725	1,025	1,389	1,995	2,384	2,756	3,800	5,099	7,598	11,119	13,840	....	....	....	....	99a
Consumption of Fixed Capital	48	69	86	111	131	156	329	411	514	801	997	....	....	....	....	99cf
GDP Volume 1975 Prices(Millions)	5,976	6,312	6,633	6,853	7,217	7,498	7,868	....	....	....	....	....	....	....	....	99b.*p*
GDP Volume 1993 Prices							3,873	3,999	4,160	4,351	4,533	....	....	....	....	99b.*p*
GDP Volume (1995=100)	70.7	74.7	78.5	81.1	85.4	88.7	93.1	96.1	100.0	104.6	109.0	....	....	....	....	99bv *p*
GDP Deflator (1995=100)	13.6	18.2	23.3	32.3	36.7	40.8	53.7	69.8	100.0	139.8	167.1	....	....	....	....	99bi *p*

Midyear Estimates

	1987	1988	1989	1990	1991	1992	1993	1994	1995	1996	1997	1998	1999	2000	2001	
Population	13.39	14.14	14.67	15.13	15.56	16.00	16.44	16.88	17.30	17.71	18.10	18.49	18.89	18.41	19.73	99z

(See notes in the back of the book.)

Greece

		1972	1973	1974	1975	1976	1977	1978	1979	1980	1981	1982	1983	1984	1985	1986
Exchange Rates													*Drachmas per SDR Through 2000,*			
Market Rate	aa	32.57	35.83	36.73	41.73	43.02	43.13	46.91	50.43	59.35	67.08	77.85	103.30	125.94	162.30	169.73
													Drachmas per US Dollar through 2000,			
Market Rate	ae	30.00	29.70	30.00	35.65	37.03	35.51	36.01	38.28	46.54	57.63	70.57	98.67	128.48	147.76	138.76
Market Rate	rf	30.00	29.63	30.00	32.05[e]	36.52	36.84	36.75	37.04	42.62	55.41	66.80	88.06	112.72	138.12	139.98
										Drachmas per ECU through 1998; Drachmas per Euro through 2000:						
Euro Rate	ea	....	....	....	....	....	....	....	....		62.18	68.54	81.78	91.04	131.20	148.53
Euro Rate	eb	....	....	....	....	....	....	....	....	59.24	61.62	65.30	78.09	88.44	105.66	137.41
													Index Numbers (1995=100):			
Market Rate	ahx	771.7	782.9	771.7	720.7	633.2	629.7	631.9	624.2	540.7	417.2	347.8	264.0	206.8	168.1	165.6
Nominal Effective Exchange Rate	neu	868.8	798.7	808.1	732.7	704.5	687.5	623.6	583.9	507.1	475.7	445.2	368.3	321.3	273.7	209.7
Real Effective Exchange Rate	reu							82.4	84.9	85.0	92.3	106.0	101.2	106.1	102.5	85.8
Fund Position														*Millions of SDRs:*		
Quota	2f.s	138.0	138.0	138.0	138.0	138.0	138.0	185.0	185.0	277.5	277.5	277.5	399.9	399.9	399.9	399.9
SDRs	1b.s	25.6	25.2	26.7	17.6	16.9	13.4	13.4	.8	.1		.1	.6	1.1		
Reserve Position in the Fund	1c.s	34.5	34.5	—	—	—	—	33.5	32.4	55.6	55.6	55.6	86.2	81.4	75.0	70.1
Total Fund Cred.&Loans Outstg.	2tl	—	—	36.2	189.8	247.8	176.5	185.0	147.3	78.5	13.9	—	—	—	—	—
International Liquidity										*Millions of US Dollars Unless Otherwise Indicated:*						
Total Res.Min.Gold(Eurosys.Def.)	1l.d	898.8	898.9	781.7	†963.6	880.6	1,048.3	1,305.0	1,342.8	1,345.9	1,022.0	861.1	900.5	954.2	868.0	†1,518.7
SDRs	1b.d	27.8	30.4	32.7	20.6	19.6	16.3	17.4	1.1		.1		.6	1.1		
Reserve Position in the Fund	1c.d	37.5	41.6					43.6	42.7	70.9	64.7	61.3	90.2	79.8	82.4	85.8
Foreign Exchange	1d.d	833.6	826.8	749.0	†943.0	861.0	1,032.0	1,244.0	1,299.0	1,275.0	957.2	799.8	809.7	873.3	785.6	†1,432.9
o/w: Fin.Deriv.Rel.to Reserves	1ddd	....	....	....	....	....	....	....	....	....	....	....	....	....	....	....
Other Reserve Assets	1e.d	....	....	....	....	....	....	....	....	....	....	....	....	....	....	....
Gold (Million Fine Troy Ounces)	1ad	3.495	3.502	3.610	3.629	3.651	3.730	3.770	3.808	3.835	3.853	3.872	3.880	4.106	4.123	3.308
Gold (Eurosystem Valuation)	1and	132.8	147.9	154.7	148.7	148.5	158.6	171.9	175.6	171.2	157.0	149.5	142.2	140.9	†862.8	841.3
Memo: Euro Cl. on Non-EA Res.	1dgd	....	....	....	....	....	....	....	....	....	....	....	....	....	....	....
Non-Euro Cl. on EA Res.	1dhd	....	....	....	....	....	....	....	....	....	....	....	....	....	....	....
Mon. Auth.: Other Foreign Assets	3..d	....	....	....	....	....	....	....	....	....	....	....	....	....	....	....
Foreign Liabilities	4..d	....	....	....	....	....	....	....	....	....	....	....	....	....	....	....
Banking Insts.: Foreign Assets	7a.d	159.6	252.7	236.9	280.4	348.7	445.2	407.1	738.9	1,187.9	1,666.2	1,407.6	1,386.3	1,598.3	1,980.2	1,788.0
Foreign Liab.	7b.d	403.3	561.7	751.5	982.6	1,557.7	2,259.7	3,699.5	4,536.2	5,150.8	5,922.7	6,310.6	6,595.6	6,595.5	7,588.4	9,115.8
Monetary Authorities										*Billions of Drachmas through 2000;*						
Fgn. Assets (Cl.on Non-EA Ctys)	11	32.9	32.0	33.1	38.8	40.0	42.8	51.1	52.7	74.1	72.5	79.2	114.9	152.9	265.1	331.8
Claims on General Government	12a.u	....	....	....	....	....	....	....	....	....	....	....	....	....	....	....
o/w: Claims on Gen.Govt.in Cty	12a	20.3	30.8	47.2	47.1	60.3	80.5	122.5	154.3	200.3	356.1	617.9	530.8	656.5	747.9	787.6
Claims on Banking Institutions	12e.u	....	....	....	....	....	....	....	....	....	....	....	....	....	....	....
o/w: Claims on Bank.Inst.in Cty	12e	54.8	69.3	86.2	108.6	125.9	150.1	152.0	176.4	198.0	286.3	299.6	307.5	290.1	282.2	298.3
Claims on Other Resident Sectors	12d.u	....	....	....	....	....	....	....	....	....	....	....	....	....	....	....
o/w: Cl. on Oth.Res.Sect.in Cty	12d	4.4	9.1	10.4	12.3	13.7	16.0	12.1	14.8	21.3	26.5	16.6	11.3	10.8	12.6	12.7
Currency Issued	14a	52.8	67.6	83.6	96.6	115.7	135.8	167.5	193.0	221.9	275.2	321.2	363.2	436.7	544.1	582.2
Liabilities to Banking Insts	14c.u	....	....	....	....	....	....	....	....	....	....	....	....	....	....	....
o/w: Liabs to Bank.Inst.in Cty	14c	10.0	7.5	7.3	13.2	18.2	27.5	28.6	22.6	61.0	140.9	213.1	199.6	312.7	280.7	309.3
Demand Dep. of Other Res.Sect.	14d.u	....	....	....	....	....	....	....	....	....	....	....	....	....	....	....
o/w: D.Dep.of Oth.Res.Sect.in Cty	14d	5.8	6.0	8.4	11.2	11.9	13.8	17.6	22.2	21.1	24.3	29.1	55.0	56.9	31.3	123.5
Other Dep. of Other Res.Sect.	15..u	....	....	....	....	....	....	....	....	....	....	....	....	....	....	....
o/w: O.Dep.of Oth.Res.Sect.in Cty	15	....	....	....	....	....	....	....	....	....	....	....	....	....	....	....
Money Market Instruments	16m.u	....	....	....	....	....	....	....	....	....	....	....	....	....	....	....
Bonds (Debt Securities)	16n.u	....	....	....	....	....	....	....	....	....	....	....	....	....	....	....
o/w: Bonds Held by Resid.of Cty	16n	....	....	....	....	....	....	....	....	....	....	....	....	....	....	....
Foreign Liab. (to Non-EA Ctys)	16c	....	....	....	....	....	....	....	....	....	....	....	....	....	....	....
Central Government Deposits	16d.u	....	....	....	....	....	....	....	....	....	....	....	....	....	....	....
o/w: Cent.Govt.Dep. in Cty	16d	12.8	13.2	19.5	19.3	26.9	28.2	34.4	24.7	38.1	85.4	179.8	70.3	104.9	55.2	34.5
Capital Accounts	17a	2.9	3.3	3.7	4.1	5.2	6.3	6.6	8.0	10.0	12.0	17.1	20.8	24.4	28.2	29.2
Other Items (Net)	17r	28.0	42.8	54.5	62.4	61.9	78.3	83.1	127.7	141.8	203.6	252.9	255.7	174.8	368.5	351.9
Memo: Net Claims on Eurosystem	12e.s	....	....	....	....	....	....	....	....	....	....	....	....	....	....	....
Currency Put into Circ.	14m	....	....	....	....	....	....	....	....	....	....	....	....	....	....	....
Banking Institutions										*Billions of Drachmas through 2000;*						
Claims on Monetary Authorities	20	14.9	14.8	15.0	20.6	34.1	36.7	70.7	88.4	134.1	244.1	384.5	451.3	683.2	711.2	799.5
Claims on Bk.Inst.in Oth.EA Ctys	20b.u	....	....	....	....	....	....	....	....	....	....	....	....	....	....	....
Fgn. Assets (Cl.on Non-EA Ctys)	21	4.8	7.5	7.1	10.0	12.9	15.8	14.7	28.3	55.3	96.0	99.3	136.8	205.4	292.6	248.1
Claims on General Government	22a.u	....	....	....	....	....	....	....	....	....	....	....	....	....	....	....
o/w: Claims on Gen.Govt.in Cty	22a	33.2	40.8	48.3	62.9	81.9	106.9	†233.6	285.9	365.2	510.5	672.6	927.7	1,196.5	1,631.8	1,988.4
Claims on Other Resident Sectors	22d.u	....	....	....	....	....	....	....	....	....	....	....	....	....	....	....
o/w: Cl. on Oth.Res.Sect.in Cty	22d	96.7	108.7	131.6	173.8	227.5	285.0	†626.8	740.3	889.1	1,116.7	1,392.1	1,624.1	1,970.2	2,387.4	2,880.8
Demand Deposits	24..u	....	....	....	....	....	....	....	....	....	....	....	....	....	....	....
o/w: D.Dep.of Oth.Res.Sect.in Cty	24	19.3	21.6	23.2	27.2	35.4	39.4	†61.2	73.3	92.2	113.1	157.4	169.9	222.8	259.5	291.7
Other Deposits	25..u	....	....	....	....	....	....	....	....	....	....	....	....	....	....	....
o/w: O.Dep.of Oth.Res.Sect.in Cty	25	103.1	114.6	139.1	183.5	232.8	287.5	†509.9	610.0	775.5	1,075.0	1,414.4	1,729.1	2,284.2	2,918.1	3,540.6
Money Market Instruments	26m.u	....	....	....	....	....	....	....	....	....	....	....	....	....	....	....
Bonds (Debt Securities)	26n.u	....	....	....	....	....	....	....	....	....	....	....	....	....	....	....
o/w: Bonds Held by Resid.of Cty	26n	....	....	....	....	....	....	8.1	10.4	17.2	30.6	48.3	77.1	127.4	184.6	244.3
Foreign Liab. (to Non-EA Ctys)	26c	12.1	16.7	22.5	35.0	57.7	80.2	†133.2	173.7	239.7	341.3	445.3	650.8	847.4	1,121.3	1,264.9
Central Government Deposits	26d.u	....	....	....	....	....	....	....	....	....	....	....	....	....	....	....
o/w: Cent.Govt.Dep. in Cty	26d	....	....	....	....	....	....	....	....	....	....	....	....	....	....	....
Credit from Monetary Authorities	26g	1.0	2.0	4.2	11.2	10.7	12.8	†160.7	198.5	226.4	328.7	350.1	409.5	455.5	528.2	548.6
Liab. to Bk.Inst.in Oth. EA Ctys	26h.u	....	....	....	....	....	....	....	....	....	....	....	....	....	....	....
Capital Accounts	27a	10.0	11.1	11.8	13.2	22.3	25.0	†69.9	80.2	98.2	105.7	152.5	176.0	209.0	246.6	316.9
Other Items (Net)	27r	4.1	5.8	1.3	−2.9	−2.5	−.4	†2.8	−3.2	−5.5	−27.0	−19.6	−72.4	−89.1	−235.2	−290.2

	1987	1988	1989	1990	1991	1992	1993	1994	1995	1996	1997	1998	1999	2000	2001		
Euros per SDR Thereafter End of Period																**Exchange Rates**	
	178.64	199.30	207.36	224.25	250.73	295.05	342.32	350.51	352.36	355.20	381.31	397.87	450.79	476.37	1.4260	Market Rate	aa
Euros per US Dollar Thereafter: End of Period (ae) Period Average (rf)																	
	125.93	148.10	157.79	157.63	175.28	214.58	249.22	240.10	237.04	247.02	282.61	282.57	328.44	365.62	1.1347	Market Rate	ae
	135.43	141.86	162.42	158.51	182.27	190.62	229.25	242.60	231.66	240.71	273.06	295.53	305.65	365.40	1.1175	Market Rate	rf
End of Period (ea) Period Average (eb)																	
	164.48	172.91	188.23	214.07	235.07	260.20	278.20	294.78	303.76	306.83	312.12	330.01	†330.35	340.75	....	Euro Rate	ea
	156.19	167.55	178.88	201.43	225.22	246.60	267.99	287.21	299.54	301.48	308.51	331.50	†325.76	336.66	....	Euro Rate	eb
Period Averages																	
	171.0	163.6	142.7	146.2	127.6	121.9	101.2	95.4	100.0	96.2	84.9	78.5	75.7	63.6	....	Market Rate	ahx
	186.9	174.1	161.6	146.5	130.3	119.9	110.6	103.1	100.0	98.2	96.3	90.5	90.0	84.8	84.2	Nominal Effective Exchange Rate	neu
	80.8	86.7	92.4	94.0	92.0	92.6	92.6	94.3	100.0	102.7	106.5	103.0	103.8	100.5	101.0	Real Effective Exchange Rate	reu
End of Period																**Fund Position**	
	399.9	399.9	399.9	399.9	399.9	587.6	587.6	587.6	587.6	587.6	587.6	587.6	823.0	823.0	823.0	Quota	2f. s
	—	.2	.3	.2	.3	—	.1	.2	—	.4	.2	.3	3.8	9.2	7.7	SDRs	1b. s
	70.1	71.1	89.2	74.7	74.7	116.9	113.7	113.7	113.7	113.7	113.7	191.5	285.0	227.8	284.3	Reserve Position in the Fund	1c. s
	—	—	—	—	—	—	—	—	—	—	—	—	—	—	—	Total Fund Cred.&Loans Outstg.	2tl
End of Period																**International Liquidity**	
	2,681.4	3,619.4	3,223.5	3,412.1	5,188.9	4,793.6	7,790.3	14,487.9	14,780.0	17,501.4	12,594.8	17,458.4	18,122.3	13,424.3	†5,154.0	Total Res.Min.Gold(Eurosys.Def.)	1l. d
	—	.3	.4	.3	.4	—	.2	.3	—	.6	.3	.5	5.2	12.0	9.7	SDRs	1b. d
	99.5	95.7	117.2	106.3	106.9	160.7	156.2	166.0	169.0	163.5	153.4	269.6	391.1	296.8	357.3	Reserve Position in the Fund	1c. d
	2,581.9	3,523.4	3,105.8	3,305.5	5,081.6	4,632.9	7,634.0	14,321.6	14,611.0	17,337.3	12,441.1	17,188.3	17,726.0	13,115.5	†4,787.0	Foreign Exchange	1d. d
	....	....	....	....	....	....	....	....	....	....	....	....	....	....	....	*o/w:* Fin.Deriv.Rel.to Reserves	1dd d
	....	....	....	....	....	....	....	....	....	....	....	....	....	....	....	Other Reserve Assets	1e. d
	3.342	3.395	3.395	3.400	3.425	3.433	3.443	3.448	3.461	3.469	3.644	3.623	4.237	4.262	3.940	Gold (Million Fine Troy Ounces)	1ad
	1,057.2	925.0	902.1	834.4	807.2	746.5	856.3	850.9	871.7	833.2	684.5	685.3	781.8	753.2	1,089.0	Gold (Eurosystem Valuation)	1and
	....	....	....	....	....	....	....	....	....	....	....	....	....	....	61.0	Memo: Euro Cl. on Non-EA Res.	1dgd
	....	....	....	....	....	....	....	....	....	....	....	....	....	....	5,566.0	Non-Euro Cl. on EA Res.	1dhd
	....	....	....	....	....	....	....	....	....	....	....	....	....	....	—	Mon. Auth.: Other Foreign Assets	3..d
	†316.1	279.5	1,452.1	1,948.7	586.4	1,055.1	731.4	777.5	860.4	795.5	1,336.5	888.4	733.4	179.1	665.4	Foreign Liabilities	4..d
	1,876.3	2,593.4	2,974.7	3,456.5	4,001.5	4,707.1	5,358.7	6,051.3	8,962.9	12,656.1	15,994.8	15,550.7	13,848.5	12,627.4	†14935.4	Banking Insts.: Foreign Assets	7a. d
	11,411.0	12,299.9	14,365.3	16,461.5	17,211.3	18,126.7	18,235.5	26,410.3	34,286.1	38,540.2	42,278.6	46,854.1	41,732.5	39,645.4	†9,608.8	Foreign Liab.	7b. d
Billions of Euros Beginning 2001: End of Period																**Monetary Authorities**	
	†483.1	696.0	695.2	811.8	1,351.0	1,736.7	2,975.5	4,463.9	4,333.9	5,253.9	4,020.3	5,414.0	6,434.2	4,961.0	6.97	Fgn. Assets (Cl.on Non-EA Ctys)	11
	....	....	....	....	....	....	....	....	....	....	....	....	....	....	18.45	Claims on General Government	12a. u
	†2,012.2	2,271.2	2,632.4	3,189.2	3,721.4	4,555.9	†7,966.2	7,352.3	7,059.4	6,457.6	6,012.1	5,757.9	5,911.7	5,759.1	17.23	*o/w:* Claims on Gen.Govt.in Cty	12a
	....	....	....	....	....	....	....	....	....	....	....	....	....	....	5.16	Claims on Banking Institutions	12e. u
	†700.6	662.0	768.7	984.0	875.2	1,059.7	580.3	377.8	461.4	332.8	791.9	447.2	54.4	299.3	.65	*o/w:* Claims on Bank.Inst.in Cty	12e
	....	....	....	....	....	....	....	....	....	....	....	....	....	....	.17	Claims on Other Resident Sectors	12d. u
	†6.4	6.9	9.1	8.7	7.4	4.2	3.8	4.8	14.1	19.9	21.9	24.6	27.3	37.5	.17	*o/w:* Cl. on Oth.Res.Sect.in Cty	12d
	†681.1	805.4	1,045.0	1,268.7	1,370.9	1,529.7	1,641.6	1,839.8	2,061.0	2,251.1	2,451.5	2,519.4	3,154.1	3,097.3	8.71	Currency Issued	14a
	....	....	....	....	....	....	....	....	....	....	....	....	....	....	15.79	Liabilities to Banking Insts	14c. u
	†1,742.9	1,896.9	2,056.3	2,472.7	3,009.1	3,620.9	4,236.5	5,364.8	5,084.2	5,406.7	5,189.2	6,634.0	7,033.2	5,955.8	7.70	*o/w:* Liabs to Bank.Inst.in Cty	14c
	....	....	....	....	....	....	....	....	....	....	....	....	....	....	.42	Demand Dep. of Other Res.Sect.	14d. u
	†64.8	72.7	72.6	94.1	100.7	76.0	63.9	27.3	47.3	29.7	5.2	4.5	165.8	60.8	.42	*o/w:* D.Dep.of Oth.Res.Sect.in Cty	14d
	....	....	....	....	....	....	....	....	....	....	....	....	....	....	.36	Other Dep. of Other Res.Sect.	15..u
	....	....	....	....	....	....	....	....	....	....	....	....	....	....	.36	*o/w:* O.Dep.of Oth.Res.Sect.in Cty	15
	....	....	....	....	....	....	....	....	....	....	....	....	....	....	—	Money Market Instruments	16m. u
	....	....	....	....	....	....	....	....	....	....	....	....	....	....	1.68	Bonds (Debt Securities)	16n. u
	999.5	1,145.4	1,304.0	1,436.9	1,817.9	2,482.5	3,626.6	3,342.7	2,742.2	2,102.0	1,533.9	1,065.9	1,015.0	606.0	....	*o/w:* Bonds Held by Resid.of Cty	16n
	39.8	41.4	229.1	307.2	102.8	226.4	182.3	186.7	203.9	196.5	377.7	251.0	240.9	65.5	.76	Foreign Liab. (to Non-EA Ctys)	16c
	....	....	....	....	....	....	....	....	....	....	....	....	....	....	.44	Central Government Deposits	16d. u
	†56.6	135.0	91.5	135.9	161.7	102.0	259.6	237.6	621.2	672.5	443.4	345.5	128.9	194.6	.44	*o/w:* Cent.Govt.Dep. in Cty	16d
	†30.3	39.2	45.5	47.9	51.0	57.0	62.7	69.5	71.8	74.1	166.2	196.1	290.0	293.1	2.53	Capital Accounts	17a
	†–412.6	–499.9	–738.7	–769.7	–658.9	–738.0	1,452.7	1,130.5	1,037.1	1,331.6	679.1	627.4	399.7	783.8	.08	Other Items (Net)	17r
	....	....	....	....	....	....	....	....	....	....	....	....	....	....	–7.06	*Memo: Net Claims on Eurosystem*	12e. s
	....	....	....	....	....	....	....	....	....	....	....	....	....	....	....	*Currency Put into Circ.*	14m
Billions of Euros Beginning 2001: End of Period																**Banking Institutions**	
	†1,040.0	1,271.4	1,281.2	1,483.9	1,769.8	2,125.9	2,531.4	2,905.2	5,000.4	5,080.2	5,583.7	7,464.1	8,196.2	7,034.8	11.52	Claims on Monetary Authorities	20
	....	....	....	....	....	....	....	....	....	....	....	....	....	....	9.15	Claims on Bk.Inst.in Oth.EA Ctys	20b. u
	†236.3	384.1	469.4	544.8	701.4	1,010.0	1,335.5	1,452.9	2,124.6	3,126.3	4,520.3	4,394.2	4,548.4	4,616.8	16.95	Fgn. Assets (Cl.on Non-EA Ctys)	21
	....	....	....	....	....	....	....	....	....	....	....	....	....	....	45.12	Claims on General Government	22a. u
	†2,745.3	3,584.0	4,567.8	5,342.7	5,721.5	7,039.6	8,957.3	9,522.7	10,448.8	11,082.1	11,565.5	11,354.2	12,447.7	14,506.2	45.10	*o/w:* Claims on Gen.Govt.in Cty	22a
	....	....	....	....	....	....	....	....	....	....	....	....	....	....	84.01	Claims on Other Resident Sectors	22d. u
	†3,007.9	3,467.8	4,234.6	4,823.4	5,618.7	6,356.1	6,644.9	7,531.6	9,142.9	10,371.1	11,902.0	13,721.5	17,734.0	21,775.7	82.59	*o/w:* Cl. on Oth.Res.Sect.in Cty	22d
	....	....	....	....	....	....	....	....	....	....	....	....	....	....	15.73	Demand Deposits	24..u
	†367.5	411.9	488.0	638.7	758.8	883.2	1,126.5	1,619.7	1,874.6	2,340.2	2,699.4	3,104.6	4,337.2	4,287.4	15.59	*o/w:* D.Dep.of Oth.Res.Sect.in Cty	24
	....	....	....	....	....	....	....	....	....	....	....	....	....	....	119.60	Other Deposits	25..u
	†4,449.0	5,543.3	6,831.6	7,651.6	8,313.9	9,066.3	9,760.5	11,925.5	13,684.8	15,339.1	16,704.7	16,564.0	17,975.3	19,164.2	118.42	*o/w:* O.Dep.of Oth.Res.Sect.in Cty	25
	....	....	....	....	....	....	....	....	....	....	....	....	....	....	—	Money Market Instruments	26m. u
	....	....	....	....	....	....	....	....	....	....	....	....	....	....	.29	Bonds (Debt Securities)	26n. u
	†251.6	384.7	481.2	594.0	598.7	673.8	703.5	838.4	570.8	59.8	126.7	163.6	78.7	85.3	....	*o/w:* Bonds Held by Resid.of Cty	26n
	†1,436.9	1,821.6	2,266.7	2,594.8	3,016.8	3,889.6	4,544.7	6,341.1	8,127.2	9,520.2	11,948.4	13,239.6	13,706.6	14,495.2	10.90	Foreign Liab. (to Non-EA Ctys)	26c
	....	....	....	....	....	....	....	....	....	....	....	....	....	....	1.38	Central Government Deposits	26d. u
	....	....	....	....	....	....	....	....	....	....	....	....	....	....	1.38	*o/w:* Cent.Govt.Dep. in Cty	26d
	†460.9	281.7	253.9	250.0	665.0	1,244.5	2,166.2	486.3	551.0	409.4	826.6	1,771.1	3,342.1	3,930.6	.71	Credit from Monetary Authorities	26g
	....	....	....	....	....	....	....	....	....	....	....	....	....	....	4.67	Liab. to Bk.Inst.in Oth. EA Ctys	26h. u
	367.4	521.7	640.5	847.3	1,142.7	1,294.8	1,510.2	1,481.2	1,740.7	1,881.7	2,217.3	2,860.2	5,157.3	5,876.1	19.49	Capital Accounts	27a
	†–304.0	–257.8	–409.0	–381.6	–684.5	–520.4	–342.5	–1,279.8	167.7	109.4	–951.6	–769.2	–1,670.9	94.8	–6.00	Other Items (Net)	27r

Greece

	1972	1973	1974	1975	1976	1977	1978	1979	1980	1981	1982	1983	1984	1985	1986
Banking Survey (Nat'l Residency)													*Billions of Drachmas through 2000;*		
Foreign Assets (Net) 31n	25.6	22.9	17.6	13.8	−4.8	−21.6	†−67.5	−92.7	−110.3	−172.8	−266.8	−399.1	−489.1	−563.5	−684.9
Domestic Credit 32	141.6	176.1	218.1	276.8	356.4	460.1	†960.7	1,170.6	1,437.9	1,924.3	2,519.3	3,023.7	3,729.2	4,724.4	5,635.1
Claims on General Govt. (Net) 32an	40.6	58.3	76.1	90.7	115.2	159.1	†321.7	415.5	527.5	781.2	1,110.7	1,388.2	1,748.2	2,324.4	2,741.6
Claims on Other Resident Sectors 32d	101.0	117.8	142.1	186.1	241.2	301.0	†638.9	755.1	910.4	1,143.1	1,408.6	1,635.4	1,981.0	2,399.9	2,893.5
Currency Issued.................................. 34a.n	52.8	67.6	83.6	96.6	115.7	135.8	167.5	193.0	221.9	275.2	321.2	363.2	436.7	544.1	582.2
Demand Deposits 34b.n	25.1	28.4	31.6	38.5	47.3	53.2	†78.8	95.5	113.3	137.4	186.5	224.9	279.7	290.8	415.2
Other Deposits .... 35..n	103.1	114.6	139.1	183.5	232.8	287.5	†509.9	610.0	775.5	1,075.0	1,414.4	1,729.1	2,282.4	2,918.1	3,540.6
Money Market Instruments 36m	....	....	....	....	....	....	....	....	....	....	....	....	....	....	....
Bonds (Debt Securities) 36n	....	....	....	....	....	....	....	8.1	10.4	17.2	30.6	48.3	77.1	127.4	184.6	244.3
o/w: Bonds Over Two Years 36na	....	....	....	....	....	....	....	....	....	....	....	....	....	....	....
Capital Accounts 37a	12.9	14.4	15.5	17.4	27.4	31.2	†76.5	88.1	108.2	117.6	169.7	196.8	233.4	274.7	346.1
Other Items (Net) 37r	−26.6	−26.1	−33.9	−45.2	−71.7	−69.1	†52.5	80.8	91.6	115.8	112.5	33.5	−119.4	−51.3	−178.1
Banking Survey (EA-Wide Residency)													*Billions of Euros:*		
Foreign Assets (Net) 31n.u	....														
Domestic Credit .... 32..u	....														
Claims on General Govt. (Net) .... 32an u	....														
Claims on Other Resident Sect. 32d.u	....														
Currency Issued.................................. 34a.u	....														
Demand Deposits 34b.u	....														
Other Deposits .... 35..u	....														
o/w: Other Dep. Over Two Yrs ...... 35ab u	....														
Money Market Instruments 36m.u	....														
Bonds (Debt Securities) 36n.u	....														
o/w: Bonds Over Two Years .... 36na u	....														
Capital Accounts 37a	....														
Other Items (Net) 37r.u	....														
Interest Rates													*Percent Per Annum*		
Central Bank Rate 60	6.5	9.0	8.0	10.0	10.0	11.0	14.0	19.0	20.5	20.5	20.5	20.5	20.5	20.5	20.5
Money Market Rate 60b															
Treasury Bill Rate 60c	....	....	9.1	9.5	9.8	8.3	9.3	11.6	14.3	14.3	15.3	15.3	18.0	18.5	18.5
Deposit Rate 60l	5.80	5.80	9.83	9.58	8.92	8.50	9.96	11.88	14.50	14.50	14.50	14.50	15.42	15.50	15.50
Lending Rate 60p	8.00	9.00	11.83	11.88	11.50	12.00	13.46	16.71	21.25	21.33	20.50	20.50	20.50	20.50	20.50
Government Bond Yield........................... 61													18.46	15.77	15.78
Prices, Production, Labor													*Index Numbers (1995=100):*		
Wholesale Prices 63	3.2	3.9	5.1	5.6	6.4	7.2	8.0	9.6	†12.4	....	....	21.7	26.3	31.7	36.9
Home and Import Goods.................... 63a	3.1	3.7	4.9	5.4	6.1	6.9	7.7	9.2	11.9	15.0	17.6	21.0	25.3	30.4	36.0
Consumer Prices 64	2.6	3.0	3.8	4.3	4.9	5.5	6.2	7.4	9.2	†11.4	13.8	16.6	19.7	23.5	28.9
Harmonized CPI 64h															
Wages: Hourly Earnings 65	1.5	1.8	2.2	2.8	3.6	4.3	5.4	6.5	8.2	10.5	14.0	16.7	21.1	25.3	28.5
Manufacturing Production.................... 66ey	65.0	75.3	73.9	77.1	85.2	86.5	93.1	98.8	†99.7	....	98.3	96.9	98.2	100.7	100.0
Industrial Employment 67ey	97.5	103.5	104.7	105.6	112.0	117.2	120.9	124.2	125.6	127.0	127.1	125.7	126.1	124.6	124.8
****													*Number in Thousands:*		
Labor Force.. 67d	....														
Employment 67e	....													3,589	3,601
Unemployment 67c	....														287
Unemployment Rate (%)...................... 67r	....														7.4
International Transactions													*Millions of US Dollars*		
Exports .... 70..d	870.4	1,456.1	2,029.7	2,294.3	2,561.1	2,756.3	3,367.6	3,884.9	5,153.0	4,246.4	4,298.0	4,413.2	4,811.2	4,538.8	5,647.7
Imports, c.i.f. .... 71..d	2,348.0	3,476.6	4,385.1	5,356.9	6,058.7	6,853.5	7,829.0	9,613.8	10,548.0	8,809.8	10,025.7	9,500.4	9,434.8	10,134.4	11,350.2
****													*1995=100*		
Volume of Exports 72	19.7	24.7	27.1	29.5	34.1	†33.5	38.8	40.9	45.1	38.0	38.1	43.5	52.8	†52.7	61.6
Volume of Imports.............................. 73	23.2	29.3	26.7	26.1	28.2	†29.8	31.3	34.1	31.6	31.6	35.0	38.3	38.5	†43.7	44.3
Unit Value of Exp............................... 74	5.4	6.9	9.2	10.3	11.2	†12.3	12.9	13.9	20.0	24.6	29.6	35.5	41.0	46.9	50.4
Unit Value of Imp............................... 75	5.2	6.2	9.1	10.7	12.0	†12.5	13.4	16.5	22.5	26.0	32.4	37.4	46.6	53.9	60.8
Export Prices..................................... 76	3.6	5.3	†6.3	6.5	7.7	9.2	9.7	12.2	15.4	19.3	20.8	†24.9	32.3	39.4	43.0
Import Prices..................................... 76.x	2.6	3.2	†4.4	4.9	5.6	6.3	7.1	8.5	10.9	14.3	†16.5	20.0	24.8	30.6	36.9

1987	1988	1989	1990	1991	1992	1993	1994	1995	1996	1997	1998	1999	2000	2001	
Billions of Euros Beginning 2001: End of Period															**Banking Survey (Nat'l Residency)**
†-757.3	-782.9	-1,331.2	-1,545.3	-1,067.2	-1,369.3	-416.0	-611.0	-1,872.7	-1,336.5	-3,785.5	-3,682.5	-2,965.0	-4,982.8	15.00	Foreign Assets (Net) **31n**
†7,715.1	9,194.9	11,352.3	13,228.0	14,907.4	17,853.9	†23312.6	24,173.8	26,044.0	27,258.3	29,058.1	30,512.8	35,991.7	41,884.0	143.27	Domestic Credit **32**
†4,700.8	5,720.2	7,108.7	8,396.0	9,281.3	11,493.6	†16663.9	16,637.4	16,887.0	16,867.2	17,134.2	16,766.7	18,230.5	20,070.7	60.51	Claims on General Govt. (Net) **32an**
†3,014.3	3,474.7	4,243.6	4,832.1	5,626.1	6,360.3	6,648.7	7,536.5	9,157.0	10,391.0	11,924.0	13,746.1	17,761.3	21,813.3	82.77	Claims on Other Resident Sectors **32d**
†681.1	805.4	1,045.0	1,268.7	1,370.9	1,529.7	1,641.6	1,839.8	2,061.0	2,251.0	2,451.5	2,519.4	3,154.1	3,097.3	8.71	Currency Issued **34a.n**
†432.4	484.6	560.6	732.8	859.5	959.2	1,190.3	1,647.0	1,921.9	2,369.9	2,704.5	3,109.1	4,503.0	4,348.3	16.01	Demand Deposits **34b.n**
†4,449.0	5,543.3	6,831.6	7,651.6	8,313.9	9,066.3	9,760.5	11,925.5	13,684.8	15,339.1	16,704.7	16,564.0	17,975.3	19,164.2	118.77	Other Deposits .... **35..n**
....	....	....	....	....	....	....	....	....	....	....	....	....	....	—	Money Market Instruments **36m**
†1,251.2	1,530.1	1,785.2	2,030.9	2,416.6	3,156.3	4,330.1	4,181.1	3,313.0	2,161.9	1,660.6	1,229.5	1,093.7	691.4	1.96	Bonds (Debt Securities) **36n**
														1.79	*o/w:* Bonds Over Two Years **36na**
†397.7	560.9	686.0	895.2	1,193.7	1,351.9	1,573.0	1,550.7	1,812.5	1,955.7	2,383.5	3,056.3	5,447.3	6,169.2	22.02	Capital Accounts **37a**
†-253.5	-512.5	-887.4	-896.5	-314.4	421.4	4,401.2	2,418.7	1,378.1	1,844.1	-632.1	352.0	853.5	3,431.0	-9.20	Other Items (Net) **37r**
End of Period															**Banking Survey (EA-Wide Residency)**
....	....	....	....	....	....	....	....	....	....	....	....	....	....	12.26	Foreign Assets (Net) **31n.u**
....	....	....	....	....	....	....	....	....	....	....	....	....	....	145.93	Domestic Credit .... **32..u**
....	....	....	....	....	....	....	....	....	....	....	....	....	....	61.75	Claims on General Govt. (Net) **32an u**
....	....	....	....	....	....	....	....	....	....	....	....	....	....	84.18	Claims on Other Resident Sect. **32d.u**
....	....	....	....	....	....	....	....	....	....	....	....	....	....	8.71	Currency Issued **34a.u**
....	....	....	....	....	....	....	....	....	....	....	....	....	....	16.15	Demand Deposits **34b.u**
....	....	....	....	....	....	....	....	....	....	....	....	....	....	119.95	Other Deposits .... **35..u**
....	....	....	....	....	....	....	....	....	....	....	....	....	....	2.15	*o/w:* Other Dep. Over Two Yrs **35ab u**
....	....	....	....	....	....	....	....	....	....	....	....	....	....	—	Money Market Instruments **36m.u**
....	....	....	....	....	....	....	....	....	....	....	....	....	....	1.96	Bonds (Debt Securities) **36n.u**
....	....	....	....	....	....	....	....	....	....	....	....	....	....	1.79	*o/w:* Bonds Over Two Years .. **36na u**
....	....	....	....	....	....	....	....	....	....	....	....	....	....	22.02	Capital Accounts **37a**
....	....	....	....	....	....	....	....	....	....	....	....	....	....	-10.59	Other Items (Net) **37r.u**
Percent Per Annum															**Interest Rates**
20.5	19.0	19.0	19.0	19.0	19.0	21.5	20.5	18.0	16.5	14.5	....	†11.8	8.1	....	Central Bank Rate **60**
....	....	....	....	....	....	....	24.60	16.40	13.80	12.80	13.99	....	....	....	Money Market Rate **60b**
19.5	19.0	20.0	24.0	22.5	22.5	20.3	17.5	14.2	11.2	11.4	10.3	8.3	†6.2	4.1	Treasury Bill Rate **60c**
15.33	†17.33	17.14	19.52	20.67	19.92	19.33	18.92	15.75	13.51	10.11	10.70	8.69	6.13	3.32	Deposit Rate **60l**
21.82	22.89	23.26	27.62	29.45	28.71	28.56	27.44	23.05	20.96	18.92	18.56	15.00	12.32	8.59	Lending Rate **60p**
....	16.56	....	....	....	....	....	....	....	....	....	8.48	6.30	6.10	5.30	Government Bond Yield **61**
Period Averages															**Prices, Production, Labor**
40.5	44.6	50.6	58.7	68.5	76.3	85.3	92.8	100.0	†106.1	109.6	113.9	116.3	125.4	129.8	Wholesale Prices **63**
39.6	43.6	49.1	57.8	68.2	76.5	85.7	93.1	100.0	†106.2	109.8	114.3	117.3	125.8	130.4	Home and Import Goods **63a**
33.6	†38.2	43.4	52.3	62.4	72.3	82.8	†91.8	100.0	108.2	114.2	119.6	122.8	126.6	130.9	Consumer Prices **64**
....	....	....	....	....	....	....	....	100.0	107.9	113.7	118.9	121.4	124.9	129.5	Harmonized CPI **64h**
31.2	37.0	44.6	53.2	62.1	70.7	78.1	88.3	100.0	108.6	118.3	123.9	....	....	115.5	Wages: Hourly Earnings **65**
98.0	102.9	105.3	102.3	101.4	100.1	96.8	97.9	†100.0	100.2	100.9	106.5	107.2	113.8	....	Manufacturing Production **66ey**
123.1	124.4	124.7	122.8	115.2	109.5	103.0	99.9	100.0	99.4	96.2	95.3	....	....	....	Industrial Employment **67ey**
Period Averages															
....	3,953	....	....	3,873	4,034	4,112	4,189	4,245	4,314	4,293	4,446	4,463	4,437	....	Labor Force **67d**
3,597	3,657	3,671	3,719	3,632	3,685	3,720	3,790	3,824	3,872	3,854	3,967	3,940	3,946	....	Employment **67e**
286	303	296	281	301	350	398	404	425	446	440	†479	523	491	....	Unemployment **67c**
7.4	7.7	7.5	7.0	7.7	8.7	9.7	9.6	10.0	10.3	10.3	†10.8	11.7	11.1	....	Unemployment Rate (%) **67r**
Millions of US Dollars															**International Transactions**
6,532.9	5,428.8	7,544.6	8,105.2	8,673.3	9,439.3	9,092.7	8,807.6	10,960.8	11,948.2	11,127.7	10,731.9	10,475.1	10,747.0	9,483.3	Exports .... **70..d**
13,167.6	12,320.9	16,151.0	19,777.0	21,579.8	22,818.0	20,200.3	21,381.3	26,795.2	29,672.4	27,898.7	29,388.1	28,719.5	29,221.4	29,927.7	Imports, c.i.f. .... **71..d**
1995=100															
69.6	46.8	64.4	61.0	69.9	89.5	87.1	90.7	100.0	106.8	118.7	....	....	....	....	Volume of Exports **72**
54.0	40.5	54.6	61.4	69.2	79.8	87.5	92.2	100.0	109.0	110.7	....	....	....	....	Volume of Imports **73**
53.9	65.3	75.1	†81.8	89.0	86.9	89.2	99.3	100.0	105.2	100.7	....	....	....	....	Unit Value of Exp. **74**
59.4	73.0	81.7	†89.4	97.7	98.4	99.6	98.4	100.0	105.4	112.3	....	....	....	....	Unit Value of Imp. **75**
46.3	52.9	60.5	63.6	70.5	75.0	83.5	90.7	100.0	†105.6	108.7	112.0	111.9	123.7	126.8	Export Prices **76**
41.0	46.7	52.6	59.1	67.8	76.3	85.6	93.5	100.0	†101.6	103.8	109.4	110.0	116.7	120.2	Import Prices **76.x**

Greece

		1972	1973	1974	1975	1976	1977	1978	1979	1980	1981	1982	1983	1984	1985	1986
Balance of Payments															*Millions of US Dollars:*	
Current Account, n.i.e.	78al d	....	....	....	....	−929	−1,075	−955	−1,886	−2,209	−2,408	−1,892	−1,878	−2,132	−3,276	−1,676
Goods: Exports f.o.b.	78aa d	....	....	....	....	2,258	2,583	3,036	3,991	4,175	4,884	4,273	4,179	4,426	4,357	4,586
Goods: Imports f.o.b.	78ab d	....	....	....	....	−4,997	−5,728	−6,530	−8,997	−9,717	−10,221	−8,972	−8,449	−8,648	−9,370	−8,961
Trade Balance	78ac d	....	....	....	....	−2,739	−3,145	−3,494	−5,006	−5,542	−5,337	−4,699	−4,270	−4,222	−5,013	−4,375
Services: Credit	78ad d	....	....	....	....	1,808	2,133	2,705	3,436	3,947	3,953	3,360	2,857	2,724	2,600	3,213
Services: Debit	78ae d	....	....	....	....	−677	−829	−985	−1,308	−1,428	−1,720	−1,562	−1,411	−1,309	−1,401	−1,574
Balance on Goods & Services	78af d	....	....	....	....	−1,608	−1,841	−1,774	−2,878	−3,023	−3,104	−2,901	−2,824	−2,807	−3,814	−2,736
Income: Credit	78ag d	....	....	....	....	136	118	164	253	252	346	258	130	183	154	106
Income: Debit	78ah d	....	....	....	....	−267	−275	−327	−426	−525	−887	−848	−951	−1,140	−1,282	−1,413
Balance on Gds, Serv. & Inc.	78ai d	....	....	....	....	−1,739	−1,998	−1,937	−3,051	−3,296	−3,645	−3,491	−3,645	−3,764	−4,942	−4,043
Current Transfers, n.i.e.: Credit	78aj d	....	....	....	....	812	926	985	1,169	1,091	1,241	1,603	1,771	1,636	1,670	2,375
Current Transfers: Debit	78ak d	....	....	....	....	−2	−3	−3	−4	−4	−4	−4	−4	−4	−4	−8
Capital Account, n.i.e.	78bc d	....	....	....	....	—	—	—	—	—	—	—	—	—	—	—
Capital Account, n.i.e.: Credit	78ba d	....	....	....	....	—	—	—	—	—	—	—	—	—	—	—
Capital Account: Debit	78bb d	....	....	....	....	—	—	—	—	—	—	—	—	—	—	—
Financial Account, n.i.e.	78bj d	....	....	....	....	922	1,313	1,419	1,424	2,468	1,769	1,283	2,391	2,172	2,924	2,408
Direct Investment Abroad	78bd d	....	....	....	....	—	—	—	—	—	—	—	—	—	—	—
Dir. Invest. in Rep. Econ., n.i.e.	78be d	....	....	....	....	305	387	428	613	672	520	436	439	485	447	471
Portfolio Investment Assets	78bf d	....	....	....	....	—	—	—	—	—	—	—	—	—	—	—
Equity Securities	78bk d	....	....	....	....	—	—	—	—	—	—	—	—	—	—	—
Debt Securities	78bl d	....	....	....	....	—	—	—	—	—	—	—	—	—	—	—
Portfolio Investment Liab., n.i.e.	78bg d	....	....	....	....	−1	−1	—	—	—	—	—	—	—	—	—
Equity Securities	78bm d	....	....	....	....	—	—	—	—	—	—	—	—	—	—	—
Debt Securities	78bn d	....	....	....	....	−1	−1	—	—	—	—	—	—	—	—	—
Financial Derivatives Assets	78bw d	....	....	....	....	....	....									
Financial Derivatives Liabilities	78bx d	....	....	....	....	....	....									
Other Investment Assets	78bh d	....	....	....	....	−4	−54	83	−332	−399	—	—	—	—	—	—
Monetary Authorities	78bo d	....	....	....	....	....	....	....	....	....						
General Government	78bp d	....	....	....	....	65	44	46	—	—	—	—	—	—	—	—
Banks	78bq d	....	....	....	....	−69	−98	37	−332	−399	—	—	—	—	—	—
Other Sectors	78br d	....	....	....	....	—	—	—	—	—	—	—	—	—	—	—
Other Investment Liab., n.i.e.	78bi d	....	....	....	....	622	981	908	1,143	2,195	1,249	847	1,952	1,687	2,477	1,937
Monetary Authorities	78bs d	....	....	....	....	−91	113	178	8	690	243	367	499	430	1,386	650
General Government	78bt d	....	....	....	....	−28	−17	50	−33	−95	−13	−89	18	−17	28	781
Banks	78bu d	....	....	....	....	496	556	367	441	633	354	129	312	223	227	190
Other Sectors	78bv d	....	....	....	....	245	329	313	727	967	665	440	1,123	1,051	836	316
Net Errors and Omissions	78ca d	....	....	....	....	−127	−108	−270	470	−395	446	47	−313	−242	−44	−82
Overall Balance	78cb d	....	....	....	....	−134	130	194	8	−136	−193	−562	200	−202	−396	650
Reserves and Related Items	79da d	....	....	....	....	134	−130	−194	−8	136	193	562	−200	202	396	−650
Reserve Assets	79db d	....	....	....	....	5	−88	−144	92	227	234	128	−100	−131	141	−270
Use of Fund Credit and Loans	79dc d	....	....	....	....	67	−83	10	−49	−90	−75	−16	—	—	—	—
Exceptional Financing	79de d	....	....	....	....	62	41	−60	−51	−1	35	450	−100	333	255	−380
International Investment Position															*Millions of US Dollars*	
Assets	79aa d	....	....	....	....	....	....	....	....	....	....	....	....	....	....	....
Direct Investment Abroad	79ab d	....	....	....	....	....	....	....	....	....	....	....	....	....	....	....
Portfolio Investment	79ac d	....	....	....	....	....	....	....	....	....	....	....	....	....	....	....
Equity Securities	79ad d	....	....	....	....	....	....	....	....	....	....	....	....	....	....	....
Debt Securities	79ae d	....	....	....	....	....	....	....	....	....	....	....	....	....	....	....
Financial Derivatives	79al d	....	....	....	....	....	....	....	....	....	....	....	....	....	....	....
Other Investment	79af d	....	....	....	....	....	....	....	....	....	....	....	....	....	....	....
Monetary Authorities	79ag d	....	....	....	....	....	....	....	....	....	....	....	....	....	....	....
General Government	79ah d	....	....	....	....	....	....	....	....	....	....	....	....	....	....	....
Banks	79ai d	....	....	....	....	....	....	....	....	....	....	....	....	....	....	....
Other Sectors	79aj d	....	....	....	....	....	....	....	....	....	....	....	....	....	....	....
Reserve Assets	79ak d	....	....	....	....	....	....	....	....	....	....	....	....	....	....	....
Liabilities	79la d	....	....	....	....	....	....	....	....	....	....	....	....	....	....	....
Dir. Invest. in Rep. Economy	79lb d	....	....	....	....	....	....	....	....	....	....	....	....	....	....	....
Portfolio Investment	79lc d	....	....	....	....	....	....	....	....	....	....	....	....	....	....	....
Equity Securities	79ld d	....	....	....	....	....	....	....	....	....	....	....	....	....	....	....
Debt Securities	79le d	....	....	....	....	....	....	....	....	....	....	....	....	....	....	....
Financial Derivatives	79ll d	....	....	....	....	....	....	....	....	....	....	....	....	....	....	....
Other Investment	79lf d	....	....	....	....	....	....	....	....	....	....	....	....	....	....	....
Monetary Authorities	79lg d	....	....	....	....	....	....	....	....	....	....	....	....	....	....	....
General Government	79lh d	....	....	....	....	....	....	....	....	....	....	....	....	....	....	....
Banks	79li d	....	....	....	....	....	....	....	....	....	....	....	....	....	....	....
Other Sectors	79lj d	....	....	....	....	....	....	....	....	....	....	....	....	....	....	....

	1987	1988	1989	1990	1991	1992	1993	1994	1995	1996	1997	1998	1999	2000	2001	Balance of Payments	
Minus Sign Indicates Debit																	
Current Account, n.i.e.	−1,223	−958	−2,561	−3,537	−1,574	−2,140	−747	−146	−2,864	−4,554	−4,860	....	−7,295	−9,820	−9,400	Current Account, n.i.e.	**78ald**
	5,699	6,015	6,074	6,458	6,911	6,076	5,112	5,338	5,918	5,890	5,576	....	8,545	10,202	10,615	Goods: Exports f.o.b.	**78aad**
	−11,134	−12,042	−13,401	−16,564	−16,933	−17,637	−15,611	−16,611	−20,343	−21,395	−20,951	....	−26,496	−30,440	−29,702	Goods: Imports f.o.b.	**78abd**
	−5,435	−6,027	−7,327	−10,106	−10,022	−11,561	−10,499	−11,273	−14,425	−15,505	−15,375	....	−17,951	−20,239	−19,087	*Trade Balance*	**78acd**
	4,332	5,094	4,828	6,560	7,222	8,697	8,214	9,213	9,605	9,348	9,287	....	16,506	19,239	19,456	Services: Credit	**78add**
	−1,726	−2,164	−2,415	−3,000	−3,193	−3,701	−3,521	−3,774	−4,368	−4,238	−4,650	....	−9,251	−11,286	−11,589	Services: Debit	**78aed**
	−2,829	−3,097	−4,914	−6,546	−5,993	−6,565	−5,806	−5,834	−9,188	−10,395	−10,738	....	−10,696	−12,286	−11,220	*Balance on Goods & Services*	**78afd**
	185	269	283	315	421	555	927	1,099	1,312	1,156	1,208	....	2,577	2,807	1,885	Income: Credit	**78agd**
	−1,614	−1,779	−1,913	−2,024	−2,185	−2,605	−2,367	−2,347	−2,996	−3,337	−2,840	....	−3,248	−3,692	−3,652	Income: Debit	**78ahd**
	−4,258	−4,607	−6,544	−8,255	−7,757	−8,615	−7,246	−7,082	−10,872	−12,576	−12,370	....	−11,367	−13,171	−12,987	*Balance on Gds, Serv. & Inc.*	**78aid**
	3,044	3,663	3,996	4,730	6,199	6,489	6,516	6,964	8,039	8,053	7,538	....	4,957	4,116	4,592	Current Transfers, n.i.e.: Credit	**78ajd**
	−9	−14	−13	−12	−16	−14	−17	−28	−31	−31	−28	....	−884	−764	−1,005	Current Transfers: Debit	**78akd**
	—	—	—	—	—	—	—	—	—	—	—	....	2,211	2,112	2,153	Capital Account, n.i.e.	**78bcd**
	—	—	—	—	—	—	—	—	—	—	—	....	2,318	2,244	2,320	Capital Account, n.i.e.: Credit	**78bad**
	—	—	—	—	—	—	—	—	—	—	—	....	−107	−131	−167	Capital Account: Debit	**78bbd**
	1,974	1,854	2,751	4,002	3,961	2,619	4,817	6,903	3,162	8,658	119	....	7,478	10,830	537	Financial Account, n.i.e.	**78bjd**
	—	—	—	—	—	—	—	—	—	—	—	....	−542	−2,099	−611	Direct Investment Abroad	**78bdd**
	683	907	752	1,005	1,135	1,144	977	981	1,053	1,058	984	....	567	1,083	1,585	Dir. Invest. in Rep. Econ., n.i.e.	**78bed**
	—	—	—	—	—	—	—	—	—	—	—	....	−858	−1,184	−474	Portfolio Investment Assets	**78bfd**
	—	—	—	—	—	—	—	—	—	—	—	....	−166	−846	−1,020	Equity Securities	**78bkd**
	—	—	—	—	—	—	—	—	—	—	—	....	−692	−338	546	Debt Securities	**78bld**
	—	—	—	—	—	—	—	—	—	—	—	....	6,754	9,262	9,012	Portfolio Investment Liab., n.i.e.	**78bgd**
	—	—	—	—	—	—	—	—	—	—	—	....	−2,589	1,637	1,829	Equity Securities	**78bmd**
	—	—	—	—	—	—	—	—	—	—	—	....	9,343	7,625	7,183	Debt Securities	**78bnd**
	....	....	....	....	....	....	....	....	....	....	....	....	....	....	....	Financial Derivatives Assets	**78bwd**
	....	....	....	....	....	....	....	....	....	....	....	....	419	348	74	Financial Derivatives Liabilities	**78bxd**
	—	—	—	—	—	—	—	—	—	—	980	....	−2,913	6,970	−1,539	Other Investment Assets	**78bhd**
	....	....	....	....	....	....	....	....	....	....	....	....	....	....	....	Monetary Authorities	**78bod**
	—	—	—	—	—	—	—	—	—	—	980	....	−2,913	6,970	−1,539	General Government	**78bpd**
	—	—	—	—	—	—	—	—	—	—	—	....	....	....	....	Banks	**78bqd**
	—	—	—	—	—	—	—	—	—	—	—	....	....	....	....	Other Sectors	**78brd**
	1,291	947	1,999	2,997	2,826	1,475	3,840	5,922	2,109	7,600	−1,845	....	4,050	−3,551	−7,511	Other Investment Liab., n.i.e.	**78bid**
	−92	288	736	367	710	1,460	2,584	−1,791	−2,385	−2,194	−2,570	....	—	—	—	Monetary Authorities	**78bsd**
	851	−145	255	936	688	−1,773	884	4,703	3,441	3,530	7,101	....	—	—	—	General Government	**78btd**
	321	143	503	581	175	−2	78	89	−2,110	−598	−3,348	....	1,644	−3,425	−6,989	Banks	**78bud**
	211	661	505	1,113	1,253	1,790	294	2,921	3,163	6,862	−3,028	....	2,406	−126	−522	Other Sectors	**78bvd**
	223	41	−538	−185	−183	−853	−631	−448	−321	111	226	....	42	−550	1,011	Net Errors and Omissions	**78cad**
	974	937	−348	280	2,204	−374	3,439	6,309	−23	4,215	−4,515	....	2,435	2,573	−5,699	*Overall Balance*	**78cbd**
	−974	−937	348	−280	−2,204	374	−3,439	−6,309	23	−4,215	4,515	....	−2,435	−2,573	5,699	Reserves and Related Items	**79dad**
	−806	−1,148	341	−40	−1,660	188	−3,019	−6,309	23	−4,215	4,515	....	−2,435	−2,573	5,699	Reserve Assets	**79dbd**
	—	—	—	—	—	—	—	—	—	—	—	....	—	—	—	Use of Fund Credit and Loans	**79dcd**
	−168	211	7	−240	−544	186	−420	—	—	—	—	....	....	....	....	Exceptional Financing	**79ded**
Millions of US Dollars																International Investment Position	
	....	....	....	....	....	....	....	....	....	....	....	55,491	59,106	57,078	....	Assets	**79aad**
	....	....	....	....	....	....	....	....	....	....	....	2,792	3,809	5,735	....	Direct Investment Abroad	**79abd**
	....	....	....	....	....	....	....	....	....	....	....	4,503	4,777	3,847	....	Portfolio Investment	**79acd**
	....	....	....	....	....	....	....	....	....	....	....	1,177	1,147	1,345	....	Equity Securities	**79add**
	....	....	....	....	....	....	....	....	....	....	....	3,326	3,630	2,502	....	Debt Securities	**79aed**
	....	....	....	....	....	....	....	....	....	....	....	12	13	12	....	Financial Derivatives	**79ald**
	....	....	....	....	....	....	....	....	....	....	....	38,726	40,362	35,227	....	Other Investment	**79afd**
	....	....	....	....	....	....	....	....	....	....	....	7,239	6,135	477	....	Monetary Authorities	**79agd**
	....	....	....	....	....	....	....	....	....	....	....	—	—	—	....	General Government	**79ahd**
	....	....	....	....	....	....	....	....	....	....	....	18,712	20,881	20,908	....	Banks	**79aid**
	....	....	....	....	....	....	....	....	....	....	....	12,775	13,346	13,842	....	Other Sectors	**79ajd**
	....	....	....	....	....	....	....	....	....	....	....	9,458	10,145	12,257	....	Reserve Assets	**79akd**
	....	....	....	....	....	....	....	....	....	....	....	91,539	100,463	104,286	....	Liabilities	**79lad**
	....	....	....	....	....	....	....	....	....	....	....	13,084	15,387	12,480	....	Dir. Invest. in Rep. Economy	**79lbd**
	....	....	....	....	....	....	....	....	....	....	....	45,330	51,152	54,705	....	Portfolio Investment	**79lcd**
	....	....	....	....	....	....	....	....	....	....	....	12,001	15,211	9,584	....	Equity Securities	**79ldd**
	....	....	....	....	....	....	....	....	....	....	....	33,329	35,941	45,121	....	Debt Securities	**79led**
	....	....	....	....	....	....	....	....	....	....	....	—	—	—	....	Financial Derivatives	**79lld**
	....	....	....	....	....	....	....	....	....	....	....	33,125	33,924	37,101	....	Other Investment	**79lfd**
	....	....	....	....	....	....	....	....	....	....	....	—	—	—	....	Monetary Authorities	**79lgd**
	....	....	....	....	....	....	....	....	....	....	....	8,071	7,645	9,023	....	General Government	**79lhd**
	....	....	....	....	....	....	....	....	....	....	....	15,384	16,551	18,846	....	Banks	**79lid**
	....	....	....	....	....	....	....	....	....	....	....	9,670	9,728	9,232	....	Other Sectors	**79ljd**

Greece

		1972	1973	1974	1975	1976	1977	1978	1979	1980	1981	1982	1983	1984	1985	1986
Government Finance															*Billions of Drachmas:*	
Budgetary Central Government																
Deficit (-) or Surplus	80	−9.8	−11.0	−18.0	−26.3	−31.2	−35.8	−42.4	−51.5	−53.4	−176.8	−174.5	−283.3	−351.0	−586.6	−519.9
Total Revenue and Grants	81y	70.3	85.4	102.5	135.0	171.2	206.0	242.6	306.7	342.0	412.5	598.1	726.7	944.0	1,122.3	1,495.0
Revenue	81	69.4	83.9	100.8	134.2	170.4	205.2	242.0	306.2	341.3	404.2	590.4	721.0	936.5	1,114.4	1,464.9
Grants Received	81z	.9	1.4	1.7	.8	.8	.8	.6	.4	.6	8.3	7.7	5.7	7.5	7.9	30.1
Expenditure	82	80.1	96.4	120.6	161.3	202.4	241.7	285.0	358.2	395.4	589.3	772.6	1,010.0	1,295.0	1,708.9	2,014.9
Financing																
Net Borrowing	84	9.8	11.0	18.0	26.3	31.2	35.8	42.4	51.5	53.4	176.8	174.5	283.3	351.0	586.6	519.9
Borrowing: Domestic	84c	10.5	7.3	17.0	16.0	35.8	39.3	36.5	41.4	38.0	153.2	148.5	229.4	233.9	395.8	350.0
Foreign	85c	3.2	8.6	5.2	15.4	1.0	4.7	14.6	20.5	26.1	43.0	47.6	77.9	159.4	257.1	292.7
Amortization	84y	−3.9	−4.9	−4.2	−5.1	−5.6	−8.2	−8.6	−10.4	−10.6	−19.3	−21.7	−24.0	−42.2	−66.2	−122.8
General Government															*As Percent of*	
Deficit (-) or Surplus	80g	....	....	....	....	....	....	....	....	....	....	....	....	....	....	....
Debt	88g	....	....	....	....	....	....	....	....	....	....	....	....	....	....	....
National Accounts															*Billions of Drachmas*	
Househ.Cons.Expend.,incl.NPISHs	96f	248.1	307.1	381.9	454.0	542.5	634.9	756.8	904.9	1,104.6	1,383.1	1,734.2	2,053.6	2,461.4	3,025.5	3,718.9
Government Consumption Expend.	91f	45.9	55.4	78.1	102.0	124.3	153.8	185.2	233.5	280.0	368.5	471.2	579.4	742.8	942.0	1,067.2
Gross Fixed Capital Formation	93e	104.8	135.7	125.5	139.9	175.0	221.4	278.0	369.2	413.7	456.4	513.5	624.0	702.9	880.4	1,018.1
Changes in Inventories	93i	6.8	37.5	39.9	41.4	41.7	33.3	43.4	61.6	75.7	64.3	29.8	49.2	60.4	102.9	75.0
Exports of Goods and Services	90c	44.3	68.9	90.8	113.3	145.1	162.3	204.4	249.6	357.7	422.4	473.0	609.5	824.6	977.6	1,233.1
Imports of Goods and Services (-)	98c	75.7	122.1	144.7	180.6	213.1	243.3	286.1	360.8	448.9	556.1	738.3	925.4	1,139.1	1,513.5	1,703.3
Gross Domestic Product (GDP)	99b	377.7	484.1	564.2	672.2	825.0	963.7	1,161.4	1,428.7	1,711.0	2,050.1	2,574.6	3,079.2	3,805.7	4,617.8	5,514.7
Net Primary Income from Abroad	98.n	9.6	13.1	17.9	19.2	24.9	30.3	32.4	43.5	56.6	59.0	57.8	30.4	1.9	−33.8	−67.8
Gross National Income (GNI)	99a	387.3	497.2	582.1	691.4	849.9	994.0	1,193.8	1,472.2	1,767.6	2,109.1	2,632.4	3,109.6	3,807.6	4,584.0	5,446.9
Consumption of Fixed Capital	99cf	23.7	30.6	39.3	47.5	59.2	72.4	89.5	112.4	142.1	175.5	215.4	272.6	329.4	403.0	505.1
GDP Volume 1970 Prices	99b.p	348.6	374.1	360.5	382.4	406.7	420.7	448.8	465.4	473.5	473.8	475.7	477.6	490.7	506.0	514.2
GDP Volume 1995 Prices	99b.p	....	....	....	....	....	....	....	....	....	....	....	....	....	....	....
GDP Volume (1995=100)	99bvp	59.5	63.8	61.5	65.3	69.4	71.8	76.6	79.4	80.8	80.9	81.2	81.5	83.7	86.3	87.7
GDP Deflator (1995=100)	99bip	2.3	2.8	3.4	3.8	4.4	4.9	5.6	6.6	7.8	9.3	11.6	13.9	16.7	19.6	23.1
															Millions:	
Population	99z	8.89	8.93	8.96	9.05	9.17	9.27	9.36	9.45	9.64	9.73	9.79	9.85	9.90	9.93	9.97

	1987	1988	1989	1990	1991	1992	1993	1994	1995	1996	1997	1998	1999	2000	2001	
Year Ending December 31																**Government Finance**
																Budgetary Central Government
Deficit (-) or Surplus	−703.3	−1,045.1	−1,553.1	−1,814.3	−1,775.0	−1,358.4	−2,431.7	−5,050.3	−3,252.2	−2,904.2	−2,505.4	−2,125.5	−1,930.0	....	....	80
Total Revenue and Grants	1,718.1	1,992.0	2,197.8	2,991.3	3,816.9	4,821.6	5,281.7	6,191.7	7,113.6	7,956.4	9,185.4	10,412.5	11,603.0	....	....	81y
Revenue	1,707.4	1,936.0	2,134.8	2,888.0	3,679.6	4,617.6	4,989.1	5,883.4	6,753.5	7,306.9	....	....	....	....	....	81
Grants Received	10.7	56.0	63.0	103.3	137.3	204.0	292.6	308.3	360.1	649.5	....	....	....	....	....	81z
Expenditure	2,421.3	3,037.1	3,751.0	4,805.7	5,591.9	6,180.0	7,713.4	11,242.0	10,365.8	10,860.6	11,690.8	12,538.0	13,533.0	....	....	82
																Financing
Net Borrowing	703.3	1,045.1	1,553.1	1,814.3	1,775.0	1,358.4	2,431.7	5,050.3	3,252.2	2,904.2	2,505.4	2,125.5	1,930.0	....	....	84
Borrowing: Domestic	643.4	1,021.5	1,498.2	1,922.7	2,205.4	2,892.3	3,385.9	6,439.2	5,111.7	5,180.4	....	....	....	....	....	84c
Foreign	320.7	175.6	260.0	230.3	490.8	649.0	649.8	1,138.0	914.0	1,362.0	....	....	....	....	....	85c
Amortization	−260.8	−152.0	−205.1	−338.7	−921.1	−2,182.9	−1,604.0	−2,526.9	−2,773.5	−3,638.2	−3,589.4	−3,536.4	−3,362.3	....	....	84y
Gross Domestic Product																*General Government*
	....	....	....	....	....	....	....	....	....	....	....	−2.4	−1.7	−.8	.1	Deficit (-) or Surplus 80g
	....	....	....	....	....	....	....	....	....	....	....	105.0	103.8	102.8	99.7	Debt 88g
Billions of Drachmas																**National Accounts**
Househ.Cons.Expend.,incl.NPISHs	4,356.3	6,502.0	7,827.7	9,627.7	11,851.4	14,033.5	15,900.9	18,012.1	†19901.6	22,050.8	23,901.9	25,850.0	27,157.0	28,884.9	30,790.3	96f
Government Consumption Expend.	1,224.8	1,311.0	1,654.5	2,007.0	2,337.9	2,613.9	3,063.3	3,345.4	†4,174.1	4,348.0	5,013.3	5,506.8	5,879.9	6,408.4	7,049.2	91f
Gross Fixed Capital Formation	1,074.7	1,966.7	2,447.4	3,027.1	3,650.3	3,983.8	4,267.1	4,453.5	†5,066.0	5,828.1	6,558.7	7,615.1	8,346.6	9,377.6	10,420.5	93e
Changes in Inventories	28.3	†53.4	−24.1	−39.5	152.9	−60.4	−75.5	25.8	†85.7	96.5	93.2	79.7	−106.6	17.5	−198.9	93i
Exports of Goods and Services	1,536.8	1,696.4	1,982.8	2,209.8	2,620.7	3,174.5	3,355.5	3,904.0	†4,800.2	5,245.6	6,523.7	7,150.6	7,893.2	10,343.4	11,235.7	90c
Imports of Goods and Services (-)	1,993.4	2,360.5	2,993.1	3,689.0	4,382.7	4,979.2	5,375.6	5,757.2	†6,792.4	7,633.9	8,958.1	10,160.0	10,720.9	13,633.7	14,748.7	98c
Gross Domestic Product (GDP)	6,271.9	†9,169.0	10,895.2	13,143.1	16,230.5	18,766.1	21,135.7	23,983.6	†27235.2	29,935.1	33,132.7	36,042.2	38,449.2	41,406.7	44,483.7	99b
Net Primary Income from Abroad	−63.3	−17.3	−29.3	105.1	196.5	249.8	137.8	212.8	†861.7	835.2	928.2	976.5	759.3	644.3	750.0	98.n
Gross National Income (GNI)	6,208.6	†9,151.7	10,865.9	13,248.2	16,427.0	19,015.9	21,273.5	24,195.7	†28096.9	30,770.3	34,060.9	37,018.7	39,208.5	42,051.0	45,233.7	99a
Consumption of Fixed Capital	578.1	811.7	959.8	1,132.0	1,395.7	1,640.0	1,847.7	2,117.2	†2,449.8	2,707.4	2,954.2	3,235.2	3,473.9	3,831.7	4,003.5	99cf
GDP Volume 1970 Prices	511.8	534.6	553.5	550.4	569.4	571.9	566.7	575.0	586.0	....	....	....	....	....	....	99b.p
GDP Volume 1995 Prices	....	....	....	....	....	....	....	....	27,235.2	27,877.5	28,891.4	29,863.2	30,939.7	32,217.2	33,538.1	99b.p
GDP Volume (1995=100)	87.3	91.2	94.5	93.9	97.2	97.6	96.7	98.1	100.0	102.4	106.1	109.6	113.6	118.3	123.1	99bvp
GDP Deflator (1995=100)	26.4	†36.9	42.4	51.4	61.3	70.6	80.2	89.7	†100.0	107.4	114.7	120.7	124.3	128.5	132.6	99bip
Midyear Estimates																
Population	10.00	10.04	10.09	10.16	10.25	10.32	10.38	10.43	10.45	10.48	10.50	10.52	10.59	10.01	10.02	99z

(See notes in the back of the book.)

Grenada

		1972	1973	1974	1975	1976	1977	1978	1979	1980	1981	1982	1983	1984	1985	1986
Exchange Rates														*E.Caribbean Dollars per SDR: End of Period (aa)*		
Official Rate	aa	2.2194	2.4925	2.5024	2.7770	3.1369	3.2797	3.5175	3.5568	3.4436	3.1427	2.9784	2.8268	2.6466	2.9657	3.3026
Official Rate	ae	2.0442	2.0661	2.0439	2.3721	2.7000	2.7000	2.7000	2.7000	2.7000	2.7000	2.7000	2.7000	2.7000	2.7000	2.7000
														Index Numbers (1995=100):		
Official Rate	ahx	140.7	137.9	131.6	125.0	100.0	100.0	100.0	100.0	100.0	100.0	100.0	100.0	100.0	100.0	100.0
Nominal Effective Exchange Rate	ne c	....	....	....	....	....	....	....	50.3	49.0	52.9	56.4	59.4	63.8	65.5	62.7
Real Effective Exchange Rate	re c	....	....	....	....	....	....	....	88.0	91.5	105.8	112.3	118.4	126.3	126.4	117.8
Fund Position														*Millions of SDRs:*		
Quota	2f. s	....	....	....	2.00	2.00	2.00	3.00	3.00	4.50	4.50	4.50	6.00	6.00	6.00	6.00
SDRs	1b. s	....	....	....	.07	.09	.02	—	.01	—	—	.01	.14	.02	.01	—
Reserve Position in the Fund	1c. s	....	....	....	—	—	—	—	—	—	—	—	—	—	—	—
Total Fund Cred.&Loans Outstg.	2tl	....	....	....	.81	1.21	1.42	2.03	2.40	2.21	7.10	6.27	7.32	6.30	3.83	2.13
International Liquidity													*Millions of US Dollars Unless Otherwise Indicated:*			
Total Reserves minus Gold	1l. d	5.60	5.00	5.36	†5.04	8.11	7.65	9.70	12.22	12.91	16.10	9.23	14.14	14.23	20.81	20.57
SDRs	1b. d	....	....	....	.08	.10	.02	—	.01	—	—	.01	.15	.02	.01	—
Reserve Position in the Fund	1c. d	....	....	....	—	—	—	—	—	—	—	—	—	—	—	—
Foreign Exchange	1d. d	5.60	5.00	5.36	†4.95	8.01	7.63	9.70	12.21	12.91	16.10	9.22	14.00	14.21	20.80	20.57
Deposit Money Banks: Assets	7a. d	.68	1.40	4.33	6.03	5.26	4.99	5.44	11.08	10.89	12.71	6.49	7.47	8.04	7.55	9.21
Liabilities	7b. d	10.13	11.57	15.12	11.75	6.26	6.84	6.48	11.10	11.04	12.50	12.56	9.61	9.70	10.29	13.12
Monetary Authorities													*Millions of E. Caribbean Dollars:*			
Foreign Assets	11	10.32	10.34	10.96	†11.95	21.91	20.66	26.20	32.99	34.85	43.46	24.93	38.18	38.43	56.19	55.53
Claims on Central Government	12a	.70	1.59	1.89	5.53	8.36	9.44	12.56	14.89	14.90	31.84	38.85	29.95	42.91	37.62	33.78
Claims on Deposit Money Banks	12e	—	—	—	—	—	—	—	—	—	—	—	—	—	.86	.24
Reserve Money	14	11.03	11.92	12.85	†15.22	26.47	25.44	31.61	39.35	42.15	52.98	45.09	47.45	64.66	83.30	82.50
of which: Currency Outside DMBs	14a	8.28	8.39	9.71	12.65	15.32	18.33	23.67	28.50	32.58	37.41	39.95	41.36	20.58	25.07	30.69
Foreign Liabilities	16c	—	—	—	2.25	3.80	4.66	7.14	8.54	7.61	22.33	18.69	20.69	16.68	11.37	7.04
Central Government Deposits	16d	—	—	—	—	—	—	—	—	—	—	—	—	—	—	—
Other Items (Net)	17r	—	—	—	—	—	—	—	—	—	—	—	—	—	—	—
Deposit Money Banks													*Millions of E. Caribbean Dollars:*			
Reserves	20	1.96	2.64	2.38	†2.57	11.15	7.11	7.95	10.85	9.57	15.56	5.14	6.08	43.27	44.69	49.72
Foreign Assets	21	1.39	2.89	8.86	†14.30	14.20	13.48	14.70	29.93	29.39	34.32	17.52	20.17	21.71	20.39	24.85
Claims on Central Government	22a	13.43	12.13	15.33	15.45	13.26	13.14	13.34	10.12	12.42	12.05	23.53	32.57	28.53	32.09	31.87
Claims on Local Government	22b	—	—	—	—	—	—	—	—	—	—	—	—	—	—	—
Claims on Nonfin.Pub.Enterprises	22c	—	—	—	.50	.50	.50	.40	.76	1.53	2.25	10.51	8.77	7.40	7.38	7.88
Claims on Private Sector	22d	46.32	50.72	45.94	39.42	38.74	48.02	56.54	64.34	72.34	75.11	78.80	76.17	81.27	109.67	152.02
Claims on Nonbank Financial Insts	22g	.50	.50	.50	.50	.50	.49	.37	.27	.29	.50	.53	.45	1.76	.52	.51
Demand Deposits	24	6.03	7.23	6.07	6.73	11.38	11.18	14.37	17.15	15.87	15.91	19.62	16.74	30.13	29.05	38.65
Time, Savings,& Fgn.Currency Dep.	25	39.60	39.86	38.69	47.29	52.58	58.55	66.09	77.75	82.51	87.83	87.03	88.86	97.71	123.09	157.61
Foreign Liabilities	26c	20.70	23.90	30.90	†27.88	16.91	18.48	17.48	29.98	29.80	33.75	33.90	25.95	26.20	27.80	35.41
Central Government Deposits	26d	—	—	—	—	.10	.10	.40	.71	3.31	2.28	1.12	2.49	4.73	2.65	1.25
Credit from Monetary Authorities	26g	—	—	—	—	—	—	—	—	—	—	2.54	6.41	—	—	—
Capital Accounts	27a	.93	.95	1.00	.98	1.12	1.20	1.30	.88	.70	3.03	3.10	9.54	17.87	19.43	22.38
Other Items (Net)	27r	−3.66	−3.07	−3.67	−10.15	−3.76	−6.78	−6.35	−10.21	−6.64	−3.01	−11.29	−5.78	7.29	12.72	11.55
Monetary Survey													*Millions of E. Caribbean Dollars:*			
Foreign Assets (Net)	31n	−8.98	−10.67	−11.08	†−3.89	15.40	11.00	16.27	24.40	26.84	21.71	−10.15	11.72	17.26	37.42	37.92
Domestic Credit	32	60.95	64.93	63.65	61.40	61.25	71.49	82.81	89.67	98.17	119.46	151.11	145.42	157.13	184.63	224.81
Claims on Central Govt. (Net)	32an	14.13	13.71	17.21	20.98	21.51	22.47	25.50	24.31	24.01	41.61	61.27	60.04	66.71	67.05	64.40
Claims on Local Government	32b	—	—	—	—	—	—	—	—	—	—	—	—	—	—	—
Claims on Nonfin.Pub.Enterprises	32c	—	—	—	.50	.50	.50	.40	.76	1.53	2.25	10.51	8.77	7.40	7.38	7.88
Claims on Private Sector	32d	46.32	50.72	45.94	39.42	38.74	48.02	56.54	64.34	72.34	75.11	78.80	76.17	81.27	109.67	152.02
Claims on Nonbank Financial Inst	32g	.50	.50	.50	.50	.50	.49	.37	.27	.29	.50	.53	.45	1.76	.52	.51
Money	34	14.31	15.62	15.79	19.38	26.70	29.51	38.04	45.65	48.45	53.32	59.57	58.10	50.71	54.12	69.34
Quasi-Money	35	39.60	39.86	38.69	47.29	52.58	58.55	66.09	77.75	82.51	87.83	87.03	88.86	97.71	123.09	157.61
Capital Accounts	37a	.93	.95	1.00	.98	1.12	1.20	1.30	1.98	2.83	5.95	5.87	12.17	20.33	22.19	25.45
Other Items (Net)	37r	−2.87	−2.18	−2.91	−10.15	−3.76	−6.78	−6.35	−11.31	−8.77	−5.93	−11.52	−1.99	5.64	22.65	10.33
Money plus Quasi-Money	35l	53.91	55.48	54.48	66.67	79.28	88.07	104.13	123.40	130.95	141.16	146.61	146.96	148.42	177.21	226.95
Interest Rates														*Percent Per Annum*		
Treasury Bill Rate	60c	....	....	....	....	....	....	....	....	6.5	6.5	6.5	6.5	6.5	6.5	6.5
Deposit Rate	60l	....	....	....	....	....	....	....	....	4.5	4.5	4.5	5.9	7.0	7.0	6.5
Lending Rate	60p	....	....	....	....	....	....	9.0	8.5	9.5	9.5	10.5	10.5	10.5	11.7	11.5
Prices														*Index Numbers (1995=100):*		
Consumer Prices	64	....	....	....	....	25.3	30.0	35.4	42.9	52.2	62.0	66.9	70.9	74.9	76.8	77.2
International Transactions													*Millions of E. Caribbean Dollars*			
Exports	70	10.53	14.51	19.27	26.84	33.82	38.75	45.58	57.80	46.95	51.36	50.09	51.09	49.11	60.23	77.76
Imports, c.i.f.	71	42.81	42.49	37.08	52.63	66.25	87.29	96.45	117.98	135.57	146.71	152.43	154.48	151.10	187.00	218.40

	1987	1988	1989	1990	1991	1992	1993	1994	1995	1996	1997	1998	1999	2000	2001		
																Exchange Rates	
E.Caribbean Dollars per US Dollar: End of Period (ae)																	
	3.8304	3.6334	3.5482	3.8412	3.8622	3.7125	3.7086	3.9416	4.0135	3.8825	3.6430	3.8017	3.7058	3.5179	3.3932	Official Rate	**aa**
	2.7000	2.7000	2.7000	2.7000	2.7000	2.7000	2.7000	2.7000	2.7000	2.7000	2.7000	2.7000	2.7000	2.7000	2.7000	Official Rate	**ae**
Period Averages																	
	100.0	100.0	100.0	100.0	100.0	100.0	100.0	100.0	100.0	100.0	100.0	100.0	100.0	100.0	100.0	Official Rate	**ah x**
	59.4	58.0	61.1	63.4	68.6	74.4	88.4	101.1	100.0	102.2	106.3	107.9	110.3	114.9	118.9	Nominal Effective Exchange Rate	**ne c**
	105.9	102.8	107.5	99.8	99.0	98.1	103.5	103.5	100.0	101.2	103.8	104.9	105.7	109.6	113.8	Real Effective Exchange Rate	**re c**
																Fund Position	
End of Period																	
	6.00	6.00	6.00	6.00	6.00	8.50	8.50	8.50	8.50	8.50	8.50	8.50	11.70	11.70	11.70	Quota	**2f. s**
	—	—	—	—	—	—	—	.02	.02	.04	—	.03	—	—	—	SDRs	**1b. s**
	—	—	—	—	—	—	—	—	—	—	—	—	—	—	—	Reserve Position in the Fund	**1c. s**
	1.47	.91	.35	.01	—	—	—	—	—	—	—	—	—	—	—	Total Fund Cred.&Loans Outstg.	**2tl**
																International Liquidity	
End of Period																	
	22.74	16.92	15.44	17.58	17.47	25.88	26.90	31.23	36.73	35.73	42.67	46.84	50.84	57.66	63.94	Total Reserves minus Gold	**1l. d**
	—	—	—	—	—	—	—	.03	.02	.06	.01	.04	—	—	—	SDRs	**1b. d**
	—	—	—	—	—	—	—	—	—	—	—	—	—	—	—	Reserve Position in the Fund	**1c. d**
	22.74	16.92	15.44	17.58	17.47	25.88	26.90	31.20	36.71	35.67	42.66	46.80	50.84	57.66	63.94	Foreign Exchange	**1d. d**
	14.25	21.33	10.31	18.52	18.05	27.93	35.68	51.88	59.06	61.88	57.07	54.97	72.71	69.81	113.23	Deposit Money Banks: Assets	**7a. d**
	18.12	16.59	23.40	20.57	22.12	29.70	37.26	41.15	38.98	50.55	68.25	69.12	74.01	76.85	99.94	Liabilities	**7b. d**
																Monetary Authorities	
End of Period																	
	61.40	45.69	41.69	47.46	47.18	69.25	72.68	84.20	99.18	96.70	115.48	126.72	137.82	155.84	174.06	Foreign Assets	**11**
	32.19	33.28	36.16	36.52	37.71	35.02	28.34	24.30	21.70	20.60	18.40	18.39	15.85	13.51	9.67	Claims on Central Government	**12a**
	1.90	1.43	3.22	1.15	.85	.64	.48	.27	.09	.01	.02	.03	.02	.04	.01	Claims on Deposit Money Banks	**12e**
	89.86	77.10	79.84	85.09	85.74	104.91	100.79	107.24	116.31	116.76	131.28	139.70	148.04	163.46	181.41	Reserve Money	**14**
	33.07	35.13	31.40	38.05	40.35	46.68	46.56	52.96	53.83	53.18	58.35	64.08	64.75	71.14	70.20	*of which: Currency Outside DMBs*	**14a**
	5.63	3.31	1.24	.04	—	—	—	—	—	—	—	—	—	—	—	Foreign Liabilities	**16c**
	—	—	—	—	—	—	.71	1.54	4.66	.55	2.61	5.44	5.66	5.92	2.33	Central Government Deposits	**16d**
	—	—	—	—	—	—	—	—	—	—	—	—	—	—	—	Other Items (Net)	**17r**
																Deposit Money Banks	
End of Period																	
	53.80	44.15	54.19	45.53	43.15	55.55	53.14	56.10	56.87	59.35	73.43	76.10	92.36	98.26	107.62	Reserves	**20**
	38.49	57.60	27.83	50.00	48.74	75.42	96.33	140.08	159.47	167.09	154.08	148.42	196.32	188.48	305.73	Foreign Assets	**21**
	31.95	38.44	35.62	40.12	43.83	34.62	38.39	42.98	46.44	55.93	74.32	80.49	62.76	84.37	101.89	Claims on Central Government	**22a**
	—	—	—	—	—	—	—	.06	—	—	—	—	2.15	.79	3.51	Claims on Local Government	**22b**
	9.55	10.57	14.49	12.83	11.04	9.38	9.74	6.71	6.12	16.07	20.92	25.88	26.13	46.43	65.79	Claims on Nonfin.Pub.Enterprises	**22c**
	188.60	212.70	272.99	270.74	287.52	315.02	413.64	414.60	437.29	495.26	587.95	684.68	767.87	878.39	886.41	Claims on Private Sector	**22d**
	.42	.30	.32	.36	.32	2.22	4.82	4.24	6.06	10.31	10.09	15.59	23.33	31.50	39.30	Claims on Nonbank Financial Insts	**22g**
	41.24	47.87	56.59	53.04	49.17	63.44	77.51	85.95	91.52	95.26	98.27	114.31	126.28	134.20	142.68	Demand Deposits	**24**
	179.24	216.63	234.26	263.32	283.35	290.62	364.42	409.15	455.19	504.59	564.27	627.50	722.76	846.61	949.71	Time, Savings,& Fgn.Currency Dep.	**25**
	48.93	44.80	63.18	55.54	59.72	80.19	100.60	111.11	105.24	136.50	184.29	186.63	199.83	207.51	269.84	Foreign Liabilities	**26c**
	4.80	10.35	14.89	13.08	6.98	17.03	20.35	24.37	30.55	41.02	42.04	56.74	71.04	71.67	65.49	Central Government Deposits	**26d**
	3.21	1.42	2.86	1.21	.83	.79	.58	.25	.07	.02	.02	2.72	.02	.03	.01	Credit from Monetary Authorities	**26g**
	27.18	28.32	30.94	35.18	43.33	47.02	64.73	68.28	71.07	72.39	79.56	86.15	97.22	109.00	123.55	Capital Accounts	**27a**
	18.20	14.38	2.71	−1.81	−8.78	−6.87	−12.14	−34.35	−41.39	−45.76	−47.65	−42.89	−46.22	−40.78	−41.03	Other Items (Net)	**27r**
																Monetary Survey	
End of Period																	
	45.33	55.18	5.10	41.88	36.19	64.48	68.41	113.17	153.41	127.29	85.28	88.51	134.32	136.81	209.95	Foreign Assets (Net)	**31n**
	257.91	284.96	344.69	347.48	373.44	379.23	473.86	466.97	482.40	556.60	667.03	762.84	821.40	977.40	1,038.75	Domestic Credit	**32**
	59.34	61.38	56.89	63.56	74.56	52.61	45.65	41.36	32.93	34.96	48.07	36.71	1.92	20.29	43.74	Claims on Central Govt. (Net)	**32an**
	—	—	—	—	—	—	—	.06	—	—	—	—	2.15	.79	3.51	Claims on Local Government	**32b**
	9.55	10.57	14.49	12.83	11.04	9.38	9.74	6.71	6.12	16.07	20.92	25.88	26.13	46.43	65.79	Claims on Nonfin.Pub.Enterprises	**32c**
	188.60	212.70	272.99	270.74	287.52	315.02	413.64	414.60	437.29	495.26	587.95	684.68	767.87	878.39	886.41	Claims on Private Sector	**32d**
	.42	.30	.32	.36	.32	2.22	4.82	4.24	6.06	10.31	10.09	15.59	23.33	31.50	39.30	Claims on Nonbank Financial Inst	**32g**
	74.31	83.00	87.99	91.09	89.50	110.12	124.07	139.05	145.60	148.46	156.64	178.38	191.03	205.44	212.94	Money	**34**
	179.24	216.63	234.26	263.32	283.35	290.62	364.42	409.15	455.19	504.59	564.27	627.50	722.76	846.61	949.71	Quasi-Money	**35**
	30.75	31.70	34.24	38.76	46.92	50.47	68.18	71.95	74.80	76.00	82.95	89.68	100.66	112.27	126.71	Capital Accounts	**37a**
	18.95	8.80	−6.70	−3.80	−10.14	−7.49	−14.41	−40.00	−39.78	−45.16	−51.55	−44.21	−58.74	−50.10	−40.66	Other Items (Net)	**37r**
	253.55	299.63	322.25	354.42	372.86	400.74	488.49	548.20	600.78	653.05	720.91	805.88	913.80	1,052.05	1,162.65	Money plus Quasi-Money	**35l**
																Interest Rates	
Percent Per Annum																	
	6.5	6.5	6.5	6.5	6.5	6.5	6.5	6.5	6.5	6.5	6.5	6.5	6.5	6.5	6.5	Treasury Bill Rate	**60c**
	6.1	5.5	5.0	6.5	6.2	5.5	5.0	4.2	4.0	4.1	4.5	4.6	5.2	5.7	5.8	Deposit Rate	**60l**
	11.4	10.5	10.7	10.5	10.6	10.5	10.5	10.5	10.5	10.5	10.5	10.5	10.5	10.5	10.5	Lending Rate	**60p**
																Prices	
Period Averages																	
	†76.6	79.6	84.1	86.4	88.7	92.0	94.6	98.2	100.0	102.0	103.3	104.7	105.0	....	....	Consumer Prices	**64**
																International Transactions	
Millions of E. Caribbean Dollars																	
	85.30	88.60	81.90	75.30	59.30	53.90	55.10	64.30	58.70	54.00	61.50	72.50	....	....	....	Exports	**70**
	240.50	248.90	267.40	286.90	333.80	287.80	319.60	320.60	333.80	411.10	468.20	540.40	....	....	....	Imports, c.i.f.	**71**

Grenada

		1972	1973	1974	1975	1976	1977	1978	1979	1980	1981	1982	1983	1984	1985	1986
Balance of Payments														*Millions of US Dollars:*		
Current Account, n.i.e.	78al d	...	...	...	...	...	1.31	1.05	−1.11	.24	−13.95	−17.71	−15.09	1.80	2.22	−19.09
Goods: Exports f.o.b.	78aa d	...	...	...	...	...	14.26	16.90	21.40	17.40	19.00	18.50	19.30	18.20	22.30	28.96
Goods: Imports f.o.b.	78ab d	...	...	...	...	...	−28.54	−33.35	−42.64	−48.79	−56.07	−59.03	−57.88	−51.12	−65.56	−80.89
Trade Balance	78ac d	...	...	...	...	...	−14.28	−16.45	−21.24	−31.39	−37.07	−40.53	−38.58	−32.92	−43.26	−51.93
Services: Credit	78ad d	...	...	...	...	...	14.60	16.40	19.15	20.60	18.70	18.30	18.60	21.60	30.59	46.19
Services: Debit	78ae d	...	...	...	...	...	−4.35	−6.60	−12.42	−11.07	−13.39	−17.37	−15.82	−18.38	−21.07	−24.92
Balance on Goods & Services	78af d	...	...	...	...	...	−4.03	−6.65	−14.51	−21.86	−31.76	−39.60	−35.80	−29.70	−33.74	−30.66
Income: Credit	78ag d	...	...	...	...	...	.30	.30	.80	1.10	1.30	1.50	1.70	1.40	1.39	1.82
Income: Debit	78ah d	...	...	...	...	...	−.20	−.40	−.60	−3.20	−6.30	−6.50	−6.10	−2.90	−3.10	−7.37
Balance on Gds, Serv. & Inc.	78ai d	...	...	...	...	...	−3.93	−6.75	−14.31	−23.96	−36.76	−44.60	−40.20	−31.20	−35.44	−36.21
Current Transfers, n.i.e.: Credit	78aj d	...	...	...	...	...	5.24	7.80	14.90	26.10	25.11	30.19	29.61	37.20	41.96	17.81
Current Transfers: Debit	78ak d	...	...	...	...	...	—	—	−1.70	−1.90	−2.30	−3.30	−4.50	−4.20	−4.30	−.68
Capital Account, n.i.e.	78bc d	...	...	...	...	...	—	—	—	—	—	—	—	—	—	15.84
Capital Account, n.i.e.: Credit	78ba d	...	...	...	...	...	—	—	—	—	—	—	—	—	—	24.44
Capital Account: Debit	78bb d	...	...	...	...	...	—	—	—	—	—	—	—	—	—	−8.59
Financial Account, n.i.e.	78bj d	...	...	...	...	...	2.34	1.46	1.44	1.63	7.26	17.02	11.99	7.57	5.99	9.44
Direct Investment Abroad	78bd d	...	...	...	...	...	—	—	—	—	—	—	—	—	—	—
Dir. Invest. in Rep. Econ., n.i.e.	78be d	...	...	...	...	...	−.10	1.40	—	—	—	1.90	2.50	2.80	4.11	4.48
Portfolio Investment Assets	78bf d	...	...	...	...	...	—	—	—	—	—	—	—	—	—	—
Equity Securities	78bk d															
Debt Securities	78bl d															
Portfolio Investment Liab., n.i.e.	78bg d															
Equity Securities	78bm d															
Debt Securities	78bn d															
Financial Derivatives Assets	78bw d						...	...	...	...	...	...	...	...	...	...
Financial Derivatives Liabilities	78bx d						...	...	...	...	...	...	...	...	...	...
Other Investment Assets	78bh d	...	...	...	...	...	.27	−.45	−5.40	.49	−1.83	6.22	−.98	−.57	.49	1.19
Monetary Authorities	78bo d	...	...	...	...	...	—	—	—	—	—	—	—	—	—	...
General Government	78bp d	...	...	...	...	...	—	—	—	—	—	—	—	—	—	...
Banks	78bq d	...	...	...	...	...	.27	−.45	−5.40	.49	−1.83	6.22	−.98	−.57	.49	1.19
Other Sectors	78br d	...	...	...	...	...	—	—	—	—	—	—	—	—	—	...
Other Investment Liab., n.i.e.	78bi d	...	...	...	...	...	2.17	.51	6.84	1.14	9.09	8.90	10.47	5.34	1.39	3.78
Monetary Authorities	78bs d						—	—	—	—	—	—	—	—	—	—
General Government	78bt d	...	...	...	...	...	1.49	.87	1.93	1.27	7.58	8.58	11.71	3.30	.03	3.30
Banks	78bu d	...	...	...	...	...	.58	−.37	4.63	−.07	1.47	.06	−2.94	.09	.59	—
Other Sectors	78bv d	...	...	...	...	...	.10	.01	.28	−.06	.03	.26	1.70	1.95	.76	.48
Net Errors and Omissions	78ca d	...	...	...	...	...	−4.02	−1.48	1.41	−.96	2.84	−1.31	2.76	−11.65	−1.99	−4.25
Overall Balance	78cb d	...	...	...	...	...	−.37	1.03	1.74	.91	−3.85	−2.00	−.34	−2.28	6.22	1.95
Reserves and Related Items	79da d	...	...	...	...	...	.37	−1.03	−1.74	−.91	3.85	2.00	.34	2.28	−6.22	−1.95
Reserve Assets	79db d	...	...	...	...	...	.13	−1.79	−2.22	−.69	−1.98	2.90	−1.25	.31	−6.76	.01
Use of Fund Credit and Loans	79dc d	...	...	...	...	...	.24	.76	.47	−.25	5.75	−.91	1.10	−1.03	−2.51	−1.97
Exceptional Financing	79de d	...	...	...	...	...	—	—	—	.03	.08	.01	.49	3.00	3.06	...
Government Finance														*Millions of E. Caribbean Dollars:*		
Deficit (-) or Surplus	80	...	...	−5.25	−5.08	−6.37	−1.66	†−10.60	−7.80	−4.60	...	...	...	...	...	...
Revenue	81	...	...	15.76	18.41	28.18	33.65	†44.80	55.10	59.10	...	...	...	...	...	...
Grants Received	81z	...	...	2.94	2.84	1.63	1.59	†1.60	34.40	29.60	...	...	...	...	...	...
Expenditure	82	...	...	22.79	24.52	34.43	34.77	†52.70	95.40	91.00	...	...	...	...	...	...
Lending Minus Repayments	83	...	...	1.16	1.81	1.75	2.13	†4.30	1.90	2.30	...	...	...	...	...	...
Financing																
Domestic	84a	...	...	3.05	6.22	5.57	1.12	†5.40	3.00	.40	...	...	...	...	...	...
Foreign	85a	...	...	2.20	−1.14	.80	.54	†5.20	4.80	4.20	...	...	...	...	...	...
National Accounts														*Millions of E. Caribbean Dollars*		
Househ.Cons.Expend.,incl.NPISHs	96f	...	41.5	48.7	69.5	75.6	97.0	132.1	156.0	161.1	154.6	195.0	183.9	213.2	264.2	207.4
Government Consumption Expend.	91f	...	17.7	17.3	21.0	30.2	29.2	46.1	50.8	41.7	45.0	47.2	55.9	59.3	68.9	88.2
Gross Fixed Capital Formation	93e	...	15.2	13.6	6.3	13.7	14.8	13.8	31.3	52.7	91.1	107.2	106.8	80.0	97.1	117.1
Exports of Goods and Services	90c	...	36.4	32.5	58.2	67.3	80.5	92.3	109.1	106.9	106.1	103.4	105.3	112.8	149.0	204.9
Imports of Goods and Services (-)	98c	...	42.5	38.1	58.8	72.3	93.4	112.6	145.3	163.6	185.0	213.3	193.8	192.1	237.9	288.1
Gross Domestic Product (GDP)	99b	...	68.3	74.0	96.2	116.1	134.3	172.3	202.6	202.0	216.7	239.4	252.9	274.9	346.2	388.8
Net Primary Income from Abroad	98.n	...	...	...	...	...	...	...	...	...	...	...	...	...	...	...
Gross National Income (GNI)	99a	...	...	...	...	...	...	...	...	...	...	...	...	...	...	...
Net Current Transf.from Abroad	98t	...	...	...	...	...	...	...	...	...	...	...	...	...	...	...
Gross Nat'l Disposable Inc.(GNDI)	99i	...	...	...	...	...	...	...	...	...	...	...	...	...	...	...
Gross Saving	99s	...	...	...	...	...	...	...	...	...	...	...	...	...	...	...
GDP Volume 1980 prices	99b. p	...	...	...	181.7	198.1	209.4	226.4	231.8	232.2	...	...	...	...	...	...
GDP Volume 1984 Prices	99b. p	...	...	...	...	...	...	...	...	†194.5	198.5	209.1	261.7	273.9	296.3	307.9
GDP Volume (1990=100)	99bv p	...	...	...	49.6	54.1	57.2	61.8	63.3	63.4	64.7	68.2	85.3	89.3	96.6	100.4
GDP Deflator (1990=100)	99bi p	...	...	...	32.5	36.0	39.3	46.7	53.6	53.4	56.1	58.8	49.7	51.6	60.0	64.9
														Millions:		
Population	99z	.10	.10	.10	.11	.11	.11	.11	.09	.11	.09	.09	.09	.09	.09	.10

Balance of Payments

Minus Sign Indicates Debit

Item	1987	1988	1989	1990	1991	1992	1993	1994	1995	1996	1997	1998	1999	2000	2001	Code
Current Account, n.i.e.	-29.19	-27.77	-36.32	-46.24	-48.07	-32.39	-43.68	-26.93	-40.84	-55.60	-67.15	-80.43	-46.60	-79.10	....	78ald
Goods: Exports f.o.b.	32.26	33.19	31.11	29.29	25.73	23.53	22.74	25.24	24.57	24.93	32.80	45.95	74.30	84.54	....	78aad
Goods: Imports f.o.b.	-89.07	-92.19	-99.04	-106.26	-113.58	-103.18	-118.13	-119.45	-129.78	-147.41	-154.90	-183.01	-184.57	-220.94	....	78abd
Trade Balance	-56.81	-59.00	-67.93	-76.98	-87.85	-79.65	-95.38	-94.21	-105.21	-122.49	-122.10	-137.06	-110.28	-136.40	....	78acd
Services: Credit	47.52	53.00	54.22	63.81	71.82	76.04	87.68	101.53	99.19	106.69	106.14	119.77	148.49	151.30	....	78add
Services: Debit	-26.02	-27.70	-29.59	-32.54	-36.45	-35.45	-41.19	-41.26	-38.46	-45.77	-56.48	-69.27	-78.46	-83.31	....	78aed
Balance on Goods & Services	-35.31	-33.70	-43.30	-45.71	-52.48	-39.06	-48.89	-33.94	-44.48	-61.57	-72.44	-86.56	-40.25	-68.41	....	78afd
Income: Credit	1.73	2.73	2.43	2.51	2.89	3.41	2.68	3.61	4.91	4.68	4.70	4.13	4.33	5.08	....	78agd
Income: Debit	-8.37	-9.00	-11.96	-14.38	-9.77	-8.74	-11.16	-12.43	-18.36	-20.08	-20.92	-27.19	-29.87	-35.88	....	78ahd
Balance on Gds, Serv. & Inc.	-41.96	-39.98	-52.83	-57.58	-59.37	-44.40	-57.37	-42.76	-57.92	-76.97	-88.66	-109.62	-65.79	-99.21	....	78aid
Current Transfers, n.i.e.: Credit	13.70	13.04	17.39	12.46	13.25	14.26	16.10	19.75	21.58	25.46	25.53	34.19	26.76	30.35	....	78ajd
Current Transfers: Debit	-.94	-.83	-.88	-1.11	-1.96	-2.25	-2.41	-3.92	-4.50	-4.09	-4.01	-5.00	-7.57	-10.25	....	78akd
Capital Account, n.i.e.	10.22	12.93	9.87	22.10	17.51	16.38	16.89	21.67	25.84	31.41	31.78	28.58	31.18	29.63	....	78bcd
Capital Account: Credit	19.33	20.85	10.69	23.36	18.51	17.76	18.27	23.04	27.28	31.41	33.42	30.36	33.10	31.71	....	78bad
Capital Account: Debit	-9.11	-7.93	-.81	-1.26	-1.01	-1.38	-1.38	-1.38	-1.44	—	-1.64	-1.78	-1.92	-2.08	....	78bbd
Financial Account, n.i.e.	21.23	11.43	33.16	18.54	19.60	16.30	17.74	4.06	3.10	26.19	55.08	57.14	33.63	68.69	....	78bjd
Direct Investment Abroad																78bdd
Dir. Invest. in Rep. Econ., n.i.e.	14.72	14.98	10.48	12.87	15.27	22.58	20.25	19.31	19.98	16.96	33.50	48.69	41.55	37.41	....	78bed
Portfolio Investment Assets	—	—	—	—	—	-.16	.20	-.38	-.87	—	-.02	.04	-.36	-.07	....	78bfd
Equity Securities	—	—	—	—	....	....	....	....	....	....	....	....	....	....	....	78bkd
Debt Securities	....	....	....	....	....	....	....	....	....	....	....	....	....	....	....	78bld
Portfolio Investment Liab., n.i.e.	—	.15	—	.02	.05	....	....	....	....	....	—	-.11	.75	19.77	....	78bgd
Equity Securities	—	.15	—	.02	....	....	....	....	....	....	....	....	....	....	....	78bmd
Debt Securities	....	....	....	....	....	....	....	....	....	....	—	-.11	.75	19.77	....	78bnd
Financial Derivatives Assets																78bwd
Financial Derivatives Liabilities																78bxd
Other Investment Assets	-.01	-8.35	17.52	-11.48	-1.66	-12.51	-9.95	-23.59	-11.02	-6.51	-1.09	-1.71	-30.13	-11.07	....	78bhd
Monetary Authorities	....	....	....	....	....	....	....	....	....	....	....	....	....	....	....	78bod
General Government	—	—	—	—	....	....	....	....	....	....	....	....	....	....	....	78bpd
Banks	-.01	-8.35	17.52	-11.48	....	....	....	....	....	....	....	....	....	....	....	78bqd
Other Sectors	....	....	....	....	....	....	....	....	....	....	....	....	....	....	....	78brd
Other Investment Liab., n.i.e.	6.52	4.65	5.16	17.13	5.93	6.38	7.24	8.72	-4.99	15.74	22.69	10.23	21.82	22.66	....	78bid
Monetary Authorities	—	—	—	—	....	....	....	....	....	....	....	....	....	....	....	78bsd
General Government	5.59	6.19	6.56	16.19	....	....	....	....	....	....	....	....	....	....	....	78btd
Banks	....	....	....	....	....	....	....	....	....	....	....	....	....	....	....	78bud
Other Sectors	.93	-1.54	-1.40	.94	....	....	....	....	....	....	....	....	....	....	....	78bvd
Net Errors and Omissions	1.55	-1.72	-7.55	8.12	13.42	7.82	9.49	5.88	17.94	-1.55	-12.78	-1.10	-13.56	-12.61	....	78cad
Overall Balance	3.81	-5.14	-.84	2.53	2.46	8.10	.44	4.68	6.03	.45	6.93	4.18	4.65	6.61	....	78cbd
Reserves and Related Items	-3.81	5.14	.84	-2.53	-2.46	-8.10	-.44	-4.68	-6.03	-.45	-6.93	-4.18	-4.65	-6.61	....	79dad
Reserve Assets	-2.96	5.89	1.56	-2.07	-2.44	-8.10	-.44	-4.68	-6.03	-.45	-6.93	-4.18	-4.65	-6.61	....	79dbd
Use of Fund Credit and Loans	-.85	-.75	-.72	-.46	-.01	—	—	—	—	—	—	—	—	—	....	79dcd
Exceptional Financing																79ded

Government Finance

Year Ending December 31

Item	1987	1988	1989	1990	1991	1992	1993	1994	1995	1996	1997	1998	1999	2000	2001	Code
Deficit (-) or Surplus	....	....	....	....	†-12.23	1.18	-1.42	-7.86	16.79	....	....	....	....	....	....	80
Revenue	....	....	....	....	†165.55	165.59	178.27	194.26	205.00	....	....	....	....	....	....	81
Grants Received	....	....	....	....	†22.77	14.15	16.33	26.50	21.48	....	....	....	....	....	....	81z
Expenditure	....	....	....	....	†200.55	178.56	196.02	228.62	209.69	....	....	....	....	....	....	82
Lending Minus Repayments	....	....	....	....	†—	—	—	—	—	....	....	....	....	....	....	83
Financing Domestic	....	....	....	....	....	....	....	....	....	....	....	....	....	....	....	84a
Financing Foreign	....	....	....	....	....	....	....	....	....	....	....	....	....	....	....	85a

National Accounts

Millions of E. Caribbean Dollars

Item	1987	1988	1989	1990	1991	1992	1993	1994	1995	1996	1997	1998	1999	2000	2001	Code
Househ.Cons.Expend.,incl.NPISHs	309.1	330.4	373.6	370.8	405.1	455.6	472.9	420.2	503.3	551.4	590.5	697.1	544.1	758.6	....	96f
Government Consumption Expend.	92.0	94.1	129.1	128.8	137.1	127.5	123.7	126.6	123.7	130.3	137.5	150.8	147.5	161.4	....	91f
Gross Fixed Capital Formation	141.6	160.5	181.4	210.5	247.1	199.5	210.5	253.8	239.3	280.4	311.2	343.9	408.9	453.8	....	93e
Exports of Goods and Services	215.4	232.7	224.6	252.8	265.5	268.2	297.7	342.3	334.2	355.1	381.7	448.8	636.8	674.0	....	90c
Imports of Goods and Services (-)	315.0	326.8	348.4	383.9	402.6	373.4	429.7	433.9	454.5	521.6	570.7	694.0	716.2	939.2	....	98c
Gross Domestic Product (GDP)	451.5	498.2	575.3	596.9	652.2	677.5	675.1	708.9	746.0	795.6	850.2	946.7	1,021.1	1,108.5	....	99b
Net Primary Income from Abroad	....	....	....	-32.1	-18.6	-14.4	-22.6	-23.8	-36.3	-41.6	-46.8	-64.2	-80.2	-90.9	....	98.n
Gross National Income (GNI)	....	....	....	564.8	633.6	663.1	652.5	685.1	709.7	754.0	803.4	882.5	940.9	1,017.7	....	99a
Net Current Transf.from Abroad	....	....	....	30.5	30.5	32.4	37.0	42.7	46.1	51.2	53.9	78.9	75.6	78.0	....	98t
Gross Nat'l Disposable Inc.(GNDI)	....	....	....	595.3	664.1	695.5	689.5	727.9	755.8	805.2	857.3	961.4	1,016.5	1,095.6	....	99i
Gross Saving	....	....	....	....	112.3	92.9	181.1	128.8	123.5	129.3	113.4	325.0	175.6	....	....	99s
GDP Volume 1980 prices	....	....	....	....	....	....	....	....	....	....	....	....	....	....	....	99b,p
GDP Volume 1984 Prices	262.1	275.9	291.5	306.7	315.7	317.5	....	....	....	....	....	....	....	....	....	99b,p
GDP Volume (1990=100)	85.5	90.0	95.0	100.0	102.9	103.5	....	....	....	....	....	....	....	....	....	99bv,p
GDP Deflator (1990=100)	88.5	92.8	101.4	100.0	106.1	109.6	....	....	....	....	....	....	....	....	....	99bi,p

Midyear Estimates

Item	1987	1988	1989	1990	1991	1992	1993	1994	1995	1996	1997	1998	1999	2000	2001	Code
Population	.10	.09	.09	.09	.09	.09	.09	.09	.09	.10	.09	.09	.09	.10	.10	99z

(See notes in the back of the book.)

Guatemala

		1972	1973	1974	1975	1976	1977	1978	1979	1980	1981	1982	1983	1984	1985	1986
Exchange Rates																*Quetzales per SDR:*
Market Rate..........aa=..............wa	wa	1.0857	1.2064	1.2244	1.1707	1.1618	1.2147	1.3028	1.3173	1.2754	1.1640	1.1031	1.0470	.9802	1.0984	3.0580
																Quetzales per US Dollar:
Market Rate..........ae=..............we	we	1.0000	1.0000	1.0000	1.0000	1.0000	1.0000	1.0000	1.0000	1.0000	1.0000	1.0000	1.0000	1.0000	1.0000	2.5000
Market Rate..........rf=..............wf	wf	1.0000	1.0000	1.0000	1.0000	1.0000	1.0000	1.0000	1.0000	1.0000	1.0000	1.0000	1.0000	1.0000	1.0000	1.8750
Secondary Rate.............................xe	xe	....	....	....	....	....	....	....	....	....	....	....	....	1.47	2.93	1.00
Secondary Rate.............................xf	xf	....	....	....	....	....	....	....	....	....	....	....	....		2.77	1.80
Tertiary Rate...............................yf	yf	....	....	....	....	....	....	....	....	....	....	....	....	....	....	2.85
Fund Position																*Millions of SDRs:*
Quota.................................**2f. s**		36.0	36.0	36.0	36.0	36.0	36.0	51.0	51.0	76.5	76.5	76.5	108.0	108.0	108.0	108.0
SDRs..................................**1b. s**		7.6	11.5	11.5	11.5	11.4	11.5	11.6	18.4	17.7	2.2	—	—	—	—	—
Reserve Position in the Fund.......**1c. s**		9.0	9.0	9.0	9.0	12.0	12.4	12.9	14.1	21.7	8.4	—	7.9	2.0	—	—
of which: Outstg.Fund Borrowing......**2c**											8.4					
Total Fund Cred.&Loans Outstg...**2tl**		—	—	—	—	—	—	—	—	—	95.6	95.6	133.9	153.0	105.2	57.2
International Liquidity										*Millions of US Dollars Unless Otherwise Indicated:*						
Total Reserves minus Gold............**1l. d**		116.2	191.3	181.3	283.8	491.0	668.9	741.5	696.3	444.7	149.7	112.2	210.0	274.4	300.9	362.1
SDRs..................................**1b. d**		8.3	13.8	14.1	13.4	13.3	14.0	15.1	24.2	22.6	2.6	—	.6	—	—	—
Reserve Position in the Fund.......**1c. d**		9.8	10.9	11.0	10.5	13.9	15.0	16.8	18.6	27.7	9.7	—	8.2	2.0	—	—
Foreign Exchange....................**1d. d**		98.2	166.6	156.2	259.8	463.8	639.9	709.6	653.5	394.4	137.4	112.2	201.2	272.4	300.9	362.1
Gold (Million Fine Troy Ounces)....**1ad**		.492	.492	.492	.492	.492	.507	.515	.522	.522	.522	.522	.522	.522	.522	.522
Gold (National Valuation)............**1an d**		18.7	20.8	20.8	20.8	20.8	21.4	21.7	22.1	22.1	22.1	22.1	22.1	22.1	22.1	22.1
Monetary Authorities: Other Liab...**4..d**		22.2	19.2	24.2	50.1	69.8	101.5	111.4	104.6	183.7	296.5	361.7	784.1	1,124.2	1,259.6	437.4
Deposit Money Banks: Assets..........**7a. d**		5.0	7.0	8.5	8.6	14.3	16.9	16.1	27.2	20.1	23.4	46.2	72.3	53.8	76.7	18.5
Liabilities.........**7b. d**		9.2	11.7	9.8	12.7	23.5	26.4	27.5	51.6	53.6	49.3	73.8	137.1	149.0	78.7	37.2
Other Banking Insts.: Assets.........**7e. d**		.3	.3	2.9	.2	.3	1.4	.6	6.9	.3	.7	.6	.2	.4	.4	.1
Liabilities.........**7f. d**		.7	9.8	16.1	8.9	11.6	14.3	12.5	17.9	11.8	15.8	21.6	24.5	30.7	32.9	14.3
Monetary Authorities														*Millions of Quetzales:*		
Foreign Assets.............................**11**		161.6	245.8	230.2	339.3	554.7	740.5	817.4	798.7	604.3	384.9	319.5	372.9	431.4	478.2	608.4
Claims on Central Government........**12a**		70.0	55.5	125.3	102.7	203.0	254.8	291.0	268.8	461.4	860.4	1,362.1	1,619.1	1,791.8	1,931.7	1,528.2
Claims on Local Government..........**12b**		4.6	1.6	3.7	3.1	3.3	3.3	3.4	3.4	3.8	2.7	3.9	8.5	7.7	8.8	7.9
Claims on Nonfin.Pub.Enterprises....**12c**		5.6	5.7	14.1	24.4	9.9	9.0	9.4	13.6	15.3	37.9	35.0	25.6	17.3	12.2	11.4
Claims on Private Sector................**12d**																
Claims on Deposit Money Banks......**12e**		37.7	29.7	38.6	50.5	29.5	27.5	27.7	76.2	121.2	138.1	85.8	146.7	144.3	121.1	133.9
Claims on Other Banking Insts........**12f**		—	—	.1	.1	1.5	2.1	14.7	15.1	27.3	74.0	53.0	77.6	77.3	68.3	55.0
Reserve Money............................**14**		213.6	252.0	291.5	344.1	527.5	595.2	652.4	681.7	680.4	720.1	838.3	773.7	805.6	1,302.0	1,569.6
of which: Currency Outside DMBs...**14a**		114.1	137.3	158.3	175.4	236.6	284.4	324.6	365.4	381.0	405.2	404.6	437.9	460.9	697.8	804.6
Time and Foreign Currency Deposits...**15**																
Bonds...................................**16ab**																
Foreign Liabilities.......................**16c**		5.6	8.9	15.9	13.3	9.6	33.5	32.8	30.7	53.8	152.9	154.3	464.3	730.6	735.1	669.0
Long-Term Foreign Liabilities.........**16cl**		16.6	10.3	8.3	36.8	60.2	68.0	78.6	73.9	129.9	254.9	312.9	459.9	543.6	640.0	599.3
Central Government Deposits...........**16d**		31.1	38.4	62.6	82.8	141.8	264.2	288.9	206.1	171.0	171.7	420.2	443.0	284.7	355.4	568.5
Liabilities to Other Banking Insts.......**16i**																
Capital Accounts.........................**17a**		23.2	24.6	24.7	25.9	46.3	56.1	62.6	76.7	124.2	149.0	138.1	123.9	122.1	125.3	128.8
Other Items (Net).......................**17r**		−10.6	4.1	9.0	17.2	16.5	20.2	48.3	106.7	74.0	49.4	−4.5	−14.4	−16.8	−537.5	−1,190.4
Deposit Money Banks														*Millions of Quetzales:*		
Reserves....................................**20**		95.7	108.4	125.1	160.5	271.6	284.4	278.3	266.7	245.5	265.5	370.7	274.5	365.1	583.0	770.3
Foreign Assets.............................**21**		5.0	7.0	8.5	8.6	14.3	16.9	16.1	27.2	20.1	23.4	46.2	72.3	53.8	76.7	46.2
Claims on Central Government........**22a**		53.6	84.6	53.0	94.5	91.9	99.3	64.9	41.5	55.2	74.6	123.6	56.1	47.8	137.1	295.7
Claims on Local Government..........**22b**		—	—	—	—	—	—	—	—	—	—	—	—	—	—	—
Claims on Nonfin.Pub.Enterprises....**22c**		—	—	—	—	—	—	—	—	—	—	—	—	—	—	—
Claims on Private Sector................**22d**		261.3	296.0	386.2	433.1	502.8	651.1	826.9	998.4	1,222.2	1,374.4	1,476.4	1,670.3	1,867.8	2,037.1	2,242.1
Claims on Other Banking Insts........**22f**		—	—	—	—	—	—	—	—	—	—	—	—	—	—	—
Demand Deposits.........................**24**		95.8	120.4	138.2	168.7	236.7	279.9	291.9	320.4	320.5	325.3	339.7	346.2	381.6	614.5	748.6
Time, Savings,& Fgn.Currency Dep......**25**		262.5	315.5	362.9	454.9	558.0	655.0	759.6	802.3	939.6	1,128.9	1,404.1	1,321.3	1,529.7	1,846.4	2,266.7
Bonds...................................**26ab**		.2	.6	.4	.6	.4										
Foreign Liabilities.......................**26c**		7.9	11.5	9.6	12.5	23.4	26.3	27.5	51.6	53.6	49.3	73.8	137.1	149.0	78.7	93.0
Long-Term Foreign Liabilities.........**26cl**		1.3	.2	.2	.2	.1	.1									
Central Government Deposits...........**26d**		1.6	2.0	3.2	3.1	5.3	3.3	3.3	4.6	7.0	3.3	4.8	9.9	5.5	10.5	11.7
Credit from Monetary Authorities.......**26g**		19.4	15.5	19.6	17.1	7.8	8.2	31.0	80.8	130.1	132.3	92.4	153.2	147.8	121.5	111.8
Liabilities to Other Banking Insts.......**26i**		—	—	—	—	—	—	—	—	—	1.9	—	—	—	—	—
Capital Accounts.........................**27a**		53.1	56.3	64.1	68.2	91.4	114.2	131.2	160.7	155.2	166.7	171.6	189.0	208.6	236.7	270.9
Other Items (Net).......................**27r**		−26.2	−26.0	−25.4	−28.6	−42.5	−35.3	−58.3	−86.6	−63.0	−69.8	−69.5	−83.5	−87.7	−74.4	−148.4
Monetary Survey														*Millions of Quetzales:*		
Foreign Assets (Net).....................**31n**		153.1	232.4	213.2	322.1	536.0	697.6	773.2	743.6	517.0	206.1	137.6	−156.2	−394.4	−258.9	−107.4
Domestic Credit...........................**32**		362.4	403.0	516.6	572.0	665.3	752.1	918.1	1,130.1	1,607.2	2,249.0	2,629.0	3,004.3	3,519.5	3,829.3	3,560.1
Claims on Central Govt. (Net)........**32an**		90.9	99.7	112.5	111.3	147.8	86.6	63.7	99.6	338.6	760.0	1,060.7	1,222.3	1,549.4	1,702.9	1,243.7
Claims on Local Government..........**32b**		4.6	1.6	3.7	3.1	3.3	3.3	3.4	3.4	3.8	2.7	3.9	8.5	7.7	8.8	7.9
Claims on Nonfin.Pub.Enterprises....**32c**		5.6	5.7	14.1	24.4	9.9	9.0	9.4	13.6	15.3	37.9	35.0	25.6	17.3	12.2	11.4
Claims on Private Sector................**32d**		261.3	296.0	386.2	433.1	502.8	651.1	826.9	998.4	1,222.2	1,374.4	1,476.4	1,670.3	1,867.8	2,037.1	2,242.1
Claims on Other Banking Insts........**32f**		—	—	.1	.1	1.5	2.1	14.7	15.1	27.3	74.0	53.0	77.6	77.3	68.3	55.0
Money.......................................**34**		214.4	264.3	305.4	353.6	493.8	594.1	664.0	734.9	752.8	775.9	786.6	833.8	869.4	1,346.5	1,608.4
Quasi-Money...............................**35**		262.5	315.5	362.9	454.9	558.0	655.0	759.6	802.3	939.6	1,128.9	1,404.1	1,321.3	1,529.7	1,846.4	2,266.7
Bonds...................................**36ab**		.2	.6	.4	.6	.4										
Long-Term Foreign Liabilities.........**36cl**		17.9	10.5	8.5	37.0	60.3	68.1	78.6	73.9	129.9	254.9	312.9	459.9	543.6	640.0	599.3
Liabilities to Other Banking Insts.......**36i**		—	—	—	—	—	—	—	—	—	1.9	—	—	—	—	—
Capital Accounts.........................**37a**		76.3	80.9	88.8	94.1	137.7	170.3	193.8	237.4	279.4	315.7	309.7	312.9	330.7	362.0	399.7
Other Items (Net).......................**37r**		−55.8	−36.4	−36.2	−46.1	−48.9	−37.8	−4.7	25.2	22.5	−22.2	−46.7	−79.8	−148.3	−624.5	−1,421.4
Money plus Quasi-Money................**35l**		476.9	579.8	668.3	808.5	1,051.8	1,249.1	1,423.6	1,537.2	1,692.4	1,904.8	2,190.7	2,155.1	2,399.1	3,192.9	3,875.1

1987	1988	1989	1990	1991	1992	1993	1994	1995	1996	1997	1998	1999	2000	2001		
End of Period															**Exchange Rates**	
3.5467	3.6401	4.4681	7.1341	7.2142	7.2522	7.9876	8.2460	8.9810	8.5782	8.3342	9.6425	10.7342	10.0731	10.0544	Market Rate....................aa=	**wa**
End of Period (we) Period Average (wf)																
2.5000	2.7050	3.4000	5.0146	5.0434	5.2743	5.8152	5.6485	6.0418	5.9656	6.1769	6.8482	7.8208	7.7312	8.0005	Market Rate....................ae=	**we**
2.5000	2.6196	2.8161	4.4858	5.0289	5.1706	5.6354	5.7512	5.8103	6.0495	6.0653	6.3947	7.3856	7.7632	7.8586	Market Rate....................rf=	**wf**
1.00	1.00	1.00	1.00	1.00	1.00	1.00	1.00	1.00	1.00	1.00	1.00	1.00	1.00	....	Secondary Rate	**xe**
1.00	1.00	1.00	1.00	1.00	1.00	1.00	1.00	1.00	1.00	1.00	1.00	1.00	1.00	....	Secondary Rate	**xf**
2.70	2.65	....	....	....	....	....	....	....	....	....	....	....	....	....	Tertiary Rate	**yf**
End of Period															**Fund Position**	
108.0	108.0	108.0	108.0	108.0	153.8	153.8	153.8	153.8	153.8	153.8	153.8	210.2	210.2	210.2	Quota	**2f.*s***
1.2	.1	.6	—	—	11.4	11.4	11.4	10.6	10.2	9.4	8.7	8.4	7.5	6.7	SDRs	**1b.*s***
—	—	—	—	—	—	—	—	—	—	—	—	—	—	—	Reserve Position in the Fund	**1c.*s***
—	—	—	—	—	—	—	—	—	—	—	—	—	—	—	*of which:* Outstg.Fund Borrowing	**2c**
41.7	65.4	55.5	46.8	44.8	22.4	—	—	—	—	—	—	—	—	—	Total Fund Cred.&Loans Outstg.	**2tl**
End of Period															**International Liquidity**	
287.8	201.2	306.0	282.0	807.3	765.2	867.8	863.1	702.0	869.7	1,111.1	1,335.1	1,189.2	1,746.4	2,292.2	Total Reserves minus Gold	**1l.*d***
1.7	.2	.7	—	—	15.6	15.7	16.6	15.8	14.6	12.7	12.2	11.5	9.8	8.5	SDRs	**1b.*d***
—	—	—	—	—	—	—	—	—	—	—	—	—	—	—	Reserve Position in the Fund	**1c.*d***
286.1	201.0	305.3	282.0	807.3	749.6	852.1	846.5	686.2	855.1	1,098.4	1,322.9	1,177.7	1,736.6	2,283.7	Foreign Exchange	**1d.*d***
.523	.523	.542	.207	.208	.122	.209	.209	.210	.212	.213	.215	.215	.216	.217	Gold (Million Fine Troy Ounces)	**1ad**
22.1	22.1	22.9	8.8	8.8	5.1	8.8	8.8	8.9	8.9	9.0	9.1	9.1	9.1	9.2	Gold (National Valuation)	**1an*d***
436.7	257.8	209.3	146.4	127.9	115.1	89.6	66.5	55.4	48.1	184.3	152.3	126.4	102.3	90.1	Monetary Authorities: Other Liab.	**4..*d***
30.0	17.9	12.7	4.3	4.6	6.8	8.6	17.7	66.3	81.2	72.6	65.6	84.1	123.6	203.4	Deposit Money Banks: Assets	**7a.*d***
52.5	55.0	48.2	26.6	26.7	48.4	113.1	373.3	266.2	375.4	413.4	500.9	452.5	613.8	656.6	Liabilities	**7b.*d***
.1	.1	.1	.1	.3	—	.1	4.1	4.3	4.5	1.8	12.1	4.3	3.2	6.1	Other Banking Insts.: Assets	**7e.*d***
14.0	16.8	10.7	70.2	76.7	79.4	79.9	100.2	515.8	554.3	592.0	615.8	633.7	654.1	526.0	Liabilities	**7f.*d***
End of Period															**Monetary Authorities**	
510.7	492.4	530.5	567.6	1,123.7	1,149.3	1,307.4	1,292.5	1,157.7	1,341.6	†7,566.2	10,109.3	10,521.1	15,038.3	19,265.5	Foreign Assets	**11**
1,441.2	1,571.4	1,615.3	1,551.1	117.3	452.4	112.5	357.6	187.4	698.0	†78.7	.2	.2	.2	.2	Claims on Central Government	**12a**
7.1	6.2	5.3	4.4	—	—	2.6	2.0	1.3	.6	†.3	—	—	—	—	Claims on Local Government	**12b**
9.4	10.6	8.4	7.4	7.4	7.4	7.4	7.4	7.4	—	†—	—	—	—	—	Claims on Nonfin.Pub.Enterprises	**12c**
—	—	—	—	—	—	—	—	—	—	†29.7	30.0	29.9	30.6	31.5	Claims on Private Sector	**12d**
122.0	156.2	162.4	159.4	154.6	184.6	184.8	61.3	123.3	97.5	†81.9	228.5	652.6	793.8	2,227.2	Claims on Deposit Money Banks	**12e**
51.1	64.0	66.9	74.7	153.8	284.3	245.2	188.3	148.4	97.1	†44.1	12.8	41.7	7.5	7.4	Claims on Other Banking Insts	**12f**
1,578.6	1,932.7	2,301.8	3,079.7	3,946.2	4,263.2	5,255.3	5,494.3	5,689.3	6,418.2	†10746.6	10,324.2	10,608.5	12,653.6	14,702.7	Reserve Money	**14**
931.2	1,069.0	1,329.2	1,897.1	2,089.4	2,712.6	3,097.3	3,714.6	4,018.9	4,179.1	†4,890.2	5,632.5	7,752.8	7,298.2	8,360.7	*of which: Currency Outside DMBs*	**14a**
—	—	—	—	—	1,141.9	2,460.9	3,845.6	4,600.0	6,582.4	†665.2	1,103.4	1,995.1	6,872.7	8,083.6	Time and Foreign Currency Deposits	**15**
—	559.3	526.8	477.7	842.2	970.1	670.7	372.9	76.0	50.3	†212.7	67.5	60.9	58.4	57.1	Bonds	**16ab**
639.9	303.7	230.7	637.3	623.1	506.1	323.5	338.3	352.6	359.5	†13.4	9.2	8.4	4.9	3.5	Foreign Liabilities	**16c**
599.5	631.6	728.8	625.7	539.4	462.1	451.6	277.6	236.2	202.1	†1,125.2	1,034.0	980.2	785.9	717.7	Long-Term Foreign Liabilities	**16cl**
683.7	746.7	694.7	687.6	1,416.3	1,555.4	1,421.5	1,566.3	1,439.6	1,872.3	†5,293.5	7,586.1	6,405.8	5,527.8	9,162.1	Central Government Deposits	**16d**
—	—	—	—	—	—	—	—	—	—	†2.0	—	—	—	—	Liabilities to Other Banking Insts	**16i**
134.2	132.1	131.3	331.7	334.1	333.7	354.1	363.5	384.6	372.1	†330.2	366.4	396.6	3,595.0	3,958.3	Capital Accounts	**17a**
−1,494.4	−2,005.3	−2,225.3	−3,475.1	−6,144.5	−7,154.6	−9,077.7	−10,349.5	−11,152.8	−13,622.1	†−10587.9	−10,110.0	−9,210.0	−13,627.9	−15,153.2	Other Items (Net)	**17r**
End of Period															**Deposit Money Banks**	
756.4	1,048.3	1,118.7	1,450.3	2,306.2	2,346.5	2,815.2	2,175.5	4,019.2	4,794.7	†5,731.3	4,823.0	3,121.7	5,132.4	6,120.3	Reserves	**20**
74.9	48.3	43.1	21.4	23.0	35.7	50.0	100.1	400.8	484.2	†448.4	449.5	657.4	955.4	1,627.4	Foreign Assets	**21**
239.1	65.7	148.5	240.3	1,994.1	1,732.4	1,794.1	2,869.7	1,292.5	1,676.9	†2,870.0	2,389.0	2,277.1	3,361.2	4,654.9	Claims on Central Government	**22a**
—	—	—	—	—	—	—	—	—	—	†81.3	14.4	14.6	38.1	30.4	Claims on Local Government	**22b**
—	—	—	—	—	—	—	—	—	—	†—		63.1	—	—	Claims on Nonfin.Pub.Enterprises	**22c**
2,711.2	3,109.2	3,427.1	4,299.9	5,010.6	6,624.8	7,434.4	9,156.9	13,898.6	15,446.7	†16603.7	21,142.4	24,115.9	26,416.0	30,155.3	Claims on Private Sector	**22d**
—	—	—	—	—	—	—	—	—	—	†2,116.8	2,482.6	2,034.7	2,155.3	2,174.0	Claims on Other Banking Insts	**22f**
807.9	915.6	1,065.6	1,341.5	1,752.8	1,475.4	1,928.0	3,336.2	3,728.4	4,617.5	†6,856.2	7,866.9	7,614.1	11,271.5	12,512.2	Demand Deposits	**24**
2,402.2	2,976.0	3,362.8	4,054.8	7,022.1	8,912.8	8,893.9	7,450.0	8,900.3	8,802.5	†10535.8	12,976.8	13,682.8	16,506.1	20,722.1	Time, Savings,& Fgn.Currency Dep.	**25**
—	—	—	—	—	—	—	—	—	—	†5,139.9	4,480.2	4,266.1	4,286.1	3,917.4	Bonds	**26ab**
131.3	148.9	164.0	133.6	134.8	255.5	657.9	2,108.7	1,608.2	2,239.3	†2,385.2	3,261.9	3,318.0	4,659.8	5,068.2	Foreign Liabilities	**26c**
—	—	—	—	—	—	—	—	—	—	†168.4	168.6	221.0	85.3	184.8	Long-Term Foreign Liabilities	**26cl**
15.7	20.1	24.9	28.6	42.3	63.3	76.7	71.0	171.5	194.4	†410.7	677.9	1,197.0	2,675.4	3,722.9	Central Government Deposits	**26d**
96.7	132.8	147.8	172.8	164.6	187.0	185.9	66.0	123.5	97.6	†7.4	162.7	804.6	755.1	2,195.8	Credit from Monetary Authorities	**26g**
—	—	—	—	—	—	—	—	—	—	†478.9	575.9	578.0	658.0	1,277.6	Liabilities to Other Banking Insts	**26i**
293.5	385.5	440.2	666.6	884.7	1,056.3	1,293.0	1,586.7	1,821.9	2,019.8	†2,315.5	2,775.7	3,810.3	4,464.9	2,834.7	Capital Accounts	**27a**
34.3	−307.4	−467.9	−386.0	−667.4	−1,210.9	−941.7	−316.4	3,257.3	4,431.4	†−446.5	−1,645.7	−3,207.4	−7,303.8	−7,673.4	Other Items (Net)	**27r**
End of Period															**Monetary Survey**	
−185.6	88.1	178.9	−181.9	388.8	423.4	376.0	−1,054.4	−402.3	−773.0	†5,616.0	7,287.7	7,852.1	11,329.0	15,821.2	Foreign Assets (Net)	**31n**
3,759.7	4,060.3	4,551.9	5,461.6	5,824.6	7,482.6	8,098.0	10,944.6	13,924.5	15,852.6	†16120.4	17,807.4	20,974.4	23,805.7	24,168.7	Domestic Credit	**32**
980.9	870.3	1,044.2	1,075.2	652.8	566.1	408.4	1,590.0	−131.2	308.2	†−2755.5	−5,874.8	−5,325.5	−4,841.8	−8,229.9	Claims on Central Govt. (Net)	**32an**
7.1	6.2	5.3	4.4	—	—	2.6	2.0	1.3	.6	†81.6	14.4	14.6	38.1	30.4	Claims on Local Government	**32b**
9.4	10.6	8.4	7.4	7.4	7.4	7.4	7.4	7.4	—	†—	—	63.1	—	—	Claims on Nonfin.Pub.Enterprises	**32c**
2,711.2	3,109.2	3,427.1	4,299.9	5,010.6	6,624.8	7,434.4	9,156.9	13,898.6	15,446.7	†16633.4	21,172.4	24,145.8	26,446.6	30,186.8	Claims on Private Sector	**32d**
51.1	64.0	66.9	74.7	153.8	284.3	245.2	188.3	148.4	97.1	†2,160.9	2,495.4	2,076.4	2,162.8	2,181.4	Claims on Other Banking Insts	**32f**
1,765.6	2,019.0	2,437.8	3,241.5	3,843.4	4,193.2	5,048.1	7,073.6	7,771.8	8,822.4	†11997.5	13,613.5	15,467.6	18,832.2	21,059.0	Money	**34**
2,402.2	2,976.0	3,362.8	4,054.8	7,022.1	10,054.7	11,354.8	11,295.6	13,500.3	15,384.9	†11201.0	14,080.2	15,677.9	23,378.8	28,805.7	Quasi-Money	**35**
—	559.3	526.8	477.7	842.2	970.1	670.7	372.9	76.0	50.3	†5,352.6	4,547.7	4,327.0	4,344.5	3,974.5	Bonds	**36ab**
599.5	631.6	728.8	625.7	539.4	462.1	451.6	277.6	236.2	202.1	†1,293.6	1,202.6	1,201.2	871.2	902.5	Long-Term Foreign Liabilities	**36cl**
—	—	—	—	—	—	—	—	—	—	†480.9	575.9	578.0	658.0	1,277.6	Liabilities to Other Banking Insts	**36i**
427.7	517.6	571.5	998.3	1,218.8	1,390.0	1,647.1	1,950.2	2,206.5	2,391.9	†2,645.7	3,142.1	4,206.9	8,059.9	6,793.0	Capital Accounts	**37a**
−1,620.9	−2,555.1	−2,896.9	−4,118.3	−7,252.5	−9,164.2	−10,698.3	−11,079.8	−10,268.6	−11,772.0	†−11234.9	−12,066.9	−12,632.1	−21,009.9	−22,822.4	Other Items (Net)	**37r**
4,167.8	4,995.0	5,800.6	7,296.3	10,865.5	14,247.9	16,402.9	18,369.2	21,272.1	24,207.3	†23198.5	27,693.7	31,145.5	42,211.0	49,864.7	Money plus Quasi-Money	**35l**

		1972	1973	1974	1975	1976	1977	1978	1979	1980	1981	1982	1983	1984	1985	1986
Other Banking Institutions																*Millions of Quetzales:*
Reserves	40	4.9	7.3	9.9	10.7	21.9	31.2	49.1	50.7	53.0	47.2	44.5	51.9	29.9	37.1	58.5
Foreign Assets	41	.3	.3	2.9	.2	.3	1.4	.6	6.9	.3	.7	.6	.2	.2	.4	.2
Claims on Central Government	42a	2.7	5.8	6.2	2.6	10.0	13.8	13.7	4.5	6.2	7.5	1.4	5.2	1.6	14.1	31.8
Claims on Nonfin.Pub.Enterprises	42c	....	....	....	....	....	....	....	....	....	....	....	....	....	....	....
Claims on Private Sector	42d	10.8	9.9	14.0	23.7	32.7	40.5	41.0	45.0	56.2	60.3	60.4	69.2	68.6	97.5	108.5
Claims on Deposit Money Banks	42e	....	....	....	....	....	....	....	....	....	....	....	....	....	....	....
Time, Savings,& Fgn.Currency Dep.	45	....	....	....	....	....	....	....	....	....	....	....	....	....	....	....
Bonds	46ab												9.8			
Foreign Liabilities	46c	.2	9.3	15.7	8.5	11.2	14.3	.4	6.4	.9	.4	.3	.4	—	—	.1
Long-Term Foreign Liabilities	46cl	.5	.5	.4	.4	.4	—	12.1	11.5	10.9	15.4	21.3	24.1	30.7	32.2	35.6
Credit from Monetary Authorities	46g	9.8	5.5	11.8	28.5	10.7	8.4	6.0	3.6	3.0	14.1	8.6	6.8	.6	.5	.5
Credit from Deposit Money Banks	46h	.1						1.0								
Capital Accounts	47a	5.6	11.9	18.1	28.6	32.9	39.4	39.5	37.8	40.2	36.4	32.4	37.5	30.5	47.4	51.6
Other Items (Net)	47r	2.5	–3.9	–13.0	–28.8	9.7	24.8	45.4	47.8	60.7	49.4	44.3	47.9	38.5	68.3	111.2
Banking Survey																*Millions of Quetzales:*
Foreign Assets (Net)	51n	134.2	200.5	174.3	286.4	492.9	648.1	733.0	700.7	442.3	127.3	72.5	–221.8	–459.6	–334.6	–223.9
Domestic Credit	52	374.0	417.2	534.6	595.1	704.4	803.4	957.1	1,161.7	1,640.6	2,243.7	2,665.4	3,034.5	3,538.4	3,897.7	3,653.2
Claims on Central Govt. (Net)	52an	91.7	104.0	116.5	110.7	154.2	98.3	75.5	100.7	343.1	755.1	1,050.3	1,221.6	1,537.7	1,702.8	1,244.0
Claims on Local Government	52b	4.6	1.6	3.7	3.1	3.3	3.3	3.4	3.4	3.8	2.7	3.9	8.5	7.7	8.8	7.9
Claims on Nonfin.Pub.Enterprises	52c	5.6	5.7	14.1	24.4	9.9	9.0	9.4	13.6	15.3	37.9	35.0	25.6	17.3	12.2	11.4
Claims on Private Sector	52d	272.1	305.9	400.3	456.9	537.0	692.8	868.8	1,044.0	1,278.4	1,448.0	1,576.2	1,778.8	1,975.7	2,173.9	2,389.9
Liquid Liabilities	55l	483.0	591.3	674.4	827.0	1,081.9	1,284.6	1,461.0	1,568.0	1,734.4	1,948.3	2,241.8	2,211.6	2,466.0	3,276.4	3,955.8
Bonds	56ab	.2	.6	.4	.6	.4							9.8			
Long-Term Foreign Liabilities	56cl	18.4	11.0	8.9	37.4	60.7	68.1	90.7	85.4	140.8	270.3	334.2	484.0	574.3	672.2	634.9
Capital Accounts	57a	81.9	92.8	106.9	122.7	170.6	209.7	233.3	275.2	319.6	352.1	342.1	350.4	361.2	409.4	451.3
Other Items (Net)	57r	–75.3	–78.0	–81.7	–106.2	–116.3	–110.9	–94.9	–66.2	–111.9	–199.7	–180.2	–243.1	–322.7	–794.9	–1,612.7
Interest Rates																*Percent Per Annum*
Discount Rate (End of Period)	60	4.0	4.0	5.0	5.0	5.0	7.0	5.0	9.0	8.0	12.0	9.0	9.0	9.0	9.0	9.0
Money Market Rate	60b	....	....	....	....	....	....	....	....	....	....	....	....	....	....	....
Savings Rate	60k	....	....	....	....	....	....	....	....	....	....	....	....	....	....	....
Deposit Rate	60l	....	....	....	....	....	....	9.0	9.0	9.0	10.0	12.0	9.0	9.0	9.0	10.2
Lending Rate	60p	....	....	....	....	....	....	11.0	11.0	11.0	12.0	14.5	12.0	12.0	12.0	13.2
Prices and Labor																*Index Numbers (1995=100):*
Consumer Prices	64	5.3	6.0	7.0	†7.9	†8.8	9.9	10.7	11.9	13.2	14.7	14.8	15.4	16.0	18.9	25.9
																Number in Thousands:
Labor Force	67d	....	....	....	....	....	....	....	....	....	....	....	....	....	....	....
Employment	67e	....	....	....	....	....	....	....	....	....	....	....	....	....	632	660
Unemployment	67c	....	....	....	....	....	....	....	....	....	....	....	....	....	3	3
International Transactions																*Millions of US Dollars*
Exports	70..d	327.5	436.2	572.1	623.5	760.4	1,160.2	1,089.5	1,241.4	1,519.8	1,226.1	1,119.8	1,158.8	1,128.5	1,057.0	1,043.8
Imports, c.i.f.	71..d	324.0	431.0	700.5	732.7	838.9	1,052.5	1,285.7	1,503.9	1,598.2	1,688.3	1,388.0	1,126.1	1,278.5	1,174.8	958.5
Imports, f.o.b.	71.vd	289.5	389.0	624.1	669.8	766.8	926.5	1,178.9	1,395.4	1,472.6	1,539.9	1,284.2	1,054.6	1,180.3	1,076.7	875.6
Balance of Payments																*Millions of US Dollars:*
Current Account, n.i.e.	78ald	....	....	....	....	....	–35.3	–270.5	–205.6	–163.3	–572.7	–399.1	–223.9	–377.4	–246.3	–17.6
Goods: Exports f.o.b.	78aad	....	....	....	....	....	1,160.2	1,092.4	1,221.4	1,519.8	1,291.3	1,170.4	1,091.7	1,132.2	1,059.7	1,043.8
Goods: Imports f.o.b.	78abd	....	....	....	....	....	–1,087.0	–1,283.8	–1,401.7	–1,472.6	–1,540.0	–1,284.3	–1,056.0	–1,182.2	–1,076.7	–875.7
Trade Balance	78acd	....	....	....	....	....	73.2	–191.4	–180.3	47.2	–248.7	–113.9	35.7	–50.0	–17.0	168.1
Services: Credit	78add	....	....	....	....	....	161.5	183.8	228.5	211.2	155.1	107.6	80.3	96.0	101.1	123.7
Services: Debit	78aed	....	....	....	....	....	–339.5	–361.0	–383.1	–487.4	–484.3	–341.9	–257.8	–245.5	–180.0	–170.1
Balance on Goods & Services	78afd	....	....	....	....	....	–104.8	–368.6	–334.9	–229.0	–577.9	–348.2	–141.8	–199.5	–95.9	121.7
Income: Credit	78agd	....	....	....	....	....	47.9	72.9	102.1	103.0	79.5	34.2	33.0	33.0	30.5	35.7
Income: Debit	78ahd	....	....	....	....	....	–74.2	–90.4	–99.4	–147.1	–165.2	–147.8	–145.7	–239.6	–200.6	–250.1
Balance on Gds, Serv. & Inc.	78aid	....	....	....	....	....	–131.1	–386.1	–332.2	–273.1	–663.6	–461.8	–254.5	–406.1	–266.0	–92.7
Current Transfers, n.i.e.: Credit	78ajd	....	....	....	....	....	116.4	139.4	149.5	125.3	96.9	66.1	34.2	31.6	21.0	76.2
Current Transfers: Debit	78akd	....	....	....	....	....	–20.6	–23.8	–22.9	–15.5	–6.0	–3.4	–3.6	–2.9	–1.3	–1.1
Capital Account, n.i.e.	78bcd	....	....	....	....	....	—	—	—	—	—	—	—	—	—	—
Capital Account, n.i.e.: Credit	78bad	....	....	....	....	....	—	—	—	—	—	—	—	—	—	—
Capital Account: Debit	78bbd	....	....	....	....	....	—	—	—	—	—	—	—	—	—	—
Financial Account, n.i.e.	78bjd	....	....	....	....	....	222.4	377.2	205.5	–143.9	110.6	11.2	187.8	–115.4	–124.3	–329.0
Direct Investment Abroad	78bdd	....	....	....	....	....										
Dir. Invest. in Rep. Econ., n.i.e.	78bed	....	....	....	....	....	97.5	127.2	117.0	110.7	127.1	77.1	45.0	38.0	61.8	68.8
Portfolio Investment Assets	78bfd	....	....	....	....	....	.5	2.3	8.0	4.2	–.4	—	–.1	.3	–1.1	–.2
Equity Securities	78bkd	....	....	....	....	....	.5	2.3	8.0	4.2	–.4	—	–.1	.3	–1.1	–.2
Debt Securities	78bld	....	....	....	....	....	—	—	—	—	—	—	—	—	—	—
Portfolio Investment Liab., n.i.e.	78bgd	....	....	....	....	....	4.8	9.4	–2.7	–.3	.7	.5	—	–9.9	–26.5	–11.4
Equity Securities	78bmd	....	....	....	....	....	–1.0	1.4	–2.7	–.3	.7	.5	—	—	—	–1.2
Debt Securities	78bnd	....	....	....	....	....	5.8	8.0	—	—	—	—	—	–9.9	–26.5	–10.2
Financial Derivatives Assets	78bwd	....	....	....	....	....	....	....	....	....	....	....	....	....	....	....
Financial Derivatives Liabilities	78bxd	....	....	....	....	....	....	....	....	....	....	....	....	....	....	....
Other Investment Assets	78bhd	....	....	....	....	....	14.6	21.3	–217.2	–311.3	–149.1	–10.4	—	4.7	—	....
Monetary Authorities	78bod	....	....	....	....	....	—	—	—	—	—	—	—	—	—	....
General Government	78bpd	....	....	....	....	....	—	—	—	—	....	—	–1.3	—	—	....
Banks	78bqd	....	....	....	....	....	—	—	—	—	—	—	—	3.2	—	....
Other Sectors	78brd	....	....	....	....	....	14.6	21.3	–217.2	–311.3	–149.1	–9.1	—	1.5	—	....
Other Investment Liab., n.i.e.	78bid	....	....	....	....	....	105.0	217.0	300.4	52.8	132.3	–56.0	142.9	–148.5	–158.5	–386.2
Monetary Authorities	78bsd	....	....	....	....	....	–1.9	6.6	.1	17.3	2.1	24.5	–25.8	–172.1	–321.5	–450.3
General Government	78btd	....	....	....	....	....	49.0	83.0	95.1	80.5	96.6	84.8	92.8	41.9	44.9	–18.6
Banks	78bud	....	....	....	....	....	3.3	1.2	24.1	2.3	–6.9	13.6	71.0	9.1	–64.0	13.0
Other Sectors	78bvd	....	....	....	....	....	54.6	126.2	181.1	–47.3	40.5	–178.9	4.9	–27.4	182.1	69.7
Net Errors and Omissions	78cad	....	....	....	....	....	–26.5	–58.6	–44.4	–18.1	4.3	–18.0	–37.1	15.5	43.6	67.3
Overall Balance	78cbd	....	....	....	....	....	160.6	48.1	–44.5	–325.3	–457.8	–405.9	–73.2	–477.3	–327.0	–279.3
Reserves and Related Items	79dad	....	....	....	....	....	–160.6	–48.1	44.5	325.3	457.8	405.9	73.2	477.3	327.0	279.3
Reserve Assets	79dbd	....	....	....	....	....	–181.7	–68.3	25.7	257.9	189.8	38.4	–91.1	–30.9	–62.6	–56.2
Use of Fund Credit and Loans	79dcd	....	....	....	....	....	—	—	—	—	111.5	—	40.1	20.2	–48.6	–56.7
Exceptional Financing	79ded	....	....	....	....	....	21.1	20.2	18.8	67.4	156.5	367.5	124.2	487.9	438.2	392.2

1987	1988	1989	1990	1991	1992	1993	1994	1995	1996	1997	1998	1999	2000	2001	
End of Period															**Other Banking Institutions**
31.1	40.1	49.2	†11.7	51.4	51.7	66.1	31.5	48.3	69.6	†14.9	120.8	45.8	30.2	50.6	Reserves ... **40**
.2	.3	.3	†.5	1.4	.2	.4	23.4	26.2	26.6	†10.9	83.2	33.9	24.7	48.6	Foreign Assets ... **41**
22.7	11.1	48.1	†8.4	109.0	36.0	36.2	48.4	42.6	111.5	†77.0	120.0	88.7	155.6	220.0	Claims on Central Government ... **42a**
....	....	....	....	....	....	....	....	....	....	13.2	.2	.2	.2	.2	Claims on Nonfin.Pub.Enterprises ... **42c**
214.3	236.0	255.7	†565.5	641.3	1,188.9	1,489.9	2,055.3	2,512.4	2,655.5	†3,388.5	4,310.1	3,859.8	3,181.8	2,813.0	Claims on Private Sector ... **42d**
....	....	....	137.6	279.4	186.2	331.7	309.3	458.5	443.5	†555.7	550.1	453.8	540.5	567.2	Claims on Deposit Money Banks ... **42e**
....	....	....	†—	—	—	—	—	—	—	†3.8	201.4	4.5	3.3	5.9	Time, Savings,& Fgn.Currency Dep. ... **45**
—	—	—	†200.2	463.6	942.2	1,326.4	1,710.5	1,176.0	1,378.7	†2,298.6	2,692.3	2,192.6	2,314.7	2,171.6	Bonds ... **46ab**
.9	12.1	5.8	†2.0	8.4	9.0	26.4	99.7	146.1	157.7	†—	—	—	—	—	Foreign Liabilities ... **46c**
34.0	33.4	30.6	†349.9	378.6	409.9	438.0	466.4	2,970.0	3,149.1	†3,656.5	4,216.9	4,956.2	5,057.0	4,208.6	Long-Term Foreign Liabilities ... **46cl**
26.1	28.8	26.6	†94.1	170.4	295.6	259.3	195.4	144.2	102.3	†—	—	—	—	—	Credit from Monetary Authorities ... **46g**
—	—	—	†293.1	363.1	431.2	523.5	877.6	1,637.1	1,689.4	†1,584.0	1,925.9	2,110.8	1,629.1	1,436.3	Credit from Deposit Money Banks ... **46h**
55.7	58.8	65.2	†-73.3	-107.2	-107.0	-142.8	-107.4	-2,559.7	-2,667.4	†-2849.0	-3,329.4	-4,019.0	-4,242.2	-3,414.7	Capital Accounts ... **47a**
151.6	154.4	225.1	†-142.3	-194.4	-517.9	-506.5	-774.3	-425.7	-503.1	†-633.7	-522.7	-762.9	-828.9	-708.1	Other Items (Net) ... **47r**
End of Period															**Banking Survey**
-305.9	-52.9	44.2	†-183.4	381.8	414.6	350.0	-1,130.7	-522.2	-904.1	†5,626.9	7,370.9	7,886.0	11,353.7	15,869.8	Foreign Assets (Net) ... **51n**
3,973.9	4,273.1	4,816.8	†5,960.8	6,421.1	8,423.2	9,378.9	12,860.0	16,331.1	18,522.5	†17438.2	19,743.0	22,853.3	24,980.5	25,020.5	Domestic Credit ... **52**
992.6	871.8	1,081.0	†1,083.6	761.8	602.1	444.6	1,638.4	-88.6	419.7	†-2678.5	-5,754.8	-5,236.8	-4,686.2	-8,009.9	Claims on Central Govt. (Net) ... **52an**
7.1	6.2	5.3	4.4	—	—	2.6	2.0	1.3	.6	†81.6	15.1	21.2	38.1	30.4	Claims on Local Government ... **52b**
9.4	10.6	8.4	7.4	7.4	7.4	7.4	7.4	7.4	—	†13.2	.2	63.3	.2	.2	Claims on Nonfin.Pub.Enterprises ... **52c**
2,964.8	3,384.5	3,722.1	†4,865.4	5,651.9	7,813.7	8,924.3	11,212.2	16,411.0	18,102.2	†20021.9	25,482.5	28,005.6	29,628.4	32,999.8	Claims on Private Sector ... **52d**
4,285.3	5,130.6	5,968.8	†7,284.6	10,814.1	14,196.2	16,336.8	18,337.7	21,223.8	24,137.7	†23186.8	27,912.3	31,097.0	42,176.7	49,815.0	Liquid Liabilities ... **55l**
—	559.3	526.8	†677.9	1,305.8	1,912.3	1,997.1	2,083.4	1,252.0	1,429.0	†7,651.2	7,240.0	6,519.6	6,659.2	6,146.1	Bonds ... **56ab**
633.5	665.0	759.4	†975.6	918.0	872.0	889.6	744.0	3,206.2	3,351.2	†4,950.1	5,419.5	6,157.4	5,928.2	5,111.1	Long-Term Foreign Liabilities ... **56cl**
483.4	576.4	636.7	†925.0	1,111.6	1,283.0	1,504.3	1,842.8	-353.2	-275.5	†-203.3	-187.3	187.9	3,817.7	3,378.3	Capital Accounts ... **57a**
-1,734.2	-2,711.1	-3,030.7	†-4085.7	-7,346.6	-9,425.8	-10,998.9	-11,278.7	-9,519.9	-11,024.0	†-12519.7	-13,270.6	-13,222.6	-22,247.6	-23,560.2	Other Items (Net) ... **57r**
Percent Per Annum															**Interest Rates**
9.0	9.0	13.0	18.5	16.5	....	....	....	....	....	....	....	....	....	....	Discount Rate *(End of Period)* ... **60**
....	....	....	....	....	....	....	....	....	....	7.8	6.6	9.2	9.3	10.6	Money Market Rate ... **60b**
....	....	....	....	....	....	....	....	....	....	5.1	4.5	5.2	5.4	4.5	Savings Rate ... **60k**
11.0	12.2	13.0	18.2	24.4	10.4	12.6	9.7	7.9	7.7	†5.8	5.4	8.0	10.2	8.8	Deposit Rate ... **60l**
14.0	15.2	16.0	23.3	34.1	19.5	24.7	22.9	21.2	22.7	†18.6	16.6	19.5	20.9	19.0	Lending Rate ... **60p**
Period Averages															**Prices and Labor**
29.1	32.3	36.0	50.8	67.6	74.4	83.2	92.2	100.0	111.1	121.3	129.8	136.1	†144.2	155.2	Consumer Prices ... **64**
Period Averages															
....	....	2,688	....	....	....	....	2,326	....	....	....	....	3,982	4,208	....	Labor Force ... **67d**
679	780	788	786	787	796	823	830	856	831	....	....	....	....	....	Employment ... **67e**
2	2	2	2	2	2	1	1	1	....	....	....	....	....	....	Unemployment ... **67c**
Millions of US Dollars															**International Transactions**
987.3	1,021.7	1,108.0	1,163.0	1,202.2	1,295.3	1,340.4	1,521.5	2,155.5	2,030.7	2,344.1	2,581.6	2,397.5	2,695.6	2,466.0	Exports ... **70..d**
1,447.2	1,557.0	1,653.8	1,648.8	1,851.3	2,531.5	2,599.3	2,781.4	3,292.5	3,146.1	3,851.9	4,651.1	4,381.7	4,790.9	5,606.8	Imports, c.i.f. ... **71..d**
1,333.2	1,413.2	1,497.2	1,428.0	1,672.5	2,330.7	2,384.0	2,425.7	3,032.5	2,880.3	3,542.8	4,164.5	4,010.5	4,423.3	5,234.2	Imports, f.o.b. ... **71.vd**
Minus Sign Indicates Debit															Balance of Payments
-442.5	-414.0	-367.1	-232.9	-183.7	-705.9	-701.7	-625.3	-572.0	-451.5	-633.5	-1,039.1	-1,025.9	-1,049.5	....	Current Account, n.i.e. ... **78ald**
977.9	1,073.3	1,126.1	1,211.4	1,230.0	1,283.7	1,363.2	1,550.1	2,157.5	2,236.9	2,602.9	2,846.9	2,780.6	3,082.0	....	Goods: Exports f.o.b. ... **78aad**
-1,333.2	-1,413.2	-1,484.4	-1,428.0	-1,673.0	-2,327.8	-2,384.0	-2,546.6	-3,032.6	-2,880.3	-3,542.7	-4,255.7	-4,225.7	-4,742.0	....	Goods: Imports f.o.b. ... **78abd**
-355.3	-339.9	-358.3	-216.6	-443.0	-1,044.1	-1,020.8	-996.5	-875.1	-643.4	-939.8	-1,408.8	-1,445.1	-1,660.0	....	*Trade Balance* ... **78acd**
158.3	195.8	297.7	356.1	458.8	614.0	660.4	697.5	665.9	559.0	588.8	639.9	699.5	810.4	....	Services: Credit ... **78add**
-259.5	-317.9	-376.9	-383.7	-356.4	-525.3	-586.1	-644.9	-694.9	-659.7	-650.5	-791.8	-790.7	-842.0	....	Services: Debit ... **78aed**
-456.5	-462.0	-437.5	-244.2	-340.6	-955.4	-946.5	-943.9	-904.1	-744.1	-1,001.5	-1,560.7	-1,536.3	-1,691.6	....	*Balance on Goods & Services* ... **78afd**
31.1	31.6	31.0	20.9	63.9	69.1	61.1	63.6	46.6	40.2	72.4	91.4	76.2	181.6	....	Income: Credit ... **78agd**
-210.4	-207.9	-210.4	-216.6	-166.7	-210.1	-179.5	-193.6	-205.7	-270.1	-311.1	-275.1	-280.7	-407.5	....	Income: Debit ... **78ahd**
-635.8	-638.3	-616.9	-439.9	-443.4	-1,096.4	-1,064.9	-1,073.9	-1,063.2	-974.0	-1,240.2	-1,744.4	-1,740.8	-1,917.6	....	*Balance on Gds, Serv. & Inc.* ... **78aid**
195.9	227.7	255.1	217.6	276.7	406.2	371.4	456.4	508.2	537.1	628.8	742.9	754.4	911.0	....	Current Transfers, n.i.e.: Credit ... **78ajd**
-2.6	-3.4	-5.3	-10.6	-17.0	-15.7	-8.2	-7.8	-17.0	-14.6	-22.1	-37.6	-39.5	-42.9	....	Current Transfers: Debit ... **78akd**
—	—	—	—	—	—	—	—	61.6	65.0	85.0	71.0	68.4	86.6	....	Capital Account, n.i.e. ... **78bcd**
—	—	—	—	—	—	—	—	61.6	65.0	85.0	71.0	68.4	86.6	....	Capital Account, n.i.e.: Credit ... **78bad**
—	—	—	—	—	—	—	—	....	....	....	....	....	....	....	Capital Account: Debit ... **78bbd**
187.7	78.0	228.3	-46.1	731.8	610.5	816.2	655.2	494.8	672.3	737.4	1,136.7	637.5	1,869.0	....	Financial Account, n.i.e. ... **78bjd**
—	—	—	—	—	—	—	—	....	....	....	....	....	....	....	Direct Investment Abroad ... **78bdd**
150.2	329.7	76.2	47.7	90.7	94.1	142.5	65.2	75.2	76.9	84.4	672.8	154.6	230.1	....	Dir. Invest. in Rep. Econ., n.i.e. ... **78bed**
—	—	—	-1.8	-.2	1.8	112.4	-9.8	-22.2	-11.5	-18.1	-11.6	-26.0	-36.3	....	Portfolio Investment Assets ... **78bfd**
—	—	—	—	—	—	—	—	....	....	....	....	....	....	....	Equity Securities ... **78bkd**
—	—	—	-1.8	-.2	1.8	112.4	-9.8	-22.2	-11.5	-18.1	-11.6	-26.0	-36.3	....	Debt Securities ... **78bld**
-16.0	-372.2	-63.9	-19.5	71.3	9.6	-27.0	7.1	5.9	-4.5	249.7	65.8	136.5	78.9	....	Portfolio Investment Liab., n.i.e. ... **78bgd**
—	—	—	—	—	—	—	—	....	....	....	....	....	....	....	Equity Securities ... **78bmd**
-16.0	-372.2	-63.9	-19.5	71.3	9.6	-27.0	7.1	5.9	-4.5	249.7	65.8	136.5	78.9	....	Debt Securities ... **78bnd**
....	....	....	....	....	....	....	—	....	....	....	....	....	....	....	Financial Derivatives Assets ... **78bwd**
....	....	....	....	....	....	....	—	....	....	....	....	....	....	....	Financial Derivatives Liabilities ... **78bxd**
—	29.4	98.7	-78.0	68.1	57.2	-3.0	116.8	125.1	199.2	221.2	241.7	199.9	132.6	....	Other Investment Assets ... **78bhd**
....	....	....	....	....	....	....	—	....	....	....	....	....	....	....	Monetary Authorities ... **78bod**
—	29.4	98.7	-90.7	—	—	-45.9	-49.2	....	....	....	....	....	....	....	General Government ... **78bpd**
—	—	—	—	—	—	—	—	....	....	....	....	....	....	....	Banks ... **78bqd**
—	—	—	12.7	68.1	57.2	42.9	166.0	125.1	199.2	221.2	241.7	199.9	132.6	....	Other Sectors ... **78brd**
53.5	91.1	117.3	5.5	501.9	447.8	591.3	475.9	310.8	412.2	200.2	168.0	172.5	1,463.7	....	Other Investment Liab., n.i.e. ... **78bid**
-246.3	-87.8	-93.9	-102.5	-66.1	.6	-44.1	-63.9	-78.3	-56.3	-108.6	-54.2	-25.6	-24.0	....	Monetary Authorities ... **78bsd**
-17.0	31.6	60.6	3.6	-25.8	-16.3	-51.3	132.7	11.8	91.1	89.5	252.4	295.9	92.7	....	General Government ... **78btd**
38.7	16.9	-14.3	-17.0	-3.9	14.4	—	—	7.3	19.4	-4.6	3.2	23.0	-17.4	....	Banks ... **78bud**
278.1	130.4	164.9	121.4	597.7	449.1	686.7	407.1	370.0	358.0	223.9	-33.4	-120.8	1,412.4	....	Other Sectors ... **78bvd**
-72.7	-2.4	54.7	36.1	83.3	81.8	85.2	-23.6	-136.2	-71.7	40.7	66.8	195.0	-263.5	....	Net Errors and Omissions ... **78cad**
-327.5	-338.5	-84.1	-242.9	631.4	-13.6	199.7	6.3	-151.8	214.1	229.6	235.4	-125.0	642.7	....	*Overall Balance* ... **78cbd**
327.5	338.5	84.1	242.9	-631.4	13.6	-199.7	-6.3	151.8	-214.1	-229.6	-235.4	125.0	-642.7	....	Reserves and Related Items ... **79dad**
73.2	110.6	-59.0	41.8	-551.3	51.6	-120.5	-47.3	157.3	-199.0	-257.7	-263.0	125.0	-642.7	....	Reserve Assets ... **79dbd**
-20.1	30.8	-12.7	-11.9	-2.8	-31.7	-31.3	—	—	—	—	—	—	—	....	Use of Fund Credit and Loans ... **79dcd**
274.5	197.0	155.8	213.0	-77.3	-6.4	-47.9	41.0	-5.5	-15.1	28.1	27.6	....	....	....	Exceptional Financing ... **79ded**

Guatemala

		1972	1973	1974	1975	1976	1977	1978	1979	1980	1981	1982	1983	1984	1985	1986
Government Finance															*Millions of Quetzales:*	
Deficit (-) or Surplus	80	-44.9	-37.2	-45.8	-6.7	-96.6	-40.6	6.6	-167.5	-362.6	-613.0	-360.4	-295.3	....	-214.8	-218.5
Revenue	81	186.6	214.7	282.1	351.3	428.0	603.0	734.9	682.2	753.7	748.7	749.1	742.9	....	845.4	1,460.7
Grants Received	81z	....	....	....	....	....	....	....	....	....	....	....	....	....	....	....
Exp. & Lending Minus Repay.	82z															
Expenditure	82	231.5	251.9	327.9	358.0	524.6	643.6	728.3	849.7	1,116.3	1,361.7	1,109.5	1,038.2	....	1,060.2	1,679.2
Lending Minus Repayments	83	....	....	....	....	....	....	....	....	....	....	....	....	....	....	....
Adjustment to Cash Basis	82x	....	....	....	....	....	....	....	....	....	....	....	....	....	....	....
Financing (by Residence of Lender)																
Domestic	84a	....	....	....	....	....	....	....	....	....	....	....	....	....	....	....
Foreign	85a	....	....	....	....	....	....	....	....	....	....	....	....	....	....	....
Debt: Domestic	88a	....	....	....	....	....	....	....	....	....	....	....	....	....	....	....
Foreign	89a	....	....	....	....	....	....	....	....	....	....	....	....	....	....	....
Financing (by Currency)																
Net Borrowing: Quetzales	84b	20.3	19.6	48.8	24.6	125.6	95.1	21.1	-37.1	222.1	409.4	440.4	250.9	....	213.9	134.9
Foreign Currency	85b	31.5	21.4	18.7	12.9	16.7	33.0	94.5	99.7	113.3	105.3	82.4	80.3	....	84.8	75.6
Use of Cash Balances	87	-6.9	-3.8	-21.7	-30.8	-45.7	-87.5	-122.2	104.9	27.2	98.3	-162.4	-35.9	....	-83.9	8.0
National Accounts															*Millions of Quetzales*	
Househ.Cons.Expend.,incl.NPISHs	96f	1,682	2,034	2,470	2,875	3,396	4,127	4,675	5,432	6,217	7,022	7,150	7,501	7,856	9,296	12,847
Government Consumption Expend.	91f	157	167	207	250	297	354	435	488	627	680	676	688	726	777	1,124
Gross Fixed Capital Formation	93e	273	357	468	571	900	1,039	1,218	1,286	1,295	1,443	1,310	950	912	1,225	1,593
Changes in Inventories	93i	-18	-5	120	16	34	60	95	8	-44	23	-76	52	184	61	43
Exports of Goods and Services	90c	397	537	708	792	942	1,340	1,304	1,474	1,748	1,471	1,289	1,176	1,256	2,068	2,542
Imports of Goods and Services (-)	98c	389	519	811	858	1,204	1,439	1,655	1,784	1,963	2,032	1,629	1,317	1,464	2,247	2,311
Gross Domestic Product (GDP)	99b	2,102	2,569	3,162	3,646	4,365	5,481	6,071	6,903	7,879	8,608	8,717	9,050	9,470	11,180	15,838
Net Primary Income from Abroad	98.n	-48	-48	-50	-69	-74	-33	-26	-12	-71	-103	-121	-113	-207	-331	-436
Gross National Income (GNI)	99a	2,054	2,521	3,111	3,577	4,292	5,448	6,044	6,891	7,809	8,505	8,596	8,937	9,264	10,849	15,402
Consumption of Fixed Capital	99cf	....	....	....	....	....	....	....	....	295	....	398	....	445	472	509
GDP Volume 1958 Prices	99b.p	2,032	2,169	2,308	2,353	2,527	2,724	2,860	2,995	3,107	3,128	3,017	2,940	2,954	2,936	2,940
GDP Volume (1995=100)	99bvp	48.6	51.9	55.2	56.3	60.4	65.2	68.4	71.6	74.3	74.8	72.2	70.3	70.7	70.2	70.3
GDP Deflator (1995=100)	99bip	5.1	5.8	6.7	7.6	8.5	9.9	10.4	11.3	12.4	13.5	14.2	15.1	15.7	18.7	26.4
																Millions:
Population	99z	5.58	5.74	†6.05	6.24	†6.19	6.36	6.54	6.73	6.92	7.11	7.32	7.52	7.74	7.96	8.19

Government Finance

Year Ending December 31

1987	1988	1989	1990	1991	1992	1993	1994	1995	1996	1997	1998	1999	2000	2001		
−182.7	−284.6	−754.2	−406.2	242.5	407.0	−1,064.5	†−938.7	−218.4	−268.0	−2,244.3	−2,708.9	−3,804.2	−2,709.8	−3,105.0	Deficit (-) or Surplus	80
1,875.6	2,299.3	2,382.3	2,777.6	4,301.1	5,575.0	5,645.8	†5,712.3	7,227.7	8,605.1	9,730.3	12,714.0	14,735.7	16,050.5	17,656.4	Revenue	81
....	....	....	....	....	....	....	†74.3	39.1	53.0	55.1	94.2	188.2	348.5	565.7	Grants Received	81z
....	....	....	....	....	....	....	†6,725.3	7,485.2	8,926.1	12,029.7	15,517.1	18,728.1	19,108.8	21,327.1	Exp. & Lending Minus Repay.	82z
2,058.3	2,583.9	3,136.5	3,183.8	4,058.6	5,168.0	6,710.3	†6,592.2	7,512.4	8,378.5	11,408.0	15,517.1	18,728.1	19,108.8	21,327.1	Expenditure	82
....	....	....	....	....	....	....	†237.8	308.4	235.9	—	—	—	—	—	Lending Minus Repayments	83
....	....	....	....	....	....	....	†−104.7	−335.6	311.7	621.7	—	—	—	—	Adjustment to Cash Basis	82x
															Financing (by Residence of Lender)	
....	....	....	....	....	....	....	†−187.5	433.0	−54.7	92.9	1,306.7	1,541.9	2,058.4	−129.2	Domestic	84a
....	....	....	....	....	....	....	†1,126.2	−214.6	322.7	2,151.4	1,402.2	2,262.3	651.4	3,234.2	Foreign	85a
....	....	....	....	....	....	....	4,854.7	4,485.2	5,093.0	5,862.2	6,259.8	7,807.1	8,629.7	9,281.1	Debt: Domestic	88a
....	....	....	....	....	....	....	887.8	1,203.5	1,308.2	1,491.3	1,693.8	2,034.4	2,058.0	2,350.1	Foreign	89a
															Financing (by Currency)	
174.0	292.5	279.6	346.0	369.3	80.9	551.7	....	....	....	....	....	....	....	....	Net Borrowing: Quetzales	84b
78.7	152.4	122.2	126.5	−21.7	−11.2	−84.9	....	....	....	....	....	....	....	....	Foreign Currency	85b
−70.0	−160.3	352.4	−66.3	−590.1	−476.7	597.7	....	....	....	....	....	....	....	....	Use of Cash Balances	87

Millions of Quetzales

National Accounts

1987	1988	1989	1990	1991	1992	1993	1994	1995	1996	1997	1998	1999	2000	2001		
14,989	17,289	19,837	28,692	39,693	45,899	54,165	63,893	72,899	83,072	93,804	105,429	114,554	124,568	136,867	Househ.Cons.Expend.,incl.NPISHs	96f
1,400	1,640	1,870	2,324	2,714	3,482	4,151	4,468	4,692	4,851	5,391	7,041	8,552	10,458	12,501	Government Consumption Expend.	91f
2,188	2,747	3,255	4,455	5,760	8,445	10,335	10,622	12,360	12,727	16,302	20,645	24,205	24,109	25,656	Gross Fixed Capital Formation	93e
275	67	−54	213	1,002	1,448	745	1,087	460	−614	−1,540	929	−728	2,517	1,556	Changes in Inventories	93i
2,807	3,309	4,099	6,776	8,349	9,483	11,613	13,170	16,400	17,005	19,370	22,537	25,711	30,147	29,998	Exports of Goods and Services	90c
3,949	4,507	5,323	8,143	10,216	14,771	16,765	18,571	21,656	21,562	25,454	32,559	37,008	43,352	45,156	Imports of Goods and Services (-)	98c
17,711	20,545	23,685	34,317	47,302	53,985	64,243	74,669	85,157	95,479	107,873	124,022	135,287	148,447	161,421	Gross Domestic Product (GDP)	99b
−472	−471	−544	−828	−517	−426	−854	−856	926	−1,400	−1,451	−979	−1,480	−1,751	−1,303	Net Primary Income from Abroad	98.n
17,239	20,074	23,141	33,489	43,786	53,560	63,389	73,813	84,231	94,079	106,422	123,043	133,807	146,696	160,119	Gross National Income (GNI)	99a
557	622	705	802	936	1,108	1,362	1,672	1,990	2,361	2,742	3,231	3,850	4,576	5,296	Consumption of Fixed Capital	99cf
3,044	3,163	3,288	3,390	3,514	3,684	3,829	3,983	4,180	4,303	4,491	4,716	4,897	5,072	5,189	GDP Volume 1958 Prices	99b.p
72.8	75.7	78.7	81.1	84.1	88.1	91.6	95.3	100.0	102.9	107.4	112.8	117.2	121.3	124.1	GDP Volume (1995=100)	99bv p
28.6	31.9	35.4	49.7	66.1	71.9	82.4	92.0	100.0	108.9	117.9	129.1	135.6	143.7	152.7	GDP Deflator (1995=100)	99bi p

Midyear Estimates

1987	1988	1989	1990	1991	1992	1993	1994	1995	1996	1997	1998	1999	2000	2001		
8.43	8.68	8.94	8.75	8.98	9.22	9.47	9.72	9.98	10.24	10.52	10.80	11.09	11.39	11.68	Population	99z

(See notes in the back of the book.)

Guinea

		1972	1973	1974	1975	1976	1977	1978	1979	1980	1981	1982	1983	1984	1985	1986
Exchange Rates															*Francs per SDR:*	
Official Rate	aa	24.7	24.9	25.3	24.7	24.7	24.7	24.7	24.7	24.7	24.7	24.7	24.7	24.7	24.7	288.2
															Francs per US Dollar:	
Official Rate	ae	22.7	20.7	20.7	21.1	21.2	20.3	18.9	18.7	19.4	21.2	22.4	23.6	25.2	22.5	235.6
Official Rate	rf	22.7	20.7	20.6	20.7	21.4	21.1	19.7	19.1	19.0	20.9	22.4	23.1	24.1	24.3	333.5
Fund Position															*Millions of SDRs:*	
Quota	2f. s	24.00	24.00	24.00	24.00	24.00	24.00	30.00	30.00	45.00	45.00	45.00	57.90	57.90	57.90	57.90
SDRs	1b. s	2.88	1.43	3.41	3.14	2.86	2.17	—	—	—	—	.17	.02	.03	—	.32
Reserve Position in the Fund	1c. s	—	—	—	—	—	—	—	—	—	.55	1.45	—	—	—	—
Total Fund Cred.&Loans Outstg.	2tl	2.95	1.02	9.51	7.11	7.11	18.38	19.98	26.16	27.45	23.67	34.95	34.28	32.29	28.35	32.93
International Liquidity											*Millions of US Dollars Unless Otherwise Indicated:*					
Total Reserves minus Gold	1l. d															
SDRs	1b. d	3.13	1.73	4.18	3.68	3.32	2.64	....	—	....	—	.19	.02	.03	—	.39
Reserve Position in the Fund	1c. d	—	—	—	—	—	—	—	—	—	.64	1.60	—	—	—	—
Foreign Exchange	1d. d	....	....	....	....	....	....	....	....	....	....	....	....	....	....	....
Monetary Authorities: Other Liab.	4.. d	....	....	....	....	....	....	....	....	....	....	....	....	....	....	....
Deposit Money Banks: Assets	7a. d	....	....	....	....	....	....	....	....	....	....	....	....	....	....	....
Liabilities	7b. d	....	....	....	....	....	....	....	....	....	....	....	....	....	....	....
Monetary Authorities															*Millions of Francs:*	
Foreign Assets	11	....	....	....	....	....	....	....	....	....	....	....	....	....	....	....
Claims on Central Government	12a	....	....	....	....	....	....	....	....	....	....	....	....	....	....	....
Claims on Nonfin.Pub.Enterprises	12c	....	....	....	....	....	....	....	....	....	....	....	....	....	....	....
Claims on Private Sector	12d	....	....	....	....	....	....	....	....	....	....	....	....	....	....	....
Claims on Deposit Money Banks	12e	....	....	....	....	....	....	....	....	....	....	....	....	....	....	....
Claims on Other Banking Insts	12f	....	....	....	....	....	....	....	....	....	....	....	....	....	....	....
Reserve Money	14	....	....	....	....	....	....	....	....	....	....	....	....	....	....	....
of which: Currency Outside DMBs	14a	....	....	....	....	....	....	....	....	....	....	....	....	....	....	....
Foreign Liabilities	16c	....	....	....	....	....	....	....	....	....	....	....	....	....	....	....
Central Government Deposits	16d	....	....	....	....	....	....	....	....	....	....	....	....	....	....	....
Capital Accounts	17a	....	....	....	....	....	....	....	....	....	....	....	....	....	....	....
Other Items (Net)	17r	....	....	....	....	....	....	....	....	....	....	....	....	....	....	....
Deposit Money Banks															*Millions of Francs:*	
Reserves	20	....	....	....	....	....	....	....	....	....	....	....	....	....	....	....
Foreign Assets	21	....	....	....	....	....	....	....	....	....	....	....	....	....	....	....
Claims on Central Government	22a	....	....	....	....	....	....	....	....	....	....	....	....	....	....	....
Claims on Nonfin.Pub.Enterprises	22c	....	....	....	....	....	....	....	....	....	....	....	....	....	....	....
Claims on Private Sector	22d	....	....	....	....	....	....	....	....	....	....	....	....	....	....	....
Demand Deposits	24	....	....	....	....	....	....	....	....	....	....	....	....	....	....	....
Time, Savings,& Fgn.Currency Dep.	25	....	....	....	....	....	....	....	....	....	....	....	....	....	....	....
Foreign Liabilities	26c	....	....	....	....	....	....	....	....	....	....	....	....	....	....	....
Central Government Deposits	26d	....	....	....	....	....	....	....	....	....	....	....	....	....	....	....
Credit from Monetary Authorities	26g	....	....	....	....	....	....	....	....	....	....	....	....	....	....	....
Capital Accounts	27a	....	....	....	....	....	....	....	....	....	....	....	....	....	....	....
Other Items (Net)	27r	....	....	....	....	....	....	....	....	....	....	....	....	....	....	....
Monetary Survey															*Millions of Francs:*	
Foreign Assets (Net)	31n	....	....	....	....	....	....	....	....	....	....	....	....	....	....	....
Domestic Credit	32	....	....	....	....	....	....	....	....	....	....	....	....	....	....	....
Claims on Central Govt. (Net)	32an	....	....	....	....	....	....	....	....	....	....	....	....	....	....	....
Claims on Nonfin.Pub.Enterprises	32c	....	....	....	....	....	....	....	....	....	....	....	....	....	....	....
Claims on Private Sector	32d	....	....	....	....	....	....	....	....	....	....	....	....	....	....	....
Claims on Other Banking Insts	32f	....	....	....	....	....	....	....	....	....	....	....	....	....	....	....
Money	34	....	....	....	....	....	....	....	....	....	....	....	....	....	....	....
Quasi-Money	35	....	....	....	....	....	....	....	....	....	....	....	....	....	....	....
Capital Accounts	37a	....	....	....	....	....	....	....	....	....	....	....	....	....	....	....
Other Items (Net)	37r	....	....	....	....	....	....	....	....	....	....	....	....	....	....	....
Money plus Quasi-Money	35l	....	....	....	....	....	....	....	....	....	....	....	....	....	....	....
Interest Rates															*Percent Per Annum*	
Refinancing Rate *(End of Period)*	60	....	....	....	....	....	....	....	....	....	....	....	....	....	....	9.00
Savings Rate	60k	....	....	....	....	....	....	....	....	....	....	....	....	....	....	....
Deposit Rate	60l	....	....	....	....	....	....	....	....	....	....	....	....	....	....	....
Lending Rate	60p	....	....	....	....	....	....	....	....	....	....	....	....	....	....	....

1987	1988	1989	1990	1991	1992	1993	1994	1995	1996	1997	1998	1999	2000	2001		
															Exchange Rates	
End of Period																
624.2	740.1	814.8	967.4	1,148.6	1,268.3	1,335.7	1,432.1	1,483.5	1,494.2	1,544.8	1,827.7	2,382.7	2,452.4	2,498.8	Official Rate............	aa
End of Period (ae) Period Average (rf)																
440.0	550.0	620.0	680.0	803.0	922.4	972.4	981.0	998.0	1,039.1	1,145.0	1,298.0	1,736.0	1,882.3	1,988.3	Official Rate............	ae
428.4	474.4	591.6	660.2	753.9	902.0	955.5	976.6	991.4	1,004.0	1,095.3	1,236.8	1,387.4	1,746.9	1,950.6	Official Rate............	rf
															Fund Position	
End of Period																
57.90	57.90	57.90	57.90	57.90	78.70	78.70	78.70	78.70	78.70	78.70	78.70	107.10	107.10	107.10	Quota............	2f. s
.21	.18	—	.16	9.44	7.93	8.49	3.79	5.01	.54	1.97	1.02	.94	.19	.63	SDRs............	1b. s
						.03	.07	.07	.07	.08	.08	.08	.08	.08	Reserve Position in the Fund............	1c. s
40.09	36.08	46.65	36.17	38.39	46.32	44.00	48.64	63.11	57.32	73.39	90.05	92.71	86.63	98.08	Total Fund Cred.&Loans Outstg..............	2tl
															International Liquidity	
End of Period																
....	....	....	....	80.05	86.96	132.12	87.85	86.76	87.34	121.63	236.71	199.68	147.91	200.23	Total Reserves minus Gold............	1l. d
.30	.24	—	.23	13.50	10.90	11.67	5.53	7.45	.77	2.66	1.43	1.29	.25	.80	SDRs............	1b. d
						.04	.09	.10	.10	.11	.10	.11	.10	.09	Reserve Position in the Fund............	1c. d
....	....	....	....	66.55	76.01	120.36	82.22	79.21	86.46	118.88	235.17	198.29	147.56	199.34	Foreign Exchange............	1d. d
....	....	....	....	13.92	15.88	5.50	6.70	5.30	44.61	10.13	10.51	....	7.78	21.94	Monetary Authorities: Other Liab..............	4.. d
....	....	56.79	70.36	81.27	87.24	85.47	86.27	90.89	81.05	73.08	85.27	77.53	80.32	68.46	Deposit Money Banks: Assets...............	7a. d
....	....	45.42	48.79	51.31	45.68	46.81	52.39	79.93	70.17	53.86	58.75	62.70	40.88	27.33	Liabilities............	7b. d
															Monetary Authorities	
End of Period																
....	....	....	....	107,473	139,668	185,522	155,011	185,089	201,116	254,054	319,566	....	303,361	407,345	Foreign Assets............	11
....	....	....	....	145,054	168,089	183,958	225,807	332,922	429,007	532,766	662,569	....	802,821	1,421,713	Claims on Central Government...............	12a
....	....	....	....	2,428	2,359	2,352	3,059	3,685	4,063	4,659	31,740	....	33,048	33,236	Claims on Nonfin.Pub.Enterprises............	12c
....	....	....	....	189	445	42	129	108	159	3,362	5,763	....	5,313	12,924	Claims on Private Sector............	12d
....	....	....	....	15,403	9,890	8,211	8,587	8,632	8,196	26,227	6,701	....	8,090	3,043	Claims on Deposit Money Banks............	12e
....	....	....	....	86	—	—	48	493		—	439	....	193	78	Claims on Other Banking Insts............	12f
....	....	....	....	147,756	165,178	196,468	176,724	198,442	195,681	248,968	†262,015	....	385,183	442,501	Reserve Money............	14
....	....	....	....	119,409	133,028	166,609	154,748	167,144	154,420	191,635	209,682	....	288,468	310,063	of which: Currency Outside DMBs............	14a
....	....	....	....	55,262	73,396	64,127	76,223	98,912	132,011	124,978	178,215	....	227,096	288,707	Foreign Liabilities............	16c
....	....	....	....	77,036	93,479	129,003	151,170	249,942	313,926	444,141	590,113	....	576,045	1,170,909	Central Government Deposits............	16d
....	....	....	....	31,512	41,609	51,848	57,608	55,460	51,645	52,291	55,559	....	74,939	91,303	Capital Accounts............	17a
....	....	....	....	−40,937	−53,217	−61,361	−69,088	−71,830	−50,726	−49,316	−59,124	....	−110,436	−115,080	Other Items (Net)............	17r
															Deposit Money Banks	
End of Period																
....	....	3,599	7,407	13,978	17,591	20,458	15,380	28,310	31,930	46,130	50,064	59,859	66,492	101,186	Reserves............	20
....	....	35,210	47,846	65,256	80,474	83,110	84,630	90,710	84,220	83,670	110,678	134,586	151,182	136,119	Foreign Assets............	21
....	....	156	4	16	20	12,596	13,210	29,910	38,500	46,750	44,054	39,287	18,037	46,993	Claims on Central Government............	22a
....	....	1	192	21	59	124	10	270	430	260	273	54	185	60	Claims on Nonfin.Pub.Enterprises............	22c
....	....	53,138	71,648	79,397	106,487	130,322	144,410	181,410	188,270	184,070	156,383	178,654	203,379	210,107	Claims on Private Sector............	22d
....	....	30,194	42,908	53,012	76,665	86,763	94,430	104,060	112,590	130,430	144,030	139,940	177,997	226,047	Demand Deposits............	24
....	....	17,703	14,623	26,059	38,624	54,794	52,180	64,950	77,710	83,430	81,176	99,528	111,339	129,777	Time, Savings,& Fgn.Currency Dep..............	25
....	....	28,163	33,175	41,199	42,135	45,523	51,400	79,770	72,920	61,670	76,257	108,851	76,944	54,341	Foreign Liabilities............	26c
....	....	8,422	10,360	13,515	13,934	15,267	17,100	16,490	15,800	19,960	23,575	25,296	23,108	27,527	Central Government Deposits............	26d
....	....	10,611	15,820	16,291	10,622	9,601	10,360	11,580	10,360	10,660	7,239	7,822	8,995	4,775	Credit from Monetary Authorities............	26g
....	....	16,272	23,652	26,760	39,613	47,601	46,400	50,870	38,980	49,600	34,986	43,293	53,695	53,017	Capital Accounts............	27a
....	....	−19,261	−13,441	−18,168	−16,962	−12,939	−14,230	2,920	14,960	5,120	−5,811	−12,290	−12,803	−1,019	Other Items (Net)............	27r
															Monetary Survey	
End of Period																
....	....	....	....	76,269	104,610	158,982	112,018	97,118	80,405	151,077	175,772	....	150,503	200,416	Foreign Assets (Net)............	31n
....	....	....	....	136,640	170,046	185,124	218,403	282,366	330,703	307,766	287,534	....	466,370	526,693	Domestic Credit............	32
....	....	....	....	54,519	60,696	52,284	70,747	96,400	137,781	115,415	92,935	....	221,705	270,270	Claims on Central Govt. (Net)............	32an
....	....	....	....	2,449	2,418	2,476	3,069	3,955	4,493	4,919	32,013	....	33,233	33,296	Claims on Nonfin.Pub.Enterprises............	32c
....	....	....	....	79,586	106,932	130,364	144,539	181,518	188,429	187,432	162,146	....	208,692	223,031	Claims on Private Sector............	32d
....	....	....	....	86	—	—	48	493		—	439	....	193		Claims on Other Banking Insts............	32f
....	....	....	....	182,469	218,445	260,854	252,582	274,125	273,465	331,666	†361,469	....	499,885	559,993	Money............	34
....	....	17,703	14,623	26,059	38,624	54,794	52,180	64,950	77,710	83,430	81,176	99,528	111,339	129,777	Quasi-Money............	35
....	....			58,272	81,222	99,449	104,008	106,330	90,625	101,891	90,545	....	128,634	144,320	Capital Accounts............	37a
....	....			−53,896	−63,640	−70,991	−78,353	−65,895	−30,726	−58,161	−69,885	....	−122,984	−106,980	Other Items (Net)............	37r
....	....	....	....	208,528	257,069	315,648	304,762	339,075	351,175	415,096	441,858	....	610,741	....	Money plus Quasi-Money............	35l
															Interest Rates	
Percent Per Annum																
10.00	10.00	13.00	15.00	19.00	19.00	17.00	17.00	18.00	18.00	15.00	....	....	11.50	16.25	Refinancing Rate *(End of Period)*...............	60
....	12.00	12.67	16.08	19.00	21.00	17.00	16.00	15.50	....	....	6.38	5.67	7.50	8.03	Savings Rate............	60k
15.00	16.83	19.50	21.00	22.00	23.00	19.75	18.00	17.50	....	....	6.38	5.67	7.50	8.03	Deposit Rate............	60l
15.00	15.00	17.25	21.17	24.50	27.00	24.50	22.00	21.50	....	....	19.56	19.88	19.38	....	Lending Rate............	60p

Guinea

		1972	1973	1974	1975	1976	1977	1978	1979	1980	1981	1982	1983	1984	1985	1986
Balance of Payments																*Millions of US Dollars:*
Current Account, n.i.e.	78al d	...	...	...	...	...	...	...	...	...	...	...	...	...	...	−123.9
Goods: Exports f.o.b.	78aa d	...	...	...	...	...	...	...	...	...	...	...	...	...	...	506.6
Goods: Imports f.o.b.	78ab d	...	...	...	...	...	...	...	...	...	...	...	...	...	...	−422.7
Trade Balance	78ac d	...	...	...	...	...	...	...	...	...	...	...	...	...	...	83.9
Services: Credit	78ad d	...	...	...	...	...	...	...	...	...	...	...	...	...	...	55.6
Services: Debit	78ae d	...	...	...	...	...	...	...	...	...	...	...	...	...	...	−137.4
Balance on Goods & Services	78af d	...	...	...	...	...	...	...	...	...	...	...	...	...	...	2.2
Income: Credit	78ag d	...	...	...	...	...	...	...	...	...	...	...	...	...	...	4.9
Income: Debit	78ah d	...	...	...	...	...	...	...	...	...	...	...	...	...	...	−156.6
Balance on Gds, Serv. & Inc.	78ai d	...	...	...	...	...	...	...	...	...	...	...	...	...	...	−149.6
Current Transfers, n.i.e.: Credit	78aj d	...	...	...	...	...	...	...	...	...	...	...	...	...	...	37.9
Current Transfers: Debit	78ak d	...	...	...	...	...	...	...	...	...	...	...	...	...	...	−12.3
Capital Account, n.i.e.	78bc d	...	...	...	...	...	...	...	...	...	...	...	...	...	...	...
Capital Account, n.i.e.: Credit	78ba d	...	...	...	...	...	...	...	...	...	...	...	...	...	...	...
Capital Account: Debit	78bb d	...	...	...	...	...	...	...	...	...	...	...	...	...	...	...
Financial Account, n.i.e.	78bj d	...	...	...	...	...	...	...	...	...	...	...	...	...	...	−11.2
Direct Investment Abroad	78bd d	...	...	...	...	...	...	...	...	...	...	...	...	...	...	...
Dir. Invest. in Rep. Econ., n.i.e.	78be d	...	...	...	...	...	...	...	...	...	...	...	...	...	...	8.4
Portfolio Investment Assets	78bf d	...	...	...	...	...	...	...	...	...	...	...	...	...	...	...
Equity Securities	78bk d	...	...	...	...	...	...	...	...	...	...	...	...	...	...	...
Debt Securities	78bl d	...	...	...	...	...	...	...	...	...	...	...	...	...	...	...
Portfolio Investment Liab., n.i.e.	78bg d	...	...	...	...	...	...	...	...	...	...	...	...	...	...	...
Equity Securities	78bm d	...	...	...	...	...	...	...	...	...	...	...	...	...	...	...
Debt Securities	78bn d	...	...	...	...	...	...	...	...	...	...	...	...	...	...	...
Financial Derivatives Assets	78bw d	...	...	...	...	...	...	...	...	...	...	...	...	...	...	...
Financial Derivatives Liabilities	78bx d	...	...	...	...	...	...	...	...	...	...	...	...	...	...	...
Other Investment Assets	78bh d	...	...	...	...	...	...	...	...	...	...	...	...	...	...	−29.1
Monetary Authorities	78bo d	...	...	...	...	...	...	...	...	...	...	...	...	...	...	...
General Government	78bp d	...	...	...	...	...	...	...	...	...	...	...	...	...	...	...
Banks	78bq d	...	...	...	...	...	...	...	...	...	...	...	...	...	...	−25.9
Other Sectors	78br d	...	...	...	...	...	...	...	...	...	...	...	...	...	...	−3.3
Other Investment Liab., n.i.e.	78bi d	...	...	...	...	...	...	...	...	...	...	...	...	...	...	9.6
Monetary Authorities	78bs d	...	...	...	...	...	...	...	...	...	...	...	...	...	...	−15.9
General Government	78bt d	...	...	...	...	...	...	...	...	...	...	...	...	...	...	39.2
Banks	78bu d	...	...	...	...	...	...	...	...	...	...	...	...	...	...	−.5
Other Sectors	78bv d	...	...	...	...	...	...	...	...	...	...	...	...	...	...	−13.3
Net Errors and Omissions	78ca d	...	...	...	...	...	...	...	...	...	...	...	...	...	...	22.6
Overall Balance	78cb d	...	...	...	...	...	...	...	...	...	...	...	...	...	...	−112.5
Reserves and Related Items	79da d	...	...	...	...	...	...	...	...	...	...	...	...	...	...	112.5
Reserve Assets	79db d	...	...	...	...	...	...	...	...	...	...	...	...	...	...	−24.5
Use of Fund Credit and Loans	79dc d	...	...	...	...	...	...	...	...	...	...	...	...	...	...	5.2
Exceptional Financing	79de d	...	...	...	...	...	...	...	...	...	...	...	...	...	...	131.8
Government Finance																*Millions of Francs:*
Deficit (-) or Surplus	80	...	...	...	...	...	...	...	...	...	...	...	...	...	...	...
Revenue	81	...	...	...	...	...	...	...	...	...	...	...	...	...	...	...
Grants Received	81z	...	...	...	...	...	...	...	...	...	...	...	...	...	...	...
Expenditure	82	...	...	...	...	...	...	...	...	...	...	...	...	...	...	...
Lending Minus Repayments	83	...	...	...	...	...	...	...	...	...	...	...	...	...	...	...
Financing																
Domestic	84a	...	...	...	...	...	...	...	...	...	...	...	...	...	...	...
Foreign	85a	...	...	...	...	...	...	...	...	...	...	...	...	...	...	...
																Millions:
Population	99z	4.11	...	...	4.34	4.43	†5.06	5.17	5.29	5.41	4.55	4.64	†4.41	4.53	4.66	4.79

Minus Sign Indicates Debit

1987	1988	1989	1990	1991	1992	1993	1994	1995	1996	1997	1998	1999	2000	2001	Balance of Payments	
-38.3	-221.5	-179.7	-203.0	-288.8	-262.7	-56.8	-248.0	-216.5	-177.3	-91.1	-183.6	-151.6	....	....	Current Account, n.i.e.	78al *d*
544.6	511.9	595.6	671.2	687.1	517.2	561.1	515.7	582.8	636.5	630.1	693.0	677.9	....	....	Goods: Exports f.o.b.	78aa *d*
-380.3	-510.6	-531.6	-585.8	-694.9	-608.4	-582.7	-685.4	-621.7	-525.3	-512.5	-572.0	-583.4			Goods: Imports f.o.b.	78ab *d*
164.4	1.3	64.0	85.5	-7.8	-91.2	-21.6	-169.7	-39.0	111.2	117.6	121.0	94.5			*Trade Balance*	78ac *d*
53.6	52.6	103.7	157.5	144.7	159.7	186.8	152.9	117.5	124.1	110.7	110.8	113.2			Services: Credit	78ad *d*
-154.0	-230.8	-259.8	-367.3	-347.8	-322.6	-334.8	-366.0	-389.3	-422.2	-321.6	-382.7	-342.1			Services: Debit	78ae *d*
64.0	-177.0	-92.1	-124.3	-210.9	-254.0	-169.6	-382.9	-310.8	-186.8	-93.3	-150.9	-134.4			*Balance on Goods & Services*	78af *d*
4.6	11.2	8.6	12.6	15.5	7.9	9.3	6.5	12.9	12.8	7.8	9.0	24.7			Income: Credit	78ag *d*
-128.8	-142.4	-178.5	-161.5	-181.4	-148.9	-92.6	-79.8	-97.5	-105.7	-121.3	-133.5	-106.9			Income: Debit	78ah *d*
-60.2	-308.1	-261.9	-273.2	-376.8	-395.0	-252.9	-456.1	-395.5	-279.8	-206.9	-275.5	-216.6			*Balance on Gds, Serv. & Inc.*	78ai *d*
37.6	121.3	143.6	118.8	136.2	193.5	260.3	280.6	258.3	137.8	131.4	116.2	80.1			Current Transfers, n.i.e.: Credit	78aj *d*
-15.6	-34.7	-61.3	-48.6	-48.2	-61.2	-64.2	-72.5	-79.3	-35.3	-15.6	-24.3	-15.1			Current Transfers: Debit	78ak *d*
....	....	198.7	—	—	8.0	5.0	—	—	—	—	—	—	....	....	Capital Account, n.i.e.	78bc *d*
....	....	198.7	—	—	8.0	5.0	—	—	—	—	—	—			Capital Account, n.i.e.: Credit	78ba *d*
....	....	....	....	....	....	....	....	....	....	....	....	....			Capital Account: Debit	78bb *d*
-49.5	34.8	-158.9	53.8	18.8	61.7	62.6	84.2	109.2	47.5	-89.3	8.0	117.2	....	....	Financial Account, n.i.e.	78bj *d*
									-.5			—			Direct Investment Abroad	78bd *d*
12.9	15.7	12.3	17.9	38.8	19.7	2.7	.2	.8	23.8	17.3	17.8	63.4			Dir. Invest. in Rep. Econ., n.i.e.	78be *d*
											-82.7	-20.0			Portfolio Investment Assets	78bf *d*
															Equity Securities	78bk *d*
											-82.7	-20.0			Debt Securities	78bl *d*
															Portfolio Investment Liab., n.i.e.	78bg *d*
															Equity Securities	78bm *d*
															Debt Securities	78bn *d*
															Financial Derivatives Assets	78bw *d*
															Financial Derivatives Liabilities	78bx *d*
-15.8	-5.2	-39.1	-52.7	-47.0	-27.5	-20.1	-14.5	-73.7	-19.8	-99.1	-14.6	.7			Other Investment Assets	78bh *d*
							-6.5	9.0	6.0	2.4	1.2	-1.0			Monetary Authorities	78bo *d*
-5.4	3.1	-.9	-10.6	-1.1	-4.1	2.2									General Government	78bp *d*
-23.8	6.6	-7.6	-12.5	-11.4	-5.0	—	-2.2	-4.6	9.0	9.3	-12.5	7.6			Banks	78bq *d*
13.4	-15.0	-30.6	-29.6	-34.5	-18.4	-22.3	-5.8	-78.2	-34.7	-110.8	-3.3	-6.0			Other Sectors	78br *d*
-46.5	24.4	-132.1	88.7	27.0	69.6	80.0	98.5	182.2	44.0	-7.5	87.5	73.1			Other Investment Liab., n.i.e.	78bi *d*
—	—	—	—	8.4	-5.7	-.1	.1	-.5	39.1	-35.3	-3.0	.2			Monetary Authorities	78bs *d*
-38.3	-28.8	-153.8	54.3	-34.1	15.4	54.6	79.6	106.5	-14.4	48.2	37.6	84.2			General Government	78bt *d*
10.2	23.7	-2.6	9.4	2.4	-6.5	.1	8.3	26.0	-9.8	-18.1	6.7	3.7			Banks	78bu *d*
-18.4	29.5	24.2	25.0	50.3	66.4	25.4	10.5	50.2	29.0	-2.3	46.2	-15.1			Other Sectors	78bv *d*
-9.3	65.6	-44.9	52.4	112.3	18.6	-107.5	39.7	34.8	69.9	49.8	17.8	-45.0			Net Errors and Omissions	78ca *d*
-97.1	-121.1	-184.9	-96.7	-157.8	-174.4	-96.7	-124.1	-72.5	-59.9	-130.6	-157.8	-79.5			*Overall Balance*	78cb *d*
97.1	121.1	184.9	96.7	157.8	174.4	96.7	124.1	72.5	59.9	130.6	157.8	79.5			Reserves and Related Items	79da *d*
-15.0	-35.4	-13.4	-3.4	10.5	1.6	-49.9	32.4	-43.8	-6.5	-20.3	60.7	64.2			Reserve Assets	79db *d*
8.9	-5.4	13.9	-14.3	3.2	11.0	-3.2	7.0	22.1	-8.4	22.4	22.8	3.7			Use of Fund Credit and Loans	79dc *d*
103.2	162.0	184.3	114.4	144.1	161.8	149.9	84.7	94.2	74.9	128.5	74.3	11.5			Exceptional Financing	79de *d*

Year Ending December 31

1987	1988	1989	1990	1991	1992	1993	1994	1995	1996	1997	1998	1999	2000	2001	Government Finance	
....	....	-50,145	-61,090	-76,955	-83,585	....	....	....	....	....	-192,650	-116,310 [f]	.		Deficit (-) or Surplus	80
....	....	222,778	297,860	326,183	357,889	....	....	....	....	....	497,293	574,901 [f]			Revenue	81
....	....	52,500	68,300	82,500	117,300	....	....	....	....	....	106,481	320,500 [f]			Grants Received	81z
....	....	326,960	426,852	489,323	559,854	....	....	....	....	....	792,554	1,010,060 [f]			Expenditure	82
....	....	-1,537	398	-3,685	-1,080	....	....	....	....	....	3,870	1,650 [f]			Lending Minus Repayments	83
															Financing	
....	....	-15,092	-14,654	478	-26,108	....	....	....	....	....	-2,610	8,250 [f]			Domestic	84a
....	....	65,237	75,744	76,477	109,693	....	....	....	....	....	195,260	108,060 [f]			Foreign	85a

Midyear Estimates

1987	1988	1989	1990	1991	1992	1993	1994	1995	1996	1997	1998	1999	2000	2001		
4.93	5.07	5.54	5.76	6.36	6.61	6.86	7.11	7.33	7.53	7.71	7.88	8.02	8.15	8.27	**Population**	99z

(See notes in the back of the book.)

Guinea-Bissau

		1972	1973	1974	1975	1976	1977	1978	1979	1980	1981	1982	1983	1984	1985	1986
Exchange Rates															*Francs per SDR:*	
Official Rate	aa	.45	.48	.46	.49	.56	.64	.68	.68	.68	.68	.68	1.36	1.92	2.98	4.49
															Francs per US Dollar:	
Official Rate	ae	.42	.40	.38	.42	.49	.53	.52	.51	.53	.58	.61	1.29	1.96	2.71	3.67
Official Rate	rf	.42	.38	.39	.39	.47	.52	.54	.52	.52	.57	.61	.65	1.61	2.45	3.13
Fund Position															*Millions of SDRs:*	
Quota	2f. s	...	...	...	...	...	3.20	3.90	3.90	5.90	5.90	5.90	7.50	7.50	7.50	7.50
SDRs	1b. s	...	...	...	...	...	—	—	.09	—	.07	.01	.01	.09	—	—
Reserve Position in the Fund	1c. s	...	...	...	...	...	.80	—	—	.50	—	—	—	—	—	—
Total Fund Cred.&Loans Outstg.	2tl	...	...	...	...	...	—	—	1.10	1.10	2.95	2.68	2.26	3.73	2.80	1.87
International Liquidity													*Millions of US Dollars Unless Otherwise Indicated:*			
Total Reserves minus Gold	11. d	...	...	...	...	...	...	...	...	...	...	...	...	...	...	-.63
SDRs	1b. d	...	...	...	...	...	—	—	.12	—	.08	.01	.01	.09	—	—
Reserve Position in the Fund	1c. d	...	...	...	...	...	—	—	—	—	—	—	—	—	—	—
Foreign Exchange	1d. d	...	...	...	...	...	...	...	...	...	...	...	...	...	...	-.63
Monetary Authorities: Other Liab.	4.. d	...	...	...	...	...	...	...	...	...	...	...	...	...	...	79.4
Deposit Money Banks: Assets	7a. d	...	...	...	...	...	...	...	...	...	...	...	...	...	...	...
Liabilities	7b. d	...	...	...	...	...	...	...	...	...	...	...	...	...	...	...
Monetary Authorities															*Millions of Francs:*	
Foreign Assets	11	...	...	...	...	...	...	...	...	...	...	...	...	...	...	-2
Claims on Central Government	12a	...	...	...	...	...	...	...	...	...	...	...	...	...	...	328
Claims on Other Financial Insts.	12f	...	...	...	...	...	...	...	...	...	...	...	...	...	...	
Reserve Money	14	...	...	...	...	...	...	...	...	...	...	...	...	...	...	133
of which: Currency Outside DMBs	14a	...	...	...	...	...	...	...	...	...	...	...	...	...	...	84
Foreign Liabilities	16c	...	...	...	...	...	...	...	...	...	...	...	...	...	...	302
Central Government Deposits	16d	...	...	...	...	...	...	...	...	...	...	...	...	...	...	-8
Other Items (Net)	17r	...	...	...	...	...	...	...	...	...	...	...	...	...	...	-100
Deposit Money Banks															*Millions of Francs:*	
Reserves	20	...	...	...	...	...	...	...	...	...	...	...	...	...	...	
Foreign Assets	21	...	...	...	...	...	...	...	...	...	...	...	...	...	...	
Claims on Central Government	22a	...	...	...	...	...	...	...	...	...	...	...	...	...	...	
Claims on Private Sector	22d	...	...	...	...	...	...	...	...	...	...	...	...	...	...	
Claims on Other Financial Insts.	22f	...	...	...	...	...	...	...	...	...	...	...	...	...	...	—
Demand Deposits	24	...	...	...	...	...	...	...	...	...	...	...	...	...	...	
Time & Foreign Currency Deposits	25	...	...	...	...	...	...	...	...	...	...	...	...	...	...	
Foreign Liabilities	26c	...	...	...	...	...	...	...	...	...	...	...	...	...	...	
Long-Term Foreign Liabilities	26cl	...	...	...	...	...	...	...	...	...	...	...	...	...	...	
Central Government Deposits	26d	...	...	...	...	...	...	...	...	...	...	...	...	...	...	
Credit from Monetary Authorities	26g	...	...	...	...	...	...	...	...	...	...	...	...	...	...	
Other Items (Net)	27r	...	...	...	...	...	...	...	...	...	...	...	...	...	...	
Monetary Survey															*Millions of Francs:*	
Foreign Assets (Net)	31n	...	...	...	...	...	...	...	...	...	...	...	...	...	...	-302
Domestic Credit	32	...	...	...	...	...	...	...	...	...	...	...	...	...	...	310
Claims on Central Govt. (Net)	32an	...	...	...	...	...	...	...	...	...	...	...	...	...	...	164
Claims on Private Sector	32d	...	...	...	...	...	...	...	...	...	...	...	...	...	...	145
Claims on Other Financial Insts.	32f	...	...	...	...	...	...	...	...	...	...	...	...	...	...	—
Money	34	...	...	...	...	...	...	...	...	...	...	...	...	...	...	133
Quasi-Money	35	...	...	...	...	...	...	...	...	...	...	...	...	...	...	2
Long-Term Foriegn Liabilities	36cl	...	...	...	...	...	...	...	...	...	...	...	...	...	...	
Other Items (Net)	37r	...	...	...	...	...	...	...	...	...	...	...	...	...	...	-100
Money plus Quasi-Money	35l	...	...	...	...	...	...	...	...	...	...	...	...	...	...	135
Interest Rates															*Percent Per Annum*	
Discount Rate *(End of Period)*	60	...	...	...	...	...	...	...	...	...	...	...	...	...	...	
Money Market Rate	60b	...	...	...	...	7.28	7.38	7.40	7.72	10.13	13.68	14.66	12.23	11.92	10.66	8.58
Deposit Rate	60l	...	...	...	...	...	...	...	...	...	...	...	...	...	...	
Lending Rate	60p	...	...	...	...	...	...	...	...	...	...	...	...	...	...	18.00
Prices															*Index Numbers (1995=100):*	
Consumer Prices	64	...	...	...	...	...	...	...	...	...	...	...	...	...	...	

	1987	1988	1989	1990	1991	1992	1993	1994	1995	1996	1997	1998	1999	2000	2001	
Exchange Rates																
End of Period																
Official Rate ... aa	18.58	28.21	40.18	54.91	109.13	183.10	242.25	345.18	501.49	772.88	807.94	791.61	†896.19	918.49	935.39	
End of Period (ae) Period Average (rf)																
Official Rate ... ae	13.10	20.97	30.57	38.59	76.29	133.16	176.37	236.45	337.37	537.48	598.81	562.21	†652.95	704.95	744.31	
Official Rate ... rf	8.60	17.07	27.85	33.62	56.29	106.68	155.11	198.34	278.04	405.75	583.67	589.95	†615.70	711.98	733.04	
Fund Position																
End of Period																
Quota ... 2f, s	7.50	7.50	7.50	7.50	7.50	10.50	10.50	10.50	10.50	10.50	10.50	10.50	14.20	14.20	14.20	
SDRs ... 1b, s	.05	—	—	—	—	—	.01	—	.01	.01	.04	.02	.06	.03	.16	
Reserve Position in the Fund ... 1c, s															—	
Total Fund Cred.&Loans Outstg. ... 2tl	3.14	2.20	3.75	3.75	3.75	3.75	3.45	3.15	3.98	5.33	9.04	10.95	12.63	18.97	18.45	
International Liquidity																
End of Period																
Total Reserves minus Gold ... 1l, d	10.31	15.97	20.84	18.22	14.58	17.75	14.17	18.43	20.27	11.53	33.70	35.76	35.28	66.73	69.47	
SDRs ... 1b, d	.07	—	—	—	—	—	.01	—	.01	.01	.06	.03	.08	.04	.20	
Reserve Position in the Fund ... 1c, d															—	
Foreign Exchange ... 1d, d	10.24	15.97	20.84	18.22	14.58	17.75	14.16	18.43	20.26	11.52	33.65	35.73	35.21	66.69	69.28	
Monetary Authorities: Other Liab. ... 4, d	96.3	92.2	43.4	32.5	38.6	53.1	48.3	42.6	38.6	18.2	1.8	.7	1.4	-.6	1.0	
Deposit Money Banks: Assets ... 7a, d				4.5	2.8	12.1	10.8	12.1	18.7	16.7	19.2	19.3	16.6	2.3	3.8	
Liabilities ... 7b, d				1.0	.2	1.7	.7	7.2	6.9	7.5	11.7	12.9	11.1	13.7	11.5	
Monetary Authorities																
End of Period																
Foreign Assets ... 11	135	335	637	703	1,112	2,364	2,499	4,357	6,837	6,196	20,183	20,105	23,038	47,044	51,711	
Claims on Central Government ... 12a	668	1,105	2,444	2,007	1,982	2,857	3,197	4,144	4,728	7,679	10,690	12,453	13,081	20,343	20,288	
Claims on Other Financial Insts. ... 12f	—	—	—												—	
Reserve Money ... 14	258	475	647	794	1,831	3,031	4,005	5,300	6,998	9,709	21,922	19,011	25,561	47,936	55,559	
of which: Currency Outside DMBs ... 14a	143	246	384	562	839	1,603	2,039	3,015	4,278	6,370	20,137	17,642	24,186	44,245	53,054	
Foreign Liabilities ... 16c	1,405	2,114	1,676	1,461	3,354	7,752	9,360	11,157	15,012	13,878	8,359	9,055	12,251	17,006	18,019	
Central Government Deposits ... 16d	306	592	1,474	1,905	2,286	2,487	2,642	4,915	7,722	9,080	6,110	8,148	2,994	3,567	3,742	
Other Items (Net) ... 17r	-1,167	-1,741	-717	-243	-2,097	-4,808	-5,985	-8,542	-13,840	-18,793	-5,518	-3,655	-4,686	-1,122	-5,320	
Deposit Money Banks																
End of Period																
Reserves ... 20	....	....	....	230	949	1,484	2,052	2,420	3,362	2,614	4,392	2,728	2,728	6,256	2,397	
Foreign Assets ... 21	....	....	....	173	214	1,610	1,912	2,856	6,295	8,989	11,479	10,827	10,827	1,621	2,850	
Claims on Central Government ... 22a	....	....	....	443	460	624	544	576	567	77	21	21	21	—	—	
Claims on Private Sector ... 22d	....	....	....	1,518	1,787	1,751	2,859	4,617	4,612	5,305	7,651	9,859	9,859	12,121	4,436	
Claims on Other Financial Insts. ... 22f															—	
Demand Deposits ... 24	....	....	....	431	477	834	1,050	1,855	2,880	4,507	16,431	14,476	14,476	19,985	16,261	
Time & Foreign Currency Deposits ... 25	....	....	....	358	513	1,452	2,361	3,207	4,395	6,320	1,132	1,355	1,355	1,037	794	
Foreign Liabilities ... 26c	....	....	....	39	16	228	114	1,700	2,330	3,999	6,984	7,220	7,220	2,924	543	
Long-Term Foreign Liabilities ... 26cl	....	....	....	—	—	3	4	6	8	13	14	14	14	6,744	8,001	
Central Government Deposits ... 26d	....	....	....	2	7	232	132	47	14	561	820	1,014	1,014	1,066	1,144	
Credit from Monetary Authorities ... 26g	....	....	....	1,208	2,272	3,223	4,328	4,328	4,328	97	—	—	—	—	—	
Other Items (Net) ... 27r	....	....	....	324	124	-502	-622	-674	881	1,489	-1,838	-644	-644	-11,758	-17,061	
Monetary Survey																
End of Period																
Foreign Assets (Net) ... 31n	-1,184	-1,660	-839	-625	-2,044	-4,006	-5,064	-5,644	-4,211	-2,692	16,318	14,657	14,394	28,735	35,999	
Domestic Credit ... 32	446	692	1,739	6,355	1,935	2,514	3,825	4,374	2,171	3,420	11,432	13,172	18,954	27,831	19,838	
Claims on Central Govt. (Net) ... 32an	196	217	692	4,550	6	62	-542	-2,302	-3,959	-3,923	331	613	9,095	15,709	15,402	
Claims on Private Sector ... 32d	250	475	1,047	1,805	1,930	2,452	4,368	6,677	6,129	7,343	11,101	12,559	9,859	12,121	4,436	
Claims on Other Financial Insts. ... 32f	—														—	
Money ... 34	265	489	638	5,291	1,332	2,440	3,105	4,910	7,211	10,891	36,625	32,194	39,420	64,524	69,535	
Quasi-Money ... 35	86	120	199	358	513	1,452	2,361	3,207	4,395	6,320	1,132	1,355	1,355	1,037	794	
Long-Term Foriegn Liabilities ... 36cl	....	....	....	—	—	3	4	6	8	13	14	14	14	6,744	8,001	
Other Items (Net) ... 37r	-1,165	-1,739	-662	-113	-2,877	-6,775	-8,598	-11,538	-16,195	-19,639	-10,020	-5,733	-7,440	-15,739	-22,493	
Money plus Quasi-Money ... 35l	351	609	837	5,649	1,845	3,891	5,466	8,116	11,606	17,212	37,757	33,548	40,774	65,561	70,329	
Interest Rates																
Percent Per Annum																
Discount Rate *(End of Period)* ... 60	....	....	....	42.00	42.00	45.50	41.00	26.00	39.00	54.00	6.00	6.25	5.75	6.50	6.50	
Money Market Rate ... 60b	8.37	8.72	10.07	10.98	10.94	11.45	....	....	....	....	....	4.81	4.95	4.95	4.95	
Deposit Rate ... 60l	....	23.00	28.00	32.67	36.00	39.33	53.92	28.67	26.50	47.25	4.63	3.50	3.50	3.50	3.50	
Lending Rate ... 60p	18.00	30.00	38.33	45.75	47.00	50.33	63.58	36.33	32.92	51.75	....	....	....	....	....	
Prices																
Period Averages																
Consumer Prices ... 64	3.9	6.3	11.3	15.1	23.8	40.3	59.7	68.8	100.0	150.7	224.7	239.4	237.7	258.2	266.9	

Guinea-Bissau

654

International Transactions *Millions of Francs*

		1972	1973	1974	1975	1976	1977	1978	1979	1980	1981	1982	1983	1984	1985	1986
Exports	70	...	...	...	...	...	...	...	...	...	...	...	...		...	...
Imports, c.i.f.	71	...	...	...	...	...	...	...	...	...	...	...	...		...	...
Imports, f.o.b.	71.v	...	...	...	...	...	...	...	...	...	...	...	...		...	...

Balance of Payments *Millions of US Dollars:*

		1982	1983	1984	1985	1986
Current Account, n.i.e.	78ald	−79.50	−72.00	−65.50	−75.80	−62.50
Goods: Exports f.o.b.	78aad	11.80	8.60	17.40	11.60	9.70
Goods: Imports f.o.b.	78abd	−61.50	−58.40	−60.10	−59.50	−51.20
Trade Balance	78acd	−49.70	−49.80	−42.70	−47.90	−41.50
Services: Credit	78add	5.60	6.70	8.00	6.50	—
Services: Debit	78aed	−13.60	−13.20	−21.20	−25.10	−14.40
Balance on Goods & Services	78afd	−57.70	−56.30	−55.90	−66.50	−55.90
Income: Credit	78agd	—	—	—	—	—
Income: Debit	78ahd	−7.80	−4.80	−4.70	−5.90	−16.50
Balance on Gds, Serv. & Inc.	78aid	−65.50	−61.10	−60.60	−72.40	−72.40
Current Transfers, n.i.e.: Credit	78ajd					11.40
Current Transfers: Debit	78akd	−14.00	−10.90	−4.90	−3.40	−1.50
Capital Account, n.i.e.	78bcd	44.50	43.00	29.30	30.50	26.90
Capital Account, n.i.e.: Credit	78bad	44.50	43.00	29.30	30.50	26.90
Capital Account: Debit	78bbd	—	—	—	—	—
Financial Account, n.i.e.	78bjd	23.80	16.66	36.63	62.96	6.67
Direct Investment Abroad	78bdd	—	—	—	—	—
Dir. Invest. in Rep. Econ., n.i.e.	78bed	—	—	—	—	—
Portfolio Investment Assets	78bfd	—	—	—	—	—
Equity Securities	78bkd	—	—	—	—	—
Debt Securities	78bld	—	—	—	—	—
Portfolio Investment Liab., n.i.e.	78bgd	—	—	—	—	—
Equity Securities	78bmd	—	—	—	—	—
Debt Securities	78bnd	—	—	—	—	—
Financial Derivatives Assets	78bwd	...	...	...		...
Financial Derivatives Liabilities	78bxd	...	...	...		...
Other Investment Assets	78bhd	—	—	—	—	—
Monetary Authorities	78bod	...	...	...		...
General Government	78bpd	...	...	...		...
Banks	78bqd	—	—	—	—	—
Other Sectors	78brd	—	—	—	—	—
Other Investment Liab., n.i.e.	78bid	23.80	16.66	36.63	62.96	6.67
Monetary Authorities	78bsd	—	—	—	—	—
General Government	78btd	23.80	16.66	36.63	62.96	6.67
Banks	78bud	—	—	—	—	—
Other Sectors	78bvd	—	—	—	—	—
Net Errors and Omissions	78cad	−9.17	−5.35	−12.88	−9.64	−3.71
Overall Balance	78cbd	−20.37	−17.69	−12.45	8.01	−32.65
Reserves and Related Items	79dad	20.37	17.69	12.45	−8.01	32.65
Reserve Assets	79dbd	16.17	13.50	2.60	−15.61	−3.10
Use of Fund Credit and Loans	79dcd	−.29	−.45	1.48	−.94	−1.09
Exceptional Financing	79ded	4.50	4.64	8.37	8.54	36.83

Government Finance *Millions of Francs:*

		1982	1983	1984	1985	1986
Deficit (-) or Surplus	80	...	−34.1	−71.0	−110.2	−115.8
Revenue	81	...	15.6	30.6	45.2	58.9
Grants Received	81z	...	23.1	48.6	84.2	118.1
Expenditure	82	...	72.8	150.2	223.4	295.9
Lending Minus Repayments	83	...	—	—	16.2	−3.0
Financing						
Domestic	84a	...	19.4	19.3	27.1	...
Foreign	85a	...	10.4	45.3	75.6	...
Unallocated Financing	84xx	...	4.3	6.4	7.5	...

National Accounts *Millions of Francs*

		1986
Househ.Cons.Expend.,incl.NPISHs	96f	70,198
Government Consumption Expend.	91f	13,596
Gross Fixed Capital Formation	93e	15,708
Changes in Inventories	93i	3,153
Exports of Goods and Services	90c	4,525
Imports of Goods and Services (-)	98c	28,232
Gross Domestic Product (GDP)	99b	78,700
Net Primary Income from Abroad	98.n	—
Gross National Income (GNI)	99a	723
GDP Volume 1986 Prices	99b.p	78,700
GDP Volume (1995=100)	99bv p	73.3
GDP Deflator (1995=100)	99bi p	83.2

Millions:

		1972	1973	1974	1975	1976	1977	1978	1979	1980	1981	1982	1983	1984	1985	1986
Population	99z	.55	.57	.60	.63	.66	.70	.74	.78	.78	.80	.81	.83	.85	.87	.89

	1987	1988	1989	1990	1991	1992	1993	1994	1995	1996	1997	1998	1999	2000	2001	International Transactions	
Millions of Francs																	
	....	271	395	648	1,150	690	4,360	16,580	12,310	11,030	28,300	15,800	31,500	44,200	....	Exports	70
	....	1,131	2,159	2,882	4,272	10,181	9,541	32,530	36,990	35,240	51,800	40,300	42,300	44,300	....	Imports, c.i.f.	71
	....	1,006	1,919	2,289	3,798	8,908	8,348	2,857	16,092	21,150	45,043	36,636	38,455	45,818	....	Imports, f.o.b.	71.v
																Balance of Payments	
Minus Sign Indicates Debit																	
	−56.50	−68.40	−92.80	−60.49	−79.04	−104.18	−65.48	−47.63	−50.65	−60.43	−30.28	....	....	....	....	Current Account, n.i.e.	78ald
	15.40	15.90	14.20	19.26	20.44	6.47	15.96	33.21	23.90	21.61	48.86	....	....	....	....	Goods: Exports f.o.b.	78aad
	−44.70	−58.90	−68.90	−68.07	−67.47	−83.51	−53.82	−53.80	−59.34	−56.80	−62.49	....	....	....	....	Goods: Imports f.o.b.	78abd
	−29.30	−43.00	−54.70	−48.81	−47.03	−77.04	−37.86	−20.59	−35.44	−35.19	−13.63	....	....	....	....	*Trade Balance*	78acd
	—	—	6.44	6.84	13.06	11.56	9.76	5.61	5.69	6.96	8.00	....	....	....	....	Services: Credit	78add
	−15.30	−17.10	−27.39	−20.10	−27.41	−27.56	−21.14	−27.11	−29.91	−29.25	−26.15	....	....	....	....	Services: Debit	78aed
	−44.60	−60.10	−75.65	−62.07	−61.38	−93.04	−49.24	−42.09	−59.66	−57.48	−31.78	....	....	....	....	*Balance on Goods & Services*	78afd
	−17.90	−19.90	−28.05	−22.28	−32.91	−27.78	−28.98	−26.27	−21.09	−18.65	−14.30	....	....	....	....	Income: Credit	78agd
	−62.50	−80.00	−103.70	−84.35	−94.29	−120.82	−78.22	−68.36	−80.75	−76.13	−46.08	....	....	....	....	Income: Debit	78ahd
	8.00	11.60	10.90	23.86	19.39	17.28	14.39	21.79	31.42	15.70	15.80	....	....	....	....	*Balance on Gds, Serv. & Inc.*	78aid
	−2.00			−4.14	−.64	−1.65	−1.06	−1.32				....	....	....	....	Current Transfers, n.i.e.: Credit	78ajd
												....	....	....	....	Current Transfers: Debit	78akd
	32.20	26.90	41.60	28.96	32.72	28.49	36.57	44.42	49.20	40.70	32.20	....	....	....	....	Capital Account, n.i.e.	78bcd
	32.20	26.90	41.60	28.96	32.72	28.49	36.57	44.42	49.20	40.70	32.20	....	....	....	....	Capital Account, n.i.e.: Credit	78bad
	—	—	—	—	—	—	—	—	—	—	—	....	....	....	....	Capital Account: Debit	78bbd
	1.48	−3.44	−8.38	1.22	−12.50	2.13	−15.82	−26.98	−28.25	−12.30	2.03	....	....	....	....	Financial Account, n.i.e.	78bjd
	—	—	—	—	—	—	....	....	....	....	—	....	....	....	....	Direct Investment Abroad	78bdd
	—	—	—	—	—	—	....	....	....	....	—	....	....	....	....	Dir. Invest. in Rep. Econ., n.i.e.	78bed
	—	—	—	—	—	—	....	....	....	....	—	....	....	....	....	Portfolio Investment Assets	78bfd
	—	—	—	—	—	—	....	....	....	....	—	....	....	....	....	Equity Securities	78bkd
	—	—	—	—	—	—	....	....	....	....	—	....	....	....	....	Debt Securities	78bld
	—	—	—	—	—	—	....	....	....	....	—	....	....	....	....	Portfolio Investment Liab., n.i.e.	78bgd
	—	—	—	—	—	—	....	....	....	....	—	....	....	....	....	Equity Securities	78bmd
	—	—	—	—	—	—	....	....	....	....	—	....	....	....	....	Debt Securities	78bnd
	....	....	....	....	....	....	....	....	....	....	—	....	....	....	....	Financial Derivatives Assets	78bwd
	....	....	....	....	....	....	....	....	....	....	—	....	....	....	....	Financial Derivatives Liabilities	78bxd
	....	—	—	—	—	—	....	....	....	....	−5.80	....	....	....	....	Other Investment Assets	78bhd
	—	—	—	—	—	—	....	....	....	....	—	....	....	....	....	Monetary Authorities	78bod
	—	—	—	—	—	—	....	....	....	....	—	....	....	....	....	General Government	78bpd
	—	—	—	—	—	—	....	....	....	....	−5.80	....	....	....	....	Banks	78bqd
	—	—	—	—	—	—	....	....	....	....	—	....	....	....	....	Other Sectors	78brd
	1.48	−3.44	−8.38	1.22	−12.50	2.13	−15.82	−26.98	−28.25	−12.30	7.83	....	....	....	....	Other Investment Liab., n.i.e.	78bid
	—	—	−1.38	—	−3.75	—	−2.27	—	−6.88	—	.43	....	....	....	....	Monetary Authorities	78bsd
	1.48	−3.44	−7.00	1.22	−8.75	2.13	−13.55	−26.98	−21.37	−12.30	7.40	....	....	....	....	General Government	78btd
	—	—	—	—	—	—	....	....	....	....	—	....	....	....	....	Banks	78bud
	—	—	—	—	—	—	....	....	....	....	—	....	....	....	....	Other Sectors	78bvd
	−7.70	3.50	−11.60	−1.38	−16.28	22.01	−15.97	−24.34	−10.90	−11.47	−19.19	....	....	....	....	Net Errors and Omissions	78cad
	−30.52	−41.44	−71.18	−31.69	−75.10	−51.55	−60.70	−54.53	−40.60	−43.50	−15.24	....	....	....	....	*Overall Balance*	78cbd
	30.52	41.44	71.18	31.69	75.10	51.55	60.70	54.53	40.60	43.50	15.24	....	....	....	....	Reserves and Related Items	79dad
	−2.36	−11.83	6.70	−5.20	8.89	−5.10	9.02	6.24	−3.64	−8.90	−35.15	....	....	....	....	Reserve Assets	79dbd
	1.62	−1.26	1.97	—	—	—	−.42	−.43	1.19	1.94	5.11	....	....	....	....	Use of Fund Credit and Loans	79dcd
	31.26	54.53	62.51	36.89	66.21	56.65	52.10	48.72	43.05	50.46	45.28	....	....	....	....	Exceptional Financing	79ded
																Government Finance	
Year Ending December 31																	
	†−52.6	−325.5	−536.9	−1,110.5	−1,759.1	−3,655.8[P]	....									Deficit (-) or Surplus	80
	†193.5	358.5	657.5	1,502.2	1,904.5	2,592.2[P]	....									Revenue	81
	†392.2	751.2	1,620.8	1,488.2	2,120.0	3,328.3[P]	....									Grants Received	81z
	†636.6	1,198.2	2,664.3	3,622.6	5,093.4	8,552.3[P]	....									Expenditure	82
	†1.7	237.1	150.9	478.2	690.2	1,024.0[P]	....									Lending Minus Repayments	83
																Financing	
	†−146.8	−201.8	−196.3	468.5	−412.5	452.2[P]	....									Domestic	84a
	†226.2	498.5	824.3	884.3	2,001.4	3,203.2[P]	....									Foreign	85a
	†−26.8	28.8	−91.1	−242.2	170.2	.6[P]	....									Unallocated Financing	84xx
																National Accounts	
Millions of Francs																	
	49,850	47,715	63,849	64,190	63,324	51,017	58,010	119,594	117,485	132,206	141,323	....	....	....	....	Househ.Cons.Expend.,incl.NPISHs	96f
	9,235	11,938	13,904	10,547	12,623	9,748	8,573	15,645	10,033	10,891	18,118	....	....	....	....	Government Consumption Expend.	91f
	14,451	17,512	18,684	16,108	18,398	22,078	15,255	23,302	22,373	21,248	21,278	....	....	....	....	Gross Fixed Capital Formation	93e
	283	532	1,579	−119	−446	3,694	1,182	−7,021	154	5,624	27	....	....	....	....	Changes in Inventories	93i
	6,350	6,209	6,586	7,101	9,450	4,669	7,149	23,222	16,051	17,304	38,370	....	....	....	....	Exports of Goods and Services	90c
	22,619	27,356	36,161	27,140	31,404	32,537	24,490	48,871	42,122	47,932	60,154	....	....	....	....	Imports of Goods and Services (-)	98c
	57,500	53,000	68,200	70,700	70,900	60,100	65,600	129,200	128,900	127,400	154,600	....	....	....	....	Gross Domestic Product (GDP)	99b
	−7	−38	−113	340	−119	14	−131	....				....	....	....	....	Net Primary Income from Abroad	98.n
	1,414	2,608	5,408	8,188	13,034	23,553	36,264	....	....	....	....	....	....	....	....	Gross National Income (GNI)	99a
	79,900	82,000	85,800	91,000	94,500	96,200	98,600	103,500	107,300	112,500	117,900	....	....	....	....	GDP Volume 1986 Prices	99b.p
	74.5	76.4	80.0	84.8	88.1	89.7	91.9	96.5	100.0	104.8	109.9	....	....	....	....	GDP Volume (1995=100)	99bvp
	59.9	53.8	66.2	64.7	62.5	52.0	55.4	103.9	100.0	94.3	109.2	....	....	....	....	GDP Deflator (1995=100)	99bip
Midyear Estimates																	
	.91	.93	.95	.97	.97	1.00	1.03	1.05	1.08	1.10	1.13	1.15	1.17	1.12	1.23	**Population**	99z

(See notes in the back of the book.)

		1972	1973	1974	1975	1976	1977	1978	1979	1980	1981	1982	1983	1984	1985	1986
Exchange Rates														*Guyana Dollars per SDR:*		
Market Rate	aa	2.4	2.7	2.7	3.0	3.0	3.1	3.3	3.4	3.3	3.5	3.3	3.1	4.1	4.6	5.4
														Guyana Dollars per US Dollar:		
Market Rate	ae	2.2	2.2	2.2	2.6	2.6	2.6	2.6	2.6	2.6	3.0	3.0	3.0	4.2	4.2	4.4
Market Rate	rf	2.1	2.1	2.2	2.4	2.6	2.6	2.6	2.6	2.6	2.8	3.0	3.0	3.8	4.3	4.3
														Index Numbers (1995=100):		
Market Rate	ahx	6,810.5	6,675.3	6,367.4	6,049.1	5,564.0	5,564.0	5,564.0	5,564.0	5,564.0	5,076.8	4,728.8	4,728.8	3,717.1	3,340.4	3,321.8
Nominal Effective Exchange Rate	nec	....	....	....	....	....	....	....	....	1,644.3	1,672.7	1,695.4	1,749.5	1,954.5	1,774.8	1,674.0
Real Effective Exchange Rate	rec	....	....	....	....	....	....	....	....	523.8	567.4	641.8	754.3	772.2	798.0	757.3
Fund Position														*Millions of SDRs:*		
Quota	2f.s	20.00	20.00	20.00	20.00	20.00	20.00	25.00	25.00	37.50	37.50	37.50	49.20	49.20	49.20	49.20
SDRs	1b.s	4.10	4.04	3.91	3.77	3.54	2.73	2.76	2.83	—	1.04	2.59	—	—	—	—
Reserve Position in the Fund	1c.s	.57	—	1.76	5.00	—	—	—	—	—	—	—	—	—	—	—
Total Fund Cred.&Loans Outstg.	2tl	—	3.87	5.00	—	17.25	17.25	30.27	40.49	67.40	85.31	89.07	85.01	84.01	83.01	82.45
International Liquidity												*Millions of US Dollars Unless Otherwise Indicated:*				
Total Reserves minus Gold	1l.d	36.75	13.97	62.57	100.50	27.28	22.98	58.27	17.53	12.70	6.91	10.56	6.49	5.85	6.47	9.00
SDRs	1b.d	4.45	4.87	4.79	4.41	4.11	3.32	3.60	3.73	—	1.21	2.86	—	—	—	—
Reserve Position in the Fund	1c.d	.62	—	2.15	5.85	—	—	—	—	—	—	—	—	—	—	—
Foreign Exchange	1d.d	31.68	9.10	55.63	90.23	23.17	19.66	54.67	13.80	12.70	5.70	7.70	6.49	5.85	6.47	9.00
Monetary Authorities: Other Liab.	4..d	—	—	14.99	30.20	30.47	43.71	44.02	37.93	80.35	79.46	127.69	210.79	286.19	357.70	384.77
Deposit Money Banks: Assets	7a.d	1.12	5.99	6.27	17.20	10.28	8.31	13.25	21.91	23.12	12.16	10.24	9.13	6.93	8.19	9.17
Liabilities	7b.d	4.13	3.75	6.94	14.39	8.33	10.58	19.61	28.60	27.61	22.89	25.78	22.16	16.07	15.21	19.77
Other Banking Insts.: Assets	7e.d	.70	.70	.78	.74	.81	.88	.97	.98	1.10	1.05	.60	.66	.52	.58	.55
Liabilities	7f.d	.01	.01	.02	.02	.02	.02	.03	.03	.26	.26	.24	.23	.09	.12	.23
Monetary Authorities														*Millions of Guyana Dollars:*		
Foreign Assets	11	74	28	138	256	70	60	149	45	32	21	32	19	21	27	38
Claims on Central Government	12a	29	89	29	44	254	346	396	589	828	934	1,467	2,026	2,421	3,228	4,252
Claims on Nonfin.Pub.Enterprises	12c	—	—	—	—	—	—	—	—	—	—	—	—	—	—	—
Reserve Money	14	72	75	86	127	143	183	259	268	293	377	588	749	960	1,052	1,298
of which: Currency Outside DMBs	14a	48	56	64	92	105	143	156	148	167	186	231	269	336	422	509
Time, Savings,& Fgn.Currency Dep.	15	—	—	—	—	—	—	—	—	—	—	—	—	—	—	8
Restricted Deposits	16b	—	—	—	—	—	—	—	—	—	—	—	—	—	—	8
Foreign Liabilities	16c	—	10	14	—	51	79	126	146	229	304	297	468	955	1,281	1,524
Long-Term Foreign Liabilities	16cl	—	—	33	77	78	86	87	87	195	232	380	431	575	582	613
Central Government Deposits	16d	6	1	—	42	2	2	4	41	2	8	13	400	26	5	8
Capital Accounts	17a	24	26	27	29	31	33	35	46	56	72	74	76	92	106	118
Other Items (Net)	17r	1	5	7	25	20	22	34	46	85	−40	146	−78	−165	229	714
Deposit Money Banks														*Millions of Guyana Dollars:*		
Reserves	20	22	16	18	29	29	35	101	114	126	187	361	482	617	628	791
Foreign Assets	21	2	13	14	44	26	21	34	56	59	36	31	27	29	34	40
Claims on Central Government	22a	59	66	64	146	136	187	213	199	216	249	418	578	630	823	1,086
Claims on Local Government	22b	1	2	3	2	3	4	4	4	5	6	5	4	5	4	3
Claims on Nonfin.Pub.Enterprises	22c	12	20	56	57	76	119	122	173	229	376	306	613	551	838	323
Claims on Private Sector	22d	85	101	106	118	120	113	122	163	196	263	314	377	463	520	674
Claims on Other Banking Insts	22f	1	2	2	1	4	1	2	2	2	4	3	5	2	3	7
Demand Deposits	24	32	34	60	102	97	127	127	122	136	144	184	219	251	286	337
Time, Savings,& Fgn.Currency Dep.	25	139	167	180	232	257	303	345	408	478	584	738	899	1,035	1,270	1,507
Restricted Deposits	26b	—	—	—	—	—	—	1	1	1	1	285	398	458	489	562
Foreign Liabilities	26c	8	8	15	37	21	27	50	73	70	69	77	66	67	63	87
Central Government Deposits	26d	—	4	4	7	9	9	11	17	25	34	32	32	35	60	154
Liabilities to Other Banking Insts	26i	12	14	10	17	23	19	28	24	59	63	95	125	166	155	129
Capital Accounts	27a	2	3	4	5	5	8	9	14	18	24	39	63	69	93	132
Other Items (Net)	27r	−10	−9	−11	−1	−17	−15	29	50	47	204	−13	284	215	435	16
Monetary Survey														*Millions of Guyana Dollars:*		
Foreign Assets (Net)	31n	68	23	123	263	23	−25	6	−118	−208	−316	−312	−488	−972	−1,283	−1,533
Domestic Credit	32	182	276	255	321	584	758	845	1,071	1,450	1,790	2,467	3,172	4,010	5,352	6,183
Claims on Central Govt. (Net)	32an	82	151	88	142	380	522	595	729	1,018	1,141	1,839	2,172	2,989	3,987	5,177
Claims on Local Government	32b	1	2	3	2	3	4	4	4	5	6	5	4	5	4	3
Claims on Nonfin.Pub.Enterprises	32c	12	20	56	57	76	119	122	173	229	376	306	613	551	838	323
Claims on Private Sector	32d	85	101	106	118	120	113	122	163	196	263	314	377	463	520	674
Claims on Other Banking Insts	32f	1	2	2	1	4	1	2	2	2	4	3	5	2	3	7
Money	34	83	93	127	199	207	276	290	277	309	336	421	494	594	714	852
Quasi-Money	35	139	167	180	232	257	303	345	408	478	584	738	899	1,035	1,270	1,515
Restricted Deposits	36b	—	—	—	—	—	—	1	1	1	1	285	398	458	489	570
Long-Term Foreign Liabilities	36cl	—	—	33	77	78	86	87	87	195	232	380	431	575	582	613
Liabilities to Other Banking Insts	36i	12	14	10	17	23	19	28	24	59	63	95	125	166	155	129
Capital Accounts	37a	26	29	31	35	36	41	44	60	75	97	113	138	161	199	250
Other Items (Net)	37r	−10	−4	−4	24	6	7	57	96	125	162	122	198	51	660	721
Money plus Quasi-Money	35l	222	260	307	431	465	579	635	686	787	920	1,159	1,393	1,629	1,984	2,367
Other Banking Institutions														*Millions of Guyana Dollars:*		
Cash	40	1	1	—	—	1	1	4	3	—	—	—	—	1	—	—
Foreign Assets	41	1	2	2	2	2	2	3	3	3	3	2	2	2	2	2
Claims on Central Government	42a	1	1	2	5	8	9	7	9	10	18	27	46	87	161	260
Claims on Local Government	42b	—	1	1	1	1	2	1	1	1	1	1	1	1	1	9
Claims on Private Sector	42d	12	15	18	22	27	36	44	51	74	86	111	117	115	135	152
Claims on Deposit Money Banks	42e	—	—	—	—	—	—	—	—	8	13	13	19	22	13	17
Time, Savings,& Fgn.Currency Dep.	45	14	19	22	28	37	48	58	65	92	114	144	173	220	303	428
Foreign Liabilities	46c	—	—	—	—	—	—	—	—	1	1	1	1	—	1	1
Capital Accounts	47a	1	1	2	2	2	2	3	3	5	5	5	6	7	10	17
Other Items (Net)	47r	—	—	—	—	−1	−1	−1	−1	5	—	2	5	1	−2	−5
Banking Survey														*Millions of Guyana Dollars:*		
Foreign Assets (Net)	51n	69	24	125	265	25	−23	9	−116	−206	−313	−311	−486	−970	−1,282	−1,531
Domestic Credit	52	193	291	274	347	616	804	896	1,129	1,534	1,891	2,604	3,331	4,212	5,645	6,598
Claims on Central Govt. (Net)	52an	83	152	90	147	388	531	602	738	1,028	1,159	1,866	2,218	3,076	4,148	5,437
Claims on Local Government	52b	1	3	4	3	4	5	6	5	6	8	7	5	6	5	13
Claims on Nonfin.Pub.Enterprises	52c	12	20	56	57	76	119	122	173	229	376	306	613	551	838	323
Claims on Private Sector	52d	97	116	125	139	147	149	166	214	271	348	425	494	578	655	826
Liquid Liabilities	55l	235	278	329	459	501	627	688	747	878	1,033	1,302	1,566	1,847	2,287	2,795
Restricted Deposits	56b	—	—	—	—	—	—	1	1	1	1	285	398	458	489	570
Long-Term Foreign Liabilities	56cl	—	—	33	77	78	86	87	87	195	232	380	431	575	582	613
Capital Accounts	57a	27	30	33	37	38	43	47	62	79	102	119	145	168	209	267
Other Items (Net)	57r	—	7	4	39	25	25	82	117	174	209	207	304	194	797	823

1987	1988	1989	1990	1991	1992	1993	1994	1995	1996	1997	1998	1999	2000	2001		
End of Period															**Exchange Rates**	
14.2	13.5	43.4	64.0	174.5	173.3	179.6	208.0	208.9	203.1	194.3	228.5	247.7	240.7	238.2	Market Rate	aa
End of Period (ae) Period Average (rf)																
10.0	10.0	33.0	45.0	122.0	126.0	130.8	142.5	140.5	141.3	144.0	162.3	180.5	184.8	189.5	Market Rate	ae
9.8	10.0	27.2	39.5	111.8	125.0	126.7	138.3	142.0	140.4	142.4	150.5	178.0	182.4	187.3	Market Rate	rf
Period Averages																
1,467.6	1,418.7	678.2	366.7	139.2	113.0	112.0	102.7	100.0	101.1	99.4	94.5	79.8	77.8	75.7	Market Rate	ahx
733.8	749.7	410.8	207.8	94.5	89.5	102.7	104.9	100.0	103.7	108.0	105.9	90.6	92.2	93.9	Nominal Effective Exchange Rate	nec
389.3	170.9	136.3	96.6	82.5	90.6	98.9	98.2	100.0	108.0	113.8	114.5	103.8	109.4	110.5	Real Effective Exchange Rate	rec
End of Period															**Fund Position**	
49.20	49.20	49.20	49.20	49.20	67.20	67.20	67.20	67.20	67.20	67.20	67.20	90.90	90.90	90.90	Quota	2f.s
—	—	—	1.49	.99	.24	—	.05	.09	.07	.14	.17	.92	7.02	1.96	SDRs	1b.s
—	—	—	—	—	—	—	—	—	—	—	—	—	—	—	Reserve Position in the Fund	1c.s
81.74	81.74	80.91	79.38	104.46	122.17	128.60	122.25	115.60	117.11	116.44	109.50	102.15	90.12	77.67	Total Fund Cred.&Loans Outstg.	2tl
End of Period															**International Liquidity**	
8.43	4.04	13.35	28.68	124.42	188.08	247.45	247.13	268.94	329.68	315.51	276.60	268.28	304.96	287.26	Total Reserves minus Gold	1l.d
—	—	—	2.12	1.42	.33	—	.08	.14	.11	.20	.24	1.27	9.15	2.47	SDRs	1b.d
—	—	—	—	—	—	—	—	—	—	—	—	—	—	—	Reserve Position in the Fund	1c.d
8.43	4.04	13.35	26.56	123.00	187.75	247.45	247.05	268.80	329.57	315.31	276.36	267.01	295.81	284.79	Foreign Exchange	1d.d
418.61	427.85	605.64	711.78	727.42	729.66	715.25	656.62	725.00	448.57	286.86	222.56	187.68	186.51	179.00	Monetary Authorities: Other Liab.	4..d
16.05	16.42	23.06	53.38	19.74	29.83	24.40	24.88	27.03	26.55	24.29	23.91	40.13	38.77	46.36	Deposit Money Banks: Assets	7a.d
14.37	14.14	5.73	19.77	7.52	14.64	15.92	20.57	20.52	25.62	34.47	31.93	22.23	20.66	17.55	Liabilities	7b.d
.27	.40	.12	.12	.16	.72	.94	1.21	1.28	1.38	2.38	1.98	2.59	7.32	7.67	Other Banking Insts.: Assets	7e.d
.22	.23	—	—	—	—	.04	—	7.30	1.03	1.12	.69	.46	3.42	5.38	Liabilities	7f.d
End of Period															**Monetary Authorities**	
84	40	470	1,328	15,277	23,488	†31,557	35,741	38,398	46,466	43,578	40,149	44,590	54,645	53,979	Foreign Assets	11
6,664	10,463	24,199	31,301	68,417	100,839	†109,080	118,849	125,918	96,232	76,959	67,904	71,686	72,208	70,613	Claims on Central Government	12a
41	94	318	671	801	898	†762	1,098	811	2,441	3,238	3,320	4,709	4,710	4,710	Claims on Nonfin.Pub.Enterprises	12c
3,111	3,695	3,399	4,016	10,316	15,647	†12,523	16,453	19,603	20,760	24,314	27,179	26,128	29,794	33,043	Reserve Money	14
726	1,058	1,506	2,211	3,711	5,095	†6,480	8,167	8,967	9,959	11,210	11,334	13,394	14,495	15,138	*of which: Currency Outside DMBs*	14a
—	—	8	53	108	278	†378	335	561	489	749	694	1,219	1,146	921	Time, Savings,& Fgn.Currency Dep.	15
—	1	30	—	—	84	†—	—	—	—	—	—	—	—	—	Restricted Deposits	16b
3,948	3,978	18,854	27,312	79,613	86,008	†89,751	91,358	95,914	63,243	44,406	45,418	46,547	43,511	40,968	Foreign Liabilities	16c
1,398	1,401	4,641	9,800	27,361	27,094	†26,864	27,641	30,091	23,903	19,525	15,708	12,636	12,640	11,449	Long-Term Foreign Liabilities	16cl
7	—	31	70	680	1,260	†15,220	22,623	21,335	30,256	27,147	22,066	34,594	39,130	37,965	Central Government Deposits	16d
249	242	677	977	2,540	2,522	†–1,455	2,345	3,253	2,567	3,449	5,184	5,891	6,822	7,290	Capital Accounts	17a
–1,924	1,279	–2,654	–8,930	–36,124	–7,669	†–1,882	–5,068	–5,631	3,921	4,187	–4,875	–6,030	–1,482	–2,334	Other Items (Net)	17r
End of Period															**Deposit Money Banks**	
2,433	2,697	1,865	1,802	6,629	10,548	5,503	8,171	10,326	10,781	13,315	16,070	12,419	15,510	18,340	Reserves	20
161	164	761	2,402	2,409	3,759	3,190	3,546	3,798	3,750	3,497	3,880	7,243	7,163	8,786	Foreign Assets	21
352	731	2,686	4,111	7,227	12,282	20,064	15,651	14,847	17,251	18,028	15,851	13,346	20,264	20,766	Claims on Central Government	22a
6	4	10	2	2	28	36	—	36	1	4	500	48	39	1	Claims on Local Government	22b
356	552	652	755	359	835	471	188	410	254	216	410	683	420	852	Claims on Nonfin.Pub.Enterprises	22c
987	1,591	2,566	4,160	6,672	8,735	10,254	13,900	21,107	36,309	44,863	51,838	55,823	58,341	58,943	Claims on Private Sector	22d
6	5	7	1	62	5	28	13	73	183	118	195	569	660	464	Claims on Other Banking Insts	22f
558	934	1,165	1,918	3,126	3,897	4,902	4,941	6,336	7,565	8,064	7,639	9,949	11,286	10,945	Demand Deposits	24
2,173	2,733	4,479	6,742	12,003	21,483	25,271	28,764	36,661	44,708	49,032	53,981	57,049	61,514	69,109	Time, Savings,& Fgn.Currency Dep.	25
641	763	957	916	746	517	368	334	330	330	318	307	70	66	56	Restricted Deposits	26b
144	141	189	890	917	1,845	2,081	2,931	2,883	3,619	4,964	5,181	4,012	3,816	3,325	Foreign Liabilities	26c
194	248	356	515	1,064	1,612	3,161	3,246	2,071	2,920	5,662	5,782	3,857	7,284	5,488	Central Government Deposits	26d
356	676	975	1,437	2,840	3,200	2,895	1,356	1,827	2,757	3,778	5,898	5,796	8,455	8,009	Liabilities to Other Banking Insts	26i
170	247	388	797	1,397	4,045	3,660	3,968	5,392	13,712	15,054	19,385	21,477	22,277	22,722	Capital Accounts	27a
64	2	38	20	1,265	–409	–2,792	–4,072	–4,903	–7,079	–6,828	–9,429	–12,081	–12,302	–11,501	Other Items (Net)	27r
End of Period															**Monetary Survey**	
–3,846	–3,914	–17,812	–24,472	–62,845	–60,606	†–57,085	–55,003	–56,600	–16,646	–2,294	–6,570	1,274	14,480	18,472	Foreign Assets (Net)	31n
8,210	13,191	30,050	40,415	81,796	120,749	†122,314	123,830	139,796	119,495	110,619	112,172	108,412	110,227	112,896	Domestic Credit	32
6,815	10,946	26,497	34,827	73,900	110,249	†110,763	108,630	117,360	80,307	62,178	55,908	46,581	46,058	47,927	Claims on Central Govt. (Net)	32an
6	4	10	2	2	28	36	—	36	1	4	500	48	39	1	Claims on Local Government	32b
397	646	970	1,426	1,160	1,733	†1,232	1,286	1,220	2,695	3,455	3,730	5,392	5,129	5,562	Claims on Nonfin.Pub.Enterprises	32c
987	1,591	2,566	4,160	6,672	8,735	10,254	13,900	21,107	36,309	44,863	51,838	55,823	58,341	58,943	Claims on Private Sector	32d
6	5	7	1	62	5	28	13	73	183	118	195	569	660	464	Claims on Other Banking Insts	32f
1,291	1,999	2,677	4,136	6,844	8,999	†11,881	13,115	15,310	17,531	19,281	18,980	23,350	25,788	26,089	Money	34
2,173	2,733	4,487	6,795	12,112	21,762	†25,649	29,100	37,222	45,197	49,780	54,675	58,268	62,660	70,029	Quasi-Money	35
642	764	987	916	746	601	†368	334	330	330	318	307	70	66	56	Restricted Deposits	36b
1,398	1,401	4,641	9,800	27,361	27,094	†26,864	27,641	30,091	23,903	19,525	15,708	12,636	12,640	11,449	Long-Term Foreign Liabilities	36cl
356	676	975	1,437	2,840	3,200	2,895	1,356	1,827	2,757	3,778	5,898	5,796	8,455	8,009	Liabilities to Other Banking Insts	36i
419	489	1,065	1,774	3,937	6,567	†2,205	6,313	8,645	16,278	18,503	24,569	27,368	29,099	30,013	Capital Accounts	37a
–1,915	1,216	–2,594	–8,914	–34,889	–8,080	†–4,634	–9,032	–10,231	–3,146	–2,860	–14,536	–17,803	–14,000	–14,277	Other Items (Net)	37r
3,464	4,732	7,164	10,930	18,956	30,760	†37,531	42,214	52,532	62,727	69,061	73,655	81,618	88,448	96,119	Money plus Quasi-Money	35l
End of Period															**Other Banking Institutions**	
—	8	3	4	3	6	129	9	21	50	29	44	184	331	464	Cash	40
3	4	4	6	20	91	123	172	180	195	342	321	467	1,353	1,454	Foreign Assets	41
316	339	483	743	1,326	2,146	2,611	3,444	3,410	4,339	5,055	5,226	4,725	5,227	7,020	Claims on Central Government	42a
9	9	10	12	12	12	18	17	17	—	—	—	—	—	—	Claims on Local Government	42b
204	286	357	479	626	1,300	2,102	2,446	3,615	5,335	6,609	8,718	14,759	15,939	18,034	Claims on Private Sector	42d
32	73	63	173	308	437	530	131	555	460	233	287	255	1,168	1,790	Claims on Deposit Money Banks	42e
538	662	904	1,063	1,633	3,435	4,339	5,254	6,360	8,450	10,477	12,065	13,352	15,641	19,648	Time, Savings,& Fgn.Currency Dep.	45
2	2	—	—	—	—	5	—	1,025	145	162	111	83	632	1,020	Foreign Liabilities	46c
34	63	46	97	180	343	581	778	1,078	1,990	2,658	3,515	4,721	5,358	5,828	Capital Accounts	47a
–11	–8	–30	257	482	214	588	188	–665	–205	–1,027	–1,095	2,234	2,386	2,265	Other Items (Net)	47r
End of Period															**Banking Survey**	
–3,846	–3,913	–17,808	–24,466	–62,825	–60,515	†–56,967	–54,831	–57,445	–16,595	–2,114	–6,360	1,658	15,201	18,905	Foreign Assets (Net)	51n
8,733	13,820	30,893	41,648	83,698	124,202	127,017	129,724	146,764	128,986	122,165	125,921	127,328	130,733	137,487	Domestic Credit	52
7,131	11,284	26,980	35,570	75,226	112,395	†113,374	112,074	120,769	84,646	67,234	61,134	51,306	51,285	54,947	Claims on Central Govt. (Net)	52an
15	14	20	14	14	40	55	17	53	1	4	500	48	39	1	Claims on Local Government	52b
397	646	970	1,426	1,160	1,733	†1,232	1,286	1,220	2,695	3,455	3,730	5,392	5,129	5,562	Claims on Nonfin.Pub.Enterprises	52c
1,190	1,877	2,923	4,638	7,299	10,035	12,356	16,346	24,722	41,644	51,472	60,556	70,583	74,280	76,977	Claims on Private Sector	52d
4,002	5,386	8,065	11,990	20,587	34,189	†41,741	47,459	58,871	71,128	79,509	85,676	94,786	103,758	115,303	Liquid Liabilities	55l
642	764	987	916	746	601	†368	334	330	330	318	307	70	66	56	Restricted Deposits	56b
1,398	1,401	4,641	9,800	27,361	27,094	†26,864	27,641	30,091	23,903	19,525	15,708	12,636	12,640	11,449	Long-Term Foreign Liabilities	56cl
453	551	1,111	1,870	4,116	6,910	†2,786	7,091	9,723	18,268	21,161	28,084	32,089	34,457	35,841	Capital Accounts	57a
–1,608	1,806	–1,720	–7,395	–31,937	–5,107	†–1,709	–7,633	–9,697	–1,238	–461	–10,215	–10,596	–4,987	–6,257	Other Items (Net)	57r

Guyana

		1972	1973	1974	1975	1976	1977	1978	1979	1980	1981	1982	1983	1984	1985	1986
Interest Rates															*Percent Per Annum*	
Discount Rate (End of Period)	60	6.5	6.5	6.5	6.5	6.5	6.5	8.5	10.5	12.5	12.5	14.0	14.0	14.0	14.0	14.0
Treasury Bill Rate	60c	5.9	5.9	5.9	5.9	5.9	5.9	7.0	9.1	10.7	11.6	12.3	12.8	12.8	12.8	12.8
Deposit Rate	60l	....	....	4.0	4.0	4.0	4.0	7.0	9.0	11.0	11.0	11.6	12.0	12.0	12.0	12.0
Lending Rate	60p	....	....	7.5	7.5	7.5	7.5	9.5	11.5	13.5	13.5	14.4	15.0	15.0	15.0	15.0
Prices														*Index Numbers (1995=100):*		
Consumer Prices	64	....		....		....		....		....		....		....		....
International Transactions													*Millions of Guyana Dollars*			
Exports	70	306.5	288.0	600.0	858.0	711.3	661.2	753.8	746.4	992.4	974.3	724.0	566.5	807.7	705.6	953.2
Imports, c.i.f.	71	297.9	372.6	567.0	810.6	927.4	800.3	711.1	809.8	1,010.4	1,207.6	842.4	738.3	811.5	959.6	1,030.0
																1995=100
Volume of Exports	72	115	73	89	89	86	65	86	80	76	79	68	59	60	62	62
Balance of Payments													*Millions of US Dollars:*			
Current Account, n.i.e.	78al d	....		....		....	−97.5	−29.6	−82.9	−128.5	−184.5	−142.3	−157.5	−98.9	−96.6	....
Goods: Exports f.o.b.	78aa d						259.3	295.6	292.7	388.9	346.4	241.4	193.3	216.9	214.0	
Goods: Imports f.o.b.	78ab d						−286.7	−253.5	−288.8	−386.4	−399.6	−254.2	−225.7	−201.6	−209.1	
Trade Balance	78ac d						−27.4	42.1	3.9	2.4	−53.2	−12.7	−32.4	15.2	4.9	
Services: Credit	78ad d						16.2	18.2	18.5	19.8	23.0	22.6	31.5	29.2	48.0	
Services: Debit	78ae d						−60.7	−60.1	−71.4	−107.3	−98.9	−94.5	−98.1	−99.0	−104.0	
Balance on Goods & Services	78af d						−72.0	.2	−48.9	−85.1	−129.1	−84.6	−99.0	−54.6	−51.1	
Income: Credit	78ag d								3.7	1.9	3.1	.3	.3	.3		
Income: Debit	78ah d						−21.6	−23.3	−38.1	−44.5	−57.6	−49.3	−57.8	−44.9	−40.3	
Balance on Gds, Serv. & Inc.	78ai d						−93.6	−23.1	−83.3	−127.7	−183.7	−133.5	−156.5	−99.3	−91.4	
Current Transfers, n.i.e.: Credit	78aj d						3.6	3.8	10.2	8.9	8.3	3.1	5.1	3.7	2.3	
Current Transfers: Debit	78ak d						−7.5	−10.3	−9.8	−9.7	−9.1	−11.9	−6.1	−3.4	−7.5	
Capital Account, n.i.e.	78bc d						—	—	—	—	—	—	—	2.6		
Capital Account, n.i.e.: Credit	78ba d						—	—	—	—	—	—	—	2.6		
Capital Account: Debit	78bb d						—	—	—	—	—	—	—			
Financial Account, n.i.e.	78bj d						30.7	34.7	29.2	22.4	−17.7	−61.6	−131.4	−28.6	−37.6	
Direct Investment Abroad	78bd d															
Dir. Invest. in Rep. Econ., n.i.e.	78be d						−1.8		.6	.6	−1.8	4.4	4.7	4.5	1.8	
Portfolio Investment Assets	78bf d						−1.0	−1.5	3.5	2.5	—	—	—	—		
Equity Securities	78bk d						—	—	—	—	—	—	—	—		
Debt Securities	78bl d						−1.0	−1.5	3.5	2.5	—	—	—	—		
Portfolio Investment Liab., n.i.e.	78bg d						—	—	—	—	—	—	—	—		
Equity Securities	78bm d						—	—	—	—	—	—	—	—		
Debt Securities	78bn d						—	—	—	—	—	—	—	—		
Financial Derivatives Assets	78bw d						....	....	....	....	....	....	....	....		
Financial Derivatives Liabilities	78bx d						....	....	....	....	....	....	....	....		
Other Investment Assets	78bh d						−3.6	−12.7	−5.3	−1.1	9.8	−1.4	1.1	−.4	−1.2	
Monetary Authorities	78bo d															
General Government	78bp d															
Banks	78bq d						2.0	−4.9	−8.7	−1.2	8.0	1.9	1.1	−.4	−1.2	
Other Sectors	78br d						−5.6	−7.7	3.4	.1	1.8	−3.4	—			
Other Investment Liab., n.i.e.	78bi d						37.1	48.9	30.3	20.4	−25.8	−64.6	−137.3	−32.7	−38.2	
Monetary Authorities	78bs d						—	—	−6.3	−15.5	−64.3	−32.5	−72.3	—		
General Government	78bt d						8.7	20.9	26.9	46.5	36.2	−40.4	−42.8	−32.5	−37.2	
Banks	78bu d						2.3	8.9	9.0	−1.0	−.9	2.9	−3.3	−.5	−.4	
Other Sectors	78bv d						26.2	19.1	.7	−9.7	3.3	5.4	−18.9	.3	−.7	
Net Errors and Omissions	78ca d						9.6	21.4	−8.0	.1	−10.8	43.4	58.1	−12.7	−4.3	
Overall Balance	78cb d						−57.3	26.6	−61.8	−106.0	−213.1	−160.5	−230.9	−137.6	−138.6	
Reserves and Related Items	79da d						57.3	−26.6	61.8	106.0	213.1	160.5	230.9	137.6	138.6	
Reserve Assets	79db d						11.4	−32.9	44.0	8.2	10.6	−3.5	4.0	−22.9	−3.5	
Use of Fund Credit and Loans	79dc d						—	16.4	13.0	35.1	21.0	3.9	−4.4	−1.0	−1.0	
Exceptional Financing	79de d						45.8	−10.0	4.8	62.7	181.5	160.1	231.2	161.5	143.1	....
Government Finance													*Millions of Guyana Dollars:*			
Deficit (-) or Surplus	80	−39	−105	−22	−78	−313	−133	−129	−232	−440	−589	−958	−592	−756	−740	−1,306
Total Revenue and Grants	81y	163	180	323	503	399	381	404	481	540	647	627	631	701	812	1,047
Revenue	81	163	176	322	503	399	378	404	465	527	644	624	630	651	781	1,022
Grants	81z	—	3	1	—	—	2	1	16	13	3	3	1	51	31	26
Exp. & Lending Minus Repay.	82z	203	285	345	581	712	514	533	713	980	1,236	1,585	1,223	1,457	1,553	2,354
Expenditure	82	202	280	340	560	685	513	533	689	906	1,154	1,509	1,141	1,457	1,553	2,354
Lending Minus Repayments	83	1	4	5	21	27	1	—	24	74	82	76	82			
Total Financing	80h	39	105	22	78	313	133	129	232	440	589	958	592	756	740	1,306
Total Net Borrowing	84	39	147	17	160	351	167	183	225	440	659	835	440	1,066	1,036	1,706
Net Domestic	84a	33	106	−46	9	225	153	138	173	347	377	784	348	1,012	996	1,600
Net Foreign	85a	7	41	63	152	126	14	45	52	93	282	51	91	54	40	106
Use of Cash Balances	87	—	−42	5	−83	−38	−34	−55	7	—	−70	122	153	−310	−296	−400
Total Debt	88	286	451	603	892	1,211	1,414	1,599	1,892	3,676	4,046	4,801	5,914	7,142	8,707	†10,673
Domestic	88a	157	210	189	304	511	692	810	1,014	1,637	1,808	2,763	3,810	4,396	5,293	6,117
Foreign	89a	129	241	414	588	700	722	789	879	2,039	2,238	2,038	2,104	2,746	3,414	†4,557
National Accounts													*Millions of Guyana Dollars*			
Househ.Cons.Expend.,incl.NPISHs	96f	363	424	517	562	638	707	669	810	1,010	1,236	842	893	969	1,071	1,000
Government Consumption Expend.	91f	117	159	180	247	330	298	335	348	436	470	435	465	790	700	876
Gross Fixed Capital Formation	93e	119	175	252	392	425	290	241	411	449	573	380	395	390	410	586
Exports of Goods and Services	90c	300	288	595	830	711	661	750	746	992	974	775	565	831	869	920
Imports of Goods and Services (-)	98c	298	373	567	811	927	804	711	930	1,215	1,375	1,037	738	812	960	1,030
Gross Domestic Product (GDP)	99b	598	644	943	1,179	1,117	1,120	1,246	1,326	1,508	1,597	1,446	1,455	1,700	1,964	2,220
Net Primary Income from Abroad	98.n	−22	−27	−38	−44	−60	−67	−53	−73	−83	−161	−156	−173	−182	−107	−283
Gross National Income (GNI)	99a	576	617	905	1,135	1,057	1,053	1,193	1,253	1,425	1,446	1,290	1,282	1,518	1,857	1,936
Net National Income	99e	543	581	865	1,088	1,003	993	1,123	1,168	1,330	1,343	1,172	1,162	1,393	1,731	1,802
GDP Volume 1977 Prices	99b.p	955	971	1,039	1,148	1,181	†1,120	1,105	976	992	989	886	804	....		
GDP Volume 1988 Prices	99b.p	....		....		....		....		....		....	3,749	2,830	3,843	3,664
GDP Volume (1990=100)	99bv p	134.2	136.5	146.0	161.2	165.9	†158.0	155.3	137.1	139.4	138.9	124.5	113.0	85.3	115.8	110.4
GDP Deflator (1990=100)	99bi p	2.8	3.0	4.1	4.7	4.3	†4.5	5.1	6.2	6.9	7.3	7.4	8.2	12.7	10.8	12.8
																Millions:
Population	99z	.75	.76	.77	.78	.79	.81	.82	.85	.87	.77	.77	.78	.79	.79	.79

Interest Rates / Prices / International Transactions

1987	1988	1989	1990	1991	1992	1993	1994	1995	1996	1997	1998	1999	2000	2001		
Percent Per Annum															**Interest Rates**	
14.0	14.0	35.0	30.0	32.5	24.3	17.0	20.3	17.3	12.0	11.0	11.3	13.3	11.8	8.8	Discount Rate *(End of Period)*	60
11.3	11.0	15.2	30.0	30.9	25.7	16.8	17.7	17.5	11.4	8.9	8.3	11.3	9.9	7.8	Treasury Bill Rate	60c
11.1	12.0	15.8	29.2	29.5	22.5	12.3	11.4	12.9	10.5	8.6	8.1	9.1	8.7	7.6	Deposit Rate	60l
15.0	15.1	18.9	32.8	33.6	28.7	19.4	18.4	19.2	17.8	17.0	16.8	17.1	17.3	17.0	Lending Rate	60p
Period Averages															**Prices**	
....	....	....	....	....	....	....	89.1	100.0	107.1	110.9	116.0	124.7	132.4	135.9	Consumer Prices	64
Millions of Guyana Dollars															**International Transactions**	
2,596.3	2,295.6	6,123.2	10,207.7	28,107.2	36,567.2	52,506.9	63,389.8	64,581.3	72,597.9	91,808.7	73,336.3	93,138.0	90,830.4	89,593.4	Exports	70
2,590.0	2,156.0	7,012.0	12,290.0	34,274.9	55,319.8	61,376.0	70,000.6	74,911.5	83,895.0	89,746.8	....	....	....	109,362.4	Imports, c.i.f.	71
1995=100																
59	45	52	44	45	70	81	88	100	70	102	98	106	102	34,881	Volume of Exports	72

Balance of Payments

Minus Sign Indicates Debit

1992	1993	1994	1995		
				Balance of Payments	
−138.5	−140.2	−124.9	−134.8	Current Account, n.i.e.	78ald
381.7	415.5	463.4	495.7	Goods: Exports f.o.b.	78aad
−442.7	−483.8	−504.0	−536.5	Goods: Imports f.o.b.	78abd
−61.0	−68.3	−40.6	−40.8	*Trade Balance*	78acd
105.9	115.3	120.7	133.5	Services: Credit	78add
−139.8	−148.1	−160.9	−171.8	Services: Debit	78aed
−95.0	−101.1	−80.8	−79.2	*Balance on Goods & Services*	78afd
4.9	5.1	8.7	12.2	Income: Credit	78agd
−101.5	−106.8	−114.8	−129.9	Income: Debit	78ahd
−191.6	−202.9	−186.9	−196.8	*Balance on Gds, Serv. & Inc.*	78aid
62.9	70.0	68.1	67.4	Current Transfers, n.i.e.: Credit	78ajd
−9.9	−7.4	−6.2	−5.3	Current Transfers: Debit	78akd
1.6	4.4	8.3	9.5	Capital Account, n.i.e.	78bcd
3.4	6.6	11.0	12.5	Capital Account, n.i.e.: Credit	78bad
−1.8	−2.2	−2.7	−3.0	Capital Account: Debit	78bbd
63.1	88.7	126.9	71.1	Financial Account, n.i.e.	78bjd
				Direct Investment Abroad	78bdd
146.6	69.5	106.7	74.4	Dir. Invest. in Rep. Econ., n.i.e.	78bed
....	....	....	....	Portfolio Investment Assets	78bfd
....	....	....	....	Equity Securities	78bkd
....	....	....	....	Debt Securities	78bld
2.8	3.6	15.8	3.2	Portfolio Investment Liab., n.i.e.	78bgd
....	....	....	....	Equity Securities	78bmd
2.8	3.6	15.8	3.2	Debt Securities	78bnd
....	....	....	....	Financial Derivatives Assets	78bwd
....	....	....	....	Financial Derivatives Liabilities	78bxd
−19.9	8.8	−5.8	−8.9	Other Investment Assets	78bhd
....	....	....	....	Monetary Authorities	78bod
−3.4	1.4	1.3	−2.2	General Government	78bpd
−6.4	3.2	4.2	−2.8	Banks	78bqd
−10.2	4.2	−11.2	−3.9	Other Sectors	78brd
−66.4	6.7	10.2	2.3	Other Investment Liab., n.i.e.	78bid
−4.7	−13.9	1.3	18.6	Monetary Authorities	78bsd
−73.6	27.3	−1.0	−5.4	General Government	78btd
−5.5	−4.9	−2.9	−.4	Banks	78bud
17.4	−1.8	12.9	−10.5	Other Sectors	78bvd
12.2	11.0	−16.3	11.2	Net Errors and Omissions	78cad
−61.6	−36.1	−6.0	−43.0	*Overall Balance*	78cbd
61.6	36.1	6.0	43.0	Reserves and Related Items	79dad
−67.1	−57.1	−21.8	.8	Reserve Assets	79dbd
24.8	9.1	−8.8	−9.7	Use of Fund Credit and Loans	79dcd
103.9	84.2	36.6	52.0	Exceptional Financing	79ded

Government Finance / National Accounts

Year Ending December 31

1987	1988	1989	1990	1991	1992	1993	1994	1995	1996	1997		
											Government Finance	
−1,425	−1,309	−719	−3,398	−9,166	−7,994	−4,001	−5,092	−2,886	−3,115	−6,611	Deficit (-) or Surplus	80
1,291	1,790	4,241	7,536	13,545	19,464	23,901	29,133	32,428	37,180	39,071	Total Revenue and Grants	81y
1,221	1,730	3,248	5,642	13,392	18,913	23,191	28,138	30,823	34,666	36,006	Revenue	81
70	59	992	1,895	152	551	710	995	1,605	2,515	3,065	Grants	81z
2,716	3,099	4,960	10,935	22,711	27,457	27,902	34,226	35,314	40,295	45,682	Exp. & Lending Minus Repay.	82z
2,716	3,099	4,960	10,935	22,711	27,457	27,902	34,226	35,314	40,295	45,682	Expenditure	82
—	—	—									Lending Minus Repayments	83
1,425	1,309	719	3,398	9,166	7,994	4,001	5,092	2,886	3,115	6,611	Total Financing	80h
4,307	1,139	2,836	3,468	6,357	4,715	−5,398	−699	2,826	−931	4,310	Total Net Borrowing	84
4,210	1,384	2,549	737	233	1,183	−6,573	−4,394	1,627	−7,298	−162	Net Domestic	84a
97	−245	287	2,731	6,124	3,532	1,175	3,695	1,199	6,367	4,473	Net Foreign	85a
−2,882	170	−2,116	−70	2,809	3,278	9,399	5,791	60	4,046	2,301	Use of Cash Balances	87
17,984	19,419	55,208	91,687	239,708	265,920	283,213	316,419	322,444	249,167	258,325	Total Debt	88
6,810	7,084	9,275	9,782	11,958	18,053	27,793	31,490	33,252	37,478	35,888	Domestic	88a
11,174	12,335	45,933	81,905	227,750	247,867	255,420	284,929	289,191	211,688	222,436	Foreign	89a

Millions of Guyana Dollars

1987	1988	1989	1990	1991	1992	1993	1994	1995	1996	1997		
											National Accounts	
1,715	2,279	5,987	9,537	21,504	23,525	29,134	36,131	40,897	44,224	47,147	Househ.Cons.Expend.,incl.NPISHs	96f
952	1,162	1,701	2,133	4,610	6,383	8,529	11,817	14,092	17,330	21,747	Government Consumption Expend.	91f
1,123	890	3,536	6,624	13,746	25,113	30,745	34,348	40,077	43,436	47,099	Gross Fixed Capital Formation	93e
2,406	2,123	6,452	8,630	29,870	47,689	52,518	59,185	70,315	82,155	84,375	Exports of Goods and Services	90c
2,619	2,125	7,012	12,290	34,275	55,310	64,370	64,370	74,912	83,895	91,749	Imports of Goods and Services (-)	98c
3,357	4,137	10,330	15,665	38,966	46,734	59,124	75,412	88,271	99,038	105,859	Gross Domestic Product (GDP)	99b
−606	−869	−2,790	−4,239	−15,093	−13,800	−11,912	−11,473	−12,203	−7,319	−10,406	Net Primary Income from Abroad	98.n
2,751	3,268	7,540	11,426	23,873	32,934	47,212	63,939	76,068	91,719	95,399	Gross National Income (GNI)	99a
2,611	3,128	7,160	11,426	23,873	32,934	47,212	63,939	76,068	91,719	95,399	Net National Income	99e
....	....	....	....	....	....	....	....	....	....	....	GDP Volume 1977 Prices	99b.p
3,695	3,600	3,482	3,319	3,519	3,792	4,104	....	....	....	....	GDP Volume 1988 Prices	99b.p
111.3	108.5	104.9	100.0	106.0	114.3	123.7	....	....	....	....	GDP Volume (1990=100)	99bv.p
19.2	24.3	62.9	100.0	234.6	261.1	305.2	....	....	....	....	GDP Deflator (1990=100)	99bi.p

Population

Midyear Estimates

1987	1988	1989	1990	1991	1992	1993	1994	1995	1996	1997	1998	1999	2000	2001		
.79	.79	.79	.80	.73	.73	.73	.75	.76	.77	.78	.77	.77	.77	.76	Population	99z

(See notes in the back of the book.)

Haiti

		1972	1973	1974	1975	1976	1977	1978	1979	1980	1981	1982	1983	1984	1985	1986
Exchange Rates														*Gourdes per SDR:*		
Market Rate	aa	5.428	6.031	6.121	5.852	5.808	6.072	6.513	6.585	6.376	5.819	5.515	5.234	4.900	5.491	6.115
														Gourdes per US Dollar:		
Market Rate	ae	4.999	4.999	4.999	4.999	4.999	4.999	4.999	4.999	4.999	4.999	4.999	4.999	4.999	4.999	4.999
Market Rate	rf	5.000	5.000	5.000	5.000	5.000	5.000	5.000	5.000	5.000	5.000	5.000	5.000	5.000	5.000	5.000
Fund Position														*Millions of SDRs:*		
Quota	2f. s	19.0	19.0	19.0	19.0	19.0	19.0	23.0	23.0	34.5	34.5	34.5	44.1	44.1	44.1	44.1
SDRs	1b. s	3.1	1.7	2.5	2.0	1.2	1.6	3.8	5.5	—	—	1.0	1.0	—	—	5.4
Reserve Position in the Fund	1c. s	2.9	.2	—	—	—	—	2.4	4.4	—	—	.1	.1	.1	.1	.1
Total Fund Cred.&Loans Outstg.	2tl	—	—	6.6	11.0	12.4	10.5	15.5	19.3	35.7	50.6	61.4	90.1	102.3	87.4	72.8
International Liquidity												*Millions of US Dollars Unless Otherwise Indicated:*				
Total Reserves minus Gold	1l. d	17.9	17.0	19.7	12.4	27.9	33.8	38.6	55.0	16.2	24.0	4.2	9.0	13.0	6.4	15.9
SDRs	1b. d	3.3	2.0	3.0	2.3	1.4	1.9	5.0	7.2	—	—	1.0	1.0	—	—	6.6
Reserve Position in the Fund	1c. d	3.2	.2	—	—	—	—	3.1	5.8	—	—	.1	.1	.1	.1	.1
Foreign Exchange	1d. d	11.4	14.8	16.7	10.1	26.5	31.9	30.6	42.0	16.2	24.0	3.1	7.9	12.9	6.3	9.2
Gold (Million Fine Troy Ounces)	1ad	....	....	.002	.002	.002	.006	.010	.018	.018	.018	.018	.018	.018	.018	.018
Monetary Authorities: Other Liab.	4..d	6.2	7.0	7.4	17.9	33.2	59.7	82.6	103.2	114.6	124.1	132.9	143.9	157.0	139.6	154.0
Deposit Money Banks: Assets	7a. d	3.5	2.4	3.0	5.5	5.3	8.9	6.0	8.8	20.7	46.5	19.4	26.5	29.8	30.0	30.2
Liabilities	7b. d	—	4.7	17.0	23.0	19.6	16.8	16.2	13.3	13.3	12.3	15.4	11.9	8.8		2.4
Monetary Authorities														*Millions of Gourdes:*		
Foreign Assets	11	92.1	84.5	98.8	62.6	140.0	171.1	193.1	295.0	149.4	190.3	116.4	133.3	145.8	104.2	180.1
Claims on Central Government	12a	216.0	242.5	306.3	446.1	534.1	754.6	739.2	793.4	1,094.1	1,382.3	1,549.0	2,183.1	2,204.3	2,199.9	2,700.0
Claims on Local Government	12b															
Claims on Nonfin.Pub.Enterprises	12c	32.2	46.0	61.9	161.4	243.8	298.6	358.8	421.1	597.9	626.5	522.5	514.3	514.9	496.3	287.8
Claims on Private Sector	12d	57.8	84.8	111.3	149.2	184.6	226.9	370.6	315.7	346.0	394.1	374.5	266.6	314.5	363.9	336.0
Claims on Deposit Money Banks	12e	3.3	10.1	19.6	15.7	20.8	39.0	50.8	79.2	53.5	53.2	69.7	35.2	25.2	26.3	7.4
Claims on Other Banking Insts	12f	9.8	11.2	12.8	11.0	12.4	12.4	10.2	16.6	15.9	31.7	36.5	43.6	48.9	35.2	73.2
Claims on Nonbank Financial Insts	12g															
Reserve Money	14	256.5	305.0	319.0	396.7	548.8	649.5	717.7	804.6	994.3	1,157.0	1,169.7	1,153.1	1,397.9	1,569.7	1,809.1
of which: Currency Outside DMBs	14a	147.7	172.9	182.7	189.5	243.2	265.5	311.4	418.5	418.1	487.4	565.6	599.5	691.0	763.2	829.1
Time, Savings,& Fgn.Currency Dep.	15	41.2	55.1	74.1	82.2	107.1	135.1	168.6	168.9	175.2	208.4	223.4	260.9	277.9	366.4	375.4
Liabs. of Central Bank: Securities	16ac															
Foreign Liabilities	16c	2.0	2.7	45.6	66.4	76.0	68.7	107.2	136.4	234.3	309.5	357.2	485.9	560.9	479.9	445.0
Long-Term Foreign Liabilities	16cl	28.8	32.1	32.2	87.3	161.9	293.2	406.7	507.1	565.8	605.2	646.0	704.9	725.3	697.9	769.9
Central Government Deposits	16d	14.2	14.6	59.0	141.7	174.4	259.1	295.6	268.6	190.6	226.3	186.3	203.2	218.3	462.8	586.0
Capital Accounts	17a	62.1	71.3	75.7	76.9	87.5	103.3	120.7	156.0	237.8	229.7	210.6	167.4	286.5	181.1	164.9
Other Items (Net)	17r	6.4	–1.6	5.1	–5.2	–20.0	–6.3	–93.8	–120.7	–141.2	–57.9	–124.6	200.8	–213.1	–531.9	–565.9
Deposit Money Banks														*Millions of Gourdes:*		
Reserves	20	42.6	58.8	74.2	124.1	159.6	191.4	214.3	241.7	325.8	344.9	359.5	363.9	601.1	610.8	637.4
Claims on Mon.Author.: Securities	20c															
Foreign Assets	21	17.7	12.2	14.9	27.5	26.4	44.3	30.0	44.1	103.4	232.5	97.1	132.4	149.0	150.0	151.0
Claims on Central Government	22a	2.5	2.5	22.0	27.2	27.1	26.3	25.5	—	.5	3.0	2.5	48.0	40.9	27.5	26.7
Claims on Private Sector	22d	65.4	143.3	255.4	331.3	419.2	480.6	598.5	672.5	726.0	816.4	858.1	850.2	884.6	885.4	886.0
Claims on Other Banking Insts.	22f															
Demand Deposits	24	52.6	75.8	91.3	110.9	135.6	155.7	183.4	186.7	224.0	295.2	318.2	357.2	384.4	512.6	544.2
Time, Savings,& Fgn.Currency Dep.	25	69.1	99.4	167.1	250.1	358.5	452.6	545.1	602.9	817.6	800.1	859.4	912.0	990.7	1,045.3	1,111.2
Bonds	26ab															
Foreign Liabilities	26c	—	23.4	84.7	114.7	97.9	83.8	81.1	66.6	66.2	61.6	77.1	59.4	43.7	51.4	11.8
Central Government Deposits	26d	3.9	3.9	3.9	11.4	11.4	11.4	11.4	11.4	—	4.1	4.1	3.9	3.9	3.9	3.9
Credit from Monetary Authorities	26g	3.1	5.4	7.9	11.1	12.7	25.1	27.2	50.4	23.9	41.8	10.6	42.5	33.7	17.7	25.0
Capital Accounts	27a	6.8	18.5	24.1	28.9	29.4	30.9	40.4	31.5	33.5	290.1	305.5	293.8	339.2	325.5	314.1
Other Items (Net)	27r	–7.4	–9.7	–12.6	–17.1	–13.2	–16.7	–20.4	8.8	–9.7	–96.0	–257.6	–274.3	–120.0	–282.9	–309.0
Monetary Survey														*Millions of Gourdes:*		
Foreign Assets (Net)	31n	107.7	70.5	–16.6	–91.1	–7.5	63.0	34.8	136.1	–47.8	51.7	–220.7	–279.6	–309.8	–277.2	–125.6
Domestic Credit	32	365.7	511.8	706.8	976.2	1,237.6	1,530.3	1,796.2	1,939.8	2,590.2	3,024.2	3,153.2	3,699.1	3,786.0	3,541.5	3,719.8
Claims on Central Govt. (Net)	32an	200.4	226.5	265.4	320.1	375.5	510.4	457.7	513.4	904.0	1,154.9	1,361.1	2,024.0	2,023.0	1,760.7	2,136.8
Claims on Local Government	32b				3.2	2.2	1.4	.5	.5	.5	.5	.5	.5			
Claims on Nonfin.Pub.Enterprises	32c	32.2	46.0	61.9	161.4	243.8	298.6	358.8	421.1	597.9	626.5	522.5	514.3	514.9	496.3	287.8
Claims on Private Sector	32d	123.2	228.1	366.7	480.5	603.8	707.6	969.0	988.2	1,071.9	1,210.6	1,232.6	1,116.7	1,199.1	1,249.3	1,222.0
Claims on Other Banking Insts	32f	9.8	11.2	12.8	11.0	12.4	12.4	10.2	16.6	15.9	31.7	36.5	43.6	48.9	35.2	73.2
Claims on Nonbank Financial Inst	32g	—	—	—	—	—	—	—	—	—	—	—	—	—	—	—
Money	34	271.2	332.8	342.4	402.6	549.6	629.1	717.8	802.5	945.4	1,166.5	1,164.3	1,174.7	1,388.0	1,588.7	1,789.9
Quasi-Money	35	110.3	154.5	241.3	332.2	465.6	587.8	713.7	771.8	992.8	1,008.5	1,082.7	1,172.9	1,268.6	1,411.7	1,486.7
Bonds	36ab															
Long-Term Foreign Liabilities	36cl	28.9	32.2	32.3	87.4	161.9	293.2	406.7	507.1	565.8	605.2	646.0	704.9	725.3	697.9	769.9
Capital Accounts	37a	68.9	89.8	99.7	105.8	117.0	134.1	161.2	187.5	271.3	519.8	516.1	461.1	625.7	506.6	479.0
Other Items (Net)	37r	–6.0	–27.0	–25.5	–42.9	–64.0	–50.9	–168.3	–193.0	–232.9	–224.0	–476.6	–94.1	–531.4	–940.5	–931.3
Money plus Quasi-Money	35l	381.6	487.3	583.7	734.8	1,015.2	1,216.8	1,431.5	1,574.4	1,938.2	2,175.0	2,247.0	2,347.6	2,656.6	3,000.4	3,276.5
Other Banking Institutions														*Millions of Gourdes:*		
Cash	40	4.4	5.4	7.8	3.8	11.3	11.7	11.5	11.1	2.8	8.8	9.9	14.8	4.5	4.5	3.3
Claims on Private Sector	42d	23.7	25.6	26.7	31.1	32.4	57.0	44.6	52.9	72.3	96.3	68.9	85.6	105.5	....	....
Credit from Monetary Authorities	46g	8.7	8.5	11.7	12.5	14.0	14.6	12.4	14.3	17.8	32.5	50.8	60.9	55.5	54.8	58.2
Capital Accounts	47a	17.1	18.0	21.0	22.7	28.2	41.1	47.3	63.0	52.2	51.6	31.0	40.5	58.2	87.8	28.6
Other Items (Net)	47r	2.2	4.5	1.8	–.4	1.6	13.1	–3.6	–13.3	5.2	20.9	–3.0	–1.0	–3.7	....	....
Interest Rates														*Percent per Annum*		
Treasury Bill Rate	60c	....	....	....	....	....	....	....	....	....	....	....	....	....	....	....
Savings Rate	60k	....	....	....	....	....	....	....	....	....	....	....	....	....	....	....
Deposit Rate	60l	....	....	....	....	....	....	....	....	....	....	....	....	....	....	....
Lending Rate	60p	....	....	....	....	....	....	....	....	....	....	....	....	....	....	....
Prices														*Index Numbers (1995=100):*		
Consumer Prices	64	6.8	8.3	9.6	11.2	12.0	12.7	12.4	14.0	†16.5	18.3	19.6	21.7	23.0	25.5	26.3

1987	1988	1989	1990	1991	1992	1993	1994	1995	1996	1997	1998	1999	2000	2001		
End of Period															**Exchange Rates**	
7.092	6.727	6.570	7.112	†11.787	15.060	17.588	18.900	24.022	21.703	23.357	23.239	24.658	29.347	33.101	Market Rate	aa
End of Period (ae) Period Average (rf)																
4.999	4.999	4.999	4.999	†8.240	10.953	12.805	12.947	16.160	15.093	17.311	16.505	17.965	22.524	26.339	Market Rate	ae
5.000	5.000	5.000	5.000	6.034	9.802	12.823	15.040	15.110	15.701	16.655	16.766	16.938	21.171	24.429	Market Rate	rf
End of Period															**Fund Position**	
44.1	44.1	44.1	44.1	44.1	44.1	44.1	44.1	60.7	60.7	60.7	60.7	60.7	60.7	60.7	Quota	2f. s
—	—	.1	—	—	—	—	—	.4	—	.1	.4	.6	.1	.4	SDRs	1b. s
.1	.1	.1	.1	.1	.1	—	—	—	—	—	—	—	.1	.1	Reserve Position in the Fund	1c. s
51.1	33.8	30.6	25.5	23.8	23.8	23.8	3.8	18.2	31.6	31.6	40.8	32.6	30.4	30.4	Total Fund Cred.&Loans Outstg.	2tl
End of Period															**International Liquidity**	
17.0	13.0	12.6	3.2	35.1	27.1	32.1	51.1	191.6	216.1	213.1	264.6	264.9	183.1	141.6	Total Reserves minus Gold	1l. d
—	—	.1	—	—	—	—	—	.5	.1	.1	.5	.9	.1	.5	SDRs	1b. d
.1	.1	.1	.1	.1	.1	.1	.1	.1	.1	.1	.1	.1	.1	.1	Reserve Position in the Fund	1c. d
16.9	12.9	12.4	3.1	35.0	27.0	32.0	51.0	191.0	216.0	213.0	264.0	264.0	183.0	141.0	Foreign Exchange	1d. d
.018	.018	.018	.018	.018	.019	.019	.019	.019	.019	.020	.020	.001	.001	.001	Gold (Million Fine Troy Ounces)	1ad
165.3	175.2	177.7	4.8	4.8	9.0	9.7	48.3	20.6	82.1	59.6	60.4	60.7	61.4	62.2	Monetary Authorities: Other Liab.	4..d
23.4	23.1	17.1	42.4	32.4	54.0	78.3	96.1	98.1	114.9	133.1	124.4	150.7	199.1	177.0	Deposit Money Banks: Assets	7a. d
1.6	1.6	8.5	20.3	.5	—	—	.8	4.9	6.9	17.9	8.3	16.7	21.8	18.7	Liabilities	7b. d
End of Period															**Monetary Authorities**	
182.0	162.5	209.6	100.1	75.9	152.9	236.8	834.0	3,073.7	3,988.0	†4,757.2	5,308.4	5,916.0	5,549.2	6,988.4	Foreign Assets	11
2,769.8	2,848.8	2,876.1	3,243.4	3,397.2	3,985.1	4,394.6	5,860.7	7,074.0	7,238.8	†7,668.1	8,273.3	10,302.3	11,802.0	13,846.8	Claims on Central Government	12a
—	—	—	—	—	—	—	—	—	12.9	†8.5	5.0	1.7	.6	—	Claims on Local Government	12b
278.3	397.2	382.1	296.8	283.8	348.7	426.5	328.1	152.1	80.8	†50.9	85.5	84.5	1,820.3	1,996.3	Claims on Nonfin.Pub.Enterprises	12c
338.0	291.2	323.2	—	—	—	—	—	—	141.2	†163.5	233.1	304.2	358.8	452.9	Claims on Private Sector	12d
8.3	5.6	9.2	22.3	5.4	331.9	754.6	415.6	65.0	70.2	†129.2	106.2	264.6	228.5	93.4	Claims on Deposit Money Banks	12e
73.0	71.4	70.5	15.0	10.0	—	—	—	28.6	—	†—	—	—	—	—	Claims on Other Banking Insts	12f
—	—	—	—	—	—	—	—	—	4.7	†22.4	19.8	13.9	12.0	9.8	Claims on Nonbank Financial Insts	12g
2,174.8	1,595.5	2,629.4	3,081.7	3,356.7	4,346.1	5,616.6	6,954.9	7,975.8	7,645.1	†7,653.3	7,672.5	9,894.3	12,452.2	14,556.3	Reserve Money	14
979.5	205.0	1,458.8	1,382.3	1,544.6	2,074.5	2,668.8	3,029.5	3,536.7	3,435.7	†3,935.4	3,905.4	4,927.1	5,807.2	6,584.2	*of which: Currency Outside DMBs*	14a
412.4	400.0	430.8	—	—	—	—	—	—	—	†8.4	37.3	55.9	84.0	101.8	Time, Savings,& Fgn.Currency Dep.	15
....	....	....	....	....	....	....	....	....	....	857.0	1,980.0	2,335.0	944.0	2,432.0	Liabs. of Central Bank: Securities	16ac
395.0	284.2	246.0	205.1	320.6	456.9	543.7	136.0	555.9	1,595.1	†737.5	954.0	802.6	890.9	1,004.8	Foreign Liabilities	16c
793.7	818.9	843.0	—	—	—	—	560.6	212.8	—	†1,030.9	990.4	1,091.0	1,383.0	1,638.3	Long-Term Foreign Liabilities	16cl
427.5	586.6	212.6	407.7	428.0	457.3	481.3	892.7	1,983.0	1,617.2	†1,514.2	1,647.6	1,895.3	1,125.1	1,093.8	Central Government Deposits	16d
216.9	227.0	259.1	232.5	316.4	411.4	472.2	564.0	1,139.1	857.2	†1,266.5	1,313.1	1,566.8	3,974.8	4,143.9	Capital Accounts	17a
-770.8	-135.4	-750.3	-249.4	-649.4	-853.1	-1,301.3	-1,669.8	-1,473.3	-178.0	†-268.1	-563.6	-753.7	-1,082.6	-1,583.2	Other Items (Net)	17r
End of Period															**Deposit Money Banks**	
808.1	751.3	865.9	1,517.0	1,736.9	2,420.8	3,059.1	3,718.1	3,608.0	3,979.8	†3,323.6	3,411.0	4,394.1	6,297.4	7,713.6	Reserves	20
....	....	....	....	....	....	....	....	....	....	857.0	1,980.0	2,335.0	944.0	2,432.0	Claims on Mon.Author.: Securities	20c
117.0	115.6	85.3	212.2	266.6	592.0	1,002.7	1,243.6	1,584.9	1,734.2	†2,303.9	2,053.8	2,706.8	4,484.6	4,662.5	Foreign Assets	21
17.8	28.4	31.6	12.3	11.7	11.5	8.0	114.1	11.3	6.5	†6.5	6.5	169.3	164.3	99.3	Claims on Central Government	22a
957.1	1,250.5	1,503.3	1,800.6	1,862.2	2,100.2	2,516.3	3,253.2	5,072.4	5,825.0	†8,511.2	9,156.2	10,128.9	12,074.3	12,914.0	Claims on Private Sector	22d
....	....	....	....	....	....	....	....	....	....	—	—	—	170.0	—	Claims on Other Banking Insts.	22f
658.6	715.7	767.2	920.2	1,062.5	1,199.9	1,429.6	1,578.0	2,372.7	2,211.1	†2,435.2	2,544.2	3,241.3	3,251.2	3,749.2	Demand Deposits	24
1,183.3	1,277.7	1,494.4	2,371.2	2,764.5	3,671.8	4,944.8	6,486.8	8,018.7	9,064.7	†11499.7	13,209.8	15,997.4	20,102.3	22,847.1	Time, Savings,& Fgn.Currency Dep.	25
....	....	....	....	....	....	....	....	....	....	46.1	44.9	21.9	113.6	148.2	Bonds	26ab
8.2	7.9	42.5	101.5	3.8	.5	.3	10.7	78.6	104.5	†310.3	136.4	299.8	490.4	492.9	Foreign Liabilities	26c
3.9	—	—	50.9	31.0	26.3	27.0	27.6	37.5	54.5	†514.7	475.1	402.9	257.2	157.5	Central Government Deposits	26d
18.6	33.6	73.5	—	—	—	—	—	72.6	81.9	†49.0	42.8	134.7	72.1	32.1	Credit from Monetary Authorities	26g
344.7	460.9	515.1	221.3	199.1	269.7	320.9	395.7	525.7	946.2	†1,373.9	1,692.9	1,811.2	2,432.1	2,878.4	Capital Accounts	27a
-317.3	-350.1	-406.7	-123.0	-183.5	-43.7	-136.5	-169.8	-829.1	-917.4	†-1226.7	-1,538.6	-2,175.1	-2,584.1	-2,483.9	Other Items (Net)	27r
End of Period															**Monetary Survey**	
-104.3	-14.1	6.4	5.7	18.1	287.5	695.5	1,930.9	4,024.1	4,022.6	†6,013.4	6,271.8	7,520.4	8,652.5	10,153.2	Foreign Assets (Net)	31n
4,002.7	4,301.0	4,974.2	4,909.5	5,105.9	5,961.9	6,837.1	8,440.9	10,317.9	11,638.2	†14402.1	15,656.7	18,706.6	25,020.0	28,067.9	Domestic Credit	32
2,356.3	2,290.6	2,695.1	2,797.1	2,949.9	3,513.0	3,894.3	4,861.4	5,064.8	5,573.6	†5,645.7	6,157.1	8,173.4	10,584.0	12,694.8	Claims on Central Govt. (Net)	32an
—	—	—	—	—	—	—	—	—	12.9	†8.5	5.0	1.7	.6	—	Claims on Local Government	32b
278.3	397.2	382.1	296.8	283.8	348.7	426.5	326.3	152.1	80.8	†50.9	85.5	84.5	1,820.3	1,996.3	Claims on Nonfin.Pub.Enterprises	32c
1,295.2	1,541.7	1,826.5	1,800.6	1,862.2	2,100.2	2,516.3	3,253.2	5,072.4	5,966.2	†8,674.6	9,389.3	10,433.0	12,433.1	13,367.0	Claims on Private Sector	32d
73.0	71.4	70.5	15.0	10.0	—	—	—	28.6	—	†—	—	—	170.0	—	Claims on Other Banking Insts	32f
—	—	—	—	—	—	—	—	—	4.7	†22.4	19.8	13.9	12.0	9.8	Claims on Nonbank Financial Inst	32g
2,097.9	1,635.2	2,633.6	2,302.5	2,464.4	3,150.1	3,866.4	5,095.5	6,703.9	5,823.9	†6,633.5	6,650.9	8,422.8	9,220.2	10,610.2	Money	34
1,595.7	1,677.7	1,925.3	2,371.2	2,764.5	3,671.8	4,944.8	6,486.8	8,018.7	9,064.7	†11508.1	13,247.1	16,053.3	20,186.3	22,948.9	Quasi-Money	35
....	....	....	....	....	....	....	....	....	....	46.1	44.9	21.9	113.6	148.2	Bonds	36ab
793.7	818.9	843.0	—	—	—	—	560.6	212.8	—	†1,030.9	990.4	1,091.0	1,383.0	1,638.3	Long-Term Foreign Liabilities	36cl
561.6	687.9	774.2	453.8	515.5	681.1	793.1	959.7	1,664.7	1,803.4	†2,640.4	3,006.0	3,378.0	6,406.8	7,022.3	Capital Accounts	37a
-1,150.4	-532.8	-1,195.4	-212.3	-620.4	-1,253.6	-2,071.7	-2,730.8	-2,258.1	-1,031.3	†-1443.5	-2,010.8	-2,740.1	-3,637.3	-4,146.8	Other Items (Net)	37r
3,693.6	3,312.9	4,558.8	4,673.7	5,228.9	6,821.9	8,811.2	11,582.3	14,722.5	14,888.6	†18141.5	19,898.0	24,476.2	29,406.4	33,559.1	Money plus Quasi-Money	35l
End of Period															**Other Banking Institutions**	
....	....	....	....	....	....	....	....	....	....	....	....	....	....	....	Cash	40
....	....	....	....	....	....	....	....	....	....	....	....	....	....	....	Claims on Private Sector	42d
....	....	....	....	....	....	....	....	....	....	....	....	....	....	....	Credit from Monetary Authorities	46g
....	....	....	....	....	....	....	....	....	....	....	....	....	....	....	Capital Accounts	47a
....	....	....	....	....	....	....	....	....	....	....	....	....	....	....	Other Items (Net)	47r
Percent per Annum															**Interest Rates**	
....	....	....	....	....	....	....	....	....	....	14.13	16.21	7.71	12.33	13.53	Treasury Bill Rate	60c
....	....	....	....	....	....	....	....	....	....	5.36	5.50	3.51	3.57	3.35	Savings Rate	60k
....	....	....	....	....	....	....	....	....	....	10.74	13.06	7.39	11.85	13.66	Deposit Rate	60l
....	....	....	....	....	....	....	....	....	....	21.00	23.62	22.88	25.09	28.63	Lending Rate	60p
Period Averages															**Prices**	
23.3	24.3	26.0	31.5	†36.3	†43.4	56.2	78.4	100.0	120.6	145.4	160.8	174.8	198.7	226.9	Consumer Prices	64

Haiti

		1972	1973	1974	1975	1976	1977	1978	1979	1980	1981	1982	1983	1984	1985	1986
International Transactions															*Millions of Gourdes*	
Exports	70	220.0	263.6	357.7	398.8	621.7	742.8	776.7	926.9	1,131.0	757.5	888.4	830.0	896.0	842.0	922.2
Imports, c.i.f.	71	344.6	415.7	626.0	744.8	1,033.7	1,063.3	1,166.0	1,360.4	1,770.7	2,239.8	1,936.4	2,202.6	2,360.7	2,207.8	1,799.9
Balance of Payments													*Millions of US Dollars: F.Y. Ending*			
Current Account, n.i.e.	78al d	8.2	1.2	−21.0	−24.5	−12.5	−37.7	−44.9	−52.8	−101.1	−148.8	−98.5	−111.2	−103.0	−94.7	−44.9
Goods: Exports f.o.b.	78aa d	42.9	54.4	70.0	80.3	111.9	137.6	149.9	138.0	215.8	151.1	177.1	186.6	214.6	223.0	190.8
Goods: Imports f.o.b.	78ab d	−57.6	−66.5	−96.5	−122.1	−158.7	−199.9	−207.5	−220.1	−319.0	−360.1	−301.9	−325.9	−337.9	−344.7	−303.2
Trade Balance	78ac d	−14.7	−12.1	−26.5	−41.8	−46.7	−62.3	−57.5	−82.1	−103.2	−209.0	−124.8	−139.3	−123.3	−121.7	−112.5
Services: Credit	78ad d	21.0	21.6	21.8	25.6	28.8	36.4	61.3	74.9	89.9	90.4	97.7	103.3	104.5	114.2	101.3
Services: Debit	78ae d	−22.2	−27.5	−34.2	−37.3	−52.8	−63.1	−101.6	−107.9	−162.0	−156.5	−169.1	−171.3	−189.1	−212.4	−170.2
Balance on Goods & Services	78af d	−15.9	−18.0	−38.9	−53.5	−70.8	−89.0	−97.9	−115.0	−175.3	−275.1	−196.2	−207.4	−207.9	−219.9	−181.4
Income: Credit	78ag d	—	.2	.2	.3	1.0	1.3	2.0	2.6	3.1	4.1	3.6	4.7	4.5	5.1	4.6
Income: Debit	78ah d	−5.4	−6.6	−8.1	−7.4	−8.1	−13.4	−16.7	−16.0	−17.4	−17.2	−17.6	−18.9	−22.6	−24.9	−19.9
Balance on Gds, Serv. & Inc.	78ai d	−21.3	−24.3	−46.7	−60.6	−77.9	−101.0	−112.5	−128.4	−189.6	−288.1	−210.2	−221.6	−226.0	−239.7	−196.8
Current Transfers, n.i.e.: Credit	78aj d	32.7	33.3	36.5	76.9	111.8	107.4	114.9	126.3	158.5	201.2	159.0	153.9	168.0	192.3	205.3
Current Transfers: Debit	78ak d	−3.1	−7.9	−10.8	−40.8	−46.5	−44.1	−47.3	−50.7	−70.0	−61.8	−47.3	−43.5	−45.0	−47.2	−53.4
Capital Account, n.i.e.	78bc d	−1.0	−1.1	−1.0	−.3	−.4	—	—	—	—	—	—	—	—	—	—
Capital Account, n.i.e.: Credit	78ba d	—	—	—	—	—	—	—	—	—	—	—	—	—	—	—
Capital Account: Debit	78bb d	−1.0	−1.1	−1.0	−.3	−.4	—	—	—	—	—	—	—	—	—	—
Financial Account, n.i.e.	78bj d	10.0	7.4	21.1	33.8	26.5	67.3	36.4	59.8	76.0	109.8	90.5	91.2	112.7	46.0	34.4
Direct Investment Abroad	78bd d	—	—	—	—	—	—	—	—	—	—	—	—	—	—	—
Dir. Invest. in Rep. Econ., n.i.e.	78be d	4.1	7.0	7.9	2.6	7.8	8.0	10.0	12.0	13.0	8.3	7.1	8.4	4.5	4.9	4.8
Portfolio Investment Assets	78bf d	—	—	—	—	—	—	—	—	—	—	—	—	—	—	—
Equity Securities	78bk d	—	—	—	—	—	—	—	—	—	—	—	—	—	—	—
Debt Securities	78bl d	—	—	—	—	—	—	—	—	—	—	—	—	—	—	—
Portfolio Investment Liab., n.i.e.	78bg d	—	—	—	—	—	—	—	—	—	—	—	—	—	—	—
Equity Securities	78bm d	—	—	—	—	—	—	—	—	—	—	—	—	—	—	—
Debt Securities	78bn d	—	—	—	—	—	—	—	—	—	—	—	—	—	—	—
Financial Derivatives Assets	78bw d	. . . .	. . . .	. . . .	. . . .	. . . .	. . . .	. . . .	. . . .	. . . .	. . . .	. . . .	. . . .	. . . .	. . . .	. . . .
Financial Derivatives Liabilities	78bx d	. . . .	. . . .	. . . .	. . . .	. . . .	. . . .	. . . .	. . . .	. . . .	. . . .	. . . .	. . . .	. . . .	. . . .	. . . .
Other Investment Assets	78bh d	−1.5	2.0	−1.8	−1.1	−2.7	.7	−3.0	3.5	−7.5	−3.4	6.7	−.1	6.1	−7.1	−1.1
Monetary Authorities	78bo d	. . . .	. . . .	. . . .	. . . .	. . . .	. . . .	. . . .	. . . .	. . . .	. . . .	. . . .	. . . .	. . . .	. . . .	. . . .
General Government	78bp d	—	—	—	—	—	—	—	—	—	—	—	—	—	—	—
Banks	78bq d	−1.5	2.0	−1.8	−1.1	−2.7	.7	−3.0	3.5	−7.5	−3.4	6.7	−.1	6.1	−7.1	−1.1
Other Sectors	78br d	—	—	—	—	—	—	—	—	—	—	—	—	—	—	—
Other Investment Liab., n.i.e.	78bi d	7.5	−1.6	14.9	32.3	21.4	58.6	29.4	44.3	70.5	104.9	76.7	82.9	102.1	48.2	30.6
Monetary Authorities	78bs d	—	.3	−.3	.4	−.2	.1	.3	.8	−1.7	—	—	.4	10.0	6.7	5.6
General Government	78bt d	3.8	−2.9	−1.9	13.8	19.3	40.2	24.2	32.1	45.3	27.9	48.5	33.4	67.1	24.9	−.2
Banks	78bu d	.1	.9	10.9	12.2	−4.5	−1.5	−.9	−5.7	4.9	2.1	−.8	5.6	6.2	−7.4	−9.3
Other Sectors	78bv d	3.5	.1	6.3	5.9	6.8	19.8	5.9	17.1	22.1	74.9	29.0	43.5	18.9	24.0	34.5
Net Errors and Omissions	78ca d	−10.1	−6.4	−9.9	−21.7	−2.5	−19.9	15.1	−5.0	−12.4	.7	−11.6	−8.6	−29.9	46.6	14.9
Overall Balance	78cb d	7.1	1.0	−10.7	−12.7	11.1	9.7	6.6	2.0	−37.4	−38.3	−19.6	−28.6	−20.1	−2.1	4.4
Reserves and Related Items	79da d	−7.1	−1.0	10.7	12.7	−11.1	−9.7	−6.6	−2.0	37.4	38.3	19.6	28.6	20.1	2.1	−4.4
Reserve Assets	79db d	−5.9	−1.0	7.0	3.0	−12.8	−7.6	−13.5	−5.9	32.1	23.6	−9.5	3.4	−1.0	6.8	−1.3
Use of Fund Credit and Loans	79dc d	−1.3	—	3.7	9.7	1.6	−2.3	6.7	3.6	5.0	14.7	29.1	24.9	20.3	−12.1	−23.3
Exceptional Financing	79de d	—	—	—	—	.1	.2	.2	.3	.3	—	—	.2	.8	7.5	20.2
Government Finance															*Millions of Gourdes:*	
Deficit (−) or Surplus	80	2.5	1.2	−10.4	−42.2	−64.2	−143.3	−168.2	−168.0	−327.7	−446.3	−380.6	−277.1	−572.7	−217.5	−236.6
Revenue	81	278.8	302.5	333.3	475.3	644.3	784.5	986.9	623.3	789.3	759.9	858.6	952.9	1,075.7	1,279.4	1,339.8
Grants Received	81z	. . . .	. . . .	. . . .	. . . .	. . . .	. . . .	. . . .	. . . .	151.0	157.7	593.0	640.8	341.9	515.8	385.9
Expenditure	82	276.3	301.3	343.7	517.5	708.5	927.8	1,155.1	791.3	1,268.0	1,363.9	1,832.2	1,870.8	1,990.3	2,012.7	1,962.3
Financing																
Net Domestic Borrowing	84a	2.8	5.0	20.7	54.5	31.8	45.0	36.1	68.2	165.2	367.8	157.7	129.3	431.6	351.8	109.7
Monetary Authorities	84aa	3.6	5.3	23.0	50.3	34.7	46.1	22.9	66.8	161.0	364.8	154.4	109.5	435.9	356.6	111.7
Other	84ac	−.8	−.3	−2.3	4.2	−2.9	−1.1	13.2	1.4	4.2	3.0	3.3	19.8	−4.3	−4.8	−2.0
Net Foreign Borrowing	85a	−6.7	−6.5	−9.0	−9.5	49.8	185.0	130.4	117.3	156.6	105.6	171.8	150.8	159.6	33.6	229.8
Use of Cash Balances	87	1.4	.3	−2.3	−2.1	−17.3	−85.3	2.2	−17.5	5.9	−27.1	51.1	−3.0	−18.5	−167.9	35.3
Adjustment to Financing	84x	—	—	1.0	−.7	−.1	−1.4	−.5	—	—	—	—	—	—	—	−138.2
National Accounts															*Millions of Gourdes:*	
Househ.Cons.Expend.,incl.NPISHs	96f	2,160	3,013	2,604	3,149	4,101	4,592	4,690	5,245	6,835	7,535	7,202	7,835	8,174	9,471	10,472
Gross Fixed Capital Formation	93e	207	258	†410	533	678	748	857	938	1,238	1,252	1,230	1,331	1,441	1,673	1,620
Changes in Inventories	93i	13	17	†19	23	26	28	—	—	—	—	—	—	—	—	—
Exports of Goods and Services	90c	332	381	663	785	1,046	1,249	1,495	1,522	2,148	1,944	2,139	2,302	2,598	2,716	2,340
Imports of Goods and Services (−)	98c	400	508	868	1,082	1,430	1,692	1,982	2,105	3,302	3,650	3,186	3,381	3,636	3,813	3,245
Gross Domestic Product (GDP)	99b	2,312	3,129	†2,828	3,408	4,395	4,897	5,060	5,600	6,919	7,081	7,370	8,120	9,080	10,050	11,190
Net Primary Income from Abroad	98.n	−20	†−21	−28	−34	−36	−63	−76	−70	−72	−66	−72	−73	−92	−101	−100
Gross National Income (GNI)	99a	2,292	3,108	2,800	3,374	4,359	4,834	4,984	5,530	6,847	7,015	7,299	8,045	8,990	9,946	11,079
Net National Income	99e	2,241	3,062	2,739	3,300	4,251	4,715	4,847	5,380	6,650	6,815	7,102	7,833	8,760	9,680	10,822
GDP Volume 1976 Prices	99b.p	3,617	3,789	4,009	4,054	4,395	4,416	4,631	4,983	5,342	5,196	5,018	5,056	5,071	5,085	5,134
GDP Volume 1987 Prices	99b.p	. . . .	. . . .	. . . .	. . . .	. . . .	. . . .	. . . .	. . . .	. . . .	. . . .	. . . .	. . . .	. . . .	. . . .	. . . .
GDP Volume (1995=100)	99bv p	83.5	87.4	92.5	93.5	101.4	101.9	106.9	115.0	123.3	119.9	115.8	116.7	117.0	117.3	118.5
GDP Deflator (1995=100)	99bi p	7.9	10.1	†8.7	10.3	12.3	13.6	13.4	13.8	15.9	16.7	18.1	19.7	22.0	24.3	26.8
															Millions:	
Population	99z	4.37	4.44	4.51	4.58	4.67	4.75	4.83	4.92	5.01	5.46	5.56	5.66	5.76	5.86	5.99

	1987	1988	1989	1990	1991	1992	1993	1994	1995	1996	1997	1998	1999	2000	2001		
International Transactions																	
Millions of Gourdes																	
Exports	1,067.7	896.4	720.3	801.3	1,005.2	719.4	1,029.3	1,236.7	1,666.5	1,413.9	3,537.1	5,365.0	5,661.3	6,725.3	6,700.7	Exports	70
Imports, c.i.f.	1,995.9	1,721.3	1,455.0	1,661.1	2,414.2	2,727.9	4,555.7	3,783.6	9,866.2	10,448.2	10,792.1	13,365.6	17,366.9	21,936.2	24,745.7	Imports, c.i.f.	71
Balance of Payments																	
Sept 30; Minus Sign Indicates Debit																	
Current Account, n.i.e.	−31.1	−40.4	−62.7	−21.9	−91.5	7.3	−11.8	−23.4	−87.1	−137.7	−47.7	−38.1	....	....	....	Current Account, n.i.e.	78ald
Goods: Exports f.o.b.	210.1	180.4	148.3	265.8	166.6	73.4	80.3	60.3	88.3	82.5	205.4	299.3				Goods: Exports f.o.b.	78aad
Goods: Imports f.o.b.	−311.2	−283.9	−259.3	−442.6	−448.6	−212.5	−260.5	−171.5	−517.2	−498.6	−559.6	−640.7				Goods: Imports f.o.b.	78abd
Trade Balance	−101.1	−103.5	−111.0	−176.8	−282.0	−139.1	−180.2	−111.2	−428.9	−416.1	−354.2	−341.4				Trade Balance	78acd
Services: Credit	110.3	94.5	88.5	52.2	57.6	38.5	35.8	6.7	104.1	109.1	173.7	180.0				Services: Credit	78add
Services: Debit	−190.5	−197.1	−188.8	−72.0	−83.3	−35.2	−30.2	−63.9	−284.5	−283.3	−331.5	−380.6				Services: Debit	78aed
Balance on Goods & Services	−181.3	−206.1	−211.4	−196.6	−307.7	−135.8	−174.6	−168.4	−609.3	−590.3	−512.0	−542.0				Balance on Goods & Services	78afd
Income: Credit	5.2	6.2	4.6	6.9	2.0	1.0	2.0	—	—	—	—	—				Income: Credit	78agd
Income: Debit	−26.1	−33.4	−30.2	−25.1	−20.0	−12.9	−12.6	−11.2	−30.6	−9.9	−13.6	−11.7				Income: Debit	78ahd
Balance on Gds, Serv. & Inc.	−202.2	−233.2	−236.9	−214.8	−325.7	−147.7	−185.2	−179.6	−639.9	−600.2	−525.6	−553.7				Balance on Gds, Serv. & Inc.	78aid
Current Transfers, n.i.e.: Credit	228.0	253.6	237.7	192.9	234.2	155.0	173.4	156.2	552.9	462.5	477.9	515.6				Current Transfers, n.i.e.: Credit	78ajd
Current Transfers: Debit	−56.9	−60.7	−63.5	—												Current Transfers: Debit	78akd
Capital Account, n.i.e.	—	—	—	—	—	—	—	—	....	....	....	....				Capital Account, n.i.e.	78bcd
Capital Account, n.i.e.: Credit	—	—	—	—	—	—	—	—	....	....	....	....				Capital Account, n.i.e.: Credit	78bad
Capital Account: Debit	—	—	—	—	—	—	—	—	....	....	....	....				Capital Account: Debit	78bbd
Financial Account, n.i.e.	53.4	26.3	60.1	33.0	24.1	−22.8	−46.5	−15.8	99.2	67.9	61.5	193.1				Financial Account, n.i.e.	78bjd
Direct Investment Abroad				8.0	13.6											Direct Investment Abroad	78bdd
Dir. Invest. in Rep. Econ., n.i.e.	4.7	10.1	9.4	—	−1.8	−2.2	−2.8	—	7.4	4.1	4.0	10.8				Dir. Invest. in Rep. Econ., n.i.e.	78bed
Portfolio Investment Assets									....	....	....	....				Portfolio Investment Assets	78bfd
Equity Securities									....	....	....	....				Equity Securities	78bkd
Debt Securities									....	....	....	....				Debt Securities	78bld
Portfolio Investment Liab., n.i.e.									....	....	....	....				Portfolio Investment Liab., n.i.e.	78bgd
Equity Securities									....	....	....	....				Equity Securities	78bmd
Debt Securities									....	....	....	....				Debt Securities	78bnd
Financial Derivatives Assets									....	....	....	....				Financial Derivatives Assets	78bwd
Financial Derivatives Liabilities									....	....	....	....				Financial Derivatives Liabilities	78bxd
Other Investment Assets	−7.8	−3.1	21.5	−23.1	−16.2	−12.6	−30.6	−5.5	−11.2	−4.6	21.6	86.8				Other Investment Assets	78bhd
Monetary Authorities									....	....	....	....				Monetary Authorities	78bod
General Government									—	—	—	—				General Government	78bpd
Banks	−7.8	−3.1	21.5	−23.1	−16.2	−12.6	−30.6	−5.5	−11.2	−4.6	3.6	2.8				Banks	78bqd
Other Sectors									—	—	18.0	84.0				Other Sectors	78brd
Other Investment Liab., n.i.e.	56.5	19.3	29.3	48.1	28.5	−8.0	−13.1	−10.3	103.1	68.4	35.9	95.5				Other Investment Liab., n.i.e.	78bid
Monetary Authorities	4.7	−2.1	−.4	−.6		2.9	2.2	2.1	—	—	—	—				Monetary Authorities	78bsd
General Government	18.1	−4.5	2.3	48.7	28.5	−10.9	−15.3	−12.4	112.5	68.8	37.7	43.0				General Government	78btd
Banks	−1.2	8.1	9.1	—	—	—	—	—	.4	−.4	12.3	−4.5				Banks	78bud
Other Sectors	34.9	17.9	18.3	—	—	—	—	—	−9.8	.1	−14.1	57.0				Other Sectors	78bvd
Net Errors and Omissions	−16.4	14.3	−10.7	−46.3	80.1	9.2	35.3	−10.5	124.9	19.4	16.0	−120.5				Net Errors and Omissions	78cad
Overall Balance	5.9	.3	−13.2	−35.2	12.7	−6.3	−23.0	−49.7	137.1	−50.4	29.8	34.5				Overall Balance	78cbd
Reserves and Related Items	−5.9	−.3	13.2	35.2	−12.7	6.3	23.0	49.7	−137.1	50.4	−29.8	−34.5				Reserves and Related Items	79dad
Reserve Assets	11.8	1.2	3.9	39.0	−20.0	−11.3	−19.1	12.8	−175.6	48.5	−50.6	−29.1				Reserve Assets	79dbd
Use of Fund Credit and Loans	−17.7	−26.6	−5.6	−7.0	−4.5	—	—	—	−5.6	−2.6	20.8	−5.3				Use of Fund Credit and Loans	79dcd
Exceptional Financing	—	25.1	14.9	3.2	11.8	17.6	42.1	36.9	44.1	4.4	....	....				Exceptional Financing	79ded
Government Finance																	
Year Ending September 30																	
Deficit (−) or Surplus	−151.2	−424.1	−523.7	−577.5	−233.3	−590.2	−506.9	−947.1	−986.1	−329.5	−320.5	−776.5	−1,647.7	−1,774.1	−1,887.0	Deficit (-) or Surplus	80
Revenue	1,287.9	1,235.3	1,265.4	1,214.7	1,425.1	1,234.7	1,284.2	874.8	2,456.0	3,436.1	4,781.8	5,330.0	6,211.2	6,169.4	6,332.2	Revenue	81
Grants Received	564.6	146.5	16.2	7.6	45.9	14.0	1.1	2.2	696.7	354.3	694.6	644.7	47.0	197.2	369.8	Grants Received	81z
Expenditure	2,003.7	1,805.9	1,805.3	1,799.8	1,704.3	1,838.9	1,792.2	1,824.1	4,138.8	4,119.9	5,796.9	6,751.2	7,905.9	8,140.7	8,589.0	Expenditure	82
Financing																	
Net Domestic Borrowing	56.3	93.5	175.1	333.5	116.0	625.4	516.9	1,109.6	885.7	650.4	223.7	431.5	1,900.1	1,529.9	2,143.8	Net Domestic Borrowing	84a
Monetary Authorities	60.0	110.5	172.4	328.4	109.9	618.7	516.9	1,109.6	885.7	650.4	223.7	591.5	1,799.6	1,566.1	2,148.0	Monetary Authorities	84aa
Other	−3.7	−17.0	2.7	5.1	6.1	6.7	—	—	—	—	—	−160.0	100.5	−36.2	−4.2	Other	84ac
Net Foreign Borrowing	134.4	88.7	51.3	30.2	92.9	1.1	—	—	1,031.3	−260.7	−272.0	−421.7	−577.5	−389.5	−309.6	Net Foreign Borrowing	85a
Use of Cash Balances	−1.3	61.7	26.4	−110.7	−15.1	−32.2	39.1	−88.1	−975.8	−28.4	−327.3	85.5	−544.4	371.5	233.3	Use of Cash Balances	87
Adjustment to Financing	−38.2	180.2	270.9	324.5	39.5	−4.1	−49.1	−74.4	44.9	−31.8	696.1	681.2	869.5	262.2	−180.5	Adjustment to Financing	84x
National Accounts																	
Year Ending September 30																	
Househ.Cons.Expend.,incl.NPISHs	9,156	9,137	9,590	11,661	13,755	15,321	21,344	31,310	38,167	41,719	49,393	57,148	62,157	72,446	82,353	Househ.Cons.Expend.,incl.NPISHs	96f
Gross Fixed Capital Formation	1,545	1,500	1,791	1,866	2,221	1,376	1,467	1,857	4,867	13,122	13,247	16,382	19,182	21,208	22,106	Gross Fixed Capital Formation	93e
Changes in Inventories	—	—	—	—	—	—	—	—								Changes in Inventories	93i
Exports of Goods and Services	2,860	2,542	2,143	2,511	3,783	1,346	1,912	1,942	3,845	5,284	5,646	6,237	8,482	9,849	10,208	Exports of Goods and Services	90c
Imports of Goods and Services (-)	3,767	3,766	2,688	2,862	5,336	3,022	4,849	4,173	11,634	13,479	14,280	16,770	20,568	25,923	29,225	Imports of Goods and Services (-)	98c
Gross Domestic Product (GDP)	10,800	11,130	12,520	13,068	14,190	15,020	19,894	30,936	35,265	46,647	54,005	62,997	69,254	77,580	85,442	Gross Domestic Product (GDP)	99b
Net Primary Income from Abroad	−105	−135	−128	−125	−131	−153	−211	−584	....	....	....	....	....	....	....	Net Primary Income from Abroad	98.n
Gross National Income (GNI)	9,937	9,773	10,368	11,617	14,624	14,871	....	....	....	....	....	....	....	....	....	Gross National Income (GNI)	99a
Net National Income	9,697	9,534	10,083	11,328	....	....	....	....	....	....	....	....	....	....	....	Net National Income	99e
GDP Volume 1976 Prices	5,122	5,110	5,091	5,100	5,342	4,638	4,525	4,150	4,334	4,451	....	....	....	....	....	GDP Volume 1976 Prices	99b.p
GDP Volume 1987 Prices	....	....	....							12,083	12,410	12,681	13,025	13,138	12,991	GDP Volume 1987 Prices	99b.p
GDP Volume (1995=100)	118.2	117.9	117.5	117.7	123.3	107.0	104.4	95.8	100.0	102.7	105.5	107.8	110.7	111.7	110.4	GDP Volume (1995=100)	99bvp
GDP Deflator (1995=100)	25.9	26.8	30.2	31.5	32.6	39.8	54.0	91.6	100.0	128.8	145.2	165.7	177.4	197.0	219.4	GDP Deflator (1995=100)	99bip
Midyear Estimates																	
Population	6.11	6.24	6.36	6.49	6.62	6.76	6.90	7.04	7.18	7.34	7.49	7.65	7.80	7.96	8.13	Population	99z

(See notes in the back of the book.)

Honduras

		1972	1973	1974	1975	1976	1977	1978	1979	1980	1981	1982	1983	1984	1985	1986
Exchange Rates															*Lempiras per SDR:*	
Market Rate	aa	2.1714	2.4127	2.4487	2.3413	2.3237	2.4294	2.6056	2.6347	2.5508	2.3279	2.2062	2.0939	1.9604	2.1968	2.4464
															Lempiras per US Dollar:	
Market Rate	ae	2.0000	2.0000	2.0000	2.0000	2.0000	2.0000	2.0000	2.0000	2.0000	2.0000	2.0000	2.0000	2.0000	2.0000	2.0000
Market Rate	rf	2.0000	2.0000	2.0000	2.0000	2.0000	2.0000	2.0000	2.0000	2.0000	2.0000	2.0000	2.0000	2.0000	2.0000	2.0000
Fund Position															*Millions of SDRs:*	
Quota	2f. s	25.00	25.00	25.00	25.00	25.00	25.00	34.00	34.00	51.00	51.00	51.00	67.80	67.80	67.80	67.80
SDRs	1b. s	5.45	5.41	5.27	3.98	2.66	3.55	2.95	7.68	.02	1.39	1.63	2.12	.16	—	—
Reserve Position in the Fund	1c. s	—	6.25	—	—	—	—	6.25	6.06	—	—	—	4.20	—	—	—
Total Fund Cred.&Loans Outstg.	2tl	—	—	16.78	16.78	16.78	4.29	—	7.58	25.73	46.46	108.16	154.06	152.47	133.72	89.54
International Liquidity													*Millions of US Dollars Unless Otherwise Indicated:*			
Total Reserves minus Gold	1l. d	35.09	41.66	44.30	96.97	130.83	179.77	184.44	209.17	149.83	101.02	112.23	113.62	128.16	105.80	111.30
SDRs	1b. d	5.92	6.53	6.45	4.66	3.09	4.31	3.84	10.12	.03	1.62	1.80	2.22	.16	—	—
Reserve Position in the Fund	1c. d	—	7.54	—	—	—	—	8.14	7.98	—	—	—	4.40	—	—	—
Foreign Exchange	1d. d	29.17	27.59	37.85	92.31	127.74	175.46	172.45	191.07	149.80	99.40	110.43	107.00	128.00	105.80	111.30
Gold (Million Fine Troy Ounces)	1ad	.003	.003	.003	.003	.003	.014	.014	.014	.016	.016	.016	.016	.016	.016	.016
Gold (National Valuation)	1and	.10	.15	.15	.15	.15	.60	.60	.80	1.05	1.05	1.05	1.05	1.05	1.05	1.05
Monetary Authorities: Other Liab.	4..d	1.50	3.75	26.95	111.00	121.10	134.50	129.20	161.30	180.90	223.95	266.10	230.75	276.15	392.80	479.30
Deposit Money Banks: Assets	7a. d	2.50	2.25	3.75	7.05	5.10	7.00	7.70	7.90	9.15	12.65	5.10	2.85	2.85	3.30	4.60
Liabilities	7b. d	20.35	27.75	29.75	32.50	43.50	67.05	52.40	67.25	46.95	19.50	13.45	19.75	23.45	31.20	33.10
Other Banking Insts.: Assets	7e. d	.30	.65	.60	.55	1.25	1.25	2.30	2.25	1.60	2.05	.85	.60	2.35	1.20	1.80
Liabilities	7f. d	20.95	22.55	27.70	44.60	56.25	72.70	87.10	101.90	109.55	126.60	125.15	118.90	123.05	122.85	119.85
Monetary Authorities															*Millions of Lempiras:*	
Foreign Assets	11	75	89	95	201	277	381	390	440	324	237	258	265	297	203	221
Claims on Central Government	12a	60	62	79	77	86	60	144	200	276	455	509	442	593	681	643
Claims on Local Government	12b	11	12	15	17	16	21	32	62	66	66	61	65	69	67	64
Claims on Private Sector	12d	—	—	—	—	—	—	—	1	1	1	1	1	1	1	1
Claims on Deposit Money Banks	12e	19	30	47	68	62	75	80	97	140	152	161	162	237	425	517
Claims on Other Banking Insts	12f	17	24	35	50	56	51	68	71	95	147	193	234	279	302	329
Reserve Money	14	126	153	147	169	238	276	334	379	387	412	445	476	469	465	498
of which: Currency Outside DMBs	14a	90	112	109	115	173	193	215	270	275	302	314	362	384	410	426
Time, Savings,& Fgn.Currency Dep.	15	2	3	3	1	2	2	2	3	2	3	4	5	11	14	20
Foreign Liabilities	16c	1	3	88	158	158	131	81	100	140	241	438	453	492	692	763
Long-Term Foreign Liabilities	16cl	2	4	7	103	123	148	178	243	287	315	333	331	359	388	415
Central Government Deposits	16d	55	47	57	42	60	72	121	167	132	155	164	35	177	211	243
Capital Accounts	17a	41	47	51	52	51	66	86	118	170	195	213	245	268	337	361
Other Items (Net)	17r	−44	−39	−82	−113	−137	−107	−87	−139	−217	−261	−414	−377	−302	−429	−525
Deposit Money Banks															*Millions of Lempiras:*	
Reserves	20	35	38	41	54	55	78	108	111	104	111	118	80	130	129	129
Foreign Assets	21	5	5	8	14	10	14	15	16	18	25	10	6	6	7	9
Claims on Central Government	22a	55	59	67	70	91	133	144	167	193	182	276	371	449	518	691
Claims on Local Government	22b	1	3							3			44	59	14	16
Claims on Private Sector	22d	305	378	427	504	637	774	859	931	945	992	1,095	1,253	1,414	1,617	1,795
Claims on Other Banking Insts	22f	2	3	3	8	9	11	12	13	13	17	33	32	36	35	30
Demand Deposits	24	101	125	132	144	184	214	257	270	323	328	380	431	444	424	490
Time, Savings,& Fgn.Currency Dep.	25	170	202	214	241	301	379	472	490	515	586	745	895	1,051	1,036	1,140
Bonds	26ab	11	14	17	12	25	37	51	52	31	28	23	26	31	24	32
Foreign Liabilities	26c	21	25	25	30	43	65	34	97	60	24	17	32	41	45	42
Long-Term Foreign Liabilities	26cl	20	31	34	35	44	69	71	98	34	15	10	8	6	17	24
Central Government Deposits	26d	2	2	9	13	16	25	29	33	37	54	65	70	73	135	201
Credit from Monetary Authorities	26g	19	30	45	67	64	79	79	100	180	166	174	177	255	429	522
Liabilities to Other Banking Insts.	26i	....	....	....	....	....	....	....	....	....	....	....	....	....	....	....
Capital Accounts	27a	57	61	69	80	92	105	122	144	161	172	184	207	240	278	307
Other Items (Net)	27r	—	−5	—	29	35	37	25	13	−65	−48	−66	−59	−47	−68	−87
Monetary Survey															*Millions of Lempiras:*	
Foreign Assets (Net)	31n	57	66	−11	28	86	198	291	259	143	−2	−187	−214	−231	−527	−574
Domestic Credit	32	393	491	561	671	818	953	1,109	1,243	1,422	1,650	1,938	2,338	2,649	2,889	3,125
Claims on Central Govt. (Net)	32an	58	71	79	91	100	96	139	167	300	428	555	709	791	853	890
Claims on Local Government	32b	12	15	15	17	16	21	32	62	69	66	61	109	128	81	80
Claims on Private Sector	32d	305	378	428	505	638	774	859	931	946	992	1,095	1,254	1,415	1,618	1,795
Claims on Other Banking Insts	32f	18	27	38	58	65	62	80	84	107	164	226	267	315	337	359
Money	34	193	240	243	266	370	417	491	548	611	638	724	823	843	816	882
Quasi-Money	35	172	205	217	242	302	381	474	493	517	589	749	901	1,062	1,051	1,159
Bonds	36ab	11	14	17	12	25	37	51	52	31	28	23	26	31	24	32
Long-Term Foreign Liabilities	36cl	22	35	41	139	167	217	248	281	322	330	343	339	365	405	439
Liabilities to Other Banking Insts.	36i	....	....	....	....	....	....	....	....	....	....	....	....	....	....	....
Capital Accounts	37a	98	108	120	131	143	171	208	263	331	367	397	452	508	615	668
Other Items (Net)	37r	−46	−46	−89	−91	−103	−71	−72	−133	−247	−305	−485	−416	−390	−549	−630
Money plus Quasi-Money	35l	366	445	460	508	672	798	965	1,041	1,128	1,227	1,473	1,723	1,905	1,866	2,042
Other Banking Institutions															*Millions of Lempiras:*	
Reserves	40	5	6	6	8	15	14	20	16	18	19	30	36	29	39	39
Foreign Assets	41	1	1	1	1	3	3	5	5	3	4	2	1	5	2	4
Claims on Central Government	42a	1	1	2	6	9	22	11	12	17	11	12	52	59	55	70
Claims on Local Government	42b	1	1	3	4	6	12	10	18	25	41	45	54	62	75	80
Claims on Private Sector	42d	109	129	155	193	201	264	342	429	532	598	678	713	744	811	832
Claims on Deposit Money Banks	42e	1	2	12	25	26	16	18	18	13	6	7	11	14	18	8
Demand Deposits	44	6	8	7	8	6	8	6	10	9	5	7	7	9	14	9
Time, Savings,& Fgn.Currency Dep.	45	11	14	14	25	29	49	60	73	94	108	124	148	165	164	183
Bonds	46ab	4	11	15	20	8	17	27	50	38	40	44	49	58	60	61
Foreign Liabilities	46c	5	7	8	11	30	25	26	49	70	45	40	40	40	47	53
Long-Term Foreign Liabilities	46cl	37	38	48	78	82	120	148	155	149	208	210	202	206	199	187
Central Government Deposits	46d	7	5	12	20	22	11	20	36	64	78	85	101	105	119	121
Credit from Monetary Authorities	46g	17	25	35	51	56	51	62	64	92	150	211	250	290	350	403
Credit from Deposit Money Banks	46h	1	2	7	7	3	4	4	3	3	7	21	22	24	20	13
Capital Accounts	47a	63	68	78	101	121	131	143	160	153	181	302	303	312	328	329
Other Items (Net)	47r	−34	−37	−43	−82	−98	−86	−90	−102	−63	−143	−271	−250	−296	−300	−325

1987	1988	1989	1990	1991	1992	1993	1994	1995	1996	1997	1998	1999	2000	2001		
End of Period															**Exchange Rates**	
2.8373	2.6914	2.6283	7.6212	7.7243	8.0163	9.9720	13.7227	15.3751	18.5057	17.6673	19.4415	19.9067	19.7270	20.0068	Market Rate	aa
End of Period (ae) Period Average (rf)																
2.0000	2.0000	2.0000	5.3570	5.4000	5.8300	7.2600	9.4001	10.3432	12.8694	13.0942	13.8076	14.5039	15.1407	15.9197	Market Rate	ae
2.0000	2.0000	2.0000	4.1120	5.3167	5.4979	6.4716	8.4088	9.4710	11.7053	13.0035	13.3850	14.2132	14.8392	15.4737	Market Rate	rf
End of Period															**Fund Position**	
67.80	67.80	67.80	67.80	67.80	95.00	95.00	95.00	95.00	95.00	95.00	95.00	129.50	129.50	129.50	Quota	2f. s
—	—	—	.01	—	.11	.11	.15	.10	.06	.06	.05	.68	.08	.25	SDRs	1b. s
												8.63	8.63	8.63	Reserve Position in the Fund	1c. s
54.37	27.29	26.96	22.66	23.55	81.35	86.01	74.81	66.36	40.28	33.90	80.04	153.33	165.08	178.30	Total Fund Cred.&Loans Outstg.	2tl
End of Period															**International Liquidity**	
106.00	50.00	21.10	40.41	104.90	197.45	97.15	171.01	261.45	249.19	580.37	818.07	1,257.58	1,313.04	1,415.56	Total Reserves minus Gold	1l. d
—	—	—	.01	—	.15	.15	.21	.15	.09	.07	.07	.94	.10	.32	SDRs	1b. d
												11.84	11.24	10.84	Reserve Position in the Fund	1c. d
106.00	50.00	21.10	40.40	104.90	197.30	97.00	170.80	261.30	249.10	580.30	818.00	1,244.80	1,301.70	1,404.40	Foreign Exchange	1d. d
.016	.016	.016	.016	.021	.021	.021	.021	.021	.021	.021	.021	.021	.021	.021	Gold (Million Fine Troy Ounces)	1ad
1.05	1.05	1.05	1.05	7.78	7.79	8.47	8.30	8.41	8.03	6.43	6.25	6.28	5.99	6.05	Gold (National Valuation)	1and
546.96	570.73	617.12	662.67	616.98	588.14	560.88	599.86	595.09	509.27	379.96	361.89	443.44	427.88	416.92	Monetary Authorities: Other Liab.	4.. d
4.30	9.55	14.95	24.62	29.11	66.52	75.65	84.32	123.47	209.97	228.00	275.70	379.81	451.94	487.77	Deposit Money Banks: Assets	7a. d
51.90	45.15	24.40	16.33	17.28	16.95	28.71	68.89	103.20	154.84	271.39	344.95	297.64	272.02	228.04	Liabilities	7b. d
1.60	1.85	1.95	1.47	4.33	6.50	8.79	10.20	9.29	12.39	8.06	6.80	7.67	11.77	11.23	Other Banking Insts.: Assets	7e. d
128.60	120.05	111.90	112.99	17.69	17.51	13.93	15.80	16.49	13.01	15.80	17.19	9.84	38.26	56.85	Liabilities	7f. d
End of Period															**Monetary Authorities**	
196	152	95	357	748	1,343	954	1,930	3,058	3,641	†10,437	14,282	21,375	23,151	25,978	Foreign Assets	11
881	1,299	1,428	1,905	1,360	1,555	2,023	1,512	1,284	1,220	†1,462	1,534	1,014	1,109	935	Claims on Central Government	12a
62	59	54	80	75	67	63	60	53	92	†48	45	42	39	36	Claims on Local Government	12b
3	18	27	29	32	42	59	58	64	58	†1	1	1	1	1	Claims on Private Sector	12d
476	481	542	543	653	665	665	678	616	721	†136	99	60	33	215	Claims on Deposit Money Banks	12e
450	443	483	509	468	532	547	569	572	555	†157	108	108	97	74	Claims on Other Banking Insts	12f
622	714	892	1,113	1,200	1,734	1,852	2,723	3,373	4,842	†9,045	10,501	11,720	12,813	14,091	Reserve Money	14
492	570	676	882	977	1,141	1,448	1,995	2,111	2,630	†3,315	3,744	4,714	4,727	5,166	of which: Currency Outside DMBs	14a
18	21	34	128	122	39	52	86	318	219	†791	503	1,582	3,599	5,959	Time, Savings,& Fgn.Currency Dep.	15
811	779	841	2,187	2,007	2,428	3,103	4,274	4,438	4,216	†960	1,618	3,190	3,361	3,659	Foreign Liabilities	16c
437	436	464	1,536	1,507	1,599	1,692	2,206	2,216	2,456	†4,015	4,302	4,188	4,054	3,928	Long-Term Foreign Liabilities	16cl
367	541	459	1,275	1,185	1,390	1,751	1,229	1,562	2,042	†2,878	4,766	7,409	6,112	4,834	Central Government Deposits	16d
347	411	486	639	782	891	1,116	1,422	1,762	1,930	†1,623	908	945	973	1,080	Capital Accounts	17a
−535	−451	−548	−3,456	−3,467	−3,876	−5,255	−7,133	−8,022	−9,419	†−7,072	−6,528	−6,432	−6,483	−6,313	Other Items (Net)	17r
End of Period															**Deposit Money Banks**	
125	197	279	274	463	648	423	668	1,118	1,968	†5,021	6,018	6,374	7,134	8,091	Reserves	20
9	19	30	132	157	388	549	793	1,277	2,702	†2,985	3,807	5,509	6,843	7,765	Foreign Assets	21
699	715	836	919	1,202	1,045	968	1,287	1,205	867	†275	77	41	370	732	Claims on Central Government	22a
35	64	60	47	40	5	2	1	10	15	†54	147	125	136	79	Claims on Local Government	22b
2,131	2,386	2,604	3,026	3,481	4,341	5,009	6,364	7,711	10,966	†16,744	23,247	28,014	32,021	35,524	Claims on Private Sector	22d
33	31	30	28	3	6	6	37	55	29	†26	43	473	195	280	Claims on Other Banking Insts	22f
581	625	774	903	1,138	1,276	1,313	1,761	2,368	3,074	†4,287	4,841	5,666	6,180	6,344	Demand Deposits	24
1,355	1,589	1,738	1,990	2,486	3,151	3,432	4,287	5,626	8,721	†13,657	18,094	22,228	27,819	32,585	Time, Savings,& Fgn.Currency Dep.	25
41	36	32	28	23	19	16	14	29	33	†61	90	58	50	42	Bonds	26ab
83	66	30	48	32	66	74	256	459	759	†1,294	1,314	878	961	822	Foreign Liabilities	26c
21	24	19	39	62	33	135	392	609	1,234	†2,259	3,449	3,439	3,158	2,808	Long-Term Foreign Liabilities	26cl
210	272	350	465	467	649	349	300	270	331	†1,059	2,004	2,846	2,457	2,103	Central Government Deposits	26d
479	497	554	545	656	679	704	691	619	760	†156	90	60	33	215	Credit from Monetary Authorities	26g
....	....	....	....	....	....	....	....	....	....	833	1,453	2,575	2,897	3,421	Liabilities to Other Banking Insts.	26i
336	372	426	531	708	876	1,234	1,670	2,224	2,846	†3,885	4,876	5,958	7,168	8,343	Capital Accounts	27a
−74	−69	−85	−123	−225	−315	−302	−222	−829	−1,212	†−2,385	−2,872	−3,173	−4,024	−4,212	Other Items (Net)	27r
End of Period															**Monetary Survey**	
−689	−674	−747	−1,746	−1,133	−763	−1,673	−1,807	−562	1,368	†11,168	15,156	22,816	25,672	29,262	Foreign Assets (Net)	31n
3,716	4,201	4,712	4,803	5,009	5,554	6,577	8,359	9,122	11,427	†14,830	18,432	19,563	25,397	30,724	Domestic Credit	32
1,003	1,201	1,455	1,084	910	561	890	1,270	657	−287	†−2,200	−5,158	−9,200	−7,091	−5,271	Claims on Central Govt. (Net)	32an
97	123	114	127	114	72	66	61	63	107	†102	192	168	175	116	Claims on Local Government	32b
2,134	2,404	2,630	3,055	3,513	4,383	5,068	6,422	7,775	11,024	†16,745	23,247	28,015	32,021	35,525	Claims on Private Sector	32d
483	474	513	537	471	538	553	606	627	583	†183	151	581	292	354	Claims on Other Banking Insts	32f
1,117	1,250	1,501	1,855	2,060	2,523	2,825	3,845	4,678	6,053	†8,294	9,349	11,050	11,954	12,388	Money	34
1,373	1,610	1,773	2,118	2,609	3,190	3,485	4,374	5,945	8,941	†14,448	18,597	23,810	31,418	38,544	Quasi-Money	35
41	36	32	28	23	19	16	14	29	33	†61	90	58	50	42	Bonds	36ab
458	460	482	1,575	1,569	1,632	1,826	2,597	2,825	3,690	†6,274	7,751	7,626	7,212	6,737	Long-Term Foreign Liabilities	36cl
....	....	....	....	....	....	....	....	....	....	833	1,453	2,575	2,897	3,421	Liabilities to Other Banking Insts.	36i
683	783	912	1,170	1,490	1,767	2,350	3,093	3,986	4,775	†5,509	5,784	6,903	8,141	9,423	Capital Accounts	37a
−645	−611	−735	−3,689	−3,874	−4,340	−5,599	−7,370	−8,902	−10,697	†−9,420	−9,436	−9,643	−10,602	−10,569	Other Items (Net)	37r
2,490	2,860	3,273	3,973	4,668	5,713	6,309	8,219	10,623	14,994	†22,742	27,946	34,860	43,371	50,932	Money plus Quasi-Money	35l
End of Period															**Other Banking Institutions**	
32	35	40	39	48	58	75	139	124	121	†661	759	654	1,057	950	Reserves	40
3	4	4	8	23	38	64	96	96	160	†106	94	111	178	179	Foreign Assets	41
82	83	82	89	79	76	79	110	137	156	†294	79	54	46	209	Claims on Central Government	42a
67	73	73	76	73	76	80	86	93	95	†136	131	112	110	99	Claims on Local Government	42b
890	785	834	842	785	981	1,094	1,261	1,529	1,507	†3,044	3,337	3,969	4,363	5,272	Claims on Private Sector	42d
13	25	19	21	8	7	20	27	38	34	†881	1,462	2,597	2,918	3,463	Claims on Deposit Money Banks	42e
14	25	22	21	17	17	19	21	19	20	†26	18	40	38	37	Demand Deposits	44
229	226	231	258	355	557	675	744	938	1,063	†3,387	3,154	3,504	3,531	4,142	Time, Savings,& Fgn.Currency Dep.	45
65	68	65	63	4	1	1	1	1	1	†17	7	—	—	—	Bonds	46ab
70	76	85	248	3	1	—	6	18	1	†30	14	1	17	4	Foreign Liabilities	46c
187	164	139	357	93	101	101	143	153	166	†177	224	142	563	901	Long-Term Foreign Liabilities	46cl
102	122	120	142	147	194	217	326	425	407	†636	1,091	1,462	1,851	1,687	Central Government Deposits	46d
469	450	492	537	637	589	579	647	586	584	†177	110	112	102	74	Credit from Monetary Authorities	46g
17	13	10	7	2	4	5	36	54	28	†70	92	527	186	213	Credit from Deposit Money Banks	46h
321	310	368	373	328	345	301	407	449	497	†2,058	2,087	2,866	3,479	4,398	Capital Accounts	47a
−387	−450	−478	−932	−570	−574	−487	−611	−623	−693	†−1,456	−935	−1,157	−1,094	−1,285	Other Items (Net)	47r

Honduras

		1972	1973	1974	1975	1976	1977	1978	1979	1980	1981	1982	1983	1984	1985	1986
Banking Survey																*Millions of Lempiras:*
Foreign Assets (Net)	51n	53	60	−17	18	58	176	269	215	76	−43	−225	−249	−266	−572	−624
Domestic Credit	52	478	591	671	796	947	1,178	1,372	1,583	1,824	2,058	2,360	2,789	3,093	3,375	3,627
Claims on Central Govt. (Net)	52an	52	67	70	78	86	106	130	143	253	361	482	661	745	790	839
Claims on Local Government	52b	13	16	19	21	22	34	41	80	94	107	106	162	190	156	160
Claims on Private Sector	52d	414	508	582	697	839	1,038	1,201	1,360	1,477	1,590	1,773	1,966	2,159	2,429	2,627
Liquid Liabilities	55l	378	461	474	533	693	841	1,011	1,108	1,213	1,322	1,574	1,842	2,050	2,005	2,195
Bonds	56ab	15	25	32	31	32	54	78	102	69	68	67	75	89	85	94
Long-Term Foreign Liabilities	56cl	59	74	89	217	249	338	396	436	471	539	553	541	571	604	626
Capital Accounts	57a	161	176	198	232	264	302	350	422	484	548	699	755	819	943	997
Other Items (Net)	57r	−81	−85	−140	−199	−233	−181	−195	−270	−336	−461	−758	−672	−701	−834	−908
Money (National Definitions)																*Millions of Lempiras:*
Reserve Money (M0)	19ma	....	....	....	....	....	....	....	....							
M1	59ma	....	....	....	....	....	....	....	....	605	632	699	799	832	844	917
M2	59mb	....	....	....	....	....	....	....	....	1,303	1,446	1,689	1,931	2,161	2,241	2,456
M3	59mc	....	....	....	....	....	....	....	....	1,368	1,504	1,748	1,985	2,206	2,289	2,512
Interest Rates																*Percent Per Annum*
Discount Rate (*End of Period*)	60							13.0	13.5	16.0	16.0	24.0	24.0	24.0	24.0	24.0
Savings Rate	60k											7.5	7.1	7.2	7.1	7.2
Savings Rate (Fgn.Currency)	60k. f															
Deposit Rate	60l											10.6	11.3	10.3	9.9	9.7
Deposit Rate (Fgn.Currency)	60l. f															
Lending Rate	60p											16.5	16.1	16.2	16.3	16.1
Lending Rate (Fgn.Currency)	60p. f															
Government Bond Yield	61												9.4	10.3	10.4	10.4
Prices and Labor																*Index Numbers (1995=100):*
Consumer Prices	64	9.1	9.5	10.8	11.7	12.2	13.3	†14.0	15.7	18.6	20.3	22.2	24.0	25.1	26.0	27.1
																Number in Thousands:
Labor Force	67d	....	....	....	....	....	....	....	....							
Employment	67e	....	....	....	....	....	....	....	....						281	406
Unemployment	67c	....	....	....	....	....	....	....	....							
Unemployment Rate (%)	67r	....	....	....	....	....	....	....	....							
International Transactions																*Millions of US Dollars*
Exports	70..d	204.5	258.7	289.1	295.0	400.1	513.5	607.6	733.6	829.5	760.7	659.5	671.8	725.4	780.1	854.2
Imports, c.i.f.	71..d	193.3	262.3	382.2	400.1	455.9	574.7	693.0	825.9	1,008.7	949.1	700.5	802.6	893.4	888.1	875.1
Imports, f.o.b.	71.vd	171.3	235.2	348.0	364.5	414.3	520.6	628.9	748.8	912.3	860.5	636.6	722.7	810.7	803.7	791.9
																1995=100
Volume of Exports	72	93.5	96.7	74.6	98.2	116.3	133.5	136.5	161.1	162.0	156.8	154.2	146.8	142.1	158.0	140.8
Export Prices	74..d	....	....	....	45.4	56.3	81.4	74.1	70.9	84.4	76.5	74.0	74.6	79.0	81.2	97.2
Balance of Payments																*Millions of US Dollars:*
Current Account, n.i.e.	78ald	....	....	−103.9	−112.1	−104.8	−128.7	−157.2	−192.1	−316.8	−302.7	−228.3	−232.0	−374.3	−308.6	−224.6
Goods: Exports f.o.b.	78aad	....	....	303.9	313.1	415.5	534.4	631.2	763.8	860.1	793.0	685.1	707.2	746.2	805.7	902.1
Goods: Imports f.o.b.	78abd	....	....	−387.5	−372.4	−432.5	−550.1	−654.5	−783.5	−954.1	−898.6	−680.7	−756.3	−884.8	−891.7	−879.5
Trade Balance	78acd	....	....	−83.5	−59.3	−17.0	−15.7	−23.3	−19.7	−94.0	−105.7	4.4	−49.1	−138.6	−86.1	22.6
Services: Credit	78add	....	....	27.9	31.3	38.2	46.3	56.2	74.3	81.5	90.6	81.9	93.8	101.2	103.8	109.6
Services: Debit	78aed	....	....	−68.3	−73.8	−82.2	−105.4	−123.1	−148.2	−174.0	−163.7	−144.3	−158.4	−183.2	−195.3	−198.6
Balance on Goods & Services	78afd	....	....	−123.9	−101.8	−60.9	−74.9	−90.2	−93.7	−186.4	−178.7	−58.0	−113.6	−220.6	−177.6	−66.4
Income: Credit	78agd	....	....	5.0	6.5	9.7	13.2	19.1	21.2	25.9	19.7	16.6	14.0	15.8	14.9	13.1
Income: Debit	78ahd	....	....	−17.5	−34.6	−66.8	−81.2	−103.4	−140.1	−177.8	−171.2	−216.8	−164.1	−191.7	−203.0	−222.2
Balance on Gds, Serv. & Inc.	78aid	....	....	−136.5	−129.8	−118.0	−142.8	−174.5	−212.6	−338.3	−330.2	−258.3	−263.7	−396.5	−365.7	−275.5
Current Transfers, n.i.e.: Credit	78ajd	....	....	37.4	23.2	19.5	20.6	25.4	35.5	37.7	38.1	40.0	42.9	33.7	69.0	63.4
Current Transfers: Debit	78akd	....	....	−4.9	−5.5	−6.2	−6.5	−8.1	−15.0	−16.2	−10.6	−10.0	−11.1	−11.5	−11.9	−12.5
Capital Account, n.i.e.	78bcd	....	....	—	—	—	—	—	—	—	—	—	—	—	—	—
Capital Account, n.i.e.: Credit	78bad	....	....	—	—	—	—	—	—	—	—	—	—	—	—	—
Capital Account: Debit	78bbd	....	....	—	—	—	—	—	—	—	—	—	—	—	—	—
Financial Account, n.i.e.	78bjd	....	....	91.7	118.8	135.7	185.0	136.5	208.0	237.4	229.5	153.3	102.1	284.5	175.0	69.4
Direct Investment Abroad	78bdd	....	....	—	—	—	—	—	—	—	—	—	—	—	—	—
Dir. Invest. in Rep. Econ., n.i.e.	78bed	....	....	−1.2	7.0	5.3	8.9	13.2	28.2	5.8	−3.6	13.8	21.0	20.5	27.5	30.0
Portfolio Investment Assets	78bfd	....	....	—	—	—	—	−.6	−.1	−.1	−.3	−.2	.2	−1.9	1.2	−1.0
Equity Securities	78bkd	....	....	—	—	—	—	−.6	−.1	−.1	−.3	−.2	.2	−1.9	1.2	−1.0
Debt Securities	78bld	....	....	—	—	—	—	—	—	—	—	—	—	—	—	—
Portfolio Investment Liab., n.i.e.	78bgd	....	....	—	—	—	—	—	—	—	—	—	—	—	—	—
Equity Securities	78bmd	....	....	—	—	—	—	—	—	—	—	—	—	—	—	—
Debt Securities	78bnd	....	....	—	—	—	—	—	—	—	—	—	—	—	—	—
Financial Derivatives Assets	78bwd	....	....	....	....	....	....	....	....	....	....	....	....	....	....	....
Financial Derivatives Liabilities	78bxd	....	....	....	....	....	....	....	....	....	....	....	....	....	....	....
Other Investment Assets	78bhd	....	....	−5.8	−7.7	−1.6	−12.0	−12.0	−13.2	−10.6	−18.1	−.9	−6.3	−2.5	−44.8	−41.2
Monetary Authorities	78bod	....	....													
General Government	78bpd	....	....	−2.0	−1.5	−1.6	−7.3	−3.7	−3.0	−10.3	−14.1	−10.0	−8.7	−2.5	−44.6	−39.4
Banks	78bqd	....	....	−1.4	−3.3	1.3	−1.5	−1.5	−.2	−.3	−4.1	9.1	2.4	—	−.2	−1.8
Other Sectors	78brd	....	....	−2.4	−2.9	−1.3	−3.3	−6.8	−10.0							
Other Investment Liab., n.i.e.	78bid	....	....	98.6	119.4	132.0	188.1	135.9	193.1	242.2	251.4	140.6	87.2	268.4	191.1	81.5
Monetary Authorities	78bsd	....	....	.3	35.5	2.5	6.9	−9.2	8.8	−43.4	5.0	59.1	−39.7	53.2	54.8	59.2
General Government	78btd	....	....	22.8	42.6	46.1	28.1	39.1	26.2	57.8	60.1	32.6	42.0	60.0	47.2	68.4
Banks	78bud	....	....	4.1	6.0	14.4	24.2	−14.6	28.1	−6.5	−26.0	6.6	2.5	−10.5	12.9	2.3
Other Sectors	78bvd	....	....	71.5	35.5	69.1	129.1	120.6	130.1	234.3	212.3	42.3	82.5	165.6	76.3	−48.4
Net Errors and Omissions	78cad	....	....	−4.8	−.4	−1.6	−6.4	12.7	−18.5	−38.9	−18.4	−.5	12.7	−8.6	−38.6	3.2
Overall Balance	78cbd	....	....	−17.0	6.3	29.3	49.9	−8.0	−2.6	−118.4	−91.7	−75.5	−117.2	−98.4	−172.2	−152.1
Reserves and Related Items	79dad	....	....	17.0	−6.3	−29.3	−49.9	8.0	2.6	118.4	91.7	75.5	117.2	98.4	172.2	152.1
Reserve Assets	79dbd	....	....	−3.2	−53.4	−37.9	−51.8	−4.0	−20.1	62.2	47.5	7.6	−1.6	−8.9	53.9	−7.9
Use of Fund Credit and Loans	79dcd	....	....	20.2	—	—	−14.6	−5.7	9.9	23.9	23.4	67.8	49.2	−1.6	−19.2	−51.9
Exceptional Financing	79ded	....	....	—	47.1	8.6	16.6	17.6	12.9	32.3	20.7	—	69.7	108.8	137.5	212.0

	1987	1988	1989	1990	1991	1992	1993	1994	1995	1996	1997	1998	1999	2000	2001		
End of Period																**Banking Survey**	
	−756	−746	−828	−1,987	−1,112	−726	−1,610	−1,717	−484	1,527	†11,244	15,237	22,926	25,833	29,436	Foreign Assets (Net)	**51n**
	4,169	4,547	5,068	5,131	5,327	5,954	7,059	8,884	9,830	12,195	†17,484	20,737	21,655	27,774	34,263	Domestic Credit	**52**
	982	1,162	1,417	1,030	842	442	752	1,054	369	−537	†−2,542	−6,171	−10,609	−8,896	−6,749	Claims on Central Govt. (Net)	**52an**
	163	196	187	203	187	148	146	146	156	202	†238	323	280	285	215	Claims on Local Government	**52b**
	3,024	3,189	3,464	3,897	4,298	5,364	6,161	7,683	9,305	12,530	†19,788	26,584	31,983	36,384	40,797	Claims on Private Sector	**52d**
	2,701	3,076	3,486	4,213	4,993	6,229	6,928	8,845	11,455	15,956	†25,494	30,359	37,749	45,883	54,162	Liquid Liabilities	**55l**
	105	104	97	91	27	20	17	14	30	33	†78	97	58	50	42	Bonds	**56ab**
	645	624	622	1,932	1,662	1,733	1,927	2,740	2,977	3,856	†6,451	7,974	7,768	7,775	7,637	Long-Term Foreign Liabilities	**56cl**
	1,004	1,093	1,279	1,543	1,818	2,111	2,652	3,500	4,434	5,272	†7,566	7,870	9,769	11,620	13,822	Capital Accounts	**57a**
	−1,043	−1,097	−1,244	−4,635	−4,285	−4,865	−6,074	−7,932	−9,550	−11,396	†−10,861	−10,328	−10,764	−11,721	−11,964	Other Items (Net)	**57r**
End of Period																**Money (National Definitions)**	
	....	....	....	....	....	....	....	....	....	4,627	8,102	9,281	10,079	10,353	9,790	*Reserve Money (M0)*	**19ma**
	1,080	1,215	1,462	1,831	2,139	2,444	2,762	3,783	4,474	5,690	7,609	8,577	10,450	10,943	11,508	*M1*	**59ma**
	2,915	3,322	3,752	4,582	5,113	6,270	6,822	8,537	10,224	12,560	20,344	23,706	28,723	33,482	36,263	*M2*	**59mb**
	2,971	3,360	3,782	4,654	5,258	6,592	7,517	9,834	12,173	16,727	25,716	30,395	37,155	43,924	50,128	*M3*	**59mc**
Percent Per Annum																**Interest Rates**	
	24.0	24.0	24.0	28.2	30.1	26.1	....	....	....	....	....	....	....	....	....	Discount Rate *(End of Period)*	**60**
	6.6	6.9	6.4	7.8	9.4	9.6	9.2	9.4	10.0	9.9	12.6	12.3	12.0	10.9	10.0	Savings Rate	**60k**
	....	....	....	....	....	....	....	....	....	....	4.7	4.5	4.0	3.7	3.2	Savings Rate (Fgn.Currency)	**60k. f**
	9.6	8.6	8.6	8.8	11.5	12.3	11.6	11.6	12.0	16.7	21.3	18.6	20.0	15.9	14.5	Deposit Rate	**60l**
	....	....	....	....	....	....	....	....	....	....	9.9	9.5	9.1	7.5	6.4	Deposit Rate (Fgn.Currency)	**60l. f**
	15.5	15.4	15.4	17.1	21.9	21.7	22.1	24.7	27.0	29.7	32.1	30.7	30.2	26.8	23.8	Lending Rate	**60p**
	....	....	....	....	....	....	....	....	....	....	12.9	12.5	12.6	12.9	12.7	Lending Rate (Fgn.Currency)	**60p. f**
	10.4	10.4	10.4	10.4	10.4	10.4	10.4	23.1	27.2	35.6	29.6	20.3	16.0	14.8	15.3	Government Bond Yield	**61**
Period Averages																**Prices and Labor**	
	27.8	29.0	31.9	39.3	52.7	57.3	63.5	77.2	100.0	123.8	†148.8	169.2	188.9	209.8	230.1	Consumer Prices	**64**
Period Averages																	
	....	....	....	....	....	....	....	....	1,777	1,977	2,053	2,135	2,388	....	....	Labor Force	**67d**
	391	1,354	1,394	1,213	1,494	1,675	....	....	1,806	1,985	2,088	2,135	2,299	....	....	Employment	**67e**
	....	....	....	62	72	54	....	....	59	89	69	88	89	....	....	Unemployment	**67c**
	....	....	....	4.8	4.6	3.1	....	....	3.2	4.3	3.2	3.9	3.7	....	....	Unemployment Rate (%)	**67r**
Millions of US Dollars																**International Transactions**	
	791.4	841.9	858.5	831.0	792.4	801.5	814.0	842.0	1,220.2	1,316.0	1,445.7	1,532.8	1,164.4	1,369.8	1,318.0	Exports	**70..d**
	827.4	940.1	968.6	934.8	955.1	1,036.6	1,130.0	1,055.9	1,642.7	1,839.9	2,148.6	2,534.8	2,676.1	2,854.7	2,917.6	Imports, c.i.f.	**71..d**
	748.8	801.6	789.2	796.8	796.2	938.1	1,022.6	955.6	1,486.6	1,665.1	....	....	....	....	....	Imports, f.o.b.	**71.vd**
1995=100																	
	164.3	144.1	125.2	125.0	110.7	125.1	111.4	96.1	100.0	118.7	103.5	103.3	....	....	....	Volume of Exports	**72**
	88.2	93.7	94.0	94.4	92.4	72.4	74.2	77.4	100.0	92.9	96.8	94.4	....	....	....	Export Prices	**74..d**
Minus Sign Indicates Debit																Balance of Payments	
	−245.2	−161.0	−180.3	−186.4	−213.4	−298.2	−308.7	−343.3	−200.9	−335.4	−272.2	−394.8	−583.2	−509.7	....	Current Account, n.i.e.	**78ald**
	830.5	889.5	911.2	895.2	840.6	839.3	999.6	1,101.5	1,377.2	1,638.4	1,856.5	2,047.9	1,769.6	2,039.2	....	Goods: Exports f.o.b.	**78aad**
	−871.4	−923.4	−955.7	−907.0	−912.5	−990.2	−1,203.1	−1,351.1	−1,518.6	−1,925.8	−2,150.4	−2,370.5	−2,509.6	−2,697.6	....	Goods: Imports f.o.b.	**78abd**
	−40.9	−34.0	−44.5	−11.8	−71.9	−150.9	−203.5	−249.6	−141.4	−287.4	−293.9	−322.6	−740.0	−658.4	....	*Trade Balance*	**78acd**
	119.7	136.4	149.7	137.3	175.0	202.0	223.9	242.4	257.6	283.3	334.9	377.1	503.5	462.2	....	Services: Credit	**78add**
	−202.4	−217.5	−230.5	−219.8	−226.7	−243.2	−294.7	−311.0	−333.7	−327.8	−360.9	−446.8	−502.4	−577.3	....	Services: Debit	**78aed**
	−123.7	−115.1	−125.3	−94.3	−123.6	−192.1	−274.3	−318.2	−217.5	−331.9	−319.9	−392.3	−738.9	−773.5	....	*Balance on Goods & Services*	**78afd**
	15.2	22.0	24.3	20.7	39.8	61.4	16.6	24.0	32.3	61.2	70.0	59.5	79.2	79.7	....	Income: Credit	**78agd**
	−247.9	−253.3	−261.9	−257.5	−285.9	−343.4	−215.3	−238.1	−258.2	−292.0	−281.8	−263.6	−235.7	−217.9	....	Income: Debit	**78ahd**
	−356.4	−346.4	−362.9	−331.1	−369.7	−474.1	−473.0	−532.3	−443.4	−562.7	−531.7	−596.4	−895.4	−911.7	....	*Balance on Gds, Serv. & Inc.*	**78aid**
	124.2	198.4	194.6	156.2	166.3	186.1	165.5	190.2	243.7	271.7	306.8	241.7	354.6	447.4	....	Current Transfers, n.i.e.: Credit	**78ajd**
	−13.0	−13.0	−12.0	−11.5	−10.0	−10.2	−1.2	−1.2	−1.2	−44.4	−47.3	−40.1	−42.4	−45.4	....	Current Transfers: Debit	**78akd**
	—	—	—	—	—	—	—	—	—	28.5	14.6	29.4	111.1	81.7	....	Capital Account, n.i.e.	**78bcd**
	—	—	—	—	—	—	—	—	—	29.2	15.3	29.4	111.1	81.7	....	Capital Account, n.i.e.: Credit	**78bad**
	—	—	—	—	—	—	—	—	—	−.7	−.7	—	—	—	....	Capital Account: Debit	**78bbd**
	96.0	45.4	−48.6	−16.7	−98.3	22.0	22.8	157.5	114.6	70.2	243.3	113.9	275.1	73.1	....	Financial Account, n.i.e.	**78bjd**
	—	—	—	—	—	—	—	—	—	—	—	—	—	—	....	Direct Investment Abroad	**78bdd**
	38.7	48.3	51.0	43.5	52.1	47.6	26.7	34.8	50.0	90.9	121.5	99.0	237.3	282.0	....	Dir. Invest. in Rep. Econ., n.i.e.	**78bed**
	.6	−.2	.1	.1	.1	.1	—	—	—	16.0	—	—	—	−35.0	....	Portfolio Investment Assets	**78bfd**
	.6	−.2	.1	.1	.1	.1	—	....	....	16.0	—	—	—	—	....	Equity Securities	**78bkd**
	—	—	—	—	—	—	—	—	—	....	....	—	—	−35.0	....	Debt Securities	**78bld**
	—	—	—	—	—	—	—	—	—	....	....	—	—	—	....	Portfolio Investment Liab., n.i.e.	**78bgd**
	—	—	—	—	—	—	—	—	—	....	....	—	—	—	....	Equity Securities	**78bmd**
	—	—	—	—	—	—	—	—	—	....	....	—	—	—	....	Debt Securities	**78bnd**
	....	....	....	....	....	....	....	....	....	....	....	—	—	....	....	Financial Derivatives Assets	**78bwd**
	....	....	....	....	....	....	....	....	....	....	....	−25.8	−16.8	2.0	....	Financial Derivatives Liabilities	**78bxd**
	−1.6	−12.5	−6.2	−39.5	−17.4	−63.4	−139.6	8.9	−12.8	−89.4	−53.4	−61.7	−132.2	−157.2	....	Other Investment Assets	**78bhd**
	....	....	....	....	....	....	3.9	3.3	11.7	....	....	—	—	—	....	Monetary Authorities	**78bod**
	−2.1	−7.2	−.7	12.9	1.6	−26.3	−132.0	14.4	14.4	....	....	—	—	—	....	General Government	**78bpd**
	.5	−5.3	−5.5	−52.4	−19.0	−37.1	−11.5	−8.8	−38.9	−89.4	−53.4	−61.7	−132.2	−97.8	....	Banks	**78bqd**
	—	—	—	—	—	—	—	....	....	....	....	—	—	−59.4	....	Other Sectors	**78brd**
	58.4	9.8	−93.5	−20.8	−133.1	37.7	135.7	113.8	77.4	52.7	175.2	102.4	186.8	−18.7	....	Other Investment Liab., n.i.e.	**78bid**
	31.3	−9.1	−12.4	−31.2	−125.4	−84.8	−73.6	−60.7	−73.1	−180.1	−24.1	−27.2	−22.2	−33.5	....	Monetary Authorities	**78bsd**
	55.7	68.5	−1.6	128.7	184.1	104.7	224.8	96.2	101.7	141.9	−48.4	−30.3	168.8	19.9	....	General Government	**78btd**
	28.5	−6.1	−15.5	−24.6	−15.6	−7.3	1.7	−2.2	6.3	34.5	113.8	51.1	−11.5	−46.3	....	Banks	**78bud**
	−57.1	−43.6	−64.1	−93.7	−176.2	25.1	−17.2	80.5	42.5	56.4	133.9	108.8	51.7	41.2	....	Other Sectors	**78bvd**
	−33.4	−93.1	−138.9	−107.4	152.0	29.2	−47.5	115.5	45.0	157.9	196.5	96.1	6.4	16.6	....	Net Errors and Omissions	**78cad**
	−182.6	−208.7	−367.7	−310.5	−159.7	−247.0	−333.4	−70.3	−41.3	−78.8	182.2	−155.4	−190.6	−338.3	....	*Overall Balance*	**78cbd**
	182.6	208.7	367.7	310.5	159.7	247.0	333.4	70.3	41.3	78.8	−182.2	155.4	190.6	338.3	....	Reserves and Related Items	**79dad**
	−19.9	21.6	29.0	−20.1	−66.9	−92.0	99.6	−74.1	−90.3	12.7	−307.9	−229.8	−441.9	−32.3	....	Reserve Assets	**79dbd**
	−45.0	−36.0	−.4	−4.2	1.1	80.7	6.4	−16.1	−13.7	−38.0	−8.8	64.8	99.5	15.5	....	Use of Fund Credit and Loans	**79dcd**
	247.4	223.1	339.2	334.8	225.5	258.3	227.4	160.4	145.3	104.1	134.5	320.4	532.9	355.2	....	Exceptional Financing	**79ded**

Honduras

	1972	1973	1974	1975	1976	1977	1978	1979	1980	1981	1982	1983	1984	1985	1986
Government Finance														*Millions of Lempiras:*	
Deficit (-) or Surplus..............................80	−45.4	−16.0	−5.6	−48.0	−31.2	2.7	−29.7	−79.2	−396.9	−405.0	−450.4	−603.8	−678.6	−653.6	−492.2
Total Revenue and Grants...................81y	....	....	....	....	....	....	....	....	758.2	743.5	....	....	....	....	....
Revenue 81	192.9	219.5	257.0	272.0	352.7	457.1	549.5	655.9	758.2	743.5	770.0	778.1	951.0	1,064.1	1,151.8
Grants 81z	....	....	....	....	....	....	....	....	—	—	....	....	....	....	....
Exp. & Lending Minus Repay. 82z	....	....	....	....	....	....	....	....	1,155.1	1,148.5	....	....	....	....	....
Expenditure 82	238.3	235.5	262.6	320.0	383.9	454.4	579.2	735.1	1,017.6	1,003.5	1,220.4	1,381.9	1,629.6	1,717.7	1,644.0
Lending Minus Repayments 83	....	....	....	....	....	....	....	....	137.5	145.0	....	....	....	....	....
Total Financing 80h	....	....	....	....	....	....	....	....	396.9	405.1	....	....	....	....	....
Domestic 84a	....	....	....	....	....	....	....	....	142.6	151.4	....	....	....	....	....
Foreign 85a	....	....	....	....	....	....	....	....	254.3	253.7	....	....	....	....	....
Total Debt by Residence 88	333.0	355.5	410.5	506.5	615.2	698.5	942.3	1,182.0	1,642.7	2,091.2	2,538.7	2,991.8	3,510.0	4,053.8	4,531.8
Domestic 88a	136.0	141.3	153.2	162.4	198.8	218.0	296.9	347.2	544.7	742.6	817.5	1,101.6	1,250.5	1,438.0	1,640.6
Foreign 89a	197.0	214.2	257.3	344.1	416.4	480.5	645.4	834.8	1,098.0	1,348.6	1,721.2	1,890.2	2,259.5	2,615.8	2,891.2
Memorandum Item:															
Intragovernmental Debt 88s	6.0	8.9	14.0	23.7	43.7	61.0	65.4	77.3	93.7	—	129.3	160.9	186.0	212.1	208.6
National Accounts														*Millions of Lempiras*	
Househ.Cons.Expend.,incl.NPISHs 96f	1,222	1,382	1,581	1,754	1,964	2,314	2,511	2,945	3,612	4,072	4,310	4,684	5,026	5,412	5,606
Government Consumption Expend. 91f	193	186	242	278	348	417	442	520	650	721	758	807	876	953	1,087
Gross Fixed Capital Formation 93e	245	325	433	476	550	711	941	1,004	1,258	1,088	1,009	1,028	1,251	1,234	1,045
Changes in Inventories 93i	11	23	109	−50	−32	59	93	170	13	100	−190	−176	−95	27	10
Exports of Goods and Services 90c	461	579	656	680	898	1,149	1,366	1,649	1,860	1,784	1,549	1,610	1,706	1,827	2,025
Imports of Goods and Services (-) 98c	449	600	907	890	1,032	1,311	1,555	1,863	2,261	2,126	1,629	1,799	2,126	2,174	2,156
Gross Domestic Product (GDP) 99b	1,683	1,895	2,114	2,248	2,696	3,339	3,798	4,425	5,132	5,639	5,807	6,154	6,638	7,279	7,617
Net Primary Income from Abroad 98.n	−50	−62	−22	−50	−102	−124	−157	−210	−275	−319	−429	−338	−373	−384	−420
Gross National Income (GNI) 99a	1,633	1,833	2,092	2,198	2,594	3,215	3,641	4,215	4,857	5,320	5,378	5,816	6,265	6,895	7,197
Consumption of Fixed Capital 99cf	57	61	118	95	115	154	166	200	321	360	394	427	462	487	534
GDP Volume 1966 prices 99b.p	1,422	1,502	1,500	1,455	....	....	....	....	....	....	....	....	....	....	....
GDP Volume 1978 Prices.......................99b.p	....	....	....	2,876	3,178	3,508	3,798	4,038	4,066	4,169	4,111	4,073	4,250	4,428	4,460
GDP Volume (1995=100) ....99bv p	45.7	48.3	48.2	46.8	51.7	57.1	61.8	65.7	66.1	67.8	66.9	66.2	69.1	72.0	72.5
GDP Deflator (1995=100) ....99bi p	9.8	10.5	11.7	12.8	13.9	15.6	16.4	18.0	20.7	22.2	23.2	24.8	25.6	26.9	28.0
														Millions:	
Population..99z	2.81	2.90	2.99	3.09	3.20	3.32	3.44	3.56	3.69	3.82	3.96	4.09	4.23	4.37	4.51

	1987	1988	1989	1990	1991	1992	1993	1994	1995	1996	1997	1998	1999	2000	2001		
Year Ending December 31																**Government Finance**	
	−298.7	−274.3	−339.2	−854.6	†−458.0	−860.6	−1,447.7	−1,458.6	−1,326.1	−1,516.1	−1,260.2	−277.5	−1,115.4	−3,847.6	....	Deficit (-) or Surplus............................	**80**
	....	....	....	2,142.7	†3,142.7	3,772.1	4,453.1	4,952.1	7,296.6	8,512.4	11,091.2	14,012.5	16,395.1	17,128.1	....	Total Revenue and Grants	**81y**
	1,290.0	1,377.8	1,534.4	2,062.8	†2,980.4	3,500.5	4,182.2	4,809.8	7,139.5	8,256.8	10,773.8	13,641.8	15,136.2	15,872.0	....	Revenue	**81**
	....	....	....	79.9	†162.3	271.6	270.9	142.3	157.1	255.6	317.4	370.7	1,258.9	1,256.1	....	Grants	**81z**
	....	....	....	2,997.3	†3,600.7	4,632.7	5,900.8	6,410.7	8,622.7	10,028.5	12,351.4	14,290.0	17,510.5	20,975.7	....	Exp. & Lending Minus Repay.	**82z**
	1,588.7	1,652.1	1,873.6	3,041.0	†3,331.5	4,414.6	5,888.7	6,030.7	7,780.4	9,778.8	12,727.6	14,583.9	16,312.8	20,477.8	....	Expenditure	**82**
	....	....	....	−43.7	†269.2	218.1	12.1	380.0	842.3	249.7	−376.2	−293.9	1,197.7	497.9	....	Lending Minus Repayments	**83**
	....	....	....	....	†458.0	860.6	1,447.7	1,458.6	1,326.1	1,516.1	1,260.2	277.5	1,115.4	3,847.6	....	Total Financing	**80h**
	....	....	....	....	†234.3	−170.0	−322.8	505.2	−134.8	337.4	129.0	−685.8	−3,282.5	1,722.4	....	Domestic	**84a**
	....	....	....	375.0	†223.7	1,030.6	1,770.5	953.4	1,460.9	1,178.7	1,131.2	963.3	4,397.9	2,125.2	....	Foreign	**85a**
	5,196.8	5,958.2	6,819.2	14,787.1	14,853.9	16,955.2	22,597.0	30,997.1	36,435.5	44,360.1	46,672.5	50,721.6	56,112.1	58,646.1	....	Total Debt by Residence	**88**
	2,043.3	2,433.8	3,017.4	3,427.1	3,176.9	3,065.8	3,460.8	3,570.3	3,711.7	3,875.5	4,424.1	3,970.4	3,280.2	3,825.0	....	Domestic	**88a**
	3,153.5	3,524.4	3,801.8	11,360.0	11,677.0	13,889.4	19,136.2	27,426.8	32,723.8	40,484.6	42,248.4	46,751.2	52,831.9	54,821.1	....	Foreign	**89a**
Memorandum Item:																	
	285.0	276.6	256.9	477.0	−187.3	−100.7	−67.3	−332.2	−347.8	−394.1	−304.4	−330.2	−163.4	−20.3	....	Intragovernmental Debt	**88s**
Millions of Lempiras																**National Accounts**	
	5,916	6,245	7,226	8,379	11,021	12,520	14,717	18,114	23,819	30,782	39,732	46,930	53,240	62,909	71,684	Househ.Cons.Expend.,incl.NPISHs..........	**96f**
	1,181	1,308	1,475	1,621	1,769	2,171	2,405	2,780	3,495	4,556	5,422	7,117	8,726	10,475	13,624	Government Consumption Expend.	**91f**
	1,132	1,429	1,884	2,533	3,096	4,202	6,535	8,110	8,994	11,468	15,732	19,874	22,973	23,134	23,729	Gross Fixed Capital Formation	**93e**
	314	513	94	348	926	679	1,079	2,751	2,842	3,400	3,994	1,910	3,687	3,995	5,977	Changes in Inventories	**93i**
	1,907	2,432	3,204	4,664	5,632	6,048	7,869	11,498	16,390	22,378	28,217	32,699	31,627	36,480	37,755	Exports of Goods and Services	**90c**
	2,145	2,676	3,549	5,008	6,130	6,820	9,916	14,391	18,033	24,821	31,775	38,092	43,157	49,085	53,956	Imports of Goods and Services (-)	**98c**
	8,305	9,251	10,334	12,537	16,314	18,800	22,689	28,862	37,507	47,763	61,322	70,438	77,096	87,908	98,812	Gross Domestic Product (GDP)	**99b**
	−475	−570	−740	−1,136	−1,499	−1,859	−1,498	−1,843	−2,532	−3,069	−2,872	−2,845	−2,335	−2,305	−2,314	Net Primary Income from Abroad	**98.n**
	7,830	8,681	9,594	11,401	14,815	16,941	21,191	27,019	34,975	44,694	58,450	67,593	74,761	85,603	96,498	Gross National Income (GNI)	**99a**
	571	608	654	872	1,115	1,214	1,372	1,707	2,258	2,845	3,528	4,086	4,645	5,269	5,908	Consumption of Fixed Capital	**99cf**
															....	GDP Volume 1966 prices	**99b.p**
	4,729	4,947	5,161	5,166	5,334	5,634	5,985	5,907	6,148	6,368	6,686	6,880	6,750	7,083	7,266	GDP Volume 1978 Prices	**99b.p**
	76.9	80.5	83.9	84.0	86.8	91.6	97.3	96.1	100.0	103.6	108.8	111.9	109.8	115.2	118.2	GDP Volume (1995=100)	**99bv p**
	28.8	30.7	32.8	39.8	50.1	54.7	62.1	80.1	100.0	122.9	150.3	167.8	187.2	203.4	222.9	GDP Deflator (1995=100)	**99bi p**
Midyear Estimates																	
	4.66	4.80	4.60	4.76	4.92	5.08	5.25	5.42	5.60	5.79	5.98	6.18	6.39	6.42	6.58	**Population**..	**99z**

(See notes in the back of the book.)

Hungary

		1972	1973	1974	1975	1976	1977	1978	1979	1980	1981	1982	1983	1984	1985	1986
Exchange Rates															*Forint per SDR:*	
Official Rate	aa	59.996	56.400	57.241	50.934	47.984	49.317	46.351	46.868	41.084	40.075	43.694	47.315	50.186	52.007	56.177
															Forint per US Dollar:	
Official Rate	ae	55.260	46.752	46.752	43.509	41.300	40.600	35.578	35.578	32.213	34.430	39.610	45.193	51.199	47.347	45.927
Official Rate	rf	55.260	48.966	46.752	43.971	41.575	40.961	37.911	35.578	32.532	34.314	36.631	42.671	48.042	50.119	45.832
Secondary Rate	xe	27.630	23.376	23.376	20.449	20.650	20.300	17.789	20.330	23.950	....	....	....	....	....	....
Secondary Rate	xf	27.630	24.483	23.376	20.666	20.788	20.480	18.956	20.013	22.139	....	....	....	....	....	....
													Index Numbers (1995=100):			
Official Rate	ahx	226.3	256.0	267.4	284.5	300.8	305.3	330.2	351.4	384.5	364.7	342.4	293.7	260.8	249.7	272.9
Nominal Effective Exchange Rate	nec	....	....	....	....	....	....	....	243.6	267.4	304.0	319.2	299.4	298.4	302.7	267.6
Real Effective Exchange Rate	rec	....	....	....	....	....	....	....	....	83.9	90.4	93.5	88.3	89.6	92.4	83.2
Fund Position															*Millions of SDRs:*	
Quota	2f.s	....	....	....	....	....	....	....	....	....	....	375	531	531	531	531
SDRs	1b.s	....	....	....	....	....	....	....	....	....	....	2	44	—	—	—
Reserve Position in the Fund	1c.s	....	....	....	....	....	....	....	....	....	....	....	39	—	—	—
Total Fund Cred.&Loans Outstg.	2tl	....	....	....	....	....	....	....	....	....	....	215	547	972	884	843
International Liquidity												*Millions of US Dollars Unless Otherwise Indicated:*				
Total Reserves minus Gold	1l.d	....	....	....	....	....	....	....	....	....	....	....	1,231	1,560	2,153	2,302
SDRs	1b.d	....	....	....	....	....	....	....	....	....	....	3	46	—	—	—
Reserve Position in the Fund	1c.d	....	....	....	....	....	....	....	....	....	....	....	41	—	—	—
Foreign Exchange	1d.d	....	....	....	....	....	....	....	....	....	....	....	1,144	1,560	2,153	2,302
Gold (Million Fine Troy Ounces)	1ad	1.671	1.820	1.330	.951	1.322	1.282	1.978	1.777	2.069	1.685	.646	1.532	2.063	2.327	2.346
Gold (National Valuation)	1and	71	77	56	67	66	70	249	402	468	381	146	346	466	640	751
Monetary Authorities: Other Liabs.	4..d	....	....	....	....	....	....	....	....	....	....	8,689	9,002	8,922	11,394	13,931
Deposit Money Banks: Assets	7a.d	....	....	....	....	....	....	....	....	....	....	76	127	119	344	634
Liabilities	7b.d	....	....	....	....	....	....	....	....	....	....	1,128	1,148	1,015	1,197	1,725
Monetary Authorities															*Billions of Forint:*	
Foreign Assets	11	....	....	....	....	....	....	....	....	....	....	57.8	91.2	121.3	172.7	159.8
Claims on Consolidated Cent.Govt	12a	....	....	....	....	....	....	....	....	....	....	487.7	486.8	489.5	488.5	563.1
Other Claims on Residents	12d	....	....	....	....	....	....	....	....	....	....	276.2	283.2	299.7	322.5	353.8
Claims on Banking Institutions	12e	....	....	....	....	....	....	....	....	....	....	—	—	—	—	—
Reserve Money	14	....	....	....	....	....	....	....	....	....	....	360.9	324.2	289.2	330.1	352.2
of which: Currency Outside DMBs	14a	....	....	....	....	....	....	....	....	....	....	84.9	94.8	105.4	116.8	130.9
Other Liabilities to Banks	14n	....	....	....	....	....	....	....	....	....	....					
Time & Foreign Currency Deposits	15	....	....	....	....	....	....	....	....	....	....	51.4	44.4	44.3	27.8	22.5
Money Market Instruments	16aa	....	....	....	....	....	....	....	....	....	....	....	....	....	....	....
Bonds	16ab	....	....	....	....	....	....	....	....	....	....	—	—	—	—	—
Liabs. of Central Bank: Securities	16ac	....	....	....	....	....	....	....	....	....	....					
Foreign Liabilities	16c	....	....	....	....	....	....	....	....	....	....	119.1	178.8	171.0	145.4	169.6
Long-Term Foreign Liabilities	16cl	....	....	....	....	....	....	....	....	....	....	234.4	253.9	334.6	440.1	517.5
Consolidated Centr.Govt.Deposits	16d	....	....	....	....	....	....	....	....	....	....	35.9	33.6	39.7	36.2	48.5
Capital Accounts	17a	....	....	....	....	....	....	....	....	....	....	10.4	10.5	16.9	18.4	19.2
Other Items (Net)	17r	....	....	....	....	....	....	....	....	....	....	47.3	47.1	55.7	29.0	53.4
Banking Institutions															*Billions of Forint:*	
Reserves	20	....	....	....	....	....	....	....	....	....	....	181.5	143.0	103.2	117.7	120.0
Claims on Mon.Author.: Securities	20c	....	....	....	....	....	....	....	....	....	....	....	....	....	....	....
Other Claims on Monetary Author.	20n	....	....	....	....	....	....	....	....	....	....					
Foreign Assets	21	....	....	....	....	....	....	....	....	....	....	3.0	5.8	6.1	16.3	29.1
Claims on Consolidated Cent.Govt	22a	....	....	....	....	....	....	....	....	....	....	7.2	7.2	8.7	8.7	8.7
Claims on Local Government	22b	....	....	....	....	....	....	....	....	....	....	6.7	6.3	6.0	6.7	7.3
Other Claims on Residents	22d	....	....	....	....	....	....	....	....	....	....	133.6	154.3	179.6	208.6	240.6
Demand Deposits	24	....	....	....	....	....	....	....	....	....	....	8.2	11.0	14.9	27.3	34.3
Time, Savings,& Fgn.Currency Dep.	25	....	....	....	....	....	....	....	....	....	....	178.9	190.8	204.1	230.8	253.1
Bonds	26ab	....	....	....	....	....	....	....	....	....	....	8.2	11.6	26.9	30.6	34.8
Foreign Liabilities	26c	....	....	....	....	....	....	....	....	....	....	12.2	20.9	23.1	24.9	25.0
Long-Term Foreign Liabilities	26cl	....	....	....	....	....	....	....	....	....	....	32.5	31.0	28.9	31.8	54.2
Consolidated Centr.Govt.Deposits	26d	....	....	....	....	....	....	....	....	....	....					
Credit from Monetary Authorities	26g	....	....	....	....	....	....	....	....	....	....	—	—	—	—	—
Capital Accounts	27a	....	....	....	....	....	....	....	....	....	....	3.8	4.1	5.2	9.0	11.6
Other Items (Net)	27r	....	....	....	....	....	....	....	....	....	....	88.2	47.2	.5	3.7	-7.2
Banking Survey															*Billions of Forint*	
Foreign Assets (Net)	31n	....	....	....	....	....	....	....	....	....	....	-70.6	-102.8	-66.7	18.7	-5.8
Domestic Credit	32	....	....	....	....	....	....	....	....	....	....	875.5	904.2	943.8	998.9	1,125.1
Claims on Cons.Cent.Govt.(Net)	32an	....	....	....	....	....	....	....	....	....	....	459.0	460.4	458.5	461.0	523.4
Claims on Local Government	32b	....	....	....	....	....	....	....	....	....	....	6.7	6.3	6.0	6.7	7.3
Other Claims on Residents	32d	....	....	....	....	....	....	....	....	....	....	409.8	437.5	479.3	531.1	594.4
Money	34	....	....	....	....	....	....	....	....	....	....	187.6	192.2	200.9	239.7	266.5
Quasi-Money	35	....	....	....	....	....	....	....	....	....	....	230.3	235.2	248.4	258.6	275.5
Money Market Instruments	36aa	....	....	....	....	....	....	....	....	....	....					
Bonds	36ab	....	....	....	....	....	....	....	....	....	....	8.2	11.6	26.9	30.6	34.8
Long-Term Foreign Liabilities	36cl	....	....	....	....	....	....	....	....	....	....	266.8	284.9	363.5	471.8	571.7
Capital Accounts	37a	....	....	....	....	....	....	....	....	....	....	14.3	14.6	22.1	27.4	30.8
Other Items (Net)	37r	....	....	....	....	....	....	....	....	....	....	135.5	94.3	56.2	32.7	46.2
Money plus Quasi-Money	35l	....	....	....	....	....	....	....	....	....	....	417.9	427.4	449.3	498.3	542.0
Money (National Definition)															*Billions of Forint:*	
Monetary Base	19m	....	....	....	....	....	....	....	....	....	....	....	....	....	....	....
M1	39ma	....	....	....	....	....	....	....	....	....	....	....	....	....	....	....
M2	39mb	....	....	....	....	....	....	....	....	....	....	....	....	....	....	....
M3	39mc	....	....	....	....	....	....	....	....	....	....	....	....	....	....	....
M4	39md	....	....	....	....	....	....	....	....	....	....	....	....	....	....	....
Interest Rates															*Percent Per Annum*	
Discount Rate *(End of Period)*	60	....	....	....	....	....	....	....	....	....	....	....	....	....	11.5	10.5
Treasury Bill Rate	60c	....	....	....	....	....	....	....	....	....	....	....	....	....	....	....
Deposit Rate	60l	3.0	3.0	3.0	3.0	3.0	3.0	3.0	3.0	3.0	3.0	3.5	5.0	5.0	5.0	4.5
Lending Rate	60p	....	....	....	....	....	....	....	....	....	....	....	....	....	....	....

1987	1988	1989	1990	1991	1992	1993	1994	1995	1996	1997	1998	1999	2000	2001		944
End of Period															**Exchange Rates**	
65.807	70.699	82.192	87.421	108.169	115.459	138.317	161.591	207.321	237.163	274.572	308.401	346.586	370.978	350.665	Official Rate	**aa**
End of Period (ae) Period Average (rf)																
46.387	52.537	62.543	61.449	75.620	83.970	100.700	110.690	139.470	164.930	203.500	219.030	252.520	284.730	279.030	Official Rate	**ae**
46.971	50.413	59.066	63.206	74.735	78.988	91.933	105.160	125.681	152.647	186.789	214.402	237.146	282.179	286.490	Official Rate	**rf**
....	....	....	....	....	....	....	....	....	....	....	....	....	....	....	Secondary Rate	**xe**
....	....	....	....	....	....	....	....	....	....	....	....	....	....	....	Secondary Rate	**xf**
Period Averages																
266.4	248.7	212.3	198.0	167.6	158.4	136.5	119.0	100.0	82.1	67.2	58.3	52.8	44.5	43.7	Official Rate	**ahx**
230.7	215.8	202.0	178.1	158.2	151.2	144.8	128.3	100.0	85.7	79.6	71.0	66.9	63.3	64.4	Nominal Effective Exchange Rate	**nec**
75.0	76.8	77.7	80.6	89.0	96.8	105.3	104.2	100.0	102.7	108.0	107.2	109.0	109.7	118.5	Real Effective Exchange Rate	**rec**
End of Period															**Fund Position**	
531	531	531	531	531	755	755	755	755	755	755	755	1,038	1,038	1,038	Quota	**2f.s**
—	—	—	1	1	2	2	1	1	—	—	1	3	9	16	SDRs	**1b.s**
—	—	—	—	—	56	56	56	56	56	56	56	177	202	322	Reserve Position in the Fund	**1c.s**
570	471	347	232	880	876	896	782	259	119	119	—	—	—	—	Total Fund Cred.&Loans Outstg.	**2tl**
End of Period															**International Liquidity**	
1,634	1,467	1,246	1,069	3,934	4,425	6,700	6,735	11,974	9,720	8,408	9,319	10,954	11,190	10,727	Total Reserves minus Gold	**1l.d**
—	—	—	1	1	3	3	2	1	—	—	1	4	12	21	SDRs	**1b.d**
—	—	—	—	—	77	77	82	83	81	76	79	243	263	405	Reserve Position in the Fund	**1c.d**
1,634	1,467	1,246	1,068	3,933	4,345	6,620	6,652	11,890	9,639	8,332	9,239	10,707	10,915	10,302	Foreign Exchange	**1d.d**
1.641	1.593	1.497	.300	.258	.102	.114	.110	.111	.101	.101	.101	.101	.101	.101	Gold (Million Fine Troy Ounces)	**1ad**
525	510	479	97	83	33	45	42	43	37	29	29	29	28	28	Gold (National Valuation)	**1and**
16,817	16,746	17,426	17,431	16,739	14,974	17,244	19,191	20,836	16,239	11,647	11,677	9,847	8,537	6,614	Monetary Authorities: Other Liabs.	**4..d**
661	777	1,004	1,156	1,405	1,504	1,331	1,030	921	1,679	2,495	3,306	3,594	2,879	4,520	Deposit Money Banks: Assets	**7a.d**
1,766	1,839	2,045	1,689	1,813	1,831	1,783	2,379	2,878	3,092	4,702	5,574	5,931	5,728	6,160	Liabilities	**7b.d**
End of Period															**Monetary Authorities**	
138.3	138.6	162.7	140.4	362.5	385.2	689.8	784.0	1,680.7	1,614.9	1,723.3	2,054.3	2,992.4	3,463.4	3,336.2	Foreign Assets	**11**
633.0	666.7	739.4	†1,297.4	1,622.1	1,841.9	2,166.9	2,558.3	3,144.7	2,902.9	2,854.0	2,930.0	2,488.2	2,202.4	1,664.6	Claims on Consolidated Cent.Govt	**12a**
2.6	5.3	1.3	2.2	2.0	3.8	4.4	4.4	3.8	—	.1	.1	—	—	—	Other Claims on Residents	**12d**
253.8	225.4	252.5	354.0	417.4	293.4	368.8	405.8	302.6	231.4	185.3	178.4	126.6	93.8	46.9	Claims on Banking Institutions	**12e**
313.4	299.3	358.0	336.4	499.9	606.5	624.5	614.1	723.3	660.4	858.2	1,034.9	1,306.2	1,532.0	1,559.5	Reserve Money	**14**
153.8	164.5	180.6	209.8	260.2	322.3	371.2	410.7	443.9	497.7	562.6	668.9	855.3	883.7	1,037.7	*of which: Currency Outside DMBs*	**14a**
....	....	....	188.0	299.0	281.1	387.0	533.9	748.4	920.8	835.4	820.5	1,075.0	774.8	526.9	Other Liabilities to Banks	**14n**
.6	.7	.7	†1.3	2.0	2.6	3.5	6.1	7.3	4.5	5.0	18.2	12.7	10.1	6.4	Time & Foreign Currency Deposits	**15**
....	....	....	—	—	—	—	—	—	—	68.9	152.2	—	349.7	402.6	Money Market Instruments	**16aa**
—	—	—	—	—	5.6	7.6	6.4	5.2	3.5	2.3	—	—	—	—	Bonds	**16ab**
....	....	....	—	—	—	8.0	21.0	44.2	76.2	272.5	340.7	242.7	305.4	248.7	Liabs. of Central Bank: Securities	**16ac**
141.1	150.6	143.9	88.0	125.4	111.5	140.6	148.3	104.9	57.8	138.2	42.6	137.0	334.4	268.3	Foreign Liabilities	**16c**
676.5	762.5	974.5	1,003.4	1,235.6	1,247.0	1,719.9	2,102.3	2,854.7	2,648.7	2,264.7	2,515.1	2,349.6	2,096.3	1,577.2	Long-Term Foreign Liabilities	**16cl**
55.9	47.2	32.7	†97.7	228.0	255.3	341.1	316.8	561.8	389.9	328.4	194.1	555.8	434.4	745.1	Consolidated Centr.Govt.Deposits	**16d**
18.8	19.8	21.6	24.9	26.8	39.5	46.1	31.6	55.2	59.3	72.7	128.2	74.0	65.0	65.0	Capital Accounts	**17a**
17.6	5.3	85.4	54.3	–12.5	–25.1	–48.1	–28.0	26.5	–71.9	–83.4	–83.7	–145.8	–142.9	–351.9	Other Items (Net)	**17r**
End of Period															**Banking Institutions**	
151.9	126.8	169.7	118.4	228.0	274.7	234.6	194.1	273.7	154.0	291.1	365.7	447.5	646.9	520.1	Reserves	**20**
....	....	....	—	—	—	8.0	21.0	44.2	76.2	272.5	340.7	242.7	309.4	250.3	Claims on Mon.Author.: Securities	**20c**
....	....	....	188.0	299.0	281.1	387.0	533.9	748.4	920.8	835.4	820.5	1,075.0	774.6	526.9	Other Claims on Monetary Author.	**20n**
30.7	40.8	62.8	71.0	106.3	126.3	134.1	114.0	128.5	276.9	507.7	724.0	907.5	819.7	1,261.3	Foreign Assets	**21**
13.6	12.9	23.8	18.9	151.3	263.2	601.8	649.7	732.7	910.4	944.7	1,128.9	1,052.9	1,149.6	1,441.5	Claims on Consolidated Cent.Govt	**22a**
10.9	15.7	13.4	15.7	13.6	13.0	22.6	47.6	49.9	38.5	30.3	44.4	50.3	57.6	73.2	Claims on Local Government	**22b**
648.7	668.9	809.6	971.3	976.6	979.7	1,003.8	1,152.9	1,263.1	1,520.7	†2,076.9	2,441.4	2,967.5	4,247.9	5,026.6	Other Claims on Residents	**22d**
145.2	129.5	191.7	299.5	339.6	475.7	512.4	553.9	561.5	730.8	961.3	1,121.9	1,276.9	1,494.4	1,738.3	Demand Deposits	**24**
287.0	304.6	327.2	395.5	569.5	861.1	1,061.6	1,266.0	1,696.7	2,074.9	2,438.6	2,786.0	3,171.2	3,592.8	4,193.4	Time, Savings,& Fgn.Currency Dep.	**25**
53.1	58.7	67.5	95.1	186.8	71.4	41.8	26.7	15.8	30.8	36.8	29.6	51.0	70.7	114.2	Bonds	**26ab**
28.9	38.6	60.8	41.6	64.5	83.0	90.6	134.3	196.0	307.9	593.3	689.2	746.7	750.8	646.6	Foreign Liabilities	**26c**
53.1	58.0	67.1	62.1	72.6	70.8	89.0	129.1	205.4	202.1	363.6	531.7	751.1	880.2	1,072.3	Long-Term Foreign Liabilities	**26cl**
1.5	2.9	3.9	3.3	5.1	14.4	16.1	31.1	13.0	10.0	7.6	5.0	4.7	23.3	28.6	Consolidated Centr.Govt.Deposits	**26d**
253.8	225.4	252.5	354.0	417.4	293.4	368.8	405.8	302.6	231.4	185.3	178.4	126.6	91.5	44.6	Credit from Monetary Authorities	**26g**
40.4	59.0	118.8	184.4	247.3	277.5	174.0	230.8	316.7	382.9	559.8	597.0	662.8	413.0	962.6	Capital Accounts	**27a**
–7.2	–11.7	–10.1	–51.1	–128.2	–209.2	37.6	–64.5	–67.0	–73.2	–187.8	–73.1	–47.6	689.3	299.4	Other Items (Net)	**27r**
End of Period															**Banking Survey**	
–1.0	–9.8	20.9	81.8	278.9	317.1	592.7	615.4	1,508.3	1,526.2	1,499.5	2,046.6	3,016.2	3,198.0	3,682.7	Foreign Assets (Net)	**31n**
1,251.3	1,319.3	1,550.9	†2,204.4	2,532.4	2,831.8	3,442.3	4,064.9	4,619.4	4,972.7	†5,570.0	6,345.6	5,998.5	7,199.8	7,432.2	Domestic Credit	**32**
589.2	629.4	726.6	†1,215.2	1,540.2	1,835.4	2,411.4	2,860.1	3,302.6	3,413.5	3,462.7	3,859.7	2,980.6	2,894.3	2,332.4	Claims on Cons.Cent.Govt.(Net)	**32an**
10.9	15.7	13.4	15.7	13.6	13.0	22.6	47.6	49.9	38.5	30.3	44.4	50.3	57.6	73.2	Claims on Local Government	**32b**
651.2	674.2	810.9	973.5	978.6	983.4	1,008.2	1,157.2	1,266.9	1,520.8	†2,077.0	2,441.5	2,967.5	4,247.9	5,026.6	Other Claims on Residents	**32d**
306.6	302.0	379.9	517.5	611.5	807.7	901.9	973.9	1,011.3	1,237.2	1,528.3	1,791.1	2,135.6	2,378.1	2,776.1	Money	**34**
287.6	305.3	327.8	†396.8	571.5	863.7	1,065.1	1,272.1	1,704.0	2,079.4	2,443.6	2,804.2	3,183.9	3,602.9	4,199.7	Quasi-Money	**35**
....	....	....	—	—	—	—	—	—	—	68.9	152.2	—	349.7	402.6	Money Market Instruments	**36aa**
53.1	58.7	67.5	95.1	186.8	76.9	49.4	33.1	21.0	34.4	39.0	29.6	51.0	70.7	114.2	Bonds	**36ab**
729.6	820.5	1,041.7	1,065.5	1,308.2	1,317.8	1,808.9	2,231.3	3,060.1	2,850.9	2,628.3	3,046.7	3,100.7	2,976.5	2,649.6	Long-Term Foreign Liabilities	**36cl**
59.2	78.8	140.4	209.3	274.1	317.0	220.1	262.4	371.8	442.2	632.5	725.2	736.8	478.0	1,027.5	Capital Accounts	**37a**
10.4	–6.4	75.3	3.2	–140.7	–234.3	–10.5	–92.5	–40.5	–145.1	–271.2	–156.8	–193.4	541.4	–54.6	Other Items (Net)	**37r**
594.3	607.3	707.7	914.3	1,183.0	1,671.4	1,967.0	2,246.0	2,715.3	3,316.6	3,971.9	4,582.5	5,308.1	5,970.9	6,969.4	Money plus Quasi-Money	**35l**
End of Period															**Money (National Definition)**	
....	....	....	338.9	494.9	593.9	599.8	621.0	749.6	859.1	994.6	1,162.8	1,448.1	1,568.5	1,554.9	*Monetary Base*	**19m**
....	....	....	517.5	611.5	807.7	901.9	973.9	1,011.3	1,237.2	1,528.3	1,791.1	2,135.6	2,378.4	2,776.9	*M1*	**39ma**
....	....	....	914.3	1,183.0	1,671.4	1,967.0	2,246.0	2,715.3	3,316.6	3,970.6	4,595.3	5,319.6	5,955.2	6,957.3	*M2*	**39mb**
....	....	....	1,009.4	1,369.8	1,748.3	2,016.4	2,279.1	2,736.3	3,350.9	4,009.6	4,624.9	5,370.6	6,052.0	7,092.5	*M3*	**39mc**
....	....	....	....	1,415.4	1,820.1	2,223.5	2,628.1	3,285.5	4,170.2	5,293.9	6,351.0	7,535.9	8,690.1	10,062.1	*M4*	**39md**
Percent Per Annum															**Interest Rates**	
10.5	14.0	17.0	22.0	22.0	21.0	22.0	25.0	28.0	23.0	20.5	17.0	14.5	11.0	9.8	Discount Rate *(End of Period)*	**60**
....	18.0	20.5	30.1	34.5	22.7	17.2	26.9	32.0	24.0	20.1	17.8	14.7	11.0	10.8	Treasury Bill Rate	**60c**
4.0	5.3	9.4	†24.7	30.4	24.4	15.7	20.3	26.1	22.2	18.5	16.2	13.3	9.6	9.3	Deposit Rate	**60l**
....	....	20.3	28.8	35.1	33.1	25.4	27.4	32.6	27.3	21.8	19.3	16.3	12.6	12.1	Lending Rate	**60p**

Hungary

		1972	1973	1974	1975	1976	1977	1978	1979	1980	1981	1982	1983	1984	1985	1986
Prices, Production, Labor															Index Numbers (1995=100):		
Producer Prices: Industry	63	50.6	52.1	53.8	59.5	62.3	63.5	65.9	67.3	77.6	82.5	86.4	91.2	95.0	100.0	†27.2
Consumer Prices	64	7.9	8.1	8.3	8.6	9.1	9.4	9.9	10.7	11.7	12.3	13.1	14.0	15.2	†16.2	17.1
Wages: Avg. Earnings	65	8.5	9.1	9.8	10.5	11.1	12.0	13.0	13.8	14.6	15.7	16.7	17.5	18.7	20.6	22.2
Industrial Production	66	79.5	85.4	93.3	98.2	102.7	109.5	114.8	118.7	116.2	119.5	121.7	123.4	126.2	127.1	128.9
Industrial Employment	67	230.7	233.8	237.6	240.0	238.1	237.6	237.4	233.6	†227.1	222.3	218.0	213.1	212.1	210.9	209.5
															Number in Thousands:		
Labor Force	67d	....	....	....	....	....	....	....	....	....	....	....	....	....	....	....
Employment	67e	....	....	....	....	....	....	....	....	....	....	....	....	....	....	....
Unemployment	67c	....	....	....	....	....	....	....	....	....	....	....	....	....	....	....
Unemployment Rate (%)	67r	....	....	....	....	....	....	....	....	....	....	....	....	....	....	....
International Transactions															Billions of Forint		
Exports	70	132.8	164.2	184.3	198.7	204.8	238.6	240.7	282.1	281.0	299.5	324.5	374.1	414.0	424.6	420.3
Imports, c.i.f.	71	130.2	147.8	208.2	237.5	230.1	267.3	300.9	308.9	299.9	314.3	324.8	365.0	390.5	410.1	439.7
Imports, f.o.b.	71.v	127.9	145.2	204.5	233.2	225.4	262.9	295.8	304.0	294.6	307.9	319.0	359.2	384.0	402.0	432.1
															1995=100		
Volume of Exports	72	41.3	47.8	48.7	51.0	55.2	62.1	63.0	70.9	71.7	73.5	75.9	80.9	86.7	91.1	89.1
Volume of Imports	73	46.8	49.1	56.7	59.6	62.0	67.2	75.7	73.2	72.3	72.5	69.5	70.2	70.9	76.3	78.2
Export Prices	76	19.3	20.6	22.7	23.4	22.3	23.1	22.9	23.9	23.6	24.5	24.7	26.0	27.2	28.0	28.4
Import Prices	76.x	14.0	15.2	18.6	20.1	18.8	20.1	20.1	21.4	21.0	22.0	22.7	24.5	26.2	27.2	28.6
Balance of Payments																Millions of US Dollars:		
Current Account, n.i.e.	78ald	....	....	....	....	....	....	....	....	....	....	−531	−181	39	−455	−1,365
Goods: Exports f.o.b.	78aad	....	....	....	....	....	....	....	....	....	....	9,038	8,978	9,090	8,578	9,198
Goods: Imports f.o.b.	78abd	....	....	....	....	....	....	....	....	....	....	−8,628	−8,544	−8,310	−8,130	−9,663
Trade Balance	78acd	....	....	....	....	....	....	....	....	....	....	410	434	780	448	−465
Services: Credit	78add	....	....	....	....	....	....	....	....	....	....	633	589	595	622	729
Services: Debit	78aed	....	....	....	....	....	....	....	....	....	....	−524	−485	−552	−723	−713
Balance on Goods & Services	78afd	....	....	....	....	....	....	....	....	....	....	519	538	823	347	−449
Income: Credit	78agd	....	....	....	....	....	....	....	....	....	....	109	117	139	195	261
Income: Debit	78ahd	....	....	....	....	....	....	....	....	....	....	−1,222	−892	−989	−1,062	−1,252
Balance on Gds, Serv. & Inc.	78aid	....	....	....	....	....	....	....	....	....	....	−594	−237	−27	−520	−1,440
Current Transfers, n.i.e.: Credit	78ajd	....	....	....	....	....	....	....	....	....	....	63	56	66	65	75
Current Transfers: Debit	78akd	....	....	....	....	....	....	....	....	....	....	—	—	—	—	—
Capital Account, n.i.e.	78bcd	....	....	....	....	....	....	....	....	....	....	—	—	—	—	—
Capital Account, n.i.e.: Credit	78bad	....	....	....	....	....	....	....	....	....	....	—	—	—	—	—
Capital Account: Debit	78bbd	....	....	....	....	....	....	....	....	....	....	—	—	—	—	—
Financial Account, n.i.e.	78bjd	....	....	....	....	....	....	....	....	....	....	−474	646	267	1,066	1,388
Direct Investment Abroad	78bdd	....	....	....	....	....	....	....	....	....	....	—	—	—	—	—
Dir. Invest. in Rep. Econ., n.i.e.	78bed	....	....	....	....	....	....	....	....	....	....	—	—	—	—	—
Portfolio Investment Assets	78bfd	....	....	....	....	....	....	....	....	....	....	—	—	—	—	—
Equity Securities	78bkd	....	....	....	....	....	....	....	....	....	....	—	—	—	—	—
Debt Securities	78bld	....	....	....	....	....	....	....	....	....	....	—	—	—	—	—
Portfolio Investment Liab., n.i.e.	78bgd	....	....	....	....	....	....	....	....	....	....	—	—	—	—	—
Equity Securities	78bmd	....	....	....	....	....	....	....	....	....	....	—	—	—	—	—
Debt Securities	78bnd	....	....	....	....	....	....	....	....	....	....	—	—	—	—	—
Financial Derivatives Assets	78bwd	....	....	....	....	....	....	....	....	....	....	....	....	....	....	....
Financial Derivatives Liabilities	78bxd	....	....	....	....	....	....	....	....	....	....	....	....	....	....	....
Other Investment Assets	78bhd	....	....	....	....	....	....	....	....	....	....	−880	−429	−251	−424	180
Monetary Authorities	78bod	....	....	....	....	....	....	....	....	....	....					
General Government	78bpd	....	....	....	....	....	....	....	....	....	....	−528	−177	−48	−225	−127
Banks	78bqd	....	....	....	....	....	....	....	....	....	....	−76	−51	8	−225	−290
Other Sectors	78brd	....	....	....	....	....	....	....	....	....	....	−276	−201	−211	26	597
Other Investment Liab., n.i.e.	78bid	....	....	....	....	....	....	....	....	....	....	406	1,075	518	1,490	1,208
Monetary Authorities	78bsd	....	....	....	....	....	....	....	....	....	....	−177	934	−710	−612	−340
General Government	78btd	....	....	....	....	....	....	....	....	....	....	583	121	1,361	1,920	1,020
Banks	78bud	....	....	....	....	....	....	....	....	....	....	—	20	−133	182	528
Other Sectors	78bvd	....	....	....	....	....	....	....	....	....	....					
Net Errors and Omissions	78cad	....	....	....	....	....	....	....	....	....	....	465	−590	−240	−75	109
Overall Balance	78cbd	....	....	....	....	....	....	....	....	....	....	−540	−125	66	536	132
Reserves and Related Items	79dad	....	....	....	....	....	....	....	....	....	....	540	125	−66	−536	−132
Reserve Assets	79dbd	....	....	....	....	....	....	....	....	....	....	305	−228	−501	−441	−82
Use of Fund Credit and Loans	79dcd	....	....	....	....	....	....	....	....	....	....	235	353	436	−95	−49
Exceptional Financing	79ded	....	....	....	....	....	....	....	....	....	....					
International Investment Position																Millions of US Dollars		
Assets	79aad	....	....	....	....	....	....	....	....	....	....	....	....	....	....	....
Direct Investment Abroad	79abd	....	....	....	....	....	....	....	....	....	....	....	....	....	....	....
Portfolio Investment	79acd	....	....	....	....	....	....	....	....	....	....	....	....	....	....	....
Equity Securities	79add	....	....	....	....	....	....	....	....	....	....	....	....	....	....	....
Debt Securities	79aed	....	....	....	....	....	....	....	....	....	....	....	....	....	....	....
Financial Derivatives	79ald	....	....	....	....	....	....	....	....	....	....	....	....	....	....	....
Other Investment	79afd	....	....	....	....	....	....	....	....	....	....	....	....	....	....	....
Monetary Authorities	79agd	....	....	....	....	....	....	....	....	....	....	....	....	....	....	....
General Government	79ahd	....	....	....	....	....	....	....	....	....	....	....	....	....	....	....
Banks	79aid	....	....	....	....	....	....	....	....	....	....	....	....	....	....	....
Other Sectors	79ajd	....	....	....	....	....	....	....	....	....	....	....	....	....	....	....
Reserve Assets	79akd	....	....	....	....	....	....	....	....	....	....	....	....	....	....	....
Liabilities	79lad	....	....	....	....	....	....	....	....	....	....	....	....	....	....	....
Dir. Invest. in Rep. Economy	79lbd	....	....	....	....	....	....	....	....	....	....	....	....	....	....	....
Portfolio Investment	79lcd	....	....	....	....	....	....	....	....	....	....	....	....	....	....	....
Equity Securities	79ldd	....	....	....	....	....	....	....	....	....	....	....	....	....	....	....
Debt Securities	79led	....	....	....	....	....	....	....	....	....	....	....	....	....	....	....
Financial Derivatives	79lld	....	....	....	....	....	....	....	....	....	....	....	....	....	....	....
Other Investment	79lfd	....	....	....	....	....	....	....	....	....	....	....	....	....	....	....
Monetary Authorities	79lgd	....	....	....	....	....	....	....	....	....	....	....	....	....	....	....
General Government	79lhd	....	....	....	....	....	....	....	....	....	....	....	....	....	....	....
Banks	79lid	....	....	....	....	....	....	....	....	....	....	....	....	....	....	....
Other Sectors	79ljd	....	....	....	....	....	....	....	....	....	....	....	....	....	....	....

1987	1988	1989	1990	1991	1992	1993	1994	1995	1996	1997	1998	1999	2000	2001		
															Prices, Production, Labor	
Period Averages																
28.0	29.5	33.9	41.2	55.3	60.8	69.3	77.8	100.0	121.8	146.6	163.3	171.5	190.0	199.7	Producer Prices: Industry	63
18.6	21.5	25.2	32.4	43.6	†53.5	65.6	77.9	†100.0	123.4	146.0	166.7	183.5	201.4	219.8	Consumer Prices	64
24.1	26.6	†31.8	38.1	47.5	57.5	68.9	86.3	100.0	117.8	145.7	170.7	191.6	215.8	245.2	Wages: Avg. Earnings	65
132.6	†131.7	125.0	112.5	92.7	84.0	86.3	95.2	†100.0	103.3	114.8	129.1	142.4	168.3	175.1	Industrial Production	66
204.3	198.6	190.7	173.8	150.6	125.3	113.3	105.7	100.0	94.7	94.1	95.6	96.3	97.6	97.2	Industrial Employment	67
Period Averages																
....	....	....	4,525	....	4,242	....	4,144	4,095	4,048	....	4,011	4,096	4,112	....	Labor Force	67d
....	....	....	....	....	4,083	3,827	3,752	3,679	3,648	3,646	3,698	3,811	3,849	....	Employment	67e
....	....	....	....	....	444	519	449	417	400	349	313	285	263	....	Unemployment	67c
....	....	....	....	....	9.8	11.9	10.7	10.2	9.9	8.7	7.8	7.0	6.4	....	Unemployment Rate (%)	67r
															International Transactions	
Billions of Forint																
450.1	504.1	571.3	603.6	764.3	843.6	819.9	1,101.3	1,622.0	2,392.3	3,566.8	4,934.5	5,938.5	7,942.8	8,748.2	Exports	70
463.1	472.5	518.7	544.9	855.7	878.5	1,162.5	1,505.6	1,936.4	2,763.9	3,961.2	5,511.5	6,645.6	9,064.0	9,665.1	Imports, c.i.f.	71
455.1	463.8	515.1	547.5	840.5	863.0	1,141.9	1,479.0	1,902.1	2,715.0	3,891.2	5,475.8	6,558.1	8,958.4	9,534.8	Imports, f.o.b.	71.v
1995=100																
92.1	98.3	98.7	94.7	†90.0	91.0	79.0	92.2	100.0	104.6	†135.8	166.4	192.9	234.8	253.0	Volume of Exports	72
80.0	79.8	80.6	76.4	†80.6	75.3	91.0	104.2	100.0	105.5	†133.4	166.5	190.3	229.9	239.2	Volume of Imports	73
29.2	31.2	36.0	†39.6	†51.8	56.6	63.3	74.7	100.0	118.0	135.5	153.0	158.8	174.5	178.4	Export Prices	76
29.2	30.4	34.2	†37.4	†54.6	60.1	65.2	76.2	100.0	121.0	137.3	153.1	161.5	182.4	186.9	Import Prices	76.x
															Balance of Payments	
Minus Sign Indicates Debit																
-676	-572	-588	379	403	352	-4,262	-4,054	-2,530	-1,689	-982	-2,304	-2,106	-1,328	-1,097	Current Account, n.i.e.	78al d
9,967	9,989	10,493	9,151	9,688	10,097	8,119	7,648	12,864	14,184	19,640	20,747	21,848	25,747	28,071	Goods: Exports f.o.b.	78aa d
-9,887	-9,406	-9,450	-8,617	-9,330	-10,108	-12,140	-11,364	-15,297	-16,836	-21,602	-23,101	-24,037	-27,506	-30,089	Goods: Imports f.o.b.	78ab d
80	583	1,043	534	358	-11	-4,021	-3,716	-2,433	-2,652	-1,962	-2,354	-2,189	-1,760	-2,018	*Trade Balance*	78ac d
980	1,047	1,291	2,884	2,526	3,405	2,836	3,117	5,182	5,980	5,733	5,921	5,649	6,251	7,707	Services: Credit	78ad d
-814	-1,227	-1,658	-2,400	-1,991	-2,641	-2,620	-2,958	-3,616	-3,506	-3,465	-4,141	-4,263	-4,476	-5,544	Services: Debit	78ae d
246	403	676	1,019	892	753	-3,805	-3,557	-867	-178	306	-574	-803	15	146	*Balance on Goods & Services*	78af d
247	240	231	280	322	424	465	676	798	1,202	1,382	1,111	775	942	1,111	Income: Credit	78ag d
-1,274	-1,332	-1,625	-1,707	-1,678	-1,684	-1,655	-2,082	-2,602	-2,658	-2,808	-2,990	-2,417	-2,516	-2,599	Income: Debit	78ah d
-781	-689	-718	-408	-464	-506	-4,995	-4,963	-2,671	-1,634	-1,120	-2,453	-2,446	-1,559	-1,342	*Balance on Gds, Serv. & Inc.*	78ai d
105	117	130	1,595	2,604	2,866	2,694	2,871	364	160	335	379	582	520	589	Current Transfers, n.i.e.: Credit	78aj d
—	—	—	-808	-1,737	-2,008	-1,961	-1,961	-222	-214	-197	-231	-243	-289	-344	Current Transfers: Debit	78ak d
—	—	—	—	—	—	—	—	59	156	117	189	29	270	317	Capital Account, n.i.e.	78bc d
—	—	—	—	—	—	—	—	80	266	266	408	509	458	417	Capital Account, n.i.e.: Credit	78ba d
—	—	—	—	—	—	—	—	-20	-110	-149	-219	-480	-188	-101	Capital Account: Debit	78bb d
235	680	901	-801	1,474	416	6,083	3,370	7,080	-687	658	3,017	4,693	2,219	617	Financial Account, n.i.e.	78bj d
—	—	—	—	—	—	-11	-49	-43	4	-433	-478	-252	-532	-337	Direct Investment Abroad	78bd d
—	—	—	—	1,462	1,479	2,350	1,144	4,519	2,274	2,167	2,037	1,977	1,646	2,440	Dir. Invest. in Rep. Econ., n.i.e.	78be d
—	—	—	—	—	—	-8	6	-1	-35	-134	-93	-75	-309	-149	Portfolio Investment Assets	78bf d
—	—	—	—	—	—	—	-10	....	-15	-32	-45	16	-151	-55	Equity Securities	78bk d
—	—	—	—	—	—	-8	16	-1	-20	-102	-48	-91	-158	-95	Debt Securities	78bl d
—	—	—	—	—	—	3,927	2,458	2,213	-396	-914	1,925	2,065	-187	1,526	Portfolio Investment Liab., n.i.e.	78bg d
—	—	—	—	—	—	46	224	....	359	1,004	556	1,191	-416	134	Equity Securities	78bm d
—	—	—	—	—	—	3,881	2,234	2,213	-754	-1,918	1,369	874	229	1,392	Debt Securities	78bn d
....	....	....	....	....	....	....	....	....	17	12	185	852	753	579	Financial Derivatives Assets	78bw d
....	....	....	....	....	....	....	....	....	-1	-4	-38	-899	-692	-457	Financial Derivatives Liabilities	78bx d
-319	-83	-322	-524	-13	-421	881	362	592	-1,256	-584	-507	-1,170	-1,014	-3,430	Other Investment Assets	78bh d
								-15	14	1	4	—	-8	4	Monetary Authorities	78bo d
-153	-95	-95	-524	-136	-899	811	156	27	45	189	75	30	64	30	General Government	78bp d
-27	-116	-227	—	116	616	-127	191	125	-1,129	-789	-333	-430	755	-1,490	Banks	78bq d
-139	128	—	6	-138	198	15	456	-185	15	-253	-770	-1,825	-1,975		Other Sectors	78br d
554	763	1,223	-278	25	-642	-1,055	-551	-199	-1,294	549	-13	2,197	2,555	446	Other Investment Liab., n.i.e.	78bi d
-573	173	-358	-570	-431	174	54	17	-904	-1,875	-659	-15	286	613	-644	Monetary Authorities	78bs d
1,086	517	1,375	292	815	-787	-1,541	-1,761	-438	-331	-106	-288	235	-225	-33	General Government	78bt d
41	73	206	—	-359	-29	-69	365	321	394	1,123	619	522	401	294	Banks	78bu d
—	—	—	—	—	—	501	828	823	518	190	-329	1,154	1,765	829	Other Sectors	78bv d
160	50	-141	10	-82	2	724	209	789	976	32	49	-282	-109	79	Net Errors and Omissions	78ca d
-281	158	172	-413	1,795	770	2,545	-475	5,399	-1,244	-175	951	2,335	1,052	-84	*Overall Balance*	78cb d
281	-158	-172	413	-1,795	-770	-2,545	475	-5,399	1,244	175	-951	-2,335	-1,052	84	Reserves and Related Items	79da d
637	-25	-14	558	-2,700	-763	-2,574	640	-4,614	1,447	175	-790	-2,335	-1,052	84	Reserve Assets	79db d
-356	-132	-158	-145	905	-7	30	-165	-785	-203	—	-160	—	—	—	Use of Fund Credit and Loans	79dc d
....	....	....	....	....	....	....	....	....	....						Exceptional Financing	79de d
															International Investment Position	
Millions of US Dollars																
....	....	....	....	....	....	....	....	....	....	13,335	15,651	19,353	21,344	25,066	Assets	79aa d
....	....	....	....	....	....	....	....	....	....	887	1,273	1,484	1,925	2,205	Direct Investment Abroad	79ab d
....	....	....	....	....	....	....	....	....	....	171	293	367	667	814	Portfolio Investment	79ac d
....	....	....	....	....	....	....	....	....	....	32	87	73	221	271	Equity Securities	79ad d
....	....	....	....	....	....	....	....	....	....	139	206	294	447	543	Debt Securities	79ae d
....	....	....	....	....	....	....	....	....	....	—	9	880	859	1,165	Financial Derivatives	79al d
....	....	....	....	....	....	....	....	....	....	3,841	4,730	5,639	6,675	10,127	Other Investment	79af d
....	....	....	....	....	....	....	....	....	....	32	23	20	75	55	Monetary Authorities	79ag d
....	....	....	....	....	....	....	....	....	....	593	505	468	381	353	General Government	79ah d
....	....	....	....	....	....	....	....	....	....	2,323	3,083	3,387	2,559	4,067	Banks	79ai d
....	....	....	....	....	....	....	....	....	....	893	1,118	1,764	3,660	5,653	Other Sectors	79aj d
....	....	....	....	....	....	....	....	....	....	8,437	9,348	10,983	11,217	10,755	Reserve Assets	79ak d
....	....	....	....	....	....	....	....	....	....	41,180	45,574	49,955	50,318	54,297	Liabilities	79la d
....	....	....	....	....	....	....	....	....	....	16,073	18,505	19,217	19,662	22,584	Dir. Invest. in Rep. Economy	79lb d
....	....	....	....	....	....	....	....	....	....	12,496	14,534	16,934	14,839	15,721	Portfolio Investment	79lc d
....	....	....	....	....	....	....	....	....	....	2,582	2,317	4,335	3,014	2,935	Equity Securities	79ld d
....	....	....	....	....	....	....	....	....	....	9,914	12,217	12,599	11,825	12,786	Debt Securities	79le d
....	....	....	....	....	....	....	....	....	....	450	11	164	276	483	Financial Derivatives	79ll d
....	....	....	....	....	....	....	....	....	....	12,161	12,524	13,640	15,541	15,509	Other Investment	79lf d
....	....	....	....	....	....	....	....	....	....	1,216	1,094	1,322	1,863	1,165	Monetary Authorities	79lg d
....	....	....	....	....	....	....	....	....	....	1,635	1,380	1,532	1,246	1,181	General Government	79lh d
....	....	....	....	....	....	....	....	....	....	4,290	5,185	5,297	5,476	5,581	Banks	79li d
....	....	....	....	....	....	....	....	....	....	5,019	4,866	5,489	6,956	7,582	Other Sectors	79lj d

Hungary

		1972	1973	1974	1975	1976	1977	1978	1979	1980	1981	1982	1983	1984	1985	1986
Government Finance																*Billions of Forint:*
Deficit (-) or Surplus	80	...	...	...	...	...	...	...	...	...	−22.1	−16.1	−6.4	15.7	−10.1	−30.9
Total Revenue and Grants	81y	...	...	...	...	...	...	...	...	...	418.1	438.7	485.5	535.2	539.0	606.8
Revenue	81	...	...	...	...	...	...	...	...	...	418.1	438.7	485.5	535.2	539.0	606.8
Grants	81z	...	...	...	...	...	...	...	...	...	—	—	—	—	—	—
Exp. & Lending Minus Repay.	82z	...	...	...	...	...	...	...	...	...	440.2	454.8	491.9	519.5	549.1	637.7
Expenditure	82	...	...	...	...	...	...	...	...	...	438.2	453.8	492.3	519.5	549.8	636.5
Lending Minus Repayments	83	...	...	...	...	...	...	...	...	...	2.0	1.0	−.4	—	−.7	1.2
Total Financing	80h	...	...	...	...	...	...	...	...	...	22.1	16.1	6.4	−15.7	10.1	30.9
Total Net Borrowing	84	...	...	...	...	...	...	...	...	...	16.3	17.8	7.6	−3.1	.1	31.2
Net Domestic	84a	...	...	...	...	...	...	...	...	...	—	14.9	3.5	−4.4	1.2	39.8
Net Foreign	85a	...	...	...	...	...	...	...	...	...	16.3	2.9	4.1	1.3	−1.1	−8.6
Use of Cash Balances	87	...	...	...	...	...	...	...	...	...	5.8	−1.7	−1.2	−12.6	10.0	−.3
Total Debt by Residence	88	...	...	...	...	...	...	...	...	...	...	...	...	...	...	...
Domestic	88a	...	...	...	...	...	...	...	...	...	...	...	...	...	...	...
Foreign	89a	...	...	...	...	...	...	...	...	...	...	...	...	...	...	...
Memorandum Item:																
Privatization Receipts	83a	...	...	...	...	...	...	...	...	...	...	...	...	...	...	...
National Accounts																*Billions of Forint*
Househ.Cons.Expend.,incl.NPISHs	96f	223.5	241.7	261.4	286.1	307.3	334.0	361.7	401.2	441.2	477.7	515.1	551.2	600.5	649.3	695.5
Government Consumption Expend.	91f	38.6	40.5	46.9	50.2	53.2	57.8	65.8	71.3	74.2	79.1	84.2	90.9	95.3	104.6	116.0
Gross Fixed Capital Formation	93e	123.1	139.2	161.0	161.0	168.2	197.7	214.4	220.8	207.7	206.7	213.9	220.0	225.4	232.1	262.2
Changes in Inventories	93i	7.3	4.1	21.3	21.4	21.5	18.8	45.5	11.3	13.6	24.6	27.9	17.1	26.4	26.3	31.6
Exports of Goods and Services	90c	.1	.2	.2	.2	.2	.2	243.9	283.3	281.8	308.2	321.8	360.7	402.0	436.2	431.6
Imports of Goods and Services (-)	98c	.1	.1	.2	.2	.2	.3	301.6	305.6	297.4	316.4	315.0	343.6	371.1	414.8	447.0
Gross Domestic Product (GDP)	99b	391.0	429.0	448.9	482.7	528.9	582.0	629.7	682.3	721.0	779.9	847.9	896.3	978.5	1,033.7	1,088.8
Net National Income	99e	347.8	382.9	398.8	427.8	467.1	513.4	553.6	598.9	628.3	683.6	746.8	793.5	868.6	919.4	966.9
GDP Volume 1976 prices	99b.p	421.5	450.4	476.8	506.4	524.4	564.5	589.6	605.4	606.7						
GDP Volume 1981 prices	99b.p	...	...	...	...	...	...	...	...	751.0	772.6	794.5	800.3	821.5	819.4	...
GDP Volume 1988 prices	99b.p	...	...	...	...	...	...	...	...	...	...	...	...	...	...	...
GDP Volume 1991 Prices	99b.p	...	...	...	...	...	...	...	...	...	...	...	...	1,291.0	1,322.4	
GDP Volume 1995 Prices	99b.p	...	...	...	...	...	...	...	...	...	...	...	...	...	...	...
GDP Volume (1995=100)	99bv p	65.8	70.3	74.4	79.1	81.9	88.1	92.1	94.5	94.7	97.5	100.2	101.0	103.6	103.4	105.9
GDP Deflator (1995=100)	99bi p	10.6	10.9	10.7	10.9	11.5	11.8	12.2	12.9	13.6	14.3	15.1	15.8	16.8	17.8	18.3
Population	99z	10.40	10.43	10.48	10.53	10.59	10.64	10.67	10.70	10.71	10.70	10.68	10.66	10.62	10.58	*Millions:* 10.53

Year Ending December 31

Government Finance

Item	1987	1988	1989	1990	1991	1992	1993	1994	1995	1996	1997	1998	1999	2000	2001	Code
Deficit (-) or Surplus	-40.3	-3.2	-32.6	16.7	†-95.2	-214.6	-202.9	-310.8	-355.5	-213.1	-383.6	-631.5	-420.0	-449.3	-444.8	80
Total Revenue and Grants	660.4	789.9	926.6	1,105.9	†1,270.5	1,411.1	1,716.1	2,085.4	2,393.6	2,908.9	3,205.9	4,072.5	4,663.1	5,228.1	5,831.5	81y
Revenue	652.0	789.9	926.6	1,105.9	†1,270.5	1,411.1	1,716.1	2,085.2	2,393.4	2,908.5	3,205.3	4,065.5	4,649.9	5,193.7	5,801.1	81
Grants	8.4	—	—	—	†—			.2	.2	.4	.6	7.0	13.2	34.4	30.4	81z
Exp. & Lending Minus Repay.	700.7	793.1	959.2	1,089.2	†1,365.7	1,625.7	1,919.0	2,396.2	2,749.1	3,122.0	3,589.5	4,704.0	5,083.1	5,677.4	6,276.3	82z
Expenditure	700.1	792.0	957.8	1,088.8	†1,367.1	1,623.1	1,985.6	2,390.9	2,734.4	3,122.1	3,644.0	4,671.6	5,070.0	5,682.5	6,273.3	82
Lending Minus Repayments	.6	1.1	1.4	.4	†-1.4	2.6	-66.6	5.3	14.7	-.1	-54.5	32.4	13.1	-5.1	3.0	83
Total Financing	40.3	3.2	32.6	-16.7	†95.1	214.6	203.0	310.8	355.5	213.2	....	....	....	....	444.8	80h
Total Net Borrowing	40.3	4.4	32.0	-5.8	†110.8	218.4	221.8	203.9	204.4	380.6	....	....	....	....	635.9	84
Net Domestic	47.9	14.9	42.3	4.9	†112.7	217.7	216.7	202.4	198.5	373.7	....	....	....	....	408.0	84a
Net Foreign	-7.6	-10.5	-10.3	-10.7	†-1.9	.7	5.1	1.5	5.9	6.9	....	....	....	....	227.9	85a
Use of Cash Balances	—	-1.2	.6	-10.9	†-15.7	-3.8	-18.8	106.9	151.1	-167.4	....	....	....	....	-191.1	87
Total Debt by Residence	....	....	....	....	†1,850.0	2,310.8	3,181.6	3,801.0	4,781.6	4,959.1	5,405.7	6,161.5	6,890.5	7,228.7	7,721.6	88
Domestic	....	....	....	....	†1,731.2	2,176.9	2,978.9	3,564.5	4,461.7	4,669.2	5,055.4	5,867.3	5,940.0	6,144.2	6,486.1	88a
Foreign	....	....	....	....	†118.8	133.9	202.7	236.5	319.9	289.9	350.3	294.2	950.5	1,084.5	1,235.5	89a

Memorandum Item:

Item	1987	1988	1989	1990	1991	1992	1993	1994	1995	1996	1997	1998	1999	2000	2001	Code
Privatization Receipts	....	....	....	....	—	20.0	7.2	31.0	150.0	219.9	161.9	13.0	4.0	.9	....	83a

Billions of Forint

National Accounts

Item	1987	1988	1989	1990	1991	1992	1993	1994	1995	1996	1997	1998	1999	2000	2001	Code
Househ.Cons.Expend.,incl.NPISHs	778.5	†868.5	1,029.6	1,282.5	†1,746.9	2,141.1	2,639.9	3,151.7	3,724.0	4,389.8	5,270.1	6,282.8	7,272.1	8,297.0	9,502.7	96f
Government Consumption Expend.	126.3	†168.5	177.7	221.8	†264.6	336.4	491.4	527.1	617.7	703.6	900.8	1,024.6	1,156.7	1,293.7	1,636.5	91f
Gross Fixed Capital Formation	303.5	†310.8	372.5	402.4	†522.9	584.7	670.0	878.5	1,125.4	1,475.5	1,898.9	2,384.6	2,724.5	3,179.9	3,484.7	93e
Changes in Inventories	23.9	†53.9	85.6	128.0	†-11.9	38.1	90.1	218.4	399.9	467.9	607.8	523.4	909.4	571.0		93i
Exports of Goods and Services	464.4	†530.4	620.9	650.7	†818.4	925.3	937.4	1,262.5	2,073.0	2,678.7	3,885.6	5,105.9	6,038.3	8,053.5	8,995.8	90c
Imports of Goods and Services (-)	470.3	†491.7	563.5	596.1	†842.6	933.2	1,228.1	1,545.1	2,144.4	2,753.6	3,882.6	5,318.2	6,321.6	8,582.7	9,314.2	98c
Gross Domestic Product (GDP)	1,226.4	†1,440.4	1,722.8	2,089.3	†2,498.3	2,942.6	3,548.2	4,364.8	5,614.0	6,893.9	8,540.7	10,087.4	11,393.5	13,150.8	14,876.4	99b
Net National Income	1,097.7	1,278.9	....	....	....	....	....	....	....	....	....	....	....	....	....	99e
GDP Volume 1976 prices																99b.*p*
GDP Volume 1981 prices	1,372.2	†1,448.2	1,458.9	1,407.9	1,240.4	....										99b.*p*
GDP Volume 1988 prices																99b.*p*
GDP Volume 1991 Prices					2,498.3	2,421.8	2,407.8	2,478.8	2,515.7							99b.*p*
GDP Volume 1995 Prices									5,614.0	5,689.2	5,949.4	6,238.5				99b.*p*
GDP Volume (1995=100)	109.9	†115.9	116.8	112.7	99.3	96.3	95.7	98.5	100.0	101.3	106.0	111.1	115.8	121.8	126.4	99bv *p*
GDP Deflator (1995=100)	19.9	†22.1	26.3	33.0	†44.8	54.4	66.0	78.9	100.0	121.2	143.6	161.7	175.3	192.4	209.6	99bi *p*

Midyear Estimates

Item	1987	1988	1989	1990	1991	1992	1993	1994	1995	1996	1997	1998	1999	2000	2001	Code
Population	10.49	10.44	10.40	10.36	10.35	10.32	10.29	10.26	10.23	10.19	10.15	10.11	10.07	10.02	9.92	99z

(See notes in the back of the book.)

Iceland

		1972	1973	1974	1975	1976	1977	1978	1979	1980	1981	1982	1983	1984	1985	1986
Exchange Rates															*Kronur per SDR:*	
Official Rate	aa	1.063	1.013	†1.451	1.999	2.204	2.589	4.144	5.202	7.957	†9.513	18.339	30.016	39.743	46.200	49.221
															Kronur per US Dollar:	
Official Rate	ae	.979	.840	†1.185	1.708	1.897	2.131	3.181	3.949	6.239	†8.173	16.625	28.670	40.545	42.060	40.240
Official Rate	rf	.883	.901	1.000	1.537	1.822	1.989	2.711	3.526	4.798	7.224	12.352	24.843	31.694	41.508	41.104
														Index Numbers (1995=100):		
Official Rate	ahx	7,371.6	7,199.4	6,579.7	4,245.2	3,554.1	3,256.7	2,416.3	1,845.0	1,370.3	902.2	544.8	267.1	205.8	155.9	157.3
Nominal Effective Exchange Rate	ne c	....	....	....	....	....	....	....	1,516.2	1,127.3	850.1	571.8	304.6	255.4	201.4	168.8
Real Effective Exchange Rate	re c	....	....	....	....	....	....	....	112.1	117.1	124.4	113.4	104.2	111.0	110.1	109.8
Fund Position															*Millions of SDRs:*	
Quota	2f. s	23.0	23.0	23.0	23.0	23.0	23.0	29.0	29.0	43.5	43.5	43.5	59.6	59.6	59.6	59.6
SDRs	1b. s	6.4	6.3	6.3	4.8	1.8	2.7	1.8	.2	1.8	3.4	2.0	.2	.4	.4	.2
Reserve Position in the Fund	1c. s	5.8	5.8	—	—	—	—	—	5.4	9.0	9.0	—	4.0	4.0	4.0	4.0
Total Fund Cred.&Loans Outstg.	2tl	—	—	15.5	31.4	56.4	56.4	47.3	34.7	15.7	5.9	22.4	21.5	21.5	21.5	10.8
International Liquidity												*Millions of US Dollars Unless Otherwise Indicated:*					
Total Reserves minus Gold	1l. d	83.0	98.4	47.3	45.6	79.4	98.3	135.8	161.9	173.8	229.5	145.2	149.3	127.6	205.5	309.8
SDRs	1b. d	6.9	7.6	7.7	5.6	2.1	3.2	2.3	.2	2.3	4.0	2.2	.2	.4	.4	.2
Reserve Position in the Fund	1c. d	6.2	6.9						7.1	11.5	10.5		4.2	4.0	4.4	4.9
Foreign Exchange	1d. d	69.9	83.8	39.6	40.0	77.3	95.1	133.5	154.6	160.0	215.0	143.0	144.9	123.3	200.7	304.7
Gold (Million Fine Troy Ounces)	1ad	.029	.029	.030	.030	.030	.039	.044	.049	.049	.049	.049	.049	.049	.049	.049
Gold (National Valuation)	1and	1.1	1.2	1.2	1.2	1.2	1.7	2.0	2.2	2.1	2.0	1.9	1.8	1.7	1.9	2.1
Monetary Authorities: Other Liab.	4. d	18.3	21.4	28.5	56.5	54.0	31.1	39.5	32.0	26.5	36.0	42.4	55.4	69.3	13.3	25.8
Deposit Money Banks: Assets	7a. d	3.4	4.8	10.9	11.7	11.3	13.4	14.8	17.4	25.0	20.2	24.5	26.7	27.6	40.9	43.6
Liabilities	7b. d	13.8	21.4	39.6	60.8	60.3	78.1	102.9	126.5	177.9	209.1	222.4	289.4	260.4	422.0	418.5
Monetary Authorities												*Thousands of Kronur through 1974;*					
Foreign Assets	11	82,441	84,278	57,448	†80	153	213	438	648	1,106	1,889	2,441	4,324	5,234	8,723	12,532
Claims on Central Government	12a	16,322	28,600	64,550	†137	163	201	347	411	463	545	599	2,022	2,754	4,830	3,264
Claims on Private Sector	12d	1,509	1,430	1,620	†1	2	3	4	4	15	30	48	92	44	49	128
Claims on Deposit Money Banks	12e	11,467	18,390	69,690	†56	85	68	62	95	113	197	1,579	2,018	3,447	4,603	5,634
Claims on Other Financial Insts	12f	12,478	13,430	13,270	†32	38	36	36	33	38	105	153	251	594	670	859
Reserve Money	14	78,702	115,390	147,220	†198	270	410	617	939	1,577	2,612	4,059	7,243	10,009	12,362	15,463
of which: Currency Outside DMBs	14a	21,436	27,000	34,530	†44	57	88	124	160	224	406	527	770	966	1,251	1,734
Foreign Liabilities	16c	18,012	19,940	56,298	†159	227	212	322	307	290	351	1,114	2,233	3,666	1,553	1,567
Central Government Deposits	16d	29,360	36,540	52,310	†43	64	103	237	346	380	660	979	1,862	2,080	2,184	1,286
Other Items (Net)	17r	24,983	15,558	32,980	†32	40	61	109	185	480	536	1,603	2,284	3,126	3,845	4,421
Deposit Money Banks												*Thousands of Kronur through 1974;*					
Reserves	20	44,060	63,530	79,130	†108	150	233	381	559	1,045	1,771	2,626	4,277	6,134	7,365	9,955
Foreign Assets	21	3,330	4,500	12,950	†20	21	29	47	69	156	165	407	765	1,119	1,719	1,753
Claims on Central Government	22a	3,780	4,670	6,030	†6	9	9	9	20	71	146	264	525	†421	482	458
Claims on Private Sector	22d	215,240	293,230	465,430	†615	785	1,103	1,646	2,599	4,294	7,313	14,261	26,034	†35,733	46,928	54,051
Claims on Other Financial Insts	22f	13,420	16,740	21,420	†29	37	50	64	74	109	152	265	581	963	1,230	54,051
Demand Deposits	24	47,580	68,840	90,150	†123	151	217	306	469	786	1,222	1,549	2,928	†4,312	5,471	7,940
Savings Deposits	25	177,740	230,970	295,680	†375	513	732	1,110	1,792	2,993	†3,371	6,437	11,634	15,291	24,849	31,968
Bonds	26a	....	....	....	....									—	317	1,238
Restricted Deposits	26b	2,260	3,930	5,100	†6	7	9	16	8	9	13	6	11	19	24	46
Foreign Liabilities	26c	13,580	19,890	46,890	†104	114	166	327	499	1,110	1,709	3,698	8,297	10,556	17,751	16,842
Credit from Monetary Authorities	26g	38,330	58,160	151,170	†182	242	333	460	658	994	1,507	4,463	6,939	10,251	5,656	6,035
Other Items (Net)	27r	9,390	14,340	16,420	†14	11	17	1	16	−7	219	−122	−779	†2,743	2,829	1,472
Monetary Survey												*Thousands of Kronur through 1974;*					
Foreign Assets (Net)	31n	54,179	48,948	−32,790	†−163	−167	−137	−164	−90	−138	−5	−1,964	−5,441	−7,869	−8,862	−4,124
Domestic Credit	32	233,389	321,560	520,010	†777	971	1,298	1,869	2,795	4,610	7,631	14,611	27,643	†38,429	52,004	59,040
Claims on Central Govt. (Net)	32an	−9,258	−3,270	18,270	†100	108	106	118	84	154	31	−116	685	†1,095	3,128	2,436
Claims on Private Sector	32d	216,749	294,660	467,050	†616	788	1,106	1,650	2,604	4,309	7,343	14,309	26,126	†35,777	46,977	54,179
Claims on Other Financial Inst	32f	25,898	30,170	34,690	†61	76	86	100	107	147	257	418	832	1,557	1,900	2,426
Money	34	69,016	95,840	124,680	†167	208	305	430	629	1,010	1,628	2,076	3,698	†5,278	6,722	9,674
Quasi-Money	35	177,740	230,970	295,680	†375	513	732	1,110	1,792	2,993	3,371	6,437	11,634	15,291	24,849	31,968
Bonds	36a	....	....	....	....										317	1,238
Other Items (Net)	37r	76,702	98,458	†66,860	†72	83	124	156	284	469	758	1,791	2,754	15,601	11,497	10,114
Money plus Quasi-Money	35l	246,756	326,810	420,360	†542	720	1,038	1,540	2,421	4,003	4,999	8,513	15,332	†20,569	31,571	41,642
Interest Rates												*Percent Per Annum*					
Discount Rate (End of Period)	60	5.30	6.30	7.30	7.30	7.30	14.00	17.00	26.00	28.00	28.00	28.00	22.00	16.50	30.00	21.00
Money Market Rate	60b	....	....	....	....	....	....	....	....	....	....	....	....	36.90	....	....
Treasury Bill Rate	60c	....	....	....	....	....	....	....	....	....	....	....	....	....	....	....
Deposit Rate	60l	....	12.00	17.00	17.00	13.62	29.00	42.25	29.50	38.83	38.75	38.33	39.46	18.09	24.69	12.21
Housing Bond Rate	60m	....	....	....	....	....	....	....	....	....	....	....	....	....	....	....
Lending Rate	60p	....	....	....	....	....	....	33.00	42.50	45.00	40.00	45.95	42.75	22.83	32.60	18.78
Government Bond Yield	61	....	....	....	....	....	....	....	....	....	....	....	....	....	....	....
Prices, Production, Labor												*Index Numbers (1995=100):*					
Consumer Prices	64	.3	.4	.5	.8	†1.1	1.4	2.0	2.9	4.7	7.0	10.6	19.6	25.3	33.3	40.6
Wages, Hourly	65	.4	.5	.7	.9	†1.2	1.6	2.5	3.6	5.6	8.6	13.4	20.3	22.6	29.9	37.5
Total Fish Catch	66al	46.4	58.0	61.2	66.4	63.2	88.9	101.5	106.4	97.8	93.1	50.9	54.0	98.9	107.2	105.1
Labor Force	67d	....	....	....	....	....	....	....	....	....	....	....	....	....	*Number in Thousands:*	
Employment	67e	....	....	....	....	....	....	....	....	....	....	....	....	....	....	....
Unemployment	67c	....	....	....	....	....	....	....	....	....	....	....	....	....	....	....
Unemployment Rate (%)	67r	....	....	....	....	....	....	....	....	....	....	....	....	....	1	1
															.9	.7
International Transactions												*Trillions of Kronur through 1974;*					
Exports	70	167,000	260,200	328,800	†474	735	1,019	1,763	2,786	4,461	6,530	8,479	18,633	23,557	33,826	45,093
Fish	70al	78,100	107,600	146,700	†262	366	465	810	1,293	1,884	2,945	4,330	8,611	9,989	15,330	19,557
Fishmeal	70z	11,600	36,200	32,600	†39	55	121	218	269	361	423	235	335	1,547	1,879	2,671
Imports, c.i.f.	71	204,200	318,600	525,700	†751	857	1,210	1,843	2,913	4,802	7,485	11,647	20,596	26,780	37,600	45,910
Volume of Exports	72	41.9	45.3	41.8	45.1	51.7	56.2	66.1	71.7	†77.2	75.4	63.8	72.3	73.8	*1995=100*	90.4
Volume of Imports	73	60.5	70.7	76.9	65.3	66.0	74.0	80.8	81.2	†86.7	91.6	89.0	79.4	84.9	92.0	99.1
Unit Value of Exports	74	†.3	.4	.6	.8	1.1	1.4	2.1	3.1	†4.5	6.8	10.8	20.4	24.6	32.7	40.2
Unit Value of Imports	75	†.3	.4	.5	.9	1.1	1.3	1.9	3.0	†4.6	6.8	10.7	21.2	26.3	34.6	39.2

1987	1988	1989	1990	1991	1992	1993	1994	1995	1996	1997	1998	1999	2000	2001		
End of Period															**Exchange Rates**	
50.589	62.198	80.387	78.801	79.561	87.890	99.899	99.708	96.964	96.185	97.389	97.605	99.576	110.356	129.380	Official Rate	**aa**
End of Period (ae) Period Average (rf)																
35.660	46.220	61.170	55.390	55.620	63.920	72.730	68.300	65.230	66.890	72.180	69.320	72.550	84.700	102.950	Official Rate	**ae**
38.677	43.014	57.042	58.284	58.996	57.546	67.603	69.944	64.692	66.500	70.904	70.958	72.335	78.616	97.425	Official Rate	**rf**
Period Averages																
167.3	151.6	114.1	111.1	109.8	112.6	96.0	92.5	100.0	97.2	91.2	91.2	89.4	82.6	66.8	Official Rate	**ahx**
159.7	138.5	109.5	100.6	102.7	105.3	100.0	98.9	100.0	100.3	102.6	105.2	104.8	104.8	88.8	Nominal Effective Exchange Rate	**nec**
118.6	124.2	113.3	112.0	114.9	115.3	106.8	100.3	100.0	100.5	102.5	105.4	107.0	110.1	96.8	Real Effective Exchange Rate	**rec**
End of Period															**Fund Position**	
59.6	59.6	59.6	59.6	59.6	85.3	85.3	85.3	85.3	85.3	85.3	85.3	117.6	117.6	117.6	Quota	**2f.s**
1.9	1.0	—	.3	.1	—	—	.1	—	—	—	—	—	—	.1	SDRs	**1b.s**
4.0	4.0	4.0	4.0	4.0	10.5	10.5	10.5	10.5	10.5	10.5	10.5	18.6	18.6	18.6	Reserve Position in the Fund	**1c.s**
—	—	—	—	—	—	—	—	—	—	—	—	—	—	—	Total Fund Cred.&Loans Outstg.	**2tl**
End of Period															**International Liquidity**	
311.3	290.7	337.3	436.1	449.5	498.3	426.4	292.9	308.1	453.7	383.7	426.4	478.4	388.9	338.3	Total Reserves minus Gold	**1l.d**
2.7	1.3	—	.4	.1	—	.1	.1	—	—	—	—	—	—	.1	SDRs	**1b.d**
5.7	5.4	5.3	5.7	5.8	14.4	14.4	15.3	15.6	15.1	14.2	14.8	25.5	24.2	23.3	Reserve Position in the Fund	**1c.d**
302.9	284.0	332.0	430.0	443.6	483.9	412.0	277.5	292.5	438.6	369.5	411.6	452.9	364.6	314.8	Foreign Exchange	**1d.d**
.049	.049	.049	.049	.049	.049	.049	.049	.049	.049	.049	.056	.056	.059	.062	Gold (Million Fine Troy Ounces)	**1ad**
2.4	2.3	2.2	2.4	2.5	2.4	2.4	2.5	2.6	2.7	2.6	2.8	....	....	....	Gold (National Valuation)	**1and**
22.2	40.3	16.7	17.1	20.3	12.4	36.8	137.5	176.5	75.5	75.1	130.9	....	....	....	Monetary Authorities: Other Liab.	**4..d**
63.9	63.7	62.3	81.0	83.5	70.8	94.0	118.7	79.9	108.9	153.4	162.7	188.8	243.7	273.3	Deposit Money Banks: Assets	**7a.d**
629.8	754.1	696.0	705.4	714.8	682.4	593.0	464.1	419.4	639.0	875.8	1,477.8	1,989.9	2,649.4	2,479.5	Liabilities	**7b.d**
Millions of Kronur Beginning 1975: End of Period															**Monetary Authorities**	
11,167	13,563	20,797	24,261	25,248	32,017	31,318	24,347	25,961	36,151	33,274	35,136	....	....	....	Foreign Assets	**11**
6,017	10,707	10,800	5,112	10,882	6,751	12,865	24,546	18,476	10,534	12,852	5,011	....	....	....	Claims on Central Government	**12a**
357	445	922	672	412	380	330	408	413	487	142	113	....	....	....	Claims on Private Sector	**12d**
4,995	4,565	4,726	4,319	3,342	3,983	2,630	2,226	5,353	1,878	6,496	19,600	....	....	....	Claims on Deposit Money Banks	**12e**
1,091	1,196	873	1,866	603	531	639	4,490	3,380	3,443	3,472	7,770	....	....	....	Claims on Other Financial Insts	**12f**
16,489	19,087	23,550	21,097	21,637	22,328	20,333	20,949	17,164	21,691	24,153	24,690	....	....	....	Reserve Money	**14**
2,244	2,631	2,975	3,057	3,239	3,593	3,906	4,641	5,169	5,475	5,751	6,322	....	....	....	*of which: Currency Outside DMBs*	**14a**
792	1,862	1,019	950	1,127	792	2,678	9,389	11,513	5,049	5,418	9,073	....	....	....	Foreign Liabilities	**16c**
2,351	2,428	2,226	2,448	5,118	5,512	7,350	7,419	6,177	6,850	6,438	13,176	....	....	....	Central Government Deposits	**16d**
4,154	7,099	11,321	11,735	12,605	15,031	17,421	18,259	18,728	18,904	20,226	20,691	....	....	....	Other Items (Net)	**17r**
Millions of Kronur Beginning 1975: End of Period															**Deposit Money Banks**	
10,747	11,899	19,525	15,042	16,706	14,474	11,747	11,540	10,325	13,418	14,100	13,990	29,026	25,731	20,569	Reserves	**20**
2,277	2,943	3,810	4,488	4,644	4,524	6,835	8,105	5,213	7,285	11,076	11,276	13,699	20,641	28,132	Foreign Assets	**21**
1,813	2,644	8,022	18,416	18,848	20,577	26,746	19,168	11,432	13,241	10,578	6,287	7,271	4,126	12,982	Claims on Central Government	**22a**
75,386	103,457	147,389	157,123	175,155	187,675	193,643	196,262	208,982	236,720	348,883	376,127	461,004	663,599	768,288	Claims on Private Sector	**22d**
1,999	2,398	2,521	2,642	3,227	3,162	4,265	4,485	1,750	1,167	1,680	375	934	2,486	3,077	Claims on Other Financial Insts	**22f**
10,463	12,187	16,825	21,587	26,317	26,351	27,663	30,313	33,146	36,081	42,600	51,852	63,346	65,117	65,228	Demand Deposits	**24**
44,293	59,591	92,291	103,258	118,696	124,088	132,526	132,482	133,341	140,725	150,977	171,434	198,763	225,879	271,394	Savings Deposits	**25**
3,084	7,928	13,963	17,453	19,180	20,589	22,699	22,337	24,095	32,166	40,731	53,419	62,938	169,070	194,709	Bonds	**26a**
68	83	66	—	19	—	—	—	6	2	5	2	1	—	—	Restricted Deposits	**26b**
22,459	34,853	42,575	39,072	39,755	43,616	43,127	31,697	27,356	42,741	63,215	102,438	144,370	224,406	255,265	Foreign Liabilities	**26c**
5,038	4,578	4,737	3,625	3,335	2,520	1,600	4,833	4,860	1,954	6,480	21,000	30,797	39,016	53,918	Credit from Monetary Authorities	**26g**
5,384	7,155	7,291	8,437	9,282	11,210	13,689	15,563	15,018	18,287	84,827	8,053	11,718	–6,904	–7,467	Other Items (Net)	**27r**
Millions of Kronur Beginning 1975: End of Period															**Monetary Survey**	
–9,806	–20,208	–18,987	–11,272	–10,990	–7,867	–7,652	–8,635	–7,695	–4,354	–24,282	–65,099	....	....	....	Foreign Assets (Net)	**31n**
84,313	118,419	168,300	183,383	204,009	213,565	231,138	241,940	238,256	258,743	371,168	382,507	....	....	....	Domestic Credit	**32**
5,479	10,922	16,595	21,080	24,612	21,816	32,260	36,295	23,731	16,925	16,991	–1,878	....	....	....	Claims on Central Govt. (Net)	**32an**
75,743	103,902	148,311	157,795	175,567	188,055	193,973	196,670	209,395	237,207	349,025	376,240	....	....	....	Claims on Private Sector	**32d**
3,090	3,594	3,394	4,508	3,830	3,693	4,904	8,975	5,130	4,610	5,152	8,145	....	....	....	Claims on Other Financial Inst	**32f**
12,707	14,818	19,800	24,644	29,556	29,944	31,569	34,954	38,315	41,556	48,351	58,174	....	....	....	Money	**34**
44,293	59,591	92,291	103,258	118,696	124,088	132,526	132,482	133,341	140,725	150,977	171,434	198,763	225,879	271,394	Quasi-Money	**35**
3,084	7,928	13,963	17,453	19,180	20,589	22,699	22,337	24,095	32,166	40,731	53,419	62,938	169,070	194,709	Bonds	**36a**
13,148	18,907	19,739	22,476	23,592	29,039	34,760	41,197	34,930	40,067	109,344	34,524	....	....	....	Other Items (Net)	**37r**
57,000	74,409	112,091	127,902	148,252	154,032	164,095	167,436	171,656	182,281	199,328	229,608	....	....	....	Money plus Quasi-Money	**35l**
Percent Per Annum															**Interest Rates**	
49.20	24.10	38.40	21.00	21.00	†16.63	....	4.70	5.93	5.70	6.55	†8.50	10.00	12.40	12.00	Discount Rate *(End of Period)*	**60**
31.52	34.49	21.58	12.73	14.85	12.38	8.61	4.96	6.58	6.96	7.38	8.12	9.24	11.61	14.51	Money Market Rate	**60b**
....	26.39	23.00	12.92	14.25	†11.30	8.35	4.95	7.22	6.97	7.04	7.40	8.61	11.12	11.03	Treasury Bill Rate	**60c**
15.51	†25.54	23.58	12.31	12.73	5.94	6.63	3.03	3.69	4.25	4.72	4.50	4.82	7.11	....	Deposit Rate	**60l**
....	....	....	....	....	....	....	5.75	5.80	5.78	5.30	4.71	4.78	6.31	6.07	Housing Bond Rate	**60m**
26.61	30.28	27.97	16.18	17.52	13.05	14.11	10.57	11.58	12.43	12.89	12.78	13.30	16.80	17.95	Lending Rate	**60p**
....	....	....	....	....	7.75	6.80	5.02	7.18	5.61	5.49	4.73	4.28	5.35	5.33	Government Bond Yield	**61**
Period Averages															**Prices, Production, Labor**	
47.8	60.1	72.6	83.8	89.5	93.1	96.9	98.4	100.0	102.3	104.1	105.9	109.3	114.9	122.3	Consumer Prices	**64**
62.6	79.4	90.0	†96.9	98.4	98.5	96.3	96.8	100.0	....	....	....	....	....	....	Wages, Hourly	**65**
102.3	110.5	88.6	96.7	64.3	99.6	109.0	93.7	100.0	127.6	145.0	99.4	93.6	108.7	127.1	Total Fish Catch	**66al**
Period Averages																
....	....	....	....	....	....	....	145	149	148	148	152	157	160	....	Labor Force	**67d**
....	....	....	....	137	137	137	138	142	142	142	148	154	156	....	Employment	**67e**
1	1	2	2	2	4	6	6	7	6	5	4	3	2	2	Unemployment	**67c**
.4	.6	1.7	1.8	1.5	3.0	4.3	4.7	4.9	4.4	3.9	2.8	1.9	1.4	1.4	Unemployment Rate (%)	**67r**
Millions of Kronur Beginning 1975															**International Transactions**	
53,053	61,674	79,131	92,624	91,560	87,833	94,711	113,279	116,613	108,977	131,228	145,008	145,132	148,516	196,803	Exports	**70**
24,190	25,941	33,695	43,895	49,189	42,599	45,754	54,644	50,535	46,030	46,712	54,722	60,028	57,442	66,986	Fish	**70al**
2,222	3,699	3,934	3,369	1,700	4,415	5,015	4,757	4,789	8,792	9,460	9,896	7,404	9,299	12,906	Fishmeal	**70z**
61,237	68,996	80,284	97,559	104,129	96,895	90,775	102,499	113,388	135,165	141,355	176,521	181,321	203,847	218,296	Imports, c.i.f.	**71**
1995=100																
94.4	93.2	96.5	95.1	87.7	86.8	91.3	102.3	100.0	109.0	111.1	107.9	....	....	....	Volume of Exports	**72**
123.9	117.2	104.4	104.7	109.8	101.4	87.4	93.9	100.0	116.5	123.7	154.2	....	....	....	Volume of Imports	**73**
45.8	52.1	64.2	78.6	91.0	88.3	91.3	95.4	100.0	98.4	99.6	....	....	....	....	Unit Value of Exports	**74**
42.4	50.3	66.0	79.2	83.9	83.3	90.9	96.1	100.0	102.7	103.4	....	....	....	....	Unit Value of Imports	**75**

Iceland

Balance of Payments

Millions of US Dollars:

	1972	1973	1974	1975	1976	1977	1978	1979	1980	1981	1982	1983	1984	1985	1986
Current Account, n.i.e. .... 78al d	...	...	...	...	-24	-48	20	-19	-76	-148	-261	-56	-133	-115	16
Goods: Exports f.o.b. .... 78aa d	...	...	...	...	402	513	640	780	920	896	686	742	743	814	1,097
Goods: Imports f.o.b. .... 78ab d	...	...	...	...	-428	-565	-618	-754	-900	-926	-838	-722	-757	-814	-1,000
Trade Balance .... 78ac d	...	...	...	...	-26	-52	22	26	20	-29	-152	20	-13	—	97
Services: Credit .... 78ad d	...	...	...	...	173	212	262	293	280	303	341	343	347	394	453
Services: Debit .... 78ae d	...	...	...	...	-117	-150	-192	-254	-263	-282	-309	-281	-311	-363	-374
Balance on Goods & Services .... 78af d	...	...	...	...	29	10	92	65	37	-8	-120	82	23	31	176
Income: Credit .... 78ag d	...	...	...	...	3	5	6	12	14	22	28	16	16	16	20
Income: Debit .... 78ah d	...	...	...	...	-56	-63	-78	-95	-126	-159	-166	-153	-171	-163	-183
Balance on Gds, Serv. & Inc. .... 78ai d	...	...	...	...	-23	-48	20	-18	-75	-145	-258	-55	-132	-115	13
Current Transfers, n.i.e.: Credit .... 78aj d	...	...	...	...	—	1	1	1	1	1	1	1	2	3	6
Current Transfers: Debit .... 78ak d	...	...	...	...	-1	-1	-1	-2	-2	-4	-4	-3	-3	-2	-3
Capital Account, n.i.e. .... 78bc d	...	...	...	...	1	—	-1	-2	-3	—	-2	-1	1	—	1
Capital Account, n.i.e.: Credit .... 78ba d	...	...	...	...	1	1	1	1	1	2	1	1	6	3	6
Capital Account: Debit .... 78bb d	...	...	...	...	—	-1	-2	-3	-4	-3	-3	-2	-4	-4	-5
Financial Account, n.i.e. .... 78bj d	...	...	...	...	33	85	64	95	157	234	214	66	145	233	100
Direct Investment Abroad .... 78bd d	...	...	...	...											
Dir. Invest. in Rep. Econ., n.i.e. .... 78be d	...	...	...	...											-2
Portfolio Investment Assets .... 78bf d	...	...	...	...	5	4	8	3	22	53	36	-23	14	24	9
Equity Securities .... 78bk d	...	...	...	...	—	—	—	—	—	—	—	—	—	—	—
Debt Securities .... 78bl d	...	...	...	...	—	—	—	—	—	—	—	—	—	—	—
Portfolio Investment Liab., n.i.e. .... 78bg d	...	...	...	...	31	45	-5	—	—	—	—	—	—	—	—
Equity Securities .... 78bm d	...	...	...	...	—	—	—	—	—	—	—	—	—	—	—
Debt Securities .... 78bn d	...	...	...	...	31	45	-5	—	—	—	—	—	—	—	—
Financial Derivatives Assets .... 78bw d	...	...	...	...	...	...	...	...	...	...	...	...	...	...	...
Financial Derivatives Liabilities .... 78bx d	...	...	...	...	...	...	...	...	...	...	...	...	...	...	...
Other Investment Assets .... 78bh d	...	...	...	...	-11	-20	-28	-34	-56	-21	-1	-44	-26	41	—
Monetary Authorities .... 78bo d	...	...	...	...											
General Government .... 78bp d	...	...	...	...											
Banks .... 78bq d	...	...	...	...	-2	-1	1	-2	-12	2	-8	-1	-16	6	—
Other Sectors .... 78br d	...	...	...	...	-9	-19	-28	-32	-44	-23	7	-43	-10	35	—
Other Investment Liab., n.i.e. .... 78bi d	...	...	...	...	8	56	88	126	191	202	179	133	157	168	94
Monetary Authorities .... 78bs d	...	...	...	...	-12	-13	8	-5	-3	12	10	9	18	-53	2
General Government .... 78bt d	...	...	...	...	34	44	51	80	73	98	170	117	135	118	103
Banks .... 78bu d	...	...	...	...	—	6	5	29	19	30	18	29	-7	15	9
Other Sectors .... 78bv d	...	...	...	...	-13	19	25	22	102	61	-19	-22	10	89	-20
Net Errors and Omissions .... 78ca d	...	...	...	...	-6	-20	-32	-37	-44	-14	-47	2	-28	-53	-18
Overall Balance .... 78cb d	...	...	...	...	4	16	51	37	34	72	-96	11	-15	64	99
Reserves and Related Items .... 79da d	...	...	...	...	-4	-16	-51	-37	-34	-72	96	-11	15	-64	-99
Reserve Assets .... 79db d	...	...	...	...	-33	-16	-40	-20	-10	-60	78	-10	15	-64	-86
Use of Fund Credit and Loans .... 79dc d	...	...	...	...	29	—	-12	-16	-25	-12	18	-1	—	—	-13
Exceptional Financing .... 79de d	...	...	...	...	...	...	...	...	...	...	...	...	...	...	...

International Investment Position

Millions of US Dollars

	1972	1973	1974	1975	1976	1977	1978	1979	1980	1981	1982	1983	1984	1985	1986
Assets .... 79aa d	...	...	...	...	...	...	...	...	...	...	...	...	...	...	499
Direct Investment Abroad .... 79ab d	...	...	...	...	...	...	...	...	...	...	...	...	...	...	—
Portfolio Investment .... 79ac d	...	...	...	...	...	...	...	...	...	...	...	...	...	...	—
Equity Securities .... 79ad d	...	...	...	...	...	...	...	...	...	...	...	...	...	...	—
Debt Securities .... 79ae d	...	...	...	...	...	...	...	...	...	...	...	...	...	...	—
Financial Derivatives .... 79al d	...	...	...	...	...	...	...	...	...	...	...	...	...	...	—
Other Investment .... 79af d	...	...	...	...	...	...	...	...	...	...	...	...	...	...	187
Monetary Authorities .... 79ag d	...	...	...	...	...	...	...	...	...	...	...	...	...	...	150
General Government .... 79ah d	...	...	...	...	...	...	...	...	...	...	...	...	...	...	—
Banks .... 79ai d	...	...	...	...	...	...	...	...	...	...	...	...	...	...	—
Other Sectors .... 79aj d	...	...	...	...	...	...	...	...	...	...	...	...	...	...	37
Reserve Assets .... 79ak d	...	...	...	...	...	...	...	...	...	...	...	...	...	...	312
Liabilities .... 79la d	...	...	...	...	...	...	...	...	...	...	...	...	...	...	2,297
Dir. Invest. in Rep. Economy .... 79lb d	...	...	...	...	...	...	...	...	...	...	...	...	...	...	—
Portfolio Investment .... 79lc d	...	...	...	...	...	...	...	...	...	...	...	...	...	...	—
Equity Securities .... 79ld d	...	...	...	...	...	...	...	...	...	...	...	...	...	...	—
Debt Securities .... 79le d	...	...	...	...	...	...	...	...	...	...	...	...	...	...	—
Financial Derivatives .... 79ll d	...	...	...	...	...	...	...	...	...	...	...	...	...	...	—
Other Investment .... 79lf d	...	...	...	...	...	...	...	...	...	...	...	...	...	...	2,297
Monetary Authorities .... 79lg d	...	...	...	...	...	...	...	...	...	...	...	...	...	...	40
General Government .... 79lh d	...	...	...	...	...	...	...	...	...	...	...	...	...	...	756
Banks .... 79li d	...	...	...	...	...	...	...	...	...	...	...	...	...	...	419
Other Sectors .... 79lj d	...	...	...	...	...	...	...	...	...	...	...	...	...	...	1,082

Balance of Payments

Minus Sign Indicates Debit

1987	1988	1989	1990	1991	1992	1993	1994	1995	1996	1997	1998	1999	2000	2001	Item	Code
-188	-231	-102	-126	-273	-158	42	109	54	-117	-125	-560	-591	-848	....	Current Account, n.i.e.	78al d
1,376	1,425	1,402	1,588	1,552	1,529	1,398	1,561	1,804	1,890	1,855	1,927	2,009	1,902	....	Goods: Exports f.o.b.	78aa d
-1,428	-1,439	-1,267	-1,509	-1,599	-1,527	-1,217	-1,288	-1,598	-1,871	-1,850	-2,279	-2,317	-2,376	....	Goods: Imports f.o.b.	78ab d
-52	-14	134	79	-47	2	181	273	206	19	5	-352	-308	-474	....	*Trade Balance*	78ac d
542	532	517	562	569	587	602	615	689	768	844	947	941	1,049	....	Services: Credit	78ad d
-510	-536	-495	-556	-605	-591	-594	-577	-641	-739	-800	-964	-1,026	-1,164	....	Services: Debit	78ae d
-20	-18	156	85	-83	-2	189	311	254	48	49	-369	-393	-589	....	*Balance on Goods & Services*	78af d
28	26	33	86	85	101	91	73	91	113	104	123	119	154	....	Income: Credit	78ag d
-198	-229	-270	-295	-266	-254	-235	-267	-286	-272	-273	-298	-307	-403	....	Income: Debit	78ah d
-190	-220	-81	-124	-264	-155	45	117	59	-111	-120	-544	-580	-839	....	*Balance on Gds, Serv. & Inc.*	78ai d
7	9	11	26	13	19	18	12	15	10	17	4	5	6	....	Current Transfers, n.i.e.: Credit	78aj d
-5	-20	-32	-28	-22	-22	-21	-20	-20	-16	-22	-20	-15	-16	....	Current Transfers: Debit	78ak d
-3	10	18	2	3	-2	1	-6	-3	-1	1	-5	-1	-3	....	Capital Account, n.i.e.	78bc d
10	18	26	17	15	11	12	6	13	10	11	9	17	18	....	Capital Account, n.i.e.: Credit	78ba d
-13	-9	-8	-15	-12	-13	-11	-12	-16	-11	-10	-14	-18	-21	....	Capital Account: Debit	78bb d
232	227	125	240	264	242	-55	-293	-17	303	195	679	908	853	....	Financial Account, n.i.e.	78bj d
-1	-1	-8	-13	-31	-10	-14	-23	-25	-62	-50	-74	-107	-368	....	Direct Investment Abroad	78bd d
2	-15	-27	22	19	-11	-1	1	-10	80	144	150	64	145	....	Dir. Invest. in Rep. Econ., n.i.e.	78be d
—	—	1	—	-4	-4	-34	-73	-76	-64	-201	-302	-448	-668	....	Portfolio Investment Assets	78bf d
—	—	—	....	-4	-4	-15	-25	-55	-81	-180	-253	-369	-651	....	Equity Securities	78bk d
—	—	1	—	—	—	-19	-48	-21	17	-21	-49	-79	-17	....	Debt Securities	78bl d
—	—	—	26	187	286	303	242	214	176	-38	66	1,029	1,142	....	Portfolio Investment Liab., n.i.e.	78bg d
—	—	—	—	—	—	—	—	—	1	-1	14	56	-44	....	Equity Securities	78bm d
—	—	—	26	187	286	303	242	214	175	-37	52	973	1,186	....	Debt Securities	78bn d
....	....	....	—	—	7	....	-49	-17	-1	-1	-1	59	15	....	Financial Derivatives Assets	78bw d
....	....	....		-7		54	16	—	—	—	-57	-16		....	Financial Derivatives Liabilities	78bx d
-55	-65	12	-47	4	30	-28	-31	22	-30	-162	3	-174	-80	....	Other Investment Assets	78bh d
....	....	....	....	....	....	....	....	....	....	....	....	....	....	....	Monetary Authorities	78bo d
—	—	....												....	General Government	78bp d
-11	-7	3	-26	-3	13	-28	—	47	-37	-86	28	-92	-71	....	Banks	78bq d
-44	-58	9	-21	7	17	—	-15	-25	7	-76	-25	-82	-9	....	Other Sectors	78br d
285	308	148	252	89	-49	-281	-414	-141	204	503	837	541	684	....	Other Investment Liab., n.i.e.	78bi d
-16	20	-25	-1	2	1	23	39	21	-100	-1	55	-3	142	....	Monetary Authorities	78bs d
83	144	192	21	72	-117	-46	-76	58	-17	34	81	43	25	....	General Government	78bt d
76	74	63	-21	10	-9	-69	-158	-54	288	306	422	441	332	....	Banks	78bu d
142	69	-82	253	5	76	-189	-219	-166	33	164	279	61	184	....	Other Sectors	78bv d
-59	-4	13	-42	15	-3	-47	40	-30	-32	-115	-82	-231	-71	....	Net Errors and Omissions	78ca d
-18	1	55	74	9	79	-59	-150	4	153	-44	32	86	-69	....	*Overall Balance*	78cb d
18	-1	-55	-74	-9	-79	59	150	-4	-153	44	-32	-86	69	....	Reserves and Related Items	79da d
32	-1	-55	-74	-9	-79	59	150	-4	-153	44	-32	-86	69	....	Reserve Assets	79db d
-14	—	—	—	—	—	—	—	—	—	—	—	—	—	....	Use of Fund Credit and Loans	79dc d
														....	Exceptional Financing	79de d

International Investment Position

Millions of US Dollars

1987	1988	1989	1990	1991	1992	1993	1994	1995	1996	1997	1998	1999	2000	2001	Item	Code
571	588	648	759	777	783	786	872	1,008	1,319	1,601	2,196	3,370	3,741	....	Assets	79aa d
—	57	58	75	101	99	114	149	180	242	275	339	452	667	....	Direct Investment Abroad	79ab d
—	—	—	—	4	9	41	118	198	264	488	967	1,902	2,205	....	Portfolio Investment	79ac d
—	—	—	—	4	9	22	48	103	183	398	830	1,718	2,128	....	Equity Securities	79ad d
—	—	—	—	—	—	19	71	95	81	90	137	184	78	....	Debt Securities	79ae d
—	—	—	12	13	4	4	59	81	81	76	78	16	—	....	Financial Derivatives	79al d
258	241	261	245	218	175	201	248	235	259	376	384	505	463	....	Other Investment	79af d
—	3	10	—	—	—	—	—	—	—	—	—	—	—	....	Monetary Authorities	79ag d
														....	General Government	79ah d
54	59	57	90	80	61	94	119	80	115	165	142	184	229	....	Banks	79ai d
204	179	194	155	138	114	107	129	155	143	212	243	321	234	....	Other Sectors	79aj d
313	290	329	427	441	496	426	298	315	474	386	427	495	405	....	Reserve Assets	79ak d
2,891	3,142	3,266	3,771	4,089	4,135	4,123	4,245	4,478	4,719	5,020	6,363	7,597	9,027	....	Liabilities	79la d
—	95	109	147	166	124	117	127	129	199	332	458	477	483	....	Dir. Invest. in Rep. Economy	79lb d
—	—	—	844	1,028	1,251	1,550	1,882	2,129	2,213	2,039	2,200	3,127	4,107	....	Portfolio Investment	79lc d
—	—	—	—	—	—	—	—	—	1	—	14	66	17	....	Equity Securities	79ld d
—	—	—	844	1,028	1,251	1,550	1,882	2,128	2,212	2,039	2,186	3,061	4,090	....	Debt Securities	79le d
—	—	—	12	12	4	4	56	74	74	74	74	16	—	....	Financial Derivatives	79ll d
2,891	3,047	3,157	2,768	2,883	2,756	2,452	2,180	2,146	2,233	2,575	3,631	3,976	4,436	....	Other Investment	79lf d
23	41	17	6	12	12	32	82	103	2	1	57	51	187	....	Monetary Authorities	79lg d
879	904	1,004	347	468	395	333	287	377	334	345	446	442	446	....	General Government	79lh d
609	748	686	702	712	676	592	459	421	660	903	1,427	1,814	2,269	....	Banks	79li d
1,380	1,354	1,450	1,713	1,691	1,673	1,495	1,352	1,246	1,238	1,326	1,701	1,669	1,534	....	Other Sectors	79lj d

Iceland

		1972	1973	1974	1975	1976	1977	1978	1979	1980	1981	1982	1983	1984	1985	1986
Government Finance													*Thousands of Kronur through 1974;*			
Deficit (-) or Surplus	80	†−17,950	−29,960	−66,330	†−122	−69	−173	−156	−193	−193	−172	−958	−1,998	−1,610	−4,719	−7,639
Total Revenue and Grants	81y	193,500	285,620	417,480	†588	773	1,071	1,720	2,630	4,091	6,624	10,772	17,513	23,634	31,256	41,938
Revenue	81	†193,400	271,940	410,500	†586	773	1,071	1,719	2,629	4,090	6,621	10,767	17,510	23,628	31,249	41,938
Grants	81z	100	13,680	6,980	†2	—	—	1	1	1	3	5	4	6	8	
Exp. & Lending Minus Repay.	82z	211,450	315,580	483,810	†710	842	1,244	1,876	2,823	4,284	6,796	11,730	19,511	25,244	35,975	49,577
Expenditure	82	†188,920	286,160	451,460	†638	741	1,086	1,720	2,644	4,015	6,383	10,454	19,094	22,754	33,551	48,381
Lending Minus Repayments	83	22,530	29,420	32,350	†72	100	159	155	179	268	413	1,276	417	2,490	2,424	1,196
Financing																
Total Financing	80h	....	....	....	....	....										
Total Net Borrowing	84	17,920	29,960	66,330	†122	69	173	156	193	193	172	958	1,998	1,610	4,719	7,639
Net Domestic	84a	−1,780	14,480	49,250	†84	15	51	115	47	76	−22	−63	733	−810	1,508	3,859
Net Foreign	85a	19,700	15,480	17,080	†38	54	122	42	146	117	194	1,021	1,265	2,421	3,211	3,780
Use of Cash Balances	87	....	....	....	....											
Total Debt by Residence	88	109,520	122,460	192,180	†359	515	808	1,331	2,081	3,648	5,039	10,256	19,012	27,010	35,978	44,426
Domestic	88a	36,600	42,360	57,280	†137	200	286	411	777	1,530	2,284	3,515	6,525	7,513	10,348	15,122
Foreign	89a	72,920	80,100	134,900	†222	316	522	920	1,304	2,118	2,756	6,741	12,487	19,498	25,631	29,304
National Accounts													*Thousands of Kronur through 1974;*			
Househ.Cons.Expend.,incl.NPISHs	96f	419,000	556,830	845,400	†1,188	1,626	2,342	3,656	5,501	8,937	14,361	23,864	41,016	55,872	77,240	99,196
Government Consumption Expend.	91f	104,170	141,600	229,200	†335	449	653	1,074	1,638	2,546	4,195	6,942	12,050	14,701	21,130	28,776
Gross Fixed Capital Formation	93e	194,000	291,260	455,000	†636	780	1,090	1,546	2,248	3,927	5,929	9,726	14,839	19,337	25,528	30,911
Changes in Inventories	93i	−10,000	−3,000	25,340	†37	−18	66	−39	51	80	253	913	−1,070	−661	−3,111	−3,748
Exports of Goods and Services	90c	259,000	369,300	474,750	†718	1,048	1,443	2,482	3,810	5,746	8,724	12,466	26,683	33,765	48,774	61,961
Imports of Goods and Services (-)	98c	267,600	383,850	610,900	†883	1,019	1,452	2,242	3,631	5,648	8,936	14,329	25,275	33,871	48,663	55,880
Gross Domestic Product (GDP)	99b	698,000	972,000	1,418,000	†2,031	2,866	4,142	6,477	9,617	15,588	24,526	39,582	68,243	89,143	120,898	161,216
Net Primary Income from Abroad	98.n	−8,902	−11,803	−19,205	†−49	−73	−88	−161	−244	−411	−811	−1,247	−2,671	−4,024	−4,824	−5,302
Gross National Income (GNI)	99a	689,000	960,000	1,399,000	†1,982	2,793	4,054	6,316	9,373	15,177	23,715	38,335	65,572	85,119	116,074	155,914
Consumption of Fixed Capital	99cf	84,580	114,000	172,000	†283	371	489	753	1,138	1,810	2,898	5,100	9,330	11,409	15,483	19,696
GDP Volume 1985 Prices(Millions)	99b.p	67,365	71,257	75,761	76,450	81,097	88,325	94,483	99,641	106,621	111,256	113,478	....	....		
GDP Volume 1990 Prices	99b.p	....	....	....	....	....	....	....	....	....	....	295,794	289,609	301,394	311,329	331,277
GDP Volume (1995=100)	99bv p	46.5	49.2	52.3	52.8	56.0	61.0	65.2	68.8	73.6	76.8	78.3	76.7	79.8	82.4	87.7
GDP Deflator (1995=100)	99bi p	.3	.4	.6	.9	1.1	1.5	2.2	3.1	4.7	7.1	11.2	19.7	24.7	32.5	40.7
Population	99z	.21	.21	.22	.22	.22	.22	.22	.23	.23	.23	.23	.24	.24	.24	*Millions:* .24

	1987	1988	1989	1990	1991	1992	1993	1994	1995	1996	1997	1998	1999	2000	2001		
Government Finance																	

Millions of Kronur Beginning 1975: Year Ending December 31

	1987	1988	1989	1990	1991	1992	1993	1994	1995	1996	1997	1998	1999	2000	2001		
Deficit (-) or Surplus	-4,278	-9,702	-7,962	-8,953	-17,342	-12,490	-16,844	-21,972	-20,270	-4,389	1,863	†16,284	20,435	9,548	-16,866		80
Total Revenue and Grants	55,575	73,424	95,084	107,838	117,438	122,859	122,810	130,008	135,715	150,816	155,200	†167,388	194,993	207,561	219,567		81y
Revenue	54,330	71,782	92,993	107,612	117,438	122,284	122,285	129,409	135,715	150,816	155,200	†166,529	194,250	206,993	218,848		81
Grants	1,245	1,643	2,091	226	—	575	525	599	—	—	—	†859	743	568	719		81z
Exp. & Lending Minus Repay.	59,853	83,126	103,045	116,790	134,780	135,349	139,655	151,980	155,985	155,205	153,337	†151,104	174,558	198,013	236,433		82z
Expenditure	60,199	82,334	105,933	117,531	132,473	133,466	135,537	142,756	146,826	156,454	152,990	†159,651	177,964	195,411	218,208		82
Lending Minus Repayments	-347	792	-2,888	-740	2,308	1,883	4,117	9,224	9,159	-1,248	347	†-8,547	-3,406	2,602	18,225		83
Financing																	
Total Financing	....	....	....	....	....	....	....	....	....	....	....	†-16,284	-20,435	-9,548	16,865		80h
Total Net Borrowing	4,278	9,702	7,962	8,953	17,342	12,489	16,844	21,972	20,270	4,389	-1,863	†-10,498	-20,691	-9,246	27,738		84
Net Domestic	3,678	4,878	2,912	6,281	9,633	2,118	13,866	10,493	5,185	-2,254	4,660	†48	-19,586	-17,443	-3,688		84a
Net Foreign	600	4,823	5,050	2,672	7,709	10,371	2,979	11,479	15,085	6,643	-6,523	†-10,546	-1,105	8,197	31,426		85a
Use of Cash Balances	....	....	....	....	....	....	....	....	....	....	....	†-5,786	256	-302	-10,873		87
Total Debt by Residence	52,026	68,273	97,183	112,784	127,656	153,412	181,030	197,106	213,575	225,677	226,111	†209,020	190,693	187,972	242,353		88
Domestic	22,071	28,068	38,671	53,005	59,703	66,139	78,725	83,473	86,314	93,459	99,483	†92,938	74,480	61,643	69,160		88a
Foreign	29,955	40,205	58,512	59,779	67,953	87,273	102,305	113,633	127,261	132,218	126,628	†116,082	116,213	126,329	173,193		89a
National Accounts																	

Millions of Kronur Beginning 1975

	1987	1988	1989	1990	1991	1992	1993	1994	1995	1996	1997	1998	1999	2000	2001		
Househ.Cons.Expend.,incl.NPISHs	133,557	161,068	190,254	218,091	239,517	240,278	237,402	247,821	258,215	278,656	298,170	332,239	365,909	398,740	417,717		96f
Government Consumption Expend.	38,981	50,537	60,341	73,055	81,501	83,927	88,618	93,823	98,961	105,563	112,775	127,754	142,088	156,740	175,190		91f
Gross Fixed Capital Formation	42,639	50,498	58,698	76,596	83,940	76,885	71,776	74,398	75,386	97,868	109,858	138,850	134,980	156,481	163,055		93e
Changes in Inventories	-3,779	-3,080	-8,143	-4,247	-891	-486	1,016	-26	2,285	-1,202	102	908	120	2,494	-2,083		93i
Exports of Goods and Services	71,681	81,721	106,282	124,937	125,671	121,597	135,694	157,436	161,250	176,836	190,948	203,726	212,981	231,697	303,557		90c
Imports of Goods and Services (-)	73,965	84,100	99,240	119,959	130,491	121,784	122,466	134,631	144,725	173,755	187,717	230,055	241,482	278,637	307,282		98c
Gross Domestic Product (GDP)	209,114	256,645	308,192	368,474	399,248	400,417	412,039	438,822	451,372	483,966	524,135	573,421	614,596	667,515	750,354		99b
Net Primary Income from Abroad	-4,799	-6,506	-11,164	-12,481	-10,655	-8,952	-9,890	-13,635	-12,828	-11,349	-11,864	-12,741	-13,407	-19,781	-28,478		98.n
Gross National Income (GNI)	204,315	250,138	297,028	355,993	388,593	391,465	402,149	425,187	439,311	473,843	512,271	560,680	601,189	647,734	721,876		99a
Consumption of Fixed Capital	23,473	28,905	37,267	46,898	53,308	56,875	61,028	63,429	64,960	67,526	70,897	75,053	81,397	87,000	101,953		99cf
GDP Volume 1985 Prices(Millions)	....	....	....	....	....	....	....	....	....	....	....	....	....	....	....		99b. p
GDP Volume 1990 Prices	359,590	359,263	360,174	368,474	371,181	358,920	361,005	377,182	377,626	397,047	415,382	431,361	447,148	471,618	485,862		99b. p
GDP Volume (1995=100)	95.2	95.1	95.4	97.6	98.3	95.0	95.6	99.9	100.0	105.1	110.0	114.2	118.4	124.9	128.7		99bv p
GDP Deflator (1995=100)	48.7	59.8	71.6	83.7	90.0	93.3	95.5	97.3	100.0	102.0	105.6	111.2	115.0	118.4	129.2		99bi p

Midyear Estimates

	1987	1988	1989	1990	1991	1992	1993	1994	1995	1996	1997	1998	1999	2000	2001		
Population	.25	.25	.25	.25	.26	.26	.26	.27	.27	.27	.27	.27	.28	.28	....		99z

(See notes in the back of the book.)

India

		1972	1973	1974	1975	1976	1977	1978	1979	1980	1981	1982	1983	1984	1985	1986
Exchange Rates														*Rupees per SDR:*		
Market Rate	aa	8.773	9.896	†9.978	10.462	10.318	9.971	10.668	10.416	10.114	10.591	10.627	10.986	12.205	13.363	16.051
														Rupees per US Dollar:		
Market Rate	ae	8.080	8.203	†8.150	8.937	8.881	8.209	8.188	7.907	7.930	9.099	9.634	10.493	12.451	12.166	13.122
Market Rate	rf	7.594	7.742	8.102	8.376	8.960	8.739	8.193	8.126	7.863	8.659	9.455	10.099	11.363	12.369	12.611
Fund Position														*Millions of SDRs:*		
Quota	2f. s	940	940	940	940	940	940	1,145	1,145	1,718	1,718	1,718	2,208	2,208	2,208	2,208
SDRs	1b. s	246	245	240	212	189	149	226	371	377	468	339	105	338	306	291
Reserve Position in the Fund	1c. s	76	76	—	—	—	—	69	162	330	330	364	487	487	487	487
Total Fund Cred.&Loans Outstg.	2tl	—	—	497	698	406	125	—	—	791	1,095	2,595	4,062	4,529	4,354	3,918
International Liquidity										*Millions of US Dollars Unless Otherwise Indicated:*						
Total Reserves minus Gold	1l. d	916	849	1,028	1,089	2,792	4,872	6,426	7,432	6,944	4,693	4,315	4,937	5,842	6,420	6,396
SDRs	1b. d	268	296	294	248	220	181	294	489	480	545	374	110	331	336	356
Reserve Position in the Fund	1c. d	83	92	—	—	—	—	90	213	420	384	402	510	477	535	596
Foreign Exchange	1d. d	566	461	734	841	2,572	4,691	6,042	6,731	6,043	3,764	3,539	4,318	5,034	5,549	5,444
Gold (Million Fine Troy Ounces)	1ad	6.954	6.954	6.954	6.954	6.954	7.356	8.362	8.560	8.594	8.594	8.594	8.594	8.737	9.397	10.449
Gold (National Valuation)	1an d	226	222	228	204	205	235	268	284	284	248	234	215	184	203	209
Other Banking Insts.: Liabilities	7f. d	145	162	176	215	234	273	303	306	293	371	422	447	470	623	826
Monetary Authorities														*Billions of Rupees:*		
Foreign Assets	11	10.3	11.0	13.0	17.7	27.3	43.7	55.4	63.0	57.2	46.6	44.1	54.3	76.2	79.2	88.0
Claims on Central Government	12a	54.4	64.7	71.4	75.5	72.6	79.3	84.4	102.4	144.3	187.1	237.9	273.7	330.7	406.4	480.7
Claims on Deposit Money Banks	12e	3.6	6.7	7.5	11.4	15.9	10.9	10.3	13.9	10.9	13.6	8.3	8.7	16.5	6.2	5.8
Claims on Other Financial Insts	12f	1.3	1.9	3.4	4.6	6.3	7.9	10.4	13.6	15.9	18.4	29.9	33.9	49.0	52.7	56.5
Reserve Money	14	55.6	68.1	70.4	74.3	86.8	105.1	126.6	153.2	176.5	195.1	230.3	260.2	303.9	375.3	436.5
of which: Currency Outside DMBs	14a	49.1	57.8	61.4	64.4	73.2	84.2	94.6	108.0	126.3	137.4	157.4	181.3	218.1	239.4	268.0
Foreign Liabilities	16c	—	—	5.0	7.3	4.2	1.2	—	—	2.7	6.0	22.0	38.8	48.8	51.1	56.1
Central Government Deposits	16d	.8	.6	.6	.7	1.1	.7	.5	.6	.8	.7	.6	18.9	30.7	.7	.6
Capital Accounts	17a	8.7	10.1	11.2	13.6	15.8	18.6	22.2	27.3	32.9	38.9	34.2	36.6	39.3	42.3	46.8
Other Items (Net)	17r	4.6	5.6	8.0	13.5	14.2	16.2	11.2	11.7	15.4	25.0	33.1	16.1	49.8	75.0	91.2
Deposit Money Banks														*Billions of Rupees:*		
Reserves	20	5.3	9.4	8.9	8.8	12.0	23.0	28.6	41.6	47.7	54.8	70.4	76.6	81.9	130.7	143.3
Claims on Central Government	22a	22.2	24.5	28.7	32.5	40.1	49.9	63.3	76.7	92.5	103.9	114.5	148.8	188.7	194.2	245.0
Claims on Private Sector	22d	71.4	88.0	102.5	127.3	164.2	187.7	221.9	258.9	302.1	366.7	438.5	515.3	612.4	698.9	821.4
Demand Deposits	24	36.5	42.9	49.4	57.3	78.7	93.6	†61.2	65.8	76.1	93.2	113.8	125.7	144.5	170.1	207.8
Time Deposits	25	49.0	60.5	70.0	84.4	104.6	128.2	†213.9	260.5	302.3	362.9	424.0	507.0	596.7	712.3	847.7
Credit from Monetary Authorities	26g	3.6	6.6	7.5	11.4	15.5	14.4	13.3	13.9	10.9	13.5	18.0	8.8	16.5	6.2	7.7
Other Items (Net)	27r	9.7	11.9	13.1	16.1	17.6	24.4	25.5	37.0	53.0	55.9	67.6	99.2	125.3	135.2	146.6
Monetary Survey														*Billions of Rupees:*		
Foreign Assets (Net)	31n	10.3	11.0	8.0	10.4	23.1	42.5	55.4	63.0	54.5	40.6	22.1	15.5	27.4	28.1	31.9
Domestic Credit	32	148.5	178.6	205.4	239.3	282.1	324.1	379.5	451.0	554.1	675.5	820.1	952.7	1,150.1	1,351.4	1,603.0
Claims on Central Govt. (Net)	32an	75.9	88.6	99.5	107.4	111.5	128.5	147.2	178.5	236.1	290.3	351.8	403.5	488.7	599.9	725.0
Claims on Private Sector	32d	71.4	88.0	102.5	127.3	164.2	187.7	221.9	258.9	302.1	366.7	438.5	515.3	612.4	698.9	821.4
Claims on Other Financial Insts	32f	1.3	1.9	3.4	4.6	6.3	7.9	10.4	13.6	15.9	18.4	29.9	33.9	49.0	52.7	56.5
Money	34	86.2	101.0	111.3	122.3	152.8	178.5	†157.6	176.9	204.6	232.5	273.7	308.6	365.6	412.4	478.7
Quasi-Money	35	49.0	60.5	70.0	84.4	104.6	128.2	†213.9	260.5	302.3	362.9	424.0	507.0	596.7	712.3	847.7
Other Items (Net)	37r	23.6	28.0	32.1	43.6	47.8	59.9	63.4	76.6	101.7	120.7	144.5	152.6	215.3	254.8	308.7
Money plus Quasi-Money	35l	135.2	161.5	181.3	206.7	257.4	306.7	†371.5	437.3	506.9	595.3	697.7	815.6	962.3	1,124.7	1,326.3
Other Banking Institutions														*Billions of Rupees:*		
Claims on Private Sector	42d	8.20	9.35	11.57	14.03	17.57	21.72	27.37	34.51	42.81	55.58	68.35	85.02	102.69	124.35	151.36
Bonds	46ab	2.14	2.47	3.07	4.13	5.78	7.70	10.40	14.27	20.15	27.34	35.93	43.94	56.81	71.00	86.24
Long-Term Foreign Liabilities	46cl	1.17	1.33	1.43	1.92	2.08	2.24	2.48	2.42	2.33	3.38	4.06	4.69	5.85	7.58	10.84
Central Govt. Lending Funds	46f	2.69	2.53	2.36	2.15	2.00	1.95	1.78	1.68	1.57	2.10	3.97	4.15	4.99	5.13	5.56
Capital Accounts	47a	1.30	1.41	1.61	1.76	1.92	2.27	2.73	3.38	4.01	5.25	6.92	8.39	11.12	13.10	15.87
Other Items (Net)	47r	.90	1.61	3.10	4.06	5.79	7.57	9.98	12.75	14.75	17.52	17.47	23.86	23.92	27.54	32.86
Post Office: Savings Deposits	45.. i	10.37	11.31	11.62	11.66	14.34	15.23	16.78	18.53	20.83	22.68	23.20	24.86	26.14	27.76	29.62
Nonbank Financial Institutions														*Billions of Rupees:*		
Claims on Central Government	42a. s	14.92	16.88	19.26	21.81	24.68	28.55	32.33	36.64	43.11	50.14	57.25	65.71	....	....	....
Claims on Local Government	42b. s	.37	.37	.37	.35	.34	.33	.34	.43	.53	.62	.62	.57	....	....	....
Claims on Private Sector	42d. s	7.50	8.46	9.86	10.94	12.25	13.42	14.46	19.35	20.58	22.74	26.62	28.37	....	....	....
Incr.in Total Assets(Within Per.)	49z. s	3.06	3.66	3.61	4.05	5.21	5.80	6.78	7.56	9.14	9.77	10.34	11.54	....	....	....
Liquid Liabilities	55l	145.33	172.58	192.81	218.15	271.53	322.09	†385.92	455.88	527.71	618.01	720.95	840.44	988.40	1,152.48	1,346.51
Interest Rates														*Percent Per Annum*		
Bank Rate *(End of Period)*	60	6.00	7.00	9.00	9.00	9.00	9.00	9.00	9.00	9.00	10.00	10.00	10.00	10.00	10.00	10.00
Money Market Rate	60b	4.69	6.64	13.52	10.40	11.28	10.18	8.05	8.47	7.24	8.61	7.27	8.30	9.95	10.00	9.97
Lending Rate	60p							13.50	14.50	16.50	16.50	16.50	16.50	16.50	16.50	16.50
Government Bond Yield	61	5.65	5.65	6.04	6.35	6.29	6.32	6.37	6.45	6.71	7.15	7.59	7.99	8.65	8.99	....
Prices, Production, Labor														*Index Numbers (1995=100):*		
Share Prices	62	4.9	†5.4	6.0	4.9	5.2	5.3	6.2	7.1	7.7	9.4	9.2	9.7	†10.3	15.4	18.7
Wholesale Prices	63	13.9	16.2	20.9	21.7	21.2	22.9	22.8	25.5	30.6	34.3	35.1	†37.9	40.5	42.4	44.8
Consumer Prices	64	13.5	15.8	20.3	21.4	19.8	21.4	22.0	23.4	26.0	29.4	31.8	35.5	38.5	40.6	44.2
Industrial Production	66	26.8	27.2	27.8	29.1	32.0	33.6	35.9	36.4	36.6	†39.9	40.7	42.8	46.8	51.1	54.5
															Number in Thousands:	
Labor Force	67d	....	....	....	....	....	....	....	....	....	....	....	....	....	....	....
Employment	67e	....	....	....	....	....	....	....	....	....	....	....	....	....	24,578	25,056
Unemployment	67c	....	....	....	....	....	....	....	....	....	....	....	....	....	24,861	28,261

1987	1988	1989	1990	1991	1992	1993	1994	1995	1996	1997	1998	1999	2000	2001		
End of Period															**Exchange Rates**	
18.268	20.117	22.387	25.712	36.953	36.025	43.102	45.810	52.295	51.666	52.999	59.813	59.690	60.911	60.549	Market Rate	aa
End of Period (ae)		*Period Average (rf)*													Market Rate	ae
12.877	14.949	17.035	18.073	25.834	26.200	31.380	31.380	35.180	35.930	39.280	42.480	43.490	46.750	48.180	Market Rate	ae
12.962	13.917	16.226	17.504	22.742	25.918	30.493	31.374	32.427	35.433	36.313	41.259	43.055	44.942	47.186	Market Rate	rf
End of Period															**Fund Position**	
2,208	2,208	2,208	2,208	2,208	3,056	3,056	3,056	3,056	3,056	3,056	3,056	4,158	4,158	4,158	Quota	2f. s
112	71	86	222	32	3	73	1	93	85	57	59	3	1	4	SDRs	1b. s
487	487	487	—	—	213	213	213	213	213	213	213	489	489	489	Reserve Position in the Fund	1c. s
3,175	2,282	1,440	804	2,426	3,260	3,585	2,763	1,967	1,085	590	285	39	—	—	Total Fund Cred.&Loans Outstg.	2tl
End of Period															**International Liquidity**	
6,454	4,899	3,859	1,521	3,627	5,757	10,199	19,698	17,922	20,170	24,688	27,341	32,667	37,902	45,870	Total Reserves minus Gold	1l. d
159	96	113	316	46	4	100	2	139	122	77	83	4	2	5	SDRs	1b. d
691	656	640	—	—	292	292	310	316	306	287	300	671	637	614	Reserve Position in the Fund	1c. d
5,603	4,148	3,105	1,205	3,580	5,461	9,807	19,386	17,467	19,742	24,324	26,958	31,992	37,264	45,251	Foreign Exchange	1d. d
10.449	10.449	10.449	10.692	11.282	11.348	11.457	11.800	12.780	12.781	12.740	11.487	11.502	11.502	11.502	Gold (Million Fine Troy Ounces)	1ad
213	183	161	3,667	3,168	2,908	3,325	3,355	3,669	3,614	2,880	2,492	2,403	2,252	2,329	Gold (National Valuation)	1an d
1,268	1,566	1,641	1,926	1,718	....	....	....	....	....		332	303	294	....	Other Banking Insts.: Liabilities	7f. d
Last Friday of Period															**Monetary Authorities**	
83.8	77.1	68.4	96.4	177.9	230.6	413.0	721.3	749.0	847.8	1,058.1	1,256.4	1,525.2	1,876.8	2,326.0	Foreign Assets	11
552.2	649.2	758.7	896.5	1,056.0	1,020.6	1,155.7	1,034.9	1,128.0	1,360.6	1,373.8	1,571.3	1,631.0	1,538.5	1,553.0	Claims on Central Government	12a
16.7	16.5	24.4	18.2	4.1	37.7	13.2	25.2	60.1	7.9	12.7	31.9	26.8	68.0	70.8	Claims on Deposit Money Banks	12e
65.4	76.4	86.4	91.6	97.8	105.4	103.8	120.7	125.2	124.0	134.9	146.2	158.6	210.4	194.9	Claims on Other Financial Insts	12f
516.0	599.9	712.1	809.7	961.1	1,042.2	1,268.0	1,543.8	1,737.8	1,903.2	2,116.1	2,378.7	2,649.3	2,854.2	3,145.1	Reserve Money	14
315.6	356.4	434.5	501.9	591.3	645.8	783.3	948.5	1,136.2	1,295.2	1,443.0	1,624.4	1,925.0	2,038.5	2,301.8	of which: Currency Outside DMBs	14a
52.2	41.6	29.8	20.6	89.7	117.5	154.5	126.6	102.8	56.1	31.3	17.0	2.3	—	—	Foreign Liabilities	16c
.6	1.6	.8	2.1	1.1	.6	.7	.7	.7	.6	.6	.6	1.4	1.4	1.4	Central Government Deposits	16d
51.2	57.0	63.8	135.3	148.7	148.1	152.9	154.8	159.2	158.8	166.8	167.4	164.3	161.7	157.5	Capital Accounts	17a
98.1	119.2	131.3	135.0	135.1	86.0	109.5	76.4	61.7	221.5	264.7	442.0	524.2	676.2	840.7	Other Items (Net)	17r
Last Friday of Period															**Deposit Money Banks**	
194.8	239.1	263.5	287.4	352.0	379.9	483.9	628.8	646.9	568.7	604.3	783.7	661.7	747.4	769.8	Reserves	20
308.4	366.1	422.3	508.0	617.1	761.2	922.1	1,223.3	1,291.1	1,545.9	1,896.4	2,237.7	2,768.1	3,333.8	4,082.5	Claims on Central Government	22a
918.5	1,085.2	1,311.6	1,435.5	1,577.6	1,880.0	2,087.7	2,429.9	2,713.9	3,264.2	3,640.0	4,196.4	5,054.7	6,064.3	6,626.1	Claims on Private Sector	22d
224.1	272.7	307.0	337.4	445.8	466.4	530.6	710.8	686.2	808.5	933.1	1,039.1	1,203.4	1,435.5	1,523.9	Demand Deposits	24
999.6	1,192.2	1,365.1	1,576.7	1,829.3	2,239.4	2,601.5	3,034.0	3,366.2	4,084.4	4,914.7	5,963.9	6,991.9	8,197.5	9,522.0	Time Deposits	25
16.5	16.5	25.7	18.1	4.0	37.4	16.2	77.6	138.4	18.1	7.7	63.1	25.5	66.9	69.9	Credit from Monetary Authorities	26g
181.4	209.1	299.6	298.6	267.7	277.9	345.3	459.7	461.1	467.8	285.2	152.3	263.6	445.6	362.6	Other Items (Net)	27r
Last Friday of Period															**Monetary Survey**	
31.6	35.5	38.6	75.9	88.3	113.2	258.4	594.8	646.2	791.7	1,026.8	1,239.3	1,522.9	1,876.8	2,326.0	Foreign Assets (Net)	31n
1,843.8	2,175.4	2,578.2	2,929.5	3,347.4	3,766.6	4,268.6	4,808.2	5,257.5	6,294.0	7,044.4	8,151.0	9,610.9	11,145.5	12,455.1	Domestic Credit	32
859.9	1,013.7	1,180.2	1,402.4	1,672.0	1,781.2	2,077.1	2,257.6	2,418.4	2,905.9	3,269.6	3,808.4	4,397.6	4,870.8	5,634.1	Claims on Central Govt. (Net)	32an
918.5	1,085.2	1,311.6	1,435.5	1,577.6	1,880.0	2,087.7	2,429.9	2,713.9	3,264.2	3,640.0	4,196.4	5,054.7	6,064.3	6,626.1	Claims on Private Sector	32d
65.4	76.4	86.4	91.6	97.8	105.4	103.8	120.7	125.2	124.0	134.9	146.2	158.6	210.4	194.9	Claims on Other Financial Insts	32f
543.2	632.8	746.9	853.6	1,046.1	1,120.9	1,330.2	1,695.0	1,883.5	2,148.9	2,419.3	2,703.5	3,161.2	3,495.9	3,850.9	Money	34
999.6	1,192.2	1,365.1	1,576.7	1,829.3	2,239.4	2,601.5	3,034.0	3,366.2	4,084.4	4,914.7	5,963.9	6,991.9	8,197.5	9,522.0	Quasi-Money	35
332.7	385.9	504.7	575.1	560.2	519.5	595.3	673.9	653.9	852.4	737.3	723.6	980.7	1,328.9	1,408.2	Other Items (Net)	37r
1,542.8	1,825.0	2,112.0	2,430.2	2,875.4	3,360.3	3,931.8	4,729.0	5,249.7	6,233.4	7,334.0	8,666.8	10,153.0	11,693.4	13,372.9	Money plus Quasi-Money	35l
End of Period															**Other Banking Institutions**	
186.09	228.99	....	....	....	....	....	....	....	....	....	....	....	....	....	Claims on Private Sector	42d
107.16	127.26	....	....	....	....	....	....	....	....	....	....	....	....	....	Bonds	46ab
16.33	23.41	27.95	34.80	44.39							14.11	13.17	13.76	....	Long-Term Foreign Liabilities	46cl
5.28	5.11	....	....	....										....	Central Govt. Lending Funds	46f
19.08	23.91	....	....	....										....	Capital Accounts	47a
38.25	49.15	....	....	....										....	Other Items (Net)	47r
32.63	34.02	37.36	39.92	42.45											Post Office: Savings Deposits	45.. i
Year Beginning April 1															**Nonbank Financial Institutions**	
....	....	....	....												Claims on Central Government	42a. s
....	....	....	....												Claims on Local Government	42b. s
....	....	....	....												Claims on Private Sector	42d. s
....	....	....	....												Incr.in Total Assets(Within Per.)	49z. s
1,564.04	1,844.95	2,133.28	2,452.97	2,898.59											Liquid Liabilities	55l
Percent Per Annum															**Interest Rates**	
10.00	10.00	10.00	10.00	12.00	12.00	12.00	12.00	12.00	12.00	9.00	9.00	8.00	8.00	6.50	Bank Rate (End of Period)	60
9.83	9.73	11.39	15.57	19.35	15.23	8.64	7.14	15.57	11.04	5.29	....	12.54	12.29	12.08	Money Market Rate	60b
16.50	16.50	16.50	16.50	17.88	18.92	16.25	14.75	15.46	15.96	13.83	13.54				Lending Rate	60p
....	....	....	....	....	....	....	....	....	....	....	....	....	....	....	Government Bond Yield	61
Period Averages															**Prices, Production, Labor**	
17.2	17.7	26.7	37.0	49.9	91.6	75.1	119.3	100.0	91.3	84.5	76.8	....	....	127.5	Share Prices	62
47.9	52.1	55.6	60.6	68.8	77.0	82.7	91.5	†100.0	104.5	109.2	115.6	119.6	127.5	133.6	Wholesale Prices	63
48.0	†52.6	55.8	60.8	69.2	77.4	82.3	90.7	100.0	109.0	116.8	132.2	138.4	144.0	149.3	Consumer Prices	64
60.6	65.0	68.6	76.2	77.4	79.6	81.1	88.7	†100.0	108.6	114.5	118.4	127.3	136.8	139.7	Industrial Production	66
Period Averages																
....	....	....	....	302,204								....	....	....	Labor Force	67d
25,388	25,712	25,962	26,353	26,733	27,056	27,177	27,375	27,987	27,941	28,245	28,166	....	....	....	Employment	67e
30,542	†30,050	32,776	34,632	36,300	†36,758	36,276	36,692	36,742	37,430	39,140	40,090	40,371	....	....	Unemployment	67c

India

		1972	1973	1974	1975	1976	1977	1978	1979	1980	1981	1982	1983	1984	1985	1986
International Transactions															*Billions of Rupees*	
Exports	70	19	23	32	36	50	56	55	63	68	72	88	92	107	113	119
Imports, c.i.f.	71	17	25	42	53	51	58	64	80	117	133	140	142	173	197	195
																1995=100
Unit Value of Exports	74	†10	11	13	16	17	18	21	21	22	23	26	27	31	35	35
Unit Value of Imports	75	†9	10	14	24	28	27	25	28	32	37	38	39	36	46	46
Balance of Payments															*Millions of US Dollars:*	
Current Account, n.i.e.	78al d	...	...	...	−148	1,571	2,108	683	48	−1,785	−2,698	−2,524	−1,953	−2,343	−4,177	−4,598
Goods: Exports f.o.b.	78aa d	...	...	...	4,666	5,410	6,249	6,518	7,597	8,303	8,437	9,226	9,770	10,192	9,465	10,248
Goods: Imports f.o.b.	78ab d	...	...	...	−4,952	−4,623	−5,317	−7,402	−9,819	−13,947	−14,149	−14,046	−13,868	−14,216	−15,081	−15,686
Trade Balance	78ac d	...	...	...	−286	787	932	−884	−2,222	−5,644	−5,711	−4,820	−4,098	−4,025	−5,616	−5,438
Services: Credit	78ad d	...	...	...	841	1,056	1,316	1,607	2,083	2,971	2,797	2,933	3,290	3,232	3,384	3,228
Services: Debit	78ae d	...	...	...	−1,054	−1,140	−1,286	−1,555	−2,120	−2,981	−3,249	−3,471	−3,705	−3,641	−3,903	−3,945
Balance on Goods & Services	78af d	...	...	...	−500	703	962	−832	−2,258	−5,654	−6,163	−5,359	−4,513	−4,434	−6,135	−6,156
Income: Credit	78ag d	...	...	...	130	195	275	390	749	1,058	972	608	480	487	528	518
Income: Debit	78ah d	...	...	...	−388	−355	−425	−492	−485	−523	−513	−690	−982	−1,166	−1,347	−1,581
Balance on Gds, Serv. & Inc.	78ai d	...	...	...	−758	543	813	−935	−1,995	−5,119	−5,704	−5,441	−5,014	−5,113	−6,953	−7,219
Current Transfers, n.i.e.: Credit	78aj d	...	...	...	636	1,043	1,306	1,637	2,065	3,347	3,026	2,939	3,075	2,789	2,799	2,638
Current Transfers: Debit	78ak d	...	...	...	−26	−16	−11	−20	−23	−14	−21	−22	−13	−19	−23	−17
Capital Account, n.i.e.	78bc d	...	...	...	—	—	—	—	—	—	—	—	—	—	—	—
Capital Account, n.i.e.: Credit	78ba d	...	...	...	—	—	—	—	—	—	—	—	—	—	—	—
Capital Account: Debit	78bb d	...	...	...	—	—	—	—	—	—	—	—	—	—	—	—
Financial Account, n.i.e.	78bj d	...	...	...	944	930	430	806	483	483	845	456	2,051	3,044	3,281	3,992
Direct Investment Abroad	78bd d	...	...	...	—	—	—	—	—	—	—	—	—	—	—	—
Dir. Invest. in Rep. Econ., n.i.e.	78be d	...	...	...	−10	−8	—	—	—	—	—	—	—	—	—	—
Portfolio Investment Assets	78bf d	...	...	...	—	—	—	—	—	—	—	—	—	—	—	—
Equity Securities	78bk d	...	...	...	—	—	—	—	—	—	—	—	—	—	—	—
Debt Securities	78bl d	...	...	...	—	—	—	—	—	—	—	—	—	—	—	—
Portfolio Investment Liab., n.i.e.	78bg d	...	...	...	—	—	—	—	—	—	—	—	—	—	—	—
Equity Securities	78bm d	...	...	...	—	—	—	—	—	—	—	—	—	—	—	—
Debt Securities	78bn d	...	...	...	—	—	—	—	—	—	—	—	—	—	—	—
Financial Derivatives Assets	78bw d	...	...	...	...	...	...	...	...	...	...	...	...	...	...	...
Financial Derivatives Liabilities	78bx d	...	...	...	...	...	...	...	...	...	...	...	...	...	...	...
Other Investment Assets	78bh d	...	...	...	3	−51	−210	95	−19	−318	−47	−691	541	−254	53	−250
Monetary Authorities	78bo d	...	...	...	...	...	...	...	...	...	...	...	...	...	...	...
General Government	78bp d	...	...	...	19	−91	−138	1	29	42	−104	−591	496	−156	2	−213
Banks	78bq d	...	...	...	−20	35	−72	102	−20	−342	61	−93	51	−89	52	−37
Other Sectors	78br d	...	...	...	4	5	1	−7	−28	−18	−4	−7	−5	−9	−2	...
Other Investment Liab., n.i.e.	78bi d	...	...	...	952	989	640	711	502	802	893	1,147	1,510	3,298	3,228	4,242
Monetary Authorities	78bs d	...	...	...	−8	−92	223	−55	89	−23	−68	−82	−54	308	−149	−217
General Government	78bt d	...	...	...	997	1,068	264	662	416	627	781	995	930	1,911	1,839	2,674
Banks	78bu d	...	...	...	18	43	96	58	13	135	68	92	5	188	19	−51
Other Sectors	78bv d	...	...	...	−56	−31	57	46	−15	62	111	142	629	890	1,519	1,836
Net Errors and Omissions	78ca d	...	...	...	−439	−291	−456	431	301	−361	−325	369	−850	368	500	197
Overall Balance	78cb d	...	...	...	357	2,210	2,081	1,920	832	−1,663	−2,178	−1,698	−752	1,070	−397	−409
Reserves and Related Items	79da d	...	...	...	−357	−2,210	−2,081	−1,920	−832	1,663	2,178	1,698	752	−1,070	397	409
Reserve Assets	79db d	...	...	...	−597	−1,881	−2,090	−1,772	−835	624	1,824	43	−840	−1,595	538	891
Use of Fund Credit and Loans	79dc d	...	...	...	239	−337	−330	−158	—	1,039	354	1,656	1,576	494	−177	−512
Exceptional Financing	79de d	...	...	...	—	8	338	9	3	—	—	—	16	31	37	30
Government Finance															*Billions of Rupees:*	
Deficit (-) or Surplus	80	−21.8	−17.0	†−23.6	−32.0	−36.9	−37.9	−50.8	−63.0	−88.6	−87.3	−107.3	−133.3	−175.8	−222.5	−272.0
Revenue	81	45.7	49.7	†75.3	91.7	102.6	113.5	129.6	144.0	161.1	195.9	225.1	255.2	296.1	361.2	420.7
Grants Received	81z	...	...	†1.0	2.8	2.7	3.2	2.7	3.9	4.4	3.8	4.0	3.3	4.8	4.9	4.4
Expenditure	82	55.2	58.1	†77.0	93.3	104.1	114.8	133.5	159.0	180.3	208.4	244.2	287.2	351.3	430.7	518.1
Lending Minus Repayments	83	12.3	8.6	†22.9	33.3	38.1	39.9	49.6	51.8	73.9	78.7	92.1	104.6	125.3	157.9	178.9
Financing																
Net Borrowing: Domestic	84a	...	...	†17.6	22.0	20.9	58.3	21.2	60.0	83.4	73.5	133.0	85.5	161.5	208.9	258.5
Rupees	84b	19.4	−3.3	...	...	...	...	...	...	...	...	...	...	...	...	...
Foreign	85a	...	...	†6.5	14.7	11.2	3.8	4.5	5.0	7.0	9.2	11.9	12.9	13.8	13.7	19.4
Foreign Currency	85b	2.9	4.7	...	...	...	...	...	...	...	...	...	...	...	...	...
Finance from Foreign Aid	86a	.3	16.7	...	...	...	...	...	...	...	...	...	...	...	...	...
Use of Cash Balances	87	−.9	−1.1	†−.6	−4.8	4.7	−24.2	25.2	−2.1	−1.8	4.7	−37.6	34.9	.5	—	−6.0
Debt: Domestic	88a	...	...	†174.0	201.3	221.6	281.1	305.8	367.8	453.4	527.7	673.6	746.8	887.8	1,083.6	1,315.4
Rupees	88b	168.2	184.0	...	...	...	...	...	...	...	...	...	...	...	...	...
Foreign	89a	...	...	†64.2	76.0	86.1	89.9	93.8	99.6	107.6	117.9	131.4	145.8	161.0	181.5	203.0
Foreign Currency	89b	71.2	58.7	...	...	...	...	...	...	...	...	...	...	...	...	...
National Accounts															*Billions of Rupees:*	
Househ.Cons.Expend.,incl.NPISHs	96f	386.9	434.3	565.1	578.2	600.8	691.8	752.4	817.0	992.9	1,137.7	1,251.7	1,459.7	1,614.6	1,768.5	1,986.0
Government Consumption Expend.	91f	47.3	51.6	62.4	73.0	82.3	87.6	97.2	111.7	130.8	153.6	182.7	211.4	243.5	291.7	346.3
Gross Fixed Capital Formation	93e	81.3	90.7	110.0	133.3	153.0	172.2	188.8	213.1	262.8	314.6	357.7	399.9	455.7	542.6	620.5
Changes in Inventories	93i	5.9	22.6	34.7	30.8	24.7	18.0	41.1	48.4	21.8	85.6	50.2	38.0	34.4	91.9	58.5
Exports of Goods and Services	90c	21.5	26.6	36.9	49.5	61.3	64.0	71.2	83.4	90.3	102.6	115.6	131.4	158.5	149.5	165.4
Imports of Goods and Services (-)	98c	20.5	31.8	47.8	56.6	56.1	65.2	74.2	100.9	136.0	148.1	157.4	176.8	194.8	217.5	223.6
Gross Domestic Product (GDP)	99b	510.1	620.1	732.4	787.6	848.9	960.7	1,041.9	1,143.6	1,360.1	1,597.6	1,781.3	2,075.9	2,313.4	2,622.4	2,929.5
Net Primary Income from Abroad	98.n	−3.1	−3.0	−2.5	−2.6	−2.3	−2.4	−1.6	1.5	3.5	.4	−6.3	−9.4	−14.2	−14.3	−18.1
Gross National Income (GNI)	99a	507.0	616.8	729.4	785.1	846.6	958.3	1,040.3	1,145.1	1,363.6	1,598.0	1,775.0	2,066.5	2,299.2	2,608.1	2,911.4
Gross Nat'l Disposable Inc.(GNDI)	99i	...	...	...	...	...	...	...	...	...	...	...	...	...	...	...
Gross Saving	99s	...	...	...	...	...	...	...	...	...	...	...	...	...	...	...
Consumption of Fixed Capital	99cf	37.9	43.9	55.5	64.2	69.0	74.5	84.7	102.8	120.9	144.6	168.9	192.3	220.9	262.4	298.2
GDP at Factor Cost	99ba	...	...	...	...	...	...	...	...	...	...	...	...	...	...	...
GDP Vol.,Fact.Cost,93/94 Prices	99ba p	...	...	...	...	...	...	...	...	...	...	...	...	...	...	...
GDP Volume 1980 Prices	99b. p	1,025.7	1,056.0	1,068.5	1,166.8	1,187.5	1,272.9	1,346.4	1,275.7	1,360.1	1,449.0	1,503.8	1,615.5	1,674.9	1,766.5	1,852.5
GDP Volume 1993/94 Prices	99b. p	...	...	...	...	...	...	...	...	...	...	...	...	...	...	...
GDP Volume (1995=100)	99bv p	33.3	34.3	34.7	37.9	38.6	41.3	43.7	41.4	44.2	47.0	48.8	52.5	54.4	57.4	60.1
GDP Deflator (1995=100)	99bi p	12.9	15.2	17.8	17.5	18.5	19.6	20.1	23.2	25.9	28.6	30.7	33.3	35.8	38.5	41.0
																Millions:
Population	99z	563.53	575.89	588.30	600.76	613.27	625.82	†646.00	660.00	675.00	690.00	705.00	720.00	736.00	750.86	767.20

		1987	1988	1989	1990	1991	1992	1993	1994	1995	1996	1997	1998	1999	2000	2001
International Transactions		*Billions of Rupees*														
Exports	70	146	184	258	314	401	509	657	785	995	1,172	1,271	1,379	1,536	1,907	2,057
Imports, c.i.f.	71	216	266	334	414	459	611	694	842	1,127	1,344	1,505	1,772	2,024	2,306	2,341
		1995=100														
Unit Value of Exports	74	37	48	57	61	76	87	98	102	100	104	122	126	125	129	....
Unit Value of Imports	75	40	53	65	76	88	95	93	93	100	114	115	116	128	139	....
Balance of Payments		*Minus Sign Indicates Debit*														
Current Account, n.i.e.	78al*d*	-5,192	-7,172	-6,826	-7,037	-4,292	-4,485	-1,876	-1,676	-5,563	-5,956	-2,965	-6,903	-3,228	-4,198	....
Goods: Exports f.o.b.	78aa*d*	11,884	13,510	16,144	18,286	18,095	20,019	22,016	25,523	31,239	33,737	35,702	34,076	36,877	43,132	....
Goods: Imports f.o.b.	78ab*d*	-17,661	-20,091	-22,254	-23,437	-21,087	-22,931	-24,108	-29,673	-37,957	-43,789	-45,730	-44,828	-45,556	-55,325	....
Trade Balance	78ac*d*	-5,777	-6,581	-6,110	-5,151	-2,992	-2,911	-2,093	-4,150	-6,719	-10,052	-10,028	-10,752	-8,679	-12,193	....
Services: Credit	78ad*d*	3,363	3,791	4,140	4,625	4,925	4,934	5,107	6,038	6,775	7,238	9,111	11,691	14,509	18,331	....
Services: Debit	78ae*d*	-4,629	-5,321	-5,874	-6,090	-5,945	-6,735	-6,497	-8,200	-10,268	-11,171	-12,443	-14,540	-17,271	-19,913	....
Balance on Goods & Services	78af*d*	-7,043	-8,112	-7,844	-6,616	-4,012	-4,712	-3,482	-6,312	-10,212	-13,984	-13,360	-13,601	-11,441	-13,775	....
Income: Credit	78ag*d*	450	427	446	436	232	377	375	821	1,486	1,411	1,484	1,806	1,919	2,280	....
Income: Debit	78ah*d*	-1,605	-2,211	-2,498	-3,693	-4,235	-4,289	-4,121	-4,370	-5,219	-4,667	-5,002	-5,443	-5,629	-6,156	....
Balance on Gds, Serv. & Inc.	78ai*d*	-8,198	-9,895	-9,896	-9,873	-8,015	-8,624	-7,228	-9,861	-13,945	-17,240	-16,878	-17,238	-15,151	-17,651	....
Current Transfers, n.i.e.: Credit	78aj*d*	3,034	2,739	3,093	2,853	3,736	4,157	5,375	8,208	8,410	11,350	13,975	10,402	11,958	13,504	....
Current Transfers: Debit	78ak*d*	-28	-16	-23	-17	-13	-18	-23	-23	-27	-66	-62	-67	-35	-51	....
Capital Account, n.i.e.	78bc*d*	—	—	—	—	....	....	....	....	....	....	—	—	....	....	....
Capital Account, n.i.e.: Credit	78ba*d*	—	—	—	—	....	....	....	....	....	....	—	—	....	....	....
Capital Account: Debit	78bb*d*	—	—	—	—	....	....	....	....	....	....	—	—	....	....	....
Financial Account, n.i.e.	78bj*d*	5,734	7,175	7,212	5,528	3,450	4,075	7,074	10,576	3,861	11,848	9,635	8,584	9,579	9,616	....
Direct Investment Abroad	78bd*d*	—	—	—	—	....	....	—	-83	-117	-239	-113	-48	-79	-335	....
Dir. Invest. in Rep. Econ., n.i.e.	78be*d*	—	—	—	—	74	277	550	973	2,144	2,426	3,577	2,635	2,169	2,315	....
Portfolio Investment Assets	78bf*d*	—	—	—	—	....	....	....	....	....	....	—	—	....	....	....
Equity Securities	78bk*d*	—	—	—	—	....	....	....	....	....	....	—	—	....	....	....
Debt Securities	78bl*d*	—	—	—	—	....	....	....	....	....	....	—	—	....	....	....
Portfolio Investment Liab., n.i.e.	78bg*d*	—	—	—	—	5	284	1,369	5,491	1,590	3,958	2,556	-601	2,317	1,619	....
Equity Securities	78bm*d*	—	—	—	—	5	284	1,369	5,491	1,590	3,958	2,556	-601	2,317	1,619	....
Debt Securities	78bn*d*	—	—	—	—	....	....	....	....	....	....	—	—	....	....	....
Financial Derivatives Assets	78bw*d*	....	....	....	....	....	....	....	....	....	....	—	—	....	....	....
Financial Derivatives Liabilities	78bx*d*	....	....	....	....	....	....	....	....	....	....	—	—	....	....	....
Other Investment Assets	78bh*d*	125	276	114	-611	-808	929	1,830	1,170	-1,179	-4,710	-4,743	-3,239	-450	-1,136	....
Monetary Authorities	78bo*d*	....	....	....	....	....	1	3	1	....	....	—	—	-498	-473	....
General Government	78bp*d*	90	43	-186	-868	183	-791	309	9	-29	-5	67	11	33	-15	....
Banks	78bq*d*	31	240	310	333	-1,003	1,732	-148	-1,029	-92	-1,642	-2,156	-1,355	1,140	-1,688	....
Other Sectors	78br*d*	3	-6	-10	-76	12	-13	1,667	2,189	-1,058	-3,063	-2,653	-1,896	-1,126	1,041	....
Other Investment Liab., n.i.e.	78bi*d*	5,609	6,899	7,099	6,139	4,180	2,587	3,325	3,024	1,423	10,413	8,357	9,837	5,623	7,152	....
Monetary Authorities	78bs*d*	1,163	1,296	1,344	1,867	-297	407	81	142	-65	45	233	122	1,344	272	....
General Government	78bt*d*	2,955	3,877	3,605	2,999	1,319	-1,345	141	92	1,483	1,698	397	-72	237	-416	....
Banks	78bu*d*	-76	-297	-281	-450	69	1,947	2,045	1,307	266	2,989	1,098	1,739	2,458	1,396	....
Other Sectors	78bv*d*	1,566	2,023	2,431	1,723	3,090	1,578	1,058	1,483	-261	5,680	6,629	8,047	1,584	5,900	....
Net Errors and Omissions	78ca*d*	-409	-18	-150	-432	607	1,482	-987	1,492	970	-1,934	-1,348	1,390	313	670	....
Overall Balance	78cb*d*	133	-16	237	-1,941	-235	1,072	4,211	10,391	-733	3,958	5,321	3,071	6,664	6,087	....
Reserves and Related Items	79da*d*	-133	16	-237	1,941	235	-1,072	-4,211	-10,391	733	-3,958	-5,321	-3,071	-6,664	-6,087	....
Reserve Assets	79db*d*	800	1,184	836	2,798	-2,040	-2,253	-4,663	-9,238	1,956	-2,676	-4,637	-2,659	-6,327	-6,035	....
Use of Fund Credit and Loans	79dc*d*	-954	-1,197	-1,086	-858	2,275	1,181	451	-1,153	-1,223	-1,282	-684	-412	-337	-52	....
Exceptional Financing	79de*d*	21	29	13	1	....	....	....	....	....	....	—	—	....	....	....
Government Finance		*Year Beginning April 1*														
Deficit (-) or Surplus	80	-278.8	-320.6	-361.8	-434.6	-358.2	-399.0	-605.3	-567.5	-598.5	-668.8	-741.8	-917.2	-1,113.8[p]	-1,118.3[f]	....
Revenue	81	480.8	557.4	675.4	723.6	892.1	1,004.6	1,011.7	1,283.2	1,488.8	1,717.1	1,864.5	2,015.3	2,336.4[p]	2,825.1[f]	....
Grants Received	81z	4.9	6.0	7.5	5.9	9.5	9.2	9.9	10.4	11.4	11.9	10.2	9.9	8.5[p]	7.3[f]	....
Expenditure	82	597.1	694.9	818.3	924.6	1,050.5	1,189.3	1,363.7	1,540.6	1,763.1	2,010.6	2,305.8	2,610.5	3,069.6[p]	3,547.2[f]	....
Lending Minus Repayments	83	167.4	189.0	226.4	239.5	209.3	223.5	263.2	320.5	335.6	387.2	310.7	331.9	389.1[p]	403.5[f]	....
Financing																
Net Borrowing: Domestic	84a	244.4	302.0	335.8	407.0	304.4	340.5	564.7	519.4	611.9	634.3	740.1	900.4	1,070.0[p]	1,118.7[f]	....
Rupees	84b	....	....	....	....	....	....	....	....	....	....	....	....	....	....	....
Foreign	85a	32.7	24.6	26.0	31.8	54.2	53.2	50.7	35.8	3.2	29.9	10.9	19.2	9.1[p]	-.4[f]	....
Foreign Currency	85b	....	....	....	....	....	....	....	....	....	....	....	....	....	....	....
Finance from Foreign Aid	86a	....	....	....	....	....	....	....	....	....	....	....	....	....	....	....
Use of Cash Balances	87	1.6	-6.0	—	-4.2	-.3	5.4	-10.2	12.3	-16.6	4.6	-9.1	-2.4	34.7[p]	—[f]	....
Debt: Domestic	88a	1,532.9	1,830.4	2,202.6	2,610.4	2,942.5	3,359.0	4,060.7	4,586.9	5,213.0	5,835.2	7,229.6	8,345.5	9,731.4[p]	11,229.0[f]	....
Rupees	88b	....	....	....	....	....	....	....	....	....	....	....	....	....	....	....
Foreign	89a	232.2	257.5	283.4	315.3	369.5	422.7	473.5	509.3	512.5	542.4	553.3	572.5	576.0[p]	569.0[f]	....
Foreign Currency	89b	....	....	....	....	....	....	....	....	....	....	....	....	....	....	....
National Accounts		*Year Beginning April 1*														
Househ.Cons.Expend.,incl.NPISHs	96f	2,225.5	2,992.6	3,387.5	3,871.4	4,462.6	5,009.8	5,747.7	6,641.6	7,658.0	9,036.5	9,748.0	11,412.1	12,653.5	13,409.6	....
Government Consumption Expend.	91f	408.4	507.0	579.1	660.3	742.9	839.6	977.3	1,086.4	1,288.2	1,457.3	1,721.9	2,117.7	2,481.3	2,759.0	....
Gross Fixed Capital Formation	93e	721.9	856.7	1,088.8	1,304.0	1,438.6	1,679.7	1,842.9	2,222.4	2,894.1	3,118.5	3,304.2	3,743.4	4,169.4	4,569.8	....
Changes in Inventories	93i	26.9	107.4	61.6	64.5	-6.0	100.5	-16.7	145.5	257.7	-139.9	132.9	-21.3	322.2	212.2	....
Exports of Goods and Services	90c	202.8	259.1	346.1	406.4	562.5	673.1	861.5	1,016.1	1,307.3	1,448.5	1,652.0	1,952.8	2,311.1		....
Imports of Goods and Services (-)	98c	252.6	320.1	402.1	487.0	562.5	730.0	860.0	1,047.1	1,449.5	1,610.2	1,843.3	2,247.4	2,560.1	....	....
Gross Domestic Product (GDP)	99b	3,332.0	4,235.0	4,861.8	5,686.7	6,531.2	7,483.7	8,592.2	10,127.7	11,880.1	13,682.1	15,225.5	17,409.4	19,296.4	20,879.9	....
Net Primary Income from Abroad	98.n	-26.2	-45.0	-57.3	-75.5	-100.8	-116.5	-120.8	-130.8	-134.8	-130.8	-132.1	-149.7	-154.3	-174.2	....
Gross National Income (GNI)	99a	3,305.8	4,190.0	4,804.5	5,611.3	6,430.4	7,367.2	8,471.4	9,996.9	11,745.3	13,551.3	15,092.4	17,433.1	19,142.1	20,705.7	....
Gross Nat'l Disposable Inc.(GNDI)	99i	3,340.8	3,959.0	4,842.5	5,648.4	6,524.2	7,479.5	8,636.5	10,251.0	11,966.4	13,990.9	15,530.0	17,865.5	19,675.5	21,292.9	....
Gross Saving	99s	696.3	879.1	1,069.8	1,313.4	1,439.1	1,629.1	1,936.2	2,514.6	2,987.5	3,172.6	3,521.8	3,772.7	4,471.9	4,883.3	....
Consumption of Fixed Capital	99cf	333.4	396.9	465.6	532.6	644.0	745.1	833.5	979.9	1,179.3	1,365.0	1,520.5	1,666.1	1,824.3	1,984.5	....
GDP at Factor Cost	99ba	....	3,804.2	4,380.2	5,109.5	5,890.9	6,732.2	7,813.5	9,170.6	10,732.7	12,435.5	13,901.5	15,980.8	17,556.4	18,958.4	....
GDP Vol.,Fact.Cost,93/94 Prices	99ba*p*	....	6,198.1	6,563.3	6,928.7	7,018.6	7,377.9	7,813.5	8,380.3	8,995.6	9,700.8	10,164.0	10,824.7	11,485.0	11,939.2	....
GDP Volume 1980 Prices	99b.*p*	1,940.9	2,133.5	....	....	....	....	....	....	....	....	....	....	....	....	....
GDP Volume 1993/94 Prices	99b.*p*	....	6,895.4	7,289.5	7,713.0	7,782.9	8,193.2	8,592.2	9,244.6	9,954.5	10,674.5	11,149.2	11,818.8	12,656.1	13,152.0	....
GDP Volume (1995=100)	99bv*p*	63.0	69.3	73.2	77.5	78.2	82.3	86.3	92.9	100.0	107.2	112.0	118.7	127.1	132.1	....
GDP Deflator (1995=100)	99bi*p*	44.5	51.5	55.9	61.8	70.3	76.5	83.8	91.8	100.0	107.4	114.4	123.4	127.8	133.0	....
		Midyear Estimates														
Population	99z	783.73	800.50	817.49	835.13	851.90	868.90	886.25	903.94	921.99	939.54	955.22	970.93	986.61	1,002.14	1,017.54

(See notes in the back of the book.)

Indonesia

		1972	1973	1974	1975	1976	1977	1978	1979	1980	1981	1982	1983	1984	1985	1986
Exchange Rates																*Rupiah per SDR:*
Market Rate	aa	450.6	500.6	508.1	485.8	482.2	504.1	814.2	826.0	799.4	749.6	763.9	1,040.7	1,052.7	1,235.7	2,007.3
														Rupiah per US Dollar:		
Market Rate	ae	415.0	415.0	415.0	415.0	415.0	415.0	625.0	627.0	626.8	644.0	692.5	994.0	1,074.0	1,125.0	1,641.0
Market Rate	rf	415.0	415.0	415.0	415.0	415.0	415.0	442.0	623.1	627.0	631.8	661.4	909.3	1,025.9	1,110.6	1,282.6
Fund Position																*Millions of SDRs:*
Quota	2f. s	260	260	260	260	260	260	480	480	720	720	720	1,010	1,010	1,010	1,010
SDRs	1b. s	36	43	56	6	4	22	57	129	137	227	282	4	1	51	36
Reserve Position in the Fund	1c. s	—	—	29	—	—	68	69	74	161	196	218	72	72	72	72
Total Fund Cred.&Loans Outstg.	2tl	107	19	—	—	—	—	—	—	—	—	—	425	421	42	42
International Liquidity												*Millions of US Dollars Unless Otherwise Indicated:*				
Total Reserves minus Gold	1l. d	572	805	1,490	584	1,497	2,509	2,626	4,062	5,392	5,014	3,144	3,718	4,773	4,974	4,051
SDRs	1b. d	39	52	68	7	5	26	75	170	175	264	311	4	1	56	43
Reserve Position in the Fund	1c. d	—	—	35	—	—	83	90	97	205	228	241	4	71	80	89
Foreign Exchange	1d. d	533	753	1,386	577	1,492	2,400	2,461	3,795	5,012	4,521	2,593	3,639	4,702	4,838	3,919
Gold (Million Fine Troy Ounces)	1ad	.121	.057	.057	.057	.057	.169	.224	.280	2.394	3.104	3.104	3.104	3.104	3.104	3.104
Gold (National Valuation)	1an d	5	2	2	2	2	7	37	105	1,108	1,062	1,052	1,096	947	906	1,360
Monetary Authorities: Other Liab.	4.. d	....	....	....	....	....	....	....	....	—	—	—	1	—	—	—
Deposit Money Banks: Assets	7a. d	....	....	....	....	....	....	....	....	4,364	5,059	3,776	4,547	4,777	5,546	4,993
Liabilities	7b. d	....	....	....	....	....	....	....	....	618	676	966	973	713	523	329
Monetary Authorities													*Billions of Rupiah:*			
Foreign Assets	11	....	....	....	....	....	....	....	....	4,217	4,037	3,685	5,309	8,041	8,507	8,352
Claims on Central Government	12a	....	....	....	....	....	....	....	....	716	925	1,154	1,521	1,670	1,237	3,106
Claims on Official Entities	12bx	....	....	....	....	....	....	....	....	2,370	2,467	2,453	1,864	203	32	24
Claims on Private Sector	12d	....	....	....	....	....	....	....	....	69	107	409	444	652	823	1,133
Claims on Deposit Money Banks	12e	....	....	....	....	....	....	....	....	1,722	2,548	5,050	5,866	9,521	10,041	12,552
Claims on Nonbank Financial Insts	12g	....	....	....	....	....	....	....	....	44	117	215	366	518	729	877
Reserve Money	14	....	....	....	....	....	....	....	....	3,375	3,920	4,107	5,138	5,701	6,721	8,170
of which: Currency Outside DMBs	14a	....	....	....	....	....	....	....	....	2,169	2,546	2,934	3,340	3,712	4,460	5,338
Time & Foreign Currency Deposits	15	....	....	....	....	....	....	....	....	41	104	57	110	25	69	42
Liabs. of Central Bank: Securities	16ac	....	....	....	....	....	....	....	....	....	....	....	....	....	....	....
Restricted Deposits	16b	....	....	....	....	....	....	....	....	119	134	46	74	33	23	24
Foreign Liabilities	16c	....	....	....	....	....	....	....	....	30	27	23	471	467	74	111
Central Government Deposits	16d	....	....	....	....	....	....	....	....	2,755	4,770	5,796	5,946	8,745	8,970	10,643
Capital Accounts	17a	....	....	....	....	....	....	....	....	1,182	1,040	601	596	1,179	1,192	2,409
Other Items (Net)	17r	....	....	....	....	....	....	....	....	1,636	206	2,336	3,034	4,455	4,320	4,643
Deposit Money Banks													*Billions of Rupiah:*			
Reserves	20	....	....	....	....	....	....	....	....	1,262	1,430	1,988	1,815	2,273	2,940	2,935
Claims on Mon.Author.: Securities	20c	....	....	....	....	....	....	....	....	....	....	....	....	....	....	....
Foreign Assets	21	....	....	....	....	....	....	....	....	2,741	3,233	2,591	4,520	5,107	6,239	8,193
Claims on Central Government	22a	....	....	....	....	....	....	....	....	28	69	139	266	440	530	683
Claims on Prov. and Local Govts	22b	....	....	....	....	....	....	....	....	....	....	....	....	....	....	....
Claims on Official Entities	22bx	....	....	....	....	....	....	....	....	1,359	1,791	2,427	2,819	4,515	4,981	5,080
Claims on Nonfin.Pub.Enterprises	22c	....	....	....	....	....	....	....	....	....	....	....	....	....	....	....
Claims on Private Sector	22d	....	....	....	....	....	....	....	....	4,254	5,942	8,106	10,490	14,086	17,281	21,731
Claims on Other Banking Insts	22f	....	....	....	....	....	....	....	....	....	....	....	....	....	....	....
Claims on Nonbank Financial Insts	22g	....	....	....	....	....	....	....	....	19	26	20	25	37	41	25
Demand Deposits	24	....	....	....	....	....	....	....	....	2,795	3,847	4,133	4,177	4,817	5,560	6,082
Time, Savings,& Fgn. Currency Dep.	25	....	....	....	....	....	....	....	....	2,654	3,127	3,897	6,983	9,331	12,985	15,942
Money Market Instruments	26aa	....	....	....	....	....	....	....	....	....	....	....	....	....	....	....
Restricted Deposits	26b	....	....	....	....	....	....	....	....	366	298	300	242	218	268	402
Foreign Liabilities	26c	....	....	....	....	....	....	....	....	388	432	663	968	762	588	541
Central Government Deposits	26d	....	....	....	....	....	....	....	....	735	914	691	779	1,397	1,884	1,687
Central Govt. Lending Funds	26f	....	....	....	....	....	....	....	....	....	....	....	....	....	....	....
Credit from Monetary Authorities	26g	....	....	....	....	....	....	....	....	1,636	2,596	3,890	4,264	7,045	7,039	7,747
Liab. to Nonbank Financial Insts	26j	....	....	....	....	....	....	....	....	....	....	....	....	....	....	....
Capital Accounts	27a	....	....	....	....	....	....	....	....	803	1,014	1,268	1,630	2,211	2,541	3,049
Other Items (Net)	27r	....	....	....	....	....	....	....	....	285	262	427	893	677	1,146	3,197
Monetary Survey													*Billions of Rupiah:*			
Foreign Assets (Net)	31n	117	296	659	-345	525	1,061	1,844	3,483	6,540	6,811	5,590	8,391	11,919	14,083	15,892
Domestic Credit	32	†633	1,086	1,388	2,803	3,283	3,299	4,522	4,616	5,369	5,759	8,434	11,069	11,978	14,799	20,329
Claims on Central Govt. (Net)	32an	-12	-32	-151	18	-279	-613	-878	-1,711	-2,746	-4,691	-5,195	-4,938	-8,031	-9,087	-8,541
Claims on Prov. and Local Govts	32b	....	....	....	....	....	....	....	....	....	....	....	....	....	....	....
Claims on Official Entities	32bx	105	70	146	125	84	84	140	133	3,729	4,258	4,879	4,682	4,717	5,013	5,104
Claims on Nonfin.Pub.Enterprises	32c	....	....	....	....	....	....	....	....	....	....	....	....	....	....	....
Claims on Private Sector	32d	†540	1,048	1,394	2,660	3,477	3,828	5,260	6,194	4,323	6,049	8,515	10,934	14,737	18,104	22,864
Claims on Other Banking Insts	32f	....	....	....	....	....	....	....	....	....	....	....	....	....	....	....
Claims on Nonbank Financial Inst	32g	....	....	....	....	....	....	....	....	62	143	235	391	555	770	902
Money	34	471	669	940	1,250	1,601	2,006	2,488	3,379	5,011	6,474	7,120	7,576	8,581	10,124	11,631
Quasi-Money	35	190	319	515	747	1,019	1,125	1,320	1,837	2,696	3,231	3,954	7,093	9,356	13,054	15,984
Money Market Instruments	36aa	....	....	....	....	....	....	....	....	....	....	....	....	....	....	....
Restricted Deposits	36b	....	....	....	....	....	....	....	....	484	432	346	316	251	291	426
Central Govt. Lending Funds	36f	....	....	....	....	....	....	....	....	....	....	....	....	....	....	....
Liab. to Nonbank Financial Insts	36j	....	....	....	....	....	....	....	....	....	....	....	....	....	....	....
Capital Accounts	37a	....	....	....	....	....	....	....	....	....	....	....	....	....	....	....
Other Items (Net)	37r	90	394	592	460	1,188	1,228	2,557	2,883	3,717	2,433	2,604	4,475	5,709	5,414	8,180
Money plus Quasi-Money	35l	661	988	1,455	1,997	2,620	3,131	3,808	5,216	7,707	9,705	11,074	14,670	17,937	23,177	27,615

1987	1988	1989	1990	1991	1992	1993	1994	1995	1996	1997	1998	1999	2000	2001	Item	Code
															Exchange Rates	
End of Period																
2,340.8	2,329.4	2,361.5	2,704.5	2,849.4	2,835.3	2,898.2	3,211.7	3,430.8	3,426.7	6,274.0	11,299.4	9,724.2	12,501.4	13,070.0	Market Rate	aa
End of Period (ae) Period Average (rf)																
1,650.0	1,731.0	1,797.0	1,901.0	1,992.0	2,062.0	2,110.0	2,200.0	2,308.0	2,383.0	4,650.0	8,025.0	7,085.0	9,595.0	10,400.0	Market Rate	ae
1,643.8	1,685.7	1,770.1	1,842.8	1,950.3	2,029.9	2,087.1	2,160.8	2,248.6	2,342.3	2,909.4	10,013.6	7,855.2	8,421.8	10,260.9	Market Rate	rf
															Fund Position	
End of Period																
1,010	1,010	1,010	1,010	1,010	1,498	1,498	1,498	1,498	1,498	1,498	1,498	2,079	2,079	2,079	Quota	2f. s
4	2	1	2	3	—	—	—	1	2	370	222	—	24	13	SDRs	1b. s
72	72	72	72	72	194	200	214	270	298	—	—	145	145	145	Reserve Position in the Fund	1c. s
505	463	463	347	116	—	—	—	—	—	2,201	6,456	7,467	8,318	7,252	Total Fund Cred.&Loans Outstg.	2tl
															International Liquidity	
End of Period																
5,592	5,048	5,454	7,459	9,258	10,449	11,263	12,133	13,708	18,251	16,587	22,713	26,445	28,502	27,246	Total Reserves minus Gold	1l. d
6	3	1	3	4	—	—	—	1	2	499	312	—	32	16	SDRs	1b. d
103	97	95	103	104	267	274	312	401	429	—	—	200	190	183	Reserve Position in the Fund	1c. d
5,483	4,948	5,357	7,353	9,151	10,181	10,988	11,820	13,306	17,820	16,088	22,401	26,245	28,280	27,048	Foreign Exchange	1d. d
3.104	3.104	3.107	3.111	3.111	3.101	3.101	3.101	3.101	3.101	3.101	3.101	3.101	3.101	3.101	Gold (Million Fine Troy Ounces)	1ad
1,319	1,158	1,044	1,061	992	946	1,092	1,067	1,079	1,030	809	803	812	766	772	Gold (National Valuation)	1and
—	—	—	28	24	26	22	20	21	21	419	3,356	3,517	2,142	2,078	Monetary Authorities: Other Liab.	4..d
4,731	4,815	5,985	6,223	5,589	6,337	5,374	5,852	7,407	8,737	10,067	14,412	16,967	10,649	10,555	Deposit Money Banks: Assets	7a. d
456	664	1,781	6,737	6,025	7,894	9,691	11,311	11,678	12,482	15,147	12,192	14,167	9,659	6,577	Liabilities	7b. d
															Monetary Authorities	
End of Period																
12,458	11,732	11,835	17,950	25,155	†32,795	37,643	36,444	40,163	59,886	94,202	179,439	183,866	286,157	289,561	Foreign Assets	11
3,518	4,427	4,589	5,221	6,258	†7,528	8,591	6,632	3,726	3,775	4,996	34,895	247,289	233,629	267,414	Claims on Central Government	12a
36	58	830	759	35	....	....	....	....	....	....	....	....	....	....	Claims on Official Entities	12bx
1,676	1,724	1,307	1,732	953	†—	—	—	—	—	—	—	—	—	—	Claims on Private Sector	12d
14,562	20,375	15,240	20,990	14,867	†11,054	10,885	13,607	16,456	15,182	67,313	—	—	—	—	Claims on Deposit Money Banks	12e
978	950	988	992	1,012	†6	—	—	—	—	—	41,294	23,117	23,126	23,126	Claims on Nonbank Financial Insts	12g
9,032	8,381	10,788	12,549	12,961	†16,997	18,414	23,053	27,160	36,896	51,014	81,448	102,043	132,254	129,240	Reserve Money	14
5,802	6,245	7,908	9,094	9,346	†11,465	14,430	18,634	20,807	22,487	28,424	41,394	58,353	72,371	76,342	of which: Currency Outside DMBs	14a
305	143	11	18	21	†—	—	—	—	—	—	—	—	—	126	Time & Foreign Currency Deposits	15
					20,595	23,339	15,051	11,851	18,553	14,885	49,590	63,049	60,076	55,742	Liabs. of Central Bank: Securities	16ac
24	25	26	26	24	†382	534	497	461	436	267	660	244	290	505	Restricted Deposits	16b
3,308	5,219	6,804	6,327	7,013	†54	46	43	49	50	15,761	99,879	97,526	124,541	116,390	Foreign Liabilities	16c
9,713	10,435	10,545	13,460	14,509	†11,206	13,016	13,536	15,558	16,856	33,472	35,438	83,990	72,266	65,900	Central Government Deposits	16d
3,715	3,624	3,825	3,587	4,594	†3,157	2,475	2,575	2,891	3,408	4,397	9,693	17,794	142,713	110,374	Capital Accounts	17a
7,132	11,438	2,789	11,678	9,158	†-1,008	-705	1,928	2,375	2,645	46,715	104,678	110,936	36,251	126,378	Other Items (Net)	17r
															Deposit Money Banks	
End of Period																
3,433	5,151	5,615	4,893	12,300	†4,112	4,591	5,051	7,371	14,896	24,172	48,090	59,290	66,536	74,802	Reserves	20
....	....	....	....	....	11,782	14,799	7,619	5,152	11,225	6,318	47,103	72,238	58,700	74,296	Claims on Mon.Author.: Securities	20c
7,807	8,397	10,731	11,661	11,076	†13,009	11,340	12,874	17,096	20,820	46,810	115,657	120,209	102,177	109,774	Foreign Assets	21
1,093	1,069	960	933	1,027	†3,541	4,004	2,843	4,165	5,727	8,571	10,230	274,551	433,266	415,980	Claims on Central Government	22a
....	....	....	....	....	1,032	256	113	276	290	292	319	214	376	446	Claims on Prov. and Local Govts	22b
....	....	....	....	....	....	....	....	....	....	....	....	....	....	....	Claims on Official Entities	22bx
4,782	6,292	7,730	6,950	9,671	....	....	....	....	....	....	....	....	....	....	Claims on Official Entities	22bx
....	....	....	....	....	6,000	6,492	6,866	8,423	9,248	11,036	15,128	11,854	10,343	10,748	Claims on Nonfin.Pub.Enterprises	22c
28,034	38,809	58,404	97,145	114,453	†128,521	161,273	198,311	243,067	295,195	381,741	508,558	225,236	270,303	298,901	Claims on Private Sector	22d
....	....	....	....	....	97	190	236	312	370	364	277	100	101	130	Claims on Other Banking Insts	22f
115	170	246	345	590	†1,934	1,276	2,329	2,785	4,897	6,353	5,763	1,998	2,554	4,025	Claims on Nonbank Financial Insts	22g
6,776	8,032	12,477	14,532	17,103	†14,206	19,057	22,710	26,202	28,883	40,232	45,717	55,327	78,102	93,146	Demand Deposits	24
20,895	27,538	37,956	60,793	72,696	†91,570	109,402	130,280	171,257	226,097	279,073	481,350	525,227	584,847	666,398	Time, Savings,& Fgn. Currency Dep.	25
....	....	....	....	....	1,730	2,435	2,437	4,162	3,353	4,306	3,223	2,986	2,253	1,847	Money Market Instruments	26aa
425	684	632	1,048	966	†1,370	1,699	1,541	1,779	2,099	1,419	2,417	1,659	4,783	7,966	Restricted Deposits	26b
752	1,159	3,193	12,645	11,935	†16,206	20,448	24,885	26,952	29,744	70,434	97,842	100,375	92,674	68,406	Foreign Liabilities	26c
1,779	2,227	3,943	4,719	5,487	†7,442	11,683	10,344	11,844	13,858	16,929	23,169	23,336	47,245	44,563	Central Government Deposits	26d
....	....	....	....	....	....	3,307	3,801	3,871	5,029	1,653	1,416	4,508	9,178	9,450	Central Govt. Lending Funds	26f
8,100	11,711	12,936	11,144	11,692	†10,554	16,237	11,432	10,394	11,622	23,008	112,947	33,360	16,547	15,225	Credit from Monetary Authorities	26g
....	....	....	....	....	10,974	1,153	1,326	1,564	2,533	7,536	39,332	14,725	14,690	2,845	Liab. to Nonbank Financial Insts	26j
3,650	4,464	7,376	11,255	9,075	†15,196	21,973	26,775	36,506	42,523	53,408	-94,556	-17,346	52,327	66,988	Capital Accounts	27a
2,888	4,072	5,171	5,811	20,161	†780	-3,173	711	-5,884	-3,073	-12,341	38,268	21,533	41,710	12,268	Other Items (Net)	27r
															Monetary Survey	
End of Period																
16,206	13,751	12,568	10,659	17,283	†29,544	28,489	24,390	30,258	50,912	54,817	97,374	106,174	171,119	214,539	Foreign Assets (Net)	31n
28,739	40,835	60,564	95,898	114,002	†130,030	157,396	193,458	235,356	288,788	362,952	557,857	677,033	854,727	911,252	Domestic Credit	32
-6,882	-7,167	-8,941	-12,024	-12,711	†-7,579	-12,104	-14,405	-19,511	-21,212	-36,834	-13,482	414,514	547,384	572,931	Claims on Central Govt. (Net)	32an
....	....	....	....	....	1,032	256	113	276	290	292	319	214	376	446	Claims on Prov. and Local Govts	32b
4,818	6,350	8,560	7,709	9,706	....	....	....	....	....	....	....	....	....	....	Claims on Official Entities	32bx
....	....	....	....	....	6,019	6,505	6,874	8,427	9,248	11,036	15,128	11,854	10,883	11,693	Claims on Nonfin.Pub.Enterprises	32c
29,710	40,532	59,711	98,877	115,406	†128,521	161,273	198,311	243,067	295,195	381,741	508,558	225,236	270,303	298,901	Claims on Private Sector	32d
....	....	....	....	....	97	190	236	312	370	364	277	100	101	130	Claims on Other Banking Insts	32f
1,093	1,120	1,234	1,337	1,601	†1,940	1,276	2,329	2,785	4,897	6,353	47,057	25,115	25,680	27,150	Claims on Nonbank Financial Inst	32g
12,705	14,392	20,559	23,819	26,693	†27,485	33,739	41,462	47,135	51,652	68,785	87,301	114,562	156,785	170,509	Money	34
21,200	27,681	37,967	60,811	72,717	†91,570	109,402	130,280	171,257	226,097	279,073	481,350	525,227	585,039	666,525	Quasi-Money	35
....	....	....	....	....	1,730	2,435	2,437	4,162	3,353	4,306	3,223	2,986	2,253	1,847	Money Market Instruments	36aa
449	709	658	1,074	990	†1,752	2,233	2,038	2,240	2,535	1,686	3,077	1,903	5,073	8,472	Restricted Deposits	36b
....	....	....	....	....	....	3,307	3,801	3,871	5,029	1,653	1,416	4,508	9,178	9,450	Central Govt. Lending Funds	36f
....	....	....	....	....	10,974	1,153	1,326	1,564	2,533	7,536	39,332	14,725	14,690	2,845	Liab. to Nonbank Financial Insts	36j
....	....	....	....	....	18,353	24,448	29,350	39,397	45,931	57,805	-84,863	448	195,040	177,362	Capital Accounts	37a
10,592	11,806	13,948	20,854	†30,885	†7,710	9,168	7,154	-4,012	2,571	-3,075	124,395	118,848	57,789	88,780	Other Items (Net)	37r
33,904	42,073	58,526	84,630	99,410	†119,055	143,141	171,742	218,392	277,749	347,858	568,651	639,789	741,824	837,034	Money plus Quasi-Money	35l

Indonesia

		1972	1973	1974	1975	1976	1977	1978	1979	1980	1981	1982	1983	1984	1985	1986
Other Banking Institutions																*Billions of Rupiah:*
Cash	40	1	2	6	8	10	16	22	30	42	61	75	101	130	74	63
Savings Deposits	45	1	2	3	5	8	13	17	20	36	46	54	75	98	134	220
Credit from Monetary Authorities	46g	1	1	—	3	5	6	6	11	44	122	222	389	523	734	882
Other Items (Net)	47r	−1	−1	3	—	−3	−3	—	−2	−38	−107	−200	−362	−492	−793	−1,038
Liquid Liabilities	55l	661	988	1,452	1,994	2,618	3,127	3,802	5,206	7,701	9,690	11,052	14,643	17,905	23,237	27,772
Interest Rates																*Percent Per Annum*
Discount Rate *(End of Period)*	60	....	....													
Money Market Rate	60b	....	....	11.42	13.41	14.17	7.23	7.29	13.23	12.87	16.26	17.24	13.17	18.63	10.33	....
Deposit Rate	60l	15.00	12.00	12.00	12.00	12.00	9.00	6.00	6.00	6.00	6.00	6.00	6.00	16.00	18.00	15.39
Lending Rate	60p	....	....	....	....	....	....	....	....	....	....	....	....	....	....	21.49
Prices, Production, Labor																*Index Numbers (1995=100):*
Wholesale Prices: Incl. Petroleum	63	5.0	6.9	10.3	10.9	12.5	14.3	†15.6	23.4	29.7	32.9	35.4	†41.7	46.3	48.6	49.7
Excl. Petroleum	63a	5.4	7.3	9.4	10.4	12.3	14.0	†15.4	20.6	24.4	26.8	29.1	34.8	39.4	†41.1	44.5
Consumer Prices	64	6.6	8.7	12.2	14.5	17.4	19.3	20.9	†24.3	28.6	32.2	35.2	39.4	43.5	45.5	48.2
Crude Petroleum Production	66aa	67.6	83.3	85.5	81.3	93.8	104.8	101.7	98.9	98.3	99.7	83.2	83.6	88.1	82.5	86.5
																Number in Thousands:
Labor Force	67d	....	....	....	....	....	....	....	....	....	....	....	....	....		
Employment	67e	....	....	....	....	....	....	....	....	....	....	....	....	....	62,457	68,338
Unemployment	67c	....	....	....	....	....	....	....	....	....	....	....	....	....	1,369	1,855
Unemployment Rate (%)	67r	....	....	....	....	....	....	....	....	....	....	....	....	....	2.1	2.6
International Transactions																*Millions of US Dollars*
Exports	70..d	1,777	3,211	7,426	7,102	8,547	10,853	11,643	15,591	21,909	25,165	22,328	21,146	21,888	18,587	14,805
Crude Petroleum & Products	70a.d	913	1,609	5,211	5,311	6,004	7,298	7,439	8,871	12,850	14,390	14,861	13,478	12,097	7,670	5,167
Crude Petroleum	70aad	834	1,359	4,680	4,933	5,652	6,827	7,015	8,124	11,671	13,183	14,002	11,646	10,214	7,217	4,721
Imports, c.i.f.	71..d	1,562	2,729	3,842	4,770	5,673	6,230	6,690	7,202	10,834	13,272	16,859	16,352	13,882	10,259	10,718
																1995=100
Volume of Exports	72	31.0	37.6	38.9	40.3	46.1	52.5	55.8	54.1	51.0	41.8	39.7	47.9	48.1	53.4	57.7
Crude Petroleum	72aa	100.8	123.9	127.6	128.4	146.5	167.2	171.0	148.5	122.2	127.4	104.5	122.6	115.0	85.2	100.1
Export Prices																*1995=100:*
Exports (Unit Value)	74..d	18.6	27.0	59.0	62.4	65.6	73.2	74.2	104.3	152.4	152.6	148.9	132.1	130.6	112.4	74.8
Crude Petroleum (Unit Value)	74aad	12.7	17.3	53.0	58.2	59.0	62.1	62.4	84.3	141.6	162.4	162.8	141.9	135.2	128.5	83.1
Crude Petroleum (Ofc.Price)	76aad	16.0	23.0	68.5	72.7	73.9	77.9	77.9	105.7	175.6	201.1	200.7	174.0	169.7	164.4	164.0
Balance of Payments																*Millions of US Dollars:*
Current Account, n.i.e.	78ald	....	....	....	....	....	....	....	....	....	−566	−5,324	−6,338	−1,856	−1,923	−3,911
Goods: Exports f.o.b.	78aad	....	....	....	....	....	....	....	....	....	23,348	19,747	18,689	20,754	18,527	14,396
Goods: Imports f.o.b.	78abd	....	....	....	....	....	....	....	....	....	−16,542	−17,854	−17,726	−15,047	−12,705	−11,938
Trade Balance	78acd	....	....	....	....	....	....	....	....	....	6,806	1,893	963	5,707	5,822	2,458
Services: Credit	78add	....	....	....	....	....	....	....	....	....	449	504	546	570	844	844
Services: Debit	78aed	....	....	....	....	....	....	....	....	....	−4,998	−4,862	−4,311	−4,239	−5,135	−4,256
Balance on Goods & Services	78afd	....	....	....	....	....	....	....	....	....	2,257	−2,465	−2,802	2,038	1,531	−954
Income: Credit	78agd	....	....	....	....	....	....	....	....	....	1,081	1,023	631	828	768	732
Income: Debit	78ahd	....	....	....	....	....	....	....	....	....	−4,154	−4,016	−4,281	−4,889	−4,310	−3,948
Balance on Gds, Serv. & Inc.	78aid	....	....	....	....	....	....	....	....	....	−816	−5,458	−6,452	−2,023	−2,011	−4,170
Current Transfers, n.i.e.: Credit	78ajd	....	....	....	....	....	....	....	....	....	250	134	114	167	88	259
Current Transfers: Debit	78akd	....	....	....	....	....	....	....	....	....						
Capital Account, n.i.e.	78bcd	....	....	....	....	....	....	....	....	....	—	—	—	—	—	—
Capital Account, n.i.e.: Credit	78bad	....	....	....	....	....	....	....	....	....	—	—	—	—	—	—
Capital Account: Debit	78bbd	....	....	....	....	....	....	....	....	....	—	—	—	—	—	—
Financial Account, n.i.e.	78bjd	....	....	....	....	....	....	....	....	....	1,861	5,622	6,054	3,457	1,782	4,177
Direct Investment Abroad	78bdd	....	....	....	....	....	....	....	....	....						
Dir. Invest. in Rep. Econ., n.i.e.	78bed	....	....	....	....	....	....	....	....	....	133	225	292	222	310	258
Portfolio Investment Assets	78bfd	....	....	....	....	....	....	....	....	....						
Equity Securities	78bkd	....	....	....	....	....	....	....	....	....	—	—	—	—	—	—
Debt Securities	78bld	....	....	....	....	....	....	....	....	....	—	—	—	—	—	—
Portfolio Investment Liab., n.i.e.	78bgd	....	....	....	....	....	....	....	....	....	47	315	368	−10	−35	268
Equity Securities	78bmd	....	....	....	....	....	....	....	....	....	—	—	—	—	—	—
Debt Securities	78bnd	....	....	....	....	....	....	....	....	....	47	315	368	−10	−35	268
Financial Derivatives Assets	78bwd	....	....	....	....	....	....	....	....	....	....	....		....	....	....
Financial Derivatives Liabilities	78bxd	....	....	....	....	....	....	....	....	....	....	....		....	....	....
Other Investment Assets	78bhd	....	....	....	....	....	....	....	....	....						
Monetary Authorities	78bod	....	....	....	....	....	....	....	....	....	—	—	—	—	—	—
General Government	78bpd	....	....	....	....	....	....	....	....	....	—	—	—	—	—	—
Banks	78bqd	....	....	....	....	....	....	....	....	....	—	—	—	—	—	—
Other Sectors	78brd	....	....	....	....	....	....	....	....	....	—	—	—	—	—	—
Other Investment Liab., n.i.e.	78bid	....	....	....	....	....	....	....	....	....	1,681	5,082	5,394	3,245	1,507	3,651
Monetary Authorities	78bsd	....	....	....	....	....	....	....	....	....						
General Government	78btd	....	....	....	....	....	....	....	....	....	1,666	3,668	3,860	2,918	1,747	2,618
Banks	78bud	....	....	....	....	....	....	....	....	....						
Other Sectors	78bvd	....	....	....	....	....	....	....	....	....	15	1,414	1,534	327	−240	1,033
Net Errors and Omissions	78cad	....	....	....	....	....	....	....	....	....	−1,669	−2,151	467	−620	651	−1,269
Overall Balance	78cbd	....	....	....	....	....	....	....	....	....	−374	−1,853	183	981	510	−1,003
Reserves and Related Items	79dad	....	....	....	....	....	....	....	....	....	374	1,853	−183	−981	−510	1,003
Reserve Assets	79dbd	....	....	....	....	....	....	....	....	....	374	1,853	−633	−977	−126	1,003
Use of Fund Credit and Loans	79dcd	....	....	....	....	....	....	....	....	....	—	—	450	−4	−385	—
Exceptional Financing	79ded	....	....	....	....	....	....	....	....	....	....	....		....	....	....

Other Banking Institutions — *End of Period*

1987	1988	1989	1990	1991	1992	1993	1994	1995	1996	1997	1998	1999	2000	2001		
72	76	65	162	99	....	....	....	....	....	....	....	....	....	....	Cash	40
348	492	289	740	919	....	....	....	....	....	....	....	....	....	....	Savings Deposits	45
1,157	951	1,827	1,412	1,338	....	....	....	....	....	....	....	....	....	....	Credit from Monetary Authorities	46g
−1,433	−1,368	−2,051	−1,990	−2,158	....	....	....	....	....	....	....	....	....	....	Other Items (Net)	47r
34,181	42,489	58,750	85,208	100,230	....	....	....	....	....	....	....	....	....	....	Liquid Liabilities	55l

Interest Rates — *Percent Per Annum*

1987	1988	1989	1990	1991	1992	1993	1994	1995	1996	1997	1998	1999	2000	2001		
....	....	....	18.83	18.47	13.50	8.82	12.44	13.99	12.80	20.00	38.44	12.51	14.53	17.62	Discount Rate (End of Period)	60
14.52	15.00	12.57	13.97	14.91	11.99	8.66	9.74	13.64	13.96	27.82	62.79	23.58	10.32	15.03	Money Market Rate	60b
16.78	17.72	18.63	†17.53	23.32	19.60	14.55	12.53	16.72	17.26	20.01	39.07	25.74	12.50	15.48	Deposit Rate	60l
21.67	22.10	21.70	20.83	25.53	24.03	20.59	17.76	18.85	19.22	21.82	32.15	27.66	18.46	18.55	Lending Rate	60p

Prices, Production, Labor — *Period Averages*

1987	1988	1989	1990	1991	1992	1993	1994	1995	1996	1997	1998	1999	2000	2001		
59.2	62.2	67.5	74.3	78.1	82.1	85.2	89.8	100.0	107.9	117.5	237.2	†262.0	294.7	336.4	Wholesale Prices: Incl. Petroleum	63
51.2	56.5	60.9	65.1	69.9	74.1	79.5	87.8	100.0	106.2	114.4	206.3	†243.3	257.2	301.2	Excl. Petroleum	63a
52.6	56.9	60.5	65.3	71.4	†76.8	84.2	91.4	100.0	†108.0	115.2	181.7	218.9	227.0	253.1	Consumer Prices	64
81.7	83.8	87.6	90.9	99.1	93.9	95.1	100.3	100.0	99.5	73.7	96.9	....	....	....	Crude Petroleum Production	66aa

Period Averages

1987	1988	1989	1990	1991	1992	1993	1994	1995	1996	1997	1998	1999	2000	2001		
....	....	....	....	....	....	....	....	....	88,187	89,603	94,735	95,793	....	....	Labor Force	67d
70,402	72,518	73,425	75,850	76,423	78,104	79,201	80,110	82,038	85,702	87,050	87,674	88,817	89,824	....	Employment	67e
1,843	2,106	2,083	1,952	2,032	2,199	2,246	3,738	....	3,625	4,197	5,063	6,030	5,872	....	Unemployment	67c
2.6	2.8	2.8	2.5	2.6	2.7	2.8	4.4	....	4.0	4.7	5.5	....	....	....	Unemployment Rate (%)	67r

International Transactions — *Millions of US Dollars*

1987	1988	1989	1990	1991	1992	1993	1994	1995	1996	1997	1998	1999	2000	2001		
17,136	19,219	22,160	25,675	29,142	33,967	36,823	40,055	45,417	49,814	53,443	48,847	48,665	62,124	....	Exports	70..d
5,919	....	4,964	6,481	5,745	5,850	5,009	6,006	6,441	7,243	6,822	4,264	....	....	....	Crude Petroleum & Products	70a.d
4,590	4,396	4,349	5,313	4,999	4,648	4,259	5,072	5,146	5,712	5,479	3,349	....	....	....	Crude Petroleum	70aa d
12,370	13,249	16,360	21,837	25,869	27,280	28,328	31,983	40,630	42,929	41,694	27,337	24,004	33,515	....	Imports, c.i.f.	71..d

1995=100

1987	1988	1989	1990	1991	1992	1993	1994	1995	1996	1997	1998	1999	2000	2001		
59.2	54.7	59.6	†58.6	....	82.9	86.9	95.7	100.0	105.1	135.0	125.5	....	....	....	Volume of Exports	72
98.0	78.4	82.1	81.4	86.7	84.4	71.0	107.4	100.0	94.0	95.8	90.4	....	....	....	Crude Petroleum	72aa

Indices of Unit Values in US Dollars — **Export Prices**

1987	1988	1989	1990	1991	1992	1993	1994	1995	1996	1997	1998	1999	2000	2001		
73.4	69.9	74.2	†90.3	91.0	90.3	88.3	87.6	100.0	105.8	100.5	78.4	....	....	....	Exports (Unit Value)	74..d
77.9	72.9	76.0	129.9	113.2	110.0	104.8	91.8	100.0	117.6	113.5	72.2	....	....	....	Crude Petroleum (Unit Value)	74aa d
106.2	88.8	88.0	127.7	108.8	108.8	100.3	92.3	100.0	116.9	109.4	70.9	101.1	164.0	137.9	Crude Petroleum (Ofc.Price)	76aa d

Balance of Payments — *Minus Sign Indicates Debit*

1987	1988	1989	1990	1991	1992	1993	1994	1995	1996	1997	1998	1999	2000	2001		
−2,098	−1,397	−1,108	−2,988	−4,260	−2,780	−2,106	−2,792	−6,431	−7,663	−4,889	4,096	5,785	7,985	....	Current Account, n.i.e.	78al d
17,206	19,509	22,974	26,807	29,635	33,796	36,607	40,223	47,454	50,188	56,298	50,371	51,242	65,406	....	Goods: Exports f.o.b.	78aa d
−12,532	−13,831	−16,310	−21,455	−24,834	−26,774	−28,376	−32,322	−40,921	−44,240	−46,223	−31,942	−30,598	−40,366	....	Goods: Imports f.o.b.	78ab d
4,674	5,678	6,664	5,352	4,801	7,022	8,231	7,901	6,533	5,948	10,075	18,429	20,644	25,040	....	*Trade Balance*	78ac d
1,065	1,369	1,875	2,488	2,822	3,391	3,959	4,797	5,469	6,599	6,941	4,479	4,599	5,213	....	Services: Credit	78ad d
−4,440	−4,606	−5,439	−6,056	−6,564	−8,100	−9,846	−11,416	−13,540	−15,139	−16,607	−11,961	−11,573	−15,011	....	Services: Debit	78ae d
1,299	2,441	3,100	1,784	1,059	2,313	2,344	1,282	−1,538	−2,592	409	10,947	13,670	15,242	....	*Balance on Goods & Services*	78af d
561	492	562	409	917	818	1,028	1,048	1,306	1,210	1,855	1,910	1,891	2,456	....	Income: Credit	78ag d
−4,215	−4,584	−5,109	−5,599	−6,498	−6,482	−6,015	−5,741	−7,180	−7,218	−8,187	−10,099	−11,690	−11,529	....	Income: Debit	78ah d
−2,355	−1,651	−1,447	−3,406	−4,522	−3,351	−2,643	−3,411	−7,412	−8,600	−5,923	2,758	3,871	6,169	....	*Balance on Gds, Serv. & Inc.*	78ai d
257	254	339	418	262	571	537	619	981	937	1,034	1,338	1,914	1,816	....	Current Transfers, n.i.e.: Credit	78aj d
—	—	—	—	—	—	—	—	—	—	—	—	—	—	....	Current Transfers: Debit	78ak d
—	—	—	—	—	—	—	—	—	—	—	—	—	—	....	Capital Account, n.i.e.	78bc d
														....	Capital Account, n.i.e.: Credit	78ba d
—	—	—	—	—	—	—	—	—	—	—	—	—	—	....	Capital Account: Debit	78bb d
3,481	2,217	2,918	4,495	5,697	6,129	5,632	3,839	10,259	10,847	−603	−9,638	−5,941	−7,896	....	Financial Account, n.i.e.	78bj d
—	—	—	—	—	—	−356	−609	−603	−600	−178	—	—	—	....	Direct Investment Abroad	78bd d
385	576	682	1,093	1,482	1,777	2,004	2,109	4,346	6,194	4,677	−356	−2,745	−4,550	....	Dir. Invest. in Rep. Econ., n.i.e.	78be d
—	—	—	—	—	—	—	—	....	—	—	—	—	—	....	Portfolio Investment Assets	78bf d
														....	Equity Securities	78bk d
														....	Debt Securities	78bl d
−88	−98	−173	−93	−12	−88	1,805	3,877	4,100	5,005	−2,632	−1,878	−1,792	−1,909	....	Portfolio Investment Liab., n.i.e.	78bg d
						1,805	1,900	1,493	1,819	−4,987	−4,371	−782	−1,020	....	Equity Securities	78bm d
−88	−98	−173	−93	−12	−88	—	1,977	2,607	3,186	2,355	2,493	−1,010	−889	....	Debt Securities	78bn d
....	....	....	....	....	....	....	....	....	....	....	....	....	....	....	Financial Derivatives Assets	78bw d
....	....	....	....	....	....	....	....	....	....	....	....	....	....	....	Financial Derivatives Liabilities	78bx d
....	....	....	....	....	....	—	—	—	—	—	—	−44	−72	−150	Other Investment Assets	78bh d
															Monetary Authorities	78bo d
															General Government	78bp d
															Banks	78bq d
....	....	....	....	....	....	—	—	—	—	—	—	−44	−72	−150	Other Sectors	78br d
3,184	1,739	2,409	3,495	4,227	4,440	2,179	−1,538	2,416	248	−2,470	−7,360	−1,332	−1,287	....	Other Investment Liab., n.i.e.	78bi d
															Monetary Authorities	78bs d
2,021	1,908	2,777	474	1,299	858	552	137	6	−663	−265	4,209	3,979	2,093	....	General Government	78bt d
						1,357	527	1,953	−758	−276	−2,270	126	−1,420	....	Banks	78bu d
1,163	−169	−368	3,021	2,928	3,582	270	−2,202	457	1,669	−1,929	−9,299	−5,437	−1,960	....	Other Sectors	78bv d
−753	−933	−1,315	744	91	−1,279	−2,932	−263	−2,255	1,319	−2,645	1,849	2,128	3,637	....	Net Errors and Omissions	78ca d
630	−113	495	2,251	1,528	2,070	594	784	1,573	4,503	−8,137	−3,693	1,972	3,726	....	*Overall Balance*	78cb d
−630	113	−495	−2,251	−1,528	−2,070	−594	−784	−1,573	−4,503	8,137	3,693	−1,972	−3,726	....	Reserves and Related Items	79da d
−1,233	167	−495	−2,088	−1,210	−1,909	−594	−784	−1,573	−4,503	5,113	−2,090	−3,342	−4,851	....	Reserve Assets	79db d
604	−54	—	−163	−319	−161	—	—	—	—	3,025	5,782	1,371	1,125	....	Use of Fund Credit and Loans	79dc d
....	....	....	....	....	....	....	....	....	....	....	....	....	....	....	Exceptional Financing	79de d

Indonesia

		1972	1973	1974	1975	1976	1977	1978	1979	1980	1981	1982	1983	1984	1985	1986
Government Finance																*Billions of Rupiah:*
Deficit (-) or Surplus	80	†–117	–163	–168	–468	–693	–393	–754	–764	–1,102	–1,172	–1,191	–1,862	1,219	–948	–3,621
Revenue	81	†644	1,020	1,832	2,300	2,968	3,634	4,378	7,050	10,406	13,763	12,815	15,511	18,724	20,347	21,324
Grants Received	81z	—	—	—	—	—	—	—	—	—	—	—	—	—	—	—
Expenditure	82	†718	1,103	1,857	2,592	3,375	3,707	4,870	7,284	10,827	14,246	13,568	16,359	16,803	20,770	24,844
Lending Minus Repayments	83	43	80	143	176	286	320	262	530	681	689	438	1,014	702	525	101
Financing																
Net Borrowing: Domestic	84a	†5	–2	–15	28	–37	64	42	41	43	145	–155	960	–1,088	348	836
Foreign	85a	†112	165	182	454	750	460	701	868	1,024	1,094	1,277	1,082	207	705	2,889
Use of Cash Balances	87	†—	—	—	–14	–20	–131	11	–145	35	–67	69	–180	–338	–105	–104
Debt: Domestic	88a	111	115	115	143	106	170	212	252	229	371	216	1,176	115	462	1,298
Foreign	89a	1,890	2,170	2,358	2,671	3,317	3,831	7,144	7,392	8,211	9,462	17,254	21,018	22,972	30,747	52,298
National Accounts																*Billions of Rupiah*
Househ.Cons.Expend.,incl.NPISHs	96f	3,402	4,791	7,259	8,745	10,464	12,458	13,850	19,514	27,503	32,293	37,924	47,063	54,067	57,985	68,453
Government Consumption Expend.	91f	414	716	841	1,254	1,591	2,077	2,659	3,733	4,688	6,452	7,229	8,077	9,122	11,067	12,167
Gross Fixed Capital Formation	93e	....	....	....	....	....	....	4,671	6,704	9,485	14,135	15,822	19,468	20,136	22,700	26,760
Changes in Inventories	93i	....	....	....	....	....	....	—	—	—	3,190	1,583	2,794	3,406	4,931	4,476
Exports of Goods and Services	90c	754	1,354	3,105	2,851	3,430	4,466	4,935	9,629	13,849	16,177	15,103	19,847	22,999	21,867	21,486
Imports of Goods and Services (-)	98c	862	1,316	2,294	2,778	3,222	3,817	3,370	7,555	10,080	14,119	15,186	19,626	19,845	20,142	22,645
Gross Domestic Product (GDP)	99b	4,564	6,753	10,708	12,643	15,467	19,011	22,746	32,025	45,446	58,127	62,476	77,623	89,885	98,406	110,697
Net Primary Income from Abroad	98.n	–159	–246	–507	–556	–432	–679	–892	–1,484	–2,011	–1,930	–1,980	–3,283	–4,183	–3,941	–4,193
Gross National Income (GNI)	99a	4,405	6,508	10,201	12,087	15,035	18,332	21,854	30,541	43,435	56,197	60,496	74,340	85,702	94,465	106,504
Consumption of Fixed Capital	99cf	296	439	696	821	1,006	1,236	1,483	2,089	2,962	3,512	3,876	3,881	4,494	4,850	5,234
GDP Volume 1973 Prices	99b.p	6,067	6,753	7,269	7,631	8,156	8,871	9,567	10,165	11,169	12,055	12,325	12,842			
GDP Volume 1983 Prices	99b.p	....	....	....	....	....	....	....	....	....	....	....	77,623	83,037	85,082	90,081
GDP Volume 1993 Prices	99b.p	....	....	....	....	....	....	....	....	....	....	....	....	....	....	....
GDP Volume (1995=100)	99bvp	22.6	25.1	27.0	28.4	30.3	33.0	35.6	37.8	41.5	44.8	45.8	47.7	51.1	52.3	55.4
GDP Deflator (1995=100)	99bip	4.5	5.9	8.7	9.8	11.2	12.7	14.1	18.6	24.1	28.5	30.0	35.8	38.7	41.4	44.0
																Millions:
Population	99z	125.64	128.80	132.00	135.67	†133.53	136.63	139.80	143.04	147.49	151.31	154.66	158.08	161.58	164.63	168.35

Government Finance

Year Beginning April 1

	1987	1988	1989	1990	1991	1992	1993	1994	1995	1996	1997	1998	1999	2000	2001	
Deficit (-) or Surplus	-1,037	-4,388	-3,362	798	982	-1,096	2,018	3,581	10,085	6,180	-4,211	-28,191	-12,645	....	....	80
Revenue	24,781	24,088	29,093	39,566	42,415	50,645	56,318	69,402	80,427	90,298	113,882	157,412	198,673	....	....	81
Grants Received	—	—	—	—	—	—	—	67	—	—	—	—	—	....	....	81z
Expenditure	26,056	28,691	32,545	38,720	41,319	52,200	54,983	61,866	66,723	77,964	112,893	174,097	223,462	....	....	82
Lending Minus Repayments	-238	-215	-90	48	114	-459	-683	4,022	3,619	6,154	5,200	11,506	-12,144	....	....	83
Financing																
Net Borrowing: Domestic	610	1,424	336	-147	594	-1,225	444	-4,295	....	-3,058	5,210	9,593	-7,227	....	....	84a
Foreign	456	3,354	2,882	1,515	1,798	1,159	-451	-303	-1,677	-2,659	-4,674	49,705	15,942	....	....	85a
Use of Cash Balances	-29	-390	144	-2,166	-3,374	1,162	-2,011	1,017	....	-463	3,676	-31,106	3,930	....	....	87
Debt: Domestic	1,908	3,343	3,686	3,578	4,172	5,449	4,861	939	3,229	83	4,097	13,481	6,481	....	....	88a
Foreign	63,297	76,902	74,817	85,891	87,435	105,546	118,797	138,841	136,781	127,324	450,890	514,134	490,685	....	....	89a

National Accounts

Billions of Rupiah

	1987	1988	1989	1990	1991	1992	1993	1994	1995	1996	1997	1998	1999	2000	2001	
Househ.Cons.Expend.,incl.NPISHs	74,246	85,318	95,414	114,693	137,469	147,709	†192,958	228,119	279,876	332,094	387,108	647,824	813,183	867,997	....	96f
Government Consumption Expend.	12,126	13,421	16,872	18,953	22,830	26,879	†29,757	31,014	35,584	40,299	42,952	54,416	72,631	90,780	....	91f
Gross Fixed Capital Formation	31,974	38,771	49,193	59,708	70,200	76,965	86,667	105,381	129,218	157,653	177,686	243,043	240,322	313,915	....	93e
Changes in Inventories	8,272	8,222	13,929	16,488	18,471	24,229	10,546	13,326	15,900	5,800	21,615	-82,716	-105,063	-83,319	....	93i
Exports of Goods and Services	30,837	36,493	45,764	55,852	68,452	83,050	†88,231	101,332	119,593	137,533	174,871	506,245	390,560	497,519	....	90c
Imports of Goods and Services (-)	28,825	32,830	41,564	54,827	67,453	76,438	†78,383	96,953	125,657	140,812	176,600	413,059	301,654	396,208	....	98c
Gross Domestic Product (GDP)	128,630	149,395	179,608	210,866	249,969	282,395	†329,776	382,220	454,514	532,568	627,695	955,754	1,109,980	1,290,684	....	99b
Net Primary Income from Abroad	-6,022	-6,922	-8,074	-9,616	-10,899	-12,447	†-12,553	-10,248	-13,366	-14,272	-18,355	-53,894	-78,897	-89,256	....	98.n
Gross National Income (GNI)	122,607	142,472	171,533	201,249	239,069	269,947	†296,095	348,072	413,661	489,377	571,512	895,379	1,013,133	1,239,248	....	99a
Consumption of Fixed Capital	6,241	7,105	8,365	9,784	11,380	13,045	16,489	19,111	22,725	26,629	31,385	47,788	55,499	64,534	....	99cf
GDP Volume 1973 Prices	....	....	....	....	....	....	....	....	....	....	....	....	....	....	....	99b.p
GDP Volume 1983 Prices	94,518	99,981	107,437	115,217	123,225	131,185	139,707	....	....	....	....	....	....	....	....	99b.p
GDP Volume 1993 Prices	....	....	....	....	....	....	329,776	354,641	383,792	413,798	433,246	376,375	379,558	397,666	....	99b.p
GDP Volume (1995=100)	58.1	61.5	66.1	70.9	75.8	80.7	85.9	92.4	100.0	107.8	112.9	98.1	98.9	103.6	....	99bv p
GDP Deflator (1995=100)	48.7	53.5	59.8	65.5	72.6	77.0	†84.4	91.0	100.0	108.7	122.3	214.4	246.9	274.1	....	99bi p

Midyear Estimates

	1987	1988	1989	1990	1991	1992	1993	1994	1995	1996	1997	1998	1999	2000	2001	
Population	172.01	175.59	179.14	†179.48	181.39	184.49	187.59	190.68	194.75	196.81	199.87	†204.42	207.44	210.49	214.84	99z

(See notes in the back of the book.)

		1972	1973	1974	1975	1976	1977	1978	1979	1980	1981	1982	1983	1984	1985	1986
Exchange Rates															*Rials per SDR:*	
Official Rate	aa	82.93	81.58	82.80	81.10	82.05	85.61	91.81	92.84	92.30	92.30	92.30	92.30	92.30	92.30	92.30
															Rials per US Dollar:	
Official Rate	ae	76.38	67.63	67.63	69.28	70.63	70.48	70.48	70.48	72.32	79.45	83.43	88.16	93.99	84.23	75.64
Official Rate	rf	75.75	68.88	67.63	67.64	70.22	70.62	70.48	70.48	70.61	78.33	83.60	86.36	90.03	91.05	78.76
															Rials per US Dollar:	
Market Rate	ae a	....	....	....	....	....	....	....	....	....	....	....	....	....	....	....
															Rials per US Dollar:	
Weighted Average	yf	....	....	....	....	....	....	....	....	....	....	....	....	....	207.300	217.500
															Index Numbers (1995=100):	
Nominal Effective Exchange Rate	ne c	....	....	....	....	....	....	....	1,566.10	1,607.99	1,697.21	1,811.43	1,907.28	2,032.36	1,218.48	726.53
Real Effective Exchange Rate	re c	....	....	....	....	....	....	....	238.83	260.87	310.50	363.31	430.18	485.02	287.93	192.68
Fund Position															*Millions of SDRs:*	
Quota	2f. s	192	192	192	192	192	192	660	660	660	660	660	660	660	660	660
SDRs	1b. s	34	37	45	56	64	70	96	167	240	291	300	309	320	328	335
Reserve Position in the Fund	1c. s	19	48	422	959	998	986	725	325	235	141	76	71	71	71	71
Total Fund Cred.&Loans Outstg.	2tl	—	—	—	—	—	—	—	—	—	—	—	—	—	—	—
International Liquidity											*Millions of US Dollars Unless Otherwise Indicated:*					
Total Reserves minus Gold	1l. d	818	1,078	8,223	8,744	8,681	12,106	11,977	15,210	10,223	1,605	5,701	....	....	....	600
SDRs	1b. d	37	45	55	65	75	85	125	220	307	339	331	324	314	361	410
Reserve Position in the Fund	1c. d	21	58	517	1,122	1,160	1,197	945	428	299	165	84	74	69	78	87
Foreign Exchange	1d. d	760	976	7,652	7,556	7,447	10,824	10,907	14,561	9,617	1,102	5,287	....	....	....	....
Gold (Million Fine Troy Ounces)	1ad	3.743	3.743	3.738	3.738	3.738	3.779	3.820	3.903	4.343	4.343	4.343	4.343	4.343	4.343	4.343
Gold (National Valuation)	1an d	142	158	160	153	152	161	174	180	194	177	168	159	149	167	186
Monetary Authorities: Other Assets	3.. d	33	48	28	27	51	58	....	209	203	185	176	1,143			
Deposit Money Banks: Assets	7a. d	183	233	458	637	583	618	969	1,409	2,218	1,824	3,090	2,191	1,626	2,004	2,083
Liabilities	7b. d	161	321	639	1,069	1,419	1,830	1,500	653	693	743	798	730	622	....	997
Other Banking Insts.: Liabilities	7f. d	206	305	383	578	1,192	1,913	2,200	2,133	1,778	1,473	1,363	1,197	—	—	
Monetary Authorities															*Billions of Rials:*	
Foreign Assets	11	75	87	569	628	660	903	....	1,109	837	479	1,232	720	....	....	569
Claims on Central Government	12a	149	208	124	156	101	176	....	480	1,636	3,003	4,003	3,758	....	....	6,290
Claims on Official Entities	12bx	15	32	128	268	445	473	....	723	720	892	954	1,005	....	....	942
Claims on Deposit Money Banks	12e	20	38	37	82	101	80	....	80	100	127	110	120	116	....	82
Reserve Money	14	179	246	330	412	573	733	....	1,444	1,833	2,421	3,408	3,823	....	....	5,798
of which: Currency Outside DMBs	14a	56	70	102	148	206	252	....	769	1,108	1,248	1,465	1,757	....	....	2,354
Nonfin.Pub.Ent. Deps.	14e	57	82	96	77	102	139	....	220	169	167	329	335	....	....	290
Restricted Deposits	16b	25	46	147	131	124	151	....	163	201	185	201	335	....	....	241
Foreign Liabilities	16c	20	2	12	11	12	12	....	14	53	56	26	92	....	....	51
Central Government Deposits	16d	22	48	296	423	408	513	....	528	588	796	836	1,005	....	....	1,164
Capital Accounts	17a	12	12	14	39	54	61	....	106	112	117	178	218	....	....	244
Other Items (Net)	17r	1	10	59	117	137	162	....	136	507	926	1,649	130	....	....	385
Deposit Money Banks															*Billions of Rials:*	
Reserves	20	66	86	132	187	265	342	....	455	556	1,006	1,614	1,731	2,056	2,909	3,068
Foreign Assets	21	14	16	31	44	41	44	....	99	160	145	258	193	153	169	158
Claims on Central Government	22a	18	32	83	148	229	349	....	479	496	543	763	943	1,179	1,194	1,194
Claims on Private Sector	22d	266	369	480	738	1,041	1,223	....	1,639	2,006	2,104	2,199	2,703	2,730	3,045	3,647
Demand Deposits	24	101	126	183	233	360	431	....	700	981	1,222	1,499	1,830	2,296	....	2,865
Time and Savings Deposits	25	204	268	398	592	843	1,083	....	1,497	1,767	2,046	2,591	3,061	2,986	....	4,339
Foreign Liabilities	26c	12	22	43	74	100	129	....	46	50	59	67	64	59	....	75
Credit from Monetary Authorities	26g	20	38	37	82	101	80	....	80	100	127	110	120	116	....	82
Capital Accounts	27a	17	26	33	73	96	129	....	162	—	—	—	—	85	100	84
Other Items (Net)	27r	10	24	32	63	76	105	....	188	320	344	567	495	576	....	620
Monetary Survey															*Billions of Rials:*	
Foreign Assets (Net)	31n	57	79	544	587	590	805	....	1,147	895	509	1,397	756	....	....	600
Domestic Credit	32	427	594	520	838	1,368	1,661	....	2,724	4,236	5,689	7,132	7,141	....	....	10,874
Claims on Central Govt. (Net)	32an	146	193	−88	−168	−124	−44	....	352	1,504	2,688	3,916	3,414	....	....	6,257
Claims on Official Entities	32bx	15	32	128	268	450	482	....	732	726	898	1,017	1,024	....	....	971
Claims on Private Sector	32d	266	369	480	738	1,041	1,223	....	1,639	2,006	2,104	2,199	2,703	2,730	3,045	3,647
Money	34	214	278	381	458	668	822	1,078 [e]	1,689	2,258	2,637	3,293	3,922	....	....	5,509
Quasi-Money	35	204	268	398	592	843	1,083	1,273	1,497	1,767	2,046	2,591	3,061	2,986	....	4,339
Restricted Deposits	36b	25	46	147	131	124	151	....	163	201	185	201	335	....	....	241
Other Items (Net)	37r	39	81	138	244	323	411	....	522	906	1,330	2,444	579	....	....	1,385
Money plus Quasi-Money	35l	419	546	779	1,050	1,511	1,905	2,351	3,186	4,025	4,683	5,884	6,983	....	....	9,848
Other Banking Institutions															*Billions of Rials:*	
Cash	40	4	5	7	19	25	28	....	26	16	22	29	33	33	37	40
Claims on Central Government	42a	4	5	6	14	13	13	....	7	7	4	4	3	122	2	2
Claims on Official Entities	42bx	13	17	20	22	22	20	....	18	17	17	14	12	19	13	16
Claims on Private Sector	42d	68	83	134	233	360	497	....	697	896	1,014	1,174	1,403	1,594	1,765	1,874
Demand Deposits	44	11	14	35	45	51	50	....	50	54	74	83	111	103	143	184
Private Sector	44x	4	5	9	14	18	21	....	27	43	63	83	111	103	143	184
Official Entities	44y	7	9	26	32	33	30	....	23	11	11	—	—	—	—	—
Time and Savings Deposits	45	11	15	20	30	48	67	....	99	166	203	236	302	385	345	336
Foreign Liabilities	46c	16	21	26	40	84	135	....	150	129	117	114	106	—	—	
Central Government Deposits	46d	20	26	31	64	75	83	....	78	109	139	83	139	269	160	118
Credit from Monetary Authorities	46g	1	2	11	23	42	95	....	163	214	299	365	336	332	319	248
Capital Accounts	47a	33	39	53	79	98	118	....	171	200	153	....	231	273	270	212
Other Items (Net)	47r	−1	−5	−8	7	21	11	....	37	65	72	340	228	404	582	835
Liquid Liabilities	55l	436	569	826	1,106	1,584	1,994	....	3,309	4,228	4,937	6,174	7,363	....	....	10,327
Interest Rates															*Percent Per Annum*	
Discount Rate *(End of Period)*	60	7.50	9.00	9.00	8.00	8.00	8.00	10.00	9.00	....	....	....	....	....	....	....
Prices and Production															*Index Numbers (1995=100):*	
Share Prices	62	....	....	....	....	....	....	....	....	....	....	....	....	....	....	....
Producer Prices	63	1.4	1.6	1.9	2.0	2.2	2.6	2.8	3.2	4.3	5.3	5.9	6.8	7.3	†7.7	9.2
Home Goods	63a	1.4	1.5	1.8	2.0	2.2	2.6	2.8	3.3	4.4	5.5	6.3	7.3	7.9	†8.3	9.8
Consumer Prices	64	1.8	2.0	2.2	2.5	2.8	3.6	4.0	4.4	5.3	6.6	7.8	9.4	10.6	†11.0	13.1
Wages	65ey	5.0	6.3	8.3	†11.7	16.3	21.1	27.7	41.0	†55.5	60.2	66.0	76.9	88.1	100.0	....
Crude Petroleum Production	66aa	139.5	162.3	166.7	148.1	163.3	156.8	148.4	85.7	46.3	39.8	67.4	75.4	65.6	69.3	60.2

1987	1988	1989	1990	1991	1992	1993	1994	1995	1996	1997	1998	1999	2000	2001		
End of Period															**Exchange Rates**	
92.30	92.30	92.30	92.30	92.30	92.30	2,415.49	2,534.26	2,597.64	2,515.19	2,366.94	2,465.36	2,405.04	2,948.39	2,200.47	Official Rate	aa
End of Period (ae) Period Average (rf)																
65.62	68.59	70.24	65.31	64.59	67.04	1,758.56	1,735.97	1,747.50	1,749.14	1,754.26	1,750.93	1,752.29	2,262.93	1,750.95	Official Rate	ae
71.46	68.68	72.01	68.10	67.51	65.55	1,267.77	1,748.75	1,747.93	1,750.76	1,752.92	1,751.86	1,752.93	1,764.43	1,753.56	Official Rate	rf
End of Period																
....	....	....	....	....	....	....	....	....	....	4,645	5,721	8,135	7,909	7,924	Market Rate	ae a
Year Ending December 20																
221.600	237.100	299.100	394.200	511.700	655.100	890.083	1,221.700	1,725.800	2,194.000	2,779.500	3,206.000	4,172.000	5,731.000	....	Weighted Average	yf
Period Averages																
607.08	570.16	515.62	360.12	304.80	271.31	183.04	105.13	100.00	111.42	126.52	133.92	139.13	153.81	167.59	Nominal Effective Exchange Rate	ne c
202.05	232.65	245.38	166.27	150.01	152.09	111.21	74.37	100.00	135.36	171.18	203.77	245.34	297.68	345.78	Real Effective Exchange Rate	re c
End of Period															**Fund Position**	
660	660	660	660	660	1,079	1,079	1,079	1,079	1,079	1,079	1,079	1,497	1,497	1,497	Quota	2f. s
342	116	305	310	216	7	105	98	90	240	245	1	101	267	267	SDRs	1b. s
71	—	—	—	—	105	—	—	—	—	—	—	—	—	—	Reserve Position in the Fund	1c. s
—	—	—	—	—	—	—	—	—	—	—	—	—	—	—	Total Fund Cred.&Loans Outstg.	2tl
End of Period															**International Liquidity**	
....	....	....	....	....	....	....	....	....	....	....	....	....	....	....	Total Reserves minus Gold	1l. d
486	156	400	442	309	10	144	143	134	345	330	2	139	349	336	SDRs	1b. d
100	—	—	—	—	144	—	—	—	—	—	—	—	—	—	Reserve Position in the Fund	1c. d
....	....	....	....	....	....	....	....	....	....	....	....	....	....	....	Foreign Exchange	1d. d
4.343	4.343	4.343	4.343	4.343	4.343	4.765	4.740	4.842	....	....	....	....	....	....	Gold (Million Fine Troy Ounces)	1ad
216	205	200	216	217	209	229	242	252	....	....	....	....	....	....	Gold (National Valuation)	1and
....	....	....	....	....	....	....	....	....	....	....	....	....	....	....	Monetary Authorities: Other Assets	3.. d
1,518	1,448	2,029	3,110	2,912	3,070	1,459	3,321	3,354	4,319	4,403	4,648	2,258	3,112	6,298	Deposit Money Banks: Assets	7a. d
1,067	1,077	1,242	1,860	2,262	4,053	3,397	5,589	4,015	2,668	2,128	2,771	3,410	3,486	6,695	Liabilities	7b. d
—	—	10	3	5	227	71	53	118	110	66	136	250	266	403	Other Banking Insts.: Liabilities	7f. d
Year Ending December 20															**Monetary Authorities**	
758	602	731	696	1,238	1,349	7,916	9,681	14,413	19,454	15,669	9,827	11,413	24,478	28,151	Foreign Assets	11
8,095	10,156	11,954	12,818	14,267	14,651	16,002	28,169	32,648	42,461	42,624	55,710	61,731	60,207	64,673	Claims on Central Government	12a
1,036	1,072	1,137	1,651	2,384	2,520	3,792	5,549	10,704	18,826	15,618	18,842	19,794	23,189	16,287	Claims on Official Entities	12bx
99	128	162	194	379	742	3,751	1,967	10,462	2,056	11,162	9,565	13,392	17,567	18,589	Claims on Deposit Money Banks	12e
7,240	9,063	10,254	10,577	12,293	13,901	16,511	22,165	32,805	41,708	51,298	60,533	70,911	82,726	88,015	Reserve Money	14
2,712	3,068	3,225	3,518	3,862	4,088	4,925	6,199	7,949	9,598	11,271	14,050	16,652	20,020	21,840	of which: Currency Outside DMBs	14a
281	214	151	183	553	559	862	1,604	2,020	2,639	2,642	4,662	5,304	7,859	4,552	Nonfin.Pub.Ent. Deps.	14e
364	289	377	611	568	352	1,158	4,004	7,085	8,764	6,789	3,810	4,066	3,351	4,133	Restricted Deposits	16b
26	28	64	148	129	166	2,924	2,883	2,679	3,466	5,057	8,012	6,562	7,094	13,991	Foreign Liabilities	16c
1,269	1,515	1,788	2,426	2,779	3,077	4,965	6,752	9,738	13,035	13,837	13,814	18,275	28,645	37,312	Central Government Deposits	16d
261	261	265	275	281	294	801	903	989	1,004	1,003	1,012	1,097	1,064	1,235	Capital Accounts	17a
828	800	1,236	1,322	2,220	1,472	5,104	8,658	14,929	14,820	7,089	6,763	5,420	2,561	-16,986	Other Items (Net)	17r
Year Ending December 20															**Deposit Money Banks**	
4,207	5,715	6,797	6,780	7,764	9,134	10,586	14,179	22,519	28,865	36,563	40,385	47,190	51,536	58,559	Reserves	20
100	99	143	203	188	206	2,566	5,766	5,861	7,555	7,724	8,138	3,957	7,043	11,027	Foreign Assets	21
1,249	1,247	1,347	1,346	1,338	1,343	1,236	1,232	1,827	1,823	1,821	1,821	7,494	5,800	5,648	Claims on Central Government	22a
4,184	4,672	6,184	8,729	12,059	16,665	22,131	27,535	32,938	41,043	52,579	63,716	85,701	112,986	155,268	Claims on Private Sector	22d
3,469	3,836	4,862	6,028	7,851	9,434	12,519	18,120	24,373	33,628	41,064	48,732	59,996	74,291	99,275	Demand Deposits	24
5,283	6,988	9,045	10,663	13,342	17,770	23,181	29,377	37,599	49,426	62,881	74,438	90,435	108,884	143,689	Time and Savings Deposits	25
70	74	87	122	146	272	5,973	9,703	7,016	4,667	3,734	4,851	5,975	7,890	11,723	Foreign Liabilities	26c
99	128	162	194	379	742	3,751	1,967	10,462	2,056	11,162	9,565	13,392	17,567	18,589	Credit from Monetary Authorities	26g
134	134	134	134	134	134	3,719	3,724	3,724	3,724	3,724	3,724	3,764	3,764	8,564	Capital Accounts	27a
685	573	180	-83	-502	-1,003	-12,625	-14,180	-20,030	-14,215	-23,878	-27,250	-29,220	-35,031	-51,338	Other Items (Net)	27r
Year Ending December 20															**Monetary Survey**	
762	599	723	629	1,152	1,118	1,585	2,860	10,578	18,876	14,603	5,102	2,833	16,538	13,465	Foreign Assets (Net)	31n
13,414	15,807	19,199	22,751	28,030	33,915	43,385	59,484	74,426	101,566	115,511	151,740	187,227	211,234	246,942	Domestic Credit	32
7,972	9,746	11,367	11,636	12,727	12,816	12,211	22,556	24,674	31,026	30,370	43,463	48,057	34,512	30,557	Claims on Central Govt. (Net)	32an
1,258	1,389	1,647	2,386	3,244	4,434	9,043	9,393	16,814	29,498	32,562	44,561	53,469	63,736	61,117	Claims on Official Entities	32bx
4,184	4,672	6,184	8,729	12,059	16,665	22,131	27,535	32,938	41,043	52,579	63,716	85,701	112,986	155,268	Claims on Private Sector	32d
6,462	7,118	8,238	9,729	12,266	14,081	18,305	25,923	34,342	45,865	54,977	67,444	81,952	102,170	125,667	Money	34
5,283	6,988	9,045	10,663	13,342	17,770	23,181	29,377	37,599	49,426	62,881	74,438	90,435	108,884	143,689	Quasi-Money	35
364	289	377	611	568	352	1,158	4,004	7,085	8,764	6,789	3,810	4,066	3,351	4,133	Restricted Deposits	36b
2,066	2,011	2,262	2,377	3,007	2,829	2,327	3,040	5,977	16,387	5,467	11,150	13,608	13,367	-13,082	Other Items (Net)	37r
11,745	14,106	17,283	20,392	25,607	31,851	41,486	55,299	71,941	95,291	117,858	141,883	172,387	211,054	269,356	Money plus Quasi-Money	35l
Year Ending December 20															**Other Banking Institutions**	
46	75	93	109	132	147	166	218	361	671	912	1,549	1,901	3,417	3,094	Cash	40
2	2	2	2	2	2	2	2	2	2	2	2	941	1,249	1,755	Claims on Central Government	42a
17	16	21	67	75	58	113	141	90	163	591	1,002	195	208	222	Claims on Official Entities	42bx
1,948	2,130	2,577	3,191	4,214	5,134	6,159	7,504	9,831	13,506	18,611	25,812	36,411	51,503	66,108	Claims on Private Sector	42d
157	155	213	281	408	476	767	870	1,287	2,129	3,325	4,002	4,001	6,023	6,948	Demand Deposits	44
157	155	213	281	408	476	767	870	1,287	2,129	3,325	4,002	4,001	6,023	6,948	Private Sector	44x
—	—	—	—	—	—	—	—	—	—	—	—	—	—	—	Official Entities	44y
342	408	484	549	682	729	914	1,409	2,367	3,327	5,591	9,157	12,584	15,831	24,110	Time and Savings Deposits	45
—	—	—	1	—	15	125	91	207	192	116	238	438	601	705	Foreign Liabilities	46c
177	148	144	65	95	138	139	114	124	175	158	106	69	87	112	Central Government Deposits	46d
270	257	275	307	307	509	215	795	3,437	8,126	3,518	4,635	5,895	9,358	652	Credit from Monetary Authorities	46g
259	260	260	280	300	567	870	1,928	1,928	1,940	1,940	1,940	1,940	2,960	6,385	Capital Accounts	47a
807	995	1,316	1,888	2,632	2,907	3,409	2,658	935	-1,548	5,469	8,287	14,522	21,517	32,267	Other Items (Net)	47r
12,198	14,594	17,887	21,112	26,565	32,908	43,002	57,360	75,232	100,077	125,862	153,493	187,070	229,491	297,320	Liquid Liabilities	55l
Year Ending December 20															**Interest Rates**	
....	....	....	....	....	....	....	....	....	....	....	....	....	....	....	Discount Rate (End of Period)	60
Year Ending December 20															**Prices and Production**	
....	....	....	....	....	51.9	46.0	49.8	100.0	209.1	200.7	177.2	190.6	271.9	363.8	Share Prices	62
12.1	14.8	17.9	†21.5	27.1	36.0	45.3	62.3	100.0	132.9	147.1	164.7	196.3	†231.3	....	Producer Prices	63
12.6	15.3	18.7	†22.5	27.7	37.8	47.4	65.1	100.0	130.8	146.3	171.1	205.2	†239.9	257.4	Home Goods	63a
16.8	21.6	26.4	28.5	†33.3	41.9	50.8	66.8	100.0	128.9	151.3	178.3	214.1	245.1	272.8	Consumer Prices	64
....	....	....	....	....	....	....	....	....	....	....	....	....	....	....	Wages	65ey
68.1	70.8	81.6	88.6	92.6	95.2	101.0	99.5	100.0	101.6	100.4	99.4	97.0	104.1	....	Crude Petroleum Production	66aa

Iran, I.R. of

	1972	1973	1974	1975	1976	1977	1978	1979	1980	1981	1982	1983	1984	1985	1986
International Transactions															*Millions of US Dollars*
Exports .... 70..d	1,799	2,669	8,401	7,963	8,935	9,216	8,560	8,310	†7,109	†3,947	12,968	19,378	12,422	13,328	7,171
Imports, c.i.f. .... 71..d	2,409	3,393	5,433	10,343	12,894	14,070	13,549	9,738	†12,246	14,693	11,955	18,320	15,370	11,635	10,521
Imports, f.o.b. 71.vd	2,096	2,925	4,563	8,526	10,857	12,122	11,681	8,395	†10,557	12,667	10,306	15,793	13,250	10,030	9,070
Volume of Exports															*1995=100*
Petroleum 72a	183.2	208.8	212.1	187.4	201.9	188.9	174.1	98.7	†43.3	†27.2	64.9	68.1	62.3	56.6	44.9
Crude Petroleum 72aa	184.8	216.3	220.0	191.5	213.7	200.0	184.9	95.4	†32.6	†29.2	66.5	74.9	65.9	60.5	51.2
Export Prices 76	....	....	....	....	....	....	....	....	....	....	....	....	....	....	
Import Prices 76.x	....	....	....	....	....	....	....	....	....	....	....	....	....	....	
															1990=100
Export Prices 76	....	....	....	....	....	....	....	....	....	....	....	....	....	....	
Import Prices 76.x	....	....	....	....	....	....	....	....	....	....	....	....	....	....	
Balance of Payments															*Millions of US$:*
Current Account, n.i.e. 78ald	....	....	....	....	7,660	2,816	104	11,968	−2,438	−3,446	5,733	358	−414	−476	−5,155
Goods: Exports f.o.b. 78aad	....	....	....	....	24,719	24,076	17,675	24,171	12,338	11,831	20,452	21,507	17,087	14,175	7,171
Goods: Imports f.o.b. 78abd	....	....	....	....	−13,860	−16,718	−11,803	−8,521	−10,888	−13,138	−12,552	−18,027	−14,729	−12,006	−10,585
Trade Balance 78acd	....	....	....	....	10,859	7,358	5,872	15,650	1,450	−1,307	7,900	3,480	2,358	2,169	−3,414
Services: Credit 78add	....	....	....	....	2,651	3,699	3,104	1,580	731	556	509	540	475	370	242
Services: Debit 78aed	....	....	....	....	−5,773	−8,201	−9,177	−5,690	−5,223	−3,315	−3,061	−4,273	−3,698	−3,308	−2,282
Balance on Goods & Services .. 78afd	....	....	....	....	7,737	2,856	−201	11,540	−3,042	−4,066	5,348	−253	−865	−769	−5,454
Income: Credit 78agd	....	....	....	....	610	769	1,100	1,240	1,004	895	612	795	594	393	365
Income: Debit 78ahd	....	....	....	....	−670	−684	−780	−797	−398	−275	−227	−184	−143	−100	−66
Balance on Gds, Serv. & Inc. .. 78aid	....	....	....	....	7,677	2,941	119	11,983	−2,436	−3,446	5,733	358	−414	−476	−5,155
Current Transfers, n.i.e.: Credit .. 78ajd	....	....	....	....	—	—	—	—	—	—	—	—	—	—	—
Current Transfers: Debit 78akd	....	....	....	....	−17	−125	−15	−15	−2	—	—	—	—	—	—
Capital Account, n.i.e. 78bcd	....	....	....	....	—	—	—	—	—	—	—	—	—	—	—
Capital Account, n.i.e.: Credit .. 78bad	....	....	....	....	—	—	—	—	—	—	—	—	—	—	—
Capital Account: Debit 78bbd	....	....	....	....	—	—	—	—	—	—	—	—	—	—	—
Financial Account, n.i.e. 78bjd	....	....	....	....	−4,957	−366	−165	−8,023	−8,238	1,441	−1,847	−2,474	−2,818	544	3,127
Direct Investment Abroad 78bdd	....	....	....	....	—	—	—	—	—	—	—	—	—	—	—
Dir. Invest. in Rep. Econ., n.i.e. .. 78bed	....	....	....	....	—	—	—	—	—	—	—	—	—	—	—
Portfolio Investment Assets 78bfd	....	....	....	....	—	—	—	—	—	—	—	—	—	—	—
Equity Securities 78bkd	....	....	....	....	—	—	—	—	—	—	—	—	—	—	—
Debt Securities 78bld	....	....	....	....	—	—	—	—	—	—	—	—	—	—	—
Portfolio Investment Liab., n.i.e. .. 78bgd	....	....	....	....	—	—	—	—	—	—	—	—	—	—	—
Equity Securities 78bmd	....	....	....	....	—	—	—	—	—	—	—	—	—	—	—
Debt Securities 78bnd	....	....	....	....	—	—	—	—	—	—	—	—	—	—	—
Financial Derivatives Assets 78bwd	....	....	....	....											
Financial Derivatives Liabilities .. 78bxd	....	....	....	....											
Other Investment Assets 78bhd	....	....	....	....	−5,623	−3,663	−879	−4,396	91	1,968	−157	−915	504	−334	1,164
Monetary Authorities 78bod	....	....	....	....	—	—	—	—	—	—	—	—	—	—	—
General Government 78bpd	....	....	....	....	−1,254	−126	195	945	636	618	160	282	121	205	1,030
Banks 78bqd	....	....	....	....	48	−281	68	−999	−685	311	−200	−438	591	−539	134
Other Sectors 78brd	....	....	....	....	−4,417	−3,256	−1,142	−4,342	140	1,039	−117	−759	−208		
Other Investment Liab., n.i.e. 78bid	....	....	....	....	666	3,297	714	−3,627	−8,329	−527	−1,690	−1,559	−3,322	878	1,963
Monetary Authorities 78bsd	....	....	....	....	38	−20	51	130	212	−202	−468	752	−1,605	−1,000	1,076
General Government 78btd	....	....	....	....	−151	822	15	−935	−5,882	−496	−2,027	−433	−427	−320	−190
Banks 78bud	....	....	....	....	893	754	220	−1,177	−342	135	−55	−45	−1,095	188	157
Other Sectors 78bvd	....	....	....	....	−114	1,741	428	−1,645	−2,317	36	860	−1,833	−195	2,010	920
Net Errors and Omissions 78cad	....	....	....	....	−192	−339	−516	−1,005	828	1,633	980	860	−904	486	814
Overall Balance 78cbd	....	....	....	....	2,511	2,111	−577	2,940	−9,848	−372	4,866	−1,256	−4,136	554	−1,214
Reserves and Related Items 79dad	....	....	....	....	−2,511	−2,111	577	−2,940	9,848	372	−4,866	1,256	4,136	−554	1,214
Reserve Assets 79dbd	....	....	....	....	−2,511	−2,111	577	−2,940	9,848	372	−4,866	1,256	4,136	−554	1,214
Use of Fund Credit and Loans .. 79dcd	....	....	....	....	—	—	—	—	—	—	—	—	—	—	—
Exceptional Financing 79ded	....	....	....	....	....	....	....	....	....	....	....	....	....	....	....
Government Finance															*Billions of Rials:*
Deficit (-) or Surplus 80	−54	−13	140	12	−38	−262	−450	−231	−915	−841	−603	−842	−597	−594	−1,353
Revenue 81	323	491	1,427	1,627	1,896	2,193	1,736	1,781	1,430	1,923	2,698	2,994	2,989	2,964	2,017
Grants 81z	....	....	....	....	....	....	....	....	....	....	....	....	....	....	....
Exp. & Lending Minus Repay. 82z	378	504	1,287	1,615	1,933	2,455	2,186	2,012	2,345	2,763	3,302	3,836	3,586	3,558	3,370
Expenditure 82	378	504	1,287	1,615	1,933	2,455	2,286	2,104	2,368	2,814	3,317	3,857	3,598	3,583	3,438
Lending Minus Repayments 83	—	—	—	—	—	—	−100	−92	−23	−51	−16	−21	−12	−25	−68
Total Financing 80h	54	13	−140	−12	38	262	450	231	915	841	603	842	597	594	1,353
Total Net Borrowing 84	54	13	−140	−12	38	262	450	231	915	841	603	842	597	594	1,353
Net Domestic 84a	44	16	34	124	130	331	505	267	952	886	641	878	627	625	1,375
Net Foreign 85a	11	−3	−174	−136	−93	−69	−56	−35	−37	−45	−38	−36	−30	−31	−22
Debt: Domestic 88a	....	....	....	368	391	738	....	....	....	....	....	....	....	....	....
National Accounts															*Billions of Rials:*
Househ.Cons.Expend.,incl.NPISHs .. 96f	592	743	1,028	1,439	1,628	2,146	2,472	2,990	3,488	4,596	5,870	7,676	8,817	9,509	10,311
Government Consumption Expend. .. 91f	250	322	659	842	1,029	1,158	1,282	1,259	1,420	1,726	1,966	2,215	2,254	2,515	2,440
Gross Fixed Capital Formation 93e	422	543	832	1,500	2,180	2,627	2,182	1,644	1,973	2,175	2,635	4,105	4,482	3,888	3,354
Changes in Inventories 93i	−92	−86	−10	100	85	44	168	16	−424	−240	135	−184	−414	−458	−896
Exports of Goods and Services 90c	299	642	1,478	1,440	1,788	1,754	1,292	1,706	932	997	1,821	1,982	1,657	1,320	584
Imports of Goods and Services (-) .. 98c	251	345	676	1,127	1,237	1,501	1,103	921	1,745	2,019	2,005	2,966	2,572	2,029	1,498
Gross Domestic Product (GDP) 99b	1,122	1,645	2,862	3,176	4,264	5,038	4,939	5,818	6,179	7,428	9,806	12,379	13,606	14,501	14,787
Net Primary Income from Abroad .. 98.n	−29	−36	−11	−15	−16	−52	−186	55	423	412	287	338	275	142	107
Gross National Income (GNI) 99a	1,093	1,610	2,852	3,162	4,248	4,986	4,753	5,872	6,602	7,840	10,093	12,717	13,881	14,642	14,894
GDP Volume 1974 Prices 99b.p	2,614	2,838	3,090	3,176	3,758	4,043	3,191	2,895	2,491	2,688	3,075	3,391	3,504	3,651	3,344
GDP Volume 1982 Prices 99b.p	....	....	....	....	....	....	....	....	....	....	....	....	....	....	....
GDP Volume (1995=100) 99bvp	73.0	79.2	86.3	88.7	104.9	112.9	89.1	80.8	69.5	67.8	76.7	86.9	87.6	87.9	74.6
GDP Deflator (1995=100) 99bip	.8	1.1	1.8	1.9	2.2	2.4	3.0	3.9	4.8	5.9	6.9	7.6	8.3	8.9	10.6
															Millions:
Population 99z	30.41	31.23	32.50	33.38	33.71	34.69	36.11	37.20	39.30	40.85	42.48	44.08	45.80	47.82	49.44

		1987	1988	1989	1990	1991	1992	1993	1994	1995	1996	1997	1998	1999	2000	2001
International Transactions		*Year Ending March 20*														
Exports	70..d	11,916	10,709	13,081	19,305	18,661	19,868	18,080	19,434	18,360	22,391	18,381	13,118	21,030	28,345	....
Imports, c.i.f.	71..d	9,570	9,454	14,794	20,322	27,927	25,860	21,427	13,774	13,882	16,274	14,196	14,323	12,683	14,296	....
Imports, f.o.b.	71.vd	8,250	8,150	12,753	17,519	24,075	22,293	18,472	11,874	11,967	14,029	12,238	12,347	10,934	12,324	....
Volume of Exports		*Year Ending December 20*														
Petroleum	72a	55.1	58.7	69.8	79.3	94.8	102.4	99.2	95.8	100.0	100.8	....	....	....	....	....
Crude Petroleum	72aa	63.4	67.5	77.0	85.9	101.3	109.5	103.5	98.6	100.0	100.0	96.0	94.3	85.2	103.3	....
Export Prices	76	....	....	....	....	....	....	....	....	100.0	94.8	71.2	44.7	61.9	55.9	....
Import Prices	76.x	....	....	....	....	....	....	....	....	100.0	115.9	104.7	141.5	111.4	97.6	....
		1990=100														
Export Prices	76	....	....	....	....	....	....	....	....	100.0	94.8	71.2	44.7	61.9	55.9	....
Import Prices	76.x	....	....	....	....	....	....	....	....	100.0	115.9	104.7	141.5	111.4	97.6	....
Balance of Payments		*Minus Sign Indicates Debit*														
Current Account, n.i.e.	78ald	-2,090	-1,869	-191	327	-9,448	-6,504	-4,215	4,956	3,358	5,232	2,213	-2,139	6,589	12,645	....
Goods: Exports f.o.b.	78aad	11,916	10,709	13,081	19,305	18,661	19,868	18,080	19,434	18,360	22,391	18,381	13,118	21,030	28,345	....
Goods: Imports f.o.b.	78abd	-12,005	-10,608	-13,448	-18,330	-25,190	-23,274	-19,287	-12,617	-12,774	-14,989	-14,123	-14,286	-13,433	-15,207	....
Trade Balance	78acd	-89	101	-367	975	-6,529	-3,406	-1,207	6,817	5,586	7,402	4,258	-1,168	7,597	13,138	....
Services: Credit	78add	231	244	446	436	668	559	1,084	438	593	860	1,192	1,793	1,216	1,382	....
Services: Debit	78aed	-2,372	-2,355	-3,018	-3,962	-5,715	-5,783	-5,600	-3,226	-2,339	-3,083	-3,371	-2,760	-2,457	-2,296	....
Balance on Goods & Services	78afd	-2,230	-2,010	-2,939	-2,551	-11,576	-8,630	-5,723	4,029	3,840	5,179	2,079	-2,135	6,356	12,224	....
Income: Credit	78agd	206	223	352	456	213	287	151	142	316	488	466	230	181	404	....
Income: Debit	78ahd	-66	-82	-104	-78	-85	-157	-143	-413	-794	-898	-725	-731	-473	-604	....
Balance on Gds, Serv. & Inc.	78aid	-2,090	-1,869	-2,691	-2,173	-11,448	-8,500	-5,715	3,758	3,362	4,769	1,820	-2,636	6,064	12,024	....
Current Transfers, n.i.e.: Credit	78ajd	—	—	2,500	2,500	2,000	1,996	1,500	1,200	—	471	400	500	508	539	....
Current Transfers: Debit	78akd	—	—	—	—	—	—	—	-2	-4	-8	-7	-3	17	82	....
Capital Account, n.i.e.	78bcd	—	—	—	—	—	—	—	—	—	—	—	—	—	—	....
Capital Account, n.i.e.: Credit	78bad	—	—	—	—	—	—	—	—	—	—	—	—	—	—	....
Capital Account: Debit	78bbd	—	—	—	—	—	—	—	—	—	—	—	—	—	—	....
Financial Account, n.i.e.	78bjd	1,711	320	3,261	295	6,033	4,703	5,563	-346	-774	-5,508	-4,822	2,270	-5,894	-10,189	....
Direct Investment Abroad	78bdd	—	—	—	—	—	—	—	—	—	—	—	—	—	—	....
Dir. Invest. in Rep. Econ., n.i.e.	78bed	—	—	—	—	—	—	—	2	17	26	53	24	35	39	....
Portfolio Investment Assets	78bfd	—	—	—	—	—	—	—	—	—	—	—	—	—	—	....
Equity Securities	78bkd	—	—	—	—	—	—	—	—	—	—	—	—	—	—	....
Debt Securities	78bld	—	—	—	—	—	—	—	—	—	—	—	—	—	—	....
Portfolio Investment Liab., n.i.e.	78bgd	—	—	—	—	—	—	—	—	—	—	—	—	—	—	....
Equity Securities	78bmd	—	—	—	—	—	—	—	—	—	—	—	—	—	—	....
Debt Securities	78bnd	—	—	—	—	—	—	—	—	—	—	—	—	—	—	....
Financial Derivatives Assets	78bwd	....	....	....	....	....	....	....	....	....	....	....	—	—	—	....
Financial Derivatives Liabilities	78bxd	....	....	....	....	....	....	....	....	....	....	....	—	—	—	....
Other Investment Assets	78bhd	1,248	10	539	-1,510	1,082	1,000	1,250	-1,258	-419	-1,305	2,293	963	-1,650	-8,257	....
Monetary Authorities	78bod	....	....	....	....	....	....	....	....	....	....	....	—	—	—	....
General Government	78bpd	899	140	1,099	142	910	342	44	-42	235	-48	-99	-21	-6	-5,932	....
Banks	78bqd	349	-130	-560	-1,652	172	658	1,206	-1,216	-654	-1,257	2,392	984	-1,638	-1,783	....
Other Sectors	78brd	—	—	—	—	—	—	—	—	—	—	—	—	-6	-542	....
Other Investment Liab., n.i.e.	78bid	463	310	2,722	1,805	4,951	3,703	4,313	910	-372	-4,229	-7,168	1,283	-4,279	-1,971	....
Monetary Authorities	78bsd	-192	117	501	387	-372	63	68	-252	-64	-283	179	93	-5,517	-1,410	....
General Government	78btd	-142	-144	-71	-41	440	4,556	-1,358	10,447	1,684	-4,523	-4,035	-489	-402	-621	....
Banks	78bud	197	-29	344	1,101	489	—	—	—	—	—	—	—	506	—	....
Other Sectors	78bvd	600	366	1,948	358	4,394	-916	5,603	-9,285	-1,992	577	-3,312	1,679	1,134	60	....
Net Errors and Omissions	78cad	155	405	-635	-947	1,324	1,640	-1,120	-3,702	202	2,717	-1,088	-1,122	-244	-1,373	....
Overall Balance	78cbd	-224	-1,144	2,435	-325	-2,091	-161	228	908	2,786	2,441	-3,697	-991	451	1,083	....
Reserves and Related Items	79dad	224	1,144	-2,435	325	2,091	161	-228	-908	-2,786	-2,441	3,697	991	-451	-1,083	....
Reserve Assets	79dbd	224	1,144	-2,435	325	2,091	161	-228	-908	-2,786	-2,441	3,697	991	-451	-1,083	....
Use of Fund Credit and Loans	79dcd	—	—	—	—	—	—	—	—	—	—	—	—	—	—	....
Exceptional Financing	79ded	....	....	....	....	....	....	....	....	....	....	....	—	—	—	....
Government Finance		*Year Beginning March 21*														
Deficit (-) or Surplus	80	-1,419	†-2,041	-1,089	-665	-1,157	-872	-636	332	245	493	-2,869	-17,208	-691	-3,675	....
Revenue	81	2,511	†2,656	3,830	6,617	6,934	9,885	20,251	29,245	41,575	57,276	62,569	53,762	92,470	104,641	....
Grants	81z	....	....	....	—	—	—	†—	—	—	—	—	—	—	—	....
Exp. & Lending Minus Repay.	82z	3,930	†4,697	4,919	7,282	....	....	....	....	....	....	....	....	....	....	....
Expenditure	82	3,966	†4,703	4,924	7,288	8,091	10,757	20,887	28,912	41,331	56,783	65,438	70,970	93,161	108,316	....
Lending Minus Repayments	83	-36	†-6	-5	-6	-39	-6	†-108	-85	-275	-68	-331	-188	-272	....	....
Total Financing	80h	1,419	†2,041	1,089	665	1,158	872	638	-331	-244	-492	2,869	17,208	691	1,311	....
Total Net Borrowing	84	1,419	†2,041	1,089	665	....	....	....	....	....	....	....	....	....	....	....
Net Domestic	84a	1,430	†2,048	1,093	670	1,131	966	†439	247	-2,473	-2,279	838	18,585	4,895	....	....
Net Foreign	85a	-11	†-7	-4	-5	-2	-2	†-2	-4	144	153	187	108	339	....	....
Debt: Domestic	88a	....	....	....	....	....	....	....	....	....	....	....	....	....	....	....
National Accounts		*Year Beginning March 21*														
Househ.Cons.Expend.,incl.NPISHs	96f	12,076	15,567	18,506	21,478	28,380	36,039	46,274	64,056	95,702	117,271	148,833	190,745	241,647	263,936	....
Government Consumption Expend.	91f	2,787	3,269	3,523	5,266	5,302	9,507	15,708	19,066	26,095	36,993	41,829	51,444	71,043	83,795	....
Gross Fixed Capital Formation	93e	3,599	4,322	6,043	11,046	18,341	23,394	23,523	29,081	41,182	70,789	83,821	99,669	148,888	157,556	....
Changes in Inventories	93i	-1,970	-1,057	-116	3,328	4,125	8,135	4,804	-2,426	8,598	14,239	14,328	1,895	748	4,952	....
Exports of Goods and Services	90c	883	1,885	2,684	5,979	7,885	22,135	18,578	45,818	41,473	53,831	47,114	53,844	95,945	188,897	....
Imports of Goods and Services (-)	98c	1,523	2,515	5,210	10,569	14,039	22,058	15,899	19,460	26,396	40,757	46,325	50,300	68,251	94,866	....
Gross Domestic Product (GDP)	99b	18,085	21,930	26,364	37,018	51,757	77,375	91,451	137,063	186,412	251,131	283,914	339,844	477,732	582,050	....
Net Primary Income from Abroad	98.n	22	9	175	360	-63	-308	-359	-1,494	-790	-1,425	-1,292	581	56	-2,765	....
Gross National Income (GNI)	99a	18,107	20,136	25,191	34,038	47,650	62,977	95,069	124,498	171,743	237,760	279,782	317,665	415,804	....	....
GDP Volume 1974 Prices	99b.p	3,307	3,147	....	....	....	....	....	....	....	....	....	....	....	....	....
GDP Volume 1982 Prices	99b.p	....	9,468	9,782	10,930	12,181	12,879	13,084	13,181	13,741	14,661	15,203	15,479	....	....	....
GDP Volume (1995=100)	99bvp	75.5	68.9	71.2	79.5	88.6	93.7	95.2	95.9	100.0	106.7	110.6	112.6	....	....	....
GDP Deflator (1995=100)	99bip	12.9	17.1	19.9	25.0	31.3	44.3	51.5	76.7	100.0	126.3	137.7	161.8	....	....	....
		Midyear Estimates														
Population	99z	50.66	51.91	53.19	54.50	55.84	56.66	57.49	58.33	59.19	60.06	60.94	61.84	62.75	63.66	64.53

(See notes in the back of the book.)

Iraq

		1972	1973	1974	1975	1976	1977	1978	1979	1980	1981	1982	1983	1984	1985	1986
Exchange Rates															*SDRs per Dinar:*	
Principal Rate	ac	2.7440	2.8070	2.7657	2.8926	2.9145	2.7877	2.5992	2.5705	2.6550	2.9092	2.9162	3.0726	3.2818	2.9287	2.6299
															US Dollars per Dinar:	
Principal Rate	ag	2.9792	3.3862	3.3862	3.3862	3.3862	3.3862	3.3862	3.3862	3.3862	3.3862	3.2169	3.2169	3.2169	3.2169	3.2169
Principal Rate	rh	3.0039	3.3064	3.3862	3.3862	3.3862	3.3862	3.3862	3.3862	3.3862	3.3862	3.3513	3.2169	3.2169	3.2169	3.2169
													Index Numbers (1995=100):			
Principal Rate	ahx	93.4	102.8	105.3	105.3	105.3	105.3	105.3	105.3	105.3	105.3	104.2	100.0	100.0	100.0	100.0
Nominal Effective Exchange Rate	ne c	.....	.....	.....	.....	.....	.....	.....	56.9	58.0	67.4	75.7	77.6	85.2	88.4	69.1
Fund Position															*Millions of SDRs:*	
Quota	2f. s	109.0	109.0	109.0	109.0	109.0	109.0	141.0	141.0	234.1	234.1	234.1	234.1	504.0	504.0	504.0
SDRs	1b. s	23.2	20.1	23.0	23.0	28.0	34.2	45.5	82.2	87.2	113.7	74.2	8.6	.1	—	—
Reserve Position in the Fund	1c. s	17.3	27.3	27.3	27.3	27.3	27.5	27.7	47.8	111.9	111.9	111.9	111.9			
Total Fund Cred.&Loans Outstg.	2tl	—	—	—	—	—	—	—	—	—	—	—				
International Liquidity											*Millions of US Dollars Unless Otherwise Indicated:*					
Total Reserves minus Gold	11. d	625.7	1,380.0	3,097.5	2,559.3	4,434.0	6,819.6									
SDRs	1b. d	25.2	24.2	28.2	26.9	32.5	41.5	59.3	108.3	111.2	132.3	81.9	9.0	—	—	—
Reserve Position in the Fund	1c. d	18.7	32.9	33.4	31.9	31.7	33.4	36.0	63.0	142.7	130.3	123.5		—	—	—
Foreign Exchange	1d. d	581.8	1,322.9	3,035.9	2,500.5	4,369.8	6,744.7	.....	.....	.....	.....	.....	.....	.....	.....	.....
Gold (Million Fine Troy Ounces)	1ad	4.099	4.099	4.099	4.099	4.099	4.144	.....	.....	.....	.....	.....	.....	.....	.....	.....
Monetary Authorities: Other Assets	3.. d	9.1	7.9	13.3	12.5	10.0	.....	.....	.....	.....	.....	.....	.....	.....	.....	.....
Other Liab.	4.. d	49.6	176.0	284.3	43.4	1.4	.....	.....	.....	.....	.....	.....	.....	.....	.....	.....
Deposit Money Banks: Assets	7a. d	26.4	121.4	348.7	269.3	333.8	.....	.....	.....	.....	.....	.....	.....	.....	.....	.....
Liabilities	7b. d	2.4	4.5	47.1	42.0	54.6	.....	.....	.....	.....	.....	.....	.....	.....	.....	.....
Monetary Authorities															*Millions of Dinars:*	
Foreign Assets	11	260.1	462.1	993.9	805.7	1,356.8	.....	.....	.....	.....	.....	.....	.....	.....	.....	.....
Claims on Central Government	12a	110.7	69.5	90.0	130.5	64.2	.....	.....	.....	.....	.....	.....	.....	.....	.....	.....
Claims on Deposit Money Banks	12e	.4	.1	—	295.7		.....	.....	.....	.....	.....	.....	.....	.....	.....	.....
Reserve Money	14	257.2	344.5	444.6	571.8	726.6	.....	.....	.....	.....	.....	.....	.....	.....	.....	.....
of which: Currency Outside DMBs	14a	206.9	252.2	358.2	472.6	565.9	.....	.....	.....	.....	.....	.....	.....	.....	.....	.....
Foreign Liabilities	16c	16.3	52.1	84.0	12.8	.4	.....	.....	.....	.....	.....	.....	.....	.....	.....	.....
Central Government Deposits	16d	43.8	73.7	393.9	480.6	486.5	.....	.....	.....	.....	.....	.....	.....	.....	.....	.....
Capital Accounts	17a	59.7	68.1	132.9	130.7	145.0	.....	.....	.....	.....	.....	.....	.....	.....	.....	.....
Other Items (Net)	17r	−5.9	−6.7	28.6	36.0	62.6	.....	.....	.....	.....	.....	.....	.....	.....	.....	.....
Deposit Money Banks															*Millions of Dinars:*	
Reserves	20	46.3	78.8	65.6	95.8	150.0	.....	.....	.....	.....	.....	.....	.....	.....	.....	.....
Foreign Assets	21	8.7	36.0	103.0	79.5	98.6	.....	.....	.....	.....	.....	.....	.....	.....	.....	.....
Claims on Central Government	22a	114.5	151.3	316.2	621.4	620.4	.....	.....	.....	.....	.....	.....	.....	.....	.....	.....
Claims on Private Sector	22d	82.5	81.1	102.5	118.2	132.8	.....	.....	.....	.....	.....	.....	.....	.....	.....	.....
Demand Deposits	24	50.5	64.3	92.7	149.5	184.9	.....	.....	.....	.....	.....	.....	.....	.....	.....	.....
Time and Savings Deposits	25	95.2	122.4	172.8	257.0	315.0	.....	.....	.....	.....	.....	.....	.....	.....	.....	.....
Central Government Deposits	26d	75.1	118.7	201.4	301.2	399.4	.....	.....	.....	.....	.....	.....	.....	.....	.....	.....
Credit from Monetary Authorities	26g	.4	.1	—	130.5	—	.....	.....	.....	.....	.....	.....	.....	.....	.....	.....
Capital Accounts	27a	28.7	33.1	51.1	74.5	89.9	.....	.....	.....	.....	.....	.....	.....	.....	.....	.....
Other Items (Net)	27r	2.2	8.4	69.3	2.3	12.6	.....	.....	.....	.....	.....	.....	.....	.....	.....	.....
Monetary Survey															*Millions of Dinars:*	
Foreign Assets (Net)	31n	251.7	444.7	999.0	860.0	1,438.8	.....	.....	.....	.....	.....	.....	.....	.....	.....	.....
Domestic Credit	32	197.8	117.8	−74.4	107.8	−37.7	.....	.....	.....	.....	.....	.....	.....	.....	.....	.....
Claims on Central Govt. (Net)	32an	106.3	28.3	−189.1	−29.9	−201.3	.....	.....	.....	.....	.....	.....	.....	.....	.....	.....
Claims on Private Sector	32d	82.5	81.1	102.5	118.2	132.8	.....	.....	.....	.....	.....	.....	.....	.....	.....	.....
Claims on Other Banking Insts.	32f	9.0	8.3	12.3	19.5	30.8	.....	.....	.....	.....	.....	.....	.....	.....	.....	.....
Money	34	259.7	322.7	462.3	625.5	754.8	.....	.....	.....	.....	.....	.....	.....	.....	.....	.....
Quasi-Money	35	95.2	122.4	172.8	257.0	315.0	.....	.....	.....	.....	.....	.....	.....	.....	.....	.....
Other Items (Net)	37r	94.5	117.3	289.5	85.3	331.4	.....	.....	.....	.....	.....	.....	.....	.....	.....	.....
Money plus Quasi-Money	35l	354.9	445.1	635.1	882.6	1,069.8	.....	.....	.....	.....	.....	.....	.....	.....	.....	.....
Other Banking Institutions																
Specialized Banks															*Millions of Dinars:*	
Cash	40	4.1	7.9	14.2	12.6	14.8	.....	.....	.....	.....	.....	.....	.....	.....	.....	.....
Claims on Private Sector	42d	84.1	96.6	122.0	150.9	189.5	.....	.....	.....	.....	.....	.....	.....	.....	.....	.....
Central Government Deposits	46d	38.2	44.4	52.3	64.2	79.4	.....	.....	.....	.....	.....	.....	.....	.....	.....	.....
Credit from Monetary Authorities	46g	3.2	1.9	1.2	2.9	10.5	.....	.....	.....	.....	.....	.....	.....	.....	.....	.....
Credit from Deposit Money Banks	46h	5.5	5.7	10.6	17.3	17.4	.....	.....	.....	.....	.....	.....	.....	.....	.....	.....
Capital Accounts	47a	43.4	52.7	70.7	74.5	87.7	.....	.....	.....	.....	.....	.....	.....	.....	.....	.....
Other Items (Net)	47r	−2.0	−.1	1.4	4.6	9.2	.....	.....	.....	.....	.....	.....	.....	.....	.....	.....
Post Office: Savings Deposits	45.. i	6.9	8.4	12.4	16.6	21.3	.....	.....	.....	.....	.....	.....	.....	.....	.....	.....
Nonbank Financial Institutions															*Millions of Dinars:*	
Cash	40.. s	1.60	2.04	2.68	3.80	4.61	.....	.....	.....	.....	.....	.....	.....	.....	.....	.....
Claims on Central Government	42a. s	1.11	1.09	.86	.86	.86	.....	.....	.....	.....	.....	.....	.....	.....	.....	.....
Claims on Private Sector	42d. s	.96	1.07	1.18	1.25	1.40	.....	.....	.....	.....	.....	.....	.....	.....	.....	.....
Incr.in Total Assets(Within Per.)	49z. s	.52	.58	.81	1.11	1.31	.....	.....	.....	.....	.....	.....	.....	.....	.....	.....
Production															*Index Numbers (1995=100):*	
Wholesale Prices (1975=100)	63	76.9	80.5	90.6	100.0	111.2	118.6[e]	.....	.....	.....	.....	.....	.....	.....	.....	.....
Consumer Prices (1975=100)	64	80.8	84.7[e]	91.3[e]	100.0[e]	112.8[e]	123.1[e]	128.8	.....	.....	.....	.....	.....	.....	.....	.....
Crude Petroleum	66aa	73.2	100.6	98.1	112.6	120.5	114.4	130.9	171.9	132.2	44.7	45.9	50.1	60.1	71.4	84.1

	1987	1988	1989	1990	1991	1992	1993	1994	1995	1996	1997	1998	1999	2000	2001		
																Exchange Rates	
End of Period																	
	2.2676	2.3905	2.4479	2.2612	2.2489	2.3396	2.3420	2.2036	2.1641	2.2371	2.3842	2.2847	2.3438	2.4690	2.5597	Principal Rate	**ac**
End of Period (ag) Period Average (rh)																	
	3.2169	3.2169	3.2169	3.2169	3.2169	3.2169	3.2169	3.2169	3.2169	3.2169	3.2169	3.2169	3.2169	3.2169	3.2169	Principal Rate	**ag**
	3.2169	3.2169	3.2169	3.2169	3.2169	3.2169	3.2169	3.2169	3.2169	3.2169	3.2169	3.2169	3.2169	3.2169	3.2169	Principal Rate	**rh**
Period Averages																	
	100.0	100.0	100.0	100.0	100.0	100.0	100.0	100.0	100.0	100.0	100.0	100.0	100.0	100.0	100.0	Principal Rate	**ah** *x*
	60.4	58.3	62.7	61.4	68.0	73.9	87.8	101.1	100.0	108.1	123.4	131.2	140.1	156.6	172.0	Nominal Effective Exchange Rate	**ne** *c*
End of Period																**Fund Position**	
	504.0	504.0	504.0	504.0	504.0	504.0	504.0	504.0	504.0	504.0	504.0	504.0	504.0	504.0	504.0	Quota	**2f.** *s*
	5.1	—	—	—	—	—	—	—	—	—	—	—	—	—	—	SDRs	**1b.** *s*
	—	—	—	—	—	—	—	—	—	—	—	—	—	—	—	Reserve Position in the Fund	**1c.** *s*
	—	—	—	—	—	—	—	—	—	—	—	—	—	—	—	Total Fund Cred.&Loans Outstg.	**2tl**
End of Period																**International Liquidity**	
	....	....	....	....	....										....	Total Reserves minus Gold	**1l.** *d*
	7.2	—	—	—	—	—	—	—	—	—	—	—	—	—	—	SDRs	**1b.** *d*
	—	—	—	—	—	—	—	—	—	—	—	—	—	—	—	Reserve Position in the Fund	**1c.** *d*
	....	....	....	....	....										....	Foreign Exchange	**1d.** *d*
	....	....	....	....	....										....	Gold (Million Fine Troy Ounces)	**1ad**
	....	....	....	....	....										....	Monetary Authorities: Other Assets	**3..** *d*
																Other Liab.	**4..** *d*
	....	....	....	....	....										....	Deposit Money Banks: Assets	**7a.** *d*
																Liabilities	**7b.** *d*
End of Period																**Monetary Authorities**	
	....	....	....	....	....										....	Foreign Assets	**11**
	....	....	....	....	....										....	Claims on Central Government	**12a**
	....	....	....	....	....										....	Claims on Deposit Money Banks	**12e**
	....	....	....	....	....										....	Reserve Money	**14**
	....	....	....	....	....										....	*of which: Currency Outside DMBs*	**14a**
	....	....	....	....	....										....	Foreign Liabilities	**16c**
	....	....	....	....	....										....	Central Government Deposits	**16d**
	....	....	....	....	....										....	Capital Accounts	**17a**
	....	....	....	....	....										....	Other Items (Net)	**17r**
End of Period																**Deposit Money Banks**	
	....	....	....	....	....										....	Reserves	**20**
	....	....	....	....	....										....	Foreign Assets	**21**
	....	....	....	....	....										....	Claims on Central Government	**22a**
	....	....	....	....	....										....	Claims on Private Sector	**22d**
	....	....	....	....	....										....	Demand Deposits	**24**
	....	....	....	....	....										....	Time and Savings Deposits	**25**
	....	....	....	....	....										....	Central Government Deposits	**26d**
	....	....	....	....	....										....	Credit from Monetary Authorities	**26g**
	....	....	....	....	....										....	Capital Accounts	**27a**
	....	....	....	....	....										....	Other Items (Net)	**27r**
End of Period																**Monetary Survey**	
	....	....	....	....	....										....	Foreign Assets (Net)	**31n**
	....	....	....	....	....										....	Domestic Credit	**32**
	....	....	....	....	....										....	Claims on Central Govt. (Net)	**32an**
	....	....	....	....	....										....	Claims on Private Sector	**32d**
	....	....	....	....	....										....	Claims on Other Banking Insts.	**32f**
	....	....	....	....	....										....	Money	**34**
	....	....	....	....	....										....	Quasi-Money	**35**
	....	....	....	....	....										....	Other Items (Net)	**37r**
	....	....	....	....	....										....	Money plus Quasi-Money	**35l**
End of Period																**Other Banking Institutions**	
																Specialized Banks	
	....	....	....	....	....										....	Cash	**40**
	....	....	....	....	....										....	Claims on Private Sector	**42d**
	....	....	....	....	....										....	Central Government Deposits	**46d**
	....	....	....	....	....										....	Credit from Monetary Authorities	**46g**
	....	....	....	....	....										....	Credit from Deposit Money Banks	**46h**
	....	....	....	....	....										....	Capital Accounts	**47a**
	....	....	....	....	....										....	Other Items (Net)	**47r**
	....	....	....	....	....										....	Post Office: Savings Deposits	**45..** *i*
End of Period																*Nonbank Financial Institutions*	
	....	....	....	....	....										....	Cash	**40..** *s*
	....	....	....	....	....										....	Claims on Central Government	**42a.** *s*
	....	....	....	....	....										....	Claims on Private Sector	**42d.** *s*
	....	....	....	....	....										....	*Incr.in Total Assets(Within Per.)*	**49z.** *s*
Period Averages																**Production**	
	....	....	....	....	....										....	Wholesale Prices (1975=100)	**63**
	....	....	....	....	....										....	Consumer Prices (1975=100)	**64**
	103.5	130.5	140.6	100.0	14.9	21.9	29.9	29.9	29.9	31.3	60.5	105.4	124.7	....	....	Crude Petroleum	**66aa**

Iraq

	1972	1973	1974	1975	1976	1977	1978	1979	1980	1981	1982	1983	1984	1985	1986
International Transactions														*Millions of Dinars*	
Exports 70	362.0	251.4	706.5	4,705.5	5,389.5	5,614.6	6,422.7	12,522.0	....	....					
Crude Petroleum 70aa	658.6	1,102.3	3,813.8	4,669.9	5,342.9	5,571.9	6,360.5	12,480.0	15,321.3	6,089.6	5,982.4	5,954.8	6,937.0	8,142.5	5,126.2
Imports, c.i.f. 71	234.6	270.3	700.1	1,244.7	1,150.9	1,323.2	1,244.1	1,738.9	2,208.1	2,333.8	....				
Imports, c.i.f., from DOTS 71y	....	....	....	....	....	....	....	....	....	6,013.0	6,309.0	3,086.2	3,032.4	3,285.7	2,773.0
Volume of Exports															*1985=100*
Crude Petroleum 72aa	103.1	142.4	138.7	149.8	166.7	161.0	184.2	241.7	187.7	62.9	64.6	70.4	84.5	100.0	117.7
Export Prices															*1985=100:*
Crude Petroleum .... 76aa *d*	7.3	9.8	35.6	38.1	40.7	44.7	44.6	65.9	107.2	125.5	118.4	104.4	100.7	100.0	54.0
Balance of Payments														*Millions of US Dollars:*	
Current Account, n.i.e. .... 78al *d*	....	....	....	....	2,495	2,988	....	....	....	....	....	....	....	....	....
Goods: Exports f.o.b. .... 78aa *d*	....	....	....	....	7,854	10,838	....	....	....	....	....	....	....	....	....
Goods: Imports f.o.b. .... 78ab *d*	....	....	....	....	−4,269	−5,867	....	....	....	....	....	....	....	....	....
Trade Balance .... 78ac *d*	....	....	....	....	3,585	4,971	....	....	....	....	....	....	....	....	....
Services: Credit .... 78ad *d*	....	....	....	....	582	760	....	....	....	....	....	....	....	....	....
Services: Debit .... 78ae *d*	....	....	....	....	−1,540	−2,708	....	....	....	....	....	....	....	....	....
Balance on Goods & Services ..... 78af *d*	....	....	....	....	2,627	3,023	....	....	....	....	....	....	....	....	....
Income: Credit .... 78ag *d*	....	....	....	....	....	....	....	....	....	....	....	....	....	....	....
Income: Debit .... 78ah *d*	....	....	....	....	....	....	....	....	....	....	....	....	....	....	....
Balance on Gds, Serv. & Inc. .... 78ai *d*	....	....	....	....	2,627	3,023	....	....	....	....	....	....	....	....	....
Current Transfers, n.i.e.: Credit .... 78aj *d*	....	....	....	....	....	....	....	....	....	....	....	....	....	....	....
Current Transfers: Debit .... 78ak *d*	....	....	....	....	−132	−35	....	....	....	....	....	....	....	....	....
Capital Account, n.i.e. .... 78bc *d*	....	....	....	....	—	—	....	....	....	....	....	....	....	....	....
Capital Account, n.i.e.: Credit ..... 78ba *d*	....	....	....	....	—	—	....	....	....	....	....	....	....	....	....
Capital Account: Debit .... 78bb *d*	....	....	....	....	—	—	....	....	....	....	....	....	....	....	....
Financial Account, n.i.e. .... 78bj *d*	....	....	....	....	−1,053	−7	....	....	....	....	....	....	....	....	....
Direct Investment Abroad .... 78bd *d*	....	....	....	....	—	—	....	....	....	....	....	....	....	....	....
Dir. Invest. in Rep. Econ., n.i.e. ..... 78be *d*	....	....	....	....	—	—	....	....	....	....	....	....	....	....	....
Portfolio Investment Assets ...... 78bf *d*	....	....	....	....	—	—	....	....	....	....	....	....	....	....	....
Equity Securities .... 78bk *d*	....	....	....	....	—	—	....	....	....	....	....	....	....	....	....
Debt Securities .... 78bl *d*	....	....	....	....	—	—	....	....	....	....	....	....	....	....	....
Portfolio Investment Liab., n.i.e. .. 78bg *d*	....	....	....	....	—	—	....	....	....	....	....	....	....	....	....
Equity Securities .... 78bm *d*	....	....	....	....	—	—	....	....	....	....	....	....	....	....	....
Debt Securities .... 78bn *d*	....	....	....	....	—	—	....	....	....	....	....	....	....	....	....
Financial Derivatives Assets ...... 78bw *d*	....	....	....	....	....	....	....	....	....	....	....	....	....	....	....
Financial Derivatives Liabilities ..... 78bx *d*	....	....	....	....	....	....	....	....	....	....	....	....	....	....	....
Other Investment Assets .... 78bh *d*	....	....	....	....	−201	−152	....	....	....	....	....	....	....	....	....
Monetary Authorities .... 78bo *d*	....	....	....	....	....	....	....	....	....	....	....	....	....	....	....
General Government .... 78bp *d*	....	....	....	....	−137	−80	....	....	....	....	....	....	....	....	....
Banks .... 78bq *d*	....	....	....	....	−65	−72	....	....	....	....	....	....	....	....	....
Other Sectors .... 78br *d*	....	....	....	....	....	....	....	....	....	....	....	....	....	....	....
Other Investment Liab., n.i.e. ..... 78bi *d*	....	....	....	....	−852	145	....	....	....	....	....	....	....	....	....
Monetary Authorities .... 78bs *d*	....	....	....	....	−41	12	....	....	....	....	....	....	....	....	....
General Government .... 78bt *d*	....	....	....	....	−231	−121	....	....	....	....	....	....	....	....	....
Banks .... 78bu *d*	....	....	....	....	—	57	....	....	....	....	....	....	....	....	....
Other Sectors .... 78bv *d*	....	....	....	....	−579	197	....	....	....	....	....	....	....	....	....
Net Errors and Omissions .... 78ca *d*	....	....	....	....	423	−508	....	....	....	....	....	....	....	....	....
Overall Balance .... 78cb *d*	....	....	....	....	1,865	2,473	....	....	....	....	....	....	....	....	....
Reserves and Related Items .... 79da *d*	....	....	....	....	−1,865	−2,473	....	....	....	....	....	....	....	....	....
Reserve Assets .... 79db *d*	....	....	....	....	−1,865	−2,473	....	....	....	....	....	....	....	....	....
Use of Fund Credit and Loans ..... 79dc *d*	....	....	....	....	—	—	....	....	....	....	....	....	....	....	....
Exceptional Financing .... 79de *d*	....	....	....	....	....	....	....	....	....	....	....	....	....	....	....
National Accounts														*Millions of Dinars*	
Househ.Cons.Expend.,incl.NPISHs 96f	956.1	929.4	1,427.1	2,266.7	2,611.9	3,669.9	2,628.9	2,971.8	3,601.9	4,156.2	6,035.6	6,848.9	7,815.2	8,098.7	8,397.7
Government Consumption Expend. 91f	....	....	....	755.6	870.6	1,223.3	1,584.1	1,646.3	2,451.2	3,446.2	4,468.2	5,475.3	4,989.1	4,431.8	5,252.8
Gross Fixed Capital Formation 93e	217.1	288.6	628.6	1,067.9	1,336.4	1,478.6	1,993.0	2,714.3	3,807.1	5,708.1	6,536.5	5,513.2	4,433.4	4,301.2	3,859.2
Changes in Inventories 93i	56.2	70.6	320.2	150.8	−301.2	—	−537.4	564.3	1,053.3	1,313.6	833.6	−3,533.3	−1,733.2	−636.5	−990.9
Exports of Goods and Services 90c	505.7	720.5	2,075.9	2,329.0	2,491.0	3,425.6	3,977.1	6,974.3	10,012.4	3,587.8	3,350.5	3,107.9	3,734.3	3,774.7	2,417.8
Imports of Goods and Services (-) 98c	294.2	382.7	1,073.8	1,792.0	1,479.0	2,532.0	2,220.8	3,480.1	4,977.6	7,068.3	8,447.4	4,156.3	4,316.4	4,476.0	3,873.6
Gross Domestic Product (GDP) 99b	1,440.9	1,626.4	3,378.0	4,022.4	4,659.1	6,042.1	7,224.9	11,390.9	15,948.4	11,143.6	12,777.0	13,255.7	14,922.4	15,493.8	15,063.0
Net Primary Income from Abroad 98.n	−136.5	−82.0	−242.0	−115.0	37.7	80.7	139.0	90.4	474.2	−401.0	−729.1	−589.6	−470.5	−558.8	−692.4
Gross National Income (GNI) 99a	1,304.4	1,544.4	3,136.0	3,907.4	....	....	7,363.9	11,481.3	16,422.6	10,742.6	12,051.9	12,666.1	14,451.9	14,935.0	14,370.6
Net National Income 99e	1,219.0	1,451.0	3,033.0	3,802.0	....	....	....	....	....	....	....	....	....	....	....
															Millions:
Population 99z	10.07	10.41	10.77	11.12	11.51	12.03	12.41	12.82	13.24	13.67	14.11	14.59	15.08	15.58	16.11

	1987	1988	1989	1990	1991	1992	1993	1994	1995	1996	1997	1998	1999	2000	2001		
International Transactions																	
Millions of Dinars																	
Exports	....	....	....	....	....	....	....	....	....	....	....	....	....	....	....		70
Crude Petroleum	6,988.9	7,245.8	....	....	....	....	....	....	....	....	....	....	....	....	....		70aa
Imports, c.i.f.	....	....	....	....	....	....	....	....	....	....	....	....	....	....	....		71
Imports, c.i.f., from DOTS	2,268.7	2,888.8	3,077.1	2,028.5	131.5	187.3	165.6	158.3	206.9	176.7	356.5	579.1	672.9	910.5	1,165.1		71y
1985=100																Volume of Exports	
Crude Petroleum	143.5	180.5	197.2	....	....	....	....	....	....	....	....	....	....	....	....		72aa
Index of Prices in US Dollars																Export Prices	
Crude Petroleum	59.8	49.2	....	....	....	....	....	....	....	....	....	....	....	....	....		76aa *d*
Minus Sign Indicates Debit																Balance of Payments	
Current Account, n.i.e.	....	....	....	....	....	....	....	....	....	....	....	....	....	....	....		78al *d*
Goods: Exports f.o.b.	....	....	....	....	....	....	....	....	....	....	....	....	....	....	....		78aa *d*
Goods: Imports f.o.b.	....	....	....	....	....	....	....	....	....	....	....	....	....	....	....		78ab *d*
Trade Balance	....	....	....	....	....	....	....	....	....	....	....	....	....	....	....		78ac *d*
Services: Credit	....	....	....	....	....	....	....	....	....	....	....	....	....	....	....		78ad *d*
Services: Debit	....	....	....	....	....	....	....	....	....	....	....	....	....	....	....		78ae *d*
Balance on Goods & Services	....	....	....	....	....	....	....	....	....	....	....	....	....	....	....		78af *d*
Income: Credit	....	....	....	....	....	....	....	....	....	....	....	....	....	....	....		78ag *d*
Income: Debit	....	....	....	....	....	....	....	....	....	....	....	....	....	....	....		78ah *d*
Balance on Gds, Serv. & Inc.	....	....	....	....	....	....	....	....	....	....	....	....	....	....	....		78ai *d*
Current Transfers, n.i.e.: Credit	....	....	....	....	....	....	....	....	....	....	....	....	....	....	....		78aj *d*
Current Transfers: Debit	....	....	....	....	....	....	....	....	....	....	....	....	....	....	....		78ak *d*
Capital Account, n.i.e.	....	....	....	....	....	....	....	....	....	....	....	....	....	....	....		78bc *d*
Capital Account, n.i.e.: Credit	....	....	....	....	....	....	....	....	....	....	....	....	....	....	....		78ba *d*
Capital Account: Debit	....	....	....	....	....	....	....	....	....	....	....	....	....	....	....		78bb *d*
Financial Account, n.i.e.	....	....	....	....	....	....	....	....	....	....	....	....	....	....	....		78bj *d*
Direct Investment Abroad	....	....	....	....	....	....	....	....	....	....	....	....	....	....	....		78bd *d*
Dir. Invest. in Rep. Econ., n.i.e.	....	....	....	....	....	....	....	....	....	....	....	....	....	....	....		78be *d*
Portfolio Investment Assets	....	....	....	....	....	....	....	....	....	....	....	....	....	....	....		78bf *d*
Equity Securities	....	....	....	....	....	....	....	....	....	....	....	....	....	....	....		78bk *d*
Debt Securities	....	....	....	....	....	....	....	....	....	....	....	....	....	....	....		78bl *d*
Portfolio Investment Liab., n.i.e.	....	....	....	....	....	....	....	....	....	....	....	....	....	....	....		78bg *d*
Equity Securities	....	....	....	....	....	....	....	....	....	....	....	....	....	....	....		78bm *d*
Debt Securities	....	....	....	....	....	....	....	....	....	....	....	....	....	....	....		78bn *d*
Financial Derivatives Assets	....	....	....	....	....	....	....	....	....	....	....	....	....	....	....		78bw *d*
Financial Derivatives Liabilities	....	....	....	....	....	....	....	....	....	....	....	....	....	....	....		78bx *d*
Other Investment Assets	....	....	....	....	....	....	....	....	....	....	....	....	....	....	....		78bh *d*
Monetary Authorities	....	....	....	....	....	....	....	....	....	....	....	....	....	....	....		78bo *d*
General Government	....	....	....	....	....	....	....	....	....	....	....	....	....	....	....		78bp *d*
Banks	....	....	....	....	....	....	....	....	....	....	....	....	....	....	....		78bq *d*
Other Sectors	....	....	....	....	....	....	....	....	....	....	....	....	....	....	....		78br *d*
Other Investment Liab., n.i.e.	....	....	....	....	....	....	....	....	....	....	....	....	....	....	....		78bi *d*
Monetary Authorities	....	....	....	....	....	....	....	....	....	....	....	....	....	....	....		78bs *d*
General Government	....	....	....	....	....	....	....	....	....	....	....	....	....	....	....		78bt *d*
Banks	....	....	....	....	....	....	....	....	....	....	....	....	....	....	....		78bu *d*
Other Sectors	....	....	....	....	....	....	....	....	....	....	....	....	....	....	....		78bv *d*
Net Errors and Omissions	....	....	....	....	....	....	....	....	....	....	....	....	....	....	....		78ca *d*
Overall Balance	....	....	....	....	....	....	....	....	....	....	....	....	....	....	....		78cb *d*
Reserves and Related Items	....	....	....	....	....	....	....	....	....	....	....	....	....	....	....		79da *d*
Reserve Assets	....	....	....	....	....	....	....	....	....	....	....	....	....	....	....		79db *d*
Use of Fund Credit and Loans	....	....	....	....	....	....	....	....	....	....	....	....	....	....	....		79dc *d*
Exceptional Financing	....	....	....	....	....	....	....	....	....	....	....	....	....	....	....		79de *d*
National Accounts																	
Millions of Dinars																	
Househ.Cons.Expend.,incl.NPISHs	9,204.4	10,101.4	11,232.4	11,760.5	9,611.1	40,929.8	81,106.0										96f
Government Consumption Expend.	5,673.8	6,645.8	5,990.1	6,142.0	7,033.3	8,898.0	15,576.3										91f
Gross Fixed Capital Formation	3,657.5	2,899.2	6,305.5	6,220.0	3,289.1	10,782.0	16,258.7										93e
Changes in Inventories	-124.1	1,193.5	-2,317.5	-976.9	520.0	-2,379.0	1,102.0										93i
Exports of Goods and Services	4,087.1	3,824.5	4,482.6	4,305.4	547.8	670.3	1,474.0										90c
Imports of Goods and Services (-)	4,598.4	5,038.1	4,667.3	4,154.2	1,061.6	1,540.6	3,375.0										98c
Gross Domestic Product (GDP)	17,900.6	19,626.3	21,025.8	23,296.8	19,939.7	57,360.5	112,142.0										99b
Net Primary Income from Abroad	-704.7	-700.4	-678.2														98.n
Gross National Income (GNI)	17,195.9	19,332.1	19,331.6	....	....	....	....										99a
Net National Income	....	....	....	....	....	....	....										99e
Midyear Estimates																	
Population	16.33	16.88	17.43	18.08	17.77	18.31	18.89	19.47	20.04	20.62	21.18	21.75	22.34	22.95	23.58		99z

(See notes in the back of the book.)

Ireland

		1972	1973	1974	1975	1976	1977	1978	1979	1980	1981	1982	1983	1984	1985	1986
Exchange Rates													*SDRs per Pound through 1998,*			
Market Rate	ac	2.1627	1.9258	1.9182	1.7285	1.4653	1.5691	1.5616	1.6283	1.4878	1.3574	1.2660	1.0841	1.0115	1.1321	1.1441
													US Dollars per Pound through 1998,			
Market Rate	ag	2.3481	2.3232	2.3485	2.0235	1.7024	1.9060	2.0345	2.1450	1.8975	1.5800	1.3965	1.1350	.9915	1.2435	1.3995
Market Rate	rh	2.5018	2.4522	2.3390	2.2218	1.8062	1.7455	1.9195	2.0475	2.0580	1.6167	1.4222	1.2482	1.0871	1.0656	1.3415
													ECUs per Pound:			
ECU Rate	ec	....	....	....	....	....	....	....	1.4913	1.4537	1.4560	1.4432	1.3718	1.3986	1.4005	1.3075
ECU Rate	ed	....	....	....	....	....	....	1.5063	1.4938	1.4793	1.4470	1.4502	1.3996	1.3773	1.3982	1.3661
													Index Numbers (1995=100):			
Market Rate	ahx	156.0	152.9	145.8	138.5	112.6	108.8	119.7	127.7	128.3	100.8	88.7	77.8	67.8	66.4	83.6
Nominal Effective Exchange Rate	neu	159.08	146.40	143.08	134.11	120.95	116.56	116.97	117.17	114.60	104.98	103.81	100.14	96.42	97.23	101.64
Fund Position													*Millions of SDRs:*			
Quota	2f. s	121	121	121	121	121	121	155	155	233	233	233	343	343	343	343
SDRs	1b. s	39	39	41	41	45	46	48	71	71	91	96	65	89	99	113
Reserve Position in the Fund	1c. s	40	40	42	39	69	66	60	61	77	75	75	116	124	121	131
Total Fund Cred.&Loans Outstg.	2tl	—														
International Liquidity													*Millions of US Dollars Unless Otherwise Indicated:*			
Total Res.Min.Gold (Eurosys.Def)	1l. d	1,109	1,007	1,247	1,513	1,818	2,351	2,668	2,212	2,860	2,651	2,622	2,640	2,352	2,940	3,236
SDRs	1b. d	43	48	50	48	53	55	63	93	91	106	106	68	88	109	139
Reserve Position in the Fund	1c. d	44	49	52	46	80	80	78	80	98	87	83	121	122	133	160
Foreign Exchange	1d. d	1,023	911	1,146	1,419	1,686	2,216	2,528	2,039	2,672	2,458	2,433	2,450	2,143	2,698	2,938
o/w: Fin.Deriv.Rel.to Reserves	1dd d	....	....	....	....	....	....	....	....	....	....	....	....	....	....	....
Other Reserve Assets	1e. d	....	....	....	....	....	....	....	....	....	....	....	....	....	....	....
Gold (Million Fine Troy Ounces)	1ad	.457	.429	.447	.447	.447	.473	.447	.383	.357	.359	.360	.360	.360	.359	.359
Gold (Eurosystem Valuation)	1an d	17	18	19	18	18	20	20	18	16	117	96	106	88	95	105
Memo: Euro Cl. on Non-EA Res.	1dg d	....	....	....	....	....	....	....	....	....	....	....	....	....	....	....
Non-Euro Cl. on EA Res.	1dh d	....	....	....	....	....	....	....	....	....	....	....	....	....	....	....
Mon. Auth.: Other Foreign Assets	3.. d	....	....	....	....	....	....	....	....	....	....	....	....	....	....	....
Foreign Liabilities	4.. d	....	....	....	....	....	....	....	....	....	....	....	....	....	....	....
Banking Insts.: Foreign Assets	7a. d	1,727	2,625	3,328	3,138	3,203	4,216	5,321	7,084	8,781	8,583	2,774	2,579	2,631	3,213	3,829
Foreign Liab.	7b. d	2,174	2,964	3,736	3,573	3,577	5,331	6,528	8,549	10,720	10,363	†5,075	5,116	5,127	6,323	8,318
Monetary Authorities													*Millions of Pounds through 1998;*			
Fgn. Assets (Cl.on Non-EA Ctys)	11	432	443	504	689	978	1,218	1,270	989	1,369	1,507	1,637	2,061	2,160	2,326	2,259
Claims on General Government	12a. u	....	....	....	....	....	....	....	....	....	....	....	....	....	....	....
o/w: Claims on Gen.Govt.in Cty	12a	33	61	63	114	108	111	136	278	342	334	398	412	513	454	442
Claims on Banking Institutions	12e. u	....	....	....	....	....	....	....	....	....	....	....	....	....	....	....
o/w: Claims on Bank.Inst.in Cty	12e	....	....	....	....	....	....	....	....	....	....	....	....	....	....	....
Claims on Other Resident Sectors	12d. u	....	....	....	....	....	....	....	....	....	....	....	....	....	....	....
o/w: Cl. on Oth.Res.Sect.in Cty	12d	—	—	—	—	67	10	26	15	—	—	55	—	4	2	—
Currency Issued	14a	205	240	268	321	369	422	512	633	721	797	879	985	1,035	1,073	1,130
Liabilities to Banking Insts	14c. u	....	....	....	....	....	....	....	....	....	....	....	....	....	....	....
o/w: Liabs to Bank.Inst.in Cty	14c	138	188	265	299	357	405	525	508	603	484	517	565	636	727	731
Demand Dep. of Other Res.Sect.	14d. u	....	....	....	....	....	....	....	....	....	....	....	....	....	....	....
o/w: D.Dep.of Oth.Res.Sect.in Cty	14d	....	....	....	....	....	....	....	....	....	....	....	....	....	....	....
Other Dep. of Other Res.Sect.	15.. u	....	....	....	....	....	....	....	....	....	....	....	....	....	....	....
o/w: O.Dep.of Oth.Res.Sect.in Cty	15	....	....	....	....	....	....	....	....	....	....	....	....	....	....	....
Money Market Instruments	16m. u	....	....	....	....	....	....	....	....	....	....	....	....	....	....	....
o/w: MMI Held by Resid.of Cty	16m	....	....	....	....	....	....	....	....	....	....	....	....	....	....	....
Bonds (Debt Securities)	16n. u	....	....	....	....	....	....	....	....	....	....	....	....	....	....	....
o/w: Bonds Held by Resid.of Cty	16n	....	....	....	....	....	....	....	....	....	....	....	....	....	....	....
Foreign Liab. (to Non-EA Ctys)	16c	—	—	—	—	—	—	—	—	—	—	—	—	—	—	—
Central Government Deposits	16d. u	....	....	....	....	....	....	....	....	....	....	....	....	....	....	....
o/w: Cent.Govt.Dep. in Cty	16d	85	40	28	135	232	297	193	117	138	130	186	222	198	193	274
Capital Accounts	17a	43	41	62	84	183	202	183	203	248	382	434	654	796	793	824
Other Items (Net)	17r	-7	-4	-56	-37	12	15	19	-180	1	48	73	47	13	-5	-257
Memo: Currency Put into Circ.	14m	....	....	....	....	....	....	....	....	....	....	....	....	....	....	....
Banking Institutions													*Millions of Pounds through 1998;*			
Claims on Monetary Authorities	20	164	229	302	341	402	476	620	622	770	953	567	639	742	827	833
Claims on Bk.Inst.in Oth.EA Ctys	20b. u	....	....	....	....	....	....	....	....	....	....	....	....	....	....	....
Fgn. Assets (Cl.on Non-EA Ctys)	21	663	1,130	1,417	1,551	1,882	2,212	2,615	3,302	4,628	5,432	1,986	2,272	2,654	2,584	2,736
Claims on General Government	22a. u	....	....	....	....	....	....	....	....	....	....	....	....	....	....	....
o/w: Claims on Gen.Govt.in Cty	22a	293	348	488	656	722	879	930	1,056	1,275	1,443	1,844	2,161	2,740	2,939	3,045
Claims on Other Resident Sectors	22d. u	....	....	....	....	....	....	....	....	....	....	....	....	....	....	....
o/w: Cl. on Oth.Res.Sect.in Cty	22d	917	1,088	1,256	1,470	1,747	2,304	3,037	3,669	4,300	5,224	†6,423	7,229	7,891	8,197	8,805
Demand Deposits	24.. u	....	....	....	....	....	....	....	....	....	....	....	....	....	....	....
o/w: D.Dep.of Oth.Res.Sect.in Cty	24	512	645	757	894	1,025	1,214	1,673	1,988	2,407	3,064	†1,318	1,450	1,779	1,765	1,828
Other Deposits	25.. u	....	....	....	....	....	....	....	....	....	....	....	....	....	....	....
o/w: O.Dep.of Oth.Res.Sect.in Cty	25	654	824	1,042	1,280	1,417	1,693	2,047	2,400	2,993	3,439	†4,932	5,161	5,587	6,026	5,794
Money Market Instruments	26m. u	....	....	....	....	....	....	....	....	....	....	....	....	....	....	....
o/w: MMI Held by Resid.of Cty	26m	....	....	....	....	....	....	....	....	....	....	....	....	....	....	....
Bonds (Debt Securities)	26n. u	....	....	....	....	....	....	....	....	....	....	....	....	....	....	....
o/w: Bonds Held by Resid.of Cty	26n	....	....	....	....	....	....	....	....	....	....	....	....	....	....	....
Foreign Liab. (to Non-EA Ctys)	26c	834	1,276	1,591	1,766	2,101	2,797	3,209	3,986	5,650	6,559	†3,634	4,508	5,171	5,085	5,943
Central Government Deposits	26d. u	....	....	....	....	....	....	....	....	....	....	....	....	....	....	....
o/w: Cent.Govt.Dep. in Cty	26d	9	17	13	15	27	34	30	38	22	43	†46	60	84	55	93
Credit from Monetary Authorities	26g	....	....	....	....	....	....	....	....	....	....	105	70	143	87	369
Liab. to Bk.Inst.in Oth. EA Ctys	26h. u	....	....	....	....	....	....	....	....	....	....	....	....	....	....	....
Capital Accounts	27a	16	23	36	38	49	68	91	115	142	184	1,188	1,372	1,607	1,686	1,584
Other Items (Net)	27r	9	—	25	26	32	66	152	123	-241	-238	†-403	-321	-345	-157	-192

1987	1988	1989	1990	1991	1992	1993	1994	1995	1996	1997	1998	1999	2000	2001	
															Exchange Rates
SDRs per Euro Thereafter: End of Period															
1.1810	1.1202	1.1843	1.2480	1.2233	1.1850	1.0271	1.0598	1.0801	1.1691	1.0601	1.0563	.7319	.7142	.7013	Market Rate .... **ac**
US Dollars per Euro Thereafter: End of Period (ag) Period Average (rh)															
1.6755	1.5075	1.5563	1.7755	1.7498	1.6294	1.4108	1.5471	1.6055	1.6811	1.4304	1.4873	1.0046	.9305	.8813	Market Rate .... **ag**
1.4881	1.5261	1.4190	1.6585	1.7053	1.4671	1.4978	1.6038	1.6006	1.5180	1.4257		1.0668	.9240	.8956	Market Rate .... **rh**
End of Period (ec) Period Average (ed)															
1.2855	1.2846	1.3002	1.3024	1.3049	1.3456	1.2630	1.2578	1.2218	1.3417	1.2960	1.2697	....	....	....	ECU Rate .... **ec**
1.2896	1.2892	1.2873	1.3026	1.3024	1.3146	1.2514	1.2604	1.2263	1.2611	1.3380	1.2717	....	....	....	ECU Rate .... **ed**
Period Averages															
92.8	95.2	88.5	103.4	100.7	106.3	91.5	93.4	100.0	99.8	94.7	88.9	....	....	....	Market Rate .... **ahx**
99.75	98.00	96.96	102.76	101.37	104.51	99.14	99.44	100.00	102.07	102.33	97.01	94.17	88.97	89.73	Nominal Effective Exchange Rate .... **neu**
															Fund Position
End of Period															
343	343	343	343	343	525	525	525	525	525	525	525	838	838	838	Quota **2f.s**
126	134	145	158	170	90	97	101	107	115	123	137	29	37	43	SDRs **1b.s**
131	134	125	105	124	171	155	152	197	226	252	414	303	252	268	Reserve Position in the Fund **1c.s**
—	—	—	—	—	—	—	—	—	—	—	—	—	—	—	Total Fund Cred.&Loans Outstg. **2tl**
															International Liquidity
End of Period															
4,796	5,087	4,057	5,223	5,740	3,440	5,925	6,115	8,630	8,205	6,526	9,397	†5,282	5,360	5,587	Total Res.Min.Gold (Eurosys.Def) **1l.d**
179	181	191	225	243	124	133	148	159	165	166	193	40	48	55	SDRs **1b.d**
186	181	165	149	177	236	213	222	294	325	340	582	416	329	336	Reserve Position in the Fund **1c.d**
4,431	4,725	3,702	4,849	5,320	3,080	5,579	5,745	8,178	7,715	6,020	8,622	4,826	4,983	5,196	Foreign Exchange **1d.d**
															o/w: Fin.Deriv.Rel.to Reserves .... **1dd d**
															Other Reserve Assets **1e.d**
.359	.359	.359	.359	.359	.360	.360	.360	.361	.361	.361	.451	.176	.176	.176	Gold (Million Fine Troy Ounces) **1ad**
139	114	109	109	104	109	123	141	137	143	116	132	52	48	49	Gold (Eurosystem Valuation) .... **1an d**
												43.17	19.54	185.07	Memo: Euro Cl. on Non-EA Res. .... **1dg d**
												94.00	303.00	358.00	Non-Euro Cl. on EA Res. .... **1dh d**
															Mon. Auth.: Other Foreign Assets .... **3..d**
				1,167								†1,389		78	Foreign Liabilities .... **4..d**
5,862	6,103	9,704	13,445	14,338	18,428	21,381	30,088	46,679	70,324	101,447	142,089	†78,106	135,339	173,199	Banking Insts.: Foreign Assets **7a.d**
10,754	10,750	12,823	17,740	17,053	18,727	19,146	28,127	49,100	70,169	99,225	142,772	†77,733	93,119	104,054	Foreign Liab. **7b.d**
															Monetary Authorities
Millions of Euros Beginning 1999: End of Period															
2,868	3,220	2,565	2,926	3,294	2,158	4,283	4,173	5,471	4,959	4,634	6,445	5,411	6,333	6,617	Fgn. Assets (Cl.on Non-EA Ctys) **11**
												2,109	2,183	2,029	Claims on General Government **12a.u**
439	492	484	496	361	361	315	254	183	132	132	132	279	229	29	*o/w:* Claims on Gen.Govt.in Cty **12a**
												8,662	9,012	13,977	Claims on Banking Institutions **12e.u**
												5,062	8,407	13,201	*o/w:* Claims on Bank.Inst.in Cty **12e**
												—	—	—	Claims on Other Resident Sectors **12d.u**
5	—	—	—	—	—	—	—	—	—	—	—	—	—	—	*o/w:* Cl. on Oth.Res.Sect.in Cty **12d**
1,215	1,347	1,460	1,550	1,568	1,604	1,776	1,907	2,092	2,287	2,619	3,040	4,848	5,368	4,704	Currency Issued **14a**
												4,228	6,426	8,619	Liabilities to Banking Insts **14c.u**
843	774	764	912	679	457	709	685	1,188	1,030	1,326	2,258	2,074	2,426	3,506	*o/w:* Liabs to Bank.Inst.in Cty **14c**
												—	—	—	Demand Dep. of Other Res.Sect. **14d.u**
												—	—	—	*o/w:* D.Dep.of Oth.Res.Sect.in Cty **14d**
												—	—	—	Other Dep. of Other Res.Sect. .... **15..u**
												—	—	—	*o/w:* O.Dep.of Oth.Res.Sect.in Cty **15**
												—	—	—	Money Market Instruments **16m.u**
														....	*o/w:* MMI Held by Resid.of Cty **16m**
												—	—	—	Bonds (Debt Securities) **16n.u**
														....	*o/w:* Bonds Held by Resid.of Cty **16n**
—	—	—	—	—	716	—	—	—	—	—	—	1,383	616	89	Foreign Liab. (to Non-EA Ctys) **16c**
												3,546	2,139	5,151	Central Government Deposits **16d.u**
648	883	1,133	979	1,248	639	1,426	836	1,082	1,178	1,191	1,674	3,546	2,139	5,151	*o/w:* Cent.Govt.Dep. in Cty **16d**
864	863	933	807	822	999	1,366	1,416	1,264	841	1,265	1,248	2,593	2,923	3,073	Capital Accounts **17a**
−258	−156	−1,241	−827	−662	−1,897	−679	−417	28	−245	−1,635	−1,642	−416	58	985	Other Items (Net) **17r**
															Memo: Currency Put into Circ. **14m**
															Banking Institutions
Millions of Euros Beginning 1999: End of Period															
946	906	910	1,138	857	642	775	675	1,436	1,348	1,686	2,706	2,486	....	13,316	Claims on Monetary Authorities **20**
												34,495	49,609	63,850	Claims on Bk.Inst.in Oth.EA Ctys **20b.u**
3,499	4,048	6,235	7,573	8,194	11,310	15,155	19,448	29,074	41,832	70,922	95,535	77,748	145,448	196,527	Fgn. Assets (Cl.on Non-EA Ctys) **21**
												29,909	30,698	38,230	Claims on General Government **22a.u**
3,237	2,966	2,695	2,773	2,786	3,260	3,196	3,581	4,637	4,049	4,220	4,676	6,335	5,465	5,363	*o/w:* Claims on Gen.Govt.in Cty **22a**
												109,999	136,032	161,126	Claims on Other Resident Sectors **22d.u**
9,222	10,551	12,199	13,615	13,276	14,321	14,835	16,571	29,106	33,978	44,058	54,020	91,795	110,652	129,079	*o/w:* Cl. on Oth.Res.Sect.in Cty **22d**
												12,711	15,117	18,871	Demand Deposits .... **24..u**
1,915	2,122	2,349	2,674	2,658	2,783	3,103	3,539	6,808	7,552	5,199	6,802	12,649	15,032	18,768	*o/w:* D.Dep.of Oth.Res.Sect.in Cty **24**
												67,614	76,097	81,626	Other Deposits .... **25..u**
6,584	6,930	7,089	8,405	9,031	9,744	12,693	13,848	20,494	24,324	32,890	38,108	59,223	67,035	71,694	*o/w:* O.Dep.of Oth.Res.Sect.in Cty **25**
												—	59,744	108,439	Money Market Instruments **26m.u**
														....	*o/w:* MMI Held by Resid.of Cty **26m**
												24,237	28,224	41,322	Bonds (Debt Securities) **26n.u**
														....	*o/w:* Bonds Held by Resid.of Cty **26n**
6,418	7,131	8,240	9,991	9,746	11,493	13,571	18,180	30,582	41,740	69,369	95,994	77,377	100,074	118,069	Foreign Liab. (to Non-EA Ctys) **26c**
												1,274	1,970	1,471	Central Government Deposits **26d.u**
83	99	110	124	125	121	119	360	239	248	299	332	1,274	1,970	1,454	*o/w:* Cent.Govt.Dep. in Cty **26d**
338	240	1,302	884	817	2,065	737	403	37	261	1,637	1,755	5,245	....	4,324	Credit from Monetary Authorities **26g**
												44,248	44,476	50,923	Liab. to Bk.Inst.in Oth. EA Ctys **26h.u**
1,768	2,293	3,130	3,390	3,509	3,934	4,322	4,854	6,486	7,249	10,280	12,881	22,091	26,993	31,133	Capital Accounts **27a**
−202	−343	−180	−371	−774	−607	−584	−909	−394	−167	1,211	1,067	−158	....	16,871	Other Items (Net) **27r**

Ireland

		1972	1973	1974	1975	1976	1977	1978	1979	1980	1981	1982	1983	1984	1985	1986
Banking Survey (Nat'l Residency)												*Millions of Pounds through 1998;*				
Foreign Assets (Net)	31n	261	298	330	474	758	633	677	306	347	380	†−11	−175	−358	−174	−949
Domestic Credit	32	1,148	1,440	1,766	2,090	2,385	2,973	3,906	4,864	5,757	6,829	†8,488	9,519	10,867	11,344	11,927
Claims on General Govt. (Net)	32an	231	352	510	620	571	659	843	1,179	1,457	1,605	†2,010	2,290	2,971	3,145	3,121
Claims on Other Resident Sectors	32d	917	1,088	1,256	1,470	1,814	2,314	3,063	3,684	4,300	5,224	†6,478	7,229	7,896	8,199	8,805
Currency Issued	34a.n	205	240	268	321	369	422	512	633	721	797	879	985	1,035	1,073	1,130
Demand Deposits	34b.n	512	645	757	894	1,025	1,214	1,673	1,988	2,407	3,064	†1,318	1,450	1,779	1,765	1,828
Other Deposits	35..n	654	824	1,042	1,280	1,417	1,693	2,047	2,400	2,993	3,439	†4,932	5,161	5,587	6,026	5,794
Money Market Instruments	36m	....	....	....	....	....	....	....	....	....	....	....	....	....	....	....
Bonds (Debt Securities)	36n	....	....	....	....	....	....	....	....	....	....	....	....	....	....	....
o/w: Bonds Over Two Years	36na	....	....	....	....	....	....	....	....	....	....	....	....	....	....	....
Capital Accounts	37a	59	64	98	122	232	270	275	318	390	565	†1,622	2,026	2,403	2,479	2,408
Other Items (Net)	37r	−24	−45	−68	−52	−1	9	76	−170	−406	−659	†−275	−278	−295	−174	−182
Banking Survey (EA-Wide Residency)													*Millions of Euros:*			
Foreign Assets (Net)	31n.u	....	....	....	....	....	....	....	....	....	....	....	....	....	....	....
Domestic Credit	32..u	....	....	....	....	....	....	....	....	....	....	....	....	....	....	....
Claims on General Govt. (Net)	32anu	....	....	....	....	....	....	....	....	....	....	....	....	....	....	....
Claims on Other Resident Sect.	32d.u	....	....	....	....	....	....	....	....	....	....	....	....	....	....	....
Currency Issued	34a.u	....	....	....	....	....	....	....	....	....	....	....	....	....	....	....
Demand Deposits	34b.u	....	....	....	....	....	....	....	....	....	....	....	....	....	....	....
Other Deposits	35..u	....	....	....	....	....	....	....	....	....	....	....	....	....	....	....
o/w: Other Dep. Over Two Yrs	35abu	....	....	....	....	....	....	....	....	....	....	....	....	....	....	....
Money Market Instruments	36m.u	....	....	....	....	....	....	....	....	....	....	....	....	....	....	....
Bonds (Debt Securities)	36n.u	....	....	....	....	....	....	....	....	....	....	....	....	....	....	....
o/w: Bonds Over Two Years	36nau	....	....	....	....	....	....	....	....	....	....	....	....	....	....	....
Capital Accounts	37a	....	....	....	....	....	....	....	....	....	....	....	....	....	....	....
Other Items (Net)	37r.u	....	....	....	....	....	....	....	....	....	....	....	....	....	....	....
Nonbank Financial Institutions														*Millions of Pounds:*		
Cash	40..k	7	9	13	26	28	30	38	74	91	111	†300	319	402	463	437
Foreign Assets	41..k	1	2	1	1	1	1	1	1	1	—	†11	10	15	5	5
Claims on Central Government	42a.k	270	306	363	444	544	721	868	1,024	1,155	1,285	†923	980	1,560	1,383	1,344
Claims on Private Sector	42d.k	152	191	218	266	354	458	585	776	987	1,264	†2,357	2,680	3,021	3,325	3,577
Quasi-Monetary Liabilities	45..k	386	458	535	673	847	1,108	1,357	1,699	2,061	2,442	†2,794	3,163	3,697	4,280	4,393
Foreign Liabilities	46c.k	16	18	29	24	29	34	44	38	36	33	†460	487	528	530	547
Cred.from Deposit Money Banks	46h.k	16	19	24	20	23	30	41	70	67	89	†203	183	184	185	198
Capital Accounts	47a.k	7	8	11	15	16	20	30	39	50	66	†131	159	184	209	268
Other Items (Net)	47r.k	5	5	−3	6	11	19	21	29	22	31	−11	−2	18	−28	−43
Interest Rates														*Percent Per Annum*		
Discount Rate *(End of Period)*	60	8.00	12.75	12.00	10.00	14.75	6.75	11.85	†16.50	14.00	16.50	14.00	12.25	14.00	10.25	13.25
Money Market Rate	60b	8.75	12.12	13.81	10.71	14.94	8.27	12.44	16.11	16.39	16.20	17.65	14.45	12.93	11.87	12.28
Treasury Bill Rate	60c	7.98	9.52	11.58	10.33	14.28	8.15	11.83	12.96	15.13	15.20	16.33	13.26	13.13	11.78	11.85
Deposit Rate	60l	3.33	7.06	9.63	7.75	7.54	6.17	6.33	10.96	12.00	11.33	12.73	9.27	7.83	6.98	6.50
Lending Rate	60p				11.25	13.25	9.65	13.00	15.50	15.96	15.50	17.04	14.13	12.92	12.44	12.23
Government Bond Yield	61	9.46	12.33	16.86	14.64	15.49	11.30	12.83	15.07	15.35	17.26	17.06	13.90	14.62	12.64	11.07
Prices, Production, Labor														*Index Numbers (1995=100):*		
Share Prices	62	12.8	†15.1	10.1	10.0	10.4	13.1	19.8	21.2	20.9	21.7	17.7	20.2	29.2	†31.2	49.0
Wholesale Prices	63	17.8	21.0	23.8	†29.6	35.4	41.5	45.2	50.7	56.1	65.8	73.2	77.7	83.6	†86.3	84.4
Output Manufacturing Industry	63a	17.2	20.4	22.8	†28.5	33.8	39.8	43.4	48.5	53.8	62.8	70.2	74.8	80.3	†83.4	82.4
Consumer Prices	64	13.8	15.4	18.0	21.8	†25.7	29.2	31.5	35.6	†42.1	50.7	59.3	65.6	71.2	†75.1	77.9
Harmonized CPI	64h	....	....	....	....	....	....	....	....	....	....	....	....	....	....	....
Wages: Weekly Earnings	65ey	9.0	10.8	12.7	16.6	19.9	23.5	27.0	30.9	36.5	42.6	48.0	53.7	60.2	65.0	69.9
Industrial Production	66..c	53.2	58.5	60.2	57.8	62.9	67.9	73.3	79.0	†78.0	82.3	81.6	88.2	96.7	100.0	102.2
Manufacturing Employment	67ey	93.3	97.8	99.4	93.3	93.0	95.9	97.8	107.2	107.4	104.3	101.1	95.0	92.2	88.4	87.1
														Number in Thousands:		
Labor Force	67d	....	....	....	....	....	....	....	....	....	....	....	....	....	....	....
Employment	67e	....	....	....	....	....	....	....	....	....	....	....	....	....	....	1,095
Unemployment	67c	....	....	....	....	....	....	....	....	....	....	....	....	214	231	236
Unemployment Rate (%)	67r	....	....	....	....	....	....	....	....	....	....	....	....	16.4	17.7	18.1
International Transactions													*Millions of Pounds through 1998;*			
Exports	70	645	869	1,136	1,447	1,859	2,518	2,963	3,483	4,082	4,778	5,691	6,944	8,898	9,743	9,374
Imports, c.i.f.	71	843	1,137	1,627	1,704	2,341	3,091	3,713	4,828	5,421	6,578	6,816	7,367	8,912	9,428	8,621
															1995=100	
Volume of Exports	72	11.9	12.5	14.0	†15.0	15.6	18.4	20.6	22.2	23.4	24.0	25.5	28.6	33.7	35.4	36.9
Volume of Imports	73	25.6	29.1	29.4	†26.5	30.5	34.4	40.2	45.8	43.5	44.1	42.3	43.8	47.9	†49.5	51.0
Unit Value of Exports	74	19.6	24.9	29.1	†34.6	42.7	49.2	51.6	56.4	62.7	72.0	80.1	86.9	94.7	†98.7	91.5
Unit Value of Imports	75	15.7	17.7	25.9	†31.3	37.2	43.6	44.8	51.2	60.8	72.5	78.4	81.8	90.6	†92.8	82.4

Millions of Euros Beginning 1999: End of Period — **Banking Survey (Nat'l Residency)**

	1987	1988	1989	1990	1991	1992	1993	1994	1995	1996	1997	1998	1999	2000	2001	
Foreign Assets (Net)	-51	137	560	507	1,742	1,258	5,867	5,440	3,963	5,051	6,187	5,986	31,539	....	151,029	31n
Domestic Credit	12,173	13,027	14,135	15,780	15,049	17,182	16,801	19,210	32,604	36,733	46,920	56,822	93,589	112,237	127,866	32
Claims on General Govt. (Net)	2,945	2,476	1,936	2,165	1,773	2,861	1,966	2,639	3,498	2,755	2,862	2,802	1,794	1,585	-1,213	32an
Claims on Other Resident Sectors	9,227	10,551	12,199	13,615	13,276	14,321	14,835	16,571	29,106	33,978	44,058	54,020	91,795	110,652	129,079	32d
Currency Issued	1,215	1,347	1,460	1,550	1,568	1,604	1,776	1,907	2,092	2,287	2,619	3,040	5,528	5,368	4,704	34a.n
Demand Deposits	1,915	2,122	2,349	2,674	2,658	2,783	3,103	3,539	6,808	7,552	5,199	6,802	12,649	15,032	18,768	34b.n
Other Deposits	6,584	6,930	7,089	8,405	9,031	9,744	12,693	13,848	20,494	24,324	32,890	38,108	59,223	67,035	71,694	35..n
Money Market Instruments	....	....	....	....	....	....	....	....	....	....	....	....	—	59,744	108,439	36m
Bonds (Debt Securities)													24,237	28,224	41,322	36n
o/w: Bonds Over Two Years													10,200	11,038	12,563	36na
Capital Accounts	2,632	3,155	4,063	4,197	4,331	4,934	5,688	6,271	7,750	8,090	11,545	14,129	24,684	29,916	34,206	37a
Other Items (Net)	-225	-390	-264	-540	-798	-625	-591	-914	-577	-469	853	732	-1,191	....	-240	37r

End of Period — **Banking Survey (EA-Wide Residency)**

	1999	2000	2001	
Foreign Assets (Net)	4,399	51,091	84,986	31n.u
Domestic Credit	137,197	164,804	194,763	32..u
Claims on General Govt. (Net)	27,198	28,772	33,637	32an u
Claims on Other Resident Sect.	109,999	136,032	161,126	32d.u
Currency Issued	5,528	5,368	4,704	34a.u
Demand Deposits	12,711	15,117	18,871	34b.u
Other Deposits	67,614	76,097	81,626	35..u
o/w: Other Dep. Over Two Yrs	7,633	8,496	9,904	35ab u
Money Market Instruments	—	59,744	108,439	36m.u
Bonds (Debt Securities)	24,237	28,224	41,322	36n.u
o/w: Bonds Over Two Years	10,200	11,038	12,563	36na u
Capital Accounts	24,684	29,916	34,206	37a
Other Items (Net)	6,824	....	-9,421	37r.u

End of Period — **Nonbank Financial Institutions**

	1987	1988	1989	1990	1991	1992	1993	1994	1995	1996	1997	1998	
Cash	632	607	676	679	830	915	1,559	1,676	†18	6	5	5	40..k
Foreign Assets	23	103	103	55	20	112	241	704	†2	5	8	11	41..k
Claims on Central Government	1,498	1,598	1,592	1,882	2,022	2,147	1,801	1,777	†717	762	786	819	42a.k
Claims on Private Sector	3,626	4,006	4,627	5,251	5,894	6,836	7,634	8,438	†644	703	878	1,051	42d.k
Quasi-Monetary Liabilities	4,793	5,103	5,385	6,175	6,894	7,927	8,682	9,274	†917	1,039	1,154	1,237	45..k
Foreign Liabilities	610	674	849	895	1,114	1,456	1,690	2,233	†2	5	8	10	46c.k
Cred.from Deposit Money Banks	176	278	383	475	627	653	1,009	1,285	†394	339	448	564	46h.k
Capital Accounts	282	334	382	426	495	607	795	928	†35	78	53	56	47a.k
Other Items (Net)	-81	-75	—	-104	-365	-634	-941	-1,125	†33	15	15	18	47r.k

Percent Per Annum — **Interest Rates**

	1987	1988	1989	1990	1991	1992	1993	1994	1995	1996	1997	1998	1999	2000	2001	
Discount Rate (End of Period)	9.25	8.00	12.00	11.25	10.75	....	7.00	6.25	6.50	6.25	6.75	4.06	....	....	....	60
Money Market Rate	10.84	7.84	9.55	11.10	10.45	15.12	10.49	†5.75	5.45	5.74	6.43	3.23	3.14	4.84	3.31	60b
Treasury Bill Rate	10.70	7.81	9.70	10.90	10.12	....	†9.06	5.87	6.19	5.36	6.03	5.37				60c
Deposit Rate	6.21	3.63	4.54	6.29	5.21	5.42	2.27	.33	.44	.29	.46	.43	.10	.10	.10	60l
Lending Rate	11.15	8.29	9.42	11.29	10.63	†12.66	9.93	6.13	6.56	5.85	6.57	6.22	3.34	4.77	4.84	60p
Government Bond Yield	11.27	9.49	8.95	10.08	9.17	9.11	7.72	8.19	8.30	7.48	6.49	4.99				61

Period Averages — **Prices, Production, Labor**

	1987	1988	1989	1990	1991	1992	1993	1994	1995	1996	1997	1998	1999	2000	2001	
Share Prices	70.7	69.4	†82.4	75.0	69.0	64.1	80.1	91.4	100.0	125.1	169.8	238.7	245.9	262.7	284.3	62
Wholesale Prices	84.9	88.4	93.3	90.7	91.8	92.6	97.0	97.9	100.0	100.5	100.0	101.5	102.6	108.9		63
Output Manufacturing Industry	83.8	87.2	91.4	89.9	90.7	92.2	96.4	97.5	100.0	100.6	100.1	100.9	101.9	107.7	109.9	63a
Consumer Prices	80.4	82.1	85.5	88.3	91.1	†94.0	95.3	97.5	100.0	101.7	103.2	105.7	107.4	113.4	118.9	64
Harmonized CPI	....	....	....	....	....	....	....	....	....	....	....	105.6	108.2	113.9	118.5	64h
Wages: Weekly Earnings	73.4	76.9	80.0	83.1	86.7	90.2	95.1	97.8	100.0	102.5	107.5	111.9	118.4	126.4	136.4	65ey
Industrial Production	111.4	126.5	141.8	148.2	152.4	69.5	73.2	82.5	100.0	108.4	†129.4	149.2	164.9	218.7	241.4	66..c
Manufacturing Employment	86.2	86.4	88.4	90.7	91.7	90.8	90.9	94.2	100.0	104.8	110.9	114.1	113.1	117.6		67ey

Period Averages

	1987	1988	1989	1990	1991	1992	1993	1994	1995	1996	1997	1998	1999	2000	2001	
Labor Force									1,443	1,494	1,539	1,621	1,688	....	....	67d
Employment	1,111	1,111	1,111	1,160	1,156	1,165	1,183	1,221	†1,282	1,329	1,380	1,495	1,591	....	....	67e
Unemployment	247	241	322	225	254	283	294	282	277	279	254	227	192	....	....	67c
Unemployment Rate (%)	18.8	18.4	17.9	17.2	19.0	16.3	16.7	15.1	14.1	11.8	10.1	7.6	5.8	....	....	67r

Millions of Euros Beginning 1999 — **International Transactions**

	1987	1988	1989	1990	1991	1992	1993	1994	1995	1996	1997	1998	1999	2000	2001	
Exports	10,723	12,305	14,597	14,337	15,019	21,260	25,179	28,891	35,330	38,609	44,868	57,322	†66,956	83,889	92,730	70
Imports, c.i.f.	9,155	10,215	12,284	12,469	12,851	16,754	18,900	21,945	26,181	28,479	32,863	39,715	†44,327	55,909	57,230	71

1995=100

	1987	1988	1989	1990	1991	1992	1993	1994	1995	1996	1997	1998	1999	2000	2001	
Volume of Exports	42.1	45.0	†50.1	54.3	57.4	65.8	72.5	83.3	100.0	109.9	126.3	157.2	182.9	218.2	229.1	72
Volume of Imports	54.1	56.7	†64.0	68.4	68.9	72.2	77.2	87.4	100.0	110.0	126.3	149.2	161.7	188.1	186.9	73
Unit Value of Exports	91.5	98.0	104.5	†94.6	93.9	91.4	98.3	98.2	100.0	99.4	100.6	103.2	108.8	114.4	115.7	74
Unit Value of Imports	82.4	87.8	†93.4	88.7	90.8	88.9	93.5	95.9	100.0	98.8	99.4	101.7	104.7	113.6	116.9	75

Ireland

	1972	1973	1974	1975	1976	1977	1978	1979	1980	1981	1982	1983	1984	1985	1986
Balance of Payments															*Millions of US Dollars:*
Current Account, n.i.e. .... 78al d	...	...	−688	−124	−428	−522	−849	−2,100	−2,132	−2,601	−1,935	−1,219	−1,038	−736	−847
Goods: Exports f.o.b. .... 78aa d	...	...	2,479	3,032	3,326	4,229	5,604	6,949	8,229	7,696	7,933	8,438	9,421	10,131	12,366
Goods: Imports f.o.b. .... 78ab d	...	...	−3,561	−3,518	−3,935	−5,049	−6,669	−9,269	−10,452	−9,950	−9,096	−8,690	−9,183	−9,500	−11,221
Trade Balance .... 78ac d	...	...	−1,082	−486	−609	−820	−1,065	−2,320	−2,222	−2,255	−1,162	−252	237	631	1,145
Services: Credit .... 78ad d	...	...	508	568	561	715	896	1,169	1,381	1,209	1,219	1,174	1,166	1,302	1,595
Services: Debit .... 78ae d	...	...	−407	−550	−572	−739	−1,024	−1,372	−1,593	−1,435	−1,375	−1,372	−1,435	−1,547	−2,192
Balance on Goods & Services .... 78af d	...	...	−982	−467	−620	−844	−1,193	−2,523	−2,434	−2,481	−1,318	−450	−32	386	548
Income: Credit .... 78ag d	...	...	331	347	360	343	442	565	808	776	712	584	663	756	934
Income: Debit .... 78ah d	...	...	−342	−395	−485	−608	−984	−1,288	−1,710	−1,734	−2,162	−2,179	−2,468	−2,878	−3,595
Balance on Gds, Serv. & Inc. .... 78ai d	...	...	−992	−515	−744	−1,109	−1,735	−3,246	−3,336	−3,439	−2,768	−2,045	−1,837	−1,736	−2,112
Current Transfers, n.i.e.: Credit .... 78aj d	...	...	335	468	431	736	1,039	1,336	1,442	1,064	1,082	1,113	1,075	1,314	1,730
Current Transfers: Debit .... 78ak d	...	...	−31	−77	−114	−149	−153	−190	−238	−226	−248	−286	−276	−314	−465
Capital Account, n.i.e. .... 78bc d	...	...	—	—	—	—	—	—	—	—	—	—	4	55	42
Capital Account, n.i.e.: Credit .... 78ba d	...	...	—	—	—	—	—	—	—	—	—	—	92	117	134
Capital Account: Debit .... 78bb d	...	...	—	—	—	—	—	—	—	—	—	—	−87	−62	−93
Financial Account, n.i.e. .... 78bj d	...	...	717	485	990	1,397	1,164	1,671	2,724	2,392	2,371	1,752	1,208	1,127	1,790
Direct Investment Abroad .... 78bd d	...	...	—	—	—	—	—	—	—	—	—	—	—	—	—
Dir. Invest. in Rep. Econ., n.i.e. .... 78be d	...	...	51	158	173	136	375	337	286	203	242	170	121	164	−40
Portfolio Investment Assets .... 78bf d	...	...	2	−1	9	56	−58	−32	−44	−116	−108	−90	−91	−134	−239
Equity Securities .... 78bk d	...	...	—	—	—	—	—	—	—	—	—	—	—	—	—
Debt Securities .... 78bl d	...	...	2	−1	9	56	−58	−32	−44	−116	−108	−90	−91	−134	−239
Portfolio Investment Liab., n.i.e. .... 78bg d	...	...	155	114	139	275	537	−86	224	605	279	467	1,268	1,104	1,986
Equity Securities .... 78bm d	...	...	—	—	—	—	—	—	—	—	—	—	—	—	—
Debt Securities .... 78bn d	...	...	155	114	139	275	537	−86	224	605	279	467	1,268	1,104	1,986
Financial Derivatives Assets .... 78bw d	...	...	....	....	....	....	....	....	....	....	....	....	....	....	....
Financial Derivatives Liabilities .... 78bx d	...	...	....	....	....	....	....	....	....	....	....	....	....	....	....
Other Investment Assets .... 78bh d	...	...	−519	−452	−9	−22	−301	−117	−500	−229	−649	−423	−634	44	−443
Monetary Authorities .... 78bo d	...	...	....	....	....	....	....	....	....	....	....	....	....	....	....
General Government .... 78bp d	...	...	—	—	—	—	−9	—	—	—	—	—	—	—	—
Banks .... 78bq d	...	...	−679	−319	−58	−295	−277	−336	−583	−530	−872	−423	−452	197	−187
Other Sectors .... 78br d	...	...	159	−133	49	274	−16	220	83	301	223	—	−183	−153	−255
Other Investment Liab., n.i.e. .... 78bi d	...	...	1,029	666	679	951	611	1,569	2,757	1,929	2,607	1,628	545	−50	526
Monetary Authorities .... 78bs d	...	...	....	....	....	....	....	....	....	....	....	....	....	....	....
General Government .... 78bt d	...	...	170	248	401	111	123	851	945	1,299	1,471	448	−317	−145	−397
Banks .... 78bu d	...	...	859	418	278	841	488	717	1,813	630	1,136	1,180	862	95	924
Other Sectors .... 78bv d	...	...	....	....	....	....	....	....	....	....	....	....	....	....	....
Net Errors and Omissions .... 78ca d	...	...	103	−12	−233	−467	−172	−157	120	201	−315	−345	−218	−399	−1,079
Overall Balance .... 78cb d	...	...	132	350	329	408	142	−586	712	−8	121	188	−43	48	−94
Reserves and Related Items .... 79da d	...	...	−132	−350	−329	−408	−142	586	−712	8	−121	−188	43	−48	94
Reserve Assets .... 79db d	...	...	−132	−350	−329	−408	−142	586	−712	8	−121	−188	43	−48	94
Use of Fund Credit and Loans .... 79dc d	...	...	—	—	—	—	—	—	—	—	—	—	—	—	—
Exceptional Financing .... 79de d	...	...	....	....	....	....	....	....	....	....	....	....	....	....	....
Government Finance															
Central Government														*Millions of Pounds through 1998;*	
Deficit (-) or Surplus 80	−127.6	−170.5	−352.2	−499.4	−491.3	−555.6	−856.3	−1,055.2	−1,284.7	−1,789.1	−2,027.8	−1,835.3	−1,821.7	−2,129.1	−2,115.2
Revenue 81	634.0	758.6	911.7	1,295.5	1,550.9	1,779.3	2,076.1	2,483.6	3,256.2	4,064.2	5,158.7	5,878.2	6,138.7	6,601.7	6,936.7
Expenditure 82	761.6	929.1	1,263.9	1,794.9	2,042.2	2,334.9	2,932.4	3,538.8	4,540.9	5,853.3	7,186.5	7,713.5	7,960.4	8,730.8	9,051.9
Financing															
Net Borrowing 84	127.6	170.5	352.2	499.4	491.3	555.6	856.3	1,055.2	1,284.7	1,789.1	2,027.8	1,835.3	1,821.7	2,129.1	2,192.1
Use of Cash Balances 87	—	—	—	—	—	—	—	—	—	—	—	—	—	—	−76.9
Total Debt *(Yr. Beg. April 1)* 88	1,421.1	1,622.2	1,957.9	2,743.8	3,612.0	4,208.2	....	....	....	....	....	....	....	....	....
General Government															*As Percent of*
Deficit (-) or Surplus 80g	....	....	....	....	....	....	....	....	....	....	....	....	....	....	....
Debt 88g	....	....	....	....	....	....	....	....	....	....	....	....	....	....	....
National Accounts															*Millions of Pounds through 1998;*
Househ.Cons.Expend.,incl.NPISHs 96f	1,455	1,738	2,045	2,434	3,004	3,661	4,309	5,170	6,158	7,490	8,001	8,950	9,801	10,777	12,138
Government Consumption Expend. 91f	342	422	512	703	838	970	1,156	1,431	1,860	2,260	2,646	2,857	3,067	3,301	3,542
Gross Fixed Capital Formation 93e	497	671	753	885	1,157	1,414	1,862	2,430	2,718	3,350	3,531	3,414	3,506	3,377	3,456
Changes in Inventories 93i	64	83	118	—	24	178	99	184	−128	185	106	228	173	118
Exports of Goods and Services 90c	773	1,026	1,272	1,619	2,152	2,817	3,374	3,936	4,639	5,504	6,433	7,752	9,770	10,738	10,377
Imports of Goods and Services (-) 98c	893	1,211	1,708	1,849	2,522	3,337	4,043	5,235	5,900	7,117	7,414	8,164	9,815	10,397	9,929
Gross Domestic Product (GDP) 99b	2,238	2,729	2,991	3,792	4,653	5,703	6,757	7,917	9,361	11,359	13,382	14,916	16,556	17,969	19,703
Net Primary Income from Abroad 98.n	30	12	19	4	−36	−108	−228	−283	−358	−505	−928	−1,184	−1,639	−1,966	−2,017
Gross National Income (GNI) 99a	2,267	2,742	3,010	3,796	4,617	5,595	6,529	7,634	9,003	10,854	12,455	13,732	14,917	16,003	17,686
Net National Income 99e	2,083	2,527	2,751	3,493	4,223	5,095	5,872	6,835	7,969	9,690	11,089	12,203	13,320	14,279	15,801
GDP Volume 1975 Prices 99b.p	3,351	3,560	....	....	....	....	....	....	....	....	....	....	....	....	....
GDP Volume 1980 Prices 99b.p	....	7,034	7,319	7,491	7,596	8,220	8,810	9,081	9,361	9,672	....	....	....	....	....
GDP Volume 1990 Prices 99b.p	....	....	....	....	....	....	....	....	....	....	19,139	19,572	19,525	20,372	21,004	21,777
GDP Volume 1995 Prices 99b.p	....	....	....	....	....	....	....	....	....	....	....	....	....	....	....
GDP Volume (1995=100) .... 99bv p	38.4	40.8	42.4	43.4	44.0	47.7	51.1	52.6	54.3	56.1	57.3	57.2	59.7	61.5	63.8
GDP Deflator (1995=100) .... 99bi p	14.1	16.2	17.1	21.1	25.6	29.0	32.0	36.4	41.8	49.0	56.5	63.1	67.1	70.7	74.7
															Millions:
Population 99z	3.02	3.07	3.12	3.18	3.23	3.27	3.31	3.37	3.40	3.44	3.48	3.50	3.53	3.54	3.54

1987	1988	1989	1990	1991	1992	1993	1994	1995	1996	1997	1998	1999	2000	2001		
Minus Sign Indicates Debit															Balance of Payments	
−76	−25	−581	−361	284	607	1,765	1,577	1,721	2,049	1,866	1,016	354	−593	−1,043	Current Account, n.i.e.	78al*d*
15,566	18,389	20,356	23,341	23,659	28,107	28,728	33,642	44,423	49,184	55,293	78,562	68,540	73,433	78,371	Goods: Exports f.o.b.	78aa*d*
−12,952	−14,567	−16,352	−19,397	−19,366	−21,062	−20,553	−24,275	−30,866	−33,430	−36,668	−53,172	−44,284	−48,017	−48,369	Goods: Imports f.o.b.	78ab*d*
2,614	3,822	4,003	3,944	4,294	7,045	8,175	9,366	13,557	15,754	18,625	25,390	24,256	25,416	30,003	*Trade Balance*	78ac*d*
2,069	2,414	2,533	3,445	3,667	4,054	3,769	4,319	5,017	5,749	6,186	16,735	15,522	16,788	20,194	Services: Credit	78ad*d*
−3,015	−3,837	−4,342	−5,178	−5,662	−7,084	−6,760	−8,452	−11,303	−13,448	−15,195	−29,626	−26,637	−28,745	−34,853	Services: Debit	78ae*d*
1,668	2,399	2,194	2,211	2,298	4,015	5,185	5,233	7,270	8,055	9,616	12,499	13,142	13,459	15,344	*Balance on Goods & Services*	78af*d*
1,085	1,411	1,795	3,280	3,259	3,282	2,780	3,513	5,110	5,576	7,353	25,430	24,442	29,973	28,697	Income: Credit	78ag*d*
−4,152	−5,282	−6,075	−8,235	−7,858	−8,827	−8,116	−8,919	−12,435	−13,772	−17,059	−38,800	−38,484	−44,974	−45,562	Income: Debit	78ah*d*
−1,399	−1,473	−2,086	−2,745	−2,301	−1,530	−151	−173	−55	−141	−90	−870	−899	−1,542	−1,520	*Balance on Gds, Serv. & Inc.*	78ai*d*
1,792	1,908	1,976	3,089	3,395	3,033	2,858	2,850	3,009	3,538	3,083	7,428	5,308	4,304	4,295	Current Transfers, n.i.e.: Credit	78aj*d*
−469	−460	−471	−705	−809	−896	−941	−1,100	−1,233	−1,349	−1,128	−5,543	−4,055	−3,355	−3,818	Current Transfers: Debit	78ak*d*
−16	95	103	387	601	787	775	387	817	785	871	1,218	593	1,097	598	Capital Account, n.i.e.	78bc*d*
179	247	231	486	698	889	863	477	914	881	962	1,327	674	1,167	667	Capital Account, n.i.e.: Credit	78ba*d*
−195	−152	−127	−99	−97	−102	−89	−90	−96	−96	−91	−108	−81	−70	−69	Capital Account: Debit	78bb*d*
632	200	−1,574	−2,009	−2,002	−3,962	−901	−3,963	−33	−2,780	−7,484	4,686	−3,893	8,901	37	Financial Account, n.i.e.	78bj*d*
—	—	—	−365	−195	−215	−220	−438	−820	−727	−1,008	−4,955	−6,102	−3,983	−5,405	Direct Investment Abroad	78bd*d*
89	92	85	627	1,357	1,442	1,121	838	1,447	2,618	2,743	11,035	18,615	22,778	9,865	Dir. Invest. in Rep. Econ., n.i.e.	78be*d*
−316	−485	−1,120	−465	−1,717	−439	−272	−1,019	−1,056	−183	−716	−66,738	−82,813	−78,817	−108,535	Portfolio Investment Assets	78bf*d*
—	—	—	—	—	—	—	—	—	—	—	−27,624	−36,357	−28,163	−23,886	Equity Securities	78bk*d*
−316	−485	−1,120	−465	−1,717	−439	−272	−1,019	−1,056	−183	−716	−39,114	−46,457	−50,654	−84,650	Debt Securities	78bl*d*
109	1,475	1,770	266	648	−2,750	2,723	−379	771	982	−2,505	54,735	67,377	80,255	91,128	Portfolio Investment Liab., n.i.e.	78bg*d*
—	—	—	—	—	—	—	—	—	—	—	47,948	52,061	67,533	78,250	Equity Securities	78bm*d*
109	1,475	1,770	266	648	−2,750	2,723	−379	771	982	−2,505	6,787	15,316	12,721	12,878	Debt Securities	78bn*d*
....	....	....	....	....	....	....	....	....	....	....	....	....	416	−867	Financial Derivatives Assets	78bw*d*
....	....	....	—	—	—	—	—	—	—	—	....	....	−42	919	Financial Derivatives Liabilities	78bx*d*
−1,906	−1,941	−4,483	−5,284	−1,860	−8,489	−10,642	−4,483	−16,572	−22,162	−48,337	−25,211	−38,545	−41,048	−12,101	Other Investment Assets	78bh*d*
....	....	....	—	—	—	—	—	—	—	—	....	....	3,311	−310	Monetary Authorities	78bo*d*
—	—	—	—	—	—	—	−76	76	—	—	....	....	−2,057	725	General Government	78bp*d*
−1,158	−1,214	−2,942	−2,310	−662	−6,414	−9,486	−2,919	−14,083	−19,623	−43,421	....	....	−15,526	−6,779	Banks	78bq*d*
−748	−727	−1,541	−2,973	−1,197	−2,075	−1,157	−1,489	−2,565	−2,539	−4,916	....	....	−26,776	−5,735	Other Sectors	78br*d*
2,655	1,060	2,175	3,212	−235	6,489	6,389	1,519	16,197	16,691	42,340	35,820	37,576	29,343	25,033	Other Investment Liab., n.i.e.	78bi*d*
—	—	—	—	—	1,376	−1,255	—	—	—	—	—	—	165	1,111	Monetary Authorities	78bs*d*
1,696	−615	−413	−195	−239	1,142	−580	−1,585	−808	−947	−812	....	....	−135	−1	General Government	78bt*d*
960	1,675	2,588	3,406	4	3,972	8,224	3,103	17,005	17,639	43,152	....	....	14,540	17,735	Banks	78bu*d*
—	—	—	—	—	—	—	—	—	—	—	....	....	14,772	6,187	Other Sectors	78bv*d*
346	322	1,115	2,608	1,579	402	1,021	1,823	−167	−106	3,639	−3,708	972	−9,284	803	Net Errors and Omissions	78ca*d*
886	592	−937	626	463	−2,166	2,660	−176	2,339	−52	−1,109	3,212	−1,973	121	395	*Overall Balance*	78cb*d*
−886	−592	937	−626	−463	2,166	−2,660	176	−2,339	52	1,109	−3,212	1,973	−121	−395	Reserves and Related Items	79da*d*
−886	−592	937	−626	−463	2,166	−2,660	176	−2,339	52	1,109	−3,212	1,973	−121	−395	Reserve Assets	79db*d*
—	—	—	—	—	—	—	—	—	—	—	—	—	—	—	Use of Fund Credit and Loans	79dc*d*
....	....	....	....	....	....	....	....	....	....	....	....	....	....	....	Exceptional Financing	79de*d*
															Government Finance	
Millions of Euros Beginning 1999: Year Ending December 31															*Central Government*	
−1,803.4	−640.3	−484.7	−471.9	−235.4	−700.5	−260.4	−322.6	−259.5	102.0	289.7	1,226.2	1,513.0	3,171.2	2,104.3	Deficit (-) or Surplus	80
7,467.5	8,160.2	8,145.2	8,586.2	9,457.5	9,812.9	10,872.8	11,676.6	12,423.4	13,422.3	15,108.6	17,175.6	29,441.7	29,865.1	37,184.3	Revenue	81
9,270.9	8,800.5	8,629.9	9,058.1	9,692.9	10,513.4	11,133.2	11,999.2	12,682.9	13,320.3	14,818.9	15,949.4	27,928.7	26,693.9	35,080.0	Expenditure	82
															Financing	
2,042.2	1,045.5	737.8	347.0	527.3	−440.0	850.2	−18.6	535.0	164.5	−109.3	−881.8	−1,686.3	−3,177.3	−2,574.0	Net Borrowing	84
−238.8	−405.2	−253.1	124.9	−291.9	1,140.5	−589.8	341.2	−275.5	−266.5	−180.4	−344.4	173.3	6.1	309.7	Use of Cash Balances	87
....	....	....	....	....	....	....	....	....	....	....	....	....	....	....	Total Debt *(Yr. Beg. April 1)*	88
Gross Domestic Product															*General Government*	
....	....	....	−2.3	−2.3	−2.5	−2.4	−1.7	−2.1	−.6	.7	2.3	2.3	4.5	1.7	Deficit (-) or Surplus	80g
....	....	....	96.0	95.3	92.3	96.3	88.2	78.9	74.1	65.1	55.1	49.6	39.0	36.6	Debt	88g
															National Accounts	
Millions of Euros Beginning in 1999																
12,845	13,946	15,403	†17,293	18,085	19,161	20,162	21,621	23,192	25,311	27,900	31,219	†42,943	49,560	56,001	Househ.Cons.Expend.,incl.NPISHs	96f
3,575	3,540	3,683	†4,308	4,742	5,155	5,495	5,838	6,177	6,514	7,274	7,978	†12,464	13,880	14,312	Government Consumption Expend.	91f
3,453	3,568	4,294	†5,287	5,072	5,211	5,259	6,043	7,072	8,512	10,650	13,275	†20,908	24,442	26,643	Gross Fixed Capital Formation	93e
28	−47	262	†727	631	−87	−112	−135	428	427	683	886	†−20	312	388	Changes in Inventories	93i
11,855	13,634	16,137	†16,294	17,178	19,179	22,475	25,923	31,679	35,453	42,121	52,585	†79,006	98,165	110,120	Exports of Goods and Services	90c
10,681	11,921	14,360	†14,972	15,701	16,775	18,860	22,301	26,936	30,142	35,442	45,678	†66,617	83,484	92,915	Imports of Goods and Services (-)	98c
21,075	22,718	25,418	†28,598	29,675	31,529	34,054	36,624	41,409	45,634	52,760	60,582	†89,029	103,470	115,437	Gross Domestic Product (GDP)	99b
−2,112	−2,662	−3,233	†−3,258	−3,215	−3,537	−3,671	−3,716	−4,685	−5,147	−6,332	−7,389	†−12,243	−15,480	−18,690	Net Primary Income from Abroad	98.n
18,963	20,056	22,185	†25,339	26,460	27,992	30,383	32,908	36,725	40,487	46,428	53,193	†76,787	87,990	96,747	Gross National Income (GNI)	99a
16,900	17,894	19,806	22,944	23,476	25,094	27,037	29,170	32,366	35,618	40,392	46,109	....	....	....	Net National Income	99e
....	....	....	....	....	....	....	....	....	....	....	....	....	....	....	GDP Volume 1975 Prices	99b.*p*
....	....	....	....	....	....	....	....	....	....	....	....	....	....	....	GDP Volume 1980 Prices	99b.*p*
22,793	23,765	25,219	27,190	....	....	....	....	....	....	....	....	....	....	....	GDP Volume 1990 Prices	99b.*p*
....	....	....	32,986	33,622	34,746	35,682	37,736	41,409	44,594	49,382	53,609	†75,767	84,452	89,392	GDP Volume 1995 Prices	99b.*p*
66.8	69.6	73.9	79.7	81.2	83.9	86.2	91.1	100.0	107.7	119.3	129.5	†144.1	160.6	170.0	GDP Volume (1995=100)	99bv*p*
76.4	79.0	83.3	†86.9	88.5	90.9	95.7	97.3	100.0	102.3	106.7	112.8	†117.8	122.8	129.4	GDP Deflator (1995=100)	99bi*p*
Midyear Estimates																
3.54	3.54	3.51	3.50	3.53	3.55	3.57	3.59	3.60	3.63	3.66	3.70	3.75	3.79	3.84	**Population**	99z

(See notes in the back of the book.)

		1972	1973	1974	1975	1976	1977	1978	1979	1980	1981	1982	1983	1984	1985	1986
Exchange Rates													*New Sheqalim per Thousand SDRs through 1980*			
Market Rate	aa	.4555	.5061	.7338	.8303	1.0158	1.8672	2.4746	4.6517	9.6268	†.0182	.0371	.1128	.6261	1.6471	1.8181
												New Sheqalim per Thousand US Dollars through 1980				
Market Rate	ae	.4195	.4195	.5994	.7092	.8743	1.5372	1.8995	3.5311	7.5480	†.0156	.0337	.1078	.6387	1.4995	1.4864
Market Rate	rf	.4180	.4195	.4452	.6336	.7926	1.0445	1.7435	2.5406	5.1243	†.0114	.0243	.0562	.2932	1.1788	1.4878
														Index Numbers (1995=100):		
Nominal Effective Exchange Rate	ne c	....	....	....	....	....	....	....	....	60,531.99	30,650.05	15,931.25	7,755.53	1,895.64	414.71	247.80
Real Effective Exchange Rate	re c	....	....	....	....	....	....	....	90.42	92.31	93.77	98.17	106.82	100.39	97.20	94.79
Fund Position														*Millions of SDRs:*		
Quota	2f. s	130.0	130.0	130.0	130.0	130.0	130.0	205.0	205.0	307.5	307.5	307.5	446.6	446.6	446.6	446.6
SDRs	1b. s	29.2	27.9	2.5	2.0	8.7	22.2	21.0	4.8	8.8	.6	.5	1.6	.1	.1	—
Reserve Position in the Fund	1c. s	—	32.5							31.6	25.6		34.8			
Total Fund Cred.&Loans Outstg.	2tl	—	—	32.5	208.3	285.3	285.2	271.3	224.2	156.4	87.5	27.2	—	—	—	—
International Liquidity													*Millions of US Dollars Unless Otherwise Indicated:*			
Total Reserves minus Gold	1l. d	1,178.8	1,768.3	1,153.4	1,137.1	1,328.3	1,521.6	2,625.1	3,063.5	3,351.4	3,496.7	3,839.3	3,651.2	3,060.3	3,680.2	4,659.6
SDRs	1b. d	31.7	33.6	3.1	2.4	10.0	27.0	27.3	6.3	11.2	.7	.6	1.7	.1	.1	—
Reserve Position in the Fund	1c. d	—	39.2						41.6	32.7			36.4			
Foreign Exchange	1d. d	1,147.1	1,695.4	1,150.3	1,134.7	1,318.3	1,494.6	2,597.8	3,015.6	3,307.5	3,496.0	3,838.7	3,613.1	3,060.2	3,680.1	4,659.6
Gold (Million Fine Troy Ounces)	1ad	1.143	1.097	1.099	1.101	1.103	1.164	1.171	1.231	1.194	1.193	1.084	1.015	1.017	1.017	1.017
Gold (National Valuation)	1an d	43.4	46.3	47.1	45.1	44.9	49.5	53.4	56.8	53.3	48.6	41.9	37.2	34.9	39.1	43.5
Monetary Authorities: Other Assets	3.. d	95.2	119.0	100.1	84.6	228.8	214.7	279.0	36.8	90.1	6.4	218.4	70.0	1.6	1.3	161.5
Monetary Authorities: Other Liab.	4.. d	150.0	116.7	133.5	145.2	209.3	214.7	7.9	25.2	17.2	17.2	14.6	13.5	17.4	17.3	19.5
Deposit Money Banks: Assets	7a. d	1,250.9	1,695.2	1,818.6	1,876.7	1,989.0	2,472.7	3,452.0	4,318.7	5,522.5	6,270.8	7,193.3	6,848.9	6,637.2	6,256.3	6,575.0
Liabilities	7b. d	1,357.1	1,876.2	2,230.7	2,638.1	2,917.8	3,190.3	4,679.2	6,215.6	7,593.4	8,662.5	10,965.1	10,631.4	10,308.9	10,038.0	10,313.0
Monetary Authorities													*Thousands of New Sheqalim through 1982;*			
Foreign Assets	11	570	826	778	902	1,416	2,784	5,673	11,332	26,625	55,386	136,370	†410	1,980	5,578	7,230
Claims on Central Government	12a	424	428	695	829	1,249	2,558	3,540	5,688	9,383	34,104	104,040	†493	3,104	8,498	8,144
Claims on Deposit Money Banks	12e	172	279	460	639	796	1,809	3,308	7,989	19,283	27,378	18,360	†83	294	392	500
Reserve Money	14	760	957	1,157	1,378	2,021	6,492	11,189	21,741	46,832	96,666	224,030	†832	4,596	11,366	11,926
of which: Currency Outside DMBs	14a	198	271	317	397	477	632	878	1,205	2,100	4,413	8,430	†25	123	481	974
Foreign Cur.Deps.	14cf	220	268	435	554	898	4,891	9,142	19,461	42,288	86,042	199,000	†775	4,288	9,158	8,978
Foreign Liabilities	16c	63	49	104	276	473	863	686	1,132	1,636	1,858	1,498	†1	11	26	29
Central Government Deposits	16d	48	103	30	32	46	223	644	1,040	2,334	4,281	14,870	†87	473	1,369	2,620
Other Items (Net)	17r	296	424	643	685	921	−426	2	1,096	4,490	14,063	18,372	†65	297	1,707	1,299
Deposit Money Banks													*Thousands of New Sheqalim through 1982;*			
Reserves	20	†825	1,021	1,472	1,721	2,743	5,822	10,321	20,540	44,756	96,171	228,692	†836	4,601	11,107	11,227
Foreign Assets	21	†48	61	143	124	141	1,143	1,863	5,294	12,617	97,851	242,053	†738	4,239	9,381	9,773
Claims on Central Government	22a	†225	506	1,220	2,233	3,388	6,502	10,730	24,402	64,023	173,753	456,180	†1,353	9,000	25,939	30,034
Claims on Other Banking Insts	22f	†51	84	134	297	531	899	1,462	3,176	7,356	15,712	39,723	†119	777	2,361	2,971
Claims on Private Sector	22d	†1,027	1,424	2,254	3,172	4,260	7,379	15,313	33,051	79,029	164,099	409,170	†1,097	6,236	17,051	23,267
Demand Deposits	24	†359	470	554	666	871	1,240	1,818	2,343	4,879	8,101	17,880	†38	154	508	1,203
Time and Savings Deposits	25	†557	624	1,063	1,590	2,383	4,217	3,553	5,985	15,346	205,775	496,798	†1,554	9,640	24,243	27,989
Restricted Deposits	26b	†459	904	1,786	2,905	4,632	7,932	13,010	29,072	76,059	175,826	435,335	†1,227	7,115	20,518	24,625
Foreign Liabilities	26c	†—						3,628	9,838	25,663	135,170	368,976	†1,146	6,584	15,052	15,329
Central Government Deposits	26d	†245	302	415	604	816	1,208	1,701	3,115	6,595	16,713	47,388	†149	922	2,661	3,974
Credit from Monetary Authorities	26g	†138	243	421	623	795	1,834	3,341	7,964	19,181	26,716	33,340	†111	433	665	832
Other Items (Net)	27r	†418	552	985	1,160	1,566	5,314	12,638	28,147	60,056	−20,715	−23,900	†−83	5	2,192	3,321
Monetary Survey													*Thousands of New Sheqalim through 1982;*			
Foreign Assets (Net)	31n	†555	837	817	750	1,084	3,065	3,221	5,656	11,943	16,209	7,950	†1	−376	−119	1,645
Domestic Credit	32	†1,434	2,037	3,859	5,895	8,567	15,907	28,700	62,163	150,861	366,674	946,854	†2,827	17,722	49,819	57,822
Claims on Central Govt. (Net)	32an	†356	529	1,471	2,426	3,776	7,629	11,925	25,935	64,477	186,864	497,961	†1,611	10,709	30,406	31,584
Claims on Other Banking Insts	32f	†51	84	134	297	531	899	1,462	3,176	7,356	15,712	39,723	†119	777	2,361	2,971
Claims on Private Sector	32d	†1,027	1,424	2,254	3,172	4,260	7,379	15,313	33,051	79,029	164,099	409,170	†1,097	6,236	17,051	23,267
Money	34	†557	741	871	1,063	1,348	1,872	2,696	3,548	6,979	13,354	27,930	†67	304	1,052	2,238
Quasi-Money	35	†557	624	1,063	1,590	2,383	4,217	3,631	6,432	17,230	211,629	516,186	†1,602	9,884	26,309	30,800
Restricted Deposits	36b	†459	904	1,786	2,905	4,632	7,932	13,010	29,072	76,059	175,826	435,335	†1,227	7,115	20,518	24,625
Other Items (Net)	37r	†418	604	957	1,089	1,287	4,951	12,585	28,768	62,536	−17,925	−24,647	†−70	42	1,821	1,804
Money plus Quasi-Money	35l	†1,114	1,366	1,935	2,652	3,732	6,089	6,327	9,979	24,210	224,983	544,116	†1,670	10,188	27,361	33,038
Interest Rates														*Percent Per Annum*		
Discount Rate	60	'	....	....	....	....	....	....	....	....	....	108.2	†311.0	690.3	79.6	31.4
Treasury Bill Rate	60c	....	....	....	....	....	....	....	....	....	....	....		217.3	210.1	19.9
Deposit Rate	60l	....	....	....	....	....	....	....	....	....	....	....	132.9	438.4	178.8	18.6
Lending Rate	60p	....	....	....	....	....	....	....	89.2	176.9	170.6	140.2	186.2	823.0	503.4	60.3
Prices, Production, Labor														*Index Numbers (1995=100):*		
Share Prices	62	—	—	—	—	—	—	—	—	†—	†—	†—	1	†2	†11	14
Prices: Industrial Products	63	—	—	—	†—	—	—	—	—	.1	.2	.5	1.2	†6.1	22.2	†32.2
Consumer Prices	64	—	—	—	†—	—	—	—	—	†.1	.2	.4	1.0	†4.7	†18.8	†27.9
Wages: Daily Earnings	65	—	—	—	—	—	†—	—	—	.1	.2	.3	†.9	4.3	15.3	24.7
Industrial Production	66.. c	39.0	40.6	42.9	†44.2	45.8	48.1	51.6	54.3	52.6	56.0	56.6	58.8	61.3	63.3	65.4
Industrial Employment	67	75.2	76.0	78.1	78.7	80.7	82.3	†83.8	86.6	83.3	85.5	87.1	†88.6	89.5	89.2	90.0
														Number in Thousands:		
Labor Force	67d	....	....	....	....	....	....	....	....	....	....	....	....	....		
Employment	67e	....	....	....	....	....	....	....	....	....	....	....	....	....	1,349	1,368
Unemployment	67c	....	....	....	....	....	....	....	....	....	....	....	....	....	97	104
Unemployment Rate (%)	67r	....	....	....	....	....	....	....	....	....	....	....	....	....	6.7	7.1
International Transactions														*Millions of US Dollars*		
Exports	70.. d	1,147	1,449	1,825	1,941	2,415	3,082	3,921	4,546	5,538	5,670	5,255	5,108	5,807	6,260	7,154
Imports, c.i.f.	71.. d	2,473	4,240	5,437	5,997	5,669	5,787	7,415	8,576	9,784	10,235	9,655	9,574	9,819	9,875	10,806
Imports,c.i.f.,excl. Military Gds	71.m d	1,987	2,987	4,215	4,173	4,140	4,807	5,843	7,511	7,995	7,960	8,071	8,599	8,413	8,320	9,645
														1995=100		
Volume of Exports	72	†22.7	23.2	24.8	25.2	30.9	33.8	33.8	34.8	†37.9	40.2	39.5	39.8	45.9	50.1	55.4
Volume of Imports	73	†26.9	31.7	32.5	30.9	31.2	33.6	35.0	36.6	†32.5	33.2	36.8	40.3	40.1	40.4	47.7
Unit Value of Exports(US$)	74.. d	†24.3	30.3	35.4	37.0	†37.6	44.5	†58.8	†67.6	†76.1	†73.5	69.5	†67.8	†66.6	65.9	68.1
Unit Value of Imports(US$)	75.. d	†23.9	30.8	41.8	43.7	†42.7	46.5	†57.1	†70.9	†87.1	†84.3	77.1	†73.6	†73.6	72.0	71.6

1987	1988	1989	1990	1991	1992	1993	1994	1995	1996	1997	1998	1999	2000	2001		
															Exchange Rates	
and per SDR thereafter: End of Period																
2.1828	2.2675	2.5797	2.9136	3.2657	3.8005	4.1015	4.4058	4.6601	4.6748	4.7709	5.8588	5.7000	5.2651	5.5497	Market Rate	**aa**
and per US Dollar thereafter: End of Period (ae) Period Average (rf)																
1.5386	1.6850	1.9630	2.0480	2.2830	2.7640	2.9860	3.0180	3.1350	3.2510	3.5360	4.1610	4.1530	4.0410	4.4160	Market Rate	**ae**
1.5946	1.5989	1.9164	2.0162	2.2791	2.4591	2.8301	3.0111	3.0113	3.1917	3.4494	3.8001	4.1397	4.0773	4.2057	Market Rate	**rf**
Period Averages																
207.18	201.58	177.34	155.61	139.12	125.48	115.24	106.52	100.00	97.35	97.57	91.32	84.29	92.00	92.61	Nominal Effective Exchange Rate	**ne c**
92.50	101.45	102.47	100.07	101.93	99.35	98.14	99.20	100.00	105.87	113.27	109.92	105.68	114.16	113.81	Real Effective Exchange Rate	**re c**
End of Period															**Fund Position**	
446.6	446.6	446.6	446.6	446.6	666.2	666.2	666.2	666.2	666.2	666.2	666.2	928.2	928.2	928.2	Quota	**2f.** ***s***
.1	.1	.1	.2	.3	.2	.4	.2	.4	1.0	—	.2	.1	.8	1.4	SDRs	**1b.** ***s***
—	—	—	—	—	—	—	—	—	—	—	—	65.5	89.9	157.4	Reserve Position in the Fund	**1c.** ***s***
—	—	—	—	—	178.6	178.6	178.6	111.7	22.3	—	—	—	—	—	Total Fund Cred.&Loans Outstg.	**2tl**
End of Period															**International Liquidity**	
5,876.1	4,015.6	5,276.2	6,275.1	6,279.1	5,127.4	6,382.6	6,792.4	8,119.3	11,414.6	20,332.1	22,674.3	22,604.9	23,281.2	23,378.6	Total Reserves minus Gold	**1l.** ***d***
.1	.1	.1	.2	.4	.3	.5	.4	.6	1.4	—	.3	.2	1.1	1.7	SDRs	**1b.** ***d***
—	—	—	—	—	—	—	—	—	—	—	—	89.9	117.1	197.8	Reserve Position in the Fund	**1c.** ***d***
5,876.0	4,015.5	5,276.1	6,274.9	6,278.7	5,127.1	6,382.1	6,792.0	8,118.7	11,413.2	†20332.0	22,674.0	22,514.8	23,163.0	23,179.1	Foreign Exchange	**1d.** ***d***
1.017	1.018	1.017	.839	.421	.009	.009	.009	.009	.009	.009	—	—	—	—	Gold (Million Fine Troy Ounces)	**1ad**
50.5	47.9	46.8	41.8	21.1	.4	.4	.4	.5	.4	.4	—	—	—	—	Gold (National Valuation)	**1an** ***d***
—	—	—	—	—	—	—	—	—	—	—	....	....	....	....	Monetary Authorities: Other Assets	**3..** ***d***
29.2	36.2	32.6	28.8	28.9	37.7	38.5	37.8	38.6	38.1	30.0	21.9	17.8	18.1	17.0	Monetary Authorities: Other Liab.	**4..** ***d***
6,447.3	7,264.4	7,360.8	8,316.7	8,896.8	10,608.7	10,137.7	11,330.0	12,055.9	12,945.4	10,823.5	12,746.6	14,146.6	16,095.4	15,644.9	Deposit Money Banks: Assets	**7a.** ***d***
10,264.4	10,676.4	9,982.2	11,024.5	11,480.4	12,093.0	12,159.1	13,098.9	14,514.4	15,113.4	16,738.3	18,334.0	20,452.0	21,872.6	22,106.4	Liabilities	**7b.** ***d***
Millions of New Sheqalim Beginning 1983: End of Period															**Monetary Authorities**	
9,377	7,391	10,464	12,935	14,380	14,186	19,065	20,508	25,578	37,130	70,970	94,326	93,878	94,084	103,248	Foreign Assets	**11**
8,029	9,905	10,086	10,300	10,285	10,419	10,338	9,976	10,818	12,304	12,199	12,288	12,416	12,530	12,204	Claims on Central Government	**12a**
1,205	3,853	4,711	3,066	5,475	11,053	16,972	15,555	4,503	1,236	1,519	838	810	787	802	Claims on Deposit Money Banks	**12e**
14,128	15,059	16,530	18,815	20,488	21,901	28,051	26,166	19,157	25,838	56,659	64,802	80,218	80,706	81,237	Reserve Money	**14**
1,365	1,643	2,225	2,817	3,228	†4,113	4,852	5,467	6,731	7,772	8,767	10,051	12,178	12,347	14,580	*of which: Currency Outside DMBs*	**14a**
9,919	11,796	12,700	14,442	15,364	15,893	20,203	16,413	10,119	7,982	7,633	7,931	10,741	9,100	10,773	*Foreign Cur.Deps.*	**14cf**
45	61	64	59	66	783	848	901	641	228	106	91	74	73	75	Foreign Liabilities	**16c**
3,469	5,025	7,503	6,108	8,383	11,694	16,165	17,456	19,325	23,013	26,509	39,407	32,242	37,369	39,290	Central Government Deposits	**16d**
969	1,004	1,164	1,319	1,203	1,280	1,311	1,516	1,775	1,591	1,414	3,152	–5,430	–10,747	–4,348	Other Items (Net)	**17r**
Millions of New Sheqalim Beginning 1983: End of Period															**Deposit Money Banks**	
13,026	13,313	14,223	15,911	17,053	†17,854	23,223	20,743	12,425	18,085	48,103	54,578	68,029	67,882	65,788	Reserves	**20**
9,920	12,241	14,449	17,033	20,311	29,322	30,271	34,194	37,795	42,086	38,272	53,038	58,751	65,041	69,088	Foreign Assets	**21**
34,588	40,937	46,860	49,814	56,836	†62,094	65,080	66,289	69,960	77,542	66,136	63,806	61,984	44,464	43,883	Claims on Central Government	**22a**
3,661	4,299	5,289	5,605	7,515	....	....	....	....	....	....	....	....	....	....	Claims on Other Banking Insts	**22f**
31,698	40,720	49,464	60,957	75,468	†94,092	121,800	154,285	185,123	219,842	254,886	303,434	347,382	390,938	439,228	Claims on Private Sector	**22d**
1,922	2,012	3,079	4,133	4,680	†6,324	8,526	8,946	9,870	12,227	13,502	14,937	17,933	18,536	23,053	Demand Deposits	**24**
34,595	45,136	52,273	60,780	71,643	†89,564	104,678	139,899	171,485	217,117	251,747	306,960	352,568	381,425	412,502	Time and Savings Deposits	**25**
27,206	29,937	32,830	35,500	37,855	†29,879	28,775	28,730	22,979	21,481	19,368	17,063	13,593	11,002	6,813	Restricted Deposits	**26b**
15,793	17,990	19,595	22,578	26,210	33,425	36,307	39,533	45,503	49,134	59,187	76,288	84,937	88,387	97,622	Foreign Liabilities	**26c**
4,781	5,648	6,606	8,145	12,149	†15,147	19,604	23,211	26,684	27,590	28,190	24,286	24,300	21,082	22,058	Central Government Deposits	**26d**
1,546	3,828	4,685	3,056	5,453	†11,053	16,896	15,569	4,212	1,186	1,506	835	814	787	806	Credit from Monetary Authorities	**26g**
7,051	6,960	11,215	15,127	19,194	†17,972	25,587	19,621	24,570	28,821	33,895	34,486	42,001	47,106	55,137	Other Items (Net)	**27r**
Millions of New Sheqalim Beginning 1983: End of Period															**Monetary Survey**	
3,459	1,581	5,254	7,331	8,415	9,300	12,181	14,268	17,229	29,854	49,949	70,986	67,618	70,665	74,639	Foreign Assets (Net)	**31n**
69,726	85,188	97,589	112,424	129,573	†139,765	161,448	189,882	219,891	259,086	278,521	315,834	365,240	389,482	433,967	Domestic Credit	**32**
34,368	40,169	42,837	45,861	46,589	†45,673	39,649	35,598	34,768	39,244	23,635	12,401	17,858	–1,457	–5,261	Claims on Central Govt. (Net)	**32an**
3,661	4,299	5,289	5,605	7,515	....	....	....	....	....	....	....	....	....	....	Claims on Other Banking Insts	**32f**
31,698	40,720	49,464	60,957	75,468	†94,092	121,800	154,285	185,123	219,842	254,886	303,434	347,382	390,938	439,228	Claims on Private Sector	**32d**
3,346	3,723	5,376	7,022	7,988	†10,541	13,486	14,523	16,716	20,131	22,401	25,145	30,263	31,030	37,796	Money	**34**
38,691	47,668	56,842	67,280	79,486	†100,085	121,441	153,587	187,829	235,519	271,480	326,491	376,013	407,831	442,567	Quasi-Money	**35**
27,206	29,937	32,830	35,500	37,855	†29,879	28,775	28,730	22,979	21,481	19,368	17,063	13,593	11,002	6,813	Restricted Deposits	**36b**
3,943	5,441	7,796	9,952	12,660	†8,560	9,928	7,310	9,596	11,809	15,221	18,120	12,990	10,283	21,434	Other Items (Net)	**37r**
42,037	51,391	62,218	74,303	87,473	†110,626	134,926	168,109	204,545	255,650	293,881	351,636	406,276	438,862	480,363	Money plus Quasi-Money	**35l**
Percent Per Annum															**Interest Rates**	
26.8	30.9	15.0	13.0	14.2	10.4	9.8	17.0	14.2	....	....	....	....	....	....	Discount Rate	**60**
20.0	16.0	12.9	15.1	14.5	11.8	10.5	11.8	14.4	15.5	13.9	12.2	....	....	....	Treasury Bill Rate	**60c**
19.4	14.5	14.1	14.4	13.9	11.3	10.4	12.2	14.1	14.5	13.1	11.0	11.3	8.6	6.2	Deposit Rate	**60l**
61.4	41.7	31.6	26.4	26.4	19.9	16.4	17.4	20.2	20.7	18.7	16.2	16.4	12.9	10.0	Lending Rate	**60p**
Period Averages															**Prices, Production, Labor**	
17	17	30	35	54	103	145	88	100	99	134	138	227	228	212	Share Prices	**62**
38.2	44.8	54.3	60.5	†70.3	77.4	83.7	90.3	100.0	108.6	115.4	120.3	128.7	133.4	133.3	Prices: Industrial Products	**63**
33.4	38.8	46.7	54.7	65.1	72.9	†80.9	†90.9	100.0	111.3	121.3	127.9	134.5	†136.0	137.6	Consumer Prices	**64**
32.4	39.4	†47.7	†56.0	63.2	71.5	78.8	87.1	100.0	113.9	130.8	143.9	155.4	165.2	....	Wages: Daily Earnings	**65**
68.6	66.5	†65.5	69.8	74.9	81.1	86.3	†92.8	100.0	105.1	107.3	110.2	111.5	122.5	116.4	Industrial Production	**66..** ***c***
91.8	88.6	†83.1	82.4	85.8	89.3	93.1	†96.4	100.0	101.6	100.5	99.6	98.2	99.4	96.7	Industrial Employment	**67**
Period Averages																
....	....	....	1,650	1,770	1,858	1,946	2,030	†2,110	2,157	2,210	†2,266	2,345	2,435	....	Labor Force	**67d**
1,404	1,453	1,461	1,492	1,583	1,650	1,751	1,871	†1,965	2,013	2,040	†2,073	2,137	2,221	....	Employment	**67e**
90	100	143	158	187	208	195	158	†145	144	170	†193	208	214	233	Unemployment	**67c**
6.1	6.4	8.9	9.6	10.6	11.2	10.0	7.8	†6.9	6.7	7.7	†8.6	8.9	8.8	9.3	Unemployment Rate (%)	**67r**
Millions of US Dollars															**International Transactions**	
8,454	8,198	10,738	11,576	11,921	10,019	14,826	16,884	19,046	20,610	22,503	22,993	25,794	31,404	29,019	Exports	**70..** ***d***
14,348	15,018	14,347	16,794	18,658	15,535	22,624	25,237	29,579	31,620	30,781	29,342	33,166	31,404	35,465	Imports, c.i.f.	**71..** ***d***
11,921	12,960	13,197	15,312	16,839	18,814	20,518	23,776	28,287	29,951	29,084	27,470	31,090	35,750	33,319	Imports,c.i.f.,excl. Military Gds	**71.m** ***d***
1995=100																
61.5	63.4	66.3	†66.7	65.3	71.6	80.5	93.0	100.0	†107.4	118.2	125.6	135.8	170.5	163.6	Volume of Exports	**72**
53.5	53.6	51.2	†55.1	64.0	71.1	80.2	91.0	100.0	†106.6	108.0	108.3	124.2	141.1	130.7	Volume of Imports	**73**
72.5	82.7	88.0	†95.3	95.7	96.4	96.8	95.4	100.0	†99.9	99.1	96.1	97.3	97.3	93.9	Unit Value of Exports(US$)	**74..** ***d***
78.8	85.4	91.1	†98.1	93.4	93.5	90.3	92.2	100.0	†99.3	94.8	89.6	87.0	89.7	88.4	Unit Value of Imports(US$)	**75..** ***d***

Israel

		1972	1973	1974	1975	1976	1977	1978	1979	1980	1981	1982	1983	1984	1985	1986
Balance of Payments															*Millions of US Dollars:*	
Current Account, n.i.e.	78al d	−216	−525	−1,563	−1,822	−676	−356	−1,009	−920	−871	−1,361	−2,257	−2,373	−1,578	988	1,277
Goods: Exports f.o.b.	78aa d	1,227	1,571	2,029	2,192	2,688	3,422	4,104	4,841	5,946	6,095	5,750	5,722	6,380	6,826	7,894
Goods: Imports f.o.b.	78ab d	−2,307	−3,987	−5,060	−5,600	−5,345	−5,484	−6,814	−8,088	−9,201	−9,694	−8,986	−8,971	−8,959	−9,202	−9,735
Trade Balance	78ac d	−1,080	−2,416	−3,031	−3,408	−2,657	−2,062	−2,710	−3,247	−3,255	−3,599	−3,237	−3,250	−2,579	−2,376	−1,841
Services: Credit	78ad d	727	848	1,140	1,126	1,338	1,606	1,954	2,318	2,722	2,724	2,643	2,750	2,818	3,152	3,122
Services: Debit	78ae d	−634	−880	−1,092	−1,198	−1,365	−1,538	−1,851	−2,133	−2,310	−2,663	−2,586	−2,799	−2,807	−2,404	−2,741
Balance on Goods & Services	78af d	−987	−2,448	−2,983	−3,480	−2,684	−1,994	−2,607	−3,062	−2,843	−3,538	−3,180	−3,298	−2,567	−1,629	−1,460
Income: Credit	78ag d	166	278	394	370	371	431	561	916	1,190	1,735	1,808	1,529	1,318	1,003	902
Income: Debit	78ah d	−278	−396	−604	−739	−756	−796	−1,047	−1,369	−1,947	−2,253	−3,077	−3,043	−3,339	−3,122	−3,066
Balance on Gds, Serv. & Inc.	78ai d	−1,099	−2,566	−3,193	−3,849	−3,069	−2,359	−3,093	−3,515	−3,600	−4,056	−4,449	−4,812	−4,588	−3,748	−3,624
Current Transfers, n.i.e.: Credit	78aj d	933	2,101	1,651	2,065	2,492	2,103	2,212	2,733	2,864	2,894	2,417	2,693	3,242	4,871	5,026
Current Transfers: Debit	78ak d	−50	−60	−21	−38	−99	−100	−128	−138	−135	−199	−225	−254	−232	−136	−126
Capital Account, n.i.e.	78bc d	166	148	100	64	40	69	141	242	296	403	262	258	260	271	534
Capital Account, n.i.e.: Credit	78ba d	166	148	100	64	40	69	141	242	296	403	262	258	260	271	534
Capital Account: Debit	78bb d	—	—	—	—	—	—	—	—	—	—	—	—	—	—	—
Financial Account, n.i.e.	78bj d	581	1,111	908	1,728	418	381	1,331	1,668	1,082	2,277	3,140	1,784	1,428	377	60
Direct Investment Abroad	78bd d	—	—	—	2	−6	−6	−7	−1	3	−114	−189	−100	−24	−96	−127
Dir. Invest. in Rep. Econ., n.i.e.	78be d	114	149	84	45	47	81	39	11	51	114	21	79	90	112	143
Portfolio Investment Assets	78bf d	—	−14	−9	14	−6	−2	−107	−149	−173	−155	−37	−265	153	119	126
Equity Securities	78bk d	−2	−6	−5	9	3	1	−64	−68	−58	−42	−4	−259	56	61	67
Debt Securities	78bl d	2	−8	−4	5	−9	−3	−43	−81	−115	−113	−33	−6	97	58	60
Portfolio Investment Liab., n.i.e.	78bg d	221	399	187	162	169	193	248	127	148	93	−102	862	−101	−8	36
Equity Securities	78bm d	—	—	—	—	—	—	—	—	—	—	−70	757	−87	1	26
Debt Securities	78bn d	221	399	187	162	169	193	248	127	148	93	−32	106	−14	−10	10
Financial Derivatives Assets	78bw d	....	....	....	....	....	....	....	....	....	....	....	....	....	....	....
Financial Derivatives Liabilities	78bx d	....	....	....	....	....	....	....	....	....	....	....	....	....	....	....
Other Investment Assets	78bh d	−484	−301	−55	−301	−819	−1,122	−1,015	−1,607	−1,694	−347	−502	−464	250	449	−923
Monetary Authorities	78bo d	—	—	—	—	—	—	—	—	—	—	—	—	—	—	—
General Government	78bp d	15	59	60	163	−388	−452	49	−468	−177	398	152	−802	448	−5	−657
Banks	78bq d	−450	−327	90	−358	−224	−479	−851	−782	−1,198	−685	−717	348	−2	538	−145
Other Sectors	78br d	−49	−33	−205	−106	−207	−191	−213	−357	−319	−59	63	−10	−197	−85	−121
Other Investment Liab., n.i.e.	78bi d	730	878	701	1,806	1,033	1,237	2,173	3,287	2,747	2,685	3,950	1,672	1,061	−199	804
Monetary Authorities	78bs d	—	—	—	—	—	—	—	—	—	1	—	—	—	—	—
General Government	78bt d	215	276	413	948	913	758	719	912	1,280	1,211	1,189	1,479	1,113	136	314
Banks	78bu d	341	422	244	660	50	446	1,290	1,484	1,260	1,272	2,402	−318	−254	−598	−8
Other Sectors	78bv d	174	180	44	198	70	33	164	891	207	201	359	511	203	263	498
Net Errors and Omissions	78ca d	17	−186	−287	−126	402	120	482	−779	34	−768	−228	−167	−663	−1,236	−877
Overall Balance	78cb d	548	548	−842	−156	184	214	945	211	541	550	918	−498	−552	399	994
Reserves and Related Items	79da d	−548	−548	842	156	−184	−214	−945	−211	−541	−550	−918	498	552	−399	−994
Reserve Assets	79db d	−513	−548	802	−57	−273	−214	−929	−151	−453	−468	−851	527	552	−399	−994
Use of Fund Credit and Loans	79dc d	−35	—	39	213	88	—	−16	−61	−89	−82	−67	−29	—	—	—
Exceptional Financing	79de d	....	....	....	....	....	....	....	....	....	....	....	....	....	....	....
International Investment Position															*Millions of US Dollars*	
Assets	79aa d	....	....	....	....	....	....	....	....	....	....	....	....	....	....	....
Direct Investment Abroad	79ab d	....	....	....	....	....	....	....	....	....	....	....	....	....	....	....
Portfolio Investment	79ac d	....	....	....	....	....	....	....	....	....	....	....	....	....	....	....
Equity Securities	79ad d	....	....	....	....	....	....	....	....	....	....	....	....	....	....	....
Debt Securities	79ae d	....	....	....	....	....	....	....	....	....	....	....	....	....	....	....
Financial Derivatives	79al d	....	....	....	....	....	....	....	....	....	....	....	....	....	....	....
Other Investment	79af d	....	....	....	....	....	....	....	....	....	....	....	....	....	....	....
Monetary Authorities	79ag d	....	....	....	....	....	....	....	....	....	....	....	....	....	....	....
General Government	79ah d	....	....	....	....	....	....	....	....	....	....	....	....	....	....	....
Banks	79ai d	....	....	....	....	....	....	....	....	....	....	....	....	....	....	....
Other Sectors	79aj d	....	....	....	....	....	....	....	....	....	....	....	....	....	....	....
Reserve Assets	79ak d	....	....	....	....	....	....	....	....	....	....	....	....	....	....	....
Liabilities	79la d	....	....	....	....	....	....	....	....	....	....	....	....	....	....	....
Dir. Invest. in Rep. Economy	79lb d	....	....	....	....	....	....	....	....	....	....	....	....	....	....	....
Portfolio Investment	79lc d	....	....	....	....	....	....	....	....	....	....	....	....	....	....	....
Equity Securities	79ld d	....	....	....	....	....	....	....	....	....	....	....	....	....	....	....
Debt Securities	79le d	....	....	....	....	....	....	....	....	....	....	....	....	....	....	....
Financial Derivatives	79ll d	....	....	....	....	....	....	....	....	....	....	....	....	....	....	....
Other Investment	79lf d	....	....	....	....	....	....	....	....	....	....	....	....	....	....	....
Monetary Authorities	79lg d	....	....	....	....	....	....	....	....	....	....	....	....	....	....	....
General Government	79lh d	....	....	....	....	....	....	....	....	....	....	....	....	....	....	....
Banks	79li d	....	....	....	....	....	....	....	....	....	....	....	....	....	....	....
Other Sectors	79lj d	....	....	....	....	....	....	....	....	....	....	....	....	....	....	....

Balance of Payments

Minus Sign Indicates Debit

	1987	1988	1989	1990	1991	1992	1993	1994	1995	1996	1997	1998	1999	2000	2001
Current Account, n.i.e. 78al d	-1,407	-838	208	163	-1,278	-875	-2,480	-3,447	-4,972	-5,498	-3,845	-1,325	-3,277	-1,974	-1,852
Goods: Exports f.o.b. 78aa d	9,311	10,350	11,142	12,743	12,233	13,621	14,926	17,242	19,663	21,333	22,698	22,974	25,577	30,947	27,678
Goods: Imports f.o.b. 78ab d	-13,018	-13,241	-13,047	-15,307	-17,093	-18,389	-20,533	-22,728	-26,890	-28,469	-27,875	-26,241	-30,041	-34,036	-30,942
Trade Balance 78ac d	-3,707	-2,890	-1,905	-2,564	-4,861	-4,769	-5,607	-5,486	-7,227	-7,136	-5,177	-3,267	-4,464	-3,089	-3,264
Services: Credit 78ad d	3,798	4,124	4,348	4,569	4,671	5,811	5,967	6,579	7,786	8,071	8,531	9,445	11,447	15,181	11,991
Services: Debit 78ae d	-3,390	-3,827	-4,276	-4,921	-5,178	-5,545	-6,397	-7,590	-8,401	-9,107	-9,288	-9,636	-10,708	-12,529	-12,563
Balance on Goods & Services 78af d	-3,298	-2,593	-1,833	-2,916	-5,368	-4,502	-6,037	-6,497	-7,842	-8,173	-5,934	-3,457	-3,726	-437	-3,836
Income: Credit 78ag d	950	1,099	1,370	1,590	1,685	1,599	1,295	1,160	1,730	1,806	2,093	2,756	2,553	3,353	3,545
Income: Debit 78ah d	-3,204	-3,393	-3,403	-3,571	-3,329	-3,651	-3,344	-3,711	-4,533	-5,268	-6,053	-6,704	-8,420	-11,360	-7,959
Balance on Gds, Serv. & Inc. 78ai d	-5,553	-4,887	-3,866	-4,897	-7,011	-6,553	-8,087	-9,048	-10,645	-11,635	-9,894	-7,405	-9,592	-8,443	-8,251
Current Transfers, n.i.e.: Credit 78aj d	4,357	4,255	4,238	5,268	6,087	6,002	5,911	5,850	5,941	6,441	6,374	6,686	7,125	7,483	7,531
Current Transfers: Debit 78ak d	-211	-207	-163	-207	-354	-324	-304	-250	-268	-304	-325	-606	-809	-1,015	-1,132
Capital Account, n.i.e. 78bc d	671	604	357	728	857	1,070	863	786	809	774	723	577	569	455	681
Capital Account, n.i.e.: Credit 78ba d	671	604	357	728	857	1,070	863	786	809	774	723	577	569	455	681
Capital Account: Debit 78bb d															
Financial Account, n.i.e. 78bj d	1,679	-6,157	-464	593	641	-451	1,041	-959	4,217	4,535	7,238	-650	2,040	2,982	-110
Direct Investment Abroad 78bd d	-167	-147	-109	-199	-331	-580	-615	-742	-820	-815	-923	-1,125	-933	-2,859	-1,135
Dir. Invest. in Rep. Econ., n.i.e. 78be d	224	267	160	151	346	589	605	442	1,351	1,398	1,635	1,737	2,873	4,524	3,224
Portfolio Investment Assets 78bf d	67	-566	-106	-368	-208	-1,183	-812	-1,772	98	368	215	107	-830	-2,139	-1,199
Equity Securities 78bk d	32	5	-3	14	-345	-926	80	303	16	160	166	154	383	-1,538	-493
Debt Securities 78bl d	36	-571	-104	-382	137	-257	-891	-2,075	82	208	49	-47	-1,213	-601	-707
Portfolio Investment Liab., n.i.e. 78bg d	-49	-772	-20	-36	-10	-40	276	481	989	1,436	1,743	425	1,499	4,361	656
Equity Securities 78bm d	-41	-768	-17	-18	17	-32	284	469	991	1,440	1,719	476	1,500	4,397	664
Debt Securities 78bn d	-8	-4	-4	-18	-26	-8	-7	13	-2	-4	25	-51	-1	-37	-8
Financial Derivatives Assets 78bw d	....	....	—	—	—	—	—	—	—	—	—	—	—	—	—
Financial Derivatives Liabilities 78bx d	....	....	—	—	—	—	—	—	—	—	—	—	—	—	—
Other Investment Assets 78bh d	881	-269	-783	-632	-545	-1,143	1,003	-1,063	-586	845	1,600	-2,152	-3,948	-2,854	-2,850
Monetary Authorities 78bo d															
General Government 78bp d	735	397	-222	-190	-180	78	261	-28	-1,230	864	-19	-13	-188	-142	-667
Banks 78bq d	430	-413	-538	-244	-604	-1,657	940	-1,736	-216	-1,165	1,686	-1,808	-753	-1,198	-361
Other Sectors 78br d	-285	-252	-23	-198	240	436	-197	701	860	1,146	-66	-332	-3,007	-1,513	-1,821
Other Investment Liab., n.i.e. 78bi d	724	-4,671	394	1,677	1,389	1,907	583	1,695	3,185	1,303	2,969	359	3,379	1,950	1,194
Monetary Authorities 78bs d															
General Government 78bt d	68	-4,483	-713	102	403	905	225	-64	215	77	-272	-307	-168	560	314
Banks 78bu d	-415	-57	-22	389	177	692	280	1,000	1,219	612	2,352	1,525	2,385	1,657	1,643
Other Sectors 78bv d	1,071	-131	1,129	1,186	810	310	78	760	1,751	615	889	-859	1,162	-267	-763
Net Errors and Omissions 78ca d	-293	441	578	-838	-623	-1,220	249	1,510	426	1,396	2,960	1,305	677	-1,591	1,477
Overall Balance 78cb d	650	-5,950	679	646	-404	-1,476	-327	-2,111	480	1,206	7,077	-93	9	-128	196
Reserves and Related Items 79da d	-650	5,950	-679	-646	404	1,476	327	2,111	-480	-1,206	-7,077	93	-9	128	-196
Reserve Assets 79db d	-650	1,172	-1,403	-511	173	1,444	-1,533	-124	-1,123	-3,413	-9,378	-1,880	-1,109	-597	170
Use of Fund Credit and Loans 79dc d	—	—	—	—	—	245	—	—	-101	-129	-31	—	—	—	—
Exceptional Financing 79de d	....	4,778	723	-136	230	-212	1,861	2,235	745	2,336	2,332	1,973	1,099	725	-366

International Investment Position

Millions of US Dollars

	1987	1988	1989	1990	1991	1992	1993	1994	1995	1996	1997	1998	1999	2000	2001
Assets 79aa d	....	....	14,682	16,928	19,637	19,720	21,944	26,345	30,754	34,751	44,556	50,468	56,967	65,271	68,990
Direct Investment Abroad 79ab d	....	....	—	—	—	—	—	—	2,867	3,283	5,223	5,376	6,180	8,735	9,727
Portfolio Investment 79ac d	....	....	761	1,073	934	1,219	2,518	2,866	2,801	2,609	2,711	3,027	5,001	7,294	8,033
Equity Securities 79ad d	....	....	—	—	—	—	—	374	430	356	447	499	1,449	2,518	2,067
Debt Securities 79ae d	....	....	761	1,073	934	1,219	2,518	2,492	2,371	2,253	2,264	2,528	3,552	4,776	5,966
Financial Derivatives 79al d															
Other Investment 79af d	....	....	8,591	9,540	12,296	13,168	12,656	16,315	16,476	17,107	16,022	19,022	22,515	25,370	27,358
Monetary Authorities 79ag d	....	....	—	—	—	—	—	—	—	—	—	—	—	—	—
General Government 79ah d	....	....	—	—	—	—	—	—	—	—	—	—	—	—	—
Banks 79ai d	....	....	6,424	6,940	7,530	8,935	7,776	9,789	10,262	11,223	9,155	11,070	11,571	12,613	12,887
Other Sectors 79aj d	....	....	2,167	2,600	4,766	4,233	4,880	6,526	6,214	5,884	6,867	7,951	10,944	12,756	14,471
Reserve Assets 79ak d	....	....	5,330	6,316	6,406	5,333	6,770	7,164	8,609	11,752	20,599	23,043	23,271	23,872	23,872
Liabilities 79la d	....	....	32,031	33,773	34,666	39,086	40,969	47,586	52,953	57,819	74,593	77,568	104,809	115,288	105,628
Dir. Invest. in Rep. Economy 79lb d	....	....	329	365	315	353	402	474	636	774	9,315	10,507	18,442	21,559	23,206
Portfolio Investment 79lc d	....	....	5,622	5,477	5,681	5,461	7,315	12,437	14,968	19,399	25,694	26,863	43,729	49,759	37,011
Equity Securities 79ld d	....	....	—	—	—	—	—	2,893	4,706	6,806	10,789	9,912	25,655	31,119	18,882
Debt Securities 79le d	....	....	5,622	5,477	5,681	5,461	7,315	9,544	10,262	12,593	14,905	16,951	18,074	18,640	18,129
Financial Derivatives 79ll d															
Other Investment 79lf d	....	....	26,081	27,932	28,670	33,272	33,253	34,676	37,350	37,647	39,584	40,198	42,637	43,970	45,411
Monetary Authorities 79lg d	....	....	33	29	29	284	284	317	235	98	89	83	39	54	50
General Government 79lh d	....	....	11,464	11,801	12,168	12,946	13,023	12,944	13,335	13,289	12,724	12,549	12,554	12,718	12,940
Banks 79li d	....	....	10,507	11,389	11,540	11,986	12,211	13,500	14,958	15,428	17,470	19,129	21,218	22,668	24,162
Other Sectors 79lj d	....	....	4,077	4,713	4,934	8,057	7,736	7,915	8,822	8,832	9,300	8,436	8,827	8,530	8,260

Israel

		1972	1973	1974	1975	1976	1977	1978	1979	1980	1981	1982	1983	1984	1985	1986
Government Finance												*Thousands of New Sheqalim through 1982; Millions Beginning 1983;*				
Deficit (-) or Surplus	80	†−463	−745	†−1,329	−1,561	−1,818	−2,798	−2,990	−6,730	−18,107	−58,218	−100,501	†−412	−1,440	−951	333
Revenue	81	†1,018	1,442	†2,369	3,588	5,206	7,700	12,300	25,900	58,300	133,800	354,800	†954	4,490	15,503	23,094
Grants Received	81z	†22	500	†206	609	1,005	1,318	2,132	4,633	11,437	24,181	26,605	†154	1,301	5,446	6,010
Expenditure	82	†1,403	2,521	†3,611	5,251	7,356	10,900	16,055	34,037	81,229	198,568	443,100	†1,373	6,803	19,817	26,696
Lending Minus Repayments	83	†100	166	†293	507	673	916	1,367	3,226	6,615	17,631	38,806	†148	429	2,083	2,076
Financing																
Domestic	84a	†341	560	†700	896	1,500	1,900	1,600	2,800	9,000	46,900	48,400	†280	1,137	807	−11
Foreign	85a	†178	236	†553	665	417	925	1,461	3,922	9,100	11,277	52,111	†132	302	144	−322
Debt: Domestic	88a	2,500	3,700	5,300	7,600	10,500	16,774	26,100	51,700	190,000	491,400	884,500	†4,328	20,321	47,205	58,138
Foreign	89a	1,500	1,700	3,000	4,532	6,900	13,810	20,200	46,200	107,200	251,600	588,100	†2,396	13,838	25,314	27,992
National Accounts												*Thousands of New Sheqalim through 1982;*				
Househ.Cons.Expend.,incl.NPISHs	96f	1,669	2,182	3,264	4,628	6,192	8,795	14,576	27,956	†58,891	145,250	342,832	†910	4,160	16,490	27,801
Government Consumption Expend.	91f	924	1,640	2,207	3,393	4,027	5,101	9,022	15,187	44,701	109,973	228,133	†545	2,919	10,313	13,641
Gross Fixed Capital Formation	93e	920	1,260	1,750	2,300	2,550	3,100	5,540	11,510	24,543	59,002	136,006	†360	1,568	5,338	8,051
Changes in Inventories	93i	50	30	20	190	140	320	660	750	840	−2,768	4,968	†5	100	117	401
Exports of Goods and Services	90c	939	1,165	1,683	2,551	3,851	6,413	11,771	21,104	†48,863	112,684	227,483	†546	3,099	12,700	17,434
Imports of Goods and Services (-)	98c	1,512	2,182	3,264	5,262	6,816	9,431	18,047	31,813	†66,226	158,993	343,990	†824	4,210	16,570	23,136
Gross Domestic Product (GDP)	99b	2,999	3,877	5,595	7,817	9,888	14,390	23,745	44,490	†111,612	265,148	596,306	†1,542	7,636	28,437	44,191
Net Primary Income from Abroad	98.n	−52	−115	−167	−284	−356	−361	−710	−1,758	−3,802	−6,350	−17,747	†−48	−333	−1,119	−1,561
Gross National Income (GNI)	99a	2,947	3,762	5,427	7,533	9,532	14,029	23,035	42,732	107,809	258,795	578,559	†1,494	7,303	27,318	42,630
Consumption of Fixed Capital	99cf	291	410	630	920	1,270	1,920	....	....	16,868	40,800	92,208	†233	1,210	4,744	7,343
Net National Income	99e	2,656	3,375	4,820	6,556	8,330	12,105	20,970	39,170	90,941	217,995	486,351	†1,261	6,093	22,575	35,288
GDP Volume 1970 prices (thousands)	99b.p	40	60	60	70	....	....	....	....	....	....	....	....	....	....	....
GDP Volume 1975 prices (thousands)	99b.p	....	....	....	270	280	220	250	310	320	210	....	....	....	....	....
GDP Volume 1980 prices (thousands)	99b.p	....	....	....	....	....	....	....	....	111,608	116,646	118,174	121,176	123,766	128,726	134,052
GDP Volume 1986 prices (millions)	99b.p	....	....	....	....	....	....	....	....	....	....	....	....	....	....	44,561
GDP Volume 1990 Prices (millions)	99b.p	....	....	....	....	....	....	....	....	....	....	....	....	....	....	....
GDP Volume 1995 Ref.,Chained (mil.)	99b.p	....	....	....	....	....	....	....	....	....	....	....	....	....	....	....
GDP Volume (1995=100)	99bv p	25.6	38.5	38.5	44.9	46.5	36.6	41.6	51.5	53.2	55.6	56.3	57.8	59.0	61.4	63.9
GDP Deflator (1995=100)	99bi p	—	—	—	—	—	—	—	—	†.1	.2	.4	1.0	4.8	17.1	25.6
																Millions:
Population	99z	3.15	3.28	3.38	3.46	3.53	3.61	3.69	3.79	3.88	3.95	4.03	4.11	4.16	4.23	4.30

Year Ending March 31 through 1991, Year Ending December 31 thereafter

1987	1988	1989	1990	1991	1992	1993	1994	1995	1996	1997	1998	1999	2000	2001		
															Government Finance	
-2,000	-5,897	-3,677	-5,641	†-9,160	†-6,949	-4,675	-6,882	-11,971	-13,253	1,017	-5,519	-8,698	....	....	Deficit (-) or Surplus	80
27,862	29,582	34,355	42,286	†39,758	†63,295	73,482	88,559	108,032	123,796	145,110	159,911	173,187	....	....	Revenue	81
5,193	5,020	5,816	6,941	†6,458	†9,074	8,229	7,927	6,340	12,953	11,437	12,158	12,327	....	....	Grants Received	81z
32,487	35,010	42,649	53,702	†50,818	†78,163	86,273	102,350	125,369	149,571	165,250	183,046	197,954	....	....	Expenditure	82
2,568	5,488	1,199	1,165	†4,558	†1,155	113	1,018	974	431	-9,720	-5,458	-3,742	....	....	Lending Minus Repayments	83
															Financing	
2,056	4,196	4,138	4,837	†8,307	†4,864	-273	655	12,615	7,431	-5,091	538	11,602	....	....	Domestic	84a
-56	1,701	-461	804	†853	†2,085	4,948	6,227	-644	5,822	4,074	4,981	-2,904	....	....	Foreign	85a
68,827	87,275	103,729	123,837	147,861	168,248	188,706	211,726	240,333	277,034	292,401	318,398	330,062	....	....	Debt: Domestic	88a
26,701	32,655	35,659	41,362	42,638	54,742	64,112	71,069	75,083	83,673	92,523	114,261	113,472	....	....	Foreign	89a
															National Accounts	

Millions of New Sheqalim Beginning 1983

1987	1988	1989	1990	1991	1992	1993	1994	1995	1996	1997	1998	1999	2000	2001		
36,393	44,257	53,168	64,745	81,484	97,915	116,475	142,478	†157,394	181,417	201,728	221,189	240,503	259,424	271,737	Househ.Cons.Expend.,incl.NPISHs	96f
19,214	22,199	25,108	31,745	40,015	45,783	53,188	62,634	†79,242	93,382	102,756	112,189	122,274	129,379	137,293	Government Consumption Expend.	91f
11,294	12,776	14,554	20,234	32,280	38,068	42,485	52,014	†68,599	79,249	83,963	85,922	92,556	92,657	87,239	Gross Fixed Capital Formation	93e
-204	113	258	422	1,960	2,138	4,505	2,220	†3,806	2,146	2,206	-73	5,293	5,397	9,761	Changes in Inventories	93i
22,179	24,635	31,461	36,715	40,299	49,544	60,536	73,334	†82,896	93,706	107,319	122,424	151,485	184,492	163,032	Exports of Goods and Services	90c
32,302	33,799	39,078	48,030	61,183	71,709	90,613	107,843	†121,424	136,856	145,552	154,694	189,257	211,256	....	Imports of Goods and Services (-)	98c
56,572	70,181	85,471	105,831	134,855	161,738	186,576	224,838	†270,297	313,001	352,331	387,211	405,021	443,048	481,385	Gross Domestic Product (GDP)	99b
-1,804	-1,779	-2,204	-2,496	-2,490	-3,209	-2,952	-3,329	†-4,910	-7,106	-10,389	-11,158	-16,204	-21,604	-10,933	Net Primary Income from Abroad	98.n
54,768	68,402	83,267	103,335	132,365	158,529	183,624	221,509	†265,387	305,895	341,942	376,053	406,923	437,204	454,304	Gross National Income (GNI)	99a
8,977	10,455	12,971	15,661	19,189	22,061	26,281	31,474	†37,956	43,896	50,185	55,875	61,845	63,856	68,129	Consumption of Fixed Capital	99cf
45,791	57,946	70,296	87,674	113,176	136,468	157,343	190,035	†227,431	261,999	291,757	320,178	345,078	373,348	386,175	Net National Income	99e
....	....	....	....	....	....	....	....	....	....	....	....	....	....	....	GDP Volume 1970 prices (thousands)	99b.p
....	....	....	....	....	....	....	....	....	....	....	....	....	....	....	GDP Volume 1975 prices (thousands)	99b.p
....	....	....	....	....	....	....	....	....	....	....	....	....	....	....	GDP Volume 1980 prices (thousands)	99b.p
47,299	48,758	49,372	52,217												GDP Volume 1986 prices (millions)	99b.p
			105,805	111,787	119,157	122,965	131,280	140,540							GDP Volume 1990 Prices (millions)	99b.p
								†270,295	282,493	290,613	298,341	307,324	328,669	....	GDP Volume 1995 Ref.,Chained (mil.)	99b.p
67.8	69.9	70.8	74.9	79.5	84.8	87.5	93.4	100.0	104.5	107.5	110.4	113.7	121.6	....	GDP Volume (1995=100)	99bv.p
30.9	37.1	44.7	52.3	62.7	70.6	78.9	89.0	†100.0	110.8	121.2	129.8	131.8	134.8	....	GDP Deflator (1995=100)	99bi.p

Midyear Estimates

1987	1988	1989	1990	1991	1992	1993	1994	1995	1996	1997	1998	1999	2000	2001		
4.37	4.44	4.52	4.66	4.95	5.12	5.26	5.40	5.54	5.70	5.83	5.97	6.10	6.29	6.45	Population	99z

(See notes in the back of the book.)

Italy

136	1972	1973	1974	1975	1976	1977	1978	1979	1980	1981	1982	1983	1984	1985	1986
Exchange Rates															*Lire per SDR through 1998,*
Market Rate ... aa	632.4	733.4	795.1	800.2	1,016.6	1,058.7	1,081.0	1,059.1	1,186.8	1,396.8	1,511.3	1,737.4	1,897.6	1,843.7	1,661.3
															Lire per US Dollar through 1998,
Market Rate ... ae	582.5	607.9	649.4	683.6	875.0	871.6	829.8	804.0	930.5	1,200.0	1,370.0	1,659.5	1,935.9	1,678.5	1,358.1
Market Rate ... rf	583.2	583.0	650.3	652.8	832.3	882.4	848.7	830.9	856.4	1,136.8	1,352.5	1,518.8	1,757.0	1,909.4	1,490.8
															Lire per ECU:
ECU Rate ... ea	....	....	....	....	....	....	....	1,157.2	1,215.0	1,303.6	1,325.7	1,372.0	1,371.1	1,489.9	1,446.2
ECU Rate ... eb	....	....	....	....	929.8	1,006.9	1,080.6	1,138.5	1,189.1	1,263.1	1,323.6	1,349.7	1,376.0	1,430.7	1,462.1
															Index Numbers (1995=100):
Market Rate ... ahx	279.1	279.4	249.7	249.7	196.4	184.5	191.9	196.0	190.4	144.2	120.7	107.6	93.0	85.6	109.6
Nominal Effective Exchange Rate ... neu	373.2	333.1	300.1	286.3	240.3	221.1	206.9	197.8	190.8	172.8	162.1	158.4	151.7	144.0	146.1
Real Effective Exchange Rate ... reu	....	....	....	104.5	96.2	92.8	120.0	121.9	†120.7	119.0	118.6	124.7	126.3	122.9	125.7
Fund Position															*Millions of SDRs:*
Quota ... 2f.s	1,000	1,000	1,000	1,000	1,000	1,000	1,240	1,240	1,860	1,860	1,860	2,909	2,909	2,909	2,909
SDRs ... 1b.s	341	343	181	83	78	119	226	449	521	673	711	565	645	297	480
Reserve Position in the Fund ... 1c.s	330	297	—	—	—	—	243	237	646	631	631	945	1,096	1,056	1,037
of which: Outstg.Fund Borrowing ... 2c	—	—	—	—	—	—	—	—	—	—	—	—	—	—	—
Total Fund Cred.&Loans Outstg. ... 2tl	—	—	1,377	2,457	2,457	1,581	880	—	—	—	—	—	—	—	—
International Liquidity															*Millions of US Dollars Unless Otherwise Indicated:*
Total Res.Min.Gold (Eurosys.Def) ... 1l.d	2,954	2,953	3,406	1,306	3,223	8,104	11,109	18,197	23,126	20,134	14,091	20,105	20,795	15,595	19,987
SDRs ... 1b.d	371	414	221	97	91	144	294	592	665	783	785	591	633	326	587
Reserve Position in the Fund ... 1c.d	359	359	—	—	—	—	316	312	823	734	696	990	1,074	1,160	1,268
Foreign Exchange ... 1d.d	2,225	2,181	3,185	1,209	3,132	7,960	10,499	17,294	21,638	18,617	12,611	18,524	19,088	14,109	18,132
o/w: Fin.Deriv.Rel.to Reserves ... 1ddd	....	....	....	....	....	....	....	....	....	....	....	....	....	....	....
Other Reserve Assets ... 1e.d	....	....	....	....	....	....	....	....	....	....	....	....	....	....	....
Gold (Million Fine Troy Ounces) ... 1ad	82.37	82.48	82.48	82.48	82.48	82.91	83.12	66.71	66.67	66.67	66.67	66.67	66.67	66.67	66.67
Gold (Eurosystem Valuation) ... 1and	3,130	3,482	3,482	3,482	9,321	11,260	14,334	20,125	36,722	28,993	23,685	26,152	21,637	23,558	26,055
Memo: Euro Cl. on Non-EA Res. ... 1dgd	....	....	....	....	....	....	....	....	....	....	....	....	....	....	....
Non-Euro Cl. on EA Res. ... 1dhd	....	....	....	....	....	....	....	....	....	....	....	....	....	....	....
Mon. Auth.: Other Foreign Assets ... 3..d	....	....	....	....	....	....	....	....	....	....	....	....	....	....	....
Foreign Liabilities ... 4..d	442	717	4,344	3,797	4,620	5,029	2,152	1,937	2,164	1,971	1,342	1,249	824	894	1,065
Banking Insts.: Foreign Assets ... 7a.d	22,418	30,767	20,724	22,336	19,063	21,385	28,586	33,830	35,087	39,385	36,484	36,354	40,138	50,444	60,532
Foreign Liab. ... 7b.d	22,196	30,246	22,520	22,790	22,769	29,298	36,152	42,598	51,411	54,282	52,006	55,508	61,811	72,831	90,957
Monetary Authorities															*Trillions of Lire through 1998;*
Fgn. Assets (Cl.on Non-EA Ctys) ... 11	3.80	3.86	4.34	3.19	11.72	17.94	22.39	32.10	57.05	60.38	53.01	78.11	83.41	66.71	62.86
Claims on General Government ... 12a.u	....	....	....	....	....	....	....	....	....	....	....	....	....	....	....
o/w: Claims on Gen.Govt.in Cty ... 12a	4.12	5.22	22.19	29.87	39.88	36.04	40.81	41.48	53.43	66.34	78.23	83.93	91.83	114.40	123.45
Claims on Banking Institutions ... 12e.u	....	....	....	....	....	....	....	....	....	....	....	....	....	....	....
o/w: Claims on Bank.Inst.in Cty ... 12e	2.89	3.18	3.59	4.25	2.63	2.83	2.75	5.34	2.72	2.94	3.99	3.88	4.65	14.08	11.50
Claims on Other Resident Sectors ... 12d.u	....	....	....	....	....	....	....	....	....	....	....	....	....	....	....
o/w: Cl. on Oth.Res.Sect.in Cty ... 12d	—	—	—	—	—	—	—	—	—	—	—	—	—	—	—
Currency Issued ... 14a	9.00	10.30	11.45	13.23	14.94	16.91	20.10	23.23	27.01	31.41	35.07	39.36	44.22	48.05	51.60
Liabilities to Banking Insts ... 14c.u	....	....	....	....	....	....	....	....	....	....	....	....	....	....	....
o/w: Liabs to Bank.Inst.in Cty ... 14c	5.51	6.47	8.29	14.45	18.38	22.84	29.47	33.31	36.75	40.17	47.38	56.64	65.64	80.67	87.38
Demand Dep. of Other Res.Sect. ... 14d.u	....	....	....	....	....	....	....	....	....	....	....	....	....	....	....
o/w: D.Dep.of Oth.Res.Sect.in Cty ... 14d	....	....	....	....	....	....	....	....	....	....	....	....	....	....	....
Other Dep. of Other Res.Sect. ... 15..u	....	....	....	....	....	....	....	....	....	....	....	....	....	....	....
o/w: O.Dep.of Oth.Res.Sect.in Cty ... 15	....	....	....	....	....	....	....	....	....	....	....	....	....	....	....
Money Market Instruments ... 16m.u	....	....	....	....	....	....	....	....	....	....	....	....	....	....	....
o/w: MMI Held by Resid.of Cty ... 16m	....	....	....	....	....	....	....	....	....	....	....	....	....	....	....
Bonds (Debt Securities) ... 16n.u	....	....	....	....	....	....	....	....	....	....	....	....	....	....	....
o/w: Bonds Held by Resid.of Cty ... 16n	.04	.05	.06	.08	.09	.11	.19	.27	.26	.33	.41	.40	.56	.67	.74
Foreign Liab. (to Non-EA Ctys) ... 16c	.26	.44	3.92	4.56	6.54	6.06	2.74	1.56	2.01	2.37	1.84	2.07	1.60	1.50	1.45
Central Government Deposits ... 16d.u	....	....	....	....	....	....	....	....	....	....	....	....	....	....	....
o/w: Cent.Govt.Dep. in Cty ... 16d	—	—	—	—	—	—	—	—	—	—	—	—	—	—	—
Capital Accounts ... 17a	—	—	—	—	—	—	—	—	44.79	48.90	47.08	63.47	64.49	64.16	59.67
Other Items (Net) ... 17r	–4.00	–4.99	6.41	5.00	14.27	10.91	13.46	20.55	2.38	6.49	3.44	3.99	3.40	.13	–3.04
Memo: Net Claims on Eurosystem ... 12e.s	....	....	....	....	....	....	....	....	....	....	....	....	....	....	....
Currency Put into Circ. ... 14m	....	....	....	....	....	....	....	....	....	....	....	....	....	....	....
Banking Institutions															*Trillions of Lire through 1998;*
Claims on Monetary Authorities ... 20	6.03	7.15	8.95	15.13	19.08	23.65	30.56	34.88	39.07	43.30	50.13	58.67	68.66	83.73	90.79
Claims on Bk.Inst.in Oth.EA Ctys ... 20b.u	....	....	....	....	....	....	....	....	....	....	....	....	....	....	....
Fgn. Assets (Cl.on Non-EA Ctys) ... 21	13.04	18.70	13.46	15.27	16.68	18.64	23.72	27.20	32.65	47.26	49.98	†60.33	77.70	84.67	82.21
Claims on General Government ... 22a.u	....	....	....	....	....	....	....	....	....	....	....	....	....	....	....
o/w: Claims on Gen.Govt.in Cty ... 22a	10.66	13.78	18.58	26.59	25.46	42.67	56.38	64.50	69.83	73.80	103.65	129.84	141.94	161.62	168.62
Claims on Other Resident Sectors ... 22d.u	....	....	....	....	....	....	....	....	....	....	....	....	....	....	....
o/w: Cl. on Oth.Res.Sect.in Cty ... 22d	63.22	76.13	88.57	102.86	122.67	142.54	158.26	183.10	215.23	249.52	282.29	315.80	371.49	411.45	455.64
Demand Deposits ... 24..u	....	....	....	....	....	....	....	....	....	....	....	....	....	....	....
o/w: D.Dep.of Oth.Res.Sect.in Cty ... 24	31.86	38.91	†44.10	50.71	62.09	76.31	98.74	122.54	140.07	153.71	181.73	203.94	230.32	254.23	285.29
Other Deposits ... 25..u	....	....	....	....	....	....	....	....	....	....	....	....	....	....	....
o/w: O.Dep.of Oth.Res.Sect.in Cty ... 25	31.94	38.64	†39.60	54.71	65.81	80.47	95.95	109.90	122.04	136.36	168.90	192.41	215.14	237.78	250.09
Money Market Instruments ... 26m.u	....	....	....	....	....	....	....	....	....	....	....	....	....	....	....
o/w: MMI Held by Resid.of Cty ... 26m	....	....	....	....	....	....	....	....	....	....	....	....	....	....	....
Bonds (Debt Securities) ... 26n.u	....	....	....	....	....	....	....	....	....	....	....	....	....	....	....
o/w: Bonds Held by Resid.of Cty ... 26n	17.16	23.86	26.36	32.78	38.17	43.73	49.44	54.69	60.98	68.86	77.17	85.13	89.55	95.02	102.19
Foreign Liab. (to Non-EA Ctys) ... 26c	12.91	18.39	14.63	15.58	19.92	25.54	30.00	34.25	47.84	65.14	71.25	92.12	119.66	122.25	123.53
Central Government Deposits ... 26d.u	....	....	....	....	....	....	....	....	....	....	....	....	....	....	....
o/w: Cent.Govt.Dep. in Cty ... 26d	1.83	2.09	14.36	16.74	16.81	16.68	16.43	16.30	15.86	16.12	16.15	15.70	14.91	14.39	14.84
Credit from Monetary Authorities ... 26g	1.84	2.10	3.19	2.53	1.02	1.00	.31	3.60	.50	.97	2.02	4.79	1.24	6.91	3.55
Liab. to Bk.Inst.in Oth. EA Ctys ... 26h.u	....	....	....	....	....	....	....	....	....	....	....	....	....	....	....
Capital Accounts ... 27a	1.46	1.83	2.08	2.40	2.89	3.48	1.74	5.65	6.77	8.36	10.03	12.59	15.32	18.11	21.23
Other Items (Net) ... 27r	–6.05	–10.07	†–14.75	–15.61	–22.83	–19.69	–23.68	–37.25	–37.28	–35.64	–41.20	†–42.04	–26.35	–7.24	–3.46
Post Office: Checking Deposits ... 24..i	1.06	.99	1.21	1.47	1.84	2.53	3.60	5.93	4.34	5.10	5.86	7.12	7.44	8.76	9.44
Post Office: Savings Deposits ... 25..i	....	....	2.30	2.84	3.36	3.87	4.56	5.43	6.12	6.70	7.30	7.91	8.57	9.51	11.05
Savings Certif. ... 26ab i	5.16	6.23	6.45	7.62	9.04	10.29	12.51	15.11	17.13	17.80	19.00	20.86	24.73	28.57	33.82

1987	1988	1989	1990	1991	1992	1993	1994	1995	1996	1997	1998	1999	2000	2001	
Euros per SDR Thereafter: End of Period															**Exchange Rates**
1,658.8	1,757.2	1,669.6	1,607.8	1,646.5	2,022.4	2,340.5	2,379.2	2,355.7	2,200.9	2,373.6	2,327.6	1.3662	1.4002	1.4260	Market Rate **aa**
Euros per US Dollar Thereafter: End of Period (ae) Period Average (rf)															
1,169.3	1,305.8	1,270.5	1,130.2	1,151.1	1,470.9	1,704.0	1,629.7	1,584.7	1,530.6	1,759.2	1,653.1	.9954	1.0747	1.1347	Market Rate **ae**
1,296.1	1,301.6	1,372.1	1,198.1	1,240.6	1,232.4	1,573.7	1,612.4	1,628.9	1,542.9	1,703.1	1,736.2	.9386	1.0854	1.1175	Market Rate **rf**
End of Period (ea) Period Average (eb)															
1,521.7	1,531.1	1,517.6	1,540.3	1,542.4	1,787.4	1,908.4	1,997.5	2,082.7	1,913.7	1,940.7	1,936.3	....	....	....	ECU Rate **ea**
1,494.7	1,537.3	1,510.7	1,521.9	1,533.3	1,587.5	1,841.6	1,913.9	2,131.3	1,958.6	1,929.7	1,943.7	....	....	....	ECU Rate **eb**
Period Averages															
125.7	125.4	118.7	136.1	131.7	132.7	103.6	101.1	100.0	105.5	95.7	93.9	....	....	....	Market Rate **ahx**
145.7	140.8	142.0	144.2	142.2	137.8	116.0	110.9	100.0	109.3	110.1	109.6	107.7	104.2	104.6	Nominal Effective Exchange Rate **neu**
126.8	125.4	131.4	135.8	138.1	134.7	114.9	108.7	100.0	114.6	117.1	114.8	114.3	110.4	109.7	Real Effective Exchange Rate **reu**
End of Period															**Fund Position**
2,909	2,909	2,909	2,909	2,909	4,591	4,591	4,591	4,591	4,591	4,591	4,591	7,056	7,056	7,056	Quota **2f.s**
668	705	759	729	650	173	175	86	—	20	50	79	122	182	236	SDRs **1b.s**
1,020	941	1,099	1,205	1,576	1,774	1,575	1,393	1,321	1,290	1,661	3,075	2,584	2,230	2,560	Reserve Position in the Fund **1c.s**
—	—	—	—	—	—	—	—	—	—	—	257	—	—	—	*of which:* Outstg.Fund Borrowing **2c**
—	—	—	—	—	—	—	—	—	—	—	—	—	—	—	Total Fund Cred.&Loans Outstg. **2tl**
End of Period															**International Liquidity**
30,214	34,715	46,720	62,927	48,679	27,643	27,545	32,265	34,905	45,948	55,739	29,888	†22,421	25,566	24,419	Total Res.Min.Gold (Eurosys.Def) **1l.d**
948	949	998	1,037	930	238	241	125	—	29	67	111	168	238	297	SDRs **1b.d**
1,447	1,266	1,444	1,714	2,255	2,439	2,164	2,033	1,963	1,855	2,241	4,330	3,546	2,906	3,217	Reserve Position in the Fund **1c.d**
27,819	32,500	44,278	60,176	45,495	24,966	25,140	30,107	32,942	44,064	53,431	25,447	†18,623	22,423	20,905	Foreign Exchange **1d.d**
....	....	....	....	....	....	....	....	....	....	....	....	—	—	—	*o/w:* Fin.Deriv.Rel.to Reserves **1ddd**
....	....	....	....	....	....	....	....	....	....	....	....	84	—	—	Other Reserve Assets **1e.d**
66.67	66.67	66.67	66.67	66.67	66.67	66.67	66.67	66.67	66.67	66.67	83.36	78.83	78.83	78.83	Gold (Million Fine Troy Ounces) **1ad**
34,050	28,521	26,496	24,913	23,230	23,175	23,593	26,342	25,570	25,369	21,806	24,711	22,880	21,635	21,796	Gold (Eurosystem Valuation) **1and**
....	....	....	....	....	....	....	....	....	....	....	....	1	476	451	Memo: Euro Cl. on Non-EA Res. **1dgd**
....	....	....	....	....	....	....	....	....	....	....	....	3,620	2,812	4,814	Non-Euro Cl. on EA Res. **1dhd**
....	....	....	....	....	....	....	....	....	....	....	....	....	....	....	Mon. Auth.: Other Foreign Assets **3..d**
1,105	1,092	1,238	1,353	1,368	6,282	1,543	1,510	2,598	1,249	1,123	1,045	†6,315	235	2,198	Foreign Liabilities **4..d**
68,514	66,859	86,872	102,731	108,509	112,306	134,425	123,919	145,842	193,215	177,149	193,743	†90,837	85,886	75,040	Banking Insts.: Foreign Assets **7a.d**
114,421	122,171	161,774	205,376	243,066	249,851	217,128	230,505	216,808	237,872	223,249	236,896	†136,362	146,749	150,809	Foreign Liab. **7b.d**
Billions of Euros Beginning 1999: End of Period															**Monetary Authorities**
75.59	84.20	94.81	104.93	95.91	76.54	86.57	93.90	95.59	108.65	135.62	90.33	45.80	50.49	52.42	Fgn. Assets (Cl.on Non-EA Ctys) **11**
....	....	....	....	....	....	....	....	....	....	....	....	60.12	63.25	65.06	Claims on General Government **12a.u**
136.31	139.76	141.49	140.27	140.40	161.75	170.23	195.88	196.42	168.95	174.17	156.37	60.12	63.25	65.06	*o/w:* Claims on Gen.Govt.in Cty **12a**
....	....	....	....	....	....	....	....	....	....	....	....	51.35	36.49	33.51	Claims on Banking Institutions **12e.u**
6.87	5.79	11.24	14.82	34.71	49.28	44.94	42.50	41.04	50.03	32.30	11.04	36.01	26.53	10.70	*o/w:* Claims on Bank.Inst.in Cty **12e**
....	....	....	....	....	....	....	....	....	....	....	....	7.36	8.29	6.75	Claims on Other Resident Sectors **12d.u**
—	—	—	—	—	.10	4.35	.56	2.64	—	—	—	7.13	8.06	6.49	*o/w:* Cl. on Oth.Res.Sect.in Cty **12d**
55.62	60.20	71.36	74.81	82.02	90.85	95.23	101.86	105.22	108.16	116.27	124.88	71.96	76.42	65.89	Currency Issued **14a**
....	....	....	....	....	....	....	....	....	....	....	....	24.84	25.52	26.28	Liabilities to Banking Insts **14c.u**
96.29	105.23	113.84	122.35	128.38	127.97	104.19	87.54	72.30	73.69	79.08	13.78	9.23	7.75	26.28	*o/w:* Liabs to Bank.Inst.in Cty **14c**
....	....	....	....	....	....	....	....	....	....	....	....	.39	.08	.23	Demand Dep. of Other Res.Sect. **14d.u**
....	....	....	....	....	....	....	....	....	....	....	....	.39	.08	.23	*o/w:* D.Dep.of Oth.Res.Sect.in Cty **14d**
....	....	....	....	....	....	....	....	....	....	....	....	—	—	—	Other Dep. of Other Res.Sect. **15..u**
....	....	....	....	....	....	....	....	....	....	....	....	—	—	—	*o/w:* O.Dep.of Oth.Res.Sect.in Cty **15**
....	....	....	....	....	....	....	....	....	....	....	....	—	—	—	Money Market Instruments **16m.u**
....	....	....	....	....	....	....	....	....	....	....	....	....	....	....	*o/w:* MMI Held by Resid.of Cty **16m**
....	....	....	....	....	....	....	....	....	....	....	....	—	—	—	Bonds (Debt Securities) **16n.u**
.77	.82	1.55	1.54	1.55	1.30	1.22	1.47	1.99	1.66	1.20	.92	....	....	....	*o/w:* Bonds Held by Resid.of Cty **16n**
1.29	1.43	1.57	1.53	1.58	9.24	2.63	2.46	4.12	1.91	1.98	1.73	6.29	.25	2.49	Foreign Liab. (to Non-EA Ctys) **16c**
....	....	....	....	....	....	....	....	....	....	....	....	29.08	19.37	23.46	Central Government Deposits **16d.u**
—	—	—	—	—	—	30.67	63.94	72.13	54.76	57.78	42.21	29.08	19.37	23.46	*o/w:* Cent.Govt.Dep. in Cty **16d**
66.31	66.61	64.35	64.29	66.12	69.80	84.36	90.66	94.79	99.84	98.93	75.85	35.37	40.44	41.46	Capital Accounts **17a**
–1.52	–4.53	–5.13	–4.50	–8.62	–11.51	–12.21	–15.09	–14.85	–12.39	–13.15	–1.61	–3.30	–3.56	–2.09	Other Items (Net) **17r**
....	....	....	....	....	....	....	....	....	....	....	....	–3.85	–10.31	18.16	*Memo: Net Claims on Eurosystem* **12e.s**
....	....	....	....	....	....	....	....	....	....	....	....	....	....	....	*Currency Put into Circ.* **14m**
Billions of Euros Beginning 1999: End of Period															**Banking Institutions**
100.11	108.56	†119.08	129.97	134.15	133.29	109.65	93.29	79.31	81.70	87.81	23.65	9.90	8.16	25.73	Claims on Monetary Authorities **20**
....	....	....	....	....	....	....	....	....	....	....	....	67.89	69.20	62.36	Claims on Bk.Inst.in Oth.EA Ctys **20b.u**
80.11	87.30	†110.37	116.10	124.90	165.19	229.06	201.96	231.12	295.73	311.64	320.28	90.42	92.30	85.15	Fgn. Assets (Cl.on Non-EA Ctys) **21**
....	....	....	....	....	....	....	....	....	....	....	....	243.13	211.34	211.95	Claims on General Government **22a.u**
165.04	161.02	†206.73	217.66	293.45	355.88	404.16	434.80	413.46	442.92	408.43	395.40	240.00	206.65	207.15	*o/w:* Claims on Gen.Govt.in Cty **22a**
....	....	....	....	....	....	....	....	....	....	....	....	811.05	926.19	997.04	Claims on Other Resident Sectors **22d.u**
503.74	584.90	645.11	745.89	850.93	942.92	969.94	983.66	1,027.70	1,060.42	1,123.53	1,224.36	788.23	896.82	966.60	*o/w:* Cl. on Oth.Res.Sect.in Cty **22d**
....	....	....	....	....	....	....	....	....	....	....	....	386.95	410.65	449.75	Demand Deposits **24..u**
308.00	334.81	†353.67	385.62	430.80	426.20	454.92	471.38	471.06	498.87	531.72	601.15	384.91	407.91	446.12	*o/w:* D.Dep.of Oth.Res.Sect.in Cty **24**
....	....	....	....	....	....	....	....	....	....	....	....	194.71	194.55	192.43	Other Deposits **25..u**
265.13	294.07	†321.74	363.97	389.56	430.86	469.88	458.91	476.50	469.39	359.51	287.75	190.61	190.26	190.54	*o/w:* O.Dep.of Oth.Res.Sect.in Cty **25**
....	....	....	....	....	....	....	....	....	....	....	....	13.07	10.08	26.16	Money Market Instruments **26m.u**
....	....	10.02	14.14	53.30	99.36	95.80	87.71	126.67	119.76	132.48	108.68	....	....	....	*o/w:* MMI Held by Resid.of Cty **26m**
....	....	....	....	....	....	....	....	....	....	....	....	271.55	302.48	334.67	Bonds (Debt Securities) **26n.u**
113.68	121.24	129.64	135.87	153.17	166.41	194.11	215.68	215.29	280.21	377.74	435.32	....	....	....	*o/w:* Bonds Held by Resid.of Cty **26n**
133.79	159.53	†205.53	232.11	279.78	367.50	369.98	375.66	343.58	364.08	392.74	391.61	135.74	157.71	171.12	Foreign Liab. (to Non-EA Ctys) **26c**
....	....	....	....	....	....	....	....	....	....	....	....	7.96	7.00	7.51	Central Government Deposits **26d.u**
15.41	15.22	11.43	11.06	11.22	10.73	13.40	13.23	9.29	11.15	12.73	13.40	7.92	6.96	7.21	*o/w:* Cent.Govt.Dep. in Cty **26d**
3.88	4.47	†12.69	16.27	34.71	49.28	44.94	42.50	41.04	50.03	32.30	11.04	33.29	26.46	10.81	Credit from Monetary Authorities **26g**
....	....	....	....	....	....	....	....	....	....	....	....	98.65	107.61	109.57	Liab. to Bk.Inst.in Oth. EA Ctys **26h.u**
23.61	25.96	†115.83	126.56	162.50	189.99	206.02	219.39	232.44	250.19	257.05	280.93	118.27	123.93	133.63	Capital Accounts **27a**
–14.49	–13.50	†–79.28	–75.99	–111.62	–143.06	–136.25	–170.74	–164.29	–162.91	–164.86	–166.20	–37.79	–33.28	–53.44	Other Items (Net) **27r**
10.21	7.70	9.39	7.83	7.02	9.34	9.48	8.16	8.49	7.28	6.67	1.66	....	....	....	Post Office: Checking Deposits **24..i**
13.43	16.37	19.73	23.59	26.92	29.06	30.86	39.15	43.94	46.26	52.00	58.33	....	....	....	Post Office: Savings Deposits **25..i**
40.13	46.54	52.10	57.22	61.87	66.58	72.16	87.05	97.77	110.61	117.35	121.65	....	....	....	Savings Certif. **26ab i**

Italy

		1972	1973	1974	1975	1976	1977	1978	1979	1980	1981	1982	1983	1984	1985	1986
Banking Survey (Nat'l Residency)													*Trillions of Lire through 1998;*			
Foreign Assets (Net)	31n	3.67	3.74	−.74	−1.68	1.94	4.99	13.38	23.49	39.84	40.14	29.90	†44.25	39.86	27.63	20.09
Domestic Credit	32	82.39	100.25	†124.93	154.51	185.42	221.26	259.69	299.23	350.21	403.14	480.17	549.77	631.07	719.91	787.18
Claims on General Govt. (Net)	32an	19.17	12.90	†36.37	51.65	62.75	78.72	101.43	116.14	134.98	153.61	197.88	233.96	259.60	308.46	331.54
Claims on Other Resident Sectors	32d	63.22	76.13	88.57	102.86	122.67	142.54	158.26	183.10	215.23	249.52	282.29	315.80	371.49	411.45	455.64
Currency Issued	34a.n	10.06	11.29	12.66	14.70	16.78	19.44	23.70	29.16	31.34	36.51	40.94	46.48	51.66	56.81	61.04
Demand Deposits	34b.n	31.86	38.91	44.10	50.71	62.09	76.31	98.74	122.54	140.07	153.71	181.73	203.94	230.32	254.23	285.29
Other Deposits	35..n	31.94	38.64	†41.90	57.55	69.17	84.33	100.51	115.33	128.16	143.06	176.19	200.32	223.70	247.29	261.13
Money Market Instruments	36m	....	....	....	....	....	....	....	....	....	....	....	....	....	....	....
Bonds (Debt Securities)	36	22.36	30.13	32.86	40.47	47.29	54.13	62.14	70.07	78.37	86.99	96.59	106.39	114.84	124.26	136.75
o/w: Bonds Over Two Years	36na															
Capital Accounts	37a	1.46	1.83	2.08	2.40	2.89	3.48	1.74	5.65	51.56	57.26	57.11	76.06	79.81	82.28	80.90
Other Items (Net)	37r	−11.62	−16.82	†−9.40	−13.01	−10.87	−11.44	−13.76	−20.01	−39.44	−34.25	−42.49	†−39.18	−29.39	−17.33	−17.84
Banking Survey (EA-Wide Residency)													*Billions of Euros:*			
Foreign Assets (Net)	31n.u	....	....	....	....	....	....	....	....	....	....	....	....	....	....	....
Domestic Credit	32..u	....	....	....	....	....	....	....	....	....	....	....	....	....	....	....
Claims on General Govt. (Net)	32an u	....	....	....	....	....	....	....	....	....	....	....	....	....	....	....
Claims on Other Resident Sect.	32d.u	....	....	....	....	....	....	....	....	....	....	....	....	....	....	....
Currency Issued	34a.u	....	....	....	....	....	....	....	....	....	....	....	....	....	....	....
Demand Deposits	34b.u	....	....	....	....	....	....	....	....	....	....	....	....	....	....	....
Other Deposits	35..u	....	....	....	....	....	....	....	....	....	....	....	....	....	....	....
o/w: Other Dep. Over Two Yrs	35ab u	....	....	....	....	....	....	....	....	....	....	....	....	....	....	....
Money Market Instruments	36m.u	....	....	....	....	....	....	....	....	....	....	....	....	....	....	....
Bonds (Debt Securities)	36n.u	....	....	....	....	....	....	....	....	....	....	....	....	....	....	....
o/w: Bonds Over Two Years	36na u	....	....	....	....	....	....	....	....	....	....	....	....	....	....	....
Capital Accounts	37a	....	....	....	....	....	....	....	....	....	....	....	....	....	....	....
Other Items (Net)	37r.u	....	....	....	....	....	....	....	....	....	....	....	....	....	....	....
Money (National Definitions)													*Trillions of Lire:*			
M2	39m	....	....	94.61	118.13	142.63	173.56	214.95	258.48	290.05	321.54	378.50	429.84	479.85	530.74	575.96
Liquid Liabilities	55l	80.23	96.46	†106.73	132.73	159.71	193.40	238.91	285.96	321.12	356.07	423.33	477.48	535.92	593.34	648.98
Interest Rates													*Percent Per Annum*			
Discount Rate (End of Period)	60	4.00	6.50	8.00	6.00	15.00	11.50	10.50	15.00	16.50	19.00	18.00	17.00	16.50	15.00	12.00
Money Market Rate	60b	5.18	6.93	14.57	10.64	15.68	14.03	11.49	11.86	17.17	19.60	20.16	18.44	17.27	15.25	13.41
Treasury Bill Rate	60c	....	....	....	....	....	12.34	11.99	12.51	15.92	19.70	19.44	17.89	15.37	13.71	11.40
Deposit Rate	60l	....	....	....	....	....		10.82	10.59	12.70	14.31	15.28	12.91	11.75	11.00	8.89
Lending Rate	60p	....	....	....	....	....		16.05	14.64	19.03	18.36	17.37	22.27	21.97	18.06	15.93
Govt Bond Yield (Long-Term)	61	7.47	7.42	9.87	11.54	13.08	14.62	13.70	14.05	16.11	20.56	20.90	18.02	14.95	13.00	10.52
Govt Bond Yield (Medium-Term)	61b	6.59	6.92	9.61	10.04	12.66	14.71	13.05	13.02	15.25	19.36	20.22	18.30	15.60	13.71	11.47
Prices, Production, Labor													*Index Numbers (1995=100):*			
Share Prices	62	12.3	15.8	14.5	†10.8	9.4	7.8	8.3	10.6	17.0	33.3	27.8	30.1	33.1	52.0	109.9
Producer Prices	63	....	....	....	....	....	....	....	....	....	46.6	52.7	58.5	64.5	69.5	69.6
Consumer Prices	64	9.5	10.5	12.5	14.6	17.1	20.0	22.5	25.8	31.2	36.8	42.8	49.1	54.4	59.4	62.8
Harmonized CPI	64h	....	....	....	....	....	....	....	....	....	....	....	....	....	....	....
Wages: Contractual	65ey	5.7	7.0	8.4	10.8	13.0	16.6	19.4	23.0	28.1	34.8	40.9	47.0	52.3	58.1	60.9
Industrial Production	66..c	60.6	66.5	69.5	63.1	70.9	71.7	73.1	77.9	82.2	80.9	78.5	75.9	78.5	79.4	82.2
Industrial Employment	67	121.6	121.9	125.1	125.1	123.2	124.4	123.0	123.3	123.9	122.6	119.9	116.6	111.6	109.1	107.3
														Number in Thousands:		
Labor Force	67d	....	....	....	....	....	....	....	....	....	....	....	....	....	....	....
Employment	67e	....	....	....	....	....	....	....	....	....	....	....	....	....	20,894	21,006
Unemployment	67c	....	....	....	....	....	....	....	....	....	....	....	....	....	2,382	2,611
Unemployment Rate (%)	67r	....	....	....	....	....	....	....	....	....	....	....	....	....	10.3	11.1
International Transactions													*Billions of Lire through 1998;*			
Exports	70	10,850	12,971	19,825	22,867	31,170	39,968	47,506	59,927	66,869	87,716	99,596	110,599	130,836	145,888	144,460
Imports, c.i.f.	71	11,265	16,225	26,715	25,199	36,730	42,430	47,867	64,598	86,215	106,574	117,802	121,078	149,469	167,095	150,196
														1995=100		
Volume of Exports	72	30.7	31.2	33.7	34.4	38.7	41.7	46.2	49.5	†45.6	48.5	47.8	49.4	53.3	55.1	57.1
Volume of Imports	73	40.4	45.4	42.8	38.0	44.1	43.7	47.0	53.3	†54.5	52.2	51.2	50.1	55.6	57.9	62.3
Unit Value of Exports	74	9.4	11.1	15.7	17.4	21.3	25.4	27.2	31.9	†38.5	47.4	54.7	58.7	64.3	69.5	66.3
Unit Value of Imports	75	8.5	11.1	18.9	20.0	25.2	29.2	30.7	36.6	†47.2	61.0	68.7	72.0	80.1	86.1	70.8

1987	1988	1989	1990	1991	1992	1993	1994	1995	1996	1997	1998	1999	2000	2001	
Billions of Euros Beginning 1999: End of Period															**Banking Survey (Nat'l Residency)**
20.62	10.55	†−1.92	−12.61	−60.55	−135.01	−56.99	−82.27	−20.99	38.39	52.54	17.26	−11.03	−27.48	−23.54	Foreign Assets (Net) **31n**
853.46	941.07	1,063.11	1,181.38	1,369.36	1,554.88	1,617.11	1,672.10	1,708.99	1,770.52	1,811.64	1,902.18	1,058.49	1,148.44	1,214.62	Domestic Credit **32**
349.72	356.17	418.01	435.49	518.44	611.86	642.82	687.88	678.65	710.10	688.11	677.82	263.13	243.56	241.53	Claims on General Govt. (Net)........... **32an**
503.74	584.90	645.11	745.89	850.93	943.01	974.29	984.22	1,030.34	1,060.42	1,123.53	1,224.36	795.36	904.89	973.09	Claims on Other Resident Sectors **32d**
65.83	67.90	80.75	82.63	89.04	100.19	104.71	110.02	113.71	115.44	122.94	126.54	71.96	76.42	65.89	Currency Issued **34a.n**
308.00	334.81	353.67	385.62	430.80	426.20	454.92	471.38	471.06	498.87	531.72	601.15	385.30	407.99	446.35	Demand Deposits **34b.n**
278.56	310.45	341.48	387.56	416.49	459.92	500.75	498.06	520.44	515.65	411.52	346.08	190.61	190.26	190.54	Other Deposits .... **35..n**
....	....	10.02	14.14	53.30	99.36	95.80	87.71	126.67	119.76	132.48	108.68	13.07	10.08	26.16	Money Market Instruments **36m**
154.58	168.60	183.29	194.63	216.58	234.29	267.50	304.20	315.05	392.48	496.29	557.89	271.55	302.48	334.67	Bonds (Debt Securities).................... **36n**
												259.05	289.12	322.13	o/w: Bonds Over Two Years **36na**
89.92	92.57	†180.18	190.85	228.62	259.79	290.37	310.05	327.22	350.03	355.99	356.78	153.63	164.37	175.10	Capital Accounts **37a**
−22.82	−22.69	†−88.19	−86.65	−126.01	−159.89	−153.92	−191.58	−186.14	−183.31	−186.74	−177.68	−38.66	−30.63	−47.64	Other Items (Net) **37r**
End of Period															**Banking Survey (EA-Wide Residency)**
....	....	....	....	....	....	....	....	....	....	....	....	−5.80	−15.17	−36.04	Foreign Assets (Net) **31n.u**
....	....	....	....	....	....	....	....	....	....	....	....	1,084.62	1,182.69	1,249.82	Domestic Credit .... **32..u**
....	....	....	....	....	....	....	....	....	....	....	....	266.21	248.22	246.04	Claims on General Govt. (Net)........... **32an u**
....	....	....	....	....	....	....	....	....	....	....	....	818.41	934.47	1,003.78	Claims on Other Resident Sect. **32d.u**
....	....	....	....	....	....	....	....	....	....	....	....	71.96	76.42	65.89	Currency Issued **34a.u**
....	....	....	....	....	....	....	....	....	....	....	....	387.33	410.74	449.98	Demand Deposits .... **34b..u**
....	....	....	....	....	....	....	....	....	....	....	....	194.71	194.55	192.43	Other Deposits .... **35..u**
....	....	....	....	....	....	....	....	....	....	....	....	17.00	11.49	6.41	o/w: Other Dep. Over Two Yrs ..... **35ab u**
....	....	....	....	....	....	....	....	....	....	....	....	13.07	10.08	26.16	Money Market Instruments **36m.u**
....	....	....	....	....	....	....	....	....	....	....	....	271.55	302.48	334.67	Bonds (Debt Securities).................... **36n.u**
....	....	....	....	....	....	....	....	....	....	....	....	259.05	289.12	322.13	o/w: Bonds Over Two Years .... **36na u**
....	....	....	....	....	....	....	....	....	....	....	....	153.63	164.37	175.10	Capital Accounts **37a**
....	....	....	....	....	....	....	....	....	....	....	....	−13.44	8.89	−30.46	Other Items (Net) **37r.u**
End of Period															**Money (National Definitions)**
618.61	654.29	711.48	759.41	807.84	814.20	841.32	847.42	834.15	863.29	930.99	975.34	....	....	....	*M2* **39m**
703.04	772.92	†844.01	931.22	1,019.40	1,076.88	....	....	....	....	....	....	....	....	....	Liquid Liabilities **551**
Percent Per Annum															**Interest Rates**
12.00	12.50	13.50	12.50	12.00	12.00	8.00	7.50	9.00	7.50	5.50	3.00	....	....	....	Discount Rate *(End of Period)*.................... **60**
11.51	11.29	12.69	12.38	†12.21	14.02	10.20	8.51	10.46	8.82	6.88	4.99	2.95	4.39	4.26	Money Market Rate **60b**
10.73	11.19	12.58	12.38	12.54	14.32	10.58	9.17	10.85	8.46	6.33	4.59	3.01	4.53	4.05	Treasury Bill Rate **60c**
7.01	6.69	6.93	6.80	6.64	7.11	†7.79	6.20	6.45	6.49	4.83	3.16	1.61	1.84	1.96	Deposit Rate **60l**
13.58	13.57	14.21	†14.09	13.90	15.76	13.87	11.22	12.47	12.06	9.75	7.88	5.58	6.26	6.53	Lending Rate **60p**
9.68	10.16	10.72	11.51	†13.18	13.27	11.31	10.56	12.21	9.40	6.86	4.90	4.73	5.58	5.19	Govt Bond Yield (Long-Term) **61**
10.58	10.54	11.61	11.87	†13.37	13.67	11.21	10.57	11.98	8.93	6.47	4.55	4.04	5.29	4.64	Govt Bond Yield (Medium-Term)...... **61b**
Period Averages															**Prices, Production, Labor**
104.5	84.2	104.1	104.8	88.8	73.9	87.5	109.1	100.0	100.6	137.7	220.5	245.5	319.0	258.8	Share Prices **62**
71.7	74.2	78.6	81.8	84.6	86.2	89.4	92.7	100.0	101.9	103.2	103.3	103.1	109.3	111.4	Producer Prices **63**
65.8	69.2	73.5	78.3	83.2	87.4	91.3	95.0	†100.0	104.0	106.1	108.2	110.0	112.8	115.9	Consumer Prices **64**
....	....	....	....	....	....	....	....	100.0	104.0	106.0	108.0	109.8	112.7	115.3	Harmonized CPI **64h**
64.8	68.8	72.9	78.2	85.9	90.6	93.7	97.0	100.0	103.2	106.9	109.9	112.4	114.7	116.6	Wages: Contractual **65ey**
85.4	90.5	93.4	93.5	92.6	92.4	90.2	94.9	100.0	99.1	102.4	104.3	104.1	108.2	....	Industrial Production .... **66..c**
105.6	106.1	106.1	107.7	108.6	106.8	104.5	102.3	100.0	98.9	98.5	99.5	99.6	99.7	100.7	Industrial Employment **67**
Period Averages															
....	....	....	24,245	....	....	22,680	22,734	22,779	22,895	23,180	23,361	23,575	23,781		Labor Force **67d**
20,986	21,253	21,154	21,454	21,595	21,459	†20,427	20,119	20,010	20,125	20,208	20,435	20,692	21,080	21,514	Employment................................ **67e**
2,832	2,885	2,865	2,621	2,653	2,799	†2,299	2,508	2,638	2,653	2,688	2,745	2,669	2,495	....	Unemployment............................ **67c**
11.9	12.0	12.0	11.0	10.9	11.4	†9.6	10.7	11.3	11.4	11.5	11.7	11.4	10.5	....	Unemployment Rate (%) **67r**
Millions of Euros Beginning 1999															**International Transactions**
150,880	166,379	192,797	203,718	209,741	219,436	266,213	308,045	381,175	388,885	409,128	426,182	†221,040	260,414	270,295	Exports..................................... **70**
162,353	180,014	209,910	217,704	225,751	232,200	232,991	272,382	335,661	321,286	357,587	378,784	†207,016	258,507	260,361	Imports, c.i.f. **71**
1995=100															
59.0	61.9	67.5	69.8	69.9	72.5	79.0	88.2	100.0	†97.8	102.4	105.6	105.9	118.2	117.9	Volume of Exports **72**
69.4	73.8	79.9	83.5	87.2	90.2	81.1	91.1	100.0	†95.2	104.6	113.8	121.5	133.1	131.8	Volume of Imports **73**
67.0	70.4	74.8	76.4	78.7	79.3	88.3	91.5	100.0	†104.3	104.8	105.8	105.5	111.3	116.1	Unit Value of Exports..................... **74**
69.8	72.7	78.2	77.6	77.1	76.6	85.6	89.0	100.0	†100.0	101.4	98.7	97.7	111.5	113.9	Unit Value of Imports..................... **75**

Italy

		1972	1973	1974	1975	1976	1977	1978	1979	1980	1981	1982	1983	1984	1985	1986
Balance of Payments														*Millions of US Dollars:*		
Current Account, n.i.e.	78ald	1,984	−2,841	−8,275	−635	−2,849	2,347	6,054	5,914	−10,587	−10,467	−7,380	699	−3,190	−4,084	2,462
Goods: Exports f.o.b.	78aad	18,635	22,261	30,495	34,998	37,269	45,312	56,050	72,218	78,106	77,071	73,791	72,877	74,564	76,718	97,207
Goods: Imports f.o.b.	78abd	−18,392	−26,013	−38,556	−35,656	−41,011	−44,926	−52,595	−72,372	−94,016	−88,386	−81,771	−74,588	−79,696	−82,086	−92,159
Trade Balance	78acd	243	−3,752	−8,061	−658	−3,741	386	3,455	−155	−15,910	−11,315	−7,981	−1,711	−5,132	−5,367	5,048
Services: Credit	78add	5,339	6,277	6,910	8,167	8,343	10,630	13,339	17,129	19,192	16,359	16,891	17,723	18,010	19,818	23,645
Services: Debit	78aed	−4,613	−5,848	−6,736	−7,970	−7,323	−8,797	−10,615	−13,175	−16,249	−14,488	−14,598	−14,090	−14,726	−16,406	−20,189
Balance on Goods & Services	78afd	969	−3,323	−7,887	−461	−2,721	2,219	6,179	3,799	−12,967	−9,444	−5,688	1,922	−1,848	−1,955	8,503
Income: Credit	78agd	2,115	2,540	3,329	2,564	2,081	2,585	3,787	5,849	7,681	7,842	7,694	6,069	6,648	6,960	8,159
Income: Debit	78ahd	−1,470	−2,138	−3,632	−3,059	−2,594	−2,671	−3,429	−4,546	−6,402	−9,470	−10,148	−8,579	−9,196	−9,692	−12,398
Balance on Gds, Serv. & Inc.	78aid	1,614	−2,922	−8,190	−956	−3,234	2,133	6,537	5,102	−11,689	−11,072	−8,142	−588	−4,396	−4,687	4,264
Current Transfers, n.i.e.: Credit	78ajd	1,588	1,656	1,277	1,917	1,879	2,299	2,896	4,469	5,457	4,839	5,080	5,655	5,775	5,398	6,739
Current Transfers: Debit	78akd	−1,218	−1,575	−1,362	−1,596	−1,494	−2,085	−3,379	−3,657	−4,356	−4,233	−4,317	−4,369	−4,570	−4,795	−8,541
Capital Account, n.i.e.	78bcd	−31	−38	−83	−120	24	4	−19	−100	205	166	253	201	290	244	−56
Capital Account, n.i.e.: Credit	78bad	15	12	12	14	125	118	88	223	497	380	484	461	530	526	751
Capital Account: Debit	78bbd	−46	−50	−95	−133	−101	−113	−108	−323	−292	−214	−231	−260	−240	−282	−807
Financial Account, n.i.e.	78bjd	−2,298	3,275	7,054	−1,931	5,711	4,073	−2,858	−2,160	12,030	8,259	2,513	3,916	2,848	117	1,971
Direct Investment Abroad	78bdd	−221	−276	−203	−343	−159	−560	−160	−538	−740	−1,392	−969	−2,022	−1,882	−1,736	−2,456
Dir. Invest. in Rep. Econ., n.i.e.	78bed	674	664	596	645	109	1,128	476	415	577	1,127	617	1,190	1,321	1,072	−172
Portfolio Investment Assets	78bfd	−706	−715	124	195	271	318	21	48	−410	−561	57	−163	−222	−780	−2,216
Equity Securities	78bkd	−74	−62	−24	26	28	48	−27	−96	−484	−535	−100	−322	−344	−347	110
Debt Securities	78bld	−633	−653	148	169	243	270	48	144	74	−26	157	158	122	−434	−2,327
Portfolio Investment Liab., n.i.e.	78bgd	53	−387	−174	−109	−133	22	−107	66	−526	159	−448	403	320	1,029	1,118
Equity Securities	78bmd	—	—	—	—	—	—	—	—	—	—	—	—	—	—	—
Debt Securities	78bnd	53	−387	−174	−109	−133	22	−107	66	−526	159	−448	403	320	1,029	1,118
Financial Derivatives Assets	78bwd	—	—	—	—	—	—	—	—	—	—	—	—	—	—	—
Financial Derivatives Liabilities	78bxd	—	—	—	—	—	—	—	—	—	—	—	—	—	—	—
Other Investment Assets	78bhd	−9,495	−7,657	7,050	−4,402	−2,475	−2,999	−9,319	−12,113	−8,218	−16,114	−1,582	−9,400	−9,669	−5,810	−1,211
Monetary Authorities	78bod	. . . .	. . . .	. . . .	. . . .	. . . .	. . . .									
General Government	78bpd	−11	−49	23	11	−19	−15	−74	−105	−224	−182	−541	−651	−765	−912	−1,109
Banks	78bqd	−6,638	−6,412	9,893	−2,733	−205	−2,555	−7,005	−6,180	−4,579	−12,313	−1,274	−5,972	−6,160	−5,060	198
Other Sectors	78brd	−2,846	−1,195	−2,866	−1,680	−2,251	−430	−2,239	−5,828	−3,416	−3,619	232	−2,776	−2,744	163	−299
Other Investment Liab., n.i.e.	78bid	7,398	11,646	−339	2,082	8,098	6,164	6,230	9,962	21,347	25,041	4,839	13,908	12,980	6,342	6,908
Monetary Authorities	78bsd	−6	307	3,587	−539	867	377	−2,945	−418	136	−220	−531	94	−348	−9	67
General Government	78btd	−290	973	113	191	163	259	1,470	1,539	3,820	4,611	2,878	2,355	3,217	3,128	2,797
Banks	78bud	7,035	6,438	−8,847	2,329	3,304	6,420	5,693	7,393	12,491	10,925	−971	9,443	9,167	1,956	3,928
Other Sectors	78bvd	659	3,928	4,807	102	3,764	−892	2,011	1,448	4,899	9,724	3,463	2,016	944	1,268	116
Net Errors and Omissions	78cad	−495	−482	90	−396	−806	−200	859	−676	−851	1,083	−91	1,060	2,612	−3,863	−2,030
Overall Balance	78cbd	−840	−85	−1,214	−3,081	2,080	6,225	4,035	2,977	797	−958	−4,704	5,875	2,560	−7,585	2,348
Reserves and Related Items	79dad	840	85	1,214	3,081	−2,080	−6,225	−4,035	−2,977	−797	958	4,704	−5,875	−2,560	7,585	−2,348
Reserve Assets	79dbd	840	85	−432	1,786	−2,080	−5,201	−3,151	−1,835	−797	958	4,704	−5,875	−2,560	7,585	−2,348
Use of Fund Credit and Loans	79dcd	—	—	1,646	1,295	—	−1,024	−885	−1,142	—	—	—	—	—	—	—
Exceptional Financing	79ded	. . . .	. . . .	. . . .	. . . .	. . . .	. . . .	. . . .	. . . .	. . . .	. . . .	. . . .	. . . .	. . . .	. . . .	—
International Investment Position														*Millions of US Dollars*		
Assets	79aad	53,258	59,141	47,781	47,706	52,663	65,237	85,761	113,821	135,630	126,887	111,658	122,178	125,716	143,474	182,393
Direct Investment Abroad	79abd	3,373	3,247	3,574	3,359	3,408	4,478	5,141	6,236	7,319	7,718	8,424	8,743	13,099	16,600	26,080
Portfolio Investment	79acd	3,224	3,839	3,934	3,720	2,691	3,381	4,891	5,091	5,222	4,183	4,129	3,890	4,646	7,464	14,334
Equity Securities	79add	707	707	707	683	574	704	1,103	999	2,199	2,187	2,318	2,219	3,153	5,166	7,941
Debt Securities	79aed	2,517	3,132	3,227	3,037	2,118	2,677	3,788	4,092	3,023	1,997	1,812	1,670	1,494	2,298	6,393
Financial Derivatives	79ald	—	—	—	—	—	—	—	—	—	—	—	—	—	—	—
Other Investment	79afd	40,369	45,807	33,770	36,111	33,301	36,914	48,853	62,670	61,869	64,754	60,513	62,611	65,029	79,944	95,967
Monetary Authorities	79agd	—	—	—	—	—	—	—	—	—	—	—	—	—	—	—
General Government	79ahd	345	354	308	259	179	414	480	600	607	903	1,073	2,678	3,232	4,343	6,160
Banks	79aid	19,597	24,987	13,485	15,693	12,825	15,438	23,179	30,144	31,378	37,341	35,072	35,930	37,513	48,398	57,825
Other Sectors	79ajd	20,427	20,467	19,978	20,159	20,296	21,061	25,194	31,927	29,884	26,511	24,368	24,003	24,284	27,203	31,982
Reserve Assets	79akd	6,292	6,247	6,503	4,515	13,263	20,464	26,876	39,823	61,220	50,231	38,592	46,934	42,942	39,466	46,012
Liabilities	79lad	43,356	56,270	47,469	51,212	50,717	58,129	69,388	82,230	98,697	110,823	108,491	112,891	120,149	151,518	192,024
Dir. Invest. in Rep. Economy	79lbd	6,647	7,299	8,364	8,999	6,245	7,442	8,682	9,888	9,711	8,456	8,121	8,051	12,291	19,949	26,930
Portfolio Investment	79lcd	3,820	3,968	2,946	2,800	1,819	2,190	2,209	3,418	5,239	4,671	3,882	3,694	2,580	5,644	9,379
Equity Securities	79ldd	—	—	—	—	—	—	—	—	—	—	—	—	—	—	5
Debt Securities	79led	3,820	3,968	2,946	2,800	1,819	2,190	2,209	3,418	5,239	4,671	3,882	3,694	2,580	5,644	9,374
Financial Derivatives	79lld	—	—	—	—	—	—	—	—	—	—	—	—	—	—	—
Other Investment	79lfd	32,889	45,003	36,159	39,413	42,653	48,497	58,497	68,924	83,747	97,697	96,488	101,145	105,279	125,924	155,716
Monetary Authorities	79lgd	99	389	1,756	2,917	2,963	2,137	1,329	164	292	153	105	214	136	122	210
General Government	79lhd	1,555	2,420	3,049	2,464	3,251	3,631	5,537	7,679	11,192	15,289	17,848	19,482	21,248	28,371	35,602
Banks	79lid	20,433	25,921	15,286	17,026	16,881	23,518	30,271	38,683	47,229	50,732	45,703	48,800	52,652	62,988	79,544
Other Sectors	79ljd	10,802	16,274	16,068	17,007	19,558	19,211	21,361	22,398	25,034	31,523	32,832	32,650	31,243	34,443	40,360

Minus Sign Indicates Debit

1987	1988	1989	1990	1991	1992	1993	1994	1995	1996	1997	1998	1999	2000	2001	Balance of Payments	
-2,635	-7,181	-12,812	-16,479	-24,463	-29,217	7,802	13,209	25,076	39,999	32,403	19,998	8,111	-5,781	-163	Current Account, n.i.e.	78al *d*
116,712	127,860	140,556	170,304	169,465	178,155	169,153	191,421	233,998	252,039	240,404	242,572	235,856	240,473	242,430	Goods: Exports f.o.b.	78aa *d*
-116,628	-128,784	-142,219	-171,778	-172,049	-178,355	-140,264	-159,854	-195,269	-197,921	-200,527	-206,941	-212,420	-230,925	-226,568	Goods: Imports f.o.b.	78ab *d*
83	-924	-1,664	-1,474	-2,584	-200	28,889	31,568	38,729	54,118	39,878	35,631	23,437	9,549	15,862	*Trade Balance*	78ac *d*
29,715	30,187	31,790	49,666	46,911	58,545	52,284	53,681	61,619	65,660	66,991	67,549	58,788	56,556	57,548	Services: Credit	78ad *d*
-26,252	-29,060	-32,121	-46,795	-44,379	-58,134	-48,939	-48,238	-55,050	-57,605	-59,227	-63,379	-57,707	-55,601	-57,345	Services: Debit	78ae *d*
3,546	203	-1,995	1,397	-52	211	32,235	37,011	45,299	62,173	47,642	39,801	24,517	10,504	16,065	*Balance on Goods & Services*	78af *d*
9,193	11,025	14,585	18,997	21,930	28,757	31,844	28,599	34,168	40,142	45,734	51,319	46,361	38,671	38,649	Income: Credit	78ag *d*
-14,108	-16,536	-21,906	-33,709	-39,477	-50,644	-49,062	-45,289	-49,812	-55,101	-56,936	-63,636	-57,411	-50,680	-48,929	Income: Debit	78ah *d*
-1,370	-5,308	-9,315	-13,315	-17,598	-21,676	15,017	20,321	29,655	47,213	36,440	27,483	13,467	-1,506	5,785	*Balance on Gds, Serv. & Inc.*	78ai *d*
8,872	10,394	11,214	12,562	13,743	14,198	12,925	12,254	14,287	14,320	15,552	14,402	16,776	15,797	16,176	Current Transfers, n.i.e.: Credit	78aj *d*
-10,138	-12,267	-14,710	-15,726	-20,607	-21,739	-20,140	-19,366	-18,866	-21,535	-19,588	-21,887	-22,132	-20,073	-22,125	Current Transfers: Debit	78ak *d*
236	580	912	759	589	807	1,659	1,026	1,671	66	3,434	2,358	2,964	2,879	846	Capital Account, n.i.e.	78bc *d*
984	1,514	1,608	1,823	1,718	2,266	2,807	2,213	2,797	1,414	4,582	3,359	4,572	4,172	2,098	Capital Account, n.i.e.: Credit	78ba *d*
-749	-934	-696	-1,063	-1,129	-1,459	-1,149	-1,187	-1,125	-1,348	-1,148	-1,001	-1,608	-1,293	-1,252	Capital Account: Debit	78bb *d*
8,910	16,710	24,738	42,639	24,212	11,550	5,260	-14,207	-2,889	-7,982	-6,878	-18,074	-17,415	7,504	-3,211	Financial Account, n.i.e.	78bj *d*
-2,094	-4,703	-2,160	-7,394	-7,534	-4,148	-7,329	-5,239	-7,024	-8,697	-10,414	-12,407	-6,723	-12,077	-21,758	Direct Investment Abroad	78bd *d*
4,175	6,801	2,166	6,411	2,401	3,105	3,749	2,199	4,842	3,546	3,700	2,635	6,943	13,176	14,874	Dir. Invest. in Rep. Econ., n.i.e.	78be *d*
-3,642	-5,498	-9,062	-19,325	-23,490	-16,827	12,187	-37,718	-4,938	-25,598	-61,857	-109,064	-129,624	-80,263	-36,167	Portfolio Investment Assets	78bf *d*
132	924	-4,742	-6,135	429	3,699	385	-3,360	1,014	-1,036	-15,116	-26,570	-63,277	-77,036	-9,988	Equity Securities	78bk *d*
-3,774	-6,422	-4,319	-13,190	-23,918	-20,526	11,802	-34,358	-5,952	-24,562	-46,741	-82,493	-66,347	-3,227	-26,179	Debt Securities	78bl *d*
-3,678	5,805	18,262	19,216	18,720	25,237	62,107	29,895	45,583	74,655	73,375	111,987	104,607	57,020	29,329	Portfolio Investment Liab., n.i.e.	78bg *d*
—	—	4,242	3,950	70	-432	4,133	-1,395	5,358	9,331	9,414	14,423	-4,537	-2,426	-245	Equity Securities	78bm *d*
-3,678	5,805	8,020	15,266	18,650	25,670	57,974	31,290	40,225	65,324	63,962	97,565	109,144	59,446	29,573	Debt Securities	78bn *d*
—	1	-7	39	-18	-148	-8	87	-852	-1,009	-1,118	-850	161	744	-2,277	Financial Derivatives Assets	78bw *d*
2	4	-17	43	-18	-108	-221	628	1,079	1,272	1,273	1,041	1,709	1,588	1,839	Financial Derivatives Liabilities	78bx *d*
1,804	-10,938	-21,492	-13,894	-16,293	-28,863	-44,197	2,092	-28,947	-68,358	-25,541	-21,232	-33,573	242	717	Other Investment Assets	78bh *d*
....	....	....	....	....	....	....	....	....	....	....	....	5,396	3,034	-27,626	Monetary Authorities	78bo *d*
-1,421	-2,556	-1,365	-1,341	-1,772	-1,820	-1,539	-2,023	-2,148	-1,112	-62	-1,101	-163	-649	-359	General Government	78bp *d*
3,343	-7,281	-16,818	-4,384	-5,831	-8,691	-33,300	22,599	-18,689	-45,046	-1,602	-7,052	-9,643	2,388	12,091	Banks	78bq *d*
-118	-1,101	-3,310	-8,169	-8,691	-10,953	-9,358	-18,483	-8,110	-22,199	-23,877	-13,078	-29,163	-4,532	16,611	Other Sectors	78br *d*
12,343	25,239	43,047	57,542	50,444	33,301	-21,027	-6,152	-12,632	16,206	13,703	9,816	39,085	27,074	10,233	Other Investment Liab., n.i.e.	78bi *d*
-140	68	161	7	43	7,198	-4,602	-95	1,062	-1,269	-48	-128	916	-690	1,928	Monetary Authorities	78bs *d*
5,729	3,870	2,318	5,814	87	1,423	765	-1,812	4,893	-2,583	-1,798	-5,739	-3,255	-3,549	-766	General Government	78bt *d*
1,104	15,350	27,906	23,589	38,167	17,005	-16,752	-1,527	-22,716	26,613	6,861	12,780	1,109	24,875	12,783	Banks	78bu *d*
5,650	5,950	12,662	28,132	12,147	7,675	-439	-2,719	4,129	-6,555	8,688	2,903	40,315	6,438	-3,712	Other Sectors	78bv *d*
-1,040	-1,693	-1,480	-15,296	-7,055	-7,132	-17,856	1,547	-21,054	-20,176	-15,810	-21,472	-1,711	-1,355	1,940	Net Errors and Omissions	78ca *d*
5,470	8,417	11,358	11,623	-6,718	-23,992	-3,135	1,575	2,804	11,907	13,150	-21,472	-8,051	3,247	-588	*Overall Balance*	78cb *d*
-5,470	-8,417	-11,358	-11,623	6,718	23,992	3,135	-1,575	-2,804	-11,907	-13,150	21,472	8,051	-3,247	588	Reserves and Related Items	79da *d*
-5,470	-8,417	-11,358	-11,623	6,718	23,992	3,135	-1,575	-2,804	-11,907	-13,150	21,472	8,051	-3,247	588	Reserve Assets	79db *d*
—	—	—	—	—	—	—	—	—	—	—	—	—	—	—	Use of Fund Credit and Loans	79dc *d*
....	....	....	....	....	....	....	....	....	....	....	....	....	....	....	Exceptional Financing	79de *d*

Millions of US Dollars

1987	1988	1989	1990	1991	1992	1993	1994	1995	1996	1997	1998	1999	2000	2001	International Investment Position	
230,042	238,415	296,776	380,737	424,364	410,960	450,985	516,329	597,810	727,498	809,597	1,002,865	1,081,099	1,114,466	....	Assets	79aa *d*
32,332	37,432	43,462	57,261	67,233	71,004	81,892	91,097	109,176	113,251	130,668	165,412	181,853	180,184	....	Direct Investment Abroad	79ab *d*
18,444	24,411	38,054	62,843	94,849	111,125	130,670	150,426	171,793	192,351	257,494	394,501	546,906	580,883	....	Portfolio Investment	79ac *d*
9,051	8,327	14,070	15,730	15,143	12,170	11,723	14,015	13,982	16,915	26,600	37,690	210,930	260,383	....	Equity Securities	79ad *d*
9,393	16,084	23,983	47,113	79,706	98,954	118,947	136,411	157,811	175,436	230,894	356,811	335,976	320,500	....	Debt Securities	79ae *d*
—	—	—	—	—	—	—	—	—	—	—	—	2,952	3,533	....	Financial Derivatives	79al *d*
114,838	112,179	140,633	167,787	178,953	176,794	187,620	217,192	256,520	350,907	344,344	388,310	304,087	302,808	....	Other Investment	79af *d*
—	—	—	—	—	—	—	—	—	—	—	—	-4,190	-6,715	....	Monetary Authorities	79ag *d*
8,639	8,031	10,814	12,798	14,302	13,455	13,641	16,459	19,542	21,777	20,180	22,567	20,417	23,304	....	General Government	79ah *d*
63,664	70,064	90,098	102,381	106,122	106,045	116,107	121,726	146,945	214,524	198,520	225,089	138,719	140,447	....	Banks	79ai *d*
42,535	34,084	39,720	52,608	58,529	57,294	57,872	79,006	90,034	114,606	125,644	140,653	149,141	145,772	....	Other Sectors	79aj *d*
64,428	64,394	74,627	92,845	83,329	52,037	50,803	57,615	60,321	70,989	77,091	54,642	45,302	47,058	....	Reserve Assets	79ak *d*
239,467	257,710	342,678	465,424	530,368	521,563	535,352	587,612	650,102	761,656	807,436	1,022,771	1,027,734	1,070,915	....	Liabilities	79la *d*
32,952	38,529	50,937	59,997	61,576	50,730	54,538	60,955	65,980	74,640	83,158	105,397	108,699	113,119	....	Dir. Invest. in Rep. Economy	79lb *d*
9,604	15,900	32,098	53,319	91,395	101,229	160,403	188,595	237,861	333,422	385,388	544,602	549,252	570,237	....	Portfolio Investment	79lc *d*
202	451	5,129	9,872	9,938	7,724	11,123	11,118	16,434	27,245	35,500	65,833	53,380	53,182	....	Equity Securities	79ld *d*
9,402	15,449	26,969	43,447	81,457	93,504	149,280	177,477	221,427	306,177	349,888	478,769	495,872	517,056	....	Debt Securities	79le *d*
—	—	—	—	—	—	—	—	—	—	—	—	3,244	2,641	....	Financial Derivatives	79ll *d*
196,912	203,282	259,644	352,107	377,396	369,604	320,411	338,063	346,261	353,593	338,891	372,772	366,539	384,918	....	Other Investment	79lf *d*
109	147	315	354	363	5,316	578	485	1,554	239	175	56	950	234	....	Monetary Authorities	79lg *d*
48,145	30,705	37,702	47,179	25,542	21,579	21,506	21,551	26,328	22,187	21,470	15,595	8,881	7,252	....	General Government	79lh *d*
93,554	129,264	161,942	202,898	239,554	242,770	213,524	229,119	228,859	247,732	239,171	268,935	241,670	265,042	....	Banks	79li *d*
55,105	43,165	59,686	101,677	111,938	99,939	84,803	86,907	89,521	83,436	78,075	88,186	115,039	112,390	....	Other Sectors	79lj *d*

Italy

		1972	1973	1974	1975	1976	1977	1978	1979	1980	1981	1982	1983	1984	1985	1986
Government Finance																
Central Government														*Trillions of Lire through 1998;*		
Deficit (-) or Surplus	**80**	−5.9	−8.0	−9.1	−16.8	−14.7	−22.2	−34.3	−30.4	−37.0	−53.3	−72.8	−88.3	†−94.0	−118.7	−107.6
Revenue	**81**	12.1	14.1	18.2	23.4	31.6	41.4	52.7	63.5	89.2	106.8	151.7	177.2	†199.7	221.5	253.8
Expenditure	**82**	16.4	19.9	25.0	37.3	42.1	52.5	79.8	90.3	118.3	150.9	210.8	249.1	†280.5	325.0	348.7
Lending Minus Repayments	**83**	1.6	2.2	2.3	2.8	4.2	11.1	7.1	3.6	8.0	9.2	13.7	16.4	†13.2	15.3	12.7
Financing	**80h**	5.8	8.1	8.9	16.4	15.1	22.6	34.1	30.3	37.2	53.2	72.5	87.4	95.5	121.7	111.3
Domestic	**84a**	....	....	....	....	....	....	....	....	....	....	....	....	....	....	....
Foreign	**85a**	....	....	....	....	....	....	....	....	....	....	....	....	....	....	....
Total Debt by Residence	**88**	33.9	42.5	53.7	69.1	85.2	109.9	144.5	175.3	212.6	267.5	341.7	432.3	†521.2	642.3	750.3
Debt: Domestic	**88a**	....	....	....	....	....	....	....	....	....	....	....	....	....	....	....
Foreign	**89a**	....	....	....	....	....	....	....	....	....	....	....	....	....	....	....
Net Borrowing: Lire	**84b**	5.8	7.9	8.9	16.4	14.8	22.5	33.6	29.7	36.3	50.6	69.8	86.0	93.1	118.8	110.4
Net Borrowing: Foreign Currency	**85b**	—	.1	—	—	.2	.1	.3	.6	.8	2.5	2.6	1.3	2.3	2.9	.9
Monetary Operations	**86c**	—	—	—	—	—	.1	.1	.1	.1	.1	.1	.1	.1		
General Government															*As Percent of*	
Deficit (-) or Surplus	**80g**	....	....	....	....	....	....	....	....	....	....	....	....	....	....	....
Debt	**88g**	....	....	....	....	....	....	....	....	....	....	....	....	....	....	....
National Accounts														*Trillions of Lire through 1998;*		
Househ.Cons.Expend.,incl.NPISHs	**96f.** *c*	48.6	59.2	74.5	87.1	107.8	131.9	154.3	189.7	241.4	289.1	315.8	364.0	418.4	470.2	520.8
Government Consumption Expend.	**91f.** *c*	12.3	14.2	17.1	19.9	24.0	30.1	36.5	45.7	58.1	75.4	102.1	121.2	137.5	156.0	169.6
Gross Fixed Capital Formation	**93e.** *c*	18.5	24.1	31.7	34.6	41.8	50.3	57.7	70.8	94.1	110.7	129.4	143.1	162.1	177.4	188.5
Changes in Inventories	**93i.** *c*	.7	2.2	5.2	−1.4	5.3	3.0	3.5	5.6	10.5	4.1	4.0	2.3	11.0	14.4	9.5
Exports of Goods and Services	**90c.** *c*	12.7	15.2	22.9	26.3	35.9	45.6	54.0	68.3	77.3	100.0	122.2	137.1	162.0	182.8	178.8
Imports of Goods and Services (-)	**98c.** *c*	13.0	18.1	29.1	27.9	39.9	46.6	52.5	70.3	93.5	115.3	129.7	134.2	165.3	186.9	166.8
Gross Domestic Product (GDP)	**99b.** *c*	79.8	96.7	122.2	138.6	174.9	214.4	253.5	309.8	387.7	464.0	543.8	633.4	725.7	813.9	900.4
Net Primary Income from Abroad	**98.n**	.3	.1	−.3	−.4	−.6	−.2	—	1.0	1.0	−2.0	−3.5	−4.1	−4.8	−5.4	−6.6
Gross National Income (GNI)	**99a**	80.1	96.7	121.7	138.1	174.0	212.5	251.0	308.8	386.3	459.1	538.6	627.6	718.0	804.6	891.7
Net Current Transf.from Abroad	**98t**	....	....	....	....	....	....	....	....	....	....	....	....	....	....	....
Gross Nat'l Disposable Inc.(GNDI)	**99i**	....	....	....	....	....	....	....	....	....	....	....	....	....	....	....
Gross Saving	**99s**	....	....	....	....	....	....	....	....	....	....	....	....	....	....	....
Net National Income	**99e**	61.0	75.3	101.7	129.2	157.9	194.4	223.6	264.3	341.7	402.6	470.9	549.6	629.4	704.5	783.7
GDP Volume 1990 Prices	**99b.** *r*	774.4	825.1	863.8	845.2	900.2	926.2	960.7	1,015.2	1,051.0	1,056.0	1,060.9				
GDP Volume 1995 Prices	**99b.** *r*	....	....	....	....	....	....	....	....	....	....	1,360.4	1,377.2	1,415.2	1,457.3	1,494.1
GDP Volume (1995=100)	**99bv** *r*	55.6	59.2	62.0	60.6	64.6	66.5	68.9	72.8	75.4	75.8	76.1	77.1	79.2	81.5	83.6
GDP Deflator (1995=100)	**99bi** *r*	8.0	9.1	11.0	12.8	15.1	18.1	20.6	23.8	28.8	34.3	40.0	46.0	51.3	55.8	60.3
																Millions:
Population	**99z**	54.41	54.80	55.10	55.40	55.70	55.93	56.13	56.29	56.43	56.51	56.64	56.84	57.00	57.14	57.25

	1987	1988	1989	1990	1991	1992	1993	1994	1995	1996	1997	1998	1999	2000	2001		
Government Finance																	
Central Government																	
Billions of Euros Beginning 1999: Year Ending December 31																	
Deficit (-) or Surplus	-111.0	-121.7	-128.3	-138.6	-146.5	-162.8	†-157.8	-152.9	-122.6	-136.1	-31.0	548.7	.3	-14.6	-35.5	Deficit (-) or Surplus	80
	281.4	311.9	353.6	406.5	445.4	499.1	†470.1	477.1	524.8	549.7	621.3	611.3	353.1	350.6	356.7	Revenue	81
	380.3	418.6	466.2	526.3	581.8	651.4	†610.3	601.8	619.3	652.8	602.6	31.3	327.5	341.3	372.8	Expenditure	82
	12.1	15.0	15.7	18.8	10.1	10.4	†17.6	28.2	28.0	32.9	49.7	31.3	25.3	24.0	19.4	Lending Minus Repayments	83
	114.4	125.9	133.2	144.2	151.2	164.1	164.8	153.0	122.7	136.1	31.3	48.0	-.4	14.7	35.6	Financing	80h
	....	....	....	....	....	....	....	109.5	61.6	34.4	-72.3	-91.9	-92.9	-34.4	23.5	Domestic	84a
	....	....	....	....	....	....	....	43.5	61.1	101.7	103.6	139.9	92.5	49.1	12.1	Foreign	85a
	864.2	987.8	1,116.8	1,260.0	1,412.0	1,595.1	1,765.5	†1,931.8	2,073.7	2,206.1	2,250.8	2,290.5	1188.0	1212.8	1249.8	Total Debt by Residence	88
	....	....	....	....	....	....	....	1,621.8	1,720.3	1,769.8	1,719.1	1,630.0	756.0	742.5	770.5	Debt: Domestic	88a
	....	....	....	....	....	....	....	310.0	353.4	436.3	531.7	660.5	432.0	470.3	479.3	Foreign	89a
	108.2	121.6	124.7	129.2	145.5	163.8	150.3	147.5	100.9	129.9	....	....	....	....	....	Net Borrowing: Lire	84b
	6.1	4.2	8.4	14.9	5.5	.2	14.4	9.2	25.8	12.9	....	....	....	....	....	Net Borrowing: Foreign Currency	85b
	.1	.1	.1	.1	.2	.1	.1	.1	.1	.1	....	....	....	....	....	Monetary Operations	86c
Gross Domestic Product																*General Government*	
				-11.1	-10.1	-9.6	-9.5	-9.2	-7.7	-7.1	-2.7	-2.8	-1.8	-.5	-1.4	Deficit (-) or Surplus	80g
	....	....	....	98.0	101.5	108.7	119.1	124.9	125.3	122.1	120.1	116.4	114.5	110.6	109.4	Debt	88g
Millions of Euros Beginning 1999																**National Accounts**	
	569.1	627.1	694.4	754.1	829.9	892.5	906.8	966.5	1,041.9	1,101.2	1,162.0	1,223.5	†662.0	698.8	727.0	Housel.Cons.Expend.,incl.NPISHs	96f. c
	192.6	218.5	236.6	272.7	298.8	311.0	318.6	323.5	326.9	352.0	369.9	382.2	†205.0	217.5	230.0	Government Consumption Expend.	91f. c
	205.7	†232.6	255.4	283.3	303.1	310.7	288.2	297.6	327.9	348.8	362.8	384.8	†212.1	231.0	241.0	Gross Fixed Capital Formation	93e. c
	12.5	13.9	12.6	10.2	9.4	4.7	-1.1	8.1	17.8	6.4	12.0	16.1	†7.1	6.2	-.7	Changes in Inventories	93i. c
	188.7	205.0	235.5	260.8	267.1	289.2	347.9	394.4	483.2	491.1	524.1	548.1	†283.1	330.3	344.0	Exports of Goods and Services	90c. c
	184.0	204.2	237.7	260.2	267.5	290.4	297.2	336.8	410.5	397.3	443.6	477.3	†260.3	319.0	324.5	Imports of Goods and Services (-)	98c. c
	984.7	1,092.8	1,196.8	1,320.8	1,440.6	1,517.6	1,563.3	1,653.4	1,787.3	1,902.3	1,987.2	2,077.4	†1,108.5	1,164.8	1,216.6	Gross Domestic Product (GDP)	99b. c
	-6.6	†-6.9	-9.9	-17.3	-21.6	-26.8	-26.7	-26.6	-25.5	-22.7	-18.2	-19.7	†-6.8	-8.5	-5.5	Net Primary Income from Abroad	98.n
	976.1	†1,086.0	1,186.9	1,303.5	1,419.1	1,490.8	1,536.6	1,626.8	1,761.7	1,879.5	1,968.9	2,057.6	†1,101.7	1,156.2	1,211.0	Gross National Income (GNI)	99a
	....	-.7	-3.8	-.8	-5.4	-6.7	-8.5	-5.7	-2.4	-6.6	-7.1	-9.4	†-4.4	-3.9	-5.2	Net Current Transf.from Abroad	98t
	....	1,083.3	1,181.8	1,299.7	1,410.6	1,481.0	1,525.2	1,615.7	1,754.5	1,869.5	1,961.8	2,044.8	†1,096.6	1,151.5	1,204.7	Gross Nat'l Disposable Inc.(GNDI)	99i
	....	237.7	250.8	272.9	282.0	277.4	299.7	325.7	385.7	416.3	429.9	439.1	†230.2	235.2	247.8	Gross Saving	99s
	859.3	†945.7	1,033.5	1,135.3	1,235.8	1,294.7	1,328.3	1,407.4	1,527.7	1,633.3	1,709.1	1,779.8	†947.2	....	....	Net National Income	99e
																GDP Volume 1990 Prices	99b. r
	1,538.7	1,599.5	1,645.4	1,677.9	1,701.2	1,714.1	1,699.0	1,736.5	1,787.3	1,806.8	1,843.4	1,876.8	†985.0	1,013.0	1,031.0	GDP Volume 1995 Prices	99b. r
	86.1	89.5	92.1	93.9	95.2	95.9	95.1	97.2	100.0	101.1	103.1	105.0	†106.7	109.7	111.7	GDP Volume (1995=100)	99bv r
	64.0	68.3	72.7	78.7	84.7	88.5	92.0	95.2	100.0	105.3	107.8	110.7	†112.5	115.0	118.0	GDP Deflator (1995=100)	99bi r
Midyear Estimates																	
	57.34	57.44	57.54	57.66	56.75	56.86	57.05	57.20	57.30	57.40	57.52	57.59	57.65	57.76	57.95	**Population**	99z

(See notes in the back of the book.)

Jamaica

		1972	1973	1974	1975	1976	1977	1978	1979	1980	1981	1982	1983	1984	1985	1986
Exchange Rates														Jamaica Dollars per SDR:		
Market Rate.........aa=	wa	.925	1.097	1.113	1.064	1.056	1.104	2.208	2.347	2.272	2.074	1.965	3.432	4.832	6.019	6.703
													Jamaica Dollars per US Dollar:			
Market Rate.........ae=	we	.852	.909	.909	.909	.909	.909	1.695	1.781	1.781	1.781	1.781	3.278	4.930	5.480	5.480
Market Rate.........rf=	wf	.767	.902	.909	.909	.909	.909	1.413	1.765	1.781	1.781	1.781	1.932	3.943	5.559	5.478
Fund Position														Millions of SDRs:		
Quota.............................2f. s		53.0	53.0	53.0	53.0	53.0	53.0	74.0	74.0	111.0	111.0	111.0	111.0	145.5	145.5	145.5
SDRs.............................1b. s		6.9	6.4	5.1	4.3	.8	14.3	4.5	.4	—	1.1	.1	—	—	—	.3
Reserve Position in the Fund ....1c. s		—	—	—	—	—	—	—	—	—	—	—	2.4	3.8	—	—
Total Fund Cred.&Loans Outstg. 2tl		—	13.3	13.3	13.3	68.9	88.1	138.6	266.8	242.5	403.5	528.4	599.1	641.4	631.1	554.4
International Liquidity													Millions of US Dollars Unless Otherwise Indicated:			
Total Reserves minus Gold ....1l. d		159.7	127.4	190.4	125.6	32.4	47.8	58.8	63.8	105.0	85.2	109.0	63.2	96.9	161.3	98.4
SDRs.............................1b. d		7.5	7.7	6.3	5.0	.9	17.4	5.8	.5	—	1.3	.1	—	—	—	.4
Reserve Position in the Fund ....1c. d		—	—	—	—	—	—	—	—	—	2.8	4.1	—	—	—	—
Foreign Exchange ....1d. d		152.2	119.7	184.1	120.6	31.5	30.4	53.0	63.3	105.0	81.1	104.7	63.2	96.9	161.3	98.0
Other Official Insts.: Assets ....3b. d		2.8	5.3	14.1	33.5	1.4	.8	1.2	1.1	.8	10.8	14.5	—	37.1	37.6	49.4
Monetary Authorities: Other Liab. ....4..d		—	—	20.0	51.2	116.6	132.7	205.8	161.8	320.2	411.4	415.0	834.6	529.7	667.6	608.4
Deposit Money Banks: Assets ....7a. d		30.4	51.4	44.0	38.2	36.3	40.1	32.2	28.4	37.8	45.8	60.8	82.4	56.7	59.9	62.1
Liabilities ....7b. d		71.1	125.9	111.4	109.7	115.2	119.0	73.5	67.1	65.1	91.5	94.7	53.7	48.2	71.1	81.0
Other Banking Insts.: Assets ....7e. d		.6	.2	.8	.9	1.0	2.7	3.5	1.9	.3	.4	.6	.4	.2	.4	.5
Liabilities ....7f. d		22.6	24.5	45.1	63.3	49.5	38.9	31.4	31.3	8.0	12.8	12.6	4.7	.1	.1	—
Monetary Authorities														Millions of Jamaica Dollars:		
Foreign Assets 11		118	117	174	115	35	44	99	122	200	324	203	244	475	1,087	573
Claims on Central Government 12a		33	51	72	204	505	469	616	1,347	1,539	1,989	2,235	3,164	3,919	3,598	4,294
Claims on Deposit Money Banks 12e		10	32	46	11	16	6	10	18	64	10	15	—	49	47	38
Reserve Money...........................14		109	140	170	202	234	273	302	362	510	489	433	744	1,427	1,926	2,285
of which: Currency Outside DMBs.........14a		72	82	102	127	138	182	173	220	260	282	316	375	436	540	729
Foreign Liabilities........................16c		—	15	33	61	179	218	655	914	1,121	1,570	1,778	4,792	5,711	7,457	7,050
Central Government Deposits 16d		27	21	74	58	138	50	15	119	406	243	349	448	833	1,349	1,855
Capital Accounts 17a		23	26	28	27	35	36	44	65	79	88	84	143	200	248	276
Other Items (Net) 17r		3	−2	−12	−18	−30	−57	−290	27	−314	−66	−192	−2,719	−3,730	−6,249	−6,561
Deposit Money Banks														Millions of Jamaica Dollars:		
Reserves......................................20		40	58	70	70	95	93	198	156	392	302	59	372	1,015	1,304	2,340
Foreign Assets 21		23	47	40	35	33	36	55	51	67	82	108	270	280	328	340
Claims on Central Government 22a		79	74	77	107	133	288	355	384	378	553	705	794	744	1,069	1,920
Claims on Nonfin.Pub.Enterprises 22c		—	35	33	47	58	92	105	129	195	274	330	368	380	558	157
Claims on Private Sector 22d		416	471	549	641	622	544	654	775	904	1,231	1,683	2,123	2,483	2,602	3,109
Claims on Other Banking Insts........22f		9	5	9	4	16	3	13	—	—	11	21	74	123	125	71
Demand Deposits............................24		101	†136	156	195	200	292	397	410	457	492	560	691	882	980	1,410
Time and Savings Deposits.................25		356	†359	428	506	558	570	665	793	996	1,422	1,897	2,461	2,878	3,718	4,548
Foreign Liabilities........................26c		55	†114	101	100	105	108	125	120	116	163	169	176	237	390	444
Central Government Deposits 26d		3	9	10	10	13	13	17	32	35	45	44	88	101	141	139
Credit from Monetary Authorities 26g		—	33	1	7	8	—	3	18	64	2	3	1	26	23	42
Capital Accounts............................27a		36	69	109	119	115	104	141	158	182	205	224	327	490	522	788
Other Items (Net)..........................27r		16	−31	−27	−32	−42	−32	32	−36	87	123	10	256	409	212	567
Monetary Survey														Millions of Jamaica Dollars:		
Foreign Assets (Net) 31n		87	†34	80	−11	−215	−246	−626	−861	−970	−1,327	−1,635	−4,454	−5,194	−6,432	−6,580
Domestic Credit 32		511	610	667	950	1,201	1,348	1,735	2,527	2,649	3,797	4,605	6,012	6,736	6,482	7,597
Claims on Central Govt. (Net) 32an		82	95	66	243	487	693	939	1,581	1,476	2,255	2,548	3,422	3,729	3,178	4,220
Claims on Local Government 32b		—	—	1	3	3	3	3	10	6	2	7	6	5	4	—
Claims on Nonfin.Pub.Enterprises 32c		—	35	33	47	58	92	105	129	195	274	330	368	380	558	157
Claims on Private Sector 32d		420	475	558	650	630	552	663	785	914	1,241	1,692	2,135	2,494	2,613	3,146
Claims on Other Banking Insts 32f		9	5	9	7	23	8	25	22	59	26	29	81	128	129	74
Money.......................................34		173	†218	258	322	339	474	570	629	717	775	876	1,066	1,319	1,520	2,140
Quasi-Money.................................35		356	†359	428	506	558	570	665	793	996	1,422	1,897	2,461	2,878	3,718	4,548
Capital Accounts...........................37a		59	95	136	146	149	139	185	223	261	293	308	471	690	771	1,064
Other Items (Net).........................37r		11	−28	−77	−35	−61	−82	−310	20	−293	−20	−111	−2,440	−3,346	−5,958	−6,735
Money plus Quasi-Money.....................35l		528	†578	687	828	897	1,044	1,235	1,422	1,712	2,197	2,773	3,527	4,197	5,238	6,687
Other Banking Institutions														Millions of Jamaica Dollars:		
Reserves......................................40		1	—	—	—	—	—	—	—	—	—	—	2	—	12	45
Foreign Assets 41		—	—	1	1	1	2	1	3	—	1	1	1	1	2	3
Claims on Central Government 42a		—	—	—	—	—	8	5	23	9	7	10	7	9	52	103
Claims on Private Sector 42d		43	92	136	160	159	141	168	169	134	170	258	347	476	615	768
Claims on Deposit Money Banks 42e		31	29	98	73	61	54	66	50	55	57	42	77	130	96	103
Demand Deposits............................44		—	7	95	—	—	—	—	—	1	3	—	10	12	—	19
Time and Savings Deposits.................45		53	81	86	135	133	101	119	116	129	158	242	362	483	771	917
Foreign Liabilities........................46c		17	21	41	56	44	34	52	54	14	22	10	—	—	—	—
Long-Term Foreign Liabilities..............46cl		—	1	—	1	1	1	1	2	1	1	12	15	—	—	—
Credit from Deposit Money Banks 46h		2	3	—	6	10	27	24	39	17	22	36	30	113	65	120
Capital Accounts............................47a		5	6	6	14	14	15	15	17	18	19	25	29	54	67	90
Other Items (Net)..........................47r		−2	1	7	22	20	27	29	18	18	9	−14	−12	−46	−127	−124
Banking Survey														Millions of Jamaica Dollars:		
Foreign Assets (Net) 51n		70	†13	39	−66	−259	−278	−676	−911	−983	−1,348	−1,645	−4,453	−5,193	−6,430	−6,578
Domestic Credit 52		545	698	795	1,103	1,338	1,488	1,883	2,697	2,733	3,948	4,845	6,285	7,092	7,020	8,395
Claims on Central Govt. (Net) 52an		82	95	66	243	487	701	944	1,604	1,485	2,262	2,558	3,429	3,737	3,230	4,324
Claims on Local Government 52b		—	—	1	3	3	3	3	10	6	2	7	6	5	4	—
Claims on Nonfin.Pub.Enterprises 52c		—	35	33	47	58	92	105	129	195	274	330	368	380	558	157
Claims on Private Sector 52d		463	567	694	810	789	692	831	954	1,047	1,411	1,950	2,482	2,971	3,228	3,914
Liquid Liabilities 55l		581	†667	868	962	1,030	1,145	1,353	1,538	1,842	2,358	3,015	3,897	4,692	5,997	7,579
Long-Term Foreign Liabilities................56cl		—	1	—	1	1	1	1	2	1	1	12	15	—	—	—
Capital Accounts.............................57a		64	101	142	161	163	154	200	240	279	312	333	500	744	838	1,154
Other Items (Net).........................57r		−30	−57	−176	−87	−115	−90	−348	5	−372	−71	−160	−2,580	−3,537	−6,245	−6,916

1987	1988	1989	1990	1991	1992	1993	1994	1995	1996	1997	1998	1999	2000	2001		
End of Period															**Exchange Rates**	
7.803	7.374	8.516	11.435	30.744	30.504	44.606	48.469	58.889	50.135	49.033	52.174	56.672	59.172	59.426	Market Rate.........aa= ....wa	
End of Period (we)		*Period Average (wf)*														
5.500	5.480	6.480	8.038	21.493	22.185	32.475	33.202	39.616	34.865	36.341	37.055	41.291	45.415	47.286	Market Rate.........ae= ....we	
5.487	5.489	5.745	7.184	12.116	22.960	24.949	33.086	35.142	37.120	35.404	36.550	39.044	42.701	45.996	Market Rate.........rf= ....wf	
End of Period															**Fund Position**	
145.5	145.5	145.5	145.5	145.5	200.9	200.9	200.9	200.9	200.9	200.9	200.9	273.5	273.5	273.5	Quota	2f. s
1.0	—	—	.3	—	9.0	9.1	—	.3	—	.2	.5	.5	.1	1.2	SDRs	1b. s
—	—	—	—	—	—	—	—	—	—	—	—	—	—	—	Reserve Position in the Fund	1c. s
478.2	358.8	291.8	250.7	273.6	259.7	244.2	217.6	161.7	112.2	87.1	74.7	60.8	46.3	31.9	Total Fund Cred.&Loans Outstg.	2tl
End of Period															**International Liquidity**	
174.3	147.2	107.5	168.2[e]	106.1	324.1	417.0	735.9	681.3	880.0	682.1	709.5	554.5	1,053.7	1,900.9	Total Reserves minus Gold	1l. d
1.4	—	—	.5	.1	12.3	12.4	—	.5	.1	.2	.7	.7	.1	1.5	SDRs	1b. d
—	—	—	—	—	—	—	—	—	—	—	—	—	—	—	Reserve Position in the Fund	1c. d
172.9	147.2	107.5	167.7[e]	106.0	311.8	404.6	735.9	680.8	879.9	681.9	708.8	553.8	1,053.6	1,899.4	Foreign Exchange	1d. d
54.1	59.7	52.9	....	—	14.9	17.5	8.3	7.7	8.0	1.1	1.0	3.2	3.1	2.5	Other Official Insts.: Assets	3b. d
493.9	535.1	523.4	492.1	232.0	109.8	65.1	58.2	....	....	....	....	....	....	....	Monetary Authorities: Other Liab.	4.. d
66.1	99.0	122.2	113.0	236.2	307.0	292.6	449.5	489.0	464.6	542.0	457.9	571.8	593.8	811.8	Deposit Money Banks: Assets	7a. d
104.1	155.4	161.5	138.4	204.0	253.4	238.3	393.2	336.2	370.2	371.6	328.0	267.2	219.7	368.7	Liabilities	7b. d
—	2.3	2.4	2.9	2.6	7.6	1.8	34.1	7.0	9.1	16.7	23.8	33.7	37.8	133.7	Other Banking Insts.: Assets	7e. d
—	.6	.3	3.5	.7	.1	3.9	53.8	47.0	43.5	11.7	6.4	5.4	12.9	53.5	Liabilities	7f. d
End of Period															**Monetary Authorities**	
930	806	692	1,352	2,311	6,912	12,618	24,486	27,084	30,663	24,739	26,280	22,850	47,664	89,818	Foreign Assets	11
2,829	2,940	3,343	3,316	2,614	2,562	7,055	7,466	15,702	20,751	39,777	51,219	57,268	54,930	56,038	Claims on Central Government	12a
—	150	127	12	—	—	—	—	—	—	—	—	—	—	—	Claims on Deposit Money Banks	12e
2,736	3,752	4,604	5,321	6,820	12,859	18,588	24,969	32,381	33,668	38,770	47,324	45,343	48,887	45,735	Reserve Money	14
844	1,288	1,378	1,640	2,632	3,741	5,228	7,118	9,516	10,760	12,449	13,504	17,821	17,607	18,783	*of which: Currency Outside DMBs*	14a
6,448	5,578	5,876	6,822	13,398	10,357	13,007	12,480	8,077	2,136	1,588	1,345	906	685	448	Foreign Liabilities	16c
2,261	3,707	4,452	6,410	9,188	12,682	17,255	26,512	28,948	37,755	41,571	45,837	48,058	64,072	110,622	Central Government Deposits	16d
321	303	350	468	1,252	1,243	1,815	1,972	2,396	2,060	2,015	2,143	2,326	2,427	2,437	Capital Accounts	17a
–8,007	–9,444	–11,121	–14,341	–25,734	–27,668	–30,993	–33,981	–29,015	–24,205	–19,427	–19,150	–16,515	–13,477	–13,386	Other Items (Net)	17r
End of Period															**Deposit Money Banks**	
2,323	3,270	3,838	4,273	5,059	11,113	13,681	18,794	25,623	23,568	29,167	30,812	26,972	32,236	40,378	Reserves	20
364	543	792	908	5,076	6,810	9,501	14,924	19,373	16,197	19,667	16,966	23,608	26,967	38,388	Foreign Assets	21
2,049	1,977	1,150	1,539	1,843	8,134	7,580	16,967	13,716	22,281	23,898	23,280	30,373	34,886	93,576	Claims on Central Government	22a
276	285	423	335	222	159	730	1,016	2,081	1,902	3,326	3,462	3,236	4,269	6,094	Claims on Nonfin.Pub.Enterprises	22c
4,046	5,549	7,290	8,583	11,940	14,358	23,326	32,164	44,408	52,006	57,482	74,777	84,593	102,602	42,312	Claims on Private Sector	22d
10	82	86	66	233	488	281	686	803	380	512	342	579	1,059	42	Claims on Other Banking Insts	22f
1,407	2,157	1,775	2,376	5,185	9,650	11,675	14,134	19,804	22,788	22,022	23,160	27,221	30,289	35,359	Demand Deposits	24
5,275	6,513	7,460	8,875	11,698	20,908	29,725	44,300	57,075	62,243	74,017	80,138	86,054	100,215	106,772	Time and Savings Deposits	25
572	852	1,046	1,113	4,384	5,622	7,740	13,055	13,319	12,905	13,504	12,153	11,031	9,978	17,436	Foreign Liabilities	26c
206	262	366	378	563	1,814	2,304	6,529	6,945	6,690	8,086	5,736	8,075	15,816	11,261	Central Government Deposits	26d
21	145	148	108	8	442	38	283	3,721	8,120	5,239	101	1,527	3,044	83	Credit from Monetary Authorities	26g
958	1,232	1,560	1,876	2,510	3,902	5,139	8,615	10,613	14,140	16,469	33,180	32,567	30,751	31,232	Capital Accounts	27a
628	545	1,223	979	23	–1,275	–1,522	–2,363	–5,474	–10,554	–5,254	–4,830	2,887	11,925	18,647	Other Items (Net)	27r
End of Period															**Monetary Survey**	
–5,727	–5,081	–5,440	–5,675	–10,396	–2,257	1,372	13,876	25,061	31,818	29,345	29,748	34,521	63,967	110,322	Foreign Assets (Net)	31n
6,808	7,006	7,616	7,227	7,273	11,378	19,442	25,492	41,074	53,129	75,593	101,760	120,167	118,003	76,315	Domestic Credit	32
2,411	948	–325	–1,932	–5,294	–3,800	–4,924	–8,608	–6,475	–1,413	14,019	22,926	31,508	9,928	27,732	Claims on Central Govt. (Net)	32an
—	—	—	—	—	—	—	6	6	2	3	1	—	—	—	Claims on Local Government	32b
276	285	423	335	222	159	730	1,016	2,081	1,902	3,326	3,462	3,236	4,269	6,094	Claims on Nonfin.Pub.Enterprises	32c
4,046	5,689	7,430	8,756	12,113	14,531	23,355	32,391	44,660	52,258	57,734	75,029	84,845	102,747	42,447	Claims on Private Sector	32d
76	84	88	68	233	488	281	686	803	380	512	342	579	1,059	42	Claims on Other Banking Insts	32f
2,252	3,445	3,153	4,016	7,818	13,391	16,903	21,252	29,320	33,548	34,470	36,664	45,042	47,897	54,142	Money	34
5,275	6,513	7,460	8,875	11,698	20,908	29,725	44,300	57,075	62,243	74,017	80,138	86,054	100,215	106,772	Quasi-Money	35
1,279	1,535	1,910	2,344	3,763	5,145	6,954	10,587	13,009	16,200	18,484	35,323	34,893	33,178	33,669	Capital Accounts	37a
–7,724	–9,567	–10,346	–13,683	–26,401	–30,322	–32,768	–36,771	–33,269	–27,043	–22,033	–20,618	–11,299	680	–7,946	Other Items (Net)	37r
7,527	9,958	10,612	12,891	19,516	34,299	46,628	65,552	86,396	95,791	108,487	116,803	131,095	148,112	160,914	Money plus Quasi-Money	35l
End of Period															**Other Banking Institutions**	
71	187	196	257	406	870	1,396	1,276	1,287	1,390	1,233	1,279	765	454	828	Reserves	40
—	13	15	23	55	168	59	1,133	277	318	608	882	1,393	1,718	6,322	Foreign Assets	41
214	328	334	323	471	832	312	1,681	2,818	4,404	4,281	1,894	1,500	2,004	4,167	Claims on Central Government	42a
1,122	1,843	2,724	3,149	4,257	6,902	7,468	7,627	9,890	10,662	7,069	5,781	4,354	2,855	3,372	Claims on Private Sector	42d
100	115	153	409	332	1,019	686	1,148	932	865	1,442	379	299	143	251	Claims on Deposit Money Banks	42e
—	—	—	—	—	—	—	—	—	—	—	—	—	—	—	Demand Deposits	44
1,403	2,140	2,635	2,929	3,229	6,580	7,306	6,998	7,077	6,996	6,862	5,759	4,938	3,966	7,290	Time and Savings Deposits	45
—	—	—	—	—	—	—	—	—	—	—	15	24	—	—	Foreign Liabilities	46c
—	3	2	28	16	2	127	1,786	1,863	1,516	410	213	224	586	2,531	Long-Term Foreign Liabilities	46cl
41	117	336	402	661	843	949	1,312	1,096	5,463	4,098	1,120	—	170	160	Credit from Deposit Money Banks	46h
125	198	202	252	491	1,189	1,738	2,521	2,924	3,013	1,688	2,946	4,259	2,820	4,117	Capital Accounts	47a
–62	29	246	550	1,124	1,177	–200	249	2,244	649	1,559	153	–1,111	–367	844	Other Items (Net)	47r
End of Period															**Banking Survey**	
–5,727	–5,068	–5,424	–5,651	–10,341	–2,090	1,432	15,009	25,339	32,136	29,937	30,606	35,914	65,686	116,644	Foreign Assets (Net)	51n
8,069	9,093	10,586	10,631	11,768	18,624	26,940	34,114	52,979	67,815	86,431	109,094	125,442	121,804	83,813	Domestic Credit	52
2,626	1,276	9	–1,609	–4,824	–2,968	–4,612	–6,927	–3,658	2,991	18,299	24,821	33,008	11,932	31,899	Claims on Central Govt. (Net)	52an
—	—	—	—	—	—	—	6	6	2	3	1	—	—	—	Claims on Local Government	52b
276	285	423	335	222	159	730	1,016	2,081	1,902	3,326	3,462	3,236	4,269	6,094	Claims on Nonfin.Pub.Enterprises	52c
5,167	7,532	10,154	11,904	16,370	21,433	30,823	40,018	54,550	62,920	64,803	80,810	89,198	105,603	45,819	Claims on Private Sector	52d
8,859	11,910	13,051	15,563	22,339	40,008	52,538	71,273	92,186	101,398	114,116	121,282	135,267	151,624	167,375	Liquid Liabilities	55l
—	3	2	28	16	2	127	1,786	1,863	1,516	410	213	224	586	2,531	Long-Term Foreign Liabilities	56cl
1,403	1,733	2,113	2,596	4,254	6,334	8,692	13,108	15,933	19,213	20,172	38,270	39,152	35,999	37,786	Capital Accounts	57a
–7,921	–9,621	–10,004	–13,208	–25,181	–29,810	–32,986	–37,045	–31,663	–22,175	–18,330	–20,066	–13,288	–718	–7,236	Other Items (Net)	57r

Jamaica

343		1972	1973	1974	1975	1976	1977	1978	1979	1980	1981	1982	1983	1984	1985	1986
Interest Rates																*Percent Per Annum*
Bank Rate *(End of Period)*	**60**	6.00	7.00	9.00	8.00	9.00	9.00	9.00	9.00	11.00	11.00	11.00	11.00	16.00	21.00	21.00
Treasury Bill Rate	**60c**	4.32	5.54	7.19	6.94	7.23	7.21	8.26	9.25	9.97	9.83	8.61	12.38	13.29	19.03	20.88
Deposit Rate	**60l**	....	....	....	....	10.78	7.08	5.68	8.28	9.53	10.55	10.71	13.60	15.86	19.58	18.76
Lending Rate	**60p**	....	....	....	....	13.76	13.86	13.68	13.81	15.63	16.07	16.44	16.97	18.53	24.92	27.34
Government Bond Yield	**61**	8.35	8.81	10.41	11.10	11.60	11.70	11.70	12.28	13.61	13.68	13.68	15.16	17.14	22.48	22.62
Prices, Production, Labor																*Index Numbers (1995=100):*
Industrial Share Prices	**62**	.6	.6	.4	.4	.3	.2	.2	.3	.3	.7	1.0	1.3	2.1	3.4	6.5
Consumer Prices	**64**	1.0	1.2	1.5	1.7	1.9	2.1	2.9	3.7	4.7	5.3	5.7	6.3	8.1	10.2	11.7
Industrial Production	**66**	....	....	....	....	....	....	....	....	....	....	....	....	....	....	75.2
																Number in Thousands:
Labor Force	**67d**	....	....	....	....	....	....	....	....	....	....	....	....	....	....	....
Employment	**67e**	....	....	....	....	....	....	....	....	....	....	....	....	....	782	821
Unemployment	**67c**	....	....	....	....	....	....	....	....	....	....	....	....	....	261	251
Unemployment Rate (%)	**67r**	....	....	....	....	....	....	....	....	....	....	....	....	....	25.0	23.6
International Transactions																*Millions of Jamaica Dollars*
Exports	**70**	300	355	549	690	573	699	1,143	1,446	1,715	1,735	1,367	1,392	2,733	3,128	3,226
Imports, c.i.f.	**71**	489	615	851	1,021	830	782	1,260	1,754	2,087	2,623	2,460	2,841	4,510	6,147	5,322
																1995=100
Volume of Exports	**72**	113.9	104.0	49.2	97.5	77.5	87.5	89.0	86.3	88.8	91.1	65.8	70.8	65.1	59.2	57.9
Balance of Payments																*Millions of US Dollars:*
Current Account, n.i.e.	**78al*d***	....	....	....	....	-263.8	-12.7	-21.7	-106.5	-136.1	-306.8	-383.3	-338.6	-315.2	-273.4	-17.9
Goods: Exports f.o.b.	**78aa*d***	....	....	....	....	656.4	737.8	831.1	818.2	962.7	974.0	767.4	685.7	702.3	568.6	589.5
Goods: Imports f.o.b.	**78ab*d***	....	....	....	....	-791.6	-666.7	-750.1	-882.5	-1,038.2	-1,296.7	-1,208.9	-1,124.2	-1,037.0	-1,004.2	-837.4
Trade Balance	**78ac*d***	....	....	....	....	-135.2	71.1	81.0	-64.3	-75.5	-322.7	-441.5	-438.5	-334.7	-435.6	-247.9
Services: Credit	**78ad*d***	....	....	....	....	232.7	217.2	285.4	351.8	400.7	430.9	493.0	540.1	566.3	609.5	753.5
Services: Debit	**78ae*d***	....	....	....	....	-332.8	-257.0	-299.7	-339.5	-369.9	-407.1	-430.0	-403.3	-418.0	-414.9	-411.4
Balance on Goods & Services	**78af*d***	....	....	....	....	-235.3	31.3	66.7	-52.0	-44.7	-298.9	-378.5	-301.7	-186.4	-241.0	94.2
Income: Credit	**78ag*d***	....	....	....	....	53.8	52.0	53.3	50.9	58.2	94.9	110.7	106.4	66.6	88.1	68.0
Income: Debit	**78ah*d***	....	....	....	....	-127.0	-145.5	-195.8	-217.9	-270.2	-257.1	-285.9	-261.3	-332.9	-369.9	-348.7
Balance on Gds, Serv. & Inc.	**78ai*d***	....	....	....	....	-308.5	-62.2	-75.8	-219.0	-256.7	-461.1	-553.7	-456.6	-452.7	-522.8	-186.5
Current Transfers, n.i.e.: Credit	**78aj*d***	....	....	....	....	94.2	92.3	93.3	152.7	162.7	199.3	219.0	174.8	178.5	294.4	209.4
Current Transfers: Debit	**78ak*d***	....	....	....	....	-49.5	-42.8	-39.2	-40.2	-42.1	-45.0	-48.6	-56.8	-41.0	-45.0	-40.8
Capital Account, n.i.e.	**78bc*d***	....	....	....	....	-38.8	-29.4	-28.3	-32.4	-29.9	-30.0	-25.2	-20.0	-20.0	-31.0	-22.3
Capital Account, n.i.e.: Credit	**78ba*d***	....	....	....	....	—	—	—	—	—	—	—	—	—	—	—
Capital Account: Debit	**78bb*d***	....	....	....	....	-38.8	-29.4	-28.3	-32.4	-29.9	-30.0	-25.2	-20.0	-20.0	-31.0	-22.3
Financial Account, n.i.e.	**78bj*d***	....	....	....	....	58.0	-6.7	-139.4	-14.1	117.9	95.0	199.7	-27.2	552.6	216.5	-118.0
Direct Investment Abroad	**78bd*d***	....	....	....	....	—	—	—	—	—	—	—	—	—	—	—
Dir. Invest. in Rep. Econ., n.i.e.	**78be*d***	....	....	....	....	-.6	-9.7	-26.6	-26.4	27.7	-11.5	-15.8	-18.7	12.2	-9.0	-4.6
Portfolio Investment Assets	**78bf*d***	....	....	....	....	3.8	—	—	—	—	—	—	—	—	—	—
Equity Securities	**78bk*d***	....	....	....	....	—	—	—	—	—	—	—	—	—	—	—
Debt Securities	**78bl*d***	....	....	....	....	3.8	—	—	—	—	—	—	—	—	—	—
Portfolio Investment Liab., n.i.e.	**78bg*d***	....	....	....	....	—	—	—	—	—	—	—	—	—	—	—
Equity Securities	**78bm*d***	....	....	....	....	—	—	—	—	—	—	—	—	—	—	—
Debt Securities	**78bn*d***	....	....	....	....	—	—	—	—	—	—	—	—	—	—	—
Financial Derivatives Assets	**78bw*d***	....	....	....	....	....	....	....	....	....	....	....	....	....	....	....
Financial Derivatives Liabilities	**78bx*d***	....	....	....	....	....	....	....	....	....	....	....	....	....	....	....
Other Investment Assets	**78bh*d***	....	....	....	....	13.1	.1	2.5	.1	-11.6	-16.7	-21.6	-14.7	-33.9	-5.2	-8.4
Monetary Authorities	**78bo*d***	....	....	....	....	....	....	....	....	....	....	....	....	....	....	....
General Government	**78bp*d***	....	....	....	....	-1.8	-1.1	-2.3	-2.6	-2.1	-8.7	-6.6	-7.0	-8.6	-9.1	-8.8
Banks	**78bq*d***	....	....	....	....	3.9	-4.3	4.8	2.7	-9.5	-8.0	-15.0	-7.7	-25.3	3.9	.4
Other Sectors	**78br*d***	....	....	....	....	11.0	5.5	—	—	—	—	—	—	—	—	—
Other Investment Liab., n.i.e.	**78bi*d***	....	....	....	....	41.7	2.9	-115.3	12.2	101.8	123.2	237.1	6.2	574.3	230.7	-105.0
Monetary Authorities	**78bs*d***	....	....	....	....	9.2	15.8	-8.4	-13.3	14.4	30.4	-73.8	59.2	109.1	7.2	-33.0
General Government	**78bt*d***	....	....	....	....	75.5	52.5	85.3	72.6	188.2	101.5	276.8	61.4	356.5	141.1	-126.7
Banks	**78bu*d***	....	....	....	....	1.0	4.2	—	—	-4.1	13.1	-13.3	-17.8	1.1	13.4	8.0
Other Sectors	**78bv*d***	....	....	....	....	-44.0	-69.6	-192.2	-47.1	-96.7	-21.8	47.4	-96.6	107.6	69.0	46.7
Net Errors and Omissions	**78ca*d***	....	....	....	....	43.5	-1.1	35.8	-4.2	-28.4	3.9	18.0	-.9	-64.0	17.0	80.0
Overall Balance	**78cb*d***	....	....	....	....	-201.1	-49.9	-153.6	-157.2	-76.5	-237.8	-190.8	-386.7	153.3	-70.8	-78.2
Reserves and Related Items	**79da*d***	....	....	....	....	201.1	49.9	153.6	157.2	76.5	237.8	190.8	386.7	-153.3	70.8	78.2
Reserve Assets	**79db*d***	....	....	....	....	119.9	-8.4	-9.8	-.4	-41.6	25.1	-19.7	56.6	-65.9	-18.7	-14.1
Use of Fund Credit and Loans	**79dc*d***	....	....	....	....	64.4	22.5	63.3	165.8	-31.0	190.3	137.3	76.6	44.3	-10.5	-88.6
Exceptional Financing	**79de*d***	....	....	....	....	16.8	35.8	100.1	-8.2	149.1	22.4	73.3	253.5	-131.7	100.1	180.9
Government Finance																*Millions of Jamaica Dollars:*
Deficit (-) or Surplus	**80**	....	....	....	-253.0	-394.9	-496.5	-514.1	-542.6	-739.3	-720.6	-893.3	-1,389.9	-547.0	-963.4	....
Revenue	**81**	....	....	....	682.0	709.9	734.1	1,129.7	1,149.9	1,381.9	1,671.7	1,719.4	1,840.8	2,882.2	3,740.8	....
Grants Received	**81z**	....	....	....	—	—	—	—	—	—	—	—	—	—	—	....
Expenditure	**82**	....	....	....	805.6	946.2	1,064.5	1,427.7	1,426.4	1,980.9	2,116.6	2,263.2	2,847.3	3,168.2	4,492.6	....
Lending Minus Repayments	**83**	....	....	....	129.4	158.6	166.1	216.1	266.1	140.3	275.7	349.5	383.4	261.0	211.6	....
Debt: Domestic	**88a**	....	....	....	....	....	....	....	....	2,253.1	2,585.3	3,158.4	6,178.1	5,871.8	6,831.0	....
Foreign	**89a**	....	....	....	....	....	....	....	....	1,700.1	2,232.1	2,605.9	4,681.2	8,417.5	10,404.4	....
National Accounts																*Millions of Jamaica Dollars*
Househ.Cons.Expend.,incl.NPISHs	**96f**	968	1,063	1,469	1,723	1,887	2,030	2,387	2,714	3,147	3,682	4,034	4,874	6,271	8,247	9,936
Government Consumption Expend.	**91f**	197	280	386	477	562	612	750	825	966	1,095	1,288	1,406	1,548	1,738	2,151
Gross Fixed Capital Formation	**93e**	367	448	478	610	451	350	499	748	690	954	1,168	1,436	1,981	2,581	2,432
Changes in Inventories	**93i**	27	94	47	60	40	12	63	74	69	123	57	120	183	256	125
Exports of Goods and Services	**90c**	472	543	770	917	783	928	1,575	2,065	2,426	2,510	2,240	2,621	4,956	6,521	7,370
Imports of Goods and Services (-)	**98c**	591	707	991	1,186	1,022	972	1,525	2,133	2,525	3,058	2,919	3,465	5,580	7,669	6,924
Gross Domestic Product (GDP)	**99b**	1,439	1,720	2,159	2,600	2,696	2,954	3,737	4,297	4,773	5,307	5,867	6,993	9,359	11,674	15,089
Net Primary Income from Abroad	**98.n**	-25	-27	52	20	-69	-98	-152	-257	-318	-293	-289	-248	-902	-1,488	-1,505
Gross National Income (GNI)	**99a**	1,414	1,693	2,211	2,620	2,632	2,862	3,598	4,037	4,455	5,014	5,578	6,745	8,456	10,186	13,584
GDP Volume 1974 prices	**99b.*p***	2,231.3	2,293.4	2,159.0	2,143.8	2,009.5	1,961.8	1,976.0	1,940.0	1,828.8	1,875.5	1,898.7	1,942.2	1,925.0	1,836.1	1,867.2
GDP Volume 1986 Prices	**99b.*p***	....	....	....	....	....	....	....	....	....	....	....	....	....	....	15,089
GDP Volume (1995=100)	**99bv*p***	89.3	91.8	86.5	85.8	80.5	78.6	79.1	77.7	73.2	75.1	76.0	77.8	77.1	73.5	74.8
GDP Deflator (1995=100)	**99bi*p***	.8	.9	1.2	1.5	1.7	1.9	2.4	2.8	3.3	3.5	3.9	4.5	6.1	7.9	10.1
																Millions:
Population	**99z**	1.93	1.97	2.01	2.04	2.07	2.09	2.10	2.11	2.13	2.18	2.19	2.24	2.28	2.31	2.34

1987	1988	1989	1990	1991	1992	1993	1994	1995	1996	1997	1998	1999	2000	2001		
Percent Per Annum															**Interest Rates**	
21.00	21.00	21.00	21.00	....	....	....	....	....	....	....	....	....	....	....	Bank Rate *(End of Period)*	60
18.16	18.50	19.10	26.21	25.56	34.36	28.85	42.98	27.65	37.95	21.14	25.65	20.75	18.24	16.71	Treasury Bill Rate	60c
15.64	15.80	15.95	23.88	24.67	33.63	27.59	36.41	23.21	25.16	13.95	15.61	13.48	11.62	9.64	Deposit Rate	60l
25.45	25.19	25.22	30.50	31.51	44.81	43.71	49.46	43.58	39.83	32.86	31.59	27.01	23.35	20.61	Lending Rate	60p
20.83	20.40	20.17	25.46	26.33	30.50	24.82	26.82	26.85	26.87	26.85	....	....	....	....	Government Bond Yield	61
Period Averages															**Prices, Production, Labor**	
9.9	8.1	11.6	12.6	29.2	67.9	122.4	83.4	100.0	81.2	97.3	122.5	115.0	166.0	183.7	Industrial Share Prices	62
12.5	†13.5	15.5	18.9	28.5	50.6	61.7	83.4	100.0	126.4	138.6	150.6	159.5	172.6	184.6	Consumer Prices	64
80.2	80.1	93.0	100.0	....	....	....	....	....	....	....	....	....	....	....	Industrial Production	66
Period Averages																
....	....	....	1,060	....	....	....	....	....	....	....	1,129	....	....	....	Labor Force	67d
845	872	881	896	908	906	906	923	963	960	956	954	....	....	....	Employment	67e
224	203	177	167	169	169	177	167	187	183	187	175	....	....	....	Unemployment	67c
21.0	18.9	16.8	15.7	15.7	15.4	16.3	15.4	16.2	16.0	....	....	....	....	....	Unemployment Rate (%)	67r
Millions of Jamaica Dollars															**International Transactions**	
3,874	4,830	5,747	8,305	13,079	24,099	26,421	40,121	49,916	51,513	48,971	47,940	48,425	55,289	56,298	Exports	70
6,791	7,983	10,668	13,923	20,830	38,267	53,737	73,631	99,418	109,687	110,932	110,926	113,472	137,308	153,175	Imports, c.i.f.	71
1995=100																
58.7	62.5	78.0	98.3	103.1	99.0	99.3	106.9	100.0	110.1	112.3	115.3	116.5	116.6	115.7	Volume of Exports	72
															Balance of Payments	
Minus Sign Indicates Debit																
–125.7	46.6	–282.6	–312.1	–240.1	28.5	–184.0	81.6	–98.7	–142.6	–332.2	–327.8	–211.4	–274.6	....	Current Account, n.i.e.	78al*d*
725.2	898.4	1,028.9	1,190.6	1,196.7	1,116.5	1,105.4	1,548.0	1,796.0	1,721.0	1,700.3	1,613.4	1,499.1	1,554.6	....	Goods: Exports f.o.b.	78aa*d*
–1,077.3	–1,255.3	–1,618.7	–1,692.7	–1,588.3	–1,541.1	–1,920.5	–2,099.2	–2,625.3	–2,715.2	–2,832.6	–2,743.9	–2,685.6	–2,908.1	....	Goods: Imports f.o.b.	78ab*d*
–352.1	–356.9	–589.8	–502.1	–391.6	–424.6	–815.1	–551.2	–829.3	–994.2	–1,132.3	–1,130.5	–1,186.5	–1,353.5	....	*Trade Balance*	78ac*d*
837.5	785.3	876.1	1,026.5	992.1	1,104.0	1,260.7	1,480.2	1,597.9	1,601.9	1,698.9	1,770.4	1,978.4	2,025.8	....	Services: Credit	78ad*d*
–455.0	–567.6	–720.8	–697.4	–670.3	–714.4	–823.5	–955.3	–1,103.6	–1,149.2	–1,231.7	–1,293.5	–1,323.0	–1,431.9	....	Services: Debit	78ae*d*
30.4	–139.2	–434.5	–173.0	–69.8	–35.0	–377.9	–26.3	–335.0	–541.5	–665.1	–653.6	–531.1	–759.6	....	*Balance on Goods & Services*	78af*d*
71.5	88.0	104.0	107.6	59.7	75.0	117.0	104.6	146.6	141.8	147.3	156.3	165.8	193.1	....	Income: Credit	78ag*d*
–414.8	–423.2	–454.1	–537.6	–498.5	–368.9	–312.9	–456.6	–517.3	–366.5	–439.2	–464.4	–498.3	–528.7	....	Income: Debit	78ah*d*
–312.9	–474.4	–784.6	–603.0	–508.6	–328.9	–573.8	–378.3	–705.7	–766.2	–957.0	–961.7	–863.6	–1,095.2	....	*Balance on Gds, Serv. & Inc.*	78ai*d*
217.7	587.8	523.8	314.9	294.8	387.2	415.9	504.2	669.6	709.3	705.7	733.5	762.8	969.2	....	Current Transfers, n.i.e.: Credit	78aj*d*
–30.5	–66.8	–21.8	–24.0	–26.3	–29.8	–26.1	–44.3	–62.6	–85.7	–80.9	–99.6	–110.6	–148.6	....	Current Transfers: Debit	78ak*d*
–16.5	–15.4	–15.0	–15.9	–15.7	–17.6	–12.9	10.4	10.5	16.6	–11.6	–8.7	–10.9	2.2	....	Capital Account, n.i.e.	78bc*d*
—	—	—	—	—	—	—	33.2	34.5	42.5	21.7	20.3	19.1	29.6	....	Capital Account, n.i.e.: Credit	78ba*d*
–16.5	–15.4	–15.0	–15.9	–15.7	–17.6	–12.9	–22.8	–24.0	–25.9	–33.3	–29.0	–30.0	–27.4	....	Capital Account: Debit	78bb*d*
357.5	92.8	115.8	428.2	254.9	297.3	257.1	256.1	108.4	388.6	163.5	337.2	94.8	841.7	....	Financial Account, n.i.e.	78bj*d*
—	—	—	—	—	—	—	–52.7	–66.3	–93.3	–56.6	–82.0	–94.9	–74.3	....	Direct Investment Abroad	78bd*d*
53.4	–12.0	57.1	137.9	133.2	142.4	77.9	129.7	147.4	183.7	203.3	369.1	523.7	456.0	....	Dir. Invest. in Rep. Econ., n.i.e.	78be*d*
—	—	—	—	—	—	—	—	—	—	—	–3.9	–3.7	–70.0	....	Portfolio Investment Assets	78bf*d*
—	—	—	—	—	—	—	....	....	....	....	....	—	—	....	Equity Securities	78bk*d*
—	—	—	—	—	—	—	—	—	—	—	–3.9	–3.7	–70.0	....	Debt Securities	78bl*d*
—	—	—	—	—	—	—	—	—	—	5.7	10.9	8.6	5.9	....	Portfolio Investment Liab., n.i.e.	78bg*d*
—	—	—	—	—	—	—	....	....	....	....	....	—	—	....	Equity Securities	78bm*d*
—	—	—	—	—	—	—	—	—	—	5.7	10.9	8.6	5.9	....	Debt Securities	78bn*d*
....	....	....	....	....	....	....	....	....	....	....	....	—	—	....	Financial Derivatives Assets	78bw*d*
....	....	....	....	....	....	....	....	....	....	....	....	—	—	....	Financial Derivatives Liabilities	78bx*d*
1.6	1.3	12.0	–2.5	105.7	10.2	1.1	–141.3	–148.8	–13.8	–113.2	–59.1	–122.7	–94.9	....	Other Investment Assets	78bh*d*
....	....	....	....	....	....	....	—	—	—	—	—	—	—	....	Monetary Authorities	78bo*d*
–5.5	–22.9	–6.1	–7.4	–8.0	–1.0	–1.4	—	—	—	—	—	—	—	....	General Government	78bp*d*
7.1	24.2	18.1	4.9	113.7	11.2	2.5	–177.9	–199.2	–88.1	–166.1	–142.3	–215.1	–181.5	....	Banks	78bq*d*
—	—	—	—	—	—	—	36.6	50.4	74.3	52.9	83.2	92.4	86.6	....	Other Sectors	78br*d*
302.5	103.5	46.7	292.8	16.0	144.7	178.1	320.4	176.1	312.0	124.3	102.2	–216.2	619.0	....	Other Investment Liab., n.i.e.	78bi*d*
15.3	1.9	–1.3	.5	–55.3	–50.8	–35.9	—	—	—	—	—	—	—	....	Monetary Authorities	78bs*d*
198.4	61.3	216.8	94.7	94.9	–10.0	37.8	–127.4	–97.0	–144.7	43.1	–41.3	–331.4	383.6	....	General Government	78bt*d*
–3.4	–28.8	–19.9	–21.7	–151.3	–46.4	–6.0	142.2	74.7	130.7	156.7	205.5	122.2	167.9	....	Banks	78bu*d*
92.2	69.1	–148.9	219.3	127.7	251.9	182.2	305.6	198.4	326.0	–75.5	–62.0	–7.0	67.5	....	Other Sectors	78bv*d*
84.6	–46.0	10.0	29.3	–20.4	–59.9	49.7	9.6	6.8	8.8	9.9	43.2	–8.9	–50.9	....	Net Errors and Omissions	78ca*d*
299.9	78.0	–171.8	129.5	–21.3	248.3	109.9	357.7	27.0	271.4	–170.4	43.9	–136.4	518.4	....	*Overall Balance*	78cb*d*
–299.9	–78.0	171.8	–129.5	21.3	–248.3	–109.9	–357.7	–27.0	–271.4	170.4	–43.9	136.4	–518.4	....	Reserves and Related Items	79da*d*
–69.3	25.2	39.9	–65.3	52.9	–192.2	–92.9	–321.0	55.8	–201.7	205.0	–26.9	155.3	–499.4	....	Reserve Assets	79db*d*
–96.5	–160.2	–86.0	–53.2	32.6	–19.4	–21.3	–38.2	–84.6	–71.9	–34.6	–17.0	–18.9	–19.0	....	Use of Fund Credit and Loans	79dc*d*
–134.1	57.0	217.9	–11.1	–64.2	–36.7	4.4	1.5	1.9	2.2	—	—	—	—	....	Exceptional Financing	79de*d*
Year Ending December 31															**Government Finance**	
....	....	....	....	....	....	....	....	....	....	....	....	....	....	....	Deficit (-) or Surplus	80
....	....	....	....	....	....	....	....	....	....	....	....	....	....	....	Revenue	81
....	....	....	....	....	....	....	....	....	....	....	....	....	....	....	Grants Received	81z
....	....	....	....	....	....	....	....	....	....	....	....	....	....	....	Expenditure	82
....	....	....	....	....	....	....	....	....	....	....	....	....	....	....	Lending Minus Repayments	83
....	....	....	....	....	....	....	....	....	....	....	....	....	....	....	Debt: Domestic	88a
....	....	....	....	....	....	....	....	....	....	....	....	....	....	....	Foreign	89a
Millions of Jamaica Dollars															**National Accounts**	
11,753	13,904	17,524	21,408	32,758	53,880	79,953	108,150	139,785	162,340	174,685	181,900	196,641	223,341	245,990	Househ.Cons.Expend.,incl.NPISHs	96f
2,497	3,018	3,270	4,301	5,772	7,587	13,876	16,469	22,635	32,476	40,134	46,752	48,633	53,570	55,710	Government Consumption Expend.	91f
3,545	4,865	6,538	8,362	11,825	23,953	33,781	43,499	57,901	70,022	76,494	72,660	73,531	90,338	107,118	Gross Fixed Capital Formation	93e
179	98	196	177	297	260	779	340	667	396	511	345	237	575	562	Changes in Inventories	93i
8,405	9,168	11,036	15,856	24,978	50,551	57,835	83,815	103,214	106,090	103,466	114,038	124,754	146,163	148,477	Exports of Goods and Services	90c
8,344	10,041	13,259	17,114	25,567	51,319	67,882	93,908	124,175	133,943	137,264	142,266	149,721	184,815	199,821	Imports of Goods and Services (-)	98c
18,035	21,012	25,305	32,990	50,062	84,913	118,342	158,365	200,027	237,382	258,026	273,429	294,076	329,171	358,036	Gross Domestic Product (GDP)	99b
–1,904	–1,879	–2,022	–3,122	–5,080	–6,843	–4,689	–7,952	–8,575	–4,852	–4,655	–9,847	–12,543	–14,060	–22,510	Net Primary Income from Abroad	98.n
16,131	19,133	23,283	29,868	44,982	78,070	113,653	150,413	191,452	232,530	253,371	263,583	281,533	315,111	335,526	Gross National Income (GNI)	99a
....	....	....	....	....	....	....	....	....	....	....	....	....	....	....	GDP Volume 1974 prices	99b.*p*
16,292	16,648	17,820	18,942	19,100	19,417	19,799	19,975	20,181	19,968	19,624	19,559	19,472	19,602	19,940	GDP Volume 1986 Prices	99b.*p*
80.7	82.5	88.3	93.9	94.6	96.2	98.1	99.0	100.0	98.9	97.2	96.9	96.5	97.1	98.8	GDP Volume (1995=100)	99bv*p*
11.2	12.7	14.3	17.6	26.4	44.1	60.3	80.0	100.0	119.9	132.7	141.0	152.4	169.4	181.2	GDP Deflator (1995=100)	99bi*p*
Midyear Estimates																
2.35	2.36	2.39	2.41	2.39	2.41	2.43	2.46	2.49	2.52	2.54	2.56	2.59	2.63	2.60	**Population**	99z

(See notes in the back of the book.)

Japan

	1972	1973	1974	1975	1976	1977	1978	1979	1980	1981	1982	1983	1984	1985	1986
Exchange Rates															*Yen per SDR:*
Market Rate .... aa	327.88	337.78	368.47	357.23	340.18	291.53	253.52	315.76	258.91	255.95	259.23	243.10	246.13	220.23	194.61
															Yen per US Dollar:
Market Rate .... ae	302.00	280.00	300.95	305.15	292.80	240.00	194.60	239.70	203.00	219.90	235.00	232.20	251.10	200.50	159.10
Market Rate .... rf	303.17	271.70	292.08	296.79	296.55	268.51	210.44	219.14	226.74	220.54	249.08	237.51	237.52	238.54	168.52
															Index Numbers (1995=100):
Market Rate .... ahx	30.8	34.5	32.0	31.5	31.5	34.9	44.8	42.8	41.4	42.5	37.7	39.4	39.4	39.5	55.8
Nominal Effective Exchange Rate... neu	32.6	34.7	32.4	31.4	32.7	36.1	44.3	41.1	39.5	44.2	41.4	41.4	47.8	48.8	62.4
Real Effective Exchange Rate........ reu	....	....	....	88.0	87.1	93.3	70.3	62.1	†55.6	59.5	52.5	55.7	56.8	56.1	70.7
Fund Position															*Millions of SDRs:*
Quota .... 2f. s	1,200	1,200	1,200	1,200	1,200	1,200	1,659	1,659	2,489	2,489	2,489	4,223	4,223	4,223	4,223
SDRs .... 1b. s	424	425	432	444	460	494	1,053	1,281	1,363	1,662	1,895	1,848	1,966	1,926	1,813
Reserve Position in the Fund .... 1c. s	571	529	603	686	1,143	1,329	1,642	1,121	1,044	1,339	1,878	2,199	2,264	2,071	1,947
of which: Outstg.Fund Borrowing........ 2c	—	—	—	—	—	339	369	236	381	641	825	839	793	663	487
International Liquidity														*Millions of US Dollars Unless Otherwise Indicated:*	
Total Reserves minus Gold 1l.d	17,564	11,355	12,614	11,950	15,746	22,341	32,407	19,522	24,636	28,208	23,334	24,602	26,429	26,719	42,257
SDRs 1b.d	461	513	529	520	535	600	1,372	1,688	1,738	1,934	2,091	1,935	1,927	2,116	2,218
Reserve Position in the Fund 1c.d	620	639	739	804	1,329	1,615	2,139	1,477	1,331	1,558	2,071	2,303	2,219	2,275	2,382
Foreign Exchange 1d.d	16,483	10,203	11,347	10,627	13,883	20,126	28,896	16,357	21,567	24,716	19,172	20,364	22,283	22,328	37,657
Gold (Million Fine Troy Ounces) 1ad	21.10	21.11	21.11	21.11	21.11	21.62	23.97	24.23	24.23	24.23	24.23	24.23	24.23	24.23	24.23
Gold (National Valuation)............... 1and	802	891	905	865	858	919	1,093	1,117	1,082	987	935	888	831	931	1,037
Deposit Money Banks: Assets 7a.d	8,864	†17,110	20,610	20,360	21,647	21,694	33,691	45,435	65,666	84,607	90,949	109,063	126,921	194,620	345,327
Liabilities 7b.d	8,356	†13,620	24,950	26,690	29,037	28,581	39,013	50,485	80,209	100,391	100,018	106,645	127,046	179,306	345,987
Monetary Authorities															*Trillions of Yen:*
Foreign Assets (Net) 11	5.43	3.55	3.97	3.73	4.82	6.69	6.96	3.45	5.27	5.32	4.76	5.17	5.47	5.87	6.70
Claims on Central Government 12a	1.22	1.74	4.05	7.49	7.29	6.90	8.73	9.09	10.25	13.35	14.72	14.57	14.50	12.83	11.30
Claims on Deposit Money Banks 12e	2.79	6.24	5.80	4.03	4.38	5.15	5.42	5.46	5.25	2.24	3.43	5.97	5.35	9.01	10.62
Reserve Money 14	9.15	12.29	14.28	14.86	16.13	17.48	20.08	21.58	22.96	23.57	25.03	26.39	28.63	29.71	32.12
of which: Currency Outside DMBs ... 14a	7.71	9.11	10.73	11.58	12.86	14.12	16.26	17.05	17.48	18.58	19.78	20.58	22.11	23.41	26.20
Central Government Deposits 16d	.68	1.27	.93	.66	.76	1.01	1.42	1.88	.95	1.49	1.37	3.48	1.33	2.52	1.41
Other Items (Net) 17r	−.40	−2.03	−1.38	−.27	−.40	.24	†−.40	−5.46	−3.14	−4.15	−3.50	−4.16	−4.63	−4.52	−4.90
Deposit Money Banks															*Trillions of Yen:*
Reserves 20	1.45	3.18	3.55	3.28	3.28	3.36	3.82	4.53	5.48	4.99	5.26	5.81	6.51	6.30	5.92
Foreign Assets 21	2.73	3.08	4.03	3.99	4.40	4.45	5.00	6.17	10.93	12.83	14.24	17.09	17.92	25.33	36.02
Claims on Central Government 22a	2.61	1.99	1.50	3.84	8.53	12.50	18.49	20.08	20.24	21.27	22.05	25.08	26.12	27.91	31.12
Claims on Local Government 22b	2.16	2.78	3.99	4.79	5.27	6.59	8.20	9.65	10.33	11.22	10.89	10.56	10.45	10.51	10.47
Claims on Nonfin.Pub.Enterprises 22c	1.99	2.33	2.59	2.99	3.70	4.26	4.94	6.12	7.08	8.71	9.55	10.46	11.24	11.71	13.09
Claims on Private Sector 22d	87.24	103.25	116.12	130.04	145.04	157.78	173.74	187.49	203.02	221.84	241.72	262.70	287.37	318.50	348.73
Demand Deposits 24	26.82	31.20	34.22	38.37	43.32	46.66	52.67	53.97	52.10	57.93	61.12	60.23	64.26	65.57	72.02
Time Deposits 25	49.51	57.88	64.54	75.38	86.07	97.25	109.79	122.70	137.42	152.70	165.68	182.78	195.43	217.82	237.00
Certificates of Deposit 26aa								1.29	2.00	2.84	3.88	5.11	7.91	8.14	8.58
Bonds 26ab	6.12	7.22	8.45	10.89	13.51	15.26	17.28	18.69	20.19	22.03	24.40	27.72	31.26	33.69	37.82
Foreign Liabilities............... 26c	2.57	4.15	7.60	8.14	8.74	8.27	8.60	10.34	18.87	21.13	23.32	25.43	30.05	40.89	59.60
Credit from Monetary Authorities ... 26g	2.79	6.24	5.80	4.03	4.38	5.15	5.42	5.46	5.25	2.24	3.43	5.97	5.35	9.01	10.62
Other Items (Net) 27r	10.37	9.92	11.18	12.12	14.20	16.35	20.42	21.58	21.26	21.99	21.85	24.45	25.33	25.14	19.63
Monetary Survey															*Trillions of Yen:*
Foreign Assets (Net) 31n	5.59	2.49	.40	−.42	.48	2.86	3.36	−.72	−2.67	−2.99	−4.32	−3.18	−6.67	−9.70	−16.88
Domestic Credit 32	94.54	110.82	127.33	148.49	169.07	187.02	212.67	230.55	249.97	274.90	297.55	319.88	348.34	378.94	413.31
Claims on Central Govt. (Net) 32an	3.15	2.46	4.62	10.67	15.06	18.39	25.80	27.28	29.54	33.13	35.39	36.16	39.29	38.22	41.02
Claims on Local Government 32b	2.16	2.78	3.99	4.79	5.27	6.59	8.20	9.65	10.33	11.22	10.89	10.56	10.45	10.51	10.47
Claims on Nonfin.Pub.Enterprises..... 32c	1.99	2.33	2.59	2.99	3.70	4.26	4.94	6.12	7.08	8.71	9.55	10.46	11.24	11.71	13.09
Claims on Private Sector.............. 32d	87.24	103.25	116.12	130.04	145.04	157.78	173.74	187.49	203.02	221.84	241.72	262.70	287.37	318.50	348.73
Money 34	34.53	40.31	44.95	49.95	56.18	60.79	68.93	71.02	69.57	76.51	80.80	80.80	86.38	88.98	98.21
Quasi-Money 35	49.51	57.88	64.54	75.38	86.07	97.25	109.79	122.70	137.42	152.70	165.68	182.78	195.43	217.82	237.00
Certificates of Deposit 36aa								1.29	2.00	2.84	3.88	5.11	7.91	8.14	8.58
Bonds 36ab	6.12	7.22	8.45	10.89	13.51	15.26	17.28	18.69	20.19	22.03	24.40	27.72	31.26	33.69	37.82
Other Items (Net) 37r	9.98	7.89	9.79	11.85	13.80	16.59	†20.03	16.13	18.12	17.84	18.36	20.28	20.70	20.61	14.72
Money plus Quasi-Money 35l	84.04	98.19	109.49	125.33	142.25	158.03	178.72	193.72	206.99	229.21	246.58	263.59	281.81	306.80	335.31
Other Banking Institutions															*Trillions of Yen:*
Cash 40	5.43	5.35	6.93	8.40	9.66	12.06	15.17	16.60	16.46	18.20	20.40	24.06	28.32	31.82	40.35
Claims on Central Government 42a	5.59	5.72	5.68	7.24	10.05	15.55	20.73	25.52	32.09	36.51	44.59	53.03	60.71	71.90	83.82
Claims on Local Government 42b	5.59	7.31	9.23	11.44	14.39	16.90	19.78	23.54	27.44	31.15	35.65	39.59	43.55	46.78	49.80
Claims on Nonfin.Pub.Enterprises 42c	5.78	7.81	10.14	12.99	15.90	18.52	21.98	24.63	28.09	31.09	34.58	37.11	39.83	40.20	42.25
Claims on Private Sector 42d	28.82	36.72	43.52	50.90	59.02	65.64	71.19	80.99	91.32	100.67	110.84	118.62	125.01	132.22	143.79
Demand and Time Deposits 45a	36.47	45.16	54.01	65.92	78.68	93.24	108.75	124.52	141.38	159.59	177.56	195.66	211.15	229.72	250.76
Deposits with Trust Fund Bureau........ 46b	8.42	9.99	11.65	13.59	16.09	18.76	21.58	24.43	26.96	30.91	36.00	40.32	46.12	54.06	67.21
Insurance Reserves 47d	3.50	4.29	5.22	6.37	7.73	9.23	10.86	12.68	14.70	16.96	19.50	22.22	25.00	27.98	31.29
Other Items (Net) 47r	2.83	3.47	4.62	5.10	6.52	7.46	7.65	9.65	12.35	10.16	13.00	14.20	15.09	11.16	10.75
Nonbank Financial Institutions															*Trillions of Yen:*
Cash .... 40.. s	1.11	1.22	1.56	1.73	2.07	2.69	3.48	3.94	4.33	4.75	5.57	6.62	8.61	11.34	10.29
Claims on Central Government .... 42a. s	.05	.05	.03	.19	.44	.50	.88	1.02	1.00	1.34	1.76	2.64	3.09	3.86	5.20
Claims on Local Government .... 42b. s	.07	.08	.13	.20	.30	.49	.74	1.11	1.41	1.49	1.72	1.75	1.80	1.79	2.07
Claims on Nonfin.Pub.Enterprises ...... 42c. s	.60	.64	.72	.83	.95	1.20	1.46	1.65	1.75	1.93	2.37	2.79	3.17	3.46	4.07
Claims on Private Sector.............. 42d. s	8.63	10.41	12.05	13.97	15.95	17.72	19.01	20.99	24.50	27.60	30.03	32.11	34.30	37.04	39.77
Insurance and Pension Reserves .... 47d. s	9.44	10.96	12.82	15.01	17.52	20.13	23.04	26.57	30.56	35.04	40.13	45.67	52.22	60.69	73.50
Other Items (Net) .... 47r. s	1.01	1.43	1.67	1.92	2.17	2.47	2.53	2.14	2.43	2.06	1.31	.24	−1.24	−3.20	−12.11

1987	1988	1989	1990	1991	1992	1993	1994	1995	1996	1997	1998	1999	2000	2001		
End of Period															**Exchange Rates**	
175.20	169.36	188.52	191.21	179.09	171.53	153.63	145.61	152.86	166.80	175.34	162.77	140.27	149.70	165.64	Market Rate	aa
End of Period (ae)	*Period Average (rf)*															
123.50	125.85	143.45	134.40	125.20	124.75	111.85	99.74	102.83	116.00	129.95	115.60	102.20	114.90	131.80	Market Rate	ae
144.64	128.15	137.96	144.79	134.71	126.65	111.20	102.21	94.06	108.78	120.99	130.91	113.91	107.77	121.53	Market Rate	rf
Period Averages																
64.8	73.0	67.9	64.9	69.5	73.9	84.3	91.6	100.0	86.0	77.4	71.7	82.0	86.8	77.0	Market Rate	ahx
67.7	75.1	71.8	64.7	70.2	73.6	88.3	95.2	100.0	86.8	81.7	76.5	89.4	99.5	89.8	Nominal Effective Exchange Rate	neu
74.3	79.1	75.7	68.4	73.3	75.6	89.5	95.1	100.0	85.6	81.7	76.3	86.9	93.3	82.6	Real Effective Exchange Rate	reu
End of Period															**Fund Position**	
4,223	4,223	4,223	4,223	4,223	8,242	8,242	8,242	8,242	8,242	8,242	8,242	13,313	13,313	13,313	Quota	2f.s
1,736	2,182	1,862	2,138	1,803	795	1,123	1,427	1,821	1,837	1,955	1,891	1,935	1,870	1,892	SDRs	1b.s
2,011	2,436	2,677	4,197	5,398	6,284	6,015	5,912	5,449	4,639	6,777	6,813	4,774	4,032	4,019	Reserve Position in the Fund	1c.s
294	154	134	1,866	3,000	2,985	2,985	2,913	1,137	—	—	508	—	—	—	*of which:* Outstg. Fund Borrowing	2c
End of Period															**International Liquidity**	
80,973	96,728	83,957	78,501	72,059	71,623	98,524	125,860	183,250	216,648	219,648	215,471	286,916	354,902	395,155	Total Reserves minus Gold	1l.d
2,463	2,936	2,447	3,042	2,579	1,094	1,543	2,083	2,707	2,642	2,638	2,663	2,656	2,437	2,377	SDRs	1b.d
2,853	3,278	3,518	5,971	7,722	8,641	8,261	8,631	8,100	6,671	9,144	9,593	6,552	5,253	5,051	Reserve Position in the Fund	1c.d
75,657	90,514	77,992	69,487	61,758	61,888	88,720	115,146	172,443	207,335	207,866	203,215	277,708	347,212	387,727	Foreign Exchange	1d.d
24.23	24.23	24.23	24.23	24.23	24.23	24.23	24.23	24.23	24.23	24.23	24.23	24.23	24.55	24.60	Gold (Million Fine Troy Ounces)	1ad
1,203	1,141	1,114	1,206	1,213	1,166	1,165	1,238	1,260	1,219	1,144	1,194	1,164	1,119	1,082	Gold (National Valuation)	1and
576,828	733,688	842,055	950,578	942,431	879,191	918,559	1,007,605	1,217,867	1,123,529	....	....	....	....	....	Deposit Money Banks: Assets	7a.d
592,027	772,423	879,721	958,478	845,674	708,623	688,436	723,697	738,324	695,848	....	....	....	....	....	Liabilities	7b.d
End of Period															**Monetary Authorities**	
11.82	11.78	8.86	7.63	4.11	3.40	6.73	7.25	11.54	17.49	16.86	14.47	21.56	33.01	42.25	Foreign Assets (Net)	11
12.28	12.12	13.27	21.33	15.27	19.13	21.40	21.98	25.08	31.30	32.87	37.93	50.06	44.42	71.86	Claims on Central Government	12a
10.82	11.68	15.68	12.89	20.76	20.01	14.13	12.92	11.62	9.91	13.80	15.28	14.60	8.11	21.33	Claims on Deposit Money Banks	12e
34.92	39.46	44.57	47.86	47.19	45.40	48.03	49.44	53.32	57.84	62.09	64.34	89.62	73.27	85.96	Reserve Money	14
28.58	31.52	36.68	37.25	37.97	38.10	40.85	42.35	46.23	49.08	52.73	54.31	59.40	61.95	66.68	*of which:* Currency Outside DMBs	14a
6.07	5.03	2.25	2.02	3.14	5.61	1.97	5.03	5.85	7.64	3.79	7.65	8.08	14.29	13.93	Central Government Deposits	16d
−6.07	−8.92	−9.01	−8.03	−10.21	−8.47	−7.73	−12.31	−10.93	−6.77	−2.35	−4.31	−11.48	−2.03	35.54	Other Items (Net)	17r
End of Period															**Deposit Money Banks**	
6.34	7.94	7.89	10.61	9.22	7.29	7.18	7.09	7.09	8.75	9.36	10.03	30.22	11.33	19.28	Reserves	20
48.35	63.79	81.62	96.68	86.51	77.99	102.29	98.89	110.01	104.51	128.73	109.07	77.75	84.90	93.38	Foreign Assets	21
34.26	38.71	41.48	40.02	36.76	40.25	42.89	40.14	38.50	37.04	37.68	44.39	67.07	102.47	99.11	Claims on Central Government	22a
10.54	10.26	10.75	10.73	10.98	12.01	14.95	17.38	19.78	20.72	21.39	23.75	24.79	24.33	25.28	Claims on Local Government	22b
13.69	13.95	13.88	14.12	14.04	13.58	13.47	12.55	11.57	10.06	9.01	8.34	8.06	9.99	10.58	Claims on Nonfin.Pub.Enterprises	22c
387.70	430.13	480.17	524.38	552.11	564.98	558.67	559.81	569.20	575.88	578.79	583.35	570.91	559.44	539.03	Claims on Private Sector	22d
74.39	80.32	77.79	82.37	93.07	98.04	104.77	109.31	125.31	139.06	151.55	160.09	180.13	185.91	215.11	Demand Deposits	24
269.72	297.53	343.15	375.38	376.48	370.66	372.57	382.44	377.04	373.00	374.11	387.86	383.27	381.76	361.53	Time Deposits	25
8.17	10.36	12.40	9.96	8.82	8.69	8.65	7.32	10.22	14.16	19.10	19.23	15.21	20.24	28.34	Certificates of Deposit	26aa
39.94	44.14	47.43	55.30	61.86	65.89	64.39	63.90	62.22	62.10	53.56	43.31	43.13	38.28	33.47	Bonds	26ab
80.04	97.18	116.31	134.83	108.48	89.01	77.24	71.58	75.53	80.07	92.26	80.18	54.54	61.29	68.73	Foreign Liabilities	26c
10.82	11.68	15.68	12.89	20.76	20.01	14.13	12.92	11.62	9.91	13.80	15.28	14.60	8.11	21.33	Credit from Monetary Authorities	26g
17.79	23.56	23.02	25.81	40.15	63.81	97.69	88.38	94.19	78.67	80.58	76.65	89.14	103.36	70.98	Other Items (Net)	27r
End of Period															**Monetary Survey**	
−19.88	−21.61	−25.83	−30.52	−17.86	−7.62	31.78	34.56	46.01	41.94	53.33	43.36	44.77	56.61	66.90	Foreign Assets (Net)	31n
452.40	500.13	557.29	608.57	626.01	644.34	649.41	646.82	658.28	667.36	675.96	690.11	712.82	725.37	731.92	Domestic Credit	32
40.48	45.80	52.50	59.34	48.88	53.77	62.32	57.09	57.73	60.70	66.76	74.67	109.06	132.60	157.03	Claims on Central Govt. (Net)	32an
10.54	10.26	10.75	10.73	10.98	12.01	14.95	17.38	19.78	20.72	21.39	23.75	24.79	24.33	25.28	Claims on Local Government	32b
13.69	13.95	13.88	14.12	14.04	13.58	13.47	12.55	11.57	10.06	9.01	8.34	8.06	9.99	10.58	Claims on Nonfin.Pub.Enterprises	32c
387.70	430.13	480.17	524.38	552.11	564.98	558.67	559.81	569.20	575.88	578.79	583.35	570.91	559.44	539.03	Claims on Private Sector	32d
102.97	111.84	114.47	119.63	131.04	136.14	145.61	151.67	171.54	188.15	204.28	214.40	239.54	247.86	281.79	Money	34
269.72	297.53	343.15	375.38	376.48	370.66	372.57	382.44	377.04	373.00	374.11	387.86	383.27	381.76	361.53	Quasi-Money	35
8.17	10.36	12.40	9.96	8.82	8.69	8.65	7.32	10.22	14.16	19.10	19.23	15.21	20.24	28.34	Certificates of Deposit	36aa
39.94	44.14	47.43	55.30	61.86	65.89	64.39	63.90	62.22	62.10	53.56	43.31	43.13	38.28	33.47	Bonds	36ab
11.72	14.65	14.01	17.78	29.94	55.34	89.96	76.07	83.27	71.90	78.23	72.34	77.66	101.33	106.52	Other Items (Net)	37r
372.70	409.38	457.62	495.01	507.53	506.79	518.19	534.10	548.59	561.14	578.39	602.26	622.80	629.62	643.31	Money plus Quasi-Money	35l
End of Period															**Other Banking Institutions**	
46.95	53.30	55.14	56.73	65.19	76.47	82.85	76.56	82.47	87.21	84.43	....	....	....	....	Cash	40
90.68	94.40	97.70	93.59	103.51	111.09	117.65	126.45	142.11	151.55	170.24	....	....	....	....	Claims on Central Government	42a
53.19	57.44	60.41	62.97	66.01	69.31	74.34	82.91	89.40	100.50	110.58	....	....	....	....	Claims on Local Government	42b
29.35	29.79	31.52	33.43	36.62	39.17	43.44	47.27	50.76	54.46	57.78	....	....	....	....	Claims on Nonfin.Pub.Enterprises	42c
177.81	204.74	226.60	249.06	265.12	289.22	307.76	324.62	327.79	339.87	332.09	....	....	....	....	Claims on Private Sector	42d
269.78	289.98	317.64	336.54	371.75	401.74	430.84	456.40	479.69	502.71	531.44	....	....	....	....	Demand and Time Deposits	45a
84.22	98.50	116.38	124.10	129.05	138.86	147.58	153.18	150.65	155.69	153.94	....	....	....	....	Deposits with Trust Fund Bureau	46b
35.31	39.93	44.78	49.94	55.56	62.81	71.34	79.86	88.88	88.16	95.68	....	....	....	....	Insurance Reserves	47d
8.68	11.26	−7.43	−14.79	−19.91	−18.16	−23.73	−31.64	−26.70	−12.97	−25.93	....	....	....	....	Other Items (Net)	47r
End of Period															**Nonbank Financial Institutions**	
11.03	11.95	12.36	19.45	22.14	24.62	27.30	30.88	33.05	27.86	33.77	....	....	....	....	Cash	40..s
5.60	7.13	6.86	5.36	6.14	10.39	14.86	20.86	29.58	29.72	31.36	....	....	....	....	Claims on Central Government	42a.s
2.35	2.02	1.89	2.08	2.09	2.19	2.98	4.44	6.78	7.90	8.79	....	....	....	....	Claims on Local Government	42b.s
3.38	2.56	2.78	3.30	3.42	4.38	3.62	4.42	4.44	4.83	5.20	....	....	....	....	Claims on Nonfin.Pub.Enterprises	42c.s
48.89	60.06	73.60	89.13	100.04	105.59	111.33	114.86	112.66	120.58	108.74	....	....	....	....	Claims on Private Sector	42d.s
87.58	106.50	126.94	144.16	157.62	171.50	186.38	199.49	210.48	226.01	230.02	....	....	....	....	Insurance and Pension Reserves	47d.s
−16.34	−22.78	−29.45	−24.85	−23.79	−24.34	−26.30	−24.04	−23.99	−35.12	−42.17	....	....	....	....	Other Items (Net)	47r.s

Japan

		1972	1973	1974	1975	1976	1977	1978	1979	1980	1981	1982	1983	1984	1985	1986
Financial Survey															*Trillions of Yen:*	
Foreign Assets (Net)	51n	5.59	2.49	.40	–.42	.48	2.86	3.36	–.72	–2.67	–2.99	–4.32	–3.18	–6.67	–9.70	–16.88
Domestic Credit	52	149.67	179.55	208.83	246.25	286.06	323.54	368.43	409.99	457.56	506.68	559.08	607.51	659.80	716.19	784.07
Claims on Central Govt. (Net)	52an	8.79	8.23	10.33	18.10	25.55	34.44	47.41	53.82	62.63	70.98	81.74	91.82	103.10	113.98	130.04
Claims on Local Government	52b	7.82	10.17	13.36	16.43	19.96	23.98	28.71	34.29	39.18	43.87	48.25	51.90	55.80	59.08	62.34
Claims on Nonfin.Pub.Enterprises	52c	8.37	10.77	13.46	16.81	20.55	23.98	28.37	32.40	36.92	41.73	46.50	50.36	54.23	55.37	59.41
Claims on Private Sector	52d	124.69	150.37	171.69	194.91	220.01	241.14	263.94	289.48	318.83	350.10	382.59	413.43	446.67	487.77	532.28
Liquid Liabilities	55l	115.73	139.02	158.67	185.19	213.63	242.07	275.57	306.50	337.43	376.89	411.56	443.74	477.58	519.33	567.36
Bonds	56ab	6.12	7.22	8.45	10.89	13.51	15.26	17.28	18.69	20.19	22.03	24.40	27.72	31.26	33.69	37.82
Deposits with Fiscal Loan Fund	56b	8.42	9.99	11.65	13.59	16.09	18.76	21.58	24.43	26.96	30.91	36.00	40.32	46.12	54.06	67.21
Insurance and Pension Reserves	57d	12.93	15.25	18.04	21.38	25.24	29.35	33.90	39.25	45.26	52.00	59.63	67.89	77.22	88.66	104.79
Other Items (Net)	57r	12.06	10.55	12.44	14.79	18.07	20.97	23.46	20.41	25.06	21.86	23.16	24.65	20.91	10.75	–9.99
Interest Rates															*Percent Per Annum*	
Discount Rate (End of Period)	60	4.25	9.00	9.00	6.50	6.50	4.25	3.50	6.25	7.25	5.50	5.50	5.00	5.00	5.00	3.00
Money Market Rate	60b	4.72	7.16	12.54	10.67	6.98	5.68	4.36	5.86	10.93	7.43	6.94	6.39	6.10	6.46	4.79
Private Bill Rate	60bs	....	....	....	....	....	....	....	....	....	7.69	7.12	6.72	6.32	6.70	4.99
Deposit Rate	60l	3.88	4.00	5.33	5.33	4.50	3.83	2.69	3.31	5.50	4.44	3.75	3.75	3.50	3.50	2.32
Lending Rate	60p	7.05	7.19	9.11	9.10	8.26	7.56	6.42	6.37	8.35	7.86	7.31	7.13	6.75	6.60	6.02
Government Bond Yield	61	6.70	7.26	9.26	9.20	8.72	7.33	6.09	7.69	9.22	8.66	8.06	7.42	6.81	6.34	4.94
Prices, Production, Labor														*Index Numbers (1995=100):*		
Share Prices	62	20.5	26.3	22.3	22.6	25.2	27.3	30.1	32.6	34.3	39.9	39.8	46.9	59.1	72.2	95.9
Wholesale Prices	63	54.9	63.5	81.0	83.3	87.8	90.8	90.3	94.8	109.0	110.5	111.0	110.3	110.4	109.6	104.4
Consumer Prices	64	36.0	40.2	49.5	55.4	60.6	65.5	68.3	70.8	76.3	80.1	82.2	83.8	85.7	87.4	88.0
Wages: Monthly Earnings	65	24.4	29.0	36.2	42.7	48.0	52.5	56.2	59.4	62.9	66.1	69.4	71.6	74.0	76.4	78.6
Industrial Production	66..c	52.5	60.4	58.1	51.6	57.3	59.7	63.5	68.2	71.4	72.1	72.4	74.5	81.5	84.6	84.4
Manufacturing Employment	67ey c	102.8	103.1	102.7	97.3	95.3	94.5	92.4	91.9	†92.9	93.8	94.3	94.0	95.1	†96.6	97.2
															Number in Thousands:	
Labor Force	67d	....	....	....	....	....	....	....	....	....	....	....	....	....		
Employment	67e	....	....	....	....	....	....	....	....	....	....	....	....	....	58,070	58,530
Unemployment	67c	....	....	....	....	....	....	....	....	....	....	....	....	....	1,560	1,670
Unemployment Rate (%)	67r	....	....	....	....	....	....	....	....	....	....	....	....	....	2.6	2.8
International Transactions															*Billions of Yen*	
Exports	70	8,806	10,031	16,220	16,572	19,930	21,648	20,526	22,532	29,382	33,469	34,433	34,910	40,325	41,959	35,291
Imports, c.i.f.	71	7,229	10,404	18,067	17,176	19,229	19,132	16,728	24,245	31,995	31,464	32,656	30,015	32,320	31,076	21,551
															1995=100	
Volume of Exports	72	28.2	30.2	36.4	36.3	44.0	47.7	48.0	48.1	56.4	62.3	60.9	†66.2	76.7	80.9	80.5
Volume of Imports	73	29.0	37.8	37.5	33.0	35.9	36.8	39.3	43.7	41.5	40.6	40.4	†40.9	45.2	45.6	50.0
Unit Value of Exports	74	74.7	79.3	106.5	109.0	108.3	108.6	102.5	111.9	124.7	128.4	135.1	†126.0	125.8	124.9	105.7
Unit Value of Imports	75	78.6	86.8	151.9	164.2	168.1	163.0	133.8	174.1	241.9	243.1	253.7	230.3	224.0	†216.0	136.7
Export Prices	76	101.1	111.4	149.1	143.1	142.1	135.4	126.4	140.2	152.2	154.0	160.0	150.5	151.4	149.2	†126.7
Import Prices	76.x	65.0	78.9	132.3	142.0	149.4	142.6	117.6	151.4	219.1	222.7	240.2	221.5	214.0	208.7	†133.9
Balance of Payments															*Billions of US Dollars:*	
Current Account, n.i.e.	78al d	....	....	....	....	....	10.91	16.53	–8.74	–10.75	4.77	6.85	20.80	35.00	51.13	85.88
Goods: Exports f.o.b.	78aa d	....	....	....	....	....	79.16	95.32	101.12	126.74	149.52	137.66	145.47	168.29	175.46	206.42
Goods: Imports f.o.b.	78ab d						–62.00	–71.02	–99.38	–124.61	–129.56	–119.58	–114.01	–124.03	–120.17	–115.23
Trade Balance	78ac d						17.16	24.30	1.74	2.13	19.96	18.08	31.46	44.26	55.29	91.19
Services: Credit	78ad d						11.77	13.55	16.01	20.24	23.83	22.56	21.81	23.12	21.65	23.25
Services: Debit	78ae d						–17.68	–21.51	–27.35	–32.36	–36.59	–34.01	–33.86	–35.02	–31.25	–36.22
Balance on Goods & Services	78af d						11.25	16.34	–9.60	–9.99	7.20	6.63	19.41	32.36	45.69	78.22
Income: Credit	78ag d						3.82	5.41	9.13	11.25	15.95	18.53	15.78	18.98	22.31	29.26
Income: Debit	78ah d						–3.76	–4.54	–7.15	–10.48	–16.76	–16.93	–12.84	–14.83	–15.57	–19.93
Balance on Gds, Serv. & Inc.	78ai d						11.31	17.21	–7.62	–9.22	6.39	8.23	22.35	36.51	52.43	87.55
Current Transfers, n.i.e.: Credit	78aj d						.26	.30	.37	.39	.44	.47	.48	.56	.58	.56
Current Transfers: Debit	78ak d						–.66	–.98	–1.49	–1.92	–2.06	–1.85	–2.03	–2.07	–1.88	–2.24
Capital Account, n.i.e.	78bc d						—	—	—	—	—	—	—	—	–.42	–.49
Capital Account, n.i.e.: Credit	78ba d						—	—	—	—	—	—	—	—	—	—
Capital Account: Debit	78bb d						—	—	—	—	—	—	—	—	–.42	–.49
Financial Account, n.i.e.	78bj d						–4.96	–6.70	–6.82	18.88	–1.56	–16.20	–21.32	–36.57	–55.20	–72.89
Direct Investment Abroad	78bd d						–1.65	–2.37	–2.90	–2.39	–4.90	–4.54	–3.61	–5.96	–6.49	–14.67
Dir. Invest. in Rep. Econ., n.i.e.	78be d						.02	.01	.24	.28	.19	.44	.41	–.01	.64	.23
Portfolio Investment Assets	78bf d						–1.72	–5.30	–5.87	–3.75	–8.77	–9.74	–16.02	–30.63	–60.68	–105.60
Equity Securities	78bk d						–.01	–.12	–.58	.21	–.24	–.15	–.66	–1.00	–1.00	–7.07
Debt Securities	78bl d						–1.71	–5.18	–5.29	–3.96	–8.53	–9.59	–15.36	–30.58	–59.68	–98.54
Portfolio Investment Liab., n.i.e.	78bg d						2.36	2.49	4.28	13.11	13.22	11.86	14.15	7.03	17.99	1.69
Equity Securities	78bm d						–.78	–.81	.33	6.55	5.92	2.55	6.13	–3.61	–.67	–15.71
Debt Securities	78bn d						3.14	3.30	3.95	6.56	7.30	9.31	8.02	10.64	18.66	17.39
Financial Derivatives Assets	78bw d															
Financial Derivatives Liabilities	78bx d															
Other Investment Assets	78bh d						–2.13	–13.65	–16.18	–20.14	–25.53	–14.64	–24.41	–29.33	—	—
Monetary Authorities	78bo d															
General Government	78bp d						–1.78	–2.78	–2.71	–2.70	–3.66	–3.52	–3.61	–3.42		
Banks	78bq d						1.41	–9.88	–12.44	–16.05	–17.46	–4.69	–15.64	–14.48		
Other Sectors	78br d						–1.76	–.99	–1.03	–1.39	–4.41	–6.43	–5.16	–11.43		
Other Investment Liab., n.i.e.	78bi d						–1.84	12.12	13.61	31.77	24.23	.42	8.16	22.33	–6.68	45.47
Monetary Authorities	78bs d						.74	2.12	–.23	1.02	–.24	.21	.31	.79	—	—
General Government	78bt d						–.04	–.03	–1.04	–.04	–.04	–.03	–.03	–.02		
Banks	78bu d						–1.50	8.40	12.13	28.81	22.18	1.34	7.90	23.33		
Other Sectors	78bv d						–1.04	1.63	2.75	1.98	2.33	–1.10	–.02	–1.77		
Net Errors and Omissions	78ca d						.54	.13	2.42	–3.10	.43	4.65	2.07	3.69	4.02	2.62
Overall Balance	78cb d						6.49	9.96	–13.14	5.03	3.64	–4.70	1.55	2.12	–.50	15.13
Reserves and Related Items	79da d						–6.49	–9.96	13.14	–5.03	–3.64	4.70	–1.55	–2.12	.50	–15.12
Reserve Assets	79db d						–6.49	–9.96	13.14	–5.03	–3.64	4.70	–1.55	–2.12	.50	–15.12
Use of Fund Credit and Loans	79dc d															
Exceptional Financing	79de d	....	....	....	....	....	....	....	....	....	....	....	....	....	....	....

1987	1988	1989	1990	1991	1992	1993	1994	1995	1996	1997	1998	1999	2000	2001		
End of Period															**Financial Survey**	
-19.88	-21.61	-25.83	-30.52	-17.86	-7.62	31.78	34.56	46.01	41.94	†90.22	109.48	103.15	110.55	127.28	Foreign Assets (Net)	51n
863.64	958.27	1,058.65	1,147.49	1,208.95	1,275.67	1,325.38	1,372.64	1,421.79	1,476.78	†1525.56	1,553.71	1,634.71	1,619.82	1,597.88	Domestic Credit	52
136.75	147.33	157.06	158.29	158.53	175.25	194.82	204.40	229.42	241.97	†289.14	321.51	367.44	399.01	412.04	Claims on Central Govt. (Net)	52an
66.08	69.73	73.04	75.78	79.08	83.51	92.27	104.72	115.95	129.13	†100.84	108.20	115.24	119.46	124.40	Claims on Local Government	52b
46.41	46.29	48.18	50.85	54.08	57.12	60.53	64.24	66.77	69.35	†134.05	116.74	119.13	121.86	121.55	Claims on Nonfin.Pub.Enterprises	52c
614.40	694.93	780.37	862.57	917.27	959.79	977.75	999.29	1,009.65	1,036.33	†1001.53	1,007.26	1,032.90	979.49	939.90	Claims on Private Sector	52d
619.43	675.85	756.28	806.12	847.89	868.82	900.42	945.09	976.19	1,019.37	†920.38	954.89	983.93	990.60	1,003.92	Liquid Liabilities	55l
39.94	44.14	47.43	55.30	61.86	65.89	64.39	63.90	62.22	62.10	†121.60	117.64	123.10	118.63	113.41	Bonds	56ab
84.22	98.50	116.38	124.10	129.05	138.86	147.58	153.18	150.65	155.69	†147.35	152.85	156.60	159.19	147.35	Deposits with Fiscal Loan Fund	56b
122.89	146.43	171.72	194.10	213.18	234.31	257.73	279.35	299.37	314.17	†360.26	372.72	385.72	398.25	408.05	Insurance and Pension Reserves	57d
-22.70	-28.26	-58.99	-62.65	-60.89	-39.84	-12.96	-34.33	-20.64	-32.62	†66.19	65.10	88.51	63.70	43.70	Other Items (Net)	57r
Percent Per Annum															**Interest Rates**	
2.50	2.50	4.25	6.00	4.50	3.25	1.75	1.75	.50	.50	.50	.50	.50	.50	.10	Discount Rate *(End of Period)*	60
3.51	3.62	4.87	†7.24	7.46	4.58	†3.06	2.20	1.21	.47	.48	.37	.06	.11	.06	Money Market Rate	60b
3.88	4.08	5.37	7.67	†7.31	4.40	2.97	2.24	1.22	.59	.62	.72	.15	.23	....	Private Bill Rate	60bs
1.76	1.76	1.97	3.56	†4.14	†3.35	2.14	1.70	.90	.30	.30	.27	.12	.07	.06	Deposit Rate	60l
5.21	5.03	5.29	6.95	7.53	6.15	†4.41	4.13	3.51	2.66	2.45	2.32	2.16	2.07	1.97	Lending Rate	60p
4.21	4.27	5.05	7.36	6.53	4.94	3.69	3.71	2.53	2.23	1.69	1.10	†1.77	1.75	1.33	Government Bond Yield	61
Period Averages															**Prices, Production, Labor**	
141.8	154.4	186.1	158.0	133.4	98.8	110.4	115.8	100.0	116.3	101.0	85.4	100.4	112.0	86.5	Share Prices	62
101.2	100.6	102.5	104.1	105.1	104.2	102.6	100.8	100.0	98.4	99.0	97.5	96.0	96.1	95.3	Wholesale Prices	63
88.1	88.7	90.7	93.5	96.5	98.2	99.4	100.1	100.0	100.1	101.9	102.5	102.2	101.5	100.8	Consumer Prices	64
80.2	83.0	85.6	88.9	91.9	93.9	95.7	97.9	100.0	101.9	103.4	103.1	103.6	104.6	104.7	Wages: Monthly Earnings	65
87.2	95.6	101.2	105.3	107.2	100.6	96.1	96.7	100.0	102.9	†107.3	99.7	100.1	106.4	98.2	Industrial Production	66..c
95.9	96.9	99.1	101.7	104.2	104.9	104.2	101.8	100.0	97.7	96.9	95.6	93.1	90.9	88.5	Manufacturing Employment	67ey c
Period Averages																
....	....	....	....	65,050	65,780	66,150	66,450	66,660	67,110	67,870	67,930	67,790	67,660	67,520	Labor Force	67d
59,110	60,110	61,280	62,490	63,690	64,360	64,500	64,530	64,570	64,860	65,570	65,140	64,623	64,464	64,120	Employment	67e
1,730	1,550	1,420	1,340	1,360	1,420	1,656	1,920	2,098	2,250	2,303	2,787	3,171	3,198	3,395	Unemployment	67c
2.8	2.5	2.3	2.1	2.1	2.2	2.5	2.9	3.2	3.4	3.4	4.1	4.7	4.7	5.0	Unemployment Rate (%)	67r
Billions of Yen															**International Transactions**	
33,316	33,928	37,823	41,457	42,359	43,011	40,200	40,470	41,532	44,729	50,938	50,644	47,549	51,649	49,010	Exports	70
21,739	24,007	28,981	33,854	31,900	29,527	26,824	28,051	31,534	37,992	40,956	36,653	35,270	40,915	42,402	Imports, c.i.f.	71
1995=100																
†80.7	85.5	89.2	93.8	96.2	97.6	95.2	96.9	100.0	100.6	†110.2	108.7	111.1	121.5	109.1	Volume of Exports	72
†54.6	64.4	69.5	73.4	76.4	76.1	78.2	88.9	100.0	103.4	†106.2	100.5	110.2	122.2	120.6	Volume of Imports	73
†99.3	95.6	102.2	106.3	106.0	106.0	101.6	100.7	100.0	107.0	†111.3	112.1	103.1	102.3	108.0	Unit Value of Exports	74
†126.1	118.2	132.3	146.2	132.4	123.1	108.9	100.3	100.0	116.4	†122.3	115.6	101.5	106.1	111.5	Unit Value of Imports	75
120.3	117.6	122.7	125.3	118.6	114.3	105.2	102.2	†100.0	104.8	106.7	108.2	97.2	92.7	96.1	Export Prices	76
123.0	117.4	126.1	137.1	125.9	118.2	105.9	100.1	†100.0	109.7	117.9	112.1	101.7	106.4	112.9	Import Prices	76.x
Minus Sign Indicates Debit															Balance of Payments	
84.35	79.25	63.21	44.08	68.20	112.57	131.64	130.26	111.04	65.88	94.35	120.70	106.87	116.88	89.28	Current Account, n.i.e.	78ald
225.51	260.88	270.99	282.31	308.17	332.56	352.66	385.70	428.72	400.28	409.24	374.04	403.69	459.51	383.59	Goods: Exports f.o.b.	78aad
-133.93	-168.64	-190.87	-213.02	-212.08	-207.79	-213.24	-241.51	-296.93	-316.72	-307.64	-251.66	-280.37	-342.80	-313.38	Goods: Imports f.o.b.	78abd
91.58	92.24	80.12	69.28	96.08	124.76	139.42	144.19	131.79	83.56	101.60	122.39	123.32	116.72	70.21	*Trade Balance*	78acd
28.94	35.37	40.26	41.38	44.84	49.07	53.22	58.30	65.27	67.72	69.30	62.41	61.00	69.24	64.52	Services: Credit	78add
-49.33	-65.62	-76.96	-84.28	-86.63	-93.03	-96.30	-106.36	-122.63	-129.96	-123.45	-111.83	-115.16	-116.86	-108.25	Services: Debit	78aed
71.19	61.99	43.42	26.39	54.29	80.80	96.33	96.13	74.43	21.32	47.45	72.97	69.16	69.09	26.48	*Balance on Goods & Services*	78afd
49.41	75.11	102.23	122.64	140.93	142.87	147.83	155.19	192.45	225.10	222.15	209.58	188.27	206.94	190.82	Income: Credit	78agd
-33.07	-54.49	-79.27	-100.15	-114.97	-107.27	-107.42	-114.96	-148.16	-171.55	-166.41	-153.01	-138.43	-149.31	-120.12	Income: Debit	78ahd
87.53	82.61	66.39	48.88	80.24	116.41	136.74	136.36	118.72	74.88	103.19	129.54	119.00	126.71	97.18	*Balance on Gds, Serv. & Inc.*	78aid
.82	1.36	1.30	1.29	1.42	1.67	1.58	1.83	1.98	6.04	6.01	5.53	6.21	7.38	6.15	Current Transfers, n.i.e.: Credit	78ajd
-4.00	-4.73	-4.47	-6.09	-13.46	-5.50	-6.68	-7.94	-9.66	-15.04	-14.84	-14.37	-18.35	-17.21	-14.06	Current Transfers: Debit	78akd
-.77	-1.01	-1.39	-1.06	-1.20	-1.30	-1.46	-1.85	-2.23	-3.29	-4.05	-14.45	-16.47	-9.26	-2.87	Capital Account, n.i.e.	78bcd
—	—	—	—	—	—	—	—	.01	1.22	1.51	1.57	.75	.78	.99	Capital Account, n.i.e.: Credit	78bad
-.77	-1.01	-1.39	-1.06	-1.20	-1.30	-1.46	-1.85	-2.24	-4.51	-5.57	-16.02	-17.21	-10.04	-3.86	Capital Account: Debit	78bbd
-41.36	-64.36	-53.31	-30.71	-67.66	-100.28	-102.21	-85.11	-63.98	-28.10	-118.05	-116.76	-31.11	-75.54	-49.65	Financial Account, n.i.e.	78bjd
-20.30	-35.46	-46.02	-50.50	-31.62	-17.39	-13.83	-18.09	-22.51	-23.44	-26.06	-24.62	-22.27	-31.53	-38.50	Direct Investment Abroad	78bdd
1.16	-.48	-1.04	1.78	1.29	2.76	.12	.91	.04	.20	3.20	3.27	12.31	8.23	6.19	Dir. Invest. in Rep. Econ., n.i.e.	78bed
-95.74	-98.17	-114.21	-37.80	-81.63	-33.95	-63.74	-91.97	-86.05	-100.62	-47.06	-95.24	-154.41	-83.36	-106.79	Portfolio Investment Assets	78bfd
-16.95	-2.98	-17.96	-6.24	-3.63	2.98	-15.28	-14.00	.07	-8.18	-13.73	-14.00	-32.40	-19.72	-11.28	Equity Securities	78bkd
-78.80	-95.19	-96.25	-31.56	-78.00	-36.93	-48.46	-77.97	-86.11	-92.44	-33.34	-81.24	-122.01	-63.64	-95.51	Debt Securities	78bld
-11.38	21.81	97.00	46.68	127.34	9.57	-6.11	64.53	59.79	66.81	79.19	56.06	126.93	47.39	60.50	Portfolio Investment Liab., n.i.e.	78bgd
-43.55	6.82	6.95	-13.36	46.62	8.88	19.86	48.95	50.60	49.46	27.00	16.11	103.89	-1.29	39.10	Equity Securities	78bmd
32.18	14.99	90.06	60.04	80.72	.70	-25.97	15.58	9.19	17.35	52.19	39.95	23.04	48.67	21.40	Debt Securities	78bnd
....	....	....	....	-.03	-.61	-.49	.43	-1.20	-13.96	-24.16	-18.49	-12.43	-3.00	15.06	Financial Derivatives Assets	78bwd
....	....	....	....	-1.29	-1.97	-.54	-.20	-9.12	6.63	20.77	17.64	17.53	1.10	-15.16	Financial Derivatives Liabilities	78bxd
—	—	—	—	26.46	46.56	15.07	-35.12	-102.24	5.22	-191.96	37.94	266.34	-4.15	46.59	Other Investment Assets	78bhd
....	....	....	....	....	....	....	....	....	....	....	....	....	....	....	Monetary Authorities	78bod
....	....	....	....	-12.56	-9.51	-7.80	-8.76	-8.66	-5.28	-9.12	-15.50	-11.56	-1.89	-3.95	General Government	78bpd
....	....	....	....	37.03	49.64	27.73	-10.67	-85.62	75.56	-140.18	54.14	239.40	36.51	15.59	Banks	78bqd
....	....	....	....	1.99	6.42	-4.85	-15.69	-7.96	-65.07	-42.66	-.70	38.50	-38.77	34.95	Other Sectors	78brd
84.90	47.94	10.98	9.12	-108.19	-105.24	-32.70	-5.60	97.30	31.07	68.03	-93.33	-265.12	-10.21	-17.55	Other Investment Liab., n.i.e.	78bid
—	—	—	—	—	—	—	—	—	—	—	—	—	—	—	Monetary Authorities	78bsd
....	....	....	....	-2.16	1.28	-.10	-2.00	1.18	-2.13	-.11	-1.30	.55	-.93	7.01	General Government	78btd
....	....	....	....	-126.97	-119.86	-37.90	4.87	17.27	-9.06	43.34	-23.75	-189.16	28.22	4.99	Banks	78bud
....	....	....	....	20.94	13.34	5.30	-8.47	78.86	42.26	24.80	-68.28	-76.50	-37.49	-29.54	Other Sectors	78bvd
-4.17	3.68	-21.57	-21.40	-7.73	-10.38	-.50	-18.03	13.78	.64	34.31	4.36	16.97	16.87	3.72	Net Errors and Omissions	78cad
38.05	17.56	-13.05	-9.09	-8.39	.62	27.47	25.27	58.61	35.14	6.57	-6.16	76.26	48.95	40.49	*Overall Balance*	78cbd
-38.05	-17.57	13.06	9.09	8.39	-.62	-27.47	-25.27	-58.61	-35.14	-6.57	6.16	-76.26	-48.95	-40.49	Reserves and Related Items	79dad
-38.05	-17.57	13.06	9.09	8.39	-.62	-27.47	-25.27	-58.61	-35.14	-6.57	6.16	-76.26	-48.95	-40.49	Reserve Assets	79dbd
—	—	—	—	—	—	—	—	—	—	—	—	—	—	—	Use of Fund Credit and Loans	79dcd
....	....	....	....	....	....	....	....	....	....	....	....	....	....	....	Exceptional Financing	79ded

Japan

	1972	1973	1974	1975	1976	1977	1978	1979	1980	1981	1982	1983	1984	1985	1986
International Investment Position														*Billions of US Dollars*	
Assets .... 79aa *d*	...	...	...	...	...	...	...	...	159.65	210.06	228.50	271.78	341.04	437.28	726.85
Direct Investment Abroad .... 79ab *d*									19.61	24.51	28.97	32.18	37.92	43.97	58.07
Portfolio Investment .... 79ac *d*									21.44	31.54	40.07	56.12	87.58	145.75	257.93
Equity Securities .... 79ad *d*									...	...	...	...	...	...	...
Debt Securities .... 79ae *d*									...	...	...	...	...	...	...
Financial Derivatives .... 79al *d*															
Other Investment .... 79af *d*									92.88	124.86	135.29	158.10	188.45	220.33	368.02
Monetary Authorities .... 79ag *d*									—	—	—	—	—	—	—
General Government .... 79ah *d*									21.38	27.82	29.43	32.86	37.24	36.84	51.43
Banks .... 79ai *d*									54.78	74.12	76.70	90.85	105.09	131.49	243.50
Other Sectors .... 79aj *d*									16.72	22.92	29.16	34.39	46.12	52.00	73.09
Reserve Assets .... 79ak *d*									25.72	29.15	24.17	25.38	27.09	27.23	42.83
Liabilities .... 79la *d*									147.13	197.30	202.03	233.76	265.99	306.90	545.87
Dir. Invest. in Rep. Economy .... 79lb *d*									3.27	3.92	4.00	4.36	4.46	4.74	6.51
Portfolio Investment .... 79lc *d*									42.55	68.27	73.91	97.48	107.67	117.81	186.04
Equity Securities .... 79ld *d*									14.18	27.77	29.81	47.42	48.03	45.95	78.69
Debt Securities .... 79le *d*									28.37	40.50	44.10	50.06	59.64	71.86	107.35
Financial Derivatives .... 79ll *d*									—	—	—	—	—	—	—
Other Investment .... 79lf *d*									101.31	125.11	124.12	131.92	153.86	184.35	353.32
Monetary Authorities .... 79lg *d*									5.37	5.98	5.57	5.90	6.87	7.59	11.68
General Government .... 79lh *d*									.23	.18	.15	.13	.10	.08	.07
Banks .... 79li *d*									78.06	100.98	100.41	107.63	130.43	161.27	322.50
Other Sectors .... 79lj *d*									17.65	17.97	17.99	18.26	16.46	15.41	19.07
Government Finance														*Billions of Yen:*	
Deficit (-) or Surplus 80	−1,457	−1,825	−1,798	†−7,666	−9,417	−11,916	−15,236	−16,318	−16,872	−16,826	−17,583	−18,843	−17,290	−15,603	−15,967
Revenue 81	9,681	9,868	12,200	†14,608	16,509	18,469	20,606	24,113	27,907	31,429	32,826	33,776	36,738	40,262	41,683
Grants Received 81z	...	...	...	†93	146	124	134	157	198	212	212	139	97	99	108
Expenditure 82	11,138	11,693	13,997	†21,827	25,534	29,841	35,207	39,728	44,137	47,619	49,831	52,012	53,148	55,214	56,962
Lending Minus Repayments 83	...	...	...	†540	538	668	769	860	840	848	790	746	977	750	796
Financing															
Net Borrowing: Domestic Currency 84a	...	...	...	...	...	...	...	...	...	...	...	...	...	...	...
Foreign Currency 85b	−4	−33	−4	...	...	...	...	...	...	...	...	...	...	...	...
Use of Cash Balances 87	4	288	−207	...	...	...	...	...	...	...	...	...	...	...	...
Debt: Domestic 88a	...	...	...	†23,448	33,542	46,932	63,098	78,367	97,528	113,209	127,646	144,679	159,356	173,660	196,148
Foreign 89a	...	...	...	†517	528	587	518	408	621	691	735	704	925	991	1,036
National Accounts														*Billions of Yen*	
Househ.Cons.Expend.,incl.NPISHs .... 96f. *c*	49,901	60,308	72,912	84,763	95,784	107,076	117,923	130,078	134,255	141,921	151,924	159,909	168,196	177,670	184,731
Government Consumption Expend. ...... 91f. *c*	7,537	9,336	12,240	14,890	16,417	18,243	19,753	21,486	32,422	35,407	37,813	40,157	42,516	44,742	47,417
Gross Fixed Capital Formation .... 93e. *c*	31,524	40,938	46,695	48,136	51,945	55,982	62,147	70,171	77,046	80,256	81,178	80,363	85,004	90,104	93,872
Changes in Inventories .... 93i. *c*	1,299	1,885	3,396	476	1,092	1,280	1,027	1,813	1,735	1,525	1,289	283	1,108	2,240	1,650
Exports of Goods and Services .... 90c. *c*	9,779	11,291	18,258	18,982	22,582	24,308	22,729	25,627	32,817	37,846	39,191	39,125	44,901	46,176	38,058
Imports of Goods and Services (-) ...... 98c. *c*	7,645	11,261	19,257	18,919	21,247	21,267	19,174	27,629	35,036	35,927	37,341	34,258	36,866	35,137	24,777
Gross Domestic Product (GDP) .... 99b. *c*	92,394	112,498	134,244	148,327	166,573	185,622	204,404	221,547	243,235	261,028	274,050	285,579	304,859	325,792	340,948
Net Primary Income from Abroad ...... 98.n *c*	6	21	−247	−157	−156	−92	70	278	20	−381	186	437	681	1,213	1,175
Gross National Income (GNI) .... 99a. *c*	92,401	112,520	133,997	148,170	166,417	185,530	204,475	221,825	243,255	260,647	274,236	286,016	305,540	327,005	342,123
Net Current Transf.from Abroad .... 98t. *c*	...	...	...	...	...	...	...	...	3,636	3,855	3,904	4,271	4,844	5,863	5,997
Gross Nat'l Disposable Inc.(GNDI) ..... 99i. *c*	...	...	...	...	...	...	...	...	239,619	256,792	270,332	281,745	300,696	321,142	336,126
Gross Saving .... 99s. *c*	...	...	...	...	...	...	...	...	74,727	81,211	82,703	84,062	92,616	101,697	107,027
Consumption of Fixed Capital 99cf	12,825	15,297	17,766	19,026	20,704	23,012	25,000	27,645	30,700	34,059	36,216	38,426	40,777	43,615	46,169
GDP Volume 1980 Prices .... 99b. *r*	172,309	185,882	183,620	188,393	197,406	207,845	218,449	229,785	...	...	...	...	...	...	...
GDP Volume 1985 Prices .... 99b. *r*	...	...	...	...	...	...	...	257,372	266,722	276,268	285,002	292,702	305,187	320,397	328,816
GDP Volume 1995 Prices .... 99b. *r*	...	...	...	...	...	...	...	...	...	...	...	...	...	...	...
GDP Volume (1995=100) .... 99bv *r*	45.0	48.6	48.0	49.2	51.6	54.3	57.1	†60.1	†62.2	64.2	66.2	67.7	70.3	73.3	75.5
GDP Deflator (1995=100) .... 99bi *r*	41.2	46.5	56.2	60.5	64.9	68.6	71.9	74.1	78.5	81.7	83.2	84.7	87.1	89.3	90.7
														Millions:	
Population 99z	107.19	108.71	110.16	111.57	112.77	113.86	114.90	115.87	116.81	117.66	118.48	119.31	120.08	120.84	121.49

Billions of US Dollars — International Investment Position

1987	1988	1989	1990	1991	1992	1993	1994	1995	1996	1997	1998	1999	2000	2001		
1,071.35	1,469.34	1,771.01	1,857.88	2,006.51	2,035.24	2,180.88	2,424.24	2,632.86	2,652.61	2,737.45	2,986.33	3,013.60	3,012.17	....	Assets	79aa *d*
77.02	110.78	154.37	201.44	231.79	248.06	259.80	275.57	238.45	258.61	271.90	270.04	248.78	278.44	....	Direct Investment Abroad	79ab *d*
354.55	449.31	561.85	595.84	679.18	715.45	771.11	858.69	855.07	933.20	902.26	1,056.49	1,242.37	1,244.91	....	Portfolio Investment	79ac *d*
....	....	....	....	....	....	....	....	146.26	154.90	158.77	209.38	285.34	262.23	....	Equity Securities	79ad *d*
....	....	....	....	....	....	....	....	708.81	778.30	743.49	847.11	957.04	982.68	....	Debt Securities	79ae *d*
								3.21	3.97	4.41	5.09	4.46	3.31	....	Financial Derivatives	79al *d*
557.88	811.39	969.72	980.89	1,022.27	998.94	1,050.29	1,162.87	1,351.31	1,239.23	1,338.08	1,438.88	1,230.34	1,124.52	....	Other Investment	79af *d*
														....	Monetary Authorities	79ag *d*
66.21	82.41	89.42	90.44	110.73	123.40	142.22	165.01	184.05	170.47	162.32	196.16	230.91	210.16	....	General Government	79ah *d*
389.79	585.09	716.70	725.40	729.67	690.32	701.47	752.12	911.23	773.14	861.44	876.07	630.02	565.80	....	Banks	79ai *d*
101.88	143.89	163.60	165.05	181.87	185.22	206.60	245.74	256.02	295.63	314.32	366.65	369.41	348.55	....	Other Sectors	79aj *d*
81.90	97.86	85.07	79.71	73.27	72.79	99.68	127.10	184.82	217.61	220.81	215.83	287.66	360.99	....	Reserve Assets	79ak *d*
829.63	1,176.41	1,476.62	1,528.52	1,622.17	1,520.39	1,568.84	1,733.92	1,815.26	1,761.59	1,778.72	1,832.69	2,184.48	1,854.24	....	Liabilities	79la *d*
9.02	10.42	9.16	9.85	12.29	15.51	16.89	19.17	33.51	29.94	27.08	26.07	46.12	50.32	....	Dir. Invest. in Rep. Economy	79lb *d*
229.46	317.73	431.88	395.97	527.69	513.10	545.32	630.67	545.42	556.25	582.48	632.76	1,165.44	871.76	....	Portfolio Investment	79lc *d*
66.30	113.52	162.08	90.38	141.78	124.59	171.17	250.88	306.28	315.65	279.53	304.33	833.43	558.52	....	Equity Securities	79ld *d*
163.16	204.21	269.80	305.59	385.91	388.51	374.15	379.79	239.14	240.60	302.95	328.43	332.01	313.24	....	Debt Securities	79le *d*
								2.85	2.72	4.10	4.54	3.10	3.19	....	Financial Derivatives	79ll *d*
591.15	848.26	1,035.58	1,122.70	1,082.19	991.78	1,006.63	1,084.08	1,233.48	1,172.69	1,165.06	1,169.32	969.83	928.97	....	Other Investment	79lf *d*
10.38	13.81	25.03	35.74	50.11	54.72	65.52	99.85	—	—	—	—	—	—	....	Monetary Authorities	79lg *d*
.05	.03	.01	—	—	—	—	—	14.96	11.35	10.12	9.65	11.62	9.68	....	General Government	79lh *d*
532.13	766.93	897.88	904.41	812.82	696.71	673.58	694.94	745.42	701.56	714.28	751.47	570.71	606.50	....	Banks	79li *d*
48.59	67.49	112.66	182.55	219.26	240.35	267.53	289.29	473.10	459.78	440.66	408.20	387.50	312.79	....	Other Sectors	79lj *d*

Year Beginning April 1 — Government Finance

1987	1988	1989	1990	1991	1992	1993	1994	1995	1996	1997	1998	1999	2000	2001		
−12,195	−9,657	−11,645	−6,781	†7,759	1,473[p]	−7,318[p]	....	....	....	....	....	....	....	....	Deficit (-) or Surplus	80
47,176	52,082	55,762	62,146	†104,462	99,412[p]	99,866[p]	....	....	....	....	....	....	....	....	Revenue	81
134	148	160	166	†2,883	3,278[p]	3,498[p]	....	....	....	....	....	....	....	....	Grants Received	81z
58,641	60,863	66,695	67,533	†97,478	100,642[p]	112,655[p]	....	....	....	....	....	....	....	....	Expenditure	82
864	1,024	872	1,560	†2,108	575[p]	−1,973[p]	....	....	....	....	....	....	....	....	Lending Minus Repayments	83
															Financing	
....	....	....		†−7,759	−1,473[p]	7,318[p]	....	....	....	....	....	....	....	....	Net Borrowing: Domestic Currency	84a
															Foreign Currency	85b
															Use of Cash Balances	87
210,407	220,644	231,008	238,746	†187,605	196,194[p]	212,474[p]	....	....	....	....	....	....	....	....	Debt: Domestic	88a
1,144	1,200	1,149	1,186	....											Foreign	89a

Billions of Yen — National Accounts

1987	1988	1989	1990	1991	1992	1993	1994	1995	1996	1997	1998	1999	2000	2001		
193,137	204,298	218,442	234,140	247,005	257,368	264,456	272,678	275,745	282,121	287,152	286,946	288,764	287,231	283,652	Housh.Cons.Expend.,incl.NPISHs	96f. *c*
49,521	51,766	55,008	58,809	62,462	66,008	69,046	71,285	74,698	77,356	79,201	80,735	82,876	85,731	88,312	Government Consumption Expend.	91f. *c*
101,865	114,488	126,850	142,248	149,018	146,796	142,047	138,694	138,126	145,324	146,595	138,679	134,222	132,914	129,874	Gross Fixed Capital Formation	93e. *c*
756	2,790	3,067	2,547	3,199	1,015	209	−699	2,213	3,466	3,156	34	−887	−120	−1,708	Changes in Inventories	93i. *c*
36,180	37,431	42,273	45,863	46,668	47,288	44,109	44,270	45,230	49,561	56,074	55,051	51,144	55,256	52,567	Exports of Goods and Services	90c. *c*
25,619	29,191	36,036	41,690	39,121	36,891	33,346	34,387	38,272	47,022	50,316	45,607	43,251	47,940	49,393	Imports of Goods and Services (-)	98c. *c*
355,837	381,579	409,602	441,915	469,230	481,582	486,519	491,835	497,739	510,802	521,862	515,835	511,837	513,534	503,304	Gross Domestic Product (GDP)	99b. *c*
1,981	2,210	2,720	2,770	3,070	3,988	4,161	3,811	3,834	5,469	6,755	6,938	7,077	4,722	....	Net Primary Income from Abroad	98.n *c*
357,818	383,789	412,322	444,685	472,300	485,570	490,680	495,646	501,573	516,271	528,617	522,773	518,914	518,256	....	Gross National Income (GNI)	99a. *c*
5,346	6,727	8,957	12,235	10,780	10,551	11,841	13,570	14,672	10,509	15,397	19,818	19,913	18,762	....	Net Current Transf.from Abroad	98t. *c*
352,472	377,062	403,365	432,450	461,520	475,019	478,840	482,076	486,901	505,762	513,220	502,955	499,001	499,494	....	Gross Nat'l Disposable Inc.(GNDI)	99i. *c*
113,541	125,040	134,200	144,355	158,273	159,463	155,365	150,179	148,959	157,999	157,300	147,390	139,993	140,110	....	Gross Saving	99s. *c*
48,862	52,307	57,530	68,262	75,118	80,949	83,730	86,150	88,442	91,677	93,849	95,805	95,739	97,952	....	Consumption of Fixed Capital	99cf
....	....	....													GDP Volume 1980 Prices	99b. *r*
342,315	363,567	380,709	399,043	....											GDP Volume 1985 Prices	99b. *r*
			464,165	478,259	482,658	485,193	490,164	497,847	514,471	524,364	518,827	522,906	530,961	531,579	GDP Volume 1995 Prices	99b. *r*
78.9	84.0	88.5	93.2	96.1	96.9	97.5	98.5	100.0	103.3	105.3	104.2	105.0	106.7	106.8	GDP Volume (1995=100)	99bv *r*
90.6	91.2	93.0	95.2	98.1	99.8	100.3	100.4	100.0	99.3	99.5	99.4	97.9	96.7	94.7	GDP Deflator (1995=100)	99bi *r*

Midyear Estimates

1987	1988	1989	1990	1991	1992	1993	1994	1995	1996	1997	1998	1999	2000	2001		
122.09	122.58	123.07	123.48	123.96	124.42	124.83	125.18	125.47	125.76	126.07	126.41	126.65	126.87	127.34	Population	99z

(See notes in the back of the book.)

Jordan

		1972	1973	1974	1975	1976	1977	1978	1979	1980	1981	1982	1983	1984	1985	1986
Exchange Rates															*SDRs per Dinar:*	
Official Rate	ac	2.5790	2.5192	2.5929	2.5790	2.5790	2.5790	2.5790	2.5790	2.5790	2.5790	2.5790	2.5790	2.5790	2.5790	2.5790
															US Dollars per Dinar:	
Official Rate	ag	2.8000	3.0390	3.1746	3.0303	3.0211	3.1746	3.4130	3.3898	3.2415	2.9498	2.8450	2.6918	2.4691	2.7192	2.9061
Official Rate	rh	2.8000	3.0462	3.1113	3.1393	3.0122	3.0375	3.2733	3.3299	3.3543	3.0293	2.8384	2.7550	2.6036	2.5379	2.8583
Fund Position															*Millions of SDRs:*	
Quota	2f. s	23.0	23.0	23.0	23.0	23.0	23.0	30.0	30.0	45.0	45.0	45.0	73.9	73.9	73.9	73.9
SDRs	1b. s	7.6	7.5	7.4	7.4	7.4	7.4	7.4	11.0	11.7	15.5	16.5	17.4	15.8	21.9	19.6
Reserve Position in the Fund	1c. s	5.8	5.8	5.8	5.8	5.8	5.8	5.6	10.3	16.6	16.6	16.6	7.2	—	—	—
Total Fund Cred.&Loans Outstg.	2tl	4.5	1.6	—	—	—	—	—	—	—	—	—	—	—	57.4	57.4
International Liquidity														*Millions of US Dollars Unless Otherwise Indicated:*		
Total Reserves minus Gold	1l. d	241.0	270.7	312.8	458.9	471.5	643.1	885.6	1,166.1	1,142.8	1,086.7	884.1	824.2	515.0	422.8	437.1
SDRs	1b. d	8.2	9.1	9.1	8.7	8.6	9.0	9.6	14.4	14.9	18.0	18.2	18.2	15.5	24.1	23.9
Reserve Position in the Fund	1c. d	6.2	6.9	7.1	6.7	6.7	7.0	7.3	13.6	21.1	19.3	18.3	7.6	—	—	—
Foreign Exchange	1d. d	226.5	254.7	296.7	443.5	456.2	627.2	868.7	1,138.1	1,106.8	1,049.4	847.6	798.4	499.5	398.7	413.2
Gold (Million Fine Troy Ounces)	1ad	.797	.797	.797	.797	.797	.806	.811	.816	1.021	1.067	1.080	1.090	1.060	1.061	1.064
Gold (National Valuation)	1and	30.3	33.6	34.3	32.8	79.7	80.6	81.1	81.6	204.2	213.4	216.0	199.5	172.2	189.8	203.5
Monetary Authorities: Other Liab.	4.. d	.5	1.2	1.8	1.5	.5	1.2	.8	11.2	1.3	3.6	1.5	.7	1.1	1.0	1.0
Deposit Money Banks: Assets	7a. d	9.5	20.4	25.3	37.7	58.1	116.6	254.7	271.4	665.2	688.2	726.6	819.3	816.1	1,046.6	1,172.1
Liabilities	7b. d	6.8	8.1	13.5	31.4	80.4	67.4	204.6	283.6	480.5	523.3	572.1	664.2	779.3	917.9	1,011.6
Other Banking Insts.: Liabilities	7f. d	10.4	11.9	13.2	14.9	12.8	42.6	34.3	48.1	53.1	56.4	59.0	57.0	71.0	81.0	101.0
Monetary Authorities															*Millions of Dinars:*	
Foreign Assets	11	96.9	100.4	110.2	162.3	182.2	229.1	286.1	370.8	416.9	433.7	372.9	380.3	278.3	379.3	402.0
Claims on Central Government	12a	11.5	28.8	30.4	27.2	44.9	58.9	56.5	60.3	126.7	150.3	195.4	200.4	181.1	204.7	225.9
Reserve Money	14	100.7	117.2	140.5	173.5	216.4	255.2	299.9	380.3	467.3	534.1	596.5	663.6	676.2	701.7	747.2
of which: Currency Outside DMBs	14a	81.5	97.5	115.5	139.0	161.5	188.2	219.5	275.4	351.6	412.3	470.0	516.0	530.5	531.8	583.9
Foreign Liabilities	16c	1.9	1.0	.6	.5	.2	.4	.2	3.3	.4	1.2	.5	.3	.5	23.6	24.5
Central Government Deposits	16d	2.4	6.7	4.2	14.1	10.0	23.9	31.4	31.5	51.1	39.3	23.6	40.3	17.5	6.7	10.4
Other Items (Net)	17r	3.4	4.4	-4.6	1.2	.5	8.5	11.1	16.0	24.7	9.4	-52.3	-123.5	-234.7	-148.0	-154.1
Deposit Money Banks															*Millions of Dinars:*	
Reserves	20	19.2	18.8	24.5	35.9	54.2	67.6	81.7	101.6	116.6	115.1	118.5	134.0	136.2	161.9	180.6
Foreign Assets	21	3.4	6.6	8.0	12.5	19.2	36.7	74.6	80.1	205.2	233.3	255.4	304.4	330.5	384.9	403.3
Claims on Central Government	22a	16.2	16.9	14.9	24.5	23.0	32.9	68.6	73.8	59.8	80.8	102.8	147.2	208.5	228.3	275.7
Claims on Private Sector	22d	47.9	59.3	80.3	115.6	177.2	196.7	313.8	444.0	541.6	689.7	843.0	993.3	1,133.5	1,193.4	1,291.5
Demand Deposits	24	33.5	40.9	55.7	84.5	113.9	139.8	150.0	182.0	225.2	280.1	305.1	338.7	336.9	308.4	310.7
Time and Savings Deposits	25	31.1	36.6	47.3	63.6	99.1	135.1	226.8	298.2	386.4	476.8	614.5	745.2	877.4	1,023.2	1,173.8
Foreign Liabilities	26c	2.4	2.6	4.3	10.3	26.6	21.2	60.0	83.7	148.2	177.4	201.1	246.7	315.6	337.6	348.1
Central Government Deposits	26d	6.2	6.1	8.4	12.0	16.6	21.0	24.3	45.8	63.6	77.2	78.3	97.2	111.9	121.3	156.2
Capital Accounts	27a	8.0	8.0	11.6	14.9	21.0	32.7	54.7	67.9	76.8	91.7	131.2	140.3	152.9	164.4	177.5
Other Items (Net)	27r	5.3	7.4	.4	3.2	-3.6	-16.0	23.0	21.9	23.0	15.7	-10.5	10.7	14.1	13.6	-15.3
Monetary Survey															*Millions of Dinars:*	
Foreign Assets (Net)	31n	95.9	103.4	113.3	163.8	174.7	244.2	300.6	363.9	473.4	488.4	426.7	437.7	292.8	403.1	432.7
Domestic Credit	32	71.4	98.1	122.0	152.6	240.0	275.7	425.2	545.9	666.7	883.9	1,162.1	1,360.4	1,587.7	1,743.0	1,833.6
Claims on Central Govt. (Net)	32an	19.1	32.9	32.8	25.5	41.3	46.8	69.4	56.7	71.8	114.6	196.3	210.1	260.2	305.0	335.0
Claims on Nonfin.Pub.Enterprises	32c	4.4	5.8	9.0	11.5	21.4	31.6	42.0	44.2	53.3	78.2	122.8	157.0	173.5	218.7	175.1
Claims on Private Sector	32d	47.9	59.3	80.3	115.6	177.2	197.3	313.8	445.0	541.6	691.1	843.0	993.3	1,133.5	1,197.1	1,296.2
Money	34	115.0	139.2	172.0	224.7	276.7	329.0	370.5	465.6	580.7	701.7	787.5	869.4	878.4	848.2	897.1
Quasi-Money	35	31.6	37.2	48.5	67.5	110.8	144.9	237.1	301.6	399.5	482.0	619.4	748.5	883.8	1,030.9	1,181.7
Other Items (Net)	37r	20.7	25.0	14.8	24.4	27.2	46.0	118.2	142.7	159.9	188.6	181.9	180.2	118.3	267.0	187.6
Money plus Quasi-Money	35l	146.6	176.4	220.5	292.1	387.5	473.9	607.6	767.2	980.3	1,183.6	1,406.9	1,617.9	1,762.2	1,879.1	2,078.8
Other Banking Institutions															*Millions of Dinars:*	
Cash	40	.8	1.3	1.3	.9	2.1	2.3	3.4	7.0	9.2	18.3	12.5	12.2	13.6	22.9	19.8
Claims on Private Sector	42d	16.2	17.5	21.5	25.1	30.5	36.0	43.4	50.0	59.9	71.5	95.9	119.9	128.0	138.4	144.0
Deposits	45	—	—	—	—	2.1	—	—	—	—	10.2	10.4	12.4	16.5	18.6	28.7
Foreign Liabilities	46c	3.7	3.8	4.2	4.9	4.2	13.4	10.0	14.2	16.4	19.1	20.6	25.3	28.8	30.0	34.6
Central Govt. Lending Funds	46f	1.8	1.7	1.6	1.7	1.7	1.5	1.5	1.5	1.3	1.2	2.1	2.0	2.1	2.2	2.3
Capital Accounts	47a	13.0	14.1	15.0	17.9	19.5	22.4	24.4	28.1	31.7	39.5	48.5	55.4	62.3	63.9	69.1
Other Items (Net)	47r	-1.5	-.8	2.0	1.5	5.1	1.0	10.9	13.2	19.7	19.8	26.7	37.0	31.8	46.7	29.1
Liquid Liabilities	55l	145.7	175.1	218.6	287.5	387.5	471.6	604.2	760.2	971.0	1,175.5	1,404.8	1,618.1	1,765.1	1,874.8	2,087.6
Interest Rates															*Percent Per Annum*	
Discount Rate *(End of Period)*	60	5.00	5.00	5.00	5.00	5.50	5.50	5.50	6.00	6.00	6.50	6.50	6.25	6.25	6.25	6.25
Deposit Rate *(Period Average)*	60l	....	....	....	....	....	....	....	....	....	....	....	....	....	....	....
Lending Rate *(Period Average)*	60p	....	....	....	....	....	....	....	....	....	....	....	....	....	....	....
Prices and Production															*Index Numbers (1995=100):*	
Wholesale Prices	63	....	....	....	27.0	30.8	32.9	34.7	36.9	42.4	46.3	47.7	49.6	50.5	51.2	51.1
Consumer Prices	64	15.6	17.3	20.7	†23.2	25.9	29.6	31.7	†36.2	40.2	43.3	46.5	48.9	50.7	†52.3	52.3
Industrial Production	66	15.7	17.3	18.0	†19.3	24.1	25.0	30.8	36.8	44.0	51.3	53.0	55.6	63.7	68.2	69.2
International Transactions															*Millions of Dinars*	
Exports	70	17.0	24.0	49.8	48.9	68.7	82.1	90.9	120.9	171.4	242.6	264.5	210.6	290.7	310.9	256.0
Imports, c.i.f.	71	97.7	108.2	156.8	234.0	334.1	454.4	458.8	589.5	716.1	1,047.5	1,142.5	1,103.3	1,071.4	1,074.4	850.2
															1995=100	
Volume of Exports	72	10.7	11.6	16.5	†14.2	17.2	20.7	22.3	27.5	34.3	40.0	41.0	†40.7	57.1	59.5	61.0
Volume of Imports	73	17.1	17.5	19.5	†24.8	37.2	43.4	49.6	58.2	57.1	67.8	74.4	†75.1	70.4	72.1	75.7
Unit Value of Exports	74	14.5	14.6	29.7	†33.7	31.4	31.4	30.2	30.4	36.1	41.5	45.3	†41.4	45.1	43.8	37.7
Unit Value of Imports	75	20.5	21.5	27.3	†37.4	36.5	37.2	36.1	38.7	48.0	58.5	59.4	†54.3	60.0	58.5	44.0

	1987	1988	1989	1990	1991	1992	1993	1994	1995	1996	1997	1998	1999	2000	2001		
End of Period																**Exchange Rates**	
	2.5790	1.5579	1.1743	1.0570	1.0357	1.0525	1.0341	.9772	.9488	.9809	1.0454	1.0017	1.0276	1.0825	1.1223	Official Rate	**ac**
End of Period (ag) Period Average (rh)																	
	3.0395	2.0964	1.5432	1.5038	1.4815	1.4472	1.4205	1.4265	1.4104	1.4104	1.4104	1.4104	1.4104	1.4104	1.4104	Official Rate	**ag**
	2.9522	2.6916	1.7532	1.5069	1.4689	1.4712	1.4434	1.4312	1.4276	1.4104	1.4104	1.4104	1.4104	1.4104	1.4105	Official Rate	**rh**
End of Period																**Fund Position**	
	73.9	73.9	73.9	73.9	73.9	121.7	121.7	121.7	121.7	121.7	121.7	121.7	170.5	170.5	170.5	Quota	**2f. s**
	8.5	—	8.4	.7	.8	.4	4.0	.5	.8	.6	.1	.6	.2	.5	.9	SDRs	**1b. s**
	—	—	—	—	—	12.0	—	—	—	—	—	—	—	—	.1	Reserve Position in the Fund	**1c. s**
	57.4	35.9	73.4	66.2	66.2	81.2	59.2	98.9	169.2	236.1	316.6	333.4	362.9	354.3	344.5	Total Fund Cred.&Loans Outstg.	**2tl**
End of Period																**International Liquidity**	
	424.7	109.6	470.7	848.8	825.8	767.2	†1,637.4	1,692.6	1,972.9	1,759.3	2,200.3	1,750.4	2,629.1	3,331.3	3,062.2	Total Reserves minus Gold	**1l. d**
	12.1	.1	11.0	1.0	1.1	.6	5.5	.7	1.2	.8	.2	.8	.3	.6	1.2	SDRs	**1b. d**
	—	—	—	—	—	16.4	—	—	—	—	—	—	—	.1	.1	Reserve Position in the Fund	**1c. d**
	412.6	109.5	459.7	847.8	824.7	750.2	†1,631.9	1,691.9	1,971.7	1,758.5	2,200.1	1,749.6	2,628.8	3,330.6	3,061.0	Foreign Exchange	**1d. d**
	1.002	.743	.748	.753	.789	.789	.791	.794	.793	.800	.812	.827	.486	.401	.405	Gold (Million Fine Troy Ounces)	**1ad**
	200.1	138.3	102.5	100.6	103.8	101.4	99.8	198.5	195.9	197.7	200.7	204.3	120.0	99.1	112.2	Gold (National Valuation)	**1and**
	176.2	25.5	15.4	10.6	.5	.8	125.6	117.5	82.3	71.3	43.8	32.8	230.6	177.6	181.3	Monetary Authorities: Other Liab.	**4.. d**
	1,374.0	1,200.4	976.0	986.9	1,922.5	2,137.9	2,216.3	2,399.3	2,655.3	2,845.0	3,077.5	3,607.1	4,101.5	5,235.2	6,104.3	Deposit Money Banks: Assets	**7a. d**
	1,160.5	1,157.8	779.2	691.5	1,367.1	2,310.5	2,166.6	2,518.5	2,926.5	3,100.7	3,084.7	3,079.7	3,285.2	3,819.1	4,213.5	Liabilities	**7b. d**
	110.0	77.0	61.0	75.0	86.0	98.0	112.3	120.6	130.3	117.0	126.0	124.7	120.9	114.9	....	Other Banking Insts.: Liabilities	**7f. d**
End of Period																**Monetary Authorities**	
	391.7	346.9	601.4	788.0	949.5	999.7	†1,688.7	1,904.3	2,185.2	2,253.9	2,557.1	2,297.7	2,889.6	3,267.4	3,064.2	Foreign Assets	**11**
	351.6	663.7	741.3	747.5	685.9	688.9	772.5	905.3	867.1	930.9	989.4	1,033.4	1,015.8	1,125.7	1,097.0	Claims on Central Government	**12a**
	779.9	959.1	1,135.9	1,279.7	1,665.6	1,771.3	†2,236.0	2,349.5	2,498.9	2,164.4	2,104.0	2,005.0	2,246.9	2,264.8	2,135.7	Reserve Money	**14**
	655.8	811.2	871.1	1,006.2	992.4	1,003.9	1,047.9	1,072.6	1,050.9	952.1	987.6	952.8	1,106.6	1,239.9	1,202.4	*of which: Currency Outside DMBs*	**14a**
	84.8	35.2	72.5	69.7	64.3	77.7	†145.7	183.6	236.7	291.3	333.9	356.1	516.6	453.2	435.5	Foreign Liabilities	**16c**
	1.7	—	21.4	5.7	210.7	137.6	101.3	225.1	163.5	323.7	321.0	137.7	145.9	420.7	401.6	Central Government Deposits	**16d**
	–123.1	16.2	112.9	180.3	–305.2	–297.9	†–21.8	51.4	153.1	405.4	787.5	832.3	995.9	1,254.4	1,188.4	Other Items (Net)	**17r**
End of Period																**Deposit Money Banks**	
	181.0	248.8	456.4	566.6	1,318.2	1,584.9	1,477.1	1,576.9	1,799.6	1,854.9	2,163.8	2,015.9	2,389.2	2,518.1	2,383.3	Reserves	**20**
	452.0	572.6	632.4	656.3	1,297.7	1,477.3	1,560.3	1,681.9	1,882.6	2,017.1	2,182.0	2,557.5	2,907.9	3,711.7	4,328.0	Foreign Assets	**21**
	345.9	334.9	369.0	388.8	424.1	457.9	358.7	307.0	240.0	238.1	163.0	412.5	618.5	733.0	902.5	Claims on Central Government	**22a**
	1,349.9	1,461.5	1,565.0	1,716.1	1,841.0	2,013.7	2,310.5	2,763.4	3,192.5	3,354.9	3,526.5	3,803.2	4,050.2	4,230.7	4,709.9	Claims on Private Sector	**22d**
	322.8	353.7	425.4	413.8	640.3	685.9	†669.6	666.0	664.7	578.1	636.1	648.5	658.0	774.2	888.4	Demand Deposits	**24**
	1,391.4	1,459.3	1,638.5	1,673.0	2,361.1	2,448.8	†2,510.0	2,782.4	3,040.5	3,209.8	3,469.3	3,734.4	4,212.9	4,651.9	4,963.3	Time and Savings Deposits	**25**
	381.6	552.3	504.9	459.8	922.8	1,596.5	1,525.3	1,765.5	2,074.9	2,198.4	2,187.1	2,183.5	2,329.2	2,707.7	2,987.4	Foreign Liabilities	**26c**
	127.3	110.6	161.1	168.8	212.4	91.5	†424.8	499.8	550.9	634.6	736.3	848.3	1,011.0	1,062.8	1,071.4	Central Government Deposits	**26d**
	185.6	194.4	204.2	75.9	88.7	348.5	492.6	582.8	701.7	771.0	1,047.1	1,181.3	1,316.6	1,377.9	1,436.2	Capital Accounts	**27a**
	–80.0	–52.5	88.8	536.4	655.6	362.7	†84.3	32.9	82.0	73.2	–41.3	193.2	438.0	619.1	976.9	Other Items (Net)	**27r**
End of Period																**Monetary Survey**	
	377.4	332.0	656.5	914.7	1,260.1	802.7	†1,578.0	1,637.2	1,756.2	1,781.3	2,218.1	2,315.6	2,951.7	3,818.2	3,969.3	Foreign Assets (Net)	**31n**
	2,190.5	2,637.3	2,780.7	2,935.1	2,759.1	3,220.9	†3,324.8	3,723.1	4,089.0	4,114.2	4,184.4	4,780.0	4,925.6	5,016.0	5,613.0	Domestic Credit	**32**
	568.5	888.0	927.7	961.7	686.9	917.8	†605.1	487.4	392.7	210.8	95.1	459.9	477.3	375.2	526.4	Claims on Central Govt. (Net)	**32an**
	237.9	253.0	251.4	250.5	225.4	235.0	†296.8	341.9	362.2	408.9	425.3	381.2	307.9	316.9	284.3	Claims on Nonfin.Pub.Enterprises	**32c**
	1,354.7	1,467.4	1,568.4	1,719.5	1,844.7	2,018.1	2,316.1	2,769.9	3,200.1	3,363.0	3,535.2	3,812.7	4,062.1	4,243.9	4,723.6	Claims on Private Sector	**32d**
	979.8	1,166.8	1,302.3	1,425.3	1,646.6	1,716.0	†1,719.4	1,741.6	1,738.7	1,532.8	1,626.1	1,612.6	1,766.1	2,017.4	2,094.8	Money	**34**
	1,424.4	1,611.2	1,935.3	2,080.1	2,412.8	2,479.0	†2,664.7	2,788.6	3,051.0	3,213.3	3,482.7	3,818.8	4,507.2	4,734.3	5,204.0	Quasi-Money	**35**
	163.7	191.3	199.5	344.4	–40.2	–171.4	†518.8	830.1	1,055.6	1,149.4	1,293.6	1,664.1	1,603.9	2,082.6	2,283.5	Other Items (Net)	**37r**
	2,404.2	2,778.0	3,237.6	3,505.4	4,059.4	4,195.0	†4,384.1	4,530.2	4,789.7	4,746.1	5,108.8	5,431.4	6,273.3	6,751.7	7,298.7	Money plus Quasi-Money	**35l**
End of Period																**Other Banking Institutions**	
	26.8	25.1	42.3	39.1	65.9	49.8	†70.6	59.9	63.3	54.3	53.0	41.2	22.5	71.2	....	Cash	**40**
	191.2	213.0	210.5	209.8	219.8	256.2	†294.9	284.8	306.2	315.0	334.9	349.3	362.2	343.0	....	Claims on Private Sector	**42d**
	35.9	29.4	32.2	35.4	58.9	44.9	†66.5	47.4	32.7	24.5	17.0	11.8	8.8	9.5	....	Deposits	**45**
	36.3	36.8	39.8	50.0	57.8	67.5	†79.0	84.6	92.4	83.0	89.3	88.4	85.7	81.5	....	Foreign Liabilities	**46c**
	2.2	3.0	2.8	2.9	3.1	.9	†17.1	16.2	16.2	15.0	14.3	13.7	13.1	50.3	....	Central Govt. Lending Funds	**46f**
	70.7	76.6	80.9	88.1	78.5	104.0	†90.9	91.6	111.5	132.0	153.2	164.5	177.4	186.4	....	Capital Accounts	**47a**
	73.0	92.4	97.1	72.9	87.4	88.7	†111.9	104.9	116.8	114.9	114.2	112.0	99.7	86.4	....	Other Items (Net)	**47r**
	2,413.3	2,782.2	3,227.5	3,501.6	4,052.4	4,190.1	†4,380.0	4,517.8	4,759.1	4,716.3	5,072.7	5,402.0	6,259.6	6,690.0	....	Liquid Liabilities	**55l**
Percent Per Annum																**Interest Rates**	
	6.25	6.25	8.00	8.50	8.50	8.50	8.50	8.50	8.50	8.50	7.75	9.00	8.00	6.50	5.00	Discount Rate (End of Period)	**60**
	....	....	....	8.15	8.13	7.20	6.88	7.09	7.68	8.50	9.10	8.21	8.30	6.97	5.81	Deposit Rate (Period Average)	**60l**
	....	....	....	10.31	10.37	10.16	10.23	10.45	10.66	11.25	12.25	12.61	12.33	11.80	10.92	Lending Rate (Period Average)	**60p**
Period Averages																**Prices and Production**	
	51.6	56.4	75.4	86.3	90.7	†94.5	97.7	102.5	100.0	102.0	103.6	104.3	99.9	95.8	98.5	Wholesale Prices	**63**
	52.2	55.6	69.9	81.2	87.8	†91.4	94.4	97.7	100.0	106.5	†109.7	113.1	113.8	114.6	116.6	Consumer Prices	**64**
	75.6	69.4	72.9	73.3	72.5	†78.1	84.3	†89.0	100.0	94.8	98.2	100.2	102.6	106.6	117.3	Industrial Production	**66**
Millions of Dinars																**International Transactions**	
	315.7	381.5	637.6	706.1	770.8	829.3	864.7	995.2	1,241.1	1,288.2	1,301.4	1,277.9	1,298.8	1,345.3	1,625.8	Exports	**70**
	915.6	1,022.5	1,230.0	1,725.8	1,710.5	2,214.0	2,453.6	2,362.6	2,590.3	3,043.6	2,908.1	2,714.4	2,635.2	3,218.1	3,434.4	Imports, c.i.f.	**71**
1995=100																	
	72.5	81.2	85.6	82.4	72.4	79.6	85.9	†92.0	100.0	97.3	104.0	106.9	109.9	118.4	146.0	Volume of Exports	**72**
	78.6	82.9	68.8	71.7	70.8	97.1	105.9	†103.2	100.0	107.7	105.3	99.5	98.3	117.1	122.6	Volume of Imports	**73**
	35.0	40.7	63.6	75.7	84.2	81.2	82.0	†85.9	100.0	106.4	103.3	97.5	95.1	91.0	92.1	Unit Value of Exports	**74**
	45.7	48.3	70.2	94.4	94.7	89.4	90.9	†88.3	100.0	109.1	106.7	105.8	103.3	105.9	108.2	Unit Value of Imports	**75**

Jordan

Balance of Payments		1972	1973	1974	1975	1976	1977	1978	1979	1980	1981	1982	1983	1984	1985	1986
																Millions of US Dollars:
Current Account, n.i.e.	78al d	6.4	12.5	3.4	44.7	36.1	−16.5	−288.4	−6.5	373.9	−38.9	−332.7	−390.7	−264.7	−260.5	−39.8
Goods: Exports f.o.b.	78aa d	47.6	73.7	154.3	152.9	206.9	248.9	297.4	402.2	575.2	733.2	751.6	580.0	751.9	788.9	732.0
Goods: Imports f.o.b.	78ab d	−236.6	−291.9	−430.3	−648.2	−907.9	−1,225.2	−1,339.2	−1,743.2	−2,136.1	−2,815.3	−2,878.6	−2,700.1	−2,472.6	−2,426.7	−2,158.4
Trade Balance	78ac d	−189.0	−218.2	−276.0	−495.3	−700.9	−976.3	−1,041.8	−1,341.0	−1,560.9	−2,082.0	−2,127.0	−2,120.1	−1,720.7	−1,637.9	−1,426.4
Services: Credit	78ad d	65.0	96.2	98.1	226.4	344.3	442.5	572.4	731.3	1,002.9	1,160.0	1,112.1	1,124.5	1,131.0	1,167.1	1,058.8
Services: Debit	78ae d	−90.7	−122.0	−172.3	−293.3	−387.4	−426.0	−650.5	−1,001.7	−1,094.3	−1,386.1	−1,376.9	−1,159.5	−1,330.2	−1,286.9	−1,150.5
Balance on Goods & Services	78af d	−214.8	−244.1	−350.2	−562.2	−744.0	−959.8	−1,119.9	−1,611.3	−1,652.4	−2,308.2	−2,391.8	−2,155.1	−1,920.0	−1,757.7	−1,518.1
Income: Credit	78ag d	12.3	19.2	27.3	35.3	39.2	40.4	51.5	88.1	126.1	200.4	204.7	173.0	100.7	101.1	100.1
Income: Debit	78ah d	−2.8	−4.0	−6.5	−9.7	−14.2	−18.2	−24.7	−49.0	−78.9	−113.0	−112.0	−127.9	−161.4	−189.6	−240.4
Balance on Gds, Serv. & Inc.	78ai d	−205.2	−228.9	−329.4	−536.6	−719.0	−937.6	−1,093.1	−1,572.2	−1,605.1	−2,220.8	−2,299.1	−2,110.0	−1,980.6	−1,846.2	−1,658.4
Current Transfers, n.i.e.: Credit	78aj d	211.7	241.3	333.1	583.2	779.6	975.5	872.4	1,666.3	2,140.8	2,344.2	2,149.3	1,925.0	1,979.5	1,828.3	1,872.7
Current Transfers: Debit	78ak d	—	—	−.3	−1.9	−24.4	−54.4	−67.7	−100.6	−161.8	−162.3	−183.0	−205.7	−263.7	−242.5	−254.1
Capital Account, n.i.e.	78bc d	—	—	—	—	—	—	—	—	—	—	—	—	—	—	—
Capital Account, n.i.e.: Credit	78ba d	—	—	—	—	—	—	—	—	—	—	—	—	—	—	—
Capital Account: Debit	78bb d	—	—	—	—	—	—	—	—	—	—	—	—	—	—	—
Financial Account, n.i.e.	78bj d	17.4	23.1	39.4	164.5	16.0	134.8	426.5	268.2	328.2	299.5	385.5	483.7	123.7	248.2	99.5
Direct Investment Abroad	78bd d	−1.7	−5.5	−3.4	−6.3	−2.7	—	—	—	−3.1	7.0	−3.4	−4.8	−2.7	.7	−3.9
Dir. Invest. in Rep. Econ., n.i.e.	78be d	.6	2.1	6.8	25.6	−7.5	11.2	56.4	26.4	33.8	140.8	59.4	34.9	77.5	24.9	22.8
Portfolio Investment Assets	78bg d	—	—	—	—	—	—	—	—	—	—	—	—	—	—	—
Equity Securities	78bk d	—	—	—	—	—	—	—	—	—	—	—	—	—	—	—
Debt Securities	78bl d	—	—	—	—	—	—	—	—	—	—	—	—	—	—	—
Portfolio Investment Liab., n.i.e.	78bg d	—	—	—	—	—	—	—	—	—	—	—	—	—	—	—
Equity Securities	78bm d	—	—	—	—	—	—	—	—	—	—	—	—	—	—	—
Debt Securities	78bn d	—	—	—	—	—	—	—	—	—	—	—	—	—	—	—
Financial Derivatives Assets	78bw d	....	....	....	....	....	....	....	....	....	....	....	....	....	....	....
Financial Derivatives Liabilities	78bx d	....	....	....	....	....	....	....	....	....	....	....	....	....	....	....
Other Investment Assets	78bh d	.3	.3	.6	−1.9	.3	−7.8	−2.6	−38.0	−170.8	−244.4	−104.2	−198.1	−246.2	−190.2	−84.9
Monetary Authorities	78bo d	....	....	....	....	....	....	....	....	....	....	....	−76.6	−212.9	−112.4	−77.1
General Government	78bp d	.3	.3	.6	−1.9	.3	−7.8	−2.6	−38.0	−170.8	−244.4	−104.2	−121.6	−33.2	−77.8	−7.8
Banks	78bq d															
Other Sectors	78br d															
Other Investment Liab., n.i.e.	78bi d	18.2	26.2	35.4	147.0	25.9	131.4	372.6	279.8	468.3	396.1	433.7	651.7	295.0	412.7	165.6
Monetary Authorities	78bs d		2.7	.3	7.8	22.0	−11.2	2.7	−9.1	6.2	−3.3	−.3		−.5		
General Government	78bt d	18.5	22.8	30.1	120.1	−34.3	148.4	239.5	209.4	246.5	313.4	367.9	524.0	122.5	355.2	135.5
Banks	78bu d	−.3	.6	5.0	19.1	38.3	−5.8	130.3	79.4	215.7	86.0	66.1	127.7	173.0	57.5	30.0
Other Sectors	78bv d															
Net Errors and Omissions	78ca d	−5.1	3.8	−16.9	−36.3	−24.7	67.6	113.9	59.2	−257.3	−99.6	−152.3	−40.0	−47.9	−29.6	−17.2
Overall Balance	78cb d	18.7	39.4	26.0	172.9	27.4	185.9	251.9	320.9	444.8	161.0	−99.5	53.0	−189.0	−41.9	42.5
Reserves and Related Items	79da d	−18.7	−39.4	−26.0	−172.9	−27.4	−185.9	−251.9	−320.9	−444.8	−161.0	99.5	−53.0	189.0	41.9	−42.5
Reserve Assets	79db d	−18.7	−35.6	−24.1	−172.9	−27.4	−185.9	−251.9	−320.9	−444.8	−161.0	99.5	−53.0	189.0	−14.1	−42.5
Use of Fund Credit and Loans	79dc d	—	−3.8	−1.9	—	—	—	—	—	—	—	—	—	—	56.0	—
Exceptional Financing	79de d	—	—	—	—	—	—	—	—	—	—	—	—	—	—	—

International Investment Position																*Millions of US Dollars*
Assets	79aa d	....	....	....	....	....	....	....	....	....	....	....	....	....	....	....
Direct Investment Abroad	79ab d	....	....	....	....	....	....	....	....	....	....	....	....	....	....	....
Portfolio Investment	79ac d	....	....	....	....	....	....	....	....	....	....	....	....	....	....	....
Equity Securities	79ad d	....	....	....	....	....	....	....	....	....	....	....	....	....	....	....
Debt Securities	79ae d	....	....	....	....	....	....	....	....	....	....	....	....	....	....	....
Financial Derivatives	79al d	....	....	....	....	....	....	....	....	....	....	....	....	....	....	....
Other Investment	79af d	....	....	....	....	....	....	....	....	....	....	....	....	....	....	....
Monetary Authorities	79ag d	....	....	....	....	....	....	....	....	....	....	....	....	....	....	....
General Government	79ah d	....	....	....	....	....	....	....	....	....	....	....	....	....	....	....
Banks	79ai d	....	....	....	....	....	....	....	....	....	....	....	....	....	....	....
Other Sectors	79aj d	....	....	....	....	....	....	....	....	....	....	....	....	....	....	....
Reserve Assets	79ak d	....	....	....	....	....	....	....	....	....	2,016.6	1,967.6	1,787.6	....	....	....
Liabilities	79la d	....	....	....	....	....	....	....	....	....	....	....	....	....	....	....
Dir. Invest. in Rep. Economy	79lb d	....	....	....	....	....	....	....	....	....	....	....	....	....	....	....
Portfolio Investment	79lc d	....	....	....	....	....	....	....	....	....	....	....	....	....	....	....
Equity Securities	79ld d	....	....	....	....	....	....	....	....	....	....	....	....	....	....	....
Debt Securities	79le d	....	....	....	....	....	....	....	....	....	....	....	....	....	....	....
Financial Derivatives	79ll d	....	....	....	....	....	....	....	....	....	....	....	....	....	....	....
Other Investment	79lf d	....	....	....	....	....	....	....	....	....	....	....	....	....	....	....
Monetary Authorities	79lg d	....	....	....	....	....	....	....	....	....	....	....	....	....	....	....
General Government	79lh d	....	....	....	....	....	....	....	....	....	....	....	....	....	....	....
Banks	79li d	....	....	....	....	....	....	....	....	....	....	....	....	....	....	....
Other Sectors	79lj d	....	....	....	....	....	....	....	....	....	....	....	....	....	....	....

	1987	1988	1989	1990	1991	1992	1993	1994	1995	1996	1997	1998	1999	2000	2001		
Minus Sign Indicates Debit																**Balance of Payments**	
Current Account, n.i.e.	−351.8	−293.7	384.9	−227.1	−393.5	−835.2	−629.1	−398.0	−258.6	−221.9	29.3	14.1	404.9	....	....	Current Account, n.i.e.	78ald
	933.1	1,007.4	1,109.4	1,063.8	1,129.5	1,218.9	1,246.3	1,424.5	1,769.6	1,816.9	1,835.5	1,802.4	1,831.9	....	....	Goods: Exports f.o.b.	78aa d
	−2,400.1	−2,418.7	−1,882.5	−2,300.7	−2,302.2	−2,998.7	−3,145.2	−3,003.8	−3,287.8	−3,818.1	−3,648.5	−3,403.9	−3,292.0	....	....	Goods: Imports f.o.b.	78ab d
	−1,467.0	−1,411.3	−773.1	−1,236.9	−1,172.7	−1,779.7	−1,898.8	−1,579.4	−1,518.2	−2,001.1	−1,813.0	−1,601.6	−1,460.1	....	....	*Trade Balance*	78ac d
	1,291.7	1,420.6	1,239.2	1,447.2	1,351.2	1,449.2	1,573.7	1,562.0	1,709.2	1,846.3	1,736.8	1,825.1	1,701.7	....	....	Services: Credit	78ad d
	−1,298.3	−1,340.5	−1,063.3	−1,267.9	−1,122.5	−1,324.7	−1,347.2	−1,392.7	−1,614.9	−1,597.7	−1,537.2	−1,783.8	−1,698.0	....	....	Services: Debit	78ae d
	−1,473.6	−1,331.1	−597.1	−1,057.6	−944.0	−1,655.2	−1,672.3	−1,410.1	−1,424.0	−1,752.6	−1,613.4	−1,560.2	−1,456.4	....	....	*Balance on Goods & Services*	78af d
	58.3	40.6	39.0	67.3	114.3	112.4	99.0	72.7	115.7	111.7	248.2	306.9	301.1	....	....	Income: Credit	78ag d
	−278.6	−354.8	−235.6	−281.8	−447.7	−460.0	−409.4	−387.5	−394.5	−412.7	−457.0	−445.0	−455.6	....	....	Income: Debit	78ah d
	−1,693.8	−1,645.2	−793.7	−1,272.1	−1,277.4	−2,002.8	−1,982.8	−1,724.9	−1,702.8	−2,053.6	−1,822.1	−1,698.3	−1,610.9	....	....	*Balance on Gds, Serv. & Inc.*	78ai d
	1,547.1	1,532.0	1,284.5	1,123.1	949.5	1,263.6	1,441.1	1,447.4	1,591.8	1,970.2	2,096.1	1,984.3	2,321.3	....	....	Current Transfers, n.i.e.: Credit	78aj d
	−205.1	−180.5	−105.8	−78.2	−65.7	−96.1	−87.4	−120.5	−147.6	−138.5	−244.6	−271.9	−305.5	....	....	Current Transfers: Debit	78ak d
	—	—	—	—	—	—	—	—	197.2	157.7	163.8	81.1	90.3	....	....	Capital Account, n.i.e.	78bc d
	—	—	—	—	—	—	—	—	197.2	157.7	163.8	81.1	90.3	....	....	Capital Account, n.i.e.: Credit	78ba d
	—	—	—	—	—	—	—	—	—	—	—	—	—	....	....	Capital Account: Debit	78bb d
	465.2	374.2	79.5	572.7	2,097.3	615.1	−530.0	188.9	230.0	233.9	242.3	−177.3	487.9	....	....	Financial Account, n.i.e.	78bj d
	−1.2	.1	−16.7	31.5	−13.7	3.4	53.0	23.1	27.3	43.3	—	—	−4.5	....	....	Direct Investment Abroad	78bd d
	39.5	23.7	−1.3	37.6	−11.9	40.7	−33.5	2.9	13.3	15.5	360.9	310.0	158.0	....	....	Dir. Invest. in Rep. Econ., n.i.e.	78be d
	—	—	—	—	—	—	—	—	....	....	....	....	32.2	....	....	Portfolio Investment Assets	78bf d
	—	—	—	—	—	—	—	—	....	....	....	....	32.2	....	....	Equity Securities	78bk d
	—	—	—	—	—	—	—	—	....	....	....	....	—	....	....	Debt Securities	78bl d
	—	—	—	—	—	—	—	—	—	—	....	....	21.9	....	....	Portfolio Investment Liab., n.i.e.	78bg d
	—	—	—	—	—	—	—	—	—	—	....	....	21.9	....	....	Equity Securities	78bm d
	—	—	—	—	—	—	—	—	—	—	....	....	—	....	....	Debt Securities	78bn d
	....	....	....	....	....	....	....	....	....	....	....	....	....	....	....	Financial Derivatives Assets	78bw d
	....	....	....	....	....	....	....	....	....	....	....	....	....	....	....	Financial Derivatives Liabilities	78bx d
	−9.0	—	....	222.2	561.5	609.2	384.8	62.5	−313.4	−5.9	16.4	−80.3	−73.5	....	....	Other Investment Assets	78bh d
	−13.8	—	—	110.1	−241.7	−113.6	−94.9	−163.5	−313.4	−5.9	16.4	−80.3	−40.5	....	....	Monetary Authorities	78bo d
	4.8	—	—	—	—	—	−.3	....	....	....	....	....	....	....	....	General Government	78bp d
	—	—	—	—	—	—	—	....	....	....	....	....	....	....	....	Banks	78bq d
	—	—	—	112.1	803.2	722.8	480.0	225.9	....	....	....	....	−33.0	....	....	Other Sectors	78br d
	435.9	350.4	97.6	281.4	1,561.4	−38.3	−934.3	100.4	502.8	181.0	−135.0	−407.1	353.9	....	....	Other Investment Liab., n.i.e.	78bi d
	169.9	−133.2	5.2	.2	—	.6	.7	−8.7	−34.4	−11.0	−27.6	−11.0	165.9	....	....	Monetary Authorities	78bs d
	183.4	13.4	202.6	353.2	296.5	−532.1	−675.8	−235.4	96.8	17.8	−91.4	−391.0	6.3	....	....	General Government	78bt d
	100.0	457.2	−75.9	−66.7	1,267.9	495.1	−257.5	344.5	440.5	174.2	−15.9	−5.1	205.5	....	....	Banks	78bu d
	−17.5	13.0	−34.3	−5.3	−3.1	−1.9	−1.7	—	—	—	—	—	−23.8	....	....	Other Sectors	78bv d
	27.9	123.4	.3	75.4	321.4	83.1	298.0	−55.8	−339.9	−357.9	−160.8	−454.0	−10.2	....	....	Net Errors and Omissions	78ca d
	141.3	203.9	464.7	421.0	2,025.2	−137.1	−861.1	−264.9	−171.3	−188.2	274.6	−536.1	972.9	....	....	*Overall Balance*	78cb d
	−141.3	−203.9	−464.7	−421.0	−2,025.2	137.1	861.1	264.9	171.3	188.2	−274.6	536.1	−972.9	....	....	Reserves and Related Items	79da d
	−141.3	−175.2	−512.0	−411.5	−2,025.2	−432.0	402.9	−216.8	−371.5	−280.7	−677.1	−83.4	−1,288.7	....	....	Reserve Assets	79db d
	—	−28.7	47.2	−9.5	—	21.1	−31.0	57.6	106.5	97.6	110.3	22.4	39.7	....	....	Use of Fund Credit and Loans	79dc d
	—	—	—	—	—	548.0	489.1	424.1	436.3	371.4	292.2	597.0	276.2	....	....	Exceptional Financing	79de d
Millions of US Dollars																**International Investment Position**	
	....	....	....	....	....	....	....	....	....	7,826.9	8,854.4	6,892.9	8,221.7	....	....	Assets	79aa d
	....	....	....	....	....	....	....	....	....	—	—	—	—	....	....	Direct Investment Abroad	79ab d
	....	....	....	....	....	....	....	....	....	209.0	270.9	279.8	290.1	....	....	Portfolio Investment	79ac d
	....	....	....	....	....	....	....	....	....	89.1	110.6	109.7	93.1	....	....	Equity Securities	79ad d
	....	....	....	....	....	....	....	....	....	119.9	160.4	170.1	197.0	....	....	Debt Securities	79ae d
	....	....	....	....	....	....	....	....	....	—	—	—	—	....	....	Financial Derivatives	79al d
	....	....	....	....	....	....	....	....	....	5,660.8	6,257.0	6,407.9	7,811.3	....	....	Other Investment	79af d
	....	....	....	....	....	....	....	....	....	2,890.1	3,323.4	2,946.0	3,849.4	....	....	Monetary Authorities	79ag d
	....	....	....	....	....	....	....	....	....	—	—	—	—	....	....	General Government	79ah d
	....	....	....	....	....	....	....	....	....	2,770.7	2,933.6	3,461.9	3,961.9	....	....	Banks	79ai d
	....	....	....	....	....	....	....	....	....	—	—	—	—	....	....	Other Sectors	79aj d
	....	....	....	....	....	....	....	....	....	1,957.1	2,326.5	205.2	120.3	....	....	Reserve Assets	79ak d
	....	....	....	....	....	....	....	....	....	9,833.2	9,611.8	10,169.3	10,830.1	....	....	Liabilities	79la d
	....	....	....	....	....	....	....	....	....	—	—	—	—	....	....	Dir. Invest. in Rep. Economy	79lb d
	....	....	....	....	....	....	....	....	....	—	—	—	—	....	....	Portfolio Investment	79lc d
	....	....	....	....	....	....	....	....	....	—	—	—	—	....	....	Equity Securities	79ld d
	....	....	....	....	....	....	....	....	....	—	—	—	—	....	....	Debt Securities	79le d
	....	....	....	....	....	....	....	....	....	—	—	—	—	....	....	Financial Derivatives	79ll d
	....	....	....	....	....	....	....	....	....	9,833.2	9,611.8	10,169.3	10,830.1	....	....	Other Investment	79lf d
	....	....	....	....	....	....	....	....	....	410.9	470.9	502.2	728.6	....	....	Monetary Authorities	79lg d
	....	....	....	....	....	....	....	....	....	6,321.6	6,056.1	6,587.6	6,816.4	....	....	General Government	79lh d
	....	....	....	....	....	....	....	....	....	3,100.7	3,084.8	3,079.6	3,285.1	....	....	Banks	79li d
	....	....	....	....	....	....	....	....	....	—	—	—	—	....	....	Other Sectors	79lj d

Jordan

		1972	1973	1974	1975	1976	1977	1978	1979	1980	1981	1982	1983	1984	1985	1986
Government Finance															*Millions of Dinars:*	
Deficit (-) or Surplus	80	22.0	−23.1	−15.1	−14.8	−81.4	−61.1	−110.8	−104.1	−103.9	−100.8	−113.0	−68.2	−142.0	−111.7	−153.1
Revenue	81	42.6	46.2	65.7	82.6	107.6	142.3	158.5	187.9	226.2	309.2	362.0	400.6	415.0	440.8	514.4
Grants Received	81z	45.6	43.6	57.7	97.1	66.2	122.2	81.7	210.3	209.3	206.3	199.6	197.0	106.1	187.8	143.7
Expenditure	82	66.1	112.7	138.2	183.6	244.0	307.9	340.1	475.4	512.5	576.2	643.7	630.0	640.6	713.4	770.1
Lending Minus Repayments	83	.1	.2	.3	11.0	11.3	17.6	10.9	26.9	26.8	40.1	31.0	35.8	22.5	27.0	41.1
Financing																
Net Borrowing: Dinars	84b	4.3	9.3	8.1	9.8	12.9	9.6	13.3	26.9	11.2	16.1	19.2	8.0	14.2	25.9	−8.9
Foreign Currency	85b	3.9	8.2	9.4	9.3	12.8	51.6	82.9	29.7	54.6	54.7	55.5	60.4	85.4	125.0	86.1
Use of Cash Balances	87	−30.2	5.6	−2.3	−4.2	55.8	−.1	14.6	47.5	38.1	30.0	38.3	−.2	42.4	−39.1	75.9
Debt: Domestic	88a	36.00	49.80	56.00	65.40	89.30	105.90	135.20	139.40	177.80	209.50	250.00	287.90	316.50	347.20	392.70
Foreign	89a	62.90	68.90	79.80	91.70	114.10	147.30	187.80	233.70	255.90	350.20	441.50	536.50	653.60	773.20	884.50
National Accounts															*Millions of Dinars*	
Househ.Cons.Expend..incl.NPISHs	96f	177.4	183.1	199.8	261.9	325.5	412.8	517.4	736.8	858.3	1,074.5	1,457.9	†1,579.1	1,648.4	1,794.8	1,718.2
Government Consumption Expend.	91f	68.3	80.0	97.7	110.1	155.9	156.6	190.0	235.3	342.7	455.5	477.9	†473.4	534.6	531.7	566.5
Gross Fixed Capital Formation	93e	36.3	47.2	63.2	87.9	138.0	201.0	229.1	294.5	452.9	672.6	626.9	†535.9	526.8	384.8	409.3
Changes in Inventories	93i	6.0	−8.0	2.4	.9	12.2	5.5	−6.1	−14.5	11.0	28.4	23.9	†53.9	44.4	30.1	35.0
Exports of Goods and Services	90c	37.0	52.4	80.3	118.9	192.1	242.0	264.3	339.5	448.0	588.5	670.2	†639.6	746.3	781.5	634.1
Imports of Goods and Services (-)	98c	117.8	136.4	196.1	301.1	422.0	540.3	605.6	824.5	961.7	1,392.7	1,555.7	†1,453.2	1,519.1	1,502.7	1,199.5
Gross Domestic Product (GDP)	99b	251.7	265.2	300.4	379.1	512.1	624.6	767.9	914.6	1,151.2	1,426.7	1,701.1	†1,828.7	1,981.4	2,020.2	2,163.6
Net Primary Income from Abroad	98.n	13.8	23.2	32.0	63.9	140.8	145.9	148.8	168.3	32.4	57.5	64.4	†49.2	13.6	−4.7	−17.3
Gross National Income (GNI)	99a	221.9	242.4	280.4	377.5	564.5	662.7	784.0	924.9	1,183.6	1,484.2	1,765.5	†1,877.9	1,995.0	2,015.5	2,146.3
Net National Income	99e	210.7	231.0	268.7	360.2	545.0	639.1	754.0	882.8	1,096.3	1,371.2	1,608.1	†1,699.2	1,795.3	1,809.0	1,949.1
GDP Volume 1985 Prices	99b.*p*	....	....	....	....	....	....	....	....	....	....	....	....	....	2,020.2	2,161.9
GDP Volume 1994 Prices	99b.*p*	....	....	....	....	....	....	....	....	....	....	....	....	....		
GDP Volume (1995=100)	99bv*p*	....	....	....	....	....	....	....	....	....	....	....	....	....	75.7	81.0
GDP Deflator (1995=100)	99bi*p*	....	....	....	....	....	....	....	....	....	....	....	....	....	55.9	56.0
																Millions:
Population	99z	2.46	2.54	2.62	2.70	2.78	†2.71	2.77	2.84	2.92	3.01	3.10	3.20	†3.36	3.83	3.94

Year Ending December 31

	1987	1988	1989	1990	1991	1992	1993	1994	1995	1996	1997	1998	1999	2000	2001		
Government Finance																	
Deficit (-) or Surplus	-198.2	-204.6	-137.1	-94.4	12.4	181.0	69.7	105.0	15.2	75.9	-102.6	-296.6	-136.8	....	....	80	
Revenue	531.5	544.3	565.4	744.1	828.8	1,168.9	1,191.5	1,306.4	1,389.1	1,518.0	1,425.7	1,496.5	1,589.4	....	....	81	
Grants Received	127.5	155.4	261.7	164.3	225.2	137.4	163.3	175.6	182.8	191.3	225.0	203.0	198.5	....	....	81z	
Expenditure	825.7	910.9	947.9	1,000.9	1,077.4	1,140.5	1,306.4	1,396.6	1,561.9	1,648.3	1,763.3	1,951.1	1,859.4	....	....	82	
Lending Minus Repayments	31.6	-6.5	16.3	1.9	-35.8	-15.2	-21.3	-19.6	-5.2	-14.9	-10.0	45.0	65.3	....	....	83	
Financing																	
Net Borrowing: Dinars	95.1	115.3	22.3	14.4	-7.1	-51.2	-47.7	-15.5	-119.0	-15.2	-47.2	321.0	69.1	....	....	84b	
Foreign Currency	7.2	-10.9	96.0	129.7	211.4	208.6	-133.2	75.4	287.8	296.5	-2.6	-46.0	122.8	....	....	85b	
Use of Cash Balances	95.8	100.2	18.8	-49.7	-216.8	-338.4	111.2	-164.9	-184.0	-357.2	152.4	21.6	-55.1	....	....	87	
Debt: Domestic	604.20	903.60	976.60	1,019.30	1,021.39	1,004.19	1,106.50	1,144.00	928.85	961.50	914.20	1,339.40	899.30	....	....	88a	
Foreign	951.40	3,859.60	3,576.51	4,454.37	4,392.83	3,988.38	3,693.12	3,955.45	4,076.20	....	....	4,677.20	5,539.60	....	....	89a	

Millions of Dinars

	1987	1988	1989	1990	1991	1992	1993	1994	1995	1996	1997	1998	1999	2000	2001		
National Accounts																	
Househ.Cons.Expend.,incl.NPISHs	1,669.8	1,626.5	1,635.1	1,976.5	2,052.8	†2,803.6	2,834.6	2,977.6	3,104.7	3,523.6	3,702.2	4,143.5	4,256.3	4,770.2	....	96f	
Government Consumption Expend.	586.7	604.3	618.8	663.9	742.0	†790.6	857.9	985.6	1,111.3	1,204.1	1,312.5	1,367.0	1,412.3	1,493.3	....	91f	
Gross Fixed Capital Formation	448.5	513.4	554.1	694.0	678.0	†1,049.2	1,303.5	1,391.0	1,395.0	1,445.3	1,325.1	1,189.8	1,087.8	1,199.0	....	93e	
Changes in Inventories	67.1	19.1	9.1	156.1	60.5	†159.6	119.2	60.0	159.3	52.1	-3.3	35.6	—	—	....	93i	
Exports of Goods and Services	756.2	1,020.8	1,359.5	1,652.1	1,697.6	†1,819.9	1,962.1	2,093.4	2,438.5	2,597.2	2,532.8	2,515.7	2,505.4	2,505.7	....	90c	
Imports of Goods and Services (-)	1,319.7	1,519.7	1,804.5	2,474.3	2,362.6	†2,974.7	3,151.7	3,107.6	3,435.2	3,839.9	3,676.7	3,608.7	3,537.9	4,055.3	....	98c	
Gross Domestic Product (GDP)	2,208.6	2,264.4	2,372.1	2,668.3	2,868.3	†3,648.2	3,925.6	4,400.0	4,773.6	4,982.4	5,192.4	5,646.9	5,723.9	5,912.9	....	99b	
Net Primary Income from Abroad	-50.2	-88.5	-191.4	-239.5	-221.1	†-186.2	-149.1	-151.4	-116.8	-112.3	-47.4	-5.8	-8.7	95.5	....	98.n	
Gross National Income (GNI)	2,158.4	2,175.9	2,180.7	2,428.8	2,647.2	†3,462.0	3,776.5	4,248.6	4,656.8	4,870.1	5,145.0	5,637.1	5,715.2	6,008.4	....	99a	
Net National Income	1,955.1	1,955.3	1,942.5	2,195.4	2,344.5	†3,138.3	3,424.1	3,858.2	4,223.2	4,352.6	4,583.1	5,029.8	....	....	....	99e	
GDP Volume 1985 Prices	2,224.5	2,183.2	1,889.6	1,908.0	1,951.9	2,283.7	2,417.0	2,601.5	2,702.2	2,729.6	2,764.5	2,824.9	....	....	....	99b.p	
GDP Volume 1994 Prices	....	....	....	....	....	4,005.8	4,192.0	4,400.6	4,681.5	4,779.8	4,926.1	5,070.9	....	....	....	99b.p	
GDP Volume (1995=100)	83.3	81.8	70.8	71.5	73.1	85.6	89.5	94.0	100.0	102.1	105.2	108.3	....	....	....	99bv p	
GDP Deflator (1995=100)	55.5	58.0	70.2	78.2	82.2	†89.3	91.8	98.1	100.0	102.2	103.4	109.2	....	....	....	99bi p	

Midyear Estimates

	1987	1988	1989	1990	1991	1992	1993	1994	1995	1996	1997	1998	1999	2000	2001		
Population	4.00	4.06	4.50	4.62	4.80	5.02	5.26	5.51	5.73	5.94	6.13	6.30	6.48	....	....	99z	

(See notes in the back of the book.)

Kazakhstan

916		1972	1973	1974	1975	1976	1977	1978	1979	1980	1981	1982	1983	1984	1985	1986
Exchange Rates																*Tenge per SDR:*
Official Rate	aa	....	....	....	....	....	....	....	....	....	....	....	....	....	....	....
																Tenge per US Dollar:
Official Rate	ae	....	....	....	....	....	....	....	....	....	....	....	....	....	....	....
Official Rate	rf	....	....	....	....	....	....	....	....	....	....	....	....	....	....	....
Fund Position																*Millions of SDRs:*
Quota	2f.s	....	....	....	....	....	....	....	....	....	....	....	....	....	....	....
SDRs	1b.s	....	....	....	....	....	....	....	....	....	....	....	....	....	....	....
Reserve Position in the Fund	1c.s	....	....	....	....	....	....	....	....	....	....	....	....	....	....	....
Total Fund Cred.&Loans Outstg.	2tl	....	....	....	....	....	....	....	....	....	....	....	....	....	....	....
International Liquidity																*Millions of US Dollars Unless Otherwise Indicated:*
Total Reserves minus Gold	1l.d	....	....	....	....	....	....	....	....	....	....	....	....	....	....	....
SDRs	1b.d	....	....	....	....	....	....	....	....	....	....	....	....	....	....	....
Reserve Position in the Fund	1c.d	....	....	....	....	....	....	....	....	....	....	....	....	....	....	....
Foreign Exchange	1d.d	....	....	....	....	....	....	....	....	....	....	....	....	....	....	....
Gold (Million Fine Troy Ounces)	1ad	....	....	....	....	....	....	....	....	....	....	....	....	....	....	....
Gold (National Valuation)	1and	....	....	....	....	....	....	....	....	....	....	....	....	....	....	....
Monetary Authorities: Other Assets	3..d	....	....	....	....	....	....	....	....	....	....	....	....	....	....	....
Other liab.	4..d	....	....	....	....	....	....	....	....	....	....	....	....	....	....	....
Deposit Money Banks: Assets	7a.d	....	....	....	....	....	....	....	....	....	....	....	....	....	....	....
Liabilities	7b.d	....	....	....	....	....	....	....	....	....	....	....	....	....	....	....
Monetary Authorities																*Millions of Tenge:*
Foreign Assets	11	....	....	....	....	....	....	....	....	....	....	....	....	....	....	....
Claims on Central Government	12a	....	....	....	....	....	....	....	....	....	....	....	....	....	....	....
Claims on Rest of the Economy	12d	....	....	....	....	....	....	....	....	....	....	....	....	....	....	....
Claims on Deposit Money Banks	12e	....	....	....	....	....	....	....	....	....	....	....	....	....	....	....
Reserve Money	14	....	....	....	....	....	....	....	....	....	....	....	....	....	....	....
of which: Currency Outside Banks	14a	....	....	....	....	....	....	....	....	....	....	....	....	....	....	....
Other Deposits	15	....	....	....	....	....	....	....	....	....	....	....	....	....	....	....
Liabs. of Central Bank: Securities	16ac	....	....	....	....	....	....	....	....	....	....	....	....	....	....	....
Foreign Liabilities	16c	....	....	....	....	....	....	....	....	....	....	....	....	....	....	....
Central Government Deposits	16d	....	....	....	....	....	....	....	....	....	....	....	....	....	....	....
Capital Accounts	17a	....	....	....	....	....	....	....	....	....	....	....	....	....	....	....
Other Items (Net)	17r	....	....	....	....	....	....	....	....	....	....	....	....	....	....	....
Deposit Money Banks																*Millions of Tenge:*
Reserves	20	....	....	....	....	....	....	....	....	....	....	....	....	....	....	....
Claims on Central Bank: Securities	20c	....	....	....	....	....	....	....	....	....	....	....	....	....	....	....
Other Claims on Central Bank	20n	....	....	....	....	....	....	....	....	....	....	....	....	....	....	....
Foreign Assets	21	....	....	....	....	....	....	....	....	....	....	....	....	....	....	....
Claims on Central Government	22a	....	....	....	....	....	....	....	....	....	....	....	....	....	....	....
Claims on Local Government	22b	....	....	....	....	....	....	....	....	....	....	....	....	....	....	....
Claims on Nonfin.Pub.Enterprises	22c	....	....	....	....	....	....	....	....	....	....	....	....	....	....	....
Claims on Rest of the Economy	22d	....	....	....	....	....	....	....	....	....	....	....	....	....	....	....
Claims on Nonbank Financial Insts.	22g	....	....	....	....	....	....	....	....	....	....	....	....	....	....	....
Demand Deposits	24	....	....	....	....	....	....	....	....	....	....	....	....	....	....	....
Other Deposits	25	....	....	....	....	....	....	....	....	....	....	....	....	....	....	....
Bonds	26ab	....	....	....	....	....	....	....	....	....	....	....	....	....	....	....
Restricted Deposits	26b	....	....	....	....	....	....	....	....	....	....	....	....	....	....	....
Foreign Liabilities	26c	....	....	....	....	....	....	....	....	....	....	....	....	....	....	....
Central Government Deposits	26d	....	....	....	....	....	....	....	....	....	....	....	....	....	....	....
Liabilities to Local Government	26db	....	....	....	....	....	....	....	....	....	....	....	....	....	....	....
Credit from Central Bank	26g	....	....	....	....	....	....	....	....	....	....	....	....	....	....	....
Capital Accounts	27a	....	....	....	....	....	....	....	....	....	....	....	....	....	....	....
Other Items (Net)	27r	....	....	....	....	....	....	....	....	....	....	....	....	....	....	....
Monetary Survey																*Millions of Tenge:*
Foreign Assets (Net)	31n	....	....	....	....	....	....	....	....	....	....	....	....	....	....	....
Domestic Credit	32	....	....	....	....	....	....	....	....	....	....	....	....	....	....	....
Claims on General Govt. (Net)	32an	....	....	....	....	....	....	....	....	....	....	....	....	....	....	....
Claims on Local Government	32b	....	....	....	....	....	....	....	....	....	....	....	....	....	....	....
Claims on Nonfin.Pub.Enterprises	32c	....	....	....	....	....	....	....	....	....	....	....	....	....	....	....
Claims on Rest of the Economy	32d	....	....	....	....	....	....	....	....	....	....	....	....	....	....	....
Claims on Nonbank Financial Insts.	32g	....	....	....	....	....	....	....	....	....	....	....	....	....	....	....
Money	34	....	....	....	....	....	....	....	....	....	....	....	....	....	....	....
Quasi-Money	35	....	....	....	....	....	....	....	....	....	....	....	....	....	....	....
Bonds	36ab	....	....	....	....	....	....	....	....	....	....	....	....	....	....	....
Liabs. of Central Bank: Securities	36ac	....	....	....	....	....	....	....	....	....	....	....	....	....	....	....
Restricted Deposits	36b	....	....	....	....	....	....	....	....	....	....	....	....	....	....	....
Capital Accounts	37a	....	....	....	....	....	....	....	....	....	....	....	....	....	....	....
Other Items (Net)	37r	....	....	....	....	....	....	....	....	....	....	....	....	....	....	....
Money plus Quasi-Money	35l	....	....	....	....	....	....	....	....	....	....	....	....	....	....	....
Interest Rates																*Percent Per Annum*
Refinancing Rate *(End of Per.)*	60	....	....	....	....	....	....	....	....	....	....	....	....	....	....	....
Treasury Bill Rate	60c	....	....	....	....	....	....	....	....	....	....	....	....	....	....	....
Prices and Labor																*Index Numbers:*
Producer Prices	63	....	....	....	....	....	....	....	....	....	....	....	....	....	....	....
Consumer Prices	64	....	....	....	....	....	....	....	....	....	....	....	....	....	....	....
Wages: Monthly Earnings	65	....	....	....	....	....	....	....	....	....	....	....	....	....	....	....
Total Employment	67	....	....	....	....	....	....	....	....	....	....	....	....	....	....	....
																Number in Thousands:
Employment	67e	....	....	....	....	....	....	....	....	....	....	....	....	....	....	....
Unemployment	67c	....	....	....	....	....	....	....	....	....	....	....	....	....	....	....
Unemployment Rate (%)	67r	....	....	....	....	....	....	....	....	....	....	....	....	....	....	....
International Transactions																*Millions of US Dollars*
Exports	70..d	....	....	....	....	....	....	....	....	....	....	....	....	....	....	....
Imports, c.i.f.	71..d	....	....	....	....	....	....	....	....	....	....	....	....	....	....	....

1987	1988	1989	1990	1991	1992	1993	1994	1995	1996	1997	1998	1999	2000	2001		Code
															Exchange Rates	
															End of Period	
						8.67	79.21	95.06	105.40	101.94	117.99	189.68	188.27	188.76	Official Rate	aa
															End of Period (ae) Period Average (rf)	
						6.31	54.26	63.95	73.30	75.55	83.80	138.20	144.50	150.20	Official Rate	ae
							35.54	60.95	67.30	75.44	78.30	119.52	142.13	146.74	Official Rate	rf
															Fund Position	
															End of Period	
					247.50	247.50	247.50	247.50	247.50	247.50	247.50	365.70	365.70	365.70	Quota	2f. s
						13.98	69.54	154.87	240.19	327.15	275.08	164.24	.01	—	SDRs	1b. s
					.01	.01	.01	.01	.01	.01	.01	.01	.01	.01	Reserve Position in the Fund	1c. s
					—	61.88	198.00	290.82	383.60	378.96	463.66	335.15	—	—	Total Fund Cred.&Loans Outstg.	2tl
															International Liquidity	
						455.7	837.5	1,135.6	1,294.7	1,697.1	1,461.2	1,479.2	1,594.1	1,997.2	Total Reserves minus Gold	1l. d
						19.2	101.5	230.2	345.4	441.4	387.3	225.4	—	—	SDRs	1b. d
					.01	.01	.01	.01	.01	.01	.01	.01	.01	.01	Reserve Position in the Fund	1c. d
						436.5	736.0	905.3	949.3	1,255.7	1,073.9	1,253.8	1,594.1	1,997.2	Foreign Exchange	1d. d
						.65	.99	1.36	1.80	1.81	1.75	1.80	1.84	1.84	Gold (Million Fine Troy Ounces)	1ad
						255.5	378.0	524.3	949.3	523.9	503.6	522.8	501.5	510.7	Gold (National Valuation)	1an d
						133.1	3.5	2.4							Monetary Authorities: Other Assets	3.. d
							26.3	60.9							Other liab.	4.. d
						345.6	271.9	440.9	330.1	273.8	344.6	570.6	383.5	556.0	Deposit Money Banks: Assets	7a. d
						563.5	1,195.8	414.2	138.1	207.5	390.5	232.2	379.6	982.2	Liabilities	7b. d
															Monetary Authorities	
															End of Period	
						5,328	66,143	106,300	129,801	†172,971	164,663	276,713	302,950	565,816	Foreign Assets	11
						1,696	20,236	39,467	39,265	†77,078	87,931	109,304	41,568	19,134	Claims on Central Government	12a
						197	760	332	16,906	†620	7,277	12,657	2,146	3,587	Claims on Rest of the Economy	12d
						6,095	13,355	10,487	9,059	†8,248	2,084	4,634	2,774	1,810	Claims on Deposit Money Banks	12e
						4,309	31,171	66,550	84,354	†115,389	81,427	126,749	134,416	175,551	Reserve Money	14
						2,273	20,255	47,998	62,811	†92,796	68,728	103,486	106,428	131,175	*of which: Currency Outside Banks*	14a
						127	738	445	3,068	†18	47	1,107	702	750	Other Deposits	15
										6,855	12,046	6,206	49,180	17,796	Liabs. of Central Bank: Securities	16ac
						2,660	16,548	31,444	46,001	†42,409	56,354	66,097	286	345	Foreign Liabilities	16c
						2,016	8,337	14,641	13,908	†53,647	59,766	93,898	57,507	256,768	Central Government Deposits	16d
						2,744	47,653	62,822	64,993	†52,611	63,480	121,957	118,963	134,375	Capital Accounts	17a
						1,460	−3,953	−19,317	−17,293	†−12,012	−11,167	−12,707	−11,615	4,762	Other Items (Net)	17r
															Deposit Money Banks	
															End of Period	
						1,914	8,638	14,771	16,891	†22,361	12,144	21,793	24,359	42,343	Reserves	20
											2,018	4,235	41,591	7,182	Claims on Central Bank: Securities	20c
											—	6,390	3,700	16,748	Other Claims on Central Bank	20n
						2,181	14,755	28,197	24,196	†20,685	28,874	78,863	55,410	83,512	Foreign Assets	21
						514	426	5,104	8,691	†25,303	21,184	34,752	59,512	†75,847	Claims on Central Government	22a
													5,205		Claims on Local Government	22b
														14,564	Claims on Nonfin.Pub.Enterprises	22c
						14,310	111,747	71,988	72,448	†85,866	102,887	153,534	288,856	†515,735	Claims on Rest of the Economy	22d
											2,195	2,904	3,703	16,079	Claims on Nonbank Financial Insts.	22g
						5,593	32,894	63,930	71,938	†57,998	49,511	101,050	126,124	137,014	Demand Deposits	24
										†22,073	29,767	66,844	160,150	†285,867	Other Deposits	25
						—	92	1,902	119	†30		32	1,173	1,613	Bonds	26ab
														19,397	Restricted Deposits	26b
						3,556	64,883	26,485	10,120	†15,674	32,727	32,087	54,857	147,524	Foreign Liabilities	26c
						111	1,494	5,416	11,494	†26,484	10,986	15,178	17,242	†14,699	Central Government Deposits	26d
														2,627	Liabilities to Local Government	26db
						6,049	14,204	5,883	11,482	†8,208	5,092	4,699	2,915	1,888	Credit from Central Bank	26g
						1,091	14,662	29,259	39,289	†40,183	59,735	89,539	107,159	159,897	Capital Accounts	27a
						2,521	7,338	−12,815	−22,216	†−16,436	−18,517	−6,957	7,509	6,690	Other Items (Net)	27r
															Monetary Survey	
															End of Period	
						1,293	−533	76,568	97,876	†135,572	104,455	257,392	303,217	501,460	Foreign Assets (Net)	31n
						14,590	123,338	96,834	111,908	†108,737	150,721	204,074	321,036	376,057	Domestic Credit	32
						83	10,831	24,514	22,554	†22,250	38,363	34,979	26,331	†−176487	Claims on General Govt. (Net)	32an
														2,578	Claims on Local Government	32b
														14,564	Claims on Nonfin.Pub.Enterprises	32c
						14,507	112,507	72,320	89,354	†86,487	110,163	166,191	291,002	†519,321	Claims on Rest of the Economy	32d
											2,195	2,904	3,703	16,079	Claims on Nonbank Financial Insts.	32g
						8,198	55,417	115,384	139,452	†150,908	118,735	205,929	236,163	270,009	Money	34
										22,091	29,815	67,951	160,852	†286,617	Quasi-Money	35
						—	92	1,902	119	†30	—	32	1,173	1,613	Bonds	36ab
						—	92	1,902	119	6,855	†10,028	1,971	7,589	10,614	Liabs. of Central Bank: Securities	36ac
														19,397	Restricted Deposits	36b
						3,835	62,315	92,081	104,282	†92,794	123,215	211,495	226,122	294,271	Capital Accounts	37a
						3,852	4,982	−35,966	−34,069	†−28,369	−26,617	−25,912	−7,647	−5,006	Other Items (Net)	37r
						8,198	55,417	115,384	139,452	†172,999	148,549	273,880	397,015	479,477	Money plus Quasi-Money	35l
															Interest Rates	
															Percent Per Annum	
						170.00	230.00	†52.50	35.00	18.50	25.00	18.00	14.00	9.00	Refinancing Rate (End of Per.)	60
							214.34	48.98	28.91	15.15	23.59	15.63	6.59	5.28	Treasury Bill Rate	60c
															Prices and Labor	
															Period Averages	
								100.0	123.9	142.8	144.0	171.4	236.6	237.4	Producer Prices	63
						1.8	36.2	100.0	139.3	163.4	175.0	189.6	214.6	232.5	Consumer Prices	64
						2.7	36.1	100.0	142.9	178.5	202.3	229.2	288.5	362.5	Wages: Monthly Earnings	65
						122.6	114.7	100.0	96.4	80.0	67.3	59.9	53.9	55.2	Total Employment	67
															Period Averages	
		7,467	7,563	7,494	7,356	6,565	5,853	5,329	4,794	3,874					Employment	67e
					34	41	70	140	282	258	252	251			Unemployment	67c
					.4	.6	1.1	2.1	4.2	3.8	3.7	3.9			Unemployment Rate (%)	67r
															International Transactions	
															Millions of US Dollars	
						3,277.0	3,230.8	5,250.2	5,911.0	6,497.0	5,435.8	5,598.0	9,125.9	8,646.9	Exports	70.. d
						3,887.4	3,561.2	3,806.7	4,241.1	4,300.8	4,349.6	3,686.5	5,050.7	6,363.0	Imports, c.i.f.	71.. d

Kazakhstan

916

		1972	1973	1974	1975	1976	1977	1978	1979	1980	1981	1982	1983	1984	1985	1986
Balance of Payments																*Millions of US Dollars:*
Current Account, n.i.e.	78al d	....	....	....	....	....	....	....	....	....	....	....	....	....	....	....
Goods: Exports f.o.b.	78aa d	....	....	....	....	....	....	....	....	....	....	....	....	....	....	....
Goods: Imports f.o.b.	78ab d	....	....	....	....	....	....	....	....	....	....	....	....	....	....	....
Trade Balance	78ac d	....	....	....	....	....	....	....	....	....	....	....	....	....	....	....
Services: Credit	78ad d	....	....	....	....	....	....	....	....	....	....	....	....	....	....	....
Services: Debit	78ae d	....	....	....	....	....	....	....	....	....	....	....	....	....	....	....
Balance on Goods & Services	78af d	....	....	....	....	....	....	....	....	....	....	....	....	....	....	....
Income: Credit	78ag d	....	....	....	....	....	....	....	....	....	....	....	....	....	....	....
Income: Debit	78ah d	....	....	....	....	....	....	....	....	....	....	....	....	....	....	....
Balance on Gds, Serv. & Inc.	78ai d	....	....	....	....	....	....	....	....	....	....	....	....	....	....	....
Current Transfers, n.i.e.: Credit	78aj d	....	....	....	....	....	....	....	....	....	....	....	....	....	....	....
Current Transfers: Debit	78ak d	....	....	....	....	....	....	....	....	....	....	....	....	....	....	....
Capital Account, n.i.e.	78bc d	....	....	....	....	....	....	....	....	....	....	....	....	....	....	....
Capital Account, n.i.e.: Credit	78ba d	....	....	....	....	....	....	....	....	....	....	....	....	....	....	....
Capital Account: Debit	78bb d	....	....	....	....	....	....	....	....	....	....	....	....	....	....	....
Financial Account, n.i.e.	78bj d	....	....	....	....	....	....	....	....	....	....	....	....	....	....	....
Direct Investment Abroad	78bd d	....	....	....	....	....	....	....	....	....	....	....	....	....	....	....
Dir. Invest. in Rep. Econ., n.i.e.	78be d	....	....	....	....	....	....	....	....	....	....	....	....	....	....	....
Portfolio Investment Assets	78bf d	....	....	....	....	....	....	....	....	....	....	....	....	....	....	....
Equity Securities	78bk d	....	....	....	....	....	....	....	....	....	....	....	....	....	....	....
Debt Securities	78bl d	....	....	....	....	....	....	....	....	....	....	....	....	....	....	....
Portfolio Investment Liab., n.i.e.	78bg d	....	....	....	....	....	....	....	....	....	....	....	....	....	....	....
Equity Securities	78bm d	....	....	....	....	....	....	....	....	....	....	....	....	....	....	....
Debt Securities	78bn d	....	....	....	....	....	....	....	....	....	....	....	....	....	....	....
Financial Derivatives Assets	78bw d	....	....	....	....	....	....	....	....	....	....	....	....	....	....	....
Financial Derivatives Liabilities	78bx d	....	....	....	....	....	....	....	....	....	....	....	....	....	....	....
Other Investment Assets	78bh d	....	....	....	....	....	....	....	....	....	....	....	....	....	....	....
Monetary Authorities	78bo d	....	....	....	....	....	....	....	....	....	....	....	....	....	....	....
General Government	78bp d	....	....	....	....	....	....	....	....	....	....	....	....	....	....	....
Banks	78bq d	....	....	....	....	....	....	....	....	....	....	....	....	....	....	....
Other Sectors	78br d	....	....	....	....	....	....	....	....	....	....	....	....	....	....	....
Other Investment Liab., n.i.e.	78bi d	....	....	....	....	....	....	....	....	....	....	....	....	....	....	....
Monetary Authorities	78bs d	....	....	....	....	....	....	....	....	....	....	....	....	....	....	....
General Government	78bt d	....	....	....	....	....	....	....	....	....	....	....	....	....	....	....
Banks	78bu d	....	....	....	....	....	....	....	....	....	....	....	....	....	....	....
Other Sectors	78bv d	....	....	....	....	....	....	....	....	....	....	....	....	....	....	....
Net Errors and Omissions	78ca d	....	....	....	....	....	....	....	....	....	....	....	....	....	....	....
Overall Balance	78cb d	....	....	....	....	....	....	....	....	....	....	....	....	....	....	....
Reserves and Related Items	79da d	....	....	....	....	....	....	....	....	....	....	....	....	....	....	....
Reserve Assets	79db d	....	....	....	....	....	....	....	....	....	....	....	....	....	....	....
Use of Fund Credit and Loans	79dc d	....	....	....	....	....	....	....	....	....	....	....	....	....	....	....
Exceptional Financing	79de d	....	....	....	....	....	....	....	....	....	....	....	....	....	....	....
International Investment Position																*Millions of US Dollars*
Assets	79aa d	....	....	....	....	....	....	....	....	....	....	....	....	....	....	....
Direct Investment Abroad	79ab d	....	....	....	....	....	....	....	....	....	....	....	....	....	....	....
Portfolio Investment	79ac d	....	....	....	....	....	....	....	....	....	....	....	....	....	....	....
Equity Securities	79ad d	....	....	....	....	....	....	....	....	....	....	....	....	....	....	....
Debt Securities	79ae d	....	....	....	....	....	....	....	....	....	....	....	....	....	....	....
Financial Derivatives	79al d	....	....	....	....	....	....	....	....	....	....	....	....	....	....	....
Other Investment	79af d	....	....	....	....	....	....	....	....	....	....	....	....	....	....	....
Monetary Authorities	79ag d	....	....	....	....	....	....	....	....	....	....	....	....	....	....	....
General Government	79ah d	....	....	....	....	....	....	....	....	....	....	....	....	....	....	....
Banks	79ai d	....	....	....	....	....	....	....	....	....	....	....	....	....	....	....
Other Sectors	79aj d	....	....	....	....	....	....	....	....	....	....	....	....	....	....	....
Reserve Assets	79ak d	....	....	....	....	....	....	....	....	....	....	....	....	....	....	....
Liabilities	79la d	....	....	....	....	....	....	....	....	....	....	....	....	....	....	....
Dir. Invest. in Rep. Economy	79lb d	....	....	....	....	....	....	....	....	....	....	....	....	....	....	....
Portfolio Investment	79lc d	....	....	....	....	....	....	....	....	....	....	....	....	....	....	....
Equity Securities	79ld d	....	....	....	....	....	....	....	....	....	....	....	....	....	....	....
Debt Securities	79le d	....	....	....	....	....	....	....	....	....	....	....	....	....	....	....
Financial Derivatives	79ll d	....	....	....	....	....	....	....	....	....	....	....	....	....	....	....
Other Investment	79lf d	....	....	....	....	....	....	....	....	....	....	....	....	....	....	....
Monetary Authorities	79lg d	....	....	....	....	....	....	....	....	....	....	....	....	....	....	....
General Government	79lh d	....	....	....	....	....	....	....	....	....	....	....	....	....	....	....
Banks	79li d	....	....	....	....	....	....	....	....	....	....	....	....	....	....	....
Other Sectors	79lj d	....	....	....	....	....	....	....	....	....	....	....	....	....	....	....

Minus Sign Indicates Debit — Balance of Payments

1987	1988	1989	1990	1991	1992	1993	1994	1995	1996	1997	1998	1999	2000	2001		
....	....	....	....	....	....	....	....	−213.1	−751.0	−799.3	−1,224.9	−171.0	412.9	−1,749.0	Current Account, n.i.e.	78al *d*
....	....	....	....	....	....	....	....	5,440.0	6,291.6	6,899.3	5,870.5	5,988.7	9,288.1	9,119.7	Goods: Exports f.o.b.	78aa *d*
....	....	....	....	....	....	....	....	−5,325.9	−6,626.7	−7,175.7	−6,671.7	−5,645.0	−6,848.2	−8,224.1	Goods: Imports f.o.b.	78ab *d*
....	....	....	....	....	....	....	....	114.1	−335.1	−276.4	−801.2	343.7	2,439.9	895.6	*Trade Balance*	78ac *d*
....	....	....	....	....	....	....	....	535.1	674.4	841.9	904.3	932.5	1,132.8	1,273.8	Services: Credit	78ad *d*
....	....	....	....	....	....	....	....	−775.8	−928.3	−1,124.4	−1,154.1	−1,104.2	−2,156.6	−2,853.2	Services: Debit	78ae *d*
....	....	....	....	....	....	....	....	−126.6	−589.0	−558.9	−1,051.0	172.0	1,416.1	−683.8	*Balance on Goods & Services*	78af *d*
....	....	....	....	....	....	....	....	44.6	56.7	73.8	95.5	108.6	138.8	227.2	Income: Credit	78ag *d*
....	....	....	....	....	....	....	....	−190.1	−277.1	−388.8	−391.8	−608.3	−1,333.0	−1,442.2	Income: Debit	78ah *d*
....	....	....	....	....	....	....	....	−272.1	−809.4	−873.9	−1,347.3	−327.7	221.9	−1,898.8	*Balance on Gds, Serv. & Inc.*	78ai *d*
....	....	....	....	....	....	....	....	79.9	83.4	104.7	141.4	174.7	294.2	312.7	Current Transfers, n.i.e.: Credit	78aj *d*
....	....	....	....	....	....	....	....	−20.9	−25.0	−30.1	−19.0	−18.0	−103.2	−162.9	Current Transfers: Debit	78ak *d*
....	....	....	....	....	....	....	....	−380.6	−315.5	−439.8	−369.1	−234.0	−290.6	−197.4	Capital Account, n.i.e.	78bc *d*
....	....	....	....	....	....	....	....	116.1	87.9	58.3	65.9	61.1	66.3	89.1	Capital Account, n.i.e.: Credit	78ba *d*
....	....	....	....	....	....	....	....	−496.7	−403.4	−498.1	−435.0	−295.1	−356.9	−286.5	Capital Account: Debit	78bb *d*
....	....	....	....	....	....	....	....	1,162.5	2,005.1	2,901.6	2,229.1	1,299.2	1,299.9	2,480.6	Financial Account, n.i.e.	78bj *d*
....	....	....	....	....	....	....	....	−.3	....	−1.4	−8.1	−3.6	−4.4	28.8	Direct Investment Abroad	78bd *d*
....	....	....	....	....	....	....	....	964.2	1,137.0	1,321.4	1,151.4	1,587.0	1,281.9	2,731.2	Dir. Invest. in Rep. Econ., n.i.e.	78be *d*
....	....	....	....	....	....	....	....	....	....	−1.2	−5.3	−5.6	−85.5	−1,354.0	Portfolio Investment Assets	78bf *d*
....	....	....	....	....	....	....	....	....	....	−1.2	−.4	−1.8	.7	−10.4	Equity Securities	78bk *d*
....	....	....	....	....	....	....	....				−4.9	−3.8	−86.2	−1,343.6	Debt Securities	78bl *d*
....	....	....	....	....	....	....	....	7.2	223.5	405.4	66.2	−39.9	23.3	39.0	Portfolio Investment Liab., n.i.e.	78bg *d*
....	....	....	....	....	....	....	....	....	....	....	....	....	12.0	62.6	Equity Securities	78bm *d*
....	....	....	....	....	....	....	....	7.2	223.5	405.4	66.2	−39.9	11.3	−23.6	Debt Securities	78bn *d*
....	....	....	....	....	....	....	....	....	....	....	....	....	—	....	Financial Derivatives Assets	78bw *d*
....	....	....	....	....	....	....	....	....	....	....	....	....	—	....	Financial Derivatives Liabilities	78bx *d*
....	....	....	....	....	....	....	....	−657.4	243.8	−139.5	−220.5	−778.4	43.1	407.8	Other Investment Assets	78bh *d*
....	....	....	....	....	....	....	....	21.3	2.1	....	....	−.3	−.4	.3	Monetary Authorities	78bo *d*
....	....	....	....	....	....	....	....	—	27.8	.3	−41.1	16.3	—	210.0	General Government	78bp *d*
....	....	....	....	....	....	....	....	−152.3	174.4	−66.0	−67.9	−205.8	154.4	−63.6	Banks	78bq *d*
....	....	....	....	....	....	....	....	−526.4	39.5	−73.8	−111.5	−588.6	−110.9	261.1	Other Sectors	78br *d*
....	....	....	....	....	....	....	....	848.8	400.8	1,316.9	1,245.4	539.7	41.5	627.8	Other Investment Liab., n.i.e.	78bi *d*
....	....	....	....	....	....	....	....	−4.9	12.1	−5.0	−37.7	....	−2.6	.5	Monetary Authorities	78bs *d*
....	....	....	....	....	....	....	....	331.3	323.4	317.2	673.3	291.5	88.2	55.1	General Government	78bt *d*
....	....	....	....	....	....	....	....	−251.5	−125.7	161.4	60.2	−20.2	165.1	366.8	Banks	78bu *d*
....	....	....	....	....	....	....	....	773.9	191.0	843.3	549.6	268.4	−209.2	205.4	Other Sectors	78bv *d*
....	....	....	....	....	....	....	....	−270.1	−780.0	−1,114.1	−1,078.4	−641.6	−851.9	−149.6	Net Errors and Omissions	78ca *d*
....	....	....	....	....	....	....	....	298.7	158.6	548.4	−443.3	252.6	570.3	384.6	*Overall Balance*	78cb *d*
....	....	....	....	....	....	....	....	−298.7	−158.6	−548.4	443.3	−252.6	−570.3	−384.6	Reserves and Related Items	79da *d*
....	....	....	....	....	....	....	....	−440.1	−293.7	−542.0	321.7	−77.1	−129.2	−384.6	Reserve Assets	79db *d*
....	....	....	....	....	....	....	....	141.4	135.1	−6.4	121.6	−175.5	−441.0	—	Use of Fund Credit and Loans	79dc *d*
....	....	....	....	....	....	....	....	....	....	....	....	....			Exceptional Financing	79de *d*

Millions of US Dollars — International Investment Position

1987	1988	1989	1990	1991	1992	1993	1994	1995	1996	1997	1998	1999	2000	2001		
....	....	....	....	....	....	....	....	....	....	2,629.1	2,391.8	2,598.4	4,217.6	5,784.0	Assets	79aa *d*
....	....	....	....	....	....	....	....	....	....	2.6	3.1	3.1	13.3	−15.1	Direct Investment Abroad	79ab *d*
....	....	....	....	....	....	....	....	....	....	2.0	4.2	1.0	69.5	1,435.9	Portfolio Investment	79ac *d*
....	....	....	....	....	....	....	....	....	....	—	—	—	3.2	15.1	Equity Securities	79ad *d*
....	....	....	....	....	....	....	....	....	....	2.0	4.2	1.0	66.3	1,420.8	Debt Securities	79ae *d*
....	....	....	....	....	....	....	....	....	....	—	2.0	—	—	—	Financial Derivatives	79al *d*
....	....	....	....	....	....	....	....	....	....	335.3	417.7	592.2	2,039.2	1,855.3	Other Investment	79af *d*
....	....	....	....	....	....	....	....	....	....	.3	.1	.3	.7	.3	Monetary Authorities	79ag *d*
....	....	....	....	....	....	....	....	....	....	46.8	46.8	46.8	466.8	256.8	General Government	79ah *d*
....	....	....	....	....	....	....	....	....	....	288.2	370.8	545.1	359.9	423.0	Banks	79ai *d*
....	....	....	....	....	....	....	....	....	....	—	—	—	1,211.8	1,175.2	Other Sectors	79aj *d*
....	....	....	....	....	....	....	....	....	....	2,289.2	1,964.8	2,002.1	2,095.6	2,507.9	Reserve Assets	79ak *d*
....	....	....	....	....	....	....	....	....	....	2,595.3	3,594.3	3,678.4	15,676.2	18,986.8	Liabilities	79la *d*
....	....	....	....	....	....	....	....	....	....	50.1	122.3	115.9	9,992.1	12,646.9	Dir. Invest. in Rep. Economy	79lb *d*
....	....	....	....	....	....	....	....	....	....	623.9	663.4	617.2	690.3	725.0	Portfolio Investment	79lc *d*
....	....	....	....	....	....	....	....	....	....	53.9	49.9	37.7	93.9	145.9	Equity Securities	79ld *d*
....	....	....	....	....	....	....	....	....	....	570.0	613.5	579.5	596.4	579.1	Debt Securities	79le *d*
....	....	....	....	....	....	....	....	....	....						Financial Derivatives	79ll *d*
....	....	....	....	....	....	....	....	....	....	1,921.3	2,808.6	2,945.3	4,993.8	5,614.9	Other Investment	79lf *d*
....	....	....	....	....	....	....	....	....	....	553.0	655.4	462.6	—	.2	Monetary Authorities	79lg *d*
....	....	....	....	....	....	....	....	....	....	1,175.3	1,896.4	2,231.3	2,272.0	2,249.0	General Government	79lh *d*
....	....	....	....	....	....	....	....	....	....	193.0	256.8	251.4	402.5	806.5	Banks	79li *d*
....	....	....	....	....	....	....	....	....	....	—	—	—	2,319.3	2,559.2	Other Sectors	79lj *d*

Kazakhstan

		1972	1973	1974	1975	1976	1977	1978	1979	1980	1981	1982	1983	1984	1985	1986
Government Finance															*Millions of Tenge:*	
Deficit (-) or Surplus	80	....	....	....	....	....	....	....	....	....	....	....	....	....	....	....
Total Revenue and Grants	81y	....	....	....	....	....	....	....	....	....	....	....	....	....	....	....
Revenue	81	....	....	....	....	....	....	....	....	....	....	....	....	....	....	....
Grants Received	81z	....	....	....	....	....	....	....	....	....	....	....	....	....	....	....
Exp. & Lending Minus Repay	82z	....	....	....	....	....	....	....	....	....	....	....	....	....	....	....
Expenditure	82	....	....	....	....	....	....	....	....	....	....	....	....	....	....	....
Lending Minus Repayments	83	....	....	....	....	....	....	....	....	....	....	....	....	....	....	....
Total Financing																
Domestic	84a	....	....	....	....	....	....	....	....	....	....	....	....	....	....	....
Foreign	85a	....	....	....	....	....	....	....	....	....	....	....	....	....	....	....
National Accounts															*Billions of Tenge*	
Househ.Cons.Expend.,incl.NPISHs	96f	....	....	....	....	....	....	....	....	....	....	....	....	....	....	....
Government Consumption Expend.	91f	....	....	....	....	....	....	....	....	....	....	....	....	....	....	....
Gross Fixed Capital Formation	93e	....	....	....	....	....	....	....	....	....	....	....	....	....	....	....
Changes in Inventories	93i	....	....	....	....	....	....	....	....	....	....	....	....	....	....	....
Exports of Goods and Services	90c	....	....	....	....	....	....	....	....	....	....	....	....	....	....	....
Imports of Goods and Services (-)	98c	....	....	....	....	....	....	....	....	....	....	....	....	....	....	....
Gross Domestic Product (GDP)	99b	....	....	....	....	....	....	....	....	....	....	....	....	....	....	....
Net Primary Income from Abroad	98.n	....	....	....	....	....	....	....	....	....	....	....	....	....	....	....
Gross National Income (GNI)	99a	....	....	....	....	....	....	....	....	....	....	....	....	....	....	....
Net Current Transf.from Abroad	98t	....	....	....	....	....	....	....	....	....	....	....	....	....	....	....
Gross Nat'l Disposable Inc.(GNDI)	99i	....	....	....	....	....	....	....	....	....	....	....	....	....	....	....
Gross Saving	99s	....	....	....	....	....	....	....	....	....	....	....	....	....	....	....
Consumption of Fixed Capital	99cf	....	....	....	....	....	....	....	....	....	....	....	....	....	....	....
GDP, Production Based	99bp	....	....	....	....	....	....	....	....	....	....	....	....	....	....	....
Statistical Discrepancy	99bs	....	....	....	....	....	....	....	....	....	....	....	....	....	....	....
GDP Volume (1995=100)	99bv p	....	....	....	....	....	....	....	....	....	....	....	....	....	....	....
GDP Deflator (1995=100)	99bi p	....	....	....	....	....	....	....	....	....	....	....	....	....	....	....
															Millions:	
Population	99z	....	....	....	....	....	....	....	....	....	....	....	....	....	....	....

	1987	1988	1989	1990	1991	1992	1993	1994	1995	1996	1997	1998	1999	2000	2001		
Year Ending December 31																**Government Finance**	
	...	...	...	...	...	...	...	−30,382	−25,181	−59,564	−63,998	−72,073	−69,830	−3,279	−5,543	Deficit (-) or Surplus	80
	...	...	...	...	...	...	...	79,474	178,347	306,943	405,624	379,521	395,580	590,236	730,829	Total Revenue and Grants	81y
	...	...	...	...	...	...	...	79,413	178,347	306,943	405,342	379,311	392,951	587,039	730,596	Revenue	81
	...	...	...	...	...	...	...	61	—	—	282	210	2,629	3,197	233	Grants Received	81z
	...	...	...	...	...	...	...	109,856	203,528	366,507	469,622	451,594	465,410	593,515	736,372	Exp. & Lending Minus Repay	82z
	...	...	...	...	...	...	...	109,672	210,603	381,602	439,476	426,142	447,426	576,182	716,125	Expenditure	82
	...	...	...	...	...	...	...	184	−7,075	−15,095	30,146	25,452	17,984	17,333	20,247	Lending Minus Repayments	83
																Total Financing	
	...	...	...	...	...	...	...	....	....	....	17,170	20,504	20,671	−28,515	777	Domestic	84a
	...	...	...	...	...	...	...	....	....	....	46,828	51,569	49,159	31,794	4,766	Foreign	85a
Billions of Tenge																**National Accounts**	
	...	...	...	...	...	...	20.85	328.85	721.13	952.79	1,179.14	1,270.02	1,460.12	1,620.18	1,926.12	Househ.Cons.Expend.,incl.NPISHs	96f
	...	...	...	...	...	...	4.09	45.23	137.75	182.79	207.02	186.87	232.71	384.82	540.58	Government Consumption Expend.	91f
	...	...	...	...	...	...	8.21	110.65	233.81	243.88	271.77	272.44	326.26	442.82	744.48	Gross Fixed Capital Formation	93e
	...	...	...	...	...	...	−2.32	10.90	2.69	−15.28	−10.94	1.49	32.19	21.34	102.38	Changes in Inventories	93i
	...	...	...	...	...	...	11.15	156.96	395.27	499.32	583.86	525.95	856.23	1,529.35	1,522.03	Exports of Goods and Services	90c
	...	...	...	...	...	...	13.75	199.53	441.67	509.74	626.10	604.22	808.94	1,282.98	1,599.33	Imports of Goods and Services (-)	98c
	...	...	...	...	...	...	28.23	453.07	1,048.99	1,353.75	1,604.76	1,652.55	2,098.57	2,715.52	3,236.26	Gross Domestic Product (GDP)	99b
	...	...	...	...	...	...	−.07	−2.17	−9.11	−12.28	−23.38	−23.33	−62.78	−169.55	....	Net Primary Income from Abroad	98.n
	...	...	...	...	...	...	29.35	421.30	1,005.08	1,403.47	1,648.76	1,709.93	1,953.68	2,430.36	....	Gross National Income (GNI)	99a
	...	...	...	...	...	...	.34	7.36	7.88	9.81	5.63	6.11	18.39	28.57	....	Net Current Transf.from Abroad	98t
	...	...	...	...	...	...	29.69	428.66	1,012.96	1,413.29	1,654.40	1,716.05	1,972.06	2,458.92	....	Gross Nat'l Disposable Inc.(GNDI)	99i
	...	...	...	...	...	...	4.75	54.58	154.09	277.71	268.23	259.16	279.23	453.93	....	Gross Saving	99s
	...	...	...	...	...	...	5.29	84.31	204.50	241.13	283.71	238.76	....	....	....	Consumption of Fixed Capital	99cf
	...	...	...	...	...	1,217.69	29.42	423.47	1,014.19	1,415.75	1,672.14	1,733.26	2,016.46	2,599.90	....	GDP, Production Based	99bp
	...	...	...	...	...	151.86	1.19	−29.60	−34.80	61.99	67.39	80.71	−82.11	−115.62	....	Statistical Discrepancy	99bs
	...	...	...	...	...	...	....	†108.9	100.0	100.5	102.2	100.3	103.0	113.1	....	GDP Volume (1995=100)	99bv p
	...	...	...	...	...	...	....	†39.7	100.0	128.4	149.7	157.1	194.2	228.9	....	GDP Deflator (1995=100)	99bi p
Midyear Estimates																	
	...	...	...	...	16.45	16.52	16.48	16.30	16.07	15.92	15.75	15.07	14.93	14.90	14.83	Population	99z

(See notes in the back of the book.)

Kenya

	1972	1973	1974	1975	1976	1977	1978	1979	1980	1981	1982	1983	1984	1985	1986
Exchange Rates														*Shillings per SDR:*	
Principal Rate................................... aa	7.755	8.324	8.745	9.660	9.660	9.660	9.660	9.660	9.660	11.950	14.060	14.417	15.187	17.738	19.135
														Shillings per US Dollar:	
Principal Rate................................... ae	7.143	6.900	7.143	8.260	8.310	7.947	7.404	7.328	7.569	10.286	12.725	13.796	15.781	16.284	16.042
Principal Rate................................... rf	7.143	7.020	7.143	7.343	8.367	8.277	7.729	7.475	7.420	9.047	10.922	13.312	14.414	16.432	16.226
Fund Position														*Millions of SDRs:*	
Quota...................................... 2f. s	48.0	48.0	48.0	48.0	48.0	48.0	69.0	69.0	103.5	103.5	103.5	142.0	142.0	142.0	142.0
SDRs...................................... 1b. s	18.5	17.1	1.9	3.8	2.8	14.4	11.0	82.1	20.2	9.4	14.0	16.6	2.2	.8	9.9
Reserve Position in the Fund .... 1c. s	12.0	12.3	—	—	—	—	—	—	—	.2	1.5	9.6	10.9	12.2	12.2
Total Fund Cred.&Loans Outstg. 2tl	—	—	32.1	68.6	85.0	52.8	72.2	142.7	199.1	222.2	356.7	443.5	428.3	474.7	375.9
International Liquidity										*Millions of US Dollars Unless Otherwise Indicated:*					
Total Reserves minus Gold .... 1l. d	202.0	233.0	193.3	173.4	275.5	522.4	352.6	627.7	491.7	231.1	211.7	376.0	389.8	390.6	413.3
SDRs.. 1b. d	18.5	20.6	2.3	4.4	3.2	17.5	14.3	108.1	25.7	10.9	15.4	17.4	2.1	.9	12.1
Reserve Position in the Fund .... 1c. d	13.1	14.8	—	—	—	—	—	—	—	.2	1.6	10.1	10.7	13.4	14.9
Foreign Exchange........................... 1d. d	170.4	197.6	191.0	169.0	272.3	504.9	338.3	519.6	466.0	220.0	194.6	348.5	377.0	376.4	386.3
Gold (Million Fine Troy Ounces) 1ad	....	— e	—	—	—	.021	.072	.080	.080	.080	.080	.080	.080	.080	.080
Gold (National Valuation)................. 1an d	....	— e	1.3	—	—	.9	9.4	9.7	9.4	18.6	17.4	16.6	13.6	12.6	14.0
Monetary Authorities: Other Liab. .... 4.. d	2.9	.8	1.3	10.5	2.8	7.6	9.0	13.4	6.0	4.2	14.4	4.7	.8	11.3	7.0
Deposit Money Banks: Assets .... 7a. d	16.4	32.1	42.6	40.7	48.3	42.0	50.4	68.8	70.4	67.5	49.3	44.6	40.1	39.3	45.9
Liabilities .... 7b. d	25.4	39.5	56.0	58.1	49.7	52.0	52.5	72.7	68.7	42.8	44.1	45.3	51.5	50.0	53.2
Other Banking Insts.: Liabilities .... 7f. d	1.9	2.7	7.5	6.2	8.3	8.7	11.1	11.3	17.8	14.5	11.1	9.9	7.5	8.7	7.9
Monetary Authorities														*Millions of Shillings:*	
Foreign Assets............................... 11	1,416	1,603	1,347	1,427	2,301	4,259	2,732	4,780	3,784	2,577	2,957	5,459	6,444	6,807	7,115
Claims on Central Government............... 12a	194	237	526	1,169	834	1,217	1,639	1,783	2,663	4,955	8,725	7,028	7,089	8,884	11,260
Claims on Deposit Money Banks 12e	—	—	236	34	9	18	130	—	211	127	20	—	20	—	—
Reserve Money................................. 14	1,264	1,395	1,789	1,613	2,001	3,233	3,466	4,325	4,422	4,605	5,787	5,659	6,304	7,257	10,132
of which: Currency Outside DMBs 14a	894	982	1,086	1,235	1,625	2,182	2,305	2,673	3,032	3,569	3,724	4,083	4,370	5,038	6,371
Foreign Liabilities........................... 16c	21	6	289	750	845	570	763	1,476	1,967	2,704	5,190	6,470	6,637	8,607	7,410
Long-Term Foreign Liabilities............... 16cl	—	—	—	—	—	—	—	—	—	—	—	—	—	68	78
Central Government Deposits 16d	241	330	37	—	55	1,253	—	—	—	103	—	—	—	—	—
Counterpart Funds 16e	—	—	—	—	—	—	—	—	—	—	—	—	—	34	33
Capital Accounts............................. 17a	52	182	186	186	186	186	186	312	364	391	431	525	618	708	805
Other Items (Net)............................ 17r	32	−73	−192	82	57	251	85	449	−96	−143	294	−167	−6	−982	−83
Deposit Money Banks														*Millions of Shillings:*	
Reserves...................................... 20	343	372	514	298	313	972	833	1,184	1,204	985	1,834	1,323	1,635	2,272	3,420
Foreign Assets............................... 21	117	222	304	336	401	334	373	504	533	695	627	609	632	640	737
Claims on Central Government............... 22a	452	650	510	677	1,192	1,963	1,805	2,216	1,542	2,133	2,544	2,121	3,093	2,407	5,252
Claims on Local Government................. 22b	26	42	38	34	25	24	29	33	28	15	25	23	24	25	33
Claims on Nonfin.Pub.Enterprises 22c	157	188	185	269	190	235	182	207	337	333	540	1,138	1,526	1,735	1,757
Claims on Private Sector 22d	2,481	3,143	3,814	4,149	4,892	6,513	8,901	9,774	11,759	13,025	14,357	15,380	16,944	19,491	22,684
Claims on Other Financial Insts 22f	—	—	—	196	471	684	235	692	147	117	434	693	563	560	1,000
Demand Deposits............................. 24	1,880	2,413	2,620	2,851	3,525	5,095	5,445	6,327	5,814	6,374	6,798	7,640	8,901	9,219	11,314
Time & Foreign Currency Deposits......... 25	1,492	1,907	2,064	2,672	3,335	5,193	6,277	6,833	7,702	8,872	10,735	10,953	12,198	13,976	18,172
Foreign Liabilities........................... 26c	181	273	400	480	413	413	388	533	520	440	561	626	813	814	854
Central Government Deposits 26d	58	76	70	81	72	128	219	353	246	212	566	440	613	928	961
Credit from Monetary Authorities 26g	—	—	254	19	—	—	120	—	197	75	—	4	165	165	1
Credit from Other Financial Insts 26i	—	—	—	—	—	—	—	—	—	—	—	—	—	—	—
Capital Accounts............................. 27a	273	307	373	433	537	750	983	1,056	1,360	1,718	1,964	2,099	2,454	2,806	3,386
Other Items (Net)............................ 27r	−309	−359	−416	−578	−398	−855	−1,074	−493	−289	−387	−263	−474	−727	−779	196
Monetary Survey														*Millions of Shillings:*	
Foreign Assets (Net)......................... 31n	1,331	1,546	962	534	1,446	3,610	1,954	3,275	1,830	128	−2,167	−1,027	−374	−1,975	−411
Domestic Credit............................... 32	3,019	3,861	4,966	6,413	7,476	9,254	12,571	14,351	16,230	20,264	26,059	25,944	28,626	32,173	41,025
Claims on Central Govt. (Net) 32an	346	480	929	1,765	1,898	1,799	3,225	3,646	3,959	6,773	10,703	8,710	9,569	10,363	15,552
Claims on Local Government............. 32b	26	42	38	34	25	24	29	33	28	15	25	23	24	25	33
Claims on Nonfin.Pub.Enterprises....... 32c	157	188	185	269	190	235	182	207	337	333	540	1,138	1,526	1,735	1,757
Claims on Private Sector 32d	2,481	3,143	3,814	4,149	4,892	6,513	8,901	9,774	11,759	13,025	14,357	15,380	16,944	19,491	22,684
Claims on Other Financial Insts 32f	8	7	—	196	471	684	235	692	147	117	434	693	563	560	1,000
Money.. 34	2,804	3,449	3,755	4,143	5,120	7,333	7,879	9,178	8,434	9,409	10,635	11,473	13,095	12,923	17,522
Quasi-Money................................. 35	1,492	1,907	2,064	2,672	3,335	5,193	6,277	6,833	7,702	8,872	10,735	10,953	12,198	13,976	18,172
Long-Term Foreign Liabilities............... 36cl	—	—	—	—	—	—	—	—	—	—	—	—	—	68	78
Counterpart Funds 36e	—	—	—	—	—	—	—	—	—	—	—	—	—	34	33
Capital Accounts............................. 37a	325	489	559	620	723	936	1,169	1,368	1,724	2,108	2,395	2,625	3,072	3,514	4,191
Other Items (Net)............................ 37r	−270	−438	−450	−487	−256	−599	−799	248	200	3	126	−134	−113	−316	618
Money plus Quasi-Money..................... 35l	4,295	5,356	5,819	6,814	8,455	12,527	14,155	16,011	16,136	18,281	21,370	22,426	25,293	26,898	35,694
Other Banking Institutions														*Millions of Shillings:*	
Cash... 40	....	40	44	163	206	458	527	682	847	642	1,390	1,281	2,065	1,978	2,470
Claims on Central Government............... 42a	....	131	173	166	166	191	257	286	577	854	1,073	2,340	2,464	3,420	4,021
Claims on Local Government................. 42b	....	2	2	—	13	—	—	—	—	1	—	1	1	—	—
Claims on Nonfin.Pub.Enterprises 42c	....	33	17	16	1	13	13	39	34	35	118	79	70	71	152
Claims on Private Sector 42d	....	712	842	1,059	1,409	1,772	2,406	2,935	4,136	5,209	6,710	7,978	10,324	12,290	12,856
Claims on Deposit Money Banks 42e	....	....	....	....	....	....	....	....	....	....	....	....	....	....	....
Claims on Other Financial Insts 42f	....	19	20	3	31	124	153	193	169	320	714	683	1,714	1,506	1,980
Demand Deposits............................. 44	....	14	3	105	35	450	307	376	104	324	323	488	919	1,455	1,976
Time and Savings Deposits.................. 45	....	790	952	1,295	1,536	1,837	2,636	3,548	5,037	5,745	7,281	8,623	11,714	13,112	14,779
Foreign Liabilities........................... 46c	....	19	54	51	69	69	82	83	134	149	141	137	119	142	126
Central Government Deposits 46d	....	22	63	73	116	118	220	172	166	169	185	229	238	258	280
Credit from Deposit Money Banks 46h	....	122	51	8	26	36	112	214	124	377	854	1,150	1,046	1,047	899
Capital Accounts............................. 47a	....	91	90	117	136	171	233	293	455	589	742	878	1,003	1,082	1,350
Other Items (Net)............................ 47r	....	−122	−115	−242	−92	−124	−235	−551	−258	−293	478	857	1,600	2,171	2,068

	1987	1988	1989	1990	1991	1992	1993	1994	1995	1996	1997	1998	1999	2000	2001	
Exchange Rates																
End of Period																
Principal Rate	23.429	25.029	28.387	34.263	40.158	49.797	93.626	65.458	83.153	79.118	84.568	87.165	100.098	101.674	98.779	aa
End of Period (ae) Period Average (rf)																
Principal Rate	16.515	18.599	21.601	24.084	28.074	36.216	68.163	44.839	55.939	55.021	62.678	61.906	72.931	78.036	78.600	ae
Principal Rate	16.454	17.747	20.572	22.915	27.508	32.217	58.001	56.051	51.430	57.115	58.732	60.367	70.326	76.176	78.563	rf
Fund Position																
End of Period																
Quota	142.0	142.0	142.0	142.0	142.0	199.4	199.4	199.4	199.4	199.4	199.4	199.4	271.4	271.4	271.4	2f. s
SDRs	11.4	.4	8.7	2.8	1.0	.6	.8	.5	.2	.5	.5	.4	1.7	.2	.8	1b. s
Reserve Position in the Fund	12.2	12.2	12.2	12.2	12.2	12.2	12.2	12.3	12.3	12.3	12.4	12.4	12.4	12.5	12.5	1c. s
Total Fund Cred.&Loans Outstg.	282.9	338.4	316.1	338.9	344.8	286.1	264.3	277.3	251.5	234.5	185.6	139.5	95.8	97.2	78.6	2tl
International Liquidity																
End of Period																
Total Reserves minus Gold	255.8	263.7	284.6	205.4	116.9	53.0[e]	405.6	557.6	353.4	746.5	787.9	783.1	791.6	897.7	1,064.9	1l. d
SDRs	16.2	.6	11.5	3.9	1.4	.8	1.1	.7	.3	.8	.7	.6	2.4	.3	1.0	1b. d
Reserve Position in the Fund	17.3	16.4	16.1	17.4	17.5	16.8	16.8	18.0	18.3	17.7	16.7	17.5	17.1	16.2	15.8	1c. d
Foreign Exchange	222.3	246.7	257.1	184.1	98.1	35.4[e]	387.7	538.9	334.8	728.0	770.6	765.0	772.2	881.2	1,048.1	1d. d
Gold (Million Fine Troy Ounces)	.080	.080	.080	.080	.080	.080	.080	.080	.080	.080	.080	—	—	—	—	1ad
Gold (National Valuation)	17.8	16.9	14.5	13.5	15.0	12.2	14.3	15.2	15.4	14.8	23.1	—	—	—	.1	1and
Monetary Authorities: Other Liab.	5.9	3.2	72.3	175.7	211.6	203.0	232.0	278.1	265.7	261.6	205.8	174.8	126.5	127.9	99.2	4..d
Deposit Money Banks: Assets	39.8	46.1	64.8	68.7	70.4	108.2	348.9	425.4	439.6	444.2	594.2	501.6	313.6	500.7	395.0	7a. d
Liabilities	54.4	83.8	77.9	70.5	49.5	53.1	49.8	293.1	103.8	103.3	165.2	195.8	218.2	173.0	162.3	7b. d
Other Banking Insts.: Liabilities	17.1	14.5	19.8	15.3	16.5	13.4	10.2	11.0	8.7	7.0	18.9	1.2	.8	.5	.4	7f. d
Monetary Authorities																
End of Period																
Foreign Assets	4,753	5,558	7,310	6,630	5,339	6,315	34,527	28,227	25,683	47,266	44,499	47,103	57,816	71,245	83,499	11
Claims on Central Government	14,491	15,078	13,225	20,963	24,900	16,074	49,275	53,857	98,401	57,287	47,905	43,585	39,028	36,742	37,421	12a
Claims on Deposit Money Banks	—	223	1,019	208	864	12,717	11,484	10,072	9,766	9,056	9,124	1,140	904	4,884	1,362	12e
Reserve Money	12,093	12,342	14,434	17,585	20,341	31,230	47,628	58,472	76,610	82,903	84,621	84,269	89,341	88,758	87,859	14
of which: Currency Outside DMBs	7,688	8,536	9,655	10,829	12,761	17,205	21,355	24,817	28,887	30,390	36,178	38,713	42,963	43,466	45,349	14a
Foreign Liabilities	6,673	8,507	9,399	12,035	13,871	14,287	24,771	18,252	20,923	18,590	15,715	12,244	9,653	9,982	7,796	16c
Long-Term Foreign Liabilities	53	23	62	42	89	81	83	25	21	14	5	2	2	—	—	16cl
Central Government Deposits	—	—	—	—	—	—	38,289	32,920	55,239	27,349	11,698	17,172	18,922	26,526	28,537	16d
Counterpart Funds	38	46	49	42	58	73	73	127	6	—	—	—	—	—	—	16e
Capital Accounts	898	1,049	1,229	1,479	1,820	2,278	720	813	1,079	1,892	2,484	4,057	5,097	5,561	5,968	17a
Other Items (Net)	-510	-1,108	-3,619	-3,383	-5,075	-12,843	-16,279	-18,454	-20,028	-17,139	-12,995	-25,916	-25,267	-17,963	-7,889	17r
Deposit Money Banks																
End of Period																
Reserves	3,475	3,430	4,119	5,353	6,571	8,956	20,870	31,790	35,316	42,460	39,736	34,970	36,081	31,762	37,062	20
Foreign Assets	658	857	1,401	1,653	1,975	3,919	23,783	19,073	24,594	24,440	37,240	31,051	22,871	39,072	31,049	21
Claims on Central Government	7,046	5,383	7,737	9,548	11,562	18,010	21,136	38,088	26,417	42,576	46,121	70,550	68,415	71,206	89,091	22a
Claims on Local Government	49	80	50	62	64	148	219	249	304	358	582	595	895	1,143	659	22b
Claims on Nonfin.Pub.Enterprises	3,516	3,372	2,735	3,198	3,960	4,003	3,885	5,174	4,987	5,290	7,572	6,922	6,479	7,013	6,839	22c
Claims on Private Sector	24,154	28,064	32,759	36,648	44,752	58,587	61,705	78,809	117,351	145,926	182,253	182,976	202,657	210,268	201,934	22d
Claims on Other Financial Insts	1,507	2,638	2,725	3,036	3,907	4,809	3,793	6,835	11,347	14,620	16,255	32,507	50,317	53,116	53,500	22f
Demand Deposits	11,281	11,551	14,931	16,773	19,155	26,621	33,664	39,294	38,994	43,094	46,258	47,273	56,849	65,206	76,220	24
Time & Foreign Currency Deposits	20,750	23,696	26,746	30,571	37,804	50,003	64,332	95,755	133,520	175,401	210,888	215,615	218,788	224,051	225,233	25
Foreign Liabilities	898	1,558	1,682	1,698	1,388	1,922	3,392	13,144	5,807	5,681	10,356	12,122	15,914	13,501	12,756	26c
Central Government Deposits	1,624	2,086	3,470	3,098	5,323	3,078	4,790	4,950	5,531	3,822	4,226	9,592	8,754	8,385	5,310	26d
Credit from Monetary Authorities	—	183	864	25	1,342	4,921	252	—	—	—	448	4,335	1,614	3,635	2,974	26g
Credit from Other Financial Insts	6	—	—	—	—	—	—	—	2	—	—	—	—	—	—	26i
Capital Accounts	5,572	6,456	8,465	10,098	12,360	17,398	24,328	31,942	45,104	56,111	72,324	78,930	91,311	79,289	80,284	27a
Other Items (Net)	275	-1,706	-4,633	-2,764	-4,583	-5,510	4,634	-5,068	-8,643	-8,439	-14,740	-8,298	-5,513	19,513	17,357	27r
Monetary Survey																
End of Period																
Foreign Assets (Net)	-2,159	-3,651	-2,370	-5,450	-7,945	-5,975	30,146	15,903	23,546	47,434	55,669	53,787	55,121	86,833	93,996	31n
Domestic Credit	49,139	52,529	55,761	70,356	83,821	98,554	96,935	145,142	198,876	236,037	285,817	311,661	341,495	345,964	357,106	32
Claims on Central Govt. (Net)	19,912	18,375	17,492	27,412	31,138	31,007	27,332	54,075	64,048	68,693	78,101	87,370	79,767	73,037	92,665	32an
Claims on Local Government	49	80	50	62	64	148	219	249	304	358	582	595	895	1,143	659	32b
Claims on Nonfin.Pub.Enterprises	3,516	3,372	2,735	3,198	3,960	4,003	3,885	5,174	4,987	5,290	7,572	6,922	6,479	7,013	6,839	32c
Claims on Private Sector	24,154	28,064	32,759	36,648	44,752	58,587	61,705	78,809	118,189	147,077	183,306	184,267	204,037	211,654	203,443	32d
Claims on Other Financial Insts	1,507	2,638	2,725	3,036	3,907	4,809	3,793	6,835	11,347	14,620	16,255	32,507	50,317	53,116	53,500	32f
Money	18,917	19,160	21,647	27,529	31,667	46,577	59,322	66,792	69,333	78,995	91,037	94,092	109,506	118,968	126,332	34
Quasi-Money	20,750	23,696	26,746	30,571	37,804	50,003	64,332	95,755	133,520	175,401	210,888	215,615	218,788	224,051	225,233	35
Long-Term Foreign Liabilities	53	23	62	42	89	81	83	25	21	14	5	2	2	—	—	36cl
Counterpart Funds	38	46	49	42	58	73	73	127	6	—	—	—	—	—	—	36e
Capital Accounts	6,469	7,504	9,694	11,577	14,180	19,675	25,048	32,756	46,183	58,004	74,808	82,987	96,408	84,850	86,252	37a
Other Items (Net)	754	-1,551	-4,807	-4,854	-7,922	-23,830	-21,778	-34,409	-26,641	-28,941	-35,252	-27,248	-28,087	4,921	13,275	37r
Money plus Quasi-Money	39,667	42,856	48,393	58,099	69,471	96,579	123,654	162,547	202,853	254,395	301,924	309,707	328,293	343,019	351,565	35l
Other Banking Institutions																
End of Period																
Cash	1,325	2,287	2,845	4,033	4,196	5,502	5,781	8,762	12,988	11,937	5,148	6,900	4,920	4,671	2,325	40
Claims on Central Government	4,206	3,906	4,734	4,507	5,971	8,915	20,933	24,065	10,748	7,193	8,826	7,163	8,122	9,323	10,454	42a
Claims on Local Government	11	12	37	44	39	47	39	35	35	16	7	8	8	—	—	42b
Claims on Nonfin.Pub.Enterprises	184	314	133	583	601	434	348	1,031	48	34	10	6	6	6	—	42c
Claims on Private Sector	13,819	17,655	20,715	27,523	30,921	33,557	35,734	37,808	40,629	36,398	27,632	28,723	24,378	25,860	16,460	42d
Claims on Deposit Money Banks	67	133	83	82	68	92	150	446	27	423	—	—	—	4	30	42e
Claims on Other Financial Insts	1,139	671	1,212	1,375	1,336	2,083	578	1,024	541	151	124	106	96	114	97	42f
Demand Deposits	2,199	2,019	2,979	5,578	6,421	6,062	7,763	12,738	6,687	3,276	2,432	2,261	1,921	1,726	1,605	44
Time and Savings Deposits	15,111	17,476	20,266	25,111	28,355	32,764	37,939	43,266	42,335	36,447	22,385	24,752	23,335	23,586	20,349	45
Foreign Liabilities	282	269	428	368	462	484	697	494	487	384	1,185	75	58	41	33	46c
Central Government Deposits	388	412	441	937	724	511	403	908	572	459	667	661	775	775	486	46d
Credit from Deposit Money Banks	724	1,283	1,852	1,626	1,489	1,687	661	674	1,672	2,417	1,327	1,442	229	469	160	46h
Capital Accounts	1,525	1,988	2,308	2,996	3,393	4,154	6,315	7,773	7,148	6,423	4,347	4,278	4,410	3,556	2,343	47a
Other Items (Net)	520	1,531	1,484	1,532	2,288	4,968	9,785	7,318	6,114	6,744	9,405	9,437	6,806	9,852	4,367	47r

Kenya

		1972	1973	1974	1975	1976	1977	1978	1979	1980	1981	1982	1983	1984	1985	1986
Banking Survey															*Millions of Shillings:*	
Foreign Assets (Net)	51n	....	1,531	911	483	1,377	3,541	1,871	3,193	1,695	−21	−2,308	−1,164	−492	−2,117	−537
Domestic Credit	52	....	4,733	5,957	7,584	8,981	11,235	15,181	17,633	20,981	26,513	34,489	36,796	42,962	49,204	59,754
Claims on Central Govt. (Net)	52an	....	589	1,040	1,858	1,949	1,872	3,263	3,760	4,370	7,458	11,591	10,821	11,796	13,525	19,292
Claims on Local Government	52b	....	43	40	35	38	24	30	33	28	16	25	24	25	25	33
Claims on Nonfin.Pub.Enterprises	52c	....	221	203	284	192	247	195	245	371	368	658	1,217	1,596	1,806	1,909
Claims on Private Sector	52d	....	3,855	4,655	5,208	6,301	8,285	11,306	12,709	15,895	18,234	21,067	23,358	27,268	31,781	35,540
Claims on Nonbank Financial Inst	52f	....	26	20	199	502	807	388	885	316	437	1,148	1,376	2,277	2,066	2,980
Liquid Liabilities	55l	....	6,120	6,731	8,051	9,820	14,355	16,571	19,253	20,431	23,708	27,585	30,256	35,862	39,488	49,979
Long-Term Foreign Liabilities	56cl	....	—	—	—	—	—	—	—	—	—	—	—	—	68	78
Counterpart Funds	56e	....	—	—	—	—	—	—	—	—	—	—	—	—	34	33
Capital Accounts	57a	....	580	649	737	859	1,108	1,402	1,661	2,179	2,697	3,137	3,503	4,075	4,596	5,541
Other Items (Net)	57r	....	−435	−511	−721	−322	−686	−921	−89	66	87	1,459	1,873	2,533	2,902	3,586
Interest Rates															*Percent Per Annum*	
Discount Rate *(End of Period)*	60	6.50	6.50	6.50	7.00	7.00	6.50	7.50	7.50	8.00	12.50	15.00	15.00	12.50	12.50	12.50
Treasury Bill Rate	60c	3.45	1.92	4.63	6.08	5.54	2.13	4.29	6.01	5.26	7.61	12.58	14.15	13.24	13.90	13.23
Deposit Rate	60l	3.50	3.50	4.32	5.13	5.13	5.13	5.13	5.13	5.75	8.85	12.20	13.27	11.77	11.25	11.25
Lending Rate	60p	9.00	9.00	9.50	10.00	10.00	10.00	10.00	10.00	10.58	12.42	14.50	15.83	14.42	14.00	14.00
Prices, Production, Labor															*Index Numbers (1995=100):*	
Consumer Prices	64	3.9	4.2	†5.0	5.9	6.6	7.6	8.9	9.6	†10.9	12.2	14.7	16.4	18.1	20.4	21.0
Industrial Production	66	17.4	19.9	21.0	†20.9	24.9	28.9	32.6	35.0	36.9	38.7	39.0	40.8	42.5	44.5	47.1
															Number in Thousands:	
Employment	67e	....	....	....	....	....	....	....	....	....	....	....	....	....	1,174	1,221
International Transactions															*Millions of Shillings*	
Exports	70	2,567	3,335	4,305	4,464	6,610	9,824	7,914	8,144	9,248	10,248	11,146	11,579	15,415	15,725	19,459
Imports, c.i.f	71	3,822	4,316	7,327	6,948	8,113	10,663	13,225	12,228	15,747	17,413	17,809	17,802	21,180	23,589	26,163
															1995=100	
Volume of Exports	72	....	....	....	....	....	....	....	....	....	....	....	....	....	....	....
Volume of Imports	73	86	83	94	†70	68	82	96	78	†90	70	60	47	55	51	60
Export Prices	74	5	5	7	†8	11	16	13	14	†17	19	20	25	29	29	31
Unit Value of Imports	75	3	3	5	†7	8	8	9	10	†13	17	19	25	26	30	29
Balance of Payments															*Millions of US Dollars:*	
Current Account, n.i.e.	78al *d*	....	....	....	−220.2	−120.2	35.1	−661.0	−494.6	−877.7	−563.4	−307.9	−50.4	−129.8	−117.6	−46.8
Goods: Exports f.o.b.	78aa *d*	....	....	....	688.0	811.4	1,222.5	1,056.4	1,120.2	1,430.7	1,192.7	1,045.7	984.0	1,081.7	991.0	1,219.4
Goods: Imports f.o.b.	78ab *d*	....	....	....	−846.9	−809.7	−1,112.8	−1,631.8	−1,594.2	−2,344.8	−1,834.0	−1,467.7	−1,197.9	−1,348.2	−1,269.8	−1,454.6
Trade Balance	78ac *d*	....	....	....	−158.9	1.7	109.7	−575.5	−474.0	−914.1	−641.3	−422.0	−214.0	−266.5	−278.7	−235.2
Services: Credit	78ad *d*	....	....	....	266.8	296.2	330.6	439.9	448.7	576.7	568.9	562.3	512.2	542.4	577.3	646.0
Services: Debit	78ae *d*	....	....	....	−283.8	−294.6	−320.9	−428.4	−376.6	−501.6	−503.0	−398.4	−341.5	−377.0	−359.5	−415.2
Balance on Goods & Services	78af *d*	....	....	....	−175.9	3.2	119.4	−564.0	−401.9	−839.1	−575.4	−258.0	−43.3	−101.1	−60.9	−4.4
Income: Credit	78ag *d*	....	....	....	56.4	35.4	40.8	47.4	60.5	53.9	37.0	21.9	28.7	39.0	38.2	36.9
Income: Debit	78ah *d*	....	....	....	−149.3	−177.4	−199.1	−234.9	−248.3	−248.2	−238.1	−201.4	−213.2	−240.8	−281.8	−277.8
Balance on Gds, Serv. & Inc.	78ai *d*	....	....	....	−268.8	−138.8	−38.9	−751.5	−589.7	−1,033.4	−776.5	−437.5	−227.8	−302.9	−304.5	−245.3
Current Transfers, n.i.e.: Credit	78aj *d*	....	....	....	91.1	67.8	93.8	115.4	114.6	163.0	241.4	157.2	209.2	208.4	214.4	232.0
Current Transfers: Debit	78ak *d*	....	....	....	−42.5	−49.2	−19.8	−24.8	−19.5	−7.3	−28.4	−27.6	−31.9	−35.3	−27.4	−33.5
Capital Account, n.i.e.	78bc *d*	....	....	....	−3.5	−5.7	−9.2	−1.3	−5.6	−9.7	3.2	3.2	2.3	3.5	4.7	8.4
Capital Account, n.i.e.: Credit	78ba *d*	....	....	....	1.9	1.7	3.6	7.8	8.0	2.4	7.1	6.8	5.5	5.6	6.1	9.8
Capital Account: Debit	78bb *d*	....	....	....	−5.4	−7.4	−12.8	−9.1	−13.6	−12.1	−3.9	−3.6	−3.2	−2.1	−1.5	−1.4
Financial Account, n.i.e.	78bj *d*	....	....	....	197.3	209.3	240.2	435.4	566.9	506.6	185.9	99.6	130.7	179.1	32.0	132.6
Direct Investment Abroad	78bd *d*	....	....	....	−1.4	−4.3	−2.7	−2.3	−5.9	−1.1	−5.9	−9.6	−14.5	−6.9	−5.4	−4.9
Dir. Invest. in Rep. Econ., n.i.e.	78be *d*	....	....	....	17.2	46.4	56.5	34.4	84.0	79.0	14.1	13.0	23.7	10.8	28.8	32.7
Portfolio Investment Assets	78bf *d*	....	....	....	−2.2	—	—	—	—	—	—	—	—	—	—	—
Equity Securities	78bk *d*	....	....	....	.3	—	—	—	—	—	—	—	—	—	—	—
Debt Securities	78bl *d*	....	....	....	−2.5	—	—	—	—	—	—	—	—	—	—	—
Portfolio Investment Liab., n.i.e.	78bg *d*	....	....	....	−.5	−4.3	.7	—	—	.8	—	—	—	—	—	—
Equity Securities	78bm *d*	....	....	....	.3	1.7	.7	—	—	.3	—	—	—	—	—	—
Debt Securities	78bn *d*	....	....	....	−.8	−6.0	—	—	—	.5	—	—	—	—	—	—
Financial Derivatives Assets	78bw *d*	....	....	....	....	....	....	....	....	....	....	....	....	....	....	....
Financial Derivatives Liabilities	78bx *d*	....	....	....	....	....	....	....	....	....	....	....	....	....	....	....
Other Investment Assets	78bh *d*	....	....	....	−13.9	−31.2	11.5	−18.8	−41.5	−15.4	−94.7	−77.7	−61.5	−64.1	−58.5	−83.1
Monetary Authorities	78bo *d*	....	....	....	....	....	....	....	....	....	....	....	....	....	....	....
General Government	78bp *d*	....	....	....	−1.9	−.5	—	−5.0	—	−.8	−5.7	−8.7	−5.0	−18.8	3.1	−4.4
Banks	78bq *d*	....	....	....	−9.3	−4.2	8.8	−5.0	−19.3	−5.1	−16.7	7.2	1.3	−1.6	—	−6.0
Other Sectors	78br *d*	....	....	....	−2.7	−26.5	2.7	−13.7	−22.2	−9.4	−72.3	−76.3	−57.7	−43.7	−61.6	−72.8
Other Investment Liab., n.i.e.	78bi *d*	....	....	....	198.1	202.7	174.1	422.0	530.3	443.3	272.3	174.0	182.9	239.4	67.1	187.9
Monetary Authorities	78bs *d*	....	....	....	9.7	−7.8	4.8	1.3	4.3	−7.1	—	—	—	—	4.9	—
General Government	78bt *d*	....	....	....	85.5	76.3	81.9	278.0	185.5	226.0	137.7	57.8	96.8	142.8	−15.3	18.2
Banks	78bu *d*	....	....	....	10.9	−8.0	—	−3.2	19.4	−1.8	−8.8	11.1	4.9	13.0	—	2.5
Other Sectors	78bv *d*	....	....	....	92.1	142.2	87.4	145.9	321.1	226.1	143.5	105.1	81.2	83.5	77.4	167.2
Net Errors and Omissions	78ca *d*	....	....	....	−16.6	.6	3.0	4.8	4.8	9.4	68.4	45.2	15.0	8.6	28.8	43.2
Overall Balance	78cb *d*	....	....	....	−43.0	83.9	269.1	−220.2	71.6	−371.4	−305.9	−159.9	97.6	61.5	−52.1	137.4
Reserves and Related Items	79da *d*	....	....	....	43.0	−83.9	−269.1	220.2	−71.6	371.4	305.9	159.9	−97.6	−61.5	52.1	−137.4
Reserve Assets	79db *d*	....	....	....	−6.3	−104.5	−233.2	194.3	−263.2	144.8	160.6	5.8	−194.0	−48.9	−.9	−23.0
Use of Fund Credit and Loans	79dc *d*	....	....	....	44.0	18.8	−37.6	24.1	91.5	72.7	28.7	151.6	93.2	−15.5	48.6	−116.2
Exceptional Financing	79de *d*	....	....	....	5.3	1.7	1.6	1.8	100.1	154.0	116.6	2.5	3.2	2.9	4.5	1.8

Banking Survey

End of Period

Item	Code	1987	1988	1989	1990	1991	1992	1993	1994	1995	1996	1997	1998	1999	2000	2001
Foreign Assets (Net)	51n	-2,441	-3,919	-2,798	-5,817	-8,407	-6,458	29,449	15,411	23,067	47,060	54,493	53,771	55,064	86,929	93,973
Domestic Credit	52	68,109	74,675	82,150	103,451	121,965	143,079	154,164	208,196	250,305	279,369	321,748	347,007	373,330	380,492	383,632
Claims on Central Govt. (Net)	52an	23,730	21,870	21,785	30,982	36,386	39,411	47,862	77,232	74,224	75,427	86,260	93,872	87,114	81,585	102,633
Claims on Local Government	52b	60	91	86	106	103	195	258	284	339	374	589	603	903	1,143	659
Claims on Nonfin.Pub.Enterprises	52c	3,700	3,686	2,869	3,781	4,561	4,438	4,233	6,204	5,035	5,324	7,582	6,928	6,485	7,019	6,839
Claims on Private Sector	52d	37,973	45,719	53,475	64,171	75,673	92,144	97,440	116,617	158,818	183,475	210,938	212,990	228,415	237,514	219,903
Claims on Nonbank Financial Inst	52f	2,646	3,308	3,936	4,411	5,242	6,892	4,371	7,859	11,889	14,770	16,379	32,613	50,413	53,230	53,597
Liquid Liabilities	55l	55,653	60,064	68,794	84,755	100,051	129,903	163,575	209,789	238,888	282,181	321,592	329,821	348,628	363,660	371,193
Long-Term Foreign Liabilities	56cl	53	23	62	42	89	81	83	25	21	14	5	2	2	—	—
Counterpart Funds	56e	38	46	49	42	58	73	73	127	6	—	—	—	—	—	—
Capital Accounts	57a	7,994	9,492	12,001	14,573	17,573	23,830	31,364	40,529	53,331	64,427	79,155	87,265	100,818	88,406	88,595
Other Items (Net)	57r	1,931	1,131	-1,553	-1,778	-4,212	-17,267	-11,481	-26,863	-18,874	-20,192	-24,511	-16,311	-21,054	15,349	17,806

Interest Rates

Percent Per Annum

Item	Code	1987	1988	1989	1990	1991	1992	1993	1994	1995	1996	1997	1998	1999	2000	2001
Discount Rate (*End of Period*)	60	12.50	16.02	16.50	19.43	20.27	20.46	45.50	21.50	24.50	26.88	32.27	17.07	26.46	19.47	16.81
Treasury Bill Rate	60c	12.86	13.48	13.86	14.78	16.59	16.53	49.80	23.32	18.29	22.25	22.87	22.83	13.87	12.05	12.59
Deposit Rate	60l	10.31	10.33	12.00	13.67	....	....	....	....	13.60	17.59	16.72	18.40	9.55	8.10	6.64
Lending Rate	60p	14.00	15.00	17.25	18.75	19.00	21.07	29.99	36.24	28.80	33.79	30.25	29.49	22.38	22.34	19.67

Prices, Production, Labor

Period Averages

Item	Code	1987	1988	1989	1990	1991	1992	1993	1994	1995	1996	1997	1998	1999	2000	2001
Consumer Prices	64	22.8	25.6	29.1	34.2	41.1	52.4	76.4	98.5	100.0	108.9	121.2	129.3	133.8	142.1	143.2
Industrial Production	66	49.7	†52.7	58.9	61.7	63.7	70.0	73.8	83.2	100.0	111.0	....	....	....	....	....

Period Averages

Item	Code	1987	1988	1989	1990	1991	1992	1993	1994	1995	1996	1997	1998	1999	2000	2001
Employment	67e	1,265	1,311	1,356	1,409	1,442	1,463	1,475	1,506	1,557	1,607	1,647	....	....	....	....

International Transactions

Millions of Shillings

Item	Code	1987	1988	1989	1990	1991	1992	1993	1994	1995	1996	1997	1998	1999	2000	2001
Exports	70	15,790	18,934	19,510	23,697	30,386	43,756	77,919	87,142	97,284	118,226	119,960	121,252	122,067	132,183	152,712
Imports, c.i.f.	71	28,618	35,303	44,779	50,913	52,918	59,097	101,128	115,080	155,168	168,486	190,674	193,032	198,313	236,613	250,782

1995=100

Item	Code	1987	1988	1989	1990	1991	1992	1993	1994	1995	1996	1997	1998	1999	2000	2001
Volume of Exports	72	....	....	....	54	57	66	73	83	100	....	....	....	....	....	....
Volume of Imports	73	63	71	74	71	66	64	69	86	100	99	105	107	96	111	....
Export Prices	74	26	30	32	35	44	50	90	92	100	106	124	126	118	127	....
Unit Value of Imports	75	29	32	39	46	52	60	95	87	100	109	117	120	130	144	....

Balance of Payments

Minus Sign Indicates Debit

Item	Code	1987	1988	1989	1990	1991	1992	1993	1994	1995	1996	1997	1998	1999	2000	2001
Current Account, n.i.e.	78al d	-503.0	-472.1	-590.6	-527.1	-213.3	-180.2	71.2	97.9	-400.4	-73.5	-456.8	-475.3	-97.7	-238.2	....
Goods: Exports f.o.b.	78aa d	962.5	1,072.7	1,001.5	1,090.2	1,185.3	1,108.5	1,262.6	1,537.0	1,923.7	2,083.3	2,062.6	2,017.0	1,748.6	1,773.4	....
Goods: Imports f.o.b.	78ab d	-1,622.6	-1,802.2	-1,963.4	-2,005.3	-1,697.3	-1,608.7	-1,509.6	-1,775.3	-2,673.9	-2,598.2	-2,948.4	-3,028.7	-2,731.8	-3,044.0	....
Trade Balance	78ac d	-660.1	-729.5	-961.9	-915.2	-511.9	-500.2	-247.0	-238.4	-750.1	-514.8	-885.9	-1,011.7	-983.2	-1,270.6	....
Services: Credit	78ad d	738.7	798.9	921.4	1,138.3	1,014.4	1,042.2	1,063.5	1,117.3	1,024.5	936.2	914.5	830.4	934.5	967.6	....
Services: Debit	78ae d	-504.7	-530.0	-603.1	-699.7	-632.7	-563.7	-569.4	-686.8	-868.1	-854.0	-826.0	-694.7	-570.4	-724.5	....
Balance on Goods & Services	78af d	-426.1	-460.5	-643.7	-476.5	-130.2	-21.7	247.0	192.2	-593.7	-432.6	-797.4	-876.0	-619.1	-1,027.5	....
Income: Credit	78ag d	37.4	20.1	11.8	4.8	5.9	1.7	3.3	20.9	25.6	21.4	23.0	41.2	31.7	45.0	....
Income: Debit	78ah d	-319.9	-365.5	-330.1	-423.2	-434.7	-359.6	-392.2	-385.7	-350.5	-242.2	-254.9	-214.7	-190.9	-178.1	....
Balance on Gds, Serv. & Inc.	78ai d	-708.6	-805.9	-962.0	-894.9	-559.0	-379.6	-141.8	-172.6	-918.6	-653.4	-1,029.4	-1,049.4	-778.3	-1,160.6	....
Current Transfers, n.i.e.: Credit	78aj d	246.1	372.9	420.6	422.9	396.7	392.9	276.0	333.7	563.6	585.4	572.5	578.6	685.3	926.6	....
Current Transfers: Debit	78ak d	-40.4	-39.1	-49.1	-55.1	-51.1	-193.5	-63.0	-63.2	-45.5	-5.4	—	-4.5	-4.7	-4.2	....
Capital Account, n.i.e.	78bc d	8.0	11.5	11.0	6.8	3.2	83.1	28.1	-.4	-.4	-.4	76.8	84.3	55.4	49.6	....
Capital Account, n.i.e.: Credit	78ba d	10.3	11.8	11.2	7.6	3.6	83.5	28.5	—	....	....	76.8	84.3	55.4	49.6	....
Capital Account: Debit	78bb d	-2.2	-.3	-.2	-.8	-.4	-.4	-.4	-.4	-.4	-.4	....	....	....	....	....
Financial Account, n.i.e.	78bj d	325.4	382.3	633.9	360.9	96.6	-270.1	55.1	-41.7	247.9	589.1	362.6	562.1	222.9	109.7	....
Direct Investment Abroad	78bd d	-30.8	-2.2	-1.4	—	—	—	—	—	.5	-2.1					
Dir. Invest. in Rep. Econ., n.i.e.	78be d	39.4	.4	62.2	57.1	18.8	6.4	1.6	3.7	32.5	12.7	19.7	11.4	13.8	110.9	
Portfolio Investment Assets	78bf d	—	—	—	—	—	—	—	—							-10.9
Equity Securities	78bk d	—	—	—	—	—	—	—	—							-.5
Debt Securities	78bl d	—	—	—	—	—	—	—	—							-10.4
Portfolio Investment Liab., n.i.e.	78bg d	—	—	—	—	—	—	—	—	6.0	7.5	34.2	1.3	-8.0	-6.0	
Equity Securities	78bm d	—	—	—	—	—	—	—	—	6.0	7.5	26.9	1.3	-8.0	-6.0	
Debt Securities	78bn d											7.3	—			
Financial Derivatives Assets	78bw d	....	....	....												
Financial Derivatives Liabilities	78bx d	....	....	....												
Other Investment Assets	78bh d	-5.5	-14.4	-56.5	72.7	-77.5	-125.0	-31.4	171.1	277.1	628.2	-53.6	-58.6	-89.8	-55.7	....
Monetary Authorities	78bo d	....	....	....												
General Government	78bp d	-6.0	—	—	—	—	-4.3	—	—			-4.7				....
Banks	78bq d	4.8	-11.2	-26.4	-7.8	-11.7	-117.5	-310.7	-61.2	....	....	-44.2	-44.4	-74.3	-5.3	....
Other Sectors	78br d	-4.3	-3.2	-30.1	80.5	-65.8	-3.2	279.3	232.3	277.1	628.2	-4.7	-14.3	-15.5	-50.4	....
Other Investment Liab., n.i.e.	78bi d	322.2	398.4	629.6	231.1	155.3	-151.5	85.0	-216.5	-67.7	-59.9	364.6	608.0	306.9	71.3	....
Monetary Authorities	78bs d															
General Government	78bt d	197.2	289.0	378.8	91.8	83.8	-64.8	152.7	-113.3	-5.7	5.0	-110.9	-109.4	-190.3	-172.6	....
Banks	78bu d	37.3	5.1	5.8	-3.5	-11.2	13.8	25.4	32.1	....	....	....	22.6	21.0	....	....
Other Sectors	78bv d	87.7	104.4	245.0	142.8	82.7	-100.5	-93.0	-135.3	-61.9	-64.9	475.5	694.8	476.1	244.0	....
Net Errors and Omissions	78ca d	144.3	34.7	67.7	66.9	69.6	110.3	257.5	5.8	11.4	-128.2	32.8	-88.6	-214.6	43.0	....
Overall Balance	78cb d	-25.3	-43.6	121.9	-92.5	-43.9	-256.9	411.8	61.6	-141.6	387.0	15.5	82.6	-34.0	-36.0	....
Reserves and Related Items	79da d	25.3	43.6	-121.9	92.5	43.9	256.9	-411.8	-61.6	141.6	-387.0	-15.5	-82.6	34.0	36.0	....
Reserve Assets	79db d	145.1	-30.8	-92.9	58.8	36.9	-27.4	-477.3	-95.3	174.2	-378.1	70.8	5.4	-9.2	-107.1	....
Use of Fund Credit and Loans	79dc d	-120.7	73.6	-29.2	33.7	7.0	-82.9	-30.6	19.3	-39.1	-24.6	-67.3	-62.8	-59.5	1.3	....
Exceptional Financing	79de d	.9	.8	.2	—	—	367.1	96.2	14.4	6.5	15.8	-19.0	-25.2	102.7	141.8	....

Kenya

		1972	1973	1974	1975	1976	1977	1978	1979	1980	1981	1982	1983	1984	1985	1986
Government Finance																*Millions of Shillings:*
Deficit (-) or Surplus	80	−782	−696	−558	−1,259	−1,558	−1,020	−871	−2,411	−1,122	−3,897	−4,462	−1,597	−2,710	−3,775	−5,586
Total Revenue and Grants	81y	2,554	2,616	3,386	4,438	5,037	5,863	9,166	10,543	12,717	14,351	15,589	16,025	18,434	19,942	23,946
Revenue	81	2,539	2,612	3,380	4,438	5,037	5,863	9,166	10,376	12,508	13,853	15,137	15,706	17,844	19,428	22,956
Grants	81z	15	4	6	—	—	—	—	167	209	498	452	319	590	514	990
Expenditure	82	3,336	3,312	3,944	5,697	6,595	6,883	10,037	12,954	13,839	18,248	20,051	17,622	21,144	23,717	29,532
Statistical Discrepancy	80xx	....	....	....	....	....	....	....	....	....	....	....	....	....	....	....
Total Financing	80h	782	696	558	1,259	1,558	1,020	871	2,411	1,122	3,897	4,462	1,597	2,710	3,775	5,585
Domestic	84a	593	390	308	879	791	501	266	2,194	994	2,681	3,647	1,474	3,689	5,386	7,851
Foreign	85a	189	306	250	380	767	519	605	217	128	1,216	815	123	−979	−1,611	−2,266
Total Debt	88	....	....	....	....	....	....	....	....	....	....	....	....	....	....	....
Domestic	88a	....	....	....	....	....	....	....	....	....	....	....	....	....	....	....
Foreign	89a	....	....	....	....	....	....	....	....	....	....	....	....	....	....	....
National Accounts																*Millions of Shillings*
Househ.Cons.Expend.,incl.NPISHs	96f	9,003	10,848	12,554	16,240	17,908	20,680	24,977	28,896	32,178	37,203	44,612	48,734	56,481	58,435	70,385
Government Consumption Expend.	91f	2,573	2,796	3,530	4,386	5,075	6,441	7,972	8,946	10,675	11,528	12,949	14,662	15,512	17,602	21,518
Gross Fixed Capital Formation	93e	3,302	3,645	4,075	4,837	5,808	7,800	10,280	10,809	12,451	14,508	13,364	14,349	16,143	17,631	23,064
Changes in Inventories	93i	−111	−304	1,715	−496	79	1,024	1,932	−484	3,333	2,663	1,990	2,237	2,372	8,119	2,504
Exports of Goods and Services	90c	4,002	4,812	7,144	7,138	9,434	13,004	11,862	12,002	15,066	15,474	17,552	19,927	23,410	25,524	30,334
Imports of Goods and Services (-)	98c	4,323	5,036	8,676	8,260	9,232	11,752	15,860	14,732	21,054	20,914	20,188	20,284	24,639	26,540	30,129
Gross Domestic Product (GDP)	99b	13,776	15,790	18,776	21,140	25,562	32,699	35,601	39,543	44,648	51,641	58,214	66,218	72,550	100,831	117,472
Net Primary Income from Abroad	98.n	−434	−879	−846	−1,271	−1,362	−1,574	−1,812	−1,672	−1,680	−1,942	−2,787	−2,544	−3,043	−3,665	−4,183
Gross National Income (GNI)	99a	14,013	15,882	19,496	22,575	27,710	35,623	39,351	43,765	50,969	58,520	68,085	73,860	86,170	97,062	113,287
GDP Volume 1976 Prices	99b.p	22,744	....	....	....	....	....	....	....	....	....	....	....	....	....	....
GDP Volume 1982 Prices	99b.p	24,161	25,811	26,195	27,089	28,993	45,855	34,024	51,905	53,965	57,203	58,213	60,716	61,286	75,621	81,023
GDP Volume (1995=100)	99bv p	22.5	24.0	24.3	25.2	26.9	42.6	31.6	48.2	50.2	53.2	54.1	56.4	57.0	70.3	75.3
GDP Deflator (1995=100)	99bi p	13.2	14.1	16.6	18.0	20.4	16.5	24.2	17.6	19.1	20.9	23.1	25.2	27.4	30.8	33.5
																Millions:
Population	99z	12.07	12.48	12.91	13.41	13.85	14.35	14.88	15.33	16.67	17.34	18.04	18.77	19.54	20.33	21.16

	1987	1988	1989	1990	1991	1992	1993	1994	1995	1996	1997	1998	1999	2000	2001		
Government Finance																	
Year Ending June 30																	
Deficit (-) or Surplus	-9,841	-5,526	-6,574	-8,374	-11,171	-3,443	-14,931	-23,415	-6,172	6,228	†-13,605	-5,304	-5,189	7,196	-14,705		80
Total Revenue and Grants	27,513	32,427	39,211	46,703	54,582	67,321	78,469	112,413	138,181	156,804	†156,167	179,055	201,177	188,350	216,393		81y
Revenue	26,585	30,898	36,770	41,547	49,474	58,580	69,661	103,250	125,312	145,558	†150,384	173,783	196,257	184,103	192,313		81
Grants	928	1,529	2,441	5,156	5,108	8,741	8,808	9,163	12,869	11,246	5,783	5,272	4,920	4,247	24,080		81z
Expenditure	37,354	37,953	45,785	55,077	65,753	70,764	93,400	135,828	144,353	150,576	†169,772	184,359	206,366	181,154	231,098		82
Statistical Discrepancy	....	....	....	....	....	....	....	....	....	—	†-1,048	64	2,740	266	1,600		80xx
Total Financing	9,841	5,526	6,574	8,374	11,171	3,443	14,931	23,415	6,172	-6,228	†14,653	5,240	2,449	-7,462	13,105		80h
Domestic	11,994	6,514	5,173	3,824	6,662	4,958	8,571	21,962	16,977	-5,437	†21,287	12,441	11,194	11,876	616		84a
Foreign	-2,153	-988	1,401	4,550	4,509	-1,515	6,360	1,453	-10,805	-791	-6,634	-7,201	-8,745	-19,338	12,489		85a
Total Debt	....	....	....	....	....	....	....	....	....	....	....	441,561	455,050	550,185	572,963		88
Domestic												145,541	150,499	163,405	159,194		88a
Foreign												296,020	304,551	386,780	413,769		89a
National Accounts																	
Millions of Shillings																	
Househ.Cons.Expend.,incl.NPISHs	81,654	94,127	111,149	121,655	139,437	178,571	210,596	250,098	322,622	360,177	450,664	511,235	536,389	602,353	....		96f
Government Consumption Expend.	24,354	27,293	30,769	36,620	37,606	41,475	48,307	60,719	69,057	81,960	100,770	113,568	127,040	142,134	....		91f
Gross Fixed Capital Formation	25,735	30,359	33,156	40,560	42,671	43,777	56,505	75,616	99,497	104,469	109,870	113,858	113,215	116,555	....		93e
Changes in Inventories	6,116	7,417	9,209	6,906	4,351	898	2,245	1,683	2,020	3,000	5,400	6,210	7,142	6,142	....		93i
Exports of Goods and Services	27,992	33,084	39,554	51,186	60,512	69,287	134,918	148,225	152,596	173,531	174,835	173,094	186,940	208,800	....		90c
Imports of Goods and Services (-)	34,682	41,086	52,247	61,391	63,327	69,041	118,958	135,641	180,139	195,170	220,596	225,805	221,803	287,067	....		98c
Gross Domestic Product (GDP)	131,169	151,194	171,589	195,536	221,250	264,967	333,613	400,722	465,653	527,967	623,354	692,120	748,925	788,917	....		99b
Net Primary Income from Abroad	-5,030	-6,412	-7,097	-10,179	-12,572	-12,548	-24,380	-23,074	-19,832	-15,837	-13,623	-10,468	-11,457	-10,140	....		98.n
Gross National Income (GNI)	126,139	144,782	164,492	185,357	208,678	252,419	309,233	377,626	445,821	512,130	609,730	681,652	760,382	778,777	....		99a
GDP Volume 1976 Prices																	99b.p
GDP Volume 1982 Prices	85,833	91,157	95,433	99,431	100,864	100,057	100,411	103,054	107,595	112,058	115,469	116,444	....	....	....		99b.p
GDP Volume (1995=100)	79.8	84.7	88.7	92.4	93.7	93.0	93.3	95.8	100.0	104.1	107.3	108.2	....	....	....		99bv p
GDP Deflator (1995=100)	35.3	38.3	41.5	45.4	50.7	61.2	76.8	89.8	100.0	108.9	124.7	137.3	....	....	....		99bi p
Midyear Estimates																	
Population	22.94	23.88	24.87	†24.03	25.91	25.70	†28.11	29.29	30.52	31.80	†28.41	29.34	30.03	30.67	31.29		99z

(See notes in the back of the book.)

Korea

	1972	1973	1974	1975	1976	1977	1978	1979	1980	1981	1982	1983	1984	1985	1986
Exchange Rates														Won per SDR:	
Market Rate .... **aa**	433.09	479.52	592.59	566.60	562.33	587.92	630.55	637.59	841.64	815.35	826.01	832.85	811.03	977.81	1,053.66
														Won per US Dollar:	
Market Rate .... **ae**	398.90	397.50	484.00	484.00	484.00	484.00	484.00	484.00	659.90	700.50	748.80	795.50	827.40	890.20	861.40
Market Rate .... **rf**	392.89	398.32	404.47	484.00	484.00	484.00	484.00	484.00	607.43	681.03	731.08	775.75	805.98	870.02	881.45
Fund Position														Millions of SDRs:	
Quota .... **2f. s**	80.0	80.0	80.0	80.0	80.0	80.0	160.0	160.0	255.9	255.9	255.9	462.8	462.8	462.8	462.8
SDRs .... **1b. s**	26.1	26.1	1.4	3.4	6.8	10.0	11.4	18.9	9.9	54.1	57.8	60.2	30.9	36.2	14.4
Reserve Position in the Fund .... **1c. s**	12.5	20.0	—	—	—	—	10.4	18.8	—	—	—	51.7	—	.7	.7
of which: Outstg.Fund Borrowing **2c**															
Total Fund Cred.&Loans Outstg. **2tl**	—	—	110.0	217.3	301.7	280.4	201.8	104.4	535.4	1,070.6	1,141.7	1,292.8	1,598.9	1,373.0	1,266.3
International Liquidity												Millions of US Dollars Unless Otherwise Indicated:			
Total Reserves minus Gold .... **1l. d**	523.0	884.8	277.2	781.3	1,970.0	2,967.1	2,763.9	2,959.2	2,924.9	2,681.7	2,807.3	2,346.7	2,753.6	2,869.3	3,319.6
SDRs .... **1b. d**	28.3	31.5	1.7	3.9	7.9	12.2	14.9	24.9	12.6	63.0	63.7	63.0	30.3	39.8	17.7
Reserve Position in the Fund .... **1c. d**	13.6	24.1	—	—	—	—	13.6	24.8	—	—	—	54.1	—	.7	.8
Foreign Exchange .... **1d. d**	481.1	829.2	275.5	777.4	1,962.1	2,954.9	2,735.5	2,909.5	2,912.3	2,618.7	2,743.6	2,229.5	2,723.3	2,828.8	3,301.1
Gold (Million Fine Troy Ounces) **1ad**	.107	.110	.110	.111	.112	.147	.275	.295	.299	.303	.303	.304	.309	.313	.317
Gold (National Valuation) **1and**	4.0	4.6	4.7	4.7	4.7	6.2	29.7	30.6	30.8	32.2	30.9	31.0	31.1	31.4	31.5
Monetary Authorities: Other Liab. ...... **4.. d**	11.4	11.4	114.5	218.4	247.4	182.8	49.7	54.2	52.1	52.9	59.7	59.8	62.5	71.5	83.1
Deposit Money Banks: Assets ...... **7a. d**	212.7	204.9	773.8	764.2	986.0	1,333.4	2,143.8	2,718.6	3,615.8	4,176.2	4,146.9	4,531.0	4,865.0	4,848.0	4,692.0
Liabilities .... **7b. d**	447.0	376.4	1,073.1	1,514.0	1,740.7	2,295.7	3,217.1	5,106.8	7,145.9	9,288.9	11,976.0	10,751.0	14,188.0	15,867.0	14,536.0
Other Banking Insts.: Assets .... **7e. d**	....	....	....	....	....	....	111.0	232.0	144.0	210.0	402.0	306.0	389.0	385.0	179.0
Liabilities .... **7f. d**	....	....	....	....	....	....	1,255.0	2,375.0	2,821.0	3,636.0	4,628.0	5,353.0	6,322.0	8,396.0	8,606.0
Monetary Authorities														Billions of Won:	
Foreign Assets **11**	135	268	102	367	927	1,514	1,320	1,447	1,939	1,897	2,162	1,869	2,288	2,481	2,806
Claims on Central Government **12a**	189	208	409	682	818	925	1,191	1,177	1,176	1,712	1,922	2,217	2,176	2,188	2,193
Claims on Official Entities **12bx**	34	43	20	110	110	210	240	240	270	370	470	570	570	570	572
Claims on Deposit Money Banks **12e**	179	280	667	686	686	849	1,493	2,339	2,917	3,627	4,193	5,244	7,095	9,078	10,849
Reserve Money **14**	428	624	775	1,077	1,438	2,072	2,802	3,468	3,244	2,802	3,825	4,095	4,248	4,319	5,017
of which: Currency Outside DMBs **14a**	218	311	411	507	677	953	1,364	1,604	1,856	2,025	2,574	2,874	3,109	3,286	3,679
Bonds **16ab**	8	18	1	94	150	429	426	532	580	1,934	2,538	3,737	5,651	8,418	9,677
Foreign Liabilities **16c**	5	5	121	229	289	253	151	93	485	910	988	1,124	1,348	1,406	1,406
Central Government Deposits **16d**	88	104	154	217	388	711	914	902	780	544	627	764	1,121	1,187	1,447
Other Items (Net) **17r**	8	49	147	228	277	34	−49	208	1,213	1,416	769	180	−240	−1,013	−1,128
Deposit Money Banks														Billions of Won:	
Reserves **20**	166	276	352	557	755	1,110	1,401	1,815	1,324	738	1,196	1,129	856	1,016	1,307
Claims on Mon.Author.: Securities **20c**	44	61	1	68	68	381	339	319	555	1,566	2,386	2,831	4,125	5,558	5,023
Foreign Assets **21**	163	195	483	698	767	1,313	1,427	1,657	3,074	3,601	3,659	4,336	4,861	5,139	4,928
Claims on Central Government **22a**	4	28	47	104	228	371	518	632	1,030	1,407	2,229	2,395	2,897	2,968	3,595
Claims on Private Sector **22d**	1,453	1,890	2,789	3,481	4,374	5,465	8,082	11,303	15,788	19,923	25,050	29,429	33,649	39,991	46,014
Demand Deposits **24**	332	440	533	668	866	1,233	1,325	1,648	1,920	1,969	3,306	3,872	3,777	4,302	5,223
Time, Savings,& Fgn.Currency Dep. **25**	929	1,245	1,506	1,965	2,660	3,699	5,211	6,603	8,727	11,688	14,105	16,154	17,885	21,001	25,023
Bonds **26ab**	11	24	36	52	82	151	176	235	316	44	90	180	200	218	96
Restricted Deposits **26b**	77	168	173	258	327	298	329	370	617	592	281	306	287	359	725
Foreign Liabilities **26c**	178	150	519	733	842	1,111	1,557	2,472	4,716	6,507	8,968	9,956	11,739	14,124	12,521
Central Government Deposits **26d**	2	1	13	31	57	—	—	33	23	4	321	569	521	240	187
Central Govt. Lending Funds **26f**	116	127	168	209	299	394	531	738	882	1,130	1,434	1,742	1,928	2,172	2,554
Credit from Monetary Authorities **26g**	179	280	666	673	686	849	1,496	2,340	2,918	3,627	4,197	5,245	7,098	9,112	10,860
Capital Accounts **27a**	126	173	215	348	445	545	829	1,134	1,404	1,689	1,907	2,383	2,706	3,031	3,462
Other Items (Net) **27r**	−121	−159	−157	−29	−74	360	311	154	248	−15	−88	−286	248	113	216
Monetary Survey														Billions of Won:	
Foreign Assets (Net) **31n**	114	309	−54	103	562	1,462	1,039	540	−188	−1,919	−4,134	−4,875	−5,939	−7,910	−6,193
Domestic Credit **32**	1,600	2,074	3,171	4,201	5,165	6,395	9,295	12,605	17,719	23,215	29,044	33,683	38,087	44,847	51,384
Claims on Central Govt. (Net) **32an**	103	131	289	538	602	586	795	874	1,403	2,572	3,204	3,279	3,431	3,729	4,153
Claims on Official Entities **32bx**	34	43	20	110	110	210	240	240	270	370	470	570	570	570	572
Claims on Private Sector **32d**	1,463	1,900	2,863	3,554	4,454	5,599	8,260	11,491	16,047	20,273	25,371	29,834	34,086	40,548	46,659
Money **34**	519	730	946	1,182	1,544	2,173	2,714	3,275	3,807	3,982	5,799	6,783	6,821	7,558	8,809
Quasi-Money **35**	932	1,250	1,511	1,968	2,661	3,702	5,215	6,603	8,727	11,689	14,105	16,155	17,885	21,007	25,024
Bonds **36ab**	−24	−19	36	78	164	199	264	448	341	412	243	1,086	1,725	3,078	4,750
Restricted Deposits **36b**	77	168	173	258	327	298	329	370	617	592	281	306	287	359	725
Central Govt. Lending Funds **36f**	121	133	178	219	310	402	534	738	882	1,130	1,435	1,742	1,928	2,173	2,554
Other Items (Net) **37r**	47	74	274	599	721	1,084	1,279	1,711	3,157	3,490	3,048	2,737	3,503	2,763	3,329
Money plus Quasi-Money **35l**	1,452	1,980	2,457	3,150	4,205	5,874	7,929	9,878	12,534	15,671	19,904	22,938	24,706	28,565	33,833
Other Banking Institutions															
Development Institutions														Billions of Won:	
Claims on Private Sector **42d**	311	386	502	723	918	1,249	1,743	2,470	3,620	4,449	5,311	6,049	6,699	7,740	8,315
Bonds **46ab**	51	82	88	67	115	176	235	299	510	610	786	900	1,160	1,710	2,229
Counterpart Funds **46e**	17	16	16	15	15	14	14	13	12	12	3	2	2	2	2
Central Govt. Lending Funds **46f**	85	100	162	251	361	486	786	1,108	1,468	1,925	2,333	2,728	2,779	2,948	2,650
Credit from Deposit Money Banks **46h**	40	40	34	36	23	35	29	32	31	39	12	20	9	36	55
Capital Accounts **47a**	125	129	143	237	330	365	449	480	618	666	685	781	768	786	825
Other Items (Net) **47r**	2	27	62	117	75	172	231	538	981	1,197	1,493	1,617	1,982	2,256	2,554
Trust Accounts of Coml. Banks														Billions of Won:	
Claims on Private Sector .... **42d. g**	131	167	149	160	256	507	765	1,062	1,826	2,873	4,044	5,190	6,493	9,425	13,358
Claims on Deposit Money Banks .... **42e. g**	18	5	21	27	46	23	7	24	36	28	117	120	100	375	259
Quasi-Monetary Liabilities .... **45.. g**	158	183	191	186	251	355	429	588	1,043	1,448	1,581	1,721	2,236	3,928	5,095
Other Items (Net) .... **47r. g**	−9	−10	−20	—	51	175	344	498	819	1,453	2,580	3,589	4,356	5,872	8,522
Postal Savings Deposits .... **45.. h**	25	32	40	47	62	35	30	41	85	93	282	439	586	475	512

1987	1988	1989	1990	1991	1992	1993	1994	1995	1996	1997	1998	1999	2000	2001		
															Exchange Rates	
End of Period																
1,124.00	920.59	893.10	1,019.19	1,088.27	1,084.05	1,109.97	1,151.38	1,151.58	1,213.93	2,286.98	1,695.27	1,561.92	1,647.53	1,650.71	Market Rate	aa
End of Period (ae)	*Period Average (rf)*															
792.30	684.10	679.60	716.40	760.80	788.40	808.10	788.70	774.70	844.20	1,695.00	1,204.00	1,138.00	1,264.50	1,313.50	Market Rate	ae
822.57	731.47	671.46	707.76	733.35	780.65	802.67	803.45	771.27	804.45	951.29	1,401.44	1,188.82	1,130.96	1,290.99	Market Rate	rf
															Fund Position	
End of Period																
462.8	462.8	462.8	462.8	462.8	799.6	799.6	799.6	799.6	799.6	799.6	799.6	1,633.6	1,633.6	1,633.6	Quota	2f. s
11.6	4.2	1.2	10.1	20.9	30.6	42.3	52.3	65.7	82.3	43.6	8.1	.5	2.7	2.7	SDRs	1b. s
.7	.7	178.2	224.5	255.4	319.1	339.2	363.6	438.5	474.3	443.7	.1	208.6	208.6	208.8	Reserve Position in the Fund	1c. s
—	—	—	—	—	—	—	—	—	—	—	—	—	—	—	of which: Outstg.Fund Borrowing	2c
369.8	—	—	—	—	—	—	—	—	—	—	8,200.0	12,000.0	4,462.5	4,462.5	Total Fund Cred.&Loans Outstg.	2tl
															International Liquidity	
End of Period																
3,583.7	12,346.7	15,213.6	14,793.0	13,701.1	17,120.6	20,228.2	25,639.3	32,677.7	34,037.1	20,367.9	51,974.5	73,987.3	96,130.5	102,753.3	Total Reserves minus Gold	1l. d
16.4	5.7	1.6	14.4	29.8	42.0	58.1	76.3	97.7	118.4	58.8	11.4	.7	3.5	3.3	SDRs	1b. d
1.0	.9	234.2	319.4	365.3	438.7	465.9	530.8	651.8	682.0	598.7	.1	286.3	271.8	262.4	Reserve Position in the Fund	1c. d
3,566.3	12,340.1	14,977.8	14,459.2	13,306.0	16,639.9	19,704.2	25,032.1	31,928.2	33,236.7	19,710.4	51,963.0	73,700.3	95,855.1	102,487.5	Foreign Exchange	1d. d
.320	.320	.320	.320	.321	.323	.324	.325	.327	.327	.335	.435	.437	.439	.442	Gold (Million Fine Troy Ounces)	1ad
31.6	31.6	31.6	31.6	32.2	32.6	33.3	33.6	34.4	36.0	36.9	66.3	67.1	67.6	68.3	Gold (National Valuation)	1an d
112.0	143.5	-77.0	166.1	178.6	46.4	95.4	442.4	158.6	381.1	140.1	1,670.7	1,588.5	1,426.0	4,877.1	Monetary Authorities: Other Liab.	4.. d
5,578.0	†8,513.0	7,868.0	9,532.0	10,705.0	12,905.0	16,211.0	20,938.0	27,806.0	33,136.0	32,749.0	34,310.0	34,748.0	34,562.0	28,086.0	Deposit Money Banks: Assets	7a. d
11,591.0	10,246.0	9,686.0	10,181.0	13,896.0	14,665.0	14,795.0	21,170.0	31,446.0	42,197.0	27,975.0	29,455.0	27,547.0	24,805.0	21,290.0	Liabilities	7b. d
150.0	357.0	659.0	1,064.0	1,788.0	1,963.0	5,365.0	7,897.0	4,136.0	7,144.0	10,761.0	10,027.0	8,975.0	11,926.0	13,058.0	Other Banking Insts.: Assets	7e. d
5,204.0	3,803.0	3,368.0	4,653.0	7,609.0	9,780.0	15,834.0	21,692.0	21,816.0	26,857.0	29,661.0	22,466.0	18,033.0	15,222.0	13,387.0	Liabilities	7f. d
															Monetary Authorities	
End of Period																
2,802	8,458	10,360	10,820	10,712	13,684	16,672	20,880	25,390	28,173	29,227	64,832	85,342	121,558	142,589	Foreign Assets	11
2,312	2,841	2,738	2,237	2,498	2,333	2,659	2,628	1,951	2,235	5,562	5,961	6,382	4,614	5,225	Claims on Central Government	12a
572	570	570	570	570	570	570	570	570	370	2,370	8,640	2,370	2,370	2,370	Claims on Official Entities	12bx
14,890	15,958	16,144	19,553	21,122	25,571	29,169	28,971	28,076	24,378	62,442	37,830	26,003	15,563	11,637	Claims on Deposit Money Banks	12e
7,469	9,728	12,819	13,811	16,322	18,107	23,080	25,204	29,306	25,723	22,519	20,703	28,487	28,238	32,827	Reserve Money	14
4,443	5,133	6,140	7,011	7,913	8,581	12,109	13,127	15,061	15,453	15,448	13,670	19,475	17,636	18,702	of which: Currency Outside DMBs	14a
13,635	20,470	19,371	18,403	17,651	23,614	27,148	29,114	29,598	29,068	26,701	53,580	61,389	79,142	93,120	Bonds	16ab
504	98	-52	119	136	37	77	349	123	322	18,991	22,355	8,778	9,155	6,406	Foreign Liabilities	16c
3,408	5,766	7,276	7,424	5,770	4,524	5,059	6,477	6,917	6,684	5,410	5,917	9,126	10,608	7,347	Central Government Deposits	16d
-4,441	-8,236	-9,601	-6,577	-4,976	-4,124	-6,293	-8,095	-9,956	-6,640	25,980	14,708	12,318	16,961	22,121	Other Items (Net)	17r
															Deposit Money Banks	
End of Period																
3,017	4,535	6,613	6,717	8,304	9,399	10,836	11,947	14,092	10,181	6,798	6,610	8,958	10,434	14,063	Reserves	20
4,474	4,606	3,296	2,761	4,052	7,068	8,865	12,700	15,775	18,419	20,996	29,559	27,375	33,073	36,239	Claims on Mon.Author.: Securities	20c
5,206	5,824	5,400	6,829	8,145	10,174	13,100	16,514	21,542	28,627	55,509	41,309	39,543	43,704	36,891	Foreign Assets	21
4,426	5,120	4,927	5,131	5,394	4,921	4,912	5,196	5,373	4,897	6,341	13,564	21,372	23,677	22,959	Claims on Central Government	22a
52,425	59,018	74,383	94,332	113,936	128,230	144,828	173,903	200,769	240,936	293,812	318,667	383,884	457,258	520,733	Claims on Private Sector	22d
5,829	7,112	8,419	9,218	14,009	16,182	17,344	19,593	23,672	24,221	19,331	21,569	25,139	29,193	34,918	Demand Deposits	24
30,172	36,786	44,308	52,800	61,984	71,660	83,178	100,668	115,072	138,769	168,482	222,926	284,916	366,041	414,031	Time, Savings,& Fgn.Currency Dep.	25
24	70	794	1,533	1,381	1,896	2,270	2,923	4,782	6,167	5,954	17,072	11,287	14,699	19,920	Bonds	26ab
1,305	1,694	1,286	1,052	1,723	1,693	635	792	904	988	1,214	772	803	1,030	908	Restricted Deposits	26b
9,184	7,009	6,647	7,294	10,495	11,552	11,957	16,697	24,361	36,454	47,418	35,464	31,348	31,366	27,964	Foreign Liabilities	26c
67	356	23	305	123	400	424	286	948	1,030	3,290	4,499	5,493	9,442	10,446	Central Government Deposits	26d
3,132	3,925	4,553	5,300	6,904	7,708	9,234	11,032	13,493	14,828	23,193	26,703	29,946	29,182	29,340	Central Govt. Lending Funds	26f
14,858	15,948	16,103	19,664	21,207	25,874	29,420	29,256	28,429	24,460	63,076	38,738	26,242	17,191	13,515	Credit from Monetary Authorities	26g
4,069	6,205	11,803	12,939	14,504	15,641	17,110	20,406	22,523	24,877	22,673	21,891	28,152	29,883	34,792	Capital Accounts	27a
908	-2	680	5,665	7,500	7,186	10,970	18,605	23,366	30,663	28,825	20,075	37,807	40,120	45,051	Other Items (Net)	27r
															Monetary Survey	
End of Period																
-1,679	7,174	9,165	10,236	8,226	12,269	17,739	20,347	22,448	20,024	18,327	48,322	84,759	124,741	145,110	Foreign Assets (Net)	31n
59,767	66,685	81,732	102,194	125,074	139,463	157,358	186,520	213,688	255,240	314,581	351,179	412,126	479,436	545,712	Domestic Credit	32
3,262	1,839	367	-361	1,999	2,329	2,089	1,061	-541	-1,183	3,204	9,108	13,135	8,242	10,391	Claims on Central Govt. (Net)	32an
572	570	570	570	570	570	570	570	570	370	2,370	8,640	2,370	2,370	2,370	Claims on Official Entities	32bx
55,934	64,276	80,795	101,985	122,505	136,564	154,699	184,888	213,658	256,054	309,008	333,431	396,621	468,825	532,951	Claims on Private Sector	32d
10,107	12,152	14,328	15,905	21,752	24,586	29,041	32,511	38,873	39,542	35,036	35,583	44,375	46,997	53,506	Money	34
30,172	36,787	44,309	52,802	61,994	71,672	83,178	100,668	115,073	138,770	168,495	222,956	284,943	366,052	414,072	Quasi-Money	35
9,185	15,934	16,869	17,174	14,980	18,442	20,553	19,338	18,606	16,817	11,659	41,092	45,301	60,767	76,802	Bonds	36ab
1,305	1,694	1,286	1,052	1,723	1,693	635	792	904	988	1,214	772	803	1,030	908	Restricted Deposits	36b
3,133	3,925	4,553	5,300	6,906	7,713	9,234	11,032	13,493	14,828	23,193	26,703	29,946	29,182	29,340	Central Govt. Lending Funds	36f
4,185	3,368	9,550	20,196	25,945	27,625	32,455	42,526	49,187	64,320	93,311	72,396	91,518	100,149	116,194	Other Items (Net)	37r
40,280	48,939	58,637	68,708	83,746	96,259	112,219	133,179	153,946	178,312	203,532	258,538	329,317	413,049	467,577	Money plus Quasi-Money	35l
															Other Banking Institutions	
															Development Institutions	
End of Period																
9,760	10,447	12,403	15,187	18,665	21,102	23,874	26,771	30,616	35,600	48,097	55,361	55,283	58,351	55,843	Claims on Private Sector	42d
2,688	2,896	3,404	4,612	7,974	10,412	13,921	16,617	19,639	23,764	34,782	36,096	34,666	35,251	34,317	Bonds	46ab
2	1	1	1	1	1	1	1	1	1	1	1	1	—	—	Counterpart Funds	46e
2,661	2,829	2,927	3,085	3,117	3,121	3,045	2,967	3,018	3,336	3,822	14,549	15,380	16,889	14,533	Central Govt. Lending Funds	46f
2,328	3,640	4,663	5,183	5,480	4,910	5,110	5,450	5,710	5,564	2,130	2,397	1,358	704	1,594	Credit from Deposit Money Banks	46h
946	1,023	1,059	1,242	1,387	1,285	1,382	1,615	1,614	1,814	2,909	4,486	6,247	3,773	6,931	Capital Accounts	47a
1,135	58	348	1,064	706	1,372	414	121	634	1,122	4,454	-2,168	-2,367	1,734	-1,532	Other Items (Net)	47r
															Trust Accounts of Coml. Banks	
End of Period																
18,008	27,344	38,990	47,578	56,964	79,724	112,416	143,539	182,319	216,569	253,305	307,920	273,872	178,537	181,683	Claims on Private Sector	42d. g
356	356	879	854	833	1,259	1,000	1,118	1,475	1,982	2,797	8,570	9,366	6,787	10,967	Claims on Deposit Money Banks	42e. g
8,741	13,453	22,119	29,175	36,619	53,022	71,319	93,415	124,891	151,093	171,456	138,941	115,360	77,594	81,330	Quasi-Monetary Liabilities	45.. g
9,622	14,246	17,750	19,257	21,178	27,961	42,096	51,242	58,903	67,458	84,646	177,549	167,878	107,730	111,319	Other Items (Net)	47r. g
1,052	1,566	1,710	1,973	2,346	3,578	4,078	5,948	5,321	6,421	7,280	11,491	14,980	22,150	26,111	Postal Savings Deposits	45.. h

Korea

	1972	1973	1974	1975	1976	1977	1978	1979	1980	1981	1982	1983	1984	1985	1986
Nonbank Financial Institutions														*Billions of Won:*	
Cash ....40..s	3	4	5	5	7	8	14	22	40	59	87	127	208	328	549
Claims on Central Government 42a.s	1	1	5	13	21	25	44	52	72	113	152	172	252	286	213
Claims on Private Sector 42d.s	16	29	39	50	70	137	227	494	728	1,061	1,519	2,356	3,447	4,575	5,653
Real Estate 42h.s	15	17	21	23	35	28	48	71	111	176	332	484	644	748	839
Incr.in Total Assets(Within Per.) 49z.s	8	17	22	25	38	70	141	314	322	479	817	1,138	1,455	1,703	1,901
Liquid Liabilities 55l	1,632	2,191	2,682	3,379	4,511	6,256	8,374	10,484	13,622	17,153	21,680	24,972	27,320	32,640	38,892
Interest Rates														*Percent Per Annum*	
Discount Rate *(End of Period)* 60	11.0	11.0	11.0	14.0	14.0	14.0	15.0	15.0	16.0	11.0	5.0	5.0	5.0	5.0	7.0
Money Market Rate...............................60b	....	....	....	....	....	18.1	19.3	18.9	22.9	18.1	14.2	13.0	11.4	9.4	9.7
Corporate Bond Rate 60bc											17.4	19.3	14.4	13.6	13.4	13.3
Deposit Rate 60l	12.0	12.0	15.0	15.0	16.2	14.4	18.6	18.6	19.5	16.2	8.0	8.0	9.2	10.0	10.0
Lending Rate 60p	....	....	....	....	....	....	....	....	18.0	17.4	11.8	10.0	10.0	10.0	10.0
Government Bond Yield 61	....	....	21.0	21.1	21.6	21.5	21.6	25.2	28.8	23.6	17.4	13.1	14.3	13.6	11.6
Prices, Production, Labor														*Index Numbers (1995=100):*	
Share Prices 62	4.6	8.7	8.6	9.5	11.7	†12.3	15.6	13.1	11.8	13.7	13.3	13.2	14.3	15.1	24.7
Producer Prices 63	14.3	15.3	21.8	27.6	†30.9	33.7	37.6	44.7	62.1	74.8	78.3	†78.4	78.9	79.7	78.5
Consumer Prices 64	11.3	11.7	14.5	18.2	†21.0	23.2	26.5	31.3	40.3	48.9	52.5	†54.3	55.5	56.9	58.4
Wages: Monthly Earnings 65ey	1.8	2.0	2.7	3.4	4.6	6.1	8.3	10.7	13.1	15.7	18.0	20.2	21.8	24.0	26.2
Industrial Production ....66..c	5.2	7.0	8.9	10.6	13.8	16.5	20.3	22.7	22.3	25.1	26.4	†30.5	35.1	36.7	44.2
Manufacturing Employment 67ey	30.1	37.0	41.9	46.0	55.8	58.3	62.9	65.2	61.9	59.9	63.0	68.3	69.9	73.2	79.8
														Number in Thousands:	
Labor Force..67d	....	....	....	....	....	....	....	....	....	....	....	....	....		
Employment 67e	....	....	....	....	....	....	....	....	....	....	....	....	....	14,970	15,505
Unemployment 67c	....	....	....	....	....	....	....	....	....	....	....	....	....	622	611
Unemployment Rate (%) 67r	....	....	....	....	....	....	....	....	....	....	....	....	....	4.0	3.8
International Transactions														*Millions of US Dollars*	
Exports ....70..d	1,625	3,221	4,462	4,945	7,716	10,048	12,722	15,057	17,512	21,268	21,853	24,446	29,245	30,282	34,715
Imports, c.i.f. ....71..d	2,522	4,240	6,852	7,274	8,774	10,811	14,972	20,339	22,292	26,131	24,251	26,192	30,631	31,136	31,585
															1995=100	
Volume of Exports 72	4.2	6.6	7.2	8.9	12.1	14.4	16.5	16.3	18.2	21.3	22.8	26.4	30.6	32.9	36.9
Volume of Imports 73	6.6	8.5	8.7	9.0	11.1	13.4	17.5	19.5	17.7	19.7	19.9	22.6	26.1	27.6	29.8
Unit Value of Exports 74	15.7	20.1	25.8	28.7	32.1	35.1	38.8	46.4	60.8	70.4	73.0	74.5	80.1	83.2	86.1
Unit Value of Imports 75	14.2	19.2	30.4	37.4	36.6	37.4	39.5	48.3	72.9	86.2	85.7	86.6	91.1	94.2	89.6
Export Prices 76	18.2	20.9	22.5	26.9	30.3	32.5	36.9	43.3	56.4	65.5	67.7	69.8	73.9	77.8	81.5
Import Prices 76.x	14.1	18.0	25.4	29.5	30.3	30.7	31.9	40.5	64.3	75.4	76.8	77.9	81.0	84.0	80.4
Balance of Payments														*Millions of US Dollars:*	
Current Account, n.i.e. 78ald	....	....	....	....	–310	12	–1,085	–4,151	–5,312	–4,607	–2,551	–1,524	–1,293	–795	4,709
Goods: Exports f.o.b. 78aad					7,814	10,046	12,711	14,705	17,245	20,747	20,934	23,272	26,486	26,633	34,128
Goods: Imports f.o.b. 78abd					–8,404	–10,523	–14,491	–19,100	–21,859	–24,596	–23,762	–25,120	–27,575	–26,653	–29,829
Trade Balance.....................................78acd					–590	–477	–1,780	–4,395	–4,613	–3,849	–2,827	–1,849	–1,089	–20	4,299
Services: Credit 78add					1,527	2,784	4,059	4,392	2,570	3,068	3,627	3,901	3,973	3,823	5,281
Services: Debit 78aed					–1,191	–2,025	–3,195	–3,503	–3,293	–3,554	–3,362	–3,507	–3,600	–3,364	–3,929
Balance on Goods & Services 78afd					–254	282	–916	–3,506	–5,336	–4,335	–2,562	–1,455	–716	438	5,651
Income: Credit 78agd					116	243	391	433	2,149	2,772	3,194	2,635	2,699	1,907	1,725
Income: Debit 78ahd					–518	–736	–1,031	–1,517	–2,660	–3,659	–3,839	–3,428	–3,963	–3,993	–4,035
Balance on Gds, Serv. & Inc. 78aid					–656	–211	–1,556	–4,590	–5,848	–5,222	–3,207	–2,248	–1,979	–1,647	3,341
Current Transfers, n.i.e.: Credit 78ajd					461	388	574	560	720	770	795	822	790	997	1,475
Current Transfers: Debit 78akd					–115	–165	–103	–121	–185	–155	–139	–99	–104	–145	–106
Capital Account, n.i.e. 78bcd					—	—	—	—	4	–35	–97	–80	–82	–93	–96
Capital Account, n.i.e.: Credit 78bad					—	—	—	—	4	3	5	6	8	8	6
Capital Account: Debit 78bbd					—	—	—	—	—	–39	–101	–85	–90	–101	–102
Financial Account, n.i.e.......................78bjd					1,866	1,390	2,129	5,353	5,925	4,720	3,950	2,311	2,822	1,960	–3,994
Direct Investment Abroad 78bdd					–6	–21	–28	–19	–26	–48	–151	–130	–52	–591	–1,227
Dir. Invest. in Rep. Econ., n.i.e. 78bed					81	94	89	35	6	102	69	69	110	234	460
Portfolio Investment Assets 78bfd					—	—	—	—	—	—	—	—	—	—	—
Equity Securities................................78bkd					—	—	—	—	—	—	—	—	—	—	—
Debt Securities 78bld					—	—	—	—	—	—	—	—	—	—	—
Portfolio Investment Liab., n.i.e. 78bgd					74	70	42	8	134	24	–15	546	836	1,737	–333
Equity Securities...............................78bmd					—	—	—	—	—	—	—	—	—	—	—
Debt Securities 78bnd					74	70	42	8	134	24	–15	546	836	1,737	–333
Financial Derivatives Assets 78bwd					....	....	....	....							
Financial Derivatives Liabilities 78bxd					....	....	....	....							
Other Investment Assets 78bhd					–289	–924	–175	–687	–492	–19	–794	–547	296	–1,108	–682
Monetary Authorities 78bod					....	....	....	....		–24	–12	–13	–7	–9	–20	–15
General Government 78bpd					–11	–14	–15	–8	—	—	—	—	—	—	—
Banks 78bqd					–128	–377	265	–125	–108	–70	–474	66	56	–49	–255
Other Sectors 78brd					–150	–533	–425	–554	–361	64	–307	–606	250	–1,040	–412
Other Investment Liab., n.i.e. 78bid					2,006	2,171	2,201	6,016	6,303	4,660	4,840	2,374	1,632	1,689	–2,213
Monetary Authorities 78bsd					6	10	9	5	16	4	5	2	8	18	13
General Government 78btd					608	388	326	1,497	1,223	1,269	1,355	852	669	375	–214
Banks 78bud					263	479	1,002	1,967	2,228	1,989	3,211	48	1,073	946	–1,475
Other Sectors 78bvd					1,129	1,294	864	2,547	2,836	1,399	269	1,472	–118	350	–536
Net Errors and Omissions.....................78cad					–243	–32	–313	–328	–433	–328	–1,292	–831	–1,062	–862	–585
Overall Balance 78cbd					1,313	1,370	731	874	184	–250	10	–124	385	211	34
Reserves and Related Items 79dad					–1,313	–1,370	–731	–874	–184	250	–10	124	–385	–211	–34
Reserve Assets 79dbd					–1,410	–1,345	–630	–749	–747	–379	–94	–36	–703	22	93
Use of Fund Credit and Loans 79dcd					97	–25	–100	–125	564	629	84	160	318	–232	–127
Exceptional Financing 79ded					....	....	....	....	....	....	....	....	....	....	....

1987	1988	1989	1990	1991	1992	1993	1994	1995	1996	1997	1998	1999	2000	2001		
End of Period															**Nonbank Financial Institutions**	
870	1,324	1,850	2,304	3,247	4,496	3,186	3,633	5,984	8,310	12,071	7,906	5,836	6,638	6,602	Cash	40..s
137	22	63	108	324	401	452	269	107	123	163	510	1,677	2,571	4,536	Claims on Central Government	42a.s
7,937	10,608	14,411	19,279	24,337	28,656	33,091	38,931	43,207	51,210	55,510	43,442	42,937	53,578	58,010	Claims on Private Sector	42d.s
917	1,147	1,489	2,210	2,798	3,333	3,842	4,504	5,124	6,173	7,333	8,703	9,752	10,113	9,757	Real Estate	42h.s
3,163	3,933	5,223	7,657	8,196	6,528	5,607	7,230	10,951	13,101	12,461	357	15,997	13,896	16,280	*Incr.in Total Assets(Within Per.)*	49z.s
49,202	62,634	80,616	97,551	119,465	148,364	184,430	228,909	278,174	327,515	370,197	401,064	453,822	506,155	568,417	Liquid Liabilities	55l
Percent Per Annum															**Interest Rates**	
7.0	8.0	7.0	7.0	7.0	7.0	5.0	5.0	5.0	5.0	5.0	3.0	3.0	3.0	....	Discount Rate *(End of Period)*	60
8.9	9.6	13.3	14.0	17.0	14.3	12.1	12.5	12.6	12.4	13.2	15.0	5.0	5.2	4.7	Money Market Rate	60b
12.9	12.8	15.7	13.3	13.4	†16.2	12.6	12.9	13.8	11.8	13.4	15.1	8.9	9.4	7.1	Corporate Bond Rate	60bc
10.0	10.0	10.0	10.0	10.0	10.0	8.6	8.5	8.8	7.5	†10.8	13.3	7.9	7.9	5.8	Deposit Rate	60l
10.0	10.1	11.3	10.0	10.0	10.0	8.6	8.5	9.0	8.8	†11.9	15.3	9.4	8.5	7.7	Lending Rate	60p
12.4	13.0	14.7	15.0	16.5	15.1	12.1	12.3	12.4	10.9	11.7	12.8	8.7	8.5	6.7	Government Bond Yield	61
Period Averages															**Prices, Production, Labor**	
45.3	75.3	99.7	81.1	71.4	63.8	79.7	105.1	100.0	90.3	70.9	44.4	87.0	79.5	62.2	Share Prices	62
78.8	81.0	†82.2	85.6	89.6	91.6	93.0	95.5	†100.0	103.2	107.2	120.3	117.8	120.2	122.5	Producer Prices	63
60.2	64.5	†68.2	74.1	80.9	†86.0	90.1	95.7	100.0	104.9	109.6	117.8	118.8	121.5	†126.7	Consumer Prices	64
29.2	35.0	43.7	52.6	61.4	71.1	78.8	91.0	100.0	112.2	118.0	114.3	131.3	142.5	151.5	Wages: Monthly Earnings	65ey
†52.2	59.2	61.1	66.5	72.8	†77.1	80.5	89.3	100.0	108.4	113.5	106.1	131.7	154.0	156.6	Industrial Production	66..c
92.1	97.3	101.8	102.4	104.1	100.6	97.0	97.9	100.0	97.8	93.4	81.3	83.5	88.5	87.5	Manufacturing Employment	67ey
Period Averages																
....	....	....	....	....	....	....	20,326	20,798	21,188	21,604	21,390	21,634	....	....	Labor Force	67d
16,354	16,870	17,560	18,085	18,612	18,961	19,253	19,837	20,379	20,764	21,048	19,926	20,281	21,061	....	Employment	67e
519	435	463	454	436	465	550	489	419	425	557	1,463	1,353	889	819	Unemployment	67c
3.1	2.5	2.6	2.4	2.3	2.4	2.8	2.4	2.0	2.0	2.6	6.8	6.3	4.1	3.7	Unemployment Rate (%)	67r
Millions of US Dollars															**International Transactions**	
47,281	60,696	62,377	65,016	71,870	76,632	82,236	96,013	125,058	129,715	136,164	132,313	143,686	172,268	150,439	Exports	70..d
41,020	51,811	61,465	69,844	81,525	81,775	83,800	102,348	135,119	150,339	144,616	93,282	119,752	160,481	141,098	Imports, c.i.f.	71..d
1995=100																
45.7	†51.6	52.0	55.2	60.7	†65.8	70.2	80.7	100.0	117.5	134.7	160.5	179.8	217.4	....	Volume of Exports	72
36.1	†41.2	47.9	53.6	62.6	†63.8	67.9	82.5	100.0	115.6	117.8	88.3	114.0	135.6	....	Volume of Imports	73
88.5	89.4	83.5	86.4	90.0	94.3	97.4	99.2	100.0	90.5	90.3	110.8	94.8	90.6	....	Unit Value of Exports	74
89.8	88.3	82.7	88.5	91.7	96.1	95.0	95.6	100.0	100.0	115.5	138.8	114.8	125.7	....	Unit Value of Imports	75
83.3	86.9	85.5	87.9	91.3	93.7	†96.0	98.7	100.0	95.8	102.1	134.1	108.8	107.7	114.4	Export Prices	76
86.1	91.1	87.8	86.9	86.6	87.9	†91.0	94.6	100.0	100.6	110.2	141.4	124.2	133.7	140.4	Import Prices	76.x
Minus Sign Indicates Debit															Balance of Payments	
10,058	14,505	5,361	-2,003	-8,317	-3,944	990	-3,867	-8,507	-23,006	-8,167	40,365	24,477	12,241	8,617	Current Account, n.i.e.	78ald
46,560	59,973	61,832	63,659	70,541	76,199	82,089	94,964	124,632	129,968	138,619	132,122	145,164	175,948	151,371	Goods: Exports f.o.b.	78aad
-39,031	-48,690	-57,471	-66,109	-77,344	-77,954	-79,771	-97,824	-129,076	-144,933	-141,798	-90,495	-116,793	-159,076	-137,979	Goods: Imports f.o.b.	78abd
7,529	11,283	4,361	-2,450	-6,803	-1,755	2,319	-2,860	-4,444	-14,965	-3,179	41,627	28,371	16,872	13,392	*Trade Balance*	78acd
6,810	8,375	8,958	9,637	10,014	10,722	12,950	16,805	22,827	23,412	26,301	25,565	26,529	30,534	29,602	Services: Credit	78add
-4,533	-6,118	-8,514	-10,252	-12,167	-13,605	-15,076	-18,606	-25,806	-29,592	-29,502	-24,541	-27,180	-33,423	-33,129	Services: Debit	78aed
9,806	13,540	4,805	-3,065	-8,956	-4,639	192	-4,661	-7,423	-21,144	-6,379	42,651	27,720	13,982	9,866	*Balance on Goods & Services*	78afd
1,992	1,745	2,387	2,895	2,911	2,450	2,509	2,836	3,486	3,666	3,878	2,675	3,245	6,375	7,040	Income: Credit	78agd
-3,578	-3,073	-2,964	-2,982	-3,075	-2,846	-2,900	-3,322	-4,787	-5,482	-6,333	-8,313	-8,404	-8,797	-7,926	Income: Debit	78ahd
8,219	12,213	4,228	-3,152	-9,120	-5,035	-199	-5,147	-8,725	-22,960	-8,834	37,013	22,561	11,561	8,980	*Balance on Gds, Serv. & Inc.*	78aid
1,931	2,551	2,097	2,454	2,837	3,239	3,382	3,672	4,104	4,279	5,288	6,737	6,421	6,500	6,548	Current Transfers, n.i.e.: Credit	78ajd
-92	-259	-964	-1,305	-2,034	-2,147	-2,194	-2,392	-3,886	-4,325	-4,621	-3,384	-4,506	-5,820	-6,911	Current Transfers: Debit	78akd
-209	-353	-318	-331	-330	-407	-475	-437	-488	-598	-608	171	-389	-615	-443	Capital Account, n.i.e.	78bcd
5	6	8	7	7	5	2	8	15	19	17	464	95	98	29	Capital Account, n.i.e.: Credit	78bad
-215	-359	-327	-338	-336	-412	-477	-445	-502	-617	-624	-293	-484	-713	-471	Capital Account: Debit	78bbd
-8,937	-4,222	-2,568	2,895	6,741	6,994	3,217	10,733	17,273	23,924	-9,195	-8,381	12,709	12,725	2,543	Financial Account, n.i.e.	78bjd
-515	-643	-598	-1,052	-1,489	-1,162	-1,340	-2,461	-3,552	-4,671	-4,449	-4,740	-4,198	-4,999	-2,600	Direct Investment Abroad	78bdd
616	1,014	1,118	788	1,180	728	589	810	1,776	2,326	2,844	5,412	9,333	9,283	3,198	Dir. Invest. in Rep. Econ., n.i.e.	78bed
—	-473	-709	-500	198	76	-986	-2,481	-2,907	-6,413	1,076	-1,999	1,282	-520	-5,499	Portfolio Investment Assets	78bfd
—	-61	-105	-55	10	8	-204	-382	-238	-653	-320	42	-271	-480	-273	Equity Securities	78bkd
—	-412	-603	-445	188	68	-781	-2,098	-2,669	-5,760	1,395	-2,041	1,553	-40	-5,226	Debt Securities	78bld
-297	-607	-2	662	2,906	5,875	11,088	8,713	14,619	21,514	13,308	775	7,908	12,697	11,856	Portfolio Investment Liab., n.i.e.	78bgd
—	—	—	381	200	2,482	6,615	3,614	4,219	5,954	2,525	3,856	12,072	13,094	10,165	Equity Securities	78bmd
-297	-607	-2	281	2,706	3,392	4,473	5,099	10,400	15,561	10,783	-3,081	-4,164	-397	1,691	Debt Securities	78bnd
—	—	—	366	519	773	448	452	623	414	932	412	401	532	272	Financial Derivatives Assets	78bwd
—	—	—	-444	-568	-921	-535	-565	-744	-331	-1,021	-1,066	-915	-711	-378	Financial Derivatives Liabilities	78bxd
-112	-1,463	-963	-2,425	-3,006	-3,299	-4,592	-7,369	-13,991	-13,487	-13,568	6,693	-2,606	-2,289	7,458	Other Investment Assets	78bhd
-29	-27	-17	-26	-31	-24	-42	-72	-36	—	-86	-36	-164	-44	-56	Monetary Authorities	78bod
—	—	-82	49	-344	-213	-625	-296	-156	-543	-149	-46	-169	-155	-485	General Government	78bpd
-307	-1,616	192	-2,244	-1,810	-3,291	-3,993	-5,061	-9,199	-8,173	-8,336	6,970	-203	-1,219	9,048	Banks	78bqd
223	180	-1,056	-204	-822	228	68	-1,940	-4,600	-4,770	-4,996	-194	-2,071	-871	-1,048	Other Sectors	78brd
-8,629	-2,050	-1,414	5,500	7,001	4,924	-1,455	13,632	21,450	24,571	-8,317	-13,868	1,502	-1,268	-11,764	Other Investment Liab., n.i.e.	78bid
25	20	9	22	2	7	15	-2	-10	-29	23	25	148	28	63	Monetary Authorities	78bsd
-1,473	-1,256	-1,238	-817	-705	-700	-1,842	-335	-593	-493	4,671	4,628	3,309	110	-400	General Government	78btd
-2,731	-803	639	1,942	4,247	1,820	720	7,368	11,389	9,952	-9,785	-6,233	1,418	-4,538	-5,315	Banks	78bud
-4,450	-10	-824	4,353	3,458	3,798	-348	6,600	10,664	15,142	-3,226	-12,288	-3,372	3,132	-6,112	Other Sectors	78bvd
1,187	-603	1,164	-1,769	758	1,080	-722	-1,816	-1,240	1,095	-5,010	-6,225	-3,536	-561	2,698	Net Errors and Omissions	78cad
2,100	9,327	3,639	-1,208	-1,147	3,724	3,009	4,614	7,039	1,416	-22,979	25,930	33,260	23,790	13,416	*Overall Balance*	78cbd
-2,100	-9,327	-3,639	1,208	1,147	-3,724	-3,009	-4,614	-7,039	-1,416	22,979	-25,930	-33,260	-23,790	-13,416	Reserves and Related Items	79dad
-882	-8,837	-3,639	1,208	1,147	-3,724	-3,009	-4,614	-7,039	-1,416	11,875	-30,968	-22,989	-23,790	-7,724	Reserve Assets	79dbd
-1,218	-490	—	—	—	—	—	—	—	—	11,104	5,038	-10,271	—	-5,692	Use of Fund Credit and Loans	79dcd
....	....	....	....	....	....	....	....	....	....	....	....	....	....	....	Exceptional Financing	79ded

Korea

	1972	1973	1974	1975	1976	1977	1978	1979	1980	1981	1982	1983	1984	1985	1986
International Investment Position															*Millions of US Dollars*
Assets .... 79aa d	....	....	....	....	....	....	....	....	8,891	9,285	9,861	9,751	10,432	10,779	11,300
Direct Investment Abroad .... 79ab d	....	....	....	....	....	....	....	....	142	184	329	455	492	526	636
Portfolio Investment .... 79ac d	....	....	....	....	....	....	....	....	—	—	—	—	—	—	—
Equity Securities .... 79ad d	....	....	....	....	....	....	....	....	—	—	—	—	—	—	—
Debt Securities .... 79ae d	....	....	....	....	....	....	....	....	—	—	—	—	—	—	—
Financial Derivatives .... 79al d	....	....	....	....	....	....	....	....							
Other Investment .... 79af d	....	....	....	....	....	....	....	....	2,145	2,178	2,522	2,363	2,266	2,479	2,685
Monetary Authorities .... 79ag d	....	....	....	....	....	....	....	....	—	—	—	—	—	—	—
General Government .... 79ah d	....	....	....	....	....	....	....	....	—	—	—	—	—	—	—
Banks .... 79ai d	....	....	....	....	....	....	....	....	497	536	922	860	849	934	1,095
Other Sectors .... 79aj d	....	....	....	....	....	....	....	....	1,648	1,642	1,600	1,503	1,417	1,545	1,590
Reserve Assets .... 79ak d	....	....	....	....	....	....	....	....	6,604	6,923	7,010	6,933	7,674	7,774	7,979
Liabilities .... 79la d	....	....	....	....	....	....	....	....	9,236	12,012	15,322	15,758	17,885	20,543	19,973
Dir. Invest. in Rep. Economy .... 79lb d	....	....	....	....	....	....	....	....	867	969	1,038	1,107	1,217	1,451	1,886
Portfolio Investment .... 79lc d	....	....	....	....	....	....	....	....	267	327	342	530	863	1,845	2,146
Equity Securities .... 79ld d	....	....	....	....	....	....	....	....	—	44	44	44	65	186	225
Debt Securities .... 79le d	....	....	....	....	....	....	....	....	267	283	298	486	798	1,659	1,921
Financial Derivatives .... 79ll d	....	....	....	....	....	....	....	....	—	—	—	—	—	—	—
Other Investment .... 79lf d	....	....	....	....	....	....	....	....	8,102	10,716	13,942	14,121	15,805	17,247	15,941
Monetary Authorities .... 79lg d	....	....	....	....	....	....	....	....	752	1,319	1,337	1,433	1,653	1,612	1,666
General Government .... 79lh d	....	....	....	....	....	....	....	....	—	—	—	—	—	—	—
Banks .... 79li d	....	....	....	....	....	....	....	....	7,350	9,397	12,605	12,688	14,152	15,635	14,275
Other Sectors .... 79lj d	....	....	....	....	....	....	....	....	—	—	—	—	—	—	—
Government Finance															*Billions of Won:*
Deficit (-) or Surplus............................. 80	−161	−27	−164	−202	−192	−316	−300	−545	−849	−1,585	−1,656	−663	−841	−943	−86
Revenue 81	558	679	1,026	1,549	2,325	2,958	4,108	5,446	6,834	8,605	9,983	11,538	12,604	13,923	15,840
Grants Received 81z	27	16	13	15	2	—	—	—	—	—	—	—	—	—	—
Expenditure 82	751	707	1,065	1,601	2,294	2,804	3,781	5,225	6,563	8,045	10,115	10,682	11,875	13,336	14,948
Lending Minus Repayments 83	−5	14	138	165	225	470	627	766	1,120	2,145	1,524	1,519	1,570	1,530	978
Financing															
Domestic 84a	105	−38	69	46	−22	38	−65	272	524	1,046	974	260	527	501	233
Foreign... 85a	56	64	95	156	215	278	365	273	325	539	682	403	314	442	−147
Debt 88	647	775	1,107	1,505	1,867	2,347	2,980	3,530	5,328	7,346	9,343	10,715	11,614	12,751	13,576
Domestic 88a	190	195	276	384	539	652	861	1,183	1,511	2,851	4,020	4,743	5,241	5,422	5,759
Foreign... 89a	456	580	831	1,121	1,328	1,695	2,119	2,347	3,817	4,495	5,323	5,972	6,373	7,329	7,817
National Accounts															*Billions of Won*
Househ.Cons.Expend.,incl.NPISHs 96f	3,055	3,705	5,323	7,248	9,235	11,250	14,786	19,367	24,585	30,633	34,554	38,892	43,443	48,027	52,822
Government Consumption Expend. 91f	411	444	724	1,114	1,517	1,929	2,534	3,132	4,428	5,582	6,352	6,976	7,392	8,383	9,688
Gross Fixed Capital Formation 93e	871	1,298	2,069	2,745	3,594	5,107	7,924	10,573	12,230	13,369	15,586	18,944	21,381	23,435	26,976
Changes in Inventories 93i	22	80	380	191	167	51	110	684	−162	66	40	−340	794	963	611
Exports of Goods and Services 90c	815	1,561	2,074	2,785	4,281	5,560	7,010	8,399	42,373	16,613	18,467	21,539	24,969	26,744	34,825
Imports of Goods and Services (-) 98c	1,011	1,725	2,929	3,652	4,536	5,681	7,894	10,581	15,335	19,182	19,855	22,234	25,132	26,135	29,745
Statistical Discrepancy 99bs	−9	1	17	−26	−11	42	112	161	293	429	−64	931	1,215	1,184	1,111
Gross Domestic Product (GDP) 99b	4,172	5,378	7,597	10,228	13,998	17,946	24,233	31,036	37,789	47,383	54,431	63,858	73,004	81,312	94,862
Net Primary Income from Abroad 98.n	−8	−25	−20	−124	−131	−158	−114	−269	−756	−1,224	−1,292	−1,284	−1,672	−2,142	−2,223
Gross National Income (GNI) 99a	4,164	5,353	7,577	10,104	13,867	17,788	24,119	30,767	37,032	46,149	53,140	62,574	71,332	79,170	92,638
Consumption of Fixed Capital 99cf	302	426	595	753	1,070	1,395	1,778	2,427	3,030	3,898	4,942	5,989	7,104	8,001	9,244
GDP Volume 1995 Prices 99b.p	64,001	71,898	77,212	82,258	91,468	100,622	109,687	117,435	114,978	122,412	131,286	145,331	157,318	167,502	185,869
GDP Volume (1995=100) .... 99bv p	17.0	19.1	20.5	21.8	24.2	26.7	29.1	31.1	30.5	32.4	34.8	38.5	41.7	44.4	49.3
GDP Deflator (1995=100)................. 99bi p	6.5	7.5	9.8	12.4	15.3	17.8	22.1	26.4	32.9	38.7	41.5	43.9	46.4	48.5	51.0
															Millions:
Population.. 99z	33.51	34.10	34.69	35.28	35.85	36.41	36.97	37.53	38.12	38.72	39.33	39.91	40.41	40.81	41.21

Millions of US Dollars — International Investment Position

	1987	1988	1989	1990	1991	1992	1993	1994	1995	1996	1997	1998	1999	2000	2001		
Assets	13,075	24,093	26,915	28,639	30,369	38,068	46,762	60,612	....	....	....	....	....	....	....	International Investment Position	79aa d
Direct Investment Abroad	819	970	1,275	2,095	3,452	4,499	5,555	7,630	....	....	....	....	....	....	....		79ab d
Portfolio Investment	—	22	80	168	206	225	522	992	....	....	....	....	....	....	....		79ac d
Equity Securities	—								....	....	....	....	....	....	....		79ad d
Debt Securities	—	22	80	168	206	225	522	992	....	....	....	....	....	....	....		79ae d
Financial Derivatives									....	....	....	....	....	....	....		79al d
Other Investment	3,038	10,723	10,315	11,552	12,979	16,192	20,423	26,317	....	....	....	....	....	....	....		79af d
Monetary Authorities					18				....	....	....	....	....	....	....		79ag d
General Government	1,447	8,924	8,163	9,068	9,989	12,081	15,389	19,944	....	....	....	....	....	....	....		79ah d
Banks	1,591	1,799	2,152	2,484	2,972	4,111	5,034	6,373	....	....	....	....	....	....	....		79ai d
Other Sectors	9,218	12,378	15,245	14,824	13,732	17,152	20,262	25,673	....	....	....	....	....	....	....		79aj d
Reserve Assets																	79ak d
Liabilities	16,652	15,710	17,463	20,564	33,264	41,508	53,706	69,830	....	....	....	....	....	....	....		79la d
Dir. Invest. in Rep. Economy	2,487	3,358	4,116	4,831	5,947	6,482	6,984	7,715	....	....	....	....	....	....	....		79lb d
Portfolio Investment	2,033	1,573	1,602	2,501	5,655	11,416	22,438	29,714	....	....	....	....	....	....	....		79lc d
Equity Securities	263	292	322	702	702	3,030	9,316	11,796	....	....	....	....	....	....	....		79ld d
Debt Securities	1,770	1,281	1,280	1,799	4,953	8,386	13,122	17,918	....	....	....	....	....	....	....		79le d
Financial Derivatives									....	....	....	....	....	....	....		79ll d
Other Investment	12,132	10,779	11,745	13,232	21,662	23,610	24,284	32,401	....	....	....	....	....	....	....		79lf d
Monetary Authorities	667	162	162	184	186	193	208	207	....	....	....	....	....	....	....		79lg d
General Government									....	....	....	....	....	....	....		79lh d
Banks	11,465	10,617	11,583	13,048	21,476	23,417	24,076	32,194	....	....	....	....	....	....	....		79li d
Other Sectors									....	....	....	....	....	....	....		79lj d

Year Ending December 31 — Government Finance

	1987	1988	1989	1990	1991	1992	1993	1994	1995	1996	1997	1998	1999	2000	2001		
Deficit (-) or Surplus	478	2,009	285	-1,207	-3,494	-1,188	1,704	984	1,035	431	-5,747	....	....	....	....		80
Revenue	18,658	22,890	25,962	32,089	36,818	43,805	50,750	61,109	72,087	84,272	91,979	....	....	....	....		81
Grants Received												....	....	....	....		81z
Expenditure	16,944	19,454	23,776	29,004	35,619	40,776	45,010	53,887	62,320	72,600	79,004	....	....	....	....		82
Lending Minus Repayments	1,236	1,427	1,901	4,292	4,693	4,217	4,036	6,238	8,732	11,241	18,722	....	....	....	....	Financing	83
Domestic	-489	-1,297	315	1,535	3,776	1,499	-1,257	-589	-678	-136	-1,214	....	....	....	....		84a
Foreign	11	-712	-600	-328	-282	-311	-447	-395	-357	-295	6,961	....	....	....	....		85a
Debt	14,417	13,516	14,144	14,927	24,837	27,737	28,998	30,466	31,537	33,687	47,045	....	....	....	....		88
Domestic	6,562	7,548	9,034	9,369	19,137	22,216	23,504	24,800	26,296	28,636	31,724	....	....	....	....		88a
Foreign	7,855	5,968	5,110	5,558	5,700	5,521	5,494	5,666	5,241	5,051	15,321	....	....	....	....		89a

Billions of Won — National Accounts

	1987	1988	1989	1990	1991	1992	1993	1994	1995	1996	1997	1998	1999	2000	2001		
Househ.Cons.Expend.,incl.NPISHs	59,031	66,078	77,132	93,505	113,226	130,028	148,264	175,970	206,407	233,644	254,987	242,834	271,137	299,122	324,226		96f
Government Consumption Expend.	11,000	12,877	15,588	18,702	22,691	26,506	29,250	32,857	36,434	42,477	45,660	48,782	50,089	52,480	56,785		91f
Gross Fixed Capital Formation	32,600	39,451	47,673	66,689	84,507	90,809	100,354	116,436	138,439	153,976	159,110	132,308	134,152	148,203	147,498		93e
Changes in Inventories	982	1,965	2,554	736	1,773	931	-1,804	1,636	1,826	4,793	-3,933	-38,253	-5,381	-1,034	-2,043		93i
Exports of Goods and Services	43,972	49,853	47,556	52,020	59,226	67,942	76,423	89,986	113,972	123,468	157,413	220,961	204,378	233,792	233,857		90c
Imports of Goods and Services (-)	35,726	39,972	44,295	54,101	65,741	71,600	76,278	93,668	119,534	140,659	162,031	161,144	171,278	217,845	221,052		98c
Statistical Discrepancy	922	1,859	1,989	1,245	830	1,084	1,287	190	-192	779	2,071	-1,122	-353	7,242	5,741		99bs
Gross Domestic Product (GDP)	111,198	132,112	148,197	178,797	216,511	245,700	277,497	323,407	377,350	418,479	453,276	444,367	482,744	521,959	545,013		99b
Net Primary Income from Abroad	-1,610	-1,051	-427	-169	-208	-312	-389	-596	-1,033	-1,371	-2,423	-7,725	-6,147	-2,732	-1,139		98.n
Gross National Income (GNI)	109,588	131,061	147,770	178,628	216,303	245,388	277,108	322,812	376,316	417,108	450,853	436,642	476,598	519,227	543,875		99a
Consumption of Fixed Capital	11,320	13,799	15,392	18,884	22,025	25,005	28,721	32,278	40,847	46,671	51,173	58,248	60,904	61,656	63,185		99cf
GDP Volume 1995 Prices	206,287	227,864	241,726	263,431	287,738	303,384	320,044	346,448	377,350	402,821	423,007	394,710	437,709	478,533	493,026		99b.p
GDP Volume (1995=100)	54.7	60.4	64.1	69.8	76.3	80.4	84.8	91.8	100.0	106.8	112.1	104.6	116.0	126.8	130.7		99bv p
GDP Deflator (1995=100)	53.9	58.0	61.3	67.9	75.2	81.0	86.7	93.3	100.0	103.9	107.2	112.6	110.3	109.1	110.5		99bi p

Midyear Estimates

	1987	1988	1989	1990	1991	1992	1993	1994	1995	1996	1997	1998	1999	2000	2001		
Population	41.62	42.03	42.45	42.87	43.30	43.75	44.19	44.64	45.09	45.54	45.99	46.43	46.86	47.27	47.34		99z

(See notes in the back of the book.)

Kuwait

		1972	1973	1974	1975	1976	1977	1978	1979	1980	1981	1982	1983	1984	1985	1986
Exchange Rates															*SDRs per Dinar:*	
Official Rate	ac	2.8102	2.7940	2.8199	2.9040	2.9995	2.9392	2.8241	2.7795	2.8901	3.0529	3.1400	3.2648	3.3508	3.1501	2.7965
															US Dollars per Dinar:	
Official Rate	ag	3.0511	3.3705	3.4526	3.3996	3.4849	3.5703	3.6792	3.6615	3.6860	3.5535	3.4638	3.4181	3.2845	3.4601	3.4206
Official Rate	rh	3.0400	3.3770e	3.4115	3.4483	3.4203	3.4898	3.6362	3.6203	3.6993	3.5878	3.4737	3.4309	3.3785	3.3261	3.4412
Fund Position															*Millions of SDRs:*	
Quota	2f.s	65.0	65.0	65.0	65.0	65.0	65.0	235.0	235.0	393.3	393.3	393.3	635.3	635.3	635.3	635.3
SDRs	1b.s	—	—	—	—	—	—	—	—	—	35.4	62.3	35.6	76.0	104.3	128.4
Reserve Position in the Fund	1c.s	20.7	19.7	255.8	573.6	742.7	722.2	588.4	389.7	410.5	409.7	461.0	696.7	716.4	639.4	515.8
of which: Outstg.Fund Borrowing	2c	—	—	225.0	523.9	685.0	676.2	543.9	339.6	313.0	287.4	291.2	358.7	362.1	309.2	228.8
International Liquidity												*Millions of US Dollars Unless Otherwise Indicated:*					
Total Reserves minus Gold	1l.d	269.0	380.8	1,249.2	1,491.5	1,701.8	2,883.1	2,500.4	2,870.1	3,928.5	4,067.5	5,913.2	5,192.1	4,590.2	5,470.7	5,501.1
SDRs	1b.d	—	—	—	—	—	—	—	—	—	41.2	68.7	37.3	74.5	114.6	157.1
Reserve Position in the Fund	1c.d	22.5	23.8	313.2	671.5	862.9	877.2	766.6	513.4	523.6	476.9	508.6	729.4	702.3	702.3	631.0
Foreign Exchange	1d.d	246.5	357.0	936.0	820.0	838.9	2,005.9	1,733.8	2,356.7	3,404.9	3,549.4	5,335.9	4,425.4	3,813.4	4,653.8	4,713.1
Gold (Million Fine Troy Ounces)	1ad	2.480	2.846	3.504	3.988	5.578	2.511	2.525	2.539	2.539	2.539	2.539	2.539	2.539	2.539	2.539
Gold (National Valuation)	1and	94.2	....	150.5	169.6	242.9	112.1	116.3	116.1	116.8	112.6	109.8	108.4	104.1	109.7	108.4
Deposit Money Banks: Assets	7a.d	1,560.7	1,618.0	1,938.3	2,088.7	2,352.0	2,936.2	4,468.0	5,154.3	6,930.0	8,923.9	8,765.1	9,267.5	9,810.5	9,537.1	9,385.4
Liabilities	7b.d	314.9	459.7	495.1	574.5	1,129.5	1,498.8	2,213.0	2,943.5	4,181.0	4,969.9	5,651.5	5,816.6	5,685.5	5,258.3	4,633.9
Other Financial Insts.: Assets	7e.d	....	....	....	....	695.6	980.0	1,322.7	1,571.9	2,010.3	2,681.8	2,916.2	3,514.5	3,299.9	3,055.6	2,615.0
Liab.	7f.d									1,360.1	2,170.5	2,626.3	2,965.2	2,195.0	2,193.7	1,638.5
Monetary Authorities															*Millions of Dinars:*	
Foreign Assets	11	119.6	148.5	395.0	482.4	547.0	821.9	709.8	814.1	1,092.0	1,162.6	1,720.1	1,537.2	1,405.5	1,579.6	1,564.4
Claims on Central Government	12a	....	....	....		....	....									
Claims on Deposit Money Banks	12e	—	—	—	4.5	2.0	20.7	30.6	195.3	298.6	282.4	276.7	334.6	547.0	407.2	520.2
Reserve Money	14	71.0	95.8	129.2	169.2	224.8	431.5	318.7	379.2	506.2	679.3	1,097.7	841.0	743.9	729.6	667.7
of which: Currency Outside DMBs	14a	57.1	71.1	81.7	101.7	129.1	150.9	177.0	215.9	251.3	284.5	342.4	340.1	324.7	327.5	336.6
Central Government Deposits	16d	36.5	28.4	213.1	271.5	270.8	325.1	274.8	446.1	668.7	536.5	649.3	537.6	683.1	666.7	390.2
Capital Accounts	17a	5.0	5.0	5.0	5.0	5.0	8.0	27.9	27.9	30.0	32.8	33.7	138.2	188.7	194.6	188.1
Other Items (Net)	17r	7.1	19.2	47.7	41.2	48.4	78.0	119.0	156.3	185.7	196.5	216.1	354.9	336.9	396.0	838.7
Deposit Money Banks															*Millions of Dinars:*	
Reserves	20	13.8	26.9	57.9	67.2	92.4	271.0	122.7	143.3	221.7	382.5	744.1	485.1	397.6	376.4	306.8
Foreign Assets	21	513.4	479.0	561.4	614.4	674.9	822.4	1,214.4	1,407.7	1,880.1	2,511.3	2,530.5	2,711.3	2,986.9	2,756.3	2,743.8
Claims on Central Government	22a	.7	1.9	3.6	5.9	12.5	15.2	20.6	35.3	47.4	176.7	318.5	1,005.0	1,200.8	1,209.9	1,200.5
Claims on Private Sector	22d	175.7	247.6	351.7	500.8	921.8	1,221.5	1,543.5	2,088.3	2,629.1	†3,663.3	4,484.5	4,367.0	4,653.4	4,736.0	4,867.0
Demand Deposits	24	84.9	101.3	113.9	188.6	264.6	339.8	459.4	453.5	469.5	1,002.1	940.0	874.3	667.9	695.7	688.7
Time and Savings Deposits	25	351.6	363.9	489.0	600.8	826.4	1,078.0	1,314.0	1,593.2	2,136.8	2,755.0	3,267.9	3,683.7	4,176.9	4,066.6	4,085.2
Foreign Liabilities	26c	103.6	136.1	143.4	169.0	324.1	419.8	601.5	803.9	1,134.3	1,398.6	1,631.6	1,701.7	1,731.0	1,519.7	1,354.7
Central Government Deposits	26d	71.2	58.2	83.7	87.3	71.0	114.9	99.2	139.9	164.9	444.4	653.3	613.5	638.0	748.6	629.7
Credit from Monetary Authorities	26g	—	—	10.0	10.5	8.1	28.7	34.1	188.8	277.0	292.4	287.0	344.6	571.9	479.4	928.0
Capital Accounts	27a	40.8	45.6	51.0	63.8	89.2	197.4	218.4	268.6	337.0	490.4	698.7	792.9	958.1	978.0	1,042.7
Other Items (Net)	27r	51.6	50.4	83.6	68.3	118.2	151.5	174.5	226.6	258.8	351.0	599.2	557.6	494.9	591.3	389.4
Monetary Survey															*Millions of Dinars:*	
Foreign Assets (Net)	31n	529.4	491.4	813.0	927.8	897.8	1,224.5	1,322.7	1,417.9	1,837.8	2,275.3	2,619.0	2,546.8	2,661.4	2,816.2	2,953.5
Domestic Credit	32	68.7	162.9	58.5	147.9	592.5	796.7	1,190.1	1,537.6	1,842.9	2,859.1	3,500.4	4,220.9	4,533.1	4,530.6	5,047.6
Claims on Central Govt. (Net)	32an	–107.0	–84.7	–293.2	–352.9	–329.3	–424.8	–353.4	–550.7	–786.2	–804.2	–984.1	–146.1	–120.3	–205.4	180.6
Claims on Private Sector	32d	175.7	247.6	351.7	500.8	921.8	1,221.5	1,543.5	2,088.3	2,629.1	†3,663.3	4,484.5	4,367.0	4,653.4	4,736.0	4,867.0
Money	34	142.0	172.4	195.6	290.3	393.7	490.7	636.4	669.4	720.8	1,286.6	1,282.4	1,214.4	992.6	1,023.2	1,025.3
Quasi-Money	35	351.6	363.9	489.0	600.8	826.4	1,078.0	1,314.0	1,593.3	2,136.8	2,755.0	3,267.9	3,683.7	4,176.9	4,066.6	4,085.2
Other Items (Net)	37r	104.6	118.0	186.9	184.6	270.2	452.5	562.3	692.9	823.1	1,093.0	1,569.2	1,869.4	2,025.1	2,257.8	2,891.0
Money plus Quasi-Money	35l	493.6	536.3	684.6	891.1	1,220.1	1,568.7	1,950.4	2,262.7	2,857.6	4,041.6	4,550.3	4,898.1	5,169.5	5,089.8	5,110.5
Other Financial Institutions															*Millions of Dinars:*	
Cash	40	....	....	....	....	34.4	63.4	75.0	22.3	39.1	35.4	40.9	50.0	54.7	76.7	48.1
Foreign Assets	41	....	....	....	....	199.6	274.5	359.5	429.3	545.4	754.7	841.9	1,028.2	1,004.7	883.1	764.5
Claims on Private Sector	42d	....	....	....	....	62.9	90.8	130.0	196.0	285.6	453.9	808.0	717.7	596.5	518.2	560.7
Foreign Liabilities	46c	....	....	....	....	—	—	—	—	369.0	610.8	758.2	867.5	668.3	634.0	479.0
Central Government Deposits	46d	....	....	....	....	51.0	67.7	111.3	126.8	99.8	99.9	169.5	150.6	276.1	197.0	195.1
Credit from Deposit Money Banks	46h	....	....	....	....	22.1	69.9	83.9	90.2	126.6	182.8	231.1	166.1	147.1	145.6	88.5
Capital Accounts	47a	....	....	....	....	76.9	87.8	103.1	155.4	162.0	222.0	458.2	425.3	325.5	282.6	248.4
Other Items (Net)	47r	....	....	....	....	82.9	72.6	48.4	20.1	112.7	128.5	75.7	186.3	238.8	218.8	362.3
Interest Rates															*Percent Per Annum:*	
Discount Rate *(End of Period)*	60	....	....	....	5.50	5.50	5.50	5.50	6.00	6.00	6.00	6.00	6.00	6.00	6.00	6.00
Money Market Rate	60b	....	....	....					8.58	10.94	10.13	10.25	6.78	8.91	7.59	7.52
Treasury Bill Rate	60c	....	....	....						6.50	6.50	6.42	5.69	5.69	5.69	5.69
Deposit Rate	60l	....	....	....							4.50	9.21	9.21	7.13	7.73	7.25	6.80
Lending Rate	60p	....	....	....					6.30	6.80	9.28	9.39	8.35	7.73	8.58	8.75	8.63
Prices, Production, Labor															*Index Numbers (1995=100):*	
Wholesale Prices	63	31.7	38.7	42.7	46.0	49.5	52.9	52.3	55.7	61.5	65.8	†66.5	67.7	67.3	66.4	66.8
Consumer Prices	64	31.4	34.0	38.4	41.6	43.8	48.1	†52.3	56.0	59.9	64.3	69.3	72.6	73.4	74.5	75.2
Crude Petroleum Production	66aa	161.4	148.0	124.8	102.1	105.4	96.4	104.3	122.4	81.5	55.2	40.3	51.6	57.0	52.0	69.1
Labor Force	67d	....	....	....	....	....	....	....	....	....	....	....	....	....	....	....

1987	1988	1989	1990	1991	1992	1993	1994	1995	1996	1997	1998	1999	2000	2001		
															Exchange Rates	
End of Period																
2.6117	2.6294	2.6062	....	2.4593	2.4026	2.4396	2.2824	2.2504	2.3190	2.4308	2.3551	2.3953	2.5130	2.5905	Official Rate	ac
End of Period (ag) Period Average (rh)																
3.7051	3.5384	3.4250	....	3.5178	3.3036	3.3510	3.3320	3.3453	3.3346	3.2798	3.3161	3.2875	3.2742	3.2556	Official Rate	ag
3.5896	3.5848	3.4049	....	....	3.4087	3.3147	3.3600	3.3509	3.3399	3.2966	3.2814	3.2850	3.2600	3.2620	Official Rate	rh
															Fund Position	
End of Period																
635.3	635.3	635.3	635.3	635.3	635.3	995.2	995.2	995.2	995.2	995.2	995.2	1,381.1	1,381.1	1,381.1	Quota	2f.s
148.8	166.8	97.8	113.9	128.3	130.4	49.1	55.0	61.3	68.2	74.1	82.5	53.7	69.8	85.9	SDRs	1b.s
378.0	247.3	158.2	123.5	111.1	96.7	167.8	142.6	139.0	136.5	167.5	244.8	368.3	373.8	476.1	Reserve Position in the Fund	1c.s
140.2	70.9	23.9	4.3	—	—	—	—	—	—	—	31.8	—	—	—	*of which:* Outstg.Fund Borrowing	2c
															International Liquidity	
End of Period																
4,141.6	1,923.5	3,101.9	1,951.7	3,409.0	5,146.9	4,214.1	3,500.7	3,560.8	3,515.1	3,451.8	3,947.1	4,823.7	7,082.4	9,897.3	Total Reserves minus Gold	1l.d
211.1	224.4	128.6	162.1	183.5	179.2	67.4	80.3	91.1	98.0	100.0	116.2	73.8	90.9	108.0	SDRs	1b.d
536.2	332.8	207.9	175.7	158.9	132.9	230.5	208.2	206.6	196.3	226.1	344.6	505.5	487.0	598.3	Reserve Position in the Fund	1c.d
3,394.3	1,366.3	2,765.4	1,613.9	3,066.6	4,834.8	3,916.3	3,212.2	3,263.2	3,220.8	3,125.7	3,486.3	4,244.4	6,504.4	9,191.1	Foreign Exchange	1d.d
2.539	2.539	2.539	2.539	2.539	2.539	2.539	2.539	2.539	2.539	2.539	2.539	2.539	2.539	2.539	Gold (Million Fine Troy Ounces)	1ad
117.5	112.2	108.6	....	111.5	104.7	106.2	105.6	106.0	105.7	104.0	105.1	104.2	103.9	103.2	Gold (National Valuation)	1and
10,451.7	10,893.0	11,839.9	....	7,082.0	5,449.0	5,946.6	6,419.1	7,127.7	7,230.3	6,945.2	5,928.5	5,873.8	6,444.9	6,602.4	Deposit Money Banks: Assets	7a.d
5,005.6	5,163.6	5,730.7	....	1,303.7	1,936.9	1,803.2	2,377.0	2,239.0	2,536.6	4,009.2	3,595.3	3,971.0	3,913.3	5,112.9	Liabilities	7b.d
3,123.8	4,206.4	5,027.6	....	4,436.3	4,115.3	3,772.2	3,706.5	3,667.7	3,556.0	4,339.1	5,498.4	6,013.2	7,184.2	6,811.4	Other Financial Insts.: Assets	7e.d
1,520.6	1,875.7	2,255.7	....	2,288.7	2,381.2	1,790.8	1,533.7	1,584.6	1,592.9	2,330.6	3,504.4	3,693.2	4,582.2	4,639.2	Liab.	7f.d
															Monetary Authorities	
End of Period																
1,059.1	511.8	917.6	....	1,017.7	1,564.5	1,151.4	1,168.2	1,124.1	1,112.0	1,108.7	1,186.3	1,476.1	2,157.3	3,037.3	Foreign Assets	11
62.5	483.5	505.2	....	43.8	152.9	87.1	59.2	2.3	41.2	39.3	.1	45.1	—	—	Claims on Central Government	12a
404.0	346.4	188.7	....	157.1	77.6	142.4	90.8	—	—	6.0	—	—	14.0	—	Claims on Deposit Money Banks	12e
547.5	394.3	390.0	....	570.4	537.4	503.4	504.0	470.9	474.7	426.9	448.4	582.9	534.6	521.4	Reserve Money	14
337.8	342.0	333.7	....	445.6	379.1	355.2	351.3	311.5	350.1	345.3	348.7	442.9	416.6	401.2	*of which:* Currency Outside DMBs	14a
381.5	565.5	909.9	....	322.7	863.7	497.2	368.8	163.9	265.7	298.7	229.0	450.8	547.8	602.3	Central Government Deposits	16d
194.5	194.0	198.5	....	204.1	208.0	210.3	209.7	193.7	188.5	189.6	186.1	186.5	188.0	187.5	Capital Accounts	17a
402.1	188.0	113.2	....	121.3	186.0	170.0	236.1	298.0	224.2	238.9	322.9	301.0	900.9	1,726.2	Other Items (Net)	17r
															Deposit Money Banks	
200.7	53.7	55.0	....	120.6	160.9	146.0	151.8	158.1	123.0	79.0	98.0	141.2	119.3	119.5	Reserves	20
2,820.9	3,078.5	3,456.9	....	2,013.2	1,649.4	1,774.6	1,926.5	2,130.7	2,168.3	2,117.6	1,787.8	1,786.7	1,968.4	2,028.0	Foreign Assets	21
1,740.8	2,042.3	2,275.9	....	6,815.3	7,111.6	5,989.9	5,881.7	5,760.3	4,901.3	4,782.8	4,641.5	4,619.6	4,246.8	4,128.0	Claims on Central Government	22a
5,175.0	5,244.7	5,264.9	....	836.6	1,032.7	1,240.9	1,703.2	2,436.3	3,173.1	4,324.2	4,801.6	5,015.1	5,251.7	6,125.9	Claims on Private Sector	22d
747.5	663.7	635.8	....	755.6	729.4	758.8	774.7	873.5	892.5	902.2	794.7	928.5	1,051.1	1,240.2	Demand Deposits	24
4,155.0	4,594.0	4,897.7	....	4,815.5	4,950.0	5,282.5	5,616.9	6,189.8	6,088.3	6,368.5	6,413.1	6,306.6	6,695.5	7,567.3	Time and Savings Deposits	25
1,351.0	1,459.3	1,673.2	....	370.6	586.3	538.1	713.4	669.3	760.7	1,222.4	1,084.2	1,207.9	1,195.2	1,570.5	Foreign Liabilities	26c
642.8	520.9	520.8	....	563.9	613.5	555.9	421.3	459.4	374.1	343.6	256.8	195.0	185.1	230.9	Central Government Deposits	26d
1,090.0	1,037.1	1,160.0	....	1,707.3	1,384.2	196.4	112.0	6.0	—	6.0	.7	—	14.0	—	Credit from Monetary Authorities	26g
1,153.5	1,211.8	1,260.4	....	952.5	977.1	1,059.8	1,090.1	1,201.5	1,259.0	1,407.8	1,469.9	1,511.9	1,776.3	1,684.0	Capital Accounts	27a
797.6	932.4	904.9	....	620.9	714.3	760.0	935.0	1,086.2	991.2	1,053.1	1,309.7	1,412.4	669.0	108.4	Other Items (Net)	27r
															Monetary Survey	
End of Period																
2,529.0	2,131.0	2,701.3	....	2,660.3	2,627.6	2,387.9	2,381.3	2,585.5	2,519.6	2,003.9	1,889.9	2,054.9	2,930.5	3,494.8	Foreign Assets (Net)	31n
5,954.0	6,684.1	6,615.3	....	6,809.1	6,820.0	6,264.8	6,854.0	7,575.6	7,475.8	8,504.0	8,957.4	9,034.0	8,765.6	9,420.7	Domestic Credit	32
779.0	1,439.4	1,350.4	....	5,972.5	5,787.3	5,023.9	5,150.8	5,139.3	4,302.7	4,179.8	4,155.8	4,018.9	3,513.9	3,294.8	Claims on Central Govt. (Net)	32an
5,175.0	5,244.7	5,264.9	....	836.6	1,032.7	1,240.9	1,703.2	2,436.3	3,173.1	4,324.2	4,801.6	5,015.1	5,251.7	6,125.9	Claims on Private Sector	32d
1,085.3	1,005.7	969.5	....	1,201.2	1,108.5	1,114.0	1,126.0	1,185.0	1,242.6	1,247.5	1,143.4	1,371.4	1,467.7	1,641.4	Money	34
4,155.0	4,594.0	4,897.7	....	4,815.5	4,950.0	5,282.5	5,616.9	6,189.8	6,088.3	6,368.5	6,413.1	6,306.6	6,695.5	7,567.3	Quasi-Money	35
3,242.7	3,215.5	3,449.6	....	3,453.2	3,389.4	2,256.3	2,493.0	2,786.7	2,664.5	2,892.0	3,291.0	3,410.6	3,532.9	3,706.8	Other Items (Net)	37r
5,240.3	5,599.7	5,867.2	....	6,016.7	6,058.5	6,396.5	6,742.9	7,374.8	7,330.9	7,616.0	7,556.5	7,678.0	8,163.2	9,208.7	Money plus Quasi-Money	35l
															Other Financial Institutions	
End of Period																
70.9	168.5	139.4	....	163.4	141.6	132.6	120.5	95.7	125.8	153.9	258.7	207.8	154.1	167.7	Cash	40
843.1	1,188.8	1,467.9	....	1,261.1	1,245.7	1,125.7	1,112.4	1,096.1	1,064.4	1,323.0	1,658.1	1,829.1	2,194.2	2,092.2	Foreign Assets	41
582.1	744.9	741.7	....	795.5	878.8	713.1	596.6	632.9	707.6	904.0	1,244.9	931.7	766.0	851.4	Claims on Private Sector	42d
410.4	530.1	658.6	....	650.6	720.8	534.4	460.3	473.7	477.7	710.6	1,056.8	1,123.4	1,399.5	1,425.0	Foreign Liabilities	46c
228.5	333.2	247.6	....	202.2	267.3	181.0	119.9	101.1	142.7	94.5	84.8	7.5	7.0	7.5	Central Government Deposits	46d
102.7	136.6	157.1	....	245.9	230.7	186.5	134.7	185.5	158.5	206.9	296.1	207.7	239.8	392.6	Credit from Deposit Money Banks	46h
304.9	550.3	661.8	....	522.8	594.0	609.7	686.0	769.1	861.6	1,018.3	1,325.5	1,255.0	1,294.7	987.0	Capital Accounts	47a
449.6	551.9	623.8	....	598.5	453.3	460.0	428.5	295.3	259.4	350.8	398.6	374.9	173.8	299.2	Other Items (Net)	47r
															Interest Rates	
Percent Per Annum																
6.00	7.50	7.50	....	7.50	7.50	5.75	7.00	7.25	7.25	7.50	7.00	6.75	7.25	4.25	Discount Rate (*End of Period*)	60
6.08	6.12	8.70	....	....	....	7.43	6.31	7.43	6.98	7.05	7.24	6.32	6.82	4.62	Money Market Rate	60b
5.48	6.01	8.28	....	....	....	6.32	7.35	6.93	6.98	6.98	....	....	....	....	Treasury Bill Rate	60c
5.73	5.30	7.40	....	....	7.59	7.07	5.70	6.53	6.05	5.93	6.32	5.76	5.89	4.46	Deposit Rate	60l
7.86	6.72	8.38	....	....	8.00	7.95	7.61	8.37	8.77	8.80	8.93	8.56	8.87	7.88	Lending Rate	60p
															Prices, Production, Labor	
Period Averages																
69.0	72.2	78.5	81.5	96.6	97.1	98.8	98.6	100.0	105.2	103.8	102.1	100.9	101.3	103.3	Wholesale Prices	63
75.7	76.9	79.4	87.2	95.1	94.6	95.0	97.4	100.0	103.6	104.2	104.4	107.5	109.5	111.3	Consumer Prices	64
65.4	68.6	87.3	59.1	9.0	50.5	91.7	99.6	100.0	101.3	102.2	102.3	92.8	....	....	Crude Petroleum Production	66aa
Period Averages																
....	730	....	....	....	....	....	748	....	....	....	....	....	....	....	Labor Force	67d

Kuwait

		1972	1973	1974	1975	1976	1977	1978	1979	1980	1981	1982	1983	1984	1985	1986
International Transactions																*Millions of Dinars*
Exports	70	841.3	1,129.7	3,214.8	2,663.0	2,874.4	2,792.6	2,864.1	5,088.5	5,368.9	4,530.8	3,156.4	3,373.6	3,632.4	3,185.0	2,105.0
Oil Exports	70a	791.7	1,059.9	3,098.0	2,492.6	2,658.7	2,557.1	2,628.7	4,781.0	4,960.8	3,969.2	2,611.5	2,938.2	3,256.9	2,843.0	1,853.4
Imports, c.i.f.	71	262.2	310.6	455.1	693.2	972.0	1,387.1	1,263.9	1,437.0	1,764.9	1,945.4	2,384.6	2,149.1	2,041.7	1,806.0	1,661.2
Balance of Payments																*Millions of US Dollars:*
Current Account, n.i.e.	78al d	....	....	....	5,930	6,929	4,561	6,130	14,032	15,302	13,699	4,963	5,311	6,428	4,798	5,616
Goods: Exports f.o.b.	78aa d				8,485	9,621	9,561	10,234	18,114	20,633	16,023	10,819	11,473	12,156	10,374	7,216
Goods: Imports f.o.b.	78ab d				−2,400	−3,300	−4,735	−4,326	−4,870	−6,756	−6,736	−7,811	−6,889	−6,549	−5,719	−5,265
Trade Balance	78ac d				6,086	6,320	4,826	5,908	13,243	13,877	9,287	3,008	4,584	5,607	4,655	1,951
Services: Credit	78ad d				521	612	625	702	1,183	1,225	1,392	941	868	888	1,137	1,053
Services: Debit	78ae d				−759	−975	−1,406	−1,854	−2,265	−3,067	−2,905	−3,491	−3,620	−3,705	−4,086	−3,861
Balance on Goods & Services	78af d				5,848	5,958	4,044	4,755	12,161	12,035	7,773	458	1,832	2,790	1,706	−857
Income: Credit	78ag d				1,283	1,631	1,965	2,901	3,575	5,487	8,325	6,780	5,712	5,854	5,330	8,352
Income: Debit	78ah d				−131	−123	−199	−294	−416	−640	−739	−754	−683	−838	−665	−613
Balance on Gds, Serv. & Inc.	78ai d				6,999	7,466	5,810	7,362	15,320	16,881	15,359	6,485	6,862	7,806	6,371	6,882
Current Transfers, n.i.e.: Credit	78aj d				—	—	—	—	—	—	—	—	—	—	—	—
Current Transfers: Debit	78ak d				−1,069	−537	−1,249	−1,232	−1,288	−1,580	−1,661	−1,521	−1,551	−1,378	−1,573	−1,266
Capital Account, n.i.e.	78bc d	....	....	....												
Capital Account, n.i.e.: Credit	78ba d				—	—	—	—	—	—	—	—	—	—	—	—
Capital Account: Debit	78bb d				—	—	—	—	—	—	—	—	—	—	—	—
Financial Account, n.i.e.	78bj d	....	....	....	−6,648	−8,752	−4,030	−5,148	−9,929	−11,306	−8,300	−3,032	124	−7,451	−2,334	−7,505
Direct Investment Abroad	78bd d				−93	−109	−52	−95	188	−407	151	−108	−240	−95	−70	−248
Dir. Invest. in Rep. Econ., n.i.e.	78be d				—	—	—	—	—	—	—	—	—	—	—	—
Portfolio Investment Assets	78bf d				−90	−174	−157	−80	−586	−329	−140	—	−213	−7	−392	−506
Equity Securities	78bk d				—	—	—	—	—	—	—	—	—	—	—	—
Debt Securities	78bl d				−90	−174	−157	−80	−586	−329	−140	—	−213	−7	−392	−506
Portfolio Investment Liab., n.i.e.	78bg d				—	—	—	15	—	—	14	184	—	216	47	21
Equity Securities	78bm d				—	—	—	—	—	—	—	—	—	—	—	—
Debt Securities	78bn d				—	—	—	15	—	—	14	184	—	216	47	21
Financial Derivatives Assets	78bw d				....	....	....	....	....	....	....	....	....	....	....	....
Financial Derivatives Liabilities	78bx d				....	....	....	....	....	....	....	....	....	....	....	....
Other Investment Assets	78bh d				−6,368	−8,920	−4,086	−5,526	−10,334	−12,198	−8,810	−4,088	628	−7,431	−1,184	−6,235
Monetary Authorities	78bo d				−5,430	−7,333	−3,518	−4,112	−9,354	−10,377	−7,942	−4,435	1,431	−5,641	−1,902	−6,105
General Government	78bp d				−714	−1,413	−94	−276	−119	−118	538	483	−744	−476	−336	−496
Banks	78bq d				−183	−209	−516	−1,425	−738	−1,709	−1,309	−21	−172	−699	924	179
Other Sectors	78br d				−41	34	42	287	−123	7	−97	−115	113	−615	130	186
Other Investment Liab., n.i.e.	78bi d				−97	451	265	538	803	1,628	484	979	−51	−135	−735	−537
Monetary Authorities	78bs d				—	—	—	—	—	—	—	—	—	—	—	—
General Government	78bt d				—	—	—	—	—	—	—	—	—	—	—	—
Banks	78bu d				90	530	335	662	731	1,221	466	910	69	34	−665	−502
Other Sectors	78bv d				−186	−79	−70	−124	72	407	18	69	−120	−169	−70	−34
Net Errors and Omissions	78ca d				1,032	2,070	412	−1,424	−3,737	−2,950	−5,116	44	−4,432	1,140	−1,919	1,806
Overall Balance	78cb d				315	247	943	−443	366	1,045	283	1,975	1,002	117	545	−83
Reserves and Related Items	79da d	....	....	....	−315	−247	−943	443	−366	−1,045	−283	−1,975	−1,002	−117	−545	83
Reserve Assets	79db d				−315	−247	−943	443	−366	−1,045	−283	−1,975	−1,002	−117	−545	83
Use of Fund Credit and Loans	79dc d				—	—	—	—	—	—	—	—	—	—	—	—
Exceptional Financing	79de d				....	....	....	....	....	....	....	....	....	....	....	....
Government Finance																*Millions of Dinars:*
Deficit (-) or Surplus	80	†192	162	†529	2,393	1,911	924	1,093	2,938	3,035	1,240	377	−94	145	−229	−939
Total Revenue and Grants	81y	†609	696	†1,129	3,324	2,839	2,330	2,791	4,955	5,452	3,895	2,968	2,767	2,919	2,703	1,676
Revenue	81	†609	696	†1,129	3,324	2,839	2,330	2,791	4,955	5,452	3,895	2,968	2,767	2,919	2,703	1,676
Grants	81z	†—	—	†—	—	—	—	—	—	—	—	—	—	—	—	—
Exp. & Lending Minus Repay.	82z	†402	421	†600	931	927	1,406	1,698	2,017	2,417	2,655	2,591	2,860	2,774	2,932	2,614
Expenditure	82	†379	458	†600	931	927	1,406	1,698	2,017	2,417	2,655	2,591	2,860	2,774	2,932	2,614
Lending Minus Repayments	83	†38	76	†—	—	—	—	—	—	—	—	—	—	—	—	—
National Accounts																*Millions of Dinars*
Househ.Cons.Expend.,incl.NPISHs	96f	427	439	563	756	1,027	1,363	1,478	1,734	2,325	2,630	3,344	2,694	2,735	3,084	2,744
Government Consumption Expend.	91f	199	215	279	386	432	586	616	764	865	993	1,190	1,287	1,345	1,445	1,403
Gross Capital Formation	93	136	153	259	444	635	944	863	934	1,078	1,162	1,426	1,508	1,351	1,216	1,150
Gross Fixed Capital Formation	93e	127	146	222	418	563	815	794	790	973	1,073	1,297	1,527	1,359	1,277	1,127
Changes in Inventories	93i	9	7	37	26	72	129	69	144	105	89	129	−19	−8	−61	23
Exports of Goods and Services	90c	1,004	1,154	3,239	2,806	2,992	2,918	3,008	5,333	6,065	4,855	3,386	3,597	3,862	3,462	2,403
Imports of Goods and Services (-)	98c	303	356	528	907	1,250	1,760	1,700	1,902	2,577	2,601	3,132	3,002	2,868	2,757	2,498
Gross Domestic Product (GDP)	99b	1,464	1,604	3,812	3,485	3,837	4,052	4,264	6,862	7,755	7,039	6,214	6,083	6,425	6,450	5,203
Net Primary Income from Abroad	98.n	−362	−342	−281	224	441	506	717	873	1,310	2,137	1,709	1,466	1,485	1,403	2,249
Gross National Income (GNI)	99a	1,103	1,262	3,532	3,709	4,277	4,558	4,981	7,735	9,065	9,176	7,923	7,549	7,910	7,853	7,452
Consumption of Fixed Capital	99cf	70	76	81	93	107	130	169	217	263	290	337	347	424	475	486
GDP Volume 1984 Prices	99b.p	11,090	10,370	9,044	7,951	8,964	8,140	8,728	9,926	7,905	6,409	5,656	6,105	6,425	6,151	6,678
GDP Volume (1995=100)	99bv p	115.7	108.2	94.4	83.0	93.5	84.9	91.1	103.6	82.5	66.9	59.0	63.7	67.0	64.2	69.7
GDP Deflator (1995=100)	99bi p	16.0	18.7	51.0	53.0	51.8	60.2	59.1	83.6	118.6	132.8	132.9	120.5	120.9	126.8	94.2
																Millions:
Population	99z	.84	.89	.94	1.01	1.07	1.14	1.21	1.29	1.37	1.43	1.50	1.57	1.64	1.72	1.80

	1987	1988	1989	1990	1991	1992	1993	1994	1995	1996	1997	1998	1999	2000	2001		
																International Transactions	
Millions of Dinars																	
	2,304.4	2,166.0	3,378.0	2,031.4	309.4	1,931.1	3,091.2	3,342.3	3,814.5	4,458.0	4,314.3	2,911.6	3,719.2	5,962.8	4,948.4	Exports	70
	2,096.7	1,908.4	3,064.9	1,842.0	248.6	1,824.9	2,929.6	3,112.7	3,597.1	4,231.3	4,085.4	2,581.8	3,356.4	5,578.4	4,590.8	Oil Exports	70a
	1,530.7	1,714.2	1,849.4	1,145.7	1,353.3	2,129.2	2,123.8	1,988.2	2,323.1	2,507.2	2,501.6	2,626.2	2,318.3	2,195.4	2,370.9	Imports, c.i.f.	71
																Balance of Payments	
Minus Sign Indicates Debit																	
	4,561	4,602	9,136	3,886	−26,478	−450	2,499	3,227	5,016	7,107	7,934	2,215	5,062	14,670	8,566	Current Account, n.i.e.	78al *d*
	8,221	7,709	11,396	6,989	1,080	6,548	10,264	11,284	12,833	14,946	14,281	9,618	12,276	19,478	16,173	Goods: Exports f.o.b.	78aa *d*
	−4,938	−5,999	−6,410	−3,810	−5,073	−7,237	−6,940	−6,616	−7,254	−7,949	−7,747	−7,715	−6,708	−6,451	−6,932	Goods: Imports f.o.b.	78ab *d*
	3,284	1,709	4,987	3,179	−3,993	−689	3,324	4,669	5,579	6,997	6,533	1,903	5,568	13,027	9,241	*Trade Balance*	78ac *d*
	1,030	1,158	1,345	1,279	992	1,494	1,242	1,415	1,401	1,520	1,760	1,762	1,560	1,822	1,788	Services: Credit	78ad *d*
	−4,077	−4,204	−4,119	−3,359	−5,090	−4,590	−4,589	−4,531	−5,381	−5,100	−5,129	−5,542	−5,171	−4,923	−5,340	Services: Debit	78ae *d*
	237	−1,337	2,213	1,099	−8,091	−3,786	−23	1,553	1,598	3,417	3,164	−1,877	1,958	9,926	5,689	*Balance on Goods & Services*	78af *d*
	6,129	7,863	9,211	8,584	6,093	5,907	4,489	4,174	6,125	6,409	7,744	7,163	6,094	7,315	5,483	Income: Credit	78ag *d*
	−545	−606	−793	−846	−682	−662	−663	−1,004	−1,243	−1,229	−1,467	−1,296	−985	−616	−525	Income: Debit	78ah *d*
	5,821	5,921	10,630	8,837	−2,681	1,460	3,804	4,723	6,480	8,597	9,441	3,990	7,066	16,626	10,647	*Balance on Gds, Serv. & Inc.*	78ai *d*
						17	109	94	54	53	79	98	99	85	52	Current Transfers, n.i.e.: Credit	78aj *d*
	−1,260	−1,319	−1,494	−4,951	−23,798	−1,927	−1,415	−1,590	−1,518	−1,543	−1,586	−1,874	−2,102	−2,041	−2,133	Current Transfers: Debit	78ak *d*
	. . . .	. . . .	. . . .	. . . .	. . . .	. . . .	−205	−205	−194	−204	−96	79	703	2,217	2,933	Capital Account, n.i.e.	78bc *d*
	. . . .	. . . .	. . . .	. . . .	. . . .	. . . .				3	115	289	716	2,236	2,952	Capital Account, n.i.e.: Credit	78ba *d*
	. . . .	. . . .	. . . .	. . . .	. . . .	. . . .	−205	−205	−194	−207	−211	−210	−13	−20	−20	Capital Account: Debit	78bb *d*
	−5,566	−7,340	−8,323	413	38,766	11,067	421	3,304	157	−7,632	−6,211	−2,920	−5,706	−13,307	−6,038	Financial Account, n.i.e.	78bj *d*
	−775	−477	−994	−239	186	−1,211	−653	1,519	1,022	−1,740	969	1,867	−23	303	−323	Direct Investment Abroad	78bd *d*
							13		7	347	20	59	72	16	−39	Dir. Invest. in Rep. Econ., n.i.e.	78be *d*
	−179	−720	−623	−919	−813	−3	−931	394	−2,064	−788	−6,926	−4,768	−2,638	−12,923	−7,375	Portfolio Investment Assets	78bf *d*
																Equity Securities	78bk *d*
	−179	−720	−623	−919	−813	−3	−931	394	−2,064	−788	−6,926	−4,768	−2,638	−12,923	−7,375	Debt Securities	78bl *d*
	219	280	24	537	211	276	—	—	−50	27	—	—	79	254	−78	Portfolio Investment Liab., n.i.e.	78bg *d*
																Equity Securities	78bm *d*
	219	280	24	537	211	276	—	—	−50	27	—	—	79	254	−78	Debt Securities	78bn *d*
							—	—	—	—	—	—	—	—	—	Financial Derivatives Assets	78bw *d*
							—	—	—	—	—	—	—	—	—	Financial Derivatives Liabilities	78bx *d*
	−4,389	−6,042	−7,295	829	43,061	11,261	−669	529	−221	−745	3,356	646	−3,512	−1,108	431	Other Investment Assets	78bh *d*
	−3,865	−5,121	−5,647	−281	38,745	10,490										Monetary Authorities	78bo *d*
	−187	−434	−701	783	—	−634	−523	825	724	−1,122	2,993	−10	−3,288	−284	917	General Government	78bp *d*
	−370	−699	−1,236	55	3,785	1,385	−301	−401	−734	−23	260	929	−161	−1,004	238	Banks	78bq *d*
	32	211	289	270	531	20	156	104	−211	401	102	−272	−62	179	−724	Other Sectors	78br *d*
	−441	−380	565	205	−3,880	743	2,660	862	1,464	−4,733	−3,629	−725	315	150	1,347	Other Investment Liab., n.i.e.	78bi *d*
							7	−3	−54	−17	3	−10	—	7	—	Monetary Authorities	78bs *d*
							3,429	525	1,541	−5,371	−6,290	−1,316	−115	−372	7	General Government	78bt *d*
	−29	201	742	205	−4,176	720	−159	589	−97	304	1,523	−456	302	−297	1,302	Banks	78bu *d*
	−413	−581	−177	. . . .	295	24	−616	−249	74	351	1,134	1,057	128	812	39	Other Sectors	78bv *d*
	−842	810	462	−5,196	−11,012	−8,765	−4,192	−6,276	−5,120	704	−1,622	885	859	−1,311	−2,554	Net Errors and Omissions	78ca *d*
	−1,847	−1,928	1,275	−897	1,276	1,851	−1,478	50	−141	−25	6	258	918	2,268	2,906	*Overall Balance*	78cb *d*
	1,847	1,928	−1,275	897	−1,276	−1,851	1,478	−50	141	25	−6	−258	−918	−2,268	−2,906	Reserves and Related Items	79da *d*
	1,847	1,928	−1,275	897	−1,276	−1,851	1,478	−50	141	25	−6	−258	−918	−2,268	−2,906	Reserve Assets	79db *d*
															—	Use of Fund Credit and Loans	79dc *d*
	. . . .	. . . .	. . . .	. . . .	. . . .										—	Exceptional Financing	79de *d*
																Government Finance	
Year Ending December 31																	
	159	−623	251	. . . .	. . . .	. . . .		−977	−656	1,031	1,050	−456	385	3,055	3,945	Deficit (-) or Surplus	80
	2,518	1,874	3,024	. . . .	. . . .	. . . .		2,787	3,076	4,198	4,179	2,859	3,710	6,434	5,632	Total Revenue and Grants	81y
	2,518	1,874	3,024	. . . .	. . . .	. . . .		2,787	3,076	4,198	4,179	2,859	3,710	6,434	5,632	Revenue	81
				. . . .	. . . .	. . . .		—	—	—	—	—	—	—	—	Grants	81z
	2,359	2,497	2,773	. . . .	. . . .	. . . .		3,763	3,732	3,167	3,129	3,315	3,325	3,379	1,688	Exp. & Lending Minus Repay.	82z
	2,359	2,497	2,773	. . . .	. . . .	. . . .		3,763	3,732	3,167	3,129	3,315	3,325	3,379	1,688	Expenditure	82
				. . . .	. . . .	. . . .		—	—	—	—	—	—	—	—	Lending Minus Repayments	83
																National Accounts	
Millions of Dinars																	
	2,805	3,083	3,662	3,123	2,920	2,233	3,143	3,029	3,272	4,073	4,131	4,309	4,490	4,633	4,801	Househ.Cons.Expend.,incl.NPISHs	96f
	1,374	1,517	1,814	2,056	6,294	3,237	2,593	2,503	2,612	2,570	2,451	2,412	2,463	2,485	2,646	Government Consumption Expend.	91f
	1,094	906	878	846	1,230	1,158	1,243	1,192	1,197	1,424	1,256	1,594	1,335	827	866	Gross Capital Formation	93
	1,056	790	733	833	1,150	1,013	1,094	982	1,100	1,318	1,240	1,594	1,335	827	866	Gross Fixed Capital Formation	93e
	37	116	145	13	80	145	149	210	97	106	15	. . . .	. . . .	. . . .	. . . .	Changes in Inventories	93i
	3,275	2,746	3,743	2,385	529	2,358	3,454	3,753	4,248	4,930	4,866	3,468	4,212	6,534	5,506	Exports of Goods and Services	90c
	2,314	2,479	2,955	3,082	7,843	3,159	3,202	3,098	3,405	3,695	3,645	4,040	3,616	3,488	3,762	Imports of Goods and Services (-)	98c
	6,233	5,773	7,143	5,328	3,131	5,826	7,231	7,380	7,925	9,303	9,060	7,742	8,884	10,991	10,057	Gross Domestic Product (GDP)	99b
	1,556	2,025	2,473	2,232	1,538	1,538	1,155	941	1,457	1,551	1,904	1,788	1,555	2,055	1,520	Net Primary Income from Abroad	98.n
	7,789	7,798	9,616	7,560	4,669	7,364	8,386	8,321	9,382	10,854	10,964	9,530	10,439	13,046	11,577	Gross National Income (GNI)	99a
	519	554	573	532	497	532	571	639	711	671	701	707	614	443	475	Consumption of Fixed Capital	99cf
	7,222	6,496	8,178	. . . .	. . . .	6,506	8,702	9,453	9,583	9,324	9,435	9,733	9,577	9,946	9,844	GDP Volume 1984 Prices	99b. *p*
	75.4	67.8	85.3	. . . .	. . . .	67.9	90.8	98.6	100.0	97.3	98.5	101.6	99.9	103.8	102.7	GDP Volume (1995=100)	99bv *p*
	104.4	107.5	105.6	. . . .	. . . .	108.3	100.5	94.4	100.0	120.6	116.1	96.2	112.2	133.6	123.5	GDP Deflator (1995=100)	99bi *p*
Midyear Estimates																	
	1.88	1.97	2.05	2.14	†2.09	1.42	1.46	1.62	1.80	1.89	1.98	2.03	2.11	2.19	†1.97	**Population**	99z

(See notes in the back of the book.)

Kyrgyz Republic

917

		1972	1973	1974	1975	1976	1977	1978	1979	1980	1981	1982	1983	1984	1985	1986
Exchange Rates															*Soms per SDR:*	
Official Rate	aa	....	....	....	....	....	....	....	....	....	....	....	....	....	....	....
Official Rate	ae														*Soms per US Dollar:*	
Official Rate	rf	....	....	....	....	....	....	....	....	....	....	....	....	....	....	....
Fund Position															*Millions of SDRs:*	
Quota	2f. s	....	....	....	....	....	....	....	....	....	....	....	....	....	....	....
SDRs	1b. s	....	....	....	....	....	....	....	....	....	....	....	....	....	....	....
Reserve Position in the Fund	1c. s	....	....	....	....	....	....	....	....	....	....	....	....	....	....	....
Total Fund Cred.&Loans Outstg.	2tl	....	....	....	....	....	....	....	....	....	....	....	....	....	....	....
International Liquidity												*Millions of US Dollars Unless Otherwise Indicated:*				
Total Reserves minus Gold	1l. d	....	....	....	....	....	....	....	....	....	....	....	....	....	....	....
SDRs	1b. d	....	....	....	....	....	....	....	....	....	....	....	....	....	....	....
Reserve Position in the Fund	1c. d	....	....	....	....	....	....	....	....	....	....	....	....	....	....	....
Foreign Exchange	1d. d	....	....	....	....	....	....	....	....	....	....	....	....	....	....	....
Gold (Million Fine Troy Ounces)	1ad	....	....	....	....	....	....	....	....	....	....	....	....	....	....	....
Gold (National Valuation)	1an d	....	....	....	....	....	....	....	....	....	....	....	....	....	....	....
Monetary Authorities: Other Liab.	4..d	....	....	....	....	....	....	....	....	....	....	....	....	....	....	....
Banking Institutions: Assets	7a. d	....	....	....	....	....	....	....	....	....	....	....	....	....	....	....
Liabilities	7b. d	....	....	....	....	....	....	....	....	....	....	....	....	....	....	....
Monetary Authorities															*Millions of Soms:*	
Foreign Assets	11	....	....	....	....	....	....	....	....	....	....	....	....	....	....	....
Claims on General Government	12a	....	....	....	....	....	....	....	....	....	....	....	....	....	....	....
Claims on Banking Institutions	12e	....	....	....	....	....	....	....	....	....	....	....	....	....	....	....
Reserve Money	14	....	....	....	....	....	....	....	....	....	....	....	....	....	....	....
of which: Currency Outside Banks	14a	....	....	....	....	....	....	....	....	....	....	....	....	....	....	....
Other Liabilities to DMBs	14n	....	....	....	....	....	....	....	....	....	....	....	....	....	....	....
Foreign Liabilities	16c	....	....	....	....	....	....	....	....	....	....	....	....	....	....	....
General Government Deposits	16d	....	....	....	....	....	....	....	....	....	....	....	....	....	....	....
Capital Accounts	17a	....	....	....	....	....	....	....	....	....	....	....	....	....	....	....
Other Items (Net)	17r	....	....	....	....	....	....	....	....	....	....	....	....	....	....	....
Banking Institutions															*Millions of Soms:*	
Reserves	20	....	....	....	....	....	....	....	....	....	....	....	....	....	....	....
Other Claims on Monetary Author.	20n	....	....	....	....	....	....	....	....	....	....	....	....	....	....	....
Foreign Assets	21	....	....	....	....	....	....	....	....	....	....	....	....	....	....	....
Claims on General Government	22a	....	....	....	....	....	....	....	....	....	....	....	....	....	....	....
Claims on Rest of the Economy	22d	....	....	....	....	....	....	....	....	....	....	....	....	....	....	....
Demand Deposits	24	....	....	....	....	....	....	....	....	....	....	....	....	....	....	....
Time & Foreign Currency Deposits	25	....	....	....	....	....	....	....	....	....	....	....	....	....	....	....
Foreign Liabilities	26c	....	....	....	....	....	....	....	....	....	....	....	....	....	....	....
General Government Deposits	26d	....	....	....	....	....	....	....	....	....	....	....	....	....	....	....
Credit from Monetary Authorities	26g	....	....	....	....	....	....	....	....	....	....	....	....	....	....	....
Capital Accounts	27a	....	....	....	....	....	....	....	....	....	....	....	....	....	....	....
Other Items (Net)	27r	....	....	....	....	....	....	....	....	....	....	....	....	....	....	....
Banking Survey															*Millions of Soms:*	
Foreign Assets (Net)	31n	....	....	....	....	....	....	....	....	....	....	....	....	....	....	....
Domestic Credit	32	....	....	....	....	....	....	....	....	....	....	....	....	....	....	....
Claims on General Govt. (Net)	32an	....	....	....	....	....	....	....	....	....	....	....	....	....	....	....
Claims on Rest of the Economy	32d	....	....	....	....	....	....	....	....	....	....	....	....	....	....	....
Money	34	....	....	....	....	....	....	....	....	....	....	....	....	....	....	....
Quasi-Money	35	....	....	....	....	....	....	....	....	....	....	....	....	....	....	....
Capital Accounts	37a	....	....	....	....	....	....	....	....	....	....	....	....	....	....	....
Other Items (Net)	37r	....	....	....	....	....	....	....	....	....	....	....	....	....	....	....
Money plus Quasi-Money	35l	....	....	....	....	....	....	....	....	....	....	....	....	....	....	....
Interest Rates															*Percent per Annum*	
Lombard Rate	60.a	....	....	....	....	....	....	....	....	....	....	....	....	....	....	....
Money Market Rate	60b	....	....	....	....	....	....	....	....	....	....	....	....	....	....	....
Treasury Bill Rate	60c	....	....	....	....	....	....	....	....	....	....	....	....	....	....	....
Deposit Rate	60l	....	....	....	....	....	....	....	....	....	....	....	....	....	....	....
Lending Rate	60p	....	....	....	....	....	....	....	....	....	....	....	....	....	....	....
Prices, Production, Labor															*Index Numbers (1995=100):*	
Producer Prices	63	....	....	....	....	....	....	....	....	....	....	....	....	....	....	....
Consumer Prices	64	....	....	....	....	....	....	....	....	....	....	....	....	....	....	....
Wages: Average Earnings	65	....	....	....	....	....	....	....	....	....	....	....	....	....	....	....
															Number in Thousands:	
Employment	67e	....	....	....	....	....	....	....	....	....	....	....	....	....	....	....
Unemployment	67c	....	....	....	....	....	....	....	....	....	....	....	....	....	....	....
International Transactions															*Millions of US Dollars*	
Exports	70..d	....	....	....	....	....	....	....	....	....	....	....	....	....	....	....
Imports, c.i.f.	71..d	....	....	....	....	....	....	....	....	....	....	....	....	....	....	....

1987	1988	1989	1990	1991	1992	1993	1994	1995	1996	1997	1998	1999	2000	2001		
End of Period															**Exchange Rates**	
....	....	....	....	....	....	11.030	15.547	16.649	24.014	23.443	41.362	62.352	62.936	59.969	Official Rate	**aa**
End of Period (ae) Period Average (rf)																
....	....	....	....	....	....	8.030	10.650	11.200	16.700	17.375	29.376	45.429	48.304	47.719	Official Rate	**ae**
....	....	....	....	....	....	....	10.842	10.822	12.810	17.362	20.838	39.008	47.704	48.378	Official Rate	**rf**
End of Period															**Fund Position**	
....	....	....	....	....	64.5	64.5	64.5	64.5	64.5	64.5	64.5	88.8	88.8	88.8	Quota	**2f. s**
....	....	....	....	....	—	9.4	.7	9.6	5.1	.7	.2	3.7	.5	1.1	SDRs	**1b. s**
....	....	....	....	....	—	—	—	—	—	—	—	—	—	—	Reserve Position in the Fund	**1c. s**
....	....	....	....	....	—	43.9	53.3	83.6	97.1	122.2	124.4	138.7	144.3	142.7	Total Fund Cred.&Loans Outstg.	**2tl**
End of Period															**International Liquidity**	
....	....	....	....	....	....	48.2	26.2	81.0	94.6	169.8	163.8	229.7	239.0	263.5	Total Reserves minus Gold	**1l. d**
....	....	....	....	....	—	12.9	1.0	14.3	7.4	.9	.3	5.1	.7	1.3	SDRs	**1b. d**
....	....	....	....	....	—	—	—	—	—	—	—	—	—	—	Reserve Position in the Fund	**1c. d**
....	....	....	....	....	....	35.4	25.2	66.7	87.2	168.9	163.4	224.6	238.3	262.2	Foreign Exchange	**1d. d**
....	....	....	....	....	....	....	....	....	....	....	.0831	.0831	.0831	.0831	Gold (Million Fine Troy Ounces)	**1ad**
....	....	....	....	....	....	....	....	43.22	28.13	24.11	23.88	24.17	22.80	22.97	Gold (National Valuation)	**1an d**
....	....	....	....	....	....	....	....	73.5	65.8	59.2	39.7	44.1	55.5	57.4	Monetary Authorities: Other Liab	**4.. d**
....	....	....	....	....	....	....	....	19.6	13.1	34.3	17.1	15.8	18.0	32.8	Banking Institutions: Assets	**7a. d**
....	....	....	....	....	....	....	....	2.8	1.8	13.1	8.3	1.8	3.0	3.4	Liabilities	**7b. d**
End of Period															**Monetary Authorities**	
....	....	....	....	....	....	....	....	1,393	2,035	3,368	5,517	11,338	12,687	13,632	Foreign Assets	**11**
....	....	....	....	....	....	....	....	2,049	3,911	4,473	4,940	5,787	6,144	6,186	Claims on General Government	**12a**
....	....	....	....	....	....	....	....	1,153	124	92	333	543	609	506	Claims on Banking Institutions	**12e**
....	....	....	....	....	....	....	....	2,044	2,533	3,069	3,303	4,317	4,821	5,375	Reserve Money	**14**
....	....	....	....	....	....	....	....	1,938	2,416	2,678	2,829	3,578	4,102	5,016	*of which: Currency Outside Banks*	**14a**
....	....	....	....	....	....	....	....	—	—	200	36	243	189	—	Other Liabilities to DMBs	**14n**
....	....	....	....	....	....	....	....	2,216	3,430	3,893	6,314	10,652	11,763	11,296	Foreign Liabilities	**16c**
....	....	....	....	....	....	....	....	28	174	305	322	1,239	1,185	2,235	General Government Deposits	**16d**
....	....	....	....	....	....	....	....	136	243	506	949	1,118	989	1,096	Capital Accounts	**17a**
....	....	....	....	....	....	....	....	171	–311	–40	–133	98	493	323	Other Items (Net)	**17r**
End of Period															**Banking Institutions**	
....	....	....	....	....	....	....	....	113	110	381	449	739	700	343	Reserves	**20**
....	....	....	....	....	....	....	....	—	—	162	107	172	172	3	Other Claims on Monetary Author.	**20n**
....	....	....	....	....	....	....	....	219	219	596	503	719	870	1,563	Foreign Assets	**21**
....	....	....	....	....	....	....	....	83	93	323	378	150	202	487	Claims on General Government	**22a**
....	....	....	....	....	....	....	....	2,024	2,026	1,047	1,804	2,448	2,679	2,780	Claims on Rest of the Economy	**22d**
....	....	....	....	....	....	....	....	545	478	442	379	624	504	542	Demand Deposits	**24**
....	....	....	....	....	....	....	....	295	295	1,095	1,745	2,418	2,791	2,676	Time & Foreign Currency Deposits	**25**
....	....	....	....	....	....	....	....	31	31	228	245	84	143	164	Foreign Liabilities	**26c**
....	....	....	....	....	....	....	....	—	—	30	45	64	49	71	General Government Deposits	**26d**
....	....	....	....	....	....	....	....	1,188	1,188	118	318	605	619	597	Credit from Monetary Authorities	**26g**
....	....	....	....	....	....	....	....	120	149	735	980	1,125	1,229	1,802	Capital Accounts	**27a**
....	....	....	....	....	....	....	....	261	307	–138	–471	–694	–712	–676	Other Items (Net)	**27r**
End of Period															**Banking Survey**	
....	....	....	....	....	....	....	....	–635	–1,207	–157	–539	1,321	1,651	3,736	Foreign Assets (Net)	**31n**
....	....	....	....	....	....	....	....	4,129	5,856	5,528	6,780	7,120	7,831	7,196	Domestic Credit	**32**
....	....	....	....	....	....	....	....	2,105	3,830	4,462	4,951	4,634	5,112	4,367	Claims on General Govt. (Net)	**32an**
....	....	....	....	....	....	....	....	2,024	2,026	1,066	1,828	2,487	2,720	2,829	Claims on Rest of the Economy	**32d**
....	....	....	....	....	....	....	....	2,482	2,893	3,119	3,208	4,203	4,606	5,558	Money	**34**
....	....	....	....	....	....	....	....	295	295	1,095	1,745	2,418	2,791	2,676	Quasi-Money	**35**
....	....	....	....	....	....	....	....	256	392	1,242	1,929	2,243	2,218	2,898	Capital Accounts	**37a**
....	....	....	....	....	....	....	....	461	1,069	–85	–641	–423	–131	–200	Other Items (Net)	**37r**
....	....	....	....	....	....	....	....	2,777	3,188	4,214	4,953	6,621	7,397	8,234	Money plus Quasi-Money	**35l**
Percent per Annum															**Interest Rates**	
....	....	....	....	....	....	265.5	94.1	64.1	43.1	43.2	54.0	51.6	32.8	10.7	Lombard Rate	**60.a**
....	....	....	....	....	....	....	....	....	....	....	44.0	43.7	24.3	11.9	Money Market Rate	**60b**
....	....	....	....	....	....	....	143.1	34.9	40.1	35.8	43.7	47.2	32.3	19.1	Treasury Bill Rate	**60c**
....	....	....	....	....	....	....	....	....	36.7	39.6	35.8	35.6	18.4	12.5	Deposit Rate	**60l**
....	....	....	....	....	....	....	....	....	65.0	49.4	73.4	60.9	51.9	37.3	Lending Rate	**60p**
Period Averages															**Prices, Production, Labor**	
....	....	....	....	....	....	26.0	82.1	100.0	123.0	155.3	167.6	257.6	336.7	377.1	Producer Prices	**63**
....	....	....	....	....	....	....	....	100.0	131.9	162.9	179.9	244.5	290.2	310.3	Consumer Prices	**64**
....	....	....	....	....	....	22.8	63.4	100.0	133.3	184.7	228.3	285.1	328.6	....	Wages: Average Earnings	**65**
Period Averages																
....	....	....	....	....	1,836	1,681	1,645	1,642	1,652	1,689	1,705	1,764	1,767	....	Employment	**67e**
....	....	....	....	....	....	3	13	50	77	55	56	55	....	....	Unemployment	**67c**
Millions of US Dollars															**International Transactions**	
....	....	....	....	....	....	339.7	340.0	408.9	505.4	603.8	513.6	453.8	504.5	476.1	Exports	**70.. d**
....	....	....	....	....	418.0	429.5	315.9	522.3	837.7	709.3	841.5	599.7	554.1	467.5	Imports, c.i.f.	**71.. d**

Kyrgyz Republic

		1972	1973	1974	1975	1976	1977	1978	1979	1980	1981	1982	1983	1984	1985	1986
Balance of Payments														*Millions of US Dollars:*		
Current Account, n.i.e.	78al d	...	...	...	...	...	...	...	...	...	...	...	...	...	...	...
Goods: Exports f.o.b.	78aa d	...	...	...	...	...	...	...	...	...	...	...	...	...	...	...
Goods: Imports f.o.b.	78ab d	...	...	...	...	...	...	...	...	...	...	...	...	...	...	...
Trade Balance	78ac d	...	...	...	...	...	...	...	...	...	...	...	...	...	...	...
Services: Credit	78ad d	...	...	...	...	...	...	...	...	...	...	...	...	...	...	...
Services: Debit	78ae d	...	...	...	...	...	...	...	...	...	...	...	...	...	...	...
Balance on Goods & Services	78af d	...	...	...	...	...	...	...	...	...	...	...	...	...	...	...
Income: Credit	78ag d	...	...	...	...	...	...	...	...	...	...	...	...	...	...	...
Income: Debit	78ah d	...	...	...	...	...	...	...	...	...	...	...	...	...	...	...
Balance on Gds, Serv. & Inc.	78ai d	...	...	...	...	...	...	...	...	...	...	...	...	...	...	...
Current Transfers, n.i.e.: Credit	78aj d	...	...	...	...	...	...	...	...	...	...	...	...	...	...	...
Current Transfers: Debit	78ak d	...	...	...	...	...	...	...	...	...	...	...	...	...	...	...
Capital Account, n.i.e.	78bc d	...	...	...	...	...	...	...	...	...	...	...	...	...	...	...
Capital Account, n.i.e.: Credit	78ba d	...	...	...	...	...	...	...	...	...	...	...	...	...	...	...
Capital Account: Debit	78bb d	...	...	...	...	...	...	...	...	...	...	...	...	...	...	...
Financial Account, n.i.e.	78bj d	...	...	...	...	...	...	...	...	...	...	...	...	...	...	...
Direct Investment Abroad	78bd d	...	...	...	...	...	...	...	...	...	...	...	...	...	...	...
Dir. Invest. in Rep. Econ., n.i.e.	78be d	...	...	...	...	...	...	...	...	...	...	...	...	...	...	...
Portfolio Investment Assets	78bf d	...	...	...	...	...	...	...	...	...	...	...	...	...	...	...
Equity Securities	78bk d	...	...	...	...	...	...	...	...	...	...	...	...	...	...	...
Debt Securities	78bl d	...	...	...	...	...	...	...	...	...	...	...	...	...	...	...
Portfolio Investment Liab., n.i.e.	78bg d	...	...	...	...	...	...	...	...	...	...	...	...	...	...	...
Equity Securities	78bm d	...	...	...	...	...	...	...	...	...	...	...	...	...	...	...
Debt Securities	78bn d	...	...	...	...	...	...	...	...	...	...	...	...	...	...	...
Financial Derivatives Assets	78bw d	...	...	...	...	...	...	...	...	...	...	...	...	...	...	...
Financial Derivatives Liabilities	78bx d	...	...	...	...	...	...	...	...	...	...	...	...	...	...	...
Other Investment Assets	78bh d	...	...	...	...	...	...	...	...	...	...	...	...	...	...	...
Monetary Authorities	78bo d	...	...	...	...	...	...	...	...	...	...	...	...	...	...	...
General Government	78bp d	...	...	...	...	...	...	...	...	...	...	...	...	...	...	...
Banks	78bq d	...	...	...	...	...	...	...	...	...	...	...	...	...	...	...
Other Sectors	78br d	...	...	...	...	...	...	...	...	...	...	...	...	...	...	...
Other Investment Liab., n.i.e.	78bi d	...	...	...	...	...	...	...	...	...	...	...	...	...	...	...
Monetary Authorities	78bs d	...	...	...	...	...	...	...	...	...	...	...	...	...	...	...
General Government	78bt d	...	...	...	...	...	...	...	...	...	...	...	...	...	...	...
Banks	78bu d	...	...	...	...	...	...	...	...	...	...	...	...	...	...	...
Other Sectors	78bv d	...	...	...	...	...	...	...	...	...	...	...	...	...	...	...
Net Errors and Omissions	78ca d	...	...	...	...	...	...	...	...	...	...	...	...	...	...	...
Overall Balance	78cb d	...	...	...	...	...	...	...	...	...	...	...	...	...	...	...
Reserves and Related Items	79da d	...	...	...	...	...	...	...	...	...	...	...	...	...	...	...
Reserve Assets	79db d	...	...	...	...	...	...	...	...	...	...	...	...	...	...	...
Use of Fund Credit and Loans	79dc d	...	...	...	...	...	...	...	...	...	...	...	...	...	...	...
Exceptional Financing	79de d	...	...	...	...	...	...	...	...	...	...	...	...	...	...	...
International Investment Position															*Millions of US Dollars*	
Assets	79aa d	...	...	...	...	...	...	...	...	...	...	...	...	...	...	...
Direct Investment Abroad	79ab d	...	...	...	...	...	...	...	...	...	...	...	...	...	...	...
Portfolio Investment	79ac d	...	...	...	...	...	...	...	...	...	...	...	...	...	...	...
Equity Securities	79ad d	...	...	...	...	...	...	...	...	...	...	...	...	...	...	...
Debt Securities	79ae d	...	...	...	...	...	...	...	...	...	...	...	...	...	...	...
Financial Derivatives	79al d	...	...	...	...	...	...	...	...	...	...	...	...	...	...	...
Other Investment	79af d	...	...	...	...	...	...	...	...	...	...	...	...	...	...	...
Monetary Authorities	79ag d	...	...	...	...	...	...	...	...	...	...	...	...	...	...	...
General Government	79ah d	...	...	...	...	...	...	...	...	...	...	...	...	...	...	...
Banks	79ai d	...	...	...	...	...	...	...	...	...	...	...	...	...	...	...
Other Sectors	79aj d	...	...	...	...	...	...	...	...	...	...	...	...	...	...	...
Reserve Assets	79ak d	...	...	...	...	...	...	...	...	...	...	...	...	...	...	...
Liabilities	79la d	...	...	...	...	...	...	...	...	...	...	...	...	...	...	...
Dir. Invest. in Rep. Economy	79lb d	...	...	...	...	...	...	...	...	...	...	...	...	...	...	...
Portfolio Investment	79lc d	...	...	...	...	...	...	...	...	...	...	...	...	...	...	...
Equity Securities	79ld d	...	...	...	...	...	...	...	...	...	...	...	...	...	...	...
Debt Securities	79le d	...	...	...	...	...	...	...	...	...	...	...	...	...	...	...
Financial Derivatives	79ll d	...	...	...	...	...	...	...	...	...	...	...	...	...	...	...
Other Investment	79lf d	...	...	...	...	...	...	...	...	...	...	...	...	...	...	...
Monetary Authorities	79lg d	...	...	...	...	...	...	...	...	...	...	...	...	...	...	...
General Government	79lh d	...	...	...	...	...	...	...	...	...	...	...	...	...	...	...
Banks	79li d	...	...	...	...	...	...	...	...	...	...	...	...	...	...	...
Other Sectors	79lj d	...	...	...	...	...	...	...	...	...	...	...	...	...	...	...

Minus Sign Indicates Debit — Balance of Payments

1987	1988	1989	1990	1991	1992	1993	1994	1995	1996	1997	1998	1999	2000	2001		
...	...	...	...	...	...	−87.6	−84.0	−234.7	−424.8	−138.5	−412.5	−247.8	−158.3	...	Current Account, n.i.e.	78ald
...	...	...	...	...	...	339.6	340.0	408.9	531.2	630.8	535.1	462.6	510.9	...	Goods: Exports f.o.b.	78aad
...	...	...	...	...	...	−446.7	−426.1	−531.0	−782.9	−646.1	−755.7	−546.9	−502.1	...	Goods: Imports f.o.b.	78abd
...	...	...	...	...	...	−107.1	−86.1	−122.0	−251.7	−15.3	−220.7	−84.4	8.8	...	*Trade Balance*	78acd
...	...	...	...	...	...	8.7	32.7	39.2	31.5	45.0	62.8	65.0	61.8	...	Services: Credit	78add
...	...	...	...	...	...	−50.7	−71.1	−195.1	−249.0	−171.2	−175.7	−154.4	−148.8	...	Services: Debit	78aed
...	...	...	...	...	...	−149.1	−124.6	−278.0	−469.2	−141.4	−333.6	−173.8	−78.2	...	*Balance on Goods & Services*	78afd
...	...	...	...	...	...			3.7	4.4	6.8	12.6	10.9	17.0	...	Income: Credit	78agd
...	...	...	...	...	...	−5.7	−22.0	−39.2	−43.9	−71.4	−91.7	−84.9	−97.1	...	Income: Debit	78ahd
...	...	...	...	...	...	−154.8	−146.6	−313.4	−508.7	−206.1	−412.7	−247.8	−158.4	...	*Balance on Gds, Serv. & Inc.*	78aid
...	...	...	...	...	...	68.0	63.4	80.4	85.9	69.8	2.2	1.2	2.2	...	Current Transfers, n.i.e.: Credit	78ajd
...	...	...	...	...	...	−.8	−.8	−1.7	−1.9	−2.2	−2.0	−1.2	−2.2	...	Current Transfers: Debit	78akd
...	...	...	...	...	...	−107.1	−62.4	−29.0	−15.9	−8.4	−8.1	−15.2	−11.3	...	Capital Account, n.i.e.	78bcd
...	...	...	...	...	...		.3	2.2	9.0	6.2	3.9	14.6	22.8	...	Capital Account, n.i.e.: Credit	78bad
...	...	...	...	...	...	−107.1	−62.7	−31.3	−25.0	−14.6	−12.0	−29.8	−34.1	...	Capital Account: Debit	78bbd
...	...	...	...	...	...	181.2	103.4	259.9	362.5	250.7	284.5	220.2	61.6	...	Financial Account, n.i.e.	78bjd
...	...	...	...	...	...						−22.6	−6.1	−4.5	...	Direct Investment Abroad	78bdd
...	...	...	...	...	...	10.0	38.2	96.1	47.2	83.8	109.2	44.4	−2.4	...	Dir. Invest. in Rep. Econ., n.i.e.	78bed
...	...	...	...	...	...			−.1	.1	.6	−.2	—	−1.6	...	Portfolio Investment Assets	78bfd
...	...	...	...	...	...									...	Equity Securities	78bkd
...	...	...	...	...	...			−.1	.1	.6	−.2	—	−1.6	...	Debt Securities	78bld
...	...	...	...	...	...			1.8	−1.8	5.0	−4.1	−.1	.3	...	Portfolio Investment Liab., n.i.e.	78bgd
...	...	...	...	...	...							.2	.3	...	Equity Securities	78bmd
...	...	...	...	...	...			1.8	−1.8	5.0	−4.1	−.3	—	...	Debt Securities	78bnd
...	...	...	...	...	...					19.0	30.6	26.4	25.8	...	Financial Derivatives Assets	78bwd
...	...	...	...	...	...									...	Financial Derivatives Liabilities	78bxd
...	...	...	...	...	...	−53.0	−43.2	11.9	1.9	−43.1	−84.1	−1.1	−28.4	...	Other Investment Assets	78bhd
...	...	...	...	...	...			−1.0		−3.0		—	7.6	...	Monetary Authorities	78bod
...	...	...	...	...	...		−1.7	−2.1	13.3	—	−57.4	−6.9	−31.9	...	General Government	78bpd
...	...	...	...	...	...	−13.4	1.3	−1.2	1.6	−18.7	9.6	−1.8	−1.6	...	Banks	78bqd
...	...	...	...	...	...	−39.6	−42.9	16.2	−13.0	−21.5	−36.3	7.6	−2.5	...	Other Sectors	78brd
...	...	...	...	...	...	224.2	108.5	150.2	315.1	185.4	255.7	156.6	72.3	...	Other Investment Liab., n.i.e.	78bid
...	...	...	...	...	...	17.9	−17.7	.2	.2	—	−.1	−.1		...	Monetary Authorities	78bsd
...	...	...	...	...	...	179.5	110.9	102.0	104.7	137.5	177.1	224.5	96.8	...	General Government	78btd
...	...	...	...	...	...	5.7	3.6	−3.3	−2.1	14.0	1.0	−2.8	−.4	...	Banks	78bud
...	...	...	...	...	...	21.1	11.7	51.2	212.2	33.9	77.7	−65.0	−24.1	...	Other Sectors	78bvd
...	...	...	...	...	...	−16.2	48.0	−76.9	58.4	−57.7	63.5	−7.0	11.2	...	Net Errors and Omissions	78cad
...	...	...	...	...	...	−29.6	5.0	−80.7	−19.8	46.2	−72.7	−49.7	−96.9	...	*Overall Balance*	78cbd
...	...	...	...	...	...	29.6	−5.0	80.7	19.8	−46.2	72.7	49.7	96.9	...	Reserves and Related Items	79dad
...	...	...	...	...	...	−35.5	−31.9	.1	−18.6	−82.8	5.9	−61.3	−21.4	...	Reserve Assets	79dbd
...	...	...	...	...	...	62.1	13.8	46.3	19.6	34.1	2.8	19.4	7.4	...	Use of Fund Credit and Loans	79dcd
...	...	...	...	...	...	3.0	13.1	34.4	18.8	2.6	64.1	91.7	110.9	...	Exceptional Financing	79ded

Millions of US Dollars — International Investment Position

1987	1988	1989	1990	1991	1992	1993	1994	1995	1996	1997	1998	1999	2000	2001		
...	...	...	...	...	32.0	118.6	190.3	202.5	203.2	309.5	358.3	398.0	452.2	...	Assets	79aad
...	...	...	...	...	—	—	—	—	—	—	22.6	28.7	33.2	...	Direct Investment Abroad	79abd
...	...	...	...	...	—	—	—	.1	—	—	.2	.2	1.8	...	Portfolio Investment	79acd
...	...	...	...	...	—	—	—		—					...	Equity Securities	79add
...	...	...	...	...	—	—	—	.1	—	—	.2	.2	1.8	...	Debt Securities	79aed
...	...	...	...	...										...	Financial Derivatives	79ald
...	...	...	...	...	32.0	55.1	92.3	88.6	75.7	113.6	146.9	120.3	156.1	...	Other Investment	79afd
...	...	...	...	...										...	Monetary Authorities	79agd
...	...	...	...	...	24.2	33.9	72.4	67.7	56.2	75.5	69.1	53.2	76.2	...	General Government	79ahd
...	...	...	...	...	7.8	21.2	19.9	20.9	19.5	38.1	29.2	30.8	1.4	...	Banks	79aid
...	...	...	...	...							48.6	36.3	78.5	...	Other Sectors	79ajd
...	...	...	...	...	—	63.5	98.0	113.8	127.5	195.9	188.6	248.8	261.1	...	Reserve Assets	79akd
...	...	...	...	...	34.2	193.2	370.8	713.9	1,069.7	1,450.1	1,721.3	1,867.9	2,286.6	...	Liabilities	79lad
...	...	...	...	...	—	10.0	48.2	144.3	191.0	274.0	383.3	427.8	419.2	...	Dir. Invest. in Rep. Economy	79lbd
...	...	...	...	...	—	—	—	1.8	—	5.0	.9	.8	1.1	...	Portfolio Investment	79lcd
...	...	...	...	...	—	—	—		—					...	Equity Securities	79ldd
...	...	...	...	...	—	—	—	1.8	—	5.0	.9	.8	1.1	...	Debt Securities	79led
...	...	...	...	...										...	Financial Derivatives	79lld
...	...	...	...	...	34.2	183.2	322.6	567.8	878.7	1,171.1	1,337.1	1,439.3	1,866.3	...	Other Investment	79lfd
...	...	...	...	...	—	60.2	77.8	124.3	139.6	164.9	175.2	190.3	188.0	...	Monetary Authorities	79lgd
...	...	...	...	...	34.2	117.3	235.5	347.8	442.2	684.6	738.2	926.8	1,279.8	...	General Government	79lhd
...	...	...	...	...	—	5.7	9.3	6.0	3.9	18.0	18.9	16.1	1.7	...	Banks	79lid
...	...	...	...	...	—	—	—	89.7	293.0	303.6	404.8	306.1	396.8	...	Other Sectors	79ljd

Kyrgyz Republic

917

		1972	1973	1974	1975	1976	1977	1978	1979	1980	1981	1982	1983	1984	1985	1986
Government Finance																*Millions of Soms:*
Deficit (-) or Surplus	80	...	...	...	...	...	...	...	...	...	...	...	...	...	...	...
Total Revenue and Grants	81y	...	...	...	...	...	...	...	...	...	...	...	...	...	...	...
Exp. & Lending Minus Repay.	82z	...	...	...	...	...	...	...	...	...	...	...	...	...	...	...
Financing																
Domestic	84a	...	...	...	...	...	...	...	...	...	...	...	...	...	...	...
Foreign	85a	...	...	...	...	...	...	...	...	...	...	...	...	...	...	...
National Accounts																*Millions of Soms*
Househ.Cons.Expend.,incl.NPISHs	96f	...	...	...	...	...	...	...	...	...	...	...	...	...	...	...
Government Consumption Expend.	91f	...	...	...	...	...	...	...	...	...	...	...	...	...	...	...
Gross Fixed Capital Formation	93e	...	...	...	...	...	...	...	...	...	...	...	...	...	...	...
Changes in Inventories	93i	...	...	...	...	...	...	...	...	...	...	...	...	...	...	...
Exports of Goods and Services	90c	...	...	...	...	...	...	...	...	...	...	...	...	...	...	...
Imports of Goods and Services (-)	98c	...	...	...	...	...	...	...	...	...	...	...	...	...	...	...
Gross Domestic Product (GDP)	99b	...	...	...	...	...	...	...	...	...	...	...	...	...	...	...
Net Primary Income from Abroad	98.n	...	...	...	...	...	...	...	...	...	...	...	...	...	...	...
Gross National Income (GNI)	99a	...	...	...	...	...	...	...	...	...	...	...	...	...	...	...
Net Current Transf.from Abroad	98t	...	...	...	...	...	...	...	...	...	...	...	...	...	...	...
Gross Nat'l Disposable Inc.(GNDI)	99i	...	...	...	...	...	...	...	...	...	...	...	...	...	...	...
Gross Saving	99s	...	...	...	...	...	...	...	...	...	...	...	...	...	...	...
GDP Volume 1995 Prices	99b.*p*	...	...	...	...	...	...	...	...	...	...	...	...	...	...	...
GDP Volume (1995=100)	99bv*p*	...	...	...	...	...	...	...	...	...	...	...	...	...	...	...
GDP Deflator (1995=100)	99bi*p*	...	...	...	...	...	...	...	...	...	...	...	...	...	...	...
																Millions:
Population	99z	...	...	...	...	...	...	...	...	...	...	...	...	...	...	...

	1987	1988	1989	1990	1991	1992	1993	1994	1995	1996	1997	1998	1999	2000	2001	
Year Ending December 31																**Government Finance**
	...	...	...	...	....	....	−377.8	−921.6	−1,864.6	−1,269.3	−1,605.4	−1,035.8	−1,213.5	−1,244.8	286.7	Deficit (-) or Surplus **80**
	...	...	...	...	....	....	847.9	1,891.2	2,745.9	3,933.1	5,090.3	6,262.6	7,828.7	10,039.6	12,543.6	Total Revenue and Grants **81y**
	...	...	...	...	....	....	1,225.8	2,812.8	4,610.5	5,202.4	6,695.7	7,298.4	9,042.2	11,284.4	12,256.9	Exp. & Lending Minus Repay. **82z**
																Financing
	...	...	...	...	....	....	297.8	406.5	995.1	604.8	287.9	68.7	−379.6	−334.1	−377.5	Domestic **84a**
	...	...	...	...	....	....	80.0	515.1	851.1	664.5	1,317.5	966.8	1,593.1	1,579.0	90.8	Foreign **85a**
Millions of Soms																**National Accounts**
	...	...	...	...	59.3	524.3	†4,053.1	9,421.8	12,110.6	19,211.8	21,150.9	30,163.0	37,848.2	....	....	Househ.Cons.Expend.,incl.NPISHs.......... **96f**
	...	...	...	...	20.2	158.4	†1,086.2	2,272.1	3,154.5	4,333.1	5,307.3	6,103.0	9,320.1	....	....	Government Consumption Expend. **91f**
	...	...	...	...	...	108.1	†714.5	1,492.7	3,337.9	5,296.0	3,871.5	4,499.5	7,793.8	....	....	Gross Fixed Capital Formation **93e**
	...	...	...	...	...	39.6	†−89.8	−409.4	−376.8	600.0	2,781.2	779.5	992.9	....	....	Changes in Inventories **93i**
	...	...	...	...	...	263.8	†1,795.5	4,057.9	4,757.5	7,192.5	11,748.6	12,470.5	20,571.4	....	....	Exports of Goods and Services **90c**
	...	...	...	...	...	352.9	†2,204.8	4,815.9	6,838.6	13,234.1	14,173.8	19,834.1	27,782.4	....	....	Imports of Goods and Services (-) **98c**
	...	...	...	...	...	741.3	†5,354.7	12,019.2	16,145.1	22,467.7	30,685.7	34,181.4	48,744.0	....	....	Gross Domestic Product (GDP) **99b**
	...	...	...	...	...	−4.1	†−68.3	−189.6	−200.2	−485.2	−1,003.9	−1,748.4	−2,940.4	....	....	Net Primary Income from Abroad **98.n**
	...	...	...	...	...	737.1	†5,286.0	11,829.6	15,944.9	22,914.1	29,681.8	32,433.0	45,803.6	....	....	Gross National Income (GNI) **99a**
	...	...	...	—	—	40.0	521.1	665.4	819.8	1,437.8	1,161.4	1,042.7	1,969.3	....	....	Net Current Transf.from Abroad............ **98t**
	...	...	...	42.8	92.4	777.2	5,807.5	12,495.0	16,764.7	24,351.9	30,843.2	33,475.7	47,772.9	....	....	Gross Nat'l Disposable Inc.(GNDI) **99i**
	...	...	...	1.6	12.9	94.4	668.2	801.1	1,499.6	807.0	4,385.0	−2,790.3	604.6	....	....	Gross Saving **99s**
	...	...	...	...	...	25,278.2	†21360.1	17,066.7	16,145.1	17,288.9	19,003.3	19,406.4	20,100.6	....	....	GDP Volume 1995 Prices **99b,p**
	...	...	...	...	...	156.6	†132.3	105.7	100.0	107.1	117.7	120.2	124.5	....	....	GDP Volume (1995=100) .... **99bv p**
	...	...	...	...	...	2.9	†25.1	70.4	100.0	130.0	161.5	176.1	242.5	....	....	GDP Deflator (1995=100) .... **99bi p**
Midyear Estimates																
	...	...	...	...	4.49	4.55	4.54	4.54	4.59	4.66	4.72	4.76	4.83	4.90	4.95	Population.. **99z**

(See notes in the back of the book.)

Lao People's Dem.Rep

		1972	1973	1974	1975	1976	1977	1978	1979	1980	1981	1982	1983	1984	1985	1986
Exchange Rates															*Kip per SDR:*	
Official Rate	aa	651.43	723.81	734.61	†877.99	232.37	242.94	521.12	†13.17	12.75	34.92	38.61	36.64	34.31	104.35	116.20
															Kip per US Dollar:	
Official Rate	ae	600.00	600.00	600.00	†750.00	200.00	200.00	400.00	†10.00	10.00	30.00	35.00	35.00	35.00	95.00	95.00
Official Rate	rf	510.00	600.00	600.00	†725.00	429.17	200.00	333.33	†367.50	10.00	21.67	35.00	35.00	35.00	55.00	95.00
Fund Position															*Millions of SDRs:*	
Quota	2f. s	13.00	13.00	13.00	13.00	13.00	13.00	16.00	16.00	24.00	24.00	24.00	24.00	29.30	29.30	29.30
SDRs	1b. s	1.34	1.29	1.25	1.63	1.46	1.54	1.02	.78	.01	.56	.04	.14	.02	.01	.17
Reserve Position in the Fund	1c. s	2.80	2.80	3.25	—	—	—	—	—	—	—	—	—	—	—	—
Total Fund Cred.&Loans Outstg.	2tl	—	—	—	3.25	6.50	6.50	15.89	18.30	21.22	25.64	25.64	25.64	19.88	11.36	6.96
International Liquidity													*Millions of US Dollars Unless Otherwise Indicated:*			
Total Reserves minus Gold	1l. d	...	...	...	...	...	...	...	...	...	...	...	...	...	...	...
SDRs	1b. d	1.45	1.56	1.53	1.91	1.70	1.87	1.33	1.03	.01	.65	.04	.15	.02	.01	.21
Reserve Position in the Fund	1c. d	3.04	3.38	3.98	—	—	—	—	—	—	—	—	—	—	—	—
Foreign Exchange	1d. d	...	...	...	...	...	...	...	...	...	...	...	...	...	...	...
Gold (Million Fine Troy Ounces)	1ad	...	...	...	...	...	...	...	...	...	...	...	...	...	...	...
Gold (National Valuation)	1an d	...	...	...	...	...	...	...	...	...	...	...	...	...	...	...
Deposit Money Banks: Assets	7a. d	...	...	...	...	...	...	...	...	...	...	...	...	...	...	...
Liabilities	7b. d	...	...	...	...	...	...	...	...	...	...	...	...	...	...	...
Monetary Authorities															*Billions of Kip:*	
Foreign Assets	11	...	...	...	...	...	...	...	...	...	...	...	...	...	...	...
Claims on Central Government	12a	...	...	...	...	...	...	...	...	...	...	...	...	...	...	...
Claims on Nonfin.Pub.Enterprises	12c	...	...	...	...	...	...	...	...	...	...	...	...	...	...	...
Claims on Private Sector	12d	...	...	...	...	...	...	...	...	...	...	...	...	...	...	...
Claims on Deposit Money Banks	12e	...	...	...	...	...	...	...	...	...	...	...	...	...	...	...
Reserve Money	14	...	...	...	...	...	...	...	...	...	...	...	...	...	...	...
of which: Currency Outside DMBs	14a	...	...	...	...	...	...	...	...	...	...	...	...	...	...	...
Foreign Liabilities	16c	...	...	...	...	...	...	...	...	...	...	...	...	...	...	...
Central Government Deposits	16d	...	...	...	...	...	...	...	...	...	...	...	...	...	...	...
Government Lending Funds	16f	...	...	...	...	...	...	...	...	...	...	...	...	...	...	...
Capital Accounts	17a	...	...	...	...	...	...	...	...	...	...	...	...	...	...	...
Other Items (Net)	17r	...	...	...	...	...	...	...	...	...	...	...	...	...	...	...
Deposit Money Banks															*Billions of Kip:*	
Reserves	20	...	...	...	...	...	...	...	...	...	...	...	...	...	...	...
Foreign Assets	21	...	...	...	...	...	...	...	...	...	...	...	...	...	...	...
Claims on Central Government	22a	...	...	...	...	...	...	...	...	...	...	...	...	...	...	...
Claims on Nonfin.Pub.Enterprises	22c	...	...	...	...	...	...	...	...	...	...	...	...	...	...	...
Claims on Private Sector	22d	...	...	...	...	...	...	...	...	...	...	...	...	...	...	...
Demand Deposits	24	...	...	...	...	...	...	...	...	...	...	...	...	...	...	...
Time, Savings,& Fgn.Currency Dep.	25	...	...	...	...	...	...	...	...	...	...	...	...	...	...	...
Foreign Liabilities	26c	...	...	...	...	...	...	...	...	...	...	...	...	...	...	...
Central Government Deposits	26d	...	...	...	...	...	...	...	...	...	...	...	...	...	...	...
Credit from Monetary Authorities	26g	...	...	...	...	...	...	...	...	...	...	...	...	...	...	...
Capital Accounts	27a	...	...	...	...	...	...	...	...	...	...	...	...	...	...	...
Other Items (Net)	27r	...	...	...	...	...	...	...	...	...	...	...	...	...	...	...
Monetary Survey															*Billions of Kip:*	
Foreign Assets (Net)	31n	...	...	...	...	...	...	...	...	...	...	...	...	...	...	...
Domestic Credit	32	...	...	...	...	...	...	...	...	...	...	...	...	...	...	...
Claims on Central Govt. (Net)	32an	...	...	...	...	...	...	...	...	...	...	...	...	...	...	...
Claims on Nonfin.Pub.Enterprises	32c	...	...	...	...	...	...	...	...	...	...	...	...	...	...	...
Claims on Private Sector	32d	...	...	...	...	...	...	...	...	...	...	...	...	...	...	...
Money	34	...	...	...	...	...	...	...	...	...	...	...	...	...	...	...
Quasi-Money	35	...	...	...	...	...	...	...	...	...	...	...	...	...	...	...
Other Items (Net)	37r	...	...	...	...	...	...	...	...	...	...	...	...	...	...	...
Money plus Quasi-Money	35l	...	...	...	...	...	...	...	...	...	...	...	...	...	...	...
Interest Rates															*Percent Per Annum*	
Bank Rate *(End of Period)*	60	...	...	...	...	...	...	...	...	...	...	...	...	...	...	...
Treasury Bill Rate	60c	...	...	...	...	...	...	...	...	...	...	...	...	...	...	...
Deposit Rate	60l	...	...	...	...	...	...	...	...	...	...	...	...	...	...	...
Lending Rate	60p	...	...	...	...	...	...	...	...	...	...	...	...	...	...	...
Prices															*Index Numbers (1995=100):*	
Consumer Prices	64	...	...	...	...	...	...	...	...	...	...	...	...	...	...	...
International Transactions															*Millions of US Dollars*	
Exports	70..d	42.4	54.0	95.5	11.5	11.7	4.2	3.2	19.0	28.0	23.0	40.0	41.0	44.0	54.0	55.1
Imports, c.i.f.	71..d	63.0	57.2	64.8	45.1	44.6	13.8	16.3	70.0	92.0	110.0	132.0	150.0	162.0	193.0	186.0

1987	1988	1989	1990	1991	1992	1993	1994	1995	1996	1997	1998	1999	2000	2001		
															Exchange Rates	
End of Period																
549.73	608.93	937.65	989.46	1,017.75	985.88	986.22	1,049.63	†1372.03	1,344.49	3,554.60	6,017.92	10,431.08	10,707.31	11,926.37	Official Rate	**aa**
End of Period (ae) Period Average (rf)																
387.50	452.50	713.50	695.50	711.50	717.00	718.00	719.00	†923.00	935.00	2,634.50	4,274.00	7,600.00	8,218.00	9,490.00	Official Rate	**ae**
187.50	400.37	591.50	707.75	702.08	716.08	716.25	717.67	†804.69	921.02	1,259.98	3,298.33	7,102.03	7,887.64	8,954.58	Official Rate	**rf**
															Fund Position	
End of Period																
29.30	29.30	29.30	29.30	29.30	39.10	39.10	39.10	39.10	39.10	39.10	39.10	39.10	39.10	52.90	Quota	**2f.s**
—	—	.01	.01	.34	.57	1.90	7.46	9.49	7.17	9.31	4.32	.05	.07	2.72	SDRs	**1b.s**
—	—	—	—	—	—	—	—	—	—	—	—	—	—	—	Reserve Position in the Fund	**1c.s**
4.43	1.90	6.30	5.91	14.65	20.51	26.38	32.24	42.80	46.61	48.96	44.27	38.41	32.55	29.75	Total Fund Cred.&Loans Outstg.	**2tl**
															International Liquidity	
End of Period																
—	.64	1.42	1.78	28.65e	40.31e	62.96e	60.93e	92.11	169.50	112.18	112.21	101.19	138.97	130.93	Total Reserves minus Gold	**1l.d**
—	—	.01	.01	.49	.78	2.61	10.89	14.10	10.31	12.56	6.09	.07	.10	3.42	SDRs	**1b.d**
—	—	—	—	—	—	—	—	—	—	—	—	—	—	—	Reserve Position in the Fund	**1c.d**
—	.64	1.41	1.76	28.16e	39.52e	60.34e	50.03e	78.01	159.19	99.62	106.13	101.12	138.87	127.51	Foreign Exchange	**1d.d**
....	....	.0171	.0171	.0171	.0171	.0171	.0171	.0171	.0171	.0171	.0171	.1171	.0169	.0691	Gold (Million Fine Troy Ounces)	**1ad**
....	....	.60	.60	.60	.60	.60	.60	.60	.60	.60	.60	4.10	.59	2.42	Gold (National Valuation)	**1and**
.03	.03	.06	.06	.03	.04	.09	.10	.10	.11	.07	.11	.15	.13	.09	Deposit Money Banks: Assets	**7a.d**
.03	.03	.02	.03	—	.01	.01	.03	.04	.05	.03	.04	.04	.04	.04	Liabilities	**7b.d**
															Monetary Authorities	
End of Period																
....	....	1.20	1.59	20.54	29.06	45.36	43.96	85.18	158.64	295.70	479.76	799.78	1,146.86	1,265.54	Foreign Assets	**11**
....	....	7.09	5.89	5.89	10.83	8.96	12.16	4.25	4.25	4.70	91.27	198.83	158.51	184.98	Claims on Central Government	**12a**
....	....	12.25	4.01	1.59	1.44	.86	1.86	6.98	10.87	59.54	112.80	223.71	346.10	488.49	Claims on Nonfin.Pub.Enterprises	**12c**
....	....	3.01	1.72	.41	1.15	3.01	6.83	10.40	13.90	38.22	72.05	143.25	143.23	150.82	Claims on Private Sector	**12d**
....	....	27.73	10.95	11.51	15.18	34.62	37.05	46.59	52.37	57.94	80.35	301.90	445.60	347.66	Claims on Deposit Money Banks	**12e**
....	....	20.38	22.09	26.26	36.90	60.70	74.23	84.17	104.37	150.09	281.75	481.75	766.65	822.49	Reserve Money	**14**
....	....	16.84	18.57	19.22	22.83	33.24	38.61	41.95	42.97	53.31	63.16	77.79	67.83	113.08	of which: Currency Outside DMBs	**14a**
....	....	5.92	5.85	14.91	20.22	26.01	33.84	58.72	62.67	174.04	266.43	400.67	348.51	354.80	Foreign Liabilities	**16c**
....	....	1.62	.85	.02	.81	8.59	13.52	7.45	64.82	52.74	77.51	235.23	505.77	281.32	Central Government Deposits	**16d**
....	....	—	.58	8.81	16.31	18.34	12.07	16.17	18.04	31.09	54.37	87.33	211.05	346.68	Government Lending Funds	**16f**
....	....	11.08	14.40	14.81	14.38	13.85	15.23	26.44	25.21	91.25	172.61	456.94	463.05	706.21	Capital Accounts	**17a**
....	....	12.27	-19.62	-24.87	-30.97	-34.68	-47.02	-39.56	-35.08	-43.10	-16.43	5.55	-54.73	-73.99	Other Items (Net)	**17r**
															Deposit Money Banks	
End of Period																
....	....	1.23	2.82	5.97	13.75	30.66	36.45	44.16	59.24	77.70	212.42	402.96	688.77	714.46	Reserves	**20**
....	....	41.45	43.50	20.11	31.78	62.82	69.79	91.20	107.47	180.35	452.00	1,142.98	1,075.88	865.78	Foreign Assets	**21**
....	....	-.55	—	—	—	—	26.81	19.38	39.18	40.78	37.86	11.35	7.64	29.74	Claims on Central Government	**22a**
....	....	24.40	35.73	18.83	16.40	17.47	15.57	20.69	26.06	60.88	110.75	221.69	296.54	528.24	Claims on Nonfin.Pub.Enterprises	**22c**
....	....	1.40	4.18	20.89	36.54	62.90	92.02	118.46	141.79	247.35	460.77	728.69	1,074.91	1,354.49	Claims on Private Sector	**22d**
....	....	6.55	5.96	8.57	12.05	18.99	22.73	25.22	32.59	26.62	105.82	141.19	272.23	256.88	Demand Deposits	**24**
8.89	9.48	15.76	19.11	23.09	41.32	73.61	104.69	126.09	169.37	326.07	696.95	1,325.52	1,911.25	2,193.15	Time, Savings,& Fgn.Currency Dep.	**25**
10.66	....	16.99	18.44	3.09	3.96	9.28	21.51	39.76	46.87	77.24	169.34	281.96	349.38	376.08	Foreign Liabilities	**26c**
....	....	19.13	19.47	6.62	9.32	9.79	12.69	15.41	21.60	36.34	103.46	247.16	79.93	51.42	Central Government Deposits	**26d**
....	....	27.72	10.56	6.28	10.84	29.57	35.04	41.93	49.12	51.46	81.67	314.49	489.84	383.78	Credit from Monetary Authorities	**26g**
2.71	6.92	3.58	6.16	7.78	14.80	33.83	47.45	56.55	66.51	126.78	215.97	457.31	519.89	574.10	Capital Accounts	**27a**
1.61	4.86	-21.81	6.50	10.39	6.18	-1.23	-3.47	-11.05	-12.31	-37.46	-99.42	-259.97	-478.79	-342.73	Other Items (Net)	**27r**
															Monetary Survey	
End of Period																
....	....	19.74	20.80	22.66	36.66	72.89	58.40	77.90	156.57	224.77	496.00	1,260.13	1,524.85	1,400.44	Foreign Assets (Net)	**31n**
....	....	26.83	31.20	40.97	56.22	74.82	129.04	157.30	149.62	362.39	704.53	1,045.12	1,441.22	2,404.02	Domestic Credit	**32**
....	....	-14.22	-14.43	-.75	.69	-9.42	12.77	.78	-43.00	-43.61	-51.84	-272.21	-419.56	-118.02	Claims on Central Govt. (Net)	**32an**
....	....	36.65	39.73	20.42	17.84	18.33	17.43	27.67	36.93	120.42	223.55	445.39	642.63	1,016.73	Claims on Nonfin.Pub.Enterprises	**32c**
....	....	4.40	5.90	21.30	37.68	65.91	98.85	128.86	155.69	285.58	532.82	871.94	1,218.14	1,505.31	Claims on Private Sector	**32d**
....	....	25.13	25.09	28.23	35.14	52.24	61.34	67.18	75.56	79.94	168.98	218.98	344.35	371.84	Money	**34**
8.95	9.56	15.99	19.25	23.09	41.32	73.61	104.69	126.09	169.37	326.07	696.95	1,325.52	1,911.25	2,193.15	Quasi-Money	**35**
....	....	5.45	7.65	12.32	16.41	21.87	21.41	41.93	61.27	181.15	334.60	760.75	710.46	1,239.46	Other Items (Net)	**37r**
....	....	41.11	44.34	51.32	76.46	125.85	166.03	193.27	244.93	406.00	865.93	1,544.50	2,255.60	2,564.99	Money plus Quasi-Money	**35l**
															Interest Rates	
Percent Per Annum																
....	....	....	....	23.67	25.00	30.00	32.08	35.00	....	35.00	34.89	35.17	35.00		Bank Rate (*End of Period*)	**60**
....	....	....	....	....	....	....	20.46	....	....	23.66	30.00	29.94	22.70		Treasury Bill Rate	**60c**
....	....	30.00	30.00	†23.50	15.00	13.33	12.00	14.00	16.00	....	17.79	13.42	12.00	6.50	Deposit Rate	**60l**
....	....	....	26.00	26.00	†25.33	24.00	†25.67	27.00	....	29.28	32.00	32.00	26.17		Lending Rate	**60p**
															Prices	
Period Averages																
....	27.0	43.6	59.1	67.1	73.7	78.3	83.6	100.0	†113.0	144.1	275.2	†628.7	786.4	847.8	Consumer Prices	**64**
															International Transactions	
Millions of US Dollars																
64.1	58.0	63.3	78.7	96.6	132.6	241.0	300.5	311.0	322.8	359.0	369.5	310.8	330.3	331.3	Exports	**70..d**
216.0	149.0	194.0	185.0	170.0	270.0	432.0	564.1	588.8	689.6	706.0	552.8	524.8	535.3	551.0	Imports, c.i.f.	**71..d**

Lao People's Dem.Rep

		1972	1973	1974	1975	1976	1977	1978	1979	1980	1981	1982	1983	1984	1985	1986
Balance of Payments														*Millions of US Dollars:*		
Current Account, n.i.e.	78al d	...	...	...	...	...	...	...	...	...	...	...	...	−163.6	−163.6	−141.6
Goods: Exports f.o.b.	78aa d	...	...	...	...	...	...	...	...	...	...	...	...	43.8	53.6	55.0
Goods: Imports f.o.b.	78ab d	...	...	...	...	...	...	...	...	...	...	...	...	−161.9	−193.2	−185.7
Trade Balance	78ac d	...	...	...	...	...	...	...	...	...	...	...	...	−118.1	−139.6	−130.7
Services: Credit	78ad d	...	...	...	...	...	...	...	...	...	...	...	...	15.1	21.3	24.4
Services: Debit	78ae d	...	...	...	...	...	...	...	...	...	...	...	...	−57.5	−42.9	−33.8
Balance on Goods & Services	78af d	...	...	...	...	...	...	...	...	...	...	...	...	−160.5	−161.2	−140.1
Income: Credit	78ag d	...	...	...	...	...	...	...	...	...	...	...	...	—	—	—
Income: Debit	78ah d	...	...	...	...	...	...	...	...	...	...	...	...	−3.1	−2.4	−1.5
Balance on Gds, Serv. & Inc.	78ai d	...	...	...	...	...	...	...	...	...	...	...	...	−163.6	−163.6	−141.6
Current Transfers, n.i.e.: Credit	78aj d	...	...	...	...	...	...	...	...	...	...	...	...	—	—	—
Current Transfers: Debit	78ak d	...	...	...	...	...	...	...	...	...	...	...	...			
Capital Account, n.i.e.	78bc d	...	...	...	...	...	...	...	...	...	...	...	...	2.8	3.5	3.7
Capital Account, n.i.e.: Credit	78ba d	...	...	...	...	...	...	...	...	...	...	...	...	2.8	3.5	3.7
Capital Account: Debit	78bb d	...	...	...	...	...	...	...	...	...	...	...	...	—	—	—
Financial Account, n.i.e.	78bj d	...	...	...	...	...	...	...	...	...	...	...	...	−4.4	−11.1	−6.7
Direct Investment Abroad	78bd d	...	...	...	...	...	...	...	...	...	...	...	...	—	—	—
Dir. Invest. in Rep. Econ., n.i.e.	78be d	...	...	...	...	...	...	...	...	...	...	...	...	—	—	—
Portfolio Investment Assets	78bf d	...	...	...	...	...	...	...	...	...	...	...	...	—	—	—
Equity Securities	78bk d	...	...	...	...	...	...	...	...	...	...	...	...	—	—	—
Debt Securities	78bl d	...	...	...	...	...	...	...	...	...	...	...	...	—	—	—
Portfolio Investment Liab., n.i.e.	78bg d	...	...	...	...	...	...	...	...	...	...	...	...	—	—	—
Equity Securities	78bm d	...	...	...	...	...	...	...	...	...	...	...	...	—	—	—
Debt Securities	78bn d	...	...	...	...	...	...	...	...	...	...	...	...	—	—	—
Financial Derivatives Assets	78bw d	...	...	...	...	...	...	...	...	...	...	...	...	...	...	...
Financial Derivatives Liabilities	78bx d	...	...	...	...	...	...	...	...	...	...	...	...	...	...	...
Other Investment Assets	78bh d	...	...	...	...	...	...	...	...	...	...	...	...	—	—	—
Monetary Authorities	78bo d	...	...	...	...	...	...	...	...	...	...	...	...	—	—	—
General Government	78bp d	...	...	...	...	...	...	...	...	...	...	...	...	—	—	—
Banks	78bq d	...	...	...	...	...	...	...	...	...	...	...	...	—	—	—
Other Sectors	78br d	...	...	...	...	...	...	...	...	...	...	...	...	—	—	—
Other Investment Liab., n.i.e.	78bi d	...	...	...	...	...	...	...	...	...	...	...	...	−4.4	−11.1	−6.7
Monetary Authorities	78bs d	...	...	...	...	...	...	...	...	...	...	...	...	—	—	—
General Government	78bt d	...	...	...	...	...	...	...	...	...	...	...	...	−10.0	−14.4	−10.3
Banks	78bu d	...	...	...	...	...	...	...	...	...	...	...	...	—	—	—
Other Sectors	78bv d	...	...	...	...	...	...	...	...	...	...	...	...	5.6	3.3	3.6
Net Errors and Omissions	78ca d	...	...	...	...	...	...	...	...	...	...	...	...	32.5	35.7	15.0
Overall Balance	78cb d	...	...	...	...	...	...	...	...	...	...	...	...	−132.7	−135.5	−129.6
Reserves and Related Items	79da d	...	...	...	...	...	...	...	...	...	...	...	...	132.7	135.5	129.6
Reserve Assets	79db d	...	...	...	...	...	...	...	...	...	...	...	...	8.4	−14.8	−6.6
Use of Fund Credit and Loans	79dc d	...	...	...	...	...	...	...	...	...	...	...	...	−5.9	−8.6	−5.1
Exceptional Financing	79de d	...	...	...	...	...	...	...	...	...	...	...	...	130.2	158.9	141.3
National Accounts															*Billions of Kip*	
Gross Domestic Product (GDP)	99b	...	...	...	...	...	...	...	...	...	...	11.0	20.0	29.0	84.0	124.3
GDP Volume 1990 Prices	99b.p	...	...	...	...	...	...	...	...	355.9	410.4	429.8	442.7	471.2	514.2	539.0
GDP Volume (1995=100)	99bv p	...	...	...	...	...	...	...	...	42.6	49.1	51.4	53.0	56.4	61.5	64.5
GDP Deflator (1995=100)	99bi p	...	...	...	...	...	...	...	...	...	...	1.5	2.7	3.6	9.6	13.6
															Millions:	
Population	99z	3.11	3.18	3.26	†3.43	3.48	3.53	3.58	†3.16	3.21	3.26	3.33	3.41	3.50	3.59	3.70

	1987	1988	1989	1990	1991	1992	1993	1994	1995	1996	1997	1998	1999	2000	2001	
	Minus Sign Indicates Debit															**Balance of Payments**
Current Account, n.i.e.	−165.1	−103.2	−136.5	−110.8	−115.1	−111.3	−139.2	−284.0	−346.2	−346.8	−305.5	−150.1	−121.1	....	....	78al *d*
Goods: Exports f.o.b.	64.3	57.8	63.3	78.7	96.6	132.6	247.9	305.5	310.9	322.8	318.3	342.1	338.2	....	....	78aa *d*
Goods: Imports f.o.b.	−216.2	−149.4	−193.8	−185.5	−197.9	−232.8	−397.4	−519.2	−626.8	−643.7	−601.3	−506.8	−527.7	....	....	78ab *d*
Trade Balance	−151.9	−91.6	−130.5	−106.8	−101.3	−100.2	−149.5	−213.7	−315.9	−320.9	−283.0	−164.7	−189.5	....	....	78ac *d*
Services: Credit	26.3	17.8	22.5	23.7	37.8	61.4	85.2	87.0	96.8	104.4	105.8	145.0	130.0	....	....	78ad *d*
Services: Debit	−38.1	−26.7	−25.8	−26.4	−47.6	−71.3	−75.9	−152.1	−121.6	−126.0	−110.5	−95.5	−51.8	....	....	78ae *d*
Balance on Goods & Services	−163.7	−100.5	−133.8	−109.5	−111.1	−110.1	−140.2	−278.8	−340.7	−342.5	−287.7	−115.2	−111.3	....	....	78af *d*
Income: Credit	—	.4	.8	2.2	3.3	5.6	8.6	7.2	7.4	9.2	11.1	6.9	10.5	....	....	78ag *d*
Income: Debit	−1.4	−2.5	−3.1	−3.2	−4.4	−4.6	−5.6	−9.2	−12.9	−13.5	−28.9	−41.8	−49.9	....	....	78ah *d*
Balance on Gds, Serv. & Inc.	−165.1	−102.6	−136.1	−110.5	−112.2	−109.1	−137.2	−280.8	−346.2	−346.8	−305.5	−150.1	−150.7	....	....	78ai *d*
Current Transfers, n.i.e.: Credit	—	—	—	—	—	—	—	—	—	—	—	—	80.2	....	....	78aj *d*
Current Transfers: Debit	—	−.6	−.4	−.3	−2.9	−2.2	−2.0	−3.2	—	—	—	—	−50.6	....	....	78ak *d*
Capital Account, n.i.e.	3.5	6.7	8.3	10.9	10.4	8.6	9.5	9.5	13.2	35.0	33.4	43.1	—	....	....	78bc *d*
Capital Account, n.i.e.: Credit	3.5	6.7	8.3	10.9	10.4	8.6	9.5	9.5	21.7	44.9	40.3	49.4	—	....	....	78ba *d*
Capital Account: Debit	—	—	—	—	—	—	—	—	−8.5	−9.9	−6.9	−6.3	—	....	....	78bb *d*
Financial Account, n.i.e.	−5.6	−25.2	−4.4	14.2	39.5	−3.0	−21.0	24.3	90.0	135.7	3.5	−43.4	−46.9	....	....	78bj *d*
Direct Investment Abroad	—	—	—	—	—	—	—	—	—	—	—	—	—	....	....	78bd *d*
Dir. Invest. in Rep. Econ., n.i.e.	—	2.0	4.0	6.0	6.9	7.8	29.9	59.2	95.1	159.8	—	—	—	....	....	78be *d*
Portfolio Investment Assets	—	—	—	—	—	—	—	—	....	....	—	—	—	....	....	78bf *d*
Equity Securities	—	—	—	—	—	—	—	—	....	....	—	—	—	....	....	78bk *d*
Debt Securities	—	—	—	—	—	—	—	—	....	....	—	—	—	....	....	78bl *d*
Portfolio Investment Liab., n.i.e.	—	—	—	1.1	1.2	—	—	—	—	—	—	—	—	....	....	78bg *d*
Equity Securities	—	—	—	1.1	1.2	—	—	—	—	—	—	—	—	....	....	78bm *d*
Debt Securities	—	—	—	—	—	—	—	—	—	—	....	....	—	....	....	78bn *d*
Financial Derivatives Assets	....	....	....	....	....	....	....	....	....	....	....	....	....	....	....	78bw *d*
Financial Derivatives Liabilities	....	....	....	....	....	....	....	....	....	....	....	....	....	....	....	78bx *d*
Other Investment Assets	—	−28.7	−29.4	−4.5	34.2	−16.1	−43.2	−9.6	−1.5	−14.1	39.5	−22.8	−43.2	....	....	78bh *d*
Monetary Authorities	....	....	....	....	....	....	....	....	....	....	....	....	....	....	....	78bo *d*
General Government	—	—	—	—	—	—	—	—	—	—	—	—	—	....	....	78bp *d*
Banks	—	−28.7	−29.4	−4.5	34.2	−16.1	−43.2	−9.6	−1.5	−14.1	39.5	−22.8	−43.2	....	....	78bq *d*
Other Sectors	—	—	—	—	—	—	—	—	—	—	—	—	—	....	....	78br *d*
Other Investment Liab., n.i.e.	−5.6	1.5	21.0	12.7	−2.7	4.1	−7.7	−25.3	−3.6	−10.0	−36.0	−20.6	−3.7	....	....	78bi *d*
Monetary Authorities	—	—	—	—	—	—	—	—	−15.4	−17.5	−18.2	−25.3	—	....	....	78bs *d*
General Government	−9.1	−9.2	−10.6	−7.3	−12.0	−9.0	−9.3	−8.3	—	—	—	—	—	....	....	78bt *d*
Banks	—	1.5	−1.2	−.9	−.7	−1.2	−7.4	−17.0	11.8	7.5	−17.8	4.7	−3.7	....	....	78bu *d*
Other Sectors	3.5	9.2	32.8	20.9	10.0	14.3	9.0	—	—	—	—	—	....	....	....	78bv *d*
Net Errors and Omissions	15.1	17.4	−31.2	−40.2	−60.3	−16.3	13.2	71.8	92.4	17.7	−100.5	−103.8	−165.1	....	....	78ca *d*
Overall Balance	−152.1	−104.3	−163.8	−125.9	−125.5	−122.0	−137.5	−178.4	−150.6	−158.4	−369.1	−254.2	−333.1	....	....	78cb *d*
Reserves and Related Items	152.1	104.3	163.8	125.9	125.5	122.0	137.5	178.4	150.6	158.4	369.1	254.2	333.1	....	....	79da *d*
Reserve Assets	11.4	−.7	−1.0	−.7	−27.0	−12.8	−24.1	−5.6	−73.0	−70.7	25.4	28.1	12.4	....	....	79db *d*
Use of Fund Credit and Loans	−3.3	−3.4	5.4	−.5	11.8	8.1	8.3	8.1	15.6	5.5	3.3	−6.4	−8.0	....	....	79dc *d*
Exceptional Financing	144.0	108.4	159.4	127.1	140.7	126.7	153.3	175.9	208.0	223.6	340.4	232.5	328.7	....	....	79de *d*
	Billions of Kip															**National Accounts**
Gross Domestic Product (GDP)	160.9	228.6	431.3	612.6	722.0	844.4	950.9	1,107.8	1,419.0	1,725.7	2,200.0	4,240.0	10,329.0	13,671.0	15,670.0	99b
GDP Volume 1990 Prices	533.8	522.6	574.2	612.7	637.1	681.7	712.8	780.6	835.6	893.2	955.0	993.1	1,065.4	1,126.6	1,127.0	99b.*p*
GDP Volume (1995=100)	63.9	62.5	68.7	73.3	76.2	81.6	85.3	93.4	100.0	106.9	114.3	118.8	127.5	134.8	134.9	99bv *p*
GDP Deflator (1995=100)	17.7	25.8	44.2	58.9	66.7	72.9	78.6	83.6	100.0	113.8	135.7	251.4	570.9	714.6	515.0	99bi *p*
	Midyear Estimates															
Population	3.82	3.94	4.03	4.15	4.24	4.35	4.46	4.57	4.69	4.80	4.92	5.03	5.16	5.22	5.40	99z

(See notes in the back of the book.)

Latvia

	1972	1973	1974	1975	1976	1977	1978	1979	1980	1981	1982	1983	1984	1985	1986

Exchange Rates — *Lats per SDR:*
Official Rate .... **aa** ....

Lats per US Dollar:
Official Rate .... **ae** ....
Official Rate .... **rf** ....

Fund Position — *Millions of SDRs:*
Quota .... **2f. s** ....
SDRs .... **1b. s** ....
Reserve Position in the Fund .... **1c. s** ....
Total Fund Cred.&Loans Outstg. **2tl**

International Liquidity — *Millions of US Dollars Unless Otherwise Indicated:*
Total Reserves minus Gold .... **1l. d** ....
SDRs .... **1b. d** ....
Reserve Position in the Fund .... **1c. d** ....
Foreign Exchange .... **1d. d** ....
Gold (Million Fine Troy Ounces) .... **1ad** ....
Gold (National Valuation) .... **1and** ....
Monetary Authorities: Other Assets .... **3..d** ....
Other Liab. .... **4..d** ....
Deposit Money Banks: Assets .... **7a. d** ....
Liabilities .... **7b. d** ....

Monetary Authorities — *Millions of Lats:*
Foreign Assets .... **11** ....
Claims on Central Government .... **12a** ....
Claims on Banks .... **12e** ....
Reserve Money .... **14** ....
of which: Currency Outside Banks .... **14a** ....
Foreign Liabilities .... **16c** ....
Central Government Deposits .... **16d** ....
Capital Accounts .... **17a** ....
Other Items (Net) .... **17r** ....

Banking Institutions — *Millions of Lats:*
Reserves .... **20** ....
Foreign Assets .... **21** ....
Claims on Central Government .... **22a** ....
Claims on Local Government .... **22b** ....
Claims on Nonfin.Pub.Enterprises .... **22c** ....
Claims on Private Sector .... **22d** ....
Claims on Nonbank Financial Insts. ...... **22g** ....
Demand Deposits .... **24** ....
Time, Savings,& Fgn.Currency Dep. ...... **25** ....
Money Market Instruments .... **26aa** ....
Foreign Liabilities .... **26c** ....
Central Government Deposits .... **26d** ....
Government Lending Funds .... **26f** ....
Credit from Central Bank .... **26g** ....
Capital Accounts .... **27a** ....
Other Items (Net) .... **27r** ....

Banking Survey — *Millions of Lats:*
Foreign Assets (Net) .... **31n** ....
Domestic Credit .... **32** ....
Claims on Central Govt. (Net) .... **32an** ....
Claims on Local Government .... **32b** ....
Claims on Nonfin.Pub.Enterprises ...... **32c** ....
Claims on Private Sector .... **32d** ....
Claims on Nonbank Financial Insts. .... **32g** ....
Money.. **34** ....
Quasi-Money .... **35** ....
Money Market Instruments .... **36aa** ....
Government Lending Funds .... **36f** ....
Capital Accounts .... **37a** ....
Other Items (Net) .... **37r** ....

Money plus Quasi-Money........................ **35l** ....

Interest Rates — *Percent Per Annum*
Discount Rate *(End of Period)* .... **60** ....
Money Market Rate .... **60b** ....
Treasury Bill Rate .... **60c** ....
Deposit Rate .... **60l** ....
Lending Rate .... **60p** ....

Prices, Production, Labor — *Index Numbers (1995=100):*
Producer Prices .... **63** ....
Consumer Prices .... **64** ....
Wages: Average Earnings........................ **65** ....
Industrial Employment .... **67** ....

Number in Thousands:
Labor Force.. **67d** ....
Employment .... **67e** ....
Unemployment .... **67c** ....
Unemployment Rate (%) .... **67r** ....

International Transactions — *Millions of Lats*
Exports .... **70** ....
Imports, c.i.f. .... **71** ....
Imports, f.o.b. .... **71.v** ....

(1995=100)
Volume of Exports .... **72** ....
Unit Value of Exports............................ **74** ....

	1987	1988	1989	1990	1991	1992	1993	1994	1995	1996	1997	1998	1999	2000	2001	
Exchange Rates	*End of Period*															
Official Rate	....	....	....	....	....	1.148	.817	.800	.798	.800	.796	.801	.800	.799	.802	aa
	End of Period (ae) Period Average (rf)															
Official Rate	....	....	....	....	....	.835	.595	.548	.537	.556	.590	.569	.583	.613	.638	ae
Official Rate	....	....	....	....	....	.736	.675	.560	.528	.551	.581	.590	.585	.607	.628	rf
Fund Position	*End of Period*															
Quota	....	....	....	....	....	91.50	91.50	91.50	91.50	91.50	91.50	91.50	126.80	126.80	126.80	2f.s
SDRs	....	....	....	....	....	19.33	71.10	.21	1.49	1.56	1.50	.21	2.24	—	.07	1b.s
Reserve Position in the Fund	....	....	....	....	....	.01	.01	.01	.01	.01	.01	.01	.01	.06	.06	1c.s
Total Fund Cred.&Loans Outstg.	....	....	....	....	....	25.16	77.78	109.80	107.89	90.36	63.67	45.37	34.31	26.69	19.06	2tl
International Liquidity	*End of Period*															
Total Reserves minus Gold	....	....	....	....	....	....	431.55	545.18	505.70	654.07	703.96	728.24	840.17	850.91	1,148.74	1l.d
SDRs	....	....	....	....	....	26.58	97.66	.31	2.22	2.25	2.03	.29	3.07	.01	.09	1b.d
Reserve Position in the Fund	....	....	....	....	....	.01	.01	.01	.01	.01	.01	.01	.01	.07	.07	1c.d
Foreign Exchange	....	....	....	....	....	....	333.88	544.86	503.47	651.81	701.93	727.94	837.09	850.83	1,148.59	1d.d
Gold (Million Fine Troy Ounces)	....	....	....	....	....	.0675	.2428	.2492	.2492	.2493	.2491	.2493	.2493	.2487	.2486	1ad
Gold (National Valuation)	....	....	....	....	....	20.20	72.80	74.80	74.77	74.78	74.11	76.91	72.41	68.38	69.66	1and
Monetary Authorities: Other Assets	....	....	....	....	....	....	.01	—	—	—	—	.01	.01	.01	—	3..d
Other Liab.	....	....	....	....	....	....	.01	—	—	—	—	—	.01	.01	.01	4..d
Deposit Money Banks: Assets	....	....	....	....	....	....	229.93	664.25	599.56	1,021.16	1,546.56	1,258.96	1,489.19	2,112.97	2,271.57	7a.d
Liabilities	....	....	....	....	....	....	92.26	448.07	452.38	852.57	1,297.97	1,342.03	1,767.48	2,141.32	2,649.83	7b.d
Monetary Authorities	*End of Period*															
Foreign Assets	....	....	....	....	....	....	307.13	341.98	313.52	407.63	461.47	461.23	535.64	568.45	780.39	11
Claims on Central Government	....	....	....	....	....	....	—	6.59	39.38	22.33	72.88	81.00	57.70	73.47	43.33	12a
Claims on Banks	....	....	....	....	....	....	13.31	21.40	22.04	20.22	7.55	52.04	63.32	42.53	18.83	12e
Reserve Money	....	....	....	....	....	....	225.56	269.43	273.62	336.66	441.74	471.45	526.28	566.72	641.88	14
of which: Currency Outside Banks	....	....	....	....	....	....	152.75	213.06	209.54	264.00	332.65	340.19	377.41	427.66	485.19	14a
Foreign Liabilities	....	....	....	....	....	....	67.11	88.46	86.56	72.55	51.17	36.66	31.54	28.35	21.58	16c
Central Government Deposits	....	....	....	....	....	....	3.08	10.78	3.62	35.40	24.91	42.03	79.03	45.93	119.59	16d
Capital Accounts	....	....	....	....	....	....	14.70	8.02	11.00	20.89	36.60	47.22	47.23	52.02	61.64	17a
Other Items (Net)	....	....	....	....	....	....	10.00	–6.71	.15	–15.32	–12.52	–3.09	–27.40	–8.56	–2.13	17r
Banking Institutions	*End of Period*															
Reserves	....	....	....	....	....	....	69.31	57.29	64.15	71.69	107.23	129.93	144.46	135.11	153.25	20
Foreign Assets	....	....	....	....	....	....	136.81	364.01	321.96	567.77	912.47	716.35	868.20	1,295.25	1,449.26	21
Claims on Central Government	....	....	....	....	....	....	520.53	†97.14	120.81	140.09	113.01	71.41	114.01	138.36	170.10	22a
Claims on Local Government	....	....	....	....	....	....	—	6.66	11.51	15.52	2.66	4.41	15.77	36.22	51.71	22b
Claims on Nonfin.Pub.Enterprises	....	....	....	....	....	....	16.94	39.59	24.99	17.71	28.15	23.82	30.61	52.53	81.21	22c
Claims on Private Sector	....	....	....	....	....	....	253.97	335.67	184.13	202.99	344.28	533.10	612.18	804.74	1,100.54	22d
Claims on Nonbank Financial Insts.	....	....	....	....	....	....	—	—	—	—	19.24	25.34	25.90	56.69	190.68	22g
Demand Deposits	....	....	....	....	....	....	115.03	138.08	144.24	156.36	232.76	259.75	257.52	332.97	374.97	24
Time, Savings,& Fgn.Currency Dep.	....	....	....	....	....	....	196.49	346.82	195.06	230.50	331.56	357.60	398.73	554.19	716.43	25
Money Market Instruments	....	....	....	....	....	....	—	—	—	—	—	—	—	—	—	26aa
Foreign Liabilities	....	....	....	....	....	....	54.90	245.54	242.93	474.03	765.80	763.61	1,030.44	1,312.63	1,690.59	26c
Central Government Deposits	....	....	....	....	....	....	520.57	†13.92	36.98	6.31	50.33	32.83	18.10	10.14	31.37	26d
Government Lending Funds	....	....	....	....	....	....	16.94	61.43	39.68	22.00	19.66	16.73	22.48	22.55	21.26	26f
Credit from Central Bank	....	....	....	....	....	....	—	1.44	3.52	4.32	6.94	54.94	63.18	42.53	18.83	26g
Capital Accounts	....	....	....	....	....	....	73.52	96.79	77.58	118.67	117.56	62.05	40.07	230.18	314.26	27a
Other Items (Net)	....	....	....	....	....	....	20.12	–3.64	–12.44	3.58	2.43	–43.16	–19.39	13.70	29.04	27r
Banking Survey	*End of Period*															
Foreign Assets (Net)	....	....	....	....	....	....	321.94	371.98	306.00	428.82	556.97	377.31	341.86	522.72	517.48	31n
Domestic Credit	....	....	....	....	....	....	267.79	†460.96	340.22	356.93	504.98	664.22	759.05	1,105.94	1,486.61	32
Claims on Central Govt. (Net)	....	....	....	....	....	....	–3.12	†79.04	119.59	120.71	110.66	77.55	74.60	155.77	62.46	32an
Claims on Local Government	....	....	....	....	....	....	—	6.66	11.51	15.52	2.66	4.41	15.77	36.22	51.71	32b
Claims on Nonfin.Pub.Enterprises	....	....	....	....	....	....	16.94	39.59	24.99	17.71	28.15	23.82	30.61	52.53	81.21	32c
Claims on Private Sector	....	....	....	....	....	....	253.97	335.67	184.13	202.99	344.28	533.10	612.18	804.74	1,100.54	32d
Claims on Nonbank Financial Insts.	....	....	....	....	....	....	—	—	—	—	19.24	25.34	25.90	56.69	190.68	32g
Money	....	....	....	....	....	....	267.78	351.13	353.78	425.65	567.27	601.27	639.34	764.57	863.59	34
Quasi-Money	....	....	....	....	....	....	196.49	346.82	195.06	230.50	331.56	357.60	398.73	554.19	716.43	35
Money Market Instruments	....	....	....	....	....	....	—	—	—	—	—	—	—	—	—	36aa
Government Lending Funds	....	....	....	....	....	....	16.94	61.43	39.68	22.00	19.66	16.73	22.48	22.55	21.26	36f
Capital Accounts	....	....	....	....	....	....	88.23	104.81	88.58	139.56	154.16	109.27	87.30	282.19	375.89	37a
Other Items (Net)	....	....	....	....	....	....	20.30	–31.24	–30.88	–31.97	–10.69	–43.34	–46.94	5.14	26.91	37r
Money plus Quasi-Money	....	....	....	....	....	....	464.27	697.95	548.84	656.15	898.83	958.87	1,038.07	1,318.77	1,580.02	35l
Interest Rates	*Percent Per Annum*															
Discount Rate *(End of Period)*	....	....	....	....	....	....	27.00	25.00	24.00	9.50	4.00	4.00	4.00	3.50	3.50	60
Money Market Rate	....	....	....	....	....	....	....	37.18	22.39	13.08	3.76	4.42	4.72	2.97	5.23	60b
Treasury Bill Rate	....	....	....	....	....	....	....	....	28.24	16.27	4.73	5.27	6.23	3.83	5.14	60c
Deposit Rate	....	....	....	....	....	....	34.78	31.68	14.79	11.71	5.90	5.33	5.04	4.38	5.24	60l
Lending Rate	....	....	....	....	....	....	86.36	55.86	34.56	25.78	15.25	14.29	14.20	11.87	11.17	60p
Prices, Production, Labor	*Period Averages*															
Producer Prices	....	....	....	....	....	35.2	76.5	89.4	100.0	113.7	118.4	120.6	115.7	116.5	118.5	63
Consumer Prices	....	....	....	....	8.2	†28.2	58.9	80.0	100.0	117.6	127.5	133.5	136.6	140.3	143.7	64
Wages: Average Earnings	....	....	....	....	....	23.8	50.4	80.6	100.0	114.9	139.7	148.8	154.7	159.7	167.5	65
Industrial Employment	....	....	....	....	....	153.3	129.9	106.1	100.0	94.4	97.7	89.7	86.4	87.9	87.6	67
	Period Averages															
Labor Force	....	....	....	....	....	1,367	1,320	1,300	....	1,182	1,186	1,168	1,157	1,132	....	67d
Employment	....	....	....	....	....	1,294	1,205	1,083	1,046	1,018	1,037	1,043	1,038	1,038	....	67e
Unemployment	....	....	....	....	....	31	77	84	83	91	85	111	110	93	....	67c
Unemployment Rate (%)	....	....	....	....	....	2.3	5.8	6.5	6.6	7.2	7.0	9.2	9.1	7.8	....	67r
International Transactions	*Millions of Lats*															
Exports	....	....	....	....	....	573	676	553	688	795	972	1,069	1,008	1,131	1,256	70
Imports, c.i.f.	....	....	....	....	....	....	....	....	960	1,278	1,582	1,881	1,724	1,934	2,202	71
Imports, f.o.b.	....	....	....	....	....	....	639	695	923	1,223	1,513	1,796	1,652	....	....	71.v
	Period Averages															
Volume of Exports	....	....	....	....	....	....	129.7	87.9	100.0	108.0	143.2	144.9	147.7	169.1	173.3	72
Unit Value of Exports	....	....	....	....	....	....	74.7	86.1	100.0	106.2	107.9	107.8	103.8	102.5	105.2	74

Latvia

		1972	1973	1974	1975	1976	1977	1978	1979	1980	1981	1982	1983	1984	1985	1986
Balance of Payments																*Millions of US Dollars:*
Current Account, n.i.e.	78al d	....	....	....	....	....	....	....	....	....	....	....	....	....	....	....
Goods: Exports f.o.b.	78aa d	....	....	....	....	....	....	....	....	....	....	....	....	....	....	....
Goods: Imports f.o.b.	78ab d	....	....	....	....	....	....	....	....	....	....	....	....	....	....	....
Trade Balance	78ac d	....	....	....	....	....	....	....	....	....	....	....	....	....	....	....
Services: Credit	78ad d	....	....	....	....	....	....	....	....	....	....	....	....	....	....	....
Services: Debit	78ae d	....	....	....	....	....	....	....	....	....	....	....	....	....	....	....
Balance on Goods & Services	78af d	....	....	....	....	....	....	....	....	....	....	....	....	....	....	....
Income: Credit	78ag d	....	....	....	....	....	....	....	....	....	....	....	....	....	....	....
Income: Debit	78ah d	....	....	....	....	....	....	....	....	....	....	....	....	....	....	....
Balance on Gds, Serv. & Inc.	78ai d	....	....	....	....	....	....	....	....	....	....	....	....	....	....	....
Current Transfers, n.i.e.: Credit	78aj d	....	....	....	....	....	....	....	....	....	....	....	....	....	....	....
Current Transfers: Debit	78ak d	....	....	....	....	....	....	....	....	....	....	....	....	....	....	....
Capital Account, n.i.e.	78bc d	....	....	....	....	....	....	....	....	....	....	....	....	....	....	....
Capital Account, n.i.e.: Credit	78ba d	....	....	....	....	....	....	....	....	....	....	....	....	....	....	....
Capital Account: Debit	78bb d	....	....	....	....	....	....	....	....	....	....	....	....	....	....	....
Financial Account, n.i.e.	78bj d	....	....	....	....	....	....	....	....	....	....	....	....	....	....	....
Direct Investment Abroad	78bd d	....	....	....	....	....	....	....	....	....	....	....	....	....	....	....
Dir. Invest. in Rep. Econ., n.i.e.	78be d	....	....	....	....	....	....	....	....	....	....	....	....	....	....	....
Portfolio Investment Assets	78bf d	....	....	....	....	....	....	....	....	....	....	....	....	....	....	....
Equity Securities	78bk d	....	....	....	....	....	....	....	....	....	....	....	....	....	....	....
Debt Securities	78bl d	....	....	....	....	....	....	....	....	....	....	....	....	....	....	....
Portfolio Investment Liab., n.i.e.	78bg d	....	....	....	....	....	....	....	....	....	....	....	....	....	....	....
Equity Securities	78bm d	....	....	....	....	....	....	....	....	....	....	....	....	....	....	....
Debt Securities	78bn d	....	....	....	....	....	....	....	....	....	....	....	....	....	....	....
Financial Derivatives Assets	78bw d	....	....	....	....	....	....	....	....	....	....	....	....	....	....	....
Financial Derivatives Liabilities	78bx d	....	....	....	....	....	....	....	....	....	....	....	....	....	....	....
Other Investment Assets	78bh d	....	....	....	....	....	....	....	....	....	....	....	....	....	....	....
Monetary Authorities	78bo d	....	....	....	....	....	....	....	....	....	....	....	....	....	....	....
General Government	78bp d	....	....	....	....	....	....	....	....	....	....	....	....	....	....	....
Banks	78bq d	....	....	....	....	....	....	....	....	....	....	....	....	....	....	....
Other Sectors	78br d	....	....	....	....	....	....	....	....	....	....	....	....	....	....	....
Other Investment Liab., n.i.e.	78bi d	....	....	....	....	....	....	....	....	....	....	....	....	....	....	....
Monetary Authorities	78bs d	....	....	....	....	....	....	....	....	....	....	....	....	....	....	....
General Government	78bt d	....	....	....	....	....	....	....	....	....	....	....	....	....	....	....
Banks	78bu d	....	....	....	....	....	....	....	....	....	....	....	....	....	....	....
Other Sectors	78bv d	....	....	....	....	....	....	....	....	....	....	....	....	....	....	....
Net Errors and Omissions	78ca d	....	....	....	....	....	....	....	....	....	....	....	....	....	....	....
Overall Balance	78cb d	....	....	....	....	....	....	....	....	....	....	....	....	....	....	....
Reserves and Related Items	79da d	....	....	....	....	....	....	....	....	....	....	....	....	....	....	....
Reserve Assets	79db d	....	....	....	....	....	....	....	....	....	....	....	....	....	....	....
Use of Fund Credit and Loans	79dc d	....	....	....	....	....	....	....	....	....	....	....	....	....	....	....
Exceptional Financing	79de d	....	....	....	....	....	....	....	....	....	....	....	....	....	....	....
International Investment Position																*Millions of US Dollars*
Assets	79aa d	....	....	....	....	....	....	....	....	....	....	....	....	....	....	....
Direct Investment Abroad	79ab d	....	....	....	....	....	....	....	....	....	....	....	....	....	....	....
Portfolio Investment	79ac d	....	....	....	....	....	....	....	....	....	....	....	....	....	....	....
Equity Securities	79ad d	....	....	....	....	....	....	....	....	....	....	....	....	....	....	....
Debt Securities	79ae d	....	....	....	....	....	....	....	....	....	....	....	....	....	....	....
Financial Derivatives	79al d	....	....	....	....	....	....	....	....	....	....	....	....	....	....	....
Other Investment	79af d	....	....	....	....	....	....	....	....	....	....	....	....	....	....	....
Monetary Authorities	79ag d	....	....	....	....	....	....	....	....	....	....	....	....	....	....	....
General Government	79ah d	....	....	....	....	....	....	....	....	....	....	....	....	....	....	....
Banks	79ai d	....	....	....	....	....	....	....	....	....	....	....	....	....	....	....
Other Sectors	79aj d	....	....	....	....	....	....	....	....	....	....	....	....	....	....	....
Reserve Assets	79ak d	....	....	....	....	....	....	....	....	....	....	....	....	....	....	....
Liabilities	79la d	....	....	....	....	....	....	....	....	....	....	....	....	....	....	....
Dir. Invest. in Rep. Economy	79lb d	....	....	....	....	....	....	....	....	....	....	....	....	....	....	....
Portfolio Investment	79lc d	....	....	....	....	....	....	....	....	....	....	....	....	....	....	....
Equity Securities	79ld d	....	....	....	....	....	....	....	....	....	....	....	....	....	....	....
Debt Securities	79le d	....	....	....	....	....	....	....	....	....	....	....	....	....	....	....
Financial Derivatives	79ll d	....	....	....	....	....	....	....	....	....	....	....	....	....	....	....
Other Investment	79lf d	....	....	....	....	....	....	....	....	....	....	....	....	....	....	....
Monetary Authorities	79lg d	....	....	....	....	....	....	....	....	....	....	....	....	....	....	....
General Government	79lh d	....	....	....	....	....	....	....	....	....	....	....	....	....	....	....
Banks	79li d	....	....	....	....	....	....	....	....	....	....	....	....	....	....	....
Other Sectors	79lj d	....	....	....	....	....	....	....	....	....	....	....	....	....	....	....

Minus Sign Indicates Debit

Balance of Payments

1987	1988	1989	1990	1991	1992	1993	1994	1995	1996	1997	1998	1999	2000	2001		
....	....	....	....	....	191	417	201	−16	−280	−345	−650	−654	−494	−758	Current Account, n.i.e.	78al *d*
....	....	....	....	....	800	1,054	1,022	1,368	1,488	1,838	2,011	1,889	2,058	2,216	Goods: Exports f.o.b.	78aa *d*
....	....	....	....	....	−840	−1,051	−1,322	−1,947	−2,286	−2,686	−3,141	−2,916	−3,116	−3,566	Goods: Imports f.o.b.	78ab *d*
....	....	....	....	....	−40	3	−301	−580	−798	−848	−1,130	−1,027	−1,058	−1,351	*Trade Balance*	78ac *d*
....	....	....	....	....	291	533	657	720	1,126	1,033	1,108	1,024	1,212	1,235	Services: Credit	78ad *d*
....	....	....	....	....	−156	−205	−297	−246	−742	−662	−806	−689	−770	−752	Services: Debit	78ae *d*
....	....	....	....	....	94	332	60	−106	−414	−477	−827	−691	−616	−867	*Balance on Goods & Services*	78af *d*
....	....	....	....	....	3	17	51	71	140	177	207	158	215	278	Income: Credit	78ag *d*
....	....	....	....	....	−1	−10	−42	−53	−99	−122	−154	−214	−191	−249	Income: Debit	78ah *d*
....	....	....	....	....	95	339	68	−87	−373	−422	−774	−747	−592	−838	*Balance on Gds, Serv. & Inc.*	78ai *d*
....	....	....	....	....	97	81	136	75	98	91	137	114	203	221	Current Transfers, n.i.e.: Credit	78aj *d*
....	....	....	....	....	−1	−3	−3	−5	−5	−14	−13	−21	−105	−141	Current Transfers: Debit	78ak *d*
....	....	....	....	....	....	....	....	....	....	14	14	13	30	37	Capital Account, n.i.e.	78bc *d*
....	....	....	....	....						14	14	13	39	49	Capital Account, n.i.e.: Credit	78ba *d*
....	....	....	....	....						—	—	—	−9	−12	Capital Account: Debit	78bb *d*
....	....	....	....	....	−110	67	363	636	537	347	601	768	514	997	Financial Account, n.i.e.	78bj *d*
....	....	....	....	....	−2	5	65	65	−3	−6	−54	−17	−9	−7	Direct Investment Abroad	78bd *d*
....	....	....	....	....	29	45	214	180	382	521	357	348	407	201	Dir. Invest. in Rep. Econ., n.i.e.	78be *d*
....	....	....	....	....	—	—	−22	−37	−165	−539	−33	58	−346	−57	Portfolio Investment Assets	78bf *d*
....	....	....	....	....	....	—	−12	−7	12	−113	7	77	−40	6	Equity Securities	78bk *d*
....	....	....	....	....	—	—	−10	−30	−177	−426	−40	−19	−306	−64	Debt Securities	78bl *d*
....	....	....	....	....	....	....	....	—	24	−32	27	215	25	189	Portfolio Investment Liab., n.i.e.	78bg *d*
....	....	....	....	....				—	−2	6	30	7	−7	5	Equity Securities	78bm *d*
....	....	....	....	....					26	−39	−3	209	32	183	Debt Securities	78bn *d*
....	....	....	....	....						—	—	—	2	3	Financial Derivatives Assets	78bw *d*
....	....	....	....	....										−3	Financial Derivatives Liabilities	78bx *d*
....	....	....	....	....	−371	−129	−387	−31	−214	−326	75	−214	−338	−57	Other Investment Assets	78bh *d*
....	....	....	....	....	−24	39	5	1	−1	—	—	36	25	—	Monetary Authorities	78bo *d*
....	....	....	....	....	3				—	—	—	—	—	−7	General Government	78bp *d*
....	....	....	....	....	−59	−119	−400	99	−261	−253	67	−275	−370	−107	Banks	78bq *d*
....	....	....	....	....	−291	−50	8	−130	48	−73	9	25	8	56	Other Sectors	78br *d*
....	....	....	....	....	234	146	493	458	513	730	229	379	773	729	Other Investment Liab., n.i.e.	78bi *d*
....	....	....	....	....	10	−4	−5	—	—	—	—	6	—	1	Monetary Authorities	78bs *d*
....	....	....	....	....	22	99	54	55	45	20	45	14	−8	7	General Government	78bt *d*
....	....	....	....	....	5	76	272	88	385	558	69	354	719	529	Banks	78bu *d*
....	....	....	....	....	198	−25	172	315	84	152	115	4	62	191	Other Sectors	78bv *d*
....	....	....	....	....	−44	−186	−508	−653	−46	87	97	38	−21	38	Net Errors and Omissions	78ca *d*
....	....	....	....	....	37	298	57	−33	211	102	63	165	28	314	*Overall Balance*	78cb *d*
....	....	....	....	....	−37	−298	−57	33	−211	−102	−63	−165	−28	−314	Reserves and Related Items	79da *d*
....	....	....	....	....	−73	−371	−103	36	−186	−65	−38	−150	−18	−305	Reserve Assets	79db *d*
....	....	....	....	....	36	74	47	−3	−25	−37	−25	−15	−10	−10	Use of Fund Credit and Loans	79dc *d*
....	....	....	....	....	....	....	....	....	....	....	....	....	....	....	Exceptional Financing	79de *d*

Millions of US Dollars

International Investment Position

1987	1988	1989	1990	1991	1992	1993	1994	1995	1996	1997	1998	1999	2000	2001		
....	....	....	....	....	....	....	....	1,851	2,366	3,244	3,050	3,262	3,964	3,989	Assets	79aa *d*
....	....	....	....	....	....	....	....	231	209	222	281	215	242	42	Direct Investment Abroad	79ab *d*
....	....	....	....	....	....	....	....	62	227	755	590	533	854	665	Portfolio Investment	79ac *d*
....	....	....	....	....	....	....	....	21	9	122	113	37	63	56	Equity Securities	79ad *d*
....	....	....	....	....	....	....	....	41	218	633	477	495	791	610	Debt Securities	79ae *d*
....	....	....	....	....	....	....	....	—	—	—	—	—	—	3	Financial Derivatives	79al *d*
....	....	....	....	....	....	....	....	972	1,158	1,442	1,298	1,602	1,950	2,061	Other Investment	79af *d*
....	....	....	....	....	....	....	....	2	3	2	1	36	1	1	Monetary Authorities	79ag *d*
....	....	....	....	....	....	....	....	—	—	—	—	—	3	9	General Government	79ah *d*
....	....	....	....	....	....	....	....	542	800	1,047	871	1,135	1,516	1,615	Banks	79ai *d*
....	....	....	....	....	....	....	....	429	356	392	426	431	430	436	Other Sectors	79aj *d*
....	....	....	....	....	....	....	....	586	772	825	881	913	919	1,218	Reserve Assets	79ak *d*
....	....	....	....	....	....	....	....	1,932	2,717	3,707	4,250	5,235	6,109	6,927	Liabilities	79la *d*
....	....	....	....	....	....	....	....	616	936	1,272	1,558	1,885	2,081	2,216	Dir. Invest. in Rep. Economy	79lb *d*
....	....	....	....	....	....	....	....	23	46	13	43	275	259	434	Portfolio Investment	79lc *d*
....	....	....	....	....	....	....	....	7	5	9	42	51	40	45	Equity Securities	79ld *d*
....	....	....	....	....	....	....	....	16	41	4	1	224	219	389	Debt Securities	79le *d*
....	....	....	....	....	....	....	....	—	—	—	—	—	—	7	Financial Derivatives	79ll *d*
....	....	....	....	....	....	....	....	1,294	1,735	2,422	2,650	3,076	3,769	4,270	Other Investment	79lf *d*
....	....	....	....	....	....	....	....	161	130	87	64	54	36	27	Monetary Authorities	79lg *d*
....	....	....	....	....	....	....	....	242	279	284	343	346	326	324	General Government	79lh *d*
....	....	....	....	....	....	....	....	399	782	1,332	1,278	1,618	2,328	2,615	Banks	79li *d*
....	....	....	....	....	....	....	....	492	544	719	965	1,058	1,079	1,304	Other Sectors	79lj *d*

Latvia

	1972	1973	1974	1975	1976	1977	1978	1979	1980	1981	1982	1983	1984	1985	1986
Government Finance															*Millions of Lats:*
Deficit (-) or Surplus ... 80	....	....	....	....	....	....	....	....	....	....	....	....	....	....	....
Total Revenue and Grants ... 81y	....	....	....	....	....	....	....	....	....	....	....	....	....	....	....
Revenue ... 81	....	....	....	....	....	....	....	....	....	....	....	....	....	....	....
Grants ... 81z	....	....	....	....	....	....	....	....	....	....	....	....	....	....	....
Exp. & Lending Minus Repay. ... 82z	....	....	....	....	....	....	....	....	....	....	....	....	....	....	....
Expenditure ... 82	....	....	....	....	....	....	....	....	....	....	....	....	....	....	....
Lending Minus Repayments ... 83	....	....	....	....	....	....	....	....	....	....	....	....	....	....	....
Total Financing ... 80h	....	....	....	....	....	....	....	....	....	....	....	....	....	....	....
Domestic ... 84a	....	....	....	....	....	....	....	....	....	....	....	....	....	....	....
Foreign ... 85a	....	....	....	....	....	....	....	....	....	....	....	....	....	....	....
National Accounts															*Millions of Lats*
Househ.Cons.Expend.,incl.NPISHs ... 96f	....	....	....	....	....	....	....	....	....	....	....	....	....	....	....
Government Consumption Expend. ... 91f	....	....	....	....	....	....	....	....	....	....	....	....	....	....	....
Gross Fixed Capital Formation ... 93e	....	....	....	....	....	....	....	....	....	....	....	....	....	....	....
Changes in Inventories ... 93i	....	....	....	....	....	....	....	....	....	....	....	....	....	....	....
Exports of Goods and Services (-) ... 90c	....	....	....	....	....	....	....	....	....	....	....	....	....	....	....
Imports of Goods and Services (-) ... 98c	....	....	....	....	....	....	....	....	....	....	....	....	....	....	....
Gross Domestic Product (GDP) ... 99b	....	....	....	....	....	....	....	....	....	....	....	....	....	....	....
Net Primary Income from Abroad ... 98.n	....	....	....	....	....	....	....	....	....	....	....	....	....	....	....
Gross National Income (GNI) ... 99a	....	....	....	....	....	....	....	....	....	....	....	....	....	....	....
Net Current Transf.from Abroad ... 98t	....	....	....	....	....	....	....	....	....	....	....	....	....	....	....
Gross Nat'l Disposable Inc.(GNDI) ... 99i	....	....	....	....	....	....	....	....	....	....	....	....	....	....	....
Gross Saving ... 99s	....	....	....	....	....	....	....	....	....	....	....	....	....	....	....
Consumption of Fixed Capital ... 99cf	....	....	....	....	....	....	....	....	....	....	....	....	....	....	....
GDP Volume 1995 Prices ... 99b.*p*	....	....	....	....	....	....	....	....	....	....	....	....	....	....	....
GDP Volume (1995=100) ... 99bv*p*	....	....	....	....	....	....	....	....	....	....	....	....	....	....	....
GDP Deflator (1995=100) ... 99bi*p*	....	....	....	....	....	....	....	....	....	....	....	....	....	....	....
Population ... 99z	....	....	....	....	....	....	....	....	....	....	....	....	....	....	*Millions:* ....

1987	1988	1989	1990	1991	1992	1993	1994	1995	1996	1997	1998	1999	2000	2001		
Year Ending December 31															**Government Finance**	
...	...	...	...	...	...	...	...	....	†−44.13	†23.34	†5.32	−140.15	−118.96	−67.96	Deficit (-) or Surplus	80
...	...	...	...	...	...	...	...	357.10	†874.92	1,174.54	†1289.69	1,291.17	1,305.64	1,383.04	Total Revenue and Grants	81y
...	...	...	...	...	...	...	...	....						....	Revenue	81
...	...	...	...	...	...	...	...								Grants	81z
...	...	...	...	...	...	...	...	....	†919.05	†1151.20	†1284.37	1,431.32	1,424.60	1,451.00	Exp. & Lending Minus Repay.	82z
...	...	...	...	...	...	...	...	445.60	†907.14	†1116.81	†1283.65	1,419.29	1,412.14	1,442.07	Expenditure	82
...	...	...	...	...	...	...	...	....	†11.91	34.39	†.72	12.03	12.46	8.93	Lending Minus Repayments	83
...	...	...	...	...	...	...	...	....	†44.13	−23.34	†−5.32	140.15	118.96	67.96	Total Financing	80h
...	...	...	...	...	...	...	...	....	†31.81	−41.06	†−18.38	13.28	130.97	−37.57	Domestic	84a
...	...	...	...	...	...	...	...	....	†12.32	17.72	†13.06	126.87	−12.01	105.53	Foreign	85a
Millions of Lats															**National Accounts**	
...	...	...	328.9	662.5	407.9	794.0	1,240.1	1,485.3	1,975.5	2,248.8	2,387.9	2,489.7	2,759.5	2,951.9	Househ.Cons.Expend.,incl.NPISHs	96f
...	...	...	5.4	14.7	125.4	324.1	410.6	521.8	612.3	626.2	768.1	800.2	859.3	950.0	Government Consumption Expend.	91f
...	...	...	14.4	8.8	112.3	201.8	303.9	354.9	512.8	613.7	979.5	980.0	1,151.5	1,219.4	Gross Fixed Capital Formation	93e
...	...	...	10.7	39.5	301.9	−67.2	86.9	58.7	19.9	132.6	11.3	73.0	8.0	153.4	Changes in Inventories	93i
...	...	...	29.8	50.5	803.1	1,074.4	948.8	1,101.0	1,440.1	1,669.1	1,841.4	1,708.1	1,983.8	2,167.4	Exports of Goods and Services	90c
...	...	...	30.6	36.5	734.0	835.9	906.8	1,157.8	1,668.8	1,947.3	2,326.8	2,109.8	2,360.0	2,712.9	Imports of Goods and Services (-)	98c
...	...	...	62.4	143.3	1,004.6	1,467.0	2,042.6	2,349.2	2,829.1	3,275.5	3,589.5	3,897.0	4,336.1	4,740.8	Gross Domestic Product (GDP)	99b
...	...	...	1.0	2.2	1.1	−1.3	−4.0	11.5	22.9	32.1	31.9	−27.6	15.8	18.6	Net Primary Income from Abroad	98.n
...	...	...	63.5	145.5	1,005.7	1,465.7	2,038.5	2,360.7	2,852.1	3,307.5	3,621.3	3,869.4	4,351.9	4,759.4	Gross National Income (GNI)	99a
...	...	...	...	...	70.8	51.8	74.3	35.8	51.6	45.0	73.2	54.3	....	....	Net Current Transf.from Abroad	98t
...	...	...	...	...	1,076.5	1,517.5	2,112.9	2,396.5	2,903.7	3,352.5	3,694.5	3,923.7	....	....	Gross Nat'l Disposable Inc.(GNDI)	99i
...	...	...	25.1	65.2	555.2	423.6	503.2	404.2	378.4	545.2	310.4	678.0	....	....	Gross Saving	99s
...	...	...	5.2	5.7	14.9	143.4	254.7	286.9	304.3	344.5	469.5	490.0	....	....	Consumption of Fixed Capital	99cf
...	...	...	4,736.6	4,243.4	2,764.2	2,353.2	2,368.4	2,349.2	2,427.7	2,636.8	2,739.1	2,768.6	2,957.8	3,181.5	GDP Volume 1995 Prices	99b.*p*
...	...	...	201.6	180.6	117.7	100.2	100.8	100.0	103.3	112.2	116.6	117.9	125.9	....	GDP Volume (1995=100)	99bv *p*
...	...	...	1.3	3.4	36.3	62.3	86.2	100.0	116.5	124.2	131.0	140.8	146.6	149.0	GDP Deflator (1995=100)	99bi *p*
Midyear Estimates																
...	...	...		2.66	2.63	2.59	2.55	2.51	2.49	2.47	2.45	2.43	2.43	2.36	**Population**	99z

(See notes in the back of the book.)

Lebanon

446		1972	1973	1974	1975	1976	1977	1978	1979	1980	1981	1982	1983	1984	1985	1986
Exchange Rates																*Pounds per SDR:*
Market Rate	**aa**	3.3	3.0	2.8	2.8	3.4	3.6	3.9	4.3	4.7	5.4	4.2	5.7	8.7	19.9	106.4
																Pounds per US Dollar:
Market Rate	**ae**	3.0	2.5	2.3	2.4	2.9	3.0	3.0	3.3	3.6	4.6	3.8	5.5	8.9	18.1	87.0
Market Rate	**rf**	3.1	2.6	2.3	2.3[e]	2.9	3.1	3.0	3.2	3.4	4.3	4.7	4.5	6.5	16.4	38.4
																Index Numbers (1995=100):
Market Rate	**ahx**	53,258.45	62,478.04	69,839.43	70,616.98[e]	57,236.80	52,932.74	54,967.03	50,131.55	47,314.24	37,857.06	34,465.79	36,312.94	25,471.03	10,138.06	5,017.24
Nominal Effective Exchange Rate	**nec**	....	....	....	....	....	....	....	35,017.78	33,082.87	31,202.85	31,990.65	36,263.01	27,922.17	11,650.42	4,696.38
Fund Position																*Millions of SDRs:*
Quota	**2f.s**	9.0	9.0	9.0	9.0	9.0	9.0	12.0	12.0	27.9	27.9	27.9	78.7	78.7	78.7	78.7
SDRs	**1b.s**	—	—	—	—	—	—	—	1.3	—	1.9	2.0	—	.8	1.8	2.6
Reserve Position in the Fund	**1c.s**	2.3	2.3	2.3	2.3	2.3	2.3	2.3	2.1	6.1	6.1	6.1	18.8	18.8	18.8	18.8
Total Fund Cred.&Loans Outstg.	**2tl**	—	—	—	—	—	—	—	—	—	—	—	—	—	—	—
International Liquidity																*Millions of US Dollars Unless Otherwise Indicated:*
Total Reserves minus Gold	**1l.d**	324.9	472.4	1,278.8	1,201.7	1,302.6	1,568.8	1,834.9	1,531.5	1,588.2	1,516.4	2,608.1	1,902.5	671.6	1,073.8	488.0
SDRs	**1b.d**	—	—	—	—	—	—	—	1.6	—	2.2	2.3	—	.8	1.9	3.2
Reserve Position in the Fund	**1c.d**	2.5	2.7	2.8	2.7	2.6	2.8	3.0	2.8	7.8	7.1	6.8	19.7	18.5	20.7	23.0
Foreign Exchange	**1d.d**	322.4	469.7	1,276.0	1,199.0	1,300.0	1,566.0	1,831.9	1,527.0	1,580.4	1,507.0	2,599.1	1,882.8	652.3	1,051.2	461.8
Gold (Million Fine Troy Ounces)	**1ad**	9.211	9.217	9.215	9.215	9.215	9.218	9.218	9.222	9.222	9.222	9.222	9.222	9.222	9.222	9.222
Gold (National Valuation)	**1and**	350.2	389.1	386.1	389.1	389.0	389.2	389.2	389.4	389.4	389.4	†389.4	389.4	389.4	389.4	389.4
Monetary Authorities: Other Liab.	**4..d**	1.6	2.1	2.5	2.7	19.7	21.5	24.8	21.4	21.9	22.0	17.1	1.6	1.3	1.1	1.1
Deposit Money Banks: Assets	**7a.d**	1,056.0	1,443.8	1,730.5	2,103.8	1,544.2	1,923.5	2,017.6	2,879.3	3,673.9	4,336.7	3,695.9	3,284.8	2,948.0	2,559.0	2,753.2
Liabilities	**7b.d**	389.9	605.4	881.5	1,178.1	958.0	852.5	1,030.3	1,200.1	1,577.1	1,594.8	1,782.6	1,603.7	1,390.4	1,019.0	745.6
Monetary Authorities																*Millions of Pounds through 1985;*
Foreign Assets	**11**	2,048.5	2,165.7	3,810.7	3,865.2	4,957.2	5,872.9	6,683.4	6,251.8	7,213.4	8,803.1	11,411.9	12,582.4	9,423.7	26,450.4	†76.1
Claims on Central Government	**12a**	12.9	197.4	300.8	144.5	802.6	891.4	843.1	1,476.2	1,924.1	1,957.3	3,090.2	5,198.3	12,481.2	15,642.2	†34.8
Claims on Private Sector	**12d**	52.4	50.7	37.6	44.8	45.4	32.9	76.4	110.3	128.7	147.6	267.3	323.1	515.6	371.0	†.5
Claims on Deposit Money Banks	**12e**	100.1	172.8	71.2	109.2	164.6	100.9	77.3	71.9	60.3	125.7	116.2	127.3	1,122.1	1,262.0	†1.4
Reserve Money	**14**	1,643.1	1,877.1	3,131.3	3,171.6	4,228.7	4,751.1	5,384.2	5,208.9	6,197.3	7,156.4	10,147.0	11,583.5	13,169.8	18,642.0	†25.1
of which: Currency Outside DMBs	**14a**	1,032.7	1,226.0	1,353.0	2,240.9	3,083.5	2,729.1	3,286.2	3,506.2	3,982.4	4,625.1	5,582.3	7,057.7	7,668.7	10,267.2	†14.7
Foreign Liabilities	**16c**	4.8	5.2	5.7	6.5	57.8	64.4	74.4	69.8	79.8	101.8	65.3	8.8	11.4	20.6	†.1
Long-Term Foreign Liabilities	**16cl**	....	....	....	....	....	....	....	....	....	....	....	....	....	....	....
Central Government Deposits	**16d**	465.6	593.1	978.0	901.9	1,491.2	1,843.4	1,716.4	1,828.8	1,448.5	1,543.6	3,862.6	3,142.6	4,019.6	9,561.0	†18.6
Capital Accounts	**17a**	41.4	58.7	58.7	126.0	161.2	212.8	212.8	278.1	369.6	494.0	665.2	858.5	858.5	1,267.0	†1.7
Other Items (Net)	**17r**	59.1	52.6	46.4	–42.2	30.9	26.4	292.6	524.6	1,231.3	1,738.0	145.5	2,637.7	5,483.3	14,235.0	†67.1
of which: Valuation Adjustment	**17rv**	....	....	....	....	....	....	....	....	604.0	1,430.0	–1,366.0	1,927.0	4,102.0	12,278.0	†62.2
Deposit Money Banks																*Millions of Pounds through 1985;*
Reserves	**20**	576.8	625.5	1,666.9	808.2	1,073.9	1,897.7	2,031.6	1,389.9	2,168.1	2,534.9	4,567.6	4,395.9	5,291.6	8,847.8	†9.7
Foreign Assets	**21**	3,178.5	3,624.0	3,980.2	5,112.2	4,524.5	5,770.4	6,063.0	9,379.3	13,400.4	20,057.1	14,081.3	18,033.3	26,207.8	46,317.3	†239.5
Claims on Central Government	**22a**	77.5	60.0	36.3	15.7	10.1	474.6	982.0	1,065.9	2,027.2	4,175.7	11,048.9	14,711.8	15,241.3	28,057.2	†37.1
Claims on Private Sector	**22d**	3,272.0	4,671.1	5,733.3	6,854.9	7,247.1	8,031.3	10,009.0	13,030.3	16,165.9	21,292.0	25,728.9	33,604.1	43,267.8	57,707.0	†127.1
Demand Deposits	**24**	1,239.3	1,389.9	1,642.2	1,587.7	1,803.6	2,299.6	2,838.0	3,151.7	3,668.4	4,359.7	5,467.8	5,867.7	6,089.0	9,852.0	†15.6
Time & Foreign Currency Deposits	**25**	4,105.5	5,112.1	6,578.2	6,813.9	6,299.2	9,309.3	11,078.0	15,182.2	21,157.9	31,388.7	37,485.2	48,773.1	62,492.1	98,947.9	†293.6
Foreign Liabilities	**26c**	1,173.5	1,519.5	2,027.4	2,862.8	2,806.8	2,557.6	3,096.0	3,909.3	5,752.4	7,376.1	6,791.8	8,804.5	12,360.7	18,444.7	†64.9
Central Government Deposits	**26d**	176.4	259.3	344.0	406.8	418.6	490.1	517.0	584.8	585.6	803.1	826.1	733.7	745.3	704.9	†.9
Credit from Monetary Authorities	**26g**	100.1	172.8	71.2	109.2	164.6	100.9	77.3	71.9	60.3	125.7	116.2	127.3	1,122.1	1,262.0	†1.4
Capital Accounts	**27a**	413.1	437.4	496.2	551.2	583.1	618.8	683.0	878.4	1,180.4	1,668.0	2,161.6	2,978.0	3,384.0	3,782.6	†4.2
Other Items (Net)	**27r**	–103.2	89.7	257.8	459.5	779.6	797.7	796.7	1,087.5	1,356.5	2,338.4	2,578.0	3,460.8	3,815.3	7,935.2	†33.0
Monetary Survey																*Millions of Pounds through 1985;*
Foreign Assets (Net)	**31n**	4,048.7	4,265.0	5,757.8	6,108.1	6,617.1	9,021.3	9,576.0	11,652.0	14,781.6	21,382.3	18,636.1	21,802.4	23,259.4	54,302.4	†250.6
Domestic Credit	**32**	2,772.8	4,126.8	4,786.0	5,751.2	6,195.4	7,096.7	9,677.1	13,269.1	18,211.8	25,225.9	35,446.6	49,961.0	66,741.0	91,511.5	†180.0
Claims on Central Govt. (Net)	**32an**	–551.6	–595.0	–984.9	–1,148.5	–1,097.1	–967.5	–408.3	128.5	1,917.2	3,786.3	9,450.4	16,033.8	22,957.6	33,433.5	†52.4
Claims on Private Sector	**32d**	3,324.4	4,721.8	5,770.9	6,899.7	7,292.5	8,064.2	10,085.4	13,140.6	16,294.6	21,439.6	25,996.2	33,927.2	43,783.4	58,078.0	†127.6
Money	**34**	2,274.7	2,618.9	2,998.2	3,835.9	4,904.8	5,061.5	6,147.8	6,683.8	7,666.6	9,005.1	11,069.8	12,945.0	13,783.6	20,154.2	†30.3
Quasi-Money	**35**	4,107.5	5,114.4	6,580.0	6,816.4	6,302.0	9,311.3	11,080.8	15,184.3	21,159.7	31,392.1	37,487.0	48,774.9	62,493.8	98,947.9	†293.6
Other Items (Net)	**37r**	439.3	658.7	965.7	1,207.2	1,605.6	1,745.2	2,025.1	3,053.4	4,167.0	6,211.1	5,525.9	10,043.5	13,723.0	26,711.8	†106.7
Money plus Quasi-Money	**35l**	6,382.2	7,733.3	9,578.2	10,652.3	11,206.8	14,372.8	17,228.6	21,868.1	28,826.3	40,397.2	48,556.8	61,719.9	76,277.4	119,102.1	†323.9
Interest Rates																*Percent Per Annum*
Discount Rate *(End of Period)*	**60**	3.00	5.00	7.00	7.00	6.00	6.00	6.00	8.50	10.00	13.00	12.00	12.00	12.00	19.70	21.85
Treasury Bill Rate	**60c**	....	....	....	....	....	....	....	9.50	10.40	14.00	14.02	9.52	13.08	14.96	†18.67
Deposit Rate	**60l**	....	....	....	....	....	....	....	....	....	....	12.94	10.01	11.53	13.24	16.42
Lending Rate	**60p**	....	....	....	....	....	....	....	....	....	....	16.83	14.53	15.58	17.29	22.21
International Transactions																*Billions of US Dollars*
Exports	**70..d**	377	921	1,636	1,233	546	760	830	850	955	920	800	760	378	288	550
Imports, c.i.f.	**71..d**	924	1,286	2,355	2,048	612	1,539	1,922	2,700	3,650	3,499	3,391	3,661	2,948	2,203	2,203
Government Finance																*Billions of Pounds:*
Deficit (-) or Surplus	**80**	....	....	....	....	....	....	....	....	....	....	....	....	....	....	....
Revenue	**81**	....	....	....	....	....	....	....	....	....	....	....	....	....	....	....
Grants Received	**81z**	....	....	....	....	....	....	....	....	....	....	....	....	....	....	....
Expenditure	**82**	....	....	....	....	....	....	....	....	....	....	....	....	....	....	....
Lending Minus Repayments	**83**	....	....	....	....	....	....	....	....	....	....	....	....	....	....	....
Financing																
Domestic	**84a**	....	....	....	....	....	....	....	....	....	....	....	....	....	....	....
Foreign	**85a**	....	....	....	....	....	....	....	....	....	....	....	....	....	....	....
Adj. to Total Financing	**84x**	....	....	....	....	....	....	....	....	....	....	....	....	....	....	....
Debt: Domestic	**88a**	....	....	....	....	....	....	....	....	....	....	....	....	....	....	....
Foreign	**89a**	....	....	....	....	....	....	....	....	....	....	....	....	....	....	....
																Millions:
Population	**99z**	2.60	2.66	2.73	2.77	2.77	2.76	2.73	2.70	2.67	2.66	2.66	2.66	2.68	2.67	2.64

1987	1988	1989	1990	1991	1992	1993	1994	1995	1996	1997	1998	1999	2000	2001		
															Exchange Rates	
End of Period																
645.5	713.2	663.7	1,197.9	1,257.3	2,527.3	2,350.2	2,404.4	2,372.4	2,231.7	2,060.3	2,123.3	2,069.1	1,964.1	1,894.5	Market Rate	aa
End of Period (ae) Period Average (rf)																
455.0	530.0	505.0	842.0	879.0	1,838.0	1,711.0	1,647.0	1,596.0	1,552.0	1,527.0	1,508.0	1,507.5	1,507.5	1,507.5	Market Rate	ae
224.6	409.2	496.7	695.1	928.2	1,712.8	1,741.4	1,680.1	1,621.4	1,571.4	1,539.5	1,516.1	1,507.8	1,507.5	1,507.5	Market Rate	rf
Period Averages																
1,030.18	404.68	328.61	241.64	175.54	105.91	93.16	96.53	100.00	103.18	105.35	106.93	107.53	107.55	107.63	Market Rate	ahx
846.41	320.57	274.59	191.63	147.07	90.64	91.61	100.89	100.00	106.66	120.40	127.58	131.78	144.14	151.67	Nominal Effective Exchange Rate	nec
															Fund Position	
End of Period																
78.7	78.7	78.7	78.7	78.7	78.7	78.7	146.0	146.0	146.0	146.0	146.0	203.0	203.0	203.0	Quota	2f. s
3.4	4.2	5.4	6.9	8.3	9.5	10.5	11.4	12.3	13.3	14.3	15.4	16.4	18.2	19.4	SDRs	1b. s
18.8	18.8	18.8	18.8	18.8	18.8	18.8	18.8	18.8	18.8	18.8	18.8	18.8	18.8	18.8	Reserve Position in the Fund	1c. s
														—	Total Fund Cred.&Loans Outstg.	2tl
															International Liquidity	
End of Period																
367.9	977.8	938.2	659.9	1,275.5	1,496.4	2,260.3	3,884.2	4,533.3	5,931.9	5,976.4	6,556.3	7,775.6	5,943.7	5,013.8	Total Reserves minus Gold	1l. d
4.8	5.7	7.1	9.8	11.8	13.0	14.4	16.6	18.3	19.2	19.3	21.7	22.5	23.7	24.3	SDRs	1b. d
26.7	25.3	24.7	26.8	26.9	25.9	25.9	27.5	28.0	27.1	25.4	26.5	25.8	24.5	23.7	Reserve Position in the Fund	1c. d
336.4	946.8	906.3	623.3	1,236.7	1,457.5	2,220.0	3,840.1	4,487.0	5,885.6	5,931.6	6,508.0	7,727.3	5,895.4	4,965.8	Foreign Exchange	1d. d
9.222	9.222	9.222	9.222	9.222	9.222	9.222	9.222	9.222	9.222	9.222	9.222	9.222	9.222	9.222	Gold (Million Fine Troy Ounces)	1ad
389.4	3,781.2	3,696.8	3,554.0	3,260.1	3,066.4	3,603.6	3,534.5	3,571.8	3,410.0	2,670.3	2,651.0	2,678.0	2,524.6	2,561.1	Gold (National Valuation)	1and
3.3	1.8	3.0	3.2	3.2	3.3	5.6	29.5	71.3	54.4	72.9	174.0	156.3	138.4	152.0	Monetary Authorities: Other Liab.	4.. d
3,153.1	3,198.9	2,887.6	2,820.1	3,482.6	3,169.1	4,114.9	3,806.5	3,970.7	4,329.2	6,014.4	6,620.8	5,910.8	8,159.3	8,615.7	Deposit Money Banks: Assets	7a. d
899.9	943.0	887.5	901.3	1,019.1	950.5	1,198.6	1,579.7	2,063.4	2,989.5	4,189.3	5,908.2	6,392.5	7,190.2	7,347.2	Liabilities	7b. d
															Monetary Authorities	
Billions of Pounds Beginning 1986: End of Period																
342.4	2,519.2	2,337.0	3,539.9	3,976.3	8,362.5	10,025.9	12,208.7	12,923.9	14,486.2	13,191.4	13,851.8	15,725.0	12,730.1	10,531.7	Foreign Assets	11
119.0	98.1	151.0	589.1	252.5	236.3	427.8	31.6	57.2	63.6	354.8	113.0	147.5	2,060.8	6,835.9	Claims on Central Government	12a
1.0	1.2	6.8	17.9	20.1	95.1	44.4	73.1	120.0	338.7	587.7	640.3	578.7	628.8	696.1	Claims on Private Sector	12d
1.5	2.0	93.3	169.1	189.2	163.9	187.1	166.8	289.9	105.1	96.8	346.1	405.9	734.8	781.0	Claims on Deposit Money Banks	12e
57.7	196.0	332.0	509.1	800.1	1,521.9	2,159.8	3,816.7	4,624.5	5,604.4	8,404.0	7,944.3	8,378.2	8,927.4	12,246.5	Reserve Money	14
39.2	116.2	192.4	332.9	484.6	798.0	714.7	938.8	1,046.2	1,160.7	1,210.1	1,241.3	1,369.3	1,423.4	1,381.7	*of which: Currency Outside DMBs*	14a
1.5	.9	1.5	2.7	2.8	6.0	9.6	48.6	113.8	84.4	111.3	262.3	235.6	208.7	229.1	Foreign Liabilities	16c
....	....	....	....	....	....	....	....	....	....	....	1,068.1	1,068.1	1,068.1	1,386.2	Long-Term Foreign Liabilities	16cl
96.6	186.6	104.5	200.6	289.4	927.4	1,237.3	2,383.5	2,440.5	3,585.5	1,189.3	1,795.8	3,304.4	1,910.2	1,401.9	Central Government Deposits	16d
2.7	14.5	14.5	26.7	60.1	79.9	95.7	88.5	134.1	312.7	328.1	796.7	883.1	911.9	1,049.2	Capital Accounts	17a
305.3	2,222.5	2,135.6	3,576.8	3,285.8	6,322.6	7,182.8	6,142.7	6,078.2	5,406.6	4,197.8	3,084.2	2,987.8	3,128.2	2,531.7	Other Items (Net)	17r
289.5	2,236.4	2,103.6	3,429.0	3,227.8	6,252.5	6,630.3	6,094.0	5,912.1	5,222.7	3,616.3	3,046.4	2,918.3	2,521.6	2,742.2	*of which: Valuation Adjustment*	17rv
															Deposit Money Banks	
Billions of Pounds Beginning 1986: End of Period																
18.7	72.5	130.9	178.0	282.5	669.2	1,434.9	2,786.4	3,541.5	4,377.9	6,224.6	6,513.4	6,826.7	7,330.8	10,655.9	Reserves	20
1,434.7	1,695.4	1,458.2	2,374.5	3,061.2	5,824.9	7,040.6	6,269.3	6,337.3	6,718.9	9,184.0	9,984.2	8,910.5	12,300.2	12,988.2	Foreign Assets	21
51.8	302.3	558.3	688.4	1,309.4	3,098.4	4,013.3	6,908.6	7,948.9	12,060.3	13,234.2	17,942.1	21,840.8	23,271.3	23,066.8	Claims on Central Government	22a
530.1	738.5	878.1	1,548.3	1,971.1	4,804.1	5,897.9	7,799.8	10,320.0	12,687.0	15,451.3	18,681.5	20,994.3	22,243.2	22,192.0	Claims on Private Sector	22d
29.5	65.8	92.5	115.3	202.0	393.5	422.4	492.7	508.0	568.7	685.5	758.3	845.8	862.2	889.6	Demand Deposits	24
1,402.4	1,991.8	2,178.0	3,372.4	4,810.1	10,574.9	13,986.8	18,193.7	21,297.8	26,935.9	32,621.4	38,067.1	42,458.0	46,720.0	50,344.6	Time & Foreign Currency Deposits	25
409.4	499.8	448.2	758.9	895.7	1,746.9	2,050.9	2,601.7	3,293.1	4,639.8	6,397.1	8,909.6	9,636.7	10,839.2	11,075.9	Foreign Liabilities	26c
3.0	5.7	11.3	26.1	40.0	106.5	151.7	255.4	261.0	285.1	216.6	346.1	701.7	720.9	525.5	Central Government Deposits	26d
1.5	2.0	93.3	169.1	189.2	163.9	187.1	166.8	289.9	105.1	96.8	346.1	405.9	734.8	781.0	Credit from Monetary Authorities	26g
5.4	11.3	23.7	58.9	94.1	215.4	444.1	675.8	1,145.9	1,943.5	2,990.1	3,619.9	4,019.3	4,376.3	4,463.2	Capital Accounts	27a
183.9	232.4	178.5	288.5	393.2	1,195.3	1,143.6	1,378.0	1,351.9	1,366.1	1,086.5	1,074.0	504.8	892.1	823.1	Other Items (Net)	27r
															Monetary Survey	
Billions of Pounds Beginning 1986: End of Period																
1,366.1	3,714.0	3,345.6	5,152.8	6,139.0	12,434.4	15,006.0	15,827.6	15,854.3	16,481.0	15,866.9	13,596.1	13,695.1	12,914.3	10,828.7	Foreign Assets (Net)	31n
602.2	947.7	1,478.4	2,616.8	3,223.7	7,199.9	8,994.3	12,174.1	15,744.6	21,279.0	28,222.0	35,235.0	39,555.2	45,573.0	50,863.4	Domestic Credit	32
71.1	208.0	593.5	1,050.7	1,232.5	2,300.8	3,052.0	4,301.3	5,304.6	8,253.3	12,183.0	15,913.2	17,982.2	22,701.0	27,975.3	Claims on Central Govt. (Net)	32an
531.1	739.7	884.9	1,566.1	1,991.2	4,899.2	5,942.3	7,872.9	10,440.0	13,025.7	16,039.0	19,321.8	21,573.0	22,872.0	22,888.1	Claims on Private Sector	32d
68.9	182.9	287.2	449.9	689.4	1,199.4	1,143.2	1,436.8	1,560.6	1,753.4	1,929.4	2,051.5	2,260.8	2,389.3	2,365.3	Money	34
1,402.4	1,991.8	2,178.0	3,372.4	4,810.1	10,576.4	14,535.2	18,214.5	21,322.7	27,161.6	32,640.2	38,087.2	42,564.3	46,845.5	50,545.1	Quasi-Money	35
497.0	2,487.1	2,358.8	3,947.3	3,863.2	7,858.5	8,321.8	8,350.4	8,715.5	8,844.9	9,519.2	8,692.3	8,425.2	9,252.5	8,781.6	Other Items (Net)	37r
1,471.3	2,174.6	2,465.2	3,822.3	5,499.5	11,775.8	15,678.5	19,651.3	22,883.3	28,915.1	34,569.6	40,138.8	44,825.1	49,234.8	52,910.4	Money plus Quasi-Money	35l
															Interest Rates	
Percent Per Annum																
21.85	21.84	21.84	21.84	18.04	16.00	20.22	16.49	19.01	25.00	30.00	30.00	25.00	20.00	20.00	Discount Rate (End of Period)	60
26.91	25.17	18.84	18.84	17.47	22.40	18.27	15.09	19.40	15.19	13.42	12.70	11.57	11.18	11.18	Treasury Bill Rate	60c
21.18	21.96	17.54	16.86	16.76	17.09	15.56	14.80	16.30	15.54	13.37	13.61	12.50	11.21	10.85	Deposit Rate	60l
36.54	44.46	39.86	39.94	38.01	40.21	28.53	23.88	24.69	25.21	20.29	....	19.48	18.15	17.19	Lending Rate	60p
															International Transactions	
Billions of US Dollars																
650	780	485	494	539	560	452	470	656	736	643	662	677	715	870	Exports	70.. d
1,880	2,457	2,235	2,525	3,743	4,202	†2,215	2,598	5,480	7,540	7,467	7,070	6,207	6,230	7,293	Imports, c.i.f.	71.. d
															Government Finance	
Year Ending December 31																
....	....	....	....	....	....	-1,017.0	-2,631.0	-3,309.3	-4,198.3	-5,902.8	-3,944.6	....	....	....	Deficit (-) or Surplus	80
						1,855.0	2,241.0	3,032.7	3,533.7	3,753.2	4,440.9				Revenue	81
						197.0	507.0	—	—	72.0	—				Grants Received	81z
						3,069.0	5,379.0	6,342.0	7,732.0	9,728.0	8,385.5				Expenditure	82
						—	—	—	—	—	—				Lending Minus Repayments	83
															Financing	
						868.0	1,946.0	2,452.3	3,334.3	5,022.9	1,162.8				Domestic	84a
						149.0	685.0	857.0	864.0	744.5	2,470.0				Foreign	85a
										135.4	311.8				Adj. to Total Financing	84x
						6,089.4	9,347.5	11,997.2	17,228.8	19,787.1	21,685.7				Debt: Domestic	88a
						563.6	1,286.0	2,157.8	2,960.6	3,713.3	6,282.6				Foreign	89a
Midyear Estimates																
2.60	2.56	2.54	2.56	2.78	2.87	2.97	3.08	3.17	3.25	3.33	3.38	3.44	3.50	3.56	**Population**	99z

(See notes in the back of the book.)

Lesotho

		1972	1973	1974	1975	1976	1977	1978	1979	1980	1981	1982	1983	1984	1985	1986
Exchange Rates														*Loti per SDR:*		
Principal Rate	aa	.85000	.80966	.84435	1.01797	1.01029	1.05627	1.13286	1.08924	.95066	1.11341	1.18729	1.27926	1.94563	2.80926	2.67072
														Loti per US Dollar:		
Principal Rate	ae	.78290	.67116	.68963	.86957	.86957	.86957	.86957	.82686	.74538	.95657	1.07631	1.22190	1.98491	2.55754	2.18341
Principal Rate	rf	.76873	.69396	.67948	.73951	.86957	.86957	.86957	.84202	.77883	.87753	1.08582	1.11410	1.47528	2.22868	2.28503
														Index Numbers (1995=100):		
Principal Rate	ahx	469.7	523.6	533.9	495.5	417.1	417.1	417.1	430.8	466.2	416.7	335.3	326.1	252.2	165.5	159.9
Nominal Effective Exchange Rate	ne c	....	....	....	....	....	....	....	147.3	147.7	148.1	147.3	147.7	146.6	144.1	142.5
Real Effective Exchange Rate	re c	....	....	....	....	....	....	....	100.3	102.5	100.3	98.4	102.9	102.1	98.8	97.2
Fund Position														*Millions of SDRs:*		
Quota	2f. s	5.00	5.00	5.00	5.00	5.00	5.00	7.00	7.00	10.50	10.50	10.50	15.10	15.10	15.10	15.10
SDRs	1b. s	.86	.66	.58	.54	.50	.45	.41	1.09	.85	1.41	1.10	1.04	.97	.99	.80
Reserve Position in the Fund	1c. s	.23	.43	.63	1.25	1.25	1.25	1.14	1.14	1.98	2.01	.08	1.24	1.25	1.25	1.26
Total Fund Cred.&Loans Outstg.	2tl	—	—	—	—	—	.54	2.08	3.59	4.87	4.89	4.89	4.75	4.33	3.51	2.54
International Liquidity												*Millions of US Dollars Unless Otherwise Indicated:*					
Total Reserves minus Gold	1l. d	....	....	....	....	....	....	....	....	50.27	43.40	47.54	66.68	48.58	43.52	60.26
SDRs	1b. d	.93	.80	.71	.63	.58	.55	.53	1.44	1.08	1.64	1.21	1.09	.95	1.09	.98
Reserve Position in the Fund	1c. d	.25	.52	.77	1.46	1.45	1.52	1.49	1.50	2.53	2.34	.09	1.30	1.23	1.37	1.54
Foreign Exchange	1d. d	....	....	....	....	....	....	....	....	46.66	39.41	46.23	64.29	46.40	41.06	57.74
Monetary Authorities: Other Liab.	4.. d	....	....	....	....	....	....	....	....	.08	21.17	23.52	13.22	1.42	.79	.95
Deposit Money Banks: Assets	7a. d	....	20.72	22.11	20.87	21.56	28.22	48.42	61.89	45.21	37.33	51.03	58.95	44.79	43.93	38.17
Liabilities	7b. d	....	6.68	1.83	.87	1.54	1.58	3.02	2.08	8.25	5.89	3.23	18.98	3.78	3.09	4.54
Monetary Authorities														*Millions of Maloti:*		
Foreign Assets	11	....	....	....	....	....	....	....	....	41.23	45.58	52.62	83.40	100.20	116.06	135.48
Claims on Central Government	12a	....	....	....	....	....	....	....	....	4.63	26.45	34.60	24.94	13.82	36.15	44.33
Claims on Private Sector	12d	....	....	....	....	....	....	....	....	....	....	....	....	....	....	....
Claims on Deposit Money Banks	12e	....	....	....	....	....	....	....	....	....	....	....	....	....	....	....
Reserve Money	14	....	....	....	....	....	....	....	....	40.20	42.59	46.07	72.57	85.35	110.61	137.09
of which: Currency Outside DMBs	14a	....	....	....	....	....	....	....	....	6.92	10.62	17.77	23.14	23.67	25.23	32.55
Foreign Liabilities	16c	....	....	....	....	....	....	....	....	4.69	25.69	31.12	22.22	11.25	11.89	8.87
Central Government Deposits	16d	....	....	....	....	....	....	....	....	.01	.74	5.38	6.09	2.33	2.93	7.19
Capital Accounts	17a	....	....	....	....	....	....	....	....	3.89	5.40	5.72	7.62	15.79	27.28	20.82
Other Items (Net)	17r	....	....	....	....	....	....	....	....	-2.92	-2.39	-1.07	-.15	-.70	-.50	5.86
Deposit Money Banks														*Millions of Maloti:*		
Reserves	20	....	1.16	1.67	1.20	2.69	3.55	4.72	6.67	32.87	28.60	28.48	48.85	54.03	77.94	97.55
Foreign Assets	21	....	14.60	15.25	18.15	18.74	24.54	42.11	51.17	33.70	35.71	54.92	72.03	88.91	112.36	83.34
Claims on Central Government	22a	1.48	1.04	1.75	4.14	9.45	10.79	17.55	38.40	42.65	54.50	64.91	62.28	74.00	126.06	
Claims on Nonfin.Pub.Enterprises	22c	.95	1.57	1.40	2.34	4.29	10.21	8.55	9.24	10.44	10.92	14.30	13.38	11.26	11.07	
Claims on Private Sector	22d	5.74	8.61	8.43	11.57	13.64	18.44	23.85	21.45	37.15	46.97	51.75	68.34	89.16	90.47	
Claims on Other Banking Insts.	22f	—	—	—	—	—	—	—	—	—	—	—	—	—	.17	.39
Demand Deposits	24	....	4.71	5.46	7.41	11.37	18.78	28.08	39.81	41.55	48.00	59.40	61.52	79.60	107.91	122.09
Time and Savings Deposits	25	....	13.39	14.73	18.70	23.24	29.24	47.83	55.77	68.17	85.58	108.24	132.36	147.04	177.58	197.47
Foreign Liabilities	26c	....	4.71	1.26	.76	1.34	1.38	2.62	1.72	6.15	5.63	3.48	23.20	7.51	7.91	9.90
Central Government Deposits	26d	....	2.70	7.18	2.56	2.67	3.16	7.09	9.36	15.57	12.41	12.47	13.14	12.43	20.62	24.19
Capital Accounts	27a	....	1.48	1.81	3.20	3.76	5.58	6.40	8.48	11.30	13.21	18.53	33.15	39.82	53.87	62.22
Other Items (Net)	27r	....	-3.06	-2.32	-1.69	-2.89	-2.66	-5.75	-7.35	-7.08	-10.29	-6.33	-11.54	.54	-3.01	-7.01
Monetary Survey														*Millions of Maloti:*		
Foreign Assets (Net)	31n	....	....	....	....	....	....	....	....	64.09	49.96	72.94	110.01	170.35	208.62	200.05
Domestic Credit	32	....	....	....	....	....	....	....	....	58.13	103.54	129.14	136.67	143.07	187.19	240.93
Claims on Central Govt. (Net)	32an	....	....	....	....	....	....	....	....	27.44	55.95	71.25	70.62	61.34	86.60	139.01
Claims on Nonfin.Pub.Enterprises	32c	....	....	....	....	....	....	....	....	9.24	10.44	10.92	14.30	13.38	11.26	11.07
Claims on Private Sector	32d	....	....	....	....	....	....	....	....	21.45	37.15	46.97	51.75	68.34	89.16	90.47
Claims on Other Banking Insts.	32f	....	....	....	....	....	....	....	....	....	....	....	....	....	.17	.39
Money	34	....	....	....	....	....	....	....	....	48.47	58.62	77.17	84.67	103.28	133.14	154.64
Quasi-Money	35	....	....	....	....	....	....	....	....	68.17	85.58	108.24	132.36	147.04	177.58	197.47
Capital Accounts	37a	....	....	....	....	....	....	....	....	15.18	18.61	24.25	40.77	55.61	81.16	83.04
Other Items (Net)	37r	....	....	....	....	....	....	....	....	-9.59	-9.31	-7.58	-11.12	7.49	3.94	5.84
Money plus Quasi-Money	35l	....	....	....	....	....	....	....	....	116.64	144.20	185.41	217.03	250.32	310.72	352.11
Other Banking Institutions														*Millions of Maloti:*		
Cash	40	....	....	....	....	....	.33	.99	1.33	—	.52	.53	1.24	1.99	2.64	2.26
Claims on Private Sector	42d	....	....	....	....	....	.01	.50	1.79	6.61	7.99	8.08	7.93	11.68	12.49	13.70
Time and Savings Deposits	45	....	....	....	....	....	.01	.03	.58	1.97	1.96	2.26	4.37	3.18	3.17	5.54
Capital Accounts	47a	....	....	....	....	....	.25	1.25	2.25	3.52	5.29	5.44	5.44	6.97	7.63	8.43
Other Items (Net)	47r	....	....	....	....	....	.08	.20	.29	1.12	1.26	.92	-.64	3.51	4.33	1.99
Liquid Liabilities	55l	....	....	....	....	....	....	....	....	118.60	145.64	187.14	220.16	251.52	311.25	355.39
Interest Rates														*Percent Per Annum*		
Discount Rate (End of Period)	60	....	....	....	....	....	....	....	8.00	12.00	12.00	12.00	15.00	12.00	9.50	
Treasury Bill Rate	60c	....	....	....	....	....	....	....	....	7.00	10.67	18.00	18.42	17.60	11.21	
Deposit Rate	60l	....	....	....	....	....	....	....	....	9.63	11.75	9.38	9.90	10.42	10.04	
Lending Rate	60p	....	....	....	....	....	....	....	11.00	15.00	17.00	15.42	17.58	19.67	13.42	
Prices														*Index Numbers (1995=100):*		
Consumer Prices	64	....	6.0	6.8	7.8	8.7	10.1	†11.5	13.3	†15.5	17.4	19.5	22.9	25.4	28.8	34.0

1987	1988	1989	1990	1991	1992	1993	1994	1995	1996	1997	1998	1999	2000	2001		
															Exchange Rates	
End of Period																
2.73793	3.19971	3.33272	3.64560	3.92372	4.19788	4.66667	5.17298	5.42197	6.73325	6.56747	8.25106	8.44711	9.86107	15.23974	Principal Rate	aa
End of Period (ae) Period Average (rf)																
1.92994	2.37773	2.53601	2.56253	2.74303	3.05300	3.39750	3.54350	3.64750	4.68250	4.86750	5.86000	6.15450	7.56850	12.12650	Principal Rate	ae
2.03603	2.27347	2.62268	2.58732	2.76132	2.85201	3.26774	3.55080	3.62709	4.29935	4.60796	5.52828	6.10948	6.93983	8.60918	Principal Rate	rf
Period Averages																
178.2	160.4	138.6	140.2	131.6	127.3	111.1	102.2	100.0	84.9	78.8	66.2	59.4	52.5	42.7	Principal Rate	ahx
142.4	141.6	141.2	136.2	130.5	125.5	115.1	105.8	100.0	86.4	84.2	72.3	66.3	61.7	51.3	Nominal Effective Exchange Rate	nec
94.1	93.0	93.2	91.4	97.9	105.7	105.0	100.0	100.0	91.1	93.8	85.3	83.6	80.2	69.5	Real Effective Exchange Rate	rec
															Fund Position	
End of Period																
15.10	15.10	15.10	15.10	15.10	23.90	23.90	23.90	23.90	23.90	23.90	23.90	34.90	34.90	34.90	Quota	2f.s
.62	.97	.74	.46	.20	.48	.41	.33	.24	.92	.89	.86	.85	.51	.46	SDRs	1b.s
1.27	1.29	1.29	1.30	1.31	3.51	3.51	3.51	3.51	3.51	3.52	3.53	3.53	3.54	3.54	Reserve Position in the Fund	1c.s
1.56	3.75	7.72	10.59	12.84	18.12	24.92	27.63	25.82	23.48	20.39	16.76	12.46	8.53	12.13	Total Fund Cred.&Loans Outstg.	2tl
															International Liquidity	
End of Period																
67.53	56.28	49.00	72.37	115.04	157.49	252.69	372.62	456.74	460.51	571.74	575.08	499.56	417.89	386.49	Total Reserves minus Gold	1l.d
.88	1.31	.97	.65	.29	.66	.56	.47	.35	1.33	1.20	1.22	1.17	.66	.58	SDRs	1b.d
1.80	1.74	1.70	1.85	1.87	4.83	4.82	5.13	5.22	5.05	4.75	4.98	4.85	4.61	4.45	Reserve Position in the Fund	1c.d
64.85	53.24	46.33	69.87	112.88	152.00	247.30	367.02	451.17	454.13	565.78	568.89	493.54	412.62	381.46	Foreign Exchange	1d.d
1.13	1.02	.99	.73	2.11	1.80	1.63	1.85	33.39	28.73	26.79	24.79	42.72	37.78	27.16	Monetary Authorities: Other Liab.	4..d
35.31	41.23	43.40	79.88	71.89	95.26	65.84	48.52	65.04	58.36	41.80	72.97	80.37	80.48	65.11	Deposit Money Banks: Assets	7a.d
6.85	13.78	16.36	9.60	11.34	7.99	9.64	10.29	16.51	12.83	11.69	8.05	6.48	18.50	8.48	Liabilities	7b.d
															Monetary Authorities	
End of Period																
135.64	140.21	129.85	197.29	322.48	483.08	869.28	1,337.58	1,802.01	2,310.26	2,929.82	3,549.85	3,349.33	3,486.14	5,138.38	Foreign Assets	11
92.18	272.37	319.18	334.22	643.20	213.38	375.85	381.63	287.92	318.78	166.39	145.88	110.39	105.04	250.96	Claims on Central Government	12a
—	—	—	—	—	—	—	—	8.91	8.69	10.52	11.54	12.20	13.90	13.56	Claims on Private Sector	12d
—	—	—	—	—	6.25	.39	.44	—							Claims on Deposit Money Banks	12e
161.05	236.47	222.20	208.59	245.81	191.77	233.68	249.15	329.83	346.37	388.95	540.13	717.32	669.79	499.36	Reserve Money	14
33.19	41.87	53.36	59.79	37.01	39.86	43.75	52.57	74.11	84.09	92.51	134.50	122.66	139.34	147.14	*of which: Currency Outside DMBs*	14a
6.45	14.43	28.24	40.48	56.14	81.55	121.82	149.49	261.78	292.62	264.26	283.56	368.13	370.06	514.22	Foreign Liabilities	16c
29.36	125.94	155.88	210.11	593.50	349.19	790.87	1,134.25	1,350.19	1,659.50	2,062.82	2,125.51	1,602.59	1,356.38	1,502.35	Central Government Deposits	16d
21.62	23.35	24.69	54.14	53.10	54.30	77.86	82.34	185.68	368.79	409.22	735.54	805.41	1,208.99	2,858.28	Capital Accounts	17a
9.34	12.38	18.01	18.19	17.14	25.90	21.30	104.42	-28.64	-29.55	-18.54	22.52	-21.54	-.14	28.69	Other Items (Net)	17r
															Deposit Money Banks	
End of Period																
118.47	189.37	161.57	136.40	189.68	135.95	179.47	180.45	165.68	245.58	245.22	490.59	573.72	506.81	127.06	Reserves	20
68.15	98.04	110.05	204.69	197.19	290.84	223.69	171.94	237.24	273.27	203.46	427.59	494.65	609.09	789.61	Foreign Assets	21
135.02	128.54	189.66	153.29	131.07	108.45	99.72	103.95	74.91	74.35	74.23	51.53	586.38	586.20	693.91	Claims on Central Government	22a
7.61	24.05	24.62	26.24	35.86	28.91	29.31	30.92	80.53	141.33	127.62	225.53	105.28	79.22	46.39	Claims on Nonfin.Pub.Enterprises	22c
112.70	145.32	170.85	208.78	273.79	316.37	502.61	699.24	665.46	667.27	979.29	829.70	845.29	869.11	927.44	Claims on Private Sector	22d
.80	.98	1.38	.14	.62	2.77	10.00	10.39	—							Claims on Other Banking Insts.	22f
123.62	178.01	191.82	204.43	275.77	311.29	389.43	434.02	445.91	548.00	686.57	836.92	821.27	873.73	939.04	Demand Deposits	24
230.26	270.12	310.63	338.41	345.45	371.62	501.99	550.42	601.05	692.40	743.97	785.67	720.52	664.94	700.44	Time and Savings Deposits	25
13.22	32.76	41.50	24.60	31.11	24.40	32.74	36.47	60.23	60.06	56.89	47.20	39.89	140.01	102.82	Foreign Liabilities	26c
19.28	17.24	23.08	32.21	26.85	39.85	48.30	39.59	37.53	43.66	46.04	76.77	77.12	68.38	63.31	Central Government Deposits	26d
63.82	79.94	91.61	122.24	143.55	160.67	189.51	233.51	119.12	56.11	-74.15	-38.31	209.92	318.90	279.18	Capital Accounts	27a
-7.47	8.20	-.51	7.65	5.47	-24.54	-117.17	-97.12	-40.02	1.56	170.50	316.70	736.60	584.47	499.63	Other Items (Net)	27r
															Monetary Survey	
End of Period																
184.12	191.05	170.16	336.90	432.43	667.97	938.41	1,323.56	1,717.24	2,230.85	2,812.12	3,646.68	3,435.95	3,585.17	5,310.96	Foreign Assets (Net)	31n
299.65	428.06	526.73	480.35	464.17	280.84	178.33	52.29	-270.00	-492.76	-750.82	-938.11	-20.17	228.70	366.59	Domestic Credit	32
178.55	257.72	329.88	245.19	153.91	-67.21	-363.59	-688.26	-1,024.89	-1,310.03	-1,868.24	-2,004.88	-982.95	-733.52	-620.79	Claims on Central Govt. (Net)	32an
7.61	24.05	24.62	26.24	35.86	28.91	29.31	30.92	80.53	141.33	127.62	225.53	105.28	79.22	46.39	Claims on Nonfin.Pub.Enterprises	32c
112.70	145.32	170.85	208.78	273.79	316.37	502.61	699.24	674.37	675.95	989.81	841.24	857.49	883.00	941.00	Claims on Private Sector	32d
.80	.98	1.38	.14	.62	2.77	10.00	10.39	—							Claims on Other Banking Insts.	32f
156.81	219.88	245.18	264.22	312.78	351.15	433.18	486.59	537.70	641.62	787.03	983.17	957.32	1,035.96	1,292.27	Money	34
230.26	270.12	310.63	338.41	345.45	371.62	501.99	550.42	601.05	692.40	743.97	785.67	720.52	664.94	700.44	Quasi-Money	35
85.44	103.29	116.30	176.38	196.64	214.97	267.37	315.85	304.80	424.89	335.07	697.22	1,015.34	1,527.89	3,137.46	Capital Accounts	37a
11.25	25.83	24.77	38.24	41.73	11.07	-85.81	23.00	3.70	-20.83	195.23	242.51	722.60	585.07	547.38	Other Items (Net)	37r
387.08	490.00	555.82	602.64	658.23	722.77	935.17	1,037.01	1,138.74	1,334.02	1,531.00	1,768.83	1,677.84	1,700.90	1,992.71	Money plus Quasi-Money	35l
															Other Banking Institutions	
End of Period																
2.12	2.88	2.95	2.86	2.48	8.00	....	....	....	....	....	....	....	....	....	Cash	40
17.63	24.04	31.65	42.57	52.08	64.91	....	....	....	....	....	....	....	....	....	Claims on Private Sector	42d
7.77	10.09	15.11	24.38	32.29	41.52	....	....	....	....	....	....	....	....	....	Time and Savings Deposits	45
8.54	9.34	9.59	9.23	9.46	9.23	....	....	....	....	....	....	....	....	....	Capital Accounts	47a
3.44	7.50	9.89	11.83	12.80	22.16	....	....	....	....	....	....	....	....	....	Other Items (Net)	47r
392.73	497.21	567.98	624.16	688.04	756.29	....	....	....	....	....	....	....	....	....	Liquid Liabilities	55l
															Interest Rates	
Percent Per Annum																
9.00	15.50	17.00	15.75	18.00	15.00	13.50	13.50	15.50	17.00	15.60	19.50	19.00	15.00	13.00	Discount Rate (End of Period)	60
10.75	11.42	15.75	16.33	15.75	14.20	†10.01	9.44	12.40	13.89	14.83	15.47	12.45	9.06	9.49	Treasury Bill Rate	60c
7.00	9.58	12.82	13.00	13.00	10.63	8.06	8.43	13.34	12.73	11.81	10.73	7.45	4.92	4.83	Deposit Rate	60l
11.13	13.67	18.75	20.42	20.00	18.25	15.83	14.25	16.38	17.71	18.03	20.06	19.06	17.11	16.55	Lending Rate	60p
															Prices	
Period Averages																
38.0	42.3	48.5	54.2	63.8	74.7	84.6	91.5	100.0	109.3	....	....	†138.6	147.1	132.9	Consumer Prices	64

Lesotho

666

	1972	1973	1974	1975	1976	1977	1978	1979	1980	1981	1982	1983	1984	1985	1986
International Transactions														*Millions of Maloti*	
Exports 70	6.1	8.8	9.8	9.2	14.6	12.2	28.7	38.9	46.6	44.6	40.6	34.6	41.8	50.0	58.0
Imports, c.i.f. 71	43.0	60.5	81.7	122.2	184.4	203.3	244.2	275.3	331.5	405.5	497.8	539.7	634.5	751.0	803.3
Balance of Payments															
														Millions of US Dollars:	
Current Account, n.i.e. .... 78al d	....	....	....	−1.1	−34.2	−9.2	8.5	—	56.3	4.3	22.1	40.7	6.5	−12.1	−2.8
Goods: Exports f.o.b. .... 78aa d				13.5	17.9	15.2	33.0	39.1	58.2	45.2	37.4	31.1	28.3	22.4	25.4
Goods: Imports f.o.b. .... 78ab d				−151.5	−189.4	−210.8	−243.1	−316.7	−424.5	−448.6	−446.9	−482.5	−433.2	−324.0	−341.5
Trade Balance .... 78ac d				−137.9	−171.5	−195.6	−210.1	−277.7	−366.3	−403.4	−409.6	−451.4	−404.9	−301.6	−316.2
Services: Credit .... 78ad d				12.0	12.0	14.1	16.8	18.6	32.2	34.3	26.2	27.9	24.4	18.3	20.2
Services: Debit .... 78ae d				−19.1	−20.9	−24.8	−29.9	−35.3	−50.3	−55.2	−46.7	−50.2	−45.1	−35.5	−46.2
Balance on Goods & Services ... 78af d				−145.0	−180.4	−206.3	−223.2	−294.3	−384.4	−424.3	−430.0	−473.7	−425.6	−318.8	−342.1
Income: Credit .... 78ag d				127.0	142.7	170.7	183.5	219.7	273.1	301.9	361.4	395.0	343.5	242.0	268.6
Income: Debit .... 78ah d				−4.5	−4.1	−5.1	−5.8	−6.1	−7.6	−9.1	−15.1	−12.4	−11.1	−9.0	−10.3
Balance on Gds, Serv. & Inc. .. 78ai d				−22.4	−41.9	−40.7	−45.4	−80.6	−118.9	−131.5	−83.8	−91.2	−93.2	−85.8	−83.8
Current Transfers, n.i.e.: Credit ... 78aj d				21.4	16.2	31.5	53.9	80.8	222.1	184.8	163.1	192.8	147.5	104.4	116.9
Current Transfers: Debit .... 78ak d				—	−8.5	—	—	−.1	−46.9	−49.0	−57.3	−60.9	−47.8	−30.7	−35.8
Capital Account, n.i.e. .... 78bc d				—	—	—	—	—	—	—	—	—	—	—	—
Capital Account, n.i.e.: Credit .... 78ba d				—	—	—	—	—	—	—	—	—	—	—	—
Capital Account: Debit .... 78bb d				—	—	—	—	—	—	—	—	—	—	—	—
Financial Account, n.i.e. .... 78bj d	....	....	....	−.1	1.6	.2	3.1	8.3	−3.7	7.2	7.2	−1.7	−28.4	16.0	16.8
Direct Investment Abroad .... 78bd d				−.1	1.6	.2	3.1	8.3	−3.7	7.2	7.2	−1.7	−28.4	16.0	16.8
Dir. Invest. in Rep. Econ., n.i.e. ...... 78be d				—	—	—	—	—	4.5	4.8	3.0	4.8	2.3	—	2.1
Portfolio Investment Assets .... 78bf d				—	—	—	—	—	—	—	—	—	—	—	—
Equity Securities .... 78bk d				—	—	—	—	—	—	—	—	—	—	—	—
Debt Securities .... 78bl d				—	—	—	—	—	—	—	—	—	—	—	—
Portfolio Investment Liab., n.i.e. ...... 78bg d				—	—	—	—	—	—	—	—	—	—	—	—
Equity Securities .... 78bm d				—	—	—	—	—	—	—	—	—	—	—	—
Debt Securities .... 78bn d				—	—	—	—	—	—	—	—	—	—	—	—
Financial Derivatives Assets .... 78bw d									....	....	....	....	....	....	....
Financial Derivatives Liabilities .... 78bx d									....	....	....	....	....	....	....
Other Investment Assets .... 78bh d				−3.8	−1.6	−9.7	−7.5	−13.7	−41.9	−53.4	−31.2	−53.0	−17.9	−9.0	−1.6
Monetary Authorities .... 78bo d				—	—	—	—	—	—	—	—	—	—	—	—
General Government .... 78bp d				−.4	−.5	−.5	−.5	−.6	−68.1	−50.7	−15.8	−37.3	−5.2	1.9	−15.5
Banks .... 78bq d				−3.4	−1.2	−9.2	−7.0	−13.1	26.2	−2.7	−15.4	−15.7	−12.7	−10.8	13.9
Other Sectors .... 78br d				—	—	—	—	—	—	—	—	—	—	—	—
Other Investment Liab., n.i.e. .... 78bi d				3.7	3.2	9.9	10.6	21.9	33.7	55.8	35.4	46.5	−12.8	24.9	16.3
Monetary Authorities .... 78bs d				—	—	—	—	—	—	—	—	—	—	—	—
General Government .... 78bt d				4.3	2.5	9.9	9.1	23.0	30.0	54.7	37.4	28.8	−2.2	24.7	15.5
Banks .... 78bu d				−.7	.7	—	1.5	−1.1	3.7	1.1	−2.0	17.7	−10.6	.2	.9
Other Sectors .... 78bv d				—	—	—	—	—	—	—	—	—	—	—	—
Net Errors and Omissions .... 78ca d				1.9	32.5	8.3	−13.7	−11.1	−11.2	−10.9	−21.3	−12.9	30.5	1.7	−1.4
Overall Balance .... 78cb d				.7	—	−.7	−2.1	−2.9	41.4	.6	8.0	26.1	8.6	5.6	12.6
Reserves and Related Items .... 79da d				−.7	—	.7	2.1	2.9	−41.4	−.6	−8.0	−26.1	−8.6	−5.6	−12.6
Reserve Assets .... 79db d				−.7	—	.1	.2	.9	−43.1	−.6	−8.0	−26.0	−8.1	−4.8	−11.5
Use of Fund Credit and Loans .... 79dc d				—	—	.6	1.9	2.0	1.7	—	—	−.2	−.4	−.8	−1.1
Exceptional Financing .... 79de d				....	....								....	....	
International Investment Position															
														Millions of US Dollars	
Assets .... 79aa d	....	....	....	....	....	....	....	....	....	....	....	....	....	....	....
Direct Investment Abroad .... 79ab d	....	....	....	....	....	....	....	....	....	....	....	....	....	....	....
Portfolio Investment .... 79ac d	....	....	....	....	....	....	....	....	....	....	....	....	....	....	....
Equity Securities .... 79ad d	....	....	....	....	....	....	....	....	....	....	....	....	....	....	....
Debt Securities .... 79ae d	....	....	....	....	....	....	....	....	....	....	....	....	....	....	....
Financial Derivatives................. 79al d	....	....	....	....	....	....	....	....	....	....	....	....	....	....	....
Other Investment .... 79af d	....	....	....	....	....	....	....	....	....	....	....	....	....	....	....
Monetary Authorities .... 79ag d	....	....	....	....	....	....	....	....	....	....	....	....	....	....	....
General Government .... 79ah d	....	....	....	....	....	....	....	....	....	....	....	....	....	....	....
Banks .... 79ai d	....	....	....	....	....	....	....	....	....	....	....	....	....	....	....
Other Sectors .... 79aj d	....	....	....	....	....	....	....	....	....	....	....	....	....	....	....
Reserve Assets .... 79ak d	....	....	....	....	....	....	....	....	....	....	....	....	....	....	....
Liabilities .... 79la d	....	....	....	....	....	....	....	....	....	....	....	....	....	....	....
Dir. Invest. in Rep. Economy .... 79lb d	....	....	....	....	....	....	....	....	....	....	....	....	....	....	....
Portfolio Investment .... 79lc d	....	....	....	....	....	....	....	....	....	....	....	....	....	....	....
Equity Securities .... 79ld d	....	....	....	....	....	....	....	....	....	....	....	....	....	....	....
Debt Securities .... 79le d	....	....	....	....	....	....	....	....	....	....	....	....	....	....	....
Financial Derivatives .... 79ll d	....	....	....	....	....	....	....	....	....	....	....	....	....	....	....
Other Investment .... 79lf d	....	....	....	....	....	....	....	....	....	....	....	....	....	....	....
Monetary Authorities .... 79lg d	....	....	....	....	....	....	....	....	....	....	....	....	....	....	....
General Government .... 79lh d	....	....	....	....	....	....	....	....	....	....	....	....	....	....	....
Banks .... 79li d	....	....	....	....	....	....	....	....	....	....	....	....	....	....	....
Other Sectors .... 79lj d	....	....	....	....	....	....	....	....	....	....	....	....	....	....	....

International Transactions

Millions of Maloti

	1987	1988	1989	1990	1991	1992	1993	1994	1995	1996	1997	1998	1999	2000	2001		
Exports	94.7	144.9	173.0	153.0	186.0	310.0	438.0	509.0	581.0	812.0	904.0	1,071.0	1,053.3	1,528.0	2,426.2		70
Imports, c.i.f.	954.8	1,327.5	1,552.0	1,738.0	2,242.0	2,564.0	2,839.0	3,000.0	3,576.0	4,303.0	4,722.0	4,699.0	4,773.2	5,048.0	5,823.8		71

Balance of Payments

Minus Sign Indicates Debit

	1987	1988	1989	1990	1991	1992	1993	1994	1995	1996	1997	1998	1999	2000	2001		
Current Account, n.i.e.	23.6	−24.6	10.4	65.0	83.1	37.6	29.3	108.1	−323.0	−302.5	−269.2	−280.2	−220.8	−151.4	....		78al d
Goods: Exports f.o.b.	46.5	63.7	66.4	59.5	67.2	109.2	134.0	143.5	160.0	186.9	196.1	193.4	172.5	211.1	....		78aa d
Goods: Imports f.o.b.	−451.5	−559.4	−592.6	−672.6	−803.5	−932.6	−868.1	−810.2	−985.2	−998.6	−1,024.4	−866.0	−779.2	−727.6	....		78ab d
Trade Balance	−405.0	−495.7	−526.2	−613.2	−736.4	−823.4	−734.1	−666.7	−825.2	−811.8	−828.3	−672.5	−606.7	−516.5	....		78ac d
Services: Credit	27.5	32.1	32.9	40.6	40.9	41.3	37.0	37.8	39.0	42.6	86.9	53.6	43.7	42.7	....		78ad d
Services: Debit	−60.7	−69.1	−70.9	−81.4	−83.9	−82.8	−70.5	−64.2	−61.1	−55.9	−67.6	−52.2	−50.1	−42.5	....		78ae d
Balance on Goods & Services	−438.2	−532.7	−564.2	−654.0	−779.5	−864.9	−767.6	−693.2	−847.3	−825.1	−809.0	−671.2	−613.1	−516.4	....		78af d
Income: Credit	364.8	384.9	380.0	455.0	476.8	496.3	444.5	369.6	471.6	453.0	447.4	357.7	325.0	288.8	....		78ag d
Income: Debit	−15.0	−14.9	−20.3	−21.8	−20.4	−32.6	−22.8	−39.4	−157.4	−119.5	−110.0	−123.6	−80.6	−62.6	....		78ah d
Balance on Gds, Serv. & Inc.	−88.4	−162.8	−204.5	−220.9	−323.1	−401.1	−345.9	−363.0	−533.2	−491.6	−471.6	−437.1	−368.6	−290.2	....		78ai d
Current Transfers, n.i.e.: Credit	160.8	197.0	281.7	362.3	492.8	542.1	376.5	472.1	211.3	190.2	202.9	158.0	149.4	139.8	....		78aj d
Current Transfers: Debit	−48.7	−58.8	−66.8	−76.4	−86.6	−103.3	−1.3	−.9	−1.2	−1.1	−.5	−1.2	−1.6	−1.0	....		78ak d
Capital Account, n.i.e.	—	—	—	—	—	—	—	—	43.7	45.5	44.5	22.9	15.2	22.0	....		78bc d
Capital Account, n.i.e.: Credit	—	—	—	—	—	—	—	—	43.7	45.5	44.5	22.9	15.2	22.0	....		78ba d
Capital Account: Debit	—	—	—	—	—	—	—	—							....		78bb d
Financial Account, n.i.e.	3.3	−8.0	−20.2	−45.0	−60.8	−67.0	55.2	33.0	349.1	350.6	323.7	316.1	135.8	85.2	....		78bj d
Direct Investment Abroad	—	−.1	—	—	—	—	—	—	....	....	....	....	....	....	....		78bd d
Dir. Invest. in Rep. Econ., n.i.e.	5.7	21.0	13.4	17.1	7.5	2.7	15.0	18.7	275.3	287.5	268.1	264.8	163.3	117.8	....		78be d
Portfolio Investment Assets	—	—	—	—	—	—	—	—	....	....	....	....	....	....	....		78bf d
Equity Securities	—	—	—	—	—	—	—	—	....	....	....	....	....	....	....		78bk d
Debt Securities	—	—	—	—	—	—	—	—	....	....	....	....	....	....	....		78bl d
Portfolio Investment Liab., n.i.e.	—	—	—	—	—	—	—	—	....	....	....	....	....	....	....		78bg d
Equity Securities	—	—	—	—	—	—	—	—	....	....	....	....	....	....	....		78bm d
Debt Securities	—	—	—	—	—	—	—	—	....	....	....	....	....	....	....		78bn d
Financial Derivatives Assets															....		78bw d
Financial Derivatives Liabilities															....		78bx d
Other Investment Assets	−39.0	−80.0	−64.8	−109.7	−103.6	−106.4	8.9	−13.4	18.8	−7.0	−5.0	−1.7	−11.0	−19.1	....		78bh d
Monetary Authorities									....	....	....	....	....	....	....		78bo d
General Government	−45.5	−64.6	−61.4	−71.5	−105.1	−73.2	—	—	....	....	....	....	....	....	....		78bp d
Banks	6.6	−15.4	−3.5	−38.2	1.5	−33.3	8.9	−13.4	18.8	−7.0	−5.0	−1.7	−11.0	−19.1	....		78bq d
Other Sectors									....	....	....	....	....	....	....		78br d
Other Investment Liab., n.i.e.	36.6	51.0	31.3	47.6	35.4	36.8	31.3	27.6	55.0	70.1	60.5	53.0	−16.6	−13.5	....		78bi d
Monetary Authorities	—	.1	—	6.0	1.4	−.1	—	.3	6.3	−.2	—	.1	−5.4	−3.5	....		78bs d
General Government	34.9	41.3	33.0	43.4	36.0	37.1	27.7	26.0	49.2	71.8	68.6	59.8	−9.3	−15.1	....		78bt d
Banks	1.7	12.8	−1.2	−2.6	−1.3	.5	1.5	1.9	....		−7.2	−6.7	−1.2	5.2	....		78bu d
Other Sectors	—	−3.2	−.5	.8	−.7	−.7	2.1	−.5	−.5	−1.4	−.9	−.1	−.6	−.1	....		78bv d
Net Errors and Omissions	−26.0	26.5	1.9	−2.8	20.1	79.2	17.8	−20.3	28.1	23.3	42.1	56.8	29.0	62.1	....		78ca d
Overall Balance	.9	−6.1	−7.9	17.2	42.4	49.9	102.3	120.9	97.8	116.9	141.0	115.6	−40.8	17.8	....		78cb d
Reserves and Related Items	−.9	6.1	7.9	−17.2	−42.4	−49.9	−102.3	−120.9	−97.8	−116.9	−141.0	−115.6	40.8	−17.8	....		79da d
Reserve Assets	.3	3.3	3.0	−21.0	−45.4	−57.3	−111.7	−124.6	−95.1	−113.5	−136.8	−110.7	46.7	−12.6	....		79db d
Use of Fund Credit and Loans	−1.2	2.8	4.9	3.8	3.0	7.5	9.5	3.8	−2.7	−3.4	−4.3	−4.9	−5.9	−5.2	....		79dc d
Exceptional Financing															....		79de d

International Investment Position

Millions of US Dollars

	1987	1988	1989	1990	1991	1992	1993	1994	1995	1996	1997	1998	1999	2000	2001		
Assets	....	....	....	....	....	....	....	....	528.6	522.4	686.2	658.8	579.5	500.3	....		79aa d
Direct Investment Abroad	....	....	....	....	....	....	....	....	—	—	—	—	—	—	....		79ab d
Portfolio Investment	....	....	....	....	....	....	....	....	—	—	—	—	—	—	....		79ac d
Equity Securities	....	....	....	....	....	....	....	....	—	—	—	—	—	—	....		79ad d
Debt Securities	....	....	....	....	....	....	....	....	—	—	—	—	—	—	....		79ae d
Financial Derivatives	....	....	....	....	....	....	....	....							....		79al d
Other Investment	....	....	....	....	....	....	....	....	71.8	61.9	114.5	83.8	79.6	80.5	....		79af d
Monetary Authorities	....	....	....	....	....	....	....	....	—	—	—	—	—	—	....		79ag d
General Government	....	....	....	....	....	....	....	....							....		79ah d
Banks	....	....	....	....	....	....	....	....	71.8	61.9	114.5	83.8	79.6	80.5	....		79ai d
Other Sectors	....	....	....	....	....	....	....	....							....		79aj d
Reserve Assets	....	....	....	....	....	....	....	....	456.7	460.5	571.7	575.1	499.8	419.8	....		79ak d
Liabilities	....	....	....	....	....	....	....	....	566.8	535.6	512.6	590.7	559.5	600.9	....		79la d
Dir. Invest. in Rep. Economy	....	....	....	....	....	....	....	....	—	—	—	—	—	—	....		79lb d
Portfolio Investment	....	....	....	....	....	....	....	....	—	—	—	—	—	—	....		79lc d
Equity Securities	....	....	....	....	....	....	....	....	—	—	—	—	—	—	....		79ld d
Debt Securities	....	....	....	....	....	....	....	....	—	—	—	—	—	—	....		79le d
Financial Derivatives	....	....	....	....	....	....	....	....							....		79ll d
Other Investment	....	....	....	....	....	....	....	....	566.8	535.6	512.6	590.7	559.5	600.9	....		79lf d
Monetary Authorities	....	....	....	....	....	....	....	....	39.9	35.1	28.8	24.7	18.2	11.7	....		79lg d
General Government	....	....	....	....	....	....	....	....	510.3	487.7	475.3	543.5	534.8	570.7	....		79lh d
Banks	....	....	....	....	....	....	....	....	16.5	12.8	8.5	22.4	6.5	18.5	....		79li d
Other Sectors	....	....	....	....	....	....	....	....	—	—	—	—	—	—	....		79lj d

Lesotho

		1972	1973	1974	1975	1976	1977	1978	1979	1980	1981	1982	1983	1984	1985	1986
Government Finance															*Millions of Maloti:*		
Deficit (-) or Surplus	80	-.8	4.7	8.7	-8.7	-12.9	-3.0	....	....	....	....	...	135.8	167.9	216.4	238.2	260.2
Revenue	81	11.2	20.4	28.5	28.4	38.1	60.2	....	....	....	....	135.8	167.9	216.4	238.2	260.2
Grants Received	81z	3.8	3.5	3.5	4.0	2.2	10.0	....	....	....	....	....	....	23.1	....	27.1
Exp. & Lending Minus Repay.	82z	15.8	19.2	23.3	41.1	53.2	73.1	....	....	....	....	....	....	....	....	....
Expenditure	82	15.9	19.2	23.1	40.6	53.2	71.2	....	....	....	....	....	....	....	....	....
Lending Minus Repayments	83	-.1	—	.2	.5	—	2.0	....	....	....	....	....	....	....	....	....
Financing																	
Domestic	84a	....	....	-6.7	2.3	10.4	-1.5	....	....	....	....	18.0	-6.1	6.6	33.2	50.1
Foreign	85a	....	....	-2.0	6.4	2.5	4.5	....	....	....	....	....	....	....	....	....
Debt: Domestic	88a	....	....	....	....	....	....	....	....	....	....	....	....	52.0	....	....
Foreign	89a	....	....	....	....	....	....	....	....	....	....	....	....	398.6	....	....
National Accounts															*Millions of Maloti:*		
Househ.Cons.Expend.,incl.NPISHs	96f	86.4	115.5	146.9	167.2	210.5	264.2	300.7	353.7	387.2	471.0	557.1	686.2	783.4	837.9	935.9
Government Consumption Expend.	91f	9.3	9.6	15.8	21.3	24.9	29.2	40.9	52.4	74.0	81.0	89.9	91.7	98.6	135.9	159.3
Gross Fixed Capital Formation	93e	6.0	10.4	14.5	20.7	45.5	40.3	51.0	73.7	115.8	133.2	186.8	130.9	184.7	273.3	277.3
Changes in Inventories	93i	1.2	5.6	2.8	—	.9	1.7	9.1	10.9	6.3	8.3	-2.9	.6	5.2	-.9	13.6
Exports of Goods and Services	90c	5.8	9.0	14.1	14.6	21.3	18.0	36.4	50.0	58.0	58.2	55.4	50.8	60.5	70.1	80.4
Imports of Goods and Services (-)	98c	46.5	66.1	91.6	113.2	174.7	185.3	206.3	296.4	350.2	423.3	513.4	569.6	676.8	765.2	835.3
Gross Domestic Product (GDP)	99b	62.2	84.1	102.5	110.6	128.4	168.1	231.8	244.3	287.0	328.4	372.9	390.6	455.5	551.1	631.2
Net Primary Income from Abroad	98.n	20.7	29.7	60.1	89.1	119.3	139.9	153.3	178.2	205.0	254.8	372.9	423.1	487.2	514.3	583.3
Gross National Income (GNI)	99a	82.9	113.8	162.6	199.7	247.7	308.0	385.1	422.5	492.0	583.2	745.8	813.7	942.6	1,065.4	1,214.6
Net National Income	99e	81.7	112.9	153.2	210.7	260.8	326.5	413.9	492.1	570.5	650.6	789.2	897.8	1,073.5	1,230.3	1,366.1
GDP Volume 1995 Prices	99b.p	....	....	....	....	....	....	....	....	....	....	....	....	....	....	....
GDP Volume (1995=100)	99bv p	....	....	....	....	....	....	....	....	....	....	....	....	....	....	....
GDP Deflator (1995=100)	99bi p	....	....	....	....	....	....	....	....	100.0	113.3	124.2	142.3	153.1	178.9	201.0
																Millions:	
Population	99z	1.11	1.14	1.16	1.19	1.21	1.24	1.28	1.31	1.34	1.37	1.41	1.43	1.47	1.50	1.58

	1987	1988	1989	1990	1991	1992	1993	1994	1995	1996	1997	1998	1999	2000	2001	
Government Finance																
Year Beginning April 1																
Deficit (-) or Surplus 80	-160.5	-181.2	-103.4	-16.8	-9.9	81.5	147.2	149.3	108.6	137.4	88.8	-188.8	-235.0	-79.2	....	80
Revenue 81	300.1	369.2	525.2	627.7	820.0	1,003.1	1,269.4	1,438.5	1,681.6	2,034.6	2,353.4	2,158.7	2,327.5	2,752.2	....	81
Grants Received 81z	62.6	96.6	151.9	188.0	149.2	141.8	137.4	143.6	163.2	203.4	178.7	120.0	130.0	125.6	....	81z
Exp. & Lending Minus Repay. 82z	523.2	647.1	780.5	832.5	979.0	1,063.4	1,259.6	1,432.8	1,736.2	2,100.6	2,443.3	2,467.5	2,692.5	2,957.0	....	82z
Expenditure 82	518.0	636.9	770.2	823.5	970.0	1,050.9	1,169.4	994.1	1,118.1	1,179.0	1,537.6	1,971.7	2,311.5	2,457.9	....	82
Lending Minus Repayments 83	5.2	10.2	10.3	9.0	9.1	12.6	90.2	438.7	618.1	921.6	905.7	495.8	381.0	499.1	....	83
Financing																
Domestic 84a	90.2	110.0	-8.4	-110.6	-116.6	-253.6	-298.9	-252.5	-319.5	-537.3	-559.8	155.1	386.3	426.5	....	84a
Foreign 85a	70.3	71.2	111.8	127.4	126.5	172.1	151.7	103.2	210.9	399.9	471.0	33.7	-99.8	-221.7	....	85a
Debt: Domestic 88a	271.7	381.4	372.8	262.2	....	....	....	....	....	....	....	....	....	724.0	....	88a
Foreign 89a	522.6	685.3	815.0	978.1	1,113.8	1,345.7	....	1,704.4	1,861.5	2,255.1	2,568.8	3,180.8	3,724.2	4,317.1	....	89a
National Accounts																
Year Beginning April 1																
Househ.Cons.Expend.,incl.NPISHs 96f	1,256.0	1,614.2	2,005.8	2,211.3	2,545.3	2,811.0	3,472.3	3,544.9	4,075.3	4,834.8	5,359.0	5,543.7	5,723.1	6,351.9	6,442.3	96f
Government Consumption Expend. 91f	163.9	208.9	215.6	224.0	295.8	346.4	403.6	486.5	607.2	658.6	800.0	1,023.4	1,087.8	1,144.4	1,163.7	91f
Gross Fixed Capital Formation 93e	348.5	523.4	664.6	857.9	1,236.4	1,533.1	1,476.5	1,693.1	2,071.2	2,360.2	2,593.5	2,411.0	2,651.0	2,657.1	2,743.1	93e
Changes in Inventories 93i	4.4	7.3	-17.6	-1.8	-14.3	22.2	-16.1	-44.6	-24.3	7.8	-47.1	-93.4	-56.8	-178.2	—	93i
Exports of Goods and Services 90c	141.7	217.5	256.5	267.6	299.1	430.7	559.6	642.8	720.4	965.6	1,261.3	1,320.7	1,322.4	1,775.6	2,767.6	90c
Imports of Goods and Services (-) 98c	1,032.5	1,427.2	1,733.8	1,949.4	2,473.3	2,800.3	3,231.9	3,357.4	4,066.1	4,801.8	5,287.7	5,284.6	5,275.6	5,511.9	6,107.9	98c
Gross Domestic Product (GDP) 99b	881.9	1,144.0	1,376.6	1,592.1	1,888.9	2,343.0	2,664.1	2,965.3	3,383.7	4,053.6	4,719.6	4,920.7	5,564.9	6,238.8	7,008.9	99b
Net Primary Income from Abroad 98.n	705.8	825.2	899.7	1,050.7	1,061.2	1,215.1	1,325.2	1,348.5	1,410.9	1,421.5	1,538.9	1,384.7	1,492.5	1,522.3	1,514.0	98.n
Gross National Income (GNI) 99a	1,557.8	1,969.2	2,276.3	2,642.8	2,950.1	3,558.1	3,989.3	4,310.8	4,794.6	5,475.1	6,258.5	6,305.4	7,057.4	7,761.1	8,522.9	99a
Net National Income 99e	1,603.7	2,092.1	2,610.6	3,055.4	3,392.0	4,190.8	4,664.4	5,103.1	5,713.2	6,473.4	7,396.4	7,272.7	8,055.6	8,804.9	9,670.7	99e
GDP Volume 1995 Prices 99b.p	2,160.0	2,418.0	2,609.5	2,771.1	2,876.7	3,016.0	3,129.9	3,237.1	3,383.7	3,720.6	4,023.8	3,837.0	3,920.4	4,048.0	....	99b.p
GDP Volume (1995=100) 99bv.p	63.8	71.5	77.1	81.9	85.0	89.1	92.5	95.7	100.0	110.0	118.9	112.6	114.8	117.7	....	99bv.p
GDP Deflator (1995=100) 99bi.p	40.8	47.3	52.8	57.5	65.7	77.7	85.1	91.6	100.0	109.0	117.3	128.2	141.9	154.1	....	99bi.p
Midyear Estimates																
Population 99z	1.62	1.69	1.70	1.72	1.72	1.76	1.79	1.83	1.87	1.97	2.01	2.06	2.10	2.14	2.19	99z

(See notes in the back of the book.)

Liberia

		1972	1973	1974	1975	1976	1977	1978	1979	1980	1981	1982	1983	1984	1985	1986
Exchange Rates													*Liberian Dollars per SDR:*			
Market Rate	aa	1.0857	1.2064	1.2244	1.1707	1.1618	1.2147	1.3028	1.3173	1.2754	1.1640	1.1031	1.0470	.9802	1.0984	1.2232
														Liberian Dollars per US Dollar:			
Market Rate	ae	1.0000	1.0000	1.0000	1.0000	1.0000	1.0000	1.0000	1.0000	1.0000	1.0000	1.0000	1.0000	1.0000	1.0000	1.0000
Market Rate	rf	1.0000	1.0000	1.0000	1.0000	1.0000	1.0000	1.0000	1.0000	1.0000	1.0000	1.0000	1.0000	1.0000	1.0000	1.0000
Fund Position														*Millions of SDRs:*		
Quota	2f. s	29.00	29.00	29.00	29.00	29.00	29.00	37.00	37.00	55.50	55.50	55.50	71.30	71.30	71.30	71.30
SDRs	1b. s	1.63	3.28	3.18	2.90	3.52	3.33	3.34	6.52	—	1.08	.01	—	.03	—	—
Reserve Position in the Fund	1c. s	.31	—	1.36	1.78	—	—	—	—	—	.01	—	—	—	.02	.02
Total Fund Cred.&Loans Outstg.	2tl	—	.06	—	—	—	3.11	12.02	50.98	69.78	115.27	176.82	223.75	237.25	230.40	230.40
International Liquidity														*Millions of US Dollars:*		
Total Reserves minus Gold	1l. d	....	....	18.72	19.19	17.17	27.34	18.02	54.98	5.45	8.34	6.47	20.40	3.48	1.52	2.66
SDRs	1b. d	1.77	3.96	3.89	3.39	4.09	4.04	4.35	8.59	—	1.26	.01	—	.03	—	—
Reserve Position in the Fund	1c. d	.34	—	1.67	2.08	—	—	—	—	—	.01	—	—	—	.02	.02
Foreign Exchange	1d. d	....	....	13.16	13.71	13.08	23.30	13.67	46.39	5.45	7.07	6.46	20.40	3.45	1.50	2.64
Monetary Authorities: Other Liab.	4.. d	....	....	—	.03	3.61	.94	5.03	27.67	25.54	13.44	7.53	16.69	.14	1.22	.97
Banking Institutions: Assets	7a. d	11.86	16.80	33.68	33.98	54.98	38.77	35.36	49.34	24.27	15.53	26.37	24.50	11.66	18.50	
Liabilities	7b. d	16.31	13.90	27.38	25.03	15.65	20.31	29.58	62.75	49.36	56.35	54.55	40.59	35.61	46.22	34.45
Monetary Authorities														*Millions of Liberian Dollars:*		
Foreign Assets	11	....	....	13.6	13.9	17.2	27.3	18.0	55.0	†5.5	8.3	6.5	20.4	3.5	1.5	2.7
Claims on Central Government	12a	....	....	21.3	21.0	27.9	30.7	75.4	118.4	†173.5	214.2	284.2	352.1	347.7	428.0	477.0
Claims on Nonfin.Pub.Enterprises	12c	....	....							†2.3	4.2	4.4	5.6	5.3	1.0	—
Claims on Private Sector	12d	....	....	—	1.9	1.5	1.5	.3	.3	†.5	.5	.6	.7	1.8	.7	.8
Claims on Banking Institutions	12e	....	....	2.7	2.9	3.7	2.7	3.0	2.4	†1.7	1.1	1.2	2.3	.9	.8	2.0
Claims on Nonbank Financial Insts.	12g	....	....	—	—	—	—	—	—	†.5	1.6	2.0	2.1	2.0	2.0	2.0
Reserve Money	14	....	....	12.4	13.1	15.5	18.5	31.8	30.5	†42.7	41.1	57.4	71.8	86.9	121.6	169.1
of which: Currency Outside Banks	14a	....	....	8.5	8.0	8.4	9.2	10.2	11.0	11.3	11.6	15.7	19.8	28.6	46.2	66.1
Time Deposits	15	....	....	—	—	—	—	—	—	†—	—	.8	.5	.5	.9	1.0
Foreign Liabilities	16c	....	....	—	—	3.6	4.7	20.7	94.8	†114.6	147.6	202.6	250.9	232.7	264.6	317.4
Central Government Deposits	16d	....	....	5.8	8.9	12.9	19.8	22.8	28.8	†25.5	25.3	28.3	25.8	7.7	9.4	15.4
Capital Accounts	17a	....	....	16.7	16.5	16.2	16.9	17.8	22.9	†29.3	35.3	41.9	50.5	63.7	78.5	27.1
Other Items (Net)	17r	....	....	2.6	1.1	2.0	2.3	2.6	−1.0	†−28.2	−19.4	−32.2	−16.2	−30.2	−40.8	−44.6
Banking Institutions														*Millions of Liberian Dollars:*		
Reserves	20	.7	1.1	3.5	4.7	6.2	9.1	19.1	14.4	29.6	27.7	39.9	53.3	57.2	70.6	79.2
Foreign Assets	21	11.9	16.8	33.7	34.0	55.0	38.8	35.4	49.3	24.3	15.5	26.4	24.5	11.7	14.7	18.5
Claims on Central Government	22a	17.4	8.3	4.0	2.2	1.0	4.8	9.4	2.8	2.9	3.9	4.1	2.8	3.5	4.2	10.0
Claims on Nonfin.Pub.Enterprises	22c		.8	.8	1.8	.7	1.1	11.3	38.0	40.9	33.1	42.4	44.4	47.9	45.9	52.9
Claims on Private Sector	22d	47.3	54.3	72.7	76.8	83.1	109.2	132.2	146.3	88.7	91.5	75.0	71.3	74.8	77.5	74.3
Claims on Nonbank Financial Insts.	22g					.5	.9					1.3	.2	.4	.4	1.4
Demand Deposits	24	21.4	27.9	38.8	33.8	53.6	47.0	63.9	66.2	58.0	41.3	48.9	55.7	62.5	68.5	83.4
Time and Savings Deposits	25	28.4	31.0	30.1	35.0	49.6	69.1	77.5	82.2	48.9	51.1	64.2	68.6	54.5	56.2	53.7
Foreign Liabilities	26c	16.3	13.9	27.4	25.0	15.6	20.3	29.6	62.8	49.4	56.4	54.6	40.6	35.6	46.2	34.5
Central Government Deposits	26d	11.9	5.6	2.9	4.2	1.0	.8	—	.1	.1	.1	.1	1.5	6.3	10.6	18.8
Credit from Monetary Authorities	26g	—	—	2.5	2.4	3.1	2.1	1.4	1.5	.5	.5	.6	1.1	.5	1.9	.2
Capital Accounts	27a	4.9	8.7	8.9	5.8	8.8	14.5	17.2	18.6	17.9	18.3	19.7	22.6	25.1	22.0	25.0
Other Items (Net)	27r	−5.6	−5.9	4.0	13.3	14.8	10.0	17.8	19.6	11.6	4.1	.9	6.5	11.0	7.9	20.8
Banking Survey														*Millions of Liberian Dollars:*		
Foreign Assets (Net)	31n	....	....	19.9	22.9	52.9	41.1	3.1	−53.3	†−134.3	−180.1	−224.3	−246.6	−253.2	−294.6	−330.7
Domestic Credit	32	....	....	90.0	90.6	100.8	127.6	205.7	277.0	†283.7	323.6	385.4	452.0	469.5	539.8	584.4
Claims on Central Govt. (Net)	32an	....	....	16.5	10.1	15.0	14.9	62.0	92.4	†150.8	192.7	259.9	327.6	337.3	412.2	452.8
Claims on Nonfin.Pub.Enterprises	32c	....	....	.8	1.8	.7	1.1	11.3	38.0	†43.3	37.3	46.8	50.0	53.2	46.9	52.9
Claims on Private Sector	32d	....	....	72.7	78.7	84.6	110.7	132.4	146.6	†89.2	92.0	75.5	72.0	76.6	78.3	75.1
Claims on Nonbank Fin. Insts.	32g	....	....	—	—	.5	.9			†.5	1.6	3.2	2.3	2.4	2.4	3.5
Money	34	....	....	44.9	39.0	59.3	53.2	72.5	72.6	†69.8	54.0	66.2	76.1	91.3	115.2	150.4
Quasi-Money	35	....	....	30.1	35.0	49.6	69.1	78.5	82.2	†48.9	51.1	65.0	69.1	55.0	57.0	53.9
Capital Accounts	37a	....	....	25.6	22.2	25.0	31.4	34.9	41.5	†47.2	53.5	61.6	73.1	88.8	100.5	52.1
Other Items (Net)	37r	....	....	9.3	17.3	19.9	15.0	22.9	27.5	†−16.4	−15.1	−31.7	−12.9	−18.7	−27.5	−2.7
Money plus Quasi-Money	35l	....	....	75.0	73.9	108.9	122.3	151.0	154.7	†118.7	105.1	131.2	145.2	146.3	172.2	204.3
Interest Rates														*Percent Per Annum:*		
Savings Rate	60k	....	....	....	....	....	....	....	....			8.00	8.00	8.05	8.09	7.79
Deposit Rate	60l	....	....	....	....	....	....	....	....	10.30	11.50	10.21	10.25	9.81	9.34	7.25
Lending Rate	60p	....	....	....	....	....	....	....	....	18.40	21.50	18.23	20.69	20.63	19.34	14.45
Prices														*Index Numbers (1985=100):*		
Consumer Prices	64	34.1	40.8	48.5	55.3	58.4	62.0	66.6	74.3	85.2	91.7	97.1	99.8	101.0	100.0	104.0

	1987	1988	1989	1990	1991	1992	1993	1994	1995	1996	1997	1998	1999	2000	2001		
Exchange Rates																	
End of Period																	
	1.4187	1.3457	1.3142	1.4227	1.4304	1.3750	1.3736	1.4599	1.4865	1.4380	1.3493	†60.8973	54.2141	55.6994	62.2081	Market Rate	aa
End of Period (ae) Period Average (rf)																	
	1.0000	1.0000	1.0000	1.0000	1.0000	1.0000	1.0000	1.0000	1.0000	1.0000	1.0000	†43.2500	39.5000	42.7500	49.5000	Market Rate	ae
	1.0000	1.0000	1.0000	1.0000	1.0000	1.0000	1.0000	1.0000	1.0000	1.0000	1.0000	41.5075	41.9025	40.9525	48.5833	Market Rate	rf
Fund Position																	
End of Period																	
	71.30	71.30	71.30	71.30	71.30	71.30	71.30	71.30	71.30	71.30	71.30	71.30	71.30	71.30	71.30	Quota	2f. s
	—	—	—	—	—	—	—	—	—	—	—	—	—	—	—	SDRs	1b. s
	.03	.03	.03	.03	.03	.03	.03	.03	.03	.03	.03	.03	.03	.03	.03	Reserve Position in the Fund	1c. s
	230.40	229.36	227.20	226.52	226.52	226.52	226.52	225.83	225.74	225.74	225.70	225.26	224.82	224.36	223.91	Total Fund Cred.&Loans Outstg.	2tl
International Liquidity																	
End of Period																	
	.51	.38	7.88	....	1.31	.98	2.36	5.07	28.09	.38	.42	.62	.43	.27	.48	Total Reserves minus Gold	1l. d
	.04	.04	.04	.04	.04	.04	.04	.04	.04	.04	.04	.04	.04	.04	.04	SDRs	1b. d
	.47	.34	7.84	....	1.27	.94	2.32	5.03	28.05	.34	.38	.58	.39	.23	.44	Reserve Position in the Fund	1c. d
	.18	.40	.12	....	8.87	3.13	9.45	9.08	9.68	12.40	12.56	10.87	10.48	9.78	6.38	Foreign Exchange	1d. d
	18.57	23.05	34.05	....	17.53	13.78	49.05	9.46	12.04	9.49	15.59	10.36	16.71	12.39	11.04	Monetary Authorities: Other Liab.	4..d
	39.32	39.47	43.17	....	48.32	36.97	17.86	46.33	15.35	5.12	8.44	2.47	3.01	10.01	11.87	Banking Institutions: Assets	7a. d
																Liabilities	7b. d
Monetary Authorities																	
End of Period																	
	.5	.4	7.9	....	1.3	1.0	2.4	5.1	28.1	.4	.4	26.7	17.0	†11.4	23.8	Foreign Assets	11
	563.0	733.8	841.1	....	985.3	1,072.9	1,264.1	1,284.9	1,513.0	1,803.1	1,916.2	35,687.0	32,605.1	†36643.0	41,690.6	Claims on Central Government	12a
	—	—	4.1	....	4.8	4.8	4.8	4.8	4.8	5.6	5.6	5.8	5.5	† —	—	Claims on Nonfin.Pub.Enterprises	12c
	1.0	1.0	1.1	....	11.0	12.0	17.8	15.5	15.4	20.5	20.2	25.5	24.6	†48.9	16.5	Claims on Private Sector	12d
	.9	1.9	2.5	....	24.4	23.8	23.4	51.4	61.5	2.5	2.3	4.3	1.7	†77.3	134.9	Claims on Banking Institutions	12e
	3.8	3.6	3.8	....	3.8	3.8	.7	.7	—	.2	.2	1.5	1.5	† —	—	Claims on Nonbank Financial Insts.	12g
	217.2	259.2	337.5	....	406.1	411.0	522.9	551.1	723.4	852.6	920.5	938.4	979.1	†1,384.7	1,548.2	Reserve Money	14
	82.5	96.5	101.6	....	189.3	154.9	274.1	302.9	485.8	568.4	576.6	565.5	556.9	†698.3	845.1	*of which: Currency Outside Banks*	14a
	.7	1.1	1.5	....	.4	1.4	2.2	2.1	2.7	3.9	4.8	3.0	1.7	†533.2	716.9	Time Deposits	15
	391.9	396.2	414.3	....	540.9	543.9	571.5	622.4	651.1	646.9	622.4	28,629.2	25,893.0	†27242.9	30,922.3	Foreign Liabilities	16c
	17.2	17.0	25.3	....	15.9	7.8	71.6	74.2	15.1	18.6	20.0	137.4	71.0	† —	34.0	Central Government Deposits	16d
	31.4	-6.1	81.6	....	104.6	73.2	69.6	60.8	12.7	42.3	61.8	9,259.2	7,735.2	†7,675.1	8,876.7	Capital Accounts	17a
	-89.2	73.4	.2	....	-37.2	81.1	75.4	51.8	217.7	267.8	315.3	-3,216.4	-2,025.2	†-55.2	-232.4	Other Items (Net)	17r
Banking Institutions																	
End of Period																	
	106.4	126.1	190.1	....	113.9	143.9	217.3	215.4	201.8	188.4	240.0	768.5	815.2	†1,174.5	1,402.8	Reserves	20
	18.6	23.0	34.1	....	17.5	13.8	49.1	9.5	12.0	9.5	15.6	447.9	660.2	†529.8	546.7	Foreign Assets	21
	10.9	17.6	9.8	....	7.2	3.1	8.8	5.4	5.1	3.5	—	306.2	358.1	†425.3	580.9	Claims on Central Government	22a
	38.7	49.7	42.0	....	47.9	55.6	82.7	63.1	21.0	5.7	7.9	12.2	44.5	†39.5	64.6	Claims on Nonfin.Pub.Enterprises	22c
	89.9	74.4	123.3	....	96.6	152.8	127.2	222.7	176.0	55.4	82.7	1,148.1	900.9	†663.2	877.0	Claims on Private Sector	22d
	.1	1.2	.3	....	6.3	.3	.3	—	2.1	5.3	—	—	—	†123.6	181.2	Claims on Nonbank Financial Insts.	22g
	94.6	93.8	135.0	....	92.8	111.4	151.6	155.3	167.0	127.4	110.0	1,005.5	1,247.9	†898.8	851.6	Demand Deposits	24
	56.7	66.4	73.9	....	72.0	156.3	274.5	324.4	360.9	195.5	235.5	335.8	324.7	†391.5	422.4	Time and Savings Deposits	25
	39.3	39.5	43.2	....	48.3	37.0	17.9	46.3	15.3	5.1	8.4	106.9	119.0	†427.9	587.4	Foreign Liabilities	26c
	13.1	20.3	26.0	....	35.1	29.9	30.5	35.3	30.3	10.6	51.1	112.0	165.4	†134.1	122.8	Central Government Deposits	26d
	.6	1.1	1.2	....	14.2	20.7	20.0	23.7	16.9	—	—	1.9	2.0	†104.3	115.8	Credit from Monetary Authorities	26g
	29.8	35.0	48.7	....	44.6	48.3	22.7	33.5	3.8	3.4	-5.5	36.3	685.6	†889.9	1,247.7	Capital Accounts	27a
	30.3	35.9	71.6	....	-17.7	-33.9	-31.7	-102.4	-176.3	-74.1	-53.4	1,084.5	234.3	†109.3	305.4	Other Items (Net)	27r
Banking Survey																	
End of Period																	
	-412.2	-412.2	-415.6	....	-570.4	-566.1	-538.0	-654.2	-626.3	-642.2	-614.9	-28,261.6	-25,334.9	†-27129.6	-30,939.3	Foreign Assets (Net)	31n
	677.0	844.1	974.4	....	1,112.0	1,267.8	1,404.4	1,487.6	1,692.0	1,870.1	1,961.7	36,936.9	33,703.9	†37809.3	43,253.9	Domestic Credit	32
	543.5	714.1	799.6	....	941.5	1,038.4	1,170.8	1,180.7	1,472.6	1,777.4	1,845.0	35,743.8	32,726.8	†36934.3	42,114.7	Claims on Central Govt. (Net)	32an
	38.7	49.7	46.2	....	52.7	60.4	87.5	68.0	25.8	11.3	13.5	18.0	50.1	†39.5	64.6	Claims on Nonfin.Pub.Enterprises	32c
	90.9	75.4	124.4	....	107.6	164.9	145.1	238.2	191.5	75.8	102.9	1,173.6	925.5	†712.1	893.5	Claims on Private Sector	32d
	3.9	4.8	4.2	....	10.1	4.1	1.0	.7	2.1	5.5	.2	1.5	1.5	†123.6	181.2	Claims on Nonbank Fin. Insts.	32g
	177.5	190.4	236.7	....	282.1	266.4	425.8	458.3	652.8	696.2	686.8	1,571.0	1,804.8	†1,597.0	1,703.4	Money	34
	57.5	67.5	75.4	....	72.4	157.7	276.7	326.5	363.6	199.4	240.3	338.8	326.4	†924.7	1,139.3	Quasi-Money	35
	61.2	28.9	130.3	....	149.3	121.5	92.2	94.3	16.6	45.7	56.3	9,295.6	8,420.7	†8,565.0	10,124.4	Capital Accounts	37a
	-31.3	145.2	116.3	....	37.8	156.1	71.7	-45.7	32.7	286.6	363.5	-2,530.0	-2,182.9	†-407.0	-652.5	Other Items (Net)	37r
	234.9	257.8	312.2	....	354.5	424.1	702.5	784.8	1,016.4	895.6	927.0	1,909.8	2,131.2	†2,521.8	2,842.7	Money plus Quasi-Money	35l
Interest Rates																	
Percent Per Annum																	
	6.82	6.68	6.78	....	....	....	....	6.16	6.12	....	6.08	6.00	6.02	5.83	5.63	Savings Rate	60k
	5.88	5.43	6.77	....	....	....	....	6.34	6.37	....	6.43	6.22	6.25	6.18	5.94	Deposit Rate	60l
	13.63	13.36	13.82	....	....	....	....	14.53	15.57	....	16.83	†21.74	16.72	20.53	22.14	Lending Rate	60p
Prices																	
Period Averages																	
	109.2	119.8	130.6	....	....	....	....	....	....	....	....	....	....	....	....	Consumer Prices	64

Liberia

		1972	1973	1974	1975	1976	1977	1978	1979	1980	1981	1982	1983	1984	1985	1986
International Transactions															*Millions of Liberian Dollars*	
Exports	70	244.40	324.00	400.27	393.83	459.96	447.42	504.05	536.56	600.40	529.16	477.44	427.60	452.12	435.60	408.37
Imports, c.i.f.	71	178.68	193.45	288.44	331.20	399.22	463.53	480.87	506.55	534.62	447.38	428.32	411.58	363.21	284.40	259.04
																1985=100
Unit Value of Exports	74	42.8	47.5	62.5	†81.8	84.2	98.1	88.3	103.9	121.1	†100.6	109.1	101.9	100.5	100.0	98.2
Unit Value of Imports	75	37	42	62	†67	64	79	81	94	109	†98	104	99	108	100	105
Balance of Payments															*Millions of US Dollars:*	
Current Account, n.i.e.	78al d	....	....	....	....	....	....	....	16.2	46.0	75.1	2.5	-104.0	-2.1	55.3	-17.7
Goods: Exports f.o.b.	78aa d	....	....	....	....	....	....	....	536.6	600.4	529.2	477.4	420.8	446.7	430.4	407.9
Goods: Imports f.o.b.	78ab d	....	....	....	....	....	....	....	-457.5	-478.0	-423.9	-390.2	-374.8	-325.4	-263.8	-258.8
Trade Balance	78ac d	....	....	....	....	....	....	....	79.1	122.4	105.3	87.2	46.0	121.3	166.6	149.1
Services: Credit	78ad d	....	....	....	....	....	....	....	17.0	13.1	11.5	32.7	38.5	36.9	34.6	56.9
Services: Debit	78ae d	....	....	....	....	....	....	....	-68.9	-72.7	-58.7	-92.0	-108.7	-92.5	-80.2	-80.5
Balance on Goods & Services	78af d	....	....	....	....	....	....	....	27.2	62.8	58.1	27.9	-24.2	65.7	121.0	125.5
Income: Credit	78ag d	....	....	....	....	....	....	....				1.8	1.8	2.6	3.7	2.1
Income: Debit	78ah d	....	....	....	....	....	....	....	-13.7	-24.0	-21.1	-74.1	-155.4	-129.4	-131.8	-183.3
Balance on Gds, Serv. & Inc.	78ai d	....	....	....	....	....	....	....	13.5	38.8	37.0	-44.4	-177.8	-61.1	-7.1	-55.7
Current Transfers, n.i.e.: Credit	78aj d	....	....	....	....	....	....	....	37.7	39.2	71.1	124.9	146.5	142.6	130.0	97.9
Current Transfers: Debit	78ak d	....	....	....	....	....	....	....	-35.0	-32.0	-33.0	-78.0	-72.7	-83.6	-67.6	-59.9
Capital Account, n.i.e.	78bc d								—	—	—	—	—	—	—	—
Capital Account, n.i.e.: Credit	78ba d								—	—	—	—	—	—	—	—
Capital Account: Debit	78bb d								—	—	—	—	—	—	—	—
Financial Account, n.i.e.	78bj d								122.1	82.2	58.7	139.6	-16.6	-16.4	-150.0	-202.9
Direct Investment Abroad	78bd d								—	—	—	—	—	—	—	—
Dir. Invest. in Rep. Econ., n.i.e.	78be d								—	—	—	34.8	49.1	36.2	-16.2	-16.5
Portfolio Investment Assets	78bf d								—	—	—	—	5.0	6.8	4.4	5.6
Equity Securities	78bk d								—	—	—	—	—	—	—	—
Debt Securities	78bl d								—	—	—	—	5.0	6.8	4.4	5.6
Portfolio Investment Liab., n.i.e.	78bg d								—	—	—	—	—	—	—	—
Equity Securities	78bm d								—	—	—	—	—	—	—	—
Debt Securities	78bn d								—	—	—	—	—	—	—	—
Financial Derivatives Assets	78bw d															
Financial Derivatives Liabilities	78bx d															
Other Investment Assets	78bh d	....	....	....	....	....	....	....	-14.0	25.1	8.7	10.8	-3.3	-28.7	-9.3	7.1
Monetary Authorities	78bo d	....	....	....	....	....	....	....	—	—	—	—	—	—	—	—
General Government	78bp d	....	....	....	....	....	....	....	—	—	—	—	—	-4.3	—	—
Banks	78bq d	....	....	....	....	....	....	....	-14.0	25.1	8.7	10.8	1.9	12.8	-3.1	7.1
Other Sectors	78br d	....	....	....	....	....	....	....	—	—	—	—	-5.2	-37.2	-6.2	—
Other Investment Liab., n.i.e.	78bi d	....	....	....	....	....	....	....	136.1	57.1	50.0	94.0	-67.4	-30.7	-128.9	-199.1
Monetary Authorities	78bs d	....	....	....	....	....	....	....	—	—	-.9	—	-7.3	-16.7	-12.1	-2.6
General Government	78bt d	....	....	....	....	....	....	....	102.9	70.5	43.9	86.3	74.5	19.3	-84.6	-91.3
Banks	78bu d	....	....	....	....	....	....	....	33.2	-13.4	7.0	-1.8	-11.5	-3.2	12.3	1.7
Other Sectors	78bv d	....	....	....	....	....	....	....	—	—	—	9.5	-123.2	-30.1	-44.5	-107.0
Net Errors and Omissions	78ca d	....	....	....	....	....	....	....	-211.1	-175.0	-182.7	-265.8	-7.0	-134.3	-108.7	-73.4
Overall Balance	78cb d	....	....	....	....	....	....	....	-72.8	-46.8	-48.9	-123.7	-127.6	-152.8	-203.4	-294.0
Reserves and Related Items	79da d	....	....	....	....	....	....	....	72.8	46.8	48.9	123.7	127.6	152.8	203.4	294.0
Reserve Assets	79db d	....	....	....	....	....	....	....	-.5	25.9	1.4	1.2	-14.2	16.9	2.0	2.6
Use of Fund Credit and Loans	79dc d	....	....	....	....	....	....	....	50.7	24.4	53.0	67.1	50.1	14.1	-7.0	—
Exceptional Financing	79de d	....	....	....	....	....	....	....	22.6	-3.5	-5.5	55.5	91.6	121.8	208.4	291.4
Government Finance															*Millions of Liberian Dollars:*	
Deficit (-) or Surplus	80	13.2	10.5	6.8	3.4	-16.0	†-24.2	-56.2	-141.2	-88.3	-110.3	-116.6	-102.9	-61.0	-87.1	-90.9
Revenue	81	75.1	88.8	104.6	121.0	147.9	†165.4	181.7	201.3	202.3	218.0	236.9	229.7	223.7	206.8	180.7
Grants Received	81z	11.3	11.0	12.3	11.3	16.0	†16.0	16.0	23.0	23.0	24.5	41.4	33.0	36.0	22.5	25.0
Exp. & Lending Minus Repay.	82z	73.2	89.3	110.1	128.9	179.9	†205.6	253.9	365.5	313.6	352.8	394.9	365.6	320.7	316.4	296.6
Expenditure	82	....	....	102.3	119.9	178.4	†182.6	232.7	344.3	281.0	323.2	371.0	338.3	298.4	291.0	273.9
Lending Minus Repayments	83	....	....	7.8	9.0	1.5	†23.0	21.2	21.2	32.6	29.6	23.9	27.3	22.3	25.4	22.7
Financing	84x	-13.2	-10.5	-6.8	-3.4	16.0	†24.2	56.2	141.2	88.3	110.3	116.6	102.9	61.0	87.1	90.9
Domestic	84a	....	....	-1.6	-5.7	....	†-13.5	41.3	30.8	58.0	48.9	75.6	63.2	41.1	34.8	22.1
Foreign	85a	....	....	-5.2	2.3	....	†37.7	14.9	110.4	30.3	61.4	41.0	39.7	19.9	52.3	68.8
Debt: Domestic	88a	....	7.7	13.2	10.9	....	†35.9	63.5	95.1	156.0	206.1	258.3	335.0	363.0	378.5	412.6
Foreign	89a	....	143.2	138.7	141.9	....	†215.2	223.7	350.5	435.8	498.2	511.4	559.7	585.1	982.1	1,121.0
National Accounts															*Millions of Liberian Dollars*	
Househ.Cons.Expend.,incl.NPISHs	96f	176.4	197.1	245.8	257.6	281.7	363.1	402.8	436.2	430.0	647.2	650.4	723.0	710.2	706.8	662.6
Government Consumption Expend.	91f	55.4	56.9	64.5	73.2	89.3	120.0	139.0	156.6	182.0	229.5	231.1	197.0	152.2	149.9	131.0
Gross Fixed Capital Formation	93e	88.7	85.5	116.7	161.2	206.4	234.3	260.1	277.6	196.1	179.6	193.1	183.1	168.9	126.5	115.0
Changes in Inventories	93i	15.4	-13.9	5.1	85.8	33.4	51.7	20.4	43.9	109.0	18.5	42.9	47.2	25.7	7.8	7.8
exports of goods and services	90c	274.8	329.9	407.2	403.7	467.1	459.0	500.0	553.6	613.5	540.7	487.4	466.1	489.0	470.2	462.2
Imports of Goods and Services (-)	98c	204.8	240.9	332.1	371.9	446.2	521.9	548.6	587.4	614.0	560.9	478.5	479.2	411.5	322.8	299.7
Gross Domestic Product (GDP)	99b	405.9	414.6	507.2	609.6	631.7	706.2	773.7	880.5	916.6	1,022.3	1,119.5	1,128.9	1,058.0	1,069.2	1,051.2
Net Primary Income from Abroad	98.n	-68.0	-92.0	-85.4	-122.8	-86.0	-80.0	-95.9	-87.7	-83.7	-125.2	-145.9	-153.6	-126.8	-123.6	-180.5
Gross National Income (GNI)	99a	337.9	322.6	421.8	486.8	545.7	626.2	677.8	792.8	832.9	942.1	973.6	975.3	931.2	945.6	820.7
GDP Volume 1971 prices	99b.p	386.6	376.8	404.7	343.5	357.2	354.2	368.2	384.4	366.2	350.1	342.4	331.3	321.3	318.5	....
GDP Volume (1985=100)	99bv p	109.6	106.8	114.7	97.4	101.2	100.4	104.4	109.0	103.8	106.1	103.1	102.3	101.4	100.0	102.9
GDP Deflator (1985=100)	99bi p	34.6	36.3	41.4	58.6	58.4	65.8	69.3	75.6	82.6	90.1	101.6	103.2	97.6	100.0	95.5
																Millions:
Population	99z	1.42	1.47	1.50	1.55	1.61	1.67	1.72	1.78	1.85	1.91	1.98	2.04	2.11	2.16	2.22

	1987	1988	1989	1990	1991	1992	1993	1994	1995	1996	1997	1998	1999	2000	2001		
International Transactions																	
Millions of Liberian Dollars																	
Exports	382.20	396.33	460.11	....	....	....	....	....	....	....	....	....	....	....	....	Exports	70
Imports, c.i.f.	307.60	272.32	....	....	....	....	....	....	....	....	....	....	....	....	....	Imports, c.i.f.	71
1985=100																	
Unit Value of Exports	93.6	....	....	....	....	....	....	....	....	....	....	....	....	....	....	Unit Value of Exports	74
Unit Value of Imports	112	....	....	....	....	....	....	....	....	....	....	....	....	....	....	Unit Value of Imports	75
Balance of Payments																	
Minus Sign Indicates Debit																	
Current Account, n.i.e.	−145.1	....	....	....	....	....	....	....	....	....	....	....	....	....	....	Current Account, n.i.e.	78al *d*
Goods: Exports f.o.b.	374.9	....	....	....	....	....	....	....	....	....	....	....	....	....	....	Goods: Exports f.o.b.	78aa *d*
Goods: Imports f.o.b.	−311.7	....	....	....	....	....	....	....	....	....	....	....	....	....	....	Goods: Imports f.o.b.	78ab *d*
Trade Balance	63.2	....	....	....	....	....	....	....	....	....	....	....	....	....	....	*Trade Balance*	78ac *d*
Services: Credit	52.5	....	....	....	....	....	....	....	....	....	....	....	....	....	....	Services: Credit	78ad *d*
Services: Debit	−74.2	....	....	....	....	....	....	....	....	....	....	....	....	....	....	Services: Debit	78ae *d*
Balance on Goods & Services	41.5	....	....	....	....	....	....	....	....	....	....	....	....	....	....	*Balance on Goods & Services*	78af *d*
Income: Credit	5.2	....	....	....	....	....	....	....	....	....	....	....	....	....	....	Income: Credit	78ag *d*
Income: Debit	−188.3	....	....	....	....	....	....	....	....	....	....	....	....	....	....	Income: Debit	78ah *d*
Balance on Gds, Serv. & Inc.	−141.6	....	....	....	....	....	....	....	....	....	....	....	....	....	....	*Balance on Gds, Serv. & Inc.*	78ai *d*
Current Transfers, n.i.e.: Credit	50.0	....	....	....	....	....	....	....	....	....	....	....	....	....	....	Current Transfers, n.i.e.: Credit	78aj *d*
Current Transfers: Debit	−53.5	....	....	....	....	....	....	....	....	....	....	....	....	....	....	Current Transfers: Debit	78ak *d*
Capital Account, n.i.e.	—	....	....	....	....	....	....	....	....	....	....	....	....	....	....	Capital Account, n.i.e.	78bc *d*
Capital Account, n.i.e.: Credit	—	....	....	....	....	....	....	....	....	....	....	....	....	....	....	Capital Account, n.i.e.: Credit	78ba *d*
Capital Account: Debit	—	....	....	....	....	....	....	....	....	....	....	....	....	....	....	Capital Account: Debit	78bb *d*
Financial Account, n.i.e.	−185.3	....	....	....	....	....	....	....	....	....	....	....	....	....	....	Financial Account, n.i.e.	78bj *d*
Direct Investment Abroad	—	....	....	....	....	....	....	....	....	....	....	....	....	....	....	Direct Investment Abroad	78bd *d*
Dir. Invest. in Rep. Econ., n.i.e.	38.5	....	....	....	....	....	....	....	....	....	....	....	....	....	....	Dir. Invest. in Rep. Econ., n.i.e.	78be *d*
Portfolio Investment Assets	—	....	....	....	....	....	....	....	....	....	....	....	....	....	....	Portfolio Investment Assets	78bf *d*
Equity Securities	—	....	....	....	....	....	....	....	....	....	....	....	....	....	....	Equity Securities	78bk *d*
Debt Securities	—	....	....	....	....	....	....	....	....	....	....	....	....	....	....	Debt Securities	78bl *d*
Portfolio Investment Liab., n.i.e.	—	....	....	....	....	....	....	....	....	....	....	....	....	....	....	Portfolio Investment Liab., n.i.e.	78bg *d*
Equity Securities	—	....	....	....	....	....	....	....	....	....	....	....	....	....	....	Equity Securities	78bm *d*
Debt Securities	—	....	....	....	....	....	....	....	....	....	....	....	....	....	....	Debt Securities	78bn *d*
Financial Derivatives Assets		....	....	....	....	....	....	....	....	....	....	....	....	....	....	Financial Derivatives Assets	78bw *d*
Financial Derivatives Liabilities		....	....	....	....	....	....	....	....	....	....	....	....	....	....	Financial Derivatives Liabilities	78bx *d*
Other Investment Assets	4.3	....	....	....	....	....	....	....	....	....	....	....	....	....	....	Other Investment Assets	78bh *d*
Monetary Authorities	—	....	....	....	....	....	....	....	....	....	....	....	....	....	....	Monetary Authorities	78bo *d*
General Government	—	....	....	....	....	....	....	....	....	....	....	....	....	....	....	General Government	78bp *d*
Banks	—	....	....	....	....	....	....	....	....	....	....	....	....	....	....	Banks	78bq *d*
Other Sectors	4.3	....	....	....	....	....	....	....	....	....	....	....	....	....	....	Other Sectors	78br *d*
Other Investment Liab., n.i.e.	−228.1	....	....	....	....	....	....	....	....	....	....	....	....	....	....	Other Investment Liab., n.i.e.	78bi *d*
Monetary Authorities	−.7	....	....	....	....	....	....	....	....	....	....	....	....	....	....	Monetary Authorities	78bs *d*
General Government	−120.0	....	....	....	....	....	....	....	....	....	....	....	....	....	....	General Government	78bt *d*
Banks	.2	....	....	....	....	....	....	....	....	....	....	....	....	....	....	Banks	78bu *d*
Other Sectors	−107.6	....	....	....	....	....	....	....	....	....	....	....	....	....	....	Other Sectors	78bv *d*
Net Errors and Omissions	30.3	....	....	....	....	....	....	....	....	....	....	....	....	....	....	Net Errors and Omissions	78ca *d*
Overall Balance	−300.1	....	....	....	....	....	....	....	....	....	....	....	....	....	....	*Overall Balance*	78cb *d*
Reserves and Related Items	300.1	....	....	....	....	....	....	....	....	....	....	....	....	....	....	Reserves and Related Items	79da *d*
Reserve Assets	.5	....	....	....	....	....	....	....	....	....	....	....	....	....	....	Reserve Assets	79db *d*
Use of Fund Credit and Loans	—	....	....	....	....	....	....	....	....	....	....	....	....	....	....	Use of Fund Credit and Loans	79dc *d*
Exceptional Financing	299.6	....	....	....	....	....	....	....	....	....	....	....	....	....	....	Exceptional Financing	79de *d*
Government Finance																	
Year Ending December 31																	
Deficit (-) or Surplus	−83.9	†−91.9	....													Deficit (-) or Surplus	80
Revenue	180.6	†212.8	....													Revenue	81
Grants Received	18.0	† —	....													Grants Received	81z
Exp. & Lending Minus Repay.	282.5	†304.7	....													Exp. & Lending Minus Repay.	82z
Expenditure	263.5	†283.4	....													Expenditure	82
Lending Minus Repayments	19.0	†21.3	....													Lending Minus Repayments	83
Financing	83.9	†91.9	....													Financing	84x
Domestic	42.3	†71.9	....													Domestic	84a
Foreign	41.6	†20.0	....													Foreign	85a
Debt: Domestic	459.4	†507.0	....													Debt: Domestic	88a
Foreign	1,306.4	†1,427.1	....													Foreign	89a
National Accounts																	
Millions of Liberian Dollars																	
Househ.Cons.Expend.,incl.NPISHs	713.9	733.3	656.8	....	....	....	....	....	....	....	....	....	....	....	....	Househ.Cons.Expend.,incl.NPISHs	96f
Government Consumption Expend.	163.2	142.8	160.0	....	....	....	....	....	....	....	....	....	....	....	....	Government Consumption Expend.	91f
Gross Fixed Capital Formation	120.4	115.3	96.8	....	....	....	....	....	....	....	....	....	....	....	....	Gross Fixed Capital Formation	93e
Changes in Inventories	7.0	3.5	4.0	....	....	....	....	....	....	....	....	....	....	....	....	Changes in Inventories	93i
exports of goods and services	427.4	448.9	521.9	....	....	....	....	....	....	....	....	....	....	....	....	exports of goods and services	90c
Imports of Goods and Services (-)	356.8	321.5	275.2	....	....	....	....	....	....	....	....	....	....	....	....	Imports of Goods and Services (-)	98c
Gross Domestic Product (GDP)	1,120.9	1,174.4	1,182.8	....	....	....	....	....	....	....	....	....	....	....	....	Gross Domestic Product (GDP)	99b
Net Primary Income from Abroad	−183.1	−193.8	−199.1	....	....	....	....	....	....	....	....	....	....	....	....	Net Primary Income from Abroad	98.n
Gross National Income (GNI)	937.8	980.6	983.8	....	....	....	....	....	....	....	....	....	....	....	....	Gross National Income (GNI)	99a
GDP Volume 1971 prices	....		....													GDP Volume 1971 prices	99b.*p*
GDP Volume (1985=100)	105.7	105.7	....													GDP Volume (1985=100)	99bv *p*
GDP Deflator (1985=100)	99.2	103.9	....													GDP Deflator (1985=100)	99bi *p*
Midyear Estimates																	
Population	2.28	2.34	2.40	2.46	2.52	2.58	2.64	2.70	2.76	2.81	2.88	†2.50	2.71	2.91	3.11	Population	99z

(See notes in the back of the book.)

Libya

672		1972	1973	1974	1975	1976	1977	1978	1979	1980	1981	1982	1983	1984	1985	1986
Exchange Rates																*SDRs per Dinar: End of Period (ac)*
Official Rate	ac	2.8000	2.8000	2.7589	2.8854	2.9073	2.7807	2.5927	2.5641	2.6484	2.9020	3.0621	3.2263	3.4460	3.0751	2.6047[e]
Official Rate	ag	3.0400	3.3778	3.3778	3.3778	3.3778	3.3778	3.3778	3.3778	3.3778	3.3778	3.3778	3.3778	3.3778	3.3778	3.1860[e]
Fund Position																*Millions of SDRs:*
Quota	2f.s	24	24	24	24	24	24	185	185	298	298	298	298	516	516	516
SDRs	1b.s	—	—	—	—	—	—	—	31	47	104	129	158	133	156	178
Reserve Position in the Fund	1c.s	6	6	6	6	6	6	6	42	148	189	189	189	244	244	244
Total Fund Cred.&Loans Outstg.	2tl	—	—	—	—	—	—	—	—	—	—	—	—	—	—	—
International Liquidity																*Millions of US Dollars Unless Otherwise Indicated:*
Total Reserves minus Gold	1l.d	2,832	2,024	3,511	2,095	3,106	4,786	4,105	6,344	13,091	9,003	7,059	5,219	3,634	5,904	5,953[e]
SDRs	1b.d	—	—	—	—	—	—	—	40	59	121	143	165	130	172	217
Reserve Position in the Fund	1c.d	7	7	7	7	7	7	8	56	189	220	209	198	239	267	298
Foreign Exchange	1d.d	2,826	2,017	3,504	2,088	3,099	4,779	4,097	6,248	12,842	8,662	6,708	4,856	3,266	5,465	5,438[e]
Gold (Million Fine Troy Ounces)	1ad	2.437	2.437	2.438	2.438	2.438	2.448	2.448	2.464	3.078	3.578	3.578	3.578	3.648	3.600	3.600
Gold (National Valuation)	1and	95	107	103	103	103	103	103	104	130	151	151	151	154	152	152
Deposit Money Banks: Assets	7a.d	46	121	131	138	197	258	224	417	1,052	929	894	683	665	522	458
Liabilities	7b.d	19	40	15	82	52	148	156	120	113	256	239	203	146	1	171
Monetary Authorities																*Millions of Dinars:*
Foreign Assets	11	962.3	629.6	1,244.7	753.0	1,064.2	1,623.6	1,492.4	2,219.2	4,223.2	2,808.1	2,158.0	1,643.0	1,114.2	1,897.4	1,978.6
Claims on Central Government	12a	—	163.8	249.3	584.2	533.5	353.8	1,106.6	1,129.1	340.3	1,192.0	1,825.2	932.3	1,151.4	828.2	686.4
Claims on Nonfin.Pub.Enterprises	12c	53.1	152.8	368.7	421.6	443.1	501.4	789.7	1,161.4	1,594.8	2,365.0	1,816.7	1,541.4	1,640.7	1,228.4	960.5
Claims on Private Sector	12d	.3	.5	.7	.8	1.0	1.4	2.0	2.5	2.8	3.9	4.1	4.3	4.3	4.4	4.1
Claims on Deposit Money Banks	12e	—	—	—	157.6	161.7	156.0	161.1	180.7	180.7	272.7	272.7	292.7	339.2	319.2	317.4
Reserve Money	14	367.8	402.0	590.1	673.4	829.6	1,051.5	1,355.9	1,793.9	2,297.2	2,166.8	2,261.1	1,798.9	1,717.9	2,221.6	2,113.2
of which: Currency Outside DMBs	14a	147.4	202.6	262.2	346.0	436.0	585.0	868.5	1,053.7	685.7	791.1	889.9	838.2	767.5	985.0	1,023.7
Nonfin.Pub.Enterp.Dep.	14e	112.3	133.0	180.6	185.8	210.5	265.9	260.0	488.7	783.1	833.4	748.0	377.6	308.1	394.9	182.0
Time & Foreign Currency Deposits	15	40.5	68.6	151.9	101.2	120.9	142.0	166.9	184.3	227.0	188.2	202.9	239.0	287.2	297.6	289.1
Restricted Deposits	16b	39.8	75.1	170.9	144.8	140.2	144.1	133.0	150.4	221.0	226.7	259.1	269.6	354.8	307.8	284.3
Foreign Liabilities	16c	.7	1.0	.5	1.5	.9	.6	1.1	2.6	2.9	3.2	7.1	—	—	—	—
Central Government Deposits	16d	520.8	325.7	376.3	308.3	321.6	312.1	423.4	490.0	847.3	716.9	681.1	653.7	648.4	641.6	639.0
Capital Accounts	17a	8.0	8.0	8.0	8.0	8.0	8.0	8.0	15.5	22.5	127.3	184.2	241.2	254.1	270.1	280.6
Other Items (Net)	17r	38.0	66.2	565.7	680.0	782.3	978.0	1,463.4	2,056.2	2,723.7	3,212.6	2,481.2	1,211.4	987.4	538.9	340.9
Deposit Money Banks																*Millions of Dinars:*
Reserves	20	135.0	97.9	148.7	157.1	186.5	225.9	234.0	291.7	875.6	563.2	597.6	595.0	632.3	851.9	902.7
Foreign Assets	21	15.1	35.8	38.7	40.7	58.3	76.5	66.2	123.5	311.4	275.1	264.6	202.2	196.9	154.4	143.7
Claims on Central Government	22a	—	—	3.0	10.4	95.7	219.2	183.1	455.2	828.5	535.5	325.1	561.5	1,097.5	1,406.5	1,546.5
Claims on Nonfin. Pub. Enterprises	22c	15.3	59.5	40.4	46.1	39.0	56.5	58.6	57.2	59.7	139.1	182.5	76.1	117.7	107.1	151.6
Claims on Private Sector	22d	132.7	216.8	411.9	599.2	705.0	800.4	880.1	1,004.9	1,087.1	2,048.9	1,395.4	2,143.6	2,053.3	1,942.7	1,894.0
Claims on Other Banking Insts	22f	....	....	....	....	....	....	....	....	....	....	....	....	....	....	....
Claims on Nonbank Financial Insts	22g	....	....	....	....	....	....	....	....	....	....	....	....	....	....	....
Demand Deposits	24	153.3	178.4	311.1	335.7	492.9	592.9	559.3	705.0	1,430.1	1,887.6	1,594.4	1,668.6	1,635.7	2,112.3	1,835.7
Time & Foreign Currency Deposits	25	64.6	90.2	146.9	134.9	173.0	212.9	211.4	375.6	428.9	413.9	354.4	475.6	606.8	790.6	956.8
Restricted Deposits	26b	30.7	63.0	110.8	112.0	121.5	185.3	174.6	242.3	328.8	305.9	256.8	258.2	215.2	165.4	239.7
Foreign Liabilities	26c	5.5	8.7	4.3	24.3	15.5	43.7	46.3	35.5	33.3	75.7	70.8	60.0	43.2	.3	53.6
Central Government Deposits	26d	8.2	30.0	19.5	27.8	29.5	45.0	41.5	78.2	195.1	198.7	286.5	160.4	387.6	164.8	437.2
Credit from Monetary Authorities	26g	—	—	.9	157.6	161.7	156.0	161.1	181.4	180.7	272.7	272.7	293.4	339.2	319.2	317.4
Capital Accounts	27a	20.2	24.2	31.1	43.6	47.9	65.3	90.5	117.7	148.6	164.3	220.5	237.1	188.9	208.8	225.6
Other Items (Net)	27r	13.1	12.4	12.1	22.2	41.7	79.6	141.8	210.6	417.2	243.0	−287.6	432.9	684.3	704.8	574.2
Monetary Survey																*Millions of Dinars:*
Foreign Assets (Net)	31n	971.1	655.6	1,278.6	768.0	1,106.1	1,655.8	1,511.2	2,304.6	4,498.4	3,004.3	2,344.8	1,785.2	1,267.8	2,051.6	2,068.7
Domestic Credit	32	−327.6	237.7	678.2	1,326.2	1,466.3	1,575.7	2,555.1	3,242.1	2,870.7	5,368.7	4,581.3	4,445.1	5,028.7	4,710.8	4,166.9
Claims on Central Govt. (Net)	32an	−529.0	−191.9	−143.5	258.5	278.2	216.0	824.8	1,016.1	126.4	811.9	1,182.7	679.7	1,212.7	1,428.2	1,156.7
Claims on Nonfin.Pub.Enterprises	32c	68.4	212.3	409.1	467.7	482.1	558.0	848.3	1,218.6	1,654.5	2,504.1	1,999.2	1,617.5	1,758.5	1,335.5	1,112.1
Claims on Private Sector	32d	133.0	217.3	412.6	600.0	706.0	801.8	882.0	1,007.4	1,089.9	2,052.7	1,399.4	2,147.9	2,057.5	1,947.1	1,898.1
Claims on Other Banking Insts	32f	....	....	....	....	....	....	....	....	....	....	....	....	....	....	....
Claims on Nonbank Fin. Insts	32g	....	....	....	....	....	....	....	....	....	....	....	....	....	....	....
Money	34	413.0	514.0	753.8	867.6	1,139.4	1,443.8	1,687.8	2,247.3	2,898.9	3,512.2	3,232.3	2,884.5	2,711.3	3,492.2	3,041.4
Quasi-Money	35	105.1	158.8	298.8	236.1	293.9	354.9	378.3	559.8	655.9	602.1	557.3	714.6	894.0	1,088.2	1,246.0
Restricted Deposits	36b	70.5	138.1	281.7	256.8	261.7	329.5	307.6	392.7	549.8	532.6	515.9	527.8	570.0	473.2	524.0
Capital Accounts	37a	28.2	32.2	39.1	51.6	55.9	73.3	98.5	133.2	171.1	291.5	404.7	478.3	442.9	478.9	506.2
Other Items (Net)	37r	24.1	47.1	577.4	686.6	820.7	1,032.3	1,598.7	2,227.4	3,093.8	3,434.8	2,219.2	1,633.2	1,681.7	1,233.4	919.8
Money plus Quasi-Money	35l	518.1	672.8	1,052.6	1,103.7	1,433.2	1,798.7	2,066.1	2,807.2	3,554.8	4,114.2	3,789.6	3,599.0	3,605.3	4,580.4	4,287.4
Other Banking Institutions																*Millions of Dinars:*
Cash	40	6.48	6.45	9.06	16.38	17.02	22.66	20.66	19.97	48.25	25.72	28.69	1.46	1.55	4.19	3.51
Claims on Private Sector	42d	22.11	25.26	29.50	30.54	32.24	38.66	40.62	45.17	38.25	46.00	46.09	45.10	47.49	48.27	57.83
Capital Accounts	47a	8.37	11.81	12.75	12.76	44.98	45.98	45.98	45.98	45.98	46.07	46.60	63.51	66.10	74.75	92.15
Other Items (Net)	47r	20.22	19.88	25.81	34.17	4.28	15.35	15.30	19.16	40.43	25.64	28.19	−16.94	−17.06	−22.33	−30.82
Interest Rates																*Percent Per Annum*
Discount Rate *(End of Period)*	60	5.0	5.0	5.0	5.0	5.0	5.0	5.0	5.0	5.0	5.0	5.0	5.0	5.0	5.0	5.0
Money Market Rate	60b	4.0	4.0	4.0	4.0	4.0	4.0	4.0	4.0	4.0	4.0	4.0	4.0	4.0	4.0	4.0
Deposit Rate	60l	4.0	4.0	4.0	4.0	4.0	4.0	4.0	4.0	5.1	5.5	5.5	5.5	5.5	5.5	5.5
Lending Rate	60p	7.0	7.0	7.0	7.0	7.0	7.0	7.0	7.0	7.0	7.0	7.0	7.0	7.0	7.0	7.0
Production																*Index Numbers (1995=100):*
Consumer Prices (1975=100)	64	79.0	85.3	91.6	100.0	105.5	112.1	145.0	136.3	....	....	....	....	....	....	....
Foodstuffs (1975=100)	64a	95.9	87.8	93.9	100.0	113.5	127.3	142.2	180.7	....	....	....	....	....	....	....
Crude Petroleum Production	66aa	161.5	155.8	109.5	106.5	139.6	148.4	142.3	148.2	129.0	79.8	82.7	77.4	77.4	76.0	74.4
International Transactions																*Millions of Dinars*
Exports	70	966.3	1,196.4	2,445.2	2,023.2	2,828.5	3,378.2	2,929.3	4,759.3	6,486.4	4,609.8	3,908.8	3,616.6	3,300.4	3,645.6	2,432.0
Crude Petroleum	70aa	949.2	1,161.7	2,388.3	1,925.3	2,711.2	3,189.7	2,719.5	4,419.2	6,287.3	4,384.3	3,718.0	3,370.7	3,020.8	3,184.3	1,572.0
Imports, c.i.f.	71	343.2	539.9	817.8	1,048.7	950.8	1,117.1	1,362.6	1,572.4	2,006.2	2,481.4	2,124.3	1,785.0	1,842.0	1,214.0	1,316.0
Imports, c.i.f., from DOTS	71y	....	....	....	....	....	....	....	....	....	2,481.4	2,548.4	2,287.1	2,148.6	1,658.9	1,121.8
																1995=100
Volume of Exports	72	....	....	....	....	....	....	....	....	....	....	76.6	76.1	74.6	†83.1	83.4
Volume of Imports	73	....	....	....	....	....	....	....	....	....	....	125.8	123.7	132.6	†96.2	96.7
Unit Value of Exports	74	....	....	....	....	....	....	....	....	....	....	170.5	156.8	145.4	†144.4	94.8
Unit Value of Imports	75	....	....	....	....	....	....	....	....	....	....	81.6	76.5	72.4	†70.9	82.7
Export Prices																*1985=100:*
Crude Petroleum	76aad	10.2	14.5	43.3	38.8	41.0	46.0	45.5	70.0	119.5	132.8	117.8	102.5	100.0	100.0	....

1987	1988	1989	1990	1991	1992	1993	1994	1995	1996	1997	1998	1999	2000	2001		
US Dollars per Dinar: End of Period (ag)															**Exchange Rates**	
2.6046[e]	2.6047[e]	2.6046[e]	2.6046[e]	2.6047[e]	2.4138[e]	2.2400	1.9048	1.9048	1.9048	1.9048	1.8765	1.3484	1.4204	1.2240	Official Rate	ac
3.6951[e]	3.5051[e]	3.4229[e]	3.7055[e]	3.7258[e]	3.3190[e]	3.0768	2.7807	2.8314	2.7390	2.5700	2.6421	1.8507	1.8507	1.5330	Official Rate	ag
End of Period															**Fund Position**	
516	516	516	516	516	818	818	818	818	818	818	818	1,124	1,124	1,124	Quota	2f. *s*
198	219	249	287	323	278	303	325	350	374	398	426	373	413	441	SDRs	1b. *s*
244	244	244	244	244	319	319	319	319	319	319	319	396	396	396	Reserve Position in the Fund	1c. *s*
—	—	—	—	—	—	—	—	—	—	—	—	—	—	—	Total Fund Cred.&Loans Outstg.	2tl
End of Period															**International Liquidity**	
5,838[e]	4,322[e]	4,333[e]	5,839[e]	5,695[e]	6,182[e]	....	....	....	....	....	7,270	7,280	12,461	14,800	Total Reserves minus Gold	1l. *d*
280	294	328	409	461	383	417	474	520	538	538	600	511	538	554	SDRs	1b. *d*
345	328	320	346	348	439	438	466	474	459	430	449	543	515	497	Reserve Position in the Fund	1c. *d*
5,212[e]	3,699[e]	3,685[e]	5,084[e]	4,885[e]	5,361[e]	....	....	....	....	....	6,221	6,226	11,408	13,749	Foreign Exchange	1d. *d*
3.600	3.600	3.600	3.600	3.600	3.600	....	....	....	....	....	4.616	4.624	4.624	4.624	Gold (Million Fine Troy Ounces)	1ad
152	152	152	152	152	152	....	....	....	....	....	194	194	194	194	Gold (National Valuation)	1an *d*
339	109	160	273	257	435	401	385	459	583	1,183	736	629	937	925	Deposit Money Banks: Assets	7a. *d*
46	540	906	1,017	1,103	694	171	169	109	207	3,581	2,576	1,568	1,461	2,169	Liabilities	7b. *d*
End of Period															**Monetary Authorities**	
1,696.5	1,358.5	1,475.7	1,872.4	1,745.1	2,037.8	1,435.5	1,674.7	2,414.5	2,740.3	3,580.3	3,583.1	3,895.9	7,295.9	9,491.5	Foreign Assets	11
650.8	625.1	3,728.8	4,216.0	4,630.9	4,726.5	4,740.0	4,815.0	5,064.6	5,107.4	5,406.7	5,927.2	5,320.1	6,832.6	6,789.0	Claims on Central Government	12a
926.7	798.1	879.6	1,147.5	1,545.3	1,168.0	1,230.0	1,890.1	2,208.3	2,336.3	1,671.4	1,559.2	1,704.0	2,567.9	2,694.2	Claims on Nonfin.Pub.Enterprises	12c
5.0	5.6	6.0	6.2	6.4	6.3	6.3	6.7	6.6	6.4	6.4	6.4	7.1	8.0	9.5	Claims on Private Sector	12d
352.2	352.2	304.7	298.8	298.8	298.8	298.8	283.5	283.5	200.0	144.4	144.4	144.4	115.5	86.6	Claims on Deposit Money Banks	12e
2,250.7	1,912.9	2,371.1	3,185.9	3,185.5	4,092.3	3,992.6	4,627.4	4,985.7	5,434.8	†5,821.2	5,760.4	5,455.4	5,404.8	5,946.9	Reserve Money	14
1,068.2	899.6	1,131.6	1,461.0	1,620.8	1,982.2	2,216.8	1,989.8	2,035.4	2,419.8	2,534.2	2,698.6	2,657.5	2,711.0	2,577.4	*of which: Currency Outside DMBs*	14a
162.1	131.4	298.2	751.6	392.9	312.0	264.3	478.8	603.9	414.5	536.2	176.3	133.7	200.8	297.8	*Nonfin.Pub.Enterp.Dep.*	14e
288.2	333.5	520.8	462.1	337.4	419.8	529.5	615.0	701.4	522.8	†62.6	65.3	19.4	38.9	245.2	Time & Foreign Currency Deposits	15
356.9	290.7	210.8	341.4	240.6	175.6	248.6	988.1	344.8	414.2	414.2	332.0	428.1	561.9	738.0	Restricted Deposits	16b
—	—	—	—	—	—	—	—	—	—	618.3	476.9	623.8	1,501.5	1,673.2	Foreign Liabilities	16c
662.2	665.6	681.2	696.1	887.0	694.1	676.6	678.2	708.3	741.2	†3,368.6	3,696.4	4,450.6	6,941.0	7,439.1	Central Government Deposits	16d
312.6	332.6	347.6	352.6	352.6	354.3	356.2	360.9	360.9	360.9	†1,207.9	1,244.0	1,082.9	1,520.0	2,634.8	Capital Accounts	17a
−239.4	−395.6	2,263.4	2,502.5	3,223.5	2,501.3	1,907.1	1,400.5	2,876.4	2,916.6	−683.3	−354.7	−988.7	851.9	393.4	Other Items (Net)	17r
End of Period															**Deposit Money Banks**	
1,025.4	846.9	944.7	1,073.1	1,232.2	1,786.3	1,506.6	2,204.6	2,336.6	2,606.1	2,705.8	2,776.1	2,428.4	2,357.2	2,345.9	Reserves	20
91.7	31.0	46.7	73.6	69.1	131.1	130.3	138.6	162.2	212.8	460.3	278.6	339.7	506.4	603.1	Foreign Assets	21
1,319.1	1,597.7	1,437.7	1,436.5	1,436.5	1,444.1	1,444.1	1,451.1	1,451.1	1,436.5	1,387.5	1,387.5	1,387.5	1,392.5	1,810.5	Claims on Central Government	22a
417.7	80.9	73.9	72.8	104.6	109.1	127.1	146.2	153.2	328.8	†1,440.7	1,491.9	1,866.4	1,776.5	3,163.7	Claims on Nonfin. Pub. Enterprises	22c
2,021.2	2,252.3	2,391.4	2,484.8	2,546.4	2,737.3	3,001.2	3,223.6	3,468.1	2,878.4	3,109.1	3,123.4	3,989.1	4,004.0	4,039.0	Claims on Private Sector	22d
....	....	....	....	....	....	....	....	....	....	....	....	40.3	49.7	27.3	Claims on Other Banking Insts	22f
....	....	....	....	....	....	....	....	....	....	....	....	124.2	506.7	75.6	Claims on Nonbank Financial Insts	22g
2,208.3	1,980.6	2,091.6	2,239.6	2,279.1	2,693.0	2,728.2	3,417.3	3,612.1	3,489.4	3,556.5	3,753.4	4,162.8	4,363.1	4,370.1	Demand Deposits	24
689.2	866.9	645.1	662.7	886.2	1,019.3	1,069.4	1,260.5	1,550.4	1,744.0	1,555.2	1,838.0	†2,202.1	2,156.7	2,271.6	Time & Foreign Currency Deposits	25
300.3	251.9	258.4	282.7	234.1	236.9	208.7	173.9	271.7	277.3	368.1	331.0	266.5	341.0	709.1	Restricted Deposits	26b
12.4	154.1	202.8	202.2	296.0	209.0	55.7	60.8	38.5	75.7	†1,393.3	975.0	847.4	789.5	1,414.8	Foreign Liabilities	26c
187.1	136.6	160.4	193.1	149.8	181.0	175.5	171.5	114.3	340.0	385.0	354.9	284.6	267.9	259.0	Central Government Deposits	26d
199.2	352.2	304.7	298.8	319.0	291.5	299.9	283.5	283.5	203.6	147.9	147.9	147.9	119.1	90.2	Credit from Monetary Authorities	26g
249.8	293.0	287.3	311.8	356.1	373.3	391.2	405.2	411.8	491.5	601.3	659.7	728.5	793.9	962.4	Capital Accounts	27a
861.7	842.8	881.8	877.6	868.5	1,204.0	1,280.6	1,391.7	1,289.9	841.1	1,096.3	997.9	1,535.8	1,761.8	1,987.8	Other Items (Net)	27r
End of Period															**Monetary Survey**	
1,775.8	1,235.5	1,319.6	1,743.8	1,518.2	1,960.0	1,510.1	1,752.5	2,538.2	2,877.4	2,029.0	2,409.8	2,764.4	5,511.3	7,006.6	Foreign Assets (Net)	31n
4,491.1	4,557.6	7,675.8	8,474.5	9,233.3	9,316.2	9,696.7	10,683.0	11,529.3	11,012.6	†9,268.2	9,444.3	9,703.5	9,929.0	10,910.7	Domestic Credit	32
1,120.5	1,420.7	4,324.9	4,763.2	5,030.6	5,295.5	5,332.1	5,416.4	5,693.1	5,462.7	†3,040.6	3,263.4	1,972.4	1,016.2	901.4	Claims on Central Govt. (Net)	32an
1,344.4	879.0	953.5	1,220.3	1,649.9	1,277.1	1,357.1	2,036.3	2,361.5	2,665.1	†3,112.1	3,051.1	3,570.4	4,344.4	5,857.9	Claims on Nonfin.Pub.Enterprises	32c
2,026.2	2,257.9	2,397.4	2,491.0	2,552.8	2,743.7	3,007.5	3,230.3	3,474.7	2,884.8	3,115.5	3,129.8	3,996.2	4,012.0	4,048.5	Claims on Private Sector	32d
....	....	....	....	....	....	....	....	....	....	—	—	40.3	49.7	27.3	Claims on Other Banking Insts	32f
....	....	....	....	....	....	....	....	....	....	—	—	124.2	506.7	75.6	Claims on Nonbank Fin. Insts	32g
3,438.6	3,011.6	3,521.4	4,452.2	4,292.8	4,987.2	5,209.3	5,885.9	6,251.4	6,323.7	6,654.5	6,683.8	7,001.2	7,313.5	7,402.7	Money	34
977.3	1,200.3	1,165.8	1,124.8	1,223.6	1,439.0	1,598.9	1,875.5	2,251.8	2,266.8	1,617.8	1,903.3	2,221.5	2,195.6	2,516.8	Quasi-Money	35
657.2	542.6	469.2	624.1	474.8	412.5	457.3	1,162.0	616.5	691.5	782.3	663.0	694.6	902.9	1,447.1	Restricted Deposits	36b
562.4	625.5	634.9	664.3	708.6	727.6	747.4	766.1	772.7	852.4	1,809.2	1,903.7	1,811.4	2,313.9	3,597.2	Capital Accounts	37a
464.2	482.2	3,141.8	3,280.3	4,051.8	3,709.9	3,193.7	2,746.3	4,176.1	3,755.7	433.9	700.6	739.2	2,714.5	2,953.2	Other Items (Net)	37r
4,416.0	4,211.9	4,687.3	5,577.0	5,516.3	6,426.2	6,808.2	7,761.4	8,503.2	8,590.5	8,272.3	8,587.1	9,222.7	9,509.1	9,919.5	Money plus Quasi-Money	35l
End of Period															**Other Banking Institutions**	
85.30	94.20	81.90	69.60	70.60	75.70	73.10	53.60	41.40	40.80	54.40	29.40	85.50	96.40	....	Cash	40
42.40	45.80	46.50	47.10	42.90	43.40	40.30	38.80	48.90	51.00	63.90	63.50	97.40	118.70	....	Claims on Private Sector	42d
67.00	67.00	72.10	77.10	78.70	80.20	82.80	84.70	85.50	86.40	89.60	90.70	84.40	88.40	....	Capital Accounts	47a
60.70	73.00	56.30	39.60	34.50	38.90	30.60	7.60	4.80	5.40	28.70	2.20	98.50	126.70	....	Other Items (Net)	47r
Percent Per Annum															**Interest Rates**	
5.0	5.0	5.0	5.0	5.0	5.0	5.0	....	....	....	....	3.0	5.0	5.0	5.0	Discount Rate *(End of Period)*	60
4.0	4.0	4.0	4.0	4.0	4.0	4.0	....	....	....	....	4.0	4.0	4.0	4.0	Money Market Rate	60b
5.5	5.5	5.5	5.5	5.5	5.5	5.5	....	....	....	....	....	3.2	3.0	3.0	Deposit Rate	60l
7.0	7.0	7.0	7.0	7.0	7.0	7.0	....	....	....	....	....	7.0	7.0	7.0	Lending Rate	60p
Period Averages															**Production**	
....	....	....	....	....	....	....	....	....	....	....	....	....	....	....	Consumer Prices (1975=100)	64
....	....	....	....	....	....	....	....	....	....	....	....	....	....	....	Foodstuffs (1975=100)	64a
70.0	73.1	78.9	97.1	107.1	107.0	99.1	99.2	100.0	101.1	101.7	99.1	94.7	95.7	....	Crude Petroleum Production	66aa
Millions of Dinars															**International Transactions**	
2,372.0	1,907.0	2,407.0	3,745.0	3,154.0	....	....	2,873.0	3,107.2	3,581.6	3,684.2	2,620.6	3,682.2	5,221.5	....	Exports	70
....	....	....	....	....	....	....	....	....	....	....	....	....	....	....	Crude Petroleum	70aa
1,278.0	1,677.0	1,475.0	1,511.0	1,505.0	....	....	1,780.0	1,866.8	2,124.1	2,336.2	2,151.1	1,928.2	1,911.4	....	Imports, c.i.f.	71
1,279.7	1,689.0	1,316.1	1,603.6	1,498.9	1,470.4	1,694.0	1,387.0	1,781.8	2,020.7	2,111.7	2,206.3	2,145.9	2,099.0	2,600.9	Imports, c.i.f., from DOTS	71y
1995=100																
82.0	77.5	85.6	104.6	110.8	100.0	95.6	100.7	100.0	94.6	99.9	71.0	99.8	141.5	....	Volume of Exports	72
87.9	126.9	109.3	109.4	114.5	97.0	110.3	95.3	100.0	108.6	122.6	112.8	101.2	100.3	....	Volume of Imports	73
91.3	75.4	87.0	110.9	89.8	90.4	79.2	94.8	100.0	124.5	109.9	....	....	....	....	Unit Value of Exports	74
80.5	78.6	80.5	81.1	74.1	83.1	84.4	89.7	100.0	101.3	102.7	....	....	....	....	Unit Value of Imports	75
Index of Prices in US Dollars															Export Prices	
....	....	....	....	....	....	....	....	....	....	....	....	....	....	....	Crude Petroleum	76aa *d*

Libya

	1972	1973	1974	1975	1976	1977	1978	1979	1980	1981	1982	1983	1984	1985	1986
Balance of Payments														*Millions of US Dollars:*	
Current Account, n.i.e. .... 78al *d*	...	...	...	...	...	2,159	738	3,771	8,214	−3,963	−1,560	−1,643	−1,456	1,906	−166
Goods: Exports f.o.b. .... 78aa *d*	...	...	...	...	...	10,406	9,900	15,981	21,919	14,731	13,701	12,348	11,028	10,353	6,186
Goods: Imports f.o.b. .... 78ab *d*	...	...	...	...	...	−4,929	−5,764	−8,647	−10,368	−14,563	−10,976	−8,978	−8,464	−5,754	−4,718
Trade Balance............... 78ac *d*	...	...	...	...	...	5,476	4,136	7,334	11,551	168	2,725	3,370	2,564	4,599	1,468
Services: Credit .... 78ad *d*	...	...	...	...	...	136	153	143	164	163	163	161	170	63	87
Services: Debit .... 78ae *d*	...	...	...	...	...	−1,301	−1,448	−1,953	−2,303	−2,757	−2,265	−2,315	−2,202	−1,775	−1,114
Balance on Goods & Services .... 78af *d*	...	...	...	...	...	4,311	2,841	5,523	9,413	−2,427	624	1,216	532	2,887	442
Income: Credit .... 78ag *d*	...	...	...	...	...	244	317	424	1,282	1,627	868	676	550	463	582
Income: Debit .... 78ah *d*	...	...	...	...	...	−1,459	−1,370	−1,273	−1,347	−1,517	−1,376	−1,433	−1,218	−540	−629
Balance on Gds, Serv. & Inc. .... 78ai *d*	...	...	...	...	...	3,096	1,788	4,673	9,348	−2,317	115	459	−135	2,811	395
Current Transfers, n.i.e.: Credit .... 78aj *d*	...	...	...	...	...	15	17	18	20	26	32	29	14	9	7
Current Transfers: Debit .... 78ak *d*	...	...	...	...	...	−952	−1,067	−920	−1,154	−1,672	−1,706	−2,131	−1,335	−913	−567
Capital Account, n.i.e. .... 78bc *d*	...	...	...	...	...	—	—	—	—	—	—	—	—	—	—
Capital Account, n.i.e.: Credit .... 78ba *d*	...	...	...	...	...	—	—	—	—	—	—	—	—	—	—
Capital Account: Debit .... 78bb *d*	...	...	...	...	...	—	—	—	—	—	—	—	—	—	—
Financial Account, n.i.e. .... 78bj *d*	...	...	...	...	...	−518	−1,406	−1,298	−1,703	−511	−625	93	831	784	−458
Direct Investment Abroad .... 78bd *d*	...	...	...	...	...	−60	−28	−21	−47	−25	−19	—	—	—	—
Dir. Invest. in Rep. Econ., n.i.e. .... 78be *d*	...	...	...	...	...	−451	−692	−588	−1,089	−744	−392	−327	−17	119	−188
Portfolio Investment Assets .... 78bf *d*	...	...	...	...	...	−220	−146	−23	−113	−430	−255	−107	47	55	−72
Equity Securities .... 78bk *d*	...	...	...	...	...	−220	−45	−23	−113	−421	−243	−98	47	55	−72
Debt Securities .... 78bl *d*	...	...	...	...	...	—	−101	—	—	−9	−12	−8	—	—	—
Portfolio Investment Liab., n.i.e. .... 78bg *d*	...	...	...	...	...	—	—	—	—	—	—	—	—	—	—
Equity Securities .... 78bm *d*	...	...	...	...	...	—	—	—	—	—	—	—	—	—	—
Debt Securities .... 78bn *d*	...	...	...	...	...	—	—	—	—	—	—	—	—	—	—
Financial Derivatives Assets .... 78bw *d*	...	...	...	...	...	...	...	...	...	...	...	...	...	...	...
Financial Derivatives Liabilities .... 78bx *d*	...	...	...	...	...	...	...	...	...	...	...	...	...	...	...
Other Investment Assets .... 78bh *d*	...	...	...	...	...	−232	−716	−839	−1,275	52	−578	38	324	505	−404
Monetary Authorities .... 78bo *d*	...	...	...	...	...	−7	−7	—	—	—	—	−49	100	−112	−6
General Government .... 78bp *d*	...	...	...	...	...	−326	−218	−298	−123	−514	372	−83	50	29	12
Banks .... 78bq *d*	...	...	...	...	...	−53	−3	−235	−623	153	49	207	21	150	42
Other Sectors .... 78br *d*	...	...	...	...	...	155	−488	−306	−530	412	−999	−37	153	438	−453
Other Investment Liab., n.i.e. .... 78bi *d*	...	...	...	...	...	446	177	173	821	637	619	488	477	105	206
Monetary Authorities .... 78bs *d*	...	...	...	...	...	7	7	75	22	133	86	−49	100	−112	−6
General Government .... 78bt *d*	...	...	...	...	...	—	−78	—	—	—	—	—	—	—	—
Banks .... 78bu *d*	...	...	...	...	...	113	−4	8	−56	144	−22	315	−57	−145	180
Other Sectors .... 78bv *d*	...	...	...	...	...	326	253	90	855	361	554	223	434	362	32
Net Errors and Omissions .... 78ca *d*	...	...	...	...	...	33	47	−253	−104	329	172	−236	−1,096	−328	847
Overall Balance .... 78cb *d*	...	...	...	...	...	1,674	−621	2,220	6,407	−4,145	−2,013	−1,786	−1,721	2,362	224
Reserves and Related Items .... 79da *d*	...	...	...	...	...	−1,674	621	−2,220	−6,407	4,145	2,013	1,786	1,721	−2,362	−224
Reserve Assets .... 79db *d*	...	...	...	...	...	−1,674	621	−2,220	−6,407	4,145	2,013	1,786	1,721	−2,362	−224
Use of Fund Credit and Loans .... 79dc *d*	...	...	...	...	...	—	—	—	—	—	—	—	—	—	—
Exceptional Financing .... 79de *d*	...	...	...	...	...	...	...	...	...	...	...	...	...	...	...
National Accounts														*Millions of Dinars:*	
Househ.Cons.Expend.,incl.NPISHs 96f	543	703	927	1,194	1,337	1,482	1,665	1,895	2,795	4,673	3,908	3,591	3,038	3,224	3,009
Government Consumption Expend.......... 91f	359	465	865	1,044	1,185	1,400	1,692	2,007	2,442	2,552	2,456	2,381	3,159	2,229	2,055
Gross Fixed Capital Formation 93e	437	636	979	1,055	1,226	1,383	1,532	1,855	2,757	2,660	2,772	2,524	2,128	1,558	1,376
Changes in Inventories 93i	14	28	50	100	−50	58	20	110	101	235	53	76	75	30	129
Exports of Goods and Services 90c	998	1,240	2,490	2,053	2,881	3,431	2,978	4,801	6,538	4,410	4,105	3,703	3,351	3,673	2,459
Imports of Goods and Services (-) 98c	552	826	1,428	1,666	1,671	1,948	2,199	2,822	3,752	5,128	3,920	3,343	3,386	2,488	1,896
Gross Domestic Product (GDP) 99b	1,798	2,246	3,883	3,780	4,907	5,763	5,688	7,846	10,882	9,401	9,373	8,932	8,364	8,227	7,132
Net Primary Income from Abroad 98.n	−275	−318	−439	−400	−517	−517	−505	...	...	...	...	...	...	...	...
Gross National Income (GNI) 99a	1,524	1,928	3,444	3,380	4,390	5,304	5,183	...	...	...	...	...	...	...	...
Net National Income 99e	1,412	1,816	3,296	3,214	4,198	5,096	4,946	7,030	9,908	8,570	7,790	...	...	...	...
GDP Volume 1964 prices 99b.*p*	1,136	1,158	1,415	†1,472	...	...	...	...	...	...	...	...	...	...	...
GDP Volume 1975 Prices 99b.*p*	...	...	...	3,674	4,506	4,906	5,032	5,448	5,481						
GDP Volume (1980=100) .... 99bv *p*	51.7	52.7	64.4	67.0	82.2	89.5	91.8	99.4	100.0	...	...	...	...	...	...
GDP Deflator (1980=100) .... 99bi *p*	31.9	39.1	55.4	51.8	54.9	59.2	56.9	72.5	100.0	...	...	...	...	...	...
															Millions:
Population............ 99z	2.15	2.24	2.33	2.43	†2.56	2.67	2.79	2.91	2.76	2.87	2.99	3.11	3.24	3.37	3.52

1987	1988	1989	1990	1991	1992	1993	1994	1995	1996	1997	1998	1999	2000	2001		
Minus Sign Indicates Debit															**Balance of Payments**	
−1,043	−1,826	−1,026	2,201	−219	1,392	−1,362	29	1,998	1,477	1,875	−391	1,984	....	....	Current Account, n.i.e.	78al *d*
5,821	5,653	7,274	11,352	10,702	10,078	8,522	8,365	9,038	9,578	9,876	6,328	6,758	....	....	Goods: Exports f.o.b.	78aa *d*
−5,384	−5,762	−6,509	−7,575	−8,038	−7,461	−8,409	−7,339	−6,257	−7,059	−7,160	−5,857	−3,996	....	....	Goods: Imports f.o.b.	78ab *d*
437	−109	765	3,777	2,664	2,617	113	1,026	2,781	2,519	2,716	471	2,762	....	....	*Trade Balance*	78ac *d*
114	128	117	117	99	99	55	40	37	31	33	47	55	....	....	Services: Credit	78ae *d*
−1,436	−1,637	−1,481	−1,385	−2,696	−1,192	−1,171	−780	−716	−951	−920	−1,016	−918	....	....	Services: Debit	78ae *d*
−885	−1,617	−598	2,508	67	1,524	−1,003	286	2,102	1,599	1,829	−498	1,899	....	....	*Balance on Goods & Services*	78af *d*
730	762	447	666	651	767	569	487	526	573	640	633	507	....	....	Income: Credit	78ag *d*
−363	−437	−388	−493	−502	−447	−600	−438	−365	−356	−354	−259	−218	....	....	Income: Debit	78ah *d*
−518	−1,292	−539	2,682	215	1,844	−1,034	335	2,263	1,816	2,115	−124	2,187	....	....	*Balance on Gds, Serv. & Inc.*	78ai *d*
5	7	6	7	8	7	8	5	5	3	4	5	6	....	....	Current Transfers, n.i.e.: Credit	78aj *d*
−531	−541	−493	−488	−442	−460	−336	−311	−270	−342	−244	−272	−210	....	....	Current Transfers: Debit	78ak *d*
															Capital Account, n.i.e.	78bc *d*
—	—	—	—	—	—	—	—	....	....	....	....	....	....	....	Capital Account, n.i.e.: Credit	78ba *d*
—	—	—	—	—	—	—	—	....	....	....	....	....	....	....	Capital Account: Debit	78bb *d*
−127	163	1,188	−1,006	131	329	−201	160	−250	224	−884	−555	−971	....	....	Financial Account, n.i.e.	78bj *d*
−114	−56	−35	−105	−174	149	478	−28	−83	−63	−282	−304	−210	....	....	Direct Investment Abroad	78bd *d*
−98	98	125	159	92	98	58	−79	−107	−135	−82	−152	−119	....	....	Dir. Invest. in Rep. Econ., n.i.e.	78be *d*
−2,972	−222	−52	−115	297	−54	−62	−137	−128	—	−774	−212	−3	....	....	Portfolio Investment Assets	78bf *d*
−2,972	−222	−52	−115	297	−54	−62	−137	−128	—	−774	−212	−3	....	....	Equity Securities	78bk *d*
—	—	—	—	—	—	—	—	....	....	....	....	....	....	....	Debt Securities	78bl *d*
—	—	—	—	—	—	—	—	....	....	....	....	....	....	....	Portfolio Investment Liab., n.i.e.	78bg *d*
—	—	—	—	—	—	—	—	....	....	....	....	....	....	....	Equity Securities	78bm *d*
—	—	—	—	—	—	—	—	....	....	....	....	....	....	....	Debt Securities	78bn *d*
....	....	....	....	....	....	....	....	....	....	....	....	....	....	....	Financial Derivatives Assets	78bw *d*
....	....	....	....	....	....	....	....	....	....	....	....	....	....	....	Financial Derivatives Liabilities	78bx *d*
3,494	−670	320	−715	342	185	−485	−1,904	−1,646	−1,734	−1,040	−164	−293	....	....	Other Investment Assets	78bh *d*
				16	2	241	−10	46	−33	46	−7	−604	....	....	Monetary Authorities	78bo *d*
91	−150	−109	−230	305	−35	−729	−1,876	−1,657	−1,540	−678	−591	461	....	....	General Government	78bp *d*
171	−26	186	−90	21	218	3	−18	−35	−161	−408	434	−150	....	....	Banks	78bq *d*
3,233	−494	242	−395			−190	2,308	1,714	2,156	1,294	277	−346	....	....	Other Sectors	78br *d*
−436	1,013	830	−230	−426	−49	−190	2,308	1,714	2,156	1,294	277	−346	....	....	Other Investment Liab., n.i.e.	78bi *d*
−137	196	598	−130	−159	−31	96	184	207	443	−219	−6	−72	....	....	Monetary Authorities	78bs *d*
				37	81	212	2,109	1,571	1,681	1,576	263	−214	....	....	General Government	78bt *d*
−119	486	214	21	−304	−99	−498	15	−64	32	−63	20	−60	....	....	Banks	78bu *d*
−181	331	18	−121	....	....	....	....	....	....	....	....	....	....	....	Other Sectors	78bv *d*
172	271	130	−37	343	38	−148	106	299	−234	878	432	−372	....	....	Net Errors and Omissions	78ca *d*
−999	−1,392	292	1,158	255	1,759	−1,712	295	2,047	1,467	1,869	−513	641	....	....	*Overall Balance*	78cb *d*
999	1,392	−292	−1,158	−255	−1,759	1,712	−295	−2,047	−1,467	−1,869	513	−641	....	....	Reserves and Related Items	79da *d*
999	1,392	−292	−1,158	−255	−1,759	1,712	−295	−2,047	−1,467	−1,869	513	−641	....	....	Reserve Assets	79db *d*
—	—	—	—	—	—	—	—	—	—	—	—	—	....	....	Use of Fund Credit and Loans	79dc *d*
....	....	....	....	....	....	....	....	....	....	....	....	....	....	....	Exceptional Financing	79de *d*
Millions of Dinars															**National Accounts**	
3,873	3,789	3,913	3,964	5,153	5,137	5,989	5,993	6,276	6,809	8,368	8,072	8,514	7,962	....	Househ.Cons.Expend.,incl.NPISHs	96f
1,616	2,196	2,520	1,997	2,376	2,755	2,132	2,254	2,383	2,903	3,333	3,339	3,102	3,616	....	Government Consumption Expend.	91f
950	1,050	1,157	1,135	1,034	1,008	1,504	1,622	1,245	1,640	1,685	1,397	1,536	2,281	....	Gross Fixed Capital Formation	93e
126	218	128	388	143	152	15	6	54	248	64	127	46	40	....	Changes in Inventories	93i
1,697	1,652	2,213	3,248	3,038	2,919	2,636	2,695	3,116	3,490	3,790	2,468	3,374	6,186	....	Exports of Goods and Services	90c
2,009	2,114	2,394	2,547	2,763	2,430	2,944	2,603	2,394	2,910	3,091	2,661	2,433	2,690	....	Imports of Goods and Services (-)	98c
6,253	6,791	7,537	8,185	8,981	9,541	9,332	9,967	10,680	12,180	14,149	12,742	14,139	17,395	....	Gross Domestic Product (GDP)	99b
−133	−49	−143	−185	−165	−222	−91	−114	−146	−202	−201	−248	−341	....	....	Net Primary Income from Abroad	98.n
....	....	....	....	....	....	....	....	10,386	12,099	13,189	12,601	15,051	....	....	Gross National Income (GNI)	99a
....	....	....	....	....	....	....	....	10,386	12,099	13,189	12,601	15,051	....	....	Net National Income	99e
....	....	....	....	....	....	....	....	....	....	....	....	....	....	....	GDP Volume 1964 prices	99b. *p*
....	....	....	....	....	....	....	....	....	....	....	....	....	....	....	GDP Volume 1975 Prices	99b. *p*
....	....	....	....	....	....	....	....	....	....	....	....	....	....	....	GDP Volume (1980=100)	99bv *p*
....	....	....	....	....	....	....	....	....	....	....	....	....	....	....	GDP Deflator (1980=100)	99bi *p*
Midyear Estimates																
3.67	3.82	3.98	4.15	4.33	4.51	4.70	4.90	†4.76	4.85	4.96	5.06	5.18	5.29	5.41	**Population**	99z

(See notes in the back of the book.)

Lithuania

		1972	1973	1974	1975	1976	1977	1978	1979	1980	1981	1982	1983	1984	1985	1986
Exchange Rates																*Litai per SDR:*
Official Rate	aa	....	....	....	....	....	....	....	....	....	....	....	....	....	....	....
																Litai per US Dollar:
Official Rate	ae	....	....	....	....	....	....	....	....	....	....	....	....	....	....	....
Official Rate	rf	....	....	....	....	....	....	....	....	....	....	....	....	....	....	....
Fund Position																*Millions of SDRs:*
Quota	2f. s	....	....	....	....	....	....	....	....	....	....	....	....	....	....	....
SDRs	1b. s	....	....	....	....	....	....	....	....	....	....	....	....	....	....	....
Reserve Position in the Fund	1c. s	....	....	....	....	....	....	....	....	....	....	....	....	....	....	....
Total Fund Cred.&Loans Outstg.	2tl	....	....	....	....	....	....	....	....	....	....	....	....	....	....	....
International Liquidity										*Millions of US Dollars Unless Otherwise Indicated:*						
Total Reserves minus Gold	1l. d	....	....	....	....	....	....	....	....	....	....	....	....	....	....	....
SDRs	1b. d	....	....	....	....	....	....	....	....	....	....	....	....	....	....	....
Reserve Position in the Fund	1c. d	....	....	....	....	....	....	....	....	....	....	....	....	....	....	....
Foreign Exchange	1d. d	....	....	....	....	....	....	....	....	....	....	....	....	....	....	....
Gold (Million Fine Troy Ounces)	1ad	....	....	....	....	....	....	....	....	....	....	....	....	....	....	....
Gold (National Valuation)	1an d	....	....	....	....	....	....	....	....	....	....	....	....	....	....	....
Monetary Authorities: Other Liab.	4..d	....	....	....	....	....	....	....	....	....	....	....	....	....	....	....
Banking Institutions: Assets	7a.d	....	....	....	....	....	....	....	....	....	....	....	....	....	....	....
Liabilities	7b.d	....	....	....	....	....	....	....	....	....	....	....	....	....	....	....
Monetary Authorities																*Millions of Litai:*
Foreign Assets	11	....	....	....	....	....	....	....	....	....	....	....	....	....	....	....
Claims on Central Government	12a	....	....	....	....	....	....	....	....	....	....	....	....	....	....	....
Claims on Private Sector	12d	....	....	....	....	....	....	....	....	....	....	....	....	....	....	....
Claims on Banking Institutions	12e	....	....	....	....	....	....	....	....	....	....	....	....	....	....	....
Claims on Nonbank Financial Insts.	12g	....	....	....	....	....	....	....	....	....	....	....	....	....	....	....
Reserve Money	14	....	....	....	....	....	....	....	....	....	....	....	....	....	....	....
of which: Currency Outside Banks	14a	....	....	....	....	....	....	....	....	....	....	....	....	....	....	....
Foreign Currency Deposits	15	....	....	....	....	....	....	....	....	....	....	....	....	....	....	....
Foreign Liabilities	16c	....	....	....	....	....	....	....	....	....	....	....	....	....	....	....
Central Government Deposits	16d	....	....	....	....	....	....	....	....	....	....	....	....	....	....	....
Counterpart Funds	16e	....	....	....	....	....	....	....	....	....	....	....	....	....	....	....
Central Government Lending Funds	16f	....	....	....	....	....	....	....	....	....	....	....	....	....	....	....
Capital Accounts	17a	....	....	....	....	....	....	....	....	....	....	....	....	....	....	....
Other Items (Net)	17r	....	....	....	....	....	....	....	....	....	....	....	....	....	....	....
Banking Institutions																*Millions of Litai:*
Reserves	20	....	....	....	....	....	....	....	....	....	....	....	....	....	....	....
Foreign Assets	21	....	....	....	....	....	....	....	....	....	....	....	....	....	....	....
Claims on Central Government	22a	....	....	....	....	....	....	....	....	....	....	....	....	....	....	....
Claims on State and Local Govts.	22b	....	....	....	....	....	....	....	....	....	....	....	....	....	....	....
Claims on Nonfin.Pub.Enterprises	22c	....	....	....	....	....	....	....	....	....	....	....	....	....	....	....
Claims on Private Sector	22d	....	....	....	....	....	....	....	....	....	....	....	....	....	....	....
Claims on Nonbank Financial Insts.	22g	....	....	....	....	....	....	....	....	....	....	....	....	....	....	....
Demand Deposits	24	....	....	....	....	....	....	....	....	....	....	....	....	....	....	....
Time, Savings,& Fgn.Currency Dep.	25	....	....	....	....	....	....	....	....	....	....	....	....	....	....	....
Foreign Liabilities	26c	....	....	....	....	....	....	....	....	....	....	....	....	....	....	....
Central Government Deposits	26d	....	....	....	....	....	....	....	....	....	....	....	....	....	....	....
Counterpart Funds	26e	....	....	....	....	....	....	....	....	....	....	....	....	....	....	....
Central Government Lending Funds	26f	....	....	....	....	....	....	....	....	....	....	....	....	....	....	....
Credit from Monetary Authorities	26g	....	....	....	....	....	....	....	....	....	....	....	....	....	....	....
Capital Accounts	27a	....	....	....	....	....	....	....	....	....	....	....	....	....	....	....
Other Items (Net)	27r	....	....	....	....	....	....	....	....	....	....	....	....	....	....	....
Banking Survey																*Millions of Litai:*
Foreign Assets (Net)	31n	....	....	....	....	....	....	....	....	....	....	....	....	....	....	....
Domestic Credit	32	....	....	....	....	....	....	....	....	....	....	....	....	....	....	....
Claims on Central Govt. (Net)	32an	....	....	....	....	....	....	....	....	....	....	....	....	....	....	....
Claims on State and Local Govts.	32b	....	....	....	....	....	....	....	....	....	....	....	....	....	....	....
Claims on Nonfin.Pub.Enterprises	32c	....	....	....	....	....	....	....	....	....	....	....	....	....	....	....
Claims on Private Sector	32d	....	....	....	....	....	....	....	....	....	....	....	....	....	....	....
Claims on Nonbank Fin. Insts.	32g	....	....	....	....	....	....	....	....	....	....	....	....	....	....	....
Money	34	....	....	....	....	....	....	....	....	....	....	....	....	....	....	....
Quasi-Money	35	....	....	....	....	....	....	....	....	....	....	....	....	....	....	....
of which: Fgn. Currency Deposits	35b	....	....	....	....	....	....	....	....	....	....	....	....	....	....	....
Counterpart Funds	36e	....	....	....	....	....	....	....	....	....	....	....	....	....	....	....
Central Government Lending Funds	36f	....	....	....	....	....	....	....	....	....	....	....	....	....	....	....
Capital Accounts	37a	....	....	....	....	....	....	....	....	....	....	....	....	....	....	....
Other Items (Net)	37r	....	....	....	....	....	....	....	....	....	....	....	....	....	....	....
Money plus Quasi-Money	35l	....	....	....	....	....	....	....	....	....	....	....	....	....	....	....
Interest Rates																*Percent Per Annum*
Money Market Rate	60b	....	....	....	....	....	....	....	....	....	....	....	....	....	....	....
Treasury Bill Rate	60c	....	....	....	....	....	....	....	....	....	....	....	....	....	....	....
Deposit Rate	60l	....	....	....	....	....	....	....	....	....	....	....	....	....	....	....
Lending Rate	60p	....	....	....	....	....	....	....	....	....	....	....	....	....	....	....
Prices, Production, Labor																*Index Numbers (1995=100):*
Producer Prices	63	....	....	....	....	....	....	....	....	....	....	....	....	....	....	....
Consumer Prices	64	....	....	....	....	....	....	....	....	....	....	....	....	....	....	....
Wages: Average Earnings	65	....	....	....	....	....	....	....	....	....	....	....	....	....	....	....
Manufacturing Production	66	....	....	....	....	....	....	....	....	....	....	....	....	....	....	....
Manufacturing Employment	67	....	....	....	....	....	....	....	....	....	....	....	....	....	....	....
																Number in Thousands:
Labor Force	67d	....	....	....	....	....	....	....	....	....	....	....	....	....	....	....
Employment	67e	....	....	....	....	....	....	....	....	....	....	....	....	....	....	....
Unemployment	67c	....	....	....	....	....	....	....	....	....	....	....	....	....	....	....
Unemployment Rate (%)	67r	....	....	....	....	....	....	....	....	....	....	....	....	....	....	....
International Transactions																*Millions of Litai*
Exports	70	....	....	....	....	....	....	....	....	....	....	....	....	....	....	....
Imports, c.i.f.	71	....	....	....	....	....	....	....	....	....	....	....	....	....	....	....

	1987	1988	1989	1990	1991	1992	1993	1994	1995	1996	1997	1998	1999	2000	2001		
End of Period																**Exchange Rates**	
	....	....	....	....	....	5.211	5.357	5.839	5.946	5.752	5.397	5.632	5.490	5.212	5.027	Official Rate	aa
End of Period (ae) Period Average (rf)																	
	....	....	....	....	....	3.790	3.900	4.000	4.000	4.000	4.000	4.000	4.000	4.000	4.000	Official Rate	ae
	....	....	....	....	....	1.773	4.344	3.978	4.000	4.000	4.000	4.000	4.000	4.000	4.000	Official Rate	rf
End of Period																**Fund Position**	
	....	....	....	....	....	103.50	103.50	103.50	103.50	103.50	103.50	103.50	144.20	144.20	144.20	Quota	2f.*s*
	....	....	....	....	....	.94	54.71	10.38	12.22	7.09	7.95	11.50	3.19	1.01	14.67	SDRs	1b.*s*
	....	....	....	....	....	.01	.01	.01	.01	.01	.01	.02	.02	.02	.02	Reserve Position in the Fund	1c.*s*
	....	....	....	....	....	17.25	87.98	134.55	175.95	190.11	200.46	179.83	167.76	147.06	120.32	Total Fund Cred.&Loans Outstg.	2tl
End of Period																**International Liquidity**	
	....	....	....	....	....	45.34	350.32	525.48	757.05	772.25	1,009.95	1,409.13	1,195.01	1,311.55	1,617.72	Total Reserves minus Gold	1l.*d*
	....	....	....	....	....	1.29	75.14	15.15	18.16	10.20	10.73	16.19	4.38	1.32	18.43	SDRs	1b.*d*
	....	....	....	....	....	.01	.01	.01	.01	.01	.01	.02	.02	.02	.02	Reserve Position in the Fund	1c.*d*
	....	....	....	....	....	44.03	275.17	510.33	738.88	762.04	999.21	1,392.92	1,190.61	1,310.21	1,599.27	Foreign Exchange	1d.*d*
	....	....	....	....	....	.1859	.1859	.1858	.1860	.1863	.1864	.1861	.1863	.1863	.1861	Gold (Million Fine Troy Ounces)	1ad
	....	....	....	....	....	61.90	61.90	61.86	61.95	62.04	52.74	50.87	47.10	47.10	51.47	Gold (National Valuation)	1an*d*
	....	....	....	....	....	....	28.05	26.38	.28	1.33	.35	.33	.25	.18	51.85	Monetary Authorities: Other Liab.	4..*d*
	....	....	....	....	....	....	77.77	96.68	123.35	293.60	370.63	302.15	423.30	693.30	751.85	Banking Institutions: Assets	7a.*d*
	....	....	....	....	....	....	9.54	82.70	88.45	195.83	292.48	438.15	522.70	503.05	599.83	Liabilities	7b.*d*
End of Period																**Monetary Authorities**	
	....	....	....	....	....	....	1,904.6	2,618.1	3,284.7	3,345.3	4,258.5	5,847.8	4,976.2	5,375.6	6,629.3	Foreign Assets	11
	....	....	....	....	....	....	—	—	19.2	—	—	—	6.8	6.8	6.8	Claims on Central Government	12a
	....	....	....	....	....	....	1.4	5.9	12.1	9.9	7.6	6.9	6.1	5.5	6.4	Claims on Private Sector	12d
	....	....	....	....	....	....	292.0	157.0	168.1	142.0	70.3	52.3	30.1	23.7	15.4	Claims on Banking Institutions	12e
	....	....	....	....	....	....	—	—	.3	3.1	19.4	6.9	20.0	—	—	Claims on Nonbank Financial Insts.	12g
	....	....	....	....	....	....	1,256.8	1,812.5	2,446.3	2,499.3	3,308.7	4,260.5	4,088.3	3,952.4	4,279.6	Reserve Money	14
	....	....	....	....	....	....	791.3	1,334.3	1,907.0	1,899.3	2,535.5	2,800.5	2,738.7	2,658.3	2,919.9	*of which: Currency Outside Banks*	14a
	....	....	....	....	....	....	—	1.9	43.8	19.8	8.2	6.5	1.5	.1	.1	Foreign Currency Deposits	15
	....	....	....	....	....	....	580.7	891.2	1,047.3	1,098.8	1,083.3	1,014.1	922.0	767.1	812.2	Foreign Liabilities	16c
	....	....	....	....	....	....	93.1	45.1	111.1	66.0	268.7	904.4	302.1	781.8	1,488.2	Central Government Deposits	16d
	....	....	....	....	....	....	—	14.7	37.5	41.9	38.1	40.8	30.8	29.2	28.2	Counterpart Funds	16e
	....	....	....	....	....	....		.6	.7	—	.6	1.5	—	—	—	Central Government Lending Funds	16f
	....	....	....	....	....	....	1,029.6	54.8	−77.8	−48.4	−247.3	−111.8	−90.4	117.2	270.4	Capital Accounts	17a
	....	....	....	....	....	....	−762.2	−39.8	−124.5	−177.1	−104.4	−202.1	−215.1	−236.2	−220.8	Other Items (Net)	17r
End of Period																**Banking Institutions**	
	....	....	....	....	....	....	469.0	464.1	522.7	583.6	742.1	1,447.5	1,342.3	1,282.4	1,343.1	Reserves	20
	....	....	....	....	....	....	303.3	386.7	493.4	1,174.4	1,482.5	1,208.6	1,693.2	2,773.2	3,007.4	Foreign Assets	21
	....	....	....	....	....	....	—	240.8	505.2	860.7	1,890.0	1,965.5	1,665.9	2,151.1	2,637.3	Claims on Central Government	22a
	....	....	....	....	....	....	—	2.0	7.7	37.1	51.9	123.8	212.3	273.5	279.6	Claims on State and Local Govts.	22b
	....	....	....	....	....	....	409.3	398.6	237.5	134.4	109.4	272.7	276.9	304.5	253.1	Claims on Nonfin.Pub.Enterprises	22c
	....	....	....	....	....	....	1,603.5	†2,974.6	3,654.8	3,496.2	4,161.9	4,866.7	5,538.7	5,203.2	5,531.7	Claims on Private Sector	22d
	....	....	....	....	....	....	5.0	20.6	49.5	44.7	150.2	462.8	448.3	513.5	791.3	Claims on Nonbank Financial Insts.	22g
	....	....	....	....	....	....	954.4	1,134.8	1,566.5	1,694.3	2,543.1	2,757.9	2,528.9	3,002.6	3,808.0	Demand Deposits	24
	....	....	....	....	....	....	926.8	1,879.5	2,086.2	1,793.3	2,153.8	2,750.0	3,695.5	4,782.8	5,946.2	Time, Savings,& Fgn.Currency Dep.	25
	....	....	....	....	....	....	37.2	330.8	353.8	783.3	1,169.9	1,752.6	2,090.8	2,012.2	2,399.3	Foreign Liabilities	26c
	....	....	....	....	....	....	122.5	357.6	683.7	779.3	1,008.1	792.0	778.4	740.7	438.9	Central Government Deposits	26d
	....	....	....	....	....	....	16.4	28.2	52.6	59.3	50.7	22.8	19.5	23.3	2.0	Counterpart Funds	26e
	....	....	....	....	....	....	174.5	337.7	480.3	473.3	615.4	754.1	555.5	287.3	19.6	Central Government Lending Funds	26f
	....	....	....	....	....	....	285.5	157.0	168.1	142.0	70.3	52.3	30.2	23.8	15.4	Credit from Monetary Authorities	26g
	....	....	....	....	....	....	467.7	936.1	996.7	1,448.1	2,021.4	2,690.4	2,849.7	2,928.6	1,992.6	Capital Accounts	27a
	....	....	....	....	....	....	−194.9	†−674.3	−917.1	−841.8	−1,044.7	−1,224.5	−1,370.9	−1,299.9	−778.5	Other Items (Net)	27r
End of Period																**Banking Survey**	
	....	....	....	....	....	....	1,590.0	1,782.8	2,377.0	2,637.6	3,487.9	4,289.7	3,656.6	5,369.5	6,425.2	Foreign Assets (Net)	31n
	....	....	....	....	....	....	1,803.6	†3,239.8	3,691.5	3,740.8	5,113.6	6,008.9	7,094.5	6,935.6	7,579.1	Domestic Credit	32
	....	....	....	....	....	....	−215.6	−161.9	−270.4	15.4	613.2	269.1	592.2	635.4	717.0	Claims on Central Govt. (Net)	32an
	....	....	....	....	....	....	—	2.0	7.7	37.1	51.9	123.8	212.3	273.5	279.6	Claims on State and Local Govts.	32b
	....	....	....	....	....	....	409.3	398.6	237.5	134.4	109.4	272.7	276.9	304.5	253.1	Claims on Nonfin.Pub.Enterprises	32c
	....	....	....	....	....	....	1,604.9	†2,980.5	3,666.9	3,506.1	4,169.5	4,873.6	5,544.8	5,208.7	5,538.1	Claims on Private Sector	32d
	....	....	....	....	....	....	5.0	20.6	49.8	47.8	169.6	469.7	468.3	513.5	791.3	Claims on Nonbank Fin. Insts.	32g
	....	....	....	....	....	....	1,746.4	2,475.7	3,488.4	3,610.9	5,109.9	5,570.9	5,275.0	5,672.6	6,744.5	Money	34
	....	....	....	....	....	....	926.8	1,881.4	2,130.0	1,813.1	2,162.0	2,756.5	3,697.0	4,782.9	5,946.3	Quasi-Money	35
	....	....	....	....	....	....	681.4	1,169.6	1,462.9	1,325.4	1,539.0	2,006.8	2,724.6	3,554.5	4,181.5	*of which: Fgn. Currency Deposits*	35b
	....	....	....	....	....	....	16.4	42.9	90.1	101.2	88.8	63.6	50.3	52.5	30.2	Counterpart Funds	36e
	....	....	....	....	....	....	174.5	338.3	481.0	473.3	616.0	755.6	555.5	287.3	19.6	Central Government Lending Funds	36f
	....	....	....	....	....	....	1,497.3	990.9	918.9	1,399.7	1,774.1	2,578.6	2,759.3	3,045.8	2,263.0	Capital Accounts	37a
	....	....	....	....	....	....	−967.8	†−706.6	−1,039.9	−1,019.8	−1,149.3	−1,426.6	−1,586.0	−1,536.0	−999.3	Other Items (Net)	37r
	....	....	....	....	....	....	2,673.2	4,357.1	5,618.4	5,424.0	7,271.9	8,327.4	8,972.0	10,455.5	12,690.8	Money plus Quasi-Money	35l
Percent Per Annum																**Interest Rates**	
	....	....	....	....	....	....	....	69.48	26.73	20.26	9.55	6.12	6.26	3.60	3.37	Money Market Rate	60b
	....	....	....	....	....	....	....	....	26.82	20.95	8.64	10.69	11.14	....	....	Treasury Bill Rate	60c
	....	....	....	....	....	....	88.29	48.43	20.05	13.95	7.89	5.98	4.94	3.86	3.00	Deposit Rate	60l
	....	....	....	....	....	....	91.84	62.30	27.08	21.56	14.39	12.21	13.09	12.14	9.63	Lending Rate	60p
Period Averages																**Prices, Production, Labor**	
	....	....	....	....	....	10.9	53.8	77.9	100.0	117.3	122.2	114.1	117.6	140.4	138.0	Producer Prices	63
	....	....	....	....	....	8.2	†41.6	71.6	100.0	124.6	135.7	142.6	143.6	145.1	146.9	Consumer Prices	64
	....	....	....	....	....	13.0	42.4	69.7	100.0	135.1	166.7	187.7	198.6	197.2	198.2	Wages: Average Earnings	65
	....	....	....	....	....	216.0	141.0	99.1	†100.0	103.5	111.8	122.2	110.8	121.9	141.0	Manufacturing Production	66
	....	....	....	....	....	186.3	146.2	116.7	†100.0	95.8	96.0	95.0	93.5	91.7	89.0	Manufacturing Employment	67
Period Averages																	
	....	....	....	....	....	1,879	1,859	1,741	1,753	1,784	1,774	1,835	1,862	1,794	....	Labor Force	67d
	....	....	....	....	....	1,855	1,778	1,656	1,632	1,620	1,571	1,598	1,598	1,518	....	Employment	67e
	....	....	....	....	5	67	66	78	128	109	120	123	177	226	....	Unemployment	67c
	....	....	....	....	.3	3.5	3.5	4.5	7.3	6.2	6.7	6.5	10.0	12.6	....	Unemployment Rate (%)	67r
Millions of Litai																**International Transactions**	
	....	....	....	....	....	....	8,707	8,077	10,820	13,420	15,441	14,842	12,015	15,238	18,332	Exports	70
	....	....	....	....	....	....	9,798	9,355	14,594	18,235	22,577	23,174	19,338	21,826	25,413	Imports, c.i.f.	71

	1972	1973	1974	1975	1976	1977	1978	1979	1980	1981	1982	1983	1984	1985	1986
Balance of Payments															*Millions of US Dollars:*
Current Account, n.i.e. 78ald	....	....	....	....	....	....	....	....	....	....	....	....	....	....	....
Goods: Exports f.o.b. 78aad	....	....	....	....	....	....	....	....	....	....	....	....	....	....	....
Goods: Imports f.o.b. 78abd	....	....	....	....	....	....	....	....	....	....	....	....	....	....	....
Trade Balance.................... 78acd	....	....	....	....	....	....	....	....	....	....	....	....	....	....	....
Services: Credit.................. 78add	....	....	....	....	....	....	....	....	....	....	....	....	....	....	....
Services: Debit................... 78aed	....	....	....	....	....	....	....	....	....	....	....	....	....	....	....
Balance on Goods & Services 78afd	....	....	....	....	....	....	....	....	....	....	....	....	....	....	....
Income: Credit.................... 78agd	....	....	....	....	....	....	....	....	....	....	....	....	....	....	....
Income: Debit..................... 78ahd	....	....	....	....	....	....	....	....	....	....	....	....	....	....	....
Balance on Gds, Serv. & Inc............... 78aid	....	....	....	....	....	....	....	....	....	....	....	....	....	....	....
Current Transfers, n.i.e.: Credit 78ajd	....	....	....	....	....	....	....	....	....	....	....	....	....	....	....
Current Transfers: Debit 78akd	....	....	....	....	....	....	....	....	....	....	....	....	....	....	....
Capital Account, n.i.e. 78bcd	....	....	....	....	....	....	....	....	....	....	....	....	....	....	....
Capital Account, n.i.e.: Credit 78bad	....	....	....	....	....	....	....	....	....	....	....	....	....	....	....
Capital Account: Debit 78bbd	....	....	....	....	....	....	....	....	....	....	....	....	....	....	....
Financial Account, n.i.e. 78bjd	....	....	....	....	....	....	....	....	....	....	....	....	....	....	....
Direct Investment Abroad 78bdd	....	....	....	....	....	....	....	....	....	....	....	....	....	....	....
Dir. Invest. in Rep. Econ., n.i.e. 78bed	....	....	....	....	....	....	....	....	....	....	....	....	....	....	....
Portfolio Investment Assets 78bfd	....	....	....	....	....	....	....	....	....	....	....	....	....	....	....
Equity Securities............................ 78bkd	....	....	....	....	....	....	....	....	....	....	....	....	....	....	....
Debt Securities............................. 78bld	....	....	....	....	....	....	....	....	....	....	....	....	....	....	....
Portfolio Investment Liab., n.i.e. 78bgd	....	....	....	....	....	....	....	....	....	....	....	....	....	....	....
Equity Securities............................ 78bmd	....	....	....	....	....	....	....	....	....	....	....	....	....	....	....
Debt Securities............................. 78bnd	....	....	....	....	....	....	....	....	....	....	....	....	....	....	....
Financial Derivatives Assets 78bwd	....	....	....	....	....	....	....	....	....	....	....	....	....	....	....
Financial Derivatives Liabilities 78bxd	....	....	....	....	....	....	....	....	....	....	....	....	....	....	....
Other Investment Assets 78bhd	....	....	....	....	....	....	....	....	....	....	....	....	....	....	....
Monetary Authorities 78bod	....	....	....	....	....	....	....	....	....	....	....	....	....	....	....
General Government...................... 78bpd	....	....	....	....	....	....	....	....	....	....	....	....	....	....	....
Banks 78bqd	....	....	....	....	....	....	....	....	....	....	....	....	....	....	....
Other Sectors 78brd	....	....	....	....	....	....	....	....	....	....	....	....	....	....	....
Other Investment Liab., n.i.e. 78bid	....	....	....	....	....	....	....	....	....	....	....	....	....	....	....
Monetary Authorities 78bsd	....	....	....	....	....	....	....	....	....	....	....	....	....	....	....
General Government...................... 78btd	....	....	....	....	....	....	....	....	....	....	....	....	....	....	....
Banks 78bud	....	....	....	....	....	....	....	....	....	....	....	....	....	....	....
Other Sectors 78bvd	....	....	....	....	....	....	....	....	....	....	....	....	....	....	....
Net Errors and Omissions.................... 78cad	....	....	....	....	....	....	....	....	....	....	....	....	....	....	....
Overall Balance 78cbd	....	....	....	....	....	....	....	....	....	....	....	....	....	....	....
Reserves and Related Items 79dad	....	....	....	....	....	....	....	....	....	....	....	....	....	....	....
Reserve Assets 79dbd	....	....	....	....	....	....	....	....	....	....	....	....	....	....	....
Use of Fund Credit and Loans 79dcd	....	....	....	....	....	....	....	....	....	....	....	....	....	....	....
Exceptional Financing 79ded	....	....	....	....	....	....	....	....	....	....	....	....	....	....	....
International Investment Position															*Millions of US Dollars*
Assets 79aad	....	....	....	....	....	....	....	....	....	....	....	....	....	....	....
Direct Investment Abroad 79abd	....	....	....	....	....	....	....	....	....	....	....	....	....	....	....
Portfolio Investment 79acd	....	....	....	....	....	....	....	....	....	....	....	....	....	....	....
Equity Securities 79add	....	....	....	....	....	....	....	....	....	....	....	....	....	....	....
Debt Securities 79aed	....	....	....	....	....	....	....	....	....	....	....	....	....	....	....
Financial Derivatives 79ald	....	....	....	....	....	....	....	....	....	....	....	....	....	....	....
Other Investment 79afd	....	....	....	....	....	....	....	....	....	....	....	....	....	....	....
Monetary Authorities...................... 79agd	....	....	....	....	....	....	....	....	....	....	....	....	....	....	....
General Government 79ahd	....	....	....	....	....	....	....	....	....	....	....	....	....	....	....
Banks 79aid	....	....	....	....	....	....	....	....	....	....	....	....	....	....	....
Other Sectors 79ajd	....	....	....	....	....	....	....	....	....	....	....	....	....	....	....
Reserve Assets 79akd	....	....	....	....	....	....	....	....	....	....	....	....	....	....	....
Liabilities 79lad	....	....	....	....	....	....	....	....	....	....	....	....	....	....	....
Dir. Invest. in Rep. Economy............ 79lbd	....	....	....	....	....	....	....	....	....	....	....	....	....	....	....
Portfolio Investment 79lcd	....	....	....	....	....	....	....	....	....	....	....	....	....	....	....
Equity Securities 79ldd	....	....	....	....	....	....	....	....	....	....	....	....	....	....	....
Debt Securities 79led	....	....	....	....	....	....	....	....	....	....	....	....	....	....	....
Financial Derivatives 79lld	....	....	....	....	....	....	....	....	....	....	....	....	....	....	....
Other Investment 79lfd	....	....	....	....	....	....	....	....	....	....	....	....	....	....	....
Monetary Authorities...................... 79lgd	....	....	....	....	....	....	....	....	....	....	....	....	....	....	....
General Government...................... 79lhd	....	....	....	....	....	....	....	....	....	....	....	....	....	....	....
Banks 79lid	....	....	....	....	....	....	....	....	....	....	....	....	....	....	....
Other Sectors 79ljd	....	....	....	....	....	....	....	....	....	....	....	....	....	....	....

Minus Sign Indicates Debit

1987	1988	1989	1990	1991	1992	1993	1994	1995	1996	1997	1998	1999	2000	2001	Balance of Payments	
....	....	....	....	....	....	−85.7	−94.0	−614.4	−722.6	−981.3	−1,298.2	−1,194.0	−674.9	−573.6	Current Account, n.i.e.	78al *d*
....	....	....	....	....	....	2,025.8	2,029.2	2,706.1	3,413.2	4,192.4	3,961.6	3,146.7	4,050.4	4,889.0	Goods: Exports f.o.b.	78aa *d*
....	....	....	....	....	....	−2,180.5	−2,234.1	−3,404.0	−4,309.3	−5,339.9	−5,479.9	−4,551.2	−5,154.1	−5,997.0	Goods: Imports f.o.b.	78ab *d*
....	....	....	....	....	....	−154.7	−204.9	−697.9	−896.2	−1,147.5	−1,518.3	−1,404.6	−1,103.8	−1,108.0	*Trade Balance*	78ac *d*
....	....	....	....	....	....	197.8	321.9	485.2	797.5	1,031.8	1,109.0	1,091.5	1,058.8	1,157.0	Services: Credit	78ad *d*
....	....	....	....	....	....	−252.9	−376.5	−498.1	−676.7	−897.4	−868.5	−786.1	−678.7	−700.3	Services: Debit	78ae *d*
....	....	....	....	....	....	−209.8	−259.4	−710.8	−775.4	−1,013.0	−1,277.8	−1,099.1	−723.7	−651.4	*Balance on Goods & Services*	78af *d*
....	....	....	....	....	....	12.5	21.4	50.9	52.0	80.4	124.6	114.8	185.5	205.7	Income: Credit	78ag *d*
....	....	....	....	....	....	−4.3	−12.8	−63.7	−143.0	−278.8	−380.0	−372.6	−379.3	−385.5	Income: Debit	78ah *d*
....	....	....	....	....	....	−201.5	−250.8	−723.7	−866.4	−1,211.4	−1,533.2	−1,356.8	−917.5	−831.1	*Balance on Gds, Serv. & Inc.*	78ai *d*
....	....	....	....	....	....	115.9	161.6	112.3	149.4	237.0	240.4	167.4	246.8	262.0	Current Transfers, n.i.e.: Credit	78aj *d*
....	....	....	....	....	....	—	−4.8	−3.0	−5.6	−7.0	−5.4	−4.6	−4.3	−4.5	Current Transfers: Debit	78ak *d*
....	....	....	....	....	....	—	12.9	−39.0	5.5	4.1	−1.7	−3.3	2.1	1.4	Capital Account, n.i.e.	78bc *d*
....	....	....	....	....	....	—	12.9	3.3	5.5	4.5	.9	2.7	2.6	1.5	Capital Account, n.i.e.: Credit	78ba *d*
....	....	....	....	....	....	—	—	−42.3	—	−.4	−2.6	−6.0	−.4	−.1	Capital Account: Debit	78bb *d*
....	....	....	....	....	....	301.5	240.9	534.4	645.6	1,005.6	1,443.9	1,060.7	702.4	517.0	Financial Account, n.i.e.	78bj *d*
....	....	....	....	....	....	....	....	−1.0	−.1	−26.9	−4.2	−8.6	−3.7	−7.1	Direct Investment Abroad	78bd *d*
....	....	....	....	....	....	30.2	31.3	72.6	152.4	354.5	925.5	486.5	378.9	185.2	Dir. Invest. in Rep. Econ., n.i.e.	78be *d*
....	....	....	....	....	....	−.9	−.2	−10.5	−26.9	7.7	−10.1	−1.9	−141.4	26.2	Portfolio Investment Assets	78bf *d*
....	....	....	....	....	....	−.9	−.2	−3.0	.8	.1	−.3	−3.0	−1.4	1.1	Equity Securities	78bk *d*
....	....	....	....	....	....	....	....	−7.5	−27.7	7.6	−9.8	1.1	−140.0	25.1	Debt Securities	78bl *d*
....	....	....	....	....	....	.6	4.6	26.6	89.6	180.5	−42.7	507.5	405.9	238.1	Portfolio Investment Liab., n.i.e.	78bg *d*
....	....	....	....	....	....	.6	4.6	6.2	15.9	30.5	11.4	8.9	121.5	−16.3	Equity Securities	78bm *d*
....	....	....	....	....	....	—	—	20.4	73.7	150.1	−54.1	498.6	284.4	254.3	Debt Securities	78bn *d*
....	....	....	....	....	....	....	....	....	....	....	—	—	—	18.3	Financial Derivatives Assets	78bw *d*
....	....	....	....	....	....	....	....	....	....	....	—	—	—	−19.6	Financial Derivatives Liabilities	78bx *d*
....	....	....	....	....	....	95.3	−26.4	−36.1	−170.4	−219.3	−24.0	−182.5	39.9	−225.0	Other Investment Assets	78bh *d*
....	....	....	....	....	....	....	....	67.0	.2	.1	—	—	—	−2.6	Monetary Authorities	78bo *d*
....	....	....	....	....	....	....	....	....	....	....	—	—	—	—	General Government	78bp *d*
....	....	....	....	....	....	108.9	−17.3	−18.0	−139.5	−88.1	57.2	−125.7	−142.2	−158.2	Banks	78bq *d*
....	....	....	....	....	....	−13.6	−9.2	−85.0	−31.1	−131.3	−81.2	−56.7	182.1	−64.2	Other Sectors	78br *d*
....	....	....	....	....	....	176.5	231.6	482.8	601.0	709.1	599.3	259.7	22.8	300.9	Other Investment Liab., n.i.e.	78bi *d*
....	....	....	....	....	....	—	−.9	−25.1	1.0	−1.0	—	−.1	−102.0	51.7	Monetary Authorities	78bs *d*
....	....	....	....	....	....	255.7	85.5	178.5	228.5	42.9	129.3	212.0	—	−53.7	General Government	78bt *d*
....	....	....	....	....	....	−62.9	75.8	10.8	108.5	104.3	177.9	99.9	53.1	169.4	Banks	78bu *d*
....	....	....	....	....	....	−16.3	71.2	318.5	263.1	562.8	292.1	−52.1	71.7	133.5	Other Sectors	78bv *d*
....	....	....	....	....	....	−7.4	−46.9	287.2	66.7	195.8	282.9	−42.1	128.3	153.6	Net Errors and Omissions	78ca *d*
....	....	....	....	....	....	208.5	112.8	168.3	−4.8	224.2	426.8	−178.7	158.0	98.4	*Overall Balance*	78cb *d*
....	....	....	....	....	....	−208.5	−112.8	−168.3	4.8	−224.2	−426.8	178.7	−158.0	−98.4	Reserves and Related Items	79da *d*
....	....	....	....	....	....	−308.0	−179.7	−231.3	−15.9	−238.2	−398.8	195.3	−130.7	−325.0	Reserve Assets	79db *d*
....	....	....	....	....	....	99.5	66.9	63.0	20.7	14.1	−28.0	−16.6	−27.3	−34.0	Use of Fund Credit and Loans	79dc *d*
....	....	....	....	....	....	....	—	—	—	—	—	—	—	260.6	Exceptional Financing	79de *d*

Millions of US Dollars

1987	1988	1989	1990	1991	1992	1993	1994	1995	1996	1997	1998	1999	2000	2001	International Investment Position	
....	....	....	....	....	....	....	997.6	1,274.6	1,692.7	2,148.6	2,472.2	2,452.7	2,677.7	3,126.2	Assets	79aa *d*
....	....	....	....	....	....	....	.2	1.2	2.8	26.0	16.5	25.9	29.3	47.9	Direct Investment Abroad	79ab *d*
....	....	....	....	....	....	....	.6	11.1	38.1	29.7	38.0	32.5	172.3	138.2	Portfolio Investment	79ac *d*
....	....	....	....	....	....	....	.2	3.1	2.6	2.9	2.9	5.9	6.0	4.9	Equity Securities	79ad *d*
....	....	....	....	....	....	....	.5	7.9	35.5	26.8	35.1	26.7	166.4	133.2	Debt Securities	79ae *d*
....	....	....	....	....	....	....	....	....	....	....	....	....	....	....	Financial Derivatives	79al *d*
....	....	....	....	....	....	....	409.4	443.4	817.5	1,030.2	957.7	1,152.1	1,117.4	1,271.1	Other Investment	79af *d*
....	....	....	....	....	....	....	67.2	.2	.1						Monetary Authorities	79ag *d*
....	....	....	....	....	....	....									General Government	79ah *d*
....	....	....	....	....	....	....	103.3	119.2	243.3	331.3	273.7	390.5	539.7	636.5	Banks	79ai *d*
....	....	....	....	....	....	....	238.9	323.9	574.1	699.0	684.0	761.7	577.7	634.5	Other Sectors	79aj *d*
....	....	....	....	....	....	....	587.4	819.0	834.3	1,062.7	1,460.0	1,242.1	1,358.7	1,669.2	Reserve Assets	79ak *d*
....	....	....	....	....	....	....	1,115.8	1,795.8	2,813.2	3,964.8	4,928.8	6,114.1	6,693.3	7,331.4	Liabilities	79la *d*
....	....	....	....	....	....	....	262.2	353.9	700.3	1,040.6	1,625.3	2,063.0	2,334.3	2,665.5	Dir. Invest. in Rep. Economy	79lb *d*
....	....	....	....	....	....	....	12.9	40.5	306.8	416.1	368.2	833.6	1,140.4	1,312.6	Portfolio Investment	79lc *d*
....	....	....	....	....	....	....	5.8	12.4	31.5	61.3	67.1	62.0	128.1	95.6	Equity Securities	79ld *d*
....	....	....	....	....	....	....	7.2	28.1	275.3	354.7	301.1	771.6	1,012.3	1,217.1	Debt Securities	79le *d*
....	....	....	....	....	....	....	....	....	....	....	....	....	....	....	Financial Derivatives	79ll *d*
....	....	....	....	....	....	....	840.7	1,401.4	1,806.1	2,508.1	2,935.3	3,217.5	3,218.6	3,353.3	Other Investment	79lf *d*
....	....	....	....	....	....	....	221.6	261.6	275.1	270.8	253.5	230.5	191.8	203.1	Monetary Authorities	79lg *d*
....	....	....	....	....	....	....	235.2	424.0	447.4	549.2	694.2	881.3	767.0	694.1	General Government	79lh *d*
....	....	....	....	....	....	....	86.1	99.2	182.3	282.8	463.3	539.8	568.2	691.1	Banks	79li *d*
....	....	....	....	....	....	....	297.8	616.7	901.3	1,405.4	1,524.3	1,566.0	1,691.6	1,765.0	Other Sectors	79lj *d*

Lithuania

	1972	1973	1974	1975	1976	1977	1978	1979	1980	1981	1982	1983	1984	1985	1986
Government Finance														*Millions of Litai:*	
Deficit (-) or Surplus............................. 80	...	...	...	...	...	...	...	...	...	...	...	...	...	...	...
Total Revenue and Grants................... 81y	...	...	...	...	...	...	...	...	...	...	...	...	...	...	...
Revenue 81	...	...	...	...	...	...	...	...	...	...	...	...	...	...	...
Grants 81z	...	...	...	...	...	...	...	...	...	...	...	...	...	...	...
Exp.& Lending Minus Repayments...... 82z	...	...	...	...	...	...	...	...	...	...	...	...	...	...	...
Expenditure 82	...	...	...	...	...	...	...	...	...	...	...	...	...	...	...
Lending Minus Repayments 83	...	...	...	...	...	...	...	...	...	...	...	...	...	...	...
Total Financing															
Domestic 84a	...	...	...	...	...	...	...	...	...	...	...	...	...	...	...
Foreign 85a	...	...	...	...	...	...	...	...	...	...	...	...	...	...	...
Total Debt by Currency........................ 88z	...	...	...	...	...	...	...	...	...	...	...	...	...	...	...
National 88b	...	...	...	...	...	...	...	...	...	...	...	...	...	...	...
Foreign 89b	...	...	...	...	...	...	...	...	...	...	...	...	...	...	...
National Accounts														*Millions of Litai:*	
Househ.Cons.Expend.,incl.NPISHs 96f	...	...	...	...	...	...	...	...	...	...	...	...	...	...	...
Government Consumption Expend. 91f	...	...	...	...	...	...	...	...	...	...	...	...	...	...	...
Gross Fixed Capital Formation 93e	...	...	...	...	...	...	...	...	...	...	...	...	...	...	...
Changes in Inventories 93i	...	...	...	...	...	...	...	...	...	...	...	...	...	...	...
Exports of Goods and Services 90c	...	...	...	...	...	...	...	...	...	...	...	...	...	...	...
Imports of Goods and Services (-) 98c	...	...	...	...	...	...	...	...	...	...	...	...	...	...	...
Gross Domestic Product (GDP) 99b	...	...	...	...	...	...	...	...	...	...	...	...	...	...	...
Net Primary Income from Abroad 98.n	...	...	...	...	...	...	...	...	...	...	...	...	...	...	...
Gross National Income (GNI) 99a	...	...	...	...	...	...	...	...	...	...	...	...	...	...	...
Net Current Transf.from Abroad 98t	...	...	...	...	...	...	...	...	...	...	...	...	...	...	...
Gross Nat'l Disposable Inc.(GNDI) 99i	...	...	...	...	...	...	...	...	...	...	...	...	...	...	...
Gross Saving 99s	...	...	...	...	...	...	...	...	...	...	...	...	...	...	...
Consumption of Fixed Capital 99cf	...	...	...	...	...	...	...	...	...	...	...	...	...	...	...
GDP Volume 1995 Prices...................... 99b.*p*	...	...	...	...	...	...	...	...	...	...	...	...	...	...	...
GDP Volume (1995=100) .... 99bv *p*	...	...	...	...	...	...	...	...	...	...	...	...	...	...	...
GDP Deflator (1995=100) .... 99bi *p*	...	...	...	...	...	...	...	...	...	...	...	...	...	...	...
														Millions:	
Population... 99z	...	...	...	...	...	...	...	...	...	...	...	...	...	...	...

	1987	1988	1989	1990	1991	1992	1993	1994	1995	1996	1997	1998	1999	2000	2001		
Year Ending December 31																**Government Finance**	
	....	....	....	....	5.8	....	−694.2	−797.0	−1,151.5	−1,145.1	†−735.8	−183.6	−3,006.6	−584.7	−171.8	Deficit (-) or Surplus	80
	....	....	....	....	133.8	....	2,693.6	4,034.1	5,661.1	7,157.3	†10198.6	11,474.9	11,051.0	11,135.3	11,999.1	Total Revenue and Grants	81y
	....	....	....	....	133.3	....	2,688.1	4,031.9	5,661.1	7,128.8	†10198.3	11,474.9	11,051.0	11,135.3	11,759.2	Revenue	81
	....	....	....	.5	.5	....	5.5	2.2	—	28.5	.3	—	—	—	239.9	Grants	81z
	....	....	....	....	128.0	....	3,387.8	4,831.1	6,812.6	8,302.4	†10934.4	11,658.5	14,057.6	11,720.0	12,170.9	Exp.& Lending Minus Repayments	82z
	....	....	....	....	120.0	....	2,475.3	4,292.1	6,079.1	7,894.1	†10515.0	13,037.6	13,260.8	12,447.3	12,616.8	Expenditure	82
	....	....	....	....	8.0	....	912.5	539.0	733.5	408.3	419.4	−1,379.1	796.8	−727.3	−445.9	Lending Minus Repayments	83
																Total Financing	
	....	....	....	....	....	....	71.4	518.2	417.9	138.7	†451.6	−574.1	129.1	−334.2	−307.2	Domestic	84a
	....	....	....	....	....	....	622.8	278.8	733.6	1,006.4	†284.2	757.7	2,877.5	918.9	479.0	Foreign	85a
	....	....	....	....	....	....	1,749.4	2,639.1	4,470.6	4,749.9	8,077.4	9,613.6	12,069.3	12,729.9	12,903.4	Total Debt by Currency	88z
	....	....	....	....	....	....	514.6	654.3	1,111.4	2,024.0	2,470.1	2,876.1	2,354.1	2,827.4	3,047.3	National	88b
	....	....	....	....	....	....	1,234.8	1,984.8	3,359.2	2,725.9	5,607.3	6,737.5	9,715.2	9,902.5	9,856.1	Foreign	89b
Millions of Litai																**National Accounts**	
	....	....	....	26	45	445	8,474	11,489	16,240	20,973	24,939	27,126	27,931	29,118	30,615	Househ.Cons.Expend.,incl.NPISHs	96f
	....	....	....	26	45	445	1,800	3,319	4,747	5,966	7,277	10,481	9,458	9,655	9,627	Government Consumption Expend.	91f
	....	....	....	37	93	783	2,677	3,905	5,554	7,269	9,337	10,463	9,416	8,441	9,320	Gross Fixed Capital Formation	93e
	....	....	....	7	8	−247	−455	−792	405	462	839	31	247	935	1,012	Changes in Inventories	93i
	....	....	....	70	123	795	9,567	9,361	12,765	16,843	20,897	20,282	16,953	20,437	24,182	Exports of Goods and Services	90c
	....	....	....	81	87	679	10,472	10,378	15,609	19,944	24,949	25,393	21,350	23,331	26,789	Imports of Goods and Services (-)	98c
	....	....	....	134	415	3,406	11,590	16,904	24,103	31,569	38,340	42,990	42,655	45,254	47,968	Gross Domestic Product (GDP)	99b
	....	....	....	....	....	....	34	34	−51	−364	−793	−1,022	−1,031	−775	−719	Net Primary Income from Abroad	98.n
	....	....	....	....	....	....	11,624	16,938	24,051	31,205	37,547	41,968	41,624	44,479	47,249	Gross National Income (GNI)	99a
	....	....	....	....	....	....	508	624	437	575	920	940	651	970	1,030	Net Current Transf.from Abroad	98t
	....	....	....	....	....	....	12,132	17,562	24,489	31,780	38,467	42,908	42,275	45,449	48,279	Gross Nat'l Disposable Inc.(GNDI)	99i
	....	....	....	....	....	....	1,859	2,754	3,501	4,841	6,251	5,301	4,886	6,677	8,038	Gross Saving	99s
	....	....	....	....	....	....	1,040	1,496	2,106	3,065	3,736	4,232	4,533	4,590	5,012	Consumption of Fixed Capital	99cf
	....	....	....	....	....	....	....	....	....	25,238	27,075	28,459	27,350	28,412	30,051	GDP Volume 1995 Prices	99b.p
	....	....	....	....	....	....	....	....	....	104.7	112.3	118.1	113.5	117.9	124.7	GDP Volume (1995=100)	99bvp
	....	....	....	....	....	....	....	....	....	125.1	141.6	151.1	156.0	159.3	159.6	GDP Deflator (1995=100)	99bip
Midyear Estimates																	
	....	....	....	....	3.74	3.74	3.73	3.72	3.71	3.71	3.71	3.70	3.66	3.70	3.49	**Population**	99z

(See notes in the back of the book.)

Luxembourg

137

		1972	1973	1974	1975	1976	1977	1978	1979	1980	1981	1982	1983	1984	1985	1986
Exchange Rates													*Francs per SDR through 1998,*			
Market Rate	aa	47.839	49.846	44.227	46.273	41.806	40.013	37.520	36.948	40.205	44.766	51.758	58.252	61.832	55.316	49.429
													Francs per US Dollar through 1998,			
Market Rate	ae	44.063	41.320	36.123	39.528	35.983	32.940	28.800	28.048	31.523	38.460	46.920	55.640	63.080	50.360	40.410
Market Rate	rf	44.015	38.977	38.952	36.779	38.605	35.843	31.492	29.319	29.242	37.129	45.691	51.132	57.784	59.378	44.672
													Francs per ECU:			
ECU Rate	ea	....	....	....	....	....	....	....	40.318	41.335	41.747	45.321	46.097	44.717	44.645	43.233
ECU Rate	eb	....	....	....	....	42.913	40.884	40.059	40.164	40.601	41.301	44.680	45.430	45.438	44.913	43.803
													Index Numbers (1995=100):			
Market Rate	ahx	66.9	75.8	75.7	80.3	76.4	82.2	93.6	100.5	100.8	79.7	64.8	57.8	51.1	50.0	66.2
Nominal Effective Exchange Rate	ne c	....	....	....	....	....	....	....	104.6	104.2	102.0	94.7	92.5	91.7	92.1	93.7
Real Effective Exchange Rate	re c	....	....	....	....	....	....	....	105.8	103.3	100.6	94.6	94.7	94.5	95.0	95.7
Fund Position													*Millions of SDRs:*			
Quota	2f. s	20.00	20.00	20.00	20.00	20.00	20.00	31.00	31.00	46.50	46.50	46.50	77.00	77.00	77.00	77.00
SDRs	1b. s	7.34	7.34	7.34	7.34	7.34	7.44	7.58	11.59	11.32	14.88	15.41	15.98	16.58	17.08	17.54
Reserve Position in the Fund	1c. s	5.01	5.01	5.01	5.01	9.01	8.72	9.57	9.42	12.19	12.20	12.21	12.21	12.21	12.21	12.23
of which: Outstg.Fund Borrowing	2c	—	—	—	—	—	—	—	—	—	—	—	—	—	—	—
International Liquidity													*Millions of US Dollars Unless Otherwise Indicated:*			
Total Res.Min.Gold (Eurosys.Def)	1l. d													28.56	32.71	36.43
SDRs	1b. d	7.97	8.85	8.99	8.59	8.53	9.04	9.88	15.27	14.44	17.32	17.00	16.73	16.25	18.76	21.45
Reserve Position in the Fund	1c. d	5.44	6.04	6.13	5.87	10.47	10.59	12.47	12.41	15.55	14.20	13.47	12.78	11.97	13.41	14.96
Foreign Exchange	1d. d	....	....	....	....	....	....	....	....	....	....	....	....	.34	.53	.01
o/w: Fin.Deriv.Rel.to Reserves	1dd d															
Other Reserve Assets	1e. d	.442	.442	.442	.442	.442	.451	.455	.455	.455	.455	.455	.455	.429	.429	.429
Gold (Million Fine Troy Ounces)	1ad	.442	.442	.442	.442	.442	.451	.455	.455	.455	.455	.455	.455	.429	.429	.429
Gold (Eurosystem Valuation)	1an d	18.67	18.67	18.67	18.67	18.67	19.04	19.22	19.22	19.22	19.22	19.22	19.22	18.12	18.12	18.11
Memo: Euro Cl. on Non-EA Res.	1dg d															
Non-Euro Cl. on EA Res.	1dh d															
Mon. Auth.: Other Foreign Assets	3.. d															
Foreign Liabilities	4.. d															
Banking Insts.: Foreign Assets	7a. d	9,601	17,264	24,608	30,369	38,174	51,191	68,898	95,095	104,828	114,204	109,711	103,235	101,708	130,949	171,691
Foreign Liab.	7b. d	8,954	15,608	22,108	27,890	35,123	48,206	64,010	89,507	98,454	106,698	102,572	94,967	93,349	117,205	151,901
Monetary Authorities													*Billions of Francs through 1998;*			
Fgn. Assets (Cl.on Non-EA Ctys)	11	....	....	....	....	....	....	....	....	....	....	....	2.4	3.2	3.4	5.3
Claims on General Government	12a. u	....	....	....	....	....	....	....	....	....	....	....	....	....	....	....
o/w: Claims on Gen.Govt.in Cty	12a	....	....	....	....	....	....	....	....	....	....	....	....	—	2.3	2.5
Claims on Banking Institutions	12e. u	....	....	....	....	....	....	....	....	....	....	....	....	....	....	....
o/w: Claims on Bank.Inst.in Cty	12e	....	....	....	....	....	....	....	....	....	....	....	.5	.5	.3	.3
Claims on Other Resident Sectors	12d. u															
o/w: Cl. on Oth.Res.Sect.in Cty	12d															
Currency Issued	14a	....	....	....	....	....	....	....	....	....	....	....	....	—	2.3	2.5
Liabilities to Banking Insts	14c. u															
o/w: Liabs to Bank.Inst.in Cty	14c															
Demand Dep. of Other Res.Sect.	14d. u															
o/w: D.Dep.of Oth.Res.Sect.in Cty	14d															
Other Dep. of Other Res.Sect.	15.. u															
o/w: O.Dep.of Oth.Res.Sect.in Cty	15															
Money Market Instruments	16m. u															
o/w: MMI Held by Resid.of Cty	16m															
Bonds (Debt Securities)	16n. u															
o/w: Bonds Held by Resid.of Cty	16n															
Foreign Liab. (to Non-EA Ctys)	16c	....	....	....	....	....	....	....	....	....	....	....	—	—	—	—
Central Government Deposits	16d. u															
o/w: Cent.Govt.Dep. in Cty	16d	....	....	....	....	....	....	....	....	....	....	....	1.2	.7	.7	2.7
Capital Accounts	17a	....	....	....	....	....	....	....	....	....	....	....	1.7	2.5	2.5	2.4
Other Items (Net)	17r	....	....	....	....	....	....	....	....	....	....	....	.1	.6	.4	.5
Memo: Net Claims on Eurosystem	12e. s															
Currency Put into Circ.	14m															
Banking Institutions													*Billions of Francs through 1998;*			
Claims on Monetary Authorities	20	1.1	1.5	1.1	1.2	1.1	1.5	.9	1.1	1.1	1.1	1.2	1.5	1.7	1.9	2.1
Claims on Bk.Inst.in Oth.EA Ctys	20b. u	....	....	....	....	....	....	....	....	....	....	....	....	....	....	....
Fgn. Assets (Cl.on Non-EA Ctys)	21	428.2	692.9	879.9	1,192.0	1,362.2	†1,686.2	1,984.3	2,667.2	3,304.5	4,392.3	5,147.7	5,744.0	6,415.8	6,594.6	6,938.0
Claims on General Government	22a. u	....	....	....	....	....	....	....	....	....	....	....	....	....	....	....
o/w: Claims on Gen.Govt.in Cty	22a	1.6	2.0	1.4	1.3	1.2	1.2	1.4	1.2	1.1	1.4	1.4	1.7	1.4	1.4	1.5
Claims on Other Resident Sectors	22d. u	....	....	....	....	....	....	....	....	....	....	....	....	....	....	....
o/w: Cl. on Oth.Res.Sect.in Cty	22d	38.6	48.1	64.8	74.3	86.3	†58.0	117.2	135.9	160.8	180.4	202.5	204.5	218.4	224.9	259.7
Demand Deposits	24.. u	....	....	....	....	....	....	....	....	....	....	....	....	....	....	....
o/w: D.Dep.of Oth.Res.Sect.in Cty	24	12.7	15.6	16.8	22.1	20.2	23.0	25.6	23.6	25.1	27.1	29.6	34.9	38.9	38.4	45.1
Other Deposits	25.. u	....	....	....	....	....	....	....	....	....	....	....	....	....	....	....
o/w: O.Dep.of Oth.Res.Sect.in Cty	25	37.9	54.6	76.7	85.8	103.6	112.4	141.7	160.7	191.0	222.6	246.1	272.2	300.4	402.5	470.3
Money Market Instruments	26m. u	....	....	....	....	....	....	....	....	....	....	....	....	....	....	....
o/w: MMI Held by Resid.of Cty	26m															
Bonds (Debt Securities)	26n. u	....	....	....	....	....	....	....	....	....	....	....	....	....	....	....
o/w: Bonds Held by Resid.of Cty	26n															
Foreign Liab. (to Non-EA Ctys)	26c	401.3	629.5	798.6	1,102.4	1,263.8	1,587.9	1,843.5	2,510.5	3,103.6	4,103.6	4,812.7	5,284.0	5,888.4	5,902.4	6,138.3
Central Government Deposits	26d. u	....	....	....	....	....	....	....	....	....	....	....	....	....	....	....
o/w: Cent.Govt.Dep. in Cty	26d															
Credit from Monetary Authorities	26g															
Liab. to Bk.Inst.in Oth. EA Ctys	26h. u															
Capital Accounts	27a	17.4	25.0	36.0	47.3	59.3	76.5	95.4	119.5	147.4	190.0	252.7	315.8	388.7	451.7	513.2
Other Items (Net)	27r	.2	19.8	19.0	11.1	3.9	†−52.7	−2.4	−8.8	.4	32.0	11.7	44.8	20.8	27.7	34.4
Central Govt. Monetary Liabilities	25.i u	....	....	....	....	....	....	....	....	....	....	....	....	....	....	....

1987	1988	1989	1990	1991	1992	1993	1994	1995	1996	1997	1998	1999	2000	2001		
Euros per SDR Thereafter: End of Period															**Exchange Rates**	
47.032	50.255	46.994	44.078	44.730	45.623	49.599	46.478	43.725	46.022	49.814	48.682	1.3662	1.4002	1.4260	Market Rate	**aa**
Euros per US Dollar Thereafter: End of Period (ae) Period Average (rf)																
33.153	37.345	35.760	30.983	31.270	33.180	36.110	31.838	29.415	32.005	36.920	34.575	.9954	1.0747	1.1347	Market Rate	**ae**
37.334	36.768	39.404	33.418	32.150	34.597	33.456	29.480	30.962	35.774	36.299	.9386	1.0854	1.1175		Market Rate	**rf**
End of Period (ea) Period Average (eb)																
43.154	43.576	42.592	42.184	41.931	40.178	40.266	39.161	38.697	40.102	40.781	40.340	....	....	....	ECU Rate	**ea**
43.039	43.427	43.378	42.506	42.222	41.604	40.468	39.661	38.548	39.295	40.529	40.621	....	....	....	ECU Rate	**eb**
Period Averages																
79.0	80.3	74.8	88.4	86.6	91.8	85.2	88.2	100.0	95.1	82.4	81.2				Market Rate	**ahx**
95.0	94.7	94.4	96.1	96.4	97.1	97.0	98.2	100.0	98.8	97.0	96.7	96.5	95.5	95.4	Nominal Effective Exchange Rate	**nec**
95.4	94.8	94.5	96.3	96.7	97.0	97.3	98.1	100.0	98.3	96.1	95.7	95.5	95.3	95.5	Real Effective Exchange Rate	**rec**
End of Period															**Fund Position**	
77.00	77.00	77.00	77.00	77.00	135.50	135.50	135.50	135.50	135.50	135.50	135.50	279.10	279.10	279.10	Quota	**2f.s**
17.96	18.41	19.05	19.86	20.60	6.62	5.00	7.22	7.46	7.75	8.04	8.72	1.78	3.22	5.00	SDRs	**1b.s**
12.23	12.23	12.25	12.25	12.27	25.85	23.58	23.61	22.94	23.56	21.75	59.37	54.37	55.47	78.95	Reserve Position in the Fund	**1c.s**
—	—	—	—	—	—	—	—	—	—	—	31.34	—	—	—	*of which:* Outstg.Fund Borrowing	**2c**
End of Period															**International Liquidity**	
42.84	41.24	75.24	80.53	80.42	74.13	67.38	75.73	74.98	73.68	64.07	....	†77.07	76.46	105.49	Total Res.Min.Gold (Eurosys.Def)	**1l.d**
25.48	24.77	25.03	28.25	29.47	9.10	9.59	10.54	11.09	11.14	10.85	12.28	2.45	4.19	6.28	SDRs	**1b.d**
17.35	16.46	16.10	17.43	17.55	35.54	32.38	34.46	34.10	33.87	29.35	83.60	74.62	72.27	99.21	Reserve Position in the Fund	**1c.d**
.01	.01	34.11	34.85	33.40	29.48	25.40	30.73	29.79	28.67	23.87	....	—	—	—	Foreign Exchange	**1d.d**
....	....	....	....	....	....	....	....	....	....	....	....	—	—	—	*o/w:* Fin.Deriv.Rel.to Reserves	**1dd.d**
												—	—	—	Other Reserve Assets	**1e.d**
.429	.429	†.343	.343	.343	.343	.305	.305	.305	.305	.305	.305	.076	.076	.076	Gold (Million Fine Troy Ounces)	**1ad**
18.11	18.11	†16.79	19.38	19.20	19.25	14.90	16.90	18.28	16.81	14.44	....	22.00	21.00	21.00	Gold (Eurosystem Valuation)	**1and**
....	....	....	....	....	....	....	....	....	....	....	....	....	....	....	Memo: Euro Cl. on Non-EA Res.	**1dgd**
												—	—	—	Non-Euro Cl. on EA Res.	**1dhd**
—	—	34.12	34.86	33.26	26.22	25.48	30.78	29.58	28.43	24.11	....	†2171.54	47.73	56.03	Mon. Auth.: Other Foreign Assets	**3..d**
												—	—	—	Foreign Liabilities	**4..d**
226,519	232,010	280,189	355,119	358,711	376,499	....	451,135	504,838	496,510	471,904	....	†178,653	174,954	207,513	Banking Insts.: Foreign Assets	**7a.d**
197,771	199,238	241,426	308,087	309,656	320,644	....	386,770	434,105	415,569	389,816	....	†164,243	159,292	163,497	Foreign Liab.	**7b.d**
Millions of Euros Beginning 1999: End of Period															**Monetary Authorities**	
5.4	5.7	7.1	7.0	7.1	7.0	8.3	8.5	8.3	7.5	6.2	....	952	156	333	Fgn. Assets (Cl.on Non-EA Ctys)	**11**
....	....	....	....	....	....	....	....	....	....	....	....	97	45	20	Claims on General Government	**12a.u**
2.8	3.0	3.0	3.5	3.4	3.2	5.5	5.5	4.9	4.8	4.7	....	—	—	—	*o/w:* Claims on Gen.Govt.in Cty	**12a**
....	....	....	....	....	....	....	....	....	....	....	....	13,038	19,495	16,751	Claims on Banking Institutions	**12e.u**
.3	.3	.2	.2	.3	.3	.1	.1	.2	1.0	2.6	....	9,000	19,282	16,511	*o/w:* Claims on Bank.Inst.in Cty	**12e**
....	....	....	....	....	....	....	....	....	....	....	....	163	242	217	Claims on Other Resident Sectors	**12d.u**
....	....	....	....	....	....	....	....	....	....	....	....	—	—	—	*o/w:* Cl. on Oth.Res.Sect.in Cty	**12d**
2.8	3.0	3.0	3.5	3.4	3.2	5.5	5.5	4.9	5.7	5.7	....	585	661	647	Currency Issued	**14a**
....	....	....	....	....	....	....	....	....	....	....	....	11,509	19,272	16,555	Liabilities to Banking Insts	**14c.u**
....	....	....	....	....	....	....	....	....	....	....	....	4,183	4,912	5,981	*o/w:* Liabs to Bank.Inst.in Cty	**14c**
....	....	....	....	....	....	....	....	....	....	....	....	18	16	15	Demand Dep. of Other Res.Sect.	**14d.u**
....	....	....	....	....	....	....	....	....	....	....	....	3	—	—	*o/w:* D.Dep.of Oth.Res.Sect.in Cty	**14d**
....	....	....	....	....	....	....	....	....	....	....	....	—	—	—	Other Dep. of Other Res.Sect.	**15.u**
....	....	....	....	....	....	....	....	....	....	....	....	—	—	—	*o/w:* O.Dep.of Oth.Res.Sect.in Cty	**15**
....	....	....	....	....	....	....	....	....	....	....	....	—	—	—	Money Market Instruments	**16m.u**
....	....	....	....	....	....	....	....	....	....	....	....	—	—	—	*o/w:* MMI Held by Resid.of Cty	**16m**
....	....	....	....	....	....	....	....	....	....	....	....	—	—	—	Bonds (Debt Securities)	**16n.u**
....	....	....	....	....	....	....	....	....	....	....	....	—	—	—	*o/w:* Bonds Held by Resid.of Cty	**16n**
—	—	1.2	1.1	1.0	.9	.9	1.0	.9	.9	.9	....	2,162	51	64	Foreign Liab. (to Non-EA Ctys)	**16c**
....	....	....	....	....	....	....	....	....	....	....	....	485	569	581	Central Government Deposits	**16d.u**
2.7	2.7	2.7	2.7	2.8	2.9	3.2	3.4	3.4	3.3	3.4	....	485	569	581	*o/w:* Cent.Govt.Dep. in Cty	**16d**
2.4	2.6	2.8	2.8	3.1	3.3	4.1	4.2	4.2	4.3	4.5	....	199	203	188	Capital Accounts	**17a**
.6	.7	.6	.5	.6	.2	.2	.1	—	−.9	−1.1	....	−709	−833	−730	Other Items (Net)	**17r**
....	....	....	....	....	....	....	....	....	....	....	....	−3,376	−14,211	−10,425	*Memo: Net Claims on Eurosystem*	**12e.s**
....	....	....	....	....	....	....	....	....	....	....	....	....	....	....	Currency Put into Circ.	**14m**
Millions of Euros Beginning 1999: End of Period															**Banking Institutions**	
2.4	2.4	.9	3.2	3.4	4.0	....	3.0	3.7	19.1	13.6	....	4,183	4,912	5,981	Claims on Monetary Authorities	**20**
....	....	....	....	....	....	....	....	....	....	....	....	228,490	254,464	283,512	Claims on Bk.Inst.in Oth.EA Ctys	**20b.u**
7,509.7	8,664.4	10,019.5	11,002.5	11,216.9	12,492.3	....	14,363.0	14,849.8	15,890.8	17,422.7	....	177,835	188,021	235,462	Fgn. Assets (Cl.on Non-EA Ctys)	**21**
....	....	....	....	....	....	....	....	....	....	....	....	53,469	46,551	49,303	Claims on General Government	**22a.u**
.7	.7	.6	1.0	.9	3.1	....	12.2	54.3	22.1	19.9	....	733	1,078	1,050	*o/w:* Claims on Gen.Govt.in Cty	**22a**
....	....	....	....	....	....	....	....	....	....	....	....	82,554	98,232	107,910	Claims on Other Resident Sectors	**22d.u**
280.2	323.6	372.4	446.4	476.4	578.5	....	489.7	525.4	552.9	616.0	....	19,778	22,495	29,128	*o/w:* Cl. on Oth.Res.Sect.in Cty	**22d**
....	....	....	....	....	....	....	....	....	....	....	....	42,610	50,376	50,708	Demand Deposits	**24..u**
60.9	83.5	96.6	106.9	98.1	101.8	....	78.5	72.7	79.5	81.5	....	26,687	34,188	31,842	*o/w:* D.Dep.of Oth.Res.Sect.in Cty	**24**
....	....	....	....	....	....	....	....	....	....	....	....	89,947	99,507	104,401	Other Deposits	**25..u**
604.3	838.4	930.4	1,075.0	1,052.7	1,384.6	....	1,674.0	1,677.1	1,933.2	2,155.8	....	32,027	34,711	38,855	*o/w:* O.Dep.of Oth.Res.Sect.in Cty	**25**
....	....	....	....	....	....	....	....	....	....	....	....	65,940	76,337	119,162	Money Market Instruments	**26m.u**
....	....	....	....	....	....	....	....	....	....	....	....	38,771	44,774	52,322	*o/w:* MMI Held by Resid.of Cty	**26m**
....	....	....	....	....	....	....	293.8	453.3	599.1	797.7	....	....	....	....	Bonds (Debt Securities)	**26n.u**
....	....	....	....	....	....	....	....	....	....	....	....	....	....	....	*o/w:* Bonds Held by Resid.of Cty	**26n**
6,556.6	7,440.6	8,633.4	9,545.3	9,682.9	10,639.0	....	12,313.8	12,769.2	13,300.3	14,392.0	....	163,491	171,190	185,518	Foreign Liab. (to Non-EA Ctys)	**26c**
....	....	....	....	....	....	....	....	....	....	....	....	4,595	12,745	8,819	Central Government Deposits	**26d.u**
....	....	....	....	....	....	....	53.8	59.8	72.1	79.6	....	3,377	3,213	2,118	*o/w:* Cent.Govt.Dep. in Cty	**26d**
....	....	....	....	....	....	....	3.8	35.5	3.8	4.6	....	9,000	19,282	16,511	Credit from Monetary Authorities	**26g**
....	....	....	....	....	....	....	....	....	....	....	....	105,620	93,339	119,350	Liab. to Bk.Inst.in Oth. EA Ctys	**26h.u**
545.9	599.0	636.0	686.7	750.2	860.3	....	486.3	526.5	549.0	562.0	....	16,551	34,090	37,432	Capital Accounts	**27a**
25.3	29.6	97.2	39.3	113.7	92.2	....	†−36.2	−161.0	−51.9	−1.0	....	10,005	−9,459	−12,056	Other Items (Net)	**27r**
....	....	....	....	....	....	....	....	....	....	....	12,008	12,778	327	344	438	Central Govt. Monetary Liabilities	**25.iu**

Luxembourg

		1972	1973	1974	1975	1976	1977	1978	1979	1980	1981	1982	1983	1984	1985	1986
Banking Survey (Nat'l Residency)														*Billions of Francs through 1998;*		
Foreign Assets (Net)	31n	...	...	...	...	...	...	...	...	...	...	...	462.5	530.6	695.6	805.1
Domestic Credit	32	...	...	...	...	...	...	...	...	...	...	...	205.1	219.1	227.8	261.0
Claims on General Govt. (Net)	32an	...	...	...	...	...	...	...	...	...	...	...	.6	.7	2.9	1.3
Claims on Other Resident Sectors	32d	...	...	...	...	...	...	...	...	...	...	...	204.5	218.4	224.9	259.7
Currency Issued	34a.n	...	...	...	...	...	...	...	...	...	...	...	—	—	2.3	2.5
Demand Deposits	34b.n	...	...	...	...	...	...	...	...	...	...	...	34.9	38.9	38.4	45.1
Other Deposits	35..n	...	...	...	...	...	...	...	...	...	...	...	272.2	300.4	402.5	470.3
Money Market Instruments	36m	...	...	...	...	...	...	...	...	...	...	...	...	...	...	...
Bonds (Debt Securities)	36n	...	...	...	...	...	...	...	...	...	...	...	...	...	...	...
o/w: Bonds Over Two Years	36na	...	...	...	...	...	...	...	...	...	...	...	...	...	...	...
Capital Accounts	37a	...	...	...	...	...	...	...	...	...	...	...	317.5	391.2	454.3	515.7
Capital Accounts	37a	...	...	...	...	...	...	...	...	...	...	...	...	...	...	...
Other Items (Net)	37r	...	...	...	...	...	...	...	...	...	...	...	42.9	19.2	26.0	32.5
Banking Survey (EA-Wide Residency)														*Millions of Euros:*		
Foreign Assets (Net)	31n.u	...	...	...	...	...	...	...	...	...	...	...	...	...	...	...
Domestic Credit	32..u	...	...	...	...	...	...	...	...	...	...	...	...	...	...	...
Claims on General Govt. (Net)	32an u	...	...	...	...	...	...	...	...	...	...	...	...	...	...	...
Claims on Other Resident Sect.	32d.u	...	...	...	...	...	...	...	...	...	...	...	...	...	...	...
Currency Issued	34a.u	...	...	...	...	...	...	...	...	...	...	...	...	...	...	...
Demand Deposits	34b.u	...	...	...	...	...	...	...	...	...	...	...	...	...	...	...
Other Deposits	35..u	...	...	...	...	...	...	...	...	...	...	...	...	...	...	...
o/w: Other Dep. Over Two Yrs	35ab u	...	...	...	...	...	...	...	...	...	...	...	...	...	...	...
Money Market Instruments	36m.u	...	...	...	...	...	...	...	...	...	...	...	...	...	...	...
Bonds (Debt Securities)	36n.u	...	...	...	...	...	...	...	...	...	...	...	...	...	...	...
o/w: Bonds Over Two Years	36na u	...	...	...	...	...	...	...	...	...	...	...	...	...	...	...
Capital Accounts	37a	...	...	...	...	...	...	...	...	...	...	...	...	...	...	...
Other Items (Net)	37r.u	...	...	...	...	...	...	...	...	...	...	...	...	...	...	...
Money (National Definitions)														*Billions of Francs:*		
Money	39ma	...	...	23.5	26.4	28.2	32.1	34.1	36.3	38.1	40.2	41.1	45.8	47.5	44.9	49.2
Quasi-Money	39mb	...	...	40.3	42.2	51.5	57.2	68.1	80.8	101.7	114.5	113.5	122.8	122.8	152.8	170.9
Broad Money	39mc	...	...	63.8	68.6	79.7	89.3	102.2	117.1	139.8	154.7	154.6	168.6	170.3	197.7	220.1
Interest Rates														*Percent Per Annum*		
Money Market Rate	60b	...	...	...	...	...	...	...	...	12.23	15.25	12.26	10.56	10.70	9.26	7.30
Deposit Rate	60l	...	...	...	...	...	...	...	...	6.50	6.75	7.50	7.17	7.00	6.50	5.50
Lending Rate	60p	...	...	...	...	...	...	...	...	9.25	9.63	10.00	9.38	9.25	8.75	7.75
Government Bond Yield	61	7.25	6.80	7.27	6.73	7.23	7.03e	†6.64	6.78	7.50	8.68	10.50	9.83	10.22	9.53	8.67
Prices, Production, Labor														*Index Numbers (1995=100):*		
Share Prices	62	7.9	9.6	9.8	12.7	13.2	14.1	18.8	28.9	26.5	23.0	20.6	23.2	27.1	40.2	60.9
Producer Prices in Industry	63a	...	...	...	...	...	...	...	...	68.7	76.0	89.6	94.0	99.8	102.8	†100.2
Consumer Prices	64	32.8	34.8	38.1	42.2	46.3	49.4	50.9	53.3	56.6	61.2	66.9	72.7	†76.8	79.9	80.2
Harmonized CPI	64h	...	...	...	...	...	...	...	...	...	...	...	...	...	...	...
Industrial Production	66..b	66.2	74.1	76.6	59.8	61.2	61.5	64.5	66.6	64.4	60.8	61.3	64.6	73.2	78.1	80.3
Industrial Employment	67	87.7	90.2	93.7	94.1	92.2	90.9	89.7	90.5	91.2	90.6	89.6	87.6	86.5	87.4	89.2
															Number in Thousands:	
Labor Force	67d	...	...	...	...	...	...	...	...	...	...	...	...	...	...	...
Employment	67e	...	...	...	...	...	...	...	...	...	...	...	...	...	161	165
Unemployment	67c	...	...	...	...	...	...	...	...	...	...	...	...	...	3	2
Unemployment Rate (%)	67r	...	...	...	...	...	...	...	...	...	...	...	...	...	1.7	1.5
International Transactions														*Billions of Francs through 1998;*		
Exports	70	44.03	57.63	82.54	65.29	70.64	68.56	72.31	85.80	87.88	88.56	101.90	111.47	145.56	168.07	166.23
Imports, c.i.f.	71	42.26	51.95	67.51	66.85	71.84	73.01	79.57	91.20	105.62	111.33	124.64	136.22	160.06	186.70	188.81

	1987	1988	1989	1990	1991	1992	1993	1994	1995	1996	1997	1998	1999	2000	2001	
Banking Survey (Nat'l Residency)																
Millions of Euros Beginning 1999: End of Period																
Foreign Assets (Net)	958.5	1,229.5	1,392.0	1,463.1	1,540.0	1,859.4	....	2,056.7	2,088.0	2,597.1	3,036.0	....	177,387	200,514	246,105	31n
Domestic Credit	281.0	324.6	373.2	448.2	477.9	581.9	....	†450.2	521.4	504.4	557.6	....	16,649	19,791	27,479	32
Claims on General Govt. (Net)	.8	1.0	.8	1.8	1.5	3.4	....	†−39.5	−4.0	−48.5	−58.4	....	−3,129	−2,704	−1,649	32an
Claims on Other Resident Sectors	280.2	323.6	372.4	446.4	476.4	578.5	....	489.7	525.4	552.9	616.0	....	19,778	22,495	29,128	32d
Currency Issued	2.8	3.0	3.0	3.5	3.4	3.2	5.5	5.5	4.9	5.7	5.7	....	585	661	647	34a.n
Demand Deposits	60.9	83.5	96.6	106.9	98.1	101.8	....	78.5	72.7	79.5	81.5	....	26,690	34,188	31,842	34b.n
Other Deposits	604.3	838.4	930.4	1,075.0	1,052.7	1,384.6	....	1,674.0	1,677.1	1,933.2	2,155.8	....	32,027	34,711	38,855	35..n
Money Market Instruments	....	....	....	....	....	....							65,941	76,337	119,125	36m
Bonds (Debt Securities)								293.8	453.3	599.1	797.7	....	38,771	44,775	52,252	36n
o/w: Bonds Over Two Years													31,161	34,014	37,960	36na
Capital Accounts	548.3	601.6	638.8	689.5	753.3	863.7	....	490.5	530.7	553.3	566.5	....				37a
Capital Accounts	....	....	....	....	....	....							16,750	34,292	37,620	37a
Other Items (Net)	23.2	27.6	96.6	36.4	110.6	88.1	....	†−35.4	−129.4	−69.0	−13.7	....	13,272	−4,658	−6,707	37r
Banking Survey (EA-Wide Residency)																
End of Period																
Foreign Assets (Net)	....	....	....	....	....	....	....	....	....	....	....	....	13,134	16,937	50,213	31n.u
Domestic Credit	....	....	....	....	....	....	....	....	....	....	....	....	131,203	131,756	148,048	32..u
Claims on General Govt. (Net)	....	....	....	....	....	....	....	....	....	....	....	....	48,486	33,281	39,922	32an u
Claims on Other Resident Sect.	....	....	....	....	....	....	....	....	....	....	....	....	82,717	98,474	108,127	32d.u
Currency Issued	....	....	....	....	....	....	....	....	....	....	....	....	585	661	647	34a.u
Demand Deposits	....	....	....	....	....	....	....	....	....	....	....	....	42,628	50,391	50,723	34b.u
Other Deposits	....	....	....	....	....	....	....	....	....	....	....	....	89,947	99,507	104,401	35..u
o/w: Other Dep. Over Two Yrs	....	....	....	....	....	....	....	....	....	....	....	....	6,926	3,823	5,371	35ab u
Money Market Instruments	....	....	....	....	....	....	....	....	....	....	....	....	65,940	76,337	119,162	36m.u
Bonds (Debt Securities)	....	....	....	....	....	....	....	....	....	....	....	....	38,771	44,774	52,322	36n.u
o/w: Bonds Over Two Years	....	....	....	....	....	....	....	....	....	....	....	....	31,161	34,014	38,011	36na u
Capital Accounts	....	....	....	....	....	....	....	....	....	....	....	....	16,750	34,292	37,620	37a
Other Items (Net)	....	....	....	....	....	....	....	....	....	....	....	....	−110,285	−157,271	−166,615	37r.u
Money (National Definitions)																
End of Period																
Money	54.3	58.6	66.7	72.8	80.4	81.8	....	104.5	....	111.4	115.0	....	....	....	....	39ma
Quasi-Money	200.1	235.9	286.1	338.6	378.1	406.8	....	399.6	....	423.5	396.0	....	....	....	....	39mb
Broad Money	254.4	294.5	352.8	411.4	458.5	488.6	....	504.1	....	534.9	511.0	....	....	....	....	39mc
Interest Rates																
Percent Per Annum																
Money Market Rate	6.71	7.16	10.02	9.67	9.10	8.93	8.09	5.16	4.26	3.29	3.36	3.48				60b
Deposit Rate	4.94	4.46	5.04	6.00	6.00	6.00	5.33	5.00	5.00	3.54	3.46	3.31				60l
Lending Rate	7.19	6.71	7.25	8.23	8.25	8.75	7.65	6.58	6.50	5.50	5.50	5.27	....	....	....	60p
Government Bond Yield	7.96	7.13	7.68	8.51	8.15	7.90	6.93	6.38	6.05	5.21	5.39	5.29	....	....	....	61
Prices, Production, Labor																
Period Averages																
Share Prices	†55.4	55.3	66.8	61.5	58.7	55.7	78.3	110.4	100.0	117.5	152.5	194.2	....	....	....	62
Producer Prices in Industry	93.7	96.1	103.4	101.4	98.8	96.1	94.8	†96.2	100.0	96.9	98.3	100.7	†97.6	102.3	103.4	63a
Consumer Prices	80.1	81.3	84.0	†87.1	89.9	92.7	96.0	98.1	100.0	†101.4	102.8	103.8	104.8	108.1	111.0	64
Harmonized CPI	....	....	....	....	....	....	....	....	100.0	101.2	102.6	103.6	104.6	108.6	111.2	64h
Industrial Production	80.7	90.3	97.1	97.5	97.1	96.3	93.7	99.1	100.0	100.7	106.2	114.1	116.4	122.6	126.3	66..b
Industrial Employment	90.2	93.7	96.2	100.0	95.7	....	....	....	....	....	....	....	....	....	....	67
Period Averages																
Labor Force	....	....	....	....	....	....	....	....	....	172	175	179	181	....	....	67d
Employment	170	175	182	190	197	....	....	....	214	220	227	237	248	....	....	67e
Unemployment	3	2	2	2	2	3	4	5	5	6	6	6	5	5	5	67c
Unemployment Rate (%)	1.7	1.6	1.4	1.3	1.4	1.6	2.1	2.8	3.0	3.3	3.6	3.1	2.9	2.7	2.6	67r
International Transactions																
Millions of Euros Beginning 1999																
Exports	163.32	186.36	212.81	210.70	214.15	207.96	203.60	219.10	228.40	223.20	250.10	287.30	†7.37	8.48	8.84	70
Imports, c.i.f.	195.60	213.73	244.70	253.83	274.68	264.31	265.90	280.00	287.30	299.20	335.70	370.60	†10.14	11.53	11.93	71

Luxembourg

		1972	1973	1974	1975	1976	1977	1978	1979	1980	1981	1982	1983	1984	1985	1986
Balance of Payments																*Millions of US Dollars:*
Current Account, n.i.e.	78al d	...	...	...	...	...	...	...	...	...	...	...	...	...	...	...
Goods: Exports f.o.b.	78aa d	...	...	...	...	...	...	...	...	...	...	...	...	...	...	...
Goods: Imports f.o.b.	78ab d	...	...	...	...	...	...	...	...	...	...	...	...	...	...	...
Trade Balance	78ac d	...	...	...	...	...	...	...	...	...	...	...	...	...	...	...
Services: Credit	78ad d	...	...	...	...	...	...	...	...	...	...	...	...	...	...	...
Services: Debit	78ae d	...	...	...	...	...	...	...	...	...	...	...	...	...	...	...
Balance on Goods & Services	78af d	...	...	...	...	...	...	...	...	...	...	...	...	...	...	...
Income: Credit	78ag d	...	...	...	...	...	...	...	...	...	...	...	...	...	...	...
Income: Debit	78ah d	...	...	...	...	...	...	...	...	...	...	...	...	...	...	...
Balance on Gds, Serv. & Inc.	78ai d	...	...	...	...	...	...	...	...	...	...	...	...	...	...	...
Current Transfers, n.i.e.: Credit	78aj d	...	...	...	...	...	...	...	...	...	...	...	...	...	...	...
Current Transfers: Debit	78ak d	...	...	...	...	...	...	...	...	...	...	...	...	...	...	...
Capital Account, n.i.e.	78bc d	...	...	...	...	...	...	...	...	...	...	...	...	...	...	...
Capital Account, n.i.e.: Credit	78ba d	...	...	...	...	...	...	...	...	...	...	...	...	...	...	...
Capital Account: Debit	78bb d	...	...	...	...	...	...	...	...	...	...	...	...	...	...	...
Financial Account, n.i.e.	78bj d	...	...	...	...	...	...	...	...	...	...	...	...	...	...	...
Direct Investment Abroad	78bd d	...	...	...	...	...	...	...	...	...	...	...	...	...	...	...
Dir. Invest. in Rep. Econ., n.i.e.	78be d	...	...	...	...	...	...	...	...	...	...	...	...	...	...	...
Portfolio Investment Assets	78bf d	...	...	...	...	...	...	...	...	...	...	...	...	...	...	...
Equity Securities	78bk d	...	...	...	...	...	...	...	...	...	...	...	...	...	...	...
Debt Securities	78bl d	...	...	...	...	...	...	...	...	...	...	...	...	...	...	...
Portfolio Investment Liab., n.i.e.	78bg d	...	...	...	...	...	...	...	...	...	...	...	...	...	...	...
Equity Securities	78bm d	...	...	...	...	...	...	...	...	...	...	...	...	...	...	...
Debt Securities	78bn d	...	...	...	...	...	...	...	...	...	...	...	...	...	...	...
Financial Derivatives Assets	78bw d	...	...	...	...	...	...	...	...	...	...	...	...	...	...	...
Financial Derivatives Liabilities	78bx d	...	...	...	...	...	...	...	...	...	...	...	...	...	...	...
Other Investment Assets	78bh d	...	...	...	...	...	...	...	...	...	...	...	...	...	...	...
Monetary Authorities	78bo d	...	...	...	...	...	...	...	...	...	...	...	...	...	...	...
General Government	78bp d	...	...	...	...	...	...	...	...	...	...	...	...	...	...	...
Banks	78bq d	...	...	...	...	...	...	...	...	...	...	...	...	...	...	...
Other Sectors	78br d	...	...	...	...	...	...	...	...	...	...	...	...	...	...	...
Other Investment Liab., n.i.e.	78bi d	...	...	...	...	...	...	...	...	...	...	...	...	...	...	...
Monetary Authorities	78bs d	...	...	...	...	...	...	...	...	...	...	...	...	...	...	...
General Government	78bt d	...	...	...	...	...	...	...	...	...	...	...	...	...	...	...
Banks	78bu d	...	...	...	...	...	...	...	...	...	...	...	...	...	...	...
Other Sectors	78bv d	...	...	...	...	...	...	...	...	...	...	...	...	...	...	...
Net Errors and Omissions	78ca d	...	...	...	...	...	...	...	...	...	...	...	...	...	...	...
Overall Balance	78cb d	...	...	...	...	...	...	...	...	...	...	...	...	...	...	...
Reserves and Related Items	79da d	...	...	...	...	...	...	...	...	...	...	...	...	...	...	...
Reserve Assets	79db d	...	...	...	...	...	...	...	...	...	...	...	...	...	...	...
Use of Fund Credit and Loans	79dc d	...	...	...	...	...	...	...	...	...	...	...	...	...	...	...
Exceptional Financing	79de d	...	...	...	...	...	...	...	...	...	...	...	...	...	...	...
Government Finance																
Central Government														*Millions of Francs through 1998;*		
Deficit (-) or Surplus	80	...	2,125	4,067	1,008	314	706	3,801	-294	1,673	-3,016	1,190	-3,538	10,279	21,504	16,390
Revenue	81	...	27,374	34,187	38,341	44,671	50,421	56,060	58,148	66,251	72,070	79,285	90,245	96,694	104,637	109,616
Grants Received	81z	...	140	170	222	115	111	89	102	101	161	314	144	366	543	417
Expenditure	82	...	25,077	29,439	36,761	43,137	47,958	51,058	56,921	64,818	70,985	81,389	88,971	92,095	93,197	97,962
Lending Minus Repayments	83	...	312	851	794	1,335	1,868	1,290	1,623	333	1,803	601	4,176	97	3,032	3,465
Adjustment for Complem. Period	80x	...	—	—	—	—	—	—	—	472	-2,459	3,581	-780	5,411	12,553	7,784
Financing																
Total Financing	84	...	-2,125	-4,067	-1,008	-314	-706	-3,801	294	-1,673	3,016	-1,190	3,538	-10,279	-21,504	-16,390
Domestic	84a	...	...	...	...	...	...	...	...	-1,591	3,103	-1,092	3,635	-10,940	-21,470	-16,320
Foreign	85a	...	...	...	...	...	...	...	...	-82	-87	-98	-97	661	-34	-70
Debt: Domestic	88a	...	...	8,496	8,007	8,571	8,718	8,798	8,322	8,155	9,340	10,774	12,834	14,089	14,110	15,469
Foreign	89a	...	...	763	677	609	522	442	375	294	212	129	62	750	750	4,997
General Government																*As Percent of*
Deficit (-) or Surplus	80g	...	...	...	...	...	...	...	...	...	...	...	...	...	...	...
Debt	88g	...	...	...	...	...	...	...	...	...	...	...	...	...	...	...
National Accounts																*Billions of Francs through 1998;*
Househ.Cons.Expend.,incl.NPISHs	96f	33.9	37.6	43.2	50.1	56.5	61.1	65.0	70.6	78.1	86.3	95.8	104.2	112.6	120.5	126.2
Government Consumption Expend.	91f	7.4	8.7	10.7	13.0	14.7	16.3	17.6	19.5	22.2	24.7	26.1	27.6	29.8	32.3	35.0
Gross Fixed Capital Formation	93e	17.6	21.0	23.0	24.1	24.9	25.7	27.0	29.8	36.0	36.0	39.7	37.1	38.8	35.9	49.1
Changes in Inventories	93i	.4	.2	-3.2	-4.2	-2.1	-4.8	1.0	-2.8	-2.5	-1.3	-.2	5.4	9.1	2.4	—
Exports of Goods and Services	90c	52.4	68.6	96.1	80.2	87.9	89.1	94.0	111.0	117.7	122.8	141.3	157.6	195.8	222.9	224.8
Imports of Goods and Services (-)	98c	48.5	58.8	76.2	76.4	82.1	84.8	92.3	106.0	118.5	126.8	143.8	157.2	192.3	212.1	215.0
Gross Domestic Product (GDP)	99b	63.2	76.8	93.6	86.7	99.8	102.6	112.2	122.1	132.9	141.7	158.8	174.7	193.7	229.9	249.5
Net Primary Income from Abroad	98.n	3.4	3.5	5.7	11.9	16.7	19.4	21.3	23.2	28.0	36.6	60.2	72.2	76.7	83.5	82.3
Gross National Income (GNI)	99a	66.6	80.3	99.3	98.6	116.5	122.0	133.5	145.3	160.9	178.3	218.9	246.9	270.4	288.8	305.6
Net National Income	99e	57.8	69.1	87.2	86.2	104.2	110.0	120.7	130.7	145.0	161.3	200.8	226.7	247.8	264.8	280.5
GDP Volume 1975 Prices	99b.p	53.6	57.6	60.2	58.1	...	...	...	...	...	...	...	...	...	...	...
GDP Volume 1985 Prices	99b.p	...	...	...	162.09	166.20	168.81	175.69	179.61	181.32	180.32	182.36	187.82	199.44	205.26	215.07
GDP Volume 1995 Prices	99b.p	...	...	...	...	...	...	...	...	...	...	...	...	...	...	...
GDP Volume (1995=100)	99bv p	...	...	...	...	...	...	...	...	...	...	...	...	...	...	...
GDP Deflator (1990=100)	99bi p	29.5	33.1	38.7	38.4	43.1	43.6	45.8	48.8	52.6	56.4	62.5	66.7	69.7	80.3	83.2
GDP Deflator (1995=100)	99bi p	...	...	...	...	...	...	...	...	...	...	...	...	...	...	...
																Millions:
Population	99z	.35	.35	.36	.36	.36	.36	.36	.36	.36	.37	.37	.37	.37	.37	.37

	1987	1988	1989	1990	1991	1992	1993	1994	1995	1996	1997	1998	1999	2000	2001		
Minus Sign Indicates Debit																**Balance of Payments**	
	....	....	....	....	....	....	....	....	2,453	2,207	2,005	1,631	1,277	1,617	884	Current Account, n.i.e.	78al *d*
									8,578	7,944	7,767	8,557	8,597	8,558	8,791	Goods: Exports f.o.b.	78aa *d*
									-10,269	-9,872	-9,770	-10,881	-11,175	-10,909	-11,158	Goods: Imports f.o.b.	78ab *d*
									-1,690	-1,928	-2,003	-2,324	-2,579	-2,350	-2,367	*Trade Balance*	78ac *d*
									10,619	11,930	12,583	14,084	16,761	19,200	19,092	Services: Credit	78ad *d*
									-7,519	-8,483	-8,683	-9,947	-11,840	-13,642	-13,865	Services: Debit	78ae *d*
									1,410	1,519	1,897	1,813	2,343	3,207	2,860	*Balance on Goods & Services*	78af *d*
									48,798	40,476	38,422	46,541	47,664	50,178	51,761	Income: Credit	78ag *d*
									-47,182	-39,233	-37,805	-46,300	-48,153	-51,307	-53,208	Income: Debit	78ah *d*
									3,026	2,761	2,514	2,055	1,854	2,078	1,413	*Balance on Gds, Serv. & Inc.*	78ai *d*
									1,791	2,186	1,985	2,185	2,282	2,750	2,265	Current Transfers, n.i.e.: Credit	78aj *d*
									-2,364	-2,741	-2,493	-2,608	-2,859	-3,211	-2,793	Current Transfers: Debit	78ak *d*

Capital Account, n.i.e. .... 78bc *d*
  Capital Account, n.i.e.: Credit .... 78ba *d*
  Capital Account: Debit .... 78bb *d*

Financial Account, n.i.e. .... 78bj *d*
  Direct Investment Abroad .... 78bd *d*
  Dir. Invest. in Rep. Econ., n.i.e. ...... 78be *d*
  Portfolio Investment Assets .... 78bf *d*
    Equity Securities .... 78bk *d*
    Debt Securities .... 78bl *d*
  Portfolio Investment Liab., n.i.e. ..... 78bg *d*
    Equity Securities .... 78bm *d*
    Debt Securities .... 78bn *d*
  Financial Derivatives Assets .... 78bw *d*
  Financial Derivatives Liabilities ...... 78bx *d*
  Other Investment Assets .... 78bh *d*
    Monetary Authorities .... 78bo *d*
    General Government .... 78bp *d*
    Banks .... 78bq *d*
    Other Sectors .... 78br *d*
  Other Investment Liab., n.i.e. .... 78bi *d*
    Monetary Authorities .... 78bs *d*
    General Government .... 78bt *d*
    Banks .... 78bu *d*
    Other Sectors .... 78bv *d*

Net Errors and Omissions .... 78ca *d*
  Overall Balance .... 78cb *d*

Reserves and Related Items .... 79da *d*
  Reserve Assets .... 79db *d*
  Use of Fund Credit and Loans .... 79dc *d*
  Exceptional Financing .... 79de *d*

Government Finance

Central Government

Millions of Euros Beginning 1999: Year Ending December 31

	1987	1988	1989	1990	1991	1992	1993	1994	1995	1996	1997	1998	1999	2000	2001		
	8,081	7,610	9,209	16,913	-37,189	....	....	2,656	12,573	25,846	12,609					Deficit (-) or Surplus	80
	113,922	120,852	135,738	149,854	165,523	184,524	202,183	217,830	220,074	239,082	261,696					Revenue	81
	253	264	1,403	954	613	525	944	596	797	507	7,037					Grants Received	81z
	106,519	115,421	119,200	139,122	153,408	177,525	192,807	205,656	211,557	222,710	240,847					Expenditure	82
	1,044	733	3,534	3,022	8,514	1,385	603	700	613	641	-5,563					Lending Minus Repayments	83
	1,469	2,648	-5,198	8,249	-41,403	....	....	-9,414	3,872	9,608	-20,840					Adjustment for Complem. Period	80x
																Financing	
	-8,081	-7,610	-9,209	-16,913	37,189	....	....	-2,656	-11,810	-25,846	-12,609					Total Financing	84
	-6,490	-6,642	-8,675	-16,143	37,518	....	....	-2,300	-11,776	-25,598	-12,455					Domestic	84a
	-1,591	-968	-534	-770	-329	....	....	-356	-34	-248	-154					Foreign	85a
	14,739	13,035	11,774	9,473	8,190	12,181	15,473	....	....	....	24,616					Debt: Domestic	88a
	3,316	2,402	1,951	1,289	1,053	902	512	....	....	....	6,311					Foreign	89a

General Government

Gross Domestic Product

	1987	1988	1989	1990	1991	1992	1993	1994	1995	1996	1997	1998	1999	2000	2001		
	....	....	....	5.0	1.9	.8	1.7	2.8	1.8	2.7	3.6	3.2	3.8	5.8	5.0	Deficit (-) or Surplus	80g
				4.7	4.2	5.1	6.1	5.7	5.8	6.2	6.0	6.3	6.0	5.6	5.5	Debt	88g

National Accounts

Billions of Euros Beginning 1999

	1987	1988	1989	1990	1991	1992	1993	1994	1995	1996	1997	1998	1999	2000	2001		
	134.7	143.7	154.6	166.5	234.5	240.2	254.4	269.7	†257.8	273.7	289.0	300.6	†7.7	8.2	8.8	Househ.Cons.Expend.,incl.NPISHs	96f
	38.2	40.3	43.6	49.3	49.5	53.2	57.5	60.0	†95.1	102.8	107.9	111.6	†3.1	3.3	3.7	Government Consumption Expend.	91f
	59.1	68.5	73.1	84.5	103.1	98.5	114.7	107.2	†116.9	115.1	134.5	150.0	†4.5	4.5	4.7	Gross Fixed Capital Formation	93e
	.5	2.4	1.6	4.1	3.3	1.7	.5	1.9	†-1.9	-.7	1.8	2.3	†.1	.1	.1	Changes in Inventories	93i
	223.8	249.2	285.9	291.0	398.8	427.2	456.3	425.0	†571.7	597.7	685.6	756.7	†25.3	31.9	32.3	Exports of Goods and Services	90c
	225.7	250.7	279.3	291.3	367.3	361.8	377.8	383.4	†500.9	524.3	585.6	633.2	†22.3	27.6	28.2	Imports of Goods and Services (-)	98c
	262.4	291.5	334.1	359.0	389.9	417.8	456.8	498.6	†538.5	563.5	624.6	665.7	†18.4	20.5	21.2	Gross Domestic Product (GDP)	99b
	68.2	85.7	96.0	109.1	114.3	....	....	48.2	†32.2	30.1	14.0	-11.5	†-.6	-2.0	....	Net Primary Income from Abroad	98.n
	304.7	336.0	378.8	409.5	433.1	....	....	528.0	†570.6	593.6	638.6	654.3	†17.8	18.5	....	Gross National Income (GNI)	99a
	278.3	308.2	348.5	377.8	399.1	....	....	....	†491.1	510.2	554.6	567.1	†14.3	....	....	Net National Income	99e
	....	....	....	....	....	....										GDP Volume 1975 Prices	99b. *p*
	221.39	234.04	249.62	257.56	265.46	270.30	....	....								GDP Volume 1985 Prices	99b. *p*
	....	....	....	....	....	....	....	....	538.4	552.4	602.6	638.4	†16.74	17.99	18.61	GDP Volume 1995 Prices	99b. *p*
									100.0	102.6	111.9	118.6	†125.4	134.8	139.5	GDP Volume (1995=100)	99bv *p*
	85.0	89.3	96.0	100.0	105.4	110.9	....	....								GDP Deflator (1990=100)	99bi *p*
	....	....	....	....	....	....			100.0	102.0	103.6	104.3	†109.9	111.7	....	GDP Deflator (1995=100)	99bi *p*

Midyear Estimates

	1987	1988	1989	1990	1991	1992	1993	1994	1995	1996	1997	1998	1999	2000	2001		
	.37	.37	.38	.38	.39	.39	.40	.40	.41	.42	.42	.43	.43	.44	.44	**Population**	99z

(See notes in the back of the book.)

		1972	1973	1974	1975	1976	1977	1978	1979	1980	1981	1982	1983	1984	1985	1986

Exchange Rates — *Denar per SDR:*

Market Rate ... **aa** ....

Denar per US Dollar:

Market Rate ... **ae** ....

Market Rate ... **rf** ....

Index Numbers (1995=100):

Nominal Effective Exchange Rate ... **ne c** ....

Real Effective Exchange Rate ... **re c** ....

Fund Position — *Millions of SDRs:*

Quota ... **2f. s** ....

SDRs ... **1b. s** ....

Reserve Position in the Fund ... **1c. s** ....

Total Fund Cred.&Loans Outstg. ... **2tl** ....

International Liquidity — *Millions of US Dollars Unless Otherwise Indicated:*

Total Reserves minus Gold ... **1l. d** ....

SDRs ... **1b. d** ....

Reserve Position in the Fund ... **1c. d** ....

Foreign Exchange ... **1d. d** ....

Gold (Million Fine Troy Ounces) ... **1ad** ....

Gold (National Valuation) ... **1an d** ....

Other Liab. ... **4..d** ....

Deposit Money Banks: Assets ... **7a. d** ....

Liabilities ... **7b. d** ....

Monetary Authorities — *Millions of Denar:*

Foreign Assets ... **11** ....

Claims on Central Government ... **12a** ....

Claims on Deposit Money Banks ... **12e** ....

Reserve Money ... **14** ....

of which: Currency Outside DMBs ... **14a** ....

Restricted Deposits ... **16b** ....

Foreign Liabilities ... **16c** ....

Central Government Deposits ... **16d** ....

Capital Accounts ... **17a** ....

Other Items (Net) ... **17r** ....

Deposit Money Banks — *Millions of Denar:*

Reserves ... **20** ....

Foreign Assets ... **21** ....

Claims on Central Government ... **22a** ....

Claims on Local Government ... **22b** ....

Claims on Nonfin.Pub.Enterprises ... **22c** ....

Claims on Private Sector ... **22d** ....

Demand Deposits ... **24** ....

Time, Savings,& Fgn.Currency Dep. ... **25** ....

Restricted Deposits ... **26b** ....

Foreign Liabilities ... **26c** ....

Central Government Deposits ... **26d** ....

Credit from Monetary Authorities ... **26g** ....

Capital Accounts ... **27a** ....

Other Items (Net) ... **27r** ....

Monetary Survey — *Millions of Denar:*

Foreign Assets (Net) ... **31n** ....

Domestic Credit ... **32** ....

Claims on Central Govt. (Net) ... **32an** ....

Claims on Local Government ... **32b** ....

Claims on Nonfin.Pub.Enterprises ... **32c** ....

Claims on Private Sector ... **32d** ....

Money ... **34** ....

Quasi-Money ... **35** ....

Restricted Deposits ... **36b** ....

Capital Accounts ... **37a** ....

Other Items (Net) ... **37r** ....

Money plus Quasi-Money ... **35l** ....

Interest Rates — *Percent Per Annum*

Bank Rate *(End of Period)* ... **60** ....

Deposit Rate ... **60l** ....

Lending Rate ... **60p** ....

Prices, Production, Labor — *Index Numbers (1995=100):*

Consumer Prices ... **64** ....

Wages: Average Monthly ... **65** ....

Industrial Production ... **66** ....

Number in Thousands:

Employment ... **67e** ....

Unemployment ... **67c** ....

International Transactions — *Millions of US Dollars*

Exports ... **70..d** ....

Imports, c.i.f. ... **71..d** ....

1987	1988	1989	1990	1991	1992	1993	1994	1995	1996	1997	1998	1999	2000	2001		
End of Period															**Exchange Rates**	
....	....	....	....	....	....	61.062	59.264	56.456	59.547	74.776	72.987	82.816	86.420	86.930	Market Rate..........................	**aa**
End of Period (ae) Period Average (rf)																
....	....	....	....	....	....	44.456	40.596	37.980	41.411	55.421	51.836	60.339	66.328	69.172	Market Rate..........................	**ae**
							43.263	37.882	39.981	50.004	54.462	56.902	65.904	68.037	Market Rate..........................	**rf**
Period Averages																
....	....	....	....	767.09		129.86	81.71	100.00	118.02	163.70	162.01	183.26	183.18	188.88	Nominal Effective Exchange Rate	**ne c**
					99.11	87.43	90.48	100.00	96.61	82.55	73.12	74.23	72.77	73.21	Real Effective Exchange Rate	**re c**
End of Period															**Fund Position**	
....	....	....	....	....	—	49.6	49.6	49.6	49.6	49.6	49.6	68.9	68.9	68.9	Quota	**2f. s**
....	....	....	....	....	—	—	—	.2	—	.3	.8	.9	.5	1.8	SDRs	**1b. s**
....	....	....	....	....	—	—	—	—	—	—	—	—	—	—	Reserve Position in the Fund	**1c. s**
....	....	....	....	....	—	2.8	14.0	38.1	47.4	65.3	72.7	74.1	62.3	56.3	Total Fund Cred.&Loans Outstg.	**2tl**
End of Period															**International Liquidity**	
....	....	....	....	....	....	104.59	149.05	257.49	239.55	257.00	306.11	429.92	429.38	745.17	Total Reserves minus Gold..................	**1l. d**
....	....	....	....	....	....	—	—	.2	—	.4	1.1	1.2	.7	2.2	SDRs	**1b. d**
....	....	....	....	....	....	—	—	—	—	—	—	—	—	—	Reserve Position in the Fund	**1c. d**
....	....	....	....	....	....	104.57	149.04	257.26	239.51	256.61	305.04	428.73	428.73	742.94	Foreign Exchange	**1d. d**
....	....	....	....	....	.021	.041	.045	.046	.076	.081	.100	.102	.112	.194	Gold (Million Fine Troy Ounces)	**1ad**
....	....	....	....	....	7.07	14.66	16.36	17.61	27.98	23.45	28.50	29.69	30.66	53.68	Gold (National Valuation)	**1an d**
														14.01	Other Liab..................	**4.. d**
....	....	....	....	....	....	158.20	232.98	254.61	229.70	286.84	337.78	404.22	430.92	....	Deposit Money Banks: Assets	**7a. d**
....	....	....	....	....	....	579.43	528.30	84.62	138.39	185.76	250.00	262.28	233.08	....	Liabilities............	**7b. d**
End of Period															**Monetary Authorities**	
....	....	....	....	....	....	5,303	6,715	10,732	11,453	15,894	18,977	30,072	47,910	70,945	Foreign Assets	**11**
....	....	....	....	....	....	749	2,400	2,395	3,049	8,706	8,675	8,116	5,869	8,796	Claims on Central Government	**12a**
....	....	....	....	....	....	1,830	2,333	4,673	5,642	3,672	3,538	1,918	1,259	394	Claims on Deposit Money Banks	**12e**
....	....	....	....	....	....	3,705	6,360	†8,306	8,044	9,872	10,421	13,508	19,804	21,402	Reserve Money	**14**
....	....	....	....	....	....	2,703	4,786	5,965	6,401	6,846	6,964	8,271	9,522	14,134	*of which: Currency Outside DMBs*	**14a**
....	....	....	....	....	....	—	—	114	136	9	56	271	135	588	Restricted Deposits	**16b**
....	....	....	....	....	....	172	831	2,150	2,822	4,882	5,308	6,137	6,314	4,897	Foreign Liabilities........................	**16c**
....	....	....	....	....	....	14	31	2,633	3,695	5,070	6,152	9,465	16,759	24,926	Central Government Deposits	**16d**
....	....	....	....	....	....	4,754	4,682	5,059	5,771	8,398	8,130	9,547	11,076	12,348	Capital Accounts	**17a**
....	....	....	....	....	....	−911	−360	−462	−325	41	1,123	1,178	950	15,974	Other Items (Net)	**17r**
End of Period															**Deposit Money Banks**	
....	....	....	....	....	....	678	1,470	1,836	1,125	2,158	2,379	3,861	6,192	6,195	Reserves	**20**
....	....	....	....	....	....	7,033	9,458	9,670	9,512	15,897	17,509	24,390	28,582	44,479	Foreign Assets	**21**
....	....	....	....	....	....	52,503	48,954	5,624	6,311	1,782	1,288	1,289	7,337	7,744	Claims on Central Government	**22a**
....	....	....	....	....	....	—	—	2	12	27	20	14	44	7	Claims on Local Government	**22b**
....	....	....	....	....	....	—	—	528	121	208	293	237	515	755	Claims on Nonfin.Pub.Enterprises..........	**22c**
....	....	....	....	....	....	35,107	66,392	39,181	46,826	50,711	34,531	43,611	42,157	41,151	Claims on Private Sector	**22d**
....	....	....	....	....	....	2,853	5,080	5,567	4,854	6,281	7,336	10,458	11,896	11,168	Demand Deposits	**24**
....	....	....	....	....	....	38,138	9,726	8,417	8,652	11,537	13,573	17,846	23,294	49,200	Time, Savings,& Fgn.Currency Dep.	**25**
....	....	....	....	....	....	9,613	38,938	1,039	1,111	1,006	1,099	1,185	1,373	1,708	Restricted Deposits	**26b**
....	....	....	....	....	....	25,759	21,447	3,214	5,731	10,295	12,959	15,826	15,460	13,510	Foreign Liabilities	**26c**
....	....	....	....	....	....	445	2,411	1,481	1,345	1,678	2,181	2,904	5,214	4,150	Central Government Deposits	**26d**
....	....	....	....	....	....	1,310	1,961	4,016	4,395	2,388	2,303	1,287	805	427	Credit from Monetary Authorities	**26g**
....	....	....	....	....	....	10,520	15,567	17,483	23,799	23,157	23,651	29,046	33,120	30,105	Capital Accounts	**27a**
....	....	....	....	....	....	6,687	31,132	15,624	14,021	14,441	−7,082	−5,150	−6,335	−9,937	Other Items (Net)	**27r**
End of Period															**Monetary Survey**	
....	....	....	....	....	....	−13,595	−6,106	15,038	12,412	16,614	18,219	32,499	54,718	30,969	Foreign Assets (Net)	**31n**
....	....	....	....	....	....	87,900	115,304	43,635	51,406	54,797	36,637	41,075	34,027	45,516	Domestic Credit	**32**
....	....	....	....	....	....	52,793	48,912	3,905	4,320	3,740	1,630	−2,964	−8,767	3,594	Claims on Central Govt. (Net)	**32an**
....	....	....	....	....	....	—	—	2	12	27	20	14	44	7	Claims on Local Government	**32b**
....	....	....	....	....	....	—	—	528	121	208	293	237	515	755	Claims on Nonfin.Pub.Enterprises	**32c**
....	....	....	....	....	....	35,107	66,392	39,181	46,826	50,711	34,531	43,611	42,157	41,151	Claims on Private Sector	**32d**
....	....	....	....	....	....	5,590	9,965	†12,223	11,788	13,702	14,952	19,795	22,392	11,168	Money.................................	**34**
....	....	....	....	....	....	37,510	8,507	†8,417	8,652	11,537	13,573	17,846	23,294	49,200	Quasi-Money...........................	**35**
....	....	....	....	....	....	9,613	38,938	1,153	1,247	1,015	1,155	1,456	1,508	1,708	Restricted Deposits	**36b**
....	....	....	....	....	....	15,274	20,249	22,542	29,570	31,555	31,781	38,593	44,196	30,105	Capital Accounts	**37a**
....	....	....	....	....	....	6,174	31,624	14,338	12,561	13,602	−6,605	−4,116	−2,645	−15,696	Other Items (Net)	**37r**
....	....	....	....	....	....	43,100	18,472	†20,640	20,440	25,239	28,525	37,641	45,686	60,368	Money plus Quasi-Money	**35l**
Percent Per Annum															**Interest Rates**	
....	....	....	....	....	....	295.00	33.00	15.00	9.20	8.90	8.90	8.90	7.90	10.70	Bank Rate *(End of Period)*	**60**
....	....	....	....	....	....	....	117.56	24.07	12.75	11.64	11.68	11.40	11.18	9.97	Deposit Rate	**60l**
....	....	....	....	....	....	....	159.82	45.95	21.58	21.42	21.03	20.45	18.93	19.35	Lending Rate	**60p**
Period Averages															**Prices, Production, Labor**	
....	....	....	....	....	....	37.9	85.9	100.0	102.7	103.8	104.4	103.0	....	....	Consumer Prices	**64**
....	....	....	....	....	....	....	90.6	100.0	102.8	105.7	109.5	112.5	118.8	123.0	Wages: Average Monthly	**65**
....	....	....	....	....	....	124.7	112.4	100.0	103.1	104.6	....	....	....	....	Industrial Production	**66**
Period Averages																
....	517	507	468	446	421	396	357	340	319	310	316	....	....		Employment.............................	**67e**
....	150	156	165	172	175	186	216	238	253	....	....	....	....		Unemployment..........................	**67c**
Millions of US Dollars															**International Transactions**	
....	....	....	....	....	....	1,055.3	1,086.3	1,204.0	1,148.0	1,236.8	1,310.7	1,192.0	1,318.8	1,155.0	Exports	**70.. d**
....	....	....	....	....	....	1,199.4	1,484.1	1,718.9	1,627.0	1,778.5	1,914.7	1,795.8	2,085.0	1,688.0	Imports, c.i.f.	**71.. d**

Macedonia, FYR

962		1972	1973	1974	1975	1976	1977	1978	1979	1980	1981	1982	1983	1984	1985	1986
Balance of Payments																*Millions of US Dollars:*
Current Account, n.i.e.	78al *d*	....	....	....	....	....	....	....	....	....	....	....	....	....	....	....
Goods: Exports f.o.b	78aa *d*	....	....	....	....	....	....	....	....	....	....	....	....	....	....	....
Goods: Imports f.o.b	78ab *d*	....	....	....	....	....	....	....	....	....	....	....	....	....	....	....
Trade Balance	78ac *d*	....	....	....	....	....	....	....	....	....	....	....	....	....	....	....
Services: Credit	78ad *d*	....	....	....	....	....	....	....	....	....	....	....	....	....	....	....
Services: Debit	78ae *d*	....	....	....	....	....	....	....	....	....	....	....	....	....	....	....
Balance on Goods & Services	78af *d*	....	....	....	....	....	....	....	....	....	....	....	....	....	....	....
Income: Credit	78ag *d*	....	....	....	....	....	....	....	....	....	....	....	....	....	....	....
Income: Debit	78ah *d*	....	....	....	....	....	....	....	....	....	....	....	....	....	....	....
Balance on Gds, Serv. & Inc.	78ai *d*	....	....	....	....	....	....	....	....	....	....	....	....	....	....	....
Current Transfers, n.i.e.: Credit	78aj *d*	....	....	....	....	....	....	....	....	....	....	....	....	....	....	....
Current Transfers: Debit	78ak *d*	....	....	....	....	....	....	....	....	....	....	....	....	....	....	....
Capital Account, n.i.e.	78bc *d*	....	....	....	....	....	....	....	....	....	....	....	....	....	....	....
Capital Account, n.i.e.: Credit	78ba *d*	....	....	....	....	....	....	....	....	....	....	....	....	....	....	....
Capital Account: Debit	78bb *d*	....	....	....	....	....	....	....	....	....	....	....	....	....	....	....
Financial Account, n.i.e.	78bj *d*	....	....	....	....	....	....	....	....	....	....	....	....	....	....	....
Direct Investment Abroad	78bd *d*	....	....	....	....	....	....	....	....	....	....	....	....	....	....	....
Dir. Invest. in Rep. Econ., n.i.e.	78be *d*	....	....	....	....	....	....	....	....	....	....	....	....	....	....	....
Portfolio Investment Assets	78bf *d*	....	....	....	....	....	....	....	....	....	....	....	....	....	....	....
Equity Securities	78bk *d*	....	....	....	....	....	....	....	....	....	....	....	....	....	....	....
Debt Securities	78bl *d*	....	....	....	....	....	....	....	....	....	....	....	....	....	....	....
Portfolio Investment Liab., n.i.e.	78bg *d*	....	....	....	....	....	....	....	....	....	....	....	....	....	....	....
Equity Securities	78bm *d*	....	....	....	....	....	....	....	....	....	....	....	....	....	....	....
Debt Securities	78bn *d*	....	....	....	....	....	....	....	....	....	....	....	....	....	....	....
Financial Derivatives Assets	78bw *d*	....	....	....	....	....	....	....	....	....	....	....	....	....	....	....
Financial Derivatives Liabilities	78bx *d*	....	....	....	....	....	....	....	....	....	....	....	....	....	....	....
Other Investment Assets	78bh *d*	....	....	....	....	....	....	....	....	....	....	....	....	....	....	....
Monetary Authorities	78bo *d*	....	....	....	....	....	....	....	....	....	....	....	....	....	....	....
General Government	78bp *d*	....	....	....	....	....	....	....	....	....	....	....	....	....	....	....
Banks	78bq *d*	....	....	....	....	....	....	....	....	....	....	....	....	....	....	....
Other Sectors	78br *d*	....	....	....	....	....	....	....	....	....	....	....	....	....	....	....
Other Investment Liab., n.i.e.	78bi *d*	....	....	....	....	....	....	....	....	....	....	....	....	....	....	....
Monetary Authorities	78bs *d*	....	....	....	....	....	....	....	....	....	....	....	....	....	....	....
General Government	78bt *d*	....	....	....	....	....	....	....	....	....	....	....	....	....	....	....
Banks	78bu *d*	....	....	....	....	....	....	....	....	....	....	....	....	....	....	....
Other Sectors	78bv *d*	....	....	....	....	....	....	....	....	....	....	....	....	....	....	....
Net Errors and Omissions	78ca *d*	....	....	....	....	....	....	....	....	....	....	....	....	....	....	....
Overall Balance	78cb *d*	....	....	....	....	....	....	....	....	....	....	....	....	....	....	....
Reserves and Related Items	79da *d*	....	....	....	....	....	....	....	....	....	....	....	....	....	....	....
Reserve Assets	79db *d*	....	....	....	....	....	....	....	....	....	....	....	....	....	....	....
Use of Fund Credit and Loans	79dc *d*	....	....	....	....	....	....	....	....	....	....	....	....	....	....	....
Exceptional Financing	79de *d*	....	....	....	....	....	....	....	....	....	....	....	....	....	....	....
International Investment Position																*Millions of US Dollars*
Assets	79aa *d*	....	....	....	....	....	....	....	....	....	....	....	....	....	....	....
Direct Investment Abroad	79ab *d*	....	....	....	....	....	....	....	....	....	....	....	....	....	....	....
Portfolio Investment	79ac *d*	....	....	....	....	....	....	....	....	....	....	....	....	....	....	....
Equity Securities	79ad *d*	....	....	....	....	....	....	....	....	....	....	....	....	....	....	....
Debt Securities	79ae *d*	....	....	....	....	....	....	....	....	....	....	....	....	....	....	....
Financial Derivatives	79al *d*	....	....	....	....	....	....	....	....	....	....	....	....	....	....	....
Other Investment	79af *d*	....	....	....	....	....	....	....	....	....	....	....	....	....	....	....
Monetary Authorities	79ag *d*	....	....	....	....	....	....	....	....	....	....	....	....	....	....	....
General Government	79ah *d*	....	....	....	....	....	....	....	....	....	....	....	....	....	....	....
Banks	79ai *d*	....	....	....	....	....	....	....	....	....	....	....	....	....	....	....
Other Sectors	79aj *d*	....	....	....	....	....	....	....	....	....	....	....	....	....	....	....
Reserve Assets	79ak *d*	....	....	....	....	....	....	....	....	....	....	....	....	....	....	....
Liabilities	79la *d*	....	....	....	....	....	....	....	....	....	....	....	....	....	....	....
Dir. Invest. in Rep. Economy	79lb *d*	....	....	....	....	....	....	....	....	....	....	....	....	....	....	....
Portfolio Investment	79lc *d*	....	....	....	....	....	....	....	....	....	....	....	....	....	....	....
Equity Securities	79ld *d*	....	....	....	....	....	....	....	....	....	....	....	....	....	....	....
Debt Securities	79le *d*	....	....	....	....	....	....	....	....	....	....	....	....	....	....	....
Financial Derivatives	79ll *d*	....	....	....	....	....	....	....	....	....	....	....	....	....	....	....
Other Investment	79lf *d*	....	....	....	....	....	....	....	....	....	....	....	....	....	....	....
Monetary Authorities	79lg *d*	....	....	....	....	....	....	....	....	....	....	....	....	....	....	....
General Government	79lh *d*	....	....	....	....	....	....	....	....	....	....	....	....	....	....	....
Banks	79li *d*	....	....	....	....	....	....	....	....	....	....	....	....	....	....	....
Other Sectors	79lj *d*	....	....	....	....	....	....	....	....	....	....	....	....	....	....	....
Government Finance																*Millions of Denar:*
Deficit (-) or Surplus	80	....	....	....	....	....	....	....	....	....	....	....	....	....	....	....
Total Revenue and Grants	81y	....	....	....	....	....	....	....	....	....	....	....	....	....	....	....
Revenue	81	....	....	....	....	....	....	....	....	....	....	....	....	....	....	....
Grants	81z	....	....	....	....	....	....	....	....	....	....	....	....	....	....	....
Exp. & Lending Minus Repay.	82z	....	....	....	....	....	....	....	....	....	....	....	....	....	....	....
Expenditure	82	....	....	....	....	....	....	....	....	....	....	....	....	....	....	....
Lending Minus Repayments	83	....	....	....	....	....	....	....	....	....	....	....	....	....	....	....
Total Financing	80h	....	....	....	....	....	....	....	....	....	....	....	....	....	....	....
Total Net Borrowing	84	....	....	....	....	....	....	....	....	....	....	....	....	....	....	....
Net Domestic	84a	....	....	....	....	....	....	....	....	....	....	....	....	....	....	....
Net Foreign	85a	....	....	....	....	....	....	....	....	....	....	....	....	....	....	....
Use of Cash Balances	87	....	....	....	....	....	....	....	....	....	....	....	....	....	....	....
National Accounts																*Millions of Denar*
Househ.Cons.Expend.,incl.NPISHs	96f	....	....	....	....	....	....	....	....	....	....	....	....	....	....	....
Government Consumption Expend.	91f	....	....	....	....	....	....	....	....	....	....	....	....	....	....	....
Gross Fixed Capital Formation	93e	....	....	....	....	....	....	....	....	....	....	....	....	....	....	....
Changes in Inventories	93i	....	....	....	....	....	....	....	....	....	....	....	....	....	....	....
Exports of Goods and Services	90c	....	....	....	....	....	....	....	....	....	....	....	....	....	....	....
Imports of Goods and Services (-)	98c	....	....	....	....	....	....	....	....	....	....	....	....	....	....	....
GDP, Production Based	99bp	....	....	....	....	....	....	....	....	....	....	....	....	....	....	....
Statistical Discrepancy	99bs	....	....	....	....	....	....	....	....	....	....	....	....	....	....	....
																Millions:
Population	99z	....	....	....	....	....	....	....	....	....	....	....	....	....	....	....

Minus Sign Indicates Debit

Balance of Payments

	1996	1997	1998	1999	2000	2001		Code
Current Account, n.i.e.	−288.1	−275.5	−311.7	−109.3	−107.2	....	Current Account, n.i.e.	78ald
	1,147.4	1,201.4	1,292.9	1,192.1	1,317.1	....	Goods: Exports f.o.b.	78aad
	−1,464.0	−1,589.1	−1,713.2	−1,602.2	−1,875.2	....	Goods: Imports f.o.b	78abd
	−316.5	−387.6	−420.3	−410.1	−558.0	....	*Trade Balance*	78acd
	154.3	128.3	131.3	248.4	303.1	....	Services: Credit	78add
	−309.3	−272.9	−304.3	−323.8	−357.8	....	Services: Debit	78aed
	−471.5	−532.2	−593.3	−485.5	−612.7	....	*Balance on Goods & Services*	78afd
	45.3	39.0	23.5	22.5	42.2	....	Income: Credit	78agd
	−75.0	−72.6	−68.4	−66.3	−87.3	....	Income: Debit	78ahd
	−501.2	−565.8	−638.1	−529.4	−657.8	....	*Balance on Gds, Serv. & Inc.*	78aid
	475.4	535.0	692.6	750.3	923.1	....	Current Transfers, n.i.e.: Credit	78ajd
	−262.3	−244.8	−366.2	−330.2	−372.4	....	Current Transfers: Debit	78akd
			9.4	4.4	.3	....	Capital Account, n.i.e.	78bcd
			11.2	4.4	.3	....	Capital Account, n.i.e.: Credit	78bad
			−1.8	—	—	....	Capital Account: Debit	78bbd
	174.3	186.8	449.2	189.6	385.2	....	Financial Account, n.i.e.	78bjd
				—	.6	....	Direct Investment Abroad	78bdd
	11.2	15.7	117.7	30.1	175.6	....	Dir. Invest. in Rep. Econ., n.i.e.	78bed
	−.5	−2.5	−.6	−.4	....	....	Portfolio Investment Assets	78bfd
	−.5	−2.5	−.6	−.4		....	Equity Securities	78bkd
						....	Debt Securities	78bld
	.8	4.6	8.4	.5	−.1	....	Portfolio Investment Liab., n.i.e.	78bgd
	.8	4.6	8.4	.5	−.1	....	Equity Securities	78bmd
						....	Debt Securities	78bnd
				—		....	Financial Derivatives Assets	78bwd
				—		....	Financial Derivatives Liabilities	78bxd
	−133.2	−73.0	−77.2	−81.0	−81.1	....	Other Investment Assets	78bhd
						....	Monetary Authorities	78bod
			—	−14.6		....	General Government	78bpd
	25.3	−57.5	−51.0	−66.4	−81.1	....	Banks	78bqd
	−158.5	−15.6	−26.2			....	Other Sectors	78brd
	295.9	242.0	400.9	240.4	290.2	....	Other Investment Liab., n.i.e.	78bid
				—	14.7	....	Monetary Authorities	78bsd
	59.9	−71.6	109.2	68.8	50.9	....	General Government	78btd
	−1.2	29.8	97.7	30.9	−35.1	....	Banks	78bud
	237.3	283.8	194.0	140.7	259.8	....	Other Sectors	78bvd
	18.8	−29.9	−114.8	34.5	−46.0	....	Net Errors and Omissions	78cad
	−95.1	−118.6	32.1	119.2	232.3	....	*Overall Balance*	78cbd
	95.1	118.6	−32.1	−119.2	−232.3	....	Reserves and Related Items	79dad
	7.6	−35.1	−42.0	−141.6	−234.7	....	Reserve Assets	79dbd
	13.5	24.6	9.9	1.8	−15.6	....	Use of Fund Credit and Loans	79dcd
	73.9	129.2	—	20.6	18.0	....	Exceptional Financing	79ded

Millions of US Dollars

International Investment Position

	1996	1997	1998	1999	2000	2001		Code
	496.8	567.2	704.9	903.7	1,171.4	....	Assets	79aad
	—	—	—	—	—	....	Direct Investment Abroad	79abd
	—	—	—	—	—	....	Portfolio Investment	79acd
	—	—	—	—	—	....	Equity Securities	79add
	—	—	—	—	—	....	Debt Securities	79aed
	—	—	—	—	—	....	Financial Derivatives	79ald
	229.3	286.8	337.8	425.4	458.8	....	Other Investment	79afd
	—	—	—	21.2	21.4	....	Monetary Authorities	79agd
	—	—	—	—	—	....	General Government	79ahd
	229.3	286.8	337.8	404.2	437.4	....	Banks	79aid
	—	—	—	—	—	....	Other Sectors	79ajd
	267.5	280.4	367.2	478.3	712.6	....	Reserve Assets	79akd
	1,243.1	1,259.7	1,545.0	1,603.7	1,603.0	....	Liabilities	79lad
	—	—	—	—	—	....	Dir. Invest. in Rep. Economy	79lbd
	—	—	—	—	—	....	Portfolio Investment	79lcd
	—	—	—	—	—	....	Equity Securities	79ldd
	—	—	—	—	—	....	Debt Securities	79led
	—	—	—	—	—	....	Financial Derivatives	79lld
	1,243.1	1,259.7	1,545.0	1,603.7	1,603.0	....	Other Investment	79lfd
	68.2	88.1	102.4	101.7	95.4	....	Monetary Authorities	79lgd
	1,041.2	999.3	1,126.2	1,156.3	1,216.3	....	General Government	79lhd
	121.3	156.3	289.7	321.2	217.4	....	Banks	79lid
	12.4	16.0	26.8	24.5	73.9	....	Other Sectors	79ljd

Year Ending December 31

Government Finance

	1995	1996		Code
	2,267.6	175.3	Deficit (−) or Surplus	80
	40,437.0	39,865.2	Total Revenue and Grants	81y
	39,775.8	39,766.1	Revenue	81
	661.2	99.1	Grants	81z
	38,169.4	39,689.9	Exp. & Lending Minus Repay.	82z
	36,511.0	37,423.3	Expenditure	82
	1,658.4	2,266.6	Lending Minus Repayments	83
	−2,267.6	−175.3	Total Financing	80h
	−3,445.2	−175.5	Total Net Borrowing	84
	−3,334.1	−1,200.0	Net Domestic	84a
	−111.1	1,024.5	Net Foreign	85a
	1,177.6	.2	Use of Cash Balances	87

Millions of Denar

National Accounts

	1993	1994	1995	1996	1997	1998	1999		Code
	47,182	110,847	119,381	127,253	136,350	140,878	143,605	Househ.Cons.Expend.,incl.NPISHs	96f
	12,472	27,875	31,491	31,985	31,797	33,530	33,252	Government Consumption Expend.	91f
	10,994	22,461	28,027	30,654	32,189	33,982	34,949	Gross Fixed Capital Formation	93e
	−416	182	7,162	4,790	9,168	9,831	6,082	Changes in Inventories	93i
	27,660	55,920	55,961	49,722	68,260	82,939	86,020	Exports of Goods and Services	90c
	32,360	70,876	72,501	67,961	92,783	110,333	108,623	Imports of Goods and Services (−)	98c
	59,165	146,409	169,521	176,444	184,982	190,827	195,284	GDP, Production Based	99bp
	−6,368	—	—	—	—	—		Statistical Discrepancy	99bs

Midyear Estimates

	1993	1994	1995	1996	1997	1998	1999	2000	2001		Code
	2	2	2	2	2	2	2	2	2	**Population**	99z

(See notes in the back of the book.)

Madagascar

		1972	1973	1974	1975	1976	1977	1978	1979	1980	1981	1982	1983	1984	1985	1986
Exchange Rates															*Francs per SDR:*	
Official Rate	aa	278.0	284.0	272.1	262.5	288.7	285.8	272.3	264.8	288.0	334.5	405.6	515.3	645.0	698.4	941.6
															Francs per US Dollar:	
Official Rate	ae	256.1	235.4	222.2	224.3	248.5	235.2	209.0	201.0	225.8	287.4	367.7	492.2	658.0	635.8	769.8
Official Rate	rf	252.0	222.9	240.7	214.3	238.9	245.7	225.7	212.7	211.3	271.7	349.7	430.4	576.6	662.5	676.3
Fund Position															*Millions of SDRs:*	
Quota	2f. s	26.0	26.0	26.0	26.0	26.0	26.0	34.0	34.0	51.0	51.0	51.0	66.4	66.4	66.4	66.4
SDRs	1b. s	8.7	8.7	.2	.9	1.9	6.9	8.7	—	—	.3	1.1	.1	1.5	—	—
Reserve Position in the Fund	1c. s	5.0	5.0	—	—	—	—	—	—	—	.3	1.2			—	—
Total Fund Cred.&Loans Outstg.	2tl	—	—	3.5	14.3	14.3	15.7	24.2	20.7	68.2	100.2	152.0	158.1	173.8	167.6	166.0
International Liquidity														*Millions of US Dollars Unless Otherwise Indicated:*		
Total Reserves minus Gold	1l. d	52.2	67.9	49.4	35.6	42.2	68.9	59.2	5.0	9.1	26.5	20.0	29.2	58.9	48.4	114.5
SDRs	1b. d	9.5	10.5	.2	1.1	2.2	8.3	11.3	—	—	.3	1.3	.1	1.5	—	—
Reserve Position in the Fund	1c. d	5.5	6.1								.4	1.3			—	—
Foreign Exchange	1d. d	37.3	51.3	49.2	34.5	40.0	60.6	47.9	5.0	9.1	25.8	17.4	29.1	57.4	48.4	114.5
Deposit Money Banks: Assets	7a. d	20.0	24.1	46.3	38.9	29.6	44.5	45.6	46.7	75.3	46.0	45.1	31.5	44.6	46.9	52.0
Liabilities	7b. d	8.8	11.2	6.5	7.1	4.1	5.7	6.2	67.4	111.5	103.6	68.8	42.5	33.5	27.8	31.3
Monetary Authorities															*Billions of Francs:*	
Foreign Assets	11	16.8	19.0	13.4	9.6	12.5	16.3	12.0	†.3	4.0	6.7	10.0	17.4	47.7	31.3	87.8
Claims on Central Government	12a	−1.8	−.7	10.2	17.1	26.7	46.9	82.8	†139.5	215.1	278.8	361.7	460.1	572.2	664.1	802.6
Claims on Nonfin.Pub.Enterprises	12c	....	....	....	....	....	....	....	9.8	8.6	8.6	8.3	26.9	35.9	32.4	29.7
Claims on Deposit Money Banks	12e	18.0	14.5	19.1	18.9	12.0	12.4	8.3	†9.0	2.3	1.5	—	8.2	8.9	4.8	.2
Reserve Money	14	26.0	27.4	32.4	34.7	39.5	44.3	59.0	†57.4	77.5	104.0	102.8	97.8	106.9	111.4	189.8
of which: Currency Outside DMBs	14a	25.4	27.0	31.9	34.0	35.5	42.1	48.2	†53.5	70.2	83.1	90.4	75.8	89.9	96.2	113.2
Time, Savings,& Fgn. Currency Dep.	15															
Foreign Liabilities	16c	.4	.1	3.2	4.3	4.0	9.7	8.7	†53.9	117.0	161.9	215.3	454.5	671.3	752.3	1,031.0
Central Government Deposits	16d	2.2	.5	2.2	2.1	2.1	17.7	32.6	†43.1	31.3	42.9	82.4	116.2	169.3	228.5	307.3
Counterpart Funds	16e									.2	.6	1.3	1.5	.3	.4	.1
Capital Accounts	17a	4.2	5.0	6.0	5.8	6.0	5.7	5.3	†6.2	7.2	8.2	8.2	8.2	8.2	9.2	9.2
Other Items (Net)	17r	2.5	.1	1.1	.8	1.7	15.9	30.1	†−2.1	−3.2	−21.9	−29.9	−165.5	−291.2	−369.2	−617.2
Deposit Money Banks															*Billions of Francs:*	
Reserves	20	.6	.4	.7	.6	2.0	2.7	10.8	†3.8	7.3	20.5	12.0	20.8	14.8	12.3	76.5
Foreign Assets	21	5.1	5.6	10.3	8.6	7.4	10.5	9.5	†9.4	17.0	13.2	16.6	15.5	29.4	29.8	40.1
Claims on Central Government	22a	5.4	5.7	8.5	9.7	9.7	9.9	10.0	†13.2	12.4	17.0	16.8	9.0	9.4	9.8	10.7
Claims on Private Sector	22d	55.7	55.8	65.6	67.0	70.9	86.5	91.0	†120.3	155.1	171.9	208.1	245.6	303.0	362.7	424.7
Demand Deposits	24	23.5	26.3	31.7	30.5	39.6	51.8	56.0	†70.7	81.1	110.4	117.3	116.7	149.7	142.3	176.3
Time Deposits	25	12.1	10.7	14.2	14.4	17.4	16.5	23.5	†16.4	18.3	16.4	20.9	14.3	16.3	51.0	77.7
Bonds	26ab	5.4	5.1	11.1	11.0	—	—	—	14.6	17.7	21.0	27.8	42.9	46.0	52.8	61.1
Foreign Liabilities	26c	2.2	2.6	1.5	1.6	1.0	1.3	1.3	†10.6	14.0	15.1	9.3	6.4	10.3	9.6	18.4
Long-Term Foreign Liabilities	26cl	....	....	....	....	....	....	....	2.9	11.1	14.7	16.0	14.5	11.7	8.1	5.7
Central Government Deposits	26d	4.7	8.0	10.5	11.5	13.4	14.3	14.7	†11.8	19.2	12.2	15.0	18.1	24.0	28.7	33.4
Central Govt. Lending Funds	26f								3.8	4.7	5.3	5.1	6.9	8.8	9.2	11.1
Credit from Monetary Authorities	26g	11.2	10.5	11.0	11.1	—	—	—	9.0	2.3	1.5	—	8.2	8.9	4.8	.2
Capital Accounts	27a	3.7	3.8	5.2	5.4	5.7	12.5	13.5	†15.4	23.7	27.4	33.3	47.0	64.1	86.6	131.3
Other Items (Net)	27r	20.6	16.1	21.9	22.6	12.8	13.2	12.4	†−8.5	−.5	−1.4	8.9	16.1	16.6	21.5	36.8
Treasury Claims: Private Sector	22d. i	3.8	3.9	4.4	5.5	5.3	4.9	5.1	4.7	5.6	....	....	....	....	....	3.5
Post Office: Checking Deposits	24.. i	2.0	2.2	1.9	2.1	2.2	2.4	3.0	3.9	3.8	....	....	....	....	....	4.8
Treasury: Checking Deposits	24.. r	2.6	1.8	2.5	2.8	2.4	3.8	5.7	10.1[e]	....	....	....	....	....	....	9.7
Monetary Survey															*Billions of Francs:*	
Foreign Assets (Net)	31n	19.3	21.8	19.0	12.2	14.8	15.7	11.5	†−54.9	−110.0	−157.1	−198.0	−427.9	−604.6	−700.8	−921.5
Domestic Credit	32	56.8	56.3	76.0	85.1	96.4	117.4	145.2	†227.8	340.6	421.1	497.6	607.5	727.1	811.8	927.0
Claims on Central Govt. (Net)	32an	−2.7	−3.5	6.0	12.6	20.2	26.1	49.1	†97.8	176.9	240.6	281.1	334.9	388.3	416.7	472.6
Claims on Private Sector	32d	59.5	59.8	70.0	72.5	76.2	91.3	96.1	†130.1	163.7	180.5	216.5	272.6	338.8	395.1	454.4
Money	34	53.3	57.3	67.9	69.4	79.7	100.0	112.8	†124.3	151.3	193.8	208.0	192.7	239.9	238.6	289.6
Quasi-Money	35	12.1	10.7	14.2	14.4	17.4	16.5	23.5	†16.4	18.3	16.4	20.9	15.4	18.2	53.7	77.7
Bonds	36ab	5.4	5.1	11.1	11.0	—	—	—	14.6	17.7	21.0	27.8	42.9	46.0	52.8	61.1
Long-Term Foreign Liabilities	36cl								2.9	11.1	14.7	16.0	14.5	11.7	8.1	5.7
Other Items (Net)	37r	11.4	10.1	12.7	13.6	14.2	17.9	24.0	†14.8	32.2	18.1	26.9	−86.0	−193.3	−242.2	−428.6
Money plus Quasi-Money	35l	65.4	68.0	82.2	83.7	97.1	116.4	136.3	†140.7	169.6	210.2	228.9	208.1	258.1	292.3	367.2
Liquid Liabilities	55l	67.5	70.2	85.0	86.7	100.2	122.4	....	....	....	....	....	....	†363.3	419.3	511.0
Interest Rates															*Percent Per Annum*	
Discount Rate (End of Period)	60	5.50	5.50	5.50	5.50	5.50	5.50	5.50	5.50	5.50	8.00	12.50	13.00	13.00	11.50	11.50
Base Rate (End of Period)	60a	....	....	....	....	....	....	....	....	....	....	....	....	....	....	....
Money Market Rate	60b	....	....	....	....	....	....	....	....	....	....	....	....	....	....	....
Treasury Bill Rate	60c	....	....	....	....	....	....	....	....	....	....	....	....	....	....	....
Deposit Rate	60l	....	....	....	....	....	....	....	....	....	....	....	....	....	....	....
Lending Rate	60p	....	....	....	....	....	....	....	....	....	....	....	....	....	....	....
Prices and Labor														*Index Numbers (1995=100):*		
Consumer Prices	64	3.2	3.4	4.1	4.5	4.7	4.8	5.2	5.9	7.0	9.1	12.0	14.3	15.7	17.3	19.9
															Number in Thousands:	
Labor Force	67d	....	....	....	....	....	....	....	....	....	....	....	....	....	....	....
Employment	67e	....	....	....	....	....	....	....	....	....	....	....	....	....	....	259
Unemployment	67c	....	....	....	....	....	....	....	....	....	....	....	....	....	29	24

	1987	1988	1989	1990	1991	1992	1993	1994	1995	1996	1997	1998	1999	2000	2001		
																Exchange Rates	
End of Period																	
	1,751.0	2,054.1	2,014.0	2,085.4	2,621.5	2,626.5	2,695.8	5,651.2	5,088.2	6,224.2	7,130.3	7,606.5	8,980.6	8,534.6	8,333.6	Official Rate	aa
End of Period (ae) Period Average (rf)																	
	1,234.3	1,526.4	1,532.5	1,465.8	1,832.7	1,910.2	1,962.7	3,871.1	3,423.0	4,328.5	5,284.7	5,402.2	6,543.2	6,550.4	6,631.2	Official Rate	ae
	1,069.2	1,407.1	1,603.4	1,494.1	1,835.4	1,864.0	1,913.8	3,067.3	4,265.6	4,061.3	5,090.9	5,441.4	6,283.8	6,767.5	6,588.5	Official Rate	rf
																Fund Position	
End of Period																	
	66.4	66.4	66.4	66.4	66.4	90.4	90.4	90.4	90.4	90.4	90.4	90.4	122.2	122.2	122.2	Quota	2f. s
	.1	.1	.1	.1	—	—	.1	—	—	—	—	—	.1	—	.1	SDRs	1b. s
															—	Reserve Position in the Fund	1c. s
	167.7	141.4	125.8	101.0	88.7	77.1	67.0	58.6	48.9	50.8	51.5	41.2	45.8	80.0	101.4	Total Fund Cred.&Loans Outstg.	2tl
																International Liquidity	
End of Period																	
	185.2	223.7	245.3	92.1	88.9	84.4	80.6	71.6	109.0	240.9	281.6	171.4	227.2	285.2	398.3	Total Reserves minus Gold	1l. d
	.1	.1	.1	.2	.1	—	.1	—	—	.1	.1	—	.1	—	.1	SDRs	1b. d
															—	Reserve Position in the Fund	1c. d
	185.1	223.6	245.2	91.9	88.8	84.4	80.5	71.6	108.9	240.8	281.5	171.3	227.0	285.1	398.2	Foreign Exchange	1d. d
	58.6	61.6	79.5	93.0	97.0	102.8	126.7	157.7	176.6	137.9	151.7	142.0	140.5	180.4	158.4	Deposit Money Banks: Assets	7a. d
	21.0	22.7	20.8	48.3	26.6	22.9	22.2	38.6	33.5	37.3	32.0	40.0	50.9	62.2	57.7	Liabilities	7b. d
																Monetary Authorities	
End of Period																	
	236.7	342.4	379.0	136.3	163.0	159.8	156.8	238.1	374.6	1,043.6	1,492.9	926.8	1,487.2	1,953.8	2,632.3	Foreign Assets	11
	1,083.7	1,251.9	1,310.2	1,275.8	1,265.6	1,246.9	1,252.9	1,412.3	1,445.8	1,437.0	1,360.2	1,752.2	1,881.0	2,028.4	2,096.3	Claims on Central Government	12a
	32.7	26.7	26.6	21.2	22.2	9.3	8.1	7.0	12.6	14.1	15.1	15.9	15.8	111.1	276.4	Claims on Nonfin.Pub.Enterprises	12c
	5.4	10.6	11.9	127.5	84.1	46.4	49.5	134.7	175.1	127.5	107.3	102.7	75.1	59.5	40.4	Claims on Deposit Money Banks	12e
	229.1	237.6	327.5	296.6	460.6	556.5	519.9	893.9	1,159.0	1,723.1	1,741.8	1,855.0	2,339.0	2,614.2	3,385.1	Reserve Money	14
	140.3	171.2	216.6	214.9	287.3	317.2	378.7	614.5	758.7	829.4	1,020.3	1,169.9	1,434.9	1,789.1	2,159.6	of which: Currency Outside DMBs	14a
									7.5	1.5	3.0	3.4	5.2	.1	.2	Time, Savings,& Fgn. Currency Dep.	15
	2,008.0	2,363.4	2,465.4	2,404.4	3,100.2	452.1	378.8	719.6	568.0	642.4	669.4	582.1	647.8	871.0	1,010.3	Foreign Liabilities	16c
	438.3	599.1	784.1	795.7	690.6	327.3	389.7	283.4	552.8	609.4	871.4	658.2	636.7	860.3	888.7	Central Government Deposits	16d
	.1	.1	.1	.1	.1									—	—	Counterpart Funds	16e
	9.2	9.2	9.2	9.2	9.2	42.7	42.2	43.8	122.6	33.5	93.9	94.1	107.2	93.0	121.5	Capital Accounts	17a
	-1,326.3	-1,577.9	-1,858.7	-1,945.2	-2,725.8	83.8	136.7	-148.6	-401.3	-387.7	-404.1	-395.0	-276.8	-285.8	-360.4	Other Items (Net)	17r
																Deposit Money Banks	
End of Period																	
	88.8	66.3	110.8	80.9	173.3	239.2	141.1	279.3	400.2	893.7	721.5	678.7	887.1	823.4	1,225.3	Reserves	20
	72.3	94.1	121.8	136.3	177.9	196.3	248.6	610.3	604.4	597.0	801.5	766.9	919.1	1,181.8	1,050.5	Foreign Assets	21
	10.7	15.0	78.6	61.1	25.9	19.0	220.1	250.6	174.0	206.3	356.5	436.4	481.0	606.5	1,182.4	Claims on Central Government	22a
	499.4	524.5	582.2	757.2	851.7	918.5	1,061.6	1,338.5	1,550.4	1,573.6	1,797.6	1,811.8	1,937.5	2,303.3	2,500.8	Claims on Private Sector	22d
	231.5	283.7	381.7	358.7	465.3	598.1	645.7	989.0	1,089.3	1,338.3	1,643.7	1,783.1	2,115.4	2,228.9	3,074.1	Demand Deposits	24
	63.2	77.6	113.7	169.5	222.8	277.1	456.8	656.1	770.6	875.8	1,012.0	950.2	1,100.6	1,436.7	1,520.6	Time Deposits	25
	71.4	80.0	89.2	59.7	37.3	36.5	39.7	42.6	58.5	95.5	70.4	129.8	151.8	169.3	172.7	Bonds	26ab
	18.6	29.8	28.5	69.7	47.6	37.4	37.4	128.1	94.9	136.7	135.7	191.0	262.9	346.0	267.1	Foreign Liabilities	26c
	7.3	4.9	3.4	1.1	1.1	6.3	6.3	21.2	19.9	24.9	33.3	25.1	70.2	61.7	115.2	Long-Term Foreign Liabilities	26cl
	45.3	43.8	69.4	111.5	125.4	137.9	155.5	141.3	123.9	160.4	157.5	141.2	134.9	200.5	335.2	Central Government Deposits	26d
	16.3	18.6	19.6	1.3	1.2	1.2	1.1	1.4	.9	2.9	2.4	.8	6.1	5.4	7.2	Central Govt. Lending Funds	26f
	5.4	10.6	11.9	127.5	84.1	46.4	49.5	134.7	174.4	127.5	107.3	102.7	75.1	59.5	40.4	Credit from Monetary Authorities	26g
	152.1	144.9	149.5	174.1	198.0	226.9	106.6	97.6	207.0	535.6	645.9	399.5	445.8	517.9	620.7	Capital Accounts	27a
	60.0	6.0	26.6	-37.5	46.1	5.2	173.1	266.9	189.8	-27.0	-131.0	-29.6	-138.0	-110.8	-194.2	Other Items (Net)	27r
	5.9	6.8	8.3	11.8	5.6	9.2	10.0	10.2	14.0	13.3	1.4	.5	2.1	.5	1.2	Treasury Claims: Private Sector	22d. i
	5.1	5.0	5.0	5.2	5.7	5.7	5.3	4.5	5.8	11.5	15.0	11.9	12.3	76.1	196.4	Post Office: Checking Deposits	24.. i
	9.7	9.7	9.7	9.7	9.7	9.7	9.7	9.7	9.7	9.7	9.7	9.7	9.7	9.7	9.7	Treasury: Checking Deposits	24.. r
																Monetary Survey	
End of Period																	
	-1,717.6	-1,956.7	-1,993.1	-2,201.5	-2,807.1	-133.5	-10.7	.8	316.1	861.4	1,489.3	920.6	1,495.6	1,918.6	2,405.4	Foreign Assets (Net)	31n
	1,142.7	1,175.2	1,144.1	1,208.2	1,349.5	1,728.4	1,997.5	2,583.7	2,506.2	2,461.3	2,500.4	3,216.9	3,543.7	3,988.4	4,832.0	Domestic Credit	32
	610.7	624.0	535.3	429.7	475.6	800.6	927.8	1,238.2	943.2	873.5	687.7	1,389.2	1,590.4	1,574.1	2,054.9	Claims on Central Govt. (Net)	32an
	532.1	551.2	608.8	778.4	873.9	927.8	1,069.7	1,345.5	1,563.0	1,587.8	1,812.7	1,827.6	1,953.3	2,414.3	2,777.2	Claims on Private Sector	32d
	371.8	455.0	598.3	574.5	752.6	915.3	1,024.4	1,603.5	1,848.0	2,167.7	2,663.9	2,953.2	3,550.3	4,018.0	5,233.7	Money	34
	63.2	77.6	113.7	169.5	222.8	277.1	456.8	656.1	778.1	877.3	1,015.0	953.6	1,105.8	1,436.8	1,520.8	Quasi-Money	35
	71.4	80.0	89.2	59.7	37.3	36.5	39.7	42.6	58.5	95.5	70.4	129.8	151.8	169.3	172.7	Bonds	36ab
	7.3	4.9	3.4	1.1	1.1	6.3	6.3	21.2	19.9	24.9	33.3	25.1	70.2	61.7	115.2	Long-Term Foreign Liabilities	36cl
	-1,088.6	-1,399.0	-1,653.6	-1,798.0	-2,471.2	359.8	459.6	261.0	118.3	157.3	207.2	76.1	161.2	221.3	195.0	Other Items (Net)	37r
	435.0	532.6	712.0	743.9	975.3	1,192.4	1,481.3	2,259.7	2,626.1	3,045.0	3,678.9	3,906.8	4,656.1	5,454.8	6,754.5	Money plus Quasi-Money	35l
	625.4	760.2	984.8	819.6	1,044.4	1,266.7	1,636.3	2,473.2	2,901.4	3,608.0	4,501.2	5,070.9	6,089.6	7,027.4	....	Liquid Liabilities	55l
																Interest Rates	
Percent Per Annum																	
	11.50	11.50	....	....	....								15.00	....	....	Discount Rate (End of Period)	60
	....	....	....	....	....	12.0	12.0	15.6	31.3	26.4	12.8	9.3	....	....	11.0	Base Rate (End of Period)	60a
	....	....	....	15.0	15.0	15.0	....	—	29.0	10.0	....	11.2	....	16.0		Money Market Rate	60b
	....	....	....	....	....	....	....	....	....	....	....	....	....	....	10.3	Treasury Bill Rate	60c
	....	....	17.8	20.5	20.5	20.5	19.5	19.5	18.5	19.0	14.4	8.0	15.3	15.0	12.0	Deposit Rate	60l
	....	....	22.3	25.8	24.5	25.0	26.0	30.5	37.5	32.8	30.0	27.0	28.0	26.5	25.3	Lending Rate	60p
																Prices and Labor	
Period Averages																	
	22.8	29.0	31.6	35.3	38.3	43.9	48.3	67.1	100.0	119.8	125.1	132.9	146.1	†163.7	175.0	Consumer Prices	64
Period Averages																	
	....	....	....	....	....	....	5,300	....	....	....	....	....	....	....	....	Labor Force	67d
	258	258	265	281	286	....	315	322	337	....	....	....	....	....	....	Employment	67e
	18	16	16	17	9	6	5	4	3	....	....	....	....	....	....	Unemployment	67c

Madagascar

		1972	1973	1974	1975	1976	1977	1978	1979	1980	1981	1982	1983	1984	1985	1986
International Transactions															*Billions of Francs*	
Exports	70	41.86	44.75	58.50	64.64	66.04	82.93	87.21	83.83	84.78	85.74	107.64	113.39	192.33	181.63	212.74
Imports, c.i.f.	71	51.75	45.16	67.26	78.05	68.43	85.22	99.63	135.32	126.78	147.98	148.60	166.75	213.53	265.92	238.46
Balance of Payments															*Millions of US Dollars:*	
Current Account, n.i.e.	78ald	....	....	−40	−56	−28	−15	−79	−426	−556	−363	−299	−247	−193	−184	−143
Goods: Exports f.o.b.	78aad			240	320	289	351	405	414	436	332	327	310	337	291	323
Goods: Imports f.o.b.	78abd			−238	−332	−262	−312	−404	−662	−764	−511	−452	−378	−360	−336	−331
Trade Balance	78acd			2	−12	27	39	1	−249	−328	−179	−124	−68	−23	−44	−8
Services: Credit	78add			40	62	41	35	35	74	79	62	49	45	53	59	75
Services: Debit	78aed			−107	−148	−132	−136	−169	−267	−311	−224	−200	−172	−155	−167	−205
Balance on Goods & Services	78afd			−65	−98	−63	−63	−133	−441	−559	−341	−275	−195	−125	−153	−138
Income: Credit	78agd			7	5	4	2	5	2	2	4	6	3	5	4	5
Income: Debit	78ahd			−25	−22	−21	−8	−12	−30	−46	−92	−101	−121	−151	−133	−160
Balance on Gds, Serv. & Inc.	78aid			−83	−115	−80	−68	−140	−469	−603	−430	−370	−313	−271	−282	−293
Current Transfers, n.i.e.: Credit	78ajd			64	99	87	81	94	76	86	103	102	89	95	124	183
Current Transfers: Debit	78akd			−20	−39	−34	−28	−33	−34	−39	−36	−31	−23	−18	−25	−32
Capital Account, n.i.e.	78bcd	....	....	—	—	—	−1	−1	−1	—	—	—	—	—	—	2
Capital Account, n.i.e.: Credit	78bad			—	—	—				—	—	—	—	—	—	2
Capital Account: Debit	78bbd			—	—	—	−1	−1	−1	—	—	—	—	—	—	
Financial Account, n.i.e.	78bjd			11	30	20	28	1	300	381	196	2	−21	−23	6	21
Direct Investment Abroad	78bdd			—	—	—	—	—	—	—	—	—	—	—	—	—
Dir. Invest. in Rep. Econ., n.i.e.	78bed			14	5	1	−3	−4	−7	—	—	—	—	—	—	—
Portfolio Investment Assets	78bfd															
Equity Securities	78bkd															
Debt Securities	78bld															
Portfolio Investment Liab., n.i.e.	78bgd															
Equity Securities	78bmd															
Debt Securities	78bnd															
Financial Derivatives Assets	78bwd			....	....	....	....	....	....	....	....	....	....	....	....	....
Financial Derivatives Liabilities	78bxd			....	....	....	....	....	....	....	....	....	....	....	....	....
Other Investment Assets	78bhd			−18	7	3	−15	3			7	−21	−2	8	10	42	27
Monetary Authorities	78bod							−1	−1							
General Government	78bpd															
Banks	78bqd			−18	7	3	−14	4	1	7	−21	−2	8	10	42	27
Other Sectors	78brd						—	—	—	—						
Other Investment Liab., n.i.e.	78bid			16	19	15	46	2	307	375	217	5	−29	−33	−36	−6
Monetary Authorities	78bsd			9	−8	2	22	−18	75	—	—	—	—	—	—	—
General Government	78btd			14	31	20	19	23	145	375	217	29	−21	−34	−11	26
Banks	78bud			−5	1	−2	−4	−2	2	—	—	−24	−8	—	−25	−31
Other Sectors	78bvd			−3	−5	−4	10	−1	85	—	—	—	—	—	—	—
Net Errors and Omissions	78cad			−4	−8	11	−7	49	71	−73	3	88	−1	13	10	4
Overall Balance	78cbd			−33	−34	3	6	−29	−56	−248	−165	−209	−269	−204	−167	−116
Reserves and Related Items	79dad			33	34	−3	−6	29	56	248	165	209	269	204	167	116
Reserve Assets	79dbd			29	20	−3	−8	19	60	−100	−6	−10	13	−40	28	−59
Use of Fund Credit and Loans	79dcd			4	13	—	2	10	−5	63	38	56	7	16	−6	−2
Exceptional Financing	79ded			—	—	—	—	—	—	285	133	163	249	228	146	177
Government Finance															*Billions of Francs:*	
Deficit (-) or Surplus	80	†−6.7	−7.3	−9.0	....	....	....	....	....	....	....	....	....	....	....	....
Revenue	81	†48.7	54.2	58.2	....	....	....	129.9	168.4	133.0	....	....	....	....	....	....
Grants Received	81z	†1.2	—	—												
Expenditure	82	†55.2	59.5	63.2												
Lending Minus Repayments	83	†1.3	2.1	4.1												
Adjustment to Cash Basis	80x	....														
Financing																
Domestic	84a	†5.0	3.3	5.7												
Foreign	85a	†1.8	4.0	3.4												
Adjustment to Total Financing	84x	....														
Debt: Domestic	88a	†10.0	15.2	15.8												
Foreign	89a	†20.5	24.5	27.9	....	....	....	....	....	....	....	....	....	....	....	....
National Accounts															*Billions of Francs*	
Househ.Cons.Expend.,incl.NPISHs	96f	191.7	206.7	277.7	301.1	305.2	343.1	360.6	444.3	526.1	604.6	799.0	973.4	1,460.5	1,703.1	1,884.5
Government Consumption Expend.	91f	52.6	51.0	59.0	60.4	66.6	72.8	81.6	103.0	117.8	129.1	149.5	165.3	166.8	184.8	194.9
Gross Capital Formation	93	37.9	42.6	50.8	50.6	53.9	60.2	70.4	150.8	162.4	142.5	133.0	160.7	182.4	217.7e	
Gross Fixed Capital Formation	93e	36.0	39.7	47.0	49.4	54.1	58.0	64.8	....	157.6	148.3	129.4	160.7	146.1	161.8	199.2
Changes in Inventories	93i	1.9	5.8	6.8	2.2	1.8	2.2	5.0	....	4.8	−5.8	3.6	—	—	—	
Exports of Goods and Services	90c	46.3	42.2	65.8	74.5	73.9	97.6	96.1	95.3	96.8	96.4	125.7	139.7	225.1	231.8	267.7
Imports of Goods and Services (-)	98c	55.4	47.7	83.4	91.4	81.7	105.6	122.1	198.3	213.3	183.6	211.1	218.0	303.6	388.3	342.6
Gross Domestic Product (GDP)	99b	273.1	297.6	372.9	395.2	419.9	468.1	486.6	595.1	689.8	789.0	996.1	1,221.1	1,695.0	1,893.2	2,203.7
Net Primary Income from Abroad	98.n	−2.8	−1.9	−3.7	−3.2	−1.9	−.6	−.6	−.9	....	....	....	....	....	....	....
Gross National Income (GNI)	99a	270.3	295.7	369.2	392.0	418.0	467.5	486.0	594.2	....	....	....	....	....	....	....
GDP Volume 1970 prices	99b.p	247.1	242.1	250.0	257.4	247.1	255.4	248.7	273.1	275.3	251.5	246.9	248.9	254.4	....	....
GDP Volume 1984 Prices	99b.p	....	....	....	....	....	....	....	....	....	....	....	....	1,695.0	1,714.6	1,748.2
GDP Volume (1995=100)	99bvp	85.2	83.5	86.2	88.8	85.2	88.1	85.8	94.2	95.0	86.8	85.2	85.9	87.8	88.8	90.5
GDP Deflator (1995=100)	99bip	2.4	2.6	3.2	3.3	3.7	3.9	4.2	4.7	5.4	6.7	8.7	10.6	14.3	15.8	18.1
															Millions:	
Population	99z	7.13	7.30	7.49	†7.60	7.81	8.02	8.24	8.47	8.78	8.96	9.34	9.40	†10.29	9.98	10.99

	1987	1988	1989	1990	1991	1992	1993	1994	1995	1996	1997	1998	1999	2000	2001		
																International Transactions	
Billions of Francs																	
	353.98	385.10	514.85	476.68	559.07	516.82	499.00	1,246.72	1,569.39	1,215.70	1,139.07	1,310.00	1,382.43	....	....	Exports...................................	70
	323.05	538.36	595.64	969.54	785.69	833.77	895.69	1,408.62	2,333.89	2,056.11	2,392.16	2,790.32	2,375.27	....	....	Imports, c.i.f...........................	71
																Balance of Payments	
Minus Sign Indicates Debit																	
	−141	−150	−84	−265	−230	−198	−258	−277	−276	−291	−266	−301	−252	−283	....	Current Account, n.i.e.	78al *d*
	327	284	321	318	335	327	335	450	507	509	516	538	584	824	....	Goods: Exports f.o.b.	78aa *d*
	−315	−319	−320	−566	−446	−471	−514	−546	−628	−629	−694	−693	−742	−997	....	Goods: Imports f.o.b.	78ab *d*
	11	−34	1	−249	−111	−144	−180	−96	−122	−120	−178	−154	−158	−174	....	*Trade Balance*	78ac *d*
	96	118	132	153	148	174	187	206	242	293	272	291	326	364	....	Services: Credit	78ad *d*
	−226	−250	−229	−242	−233	−260	−302	−328	−359	−373	−386	−436	−456	−522	....	Services: Debit	78ae *d*
	−119	−166	−96	−338	−196	−230	−295	−218	−238	−200	−292	−299	−289	−332	....	*Balance on Goods & Services*	78af *d*
	9	13	18	15	4	6	3	2	7	6	20	25	21	22	....	Income: Credit	78ag *d*
	−184	−193	−208	−176	−166	−153	−154	−158	−174	−169	−115	−103	−63	−64	....	Income: Debit	78ah *d*
	−294	−345	−285	−499	−357	−377	−446	−374	−405	−363	−387	−377	−331	−373	....	*Balance on Gds, Serv. & Inc.*	78ai *d*
	179	225	230	270	142	197	202	114	141	94	156	109	111	122	....	Current Transfers, n.i.e.: Credit	78aj *d*
	−26	−30	−29	−36	−15	−17	−14	−17	−12	−23	−35	−33	−32	−31	....	Current Transfers: Debit	78ak *d*
	1	1	2	3	49	50	78	62	45	5	115	103	129	115	....	Capital Account, n.i.e.	78bc *d*
	1	1	2	3	49	50	78	62	45	5	115	103	129	115	....	Capital Account, n.i.e.: Credit	78ba *d*
	—	—	—	—	—	—	—	—	—	....	....	....	....	....	....	Capital Account: Debit	78bb *d*
	−11	−21	−36	−18	−59	−100	−158	−122	−198	133	110	−76	−14	−31	....	Financial Account, n.i.e.	78bj *d*
	—	—	—	—	—	—	—	—	—	....	....	....	....	....	....	Direct Investment Abroad	78bd *d*
	—	—	13	22	14	21	15	6	10	10	14	17	58	83	....	Dir. Invest. in Rep. Econ., n.i.e.	78be *d*
				....	....	....	....	....	....	....	....	....	....	....	....	Portfolio Investment Assets	78bf *d*
				....	....	....	....	....	....	....	....	....	....	....	....	Equity Securities..........................	78bk *d*
				....	....	....	....	....	....	....	....	....	....	....	....	Debt Securities............................	78bl *d*
				....	....	....	....	....	....	....	....	....	....	....	....	Portfolio Investment Liab., n.i.e.	78bg *d*
				....	....	....	....	....	....	....	....	....	....	....	....	Equity Securities..........................	78bm *d*
				....	....	....	....	....	....	....	....	....	....	....	....	Debt Securities............................	78bn *d*
																Financial Derivatives Assets	78bw *d*
																Financial Derivatives Liabilities	78bx *d*
	37	9	−18	−7	−27	−3	−47	19	−62	37	135	−68	−73	−87	....	Other Investment Assets	78bh *d*
					−25	9	−19	38	−45	....	157	−84	−71	−40	....	Monetary Authorities	78bo *d*
				....	....	....	....	....	....	....	....	....	....	....	....	General Government	78bp *d*
	37	9	−18	−7	−3	−13	−28	−18	−12	37	−22	16	−2	−48	....	Banks	78bq *d*
								−1	−5	....	....	....	....	....	....	Other Sectors	78br *d*
	−48	−30	−31	−33	−45	−117	−126	−147	−145	86	−39	−25	1	−26	....	Other Investment Liab., n.i.e.	78bi *d*
	—	1	13	—	−204	−238	−254	−235	−230	—	—	—	—	−1	....	Monetary Authorities	78bs *d*
	−8	−1	−29	−59	180	124	123	79	91	−167	−28	−26	−3	−28	....	General Government	78bt *d*
	−40	−29	−15	26	−21	−3	5	6	−8	—	−4	9	6	15	....	Banks	78bu *d*
				....	....	....	....	3	3	253	−8	−7	−2	−12	....	Other Sectors	78bv *d*
	−11	53	−42	2	−52	−31	4	61	98	59	25	−25	32	39	....	Net Errors and Omissions	78ca *d*
	−162	−117	−161	−278	−292	−278	−334	−276	−330	−94	−16	−299	−104	−160	....	*Overall Balance*	78cb *d*
	162	117	161	278	292	278	334	276	330	94	16	299	104	160	....	Reserves and Related Items	79da *d*
	−51	−42	−26	167	28	−8	23	−14	−2	−137	−214	205	11	−30	....	Reserve Assets	79db *d*
	3	−35	−20	−34	−16	−16	−14	−12	−15	3	1	−14	6	45	....	Use of Fund Credit and Loans..........	79dc *d*
	211	195	207	145	280	303	326	303	347	228	229	108	88	145	....	Exceptional Financing	79de *d*
																Government Finance	
Year Ending December 31																	
	....	†−120.5	−166.2	−39.8	−251.3	−346.4	−307.5	−367.6	−212.8	−217.5	−428.5	−646.9	−624.6	−625.6	....	Deficit (-) or Surplus	80
	....	†448.5	455.2	538.4	425.2	557.2	633.6	762.0	1,149.6	1,407.2	1,746.8	2,077.0	2,666.8	3,067.8	....	Revenue	81
	....	†24.5	164.0	202.2	103.8	195.4	225.4	274.0	392.1	683.4	735.4	707.9	770.1	946.7	....	Grants Received	81z
	....	†519.5	716.2	737.3	743.5	1,049.7	1,267.6	1,734.3	2,344.2	2,817.2	2,879.4	3,477.5	4,068.8	4,477.7	....	Expenditure	82
	....	†68.1	66.3	34.7	57.9	71.1	55.2	44.3	29.7	66.2	8.8	−38.8	51.2	26.5	....	Lending Minus Repayments	83
	....	†−5.9	−2.9	−8.4	21.1	21.8	156.3	375.0	619.4	575.3	−22.5	6.9	58.5	−135.9	....	Adjustment to Cash Basis	80x
																Financing	
	....	†−14.1	−19.1	−57.4	60.6	194.9	121.8	213.3	−38.1	−15.0	−145.5	760.9	126.0	121.9	....	Domestic	84a
	....	†134.6	185.3	97.2	190.7	151.5	185.7	154.3	250.9	232.5	574.0	−114.0	446.8	457.4	....	Foreign	85a
	....	....	....	....									51.8	46.3	....	Adjustment to Total Financing............	84x
	....	....	....	806.5	373.0	805.5	934.8	1,124.0	1,076.7	895.4	....	....	....	....	....	Debt: Domestic	88a
	....	....	....	4,230.9	6,441.0	6,610.6	7,169.1	15,646.3	15,072.4	....	....	....	....	....	....	Foreign	89a
																National Accounts	
Billions of Francs																	
	2,378.4	2,934.0	3,271.3	3,965.1	4,493.7	4,929.9	5,751.0	8,102.8	12,120.8	14,462.9	16,294.7	17,726.0	20,038.0	23,231.0	25,399.0	Househ.Cons.Expend.,incl.NPISHs..........	96f
	250.5	279.6	350.9	383.6	436.3	498.3	561.2	723.9	904.2	731.9	1,097.7	1,621.0	1,741.1	2,063.8	2,650.0	Government Consumption Expend.	91f
																Gross Capital Formation	93
	277.2	456.9	536.3	781.4	401.4	631.9	738.5	995.6	1,474.9	1,888.0	2,139.6	2,678.0	3,374.0	4,250.0	6,114.0	Gross Fixed Capital Formation	93e
																Changes in Inventories	93i
	454.4	560.2	738.9	764.4	881.8	923.6	988.1	2,011.8	3,418.0	3,325.8	3,938.3	4,358.1	5,867.0	7,984.0	9,452.0	Exports of Goods and Services	90c
	617.4	793.9	892.0	1,290.4	1,299.6	1,390.6	1,587.9	2,702.8	4,274.3	4,184.3	5,419.4	6,034.4	7,629.4	10,710.0	12,634.0	Imports of Goods and Services (-)	98c
	2,743.1	3,436.8	4,005.4	4,604.1	4,913.8	5,593.1	6,450.9	9,131.1	13,478.7	16,224.3	18,050.9	20,349.5	23,390.0	26,820.0	30,981.0	Gross Domestic Product (GDP)	99b
																Net Primary Income from Abroad........	98.n
	....	....	....	....												Gross National Income (GNI)	99a
																GDP Volume 1970 prices	99b.*p*
	1,768.8	1,829.0	1,903.6	1,963.1	1,839.3	1,861.1	1,900.1	1,898.8	1,931.3	1,972.8	2,045.5	2,126.1	2,225.1	2,333.0	2,489.0	GDP Volume 1984 Prices	99b.*p*
	91.6	94.7	98.6	101.6	95.2	96.4	98.4	98.3	100.0	102.1	105.9	110.1	115.2	120.8	128.9	GDP Volume (1995=100)	99bv *p*
	22.2	26.9	30.1	33.6	38.3	43.1	48.6	68.9	100.0	117.8	126.4	137.1	150.6	164.7	178.3	GDP Deflator (1995=100)	99bi *p*
Midyear Estimates																	
	11.37	11.82	12.28	†11.20	11.49	12.65	13.02	13.40	13.79	14.20	14.62	15.06	15.51	15.97	16.44	Population...............................	99z

(See notes in the back of the book.)

Malawi

		1972	1973	1974	1975	1976	1977	1978	1979	1980	1981	1982	1983	1984	1985	1986
Exchange Rates																*Kwacha per SDR:*
Official Rate	aa	.9280	1.0224	1.0291	1.0541	1.0541	1.0541	1.0541	1.0541	1.0541	1.0541	1.2122	1.3577	1.5339	1.8445	2.3882
																Kwacha per US Dollar:
Official Rate	ae	.8547	.8475	.8405	.8998	.9074	.8678	.8091	.7996	.8258	.9074	1.0970	1.2992	1.5649	1.6792	1.9524
Official Rate	rf	.8016	.8193	.8412	.8638	.9130	.9029	.8437	.8169	.8121	.8953	1.0555	1.1748	1.4134	1.7191	1.8611
																Index Numbers (1995=100):
Official Rate	ahx	1,905.4	1,867.1	1,816.9	1,770.9	1,674.6	1,692.8	1,812.4	1,871.1	1,882.4	1,709.3	1,457.7	1,305.8	1,084.8	895.8	823.6
Nominal Effective Exchange Rate	nec	....	....	....	....	....	....	....	566.4	570.6	589.2	574.6	572.1	557.8	538.8	460.8
Real Effective Exchange Rate	rec	....	....	....	....	....	....	....	....	182.8	182.7	175.9	179.1	177.6	177.8	159.6
Fund Position																*Millions of SDRs:*
Quota	2f.s	15.00	15.00	15.00	15.00	15.00	15.00	19.00	19.00	28.50	28.50	28.50	37.20	37.20	37.20	37.20
SDRs	1b.s	4.60	4.60	4.59	4.56	4.31	3.87	3.29	3.05	.03	5.66	3.59	.83	2.85	.02	.37
Reserve Position in the Fund	1c.s	1.90	3.75	3.75	—	—	—	—	—	—	3.76	.01	2.18	2.20	2.20	2.20
Total Fund Cred.&Loans Outstg.	2tl				2.37	3.73	10.77	11.75	37.70	62.49	89.94	88.24	111.76	127.92	132.47	108.96
International Liquidity												*Millions of US Dollars Unless Otherwise Indicated:*				
Total Reserves minus Gold	1l.d	36.24	66.64	81.79	61.46	26.22	87.49	74.80	69.51	68.39	49.05	22.66	15.40	56.60	44.95	24.60
SDRs	1b.d	4.99	5.55	5.62	5.34	5.01	4.70	4.29	4.02	.04	6.59	3.96	.87	2.79	.02	.45
Reserve Position in the Fund	1c.d	2.06	4.52	4.59	—	—	—	—	—	—	4.38	.01	2.28	2.16	2.42	2.69
Foreign Exchange	1d.d	29.18	56.57	71.58	56.12	21.21	82.79	70.51	65.49	68.35	38.09	18.69	12.25	51.65	42.51	21.46
Gold (Million Fine Troy Ounces)	1ad	—	—	—	—	—	.006	.010	.013	.013	.013	.013	.013	.013	.013	.013
Gold (National Valuation)	1and	—	—	—	—	—	.27	.44	.59	.57	.52	.50	.49	.30	.53	.56
Monetary Authorities: Other Liab.	4..d	.30	.18	.21	27.87	30.28	32.55	42.39	56.52	36.75	50.72	57.42	40.64	.01	11.50	36.65
Deposit Money Banks: Assets	7a.d	3.44	4.07	2.58	5.80	6.27	6.53	13.36	8.30	6.84	7.18	8.23	10.51	6.06	7.76	5.31
Liabilities	7b.d	6.94	9.26	8.23	12.59	24.71	36.61	39.81	69.18	56.39	32.69	29.85	37.03	32.75	40.85	50.86
Monetary Authorities																*Millions of Kwacha:*
Foreign Assets	11	28.43	56.47	72.59	55.30	23.79	76.18	60.87	51.57	56.46	44.50	24.87	20.01	92.37	76.85	42.24
Claims on Central Government	12a	6.57	6.66	7.99	22.55	27.08	14.33	17.24	48.64	67.25	152.21	223.73	282.18	240.01	297.73	383.69
Claims on Nonfin.Pub.Enterprises	12c	—	—	—	25.43	27.73	28.18	33.79	30.68	34.52	39.33	36.35	40.12	50.63	63.45	72.21
Claims on Deposit Money Banks	12e	1.54	2.00	2.24	—	3.48	—	6.00	17.68	8.85	—	—	1.00	—	—	—
Reserve Money	14	21.68	45.42	59.16	52.50	34.58	63.65	41.70	38.55	53.31	71.79	84.80	89.63	158.06	165.97	286.42
of which: Currency Outside DMBs	14a	17.30	21.31	28.31	27.84	23.07	24.58	29.80	32.29	35.34	39.36	49.47	50.03	56.85	65.99	79.30
Restricted Deposits	16b	—	—	—	—	—	—	—	—	—	—	—	8.12	10.00	19.55	15.43
Foreign Liabilities	16c	.23	.16	.17	27.58	31.41	39.60	46.69	84.91	96.16	141.02	169.77	204.81	196.24	263.65	331.76
Central Government Deposits	16d	3.40	5.24	5.37	8.22	2.72	5.75	7.69	8.40	.29	.78	26.84	36.59	31.87	33.23	18.91
Capital Accounts	17a	6.63	6.79	8.81	9.20	9.31	9.40	9.68	13.46	16.04	18.68	20.42	22.01	22.62	22.54	29.90
Other Items (Net)	17r	4.60	7.52	9.30	5.79	4.05	.29	12.15	3.26	1.28	3.76	-16.90	-17.86	-35.79	-66.90	-184.28
Deposit Money Banks																*Millions of Kwacha:*
Reserves	20	3.80	22.16	26.62	20.67	5.13	17.47	9.86	4.81	17.63	30.94	34.43	33.44	91.55	96.42	189.72
Foreign Assets	21	2.64	3.45	2.17	5.22	5.69	5.67	10.81	6.64	5.65	6.51	9.03	13.66	9.48	13.03	10.37
Claims on Central Government	22a	7.12	12.20	14.50	20.07	21.17	26.29	37.01	29.90	25.27	24.68	24.69	27.92	86.67	97.86	97.49
Claims on Nonfin.Pub.Enterprises	22c	1.37	.71	2.48	7.35	14.68	19.76	16.91	25.77	22.39	22.70	29.12	24.38	32.02	46.78	41.09
Claims on Private Sector	22d	35.62	32.96	49.44	56.09	76.55	87.79	122.38	170.99	184.23	191.97	219.11	254.72	228.80	212.67	236.33
Demand Deposits	24	22.73	31.85	40.88	41.56	43.34	53.88	62.07	56.83	61.45	73.87	80.44	71.56	87.74	97.51	124.07
Time, Savings,& Fgn. Currency Dep.	25	22.32	29.68	42.45	48.73	48.22	60.86	74.77	79.50	94.33	126.66	145.57	165.02	234.04	217.50	268.03
Foreign Liabilities	26c	5.33	7.84	6.92	11.33	22.42	31.77	32.21	55.32	46.56	29.66	32.74	48.11	51.24	68.59	99.30
Central Government Deposits	26d	—	—	—	—	—	—	—	—	—	—	—	—	—	—	—
Credit from Monetary Authorities	26g	1.54	2.00	2.24	—	3.48	—	6.00	17.68	8.92	—	—	—	—	—	—
Capital Accounts	27a	2.23	2.87	5.05	6.17	9.09	16.35	20.29	21.95	25.85	24.94	32.40	36.24	41.27	46.36	58.67
Other Items (Net)	27r	-3.60	-2.76	-2.33	1.61	-3.34	-5.90	1.63	6.83	18.07	21.67	25.23	33.19	34.22	36.81	24.94
Monetary Survey																*Millions of Kwacha:*
Foreign Assets (Net)	31n	25.51	51.92	67.66	21.61	-24.36	10.47	-7.23	-82.01	-80.62	-119.67	-168.61	-219.25	-145.63	-242.35	-378.45
Domestic Credit	32	47.28	47.30	69.04	123.28	164.48	170.60	219.65	297.58	333.37	430.12	506.15	592.73	606.25	685.27	811.91
Claims on Central Govt. (Net)	32an	10.29	13.62	17.12	34.40	45.52	34.87	46.57	70.14	92.23	176.12	221.57	273.51	294.81	362.37	462.28
Claims on Nonfin.Pub.Enterprises	32c	1.37	.71	2.48	32.79	42.41	47.93	50.70	56.45	56.91	62.03	65.46	64.50	82.64	110.23	113.30
Claims on Private Sector	32d	35.62	32.96	49.44	56.09	76.55	87.79	122.38	170.99	184.23	191.97	219.11	254.72	228.80	212.67	236.33
Money	34	40.61	55.12	73.43	73.63	72.80	100.06	93.79	90.59	97.20	114.75	130.81	127.76	154.25	166.93	220.78
Quasi-Money	35	22.33	29.71	42.46	48.73	48.24	60.94	74.77	79.50	94.33	126.66	145.57	165.02	234.04	217.50	268.03
Restricted Deposits	36b	—	—	—	—	—	—	—	—	—	—	—	8.12	10.00	19.55	15.43
Capital Accounts	37a	8.86	9.66	13.86	15.37	18.41	25.75	29.97	35.41	41.89	43.62	52.81	58.25	63.89	68.89	88.56
Other Items (Net)	37r	.99	4.74	6.95	7.15	.68	-5.68	13.90	10.06	19.35	25.41	8.33	14.32	-1.56	-29.97	-159.35
Money plus Quasi-Money	35l	62.94	84.82	115.89	122.36	121.04	161.00	168.55	170.09	191.52	241.41	276.38	292.78	388.29	384.43	488.81
Other Banking Institutions																*Millions of Kwacha:*
Cash	40	.11	.14	.31	.25	.47	.37	.72	1.62	1.36	4.00	2.38	2.00	7.08	2.40	1.50
Claims on Central Government	42a	8.45	2.14	1.25	1.95	1.84	2.75	2.50	2.08	2.40	2.82	5.93	7.69	7.47	11.74	11.07
Claims on Private Sector	42d	3.58	5.55	8.35	8.82	10.95	12.20	16.44	17.67	23.50	27.00	30.87	33.16	33.36	41.42	47.91
Shares, Time and Savings Deposits	45	11.72	8.63	10.26	11.18	14.19	16.94	18.77	22.66	26.70	32.71	37.42	42.86	47.38	54.92	58.93
Other Items (Net)	47r	.42	-.80	-.36	-.16	-.92	-1.62	.90	-1.29	.55	1.10	1.76	-.01	.53	.64	1.55
Nonbank Financial Institutions																*Millions of Kwacha:*
Claims on Central Government	42a.s	3.92	4.88	6.03	7.17	7.16	6.61	6.88	8.23	10.11	8.29	10.63	14.69	23.58	36.53	45.15
Claims on Private Sector	42d.s	1.09	1.31	2.24	3.32	4.31	7.28	7.88	8.96	11.31	10.67	14.36	19.40	23.09	26.28	32.73
of which: Policy Loans	42dx s	.25	.44	.94	1.54	1.85	2.70	2.75	2.42	2.88	2.16	1.08	4.61	7.08	7.63	10.09
Incr.in Total Assets(Within Per.)	49z.s	3.31	2.15	2.79	2.32	2.49	5.12	4.46	4.62	14.23	-2.57	-5.84	25.40	22.33	9.92	27.57
Liquid Liabilities	55l	74.55	93.31	125.85	133.29	134.75	177.57	186.59	191.13	216.86	270.12	311.42	333.64	428.60	436.96	546.24
Interest Rates																*Percent Per Annum:*
Discount Rate (End of Period)	60	6.00	6.00	6.00	6.00	7.00	7.00	7.00	8.00	10.00	10.00	10.00	10.00	10.00	11.00	11.00
Treasury Bill Rate	60c	....	....	....	....	....	....	....	....	....	9.00	9.00	11.00	11.00	12.31	12.75
Deposit Rate	60l	....	....	....	....	....	....	....	....	7.92	9.75	9.75	9.92	11.75	12.50	12.75
Lending Rate	60p	....	....	....	....	....	....	....	....	16.67	18.50	18.50	18.33	16.50	18.38	19.00
Government Bond Yield	61	....	....	....	....	....	....	....	....	....	9.25	9.73	10.27	10.58	11.50	11.50

1987	1988	1989	1990	1991	1992	1993	1994	1995	1996	1997	1998	1999	2000	2001		
End of Period															**Exchange Rates**	
2.9136	3.4120	3.5204	3.7656	3.8104	6.0442	6.1733	22.3337	22.7479	22.0340	28.6416	61.7894	63.7362	104.3318	84.5705	Official Rate	aa
End of Period (ae) Period Average (rf)																
2.0538	2.5355	2.6788	2.6469	2.6638	4.3958	4.4944	15.2986	15.3031	15.3231	21.2278	43.8836	46.4377	80.0760	67.2941	Official Rate	ae
2.2087	2.5613	2.7595	2.7289	2.8033	3.6033	4.4028	8.7364	15.2837	15.3085	16.4442	31.0727	44.0881	59.5438	72.1973	Official Rate	rf
Period Averages																
693.8	598.0	554.1	560.9	546.1	436.0	346.6	199.3	100.0	99.8	93.5	52.5	34.7	26.8	21.4	Official Rate	ahx
366.1	334.5	359.2	382.2	406.2	347.4	326.1	207.2	100.0	104.0	104.7	62.3	43.6	36.0	30.4	Nominal Effective Exchange Rate	nec
148.2	158.0	167.1	165.7	171.6	158.1	161.4	114.6	100.0	137.7	152.9	111.2	111.8	112.8	116.8	Real Effective Exchange Rate	rec
End of Period															**Fund Position**	
37.20	37.20	37.20	37.20	37.20	50.90	50.90	50.90	50.90	50.90	50.90	50.90	69.40	69.40	69.40	Quota	2f.s
—	2.38	.28	2.23	.18	.06	.17	4.25	.59	.94	.07	4.84	.29	.36	.67	SDRs	1b.s
2.20	2.20	2.21	2.22	2.22	2.22	2.22	2.22	2.22	2.22	2.22	2.24	2.24	2.24	2.27	Reserve Position in the Fund	1c.s
82.43	78.55	76.45	80.83	80.45	66.86	62.62	76.90	78.02	83.06	78.42	72.57	63.79	63.35	57.90	Total Fund Cred.&Loans Outstg.	2tl
End of Period															**International Liquidity**	
51.83	145.57	100.31	137.16	153.20	39.95	56.88	42.79	110.01	225.73	162.24	269.73	250.61	246.91	206.74	Total Reserves minus Gold	1l.d
—	3.20	.37	3.17	.26	.08	.23	6.20	.88	1.36	.09	6.82	.39	.47	.84	SDRs	1b.d
3.12	2.96	2.90	3.16	3.18	3.05	3.05	3.25	3.31	3.20	3.00	3.15	3.07	2.91	2.85	Reserve Position in the Fund	1c.d
48.71	139.41	97.04	130.83	149.77	36.82	53.59	33.35	105.82	221.17	159.15	259.77	247.15	243.52	203.05	Foreign Exchange	1d.d
.013	.013	.013	.013	.013	.013	.013	.013	.013	.013	.013	.013	.013	.010	.010	Gold (Million Fine Troy Ounces)	1ad
.62	.50	.48	.55	.54	.54	.54	.55	.54	.54	.54	.55	.54	.54	.54	Gold (National Valuation)	1and
35.49	35.18	34.35	46.34	52.09	91.23	72.58	58.30	32.37	24.36	15.90	9.22	3.91	.49	.06	Monetary Authorities: Other Liab.	4..d
3.07	5.83	8.28	11.33	4.56	10.06	17.34	25.61	29.39	36.17	41.63	60.00	47.28	53.86	59.80	Deposit Money Banks: Assets	7a.d
27.89	17.96	18.57	21.59	19.97	29.15	24.47	27.22	9.80	10.37	10.67	13.75	16.03	16.86	15.09	Liabilities	7b.d
End of Period															**Monetary Authorities**	
106.49	370.32	277.12	367.92	399.84	215.75	255.63	613.64	1,669.97	3,387.66	3,342.41	11,327.88	11,468.61	19,500.33	13,663.87	Foreign Assets	11
498.33	417.33	491.00	440.48	459.19	803.27	958.66	1,309.48	1,266.17	710.81	876.99	3,727.89	2,559.27	445.85	6,164.45	Claims on Central Government	12a
78.11	83.35	86.81	81.26	131.82	119.72	117.51	115.47	127.02	159.25	187.46	191.41	274.60	313.74	313.74	Claims on Nonfin.Pub.Enterprises	12c
—	—	—	—	—	—	36.64	28.16	13.44	150.51	9.83	9.42	8.18	112.19	3.55	Claims on Deposit Money Banks	12e
445.33	495.67	447.50	374.50	462.12	541.75	880.71	1,244.79	2,360.57	3,269.68	3,277.01	4,542.58	6,001.42	6,349.22	8,497.68	Reserve Money	14
107.62	134.62	156.60	159.38	222.69	289.79	414.17	624.74	987.52	1,223.77	1,375.33	1,999.39	2,992.02	4,144.86	4,208.47	*of which: Currency Outside DMBs*	14a
10.40	6.57	6.57	2.74	2.74	—	—	—	—	—	—	—	—	—	—	Restricted Deposits	16b
313.06	357.22	361.15	427.03	445.31	805.13	712.77	2,609.31	2,270.20	2,203.41	2,583.48	4,888.49	4,247.57	6,648.71	4,900.32	Foreign Liabilities	16c
82.20	167.50	222.92	290.14	351.24	234.99	351.72	349.54	591.77	883.33	291.29	4,564.55	3,035.28	1,513.50	2,182.92	Central Government Deposits	16d
29.90	40.63	47.55	57.19	66.55	92.15	151.92	191.42	280.66	478.84	653.87	1,049.41	1,094.70	1,547.17	1,269.16	Capital Accounts	17a
-197.95	-196.59	-230.76	-261.94	-337.11	-535.28	-728.68	-2,328.32	-2,426.60	-2,427.03	-2,388.96	211.57	-68.31	4,313.51	3,295.53	Other Items (Net)	17r
End of Period															**Deposit Money Banks**	
303.76	288.21	225.61	221.66	174.33	209.46	380.18	591.37	1,311.74	1,814.51	1,803.58	2,176.44	2,761.90	1,985.04	3,482.57	Reserves	20
6.31	14.79	22.18	29.99	12.14	44.24	77.95	391.74	449.81	554.19	883.72	2,633.01	2,195.59	4,313.17	4,024.35	Foreign Assets	21
94.02	93.25	82.88	80.84	71.38	153.47	335.28	387.86	867.29	1,746.29	1,206.70	1,484.40	2,347.30	2,352.00	2,346.05	Claims on Central Government	22a
53.44	23.79	30.50	45.57	84.15	22.54	154.34	47.63	182.97	398.03	413.57	185.80	1,442.87	1,218.22	575.14	Claims on Nonfin.Pub.Enterprises	22c
205.09	262.38	383.16	519.05	662.63	888.56	785.11	1,207.90	1,263.76	1,414.95	1,620.91	3,208.69	3,392.69	5,145.73	5,390.97	Claims on Private Sector	22d
156.46	230.96	230.88	284.25	346.00	444.90	560.15	895.94	1,218.14	1,518.01	1,824.45	2,771.19	3,641.75	4,934.39	5,473.00	Demand Deposits	24
370.44	376.57	408.98	475.00	566.73	633.51	924.45	1,119.48	1,936.43	3,048.13	2,712.42	4,463.28	5,323.24	7,832.38	9,542.70	Time, Savings,& Fgn. Currency Dep.	25
57.29	45.53	49.75	57.15	53.19	128.14	110.00	416.48	150.01	158.84	226.44	603.48	744.41	1,349.69	1,015.73	Foreign Liabilities	26c
—	—	—	.45	.01	4.79	1.22	2.65	471.85	469.65	557.21	890.96	1,121.55	674.26	348.40	Central Government Deposits	26d
.57	—	—	—	—	3.21	6.02	6.82	9.50	7.71	3.92	2.95	—	—	—	Credit from Monetary Authorities	26g
62.93	67.43	99.29	102.50	146.30	184.50	214.20	410.50	598.16	845.24	1,113.35	1,413.43	2,152.79	2,937.65	3,208.70	Capital Accounts	27a
14.93	-38.06	-44.56	-22.23	-107.61	-80.79	-83.17	-225.37	-308.52	-119.62	-509.29	-456.93	-843.39	-2,714.21	-3,769.45	Other Items (Net)	27r
End of Period															**Monetary Survey**	
-257.55	-17.64	-111.59	-86.26	-86.51	-673.29	-489.19	-2,020.41	-300.43	1,579.60	1,416.21	8,468.92	8,672.22	15,815.10	11,772.17	Foreign Assets (Net)	31n
846.79	712.61	851.43	876.61	1,057.92	1,747.78	1,997.96	2,716.15	2,643.59	3,076.34	3,457.14	3,342.68	5,859.90	7,287.78	12,259.03	Domestic Credit	32
510.15	343.09	350.96	230.73	179.32	716.96	941.00	1,345.15	1,069.85	1,104.12	1,235.19	-243.22	749.74	610.09	5,979.18	Claims on Central Govt. (Net)	32an
131.55	107.14	117.31	126.83	215.97	142.26	271.85	163.10	309.99	557.28	601.03	377.21	1,717.47	1,531.96	888.88	Claims on Nonfin.Pub.Enterprises	32c
205.09	262.38	383.16	519.05	662.63	888.56	785.11	1,207.90	1,263.76	1,414.95	1,620.91	3,208.69	3,392.69	5,145.73	5,390.97	Claims on Private Sector	32d
298.02	435.92	452.71	482.12	633.86	756.70	1,019.90	1,535.43	2,211.21	2,742.66	3,200.64	4,999.24	6,651.15	9,096.63	9,828.85	Money	34
370.44	376.57	408.98	475.00	566.73	633.51	924.45	1,119.48	1,936.43	3,048.13	2,712.42	4,463.28	5,323.24	7,832.38	9,542.70	Quasi-Money	35
10.40	6.57	6.57	2.74	2.74	—	—	—	—	—	—	—	—	—	—	Restricted Deposits	36b
92.83	108.06	146.84	159.69	212.85	276.65	366.12	601.92	878.82	1,324.08	1,767.22	2,462.84	3,247.49	4,484.82	4,477.86	Capital Accounts	37a
-182.45	-232.15	-275.26	-329.20	-444.78	-592.37	-801.69	-2,561.09	-2,683.30	-2,458.92	-2,806.93	-113.74	-689.76	1,689.05	181.79	Other Items (Net)	37r
668.47	812.49	861.69	957.12	1,200.59	1,390.22	1,944.34	2,654.90	4,147.64	5,790.79	5,913.05	9,462.51	11,974.39	16,929.01	19,371.55	Money plus Quasi-Money	35l
End of Period															**Other Banking Institutions**	
7.75	†14.99	14.84	4.11	3.74	32.57	79.11	98.87	184.06	315.90	122.77	99.02	364.39	491.84	305.90	Cash	40
15.20	†26.13	26.64	24.22	23.79	23.74	29.23	8.88	5.40	26.38	112.22	90.71	161.66	439.48	1,177.35	Claims on Central Government	42a
51.53	†57.19	75.66	109.88	167.40	248.90	324.66	394.85	480.72	558.21	811.97	1,116.26	1,053.07	1,082.10	1,309.58	Claims on Private Sector	42d
71.28	†97.04	110.84	129.25	200.54	278.47	379.50	457.64	568.48	813.40	944.45	1,128.99	1,513.45	2,007.51	2,354.60	Shares, Time and Savings Deposits	45
3.20	†1.27	6.31	8.96	-5.60	26.75	53.51	44.96	101.70	87.10	102.51	177.00	65.67	5.91	438.24	Other Items (Net)	47r
End of Period															**Nonbank Financial Institutions**	
42.81	57.80	63.25	69.12	60.92	84.91	71.06	93.51	172.57	216.19	232.89	437.70	575.90	....	....	Claims on Central Government	42a.s
35.06	44.60	46.67	80.71	112.26	138.82	208.70	269.01	377.83	584.02	230.34	332.00	352.89	....	....	Claims on Private Sector	42d.s
8.97	9.40	7.47	8.69	10.19	12.34	11.05	12.48	15.25	16.38	22.30	33.31	23.59	....	....	*of which: Policy Loans*	42dx s
14.09	38.10	41.94	68.70	-43.13	45.49	70.20	103.28	242.14	296.06	-247.43	416.41	168.14	....	....	*Incr.in Total Assets(Within Per.)*	49z.s
732.00	†894.54	957.68	1,082.25	1,397.39	1,636.11	2,244.73	3,013.67	4,532.06	6,288.29	6,734.73	10,492.48	13,123.45	18,444.68	21,420.25	Liquid Liabilities	55l
Percent Per Annum															**Interest Rates**	
14.00	11.00	11.00	14.00	13.00	20.00	25.00	40.00	50.00	27.00	23.00	43.00	47.00	50.23	46.80	Discount Rate *(End of Period)*	60
14.25	15.75	15.75	12.92	11.50	15.62	23.54	27.68	46.30	30.83	18.31	32.98	42.85	39.52	42.41	Treasury Bill Rate	60c
14.25	13.50	12.75	12.10	12.50	16.50	21.75	25.00	37.27	26.33	10.21	19.06	33.21	33.25	34.96	Deposit Rate	60l
19.50	22.25	23.00	21.00	20.00	22.00	29.50	31.00	47.33	45.33	28.25	37.67	53.58	53.13	56.17	Lending Rate	60p
11.50	11.50	11.50	11.50	11.50	....	....	23.50	38.58	42.67	39.25	....	....	....	....	Government Bond Yield	61

Malawi

		1972	1973	1974	1975	1976	1977	1978	1979	1980	1981	1982	1983	1984	1985	1986
Prices, Production, Labor															*Index Numbers (1995=100):*	
Consumer Prices	64	....	....	....	....	....	....	....	....	5.3	6.0	6.5	7.4	8.9	9.9	11.2
Industrial Production	66	38.2	46.2	48.8	56.4	55.8	62.4	68.9	69.1	70.1	77.3	72.7	83.4	82.5	82.8	84.0
															Number in Thousands:	
Employment	67e	....	....	....	....	....	....	....	....	....	....	....	....	....	415	432
International Transactions															*Millions of Kwacha*	
Exports	70	64	80	101	122	152	180	156	190	239	256	257	271	446	422	462
Imports, c.i.f.	71	103	115	158	219	188	212	285	326	356	321	322	364	382	506	478
Imports, f.o.b.	71.v	90	101	139	192	165	186	251	289	313	283	283	319	340	304	287
															1985=100	
Volume of Exports	72	58.0	61.6	59.6	61.5	68.7	75.0	71.4	94.7	†105.5	83.6	86.9	115.2	83.8	100.0	104.3
Volume of Imports	73	89.5	83.2	87.7	98.7	75.8	84.3	112.1	113.9	†101.2	75.1	75.9	77.8	83.3	100.0	73.2
Export Prices	74	27.8	31.1	39.4	46.2	51.7	68.1	61.3	55.2	†57.1	80.0	87.7	89.5	110.7	100.0	111.9
Unit Value of Imports	75	17.0	19.8	26.7	32.5	37.1	41.3	41.5	47.3	†57.6	66.0	71.6	79.7	94.5	100.0	128.5
Balance of Payments															*Millions of US Dollars:*	
Current Account, n.i.e.	78al d	....	....	....	....	....	−61.8	−175.1	−265.6	−259.9	−146.8	−112.7	−131.8	−42.6	−127.1	−85.3
Goods: Exports f.o.b.	78aa d						199.8	184.5	222.4	280.8	272.5	239.7	246.2	311.8	245.5	248.4
Goods: Imports f.o.b.	78ab d						−183.0	−263.9	−317.6	−308.0	−244.3	−214.0	−216.2	−162.0	−176.7	−154.1
Trade Balance	78ac d						16.8	−79.4	−95.1	−27.2	28.3	25.7	30.0	149.8	68.8	94.3
Services: Credit	78ad d						13.4	25.6	34.8	31.8	43.7	27.9	28.8	27.0	25.9	20.1
Services: Debit	78ae d						−117.5	−119.3	−133.2	−178.6	−146.8	−123.0	−127.8	−141.6	−143.3	−130.5
Balance on Goods & Services	78af d						−87.3	−173.2	−193.5	−174.0	−74.8	−69.4	−69.0	35.2	−48.5	−16.1
Income: Credit	78ag d						—	1.1	1.3	2.2	1.3	1.5	1.1	2.6	4.7	3.3
Income: Debit	78ah d						—	−49.4	−127.2	−151.3	−131.5	−92.9	−101.6	−116.3	−118.9	−114.9
Balance on Gds, Serv. & Inc.	78ai d						−87.3	−221.5	−319.4	−323.1	−205.0	−160.9	−169.6	−78.5	−162.7	−127.7
Current Transfers, n.i.e.: Credit	78aj d						26.0	60.2	71.4	82.6	74.7	64.6	54.6	53.6	47.9	57.2
Current Transfers: Debit	78ak d						−.6	−13.7	−17.6	−19.5	−16.5	−16.5	−16.8	−17.6	−12.3	−14.9
Capital Account, n.i.e.	78bc d						—	—	—	—	—	—	—	—	—	—
Capital Account, n.i.e.: Credit	78ba d						—	—	—	—	—	—	—	—	—	—
Capital Account: Debit	78bb d						—	—	—	—	—	—	—	—	—	—
Financial Account, n.i.e.	78bj d						69.0	126.9	132.2	152.0	31.5	−8.7	35.2	45.3	−3.7	45.8
Direct Investment Abroad	78bd d						—	—	—	—	—	—	—	—	—	—
Dir. Invest. in Rep. Econ., n.i.e.	78be d						5.5	9.1	−1.2	9.5	1.1	—	2.6	—	.5	—
Portfolio Investment Assets	78bf d						—	—	—	—	—	—	—	—	—	—
Equity Securities	78bk d						—	—	—	—	—	—	—	—	—	—
Debt Securities	78bl d						—	—	—	—	—	—	—	—	—	—
Portfolio Investment Liab., n.i.e.	78bg d						—	16.5	19.8	.5	1.9	3.3	.4	1.0	.4	1.3
Equity Securities	78bm d						—	16.5	19.8	.5	1.9	3.3	.4	1.0	.4	1.3
Debt Securities	78bn d						—	—	—	—	—	—	—	—	—	—
Financial Derivatives Assets	78bw d						....	....	....	....	....	....	....	....	....	....
Financial Derivatives Liabilities	78bx d						....	....	....	....	....	....	....	....	....	....
Other Investment Assets	78bh d						—	28.3	5.1	1.5	−.9	−2.4	−1.9	−4.4	−2.6	13.8
Monetary Authorities	78bo d						—	—	—	—	—	—	—	—	—	—
General Government	78bp d						—	—	—	—	—	—	—	—	—	—
Banks	78bq d						—	26.3	5.1	1.1	−.9	−2.4	−1.9	−4.4	−2.6	13.8
Other Sectors	78br d						—	2.0	—	.4	—	—	—	—	—	—
Other Investment Liab., n.i.e.	78bi d						63.5	73.0	108.5	140.5	29.4	−9.7	34.0	48.7	−2.0	30.7
Monetary Authorities	78bs d						.9	—	—	—	—	—	—	—	—	—
General Government	78bt d						32.8	47.1	58.0	147.3	35.5	3.8	23.8	53.2	7.7	36.6
Banks	78bu d						10.4	.5	28.3	−30.8	−18.9	2.9	—	—	—	—
Other Sectors	78bv d						19.4	25.5	22.2	24.0	12.7	−16.4	10.2	−4.5	−9.7	−5.9
Net Errors and Omissions	78ca d						42.3	35.4	50.3	86.0	88.7	83.5	−1.4	.8	105.1	38.9
Overall Balance	78cb d						49.5	−12.7	−83.1	−22.0	−26.5	−37.9	−98.0	3.5	−25.6	−.6
Reserves and Related Items	79da d						−49.5	12.7	83.1	22.0	26.5	37.9	98.0	−3.5	25.6	.6
Reserve Assets	79db d						−57.7	11.6	49.4	−10.4	−6.1	20.5	12.5	−44.4	13.0	25.0
Use of Fund Credit and Loans	79dc d						8.2	1.1	33.7	32.1	31.4	−2.3	25.4	16.5	5.1	−27.7
Exceptional Financing	79de d						—	—	—	.3	1.2	19.7	60.1	24.4	7.5	3.3
Government Finance															*Millions of Kwacha:*	
Deficit (-) or Surplus	80	−20.0	−20.6	−29.5	−48.6	−37.6	−45.2	−74.3	−75.5	−160.3	−137.7	−95.0	−101.8	−88.3	−162.6	−217.7
Revenue	81	51.8	59.9	70.7	81.3	87.7	109.1	142.4	176.2	192.2	214.1	232.0	276.5	339.7	431.6	479.2
Grants Received	81z	3.4	2.6	2.3	12.4	10.0	16.5	26.9	35.4	43.9	43.5	39.8	34.4	41.0	29.8	52.1
Exp. & Lending Minus Repay.	82z	75.3	83.1	102.5	142.3	135.3	170.7	243.7	287.1	396.4	395.3	366.8	412.7	469.1	623.9	749.1
Expenditure	82	71.1	79.6	103.9	140.5	129.2	159.8	214.8	279.6	347.7	393.4	359.8	415.4	473.4	608.5	742.6
Lending Minus Repayments	83	4.1	3.5	−1.5	1.8	6.1	10.9	28.9	7.5	48.7	1.9	7.0	−2.7	−4.3	15.4	6.5
Financing																
Net Borrowing: Domestic	84a	6.0	5.5	11.8	13.4	.5	14.3	2.2	30.9	58.0	80.8	−6.6	56.4	73.5	96.0	−30.9
Foreign	85a	16.8	15.5	19.9	33.3	24.1	41.8	60.1	40.1	83.6	33.6	62.6	95.0	56.1	68.9	165.5
Use of Cash Balances	87	−2.9	−.4	−2.2	1.9	13.0	−10.9	12.0	4.5	18.7	23.4	39.1	−49.7	−41.3	−2.3	83.1
Debt: Domestic	88a	40.4	47.4	53.4	67.1	81.7	92.0	....	....	....	....	....	408.5	433.8	514.8	
Debt: Foreign	89a	127.7	157.6	179.0	218.6	241.5	251.6	195.1	274.0	366.7	426.9	630.0	798.7	915.3	1,196.8	1,918.4
National Accounts															*Millions of Kwacha*	
Househ.Cons.Expend.,incl.NPISHs	96f	268.4	270.0	320.2	365.2	416.6	483.4	502.2	525.6	631.2	716.2	812.0	918.8	1,186.3	1,350.2	1,541.5
Government Consumption Expend.	91f	46.8	48.7	65.7	74.7	86.3	98.6	134.2	164.2	193.9	198.0	218.3	235.9	268.0	344.0	433.8
Gross Fixed Capital Formation	93e	72.4	74.3	87.3	131.8	135.3	161.6	247.1	231.9	223.1	167.8	181.7	197.3	222.7	259.5	264.1
Changes in Inventories	93i	16.4	7.2	41.0	48.6	10.9	18.0	60.7	95.4	97.3	90.3	112.2	193.8	−2.8	102.2	5.3
Exports of Goods and Services	90c	79.4	100.6	126.2	155.4	185.6	218.4	168.9	200.5	249.7	284.4	280.2	298.2	484.4	470.5	504.7
Imports of Goods and Services (-)	98c	124.3	136.8	178.9	246.0	222.7	252.0	312.4	353.1	390.1	348.6	359.3	407.1	451.2	581.5	551.8
Gross Domestic Product (GDP)	99b	359.1	364.0	461.5	529.7	612.0	728.0	800.7	864.5	1,005.1	1,108.1	1,245.1	1,436.9	1,707.4	1,944.9	2,197.6
Net Primary Income from Abroad	98.n	−3.7	.8	12.4	10.7	−17.5	−23.0	−4.0	−34.8	−81.1	−74.3	−101.3	−139.0	−78.8	−90.9	−112.9
Gross National Income (GNI)	99a	355.4	364.8	473.9	540.4	594.5	705.0	796.7	829.7	924.0	1,033.8	1,143.8	1,297.9	1,628.6	1,854.0	2,084.7
GDP Volume 1978 Prices	99b.p	....	545.5	586.1	618.5	657.0	685.5	742.5	767.3	764.4	724.4	744.9	771.2	805.5	841.4	850.6
GDP Volume 1994 Prices	99b.p	....	....	....	....	....	....	....	....	....	....	....	....	....	....	
GDP Volume (1995=100)	99bv p	....	50.4	54.1	57.1	60.6	63.3	68.5	70.8	70.6	66.9	68.8	71.2	74.3	77.7	78.5
GDP Deflator (1995=100)	99bi p	....	3.3	3.9	4.2	4.6	5.2	5.3	5.6	6.5	7.6	8.3	9.2	10.5	11.4	12.8
															Millions:	
Population	99z	4.67	4.79	5.10	5.24	5.37	5.54	5.68	5.86	6.05	6.23	6.45	6.62	6.84	7.06	7.28

	1987	1988	1989	1990	1991	1992	1993	1994	1995	1996	1997	1998	1999	2000	2001	Ref
Prices, Production, Labor																
Period Averages																
Consumer Prices	14.1	18.8	21.2	23.7	†26.7	33.0	40.5	54.5	100.0	137.6	150.2	194.9	282.4	365.6	....	64
Industrial Production	†81.0	85.6	93.1	105.8	111.3	110.0	103.0	99.1	100.0	103.6	102.7	106.3	90.2	89.6	....	66
Period Averages																
Employment	412	427	435	468	559	546	583	563	701	....	....	....	....	....	....	67e
International Transactions																
Millions of Kwacha																
Exports	615	752	743	1,124	1,326	1,489	1,411	2,954	6,193	7,359	8,827	16,533	19,425	22,111	....	70
Imports, c.i.f.	654	1,080	1,399	1,572	1,976	2,654	2,405	4,214	7,255	9,545	12,848	17,998	30,758	33,389	....	71
Imports, f.o.b.	392	648	839	943	1,185	1,592	1,440	2,793	4,353	5,727	7,709	10,799	18,455	28,389	....	71.v
1985=100																
Volume of Exports	109.9	109.3	86.8	....	....	....	....	....	....	....	....	....	....	....	....	72
Volume of Imports	96.7	76.4	109.1	....	....	....	....	....	....	....	....	....	....	....	....	73
Export Prices	146.5	176.1	206.3	....	....	....	....	....	....	....	....	....	....	....	....	74
Unit Value of Imports	174.3	216.5	248.5	....	....	....	....	....	....	....	....	....	....	....	....	75
Balance of Payments																
Minus Sign Indicates Debit																
Current Account, n.i.e.	-60.8	-87.0	-51.2	-86.2	-227.7	-284.9	-165.6	-449.6	....	....	....	....	....	....	....	78al d
Goods: Exports f.o.b.	277.6	293.5	268.8	406.4	475.5	399.9	317.5	362.6	....	....	....	....	....	....	....	78aa d
Goods: Imports f.o.b.	-177.6	-253.0	-204.8	-280.3	-415.8	-415.0	-340.2	-639.0	....	....	....	....	....	....	....	78ab d
Trade Balance	100.0	40.4	64.0	126.1	59.7	-15.0	-22.8	-276.4	....	....	....	....	....	....	....	78ac d
Services: Credit	28.4	38.5	30.5	36.6	38.5	28.5	30.0	22.2	....	....	....	....	....	....	....	78ad d
Services: Debit	-143.6	-197.9	-231.3	-268.4	-356.5	-338.8	-260.1	-233.7	....	....	....	....	....	....	....	78ae d
Balance on Goods & Services	-15.3	-119.0	-136.8	-105.6	-258.3	-325.4	-252.9	-488.0	....	....	....	....	....	....	....	78af d
Income: Credit	3.3	9.6	10.5	9.3	7.4	6.3	2.2	1.9	....	....	....	....	....	....	....	78ag d
Income: Debit	-92.7	-108.3	-99.2	-88.9	-92.9	-83.4	-70.9	-87.8	....	....	....	....	....	....	....	78ah d
Balance on Gds, Serv. & Inc.	-104.7	-217.7	-225.4	-185.2	-343.8	-402.5	-321.6	-573.9	....	....	....	....	....	....	....	78ai d
Current Transfers, n.i.e.: Credit	70.8	169.2	208.0	134.1	159.0	155.2	167.9	139.7	....	....	....	....	....	....	....	78aj d
Current Transfers: Debit	-26.9	-38.6	-33.9	-35.1	-42.9	-37.7	-11.9	-15.4	....	....	....	....	....	....	....	78ak d
Capital Account, n.i.e.	—	—	—	—	—	—	—	—	....	....	....	....	....	....	....	78bc d
Capital Account, n.i.e.: Credit	—	—	—	—	—	—	—	—	....	....	....	....	....	....	....	78ba d
Capital Account: Debit	—	—	—	—	—	—	—	—	....	....	....	....	....	....	....	78bb d
Financial Account, n.i.e.	59.5	68.9	92.0	128.6	104.3	93.6	188.9	122.0	....	....	....	....	....	....	....	78bj d
Direct Investment Abroad									....	....	....	....	....	....	....	78bd d
Dir. Invest. in Rep. Econ., n.i.e.	.1	—	—	—	—	—	—	—	....	....	....	....	....	....	....	78be d
Portfolio Investment Assets	—	—	—	—	—	—	—	—	....	....	....	....	....	....	....	78bf d
Equity Securities	—	—	—	—					....	....	....	....	....	....	....	78bk d
Debt Securities	—	—	—	—					....	....	....	....	....	....	....	78bl d
Portfolio Investment Liab., n.i.e.	4.2	.8	2.6	.8	—	—	—	—	....	....	....	....	....	....	....	78bg d
Equity Securities	4.2	.8	2.6	.8	—	—	—	—	....	....	....	....	....	....	....	78bm d
Debt Securities					—	—			....	....	....	....	....	....	....	78bn d
Financial Derivatives Assets	....	....	....	....				....	....	....	....	....	....	....	....	78bw d
Financial Derivatives Liabilities									....	....	....	....	....	....	....	78bx d
Other Investment Assets	6.6	6.7	42.8	33.9	-5.8	11.9	-11.8	—	....	....	....	....	....	....	....	78bh d
Monetary Authorities	....	....	....	....					....	....	....	....	....	....	....	78bo d
General Government	—	—					—	—	....	....	....	....	....	....	....	78bp d
Banks	6.6	6.7	42.8	33.9	-5.8	11.9	-11.8	—	....	....	....	....	....	....	....	78bq d
Other Sectors									....	....	....	....	....	....	....	78br d
Other Investment Liab., n.i.e.	48.6	61.4	46.7	93.9	110.0	81.7	200.6	122.0	....	....	....	....	....	....	....	78bi d
Monetary Authorities									....	....	....	....	....	....	....	78bs d
General Government	43.6	44.8	38.7	68.9	62.7	41.4	150.9	98.5	....	....	....	....	....	....	....	78bt d
Banks									....	....	....	....	....	....	....	78bu d
Other Sectors	5.0	16.6	8.0	25.0	47.3	40.3	49.7	23.5	....	....	....	....	....	....	....	78bv d
Net Errors and Omissions	46.8	78.3	-92.5	-13.7	139.2	144.8	.7	292.6	....	....	....	....	....	....	....	78ca d
Overall Balance	45.4	60.2	-51.7	28.7	15.7	-46.5	24.0	-35.0	....	....	....	....	....	....	....	78cb d
Reserves and Related Items	-45.4	-60.2	51.7	-28.7	-15.7	46.5	-24.0	35.0	....	....	....	....	....	....	....	79da d
Reserve Assets	-33.6	-102.1	36.7	-34.3	-15.8	65.7	-18.1	14.2	....	....	....	....	....	....	....	79db d
Use of Fund Credit and Loans	-34.6	-5.4	-2.6	5.6	.1	-19.2	-5.9	20.8	....	....	....	....	....	....	....	79dc d
Exceptional Financing	22.8	47.4	17.7	—	—	—	—	—	....	....	....	....	....	....	....	79de d
Government Finance																
Year Beginning April 1																
Deficit (-) or Surplus	-226.1	-204.7	-118.7	-81.4	....	....	....	....	....	....	....	....	....	....	....	80
Revenue	542.8	722.9	945.5	1,018.5	....	....	....	....	....	....	....	....	....	....	....	81
Grants Received	83.7	82.3	91.5	204.3	....	....	....	....	....	....	....	....	....	....	....	81z
Exp. & Lending Minus Repay.	852.5	1,010.0	1,155.7	1,304.1	....	....	....	....	....	....	....	....	....	....	....	82z
Expenditure	841.5	1,006.5	1,159.4	1,306.1	....	....	....	....	....	....	....	....	....	....	....	82
Lending Minus Repayments	11.1	3.5	-3.8	-2.0	....	....	....	....	....	....	....	....	....	....	....	83
Financing																
Net Borrowing: Domestic	81.6	....	....													84a
Net Borrowing: Foreign	184.1	....	....													85a
Use of Cash Balances	-39.6	....	....													87
Debt: Domestic	741.5	....	....													88a
Debt: Foreign	2,266.6	....	....													89a
National Accounts																
Millions of Kwacha																
Housh.Cons.Expend.,incl.NPISHs	1,774.3	2,548.0	3,284.4	3,821.7	4,822.6	5,340.4	7,677.6	7,715.8	18,380.8	34,395.9	36,873.9	46,301.9	69,784.2	80,064.2	....	96f
Government Consumption Expend.	499.2	555.3	716.8	772.9	852.4	1,240.9	1,423.5	3,257.9	4,068.7	4,635.8	5,241.8	6,399.2	9,676.3	12,933.2	....	91f
Gross Fixed Capital Formation	352.9	524.0	699.6	820.0	1,030.0	1,077.0	1,098.0	2,764.3	3,164.7	3,404.5	4,079.7	6,035.8	9,870.5	13,563.4	....	93e
Changes in Inventories	49.2	116.5	189.0	150.0	200.0	180.0	200.0	240.0	550.0	900.0	1,000.0	1,288.6	1,600.0	1,290.0	....	93i
Exports of Goods and Services	665.1	824.3	824.1	1,220.6	1,437.2	1,504.3	1,470.7	3,033.2	7,093.9	8,321.5	9,658.2	18,022.1	21,569.2	26,276.6	....	90c
Imports of Goods and Services (-)	726.7	1,150.2	1,150.2	1,715.3	2,165.0	2,858.4	2,900.9	6,784.8	11,318.1	15,203.7	14,543.3	20,728.6	33,878.4	36,968.4	....	98c
Gross Domestic Product (GDP)	2,614.0	3,417.9	4,199.2	5,069.9	6,177.2	6,484.2	8,968.9	10,227.4	21,940.0	36,454.0	42,310.4	57,319.0	78,621.9	97,159.0	....	99b
Net Primary Income from Abroad	-125.7	-137.9	-137.6	-118.2	-130.4	-140.5	-184.0	-375.3	-725.1	-596.7	-589.7	-1,230.4	-1,185.5	-1,437.0	....	98.n
Gross National Income (GNI)	2,488.3	3,280.0	4,061.6	4,951.7	6,046.8	6,343.7	8,784.9	9,852.1	21,214.9	35,857.3	41,720.7	56,088.6	77,436.4	95,722.0	....	99a
GDP Volume 1978 Prices	868.7	898.3	934.6	979.4	1,055.7	972.1	1,077.1	952.1	....	....	....	....	....	....	....	99b. p
GDP Volume 1994 Prices								9,148.8	10,410.5	11,497.9	12,302.5	12,567.9	13,022.6	13,316.2	....	99b. p
GDP Volume (1995=100)	80.2	82.9	86.3	90.4	97.4	89.7	99.4	87.9	100.0	110.4	118.2	120.7	125.1	127.9	....	99bv p
GDP Deflator (1995=100)	14.9	18.8	22.2	25.6	28.9	32.9	41.1	53.0	100.0	150.4	163.2	216.4	286.5	346.2	....	99bi p
Midyear Estimates																
Population	7.50	7.75	8.02	8.29	8.56	8.82	9.13	9.46	9.79	10.14	10.44	10.74	11.03	11.31	11.40	99z

(See notes in the back of the book.)

Malaysia

		1972	1973	1974	1975	1976	1977	1978	1979	1980	1981	1982	1983	1984	1985	1986
Exchange Rates																*Ringgit per SDR:*
Official Rate	aa	3.0584	2.9580	2.8317	3.0300	2.9452	2.8734	2.8740	2.8836	2.8345	2.6099	2.5606	2.4481	2.3770	2.6653	3.1840
																Ringgit per US Dollar:
Official Rate	ae	2.8170	2.4520	2.3128	2.5883	2.5350	2.3655	2.2060	2.1890	2.2224	2.2423	2.3213	2.3383	2.4250	2.4265	2.6030
Official Rate	rf	2.8196	2.4433	2.4071	2.3938	2.5416	2.4613	2.3160	2.1884	2.1769	2.3041	2.3354	2.3213	2.3436	2.4830	2.5814
																Index Numbers (1995=100):
Official Rate	ahx	89.4	103.0	104.2	105.1	98.7	101.9	108.4	114.6	115.3	109.0	107.4	108.1	107.0	101.0	97.2
Nominal Effective Exchange Rate	ne c	....	....	....	....	....	....	....	106.4	107.5	107.5	114.3	120.1	125.0	122.0	103.2
Real Effective Exchange Rate	re c	....	....	....	....	....	....	....	136.5	131.5	132.0	140.4	147.0	152.7	145.1	121.8
Fund Position																*Millions of SDRs:*
Quota	2f. s	186	186	186	186	186	186	253	253	380	380	380	551	551	551	551
SDRs	1b. s	63	61	62	62	65	27	39	87	98	126	118	103	99	105	111
Reserve Position in the Fund	1c. s	39	47	50	54	54	52	54	67	116	117	117	159	159	159	159
of which: Outstg.Fund Borrowing	2c	—	—	—	—	—	—	—	—	—	—	—	—	—	—	—
Total Fund Cred.&Loans Outstg.	2tl	7	—	—	—	93	—	—	—	—	190	248	315	263	107	—
International Liquidity												*Millions of US Dollars Unless Otherwise Indicated:*				
Total Reserves minus Gold	1l. d	907	1,275	1,547	1,456	2,404	2,784	3,243	3,915	4,387	4,098	3,768	3,784	3,723	4,912	6,027
SDRs	1b. d	69	73	75	72	76	32	50	115	125	146	130	108	97	116	135
Reserve Position in the Fund	1c. d	43	56	61	63	62	64	70	89	149	136	129	167	156	175	195
Foreign Exchange	1d. d	796	1,146	1,411	1,321	2,266	2,688	3,123	3,711	4,114	3,816	3,509	3,509	3,470	4,621	5,697
Gold (Million Fine Troy Ounces)	1ad	1.660	1.660	1.660	1.660	1.660	1.740	1.890	2.130	2.320	2.330	2.330	2.330	2.330	2.340	2.340
Gold (National Valuation)	1and	63	70	71	68	68	74	86	98	104	95	90	85	80	90	100
Monetary Authorities: Other Liab.	4..d	1.5	4.6	2.5	4.8	9.1	13.3	18.3	9.3	1.6	4.9	3.1	5.5	11.0	7.5	12.9
Deposit Money Banks: Assets	7a. d	164.0	235.3	250.5	258.4	444.0	436.1	459.8	774.4	872.8	893.3	1,240.5	2,312.0	1,081.0	1,247.0	1,487.0
Liabilities	7b. d	153.6	325.5	377.9	330.3	543.5	625.9	770.7	825.7	1,302.9	1,606.0	1,690.4	2,965.0	2,470.0	2,633.0	2,371.0
Other Banking Insts.: Assets	7e. d	6.0	2.0	15.2	13.6	13.8	8.1	8.7	9.5	1.0	1.1	1.0	.7	.1	.1	.7
Liabilities	7f. d	.4	—	11.5	4.5	39.8	33.1	28.6	43.6	39.5	11.0	26.2	57.3	56.5	48.4	37.7
Monetary Authorities																*Millions of Ringgit:*
Foreign Assets	11	2,735	3,319	3,763	3,943	6,272	6,772	7,404	9,247	10,316	9,805	9,338	9,456	9,655	12,479	16,358
Claims on Central Government	12a	171	277	253	445	325	422	386	742	1,681	708	2,001	3,525	4,809	2,468	2,058
Claims on Private Sector	12d	....	....	....	....	....	....	....	....	....	....	....	....	....	....	....
Claims on Deposit Money Banks	12e	....	....	....	....	....	....	....	....	....	....	....	....	....	....	....
Claims on Nonbank Financial Insts	12g	....	....	....	....	....	....	....	....	....	....	....	....	....	....	....
Reserve Money	14	1,903	2,582	2,931	3,004	3,567	4,126	4,755	5,498	6,493	7,164	8,360	8,718	9,038	9,729	10,134
of which: Currency Outside DMBs	14a	1,269	1,718	2,030	2,239	2,628	3,112	3,578	4,094	4,758	5,100	5,727	6,025	5,974	6,773	7,146
Time and Savings Deposits	15	98	107	123	111	130	154	116	86	1,130	16	5	6	2	2	1
Liabs. of Central Bank: Securities	16ac	....	....	....	....	....	....	....	....	....	....	....	....	....	....	....
Foreign Liabilities	16c	26	12	6	13	297	33	40	20	4	506	643	784	652	304	34
Central Government Deposits	16d	649	647	529	792	1,924	2,064	1,703	3,386	2,426	1,494	1,962	2,580	2,892	989	601
Capital Accounts	17a	312	339	373	415	481	477	661	738	1,119	1,333	1,326	1,616	1,741	1,935	2,177
Other Items (Net)	17r	−82	−90	55	54	198	341	513	262	826	1	−957	−723	140	1,988	5,470
Deposit Money Banks																*Millions of Ringgit:*
Reserves	20	575	750	858	731	869	938	1,049	1,246	1,587	1,834	2,323	2,451	2,816	2,552	2,440
Claims on Mon.Author.: Securities	20c	....	....	....	....	....	....	....	....	....	....	....	....	....	....	....
Foreign Assets	21	462	597	579	669	1,126	1,032	1,014	1,695	1,940	2,003	2,880	5,390	2,451	2,995	3,821
Claims on Central Government	22a	1,186	1,375	1,746	2,148	3,036	3,583	3,379	3,843	3,972	5,552	6,301	7,588	8,333	7,823	7,644
Claims on State & Local Govts	22b	....	....	....	....	....	....	....	....	....	....	....	....	....	....	....
Claims on Nonfin.Pub.Enterprises	22c	....	....	....	....	....	....	....	....	....	....	....	....	....	....	....
Claims on Private Sector	22d	3,014	4,586	5,278	6,084	7,471	8,970	11,627	14,641	20,353	24,976	29,197	35,403	41,976	47,849	51,275
Claims on Other Banking Insts	22f	....	....	....	....	....	....	....	....	1,473	2,452	2,912	3,016	3,755	3,941	4,137
Claims on Nonbank Financial Insts	22g	....	....	....	....	....	....	....	....	....	....	....	....	....	....	....
Demand Deposits	24	1,393	1,928	1,982	2,083	2,572	2,953	3,548	4,251	4,875	5,714	6,479	7,216	7,210	7,088	7,003
Time, Savings,& Fgn.Currency Dep.	25	2,957	3,731	4,551	5,541	7,384	8,580	10,162	13,166	16,549	21,309	25,136	27,725	32,500	34,786	39,779
Money Market Instruments	26aa	....	....	....	....	....	....	....	....	....	....	....	....	....	....	....
Bonds	26ab	....	....	....	....	....	....	....	....	....	....	....	....	....	....	....
Foreign Liabilities	26c	433	826	874	855	1,378	1,481	1,700	1,808	2,896	3,601	3,924	6,924	5,968	6,358	6,157
Central Government Deposits	26d	271	440	512	495	574	729	1,045	1,899	2,678	2,475	2,358	5,100	6,104	7,934	6,300
Credit from Central Bank	26g	....	....	....	....	....	....	....	....	....	....	....	....	....	....	....
Liabilities to Other Banking Insts	26i	....	....	....	....	....	....	....	....	....	....	....	....	....	....	....
Capital Accounts	27a	209	252	255	337	375	556	613	714	965	1,595	1,997	2,995	3,588	4,143	4,431
Other Items (Net)	27r	−26	132	287	320	219	225	2	−411	†1,361	2,123	3,719	3,887	3,960	4,851	5,648
Monetary Survey																*Millions of Ringgit:*
Foreign Assets (Net)	31n	2,738	3,078	3,462	3,745	5,723	6,290	6,678	9,114	9,357	7,701	7,651	7,138	5,486	8,812	13,989
Domestic Credit	32	3,451	5,152	6,237	7,390	8,333	10,183	12,644	13,942	†22,375	29,719	36,090	41,851	49,877	53,158	58,213
Claims on Central Govt. (Net)	32an	437	566	959	1,306	862	1,213	1,017	−699	549	2,291	3,982	3,433	4,146	1,368	2,801
Claims on State & Local Govts	32b	—	—	—	—	—	—	—	—	—	—	—	—	—	—	—
Claims on Nonfin.Pub.Enterprises	32c	....	....	....	....	....	....	....	....	....	....	....	....	....	....	....
Claims on Private Sector	32d	3,014	4,586	5,278	6,084	7,471	8,970	11,627	14,641	20,353	24,976	29,197	35,403	41,976	47,849	51,275
Claims on Other Banking Insts	32f	....	....	....	....	....	....	....	....	1,473	2,452	2,912	3,016	3,755	3,941	4,137
Claims on Nonbank Financial Inst	32g	....	....	....	....	....	....	....	....	....	....	....	....	....	....	....
Money	34	2,715	3,735	4,055	4,349	5,257	6,127	7,243	8,486	9,757	11,015	12,477	13,432	13,357	14,132	14,523
Quasi-Money	35	3,055	3,838	4,674	5,652	7,514	8,734	10,278	13,252	17,680	21,325	25,141	27,731	32,502	34,788	39,779
Money Market Instruments	36aa	....	....	....	....	....	....	....	....	....	....	....	....	....	....	....
Bonds	36ab	....	....	....	....	....	....	....	....	....	....	....	....	....	....	....
Liabs. of Central Bank: Securities	36ac	....	....	....	....	....	....	....	....	....	....	....	....	....	....	....
Liabilities to Other Banking Insts	36i	....	....	....	....	....	....	....	....	....	....	....	....	....	....	....
Capital Accounts	37a	520	591	627	752	856	1,033	1,274	1,451	2,084	2,927	3,323	4,611	5,329	6,078	6,609
Other Items (Net)	37r	−102	66	342	381	430	579	526	−133	†2,211	2,153	2,800	3,215	4,175	6,972	11,291
Money plus Quasi-Money	35l	5,771	7,573	8,729	10,001	12,771	14,861	17,521	21,738	27,436	32,339	37,618	41,163	45,858	48,920	54,302

1987	1988	1989	1990	1991	1992	1993	1994	1995	1996	1997	1998	1999	2000	2001		
															Exchange Rates	
End of Period																
3.5364	3.6540	3.5526	3.8433	3.8965	3.5915	3.7107	3.7372	3.7787	3.6366	5.2511	5.3505	5.2155	4.9511	4.7756	Official Rate	aa
End of Period (ae) Period Average (rf)																
2.4928	2.7153	2.7033	2.7015	2.7240	2.6120	2.7015	2.5600	2.5420	2.5290	3.8919	3.8000	3.8000	3.8000	3.8000	Official Rate	ae
2.5196	2.6188	2.7088	2.7049	2.7501	2.5474	2.5741	2.6243	2.5044	2.5159	2.8132	3.9244	3.8000	3.8000	3.8000	Official Rate	rf
Period Averages																
99.5	95.8	92.6	92.7	91.2	98.5	97.4	95.6	100.0	99.7	91.0	64.1	66.0	66.0	66.0	Official Rate	ahx
99.3	91.9	91.5	90.7	89.9	97.1	100.8	100.0	100.0	103.1	100.3	77.1	78.0	80.0	84.7	Nominal Effective Exchange Rate	nec
115.5	105.5	103.6	98.5	95.9	102.5	103.6	99.7	100.0	104.4	103.3	82.1	84.5	86.6	91.4	Real Effective Exchange Rate	rec
															Fund Position	
End of Period																
551	551	551	551	551	833	833	833	833	833	833	833	1,487	1,487	1,487	Quota	2f.s
115	120	127	136	145	82	88	93	102	115	130	146	61	81	100	SDRs	1b.s
153	172	170	164	180	240	229	274	456	478	445	445	608	608	608	Reserve Position in the Fund	1c.s
—	—	—	—	—	—	—	—	—	—	—	—	—	—	—	of which: Outstg.Fund Borrowing	2c
—	—	—	—	—	—	—	—	—	—	—	—	—	—	—	Total Fund Cred.&Loans Outstg.	2tl
															International Liquidity	
End of Period																
7,435	6,527	7,783	9,754	10,886	17,228	27,249	25,423	23,774	27,009	20,788	25,559	30,588	29,523	30,474	Total Reserves minus Gold	1l.d
163	161	167	194	207	113	121	135	151	166	175	205	83	105	125	SDRs	1b.d
217	231	223	233	257	330	315	400	678	688	600	626	835	792	764	Reserve Position in the Fund	1c.d
7,055	6,134	7,393	9,327	10,421	16,784	26,814	24,888	22,945	26,156	20,013	24,728	29,670	28,625	29,585	Foreign Exchange	1d.d
2.350	2.350	2.370	2.350	2.350	2.390	2.390	2.390	2.390	2.390	2.350	2.350	1.180	1.170	1.170	Gold (Million Fine Troy Ounces)	1ad
117	111	109	117	118	115	115	122	124	120	111	116	57	53	51	Gold (National Valuation)	1an d
33.5	3.8	8.7	7.3	5.6	8.5	14.5	11.7	10.5	6.3	.7	.8	.5	1.3	.7	Monetary Authorities: Other Liab.	4..d
2,009.0	2,802.0	2,938.0	2,804.0	2,366.0	2,008.6	3,893.0	4,168.0	4,178.0	4,357.3	6,003.2	5,517.3	6,519.0	7,470.4	7,161.2	Deposit Money Banks: Assets	7a.d
1,999.0	1,874.0	2,783.0	3,500.0	4,957.0	7,153.1	13,956.0	8,161.0	8,242.0	11,240.9	12,339.4	9,160.5	7,296.3	6,772.2	6,079.6	Liabilities	7b.d
.8	.7	.7	....	.7	49.5	50.8	65.4	82.1	147.0	274.6	266.9	245.4	382.6	278.6	Other Banking Insts.: Assets	7e.d
10.1	30.1	....	....				11.9	24.3	346.0	445.7	348.6	244.6	201.0	134.3	Liabilities	7f.d
															Monetary Authorities	
End of Period																
19,516	18,340	21,673	27,040	30,463	47,233	76,485	68,200	63,790	†70,737	60,369	99,427	117,255	113,247	116,922	Foreign Assets	11
1,961	2,164	1,529	2,681	1,611	†561	454	980	2,155	†7,113	7,153	3,926	2,377	1,838	1,422	Claims on Central Government	12a
....	....	....	....	....	410	1,296	601	566	†8,270	9,843	16,018	22,517	29,476	27,403	Claims on Private Sector	12d
....	....	....	....	....	3,860	3,597	3,443	3,250	†3,676	27,451	2,512	2,135	1,616	1,093	Claims on Deposit Money Banks	12e
....	....	....	....	....	698	1,104	2,718	3,505	†634	508	2,114	2,282	2,157	2,219	Claims on Nonbank Financial Insts	12g
10,664	11,894	14,783	18,145	20,771	†40,732	28,253	38,482	47,970	†70,596	89,926	55,192	91,827	84,881	78,710	Reserve Money	14
7,965	9,031	9,904	11,224	12,070	†12,124	13,506	15,884	17,433	†18,979	21,360	18,162	24,757	22,263	22,148	of which: Currency Outside DMBs	14a
8	1	1	1	1	†5	25	16	5	†5,790	2,320	9,079	2,043	9,171	10,637	Time and Savings Deposits	15
									†4,968	909	4	379	7,085	7,477	Liabs. of Central Bank: Securities	16ac
84	10	23	20	15	22	39	30	27	†16	3	3	2	5	3	Foreign Liabilities	16c
1,053	1,112	1,068	5,233	5,989	†5,679	2,912	8,469	8,379	†11,401	10,545	25,281	18,514	17,845	25,237	Central Government Deposits	16d
3,248	3,416	3,578	3,892	4,100	4,155	4,172	3,507	3,513	†3,633	4,085	4,099	31,413	27,384	24,092	Capital Accounts	17a
6,421	4,070	3,748	2,430	1,198	†2,168	47,535	25,438	13,374	†−5,974	−2,466	30,339	2,389	1,962	2,903	Other Items (Net)	17r
															Deposit Money Banks	
End of Period																
2,472	2,598	4,204	6,205	7,807	†23,850	51,493	35,670	32,421	†32,911	45,197	30,814	58,148	53,269	43,115	Reserves	20
								—	†3,096	—	—	9	4,822	5,112	Claims on Mon.Author.: Securities	20c
4,863	7,267	6,841	6,672	5,500	†5,247	10,482	10,542	10,320	†11,020	23,364	20,966	24,772	28,387	27,212	Foreign Assets	21
10,544	10,384	11,811	11,851	12,376	†11,324	10,683	11,127	10,182	†10,270	12,605	17,719	15,292	19,108	21,101	Claims on Central Government	22a
....	....	....	....	....	....	—	—	—	†556	744	721	552	639	786	Claims on State & Local Govts	22b
....	....	....	....	....	....	—	—	—	†864	4,008	4,416	4,839	4,951	2,638	Claims on Nonfin.Pub.Enterprises	22c
51,308	55,763	68,219	82,657	99,668	†110,418	122,344	141,965	185,472	†234,484	289,853	298,162	303,657	322,206	336,691	Claims on Private Sector	22d
4,228	4,047	3,459	3,563	5,242	†8,252	8,770	14,463	18,631	†29,358	43,220	25,383	12,887	15,393	18,330	Claims on Other Banking Insts	22f
....	....	....	....	....	....	—	—	—	8,921	16,051	23,672	21,227	22,519	22,490	Claims on Nonbank Financial Insts	22g
8,342	9,627	11,979	14,106	15,758	†18,931	29,128	31,724	36,191	†40,406	41,970	36,032	46,841	54,520	57,787	Demand Deposits	24
39,970	41,404	47,314	51,255	61,670	†73,682	90,184	99,776	124,935	†154,338	189,878	203,465	239,207	258,524	262,406	Time, Savings,& Fgn.Currency Dep.	25
....	....	....	....	....	21,741	23,196	35,731	48,266	†39,026	50,121	50,465	28,565	30,487	32,760	Money Market Instruments	26aa
....	....	....	....	....	....	....	....	....	561	1,878	1,267	1,704	1,594	2,083	Bonds	26ab
4,981	5,084	6,317	8,129	11,755	†18,684	31,488	17,000	15,873	†28,428	48,024	34,810	27,726	25,734	23,102	Foreign Liabilities	26c
6,491	7,552	7,576	5,415	6,137	†1,495	1,903	2,795	4,149	†5,887	7,182	10,069	12,238	11,819	10,829	Central Government Deposits	26d
....	....	....	....	....	2,304	2,171	1,781	1,772	†1,710	18,055	12	4	82	55	Credit from Central Bank	26g
....	....	....	....	....	435	742	2,116	2,813	†6,723	15,148	8,474	9,386	8,218	7,167	Liabilities to Other Banking Insts	26i
5,344	5,713	6,163	6,916	7,670	†14,843	16,884	23,813	29,478	†35,933	52,930	63,061	64,329	65,172	70,312	Capital Accounts	27a
8,288	10,679	15,186	25,127	27,602	†6,976	8,076	−970	−6,452	†18,467	9,856	14,198	11,384	15,144	10,975	Other Items (Net)	27r
															Monetary Survey	
End of Period																
19,315	20,513	22,174	25,563	24,192	†33,773	55,440	61,712	58,210	†53,313	35,706	85,579	114,299	115,895	121,029	Foreign Assets (Net)	31n
60,497	63,694	76,375	90,103	106,771	†124,488	139,837	160,591	207,985	†283,180	366,257	356,783	354,878	388,623	397,015	Domestic Credit	32
4,961	3,884	4,696	3,883	1,861	†4,710	6,323	844	−190	†93	2,031	−13,705	−13,083	−8,719	−13,543	Claims on Central Govt. (Net)	32an
—	—	—	—	†—	—	—	—	—	†556	744	721	552	639	786	Claims on State & Local Govts	32b
....	....	....	....	....	....	—	—	—	†864	4,008	4,416	4,839	4,951	2,638	Claims on Nonfin.Pub.Enterprises	32c
51,308	55,763	68,219	82,657	99,668	†110,828	123,640	142,566	186,038	†242,754	299,695	314,181	326,174	351,682	364,094	Claims on Private Sector	32d
4,228	4,047	3,459	3,563	5,242	†8,252	8,770	14,463	18,631	†29,358	43,220	25,383	12,887	15,393	18,330	Claims on Other Banking Insts	32f
....	....	....	....	....	698	1,104	2,718	3,505	†9,555	16,559	25,786	23,509	24,676	24,710	Claims on Nonbank Financial Inst	32g
16,375	18,730	21,978	25,405	27,928	†35,544	48,077	56,175	63,594	†74,182	82,840	58,522	75,602	80,656	83,879	Money	34
39,977	41,405	47,315	51,256	61,671	†73,687	90,209	99,791	124,940	†160,127	192,198	212,544	241,249	267,695	273,043	Quasi-Money	35
....	....	....	....	....	21,741	23,196	35,731	48,266	†39,026	50,121	50,465	28,565	30,487	32,760	Money Market Instruments	36aa
....	....	....	....	....	....	....	....	....	561	1,878	1,267	1,704	1,594	2,083	Bonds	36ab
....	....	....	....	....	....	....	....	....	†1,872	909	4	370	2,263	2,365	Liabs. of Central Bank: Securities	36ac
....	....	....	....	....	435	742	2,116	2,813	†6,723	15,148	8,474	9,386	8,218	7,167	Liabilities to Other Banking Insts	36i
8,592	9,129	9,742	10,808	11,770	†18,998	21,056	27,321	32,991	†39,565	57,016	67,160	95,741	92,556	94,405	Capital Accounts	37a
14,868	14,942	19,514	28,197	29,594	†7,856	11,996	1,168	−6,409	†14,436	1,854	43,925	16,559	21,049	22,342	Other Items (Net)	37r
56,352	60,136	69,294	76,661	89,599	†109,231	138,286	155,966	188,533	†234,309	275,038	271,066	316,852	348,351	356,922	Money plus Quasi-Money	35l

Malaysia

		1972	1973	1974	1975	1976	1977	1978	1979	1980	1981	1982	1983	1984	1985	1986
Other Banking Institutions																*Millions of Ringgit*
Reserves	40	228	368	†671	674	802	943	1,183	1,209	1,678	2,150	2,746	3,111	4,053	4,080	4,335
Claims on Mon.Author.: Securities	40c	....	....	....												
Foreign Assets	41	17	5	†35	35	35	19	19	21	2	3	2	2	....		2
Claims on Central Government	42a	416	512	†4,086	4,651	5,410	6,398	7,430	8,747	9,881	11,507	13,677	15,831	18,654	22,204	25,793
Claims on State & Local Govts	42b	....	....													
Claims on Nonfin.Pub.Enterprises	42c	....	....													
Claims on Private Sector	42d	433	617	†1,176	1,579	2,073	2,615	3,222	4,614	6,253	8,302	....	13,856	17,599	20,460	21,368
Claims on Deposit Money Banks	42e	....	....													
Claims on Nonbank Financial Insts	42g	....	....													
Time, Savings,& Fgn.Currency Dep.	45	1,021	1,401	†4,951	5,905	7,259	8,335	10,232	12,560	15,552	19,183	....	28,683	35,366	40,276	46,475
Money Market Instruments	46aa	....	....													
Bonds	46ab	....	....													
Foreign Liabilities	46c	1	—	27	12	101	78	63	95	88	25	61	134	137	117	98
Central Government Deposits	46d	....	....	—	—	—	—	—	—	—	—	—	—	—	—	13
Credit from Monetary Authorities	46g	....	....	53	95	213	345	263	569	401	1,154	1,523	1,538	2,145	1,799	1,593
Credit from Deposit Money Banks	46h	....	....													
Capital Accounts	47a	75	98	†141	166	198	223	257	344	411	490	642	869	1,111	1,349	1,577
Other Items (Net)	47r	–3	3	†796	763	550	994	1,038	1,023	1,362	1,110	....	1,576	1,548	3,202	1,742
Banking Survey																*Millions of Ringgit:*
Foreign Assets (Net)	51n	2,754	3,083	†3,471	3,768	5,657	6,231	6,633	9,040	9,271	7,679	7,593	7,005	5,350	8,695	13,893
Domestic Credit	52	4,300	6,281	†11,499	13,620	15,817	19,196	23,295	27,303	37,035	47,076	....	68,522	82,374	91,881	101,224
Claims on Central Govt. (Net)	52an	853	1,078	†5,044	5,957	6,273	7,611	8,447	8,048	10,429	13,797	17,658	19,263	22,799	23,572	28,581
Claims on State & Local Govts	52b	—	—	—	—	—	—	—	—	—	—	—	—	—	—	—
Claims on Nonfin.Pub.Enterprises	52c															
Claims on Private Sector	52d	3,447	5,203	†6,454	7,663	9,544	11,585	14,849	19,256	26,606	33,278	....	49,259	59,575	68,309	72,644
Claims on Nonbank Financial Inst	52g															
Liquid Liabilities	55l	6,563	8,606	†13,010	15,232	19,227	22,253	26,570	33,088	41,310	49,372	....	66,735	77,171	85,116	96,442
Money Market Instruments	56aa	....	....													
Bonds	56ab	....	....													
Liabs. of Central Bank: Securities	56ac	....	....													
Capital Accounts	57a	595	689	†768	918	1,054	1,256	1,531	1,795	2,495	3,417	3,964	5,480	6,440	7,427	8,186
Other Items (Net)	57r	–104	69	†1,191	1,238	1,192	1,918	1,827	1,459	†2,501	1,965	....	3,313	4,113	8,032	10,489
Nonbank Financial Institutions																*Millions of Ringgit:*
Claims on Central Government	42a. s	104.6	123.6	136.6	159.5	187.8	222.7	244.8	279.0	327.8	398.2	442.9	421.4	450.9	580.5	541.6
Claims on Private Sector	42d. s	216.9	251.9	273.5	302.7	326.2	361.4	404.1	508.2	601.2	720.9	1,022.5	1,184.2	1,602.0	1,859.7	2,216.9
Real Estate	42h. s	31.0	36.7	40.0	45.0	52.2	56.4	64.8	70.0	76.7	85.5	105.4	124.5	166.8	188.0	206.6
Interest Rates																*Percent Per Annum*
Discount Rate (*End of Period*)	60	3.75	3.78	4.89	4.97	4.38	3.56	4.21	3.47	4.46	4.50	5.12	5.20	5.06	4.13	3.89
Money Market Rate	60b	3.20	2.80	2.70	4.20	2.60	4.83	2.47	4.37	3.31	3.47	7.90	8.97	8.96	6.76	4.19
Treasury Bill Rate	60c	....	....	4.56	4.77	4.75	3.31	4.13	3.36	4.05	4.49	4.96	5.12	5.10	4.74	4.12
Deposit Rate	60l	....	....	....	....	5.50	5.21	5.13	5.50	6.23	9.67	9.75	8.02	9.54	8.81	7.17
Lending Rate	60p					8.50	7.92	7.50	7.50	7.75	8.50	8.79	11.08	11.35	11.54	10.69
Prices, Production, Labor																*Index Numbers (1995=100):*
Producer Prices	63												....	80.9	79.3	74.3
Consumer Prices	64	35.5	39.3	46.1	48.1	49.4	51.8	54.3	56.2	†60.0	65.8	69.7	72.2	75.1	75.3	75.9
Industrial Production	66	12.6	14.4	16.0	16.0	18.5	20.0	22.0	23.9	25.3	†26.1	27.5	31.0	35.9	35.0	38.4
Total Employment	67									60.3	63.1	65.4	67.7	69.4	70.1	71.1
																Number in Thousands:
Employment	67e	....	....	....	....	....	....	....	....	....	....	....	....	....	5,653	5,760
Unemployment	67c	....	....	....	....	....	....	....	....	....	....	....	....	....	....	516
Unemployment Rate (%)	67r	....	....	....	....	....	....	....	....	....	....	....	....	....	....	8.3
International Transactions																*Millions of Ringgit*
Exports	70	4,854	7,372	10,195	9,231	13,442	14,959	17,074	24,222	28,172	27,109	28,108	32,771	38,647	38,017	35,319
Rubber	70l	1,298	2,507	2,887	2,026	3,117	3,380	3,601	4,482	4,618	3,713	2,655	3,664	3,672	2,872	3,183
Palm Oil	70dg	368	467	1,086	1,320	1,155	1,680	1,871	2,471	2,603	2,836	2,742	2,995	4,547	3,963	3,020
Tin	70q	924	897	1,515	1,206	1,527	1,704	2,022	2,316	2,505	2,138	1,484	1,718	1,162	1,648	650
Imports, c.i.f.	71	4,543	5,934	9,891	8,530	9,713	11,165	13,646	17,161	23,451	26,604	29,023	30,795	32,926	30,438	27,921
Volume of Exports																*1995=100*
Rubber	72l	135	162	155	144	160	163	159	163	151	147	136	154	157	148	150
Palm Oil	72dg	11	12	14	18	19	20	23	29	34	38	42	44	45	49	65
Tin	72q	255	235	242	221	232	189	199	205	197	189	138	162	113	163	115
Export Prices																
Rubber (Wholesale Price)	76l	23	42	45	34	50	51	58	70	78	65	50	62	56	47	52
Palm Oil (Unit Value)	74dg	34	38	79	74	60	84	81	85	75	74	63	66	99	80	45
Tin (Unit Value)	76q	67	73	121	103	122	170	186	209	231	209	194	195	188	192	99

1987	1988	1989	1990	1991	1992	1993	1994	1995	1996	1997	1998	1999	2000	2001		
															Other Banking Institutions	
End of Period																
3,637	2,816	....	....	....	†4,436	8,421	10,394	12,259	†14,978	19,713	6,403	9,716	9,209	13,720	Reserves	**40**
									†539				1,503	2,086	Claims on Mon.Author.: Securities	**40c**
2	2	2	....	2	†129	137	167	209	†372	1,069	1,014	933	1,454	1,059	Foreign Assets	**41**
30,846	35,945	....	....	....	†4,209	3,703	3,010	2,997	†4,239	3,003	5,747	6,437	5,830	7,717	Claims on Central Government	**42a**
									†36	55	42	17	9	55	Claims on State & Local Govts	**42b**
									†79	593	828	660	320	375	Claims on Nonfin.Pub.Enterprises	**42c**
21,325	24,102	....	....	....	†52,706	59,678	70,911	90,750	†116,616	146,626	134,775	122,425	129,459	134,896	Claims on Private Sector	**42d**
					5,482	7,020	9,136	9,149	†5,599	10,740	9,681	10,231	8,351	6,176	Claims on Deposit Money Banks	**42e**
									3,820	3,698	3,102	2,024	1,647	1,174	Claims on Nonbank Financial Insts	**42g**
46,648	51,706	....	....	....	†44,801	56,353	61,072	68,712	†85,518	93,802	98,003	101,224	103,873	105,841	Time, Savings,& Fgn.Currency Dep.	**45**
					7,685	7,343	10,883	16,166	†2,625	5,548	5,890	226	—	531	Money Market Instruments	**46aa**
									212	1,022	892	820	787	787	Bonds	**46ab**
25	82	....	....	....	†—	....	31	62	†875	1,735	1,325	929	764	510	Foreign Liabilities	**46c**
37	64	73	....	38	†453	722	707	1,213	†2,365	1,711	2,274	2,167	2,621	3,211	Central Government Deposits	**46d**
									†510	11,788	989	553	—	132	Credit from Monetary Authorities	**46g**
2,753	2,809	1,546	....	1,612	†—	6,085	6,981	13,267	†31,981	43,720	22,470	19,126	15,347	18,510	Credit from Deposit Money Banks	**46h**
1,678	2,087	2,264	....	3,222	†5,934	6,834	8,588	10,746	†14,721	19,572	20,446	20,523	21,638	24,250	Capital Accounts	**47a**
4,668	6,119	....	....	....	†2,006	726	-930	-630	†7,469	6,600	9,303	6,876	12,752	13,485	Other Items (Net)	**47r**
															Banking Survey	
End of Period																
19,291	20,434	....	....	24,194	†33,902	55,577	61,849	58,357	†52,809	35,040	85,269	114,303	116,585	121,578	Foreign Assets (Net)	**51n**
108,403	119,630	....	....	....	†172,698	193,725	219,341	281,887	†376,247	475,302	473,619	471,387	507,873	519,691	Domestic Credit	**52**
35,769	39,765	....	....	....	†8,466	9,304	3,146	1,594	†1,967	3,323	-10,232	-8,812	-5,510	-9,036	Claims on Central Govt. (Net)	**52an**
—	—	....	....	....	†—	—	—	—	†593	799	763	569	649	841	Claims on State & Local Govts	**52b**
									†943	4,602	5,244	5,499	5,271	3,013	Claims on Nonfin.Pub.Enterprises	**52c**
72,633	79,865	....	....	....	†163,534	183,317	213,477	276,788	†359,370	446,321	448,955	448,598	481,141	498,990	Claims on Private Sector	**52d**
					698	1,104	2,718	3,505	†13,375	20,257	28,889	25,533	26,323	25,883	Claims on Nonbank Financial Inst	**52g**
99,363	109,025	....	....	....	†149,596	186,218	206,644	244,986	†304,850	349,127	362,665	408,359	443,015	449,043	Liquid Liabilities	**55l**
					29,426	30,539	46,614	64,432	†41,651	55,669	56,356	28,792	30,487	33,292	Money Market Instruments	**56aa**
									773	2,900	2,159	2,523	2,380	2,870	Bonds	**56ab**
									†1,334	909	4	370	760	279	Liabs. of Central Bank: Securities	**56ac**
10,270	11,216	12,006	....	14,992	†24,932	27,890	35,908	43,737	†54,287	76,587	87,607	116,264	114,194	118,655	Capital Accounts	**57a**
18,061	19,822	....	....	....	†2,647	4,655	-7,976	-12,911	†26,162	25,150	50,097	29,382	33,622	37,130	Other Items (Net)	**57r**
															Nonbank Financial Institutions	
End of Period																
1,293.9	949.9	1,816.3	2,041.5	3,438.1	3,170.2	4,546.6	6,050.1	....	....	....	....	....	....	....	Claims on Central Government	**42a. s**
2,078.4	2,624.8	2,032.2	2,414.2	3,558.6	3,527.9	4,108.5	6,555.5	....	....	....	....	....	....	....	Claims on Private Sector	**42d. s**
253.8	221.8	236.7	279.9	451.0	372.8	382.4	834.7	....	....	....	....	....	....	....	Real Estate	**42h. s**
															Interest Rates	
Percent Per Annum																
3.20	4.12	4.89	7.23	7.70	7.10	5.24	4.51	6.47	7.28						Discount Rate (End of Period)	**60**
3.12	4.11	4.72	6.81	7.83	8.01	6.53	4.65	5.78	†6.98	7.61	8.46	3.38	2.66	2.79	Money Market Rate	**60b**
2.68	3.49	5.29	6.12	7.27	7.66	6.48	3.68	5.50	6.41	6.41	6.86	3.53	2.86	2.79	Treasury Bill Rate	**60c**
3.00	3.19	4.60	5.90	7.18	7.97	7.04	4.94	5.93	†7.09	7.78	8.51	4.12	3.36	3.37	Deposit Rate	**60l**
8.19	7.25	7.00	7.17	8.13	9.31	9.05	7.61	7.63	†8.89	9.53	10.61	7.29	6.77	6.66	Lending Rate	**60p**
															Prices, Production, Labor	
1995=100																
77.1	82.7	85.9	86.6	90.2	91.1	†92.5	96.1	100.0	102.3	....	116.3	....	....	....	Producer Prices	**63**
76.1	78.0	80.2	†82.3	85.9	90.0	93.2	†96.7	100.0	103.5	106.2	111.8	114.9	†116.7	118.3	Consumer Prices	**64**
41.6	†47.5	53.1	59.6	66.3	72.0	78.9	88.4	100.0	†110.4	122.3	113.5	123.7	147.4	141.3	Industrial Production	**66**
73.3	75.9	79.6	83.3	85.9	88.4	92.2	94.9	100.0	104.9	107.2	106.7	....	....	....	Total Employment	**67**
Period Averages																
5,984	6,176	6,391	6,685	....	7,048	7,383	....	7,645	8,400	8,569	8,600	8,838	9,322	....	Employment	**67e**
†473	482	389	315	314	271	317	231	248	217	215	284	314	294	....	Unemployment	**67c**
7.3	7.2	6.3	5.1	4.3	3.7	3.0	2.9	2.8	2.5	2.5	3.2	3.4	3.1	....	Unemployment Rate (%)	**67r**
															International Transactions	
Millions of Ringgit																
45,225	55,260	67,824	79,646	94,497	103,657	121,238	153,921	184,987	197,026	220,890	286,756	320,929	372,913	334,420	Exports	**70**
3,915	5,256	3,949	3,027	2,690	2,357	2,132	2,927	4,038	3,510	2,971	2,829	....	....	....	Rubber	**70l**
3,292	4,540	4,691	4,411	5,045	5,437	5,797	8,365	10,169	9,266	10,810	....	....	....	....	Palm Oil	**70dg**
839	910	1,161	902	684	121	489	507	545	533	479	....	....	....	....	Tin	**70q**
31,934	43,293	60,858	79,119	100,831	101,441	117,405	155,921	194,345	197,280	220,936	228,309	246,870	312,355	280,691	Imports, c.i.f.	**71**
1995=100																
															Volume of Exports	
160	159	147	130	112	102	93	100	100	97	101	98	....	....	....	Rubber	**72l**
62	63	75	86	84	84	89	100	100	110	115	113	....	....	....	Palm Oil	**72dg**
141	139	141	150	121	128	101	105	100	98	90	64	....	....	....	Tin	**72q**
															Export Prices	
62	78	67	57	60	57	57	72	100	90	73	72	....	....	....	Rubber (Wholesale Price)	**76l**
52	71	62	51	59	64	64	83	100	82	93	....	....	....	....	Palm Oil (Unit Value)	**74dg**
109	119	152	111	104	103	89	89	100	100	97	136	....	....	....	Tin (Unit Value)	**76q**

Malaysia

		1972	1973	1974	1975	1976	1977	1978	1979	1980	1981	1982	1983	1984	1985	1986
Balance of Payments														*Millions of US Dollars:*		
Current Account, n.i.e.	78al d	....	....	−538	−491	586	447	127	941	−266	−2,469	−3,585	−3,482	−1,657	−600	−101
Goods: Exports f.o.b.	78aa d	....	....	4,199	3,826	5,293	6,093	7,380	11,074	12,963	11,771	12,070	13,804	16,521	15,251	13,655
Goods: Imports f.o.b.	78ab d	....	....	−3,959	−3,551	−3,812	−4,552	−5,760	−7,914	−10,569	−11,886	−12,801	−13,366	−13,590	−11,677	−10,441
Trade Balance	78ac d	....	....	241	275	1,481	1,541	1,620	3,160	2,393	−115	−731	438	2,931	3,573	3,214
Services: Credit	78ad d	....	....	372	410	398	491	628	790	1,135	1,315	1,579	1,851	1,932	1,934	1,981
Services: Debit	78ae d	....	....	−698	−848	−832	−1,050	−1,359	−2,108	−2,957	−2,856	−3,269	−3,964	−4,254	−3,927	−3,575
Balance on Goods & Services	78af d	....	....	−86	−163	1,047	982	889	1,842	572	−1,655	−2,421	−1,675	609	1,581	1,621
Income: Credit	78ag d	....	....	162	156	175	257	378	555	739	792	650	562	614	591	548
Income: Debit	78ah d	....	....	−576	−456	−602	−771	−1,114	−1,460	−1,575	−1,589	−1,797	−2,375	−2,856	−2,779	−2,329
Balance on Gds, Serv. & Inc.	78ai d	....	....	−500	−463	619	468	152	937	−264	−2,452	−3,569	−3,488	−1,633	−607	−160
Current Transfers, n.i.e.: Credit	78aj d	....	....	47	59	58	70	76	75	73	74	79	77	70	93	149
Current Transfers: Debit	78ak d	....	....	−86	−87	−91	−91	−101	−71	−75	−91	−95	−72	−94	−86	−91
Capital Account, n.i.e.	78bc d	....	....	−5	−5	−6	−11	−19	−12	−19	−17	−15	−15	−15	−13	−21
Capital Account, n.i.e.: Credit	78ba d	....	....	—	—	—	—	—	—	—	—	—	—	—	—	—
Capital Account: Debit	78bb d	....	....	−5	−5	−6	−11	−19	−12	−19	−17	−15	−15	−15	−13	−21
Financial Account, n.i.e.	78bj d	....	....	818	660	516	256	630	192	1,431	2,616	3,743	3,855	3,026	1,929	1,108
Direct Investment Abroad	78bd d	....	....	—	—	—	—	—	—	—	—	—	—	—	—	—
Dir. Invest. in Rep. Econ., n.i.e.	78be d	....	....	571	350	381	406	500	573	934	1,265	1,397	1,261	797	695	489
Portfolio Investment Assets	78bf d	....	....	—	—	—	—	—	—	—	—	—	—	—	—	—
Equity Securities	78bk d	....	....	—	—	—	—	—	—	—	—	—	—	—	—	—
Debt Securities	78bl d	....	....	—	—	—	—	—	—	—	—	—	—	—	—	—
Portfolio Investment Liab., n.i.e.	78bg d	....	....	12	268	52	63	79	194	−11	1,131	601	668	1,108	1,942	30
Equity Securities	78bm d	....	....	—	—	—	—	—	—	—	—	—	—	—	—	—
Debt Securities	78bn d	....	....	12	268	52	63	79	194	−11	1,131	601	668	1,108	1,942	30
Financial Derivatives Assets	78bw d	....	....	....	....	....	....	....	....	....	....	....	....	....	....	....
Financial Derivatives Liabilities	78bx d	....	....	....	....	....	....	....	....	....	....	....	....	....	....	....
Other Investment Assets	78bh d	....	....	130	−82	−282	−449	−166	−777	−101	−276	−136	−1,471	262	155	58
Monetary Authorities	78bo d	....	....	....	....	....	....	....	....	....	....	....	....	....	....	....
General Government	78bp d	....	....	−2	−24	19	−9	−9	−9	−10	−11	−137	−65	−23	−39	−1
Banks	78bq d	....	....	7	−37	−180	38	7	−496	71	−27	−377	−1,085	831	−222	−329
Other Sectors	78br d	....	....	125	−21	−121	−479	−165	−272	−161	−237	378	−321	−546	416	389
Other Investment Liab., n.i.e.	78bi d	....	....	105	124	365	237	218	202	609	496	1,881	3,398	859	−862	531
Monetary Authorities	78bs d	....	....	−2	3	4	3	3	−9	−4	—	−2	3	6	−4	6
General Government	78bt d	....	....	80	113	96	155	154	116	153	132	1,429	1,229	265	−1,402	594
Banks	78bu d	....	....	20	−8	206	42	95	44	505	306	138	1,292	−408	156	−77
Other Sectors	78bv d	....	....	7	16	59	37	−35	51	−45	58	315	874	996	387	8
Net Errors and Omissions	78ca d	....	....	−79	−96	−293	−381	−455	−329	−682	−582	−406	−371	−863	−168	476
Overall Balance	78cb d	....	....	195	68	803	311	283	792	464	−452	−264	−13	492	1,148	1,461
Reserves and Related Items	79da d	....	....	−195	−68	−803	−311	−283	−792	−464	452	264	13	−492	−1,148	−1,461
Reserve Assets	79db d	....	....	−195	−68	−909	−204	−282	−792	−464	235	199	−60	−438	−987	−1,340
Use of Fund Credit and Loans	79dc d	....	....	—	—	107	−108	—	—	—	217	64	73	−54	−161	−121
Exceptional Financing	79de d	....	....	....	....	....	....	....	....	....	....	....	....	....	....	....
International Investment Position														*Millions of US Dollars*		
Assets	79aa d	....	....	....	....	....	....	....	....	6,302	9,603	8,583	9,019	8,859	9,419	12,528
Direct Investment Abroad	79ab d	....	....	....	....	....	....	....	....	305	475	817	1,168	281	413	535
Portfolio Investment	79ac d	....	....	....	....	....	....	....	....	512	545	714	634	633	425	383
Equity Securities	79ad d	....	....	....	....	....	....	....	....	106	112	457	381	381	340	309
Debt Securities	79ae d	....	....	....	....	....	....	....	....	406	433	257	254	252	85	73
Financial Derivatives	79af d	....	....	....	....	....	....	....	....							
Other Investment	79af d	....	....	....	....	....	....	....	....	1,052	4,445	2,995	3,140	3,599	3,199	5,210
Monetary Authorities	79ag d	....	....	....	....	....	....	....	....	—	—	—	—	—	—	—
General Government	79ah d	....	....	....	....	....	....	....	....	—	—	—	—	—	—	—
Banks	79ai d	....	....	....	....	....	....	....	....	1,047	906	1,254	2,326	1,038	1,283	1,472
Other Sectors	79aj d	....	....	....	....	....	....	....	....	5	3,539	1,741	814	2,561	1,916	3,738
Reserve Assets	79ak d	....	....	....	....	....	....	....	....	4,433	4,139	4,057	4,076	4,345	5,382	6,400
Liabilities	79la d	....	....	....	....	....	....	....	....	10,831	15,300	18,711	22,567	24,203	27,325	28,819
Dir. Invest. in Rep. Economy	79lb d	....	....	....	....	....	....	....	....	5,169	5,369	6,066	6,322	6,510	7,388	6,111
Portfolio Investment	79lc d	....	....	....	....	....	....	....	....	1,572	2,955	4,911	6,551	7,553	8,435	9,460
Equity Securities	79ld d	....	....	....	....	....	....	....	....	586	816	1,034	1,304	1,511	1,718	1,657
Debt Securities	79le d	....	....	....	....	....	....	....	....	986	2,139	3,877	5,248	6,042	6,717	7,803
Financial Derivatives	79ll d	....	....	....	....	....	....	....	....							
Other Investment	79lf d	....	....	....	....	....	....	....	....	4,091	6,975	7,734	9,694	10,140	11,502	13,247
Monetary Authorities	79lg d	....	....	....	....	....	....	....	....	—	221	274	330	258	118	—
General Government	79lh d	....	....	....	....	....	....	....	....	1,201	1,552	1,791	2,334	2,555	2,790	3,073
Banks	79li d	....	....	....	....	....	....	....	....	1,521	1,746	2,088	3,299	2,809	3,051	3,079
Other Sectors	79lj d	....	....	....	....	....	....	....	....	1,368	3,456	3,581	3,731	4,518	5,542	7,095

Minus Sign Indicates Debit

	1987	1988	1989	1990	1991	1992	1993	1994	1995	1996	1997	1998	1999	2000	2001
Balance of Payments															
Current Account, n.i.e. .... 78al d	2,575	1,867	315	-870	-4,183	-2,167	-2,991	-4,520	-8,644	-4,462	-5,935	9,529	12,603	8,409	....
Goods: Exports f.o.b. .... 78aa d	17,877	20,980	24,776	28,806	33,712	39,823	46,238	56,897	71,767	76,985	77,538	71,883	84,098	98,429	....
Goods: Imports f.o.b. .... 78ab d	-12,093	-15,553	-20,498	-26,280	-33,321	-36,673	-43,201	-55,320	-71,871	-73,137	-74,029	-54,378	-61,453	-77,576	....
Trade Balance .... 78ac d	5,783	5,427	4,277	2,525	391	3,150	3,037	1,577	-103	3,848	3,510	17,505	22,644	20,854	....
Services: Credit .... 78ad d	2,273	2,379	2,870	3,859	4,374	4,989	6,412	9,320	11,602	15,135	15,727	11,517	11,919	13,775	....
Services: Debit .... 78ae d	-3,595	-4,205	-4,792	-5,485	-6,564	-7,336	-9,516	-12,052	-14,981	-17,573	-18,297	-13,127	-14,736	-16,726	....
Balance on Goods & Services .... 78af d	4,461	3,600	2,356	900	-1,799	804	-68	-1,155	-3,483	1,411	940	15,895	19,828	17,903	....
Income: Credit .... 78ag d	834	1,090	1,172	1,849	1,425	1,609	2,007	2,308	2,623	2,693	2,485	1,542	2,003	2,098	....
Income: Debit .... 78ah d	-2,797	-3,032	-3,351	-3,721	-3,898	-4,752	-5,218	-5,903	-6,767	-7,383	-7,851	-5,446	-7,499	-9,612	....
Balance on Gds, Serv. & Inc. .... 78ai d	2,498	1,659	177	-972	-4,271	-2,339	-3,278	-4,750	-7,626	-3,279	-4,426	11,991	14,332	10,388	....
Current Transfers, n.i.e.: Credit .... 78aj d	173	288	212	249	215	296	469	411	700	766	944	728	801	720	....
Current Transfers: Debit .... 78ak d	-96	-80	-74	-147	-126	-124	-181	-182	-1,717	-1,948	-2,453	-3,190	-2,529	-2,699	....
Capital Account, n.i.e. .... 78bc d	-33	-58	-57	-48	-51	-40	-88	-82	—	—	—	—	....	....	....
Capital Account, n.i.e.: Credit .... 78ba d															
Capital Account: Debit .... 78bb d	-33	-58	-57	-48	-51	-40	-88	-82	—	—	—	—	....	....	....
Financial Account, n.i.e. .... 78bj d	-1,517	-2,001	1,335	1,784	5,621	8,746	10,805	1,288	7,643	9,477	2,198	-2,550	-6,619	-6,276	....
Direct Investment Abroad .... 78bd d													-1,422	-2,026	....
Dir. Invest. in Rep. Econ., n.i.e. .. 78be d	423	719	1,668	2,332	3,998	5,183	5,006	4,342	4,178	5,078	5,137	2,163	3,895	3,788	....
Portfolio Investment Assets .... 78bf d	—	—	—	—	—	—	—	—	—	—	—	—	....	....	....
Equity Securities .... 78bk d															
Debt Securities .... 78bl d															
Portfolio Investment Liab., n.i.e. .... 78bg d	140	-448	-107	-255	170	-1,122	-709	-1,649	-436	-268	-248	283	-1,156	-2,472	....
Equity Securities .... 78bm d															
Debt Securities .... 78bn d	140	-448	-107	-255	170	-1,122	-709	-1,649	-436	-268	-248	283	....	....	....
Financial Derivatives Assets .... 78bw d															
Financial Derivatives Liabilities .... 78bx d															
Other Investment Assets .... 78bh d	-529	-1,083	32	-205	957	1,502	-934	504	1,015	4,134	-4,604	-5,269	-7,936	-5,565	....
Monetary Authorities .... 78bo d															
General Government .... 78bp d	-6	-4	72	4	-13	-42	-64	-52	5	33	-14	-11	....	....	....
Banks .... 78bq d	-454	-920	-196	135	414	481	-2,057	-1,281	28	3,339	-979	-2,677	....	....	....
Other Sectors .... 78br d	-68	-159	157	-344	556	1,063	1,187	1,837	982	762	-3,611	-2,581	....	....	....
Other Investment Liab., n.i.e. .... 78bi d	-1,551	-1,189	-258	-89	496	3,183	7,441	-1,909	2,885	533	1,912	272	—	—	....
Monetary Authorities .... 78bs d	20	-28	5	-1	-1	3	7	-3	—	—	—	—	....	....	....
General Government .... 78bt d	-1,107	-734	-276	-36	-132	-122	-509	-163	-216	-597	-350	180	....	....	....
Banks .... 78bu d	-466	330	616	712	898	3,150	6,282	-3,789	—	—	—	—	....	....	....
Other Sectors .... 78bv d	3	-758	-602	-763	-269	153	1,662	2,047	3,102	1,130	2,263	92	....	....	....
Net Errors and Omissions .... 78ca d	114	-267	-358	1,085	-151	79	3,624	154	-762	-2,502	-137	3,039	-1,273	-3,142	....
Overall Balance .... 78cb d	1,139	-458	1,235	1,951	1,236	6,618	11,350	-3,160	-1,763	2,513	-3,875	10,018	4,712	-1,009	....
Reserves and Related Items .... 79da d	-1,139	458	-1,235	-1,951	-1,236	-6,618	-11,350	3,160	1,763	-2,513	3,875	-10,018	-4,712	1,009	....
Reserve Assets .... 79db d	-1,139	458	-1,235	-1,951	-1,236	-6,618	-11,350	3,160	1,763	-2,513	3,875	-10,018	-4,712	1,009	....
Use of Fund Credit and Loans .... 79dc d	—	—	—	—	—	—	—	—	—	—	—	—	....	....	....
Exceptional Financing .... 79de d															

International Investment Position

Millions of US Dollars

	1987	1988	1989	1990	1991	1992	1993	1994	1995	1996	1997	1998	1999	2000	2001
Assets .... 79aa d	13,984	11,032	14,967	14,000	14,817	21,600	34,063	34,122	....	....	....	....	....	....	....
Direct Investment Abroad .... 79ab d	716	1,146	967	753	763	1,058	1,437	2,635	....	....	....	....	....	....	....
Portfolio Investment .... 79ac d	373	356	999	393	429	429	391	650	....	....	....	....	....	....	....
Equity Securities .... 79ad d	315	356	371	393	429	429	391	650	....	....	....	....	....	....	....
Debt Securities .... 79ae d	58	—	628	—	—	—	—	—	....	....	....	....	....	....	....
Financial Derivatives .... 79al d									....	....	....	....	....	....	....
Other Investment .... 79af d	5,023	2,732	4,945	2,807	2,407	1,999	3,892	4,164	....	....	....	....	....	....	....
Monetary Authorities .... 79ag d	—	—	—	—	—	—	—	—	....	....	....	....	....	....	....
General Government .... 79ah d									....	....	....	....	....	....	....
Banks .... 79ai d	2,011	2,732	2,946	2,807	2,393	1,999	3,892	4,164	....	....	....	....	....	....	....
Other Sectors .... 79aj d	3,012	—	1,999	—	14	—	—	—	....	....	....	....	....	....	....
Reserve Assets .... 79ak d	7,872	6,798	8,056	10,047	11,218	18,115	28,343	26,673	....	....	....	....	....	....	....
Liabilities .... 79la d	29,693	20,494	25,674	25,008	32,059	35,247	42,898	39,757	....	....	....	....	....	....	....
Dir. Invest. in Rep. Economy .... 79lb d	6,806	7,054	8,096	10,318	12,440	16,860	20,591	22,916	....	....	....	....	....	....	....
Portfolio Investment .... 79lc d	9,533	8,335	8,151	8,504	8,808	8,136	7,777	7,238	....	....	....	....	....	....	....
Equity Securities .... 79ld d	1,936	1,976	2,094	2,514	2,680	3,223	3,485	4,300	....	....	....	....	....	....	....
Debt Securities .... 79le d	7,598	6,358	6,057	5,990	6,128	4,913	4,292	2,938	....	....	....	....	....	....	....
Financial Derivatives .... 79ll d									....	....	....	....	....	....	....
Other Investment .... 79lf d	13,354	5,105	9,427	6,185	10,810	10,252	14,530	9,604	....	....	....	....	....	....	....
Monetary Authorities .... 79lg d	—	—	—	—	—	—	—	—	....	....	....	....	....	....	....
General Government .... 79lh d	3,485	3,188	2,888	3,163	3,203	3,097	2,875	2,956	....	....	....	....	....	....	....
Banks .... 79li d	2,672	1,917	2,811	3,023	4,788	7,155	11,656	6,647	....	....	....	....	....	....	....
Other Sectors .... 79lj d	7,197	—	3,728	—	2,819	—	—	—	....	....	....	....	....	....	....

Malaysia

		1972	1973	1974	1975	1976	1977	1978	1979	1980	1981	1982	1983	1984	1985	1986
Government Finance															*Millions of Ringgit:*	
Deficit (-) or Surplus	80	−1,371	−1,049	−1,381	−1,901	−1,705	−2,476	−2,249	−1,535	−3,704	−9,015	−10,421	−6,933	−4,775	−4,407	−7,506
Revenue	81	2,920	3,399	4,791	5,117	6,157	7,760	8,841	10,505	13,926	15,806	16,690	18,608	20,805	21,115	19,518
Expenditure	82	4,291	4,448	6,172	7,018	7,862	10,236	11,090	12,040	17,630	24,821	27,111	25,541	25,580	25,522	27,024
Lending Minus Repayments	83	....	....	....	....	....	....	....	....	....	....	....	....	....	....	....
Financing																
Net Borrowing: Domestic	84a	836	877	832	1,210	1,636	1,887	1,165	2,507	2,311	4,091	6,084	4,466	3,153	3,591	4,929
Foreign	85a	354	69	223	912	638	269	541	679	310	3,419	4,893	4,569	3,093	956	1,348
Special Receipts	86	66	13	8	8	9	11	4	3	1	236	2	4	46	12	111
Use of Cash Balances	87	115	90	318	−229	−578	309	539	−1,654	1,082	1,269	−558	−2,106	−1,517	−152	1,118
Debt: Domestic	88b	5,835	6,712	7,544	8,755	10,391	12,277	13,783	16,281	18,578	22,851	28,711	33,955	37,075	40,812	45,698
Foreign	89b	1,396	1,295	1,497	2,424	2,806	3,352	3,859	4,543	4,861	8,278	13,158	17,728	20,848	23,070	28,310
National Accounts															*Millions of Ringgit*	
Househ.Cons.Expend.,incl.NPISHs	96f	8,613	10,308	12,776	13,086	14,715	16,812	19,584	22,406	26,946	30,594	33,226	36,458	39,594	40,360	36,499
Government Consumption Expend.	91f	2,738	2,934	3,516	3,924	4,301	5,388	6,090	6,475	8,811	10,425	11,469	11,015	11,741	11,844	12,127
Gross Fixed Capital Formation	93e	3,211	4,219	5,798	5,602	6,206	7,465	9,381	12,250	16,597	20,759	22,745	25,213	25,391	23,124	18,865
Changes in Inventories	93i	−179	206	974	101	192	247	723	1,173	−380	−602	593	1,253	1,306	−1,757	−261
Exports of Goods and Services	90c	5,083	7,738	11,004	10,150	14,474	16,216	18,585	26,004	30,676	30,154	31,846	35,795	43,171	42,537	40,305
Imports of Goods and Services (-)	98c	5,246	6,682	11,210	10,531	11,803	13,788	16,477	21,884	29,342	33,717	37,300	39,793	41,653	38,561	35,941
Gross Domestic Product (GDP)	99b	14,220	18,723	22,858	22,332	28,085	32,340	37,886	46,424	53,308	57,613	62,579	69,941	79,550	77,547	71,594
Net Primary Income from Abroad	98.n	−378	−659	−997	−727	−1,097	−1,276	−1,700	−2,070	−1,918	−2,011	−2,889	−4,411	−5,368	−5,508	−4,780
Gross National Income (GNI)	99a	13,842	18,064	21,861	21,605	26,988	31,064	36,186	44,354	51,390	55,602	59,690	65,530	74,182	72,039	66,814
GDP Volume 1978 Prices	99b.p	24,228	27,063	29,315	29,550	32,966	35,522	37,886	41,428	44,511	47,600	50,446	53,584	57,743	57,093	57,750
GDP Volume 1987 Prices	99b.p	....	....	....	....	....	....	....	....	....	....	....	....	....	....	....
GDP Volume (1995=100)	99bv p	19.4	21.6	23.4	23.6	26.4	28.4	†30.3	33.1	35.6	38.1	40.3	42.8	46.2	45.6	46.2
GDP Deflator (1995=100)	99bi p	33.0	38.9	43.8	42.5	47.9	51.2	56.2	63.0	67.3	68.0	69.7	73.4	77.4	76.4	69.7
																Millions:
Population	99z	11.00	11.31	11.65	11.90	12.30	12.58	12.91	13.45	13.70	14.11	14.51	14.89	15.27	15.68	16.11

1987	1988	1989	1990	1991	1992	1993	1994	1995	1996	1997	1998	1999	2000	2001	
Year Ending December 31															**Government Finance**
−6,153	−3,290	−3,410	−3,437	−2,640	−1,243	354	4,408	1,861	1,815	6,627	−5,002	−9,488	....	....	Deficit (-) or Surplus ... 80
18,143	21,967	25,273	29,521	34,053	39,250	41,691	49,446	50,954	58,279	65,736	56,710	58,675	....	....	Revenue ... 81
24,296	25,257	28,683	32,958	36,693	40,493	41,337	45,038	49,093	56,464	59,109	60,371	68,210	....	....	Expenditure ... 82
....	....	....	....	....	....	....	....	....	....	....	1,341	−47	....	....	Lending Minus Repayments ... 83
															Financing
8,693	7,857	2,368	3,798	....	1,480	375	1,751	—	1,291	−2,048	11,040	5,423	....	....	Net Borrowing: Domestic ... 84a
−2,438	−3,094	−1,038	−787	....	−3,170	−3,134	−4,757	−1,635	−2,177	−1,682	1,819	2,923	....	....	Foreign ... 85a
—	291	238	52	....	201	126	519	166	475	....	....	....	....	....	Special Receipts ... 86
−102	−1,764	1,842	374	....	2,732	2,279	−1,921	−392	−1,404	†−2,897	−7,857	1,142	....	....	Use of Cash Balances ... 87
54,796	63,097	65,763	69,988	73,655	76,083	76,536	78,260	78,038	79,211	76,968	88,197	93,750	....	....	Debt: Domestic ... 88b
27,629	25,922	24,182	24,182	25,145	20,922	19,362	14,818	13,331	10,471	12,951	14,924	18,369	....	....	Foreign ... 89b
Millions of Ringgit															**National Accounts**
†39,063	45,444	52,619	61,687	70,500	75,749	83,143	94,089	106,612	116,794	127,783	117,718	125,056	144,726	150,555	Househ.Cons.Expend.,incl.NPISHs ... 96f
†12,060	13,148	14,798	16,426	18,505	19,605	21,750	23,973	27,527	28,179	30,341	27,670	33,044	36,231	42,859	Government Consumption Expend. ... 91f
†17,904	22,726	30,599	39,348	49,126	55,191	66,936	78,663	96,967	107,825	121,494	75,982	65,841	87,729	83,345	Gross Fixed Capital Formation ... 93e
†812	1,624	835	−813	1,937	−1,906	535	1,871	120	−2,580	−398	−427	1,476	4,998	−3,661	Changes in Inventories ... 93i
†50,998	61,348	75,112	88,675	105,161	114,494	135,896	174,255	209,323	232,359	262,885	327,836	364,861	427,004	389,256	Exports of Goods and Services ... 90c
†39,752	51,920	68,730	86,241	110,107	112,450	136,068	177,389	218,077	228,842	260,310	265,536	289,514	358,530	327,765	Imports of Goods and Services (-) ... 98c
†81,085	92,370	105,223	119,081	135,123	150,681	172,193	195,460	222,472	253,732	281,795	283,243	300,764	342,157	334,589	Gross Domestic Product (GDP) ... 99b
†−4,982	−5,084	−5,903	−5,064	−6,800	−8,006	−8,265	−9,412	−10,377	−11,801	−15,095	−15,321	−20,886	−28,909	−25,623	Net Primary Income from Abroad ... 98.n
†76,104	87,286	99,330	114,017	128,324	142,676	163,928	186,049	212,095	241,931	266,699	267,922	279,878	313,248	308,966	Gross National Income (GNI) ... 99a
60,863	....	....	....	....	....	....	....	....	....	....	....	....	....	....	GDP Volume 1978 Prices ... 99b.p
81,085	89,143	97,218	105,977	116,093	126,408	138,916	151,713	166,625	183,292	196,714	182,221	192,794	209,269	210,480	GDP Volume 1987 Prices ... 99b.p
†48.7	53.5	58.3	63.6	69.7	75.9	83.4	91.1	100.0	110.0	118.1	109.4	115.7	125.6	126.3	GDP Volume (1995=100) ... 99bv p
†74.9	77.6	81.1	84.2	87.2	89.3	92.8	96.5	100.0	103.7	107.3	116.4	116.8	122.5	119.1	GDP Deflator (1995=100) ... 99bi p
Midyear Estimates															
16.53	16.94	17.66	18.10	18.55	19.04	19.56	20.11	20.67	21.17	21.66	22.18	22.71	23.27	22.63	**Population** ... 99z

(See notes in the back of the book.)

Maldives

		1972	1973	1974	1975	1976	1977	1978	1979	1980	1981	1982	1983	1984	1985	1986
Exchange Rates														*Rufiyaa per SDR:*		
Market Rate	aa	4.750	4.741	4.812	7.170	10.021	10.841	11.237	9.946	9.629	8.788	7.777	7.381	6.910	7.830	8.861
														Rufiyaa per US Dollar:		
Market Rate	ae	4.375	3.930	3.930	6.125	8.625	8.925	8.625	7.550	7.550	7.550	7.050	7.050	7.050	7.129	7.244
Market Rate	rf	4.375[e]	3.986[e]	3.930[e]	5.765[e]	8.365[e]	8.767[e]	8.969[e]	7.489	7.550	7.550	7.174	7.050	7.050	7.098	7.151
Fund Position														*Millions of SDRs:*		
Quota	2f. s	....	....	....	....	....	....	.9	.9	1.4	1.4	1.4	2.0	2.0	2.0	2.0
SDRs	1b. s	....	....	....	....	....	....	—	.1	.1	.2	.2	—	—	—	—
Reserve Position in the Fund	1c. s	....	....	....	....	....	....	.2	.2	.3	.3	.3	.5	—	—	—
Total Fund Cred.&Loans Outstg.	2tl	....						—	—	—	—	—	—	—	—	—
International Liquidity										*Millions of US Dollars Unless Otherwise Indicated:*						
Total Reserves minus Gold	1l. d	....	....	....	....	.01	.08	.57	.71	.95	1.15	8.41	4.54	5.13	4.59	6.91
SDRs	1b. d	....	....	....	....	....	....	—	.12	.08	.19	.17	—	.01	.02	.02
Reserve Position in the Fund	1c. d					....	....	.22	.22	.38	.35	.33	.47	—	—	—
Foreign Exchange	1d. d					.01	.08	.35	.37	.49	.61	7.91	4.07	5.12	4.57	6.89
Gold (Million Fine Troy Ounces)	1ad					....	....	....	....	....	....					
Gold (National Valuation)	1an d					....	....	....	....	....	.055	.042	.042	.042	.042	.042
Monetary Authorities: Other Liab.	4.. d										.23	8.20	7.71	7.21	3.48	1.87
Deposit Money Banks: Assets	7a. d					.23	.27	2.38	1.81	2.44	2.75	1.94	1.72	3.56	2.24	2.30
Liabilities	7b. d					.06	.93	.54	.24	1.58	10.43	14.31	18.32	25.55	30.66	24.84
Monetary Authorities														*Millions of Rufiyaa:*		
Foreign Assets	11					.02	.31	2.41	2.96	3.88	†6.03	63.39	36.38	36.27	33.77	51.45
Claims on Central Government	12a					111.29	121.52	90.70	111.16	142.95	†152.95	156.21	167.39	185.21	†244.78	286.44
Claims on Nonfin.Pub.Enterprises	12c														9.10	3.36
Claims on Deposit Money Banks	12e						.01	2.57	2.24	3.32	1.96	1.15	.15	.40	.17	.23
Reserve Money	14					57.44	53.71	37.72	63.10	99.87	†106.33	96.49	117.25	155.45	209.90	239.68
of which: Currency Outside DMBs	14a					13.22	14.18	17.53	23.12	27.46	32.37	41.70	50.31	56.77	68.52	91.97
Foreign Currency Deposits	15										.44	.69	.09	.24	.08	.08
Foreign Liabilities	16c										1.76	57.79	54.33	50.86	†24.80	13.54
Central Government Deposits	16d					53.87	68.14	57.96	51.97	48.47	45.82	26.74	22.37	30.32	29.63	61.39
Capital Accounts	17a					—	—	—	.45	1.86	2.34	7.18	6.06	9.62	11.22	13.16
Other Items (Net)	17r					—	—	—	.84	−.05	†4.26	31.86	3.82	−24.61	12.19	13.62
Deposit Money Banks														*Millions of Rufiyaa:*		
Reserves	20					23.71	22.68	4.25	12.08	10.31	3.87	20.05	47.29	71.24	72.38	91.08
Foreign Assets	21					1.97	2.42	20.56	13.64	18.43	20.80	13.71	12.13	25.12	15.99	16.68
Claims on Central Government	22a					—	—	—	—	—	22.83	34.40	20.14	—	4.80	2.32
Claims on Nonfin.Pub.Enterprises	22c					—	2.10	—	3.02	40.66	38.58	13.61	42.63	65.70	84.64	88.42
Claims on Private Sector	22d					2.20	16.43	13.66	17.55	16.47	51.16	97.92	126.51	187.07	184.00	181.51
Demand Deposits	24					16.16	18.16	3.91	6.23	7.29	6.31	14.28	18.60	29.37	26.23	39.45
Time, Savings,& Fgn. Currency Dep.	25					8.05	16.98	29.28	37.01	62.16	48.02	47.13	49.27	68.67	72.39	107.05
Foreign Liabilities	26c					.54	8.27	4.69	1.80	11.90	78.78	100.86	129.18	180.11	†218.54	179.98
Central Government Deposits	26d					—	—	—	—	—	.16	.63	6.55	13.99	1.73	1.09
Credit from Monetary Authorities	26g					....	....	....	....	....	3.78	1.23	.14	.40	.19	.27
Capital Accounts	27a					—	—	.84	.14	.39	.47	5.63	26.61	26.83	27.81	32.57
Other Items (Net)	27r					3.12	.21	−.26	1.13	4.12	†−.30	9.93	18.36	29.77	14.92	19.61
Monetary Survey														*Millions of Rufiyaa:*		
Foreign Assets (Net)	31n					1.45	−5.55	18.28	14.81	10.41	†−53.72	−81.55	−135.00	−169.58	†−193.58	−125.38
Domestic Credit	32					59.62	71.91	46.40	79.76	151.61	†274.77	327.75	393.67	†495.95	499.56
Claims on Central Govt. (Net)	32an					57.42	53.38	32.74	59.19	94.48	†129.80	163.24	158.61	140.90	†218.21	226.27
Claims on Nonfin.Pub.Enterprises	32c					—	2.10	—	3.02	40.66	38.58	13.61	42.63	65.70	93.74	91.78
Claims on Private Sector	32d					2.20	16.43	13.66	17.55	16.47	51.16	97.92	126.51	187.07	184.00	181.51
Money	34					53.76	46.19	37.52	53.41	80.75	†109.33	92.74	88.80	113.90	163.69	188.80
Quasi-Money	35					8.05	16.98	29.28	37.01	62.16	48.47	47.82	49.35	68.91	72.47	107.12
Capital Accounts	37a					—	—	.84	.59	2.24	2.81	12.81	32.66	36.45	39.03	45.73
Other Items (Net)	37r					−.75	3.19	−2.96	3.56	16.87	†5.22	39.85	21.94	4.84	27.18	32.52
Money plus Quasi-Money	35l					61.82	63.17	66.81	90.42	142.91	†157.79	140.56	138.16	182.81	236.15	295.92
Interest Rates														*Percent Per Annum*		
Money Market Rate	60b	....	....	....	....	....	....	....	....	....	....	....	....	11.00	9.00	9.00
Prices, Production, Labor														*Index Numbers (1995=100):*		
Consumer Prices	64	....	....	....	....	....	17.2	19.4	24.7	30.6	37.9	46.2				
Total Fish Catch	66al	....	....	....	....	....	25.2	24.7	26.5	33.1	33.4	29.0	36.9	52.7	59.2	56.7
Tourist Bed Night Index	66.t						4.8	7.5	7.9	11.0	16.3	21.8	23.7	29.1	38.6	37.9
Labor Force	67d	....												*Number in Thousands:*		
International Transactions														*Millions of US Dollars*		
Exports	70.. d	3.5	3.5	4.0	2.5	3.0	3.4	4.1	4.6	7.8	8.6	9.8	13.4	17.6	23.0	24.5
Imports, c.i.f.	71.. d	5.4	7.5	7.5	7.4	6.0	10.0	14.4	21.5	28.6	30.6	43.2	56.9	53.3	53.0	45.0
Imports, f.o.b.	71.v d	4.9	6.8	6.8	6.8	5.5	9.1	13.1	19.5	26.0	27.9	39.3	51.7	48.5	47.9	40.5

1987	1988	1989	1990	1991	1992	1993	1994	1995	1996	1997	1998	1999	2000	2001		
End of Period															**Exchange Rates**	
13.328	11.472	12.097	13.686	14.762	14.486	15.253	17.182	17.496	16.925	15.881	16.573	16.154	15.335	16.086	Market Rate	**aa**
End of Period (ae) Period Average (rf)																
9.395	8.525	9.205	9.620	10.320	10.535	11.105	11.770	11.770	11.770	11.770	11.770	11.770	11.770	12.800	Market Rate	**ae**
9.223	8.785	9.041	9.552	10.253	10.569	10.957	11.586	11.770	11.770	11.770	11.770	11.770	11.770	12.242	Market Rate	**rf**
End of Period															**Fund Position**	
2.0	2.0	2.0	2.0	2.0	5.5	5.5	5.5	5.5	5.5	5.5	5.5	8.2	8.2	8.2	Quota	**2f. s**
—	—	—	—	—	—	—	—	—	.1	.1	.1	.1	.2	.2	SDRs	**1b. s**
—	—	—	—	—	.9	.9	.9	.9	.9	.9	.9	1.6	1.6	1.6	Reserve Position in the Fund	**1c. s**
—	—	—	—	—	—	—	—	—	—	—	—	—	—	—	Total Fund Cred.&Loans Outstg.	**2tl**
End of Period															**International Liquidity**	
8.19	21.59	24.77	24.38	23.47	28.19	26.15	31.22	47.95	76.17	98.31	118.54	127.12	122.80	93.07	Total Reserves minus Gold	**1l. d**
.01	.03	.03	.03	.03	.01	.03	.05	.07	.09	.11	.14	.19	.26	.31	SDRs	**1b. d**
—	—	—	—	—	1.21	1.21	1.28	1.31	1.26	1.19	1.24	2.13	2.02	1.95	Reserve Position in the Fund	**1c. d**
8.18	21.56	24.74	24.35	23.44	26.97	24.92	29.89	46.57	74.81	97.01	117.15	124.80	120.52	90.80	Foreign Exchange	**1d. d**
—	—	—	—	—	—	—	—	—	—	—	—	—	—	—	Gold (Million Fine Troy Ounces)	**1ad**
.042	.042	.042	.042	.042	.042	.042	.042	....	....	....	....	....	....	....	Gold (National Valuation)	**1an d**
.13	.20	.19	.18	.17	.17	15.39	16.13	16.21	16.20	.86	.86	.86	.86	.79	Monetary Authorities: Other Liab.	**4.. d**
7.22	5.60	8.62	10.66	12.84	14.62	10.30	10.23	14.02	22.35	11.50	23.65	19.09	21.87	24.88	Deposit Money Banks: Assets	**7a. d**
21.29	19.08	28.83	27.95	17.81	22.08	18.37	13.61	19.03	12.83	12.20	15.06	26.90	32.42	27.58	Liabilities	**7b. d**
End of Period															**Monetary Authorities**	
78.45	187.13	226.53	230.39	237.17	292.60	293.92	376.86	580.10	912.94	1,173.55	1,411.67	1,512.69	1,460.53	1,207.23	Foreign Assets	**11**
297.26	228.24	288.13	318.43	448.23	618.97	910.65	999.33	1,076.06	987.57	920.12	1,024.38	1,156.15	1,409.01	1,584.47	Claims on Central Government	**12a**
11.92	14.84	20.06	4.45	40.68	8.86	9.75	6.16	8.42	7.86	—	3.20	2.48	1.57	1.48	Claims on Nonfin.Pub.Enterprises	**12c**
.95	.54	4.06	9.14	9.56	8.80	7.91	6.57	5.62	1.37	1.41	1.42	1.43	—	—	Claims on Deposit Money Banks	**12e**
245.79	300.50	357.95	445.16	543.28	730.74	869.86	993.09	1,008.87	1,187.93	1,371.25	1,520.08	1,624.79	1,696.13	1,861.31	Reserve Money	**14**
116.54	140.08	158.32	206.73	253.46	300.91	330.38	382.27	405.83	425.85	489.68	524.92	593.34	618.14	566.52	of which: Currency Outside DMBs	**14a**
.69	.76	.58	.64	.72	1.63	.63	5.50	17.00	26.64	32.70	20.69	26.51	37.35	10.16	Foreign Currency Deposits	**15**
1.27	1.70	1.71	1.70	1.80	1.81	170.90	189.90	190.76	190.65	10.10	10.13	10.15	10.16	10.15	Foreign Liabilities	**16c**
98.89	89.70	112.07	45.60	95.13	93.65	70.28	66.47	180.22	148.50	163.00	225.18	235.02	231.83	283.81	Central Government Deposits	**16d**
26.58	17.81	36.72	42.23	51.57	46.63	74.49	90.52	62.70	105.57	130.40	105.37	118.27	179.28	185.59	Capital Accounts	**17a**
15.36	20.28	29.76	27.08	43.14	54.77	36.07	43.44	210.65	250.45	387.63	559.22	658.01	716.36	442.16	Other Items (Net)	**17r**
End of Period															**Deposit Money Banks**	
98.56	135.98	161.75	199.35	252.79	383.00	454.02	498.55	612.78	859.80	1,173.97	1,346.56	1,553.30	1,695.24	1,563.42	Reserves	**20**
67.82	47.75	79.33	102.54	132.52	154.02	114.43	120.46	165.04	263.03	135.34	278.39	224.66	257.46	318.49	Foreign Assets	**21**
2.97	1.62	2.44	5.60	8.73	9.95	4.21	—	—	—	—	—	—	—	—	Claims on Central Government	**22a**
101.61	106.91	191.47	155.09	161.55	154.31	177.04	137.24	160.98	147.32	103.78	161.89	193.80	183.15	182.55	Claims on Nonfin.Pub.Enterprises	**22c**
180.59	159.15	195.55	255.30	247.80	256.75	398.53	507.38	655.09	717.40	996.79	1,253.18	1,302.81	1,407.08	1,827.24	Claims on Private Sector	**22d**
51.24	57.27	66.95	68.21	112.98	117.02	281.13	356.06	393.70	552.92	619.23	725.45	935.95	1,074.43	1,022.15	Demand Deposits	**24**
132.17	156.26	189.75	224.67	269.48	293.80	340.13	429.26	569.91	785.77	1,075.30	1,423.72	1,318.10	1,252.06	1,658.63	Time, Savings,& Fgn. Currency Dep.	**25**
199.99	162.68	265.41	268.85	183.76	232.62	203.95	160.22	224.00	150.98	143.65	177.25	316.60	381.62	353.07	Foreign Liabilities	**26c**
1.89	3.90	11.04	13.27	21.31	51.06	60.40	31.52	58.43	90.24	93.48	126.08	160.95	182.16	222.09	Central Government Deposits	**26d**
.85	.47	.21	8.99	9.59	8.67	7.64	6.63	5.15	1.34	.89	.89	.14	—	—	Credit from Monetary Authorities	**26g**
43.76	44.14	38.66	48.04	62.15	91.72	122.32	143.77	157.69	281.00	358.92	486.96	496.18	610.86	572.11	Capital Accounts	**27a**
21.64	26.69	58.53	85.83	144.12	163.14	132.66	136.17	185.01	125.30	118.41	99.67	46.65	41.80	63.65	Other Items (Net)	**27r**
End of Period															**Monetary Survey**	
−54.99	70.50	38.74	62.38	184.13	212.19	33.50	147.20	330.38	834.34	1,155.14	1,502.68	1,410.60	1,326.21	1,162.50	Foreign Assets (Net)	**31n**
493.57	417.15	574.54	679.99	790.55	904.13	1,369.50	1,552.12	1,661.90	1,621.41	1,764.21	2,091.39	2,259.27	2,586.82	3,089.84	Domestic Credit	**32**
199.45	136.25	167.46	265.16	340.52	484.21	784.18	901.34	837.41	748.83	663.64	673.12	760.18	995.02	1,078.57	Claims on Central Govt. (Net)	**32an**
113.53	121.75	211.53	159.54	202.23	163.17	186.79	143.40	169.40	155.18	103.78	165.09	196.28	184.72	184.03	Claims on Nonfin.Pub.Enterprises	**32c**
180.59	159.15	195.55	255.30	247.80	256.75	398.53	507.38	655.09	717.40	996.79	1,253.18	1,302.81	1,407.08	1,827.24	Claims on Private Sector	**32d**
198.45	221.67	263.14	312.86	402.05	463.88	694.54	850.87	899.06	1,059.35	1,195.60	1,384.24	1,585.18	1,760.44	1,655.91	Money	**34**
132.86	157.01	190.33	225.31	270.20	295.43	340.76	434.76	586.91	812.41	1,108.00	1,444.41	1,344.61	1,289.41	1,668.79	Quasi-Money	**35**
70.34	61.95	75.38	90.27	113.72	138.35	196.81	234.29	220.39	386.57	489.32	592.33	614.45	790.14	757.70	Capital Accounts	**37a**
36.93	47.02	84.44	113.92	188.71	218.66	170.89	179.40	285.92	197.42	126.43	173.09	125.63	73.04	169.94	Other Items (Net)	**37r**
331.31	378.68	453.47	538.17	672.25	759.31	1,035.30	1,285.63	1,485.97	1,871.76	2,303.60	2,828.65	2,929.79	3,049.85	3,324.70	Money plus Quasi-Money	**35l**
Percent Per Annum															**Interest Rates**	
8.67	8.50	7.33	7.00	7.00	7.00	5.00	5.00	6.80	6.80	6.80	6.80	6.80	6.80	6.80	Money Market Rate	**60b**
Period Averages															**Prices, Production, Labor**	
—	51.3	†55.0	57.0	65.3	†76.3	91.7	94.8	100.0	106.3	114.3	112.7	116.0	114.7	115.4	Consumer Prices	**64**
54.4	68.4	68.1	73.0	77.2	78.5	86.0	99.5	100.0	100.8	97.3	110.1	117.9	110.4	119.5	Total Fish Catch	**66al**
46.5	61.0	53.7	61.7	63.3	72.5	76.8	86.3	100.0	111.5	120.0	127.2	136.4	144.5	144.3	Tourist Bed Night Index	**66.t**
Period Averages																
....	....	....	....	....	....	....	....	67	....	....	....	....	....	....	Labor Force	**67d**
Millions of US Dollars															**International Transactions**	
30.8	40.2	44.7	52.1	53.7	40.0	34.6	45.9	49.5	59.2	73.2	74.3	63.7	75.9	76.2	Exports	**70.. d**
81.0	90.0	112.6	137.8	161.2	189.3	191.3	221.7	267.9	301.7	348.8	354.0	402.2	388.6	395.4	Imports, c.i.f.	**71.. d**
73.7	81.9	95.7	117.1	137.0	166.6	168.3	195.1	235.6	265.5	307.0	311.5	353.9	342.0	348.0	Imports, f.o.b.	**71.v d**

Maldives

		1972	1973	1974	1975	1976	1977	1978	1979	1980	1981	1982	1983	1984	1985	1986
Balance of Payments														*Millions of US Dollars:*		
Current Account, n.i.e.	78ald	....	....	....	....	....	—	1.6	-4.8	-22.2	-20.2	-19.1	-24.2	-16.3	-5.5	-.3
Goods: Exports f.o.b.	78aa d	....	....	....	....	....	5.0	7.2	10.7	12.8	15.8	17.3	19.8	23.1	25.5	31.2
Goods: Imports f.o.b.	78ab d	....	....	....	....	....	-9.9	-14.8	-21.7	-44.0	-41.7	-46.0	-57.6	-61.0	-58.0	-63.0
Trade Balance	78ac d	....	....	....	....	....	-4.9	-7.6	-11.0	-31.2	-25.9	-28.7	-37.8	-37.9	-32.5	-31.8
Services: Credit	78ad d	....	....	....	....	....	5.0	5.6	31.1	52.4	58.7	59.3	56.9	61.4	65.6	65.4
Services: Debit	78ae d	....	....	....	....	....	-1.0	-1.4	-25.0	-43.1	-51.9	-47.7	-38.9	-34.2	-27.0	-23.2
Balance on Goods & Services	78af d	....	....	....	....	....	-.9	-3.4	-4.9	-21.9	-19.1	-17.1	-19.8	-10.7	6.1	10.4
Income: Credit	78ag d	....	....	....	....	....	—	—	—	—	—	.4	.6	.4	.3	1.4
Income: Debit	78ah d	....	....	....	....	....	—	—	-1.6	-2.7	-3.5	-5.7	-10.1	-12.6	-13.5	-19.9
Balance on Gds, Serv. & Inc.	78ai d	....	....	....	....	....	-.9	-3.4	-6.5	-24.6	-22.6	-22.4	-29.3	-22.9	-7.1	-8.1
Current Transfers, n.i.e.: Credit	78aj d	....	....	....	....	....	.9	5.0	1.7	2.6	2.7	4.6	7.1	10.0	3.6	9.3
Current Transfers: Debit	78ak d	....	....	....	....	....	—	—	—	-.2	-.3	-1.3	-2.0	-3.4	-2.0	-1.5
Capital Account, n.i.e.	78bc d	....	....	....	....	....	—	—	—	—	—	—	—	—	—	—
Capital Account, n.i.e.: Credit	78ba d	....	....	....	....	....	—	—	—	—	—	—	—	—	—	—
Capital Account: Debit	78bb d	....	....	....	....	....	—	—	—	—	—	—	—	—	—	—
Financial Account, n.i.e.	78bj d	....	....	....	....	....	2.5	-.1	7.9	15.9	22.0	17.0	6.7	1.5	-4.3	-5.4
Direct Investment Abroad	78bd d	....	....	....	....	....	—	—	—	—	—	—	—	—	—	—
Dir. Invest. in Rep. Econ., n.i.e.	78be d	....	....	....	....	....	—	—	—	—	—	—	—	—	—	5.4
Portfolio Investment Assets	78bf d	....	....	....	....	....	—	—	—	—	—	—	—	—	—	—
Equity Securities	78bk d	....	....	....	....	....	—	—	—	—	—	—	—	—	—	—
Debt Securities	78bl d	....	....	....	....	....	—	—	—	—	—	—	—	—	—	—
Portfolio Investment Liab., n.i.e.	78bg d	....	....	....	....	....	—	—	—	—	—	—	—	—	—	—
Equity Securities	78bm d	....	....	....	....	....	—	—	—	—	—	—	—	—	—	—
Debt Securities	78bn d	....	....	....	....	....	....	....	....	....	....	....	....	....	....	....
Financial Derivatives Assets	78bw d	....	....	....	....	....	....	....	....	....	....	....	....	....	....	....
Financial Derivatives Liabilities	78bx d	....	....	....	....	....	....	....	....	....	....	....	....	....	....	....
Other Investment Assets	78bh d	....	....	....	....	....	—	-2.1	.6	-.6	-.3	.8	.2	-1.9	1.4	—
Monetary Authorities	78bo d	....	....	....	....	....	—	—	—	—	—	—	—	—	—	—
General Government	78bp d	....	....	....	....	....	—	—	—	—	—	—	—	—	—	—
Banks	78bq d	....	....	....	....	....	—	-2.1	.6	-.6	-.3	.8	.2	-1.9	1.4	—
Other Sectors	78br d	....	....	....	....	....	—	—	—	—	—	—	—	—	—	—
Other Investment Liab., n.i.e.	78bi d	....	....	....	....	....	2.5	2.0	7.3	16.5	22.3	16.2	6.5	3.4	-5.7	-10.8
Monetary Authorities	78bs d	....	....	....	....	....	—	—	—	4.8	-3.0	1.9	7.8	-.4	-.6	-3.5	-1.6
General Government	78bt d	....	....	....	....	....	1.6	2.4	2.8	18.1	11.5	4.5	2.9	-3.2	-3.2	-3.4
Banks	78bu d	....	....	....	....	....	.9	-.4	-.3	1.4	8.9	3.9	4.0	7.2	1.0	-5.8
Other Sectors	78bv d	....	....	....	....	....	—	—	—	—	—	—	—	—	—	—
Net Errors and Omissions	78ca d	....	....	....	....	....	-2.4	-1.3	-3.1	6.3	-2.9	8.2	13.7	9.5	11.3	8.0
Overall Balance	78cb d	....	....	....	....	....	.1	.2	—	—	-1.1	6.1	-3.8	-5.3	1.5	2.3
Reserves and Related Items	79da d	....	....	....	....	....	-.1	-.2	—	—	1.1	-6.1	3.8	5.3	-1.5	-2.3
Reserve Assets	79db d	....	....	....	....	....	-.1	-.2	—	—	-.2	-6.9	3.8	-.5	-3.0	-2.3
Use of Fund Credit and Loans	79dc d	....	....	....	....	....	—	—	—	—	—	—	—	—	—	—
Exceptional Financing	79de d	....	....	....	....	....	—	—	—	—	1.3	.8	—	5.8	1.5	—
International Investment Position														*Millions of US Dollars:*		
Assets	79aa d	....	....	....	....	....	....	....	....	....	....	....	....	....	....	9.5
Direct Investment Abroad	79ab d	....	....	....	....	....	....	....	....	....	....	....	....	....	....	—
Portfolio Investment	79ac d	....	....	....	....	....	....	....	....	....	....	....	....	....	....	—
Equity Securities	79ad d	....	....	....	....	....	....	....	....	....	....	....	....	....	....	—
Debt Securities	79ae d	....	....	....	....	....	....	....	....	....	....	....	....	....	....	—
Financial Derivatives	79al d	....	....	....	....	....	....	....	....	....	....	....	....	....	....	—
Other Investment	79af d	....	....	....	....	....	....	....	....	....	....	....	....	....	....	2.4
Monetary Authorities	79ag d	....	....	....	....	....	....	....	....	....	....	....	....	....	....	—
General Government	79ah d	....	....	....	....	....	....	....	....	....	....	....	....	....	....	—
Banks	79ai d	....	....	....	....	....	....	....	....	....	....	....	....	....	....	1.7
Other Sectors	79aj d	....	....	....	....	....	....	....	....	....	....	....	....	....	....	.7
Reserve Assets	79ak d	....	....	....	....	....	....	....	....	....	....	....	....	....	....	7.1
Liabilities	79la d	....	....	....	....	....	....	....	....	....	....	....	....	....	....	85.4
Dir. Invest. in Rep. Economy	79lb d	....	....	....	....	....	....	....	....	....	....	....	....	....	....	—
Portfolio Investment	79lc d	....	....	....	....	....	....	....	....	....	....	....	....	....	....	—
Equity Securities	79ld d	....	....	....	....	....	....	....	....	....	....	....	....	....	....	—
Debt Securities	79le d	....	....	....	....	....	....	....	....	....	....	....	....	....	....	—
Financial Derivatives	79ll d	....	....	....	....	....	....	....	....	....	....	....	....	....	....	—
Other Investment	79lf d	....	....	....	....	....	....	....	....	....	....	....	....	....	....	85.4
Monetary Authorities	79lg d	....	....	....	....	....	....	....	....	....	....	....	....	....	....	1.9
General Government	79lh d	....	....	....	....	....	....	....	....	....	....	....	....	....	....	58.6
Banks	79li d	....	....	....	....	....	....	....	....	....	....	....	....	....	....	24.9
Other Sectors	79lj d	....	....	....	....	....	....	....	....	....	....	....	....	....	....	—
Government Finance														*Millions of Rufiyaa:*		
Deficit (-) or Surplus	80	....	....	....	....	....	....	....	-27.9	-76.4	-26.4	-19.6	-72.8	-25.1	-30.6	-83.7
Revenue	81	....	....	....	....	....	....	....	16.5	46.3	74.5	96.4	109.5	128.5	155.9	179.8
Grants Received	81z	....	....	....	....	....	....	....	7.9	11.5	8.3	23.4	12.4	35.2	9.7	66.3
Expenditure	82	....	....	....	....	....	....	....	48.6	102.9	108.4	138.8	192.9	192.7	187.0	312.3
Lending Minus Repayments	83	....	....	....	....	....	....	....	3.7	31.3	.8	.6	1.8	-3.9	9.2	17.5
Financing																
Domestic	84a	....	....	....	....	....	....	....	16.4	6.0	-9.9	2.7	42.6	27.3	32.3	52.9
Foreign	85a	....	....	....	....	....	....	....	11.5	70.4	36.3	16.9	30.2	-2.2	-1.7	30.8
Debt: Domestic	88a	....	....	....	....	....	....	....	....	....	155.5	154.3	184.1	206.7	237.4	246.6
Foreign	89a	....	....	....	....	....	....	....	23.2	93.6	130.2	246.4	272.8	259.1	253.7	276.7
National Accounts														*Millions of Rufiyaa*		
Househ.Cons.Expend.,incl.NPISHs	96f	....	....	....	....	....	....	....	....	267	344	366	385	336	498	546
Government Consumption Expend.	91f	....	....	....	....	....	....	....	....	39	50	61	76	99	111	137
Gross Fixed Capital Formation	93e	....	....	....	....	....	....	....	....	76	99	106	115	165	234	253
Exports of Goods and Services	90c	....	....	....	....	....	....	....	....	59	65	74	101	124	164	179
Imports of Goods and Services (-)	98c	....	....	....	....	....	....	....	....	186	195	275	362	364	340	302
Gross Domestic Product (GDP)	99b	....	....	....	....	....	142	170	224	321	376	432	466	772	903	1,015
GDP Volume 1984 Prices	99b.p	....	....	191.9	187.9	237.1	275.3	316.7	349.3	379.4	368.0	348.0	415.0	528.0	....	....
GDP Volume 1995 Prices	99b.p	....	....	....	....	....	....	....	....	....	....	....	....	1,615.2	1,864.2	2,038.7
GDP Volume (1995=100)	99bv p	....	....	13.7	13.4	16.9	19.7	22.6	25.0	27.1	26.3	....	....	37.7	43.5	47.5
GDP Deflator (1995=100)	99bi p	....	....	....	....	....	15.3	15.9	19.0	25.1	30.3	....	....	43.5	44.1	45.3
															Millions:		
Population	99z	.11	.12	.13	.13	.13	.14	.15	.15	.15	.16	.16	.17	.18	.18	.19

	1987	1988	1989	1990	1991	1992	1993	1994	1995	1996	1997	1998	1999	2000	2001		
Minus Sign Indicates Debit																**Balance of Payments**	
	8.1	8.9	10.7	9.9	−9.0	−19.6	−53.6	−11.2	−18.3	−7.3	−34.2	−23.3	−81.7	−53.1	....	Current Account, n.i.e.	78al *d*
	39.8	54.3	63.7	78.0	76.2	65.1	52.7	75.4	85.0	80.0	93.0	95.6	91.4	108.7	....	Goods: Exports f.o.b.	78aa *d*
	−66.5	−87.3	−111.3	−121.2	−141.8	−167.9	−177.7	−195.1	−235.8	−265.5	−307.0	−311.5	−353.9	−342.0	....	Goods: Imports f.o.b.	78ab *d*
	−26.7	−33.0	−47.6	−43.2	−65.6	−102.8	−125.0	−119.7	−150.8	−185.5	−214.0	−215.9	−262.5	−233.3	....	*Trade Balance*	78ac *d*
	71.4	73.6	86.4	101.1	108.1	154.3	160.7	197.4	232.8	289.0	312.1	331.3	342.7	348.5	....	Services: Credit	78ad *d*
	−28.3	−28.5	−28.8	−38.0	−42.1	−49.4	−57.1	−62.8	−76.8	−87.8	−94.2	−98.9	−108.2	−109.7	....	Services: Debit	78ae *d*
	16.4	12.1	10.0	19.9	.4	2.1	−21.4	14.9	5.2	15.7	3.9	16.5	−28.0	5.5	....	*Balance on Goods & Services*	78af *d*
	1.3	2.0	3.8	4.7	3.8	2.9	3.0	3.8	4.5	5.9	7.5	8.6	9.1	10.3	....	Income: Credit	78ag *d*
	−16.9	−11.7	−16.3	−18.5	−18.7	−20.0	−22.0	−24.0	−24.4	−27.8	−34.9	−36.7	−40.0	−40.4	....	Income: Debit	78ah *d*
	.8	2.4	−2.5	6.1	−14.5	−15.0	−40.4	−5.3	−14.7	−6.2	−23.5	−11.6	−58.9	−24.6	....	*Balance on Gds, Serv. & Inc.*	78ai *d*
	9.7	11.5	18.3	11.2	22.1	14.3	13.3	16.3	23.0	26.2	17.2	18.9	17.7	17.7	....	Current Transfers, n.i.e.: Credit	78aj *d*
	−2.4	−5.0	−5.1	−7.4	−16.6	−18.9	−26.5	−22.2	−26.6	−27.3	−27.9	−30.6	−40.5	−46.2	....	Current Transfers: Debit	78ak *d*
	—	—	—	—	—	—	—	—	—	—	—	—	—	—	....	Capital Account, n.i.e.	78bc *d*
	—	—	—	—	—	—	—	—	—	—	—	—	—	—	....	Capital Account, n.i.e.: Credit	78ba *d*
	—	—	—	—	—	—	—	—	—	—	—	—	—	—	....	Capital Account: Debit	78bb *d*
	−5.4	−1.5	11.8	8.1	5.7	44.7	46.4	27.4	67.6	52.2	71.0	60.3	76.2	40.0	....	Financial Account, n.i.e.	78bj *d*
															....	Direct Investment Abroad	78bd *d*
	5.1	1.2	4.4	5.6	6.5	6.6	6.9	8.7	7.2	9.3	11.4	11.5	12.3	13.0	....	Dir. Invest. in Rep. Econ., n.i.e.	78be *d*
															....	Portfolio Investment Assets	78bf *d*
															....	Equity Securities	78bk *d*
															....	Debt Securities	78bl *d*
															....	Portfolio Investment Liab., n.i.e.	78bg *d*
															....	Equity Securities	78bm *d*
															....	Debt Securities	78bn *d*
	....	....	....	....	....	....	....	....	....	....	....	....	....	....	....	Financial Derivatives Assets	78bw *d*
	....	....	....	....	....	....	....	....	....	....	....	....	....	....	....	Financial Derivatives Liabilities	78bx *d*
	−4.9	1.6	−2.8	−2.2	−2.2	15.8	25.1	13.2	29.9	32.7	53.8	30.8	47.5	22.8	....	Other Investment Assets	78bh *d*
	....	....	....	....	....	....	....	....	....	....	....	....	....	....	....	Monetary Authorities	78bo *d*
	−4.0	2.1	−2.9	.7	−4.3	−1.7	2.2	1.9	−3.8	−7.3	10.8	−11.6	3.6	−4.2	....	General Government	78bp *d*
	−.9	−.5	.1	−2.9	2.1	17.5	22.9	11.3	33.7	40.0	43.0	42.4	43.9	27.0	....	Banks	78bq *d*
	−5.6	−4.3	10.2	4.7	1.4	22.3	14.4	5.5	30.5	10.2	5.8	18.0	16.4	4.2	....	Other Sectors	78br *d*
	−1.7	.1	—	—	—	—	15.2	.7	.1	—	−15.3	—	—	—	....	Other Investment Liab., n.i.e.	78bi *d*
	−.3	−2.2	1.0	5.1	11.5	17.1	3.8	8.2	24.7	17.3	21.9	14.7	5.1	−2.1	....	Monetary Authorities	78bs *d*
	−3.6	−2.2	9.2	−.4	−10.1	5.2	−4.6	−3.4	5.7	−7.1	−.8	3.3	11.3	6.3	....	General Government	78bt *d*
															....	Banks	78bu *d*
															....	Other Sectors	78bv *d*
	−1.4	6.2	−20.2	−18.3	2.3	−20.3	5.9	−10.8	−32.2	−16.6	−14.6	−16.9	14.1	8.8	....	Net Errors and Omissions	78ca *d*
	1.3	13.6	2.3	−.3	−1.0	4.8	−1.3	5.4	17.1	28.3	22.2	20.1	8.6	−4.3	....	*Overall Balance*	78cb *d*
	−1.3	−13.6	−2.3	.3	1.0	−4.8	1.3	−5.4	−17.1	−28.3	−22.2	−20.1	−8.6	4.3	....	Reserves and Related Items	79da *d*
	−1.3	−13.6	−2.3	.3	1.0	−4.8	1.3	−5.4	−17.1	−28.3	−22.2	−20.1	−8.6	4.3	....	Reserve Assets	79db *d*
	—	—	—	—	—	—	—	—	—	—	—	—	—	—	....	Use of Fund Credit and Loans	79dc *d*
	—	—	—	—	—	—	—	—	—	—	—	—	—	—	....	Exceptional Financing	79de *d*
Millions of US Dollars																**International Investment Position**	
	15.5	27.6	32.8	34.7	35.8	42.4	36.7	42.2	63.3	99.9	111.2	143.7	147.6	145.9	....	Assets	79aa *d*
	—	—	—	—	—	—	—	—	—	—	—	—	—	—	....	Direct Investment Abroad	79ab *d*
	—	—	—	—	—	—	—	—	—	—	—	—	—	—	....	Portfolio Investment	79ac *d*
	—	—	—	—	—	—	—	—	—	—	—	—	—	—	....	Equity Securities	79ad *d*
	—	—	—	—	—	—	—	—	—	—	—	—	—	—	....	Debt Securities	79ae *d*
	—	—	—	—	—	—	—	—	—	—	—	—	—	—	....	Financial Derivatives	79al *d*
	7.2	5.6	8.5	10.7	12.8	14.6	10.3	10.2	14.0	22.3	11.5	23.7	19.1	21.9	....	Other Investment	79af *d*
	—	—	—	—	—	—	—	—	—	—	—	—	—	—	....	Monetary Authorities	79ag *d*
	—	—	—	—	—	—	—	—	—	—	—	—	—	—	....	General Government	79ah *d*
	5.7	3.5	6.5	5.8	10.1	11.8	9.7	7.8	11.6	18.9	8.2	19.8	16.2	20.4	....	Banks	79ai *d*
	1.5	2.1	2.0	4.9	2.7	2.8	.6	2.4	2.4	3.4	3.3	3.9	2.9	1.5	....	Other Sectors	79aj *d*
	8.3	22.0	24.3	24.0	23.0	27.8	26.4	32.0	49.3	77.6	99.7	120.0	128.5	124.0	....	Reserve Assets	79ak *d*
	82.4	77.8	83.9	95.9	96.6	116.5	130.5	141.8	173.0	178.2	179.0	201.7	213.8	212.5	....	Liabilities	79la *d*
															....	Dir. Invest. in Rep. Economy	79lb *d*
															....	Portfolio Investment	79lc *d*
															....	Equity Securities	79ld *d*
															....	Debt Securities	79le *d*
	—	—	—	—	—	—	—	—	—	—	—	—	—	—	....	Financial Derivatives	79ll *d*
	82.4	77.8	83.9	95.9	96.6	116.5	130.5	141.8	173.0	178.2	179.0	201.7	213.8	212.5	....	Other Investment	79lf *d*
	.1	.2	.2	.2	.2	.2	15.4	16.1	16.2	16.2	.9	.9	.9	.9	....	Monetary Authorities	79lg *d*
	61.0	58.5	55.4	67.8	78.6	93.3	96.7	110.8	136.2	148.4	165.3	184.7	185.6	178.0	....	General Government	79lh *d*
	21.3	19.1	28.3	27.9	17.8	23.0	18.4	14.9	20.6	13.6	12.8	16.1	27.3	33.6	....	Banks	79li *d*
															....	Other Sectors	79lj *d*
Year Ending December 31																**Government Finance**	
	19.1	25.6	−42.7	−170.8	−238.5	−356.9	−412.6	−206.6	−300.1	−133.8	−81.3	−123.1	−281.1	−321.5	−373.0 P	Deficit (-) or Surplus	80
	273.6	315.0	406.8	460.3	568.9	684.2	765.2	981.7	1,209.5	1,324.9	1,656.1	1,765.7	2,062.6	2,206.8	2,330.2 P	Revenue	81
	89.5	101.3	165.7	85.0	226.2	151.4	153.3	162.6	199.2	242.9	168.2	164.5	162.7	165.9	183.0 P	Grants Received	81z
	327.0	377.8	600.7	699.5	1,014.4	1,166.9	1,317.4	1,357.5	1,717.8	1,692.6	1,936.9	2,113.9	2,494.9	2,739.9	2,912.9 P	Expenditure	82
	17.0	12.9	14.5	16.6	19.2	25.6	13.7	−6.6	−9.0	9.0	−30.9	−60.6	11.5	−45.7	−26.7 P	Lending Minus Repayments	83
																Financing	
	−20.2	−21.7	2.6	97.3	111.0	189.9	377.0	106.4	2.1	−29.2	−90.9	−6.2	224.4	317.9	156.3 P	Domestic	84a
	1.1	−3.9	40.1	73.5	127.5	167.0	35.6	100.2	298.0	163.0	172.2	129.3	56.7	3.6	216.7 P	Foreign	85a
	245.0	178.2	183.0	200.1	331.5	526.1	846.5	960.9	1,063.0	957.6	877.1	980.3	1,101.0	1,317.4	1,495.1 P	Debt: Domestic	88a
	321.0	325.8	358.7	432.2	559.9	726.9	762.5	862.7	1,160.7	1,323.7	1,495.9	1,625.2	1,681.9	1,685.5	1,902.2 P	Foreign	89a
Millions of Rufiyaa																**National Accounts**	
	528	523	613	621	....	....	....	....	788	859	1,060	1,184	1,386	1,599	1,619	Househ.Cons.Expend.,incl.NPISHs	96f
	230	263	347	422	....	....	....	....	859	859	1,060	1,184	1,386	1,599		Government Consumption Expend.	91f
	511	545	685	755	....	....	....	....	1,479	1,053	2,087	2,042	2,400	1,727	2,079	Gross Fixed Capital Formation	93e
	289	351	401	503	544	417	377	555	4,961	4,954	5,476	5,859	6,107	6,796	6,817	Exports of Goods and Services	90c
	726	843	1,020	1,315	1,654	2,002	2,097	2,571	3,153	3,361	4,774	4,961	5,604	5,809	6,022	Imports of Goods and Services (-)	98c
	1,303	1,480	1,713	2,054	2,506	3,011	3,533	4,125	4,714	5,419	5,894	6,070	6,683	6,608	6,089	Gross Domestic Product (GDP)	99b
	2,218.7	2,412.4	2,637.4	3,084.5	3,297.1	3,510.3	3,700.5	3,978.3	4,289.2	4,679.1	5,154.5	5,575.9	5,989.1	6,263.9	6,393.9	GDP Volume 1984 Prices	99b. *p*
																GDP Volume 1995 Prices	99b. *p*
	51.7	56.2	61.5	71.9	76.9	81.8	86.3	92.8	100.0	109.1	120.2	130.0	139.6	146.0	149.1	GDP Volume (1995=100)	99bv *p*
	53.4	55.8	59.1	60.6	69.2	78.1	86.9	94.3	100.0	105.4	104.0	99.1	101.5	96.0	86.7	GDP Deflator (1995=100)	99bi *p*
Midyear Estimates																	
	.20	.20	.21	.22	.22	.23	.24	.25	.25	.26	.27	.27	.28	.27	.28	**Population**	99z

(See notes in the back of the book.)

Mali

		1972	1973	1974	1975	1976	1977	1978	1979	1980	1981	1982	1983	1984	1985	1986
Exchange Rates															*Francs per SDR:*	
Official Rate	aa	278.00	284.00	272.08	262.55	288.70	285.76	272.28	264.78	287.99	334.52	370.92	436.97	470.11	415.26	394.78
															Francs per US Dollar:	
Official Rate	ae	256.05	235.42	222.22	224.27	248.49	235.25	209.00	201.00	225.80	287.40	336.25	417.37	479.60	378.05	322.75
Official Rate	rf	252.03	222.89	240.70	214.31	238.95	245.68	225.66	212.72	211.28	271.73	328.61	381.07	436.96	449.26	346.31
Fund Position															*Millions of SDRs:*	
Quota	2f. s	22.0	22.0	22.0	22.0	22.0	22.0	27.0	27.0	40.5	40.5	40.5	50.8	50.8	50.8	50.8
SDRs	1b. s	2.4	2.3	3.0	2.7	2.8	2.7	2.6	1.3	—	.2	.5	.1	1.7	1.7	—
Reserve Position in the Fund	1c. s	—	—	—	—	—	—	—	—	5.4	7.6	8.7	8.7	8.7	8.7	8.7
Total Fund Cred.&Loans Outstg.	2tl	8.3	7.3	10.4	10.6	12.7	11.2	19.2	22.1	30.3	28.2	52.5	65.3	84.3	89.2	80.8
International Liquidity													*Millions of US Dollars Unless Otherwise Indicated:*			
Total Reserves minus Gold	1l. d	3.7	4.2	6.1	4.2	6.9	5.4	8.2	6.0	14.5	17.4	16.7	16.2	26.6	22.5	12.3
SDRs	1b. d	2.6	2.7	3.7	3.2	3.2	3.3	3.4	1.7	—	.2	.6	.1	1.7	1.8	—
Reserve Position in the Fund	1c. d	—	—	—	—	—	—	—	—	6.8	8.8	9.6	9.1	8.5	9.5	10.6
Foreign Exchange	1d. d	1.1	1.5	2.4	1.0	3.7	2.1	4.8	4.3	7.7	8.4	6.6	7.0	16.5	11.2	1.7
Gold (Million Fine Troy Ounces)	1ad	....	....	....	....	....	.010	.014	.019	.019	.019	.019	.019	.019	.019	.019
Gold (National Valuation)	1and	....	....	....	....	....	.4	.6	.9	.9	7.9	8.0	7.3	6.3	6.1	7.6
Monetary Authorities: Other Liab.	4.. d	64.4	88.2	127.0	—	—	—	—	—	—	—	—	—	3.9	2.7	34.3
Deposit Money Banks: Assets	7a. d	9.9	10.3	14.3	12.1	12.7	21.6	11.2	10.9	9.7	10.9	13.4	19.0	24.3	15.4	24.8
Liabilities	7b. d	17.4	19.5	24.6	21.6	22.6	33.1	23.6	33.9	34.4	27.4	26.4	23.9	33.5	51.2	72.6
Monetary Authorities															*Billions of Francs:*	
Foreign Assets	11	1.0	1.0	1.4	†.9	1.7	1.4	1.8	1.8	3.5	4.8	5.8	6.8	†12.8	8.5	4.0
Claims on Central Government	12a	21.6	24.2	27.2	†31.6	34.9	46.4	50.4	53.8	55.3	60.9	78.3	93.1	†47.2	51.2	48.8
Claims on Deposit Money Banks	12e	9.3	11.7	21.0	†32.4	40.9	29.4	36.4	47.7	48.4	50.0	54.1	54.3	†12.5	20.6	38.1
Claims on Other Financial Insts	12f	—	—	—	—	—	—	—	—	—	—	—	—	—	—	—
Reserve Money	14	10.8	11.5	15.3	†18.7	22.5	27.4	30.7	38.2	40.6	40.9	45.0	50.2	†63.6	71.7	80.7
of which: Currency Outside DMBs	14a	10.5	11.1	15.1	†18.7	22.5	27.4	30.7	38.2	40.6	40.0	45.0	50.2	†50.5	59.8	66.9
Foreign Liabilities	16c	18.8	22.3	31.0	†2.8	3.7	3.2	5.2	5.8	8.7	9.4	19.5	28.5	†49.9	45.4	47.6
Central Government Deposits	16d	—	.4	—	†.7	.3	.3	1.1	.1	.9	.8	3.9	3.3	†5.9	3.7	.5
Other Items (Net)	17r	2.4	2.5	3.2	†42.7	51.1	46.3	51.6	59.1	57.0	64.5	69.9	72.1	†−46.9	−40.5	−37.9
Deposit Money Banks															*Billions of Francs:*	
Reserves	20	.2	.3	.3	.4	.7	.5	1.3	†.6	.5	.4	1.4	.9	†10.9	12.8	14.0
Foreign Assets	21	2.5	2.4	3.2	2.7	3.2	5.1	2.4	†2.2	2.2	3.1	4.5	7.9	11.7	5.8	8.0
Claims on Central Government	22a	1.8	1.6	1.8	1.2	.8	.6	1.1	†.9	1.1	1.1	1.1	1.2	2.6	2.6	3.4
Claims on Private Sector	22d	17.0	21.6	34.1	51.1	61.3	53.3	65.8	†76.1	82.0	87.4	95.0	101.6	†70.3	83.2	99.5
Claims on Other Financial Insts	22f	....	....	....	....	....	....	....	....							
Demand Deposits	24	5.1	5.6	11.3	12.5	12.6	12.8	17.3	†18.1	18.5	18.9	22.9	30.7	53.4	49.7	47.5
Time Deposits	25	.4	.3	.1	.6	.6	1.2	3.0	†3.3	3.3	4.5	4.0	6.0	10.3	13.8	17.8
Foreign Liabilities	26c	1.7	2.9	3.2	4.6	4.3	5.8	6.6	†4.3	5.3	5.4	5.7	6.7	†12.6	17.0	19.8
Long-Term Foreign Liabilities	26cl	1.9	2.1	2.3	2.1	2.5	2.7	2.6	†2.5	2.5	2.5	3.1	3.3	3.5	2.4	3.7
Central Government Deposits	26d	....	....	....	....	....	....	....	....					6.0	10.5	9.9
Credit from Monetary Authorities	26g	9.3	11.7	21.0	32.3	40.8	29.3	36.4	†47.7	48.4	50.0	54.1	54.3	6.9	20.7	38.3
Other Items (Net)	27r	3.1	3.3	1.5	3.3	5.1	7.7	4.7	†3.8	7.8	10.8	12.1	10.7	2.8	−9.7	−12.1
Treasury Claims: Private Sector	22d. i	—	—	—	—	—	—	—	—	—	—	—	—	.3	.3	.3
Post Office: Checking Deposits	24.. i	—	—	—	—	.5	.5	.5	.5	.4	.4	.4	.4	3.2	4.3	3.1
Monetary Survey															*Billions of Francs:*	
Foreign Assets (Net)	31n	−17.0	−21.9	−29.7	−42.7	−50.3	−46.4	−51.9	†−6.1	−8.4	−6.9	−14.9	−20.6	†−38.1	−48.1	−55.4
Domestic Credit	32	40.8	47.8	63.8	84.0	97.3	100.5	116.7	131.1	137.9	148.0	170.9	193.0	†111.4	127.2	144.4
Claims on Central Govt. (Net)	32an	23.5	26.2	29.6	32.9	36.0	47.2	50.9	†55.0	55.9	60.6	75.9	91.4	†40.8	43.6	44.6
Claims on Private Sector	32d	17.0	21.6	34.1	51.1	61.3	53.3	65.8	76.1	82.0	87.4	95.0	101.6	†70.6	83.5	99.8
Claims on Other Financial Insts	32f	....	....	....	....	....	....	....	† —	—	—	—	—	—	—	—
Money	34	16.0	17.5	27.0	32.0	35.6	40.7	48.5	56.8	59.5	60.2	68.3	81.2	†107.1	113.8	117.5
Quasi-Money	35	.4	.3	.1	.6	.6	1.2	3.0	†3.3	3.3	4.5	4.0	6.0	†10.3	13.8	17.8
Long-Term Foreign Liabilities	36cl	1.9	2.1	2.3	2.1	2.5	2.7	2.6	†2.5	2.5	2.5	3.1	3.3	†3.5	2.4	3.7
Other Items (Net)	37r	5.5	5.9	4.6	6.6	8.3	9.6	10.7	†62.4	64.3	73.9	80.6	81.9	†−47.6	−50.9	−50.0
Money plus Quasi-Money	35l	16.4	17.9	27.1	32.5	36.3	41.8	51.5	†60.1	62.8	64.7	72.3	87.3	117.4	127.6	135.3
Other Banking Institutions															*Billions of Francs:*	
Savings Deposits	45	.3	.3	.4	.5	.5	.5	.5	.5	.4	.4	....	....	....	....	....
Liquid Liabilities	55l	16.7	18.2	27.5	33.0	36.7	42.3	52.0	†60.6	63.2	65.1	....	....	....	....	....
Interest Rates															*Percent Per Annum*	
Discount Rate (End of Period)	60	3.50	5.50	5.50	8.00	8.00	8.00	8.00	8.00	10.50	10.50	12.50	10.50	10.50	10.50	8.50
Money Market Rate	60b	....	....	....	....	7.28	7.38	7.40	7.72	10.13	13.68	14.66	12.23	11.84	10.66	8.58
Deposit Rate	60l	3.00	5.75	5.75	5.88	6.00	6.00	6.00	6.00	6.19	6.25	7.75	7.50	7.25	7.25	6.08
Lending Rate	60p	....	....	....	....	....	12.00	12.00	12.00	14.50	14.50	16.00	14.50	14.50	14.50	13.50

	1987	1988	1989	1990	1991	1992	1993	1994	1995	1996	1997	1998	1999	2000	2001	
End of Period																**Exchange Rates**
	378.78	407.68	380.32	364.84	370.48	378.57	404.89	†780.44	728.38	753.06	807.94	791.61	†896.19	918.49	935.39	Official Rate.................................... **aa**
End of Period (ae) Period Average (rf)																
	267.00	302.95	289.40	256.45	259.00	275.32	294.77	†534.60	490.00	523.70	598.81	562.21	†652.95	704.95	744.31	Official Rate.................................... **ae**
	300.54	297.85	319.01	272.26	282.11	264.69	283.16	†555.20	499.15	511.55	583.67	589.95	†615.70	711.98	733.04	Official Rate.................................... **rf**
End of Period																**Fund Position**
	50.8	50.8	50.8	50.8	50.8	68.9	68.9	68.9	68.9	68.9	68.9	68.9	93.3	93.3	93.3	Quota .... **2f. s**
	.2	.2	.1	.3	.3	.1	.1	.1	.3	.2	—	.1	.4	.1	.3	SDRs .... **1b. s**
	8.7	8.7	8.7	8.7	8.7	8.7	8.7	8.7	8.7	8.8	8.8	8.8	8.8	8.8	8.8	Reserve Position in the Fund .... **1c. s**
	60.0	54.9	41.9	48.7	42.0	47.5	51.4	74.1	99.0	114.6	130.2	132.4	140.9	134.7	136.0	Total Fund Cred.&Loans Outstg. **2tl**
End of Period																**International Liquidity**
	15.8	36.0	115.8	190.5	319.3	307.9	332.4	221.4	323.0	431.5	414.9	402.9	349.7	381.2	348.8	Total Reserves minus Gold.................... **1l. d**
	.3	.2	.1	.5	.4	.1	.1	.2	.5	.3	.1	.1	.6	.1	.4	SDRs .... **1b. d**
	12.3	11.7	11.4	12.4	12.4	11.9	12.0	12.7	13.0	12.6	11.8	12.4	12.1	11.4	11.1	Reserve Position in the Fund .... **1c. d**
	3.3	24.1	104.2	177.7	306.5	295.9	320.3	208.5	309.5	418.6	403.0	390.4	337.0	369.7	337.4	Foreign Exchange .... **1d. d**
	.019	.019	.019	.019	.019	.019	.019	.019	.019	.019	.019	.019	.019	. . . .	. . . .	Gold (Million Fine Troy Ounces)............ **1ad**
	8.9	7.8	7.3	7.1	6.7	6.5	7.0	7.0	7.3	7.1	5.8	5.5	5.6	. . . .	. . . .	Gold (National Valuation) .... **1an d**
	51.9	6.9	7.6	4.9	16.2	2.5	6.0	9.7	1.9	−6.9	3.7	1.8	3.1	2.0	2.7	Monetary Authorities: Other Liab. ...... **4.. d**
	27.2	19.4	63.7	72.1	60.8	40.4	26.3	118.7	163.6	136.7	117.6	125.2	116.6	140.1	195.0	Deposit Money Banks: Assets .... **7a. d**
	87.4	87.0	93.1	113.0	78.4	47.3	42.2	34.3	102.1	70.0	28.2	49.1	87.9	79.6	83.9	Liabilities........... **7b. d**
End of Period																**Monetary Authorities**
	4.2	10.9	33.5	48.9	82.7	84.8	98.0	118.4	158.2	226.0	248.4	226.5	228.3	268.8	259.7	Foreign Assets **11**
	46.8	52.1	42.1	34.1	34.5	37.2	41.0	58.7	65.1	77.0	99.8	105.9	112.9	108.9	135.9	Claims on Central Government **12a**
	32.2	30.4	23.9	23.9	23.9	23.9	23.9	—	—	—	—	—	—	—	—	Claims on Deposit Money Banks **12e**
	—	—	—	—	—	—	—	—	—	—	—	—	—	—	—	Claims on Other Financial Insts **12f**
	78.1	86.4	98.9	100.3	132.0	131.7	143.8	115.9	127.7	151.1	162.8	153.7	173.1	219.0	245.2	Reserve Money **14**
	60.8	62.2	54.8	46.9	60.0	60.9	65.1	91.1	107.5	120.3	129.5	135.3	123.4	146.9	179.0	of which: Currency Outside DMBs **14a**
	39.4	25.7	18.5	19.1	19.8	18.7	22.6	63.0	73.1	82.7	107.5	105.9	128.4	125.2	129.2	Foreign Liabilities **16c**
	1.0	12.3	6.1	8.9	3.1	5.9	5.5	12.8	27.1	63.0	70.6	63.7	41.5	34.7	17.2	Central Government Deposits **16d**
	−35.2	−31.0	−23.9	−21.4	−13.6	−10.4	−9.1	−14.6	−4.6	6.2	7.4	9.2	−1.8	−1.2	4.1	Other Items (Net) **17r**
End of Period																**Deposit Money Banks**
	17.3	24.6	43.8	54.0	71.8	70.5	79.4	25.3	17.1	29.5	32.1	16.5	47.7	70.7	59.2	Reserves **20**
	7.3	5.9	18.4	18.5	15.8	11.1	7.8	63.4	80.2	71.6	70.4	70.4	76.2	98.8	145.2	Foreign Assets **21**
	2.8	4.2	2.5	3.8	2.6	3.4	3.4	28.0	19.4	24.0	21.1	13.6	14.0	17.8	27.7	Claims on Central Government **22a**
	95.2	70.2	84.1	84.1	86.2	91.9	93.8	84.9	130.3	171.2	195.9	251.0	286.5	283.6	342.2	Claims on Private Sector.................... **22d**
	—	—	—	—	—	—	—	—	—	—	—	—	—	—	—	Claims on Other Financial Insts **22f**
	45.0	48.9	47.8	47.3	47.4	47.4	52.7	83.0	90.5	119.5	126.2	131.8	142.3	143.6	197.8	Demand Deposits **24**
	20.6	26.0	31.6	36.6	45.4	49.0	52.6	63.1	56.4	76.4	89.0	91.9	97.0	116.1	110.0	Time Deposits **25**
	18.1	19.0	19.6	21.2	14.0	8.7	8.8	11.5	45.3	30.5	5.9	19.5	50.3	45.2	52.4	Foreign Liabilities........................... **26c**
	5.3	7.4	7.3	7.8	6.3	4.3	3.6	6.9	4.7	6.1	10.9	8.1	7.1	10.9	10.1	Long-Term Foreign Liabilities **26cl**
	11.1	16.9	21.4	27.2	32.7	37.1	33.0	39.3	50.8	71.5	68.2	78.0	102.3	129.8	159.2	Central Government Deposits **26d**
	32.9	30.5	24.4	24.4	24.2	24.1	23.9	—	—	.1	—	—	—	—	—	Credit from Monetary Authorities **26g**
	−10.3	−43.9	−3.3	−4.0	6.4	6.3	9.8	−2.1	−.7	−8.0	19.3	22.2	25.3	25.3	44.8	Other Items (Net) **27r**
	.4	.2	.2	.3	.1	.7	1.5	2.1	1.5	2.0	4.5	3.9	5.2	2.7	1.3	Treasury Claims: Private Sector ....**22d. i**
	3.6	3.5	7.8	4.3	—	—	—	—	—	—	—	—	—	—	—	Post Office: Checking Deposits ....**24.. i**
End of Period																**Monetary Survey**
	−46.0	−27.9	13.9	27.1	64.8	68.5	74.3	107.3	120.0	184.3	205.5	171.5	125.9	197.2	223.2	Foreign Assets (Net) **31n**
	136.4	100.8	109.0	90.2	87.5	89.4	99.7	119.5	136.9	137.6	178.0	228.8	269.5	245.8	329.4	Domestic Credit **32**
	40.8	30.4	24.7	5.8	1.2	−3.2	4.4	32.6	5.1	−35.6	−22.4	−26.1	−22.2	−40.5	−14.0	Claims on Central Govt. (Net) **32an**
	95.6	70.4	84.3	84.4	86.4	92.6	95.3	86.9	131.8	173.2	200.4	254.9	291.7	286.3	343.5	Claims on Private Sector **32d**
	—	—	—	—	—	—	—	—	—	—	—	—	—	—	—	Claims on Other Financial Insts **32f**
	109.3	114.6	110.4	98.5	107.4	108.3	117.8	174.2	198.2	240.4	256.0	267.6	266.0	291.2	377.2	Money **34**
	20.6	26.0	31.6	36.6	45.4	49.0	52.6	63.1	56.4	76.4	89.0	91.9	97.0	116.1	110.0	Quasi-Money................................. **35**
	5.3	7.4	7.3	7.8	6.3	4.3	3.6	6.9	4.7	6.1	10.9	8.1	7.1	10.9	10.1	Long-Term Foreign Liabilities **36cl**
	−44.8	−75.1	−26.4	−25.6	−6.8	−3.7	—	−17.3	−2.4	−1.0	27.5	32.8	25.2	24.9	55.4	Other Items (Net) **37r**
	129.9	140.6	142.0	135.0	152.7	157.2	170.4	237.2	254.6	316.8	345.0	359.5	363.1	407.2	487.2	Money plus Quasi-Money **35l**
End of Period																**Other Banking Institutions**
	. . . .	. . . .	. . . .	. . . .	. . . .	. . . .	. . . .	. . . .	. . . .	. . . .	. . . .	. . . .	. . . .	. . . .	. . . .	Savings Deposits............................. **45**
	. . . .	. . . .	. . . .	. . . .	. . . .	. . . .	. . . .	. . . .	. . . .	316.8	345.0	359.5	363.1	407.2	. . . .	Liquid Liabilities **55l**
Percent Per Annum																**Interest Rates**
	8.50	9.50	11.00	11.00	11.00	12.50	10.50	10.00	7.50	6.50	6.00	6.25	5.75	6.50	6.50	Discount Rate (End of Period).................. **60**
	8.37	8.72	10.07	10.98	10.94	11.44	. . . .	. . . .	. . . .	. . . .	. . . .	4.81	4.95	4.95	4.95	Money Market Rate **60b**
	5.25	5.25	6.42	7.00	7.00	7.75	. . . .	. . . .	. . . .	. . . .	. . . .	3.50	3.50	3.50	3.50	Deposit Rate **60l**
	13.50	13.58	15.08	16.00	16.00	16.75	. . . .	. . . .	. . . .	. . . .	. . . .	. . . .	. . . .	. . . .	. . . .	Lending Rate **60p**

Mali

		1972	1973	1974	1975	1976	1977	1978	1979	1980	1981	1982	1983	1984	1985	1986
Prices														*Index Numbers (1995=100):*		
Consumer Prices	64	...	...	...	...	...	...	...	...	...	...	...	...	...	...	...
International Transactions														*Billions of Francs*		
Exports	70	10.53	11.65	15.41	11.49	20.56	30.61	25.20	31.35	43.31	41.92	47.90	62.90	57.97	55.56	73.34
Imports, c.i.f.	71	19.81	28.13	43.04	37.71	36.85	39.00	64.30	76.45	93.05	104.75	109.20	134.60	121.69	134.54	153.71
Balance of Payments														*Millions of US Dollars:*		
Current Account, n.i.e.	78al *d*	...	...	...	−61.1	−42.2	5.2	−146.3	−113.6	−129.9	−143.0	−115.3	−113.2	−121.5	−209.7	−254.1
Goods: Exports f.o.b.	78aa *d*	...	...	...	71.9	94.4	124.6	94.2	145.7	204.9	154.2	145.8	166.8	192.0	176.1	205.6
Goods: Imports f.o.b.	78ab *d*	...	...	...	−136.2	−111.3	−111.1	−199.4	−270.3	−308.4	−269.0	−232.6	−240.9	−257.8	−328.4	−339.0
Trade Balance	78ac *d*	...	...	...	−64.3	−16.9	13.5	−105.2	−124.6	−103.4	−114.8	−86.9	−74.1	−65.8	−152.4	−133.4
Services: Credit	78ad *d*	...	...	...	22.9	17.8	23.9	37.2	45.6	57.7	46.2	44.4	42.0	40.7	57.3	68.1
Services: Debit	78ae *d*	...	...	...	−102.5	−78.7	−95.4	−150.7	−163.8	−211.8	−168.9	−162.7	−166.9	−172.9	−263.7	−306.7
Balance on Goods & Services	78af *d*	...	...	...	−143.9	−77.8	−58.1	−218.7	−242.8	−257.5	−237.6	−205.1	−199.0	−198.0	−358.8	−371.9
Income: Credit	78ag *d*	...	...	...											4.9	3.2
Income: Debit	78ah *d*	...	...	...	−21.7	−16.6	−19.8	−13.3	−11.8	−16.9	−32.6	−24.2	−27.5	−19.2	−18.7	−24.8
Balance on Gds, Serv. & Inc.	78ai *d*	...	...	...	−165.6	−94.4	−77.9	−232.0	−254.6	−274.4	−270.1	−229.3	−226.5	−217.2	−372.6	−393.6
Current Transfers, n.i.e.: Credit	78aj *d*	...	...	...	119.9	62.6	91.3	101.0	165.6	169.3	147.2	133.7	131.7	111.9	207.5	198.4
Current Transfers: Debit	78ak *d*	...	...	...	−15.5	−10.5	−8.3	−15.3	−24.7	−24.8	−20.1	−19.6	−18.4	−16.2	−44.5	−58.9
Capital Account, n.i.e.	78bc *d*	...	...	...	4.5	—	—	47.2	—	—	—	—	—	52.9	80.8	92.7
Capital Account, n.i.e.: Credit	78ba *d*	...	...	...	4.5	—	—	47.2	—	—	—	—	—	52.9	80.8	92.7
Capital Account: Debit	78bb *d*	...	...	...	—	—	—	—	—	—	—	—	—	—	—	—
Financial Account, n.i.e.	78bj *d*	...	...	...	4.3	6.7	22.9	49.8	120.8	127.9	107.8	76.7	88.7	68.4	120.6	127.4
Direct Investment Abroad	78bd *d*	...	...	...	−.6	−7.6	−8.0	−8.9	3.1							
Dir. Invest. in Rep. Econ., n.i.e.	78be *d*	...	...	...	2.6	2.6	3.1	−.9	—	2.4	3.7	1.5	3.1	10.1	2.9	−8.4
Portfolio Investment Assets	78bf *d*	...	...	...	—	—	—	—	—	—	—	—	—	—	—	—
Equity Securities	78bk *d*	...	...	...	—	—	—	—	—	—	—	—	—	—	—	—
Debt Securities	78bl *d*	...	...	...	—	—	—	—	—	—	—	—	—	—	—	—
Portfolio Investment Liab., n.i.e.	78bg *d*	...	...	...	—	—	—	—	—	—	—	—	—	—	—	—
Equity Securities	78bm *d*	...	...	...	—	—	—	—	—	—	—	—	—	—	—	—
Debt Securities	78bn *d*	...	...	...	—	—	—	—	—	—	—	—	—	—	—	—
Financial Derivatives Assets	78bw *d*	...	...	...	...	...	...	...	...	...	...	...	...	...	...	...
Financial Derivatives Liabilities	78bx *d*	...	...	...	...	...	...	...	...	...	...	...	...	...	...	...
Other Investment Assets	78bh *d*	...	...	...	−13.6	−12.8	−7.5	5.8	26.7	6.2	4.2	—	—	−8.6	13.0	−6.2
Monetary Authorities	78bo *d*	...	...	...	...	...	...	...	...	...	...	...	...	...	...	...
General Government	78bp *d*	...	...	...	−2.2	−.2	—	—	7.8	—	—	—	—	—	—	—
Banks	78bq *d*	...	...	...	—	—	—	—	—	—	—	—	—	−8.6	13.0	−6.2
Other Sectors	78br *d*	...	...	...	−11.4	−12.6	−7.5	5.8	19.0	6.2	4.2	—	—	—	—	—
Other Investment Liab., n.i.e.	78bi *d*	...	...	...	15.9	24.5	35.4	53.8	91.0	119.4	99.8	75.2	85.5	66.9	104.7	142.0
Monetary Authorities	78bs *d*	...	...	...	—	—	—	—	—	—	—	—	—	—	—	—
General Government	78bt *d*	...	...	...	18.2	16.6	47.7	56.9	81.6	103.5	87.5	77.1	83.0	53.4	95.0	134.0
Banks	78bu *d*	...	...	...	4.5	1.9	−6.2	2.2	5.9	11.1	7.9	1.1	2.5	13.5	9.7	8.1
Other Sectors	78bv *d*	...	...	...	−6.8	6.0	−6.1	−5.3	3.5	4.7	4.4	−3.0	—	—	—	—
Net Errors and Omissions	78ca *d*	...	...	...	−9.9	−7.5	−13.0	31.6	−27.2	−30.8	22.7	12.6	−7.3	.7	−18.4	−15.6
Overall Balance	78cb *d*	...	...	...	−62.1	−43.0	15.0	−17.7	−20.1	−32.8	−12.6	−26.0	−31.9	.5	−26.6	−49.5
Reserves and Related Items	79da *d*	...	...	...	62.1	43.0	−15.0	17.7	20.1	32.8	12.6	26.0	31.9	−.5	26.6	49.5
Reserve Assets	79db *d*	...	...	...	7.6	−4.6	.4	5.5	−1.2	4.7	9.5	−1.1	−1.5	−33.7	3.5	47.2
Use of Fund Credit and Loans	79dc *d*	...	...	...	.3	2.4	−1.8	9.9	3.8	10.6	−2.6	27.0	13.5	19.3	5.1	−9.8
Exceptional Financing	79de *d*	...	...	...	54.1	45.2	−13.7	2.3	17.5	17.6	5.7	.1	19.8	13.9	18.0	12.1
Government Finance														*Billions of Francs;*		
Deficit (-) or Surplus	80	...	...	...	...	—	.2	−4.0	−9.1	†−16.0	−14.7	†−31.6	−34.5	−35.0	−46.5	−43.2
Total Revenue and Grants	81y	...	...	...	24.2	27.1	34.7	35.2	36.0	†61.4	72.0	†83.2	95.1	107.9	119.3	116.7
Revenue	81	...	...	...	18.4	24.4	32.1	33.1	32.8	†37.5	43.7	†52.6	54.6	66.1	79.7	87.6
Grants	81z	...	...	...	5.8	2.7	2.6	2.1	3.2	†23.9	28.3	†30.6	40.5	41.8	39.6	29.1
Exp.& Lending Minus Repay	82z	...	...	...	...	27.1	34.5	39.2	45.1	†77.4	86.7	†114.8	129.7	142.9	165.8	159.9
Expenditure	82	...	...	...	...	27.1	34.5	39.2	45.1	†73.4	86.8	†114.8	129.5	142.8	165.7	159.6
Lending Minus Repay	83	...	...	...	...	—	—	—	—	†4.0	−.1	†—	.1	.1	.1	.3
Statistical Discrepancy	80xx	...	...	...	...	...	...	...	...	...	...	...	...	...	...	...
Total Financing	80h	...	...	...	...	—	−.2	4.0	9.1	†16.0	14.7	†31.6	34.5	35.0	46.5	45.2
Domestic	84a	...	...	...	...	.4	.3	...	...	†1.3	−1.4	†3.3	4.7	2.5	5.4	1.4
Foreign	85a	...	...	...	...	−.4	−.6	...	...	†14.7	16.1	†28.3	29.9	32.5	41.1	43.8
Debt																
Total Debt	88	...	...	...	...	...	...	...	...	†163.7	...	†308.2	334.1	...	...	570.4
Domestic	88a	...	...	...	...	...	...	...	...	†26.5	28.2	†43.2	44.4	...	...	23.6
Foreign	89a	...	...	...	...	...	...	...	...	†137.2	...	†264.9	289.6	...	...	546.8
National Accounts														*Billions of Francs*		
Househ.Cons.Expend.,incl.NPISHs	96f	...	...	...	...	135.4	149.9	172.8	213.6	246.5	315.6	360.4	374.7	452.4	522.2	519.2
Government Consumption Expend.	91f	...	...	...	...	6.5	8.3	9.4	11.3	12.6	36.6	39.6	69.0	69.1	78.6	86.9
Gross Fixed Capital Formation	93e	...	...	...	...	...	...	...	...	...	93.0	71.4	90.7	69.8	90.8	122.2
Changes in Inventories	93i	...	...	...	...	...	...	...	...	...	...	−.4	2.5	12.6	−10.5	−15.5
Exports of Goods and Services	90c	...	...	...	...	30.4	39.2	30.0	37.2	50.3	55.6	62.6	78.8	112.2	104.0	87.4
Imports of Goods and Services (-)	98c	...	...	...	...	46.2	51.3	65.4	76.9	90.0	120.6	130.0	145.5	175.7	227.2	207.2
Gross Domestic Product (GDP)	99b	88.4	92.1	97.7	129.5	178.6	204.5	217.8	259.6	300.5	380.2	403.6	470.2	540.4	554.5	593.0
																Millions:
Population	99z	5.26	5.38	5.66	†6.29	6.32	†6.51	6.70	6.90	7.10	7.29	7.51	7.74	7.97	8.21	†7.57

	1987	1988	1989	1990	1991	1992	1993	1994	1995	1996	1997	1998	1999	2000	2001		
Period Averages																**Prices**	
	....	74.8	74.7	75.2	76.5	71.8	71.6	88.2	100.0	106.8	†106.4	110.7	109.4	108.6	114.3	Consumer Prices	**64**
Billions of Francs																**International Transactions**	
	53.79	63.89	78.78	97.68	88.06	90.72	135.30	185.95	220.50	221.41	327.70	328.13	351.57	388.13	542.29	Exports	**70**
	112.44	150.23	108.47	164.02	129.90	160.81	179.43	327.22	385.40	395.17	431.20	445.90	504.70	421.54	481.41	Imports, c.i.f.	**71**
Minus Sign Indicates Debit																**Balance of Payments**	
	−219.2	−242.8	−155.1	−221.1	−172.5	−240.5	−188.6	−162.6	−283.8	−273.2	−178.4	....	....	....	....	Current Account, n.i.e.	**78al***d*
	255.9	247.1	268.5	334.9	370.6	364.0	371.9	334.9	441.8	433.5	561.6					Goods: Exports f.o.b.	**78aa***d*
	−335.4	−387.2	−362.1	−455.4	−516.9	−526.8	−492.4	−449.2	−556.8	−551.5	−551.9					Goods: Imports f.o.b.	**78ab***d*
	−79.5	−140.1	−93.6	−120.5	−146.3	−162.8	−120.4	−114.3	−115.0	−118.0	9.7					*Trade Balance*	**78ac***d*
	82.5	69.2	76.5	84.9	71.0	78.3	74.8	69.0	87.6	87.6	82.1					Services: Credit	**78ad***d*
	−327.1	−312.2	−270.7	−374.1	−334.6	−428.6	−360.8	−317.0	−434.5	−382.8	−345.6					Services: Debit	**78ae***d*
	−324.1	−383.1	−287.8	−409.8	−409.8	−513.0	−406.4	−362.3	−461.9	−413.2	−253.8					*Balance on Goods & Services*	**78af***d*
	3.1	4.9	7.8	22.6	24.7	27.8	30.2	9.3	8.3	10.9	10.6					Income: Credit	**78ag***d*
	−28.0	−37.4	−38.7	−59.3	−48.8	−56.1	−43.2	−49.7	−48.9	−67.1	−61.7					Income: Debit	**78ah***d*
	−349.0	−415.7	−318.7	−446.5	−434.0	−541.2	−419.4	−402.7	−502.6	−469.3	−304.8					*Balance on Gds, Serv. & Inc.*	**78ai***d*
	209.3	221.1	211.2	282.2	320.1	380.0	294.6	281.3	266.8	246.1	170.0					Current Transfers, n.i.e.: Credit	**78aj***d*
	−79.5	−48.2	−47.7	−56.8	−58.6	−79.3	−63.7	−41.2	−48.0	−50.0	−43.5					Current Transfers: Debit	**78ak***d*
	116.8	142.0	102.5	105.8	137.5	143.6	111.9	99.1	126.2	136.4	108.6					Capital Account, n.i.e.	**78bc***d*
	116.8	142.0	102.5	105.8	137.5	143.6	111.9	99.1	126.2	136.4	108.6					Capital Account, n.i.e.: Credit	**78ba***d*
	—	—	—	—	—	—	—	—	—	—	—					Capital Account: Debit	**78bb***d*
	86.6	135.7	79.6	57.8	34.3	−5.6	−14.5	−7.0	118.6	174.6	52.7					Financial Account, n.i.e.	**78bj***d*
	—	—	—	—	—	—	—	—	—	—	—					Direct Investment Abroad	**78bd***d*
	−6.0	7.1	6.4	5.7	1.2	−21.9	4.1	17.4	111.4	84.1	39.4					Dir. Invest. in Rep. Econ., n.i.e.	**78be***d*
	—	—	—	—	—	—	—	—	—	—	—					Portfolio Investment Assets	**78bf***d*
	—	—	—	—	—	—	—	—	....	....	....					Equity Securities	**78bk***d*
	—	—	—	—	—	—	—	—	....	....	....					Debt Securities	**78bl***d*
	—	—	—	—	—	—	—	—	....	....	....					Portfolio Investment Liab., n.i.e.	**78bg***d*
	—	—	—	—	—	—	—	—	....	....	....					Equity Securities	**78bm***d*
	—	—	—	—	—	—	—	—	....	....	....					Debt Securities	**78bn***d*
									....	....	....					Financial Derivatives Assets	**78bw***d*
									....	....	....					Financial Derivatives Liabilities	**78bx***d*
	2.4	−24.6	−61.6	−30.2	−28.7	5.8	−21.4	−104.0	−52.3	4.1	−12.4					Other Investment Assets	**78bh***d*
																Monetary Authorities	**78bo***d*
	....	....	....	....	....	....	....	....	....	....	....					General Government	**78bp***d*
	2.4	4.6	−39.4	−.1	9.6	17.5	11.9	−100.3	−33.2	16.8	2.0					Banks	**78bq***d*
	—	−29.2	−22.2	−30.0	−38.4	−11.7	−33.3	−3.7	−19.2	−12.7	−14.4					Other Sectors	**78br***d*
	90.2	153.2	134.8	82.2	61.9	10.5	2.8	79.6	59.6	86.4	25.7					Other Investment Liab., n.i.e.	**78bi***d*
																Monetary Authorities	**78bs***d*
	95.8	122.5	121.3	82.6	65.2	12.8	−18.0	33.1	89.8	80.5	57.7					General Government	**78bt***d*
	−5.6	6.9	−.1	1.7	−25.6	−19.8	.4	11.9	−1.4	−10.6	6.7					Banks	**78bu***d*
	—	23.8	13.6	−2.2	22.2	17.4	20.4	34.5	−28.7	16.5	−38.7					Other Sectors	**78bv***d*
	1.5	−16.5	−26.1	−7.4	30.5	−35.3	−6.0	5.6	−13.0	−8.8	7.9					Net Errors and Omissions	**78ca***d*
	−14.3	18.4	.8	−65.0	29.8	−137.9	−97.2	−65.0	−52.0	29.0	−9.2					*Overall Balance*	**78cb***d*
	14.3	−18.4	−.8	65.0	−29.8	137.9	97.2	65.0	52.0	−29.0	9.2					Reserves and Related Items	**79da***d*
	7.5	−34.6	−60.1	−55.3	−120.6	−7.2	−45.8	−37.6	−80.2	−131.6	−38.3					Reserve Assets	**79db***d*
	−26.8	−7.6	−16.6	8.3	−9.2	8.4	5.6	32.7	38.4	22.4	21.3					Use of Fund Credit and Loans	**79dc***d*
	33.6	23.9	75.9	112.0	100.0	136.8	137.4	69.9	93.8	80.1	26.2					Exceptional Financing	**79de***d*
Year Ending December 31																**Government Finance**	
	−30.9	−27.6	†−28.4	−18.0	−26.5	−29.1	−30.6	−43.4	−36.7	−11.1	−29.9	†−38.7	−61.4	−69.1 [P]	−170.5	Deficit (−) or Surplus	**80**
	127.2	149.8	†143.0	155.7	165.8	154.3	146.7	236.7	269.7	314.0	320.5	†344.8	356.1	371.1 [P]	387.1	Total Revenue and Grants	**81y**
	89.4	114.3	†109.6	116.1	109.6	100.7	104.7	138.9	177.3	217.5	236.3	†254.9	272.7	269.9 [P]	314.3	Revenue	**81**
	37.8	35.5	†33.4	39.6	56.2	53.6	42.0	97.8	92.4	96.5	84.2	†89.9	83.4	101.2 [P]	72.8	Grants	**81z**
	158.1	177.4	....									†383.5	417.5	440.2 [P]	....	Exp.& Lending Minus Repay	**82z**
	157.9	174.8	†171.4	173.7	192.3	183.4	177.3	280.1	306.4	325.1	350.4	†387.1	419.7	442.7 [P]	557.6	Expenditure	**82**
	.2	2.6	....									†−3.6	−2.2	−2.5 [P]	....	Lending Minus Repay	**83**
	6.2	—	−36.1	−4.8	−3.6	4.9	8.1	−29.7	−14.0	−18.9	−8.5	−10.1	2.2	1.6 [P]	....	Statistical Discrepancy	**80xx**
	24.7	27.6	64.5	22.8	30.1	24.2	22.5	73.1	50.7	30.0	38.4	48.8	59.2	67.5 [P]	....	Total Financing	**80h**
	−5.1	4.7	−11.7	−17.3	−12.1	−8.6	−3.0	−3.6	−40.1	−52.1	−10.6	−9.2	−1.1	3.1 [P]	....	Domestic	**84a**
	29.8	22.9	76.2	40.1	42.2	32.8	25.5	76.7	90.8	82.1	49.0	58.0	60.3	64.4 [P]	....	Foreign	**85a**
																Debt	
																Total Debt	**88**
	....	....	....													Domestic	**88a**
	604.0	726.8	....	673.8	700.9	730.3	773.9	1,576.6	1,395.2	1,498.4	1,614.8	1,684.3	1,618.0	1,701.6	1,767.0	Foreign	**89a**
Billions of Francs																**National Accounts**	
	464.7	472.6	497.6	536.1	541.6	546.3	560.5	749.0	928.3	1,055.4	1,001.0	1,138.0	1,203.0	1,384.8	....	Househ.Cons.Expend.,incl.NPISHs	**96f**
	88.2	91.2	98.5	95.6	118.1	130.2	123.4	187.9	204.4	210.5	221.6	249.8	249.0	236.8	....	Government Consumption Expend.	**91f**
	121.5	116.9	132.7	128.3	141.9	143.7	144.7	249.3	299.7	316.5	347.7	305.1	312.7	318.2	....	Gross Fixed Capital Formation	**93e**
	5.1	2.7	15.9	11.2	−10.2	12.6	−21.1	−10.8	−14.2	−41.3	−22.9	31.6	21.8	42.4	....	Changes in Inventories	**93i**
	94.3	95.1	106.6	113.9	124.5	116.7	129.9	224.7	259.9	264.7	361.6	366.2	376.4	419.8	....	Exports of Goods and Services	**90c**
	183.3	192.3	206.4	211.9	225.6	229.5	226.6	421.2	491.8	487.2	486.2	498.3	544.4	618.8	....	Imports of Goods and Services (−)	**98c**
	590.5	589.1	644.9	673.4	692.5	721.4	712.1	978.7	1,187.1	1,319.3	1,422.9	1,593.6	1,670.7	1,799.8	....	Gross Domestic Product (GDP)	**99b**
Midyear Estimates																	
	7.70	7.83	7.96	8.16	9.00	9.22	9.45	9.68	9.93	10.19	10.46	10.74	11.04	11.35	†10.40	Population	**99z**

(See notes in the back of the book.)

Malta

		1972	1973	1974	1975	1976	1977	1978	1979	1980	1981	1982	1983	1984	1985	1986
Exchange Rates															*SDRs per Lira:*	
Official Rate	ac	2.3220	2.1437	2.1754	2.1161	2.0175	2.0864	2.1105	2.2076	2.2140	2.2185	2.1821	2.1440	2.0744	2.1479	2.2147
															US Dollars per Lira:	
Official Rate	ag	2.5210	2.5860	2.6635	2.4772	2.3440	2.5344	2.7495	2.9082	2.8237	2.5823	2.4071	2.2447	2.0333	2.3593	2.7090
Official Rate	rh	2.6095	2.7232	2.5947	2.6202	2.3534	2.3688	2.5974	2.7911	2.8962	2.5894	2.4282	2.3135	2.1718	2.1385	2.5481
															Index Numbers (1995=100):	
Official Rate	ahx	92.1	96.1	91.6	92.5	83.1	83.6	91.7	98.5	102.2	91.4	85.7	81.7	76.7	75.5	89.9
Nominal Effective Exchange Rate	nec	....	....	....	....	....	....	....	85.9	87.9	94.5	100.5	105.0	109.8	112.0	106.5
Real Effective Exchange Rate	rec	....	....	....	....	....	....	....	115.8	122.0	131.9	136.4	132.8	131.1	127.1	120.3
Fund Position															*Millions of SDRs:*	
Quota	2f.s	16.0	16.0	16.0	16.0	16.0	16.0	20.0	20.0	30.0	30.0	30.0	45.1	45.1	45.1	45.1
SDRs	1b.s	5.1	5.1	5.1	5.1	5.2	5.5	5.8	9.4	11.3	14.6	21.2	31.0	35.7	39.6	43.1
Reserve Position in the Fund	1c.s	4.0	4.0	4.0	7.8	13.8	12.2	13.2	13.3	15.8	23.7	25.8	28.8	30.9	29.7	32.4
International Liquidity												*Millions of US Dollars Unless Otherwise Indicated:*					
Total Reserves minus Gold	1l.d	261.7	310.4	386.7	485.8	607.8	719.6	925.1	1,012.7	990.1	1,073.8	1,083.6	1,112.3	990.2	986.9	1,145.4
SDRs	1b.d	5.5	6.1	6.2	6.0	6.0	6.7	7.6	12.4	14.5	17.0	23.4	32.4	35.0	43.5	52.8
Reserve Position in the Fund	1c.d	4.4	4.9	4.9	9.1	16.0	14.8	17.2	17.5	20.1	27.6	28.4	30.2	30.3	32.6	39.6
Foreign Exchange	1d.d	251.8	299.4	375.5	470.7	585.8	698.1	900.4	982.8	955.5	1,029.3	1,031.8	1,049.7	925.0	910.9	1,053.0
Gold (Million Fine Troy Ounces)	1ad	.353	.353	.353	.353	.353	.360	.360	.366	.434	.456	.462	.472	.466	.466	.466
Gold (National Valuation)	1and	12.3	12.3	12.3	12.3	12.3	12.6	12.7	12.8	51.4	60.8	62.9	66.7	64.5	134.8	163.9
Monetary Authorities: Other Assets	3..d	....	....	....	....	....	....	....	....	....	45.7	47.8	62.4	75.4	90.1	84.8
Other Official Insts.: Assets	3b.d	.2	.2	9.3	.1	.1	.1	4.9	5.4	6.1	39.3	33.5	40.2	37.4	52.7	65.5
Deposit Money Banks: Assets	7a.d	96.6	112.3	118.4	116.9	123.0	133.9	137.7	165.9	162.6	148.5	144.2	127.7	120.9	209.7	249.6
Liabilities	7b.d	15.3	3.0	1.6	4.8	8.7	13.9	17.7	18.5	19.1	24.6	25.4	30.3	26.6	67.4	64.9
Other Banking Insts.: Assets	7e.d	26.0	16.4	15.5	14.8	5.4	3.2	3.1	3.7	3.7	3.5	3.6	2.7	2.7	52.4	51.0
Liabilities	7f.d	.1	.1	.1	.1	.1	.1	.1	.2	.1	—	—	.1	25.3	15.8	
Monetary Authorities															*Millions of Liri:*	
Foreign Assets	11	103.14	118.32	131.08	183.93	238.61	271.51	322.59	342.74	370.66	416.41	444.09	489.92	529.57	513.86	514.57
Claims on Central Government	12a	2.05	.23	.37	.06	8.77	.04	.04	.02	.16	.18	.23	.62	.67	.25	.30
Reserve Money	14	98.66	95.07	110.32	158.04	200.86	222.03	267.66	297.45	302.84	338.76	347.23	369.75	409.77	413.36	417.22
of which: Currency Outside DMBs	14a	62.27	72.69	79.57	98.88	119.64	137.83	155.02	176.25	206.08	239.16	259.73	279.63	283.69	273.34	273.79
Central Government Deposits	16d	.56	11.31	3.25	3.34	3.22	6.25	16.15	19.52	28.43	35.34	31.82	37.42	35.44	56.91	32.86
Other Items (Net)	17r	5.98	12.19	17.90	22.61	43.30	43.26	38.83	25.79	39.54	42.50	65.27	83.38	85.03	43.84	64.79
Banking Institutions															*Millions of Liri:*	
Reserves	20	36.31	27.41	37.41	66.13	97.95	105.27	131.82	133.11	115.52	117.47	109.10	116.42	118.18	131.45	132.30
Foreign Assets	21	36.17	43.44	44.45	47.17	52.49	52.82	50.09	57.04	57.59	57.52	59.92	56.89	59.46	88.88	92.15
Claims on Central Government	22a	13.23	16.09	16.25	16.59	16.59	16.60	16.82	16.94	17.65	18.56	18.97	19.02	19.39	20.08	20.13
Claims on Private Sector	22d	57.83	55.21	59.89	58.86	62.61	64.77	70.01	85.12	117.44	139.20	168.78	204.45	230.26	262.30	298.82
Demand Deposits	24	12.01	10.29	13.00	17.51	22.73	21.35	27.05	30.58	32.62	31.94	29.60	30.39	30.93	35.48	36.66
Time and Savings Deposits	25	114.95	119.43	127.60	148.04	175.77	186.97	207.39	221.50	230.94	248.56	266.39	286.58	309.29	347.60	384.37
Foreign Liabilities	26c	5.72	1.16	.61	1.94	3.73	5.50	6.45	6.37	6.75	9.53	10.54	13.51	13.08	28.55	23.97
Capital Accounts	27a	4.99	4.56	4.62	8.03	8.74	9.21	10.59	11.31	13.13	10.82	11.99	12.99	14.18	14.44	14.45
Other Items (Net)	27r	5.88	6.71	12.16	13.23	18.67	16.43	17.26	22.45	24.76	31.91	38.24	53.30	59.80	76.66	83.95
Banking Survey															*Millions of Liri:*	
Foreign Assets (Net)	31n	133.79	160.60	174.91	229.16	287.37	318.82	366.23	393.40	421.49	464.40	493.46	533.31	575.94	574.19	582.75
Domestic Credit	32	72.40	60.16	72.81	71.79	84.75	75.16	70.58	82.51	106.75	122.47	156.01	186.54	214.70	225.54	286.24
Claims on Central Govt. (Net)	32an	14.57	4.95	12.92	12.94	22.14	10.39	.57	-2.61	-10.69	-16.74	-12.77	-17.91	-15.57	-36.76	-12.57
Claims on Private Sector	32d	57.83	55.21	59.89	58.86	62.61	64.77	70.01	85.12	117.44	139.20	168.78	204.45	230.26	262.30	298.82
Money	34	80.08	87.16	99.04	123.75	148.34	165.64	194.57	231.64	258.80	293.73	306.28	324.63	325.92	321.21	323.25
Quasi-Money	35	114.95	124.47	134.64	155.08	193.72	210.97	232.39	246.50	255.94	273.56	295.39	318.58	309.29	347.60	384.37
Other Items (Net)	37r	11.18	9.15	14.06	22.12	30.06	17.37	9.85	-2.22	13.51	19.58	47.79	76.64	155.42	130.92	161.38
Money plus Quasi-Money	35l	195.03	211.63	233.68	278.83	342.06	376.61	426.96	478.13	514.74	567.29	601.67	643.21	635.22	668.81	707.61
Interest Rates															*Percent Per Annum*	
Discount Rate (End of Period)	60	5.50	5.50	5.50	5.50	5.50	5.50	5.50	5.50	5.50	5.50	6.50	6.50	6.50	6.00	6.00
Treasury Bill Rate	60c	....	....	....	....	....	....	....	....	....	....	....	....	....	....	....
Deposit Rate	60l	....	....	....	....	....	5.00	5.00	5.00	5.00	5.00	5.00	5.00	5.00	4.96	4.50
Lending Rate	60p	....	....	....	8.00	8.00	8.00	8.00	8.00	8.00	8.00	8.00	8.00	8.00	8.00	8.00
Prices and Labor															*Index Numbers (1995=100):*	
Consumer Prices	64	37.8	40.7	†43.6	47.5	47.7	52.5	55.0	58.9	68.2	76.0	80.5	†79.7	79.4	79.2	80.8
Industrial Production (1990=100)	66	....	....	....	29.0	33.6	39.8	41.7	44.4	52.8	53.7	56.3	57.9	†62.4	63.7	67.0
															Number in Thousands:	
Labor Force	67d	....	....	....	....	....	....	....	....	....	....	121	121	122	122	124
Employment	67e	....	....	....	....	....	....	....	....	....	....	....	....	....	113	115
Unemployment	67c	....	....	....	....	....	....	....	....	....	....	....	....	....	10	9
Unemployment Rate (%)	67r	....	....	....	....	....	....	....	....	....	....	....	....	....	8.1	6.8
International Transactions															*Millions of Liri*	
Exports	70	25.72	35.96	51.58	63.90	97.41	121.79	131.95	152.17	166.72	173.73	169.04	156.75	181.36	187.10	194.67
Imports, c.i.f.	71	67.21	88.10	138.97	144.45	179.92	217.68	221.50	271.96	323.74	332.27	325.07	316.63	330.49	354.14	348.11
															1985=100	
Volume of Exports	72	28.6	38.3	40.2	44.8	63.9	80.1	83.0	89.7	†93.6	92.3	85.3	85.5	97.7	100.0	104.4
Volume of Imports	73	56.8	59.9	69.3	67.4	77.3	86.0	82.4	89.7	†98.8	88.8	88.8	86.5	92.0	100.0	102.1
Unit Value of Exports	74	44.7	49.4	62.7	66.7	74.3	77.1	83.8	90.5	†94.5	101.3	104.3	98.0	99.7	100.0	102.5
Unit Value of Imports	75	33.3	41.5	56.7	60.5	65.7	71.5	75.9	85.6	†92.5	102.2	103.3	103.3	101.4	100.0	96.2

1987	1988	1989	1990	1991	1992	1993	1994	1995	1996	1997	1998	1999	2000	2001		
															Exchange Rates	
End of Period																
2.2614	2.2373	2.2589	2.3371	2.2877	1.9436	1.8426	1.8609	1.9090	1.9338	1.8969	1.8818	1.7681	1.7532	1.7602	Official Rate	**ac**
End of Period (ag) Period Average (rh)																
3.2081	3.0107	2.9686	3.3249	3.2724	2.6725	2.5309	2.7166	2.8377	2.7807	2.5594	2.6496	2.4268	2.2843	2.2121	Official Rate	**ag**
2.8981	3.0251	2.8712	3.1527	3.1002	3.1462	2.6171	2.6486	2.8333	2.7745	2.5924	2.5743	2.5039	2.2851	2.2226	Official Rate	**rh**
Period Averages																
102.3	106.8	101.3	111.3	109.4	111.0	92.4	93.5	100.0	97.9	91.5	90.9	88.4	80.7	78.4	Official Rate	**ahx**
105.3	106.1	107.4	105.8	106.0	104.7	98.3	98.8	100.0	98.8	100.3	101.4	101.4	103.0	103.9	Nominal Effective Exchange Rate	**nec**
116.5	114.9	111.9	107.6	105.7	101.8	96.3	97.9	100.0	98.8	101.3	103.1	104.0	105.7	107.3	Real Effective Exchange Rate	**rec**
															Fund Position	
End of Period																
45.1	45.1	45.1	45.1	45.1	67.5	67.5	67.5	67.5	67.5	67.5	67.5	102.0	102.0	102.0	Quota	**2f.s**
46.6	50.1	53.6	59.1	64.2	33.1	35.3	35.6	37.6	39.7	41.9	44.4	22.5	24.5	26.4	SDRs	**1b.s**
31.2	27.3	23.5	19.6	20.8	25.3	25.3	25.4	27.3	30.7	31.6	31.6	40.3	40.3	40.3	Reserve Position in the Fund	**1c.s**
															International Liquidity	
End of Period																
1,414.6	1,364.7	1,355.1	1,431.8	1,333.3	1,268.3	1,362.4	1,849.6	1,604.5	1,619.8	1,487.6	1,662.7	1,788.0	1,470.2	1,666.2	Total Reserves minus Gold	**1l.d**
66.1	67.5	70.4	84.1	91.8	45.5	48.4	52.0	56.0	57.2	56.6	62.5	30.9	31.9	33.2	SDRs	**1b.d**
44.3	36.7	30.9	27.9	29.8	34.8	34.7	37.1	40.5	44.1	42.7	44.5	55.3	52.5	50.6	Reserve Position in the Fund	**1c.d**
1,304.2	1,260.5	1,253.8	1,319.8	1,211.7	1,188.0	1,279.3	1,760.5	1,508.0	1,518.6	1,388.3	1,555.7	1,701.9	1,385.8	1,582.4	Foreign Exchange	**1d.d**
.466	.466	.226	.157	.117	.120	.100	.105	.041	.044	.011	.006	.006	.004	.005	Gold (Million Fine Troy Ounces)	**1ad**
163.9	200.0	93.7	59.4	42.4	40.3	38.5	40.0	15.9	7.2	3.3	1.8	1.8	1.0	1.4	Gold (National Valuation)	**1and**
84.4	80.4	78.5	30.5	33.4	29.6	26.8	27.2	.1	.1	—	.1	....	....	....	Monetary Authorities: Other Assets	**3..d**
84.4	80.4	78.5	30.5	33.4	29.6	26.8	27.2	.1	.1	—	.1	—	—	....	Other Official Insts.: Assets	**3b.d**
370.9	490.1	645.1	956.1	1,127.1	1,163.1	1,233.9	1,129.8	†2,235.5	2,875.5	3,415.0	5,850.0	6,815.0	8,595.6	6,890.9	Deposit Money Banks: Assets	**7a.d**
142.5	254.6	321.4	491.1	574.5	632.0	758.9	621.5	†1,576.0	2,333.9	2,972.8	5,242.4	6,339.0	7,905.0	6,164.1	Liabilities	**7b.d**
110.9	181.8	220.0	298.5	321.0	303.1	294.0	13.7	11.0	9.1	18.0	18.6	15.9	15.6	....	Other Banking Insts.: Assets	**7e.d**
65.9	151.4	197.1	271.3	273.0	467.8	496.3	366.3	—	—	—	.5	—	—	....	Liabilities	**7f.d**
															Monetary Authorities	
End of Period																
529.59	534.00	509.97	452.63	423.81	494.46	559.11	698.01	593.74	568.12	575.53	639.77	740.30	644.17	753.93	Foreign Assets	**11**
4.12	1.85	2.88	22.21	58.17	62.30	18.08	39.22	67.73	74.28	59.16	24.32	6.15	9.18	5.80	Claims on Central Government	**12a**
429.05	430.10	412.82	389.84	416.51	442.60	443.58	584.20	512.98	491.66	498.99	514.05	549.32	568.41	589.40	Reserve Money	**14**
300.24	314.31	319.41	330.32	344.34	337.64	353.26	365.91	352.47	362.97	364.42	368.97	385.57	397.36	419.14	*of which: Currency Outside DMBs*	**14a**
33.73	47.35	25.98	22.96	16.74	17.00	21.04	22.25	42.01	33.53	35.70	47.61	96.21	56.18	69.08	Central Government Deposits	**16d**
70.94	58.50	74.05	62.04	48.73	97.17	112.56	130.78	106.48	117.22	100.01	102.44	100.92	28.76	101.25	Other Items (Net)	**17r**
															Banking Institutions	
End of Period																
117.39	105.34	87.03	58.99	62.80	93.82	83.26	194.50	†101.31	97.78	126.14	141.73	172.17	153.63	173.57	Reserves	**20**
115.62	162.77	217.30	287.56	344.60	435.23	487.52	415.89	†787.78	1,034.11	1,334.30	2,207.90	2,808.27	3,762.92	3,115.08	Foreign Assets	**21**
45.06	73.80	82.52	93.74	79.50	78.25	142.65	135.88	†149.80	196.50	297.01	391.72	463.02	466.15	550.96	Claims on Central Government	**22a**
339.66	388.81	464.78	575.39	686.25	772.21	879.53	985.51	†1097.10	1,261.33	1,350.46	1,492.26	1,658.93	1,822.57	1,976.37	Claims on Private Sector	**22d**
39.01	38.62	42.04	49.75	53.22	57.43	59.42	72.15	†80.93	87.31	111.39	146.77	190.52	194.40	215.70	Demand Deposits	**24**
423.37	482.04	562.59	651.93	723.33	827.13	940.86	1,105.35	†1254.60	1,414.07	1,567.09	1,698.96	1,860.65	1,944.22	2,117.15	Time and Savings Deposits	**25**
44.41	84.57	108.28	147.70	175.55	236.47	299.86	228.78	†555.36	839.34	1,161.54	1,978.55	2,612.12	3,460.58	2,786.53	Foreign Liabilities	**26c**
15.31	15.50	18.15	28.31	34.05	37.21	39.09	40.98	†128.61	147.62	198.02	299.97	336.14	372.76	447.91	Capital Accounts	**27a**
95.63	109.99	120.58	137.99	187.01	221.26	253.73	284.51	†116.48	101.40	69.86	109.36	102.95	233.31	248.67	Other Items (Net)	**27r**
															Banking Survey	
End of Period																
600.80	612.20	618.99	592.49	592.87	693.22	746.77	885.12	†826.16	762.89	748.29	869.13	936.44	946.51	1,082.47	Foreign Assets (Net)	**31n**
354.97	417.07	523.05	666.57	805.79	893.80	1,016.85	1,136.14	†1265.87	1,489.64	1,660.93	1,848.85	2,017.02	2,228.28	2,451.52	Domestic Credit	**32**
15.31	28.26	58.27	91.18	119.54	121.59	137.33	150.63	†168.77	228.31	310.47	356.59	358.09	405.71	475.16	Claims on Central Govt. (Net)	**32an**
339.66	388.81	464.78	575.39	686.25	772.21	879.53	985.51	†1097.10	1,261.33	1,350.46	1,492.26	1,658.93	1,822.57	1,976.37	Claims on Private Sector	**32d**
354.59	363.95	368.64	384.63	406.70	408.56	425.07	463.55	†498.91	489.66	489.63	525.09	580.70	595.72	635.61	Money	**34**
423.37	482.04	562.59	651.93	723.33	827.13	940.86	1,105.35	†1254.60	1,414.07	1,567.09	1,698.96	1,860.65	1,944.22	2,117.15	Quasi-Money	**35**
177.82	183.28	210.80	222.50	268.63	351.33	397.70	452.35	†338.52	348.80	352.50	493.93	512.11	634.85	781.24	Other Items (Net)	**37r**
777.96	845.99	931.24	1,036.56	1,130.03	1,235.69	1,365.93	1,568.90	†1753.51	1,903.73	2,056.72	2,224.05	2,441.35	2,539.94	2,752.76	Money plus Quasi-Money	**35l**
															Interest Rates	
Percent Per Annum																
5.50	5.50	5.50	5.50	5.50	5.50	5.50	5.50	5.50	5.50	5.50	5.50	4.75	4.75	4.25	Discount Rate (*End of Period*)	**60**
4.50	4.24	4.24	4.25	4.46	4.58	4.60	4.29	4.65	4.99	5.08	5.41	5.15	4.89	4.93	Treasury Bill Rate	**60c**
4.50	4.50	4.50	4.50	4.50	4.50	4.50	4.50	4.50	4.50	4.56	4.64	4.66	4.86	4.84	Deposit Rate	**60l**
8.00	8.46	8.50	8.50	8.50	8.50	8.50	8.50	†7.38	7.77	7.99	8.09	7.70	7.28	6.90	Lending Rate	**60p**
															Prices and Labor	
Period Averages																
81.2	81.9	82.6	85.1	†87.3	†88.7	92.4	96.2	100.0	102.5	105.7	108.2	110.5	113.1	116.4	Consumer Prices	**64**
69.6	75.4	88.6	100.0	112.9	128.4	132.8	149.7	....	....	....	....	....	....	....	Industrial Production (1990=100)	**66**
Period Averages																
126	128	130	132	134	136	138	136	140	142	144	144	146	147	....	Labor Force	**67d**
122	125	126	127	130	132	132	134	149	140	137	137	138	....	....	Employment	**67e**
6	5	5	5	5	6	6	6	5	6	7	7	8	7	6	Unemployment	**67c**
4.4	4.0	3.7	3.9	3.6	4.0	4.5	4.1	3.7	4.4	5.0	5.1	5.3	5.3	....	Unemployment Rate (%)	**67r**
															International Transactions	
Millions of Liri																
208.59	235.92	294.41	357.90	405.50	490.90	518.30	592.40	674.90	624.10	628.90	712.10	712.30	1,027.90	861.90	Exports	**70**
392.88	447.40	515.80	620.50	684.00	747.80	830.90	918.80	1,037.70	1,007.80	984.20	1,034.90	1,136.20	1,500.00	1,165.70	Imports, c.i.f.	**71**
1985=100																
105.4	108.4	130.4	....	....	....	....	....	....	....	....	....	....	....	....	Volume of Exports	**72**
114.6	129.1	144.2	....	....	....	....	....	....	....	....	....	....	....	....	Volume of Imports	**73**
107.4	118.8	124.3	....	....	....	....	....	....	....	....	....	....	....	....	Unit Value of Exports	**74**
96.8	97.9	101.0	....	....	....	....	....	....	....	....	....	....	....	....	Unit Value of Imports	**75**

Malta

		1972	1973	1974	1975	1976	1977	1978	1979	1980	1981	1982	1983	1984	1985	1986
Balance of Payments																*Millions of US Dollars:*
Current Account, n.i.e.	78al d	22.5	30.4	5.2	59.3	55.0	40.0	72.7	46.6	38.8	86.4	12.4	−4.9	8.2	−25.8	6.9
Goods: Exports f.o.b.	78aa d	81.5	113.9	171.0	199.3	254.7	319.0	362.2	462.2	537.6	499.9	445.5	406.1	426.4	435.5	534.1
Goods: Imports f.o.b.	78ab d	−155.9	−212.9	−313.6	−332.4	−376.6	−456.8	−507.3	−674.3	−884.7	−778.1	−709.2	−659.5	−639.2	−672.1	−786.5
Trade Balance	78ac d	−74.4	−99.0	−142.7	−133.1	−121.8	−137.8	−145.1	−212.0	−347.1	−278.3	−263.7	−253.4	−212.8	−236.6	−252.4
Services: Credit	78ad d	90.4	133.7	151.0	188.9	178.8	197.0	264.2	344.8	481.1	411.9	306.0	282.6	250.5	273.7	370.5
Services: Debit	78ae d	−44.6	−51.8	−73.2	−80.0	−85.9	−114.8	−140.1	−184.1	−242.9	−243.6	−246.0	−207.2	−209.7	−218.5	−280.4
Balance on Goods & Services	78af d	−28.6	−17.1	−64.9	−24.2	−28.9	−55.6	−21.0	−51.3	−108.9	−109.9	−203.8	−178.1	−172.0	−181.4	−162.3
Income: Credit	78ag d	32.2	35.0	48.0	63.7	61.6	70.1	78.9	102.1	153.1	161.6	174.0	133.0	138.6	126.6	146.3
Income: Debit	78ah d	−10.7	−13.3	−15.0	−14.6	−16.0	−19.7	−31.7	−61.4	−57.6	−50.9	−28.6	−22.9	−20.0	−22.8	−44.0
Balance on Gds, Serv. & Inc.	78ai d	−7.1	4.6	−31.9	24.9	16.7	−5.2	26.2	−10.6	−13.3	.8	−58.5	−68.0	−53.4	−77.6	−60.1
Current Transfers, n.i.e.: Credit	78aj d	34.9	31.5	41.2	39.0	44.0	49.0	52.7	64.7	60.5	93.9	76.7	68.2	68.5	57.1	73.5
Current Transfers: Debit	78ak d	−5.2	−5.7	−4.2	−4.7	−5.6	−3.8	−6.2	−7.5	−8.4	−8.3	−5.8	−5.1	−6.9	−5.3	−6.6
Capital Account, n.i.e.	78bc d	2.6	6.2	7.5	6.8	7.5	6.4	7.0	6.1	5.8	4.7	3.9	3.2	3.0	3.0	4.3
Capital Account, n.i.e.: Credit	78ba d	2.6	6.2	7.5	6.8	7.5	6.4	7.0	6.1	5.8	4.7	3.9	3.2	3.0	3.0	4.3
Capital Account: Debit	78bb d	—	—	—	—	—	—	—	—	—	—	—	—	—	—	—
Financial Account, n.i.e.	78bj d	45.3	−3.3	27.2	34.8	41.2	18.2	50.9	−.8	24.9	41.9	24.3	88.8	22.1	−24.7	−18.3
Direct Investment Abroad	78bd d	—	—	—	—	—	—	—	—	—	—	—	—	—	—	—
Dir. Invest. in Rep. Econ., n.i.e.	78be d	4.5	5.2	10.6	15.9	14.1	18.5	21.5	16.2	26.6	39.0	20.9	24.5	26.2	19.0	21.9
Portfolio Investment Assets	78bf d	14.9	22.2	7.3	−9.1	−1.9	−13.7	−18.9	−30.4	−8.7	3.9	−3.4	−27.1	.9	−32.8	44.0
Equity Securities	78bk d									−9.8		.7	−18.5			2.3
Debt Securities	78bl d	14.9	22.2	7.3	−9.1	−1.9	−13.7	−18.9	−30.4	1.2	3.9	−4.1	−8.6	.9	−32.8	41.7
Portfolio Investment Liab., n.i.e.	78bg d	—	—	—	—	—	—	—	—	—	—	—	—	—	—	—
Equity Securities	78bm d	—	—	—	—	—	—	—	—	—	—	—	—	—	—	—
Debt Securities	78bn d	—	—	—	—	—	—	—	—	—	—	—	—	—	—	—
Financial Derivatives Assets	78bw d	....	....	....	....	....	....	....	....	....	....	....	....	....	....	....
Financial Derivatives Liabilities	78bx d	....	....	....	....	....	....	....	....	....	....	....	....	....	....	....
Other Investment Assets	78bh d	12.8	−32.0	−13.5	1.8	−15.5	4.3	18.9	.8	−13.6	−17.3	−21.6	−13.6	3.7	−1.1	−59.0
Monetary Authorities	78bo d	....	....	....	....	....	....	....	....	....	....	....	....	....	....	....
General Government	78bp d	—	—	—	—	—	—	—	—	—	—	—	—	—	—	—
Banks	78bq d	13.6	−29.6	−14.0	−10.1	−14.8	9.0	19.2	3.3	−2.6	−16.0	−12.9	−16.0	10.4	1.7	−49.9
Other Sectors	78br d	−.8	−2.4	.5	12.0	−.7	−4.7	−.3	−2.5	−11.0	−1.3	−8.7	2.3	−6.7	−2.8	−9.2
Other Investment Liab., n.i.e.	78bi d	13.1	1.4	22.8	26.2	44.5	9.2	29.3	12.6	20.6	16.3	28.4	105.0	−8.7	−9.8	−25.2
Monetary Authorities	78bs d															
General Government	78bt d	−.8	4.6	3.9	2.6	12.2	1.4	3.6	4.5	11.9	8.8	2.2	22.7	7.4	5.1	−9.4
Banks	78bu d	5.8	−17.1	−1.6	3.4	4.0	.7	5.4	.8	5.2	4.9	22.8	27.1	−2.0	−7.9	−11.7
Other Sectors	78bv d	8.1	13.8	20.5	20.3	28.2	7.1	20.2	7.3	3.5	2.6	3.4	55.3	−14.1	−7.0	−4.1
Net Errors and Omissions	78ca d	1.6	6.0	2.1	12.0	−9.5	−4.6	−5.3	3.5	−18.1	14.9	11.6	17.0	−1.5	−19.6	2.6
Overall Balance	78cb d	72.1	39.3	42.0	112.8	94.2	60.1	125.2	55.4	51.4	147.8	52.1	104.2	31.9	−67.1	−4.6
Reserves and Related Items	79da d	−72.1	−39.3	−42.0	−112.8	−94.2	−60.1	−125.2	−55.4	−51.4	−147.8	−52.1	−104.2	−31.9	67.1	4.6
Reserve Assets	79db d	−72.1	−39.3	−42.0	−112.8	−94.2	−60.1	−125.2	−55.4	−51.4	−147.8	−52.1	−104.2	−31.9	67.1	4.6
Use of Fund Credit and Loans	79dc d	—	—	—	—	—	—	—	—	—	—	—	—	—	—	—
Exceptional Financing	79de d	....	....	....	....	....	....	....	....	....	....	....	....	....	....	....
International Investment Position																*Millions of US Dollars*
Assets	79aa d	....	....	....	....	....	....	....	....	....	....	....	....	....	....	....
Direct Investment Abroad	79ab d	....	....	....	....	....	....	....	....	....	....	....	....	....	....	....
Portfolio Investment	79ac d	....	....	....	....	....	....	....	....	....	....	....	....	....	....	....
Equity Securities	79ad d	....	....	....	....	....	....	....	....	....	....	....	....	....	....	....
Debt Securities	79ae d	....	....	....	....	....	....	....	....	....	....	....	....	....	....	....
Financial Derivatives	79al d	....	....	....	....	....	....	....	....	....	....	....	....	....	....	....
Other Investment	79af d	....	....	....	....	....	....	....	....	....	....	....	....	....	....	....
Monetary Authorities	79ag d	....	....	....	....	....	....	....	....	....	....	....	....	....	....	....
General Government	79ah d	....	....	....	....	....	....	....	....	....	....	....	....	....	....	....
Banks	79ai d	....	....	....	....	....	....	....	....	....	....	....	....	....	....	....
Other Sectors	79aj d	....	....	....	....	....	....	....	....	....	....	....	....	....	....	....
Reserve Assets	79ak d	....	....	....	....	....	....	....	....	1,041.5	1,134.5	1,146.3	1,178.9	3,884.6	4,116.8	4,382.9
Liabilities	79la d	....	....	....	....	....	....	....	....	....	....	....	....	....	....	....
Dir. Invest. in Rep. Economy	79lb d	....	....	....	....	....	....	....	....	....	....	....	....	....	....	....
Portfolio Investment	79lc d	....	....	....	....	....	....	....	....	....	....	....	....	....	....	....
Equity Securities	79ld d	....	....	....	....	....	....	....	....	....	....	....	....	....	....	....
Debt Securities	79le d	....	....	....	....	....	....	....	....	....	....	....	....	....	....	....
Financial Derivatives	79ll d	....	....	....	....	....	....	....	....	....	....	....	....	....	....	....
Other Investment	79lf d	....	....	....	....	....	....	....	....	....	....	....	....	....	....	....
Monetary Authorities	79lg d	....	....	....	....	....	....	....	....	....	....	....	....	....	....	....
General Government	79lh d	....	....	....	....	....	....	....	....	....	....	....	....	....	....	....
Banks	79li d	....	....	....	....	....	....	....	....	....	....	....	....	....	....	....
Other Sectors	79lj d	....	....	....	....	....	....	....	....	....	....	....	....	....	....	....

Balance of Payments

Minus Sign Indicates Debit

1987	1988	1989	1990	1991	1992	1993	1994	1995	1996	1997	1998	1999	2000	2001		
22.6	61.1	-9.5	-55.8	-7.4	30.2	-84.3	-131.5	-360.8	-404.0	-200.9	-221.5	-121.7	-468.6	-172.4	Current Account, n.i.e.	78al *d*
653.0	780.1	891.3	1,198.1	1,330.7	1,609.8	1,408.1	1,618.5	1,949.4	1,772.8	1,663.2	1,824.3	2,016.9	2,478.3	2,002.8	Goods: Exports f.o.b.	78aa *d*
-1,024.6	-1,222.3	-1,327.7	-1,769.2	-1,913.1	-2,122.9	-1,976.4	-2,221.0	-2,673.1	-2,536.2	-2,320.7	-2,417.0	-2,588.4	-3,096.2	-2,492.4	Goods: Imports f.o.b.	78ab *d*
-371.6	-442.2	-436.5	-571.1	-582.4	-513.0	-568.3	-602.5	-723.7	-763.4	-657.4	-592.7	-571.4	-617.9	-489.6	*Trade Balance*	78ac *d*
557.2	653.2	644.5	752.0	814.0	883.8	912.4	994.6	1,047.5	1,070.7	1,111.5	1,181.4	1,218.9	1,106.1	1,103.5	Services: Credit	78ad *d*
-358.9	-412.3	-433.3	-514.3	-528.9	-588.6	-604.2	-686.5	-750.8	-754.1	-719.7	-800.4	-845.5	-869.6	-788.4	Services: Debit	78ae *d*
-173.4	-201.3	-225.3	-333.3	-297.2	-217.8	-260.2	-294.5	-427.0	-446.8	-265.5	-211.7	-198.1	-381.4	-174.4	*Balance on Goods & Services*	78af *d*
139.5	156.6	190.5	269.0	268.3	271.2	241.8	219.4	287.7	309.7	360.4	510.6	1,234.9	895.7	814.9	Income: Credit	78ag *d*
-25.8	-53.5	-73.2	-78.9	-93.9	-116.9	-126.8	-150.6	-247.7	-298.0	-351.2	-578.4	-1,200.7	-1,008.4	-820.6	Income: Debit	78ah *d*
-59.6	-98.2	-107.9	-143.2	-122.9	-63.5	-145.2	-225.7	-387.0	-435.0	-256.3	-279.5	-163.9	-494.2	-180.1	*Balance on Gds, Serv. & Inc.*	78ai *d*
91.2	170.5	114.5	110.6	120.6	98.6	64.9	101.2	80.5	87.1	122.4	114.9	120.1	101.7	190.4	Current Transfers, n.i.e.: Credit	78aj *d*
-9.0	-11.2	-16.1	-23.1	-5.1	-4.8	-4.1	-7.1	-54.3	-56.1	-66.9	-56.9	-77.8	-76.1	-182.7	Current Transfers: Debit	78ak *d*
4.3	7.0	6.0	—	—	—	13.1	—	12.5	58.1	8.4	28.5	25.5	18.2	1.6	Capital Account, n.i.e.	78bc *d*
4.3	7.0	6.0	—	—	—	13.1	—	16.8	64.2	32.9	33.1	31.0	23.8	4.4	Capital Account, n.i.e.: Credit	78ba *d*
—	—	—	—	—	—	—	—	-4.3	-6.1	-24.5	-4.6	-5.5	-5.6	-2.9	Capital Account: Debit	78bb *d*
-2.6	17.2	-46.8	-43.1	13.3	27.0	188.7	480.9	23.3	202.3	105.1	293.6	399.5	155.2	261.8	Financial Account, n.i.e.	78bj *d*
						-.9	1.0	-5.0	-6.1	-16.2	-14.4	-44.5	-29.0	-6.5	Direct Investment Abroad	78bd *d*
19.4	40.8	51.7	45.8	77.0	39.5	56.4	151.7	131.7	276.8	80.8	273.3	814.6	607.2	303.1	Dir. Invest. in Rep. Econ., n.i.e.	78be *d*
-7.5	-38.4	-57.7	-1.9	-245.2	-214.1	-266.6	304.4	-459.7	-120.1	107.9	-141.3	-471.4	-744.5	-445.8	Portfolio Investment Assets	78bf *d*
.3	-5.4		.7	4.0	4.7	13.2	247.2	—	-.9	-10.1	6.3	-11.7	-17.5	-37.0	Equity Securities	78bk *d*
-7.8	-32.9	-57.7	-2.6	-249.3	-218.8	-279.8	57.2	-459.7	-119.2	118.0	-147.6	-459.7	-727.1	-408.8	Debt Securities	78bl *d*
—	—	—	—	—	—	—	—	1.9	3.3	.3	58.9	-32.8	-8.5	-6.7	Portfolio Investment Liab., n.i.e.	78bg *d*
—	—	—	—	—	—	—	—	-4.2	3.1	.3	-1.5	-7.5	1.3	-1.8	Equity Securities	78bm *d*
—	—	—	—	—	—	—	—	6.1	.3	—	60.5	-25.3	-9.8	-4.9	Debt Securities	78bn *d*
....	....							-.3	-3.6	-2.4	-1.2	-2.4	-1.4	—	Financial Derivatives Assets	78bw *d*
								-1.4							Financial Derivatives Liabilities	78bx *d*
-62.5	-105.5	-100.1	-242.6	67.5	-96.1	131.1	103.4	-286.0	-619.1	-1,003.0	-2,052.2	-1,593.5	-928.6	1,823.3	Other Investment Assets	78bh *d*
....	....	....					—	—	—	—	—	—	....	....	Monetary Authorities	78bo *d*
						—	-.5	—	—	—	—	—	....	....	General Government	78bp *d*
-59.6	-111.5	-98.1	-218.4	77.8	-99.7	146.4	79.6	-280.5	-581.5	-934.3	-2,077.4	-1,606.0	-965.5	1,825.2	Banks	78bq *d*
-2.9	6.0	-2.0	-24.1	-10.3	3.6	-15.3	24.4	-5.5	-37.6	-68.7	25.2	12.5	36.9	-1.9	Other Sectors	78br *d*
48.0	120.3	59.4	155.6	114.0	297.7	268.7	-79.7	642.0	671.1	937.8	2,170.5	1,729.5	1,259.9	-1,405.7	Other Investment Liab., n.i.e.	78bi *d*
....	....	....					—	—	—	—	—	—	....	....	Monetary Authorities	78bs *d*
3.5	-4.5	4.0	38.6	26.6	102.8	35.3	6.0	-40.8	51.8	-26.3	-9.4	222.8	-23.1	12.5	General Government	78bt *d*
47.2	94.6	39.3	53.2	25.8	48.5	111.2	-274.6	680.6	597.5	903.4	2,183.7	1,807.4	1,267.5	-1,416.9	Banks	78bu *d*
-2.6	30.2	16.1	63.7	61.6	146.4	122.2	188.8	2.2	21.7	60.7	-3.9	-300.6	15.5	-1.3	Other Sectors	78bv *d*
-28.8	-50.4	64.4	2.5	-84.7	-12.7	17.4	33.4	17.9	58.7	94.2	90.4	-64.9	73.6	164.1	Net Errors and Omissions	78ca *d*
-4.5	34.8	14.2	-96.3	-78.8	44.6	134.8	382.8	-307.1	-84.9	6.8	190.9	238.4	-221.6	255.1	*Overall Balance*	78cb *d*
4.5	-34.8	-14.2	96.3	78.8	-44.6	-134.8	-382.8	307.1	84.9	-6.8	-190.9	-238.4	221.6	-255.1	Reserves and Related Items	79da *d*
4.5	-34.8	-14.2	96.3	78.8	-44.6	-134.8	-382.8	307.1	84.9	-6.8	-190.9	-238.4	221.6	-255.1	Reserve Assets	79db *d*
—	—	—	—	—	—	—	—	—	—	—	—	—	—	—	Use of Fund Credit and Loans	79dc *d*
....	....	....	....	....	....	....	....	....	....	....	....	....	....	....	Exceptional Financing	79de *d*

International Investment Position

Millions of US Dollars

1987	1988	1989	1990	1991	1992	1993	1994	1995	1996	1997	1998	1999	2000	2001		
....	....	....	....	....	....	....	3,479.5	4,102.2	4,754.5	5,296.6	8,018.2	9,726.1	....	....	Assets	79aa *d*
							28.3	32.3	107.6	140.0	170.4	185.2			Direct Investment Abroad	79ab *d*
							886.4	1,394.4	1,505.2	1,286.1	1,496.0	1,911.3			Portfolio Investment	79ac *d*
							2.4	4.0	4.7	15.1	6.6	24.5			Equity Securities	79ad *d*
							884.0	1,390.5	1,500.5	1,271.0	1,489.3	1,886.8			Debt Securities	79ae *d*
															Financial Derivatives	79al *d*
							689.2	1,027.5	1,600.8	2,433.5	4,656.1	5,833.2			Other Investment	79af *d*
															Monetary Authorities	79ag *d*
							2.7	2.0	2.5	2.6	2.6	2.4			General Government	79ah *d*
							396.1	694.1	1,262.4	2,073.1	4,299.2	5,491.0			Banks	79ai *d*
							290.4	331.4	335.9	357.8	354.3	339.7			Other Sectors	79aj *d*
							1,875.6	1,647.8	1,540.8	1,437.0	1,695.7	1,796.5			Reserve Assets	79ak *d*
							2,126.0	2,947.2	3,877.4	4,578.3	7,295.4	9,139.9			Liabilities	79la *d*
							415.9	562.1	844.2	857.9	1,174.3	1,860.6			Dir. Invest. in Rep. Economy	79lb *d*
							17.4	24.1	23.9	65.0	129.8	94.4			Portfolio Investment	79lc *d*
															Equity Securities	79ld *d*
							17.4	24.1	23.9	65.0	129.8	94.4			Debt Securities	79le *d*
															Financial Derivatives	79ll *d*
							1,692.7	2,361.0	3,009.3	3,655.3	5,991.3	7,184.9			Other Investment	79lf *d*
							152.9	151.5	144.0	129.0	123.2	107.5			Monetary Authorities	79lg *d*
							702.0	1,376.0	1,947.9	2,626.7	4,955.0	6,256.6			General Government	79lh *d*
							837.8	833.4	917.4	899.6	913.1	820.7			Banks	79li *d*
															Other Sectors	79lj *d*

Malta

	1972	1973	1974	1975	1976	1977	1978	1979	1980	1981	1982	1983	1984	1985	1986
Government Finance														*Millions of Liri:*	
Deficit (-) or Surplus............................ **80**	-4.76	3.07	4.83	-6.22	4.50	3.47	11.75	....	†4.29	5.55	-7.63	7.33	2.06	-19.21	-19.50
Total Revenue and Grants.................. **81y**	40.85	57.60	74.25	92.23	105.10	105.56	125.54	....	†143.37	183.15	193.38	199.66	193.78	197.06	189.88
Revenue.. **81**	37.75	57.35	74.08	91.79	104.78	105.24	125.29	....	†139.92	167.40	186.35	192.88	186.83	196.81	189.59
Grants... **81z**	3.10	.25	.17	.44	.32	.32	.25	....	†3.45	15.75	7.03	6.78	6.95	.25	.29
Exp. & Lending Minus Repay. **82z**	45.61	54.53	69.42	98.45	100.60	102.09	113.79	....	†139.08	177.60	201.01	192.33	191.72	216.27	209.38
Expenditure.................................. **82**	43.42	47.19	67.57	83.35	92.46	96.30	106.44	....	†131.29	155.54	175.02	180.31	187.40	190.77	204.00
Lending Minus Repayments.............. **83**	2.19	7.34	1.85	15.10	8.14	5.79	7.35	....	†7.79	22.06	25.99	12.02	4.32	25.50	5.38
Total Financing............................... **80h**	4.76	-3.07	-4.83	6.22	-4.50	-3.47	-11.75	....	†-4.29	-5.55	7.63	-7.33	-2.06	19.21	19.50
Total Net Borrowing..................... **84**	.62	.09	.65	7.51	2.41	-1.02	2.53	....	†7.70	1.76	.96	10.02	2.26	-.09	-3.79
Net Domestic............................. **84b**	-1.78	-.49	-.57	-.61	-.64	-.58	-1.21	....	†—	.01	—	—	—		
Net Foreign............................... **85b**	2.40	.58	1.22	8.12	3.05	-.44	3.74	....	†7.70	1.75	.96	10.02	2.26	-.09	-3.79
Use of Cash Balances................... **87**	4.14	-3.16	-5.48	-1.29	-6.91	-2.45	-14.28	....	†-11.99	-7.31	6.67	-17.35	-4.32	19.30	23.29
Total Debt by Residence **88**	36.37	36.90	37.90	43.96	46.52	46.38	50.52	....	†58.27	57.91	57.80	67.64	70.55	67.78	60.69
Domestic.. **88a**	27.46	27.46	27.46	27.46	27.46	27.46	27.46	....	†25.21	25.22	25.24	25.23	25.24	25.26	25.25
Foreign... **89a**	8.91	9.44	10.44	16.50	19.06	18.92	23.06	....	†33.06	32.69	32.56	42.41	45.31	42.52	35.44
National Accounts														*Millions of Liri*	
Househ.Cons.Expend.,incl.NPISHs **96f**	80.4	90.1	107.0	118.7	135.7	172.4	186.4	206.0	253.5	279.4	305.7	306.7	317.5	333.2	343.4
Government Consumption Expend......... **91f**	19.8	22.8	26.9	30.5	35.9	39.7	46.1	53.7	63.4	75.4	85.2	82.3	80.3	84.3	89.5
Gross Fixed Capital Formation **93e**	22.5	22.3	31.2	37.5	54.1	60.0	60.3	78.2	87.1	105.6	120.1	131.6	126.5	125.9	122.3
Changes in Inventories **93i**	3.0	3.3	4.5	1.5	1.9	2.3	4.8	4.8	9.4	12.6	25.5	5.5	6.8	7.9	8.2
Exports of Goods and Services **90c**	53.5	75.3	110.4	137.3	172.7	207.4	229.6	290.8	356.6	355.9	319.8	307.6	323.5	345.2	370.2
Imports of Goods and Services (-) **98c**	76.9	98.0	148.4	159.7	196.6	242.0	249.5	307.7	378.0	392.5	394.6	376.1	393.5	420.5	421.7
Gross Domestic Product (GDP) **99b**	102.2	115.7	131.6	165.8	203.7	239.8	277.6	325.8	392.0	436.5	461.8	457.6	461.1	476.0	511.9
Net Primary Income from Abroad **98.n**	8.3	7.5	12.5	18.3	18.1	19.1	16.9	13.0	30.6	41.2	52.0	38.1	45.5	38.8	28.1
Gross National Income (GNI) **99a**	110.5	123.2	144.0	184.0	221.9	258.9	294.6	338.7	422.5	477.7	513.8	495.7	506.5	514.8	539.9
Consumption of Fixed Capital **99cf**	3.7	4.0	4.6	5.4	6.9	8.5	10.0	11.1	12.9	14.4	15.7	19.8	21.0	21.4	23.2
Net National Income **99e**	106.8	119.2	139.4	178.6	215.0	250.4	284.6	327.6	409.6	463.3	498.1	475.9	485.5	493.4	516.7
GDP Volume 1954 prices **99b.p**	71	78	....	....	....	....	....	....	....	....	....	....	....		
GDP Volume 1973 prices **99b.p**	....	115.7	127.3	152.2	178.1	199.8	222.1	245.4	262.7	271.4	277.6	275.9	278.5	285.7	296.8
GDP Volume 1995 prices **99b.p**	....	....	....	....	....	....	....	....	....	....	....	....			
GDP Volume (1995=100) .... **99bv p**	21.0	23.0	25.3	30.3	35.4	39.7	44.2	48.8	52.2	54.0	55.2	54.9	55.4	56.8	59.0
GDP Deflator (1995=100)................. **99bi p**	42.6	43.9	45.4	47.8	50.2	52.7	54.9	58.3	65.5	70.6	73.0	72.8	72.7	73.1	75.7
														Millions:	
Population....................................... **99z**	.30	.30	.30	†.33	.33	.33	.34	†.32	.32	.32	.32	.33	.33	.34	.34

	1987	1988	1989	1990	1991	1992	1993	1994	1995	1996	1997	1998	1999	2000	2001		
Government Finance																	
Year Ending December 31																	
Deficit (-) or Surplus	-36.68	-.18	-31.13	-38.06	-40.76	-27.19	-27.56	-37.57	-30.87	-92.92	-125.99	-76.49	....	....	....	Deficit (-) or Surplus	80
Total Revenue and Grants	188.87	234.07	238.95	288.22	319.18	309.30	335.53	358.31	406.84	407.43	450.75	460.30	....	....	....	Total Revenue and Grants	81y
Revenue	188.87	219.82	230.76	280.54	302.81	292.91	327.10	345.46	402.32	386.63	440.94	450.26	....	....	....	Revenue	81
Grants	—	14.25	8.19	7.68	16.37	16.39	8.43	12.85	4.52	20.80	9.81	10.04	....	....	....	Grants	81z
Exp. & Lending Minus Repay.	225.55	234.25	270.08	326.28	359.94	336.49	363.09	395.88	437.71	500.35	576.74	536.79	....	....	....	Exp. & Lending Minus Repay.	82z
Expenditure	223.71	229.85	274.41	327.20	360.38	333.79	367.78	402.47	447.46	500.00	535.42	576.32	....	....	....	Expenditure	82
Lending Minus Repayments	1.84	4.40	-4.33	-.92	-.44	2.70	-4.69	-6.59	-9.75	.35	41.32	-39.53	....	....	....	Lending Minus Repayments	83
Total Financing	36.68	.18	31.13	38.06	40.76	27.19	27.56	37.57	30.87	92.92	125.99	76.49	....	....	....	Total Financing	80h
Total Net Borrowing	26.32	23.06	8.79	61.95	37.05	25.72	28.17	35.61	32.89	104.04	145.16	95.87	....	....	....	Total Net Borrowing	84
Net Domestic	29.28	25.57	10.35	50.21	30.40	29.78	28.66	28.70	35.44	105.44	146.70	100.01	....	....	....	Net Domestic	84b
Net Foreign	-2.96	-2.51	-1.56	11.74	6.65	-4.06	-.49	6.91	-2.55	-1.40	-1.54	-4.14	....	....	....	Net Foreign	85b
Use of Cash Balances	10.36	-22.88	22.34	-23.89	3.71	1.47	-.61	1.96	-2.02	-11.12	-19.17	-19.38	....	....	....	Use of Cash Balances	87
Total Debt by Residence	84.73	108.54	117.84	163.03	201.99	235.33	296.30	339.59	410.79	514.47	661.35	761.59	....	....	....	Total Debt by Residence	88
Domestic	54.89	80.40	90.95	125.54	157.28	186.93	245.82	283.33	357.36	462.68	610.90	715.08	....	....	....	Domestic	88a
Foreign	29.84	28.14	26.89	37.49	44.71	48.40	50.48	56.26	53.43	51.79	50.45	46.51	....	....	....	Foreign	89a
National Accounts																	
Millions of Liri																	
Househ.Cons.Expend.,incl.NPISHs	351.2	387.6	425.5	460.8	494.5	531.4	561.5	608.3	700.4	764.9	803.5	846.0	915.0	998.3	1,039.3	Househ.Cons.Expend.,incl.NPISHs	96f
Government Consumption Expend.	98.2	105.2	119.6	129.2	147.1	164.3	188.9	209.5	235.2	259.8	264.1	269.0	272.6	291.1	328.1	Government Consumption Expend.	91f
Gross Fixed Capital Formation	153.5	166.4	188.4	232.6	239.1	240.9	276.8	305.4	365.2	345.3	326.4	333.6	340.0	411.2	376.9	Gross Fixed Capital Formation	93e
Changes in Inventories	-2.4	8.2	9.9	12.7	15.6	.1	3.7	10.0	1.2	-1.4	3.0	-10.7	9.4	30.4	-44.3	Changes in Inventories	93i
Exports of Goods and Services	429.6	480.0	543.5	626.4	701.9	804.1	896.3	994.4	1,074.7	1,045.6	1,095.8	1,194.7	1,321.3	1,605.2	1,427.8	Exports of Goods and Services	90c
Imports of Goods and Services (-)	480.9	540.9	616.8	726.9	791.2	866.0	987.2	1,099.0	1,231.2	1,212.8	1,204.6	1,270.3	1,402.2	1,776.3	1,501.2	Imports of Goods and Services (-)	98c
Gross Domestic Product (GDP)	549.2	606.5	670.1	734.7	806.9	874.8	940.0	1,028.5	1,145.5	1,201.3	1,288.2	1,362.3	1,456.1	1,562.3	1,626.7	Gross Domestic Product (GDP)	99b
Net Primary Income from Abroad	30.7	28.3	35.8	55.0	49.7	41.7	35.5	19.3	12.0	3.2	4.0	-27.4	12.4	-70.2	-2.2	Net Primary Income from Abroad	98.n
Gross National Income (GNI)	579.8	634.8	705.9	789.8	856.5	916.4	975.5	1,047.9	1,157.5	1,204.5	1,292.2	1,334.9	1,468.5	1,488.1	1,624.5	Gross National Income (GNI)	99a
Consumption of Fixed Capital	26.0	28.9	32.0	35.3	37.7	42.2	53.4	60.0	77.1	86.9	95.7	98.7	....	....	....	Consumption of Fixed Capital	99cf
Net National Income	553.8	605.9	673.9	754.5	818.8	874.2	922.1	983.0	1,080.0	1,117.6	1,196.6	1,236.2	....	....	....	Net National Income	99e
GDP Volume 1954 prices	....	....	....	....	....	....	....	....								GDP Volume 1954 prices	99b.p
GDP Volume 1973 prices	309.0	335.0	362.4	385.2	409.3	428.5	447.7	473.3	502.8							GDP Volume 1973 prices	99b.p
GDP Volume 1995 prices	....	....	....	....	....	....	....	....	1,145.5	1,191.2	1,249.0	1,291.8	1,344.2	1,418.6	1,407.9	GDP Volume 1995 prices	99b.p
GDP Volume (1995=100)	61.5	66.6	72.1	76.6	81.4	85.2	89.0	94.1	100.0	104.0	109.0	112.8	117.3	123.8	122.9	GDP Volume (1995=100)	99bv p
GDP Deflator (1995=100)	78.0	79.5	81.2	83.7	86.5	89.6	92.2	95.4	100.0	100.8	103.1	105.5	108.3	110.1	115.5	GDP Deflator (1995=100)	99bi p
Midyear Estimates																	
Population	.34	.35	.35	.35	.36	.36	.36	.36	.37	.37	.38	.38	.39	.39	.39	Population	99z

(See notes in the back of the book.)

Mauritania

		1972	1973	1974	1975	1976	1977	1978	1979	1980	1981	1982	1983	1984	1985	1986
Exchange Rates																*Ouguiyas per SDR:*
Official Rate	aa	55.599	†56.801	53.014	52.855	50.702	55.937	60.130	60.393	58.707	56.964	58.421	59.708	65.958	84.655	90.614
																Ouguiyas per US Dollar
Official Rate	ae	51.210	†47.085	43.300	45.150	43.640	46.050	46.155	45.845	46.030	48.940	52.960	57.030	67.290	77.070	74.080
Official Rate	rf	50.405	44.578	45.333^e	43.104^e	45.022^e	45.587	46.163	45.893	45.914	48.296	51.769	54.812	63.803	77.085	74.375
Fund Position																*Millions of SDRs:*
Quota	2f. s	13.0	13.0	13.0	13.0	13.0	13.0	17.0	17.0	25.5	25.5	25.5	33.9	33.9	33.9	33.9
SDRs	1b. s	2.2	2.1	2.0	1.7	1.2	.6	.7	1.3	—	1.1	—	.7	—	3.9	2.6
Reserve Position in the Fund	1c. s	.8	.9													
Total Fund Cred.&Loans Outstg.	2tl	—	—	—	—	11.8	17.9	22.0	25.1	39.1	42.5	56.4	51.7	41.4	36.5	42.7
International Liquidity													*Millions of US Dollars Unless Otherwise Indicated:*			
Total Reserves minus Gold	1l. d	13.5	42.2	103.8	47.7	82.0	50.0	79.5	113.7	139.9	161.8	139.1	105.9	77.5	59.2	48.2
SDRs	1b. d	2.3	2.6	2.4	2.0	1.4	.7	.9	1.7	—	—	—	—	—	4.3	3.1
Reserve Position in the Fund	1c. d	.8	1.1	—	—	—	—	—	—	—	1.3	—	.7	—	—	—
Foreign Exchange	1d. d	10.3	38.6	101.4	45.7	80.6	49.3	78.6	112.0	139.9	160.5	139.1	105.2	77.5	54.9	45.1
Gold (Million Fine Troy Ounces)	1ad	....	....	—	—	—	.006	.008	.008	.011	.011	.011	.011	.011	.011	.012
Gold (National Valuation)	1an d	....	....	—	—	—	.2	.2	1.7	6.9	4.5	4.1	4.5	3.6	3.7	4.5
Monetary Authorities: Other Liab.	4..d	—	19.8	35.9	36.8	55.9	57.5	81.0	88.1	79.2	98.2	93.9	88.5	89.3	89.6	89.9
Deposit Money Banks: Assets	7a. d	.6	1.1	1.0	.4	18.5	21.9	11.5	3.1	9.2	14.5	4.4	4.8	1.5	3.3	11.0
Liabilities	7b. d	5.5	7.9	24.1	11.4	29.5	40.0	67.7	70.1	81.3	79.3	98.0	78.7	93.4	56.8	77.5
Monetary Authorities																*Millions of Ouguiyas:*
Foreign Assets	11	691	1,948	4,500	2,159	3,582	2,519	3,655	5,330	6,953	8,650	6,545	5,018	4,929	3,954	3,714
Claims on Central Government	12a	10	334	25	749	369	1,749	1,459	1,752	1,965	2,726	4,515	4,535	5,052	3,839	4,476
Claims on Nonfin.Pub.Enterprises	12c	....														
Claims on Private Sector	12d	—	—	—	921	788	766	766	766	926	926	926	926	926	925	....
Claims on Deposit Money Banks	12e	280	822	490	1,348	1,428	2,255	2,103	1,781	1,770	1,679	1,952	3,105	4,029	6,471	4,303
Claims on Nonbank Financial Insts	12g	....														
Reserve Money	14	662	788	1,833	1,653	1,796	2,038	2,210	2,963	3,163	4,178	4,138	4,023	4,045	5,636	5,386
of which: Currency Outside DMBs	14a	618	630	954	1,214	1,464	1,529	1,729	2,311	2,376	2,678	2,950	3,024	3,658	4,700	4,418
Restricted Deposits	16b															
Foreign Liabilities	16c	—	933	1,555	1,663	3,040	3,574	4,738	4,990	5,195	6,500	7,528	7,394	8,009	9,236	9,951
Long-Term Foreign Liabilities	16cl	....														
Central Government Deposits	16d	62	512	599	1,161	320	153	128	177	277	135	155	164	167	191	425
Capital Accounts	17a	247	454	506	552	751	869	871	1,131	1,818	2,230	2,708	3,130	3,380	3,403	3,813
Other Items (Net)	17r	10	417	522	148	260	654	38	367	1,162	939	−591	−1,126	−663	−3,277	−7,081
Deposit Money Banks																*Millions of Ouguiyas:*
Reserves	20	432	1,106	7,964	3,202	344	504	476	638	719	890	697	999	627	1,226	938
Foreign Assets	21	29	50	44	19	808	1,008	533	142	424	708	235	276	100	256	815
Claims on Central Government	22a	116	20	74	48	111	26	59	57	31	24	85	17	50	154	213
Claims on Nonfin.Pub.Enterprises	22c	....														
Claims on Private Sector	22d	1,789	2,740	3,041	4,616	5,488	7,112	7,712	7,835	8,869	10,051	11,425	12,735	13,855	15,519	17,202
Claims on Nonbank Financial Insts	22g	....														
Demand Deposits	24	708	778	1,407	1,564	2,068	2,386	2,226	2,598	2,990	4,845	4,049	4,941	5,891	7,376	6,853
Time Deposits	25	160	531	694	1,052	1,131	964	1,025	1,212	1,403	1,777	2,437	1,995	1,682	1,674	3,471
Foreign Liabilities	26c	281	370	1,045	513	1,225	1,783	2,242	2,610	3,326	3,681	5,114	4,374	6,187	4,321	5,662
Long-Term Foreign Liabilities	26cl	....				62	57	882	604	414	201	74	116	100	55	78
Central Government Deposits	26d	317	89	162	277	267	217	143	75	115	25	491	89	105	130	160
Central Govt. Lending Funds	26f	....							69	1,162	1,223	605	820	1,448	608	159
Credit from Monetary Authorities	26g	281	822	161	1,296	1,428	2,255	2,109	1,781	1,770	1,574	2,036	2,406	3,784	4,879	5,331
Capital Accounts	27a	204	367	562	626	752	832	855	888	908	924	957	1,023	1,405	1,759	1,960
Other Items (Net)	27r	414	960	7,092	2,557	−182	157	−701	−1,164	−2,045	−2,575	−3,322	−1,737	−5,970	−3,648	−4,505
Monetary Survey																*Millions of Ouguiyas:*
Foreign Assets (Net)	31n	439	695	1,944	1	63	−1,888	−3,674	−2,732	−1,558	−1,025	−5,937	−6,590	−9,267	−9,402	−11,162
Domestic Credit	32	1,638	2,580	2,470	5,043	6,320	9,464	9,907	10,330	11,711	13,699	16,441	18,085	19,703	20,212	21,428
Claims on Central Govt. (Net)	32an	−216	−279	−709	−719	−241	1,394	1,052	1,443	1,630	2,436	3,683	4,216	4,715	3,561	3,966
Claims on Nonfin.Pub.Enterprises	32c	....														
Claims on Private Sector	32d	1,854	2,858	3,179	5,762	6,561	8,071	8,855	8,887	10,081	11,263	12,758	13,869	14,989	16,651	17,462
Claims on Nonbank Financial Inst.	32g	....														
Money	34	1,428	1,494	2,451	2,926	3,683	4,095	4,134	5,081	5,677	7,653	7,135	8,090	9,641	12,173	11,393
Quasi-Money	35	160	531	694	1,052	1,131	964	1,025	1,212	1,403	1,777	2,437	1,995	1,682	1,674	3,471
Restricted Deposits	36b	....														
Central Govt. Lending Funds	36f	—	—	—	—	—	—	—	69	1,162	1,223	605	820	1,448	608	159
Other Items (Net)	37r	489	1,250	1,268	1,066	1,569	2,518	1,073	1,236	1,911	2,021	327	590	−2,334	−3,645	−4,757
Money plus Quasi-Money	35l	1,588	2,024	3,145	3,979	4,964	5,239	5,340	6,465	7,392	9,560	9,708	10,209	11,414	13,944	14,985

	1987	1988	1989	1990	1991	1992	1993	1994	1995	1996	1997	1998	1999	2000	2001		
Exchange Rates																	
End of Period																	
Official Rate	101.576	101.910	109.798	110.740	111.316	158.263	170.541	187.401	203.813	204.837	227.146	289.744	308.815	328.724	331.994		**aa**
End of Period (ae) Period Average (rf)																	
Official Rate	71.600	75.730	83.550	77.840	77.820	115.100	124.160	128.370	137.110	142.450	168.350	205.780	225.000	252.300	264.173		**ae**
Official Rate	73.878	75.261	83.051	80.609	81.946	87.027	120.806	123.575	129.768	137.222	151.853	188.476	209.514	238.923	255.249		**rf**
Fund Position																	
End of Period																	
Quota	33.9	33.9	33.9	33.9	33.9	47.5	47.5	47.5	47.5	47.5	47.5	47.5	64.4	64.4	64.4		**2f. s**
SDRs	12.1	.1	.1	.6	.1	.1	.1	—	—	1.0	.3	—	—	.3	.2		**1b. s**
Reserve Position in the Fund	—	—	—	—	—	—	—	—	—	—	—	—	—	—	—		**1c. s**
Total Fund Cred.&Loans Outstg.	54.1	52.5	52.3	49.2	39.5	42.0	46.1	58.8	67.1	74.6	83.4	78.3	77.6	75.4	83.2		**2tl**
International Liquidity																	
End of Period																	
Total Reserves minus Gold	71.8	55.6	82.4	54.1	67.6	61.2	44.6	39.7	85.5	141.2	200.8	202.9	224.3	....	....		**1l. d**
SDRs	17.2	.1	.1	.8	.1	.1	.1	—	.1	1.4	.4	—	—	.4	.2		**1b. d**
Reserve Position in the Fund	—	—	—	—	—	—	—	—	—	—	—	—	—	—	—		**1c. d**
Foreign Exchange	54.6	55.5	82.3	53.3	67.5	61.1	44.4	39.7	85.4	139.8	200.4	202.8	224.3	....	....		**1d. d**
Gold (Million Fine Troy Ounces)	.012	.012	.012	.012	.012	.012	.012	.012	.012	.012	.012	.012	.012	.012	....		**1ad**
Gold (National Valuation)	5.7	4.8	4.6	4.4	4.2	3.8	4.5	4.3	4.4	4.2	3.3	3.3	3.3	3.1	3.1		**1and**
Monetary Authorities: Other Liab.	94.2	91.1	95.1	110.4	168.4	216.0	187.1	199.2	212.0	205.3	209.7	209.6	202.0	195.0	195.1		**4. d**
Deposit Money Banks: Assets	23.0	32.6	30.0	28.7	14.1	15.7	25.8	27.7	25.9	27.0	24.7	24.1	22.1	21.6	19.0		**7a. d**
Liabilities	79.9	87.6	106.0	120.6	181.8	110.0	106.4	105.8	67.4	35.5	26.4	15.0	13.6	12.5	12.1		**7b. d**
Monetary Authorities																	
End of Period																	
Foreign Assets	5,461	4,616	†7,386	4,136	5,308	7,598	6,218	5,746	12,425	21,030	34,425	42,546	51,335	71,429	76,028		**11**
Claims on Central Government	4,811	4,779	†10,779	11,474	12,990	14,057	18,979	17,949	17,109	17,109	17,102	17,012	16,912	16,912	16,912		**12a**
Claims on Nonfin.Pub.Enterprises	....	....	60	60	60	60	60	60	60	60	60	60	60	60	60		**12c**
Claims on Private Sector	—	—	†306	339	398	450	516	581	695	755	1,023	1,003	1,065	1,185	869		**12d**
Claims on Deposit Money Banks	5,122	6,396	†3,269	3,682	2,858	5,980	2,353	2,571	1,872	2,334	2,793	2,789	2,232	1,539	1,539		**12e**
Claims on Nonbank Financial Insts	....	....	49	49	49	49	49	49	49	49	49	49	49	49	49		**12g**
Reserve Money	6,615	7,537	†9,356	8,961	12,102	14,706	22,810	21,966	20,724	10,462	9,089	8,406	8,788	9,222	9,723		**14**
of which: Currency Outside DMBs	5,648	5,845	†6,040	6,139	7,335	7,898	9,097	8,598	7,383	5,093	5,854	5,801	5,963	6,402	6,688		**14a**
Restricted Deposits	—	—	92	5	39	86	29	91	147	91	82	55	154	225	49		**16b**
Foreign Liabilities	11,842	12,081	†6,054	5,559	4,767	13,533	10,813	12,093	14,649	15,543	19,232	23,096	23,968	24,848	27,905		**16c**
Long-Term Foreign Liabilities	....	....	7,028	6,975	11,222	15,031	15,663	16,342	16,702	15,160	17,069	20,923	22,108	24,794	23,873		**16cl**
Central Government Deposits	191	366	†1,645	1,767	2,760	4,200	7,573	8,024	13,342	30,844	42,765	51,300	55,512	68,516	68,413		**16d**
Capital Accounts	3,574	3,663	†4,475	4,149	4,177	4,496	4,946	4,888	4,415	4,059	4,821	5,161	5,594	6,339	6,912		**17a**
Other Items (Net)	−6,829	−7,855	†−6,801	−7,676	−13,404	−23,858	−33,659	−36,448	−37,769	−34,822	−37,606	−46,075	−44,471	−42,770	−41,418		**17r**
Deposit Money Banks																	
End of Period																	
Reserves	1,412	728	†2,845	2,291	4,031	5,191	10,799	12,775	12,486	5,355	3,083	2,390	2,984	2,887	3,105		**20**
Foreign Assets	1,643	2,465	†2,503	2,232	1,100	1,809	3,201	3,561	3,556	3,853	4,165	4,962	4,964	5,450	5,022		**21**
Claims on Central Government	130	166	†252	198	152	193	1,083	916	782	2,742	4,302	4,202	4,637	3,882	6,152		**22a**
Claims on Nonfin.Pub.Enterprises	—	—	—	—	—	—	—	—	—	—	—	—	—	—	—		**22c**
Claims on Private Sector	18,959	20,598	†31,202	35,411	39,314	40,101	41,191	42,500	30,722	34,634	37,279	39,835	46,942	58,486	68,939		**22d**
Claims on Nonbank Financial Insts	....	....	—	—	—	—	—	—	—	—	—	—	—	—	—		**22g**
Demand Deposits	7,630	8,068	†10,813	11,178	11,646	11,986	11,508	11,145	10,674	11,015	11,629	12,467	13,697	17,749	21,033		**24**
Time Deposits	4,244	3,971	†3,947	5,769	6,180	7,187	6,635	7,612	7,817	8,476	9,101	9,282	8,708	8,800	10,929		**25**
Foreign Liabilities	5,623	6,070	†8,858	9,387	14,145	12,656	13,216	13,583	9,246	5,054	4,451	3,078	3,058	3,164	3,195		**26c**
Long-Term Foreign Liabilities	99	563	†	—	—	—	—	—	—	—	—	—	—	—	—		**26cl**
Central Government Deposits	254	273	†580	778	814	1,093	1,330	1,552	3,198	3,428	4,058	6,487	13,596	18,085	23,365		**26d**
Central Govt. Lending Funds	1,159	1,789	†617	719	978	1,179	1,208	1,208	—	—	—	—	—	—	—		**26f**
Credit from Monetary Authorities	6,384	5,855	†2,417	2,668	1,801	4,380	3,351	3,358	7	7	7	7	7	7	7		**26g**
Capital Accounts	1,758	4,294	†12,226	12,597	13,905	14,018	20,802	21,972	20,709	22,359	23,260	24,203	25,169	28,636	29,923		**27a**
Other Items (Net)	−5,006	−6,927	†−2,656	−2,964	−4,873	−5,205	−1,776	−678	−4,105	−3,755	−3,677	−4,135	−4,708	−5,736	−5,233		**27r**
Monetary Survey																	
End of Period																	
Foreign Assets (Net)	−10,460	−11,633	†−12,051	−15,553	−23,726	−31,813	−30,273	−32,711	−24,616	−10,874	−2,162	411	7,165	24,073	26,077		**31n**
Domestic Credit	23,574	25,022	†40,423	44,986	49,389	49,617	52,975	52,479	32,877	21,077	12,992	4,374	557	−6,027	1,203		**32**
Claims on Central Govt. (Net)	4,355	4,165	†8,806	9,127	9,568	8,957	11,159	9,289	1,351	−14,421	−25,419	−36,573	−47,559	−65,807	−68,714		**32an**
Claims on Nonfin.Pub.Enterprises	....	....	60	60	60	60	60	60	60	60	60	60	60	60	60		**32c**
Claims on Private Sector	19,219	20,858	†31,508	35,750	39,712	40,551	41,707	43,081	31,417	35,389	38,302	40,838	48,007	59,671	69,808		**32d**
Claims on Nonbank Financial Inst	....	....	49	49	49	49	49	49	49	49	49	49	49	49	49		**32g**
Money	13,397	14,032	†17,028	17,622	19,376	20,202	20,938	19,816	18,202	16,227	17,579	18,504	19,675	24,151	27,721		**34**
Quasi-Money	4,244	3,971	†3,947	5,769	6,180	7,187	6,635	7,612	7,817	8,476	9,101	9,282	8,708	8,800	10,929		**35**
Restricted Deposits	....	....	92	5	39	86	29	91	147	91	82	55	154	225	49		**36b**
Central Govt. Lending Funds	1,159	1,789	†617	719	978	1,179	1,208	1,208	—	—	—	—	—	—	—		**36f**
Other Items (Net)	−5,686	−6,403	†6,688	5,318	−911	−10,850	−6,108	−8,959	−17,905	−14,591	−15,932	−23,649	−20,815	−15,130	−11,418		**37r**
Money plus Quasi-Money	17,761	18,122	†20,975	23,391	25,556	27,389	27,573	27,428	26,019	24,703	26,680	27,786	28,383	32,951	38,650		**35l**

Mauritania

		1972	1973	1974	1975	1976	1977	1978	1979	1980	1981	1982	1983	1984	1985	1986
Interest Rates														*Percent Per Annum*		
Discount Rate *(End of Period)*	60	3.50	5.50	5.50	5.00	5.00	5.00	5.00	5.00	6.00	6.00	6.00	6.00	6.00	6.50	6.50
Deposit Rate	60l	...	...	...	...	...	...	...	...	...	5.50	5.50	5.50	5.50	7.17	6.58
Lending Rate	60p	...	...	...	...	...	...	...	...	12.00	12.00	12.00	12.00	12.00	12.00	12.00
Prices														*Index Numbers (1995=100):*		
Consumer Prices	64	...	...	...	...	...	...	...	...	...	...	...	...	...	70.6	75.8
International Transactions														*Millions of Ouguiyas*		
Exports	70	5,991	6,918	8,175	7,527	8,013	7,156	5,692	6,733	8,916	12,622	12,050	15,982	18,715	28,887	25,956
Imports, c.i.f.	71	3,475	5,692	5,453	6,934	8,049	9,414	8,361	11,869	13,118	12,793	14,213	12,411	13,201	17,806	16,429
Balance of Payments														*Millions of US Dollars:*		
Current Account, n.i.e.	78ald	...	...	...	−63.2	−86.0	−122.5	−78.5	−114.7	−133.6	−147.5	−277.0	−213.6	−111.2	−116.5	−194.6
Goods: Exports f.o.b.	78aad	...	...	...	167.3	181.9	157.2	118.6	147.2	196.3	269.9	240.0	315.4	293.8	371.5	418.8
Goods: Imports f.o.b.	78abd	...	...	...	−208.5	−272.0	−295.5	−267.1	−286.0	−321.3	−386.2	−426.6	−378.2	−302.1	−333.9	−401.2
Trade Balance	78acd	...	...	...	−41.2	−90.2	−138.3	−148.5	−138.8	−125.0	−116.3	−186.5	−62.9	−8.3	37.6	17.6
Services: Credit	78add	...	...	...	18.0	19.5	21.5	33.9	45.5	56.5	48.9	47.2	30.2	28.0	27.1	23.7
Services: Debit	78aed	...	...	...	−69.2	−80.9	−67.2	−75.3	−83.2	−127.8	−128.1	−157.5	−177.2	−177.8	−201.8	−211.1
Balance on Goods & Services	78afd	...	...	...	−92.3	−151.6	−184.0	−189.9	−176.6	−196.3	−195.5	−296.8	−209.8	−158.1	−137.1	−169.9
Income: Credit	78agd	...	...	...	5.0	4.4	4.3	3.1	11.4	17.0	20.1	18.5	9.1	8.5	4.0	2.3
Income: Debit	78ahd	...	...	...	−35.1	−62.9	−47.7	−30.2	−42.8	−43.8	−70.7	−64.1	−71.4	−47.6	−96.1	−118.6
Balance on Gds, Serv. & Inc.	78aid	...	...	...	−122.4	−210.2	−227.4	−217.0	−208.0	−223.1	−246.1	−342.4	−272.1	−197.2	−229.2	−286.1
Current Transfers, n.i.e.: Credit	78ajd	...	...	...	87.5	159.1	130.3	163.2	131.6	132.4	125.8	101.4	89.6	111.9	140.1	128.9
Current Transfers: Debit	78akd	...	...	...	−28.3	−35.0	−25.5	−24.8	−38.3	−42.8	−27.2	−35.9	−31.1	−25.9	−27.4	−37.3
Capital Account, n.i.e.	78bcd	...	...	...	—	—	—	—	—	—	—	.	—	—	—	—
Capital Account, n.i.e.: Credit	78bad	...	...	...	—	—	—	—	—	—	—		—	—	—	—
Capital Account: Debit	78bbd	...	...	...	—	—	—	—	—	—	—		—	—	—	—
Financial Account, n.i.e.	78bjd	...	...	...	10.2	100.6	63.4	113.3	148.4	151.4	147.9	219.5	166.2	97.9	91.5	171.0
Direct Investment Abroad	78bdd	...	...	...	—	—	—	—	—	—	—	—	—	—	—	−1.4
Dir. Invest. in Rep. Econ., n.i.e.	78bed	...	...	...	−122.7	1.6	4.1	2.9	63.2	27.1	12.4	15.0	1.4	8.5	7.0	4.5
Portfolio Investment Assets	78bfd	...	...	...	—	—	—	—	—	—	—	—	—	—	—	—
Equity Securities	78bkd	...	...	...	—	—	—	—	—	—	—	—	—	—	—	—
Debt Securities	78bld	...	...	...	—	—	—	—	—	—	—	—	—	—	—	—
Portfolio Investment Liab., n.i.e.	78bgd	...	...	...	—	—	—	—	—	—	—	—	—	—	—	—
Equity Securities	78bmd	...	...	...	—	—	—	—	—	—	—	—	—	—	—	—
Debt Securities	78bnd	...	...	...	—	—	—	—	—	—	—	—	—	—	—	—
Financial Derivatives Assets	78bwd	...	...	...	...	...										
Financial Derivatives Liabilities	78bxd	...	...	...	...	...										
Other Investment Assets	78bhd	...	...	...	−2.7	.9	−4.5	9.1	16.6	−24.4	−13.8	7.4	1.7	−7.9	−6.8	−7.5
Monetary Authorities	78bod	...	...	...	—	—	—	—	—	—	—	—	—	—	—	—
General Government	78bpd	...	...	...	−2.2	−3.3	−1.9	−5.0	−1.3	−5.7	—	−7.3	−.5	−.3	−.4	−3.9
Banks	78bqd	...	...	...	−.2	−.2	.1	−.5	7.8	−19.1	−7.3	5.2	3.5	.7	.4	6.7
Other Sectors	78brd	...	...	...	−.4	4.4	−2.7	14.6	10.0	.3	−6.5	9.4	−1.3	−8.4	−6.8	−10.3
Other Investment Liab., n.i.e.	78bid	...	...	...	135.6	98.2	63.7	101.4	68.6	148.7	149.3	197.1	163.1	97.4	91.2	175.4
Monetary Authorities	78bsd	...	...	...	−.3	8.2	4.9	15.6	2.7	26.5	25.0	−5.6	8.4	19.4	.6	−10.8
General Government	78btd	...	...	...	28.7	149.1	45.7	71.7	58.0	113.4	73.7	81.7	68.3	54.7	76.0	144.5
Banks	78bud	...	...	...	1.2	.9	4.6	10.6	1.2	8.0	−6.3	33.2	−7.6	5.1	−2.5	−3.3
Other Sectors	78bvd	...	...	...	106.1	−60.0	8.5	3.5	6.7	.8	56.9	87.9	94.0	18.2	17.1	45.0
Net Errors and Omissions	78cad	...	...	...	−2.5	1.0	14.5	−9.9	−26.5	−32.2	−.7	−4.6	12.7	−.8	−5.6	−5.7
Overall Balance	78cbd	...	...	...	−55.6	15.7	−44.7	24.9	7.2	−14.3	−.2	−62.1	−34.7	−14.1	−30.6	−29.2
Reserves and Related Items	79dad	...	...	...	55.6	−15.7	44.7	−24.9	−7.2	14.3	.2	62.1	34.7	14.1	30.6	29.2
Reserve Assets	79dbd	...	...	...	55.3	−29.6	34.9	−30.7	−29.0	−19.0	−27.5	17.3	24.6	18.7	27.8	11.0
Use of Fund Credit and Loans	79dcd	...	...	...	—	13.7	7.1	5.1	4.0	18.6	3.6	15.7	−5.1	−10.5	−4.8	7.8
Exceptional Financing	79ded	...	...	...	.3	.3	2.7	.7	17.8	14.7	24.1	29.2	15.2	5.9	7.7	10.4
Government Finance														*Billions of Ouguiyas:*		
Deficit (-) or Surplus	80	...	...	...	−.53	−2.32	−1.69	†−.87	−1.46	...	...	...	...	...	...	...
Revenue	81	...	...	...	4.10	5.66	5.54	†6.43	6.48	...	...	...	...	...	...	...
Grants Received	81z	...	...	...	3.54	6.40	3.86	†3.34	3.18	...	...	...	...	...	...	...
Exp. & Lending Minus Repay.	82z	...	...	...	8.17	14.38	11.09	†10.64	11.13	...	...	...	...	...	...	...
Financing																
Domestic	84a	...	...	...	−.08	.27	1.74	†−.18	.43	...	...	...	...	...	...	...
Foreign	85a	...	...	...	.61	2.05	−.06	†1.05	1.04	...	...	...	...	...	...	...
Debt: Foreign	89a	...	...	...	...	...	28.71									
National Accounts														*Millions of Ouguiyas*		
Househ.Cons.Expend.,incl.NPISHs	96f	6,472	6,770	9,077	11,652	13,245	14,213	17,407	22,126	22,890	32,381	30,733	32,214	33,180	...	...
Government Consumption Expend.	91f	2,349	2,900	3,301	5,060	7,704	8,784	9,370	9,523	8,888	9,224	9,885	10,127	10,189	...	...
Gross Fixed Capital Formation	93e	4,023	4,780	6,480	7,016	10,744	9,793	4,040	5,906	7,800	9,572	10,600	11,365	14,700	...	...
Changes in Inventories	93i	362	−1,205	993	2,128	1,500	1,131	2,673	2,172	2,400	6,353	8,108	8,317	1,580	...	...
Exports of Goods and Services	90c	8,390	6,457	9,270	7,986	9,065	8,150	7,421	8,821	9,250	12,128	15,434	18,820	18,821	...	...
Imports of Goods and Services (-)	98c	8,712	6,733	11,204	13,232	18,247	17,073	16,003	17,648	19,500	26,419	32,091	34,922	33,970	...	...
Gross Domestic Product (GDP)	99b	12,884	12,919	16,660	20,595	24,105	24,998	24,908	30,853	31,728	36,125	38,838	43,014	46,068	53,230	62,699
															Millions:	
Population	99z	1.31	1.35	1.38	1.42	1.46	1.50	1.54	1.51	1.55	1.59	1.63	1.68	1.72	1.77	1.81

	1987	1988	1989	1990	1991	1992	1993	1994	1995	1996	1997	1998	1999	2000	2001		
Percent Per Annum																**Interest Rates**	
Discount Rate (End of Period)	6.50	6.50	7.00	7.00	7.00	7.00	....	....	....	....	....	....	....	....	....	Discount Rate (*End of Period*)	60
Deposit Rate	6.00	6.00	5.00	5.00	5.00	5.00	....	....	....	....	....	....	....	....	....	Deposit Rate	60l
Lending Rate	12.00	12.00	10.00	10.00	10.00	10.00	....	....	....	....	....	....	....	....	....	Lending Rate	60p
Period Averages																**Prices**	
Consumer Prices	82.0	83.1	93.8	†100.0	105.6	116.3	127.2	132.5	141.2	147.8	154.6	167.0	173.8	179.5	188.0	Consumer Prices	64
Millions of Ouguiyas																**International Transactions**	
Exports	31,608	26,655	36,332	....	....											Exports	70
Imports, c.i.f.	17,392	18,029	18,462	....	....											Imports, c.i.f.	71
Minus Sign Indicates Debit																Balance of Payments	
Current Account, n.i.e.	-147.4	-96.0	-18.6	-9.6	-29.9	-118.3	-174.0	-69.9	22.1	91.3	47.8	77.2	....	....	....	Current Account, n.i.e.	78ald
Goods: Exports f.o.b.	402.4	437.6	447.9	443.9	435.8	406.8	403.0	399.7	476.4	480.0	423.6	358.6	....	....	....	Goods: Exports f.o.b.	78aad
Goods: Imports f.o.b.	-359.2	-348.9	-349.3	-382.9	-399.1	-461.3	-400.4	-352.3	-292.6	-346.1	-316.5	-318.7	....	....	....	Goods: Imports f.o.b.	78abd
Trade Balance	43.2	88.8	98.6	61.0	36.7	-54.5	2.6	47.4	183.8	133.9	107.2	40.0				*Trade Balance*	78acd
Services: Credit	34.5	35.3	33.6	26.8	31.2	20.2	21.4	26.0	27.9	31.6	34.9	34.0				Services: Credit	78add
Services: Debit	-214.5	-217.0	-196.0	-136.8	-151.0	-179.1	-184.9	-181.1	-217.0	-231.3	-200.0	-152.5				Services: Debit	78aed
Balance on Goods & Services	-136.8	-93.0	-63.9	-49.1	-83.1	-213.4	-160.9	-107.7	-5.3	-65.8	-57.9	-78.6				*Balance on Goods & Services*	78afd
Income: Credit	2.5	4.1	5.6	3.8	2.0	1.1	.8	1.1	1.3	.9	1.4	2.5				Income: Credit	78agd
Income: Debit	-91.7	-89.7	-55.6	-50.2	-34.9	-29.9	-97.6	-47.7	-49.5	-45.9	-40.3	-34.0				Income: Debit	78ahd
Balance on Gds, Serv. & Inc.	-226.0	-178.6	-113.9	-95.5	-115.9	-242.2	-257.8	-154.3	-53.5	-110.8	-96.8	-110.2				*Balance on Gds, Serv. & Inc.*	78aid
Current Transfers, n.i.e.: Credit	115.8	123.3	130.0	120.2	118.9	157.4	110.3	113.3	94.7	217.5	157.9	198.3				Current Transfers, n.i.e.: Credit	78ajd
Current Transfers: Debit	-37.2	-40.8	-34.7	-34.3	-32.8	-33.4	-26.5	-28.9	-19.2	-15.5	-13.3	-10.8				Current Transfers: Debit	78akd
Capital Account, n.i.e.	—	—	—	—	—	—	—	—	—	—	—	—				Capital Account, n.i.e.	78bcd
Capital Account, n.i.e.: Credit	—	—	—	—	—	—	—	—	—	—	—	—				Capital Account, n.i.e.: Credit	78bad
Capital Account: Debit	—	—	—	—	—	—	—	—	—	—	—	—				Capital Account: Debit	78bbd
Financial Account, n.i.e.	117.0	48.9	16.3	-.5	26.7	77.9	-134.8	-11.4	-10.2	-86.1	-17.3	-25.9				Financial Account, n.i.e.	78bjd
Direct Investment Abroad	-.2	-.9	—	—	—	—	—	—	—	—	—	—				Direct Investment Abroad	78bdd
Dir. Invest. in Rep. Econ., n.i.e.	1.7	1.9	3.5	6.7	2.3	7.5	16.1	2.1	7.0	—	—	.1				Dir. Invest. in Rep. Econ., n.i.e.	78bed
Portfolio Investment Assets	—	—	—	—	—	—	—	—	—	—	—	—				Portfolio Investment Assets	78bfd
Equity Securities	—	—	—	—	—	—	—	—	—	—	—	—				Equity Securities	78bkd
Debt Securities	—	—	—	—	—	—	—	—	—	—	—	—				Debt Securities	78bld
Portfolio Investment Liab., n.i.e.	—	—	—	—	—	—	-.1	-.2	-.5	-.4	—	-.4				Portfolio Investment Liab., n.i.e.	78bgd
Equity Securities	—	—	—	—	—	—	—	—	—	—	—	—				Equity Securities	78bmd
Debt Securities	—	—	—	—	—	—	-.1	-.2	-.5	-.4	—	-.4				Debt Securities	78bnd
Financial Derivatives Assets	....	....	....	....	....	....	....	....	....	....	....	....				Financial Derivatives Assets	78bwd
Financial Derivatives Liabilities	....	....	....	....	....	....	....	....	....	....	....	....				Financial Derivatives Liabilities	78bxd
Other Investment Assets	8.1	2.2	-9.9	205.8	194.0	168.7	170.5	169.3	211.5	236.0	191.1	190.1				Other Investment Assets	78bhd
Monetary Authorities																Monetary Authorities	78bod
General Government	-.3	-.1	—	—	—	—	-.8	-2.2	-.4	-.2	—	—				General Government	78bpd
Banks	-8.1	11.4	-6.5	—	—	—										Banks	78bqd
Other Sectors	16.5	-9.0	-3.4	205.8	194.0	168.7	171.3	171.5	211.9	236.2	191.1	190.1				Other Sectors	78brd
Other Investment Liab., n.i.e.	107.5	45.7	22.7	-213.0	-169.6	-98.3	-321.3	-182.6	-228.2	-321.6	-208.4	-215.7				Other Investment Liab., n.i.e.	78bid
Monetary Authorities	25.5	9.4	-.6	-1.6	2.4											Monetary Authorities	78bsd
General Government	76.0	-8.9	29.0	-36.2	34.7	35.6	-137.6	-7.0	.2	-.2	5.3	.7				General Government	78btd
Banks	-3.9	5.0	-.6	-1.5	-.8	-18.8	—									Banks	78bud
Other Sectors	9.9	40.1	-11.5	-174.5	-205.1	-133.1	-164.9	-175.5	-228.4	-321.4	-213.7	-216.4				Other Sectors	78bvd
Net Errors and Omissions	-101.5	-16.0	-3.5	-62.3	19.5	57.4	26.7	-23.5	-18.1	-1.0	-3.0	-8.1	....	....	....	Net Errors and Omissions	78cad
Overall Balance	-131.8	-63.2	-5.9	-72.5	16.3	17.0	-282.1	-104.7	-6.2	4.2	27.6	43.2				*Overall Balance*	78cbd
Reserves and Related Items	131.8	63.2	5.9	72.5	-16.3	-17.0	282.1	104.7	6.2	-4.2	-27.6	-43.2				Reserves and Related Items	79dad
Reserve Assets	-12.8	10.6	-16.8	40.6	-3.1	-20.4	69.0	46.9	-42.9	-58.3	-58.8	-46.3				Reserve Assets	79dbd
Use of Fund Credit and Loans	15.4	-1.9	-.7	-4.6	-13.2	3.4	5.6	17.9	12.2	10.9	12.0	-6.9				Use of Fund Credit and Loans	79dcd
Exceptional Financing	129.2	54.5	23.3	36.4	—	—	207.5	40.0	36.9	43.3	19.3	10.0				Exceptional Financing	79ded
Year Ending December 31																**Government Finance**	
Deficit (-) or Surplus	....	....	....	†-4.26	-4.68	-2.85	-8.86	-3.19	1.58	11.26	....	....				Deficit (-) or Surplus	80
Revenue	....	....	....	†20.23	20.56	20.15	29.32	29.46	33.21	44.72	....	....				Revenue	81
Grants Received	....	....	....	†1.75	1.54	2.73	3.72	2.55	2.75	3.28	....	....				Grants Received	81z
Exp. & Lending Minus Repay.	....	....	....	†26.24	26.78	25.73	41.90	35.20	34.38	36.74	....	....				Exp. & Lending Minus Repay.	82z
Financing																Financing	
Domestic				†1.35	.86	-1.35	3.24	-1.47	-7.52	-15.81						Domestic	84a
Foreign				†2.91	3.82	4.22	5.62	4.66	5.94	4.55						Foreign	85a
Debt: Foreign				....	....											Debt: Foreign	89a
Millions of Ouguiyas																**National Accounts**	
Househ.Cons.Expend.,incl.NPISHs	....	....	....	....	67,402	76,200	87,887	87,863	79,984	99,913	111,297	113,422	....	....	....	Househ.Cons.Expend.,incl.NPISHs	96f
Government Consumption Expend.					15,473	17,545	24,814	25,883	30,072	31,111	32,456	23,525				Government Consumption Expend.	91f
Gross Fixed Capital Formation					13,756	18,080	17,314	20,147	23,684	17,326	25,094	....				Gross Fixed Capital Formation	93e
Changes in Inventories					3,652	6,170	3,963	3,590	4,308	9,015	2,626	....				Changes in Inventories	93i
Exports of Goods and Services					39,078	38,021	51,167	52,479	65,306	70,066	67,477	52,795				Exports of Goods and Services	90c
Imports of Goods and Services (-)					49,596	59,425	70,601	65,800	66,015	79,113	78,332	46,562				Imports of Goods and Services (-)	98c
Gross Domestic Product (GDP)	69,171	72,053	81,517	84,615	89,765	96,591	114,544	124,162	137,339	148,318	160,618	....				Gross Domestic Product (GDP)	99b
Midyear Estimates																	
Population	1.86	1.90	1.97	2.03	2.04	2.10	2.15	2.21	2.28	2.35	2.42	2.50	2.58	2.67	2.75	Population	99z

(See notes in the back of the book.)

Mauritius

		1972	1973	1974	1975	1976	1977	1978	1979	1980	1981	1982	1983	1984	1985	1986
Exchange Rates															*Rupees per SDR:*	
Market Rate	aa	6.165	6.923	6.951	7.714	7.714	7.714	7.714	†10.000	10.000	12.000	12.000	13.321	15.295	15.718	16.069
															Rupees per US Dollar:	
Market Rate	ae	5.678	5.739	5.677	†6.589	6.639	6.350	5.921	7.586	7.835	10.329	10.861	12.723	15.603	14.310	13.137
Market Rate	rf	5.339	5.442	5.703	6.027	6.682e	6.607e	6.163e	6.308e	7.684e	8.937e	10.873e	11.706	13.800	15.442	13.466
Fund Position															*Millions of SDRs:*	
Quota	2f. s	22.0	22.0	22.0	22.0	22.0	22.0	27.0	27.0	40.5	40.5	40.5	53.6	53.6	53.6	53.6
SDRs	1b. s	7.3	7.3	2.8	2.6	2.7	2.3	1.6	.6	—	5.6	1.7	.1	.1	—	.5
Reserve Position in the Fund	1c. s	2.5	2.5	—	5.5	5.5	—	—	—	—	—	—	—	—	—	—
Total Fund Cred.&Loans Outstg.	2tl	—	—	—	—	—	11.0	20.3	48.4	79.9	136.9	159.4	172.8	164.2	150.1	132.1
International Liquidity										*Millions of US Dollars Unless Otherwise Indicated:*						
Total Reserves minus Gold	1l. d	70.1	66.8	131.1	166.0	89.5	66.3	45.8	29.2	90.7	35.1	38.0	17.9	23.6	29.9	136.0
SDRs	1b. d	7.9	8.8	3.4	3.0	3.1	2.8	2.1	.8	—	6.5	1.9	.1	.1	—	.6
Reserve Position in the Fund	1c. d	2.7	3.0	—	6.4	6.4	—	—	—	—	—	—	—	—	—	—
Foreign Exchange	1d. d	59.5	55.0	127.7	156.5	80.0	63.5	43.7	28.4	90.7	28.6	36.1	17.8	23.5	29.9	135.4
Gold (Million Fine Troy Ounces)	1ad	....	....	....	....	—	.009	.033	.038	.038	.038	.038	.038	.038	.038	.038
Gold (National Valuation)	1an d	....	....	....	....	—	1.6	5.8	4.8	4.7	4.3	4.1	3.5	2.8	3.1	3.3
Government Assets	3ba d	.7	.8	.3	1.4	.5	.7	1.1	1.6	.9	.1	.1	—	—	—	.1
Monetary Authorities: Other Liab.	4.. d									2.0			12.0	7.0	9.0	2.9
Deposit Money Banks: Assets	7a. d	3.3	4.4	6.3	8.2	5.3	6.9	8.3	8.4	13.3	12.5	13.5	15.3	18.1	41.1	49.2
Liabilities	7b. d	1.5	2.0	1.7	1.8	1.4	15.8	15.4	16.1	19.7	16.4	2.6	6.3	8.4	6.0	2.7
Monetary Authorities															*Millions of Rupees:*	
Foreign Assets	11	393.4	383.4	743.6	1,093.5	594.2	431.1	305.5	257.9	747.0	406.1	456.3	271.5	411.9	472.5	1,830.9
Claims on Central Government	12a	33.4	13.7	17.6	5.1	338.7	823.0	1,111.8	1,541.5	1,577.3	2,943.5	3,311.1	4,059.6	4,496.4	3,868.6	2,732.0
Claims on Deposit Money Banks	12e	31.6	66.4	10.9	3.0	42.9	34.8	42.0	80.0	55.0	64.5	20.1	15.0	54.2	48.1	31.9
Reserve Money	14	217.3	258.3	475.5	653.1	774.1	917.5	1,077.8	1,041.6	1,155.0	1,203.1	1,334.5	1,417.8	1,512.5	1,787.1	2,152.6
of which: Currency Outside DMBs	14a	156.3	200.7	314.2	438.1	587.9	693.6	824.1	724.8	735.0	791.3	875.2	922.4	958.2	1,095.7	1,304.9
Money Market Instruments	16aa															
Foreign Liabilities	16c						84.9	156.5	498.9	798.0	1,645.5	1,909.1	2,454.8	2,621.0	2,488.7	2,161.7
Central Government Deposits	16d	132.2	73.3	86.4	149.8	.5	.6	1.9	3.1	3.4	1.7	1.0	2.3	.6	2.2	6.0
Capital Accounts	17a	57.5	70.7	75.9	84.9	89.8	89.9	99.9	134.7	162.8	222.2	221.6	242.7	273.7	280.4	285.9
Other Items (Net)	17r	51.4	61.2	134.3	213.9	111.3	196.1	133.2	201.0	260.1	341.6	321.4	228.6	554.7	−169.2	−11.5
Deposit Money Banks															*Millions of Rupees:*	
Reserves	20	42.9	56.7	160.6	190.1	182.0	213.0	243.2	294.4	388.0	400.9	454.9	458.3	536.2	648.5	839.9
Foreign Assets	21	17.1	25.3	35.8	54.3	34.9	43.9	49.4	63.6	104.4	129.6	146.9	194.8	282.6	588.1	645.9
Claims on Central Government	22a	127.6	145.4	479.4	518.7	247.0	338.6	502.7	637.0	989.9	717.8	1,161.2	1,225.1	1,412.0	1,616.7	2,795.0
Claims on Private Sector	22d	356.5	545.4	594.3	746.6	1,157.2	1,352.2	1,508.1	1,721.6	1,881.1	2,259.1	2,460.9	2,796.9	3,407.3	4,615.5	5,441.8
Claims on Other Banking Insts	22f															
Demand Deposits	24	201.9	265.0	468.8	530.2	506.5	525.3	615.5	683.8	953.3	731.2	861.5	844.3	1,074.0	900.2	1,119.5
Time, Savings,& Fgn.Currency Dep.	25	259.3	375.9	755.5	892.8	964.5	1,124.9	1,410.0	1,687.4	2,116.9	2,458.8	3,185.4	3,622.3	4,145.0	6,109.1	8,084.6
Foreign Liabilities	26c	7.9	11.5	9.7	11.8	9.1	100.4	91.3	122.1	154.3	169.9	28.5	79.6	130.4	85.3	35.1
Central Government Deposits	26d	2.4	6.1	9.7	10.1	4.5	5.2	4.5	3.1	9.6	16.5	34.9	28.0	45.2	16.7	15.4
Credit from Monetary Authorities	26g	31.6	66.4	10.9	3.0	25.6	33.2	35.4	71.5	45.3	56.8	10.0	9.3	34.5	25.0	15.0
Capital Accounts	27a	31.9	40.0	45.1	53.1	71.4	111.8	154.7	166.8	198.4	217.0	235.3	289.9	307.4	411.9	469.0
Other Items (Net)	27r	9.1	7.9	−29.6	8.7	39.5	46.9	−8.0	−18.1	−114.4	−142.8	−131.7	−198.3	−98.4	−79.4	−16.0
Monetary Survey															*Millions of Rupees:*	
Foreign Assets (Net)	31n	402.6	397.2	769.7	1,136.0	620.0	289.7	107.1	−299.5	−100.9	−1,279.6	−1,334.4	−2,068.0	−2,056.9	−1,513.4	280.0
Domestic Credit	32	382.9	625.1	995.2	1,110.5	1,737.9	2,508.0	3,116.2	3,893.9	4,435.3	5,902.2	6,897.3	8,051.3	9,269.9	10,081.9	10,947.4
Claims on Central Govt. (Net)	32an	26.4	79.7	400.9	363.9	580.7	1,155.8	1,608.1	2,172.3	2,554.2	3,643.1	4,436.4	5,254.4	5,862.6	5,466.4	5,505.6
Claims on Private Sector	32d	356.5	545.4	594.3	746.6	1,157.2	1,352.2	1,508.1	1,721.6	1,881.1	2,259.1	2,460.9	2,796.9	3,407.3	4,615.5	5,441.8
Claims on Other Banking Insts	32f															
Money	34	376.3	466.6	783.7	993.2	1,098.6	1,219.2	1,449.2	1,426.2	1,720.3	1,533.4	1,741.1	1,803.8	2,050.3	2,038.8	2,432.2
Quasi-Money	35	301.2	413.9	802.0	953.4	985.3	1,132.4	1,412.3	1,687.4	2,116.9	2,458.8	3,185.4	3,622.3	4,145.0	6,109.1	8,084.6
Money Market Instruments	36aa															
Capital Accounts	37a	89.4	110.7	121.0	138.0	161.2	201.7	244.6	301.5	361.2	439.2	456.9	532.6	581.1	692.3	754.9
Other Items (Net)	37r	18.6	31.1	58.2	162.0	112.7	244.5	117.2	179.2	136.0	191.1	179.6	24.6	436.6	−271.7	−44.4
Money plus Quasi-Money	35l	677.5	880.5	1,585.7	1,946.6	2,083.9	2,351.6	2,861.5	3,113.6	3,837.2	3,992.2	4,926.5	5,426.1	6,195.3	8,147.9	10,516.8
Other Banking Institutions															*Millions of Rupees:*	
Deposits	45	35.3	40.8	48.6	62.1	78.9	93.6	106.9	104.7	101.5	101.0	121.4	129.8	146.5	167.4	188.8
Liquid Liabilities	55l	712.8	921.3	1,634.3	2,008.7	2,162.8	2,445.2	2,968.4	3,218.3	3,938.7	4,093.2	5,047.9	5,555.9	6,341.8	8,315.3	10,705.6
Interest Rates															*Percent Per Annum*	
Discount Rate (End of Period)	60	6.00	6.00	6.00	6.00	6.00	7.00	9.00	10.50	10.50	12.00	12.00	11.00	11.00	11.00	11.00
Money Market Rate	60b	....	....	....	....	....	....	7.90	9.98	9.90	9.90	9.90	10.82	11.00	11.17	11.05
Deposit Rate	60l	....	....	....	....	....	....	....	....	....	9.25	11.15	12.06	10.29	9.46	9.50
Lending Rate	60p	....	....	....	....	....	....	....	....	....	12.19	13.38	15.08	13.25	13.83	14.33
Prices and Labor															*Index Numbers (1995=100):*	
Share Prices	62	....	....	....	....	....	....	....	....	....	....	....	....	....	....	....
Consumer Prices	64	8.8	10.0	12.9	†14.8	16.8	18.3	19.9	22.7	32.3	†36.9	41.2	43.5	46.7	†49.8	50.6
															Number in Thousands:	
Labor Force	67d	....	....	....	....	....	....	....	....	....	....	....	....	....	....	....
Employment	67e	....	....	....	....	....	....	....	....	....	....	....	....	....	204	223
Unemployment	67c	....	....	....	....	....	....	....	....	....	....	....	....	....	65	55
International Transactions															*Millions of Rupees:*	
Exports	70	574	748	1,788	1,839	1,770	2,042	1,987	2,433	3,341	2,999	3,989	4,311	5,180	6,729	9,062
Imports, c.i.f.	71	636	916	1,760	1,995	2,409	2,951	3,076	3,634	4,721	4,977	5,048	5,175	6,494	8,119	9,199
Imports, f.o.b.	71.v	536	787	1,533	1,688	2,046	2,459	2,572	3,004	3,902	4,260	4,319	4,473	5,662	6,988	8,294
															1995=100	
Unit Value of Exports	74	†6.0	7.1	17.6	23.1	19.0	18.6	18.2	20.6	†28.4	30.7	34.0	36.4	40.4	46.2	48.9
Unit Value of Imports	75	†7.3	9.5	15.5	17.6	19.7	21.4	22.8	27.3	†39.9	42.6	52.8	51.7	58.1	63.9	51.8

Mauritius

684

1987	1988	1989	1990	1991	1992	1993	1994	1995	1996	1997	1998	1999	2000	2001		
End of Period															**Exchange Rates**	
17.272	18.616	19.707	20.375	21.162	23.372	25.625	26.077	26.258	25.842	30.041	34.896	34.955	36.327	38.197	Market Rate	**aa**
End of Period (ae) Period Average (rf)																
12.175	13.834	14.996	14.322	14.794	16.998	18.656	17.863	17.664	17.972	22.265	24.784	25.468	27.882	30.394	Market Rate	**ae**
12.878	13.438	15.250	14.863	15.652	15.563	17.648	17.960	17.386	17.948	21.057	23.993	25.186	26.250	29.129	Market Rate	**rf**
End of Period															**Fund Position**	
53.6	53.6	53.6	53.6	53.6	73.3	73.3	73.3	73.3	73.3	73.3	73.3	101.6	101.6	101.6	Quota	**2f. s**
4.1	3.7	5.0	10.3	18.0	17.6	21.0	21.3	21.7	22.2	22.5	22.8	16.1	16.5	16.8	SDRs	**1b. s**
.1	.1	.1	.1	1.3	6.2	7.3	7.3	7.3	7.4	7.4	7.4	14.5	14.5	14.5	Reserve Position in the Fund	**1c. s**
106.9	76.5	47.6	15.5	—	—	—	—	—	—	—	—	—	—	—	Total Fund Cred.&Loans Outstg.	**2tl**
End of Period															**International Liquidity**	
343.5	442.0	517.8	737.6	893.2	820.1	757.0	747.6	863.3	896.1	693.3	559.0	731.0	897.4	835.6	Total Reserves minus Gold	**1l. d**
5.9	5.0	6.6	14.6	25.7	24.3	28.9	31.2	32.2	31.9	30.3	32.2	22.1	21.4	21.1	SDRs	**1b. d**
.1	.1	.1	.1	1.8	8.6	10.1	10.7	10.9	10.6	9.9	10.4	19.9	18.9	18.2	Reserve Position in the Fund	**1c. d**
337.5	437.0	511.2	722.9	865.8	787.3	718.1	705.7	820.2	853.7	653.0	516.5	689.1	857.1	796.3	Foreign Exchange	**1d. d**
.038	.052	.061	.061	.061	.061	.062	.062	.062	.062	.062	.062	.062	.062	.062	Gold (Million Fine Troy Ounces)	**1ad**
3.6	4.4	4.8	5.0	4.9	4.2	3.9	4.0	4.1	4.0	6.1	11.9	12.3	12.3	12.3	Gold (National Valuation)	**1an d**
.3	.3	—	—	.1	.1	.1	.1	....	....	....	....	....	....	....	Government Assets	**3ba d**
3.5	.2	.5	.5	4.4	1.9	.6	1.9	.7	1.1	.9	.6	.2	.7	.3	Monetary Authorities: Other Liab.	**4.. d**
80.0	89.0	101.7	121.9	135.8	124.2	160.4	178.3	264.2	263.6	327.4	361.0	383.8	400.2	427.0	Deposit Money Banks: Assets	**7a. d**
5.4	8.3	9.0	12.8	9.9	3.3	28.2	39.8	67.5	59.5	38.4	127.9	104.3	106.6	98.3	Liabilities	**7b. d**
End of Period															**Monetary Authorities**	
4,225.8	6,174.7	7,837.0	10,635.6	13,286.3	14,011.5	14,194.9	13,425.7	15,322.0	16,176.8	15,571.8	14,150.3	18,930.9	25,366.1	25,772.9	Foreign Assets	**11**
1,085.6	272.5	289.5	301.8	3,108.2	1,351.4	1,021.4	1,741.9	654.7	914.5	1,662.5	4,994.9	2,223.5	2,196.1	2,210.7	Claims on Central Government	**12a**
76.5	120.5	173.5	172.2	301.8	411.2	523.5	291.0	672.8	446.2	410.8	707.8	375.1	328.3	726.6	Claims on Deposit Money Banks	**12e**
2,729.0	3,387.4	4,054.3	4,816.3	11,260.0	10,207.5	9,510.3	8,837.1	10,119.2	11,360.4	9,113.6	9,759.6	10,522.3	11,763.5	12,989.7	Reserve Money	**14**
1,663.4	2,008.7	2,403.6	2,848.7	3,407.5	3,820.1	4,230.9	4,412.2	4,847.2	5,050.7	5,410.4	5,832.9	6,126.7	6,647.6	7,329.0	of which: Currency Outside DMBs	**14a**
				1,057.0	448.6	61.3	—	159.0	717.7	240.0					Money Market Instruments	**16aa**
1,890.3	1,427.5	944.6	322.7	76.0	74.7	11.1	33.2	12.1	19.9	20.7	14.8	5.7	19.2	10.4	Foreign Liabilities	**16c**
3.0	571.1	1,553.8	2,886.9	21.3	17.5	12.0	6.2	452.7	251.2	3.1	13.6	3.4	3,421.0	757.7	Central Government Deposits	**16d**
304.9	326.0	343.2	353.7	366.1	400.9	436.3	443.6	446.4	439.9	506.0	582.4	583.3	604.9	634.4	Capital Accounts	**17a**
460.7	855.7	1,404.1	2,730.0	3,916.0	4,624.9	5,708.8	6,138.6	5,460.1	4,748.5	7,761.8	9,482.6	10,414.7	12,081.9	14,318.1	Other Items (Net)	**17r**
End of Period															**Deposit Money Banks**	
1,056.9	1,366.4	1,639.5	1,954.8	7,846.3	6,381.7	5,275.5	4,416.4	5,231.8	6,304.6	3,697.1	3,899.8	4,365.3	5,030.0	5,512.9	Reserves	**20**
974.0	1,230.9	1,525.1	1,745.8	2,008.3	2,110.8	2,991.6	3,185.7	4,667.7	4,736.9	7,289.0	8,947.3	9,775.5	11,159.4	12,978.1	Foreign Assets	**21**
3,611.5	5,149.5	5,858.5	7,361.6	3,956.7	6,451.2	8,329.5	10,344.5	14,623.7	14,219.6	17,025.7	13,318.5	15,759.0	15,001.3	18,286.5	Claims on Central Government	**22a**
7,033.0	8,940.3	10,850.7	13,043.4	15,234.2	18,684.9	23,923.9	28,714.4	32,878.6	34,467.6	43,360.3	56,653.0	62,520.7	70,569.6	77,891.5	Claims on Private Sector	**22d**
			78.4	147.3	304.9	238.0	146.5	132.3	163.1	160.5	424.6	1,766.2	1,817.2	1,283.0	Claims on Other Banking Insts	**22f**
1,631.6	1,799.2	2,096.1	2,716.3	3,262.8	3,383.4	3,188.3	4,443.3	4,685.4	4,774.0	5,194.5	5,730.2	5,844.8	6,563.6	7,974.9	Demand Deposits	**24**
10,350.5	13,748.4	15,764.8	18,990.0	23,278.1	27,501.1	33,198.5	36,754.5	44,574.4	48,406.8	57,201.3	63,819.9	74,851.6	81,573.9	89,789.2	Time, Savings,& Fgn.Currency Dep.	**25**
65.5	114.4	135.6	183.9	147.1	56.7	525.7	710.7	1,192.9	1,068.8	855.5	3,169.0	2,655.5	2,971.7	2,986.4	Foreign Liabilities	**26c**
107.5	170.8	166.1	189.4	200.5	224.8	277.9	84.2	1,468.0	319.6	277.0	132.0	264.4	190.9	225.0	Central Government Deposits	**26d**
66.4	116.2	108.6	87.7	157.0	267.5	329.0	156.2	550.0	—	250.0	475.0	250.0	250.0	660.3	Credit from Monetary Authorities	**26g**
658.7	885.0	1,576.9	1,859.1	2,356.6	3,439.0	4,758.6	5,144.4	5,447.8	6,620.4	7,842.4	9,092.1	10,848.6	11,953.6	12,037.2	Capital Accounts	**27a**
-204.8	-146.9	25.7	157.6	-209.3	-939.0	-1,519.5	-485.8	-384.4	-1,297.8	-88.1	825.0	-528.2	73.8	2,279.0	Other Items (Net)	**27r**
End of Period															**Monetary Survey**	
3,244.0	5,863.7	8,282.0	11,874.7	15,071.5	15,990.9	16,649.7	15,867.5	18,784.7	19,825.0	21,984.6	19,913.8	26,045.2	33,534.6	35,754.2	Foreign Assets (Net)	**31n**
11,619.6	13,620.4	15,278.8	17,708.9	22,224.6	26,550.1	33,222.9	40,856.9	46,368.6	49,194.0	61,928.9	75,245.4	82,001.6	85,972.3	98,689.0	Domestic Credit	**32**
4,586.6	4,680.1	4,428.1	4,587.1	6,843.1	7,560.3	9,061.0	11,996.0	13,357.7	14,563.3	18,408.1	18,167.8	17,714.7	13,585.5	19,514.5	Claims on Central Govt. (Net)	**32an**
7,033.0	8,940.3	10,850.7	13,043.4	15,234.2	18,684.9	23,923.9	28,714.4	32,878.6	34,467.6	43,360.3	56,653.0	62,520.7	70,569.6	77,891.5	Claims on Private Sector	**32d**
			78.4	147.3	304.9	238.0	146.5	132.3	163.1	160.5	424.6	1,766.2	1,817.2	1,283.0	Claims on Other Banking Insts	**32f**
3,303.7	3,820.2	4,510.9	5,577.8	6,676.5	7,209.2	7,423.2	8,864.0	9,572.8	9,829.8	10,611.0	11,590.0	12,001.8	13,297.1	15,451.7	Money	**34**
10,350.5	13,748.4	15,764.8	18,990.0	23,278.1	27,501.1	33,198.5	36,754.5	44,574.4	48,406.8	57,201.3	63,819.9	74,851.6	81,573.9	89,789.2	Quasi-Money	**35**
				1,057.0	448.6	61.3	—	159.0	717.7	240.0					Money Market Instruments	**36aa**
963.6	1,211.0	1,920.1	2,212.8	2,722.7	3,839.9	5,194.9	5,588.0	5,894.2	7,060.3	8,348.4	9,674.5	11,431.9	12,558.5	12,671.6	Capital Accounts	**37a**
245.8	704.5	1,364.9	2,803.1	3,561.9	3,542.2	3,994.7	5,518.0	4,952.9	3,004.5	7,512.9	10,074.8	9,761.4	12,077.4	16,530.8	Other Items (Net)	**37r**
13,654.2	17,568.6	20,275.7	24,567.8	29,954.6	34,710.3	40,621.7	45,618.5	54,147.2	58,236.6	67,812.3	75,409.0	86,853.4	94,871.0	105,240.9	Money plus Quasi-Money	**35l**
End of Period															**Other Banking Institutions**	
196.9	228.4	266.2	295.5	311.7	346.3	373.8	397.0	420.4	448.2	494.8	557.3	611.0	670.9	762.6	Deposits	**45**
13,851.1	17,797.0	20,541.9	24,863.3	30,266.3	35,056.6	40,995.5	46,015.5	54,567.6	58,684.8	68,307.1	75,967.2	87,464.4	95,541.9	106,003.5	Liquid Liabilities	**55l**
Percent Per Annum															**Interest Rates**	
10.00	10.00	12.00	12.00	11.30	8.30	8.30	13.80	11.40	11.82	10.46	17.19	....	....	....	Discount Rate (End of Period)	**60**
10.29	10.71	11.98	13.26	12.24	9.05	7.73	10.23	10.35	9.96	9.43	8.99	10.01	7.66	7.25	Money Market Rate	**60b**
9.38	10.00	11.06	12.56	12.31	10.07	8.40	11.04	12.23	10.77	9.08	9.28	10.92	9.61	9.78	Deposit Rate	**60l**
14.13	14.96	16.13	18.00	17.75	17.13	16.58	18.92	20.81	20.81	18.92	19.92	21.63	20.77	21.10	Lending Rate	**60p**
Period Averages															**Prices and Labor**	
....	....	30.7	40.1	40.9	43.0	68.2	103.9	100.0	88.1	100.0	119.3	109.7	108.1	98.6	Share Prices	**62**
50.9	55.5	62.6	71.0	†76.0	79.5	87.9	94.3	100.0	106.6	†113.8	121.6	130.0	135.4	142.7	Consumer Prices	**64**
Period Averages																
....	....	....	....		474	485	499	484	....	....	....	....	....	....	Labor Force	**67d**
245	268	271	†281	285	292	290	292	290	....	....	....	....	....	....	Employment	**67e**
47	28	18	13	11	8	7	7	8	10	11	11	12	18	....	Unemployment	**67c**
Millions of Rupees															**International Transactions**	
11,336	13,455	15,049	17,677	18,700	20,244	22,992	24,097	26,756	32,312	33,694	39,634	39,160	....	....	Exports	**70**
13,037	17,242	20,217	24,019	24,383	25,280	30,319	34,548	34,363	41,082	46,093	49,811	56,629	....	....	Imports, c.i.f.	**71**
11,701	15,628	18,295	21,921	22,212	22,931	27,507	31,601	31,508	38,073	42,570	46,015	....	....	....	Imports, f.o.b.	**71.v**
1995=100																
54.7	†58.1	69.3	72.6	77.3	†82.6	90.1	94.2	100.0	111.2	114.9	130.0	....	....	....	Unit Value of Exports	**74**
53.6	†58.5	69.6	74.2	77.8	†79.4	88.1	94.4	100.0	106.9	109.5	110.1	....	....	....	Unit Value of Imports	**75**

		1972	1973	1974	1975	1976	1977	1978	1979	1980	1981	1982	1983	1984	1985	1986
Balance of Payments																*Millions of US Dollars:*
Current Account, n.i.e.	78al *d*	. . .	. . .	. . .	. . .	−35.2	−77.9	−117.1	−145.7	−117.1	−147.7	−42.0	−20.2	−52.1	−30.4	93.6
Goods: Exports f.o.b.	78aa *d*					264.6	307.2	319.6	384.7	433.6	334.2	366.5	371.3	376.9	453.5	698.5
Goods: Imports f.o.b.	78ab *d*					−307.4	−367.8	−418.4	−484.3	−515.9	−475.9	−396.7	−385.8	−415.0	−465.3	−622.1
Trade Balance	78ac *d*					−42.8	−60.5	−98.8	−99.6	−82.2	−141.7	−30.2	−14.5	−38.1	−11.8	76.4
Services: Credit	78ad *d*					61.2	92.8	117.8	130.1	139.9	172.5	140.7	137.3	129.6	121.2	185.5
Services: Debit	78ae *d*					−66.6	−120.6	−143.8	−173.0	−174.0	−149.9	−140.9	−126.7	−126.3	−130.5	−164.6
Balance on Goods & Services	78af *d*					−48.2	−88.4	−124.8	−142.4	−116.3	−119.1	−30.4	−3.9	−34.9	−21.0	97.4
Income: Credit	78ag *d*					14.7	5.0	5.7	3.8	5.1	7.0	4.0	2.5	2.9	1.9	5.6
Income: Debit	78ah *d*					−8.8	−7.9	−13.5	−20.6	−28.2	−52.6	−49.8	−43.9	−48.3	−47.3	−59.8
Balance on Gds, Serv. & Inc.	78ai *d*					−42.4	−91.3	−132.6	−159.2	−139.5	−164.6	−76.2	−45.4	−80.2	−66.4	43.2
Current Transfers, n.i.e.: Credit	78aj *d*					10.0	16.5	18.7	19.8	28.8	22.7	38.1	30.9	32.8	40.1	55.5
Current Transfers: Debit	78ak *d*					−2.8	−3.2	−3.2	−6.3	−6.4	−5.8	−4.0	−5.7	−4.6	−4.1	−5.2
Capital Account, n.i.e.	78bc *d*	. . .	. . .	. . .	. . .	−.9	−.9	−1.6	−1.1	−1.6	−1.3	−.9	−1.1	−.8	−.8	−1.1
Capital Account, n.i.e.: Credit	78ba *d*															
Capital Account: Debit	78bb *d*					−.9	−.9	−1.6	−1.1	−1.6	−1.3	−.9	−1.1	−.8	−.8	−1.1
Financial Account, n.i.e.	78bj *d*	. . .	. . .	. . .	. . .	−44.8	29.8	37.3	48.5	66.4	9.3	−10.9	−20.0	−12.2	−23.7	−3.6
Direct Investment Abroad	78bd *d*					.4	.8	.2	2.5	—	—	—	—	—	—	—
Dir. Invest. in Rep. Econ., n.i.e.	78be *d*					3.1	2.3	4.4	1.7	1.2	.7	1.7	1.6	4.9	8.0	7.4
Portfolio Investment Assets	78bf *d*					—	—	—	—	—	—	—	—	—	—	—
Equity Securities	78bk *d*					—	—	—	—	—	—	—	—	—	—	—
Debt Securities	78bl *d*					—	—	—	—	—	—	—	—	—	—	—
Portfolio Investment Liab., n.i.e.	78bg *d*					—	—	—	—	—	—	—	—	—	—	—
Equity Securities	78bm *d*					—	—	—	—	—	—	—	—	—	—	—
Debt Securities	78bn *d*					—	—	—	—	—	—	—	—	—	—	—
Financial Derivatives Assets	78bw *d*					. . .	. . .	. . .	. . .	. . .	. . .	. . .	. . .	. . .	. . .	. . .
Financial Derivatives Liabilities	78bx *d*					. . .	. . .	. . .	. . .	. . .	. . .	. . .	. . .	. . .	. . .	. . .
Other Investment Assets	78bh *d*					−29.9	−5.0	11.7	3.6	25.0	−17.7	−8.0	−13.1	−6.7	−24.1	−14.7
Monetary Authorities	78bo *d*					. . .	. . .	. . .	. . .	. . .	. . .	. . .	. . .	. . .	. . .	. . .
General Government	78bp *d*					—	—	—	—	—	—	—	—	—	—	—
Banks	78bq *d*					3.0	−1.4	−1.0	−2.2	−5.3	−2.8	−1.6	−4.1	−6.4	−19.8	−4.3
Other Sectors	78br *d*					−32.9	−3.6	12.7	5.9	30.3	−14.9	−6.4	−9.0	−.4	−4.3	−10.4
Other Investment Liab., n.i.e.	78bi *d*					−18.4	31.8	21.1	40.6	40.2	26.3	−4.6	−8.5	−10.4	−7.6	3.6
Monetary Authorities	78bs *d*					—	—	—	−7.1	−2.0	—	—	13.1	−3.1	−.6	−7.4
General Government	78bt *d*					3.3	6.8	16.9	25.0	18.1	31.4	7.8	−20.5	−21.4	−8.4	.1
Banks	78bu *d*					−.3	13.3	−3.7	4.8	4.2	1.7	−13.1	4.4	3.7	3.6	−11.1
Other Sectors	78bv *d*					−21.4	11.7	8.0	17.9	19.9	−6.8	.6	−5.5	10.5	−2.1	22.1
Net Errors and Omissions	78ca *d*	. . .	. . .	. . .	. . .	5.1	11.0	11.8	3.6	24.4	10.0	−6.3	9.9	21.5	52.3	32.7
Overall Balance	78cb *d*					−75.8	−38.0	−69.7	−94.6	−27.9	−129.7	−60.1	−31.4	−43.6	−2.6	121.5
Reserves and Related Items	79da *d*	. . .	. . .	. . .	. . .	75.8	38.0	69.7	94.6	27.9	129.7	60.1	31.4	43.6	2.6	−121.5
Reserve Assets	79db *d*					75.8	25.1	19.9	10.3	−59.6	43.0	−4.3	15.9	−10.2	−4.0	−100.8
Use of Fund Credit and Loans	79dc *d*					—	12.9	11.5	36.7	41.4	68.5	24.6	14.5	−8.4	−14.6	−21.2
Exceptional Financing	79de *d*					—	—	38.3	47.6	46.1	18.2	39.8	1.0	62.2	21.2	.5
International Investment Position																*Millions of US Dollars*
Assets	79aa *d*	. . .	. . .	. . .	. . .	. . .	. . .	. . .	. . .	. . .	57.8	67.6	55.1	59.9	95.8	222.9
Direct Investment Abroad	79ab *d*	. . .	. . .	. . .	. . .	. . .	. . .	. . .	. . .	. . .	—	—	—	—	—	—
Portfolio Investment	79ac *d*	. . .	. . .	. . .	. . .	. . .	. . .	. . .	. . .	. . .	—	—	—	—	—	—
Equity Securities	79ad *d*	. . .	. . .	. . .	. . .	. . .	. . .	. . .	. . .	. . .	—	—	—	—	—	—
Debt Securities	79ae *d*	. . .	. . .	. . .	. . .	. . .	. . .	. . .	. . .	. . .	—	—	—	. . .	. . .	. . .
Financial Derivatives	79al *d*	. . .	. . .	. . .	. . .	. . .	. . .	. . .	. . .	. . .	. . .	. . .	. . .	. . .	. . .	. . .
Other Investment	79af *d*	. . .	. . .	. . .	. . .	. . .	. . .	. . .	. . .	. . .	17.9	25.0	33.4	33.2	62.3	83.0
Monetary Authorities	79ag *d*	. . .	. . .	. . .	. . .	. . .	. . .	. . .	. . .	. . .	—	—	—	—	—	—
General Government	79ah *d*	. . .	. . .	. . .	. . .	. . .	. . .	. . .	. . .	. . .	—	—	—	—	—	—
Banks	79ai *d*	. . .	. . .	. . .	. . .	. . .	. . .	. . .	. . .	. . .	12.6	13.5	15.3	18.1	41.1	49.2
Other Sectors	79aj *d*	. . .	. . .	. . .	. . .	. . .	. . .	. . .	. . .	. . .	5.3	11.5	18.1	15.1	21.2	33.8
Reserve Assets	79ak *d*	. . .	. . .	. . .	. . .	. . .	. . .	. . .	. . .	. . .	39.9	42.6	21.7	26.7	33.5	140.0
Liabilities	79la *d*	. . .	. . .	. . .	. . .	. . .	. . .	. . .	. . .	. . .	535.8	577.7	551.2	556.9	609.9	600.3
Dir. Invest. in Rep. Economy	79lb *d*	. . .	. . .	. . .	. . .	. . .	. . .	. . .	. . .	. . .	—	—	—	—	—	—
Portfolio Investment	79lc *d*	. . .	. . .	. . .	. . .	. . .	. . .	. . .	. . .	. . .	—	—	—	—	—	—
Equity Securities	79ld *d*	. . .	. . .	. . .	. . .	. . .	. . .	. . .	. . .	. . .	—	—	—	—	—	—
Debt Securities	79le *d*	. . .	. . .	. . .	. . .	. . .	. . .	. . .	. . .	. . .	—	—	—	. . .	. . .	. . .
Financial Derivatives	79ll *d*	. . .	. . .	. . .	. . .	. . .	. . .	. . .	. . .	. . .	. . .	. . .	. . .	. . .	. . .	. . .
Other Investment	79lf *d*	. . .	. . .	. . .	. . .	. . .	. . .	. . .	. . .	. . .	535.8	577.7	551.2	556.9	609.9	600.3
Monetary Authorities	79lg *d*	. . .	. . .	. . .	. . .	. . .	. . .	. . .	. . .	. . .	159.3	175.8	193.0	168.0	171.9	161.6
General Government	79lh *d*	. . .	. . .	. . .	. . .	. . .	. . .	. . .	. . .	. . .	286.8	330.0	292.5	316.1	356.4	350.5
Banks	79li *d*	. . .	. . .	. . .	. . .	. . .	. . .	. . .	. . .	. . .	16.5	2.7	6.3	8.3	13.0	2.7
Other Sectors	79lj *d*	. . .	. . .	. . .	. . .	. . .	. . .	. . .	. . .	. . .	73.3	69.2	59.5	64.5	68.6	85.4

Balance of Payments

Minus Sign Indicates Debit

	1987	1988	1989	1990	1991	1992	1993	1994	1995	1996	1997	1998	1999	2000	2001	Code
Current Account, n.i.e.	64.8	−56.4	−103.5	−119.3	−16.6	−.1	−92.0	−232.1	−21.9	34.0	−88.9	3.3	−131.1	−33.3	....	78al d
Goods: Exports f.o.b.	925.8	1,030.2	1,025.3	1,238.1	1,253.4	1,334.7	1,334.4	1,376.9	1,571.7	1,810.6	1,600.1	1,669.3	1,589.2	1,559.4	....	78aa d
Goods: Imports f.o.b.	−925.4	−1,177.8	−1,217.7	−1,494.8	−1,438.5	−1,493.9	−1,576.0	−1,773.9	−1,812.2	−2,136.3	−2,036.1	−1,933.3	−2,107.9	−1,953.3	....	78ab d
Trade Balance	.4	−147.6	−192.4	−256.7	−185.1	−159.2	−241.6	−397.0	−240.5	−325.7	−436.0	−264.0	−518.7	−393.9	....	78ac d
Services: Credit	285.3	348.8	372.7	483.9	528.3	577.5	566.2	632.7	777.7	960.8	893.7	916.9	1,035.6	1,071.0	....	78ad d
Services: Debit	−247.0	−307.1	−340.3	−421.0	−448.4	−522.8	−521.7	−546.4	−641.3	−672.9	−656.3	−718.0	−728.1	−746.0	....	78ae d
Balance on Goods & Services	38.7	−105.9	−160.0	−193.8	−105.2	−104.5	−197.1	−310.6	−104.2	−37.9	−198.6	−65.1	−211.2	−69.0	....	78af d
Income: Credit	14.0	26.6	51.1	55.9	82.5	91.0	70.0	31.7	52.2	31.1	47.0	47.8	35.1	36.0	....	78ag d
Income: Debit	−55.4	−70.7	−70.9	−78.7	−76.9	−80.1	−66.5	−56.4	−71.3	−75.1	−64.6	−74.4	−58.6	−64.1	....	78ah d
Balance on Gds, Serv. & Inc.	−2.7	−150.0	−179.8	−216.6	−99.5	−93.6	−193.6	−335.3	−123.3	−81.8	−216.3	−91.7	−234.8	−97.1	....	78ai d
Current Transfers, n.i.e.: Credit	74.9	103.3	84.9	108.5	98.6	109.9	115.9	129.6	146.8	182.8	206.4	186.8	196.4	167.6	....	78aj d
Current Transfers: Debit	−7.4	−9.7	−8.7	−11.2	−15.7	−16.4	−14.4	−26.3	−45.4	−67.0	−79.0	−91.8	−92.7	−103.8	....	78ak d
Capital Account, n.i.e.	−1.8	−1.1	−.9	−.6	−1.6	−1.4	−1.5	−1.3	−1.1	−.8	−.5	−.8	−.5	−.6	....	78bc d
Capital Account, n.i.e.: Credit	—	—	—	—	—	—	—	—	—	—	—	—	—	—	....	78ba d
Capital Account: Debit	−1.8	−1.1	−.9	−.6	−1.6	−1.4	−1.5	−1.3	−1.1	−.8	−.5	−.8	−.5	−.6	....	78bb d
Financial Account, n.i.e.	59.3	121.2	50.2	138.6	40.2	−14.8	19.3	41.4	25.1	91.9	−18.6	−26.0	134.0	182.0	....	78bj d
Direct Investment Abroad	—	−.1	−.6	−.6	−10.9	−43.3	−33.2	−1.1	−3.6	−2.7	−3.2	−13.7	−6.4	−13.0	....	78bd d
Dir. Invest. in Rep. Econ., n.i.e.	17.2	23.7	35.8	41.0	17.4	14.7	14.7	20.0	18.7	36.7	55.3	12.2	49.4	265.6	....	78be d
Portfolio Investment Assets	—	—	—	−2.2	−.4	—	−2.2	−.3	—	−2.0	−96.8	43.6	59.1	23.1	....	78bf d
Equity Securities	—	—	—	—	—	—	—	—	—	—	—	−3.3	59.1	23.1	....	78bk d
Debt Securities	—	—	—	−2.2	−.4	—	−2.2	−.3	—	−2.0	−96.8	46.9	—	—	....	78bl d
Portfolio Investment Liab., n.i.e.	—	—	—	—	—	—	—	2.1	175.9	36.8	30.6	−28.7	−61.4	−143.1	....	78bg d
Equity Securities	—	—	—	—	—	—	—	2.1	22.0	36.8	30.6	5.0	−61.4	−143.1	....	78bm d
Debt Securities	—	—	—	—	—	—	—	—	154.0	—	—	−33.7	—	—	....	78bn d
Financial Derivatives Assets	....	....	....	....	....	....	....	....	....	....	....	....	....	....	....	78bw d
Financial Derivatives Liabilities	....	....	....	....	....	....	....	....	....	....	....	....	....	....	....	78bx d
Other Investment Assets	−23.6	−33.7	−49.4	−7.1	−36.2	14.3	−26.7	−64.6	−136.4	17.9	−115.7	−66.7	−245.9	−288.6	....	78bh d
Monetary Authorities	....	....	....	....	....	....	....	....	....	....	....	....	....	....	....	78bo d
General Government	—	—	−2.2	—	—	—	—	—	—	—	—	—	—	—	....	78bp d
Banks	−25.5	−19.1	−19.3	−14.9	−16.8	33.0	−49.0	−11.5	−85.2	−3.9	−121.2	−69.1	−32.9	−51.5	....	78bq d
Other Sectors	1.9	−14.6	−27.9	7.7	−19.4	−18.7	22.3	−53.1	−51.2	21.8	5.5	2.4	−213.1	−237.0	....	78br d
Other Investment Liab., n.i.e.	65.8	131.3	64.4	107.4	70.4	−.5	66.6	85.2	−29.5	5.1	111.2	27.3	339.4	337.9	....	78bi d
Monetary Authorities															....	78bs d
General Government	22.5	−15.4	1.6	−5.3	−22.0	−34.7	1.4	−14.1	−18.8	−20.4	9.0	−14.2	−11.4	−22.7	....	78bt d
Banks	2.4	3.6	1.4	3.3	−2.4	−5.8	26.6	9.2	27.7	−6.9	−10.1	96.4	−20.4	13.7	....	78bu d
Other Sectors	40.8	143.0	61.4	109.5	94.7	40.0	38.6	90.1	−38.5	32.5	112.3	−54.9	371.2	346.8	....	78bv d
Net Errors and Omissions	96.4	121.2	199.8	213.2	168.8	59.6	81.2	148.5	106.7	−76.8	73.4	−41.9	187.3	82.5	....	78ca d
Overall Balance	218.8	184.8	145.6	231.9	190.8	43.3	7.0	−43.5	108.8	48.3	−34.6	−65.4	189.7	230.6	....	78cb d
Reserves and Related Items	−218.8	−184.8	−145.6	−231.9	−190.8	−43.3	−7.0	43.5	−108.8	−48.3	34.6	65.4	−189.7	−230.6	....	79da d
Reserve Assets	−186.2	−144.0	−108.5	−188.3	−168.9	−43.3	−7.0	43.5	−108.8	−48.3	34.6	65.4	−189.7	−230.6	....	79db d
Use of Fund Credit and Loans	−32.8	−41.0	−37.1	−43.6	−21.9	—	—	—	—	—	—	—	—	—	....	79dc d
Exceptional Financing	.2	.2													....	79de d

Millions of US Dollars

International Investment Position

	1987	1988	1989	1990	1991	1992	1993	1994	1995	1996	1997	1998	1999	2000	2001	Code
Assets	462.6	580.2	696.1	929.3	1,117.2	1,001.9	947.9	994.8	1,232.3	1,243.1	1,085.6	965.7	1,395.7	1,797.0	....	79aa d
Direct Investment Abroad	—	—	—	—	—	—	—	—	—	—	—	—	—	—	....	79ab d
Portfolio Investment	—	—	—	—	....	....	....	—	—	—	—	—	—	—	....	79ac d
Equity Securities	....	....	....	....	....	....	....								....	79ad d
Debt Securities	....	....	....	....	....	....	....								....	79ae d
Financial Derivatives					....	....	....	—	—	—	—	—	—		....	
Other Investment	114.5	133.5	173.5	186.7	219.0	177.5	187.0	243.0	364.8	342.9	386.1	394.7	652.3	887.2	....	79af d
Monetary Authorities	—	—	—	—	—	—	—	—	—	—	—	—	—	—	....	79ag d
General Government	—	—	2.3	—	—	—	—	—	—	—	—	—	—	—	....	79ah d
Banks	80.0	89.0	101.7	121.9	135.7	87.9	126.4	142.5	227.9	228.4	298.8	335.1	383.8	400.2	....	79ai d
Other Sectors	34.5	44.5	69.6	64.8	83.3	89.6	60.6	100.5	136.9	114.6	87.3	59.6	268.5	487.0	....	79aj d
Reserve Assets	348.1	446.7	522.6	742.6	898.2	824.4	760.9	751.8	867.5	900.2	699.5	571.0	743.3	909.8	....	79ak d
Liabilities	726.5	780.9	810.2	923.5	970.9	922.5	937.5	1,128.3	1,345.6	1,427.1	1,318.1	1,320.0	1,601.3	1,722.5	....	79la d
Dir. Invest. in Rep. Economy	—	—	—	—	—	—	—	—	156.3	167.2	150.9	117.7	117.8	—	....	79lb d
Portfolio Investment	—	—	—	—	—	—	—	—	—	—	—	—	—	—	....	79lc d
Equity Securities	....	....	....	....	....	....	....								....	79ld d
Debt Securities	—	—	—	—	—	—	—	—	156.3	167.2	150.9	117.7	117.8	—	....	79le d
Financial Derivatives	....	....	....	....	....	....	....								....	79lf d
Other Investment	726.5	780.9	810.2	923.5	970.9	922.5	937.5	1,128.3	1,189.2	1,259.9	1,167.2	1,202.3	1,483.6	1,722.5	....	79lf d
Monetary Authorities	151.7	103.0	62.5	22.1	—	—	—	—	—	—	—	—	—	—	....	79lg d
General Government	409.8	380.6	377.2	389.0	376.8	316.2	316.6	324.8	328.3	352.6	300.1	294.1	273.4	246.2	....	79lh d
Banks	5.4	8.2	9.1	12.8	9.9	3.4	28.2	39.8	67.5	59.5	38.4	127.9	104.3	106.6	....	79li d
Other Sectors	159.6	289.1	361.4	499.7	584.2	603.0	592.7	763.7	793.4	847.9	828.7	780.3	1,105.9	1,369.7	....	79lj d

		1972	1973	1974	1975	1976	1977	1978	1979	1980	1981	1982	1983	1984	1985	1986
Government Finance														*Millions of Rupees:*		
Deficit (-) or Surplus	80	−45	†−27	−202	−186	−209	−457	−727	−882	−897	−1,293	−1,388	†−978	−649	−580	−347
Revenue	81	285	†342	456	716	1,062	1,168	1,232	1,417	1,811	2,059	2,221	†2,962	3,242	3,593	4,128
Grants Received	81z	....	†14	4	7	3	5	2	1	2	14	68	†23	53	166	233
Expenditure	82	321	†356	589	840	1,181	1,526	1,785	2,135	2,370	2,954	3,336	†3,560	3,707	4,229	4,445
Lending Minus Repayments	83	9	†27	73	69	93	105	177	165	339	413	341	†402	237	110	263
Financing																
Net Borrowing: Domestic	84a	76	†95	200	250	164	428	397	544	657	589	731	†1,132	722	−118	525
Foreign	85a	3	†11	30	44	17	69	284	316	219	701	794	†−176	−140	721	−117
Use of Cash Balances	87	−34	†−79	−29	−108	28	−40	46	22	21	4	−137	†17	68	−28	−62
Unallocated Financing	87c	....	†—	—	—	—	—	—	—	—	—	—	†4	−1	6	—
Debt: Domestic	88a	317	†416	538	794	966	1,322	1,725	2,246	2,933	3,594	4,453	†5,208	5,849	5,964	6,251
Foreign	89a	168	†139	208	247	263	323	630	911	1,432	2,218	3,540	†3,463	3,945	5,207	4,633
National Accounts														*Millions of Rupees*		
Househ.Cons.Expend.,incl.NPISHs	96f	929	1,122	1,684	1,878	2,178	3,593	4,174	5,144	6,562	7,277	8,301	8,874	9,841	11,118	12,000
Government Consumption Expend.	91f	219	235	360	443	586	798	933	1,009	1,224	1,422	1,624	1,706	1,835	1,915	2,068
Gross Fixed Capital Formation	93e	229	480	750	1,138	1,450	1,510	1,770	1,965	2,028	2,240	2,100	2,300	2,595	3,100	3,890
Changes in Inventories	93i	—	—	—	—	213	120	153	420	−225	338	30	−71	570	800	430
Exports of Goods and Services	90c	777	1,052	2,324	2,184	2,388	2,656	2,705	3,260	4,450	4,566	5,529	5,953	6,989	8,895	11,919
Imports of Goods and Services (-)	98c	722	1,037	1,902	2,227	2,712	3,235	3,477	4,158	5,342	5,634	5,859	5,999	7,470	9,210	10,607
Gross Domestic Product (GDP)	99b	1,432	1,852	3,216	3,416	4,103	5,442	6,258	7,640	8,697	10,209	11,725	12,763	14,360	16,618	19,700
Net Primary Income from Abroad	98.n	2	16	10	17	47	−17	−48	−106	−178	−408	−498	−485	−626	−700	−729
Gross National Income (GNI)	99a	1,434	1,868	3,226	3,433	4,150	5,425	6,210	7,534	8,519	9,801	11,227	12,278	13,734	15,918	18,971
GDP Volume 1987 Prices	99b.p	....	....	....	....	....	....	....	....	....	....	....	....	....	....	....
GDP Volume 1992 Prices	99b.p	....	....	....	....	....	....	....	....	....	....	....	....	....	....	....
GDP Volume (1995=100)	99bv p	29.5	32.9	35.6	36.0	42.0	44.8	46.5	48.2	43.3	45.9	48.4	48.6	50.9	54.4	59.7
GDP Deflator (1995=100)	99bi p	7.0	8.1	13.1	13.7	14.1	17.6	19.5	23.0	29.1	32.2	35.1	38.0	40.9	44.2	47.8
															Millions:	
Population	99z	.83	.84	.85	.86	.87	.88	.90	.91	.94	.95	.96	.97	.98	.99	.99

Year Ending June 30

Government Finance

	1987	1988	1989	1990	1991	1992	1993	1994	1995	1996	1997	1998	1999	2000	2001	
Deficit (-) or Surplus	54	†87	†-468	-158	2	†-358	†19	†-167	-812	-3,083	-3,427	858	-1,559	-1,458	....	80
Revenue	5,203	†6,467	†7,631	8,885	10,115	†11,378	12,364	14,076	14,398	14,469	18,277	20,327	23,082	25,587	....	81
Grants Received	188	†214	†68	116	61	†25	78	130	262	221	63	216	135	161	....	81z
Expenditure	5,125	†6,377	†7,483	8,880	9,944	†11,518	12,148	14,271	15,502	17,280	20,260	21,446	25,479	27,032	....	82
Lending Minus Repayments	211	†217	†683	279	231	†244	275	102	-31	493	1,506	-1,761	-703	174	....	83
Financing																
Net Borrowing: Domestic	-2	†71	†2,318	1,607	2,152	†-2,739	†725	†1,737	2,059	1,544	3,228	3,010	1,191	3,560	....	84a
Foreign	148	†602	†-461	-166	-284	†-331	†-313	†-113	-371	2,374	198	-274	-1,170	-510	....	85a
Use of Cash Balances	-200	†-761	†-1,389	-1,283	-1,870	†3,428	†-431	†-1,458	-874	-834	2 p	-3,594	1,538	-1,592	....	87
Unallocated Financing	—	†—	†—	—	—	†—	†—	†—								87c
Debt: Domestic	6,100	†5,999	†8,376	9,770	11,889	†10,560	11,696	14,149	17,311	19,215	21,921	22,857	24,326	29,424	....	88a
Foreign	4,844	†5,801	†5,736	5,868	5,964	†5,476	5,712	5,766	5,778	9,159	9,666	10,752	10,037	9,891	....	89a

National Accounts

Millions of Rupees

	1987	1988	1989	1990	1991	1992	1993	1994	1995	1996	1997	1998	1999	2000	2001	
Househ.Cons.Expend.,incl.NPISHs	14,690	17,565	21,280	25,370	28,085	30,999	35,915	40,482	44,631	49,325	54,865	62,436	68,711	73,938	80,942	96f
Government Consumption Expend.	2,835	3,644	4,078	4,617	5,190	5,695	6,822	7,862	8,343	9,453	10,428	12,648	14,193	15,547	16,674	91f
Gross Fixed Capital Formation	5,175	8,090	8,680	12,030	12,680	13,810	16,065	19,350	16,750	20,125	23,430	23,082	29,676	28,069	30,049	93e
Changes in Inventories	1,024	807	1,674	97	35	756	1,273	948	1,061	-915	1,888	2,556	-1,669	2,203	-618	93i
Exports of Goods and Services	15,639	18,565	21,363	25,619	27,861	29,759	33,515	36,249	41,205	50,281	54,357	65,711	69,099	73,841	89,373	90c
Imports of Goods and Services (-)	15,141	19,988	23,801	28,458	29,535	31,386	37,020	41,848	42,908	50,959	58,540	66,543	72,861	74,513	84,290	98c
Gross Domestic Product (GDP)	24,222	28,683	33,274	39,275	44,316	49,633	56,570	63,043	69,082	77,310	86,428	99,890	107,749	129,085	132,130	99b
Net Primary Income from Abroad	-533	-593	-303	-339	89	171	63	-443	-332	-789	-374	-637	-466	-783	193	98.n
Gross National Income (GNI)	23,689	28,090	32,971	38,936	44,405	49,804	56,633	62,600	68,750	76,521	86,054	99,253	107,293	118,302	132,323	99a
GDP Volume 1987 Prices	24,222	25,867	27,022	28,964	30,197	32,071	....	....	....	....	....	....	....	....	....	99b.p
GDP Volume 1992 Prices	....	....	....	....	....	49,633	52,407	54,471	57,022	60,038	63,840	67,523	69,836	....	....	99b.p
GDP Volume (1995=100)	65.7	70.2	73.3	78.6	82.0	87.0	91.9	95.5	100.0	105.3	112.0	118.4	122.5	....	....	99bv p
GDP Deflator (1995=100)	53.3	59.1	65.7	72.3	78.3	82.5	89.1	95.5	100.0	106.3	111.7	122.1	127.4	....	....	99bi p

Midyear Estimates

	1987	1988	1989	1990	1991	1992	1993	1994	1995	1996	1997	1998	1999	2000	2001	
Population	1.00	1.01	1.02	1.03	1.04	1.08	1.10	1.11	1.12	1.13	1.15	1.16	1.17	1.19	1.20	99z

(See notes in the back of the book.)

Mexico

	1972	1973	1974	1975	1976	1977	1978	1979	1980	1981	1982	1983	1984	1985	1986
Exchange Rates												*Pesos per Thousand SDRs through 1985*				
Market Rate...............aa=...............wa	13.5714	15.0794	15.3044	14.6332	23.1785	27.6180	29.6050	30.0384	29.6611	30.5294	106.4281	150.6875	188.7492	408.2827	†1.1296
												Pesos per Thousand US Dollars through 1985			
Market Rate...............ae=...............we	12.5000	12.5000	12.5000	12.5000	19.9500	22.7363	22.7243	22.8025	23.2561	26.2289	96.4800	143.9300	192.5600	371.7000	†.9235
Market Rate...............rf=...............wf	12.5000	12.5000	12.5000	12.5000	15.4259	22.5729	22.7673	22.8054	22.9510	24.5146	56.4017	120.0936	167.8276	256.8716	†.6118
Fund Position														*Millions of SDRs:*	
Quota..2f. s	370	370	370	370	370	370	535	535	803	803	803	1,166	1,166	1,166	1,166
SDRs..1b. s	128	128	129	86	1	47	43	152	113	153	5	22	3	—	7
Reserve Position in the Fund...........1c. s	98	98	98	98	—	—	—	—	100	161	—	91	—	—	—
Total Fund Cred.&Loans Outstg.......2tl	—	—	—	—	319	419	229	103	—	—	201	1,204	2,408	2,703	3,319
International Liquidity											*Millions of US Dollars Unless Otherwise Indicated:*				
Total Reserves minus Gold..............1l. d	976	1,160	1,238	1,383	1,188	1,649	1,842	2,072	2,960	4,074	834	3,913	7,272	4,906	5,670
SDRs.......................................1b. d	139	154	158	101	1	57	56	201	144	178	6	23	3	—	9
Reserve Position in the Fund.......1c. d	106	118	120	114	—	—	—	—	128	187	—	95	—	—	—
Foreign Exchange.....................1d. d	731	888	960	1,168	1,187	1,592	1,786	1,871	2,688	3,709	828	3,795	7,269	4,906	5,661
Gold (Million Fine Troy Ounces)......1ad	4.943	4.629	3.663	3.660	1.602	1.755	1.893	1.984	2.062	2.256	2.065	2.308	2.422	2.362	2.568
Monetary Authorities: Other Liab......4..d	—	—	—	—	—	48	57	13	9	8	42	—	—	3	1
Deposit Money Banks: Assets.........7a. d	....	....	....	....	....	299	414	710	1,320	984	1,433	2,179	1,912	940	833
Liabilities ....7b. d	....	....	....	....	....	1,817	2,663	3,872	7,174	10,156	9,221	10,751	10,284	2,203	2,106
Other Banking Insts.: Assets..........7e. d	....	....	....	....	....	31	31	31	47	38	156	341	386	383	484
Liabilities.........7f. d	....	....	....	....	....	10,950	11,259	12,810	13,755	21,231	22,991	23,137	23,715	25,342	27,310
Monetary Authorities											*Thousands of Pesos Through 1976;*				
Foreign Assets......................................11	16,800	17,980	18,180	20,150	28,160	†46	54	72	96	135	191	733	1,599	2,248	6,437
Claims on Central Government..........12a	38,430	60,950	95,790	127,470	133,990	†286	351	459	611	900	2,496	3,192	4,128	6,300	10,235
Claims on Nonbank Pub.Fin.Insts....12cg	....	....	....	....	....	....	....	....	....	....	99	153	219	309	481
Claims on Deposit Money Banks........12e	180	440	320	1,150	18,940	†15	9	9	16	12	235	53	54	45	51
Claims on Other Banking Insts..........12f	1,720	2,690	3,850	4,680	11,970	†5	9	12	29	35	73	73	130	79	93
Reserve Money......................................14	57,580	75,210	105,320	140,840	130,950	†296	381	513	722	1,045	2,068	3,225	4,879	5,706	8,444
of which: Currency Outside DMBs...14a	26,880	34,310	42,900	52,510	80,230	†89	115	150	195	283	505	681	1,122	1,738	3,067
Time & Foreign Currency Deposits.........15	680	1,770	1,380	1,750	11,740	†13	12	16	15	23	48	198	376	565	373
Liabs. of Central Bank: Securities....16ac	—	—	—	—	—	†—	—	—	—	—	†—	—	—	—	—
Foreign Liabilities.............................16c	—	—	—	—	7,400	†13	3	3	—	—	25	181	453	1,094	3,716
Central Government Deposits...........16d	....	....	....	....	....	2	2	2	—	7	458	15	8	—	—
Liab. to Nonbank Pub.Fin.Insts.....16dg	....	....	....	....	....	2	2	2	7	8	14	166	296	735	2,023
Capital Accounts..............................17a	....	....	....	....	....	4	4	6	7	9	31	44	55	165	373
Other Items (Net)..............................17r	−1,130	5,080	11,440	10,860	42,970	†24	14	10	—	−9	450	375	63	715	2,368
Deposit Money Banks											*Thousands of Pesos through 1976;*				
Reserves...20	17,830	26,240	32,910	40,700	37,480	†202	261	355	515	746	1,480	2,514	3,801	3,927	5,184
Claims on Mon.Author.: Securities.....20c	—	—	—	—	—	†—	—	—	—	—	†—	—	—	—	—
Foreign Assets......................................21	....	....	....	....	....	7	9	16	31	26	138	313	367	346	762
Claims on Central Government..........22a	1,950	2,290	5,500	4,480	25,780	†8	8	18	22	57	†483	707	974	2,551	8,754
Claims on State and Local Govts.......22b	....	....	....	....	....	†2	4	5	4	5	†24	20	73	73	83
Claims on Nonfin.Pub.Enterprises.....22c	....	....	....	....	....	15	21	24	37	76	228	578	1,011	397	544
Claims on Nonbank Pub.Fin.Insts....22cg	....	....	....	....	....	....	....	....	....	....	3	9	11	6	13
Claims on Private Sector....................22d	33,930	36,650	42,680	52,600	63,040	†247	353	487	696	1,015	†1,253	1,800	3,323	4,591	7,383
Claims on Other Banking Insts..........22f	5,450	7,660	7,690	9,700	13,510	†15	15	22	27	40	71	162	213	177	538
Claims on Nonbank Financial Insts.....22g	....	....	....	....	....	....	....	....	....	....	16	22	53	70	148
Demand Deposits..................................24	37,900	45,720	56,300	68,560	76,900	†106	143	197	260	315	†455	676	1,075	1,611	2,468
Time, Savings,& Fgn.Currency Dep.......25	21,310	28,640	31,630	35,680	51,360	†305	418	574	806	1,282	†1,976	3,300	5,640	7,730	14,094
Money Market Instruments................26aa	....	....	....	....	....	....	....	....	....	....	8	21	149	417	2,218
Foreign Liabilities.............................26c	....	....	....	....	....	....	....	....	....	....	71	104	140	128	259
Long-Term Foreign Liabilities...........26cl	....	....	....	....	....	41	61	88	167	266	†817	1,440	1,834	683	1,668
Central Government Deposits...........26d	....	....	....	....	....	....	....	....	....	....	8	15	24	20	63
Liab. to Nonbank Pub.Fin.Insts......26dg	....	....	....	....	....	22	35	48	60	101	202	329	519	913	1,801
Credit from Monetary Authorities.......26g	....	....	....	....	....	14	8	7	15	8	22	38	83	35	61
Liabilities to Other Banking Insts.......26i	....	....	....	....	....	....	....	....	....	....	22	38	83	35	61
Liab. to Nonbank Financial Insts......26j	....	....	....	....	....	....	....	....	....	....	33	70	122	164	316
Capital Accounts..............................27a	....	....	....	....	....	16	19	27	39	52	68	96	169	274	588
Other Items (Net)..............................27r	−50	−1,520	850	3,240	11,550	†−9	−12	−14	−15	−60	†36	36	71	163	−127
Monetary Survey											*Thousands of Pesos through 1976;*				
Foreign Assets (Net)............................31n	17,470	18,330	18,790	20,830	22,060	†41	52	83	125	160	†233	761	1,373	1,372	3,224
Domestic Credit.....................................32	80,990	108,830	155,160	197,150	239,300	†577	762	1,028	1,429	2,126	†4,180	6,528	9,879	14,228	27,731
Claims on Central Govt. (Net)..........32an	39,530	61,490	100,060	129,780	150,360	†292	357	475	633	950	†2,513	3,869	5,070	8,831	18,926
Claims on State and Local Govts.......32b	—	—	—	—	—	†2	4	5	4	5	†24	20	73	73	83
Claims on Nonfin.Pub.Enterprises.....32c	....	....	....	....	....	15	21	24	37	76	228	578	1,011	397	544
Claims on Private Sector....................32d	34,290	36,990	43,560	52,990	63,460	†248	356	490	699	1,020	†1,255	1,804	3,329	4,601	7,399
Claims on Other Banking Insts.........32f	7,170	10,350	11,540	14,380	25,480	†20	24	34	56	75	144	235	343	256	631
Claims on Nonbank Financial Inst......32g	....	....	....	....	....	....	....	....	....	....	16	22	53	70	148
Money..34	68,240	83,520	100,770	122,360	157,970	†212	270	363	481	643	†1,031	1,447	2,315	3,463	5,790
Quasi-Money...35	22,910	31,570	38,390	41,740	85,020	†317	429	588	820	1,298	†2,024	3,498	6,016	8,295	14,467
Money Market Instruments................36aa	....	....	....	....	....	....	....	....	....	....	8	21	149	417	2,218
Liabs. of Central Bank: Securities.....36ac	—	—	—	—	—	†—	—	—	—	—	†—	—	—	—	—
Long-Term Foreign Liabilities...........36cl	....	....	....	....	....	41	61	88	167	266	†817	1,440	1,834	683	1,668
Liabilities to Other Banking Insts.......36i	....	....	....	....	....	....	....	....	....	....	33	70	122	164	316
Liab. to Nonbank Financial Insts.........36j	....	....	....	....	....	....	....	....	....	....					
Capital Accounts..............................37a	....	....	....	....	....	20	23	33	46	61	99	140	224	439	961
Other Items (Net)..............................37r	7,310	12,070	34,790	53,880	18,370	†28	32	39	40	17	401	673	592	2,138	5,535
Money plus Quasi-Money.....................35l	91,150	115,090	139,160	164,100	242,990	†525	699	949	1,297	1,933	†3,055	4,945	8,331	11,758	20,257

1987	1988	1989	1990	1991	1992	1993	1994	1995	1996	1997	1998	1999	2000	2001		
															Exchange Rates	
and per SDr thereafter: End of Period																
3.1348	3.0695	3.4707	4.1903	4.3929	4.2837	4.2661	7.7737	11.3605	11.2893	10.9064	13.8902	13.0585	12.4717	11.4894	Market Rate aa=	wa
and per US Dollar thereafter: End of Period (we) Period Average (wf)																
2.2097	2.2810	2.6410	2.9454	3.0710	3.1154	3.1059	5.3250	7.6425	7.8509	8.0833	9.8650	9.5143	9.5722	9.1423	Market Rate ae=	we
1.3782	2.2731	2.4615	2.8126	3.0184	3.0949	3.1156	3.3751	6.4194	7.5994	7.9185	9.1360	9.5604	9.4556	9.3423	Market Rate rf=	wf
End of Period															**Fund Position**	
1,166	1,166	1,166	1,166	1,166	1,753	1,753	1,753	1,753	1,753	1,753	1,753	2,586	2,586	2,586	Quota	2f.s
498	293	292	293	409	399	163	121	1,074	179	490	240	575	281	283	SDRs	1b.s
—	—	—	—	—	—	—	—	—	—	—	—	—	—	—	Reserve Position in the Fund	1c.s
3,639	3,570	3,874	4,605	4,730	4,327	3,485	2,644	10,648	9,234	6,735	5,952	3,259	—	—	Total Fund Cred.&Loans Outstg.	2tl
End of Period															**International Liquidity**	
12,464	5,279	6,329	9,863	17,726	18,942	25,110	6,278	16,847	19,433	28,797	31,799	31,782	35,509	44,741	Total Reserves minus Gold	1l.d
706	394	383	417	586	548	223	177	1,597	257	661	337	790	366	356	SDRs	1b.d
—	—	—	—	—	—	—	—	—	—	—	—	—	—	—	Reserve Position in the Fund	1c.d
11,758	4,885	5,946	9,446	17,140	18,394	24,886	6,101	15,250	19,176	28,136	31,461	30,992	35,142	44,384	Foreign Exchange	1d.d
2.536	2.555	1.025	.919	.923	.688	.484	.426	.514	.255	.190	.223	.159	.249	.231	Gold (Million Fine Troy Ounces)	1ad
1	3	254	4	78	94	75	66	91	84	560	552	377	226	214	Monetary Authorities: Other Liab.	4..d
784	1,257	1,062	1,413	1,238	843	760	435	953	816	2,630	4,687	5,735	6,408	12,627	Deposit Money Banks: Assets	7a.d
336	1,060	1,251	1,340	2,291	4,410	5,410	6,771	7,948	5,414	6,909	5,462	4,141	4,422	3,064	Liabilities	7b.d
377	463	412	336	628	1,164	961	2,394	3,135	4,008	2,266	2,733	2,332	2,937	2,233	Other Banking Insts.: Assets	7e.d
29,635	28,214	26,881	20,926	22,987	25,795	31,170	37,029	36,408	32,615	28,292	28,487	26,955	26,747	25,115	Liabilities	7f.d
Millions of Pesos Beginning 1977: End of Period															**Monetary Authorities**	
30,856	15,558	18,744	30,979	56,333	60,940	79,710	34,490	122,814	140,217	†239,472	323,607	310,242	349,527	418,144	Foreign Assets	11
13,173	32,657	39,001	44,293	34,668	30,123	9,864	2,000	13,211	10,488	†—	—	—	—	—	Claims on Central Government	12a
937	1,783	3,156	5,798	9,875	14,623	21,227	38,043	78,001	70,327	†81,067	93,796	99,926	102,755	103,817	Claims on Nonbank Pub.Fin.Insts	12cg
52	171	42	37	46	13	810	97,732	43,132	11,501	†1,877	428	96,169	90,170	62,525	Claims on Deposit Money Banks	12e
126	853	142	558	1,224	2,405	2,831	4,368	1,889	382	†553	270	157	4,950	21,009	Claims on Other Banking Insts	12f
14,402	20,874	23,012	31,135	39,797	45,535	50,274	60,923	81,274	100,069	†150,907	192,511	276,315	257,223	324,869	Reserve Money	14
7,339	13,201	18,030	24,689	32,513	38,116	43,351	52,035	60,839	74,338	†94,341	116,084	164,424	182,237	199,177	*of which: Currency Outside DMBs*	14a
1,350	1,193	643	834	383	528	592	10	6	12	†4,766	3,721	7,222	13,147	4,563	Time & Foreign Currency Deposits	15
—	—	—	—	—	—	—	—	—	—	†—	—	—	21,834	156,725	Liabs. of Central Bank: Securities	16ac
11,411	10,966	14,115	19,307	21,019	18,826	15,101	20,906	121,665	104,910	†77,835	88,390	46,072	2,169	1,964	Foreign Liabilities	16c
1,958	—	304	3,389	12,871	14,145	18,678	71,270	26,195	16,124	†82,330	95,005	185,941	274,351	180,545	Central Government Deposits	16d
5,275	7,277	7,838	8,763	5,628	3,484	5,801	8,884	23,420	18,732	†21,189	27,382	15,886	10,292	4,393	Liab. to Nonbank Pub.Fin.Insts	16dg
957	938	1,055	1,263	1,322	1,313	1,309	2,327	3,367	3,346	†30,030	49,767	35,949	30,163	-4,447	Capital Accounts	17a
9,790	9,774	14,118	16,974	21,126	24,273	22,686	12,313	3,120	-10,279	†-44,089	-38,673	-60,890	-61,777	-63,118	Other Items (Net)	17r
Millions of Pesos Beginning 1977: End of Period															**Deposit Money Banks**	
6,739	7,390	5,710	6,637	7,433	7,824	6,293	9,268	114,111	230,487	†54,841	71,425	114,882	72,160	105,728	Reserves	20
—	—	—	—	—	—	—	—	—	—	†—	—	—	845	98,186	Claims on Mon.Author.: Securities	20c
1,733	2,868	2,804	4,161	3,803	2,625	2,359	2,315	7,287	6,409	†21,394	46,235	54,561	61,581	115,780	Foreign Assets	21
22,102	26,899	28,009	36,877	55,500	21,531	2,645	6,325	17,094	8,191	†375,891	371,261	471,210	579,582	543,166	Claims on Central Government	22a
227	299	1,499	2,689	3,900	4,912	9,027	14,912	5,398	4,024	†9,296	13,690	13,731	17,795	17,178	Claims on State and Local Govts	22b
604	831	2,208	961	1,241	1,078	1,525	1,817	1,208	1,310	†1,469	5,406	2,375	4,382	5,069	Claims on Nonfin.Pub.Enterprises	22c
41	53	551	572	1,045	281	123	176	64,872	192,496	†282,234	391,422	557,367	551,546	634,194	Claims on Nonbank Pub.Fin.Insts	22cg
17,798	33,574	70,682	113,321	178,954	288,066	362,508	496,078	464,075	394,723	†560,405	670,501	665,989	625,007	561,969	Claims on Private Sector	22d
1,705	869	659	307	1,637	1,936	6,544	13,835	16,309	10,697	†30,656	24,256	38,494	18,554	42,629	Claims on Other Banking Insts	22f
464	518	1,300	7,097	12,692	17,460	19,348	24,174	25,947	16,845	†66,635	37,896	59,013	94,424	93,684	Claims on Nonbank Financial Insts	22g
4,930	7,130	10,279	21,847	72,772	82,604	98,725	91,106	85,783	128,600	†169,338	190,036	229,129	266,975	317,377	Demand Deposits	24
34,907	16,813	58,336	111,961	131,668	172,687	195,852	260,570	384,294	464,112	†625,371	739,683	797,755	668,059	759,661	Time, Savings,& Fgn.Currency Dep.	25
4,671	35,348	22,637	6,327	4,933	4,253	4,705	7,055	7,176	3,180	†196,859	210,533	272,003	276,012	439,629	Money Market Instruments	26aa
419	1,400	716	774	1,001	832	731	1,525	2,525	4,237	†5,219	4,449	5,746	19,783	10,926	Foreign Liabilities	26c
323	1,018	2,588	3,172	6,034	12,906	16,072	34,530	58,215	38,270	†50,993	49,431	33,656	22,713	17,171	Long-Term Foreign Liabilities	26cl
81	156	210	441	685	956	1,188	2,024	2,190	3,894	†3,593	5,000	6,570	6,052	12,372	Central Government Deposits	26d
3,845	7,252	9,639	10,206	14,049	19,332	24,045	36,626	72,530	115,657	†231,254	331,200	339,176	278,538	304,332	Liab. to Nonbank Pub.Fin.Insts	26dg
73	198	277	241	699	712	4,208	39.697	42,129	12,185	†2,734	1,020	96,699	95,024	62,659	Credit from Monetary Authorities	26g
564	735	2,210	7,945	17,771	27,613	37,735	59,452	53,277	52,219	†64,569	68,174	59,299	112,420	82,498	Liabilities to Other Banking Insts	26i
—	—	—	—	—	—	—	—	—	—	†31	25	21	10,694	11,207	Liab. to Nonbank Financial Insts	26j
1,937	3,783	5,789	8,450	11,334	17,990	23,515	31,575	9,921	8,916	†4,067	8,638	2,646	-2,162	-22,574	Capital Accounts	27a
-337	-532	741	1,258	5,259	5,828	3,596	4,740	-1,739	33,912	†48,793	23,903	134,922	271,768	222,325	Other Items (Net)	27r
Millions of Pesos Beginning 1977: End of Period															**Monetary Survey**	
20,759	6,060	6,717	15,059	38,116	43,907	66,237	14,374	5,911	37,479	†177,812	277,004	312,985	389,156	521,033	Foreign Assets (Net)	31n
54,197	96,415	143,081	202,410	276,557	352,789	394,876	490,215	516,746	426,642	†958,982	1,023,275	1,058,458	1,064,292	1,091,787	Domestic Credit	32
33,236	59,400	66,496	77,340	76,612	36,553	-7,357	-64,969	1,920	-1,339	†289,968	271,256	278,699	299,179	350,249	Claims on Central Govt. (Net)	32an
227	299	1,499	2,689	3,900	4,912	9,027	14,912	5,398	4,024	†9,296	13,690	13,731	17,795	17,178	Claims on State and Local Govts	32b
604	831	2,208	961	1,241	1,078	1,525	1,817	1,208	1,310	†1,469	5,406	2,375	4,382	5,069	Claims on Nonfin.Pub.Enterprises	32c
17,835	33,645	70,777	113,458	179,251	288,445	362,958	496,078	464,075	394,723	†560,405	670,501	665,989	625,007	561,969	Claims on Private Sector	32d
1,831	1,722	801	865	2,861	4,341	9,375	18,203	18,198	11,079	†31,209	24,526	38,651	23,504	63,638	Claims on Other Banking Insts	32f
464	518	1,300	7,097	12,692	17,460	19,348	24,174	25,947	16,845	†66,635	37,896	59,013	94,424	93,684	Claims on Nonbank Financial Inst	32g
12,629	21,191	29,087	47,439	106,227	122,220	143,902	145,429	150,572	206,180	†267,113	308,136	395,476	450,738	527,672	Money	34
36,257	18,006	58,979	112,795	132,051	173,215	196,444	260,580	384,300	464,124	†630,137	743,404	804,977	681,206	764,224	Quasi-Money	35
4,671	35,348	22,637	6,327	4,933	4,253	4,705	7,055	7,176	3,180	†196,859	210,533	272,003	276,012	439,629	Money Market Instruments	36aa
—	—	—	—	—	—	—	—	—	—	†—	—	—	20,989	58,539	Liabs. of Central Bank: Securities	36ac
323	1,018	2,588	3,172	6,034	12,906	16,072	34,530	58,215	38,270	†50,993	49,431	33,656	22,713	17,171	Long-Term Foreign Liabilities	36cl
564	735	2,210	7,945	17,771	27,613	37,735	59,452	53,277	52,219	†64,569	68,174	59,299	112,420	82,498	Liabilities to Other Banking Insts.	36i
—	—	—	—	—	—	—	—	—	—	†31	25	21	10,694	11,207	Liab. to Nonbank Financial Insts.	36j
2,894	4,721	6,844	9,713	12,656	19,303	24,824	33,902	13,288	12,262	†34,097	58,405	38,595	28,001	-27,021	Capital Accounts	37a
17,617	21,456	27,453	30,078	35,001	37,186	37,430	-36,359	-144,171	-312,115	†-107006	-137,829	-232,583	-149,325	-261,099	Other Items (Net)	37r
48,886	39,197	88,066	160,234	238,278	295,435	340,346	406,009	534,872	670,304	†897,250	1,051,540	1,200,452	1,131,944	1,291,895	Money plus Quasi-Money	35l

Mexico

		1972	1973	1974	1975	1976	1977	1978	1979	1980	1981	1982	1983	1984	1985	1986
Other Banking Institutions													*Thousands of Pesos through 1976;*			
Reserves	40	14,950	18,800	34,500	54,280	23,790	†16	9	15	21	40	77	92	111	142	264
Claims on Mon.Author.: Securities	40c	—	—	—	—	—	† —									
Foreign Assets	41						1	1	1	1	1	15	49	74	141	443
Claims on Central Government	42a	24,940	22,160	17,400	28,450	66,490	†83	70	88	108	307	†1,055	1,595	2,248	4,823	13,354
Claims on State and Local Govts.	42b						†4	4	9	14	25	128	133	240	280	155
Claims on Nonfin.Pub.Enterprises	42c						168	186	226	295	424	1,016	1,394	1,922	3,226	7,208
Claims on Nonbank Pub.Fin.Insts.	42cg											77	98	134	317	745
Claims on Private Sector	42d	156,380	181,010	215,620	267,810	379,070	†76	98	123	167	178	†247	447	838	1,577	2,937
Claims on Deposit Money Banks	42e						6	12	15	17	43	41	96	130	183	418
Claims on Nonbank Financial Insts	42g											1	1	1	—	2
Demand Deposits	44						3	5	7	8	16	†21	28	61	78	87
Time, Savings,& Fgn.Currency Dep.	45	91,930	112,960	140,240	185,810	310,790	†38	55	73	121	192	†254	470	793	1,241	2,226
Money Market Instruments	46aa	82,390	85,700	100,390	131,200	136,830	†17	16	15	12	20	†24	36	80	197	482
Foreign Liabilities	46c											5	1	5	5	46
Long-Term Foreign Liabilities	46cl	—	—	—	—	—	†249	256	292	320	557	†2,209	3,322	4,547	9,326	24,945
Central Government Deposits	46d											180	266	384	674	430
Liab. to Nonbank Pub.Fin.Insts	46dg											39	68	46	92	201
Credit from Monetary Authorities	46g	1,560	2,370	3,630	4,020	11,780	†5	9	12	29	35	106	102	154	228	483
Credit from Deposit Money Banks	46h	13,200	18,610	24,910	32,340	37,420	†15	15	22	26	40	181	163	247	367	626
Liab. to Nonbank Financial Insts	46j															
Capital Accounts	47a	17,000	19,730	22,060	19,740	22,000	†13	16	18	19	38	86	127	234	329	541
Other Items (Net)	47r	−9,810	−17,400	−23,710	−22,570	−49,470	†13	9	39	87	119	†−448	−678	−853	−1,848	−4,541
Banking Survey													*Thousands of Pesos through 1976;*			
Foreign Assets (Net)	51n	17,470	18,330	18,790	20,830	22,060	†42	53	84	126	161	†243	809	1,442	1,508	3,621
Domestic Credit	52	255,140	301,650	376,640	479,030	659,380	†887	1,097	1,439	1,956	2,985	†6,303	9,597	14,401	23,204	50,326
Claims on Central Govt. (Net)	52an	64,470	83,650	117,460	158,230	216,850	†375	427	563	741	1,257	†3,388	5,198	6,934	12,980	31,850
Claims on State and Local Govts	52b						†6	8	13	18	30	†152	153	313	353	238
Claims on Nonfin.Pub.Enterprises	52c						183	207	250	332	500	1,244	1,972	2,933	3,623	7,752
Claims on Private Sector	52d	190,670	218,000	259,180	320,800	442,530	†323	454	613	866	1,198	†1,502	2,251	4,167	6,178	10,336
Claims on Nonbank Financial Inst	52g											17	23	54	70	150
Liquid Liabilities	55l	168,130	209,250	244,900	295,630	529,990	†554	750	1,016	1,409	2,109	†3,253	5,351	9,074	12,935	22,306
Money Market Instruments	56aa	82,390	85,700	100,390	131,200	136,830	†17	16	15	12	20	†32	57	229	614	2,700
Liabs. of Central Bank: Securities	56ac	—	—	—	—	—	† —					† —				
Long-Term Foreign Liabilities	56cl	—	—	—	—	—	†290	316	380	487	823	†3,026	4,762	6,381	10,009	26,613
Liab. to Nonbank Financial Insts	56j															
Capital Accounts	57a	17,000	19,730	22,060	19,740	22,000	†33	39	51	65	99	185	267	458	768	1,502
Other Items (Net)	57r	5,090	5,300	28,080	53,290	−7,380	†35	28	62	110	95	†50	−31	−299	385	826
Money (National Definitions)														*Millions of Pesos:*		
Reserve Money	19ma														2,741	5,424
M1	59ma														3,447	5,691
M2	59mb														15,370	31,911
M3	59mc														15,484	32,133
M4	59md														15,730	32,973
M4a	59md a														16,267	34,083
M4 National Currency	59md n														15,050	30,907
M4 Foreign Currency	59md f														680	2,066
Interest Rates														*Percent Per Annum*		
Money Market Rate	60b											45.86	57.51	49.94	62.44	88.01
Treasury Bill Rate	60c							10.53	15.02	22.46	30.77	45.75	59.07	49.32	63.20	
Savings Rate	60k															
Deposit Rate	60l						8.00	11.00	16.17	25.20	25.28	45.83	57.36	48.84	55.23	75.91
Average Cost of Funds	60n				11.92	11.83	12.88	15.13	16.35	20.71	28.62	40.40	56.65	51.08	56.07	80.88
Lending Rate	60p															
Government Bond Yield	61															
Prices, Production, Labor														*Index Numbers (1995=100):*		
Share Prices	62										—	—	.1	.2	.3	1.1
Wholesale Prices	63	.1	.1	.1	.1	.1	.2	†.2	.3	.3	.4	.6	1.3	2.2	3.4	6.5
Consumer Prices	64	.1	.1	.1	.1	.1	.2	.2	.2	.3	.4	.6	1.2	2.0	3.2	5.9
Wages, Monthly	65	.1	.1	.1	.2	.2	.3	.3	.3	.4	.6	.9	1.4	2.1	3.4	6.0
Industrial Production	66	46.3	50.9	54.7	†57.3	58.8	60.8	66.9	†73.8	81.0	88.2	86.5	79.3	82.3	86.6	†82.0
Manufacturing Production	66ey	48.0	52.4	56.0	†58.3	59.9	62.1	67.7	†73.9	79.7	85.6	82.2	76.1	79.9	85.2	†81.1
Mining Production	66zx	48.6	51.7	57.2	†54.1	57.3	57.7	59.0	†61.7	75.5	87.0	96.3	92.4	93.6	94.4	†90.4
Crude Petroleum	66aa	22.8	23.1	26.4	29.4	32.2	36.5	42.0	48.1	59.1	66.9	82.2	80.5	83.7	83.3	†80.1
														Number in Thousands:		
Labor Force	67d															
Employment	67e															
Unemployment	67c															
Unemployment Rate (%)	67r															
International Transactions																
Excluding Maquiladoras														*Millions of US Dollars*		
Exports	70n.d	1,674	2,070	2,850	2,861	3,319	4,416	5,823	8,877	15,243	19,379	20,929	21,423	24,069	21,846	16,037
Imports, f.o.b.	71nv d	2,589	3,632	5,768	6,267	5,730	5,213	7,708	11,510	19,342	25,360	14,412	9,409	12,181	14,528	12,436
Including Maquiladoras														*Millions of US Dollars*		
Exports	70..d	1,694	2,250	2,958	2,904	3,417	4,167	6,005	8,982	†18,031	23,307	24,055	25,953	29,101	26,757	21,804
Imports, f.o.b.	71.v d										21,089	27,184	17,011	11,848	15,916	18,359	16,784

1987	1988	1989	1990	1991	1992	1993	1994	1995	1996	1997	1998	1999	2000	2001		
Millions of Pesos Beginning 1977: End of Period															**Other Banking Institutions**	
632	783	875	628	670	787	1,386	1,611	3,262	10,911	†921	596	336	304	10,426	Reserves	**40**
—	—	—	—	—	—	—	—	—	—	†—	—	—	—	36,925	Claims on Mon.Author.: Securities	**40c**
834	1,057	1,089	989	1,930	3,626	2,985	12,750	23,963	31,468	†18,435	26,965	22,186	28,227	20,471	Foreign Assets	**41**
40,304	45,395	50,898	47,524	49,551	52,568	54,014	99,942	167,942	168,102	†204,551	236,664	247,604	294,286	247,089	Claims on Central Government	**42a**
239	493	531	1,178	2,592	4,816	5,593	8,861	11,176	9,008	†11,015	10,340	11,768	13,051	18,892	Claims on State and Local Govts.	**42b**
13,282	11,251	8,969	7,241	3,540	3,341	3,125	6,266	7,660	6,319	†9,438	7,794	8,451	14,653	15,229	Claims on Nonfin.Pub.Enterprises	**42c**
2,630	3,303	3,174	2,081	1,989	1,394	1,718	3,212	4,374	17,980	†40,208	58,774	60,937	21,946	57,880	Claims on Nonbank Pub.Fin.Insts.	**42cg**
7,190	12,694	14,713	15,635	19,654	27,444	36,011	54,126	73,536	80,034	†78,309	74,001	81,525	90,410	99,985	Claims on Private Sector	**42d**
1,017	2,277	3,630	11,581	19,906	25,334	42,268	69,769	75,053	69,538	†70,018	83,602	95,130	83,135	107,675	Claims on Deposit Money Banks	**42e**
2	31	100	447	1,453	6,538	14,065	20,918	22,008	8,342	†43,542	38,466	22,988	15,645	16,050	Claims on Nonbank Financial Insts	**42g**
167	255	348	437	1,088	1,360	1,824	1,974	1,912	3,132	†3,317	3,183	3,539	5,465	6,842	Demand Deposits	**44**
5,732	9,014	4,455	8,274	11,132	12,485	18,975	26,757	43,972	66,898	†84,704	97,103	133,407	126,985	140,558	Time, Savings,& Fgn.Currency Dep.	**45**
166	319	4,409	2,855	3,307	10,806	19,766	23,961	44,032	49,537	†42,789	43,288	47,904	36,384	45,788	Money Market Instruments	**46aa**
18	112	1	—	1	—	6	7	49	95	†1,727	1,475	1,464	1,222	1,033	Foreign Liabilities	**46c**
65,466	64,245	70,991	61,636	70,593	80,351	96,805	197,173	278,197	255,959	†228,454	279,546	254,992	255,807	229,261	Long-Term Foreign Liabilities	**46cl**
1,932	7,521	4,127	3,330	1,434	1,445	1,712	2,299	4,045	3,311	†9,576	12,550	2,883	3	92	Central Government Deposits	**46d**
560	1,274	1,417	874	1,602	2,780	3,277	2,882	3,510	4,018	†7,158	5,007	5,633	7,598	24,522	Liab. to Nonbank Pub.Fin.Insts	**46dg**
1,429	816	355	119	247	1,537	1,665	6,526	6,055	4,584	†4,264	5,290	5,024	6,874	22,542	Credit from Monetary Authorities	**46g**
1,046	1,557	2,377	903	949	814	894	1,510	986	2,459	†23,977	31,354	30,448	54,721	87,492	Credit from Deposit Money Banks	**46h**
—	—	—	—	—	—	—	—	—	—	†—	—	—	—	—	Liab. to Nonbank Financial Insts	**46j**
932	3,664	7,930	8,259	8,000	11,426	11,404	12,439	11,990	12,054	†23,570	24,493	29,107	25,570	12,599	Capital Accounts	**47a**
−11,318	−11,493	−12,431	617	2,932	2,844	4,837	1,927	−5,774	−345	†46,901	33,913	36,524	41,028	59,893	Other Items (Net)	**47r**
Millions of Pesos Beginning 1977: End of Period															**Banking Survey**	
21,575	7,005	7,805	16,048	40,045	47,533	69,216	27,117	29,825	68,852	†194,520	302,494	333,707	416,161	540,471	Foreign Assets (Net)	**51n**
111,451	157,036	213,364	270,240	349,052	441,710	496,597	659,826	776,825	684,057	†1265052	1,353,464	1,389,260	1,468,829	1,425,302	Domestic Credit	**52**
71,608	97,274	113,267	121,534	124,729	87,676	44,945	32,674	165,817	163,452	†484,943	495,370	523,420	593,462	597,246	Claims on Central Govt. (Net)	**52an**
466	792	2,030	3,867	6,492	9,728	14,620	23,773	16,574	13,032	20,311	24,030	25,499	30,846	36,070	Claims on State and Local Govts	**52b**
13,886	12,082	11,177	8,202	4,781	4,419	4,650	8,083	8,868	7,629	10,907	13,200	10,826	19,035	20,298	Claims on Nonfin.Pub.Enterprises	**52c**
25,025	46,339	85,490	129,093	198,905	315,889	398,969	550,204	537,611	474,757	†638,714	744,502	747,514	715,417	661,954	Claims on Private Sector	**52d**
466	549	1,400	7,544	14,145	23,998	33,413	45,092	47,955	25,187	†110,177	76,362	82,001	110,069	109,734	Claims on Nonbank Financial Inst	**52g**
54,153	47,683	91,994	168,317	249,828	308,493	359,759	433,129	577,494	729,423	†984,350	1,151,230	1,337,062	1,264,090	1,428,869	Liquid Liabilities	**55l**
4,837	35,667	27,046	9,182	8,240	15,059	24,471	31,016	51,208	52,717	†239,648	253,821	319,907	312,396	485,417	Money Market Instruments	**56aa**
—	—	—	—	—	—	—	—	—	—	†—	—	—	20,989	21,614	Liabs. of Central Bank: Securities	**56ac**
65,789	65,263	73,579	64,808	76,627	93,257	112,877	231,703	336,412	294,229	†279,447	328,977	288,648	278,520	246,432	Long-Term Foreign Liabilities	**56cl**
—	—	—	—	—	—	—	—	—	—	†31	25	21	10,694	11,207	Liab. to Nonbank Financial Insts	**56j**
3,826	8,385	14,774	17,972	20,656	30,729	36,228	46,341	25,278	24,316	†57,667	82,898	67,702	53,571	−14,422	Capital Accounts	**57a**
4,420	7,043	13,776	26,009	33,746	41,705	32,477	−55,246	−183,742	−347,777	†−101572	−160,993	−290,373	−55,270	−213,345	Other Items (Net)	**57r**
End of Period															**Money (National Definitions)**	
11,031	17,514	22,225	30,121	38,581	43,972	47,193	56,935	66,809	83,991	108,891	131,528	188,718	208,943	225,580	*Reserve Money*	**19ma**
12,759	21,433	30,835	50,958	113,634	131,732	157,044	163,828	171,638	245,260	325,391	387,897	489,136	564,233	676,646	*M1*	**59ma**
79,841	121,603	190,782	271,244	339,051	380,487	469,768	554,930	754,407	995,167	1,295,084	1,656,617	2,016,394	2,337,375	2,736,549	*M2*	**59mb**
80,276	122,459	191,640	277,790	357,973	426,852	540,875	657,103	784,495	1,025,836	1,325,560	1,683,152	2,033,275	2,365,752	2,763,792	*M3*	**59mc**
84,050	127,750	200,085	293,688	386,715	458,384	580,375	724,242	869,279	1,116,205	1,405,392	1,769,041	2,106,970	2,422,133	2,812,620	*M4*	**59md**
88,100	131,519	204,894	301,314	395,152	468,036	590,428	737,647	898,185	1,183,382	1,526,928	1,897,194	2,264,337	2,540,575	2,949,160	*M4a*	**59md *a***
76,804	110,933	179,967	263,719	345,762	417,073	527,247	530,328	754,710	985,568	1,283,497	1,627,038	1,962,766	2,285,328	2,657,640	*M4 National Currency*	**59md *n***
7,246	16,816	20,119	29,968	40,952	41,311	53,128	193,914	114,568	130,637	121,895	142,004	144,204	136,805	154,980	*M4 Foreign Currency*	**59md *f***
Percent Per Annum															**Interest Rates**	
95.59	69.01	†47.43	37.36	23.58	18.87	17.39	16.47	†53.17	33.61	21.91	26.89	24.10	16.96	12.89	Money Market Rate	**60b**
103.07	†69.15	44.99	34.76	19.28	15.62	14.99	14.10	48.44	31.39	19.80	24.76	21.41	15.24	11.31	Treasury Bill Rate	**60c**
....	....	....	....	....	....	8.41	5.38	6.67	6.58	7.57	6.38	5.85	4.86	3.26	Savings Rate	**60k**
92.44	52.70	30.85	27.88	16.57	14.48	15.06	13.32	38.12	24.70	14.66	13.75	9.61	6.27	4.74	Deposit Rate	**60l**
94.64	67.64	44.61	37.07	22.56	18.78	18.56	15.50	45.12	30.71	19.12	21.09	19.73	13.69	10.12	Average Cost of Funds	**60n**
....	....	....	....	....	....	22.04	20.38	58.59	36.89	24.55	28.70	25.87	18.23	13.87	Lending Rate	**60p**
....	....	....	....	....	....	....	....	51.74	32.81	21.44	....	....	....	....	Government Bond Yield	**61**
Period Averages															**Prices, Production, Labor**	
7.3	8.5	14.8	25.7	48.8	74.8	83.6	113.6	100.0	142.5	200.2	191.1	240.3	293.6	275.7	Share Prices	**62**
15.2	31.6	36.7	45.2	54.5	61.8	67.3	71.9	100.0	136.3	161.6	184.0	211.0	228.6	....	Wholesale Prices	**63**
13.7	29.3	35.2	44.5	54.6	†63.1	69.3	74.1	100.0	134.4	162.1	187.9	219.1	239.9	255.1	Consumer Prices	**64**
14.1	†29.8	39.9	52.1	67.2	78.9	85.7	90.9	100.0	....	156.6	....	....	....	....	Wages, Monthly	**65**
85.3	87.3	91.8	96.9	100.8	104.0	†103.5	108.5	100.0	110.1	120.3	127.9	133.3	141.5	136.5	Industrial Production	**66**
84.3	86.3	91.9	96.6	100.3	103.0	†101.0	105.0	100.0	111.0	121.7	130.7	136.1	145.5	139.8	Manufacturing Production	**66ey**
93.9	94.3	93.9	97.7	98.2	99.2	†100.2	102.7	100.0	108.3	112.9	116.0	113.6	118.0	117.3	Mining Production	**66zx**
85.2	82.7	87.5	94.4	100.7	†101.0	101.1	101.5	100.0	109.6	115.5	118.3	113.0	116.4	119.1	Crude Petroleum	**66aa**
Period Averages																
....	....	....	....	....	....	....	....	34,309	35,444	37,217	39,507	39,751	39,634	....	Labor Force	**67d**
....	28,128	....	....	30,534	....	32,833	....	33,881	35,226	37,391	38,618	39,069	38,984	....	Employment	**67e**
....	724	....	....	695	....	819	....	1,677	1,355	985	890	682	650	....	Unemployment	**67c**
....	2.5	....	....	2.2	....	2.4	....	4.7	3.7	2.6	2.3	1.7	1.6	....	Unemployment Rate (%)	**67r**
Millions of US Dollars															**International Transactions**	
															Excluding Maquiladoras	
20,527	20,449	22,701	26,830	27,098	27,529	30,003	34,318	46,864	59,084	65,266	64,376	72,954	....	....	Exports	**70n. *d***
13,207	20,068	25,362	31,221	38,146	48,180	49,054	58,362	44,893	58,961	73,475	82,816	91,655	....	....	Imports, f.o.b.	**71nv *d***
Millions of US Dollars																
															Including Maquiladoras	
27,600	30,691	35,171	40,711	42,688	46,196	51,886	60,882	79,542	96,000	110,431	117,460	136,391	166,368	158,547	Exports	**70.. *d***
18,812	28,082	34,766	41,594	49,967	62,129	65,367	79,346	72,453	89,469	109,808	125,373	141,975	174,501	168,276	Imports, f.o.b.	**71.v *d***

Mexico

273

		1972	1973	1974	1975	1976	1977	1978	1979	1980	1981	1982	1983	1984	1985	1986
Balance of Payments																*Millions of US Dollars:*
Current Account, n.i.e.	78al d	....	....	....	....	....	....	....	−5,409	−10,422	−16,240	−5,889	5,866	4,183	800	−1,377
Goods: Exports f.o.b.	78aa d	....	....	....	....	....	....	....	11,512	18,031	23,307	24,056	25,953	29,101	26,758	21,803
Goods: Imports f.o.b.	78ab d	....	....	....	....	....	....	....	−13,654	−21,087	−27,184	−17,009	−11,848	−15,915	−18,359	−16,784
Trade Balance	78ac d	....	....	....	....	....	....	....	−2,142	−3,056	−3,877	7,047	14,105	13,186	8,399	5,019
Services: Credit	78ad d	....	....	....	....	....	....	....	5,192	4,591	4,983	4,136	4,087	4,839	4,808	4,591
Services: Debit	78ae d	....	....	....	....	....	....	....	−4,901	−6,514	−8,489	−6,066	−4,477	−5,235	−5,524	−5,194
Balance on Goods & Services	78af d	....	....	....	....	....	....	....	−1,851	−4,979	−7,383	5,117	13,715	12,790	7,683	4,416
Income: Credit	78ag d	....	....	....	....	....	....	....	872	1,365	1,746	1,709	1,686	2,507	2,281	1,943
Income: Debit	78ah d	....	....	....	....	....	....	....	−4,655	−7,642	−11,621	−13,758	−10,710	−12,474	−11,148	−9,310
Balance on Gds, Serv. & Inc.	78ai d	....	....	....	....	....	....	....	−5,634	−11,256	−17,258	−6,932	4,691	2,823	−1,184	−2,951
Current Transfers, n.i.e.: Credit	78aj d	....	....	....	....	....	....	....	257	877	1,076	1,072	1,206	1,384	2,012	1,589
Current Transfers: Debit	78ak d	....	....	....	....	....	....	....	−32	−43	−58	−29	−31	−24	−28	−15
Capital Account, n.i.e.	78bc d	....	....	....	....	....	....	....	—	—	—	—	—	—	—	—
Capital Account, n.i.e.: Credit	78ba d	....	....	....	....	....	....	....	—	—	—	—	—	—	—	—
Capital Account: Debit	78bb d	....	....	....	....	....	....	....	—	—	—	—	—	—	—	—
Financial Account, n.i.e.	78bj d	....	....	....	....	....	....	....	5,120	11,508	26,601	2,923	−3,275	81	−612	1,634
Direct Investment Abroad	78bd d	....	....	....	....	....	....	....								
Dir. Invest. in Rep. Econ., n.i.e.	78be d	....	....	....	....	....	....	....	1,332	2,090	3,078	1,901	2,192	1,542	1,984	2,036
Portfolio Investment Assets	78bf d	....	....	....	....	....	....	....	−51	−17	165	275	−134	−320	−389	−709
Equity Securities	78bk d	....	....	....	....	....	....	....								
Debt Securities	78bl d	....	....	....	....	....	....	....	−51	−17	165	275	−134	−320	−389	−709
Portfolio Investment Liab., n.i.e.	78bg d	....	....	....	....	....	....	....	−342	60	996	645	−519	−435	−595	−517
Equity Securities	78bm d	....	....	....	....	....	....	....								
Debt Securities	78bn d	....	....	....	....	....	....	....	−342	60	996	645	−519	−435	−595	−517
Financial Derivatives Assets	78bw d	....	....	....	....	....	....	....	....	....	....	....	....	....	....	....
Financial Derivatives Liabilities	78bx d	....	....	....	....	....	....	....	....	....	....	....	....	....	....	....
Other Investment Assets	78bh d	....	....	....	....	....	....	....	−1,751	−1,229	−4,425	−1,101	−3,551	−1,580	−989	874
Monetary Authorities	78bo d	....	....	....	....	....	....	....	....	....	....	....	....	....	....	....
General Government	78bp d	....	....	....	....	....	....	....	—	—	—	—	—	—	—	—
Banks	78bq d	....	....	....	....	....	....	....	—	−179	−1,204	1,228	−1,091	95	−57	−363
Other Sectors	78br d	....	....	....	....	....	....	....	−1,751	−1,050	−3,221	−2,329	−2,460	−1,675	−932	1,237
Other Investment Liab., n.i.e.	78bi d	....	....	....	....	....	....	....	5,932	10,604	26,787	1,203	−1,263	874	−623	−50
Monetary Authorities	78bs d	....	....	....	....	....	....	....				1,217	−1,217			
General Government	78bt d	....	....	....	....	....	....	....	−180	768	1,881	2,319	12,251	8,800	11,586	8,568
Banks	78bu d	....	....	....	....	....	....	....	2,324	3,778	13,141	−813	1,769	658	123	846
Other Sectors	78bv d	....	....	....	....	....	....	....	3,788	6,058	11,765	−1,520	−14,066	−8,584	−12,332	−9,464
Net Errors and Omissions	78ca d	....	....	....	....	....	....	....	604	−269	−9,087	−7,454	−3,116	−2,115	−2,917	−738
Overall Balance	78cb d	....	....	....	....	....	....	....	315	817	1,274	−10,420	−525	2,149	−2,729	−481
Reserves and Related Items	79da d	....	....	....	....	....	....	....	−315	−817	−1,274	10,420	525	−2,149	2,729	481
Reserve Assets	79db d	....	....	....	....	....	....	....	−155	−684	−1,274	3,354	−3,102	−3,390	2,434	−595
Use of Fund Credit and Loans	79dc d	....	....	....	....	....	....	....	−160	−133	—	219	1,069	1,241	295	712
Exceptional Financing	79de d	....	....	....	....	....	....	....	—	—	—	6,846	2,558	—	—	364
Government Finance																*Thousands of Pesos through 1976;*
Deficit (-) or Surplus	80	....	....	....	....	....	....	....	....	−136	−401	−1,168	−1,453	−2,112	−3,559	−10,333
Total Revenue and Grants	81y	....	....	....	....	....	....	....	....	674	911	1,523	3,014	4,608	7,559	11,990
Revenue	81	....	....	....	....	....	....	....	....	674	911	1,523	3,014	4,608	7,559	11,990
Grants	81z	....	....	....	....	....	....	....	....	—	—	—	—	—	—	—
Exp.& Lending Minus Repayments	82z	....	....	....	....	....	....	....	....	810	1,312	2,691	4,467	6,720	11,118	22,323
Expenditure	82	....	....	....	....	....	....	....	....	798	1,302	2,679	4,437	6,686	11,086	22,178
Lending Minus Repayments	83	....	....	....	....	....	....	....	....	12	10	12	30	34	32	145
Total Financing	80h	....	....	....	....	....	....	....	....	136	401	1,168	1,453	2,112	3,559	10,333
Domestic	84a	....	....	....	....	....	....	....	....	153	610	1,254	828	1,624	3,463	11,077
Foreign	85a	....	....	....	....	....	....	....	....	−17	−209	−86	625	488	96	−744
Total Debt by Residence	88	88,510	116,690	156,940	217,680	372,650	....	....	....	....	....	....	3,861	6,303	10,289	19,630	51,480
Domestic	88a	74,580	99,000	127,300	177,260	282,380	....	....	....	....	....	....	2,768	3,719	5,335	9,773	23,756
Foreign	89a	13,930	17,690	29,640	40,420	90,270	....	....	....	....	....	....	1,093	2,584	4,954	9,857	27,724
National Accounts																*Thousands of Pesos through 1976;*
Househ.Cons.Expend.,incl.NPISHs	96f. c	405,600	487,000	628,300	755,900	933,400	†1,226	1,544	1,976	2,909	3,945	6,036	10,882	18,590	30,575	54,209
Government Consumption Expend.	91f. c	48,700	63,400	82,300	113,500	150,900	†199	255	334	449	660	1,026	1,574	2,722	4,374	7,208
Gross Fixed Capital Formation	93e. c	107,100	133,300	178,900	235,600	288,400	†363	492	719	1,214	1,617	2,249	3,137	5,287	9,048	15,415
Changes in Inventories	93i. c	7,600	14,400	29,700	25,000	17,200	†59	59	78	107	70	−33	577	496	762	−1,139
Exports of Goods and Services	90c. c	45,500	58,100	75,700	75,800	116,400	†191	245	343	479	638	1,502	3,397	5,122	7,305	13,732
Imports of Goods and Services (-)	98c. c	49,800	65,400	95,200	105,800	135,300	†189	258	382	580	793	1,011	1,684	2,815	4,897	10,639
Gross Domestic Product (GDP)	99b. c	564,700	690,900	899,700	1,100,100	1,371,000	†1,849	2,337	3,068	4,470	6,137	9,770	17,882	29,402	47,168	78,787
Net Primary Income from Abroad	98.n c	−7,400	−10,000	−15,000	−17,900	−29,000	†−43	−53	−77	−129	−217	−558	−1,055	−1,618	−2,122	−4,255
Gross National Income (GNI)	99a. c	557,300	680,900	884,700	1,082,100	1,342,000	†1,806	2,285	2,990	4,341	5,911	9,240	16,824	27,854	45,270	74,936
GDP Volume 1970 Prices(Millions)	99b. r	502	544	578	610	636	658	712	777	842	....	....	....	....	....	....
GDP Volume 1993 Prices(Billions)	99b. r	....	....	....	....	....	....	....	....	948	1,029	1,023	988	1,021	1,044	1,011
GDP Volume (1995=100)	99bv r	45.9	49.8	52.8	55.8	58.2	60.2	65.1	71.1	†77.0	83.6	83.1	80.2	83.0	84.8	82.2
GDP Deflator (1995=100)	99bi r	.1	.1	.1	.1	.1	.2	.2	.2	.3	.4	.6	1.2	1.9	3.0	5.2
																Millions:
Population	99z	54.27	56.16	58.12	60.15	61.98	63.81	65.66	67.52	69.66	71.35	73.02	74.67	76.31	77.94	79.57

Minus Sign Indicates Debit

	1987	1988	1989	1990	1991	1992	1993	1994	1995	1996	1997	1998	1999	2000	2001	Balance of Payments	
	4,247	−2,374	−5,825	−7,451	−14,888	−24,442	−23,400	−29,662	−1,576	−2,529	−7,696	−16,097	−14,017	−17,764	−17,708	Current Account, n.i.e.	78al d
	27,599	30,692	35,171	40,711	42,687	46,196	51,885	60,882	79,542	96,002	110,431	117,459	136,392	166,456	158,443	Goods: Exports f.o.b.	78aa d
	−18,813	−28,081	−34,766	−41,592	−49,966	−62,130	−65,366	−79,346	−72,453	−89,469	−109,808	−125,374	−141,975	−174,457	−168,398	Goods: Imports f.o.b.	78ab d
	8,786	2,611	405	−881	−7,279	−15,934	−13,481	−18,464	7,089	6,533	623	−7,915	−5,583	−8,001	−9,955	*Trade Balance*	78ac d
	5,437	6,084	7,208	8,094	8,869	9,275	9,517	10,321	9,780	10,723	11,182	11,662	11,737	13,752	12,699	Services: Credit	78ad d
	−5,310	−6,281	−7,880	−10,323	−10,959	−11,959	−12,046	−13,043	−9,715	−10,817	−12,615	−13,012	−14,473	−17,363	−17,194	Services: Debit	78ae d
	8,913	2,414	−267	−3,110	−9,369	−18,618	−16,010	−21,185	7,153	6,439	−810	−9,265	−8,319	−11,612	−14,450	*Balance on Goods & Services*	78af d
	2,397	3,049	3,160	3,273	3,523	2,789	2,694	3,347	3,713	4,033	4,431	4,911	4,476	6,049	5,098	Income: Credit	78ag d
	−8,982	−10,092	−11,261	−11,589	−11,788	−11,998	−13,724	−15,605	−16,402	−17,506	−16,537	−17,731	−16,462	−19,173	−17,672	Income: Debit	78ah d
	2,328	−4,629	−8,368	−11,426	−17,634	−27,827	−27,040	−33,444	−5,536	−7,034	−12,916	−22,085	−20,305	−24,736	−27,024	*Balance on Gds, Serv. & Inc.*	78ai d
	1,937	2,270	2,559	3,990	2,765	3,404	3,656	3,822	3,995	4,535	5,245	6,016	6,315	7,001	9,338	Current Transfers, n.i.e.: Credit	78aj d
	−18	−15	−16	−15	−19	−19	−16	−40	−35	−30	−25	−28	−27	−29	−22	Current Transfers: Debit	78ak d
	—	—	—	—	—	—	—	....	....	....	....	....	....	....	....	Capital Account, n.i.e.	78bc d
																Capital Account, n.i.e.: Credit	78ba d
																Capital Account: Debit	78bb d
	−3,067	−4,495	1,110	8,441	25,139	27,039	33,760	15,787	−10,487	4,248	25,745	12,194	14,445	25,547	22,267	Financial Account, n.i.e.	78bj d
	....	....	....	....	....	....	....	....	....	....	....	....	....	....	−3,708	Direct Investment Abroad	78bd d
	1,184	2,011	2,785	2,549	4,742	4,393	4,389	10,973	9,526	9,186	12,831	11,897	12,478	14,192	24,731	Dir. Invest. in Rep. Econ., n.i.e.	78be d
	−397	−880	−56	−7,354	−603	1,165	−564	−767	−662	544	−708	−768	−836	1,290	3,857	Portfolio Investment Assets	78bf d
										—						Equity Securities	78bk d
	−397	−880	−56	−7,354	−603	1,165	−564	−767	−662	544	−708	−768	−836	1,290	3,857	Debt Securities	78bl d
	−1,002	1,001	354	3,369	12,741	18,041	28,919	8,182	−9,715	3,537	6,002	−206	6,285	4,269	986	Portfolio Investment Liab., n.i.e.	78bg d
	....	....	494	1,995	6,331	4,783	10,716	4,084	519	2,801	3,215	−665	3,769	447	150	Equity Securities	78bm d
	−1,002	1,001	−140	1,374	6,410	13,258	18,203	4,099	−10,234	736	2,787	459	2,516	3,822	836	Debt Securities	78bn d
	....	....	....	....	....	....	....	....	....	....	....	....	....	....	....	Financial Derivatives Assets	78bw d
	....	....	....	....	....	....	....	....	....	....	....	....	....	....	....	Financial Derivatives Liabilities	78bx d
	−4,401	−874	−1,114	−1,345	−395	4,387	−3,038	−4,903	−6,694	−6,886	7,425	1,201	−3,170	5,808	−3,588	Other Investment Assets	78bh d
	....	....	....	....	....	....	....	....	....	....	....	....	....	....	....	Monetary Authorities	78bo d
								−1,400	−3,619	−22	57	26	—	—	....	General Government	78bp d
	−1,073	−338	−719	−749	−1,097	22	−1,683	−885	−1,510	−1,018	5,112	−1,209	−1,895	44	−4,666	Banks	78bq d
	−3,328	−536	−395	−596	702	4,365	−1,355	−2,618	−1,565	−5,846	2,256	2,384	−1,275	5,764	1,078	Other Sectors	78br d
	1,549	−5,753	−859	11,222	8,654	−947	4,054	2,302	−2,942	−2,133	195	70	−312	−12	−11	Other Investment Liab., n.i.e.	78bi d
									−788	−1,459	—	—	—	—	—	Monetary Authorities	78bs d
	3,881	−4,112	−104	1,657	−1,454	−5,867	−1,136	−986	210	−659	206	75	−300	—	—	General Government	78bt d
	814	320	680	9,061	7,845	1,626	3,622	2,799	−5,297	—	—	—	—	—	—	Banks	78bu d
	−3,146	−1,961	−1,435	504	2,263	3,294	1,568	488	2,933	−15	−11	−5	−12	−12	−11	Other Sectors	78bv d
	2,954	−3,193	4,504	1,228	−2,278	−852	−3,128	−3,323	−4,248	229	2,411	402	735	3,673	2,317	Net Errors and Omissions	78ca d
	4,134	−10,062	−211	2,218	7,973	1,745	7,232	−17,199	−16,312	1,948	20,460	−3,501	1,163	11,456	6,876	*Overall Balance*	78cb d
	−4,134	10,062	211	−2,218	−7,973	−1,745	−7,232	17,199	16,312	−1,948	−20,460	3,501	−1,163	−11,456	−6,876	Reserves and Related Items	79da d
	−5,986	6,721	−542	−3,261	−8,154	−1,173	−6,057	18,398	−9,648	−1,805	−10,513	−2,118	−598	−2,862	−7,339	Reserve Assets	79db d
	401	−84	364	958	161	−572	−1,175	−1,199	11,950	−2,057	−3,485	−1,075	−3,681	−4,288		Use of Fund Credit and Loans	79dc d
	1,450	3,424	389	85	20	—	—	—	14,010	1,913	−6,463	6,694	3,115	−4,306	463	Exceptional Financing	79de d

Government Finance

Millions of Pesos Beginning 1977: Year Ending December 31

	1987	1988	1989	1990	1991	1992	1993	1994	1995	1996	1997	1998	1999	2000	2001		
	−27,422	−37,007	−25,082	−18,672	27,694	46,921	6,451	−386	−9,784	−5,546	−34,161	−55,591	−71,289	−69,256	−41,818	Deficit (-) or Surplus	80
	31,476	62,170	86,939	113,317	140,636	174,278	186,644	211,434	278,626	379,573	459,047	488,959	620,135	791,040	859,834	Total Revenue and Grants	81y
	31,476	62,170	86,939	113,317	140,636	174,278	186,644	211,434	278,626	379,573	459,047	488,959	620,135	791,040	859,834	Revenue	81
																Grants	81z
	58,898	99,177	112,021	131,989	112,942	127,357	180,193	211,820	288,410	385,119	493,208	544,550	691,424	860,296	901,652	Exp.& Lending Minus Repayments	82z
	58,705	99,122	111,503	131,306	144,023	158,189	183,876	217,249	285,147	382,499	505,902	556,079	689,921	848,502	896,907	Expenditure	82
	193	55	518	683	−31,081	−30,832	−3,683	−5,429	3,263	2,620	−12,694	−11,529	1,503	11,794	4,745	Lending Minus Repayments	83
	27,422	37,007	25,082	18,672	−27,694	−46,921	−6,451	386	9,784	5,546	34,161	55,591	71,289	69,256	41,818	Total Financing	80h
	23,580	32,485	24,436	16,644	−28,934	−42,888	−1,397	4,934	−90,101	24,233	56,387	35,073	64,994	117,589	46,363	Domestic	84a
	3,842	4,522	646	2,028	1,240	−4,033	−5,054	−4,548	99,885	−18,687	−22,226	20,518	6,295	−48,333	−4,545	Foreign	85a
	133,537	197,839	257,004	342,742	361,157	316,514	317,977	417,115	751,601	787,822	821,777	1,073,220	1,175,528	1,276,451	1,306,415	Total Debt by Residence	88
	61,556	108,947	137,601	165,418	159,107	133,478	134,769	178,960	155,360	192,162	273,656	378,256	506,389	675,107	763,559	Domestic	88a
	71,981	88,892	119,403	177,324	202,050	183,036	183,208	238,155	596,241	595,660	548,121	694,964	669,139	601,344	542,856	Foreign	89a

National Accounts

Millions of Pesos Beginning 1977

	1987	1988	1989	1990	1991	1992	1993	1994	1995	1996	1997	1998	1999	2000	2001		
	127,268	281,569	377,907	514,117	669,159	808,120	†903,174	1,016,129	1,232,003	1,644,908	2,040,368	2,593,350	3,084,138	3,696,140	4,044,828	Housel.Cons.Expend.,incl.NPISHs	96f. c
	16,995	35,028	45,383	61,949	86,163	111,753	†138,565	164,161	191,981	243,706	314,622	399,956	506,459	607,479	667,011	Government Consumption Expend.	91f. c
	35,667	77,110	94,670	132,113	177,044	220,545	†233,179	274,861	296,708	451,081	619,494	804,002	973,802	1,166,096	1,132,080	Gross Fixed Capital Formation	93e. c
	1,416	16,812	31,254	38,879	44,379	41,563	†30,597	33,538	67,391	132,477	201,463	133,281	109,271	128,230	64,024	Changes in Inventories	93i. c
	37,692	82,962	104,266	137,441	155,327	171,476	†191,540	238,966	558,798	812,854	963,937	1,180,389	1,414,339	1,703,800	1,593,689	Exports of Goods and Services	90c. c
	25,877	77,174	104,622	145,603	182,924	228,123	†240,859	307,494	509,862	759,451	965,609	1,262,760	1,488,560	1,810,725	1,729,775	Imports of Goods and Services (-)	98c. c
	193,162	393,715	512,600	694,872	876,933	1,034,733	†1256196	1,423,364	1,840,431	2,529,909	3,178,954	3,848,219	4,599,449	5,491,018	5,771,858	Gross Domestic Product (GDP)	99b. c
	−8,849	−16,174	−20,190	−23,927	−25,683	−29,457	−35,859	−42,266	−84,091	−104,382	−98,787	−120,966	−122,851	−123,730	....	Net Primary Income from Abroad	98.n c
	184,462	400,131	528,668	714,971	923,465	1,095,877	1,220,337	1,377,893	1,752,929	2,421,193	3,075,488	3,725,384	4,470,835	5,361,642	....	Gross National Income (GNI)	99a. c
																GDP Volume 1970 Prices(Millions)	99b. r
	1,029	1,042	1,086	1,141	1,189	1,232	1,256	1,312	1,231	1,294	1,382	1,449	1,503	1,603	1,599	GDP Volume 1993 Prices(Billions)	99b. r
	83.6	84.7	88.2	92.7	96.6	100.1	102.1	106.6	100.0	105.2	112.3	117.8	122.2	130.3	129.9	GDP Volume (1995=100)	99bv. r
	12.6	25.3	31.6	40.7	49.3	56.2	†66.9	72.6	100.0	130.7	153.8	177.6	204.6	229.0	241.4	GDP Deflator (1995=100)	99bi. r

Midyear Estimates

	1987	1988	1989	1990	1991	1992	1993	1994	1995	1996	1997	1998	1999	2000	2001		
	81.20	82.72	81.66	83.23	84.80	87.11	88.74	90.39	91.99	93.57	95.13	96.65	98.13	100.25	101.75	Population	99z

(See notes in the back of the book.)

Micronesia, Fed.Sts.

		1972	1973	1974	1975	1976	1977	1978	1979	1980	1981	1982	1983	1984	1985	1986
Exchange Rates														*US Dollars per SDR:*		
Market Rate	aa	1.0857	1.2064	1.2244	1.1707	1.1618	1.2147	1.3028	1.3173	1.2754	1.1640	1.1031	1.0470	.9802	1.0984	1.2232
Market Rate	ae	1.0000	1.0000	1.0000	1.0000	1.0000	1.0000	1.0000	1.0000	1.0000	1.0000	1.0000	1.0000	1.0000	1.0000	1.0000
Fund Position														*Millions of SDRs:*		
Quota	2f. *s*	...	...	...	...	...	...	...	...	...	...	...	...	...	...	...
SDRs	1b. *s*	...	...	...	...	...	...	...	...	...	...	...	...	...	...	...
Reserve Position in the Fund	1c. *s*	...	...	...	...	...	...	...	...	...	...	...	...	...	...	...
Total Fund Cred.&Loans Outstg.	2tl	...	...	...	...	...	...	...	...	...	...	...	...	...	...	...
International Liquidity													*Millions of US Dollars Unless Otherwise Indicated:*			
Total Reserves minus Gold	1l. *d*	...	...	...	...	...	...	...	...	...	...	...	...	...	...	...
SDRs	1b. *d*	...	...	...	...	...	...	...	...	...	...	...	...	...	...	...
Reserve Position in the Fund	1c. *d*	...	...	...	...	...	...	...	...	...	...	...	...	...	...	...
Foreign Exchange	1d. *d*	...	...	...	...	...	...	...	...	...	...	...	...	...	...	...
Gold (Million Fine Troy Ounces)	1ad	...	...	...	...	...	...	...	...	...	...	...	...	...	...	...
Gold (National Valuation)	1an *d*	...	...	...	...	...	...	...	...	...	...	...	...	...	...	...
Monetary Authorities: Other Assets	3.. *d*	...	...	...	...	...	...	...	...	...	...	...	...	...	...	...
Banking Institutions: Assets	7a. *d*	...	...	...	...	...	...	...	...	...	...	...	...	...	...	...
Liabilities	7b. *d*	...	...	...	...	...	...	...	...	...	...	...	...	...	...	...
Monetary Authorities														*Millions of US Dollars:*		
Foreign Assets	11	...	...	...	...	...	...	...	...	...	...	...	...	...	...	...
Central Government Deposits	16d	...	...	...	...	...	...	...	...	...	...	...	...	...	...	...
Other Items (Net)	17r	...	...	...	...	...	...	...	...	...	...	...	...	...	...	...
Banking Institutions														*Millions of Us dollars:*		
Foreign Assets	21	...	...	...	...	...	...	...	...	...	...	...	...	...	...	...
Claims on Central Government	22a	...	...	...	...	...	...	...	...	...	...	...	...	...	...	...
Claims on State & Local Govts.	22b	...	...	...	...	...	...	...	...	...	...	...	...	...	...	...
Claims on Nonfin.Pub.Enterprises	22c	...	...	...	...	...	...	...	...	...	...	...	...	...	...	...
Claims on Private Sector	22d	...	...	...	...	...	...	...	...	...	...	...	...	...	...	...
Demand Deposits	24	...	...	...	...	...	...	...	...	...	...	...	...	...	...	...
Time, Savings,& Fgn. Currency Dep.	25	...	...	...	...	...	...	...	...	...	...	...	...	...	...	...
Foreign Liabilities	26c	...	...	...	...	...	...	...	...	...	...	...	...	...	...	...
Central Government Deposits	26d	...	...	...	...	...	...	...	...	...	...	...	...	...	...	...
Liab. to Nonbank Financial Insts.	26j	...	...	...	...	...	...	...	...	...	...	...	...	...	...	...
Capital Accounts	27a	...	...	...	...	...	...	...	...	...	...	...	...	...	...	...
Other Items (Net)	27r	...	...	...	...	...	...	...	...	...	...	...	...	...	...	...
Banking Survey														*Millions of US Dollars:*		
Foreign Assets (Net)	31n	...	...	...	...	...	...	...	...	...	...	...	...	...	...	...
Domestic Credit	32	...	...	...	...	...	...	...	...	...	...	...	...	...	...	...
Claims on Central Govt. (Net)	32an	...	...	...	...	...	...	...	...	...	...	...	...	...	...	...
Claims on Local Government	32b	...	...	...	...	...	...	...	...	...	...	...	...	...	...	...
Claims on Nonfin.Pub.Enterprises	32c	...	...	...	...	...	...	...	...	...	...	...	...	...	...	...
Claims on Private Sector	32d	...	...	...	...	...	...	...	...	...	...	...	...	...	...	...
Money	34	...	...	...	...	...	...	...	...	...	...	...	...	...	...	...
Quasi-Money	35	...	...	...	...	...	...	...	...	...	...	...	...	...	...	...
Liab. to Nonbank Financial Insts.	36j	...	...	...	...	...	...	...	...	...	...	...	...	...	...	...
Capital Accounts	37a	...	...	...	...	...	...	...	...	...	...	...	...	...	...	...
Other Items (Net)	37r	...	...	...	...	...	...	...	...	...	...	...	...	...	...	...
Money plus Quasi-Money	35l	...	...	...	...	...	...	...	...	...	...	...	...	...	...	...
Interest Rates														*Percent Per Annum*		
Savings Rate	60k	...	...	...	...	...	...	...	...	...	...	...	...	...	...	...
Deposit Rate	60l	...	...	...	...	...	...	...	...	...	...	...	...	...	...	...
Lending Rate	60p	...	...	...	...	...	...	...	...	...	...	...	...	...	...	...
														Millions:		
Population	99z	...	...	...	...	...	...	...	...	...	...	...	...	...	...	...

	1987	1988	1989	1990	1991	1992	1993	1994	1995	1996	1997	1998	1999	2000	2001		
																Exchange Rates	
End of Period																	
	1.4187	1.3457	1.3142	1.4227	1.4304	1.3750	1.3736	1.4599	1.4865	1.4380	1.3493	1.4080	1.3725	1.3029	1.2567	Market Rate..	aa
End of Period																	
	1.0000	1.0000	1.0000	1.0000	1.0000	1.0000	1.0000	1.0000	1.0000	1.0000	1.0000	1.0000	1.0000	1.0000	1.0000	Market Rate..	ae
																Fund Position	
End of Period																	
	....	....	...	....	....	....	3.5	3.5	3.5	3.5	3.5	3.5	5.1	5.1	5.1	Quota	2f. s
	....	....	...	....	....	....	.8	.9	.9	.9	1.0	1.0	1.1	1.1	1.1	SDRs	1b. s
	....	....	...	....	....	....	—	—	—	—	—	—	—	—	—	Reserve Position in the Fund	1c. s
	....	....	...	....	....	....	—	—	—	—	—	—	—	—	—	Total Fund Cred.&Loans Outstg.	2tl
																International Liquidity	
End of Period																	
	....	....	...	....	....	....	....	....	69.500	89.600	85.801	101.602	92.669	113.047	98.330	Total Reserves minus Gold.....................	1l. d
	....	....	...	....	....	....	1.141	1.264	1.349	1.357	1.325	1.442	1.455	1.442	1.445	SDRs	1b. d
	....	....	...	....	....	....	.001	.001	.001	.001	.001	.001	.001	.001	.001	Reserve Position in the Fund	1c. d
	....	....	...	....	....	....	—	.001	68.150	88.242	84.475	100.159	91.213	111.605	96.885	Foreign Exchange	1d. d
	....	....	...	....	....	....	....	....	—	—	—	—	—	—	—	Gold (Million Fine Troy Ounces)...........	1ad
	....	....	...	....	....	....	....	....	—	—	—	—	—	—	—	Gold (National Valuation)	1an d
	....	....	...	....	....	....	....	....	60.749	54.035	51.537	55.579	55.283	47.408	36.989	Monetary Authorities: Other Assets	3.. d
	....	....	...	....	....	....	....	....	82.200	97.210	96.273	93.042	93.472	91.259	97.967	Banking Institutions: Assets	7a. d
	....	....	...	....	....	....	....	....	1.962	1.332	.948	.131	.107	—	—	Liabilities.............	7b. d
																Monetary Authorities	
End of Period																	
	....	....	...	....	....	....	....	....	130.249	143.635	137.338	157.181	147.952	160.455	135.319	Foreign Assets	11
	....	....	...	....	....	....	....	....	130.249	143.635	137.338	157.181	147.952	160.456	135.319	Central Government Deposits	16d
	....	....	...	....	....	....	....	....	—	—	—	—	—	-.001	—	Other Items (Net)	17r
																Banking Institutions	
End of Period																	
	....	....	...	....	....	....	....	....	82.200	97.210	96.273	93.042	93.472	91.259	97.967	Foreign Assets	21
	....	....	...	....	....	....	....	....	—	—	—	—	—	—	.173	Claims on Central Government	22a
	....	....	...	....	....	....	....	....	—	—	—	—	.787	.442	—	Claims on State & Local Govts.	22b
	....	....	...	....	....	....	....	....	—	—	—	—	—	—	—	Claims on Nonfin.Pub.Enterprises...........	22c
	....	....	...	....	....	....	....	....	.699	.106	—	—	.001	—	—	Claims on Private Sector.........................	22d
	....	....	...	....	....	....	....	....	65.572	60.141	58.129	65.618	70.749	71.595	69.907	Demand Deposits	24
	....	....	...	....	....	....	....	....	19.863	19.528	21.514	21.284	19.891	18.802	21.245	Time, Savings,& Fgn. Currency Dep.	25
	....	....	...	....	....	....	....	....	87.971	82.067	83.947	84.933	89.926	89.965	94.015	Foreign Liabilities	26c
	....	....	...	....	....	....	....	....	1.962	1.332	.948	.131	.107	—	—	Central Government Deposits	26d
	....	....	...	....	....	....	....	....	4.949	14.976	11.745	11.736	11.351	10.336	7.727	Liab. to Nonbank Financial Insts.	26j
	....	....	...	....	....	....	....	....	.365	2.836	1.446	.587	2.007	.958	1.827	Capital Accounts	27a
	....	....	...	....	....	....	....	....	39.137	43.175	44.506	46.739	46.152	47.017	49.433	Other Items (Net)	27r
	....	....	...	....	....	....	....	....	-5.776	-6.457	-9.704	-6.750	-4.425	-3.782	-6.200		
																Banking Survey	
End of Period																	
	....	....	...	....	....	....	....	....	210.487	239.513	232.663	250.092	241.317	251.714	233.286	Foreign Assets (Net)	31n
	....	....	...	....	....	....	....	....	-68.927	-98.364	-90.954	-103.299	-87.766	-98.755	-72.966	Domestic Credit	32
	....	....	...	....	....	....	....	....	-135.198	-158.611	-149.083	-168.917	-159.303	-170.792	-142.873	Claims on Central Govt. (Net)	32an
	....	....	...	....	....	....	....	....	—	—	—	—	.787	.442	—	Claims on Local Government	32b
	....	....	...	....	....	....	....	....	.699	.106	—	—	.001	—	—	Claims on Nonfin.Pub.Enterprises...........	32c
	....	....	...	....	....	....	....	....	65.572	60.141	58.129	65.618	70.749	71.595	69.907	Claims on Private Sector	32d
	....	....	...	....	....	....	....	....	19.863	19.528	21.514	21.284	19.891	18.802	21.245	Money	34
	....	....	...	....	....	....	....	....	87.971	82.067	83.947	84.933	89.926	89.965	94.015	Quasi-Money..	35
	....	....	...	....	....	....	....	....	.365	2.836	1.446	.587	2.007	.958	1.827	Liab. to Nonbank Financial Insts.	36j
	....	....	...	....	....	....	....	....	39.137	43.175	44.506	46.739	46.152	47.017	49.433	Capital Accounts	37a
	....	....	...	....	....	....	....	....	-5.776	-6.457	-9.704	-6.750	-4.425	-3.783	-6.200	Other Items (Net)	37r
	....	....	...	....	....	....	....	....	107.834	101.595	105.461	106.217	109.817	108.767	115.260	Money plus Quasi-Money	35l
																Interest Rates	
Percent Per Annum																	
	...	...	...	....	...	....	....	....	3.17	3.01	3.00	2.90	2.72	2.67	2.47	Savings Rate..	60k
	...	...	...	....	...	....	....	....	5.33	4.58	4.21	3.98	3.72	4.59	3.17	Deposit Rate...	60l
	...	...	...	....	...	....	....	....	15.00	15.00	15.00	15.00	15.17	15.33	15.33	Lending Rate	60p
Midyear Estimates																	
	.10	.10	.11	.10	.11	.11	.12	†.10	.11	.11	.11	.11	.12	.12	.13	**Population**..	99z

(See notes in the back of the book.)

Moldova

921

	1972	1973	1974	1975	1976	1977	1978	1979	1980	1981	1982	1983	1984	1985	1986
Exchange Rates															*Lei per SDR:*
Official Rate ..... aa	....	....	....	....	....	....	....	....	....	....	....	....	....	....	....
															Lei per US Dollar:
Official Rate ..... ae	....	....	....	....	....	....	....	....	....	....	....	....	....	....	....
Official Rate ..... rf	....	....	....	....	....	....	....	....	....	....	....	....	....	....	....
															Index Numbers (1995=100):
Nominal Effective Exchange Rate ..... ne c	....	....	....	....	....	....	....	....	....	....	....	....	....	....	....
Real Effective Exchange Rate ..... re c	....	....	....	....	....	....	....	....	....	....	....	....	....	....	....
Fund Position															*Millions of SDRs:*
Quota ..... 2f. s	....	....	....	....	....	....	....	....	....	....	....	....	....	....	....
SDRs ..... 1b. s	....	....	....	....	....	....	....	....	....	....	....	....	....	....	....
Reserve Position in the Fund ..... 1c. s	....	....	....	....	....	....	....	....	....	....	....	....	....	....	....
Total Fund Cred.&Loans Outstg. 2tl	....	....	....	....	....	....	....	....	....	....	....	....	....	....	....
International Liquidity															*Millions of US Dollars Unless Otherwise Indicated:*
Total Reserves minus Gold ..... 1l. d	....	....	....	....	....	....	....	....	....	....	....	....	....	....	....
SDRs ..... 1b. d	....	....	....	....	....	....	....	....	....	....	....	....	....	....	....
Reserve Position in the Fund ..... 1c. d	....	....	....	....	....	....	....	....	....	....	....	....	....	....	....
Foreign Exchange ..... 1d. d	....	....	....	....	....	....	....	....	....	....	....	....	....	....	....
Gold (Million Fine Troy Ounces) 1ad	....	....	....	....	....	....	....	....	....	....	....	....	....	....	....
Gold (National Valuation) 1and	....	....	....	....	....	....	....	....	....	....	....	....	....	....	....
Monetary Authorities: Other Liab. ..... 4.. d	....	....	....	....	....	....	....	....	....	....	....	....	....	....	....
Dep.Money Banks: Assets Conv. ..... 7ax d	....	....	....	....	....	....	....	....	....	....	....	....	....	....	....
Assets Nonconv ..... 7ay d	....	....	....	....	....	....	....	....	....	....	....	....	....	....	....
Dep.Money Banks: Liab. Conv. ..... 7bx d	....	....	....	....	....	....	....	....	....	....	....	....	....	....	....
Liab. Nonconv. ..... 7by d	....	....	....	....	....	....	....	....	....	....	....	....	....	....	....
Monetary Authorities															*Millions of Lei:*
Foreign Assets 11	....	....	....	....	....	....	....	....	....	....	....	....	....	....	....
Claims on Central Government 12a	....	....	....	....	....	....	....	....	....	....	....	....	....	....	....
Claims on Private Sector 12d	....	....	....	....	....	....	....	....	....	....	....	....	....	....	....
Claims on Deposit Money Banks 12e	....	....	....	....	....	....	....	....	....	....	....	....	....	....	....
Reserve Money 14	....	....	....	....	....	....	....	....	....	....	....	....	....	....	....
of which: Currency Outside DMB 14a	....	....	....	....	....	....	....	....	....	....	....	....	....	....	....
Foreign Liabilities 16c	....	....	....	....	....	....	....	....	....	....	....	....	....	....	....
Central Government Deposits 16d	....	....	....	....	....	....	....	....	....	....	....	....	....	....	....
Capital Accounts 17a	....	....	....	....	....	....	....	....	....	....	....	....	....	....	....
Other Items (Net) 17r	....	....	....	....	....	....	....	....	....	....	....	....	....	....	....
Deposit Money Banks															*Millions of Lei:*
Reserves 20	....	....	....	....	....	....	....	....	....	....	....	....	....	....	....
Foreign Assets 21	....	....	....	....	....	....	....	....	....	....	....	....	....	....	....
Claims on Central Government 22a	....	....	....	....	....	....	....	....	....	....	....	....	....	....	....
Claims on Local Government 22b	....	....	....	....	....	....	....	....	....	....	....	....	....	....	....
Claims on Nonfin.Pub.Enterprises 22c	....	....	....	....	....	....	....	....	....	....	....	....	....	....	....
Claims on Private Sector 22d	....	....	....	....	....	....	....	....	....	....	....	....	....	....	....
Claims on Nonbank Financial Insts 22g	....	....	....	....	....	....	....	....	....	....	....	....	....	....	....
Demand Deposits 24	....	....	....	....	....	....	....	....	....	....	....	....	....	....	....
Time, Savings,& Fgn.Currency Dep. 25	....	....	....	....	....	....	....	....	....	....	....	....	....	....	....
Money Market Instruments 26aa	....	....	....	....	....	....	....	....	....	....	....	....	....	....	....
Foreign Liabilities 26c	....	....	....	....	....	....	....	....	....	....	....	....	....	....	....
Central Government Deposits 26d	....	....	....	....	....	....	....	....	....	....	....	....	....	....	....
Credit from Monetary Authorities 26g	....	....	....	....	....	....	....	....	....	....	....	....	....	....	....
Liabs. to Nonbank Financial Insts 26j	....	....	....	....	....	....	....	....	....	....	....	....	....	....	....
Capital Accounts 27a	....	....	....	....	....	....	....	....	....	....	....	....	....	....	....
Other Items (Net) 27r	....	....	....	....	....	....	....	....	....	....	....	....	....	....	....
Monetary Survey															*Millions of Lei:*
Foreign Assets (Net) 31n	....	....	....	....	....	....	....	....	....	....	....	....	....	....	....
Domestic Credit 32	....	....	....	....	....	....	....	....	....	....	....	....	....	....	....
Claims on Central Govt. (Net) 32an	....	....	....	....	....	....	....	....	....	....	....	....	....	....	....
Claims on Local Government 32b	....	....	....	....	....	....	....	....	....	....	....	....	....	....	....
Claims on Nonfin.Pub.Enterprises 32c	....	....	....	....	....	....	....	....	....	....	....	....	....	....	....
Claims on Private Sector 32d	....	....	....	....	....	....	....	....	....	....	....	....	....	....	....
Claims on Nonbank Financial Inst 32g	....	....	....	....	....	....	....	....	....	....	....	....	....	....	....
Money 34	....	....	....	....	....	....	....	....	....	....	....	....	....	....	....
Quasi-Money 35	....	....	....	....	....	....	....	....	....	....	....	....	....	....	....
Money Market Instruments 36aa	....	....	....	....	....	....	....	....	....	....	....	....	....	....	....
Liabs. to Nonbank Financial Insts 36j	....	....	....	....	....	....	....	....	....	....	....	....	....	....	....
Capital Accounts 37a	....	....	....	....	....	....	....	....	....	....	....	....	....	....	....
Other Items (Net) 37r	....	....	....	....	....	....	....	....	....	....	....	....	....	....	....
Money plus Quasi-Money 35l	....	....	....	....	....	....	....	....	....	....	....	....	....	....	....
Interest Rates															*Percent Per Annum*
Refinancing Rate 60a	....	....	....	....	....	....	....	....	....	....	....	....	....	....	....
Money Market Rate 60b	....	....	....	....	....	....	....	....	....	....	....	....	....	....	....
Money Market Rate (Fgn. Cur.) ..... 60b. f	....	....	....	....	....	....	....	....	....	....	....	....	....	....	....
Treasury Bill Rate 60c	....	....	....	....	....	....	....	....	....	....	....	....	....	....	....
Deposit Rate 60l	....	....	....	....	....	....	....	....	....	....	....	....	....	....	....
Deposit Rate (Foreign Currency) ..... 60l. f	....	....	....	....	....	....	....	....	....	....	....	....	....	....	....
Lending Rate 60p	....	....	....	....	....	....	....	....	....	....	....	....	....	....	....
Lending Rate (Foreign Currency) ..... 60p. f	....	....	....	....	....	....	....	....	....	....	....	....	....	....	....
Prices and Labor															*Index Numbers (1995=100):*
Consumer Prices 64	....	....	....	....	....	....	....	....	....	....	....	....	....	....	....
															Number in Thousands:
Labor Force 67d	....	....	....	....	....	....	....	....	....	....	....	....	....	....	....
Employment 67e	....	....	....	....	....	....	....	....	....	....	....	....	....	....	....
Unemployment 67c	....	....	....	....	....	....	....	....	....	....	....	....	....	....	....
Unemployment Rate (%) 67r	....	....	....	....	....	....	....	....	....	....	....	....	....	....	....

Exchange Rates

End of Period

1987	1988	1989	1990	1991	1992	1993	1994	1995	1996	1997	1998	1999	2000	2001		
....	....	....	....	.0024	.5698	†4.9998	6.2336	6.6877	6.7215	6.2882	11.7185	15.9077	16.1343	16.4517	Official Rate	aa

End of Period (ae) Period Average (rf)

1987	1988	1989	1990	1991	1992	1993	1994	1995	1996	1997	1998	1999	2000	2001		
....	....	....	....	.0017	.4144	†3.6400	4.2700	4.4990	4.6743	4.6605	8.3226	11.5902	12.3833	13.0909	Official Rate	ae
							4.4958	4.6045	4.6236	5.3707	10.5158	12.4342	12.8651		Official Rate	rf

Period Averages

1987	1988	1989	1990	1991	1992	1993	1994	1995	1996	1997	1998	1999	2000	2001		
						56.51	100.00	117.37	154.98	183.52	193.01	204.19	217.90		Nominal Effective Exchange Rate	ne c
						115.61	100.00	97.85	105.70	107.07	100.31	109.68	107.03		Real Effective Exchange Rate	re c

Fund Position

End of Period

1987	1988	1989	1990	1991	1992	1993	1994	1995	1996	1997	1998	1999	2000	2001		
....	....	....	....	....	90.00	90.00	90.00	90.00	90.00	90.00	90.00	123.20	123.20	123.20	Quota	2f. s
					—	25.05	14.62	8.81	5.45	.89	.50	.23	.26	.59	SDRs	1b. s
					.01	.01	.01	.01	.01	.01	.01	.01	.01	.01	Reserve Position in the Fund	1c. s
					—	63.00	112.45	154.85	172.29	172.73	125.56	127.69	118.30	116.29	Total Fund Cred.&Loans Outstg.	2tl

International Liquidity

End of Period

1987	1988	1989	1990	1991	1992	1993	1994	1995	1996	1997	1998	1999	2000	2001		
....	....	....	....	—	2.45	76.34	179.92	257.01	311.96	365.99	143.56	185.70	230.15	229.04	Total Reserves minus Gold	1l. d
					—	34.41	21.34	13.10	7.84	1.21	.70	.32	.34	.74	SDRs	1b. d
					.01	.01	.01	.01	.01	.01	.01	.01	.01	.01	Reserve Position in the Fund	1c. d
				—	2.44	41.92	158.57	243.90	304.11	364.77	142.85	185.37	229.80	228.29	Foreign Exchange	1d. d
				—	—	—	—	—	—	—	—	—	—	—	Gold (Million Fine Troy Ounces)	1ad
				—	—	—	—	—	—	—	—	—	—	—	Gold (National Valuation)	1an d
				—	138.12	12.02	10.10	7.42	4.94	4.00	2.77	10.06	9.66	1.32	Monetary Authorities: Other Liab.	4..d
				2.02	2.19	14.92	18.86	32.77	37.41	23.78	32.33	53.42	67.22	59.77	Dep.Money Banks: Assets Conv.	7ax d
				—	.20	2.14	7.79	5.24	5.55	9.25	3.44	2.23	5.16	4.92	Assets Nonconv	7ay d
				—	—	.51	1.42	10.60	50.70	58.10	67.27	41.78	44.42	41.70	Dep.Money Banks: Liab. Conv.	7bx d
				—	—	1.51	.41	3.10	1.55	4.91	7.62	3.33	5.80	5.45	Liab. Nonconv.	7by d

Monetary Authorities

End of Period

1987	1988	1989	1990	1991	1992	1993	1994	1995	1996	1997	1998	1999	2000	2001		
				—	49.32	345.41	825.14	1,198.42	†1486.91	1,716.60	1,199.82	2,207.49	2,876.49	3,008.36	Foreign Assets	11
				.48	52.24	236.21	284.01	452.92	†496.12	524.83	1,409.21	1,737.46	1,730.79	1,899.28	Claims on Central Government	12a
							1.79	†2.88	3.92	5.10	6.03	7.28	7.10		Claims on Private Sector	12d
				1.14	3.37	98.68	274.67	366.55	†362.63	286.02	233.02	130.27	105.44	91.15	Claims on Deposit Money Banks	12e
				7.74	49.04	241.14	551.94	779.85	†854.28	1,138.64	1,063.45	1,506.63	1,988.86	2,504.44	Reserve Money	14
				1.83	9.75	119.45	345.55	640.15	†731.06	972.10	†855.45	1,122.07	1,469.26	1,834.20	of which: Currency Outside DMB	14a
					57.25	358.73	744.00	1,068.96	†1181.13	1,104.75	1,494.36	2,147.89	2,028.31	1,930.53	Foreign Liabilities	16c
					.20	90.12	17.45	21.38	†126.37	9.99	60.00	85.72	277.93	100.52	Central Government Deposits	16d
				.08	.06	1.72	24.72	79.11	†95.26	91.92	161.36	215.21	296.22	416.61	Capital Accounts	17a
				-6.20	-1.62	-11.40	45.63	70.37	†91.49	186.07	67.97	125.81	128.69	53.78	Other Items (Net)	17r

Deposit Money Banks

End of Period

1987	1988	1989	1990	1991	1992	1993	1994	1995	1996	1997	1998	1999	2000	2001		
				1.48	10.60	48.87	52.44	54.38	36.54	52.05	†200.66	360.92	465.22	652.38	Reserves	20
					.99	62.11	113.76	171.03	200.79	153.90	†297.69	644.99	896.23	846.80	Foreign Assets	21
				9.46	28.16	122.13	31.56	10.31	13.68	67.58	†184.46	267.81	335.33	571.44	Claims on Central Government	22a
					4.03	10.21	22.82	2.59	13.19	23.68	†33.01	14.98	17.24	25.45	Claims on Local Government	22b
				6.79	32.81	243.28	493.91	692.37	852.27	1,120.82	†144.17	146.32	230.71	293.61	Claims on Nonfin.Pub.Enterprises	22c
				1.52	11.23	91.06	174.79	433.62	600.88	617.05	†1265.65	1,453.15	2,025.31	2,804.49	Claims on Private Sector	22d
											†23.06	37.30	28.36	5.65	Claims on Nonbank Financial Insts	22g
				7.21	49.94	121.24	173.69	244.57	263.13	326.49	†210.00	357.76	553.75	665.76	Demand Deposits	24
				9.17	23.61	106.02	228.68	358.18	435.57	624.02	†698.48	1,040.18	1,548.25	2,350.96	Time, Savings,& Fgn.Currency Dep.	25
											†1.21	2.10	.20	.29	Money Market Instruments	26aa
						7.36	7.80	61.64	244.21	293.67	†623.24	522.87	621.93	617.29	Foreign Liabilities	26c
				2.07	21.67	149.65	56.54	35.81	27.84	33.55	†13.51	44.72	57.11	270.93	Central Government Deposits	26d
				2.78	6.47	104.70	292.23	389.12	368.12	285.91	†229.83	130.27	106.44	93.15	Credit from Monetary Authorities	26g
											†.77	1.55	2.22	2.45	Liabs. to Nonbank Financial Insts	26j
				1.21	9.57	136.65	333.05	569.03	731.41	839.27	†756.20	1,242.83	1,692.04	1,896.54	Capital Accounts	27a
				-3.18	-23.44	-47.96	-202.72	-294.04	-352.93	-367.84	†-384.56	-416.81	-583.56	-697.56	Other Items (Net)	27r

Monetary Survey

End of Period

1987	1988	1989	1990	1991	1992	1993	1994	1995	1996	1997	1998	1999	2000	2001		
					-6.94	41.44	187.01	238.85	†262.37	472.08	†-620.10	181.71	1,122.48	1,307.33	Foreign Assets (Net)	31n
				16.27	107.39	463.12	933.10	1,536.40	†1824.80	2,314.34	†2991.14	3,532.62	4,039.97	5,235.57	Domestic Credit	32
				7.87	58.53	118.57	241.58	406.04	†355.59	548.88	†1520.16	1,874.84	1,731.07	2,099.27	Claims on Central Govt. (Net)	32an
					4.03	10.21	22.82	2.59	13.19	23.68	†33.01	14.98	17.24	25.45	Claims on Local Government	32b
				6.88	33.60	243.28	493.91	692.37	†852.27	1,120.82	†144.17	146.32	230.71	293.61	Claims on Nonfin.Pub.Enterprises	32c
				1.52	11.23	91.06	174.79	435.41	†603.76	620.97	†1270.75	1,459.19	2,032.59	2,811.59	Claims on Private Sector	32d
											†23.06	37.30	28.36	5.65	Claims on Nonbank Financial Inst	32g
				9.04	59.79	242.07	524.20	885.04	†994.51	1,298.83	†1065.46	1,479.84	2,023.22	2,500.00	Money	34
				9.17	23.61	107.17	229.01	360.18	†435.57	624.02	†698.48	1,040.18	1,548.25	2,350.96	Quasi-Money	35
											†1.21	2.10	.20	.29	Money Market Instruments	36aa
											†.77	1.55	2.22	2.45	Liabs. to Nonbank Financial Insts	36j
				1.29	9.63	138.37	357.77	648.15	†826.67	931.20	†917.56	1,458.04	1,988.26	2,313.16	Capital Accounts	37a
				-3.23	7.42	16.94	9.13	-118.10	†-169.58	-67.63	†-312.44	-267.37	-399.70	-623.94	Other Items (Net)	37r
				18.21	83.39	349.24	753.21	1,245.22	†1430.08	1,922.86	†1763.94	2,520.02	3,571.47	4,850.95	Money plus Quasi-Money	35l

Interest Rates

Percent Per Annum

1987	1988	1989	1990	1991	1992	1993	1994	1995	1996	1997	1998	1999	2000	2001		
							143.9	28.3	20.2	19.0	....	32.6	20.8	....	Refinancing Rate	60a
										28.1	30.9	32.6	20.8	11.0	Money Market Rate	60b
												11.9	6.9	9.1	Money Market Rate (Fgn. Cur.)	60b. f
								52.9	39.0	23.6	30.5	28.5	22.2	14.2	Treasury Bill Rate	60c
									25.4	23.5	21.7	27.5	24.9	20.9	Deposit Rate	60l
											9.9	5.3	5.1	4.1	Deposit Rate (Foreign Currency)	60l. f
									36.7	33.3	30.8	35.5	33.8	28.7	Lending Rate	60p
											22.0	20.4	17.1	14.2	Lending Rate (Foreign Currency)	60p. f

Prices and Labor

Period Averages

1987	1988	1989	1990	1991	1992	1993	1994	1995	1996	1997	1998	1999	2000	2001		
							89.2	100.0	120.9	130.6	139.2	203.2	266.8	292.9	Consumer Prices	64

Period Averages

1987	1988	1989	1990	1991	1992	1993	1994	1995	1996	1997	1998	1999	2000	2001		
					2,065				1,686		1,659	1,682	1,655	....	Labor Force	67d
		2,091	2,071	2,070	2,050	1,688	1,681	1,673	1,660	1,646	1,642	....	....		Employment	67e
					—	15	14	21	25	23	28	32	35	29	Unemployment	67c
						.7	.7	1.1	1.0	1.5	1.5	1.9	2.1	2.1	Unemployment Rate (%)	67r

Moldova

921

	Code	1972	1973	1974	1975	1976	1977	1978	1979	1980	1981	1982	1983	1984	1985	1986
International Transactions																*Millions of US Dollars*
Exports	70..d	....	....	....	....	....	....	....	....	....	....	....	....	....	....	....
Imports, c.i.f.	71..d	....	....	....	....	....	....	....	....	....	....	....	....	....	....	....
Imports, f.o.b.	71.vd	....	....	....	....	....	....	....	....	....	....	....	....	....	....	....
Balance of Payments																*Millions of US Dollars:*
Current Account, n.i.e.	78ald	....	....	....	....	....	....	....	....	....	....	....	....	....	....	....
Goods: Exports f.o.b.	78aad	....	....	....	....	....	....	....	....	....	....	....	....	....	....	....
Goods: Imports f.o.b.	78abd	....	....	....	....	....	....	....	....	....	....	....	....	....	....	....
Trade Balance	78acd	....	....	....	....	....	....	....	....	....	....	....	....	....	....	....
Services: Credit	78add	....	....	....	....	....	....	....	....	....	....	....	....	....	....	....
Services: Debit	78aed	....	....	....	....	....	....	....	....	....	....	....	....	....	....	....
Balance on Goods & Services	78afd	....	....	....	....	....	....	....	....	....	....	....	....	....	....	....
Income: Credit	78agd	....	....	....	....	....	....	....	....	....	....	....	....	....	....	....
Income: Debit	78ahd	....	....	....	....	....	....	....	....	....	....	....	....	....	....	....
Balance on Gds, Serv. & Inc.	78aid	....	....	....	....	....	....	....	....	....	....	....	....	....	....	....
Current Transfers, n.i.e.: Credit	78ajd	....	....	....	....	....	....	....	....	....	....	....	....	....	....	....
Current Transfers: Debit	78akd	....	....	....	....	....	....	....	....	....	....	....	....	....	....	....
Capital Account, n.i.e.	78bcd	....	....	....	....	....	....	....	....	....	....	....	....	....	....	....
Capital Account, n.i.e.: Credit	78bad	....	....	....	....	....	....	....	....	....	....	....	....	....	....	....
Capital Account: Debit	78bbd	....	....	....	....	....	....	....	....	....	....	....	....	....	....	....
Financial Account, n.i.e.	78bjd	....	....	....	....	....	....	....	....	....	....	....	....	....	....	....
Direct Investment Abroad	78bdd	....	....	....	....	....	....	....	....	....	....	....	....	....	....	....
Dir. Invest. in Rep. Econ., n.i.e.	78bed	....	....	....	....	....	....	....	....	....	....	....	....	....	....	....
Portfolio Investment Assets	78bfd	....	....	....	....	....	....	....	....	....	....	....	....	....	....	....
Equity Securities	78bkd	....	....	....	....	....	....	....	....	....	....	....	....	....	....	....
Debt Securities	78bld	....	....	....	....	....	....	....	....	....	....	....	....	....	....	....
Portfolio Investment Liab., n.i.e.	78bgd	....	....	....	....	....	....	....	....	....	....	....	....	....	....	....
Equity Securities	78bmd	....	....	....	....	....	....	....	....	....	....	....	....	....	....	....
Debt Securities	78bnd	....	....	....	....	....	....	....	....	....	....	....	....	....	....	....
Financial Derivatives Assets	78bwd	....	....	....	....	....	....	....	....	....	....	....	....	....	....	....
Financial Derivatives Liabilities	78bxd	....	....	....	....	....	....	....	....	....	....	....	....	....	....	....
Other Investment Assets	78bhd	....	....	....	....	....	....	....	....	....	....	....	....	....	....	....
Monetary Authorities	78bod	....	....	....	....	....	....	....	....	....	....	....	....	....	....	....
General Government	78bpd	....	....	....	....	....	....	....	....	....	....	....	....	....	....	....
Banks	78bqd	....	....	....	....	....	....	....	....	....	....	....	....	....	....	....
Other Sectors	78brd	....	....	....	....	....	....	....	....	....	....	....	....	....	....	....
Other Investment Liab., n.i.e.	78bid	....	....	....	....	....	....	....	....	....	....	....	....	....	....	....
Monetary Authorities	78bsd	....	....	....	....	....	....	....	....	....	....	....	....	....	....	....
General Government	78btd	....	....	....	....	....	....	....	....	....	....	....	....	....	....	....
Banks	78bud	....	....	....	....	....	....	....	....	....	....	....	....	....	....	....
Other Sectors	78bvd	....	....	....	....	....	....	....	....	....	....	....	....	....	....	....
Net Errors and Omissions	78cad	....	....	....	....	....	....	....	....	....	....	....	....	....	....	....
Overall Balance	78cbd	....	....	....	....	....	....	....	....	....	....	....	....	....	....	....
Reserves and Related Items	79dad	....	....	....	....	....	....	....	....	....	....	....	....	....	....	....
Reserve Assets	79dbd	....	....	....	....	....	....	....	....	....	....	....	....	....	....	....
Use of Fund Credit and Loans	79dcd	....	....	....	....	....	....	....	....	....	....	....	....	....	....	....
Exceptional Financing	79ded	....	....	....	....	....	....	....	....	....	....	....	....	....	....	....
International Investment Position																*Millions of US Dollars*
Assets	79aad	....	....	....	....	....	....	....	....	....	....	....	....	....	....	....
Direct Investment Abroad	79abd	....	....	....	....	....	....	....	....	....	....	....	....	....	....	....
Portfolio Investment	79acd	....	....	....	....	....	....	....	....	....	....	....	....	....	....	....
Equity Securities	79add	....	....	....	....	....	....	....	....	....	....	....	....	....	....	....
Debt Securities	79aed	....	....	....	....	....	....	....	....	....	....	....	....	....	....	....
Financial Derivatives	79ald	....	....	....	....	....	....	....	....	....	....	....	....	....	....	....
Other Investment	79afd	....	....	....	....	....	....	....	....	....	....	....	....	....	....	....
Monetary Authorities	79agd	....	....	....	....	....	....	....	....	....	....	....	....	....	....	....
General Government	79ahd	....	....	....	....	....	....	....	....	....	....	....	....	....	....	....
Banks	79aid	....	....	....	....	....	....	....	....	....	....	....	....	....	....	....
Other Sectors	79ajd	....	....	....	....	....	....	....	....	....	....	....	....	....	....	....
Reserve Assets	79akd	....	....	....	....	....	....	....	....	....	....	....	....	....	....	....
Liabilities	79lad	....	....	....	....	....	....	....	....	....	....	....	....	....	....	....
Dir. Invest. in Rep. Economy	79lbd	....	....	....	....	....	....	....	....	....	....	....	....	....	....	....
Portfolio Investment	79lcd	....	....	....	....	....	....	....	....	....	....	....	....	....	....	....
Equity Securities	79ldd	....	....	....	....	....	....	....	....	....	....	....	....	....	....	....
Debt Securities	79led	....	....	....	....	....	....	....	....	....	....	....	....	....	....	....
Financial Derivatives	79lld	....	....	....	....	....	....	....	....	....	....	....	....	....	....	....
Other Investment	79lfd	....	....	....	....	....	....	....	....	....	....	....	....	....	....	....
Monetary Authorities	79lgd	....	....	....	....	....	....	....	....	....	....	....	....	....	....	....
General Government	79lhd	....	....	....	....	....	....	....	....	....	....	....	....	....	....	....
Banks	79lid	....	....	....	....	....	....	....	....	....	....	....	....	....	....	....
Other Sectors	79ljd	....	....	....	....	....	....	....	....	....	....	....	....	....	....	....
National Accounts																*Millions of Lei*
Househ.Cons.Expend.,incl.NPISHs	96f	....	....	....	....	....	....	....	....	....	....	....	....	....	....	....
Government Consumption Expend.	91f	....	....	....	....	....	....	....	....	....	....	....	....	....	....	....
Gross Fixed Capital Formation	93e	....	....	....	....	....	....	....	....	....	....	....	....	....	....	....
Changes in Inventories	93i	....	....	....	....	....	....	....	....	....	....	....	....	....	....	....
Exports (Net)	90n	....	....	....	....	....	....	....	....	....	....	....	....	....	....	....
Gross Domestic Product (GDP)	99b	....	....	....	....	....	....	....	....	....	....	....	....	....	....	....
Net Primary Income from Abroad	98.n	....	....	....	....	....	....	....	....	....	....	....	....	....	....	....
Gross National Income (GNI)	99a	....	....	....	....	....	....	....	....	....	....	....	....	....	....	....
Net Current Transf.from Abroad	98t	....	....	....	....	....	....	....	....	....	....	....	....	....	....	....
Gross Nat'l Disposable Inc.(GNDI)	99i	....	....	....	....	....	....	....	....	....	....	....	....	....	....	....
Gross Saving	99s	....	....	....	....	....	....	....	....	....	....	....	....	....	....	....
																Millions:
Population	99z	....	....	....	....	....	....	....	....	....	....	....	....	....	....	....

	1987	1988	1989	1990	1991	1992	1993	1994	1995	1996	1997	1998	1999	2000	2001		
Millions of US Dollars																**International Transactions**	
	...	...	...	...	...	470	483	619	739	805	890	644	...	...	...	Exports	70..*d*
	...	...	...	...	...	640	628	703	841	1,079	1,200	1,018	...	...	...	Imports, c.i.f.	71..*d*
	...	...	...	...	...	...	...	672	794	1,077	1,238	1,032	...	...	...	Imports, f.o.b.	71.v*d*
Minus Sign Indicates Debit																Balance of Payments	
	...	...	...	...	...	...	...	−82.0	−87.8	−194.8	−274.9	−334.7	−65.6	−116.2	−118.3	Current Account, n.i.e.	78al*d*
	...	...	...	...	...	...	...	618.5	739.0	822.9	889.6	643.6	474.1	476.5	569.4	Goods: Exports f.o.b.	78aa*d*
	...	...	...	...	...	...	...	−672.4	−809.2	−1,082.5	−1,237.6	−1,031.7	−609.8	−768.3	−882.4	Goods: Imports f.o.b.	78ab*d*
	...	...	...	...	...	...	...	−53.9	−70.2	−259.7	−348.0	−388.1	−135.7	−291.8	−312.9	*Trade Balance*	78ac*d*
	...	...	...	...	...	...	...	32.8	144.5	106.0	167.7	152.0	140.9	167.9	169.9	Services: Credit	78ad*d*
	...	...	...	...	...	...	...	−79.0	−196.3	−166.4	−196.1	−198.6	−171.0	−203.2	−218.6	Services: Debit	78ae*d*
	...	...	...	...	...	...	...	−100.0	−122.0	−320.0	−376.4	−434.6	−165.8	−327.1	−361.7	*Balance on Goods & Services*	78af*d*
	...	...	...	...	...	...	...	10.8	14.2	99.3	132.7	136.8	120.4	167.3	233.3	Income: Credit	78ag*d*
	...	...	...	...	...	...	...	−26.1	−32.4	−44.2	−85.3	−102.3	−95.2	−104.2	−132.5	Income: Debit	78ah*d*
	...	...	...	...	...	...	...	−115.4	−140.2	−264.9	−329.0	−400.1	−140.6	−263.9	−260.9	*Balance on Gds, Serv. & Inc.*	78ai*d*
	...	...	...	...	...	...	...	36.9	66.6	72.9	104.1	110.9	114.7	162.9	160.7	Current Transfers, n.i.e.: Credit	78aj*d*
	...	...	...	...	...	...	...	−3.6	−14.1	−2.8	−50.0	−45.5	−39.6	−15.2	−18.1	Current Transfers: Debit	78ak*d*
	...	...	...	...	...	...	...	−1.0	−.4	−.1	−.2	−.4	1.1	1.9	−2.0	Capital Account, n.i.e.	78bc*d*
	...	...	...	...	...	...	...	—	—	.1	.1	2.1	1.5	2.8	1.1	Capital Account, n.i.e.: Credit	78ba*d*
	...	...	...	...	...	...	...	−1.0	−.4	−.1	−.3	−2.5	−.4	−.9	−3.1	Capital Account: Debit	78bb*d*
	...	...	...	...	...	...	...	211.1	−68.8	76.6	95.2	5.2	−35.9	144.9	28.0	Financial Account, n.i.e.	78bj*d*
	...	...	...	...	...	...	...	...	−.5	−.6	−.5	.7	−.1	−.1	−.1	Direct Investment Abroad	78bd*d*
	...	...	...	...	...	...	...	11.6	25.9	23.7	78.7	75.5	40.4	142.8	93.5	Dir. Invest. in Rep. Econ., n.i.e.	78be*d*
	...	...	...	...	...	...	...	−.4	—	—	—	—	—	—	−3.2	Portfolio Investment Assets	78bf*d*
	...	...	...	...	...	...	...	−.4	...	...	...	...	...	...	−3.2	Equity Securities	78bk*d*
	...	...	...	...	...	...	...	...	...	...	...	...	...	...	—	Debt Securities	78bl*d*
	...	...	...	...	...	...	...	.6	−.5	30.8	18.6	−59.1	−7.1	2.5	3.6	Portfolio Investment Liab., n.i.e.	78bg*d*
	...	...	...	...	...	...	...	.6	−.5	.8	3.7	6.5	5.5	2.6	3.6	Equity Securities	78bm*d*
	...	...	...	...	...	...	...		—	30.0	14.9	−65.6	−12.5	−.1	—	Debt Securities	78bn*d*
	...	...	...	...	...	...	...	...	...	...	...	...	...	...	...	Financial Derivatives Assets	78bw*d*
	...	...	...	...	...	...	...	...	...	...	...	...	...	...	...	Financial Derivatives Liabilities	78bx*d*
	...	...	...	...	...	...	...	−81.7	−116.4	−51.4	1.8	−86.8	−110.9	−39.4	−42.6	Other Investment Assets	78bh*d*
	...	...	...	...	...	...	...	−1.3	2.9	12.2	3.7	2.9	—	.1		Monetary Authorities	78bo*d*
	...	...	...	...	...	...	...	−4.1	11.9	12.2	1.6	−.6	−4.3	—	8.3	General Government	78bp*d*
	...	...	...	...	...	...	...	−10.1	−13.5	−6.5	10.6	−10.9	−15.4	−16.5	1.2	Banks	78bq*d*
	...	...	...	...	...	...	...	−66.2	−117.7	−57.4	−14.2	−78.2	−91.3	−23.1	−52.1	Other Sectors	78br*d*
	...	...	...	...	...	...	...	281.0	22.7	74.0	−3.4	74.8	41.7	39.2	−23.2	Other Investment Liab., n.i.e.	78bi*d*
	...	...	...	...	...	...	...	3.1	1.8	−1.9	−2.7	5.2	−2.4	1.6	−1.0	Monetary Authorities	78bs*d*
	...	...	...	...	...	...	...	147.0	−19.7	43.2	−59.2	9.7	−22.2	−4.9	−21.7	General Government	78bt*d*
	...	...	...	...	...	...	...	−.8	11.4	21.9	11.8	6.9	−20.3	2.6	−.9	Banks	78bu*d*
	...	...	...	...	...	...	...	131.6	29.2	10.7	46.6	53.1	86.6	39.9	.5	Other Sectors	78bv*d*
	...	...	...	...	...	...	...	−115.2	−18.4	15.5	−7.9	−22.8	−20.1	−4.8	23.2	Net Errors and Omissions	78ca*d*
	...	...	...	...	...	...	...	12.9	−175.4	−102.7	−187.8	−352.8	−120.4	25.8	−69.1	*Overall Balance*	78cb*d*
	...	...	...	...	...	...	...	−12.9	175.4	102.7	187.8	352.8	120.4	−25.8	69.1	Reserves and Related Items	79da*d*
	...	...	...	...	...	...	...	−103.1	−76.7	−56.9	−50.2	225.7	−48.8	−46.8	−9.6	Reserve Assets	79db*d*
	...	...	...	...	...	...	...	71.5	64.8	25.2	.8	−64.4	4.0	−12.7	−2.3	Use of Fund Credit and Loans	79dc*d*
	...	...	...	...	...	...	...	18.7	187.3	134.4	237.2	191.4	165.1	33.7	81.0	Exceptional Financing	79de*d*
Millions of US Dollars																**International Investment Position**	
	...	...	...	...	...	...	...	303.3	499.8	612.4	657.9	463.9	594.2	668.4	728.4	Assets	79aa*d*
	...	...	...	...	...	...	...	17.8	18.3	18.9	19.3	18.6	18.6	18.7	18.8	Direct Investment Abroad	79ab*d*
	...	...	...	...	...	...	...	.4	.4	.4	.4	.4	.4	.4	3.6	Portfolio Investment	79ac*d*
	...	...	...	...	...	...	...	.4	.4	.4	.4	.4	.4	.4	.4	Equity Securities	79ad*d*
	...	...	...	...	...	...	...	—	—	—	—	—	—	—	3.2	Debt Securities	79ae*d*
	...	...	...	...	...	...	...	...	...	...	...	...	...	...	...	Financial Derivatives	79al*d*
	...	...	...	...	...	...	...	105.3	224.0	279.6	276.0	308.1	394.8	426.7	477.4	Other Investment	79af*d*
	...	...	...	...	...	...	...	9.9	7.1	6.8	3.1	.1	.1	—		Monetary Authorities	79ag*d*
	...	...	...	...	...	...	...	31.8	19.9	7.6	6.2	6.8	10.1	9.1	1.6	General Government	79ah*d*
	...	...	...	...	...	...	...	27.4	40.8	47.3	36.7	44.9	58.1	74.4	72.7	Banks	79ai*d*
	...	...	...	...	...	...	...	36.3	156.3	217.9	230.0	256.4	326.6	342.4	403.1	Other Sectors	79aj*d*
	...	...	...	...	...	...	...	179.8	257.0	313.6	362.2	136.9	180.4	222.6	228.6	Reserve Assets	79ak*d*
	...	...	...	...	...	...	...	720.0	1,022.2	1,289.5	1,594.6	1,822.6	1,943.0	2,102.2	2,215.9	Liabilities	79la*d*
	...	...	...	...	...	...	...	28.6	93.2	116.9	192.7	255.3	317.8	461.9	608.5	Dir. Invest. in Rep. Economy	79lb*d*
	...	...	...	...	...	...	...	.7	.4	60.7	296.3	232.3	86.6	176.2	179.4	Portfolio Investment	79lc*d*
	...	...	...	...	...	...	...	.7	.4	.8	6.0	10.4	11.5	11.2	14.4	Equity Securities	79ld*d*
	...	...	...	...	...	...	...	—	.1	59.9	290.3	221.9	75.1	165.0	165.0	Debt Securities	79le*d*
	...	...	...	...	...	...	...	—	—	—	—	—	—	—		Financial Derivatives	79ll*d*
	...	...	...	...	...	...	...	690.7	928.6	1,111.9	1,105.7	1,335.1	1,538.6	1,464.1	1,428.0	Other Investment	79lf*d*
	...	...	...	...	...	...	...	170.6	238.5	254.1	236.7	181.2	176.4	156.7	147.6	Monetary Authorities	79lg*d*
	...	...	...	...	...	...	...	342.4	419.2	485.6	468.7	578.4	636.4	634.1	604.9	General Government	79lh*d*
	...	...	...	...	...	...	...	1.1	12.4	32.7	42.1	51.4	30.0	32.1	31.1	Banks	79li*d*
	...	...	...	...	...	...	...	176.6	258.5	339.5	358.1	524.1	695.8	641.2	644.4	Other Sectors	79lj*d*
Millions of Lei																**National Accounts**	
	...	...	...	...	14	80	728	2,486	3,616	5,243	6,017	6,876	9,137	14,031	17,037	Househ.Cons.Expend.,incl.NPISHs	96f
	...	...	...	...	5	31	290	1,087	1,755	2,113	2,663	2,327	1,954	2,472	2,812	Government Consumption Expend.	91f
	...	...	...	...	4	31	283	914	1,034	1,540	1,774	2,012	2,272	2,473	2,575	Gross Fixed Capital Formation	93e
	...	...	...	...	3	84	734	451	578	351	349	349	548	1,364	1,241	Changes in Inventories	93i
	...	...	...	...	—	−33	−213	−202	−503	−1,449	−1,887	−2,441	−1,588	−4,319	−4,646	Exports (Net)	90n
	...	...	...	...	26	192	1,821	4,737	6,480	7,798	8,917	9,122	12,322	16,020	19,019	Gross Domestic Product (GDP)	99b
	...	...	...	...	...	...	−12	−24		−114	−209	−365	...	...	...	Net Primary Income from Abroad	98.n
	...	...	...	...	...	...	1,809	4,713	6,480	8,070	9,207	9,279	12,678	16,814	...	Gross National Income (GNI)	99a
	...	...	...	...	...	...	26	125	97	317	403	438	798	1,795	...	Net Current Transf.from Abroad	98t
	...	...	...	...	...	...	1,836	4,838	6,577	8,387	9,610	9,717	13,476	18,609	...	Gross Nat'l Disposable Inc.(GNDI)	99i
	...	...	...	...	...	...	818	1,265	1,206	1,031	930	513	2,385	2,106	...	Gross Saving	99s
Midyear Estimates																	
	...	...	...	...	4.36	4.35	4.35	4.35	4.35	4.33	†3.65	3.65	3.65	3.64	4.29	**Population**	99z

(See notes in the back of the book.)

Mongolia

948

		1972	1973	1974	1975	1976	1977	1978	1979	1980	1981	1982	1983	1984	1985	1986
Exchange Rates															*Togrogs per SDR:*	
Market Rate	aa	...	...	...	...	...	...	...	...	...	...	...	...	...	...	...
															Togrogs per US Dollar:	
Market Rate	ae	...	...	...	...	...	...	...	...	...	...	...	...	...	...	...
Market Rate	rf	...	...	...	...	...	...	...	...	...	...	...	...	...	...	...
Fund Position															*Millions of SDRs:*	
Quota	2f. s	...	...	...	...	...	...	...	...	...	...	...	...	...	...	...
SDRs	1b. s	...	...	...	...	...	...	...	...	...	...	...	...	...	...	...
Reserve Position in the Fund	1c. s	...	...	...	...	...	...	...	...	...	...	...	...	...	...	...
Total Fund Cred.&Loans Outstg.	2tl	...	...	...	...	...	...	...	...	...	...	...	...	...	...	...
International Liquidity														*Millions of US Dollars Unless Otherwise Indicated:*		
Total Reserves Minus Gold	1l. d	...	...	...	...	...	...	...	...	...	...	...	...	...	...	...
SDRs	1b. d	...	...	...	...	...	...	...	...	...	...	...	...	...	...	...
Reserve Position in the Fund	1c. d	...	...	...	...	...	...	...	...	...	...	...	...	...	...	...
Foreign Exchange	1d. d	...	...	...	...	...	...	...	...	...	...	...	...	...	...	...
Gold (Million Fine Troy Ounces)	1ad	...	...	...	...	...	...	...	...	.04	.05	.04	.04	.04	.05	.03
Gold (National Valuation)	1an d	...	...	...	...	...	...	...	...	11.00	12.60	13.10	13.50	12.90	18.00	18.00
Monetary Authorities: Other Liab.	4.. d	...	...	...	...	...	...	...	...	...	...	...	...	...	...	...
Deposit Money Banks: Assets	7a. d	...	...	...	...	...	...	...	...	...	...	...	...	...	...	...
Liabilities	7b. d	...	...	...	...	...	...	...	...	...	...	...	...	...	...	...
Monetary Authorities															*Millions of Togrogs:*	
Foreign Assets	11	...	...	...	...	...	...	...	...	...	...	...	...	...	...	...
Claims on Central Government	12a	...	...	...	...	...	...	...	...	...	...	...	...	...	...	...
Claims on Deposit Money Banks	12e	...	...	...	...	...	...	...	...	...	...	...	...	...	...	...
Reserve Money	14	...	...	...	...	...	...	...	...	...	...	...	...	...	...	...
of which: Currency Outside DMBs	14a	...	...	...	...	...	...	...	...	...	...	...	...	...	...	...
Liabs. of Central Bank: Securities	16ac	...	...	...	...	...	...	...	...	...	...	...	...	...	...	...
Foreign Liabilities	16c	...	...	...	...	...	...	...	...	...	...	...	...	...	...	...
Central Government Deposits	16d	...	...	...	...	...	...	...	...	...	...	...	...	...	...	...
Capital Accounts	17a	...	...	...	...	...	...	...	...	...	...	...	...	...	...	...
Other Items (Net)	17r	...	...	...	...	...	...	...	...	...	...	...	...	...	...	...
Deposit Money Banks															*Millions of Togrogs:*	
Reserves	20	...	...	...	...	...	...	...	...	...	...	...	...	...	...	...
Claims on Mon.Author.: Securities	20c	...	...	...	...	...	...	...	...	...	...	...	...	...	...	...
Foreign Assets	21	...	...	...	...	...	...	...	...	...	...	...	...	...	...	...
Claims on Central Government	22a	...	...	...	...	...	...	...	...	...	...	...	...	...	...	...
Claims on Nonfin.Pub.Enterprises	22c	...	...	...	...	...	...	...	...	...	...	...	...	...	...	...
Claims on Private Sector	22d	...	...	...	...	...	...	...	...	...	...	...	...	...	...	...
Demand Deposits	24	...	...	...	...	...	...	...	...	...	...	...	...	...	...	...
Time, Savings,& Fgn.Currency Dep.	25	...	...	...	...	...	...	...	...	...	...	...	...	...	...	...
Money Market Instruments	26aa	...	...	...	...	...	...	...	...	...	...	...	...	...	...	...
Restricted Deposits	26b	...	...	...	...	...	...	...	...	...	...	...	...	...	...	...
Foreign Liabilities	26c	...	...	...	...	...	...	...	...	...	...	...	...	...	...	...
Central Government Deposits	26d	...	...	...	...	...	...	...	...	...	...	...	...	...	...	...
Credit from Monetary Authorities	26g	...	...	...	...	...	...	...	...	...	...	...	...	...	...	...
Capital Accounts	27a	...	...	...	...	...	...	...	...	...	...	...	...	...	...	...
Other Items (Net)	27r	...	...	...	...	...	...	...	...	...	...	...	...	...	...	...
Monetary Survey															*Millions of Togrogs:*	
Foreign Assets (Net)	31n	...	...	...	...	...	...	...	...	...	...	...	...	...	...	...
Domestic Credit	32	...	...	...	...	...	...	...	...	...	...	...	...	...	...	...
Claims on Central Govt. (Net)	32an	...	...	...	...	...	...	...	...	...	...	...	...	...	...	...
Claims on Nonfin.Pub.Enterprises	32c	...	...	...	...	...	...	...	...	...	...	...	...	...	...	...
Claims on Private Sector	32d	...	...	...	...	...	...	...	...	...	...	...	...	...	...	...
Money	34	...	...	...	...	...	...	...	...	...	...	...	...	...	...	...
Quasi-Money	35	...	...	...	...	...	...	...	...	...	...	...	...	...	...	...
Money Market Instruments	36aa	...	...	...	...	...	...	...	...	...	...	...	...	...	...	...
Liabs. of Central Bank: Securities	36ac	...	...	...	...	...	...	...	...	...	...	...	...	...	...	...
Restricted Deposits	36b	...	...	...	...	...	...	...	...	...	...	...	...	...	...	...
Capital Accounts	37a	...	...	...	...	...	...	...	...	...	...	...	...	...	...	...
Other Items (Net)	37r	...	...	...	...	...	...	...	...	...	...	...	...	...	...	...
Money plus Quasi-Money	35l	...	...	...	...	...	...	...	...	...	...	...	...	...	...	...
Interest Rates															*Percent per Annum*	
Bank Rate (End of Period)	60	...	...	...	...	...	...	...	...	...	...	...	...	...	...	...
Deposit Rate (End of Period)	60l	...	...	...	...	...	...	...	...	...	...	...	...	...	...	300.0
Lending Rate (End of Period)	60p	...	...	...	...	...	...	...	...	...	...	...	...	...	...	...
Prices, Production, Labor															*Index Numbers (1995=100):*	
Consumer Prices	64	...	...	...	...	...	...	...	...	...	...	...	...	...	...	...
Wages: Avg. Earnings ('90=100)	65	...	...	...	...	...	...	...	...	...	...	...	...	...	93.9	94.2
Industrial Production ('90=100)	66	...	...	...	...	...	...	...	...	...	...	...	...	...	88.8	95.8
Industrial Employment ('90=100)	67	...	...	...	...	...	...	...	...	...	...	...	...	...	85.9	90.2
International Transactions															*Millions of US Dollars*	
Exports	70.. d	...	...	...	...	...	...	...	...	402.8	468.8	561.7	609.8	674.4	689.1	716.1
Imports, c.i.f.	71.. d	...	...	...	...	...	...	...	...	547.8	703.7	790.8	928.1	975.2	1,095.5	1,839.7

Exchange Rates

1987	1988	1989	1990	1991	1992	1993	1994	1995	1996	1997	1998	1999	2000	2001	
End of Period															
...	...	...	19.92	56.36	144.47	†544.63	604.51	704.03	997.24	1,097.16	1,270.04	1,471.84	1,429.29	1,384.92	Market Rate .... **aa**
End of Period (ae) Period Average (rf)															
...	...	...	14.00	39.40	105.07	†396.51	414.09	473.62	693.51	813.16	902.00	1,072.37	1,097.00	1,102.00	Market Rate .... **ae**
				9.52	42.56	....	†412.72	448.61	548.40	789.99	840.83	1,021.87	1,076.67	1,097.70	Market Rate .... **rf**

Fund Position

1987	1988	1989	1990	1991	1992	1993	1994	1995	1996	1997	1998	1999	2000	2001	
End of Period															
				25.00	37.10	37.10	37.10	37.10	37.10	37.10	37.10	51.10	51.10	51.10	Quota **2f.s**
				.03	.01	.02	1.98	1.70	.30	.52	.34	.12	.01	.01	SDRs **1b.s**
				—	.01	.01	—	—	—	—	—	.02	.04	.06	Reserve Position in the Fund **1c.s**
				11.25	13.75	23.03	37.87	31.62	30.31	35.25	34.32	37.47	38.58	37.27	Total Fund Cred.&Loans Outstg. **2tl**

International Liquidity

1987	1988	1989	1990	1991	1992	1993	1994	1995	1996	1997	1998	1999	2000	2001	
End of Period															
				....	16.35	59.74	81.39	117.03	107.44	175.71	94.09	136.49	178.77	205.70	Total Reserves Minus Gold **1l.d**
				.04	.01	.03	2.89	2.52	.43	.70	.48	.16	.01	.02	SDRs **1b.d**
					.01	.01	.01	.01	.01	.01	.01	.03	.05	.08	Reserve Position in the Fund **1c.d**
				.14	16.33	59.70	78.49	114.50	107.00	175.00	93.60	136.30	178.70	205.60	Foreign Exchange **1d.d**
.03	.03	.03	.04	.14	.02	.02	.03	.10	.15	.08	.03	—	.08	.18	Gold (Million Fine Troy Ounces) **1ad**
18.50	19.70	19.00	22.90	49.70	24.20	5.31	11.00	34.50	53.60	24.60	9.10	.40	23.31	50.91	Gold (National Valuation) **1and**
				.27	.13	26.13	28.77	30.17	16.04	4.50	—	5.30	—	—	Monetary Authorities: Other Liab. .... **4..d**
				81.59	19.90	41.17	41.71	53.66	60.86	81.68	28.95	38.90	48.85	47.50	Deposit Money Banks: Assets **7a.d**
				169.52	62.02	11.67	11.90	14.06	12.38	15.06	22.14	9.13	10.20	11.58	Liabilities **7b.d**

Monetary Authorities

1987	1988	1989	1990	1991	1992	1993	1994	1995	1996	1997	1998	1999	2000	2001	
End of Period															
				1,991	1,033	25,630	40,380	60,836	67,814	113,878	114,319	174,385	210,591	227,812	Foreign Assets **11**
				714	1,985	7,477	13,661	4,520	38,953	23,980	26,111	24,136	21,443	13,570	Claims on Central Government **12a**
				1,529	6,153	6,637	10,375	7,740	1,712	3,093	5,631	6,651	4,777	7,348	Claims on Deposit Money Banks **12e**
				2,067	5,015	14,266	29,081	37,508	51,167	62,967	74,491	112,062	134,689	143,780	Reserve Money **14**
				1,694	1,839	8,751	18,946	25,591	40,136	49,768	56,446	87,281	100,910	109,131	*of which: Currency Outside DMBs* **14a**
				—	—	1,500	2,106	830	—	19,296	11,715	21,200	21,080	50,000	Liabs. of Central Bank: Securities **16ac**
				645	2,000	22,899	34,804	36,548	41,343	42,328	43,585	60,832	55,148	51,622	Foreign Liabilities **16c**
				784	1,202	580	2,465	9,500	8,388	14,417	3,673	4,833	19,289	16,930	Central Government Deposits **16d**
				3,285	3,700	2,980	4,998	7,998	24,004	37,082	41,049	37,921	44,431	41,992	Capital Accounts **17a**
				-2,548	-2,747	-2,481	-9,039	-19,289	-16,422	-35,140	-28,452	-31,676	-37,826	-55,594	Other Items (Net) **17r**

Deposit Money Banks

1987	1988	1989	1990	1991	1992	1993	1994	1995	1996	1997	1998	1999	2000	2001	
End of Period															
				345	3,023	5,690	10,319	12,531	17,848	13,457	17,921	24,171	33,858	34,637	Reserves **20**
				—	—	1,500	2,106	830	—	19,055	11,697	21,200	21,080	49,651	Claims on Mon.Author.: Securities **20c**
				3,215	2,091	16,325	17,272	25,412	42,207	66,416	26,116	41,711	53,591	52,341	Foreign Assets **21**
				1,358	2,793	513	737	643	10,472	35,451	38,328	39,269	43,371	32,458	Claims on Central Government **22a**
				9,501	11,789	16,938	12,193	10,883	8,660	7,963	10,151	4,661	5,929	9,823	Claims on Nonfin.Pub.Enterprises **22c**
				3,351	7,340	14,675	40,763	51,838	59,763	44,256	77,293	75,821	83,959	139,989	Claims on Private Sector **22d**
				5,592	5,790	9,756	14,104	17,045	20,702	26,341	26,136	27,544	29,842	46,995	Demand Deposits **24**
				2,601	5,412	24,216	43,906	59,408	58,757	93,957	84,668	105,341	128,068	174,909	Time, Savings,& Fgn.Currency Dep. **25**
				—	—	—	—	—	287	29	26	24	—	—	Money Market Instruments **26aa**
				—	—	—	—	—	15,821	6,430	6,938	3,604	5,814	7,699	Restricted Deposits **26b**
				6,679	6,517	4,629	4,926	6,660	8,585	12,246	19,973	9,794	11,193	12,758	Foreign Liabilities **26c**
				1,186	1,950	7,498	8,451	16,655	21,768	33,258	20,081	24,126	26,732	35,927	Central Government Deposits **26d**
				1,523	6,288	5,391	10,152	7,402	18,574	763	4,459	1,900	1,647	4,094	Credit from Monetary Authorities **26g**
				2,139	3,782	11,460	15,892	18,725	4,789	28,518	34,167	41,568	50,527	62,730	Capital Accounts **27a**
				-1,950	-2,702	-7,307	-14,041	-23,758	-10,334	-14,944	-14,943	-7,070	-12,034	-26,214	Other Items (Net) **27r**

Monetary Survey

1987	1988	1989	1990	1991	1992	1993	1994	1995	1996	1997	1998	1999	2000	2001	
End of Period															
				-2,119	-5,394	14,427	17,920	43,040	60,093	125,718	76,876	145,470	197,841	215,773	Foreign Assets (Net) **31n**
				12,957	20,757	31,535	56,446	41,730	93,206	67,882	137,089	119,493	109,584	144,015	Domestic Credit **32**
				102	1,627	-87	3,483	-20,992	19,270	11,755	40,685	34,446	18,793	-6,829	Claims on Central Govt. (Net) **32an**
				9,501	11,789	16,938	12,193	10,883	8,660	7,963	10,151	4,661	5,929	9,823	Claims on Nonfin.Pub.Enterprises **32c**
				3,354	7,341	14,684	40,770	51,839	65,277	48,164	86,253	80,386	84,862	141,021	Claims on Private Sector **32d**
				7,314	7,641	18,547	33,050	42,637	60,838	76,109	82,582	114,826	130,751	156,126	Money **34**
				2,601	5,412	24,216	43,906	59,408	58,757	93,957	84,668	105,341	128,068	174,909	Quasi-Money **35**
				—	—	—	—	—	287	29	26	24	—	—	Money Market Instruments **36aa**
				—	—	—	—	—	—	241	18	—	—	349	Liabs. of Central Bank: Securities **36ac**
				—	—	—	—	—	15,821	6,430	6,938	3,604	5,814	7,699	Restricted Deposits **36b**
				5,424	7,483	14,440	20,891	26,723	28,794	65,599	75,216	79,489	94,958	104,722	Capital Accounts **37a**
				-4,501	-5,172	-11,241	-23,480	-43,998	-11,198	-48,764	-35,483	-38,322	-52,165	-84,017	Other Items (Net) **37r**
				9,915	13,053	42,763	76,956	102,045	119,595	170,066	167,250	220,167	258,819	331,035	Money plus Quasi-Money **35l**

Interest Rates

1987	1988	1989	1990	1991	1992	1993	1994	1995	1996	1997	1998	1999	2000	2001	
Percent per Annum															
						628.8	180.0	150.0	109.0	45.5	23.3	11.4	8.7	8.6	Bank Rate (End of Period) **60**
300.0	300.0	300.0	300.0	400.0	500.0	125.2	101.1	60.1	36.4	37.9	24.3	19.8	13.8	13.2	Deposit Rate (End of Period) **60l**
						300.0	233.6	114.9	91.9	74.8	40.0	37.7	30.3	31.8	Lending Rate (End of Period) **60p**

Prices, Production, Labor

1987	1988	1989	1990	1991	1992	1993	1994	1995	1996	1997	1998	1999	2000	2001	
Period Averages															
					9.2	34.0	63.8	100.0	†149.3	203.9	223.0	239.9	....	....	Consumer Prices **64**
94.2	95.3	99.4	100.0	228.9	348.7	....									Wages: Avg. Earnings ('90=100) **65**
99.8	103.3	106.0	100.0	84.9	72.4	63.0	65.3	....							Industrial Production ('90=100) **66**
95.1	101.3	101.3	100.0	98.4	97.9	....									Industrial Employment ('90=100) **67**

International Transactions

1987	1988	1989	1990	1991	1992	1993	1994	1995	1996	1997	1998	1999	2000	2001	
Millions of US Dollars															
717.9	739.1	721.5	660.7	348.0	388.5	382.6	356.1	473.3	424.3	451.5	345.2	233.3	....	....	Exports .... **70..d**
1,104.6	1,113.6	963.0	924.0	360.9	418.3	379.0	258.4	415.3	450.9	468.3	503.3	425.8	....	....	Imports, c.i.f. .... **71..d**

Mongolia

		1972	1973	1974	1975	1976	1977	1978	1979	1980	1981	1982	1983	1984	1985	1986
Balance of Payments															*Millions of US Dollars:*	
Current Account, n.i.e.	78al d	...	...	...	...	...	...	...	...	...	−807.5	−845.5	−824.1	−740.0	−813.5	−1,060.6
Goods: Exports f.o.b.	78aa d	...	...	...	...	...	...	...	...	...	438.1	518.6	556.8	596.2	566.9	740.9
Goods: Imports f.o.b.	78ab d	...	...	...	...	...	...	...	...	...	−1,240.7	−1,352.5	−1,362.3	−1,308.8	−1,365.7	−1,692.0
Trade Balance	78ac d	...	...	...	...	...	...	...	...	...	−802.6	−833.9	−805.5	−712.6	−798.8	−951.1
Services: Credit	78ad d	...	...	...	...	...	...	...	...	...	37.3	48.5	55.3	52.6	70.1	84.2
Services: Debit	78ae d	...	...	...	...	...	...	...	...	...	−31.2	−39.6	−42.7	−40.6	−39.7	−191.8
Balance on Goods & Services	78af d	...	...	...	...	...	...	...	...	...	−796.5	−825.0	−792.9	−700.6	−768.4	−1,058.7
Income: Credit	78ag d	...	...	...	...	...	...	...	...	...	.2	.2	—	.1	.1	.1
Income: Debit	78ah d	...	...	...	...	...	...	...	...	...	−11.1	−20.6	−31.1	−39.1	−45.1	−1.8
Balance on Gds, Serv. & Inc.	78ai d	...	...	...	...	...	...	...	...	...	−807.4	−845.4	−824.0	−739.6	−813.4	−1,060.4
Current Transfers, n.i.e.: Credit	78aj d	...	...	...	...	...	...	...	...	...	—	—	—	—	—	—
Current Transfers: Debit	78ak d	...	...	...	...	...	...	...	...	...	−.1	−.1	−.1	−.4	−.1	−.2
Capital Account, n.i.e.	78bc d	...	...	...	...	...	...	...	...	...	—	—	—	—	—	—
Capital Account, n.i.e.: Credit	78ba d	...	...	...	...	...	...	...	...	...	—	—	—	—	—	—
Capital Account: Debit	78bb d	...	...	...	...	...	...	...	...	...	—	—	—	—	—	—
Financial Account, n.i.e.	78bj d	...	...	...	...	...	...	...	...	...	807.5	867.3	739.3	742.9	754.5	1,086.6
Direct Investment Abroad	78bd d	...	...	...	...	...	...	...	...	...	—	—	—	—	—	—
Dir. Invest. in Rep. Econ., n.i.e.	78be d	...	...	...	...	...	...	...	...	...	—	—	—	—	—	—
Portfolio Investment Assets	78bf d	...	...	...	...	...	...	...	...	...	—	—	—	—	—	—
Equity Securities	78bk d	...	...	...	...	...	...	...	...	...	—	—	—	—	—	—
Debt Securities	78bl d	...	...	...	...	...	...	...	...	...	—	—	—	—	—	—
Portfolio Investment Liab., n.i.e.	78bg d	...	...	...	...	...	...	...	...	...	—	—	—	—	—	—
Equity Securities	78bm d	...	...	...	...	...	...	...	...	...	—	—	—	—	—	—
Debt Securities	78bn d	...	...	...	...	...	...	...	...	...	—	—	—	—	—	—
Financial Derivatives Assets	78bw d	...	...	...	...	...	...	...	...	...	—	—	—	—	—	—
Financial Derivatives Liabilities	78bx d	...	...	...	...	...	...	...	...	...	—	—	—	—	—	—
Other Investment Assets	78bh d	...	...	...	...	...	...	...	...	...	—	—	—	—	—	—
Monetary Authorities	78bo d	...	...	...	...	...	...	...	...	...	—	—	—	—	—	—
General Government	78bp d	...	...	...	...	...	...	...	...	...	—	—	—	—	—	—
Banks	78bq d	...	...	...	...	...	...	...	...	...	—	—	—	—	—	—
Other Sectors	78br d	...	...	...	...	...	...	...	...	...	—	—	—	—	—	—
Other Investment Liab., n.i.e.	78bi d	...	...	...	...	...	...	...	...	...	807.5	867.3	739.3	742.9	754.5	1,086.6
Monetary Authorities	78bs d	...	...	...	...	...	...	...	...	...	.6	8.0	−1.3	−3.1	.6	29.8
General Government	78bt d	...	...	...	...	...	...	...	...	...	806.9	859.3	740.6	746.0	753.9	1,056.8
Banks	78bu d	...	...	...	...	...	...	...	...	...	—	—	—	—	—	—
Other Sectors	78bv d	...	...	...	...	...	...	...	...	...	—	—	—	—	—	—
Net Errors and Omissions	78ca d	...	...	...	...	...	...	...	...	...	−1.2	−19.9	80.4	10.7	83.6	−11.3
Overall Balance	78cb d	...	...	...	...	...	...	...	...	...	−1.2	1.9	−4.4	13.6	24.6	14.7
Reserves and Related Items	79da d	...	...	...	...	...	...	...	...	...	1.2	−1.9	4.4	−13.6	−24.6	−14.7
Reserve Assets	79db d	...	...	...	...	...	...	...	...	...	1.2	−1.9	4.4	−13.6	−24.6	−14.7
Use of Fund Credit and Loans	79dc d	...	...	...	...	...	...	...	...	...	—	—	—	—	—	—
Exceptional Financing	79de d	...	...	...	...	...	...	...	...	...	...	...				
Government Finance															*Millions of Togrogs:*	
Deficit (−) or Surplus	80	...	...	...	...	...	...	...	...	...	...	...	...	...	−783	−1,696
Total Revenue and Grants	81y	...	...	...	...	...	...	...	...	...	...	...	...	...	4,918	4,360
Revenue	81	...	...	...	...	...	...	...	...	...	...	...	...	...	4,918	4,360
Grants	81z	...	...	...	...	...	...	...	...	...	...	...	...	...	—	—
Exp. & Lending Minus Repay.	82z	...	...	...	...	...	...	...	...	...	...	...	...	...	5,701	6,056
Expenditure	82	...	...	...	...	...	...	...	...	...	...	...	...	...	5,701	6,056
Lending Minus Repayments	83	...	...	...	...	...	...	...	...	...	...	...	...	...	—	—
Total Financing	80h	...	...	...	...	...	...	...	...	...	...	...	...	...	783	1,696
Domestic	84a	...	...	...	...	...	...	...	...	...	...	...	...	...	−40	−292
Foreign	85a	...	...	...	...	...	...	...	...	...	...	...	...	...	823	1,988
Total Debt by Residence	88	...	...	...	...	...	...	...	...	...	...	...	...	...	...	...
Domestic	88a	...	...	...	...	...	...	...	...	...	...	...	...	...	...	...
Foreign	89a	...	...	...	...	...	...	...	...	...	...	...	...	...	...	...
National Accounts															*Millions of Togrogs*	
Gross Domestic Product (GDP)	99b	...	...	...	...	...	...	...	...	6,755	7,426	8,205	8,762	8,996	9,372	9,310
GDP Volume 1986 prices	99b. p	...	...	...	...	...	...	...	...	6,118	6,628	7,182	7,595	8,052	8,512	9,310
GDP Volume 1993 prices	99b. p	...	...	...	...	...	...	...	...	...	...	...	...	...	...	188,929
GDP Volume 1995 Prices	99b. p	...	...	...	...	...	...	...	...	...	...	...	...	...	...	...
GDP Volume (1995=100)	99bv p	...	...	...	...	...	...	...	...	68.7	74.4	80.6	85.3	90.4	95.6	104.5
GDP Deflator (1995=100)	99bi p	...	...	...	...	...	...	...	...	1.8	1.8	1.8	1.9	1.8	1.8	1.6
																Millions:
Population	99z	1.32	1.36	1.40	1.44	1.47	1.51	1.55	1.60	1.66	1.70	1.75	1.79	1.83	1.88	1.93

1987	1988	1989	1990	1991	1992	1993	1994	1995	1996	1997	1998	1999	2000	2001		
Minus Sign Indicates Debit															**Balance of Payments**	
−990.6	−1,033.3	−1,228.7	−639.5	−104.2	−55.7	31.1	46.4	38.9	−100.5	55.2	−128.5	−112.2	....	....	Current Account, n.i.e.	78al *d*
817.1	829.1	795.8	444.8	346.5	355.8	365.8	367.0	451.0	423.4	568.5	462.4	454.3	....	....	Goods: Exports f.o.b.	78aa *d*
−1,681.4	−1,701.9	−1,758.9	−941.7	−447.6	−384.9	−344.5	−333.3	−425.7	−459.7	−453.1	−524.2	−510.7	....	....	Goods: Imports f.o.b.	78ab *d*
−864.3	−872.8	−963.1	−496.9	−101.1	−29.1	21.3	33.7	25.3	−36.3	115.4	−61.8	−56.4	....	....	*Trade Balance*	78ac *d*
89.0	94.3	36.4	48.1	26.5	34.8	26.0	45.4	57.3	55.7	52.7	77.8	75.8	....	....	Services: Credit	78ad *d*
−203.7	−220.3	−257.0	−154.5	−66.3	−69.7	−66.9	−91.2	−95.4	−112.8	−105.1	−146.8	−145.7	....	....	Services: Debit	78ae *d*
−979.0	−998.8	−1,183.7	−603.3	−140.9	−64.0	−19.6	−12.1	−12.8	−93.4	63.0	−130.8	−126.3	....	....	*Balance on Goods & Services*	78af *d*
.2	.2	7.5	5.1	—	.2	.8	3.2	3.0	13.4	6.1	10.1	6.7	....	....	Income: Credit	78ag *d*
−11.5	−34.4	−56.4	−48.7	−4.9	−27.1	−21.0	−22.5	−28.4	−26.7	−18.1	−9.7	−6.6	....	....	Income: Debit	78ah *d*
−990.3	−1,033.0	−1,232.6	−646.9	−145.8	−90.9	−39.8	−31.4	−38.2	−106.7	51.0	−130.4	−126.2	....	....	*Balance on Gds, Serv. & Inc.*	78ai *d*
—	—	3.9	7.4	41.6	38.7	66.7	77.8	77.1	6.2	4.2	5.5	17.6	....	....	Current Transfers, n.i.e.: Credit	78aj *d*
−.3	−.3	—	—	—	−3.5	4.2	—	—	—	—	−3.6	−3.6	....	....	Current Transfers: Debit	78ak *d*
												—	....	....	Capital Account, n.i.e.	78bc *d*
												—			Capital Account, n.i.e.: Credit	78ba *d*
												—			Capital Account: Debit	78bb *d*
1,143.4	1,019.4	1,313.0	541.0	10.8	−44.0	−11.8	−39.0	−15.9	41.3	27.0	126.2	69.6	....	....	Financial Account, n.i.e.	78bj *d*
—	—	—	—	—	—	—	—	—	—	—	—	—	....	....	Direct Investment Abroad	78bd *d*
—	—	—	—	—	2.0	7.7	6.9	9.8	15.9	25.0	18.9	30.4	....	....	Dir. Invest. in Rep. Econ., n.i.e.	78be *d*
—	—	—	—	—	—	—	—	—	—	—	—		....		Portfolio Investment Assets	78bf *d*
—	—	—	—	—	—	—	—	—	—	—	—		....		Equity Securities	78bk *d*
—	—	—	—	—	—	—	—	—	—	—	—		....		Debt Securities	78bl *d*
—	—	—	—	—	—	—	—	1.0	—	—	—	—	....		Portfolio Investment Liab., n.i.e.	78bg *d*
—	—	—	—	—	—	—	—	—	—	—	—	—	....		Equity Securities	78bm *d*
—	—	—	—	—	—	—	—	1.0	—	—	—	—	....		Debt Securities	78bn *d*
—	....	—	—	—	—	—	—	....	—	—	....	—	....		Financial Derivatives Assets	78bw *d*
—	....	—	—	—	—	—	—	....	—	—	....	—	....		Financial Derivatives Liabilities	78bx *d*
—	—	—	−2.0	—	−64.0	−35.4	−51.0	−49.2	−76.4	−108.1	−54.8	−51.8	....		Other Investment Assets	78bh *d*
—	—	—	—	—	—	—	—	—	—	—	—	—	....		Monetary Authorities	78bo *d*
—	—	—	−2.0	—	—	—	—	—	—	—	—	—	....		General Government	78bp *d*
—	—	—	—	—	−11.6	−24.9	−15.3	−15.3	−9.3	−18.1	—	−14.8	....		Banks	78bq *d*
—	—	—	—	—	−52.4	−10.5	−35.7	−33.9	−67.1	−90.0	−54.8	−37.0	....		Other Sectors	78br *d*
1,143.4	1,019.4	1,313.0	543.0	10.8	18.0	15.9	5.1	22.5	101.8	110.1	162.1	91.0	....		Other Investment Liab., n.i.e.	78bi *d*
24.9	−89.1	84.6	26.3	−32.8	−69.8	−11.2	—	—	—	—	−5.2	—	....		Monetary Authorities	78bs *d*
1,118.5	1,108.5	1,228.4	516.7	36.2	45.6	32.5	7.9	22.5	56.1	79.3	80.8	91.4	....		General Government	78bt *d*
—	—	—	—	—	—	3.6	—	—	—	—	40.0	−4.8	....		Banks	78bu *d*
—	—	—	—	7.4	42.2	−9.0	−2.8	—	45.7	30.8	46.5	4.4	....		Other Sectors	78bv *d*
−76.5	14.6	45.4	−3.1	−36.4	17.4	−4.8	−1.0	9.1	−28.1	−75.6	−50.2	23.6	....		Net Errors and Omissions	78ca *d*
76.3	.7	129.7	−101.6	−129.8	−82.3	14.5	6.4	32.1	−87.3	6.6	−52.5	−19.0	....		*Overall Balance*	78cb *d*
−76.3	−.7	−129.7	101.6	129.8	82.3	−14.5	−6.4	−32.1	87.3	−6.6	52.5	19.0	....		Reserves and Related Items	79da *d*
−76.3	−.7	−129.7	101.6	51.2	72.3	−23.5	−27.4	−22.6	19.6	−61.2	−6.3	−40.6	....		Reserve Assets	79db *d*
—	—	—	—	15.3	3.5	13.1	21.1	−9.5	−1.8	6.7	−1.3	4.2	....		Use of Fund Credit and Loans	79dc *d*
—	—	—	—	63.3	6.5	−4.1	—	—	69.5	47.9	60.2	55.5	....		Exceptional Financing	79de *d*
Year Ending December 31															**Government Finance**	
−1,868	−2,061	−1,807	−1,449	−1,774	†−2,840	−27,706	−23,647	−29,185	−49,679	†−65,909	−94,913	−99,816		−63,227	Deficit (−) or Surplus	80
4,540	4,681	5,255	5,363	7,155	†9,896	48,637	65,267	113,568	126,725	†176,152	192,103	203,452		308,283	Total Revenue and Grants	81y
4,540	4,681	5,243	5,329	6,065	†8,672	45,610	62,002	108,483	122,316	†171,744	183,552	196,561		303,215	Revenue	81
—	—	12	34	1,090	†1,224	3,027	3,265	5,085	4,409	†4,408	8,551	6,891		5,068	Grants	81z
6,408	6,742	7,062	6,812	8,929	†12,736	76,343	88,914	142,753	176,404	†242,061	287,016	303,268		371,510	Exp. & Lending Minus Repay.	82z
6,408	6,742	7,062	6,812	8,929	†10,187	42,468	63,824	97,656	121,233	†176,436	201,279	232,795		306,037	Expenditure	82
—	—	—	—	—	†2,549	33,875	25,090	45,097	55,171	†65,625	85,737	70,473		65,473	Lending Minus Repayments	83
1,868	2,061	1,807	1,449	1,774	†2,840	27,707	23,648	29,185	49,679	†65,909	94,913	99,816		63,227	Total Financing	80h
−46	223	159	858	−647	†−470	−4,650	5,010	5,271	14,804	†−24,989	26,319	−6,020		−3,346	Domestic	84a
1,914	1,838	1,648	591	2,421	†3,310	32,357	18,638	23,914	34,875	†90,898	68,594	105,836		66,573	Foreign	85a
....	....	....	....	11,575	94,353	196,533	241,503	338,513	†563,499	691,175	886,401	993,940			Total Debt by Residence	88
....	....	....	....	1,063	233	5,281	233	30,393	†56,244	84,076	62,951	98,644			Domestic	88a
....	....	....	....	10,512	94,120	191,252	241,270	308,120	†507,255	607,099	823,450	895,296			Foreign	89a
Millions of Togrogs															**National Accounts**	
9,710	10,301	10,731	10,465	18,910	47,298	166,219	283,263	550,254	646,559	832,636	817,393	873,679	....	....	Gross Domestic Product (GDP)	99b
	195,461	205,440	214,028	208,642	....								....	....	GDP Volume 1986 prices	99b.*p*
....	....	....	....	....									....	....	GDP Volume 1993 prices	99b.*p*
			—	495,368	449,563	406,865	394,646	403,723	429,207	439,350	457,063	472,963	....	....	GDP Volume 1995 Prices	99b.*p*
108.1	113.6	118.4	115.4	104.7	94.8	91.9	94.1	100.0	102.4	106.5	110.2		....	....	GDP Volume (1995=100)	99bv *p*
1.6	1.6	1.6	1.6	3.3	9.1	32.9	54.7	100.0	114.8	142.1	134.8		....	....	GDP Deflator (1995=100)	99bi *p*
Midyear																
1.97	2.02	2.07	2.12	2.17	2.20	2.23	2.27	2.30	2.27	2.30	2.33	2.36	2.39	2.42	**Population**	99z

(See notes in the back of the book.)

Morocco

	1972	1973	1974	1975	1976	1977	1978	1979	1980	1981	1982	1983	1984	1985	1986
Exchange Rates														*Dirhams per SDR:*	
Official Rate .... aa	5.066	5.175	5.087	4.898	5.210	5.256	5.063	4.925	5.528	6.208	6.914	8.439	9.362	10.568	10.656
														Dirhams per US Dollar:	
Official Rate .... ae	4.666	4.290	4.155	4.184	4.484	4.327	3.886	3.739	4.334	5.333	6.268	8.061	9.551	9.621	8.712
Official Rate .... rf	4.592	4.107	4.370	4.052	4.419	4.503	4.167	3.899	3.937	5.172	6.023	7.111	8.811	10.062	9.104
												Index Numbers (1995=100):			
Official Rate .... ahx	185.9	208.3	195.4	210.8	193.3	189.6	205.2	219.0	217.2	165.9	142.1	121.0	97.2	84.9	93.8
Nominal Effective Exchange Rate ... ne c	....	....	....	....	....	....	....	103.9	105.2	97.3	97.3	94.3	87.1	82.5	76.4
Real Effective Exchange Rate ... re c	....	....	....	....	....	....	....	....	138.7	127.0	125.1	117.0	110.5	103.2	98.6
Fund Position														*Millions of SDRs:*	
Quota .... 2f. s	113	113	113	113	113	113	150	150	225	225	225	307	307	307	307
SDRs .... 1b. s	17	16	16	15	10	9	13	15	—	1	1	1	1	—	16
Reserve Position in the Fund ...... 1c. s	28	28	28	28	—	—	—	—	—	—	—	—	—	—	—
Total Fund Cred.&Loans Outstg. ... 2tl	—	—	—	—	115	128	220	232	358	497	898	985	1,107	1,161	894
International Liquidity											*Millions of US Dollars Unless Otherwise Indicated:*				
Total Reserves minus Gold .... 1l. d	214	241	391	352	467	505	618	557	399	230	218	107	49	115	211
SDRs .... 1b. d	18	20	19	17	12	10	16	20	1	2	1	1	1	—	19
Reserve Position in the Fund ...... 1c. d	31	34	35	33	—	—	—	—	—	—	—	—	—	—	—
Foreign Exchange .... 1d. d	165	187	337	302	455	495	602	537	398	228	217	106	48	115	192
Gold (Million Fine Troy Ounces) 1ad	.600	.600	.608	.608	.608	.632	.680	.704	.704	.704	.704	.704	.704	.704	.704
Gold (National Valuation) .... 1an d	....	26	26	26	24	26	31	33	29	23	20	15	13	13	14
Monetary Authorities: Other Assets .. 3.. d	13	27	16	25	17	9	15	5	4	3	3	2	2	−13	....
Monetary Authorities: Other Liab. ... 4.. d	5	1	10	13	29	23	−7	−56	−84	−52	−85	−33	−79	−44	−15
Deposit Money Banks: Assets ... 7a. d	59	75	91	86	88	97	127	215	246	326	282	266	255	322	388
Liabilities ... 7b. d	21	18	23	23	27	39	41	83	69	68	35	38	34	49	85
Other Banking Insts.: Liabilities ..... 7f. d	63	79	94	166	263	466	647	680	623	586	477	457	439	594	891
Monetary Authorities														*Millions of Dirhams:*	
Foreign Assets 11	1,162	1,241	1,795	1,714	2,276	2,340	2,584	2,226	1,871	1,366	1,507	1,001	612	1,247	1,987
Claims on Central Government 12a	1,724	1,919	2,184	3,019	3,727	5,209	6,389	7,266	†9,516	12,062	13,676	17,211	18,548	18,766	15,584
Claims on Private Sector 12d	546	670	536	655	824	627	827	1,237	†601	542	809	1,189	1,380	3,383	7,663
Claims on Deposit Money Banks ... 12e	284	411	769	592	1,153	1,200	1,160	1,931	1,631	2,662	2,870	3,041	4,123	3,753	5,315
Reserve Money 14	3,326	3,815	4,607	5,298	6,450	7,450	8,595	10,013	10,532	11,952	12,777	14,472	16,137	17,351	21,471
of which: Currency Outside DMBs 14a	3,012	3,487	4,167	4,749	5,839	6,762	7,816	9,223	10,008	11,347	12,313	13,875	15,099	16,589	19,103
Foreign Liabilities 16c	31	26	94	75	735	850	1,335	1,382	2,399	3,688	6,443	8,967	10,519	12,656	9,986
Central Government Deposits 16d	47	48	63	72	68	137	95	113	125	151	171	184	220	482	560
Capital Accounts 17a	....	....	....	....	....	....	....	....	....	....	....	....	....	....	....
Other Items (Net) 17r	313	351	520	535	727	939	934	1,152	562	841	−529	−1,181	−2,214	−3,348	−1,476
Deposit Money Banks														*Millions of Dirhams:*	
Reserves 20	246	272	334	434	511	571	674	733	389	474	417	434	816	695	2,269
Foreign Assets 21	276	315	380	358	394	421	492	803	1,066	1,737	†1,769	2,148	2,432	3,100	3,378
Claims on Central Government 22a	1,181	1,406	1,986	2,496	2,761	3,335	5,410	6,040	7,165	8,077	8,577	12,144	12,496	16,977	24,646
Claims on Private Sector 22d	2,798	3,406	4,537	5,668	6,869	8,116	8,785	9,753	11,038	13,066	†16,264	18,654	21,385	22,920	....
Claims on Other Financial Insts 22f	....	....	....	....	....	....	....	....	....	....	689	392	142	242	....
Demand Deposits 24	3,544	4,313	5,346	6,881	7,772	9,362	10,750	11,741	12,970	15,062	†15,021	18,064	19,366	21,378	25,978
Time Deposits 25	547	620	1,017	1,437	1,756	2,179	2,959	3,681	4,649	5,872	†8,691	11,412	13,491	16,592	18,819
Foreign Liabilities 26c	100	77	96	96	120	170	160	309	300	360	†217	303	323	472	740
Credit from Monetary Authorities ... 26g	284	411	769	592	1,153	1,200	1,160	1,931	1,661	2,674	2,870	3,041	3,734	3,753	7,490
Capital Accounts 27a	....	....	....	....	....	....	....	....	....	....	....	....	....	....	....
Other Items (Net) 27r	26	−23	9	−51	−266	−467	332	−334	78	−614	916	955	357	1,739	....
Post Office: Checking Deposits ..... 24.. i	362	361	547	636	687	853	912	1,118	1,169	1,371	1,468	959	1,010	951	1,001
Treasury: Checking Deposits ..... 24.. r	363	359	708	479	705	918	1,182	1,211	1,042	1,127	1,278	1,182	1,075	1,319	1,523
Monetary Survey														*Millions of Dirhams:*	
Foreign Assets (Net) 31n	1,307	1,452	1,985	1,901	1,815	1,741	1,580	1,337	239	−946	†−3,385	−6,121	−7,798	−8,781	−5,361
Domestic Credit 32	6,927	8,072	10,434	12,881	15,505	18,921	23,409	26,512	†31,215	36,939	43,719	52,321	56,759	64,938	72,114
Claims on Central Govt. (Net) 32an	3,583	3,997	5,361	6,558	7,812	10,178	13,798	15,522	†18,766	22,486	24,827	31,312	32,909	37,531	42,194
Claims on Private Sector 32d	3,344	4,076	5,073	6,323	7,693	8,743	9,612	10,990	12,449	14,453	†17,073	19,843	22,765	26,303	....
Claims on Other Financial Insts 32f	....	....	....	....	....	....	....	....	....	....	1,818	1,166	1,086	1,104	....
Money 34	7,336	8,572	10,869	12,838	15,102	18,002	20,785	23,352	25,312	29,016	†30,064	34,197	36,779	40,289	47,675
Quasi-Money 35	547	620	1,017	1,437	1,756	2,179	2,959	3,681	4,649	5,872	†8,691	11,412	13,491	16,592	18,819
Other Items (Net) 37r	352	333	534	507	461	481	1,245	816	1,493	1,106	1,579	593	−1,309	−724	259
Money plus Quasi-Money 35l	7,883	9,192	11,886	14,274	16,858	20,181	23,744	27,033	29,961	34,888	†38,755	45,608	50,270	56,881	66,494
Other Banking Institutions														*Millions of Dirhams:*	
Reserves 40	88	200	201	303	293	488	663	405	378	369	359	622	576	397	781
Claims on Central Government 42a	257	292	260	322	385	515	600	844	1,062	1,138	1,726	1,827	1,683	2,081	2,516
Claims on Official Entities............ 42bx	101	105	163	215	243	292	280	326	392	408	387	418	462	552	800
Claims on Private Sector 42d	1,699	1,809	2,236	2,966	3,815	4,853	5,981	6,769	7,578	8,782	10,024	11,418	13,267	15,702	18,096
Time Deposits 45	882	1,006	1,190	1,450	1,588	2,039	2,589	3,049	3,625	3,967	4,609	5,659	6,508	7,342	8,597
Bonds 46ab	138	206	320	436	421	480	651	822	1,038	1,617	2,251	3,179	3,556	4,219	5,138
Long-Term Foreign Liabilities........ 46cl	293	333	389	696	1,180	2,015	2,516	2,542	2,702	3,128	2,990	3,684	4,196	5,712	7,763
Central Govt. Lending Funds 46f	160	139	173	270	390	358	347	375	373	404	399	424	608	606	589
Credit from Monetary Authorities ... 46g	351	375	396	469	563	632	543	719	780	834	1,123	796	944	936	—
Credit from Deposit Money Banks ... 46h	86	76	52	71	124	151	134	110	123	337	690	392	142	242	303
Capital Accounts 47a	240	310	364	439	502	591	700	751	855	882	1,104	1,087	1,366	1,539	2,066
Other Items (Net) 47r	−5	−39	−24	−25	−32	−118	44	−24	−86	−472	−670	−936	−1,332	−1,864	−2,263
Liquid Liabilities 55l	8,677	9,998	12,875	15,421	18,153	21,732	25,670	29,677	33,208	38,486	†43,364	51,267	56,778	64,223	75,091
Interest Rates														*Percent Per Annum*	
Discount Rate (End of Period) 60	3.50	3.50	3.75	4.50	4.50	4.50	4.50	4.50	4.88	6.00	6.75	7.00	7.00	8.13	8.50
Money Market Rate.................. 60b	....	....	....	....	....	....	....	....	9.00	9.00	10.92	....	....	9.41	9.44
Deposit Rate 60l	....	....	....	....	....	....	4.5	4.5	4.9	6.0	6.4	6.5	6.5	8.0	8.5
Lending Rate 60p	....	....	....	....	....	....	7.0	7.0	7.0	7.0	7.0	7.0	7.0	7.8	8.7
Govt.Bond Yield: Long-Term 61	....	....	....	....	....	....	....	....	....	....	....	....	....	....	....
Med.-Term 61a	....	....	....	....	....	....	....	....	....	....	....	....	....	....	....

	1987	1988	1989	1990	1991	1992	1993	1994	1995	1996	1997	1998	1999	2000	2001
Exchange Rates — *End of Period*															
Official Rate ... aa	11.066	11.049	10.673	11.442	11.658	12.442	13.257	13.080	12.589	12.653	13.107	13.031	13.845	13.836	14.528
End of Period (ae) Period Average (rf)															
Official Rate ... ae	7.800	8.211	8.122	8.043	8.150	9.049	9.651	8.960	8.469	8.800	9.714	9.255	10.087	10.619	11.560
Official Rate ... rf	8.359	8.209	8.488	8.242	8.707	8.538	9.299	9.203	8.540	8.716	9.527	9.604	9.804	10.626	11.303
Period Averages															
Official Rate ... ahx	102.2	104.1	100.6	103.7	98.3	100.1	91.8	92.9	100.0	98.0	89.7	88.9	87.1	80.4	75.6
Nominal Effective Exchange Rate ... nec	75.9	78.6	84.8	84.5	85.3	87.5	92.5	98.6	100.0	100.7	102.6	103.8	105.5	108.9	106.4
Real Effective Exchange Rate ... rec	95.2	93.9	94.0	88.7	90.7	91.3	93.9	96.9	100.0	100.8	101.7	104.2	105.2	108.2	103.7
Fund Position — *End of Period*															
Quota ... 2f. s	307	307	307	307	307	428	428	428	428	428	428	428	588	588	588
SDRs ... 1b. s	3	—	—	1	103	56	25	18	17	5	1	2	62	92	98
Reserve Position in the Fund ... 1c. s	—	—	—	—	—	30	30	30	30	30	30	30	70	70	70
Total Fund Cred.&Loans Outstg. ... 2tl	789	711	647	527	402	319	207	101	35	2	—	—	—	—	—
International Liquidity — *End of Period*															
Total Reserves minus Gold ... 1l.d	411	547	488	2,066	3,100	3,584	3,655	4,352	3,601	3,794	3,993	4,435	5,689	4,823	8,474
SDRs ... 1b.d	4	—	—	1	147	77	34	26	26	7	1	3	85	119	123
Reserve Position in the Fund ... 1c.d	—	—	—	—	—	42	42	44	45	44	41	43	97	92	89
Foreign Exchange ... 1d.d	407	547	488	2,065	2,953	3,465	3,579	4,281	3,530	3,743	3,951	4,389	5,507	4,612	8,262
Gold (Million Fine Troy Ounces) ... 1ad	.704	.704	.704	.704	.704	.704	.704	.704	.704	.704	.704	.704	.704	.706	.707
Gold (National Valuation) ... 1and	16	15	15	16	15	14	202	218	230	222	201	211	193	184	169
Monetary Authorities: Other Assets ... 3..d	....	....	....	....	....	....	....	....	....	....	....	....	....	....	....
Monetary Authorities: Other Liab. ... 4..d	23	44	38	44	144	139	53	47	41	62	84	78	82	84	80
Deposit Money Banks: Assets ... 7a.d	439	495	569	781	690	598	518	755	653	665	†381	496	477	599	557
Deposit Money Banks: Liabilities ... 7b.d	70	103	127	226	267	354	386	672	442	520	†351	462	457	407	336
Other Banking Insts.: Liabilities ... 7f.d	1,170	1,171	1,187	1,448	1,585	1,523	1,450	1,534	1,589	1,452	....	....	....	....	....
Monetary Authorities — *End of Period*															
Foreign Assets ... 11	3,351	4,639	4,111	†16,760	25,410	32,570	37,243	41,001	32,509	35,402	40,808	43,070	59,392	53,224	99,920
Claims on Central Government ... 12a	13,224	13,881	13,693	†13,435	16,994	9,861	8,752	8,305	18,389	19,179	†27,860	27,459	21,129	24,310	15,993
Claims on Private Sector ... 12d	8,606	8,901	8,814	†7,661	7,535	7,611	8,803	8,416	9,129	9,075	†1,250	3,495	1,393	7,243	71
Claims on Deposit Money Banks ... 12e	5,577	5,969	10,948	†2,118	2,699	1,828	599	512	500	1,250	†—	—	—	—	—
Reserve Money ... 14	22,636	26,200	30,839	†38,341	47,847	44,023	47,796	50,746	53,384	57,467	†62,557	66,999	75,911	78,355	91,149
of which: Currency Outside DMBs ... 14a	20,502	22,446	25,413	29,543	34,298	35,745	37,202	41,107	43,261	46,581	48,662	50,644	56,713	58,169	66,025
Foreign Liabilities ... 16c	9,284	8,388	7,248	†6,381	5,853	5,227	3,256	1,745	787	577	†817	725	826	893	927
Central Government Deposits ... 16d	424	481	407	†482	517	498	523	605	633	816	†786	826	533	807	807
Capital Accounts ... 17a	....	....	....	....	....	....	....	....	....	....	4,799	4,877	4,977	5,107	5,252
Other Items (Net) ... 17r	−1,586	−1,679	−928	†−5,230	−1,579	2,122	3,822	5,139	5,722	6,046	†959	597	−332	−384	17,849
Deposit Money Banks — *End of Period*															
Reserves ... 20	2,050	3,497	5,007	†8,086	12,633	7,109	8,671	8,293	9,018	9,419	†11,936	13,380	17,100	18,980	27,466
Foreign Assets ... 21	3,428	4,068	4,618	†6,281	5,621	5,408	5,002	6,765	5,533	5,855	†3,703	4,592	4,812	6,356	6,440
Claims on Central Government ... 22a	28,810	30,428	34,453	†29,766	28,293	39,545	44,652	50,746	49,633	50,048	58,616	58,614	54,917	61,729	73,161
Claims on Private Sector ... 22d	....	....	....	†34,095	48,500	56,581	62,351	70,408	81,777	90,545	†151,203	167,602	183,531	199,576	208,026
Claims on Other Financial Insts ... 22f	....	....	....	†1,101	1,011	994	355	1,409	1,637	627	†25,580	29,834	33,017	34,309	35,883
Demand Deposits ... 24	28,390	32,128	34,732	†54,171	61,757	66,636	70,033	79,099	84,606	87,323	†116,054	126,767	140,895	156,545	181,092
Time Deposits ... 25	21,056	24,627	28,458	†24,143	30,383	36,425	42,687	45,958	50,552	54,962	†64,121	65,114	69,389	76,281	84,294
Foreign Liabilities ... 26c	549	842	1,028	†1,819	2,179	3,205	3,729	6,020	3,745	4,579	†3,409	4,276	4,605	4,322	3,881
Credit from Monetary Authorities ... 26g	7,682	8,244	12,492	†5,862	8,398	2,566	965	1,108	1,232	2,508	†1,209	3,381	1,346	7,161	7
Capital Accounts ... 27a	....	....	....	....	....	....	....	....	....	....	38,743	44,973	47,759	48,890	57,336
Other Items (Net) ... 27r	....	....	....	†−6,666	−6,659	805	3,617	5,436	7,463	7,122	†27,502	29,511	29,383	27,751	24,366
Post Office: Checking Deposits ... 24.. i	1,129	1,207	1,406	1,420	1,777	1,520	1,625	1,833	1,701	1,721	1,871	....	....	....	....
Treasury: Checking Deposits ... 24.. r	1,979	3,468	4,077	4,417	4,693	5,041	4,906	4,950	5,088	6,311	6,202	....	....	....	....
Monetary Survey — *End of Period*															
Foreign Assets (Net) ... 31n	−3,054	−523	453	†14,841	22,999	29,546	35,260	40,002	33,509	36,101	†40,285	42,661	58,773	54,365	101,552
Domestic Credit ... 32	77,243	84,026	92,644	†91,413	108,782	120,655	130,921	145,462	166,721	176,690	†263,723	286,178	293,454	326,360	332,327
Claims on Central Govt. (Net) ... 32an	44,718	48,503	53,222	†48,556	51,240	55,469	59,412	65,229	74,178	76,443	†85,690	85,247	75,513	85,232	88,347
Claims on Private Sector ... 32d	....	....	....	†41,756	56,035	64,192	71,154	78,824	90,906	99,620	†153,279	171,990	187,165	207,797	208,718
Claims on Other Financial Insts ... 32f	....	....	....	†1,101	1,507	994	355	1,409	1,637	627	†24,754	28,941	30,776	33,331	35,262
Money ... 34	52,035	59,578	66,046	†90,659	103,709	110,082	115,458	128,284	135,964	143,818	†166,843	179,795	200,597	216,503	249,726
Quasi-Money ... 35	21,056	24,627	28,458	†24,143	30,383	36,425	42,687	45,958	50,552	54,962	†64,121	65,114	69,389	76,281	84,294
Other Items (Net) ... 37r	1,098	−702	−1,407	†−8,548	−2,311	3,694	8,036	11,222	13,714	14,011	†73,044	83,930	82,241	87,941	99,859
Money plus Quasi-Money ... 35l	73,091	84,205	94,504	†114,802	134,092	146,507	158,145	174,242	186,516	198,780	†230,964	244,909	269,986	292,784	334,020
Other Banking Institutions — *End of Period*															
Reserves ... 40	464	709	474	594	899	1,428	1,938	1,383	1,301	1,469	....	....	....	....	....
Claims on Central Government ... 42a	2,662	3,545	5,421	5,881	6,567	7,191	7,980	10,966	13,063	16,164	....	....	....	....	....
Claims on Official Entities ... 42bx	204	262	162	42	1	—	—	—	—	—	....	....	....	....	....
Claims on Private Sector ... 42d	21,281	23,786	26,408	30,674	34,525	37,601	39,365	41,311	44,167	47,249	....	....	....	....	....
Time Deposits ... 45	9,294	10,890	12,978	15,014	17,410	19,670	21,836	24,606	28,574	32,745	....	....	....	....	....
Bonds ... 46ab	5,281	6,302	7,476	8,432	8,164	9,663	10,134	10,628	10,987	11,848	....	....	....	....	....
Long-Term Foreign Liabilities ... 46cl	9,124	9,613	9,641	11,643	12,917	13,779	13,997	13,744	13,461	12,776	....	....	....	....	....
Central Govt. Lending Funds ... 46f	594	610	274	143	216	617	547	393	277	271	....	....	....	....	....
Credit from Monetary Authorities ... 46g	—	—	145	53	554	14	5	8	—	—	....	....	....	....	....
Credit from Deposit Money Banks ... 46h	436	484	377	269	988	515	508	604	623	683	....	....	....	....	....
Capital Accounts ... 47a	2,715	2,903	3,978	4,713	5,271	5,958	6,911	8,093	9,122	10,068	....	....	....	....	....
Other Items (Net) ... 47r	−2,833	−2,500	−2,404	−3,076	−3,528	−3,996	−4,655	−4,416	−4,513	−3,509	....	....	....	....	....
Liquid Liabilities ... 55l	82,385	95,095	107,482	†129,816	151,502	166,177	179,981	198,848	215,090	231,525	....	....	....	....	....
Interest Rates — *Percent Per Annum*															
Discount Rate *(End of Period)* ... 60	8.50	8.50	....	....	....	....	....	7.17	....	....	....	6.04	5.42	5.00	4.71
Money Market Rate ... 60b	....	....	....	....	....	....	....	12.29	10.06	8.42	7.89	6.30	5.64	5.41	4.44
Deposit Rate ... 60l	8.5	8.5	8.5	8.5	8.5	....	....	....	....	....	....	7.3	6.4	5.2	5.0
Lending Rate ... 60p	9.0	9.0	9.0	9.0	9.0	....	....	10.0	....	....	....	13.5	13.5	13.3	13.3
Govt.Bond Yield: Long-Term ... 61	....	....	....	....	....	....	....	....	....	....	....	....	....	....	....
Med.-Term ... 61a	....	....	....	....	....	....	....	....	....	....	....	....	....	....	....

Morocco

Prices, Production, Labor		1972	1973	1974	1975	1976	1977	1978	1979	1980	1981	1982	1983	1984	1985	1986
														Index Numbers (1995=100):		
Wholesale Prices	63	16.1	18.9	23.3	24.2	25.3	†28.9	....	34.1	37.0	43.5	48.7	52.3	59.5	65.1	70.2
Consumer Prices	64	17.6	†18.4	21.6	23.3	25.3	28.5	31.2	33.8	37.0	41.6	46.0	48.9	55.0	59.2	64.4
Manufacturing Production	66ey	42.7	47.4	48.7	51.4	55.0	58.7	†63.0	66.0	67.4	67.2	69.1	72.1	71.9	†72.4	75.3
Mining Production	66zx	64.1	72.4	81.8	67.7	65.5	74.5	†80.7	84.8	80.3	78.1	81.5	88.6	92.2	92.2	90.4
Energy Production	66ze	....	....	....	....	....	....	....	....	....	....	....	....	....	....	....
														Number in Thousands:		
Labor Force	67d	....	....	....	....	....	....	....	....	....	....	....	....	....	....	....
Employment	67e	....	....	....	....	....	....	....	....	....	....	....	....	....	....	....
Unemployment	67c	....	....	....	....	....	....	....	....	....	....	....	....	....	....	....
Unemployment Rate (%)	67r	....	....	....	....	....	....	....	....	....	....	....	....	....	....	....
International Transactions															*Millions of Dirhams:*		
Exports	70	2,953	3,746	7,440	6,238	5,579	5,858	6,261	7,622	9,645	12,354	12,461	14,324	19,110	21,740	22,103
Imports, c.i.f.	71	3,577	4,683	8,292	10,398	11,555	14,400	12,361	14,328	16,793	22,692	25,983	25,542	34,397	38,675	34,604
Imports, f.o.b.	71.v	3,256	4,261	7,297	9,148	10,168	12,671	10,878	12,609	14,781	19,760	22,866	22,497	31,300	35,194	31,493
														1995=100		
Volume of Exports	72	†39	47	45	35	†40	44	37	46	46	48	48	53	56	56	59
Volume of Imports	73	†19	22	27	33	37	59	61	†64	61	64	71	61	67	65	65
Unit Value of Imports	75	†17	19	28	28	†28	22	24	32	40	51	53	61	74	82	73
Balance of Payments															*Millions of US Dollars:*		
Current Account, n.i.e.	78al d	....	....	....	−504	−1,368	−1,825	−1,311	−1,502	−1,407	−1,828	−1,867	−886	−984	−891	−209
Goods: Exports f.o.b.	78aa d	....	....	....	1,539	1,262	1,301	1,503	1,955	2,450	2,321	2,070	2,075	2,170	2,162	2,428
Goods: Imports f.o.b.	78ab d	....	....	....	−2,252	−2,287	−2,800	−2,614	−3,244	−3,771	−3,840	−3,816	−3,302	−3,571	−3,515	−3,481
Trade Balance	78ac d	....	....	....	−712	−1,025	−1,498	−1,112	−1,289	−1,321	−1,520	−1,746	−1,227	−1,401	−1,353	−1,053
Services: Credit	78ad d	....	....	....	459	434	539	636	717	783	727	849	845	830	983	1,133
Services: Debit	78ae d	....	....	....	−710	−1,192	−1,276	−1,322	−1,473	−1,436	−1,435	−1,333	−876	−781	−829	−1,156
Balance on Goods & Services	78af d	....	....	....	−963	−1,783	−2,236	−1,799	−2,044	−1,975	−2,228	−2,230	−1,257	−1,352	−1,199	−1,076
Income: Credit	78ag d	....	....	....	28	24	31	26	39	38	36	25	11	16	15	15
Income: Debit	78ah d	....	....	....	−94	−123	−189	−310	−448	−600	−738	−675	−631	−592	−781	−704
Balance on Gds, Serv. & Inc.	78ai d	....	....	....	−1,030	−1,882	−2,394	−2,082	−2,453	−2,537	−2,930	−2,880	−1,878	−1,927	−1,965	−1,765
Current Transfers, n.i.e.: Credit	78aj d	....	....	....	607	618	677	881	1,081	1,236	1,194	1,091	1,069	1,007	1,121	1,602
Current Transfers: Debit	78ak d	....	....	....	−81	−105	−108	−110	−130	−106	−91	−78	−77	−64	−47	−45
Capital Account, n.i.e.	78bc d	....	....	....	−10	−10	−9	−11	−13	−12	−12	−8	−3	−2	2	−2
Capital Account, n.i.e.: Credit	78ba d	....	....	....	—	—	1	1	1	—	—	—	1	2	5	1
Capital Account: Debit	78bb d	....	....	....	−10	−10	−9	−12	−13	−12	−12	−9	−4	−4	−4	−3
Financial Account, n.i.e.	78bj d	....	....	....	828	2,400	3,019	2,153	1,396	1,101	1,491	1,451	697	726	815	579
Direct Investment Abroad	78bd d	....	....	....	—	—	—	—	—	—	—	—	—	—	—	—
Dir. Invest. in Rep. Econ., n.i.e.	78be d	....	....	....	—	38	8	12	7	89	59	80	46	47	20	1
Portfolio Investment Assets	78bf d	....	....	....	—	—	—	—	—	—	—	—	—	—	—	—
Equity Securities	78bk d	....	....	....	—	—	—	—	—	—	—	—	—	—	—	—
Debt Securities	78bl d	....	....	....	—	—	—	—	—	—	—	—	—	—	—	—
Portfolio Investment Liab., n.i.e.	78bg d	....	....	....	—	—	—	—	—	—	—	—	—	—	—	—
Equity Securities	78bm d	....	....	....	—	—	—	—	—	—	—	—	—	—	—	—
Debt Securities	78bn d	....	....	....	—	—	—	—	—	—	—	—	—	—	—	—
Financial Derivatives Assets	78bw d	....	....	....	....	....	....	....	....	....	....	....	....	....	....	....
Financial Derivatives Liabilities	78bx d	....	....	....	....	....	....	....	....	....	....	....	....	....	....	....
Other Investment Assets	78bh d	....	....	....	81	26	−44	−64	−141	−14	−146	−99	−163	−173	−16	−212
Monetary Authorities	78bo d	....	....	....												
General Government	78bp d	....	....	....	−94	−6	−6	−14	−39	−54	−144	−122	−22	−37	−11	−4
Banks	78bq d	....	....	....	22	−6	1	−1	−35	−19	−25	−34	−53	−32	−66	−31
Other Sectors	78br d	....	....	....	153	38	−38	−49	−66	59	22	57	−88	−104	61	−177
Other Investment Liab., n.i.e.	78bi d	....	....	....	747	2,335	3,055	2,206	1,529	1,025	1,579	1,471	814	852	811	790
Monetary Authorities	78bs d	....	....	....	−7	13	10	10	−6	15	30	−29	58	−56	—	1
General Government	78bt d	....	....	....	670	2,129	2,499	1,707	1,038	1,024	1,187	1,182	622	712	564	299
Banks	78bu d	....	....	....	5	11	11	−6	39	−3	8	31	15	—	17	30
Other Sectors	78bv d	....	....	....	79	183	534	495	458	−10	353	287	120	197	230	461
Net Errors and Omissions	78ca d	....	....	....	−341	−1,024	−1,191	−893	87	45	64	7	26	97	42	−38
Overall Balance	78cb d	....	....	....	−27	−2	−6	−62	−32	−273	−284	−417	−166	−163	−32	331
Reserves and Related Items	79da d	....	....	....	27	2	6	62	32	273	284	417	166	163	32	−331
Reserve Assets	79db d	....	....	....	27	−131	−8	−55	17	110	116	−24	71	35	−17	−19
Use of Fund Credit and Loans	79dc d	....	....	....	—	133	14	116	15	163	168	441	95	128	49	−311
Exceptional Financing	79de d	....	....	....	—	—	—	—	—	—	—	—	—	—	—	−1
Government Finance															*Millions of Dirhams:*		
Deficit (-) or Surplus	80	−897	−526	−1,348	−3,341	−7,217	−7,647	−5,773	−6,039	−7,184	−10,557	−10,630	−7,680	−6,762	−9,424	−11,872
Revenue	81	4,335	5,164	8,468	9,529	9,601	12,333	13,346	15,803	17,502	20,418	24,388	24,516	26,684	30,213	32,884
Expenditure	82	5,265	5,630	9,879	12,399	16,495	19,904	18,986	21,673	24,520	30,903	34,822	32,043	33,399	39,336	44,752
Lending Minus Repayments	83	−33	60	−63	471	323	76	133	169	166	72	196	153	47	301	4
Financing																	
Net Borrowing: Domestic	84a	521	475	779	1,474	2,197	2,210	2,528	1,759	3,426	4,131	3,230	7,129	3,063	6,686	7,787
Foreign	85a	296	−2	185	1,350	4,474	5,195	3,365	4,014	3,910	7,116	6,471	3,290	5,319	4,506	−225
Use of Cash Balances	87	80	53	384	517	546	242	−120	266	−152	−690	929	−2,739	−1,620	−1,768	4,310
Debt: Domestic	88a	2,349	2,641	3,172	3,770	5,245	5,908	7,360	8,611	10,197	11,632	13,519	17,166	19,003	26,009	....
Foreign	89a	4,338	4,177	4,341	5,168	7,881	11,438	13,722	16,071	20,697	30,557	40,704	55,387	75,368	84,835	....
National Accounts															*Billions of Dirhams:*		
Househ.Cons.Expend.,incl.NPISHs	96f	16.88	18.40	22.45	24.81	27.66	31.81	36.28	40.81	50.93	55.32	63.57	69.30	81.15	89.83	110.51
Government Consumption Expend.	91f	2.96	2.99	4.04	5.92	9.21	10.25	11.47	13.23	13.59	15.08	17.00	16.63	17.48	20.52	23.75
Gross Fixed Capital Formation	93e	3.18	3.47	4.93	9.04	12.18	15.90	13.73	14.88	16.48	20.51	25.38	24.23	25.95	29.93	32.99
Changes in Inventories	93i	−.33	.13	1.99	.13	−.64	1.13	.46	.32	1.45	.13	.84	−.45	2.45	5.20	2.28
Exports of Goods and Services	90c	4.37	5.41	9.42	8.43	7.89	8.83	9.36	10.83	11.13	14.02	15.44	17.64	22.47	25.81	26.03
Imports of Goods and Services (-)	98c	4.36	5.50	9.23	11.93	15.28	18.16	16.14	18.02	19.49	26.02	29.33	28.21	37.15	41.77	40.84
Gross Domestic Product (GDP)	99b	22.68	24.92	33.60	36.39	41.01	49.76	55.15	62.04	74.09	79.03	92.90	99.14	112.34	129.51	154.73
Net Primary Income from Abroad	98.n	.24	.63	1.08	1.45	1.74	1.39	1.38	1.41	1.63	1.23	.89	1.77	2.64	2.56	7.60
Gross National Income (GNI)	99a	22.93	25.54	34.68	37.86	42.75	51.15	56.53	63.46	75.72	80.26	93.79	100.91	114.98	132.07	162.33
Net National Income	99e	22.43	24.70	33.50	36.22	42.10	49.00	54.00	60.60	67.40	72.61	85.24	89.59	....	....	....
GDP Volume 1969 prices	99b.p	20.41	21.19	24.22	23.92	26.99	28.94	29.58	31.00	32.13	....	....	....	....	....	....
GDP Volume 1980 Prices	99b.p									74.09	72.04	78.97	78.53	81.94	87.12	94.35
GDP Volume (1995=100)	99bv p	41.6	43.2	49.3	48.7	55.0	59.0	60.3	63.2	65.5	63.7	69.8	69.4	72.4	77.0	83.4
GDP Deflator (1995=100)	99bi p	19.4	20.5	24.2	26.5	26.5	30.0	32.5	34.9	40.2	44.1	47.3	50.7	55.1	59.7	65.9
															Millions:		
Population	99z	15.70	16.31	16.80	17.31	17.83	18.36	18.91	19.47	20.05	20.65	†20.31	20.91	21.33	21.84	22.35

Prices, Production, Labor

Period Averages

	1987	1988	1989	1990	1991	1992	1993	1994	1995	1996	1997	1998	1999	2000	2001	
Wholesale Prices	70.9	74.0	76.8	80.3	85.4	87.8	91.8	93.9	100.0	104.4	102.7	106.3	107.3	....	....	63
Consumer Prices	66.1	67.7	69.8	74.6	†80.6	85.2	89.6	94.2	100.0	103.0	104.1	106.9	107.7	109.7	110.4	64
Manufacturing Production	†77.2	83.8	85.5	92.7	94.9	96.5	†95.0	100.6	100.0	104.1	107.5	110.2	112.7	117.5	....	66ey
Mining Production	†100.7	115.4	86.8	101.4	88.9	90.5	†92.1	99.2	100.0	102.5	111.6	111.1	107.5	104.8	....	66zx
Energy Production	70.3	76.2	81.2	86.3	83.1	90.8	†92.6	101.1	100.0	100.0	106.4	105.8	112.6	108.9	....	66ze

Period Averages

	1987	1988	1989	1990	1991	1992	1993	1994	1995	1996	1997	1998	1999	2000	2001	
Labor Force	....	....	....	3,804	....	....	....	....	4,863	4,875	....	5,138	....	....	....	67d
Employment	....	....	3,141	3,294	3,400	3,494	3,660	....	3,870	4,034	4,224	4,168	4,175	....	....	67e
Unemployment	....	....	....	601	695	650	681	....	1,112	871	845	969	1,162	....	....	67c
Unemployment Rate (%)	14.7	13.9	16.3	15.4	17.3	16.0	15.9	....	22.9	18.1	16.9	19.1	22.0	....	....	67r

International Transactions

Millions of Dirhams

	1987	1988	1989	1990	1991	1992	1993	1994	1995	1996	1997	1998	1999	2000	2001	
Exports	23,390	29,751	28,271	35,135	37,283	33,960	28,446	50,965	58,673	60,013	67,057	68,608	72,283	73,869	80,431	70
Imports, c.i.f.	35,271	39,133	46,594	57,021	59,720	62,805	62,606	76,059	85,493	84,612	90,712	98,676	97,454	122,527	123,854	71
Imports, f.o.b.	32,097	35,604	42,401	51,890	50,859	57,146	60,579	60,168	78,654	77,843	83,455	90,782	97,457	122,527	113,946	71.v

1995=100

	1987	1988	1989	1990	1991	1992	1993	1994	1995	1996	1997	1998	1999	2000	2001	
Volume of Exports	63	73	†72	87	95	89	92	†101	100	97	104	107	112	....	....	72
Volume of Imports	71	77	†83	92	103	118	111	†89	100	93	101	124	128	....	....	73
Unit Value of Imports	72	73	†82	90	86	82	90	†102	100	106	102	89	93	....	....	75

Balance of Payments

Minus Sign Indicates Debit

	1987	1988	1989	1990	1991	1992	1993	1994	1995	1996	1997	1998	1999	2000	2001	
Current Account, n.i.e.	182	473	-787	-196	-413	-433	-521	-723	-1,296	-58	-169	-146	-171	-501	....	78al d
Goods: Exports f.o.b.	2,798	3,624	3,331	4,229	5,094	5,010	4,936	5,541	6,871	6,886	7,039	7,144	7,509	7,419	....	78aa d
Goods: Imports f.o.b.	-3,864	-4,384	-5,027	-6,338	-6,858	-7,473	-7,001	-7,648	-9,353	-9,080	-8,903	-9,463	-9,957	-10,654	....	78ab d
Trade Balance	-1,066	-760	-1,697	-2,108	-1,764	-2,463	-2,065	-2,107	-2,482	-2,193	-1,864	-2,319	-2,448	-3,235	....	78ac d
Services: Credit	1,379	1,764	1,650	2,009	1,618	2,125	2,050	2,014	2,173	2,743	2,471	2,827	3,115	3,034	....	78ad d
Services: Debit	-1,141	-1,106	-1,204	-1,445	-1,427	-1,571	-1,593	-1,730	-1,890	-1,782	-1,724	-1,963	-2,003	-1,884	....	78ae d
Balance on Goods & Services	-828	-102	-1,251	-1,544	-1,573	-1,909	-1,608	-1,822	-2,199	-1,233	-1,117	-1,455	-1,335	-2,085	....	78af d
Income: Credit	16	18	32	83	199	292	224	224	251	189	172	194	187	276	....	78ag d
Income: Debit	-782	-1,055	-1,191	-1,071	-1,315	-1,349	-1,431	-1,394	-1,569	-1,498	-1,348	-1,227	-1,172	-1,149	....	78ah d
Balance on Gds, Serv. & Inc.	-1,595	-1,139	-2,411	-2,532	-2,688	-2,966	-2,816	-2,992	-3,516	-2,541	-2,292	-2,489	-2,321	-2,958	....	78ai d
Current Transfers, n.i.e.: Credit	1,822	1,663	1,669	2,383	2,356	2,614	2,361	2,355	2,298	2,565	2,204	2,438	2,246	2,574	....	78aj d
Current Transfers: Debit	-46	-51	-46	-47	-81	-81	-66	-86	-78	-82	-81	-95	-96	-118	....	78ak d
Capital Account, n.i.e.	-6	-6	-3	-5	-5	-6	-3	-3	-6	73	-5	-10	-9	-6	....	78bc d
Capital Account, n.i.e.: Credit	2	1	—	—	—	—	—	—	—	78	1	—	—	—	....	78ba d
Capital Account: Debit	-8	-7	-3	-5	-5	-6	-3	-4	-6	-5	-5	-10	-9	-6	....	78bb d
Financial Account, n.i.e.	84	-226	822	1,889	1,371	1,239	966	1,248	-984	-897	-990	-644	-13	-719	....	78bj d
Direct Investment Abroad	—	—	—	—	-23	-32	-23	-24	-15	-30	-9	-9	-18	-59	....	78bd d
Dir. Invest. in Rep. Econ., n.i.e.	60	85	167	165	317	422	491	551	92	76	4	12	3	10	....	78be d
Portfolio Investment Assets	—	—	—	—	—	—	—	—	—	—	—	—	—	....	....	78bf d
Equity Securities	—	—	—	—	—	—	—	—	—	—	—	—	—	....	....	78bk d
Debt Securities	—	—	—	—	—	—	—	—	—	—	—	—	—	....	....	78bl d
Portfolio Investment Liab., n.i.e.	—	—	—	2	1	1	24	238	20	142	38	24	6	18	....	78bg d
Equity Securities	—	—	—	—	—	—	24	238	20	142	38	24	6	18	....	78bm d
Debt Securities	—	—	—	2	1	1	—	—	—	—	—	—	—	—	....	78bn d
Financial Derivatives Assets																78bw d
Financial Derivatives Liabilities																78bx d
Other Investment Assets	-105	-376	-94	-267	—	—	—	344	—	—	—	—	—	—	....	78bh d
Monetary Authorities	....															78bo d
General Government	-11	-10	-18	-11	—	—	—	—	—	—	—	—	—	—	....	78bp d
Banks	-6	-78	-65	-202	—	—	—	—	—	—	—	—	—	—	....	78bq d
Other Sectors	-88	-287	-11	-54	—	—	—	344	—	—	—	—	—	—	....	78br d
Other Investment Liab., n.i.e.	129	65	749	1,991	1,074	848	473	139	-1,083	-1,085	-1,022	-660	-4	-688	....	78bi d
Monetary Authorities	—	—	—	—	-7	-11	-7	19	—	—	—	—	—	—	....	78bs d
General Government	153	339	336	1,002	648	157	59	-421	-967	-867	-1,232	-954	-1,293	-1,095	....	78bt d
Banks	-27	35	25	101	—	—	—	-48	-132	-167	-123	-197	-152	-118	....	78bu d
Other Sectors	3	-308	388	887	433	702	422	588	16	-50	333	492	1,441	525	....	78bv d
Net Errors and Omissions	38	22	-11	9	3	-10	-5	-39	391	209	175	160	123	148	....	78ca d
Overall Balance	298	264	21	1,697	956	791	436	483	-1,895	-673	-988	-640	-69	-1,078	....	78cb d
Reserves and Related Items	-298	-264	-21	-1,697	-956	-791	-436	-483	1,895	673	988	640	69	1,078	....	79da d
Reserve Assets	-165	-158	63	-1,537	-785	-675	-280	-362	984	-274	-553	-248	-1,636	416	....	79db d
Use of Fund Credit and Loans	-133	-105	-83	-161	-171	-116	-156	-152	-101	-47	-3	—	—	—	....	79dc d
Exceptional Financing	—	—	—	—	—	—	—	31	1,013	995	1,544	887	1,705	663	....	79de d

Government Finance

Year Ending December 31

	1987	1988	1989	1990	1991	1992	1993	1994	1995	1996	1997	1998	1999	2000	2001	
Deficit (-) or Surplus	-7,025	-5,841	-9,951	-4,760	-5,083	-3,368	-6,509	-8,915	-12,365	-9,485	-2,201	-7,329	-8,505	-20,773	....	80
Revenue	37,089	45,454	49,238	56,635	62,437	69,907	78,653	81,442	82,018	79,180	95,115	97,327	103,221	100,907	....	81
Expenditure	44,163	51,300	59,121	61,342	67,400	73,008	84,832	90,072	93,889	88,667	97,276	106,877	112,488	122,019	....	82
Lending Minus Repayments	-49	-5	68	53	120	267	330	285	494	-2	40	-2,221	-762	-339	....	83
Financing																
Net Borrowing: Domestic	3,813	....	5,719	-2,725	427	5,816	5,682	13,949	14,843	12,914	3,301	6,333	8,250	15,035	....	84a
Net Borrowing: Foreign	1,001	3,588	3,650	8,258	4,588	-445	-958	-4,428	-2,111	-2,666	-4,632	-6,182	-5,191	-6,320	....	85a
Use of Cash Balances	2,211	....	582	-773	68	-2,003	1,785	-606	-367	-763	-4,893	7,213	-11,625	12,062	....	87
Debt: Domestic	....	51,571	58,987	57,501	58,920	67,225	76,847	93,843	93,843	110,461	121,526	131,034	136,668	149,388	....	88a
Debt: Foreign	....	156,786	161,608	159,404	115,549	136,952	141,345	134,952	129,766	131,038	130,377	125,864	123,955	118,646	....	89a

National Accounts

Billions of Dirhams

	1987	1988	1989	1990	1991	1992	1993	1994	1995	1996	1997	1998	1999	2000	2001	
Househ.Cons.Expend.,incl.NPISHs	111.84	123.91	134.67	138.70	169.00	170.14	170.67	197.17	201.70	227.34	218.61	234.26	228.10	239.39	....	96f
Government Consumption Expend.	24.63	28.04	30.41	32.98	37.69	40.85	45.05	47.85	48.99	53.82	56.61	62.00	66.30	67.83	....	91f
Gross Fixed Capital Formation	31.63	37.23	44.17	51.06	53.86	54.36	56.72	57.90	60.39	61.94	65.79	75.74	81.89	84.98	....	93e
Changes in Inventories	1.41	1.03	1.76	2.58	.96	2.01	-.74	1.72	-1.99	.60	.11	.48	-.87	1.38	....	93i
Exports of Goods and Services	27.46	35.37	42.75	52.26	53.60	54.64	56.76	60.14	77.63	69.64	73.55	77.72	84.66	93.50	....	90c
Imports of Goods and Services (-)	40.27	43.35	52.36	63.55	65.45	69.30	69.69	74.56	96.02	82.02	85.55	93.50	99.54	115.69	....	98c
Gross Domestic Product (GDP)	156.70	182.23	193.93	212.82	242.36	242.91	249.22	279.32	281.70	319.34	318.34	344.00	345.87	354.32	....	99b
Net Primary Income from Abroad	8.04	4.38	3.52	10.45	9.27	11.94	9.06	10.11	8.70	12.68	11.17	14.40	13.24	16.98	....	98.n
Gross National Income (GNI)	164.73	186.61	197.46	223.27	251.63	254.85	258.29	289.44	290.40	332.02	329.51	358.41	359.12	371.30	....	99a
Net National Income	....	....	....	....	....	....	....	....	....	....	....	....	....	....	....	99e
GDP Volume 1969 prices	....	....	....	....	....	....	....	....	....	....	....	....	....	....	....	99b.p
GDP Volume 1980 Prices	91.94	101.50	103.93	106.12	115.58	110.92	109.80	121.17	113.18	127.03	124.17	132.66	133.78	134.94	143.75	99b.p
GDP Volume (1995=100)	81.2	89.7	91.8	93.8	102.1	98.0	97.0	107.1	100.0	112.2	109.7	117.2	118.2	119.2	127.0	99bv.p
GDP Deflator (1995=100)	68.5	72.1	75.0	80.6	84.2	88.0	91.2	92.6	100.0	101.0	103.0	104.2	103.9	105.5	....	99bi.p

Midyear Estimates

	1987	1988	1989	1990	1991	1992	1993	1994	1995	1996	1997	1998	1999	2000	2001	
Population	22.88	23.23	23.70	24.18	24.65	25.12	25.58	26.07	26.39	26.85	27.31	27.78	28.24	28.71	29.17	99z

(See notes in the back of the book.)

Mozambique

		1972	1973	1974	1975	1976	1977	1978	1979	1980	1981	1982	1983	1984	1985	1986
Exchange Rates														*Meticais per SDR:*		
Market Rate	aa	29.2	31.1	30.0	32.0	36.5	39.4	42.1	42.3	41.6	41.5	42.0	42.9	42.5	45.1	48.0
														Meticais per US Dollar: End of Period (ae)		
Market Rate	ae	26.9	25.8	24.5	27.4	31.4	32.4	32.3	32.1	32.6	35.6	38.0	41.0	43.4	41.0	39.2
Market Rate	rf	27.6	25.0	25.9	26.1	30.8	33.1	33.0	32.6	33.0	36.1	38.5	41.0	43.3	44.0	41.2
Fund Position														*Millions of SDRs:*		
Quota	2f.s	....	....	....	....	....	....	....	....	....	....	....	....	61.00	61.00	61.00
SDRs	1b.s	....	....	....	....	....	....	....	....	....	....	....	....	—	—	—
Reserve Position in the Fund	1c.s	....	....	....	....	....	....	....	....	....	....	....	....	—	—	.01
Total Fund Cred.&Loans Outstg.	2tl	....	....	....	....	....	....	....	....	....	....	....	....	—	—	—
International Liquidity														*Millions of US Dollars Unless Otherwise Indicated:*		
Total Reserves minus Gold	1l.d	....	....	....	....	....	....	....	....	....	....	....	....	55.49	46.05	56.95
SDRs	1b.d	....	....	....	....	....	....	....	....	....	....	....	....	—	—	—
Reserve Position in the Fund	1c.d	....	....	....	....	....	....	....	....	....	....	....	....	—	—	.01
Foreign Exchange	1d.d	....	....	....	....	....	....	....	....	....	....	....	....	55.49	46.05	56.94
Monetary Authorities: Other Liab.	4..d	....	....	....	....	....	....	....	....	....	....	....	....	694.79	886.94	1,057.18
Banking Institutions: Assets	7a.d	....	....	....	....	....	....	....	....	....	....	....	....	1.26	1.43	1.50
Liabilities	7b.d	....	....	....	....	....	....	....	....	....	....	....	....	—	.02	.03
Monetary Authorities														*Billions of Meticais:*		
Foreign Assets	11	....	....	....	....	....	....	....	....	....	....	....	....	4.0	2.8	3.3
Claims on Central Government	12a	....	....	....	....	....	....	....	....	....	....	....	....	72.1	74.4	82.4
Claims on Local Government	12b	....	....	....	....	....	....	....	....	....	....	....	....	—	—	—
Claims on Nonfin.Pub.Enterprises	12c	....	....	....	....	....	....	....	....	....	....	....	....	—	—	—
Claims on Private Sector	12d	....	....	....	....	....	....	....	....	....	....	....	....	78.7	91.9	104.7
Claims on Banking Institutions	12e	....	....	....	....	....	....	....	....	....	....	....	....	1.8	1.5	.9
Reserve Money	14	....	....	....	....	....	....	....	....	....	....	....	....	62.9	73.8	88.1
of which: Currency Outside Banks	14a	....	....	....	....	....	....	....	....	....	....	....	....	27.0	29.8	33.5
Time & Foreign Currency Deposits	15	....	....	....	....	....	....	....	....	....	....	....	....	3.6	3.8	6.4
Liabs. of Central Bank: Securities	16ac	....	....	....	....	....	....	....	....	....	....	....	....	—	—	—
Foreign Liabilities	16c	....	....	....	....	....	....	....	....	....	....	....	....	3.0	2.3	3.0
Long-Term Foreign Liabilities	16cl	....	....	....	....	....	....	....	....	....	....	....	....	27.2	34.2	38.6
Central Government Deposits	16d	....	....	....	....	....	....	....	....	....	....	....	....	49.5	47.8	47.9
o/w: Cent.Govt.Earmarked Funds	16df	....	....	....	....	....	....	....	....	....	....	....	....	—	—	—
Capital Accounts	17a	....	....	....	....	....	....	....	....	....	....	....	....	9.5	10.5	12.0
Other Items (Net)	17r	....	....	....	....	....	....	....	....	....	....	....	....	.8	−1.8	−4.8
of which: Valuation Adjustment	17rv	....	....	....	....	....	....	....	....	....	....	....	....	....	....	....
Banking Institutions														*Billions of Meticais:*		
Reserves	20	....	....	....	....	....	....	....	....	....	....	....	....	7.7	13.6	15.8
Claims on Mon.Author.: Securities	20c	....	....	....	....	....	....	....	....	....	....	....	....	—	—	—
Foreign Assets	21	....	....	....	....	....	....	....	....	....	....	....	....	.1	.1	.1
Claims on Central Government	22a	....	....	....	....	....	....	....	....	....	....	....	....	7.9	8.4	8.4
Claims on Local Government	22b	....	....	....	....	....	....	....	....	....	....	....	....	—	—	—
Claims on Nonfin.Pub.Enterprises	22c	....	....	....	....	....	....	....	....	....	....	....	....	16.3	18.2	19.9
Claims on Private Sector	22d	....	....	....	....	....	....	....	....	....	....	....	....	6.9	7.1	8.9
Claims on Nonbank Financial Insts	22g	....	....	....	....	....	....	....	....	....	....	....	....	—	—	—
Demand Deposits	24	....	....	....	....	....	....	....	....	....	....	....	....	25.8	32.8	38.9
Time & Foreign Currency Deposits	25	....	....	....	....	....	....	....	....	....	....	....	....	3.5	4.8	5.4
Foreign Liabilities	26c	....	....	....	....	....	....	....	....	....	....	....	....	—	—	—
Long-Term Foreign Liabilities	26cl	....	....	....	....	....	....	....	....	....	....	....	....	—	—	—
Central Government Deposits	26d	....	....	....	....	....	....	....	....	....	....	....	....	8.2	8.0	8.0
o/w: Cent.Govt.Earmarked Funds	26df	....	....	....	....	....	....	....	....	....	....	....	....	—	—	—
Credit from Central Bank	26g	....	....	....	....	....	....	....	....	....	....	....	....	.6	.6	.1
Capital Accounts	27a	....	....	....	....	....	....	....	....	....	....	....	....	2.1	2.3	2.4
Other Items (Net)	27r	....	....	....	....	....	....	....	....	....	....	....	....	−1.2	−1.2	−1.7
Banking Survey														*Billions of Meticais:*		
Foreign Assets (Net)	31n	....	....	....	....	....	....	....	....	....	....	....	....	−26.2	−33.6	−38.2
Domestic Credit	32	....	....	....	....	....	....	....	....	....	....	....	....	124.2	144.2	168.4
Claims on Central Govt.(Net)	32an	....	....	....	....	....	....	....	....	....	....	....	....	22.3	27.0	34.9
Claims on Local Government	32b	....	....	....	....	....	....	....	....	....	....	....	....	—	—	—
Claims on Nonfin.Pub.Enterprises	32c	....	....	....	....	....	....	....	....	....	....	....	....	16.3	18.2	19.9
Claims on Private Sector	32d	....	....	....	....	....	....	....	....	....	....	....	....	85.7	99.0	113.6
Claims on Nonbank Financial Inst	32g	....	....	....	....	....	....	....	....	....	....	....	....	—	—	—
Money	34	....	....	....	....	....	....	....	....	....	....	....	....	80.8	92.6	109.6
Quasi-Money	35	....	....	....	....	....	....	....	....	....	....	....	....	7.1	8.6	11.8
Capital Accounts	37a	....	....	....	....	....	....	....	....	....	....	....	....	11.6	12.7	14.4
Other Items (Net)	37r	....	....	....	....	....	....	....	....	....	....	....	....	−1.5	−3.4	−5.6
Money plus Quasi-Money	35l	....	....	....	....	....	....	....	....	....	....	....	....	88.0	101.2	121.4
Money (National Definitions)														*Millions of Meticais:*		
Reserve Money	19ma	....	....	....	....	....	....	....	....	....	....	....	....	....	....	....
M1	59ma	....	....	....	....	....	....	....	....	....	....	....	....	....	....	....
M2	59mb	....	....	....	....	....	....	....	....	....	....	....	....	....	....	....
Interest Rates														*Percent Per Annum*		
Discount Rate (End of Period)	60	....	....	....	....	....	....	....	....	....	....	....	....	....	....	....
Money Market Rate	60b	....	....	....	....	....	....	....	....	....	....	....	....	....	....	....
Treasury Bill Rate	60c	....	....	....	....	....	....	....	....	....	....	....	....	....	....	....
Deposit Rate	60l	....	....	....	....	....	....	....	....	....	....	....	....	....	....	....
Lending Rate	60p	....	....	....	....	....	....	....	....	....	....	....	....	....	....	....
Prices														*Index Numbers (1995=100):*		
Consumer Prices	64	....	....	....	....	....	....	....	....	....	....	....	....	....	1.3	....
Employment	67e	....	....	....	....	....	....	....	....	....	....	....	....	*Number in Thousands:*		

1987	1988	1989	1990	1991	1992	1993	1994	1995	1996	1997	1998	1999	2000	2001	Indicator	Code
															Exchange Rates	
															End of Period	
571.1	839.7	1,073.4	1,471.7	2,630.3	†4,043.8	7,313.2	9,675.1	16,130.5	16,301.7	15,519.2	17,350.0	18,189.7	†22332.5	29,307.5	Market Rate	aa
															Period Average (rf)	
402.6	624.0	816.8	1,034.5	1,838.8	†2,940.9	5,324.2	6,627.4	10,851.4	11,336.7	11,502.1	12,322.2	13,252.9	†17140.5	23,320.4	Market Rate	ae
296.5	535.1	759.7	947.5	1,462.9	2,566.5	3,951.1	6,158.4	9,203.4	11,517.8	11,772.6	12,110.2	13,028.6	15,447.1	20,703.6	Market Rate	rf
															Fund Position	
															End of Period	
61.00	61.00	61.00	61.00	61.00	84.00	84.00	84.00	84.00	84.00	84.00	84.00	113.60	113.60	113.60	Quota	2f. s
.02	.02	.02	.02	.03	.03	.03	.03	.03	.04	.04	.04	.05	.05	.05	SDRs	1b. s
.01	.01	.01	.01	.01	.01	.01	.01	.01	.01	.01	.01	.01	.01	.01	Reserve Position in the Fund	1c. s
12.20	30.50	42.70	51.85	82.35	126.88	137.86	145.24	135.79	125.89	140.11	147.24	145.42	168.47	155.89	Total Fund Cred.&Loans Outstg.	2tl
															International Liquidity	
															End of Period	
118.44	174.22	204.22	232.57	†240.56	233.37	187.24	177.51	195.32	344.06	517.35	608.50	651.60	725.11	715.57	Total Reserves minus Gold	1l. d
.03	.03	.03	.03	.04	.04	.04	.05	.05	.05	.05	.06	.06	.06	.06	SDRs	1b. d
.01	.01	.01	.01	.01	.01	.01	.01	.01	.01	.01	.01	.01	.01	.01	Reserve Position in the Fund	1c. d
118.40	174.18	204.18	232.53	†240.50	233.31	187.19	177.45	195.26	344.00	517.29	608.43	651.53	725.04	715.50	Foreign Exchange	1d. d
1,116.50	1,070.35	1,066.29	1,073.14	1,212.29	1,062.75	1,189.84	647.90	553.36	539.82	593.77	595.47	589.97	545.92	470.15	Monetary Authorities: Other Liab.	4.. d
.21	.21	.66	5.94	14.14	97.15	148.87	221.58	275.45	251.08	242.96	205.39	192.76	315.88	341.14	Banking Institutions: Assets	7a. d
.01	.01	.38	5.26	37.20	41.93	55.44	45.10	69.30	58.26	87.88	65.74	33.64	56.30	81.89	Liabilities	7b. d
															Monetary Authorities	
															End of Period	
61.0	126.1	189.3	267.9	†486.6	769.6	1,175.2	1,367.2	2,424.4	4,359.3	6,359.0	7,928.0	9,089.9	13,018.5	17,297.2	Foreign Assets	11
89.6	129.9	173.9	190.5	†244.1	250.1	545.5	578.4	663.2	496.9	369.8	82.7	6.9	6.8	6.8	Claims on Central Government	12a
—	—	2.5	9.7	†9.8	3.8	.3	.3	.2	1.5	.2	.2	.2	.2	.2	Claims on Local Government	12b
—	—	1.6	†—	—	—	—	.5	50.5	34.0	.5	.5	.5	.5	.5	Claims on Nonfin.Pub.Enterprises	12c
136.4	183.5	242.2	315.2	†—	—	.9	2.2	.9	14.3	54.7	74.7	73.9	—	—	Claims on Private Sector	12d
.9	2.7	3.0	2.6	†27.9	94.0	478.1	781.5	734.9	768.6	566.7	589.5	552.8	682.8	491.3	Claims on Banking Institutions	12e
140.1	216.5	†312.6	383.5	†292.2	506.4	890.1	1,481.4	1,951.1	2,469.5	2,866.6	2,760.2	3,244.5	4,078.8	6,239.4	Reserve Money	14
36.6	61.4	90.9	139.3	†173.3	257.5	469.5	762.4	1,130.2	1,394.4	1,544.1	1,649.7	2,174.2	2,425.3	2,970.4	of which: Currency Outside Banks	14a
17.0	29.4	61.4	85.0	†—	.1	30.7	27.9	84.3	14.8	52.0	72.2	66.0	31.5	46.2	Time & Foreign Currency Deposits	15
....											135.0	145.0	200.0	5.0	Liabs. of Central Bank: Securities	16ac
45.1	84.9	†118.7	173.1	†216.6	513.1	1,008.2	1,405.2	2,190.3	2,052.2	2,174.4	2,554.6	2,645.2	3,762.2	4,568.7	Foreign Liabilities	16c
412.9	611.0	801.3	1,017.6	†2,229.2	3,125.5	6,335.0	4,293.9	6,004.8	6,119.8	6,829.6	7,337.5	7,818.8	9,357.4	10,964.2	Long-Term Foreign Liabilities	16cl
38.1	103.6	†206.2	262.3	†333.6	548.0	1,105.4	1,295.4	1,844.7	3,121.1	4,313.1	5,161.9	5,278.8	5,501.2	4,586.8	Central Government Deposits	16d
—	41.0	90.2	127.1	†191.1	467.8	907.9	960.6	1,258.2	2,265.6	3,068.7	3,987.4	4,345.6	3,519.9	1,989.8	o/w: Cent.Govt.Earmarked Funds	16df
25.9	26.0	51.0	125.4	†404.8	346.1	579.0	896.8	969.7	1,201.4	1,294.0	1,363.9	1,581.6	1,679.9	4,741.0	Capital Accounts	17a
-391.3	-629.3	-940.4	-1,259.1	†-2708.0	-3,921.7	-7,748.4	-6,670.5	-9,170.7	-9,304.1	-10,178.8	-10,709.7	-11,055.7	-10,902.3	-13,355.4	Other Items (Net)	17r
....	-563.0	-760.8	-1,051.0	†-1122.2	-1,621.2	-3,257.9	-5,663.9	-8,339.7	-8,683.2	-8,762.3	-9,192.1	-9,675.9	-10,916.7	-13,841.8	of which: Valuation Adjustment	17rv
															Banking Institutions	
															End of Period	
29.2	44.7	80.1	102.5	†101.4	278.6	433.1	744.6	838.6	1,111.4	1,389.9	1,310.0	1,013.1	1,545.2	3,306.8	Reserves	20
....											135.0	145.0			Claims on Mon.Author.: Securities	20c
....	.1	.5	6.2	†26.0	285.7	792.6	1,468.5	2,989.0	2,846.4	2,794.5	2,530.8	2,554.7	5,414.3	7,955.6	Foreign Assets	21
9.0	12.1	12.2	10.2	†12.7	42.7	6.6	—	.1	65.2	.1	8.3	232.7	1,610.6	2,274.1	Claims on Central Government	22a
—	—	—	.1	†—	19.7	—	.6	1.1	1.1	1.2	103.9	1.9	149.7	1.5	Claims on Local Government	22b
23.8	33.6	50.9	55.0	†63.8	42.2	121.2	170.4	111.0	65.0	223.0	181.1	46.2	85.9	12,050.1	Claims on Nonfin.Pub.Enterprises	22c
10.0	25.4	69.2	95.3	†591.0	856.2	971.3	1,538.2	2,373.3	3,440.3	5,114.8	6,467.0	8,552.7	10,987.7	1,893.1	Claims on Private Sector	22d
—	6.7	8.4	12.5	†—	—	—	.7	11.4	12.5	1.3	46.4	269.7	—		Claims on Nonbank Financial Insts	22g
40.2	71.8	129.3	178.2	†515.6	794.9	1,132.2	1,653.2	2,130.4	2,486.7	3,283.0	3,894.7	4,693.0	5,992.9	6,912.7	Demand Deposits	24
8.9	16.9	23.6	37.1	†164.5	465.8	906.9	1,380.6	2,296.8	2,791.2	3,376.6	4,132.6	5,880.9	9,315.9	12,839.2	Time & Foreign Currency Deposits	25
	—	.3	5.3	†68.2	123.3	295.2	298.9	752.0	660.4	730.8	748.3	368.9	746.3	1,835.5	Foreign Liabilities	26c
—	—	—	.2	†.2						279.9	61.8	77.0	218.8	74.2	Long-Term Foreign Liabilities	26cl
21.7	34.2	62.0	64.1	†86.1	179.5	241.4	304.0	468.7	475.1	462.2	511.2	486.6	887.0	1,853.4	Central Government Deposits	26d
.7	7.2	22.9	23.7	†23.8	23.6	25.7	97.8	235.0	248.3	208.1	290.8	221.6	336.8	586.3	o/w: Cent.Govt.Earmarked Funds	26df
.1	.2	.1	.1	†.1	92.5	.8	581.2	667.9	686.5	555.0	471.9	452.3	959.4	627.6	Credit from Central Bank	26g
2.8	4.1	7.4	10.9	†16.7	302.4	555.2	770.4	1,415.7	1,934.5	2,723.9	3,146.1	3,809.9	5,367.7	7,175.9	Capital Accounts	27a
-1.6	-4.5	-1.4	-14.1	†-56.5	-433.3	-806.9	-1,066.0	-1,417.7	-1,493.5	-1,772.7	-2,331.2	-3,028.0	-3,573.2	-3,838.8	Other Items (Net)	27r
															Banking Survey	
															End of Period	
-397.0	-569.7	†-730.5	-922.0	†-2001.6	-2,706.6	-5,670.6	-3,162.3	-3,533.6	-1,626.6	-861.2	-243.4	734.7	4,348.1	7,810.2	Foreign Assets (Net)	31n
209.0	253.4	†291.2	363.9	†501.7	487.2	299.6	691.2	887.6	533.5	1,104.3	1,144.6	3,343.8	6,574.6	9,784.5	Domestic Credit	32
38.8	4.2	†-82.0	-125.6	†-162.9	-434.7	-794.7	-1,021.0	-1,650.1	-3,034.2	-4,405.4	-5,582.1	-5,525.8	-4,770.9	-4,159.4	Claims on Central Govt.(Net)	32an
—	—	2.6	9.9	†9.8	23.5	.3	.9	1.3	2.7	104.1	2.1	149.9	1.7	.2	Claims on Local Government	32b
23.8	33.6	50.9	56.0	†63.8	42.2	121.2	170.9	161.5	99.0	223.6	181.6	46.8	86.4	12,050.6	Claims on Nonfin.Pub.Enterprises	32c
146.4	208.9	311.4	410.5	†591.0	856.2	972.2	1,540.4	2,374.2	3,454.6	5,169.5	6,541.6	8,626.6	10,987.7	1,893.1	Claims on Private Sector	32d
—	6.7	8.4	12.5	†—	—	—	.7	11.4	12.5	1.3	46.4	269.7	—		Claims on Nonbank Financial Inst	32g
152.8	244.4	†365.2	495.8	†727.0	1,056.6	1,606.1	2,417.9	3,264.0	3,917.2	4,901.7	5,613.0	6,994.4	8,557.2	10,066.0	Money	34
25.9	46.3	85.1	122.1	†164.5	465.9	937.6	1,408.5	2,381.1	2,806.0	3,428.6	4,204.7	5,946.9	9,347.5	12,885.4	Quasi-Money	35
28.6	30.1	58.4	136.3	†421.5	648.5	1,134.2	1,667.2	2,385.4	3,135.9	4,017.9	4,510.0	5,391.4	7,047.7	11,916.9	Capital Accounts	37a
-395.2	-637.1	†-948.0	-1,312.2	†-2812.9	-4,390.4	-9,048.9	-7,964.7	-10,676.5	-10,952.2	-12,105.2	-13,426.5	-14,254.2	-14,029.6	-17,273.6	Other Items (Net)	37r
178.6	290.7	†450.2	617.8	†891.5	1,522.5	2,543.7	3,826.4	5,645.1	6,723.2	8,330.3	9,817.7	12,941.3	17,904.6	22,951.4	Money plus Quasi-Money	35l
															Money (National Definitions)	
															End of Period	
....	....	....	....	....	....	....	....	....	....	2,792.1	2,691.7	3,117.3	3,939.8	6,056.5	Reserve Money	19ma
....	....	....	....	....	....	....	....	....	....	6,123.1	7,019.2	9,410.7	13,199.8	17,002.7	M1	59ma
....	....	....	....	....	....	....	....	....	....	7,413.5	8,720.0	11,721.6	16,778.7	21,814.1	M2	59mb
															Interest Rates	
															Percent Per Annum	
....	....	....	....	....	....	69.70	57.75	32.00	12.95	9.95	9.95	9.95	9.95	9.95	Discount Rate (End of Period)	60
....	....	....	....	....	....	....	....	....	....	....	9.92	16.12	33.64		Money Market Rate	60b
													16.97	24.77	Treasury Bill Rate	60c
....	....	....	....	....	....	33.38	38.84	18.14	25.43		8.22	7.86	9.70	15.10	Deposit Rate	60l
....	....	....	....	....	....	....	....	....	....		24.35	19.63	19.04	22.65	Lending Rate	60p
															Prices	
															Period Averages	
4.7	7.0	9.8	†14.4	19.2	27.9	39.7	64.8	†100.0	146.9	156.3	157.1	160.3	....	....	Consumer Prices	64
															Period Averages	
193	202	....	....	....	....	....	....	....	....	....	....	....	....	....	Employment	67e

Mozambique

International Transactions		1972	1973	1974	1975	1976	1977	1978	1979	1980	1981	1982	1983	1984	1985	1986
															Billions of Meticais	
Exports	70	...	...	...	...	...	...	...	...	...	...	...	...	...	...	...
Imports, c.i.f.	71	...	...	...	...	...	...	...	...	...	...	...	...	...	...	...
Balance of Payments															*Millions of US Dollars:*	
Current Account, n.i.e.	78al *d*	...	...	...	...	...	...	...	...	−367.0	−407.1	−496.5	−415.3	−308.4	−301.1	−409.3
Goods: Exports f.o.b.	78aa *d*	...	...	...	...	...	...	...	...	280.8	280.8	229.2	131.6	95.7	76.6	79.1
Goods: Imports f.o.b.	78ab *d*	...	...	...	...	...	...	...	...	−720.1	−721.0	−752.3	−572.8	−485.7	−381.4	−488.4
Trade Balance	78ac *d*	...	...	...	...	...	...	...	...	−439.3	−440.2	−523.1	−441.2	−390.0	−304.8	−409.3
Services: Credit	78ad *d*	...	...	...	...	...	...	...	...	117.9	114.0	107.8	90.6	61.0	66.3	62.9
Services: Debit	78ae *d*	...	...	...	...	...	...	...	...	−123.5	−137.5	−140.2	−121.4	−97.6	−100.1	−154.3
Balance on Goods & Services	78af *d*	...	...	...	...	...	...	...	...	−444.9	−463.7	−555.5	−472.0	−426.6	−338.6	−500.7
Income: Credit	78ag *d*	...	...	...	...	...	...	...	...	53.4	64.5	63.5	75.2	57.0	40.8	50.0
Income: Debit	78ah *d*	...	...	...	...	...	...	...	...	−31.4	−65.3	−83.9	−108.1	−106.6	−142.3	−177.7
Balance on Gds, Serv. & Inc.	78ai *d*	...	...	...	...	...	...	...	...	−422.9	−464.5	−575.9	−504.9	−476.2	−440.1	−628.4
Current Transfers, n.i.e.: Credit	78aj *d*	...	...	...	...	...	...	...	...	55.9	57.4	79.4	89.6	167.8	139.0	219.1
Current Transfers: Debit	78ak *d*	...	...	...	...	...	...	...	...							
Capital Account, n.i.e.	78bc *d*	...	...	...	...	...	...	...	...	—	—	—	—	—	—	—
Capital Account, n.i.e.: Credit	78ba *d*	...	...	...	...	...	...	...	...	—	—	—	—	—	—	—
Capital Account: Debit	78bb *d*	...	...	...	...	...	...	...	...	—	—	—	—	—	—	—
Financial Account, n.i.e.	78bj *d*	...	...	...	...	...	...	...	...	364.2	410.5	398.2	105.6	−113.1	−52.4	−20.2
Direct Investment Abroad	78bd *d*	...	...	...	...	...	...	...	...	—	—	—	—	—	—	—
Dir. Invest. in Rep. Econ., n.i.e.	78be *d*	...	...	...	...	...	...	...	...	—	—	—	—	—	—	1.5
Portfolio Investment Assets	78bf *d*	...	...	...	...	...	...	...	...	—	—	—	—	—	—	—
Equity Securities	78bk *d*	...	...	...	...	...	...	...	...	—	—	—	—	—	—	—
Debt Securities	78bl *d*	...	...	...	...	...	...	...	...	—	—	—	—	—	—	—
Portfolio Investment Liab., n.i.e.	78bg *d*	...	...	...	...	...	...	...	...	—	—	—	—	—	—	—
Equity Securities	78bm *d*	...	...	...	...	...	...	...	...	—	—	—	—	—	—	—
Debt Securities	78bn *d*	...	...	...	...	...	...	...	...	—	—	—	—	—	—	—
Financial Derivatives Assets	78bw *d*	...	...	...	...	...	...	...	...	...	...	...	...	...	...	...
Financial Derivatives Liabilities	78bx *d*	...	...	...	...	...	...	...	...	...	...	...	...	...	...	...
Other Investment Assets	78bh *d*	...	...	...	...	...	...	...	...	—	−2.2	−5.8	−3.3	−9.1	1.9	4.5
Monetary Authorities	78bo *d*	...	...	...	...	...	...	...	...	—	−2.2	−5.8	−3.3	−7.8	2.0	4.6
General Government	78bp *d*	...	...	...	...	...	...	...	...	—	—	—	—	—	—	—
Banks	78bq *d*	...	...	...	...	...	...	...	...	—	—	—	—	−1.3	−.1	−.1
Other Sectors	78br *d*	...	...	...	...	...	...	...	...	—	—	—	—	—	—	—
Other Investment Liab., n.i.e.	78bi *d*	...	...	...	...	...	...	...	...	364.2	412.7	404.0	108.9	−104.0	−54.3	−26.2
Monetary Authorities	78bs *d*	...	...	...	...	...	...	...	...	—	3.7	8.7	66.1	−31.0	−14.6	24.8
General Government	78bt *d*	...	...	...	...	...	...	...	...	364.2	409.0	395.3	42.8	−73.0	−39.7	−51.0
Banks	78bu *d*	...	...	...	...	...	...	...	...	—	—	—	—	—	—	—
Other Sectors	78bv *d*	...	...	...	...	...	...	...	...	—	—	—	—	—	—	—
Net Errors and Omissions	78ca *d*	...	...	...	...	...	...	...	...	−29.6	−70.1	−42.3	9.0	25.8	−12.8	457.6
Overall Balance	78cb *d*	...	...	...	...	...	...	...	...	−32.4	−66.7	−140.6	−300.7	−395.7	−366.3	28.1
Reserves and Related Items	79da *d*	...	...	...	...	...	...	...	...	32.4	66.7	140.6	300.7	395.7	366.3	−28.1
Reserve Assets	79db *d*	...	...	...	...	...	...	...	...	32.4	66.7	140.6	15.4	−23.0	20.5	−28.1
Use of Fund Credit and Loans	79dc *d*	...	...	...	...	...	...	...	...	—	—	—	—	—	—	—
Exceptional Financing	79de *d*	...	...	...	...	...	...	...	...	—	—	—	285.3	418.7	345.8	—
National Accounts															*Billions of Meticais*	
Househ.Cons.Expend.,incl.NPISHs	96f	...	...	...	...	...	...	...	...	64	65	62	57	61	83	90
Government Consumption Expend.	91f	...	...	...	...	...	...	...	...	14	17	19	22	21	23	27
Gross Fixed Capital Formation	93e	...	...	...	...	...	...	...	...	15	16	18	15	18	19	23
Changes in Inventories	93i	...	...	...	...	...	...	...	...	—	—	—	—	—	—	—
Exports of Goods and Services	90c	...	...	...	...	...	...	...	...	...	...	18	9	7	6	6
Imports of Goods and Services (-)	98c	...	...	...	...	...	...	...	...	...	...	34	28	25	21	24
Gross Domestic Product (GDP)	99b	...	...	...	...	...	...	...	...	78	82	79	75	82	111	122
Gross National Income (GNI)	99a	...	...	...	...	...	...	...	...	79	81	91	77	87	113	123
GDP Volume 1984 Prices	99b. *p*	...	...	...	...	...	...	...	...	...	...	...	...	82	83	81
GDP Volume (1995=100)	99bv *p*	...	...	...	...	...	...	...	...	...	...	...	...	71.0	71.9	70.2
GDP Deflator (1995=100)	99bi *p*	...	...	...	...	...	...	...	...	...	...	...	...	.6	.7	.8
															Millions:	
Population	99z	8.52	...	...	9.72	10.16	10.66	11.17	11.66	12.13	12.45	12.78	13.11	13.51	13.87	14.16

Billions of Meticais

1987	1988	1989	1990	1991	1992	1993	1994	1995	1996	1997	1998	1999	2000	2001	International Transactions	
...	...	...	...	...	...	...	979.3	1,573.2	2,509.2	2,614.4	2,783.1	3,429.0	...	...	Exports	70
...	...	...	...	...	...	...	3,279.0	6,527.1	8,733.7	8,704.7	9,575.9	14,859.3	...	...	Imports, c.i.f.	71

Balance of Payments

Minus Sign Indicates Debit

1987	1988	1989	1990	1991	1992	1993	1994	1995	1996	1997	1998	1999	2000	2001		
−388.8	−358.5	−460.2	−415.3	−344.3	−352.3	−446.3	−467.2	−444.7	−420.5	−295.6	−429.3	−912.0	−763.6	...	Current Account, n.i.e.	78ald
97.0	103.0	104.8	126.4	162.3	139.3	131.8	149.5	168.9	226.1	230.0	244.6	283.8	364.0	...	Goods: Exports f.o.b.	78aad
−577.8	−662.0	−726.9	−789.7	−808.8	−769.5	−859.2	−916.7	−705.2	−704.4	−684.0	−735.6	−1,090.0	−1,046.0	...	Goods: Imports f.o.b.	78abd
−480.8	−559.0	−622.1	−663.3	−646.5	−630.2	−727.4	−767.2	−536.3	−478.3	−454.0	−491.0	−806.2	−682.0	...	*Trade Balance*	78acd
79.0	85.0	95.4	103.0	147.2	164.6	180.2	191.1	242.4	253.2	278.7	286.2	295.2	325.4	...	Services: Credit	78add
−175.8	−190.9	−195.5	−206.0	−236.8	−246.4	−270.6	−323.3	−350.0	−319.0	−328.6	−396.2	−405.7	−445.8	...	Services: Debit	78aed
−577.6	−664.9	−722.2	−766.3	−736.1	−712.0	−817.8	−899.4	−643.9	−544.1	−503.9	−601.0	−916.7	−802.4	...	*Balance on Goods & Services*	78afd
58.0	71.6	71.3	70.4	55.6	58.0	59.6	54.8	59.1	61.0	63.6	46.3	57.8	79.3	...	Income: Credit	78agd
−173.4	−142.0	−196.8	−167.8	−165.5	−197.7	−191.4	−187.2	−199.1	−162.1	−168.2	−187.8	−214.8	−271.4	...	Income: Debit	78ahd
−693.0	−735.3	−847.7	−863.7	−846.0	−851.7	−949.6	−1,031.8	−783.9	−645.2	−608.5	−742.5	−1,073.7	−994.5	...	*Balance on Gds, Serv. & Inc.*	78aid
304.2	376.8	387.5	448.4	501.7	499.4	503.3	564.6	339.2	224.7	312.9	313.2	256.3	337.3	...	Current Transfers, n.i.e.: Credit	78ajd
												−94.6	−106.4	...	Current Transfers: Debit	78akd
—	—	—	—	—	—	—	—	—	—	—	—	180.3	226.8	...	Capital Account, n.i.e.	78bcd
—	—	—	—	—	—	—	—	—	—	—	—	180.3	226.8	...	Capital Account, n.i.e.: Credit	78bad
—	—	—	—	—	—	—	—	—	—	—	—			...	Capital Account: Debit	78bbd
−76.7	−126.0	−54.9	−83.4	160.9	513.7	246.9	344.4	366.7	235.0	182.2	300.4	403.9	83.2	...	Financial Account, n.i.e.	78bjd
														...	Direct Investment Abroad	78bdd
6.2	4.5	3.4	9.2	22.5	25.3	32.0	35.0	45.0	72.5	64.4	212.7	381.7	139.2	...	Dir. Invest. in Rep. Econ., n.i.e.	78bed
—	—	—	—	—	—	—	—	—	—	—	—	—	—	...	Portfolio Investment Assets	78bfd
—	—	—	—	—	—	—	—	—	—	—	—	—	—	...	Equity Securities	78bkd
—	—	—	—	—	—	—	—	—	—	—	—	—	—	...	Debt Securities	78bld
—	—	—	—	—	—	—	—	—	—	—	—	—	—	...	Portfolio Investment Liab., n.i.e.	78bgd
—	—	—	—	—	—	—	—	—	—	—	—	—	—	...	Equity Securities	78bmd
—	—	—	—	—	—	—	—	—	—	—	—	—	—	...	Debt Securities	78bnd
...	...	...	...	...	...	...	...	...	...	...	...			...	Financial Derivatives Assets	78bwd
...	...	...	...	...	...	...	...	...	...	...	...			...	Financial Derivatives Liabilities	78bxd
										—	19.0	2.6	−145.0	...	Other Investment Assets	78bhd
											1.3	1.7	—	...	Monetary Authorities	78bod
											—			...	General Government	78bpd
											17.7	13.9	−124.0	...	Banks	78bqd
											—	−13.0	−21.0	...	Other Sectors	78brd
−82.9	−130.5	−58.3	−92.6	138.4	488.4	214.9	309.4	321.7	162.5	117.8	68.7	19.6	89.0	...	Other Investment Liab., n.i.e.	78bid
												−5.8	−40.8	...	Monetary Authorities	78bsd
−82.9	−130.5	−58.3	−92.6	138.4	488.4	214.9	309.4	321.7	86.2	48.8	−.8	−261.7	−171.4	...	General Government	78btd
									76.3	69.0	20.3	−33.6	16.6	...	Banks	78bud
											49.2	320.7	284.6	...	Other Sectors	78bvd
−583.1	113.0	114.7	100.5	−274.5	−684.2	−447.4	−443.2	−308.6	−238.3	−364.8	−263.8	1.5	37.5	...	Net Errors and Omissions	78cad
−1,048.6	−371.5	−400.4	−398.2	−457.9	−522.8	−646.8	−566.0	−386.6	−423.8	−478.2	−392.7	−326.3	−416.1	...	*Overall Balance*	78cbd
1,048.6	371.5	400.4	398.2	457.9	522.8	646.8	566.0	386.6	423.8	478.2	392.7	326.3	416.1	...	Reserves and Related Items	79dad
−58.2	−50.5	−13.0	−17.9	−53.9	13.9	63.6	−12.0	16.4	161.0	162.3	91.5	−44.0	−76.8	...	Reserve Assets	79dbd
15.7	25.3	15.9	12.0	41.2	62.5	15.4	10.4	−14.4	−14.4	19.9	9.6	−2.9	31.1	...	Use of Fund Credit and Loans	79dcd
1,091.1	396.7	397.5	404.1	470.6	446.4	567.8	567.6	384.6	277.1	296.0	291.6	373.2	461.8	...	Exceptional Financing	79ded

National Accounts

Billions of Meticais

1987	1988	1989	1990	1991	1992	1993	1994	1995	1996	1997	1998	1999	2000	2001		
298	482	742	947	4,040	5,223	8,078	12,648	20,473	30,510	36,659	38,865	41,117	...	...	Househ.Cons.Expend.,incl.NPISHs	96f
68	115	195	271	427	669	1,059	2,061	2,011	2,875	3,648	4,539	5,788	...	...	Government Consumption Expend.	91f
179	362	557	791	626	952	1,537	2,608	4,931	6,357	7,222	10,389	...	...	...	Gross Fixed Capital Formation	93e
—	—	—	—	140	199	316	402	810	487	91	−19	...	...	...	Changes in Inventories	93i
51	99	149	213	320	486	714	1,514	2,582	3,901	4,422	4,758	5,537	...	...	Exports of Goods and Services	90c
202	427	652	881	1,609	2,475	3,692	5,913	10,129	11,412	11,438	12,429	20,333	...	...	Imports of Goods and Services (-)	98c
393	631	991	1,341	3,943	5,053	8,011	13,319	20,678	32,719	40,603	46,203	51,560	...	...	Gross Domestic Product (GDP)	99b
432	810	1,214	1,713	2,473	4,164	7,136	11,665	16,128	...	...	...	...	...	...	Gross National Income (GNI)	99a
93	101	106	105	107	105	123	130						...	...	GDP Volume 1984 Prices	99b.p
80.5	87.5	91.8	90.9	†92.7	84.7	90.5	96.8	100.0	106.8	118.8	133.1	145.0	...	...	GDP Volume (1995=100)	99bvp
2.4	3.5	5.2	7.1	20.6	28.8	42.8	66.5	100.0	148.2	165.3	167.9	171.9	...	...	GDP Deflator (1995=100)	99bip

Midyear Estimates

1987	1988	1989	1990	1991	1992	1993	1994	1995	1996	1997	1998	1999	2000	2001		
14.12	13.95	13.96	14.15	14.47	14.80	15.13	15.47	15.82	16.18	16.54	16.92	17.30	17.69	17.66	Population	99z

(See notes in the back of the book.)

Myanmar

		1972	1973	1974	1975	1976	1977	1978	1979	1980	1981	1982	1983	1984	1985	1986
Exchange Rates															*Kyats per SDR:*	
Official Rate	aa	5.8650	5.8653	5.8891	7.7429	7.7429	8.5085	8.5085	8.5085	8.5085	8.5085	8.5085	8.5085	8.5085	8.5085	8.5085
															Kyats per US Dollar:	
Official Rate	ae	5.4020	4.8620	4.8100	6.6777	6.7324	7.0873	6.6028	6.5186	6.7572	7.3970	7.7775	8.2231	8.7512	7.8420	7.0395
Official Rate	rf	5.4565	4.9283	4.8598	6.3676	6.7673	7.1194	6.8844	6.6538	6.5983	7.2807	7.7903	8.0355	8.3855	8.4749	7.3304
Fund Position															*Millions of SDRs:*	
Quota	2f. s	60.0	60.0	60.0	60.0	60.0	60.0	73.0	73.0	109.5	109.5	109.5	137.0	137.0	137.0	137.0
SDRs	1b. s	5.6	9.7	9.5	8.0	7.6	7.5	2.9	4.7	5.4	2.4	1.1	.2	.1	—	—
Reserve Position in the Fund	1c. s	—	—	—	—	—	—	—	—	—	9.0	13.0	6.9	6.9	—	—
Total Fund Cred.&Loans Outstg.	2tl	8.0	15.0	36.5	40.5	34.5	58.1	85.3	97.0	87.7	107.6	130.3	141.5	129.7	106.4	68.0
International Liquidity													*Millions of US Dollars Unless Otherwise Indicated:*			
Total Reserves minus Gold	1l. d	40.2	91.9	182.4	132.8	118.3	103.3	96.4	203.3	260.6	229.0	104.3	89.4	62.1	33.9	33.1
SDRs	1b. d	6.1	11.7	11.7	9.4	8.8	9.1	3.8	6.2	6.9	2.7	1.2	.2	.1	—	—
Reserve Position in the Fund	1c. d	—	—	—	—	—	—	—	—	—	10.5	14.3	7.2	6.7	—	—
Foreign Exchange	1d. d	34.1	80.2	170.7	123.4	109.5	94.2	92.6	197.1	253.7	215.8	88.8	82.0	55.3	33.9	33.1
Gold (Million Fine Troy Ounces)	1ad	.320	.200	.200	.200	.200	.226	.238	.251	.251	.251	.251	.251	.251	.251	.251
Gold (National Valuation)	1an d	12.2	8.4	8.5	8.2	8.1	9.6	10.9	11.6	11.2	10.2	9.7	9.2	8.6	9.7	10.8
Monetary Authorities: Other Assets	3.. d	....	....	....	....	10.5	25.5	21.4	47.9	75.2	47.9	45.7	19.1	26.4	30.0	13.0
Monetary Authorities: Other Liab.	4.. d	6.7	7.0	10.1	9.3	9.6	17.0	57.1	50.6	53.2	48.4	43.8	46.1	42.7	68.4	84.6
Deposit Money Banks: Assets	7a. d	—	—	—	—	.1	.1	.3	.3	.7	1.9	1.4	1.6	1.4	1.5	2.6
Liabilities	7b. d	91.5	138.8	157.7	135.2	151.8	167.3	158.6	309.6	393.8	515.6	514.7	605.0	604.9	795.6	1,155.2
Monetary Authorities															*Millions of Kyats:*	
Foreign Assets	11	366	541	1,066	1,132	841	864	908	1,705	2,201	2,125	1,242	968	850	577	400
Claims on Central Government	12a	3,399	3,553	4,608	5,378	5,500	5,083	3,883	2,846	1,123	−1,525	−3,549	−5,451	−7,878	−9,608	−5,949
Claims on Deposit Money Banks	12e	162	309	106	191	181	621	3,165	4,933	7,012	12,273	13,554	17,887	21,846	28,533	29,481
Reserve Money	14	2,322	2,947	3,620	4,538	5,981	5,712	6,403	7,671	8,561	10,291	9,753	10,823	12,361	11,042	15,627
of which: Currency Outside DMBs	14a	2,222	2,840	3,647	4,448	4,945	5,146	5,783	6,448	7,289	8,410	9,045	10,165	11,768	10,504	15,218
Other Liabilities to DMBs	14n	....	....	....	....	....	....	....	....	....	....	....	....	....	....	....
Foreign Liabilities	16c	91	137	268	378	668	1,319	1,108	1,984	1,266	1,200	1,295	1,540	1,429	1,439	1,183
Capital Accounts	17a	414	452	490	562	411	414	451	548	650	770	783	783	784	787	786
Other Items (Net)	17r	1,105	877	1,401	1,564	−538	−876	−7	−720	−142	611	368	258	243	6,234	6,336
Deposit Money Banks															*Millions of Kyats:*	
Reserves	20	817	1,272	1,173	923	1,466	1,029	1,097	2,334	2,419	2,740	1,290	1,196	1,055	879	645
Other Claims on Monetary Author.	20n	....	....	....	....	....	....	....	....	....	....	....	....	....	....	....
Foreign Assets	21	—	—	—	—	10	10	11	11	14	14	11	13	12	12	18
Claims on Central Govt. (Net)	22an	482	360	582	979	†−298	2,406	2,796	2,421	1,496	2,539	3,020	2,906	3,530	2,322	1,951
Claims on Local Government	22b	....	....	....	....	....	....	20	48	87	118	152	169	186	202	238
Claims on Nonfin.Pub.Enterprises	22c	440	618	1,033	1,151	†117	758	2,855	5,274	8,489	13,025	17,843	22,798	28,241	32,903	37,728
Claims on Private Sector	22d	685	773	580	790	1,336	1,743	2,363	2,009	2,131	2,540	2,470	2,628	2,396	2,762	3,009
Demand Deposits	24	233	253	305	388	442	439	515	555	611	696	751	894	1,002	1,040	1,112
Time, Savings,& Fgn.Currency Dep.	25	631	626	609	607	642	708	990	1,500	2,047	2,866	3,752	4,603	5,659	6,558	7,447
Restricted Deposits	26b	....	....	....	....	....	....	....	....	....	....	....	....	....	....	....
Foreign Liabilities	26c	489	668	758	903	1,022	1,186	1,047	2,018	2,661	3,814	4,003	4,975	5,294	6,239	8,132
Credit from Monetary Authorities	26g	162	309	106	191	181	621	3,165	4,933	7,012	12,273	13,554	17,887	21,846	28,533	29,481
Capital Accounts	27a	142	148	148	151	358	399	433	494	531	579	633	706	835	978	1,152
Other Items (Net)	27r	767	1,019	1,442	1,603	†−23	2,584	2,983	2,588	1,765	748	2,093	645	784	−4,268	−3,735
Monetary Survey															*Millions of Kyats:*	
Foreign Assets (Net)	31n	−214	−264	39	−149	−839	−1,631	−1,237	−2,286	−1,712	−2,875	−4,045	−5,535	−5,861	−7,089	−8,897
Domestic Credit	32	5,203	5,388	6,825	8,675	†9,972	10,524	12,599	14,506	16,448	20,827	24,179	28,761	32,110	35,660	46,552
Claims on Central Govt. (Net)	32an	3,881	3,913	5,189	6,698	†6,108	7,685	7,453	5,422	4,071	2,966	536	229	−2,150	−3,230	1,366
Claims on Local Government	32b	....	....	....	....	....	....	20	48	87	118	152	169	186	202	238
Claims on Nonfin.Pub.Enterprises	32c	637	703	1,056	1,187	†127	765	2,860	5,276	8,490	13,026	17,844	22,799	28,241	32,903	37,728
Claims on Private Sector	32d	685	773	580	790	1,336	1,743	2,363	2,009	2,131	2,540	2,470	2,628	2,396	2,762	3,009
Money	34	2,494	3,143	3,997	4,859	5,397	5,592	6,298	7,003	7,900	9,112	9,803	11,067	12,777	11,551	16,337
Quasi-Money	35	631	626	609	607	642	708	990	1,500	2,047	2,866	3,752	4,603	5,659	6,558	7,447
Restricted Deposits	36b	....	....	....	....	....	....	....	....	....	....	....	....	....	....	....
Capital Accounts	37a	556	600	638	712	769	813	884	1,042	1,181	1,349	1,416	1,489	1,619	1,765	1,938
Other Items (Net)	37r	1,308	755	1,621	2,348	†2,325	1,780	3,190	2,674	3,607	4,625	5,162	6,067	6,195	8,697	11,933
Money plus Quasi-Money	35l	3,125	3,769	4,606	5,466	6,039	6,300	7,288	8,503	9,947	11,978	13,555	15,670	18,436	18,109	23,784
Interest Rates															*Percent Per Annum*	
Central Bank Rate (End of Per.)	60	....	....	....	....	....	....	....	....	....	....	....	....	....	....	....
Deposit Rate	60l	.75	.75	.75	.75	.75	.88	1.50	1.50	1.50	1.50	1.50	1.50	1.50	1.50	1.50
Lending Rate	60p	....	....	....	....	6.00	6.33	8.00	8.00	8.00	8.00	8.00	8.00	8.00	8.00	8.00
Government Bond Yield	61	....	....	....	....	....	....	....	....	....	....	....	....	....	....	....
Prices														*Index Numbers (1995=100):*		
Consumer Prices	64	4.1	5.1	6.4	8.5	10.4	10.2	9.6	10.2	10.2	†10.3	10.8e	11.4	†12.0	12.8	14.0
															Number in Thousands:	
Employment	67e	....	....	....	....	....	....	....	....	....	....	....	....	....	14,792	15,130
Unemployment	67c	....	....	....	....	....	....	....	....	....	....	....	....	....	338	354

	1987	1988	1989	1990	1991	1992	1993	1994	1995	1996	1997	1998	1999	2000	2001		
																Exchange Rates	
End of Period																	
	8.5085	8.5085	8.5085	8.5085	8.5085	8.5085	8.5085	8.5085	8.5085	8.5085	8.5085	8.5085	8.5085	8.5085	8.5085	Official Rate	aa
End of Period (ae) Period Average (rf)																	
	6.1097	6.4104	6.4942	6.0804	6.0137	6.2411	6.2456	5.9030	5.7810	5.9877	6.3627	6.1087	6.2683	6.5985	6.8503	Official Rate	ae
	6.6535	6.3945	6.7049	6.3386	6.2837	6.1045	6.1570	5.9749	5.6670	5.9176	6.2418	6.3432	6.2858	6.5167	6.7489	Official Rate	rf
																Fund Position	
End of Period																	
	137.0	137.0	137.0	137.0	137.0	184.9	184.9	184.9	184.9	184.9	184.9	184.9	258.4	258.4	258.4	Quota	2f.s
	.1	.1	.4	.6	.1	—	.2	.1	.1	.1	.1	.2	.1	.1	.4	SDRs	1b.s
	—	—	—	—	—	—	—	—	—	—	—	—	—	—	—	Reserve Position in the Fund	1c.s
	28.9	8.0	2.0	.2	—	—	—	—	—	—	—	—	—	—	—	Total Fund Cred.&Loans Outstg.	2tl
																International Liquidity	
End of Period																	
	27.2	77.4	263.4	312.8	258.4	280.1	302.9	422.0	561.1	229.2	249.8	314.9	265.5	223.0	400.5	Total Reserves minus Gold	1l.d
	.1	.1	.6	.8	.2	—	.3	.1	.1	.1	.1	.3	.2	.1	.6	SDRs	1b.d
	—	—	—	—	—	—	—	—	—	—	—	—	—	—	—	Reserve Position in the Fund	1c.d
	27.1	77.3	262.8	312.0	258.2	280.1	302.6	421.9	561.1	229.1	249.7	314.6	265.3	222.8	399.9	Foreign Exchange	1d.d
	.251	.251	.251	.251	.251	.251	.251	.251	.231	.231	.231	.231	.231	.231	.231	Gold (Million Fine Troy Ounces)	1ad
	12.5	11.8	11.6	12.5	12.6	12.1	12.1	12.8	12.0	11.6	10.9	11.4	11.1	10.6	10.2	Gold (National Valuation)	1and
	....	....	....	....	....	....	....	....	....	....	....	....	....	....	....	Monetary Authorities: Other Assets	3..d
	114.3	120.8	352.5	341.7	357.2	311.2	328.2	348.3	318.8	328.2	333.3	346.6	336.3	328.9	518.4	Monetary Authorities: Other Liab.	4..d
	2.5	2.0	3.4	26.8	71.5	113.0	128.9	162.8	189.6	119.4	140.5	238.5	221.9	180.6	169.0	Deposit Money Banks: Assets	7a.d
	1,469.0	1,609.9	58.7	455.7	98.4	167.1	1,722.7	1,986.3	2,056.6	1,919.6	1,657.9	1,684.0	1,692.8	1,661.1	1,605.8	Liabilities	7b.d
																Monetary Authorities	
End of Period																	
	363	659	†1,537	1,796	1,640	2,259	2,030	2,656	3,587	2,119	1,690	3,663	2,494	2,933	4,149	Foreign Assets	11
	−10,366	−10,650	42,740	51,811	†60,870	74,710	91,399	116,131	142,023	182,431	214,392	281,383	331,425	447,581	675,040	Claims on Central Government	12a
	31,227	37,564	11,208	10,607	†12,543	14,138	10,375	3,639	5,923	23,785	15,553	19,602	15,918	21,576		Claims on Deposit Money Banks	12e
	8,718	15,319	42,281	51,387	†50,358	65,698	79,275	97,584	124,675	164,513	213,025	270,104	320,579	431,085	653,723	Reserve Money	14
	8,299	14,659	19,926	29,211	39,289	54,429	68,663	90,659	119,207	159,608	205,509	256,605	296,471	378,001	551,343	*of which: Currency Outside DMBs*	14a
	....	....	....	....	22,133	22,798	22,662	23,320	24,284	22,904	22,624	24,435	23,402	23,847	23,850	Other Liabilities to DMBs	14n
	1,004	841	†2,416	2,080	†2,148	1,942	2,050	2,056	1,843	1,965	2,121	2,117	2,108	2,170	3,551	Foreign Liabilities	16c
	788	787	787	636	634	666	787	788	1,086	1,082	1,681	2,882	4,874	5,282	8,952	Capital Accounts	17a
	10,713	10,625	10,001	10,111	†−220	3	−969	−1,317	−1,086	9	414	1,062	2,559	4,048	10,690	Other Items (Net)	17r
																Deposit Money Banks	
End of Period																	
	659	1,148	23,340	22,962	†7,183	2,201	5,301	7,802	14,259	23,105	25,056	51,173	64,156	78,540	107,920	Reserves	20
	....	....	....	....	22,133	22,798	22,662	23,320	24,284	22,904	22,624	24,435	23,402	23,847	23,850	Other Claims on Monetary Author.	20n
	15	13	22	163	†—	—	—	1	3	8	20	1	369	3	13	Foreign Assets	21
	−388	−365	†−8,373	−10,240	†5,605	3,367	2,751	−727	−305	−2,402	2,312	−30,179	11,960	35,659	40,485	Claims on Central Govt. (Net)	22an
	305	331	360	438	444	545	449	511	310	184	61	61	—	—	—	Claims on Local Government	22b
	41,894	46,281	560	638	†4,010	4,571	6,459	11,343	8,351	10,631	11,419	46,688	53,960	69,158	72,338	Claims on Nonfin.Pub.Enterprises	22c
	2,998	2,801	3,262	7,208	†12,406	19,173	23,076	28,262	45,956	75,346	115,505	155,761	188,649	266,966	416,676	Claims on Private Sector	22d
	1,175	1,009	1,391	1,376	†4,725	4,963	5,827	9,183	11,241	14,961	25,600	44,782	72,707	119,746	206,349	Demand Deposits	24
	8,446	7,615	9,467	11,789	†13,939	18,120	24,024	33,942	54,572	82,786	102,944	151,363	216,459	335,574	450,561	Time, Savings,& Fgn.Currency Dep.	25
	....	....	....	....	410	808	1,039	1,179	1,814	2,349	1,739	1,549	1,635	1,703	1,760	Restricted Deposits	26b
	8,975	10,320	10,538	12,472	10,234	10,355	10,759	11,725	11,889	11,494	10,549	10,287	10,611	10,961	11,000	Foreign Liabilities	26c
	31,227	37,564	11,208	10,607	†24,506	22,327	27,281	36,218	53,714	36,987	40,151	49,051	13,908	23,843	−3,655	Credit from Monetary Authorities	26g
	1,347	1,638	2,000	2,106	1,830	2,074	2,402	3,228	4,128	7,790	10,733	12,546	17,908	24,094	32,285	Capital Accounts	27a
	−5,687	−7,937	−15,397	−17,181	†−3,865	−5,991	−10,657	−24,961	−44,498	−26,592	−14,719	−21,643	9,268	−41,749	−37,013	Other Items (Net)	27r
																Monetary Survey	
End of Period																	
	−9,601	−10,489	†−11,396	−12,593	†−10,742	−10,038	−10,779	−11,124	−10,143	−11,332	−10,960	−8,740	−9,856	−10,195	−10,389	Foreign Assets (Net)	31n
	46,481	52,606	†38,549	49,855	†83,335	102,366	124,134	155,520	196,335	266,191	343,689	453,714	585,994	819,364	1,204,539	Domestic Credit	32
	−2,878	−1,639	†34,367	41,571	†66,475	78,077	94,150	115,404	141,718	180,029	216,704	251,204	343,385	483,240	715,525	Claims on Central Govt. (Net)	32an
	305	331	360	438	444	545	449	511	310	184	61	61	—	—	—	Claims on Local Government	32b
	41,894	46,281	560	638	†4,010	4,571	6,459	11,343	8,351	10,631	11,419	46,688	53,960	69,158	72,338	Claims on Nonfin.Pub.Enterprises	32c
	2,998	2,801	3,262	7,208	†12,406	19,173	23,076	28,262	45,956	75,346	115,505	155,761	188,649	266,966	416,676	Claims on Private Sector	32d
	9,474	15,668	21,317	30,587	†43,495	58,688	73,456	98,288	125,957	167,971	219,983	282,087	345,765	464,968	701,153	Money	34
	8,446	7,615	9,467	11,789	†13,939	18,120	24,024	33,942	54,572	82,786	102,944	151,363	216,459	335,574	450,561	Quasi-Money	35
	....	....	....	....	410	808	1,039	1,179	1,814	2,349	1,739	1,549	1,635	1,703	1,760	Restricted Deposits	36b
	2,135	2,425	2,787	2,742	2,464	2,740	3,189	4,016	5,213	8,871	12,413	15,428	22,782	29,376	41,237	Capital Accounts	37a
	16,825	16,409	12,413	14,681	†12,283	11,972	11,625	6,977	−1,361	−7,120	−4,354	−5,457	−10,502	−22,453	−555	Other Items (Net)	37r
	17,920	23,283	30,784	42,376	†57,434	76,808	97,480	132,230	180,528	250,757	322,927	433,451	562,224	800,542	1,151,714	Money plus Quasi-Money	351
																Interest Rates	
Percent Per Annum																	
				11.00	11.00	11.00	11.00	12.50	15.00	15.00	15.00	12.00	10.00	10.00	10.00	Central Bank Rate (End of Per.)	60
	1.50	1.50	1.50	5.88	9.00	9.00	9.00	9.00	9.75	12.50	12.50	12.50	11.00	9.75	9.50	Deposit Rate	60l
	8.00	8.00	8.00	8.00	....	8.00	....	16.50	16.50	16.50	16.50	16.50	16.13	15.25	15.00	Lending Rate	60p
							10.50	10.50	13.13	14.00	14.00	†11.00	9.00	9.00		Government Bond Yield	61
																Prices	
Period Averages																	
	17.4	20.2	25.7	30.3	40.0	48.8	64.4	79.9	100.0	116.3	150.8	228.5	†270.5	270.2	327.2	Consumer Prices	64
Period Averages																	
	15,505	15,813	16,036	15,221	....	15,737	16,469	16,817	....	....	17,964	18,359	....	....	....	Employment	67e
	331	313	486	555	559	503	518	541	....	....	535	452	425	....	....	Unemployment	67c

Myanmar

		1972	1973	1974	1975	1976	1977	1978	1979	1980	1981	1982	1983	1984	1985	1986
International Transactions															*Millions of Kyats*	
Exports	70	653.5	640.4	911.8	1,102.0	1,394.9	1,516.7	1,665.9	2,547.7	3,122.7	3,352.7	3,040.0	3,039.4	2,512.0	2,575.9	2,116.5
Imports, c.i.f.	71	723.1	522.2	855.4	1,245.0	1,198.3	1,704.6	2,114.0	2,116.1	2,337.3	2,702.5	3,178.1	2,150.8	2,016.2	2,401.5	2,245.2
Balance of Payments															*Millions of US Dollars:*	
Current Account, n.i.e.	78al d	...	...	...	...	−33.8	−100.4	−215.1	−358.5	−347.1	−314.0	−498.7	−349.8	−217.8	−205.5	−294.0
Goods: Exports f.o.b.	78aa d					172.7	206.3	272.3	362.6	428.6	533.2	422.8	375.2	364.1	310.8	330.7
Goods: Imports f.o.b.	78ab d					−212.7	−307.4	−495.4	−731.7	−788.2	−863.1	−913.0	−728.2	−564.5	−512.9	−620.9
Trade Balance	78ac d					−40.0	−101.2	−223.1	−369.1	−359.6	−329.9	−490.2	−353.0	−200.4	−202.1	−290.2
Services: Credit	78ad d					27.3	35.8	25.9	40.5	52.2	73.1	82.0	64.1	61.5	66.8	66.4
Services: Debit	78ae d					−22.8	−31.2	−27.0	−59.0	−73.3	−91.5	−105.6	−75.1	−70.6	−81.8	−56.8
Balance on Goods & Services	78af d					−35.6	−96.6	−224.2	−387.6	−380.7	−348.3	−513.8	−364.0	−209.5	−217.1	−280.6
Income: Credit	78ag d					3.5	3.8	4.8	8.7	14.0	20.1	13.3	4.0	4.9	2.2	4.2
Income: Debit	78ah d					−18.0	−18.6	−23.3	−37.6	−61.0	−69.8	−64.4	−72.1	−81.1	−71.1	−110.9
Balance on Gds, Serv. & Inc.	78ai d					−50.1	−111.4	−242.7	−416.4	−427.8	−397.9	−564.9	−432.0	−285.7	−286.0	−387.3
Current Transfers, n.i.e.: Credit	78aj d					17.6	11.9	28.5	59.7	81.3	85.3	66.5	82.4	68.1	81.8	96.7
Current Transfers: Debit	78ak d					−1.4	−.9	−.8	−1.7	−.6	−1.3	−.3	−.3	−.2	−1.3	−3.5
Capital Account, n.i.e.	78bc d					—	—	—	—	—	—	—	—	—	—	—
Capital Account, n.i.e.: Credit	78ba d					—	—	—	—	—	—	—	—	—	—	—
Capital Account: Debit	78bb d					—	—	—	—	—	—	—	—	—	—	—
Financial Account, n.i.e.	78bj d					15.8	55.7	183.6	429.1	370.8	317.7	340.2	245.6	193.8	148.7	274.0
Direct Investment Abroad	78bd d					—	—	—	—	—	—	—	—	—	—	—
Dir. Invest. in Rep. Econ., n.i.e.	78be d					—	—	—	—	—	—	—	—	—	—	—
Portfolio Investment Assets	78bf d					—	—	—	—	—	—	—	—	—	—	—
Equity Securities	78bk d					—	—	—	—	—	—	—	—	—	—	—
Debt Securities	78bl d					—	—	—	—	—	—	—	—	—	—	—
Portfolio Investment Liab., n.i.e.	78bg d					—	—	—	—	—	—	—	—	—	—	—
Equity Securities	78bm d					—	—	—	—	—	—	—	—	—	—	—
Debt Securities	78bn d					—	—	—	—	—	—	—	—	—	—	—
Financial Derivatives Assets	78bw d					...	...	...	...	...	...	...	...	...	...	...
Financial Derivatives Liabilities	78bx d					...	...	...	...	...	...	...	...	...	...	...
Other Investment Assets	78bh d					2.2	—	—	—	—	—	—	—	—	—	—
Monetary Authorities	78bo d					—	—	—	—	—	—	—	—	—	—	—
General Government	78bp d					—	—	—	—	—	—	—	—	—	—	—
Banks	78bq d					—	—	—	—	—	—	—	—	—	—	—
Other Sectors	78br d					2.2	—	—	—	—	—	—	—	—	—	—
Other Investment Liab., n.i.e.	78bi d					13.6	55.7	183.6	429.1	370.8	317.7	340.2	245.6	193.8	148.7	274.0
Monetary Authorities	78bs d					−.2	2.0	2.7	1.1	−.3	3.7	11.3	32.2	.2	1.5	2.3
General Government	78bt d					13.9	53.8	180.9	428.0	371.1	314.0	328.9	213.4	193.5	147.2	271.7
Banks	78bu d					—	—	—	—	—	—	—	—	—	—	—
Other Sectors	78bv d					—	—	—	—	—	—	—	—	—	—	—
Net Errors and Omissions	78ca d					2.8	−6.1	−32.3	−13.3	7.7	−32.6	30.3	79.9	15.3	41.7	69.3
Overall Balance	78cb d					−15.2	−50.7	−63.8	57.3	31.3	−28.9	−128.3	−24.4	−8.8	−15.0	49.3
Reserves and Related Items	79da d					15.2	50.7	63.8	−57.3	−31.3	28.9	128.3	24.4	8.8	15.0	−49.3
Reserve Assets	79db d					22.1	15.4	7.0	−95.9	−39.6	6.1	103.4	13.0	20.8	38.7	−4.4
Use of Fund Credit and Loans	79dc d					−6.9	27.8	33.7	15.1	−11.7	22.8	24.8	11.4	−12.1	−23.6	−44.9
Exceptional Financing	79de d					—	7.5	23.1	23.6	20.0	—	—	—	—	—	—
International Investment Position															*Millions of US Dollars*	
Assets	79aa d	...	...	...	...	...	...	...	...	...	...	...	...	...	...	...
Direct Investment Abroad	79ab d	...	...	...	...	...	...	...	...	...	...	...	...	...	...	...
Portfolio Investment	79ac d	...	...	...	...	...	...	...	...	...	...	...	...	...	...	...
Equity Securities	79ad d	...	...	...	...	...	...	...	...	...	...	...	...	...	...	...
Debt Securities	79ae d	...	...	...	...	...	...	...	...	...	...	...	...	...	...	...
Financial Derivatives	79al d	...	...	...	...	...	...	...	...	...	...	...	...	...	...	...
Other Investment	79af d	...	...	...	...	...	...	...	...	...	...	...	...	...	...	...
Monetary Authorities	79ag d	...	...	...	...	...	...	...	...	...	...	...	...	...	...	...
General Government	79ah d	...	...	...	...	...	...	...	...	...	...	...	...	...	...	...
Banks	79ai d	...	...	...	...	...	...	...	...	...	...	...	...	...	...	...
Other Sectors	79aj d	...	...	...	...	...	...	...	...	...	...	...	...	...	...	...
Reserve Assets	79ak d	...	...	...	...	...	...	...	...	...	...	...	...	...	...	...
Liabilities	79la d	...	...	...	...	...	...	...	...	...	...	...	...	...	...	...
Dir. Invest. in Rep. Economy	79lb d	...	...	...	...	...	...	...	...	...	...	...	...	...	...	...
Portfolio Investment	79lc d	...	...	...	...	...	...	...	...	...	...	...	...	...	...	...
Equity Securities	79ld d	...	...	...	...	...	...	...	...	...	...	...	...	...	...	...
Debt Securities	79le d	...	...	...	...	...	...	...	...	...	...	...	...	...	...	...
Financial Derivatives	79ll d	...	...	...	...	...	...	...	...	...	...	...	...	...	...	...
Other Investment	79lf d	...	...	...	...	...	...	...	...	...	...	...	...	...	...	...
Monetary Authorities	79lg d	...	...	...	...	...	...	...	...	...	...	...	...	...	...	...
General Government	79lh d	...	...	...	...	...	...	...	...	...	...	...	...	...	...	...
Banks	79li d	...	...	...	...	...	...	...	...	...	...	...	...	...	...	...
Other Sectors	79lj d	...	...	...	...	...	...	...	...	...	...	...	...	...	...	...
Government Finance															*Millions of Kyats:*	
Deficit (-) or Surplus	80	...	†−855	†−572	−678	−129	196	196	851	473	709	338	307	−93	−443	−1,482
Revenue	81	...	†1,453	†1,934	2,172	3,277	4,266	4,755	5,690	6,176	7,303	7,445	7,640	7,741	7,620	7,320
Grants Received	81z	...	73	†110	149	141	86	248	326	415	269	658	405	404	587	564
Expenditure	82	...	†2,349	†2,601	2,990	3,533	4,147	4,787	5,194	6,119	7,046	7,898	7,936	8,509	9,015	9,790
Lending Minus Repayments	83	...	32	†15	9	14	9	20	−29	−1	−183	−133	−198	−271	−365	−424
Financing																
Domestic	84a	...	941	†626	669	123	−769	−467	−1,200	−941	−1,136	−886	−779	−485	−214	690
Foreign	85a	...	−86	†−54	9	6	573	271	349	468	427	548	472	578	657	792
National Accounts															*Millions of Kyats:*	
Househ.Cons.Expend.,incl.NPISHs	96f	10,493	12,824	†17,452	21,389	24,805	26,132	27,404	28,980	31,774	35,218	39,747	42,685	47,396	49,532	53,067
Gross Fixed Capital Formation	93e	1,111	1,146	†1,525	1,681	2,320	3,753	5,364	7,389	7,228	8,635	10,044	9,057	8,476	8,649	8,618
Changes in Inventories	93i	156	352	†475	659	515	92	414	486	1,065	1,205	331	−95	−367	44	−1,139
Exports of gOods and Services	90c	680	953	†912	†1,192	1,414	1,729	1,842	2,679	3,177	3,432	3,003	3,373	3,133	2,566	2,418
Imports of Goods and Services (-)	98c	704	575	†1,016	1,443	1,628	2,087	3,224	4,201	4,635	5,611	6,314	5,197	5,041	4,802	3,936
Gross Domestic Product (GDP)	99b	11,735	14,700	†19,348	23,477	27,427	29,618	31,800	35,333	38,609	42,879	46,811	49,823	53,597	55,989	59,028
Net Primary Income from Abroad	98.n	...	...	...	−7	−18	−61	−92	−146	−160	−168	−347	−510	−517	−581	−658
Gross National Income (GNI)	99a				23,470	27,409	29,557	31,708	35,187	38,449	42,711	46,464	49,313	53,080	55,408	58,370
GDP Volume 1985/86 Prices	99b.p	...	...	...	...	35,120	39,692	39,261	41,112	44,362	47,157	49,714	51,878	54,437	55,989	55,397
GDP Volume (1995=100)	99bv p	...	...	...	...	52.6	59.5	58.8	61.6	66.5	70.7	74.5	77.7	81.6	83.9	83.0
GDP Deflator (1995=100)	99bi p	...	...	...	...	8.6	8.2	8.9	9.5	9.6	10.0	10.4	10.6	10.9	11.0	11.8
															Millions:	
Population	99z	28.26	28.89	29.52	30.17	30.83	31.51	32.21	32.91	33.64	35.09	35.91	36.75	37.61	38.54	39.41

Item	1987	1988	1989	1990	1991	1992	1993	1994	1995	1996	1997	1998	1999	2000	2001	Code
International Transactions																
Millions of Kyats																
Exports	1,449.8	1,051.4	1,410.4	2,037.0	2,633.0	3,241.1	3,609.4	4,776.7	4,825.8	4,419.5	5,415.8	6,737.2	7,073.5	10,600.5	15,344.1	70
Imports, c.i.f.	1,785.6	1,538.0	1,280.5	1,709.4	4,058.8	3,971.0	5,007.0	5,285.9	7,564.2	8,032.0	12,735.9	16,920.7	14,463.9	15,426.3	18,692.8	71
Balance of Payments																
Minus Sign Indicates Debit																
Current Account, n.i.e.	-180.0	-175.9	-68.0	-431.3	-267.4	-114.4	-227.8	-129.9	-258.5	-279.8	-412.0	-494.2	-281.9	-243.0	....	78al d
Goods: Exports f.o.b.	219.6	165.7	222.8	222.6	248.2	531.3	630.9	857.4	933.2	937.9	974.5	1,065.1	1,281.1	1,618.8	....	78aa d
Goods: Imports f.o.b.	-452.7	-370.2	-304.3	-524.3	-301.5	-636.2	-1,260.8	-1,466.7	-1,756.3	-1,869.1	-2,106.6	-2,451.2	-2,159.6	-2,134.9	....	78ab d
Trade Balance	-233.1	-204.5	-81.5	-301.7	-53.3	-104.9	-629.9	-609.4	-823.0	-931.2	-1,132.1	-1,386.1	-878.5	-516.1	....	78ac d
Services: Credit	69.1	46.9	56.6	93.5	56.0	112.4	246.6	270.7	360.9	427.7	521.7	626.1	507.1	526.5	....	78ad d
Services: Debit	-46.8	-34.5	-44.3	-72.3	-54.3	-42.4	-130.2	-128.9	-243.8	-302.0	-443.4	-364.8	-288.2	-514.4	....	78ae d
Balance on Goods & Services	-210.8	-192.0	-69.2	-280.6	-51.6	-34.9	-513.6	-467.6	-705.9	-805.4	-1,053.8	-1,124.7	-659.7	-504.1	....	78af d
Income: Credit	6.3	2.7	2.7	2.4	1.0	3.4	4.7	7.1	15.4	9.1	6.5	10.9	51.1	30.0	....	78ag d
Income: Debit	-82.5	-79.1	-57.1	-192.1	-272.2	-151.4	-63.0	-74.1	-124.2	-53.1	-20.3	-11.3	-54.0	-66.1	....	78ah d
Balance on Gds, Serv. & Inc.	-287.1	-268.4	-123.6	-470.3	-322.8	-182.9	-571.9	-534.5	-814.7	-849.4	-1,067.5	-1,125.1	-662.6	-540.1	....	78ai d
Current Transfers, n.i.e.: Credit	107.4	93.1	55.6	39.0	55.5	70.3	344.6	405.2	564.2	598.4	685.1	631.2	381.0	297.3	....	78aj d
Current Transfers, n.i.e.: Debit	-.2	-.5	—	—	-.1	-1.8	-.5	-.6	-8.0	-28.8	-29.7	-.3	-.3	-.1	....	78ak d
Capital Account, n.i.e.	—	—	84.0	232.9	—	—	—	—	—	—	....	....	....	....	....	78bc d
Capital Account, n.i.e.: Credit	—	—	84.0	232.9	—	—	—	—	—	—	....	....	....	....	....	78ba d
Capital Account: Debit	—	—	—	—	—	—	—	—	—	—	....	....	....	....	....	78bb d
Financial Account, n.i.e.	202.9	139.7	82.0	185.8	275.0	191.0	160.8	185.2	242.8	266.8	469.1	535.1	248.8	160.1	....	78bj d
Direct Investment Abroad															....	78bd d
Dir. Invest. in Rep. Econ., n.i.e.			7.8	161.1	238.1	171.6	104.7	126.1	277.2	310.4	387.2	314.5	253.1	254.8	....	78be d
Portfolio Investment Assets			—	—	—	—	—	—	—	—	—	—	—	—	....	78bf d
Equity Securities			—	—	—	—	—	—	—	—	—	—	—	—	....	78bk d
Debt Securities			—	—	—	—	—	—	—	—	—	—	—	—	....	78bl d
Portfolio Investment Liab., n.i.e.			—	—	—	—	—	—	—	—	—	—	—	—	....	78bg d
Equity Securities			—	—	—	—	—	—	—	—	—	—	—	—	....	78bm d
Debt Securities			—	—	—	—	—	—	—	—	—	—	—	—	....	78bn d
Financial Derivatives Assets															....	78bw d
Financial Derivatives Liabilities															....	78bx d
Other Investment Assets															....	78bh d
Monetary Authorities															....	78bo d
General Government															....	78bp d
Banks															....	78bq d
Other Sectors															....	78br d
Other Investment Liab., n.i.e.	202.9	139.7	74.2	24.6	37.0	19.4	56.1	59.1	-34.4	-43.6	81.9	220.7	-4.3	-94.7	....	78bi d
Monetary Authorities	-1.2	-3.3	-.6	-1.8	-2.8	-.7	—	2.6	2.3	-3.1	-5.6	-2.6	1.1	7.2	....	78bs d
General Government	204.1	143.0	74.8	26.4	39.8	20.2	56.1	56.5	-36.7	-40.6	87.5	226.9	-4.1	-105.9	....	78bt d
Banks												-3.6	-1.3	4.0	....	78bu d
Other Sectors															....	78bv d
Net Errors and Omissions	14.7	116.7	52.6	21.4	-53.9	17.7	-10.0	-10.3	-16.2	-11.7	-26.0	18.8	-12.3	59.6	....	78ca d
Overall Balance	37.7	80.5	150.6	8.7	-46.3	94.3	-77.0	45.0	-31.8	-24.7	31.0	59.7	-45.4	-23.3	....	78cb d
Reserves and Related Items	-37.7	-80.5	-150.6	-8.7	46.3	-94.3	77.0	-45.0	31.8	24.7	-31.0	-59.7	45.4	23.3	....	79da d
Reserve Assets	12.8	-52.4	-142.9	-6.3	46.6	-94.3	77.0	-45.0	31.8	24.7	-31.0	-59.7	45.4	23.3	....	79db d
Use of Fund Credit and Loans	-50.4	-28.1	-7.7	-2.4	-.3										....	79dc d
Exceptional Financing															....	79de d
International Investment Position																
Millions of US Dollars																
Assets													328.0	287.4	....	79aa d
Direct Investment Abroad													—	—	....	79ab d
Portfolio Investment													—	—	....	79ac d
Equity Securities													—	—	....	79ad d
Debt Securities													—	—	....	79ae d
Financial Derivatives													—	—	....	79al d
Other Investment													—	—	....	79af d
Monetary Authorities													—	—	....	79ag d
General Government													—	—	....	79ah d
Banks													—	—	....	79ai d
Other Sectors													—	—	....	79aj d
Reserve Assets													328.0	287.4	....	79ak d
Liabilities													8,466.7	8,198.5	....	79la d
Dir. Invest. in Rep. Economy													3,096.2	3,191.4	....	79lb d
Portfolio Investment													—	—	....	79lc d
Equity Securities													—	—	....	79ld d
Debt Securities													—	—	....	79le d
Financial Derivatives													—	—	....	79ll d
Other Investment													5,370.5	5,007.1	....	79lf d
Monetary Authorities													—	—	....	79lg d
General Government													—	—	....	79lh d
Banks													—	—	....	79li d
Other Sectors													—	—	....	79lj d
Government Finance																
Year Beginning April 1																
Deficit (-) or Surplus	-1,515	-2,300	-5,189	-7,789	-8,993	†-7,054	-7,761	-15,757	-24,924	†-25,007	-20,448	8,176	-1,580	....	....	80
Revenue	7,201	6,463	11,842	16,048	18,039	†20,313	27,329	32,029	39,429	†54,580	71,502	79,739	90,599	....	....	81
Grants Received	566	347	152	140	300	†358	456	429	744	†421	763	643	852	....	....	81z
Expenditure	9,621	9,443	17,566	24,349	27,621	†27,931	35,696	48,021	64,884	†79,929	92,628	72,097	92,880	....	....	82
Lending Minus Repayments	-339	-333	-383	-372	-289	†-206	-150	194	213	†79	85	109	151	....	....	83
Financing																
Domestic	960	2,125	5,200	7,763	9,001	†7,038	7,738	15,749	25,201	†25,185	20,726	-8,125	1,260	....	....	84a
Foreign	555	175	-11	26	-8	†16	23	8	-277	†-178	-278	-51	320	....	....	85a
National Accounts																
Year Beginning April 1																
Househ.Cons.Expend.,incl.NPISHs	63,168	67,754	113,726	134,188	160,610	217,384	319,191	417,230	523,876	701,220	987,513	1,419,709	1,906,136	....	....	96f
Gross Fixed Capital Formation	8,683	7,296	11,827	22,318	27,571	31,184	37,466	54,596	82,582	118,313	150,240	206,912	241,694	....	....	93e
Changes in Inventories	-742	2,467	-325	-1,995	1,032	2,601	7,360	3,875	3,540	-21,262	-10,276	-7,604	48,325	....	....	93i
Exports of gOods and Services	1,655	2,169	2,834	2,953	2,926	3,590	4,228	5,405	5,033	5,488	6,290	7,700	9,394	....	....	90c
Imports of Goods and Services (-)	4,066	3,443	3,395	5,523	5,337	5,365	7,923	8,332	10,302	11,779	14,258	16,941	15,248	....	....	98c
Gross Domestic Product (GDP)	68,698	76,243	124,666	151,941	186,802	249,395	360,321	472,774	604,729	791,980	1,119,509	1,609,776	2,190,301	....	....	99b
Net Primary Income from Abroad	-520	-261	-304	47	-291	-153	-429	-396	-689	-116	-69	34	-118	....	....	98.n
Gross National Income (GNI)	68,178	75,982	124,362	151,988	186,512	249,242	359,892	472,378	604,040	791,864	1,119,440	1,609,810	2,190,183	....	....	99a
GDP Volume 1985/86 Prices	53,178	47,141	48,883	50,260	49,933	54,757	58,064	62,406	66,742	71,042	75,123	79,460	88,134	93,629	....	99b.p
GDP Volume (1995=100)	79.7	70.6	73.2	75.3	74.8	82.0	87.0	93.5	100.0	106.4	112.6	119.1	132.1	140.3	....	99bv p
GDP Deflator (1995=100)	14.3	17.9	28.1	33.4	41.3	50.3	68.5	83.6	100.0	123.0	164.5	223.6	274.3	....	....	99bi p
Midyear Estimates																
Population	†39.19	39.84	40.60	40.52	41.55	42.33	43.12	43.92	44.35	45.08	45.78	46.46	47.11	47.75	48.36	99z

(See notes in the back of the book.)

Namibia

728

		1972	1973	1974	1975	1976	1977	1978	1979	1980	1981	1982	1983	1984	1985	1986
Exchange Rates													*Namibia Dollars per SDR:*			
Market Rate	aa	.85000	.80966	.84435	1.01797	1.01029	1.05627	1.13286	1.08924	.95066	1.11341	1.18729	1.27926	1.94563	2.80926	2.67072
													Namibia Dollars per US Dollar:			
Market Rate	ae	.78290	.67116	.68963	.86957	.86957	.86957	.86957	.82686	.74538	.95657	1.07631	1.22190	1.98491	2.55754	2.18341
Market Rate	rf	.77283	.69411	.67948	.73951	.86957	.86957	.86957	.84202	.77883	.87758	1.08582	1.11410	1.47528	2.22868	2.28503
Fund Position													*Millions of SDRs:*			
Quota	2f. s	...	...	...	...	...	...	...	...	...	...	...	...	...	...	...
SDRs	1b. s	...	...	...	...	...	...	...	...	...	...	...	...	...	...	...
Reserve Position in the Fund	1c. s	...	...	...	...	...	...	...	...	...	...	...	...	...	...	...
Total Fund Cred.&Loans Outstg.	2tl	...	...	...	...	...	...	...	...	...	...	...	...	...	...	...
International Liquidity													*Millions of US Dollars Unless Otherwise Indicated:*			
Total Reserves minus Gold	1l. d	...	...	...	...	...	...	...	...	...	...	...	...	...	...	...
SDRs	1b. d	...	...	...	...	...	...	...	...	...	...	...	...	...	...	...
Reserve Position in the Fund	1c. d	...	...	...	...	...	...	...	...	...	...	...	...	...	...	...
Foreign Exchange	1d. d	...	...	...	...	...	...	...	...	...	...	...	...	...	...	...
Gold (Million Fine Troy Ounces)	1ad	...	...	...	...	...	...	...	...	...	...	...	...	...	...	...
Gold (National Valuation)	1an d	...	...	...	...	...	...	...	...	...	...	...	...	...	...	...
Monetary Authorities: Other Liab.	4..d	...	...	...	...	...	...	...	...	...	...	...	...	...	...	...
Deposit Money Banks: Assets	7a. d	...	...	...	...	...	...	...	...	...	...	...	...	...	...	...
Liabilities	7b. d	...	...	...	...	...	...	...	...	...	...	...	...	...	...	...
Other Banking Insts.: Liabilities	7f. d	...	...	...	...	...	...	...	...	...	...	...	...	...	...	...
Monetary Authorities													*Millions of Namibia Dollars:*			
Foreign Assets	11	...	...	...	...	...	...	...	...	...	...	...	...	...	...	...
Claims on Central Government	12a	...	...	...	...	...	...	...	...	...	...	...	...	...	...	...
Reserve Money	14	...	...	...	...	...	...	...	...	...	...	...	...	...	...	...
Foreign Liabilities	16c	...	...	...	...	...	...	...	...	...	...	...	...	...	...	...
Central Government Deposits	16d	...	...	...	...	...	...	...	...	...	...	...	...	...	...	...
Capital Accounts	17a	...	...	...	...	...	...	...	...	...	...	...	...	...	...	...
Other Items (Net)	17r	...	...	...	...	...	...	...	...	...	...	...	...	...	...	...
Deposit Money Banks													*Millions of Namibia Dollars:*			
Reserves	20	...	...	...	...	...	...	...	...	...	...	...	...	...	...	...
Foreign Assets	21	...	...	...	...	...	...	...	...	...	...	...	...	...	...	...
Claims on Central Government	22a	...	...	...	...	...	...	...	...	...	...	...	...	...	...	...
Claims on Local Government	22b	...	...	...	...	...	...	...	...	...	...	...	...	...	...	...
Claims on Nonfin.Pub.Enterprises	22c	...	...	...	...	...	...	...	...	...	...	...	...	...	...	...
Claims on Private Sector	22d	...	...	...	...	...	...	...	...	...	...	...	...	...	...	...
Claims on Other Banking Insts	22f	...	...	...	...	...	...	...	...	...	...	...	...	...	...	...
Claims on Nonbank Financial Insts	22g	...	...	...	...	...	...	...	...	...	...	...	...	...	...	...
Demand Deposits	24	...	...	...	...	...	...	...	...	...	...	...	...	...	...	...
Time, Savings,& Fgn.Currency Dep.	25	...	...	...	...	...	...	...	...	...	...	...	...	...	...	...
Money Market Instruments	26aa	...	...	...	...	...	...	...	...	...	...	...	...	...	...	...
Bonds	26ab	...	...	...	...	...	...	...	...	...	...	...	...	...	...	...
Foreign Liabilities	26c	...	...	...	...	...	...	...	...	...	...	...	...	...	...	...
Central Government Deposits	26d	...	...	...	...	...	...	...	...	...	...	...	...	...	...	...
Credit from Monetary Authorities	26g	...	...	...	...	...	...	...	...	...	...	...	...	...	...	...
Liabilities to Other Banking Insts	26i	...	...	...	...	...	...	...	...	...	...	...	...	...	...	...
Capital Accounts	27a	...	...	...	...	...	...	...	...	...	...	...	...	...	...	...
Other Items (Net)	27r	...	...	...	...	...	...	...	...	...	...	...	...	...	...	...
Monetary Survey													*Millions of Namibia Dollars:*			
Foreign Assets (Net)	31n	...	...	...	...	...	...	...	...	...	...	...	...	...	...	...
Domestic Credit	32	...	...	...	...	...	...	...	...	...	...	...	...	...	...	...
Claims on Central Govt. (Net)	32an	...	...	...	...	...	...	...	...	...	...	...	...	...	...	...
Claims on Local Government	32b	...	...	...	...	...	...	...	...	...	...	...	...	...	...	...
Claims on Nonfin.Pub.Enterprises	32c	...	...	...	...	...	...	...	...	...	...	...	...	...	...	...
Claims on Private Sector	32d	...	...	...	...	...	...	...	...	...	...	...	...	...	...	...
Claims on Other Banking Insts	32f	...	...	...	...	...	...	...	...	...	...	...	...	...	...	...
Claims on Nonbank Financial Inst	32g	...	...	...	...	...	...	...	...	...	...	...	...	...	...	...
Money	34	...	...	...	...	...	...	...	...	...	...	...	...	...	...	...
Quasi-Money	35	...	...	...	...	...	...	...	...	...	...	...	...	...	...	...
Money Market Instruments	36aa	...	...	...	...	...	...	...	...	...	...	...	...	...	...	...
Bonds	36ab	...	...	...	...	...	...	...	...	...	...	...	...	...	...	...
Liabilities to Other Banking Insts	36i	...	...	...	...	...	...	...	...	...	...	...	...	...	...	...
Capital Accounts	37a	...	...	...	...	...	...	...	...	...	...	...	...	...	...	...
Other Items (Net)	37r	...	...	...	...	...	...	...	...	...	...	...	...	...	...	...
Money plus Quasi-Money	35l	...	...	...	...	...	...	...	...	...	...	...	...	...	...	...
Other Banking Institutions													*Millions of Namibia Dollars:*			
Reserves	40	...	...	...	...	...	...	...	...	...	...	...	...	...	...	...
Claims on Central Government	42a	...	...	...	...	...	...	...	...	...	...	...	...	...	...	...
Claims on Local Government	42b	...	...	...	...	...	...	...	...	...	...	...	...	...	...	...
Claims on Nonfin.Pub.Enterprises	42c	...	...	...	...	...	...	...	...	...	...	...	...	...	...	...
Claims on Private Sector	42d	...	...	...	...	...	...	...	...	...	...	...	...	...	...	...
Claims on Deposit Money Banks	42e	...	...	...	...	...	...	...	...	...	...	...	...	...	...	...
Claims on Nonbank Financial Insts	42g	...	...	...	...	...	...	...	...	...	...	...	...	...	...	...
Time, Savings,& Fgn.Currency Dep.	45	...	...	...	...	...	...	...	...	...	...	...	...	...	...	...
Money Market Instruments	46aa	...	...	...	...	...	...	...	...	...	...	...	...	...	...	...
Foreign Liabilities	46c	...	...	...	...	...	...	...	...	...	...	...	...	...	...	...
Central Government Deposits	46d	...	...	...	...	...	...	...	...	...	...	...	...	...	...	...
Credit from Deposit Money Banks	46h	...	...	...	...	...	...	...	...	...	...	...	...	...	...	...
Capital Accounts	47a	...	...	...	...	...	...	...	...	...	...	...	...	...	...	...
Other Items (Net)	47r	...	...	...	...	...	...	...	...	...	...	...	...	...	...	...

Exchange Rates

End of Period

1987	1988	1989	1990	1991	1992	1993	1994	1995	1996	1997	1998	1999	2000	2001		
2.73793	3.19971	3.33272	3.64557	3.92371	4.19788	4.66667	5.17298	5.42197	6.73325	6.56747	8.25106	8.44711	9.86107	15.23974	Market Rate	aa

End of Period (ae) Period Average (rf)

1987	1988	1989	1990	1991	1992	1993	1994	1995	1996	1997	1998	1999	2000	2001		
1.92994	2.37773	2.53601	2.56250	2.74303	3.05300	3.39750	3.54350	3.64750	4.68250	4.86750	5.86000	6.15450	7.56850	12.12650	Market Rate	ae
2.03603	2.27347	2.62268	2.58732	2.76132	2.85201	3.26774	3.55080	3.62709	4.29935	4.60796	5.52828	6.10948	6.93983	8.60918	Market Rate	rf

Fund Position

End of Period

1987	1988	1989	1990	1991	1992	1993	1994	1995	1996	1997	1998	1999	2000	2001		
....	....	....	70	70	100	100	100	100	100	100	100	137	137	137	Quota	2f.s
....	....	....	—	—	—	—	—	—	—	—	—	—	—	—	SDRs	1b.s
....	....	....	—	—	—	—	—	—	—	—	—	—	—	—	Reserve Position in the Fund	1c.s
....	....	....	—	—	—	—	—	—	—	—	—	—	—	—	Total Fund Cred.&Loans Outstg.	2tl

International Liquidity

End of Period

1987	1988	1989	1990	1991	1992	1993	1994	1995	1996	1997	1998	1999	2000	2001		
....	....	....	....	....	49.72	133.70	202.62	220.98	193.87	250.53	260.25	305.49	260.01	234.25	Total Reserves minus Gold	1l.d
....	....	....	—	.01	.01	.02	.02	.02	.02	.02	.02	.02	.02	.02	SDRs	1b.d
....	....	....	—	.01	.01	.01	.01	.03	.04	.04	.05	.05	.05	.05	Reserve Position in the Fund	1c.d
....	....	....	....	....	49.69	133.67	202.59	220.94	193.81	250.47	260.18	305.42	259.94	234.18	Foreign Exchange	1d.d
....	....	....			—	—	—	—	—	—	—	—	—	—	Gold (Million Fine Troy Ounces)	1ad
....	....	....			—	—	—	—	—	—	—	—	—	—	Gold (National Valuation)	1and
....	....	.03	.03	166.66	179.93	200.87	212.20	181.89	4.96	6.63	7.70	8.48		5.87	Monetary Authorities: Other Liab.	4..d
....	....	145.97	213.45	123.05	57.38	54.87	38.58	74.70	110.33	93.58	142.63	231.65		121.40	Deposit Money Banks: Assets	7a.d
....	....	107.55	46.09	32.53	47.35	110.49	137.26	63.00	172.31	116.20	67.99	129.63		129.09	Liabilities	7b.d
....	....	....	....	2.80	3.01	5.15	2.80	2.11	3.07	4.01	4.17	11.04		12.47	Other Banking Insts.: Liabilities	7f.d

Monetary Authorities

End of Period

1987	1988	1989	1990	1991	1992	1993	1994	1995	1996	1997	1998	1999	2000	2001		
....	....	....	243.0	226.0	346.8	465.9	725.8	818.1	918.0	1,236.0	1,550.1	1,885.6	2,032.0	2,715.9	Foreign Assets	11
....	....	....		510.3	619.6	720.0	783.7	856.9	—	—	—	—	—	—	Claims on Central Government	12a
....	....	....	90.0	97.1	221.8	233.3	373.6	415.6	508.3	609.3	631.4	906.7	849.6	919.7	Reserve Money	14
....	....	....	.1	.1	508.8	611.3	711.8	774.0	851.7	24.1	38.8	47.4	64.2	71.2	Foreign Liabilities	16c
....	....	....	150.4	123.1	143.5	221.7	291.2	280.8	162.4	374.4	416.1	471.8	446.3	360.5	Central Government Deposits	16d
....	....	....	10.0	21.8	31.9	40.6	71.2	119.5	303.8	316.5	513.4	562.9	783.9	1,587.9	Capital Accounts	17a
....	....	....	-7.5	-16.2	-48.9	-21.4	-2.0	11.9	-51.3	-88.4	-49.8	-103.2	-112.0	-223.3	Other Items (Net)	17r

Deposit Money Banks

End of Period

1987	1988	1989	1990	1991	1992	1993	1994	1995	1996	1997	1998	1999	2000	2001		
....	....	....	81.3	84.7	83.4	99.5	156.2	175.4	226.4	275.7	265.7	510.5	368.5	412.3	Reserves	20
....	....	....	374.1	585.5	375.7	195.0	194.4	140.7	349.8	537.0	548.4	877.8	1,753.3	1,472.2	Foreign Assets	21
....	....	....	40.0	40.8	171.6	279.2	238.8	256.2	460.9	659.8	701.7	1,020.0	949.1	904.2	Claims on Central Government	22a
....	....	....	2.2	9.3	15.2	15.0	17.2	19.2	18.6	17.4	18.8	16.3	12.4	32.8	Claims on Local Government	22b
....	....	....	4.0	50.1	42.1	42.2	42.1	72.1	72.2	148.8	142.7	136.6	234.0	119.1	Claims on Nonfin.Pub.Enterprises	22c
....	....	....	1,372.6	1,599.9	2,079.2	2,705.5	3,542.6	4,742.8	5,663.2	6,553.5	7,129.3	7,434.2	8,699.8	10,115.5	Claims on Private Sector	22d
....	....	....	47.6	13.0	21.0	10.1	95.1	74.6	7.0	23.6	14.6	.6	.4	19.7	Claims on Other Banking Insts	22f
....	....	....								10.1		10.1	45.6	2.3	Claims on Nonbank Financial Insts	22g
....	....	....	605.6	809.5	1,002.4	1,333.1	1,465.3	1,581.9	2,516.7	2,562.5	3,315.9	4,073.6	5,284.8	5,805.2	Demand Deposits	24
....	....	....	863.1	1,103.1	1,375.1	1,521.9	2,081.0	2,851.6	3,229.9	3,535.8	3,479.6	3,979.9	3,808.7	3,691.0	Time, Savings,& Fgn.Currency Dep.	25
....	....	....												103.3	Money Market Instruments	26aa
....	....	....	—	4.0	2.4	3.9	4.1	4.1	8.9	7.0	5.5	—	—	—	Bonds	26ab
....	....	....	275.6	126.4	99.3	160.9	391.5	500.6	295.0	838.7	680.9	418.4	981.1	1,565.4	Foreign Liabilities	26c
....	....	....	82.3	232.6	109.9	113.3	83.1	73.5	77.9	217.6	173.2	89.2	227.5	258.6	Central Government Deposits	26d
....	....	....									7.7	120.3	18.5	124.2	Credit from Monetary Authorities	26g
....	....	....			45.1	7.6	5.1	74.0	20.9	67.2	45.2	56.8	50.0		Liabilities to Other Banking Insts	26i
....	....	....	87.9	162.8	204.5	273.2	293.8	432.5	644.0	782.7	919.0	1,080.7	1,291.0	1,537.1	Capital Accounts	27a
....	....	....	7.3	-55.2	-50.5	-67.4	-37.6	-37.2	14.8	204.4	194.0	187.3	401.5	-6.9	Other Items (Net)	27r

Monetary Survey

End of Period

1987	1988	1989	1990	1991	1992	1993	1994	1995	1996	1997	1998	1999	2000	2001		
....	....	....	341.4	685.0	114.3	-111.3	-183.0	-315.8	121.1	910.1	1,378.7	2,297.7	2,740.0	2,551.5	Foreign Assets (Net)	31n
....	....	....	1,233.6	1,357.5	2,586.3	3,336.9	4,282.1	5,595.0	6,849.1	6,811.9	7,418.2	8,057.5	9,268.2	10,575.6	Domestic Credit	32
....	....	....	-192.7	-314.9	428.5	563.8	584.5	685.6	1,077.4	67.8	112.3	459.0	275.3	285.1	Claims on Central Govt. (Net)	32an
....	....	....	2.2	9.3	15.2	15.0	17.2	19.2	18.6	17.5	18.8	16.3	12.4	32.8	Claims on Local Government	32b
....	....	....	4.0	50.1	42.1	42.2	42.1	72.1	72.2	148.8	142.7	136.6	234.0	119.1	Claims on Nonfin.Pub.Enterprises	32c
....	....	....	1,372.6	1,599.9	2,079.2	2,705.5	3,542.6	4,742.8	5,663.2	6,553.5	7,129.3	7,434.2	8,699.8	10,115.5	Claims on Private Sector	32d
....	....	....	47.6	13.1	21.3	10.5	95.6	75.3	7.7	24.3	15.1	1.3	1.0	20.8	Claims on Other Banking Insts	32f
....	....	....								10.1		10.1	45.6	2.3	Claims on Nonbank Financial Inst	32g
....	....	....	614.3	821.9	1,002.4	1,466.8	1,682.8	1,822.2	2,799.5	2,898.1	3,680.9	4,496.3	5,766.0	6,312.7	Money	34
....	....	....	863.1	1,103.1	1,375.1	1,521.9	2,081.0	2,851.6	3,229.9	3,535.8	3,479.6	3,979.9	3,808.7	3,691.0	Quasi-Money	35
....	....	....												103.3	Money Market Instruments	36aa
....	....	....	—	4.0	2.4	3.9	4.1	4.1	8.9	7.0	5.5	—	—	—	Bonds	36ab
....	....	....			45.1	7.6	5.1	74.0	20.9	67.2	45.2	56.8	50.0	—	Liabilities to Other Banking Insts	36i
....	....	....	97.9	184.6	236.4	313.8	365.0	552.0	947.8	1,099.3	1,432.4	1,643.6	2,074.9	3,125.0	Capital Accounts	37a
....	....	....	-.2	-71.2	39.3	-88.4	-39.0	-24.5	-36.7	114.6	153.3	178.6	308.6	-104.9	Other Items (Net)	37r
....	....	....	1,477.4	1,925.0	2,377.5	2,988.8	3,763.8	4,673.7	6,029.4	6,433.9	7,160.5	8,476.2	9,574.7	10,003.7	Money plus Quasi-Money	35l

Other Banking Institutions

End of Period

1987	1988	1989	1990	1991	1992	1993	1994	1995	1996	1997	1998	1999	2000	2001		
....	....	....	....	....	138.4	43.1	.6	6.9	1.1	1.2	1.4	1.9	2.0	2.2	Reserves	40
....	....	....	....	....	3.0	6.0	31.0	5.1	140.0	166.4	151.9	209.5	34.3	138.5	Claims on Central Government	42a
....	....	....	....	....	5.8	6.1	5.5	5.3	5.3	5.2	5.1	5.0	4.9	4.6	Claims on Local Government	42b
....	....	....	....	....	2.4	7.7	16.7	7.8	4.6	4.7	7.5	8.6	211.6	63.4	Claims on Nonfin.Pub.Enterprises	42c
....	....	....	....	....	1,003.8	1,148.7	1,374.3	1,519.6	1,352.9	1,402.5	1,623.6	1,799.5	2,091.8	2,498.7	Claims on Private Sector	42d
....	....	....	....	....	—	95.8	116.8	164.1	91.3	160.6	118.8	167.6	121.5	151.6	Claims on Deposit Money Banks	42e
....	....	....	....	....	7.0	16.6	8.7	9.7	8.0	17.7	18.1	14.6	12.9	12.9	Claims on Nonbank Financial Insts	42g
....	....	....	....	....	479.8	499.4	701.7	795.1	718.1	845.4	868.8	1,123.3	1,284.2	1,531.5	Time, Savings,& Fgn.Currency Dep.	45
....	....	....	....	....	153.1	223.8	190.9	180.3	234.6	197.8	182.5	45.8	45.4	44.4	Money Market Instruments	46aa
....	....	....	....	....	8.6	10.2	18.3	10.2	9.9	15.0	23.5	25.7	83.6	151.2	Foreign Liabilities	46c
....	....	....	....	....	10.9	21.8	16.4	18.0	7.1	3.4	3.7	3.6	27.5	3.4	Central Government Deposits	46d
....	....	....	....	....	21.0	20.0	24.0	68.5	35.6	36.3	41.0	38.0	74.4	82.4	Credit from Deposit Money Banks	46h
....	....	....	....	....	563.2	634.2	763.1	821.2	792.2	894.7	960.2	1,099.9	1,237.3	1,325.0	Capital Accounts	47a
....	....	....	....	....	-76.3	-85.6	-160.8	-174.9	-194.4	-234.3	-153.3	-129.5	-273.4	-266.0	Other Items (Net)	47r

Namibia

		1972	1973	1974	1975	1976	1977	1978	1979	1980	1981	1982	1983	1984	1985	1986
Banking Survey														*Millions of Namibia Dollars:*		
Foreign Assets (Net)	51n	...	...	...	...	...	...	...	...	...	...	...	...	...	...	...
Domestic Credit	52	...	...	...	...	...	...	...	...	...	...	...	...	...	...	...
Claims on Central Govt. (Net)	52an	...	...	...	...	...	...	...	...	...	...	...	...	...	...	...
Claims on Local Government	52b	...	...	...	...	...	...	...	...	...	...	...	...	...	...	...
Claims on Nonfin.Pub.Enterprises	52c	...	...	...	...	...	...	...	...	...	...	...	...	...	...	...
Claims on Private Sector	52d	...	...	...	...	...	...	...	...	...	...	...	...	...	...	...
Claims on Nonbank Financial Inst	52g	...	...	...	...	...	...	...	...	...	...	...	...	...	...	...
Liquid Liabilities	55l	...	...	...	...	...	...	...	...	...	...	...	...	...	...	...
Money Market Instruments	56aa	...	...	...	...	...	...	...	...	...	...	...	...	...	...	...
Bonds	56ab	...	...	...	...	...	...	...	...	...	...	...	...	...	...	...
Capital Accounts	57a	...	...	...	...	...	...	...	...	...	...	...	...	...	...	...
Other Items (Net)	57r	...	...	...	...	...	...	...	...	...	...	...	...	...	...	...
Interest Rates														*Percent Per Annum*		
BoN Overdraft Rate	60	...	...	...	...	...	...	...	...	...	...	...	...	...	...	...
Treasury Bill Rate	60c	...	...	...	...	...	...	...	...	...	...	...	...	...	...	...
Deposit Rate	60l	...	...	...	...	...	...	...	...	...	...	...	...	...	...	...
Lending Rate	60p	...	...	...	...	...	...	...	...	...	...	...	...	...	...	...
Government Bond Yield	61	...	...	...	...	...	...	...	...	...	...	...	...	...	...	...
Prices														*Index Numbers (1995=100):*		
Consumer Prices	64	...	...	...	...	...	...	...	...	17.0	19.5	22.6	25.3	27.6	30.9	35.0
International Transactions														*Millions of Namibia Dollars*		
Exports	70	...	...	...	...	...	...	...	...	...	...	...	...	...	...	...
Imports, c.i.f.	71	...	...	...	...	...	...	...	...	...	...	...	...	...	...	...
Imports, f.o.b.	71.v	...	...	...	...	...	...	...	...	...	...	...	...	...	...	...
Balance of Payments														*Millions of US Dollars:*		
Current Account, n.i.e.	78al d	...	...	...	...	...	...	...	...	...	...	...	...	...	...	...
Goods: Exports f.o.b.	78aa d	...	...	...	...	...	...	...	...	...	...	...	...	...	...	...
Goods: Imports f.o.b.	78ab d	...	...	...	...	...	...	...	...	...	...	...	...	...	...	...
Trade Balance	78ac d	...	...	...	...	...	...	...	...	...	...	...	...	...	...	...
Services: Credit	78ad d	...	...	...	...	...	...	...	...	...	...	...	...	...	...	...
Services: Debit	78ae d	...	...	...	...	...	...	...	...	...	...	...	...	...	...	...
Balance on Goods & Services	78af d	...	...	...	...	...	...	...	...	...	...	...	...	...	...	...
Income: Credit	78ag d	...	...	...	...	...	...	...	...	...	...	...	...	...	...	...
Income: Debit	78ah d	...	...	...	...	...	...	...	...	...	...	...	...	...	...	...
Balance on Gds, Serv. & Inc.	78ai d	...	...	...	...	...	...	...	...	...	...	...	...	...	...	...
Current Transfers, n.i.e.: Credit	78aj d	...	...	...	...	...	...	...	...	...	...	...	...	...	...	...
Current Transfers: Debit	78ak d	...	...	...	...	...	...	...	...	...	...	...	...	...	...	...
Capital Account, n.i.e.	78bc d	...	...	...	...	...	...	...	...	...	...	...	...	...	...	...
Capital Account, n.i.e.: Credit	78ba d	...	...	...	...	...	...	...	...	...	...	...	...	...	...	...
Capital Account: Debit	78bb d	...	...	...	...	...	...	...	...	...	...	...	...	...	...	...
Financial Account, n.i.e.	78bj d	...	...	...	...	...	...	...	...	...	...	...	...	...	...	...
Direct Investment Abroad	78bd d	...	...	...	...	...	...	...	...	...	...	...	...	...	...	...
Dir. Invest. in Rep. Econ., n.i.e.	78be d	...	...	...	...	...	...	...	...	...	...	...	...	...	...	...
Portfolio Investment Assets	78bf d	...	...	...	...	...	...	...	...	...	...	...	...	...	...	...
Equity Securities	78bk d	...	...	...	...	...	...	...	...	...	...	...	...	...	...	...
Debt Securities	78bl d	...	...	...	...	...	...	...	...	...	...	...	...	...	...	...
Portfolio Investment Liab., n.i.e.	78bg d	...	...	...	...	...	...	...	...	...	...	...	...	...	...	...
Equity Securities	78bm d	...	...	...	...	...	...	...	...	...	...	...	...	...	...	...
Debt Securities	78bn d	...	...	...	...	...	...	...	...	...	...	...	...	...	...	...
Financial Derivatives Assets	78bw d	...	...	...	...	...	...	...	...	...	...	...	...	...	...	...
Financial Derivatives Liabilities	78bx d	...	...	...	...	...	...	...	...	...	...	...	...	...	...	...
Other Investment Assets	78bh d	...	...	...	...	...	...	...	...	...	...	...	...	...	...	...
Monetary Authorities	78bo d	...	...	...	...	...	...	...	...	...	...	...	...	...	...	...
General Government	78bp d	...	...	...	...	...	...	...	...	...	...	...	...	...	...	...
Banks	78bq d	...	...	...	...	...	...	...	...	...	...	...	...	...	...	...
Other Sectors	78br d	...	...	...	...	...	...	...	...	...	...	...	...	...	...	...
Other Investment Liab., n.i.e.	78bi d	...	...	...	...	...	...	...	...	...	...	...	...	...	...	...
Monetary Authorities	78bs d	...	...	...	...	...	...	...	...	...	...	...	...	...	...	...
General Government	78bt d	...	...	...	...	...	...	...	...	...	...	...	...	...	...	...
Banks	78bu d	...	...	...	...	...	...	...	...	...	...	...	...	...	...	...
Other Sectors	78bv d	...	...	...	...	...	...	...	...	...	...	...	...	...	...	...
Net Errors and Omissions	78ca d	...	...	...	...	...	...	...	...	...	...	...	...	...	...	...
Overall Balance	78cb d	...	...	...	...	...	...	...	...	...	...	...	...	...	...	...
Reserves and Related Items	79da d	...	...	...	...	...	...	...	...	...	...	...	...	...	...	...
Reserve Assets	79db d	...	...	...	...	...	...	...	...	...	...	...	...	...	...	...
Use of Fund Credit and Loans	79dc d	...	...	...	...	...	...	...	...	...	...	...	...	...	...	...
Exceptional Financing	79de d	...	...	...	...	...	...	...	...	...	...	...	...	...	...	...

End of Period — **Banking Survey**

	1987	1988	1989	1990	1991	1992	1993	1994	1995	1996	1997	1998	1999	2000	2001	Code
Foreign Assets (Net)	...	...	...	...	...	106.4	−120.8	−200.7	−325.5	111.2	895.2	1,355.2	2,272.0	2,656.4	2,400.4	51n
Domestic Credit	...	...	...	...	...	3,576.0	4,489.6	5,606.2	7,049.1	8,345.1	8,380.8	9,205.5	10,089.8	11,595.1	13,269.5	52
Claims on Central Govt. (Net)						420.6	548.0	599.1	672.7	1,210.3	230.8	260.5	664.8	282.1	420.2	52an
Claims on Local Government						20.9	21.1	22.7	24.5	23.9	22.6	23.9	21.3	17.2	37.4	52b
Claims on Nonfin.Pub.Enterprises						44.5	49.8	58.8	79.9	76.7	153.6	150.2	145.2	445.7	182.4	52c
Claims on Private Sector						3,082.9	3,854.2	4,917.0	6,262.4	7,016.1	7,956.1	8,752.8	9,233.8	10,791.7	12,614.2	52d
Claims on Nonbank Financial Inst						7.0	16.6	8.7	9.7	18.1	17.7	18.1	24.7	58.4	15.2	52g
Liquid Liabilities						2,718.9	3,445.1	4,464.9	5,461.9	6,746.4	7,278.2	8,027.9	9,597.6	10,856.9	11,533.0	55l
Money Market Instruments						153.1	223.8	190.9	180.3	234.6	197.8	182.5	45.8	45.4	147.7	56aa
Bonds						2.4	3.9	4.1	4.1	8.9	7.0	5.5	—	—	—	56ab
Capital Accounts						799.6	948.0	1,128.1	1,373.2	1,740.0	1,994.0	2,392.6	2,743.5	3,312.2	4,450.1	57a
Other Items (Net)						8.4	−252.0	−382.5	−295.9	−273.5	−201.0	−47.7	−25.1	37.0	−460.9	57r

Percent Per Annum — **Interest Rates**

	1987	1988	1989	1990	1991	1992	1993	1994	1995	1996	1997	1998	1999	2000	2001	Code
BoN Overdraft Rate	...	...	...	...	20.50	16.50	14.50	15.50	17.50	17.75	16.00	18.75	11.50	11.25	9.25	60
Treasury Bill Rate					...	13.88	12.16	11.35	13.91	15.25	15.69	17.24	13.28	10.26	9.29	60c
Deposit Rate					12.77	11.36	9.61	9.18	10.84	12.56	12.70	12.94	10.82	7.39	6.79	60l
Lending Rate					23.36	20.21	18.02	17.05	18.51	19.16	20.18	20.72	18.48	15.28	14.53	60p
Government Bond Yield						15.44	13.94	14.63	16.11	15.48	14.70	15.10	14.90	13.81	11.39	61

Period Averages — **Prices**

	1987	1988	1989	1990	1991	1992	1993	1994	1995	1996	1997	1998	1999	2000	2001	Code
Consumer Prices	39.4	44.5	51.2	57.4	64.2	75.6	82.1	90.9	100.0	108.0	117.5	124.8	135.5	147.7	161.8	64

Millions of Namibia Dollars — **International Transactions**

	1987	1988	1989	1990	1991	1992	1993	1994	1995	1996	1997	1998	1999	2000	2001	Code
Exports	...	2,400	2,943	2,809	3,351	3,826	4,214	4,692	...	...	...	...	...	...	...	70
Imports, c.i.f.				3,010	3,172	3,659	3,883	4,248								71
Imports, f.o.b.	...		1,937	2,447	2,897	3,094	3,551	3,694	...							71.v

Balance of Payments — *Minus Sign Indicates Debit*

	1987	1988	1989	1990	1991	1992	1993	1994	1995	1996	1997	1998	1999	2000	2001	Code
Current Account, n.i.e.						27.6	105.1	49.8	110.2	85.3	175.9	115.8	90.4	161.8		78al d
Goods: Exports f.o.b.						1,088.3	1,179.2	1,311.3	1,293.1	1,320.4	1,418.4	1,403.7	1,343.3	1,278.3		78aa d
Goods: Imports f.o.b.						−1,230.2	−1,228.4	−1,389.1	−1,335.0	−1,406.3	−1,548.2	−1,530.9	−1,615.0	−1,450.9		78ab d
Trade Balance						−141.9	−49.1	−77.8	−41.8	−85.8	−129.7	−127.1	−271.7	−172.6		78ac d
Services: Credit						131.8	144.6	169.8	228.1	259.0	315.3	337.4	380.1	327.0		78ad d
Services: Debit						−354.2	−462.3	−510.5	−485.4	−468.3	−551.5	−580.9	−533.7	−456.9		78ae d
Balance on Goods & Services						−364.2	−366.8	−418.4	−299.0	−295.1	−365.9	−370.7	−425.2	−302.4		78af d
Income: Credit						183.3	243.0	201.9	212.7	213.8	374.0	319.2	252.0	226.7		78ag d
Income: Debit						−145.8	−146.4	−185.4	−154.7	−159.8	−235.1	−249.0	−180.6	−165.9		78ah d
Balance on Gds, Serv. & Inc.						−326.7	−270.2	−402.0	−241.1	−241.1	−227.1	−300.5	−353.8	−241.6		78ai d
Current Transfers, n.i.e.: Credit						375.0	398.1	476.6	373.2	349.2	426.9	437.3	462.2	418.2		78aj d
Current Transfers: Debit						−20.7	−22.8	−24.9	−21.9	−22.7	−23.9	−21.0	−18.0	−14.7		78ak d
Capital Account, n.i.e.						42.2	28.9	32.0	27.0	43.2	40.1	42.1	33.5	23.8		78bc d
Capital Account, n.i.e.: Credit						46.9	33.2	32.7	27.6	43.8	40.7	42.5	33.9	24.2		78ba d
Capital Account: Debit						−4.6	−4.3	−.7	−.6	−.6	−.6	−.5	−.4	−.4		78bb d
Financial Account, n.i.e.						−202.8	−171.6	−121.2	−62.1	−102.1	−205.3	−174.0	−71.4	−145.6		78bj d
Direct Investment Abroad						−1.4	−6.4	1.6	−8.7	6.1	3.5	21.7	−.7	2.2		78bd d
Dir. Invest. in Rep. Econ., n.i.e.						29.6	120.4	118.2	55.3	98.0	153.0	128.7	91.0	96.2		78be d
Portfolio Investment Assets						−4.6	−10.8	.9	15.5	−17.0	−5.1	−8.1	−14.6	−11.1		78bf d
Equity Securities						−8.9	−12.4	−6.9	−4.9	−5.0	−3.8	−7.9	−14.6	−7.4		78bk d
Debt Securities						4.4	1.6	7.8	20.4	−12.0	−1.3	−.3	—	−3.6		78bl d
Portfolio Investment Liab., n.i.e.						15.5	−15.0	15.1	60.0	64.2	82.2	31.2	26.0	−4.4		78bg d
Equity Securities						—	−4.1	6.0	1.1	37.5	45.7	51.2	28.8	18.1		78bm d
Debt Securities						15.5	−10.9	9.0	58.9	26.7	36.5	−20.0	−2.8	−22.4		78bn d
Financial Derivatives Assets						...	...	...	...	...						78bw d
Financial Derivatives Liabilities																78bx d
Other Investment Assets						−328.4	−257.6	−231.9	−180.9	−301.0	−428.0	−411.2	−289.9	−175.5		78bh d
Monetary Authorities																78bo d
General Government						−105.6	94.7	−6.0	−9.4	9.5	−1.4	−1.2	−1.1	−.9		78bp d
Banks						−7.6	−75.5	76.4	56.5	.1	14.8	−48.6	−40.6	−2.1		78bq d
Other Sectors						−215.2	−276.8	−302.3	−228.0	−310.7	−441.5	−361.4	−248.2	−172.6		78br d
Other Investment Liab., n.i.e.						86.5	−2.4	−25.0	−3.3	47.6	−10.9	63.8	116.7	−53.1		78bi d
Monetary Authorities																78bs d
General Government						38.4	39.8	3.5	18.5	4.9	21.8	27.7	17.4	16.9		78bt d
Banks						30.0	−61.9	−14.5	18.4	66.8	4.9	−49.0	116.5	−28.5		78bu d
Other Sectors						18.1	19.7	−14.0	−40.2	−24.1	−37.7	85.0	−17.1	−41.4		78bv d
Net Errors and Omissions						169.8	25.2	32.8	16.2	48.5	13.4	39.1	15.3	15.7		78ca d
Overall Balance						36.8	−12.4	−6.6	91.3	75.0	24.2	22.9	67.8	55.8		78cb d
Reserves and Related Items						−36.8	12.4	6.6	−91.3	−75.0	−24.2	−22.9	−67.8	−55.8		79da d
Reserve Assets						−36.8	12.4	6.6	−91.3	−75.0	−24.2	−22.9	−67.8	−55.8		79db d
Use of Fund Credit and Loans						—	—	—	—	—	—	—	—	—		79dc d
Exceptional Financing						...	...	...	...	...						79de d

Namibia

	1972	1973	1974	1975	1976	1977	1978	1979	1980	1981	1982	1983	1984	1985	1986
International Investment Position														*Millions of US Dollars*	
Assets .... 79aa d	...	...	...	...	...	...	...	...	...	...	...	...	...	...	...
Direct Investment Abroad .... 79ab d	...	...	...	...	...	...	...	...	...	...	...	...	...	...	...
Portfolio Investment .... 79ac d	...	...	...	...	...	...	...	...	...	...	...	...	...	...	...
Equity Securities .... 79ad d	...	...	...	...	...	...	...	...	...	...	...	...	...	...	...
Debt Securities .... 79ae d	...	...	...	...	...	...	...	...	...	...	...	...	...	...	...
Financial Derivatives .... 79al d	...	...	...	...	...	...	...	...	...	...	...	...	...	...	...
Other Investment .... 79af d	...	...	...	...	...	...	...	...	...	...	...	...	...	...	...
Monetary Authorities.................. 79ag d	...	...	...	...	...	...	...	...	...	...	...	...	...	...	...
General Government .... 79ah d	...	...	...	...	...	...	...	...	...	...	...	...	...	...	...
Banks .... 79ai d	...	...	...	...	...	...	...	...	...	...	...	...	...	...	...
Other Sectors .... 79aj d	...	...	...	...	...	...	...	...	...	...	...	...	...	...	...
Reserve Assets .... 79ak d	...	...	...	...	...	...	...	...	...	...	...	...	...	...	...
Liabilities .... 79la d	...	...	...	...	...	...	...	...	...	...	...	...	...	...	...
Dir. Invest. in Rep. Economy............ 79lb d	...	...	...	...	...	...	...	...	...	...	...	...	...	...	...
Portfolio Investment .... 79lc d	...	...	...	...	...	...	...	...	...	...	...	...	...	...	...
Equity Securities .... 79ld d	...	...	...	...	...	...	...	...	...	...	...	...	...	...	...
Debt Securities .... 79le d	...	...	...	...	...	...	...	...	...	...	...	...	...	...	...
Financial Derivatives .... 79ll d	...	...	...	...	...	...	...	...	...	...	...	...	...	...	...
Other Investment .... 79lf d	...	...	...	...	...	...	...	...	...	...	...	...	...	...	...
Monetary Authorities.................. 79lg d	...	...	...	...	...	...	...	...	...	...	...	...	...	...	...
General Government .... 79lh d	...	...	...	...	...	...	...	...	...	...	...	...	...	...	...
Banks .... 79li d	...	...	...	...	...	...	...	...	...	...	...	...	...	...	...
Other Sectors .... 79lj d	...	...	...	...	...	...	...	...	...	...	...	...	...	...	...
Government Finance														*Millions of Namibia Dollars:*	
Deficit (-) or Surplus................ 80	...	...	...	...	...	...	...	...	...	...	...	...	...	...	200.8
Revenue 81	...	...	...	...	...	...	...	...	...	...	...	...	...	...	1,107.8
Grants Received 81z	...	...	...	...	...	...	...	...	...	...	...	...	...	...	499.6
Expenditure 82	...	...	...	...	...	...	...	...	...	...	...	...	...	...	1,408.4
Lending Minus Repayments 83	...	...	...	...	...	...	...	...	...	...	...	...	...	...	−1.8
Financing															
Domestic 84a	...	...	...	...	...	...	...	...	...	...	...	...	...	...	−162.2
Foreign............................. 85a	...	...	...	...	...	...	...	...	...	...	...	...	...	...	−38.6
National Accounts														*Millions of Namibia Dollars*	
Househ.Cons.Expend.,incl.NPISHs 96f	...	...	...	...	...	...	...	...	...	...	...	...	...	1,328	1,632
Government Consumption Expend............. 91f	...	...	...	...	...	...	...	...	...	...	...	...	...	795	959
Gross Fixed Capital Formation 93e	...	...	...	...	...	...	...	...	...	...	...	...	...	380	426
Changes in Inventories 93i	...	...	...	...	...	...	...	...	...	...	...	...	...	5	−7
Exports of Goods and Services 90c	...	...	...	...	...	...	...	...	...	...	...	...	...	1,882	2,368
Imports of Goods and Services (-) 98c	...	...	...	...	...	...	...	...	...	...	...	...	...	1,537	2,038
Gross Domestic Product (GDP) 99b	...	...	...	...	...	...	...	...	...	...	...	...	...	2,854	3,340
Statistical Discrepancy 99bs															
Net Primary Income from Abroad 98.n	...	...	...	...	...	...	...	...	...	...	...	...	...	−629	−562
Gross National Income (GNI) 99a	...	...	...	...	...	...	...	...	...	...	...	...	...	2,226	2,778
GDP Volume 1985 Prices...................... 99b.p	...	...	...	...	...	...	...	...	...	...	...	...	...	2,854	2,959
GDP Volume 1990 Prices.................... 99b.p														...	...
GDP Volume 1995 Prices.................... 99b.p														...	...
GDP Volume (1995=100) .... 99bv p	...	...	...	...	...	...	...	...	...	...	...	...	...	63.3	65.6
GDP Deflator (1995=100) .... 99bi p	...	...	...	...	...	...	...	...	...	...	...	...	...	36	40
															Millions:
Population.................................. 99z	...	...	...	...	...	...	...	...	...	...	...	1.16	1.15	1.18	1.21

	1987	1988	1989	1990	1991	1992	1993	1994	1995	1996	1997	1998	1999	2000	2001		
Millions of US Dollars																**International Investment Position**	
	....	....	1,772.9	2,107.3	2,348.2	2,264.7	2,579.9	2,788.0	2,692.6	2,095.9	....	....	....	....	....	Assets	79aa *d*
	....	....	64.3	79.6	98.1	81.6	79.2	15.8	14.8	13.0						Direct Investment Abroad	79ab *d*
	....	....	160.9	161.2	167.3	145.1	117.4	165.1	164.8	128.8						Portfolio Investment	79ac *d*
	....	....	23.7	29.7	45.2	43.6	45.6	85.2	90.2	72.8						Equity Securities	79ad *d*
	....	....	137.2	131.5	122.1	101.5	71.8	79.9	74.6	56.0						Debt Securities	79ae *d*
	—	—	—	—	—	—	—	—	—	—						Financial Derivatives	79al *d*
	....	....	1,504.3	1,786.5	2,020.4	1,988.2	2,249.6	2,404.1	2,291.4	1,760.6						Other Investment	79af *d*
	—	—	—	—	—	—	—	—	—	—						Monetary Authorities	79ag *d*
	....	....	—	106.5	4.4	9.5	17.7	7.3	8.5	7.7						General Government	79ah *d*
	....	....	129.7	128.4	208.2	106.8	46.8	38.1	29.9	67.5						Banks	79ai *d*
	....	....	1,374.6	1,551.6	1,807.9	1,871.9	2,185.1	2,358.7	2,253.1	1,685.4						Other Sectors	79aj *d*
	....	....	43.4	80.0	62.4	49.8	133.7	202.9	221.6	193.5						Reserve Assets	79ak *d*
	....	....	2,667.6	2,845.7	2,824.2	2,811.0	2,201.0	2,420.2	2,685.1	2,355.2						Liabilities	79la *d*
	....	....	1,957.8	2,046.8	2,114.8	2,141.8	1,490.8	1,601.2	1,707.7	1,492.2						Dir. Invest. in Rep. Economy	79lb *d*
	....	....	213.3	220.5	182.6	183.8	221.3	289.8	390.4	334.9						Portfolio Investment	79lc *d*
	....	....	33.1	26.5	12.4	22.6	19.1	69.1	119.0	141.8						Equity Securities	79ld *d*
	....	....	180.2	194.0	170.2	161.2	202.2	220.7	271.4	193.1						Debt Securities	79le *d*
	—	—	—	—	—	—	—	—	—	—						Financial Derivatives	79ll *d*
	....	....	496.4	578.3	526.8	485.4	488.9	529.1	587.0	528.1						Other Investment	79lf *d*
						164.4	181.9	203.2	214.9	183.0						Monetary Authorities	79lg *d*
	....	....	85.2	124.9	159.7	8.5	25.3	29.9	51.5	46.8						General Government	79lh *d*
	....	....	137.6	166.2	89.3	70.8	82.7	143.9	134.1	136.0						Banks	79li *d*
	....	....	273.7	287.2	277.8	241.7	199.0	152.1	186.4	162.3						Other Sectors	79lj *d*
Year Beginning April 1																**Government Finance**	
	−141.9	2.1	324.7	†−71.7	−189.0	−435.0 P	−402.7 f	...	...	...	...	...	...	...	...	Deficit (-) or Surplus	80
	1,219.8	1,478.0	2,011.8	†1,905.9	2,534.6	2,833.7 P	2,958.5 f	...	...	...	...	...	...	...	...	Revenue	81
	308.0	317.2	280.9	†101.1	67.8	73.5 P	70.0 f	...	...	...	...	...	...	...	...	Grants Received	81z
	1,666.4	1,800.2	1,970.8	†2,027.4	2,778.9	3,311.9 P	3,407.5 f	...	...	...	...	...	...	...	...	Expenditure	82
	3.3	−7.1	−2.8	†51.3	12.5	30.3 P	23.7 f	...	...	...	...	...	...	...	...	Lending Minus Repayments	83
																Financing	
	131.8	43.9	−248.1	†−38.8	−.9	297.8 P	391.9 f	...	...	...	...	...	...	...	...	Domestic	84a
	10.1	−46.0	−76.6	†110.5	189.9	137.2 P	10.8 f	...	...	...	...	...	...	...	...	Foreign	85a
Millions of Namibia Dollars																**National Accounts**	
	2,203	2,357	3,009	†3,351	4,157	4,476	5,493	6,355	7,189	8,653	10,160	11,185	12,235	13,636	....	Househ.Cons.Expend.,incl.NPISHs	96f
	1,164	1,330	1,442	†1,862	2,305	2,868	2,938	3,267	3,839	4,551	5,064	5,556	6,261	6,533	....	Government Consumption Expend.	91f
	504	659	829	†1,290	1,107	1,689	1,967	2,255	2,817	3,535	3,288	4,321	4,760	4,310	....	Gross Fixed Capital Formation	93e
	15	198	5	†441	183	80	−436	252	−60	−65	92	518	57	2	....	Changes in Inventories	93i
	2,194	2,636	3,244	†3,188	3,787	4,317	4,828	5,599	6,288	7,593	7,961	8,637	9,549	11,916	....	Exports of Goods and Services	90c
	2,566	2,702	3,286	†3,808	4,419	5,071	5,273	5,926	7,073	8,796	9,638	10,900	11,773	12,560	....	Imports of Goods and Services (-)	98c
	3,515	4,478	5,242	†6,323	7,119	8,358	9,302	11,549	12,706	15,011	16,752	18,791	20,691	23,786	....	Gross Domestic Product (GDP)	99b
							−213	−253	−294	−459	−176	−527	−398	−51	....	Statistical Discrepancy	99bs
	−218	−595	−342	†85	258	42	184	182	569	310	305	484	−105	−89	....	Net Primary Income from Abroad	98.n
	3,297	3,884	4,900	†6,408	7,377	8,400	9,486	11,731	13,275	15,321	17,057	19,275	20,586	23,697	....	Gross National Income (GNI)	99a
	3,026	3,294	....	....	....	....	....	...	...	...	...	...	...	...	....	GDP Volume 1985 Prices	99b.*p*
	....	5,814	5,938	†6,409	6,775	7,274	7,128	...	...	...	...	...	...	...	....	GDP Volume 1990 Prices	99b.*p*
								11,372	12,204	12,706	13,111	13,665	14,114	14,597	15,074	GDP Volume 1995 Prices	99b.*p*
	67.1	73.0	74.6	†80.5	85.1	91.3	89.5	96.0	100.0	103.2	107.5	111.1	114.9	118.6	....	GDP Volume (1995=100)	99bv *p*
	41	48	55	†62	66	72	82	95	100	114	123	133	142	158	....	GDP Deflator (1995=100)	99bi *p*
Midyear Estimates																	
	1.24	1.28	1.32	1.35	1.42	1.47	1.51	1.55	1.59	1.62	1.66	1.69	1.72	1.82	1.79	**Population**	99z

(See notes in the back of the book.)

Nepal

		1972	1973	1974	1975	1976	1977	1978	1979	1980	1981	1982	1983	1984	1985	1986
Exchange Rates															*Rupees per SDR:*	
Market Rate	aa	10.993	12.739	12.929	14.633	14.523	15.184	15.633	15.808	15.305	15.364	15.774	15.914	17.644	22.737	26.910
															Rupees per US Dollar:	
Market Rate	ae	10.125	10.560	10.560	12.500	12.500	12.500	12.000	12.000	12.000	13.200	14.300	15.200	18.000	20.700	22.000
Market Rate	rf	10.125	10.472	10.560	11.003	12.500	12.500	12.111	12.000	12.000	12.336	13.244	14.545	16.459	18.246	21.230
Fund Position															*Millions of SDRs:*	
Quota	2f. s	11.6	12.4	12.4	12.4	12.4	12.4	19.0	19.0	28.5	28.5	28.5	37.3	37.3	37.3	37.3
SDRs	1b. s	2.2	2.2	2.2	2.2	2.1	1.9	1.2	1.7	.1	—	.8	.2	.1	—	.1
Reserve Position in the Fund	1c. s	2.9	3.1	3.1	3.1	—	—	2.4	2.3	5.2	5.7	5.7	5.7	5.7	5.7	5.7
Total Fund Cred.&Loans Outstg.	2tl	—	—	—	—	4.5	6.0	15.3	18.6	32.6	32.5	27.7	22.4	15.8	19.8	19.2
International Liquidity													*Millions of US dollars Unless Otherwise Indicated:*			
Total Reserves minus Gold	1l. d	98.4	117.5	121.3	95.7	†127.5	139.5	145.1	159.2	182.8	201.9	199.2	133.3	82.0	56.0	86.7
SDRs	1b. d	2.4	2.7	2.7	2.6	2.5	2.3	1.6	2.3	.1	—	.9	.2	.1	—	.1
Reserve Position in the Fund	1c. d	3.2	3.8	3.8	3.6	—	—	3.1	3.1	6.6	6.6	6.3	6.0	5.6	6.3	7.0
Foreign Exchange	1d. d	92.8	111.1	114.8	89.5	†125.1	137.2	140.4	153.8	176.0	195.3	192.1	127.2	76.3	49.7	79.7
Gold (Million Fine Troy Ounces)	1ad	.136	.130	.130	.130	.130	.133	.146	.149	.151	.151	.151	.151	.151	.151	.151
Gold (National Valuation)	1an d	5.2	5.5	5.5	5.5	5.5	5.6	6.2	6.3	6.4	6.4	6.4	6.4	6.4	6.4	6.4
Monetary Authorities: Other Assets	3.. d	....	....	....	....	1.8	2.7	2.3	4.9	6.4	3.2	2.3	1.4	.4	—	—
Monetary Authorities: Other Liab.	4.. d	4.7	6.1	14.4	12.6	4.0	6.0	5.6	10.4	11.5	15.8	15.1	3.1	3.7	10.8	8.7
Deposit Money Banks: Assets	7a. d	17.6	17.2	18.8	26.6	34.1	45.3	52.2	55.5	59.3	71.8	57.9	81.5	71.8	83.5	65.3
Liabilities	7b. d	1.7	1.7	6.3	5.1	16.3	22.5	16.4	11.8	6.3	8.7	7.4	12.6	16.1	24.4	24.8
Monetary Authorities															*Millions of Rupees:*	
Foreign Assets	11	1,014	1,250	1,269	1,240	1,678	1,839	1,827	2,027	2,364	2,773	2,743	2,113	2,224	1,299	1,839
Claims on Central Government	12a	173	389	529	724	892	1,105	1,454	1,708	1,896	2,611	3,312	4,626	5,696	7,040	8,468
Claims on Private Sector	12d	8	19	21	21	17	18	20	34	41	53	55	64	113	254	185
Claims on Deposit Money Banks	12e	3	3	61	164	3	2	134	87	131	264	113	10	226	364	497
Claims on Other Financial Insts	12f	37	49	56	134	123	211	314	353	373	398	428	501	557	706	749
Reserve Money	14	792	1,020	1,063	1,162	1,497	1,627	1,913	2,156	2,379	2,722	3,394	3,927	4,555	5,152	6,549
of which: Currency Outside DMBs	14a	596	747	882	882	996	1,212	1,379	1,627	1,814	2,147	2,408	2,783	3,302	3,797	4,787
Private Sector Deposits	14d	44	77	82	98	127	142	164	184	229	154	270	306	351	332	391
Foreign Liabilities	16c	47	64	153	157	115	166	306	418	637	707	653	403	345	675	708
Central Government Deposits	16d	194	409	479	514	571	744	735	858	926	1,471	1,491	1,663	1,898	2,250	2,685
Capital Accounts	17a	189	230	250	405	411	497	572	681	738	890	919	1,154	2,308	2,489	2,925
Other Items (Net)	17r	14	−13	−9	46	118	140	223	95	125	309	195	166	−290	−904	−1,129
Deposit Money Banks															*Millions of Rupees:*	
Reserves	20	135	207	120	163	353	348	325	406	369	518	611	614	650	914	1,047
Foreign Assets	21	179	181	199	332	426	567	626	666	712	948	827	1,239	1,293	1,728	1,437
Claims on Central Government	22a	70	100	100	101	320	640	418	347	387	355	796	1,422	1,654	2,073	2,001
Claims on Nonfin.Pub.Enterprises	22c	23	41	222	380	307	270	604	715	780	946	874	1,075	940	1,296	1,662
Claims on Private Sector	22d	356	459	605	710	614	810	1,106	1,393	1,961	2,456	2,620	2,670	3,230	4,336	5,712
Claims on Other Financial Insts	22f	....	....	....	....	....	....	....	....	....	....	86	130	157	155	116
Demand Deposits	24	202	267	326	353	513	579	657	723	821	904	1,027	1,278	1,289	1,487	1,773
Time and Savings Deposits	25	451	573	658	847	1,175	1,468	1,870	2,178	2,661	3,375	4,283	5,228	5,899	7,398	8,592
Foreign Liabilities	26c	17	18	66	63	204	281	197	142	76	115	106	191	290	505	546
Credit from Monetary Authorities	26g	3	3	61	164	3	2	134	87	131	264	113	10	226	364	497
Other Items (Net)	27r	88	127	134	258	126	304	221	397	520	564	286	442	220	746	567
Monetary Survey															*Millions of Rupees:*	
Foreign Assets (Net)	31n	1,128	1,349	1,249	1,352	1,785	1,958	1,949	2,132	2,362	2,898	2,812	2,758	2,883	1,847	2,023
Domestic Credit	32	460	620	1,036	1,514	1,648	2,183	3,024	3,692	4,513	5,348	6,685	8,828	10,453	13,613	16,212
Claims on Central Govt. (Net)	32an	36	52	133	269	587	875	981	1,198	1,357	1,495	2,617	4,385	5,452	6,863	7,785
Claims on Nonfin.Pub.Enterprises	32c	23	41	222	380	307	270	604	715	780	946	879	1,080	945	1,301	1,667
Claims on Private Sector	32d	365	478	626	731	631	827	1,126	1,426	2,002	2,510	2,675	2,733	3,343	4,590	5,897
Claims on Other Financial Insts	32f	37	49	56	134	123	211	314	353	373	398	514	631	713	860	864
Money	34	842	1,090	1,290	1,334	1,636	1,933	2,200	2,534	2,864	3,205	3,705	4,366	4,942	5,616	6,951
Quasi-Money	35	451	573	658	847	1,175	1,468	1,870	2,178	2,661	3,375	4,283	5,228	5,899	7,398	8,592
Other Items (Net)	37r	295	306	337	685	622	740	904	1,112	1,349	1,667	1,510	1,992	2,495	2,446	2,691
Money plus Quasi-Money	35l	1,293	1,663	1,948	2,180	2,811	3,401	4,070	4,712	5,526	6,580	7,987	9,594	10,841	13,014	15,543
Interest Rates															*Percent per Annum:*	
Discount Rate	60	....	....	....	....	12.00	12.00	12.00	12.00	12.00	12.00	15.00	15.00	15.00	15.00	11.00
Treasury Bill Rate	60c	....	....	....	....	....	....	....	....	....	5.00	5.00	5.00	5.00	5.00	5.00
Deposit Rate	60l	....	....	13.63	14.58	12.17	12.00	12.00	12.00	12.00	12.00	12.29	12.50	12.50	12.50	12.50
Lending Rate	60p	....	....	12.00	13.00	14.00	14.00	14.00	14.00	14.00	14.00	15.50	17.00	17.00	17.00	15.67
Government Bond Yield	61	....	....	....	....	....	....	....	....	....	10.50	10.50	10.50	10.50	†13.00	13.00
Prices															*Index Numbers (1995=100):*	
Consumer Prices	64	11.5	12.8	†15.4	16.5	16.0	17.6	18.9	19.6	22.5	25.0	27.9	31.3	32.2	34.8	41.4
International Transactions															*Millions of Rupees*	
Exports	70	587	659	698	1,097	1,229	1,007	1,100	1,306	964	1,731	1,161	1,361	2,109	2,915	3,005
Imports, c.i.f.	71	862	1,086	1,419	1,885	2,035	2,104	2,677	3,053	4,107	4,549	5,237	6,746	6,847	8,267	9,751

	1987	1988	1989	1990	1991	1992	1993	1994	1995	1996	1997	1998	1999	2000	2001		
																Exchange Rates	
End of Period	30.643	33.912	37.585	43.249	61.079	59.400	67.634	72.817	83.243	82.007	85.408	95.288	94.326	96.806	96.108	Market Rate	aa
End of Period (ae) Period Average (rf)																	
	21.600	25.200	28.600	30.400	42.700	43.200	49.240	49.880	56.000	57.030	63.300	67.675	68.725	74.300	76.475	Market Rate	ae
	21.819	23.289	27.189	29.369	37.255	42.718	48.607	49.398	51.890	56.692	58.010	65.976	68.239	71.094	74.949	Market Rate	rf
																Fund Position	
End of Period	37.3	37.3	37.3	37.3	37.3	52.0	52.0	52.0	52.0	52.0	52.0	52.0	71.3	71.3	71.3	Quota	2f. s
	.1	.1	.1	.1	.1	.1	—	.1	—	—	.1	—	.2	—	.1	SDRs	1b. s
	5.7	5.7	5.7	5.7	5.7	5.7	5.7	5.7	5.7	5.7	5.7	5.7	5.7	5.7	5.7	Reserve Position in the Fund	1c. s
	30.3	39.2	39.9	30.9	26.9	31.7	35.8	37.7	32.5	27.2	22.0	17.2	12.9	9.5	6.2	Total Fund Cred.&Loans Outstg.	2tl
																International Liquidity	
Data as of Middle of December	178.2	220.3	211.6	295.3	397.0	467.4	640.2	693.6	586.4	571.4	626.2	756.3	845.1	945.4	1,037.7	Total Reserves minus Gold	1l. d
	.1	.1	.2	.2	.1	.2	—	.1	—	—	.1	—	.3	—	.1	SDRs	1b. d
	8.1	7.7	7.5	8.1	8.2	7.9	7.9	8.4	8.5	8.2	7.7	8.1	7.9	7.5	7.2	Reserve Position in the Fund	1c. d
	170.0	212.5	203.9	287.0	388.7	459.4	632.3	685.1	577.9	563.1	618.4	748.2	836.9	937.9	1,030.4	Foreign Exchange	1d. d
	.151	.152	.153	.153	.153	.153	.153	.153	.153	.153	.153	.153	.153	.153	.153	Gold (Million Fine Troy Ounces)	1ad
	6.4	6.4	6.4	6.5	6.5	6.5	6.5	6.5	6.5	6.6	6.6	†48.3	48.1	45.5	....	Gold (National Valuation)	1an d
	....	....	....	....	....	....	....	....	....	....	....	....	....	....	....	Monetary Authorities: Other Assets	3.. d
	31.4	18.0	38.3	39.7	32.2	51.6	55.3	62.1	54.0	45.0	32.9	27.8	19.5	17.1	11.6	Monetary Authorities: Other Liab.	4.. d
	90.1	96.8	97.1	128.9	123.1	151.0	129.9	161.6	208.9	218.1	246.1	299.0	345.3	459.9	333.9	Deposit Money Banks: Assets	7a. d
	26.0	29.4	30.7	32.8	35.8	57.8	68.6	66.1	67.4	87.7	111.3	149.7	174.9	206.8	215.2	Liabilities	7b. d
																Monetary Authorities	
Data as of Middle of December	3,830	5,816	7,492	10,329	17,894	21,320	32,721	35,627	33,960	33,883	39,767	52,331	59,155	71,427	80,535	Foreign Assets	11
	8,835	9,956	12,871	14,097	15,276	17,907	19,032	19,439	24,001	24,714	27,151	29,805	30,539	34,366	32,612	Claims on Central Government	12a
	194	167	205	349	494	501	544	503	547	895	1,145	1,356	1,460	1,478	1,856	Claims on Private Sector	12d
	341	155	—	42	34	49	39	21	12	646	6	6	6	6	6	Claims on Deposit Money Banks	12e
	876	916	818	761	837	690	499	484	844	1,122	1,477	1,631	1,613	1,560	1,666	Claims on Other Financial Insts	12f
	7,745	8,917	10,917	13,372	17,138	19,817	25,783	28,792	31,266	34,368	39,477	50,203	55,371	66,062	74,012	Reserve Money	14
	5,827	6,671	7,905	9,818	12,465	14,201	17,390	21,005	23,230	25,428	27,905	32,244	36,929	44,526	51,699	*of which: Currency Outside DMBs*	14a
	547	580	572	540	864	897	1,307	1,097	1,396	1,358	1,601	2,287	4,346	3,160	3,570	*Private Sector Deposits*	14d
	1,607	1,782	2,593	2,543	3,018	3,780	4,389	4,617	4,327	3,422	2,525	2,024	1,338	1,246	676	Foreign Liabilities	16c
	3,302	3,863	4,777	4,661	7,073	7,845	7,870	7,782	7,459	7,447	9,255	10,474	11,473	13,081	13,247	Central Government Deposits	16d
	3,207	3,998	4,383	5,774	8,344	8,259	10,633	12,077	15,982	16,128	18,580	21,545	22,953	25,752	27,982	Capital Accounts	17a
	−1,786	−1,549	−1,285	−773	−1,036	766	4,160	2,806	328	−105	−293	883	1,639	2,696	758	Other Items (Net)	17r
																Deposit Money Banks	
Data as of Middle of December	1,364	1,364	2,451	2,943	2,999	3,943	5,837	7,321	8,488	7,583	9,972	15,673	14,096	18,376	18,742	Reserves	20
	1,946	2,440	2,778	3,918	5,256	6,525	6,397	8,060	11,698	12,438	15,577	20,238	23,729	34,174	25,679	Foreign Assets	21
	3,024	3,819	4,046	4,395	8,238	9,677	10,734	8,776	6,497	7,610	8,621	8,957	13,330	15,471	28,318	Claims on Central Government	22a
	1,859	1,921	1,644	2,005	1,310	1,144	1,954	1,621	1,721	1,713	1,459	993	1,438	1,909	1,911	Claims on Nonfin.Pub.Enterprises	22c
	6,481	8,897	11,443	12,897	16,038	19,991	25,059	36,462	49,494	56,848	65,541	84,875	97,306	114,913	128,410	Claims on Private Sector	22d
	105	29	28	28	29	29	29	29	29	211	4,023	4,668	530	5,915	7,419	Claims on Other Financial Insts	22f
	2,309	2,575	3,243	3,847	4,286	5,331	6,622	8,422	8,927	8,758	9,090	10,979	13,832	15,343	16,891	Demand Deposits	24
	10,343	13,394	16,386	19,098	23,240	28,888	36,218	42,172	50,490	58,744	70,555	89,850	109,521	132,550	145,950	Time and Savings Deposits	25
	561	742	878	997	1,529	2,498	3,380	3,297	3,776	5,003	7,048	10,134	12,200	15,367	17,202	Foreign Liabilities	26c
	341	155	—	42	34	49	39	21	12	646	6	6	6	6	45	5	Credit from Monetary Authorities	26g
	1,228	1,604	1,883	2,202	4,781	4,543	3,749	8,356	14,906	17,063	19,138	20,297	20,435	28,958	31,156	Other Items (Net)	27r
																Monetary Survey	
Data as of Middle of December	3,609	5,733	6,799	10,707	18,603	21,566	31,349	35,772	37,555	37,896	45,770	60,411	69,527	88,988	88,336	Foreign Assets (Net)	31n
	18,077	21,849	26,286	29,879	35,157	42,101	49,986	59,539	75,863	89,486	100,814	117,680	140,135	164,043	189,677	Domestic Credit	32
	8,557	9,912	12,139	13,831	16,442	19,739	21,895	20,433	23,039	24,877	26,517	28,287	32,396	36,757	47,682	Claims on Central Govt. (Net)	32an
	1,864	1,928	1,652	2,012	1,317	1,152	1,961	1,628	1,721	1,720	1,446	1,000	1,446	1,917	1,918	Claims on Nonfin.Pub.Enterprises	32c
	6,675	9,064	11,648	13,246	16,532	20,492	25,602	36,965	50,041	57,742	66,685	86,231	98,766	116,391	130,267	Claims on Private Sector	32d
	981	945	846	789	866	719	527	513	1,054	5,145	6,145	2,161	7,528	8,978	9,810	Claims on Other Financial Insts	32f
	8,682	9,826	11,720	14,205	17,614	20,428	25,320	30,524	33,553	35,544	38,596	45,509	55,107	63,028	72,161	Money	34
	10,343	13,394	16,386	19,098	23,240	28,888	36,218	42,172	50,490	58,744	70,555	89,850	109,521	132,550	145,950	Quasi-Money	35
	2,662	4,362	4,978	7,282	12,907	14,351	19,797	22,615	29,376	33,093	37,433	42,732	45,034	57,453	59,903	Other Items (Net)	37r
	19,024	23,219	28,106	33,304	40,855	49,316	61,538	72,696	84,043	94,288	109,151	135,359	164,628	195,578	218,110	Money plus Quasi-Money	35l
																Interest Rates	
Data as of Middle of December	11.00	11.00	11.00	11.00	13.00	13.00	11.00	11.00	11.00	11.00	9.00	9.00	9.00	7.50	6.50	Discount Rate	60
	5.00	5.00	5.62	7.93	8.80	9.00	4.50	6.50	9.90	11.51	2.52	3.70	4.30	5.30	5.00	Treasury Bill Rate	60c
	12.50	12.50	12.50	11.92	....	....	8.75	....	9.63	9.79	8.92	7.31	5.96	4.75	Deposit Rate	60l
	15.00	15.00	15.00	14.42	....	....	....	....	12.88	14.54	14.00	11.33	9.46	7.67	Lending Rate	60p
	13.00	13.00	13.17	13.54	10.00	13.33	....	9.00	3.00	9.00	9.00	9.00	8.75	8.50	8.50	Government Bond Yield	61
																Prices	
Period Averages	45.9	†50.0	54.4	58.9	68.1	79.8	85.8	92.9	100.0	109.2	113.6	125.0	†135.1	137.1	140.9	Consumer Prices	64
																International Transactions	
Millions of Rupees	3,290	4,433	4,312	5,996	9,615	15,706	18,676	17,896	17,895	21,830	23,555	31,288	41,088	57,231	55,221	Exports	70
	12,444	15,821	15,780	19,729	27,217	33,157	43,267	57,072	69,028	79,247	97,974	81,901	97,057	111,800	110,362	Imports, c.i.f.	71

Nepal

		1972	1973	1974	1975	1976	1977	1978	1979	1980	1981	1982	1983	1984	1985	1986
Balance of Payments															*Millions of US Dollars:*	
Current Account, n.i.e.	78al *d*	...	...	...	...	18.5	−1.6	−25.7	−11.4	−38.9	−19.1	−85.4	−145.6	−95.2	−121.6	−119.2
Goods: Exports f.o.b.	78aa *d*	...	...	...	...	102.1	81.2	89.4	110.3	102.1	144.2	87.6	101.5	130.1	161.3	142.6
Goods: Imports f.o.b.	78ab *d*	...	...	...	...	−154.1	−165.7	−220.5	−251.4	−328.0	−362.4	−406.3	−468.3	−402.9	−444.0	−436.5
Trade Balance	78ac *d*					−52.0	−84.5	−131.1	−141.1	−225.9	−218.2	−318.7	−366.8	−272.8	−282.8	−293.9
Services: Credit	78ad *d*	...	...	...	...	61.4	72.2	99.1	111.5	155.0	155.5	160.2	171.0	159.2	157.4	176.6
Services: Debit	78ae *d*	...	...	...	...	−42.8	−46.0	−57.1	−74.3	−87.7	−94.0	−85.1	−88.0	−99.5	−115.7	−113.7
Balance on Goods & Services	78af *d*					−33.5	−58.3	−89.1	−103.8	−158.6	−156.6	−243.7	−283.8	−213.2	−241.1	−231.0
Income: Credit	78ag *d*	...	...	...	...	6.7	8.9	6.8	14.2	14.5	14.2	18.0	8.1	5.2	4.7	4.4
Income: Debit	78ah *d*	...	...	...	...	−1.6	−.8	−1.2	−2.9	−2.9	−3.2	−2.3	−2.4	−4.9	−3.9	−3.7
Balance on Gds, Serv. & Inc.	78ai *d*					−28.4	−50.3	−83.6	−92.6	−147.0	−145.7	−228.0	−278.1	−212.9	−240.3	−230.3
Current Transfers, n.i.e.: Credit	78aj *d*	...	...	...	...	48.3	50.4	59.0	82.4	109.5	127.6	144.9	135.3	119.7	122.2	115.7
Current Transfers: Debit	78ak *d*	...	...	...	...	−1.4	−1.7	−1.2	−1.2	−1.4	−1.0	−2.4	−2.8	−2.0	−3.4	−4.6
Capital Account, n.i.e.	78bc *d*	...	...	...	...	—	—	—	—	—	—	—	—	—	—	—
Capital Account, n.i.e.: Credit	78ba *d*					—	—	—	—	—	—	—	—	—	—	—
Capital Account: Debit	78bb *d*					—	—	—	—	—	—	—	—	—	—	—
Financial Account, n.i.e.	78bj *d*	...	...	...	...	14.2	22.7	−9.0	34.1	22.2	60.9	62.7	107.8	61.5	25.8	87.4
Direct Investment Abroad	78bd *d*					—	—	—	—	—	—	—	—	—	—	—
Dir. Invest. in Rep. Econ., n.i.e.	78be *d*					—	—	—	—	—	—	—	—	—	—	—
Portfolio Investment Assets	78bf *d*					—	—	—	—	—	—	—	—	—	—	—
Equity Securities	78bk *d*					—	—	—	—	—	—	—	—	—	—	—
Debt Securities	78bl *d*					—	—	—	—	—	—	—	—	—	—	—
Portfolio Investment Liab., n.i.e.	78bg *d*					—	—	—	—	—	—	—	—	—	—	—
Equity Securities	78bm *d*					—	—	—	—	—	—	—	—	—	—	—
Debt Securities	78bn *d*					—	—	—	—	—	—	—	—	—	—	—
Financial Derivatives Assets	78bw *d*															
Financial Derivatives Liabilities	78bx *d*															
Other Investment Assets	78bh *d*	...	...	...	...	1.5	−15.3	−20.4	3.3	−18.7	−8.1	10.1	42.3	−11.8	−96.0	.8
Monetary Authorities	78bo *d*					...	...	...	...	...	...	...	...	...	...	...
General Government	78bp *d*					—	—	—	—	—	—	—	—	—	—	—
Banks	78bq *d*					...	...	...	...	...	...	...	...	...	...	...
Other Sectors	78br *d*					1.5	−15.3	−20.4	3.3	−18.7	−8.1	10.1	42.3	−11.8	−96.0	.8
Other Investment Liab., n.i.e.	78bi *d*	...	...	...	...	12.6	38.0	11.4	30.8	40.8	69.0	52.6	65.5	73.3	121.8	86.7
Monetary Authorities	78bs *d*					−5.9	4.4	1.6	6.4	3.3	3.6	−8.4	−3.4	.1	13.0	−5.9
General Government	78bt *d*					6.0	24.3	15.6	29.6	40.5	58.9	56.7	61.5	68.9	85.2	94.2
Banks	78bu *d*					11.4	7.2	−7.1	−5.6	−3.6	3.9	.4	6.6	—	14.7	−5.7
Other Sectors	78bv *d*					1.2	2.2	1.3	.4	.6	2.7	3.9	.8	4.3	9.0	4.0
Net Errors and Omissions	78ca *d*	...	...	...	...	−4.1	−.7	10.5	4.8	3.5	9.2	24.4	30.1	12.8	2.3	−.8
Overall Balance	78cb *d*					28.6	20.4	−24.2	27.5	−13.1	51.0	1.6	−7.6	−20.9	−93.5	−32.5
Reserves and Related Items	79da *d*	...	...	...	...	−28.6	−20.4	24.2	−27.5	13.1	−51.0	−1.6	7.6	20.9	93.5	32.5
Reserve Assets	79db *d*					−33.7	−22.1	12.5	−31.7	−5.3	−50.9	3.0	13.3	27.6	88.5	33.1
Use of Fund Credit and Loans	79dc *d*					5.2	1.7	11.7	4.2	18.5	−.2	−5.3	−5.6	−6.8	4.9	−.6
Exceptional Financing	79de *d*					—	—	—	—	—	—	.8				
Government Finance															*Millions of Rupees:*	
Deficit (-) or Surplus	80	†−126	−223	−248	−236	−422	−576	−582	†−588	−705	−728	−1,591	−2,954	−2,985	−3,380	−3,637
Revenue	81	†541	602	752	995	1,088	1,291	1,522	†1,758	1,829	2,375	2,639	2,778	3,310	3,855	4,508
Grants Received	81z	†242	180	223	283	360	393	467	†564	791	859	988	1,089	877	917	1,173
Expenditure	82	†880	966	1,191	1,488	1,884	2,269	2,586	†2,928	3,340	3,967	5,221	6,852	7,238	8,209	9,445
Lending Minus Repayments	83	†29	39	31	25	−14	−10	−15	†−17	−15	−5	−4	−31	−67	−56	−128
Financing																
Net Borrowing: Domestic	84a	†87	127	162	112	212	417	230	†241	252	161	1,180	2,006	1,370	...	...
Foreign	85a	†39	47	86	95	137	153	364	†352	432	472	339	948	1,615	...	...
Use of Cash Balances	87	†—	48	−1	29	73	6	−12	†−5	21	95	72	—	—	...	...
Debt: Domestic	88a	272	359	476	605	743	1,014	1,225	†1,395	1,503	1,444	1,900	2,878	4,337	6,032	...
Foreign	89a	...	...	310	378	513	665	1,029	...	...	...	...	...	...	8,516	...
National Accounts															*Millions of Rupees:*	
Househ.Cons.Expend.,incl.NPISHs	96f	...	...	...	13,652	14,060	13,689	15,721	17,741	19,195	22,411	25,272	27,458	31,860	35,977	44,782
Government Consumption Expend.	91f	...	...	...	1,257	1,294	1,260	1,471	1,889	1,565	1,922	2,638	3,416	3,644	4,371	5,065
Gross Fixed Capital Formation	93e	...	...	...	2,223	2,443	2,580	3,294	3,263	3,681	4,299	5,465	6,576	6,907	9,386	9,431
Changes in Inventories	93i	...	...	...	179	189	188	213	251	589	509	−151	52	444	798	1,168
Exports of Goods and Services	90c	...	...	...	1,475	1,874	2,037	2,086	2,618	2,695	3,523	3,592	3,455	4,196	5,372	6,506
Imports of Goods and Services (-)	98c	...	...	...	2,215	2,466	2,474	3,053	3,547	4,374	5,357	5,828	7,196	7,661	9,317	11,218
Gross Domestic Product (GDP)	99b	10,369	9,969	12,808	†16,571	17,394	17,280	19,732	22,215	23,351	27,307	30,988	33,761	39,390	†46,587	55,734
GDP Volume 1965 prices	99b.*p*	6,487	6,456	6,865	6,965	...	...	...	...	...	...	...	...	...	...	...
GDP Volume 1975 prices	99b.*p*	...	...	...	16,571	17,300	17,822	18,607	19,048	18,606	20,158	20,920	20,297	22,262	23,630	...
GDP Volume 1985 Prices	99b.*p*	...	...	...	...	...	...	...	...	...	...	...	...	...	46,587	48,714
GDP Volume (1995=100)	99bv*p*	42.4	42.2	44.9	45.6	47.6	49.0	51.2	52.4	51.2	55.4	57.5	55.8	61.2	65.0	68.0
GDP Deflator (1995=100)	99bi*p*	11.1	10.8	13.0	†16.6	16.7	16.1	17.6	19.3	20.8	22.5	24.6	27.6	29.4	†32.7	37.4
																Millions:
Population	99z	11.81	12.06	12.32	12.59	12.86	13.14	13.42	13.71	14.01	15.02	15.42	15.83	16.25	16.69	17.13

	1987	1988	1989	1990	1991	1992	1993	1994	1995	1996	1997	1998	1999	2000	2001	
Minus Sign Indicates Debit																**Balance of Payments**
	−123.3	−271.5	−243.3	−289.2	−304.4	−181.3	−222.5	−351.9	−356.4	−326.6	−388.1	−67.2	−256.5	−277.4	....	Current Account, n.i.e. .... 78al *d*
	162.2	193.8	161.2	217.9	274.5	376.3	397.0	368.7	349.9	388.7	413.8	482.0	612.3	785.7	....	Goods: Exports f.o.b. .... 78aa *d*
	−512.4	−664.9	−568.1	−666.6	−756.9	−752.1	−858.6	−1,158.9	−1,310.8	−1,494.7	−1,691.9	−1,239.1	−1,494.2	−1,578.3	....	Goods: Imports f.o.b. .... 78ab *d*
	−350.2	−471.1	−407.0	−448.7	−482.4	−375.8	−461.6	−790.3	−961.0	−1,105.9	−1,278.1	−757.1	−881.9	−792.7	....	*Trade Balance* .... 78ac *d*
	217.7	223.8	203.1	204.4	239.8	273.8	333.2	579.2	679.0	757.5	865.7	565.1	655.1	505.9	....	Services: Credit .... 78ad *d*
	−131.2	−150.8	−147.7	−167.3	−183.9	−225.0	−251.8	−296.6	−313.3	−242.8	−224.5	−196.2	−212.5	−199.9	....	Services: Debit .... 78ae *d*
	−263.7	−398.1	−351.6	−411.7	−426.4	−327.0	−380.2	−507.6	−595.2	−591.3	−637.0	−388.1	−439.2	−486.7	....	*Balance on Goods & Services* .... 78af *d*
	6.8	16.2	21.2	25.1	27.0	33.5	28.9	34.6	43.6	33.1	31.9	45.4	55.8	72.2	....	Income: Credit .... 78ag *d*
	−6.7	−14.4	−10.5	−11.2	−16.2	−16.8	−23.7	−30.8	−34.9	−32.0	−28.6	−26.5	−28.4	−35.2	....	Income: Debit .... 78ah *d*
	−263.6	−396.3	−340.9	−397.8	−415.6	−310.3	−375.0	−503.9	−586.5	−590.2	−633.7	−369.2	−411.9	−449.7	....	*Balance on Gds, Serv. & Inc.* .... 78ai *d*
	143.6	130.5	109.2	115.7	121.3	133.6	155.5	160.7	239.2	281.6	267.4	326.0	182.3	189.0	....	Current Transfers, n.i.e.: Credit .... 78aj *d*
	−3.3	−5.6	−11.6	−7.1	−10.1	−4.6	−3.0	−8.7	−9.1	−18.0	−21.8	−24.1	−26.9	−16.7	....	Current Transfers: Debit .... 78ak *d*
	—	—	—	—	—	—	—	—	—	—	—	—	—	—	....	Capital Account, n.i.e. .... 78bc *d*
	—	—	—	—	—	—	—	—	—	—	—	—	—	—	....	Capital Account, n.i.e.: Credit .... 78ba *d*
	—	—	—	—	—	—	—	—	—	—	—	—	—	—	....	Capital Account: Debit .... 78bb *d*
	190.7	252.7	196.1	304.5	457.1	335.9	283.5	407.3	368.5	275.2	340.3	212.9	−24.5	76.1	....	Financial Account, n.i.e. .... 78bj *d*
															....	Direct Investment Abroad .... 78bd *d*
	...	...	...	...	...	...	...	...	—	19.2	23.1	12.0	—	—	....	Dir. Invest. in Rep. Econ., n.i.e. .... 78be *d*
	—	—	—	—	—	—	—	—	—	—	—	—	—	—	....	Portfolio Investment Assets .... 78bf *d*
	—	—	—	—	—	—	—	—	—	—	—	—	—	—	....	Equity Securities .... 78bk *d*
	—	—	—	—	—	—	—	—	—	—	—	—	—	—	....	Debt Securities .... 78bl *d*
	—	—	—	—	—	—	—	—	—	—	—	—	—	—	....	Portfolio Investment Liab., n.i.e. .... 78bg *d*
	—	—	—	—	—	—	—	—	—	—	—	—	—	—	....	Equity Securities .... 78bm *d*
	—	—	—	—	—	—	—	—	—	—	—	—	—	—	....	Debt Securities .... 78bn *d*
	...	...	...	...	...	...	...	...	...	...	...	...	...	...	....	Financial Derivatives Assets .... 78bw *d*
	...	...	...	...	...	...	...	...	...	...	...	...	...	...	....	Financial Derivatives Liabilities .... 78bx *d*
	59.8	38.5	−19.0	116.2	220.0	182.3	149.6	159.2	264.4	91.6	89.4	90.8	48.2	128.6	....	Other Investment Assets .... 78bh *d*
	...	...	...	...	...	...	...	...	...	...	...	...	...	...	....	Monetary Authorities .... 78bo *d*
	—	—	—	—	—	—	—	—	—	—	—	—	—	—	....	General Government .... 78bp *d*
	—	—	—	—	—	—	—	—	—	—	—	—	—	—	....	Banks .... 78bq *d*
	59.8	38.5	−19.0	116.2	220.0	182.3	149.6	159.2	264.4	91.6	89.4	90.8	48.2	128.6	....	Other Sectors .... 78br *d*
	130.9	214.2	215.1	188.3	237.1	153.7	133.9	248.0	104.1	164.5	227.8	110.0	−72.8	−52.6	....	Other Investment Liab., n.i.e. .... 78bi *d*
	13.2	−10.5	2.5	2.3	.3	1.5	−4.0	4.3	.1	−3.3	1.0	.4	−2.0	4.5	....	Monetary Authorities .... 78bs *d*
	116.4	196.8	210.3	175.7	214.6	130.1	125.7	237.5	106.8	128.4	165.9	151.8	−56.2	−61.0	....	General Government .... 78bt *d*
	−10.1	10.8	.6	6.8	12.5	22.1	11.7	5.4	−4.5	38.2	68.8	17.0	13.2	67.4	....	Banks .... 78bu *d*
	11.4	17.0	1.7	3.6	9.8	—	.4	.8	1.7	1.2	−7.8	−59.1	−27.8	−63.5	....	Other Sectors .... 78bv *d*
	−3.6	12.5	5.2	4.9	10.7	.8	4.6	7.1	2.8	82.3	216.6	134.0	58.3	124.6	....	Net Errors and Omissions .... 78ca *d*
	63.8	−6.3	−42.1	20.2	163.4	155.4	65.6	62.5	15.0	30.9	168.8	279.7	−222.7	−76.8	....	*Overall Balance* .... 78cb *d*
	−63.8	6.3	42.1	−20.2	−163.4	−155.4	−65.6	−62.5	−15.0	−30.9	−168.8	−279.7	222.7	76.8	....	Reserves and Related Items .... 79da *d*
	−78.1	−5.7	41.2	−8.1	−157.9	−162.3	−71.4	−65.0	−7.0	−23.4	−161.7	−273.0	−144.4	−291.2	....	Reserve Assets .... 79db *d*
	14.3	12.0	.9	−12.2	−5.4	6.9	5.8	2.5	−8.0	−7.5	−7.2	−6.6	−5.9	−4.4	....	Use of Fund Credit and Loans .... 79dc *d*
	—	...	...	—	—	—	—	—	...	...	...	...	373.0	372.4	....	Exceptional Financing .... 79de *d*
Year Ending July 15																**Government Finance**
	−3,902	−4,280	−8,014	−7,013	†−9,915	−10,054	−10,359	−7,463	−7,894	−10,981	−10,909	−13,846	−15,864	....	....	Deficit (−) or Surplus 80
	5,780	7,140	7,540	8,767	†10,413	13,012	14,316	18,862	23,206	26,641	29,344	31,492	34,812	....	....	Revenue 81
	1,285	2,077	1,681	1,829	†2,165	1,644	3,793	2,394	3,937	4,825	5,988	5,403	5,886	....	....	Grants Received 81z
	11,110	13,644	17,405	17,811	†22,748	25,134	29,180	29,309	36,242	43,519	47,073	51,964	58,391	....	....	Expenditure 82
	−142	−148	−170	−202	†−255	−424	−712	−590	−1,205	−1,072	−832	−1,223	−1,829	....	....	Lending Minus Repayments 83
																Financing
	1,545	1,030	2,731	1,433	†4,248	4,179	4,691	−233	2,410	3,500	3,968	5,572	4,453	....	....	Net Borrowing: Domestic 84a
	2,455	3,518	5,282	5,580	†5,667	5,875	5,668	7,696	5,484	7,481	6,941	8,274	11,411	....	....	Foreign 85a
	−98	−268	—	†—												Use of Cash Balances 87
	10,017	11,047	13,778	15,428	†20,856	23,235	24,456	30,631	32,058	34,242	35,891	38,407	49,670	....	....	Debt: Domestic 88a
	15,172	20,826	29,217	38,990	†59,505	70,924	87,421	101,967	113,000	128,044	132,087	161,208	173,861	....	....	Foreign 89a
Year Ending July 15																**National Accounts**
	50,746	62,407	70,172	86,314	97,771	121,370	133,314	154,009	166,443	191,469	216,364	231,392	264,944	287,947	309,107	Househ.Cons.Expend.,incl.NPISHs 96f
	5,797	6,895	8,947	8,959	11,085	11,908	14,900	15,987	20,267	23,018	24,987	28,015	30,529	34,579	40,973	Government Consumption Expend. 91f
	11,825	13,414	16,392	17,002	22,780	29,276	37,278	42,032	48,370	56,081	60,794	65,375	65,269	73,309	78,091	Gross Fixed Capital Formation 93e
	1,073	1,823	3,023	2,074	2,294	2,342	2,375	2,612	6,261	11,936	10,290	9,353	4,792	15,093	15,826	Changes in Inventories 93i
	7,555	8,717	9,897	10,887	14,226	23,909	30,948	47,548	53,084	55,405	73,853	68,659	78,150	90,161	93,326	Exports of Goods and Services 90c
	13,132	16,350	19,162	21,820	27,785	39,321	47,429	62,972	75,850	88,996	105,775	101,949	101,648	123,055	129,104	Imports of Goods and Services (−) 98c
	63,864	76,906	89,269	103,416	120,371	149,487	171,474	199,272	219,175	248,913	280,513	300,845	342,036	378,033	408,218	Gross Domestic Product (GDP) 99b
	...	...	...	...	...	...	...	...	...	...	...	...	...	...	...	GDP Volume 1965 prices .... 99b. *p*
	...	...	...	...	...	...	...	...	...	...	...	...	...	...	...	GDP Volume 1975 prices .... 99b. *p*
	49,540	53,353	55,662	56,151	59,768	62,531	64,586	69,686	71,685	75,773	79,388	82,116	85,789	91,317	96,612	GDP Volume 1985 Prices .... 99b. *p*
	69.1	74.4	77.6	78.3	83.4	87.2	90.1	97.2	100.0	105.7	110.7	114.6	119.7	127.4	134.8	GDP Volume (1995=100) .... 99bv *p*
	42.2	47.1	52.5	60.2	65.9	78.2	86.8	93.5	100.0	107.4	115.6	119.8	130.4	135.4	138.2	GDP Deflator (1995=100) .... 99bi *p*
Midyear Estimates																
	17.56	17.37	17.74	18.11	18.49	18.94	19.39	19.86	20.34	20.83	21.33	21.84	22.37	22.90	23.59	**Population** 99z

(See notes in the back of the book.)

Netherlands

		1972	1973	1974	1975	1976	1977	1978	1979	1980	1981	1982	1983	1984	1985	1986
Exchange Rates													*Guilders per SDR through 1998,*			
Market Rate	aa	3.5030	3.4073	3.0688	3.1473	2.8546	2.7695	2.5652	2.5102	2.7160	2.8732	2.8951	3.2084	3.4793	3.0448	2.6812
														Guilders per US Dollar through 1998,		
Market Rate	ae	3.2265	2.8245	2.5065	2.6885	2.4570	2.2800	1.9690	1.9055	2.1295	2.4685	2.6245	3.0645	3.5495	2.7720	2.1920
Market Rate	rf	3.2095	2.7956	2.6884	2.5290	2.6439	2.4543	2.1636	2.0060	1.9881	2.4952	2.6702	2.8541	3.2087	3.3214	2.4500
														Guilders per ECU:		
ECU Rate	ea	....	....	....	....				2.7460	2.7901	2.6831	2.5421	2.5371	2.5185	2.4585	2.3440
ECU Rate	eb					2.9570	2.7998	2.7535	2.7481	2.7606	2.7758	2.6153	2.5372	2.5233	2.5111	2.4015
														Index Numbers (1995=100):		
Market Rate	ahx	50.0	57.7	59.8	63.6	60.7	65.4	74.3	80.0	80.8	64.6	60.1	56.4	50.2	48.7	65.8
Nominal Effective Exchange Rate	neu	61.8	64.2	67.7	69.5	71.7	75.5	77.4	78.3	78.3	75.1	79.0	80.8	79.8	79.9	85.7
Real Effective Exchange Rate	reu	....	....	....	131.3	133.1	133.9	137.4	132.9	†123.0	109.6	110.1	108.9	103.3	100.6	105.9
Fund Position														*Millions of SDRs:*		
Quota	2f.s	700	700	700	700	700	700	948	948	1,422	1,422	1,422	2,265	2,265	2,265	2,265
SDRs	1b.s	650	475	486	520	531	564	244	394	439	592	772	502	525	569	598
Reserve Position in the Fund	1c.s	554	309	442	747	900	954	632	458	510	498	561	901	963	898	717
of which: Outstg.Fund Borrowing	2c	—	—	87	325	350	416	294	126	101	77	74	99	93	79	59
International Liquidity												*Millions of US Dollars Unless Otherwise Indicated:*				
Total Res.Min.Gold (Eurosys.Def)	1l.d	2,726	4,253	4,630	4,884	5,178	5,742	5,088	7,591	11,645	9,339	10,132	10,171	9,237	10,782	11,191
SDRs	1b.d	705	573	595	609	617	685	318	519	561	689	851	525	515	625	731
Reserve Position in the Fund	1c.d	601	373	541	874	1,045	1,158	823	603	651	579	619	943	944	987	877
Foreign Exchange	1d.d	1,420	3,306	3,495	3,401	3,515	3,899	3,947	6,469	10,434	8,071	8,662	8,702	7,778	9,170	9,583
o/w: Fin.Deriv.Rel.to Reserves	1dd d	....	....	....	....	....	....	....	....	....	....	....	....	....	....	....
Other Reserve Assets	1e.d	....	....	....	....	....	....	....	....	....	....	....	....	....	....	....
Gold (Million Fine Troy Ounces)	1ad	54.17	54.33	54.33	54.33	54.33	54.63	54.78	43.97	43.94	43.94	43.94	43.94	43.94	43.94	43.94
Gold (Eurosystem Valuation)	1an d	2,117	2,425	2,732	2,548	2,788	3,021	6,490	5,383	4,814	5,204	4,895	4,192	8,702	11,143	14,091
Memo: Euro Cl. on Non-EA Res.	1dg d	....	....	....	....	....	....	....	....	....	....	....	....	....	....	....
Non-Euro Cl. on EA Res.	1dh d	....	....	....	....	....	....	....	....	....	....	....	....	....	....	....
Mon. Auth.: Other Foreign Assets	3..d	....	....	....	....	....	....	....	....	....	....	....	....	....	....	....
Foreign Liabilities	4..d	104	705	63	69	47	270	511	114	182	111	109	133	76	110	235
Banking Insts.: Foreign Assets	7a.d	8,389	12,344	15,903	20,145	25,503	33,377	46,684	57,250	62,625	66,352	63,922	58,862	57,520	72,876	91,099
Foreign Liab.	7b.d	7,353	11,078	14,379	17,504	22,625	31,075	44,688	56,305	64,353	65,181	62,733	56,217	53,052	65,677	83,456
Monetary Authorities													*Billions of Guilders through 1998;*			
Fgn. Assets (Cl.on Non-EA Ctys)	11	15.61	18.85	18.92	20.45	20.07	20.47	23.04	24.99	35.30	36.25	39.78	44.34	64.57	61.66	56.41
Claims on General Government	12a.u	....	....	....	....	....	....	....	....	....	....	....	....	....	....	....
o/w: Claims on Gen.Govt.in Cty	12a	.98	.96	1.03	.96	1.07	1.30	1.45	1.58	1.87	2.11	2.20	2.37	2.88	2.64	2.99
Claims on Banking Institutions	12e.u	....	....	....	....	....	....	....	....	....	....	....	....	....	....	....
o/w: Claims on Bank.Inst.in Cty	12e	.53	1.15	1.26	1.84	1.65	2.20	5.21	5.17	5.80	8.08	4.70	7.54	5.80	6.75	10.91
Claims on Other Resident Sectors	12d.u	....	....	....	....	....	....	....	....	....	....	....	....	....	....	....
o/w: Cl. on Oth.Res.Sect.in Cty	12d	.14	.21	.23	.26	.28	.24	.29	.59	.42	.68	.92	.79	1.18	.84	1.54
Currency Issued	14a	11.98	12.59	13.61	15.26	16.67	18.23	19.62	21.04	22.95	23.27	25.00	28.01	29.73	30.75	31.92
Liabilities to Banking Insts	14c.u	....	....	....	....	....	....	....	....	....	....	....	....	....	....	....
o/w: Liabs to Bank.Inst.in Cty	14c	.05	.03	.04	.10	.05	.03	.04	.01	.04	.03	.02	.03	.02	.11	.05
Demand Dep. of Other Res.Sect.	14d.u	....	....	....	....	....	....	....	....	....	....	....	....	....	....	....
o/w: D.Dep.of Oth.Res.Sect.in Cty	14d	.03	.04	.04	.03	.07	.05	.07	.25	.05	.14	.20	.15	.09	.17	.19
Other Dep. of Other Res.Sect.	15..u	....	....	....	....	....	....	....	....	....	....	....	....	....	....	....
o/w: O.Dep.of Oth.Res.Sect.in Cty	15	....	....	....	....	....	....	....	....	....	....	....	....	....	....	....
Money Market Instruments	16m.u	....	....	....	....	....	....	....	....	....	....	....	....	....	....	....
o/w: MMI Held by Resid.of Cty	16m	....	....	....	....	....	....	....	....	....	....	....	....	....	....	....
Bonds (Debt Securities)	16n.u	....	....	....	....	....	....	....	....	....	....	....	....	....	....	....
o/w: Bonds Held by Resid.of Cty	16n	....	....	....	....	....	....	....	....	....	....	....	....	....	....	....
Foreign Liab. (to Non-EA Ctys)	16c	.34	1.96	.16	.19	.12	.62	1.01	.22	.39	.27	.29	.41	.27	.31	.52
Central Government Deposits	16d.u	....	....	....	....	....	....	....	....	....	....	....	....	....	....	....
o/w: Cent.Govt.Dep. in Cty	16d	3.87	5.14	6.78	5.69	5.37	5.22	4.64	2.38	3.85	3.38	3.42	3.36	1.73	3.39	5.80
Capital Accounts	17a	1.46	1.46	1.51	1.54	1.58	1.65	4.70	8.70	16.54	19.84	18.56	23.67	43.75	38.47	34.14
Other Items (Net)	17r	−.47	−.04	−.71	.70	−.78	−1.58	−.09	−.26	−.43	.21	.13	−.61	−1.17	−1.30	−.75
Memo: Net Claims on Eurosystem	12e.s	....	....	....	....	....	....	....	....	....	....	....	....	....	....	....
Currency Put into Circ.	14m	....	....	....	....	....	....	....	....	....	....	....	....	....	....	....
Banking Institutions													*Billions of Guilders through 1998;*			
Claims on Monetary Authorities	20	.58	.67	.71	.74	.81	.77	.91	1.05	1.03	.95	†1.57	1.64	1.91	2.10	2.09
Claims on Bk.Inst.in Oth.EA Ctys	20b.u	....	....	....	....	....	....	....	....	....	....	....	....	....	....	....
Fgn. Assets (Cl.on Non-EA Ctys)	21	27.22	34.33	39.86	54.16	62.66	76.10	91.92	109.09	133.36	163.79	†167.76	180.38	204.17	202.01	199.69
Claims on General Government	22a.u	....	....	....	....	....	....	....	....	....	....	....	....	....	....	....
o/w: Claims on Gen.Govt.in Cty	22a	24.10	23.88	25.45	28.06	30.37	31.60	34.74	39.49	45.40	50.07	†60.11	66.29	70.76	78.33	88.84
Claims on Other Resident Sectors	22d.u	....	....	....	....	....	....	....	....	....	....	....	....	....	....	....
o/w: Cl. on Oth.Res.Sect.in Cty	22d	57.19	71.96	85.75	97.02	117.06	147.34	178.58	204.79	224.76	236.84	†242.42	250.45	259.46	270.93	290.74
Demand Deposits	24..u	....	....	....	....	....	....	....	....	....	....	....	....	....	....	....
o/w: D.Dep.of Oth.Res.Sect.in Cty	24	23.68	23.19	26.54	32.67	35.09	40.30	41.40	41.65	43.54	41.56	†48.71	53.16	57.11	62.00	67.25
Other Deposits	25..u	....	....	....	....	....	....	....	....	....	....	....	....	....	....	....
o/w: O.Dep.of Oth.Res.Sect.in Cty	25	57.30	70.99	82.11	90.30	108.64	122.70	141.28	161.73	170.65	190.48	†195.83	201.65	214.70	229.33	239.98
Money Market Instruments	26m.u	....	....	....	....	....	....	....	....	....	....	....	....	....	....	....
o/w: MMI Held by Resid.of Cty	26m	....	....	....	....	....	....	....	....	....	....	....	....	....	....	....
Bonds (Debt Securities)	26n.u	....	....	....	....	....	....	....	....	....	....	....	....	....	....	....
o/w: Bonds Held by Resid.of Cty	26n	.97	1.46	1.67	2.63	2.93	12.11	19.43	25.79	31.47	31.01	†31.16	33.08	33.90	35.55	43.84
Foreign Liab. (to Non-EA Ctys)	26c	23.86	30.81	36.04	47.06	55.59	70.85	87.99	107.29	137.04	160.90	†164.64	172.28	188.31	182.06	182.94
Central Government Deposits	26d.u	....	....	....	....	....	....	....	....	....	....	....	....	....	....	....
o/w: Cent.Govt.Dep. in Cty	26d	.55	.56	.64	.70	.66	.75	.98	.82	.93	.85	†.78	.64	.59	.67	.95
Credit from Monetary Authorities	26g	.41	1.10	1.24	1.79	1.75	2.31	5.13	5.27	5.95	8.69	†5.26	7.03	5.85	5.67	10.70
Liab. to Bk.Inst.in Oth. EA Ctys	26h.u	....	....	....	....	....	....	....	....	....	....	....	....	....	....	....
Capital Accounts	27a	4.88	5.87	6.84	8.42	9.60	7.95	9.54	11.16	12.23	14.20	†20.23	22.24	24.35	23.57	26.79
Other Items (Net)	27r	−2.55	−3.14	−3.31	−3.59	−3.35	−1.16	.40	.80	2.75	3.97	†5.31	8.69	11.71	14.54	8.91

1987	1988	1989	1990	1991	1992	1993	1994	1995	1996	1997	1998	1999	2000	2001		
															Exchange Rates	
Euros per SDR Thereafter: End of Period																
2.5217	2.6907	2.5173	2.4043	2.4466	2.4944	2.6659	2.5330	2.3849	2.5072	2.7217	2.6595	1.3662	1.4002	1.4260	Market Rate	aa
Euros per US Dollar Thereafter: End of Period (ae) Period Average (rf)																
1.7775	1.9995	1.9155	1.6900	1.7104	1.8141	1.9409	1.6044	1.7436	2.0172	1.8888	.9954	1.0747	1.1347		Market Rate	ae
2.0257	1.9766	2.1207	1.8209	1.8697	1.7585	1.8573	1.8200	1.6057	1.6859	1.9513	1.9837	.9386	1.0854	1.1175	Market Rate	rf
End of Period (ea) Period Average (eb)																
2.3160	2.3440	2.2730	2.3125	2.2885	2.1925	2.1670	2.1280	2.0554	2.1665	2.2280	2.2037	....	....	....	ECU Rate	ea
2.3340	2.3343	2.3335	2.3162	2.3127	2.2725	2.1723	2.1528	2.0774	2.1113	2.2048	2.2227	....	....	....	ECU Rate	eb
Period Averages																
79.3	81.3	75.7	88.3	86.1	91.4	86.4	88.3	100.0	95.2	82.3	81.0	....	....	....	Market Rate	ahx
89.7	89.2	88.4	91.5	90.8	92.9	95.8	96.2	100.0	98.1	93.5	93.4	92.1	89.0	89.6	Nominal Effective Exchange Rate	neu
108.1	102.6	96.5	95.4	92.3	94.6	96.7	97.7	100.0	97.1	92.7	93.9	93.3	91.3	93.1	Real Effective Exchange Rate	reu
															Fund Position	
End of Period																
2,265	2,265	2,265	2,265	2,265	3,444	3,444	3,444	3,444	3,444	3,444	3,444	5,162	5,162	5,162	Quota	2f. s
637	576	590	504	530	403	424	442	616	566	586	644	742	501	598	SDRs	1b. s
652	563	537	519	559	834	795	802	1,169	1,275	1,625	2,113	1,880	1,524	1,872	Reserve Position in the Fund	1c. s
36	15	5	—	—	—	—	—	—	—	—	193	—	—	—	of which: Outstg.Fund Borrowing	2c
															International Liquidity	
End of Period																
16,003	16,075	16,508	17,484	17,798	21,937	31,344	34,532	33,714	26,767	24,865	21,417	†10,098	9,643	9,034	Total Res.Min.Gold (Eurosys.Def)	1l. d
903	776	776	718	758	554	583	645	916	814	791	907	1,019	653	752	SDRs	1b. d
926	757	706	738	800	1,147	1,092	1,171	1,738	1,834	2,193	2,975	2,580	1,986	2,352	Reserve Position in the Fund	1c. d
14,174	14,542	15,027	16,028	16,240	20,237	29,669	32,716	31,060	24,119	21,881	17,536	6,499	7,004	5,930	Foreign Exchange	1d. d
....	....	....	....	....	....	....	....	....	....	....	....	....	....	....	o/w: Fin.Deriv.Rel.to Reserves	1dd d
....	....	....	....	....	....	....	....	....	....	....	....	....	....	....	Other Reserve Assets	1e. d
43.94	43.94	43.94	43.94	43.94	43.94	35.05	34.77	34.77	34.77	27.07	33.83	31.57	29.32	28.44	Gold (Million Fine Troy Ounces)	1ad
15,532	13,807	14,413	14,719	14,543	13,712	7,639	8,477	9,168	8,622	5,801	7,299	9,164	8,046	7,863	Gold (Eurosystem Valuation)	1an d
												817	135	170	Memo: Euro Cl. on Non-EA Res.	1dg d
												986	491	1,314	Non-Euro Cl. on EA Res.	1dh d
....	....	....	....	....	....	....	....	....	....	....	....				Mon. Auth.: Other Foreign Assets	3.. d
94	26	87	85	245	38	152	263	141	79	64	725	†542	115	45	Foreign Liabilities	4.. d
115,975	120,572	146,271	185,921	189,048	190,591	195,752	200,374	234,141	238,726	263,592	....	†155,624	163,895	211,400	Banking Insts.: Foreign Assets	7a. d
108,672	109,884	121,329	153,434	157,364	165,530	169,204	186,977	220,964	245,746	290,784	....	†194,072	206,125	250,057	Foreign Liab.	7b. d
															Monetary Authorities	
Billions of Euros Beginning 1999: End of Period																
56.90	60.66	60.10	55.27	56.20	65.61	76.24	75.69	69.77	62.72	62.96	55.75	20.63	19.64	20.18	Fgn. Assets (Cl.on Non-EA Ctys)	11
												7.58	8.63	7.71	Claims on General Government	12a. u
3.06	4.21	6.20	6.04	6.38	6.15	4.14	4.12	4.20	4.47	4.74	4.90	1.73	1.53	1.90	o/w: Claims on Gen.Govt.in Cty	12a
												22.76	11.98	7.96	Claims on Banking Institutions	12e. e
6.84	6.45	6.39	9.18	3.06	5.35	4.46	8.26	9.97	16.05	11.37	18.68	9.88	9.20	3.71	o/w: Claims on Bank.Inst.in Cty	12e
												.31	.40	.49	Claims on Other Resident Sectors	12d. u
1.45	1.50	1.74	1.75	2.14	1.25	.60	.35	.35	.28	.22	.22	.12	.09	.10	o/w: Cl. on Oth.Res.Sect.in Cty	12d
35.42	36.89	38.65	39.42	39.91	39.89	40.41	40.93	41.30	41.67	42.10	40.90	18.98	18.73	11.39	Currency Issued	14a
												20.70	9.40	12.05	Liabilities to Banking Insts	14c. u
.08	1.83	6.11	6.62	.12	12.52	15.82	18.74	11.09	8.39	13.06	17.16	7.52	9.38	10.21	o/w: Liabs to Bank.Inst.in Cty	14c
														.01	Demand Dep. of Other Res.Sect.	14d. u
.30	.59	.60	.83	.35	.08	.13	.10	.02	.06	.06	.14	—	—	.01	o/w: D.Dep.of Oth.Res.Sect.in Cty	14d
....	....	....	....	....	....	....	....	....	....	....	....	—	—	—	Other Dep. of Other Res.Sect.	15.. u
												—	—	—	o/w: O.Dep.of Oth.Res.Sect.in Cty	15
												—	—	—	Money Market Instruments	16m. u
												—	—	—	o/w: MMI Held by Resid.of Cty	16m
												—	—	—	Bonds (Debt Securities)	16n. u
												—	—	—	o/w: Bonds Held by Resid.of Cty	16n
.17	.05	.17	.14	.42	.07	.30	.46	.23	.14	.13	1.37	.54	.12	.05	Foreign Liab. (to Non-EA Ctys)	16c
												.01	.04	.02	Central Government Deposits	16d. u
3.40	3.09	.03	1.36	3.27	3.13	7.99	9.61	14.84	14.44	.09	5.10	.01	.04	.02	o/w: Cent.Govt.Dep. in Cty	16d
29.36	30.51	29.26	24.08	24.40	23.53	21.79	20.06	17.21	19.65	24.96	17.09	12.99	14.53	15.02	Capital Accounts	17a
−.47	−.13	−.39	−.20	−.69	−.85	−1.00	−1.47	−.39	−.83	−1.10	−2.21	−1.95	−2.18	−2.20	Other Items (Net)	17r
												−1.25	2.16	.32	*Memo: Net Claims on Eurosystem*	12e. s
												....	....	....	*Currency Put into Circ.*	14m
															Banking Institutions	
Billions of Euros Beginning 1999: End of Period																
2.06	2.23	2.62	2.87	2.87	2.88	2.81	2.80	3.09	3.38	3.36	....	7.14	9.24	9.68	Claims on Monetary Authorities	20
												64.46	65.38	76.53	Claims on Bk.Inst.in Oth.EA Ctys	20b. u
206.15	241.08	280.18	314.21	323.35	345.75	379.94	347.67	375.66	416.24	531.72	....	154.91	176.14	239.87	Fgn. Assets (Cl.on Non-EA Ctys)	21
												110.03	106.62	105.40	Claims on General Government	22a. u
87.29	124.99	119.98	122.26	119.37	119.36	124.93	129.20	133.64	136.46	140.36	....	65.24	56.43	53.75	o/w: Claims on Gen.Govt.in Cty	22a
												496.17	577.35	627.59	Claims on Other Resident Sectors	22d. u
306.38	375.09	399.91	427.18	460.32	485.59	518.79	559.34	626.83	698.86	788.56	....	484.02	560.82	605.67	o/w: Cl. on Oth.Res.Sect.in Cty	22d
												118.42	131.89	150.97	Demand Deposits	24.. u
70.56	76.10	82.42	86.63	92.00	98.00	111.92	114.04	134.71	155.58	170.49	....	115.67	128.40	147.78	o/w: D.Dep.of Oth.Res.Sect.in Cty	24
												242.68	270.83	295.05	Other Deposits	25.. u
239.76	257.45	287.29	310.49	325.65	342.32	355.15	353.92	363.23	372.14	395.16	....	228.50	257.67	278.42	o/w: O.Dep.of Oth.Res.Sect.in Cty	25
												—			Money Market Instruments	26m. u
....	....	....	....	....	....	....	....	....	....	....	....				o/w: MMI Held by Resid.of Cty	26m
												154.93	172.70	207.03	Bonds (Debt Securities)	26n. u
												....	....	....	o/w: Bonds Held by Resid.of Cty	26n
50.54	138.29	143.91	149.18	150.93	150.11	154.41	169.53	187.19	193.55	196.41	....	193.18	221.52	283.74	Foreign Liab. (to Non-EA Ctys)	26c
193.17	219.71	232.41	259.30	269.16	300.29	328.41	324.42	354.51	428.48	586.57	....	1.93	.96	1.30	Central Government Deposits	26d. u
1.31	1.50	1.11	.87	1.92	1.14	1.32	.79	1.02	1.51	1.82	....	1.92	.94	1.23	o/w: Cent.Govt.Dep. in Cty	26d
7.36	6.14	4.89	9.33	3.08	6.65	4.06	7.92	10.15	13.10	14.69	....	10.21	9.97	4.19	Credit from Monetary Authorities	26g
												54.32	50.71	55.98	Liab. to Bk.Inst.in Oth. EA Ctys	26h. u
30.50	35.06	38.22	42.97	46.39	48.84	54.30	57.52	61.65	78.17	86.89	....	47.70	58.33	61.01	Capital Accounts	27a
8.67	9.14	12.44	7.74	16.79	6.24	16.90	10.88	26.74	12.40	11.97	....	9.34	17.81	−.19	Other Items (Net)	27r

Netherlands

		1972	1973	1974	1975	1976	1977	1978	1979	1980	1981	1982	1983	1984	1985	1986
Banking Survey (Nat'l Residency)												*Billions of Guilders through 1998;*				
Foreign Assets (Net)	31n	18.63	20.41	22.58	27.36	27.03	25.11	25.96	26.58	31.23	38.87	†42.62	52.04	80.16	81.31	72.65
Domestic Credit	32	78.00	91.31	105.03	119.90	142.76	174.51	209.44	243.25	267.67	285.48	†301.45	315.89	331.96	348.69	377.36
Claims on General Govt. (Net)	32an	20.67	19.14	19.05	22.63	25.42	26.93	30.58	37.87	42.59	47.95	†58.12	64.66	71.32	76.91	85.08
Claims on Other Resident Sectors	32d	57.33	72.17	85.98	97.28	117.34	147.58	178.87	205.38	225.18	237.52	†243.34	251.24	260.65	271.78	292.28
Currency Issued	34a.n	11.98	12.59	13.61	15.26	16.67	18.23	19.62	21.04	22.95	23.27	25.00	28.01	29.73	30.75	31.92
Demand Deposits	34b.n	23.71	23.22	26.58	32.70	35.16	40.35	41.47	41.90	43.59	41.70	48.91	53.31	57.20	62.17	67.44
Other Deposits	35..n	57.30	70.99	82.11	90.30	108.64	122.70	141.28	161.73	170.65	190.48	195.83	201.65	214.70	229.33	239.98
Money Market Instruments	36m	....	....	....	....	....	....	....	....	....	....	....	....	....	....	....
Bonds (Debt Securities)	36n	.97	1.46	1.67	2.63	2.93	12.11	19.43	25.79	31.47	31.01	†31.16	33.08	33.90	35.55	43.84
o/w: Bonds Over Two Years	36na	....	....	....	....	....	....	....	....	....	....	....	....	....	....	....
Capital Accounts	37a	6.33	7.32	8.35	9.96	11.18	9.60	14.24	19.86	28.77	34.04	38.79	45.91	68.10	62.04	60.93
Other Items (Net)	37r	−3.66	−3.87	−4.72	−3.58	−4.79	−3.38	−.64	−.40	1.47	3.86	†4.45	5.96	8.70	10.16	5.89
Banking Survey (EA-Wide Residency)															*Billions of Euros:*	
Foreign Assets (Net)	31n.u	....	....	....	....	....	....	....	....	....	....	....	....	....	....	....
Domestic Credit	32..u	....	....	....	....	....	....	....	....	....	....	....	....	....	....	....
Claims on General Govt. (Net)	32an.u	....	....	....	....	....	....	....	....	....	....	....	....	....	....	....
Claims on Other Resident Sect.	32d.u	....	....	....	....	....	....	....	....	....	....	....	....	....	....	....
Currency Issued	34a.u	....	....	....	....	....	....	....	....	....	....	....	....	....	....	....
Demand Deposits	34b.u	....	....	....	....	....	....	....	....	....	....	....	....	....	....	....
Other Deposits	35..u	....	....	....	....	....	....	....	....	....	....	....	....	....	....	....
o/w: Other Dep. Over Two Yrs	35ab u	....	....	....	....	....	....	....	....	....	....	....	....	....	....	....
Money Market Instruments	36m.u	....	....	....	....	....	....	....	....	....	....	....	....	....	....	....
Bonds (Debt Securities)	36n.u	....	....	....	....	....	....	....	....	....	....	....	....	....	....	....
o/w: Bonds Over Two Years	36na u	....	....	....	....	....	....	....	....	....	....	....	....	....	....	....
Capital Accounts	37a	....	....	....	....	....	....	....	....	....	....	....	....	....	....	....
Other Items (Net)	37r.u	....	....	....	....	....	....	....	....	....	....	....	....	....	....	....
Money (National Definitions)															*Billions of Guilders:*	
M3H	39m	46.90	57.19	68.66	72.58	90.74	92.29	95.71	102.88	106.82	112.46	†217.95	228.96	242.23	264.13	282.73
M3H, Seasonally Adjusted	39m.c	49.83	57.34	66.28	72.64	88.76	94.11	98.86	105.45	109.45	116.90	†221.45	233.07	247.57	267.88	283.90
Nonbank Financial Institutions																
Cash	40..l	.33	.61	.94	1.33	2.40	2.09	1.18	1.50	1.37	2.07	1.78	2.03	1.82	4.23	3.39
Foreign Assets	41..l	2.98	3.29	3.80	4.07	4.50	4.48	4.53	4.97	5.81	6.64	9.02	12.76	15.77	†28.52	37.78
Claims on Central Government	42a.l	16.29	18.25	20.79	24.18	28.62	33.36	38.38	43.11	50.22	58.42	65.32	76.24	88.96	†107.71	113.71
Claims on Local Government	42b.l	9.58	10.83	13.55	15.24	17.72	20.18	22.17	25.55	30.11	36.61	43.88	48.86	54.17	†62.15	69.10
Claims on Private Sector	42d.l	32.77	37.53	44.93	51.79	58.64	66.34	78.58	87.33	95.53	100.79	108.58	116.41	123.12	†147.59	158.36
Real Estate	42h.l	7.74	8.81	10.41	12.36	14.07	15.72	17.89	19.88	23.34	26.28	30.23	31.93	34.51	†38.41	40.33
Capital Accounts	47a.l	69.78	79.82	94.53	109.96	126.86	143.73	164.58	185.92	210.34	233.97	262.43	293.15	323.80	†376.77	408.04
Other Items (Net)	47r.l	−.11	−.50	−.12	−1.00	−.90	−1.57	−1.85	−3.58	−3.96	−3.16	−3.63	−4.91	−5.45	11.82	14.63
Interest Rates															*Percent Per Annum*	
Discount Rate (End of Period)	60	4.00	8.00	7.00	4.50	6.00	4.50	6.50	9.50	8.00	9.00	5.00	5.00	5.00	5.00	4.50
Rate on Advances	60a	....	....	....	....	....	....	....	....	....	....	....	....	....	5.50	5.00
Money Market Rate	60b	1.93	6.44	9.20	4.17	7.28	3.80	6.24	9.03	10.13	11.01	8.06	5.28	5.78	6.30	5.83
Treasury Bill Rate	60c	....	....	....	....	5.84	4.50	9.39	13.80	10.13	10.68	8.12	5.48	5.97	6.23	5.49
Deposit Rate	60l	....	....	....	....	....	....	5.04	5.54	5.96	6.06	5.88	4.03	4.10	4.10	3.93
Lending Rate	60p	....	....	....	....	....	....	13.25	16.50	13.50	14.25	11.17	8.46	8.88	9.25	8.63
Government Bond Yield	61	6.88	†7.92	9.83	8.79	8.95	8.10	7.74	8.78	10.21	11.55	10.10	8.61	8.33	7.34	6.32
Prices, Production, Labor														*Index Numbers (1995=100):*		
Share Prices: General	62	23.7	25.3	19.4	19.8	20.7	19.8	19.9	19.6	18.4	19.4	19.7	26.5	36.2	†46.8	53.8
Manufacturing	62a	54.2	59.8	46.3	46.0	44.0	39.7	39.5	35.7	30.6	32.4	33.9	51.3	63.3	47.6	60.9
Prices: Final Products	63	48.7	51.7	56.4	59.8	63.9	67.4	68.4	70.2	75.3	81.9	86.6	87.8	91.7	93.1	90.6
Consumer Prices	64	39.3	42.4	46.5	51.2	55.9	59.5	61.9	64.5	†68.7	73.4	77.7	79.9	82.5	84.3	84.4
Harmonized CPI	64h															
Wages: Hourly Rates	65	†32.9	37.2	43.6	49.5	53.9	57.7	61.0	63.7	66.5	68.7	73.4	75.3	76.2	79.9	81.2
Industrial Production	66..c	64.0	69.5	72.7	71.9	76.6	76.6	76.6	79.8	†79.0	77.3	74.0	76.7	79.8	83.1	83.1
Industrial Employment	67	139.9	136.0	134.4	130.1	125.9	121.7	118.1	†116.1	†115.0	111.7	95.5	103.6	102.5	103.6	105.7
Labor Force	67d	....	....	....	....	....	....	....	....	....	....	....	....	....	*Number in Thousands:*	
Labor Force	67d	....	....	....	....	....	....	....	....	....	....	....	....	....	....	....
Employment	67e	....	....	....	....	....	....	....	....	....	....	....	....	....	5,145	....
Unemployment	67c	....	....	....	....	....	....	....	....	....	....	....	....	....	....	711
Unemployment Rate (%)	67r	....	....	....	....	....	....	....	....	....	....	....	....	....	....	12.0
International Transactions													*Millions of Guilders through 1998;*			
Exports	70	61,490	76,039	100,322	100,761	121,662	122,914	124,292	147,395	168,850	195,259	201,921	209,954	240,081	257,267	†197,285
Imports, c.i.f.	71	66,343	79,774	104,386	103,258	123,209	129,777	132,304	154,964	175,732	188,916	193,088	194,733	221,657	241,587	†185,053
Volume of Exports	72	30.6	34.6	39.5	37.5	42.5	41.5	43.2	47.0	†47.4	47.6	47.3	49.6	†53.0	54.9	56.4
Volume of Imports	73	36.0	40.1	43.3	41.1	46.1	46.9	49.9	53.0	†51.9	48.2	48.4	49.7	52.9	56.5	58.8
Unit Value of Exports	74	51.8	55.3	70.9	†74.4	78.9	81.1	†79.6	86.5	†98.3	113.8	117.7	117.7	126.8	129.4	110.0
Unit Value of Imports	75	50.1	54.0	72.9	†76.3	80.9	83.2	†81.7	91.1	†104.7	120.6	123.3	124.6	131.2	132.6	109.4

1995=100 (header for rows 72–75)

1987	1988	1989	1990	1991	1992	1993	1994	1995	1996	1997	1998	1999	2000	2001		
Billions of Euros Beginning 1999: End of Period															**Banking Survey (Nat'l Residency)**	
69.71	81.97	107.71	110.03	109.97	111.01	127.48	98.48	90.68	50.34	7.98	....	43.19	54.60	64.91	Foreign Assets (Net)	**31n**
393.46	501.21	526.69	555.00	583.02	608.08	639.15	682.62	749.16	824.11	931.97	....	549.19	617.88	660.17	Domestic Credit	**32**
85.64	124.62	125.05	126.07	120.57	121.24	119.75	122.92	121.98	124.98	143.19	....	65.05	56.97	54.40	Claims on General Govt. (Net)	**32an**
307.83	376.59	401.64	428.93	462.45	486.84	519.40	559.69	627.18	699.13	788.78	....	484.14	560.91	605.77	Claims on Other Resident Sectors	**32d**
35.42	36.89	38.65	39.42	39.91	39.89	40.41	40.93	41.30	41.67	42.10	40.90	18.98	18.73	11.39	Currency Issued	**34a.n**
70.86	76.70	83.02	87.46	92.34	98.08	112.05	114.14	134.74	155.65	170.55	....	115.67	128.40	147.78	Demand Deposits	**34b.n**
239.76	257.45	287.29	310.49	325.65	342.32	355.15	353.92	363.23	372.14	395.16	....	228.50	257.67	278.42	Other Deposits	**35..n**
												—	—	—	Money Market Instruments	**36m**
50.54	138.29	143.91	149.18	150.93	150.11	154.41	169.53	187.19	193.55	196.41	....	154.93	172.70	207.03	Bonds (Debt Securities)	**36n**
												134.74	152.76	175.59	o/w: Bonds Over Two Years	**36na**
59.86	65.57	67.48	67.05	70.79	72.37	76.09	77.58	78.86	97.82	111.85	17.09	60.69	72.86	76.03	Capital Accounts	**37a**
6.73	8.29	14.03	11.42	13.36	16.33	28.51	25.01	34.52	13.62	23.88	....	13.59	22.10	4.42	Other Items (Net)	**37r**
End of Period															**Banking Survey (EA-Wide Residency)**	
....	....	....	....	....	....	....	....	....	....	....	....	−18.19	−25.87	−23.74	Foreign Assets (Net)	**31n.u**
....	....	....	....	....	....	....	....	....	....	....	....	612.15	692.00	739.87	Domestic Credit	**32..u**
....	....	....	....	....	....	....	....	....	....	....	....	115.67	114.25	111.79	Claims on General Govt. (Net)	**32an.u**
....	....	....	....	....	....	....	....	....	....	....	....	496.48	577.75	628.09	Claims on Other Resident Sect.	**32d.u**
....	....	....	....	....	....	....	....	....	....	....	....	18.98	18.73	11.39	Currency Issued	**34a.u**
....	....	....	....	....	....	....	....	....	....	....	....	118.42	131.89	150.98	Demand Deposits	**34b.u**
....	....	....	....	....	....	....	....	....	....	....	....	242.68	270.83	295.05	Other Deposits	**35..u**
....	....	....	....	....	....	....	....	....	....	....	....	57.62	66.15	62.61	o/w: Other Dep. Over Two Yrs	**35ab.u**
....	....	....	....	....	....	....	....	....	....	....	....	—	—	—	Money Market Instruments	**36m.u**
....	....	....	....	....	....	....	....	....	....	....	....	154.93	172.70	207.03	Bonds (Debt Securities)	**36n.u**
....	....	....	....	....	....	....	....	....	....	....	....	134.74	152.76	175.59	o/w: Bonds Over Two Years	**36na.u**
....	....	....	....	....	....	....	....	....	....	....	....	60.69	72.86	76.03	Capital Accounts	**37a**
....	....	....	....	....	....	....	....	....	....	....	....	−1.74	−.89	−24.34	Other Items (Net)	**37r.u**
End of Period															**Money (National Definitions)**	
294.21	319.81	359.72	386.02	407.19	432.15	465.08	466.02	486.57	514.99	553.24	....	....	....	....	M3H	**39m**
291.96	325.80	369.59	387.24	408.98	434.02	474.64	469.75	489.45	515.51	553.72	....	....	....	....	M3H, Seasonally Adjusted	**39m.c**
End of Period															**Nonbank Financial Institutions**	
2.85	4.13	6.38	8.87	9.73	10.06	13.77	10.87	10.99	11.58	11.90	11.81	....			Cash	**40..l**
41.06	49.05	55.38	57.16	69.33	83.26	108.54	115.34	145.81	188.36	271.83	380.97	....			Foreign Assets	**41..l**
118.01	124.01	131.04	138.87	147.12	151.57	153.09	161.40	175.66	190.88	192.82	181.40	....			Claims on Central Government	**42a.l**
76.88	25.03	25.18	26.04	27.28	28.49	30.88	31.81	31.55	30.19	27.52	25.53	....			Claims on Local Government	**42b.l**
165.15	234.57	254.30	261.42	276.86	291.20	326.30	346.67	369.32	411.29	457.37	501.60	....			Claims on Private Sector	**42d.l**
42.22	45.50	47.79	50.64	54.86	58.34	59.45	59.78	60.40	63.96	64.18	66.41	....			Real Estate	**42h.l**
433.48	468.80	506.41	526.30	566.29	604.65	673.25	702.32	767.87	871.78	994.43	1,138.09	....			Capital Accounts	**47a.l**
12.70	13.49	13.66	16.69	18.88	18.27	18.79	23.56	25.85	24.49	31.19	29.64	....			Other Items (Net)	**47r.l**
Percent Per Annum															**Interest Rates**	
3.75	4.50	7.00	7.25	8.50	7.75	5.00	....	....	....	....	....	....			Discount Rate (End of Period)	**60**
4.27	5.01	7.75	8.00	8.94	8.33	5.52	4.50	2.98	2.00	2.75	2.75	....			Rate on Advances	**60a**
5.16	4.48	6.99	8.29	9.01	9.27	7.10	5.14	4.22	2.89	3.07	3.21	....			Money Market Rate	**60b**
5.18	4.34	6.80	....	....	....	....	....	....	....	....	....	....			Treasury Bill Rate	**60c**
3.55	3.48	3.49	3.31	3.18	3.20	3.11	†4.70	4.40	3.54	3.18	3.10	2.74	2.89	3.10	Deposit Rate	**60l**
8.15	7.77	10.75	11.75	12.40	12.75	10.40	8.29	7.21	5.90	6.13	6.50	†3.46	4.79	5.00	Lending Rate	**60p**
6.40	6.42	7.22	8.92	8.74	8.10	6.51	7.20	7.20	6.49	5.81	4.87	4.92	5.51	5.17	Government Bond Yield	**61**
Period Averages															**Prices, Production, Labor**	
56.0	50.7	64.1	62.5	64.2	67.3	78.1	92.5	100.0	134.4	195.3	261.6	284.6	335.5	257.0	Share Prices: General	**62**
54.3	49.6	63.9	61.7	61.7	66.0	77.3	93.9	100.0	125.9	192.1	242.5	264.4	319.7	263.1	Manufacturing	**62a**
89.5	89.9	93.1	94.0	†96.2	97.9	98.0	†98.5	100.0	102.0	103.8	103.6	104.7	109.8	112.9	Prices: Final Products	**63**
83.8	84.4	85.3	†87.4	90.2	93.0	95.4	98.1	†100.0	102.0	104.2	106.3	108.6	111.4	116.4	Consumer Prices	**64**
....	....	....	....	....	....	....	....	100.0	101.4	103.3	105.1	107.3	109.8	115.4	Harmonized CPI	**64h**
82.3	83.4	84.5	87.0	†90.2	94.1	97.1	†98.9	100.0	101.7	104.8	108.1	111.3	115.4	120.2	Wages: Hourly Rates	**65**
84.0	86.5	89.8	91.5	†94.0	93.8	92.7	†97.2	100.0	103.8	106.6	107.7	107.7	110.5	110.1	Industrial Production	**66..c**
106.7	106.7	108.5	110.9	†111.1	110.0	106.7	102.2	100.0	98.9	100.0	....	....	....	....	Industrial Employment	**67**
Period Averages																
....	....	....	....	....	....	....	7,185	7,359	7,460	7,616	7,735	....	8,058	....	Labor Force	**67d**
†5,864	6,032	6,155	6,356	6,521	†6,597	6,448	6,692	6,835	6,971	7,194	7,398	7,601	7,731	....	Employment	**67e**
†686	†433	390	346	319	336	415	486	464	440	375	286	222	187	....	Unemployment	**67c**
†11.5	†6.5	5.8	5.0	4.5	5.3	6.5	7.6	†7.0	6.6	5.5	4.1	3.1	2.6	....	Unemployment Rate (%)	**67r**
Millions of Euros Beginning 1999															**International Transactions**	
188,016	203,730	228,544	239,181	249,051	246,541	258,343	282,209	314,693	332,920	380,018	398,686	†188,046	226,903	241,300	Exports	**70**
184,844	196,347	220,987	229,708	237,118	236,597	231,637	256,442	283,538	304,559	347,286	371,760	†178,721	214,536	217,087	Imports, c.i.f.	**71**
1995=100																
59.7	64.8	68.2	71.5	†75.4	77.5	83.1	†92.2	100.0	†104.5	113.8	122.2	127.8	138.9	139.2	Volume of Exports	**72**
62.6	67.0	70.1	73.7	†76.7	78.1	81.5	†89.3	100.0	†104.8	111.6	122.3	131.3	137.2	137.8	Volume of Imports	**73**
99.6	99.6	107.4	106.4	†104.7	101.1	97.8	†98.2	100.0	†100.3	106.5	103.1	100.4	114.6	118.9	Unit Value of Exports	**74**
102.8	102.3	112.5	109.0	†108.6	106.3	99.8	†99.8	100.0	†100.9	107.1	104.4	104.3	116.7	120.3	Unit Value of Imports	**75**

Netherlands

		1972	1973	1974	1975	1976	1977	1978	1979	1980	1981	1982	1983	1984	1985	1986
Balance of Payments																*Millions of US Dollars:*
Current Account, n.i.e.	78al d	2,101	3,224	3,040	2,394	3,587	1,413	-904	350	-855	3,826	5,025	5,089	6,380	4,248	4,318
Goods: Exports f.o.b.	78aa d	16,793	23,605	33,283	34,962	39,468	43,021	49,122	63,398	73,230	68,588	66,804	64,534	65,666	68,294	78,662
Goods: Imports f.o.b.	78ab d	-16,135	-22,314	-31,897	-33,274	-37,240	-42,510	-49,945	-64,003	-73,474	-62,912	-60,546	-58,982	-59,027	-61,590	-71,254
Trade Balance	78ac d	658	1,290	1,386	1,688	2,228	510	-823	-605	-245	5,676	6,258	5,553	6,639	6,704	7,408
Services: Credit	78ad d	4,463	5,914	7,403	8,918	9,329	10,597	12,976	14,391	17,150	15,283	15,271	13,559	13,451	13,796	17,135
Services: Debit	78ae d	-3,897	-5,237	-6,841	-7,851	-8,610	-9,985	-12,454	-14,966	-18,148	-16,061	-15,579	-14,157	-14,003	-14,948	-18,346
Balance on Goods & Services	78af d	1,225	1,967	1,949	2,754	2,947	1,122	-300	-1,180	-1,242	4,899	5,951	4,955	6,088	5,553	6,196
Income: Credit	78ag d	2,464	3,547	4,454	3,885	4,371	4,871	5,567	10,240	12,763	12,672	12,365	11,189	11,807	9,465	12,708
Income: Debit	78ah d	-1,431	-2,151	-3,009	-3,548	-3,382	-3,962	-5,330	-7,958	-11,228	-12,304	-11,986	-10,076	-10,457	-9,701	-12,900
Balance on Gds, Serv. & Inc.	78ai d	2,258	3,364	3,394	3,091	3,936	2,031	-63	1,102	293	5,267	6,330	6,068	7,438	5,317	6,004
Current Transfers, n.i.e.: Credit	78aj d	528	983	860	973	1,387	1,759	2,244	2,881	2,746	1,887	1,919	2,050	2,042	2,102	2,994
Current Transfers: Debit	78ak d	-685	-1,123	-1,213	-1,670	-1,736	-2,376	-3,086	-3,634	-3,894	-3,328	-3,224	-3,030	-3,100	-3,172	-4,680
Capital Account, n.i.e.	78bc d	27	49	-5	-6	-124	-219	-317	-216	-250	-227	-310	-148	-76	-47	-198
Capital Account, n.i.e.: Credit	78ba d	103	105	116	111	90	114	110	149	129	166	213	129	126	151	201
Capital Account: Debit	78bb d	-76	-56	-122	-117	-214	-333	-427	-366	-379	-393	-523	-278	-201	-199	-399
Financial Account, n.i.e.	78bj d	-1,431	-2,463	-2,688	-2,796	-3,061	-436	793	-816	2,411	-4,287	-2,803	-4,896	-7,559	-2,373	-2,101
Direct Investment Abroad	78bd d	-1,640	-2,117	-2,789	-2,519	-2,353	-3,038	-3,386	-6,282	-5,918	-4,527	-3,263	-3,835	-4,844	-2,705	-4,093
Dir. Invest. in Rep. Econ., n.i.e.	78be d	755	1,119	1,103	1,232	581	605	1,082	1,715	2,278	1,799	1,227	1,358	1,717	1,505	3,129
Portfolio Investment Assets	78bf d	-681	-877	-394	-565	12	-24	-322	481	176	-352	-1,470	-1,530	-1,073	-2,770	-8,000
Equity Securities	78bk d	-562	-692	-398	-472	211	179	21	523	484	268	31	-60	589	-186	-2,681
Debt Securities	78bl d	-119	-185	4	-93	-199	-203	-342	-42	-308	-620	-1,501	-1,470	-1,662	-2,584	-5,320
Portfolio Investment Liab., n.i.e.	78bg d	280	-100	128	600	-168	1,802	1,413	2,075	3,026	1,184	1,069	1,393	1,000	2,710	2,132
Equity Securities	78bm d	214	-74	-300	27	-131	274	303	297	495	225	392	533	-81	1,084	924
Debt Securities	78bn d	66	-26	428	574	-37	1,528	1,110	1,778	2,531	959	678	860	1,080	1,626	1,208
Financial Derivatives Assets	78bw d	—	—	—	-1	2	—	2	18	-54	-52	-11	-28	22	-24	-69
Financial Derivatives Liabilities	78bx d	....	....	....	....	....	....	....	....	....	....	....	....	....	....	....
Other Investment Assets	78bh d	-1,710	-3,211	-2,957	-5,836	-5,886	-5,498	-8,942	-11,137	-9,649	-7,966	-1,747	-289	-4,479	-5,171	-6,638
Monetary Authorities	78bo d	—	—	—	—	—	—	—	—	—	—	—	—	—	—	—
General Government	78bp d	-121	-142	-332	-168	-205	-273	-156	-685	-375	-577	-411	-52	-227	-154	-813
Banks	78bq d	-1,452	-2,911	-2,481	-5,339	-4,717	-4,527	-8,453	-10,251	-8,437	-6,869	-46	901	-3,007	-3,816	-3,501
Other Sectors	78br d	-138	-157	-143	-329	-963	-698	-333	-201	-837	-520	-1,290	-1,138	-1,245	-1,201	-2,325
Other Investment Liab., n.i.e.	78bi d	1,566	2,722	2,220	4,292	4,752	5,717	10,945	12,314	12,551	5,627	1,391	-1,966	99	4,082	11,439
Monetary Authorities	78bs d	65	12	-678	8	-34	208	148	-392	83	-64	13	70	-50	21	55
General Government	78bt d	-16	8	35	49	-21	49	-41	206	-73	31	290	-103	-47	66	230
Banks	78bu d	1,433	2,970	2,325	4,073	4,955	5,376	10,042	12,053	11,952	5,333	591	-2,807	475	3,700	9,765
Other Sectors	78bv d	85	-269	538	163	-148	84	797	446	589	326	497	875	-279	295	1,389
Net Errors and Omissions	78ca d	232	-75	-42	731	-108	-251	-341	-297	-43	-202	-118	-202	1,243	-1,056	-2,350
Overall Balance	78cb d	929	735	306	323	295	507	-770	-980	1,264	-891	1,795	-157	-12	771	-330
Reserves and Related Items	79da d	-929	-735	-306	-323	-295	-507	770	980	-1,264	891	-1,795	157	12	-771	330
Reserve Assets	79db d	-929	-735	-306	-323	-295	-507	770	980	-1,264	891	-1,795	157	12	-771	330
Use of Fund Credit and Loans	79dc d	—	—	—	—	—	—	—	—	—	—	—	—	—	—	—
Exceptional Financing	79de d	....	....	....	....	....	....	....	....	....	....	....	....	....	....	....
International Investment Position																*Millions of US Dollars*
Assets	79aa d	....	....	....	....	....	....	....	....	58,680	54,889	131,631	136,268	139,709	178,433	234,170
Direct Investment Abroad	79ab d	....	....	....	....	....	....	....	....	42,135	40,236	39,737	39,121	39,944	47,772	59,352
Portfolio Investment	79ac d	....	....	....	....	....	....	....	....	....	....	11,681	13,499	14,108	22,671	36,921
Equity Securities	79ad d	....	....	....	....	....	....	....	....	....	....	6,419	7,452	7,049	10,473	18,111
Debt Securities	79ae d	....	....	....	....	....	....	....	....	....	....	5,263	6,047	7,060	12,198	18,809
Financial Derivatives	79al d	....	....	....	....	....	....	....	....	....	....	....	....	....	....	....
Other Investment	79af d	....	....	....	....	....	....	....	....	—	—	65,090	69,210	67,496	85,787	109,159
Monetary Authorities	79ag d	....	....	....	....	....	....	....	....	—	—	—	—	—	—	—
General Government	79ah d	....	....	....	....	....	....	....	....	....	....	3,050	2,905	2,818	3,948	10,085
Banks	79ai d	....	....	....	....	....	....	....	....	—	—	62,040	57,314	56,488	69,871	82,635
Other Sectors	79aj d	....	....	....	....	....	....	....	....	....	....		8,991	8,191	11,968	16,438
Reserve Assets	79ak d	....	....	....	....	....	....	....	....	16,544	14,654	15,122	14,438	18,161	22,203	28,739
Liabilities	79la d	....	....	....	....	....	....	....	....	27,868	26,865	107,811	102,860	101,007	136,545	186,668
Dir. Invest. in Rep. Economy	79lb d	....	....	....	....	....	....	....	....	19,167	18,405	17,975	16,924	18,196	24,952	35,213
Portfolio Investment	79lc d	....	....	....	....	....	....	....	....	8,518	8,349	22,812	26,027	27,011	42,963	56,577
Equity Securities	79ld d	....	....	....	....	....	....	....	....	....	....	11,643	15,715	16,611	27,430	37,181
Debt Securities	79le d	....	....	....	....	....	....	....	....	8,518	8,349	11,169	10,312	10,400	15,533	19,396
Financial Derivatives	79ll d	....	....	....	....	....	....	....	....	....	....	....	....	....	....	....
Other Investment	79lf d	....	....	....	....	....	....	....	....	182	111	67,024	59,909	55,800	68,630	94,879
Monetary Authorities	79lg d	....	....	....	....	....	....	....	....	182	111	109	432	346	554	235
General Government	79lh d	....	....	....	....	....	....	....	....	....	....	406				4,286
Banks	79li d	....	....	....	....	....	....	....	....	—	—	62,678	55,429	52,695	64,537	82,084
Other Sectors	79lj d	....	....	....	....	....	....	....	....	....	....	3,831	4,048	2,760	3,539	8,274

Balance of Payments

Minus Sign Indicates Debit

1987	1988	1989	1990	1991	1992	1993	1994	1995	1996	1997	1998	1999	2000	2001	Item	Code
4,187	7,132	10,039	8,089	7,466	6,847	13,203	17,294	25,759	21,487	25,060	13,309	14,810	11,156	12,405	Current Account, n.i.e.	78al d
92,146	103,389	108,155	130,002	130,759	137,332	127,876	141,810	195,600	195,079	188,988	196,277	195,691	208,129	207,102	Goods: Exports f.o.b.	78aa d
-85,894	-93,317	-98,330	-117,944	-118,780	-125,024	-110,972	-123,124	-171,788	-172,312	-168,051	-175,222	-179,657	-186,852	-183,514	Goods: Imports f.o.b.	78ab d
6,252	10,072	9,825	12,058	11,979	12,309	16,904	18,686	23,812	22,767	20,937	21,055	16,034	21,278	23,588	*Trade Balance*	78ac d
20,673	22,318	24,745	29,302	33,000	38,274	37,923	41,523	46,920	48,495	50,155	51,661	54,102	53,312	52,627	Services: Credit	78ad d
-22,013	-24,505	-25,413	-29,708	-33,814	-38,451	-38,004	-41,303	-45,768	-46,535	-46,882	-49,185	-51,605	-53,633	-53,840	Services: Debit	78ae d
4,912	7,885	9,156	11,652	11,165	12,131	16,823	18,905	24,964	24,726	24,210	23,531	18,531	20,956	22,375	*Balance on Goods & Services*	78af d
15,840	18,365	23,602	26,249	27,282	27,230	28,117	29,466	35,755	36,292	39,197	35,970	43,646	39,623	38,363	Income: Credit	78ag d
-14,514	-17,247	-20,781	-26,869	-26,850	-28,159	-27,236	-25,799	-28,527	-32,762	-32,227	-39,011	-41,017	-43,172	-41,770	Income: Debit	78ah d
6,239	9,003	11,978	11,032	11,597	11,202	17,704	22,571	32,193	28,257	31,180	20,491	21,159	17,407	18,968	*Balance on Gds, Serv. & Inc.*	78ai d
4,051	5,592	5,142	4,478	4,603	4,642	4,359	4,197	4,725	4,319	4,346	3,799	4,566	4,366	4,636	Current Transfers, n.i.e.: Credit	78aj d
-6,103	-7,464	-7,081	-7,421	-8,733	-8,997	-8,860	-9,474	-11,159	-11,089	-10,465	-10,981	-10,916	-10,617	-11,199	Current Transfers: Debit	78ak d
-233	-198	-314	-301	-282	-631	-715	-1,006	-1,099	-2,024	-1,297	-420	-214	606	-628	Capital Account, n.i.e.	78bc d
312	293	299	314	343	369	579	564	856	1,267	1,099	1,037	1,688	2,856	1,050	Capital Account, n.i.e.: Credit	78ba d
-545	-490	-613	-615	-625	-1,000	-1,294	-1,569	-1,955	-3,291	-2,396	-1,457	-1,902	-2,249	-1,677	Capital Account: Debit	78bb d
-1,283	-668	-8,249	-4,922	-5,516	-7,279	-11,136	-9,969	-18,822	-5,465	-14,279	-14,710	-12,963	-11,234	-12,460	Financial Account, n.i.e.	78bj d
-8,658	-7,117	-14,859	-13,718	-12,835	-12,776	-9,954	-17,581	-20,181	-31,940	-24,508	-37,115	-57,296	-70,150	-44,413	Direct Investment Abroad	78bd d
3,029	4,781	8,559	10,676	5,624	6,187	6,380	7,127	12,218	16,609	11,055	37,634	41,283	56,631	55,563	Dir. Invest. in Rep. Econ., n.i.e.	78be d
-4,013	-6,947	-662	-3,547	-4,807	-13,398	-10,702	-9,570	-16,498	-25,013	-38,942	-69,292	-94,489	-65,635	-75,724	Portfolio Investment Assets	78bf d
-1,264	-1,642	-2,326	-2,521	-3,789	-2,703	-4,235	-6,595	-8,730	-2,895	-12,140	-19,890	-52,668	-23,449	-24,492	Equity Securities	78bk d
-2,749	-5,305	1,664	-1,026	-1,018	-10,696	-6,467	-2,975	-7,768	-22,119	-26,802	-49,402	-41,821	-42,186	-51,232	Debt Securities	78bl d
6,667	10,340	8,307	-1,367	4,087	3,847	12,344	-834	6,122	13,439	17,752	30,012	100,213	55,469	72,418	Portfolio Investment Liab., n.i.e.	78bg d
-245	832	2,211	-2,736	-1,336	-1,512	3,503	-1,385	-743	3,280	774	3,826	30,491	16,970	12,844	Equity Securities	78bm d
6,913	9,508	6,096	1,369	5,422	5,359	8,841	551	6,864	10,159	16,979	26,186	69,722	38,499	59,573	Debt Securities	78bn d
6	-24	-68	5,558	5,893	5,695	7,271	11,888	18,454	23,385	31,899	53,364	63,451	84,531	84,707	Financial Derivatives Assets	78bw d
			-5,624	-5,614	-5,613	-7,361	-12,256	-20,198	-24,134	-32,346	-52,388	-59,211	-88,913	-94,260	Financial Derivatives Liabilities	78bx d
-12,389	-14,054	-28,750	-25,277	-6,596	-7,819	-12,803	7,270	-8,127	1,582	-37,217	-56,321	-2,786	-32,358	-67,505	Other Investment Assets	78bh d
—	—	-1	—	-1							-235	107	-2,877	794	Monetary Authorities	78bo d
-384	-983	-658	-368	265	-324	-189	-44	7	-270	146	181	-1,442	532	-837	General Government	78bp d
-9,742	-11,337	-27,160	-22,212	-4,637	-4,200	-7,884	9,437	-3,474	2,926	-31,241	-49,373	9,488	-18,042	-57,806	Banks	78bq d
-2,263	-1,734	-932	-2,497	-2,224	-3,295	-4,730	-2,124	-4,660	-1,075	-6,122	-6,894	-10,939	-11,971	-9,656	Other Sectors	78br d
14,075	12,352	19,224	28,376	8,732	16,599	3,688	3,988	9,389	20,607	58,026	79,396	-4,102	49,191	56,755	Other Investment Liab., n.i.e.	78bi d
-167	-59	57	-9	430	-309	99	91	-137	-42	41	930	-410	7	8	Monetary Authorities	78bs d
87	239	209	-20	-185	-183	166	1,151	24	-131	-536	284	640	329	2,829	General Government	78bt d
11,125	10,962	12,984	20,914	3,940	17,023	3,122	-493	4,174	15,697	52,519	60,697	-1,541	18,367	57,759	Banks	78bu d
3,031	1,210	5,973	7,492	4,548	68	301	3,239	5,327	5,083	6,002	17,486	-2,791	30,488	-3,841	Other Sectors	78bv d
22	-4,698	-969	-2,598	-1,162	7,181	5,288	-5,819	-7,752	-19,688	-12,191	-518	-6,243	-308	332	Net Errors and Omissions	78ca d
2,693	1,568	507	268	506	6,118	6,641	500	-1,913	-5,691	-2,708	-2,339	-4,611	220	-350	Overall Balance	78cb d
-2,693	-1,568	-507	-268	-506	-6,118	-6,641	-500	1,913	5,691	2,708	2,339	4,611	-220	350	Reserves and Related Items	79da d
-2,693	-1,568	-507	-268	-506	-6,118	-6,641	-500	1,913	5,691	2,708	2,339	4,611	-220	350	Reserve Assets	79db d
—	—	—	—	—	—	—	—	—	—	—	—	—	—	—	Use of Fund Credit and Loans	79dc d
...	...	...	...	...	...	...	...	...	...	...	...	...	...	...	Exceptional Financing	79de d

International Investment Position

Millions of US Dollars

1987	1988	1989	1990	1991	1992	1993	1994	1995	1996	1997	1998	1999	2000	2001	Item	Code
297,944	301,811	352,039	427,912	461,371	464,333	498,630	547,619	651,023	696,816	746,983	957,873	1,077,477	1,141,931	...	Assets	79aa d
75,123	76,586	92,266	106,899	117,255	121,061	120,123	142,953	172,672	194,026	198,554	229,000	264,638	309,708	...	Direct Investment Abroad	79ab d
47,068	54,275	61,169	64,206	78,039	84,500	106,470	119,467	164,012	204,757	242,157	363,140	453,076	474,224	...	Portfolio Investment	79ac d
21,772	25,856	34,038	33,255	42,096	44,209	59,663	67,258	91,747	107,708	124,066	173,149	249,426	253,589	...	Equity Securities	79ad d
25,296	28,419	27,131	30,951	35,943	40,291	46,807	52,209	72,265	97,049	118,091	189,991	203,649	220,635	...	Debt Securities	79ae d
											—	39,731	29,220	...	Financial Derivatives	79al d
137,983	136,463	164,099	221,752	232,369	221,843	227,610	237,295	267,157	258,385	273,551	336,186	300,753	312,323	...	Other Investment	79af d
											252	3,230	2,528	...	Monetary Authorities	79ag d
14,875	15,553	17,536	19,425	22,113	20,804	20,492	22,441	23,984	23,124	21,255	22,597	22,292	20,919	...	General Government	79ah d
100,408	98,930	123,878	158,062	164,175	154,179	158,773	159,052	179,830	174,050	190,892	241,262	197,109	203,645	...	Banks	79ai d
22,699	21,979	22,684	44,265	46,080	46,860	48,346	55,802	63,344	61,211	61,404	72,074	78,123	85,232	...	Other Sectors	79aj d
37,771	34,487	34,504	35,054	33,708	36,928	44,427	47,904	47,182	39,649	32,721	29,547	19,280	16,456	...	Reserve Assets	79ak d
239,095	241,512	292,266	357,738	390,591	405,198	435,687	484,362	586,112	658,739	721,135	984,336	1,085,946	1,183,646	...	Liabilities	79la d
46,566	45,882	56,536	68,731	72,475	74,440	74,478	93,409	116,049	126,543	122,193	175,757	189,234	238,329	...	Dir. Invest. in Rep. Economy	79lb d
70,349	77,163	99,783	102,484	120,912	132,135	164,632	176,410	225,266	276,532	318,336	445,573	527,482	562,790	...	Portfolio Investment	79lc d
37,075	42,661	57,478	55,977	66,476	65,817	92,380	105,239	129,955	179,628	224,692	308,671	372,914	369,572	...	Equity Securities	79ld d
33,275	34,502	42,305	46,507	54,436	66,318	72,252	71,171	95,311	96,903	93,645	136,902	154,569	193,217	...	Debt Securities	79le d
											—	30,543	24,440	...	Financial Derivatives	79ll d
122,180	118,467	135,947	186,523	197,205	198,623	196,577	214,543	244,796	255,665	280,606	363,006	338,687	358,088	...	Other Investment	79lf d
94	26	87	85	245	38	152	263	141	80	64	725	3,271	115	...	Monetary Authorities	79lg d
6,313	5,806	7,492	7,919	10,490	9,300	9,504	10,864	11,536	10,971	9,891	10,232	13,089	12,785	...	General Government	79lh d
103,710	101,895	112,330	143,965	145,908	151,112	149,117	158,290	184,237	195,974	223,451	297,011	265,420	268,660	...	Banks	79li d
12,062	10,740	16,038	34,554	40,562	38,173	37,803	45,126	48,882	48,640	47,200	55,038	56,907	76,528	...	Other Sectors	79lj d

Netherlands

		1972	**1973**	**1974**	**1975**	**1976**	**1977**	**1978**	**1979**	**1980**	**1981**	**1982**	**1983**	**1984**	**1985**	**1986**
Government Finance																
Central Government															*Millions of Guilders through 1998;*	
Deficit (-) or Surplus	80	-92	467	-1,084	-6,406	-8,723	-8,068	†-9,255	-13,075	-15,282	-20,334	-26,903	-30,323	-30,045	-23,028	-6,718
Total Revenue and Grants	81y	43,896	50,291	57,749	66,908	76,961	87,200	99,803	105,834	115,362	121,101	126,104	127,433	134,130	145,605	166,488
Revenue	81	....	....	....	....	....	....	....	....	....	....	....	....	....	....	166,467
Grants	81z	....	....	....	....	....	....	....	....	....	....	....	....	....	....	21
Exp. & Lending Minus Repay.	82z	43,988	49,824	58,833	73,314	85,684	95,268	†109,058	118,909	130,644	141,435	153,007	157,756	164,175	168,633	173,206
Expenditure	82	41,024	46,782	55,790	70,423	82,056	91,919	105,501	115,988	126,486	135,204	147,583	153,073	159,047	166,351	184,565
Lending Minus Repayments	83	2,964	3,042	3,043	2,891	3,628	3,349	†3,557	2,921	4,158	6,231	5,424	4,683	5,128	2,282	-11,359
Total Financing	80h	92	-467	1,084	6,406	8,723	8,068	9,255	13,075	15,282	20,334	26,903	30,323	30,045	23,028	6,718
Total Net Borrowing	84	1,069	2,800	2,810	6,195	7,615	8,016	8,958	10,596	16,863	19,786	27,223	30,115	28,362	24,768	9,170
Net Domestic	84a	1,083	2,821	2,826	6,206	7,627	8,016	8,958	10,596	16,863	20,387	27,364	30,329	28,968	24,811	9,852
Net Foreign	85a	-14	-21	-16	-11	-12	—	—	—	—	-601	-141	-214	-606	-43	-682
Use of Cash Balances	87	-977	-3,267	-1,726	211	1,108	52	297	2,479	-1,581	548	-320	208	1,683	-1,740	-2,452
Total Debt by Currency	88z	36,548	38,774	41,301	46,735	54,996	61,704	72,529	84,394	99,518	118,457	144,653	174,795	203,100	228,283	238,735
National	88b	36,488	38,735	41,278	46,723	54,996	61,704	72,529	84,394	99,518	118,457	144,653	174,795	203,100	228,283	238,735
Foreign	89b	60	39	23	12	—	—	—	—	—	—	—	—	—	—	—
General Government																*As Percent of*
Deficit (-) or Surplus	80g	....	....	....	....	....	....	....	....	....	....	....	....	....	....	....
Debt	88g	....	....	....	....	....	....	....	....	....	....	....	....	....	....	....
National Accounts															*Billions of Guilders through 1998;*	
Househ.Cons.Expend.,incl.NPISHs	96f. c	88.5	99.8	113.4	129.0	148.0	164.3	179.2	192.4	205.8	213.2	221.8	229.9	236.8	252.9	260.2
Government Consumption Expend.	91f. c	24.4	27.4	32.5	38.3	43.5	47.9	52.6	57.2	60.3	62.8	65.1	66.6	66.4	66.9	67.7
Gross Fixed Capital Formation	93e. c	36.4	40.7	43.9	46.3	49.0	57.9	63.3	66.5	70.8	67.6	67.2	69.5	74.3	83.7	89.4
Changes in Inventories	93i. c	.7	2.5	4.6	-.9	3.0	1.5	1.8	1.5	1.7	-3.1	-1.0	.6	2.0	1.4	3.8
Exports of Goods and Services	90c. c	69.4	83.4	107.8	109.7	128.5	130.7	133.3	155.1	176.8	204.6	212.6	219.8	248.6	258.7	222.0
Imports of Goods and Services (-)	98c. c	65.2	77.8	102.3	102.3	119.9	127.4	133.2	156.7	178.6	192.2	196.8	205.2	227.8	238.3	205.4
Gross Domestic Product (GDP)	99b. c	154.3	176.0	199.8	220.0	251.9	290.4	313.0	333.2	355.8	373.0	388.4	403.3	422.4	443.1	455.9
Net Primary Income from Abroad	98.n	.7	1.3	1.7	—	.1	.2	-1.0	-1.1	-1.6	-1.9	-1.7	-.2	-.6	-.8	-.7
Gross National Income (GNI)	99a	155.0	177.3	201.5	219.9	252.1	279.0	293.6	318.8	340.4	356.3	374.9	387.0	404.1	425.5	437.2
GDP Volume 1995 Ref., Chained	99b. r	378.4	396.6	411.8	412.9	431.4	444.0	455.8	455.2	469.9	462.6	457.6	465.9	479.2	494.8	510.1
GDP Volume (1995=100)	99bv r	59.2	62.0	64.4	64.6	67.4	69.4	71.3	71.2	73.5	72.3	71.5	72.8	74.9	77.4	79.7
GDP Deflator (1995=100)	99bi r	39.2	42.6	46.6	51.2	56.1	62.8	66.0	70.3	72.7	77.4	81.5	83.1	84.7	86.0	85.8
																Millions:
Population	99z	13.33	13.44	13.54	13.65	13.77	13.85	13.94	14.03	14.14	14.25	14.31	14.36	14.42	14.48	14.56

Netherlands

Government Finance

Central Government

Millions of Euros Beginning 1999: Year Ending December 31

	1987	1988	1989	1990	1991	1992	1993	1994	1995	1996	1997	1998	1999	2000	2001	Code
Deficit (-) or Surplus	-15,013	-20,346	-20,142	-21,941	-19,106	-20,843	-8,343	2,763	-23,018	-9,626	-10,921	-3,177	†-5,815	-372	-3,500	80
Total Revenue and Grants	161,921	152,559	151,529	163,040	181,022	182,845	204,088	199,517	204,769	189,159	197,347	210,688	†105,280	108,309	115,142	81y
Revenue	161,909	152,526	151,481	162,999	181,012	182,843	204,066	199,508	204,611	188,965	196,930	210,397	†105,177	108,111	115,044	81
Grants	12	33	48	41	10	2	22	9	158	194	417	291	†103	198	98	81z
Exp. & Lending Minus Repay.	176,934	172,905	171,671	184,981	200,128	203,688	212,431	196,754	227,787	198,785	208,268	213,865	†111,095	108,681	118,642	82z
Expenditure	187,054	175,016	173,604	186,491	201,196	201,853	222,579	218,364	254,827	197,556	209,287	218,446	....	....	....	82
Lending Minus Repayments	-10,120	-2,111	-1,933	-258	297	338	-10,664	-20,508	-26,919	—	-1,314	-3,609	....	....	....	83
Total Financing	15,013	20,346	20,141	21,941	19,106	20,843	8,343	-2,763	23,018	9,626	10,921	3,177	†5,815	372	3,500	80h
Total Net Borrowing	12,545	20,663	17,038	22,962	21,782	20,088	13,220	-1,685	28,816	9,885	-4,072	13,348	†2,254	-1,032	3,521	84
Net Domestic	12,995	22,469	19,752	22,962	21,782	20,088	13,220	-1,685	28,816	9,885	-4,072	13,348	†2,254	-1,032	3,521	84a
Net Foreign	-450	-1,806	-2,714	—	—	—	—	—	—	—	—	—	†—	—	—	85a
Use of Cash Balances	2,468	-317	3,103	-1,021	-2,676	755	-4,877	-1,078	-5,798	-259	14,993	-10,171	†3,561	1,404	-21	87
Total Debt by Currency	251,157	274,473	293,842	317,666	338,535	358,007	371,209	374,645	399,825	410,989	417,467	431,383	†200,984	204,476	211,675	88z
National	251,157	274,473	293,842	317,666	338,535	358,007	371,209	374,645	399,825	410,989	417,467	431,383	†200,984	204,476	211,675	88b
Foreign												—	†	—		89b

General Government

Gross Domestic Product

	1987	1988	1989	1990	1991	1992	1993	1994	1995	1996	1997	1998	1999	2000	2001	Code
Deficit (-) or Surplus	....	....	....	-5.1	-2.9	-3.9	-3.2	-3.8	-4.0	-1.8	-1.1	-.8	.4	2.2	.2	80g
Debt	....	....	....	79.1	78.9	79.9	81.1	77.9	79.0	75.3	70.0	66.8	63.1	56.0	53.2	88g

National Accounts

Billions of Euros Beginning 1999:

	1987	1988	1989	1990	1991	1992	1993	1994	1995	1996	1997	1998	1999	2000	2001	Code
Househ.Cons.Expend.,incl.NPISHs	267.9	271.6	284.5	303.1	322.5	340.9	352.0	368.1	379.6	398.5	419.4	445.3	†186.8	199.9	210.7	96f. c
Government Consumption Expend.	69.8	70.2	71.8	74.8	77.9	83.0	84.7	86.5	89.1	92.4	97.4	102.2	†85.6	91.2	98.7	91f. c
Gross Fixed Capital Formation	91.6	97.4	104.1	107.9	110.8	113.3	111.7	117.3	124.8	131.6	142.4	149.9	†83.6	90.9	93.4	93e. c
Changes in Inventories	-.4	.3	5.4	6.5	5.2	3.1	-2.4	4.3	3.8	-3.5	1.0	2.0	†.8	-.4	-.7	93i. c
Exports of Goods and Services	219.3	240.3	267.7	279.7	293.1	294.9	292.7	312.1	336.3	354.9	384.7	414.7	†226.4	269.6	276.5	90c. c
Imports of Goods and Services (-)	207.6	222.4	248.8	255.8	267.4	269.2	259.7	279.8	298.9	318.7	346.5	364.4	†209.6	250.1	253.7	98c. c
Gross Domestic Product (GDP)	459.0	476.6	505.0	537.9	564.9	589.4	605.4	639.6	666.0	694.3	734.9	776.2	†373.6	401.1	424.8	99b. c
Net Primary Income from Abroad	-1.2	-3.5	-.2	-.9	-.9	-2.3	-.6	1.7	8.0	3.5	13.1	8.6	†3.4	3.6	3.1	98.n
Gross National Income (GNI)	439.7	454.2	484.8	515.6	541.6	563.8	580.9	616.0	674.0	697.8	748.0	784.8	†375.9	404.7	428.0	99a
GDP Volume 1995 Ref., Chained	517.2	530.3	555.2	577.4	590.3	601.9	605.8	625.0	639.7	659.6	683.7	708.9	†349.6	362.1	366.2	99b. r
GDP Volume (1995=100)	80.9	82.9	86.8	90.3	92.3	94.1	94.7	97.7	100.0	103.1	106.9	110.8	†120.4	124.7	126.1	99bv r
GDP Deflator (1995=100)	85.2	86.3	87.4	89.5	91.9	94.0	96.0	98.3	100.0	101.1	103.2	105.2	†102.6	106.4	111.4	99bi r

Midyear Estimates

	1987	1988	1989	1990	1991	1992	1993	1994	1995	1996	1997	1998	1999	2000	2001	Code
Population	14.66	14.76	14.85	14.95	15.07	15.18	15.29	15.38	15.46	15.53	15.61	15.71	15.81	15.91	16.04	99z

(See notes in the back of the book.)

Netherlands Antilles

		1972	1973	1974	1975	1976	1977	1978	1979	1980	1981	1982	1983	1984	1985	1986
Exchange Rates														*Guilders per SDR: End of Period (aa)*		
Official Rate	aa	1.954	2.171	2.204	2.107	2.091	2.186	2.345	2.371	2.296	2.095	1.986	1.885	1.764	1.977	2.202
Official Rate	ae	1.800	1.800	1.800	1.800	1.800	1.800	1.800	1.800	1.800	1.800	1.800	1.800	1.800	1.800	1.800
													Index Numbers (1995=100):			
Official Rate	ahx	99.4	99.4	99.4	99.4	99.4	99.4	99.4	99.4	99.4	99.4	99.4	99.4	99.4	99.4	99.4
Nominal Effective Exchange Rate	ne c	....	....	....	....	....	....	....	57.7	57.6	60.3	61.6	64.1	68.5	70.5	67.9
Real Effective Exchange Rate	re c	....	....	....	....	....	....	....	101.7	102.4	108.7	110.5	113.8	118.0	116.7	110.3
International Liquidity												*Millions of US Dollars Unless Otherwise Indicated:*				
Total Reserves minus Gold	1l.d	50	50	62	71	93	101	67	73	95	135	187	164	118	176	239
Foreign Exchange	1d.d	50	50	62	71	93	101	67	73	95	135	187	164	118	176	239
Gold (Million Fine Troy Ounces)	1ad	.548	.548	.548	.548	.548	.548	.548	.548	.548	.548	.548	.548	.548	.548	.548
Gold (National Valuation)	1an d	21[e]	23[e]	23	23	23	23	23	23	23	23	23	23	23	23	38
Monetary Authorities: Other Liab.	4..d	2	2	3	3	3	1	8	1	—	—	—	—	—	1	1
Deposit Money Banks: Assets	7a.d	148	125	118	125	318	584	887	1,529	2,634	3,055	3,341	2,459	1,331	1,197	361
Liabilities	7b.d	152	122	115	113	289	570	881	1,526	2,631	3,043	3,322	2,443	1,303	1,155	294
OBU: Assets	7k.d	....	....	....	....	1,228	1,799	2,283	3,588	4,759	7,513	8,512	7,788	6,377	5,417	5,610
Liabilities	7m.d	....	....	....	....	1,154	1,706	2,099	3,360	4,503	7,207	8,097	7,435	5,886	4,922	4,990
Monetary Authorities														*Millions of Guilders*		
Foreign Assets	11	125.7	127.8	149.2	168.1	206.9	217.3	161.1	172.5	211.2	285.9	375.5	337.3	253.4	367.6	501.4
Claims on Central Government	12a	14.3	26.1	56.5	94.7	96.9	93.2	134.4	131.4	111.1	101.5	100.4	111.0	119.7	188.9	130.0
Reserve Money	14	109.9	118.0	127.6	162.7	175.2	201.2	199.8	228.1	247.5	251.6	269.8	247.1	220.6	385.2	469.0
of which: Currency Outside DMBs	14a	60.4	62.8	76.8	88.0	94.7	104.9	125.8	137.7	139.2	161.6	167.0	162.6	167.8	137.5	122.2
Time Deposits	15	—	—	23.0	44.0	55.0	38.0	12.0	—	—	26.5	86.4	81.4	32.4	2.0	2.1
Foreign Liabilities	16c	3.1	3.5	6.0	6.0	6.0	2.0	14.5	1.4	.4	.1	.1	.6	.4	1.3	2.3
Central Government Deposits	16d	8.0	8.6	15.0	13.7	26.2	29.1	25.0	28.7	26.7	39.7	31.4	44.2	43.2	78.1	77.8
Capital Accounts	17a	15.0	23.1	27.1	35.2	35.4	37.2	39.9	42.3	45.9	52.1	63.8	63.8	63.8	63.8	44.6
Other Items (Net)	17r	3.9	.7	7.0	1.2	6.0	3.0	4.3	3.4	1.9	17.4	24.4	11.1	12.7	26.1	35.4
Deposit Money Banks														*Millions of Guilders:*		
Reserves	20	37.4	55.0	39.2	70.0	77.2	81.4	51.7	76.8	84.8	73.8	91.7	63.8	41.7	155.9	265.8
Foreign Assets	21	264.6	223.9	211.7	224.9	572.9	1,052.0	1,596.5	2,752.6	4,741.4	5,499.1	6,014.2	4,425.8	2,396.5	2,155.0	649.2
Claims on Local Government	22b	2.5	9.1	4.9	2.6	2.7	6.1	15.3	18.4	13.3	10.9	5.2	4.3	12.7	9.5	3.0
Claims on Private Sector	22d	305.5	327.8	379.1	374.5	409.4	492.6	624.1	658.5	746.8	895.5	979.4	1,112.1	1,112.5	1,041.1	777.8
Demand Deposits	24	91.7	98.5	98.9	115.7	135.3	159.6	197.7	192.6	197.6	221.0	269.1	280.8	251.1	260.8	271.4
Time and Savings Deposits	25a	180.1	205.4	250.3	275.6	310.1	340.4	397.7	427.5	504.1	595.9	699.6	744.2	754.0	741.8	663.5
Foreign Currency Deposits	25b	34.0	37.7	44.7	45.5	50.4	65.2	62.2	77.1	90.0	110.5	98.2	117.3	133.9	149.0	154.1
Foreign Liabilities	26c	271.5	218.5	207.8	202.5	519.7	1,026.3	1,586.1	2,746.9	4,735.8	5,476.9	5,979.9	4,398.0	2,345.5	2,079.5	529.2
Central Government Deposits	26d	4.2	5.4	4.2	4.2	4.8	5.2	5.1	4.8	7.5	5.7	7.2	7.0	6.8	9.0	14.1
Capital Accounts	27a	31.9	33.2	29.1	34.8	44.4	47.7	53.9	70.1	81.1	95.2	105.8	116.9	135.0	147.3	137.0
Other Items (Net)	27r	-3.4	17.1	-.1	-6.1	-3.2	-12.3	-15.1	-12.7	-29.8	-26.1	-69.3	-58.2	-62.9	-25.8	-73.3
Girosystem Curacao																
Private Sector Deposits	24.. i	11.1	11.3	11.1	15.5	14.6	30.4	28.0	25.5	26.2	24.2	27.6	28.8	36.7	39.0	38.9
Central Government Deposits	26d. i	6.0	2.8	6.4	5.8	3.7	3.6	8.0	41.6	37.0	32.8	31.9	32.1	32.3	34.4	32.9
Monetary Survey														*Millions of Guilders*		
Foreign Assets (Net)	31n	115.7	129.7	147.1	184.5	254.1	241.0	157.0	176.8	216.4	308.0	409.7	364.5	304.0	441.8	619.1
Domestic Credit	32	323.0	366.2	436.7	473.8	496.3	608.1	804.4	840.5	914.9	1,050.6	1,180.8	1,302.8	1,324.6	1,243.5	939.4
Claims on Central Govt. (Net)	32an	-3.7	9.6	31.0	71.2	62.6	71.6	125.3	93.6	90.2	86.0	135.6	124.5	129.5	118.6	86.1
Claims on Local Government	32b	19.6	23.6	22.6	24.2	21.0	40.6	51.8	86.0	76.9	68.3	65.1	65.5	82.0	83.2	75.0
Claims on Private Sector	32d	307.1	333.0	383.1	378.4	412.7	495.9	627.3	660.9	747.8	896.3	980.1	1,112.8	1,113.1	1,041.7	778.3
Money	34	173.7	173.9	198.3	223.6	247.9	309.8	373.8	369.4	386.5	423.0	474.8	493.0	466.7	527.7	513.5
Quasi-Money	35	214.1	243.1	318.0	365.1	415.5	443.6	471.9	504.6	594.1	732.9	884.2	942.9	920.3	892.8	819.7
Other Items (Net)	37r	50.8	78.9	67.5	69.8	86.3	95.7	115.7	143.3	150.8	202.5	231.5	231.3	241.6	264.9	225.3
Money plus Quasi-Money	35l	387.8	417.0	516.3	588.7	663.4	753.4	845.7	874.0	980.6	1,155.9	1,359.0	1,435.9	1,387.0	1,420.5	1,333.2
Interest Rates														*Percent Per Annum*		
Discount Rate (End of Period)	60	....	....	....	....	....	....	....	....	9.00	9.00	9.00	8.00	8.00	8.00	8.00
Treasury Bill Rate	60c	....	....	....	....	....	....	....	....	....	....	7.50	7.25	7.35	7.21	7.34
Deposit Rate	60l	....	....	....	....	....	....	....	....	....	....	....	5.10	5.10	5.20	5.19
Lending Rate	60p	....	....	....	9.25	9.13	9.75	9.75	11.40	11.88	11.88	11.40	11.00	11.20	11.46	11.59
Government Bond Yield	61	....	....	....	....	....	....	....	....	....	....	....	10.65	10.63	9.46	9.29
Prices and Labor														*Index Numbers (1995=100):*		
Consumer Prices	64	26.6	28.8	34.4	†39.7	41.8	44.1	47.7	53.1	60.9	68.3	72.5	†74.5	76.1	76.4	77.4
														Number in Thousands:		
Labor Force	67d	....	....	....	....	....	....	....	....	....	....	....	....	....	....	....
Employment	67e	....	....	....	....	....	....	....	....	....	....	....	....	....	60	59
Unemployment	67c	....	....	....	....	....	....	....	....	....	....	....	....	....	....	....
Unemployment Rate (%)	67r	....	....	....	....	....	....	....	....	....	....	....	....	....	....	....
International Transactions														*Millions of Guilders*		
Exports	70	1,364	2,465	5,815	4,315	4,544	4,764	5,357	7,139	9,292	9,750	8,803	7,937	6,719	1,856	†1,664
Imports, c.i.f.	71	1,565	2,868	6,536	5,088	6,601	5,631	6,284	7,911	10,216	10,551	9,157	8,148	7,258	2,498	†2,002
Crude Petroleum	71aa	988	1,977	5,409	3,490	5,207	4,129	....	....	....	....	....	....	....	....	....
Imports, f.o.b.	71.v	1,338	2,452	5,588	4,350	5,894	5,029	5,612	7,065	9,123	9,422	8,178	7,276	6,480	2,230	†1,788

Exchange Rates

Guilders per US Dollar: End of Period (ae)

	1987	1988	1989	1990	1991	1992	1993	1994	1995	1996	1997	1998	1999	2000	2001		
Official Rate	2.554	2.422	2.352	2.547	2.560	2.461	2.459	2.613	2.661	2.574	2.415	2.520	2.457	2.332	2.250		aa
Official Rate	1.800	1.800	1.790	1.790	1.790	1.790	1.790	1.790	1.790	1.790	1.790	1.790	1.790	1.790	1.790		ae

Period Averages

	1987	1988	1989	1990	1991	1992	1993	1994	1995	1996	1997	1998	1999	2000	2001		
Official Rate	99.4	99.4	99.8	100.0	100.0	100.0	100.0	100.0	100.0	100.0	100.0	100.0	100.0	100.0	100.0		ahx
Nominal Effective Exchange Rate	69.9	70.2	79.5	81.8	85.5	87.5	95.9	101.4	100.0	105.5	112.4	115.5	117.8	124.8	128.6		nec
Real Effective Exchange Rate	111.2	107.2	111.7	107.1	107.5	103.2	106.3	104.5	100.0	103.4	109.1	110.0	107.7	....	....		rec

International Liquidity

End of Period

	1987	1988	1989	1990	1991	1992	1993	1994	1995	1996	1997	1998	1999	2000	2001		
Total Reserves minus Gold	217	263	207	215	177	220	234	179	203	189	214	248	265	261	301		1l.d
Foreign Exchange	217	263	207	215	177	220	234	179	203	189	214	248	265	261	301		1d.d
Gold (Million Fine Troy Ounces)	.548	.548	.548	.548	.548	.548	.548	.548	.548	.548	.548	.548	.548	....	....		1ad
Gold (National Valuation)	38	38	38	38	38	38	38	38	117	106	106	106	106	106	106		1and
Monetary Authorities: Other Liab.	—	—	—	—	1	—	2	26	32	10	8	1	1	2	—		4..d
Deposit Money Banks: Assets	399	571	880	555	681	749	825	748	442	400	396	471	473	552	862		7a.d
Liabilities	354	532	840	548	660	722	780	720	391	402	392	421	455	568	664		7b.d
OBU: Assets	6,548	8,011	13,047	15,881	20,327	†22,952	29,155	29,152	26,085	28,106	31,393	36,430	32,792	34,466	....		7k.d
Liabilities	5,907	7,280	12,418	15,199	19,401	†21,717	27,619	28,315	15,256	26,263	29,437	33,772	30,029	31,423	....		7m.d

Monetary Authorities

	1987	1988	1989	1990	1991	1992	1993	1994	1995	1996	1997	1998	1999	2000	2001		
Foreign Assets	459.3	538.2	445.2	454.0	385.1	461.8	490.1	435.2	683.3	546.5	591.5	625.9	655.1	608.7	678.7		11
Claims on Central Government	124.0	131.0	91.5	75.4	75.3	71.0	66.2	59.9	69.2	68.6	82.0	79.1	117.5	94.8	150.5		12a
Reserve Money	426.1	434.5	302.0	355.6	294.3	380.2	401.0	375.0	449.6	385.2	445.2	489.1	460.0	497.9	678.6		14
of which: Currency Outside DMBs	124.4	128.0	144.6	160.8	168.2	178.6	184.5	198.2	209.6	195.6	188.0	186.6	197.0	188.9	218.2		14a
Time Deposits	2.3	59.2	17.5	17.6	26.8	2.9	11.0	13.2	30.3	—	—	—	—	—	—		15
Foreign Liabilities	.5	.6	.4	.8	1.2	.7	3.1	47.0	58.0	18.7	15.1	2.5	.9	3.1	.8		16c
Central Government Deposits	62.1	77.5	91.0	47.4	44.7	40.0	71.2	13.0	46.0	38.7	45.1	55.5	164.7	170.7	168.1		16d
Capital Accounts	54.7	63.5	63.5	66.4	66.4	65.8	65.8	65.8	201.6	185.4	185.4	182.4	182.4	141.5	141.6		17a
Other Items (Net)	37.7	33.8	62.3	41.6	27.0	43.2	4.2	-18.9	-33.0	-12.9	-17.3	-24.5	-35.4	-109.7	-159.9		17r

Deposit Money Banks

End of Period

	1987	1988	1989	1990	1991	1992	1993	1994	1995	1996	1997	1998	1999	2000	2001		
Reserves	216.7	234.1	127.7	138.4	74.9	122.2	176.9	128.5	209.7	164.4	232.1	263.0	251.3	304.7	432.1		20
Foreign Assets	718.5	1,027.7	1,575.5	993.0	1,219.3	1,339.9	1,476.6	1,339.5	791.7	715.9	709.7	843.6	846.0	987.5	1,542.1		21
Claims on Local Government	4.1	5.2	1.5	9.8	72.1	94.7	125.1	126.5	103.1	158.5	142.8	121.5	126.9	101.1	122.7		22b
Claims on Private Sector	982.6	1,126.5	1,371.4	1,549.5	1,679.6	1,716.6	1,796.9	2,034.4	2,130.2	2,275.8	2,262.8	2,299.8	2,529.3	2,677.4	2,686.9		22d
Demand Deposits	317.1	333.7	354.6	384.0	413.6	424.8	501.8	560.7	653.6	702.9	710.7	721.7	770.3	806.8	896.4		24
Time and Savings Deposits	697.5	784.6	789.9	869.1	912.8	1,018.6	1,136.5	1,201.7	1,231.4	1,266.4	1,325.7	1,417.1	1,484.6	1,552.9	1,743.7		25a
Foreign Currency Deposits	183.3	220.4	263.1	275.8	330.8	350.8	375.5	399.7	470.4	413.5	409.4	399.5	456.7	449.2	558.4		25b
Foreign Liabilities	637.4	958.1	1,503.1	981.8	1,181.1	1,292.9	1,396.8	1,289.6	699.0	719.1	701.5	752.9	813.6	1,017.5	1,188.7		26c
Central Government Deposits	21.9	11.1	19.6	36.9	50.9	47.5	39.0	36.0	22.6	36.5	45.7	46.2	30.0	34.5	41.8		26d
Capital Accounts	135.4	140.0	168.8	227.6	242.8	236.6	249.9	274.4	245.7	301.5	301.0	318.4	332.5	332.2	390.1		27a
Other Items (Net)	-70.6	-54.3	-23.2	-84.2	-86.1	-97.8	-124.0	-133.2	-88.0	-125.3	-146.6	-127.9	-134.2	-122.4	-35.3		27r

Girosystem Curacao

	1987	1988	1989	1990	1991	1992	1993	1994	1995	1996	1997	1998	1999	2000	2001		
Private Sector Deposits	42.6	44.3	40.5	42.0	45.7	55.5	60.1	87.1	71.4	—	....	....	....	....	....		24..i
Central Government Deposits	39.4	34.0	35.1	33.6	34.2	34.5	34.3	34.9	1.5	—	....	....	....	....	....		26d.i

Monetary Survey

End of Period

	1987	1988	1989	1990	1991	1992	1993	1994	1995	1996	1997	1998	1999	2000	2001		
Foreign Assets (Net)	539.9	607.2	517.2	464.4	422.1	508.1	566.8	438.1	718.0	524.6	584.6	714.1	686.6	575.6	1,031.3		31n
Domestic Credit	1,147.8	1,296.1	1,462.9	1,676.7	1,845.2	1,962.3	2,055.9	2,377.5	2,423.3	2,510.7	2,485.9	2,503.4	2,664.6	2,812.9	2,906.7		32
Claims on Central Govt. (Net)	78.4	85.8	13.8	25.6	7.6	59.0	39.0	86.1	87.0	76.4	80.1	67.1	-6.6	-36.4	8.1		32an
Claims on Local Government	86.3	83.6	77.2	101.1	157.5	186.2	219.5	256.5	206.0	158.5	142.8	136.5	141.9	171.9	211.7		32b
Claims on Private Sector	983.1	1,126.7	1,371.9	1,550.0	1,680.1	1,717.1	1,797.4	2,034.9	2,130.3	2,275.8	2,263.0	2,299.8	2,529.3	2,677.4	2,686.9		32d
Money	569.1	578.4	569.4	643.2	678.7	738.3	786.0	894.3	964.9	923.7	923.8	947.8	979.0	1,000.0	1,142.9		34
Quasi-Money	883.1	1,064.2	1,070.5	1,162.5	1,270.4	1,372.3	1,523.0	1,614.6	1,732.1	1,679.9	1,735.1	1,816.6	1,941.3	2,002.1	2,302.1		35
Other Items (Net)	235.7	260.7	340.0	335.7	318.2	359.8	313.7	306.7	444.3	431.7	411.6	453.1	430.9	386.4	493.0		37r
Money plus Quasi-Money	1,452.2	1,642.6	1,639.9	1,805.7	1,949.1	2,110.6	2,309.0	2,508.9	2,697.0	2,603.6	2,658.9	2,764.4	2,920.3	3,002.1	3,445.0		35l

Interest Rates

Percent Per Annum

	1987	1988	1989	1990	1991	1992	1993	1994	1995	1996	1997	1998	1999	2000	2001		
Discount Rate (End of Period)	6.00	6.00	6.00	6.00	6.00	6.00	5.00	5.00	6.00	6.00	6.00	6.00	6.00	6.00	6.00		60
Treasury Bill Rate	6.36	5.79	5.96	6.10	....	....	4.83	4.48	5.46	5.66	5.77	5.82	6.15	6.15	6.15		60c
Deposit Rate	4.82	4.63	4.71	4.97	....	....	4.33	4.05	3.75	3.67	3.66	3.58	3.59	3.63	3.65		60l
Lending Rate	11.37	11.24	11.23	9.25	....	....	12.59	12.73	12.93	13.21	13.29	13.58	13.60	9.98	10.44		60p
Government Bond Yield	10.36	10.74	10.63	10.74	....	....	8.14	7.48	8.02	8.25	8.67	8.60	8.75	8.77	9.00		61

Prices and Labor

Period Averages

	1987	1988	1989	1990	1991	1992	1993	1994	1995	1996	1997	1998	1999	2000	2001		
Consumer Prices	80.3	82.4	85.6	†88.8	92.4	93.7	95.6	97.3	100.0	†103.6	107.0	108.2	108.6	114.9	117.0		64

Period Averages

	1987	1988	1989	1990	1991	1992	1993	1994	1995	1996	1997	1998	1999	2000	2001		
Labor Force	....	....	....	57	....	....	....	....	62	66	66	65	61	....	....		67d
Employment	53	41	44	48	50	51	52	55	54	57	56	54	....	52	....		67e
Unemployment	....	13	11	10	9	8	8	8	8	9	10	11	....	9	....		67c
Unemployment Rate (%)	....	....	20.1	17.0	14.6	13.9	13.6	12.8	13.1	14.0	15.3	16.6	....	14.0	....		67r

International Transactions

Millions of Guilders

	1987	1988	1989	1990	1991	1992	1993	1994	1995	1996	1997	1998	1999	2000	2001		
Exports	2,354	2,041	2,608	3,204	2,862	2,790	2,297	2,462	....	....	....	....	....	....	....		70
Imports, c.i.f.	2,703	2,526	2,888	3,833	3,828	3,344	3,485	3,146	....	....	....	....	....	....	....		71
Crude Petroleum	....	....	....	....	....	....	....	....	....	....	....	....	....	....	....		71aa
Imports, f.o.b.	2,413	2,255	2,579	3,422	3,418	2,986	3,112	2,809	....	....	....	....	....	....	....		71.v

Netherlands Antilles

353

Balance of Payments		1972	1973	1974	1975	1976	1977	1978	1979	1980	1981	1982	1983	1984	1985	1986
														Millions of US Dollars:		
Current Account, n.i.e.	78al d	...	...	...	...	−83.0	56.6	−24.8	23.8	.6	52.9	178.0	87.6	175.4	403.1	50.7
Goods: Exports f.o.b.	78aa d	...	...	...	...	2,905.9	3,209.7	3,165.8	4,602.2	6,380.6	6,173.1	5,265.1	4,794.9	3,949.1	1,810.8	155.0
Goods: Imports f.o.b.	78ab d	...	...	...	...	−3,058.3	−3,312.7	−3,330.6	−4,459.4	−6,503.9	−6,360.2	−5,481.3	−4,966.1	−4,248.8	−2,132.3	−675.6
Trade Balance	78ac d	...	...	...	...	−152.4	−102.9	−164.7	142.8	−123.3	−187.1	−216.2	−171.1	−299.8	−321.5	−520.6
Services: Credit	78ad d	...	...	...	...	405.2	516.7	565.3	690.0	878.3	1,010.9	964.8	733.6	697.7	674.2	646.3
Services: Debit	78ae d	...	...	...	...	−289.7	−316.6	−330.0	−413.3	−529.1	−564.0	−557.6	−520.2	−454.7	−452.3	−284.4
Balance on Goods & Services	78af d	...	...	...	...	−36.9	97.1	70.6	419.5	225.9	259.8	191.0	42.3	−56.8	−99.6	−158.7
Income: Credit	78ag d	...	...	...	...	20.2	39.4	44.8	63.9	13.9	25.5	24.1	18.5	72.8	49.3	76.7
Income: Debit	78ah d	...	...	...	...	−104.5	−109.9	−192.8	−507.9	−343.1	−286.8	−118.8	−103.8	4.9	−19.5	−56.1
Balance on Gds, Serv. & Inc.	78ai d	...	...	...	...	−121.3	26.6	−77.4	−24.6	−103.3	−1.5	96.3	−43.0	20.9	−69.7	−138.2
Current Transfers, n.i.e.: Credit	78aj d	...	...	...	...	51.7	48.9	72.8	71.7	129.4	121.1	152.2	213.3	253.9	565.6	277.2
Current Transfers: Debit	78ak d	...	...	...	...	−13.4	−18.9	−20.2	−23.3	−25.6	−66.7	−70.6	−82.8	−99.4	−92.8	−88.3
Capital Account, n.i.e.	78bc d	...	...	...	...	−2.3	−3.5	−2.7	−5.0	−6.1	−3.6	−5.6	−6.3	−8.0	−11.8	−6.1
Capital Account, n.i.e.: Credit	78ba d	...	...	...	...	.6	.6	1.7	1.1	.6	1.2	1.3	.8	1.1	.5	.6
Capital Account: Debit	78bb d	...	...	...	...	−2.8	−4.1	−4.4	−6.1	−6.7	−4.7	−6.9	−7.1	−9.1	−12.3	−6.7
Financial Account, n.i.e.	78bj d	...	...	...	...	115.0	−52.2	−23.9	−23.3	20.0	−6.6	−129.3	−129.1	−193.2	−324.1	86.7
Direct Investment Abroad	78bd d	...	...	...	...	−1.1	−1.1	−2.8	−3.9	−.6	−.7	−.6	−.9	−1.7	3.3	−.8
Dir. Invest. in Rep. Econ., n.i.e.	78be d	...	...	...	...	1.1	4.4	13.3	278.3	35.0	15.1	−153.9	−95.6	3.4	−281.7	115.8
Portfolio Investment Assets	78bf d	...	...	...	...	−2.2	−3.9	−15.0	−14.4	−10.0	−28.7	−19.5	−31.3	−37.3	−48.6	−47.2
Equity Securities	78bk d	...	...	...	...											
Debt Securities	78bl d	...	...	...	...	−2.2	−3.9	−15.0	−14.4	−10.0	−28.7	−19.5	−31.3	−37.3	−48.6	−47.2
Portfolio Investment Liab., n.i.e.	78bg d	...	...	...	...	.6	—	—	1.7	.6	−3.3	−2.4	−1.6	1.0	6.1	−2.2
Equity Securities	78bm d	...	...	...	...											
Debt Securities	78bn d	...	...	...	...	.6	—	—	1.7	.6	−3.3	−2.4	−1.6	1.0	6.1	−2.2
Financial Derivatives Assets	78bw d	...	...	...	...											
Financial Derivatives Liabilities	78bx d	...	...	...	...											
Other Investment Assets	78bh d	...	...	...	...	−110.6	−337.2	−196.1	−842.2	−1,106.7	−411.8	62.6	−42.9	−117.6	76.0	−87.1
Monetary Authorities	78bo d	...	...	...	...										...	...
General Government	78bp d	...	...	...	...	.6	3.9	10.0	.6	−7.8	7.9	−3.9	4.8	−1.7	6.3	7.8
Banks	78bq d	...	...	...	...	−180.6	−272.8	−316.1	−641.1	−1,097.2	−409.4	28.2	−23.3	−24.3	80.2	−111.0
Other Sectors	78br d	...	...	...	...	69.4	−68.3	110.0	−201.7	−1.7	−10.3	38.3	−24.4	−91.7	−10.6	16.1
Other Investment Liab., n.i.e.	78bi d	...	...	...	...	227.2	285.6	176.7	557.2	1,101.7	422.8	−15.5	43.2	−40.9	−79.2	108.2
Monetary Authorities	78bs d	...	...	...	...											
General Government	78bt d	...	...	...	...	13.9	8.9	—	10.6	25.0	21.7	14.3	23.3	23.7	20.4	18.9
Banks	78bu d	...	...	...	...	180.6	281.1	310.6	645.0	1,105.0	412.2	−34.3	18.8	19.3	−84.1	110.4
Other Sectors	78bv d	...	...	...	...	32.8	−4.4	−133.9	−98.3	−28.3	−11.1	4.4	1.1	−83.9	−15.6	−21.1
Net Errors and Omissions	78ca d	...	...	...	...	4.9	−1.9	7.3	11.6	.3	10.3	7.8	21.6	−13.1	4.8	−33.4
Overall Balance	78cb d	...	...	...	...	34.7	−1.1	−44.2	7.1	14.8	53.2	50.8	−26.3	−38.9	71.9	97.9
Reserves and Related Items	79da d	...	...	...	...	−34.7	1.1	44.2	−7.1	−14.8	−53.2	−50.8	26.3	38.9	−71.9	−97.9
Reserve Assets	79db d	...	...	...	...	−34.7	1.1	44.2	−7.1	−14.8	−53.2	−50.8	26.3	38.9	−71.9	−97.9
Use of Fund Credit and Loans	79dc d	...	...	...	...	—	—	—	—	—	—	—	—	—	—	—
Exceptional Financing	79de d	...	...	...	...	...	...	...	...	...	...	...	...	...	...	...

Government Finance															*Millions of Guilders:*		
Deficit (-) or Surplus	80	...	−28.6	−35.5	−55.2	−21.4	−27.6	−71.3	−71.4	†−76.2	−100.8	−106.6	−87.9	−75.0	−20.8	†−57.5
Revenue	81	...	119.1	112.9	85.1	125.8	138.4	177.6	213.3	†253.4	275.4	343.3	345.5	355.5	356.4	†320.2
Grants Received	81z	...	19.6	16.9	27.2	27.0	21.5	26.7	33.4	†137.7	89.0	93.9	149.8	151.6	200.5	†112.0
Expenditure	82	...	167.3	163.9	159.5	140.7	171.5	245.6	255.8	†465.2	459.6	540.8	556.9	570.4	552.6	†488.5
Lending Minus Repayments	83	...	—	1.4	8.0	33.5	16.0	30.0	62.3	†2.1	5.6	3.0	26.3	11.7	25.1	†1.2
Financing																
Domestic	84a	...	8.3	20.0	41.4	−4.2	11.0	58.3	50.0	†75.5	100.7	77.4	68.5	31.3	21.7	†11.1
Foreign	85a	...	20.3	15.5	13.8	25.6	16.6	13.0	21.4	†.7	.1	29.2	19.4	43.7	−.9	†46.4
Debt: Domestic	88a	...	3.7	3.4	3.1	2.8	24.6	65.8	105.2	†238.8	296.3	282.6	311.3	416.5	217.7	†417.3
Foreign	89a	...	282.3	335.6	326.4	385.9	446.3	495.0	538.0	†525.8	499.6	449.9	542.4	403.0	541.1	†215.5
																Millions:
Population	99z	.23	.23	.24	.24	†.24	.24	.23	.23	.19	.19	.18	.17	.18	.18	.18

1987	1988	1989	1990	1991	1992	1993	1994	1995	1996	1997	1998	1999	2000	2001		
Minus Sign Indicates Debit															**Balance of Payments**	
−49.4	75.2	38.1	−44.0	−6.2	9.9	1.2	−97.9	86.5	....	....	....	....	....	....	Current Account, n.i.e.	78al *d*
157.2	225.8	313.4	302.7	301.8	332.3	306.0	351.1	354.2	....	....	....	....	....	....	Goods: Exports f.o.b.	78aa *d*
−771.7	−879.4	−1,017.8	−1,112.3	−1,118.9	−1,168.4	−1,143.8	−1,271.6	−1,318.7	....	....	....	....	....	....	Goods: Imports f.o.b.	78ab *d*
−614.4	−653.6	−704.4	−809.7	−817.2	−836.1	−837.8	−920.5	−964.4							*Trade Balance*	78ac *d*
671.1	892.6	960.8	1,161.4	1,227.9	1,339.6	1,346.0	1,414.2	1,686.8	....	....	....	....	....	....	Services: Credit	78ad *d*
−299.4	−378.2	−407.5	−518.2	−544.2	−606.9	−596.0	−670.5	−724.9	....	....	....	....	....	....	Services: Debit	78ae *d*
−242.8	−139.1	−151.1	−166.5	−133.5	−103.5	−87.8	−176.8	−2.6							*Balance on Goods & Services*	78af *d*
77.2	80.9	108.9	126.1	126.8	158.1	122.7	133.7	122.7	....	....	....	....	....	....	Income: Credit	78ag *d*
−41.1	−41.3	−73.0	−109.6	−109.6	−146.6	−140.3	−99.4	−130.9	....	....	....	....	....	....	Income: Debit	78ah *d*
−206.7	−99.5	−115.2	−149.9	−116.3	−92.0	−105.4	−142.5	−10.8							*Balance on Gds, Serv. & Inc.*	78ai *d*
241.1	268.7	260.9	213.1	228.7	217.4	250.3	217.9	245.9	....	....	....	....	....	....	Current Transfers, n.i.e.: Credit	78aj *d*
−83.9	−94.1	−107.6	−107.3	−118.6	−115.5	−143.7	−173.3	−148.5	....	....	....	....	....	....	Current Transfers: Debit	78ak *d*
−2.8	−2.9	−3.2	−1.7	−.7	−.6	−.8	−.7	−.8	....	....	....	....	....	....	Capital Account, n.i.e.	78bc *d*
.6	.4	.1	.5	.9	1.7	.8	1.0	1.4	....	....	....	....	....	....	Capital Account, n.i.e.: Credit	78ba *d*
−3.3	−3.3	−3.3	−2.2	−1.7	−2.3	−1.7	−1.7	−2.2	....	....	....	....	....	....	Capital Account: Debit	78bb *d*
−12.1	−58.3	−93.7	9.4	−41.5	41.7	32.2	−2.3	31.1	....	....	....	....	....	....	Financial Account, n.i.e.	78bj *d*
−.1	−2.8	−4.8	−2.4	−1.1	−1.5	2.2	−1.0	−.7	....	....	....	....	....	....	Direct Investment Abroad	78bd *d*
2.5	6.7	17.4	8.1	33.4	40.1	11.0	21.5	9.8	....	....	....	....	....	....	Dir. Invest. in Rep. Econ., n.i.e.	78be *d*
16.7	−55.1	−76.9	−50.3	−29.2	−21.6	−13.9	−69.1	−24.7	....	....	....	....	....	....	Portfolio Investment Assets	78bf *d*
															Equity Securities	78bk *d*
16.7	−55.1	−76.9	−50.3	−29.2	−21.6	−13.9	−69.1	−24.7	....	....	....	....	....	....	Debt Securities	78bl *d*
−2.8	−2.1	1.1	1.2	−1.5	2.8	1.5	10.9	1.7	....	....	....	....	....	....	Portfolio Investment Liab., n.i.e.	78bg *d*
															Equity Securities	78bm *d*
−2.8	−2.1	1.1	1.2	−1.5	2.8	1.5	10.9	1.7	....	....	....	....	....	....	Debt Securities	78bn *d*
....	....	....						....							Financial Derivatives Assets	78bw *d*
....	....	....						....							Financial Derivatives Liabilities	78bx *d*
−73.6	−194.2	−335.5	−249.4	−165.8	−68.7	−38.4	15.3	83.6	....	....	....	....	....	....	Other Investment Assets	78bh *d*
....	....	....						....							Monetary Authorities	78bo *d*
−1.1	.7	−13.0	24.1	−40.5	—	—	—	—							General Government	78bp *d*
−45.8	−182.1	−297.9	−290.8	−120.1	−61.0	−46.9	−55.8	−10.1	....	....	....	....	....	....	Banks	78bq *d*
−26.7	−12.8	−24.6	17.4	−5.3	−7.7	8.5	71.1	93.7	....	....	....	....	....	....	Other Sectors	78br *d*
45.3	189.1	305.0	302.1	122.7	90.6	69.8	20.1	−38.7	....	....	....	....	....	....	Other Investment Liab., n.i.e.	78bi *d*
															Monetary Authorities	78bs *d*
12.8	6.3	14.3	−3.3	−7.9	.4	−9.5	−38.3	−17.6	....	....	....	....	....	....	General Government	78bt *d*
59.7	177.6	303.9	290.1	114.6	60.6	59.7	59.7	4.4	....	....	....	....	....	....	Banks	78bu *d*
−27.2	5.2	−13.2	15.3	16.0	29.7	19.6	−1.3	−25.4	....	....	....	....	....	....	Other Sectors	78bv *d*
34.7	19.5	14.6	6.5	6.2	8.2	11.5	24.9	22.5	....	....	....	....	....	....	Net Errors and Omissions	78ca *d*
−29.6	33.4	−44.2	−29.8	−42.2	59.2	44.0	−75.9	139.3							*Overall Balance*	78cb *d*
29.6	−33.4	44.2	29.8	42.2	−59.2	−44.0	75.9	−139.3	....	....	....	....	....	....	Reserves and Related Items	79da *d*
29.6	−33.4	44.2	29.8	42.2	−59.2	−44.0	75.9	−139.3	....	....	....	....	....	....	Reserve Assets	79db *d*
—	—	—	—	—	—	—	—	....							Use of Fund Credit and Loans.........	79dc *d*
—	—	—	—	—	—	—	—	....							Exceptional Financing	79de *d*
Year Ending December 31															**Government Finance**	
−55.6	−11.1	−60.1	−51.3	−44.9	−62.0	−25.2	−40.6[P]	†−100.2	....	....	....	....	....	....	Deficit (-) or Surplus	80
334.1	365.2	337.7	438.0	463.1	517.0	587.8	663.3[P]	†462.2	....	....	....	....	....	....	Revenue	81
149.0	145.9	77.3	56.2	78.3	67.0	105.0	91.9[P]	†92.8	....	....	....	....	....	....	Grants Received	81z
536.9	521.4	475.1	536.0	586.7	638.0	719.4	795.4[P]	†655.1	....	....	....	....	....	....	Expenditure	82
1.8	.8	—	9.5	−.4	8.0	−1.4	.4[P]	†.1	....	....	....	....	....	....	Lending Minus Repayments	83
															Financing	
6.0	−24.4	75.1	−19.0	106.4	62.0	25.2	40.6[P]	†100.2	....	....	....	....	....	....	Domestic	84a
49.6	35.5	−15.0	70.3	−61.5	—	—	—[P]	†—	....	....	....	....	....	....	Foreign	85a
432.0	451.7	447.6	424.0	431.7	458.4	616.3	618.5[P]	†704.6	....	....	....	....	....	....	Debt: Domestic	88a
260.0	248.9	235.4	307.0	208.5	187.8	170.9	—[P]	†—	....	....	....	....	....	....	Foreign	89a
Midyear Estimates																
.19	.19	.19	.19	.19	.19	.19	.20	.20	.21	.21	.21	.21	.22	.22	**Population**......................	99z

(See notes in the back of the book.)

		1972	1973	1974	1975	1976	1977	1978	1979	1980	1981	1982	1983	1984	1985	1986
Exchange Rates													*SDRs per New Zealand Dollar:*				
Market Rate	ac	1.1008	1.1841	1.0744	.8915	.8177	.8395	.8187	.7486	.7545	.7083	.6640	.6252	.4872	.4538	.4280
													US Dollars per New Zealand Dollar:				
Market Rate	ag	1.1952	1.4284	1.3155	1.0437	.9500	1.0197	1.0666	.9862	.9623	.8244	.7325	.6546	.4776	.4985	.5235
Market Rate	rh	1.1952	1.3615	1.4004	1.2157	.9963	.9708	1.0378	1.0229	.9742	.8700	.7519	.6688	.5785	.4984	.5239
													Index Numbers (1995=100):				
Market Rate	ah x	182.1	207.4	213.3	185.2	151.8	147.9	158.1	155.8	148.4	132.5	114.5	101.9	88.1	75.9	79.8
Nominal Effective Exchange Rate	ne c	....	....	....	....	....	....	....	....	151.9	143.5	138.2	124.9	114.1	105.0	97.0
Real Effective Exchange Rate	re c	....	....	....	....	....	....	....	....	91.2	90.4	91.7	91.1	84.7	86.2	87.2
Fund Position													*Millions of SDRs:*				
Quota	2f. s	202	202	202	202	202	202	232	232	348	348	348	462	462	462	462
SDRs	1b. s	58	58	1	1	8	34	46	9	—	20	2	3	7	6	9
Reserve Position in the Fund	1c. s	51	51	—	—	—	—	23	—	28	28	28	28	—	—	—
Total Fund Cred.&Loans Outstg.	2tl	—	—	86	242	390	388	361	270	132	34	3	—	—	—	—
International Liquidity													*Millions of US Dollars Unless Otherwise Indicated:*				
Total Reserves minus Gold	1l. d	832	1,045	639	427	491	443	451	451	352	674	636	778	1,787	1,596	3,771
SDRs	1b. d	63	70	1	1	10	42	60	12	—	23	2	3	7	7	11
Reserve Position in the Fund	1c. d	55	61	—	—	—	—	30	—	35	32	2	30	—	—	—
Foreign Exchange	1d. d	714	914	638	426	481	401	361	439	317	619	634	745	1,780	1,589	3,760
Monetary Authorities	1da d	459	619	331	193	212	121	172	134	68	367	178	128	1,304	984	2,834
Government	1db d	255	295	307	233	269	280	189	305	249	252	456	617	476	605	926
Gold (Million Fine Troy Ounces)	1ad	.023	.023	.023	.023	.023	.044	.066	.045	.022	.022	.022	.022	.022	.022	.022
Gold (National Valuation)	1an d	1	1	1	1	1	2	3	2	1	1	1	1	1	1	1
Monetary Authorities: Other Liab.	4.. d	1	—	51	199	278	345	373	381	573	1,012	1,071	866	776	614	2,738
Banking Institutions: Assets	7a. d	117	118	163	183	185	263	321	349	435	414	402	457	338	474	579
Liabilities	7b. d	74	80	140	142	106	137	140	152	182	159	208	346	318	447	833
Monetary Authorities													*Millions of New Zealand Dollars:*				
Foreign Assets	11	685	740	488	426	555	431	378	573	381	817	873	1,240	3,762	2,936	7,375
Claims on Central Government	12a	48	141	511	621	897	1,102	1,041	1,091	1,057	1,413	1,454	1,369	2,435	1,066	1,648
Claims on Banking Institutions	12e	—	—	15	—	3	5	186	22	31	34	54	51	12	5	4
Reserve Money	14	509	749	785	637	669	729	880	956	852	972	1,048	1,172	1,263	1,409	1,227
of which: Currency Outside DMBs	14a	242	290	336	352	418	460	536	590	577	683	714	739	867	940	1,006
Liabs.of Central Bank: Securities	16ac	....	....	....	....	....	....	....	....	....	....	....	....	....	....	....
Foreign Liabilities	16c	—	—	118	462	770	801	791	747	771	1,275	1,466	1,323	1,626	1,232	5,231
Central Government Deposits	16d	398	377	348	304	343	359	366	484	419	637	1,081	1,326	4,990	2,143	2,926
Capital Accounts	17a	86	86	117	102	113	118	132	179	215	267	287	323	402	483	562
Other Items (Net)	17r	−260	−331	−354	−457	−438	−469	−563	−679	−787	−886	−1,501	−1,485	−2,071	−1,260	−919
Banking Institutions													*Millions of New Zealand Dollars:*				
Reserves	20	228	335	286	112	131	118	128	118	93	109	116	140	87	182	97
Claims on Mon.Author.: Securities	20c	....	....	....	....	....	....	....	....	....	....	....	....	....	....	....
Foreign Assets	21	96	87	124	175	195	258	301	354	452	503	549	699	707	950	1,107
Claims on Central Government	22a	540	509	213	601	646	757	1,209	1,354	1,385	1,203	1,701	2,012	2,849	4,496	4,565
Claims on Private Sector	22d	789	1,227	1,555	1,679	2,073	2,458	3,001	3,635	4,230	5,305	6,002	6,569	7,843	10,020	14,230
Demand Deposits	24	956	1,151	1,115	1,245	1,385	1,370	1,637	1,741	1,876	2,129	2,259	2,629	2,855	3,135	3,634
Time, Savings,Fgn.Currency Dep.	25	630	930	1,022	1,155	1,526	1,995	2,537	3,369	3,829	4,481	5,419	5,581	7,079	10,267	13,286
of which: Fgn Currency Deposits	25b	....	....	....	....	....	....	....	....	....	....	....	....	....	....	....
Foreign Liabilities	26c	37	29	62	86	84	116	109	129	157	164	249	488	597	773	1,120
Central Government Deposits	26d	12	12	22	38	25	20	26	33	99	55	40	56	53	52	64
Capital Accounts	27a	....	....	....	....	....	....	....	....	....	....	....	....	....	....	....
Other Items (Net)	27r	17	37	−42	43	25	91	330	188	198	289	401	666	901	1,421	1,895
Banking Survey													*Millions of New Zealand Dollars:*				
Foreign Assets (Net)	31n	743	798	432	53	−104	−227	−220	50	−96	−119	−293	128	2,246	1,882	2,131
Domestic Credit	32	1,181	1,733	2,233	2,948	3,669	4,418	5,416	6,199	6,853	7,943	9,173	9,807	9,384	14,708	18,379
Claims on Central Govt. (Net)	32an	178	261	354	880	1,176	1,480	1,858	1,929	1,924	1,923	2,033	1,998	241	3,367	3,224
Claims on Private Sector	32d	1,003	1,472	1,879	2,068	2,493	2,938	3,558	4,271	4,929	6,020	7,140	7,809	9,143	11,341	15,156
Money	34	1,219	1,545	1,601	1,749	1,910	1,946	2,378	2,458	2,535	2,926	3,030	3,426	3,761	4,104	4,668
Quasi-Money	35	630	930	1,022	1,155	1,526	1,995	2,537	3,369	3,829	4,481	5,419	5,581	7,079	10,267	13,286
Capital Accounts	37a	86	86	117	102	113	118	132	179	215	267	287	323	402	483	562
Other Items (Net)	37r	−11	−30	−74	−5	16	131	149	243	178	150	145	605	388	1,735	1,995
Money plus Quasi-Money	35l	1,850	2,474	2,623	2,905	3,436	3,941	4,915	5,827	6,364	7,407	8,448	9,007	10,840	14,371	17,953
Money (National Definitions)													*Millions of New Zealand Dollars:*				
M1	39ma	....	....	....	....	....	....	....	....	....	....	....	....	....	....	....
M2	39mb	....	....	....	....	....	....	....	....	....	....	....	....	....	....	....
M3R	39mc	....	....	....	....	....	....	....	....	....	....	....	....	....	....	....
M3	39md	....	....	....	....	....	....	....	....	....	16,009	18,066	20,669	25,020	31,397	37,807
Unused Overdrafts	39b	529	638	556	740	931	933	1,286	1,228	1,743	2,165	2,395	3,111	3,628	4,121	4,269
Other Banking Institutions													*Millions of New Zealand Dollars:*				
Claims on Central Government	42a. g	17.2	19.6	16.1	24.5	36.2	54.8	62.1	90.3	130.0	145.6	168.1	318.1	591.9	458.8[e]	432.4
Claims on Private Sector	42d. g	249.8	334.5	317.4	378.8	546.9	826.7	954.5	1,187.5	1,497.7	1,974.7	2,591.2	3,135.7	3,995.4	5,389.9	5,978.9
Time Dep. Debentures & Notes	45.. g	204.9	240.2	203.8	270.2	466.8	693.5	812.6	1,048.9	1,332.0	1,762.4	2,326.0	2,974.9	3,974.4	5,088.3	5,289.3
Foreign Liabilities	46c. g	23.6	30.4	44.3	49.8	27.5	18.1	22.9	25.3	31.9	28.4	34.6	40.5	68.9	123.7	470.8
Cred.from Deposit Money Banks	46h. g	10.6	33.5	26.4	25.8	26.5	28.4	27.7	34.8	27.2	34.0	40.1	30.5	38.8	48.1	61.5
Capital Accounts	47a. g	47.8	65.0	67.1	70.7	88.2	131.2	150.5	158.2	206.9	241.5	292.3	352.4	425.5	492.0	640.3
Other Items (Net)	47r. g	−19.9	−15.0	−8.1	−13.2	−25.9	10.3	2.9	10.6	29.7	54.0	66.3	55.5	79.7	96.6	−50.6
Post Office: Savings Deposits	45.. i	1,015.4	1,118.3	1,170.8	1,242.3	1,308.7	1,417.0	1,567.9	1,686.0	1,792.4	1,948.9	2,050.4	2,347.9	2,592.7	2,827.3	3,084.6
Trustee Savings Banks: Deposits	45.. k	590.2	707.5	758.3	850.0	944.9	1,075.7	1,357.1	1,567.6	1,872.5	2,242.1	2,493.3	2,989.5	3,399.4	3,750.3	4,202.6
Nonbank Financial Institutions													*Millions of New Zealand Dollars:*				
Claims on Central Government	42a. s	349.8	391.8	406.1	445.7	485.2	504.2	549.9	616.8	687.4	776.2	860.6	988.9	1,303.2	1,626.4	1,923.1
Claims on Local Government	42b. s	124.8	142.9	160.0	184.7	215.9	255.7	284.6	316.0	344.8	378.1	467.2	511.4	575.6	562.3	471.5
Claims on Private Sector	42d. s	918.8	989.0	1,080.7	1,153.1	1,251.2	1,359.5	1,462.3	1,584.9	1,776.9	1,997.6	2,240.0	2,517.1	2,789.6	3,007.6	4,566.1
Real Estate	42h. s	219.4	263.1	324.1	371.1	422.2	479.0	545.4	608.1	674.2	727.8	797.3	880.4	958.1	1,113.0	1,745.6
Incr.in Total Assets(Within Per.)	49z. s	154.4	174.5	188.2	185.0	218.6	233.5	258.5	295.6	343.7	419.3	477.8	585.0	770.1	921.6	3,528.4
Liquid Liabilities	55l	4,059.8	5,010.8	5,235.9	5,832.8	6,792.5	7,807.2	9,506.0	11,107.6	12,400.1	14,456.3	16,253.8	18,147.4	21,477.7	26,601.3	31,018.5

1987	1988	1989	1990	1991	1992	1993	1994	1995	1996	1997	1998	1999	2000	2001		
End of Period															**Exchange Rates**	
.4635	.4669	.4544	.4132	.3783	.3740	.4068	.4401	.4395	.4910	.4311	.3742	.3793	.3379	.3306	Market Rate	**ac**
End of Period (ag) Period Average (rh)																
.6575	.6283	.5972	.5878	.5411	.5143	.5588	.6425	.6533	.7060	.5817	.5269	.5206	.4402	.4155	Market Rate	**ag**
.5922	.6560	.5985	.5970	.5792	.5381	.5407	.5937	.6564	.6876	.6630	.5367	.5295	.4574	.4206	Market Rate	**rh**
Period Averages																
90.2	99.9	91.2	90.9	88.2	82.0	82.4	90.4	100.0	104.8	101.0	81.8	80.7	69.7	64.1	Market Rate	**ahx**
100.0	104.9	99.1	95.1	92.3	84.5	89.1	95.2	100.0	107.4	110.9	95.0	92.5	84.4	82.3	Nominal Effective Exchange Rate	**nec**
100.7	108.0	102.5	99.1	94.8	85.1	88.3	94.4	100.0	107.4	110.3	94.4	90.9	83.3	81.7	Real Effective Exchange Rate	**rec**
End of Period															**Fund Position**	
462	462	462	462	462	650	650	650	650	650	650	650	895	895	895	Quota	**2f.s**
1	1	—	—	—	—	—	—	—	1	—	1	5	10	13	SDRs	**1b.s**
—	8	40	40	54	109	104	101	110	127	132	253	309	246	308	Reserve Position in the Fund	**1c.s**
—	—	—	—	—	—	—	—	—	—	—	—	—	—	—	Total Fund Cred.&Loans Outstg.	**2tl**
End of Period															**International Liquidity**	
3,260	2,836	3,027	4,129	2,950	3,079	3,337	3,709	4,410	5,953	4,451	4,204	4,455	3,329	3,008	Total Reserves minus Gold	**1l.d**
1	1	1	1	—	—	—	—	—	1	—	2	7	13	16	SDRs	**1b.d**
—	11	52	57	77	150	142	147	164	182	178	356	424	320	387	Reserve Position in the Fund	**1c.d**
3,258	2,824	2,974	4,071	2,872	2,929	3,195	3,561	4,245	5,771	4,273	3,846	4,025	2,996	2,605	Foreign Exchange	**1d.d**
1,369	908	2,422	2,473	2,522	2,366	2,378	2,351	2,575	2,714	2,751	2,461	2,804	1,690	1,523	Monetary Authorities	**1da.d**
1,889	1,916	552	1,598	350	563	817	1,210	1,670	3,057	1,522	1,385	1,221	1,306	1,082	Government	**1db.d**
.022	.022	.001	.001	.001	.001	—	—	—	—	—	—	—	—	—	Gold (Million Fine Troy Ounces)	**1ad**
1	1	—	—	—	—	—	—	—	—	—	—	—	—	—	Gold (National Valuation)	**1and**
1,159	†82	60	6	20	100	96	—	178	299	461	383	379	605	302	Monetary Authorities: Other Liab.	**4..d**
915	†1,785	933	1,821	1,305	1,190	1,159	1,559	1,955	3,552	1,915	2,829	4,786	6,953	8,963	Banking Institutions: Assets	**7a.d**
1,294	†6,963	5,792	7,564	6,944	8,838	9,249	12,319	14,439	17,197	17,024	20,031	25,261	25,554	27,632	Liabilities	**7b.d**
End of Period															**Monetary Authorities**	
4,999	†4,545	5,083	6,979	5,454	5,967	5,974	5,772	7,024	8,856	8,544	8,799	9,077	10,330	9,310	Foreign Assets	**11**
2,216	†3,231	3,638	2,928	2,837	2,142	2,271	2,918	3,065	3,118	3,097	3,119	1,892	2,489	2,373	Claims on Central Government	**12a**
2	†26	28	313	236	789	796	301	476	1,305	1,079	451	2,178	1,802	2,247	Claims on Banking Institutions	**12e**
1,488	†1,690	1,655	1,646	1,613	1,648	1,695	1,891	2,026	1,972	2,068	2,198	3,870	2,925	3,196	Reserve Money	**14**
1,059	†969	1,110	1,007	1,118	1,173	1,199	1,367	1,489	1,497	1,633	1,724	2,077	2,069	2,241	of which: Currency Outside DMBs	**14a**
....	1,278	1,166	1,226	1,208	1,056	1,149	1,185	1,218	1,242	1,250	1,076	—	—	—	Liabs.of Central Bank: Securities	**16ac**
1,763	†131	100	11	37	194	172	—	273	424	793	726	728	1,374	727	Foreign Liabilities	**16c**
3,414	†4,373	5,156	6,649	4,896	5,297	5,342	5,219	6,319	8,959	7,871	7,574	7,751	9,463	9,129	Central Government Deposits	**16d**
584	†626	661	815	870	783	734	748	769	745	801	853	843	893	914	Capital Accounts	**17a**
-33	†-296	11	-128	-97	-80	-52	-53	-39	-62	-63	-58	-45	-34	-36	Other Items (Net)	**17r**
End of Period															**Banking Institutions**	
316	†425	480	558	471	506	491	467	606	532	409	448	1,592	818	908	Reserves	**20**
....	1,278	1,166	1,226	1,208	1,056	1,149	1,185	1,218	1,242	1,250	1,076	—	—	—	Claims on Mon.Author.: Securities	**20c**
1,392	†2,841	1,562	3,099	2,411	2,314	2,074	2,427	2,993	5,031	3,292	5,369	9,194	15,794	21,572	Foreign Assets	**21**
4,941	†6,876	5,703	7,123	7,203	8,448	7,079	5,932	4,249	3,302	3,572	4,384	6,921	7,149	5,818	Claims on Central Government	**22a**
18,315	†48,214	53,482	55,583	58,222	63,842	67,549	74,588	85,150	94,647	105,190	112,124	121,884	129,301	138,805	Claims on Private Sector	**22d**
5,579	†6,870	8,209	8,448	8,530	8,538	9,287	9,591	10,047	9,531	10,119	10,633	12,528	13,460	15,463	Demand Deposits	**24**
14,448	†37,479	40,710	46,811	47,030	48,430	51,715	55,986	61,667	74,020	77,726	78,762	81,043	82,297	86,770	Time, Savings,Fgn.Currency Dep.	**25**
....	1,499	1,798	3,100	2,660	1,970	2,535	1,849	2,030	3,764	2,806	4,198	2,521	3,296	3,194	of which: Fgn Currency Deposits	**25b**
1,555	†11,082	9,698	12,868	12,834	17,184	16,552	19,174	22,101	24,359	29,267	38,016	48,523	58,051	66,504	Foreign Liabilities	**26c**
59	† —	—	47	26	14	3	10	19	26	33	30	61	52	53	Central Government Deposits	**26d**
....	6,758	5,125	5,019	5,350	6,111	5,255	5,158	5,798	5,547	7,262	8,224	9,348	9,685	10,790	Capital Accounts	**27a**
3,321	†-2,554	-1,349	-5,604	-4,254	-4,110	-4,470	-5,320	-5,418	-8,727	-10,693	-12,263	-11,911	-10,483	-12,477	Other Items (Net)	**27r**
End of Period															**Banking Survey**	
3,072	†-3,827	-3,153	-2,801	-5,005	-9,097	-8,676	-10,976	-12,357	-10,896	-18,224	-24,575	-30,980	-33,300	-36,349	Foreign Assets (Net)	**31n**
22,054	†53,948	57,672	58,937	63,340	69,122	71,554	78,209	86,125	92,084	103,955	112,023	122,884	129,423	137,813	Domestic Credit	**32**
3,683	†5,734	4,185	3,355	5,118	5,279	4,005	3,621	976	-2,564	-1,235	-101	1,001	122	-991	Claims on Central Govt. (Net)	**32an**
18,370	†48,214	53,482	55,583	58,222	63,842	67,549	74,588	85,150	94,647	105,190	112,124	121,884	129,301	138,805	Claims on Private Sector	**32d**
6,667	†8,137	9,357	9,495	9,688	9,769	10,549	11,030	11,580	11,056	11,776	12,378	14,649	15,568	17,753	Money	**34**
14,448	†37,479	40,710	46,811	47,030	48,430	51,715	55,986	61,667	74,020	77,726	78,762	81,043	82,297	86,770	Quasi-Money	**35**
584	†7,383	5,786	5,834	6,219	6,893	5,990	5,906	6,567	6,292	8,002	9,077	10,190	10,578	11,704	Capital Accounts	**37a**
3,427	†-2,878	-1,334	-6,004	-4,603	-5,069	-5,376	-5,688	-6,045	-10,180	-11,834	-12,767	-13,977	-12,319	-14,762	Other Items (Net)	**37r**
21,115	†45,616	50,067	56,306	56,718	58,200	62,264	67,016	73,247	85,076	89,503	91,139	95,692	97,865	104,522	Money plus Quasi-Money	**35l**
End of Period															**Money (National Definitions)**	
....	....	....	....	....	....	10,948	11,516	11,003	11,718	12,887	14,880	15,800	18,052		M1	**39ma**
....	....	....	....	....	....	27,840	31,977	32,765	33,162	37,991	40,964	41,319	47,412		M2	**39mb**
....	....	....	....	....	....	58,385	65,461	73,318	78,263	78,523	84,669	86,644	92,732		M3R	**39mc**
42,932	44,418	46,137	52,832	56,489	64,239	65,873	67,948	77,800	87,568	91,023	92,120	98,748	105,179	117,213	M3	**39md**
....	....	....	....	....	....	....	....	....	....	....	....	....	....	....	Unused Overdrafts	**39b**
End of Period															**Other Banking Institutions**	
....	....	....	....	....	....	....	....	....	....	....	....	....	....	....	Claims on Central Government	**42a.g**
....	....	....	....	....	....	....	....	....	....	....	....	....	....	....	Claims on Private Sector	**42d.g**
....	....	....	....	....	....	....	....	....	....	....	....	....	....	....	Time Dep. Debentures & Notes	**45..g**
....	....	....	....	....	....	....	....	....	....	....	....	....	....	....	Foreign Liabilities	**46c.g**
....	....	....	....	....	....	....	....	....	....	....	....	....	....	....	Cred.from Deposit Money Banks	**46h.g**
....	....	....	....	....	....	....	....	....	....	....	....	....	....	....	Capital Accounts	**47a.g**
....	....	....	....	....	....	....	....	....	....	....	....	....	....	....	Other Items (Net)	**47r.g**
....	....	....	....	....	....	....	....	....	....	....	....	....	....	....	Post Office: Savings Deposits	**45..i**
....	....	....	....	....	....	....	....	....	....	....	....	....	....	....	Trustee Savings Banks: Deposits	**45..k**
End of Period															**Nonbank Financial Institutions**	
2,116.9	2,172.0	1,659.5	1,398.1	1,954.3	2,349.7	2,328.6	2,435.4	....	....	....	....	....	....	....	Claims on Central Government	**42a.s**
452.7	607.8	706.9	906.9	864.1	738.6	782.3	546.4	526.9	624.7	551.3	....	....	....	....	Claims on Local Government	**42b.s**
3,602.8	3,301.1	4,412.7	3,427.8	3,848.1	4,545.8	5,369.7	4,507.9	986.8	934.2	636.5	....	....	....	....	Claims on Private Sector	**42d.s**
2,725.3	2,746.4	3,091.8	2,580.0	2,061.4	1,740.6	1,488.7	1,590.9	....	....	....	....	....	....	....	Real Estate	**42h.s**
833.6	391.3	1,432.7	-1,559.2	522.9	765.3	2,178.4	-618.4	....	....	....	....	....	....	....	Incr.in Total Assets(Within Per.)	**49z.s**
....	....	....	....	....	....	....	....	....	....	....	....	....	....	....	Liquid Liabilities	**55l**

		1972	1973	1974	1975	1976	1977	1978	1979	1980	1981	1982	1983	1984	1985	1986
Interest Rates															*Percent Per Annum*	
Discount Rate (End of Period)	60	6.00	6.00	7.00	7.00	8.50	10.00	10.50	13.00	14.00	13.00	13.00	7.50	13.50	19.80	24.60
Money Market Rate	60b	. . .	. . .	. . .	. . .	. . .	. . .	. . .	. . .	. . .	. . .	. . .	. . .	. . .	24.74	17.70
Treasury Bill Rate	60c	. . .	. . .	. . .	. . .	. . .	. . .	8.25	10.75	11.25	11.25	11.25	10.13	9.23	. . .	19.97
Deposit Rate	60l	. . .	. . .	. . .	. . .	. . .	. . .	. . .	. . .	. . .	11.00	10.79	9.75	10.46	14.71	16.32
Lending Rate	60p	. . .	. . .	. . .	. . .	. . .	8.16	9.65	10.26	12.63	13.50	13.73	13.83	12.53	. . .	. . .
Government Bond Yield	61	5.52	5.80	6.09	6.33	8.34	9.23	9.97	12.04	13.29	12.83	12.91	12.18	12.57	17.71	16.52
Prices, Production, Labor															*Index Numbers (1995=100):*	
Share Prices	62	12.1	14.5	12.1	11.2	12.2	10.7	10.9	11.9	15.4	22.0	21.5	28.4	40.5	47.9	81.3
Input Prices: All Industry	63	12.4	14.0	15.1	17.1	20.9	†24.4	27.2	32.0	39.3	45.9	†52.9	55.8	59.8	68.9	72.9
Consumer Prices	64	11.8	12.8	14.2	16.3	19.0	21.8	24.4	27.7	32.4	37.4	43.4	46.6	49.5	†57.2	64.7
Wages: Weekly Rates (1990=100)	65	15.8	17.7	19.8	22.5	25.5	†28.8	32.2	37.2	44.1	52.6	58.8	59.0	60.4	†65.1	75.7
Labor Cost Index (Q492=100)	65a	. . .	. . .	. . .	. . .	. . .	. . .	. . .	. . .	. . .	. . .	. . .	. . .	. . .	. . .	. . .
Manufacturing Production	66ey c	. . .	. . .	. . .	. . .	. . .	76.8	75.3	80.1	79.8	83.6	87.5	85.5	97.2	95.5	94.1
Manufacturing Employment	67ey	81.9	85.6	89.3	87.9	89.3	90.4	86.7	89.4e	89.8	88.0	89.9	85.3	88.0	89.0	106.5
															Number in Thousands:	
Labor Force	67d	. . .	. . .	. . .	. . .	. . .	. . .	. . .	. . .	. . .	. . .	. . .	. . .	. . .	. . .	1,608
Employment	67e	. . .	. . .	. . .	. . .	. . .	. . .	. . .	. . .	. . .	. . .	. . .	. . .	. . .	. . .	1,544
Unemployment	67c	. . .	. . .	. . .	. . .	. . .	. . .	. . .	. . .	. . .	. . .	. . .	. . .	. . .	. . .	64
Unemployment Rate (%)	67r	. . .	. . .	. . .	. . .	. . .	. . .	. . .	. . .	. . .	. . .	. . .	. . .	. . .	. . .	4.0
International Transactions															*Millions of New Zealand Dollars*	
Exports	70	1,499.5	1,913.2	1,733.9	1,796.3	2,815.5	3,294.9	†3,603.5	4,606.7	5,568.5	6,471.2	7,414.4	8,110.0	9,584.1	11,603.2	11,225.1
Butter	70fl	163.8	137.3	119.4	166.8	227.5	254.6	257.0	318.6	354.1	489.4	683.9	545.3	567.8	670.6	498.8
Imports, c.i.f.	71	1,274.0	1,591.5	2,615.0	2,613.5	3,270.8	3,464.0	†3,359.4	4,466.1	5,615.9	6,635.5	7,699.0	7,991.9	10,939.0	12,075.5	11,622.1
Imports, f.o.b.	71.v	1,189.5	1,480.5	2,396.9	2,386.8	3,028.5	3,189.7	†3,110.6	4,052.7	5,171.2	5,587.3	7,044.8	6,928.2	8,197.9	10,966.8	10,646.5
															1995=100	
Volume of Exports	72	41.5	41.5	37.9	39.0	46.1	47.4	48.1	51.7	54.3	55.1	56.7	59.8	62.7	†69.4	68.0
Butter	72fl	75.2	82.1	73.6	77.2	89.2	83.7	76.1	91.3	90.9	85.2	102.7	77.6	82.1	107.0	89.1
Volume of Imports	73	39.9	47.5	61.5	46.6	47.7	45.9	42.0	49.7	48.3	50.0	53.1	49.5	59.4	†59.0	58.2
Unit Value of Exports	74	17.9	22.9	22.4	22.2	29.3	33.6	35.8	43.4	50.1	56.7	62.5	66.1	75.0	†81.5	79.5
Butter (Unit Value)	74fl	21.3	20.6	20.2	25.9	30.8	36.8	40.9	43.5	49.9	72.6	86.5	91.0	89.4	†86.4	77.2
Butter (Wholesale Price)	76fl	18.1	13.0	15.1	23.9	30.7	34.6	42.1	51.0	62.0	64.8	68.7	66.5	66.1	81.9	87.9
Unit Value of Imports	75	15.4	16.2	20.4	27.1	33.4	36.7	38.1	43.0	55.6	63.3	70.6	76.5	87.0	†96.3	93.9
Balance of Payments															*Millions of US Dollars:*	
Current Account, n.i.e.	78al d	153	-149	-1,847	-1,222	-794	-661	-438	-802	-973	-1,045	-1,694	-960	-3,031	-2,657	-2,826
Goods: Exports f.o.b.	78aa d	1,955	2,511	2,277	2,449	3,009	3,225	4,020	4,988	5,394	5,603	5,323	5,328	5,385	5,595	5,836
Goods: Imports f.o.b.	78ab d	-1,457	-2,148	-3,595	-3,095	-3,129	-3,116	-3,418	-4,698	-5,091	-5,346	-5,603	-4,991	-5,837	-5,656	-5,734
Trade Balance	78ac d	498	362	-1,318	-646	-119	110	602	290	303	257	-280	337	-452	-61	103
Services: Credit	78ad d	327	491	653	729	698	787	852	1,036	1,009	1,249	1,270	1,383	1,487	1,458	1,714
Services: Debit	78ae d	-549	-837	-1,060	-1,008	-962	-1,144	-1,339	-1,677	-1,843	-2,001	-2,034	-1,867	-1,860	-1,814	-2,184
Balance on Goods & Services	78af d	277	16	-1,725	-925	-384	-247	116	-351	-531	-495	-1,043	-146	-825	-417	-367
Income: Credit	78ag d	75	122	122	105	103	119	116	132	159	216	283	247	205	252	356
Income: Debit	78ah d	-225	-308	-239	-401	-523	-554	-701	-649	-697	-860	-1,024	-1,144	-2,503	-2,586	-2,950
Balance on Gds, Serv. & Inc.	78ai d	128	-170	-1,842	-1,222	-804	-682	-469	-868	-1,069	-1,139	-1,785	-1,043	-3,123	-2,752	-2,961
Current Transfers, n.i.e.: Credit	78aj d	76	90	95	109	105	126	139	181	226	220	226	222	215	211	246
Current Transfers: Debit	78ak d	-51	-69	-99	-109	-96	-105	-108	-115	-130	-126	-136	-139	-123	-116	-111
Capital Account, n.i.e.	78bc d	11	27	4	2	-24	-28	-51	-41	-38	-71	-3	2	-10	-25	-42
Capital Account, n.i.e.: Credit	78ba d	42	77	77	62	37	32	33	48	55	63	75	80	61	58	81
Capital Account: Debit	78bb d	-31	-50	-73	-60	-61	-60	-84	-89	-93	-133	-79	-79	-71	-83	-123
Financial Account, n.i.e.	78bj d	143	214	503	155	60	-199	-130	-12	-641	-708	344	48	296	-250	1
Direct Investment Abroad	78bd d	-4	-19	-21	-22	-36	-32	-56	-75	-107	-104	-69	-75	-422	-309	-592
Dir. Invest. in Rep. Econ., n.i.e.	78be d	127	208	252	138	278	154	274	351	178	275	328	175	1,263	1,266	1,214
Portfolio Investment Assets	78bf d	—	—	—	—	—	—	—	—	—	—	—	—	—	—	—
Equity Securities	78bk d	—	—	—	—	—	—	—	—	—	—	—	—	—	—	—
Debt Securities	78bl d	—	—	—	—	—	—	—	—	—	—	—	—	—	—	—
Portfolio Investment Liab., n.i.e.	78bg d	—	—	—	—	—	—	—	—	—	—	—	—	—	—	—
Equity Securities	78bm d	—	—	—	—	—	—	—	—	—	—	—	—	—	—	—
Debt Securities	78bn d	—	—	—	—	—	—	—	—	—	—	—	—	—	—	—
Financial Derivatives Assets	78bw d	. . .	. . .													
Financial Derivatives Liabilities	78bx d	. . .	. . .													
Other Investment Assets	78bh d	8	—	-42	-65	-26	-46	-40	3	-114	-34	-77	-100	26	31	-47
Monetary Authorities	78bo d															
General Government	78bp d	-2	-11	-14	-12	-7	—	-1	-3	-6	-4	-1				
Banks	78bq d	—	—	-18	-44	-19	-23	-55	-56	-146	-48	-38	-103	21	72	-47
Other Sectors	78br d	11	11	-10	-8	—	-22	16	62	38	18	-38	3	5	-40	—
Other Investment Liab., n.i.e.	78bi d	12	26	315	103	-156	-277	-307	-290	-598	-845	162	48	-571	-1,237	-574
Monetary Authorities	78bs d	—	—	—	—	—	-2	—	2	6	3	2				
General Government	78bt d	-96	-81	-32	-251	-301	-352	-317	-378	-697	-1,079	-1,293	-964	-1,351	-1,489	-1,576
Banks	78bu d	—	—	—	—	—	—	—	—	28		66	163	27	12	258
Other Sectors	78bv d	108	107	347	354	144	78	10	86	65	231	1,388	848	753	240	744
Net Errors and Omissions	78ca d	145	-65	244	66	30	216	-265	-111	230	-277	-859	-204	1,199	895	255
Overall Balance	78cb d	452	27	-1,095	-999	-728	-672	-883	-966	-1,421	-2,100	-2,213	-1,114	-1,546	-2,037	-2,612
Reserves and Related Items	79da d	-452	-27	1,095	999	728	672	883	966	1,424	2,102	2,214	1,114	1,546	2,037	2,612
Reserve Assets	79db d	-488	-30	390	-34	15	-201	235	245	314	-344	31	-209	-1,027	389	-2,044
Use of Fund Credit and Loans	79dc d	—	—	103	188	171	-2	-34	-118	-179	-116	-34	-3	—	—	—
Exceptional Financing	79de d	36	3	602	845	542	875	682	839	1,289	2,562	2,217	1,325	2,574	1,649	4,656

	1987	1988	1989	1990	1991	1992	1993	1994	1995	1996	1997	1998	1999	2000	2001		
Percent Per Annum																**Interest Rates**	
	18.55	15.10	15.00	13.25	8.30	9.15	5.70	9.75	9.80	8.80	9.70	5.60	5.00	6.50	4.75	Discount Rate *(End of Period)*	60
	21.32	15.27	13.40	13.42	9.94	6.63	6.25	6.13	8.91	9.38	7.38	6.86	4.33	6.12	5.76	Money Market Rate	60b
	20.50	14.72	13.51	13.78	9.74	6.72	6.21	6.69	8.82	9.09	7.53	7.10	4.58	6.39	5.56	Treasury Bill Rate	60c
	....	†13.41	10.92	†11.65	8.93	6.58	6.24	6.38	8.49	8.49	7.26	6.78	4.56	6.36	5.35	Deposit Rate	60l
	†20.84	17.17	15.78	16.01	14.01	11.39	10.34	9.69	12.16	12.27	11.35	11.22	8.49	10.22	9.88	Lending Rate	60p
	†16.35	13.45	12.78	12.46	10.00	7.87	6.69	7.48	7.94	8.04	7.21	6.47	6.13	6.85	6.12	Government Bond Yield	61
Period Averages																**Prices, Production, Labor**	
	†95.0	58.8	64.5	56.8	49.9	57.1	74.9	94.8	100.0	112.3	130.7	153.3	136.4	139.5	146.9	Share Prices	62
	78.7	82.8	†88.6	92.8	93.6	95.5	97.9	99.2	100.0	100.5	100.9	101.6	102.6	110.4	117.0	Input Prices: All Industry	63
	74.9	79.7	85.6	90.4	91.9	92.8	94.1	†96.4	100.0	102.3	103.5	104.8	104.7	107.4	110.3	Consumer Prices	64
	85.7	92.2	95.8	100.0	102.6	103.5	....	....	....	....	....	....	....	....	....	Wages: Weekly Rates (1990=100)	65
	....	....	....	....	....	....	97.5	98.5	100.0	101.9	104.3	106.2	107.8	109.5	111.6	Labor Cost Index (Q492=100)	65a
	93.4	89.0	88.9	85.3	81.7	85.1	90.8	96.4	100.0	100.8	102.4	99.8	101.8	....	....	Manufacturing Production	66ey c
	100.9	92.2	86.7	83.7	80.9	86.4	86.4	96.3	100.0	98.7	94.8	97.1	93.3	94.3	96.8	Manufacturing Employment	67ey
Period Averages																	
	1,623	1,597	1,581	1,606	1,628	1,636	1,653	1,698	1,742	1,797	†1,817	1,864	1,878	1,892	....	Labor Force	67d
	1,557	1,508	1,468	1,481	1,461	1,467	1,496	1,559	1,633	1,688	†1,693	1,725	1,750	1,779	....	Employment	67e
	66	89	113	125	167	169	157	138	110	110	†123	139	128	113	102	Unemployment	67c
	4.1	5.6	7.1	7.8	10.3	10.3	9.5	8.2	6.3	6.1	†6.6	7.5	6.8	6.0	....	Unemployment Rate (%)	67r
Millions of New Zealand Dollars																**International Transactions**	
	12,149.7	13,488.2	14,820.0	15,760.0	16,671.0	18,208.0	19,492.0	20,519.0	20,787.0	20,876.0	21,448.0	22,493.0	23,540.0	29,201.0	32,655.0	Exports	70
	517.7	554.9	560.4	654.2	733.7	677.3	828.4	790.5	777.9	907.7	945.9	1,073.7	972.3	1,125.3	1,040.3	Butter	70fl
	12,242.5	11,216.9	14,710.1	15,895.5	14,526.0	17,131.0	17,781.0	19,981.0	21,251.0	21,399.0	21,964.0	23,348.0	27,114.0	30,737.0	31,774.0	Imports, c.i.f.	71
	11,221.8	10,273.2	13,438.9	14,566.2	13,280.0	15,805.0	16,373.0	18,491.0	19,715.0	19,847.0	20,440.0	21,682.0	25,436.0	28,855.0	29,668.0	Imports, f.o.b.	71.v
1995=100																	
	69.9	72.7	70.7	74.8	82.6	84.7	88.2	97.2	100.0	104.8	109.9	109.6	111.3	117.7	....	Volume of Exports	72
	93.3	101.7	71.6	86.9	105.0	77.2	106.6	107.9	100.0	117.6	141.1	127.6	133.3	147.8	125.5	Butter	72fl
	64.2	59.2	72.0	77.3	69.9	77.4	80.7	93.9	100.0	103.4	107.2	109.8	124.5	121.1	....	Volume of Imports	73
	84.2	89.3	101.1	99.8	95.6	103.4	106.0	101.7	100.0	96.5	94.0	98.5	99.9	117.3	....	Unit Value of Exports	74
	71.3	72.7	94.5	97.2	95.5	110.8	108.0	97.6	100.0	100.0	99.0	89.0	106.7	95.0	100.0	Butter (Unit Value)	74fl
	76.7	85.6	98.9	98.9	97.4	111.8	104.1	94.5	100.0	....	89.1	107.8	99.9	....	....	Butter (Wholesale Price)	76fl
	89.6	89.0	96.0	96.7	97.7	104.2	103.6	100.1	100.0	97.3	96.4	100.0	102.1	119.0	....	Unit Value of Imports	75
Minus Sign Indicates Debit																**Balance of Payments**	
	−2,910	−1,863	−1,525	−1,453	−1,159	−1,071	−746	−2,384	−3,003	−3,964	−4,366	−2,162	−3,632	−2,734	−1,587	Current Account, n.i.e.	78al d
	7,245	8,831	8,846	9,190	9,555	9,735	10,468	12,176	13,554	14,338	14,246	12,256	12,595	13,484	13,918	Goods: Exports f.o.b.	78aa d
	−6,656	−6,658	−7,873	−8,375	−7,485	−8,108	−8,749	−10,769	−12,584	−13,814	−13,380	−11,333	−13,028	−12,848	−12,447	Goods: Imports f.o.b.	78ab d
	590	2,173	973	815	2,070	1,627	1,719	1,408	971	524	867	923	−433	636	1,471	*Trade Balance*	78ac d
	2,191	2,549	2,395	2,494	2,579	2,634	2,854	3,667	4,481	4,639	4,281	3,741	4,286	4,326	4,230	Services: Credit	78ad d
	−2,658	−3,153	−3,167	−3,324	−3,414	−3,582	−3,505	−4,101	−4,694	−4,900	−4,912	−4,505	−4,575	−4,511	−4,263	Services: Debit	78ae d
	123	1,569	201	−15	1,235	679	1,068	973	757	262	236	159	−722	452	1,437	*Balance on Goods & Services*	78af d
	542	451	661	719	33	117	394	358	940	372	394	879	919	590	590	Income: Credit	78ag d
	−3,719	−4,033	−2,545	−2,295	−2,566	−1,995	−2,340	−4,045	−4,895	−5,085	−5,249	−3,493	−4,036	−4,018	−3,727	Income: Debit	78ah d
	−3,053	−2,014	−1,684	−1,591	−1,298	−1,199	−877	−2,713	−3,198	−4,451	−4,618	−2,455	−3,840	−2,976	−1,700	*Balance on Gds, Serv. & Inc.*	78ai d
	278	309	314	317	321	310	310	638	558	897	705	694	622	646	584	Current Transfers, n.i.e.: Credit	78aj d
	−134	−159	−156	−179	−182	−182	−178	−309	−363	−409	−453	−402	−413	−404	−472	Current Transfers: Debit	78ak d
	−46	−49	47	213	252	292	542	617	1,224	1,335	236	−183	−218	−182	439	Capital Account, n.i.e.	78bc d
	137	228	331	507	586	602	833	995	1,652	1,838	777	260	259	236	818	Capital Account, n.i.e.: Credit	78ba d
	−182	−277	−284	−294	−334	−311	−291	−379	−427	−502	−541	−444	−477	−418	−379	Capital Account: Debit	78bb d
	10	−1,790	−740	875	−709	3,229	2,825	2,220	4,665	3,571	4,045	1,580	1,974	3,335	764	Financial Account, n.i.e.	78bj d
	−435	−373	−1,896	−1,594	−690	806	−1,276	−1,725	337	1,533	45	−928	−803	−963	−369	Direct Investment Abroad	78bd d
	1,284	1,717	1,627	1,735	1,290	2,095	2,350	2,543	3,659	2,231	2,624	1,191	1,412	3,209	2,012	Dir. Invest. in Rep. Econ., n.i.e.	78be d
	—	—	−40	−111	−68	−7	−283	−72	−284	−430	−1,612	−467	−666	−2,184	−1,079	Portfolio Investment Assets	78bf d
	—	—	−50	−97	−53	−11	−187	−152	−216	−339	−925	114	−893	−1,667	−868	Equity Securities	78bk d
	—	—	10	−14	−15	4	−97	81	−68	−90	−687	−581	227	−517	−211	Debt Securities	78bl d
	—	—	70	282	−83	−135	1,940	614	96	−104	403	425	−2,285	2,261	−1,730	Portfolio Investment Liab., n.i.e.	78bg d
	—	—	12	146	129	53	116	23	−100	175	88	22	172	−497	194	Equity Securities	78bm d
	—	—	58	136	−212	−188	1,823	591	197	−279	315	402	−2,458	2,757	−1,924	Debt Securities	78bn d
	....	....	....	....	....	....	....	....	....	....	....	....	....	....	....	Financial Derivatives Assets	78bw d
	....	....	....	....	....	....	....	....	....	....	....	....	....	....	....	Financial Derivatives Liabilities	78bx d
	−85	628	−254	−81	−207	328	−739	−78	−392	−920	991	−305	−1,282	−836	−3,260	Other Investment Assets	78bh d
	....	....	....	....	....	....	—	—	—	—	—	—	—	....	....	Monetary Authorities	78bo d
			−24	−45	−47	−11	−62	−82	−57	−94	238	55	212	....	....	General Government	78bp d
	−85	628	−411	−42	31	124	−747	66	−346	−932	819	−285	−1,591	....	....	Banks	78bq d
	—	—	181	6	−191	215	71	−61	11	106	−65	−75	97	....	−3,260	Other Sectors	78br d
	−754	−3,762	−247	644	−952	142	833	937	1,249	1,262	1,595	1,665	5,597	1,848	5,191	Other Investment Liab., n.i.e.	78bi d
	....	....	....	....	....	....	....	....	....	....	....	....	....	....	....	Monetary Authorities	78bs d
	−3,239	−2,673	−1,231	−832	−1,239	222	−117	−290	−144	−135	−73	68	13	....	....	General Government	78bt d
	228	95	−397	−58	−23	1,365	573	767	1,096	964	1,131	1,559	5,446	....	....	Banks	78bu d
	2,257	−1,183	1,381	1,534	310	−1,445	377	460	297	432	537	38	138	....	....	Other Sectors	78bv d
	697	782	1,000	544	104	−2,319	−2,695	281	−2,502	829	−1,358	279	2,065	−564	197	Net Errors and Omissions	78ca d
	−2,248	−2,921	−1,217	179	−1,511	131	−74	733	384	1,772	−1,442	−486	188	−144	−187	*Overall Balance*	78cb d
	2,248	2,921	1,217	−179	1,511	−131	74	−733	−384	−1,772	1,442	486	−188	144	187	Reserves and Related Items	79da d
	389	735	−248	−1,014	1,319	−131	74	−733	−384	−1,772	1,442	486	−188	144	187	Reserve Assets	79db d
	—	—	—	—	—	....	....	....	....	....	....	....	....	....	....	Use of Fund Credit and Loans	79dc d
	1,860	2,186	1,466	835	192	....	....	....	....	....	....	....	....	....	....	Exceptional Financing	79de d

New Zealand

		1972	1973	1974	1975	1976	1977	1978	1979	1980	1981	1982	1983	1984	1985	1986
IIP:End-March Stocks Through 1999														*Millions of US Dollars*		
Assets	79aa d	...	...	...	...	...	...	...	...	43	25	44	1	—	1	1
Direct Investment Abroad	79ab d	...	...	...	...	...	...	...	...	...	...	...	...	...	...	...
Portfolio Investment	79ac d	...	...	...	...	...	...	...	...	...	...	...	...	...	...	...
Equity Securities	79ad d	...	...	...	...	...	...	...	...	...	...	...	...	...	...	...
Debt Securities	79ae d	...	...	...	...	...	...	...	...	...	...	...	...	...	...	...
Financial Derivatives	79al d	...	...	...	...	...	...	...	...	...	...	...	...	...	...	...
Other Investment	79af d	...	...	...	...	...	...	...	...	...	...	...	...	...	...	...
Monetary Authorities	79ag d	...	...	...	...	...	...	...	...	...	...	...	...	...	...	...
General Government	79ah d	...	...	...	...	...	...	...	...	...	...	...	...	...	...	...
Banks	79ai d	...	...	...	...	...	...	...	...	...	...	...	...	...	...	...
Other Sectors	79aj d	...	...	...	...	...	...	...	...	...	...	...	...	...	...	...
Reserve Assets	79ak d	...	...	...	...	...	...	...	...	43	25	44	1	—	1	1
Liabilities	79la d	...	...	...	...	...	...	...	...	4,289	5,026	9,297	10,933	11,414	14,056	6,569
Dir. Invest. in Rep. Economy	79lb d	...	...	...	...	...	...	...	...							
Portfolio Investment	79lc d	...	...	...	...	...	...	...	...	2,625	3,243	3,919	4,193	4,506	7,660	...
Equity Securities	79ld d	...	...	...	...	...	...	...	...							
Debt Securities	79le d	...	...	...	...	...	...	...	...	2,625	3,243	3,919	4,193	4,506	7,660	...
Financial Derivatives	79ll d	...	...	...	...	...	...	...	...							
Other Investment	79lf d	...	...	...	...	...	...	...	...	1,664	1,783	5,379	6,740	6,908	6,396	6,569
Monetary Authorities	79lg d	...	...	...	...	...	...	...	...	498	268	—	—	—	—	...
General Government	79lh d	...	...	...	...	...	...	...	...	1,166	1,516	2,034	2,064	1,971	624	...
Banks	79li d	...	...	...	...	...	...	...	...							
Other Sectors	79lj d	...	...	...	...	...	...	...	...			3,345	4,676	4,937	5,772	6,569

Government Finance

		1972	1973	1974	1975	1976	1977	1978	1979	1980	1981	1982	1983	1984	1985	1986
												Millions of New Zealand Dollars:				
Deficit (-) or Surplus	80	−298	−225	−416	−1,194	−614	−789	−1,502	−1,127	−1,541	−2,111	−2,389	−3,209	−3,234	−2,082	−1,990
Revenue	81	2,146	2,632	3,124	3,503	4,283	5,153	5,651	6,827	7,877	9,753	11,207	11,724	13,705	16,933	20,843
Expenditure	82	2,231	2,614	3,107	3,873	4,276	5,232	6,404	7,338	8,802	11,075	12,880	14,108	16,155	18,330	22,711
Lending Minus Repayments	83	213	243	433	824	621	710	749	616	616	789	716	825	784	685	122
Financing																
Domestic	84a	409	341	68	755	382	576	837	919	523	1,451	2,085	2,612	1,653	1,167	†2,357
Foreign	85a	−49	−58	301	422	226	483	340	399	816	799	1,322	823	1,839	946	†−367
Use of Cash Balances	87a	−62	−58	47	17	6	−270	325	−191	202	−139	−1,018	−226	−258	−31	...
Debt: Domestic	88a	2,956	3,295	3,365	4,121	4,478	5,061	5,917	6,806	7,399	8,858	11,004	13,701	15,875	17,276	20,744
Foreign	89a	564	465	863	1,463	1,827	2,447	2,920	3,568	4,236	5,549	7,765	8,227	12,409	14,726	21,735

National Accounts

		1972	1973	1974	1975	1976	1977	1978	1979	1980	1981	1982	1983	1984	1985	1986
											Millions of New Zealand Dollars; Year Beginning April 1;					
Househ.Cons.Expend.,incl.NPISHs	96f. c	4,764	5,488	6,206	7,098	8,162	9,149	10,324	12,053	14,169	16,633	19,018	20,718	23,582	27,869	32,962
Government Consumption Expend.	91f. c	1,023	1,176	1,443	1,732	1,937	2,363	2,882	3,314	4,134	4,989	5,566	5,858	6,334	7,348	8,930
Gross Fixed Capital Formation	93e. c	1,778	2,091	2,695	3,246	3,538	3,545	3,880	4,067	4,754	6,597	7,774	8,612	9,994	11,978	12,721
Changes in Inventories	93i. c	154	452	1,036	459	810	133	−246	470	−33	165	248	375	1,111	−154	588
Exports of Goods and Services	90c. c	1,946	2,241	2,117	2,666	3,765	4,125	4,687	5,996	7,003	8,249	9,266	10,507	13,229	13,947	14,957
Imports of Goods and Services (-)	98c. c	1,710	2,233	3,344	3,430	4,057	4,378	4,647	6,256	7,272	9,168	10,318	11,063	14,539	15,311	15,076
Gross Domestic Product (GDP)	99b. c	7,901	9,199	10,095	11,668	14,101	14,970	16,958	19,795	22,992	27,891	31,409	34,839	39,346	45,282	55,848
Net Primary Income from Abroad	98.n c	−54	−37	−82	−165	−265	−336	−409	−460	−511	−615	−858	−1,275	−2,002	−2,520	−2,908
Gross National Income (GNI)	99a. c	7,847	9,162	10,013	11,503	13,836	14,634	16,549	19,335	22,481	27,276	30,551	33,564	37,344	42,762	52,940
Consumption of Fixed Capital	99cf c	613	692	797	940	1,078	1,164	1,330	1,454	1,684	1,922	2,247	2,689	3,241	3,826	†8,365
GDP Volume 1965 Prices	99b. r	4,753	5,094	5,300	5,389	5,397	5,249	...	...	...	...	...	...	...	...	...
GDP Volume 1991/92 Prices	99b. r	...	...	...	...	...	28,582	60,000	61,531	62,192	65,248	63,105	66,746	70,237	70,083	72,390
GDP Volume (1995=100)	99bv r	57.1	61.2	63.7	64.7	64.8	63.1	64.7	66.4	67.1	70.4	68.1	72.0	75.8	75.6	78.1
GDP Deflator (1995=100)	99bi r	14.9	16.2	17.1	19.4	23.5	25.6	28.3	32.2	37.0	42.7	49.8	52.2	56.0	64.6	77.1
															Millions:	
Population	99z	2.90	2.96	3.01	3.07	3.09	3.11	3.11	3.10	3.11	3.12	3.16	3.20	3.23	3.25	3.28

Millions of US Dollars — IIP:End-March Stocks Through 1999

	1987	1988	1989	1990	1991	1992	1993	1994	1995	1996	1997	1998	1999	2000	2001	
Assets	1	....	4,434	8,687	12,570	12,393	10,118	13,206	16,201	23,573	23,023	19,348	20,126	30,797	32,404	79aa d
Direct Investment Abroad	....	....	534	3,269	5,951	6,282	4,234	5,163	7,630	8,928	6,749	5,775	6,746	6,380	6,862	79ab d
Portfolio Investment	....	....	—	148	298	882	952	1,362	1,707	5,815	6,434	6,476	6,374	11,241	11,656	79ac d
Equity Securities	....	....	....	143	270	503	602	834	1,226	4,407	4,895	4,620	4,193	6,701	7,028	79ad d
Debt Securities	....	....	....	5	28	380	350	529	481	1,408	1,539	1,855	2,181	4,541	4,628	79ae d
Financial Derivatives														4,481	2,568	79al d
Other Investment	....	....	1,416	2,022	2,428	1,989	1,644	2,793	2,898	4,245	5,313	2,804	3,352	4,742	7,751	79af d
Monetary Authorities	....	....	....	....	....	....	....	....	....	....	....	....		....	....	79ag d
General Government	....	....	....	....	....	....	....	....	....	....	....	....	187	....	....	79ah d
Banks	....	....	....	....	....	....	....	....	....	....	....	....	1,980	....	....	79ai d
Other Sectors	....	....	....	....	....	....	....	....	....	....	....	....	1,185	....	....	79aj d
Reserve Assets	1	....	2,484	3,248	3,891	3,240	3,288	3,888	3,967	4,584	4,528	4,293	3,654	3,952	3,566	79ak d
Liabilities	....	....	30,835	46,936	52,728	40,971	44,240	51,100	62,339	71,631	78,547	68,752	63,782	69,677	69,316	79l a d
Dir. Invest. in Rep. Economy	....	....	5,180	7,938	10,761	12,545	14,849	19,315	25,574	33,381	37,491	34,889	31,636	21,460	19,787	79lb d
Portfolio Investment	....	....	—	11,941	12,642	14,273	15,290	17,595	19,809	19,361	20,166	17,581	16,697	25,002	22,874	79lc d
Equity Securities	....	....	....	903	1,036	468	1,320	816	1,483	288	1,045	208	227	4,542	4,164	79ld d
Debt Securities	....	....	....	11,037	11,607	13,805	13,970	16,779	18,327	19,072	19,121	17,373	16,470	20,460	18,709	79le d
Financial Derivatives														3,452	2,710	79ll d
Other Investment	....	....	25,655	27,057	29,325	14,153	14,101	14,189	16,955	18,889	20,890	16,282	15,450	19,763	23,945	79lf d
Monetary Authorities	....	....	....	....	....	....	....	....	....	....	....	....		....	....	79lg d
General Government	....	....	....	....	....	....	....	....	....	....	....	....	403	....	....	79lh d
Banks	....	....	....	....	....	....	....	....	....	....	....	....	10,300	....	....	79li d
Other Sectors	....	....	....	....	....	....	....	....	....	....	....	....	4,746	....	....	79lj d

Government Finance — Fiscal Year (see note)

	1987	1988	1989	1990	1991	1992	1993	1994	1995	1996	1997	1998	1999	2000	2001	
Deficit (-) or Surplus	642	1,354	....	†2,894	1,419	-1,677	84	679	396	4,932	3,913	484	2,049	-385	....	80
Revenue	26,668	27,160	....	†30,866	28,457	26,616	26,742	30,236	32,861	33,975	33,285	33,827	33,359	34,440	....	81
Expenditure	27,815	28,492	....	†31,758	30,084	28,598	28,440	29,662	29,954	30,593	31,465	33,005	33,869	34,386	....	82
Lending Minus Repayments	-1,789	-2,686	....	†-3,786	-3,046	-305	-1,782	-105	2,511	-1,550	-2,093	338	-2,559	439	....	83
Financing Domestic	....	....	....	....	....	....	....	....	....	....	....	....	....	....		84a
Foreign	....	....	....	....	....	....	....	....	....	....	....	....	....	....		85a
Use of Cash Balances	....	....	....	....	....	....	....	....	....	....	....	....	....	....		87a
Debt: Domestic	21,855	23,008	....	†20,452	20,981	....	24,206	20,194	21,060	19,866	15,688	18,307	19,440	20,041	....	88a
Foreign	17,257	16,593	....	†23,897	22,952	....	23,523	26,289	23,418	21,896	20,649	19,969	17,384	16,368	....	89a

National Accounts — Year Beginning April 1 Seasonally Adjusted

	1987	1988	1989	1990	1991	1992	1993	1994	1995	1996	1997	1998	1999	2000	2001	
Househ.Cons.Expend.,incl.NPISHs	†36,569	39,606	42,438	44,640	44,494	45,351	47,435	51,177	54,521	57,487	59,485	61,514	63,743	66,054	69,379	96f. c
Government Consumption Expend.	†11,633	12,543	13,252	14,058	14,319	14,865	15,109	15,337	16,378	17,041	18,601	19,024	20,230	20,344	21,097	91f. c
Gross Fixed Capital Formation	†13,904	13,647	14,857	14,421	11,973	12,571	15,034	17,747	19,890	21,110	20,709	19,972	20,806	21,189	22,605	93e. c
Changes in Inventories	†-413	-114	1,289	-154	-88	625	1,432	1,166	1,183	779	846	-116	1,292	1,115	1,380	93i. c
Exports of Goods and Services	†16,451	17,811	18,943	19,755	21,488	23,700	25,085	26,951	27,125	27,511	28,533	30,376	33,151	41,065	43,135	90c. c
Imports of Goods and Services (-)	†15,488	15,476	18,913	19,569	19,248	21,865	22,708	25,326	26,417	27,018	28,193	30,144	34,448	39,209	39,759	98c. c
Gross Domestic Product (GDP)	†62,656	68,017	71,865	73,151	72,938	75,246	81,388	87,051	92,679	96,910	99,982	100,627	104,775	110,558	120,002	99b. c
Net Primary Income from Abroad	†-3,414	-3,588	-3,722	-2,772	-4,796	-3,836	-4,408	-5,685	-5,999	-7,263	-6,751	-4,435	-5,526	-1,039	-5,662	98.n c
Gross National Income (GNI)	†59,242	64,429	68,143	70,379	68,142	71,410	76,980	81,366	86,680	89,647	93,231	96,192	99,249	109,519	114,340	99a. c
Consumption of Fixed Capital	†8,797	9,244	9,783	10,364	10,961	11,322	11,527	11,932	12,407	12,865	13,483	14,129	14,656	....	....	99cf c
GDP Volume 1965 Prices	....	....	....	....	....	....	....	....	....	....	....	....	....	....	....	99b. r
GDP Volume 1991/92 Prices	†78,522	79,936	80,122	80,118	79,198	79,995	85,006	89,375	92,679	95,523	97,968	97,567	101,577	103,630	108,128	99b. r
GDP Volume (1995=100)	†84.7	86.3	86.5	86.4	85.5	86.3	91.7	96.4	100.0	103.1	105.7	105.3	109.6	111.8	116.7	99bv r
GDP Deflator (1995=100)	†79.8	85.1	89.7	91.3	92.1	94.1	95.7	97.4	100.0	101.5	102.1	103.1	103.1	106.7	111.0	99bi r

Midyear Estimates

	1987	1988	1989	1990	1991	1992	1993	1994	1995	1996	1997	1998	1999	2000	2001	
Population	3.30	3.32	3.33	3.36	3.48	3.51	3.55	3.60	3.66	3.71	3.76	3.79	3.81	3.83	3.85	99z

(See notes in the back of the book.)

Nicaragua

278

		1972	1973	1974	1975	1976	1977	1978	1979	1980	1981	1982	1983	1984	1985	1986
Exchange Rates									*Gold Córdobas per Bill. SDRs through 1987, per Million SDRs in 1998, per*							
Principal Rate	aa	1.53	1.70	1.72	1.65	1.63	1.71	1.83	2.65	2.56	2.34	2.22	2.10	1.97	6.15	17.12
									Gold Córd.per Bill.US$ through 1987, per Mill.US$ in 1988.per Thous.US$								
Principal Rate	ae	1.41	1.41	1.41	1.41	1.41	1.41	1.41	2.01	2.01	2.01	2.01	2.01	2.01	5.60	14.00
Principal Rate	rf	2.06	2.06	2.06	2.06	2.06	2.06	2.06	2.79	2.95	2.95	2.95	2.95	2.95	7.77	19.50
													Index Numbers (1995=100):			
Principal Rate	ahx	....	....	....	....	....	....	....	....	....	....	....	....	....	....	....
Nominal Effective Exchange Rate	ne c	....	....	....	....	....	....	....	....	....	....	....	....	....	....	....
Real Effective Exchange Rate	re c	....	....	....	....	....	....	....	....	....	....	....	....	....	....	....
Fund Position													*Millions of SDRs:*			
Quota	2f. s	27.00	27.00	27.00	27.00	27.00	27.00	34.00	34.00	51.00	51.00	51.00	51.00	68.20	68.20	68.20
SDRs	1b. s	6.22	5.71	5.80	4.57	3.47	3.77	4.34	.02	—	.06	.88	—	—	—	—
Reserve Position in the Fund	1c. s	—	—	—	—	—	—	—	—	—	—	—	—	—	—	—
Total Fund Cred.&Loans Outstg.	2tl	8.25	12.24	10.06	15.50	8.74	2.00	2.01	43.51	38.67	21.19	17.54	13.29	9.04	.01	—
International Liquidity											*Millions of US Dollars Unless Otherwise Indicated:*					
Total Reserves minus Gold	1l. d	80.11	116.26	104.49	121.59	146.05	148.33	50.77	146.62	64.52	111.43	171.17	174.70	....	....	....
SDRs	1b. d	6.75	6.89	7.10	5.35	4.03	4.58	5.65	.03	—	.07	.97	—	....	....	....
Reserve Position in the Fund	1c. d	—	—	—	—	—	—	—	—	—	—	—	—	....	....	....
Foreign Exchange	1d. d	73.36	109.37	97.39	116.24	142.02	143.75	45.12	146.59	64.52	111.36	170.20	174.70	....	....	....
Gold (Million Fine Troy Ounces)	1ad	.009	.015	.019	.018	.017	.026	.027	.018	.018	.018	.018	.120	....	....	....
Gold (National Valuation)	1and	.34	.63	.80	.76	.72	1.10	1.14	.76	.76	.76	.76	5.07	....	....	....
Monetary Authorities: Other Liab.	4.. d	.74	6.35	23.56	47.24	49.42	57.99	139.05	215.29	399.74	789.78	1,099.85	1,721.93	2,351.35	2,720.96	2,819.85
Deposit Money Banks: Assets	7a. d	11.04	16.61	10.28	14.32	17.80	16.71	31.01	24.06	23.76	46.87	58.45	38.03	13.32	11.56	2.77
Liabilities	7b. d	74.14	85.03	94.25	113.97	95.87	150.19	198.68	166.00	270.54	109.00	104.28	132.92	98.25	98.39	20.97
Monetary Authorities									*Thousandths (.000) of Gold Córdobas through 1985, Gold Córd. 1986-87;*							
Foreign Assets	11	111	164	147	172	205	209	72	244	92	254	266	†369	915	2,602	†4
Claims on Central Government	12a	40	74	63	75	79	85	244	364	772	991	1,594	†3,852	5,625	11,704	†26
Claims on Nonfin.Pub.Enterprises	12c	....	....	....	....	....	....	....	....	....	....	....	70	108	206	†—
Claims on Private Sector	12d	....	....	....	....	....	....	....	....	....	....	....	†—			†—
Claims on Deposit Money Banks	12e	17	38	122	100	81	79	137	268	663	1,076	1,247	†761	840	1,271	†4
Claims on Nonbank Financial Insts	12g	....	....	....	....	....	....	....	....	....	....	....	84	316	1,962	†6
Reserve Money	14	106	150	166	171	217	230	207	472	440	691	910	†1,611	3,021	8,564	†29
of which: Currency Outside DMBs	14a	66	82	90	89	127	138	177	314	393	475	617	†1,085	2,268	5,712	†20
Time, Savings,& Fgn.Currency Dep.	15	3	2	4	5	7	5	16	5	3	2	14	†297	453	779	†2
Liabs. of Central Bank: Securities	16ac	....	....	....	....	....	....	....	....	....	....	....				
Foreign Liabilities	16c	14	27	48	67	46	44	145	305	532	883	1,128	†1,042	1,548	6,548	†13
Long-Term Foreign Liabilities	16cl	—	3	3	25	38	41	54	243	371	754	1,121	†2,447	3,196	8,690	†26
Central Government Deposits	16d	16	53	68	40	31	29	20	152	216	45	130	†34	167	470	†2
Counterpart Funds	16e	....	....	....	....	....	....	....	....	....	....	....				
Liab. to Nonbank Financial Insts	16j	....	....	....	....	....	....	....	....	....	....	....	50	87	573	†1
Capital Accounts	17a	19	21	21	21	20	21	21	38	48	57	56	†54	52	126	†—
Other Items (Net)	17r	10	20	22	18	6	3	-10	-339	-83	-111	-252	†-400	-722	-8,004	†-33
of which: Valuation Adjustment	17rv	....	....	....	....	....	....	....	....	....	....	....			-7,324	†-27
Deposit Money Banks									*Thousandths (.000) of Gold Córdobas through 1985; Gold Córd. 1986-87;*							
Reserves	20	41	68	78	84	90	95	77	82	86	200	293	†571	961	2,740	†7
Claims on Mon.Author.: Securities	20c	....	....	....	....	....	....	....	....	....	....	....				
Foreign Assets	21	15	23	14	20	25	23	44	46	48	94	117	†76	27	65	†—
Claims on Central Government	22a	7	6	17	7	5	16	7	65	622	117	65	†27	60	247	†—
Claims on Local Government	22b	....	....	....	....	....	....	....	....	....	....	....	59	82	77	†—
Claims on Nonfin.Pub.Enterprises	22c	....	....	....	....	....	....	....	....	....	....	....	1,825	2,609	4,684	†12
Claims on Private Sector	22d	293	398	531	532	594	708	775	1,393	2,010	2,573	3,132	†1,844	1,581	3,737	†14
Demand Deposits	24	83	147	172	162	195	200	183	305	427	531	664	†1,170	1,873	5,151	†18
Time, Savings,& Fgn.Currency Dep.	25	93	115	137	150	210	226	198	262	326	542	656	†1,063	1,673	3,387	†10
Money Market Instruments	26aa	....	....	....	....	....	....	....	....	....	....	....				
Foreign Liabilities	26c	24	30	43	75	59	147	227	335	443	115	124	†125	59	162	†—
Long-Term Foreign Liabilities	26cl	79	89	89	85	75	64	52	77	101	104	86	†142	139	389	†—
Central Government Deposits	26d	14	33	58	32	30	33	30	80	129	503	580	†400	229	1,102	†3
Credit from Monetary Authorities	26g	16	37	121	98	75	73	134	436	737	1,073	1,243	†754	853	1,215	†4
Liab. to Nonbank Financial Insts	26j	....	....	....	....	....	....	....	....	....	....	....	234	272	314	†1
Capital Accounts	27a	70	76	80	92	99	102	112	142	171	112	495	†665	781	788	†1
Other Items (Net)	27r	-22	-32	-60	-51	-29	-1	-32	-51	432	4	-240	†-151	-559	-960	†-4
Monetary Survey									*Thousandths (.000) of Gold Córdobas through 1985; Gold Córd. 1986-87;*							
Foreign Assets (Net)	31n	88	130	71	50	125	41	-256	-349	-834	-650	-869	†-3,311	-4,000	-13,121	†-36
Domestic Credit	32	310	391	486	541	618	748	977	1,590	3,058	3,133	4,080	†7,340	9,997	21,044	†54
Claims on Central Govt. (Net)	32an	17	-6	-45	9	24	40	202	197	1,048	560	948	†3,445	5,289	10,378	†21
Claims on Local Government	32b	....	....	....	....	....	....	....	....	....	....	....	59	82	77	†—
Claims on Nonfin.Pub.Enterprises	32c	....	....	....	....	....	....	....	....	....	....	....	1,895	2,717	4,890	†12
Claims on Private Sector	32d	293	398	531	532	594	708	775	1,393	2,010	2,573	3,132	†1,844	1,581	3,737	†14
Claims on Nonbank Financial Inst	32g	....	....	....	....	....	....	....	....	....	....	....	97	329	1,962	†6
Money	34	150	229	263	251	323	340	316	620	820	1,041	1,309	†2,271	4,169	10,955	†39
Quasi-Money	35	95	118	141	155	217	231	215	267	329	544	670	†1,360	2,126	4,166	†12
Money Market Instruments	36aa	....	....	....	....	....	....	....	....	....	....	....				
Liabs. of Central Bank: Securities	36ac	....	....	....	....	....	....	....	....	....	....	....				
Counterpart Funds	36e	....	....	....	....	....	....	....	....	....	....	....				
Liab. to Nonbank Financial Insts	36j	....	....	....	....	....	....	....	....	....	....	....	284	359	887	†2
Capital Accounts	37a	89	97	101	113	119	122	133	180	219	169	551	†718	834	914	†1
Other Items (Net)	37r	64	77	52	72	84	96	57	174	855	729	682	†-604	-1,491	-8,999	†-36
Money plus Quasi-Money	35l	245	347	403	406	540	571	530	886	1,149	1,585	1,979	†3,632	6,295	15,121	†51

Exchange Rates

Thousand SDRs in 1989-90, per SDR thereafter: End of Period

1987	1988	1989	1990	1991	1992	1993	1994	1995	1996	1997	1998	1999	2000	2001		
19.86	†247.61	10.03	853.60	†7.15	6.88	8.72	10.38	11.84	12.83	13.49	15.76	16.91	17.01	17.39	Principal Rate	aa

in 1989-90, per US$ thereafter: End of Period (ae) Period Average (rf)

1987	1988	1989	1990	1991	1992	1993	1994	1995	1996	1997	1998	1999	2000	2001		
14.00	†184.00	7.63	600.00	†5.00	5.00	6.35	7.11	7.97	8.92	10.00	11.19	12.32	13.06	13.84	Principal Rate	ae
20.53	†53.95	3.12	140.92	†4.27	5.00	5.62	6.72	7.55	8.44	9.45	10.58	11.81	12.69	13.37	Principal Rate	rf

Period Averages

1987	1988	1989	1990	1991	1992	1993	1994	1995	1996	1997	1998	1999	2000	2001		
			35,093.71	282.62	149.99	142.07	111.67	100.00	89.01	79.25	71.04	63.50	59.15	56.11	Principal Rate	ahx
		44,667.35	4,102.53	101.26	106.50	106.12	112.03	100.00	92.44	88.68	82.84	76.68	76.75	75.90	Nominal Effective Exchange Rate	nec
		17.52	53.90	99.37	114.49	116.07	108.83	100.00	98.29	100.74	103.58	104.35	113.10	116.52	Real Effective Exchange Rate	rec

Fund Position

End of Period

1987	1988	1989	1990	1991	1992	1993	1994	1995	1996	1997	1998	1999	2000	2001		
68.20	68.20	68.20	68.20	68.20	96.10	96.10	96.10	96.10	96.10	96.10	96.10	130.00	130.00	130.00	Quota	2f. s
.01	—	—	.02	.02	.06	.03	.01	—	.02	.03	.15	.16	.05	.26	SDRs	1b. s
—	—	—	—	—	—	—	—	—	—	—	—	—	—	—	Reserve Position in the Fund	1c. s
—	—	—	—	17.03	17.03	17.03	34.92	26.41	20.02	20.02	36.84	113.15	129.33	125.33	Total Fund Cred.&Loans Outstg.	2tl

International Liquidity

End of Period

1987	1988	1989	1990	1991	1992	1993	1994	1995	1996	1997	1998	1999	2000	2001		
17.41	38.10	115.80	106.63	134.13	130.48	55.04	141.01	136.20	197.32	377.94	350.41	509.71	488.46	379.93	Total Reserves minus Gold	1l. d
.01	—	—	.03	.03	.08	.04	.01	—	.02	.04	.21	.21	.06	.33	SDRs	1b. d
—	—	—	—	—	—	—	—	—	—	—	—	—	—	—	Reserve Position in the Fund	1c. d
17.40	38.10	115.80	106.60	134.10	130.40	55.00	141.00	136.20	197.30	377.90	350.20	509.50	488.40	379.60	Foreign Exchange	1d. d
.198	.312	.120	.153	.100	.475	.010	.013	.015	.015	.015	.015	.015	.015	.002	Gold (Million Fine Troy Ounces)	1ad
9.60	12.80	4.80	5.90	3.60	17.10	.42	.55	.63	.63	.63	.63	.63	.63	.08	Gold (National Valuation)	1and
3,237.13	3,637.93	3,560.99	3,809.93	4,120.70	4,340.22	3,586.21	3,470.70	2,936.22	2,113.12	2,086.84	2,046.56	1,993.95	2,134.78	1,787.42	Monetary Authorities: Other Liab.	4.. d
8.81	2.28	2.98	5.45	32.80	43.30	47.36	53.56	45.00	146.65	211.27	162.15	143.98	65.66	125.99	Deposit Money Banks: Assets	7a. d
30.94	1.09	.97	2.20	20.54	24.38	18.74	31.62	31.34	44.61	54.65	55.09	109.86	90.42	116.74	Liabilities	7b. d

Monetary Authorities

Thousands 1988-89; Millions Beginning 1990: End of Period

1987	1988	1989	1990	1991	1992	1993	1994	1995	1996	1997	1998	1999	2000	2001		
4	†11	893	†45	840	896	558	1,227	1,284	†2,199	4,036	4,202	6,468	6,625	5,451	Foreign Assets	11
119	†15	77	†52	1,080	20,498	21,646	23,257	22,469	†18,132	21,451	23,769	26,884	28,400	31,979	Claims on Central Government	12a
1	†—	17	†6	135	170	169	381	468	†98	101	113	124	77	82	Claims on Nonfin.Pub.Enterprises	12c
—	†—	—	†—	—	—	—	—	13	†206	260	315	303	307	349	Claims on Private Sector	12d
70	†23	328	†61	1,101	767	798	824	743	†152	806	99	327	2,013	6,049	Claims on Deposit Money Banks	12e
27	†3	51	†51	834	1,107	1,705	1,206	1,151	†3,168	3,004	4,028	4,203	4,453	4,705	Claims on Nonbank Financial Insts	12g
201	†23	604	†63	883	933	1,006	1,533	1,895	†2,546	3,373	4,038	4,268	4,468	6,332	Reserve Money	14
146	†13	324	†29	401	468	509	688	771	†864	1,096	1,340	1,735	1,761	1,920	of which: Currency Outside DMBs	14a
3	†—	—	—	50	18	18	18	12	†46						Time, Savings,& Fgn.Currency Dep.	15
									436	3,643	2,250	2,303	3,658	7,900	Liabs. of Central Bank: Securities	16ac
16	†234	11,522	†1,023	10,514	10,625	9,704	14,019	12,631	†12,327	12,701	13,191	19,607	23,067	21,755	Foreign Liabilities	16c
30	†435	15,648	†1,263	10,212	11,193	13,216	11,026	11,069	†6,788	8,427	10,298	6,868	7,008	5,165	Long-Term Foreign Liabilities	16cl
21	†3	37	†13	207	1,253	397	330	199	†242	175	591	1,673	1,976	643	Central Government Deposits	16d
									35	15	155	22	22	27	Counterpart Funds	16e
2	†1	4	†1	29	29	44	184	122	†119	13	—	—	—	—	Liab. to Nonbank Financial Insts	16j
—	†3	123	†13	187	183	188	213	299	†1,494	1,838	2,498	4,304	3,316	6,757	Capital Accounts	17a
-53	†-646	-26,571	†-2,162	-18,043	-828	302	-428	-97	†-76	-575	-555	-801	-2,107	-641	Other Items (Net)	17r
-26	†-576	-23,413	†-1,923	-12,718	—	—	—	—	†—	—	—	—	-1,280		of which: Valuation Adjustment	17rv

Deposit Money Banks

Thousands 1988-89; Millions Beginning 1990: End of Period

1987	1988	1989	1990	1991	1992	1993	1994	1995	1996	1997	1998	1999	2000	2001		
53	†16	249	†33	496	463	491	774	1,112	†1,681	2,324	2,753	2,627	2,729	4,593	Reserves	20
									158	1,365	1,367	1,506	2,885	6,360	Claims on Mon.Author.: Securities	20c
—	†—	23	†3	164	217	301	381	358	†1,309	2,112	1,815	1,774	857	1,744	Foreign Assets	21
1	†—	—	†—	—	—	3	—	—	†514	372	357	1,107	1,400	1,631	Claims on Central Government	22a
—	†—	—	†—	—	2	8	5	—	†35	7	7	210	243	—	Claims on Local Government	22b
116	†27	1,035	†104	728	17	12	41	10	†24	5	5	26	24	—	Claims on Nonfin.Pub.Enterprises	22c
71	†10	345	†57	1,119	2,035	3,050	4,076	5,159	†4,676	6,707	9,716	13,271	15,241	13,217	Claims on Private Sector	22d
138	†19	451	†21	324	373	295	408	471	†787	959	1,196	1,406	1,565	2,348	Demand Deposits	24
38	†8	325	†37	691	846	1,356	2,501	3,630	†5,748	9,250	12,404	14,622	15,632	22,302	Time, Savings,& Fgn.Currency Dep.	25
									365	509	360	320	270	263	Money Market Instruments	26aa
—	†—	7	†1	101	114	89	201	223	†310	443	485	1,120	758	908	Foreign Liabilities	26c
—	†—	—	†—	1	8	30	24	26	†89	103	132	233	423	707	Long-Term Foreign Liabilities	26cl
17	†2	56	†2	35	268	421	540	655	†756	1,099	798	1,662	1,382	19	Central Government Deposits	26d
70	†29	885	†75	1,054	698	759	779	752	†36	743	35	28	2,341	576	Credit from Monetary Authorities	26g
5	†—	7	†1	116	267	714	1,198	1,390	†274	484	676	879	971	1,446	Liab. to Nonbank Financial Insts	26j
—	†7	69	†48	—	—	503	649	406	†825	222	1,201	1,999	2,697	2,956	Capital Accounts	27a
-27	†-12	-149	†12	183	163	-307	-1,022	-914	†-792	-918	-1,268	-1,748	-2,660	-3,981	Other Items (Net)	27r

Monetary Survey

Thousands 1988-89; Millions Beginning 1990: End of Period

1987	1988	1989	1990	1991	1992	1993	1994	1995	1996	1997	1998	1999	2000	2001		
-42	†-658	-26,262	†-2,239	-19,824	-20,828	-22,180	-23,663	-22,307	†-16,005	-15,526	-18,089	-19,587	-23,773	-21,340	Foreign Assets (Net)	31n
298	†50	1,432	†255	3,653	22,312	25,770	28,096	28,417	†25,855	30,635	36,921	42,794	46,788	51,300	Domestic Credit	32
82	†10	-16	†37	838	18,980	20,828	22,387	21,616	†17,648	20,550	22,737	24,656	26,443	32,947	Claims on Central Govt. (Net)	32an
—	†—	—	†—	—	2	8	5	—	†35	7	7	210	243	—	Claims on Local Government	32b
117	†27	1,052	†110	862	188	180	422	478	†122	106	119	150	101	82	Claims on Nonfin.Pub.Enterprises	32c
71	†10	345	†57	1,119	2,035	3,050	4,076	5,172	†4,882	6,968	10,030	13,574	15,548	13,566	Claims on Private Sector	32d
27	†3	51	†51	834	1,107	1,705	1,206	1,151	†3,168	3,004	4,028	4,203	4,453	4,705	Claims on Nonbank Financial Inst	32g
284	†33	826	†53	758	845	806	1,097	1,242	†1,655	2,064	2,551	3,151	3,412	4,529	Money	34
41	†8	325	†37	691	896	1,374	2,518	3,641	†5,794	9,298	12,464	14,689	16,101	22,979	Quasi-Money	35
									365	509	360	320	270	263	Money Market Instruments	36aa
									278	2,278	883	797	773	1,540	Liabs. of Central Bank: Securities	36ac
									35	15	155	22	22	27	Counterpart Funds	36e
7	†1	11	†2	146	295	759	1,382	1,512	†392	497	676	879	971	1,446	Liab. to Nonbank Financial Insts	36j
—	†10	192	†61	187	183	691	862	705	†2,319	2,061	3,699	6,302	6,013	9,713	Capital Accounts	37a
-78	†-659	-26,184	†-2,137	-17,954	-735	-39	-1,426	-991	†-988	-1,614	-1,958	-2,953	-4,546	-10,538	Other Items (Net)	37r
326	†41	1,151	†90	1,450	1,741	2,179	3,616	4,884	†7,449	11,362	15,016	17,840	19,512	27,509	Money plus Quasi-Money	35l

Nicaragua

	1972	1973	1974	1975	1976	1977	1978	1979	1980	1981	1982	1983	1984	1985	1986
Nonbank Financial Institutions													*Thousands of Gold Córdobas through 1989;*		
Reserves 40	...	...	...	...	...	...	...	...	...	...	...	...	...	...	...
Foreign Assets 41	...	...	...	...	...	...	...	...	...	...	...	...	...	...	...
Claims on Central Government 42a	...	...	...	...	...	...	...	...	...	...	...	...	...	...	...
Claims on Private Sector 42d	...	...	...	...	...	...	...	...	...	...	...	...	...	...	...
Claims on Deposit Money Banks 42e	...	...	...	...	...	...	...	...	...	...	...	...	...	...	...
Foreign Liabilities 46c	...	...	...	...	...	...	...	...	...	...	...	...	...	...	...
Central Government Deposits 46d	...	...	...	...	...	...	...	...	...	...	...	...	...	...	...
Credit from Monetary Authorities 46g	...	...	...	...	...	...	...	...	...	...	...	...	...	...	...
Capital Accounts 47a	...	...	...	...	...	...	...	...	...	...	...	...	...	...	...
Other Items (Net) 47r	...	...	...	...	...	...	...	...	...	...	...	...	...	...	...
Financial Survey													*Thousands of Gold Córdobas through 1989;*		
Foreign Assets (Net) 51n	...	...	...	...	...	...	...	...	...	...	...	...	...	...	...
Domestic Credit 52	...	...	...	...	...	...	...	...	...	...	...	...	...	...	...
Claims on Central Govt. (Net) ... 52an	...	...	...	...	...	...	...	...	...	...	...	...	...	...	...
Claims on Local Government 52b	...	...	...	...	...	...	...	...	...	...	...	...	...	...	...
Claims on Nonfin.Pub.Enterprises 52c	...	...	...	...	...	...	...	...	...	...	...	...	...	...	...
Claims on Private Sector 52d	...	...	...	...	...	...	...	...	...	...	...	...	...	...	...
Liquid Liabilities 55l	...	...	...	...	...	...	...	...	...	...	...	...	...	...	...
Money Market Instruments 56aa	...	...	...	...	...	...	...	...	...	...	...	...	...	...	...
Liabs. of Central Bank: Securities 56ac	...	...	...	...	...	...	...	...	...	...	...	...	...	...	...
Counterpart Funds 56e	...	...	...	...	...	...	...	...	...	...	...	...	...	...	...
Capital Accounts 57a	...	...	...	...	...	...	...	...	...	...	...	...	...	...	...
Other Items (Net) 57r	...	...	...	...	...	...	...	...	...	...	...	...	...	...	...
Interest Rates													*Percent Per Annum*		
Discount Rate *(End of period)* 60	...	...	...	...	...	...	...	...	...	...	...	...	...	...	...
Savings Rate 60k	...	...	...	...	...	...	...	...	...	...	...	...	...	...	...
Deposit Rate 60l	...	...	...	...	...	...	...	...	...	...	...	...	...	...	...
Lending Rate 60p	...	...	...	...	...	...	...	...	...	...	...	...	...	...	...
Prices and Labor													*Index Numbers (1995=100):*		
Consumer Prices (1990=100 million) ... 64.a	19.0	24.1	27.3	29.4	30.2	33.7	35.2	52.2	70.6	87.4	109.1	143.0	193.7	618.9	4,836.0
Cons. Prices (1990=1 million) 64.b															
Consumer Prices 64.c	...	...	...	...	...	...	...	...	...	...	...	...	...	...	...
													Number in Thousands:		
Labor Force 67d	...	...	...	...	...	...	...	...	...	...	...	...	...	...	...
Employment 67e	...	...	...	...	...	...	...	...	...	...	...	...	...	290	303
Unemployment 67c	...	...	...	...	...	...	...	...	...	...	...	...	...	35	52
Unemployment Rate (%) 67r	...	...	...	...	...	...	...	...	...	...	...	...	...	3.2	4.7
International Transactions													*Millions of US Dollars*		
Exports .... 70..d	249.4	277.9	380.9	375.2	541.9	636.8	646.0	566.6	450.6	508.2	405.6	428.8	385.7	301.5	247.2
Imports, c.i.f. .... 71..d	218.5	327.0	561.7	516.9	532.1	762.0	596.0	360.2	887.3	999.4	775.6	825.6	848.4	964.3	856.8
Imports, f.o.b. 71.vd	197.2	299.4	504.7	466.1	481.9	659.4	540.4	335.5	822.3	932.5	723.6	778.1	799.6	878.2	782.0
Balance of Payments													*Millions of US Dollars:*		
Current Account, n.i.e. 78ald	...	...	...	...	...	−181.9	−24.9	180.2	−411.4	−591.6	−513.9	−507.4	−597.1	−770.9	−690.5
Goods: Exports f.o.b. 78aad	...	...	...	...	...	636.2	646.0	615.9	450.4	508.2	406.0	451.9	412.4	305.1	257.8
Goods: Imports f.o.b. 78abd	...	...	...	...	...	−704.2	−553.3	−388.9	−802.9	−922.4	−723.5	−742.3	−735.3	−794.1	−677.4
Trade Balance 78acd	...	...	...	...	...	−68.0	92.7	227.0	−352.5	−414.2	−317.5	−290.4	−322.9	−489.0	−419.6
Services: Credit 78add	...	...	...	...	...	83.1	74.2	56.3	44.4	45.1	40.8	46.1	48.4	39.3	29.5
Services: Debit 78aed	...	...	...	...	...	−139.2	−106.6	−123.6	−103.7	−110.2	−103.5	−128.2	−149.0	−129.6	−159.1
Balance on Goods & Services 78afd	...	...	...	...	...	−124.1	60.3	159.7	−411.8	−479.3	−380.2	−372.5	−423.5	−579.3	−549.2
Income: Credit 78agd	...	...	...	...	...	13.6	11.7	11.0	19.2	28.3	8.7	6.5	4.6	1.5	.7
Income: Debit 78ahd	...	...	...	...	...	−82.6	−106.4	−82.1	−142.7	−210.9	−193.9	−220.7	−268.0	−274.8	−254.3
Balance on Gds, Serv. & Inc. 78aid	...	...	...	...	...	−193.1	−34.4	88.6	−535.3	−661.9	−565.4	−586.7	−686.9	−852.6	−802.8
Current Transfers, n.i.e.: Credit 78ajd	...	...	...	...	...	12.7	10.8	92.1	124.0	70.4	51.6	79.3	89.8	81.7	112.3
Current Transfers: Debit 78akd	...	...	...	...	...	−1.5	−1.3	−.5	−.1	−.1	−.1	—	—	—	—
Capital Account, n.i.e. 78bcd	...	...	...	...	...	—	—	—	—	—	—	—	—	—	—
Capital Account, n.i.e.: Credit 78bad	...	...	...	...	...	—	—	—	—	—	—	—	—	—	—
Capital Account: Debit 78bbd	...	...	...	...	...	—	—	—	—	—	—	—	—	—	—
Financial Account, n.i.e. 78bjd	...	...	...	...	...	192.1	−104.1	−144.4	42.7	426.7	360.9	−93.0	183.6	361.7	−194.2
Direct Investment Abroad 78bdd	...	...	...	...	...	—	—	—	—	—	—	—	—	—	—
Dir. Invest. in Rep. Econ., n.i.e. 78bed	...	...	...	...	...	10.0	7.0	2.8	—	—	—	—	—	—	—
Portfolio Investment Assets 78bfd	...	...	...	...	...	—	—	—	—	—	—	—	—	—	—
Equity Securities 78bkd	...	...	...	...	...	—	—	—	—	—	—	—	—	—	—
Debt Securities 78bld	...	...	...	...	...	—	—	—	—	—	—	—	—	—	—
Portfolio Investment Liab., n.i.e. 78bgd	...	...	...	...	...	—	—	—	—	—	—	—	—	—	—
Equity Securities 78bmd	...	...	...	...	...	—	—	—	—	—	—	—	—	—	—
Debt Securities 78bnd	...	...	...	...	...	—	—	—	—	—	—	—	—	—	—
Financial Derivatives Assets 78bwd	...	...	...	...	...							...	...	...	...
Financial Derivatives Liabilities 78bxd	...	...	...	...	...							...	...	...	...
Other Investment Assets 78bhd	...	...	...	...	...	−115.7	−296.0	—	—	—	—	—	—	—	—
Monetary Authorities 78bod	...	...	...	...	...	—	—	—	—	...	...	—	—	—	—
General Government 78bpd	...	...	...	...	...	−4.4	−5.7	—	—	—	—	—	—	—	—
Banks 78bqd	...	...	...	...	...	—	—	—	—	—	—	—	—	—	—
Other Sectors 78brd	...	...	...	...	...	−111.3	−290.3	—	—	—	—	—	—	—	—
Other Investment Liab., n.i.e. 78bid	...	...	...	...	...	297.8	184.9	−147.2	42.7	426.7	360.9	−93.0	183.6	361.7	−194.2
Monetary Authorities 78bsd	...	...	...	...	...	9.4	26.3	55.1	108.8	395.0	211.9	−260.1	62.6	98.8	−104.1
General Government 78btd	...	...	...	...	...	140.5	34.1	13.8	83.5	132.3	210.0	154.4	108.0	304.2	−74.7
Banks 78bud	...	...	...	...	...	54.6	48.6	56.1	5.5	−65.0	18.1	11.8	−9.5	2.4	.5
Other Sectors 78bvd	...	...	...	...	...	93.3	75.9	−272.2	−155.1	−35.6	−79.1	.9	22.5	−43.7	−15.9
Net Errors and Omissions 78cad	...	...	...	...	...	−3.9	−10.5	−38.5	−74.7	15.8	10.8	−106.0	−38.7	−186.8	−183.6
Overall Balance 78cbd	...	...	...	...	...	6.3	−139.5	−2.7	−443.4	−149.1	−142.2	−706.3	−452.3	−596.0	−1,068.3
Reserves and Related Items 79dad	...	...	...	...	...	−6.3	139.5	2.7	443.4	149.1	142.2	706.3	452.3	596.0	1,068.3
Reserve Assets 79dbd	...	...	...	...	...	−1.0	84.4	−50.6	207.7	−64.8	−31.3	−13.7	−244.4	−7.8	211.3
Use of Fund Credit and Loans 79dcd	...	...	...	...	...	−7.9	—	53.3	−6.2	−21.4	−4.1	−4.6	−4.4	−8.9	—
Exceptional Financing 79ded	...	...	...	...	...	2.6	55.1	—	241.9	235.4	177.6	724.5	701.0	612.7	857.0

1987	1988	1989	1990	1991	1992	1993	1994	1995	1996	1997	1998	1999	2000	2001		

Millions of Gold Córdobas Beginning 1990: End of Period — **Nonbank Financial Institutions**

1987	1988	1989	1990	1991	1992	1993	1994	1995	1996	1997	1998	1999	2000	2001		
....		5	†1	21	24	39	182	122	†122	4	—	—	—	—	Reserves	40
....		4	†—	3	13	20	40	15	†2	2	—	—	—	—	Foreign Assets	41
....						....	....	....	319	367	—	—	—	—	Claims on Central Government	42a
....	3	55	†119	1,011	1,014	1,285	—	—	†442	504	690	906	1,028	1,291	Claims on Private Sector	42d
....		4	†1	113	354	742	1,199	1,391	†4	113	14	32	14	75	Claims on Deposit Money Banks	42e
....	—	—	†—	—	—	—	—	—	†303	367	1	111	122	298	Foreign Liabilities	46c
....											19	125	226	316	Central Government Deposits	46d
....	3	60	†87	1,064	1,086	1,705	1,206	1,151	†90	100	80	48	26	—	Credit from Monetary Authorities	46g
....		−53	†30	−122	117	23	134	160	†517	563	579	668	754	800	Capital Accounts	47a
....	1	62	†3	206	201	359	81	217	†−21	−40	25	−13	−85	−48	Other Items (Net)	47r

Millions of Gold Córdobas Beginning 1990: End of Period — **Financial Survey**

1987	1988	1989	1990	1991	1992	1993	1994	1995	1996	1997	1998	1999	2000	2001		
....	−658	−26,257	†−2,239	−19,821	−20,816	−22,161	−23,622	−22,292	†−16,305	−15,892	−18,090	−19,697	−23,895	−21,639	Foreign Assets (Net)	51n
....	51	1,436	†323	3,830	22,219	25,351	26,890	27,266	†23,448	28,501	33,563	39,372	43,137	47,570	Domestic Credit	52
....	10	−16	†37	838	18,980	20,828	22,387	21,616	†17,968	20,917	22,718	24,531	26,217	32,631	Claims on Central Govt. (Net)	52an
....			†—	—	2	8	5	—	35	7	7	210	243	—	Claims on Local Government	52b
....	27	1,052	†110	862	188	180	422	478	122	106	119	150	101	82	Claims on Nonfin.Pub.Enterprises	52c
....	13	400	†176	2,130	3,049	4,335	4,076	5,172	†5,323	7,472	10,720	14,480	16,576	14,857	Claims on Private Sector	52d
....	41	1,146	†89	1,428	1,717	2,140	3,434	4,762	†7,326	11,358	15,015	17,840	19,512	27,509	Liquid Liabilities	55l
....										365	509	360	320	270	263	Money Market Instruments	56aa
....										278	2,278	883	797	773	1,540	Liabs. of Central Bank: Securities	56ac
....										35	15	155	22	22	27	Counterpart Funds	56e
....	10	139	†92	66	300	714	995	865	†2,837	2,624	4,278	6,970	6,766	10,513	Capital Accounts	57a
....	−658	−26,106	†−2,096	−17,485	−613	336	−1,162	−653	†−3,699	−4,174	−5,218	−6,274	−8,101	−13,921	Other Items (Net)	57r

Percent Per Annum — **Interest Rates**

1987	1988	1989	1990	1991	1992	1993	1994	1995	1996	1997	1998	1999	2000	2001		
....	12,874.6	311.0	10.0	15.0	15.0	11.8	10.5								Discount Rate (End of period)	60
....	2,229.8	125.2	7.0	7.8	8.1	8.5	8.8	8.9	9.0	8.9	8.6	8.5	8.4	8.1	Savings Rate	60k
....	107,379.1	1,585.9	9.5	11.6	12.0	11.6	11.7	11.1	12.3	12.4	10.8	10.3	9.4	9.0	Deposit Rate	60l
....	121,906.0	558.0	22.0	17.9	19.3	20.2	20.1	19.9	20.7	21.0	21.6	22.1	21.4	22.8	Lending Rate	60p

Period Averages — **Prices and Labor**

1987	1988	1989	1990	1991	1992	1993	1994	1995	1996	1997	1998	1999	2000	2001		
48,936.4 *,***,***															Consumer Prices (1990=100 million)	64.a
	50.4	2,456.0	186,299.0												Cons. Prices (1990=1 million)	64.b
....	....	....	1.9	56.7	70.2	84.5	90.1	100.0	111.6	121.9	137.8	153.3	....		Consumer Prices	64.c

Period Averages

1987	1988	1989	1990	1991	1992	1993	1994	1995	1996	1997	1998	1999	2000	2001		
....	....	....		1,299		....		1,385	1,441	....	1,630	1,695	1,815	....	Labor Force	67d
312	296	261	258	229	215	207	203	208	221	234	260	....			....	Employment	67e
67	72	107	146	194	....	....	....	245	225	208	216	185	178	....	Unemployment	67c
5.8	6.0	8.4	11.1	14.0	....	....	....	16.9	14.9	13.3	13.3	10.9	9.8	....	Unemployment Rate (%)	67r

Millions of US Dollars — **International Transactions**

1987	1988	1989	1990	1991	1992	1993	1994	1995	1996	1997	1998	1999	2000	2001		
272.8	232.7	310.7	330.6	272.4	223.1	267.0	334.7	456.8	466.4	576.8	573.2	545.3	631.1	605.6	Exports	70..d
826.8	805.2	614.9	637.5	751.4	855.1	744.0	870.3	992.7	1,153.9	1,449.7	1,491.6	1,861.9	1,758.6	1,776.4	Imports, c.i.f.	71..d
734.4	716.6	547.3	567.3	668.7	770.9	669.6	783.8	897.1	1,043.5	1,370.7	1,396.9	1,698.5	1,593.3	1,635.5	Imports, f.o.b.	71.v d

Minus Sign Indicates Debit — **Balance of Payments**

1987	1988	1989	1990	1991	1992	1993	1994	1995	1996	1997	1998	1999	2000	2001		
−690.4	−715.4	−361.7	−385.2	−534.2	−834.0	−644.3	−714.3	−577.6	−629.2	−672.9	−503.8	−697.3	−505.0	....	Current Account, n.i.e.	78al d
295.1	235.7	318.7	332.4	268.1	223.1	267.0	338.6	470.5	470.2	581.6	580.1	552.4	652.8	....	Goods: Exports f.o.b.	78aa d
−734.4	−718.3	−547.3	−569.7	−688.0	−770.8	−659.4	−781.4	−882.3	−1,044.3	−1,371.2	−1,397.1	−1,698.2	−1,647.3	....	Goods: Imports f.o.b.	78ab d
−439.3	−482.6	−228.6	−237.3	−419.9	−547.7	−392.4	−442.8	−411.8	−574.1	−789.6	−817.0	−1,145.8	−994.5	....	Trade Balance	78ac d
29.5	37.4	22.0	59.8	70.2	86.2	100.2	125.2	141.3	171.8	213.4	248.2	283.5	300.3	....	Services: Credit	78ad d
−160.5	−138.1	−119.2	−112.3	−136.2	−148.3	−156.6	−172.9	−220.5	−252.8	−239.4	−267.8	−334.7	−338.8	....	Services: Debit	78ae d
−570.3	−583.3	−325.8	−289.8	−485.9	−609.8	−448.8	−490.5	−491.0	−655.1	−815.6	−836.6	−1,197.0	−1,033.0	....	Balance on Goods & Services	78af d
1.4	2.1	6.8	11.8	9.7	7.5	5.4	6.7	7.1	10.5	14.7	26.0	30.7	30.7	....	Income: Credit	78ag d
−245.3	−264.2	−211.6	−228.8	−373.0	−502.3	−434.5	−478.9	−379.2	−334.8	−279.4	−211.2	−227.5	−231.9	....	Income: Debit	78ah d
−814.2	−845.4	−530.6	−506.8	−849.2	−1,104.6	−877.9	−962.7	−863.1	−979.4	−1,080.3	−1,021.8	−1,393.8	−1,234.2	....	Balance on Gds, Serv. & Inc.	78ai d
123.8	130.0	168.9	121.6	315.0	270.6	233.6	248.4	285.5	350.2	407.4	518.0	696.5	729.2	....	Current Transfers: n.i.e.: Credit	78aj d
						....								....	Current Transfers: Debit	78ak d
—	—	—	—	—	—	—	—	—	—	—	—	—	—	....	Capital Account, n.i.e.	78bc d
—	—	—	—	—	—	—	—	—	—	—	—	—	—	....	Capital Account, n.i.e.: Credit	78ba d
—	—	—	—	—	—	—	—	—	—	—	—	—	—	....	Capital Account: Debit	78bb d
112.2	243.0	−89.3	−161.1	−615.7	−538.3	−502.8	−901.9	−625.0	−355.0	3.2	197.1	488.2	260.7	....	Financial Account, n.i.e.	78bj d
														....	Direct Investment Abroad	78bd d
				15.0	38.8	40.0	75.4	97.0	173.1	183.7	300.0	253.7		....	Dir. Invest. in Rep. Econ., n.i.e.	78be d
				....	....	....	....	....	....	....	....	....		....	Portfolio Investment Assets	78bf d
				....	....	....	....	....	....	....	....	....		....	Equity Securities	78bk d
				....	....	....	....	....	....	....	....	....		....	Debt Securities	78bl d
				....	....	....	....	....	....	....	....	....		....	Portfolio Investment Liab., n.i.e.	78bg d
				....	....	....	....	....	....	....	....	....		....	Equity Securities	78bm d
				....	....	....	....	....	....	....	....	....		....	Debt Securities	78bn d
														....	Financial Derivatives Assets	78bw d
														....	Financial Derivatives Liabilities	78bx d
—	—	—	−21.1	−5.9	−10.1	−1.3	−32.0	−54.3	−70.8	55.2	22.2	79.9		....	Other Investment Assets	78bh d
														....	Monetary Authorities	78bo d
—	—	—	−8.0	—	—	—	—	—	—	—	—	—		....	General Government	78bp d
—	—	—	−13.1	−6.4	−10.1	−1.3	−32.0	−54.3	−70.8	55.2	22.2	79.9		....	Banks	78bq d
														....	Other Sectors	78br d
112.2	243.0	−89.3	−161.1	−594.6	−547.4	−531.5	−940.6	−668.4	−397.7	−99.1	−41.8	166.0	−72.9	....	Other Investment Liab., n.i.e.	78bi d
−119.3	131.4	−20.1	−78.4	−131.4	−88.0	−94.9	−544.3	−221.7	−126.1	−106.0	−18.1	62.4	−39.4	....	Monetary Authorities	78bs d
230.0	132.9	−67.2	−57.9	−380.6	−459.7	−390.7	−418.7	−381.2	−295.4	−103.1	−154.8	−63.9	−73.6	....	General Government	78bt d
6.8	−10.2	−5.3	−16.9	4.2	−1.7	−16.6	14.3	5.8	6.0	25.1	.3	63.6	−19.2	....	Banks	78bu d
−5.3	−11.1	3.3	−7.9	−86.8	2.0	−29.3	8.1	−71.3	17.8	84.9	130.8	103.9	59.3	....	Other Sectors	78bv d
−78.9	51.9	−54.7	−149.2	17.2	60.2	128.1	50.4	158.8	174.1	355.1	−102.9	−251.2	−209.8	....	Net Errors and Omissions	78ca d
−657.1	−420.5	−505.7	−695.5	−1,132.7	−1,312.0	−1,019.0	−1,565.8	−1,043.8	−810.1	−314.6	−409.6	−460.3	−454.1	....	Overall Balance	78cb d
657.1	420.5	505.7	695.5	1,132.7	1,312.0	1,019.0	1,565.8	1,043.8	810.1	314.6	409.6	460.3	454.1	....	Reserves and Related Items	79da d
−6.2	−43.9	−78.6	7.3	−41.7	−.5	79.4	−84.6	11.5	−53.1	−173.2	30.3	−156.5	16.8	....	Reserve Assets	79db d
—	—	—	23.1	—	—	26.1	−12.9	−9.3	—	22.6	105.3	20.9		....	Use of Fund Credit and Loans	79dc d
663.3	464.4	584.3	688.2	1,151.3	1,312.5	939.6	1,624.3	1,045.2	872.5	487.8	356.7	511.5	416.4	....	Exceptional Financing	79de d

Nicaragua

		1972	1973	1974	1975	1976	1977	1978	1979	1980	1981	1982	1983	1984	1985	1986
Government Finance											*Thousandths (.000) of Gold Córdobas through 1985; Gold Córd. 1986-87;*					
Deficit (-) or Surplus	80	−43	−41	−117	−129	−102	−209	−230	−192	−348	−390	−654	−1,308	−2,043	−5,023	†−14
Revenue	81	130	187	273	265	305	359	320	382	922	1,192	1,456	2,057	3,169	7,461	†28
Grants Received	81z	—	—	—	—	—	—	1	—	26	45	49	123	69	135	†1
Expenditure	82	174	229	390	394	408	569	552	557	1,296	1,627	2,159	3,488	5,281	12,619	†43
Lending Minus Repayments	83	—	—	—	—	—	−1	−1	17	—	—	—	—	—	—	†—
Financing																
Domestic	84a	....	....	−9	24	63	88	218	164	186	286	533	971	1,790	4,999	†14
Foreign	85a	....	....	126	105	38	122	13	28	161	102	121	336	252	23	†—
Debt: Cordobas	88b	....	....	....	....	....	....	....	....	66	102	146	648	568	....	....
Foreign Currency	89b	....	....	....	....	....	....	....	....	41	20	40	9	111	....	....
National Accounts											*Thousandths (.000) of Gold Córdobas through 1985; Gold Córd. 1986-87;*					
Househ.Cons.Expend.,incl.NPISHs	96f	869.0	1,173.6	1,584.9	1,725.0	1,778.5	2,051.4	2,030.2	2,151.8	3,439.6	3,625.5	3,854.6	3,738.0	5,002.3	11,143.9	†48.7
Government Consumption Expend.	91f	115.5	124.3	164.0	200.9	241.0	278.5	351.5	516.8	818.4	1,071.3	1,325.6	2,064.6	3,174.1	8,224.9	†30.7
Gross Fixed Capital Formation	93e													1,740.2	4,780.6	†12.1
Changes in Inventories	93i	....	....	....	....	....	....	....	....	....	....	....	....	249.1	536.6	†2.5
Exports of Goods and Services	90c	435.2	432.0	619.0	624.4	853.6	1,006.4	1,032.0	1,220.0	1,007.8	1,094.0	906.0	1,277.4	1,480.7	3,408.1	†11.1
Imports of Goods and Services (-)	98c	365.8	579.0	907.6	822.7	824.1	1,174.1	937.6	816.9	1,800.6	2,046.7	1,477.8	1,975.6	2,653.5	5,039.7	†18.2
Gross Domestic Product (GDP)	99b	1,210.3	1,513.5	2,126.0	2,187.7	2,515.3	2,944.7	2,849.2	2,898.7	4,154.0	4,889.8	5,662.1	6,574.8	8,993.4	23,048.6	†87.0
Net Primary Income from Abroad	98.n	....	....	....	....	....	....	....	....	....	....	....	....	....	....	....
Gross National Income (GNI)	99a	....	....	....	....	....	....	....	....	....	....	....	....	....	....	....
Net National Income	99e	....	....	....	....	....	....	....	....	....	....	....	....	....	....	....
GDP Vol.1980 Prices	99b.p	†4.2	4.5	5.2	5.1	5.4	5.9	5.4	4.0	4.2	4.4	4.3	4.5	4.5	4.3	4.3
GDP Volume (1995=100)	99bvp	108.7	115.6	132.1	131.9	138.7	150.3	138.5	101.9	106.6	112.3	111.4	116.5	114.7	110.0	108.9
GDP Deflator (1995=100)	99bip	—	—	—	—	—	—	—	—	—	—	—	—	—	—	—
																Millions:
Population	99z	1.95	2.01	2.08	2.15	2.24	2.32	2.41	2.64	2.73	2.86	2.96	3.06	3.16	3.27	3.38

	1987	1988	1989	1990	1991	1992	1993	1994	1995	1996	1997	1998	1999	2000	2001		

Thousands 1988-89; Millions Beg. 1990: Year Ending December 31 — **Government Finance**

	1987	1988	1989	1990	1991	1992	1993	1994	1995	1996	1997	1998	1999	2000	2001		
	−87	†−16	−106	†−291	305	−302	−4	−4	−68	−254	−243	−415	−1,282	−2,357 P	−3,900 P	Deficit (-) or Surplus	80
	149	†13	705	†230	1,447	1,892	2,222	2,222	3,134	3,654	4,660	5,906	6,739	7,541 P	7,654 P	Revenue	81
	3	†—	103	†25	860	400	806	806	1,191	1,149	822	675	1,935	1,874 P	1,712 P	Grants Received	81z
	240	†30	914	†546	1,935	2,578	3,009	3,009	4,246	5,055	5,719	6,995	9,774	11,755 P	13,136 P	Expenditure	82
	—	†—	—	†—	67	16	23	23	147	2	6	—	182	17 P	130 P	Lending Minus Repayments	83
																Financing	
	88	†16	−3	†165	−344	−568	—	—	100	−598	−22	−1,266	−1,304	619 P	2,375 P	Domestic	84a
	—	†—	109	†126	39	870	4	4	−32	852	265	1,680	2,586	1,738 P	1,525 P	Foreign	85a
	....	....	....	....	....	....	....	....	....	....	....	....	....	....	....	Debt: Cordobas	88b
																Foreign Currency	89b

Thousands 1988-89; Millions Beginning 1990 — **National Accounts**

	1987	1988	1989	1990	1991	1992	1993	1994	1995	1996	1997	1998	1999	2000	2001		
	287.1	†54.0	2,498.3	†1,005.4	6,452.2	8,553.3	9,714.9	10,650.8	12,117.6	14,984.1	17,782.4	20,394.7	24,877.6	27,710.9	....	Househ.Cons.Expend.,incl.NPISHs	96f
	189.2	†21.4	837.2	†508.3	1,483.9	1,763.4	1,890.7	1,968.2	2,170.9	2,731.6	3,176.1	3,656.9	4,927.6	5,733.7	....	Government Consumption Expend.	91f
	72.8	†18.6	881.1	†325.8	1,358.3	1,848.1	2,133.6	2,702.9	3,408.3	4,294.8	5,787.7	7,300.8	11,258.8	10,568.8	....	Gross Fixed Capital Formation	93e
	14.5	†−.9	−16.8	†−14.4	141.9	27.5	−41.2	29.7	39.2	81.9	105.1	88.0	54.9	−110.4	....	Changes in Inventories	93i
	65.0	†11.9	1,020.4	†390.4	1,575.7	1,546.4	2,195.9	3,027.6	4,404.7	5,047.4	6,960.5	8,056.7	9,021.5	11,165.0	....	Exports of Goods and Services	90c
	76.0	†38.7	2,044.5	†698.8	3,791.7	4,774.8	5,144.5	6,406.7	8,285.3	10,936.1	15,210.8	17,615.7	24,014.5	24,658.7	....	Imports of Goods and Services (-)	98c
	552.6	†66.3	3,175.7	†1,516.7	7,220.6	8,964.0	10,749.5	11,972.4	13,855.3	16,203.7	18,601.0	21,881.4	26,125.9	30,409.3	....	Gross Domestic Product (GDP)	99b
	....	†−.5	−11.7	†−215.9	−1,687.1	−2,477.0	−2,642.2	−3,174.5	−2,801.0	−2,735.6	−2,500.9	−1,960.8	−2,324.0	−2,541.9	....	Net Primary Income from Abroad	98.n
	....	†60.8	3,553.0	†1,300.8	5,533.6	6,487.0	8,107.3	8,797.9	11,054.3	13,468.0	16,100.1	19,920.5	23,801.9	27,867.3	....	Gross National Income (GNI)	99a
	....	†58.4	3,409.7	....	....	....	....	....	....	....	....	....	....	....	....	Net National Income	99e
	4.2	3.7	3.6	3.6	3.6	3.6	3.6	3.7	3.9	4.1	4.3	4.6	4.8		....	GDP Vol.1980 Prices	99b.p
	108.1	94.6	93.0	93.0	92.8	93.1	92.8	95.9	100.0	104.7	110.1	116.8	122.7	....		GDP Volume (1995=100)	99bv p
	—	—	—	11.8	56.2	69.5	83.6	90.1	100.0	111.7	122.0	135.2	153.7	....		GDP Deflator (1995=100)	99bi p

Midyear Estimates

	1987	1988	1989	1990	1991	1992	1993	1994	1995	1996	1997	1998	1999	2000	2001		
	3.50	3.62	3.74	3.87	4.00	4.13	4.26	4.40	4.43	4.55	4.67	4.80	4.94	5.07	5.21	**Population**	99z

(See notes in the back of the book.)

Niger

		1972	1973	1974	1975	1976	1977	1978	1979	1980	1981	1982	1983	1984	1985	1986
Exchange Rates															*Francs per SDR:*	
Official Rate	aa	278.00	284.00	272.08	262.55	288.70	285.76	272.28	264.78	287.99	334.52	370.92	436.97	470.11	415.26	394.78
															Francs per US Dollar:	
Official Rate	ae	256.05	235.42	222.22	224.27	248.49	235.25	209.00	201.00	225.80	287.40	336.25	417.37	479.60	378.05	322.75
Official Rate	rf	252.03	222.89	240.70	214.31	238.95	245.68	225.66	212.72	211.28	271.73	328.61	381.07	436.96	449.26	346.31
Fund Position															*Millions of SDRs:*	
Quota	2f. s	13.0	13.0	13.0	13.0	13.0	13.0	16.0	16.0	24.0	24.0	24.0	33.7	33.7	33.7	33.7
SDRs	1b. s	4.4	4.4	4.4	4.4	4.4	4.4	4.4	6.0	5.8	7.5	7.5	4.6	2.2	—	1.0
Reserve Position in the Fund	1c. s	2.1	2.1	2.1	2.1	2.1	3.1	5.0	5.0	6.0	6.0	6.1	8.6	8.6	8.6	8.6
Total Fund Cred.&Loans Outstg.	2tl	—	—	—	—	—	—	5.4	5.4	12.7	12.7	12.7	43.5	56.8	71.3	86.8
International Liquidity												*Millions of US Dollars Unless Otherwise Indicated:*				
Total Reserves minus Gold	1l. d	41.3	50.8	45.5	50.3	82.5	101.1	128.3	131.7	125.9	105.3	29.6	53.2	88.7	136.4	189.2
SDRs	1b. d	4.8	5.3	5.4	5.1	5.1	5.3	5.7	8.0	7.4	8.8	8.2	4.8	2.2	—	1.2
Reserve Position in the Fund	1c. d	2.3	2.5	2.6	2.5	2.5	3.8	6.6	6.6	7.7	7.0	6.8	9.0	8.4	9.4	10.5
Foreign Exchange	1d. d	34.3	42.9	37.5	42.6	74.9	92.0	116.1	117.1	110.8	89.6	14.6	39.4	78.1	127.0	177.6
Gold (Million Fine Troy Ounces)	1ad	....	....	....	....	—	.006	.008	.011	.011	.011	.011	.011	.011	.011	.011
Gold (National Valuation)	1an d	....	....	....	....	—	.2	.4	.5	.5	4.7	4.7	4.3	3.7	3.6	4.5
Monetary Authorities: Other Liab.	4.. d	.1	.4	.6	1.1	6.1	3.9	3.7	5.0	4.7	1.1	3.5	12.9	7.8	10.9	14.7
Deposit Money Banks: Assets	7a. d	5.7	7.0	9.6	6.8	11.5	23.2	17.3	36.2	17.9	15.4	8.8	16.4	9.9	6.5	11.9
Liabilities	7b. d	9.4	11.1	11.8	12.0	16.7	24.5	45.5	79.9	126.9	99.3	155.5	130.7	103.6	114.7	124.4
Monetary Authorities															*Billions of Francs:*	
Foreign Assets	11	10.6	11.7	10.1	11.3	20.5	23.8	26.8	26.5	28.4	30.3	10.0	22.2	42.5	51.6	61.1
Claims on Central Government	12a	—	—	—	—	—	.6	4.4	4.6	10.9	12.2	15.9	27.9	31.1	38.9	47.7
Claims on Deposit Money Banks	12e	.1	.2	4.4	6.2	1.2	1.0	6.4	13.6	13.5	22.3	30.7	33.3	20.8	20.3	26.3
Claims on Other Financial Insts	12f	—	—	—	—	.2	.2	.2	.3	.4	.4	.4	.2	.1	—	—
Reserve Money	14	6.5	7.4	10.5	10.1	14.2	17.2	26.5	30.0	34.8	41.1	41.7	38.3	48.7	58.3	63.7
of which: Currency Outside DMBs	14a	6.2	6.7	9.4	9.4	13.4	14.8	19.7	27.3	31.1	34.8	35.3	31.5	30.7	33.3	40.5
Foreign Liabilities	16c	—	.1	.1	.2	1.5	.9	3.7	3.9	8.2	8.0	9.4	27.9	33.6	36.6	42.3
Central Government Deposits	16d	2.8	3.0	2.5	6.0	4.9	6.2	7.4	10.9	10.7	16.6	6.8	19.8	16.7	16.5	28.4
Other Items (Net)	17r	1.4	1.3	1.3	1.1	1.4	1.3	.3	.2	-.5	-.5	-.9	-2.4	-4.5	-.6	.8
Deposit Money Banks															*Billions of Francs:*	
Reserves	20	.2	.5	.9	.6	.7	2.2	6.8	2.5	3.8	6.3	4.6	6.8	17.7	24.9	23.1
Foreign Assets	21	1.5	1.6	2.1	1.5	2.9	5.5	3.6	7.3	4.0	4.4	3.0	6.8	4.8	2.4	3.9
Claims on Central Government	22a	.8	1.0	1.2	3.2	4.4	4.8	5.2	5.3	10.4	19.0	23.7	23.9	23.4	21.7	20.7
Claims on Private Sector	22d	10.3	12.2	20.7	28.1	27.5	31.3	52.5	74.2	89.1	102.6	111.3	118.3	108.3	101.2	114.0
Claims on Other Financial Insts	22f	—	—	—	—	—	—	—	.6	.6	.6	.7	.5	.3	.1	.1
Demand Deposits	24	4.7	6.4	7.6	10.1	10.7	16.6	25.9	29.0	32.3	38.8	34.5	33.8	45.9	45.6	41.1
Time Deposits	25	1.5	1.9	2.7	2.2	4.5	5.3	7.8	7.2	13.3	19.3	12.0	16.1	22.6	27.5	38.1
Foreign Liabilities	26c	1.0	1.3	1.4	1.5	3.1	4.9	8.1	12.6	19.2	12.0	32.3	26.4	21.7	16.6	13.9
Long-Term Foreign Liabilities	26cl	1.4	1.3	1.2	1.2	1.0	.9	1.4	3.5	9.5	16.6	20.0	28.1	28.0	26.7	26.3
Central Government Deposits	26d	1.4	1.6	6.2	8.8	11.7	15.4	13.3	17.2	17.8	17.1	15.3	15.3	17.4	19.1	21.8
Credit from Monetary Authorities	26g	.1	.2	4.4	6.3	1.2	1.0	6.4	13.6	13.5	22.4	30.7	33.3	20.9	20.6	26.4
Other Items (Net)	27r	2.7	2.7	1.5	3.4	3.3	-.2	5.1	6.8	2.4	6.8	-1.6	3.3	-2.2	-5.8	-5.7
Treasury Claims: Private Sector	22d. i	.4	.3	.3	.5	.8	1.1	1.5	1.2	1.6	1.6	2.3	—	.1	—	.6
Post Office: Checking Deposits	24.. i	.5	.5	.7	.6	.7	.9	.7	1.0	1.3	1.1	1.1	1.2	1.8	1.7	1.5
Monetary Survey															*Billions of Francs:*	
Foreign Assets (Net)	31n	11.0	11.9	10.7	11.0	18.7	23.4	18.6	17.3	5.1	14.7	-28.7	-25.3	-8.0	.8	8.7
Domestic Credit	32	7.3	9.2	13.8	17.1	16.2	16.3	42.4	57.9	84.2	102.3	131.1	136.9	130.8	127.9	133.8
Claims on Central Govt. (Net)	32an	-3.4	-3.3	-7.2	-11.5	-12.3	-16.4	-11.9	-18.4	-7.5	-3.0	16.3	17.9	22.0	26.6	19.1
Claims on Private Sector	32d	10.7	12.5	21.0	28.5	28.3	32.4	54.0	75.4	90.7	104.2	113.6	118.3	108.4	101.2	114.6
Claims on Other Financial Insts	32f	—	—	—	—	.2	.2	.2	.9	1.0	1.1	1.1	.7	.4	.1	.1
Money	34	11.4	13.6	17.6	20.1	24.8	32.3	46.4	57.3	64.6	74.8	70.9	66.5	78.4	80.6	83.0
Quasi-Money	35	1.5	1.9	2.7	2.2	4.5	5.3	7.8	7.2	13.3	19.3	12.0	16.1	22.6	27.5	38.1
Long-Term Foreign Liabilities	36cl	1.4	1.3	1.2	1.2	1.0	.9	1.4	3.5	9.5	16.6	20.0	28.1	28.0	26.7	26.3
Other Items (Net)	37r	4.1	4.3	3.0	4.6	4.6	1.2	5.4	7.2	1.9	6.3	-.7	.9	-6.3	-6.2	-4.8
Money plus Quasi-Money	35l	12.9	15.5	20.3	22.3	29.2	37.6	54.2	64.5	77.9	94.1	83.0	82.7	101.0	108.1	121.1
Other Banking Institutions															*Billions of Francs:*	
Savings Deposits	45	.11	.12	.14	.17	.19	.23	.28	.38	.55	.67	.76	.89	1.00	1.25	1.61
Liquid Liabilities	55l	13.0	15.6	20.5	22.5	29.4	37.9	54.5	64.9	78.5	94.7	83.7	83.6	102.0	109.4	122.7

	1987	1988	1989	1990	1991	1992	1993	1994	1995	1996	1997	1998	1999	2000	2001	
Exchange Rates																
End of Period																
Official Rate .... aa	378.78	407.68	380.32	364.84	370.48	378.57	404.89	†780.44	728.38	753.06	807.94	791.61	†896.19	918.49	935.39	
End of Period (ae) Period Average (rf)																
Official Rate .... ae	267.00	302.95	289.40	256.45	259.00	275.32	294.77	†534.60	490.00	523.70	598.81	562.21	†652.95	704.95	744.31	
Official Rate .... rf	300.54	297.85	319.01	272.26	282.11	264.69	283.16	†555.20	499.15	511.55	583.67	589.95	†615.70	711.98	733.04	
Fund Position																
End of Period																
Quota .... 2f. s	33.7	33.7	33.7	33.7	33.7	48.3	48.3	48.3	48.3	48.3	48.3	48.3	65.8	65.8	65.8	
SDRs .... 1b. s	.2	.1	.9	—	.3		.4	.3	.2	1.3	.1	.1	1.0	—	.3	
Reserve Position in the Fund .... 1c. s	8.6	8.6	8.6	8.6	8.6	8.6	8.6	8.6	8.6	8.6	8.6	8.6	8.6	8.6	8.6	
Total Fund Cred.&Loans Outstg. 2tl	86.3	70.3	64.4	59.7	51.3	44.6	37.7	41.8	35.0	36.6	45.0	54.1	49.6	56.8	64.3	
International Liquidity																
End of Period																
Total Reserves minus Gold .... 1l. d	248.5	232.1	212.3	222.2	202.8	225.0	192.0	110.3	94.7	78.5	53.3	53.1	39.2	80.3	106.9	
SDRs .... 1b. d	.2	.2	1.2	.1	.4	—	.6	.4	.3	1.9	.2	.2	1.3	—	.3	
Reserve Position in the Fund .... 1c. d	12.1	11.5	11.2	12.2	12.2	11.8	11.8	12.5	12.7	12.3	11.6	12.1	11.7	11.2	10.8	
Foreign Exchange .... 1d. d	236.1	220.4	199.8	210.0	190.1	213.2	179.7	97.4	81.7	64.3	41.5	40.8	26.1	69.1	95.8	
Gold (Million Fine Troy Ounces) 1ad	.011	.011	.011	.011	.011	.011	.011	.011	.011	.011	.011	.011	.011	....	....	
Gold (National Valuation) .... 1an d	5.2	4.6	4.3	4.2	3.9	3.8	4.1	4.1	4.3	4.2	3.4	3.3	3.3	....	....	
Monetary Authorities: Other Liab. .... 4.. d	15.6	14.2	16.8	14.7	13.1	45.7	49.8	2.9	1.5	2.2	.4	1.1	2.2	1.6	1.3	
Deposit Money Banks: Assets .... 7a. d	11.2	19.7	18.7	20.5	25.0	26.7	23.8	40.6	41.5	35.1	40.9	37.9	44.2	41.3	53.7	
Liabilities .... 7b. d	143.8	121.5	125.9	120.3	134.9	130.0	55.5	49.9	44.9	41.7	32.9	30.5	39.5	42.0	35.7	
Monetary Authorities																
End of Period																
Foreign Assets 11	66.3	70.3	61.4	57.0	52.5	61.9	56.6	58.9	46.4	41.1	31.9	29.8	25.6	56.7	79.6	
Claims on Central Government 12a	41.9	37.3	37.9	33.5	32.6	31.0	33.0	47.3	52.5	57.2	67.7	74.3	69.5	79.9	85.6	
Claims on Deposit Money Banks 12e	30.4	29.1	25.8	27.1	27.1	27.0	27.0	1.1	4.9	4.6	3.2	3.9	1.2	1.2	1.2	
Claims on Other Financial Insts 12f	—	—	—	—	—	—	—	—	—	—	—	—	—	—	—	
Reserve Money 14	65.1	79.4	80.4	82.8	81.3	83.2	79.6	60.5	68.4	64.4	50.7	32.5	43.0	44.6	66.3	
of which: Currency Outside DMBs 14a	35.6	42.3	41.8	37.6	41.0	39.5	48.3	48.7	59.6	57.7	41.7	24.5	34.1	32.2	49.3	
Foreign Liabilities 16c	39.0	34.1	30.0	25.6	22.4	29.4	30.0	34.2	26.3	28.7	36.6	43.4	45.9	53.3	61.0	
Central Government Deposits 16d	31.7	21.1	11.7	3.8	3.2	3.0	3.3	15.6	8.3	8.1	8.5	16.4	4.1	30.4	38.0	
Other Items (Net) 17r	2.9	2.0	3.1	5.5	5.3	4.2	3.6	-3.0	.9	1.7	7.1	15.7	3.3	9.5	1.1	
Deposit Money Banks																
End of Period																
Reserves 20	29.2	38.1	38.2	44.8	40.6	43.5	29.9	9.7	8.3	5.9	8.1	7.7	8.8	10.5	15.2	
Foreign Assets 21	3.0	6.0	5.4	5.3	6.5	7.3	7.0	21.7	20.3	18.4	24.5	21.3	28.9	29.1	39.9	
Claims on Central Government 22a	19.5	18.6	17.1	16.1	16.4	16.0	2.9	13.4	12.4	14.1	16.7	12.9	12.1	15.3	10.7	
Claims on Private Sector 22d	108.3	107.0	90.1	83.0	75.3	72.4	64.9	71.4	42.0	43.3	35.5	49.4	47.7	61.4	66.0	
Claims on Other Financial Insts 22f	—	—	—	—	—	—	—	—	—	—	—	—	—	—	—	
Demand Deposits 24	35.9	38.3	44.6	38.4	34.7	30.5	28.8	40.3	38.4	30.2	28.8	32.0	33.9	43.3	52.4	
Time Deposits 25	41.3	49.7	51.3	55.9	42.0	49.2	41.4	37.2	33.6	34.3	25.3	20.6	23.8	27.2	32.7	
Foreign Liabilities 26c	13.8	12.8	13.4	10.6	10.8	12.2	10.0	23.3	18.4	18.5	19.7	17.2	25.8	29.6	26.6	
Long-Term Foreign Liabilities 26cl	24.6	24.0	23.0	20.3	24.2	23.6	6.4	3.3	3.6	3.3	—	—	—	—	12.0	
Central Government Deposits 26d	20.0	23.4	20.8	21.5	27.4	24.1	21.5	21.0	19.3	19.8	3.9	9.8	8.8	10.2	1.2	
Credit from Monetary Authorities 26g	30.6	29.4	27.6	26.3	27.1	27.0	27.0	27.8	4.9	4.6	2.0	3.9	1.2	1.2	7.0	
Other Items (Net) 27r	-6.2	-7.9	-29.9	-23.8	-27.3	-27.4	-30.3	-36.8	-35.1	-29.0	5.2	7.7	4.0	4.9		
Treasury Claims: Private Sector .....22d. i	—	.2	—	—	—	—	.1	—	—	—	—	—	—	—	—	
Post Office: Checking Deposits ....24.. i	1.7	1.5	1.8	1.8	4.3	1.5	1.9	2.1	1.8	2.6	2.5	2.7	.3	1.2	1.9	
Monetary Survey																
End of Period																
Foreign Assets (Net) 31n	16.5	29.3	23.5	26.1	25.8	27.6	23.7	23.2	22.1	12.2		-9.4	-17.2	2.9	31.9	
Domestic Credit 32	119.6	119.9	114.4	109.2	98.0	93.8	77.9	97.6	81.2	89.3	110.1	113.1	116.6	117.3	114.3	
Claims on Central Govt. (Net) 32an	11.4	12.7	24.2	26.2	22.7	21.4	12.9	26.1	39.2	46.0	74.5	63.7	68.9	55.8	48.3	
Claims on Private Sector 32d	108.3	107.2	90.1	83.0	75.3	72.4	64.9	71.4	42.0	43.3	35.6	49.4	47.7	61.4	66.0	
Claims on Other Financial Insts 32f	—	—	—	—	—	—	—	—	—	—	—	—	—	—	—	
Money 34	73.1	82.1	88.2	77.9	79.9	71.6	79.5	91.8	100.2	90.7	73.1	59.6	68.8	76.9	104.0	
Quasi-Money 35	41.3	49.7	51.3	55.9	42.0	49.2	41.4	37.2	33.6	34.3	25.3	20.6	23.8	27.2	32.7	
Long-Term Foreign Liabilities 36cl	24.6	24.0	23.0	20.3	24.2	23.6	6.4	3.3	3.6	3.3	—	—	—	—	9.5	
Other Items (Net) 37r	-2.9	-6.5	-24.6	-18.7	-22.3	-23.0	-25.7	-11.6	-34.1	-26.8	11.7	23.4	6.9	16.1		
Money plus Quasi-Money 35l	114.4	131.8	139.5	133.8	122.0	120.8	120.9	129.0	133.8	125.0	98.4	80.2	92.6	104.1	136.8	
Other Banking Institutions																
End of Period																
Savings Deposits 45	2.15	2.65	3.10	....	....	....	....	....	....	....	....	....	....	....	....	
Liquid Liabilities 55l	116.6	134.5	142.6	....	....	....	....	....	....	125.0	98.4	80.2	92.6	104.1	....	

Niger

	1972	1973	1974	1975	1976	1977	1978	1979	1980	1981	1982	1983	1984	1985	1986
Interest Rates														*Percent Per Annum*	
Discount Rate (End of Period) ... 60	3.50	5.50	5.50	8.00	8.00	8.00	8.00	8.00	10.50	10.50	12.50	10.50	10.50	10.50	8.50
Money Market Rate ... 60b	...	...	...	...	7.28	7.40	7.38	7.72	10.13	13.35	14.66	12.23	11.84	10.66	8.58
Deposit Rate ... 60l	3.00	5.75	5.75	5.88	6.00	6.00	6.00	6.00	6.19	6.25	7.75	7.50	7.25	7.25	6.08
Lending Rate ... 60p	...	...	...	...	...	12.00	12.00	12.00	14.50	14.50	16.00	14.50	14.50	14.50	13.50
Prices														*Index Numbers (1995=100):*	
Consumer Prices ... 64	24.8	27.7	28.6	31.2	38.6	47.6	52.4	56.2	62.0	76.2	85.0	82.9	89.9	89.0	86.2
														Number in Thousands:	
Employment ... 67e	...	...	...	...	...	...	...	...	...	...	...	...	...	23	26
Unemployment ... 67c	...	...	...	...	...	...	...	...	...	...	...	...	...	29	28
International Transactions														*Millions of Francs*	
Exports ... 70	13,712	13,817	12,621	19,556	31,979	39,335	63,706	95,241	119,523	123,589	109,124	113,896	113,030	116,538	109,645
Imports, c.i.f. ... 71	16,576	19,098	23,144	21,889	30,383	48,221	68,896	98,058	125,426	138,512	153,214	123,287	126,034	165,935	127,559
Balance of Payments														*Millions of US Dollars:*	
Current Account, n.i.e. ... 78ald	...	...	−40.0	−39.4	−39.6	−103.5	−218.7	−143.5	−277.3	−192.6	−233.2	−63.6	−6.8	−68.5	−155.9
Goods: Exports f.o.b. ... 78aad	...	...	81.5	138.5	171.6	196.6	287.7	484.9	576.1	484.6	381.3	335.2	303.3	259.4	352.0
Goods: Imports f.o.b. ... 78abd	...	...	−144.9	−148.0	−198.4	−241.3	−410.6	−527.0	−677.4	−591.8	−515.3	−331.6	−269.9	−345.6	−379.9
Trade Balance ... 78acd	...	...	−63.4	−9.4	−26.7	−44.7	−123.0	−42.1	−101.3	−107.2	−134.0	3.7	33.4	−86.2	−27.9
Services: Credit ... 78add	...	...	17.9	23.9	23.4	26.0	31.5	35.7	40.6	39.8	41.8	40.3	31.4	38.6	46.5
Services: Debit ... 78aed	...	...	−77.1	−87.0	−103.7	−129.3	−163.4	−242.3	−279.0	−194.1	−213.0	−153.7	−124.2	−127.5	−135.6
Balance on Goods & Services ... 78afd	...	...	−122.6	−72.5	−107.0	−148.0	−254.8	−248.7	−339.7	−261.4	−305.1	−109.8	−59.5	−175.1	−117.0
Income: Credit ... 78agd	...	...	8.2	9.7	8.1	9.0	9.3	12.4	27.0	18.2	17.6	11.9	13.5	18.4	22.9
Income: Debit ... 78ahd	...	...	8.2	11.1	−11.8	−9.1	−39.1	7.4	−59.9	−46.9	−42.1	−50.6	−55.2	−60.7	−60.1
Balance on Gds, Serv. & Inc. ... 78aid	...	...	−106.2	−51.7	−110.8	−148.1	−284.6	−228.9	−372.6	−290.2	−329.7	−148.4	−101.2	−217.4	−154.2
Current Transfers, n.i.e.: Credit ... 78ajd	...	...	88.7	40.3	99.4	74.6	112.7	148.2	165.0	161.2	158.4	140.5	144.2	213.1	68.3
Current Transfers: Debit ... 78akd	...	...	−22.6	−27.9	−28.2	−29.9	−46.8	−62.8	−69.7	−63.7	−61.8	−55.7	−49.7	−64.3	−70.1
Capital Account, n.i.e. ... 78bcd	...	...	—	—	—	—	—	—	—	—	—	—	—	—	134.1
Capital Account, n.i.e.: Credit ... 78bad	...	...	—	—	—	—	—	—	—	—	—	—	—	—	134.1
Capital Account: Debit ... 78bbd	...	...	—	—	—	—	—	—	—	—	—	—	—	—	...
Financial Account, n.i.e. ... 78bjd	...	...	23.4	38.7	49.8	114.4	222.5	209.9	307.0	208.2	176.8	57.9	−38.7	−8.2	−27.5
Direct Investment Abroad ... 78bdd	...	...	−.3	−6.3	1.4	3.7	6.8	−11.2	4.2	.6	−3.3	−1.8	−.3	−1.9	−29.4
Dir. Invest. in Rep. Econ., n.i.e. ... 78bed	...	...	6.9	22.6	9.9	12.9	42.7	46.8	49.1	−6.1	28.2	1.2	1.4	−9.4	17.6
Portfolio Investment Assets ... 78bfd	...	...	—	—	—	−1.4	−3.9	—	−.3	−.4	—	—	—	—	—
Equity Securities ... 78bkd	...	...	—	—	—	−1.4	−3.9	—	−.9	−.4	—	—	—	—	—
Debt Securities ... 78bld	...	...	—	—	—	—	—	—	.6	—	—	—	—	—	—
Portfolio Investment Liab., n.i.e. ... 78bgd	...	...	—	—	—	—	—	—	—	—	—	—	—	—	—
Equity Securities ... 78bmd	...	...	—	—	—	—	—	—	—	—	—	—	—	—	—
Debt Securities ... 78bnd	...	...	—	—	—	—	—	—	—	—	—	—	—	—	—
Financial Derivatives Assets ... 78bwd	...	...	...	...	...	...	...	...	...	...	...	...	...	...	...
Financial Derivatives Liabilities ... 78bxd	...	...	...	...	...	...	...	...	...	...	...	...	...	...	...
Other Investment Assets ... 78bhd	...	...	.7	−4.0	−32.8	−3.6	−10.5	−29.0	−.5	−13.0	12.8	−15.4	−1.1	5.6	−4.2
Monetary Authorities ... 78bod	...	...	...	...	...	...	...	...	...	...	...	...	...	...	...
General Government ... 78bpd	...	...	.4	−1.2	−10.5	5.4	−8.0	.5	−1.9	4.8	−6.7	−2.8	−1.9	−.4	1.5
Banks ... 78bqd	...	...	−2.6	2.1	−6.9	−9.4	7.2	−18.9	14.6	−3.2	5.6	−5.3	−2.4	5.2	...
Other Sectors ... 78brd	...	...	2.9	−4.8	−15.4	.4	−9.7	−10.6	−13.2	−14.6	13.9	−7.3	3.2	.8	−5.7
Other Investment Liab., n.i.e. ... 78bid	...	...	16.1	26.4	71.3	102.8	187.4	203.3	254.4	227.2	139.1	73.9	−38.9	−2.4	−11.6
Monetary Authorities ... 78bsd	...	...	...	...	...	...	...	...	...	...	...	...	...	...	2.0
General Government ... 78btd	...	...	11.9	19.4	25.3	25.2	44.8	47.2	60.8	140.7	61.1	67.5	−5.1	27.9	16.6
Banks ... 78bud	...	...	.2	2.0	12.3	8.1	18.7	28.3	62.3	.2	75.7	2.6	−12.5	−14.0	−9.6
Other Sectors ... 78bvd	...	...	4.0	4.9	33.7	69.5	123.9	127.8	131.3	86.3	2.3	3.8	−21.3	−16.3	−20.5
Net Errors and Omissions ... 78cad	...	...	−2.0	−45.0	7.9	−5.3	−14.5	−75.8	−35.1	−24.0	−7.3	−7.9	14.2	26.6	−70.8
Overall Balance ... 78cbd	...	...	−18.6	−45.7	18.1	5.5	−10.7	−9.5	−5.4	−8.4	−63.7	−13.6	−31.3	−50.2	−120.2
Reserves and Related Items ... 79dad	...	...	18.6	45.7	−18.1	−5.5	10.7	9.5	5.4	8.4	63.7	13.6	31.3	50.2	120.2
Reserve Assets ... 79dbd	...	...	6.4	−5.7	−37.8	−13.4	−13.8	3.5	−5.8	−2.8	63.3	−29.8	−45.7	−19.1	29.3
Use of Fund Credit and Loans ... 79dcd	...	...	—	—	—	—	6.7	—	9.6	.1	—	32.7	13.3	15.0	18.6
Exceptional Financing ... 79ded	...	...	12.2	51.4	19.6	7.9	17.7	5.9	1.6	11.2	.3	10.7	63.7	54.3	72.4
Government Finance														*Millions of Francs:*	
Deficit (-) or Surplus ... 80	...	...	...	...	−5,468	−5,261	−12,622	−12,105	−25,241	...	...	...	...	...	...
Revenue ... 81	...	...	...	...	29,276	36,957	48,794	62,190	77,436	...	...	...	...	...	...
Grants Received ... 81z	...	...	...	...	1,213	698	1,595	369	—	...	...	...	...	...	...
Expenditure ... 82	...	...	...	...	35,388	42,511	58,552	70,819	98,727	...	...	...	...	...	...
Lending Minus Repayments ... 83	...	...	...	...	569	405	4,459	3,845	3,950	...	...	...	...	...	...
Financing															
Net Borrowing: Domestic ... 84a	...	...	...	...	4,420	2,941	4,271	1,008	8,256	...	...	...	...	...	...
Foreign ... 85a	...	...	...	...	5,813	6,307	9,925	14,278	21,616	...	...	...	...	...	...
Use of Cash Balances ... 87	...	...	...	...	−4,765	−3,987	−1,574	−3,181	−4,631	...	...	...	...	...	...
National Accounts														*Billions of Francs*	
Househ.Cons.Expend.,incl.NPISHs ... 96f	114.9	103.5	147.6	138.6	170.7	206.6	264.6	311.1	381.7	410.7	483.2	522.8	524.6	510.2	500.0
Government Consumption Expend. ... 91f	15.0	15.7	17.4	23.6	28.1	31.0	34.0	41.0	54.0	70.2	81.0	87.5	89.7	97.2	99.9
Gross Fixed Capital Formation ... 93e	8.8	15.0	18.0	36.7	43.6	65.9	90.7	112.8	136.7	163.9	155.2	119.4	55.0	92.4	82.5
Changes in Inventories ... 93i	3.5	3.8	4.1	6.3	19.1	17.7	22.9	28.2	32.4	4.5	26.0	−12.4	−21.7	6.6	1.7
Exports of Goods and Services ... 90c	23.0	28.2	26.2	†34.6	47.1	53.7	71.2	109.7	128.8	141.9	139.8	143.7	147.3	116.5	130.9
Imports of Goods and Services (-) ... 98c	29.2	38.0	54.3	†59.5	70.7	86.1	124.2	159.6	197.4	189.5	222.2	173.9	156.5	165.9	166.5
Gross Domestic Product (GDP) ... 99b	136.0	128.2	159.0	180.4	237.9	288.8	359.2	443.2	536.2	601.5	663.0	687.1	638.4	657.0	648.6
GDP Volume 1987 Prices ... 99b.p	...	...	...	...	...	...	...	...	...	...	...	...	...	...	653.6
GDP Volume (1995=100) ... 99bvp	...	...	...	...	...	...	...	...	...	...	...	...	...	...	89.3
GDP Deflator (1995=100) ... 99bip	...	...	...	...	...	...	...	...	...	...	...	...	...	...	87.0
														Millions:	
Population ... 99z	4.21	4.30	4.48	4.60	4.73	4.86	4.99	5.17	5.31	5.78	5.98	6.18	6.40	6.61	6.82

	1987	1988	1989	1990	1991	1992	1993	1994	1995	1996	1997	1998	1999	2000	2001		
Percent Per Annum																**Interest Rates**	
	8.50	8.50	11.00	11.00	11.00	12.50	10.50	10.00	7.50	6.50	6.00	6.25	5.75	6.50	6.50	Discount Rate *(End of Period)*	60
	8.37	8.72	10.07	10.98	10.94	11.44	....	....	....	....	....	4.81	4.95	4.95	4.95	Money Market Rate	60b
	5.25	5.25	6.42	7.00	7.00	7.75	....	....	....	....	....	3.50	3.50	3.50	3.50	Deposit Rate	60l
	13.50	13.58	15.13	16.00	16.00	16.75	....	....	....	....	....	....	....	....	....	Lending Rate	60p
Period Averages																**Prices**	
	80.4	79.3	77.0	76.4	†70.5	67.3	66.5	90.4	100.0	105.3	†108.4	113.3	110.7	113.9	118.5	Consumer Prices	64
Period Averages																	
	28	26	28	25	24	....	....	....	....	....	....	....	....	....	....	Employment	67e
	27	26	25	21	21	....	....	....	....	....	....	....	....	....	....	Unemployment	67c
Millions of Francs																**International Transactions**	
	93,863	85,941	77,710	76,939	86,626	88,200	81,200	125,100	143,800	166,300	158,500	197,000	176,600	201,500	....	Exports	70
	93,387	115,193	105,851	100,235	126,684	106,123	182,097	186,501	229,271	228,400	222,400	248,900	264,900	....		Imports, c.i.f.	71
Minus Sign Indicates Debit																Balance of Payments	
	−176.8	−230.5	−256.9	−235.9	−176.2	−159.2	−97.2	−126.1	−151.7	....	....	....	....	....	....	Current Account, n.i.e.	78al *d*
	477.4	426.3	390.8	488.4	351.5	347.3	300.4	226.8	288.1	....	....	....	....	....	....	Goods: Exports f.o.b.	78aa *d*
	−448.4	−459.3	−414.8	−501.7	−417.9	−396.5	−312.1	−271.3	−305.6	....	....	....	....	....	....	Goods: Imports f.o.b.	78ab *d*
	29.0	−33.0	−24.0	−13.3	−66.3	−49.2	−11.7	−44.5	−17.6	....	....	....	....	....	....	*Trade Balance*	78ac *d*
	54.1	40.7	31.7	44.4	49.6	57.7	36.5	30.4	33.3	....	....	....	....	....	....	Services: Credit	78ad *d*
	−193.0	−208.0	−202.2	−226.9	−203.2	−201.0	−185.6	−149.1	−151.8	....	....	....	....	....	....	Services: Debit	78ae *d*
	−109.8	−200.2	−194.5	−195.7	−220.0	−192.6	−160.9	−163.2	−136.0	....	....	....	....	....	....	*Balance on Goods & Services*	78af *d*
	15.7	16.7	18.0	20.4	20.1	19.7	19.3	15.6	5.8	....	....	....	....	....	....	Income: Credit	78ag *d*
	−79.1	−82.4	−59.0	−74.4	−33.7	−54.1	−30.2	−45.2	−52.9	....	....	....	....	....	....	Income: Debit	78ah *d*
	−173.3	−265.9	−235.5	−249.7	−233.6	−227.0	−171.7	−192.8	−183.2	....	....	....	....	....	....	*Balance on Gds, Serv. & Inc.*	78ai *d*
	59.8	103.3	37.2	81.4	122.2	133.6	139.5	115.1	60.6	....	....	....	....	....	....	Current Transfers, n.i.e.: Credit	78aj *d*
	−63.3	−67.9	−58.6	−67.6	−64.8	−65.7	−65.0	−48.5	−29.1	....	....	....	....	....	....	Current Transfers: Debit	78ak *d*
	132.1	116.4	149.1	117.4	103.5	109.0	109.3	88.2	65.3	....	....	....	....	....	....	Capital Account, n.i.e.	78bc *d*
	132.1	116.4	149.1	117.4	103.5	109.0	109.3	88.2	65.3	....	....	....	....	....	....	Capital Account, n.i.e.: Credit	78ba *d*
	....	....	....	....	....	....	....	....	....	....	....	....	....	....	....	Capital Account: Debit	78bb *d*
	33.3	35.9	10.3	46.5	−122.9	50.8	−123.3	29.9	−46.1	....	....	....	....	....	....	Financial Account, n.i.e.	78bj *d*
	−10.2	−4.7	−1.6	—	−2.6	−40.7	−5.8	1.8	−7.1	....	....	....	....	....	....	Direct Investment Abroad	78bd *d*
	14.8	6.9	.8	40.8	15.2	56.4	−34.4	−11.3	7.2	....	....	....	....	....	....	Dir. Invest. in Rep. Econ., n.i.e.	78be *d*
	....	....	....	....	....	....	....	....	....	....	....	....	....	....	....	Portfolio Investment Assets	78bf *d*
	....	....	....	....	....	....	....	....	....	....	....	....	....	....	....	Equity Securities	78bk *d*
	....	....	....	....	....	....	....	....	....	....	....	....	....	....	....	Debt Securities	78bl *d*
	....	....	....	....	....	....	....	....	....	....	....	....	....	....	....	Portfolio Investment Liab., n.i.e.	78bg *d*
	....	....	....	....	....	....	....	....	....	....	....	....	....	....	....	Equity Securities	78bm *d*
	....	....	....	....	....	....	....	....	....	....	....	....	....	....	....	Debt Securities	78bn *d*
	....	....	....	....	....	....	....	....	....	....	....	....	....	....	....	Financial Derivatives Assets	78bw *d*
	....	....	....	....	....	....	....	....	....	....	....	....	....	....	....	Financial Derivatives Liabilities	78bx *d*
	.9	−35.7	−13.7	−1.8	−43.0	10.4	11.2	22.3	−18.4	....	....	....	....	....	....	Other Investment Assets	78bh *d*
	....	....	....	....	....	....	....	....	....	....	....	....	....	....	....	Monetary Authorities	78bo *d*
	.6	.7	1.2	.6	.7	.1	.1	.3	—	....	....	....	....	....	....	General Government	78bp *d*
	....	....	....	....	....	....	....	....	....	....	....	....	....	....	....	Banks	78bq *d*
	.3	−36.4	−14.9	−2.4	−43.7	10.2	11.1	22.0	−18.4	....	....	....	....	....	....	Other Sectors	78br *d*
	27.8	69.3	24.8	7.5	−92.4	24.8	−94.4	17.1	−27.8	....	....	....	....	....	....	Other Investment Liab., n.i.e.	78bi *d*
	−2.0	1.4	1.2	−4.3	−1.3	34.6	7.7	−22.3	−2.3	....	....	....	....	....	....	Monetary Authorities	78bs *d*
	40.3	60.1	31.1	28.6	−18.5	31.4	−10.8	6.7	−14.8	....	....	....	....	....	....	General Government	78bt *d*
	−.4	−14.7	−5.3	−4.4	17.0	6.2	−65.0	19.4	−10.8	....	....	....	....	....	....	Banks	78bu *d*
	−10.1	22.6	−2.2	−12.3	−89.7	−47.4	−26.3	13.3	.1	....	....	....	....	....	....	Other Sectors	78bv *d*
	−66.8	11.2	86.6	−18.4	135.8	−95.5	87.2	−67.8	114.4	....	....	....	....	....	....	Net Errors and Omissions	78ca *d*
	−78.1	−67.0	−10.8	−90.3	−59.8	−94.9	−23.9	−75.8	−18.1	....	....	....	....	....	....	*Overall Balance*	78cb *d*
	78.1	67.0	10.8	90.3	59.8	94.9	23.9	75.8	18.1	....	....	....	....	....	....	Reserves and Related Items	79da *d*
	19.5	27.5	−29.2	−10.1	−6.4	31.0	−19.9	28.7	−25.8	....	....	....	....	....	....	Reserve Assets	79db *d*
	.6	−21.4	−7.8	−6.1	−11.4	−9.4	−9.6	5.4	−10.2	....	....	....	....	....	....	Use of Fund Credit and Loans	79dc *d*
	58.0	61.0	47.9	106.5	77.6	73.3	53.3	41.7	54.1	....	....	....	....	....	....	Exceptional Financing	79de *d*
Year Ending September 30																**Government Finance**	
	....	....	....	....	....	....	....	....	....	....	....	....	....	....	....	Deficit (-) or Surplus	80
	....	....	....	....	....	....	....	....	....	....	....	....	....	....	....	Revenue	81
	....	....	....	....	....	....	....	....	....	....	....	....	....	....	....	Grants Received	81z
	....	....	....	....	....	....	....	....	....	....	....	....	....	....	....	Expenditure	82
	....	....	....	....	....	....	....	....	....	....	....	....	....	....	....	Lending Minus Repayments	83
																Financing	
	....	....	....	....	....	....	....	....	....	....	....	....	....	....	....	Net Borrowing: Domestic	84a
	....	....	....	....	....	....	....	....	....	....	....	....	....	....	....	Foreign	85a
	....	....	....	....	....	....	....	....	....	....	....	....	....	....	....	Use of Cash Balances	87
Billions of Francs																**National Accounts**	
	510.0	514.7	524.9	515.2	517.7	526.2	520.1	604.5	648.8	684.5	724.2	750.9	....	....	....	Househ.Cons.Expend.,incl.NPISHs	96f
	102.5	105.5	110.5	110.4	105.0	106.0	111.6	127.4	131.9	137.5	138.8	139.8	....	....	....	Government Consumption Expend.	91f
	92.4	89.3	95.8	87.4	70.9	63.0	75.3	102.3	98.5	122.3	129.3	150.6	....	....	....	Gross Fixed Capital Formation	93e
	−25.7	17.2	−6.4	16.7	37.6	9.9	−22.6	32.0	20.9	38.6	42.7	63.6	....	....	....	Changes in Inventories	93i
	160.4	138.9	135.3	144.1	111.4	105.6	94.3	141.4	167.1	188.2	181.0	197.0	....	....	....	Exports of Goods and Services	90c
	193.2	197.8	195.6	196.5	169.9	151.7	131.3	220.6	232.6	261.5	262.5	283.6	....	....	....	Imports of Goods and Services (-)	98c
	646.4	667.8	664.5	677.2	672.7	659.0	647.4	787.1	834.6	909.7	953.5	1,018.3	....	....	....	Gross Domestic Product (GDP)	99b
	646.4	688.7	683.7	678.5	688.3	693.4	700.5	718.1	731.9	760.6	778.6	845.2	....	....	....	GDP Volume 1987 Prices	99b.*p*
	88.3	94.1	93.4	92.7	94.0	94.7	95.7	98.1	100.0	103.9	106.4	115.5	....	....	....	GDP Volume (1995=100)	99bv *p*
	87.7	85.0	85.2	87.5	85.7	83.3	81.0	96.1	100.0	104.9	107.4	105.7	....	....	....	GDP Deflator (1995=100)	99bi *p*
Midyear Estimates																	
	7.04	7.26	7.49	7.73	7.96	8.23	8.36	8.81	9.11	9.43	9.75	10.10	10.46	10.83	11.23	**Population**	99z

(See notes in the back of the book.)

Nigeria

		1972	1973	1974	1975	1976	1977	1978	1979	1980	1981	1982	1983	1984	1985	1986
Exchange Rates																*Naira per SDR:*
Principal Rate	aa	.714	.794	.754	.734	.733	.791	.844	.738	.694	.741	.739	.784	.792	1.098	4.057
																Naira per US Dollar:
Principal Rate	ae	.658	.658	.616	.627	.631	.651	.648	.561	.544	.637	.670	.749	.808	1.000	3.317
Principal Rate	rf	.658	.658	.630	.616	.627	.645	.635	.604	.547	.618	.673	.724	.767	.894	1.755
																Index Numbers (1995=100):
Principal Rate	ahx	3,327.9	3,327.9	3,482.1	3,557.4	3,494.2	3,396.8	3,447.2	3,632.5	4,006.1	3,567.0	3,252.2	3,026.4	2,864.8	2,453.4	1,625.7
Nominal Effective Exchange Rate	ne c	....	....	....	....	....	....	....	3,233.2	3,591.7	3,713.0	3,884.7	4,035.1	4,324.2	3,964.0	2,211.4
Real Effective Exchange Rate	re c	....	....	....	....	....	....	....	....	287.5	319.2	327.4	387.6	535.7	568.7	310.5
Fund Position																*Millions of SDRs:*
Quota	2f. s	135	135	135	135	135	135	360	360	540	540	540	850	850	850	850
SDRs	1b. s	46	46	48	57	61	66	67	108	133	239	40	26	11	1	—
Reserve Position in the Fund	1c. s	13	33	34	212	334	340	366	295	371	446	—	—	—	—	—
of which: Outstg.Fund Borrowing	2c	—	—	—	178	300	296	272	203	179	133	—	—	—	—	—
Total Fund Cred.&Loans Outstg.	2tl	—	—	—	—	—	—	—	—	—	—	—	—	—	—	—
International Liquidity															*Millions of US Dollars Unless Otherwise Indicated:*	
Total Reserves minus Gold	1l. d	355	559	5,602	5,586	5,180	4,232	1,887	5,548	10,235	3,895	1,613	990	1,462	1,667	1,081
SDRs	1b. d	49	55	58	67	71	80	87	142	169	278	45	27	10	1	—
Reserve Position in the Fund	1c. d	14	40	41	248	388	413	477	389	473	519	—	—	—	—	—
Foreign Exchange	1d. d	292	464	5,503	5,270	4,721	3,739	1,323	5,017	9,593	3,098	1,568	963	1,452	1,666	1,081
Gold (Million Fine Troy Ounces)	1ad	.543	.571	.571	.571	.571	.629	.629	.687	.687	.687	.687	.687	.687	.687	.687
Gold (National Valuation)	1and	....	24	26	25	25	25	28	34	35	30	28	25	24	19	6
Other Official Insts.: Assets	3b. d	38	39	44	34	35	20e	....	....	....	....	3	2	....	....	....
Monetary Authorities: Other Liab.	4.. d	2	—	2	19	2	6	3	11	60	46	24	40	14	15	19
Deposit Money Banks: Assets	7a. d	19	59	104	170	253	346	275	422	458	407	368	459	510	415	525
Liabilities	7b. d	23	14	26	20	74	39	99	119	162	206	345	351	115	260	247
Monetary Authorities																*Millions of Naira:*
Foreign Assets	11	248	385	3,452	3,584	3,218	2,693	1,308	3,065	5,479	2,457	1,058	757	1,115	1,676	3,606
Claims on Central Government	12a	157	175	20	314	512	1,827	3,197	2,521	2,861	6,053	8,148	11,871	11,068	11,522	17,722
Claims on State & Local Govts.	12b	—	—	—	—	—	—	—	—	—	—	—	—	—	—	—
Claims on Nonfin.Pub.Enterprises	12c	....	....	....	....	....	....	....	....	....	....	....	....	....	....	....
Claims on Private Sector	12d	76	10	15	89	118	171	102	96	100	106	112	91	91	91	92
Claims on Deposit Money Banks	12e	—	—	—	—	—	—	—	—	—	—	—	—	—	—	—
Claims on Nonbank Financial Insts	12g	65	98	180	169	172	244	439	638	656	804	807	972	1,213	1,332	1,534
Reserve Money	14	454	561	1,409	2,169	2,773	3,430	3,312	3,847	6,495	6,278	6,803	7,055	7,267	7,785	8,292
of which: Currency Outside DMBs	14a	385	436	570	1,031	1,351	1,941	2,157	2,351	3,186	3,862	4,223	4,843	4,884	4,910	5,178
Foreign Liabilities	16c	1	—	1	12	1	3	2	6	22	18	6	20	3	8	23
Long-Term Foreign Liabilities	16cl	—	—	—	—	—	1	1	—	11	11	10	10	9	8	41
Central Government Deposits	16d	24	19	2,098	1,732	1,088	649	820	1,442	1,885	1,459	576	1,343	1,659	2,680	2,903
Capital Accounts	17a	41	45	49	53	60	72	82	115	151	208	225	252	289	372	873
Other Items (Net)	17r	26	43	109	189	97	780	830	910	533	1,446	2,504	5,011	4,262	3,770	10,823
Deposit Money Banks																*Millions of Naira:*
Reserves	20	44	66	331	862	1,237	1,438	1,114	923	1,552	1,396	2,023	1,285	1,051	824	1,506
Foreign Assets	21	12	39	64	107	160	225	178	236	249	259	246	344	413	415	1,740
Claims on Central Government	22a	385	388	768	787	1,197	1,418	1,118	2,439	2,987	2,186	3,193	5,514	9,060	10,730	5,009
Claims on State & Local Govts.	22b	8	13	25	32	45	60	110	144	132	259	382	517	518	470	474
Claims on Private Sector	22d	601	731	907	1,475	2,063	2,934	3,861	4,362	6,046	7,977	9,503	9,765	10,302	11,253	14,916
Demand Deposits	24	337	†293	583	1,124	2,050	2,842	2,530	3,061	4,422	4,702	4,938	5,620	6,051	6,396	6,194
Time, Savings,& Fgn.Currency Dep.	25	457	†582	973	1,572	1,979	2,255	2,420	3,702	5,163	5,494	6,645	7,752	9,039	9,926	10,942
Money Market Instruments	26aa	—	—	—	—	3	2	76	31	43	34	116	108	48	20	50
Bonds	26ab	—	6	8	3	—	—	—	—	11	8	9	65	69	65	68
Foreign Liabilities	26c	15	10	16	13	47	25	64	67	88	131	231	263	93	260	820
Central Government Deposits	26d	—	138	138	142	136	138	352	205	424	481	437	567	646	1,275	1,001
Credit from Monetary Authorities	26g	4	—	—	—	—	—	—	—	—	—	—	—	—	—	4
Capital Accounts	27a	77	80	92	124	157	202	267	328	378	490	659	780	898	1,064	1,231
Other Items (Net)	27r	161	129	285	283	330	611	671	710	437	737	2,314	2,271	4,500	4,686	3,335
Monetary Survey																*Millions of Naira:*
Foreign Assets (Net)	31n	244	414	3,498	3,665	3,330	2,890	1,421	3,229	5,618	2,567	1,067	817	1,432	1,824	4,504
Domestic Credit	32	1,274	1,261	–314	1,018	2,940	5,946	7,782	8,693	10,732	15,781	21,527	27,708	30,471	31,920	36,459
Claims on Central Govt. (Net)	32an	518	407	–1,448	–774	486	2,458	3,143	3,313	3,539	6,299	10,328	15,475	17,823	18,297	18,827
Claims on State & Local Govts.	32b	8	13	25	32	45	60	110	144	132	259	382	517	518	470	474
Claims on Nonfin.Pub.Enterprises	32c	....	....	....	....	....	....	....	....	....	....	....	....	....	....	....
Claims on Private Sector	32d	678	741	921	1,564	2,180	3,105	3,963	4,458	6,147	8,083	9,615	9,856	10,393	11,345	15,008
Claims on Nonbank Fin. Insts.	32g	65	98	180	169	172	244	439	638	656	804	807	972	1,213	1,332	1,534
Money	34	747	†788	1,619	2,463	3,728	5,420	5,101	6,147	9,227	9,745	10,049	11,283	12,204	13,227	12,663
Quasi-Money	35	457	†582	973	1,572	1,979	2,255	2,420	3,702	5,163	5,494	6,645	7,752	9,039	9,926	10,942
Money Market Instruments	36aa	—	—	—	—	3	2	76	31	43	34	116	108	48	20	50
Bonds	36ab	—	6	8	3	—	—	—	—	11	8	9	65	69	65	68
Long-Term Foreign Liabilities	36cl	—	—	—	—	—	1	1	—	11	11	10	10	9	8	41
Capital Accounts	37a	117	126	141	178	217	274	349	443	529	697	884	1,032	1,186	1,435	2,104
Other Items (Net)	37r	196	173	443	468	342	885	1,256	1,599	1,366	2,359	4,881	8,276	9,348	9,062	15,096
Money plus Quasi-Money	35l	1,204	†1,370	2,592	4,035	5,708	7,675	7,521	9,849	14,390	15,239	16,694	19,034	21,243	23,153	23,605
Other Banking Institutions																*Millions of Naira:*
Reserves	40.m	1	2	5	16	20	53	59	61	94	152	306	325	152	133	178
Foreign Assets	41.m	—	—	—	4	1	8	12	21	30	53	100	92	105	136	1,135
Claims on Central Government	42a.m	6	8	12	13	14	32	14	60	59	69	175	386	894	1,132	148
Claims on Private Sector	42d.m	14	14	26	84	81	110	164	199	362	586	888	1,066	1,276	1,460	2,320
Demand Deposits	44.m	2	6	3	9	3	4	12	54	67	122	272	485	511	531	602
Time and Savings Deposits	45.m	9	9	19	55	59	82	117	117	220	328	691	794	971	1,318	1,740
Foreign Liabilities	46c.m	—	—	—	—	—	—	1	1	2	12	2	27	7	12	1
Cred.from Deposit Money Banks	46h.m	5	5	15	38	37	52	38	50	110	177	76	—	24	27	132
Capital Accounts	47a.m	2	2	7	11	10	11	14	19	26	37	63	85	132	164	192
Other Items (Net)	47r.m	4	2	—	5	9	53	73	101	120	183	365	478	783	809	1,114
Liquid Liabilities	55l	1,219	†1,387	2,614	4,089	5,756	7,716	7,593	9,967	14,589	15,545	17,351	19,988	22,572	24,869	25,769
Interest Rates																*Percent Per Annum*
Discount Rate (End of Period)	60	4.50	4.50	4.50	3.50	3.50	4.00	5.00	5.00	6.00	6.00	8.00	8.00	10.00	10.00	10.00
Treasury Bill Rate	60c	....	....	....	....	....	....	....	....	....	....	....	....	....	....	....
Deposit Rate	60l	3.04	3.00	3.00	3.00	2.67	2.83	4.15	4.47	5.27	5.72	7.60	7.41	8.25	9.12	9.24
Lending Rate	60p	7.00	7.00	7.00	6.25	6.50	6.00	6.75	7.79	8.43	8.92	9.54	9.98	10.24	9.43	9.96

1987	1988	1989	1990	1991	1992	1993	1994	1995	1996	1997	1998	1999	2000	2001		
End of Period															**Exchange Rates**	
5.874	7.204	10.055	12.805	14.107	27.014	30.056	32.113	32.534	31.471	29.530	30.816	134.437	142.734	141.948	Principal Rate	aa
End of Period (ae) Period Average (rf)																
4.141	5.353	7.651	9.001	9.862	19.646	21.882	21.997	21.887	21.886	21.886	21.886	97.950	109.550	112.950	Principal Rate	ae
4.016	4.537	7.365	8.038	9.909	17.298	22.065	21.996	21.895	21.884	21.886	21.886	92.338	101.697	111.231	Principal Rate	rf
Period Averages																
546.4	488.4	297.6	272.6	222.0	134.2	99.3	99.6	100.0	100.0	100.0	100.0	24.1	21.5	19.7	Principal Rate	ahx
666.5	546.5	366.0	367.7	301.8	192.3	146.6	192.9	100.0	96.5	104.3	106.1	51.0	49.9	47.7	Nominal Effective Exchange Rate	nec
99.0	99.5	88.6	82.2	70.0	58.0	63.6	118.0	100.0	123.7	142.0	155.8	79.0	80.9	89.8	Real Effective Exchange Rate	rec
End of Period															**Fund Position**	
850	850	850	850	850	1,282	1,282	1,282	1,282	1,282	1,282	1,282	1,753	1,753	1,753	Quota	2f.s
—	—	—	1	—	—	—	—	—	—	—	1	—	—	1	SDRs	1b.s
—	—	—	—	—	—	—	—	—	—	—	—	—	—	—	Reserve Position in the Fund	1c.s
—	—	—	—	—	—	—	—	—	—	—	—	—	—	—	*of which:* Outstg.Fund Borrowing	2c
—	—	—	—	—	—	—	—	—	—	—	—	—	—	—	Total Fund Cred.&Loans Outstg.	2tl
End of Period															**International Liquidity**	
1,165	651	1,766	3,864	4,435	967	1,372	1,386	1,443	4,075	7,582	7,101	5,450	9,911	10,457	Total Reserves minus Gold	1l.d
—	—	—	1	—	—	—	—	1	1	1	1	—	—	1	SDRs	1b.d
—	—	—	—	—	—	—	—	—	—	—	—	—	—	—	Reserve Position in the Fund	1c.d
1,165	651	1,765	3,863	4,435	967	1,372	1,386	1,443	4,075	7,581	7,100	5,450	9,910	10,456	Foreign Exchange	1d.d
.687	.687	.687	.687	.687	.687	.687	.687	.687	.687	.687	.687	.687	.687	.687	Gold (Million Fine Troy Ounces)	1ad
5	4	2	2	2	1	1	1	1	1	1	1	—	—	—	Gold (National Valuation)	1and
....	....	....	....	....	....	....	....	....	....	....	....	....	....	....	Other Official Insts.: Assets	3b.d
10	9	6	5	4	2,993	2,539	2,747	2,450	2,162	2,313	1,630	172	1,224	1,080	Monetary Authorities: Other Liab.	4..d
755	948	979	737	1,081	1,424	1,539	1,157	3,490	2,899	3,180	4,395	1,651	2,035	2,701	Deposit Money Banks: Assets	7a.d
213	64	112	28	84	122	64	130	137	148	137	299	56	138	152	Liabilities	7b.d
End of Period															**Monetary Authorities**	
4,661	3,290	11,716	34,972	44,267	†42,401	31,869	33,467	41,426	180,799	173,665	149,268	506,794	1,091,108	1,156,578	Foreign Assets	11
19,197	28,087	35,378	48,720	83,102	†139,847	211,409	308,858	438,481	313,849	406,053	456,985	532,292	513,003	716,769	Claims on Central Government	12a
—	—	—	159	3	†94	12	124	25	2	7	7	7	7	—	Claims on State & Local Govts.	12b
....	....	....	....	....	2,347	2,747	3,655	3,480	1,525	1,453	926	692	951	1,080	Claims on Nonfin.Pub.Enterprises	12c
97	176	198	47	1,468	†570	850	763	604	967	778	517	884	2,163	3,103	Claims on Private Sector	12d
54	467	313	399	—	†3,855	7,802	12,987	24,222	27,697	21,282	21,818	22,070	36,176	20,604	Claims on Deposit Money Banks	12e
1,767	1,775	792	796	862	†1,492	3,100	2,941	3,160	3,267	5,916	4,580	4,568	4,881	6,330	Claims on Nonbank Financial Insts	12g
9,853	13,982	19,195	24,570	34,892	†77,326	115,542	151,737	182,795	193,953	202,667	236,470	287,893	426,610	571,928	Reserve Money	14
6,299	9,414	12,124	14,951	23,121	†36,756	57,845	90,601	106,843	116,121	130,668	156,716	186,457	274,011	338,671	*of which: Currency Outside DMBs*	14a
4	6	1	2	—	†33,151	945	187	7,060	3,651	11,751	3,957	567	23,924	11,394	Foreign Liabilities	16c
37	42	56	40	43	†25,652	54,611	60,230	46,558	43,672	38,881	31,728	16,304	110,141	110,546	Long-Term Foreign Liabilities	16cl
4,904	6,319	18,311	25,885	55,794	†54,284	63,478	66,740	194,599	253,754	394,740	362,429	516,967	856,007	895,751	Central Government Deposits	16d
1,196	1,466	1,914	2,658	4,210	†34,589	66,251	77,543	76,542	69,618	73,083	85,212	259,537	344,995	325,030	Capital Accounts	17a
9,781	11,980	8,921	31,936	34,762	†-34,397	-43,039	6,358	3,843	-36,542	-111,968	-85,695	-13,960	-113,389	-10,186	Other Items (Net)	17r
End of Period															**Deposit Money Banks**	
2,202	2,355	2,741	4,777	13,736	†32,141	44,488	53,441	60,281	64,343	64,903	65,895	120,585	170,099	318,986	Reserves	20
3,128	5,077	7,489	6,634	10,663	†27,968	33,680	25,449	76,390	63,440	69,590	96,184	161,754	222,988	305,029	Foreign Assets	21
8,253	7,945	3,777	9,107	7,030	†6,908	39,292	47,829	22,894	56,469	46,187	58,881	202,253	292,975	182,116	Claims on Central Government	22a
501	544	755	935	937	†1,419	1,532	2,117	2,909	3,528	1,475	935	2,095	7,558	26,796	Claims on State & Local Govts.	22b
16,059	18,969	20,920	24,475	29,458	†74,037	87,249	141,400	201,181	251,325	309,883	365,609	446,959	580,442	817,690	Claims on Private Sector	22d
7,708	9,882	9,738	15,000	20,180	†36,567	55,592	74,398	85,564	104,017	131,887	150,977	209,899	356,954	448,021	Demand Deposits	24
13,989	16,960	16,707	23,014	30,360	†49,812	74,058	88,505	111,255	134,756	154,633	198,337	298,908	386,396	499,162	Time, Savings,& Fgn.Currency Dep.	25
102	72	194	213	136	†489	653	329	283	692	130	285	74	572	627	Money Market Instruments	26aa
72	87	64	100	195	†290	302	3,030	9,002	9,899	14,488	10,929	18,100	18,212	25,610	Bonds	26ab
882	345	853	248	832	†2,393	1,409	2,860	2,988	3,229	3,009	6,540	5,474	15,099	17,185	Foreign Liabilities	26c
1,389	2,223	737	762	1,870	†1,360	2,055	1,834	3,773	6,098	11,143	13,521	40,773	73,961	28,342	Central Government Deposits	26d
7	83	1,263	96	79	†233	825	10,526	15,172	17,377	8,434	7,762	6,554	5,360	14,547	Credit from Monetary Authorities	26g
1,473	1,845	2,628	3,613	4,106	†56,084	65,727	71,598	88,854	116,729	136,368	169,117	222,146	249,211	364,259	Capital Accounts	27a
4,520	3,393	3,498	2,884	4,069	†-4,753	5,621	17,158	46,766	46,308	31,946	30,038	131,719	168,296	252,864	Other Items (Net)	27r
End of Period															**Monetary Survey**	
6,902	8,016	18,352	41,357	54,098	†34,824	63,195	55,869	107,768	237,359	228,494	234,954	662,507	1,275,072	1,433,027	Foreign Assets (Net)	31n
40,311	50,752	46,021	61,665	70,609	†171,071	280,658	439,114	474,361	371,079	365,871	512,490	632,010	472,012	829,791	Domestic Credit	32
21,157	27,488	20,107	31,180	32,469	†91,112	185,168	288,114	263,003	110,466	46,358	139,916	176,805	-123,990	-25,209	Claims on Central Govt. (Net)	32an
501	544	755	1,094	940	†1,513	1,544	2,241	2,934	3,530	1,482	941	2,102	7,564	26,796	Claims on State & Local Govts.	32b
....	....	....	....	....	2,347	2,747	3,655	3,480	1,525	1,453	926	692	951	1,080	Claims on Nonfin.Pub.Enterprises	32c
16,156	19,145	21,118	24,522	30,926	†74,607	88,099	142,163	201,785	252,292	310,661	366,127	447,843	582,606	820,793	Claims on Private Sector	32d
1,767	1,775	792	796	862	†1,492	3,100	2,941	3,160	3,267	5,916	4,580	4,568	4,881	6,330	Claims on Nonbank Fin. Insts.	32g
14,906	21,446	26,664	34,540	48,708	†79,273	124,422	178,440	207,509	235,577	275,098	327,300	400,826	649,684	816,708	Money	34
13,989	16,960	16,707	23,014	30,360	†49,812	74,058	88,505	111,255	134,756	154,633	198,337	298,908	386,396	499,162	Quasi-Money	35
102	72	194	213	136	†489	653	329	283	692	130	285	74	572	627	Money Market Instruments	36aa
72	87	64	100	195	†290	302	3,030	9,002	9,899	14,488	10,929	18,100	18,212	25,610	Bonds	36ab
37	42	56	40	43	†25,652	54,611	60,230	46,558	43,672	38,881	31,728	16,304	110,141	110,546	Long-Term Foreign Liabilities	36cl
2,669	3,312	4,543	6,272	8,316	†90,672	131,979	149,141	165,396	186,347	209,452	254,328	481,682	594,207	689,289	Capital Accounts	37a
15,437	16,849	16,145	38,844	36,950	†-40,293	-42,171	15,307	42,127	-2,505	-98,317	-75,462	78,622	-12,127	120,876	Other Items (Net)	37r
28,895	38,406	43,371	57,554	79,067	†129,085	198,479	266,945	318,763	370,334	429,731	525,638	699,735	1,036,080	1,315,869	Money plus Quasi-Money	35l
End of Period															**Other Banking Institutions**	
697	2,644	1,154	1,248	2,479	....	....	....	....	....	....	....	....	....	....	Reserves	40.m
1,289	2,766	3,789	3,811	5,250	....	....	....	....	....	....	....	....	....	....	Foreign Assets	41.m
285	168	187	518	809	....	....	....	....	....	....	....	....	....	....	Claims on Central Government	42a.m
3,403	4,520	6,402	9,609	10,022	....	....	....	....	....	....	....	....	....	....	Claims on Private Sector	42d.m
560	835	1,294	989	2,022	....	....	....	....	....	....	....	....	....	....	Demand Deposits	44.m
2,823	3,983	2,515	4,104	5,046	....	....	....	....	....	....	....	....	....	....	Time and Savings Deposits	45.m
60	222	597	177	335	....	....	....	....	....	....	....	....	....	....	Foreign Liabilities	46c.m
—	1,672	4,058	4,859	6,369	....	....	....	....	....	....	....	....	....	....	Cred.from Deposit Money Banks	46h.m
253	471	853	1,484	2,186	....	....	....	....	....	....	....	....	....	....	Capital Accounts	47a.m
1,979	2,916	2,214	3,573	2,601	....	....	....	....	....	....	....	....	....	....	Other Items (Net)	47r.m
31,581	40,580	46,027	61,399	83,657	....	....	....	....	....	....	....	....	....	....	Liquid Liabilities	55l
Percent Per Annum															**Interest Rates**	
12.75	12.75	18.50	18.50	15.50	17.50	26.00	13.50	13.50	13.50	13.50	13.50	18.00	14.00	20.50	Discount Rate *(End of Period)*	60
....	....	....	....	....	17.89	24.50	12.87	12.50	12.25	12.00	12.26	17.82	15.50	....	Treasury Bill Rate	60c
13.09	12.95	14.68	19.78	14.92	18.04	23.24	13.09	13.53	13.06	7.17	10.11	12.81	11.69	....	Deposit Rate	60l
13.96	16.62	20.44	25.30	20.04	24.76	31.65	20.48	20.23	19.84	17.80	18.18	20.29	21.27	....	Lending Rate	60p

Nigeria

		1972	1973	1974	1975	1976	1977	1978	1979	1980	1981	1982	1983	1984	1985	1986
Prices and Production															*Index Numbers (1995=100):*	
Consumer Prices	64	.6	.6	.7	†1.0	1.2	†1.4	1.7	1.8	2.0	2.5	2.6	3.3	†4.5	4.9	5.2
Industrial Production	66	41.1	47.6	50.3	47.3	56.3	58.7	59.1	79.3	78.5	76.3	81.0	68.3	60.6	69.2	68.9
Crude Petroleum Production	66aa	93.0	104.9	115.1	91.1	105.9	106.9	97.4	117.7	105.5	73.5	65.6	63.0	70.7	76.4	74.7
Manufacturing Production	66ey	22.2	27.1	26.6	33.1	40.4	43.0	46.9	72.8	76.5	87.7	99.1	101.0	83.6	74.4	71.9
International Transactions															*Millions of US Dollars*	
Exports	70..d	2,180	3,462	9,205	7,834	10,566	11,839	9,938	17,334	25,946	18,231	12,196	10,298	11,843	12,537	5,923
Crude Petroleum (Naira)	70aa	1,176	1,894	5,366	4,630	6,196	7,083	5,654	9,706	13,632	10,681	8,003	7,201	8,843	10,891	8,368
Imports, c.i.f.	71..d	1,505	1,862	2,772	6,041	8,213	11,095	12,821	10,218	16,660	20,877	16,061	12,254	9,364	8,877	4,034
Volume of Exports																*1985=100*
Crude Petroleum	72aa	113	126	139	109	127	131	118	141	121	78	63	59	69	79	75
Balance of Payments															*Millions of US Dollars:*	
Current Account, n.i.e.	78ald	....	....	....	....	....	–1,016	–3,754	1,671	5,178	–6,474	–7,282	–4,332	123	2,604	211
Goods: Exports f.o.b.	78aad	....	....	....	....	....	12,373	10,441	16,733	25,945	17,845	12,149	10,356	11,856	13,114	5,085
Goods: Imports f.o.b.	78abd	....	....	....	....	....	–9,680	–11,608	–11,819	–14,728	–18,985	–14,874	–11,436	–8,856	–7,447	–3,138
Trade Balance	78acd	....	....	....	....	....	2,693	–1,166	4,914	11,217	–1,140	–2,725	–1,079	3,001	5,667	1,947
Services: Credit	78add	....	....	....	....	....	563	877	1,026	1,127	926	508	402	433	316	250
Services: Debit	78aed	....	....	....	....	....	–3,552	–2,967	–3,434	–5,285	–5,025	–3,446	–2,384	–1,799	–1,656	–1,106
Balance on Goods & Services	78afd	....	....	....	....	....	–296	–3,257	2,507	7,058	–5,239	–5,663	–3,062	1,635	4,327	1,091
Income: Credit	78agd	....	....	....	....	....	351	290	263	688	701	226	108	57	81	56
Income: Debit	78ahd	....	....	....	....	....	–887	–518	–712	–1,992	–1,374	–1,415	–983	–1,238	–1,544	–799
Balance on Gds, Serv. & Inc.	78aid	....	....	....	....	....	–833	–3,485	2,058	5,754	–5,912	–6,853	–3,937	454	2,863	348
Current Transfers, n.i.e.: Credit	78ajd	....	....	....	....	....	42	11	23	33	32	28	18	16	31	14
Current Transfers: Debit	78akd	....	....	....	....	....	–225	–280	–411	–609	–594	–457	–413	–347	–291	–152
Capital Account, n.i.e.	78bcd	....	....	....	....	....	—	—	—	—	—	—	—	—	—	—
Capital Account, n.i.e.: Credit	78bad	....	....	....	....	....	—	—	—	—	—	—	—	—	—	—
Capital Account: Debit	78bbd	....	....	....	....	....	—	—	—	—	—	—	—	—	—	—
Financial Account, n.i.e.	78bjd	....	....	....	....	....	239	1,480	1,245	–60	1,565	1,659	1,321	–1,361	–3,678	–1,087
Direct Investment Abroad	78bdd	....	....	....	....	....			–5							
Dir. Invest. in Rep. Econ., n.i.e.	78bed	....	....	....	....	....	441	211	310	–739	542	431	364	189	486	193
Portfolio Investment Assets	78bfd	....	....	....	....	....	—	—	—	—	—	—	—	—	—	—
Equity Securities	78bkd	....	....	....	....	....	—	—	—	—	—	—	—	—	—	—
Debt Securities	78bld	....	....	....	....	....	—	—	—	—	—	—	—	—	—	—
Portfolio Investment Liab., n.i.e.	78bgd	....	....	....	....	....	—	—	—	—	—	—	—	—	—	—
Equity Securities	78bmd	....	....	....	....	....	—	—	—	—	—	—	—	—	—	—
Debt Securities	78bnd	....	....	....	....	....	—	—	—	—	—	—	—	—	—	—
Financial Derivatives Assets	78bwd	....	....	....	....	....	....	....	....	....	....	....	....	....	....	....
Financial Derivatives Liabilities	78bxd	....	....	....	....	....	....	....	....	....	....	....	....	....	....	....
Other Investment Assets	78bhd	....	....	....	....	....	–149	–209	–61	–27	146	–15	–444	–686	–2,636	–388
Monetary Authorities	78bod	....	....	....	....	....	–47	–24	45	–18	–2		–237	—	1,697	1,183
General Government	78bpd	....	....	....	....	....	–102	74	–98	–24	–16	19	–137	–90	73	–259
Banks	78bqd	....	....	....	....	....	—	–260	–8	15	164	–34	–70	–596	–4,406	–1,313
Other Sectors	78brd	....	....	....	....	....										
Other Investment Liab., n.i.e.	78bid	....	....	....	....	....	–53	1,478	1,002	706	877	1,243	1,401	–864	–1,527	–893
Monetary Authorities	78bsd	....	....	....	....	....	5	6	10	—						89
General Government	78btd	....	....	....	....	....	14	1,417	930	620	777	1,071	1,332	–965	–1,823	–979
Banks	78bud	....	....	....	....	....	–26	61	5	40	70	148	44	–222	125	–14
Other Sectors	78bvd	....	....	....	....	....	–45	–6	56	46	31	24	25	324	170	11
Net Errors and Omissions	78cad	....	....	....	....	....	–46	179	233	–735	–127	4	124	267	–135	–182
Overall Balance	78cbd	....	....	....	....	....	–823	–2,096	3,148	4,382	–5,036	–5,619	–2,887	–971	–1,209	–1,059
Reserves and Related Items	79dad	....	....	....	....	....	823	2,096	–3,148	–4,382	5,036	5,619	2,887	971	1,209	1,059
Reserve Assets	79dbd	....	....	....	....	....	823	2,096	–3,148	–4,382	4,976	2,085	431	–478	–506	454
Use of Fund Credit and Loans	79dcd	....	....	....	....	....	—	—	—	—	—	—	—	—	—	—
Exceptional Financing	79ded	....	....	....	....	....	—	—	—	—	60	3,534	2,456	1,448	1,715	605
Government Finance															*Millions of Naira:*	
Deficit (-) or Surplus	80	37	404	1,487	....	–1,130	1,135	2,122	2,871	9,184	2,055	–6,559	–5,392	–2,614	–3,040	–8,254
Revenue	81	1,023	1,769	4,190	4,712	5,523	6,263	5,645	8,609	11,628	7,050	5,819	6,272	6,939	9,640	7,969
Grants Received	81z	—	—	—	—	—	—	—	—	—	—	—	—	—	—	—
Expenditure	82	898	1,207	2,684	....	6,580	5,255	3,769	5,448	2,351	4,134	12,378	11,664	9,553	12,680	16,223
Lending Minus Repayments	83	88	158	19	459	72	–127	–246	290	93	861					
Financing																
Net Borrowing: Domestic	84a	–107	–114	....	....	....	....	....	....	....	....	3,402	7,376	3,450	2,277	499
Foreign	85a	–11	5	....	....	....	....	....	....	....	....	263	1,107	1,184	1,046	708
Use of Cash Balances	87	81	–295	....	....	–222	–687	....	....	....	....	2,894	–3,091	–2,019	–283	7,047
Debt: Domestic	88a	987	1,057	1,262	1,674	2,630	3,408	5,980	7,217	7,919	11,446	14,848	22,224	25,674	27,982	28,451
Central Bank	88aa	194	175	20	314	512	457	3,197	2,484	2,859	6,047	8,023	11,347	10,701	11,522	17,722
Commercial Banks	88ab	387	388	766	801	1,197	1,683	1,196	2,542	2,979	2,155	3,169	5,460	8,998	10,699	4,968
Other	88ac	406	494	477	559	922	1,269	1,587	2,192	2,080	3,244	3,657	5,417	5,975	5,761	5,761
Debt: Foreign	89a	263	277	322	350	376	364	1,252	1,614	1,867	3,024	2,595	10,577	14,537	17,290	41,452
National Accounts															*Billions of Naira*	
Househ.Cons.Expend.,incl.NPISHs	96f	5	7	11	14	16	19	24	26	32	35	36	41	48	54	56
Government Consumption Expend.	91f	1	1	1	2	3	4	5	5	5	7	7	7	7	7	7
Gross Capital Formation	93	1	3	3	6	9	10	10	10	11	12	10	7	4	5	8
Exports of Goods and Services	90c	2	2	6	5	7	8	7	11	14	11	10	8	10	12	9
Imports of Goods and Services (-)	98c	1	2	3	5	6	8	10	8	12	14	11	7	5	6	4
Gross Domestic Product (GDP)	99b	11	12	20	23	29	34	36	43	50	51	52	57	64	72	73
Net Primary Income from Abroad	98.n	–1	–1	—	—	—	—	—	–1	–1	–1	–1	–1	–2	–2	–4
Gross National Income (GNI)	99a	7	11	18	22	27	32	36	43	50	50	51	56	62	71	69
Consumption of Fixed Capital	99cf	....	—	1	1	1	....	....	....	....	3	3	3	4	4	5
GDP Factor Cost,Vol.1977/78 pRices	99bap	....	24	27	26	29	32	29	30	32	29	....	....	....	....	....
GDP at Factor Cost,Vol.'84 Prices	99bap	....	....	....	....	....	....	....	....	....		70	70	66	63	69	71
GDP Volume (1995=100)	99bvp	....	56.8	63.7	61.8	68.5	74.1	68.7	70.4	74.2	67.9	67.7	64.1	60.8	66.5	68.6
GDP Deflator (1995=100)	99bip	.9	1.0	1.4	1.8	2.0	2.2	2.5	2.8	3.2	3.7	3.8	4.4	5.1	5.3	5.3
																Millions:
Population	99z	69.56	71.33	73.11	74.88	76.55	78.33	80.27	82.39	84.73	87.31	83.62	86.29	†93.33	95.69	98.17

	1987	1988	1989	1990	1991	1992	1993	1994	1995	1996	1997	1998	1999	2000	2001		
Prices and Production																	
Period Averages																	
	5.7	8.9	13.4	14.3	16.2	23.4	36.9	57.9	100.0	129.3	139.9	154.3	161.7	185.2	215.7	Consumer Prices	64
	†80.6	84.5	97.0	101.4	109.1	108.7	102.3	100.3	100.0	102.9	103.6	103.7	100.7	110.3	112.0	Industrial Production	66
	67.5	74.0	87.6	92.3	96.5	97.4	96.6	97.3	100.0	103.5	106.2	108.5	108.9	116.0	116.4	Crude Petroleum Production	66aa
	†96.0	99.3	113.3	119.6	130.8	132.8	106.8	105.9	100.0	101.8	101.6	97.7	101.1	101.5	104.8	Manufacturing Production	66ey
International Transactions																	
Millions of US Dollars																	
	7,344	6,916	7,876	13,596	12,264	11,886	9,908	9,415	†12,342	16,154	15,207	9,855	13,856	20,975	....	Exports	70..d
	28,209	28,436	55,017	106,627	116,857	201,384	213,779	9,171	†11,449	15,866	14,850	8,565	12,665	18,897	....	Crude Petroleum (Naira)	70aa
	3,912	4,717	4,187	5,627	8,986	8,275	5,537	6,613	†8,222	6,438	9,501	9,211	8,588	8,721	....	Imports, c.i.f.	71..d
																Volume of Exports	
1985=100																	
	68	75	91	95	100	105	102	101	100	113	117	135	111	110	....	Crude Petroleum	72aa
Balance of Payments																	
Minus Sign Indicates Debit																	
	-73	-296	1,090	4,988	1,203	2,268	-780	-2,128	-2,578	3,507	552	-4,244	506	....	....	Current Account, n.i.e.	78al d
	7,560	6,875	7,871	13,585	12,254	11,791	9,910	9,459	11,734	16,117	15,207	8,971	12,876			Goods: Exports f.o.b.	78aa d
	-4,082	-4,355	-3,693	-4,932	-7,813	-7,181	-6,662	-6,511	-8,222	-6,438	-9,501	-9,211	-8,588			Goods: Imports f.o.b.	78ab d
	3,478	2,520	4,178	8,653	4,441	4,611	3,248	2,948	3,513	9,679	5,706	-240	4,288			*Trade Balance*	78ac d
	224	364	552	965	886	1,053	1,163	371	608	733	786	884	980			Services: Credit	78ad d
	-872	-804	-1,375	-1,976	-2,448	-1,810	-2,726	-3,007	-4,619	-4,827	-4,712	-4,166	-3,476			Services: Debit	78ae d
	2,831	2,080	3,355	7,642	2,879	3,853	1,685	312	-499	5,584	1,781	-3,522	1,792			*Balance on Goods & Services*	78af d
	46	41	152	211	211	156	58	49	101	115	258	333	240			Income: Credit	78ag d
	-2,926	-2,405	-2,544	-2,949	-2,631	-2,494	-3,335	-2,986	-2,979	-3,137	-3,404	-2,624	-2,818			Income: Debit	78ah d
	-49	-285	963	4,904	458	1,515	-1,593	-2,626	-3,377	2,562	-1,365	-5,813	-786			*Balance on Gds, Serv. & Inc.*	78ai d
	4	28	157	167	877	817	857	550	804	947	1,920	1,574	1,301			Current Transfers, n.i.e.: Credit	78aj d
	-28	-40	-31	-82	-132	-64	-44	-52	-5	-2	-4	-5	-9			Current Transfers: Debit	78ak d
	—	—	—	—	—	—	—	—	-66	-68	-49	-54	-48			Capital Account, n.i.e.	78bc d
	—	—	—	—	—	—	—	—	—	—	—	—	—			Capital Account, n.i.e.: Credit	78ba d
	—	—	—	—	—	—	—	—	-66	-68	-49	-54	-48			Capital Account: Debit	78bb d
	-4,159	-4,611	-3,649	-4,182	-2,633	-7,784	-1,043	329	-46	-4,155	-425	1,502	-4,002			Financial Account, n.i.e.	78bj d
											....	....	....			Direct Investment Abroad	78bd d
	611	379	1,884	588	712	897	1,345	1,959	1,079	1,593	1,539	1,051	1,005			Dir. Invest. in Rep. Econ., n.i.e.	78be d
	—	—	—	—	—	—	—	—	—	—	9	51	50			Portfolio Investment Assets	78bf d
	—	—	—	—	—	—	—	—	—	—	—	—	—			Equity Securities	78bk d
	—	—	—	—	—	—	—	—	—	—	9	51	50			Debt Securities	78bl d
	-551	-69	-220	-197	-61	1,884	-18	-27	-82	-173	-76	-59	-39			Portfolio Investment Liab., n.i.e.	78bg d
	—	—	—	—	—	—	—	—	—	—	—	—	—			Equity Securities	78bm d
	-551	-69	-220	-197	-61	1,884	-18	-27	-82	-173	-76	-59	-39			Debt Securities	78bl d
					....											Financial Derivatives Assets	78bw d
					....											Financial Derivatives Liabilities	78bx d
	-1,851	-1,121	-2,534	-2,886	-2,487	-5,840	-1,345	-1,286	-3,295	-4,320	-2,183	-332	-3,319			Other Investment Assets	78bh d
											....	....	....			Monetary Authorities	78bo d
	-336	-174	-2,397	-2,086	-771	-2,168	-1,087	-969	-1,030							General Government	78bp d
	-48	-187	-123	-3	-171	-746	-249	320	-560	138	-80	-284	-651			Banks	78bq d
	-1,468	-760	-15	-797	-1,545	-2,926	-8	-637	-1,705	-4,458	-2,103	-48	-2,668			Other Sectors	78br d
	-2,368	-3,799	-2,779	-1,687	-797	-4,725	-1,026	-317	2,251	-1,256	286	792	-1,699			Other Investment Liab., n.i.e.	78bi d
	-393	-113	—	49												Monetary Authorities	78bs d
	-3,508	-3,448	-2,817	-1,644	-3,088	-5,180	-1,736	-1,885	-1,535	-3,039	-2,883	-1,637	-1,659			General Government	78bt d
	-34	-148	36	-79	53	33	-28	-1	—	-4	1	21	34			Banks	78bu d
	1,567	-90	2	-13	2,238	423	738	1,570	3,787	1,787	3,167	2,407	-74			Other Sectors	78bv d
	-306	-221	-107	235	-93	-122	-88	-139	-83	-45	-62	-77	7			Net Errors and Omissions	78ca d
	-4,539	-5,129	-2,667	1,041	-1,523	-5,638	-1,911	-1,938	-2,774	-761	15	-2,873	-3,538			*Overall Balance*	78cb d
	4,539	5,129	2,667	-1,041	1,523	5,638	1,911	1,938	2,774	761	-15	2,873	3,538			Reserves and Related Items	79da d
	-39	506	-1,186	-2,478	-640	3,727	-611	-327	217	-2,634	-3,507	481	1,650			Reserve Assets	79db d
													....			Use of Fund Credit and Loans	79dc d
	4,578	4,623	3,853	1,437	2,163	1,911	2,522	2,265	2,557	3,395	3,491	2,392	1,887			Exceptional Financing	79de d
Government Finance																	
Year Ending December 31																	
	-5,889	-12,224	-15,135	-22,116	-35,755	-39,532	-107,735	-70,270	1,000	37,049	-5,000	-133,389				Deficit (-) or Surplus	80
	16,129	15,525	25,893	38,152	30,829	53,265	83,494	90,623	249,768	325,144	351,262	310,174				Revenue	81
																Grants Received	81z
	22,018	27,749	41,028	60,268	66,584	92,797	191,229	160,893	248,768	288,095	356,262	443,563				Expenditure	82
	—	—	—	—	—	—	—	—	—	—	—	—				Lending Minus Repayments	83
Financing																	
	8,339	10,240	10,020	27,042	32,107	46,716	91,136	60,248	7,102	-143,190	-60,637	103,886				Net Borrowing: Domestic	84a
	832	1,919	5,719	1,564	278	-11,860	16,964	8,391	22,455	7,825	13,383	16,605				Foreign	85a
	-3,283	65	-604	-6,490	3,370	4,676	-364	1,632	-30,558	98,315	52,254	12,898				Use of Cash Balances	87
	36,790	47,030	57,050	74,093	116,200	161,900	261,093	299,361	248,774	343,674	359,028	537,489				Debt: Domestic	88a
	19,197	27,682	38,391	56,564	89,413	122,028	189,773	199,662	187,509	247,461	264,229	435,131				Central Bank	88aa
	8,400	7,896	3,768	9,273	7,526	6,908	38,798	47,829	20,113	45,107	41,450	54,114				Commercial Banks	88ab
	9,193	11,452	14,891	8,256	19,261	32,964	32,522	51,870	41,152	51,106	53,349	48,244				Other	88ac
	100,787	133,956	240,033	298,614	328,051	544,264	633,144	648,813	716,775	617,320	595,932	633,017				Debt: Foreign	89a
National Accounts																	
Millions of Naira																	
	78	113	139	146	222	404	570	694	†1,775	2,368	2,380	2,817	1,970	2,447	3,403	Househ.Cons.Expend.,incl.NPISH	96f
	7	9	10	11	13	20	28	89	†123	143	172	215	25	260	275	Government Consumption Expend.	91f
	10	9	18	31	36	59	81	85	†115	172	206	194	176	270	393	Gross Capital Formation	93
	30	32	95	130	130	197	229	217	†679	2,368	2,435	2,757	1,650	2,932	3,122	Exports of Goods and Services	90c
	16	18	37	58	76	131	174	170	†482	712	1,020	1,027	728	927	1,553	Imports of Goods and Services (-)	98c
	109	145	225	261	328	620	997	915	†1,978	2,824	2,940	2,837	3,320	4,981	5,640	Gross Domestic Product (GDP)	99b
	-12	-13	-18	-22	-25	-64	-74	-66	†-202	-213	-228	-224	-240	-365	-456	Net Primary Income from Abroad	98.n
	97	133	207	239	300	485	624	849	†1,775	2,613	2,688	2,677	3,051	4,584	5,148	Gross National Income (GNI)	99a
	7	8	11	13	15	16	17	22	†20	22	22	22	22	22	22	Consumption of Fixed Capital	99cf
	....					....			....						....	GDP Factor Cost,Vol.1977/78 pRices	99ba p
	71	78	83	90	95	98	100	101	†104	107	110	113	116	120		GDP at Factor Cost,Vol.'84 Prices	99ba p
	68.3	75.1	80.6	87.2	91.3	94.2	96.2	97.5	†100.0	103.3	106.6	109.1	112.0	116.0		GDP Volume (1995=100)	99bv p
	7.9	9.6	13.8	14.8	17.8	32.7	51.4	47.5	†100.0	134.2	134.4	....	....	....		GDP Deflator (1995=100)	99bi p
Midyear Estimates																	
	101.41	104.96	84.72	87.03	88.52	91.13	93.79	96.51	99.21	102.10	104.96	107.88	110.85	115.22	116.93	**Population**	99z

(See notes in the back of the book.)

Norway

		1972	1973	1974	1975	1976	1977	1978	1979	1980	1981	1982	1983	1984	1985	1986
Exchange Rates															*Kroner per SDR:*	
Official Rate	aa	†7.2091	6.9094	6.3727	6.5381	6.0241	6.2430	6.5433	6.4892	6.6066	6.7597	7.7813	8.0847	8.9072	8.3288	9.0516
															Kroner per US Dollar:	
Official Rate	ae	†6.6400	5.7275	5.2050	5.5850	5.1850	5.1395	5.0225	4.9260	5.1800	5.8075	7.0540	7.7222	9.0870	7.5825	7.4000
Official Rate	rf	6.5882	5.7658	5.5397	5.2269	5.4565	5.3235	5.2423	5.0641	4.9392	5.7395	6.4540	7.2964	8.1615	8.5972	7.3947
										Kroner per ECU through 1998; Kroner per Euro Beginning 1999;							
Euro Rate	ea	....	....	....	....	....	....	....	....	....	....	....	....	....	....	....
Euro Rate	ag	....	....	....	....	....	....	....	....	....	....	....	....	....	....	....
Euro Rate	eb	....	....	....	....	....	....	....	....	....	....	....	....	....	....	....
Euro Rate	rh	....	....	....	....	....	....	....	....	....	....	....	....	....	....	....
															Index Numbers (1995=100):	
Official Rate	ahx	96.1	110.2	114.6	121.5	116.1	119.0	120.9	125.0	128.2	110.6	98.7	86.8	77.9	74.0	85.7
Nominal Effective Exchange Rate	neu	104.8	109.5	115.6	118.5	121.8	123.7	116.3	113.7	115.5	118.0	119.4	116.9	115.1	112.9	105.8
Real Effective Exchange Rate	reu	....	....	....	94.7	101.8	106.0	94.5	88.4	†88.0	90.6	93.3	93.9	95.1	95.8	93.2
Fund Position															*Millions of SDRs:*	
Quota	2f.s	240.0	240.0	240.0	240.0	240.0	240.0	295.0	295.0	442.5	442.5	442.5	699.0	699.0	699.0	699.0
SDRs	1b.s	87.9	88.0	88.2	89.0	89.5	92.8	96.3	139.7	157.6	195.3	284.3	257.3	262.2	258.0	318.2
Reserve Position in the Fund	1c.s	69.0	63.4	68.9	111.8	247.4	234.7	205.7	188.1	201.4	213.8	246.4	411.0	470.4	463.7	481.8
of which: Outstg.Fund Borrowing	2c	—	—	—	29.1	100.0	97.4	82.9	66.0	51.3	31.7	8.1	—	—	—	—
International Liquidity										*Millions of US Dollars Unless Otherwise Indicated:*							
Total Reserves minus Gold	1l.d	1,287.8	1,533.5	1,886.6	2,196.5	2,189.4	2,195.6	2,860.7	4,215.2	6,048.0	6,252.9	6,873.5	6,629.2	9,365.0	13,916.7	12,524.6
SDRs	1b.d	95.4	106.1	108.0	104.2	103.9	112.8	125.4	184.1	201.1	227.3	313.7	269.3	257.0	283.4	389.2
Reserve Position in the Fund	1c.d	74.9	76.5	84.4	130.9	287.4	285.0	268.0	247.8	256.8	248.8	271.9	430.3	461.1	509.3	589.4
Foreign Exchange	1d.d	1,117.5	1,350.8	1,694.2	1,961.4	1,798.1	1,797.8	2,467.2	3,783.4	5,590.1	5,776.8	6,288.0	5,929.5	8,647.0	13,124.0	11,546.0
Gold (Million Fine Troy Ounces)	1ad	.978	.979	.979	.979	.979	1.081	1.133	1.184	1.184	1.184	1.184	1.184	1.184	1.184	1.184
Gold (National Valuation)	1and	37.2e	41.3	45.1	42.1	45.3	50.6	54.2	57.9	55.0	49.1	40.4	36.9	31.4	37.6	38.5
Deposit Money Banks: Assets	7a.d	308.5	410.8	507.2	422.6	520.7	823.8	664.4	634.4	626.8	1,882.0	2,346.5	2,539.7	2,996.5	3,643.9	6,799.7
Liabilities	7b.d	365.7	437.1	605.2	472.7	685.4	585.1	752.8	1,279.5	2,738.4	3,438.8	3,979.4	4,335.6	5,540.1	9,163.5	13,324.2
Other Banking Insts.: Liabilities	7f.d	....	....	....	....	....	1,135.5	2,049.6	3,364.0	3,311.0	2,950.3	2,674.2	2,386.0	1,955.0	2,137.0	2,309.0
Monetary Authorities															*Billions of Kroner:*	
Foreign Assets	11	8.82	8.99	9.98	12.49	†11.63	11.58	14.63	21.02	31.45	36.72	48.89	51.40	85.53	107.47	93.05
Claims on Central Government	12a	6.22	6.52	6.45	7.72	9.44	12.83	13.04	14.77	9.83	11.12	5.66	11.76	7.67	19.21	47.74
Claims on Deposit Money Banks	12e	1.01	1.32	1.92	1.22	1.39	5.53	2.31	1.49	.97	2.96	2.80	4.62	2.19	8.27	71.46
Reserve Money	14	9.60	10.23	11.64	13.66	†15.37	17.20	19.44	21.19	23.01	22.86	24.36	25.36	29.36	31.44	31.07
of which: Currency Outside DMBs	14a	8.75	9.44	10.77	12.39	14.26	16.08	17.06	17.73	18.82	20.16	20.93	21.75	22.78	25.05	26.58
Central Government Deposits	16d	4.25	5.50	5.48	6.09	5.54	7.03	6.07	8.34	10.18	11.96	8.02	19.45	35.42	81.38	144.65
Other Items (Net)	17r	2.21	1.09	1.23	1.68	†1.55	5.71	4.46	7.76	9.06	15.98	24.96	22.98	30.61	22.13	36.53
Deposit Money Banks															*Billions of Kroner:*	
Reserves	20	1.33	1.40	1.44	1.30	†1.46	1.17	1.82	5.30	2.65	1.60	2.00	3.68	4.22	4.31	3.60
Foreign Assets	21	2.05	2.34	2.64	2.36	†2.70	4.23	3.34	3.13	3.25	10.93	16.55	19.61	27.23	27.63	50.32
Claims on Central Government	22a	7.26	8.31	7.98	7.49	†20.00	23.01	28.26	37.61	48.42	48.04	47.81	49.81	67.74	74.22	84.66
Claims on Local Government	22b	....	....	....	5.21	5.89	6.46	7.10	8.29	9.50	8.90	8.85	10.30	10.58	10.18
Claims on Nonfin.Pub.Enterprises	22c	....	....	....	1.36	1.58	1.54	1.49	1.74	2.38	7.49	9.25	11.25	12.79	10.63
Claims on Private Sector	22d	38.18	43.23	49.10	57.05	†60.06	70.04	76.00	84.61	96.79	112.13	127.26	145.63	184.37	241.34	309.05
Claims on Other Financial Insts	22f	....	....	....	....	11.05	14.72	15.67	16.33	19.14	22.57	25.44	31.09	32.07	39.43	45.55
Demand Deposits	24	10.59	12.09	13.70	15.26	†17.96	20.73	22.09	24.67	25.48	31.13	36.69	42.84	57.71	71.83	73.80
Time, Savings,& Fgn.Currency Dep.	25	32.90	37.41	41.62	48.06	†61.10	72.77	82.79	96.33	109.07	122.80	135.71	149.03	173.67	195.31	198.55
Foreign Liabilities	26c	2.43	2.49	3.15	2.64	†3.55	3.01	3.78	6.30	14.19	19.97	28.07	33.48	50.34	69.48	98.60
Central Government Deposits	26d	....	....	....	7.87	7.19	9.57	10.67	12.75	11.74	11.11	11.69	15.18	20.79	22.25
Credit from Bank of Norway	26g	....	....	....	1.36	5.53	2.68	2.95	3.82	3.05	2.70	4.35	5.35	9.88	73.55
Other Items (Net)	27r	2.89	3.33	2.73	2.25	†9.97	11.38	12.16	14.63	14.95	18.44	21.17	26.53	34.93	32.85	36.19
Monetary Survey															*Billions of Kroner:*	
Foreign Assets (Net)	31n	8.29	8.67	9.21	12.01	†10.59	9.91	13.99	17.54	20.25	27.44	36.91	36.78	62.04	65.26	44.24
Domestic Credit	32	56.31	63.50	70.33	81.22	†94.18	114.31	125.84	143.37	161.72	182.48	204.01	235.20	263.29	295.87	341.53
Claims on Central Govt. (Net)	32an	14.53	16.00	15.94	18.00	†16.03	21.61	25.65	33.38	35.33	35.46	34.34	30.43	24.81	-8.74	-34.49
Claims on Local Government	32b	2.70	3.29	4.08	4.52	†5.24	5.92	6.49	7.12	8.31	9.52	8.91	8.87	10.31	10.59	10.19
Claims on Nonfin.Pub.Enterprises	32c	....	....	....	....	1.40	1.62	1.58	1.55	1.80	2.43	7.54	9.30	11.30	12.85	10.69
Claims on Private Sector	32d	39.08	44.21	50.31	58.70	†60.18	70.19	76.23	84.81	96.99	112.37	127.66	145.97	184.71	241.66	309.37
Claims on Other Financial Insts	32f	....	....	....	....	11.32	14.97	15.89	16.52	19.29	22.71	25.57	31.20	32.17	39.51	45.78
Money	34	22.39	25.81	28.88	33.65	†32.42	37.00	40.19	43.25	45.56	52.38	58.81	65.92	82.00	98.65	101.76
Quasi-Money	35	37.18	41.81	46.22	52.95	†61.29	72.91	82.85	96.42	109.17	122.88	135.79	149.72	174.99	196.82	200.12
Other Items (Net)	37r	5.02	4.59	4.48	6.62	†11.04	14.29	16.78	21.22	27.23	34.66	46.32	46.90	68.29	55.47	72.83
Money plus Quasi-Money	35l	59.56	67.62	75.10	86.60	†93.71	109.91	123.04	139.67	154.73	175.26	194.60	215.63	256.99	295.47	301.88
Money (National Definitions)															*Billions of Kroner:*	
Broad Money	39m	53.9	60.3	67.0	76.7	90.2	105.8	117.8	133.4	151.3	168.0	185.5	203.5	244.8	278.4	284.1
Broad Money, Seasonally Adj.	39m.c	....	....	....	....	....	....	....	....	....	....	....	....	....	....	....
Other Banking Institutions																
State Lending Institutions																*Billions of Kroner:*
Claims on State and Local Govts	42b	....	....	....	....	....	10.22	13.51	19.21	22.05	23.77	16.69	18.01	19.14	20.18	21.61
Claims on Private Sector	42d	24.77	28.51	32.25	37.97	45.43	†42.14	50.32	57.08	63.97	70.60	77.05	82.01	89.26	94.13	100.11
Bonds (Net)	46ab	2.21	2.72	3.15	5.41	7.45	†6.11	7.42	7.97	8.89	10.48	12.03	11.96	12.71	13.05	12.61
Foreign Liabilities	46c	....	....	....	....	....	5.84	10.29	16.19	16.68	16.67	18.41	17.97	17.28	15.77	16.64
Central Govt. Lending Funds	46f	21.91	25.11	28.52	32.12	37.11	†43.21	49.02	55.50	62.66	67.73	73.77	79.72	87.52	93.87	101.28
Capital Accounts	47a	1.73	1.80	2.11	2.31	2.65	†3.65	4.56	4.97	5.97	6.58	7.07	7.29	8.06	8.26	8.15
Other Items (Net)	47r	-1.10	-1.12	-1.53	-1.85	-1.77	†-6.45	-7.46	-8.33	-8.17	-7.09	-17.54	-16.92	-17.18	-16.64	-16.97

1987	1988	1989	1990	1991	1992	1993	1994	1995	1996	1997	1998	1999	2000	2001		
															Exchange Rates	
End of Period																
8.8418	8.8412	8.6932	8.4044	8.5440	9.5212	10.3264	9.8715	9.3931	9.2641	9.8707	10.7010	11.0343	11.5288	11.3251	Official Rate	aa
End of Period (ae) Period Average (rf)																
6.2325	6.5700	6.6150	5.9075	5.9730	6.9245	7.5180	6.7620	6.3190	6.4425	7.3157	7.6000	8.0395	8.8485	9.0116	Official Rate	ae
6.7375	6.5170	6.9045	6.2597	6.4829	6.2145	7.0941	7.0576	6.3352	6.4498	7.0734	7.5451	7.7992	8.8018	8.9917	Official Rate	rf
End of Period (ea) Period Average (eb)																
....	....	....	8.0230	8.0164	8.3848	8.3878	8.3175	8.3067	8.0615	8.0867	8.8708	†8.0765	8.2335	7.9735	Euro Rate	ea
....	....	....	....	....	....	....	....	....	....	....	....	1.0046	.9305	.8813	Euro Rate	ag
....	....	....	....	8.0186	8.0398	8.3505	8.3760	8.2859	8.1971	8.0131	8.4541	†8.3140	8.1133	8.0493	Euro Rate	eb
....	....	....	....	....	....	....	....	....	....	....	....	1.0668	.9240	.8956	Euro Rate	rh
Period Averages																
94.1	97.3	91.8	101.3	98.0	102.1	89.1	89.8	100.0	98.2	89.7	83.9	81.2	72.1	70.4	Official Rate	ahx
101.5	101.4	101.5	100.9	99.2	100.3	98.9	97.5	100.0	99.7	100.2	95.8	95.0	93.4	96.0	Nominal Effective Exchange Rate	neu
96.6	98.4	97.6	97.1	96.5	96.8	94.9	94.7	100.0	102.5	106.9	108.1	113.3	115.5	122.0	Real Effective Exchange Rate	reu
															Fund Position	
End of Period																
699.0	699.0	699.0	699.0	699.0	1,104.6	1,104.6	1,104.6	1,104.6	1,104.6	1,104.6	1,104.6	1,671.7	1,671.7	1,671.7	Quota	2f. s
311.2	362.3	345.2	315.5	315.9	139.1	288.4	266.7	311.5	247.2	257.9	294.1	298.0	235.4	282.1	SDRs	1b. s
498.1	451.3	441.9	407.8	399.0	471.4	425.5	440.9	636.2	643.8	725.5	899.1	621.2	448.1	577.3	Reserve Position in the Fund	1c. s
—	—	—	—	—	—	—	—	—	—	—	35.3	—	—	—	of which: Outstg.Fund Borrowing	2c
															International Liquidity	
End of Period																
14,276.5	13,267.7	13,784.8	15,332.3	13,232.0	11,940.4	19,622.4	19,025.5	22,517.8	26,516.7	23,400.3	18,606.7	20,400.4	20,164.1	15,488.0	Total Reserves minus Gold	1l. d
441.5	487.5	453.7	448.9	451.9	191.2	396.2	389.4	463.0	355.5	347.9	414.1	409.0	306.6	354.5	SDRs	1b. d
706.6	607.4	580.7	580.2	570.8	648.1	584.4	643.7	945.6	925.8	978.9	1,266.0	852.6	583.8	725.6	Reserve Position in the Fund	1c. d
13,128.4	12,172.9	12,750.5	14,303.2	12,209.4	11,101.0	18,641.8	17,992.4	21,109.2	25,235.5	22,073.5	16,926.7	19,138.7	19,273.7	14,408.0	Foreign Exchange	1d. d
1.184	1.184	1.184	1.184	1.184	1.184	1.184	1.184	1.184	1.184	1.184	1.184	1.184	1.184	1.184	Gold (Million Fine Troy Ounces)	1ad
45.7	43.4	43.1	48.2	47.7	41.2	37.9	42.1	45.1	44.2	38.8	37.5	274.5	257.1	260.3	Gold (National Valuation)	1and
8,507.3	6,326.0	6,428.1	7,816.8	8,954.1	11,398.8	6,597.1	7,267.4	7,473.0	9,087.8	9,781.4	12,324.9	12,418.4	15,280.1	15,092.1	Deposit Money Banks: Assets	7a. d
19,971.6	19,047.0	20,514.0	22,173.5	16,383.4	11,049.5	9,637.4	9,241.3	9,617.3	19,885.4	25,617.0	29,849.7	31,818.9	37,022.4	39,739.8	Liabilities	7b. d
2,512.0	5,531.8	5,942.9	7,725.9	7,270.6	5,946.3	5,731.3	6,040.1	6,434.6	6,198.7	7,081.2	8,179.1	8,774.8	10,659.0	13,206.4	Other Banking Insts.: Liabilities	7f. d
															Monetary Authorities	
End of Period																
89.62	87.52	91.83	90.92	78.75	82.50	151.43	143.58	142.78	225.37	284.17	312.96	408.32	620.51	812.09	Foreign Assets	11
23.93	18.24	24.05	12.56	7.98	12.58	29.25	13.69	18.06	12.41	10.65	9.43	10.77	13.83	11.88	Claims on Central Government	12a
77.27	79.83	70.77	69.04	66.25	55.40	17.48	5.86	10.09	.23	7.50	16.47	25.63	23.94	16.64	Claims on Deposit Money Banks	12e
33.39	32.56	34.45	34.12	36.73	38.52	42.66	44.09	46.39	70.96	62.79	55.89	83.95	70.29	69.75	Reserve Money	14
28.16	28.52	29.20	29.88	31.79	32.45	35.74	37.95	39.08	39.87	42.22	42.14	43.37	42.52	42.04	of which: Currency Outside DMBs	14a
119.27	116.75	121.09	109.01	85.00	67.62	106.76	87.24	98.39	131.24	201.16	222.73	290.18	482.50	696.87	Central Government Deposits	16d
38.17	36.30	31.11	29.39	31.25	44.40	48.75	31.80	26.15	35.81	38.37	60.24	70.59	105.49	73.99	Other Items (Net)	17r
															Deposit Money Banks	
End of Period																
4.31	3.10	3.27	3.00	3.34	4.57	2.88	4.32	5.15	28.06	17.28	14.07	38.36	27.82	29.75	Reserves	20
53.02	41.56	42.52	46.18	53.48	78.93	49.60	49.14	47.22	58.55	71.56	93.67	99.84	135.21	136.00	Foreign Assets	21
78.15	83.13	83.72	85.46	74.66	76.98	87.32	73.87	70.56	78.49	60.79	87.04	45.42	38.58	35.19	Claims on Central Government	22a
14.19	16.74	16.84	14.77	10.87	9.84	11.62	11.31	12.78	15.16	15.71	26.89	17.38	11.93	10.39	Claims on Local Government	22b
12.71	10.31	10.08	8.18	7.19	6.31	9.05	9.24	5.80	8.04	9.19	12.03	11.21	14.05	13.96	Claims on Nonfin.Pub.Enterprises	22c
378.46	406.09	441.17	461.68	441.38	447.36	457.14	479.68	527.46	599.82	708.01	801.58	849.70	969.64	1,075.45	Claims on Private Sector	22d
71.74	58.45	51.67	43.58	41.82	44.52	34.92	37.11	34.04	40.46	50.13	75.74	72.54	82.55	92.64	Claims on Other Financial Insts	22f
122.95	157.28	186.66	206.37	222.16	288.79	300.43	314.80	316.29	349.70	371.96	453.20	479.34	521.01	616.02	Demand Deposits	24
205.66	189.31	190.70	194.49	189.18	159.95	139.95	149.24	164.57	166.71	150.52	157.80	141.03	159.08	128.06	Time, Savings,& Fgn.Currency Dep.	25
124.47	125.14	135.70	130.99	97.86	76.51	72.45	62.49	60.77	128.11	187.41	226.86	255.81	327.59	358.12	Foreign Liabilities	26c
26.56	30.44	31.78	30.55	27.74	31.67	36.55	33.02	34.00	37.62	32.09	57.40	25.90	24.64	32.30	Central Government Deposits	26d
75.93	77.31	61.03	59.95	60.73	56.08	17.03	5.30	10.47	.45	7.88	18.79	25.94	24.70	16.90	Credit from Bank of Norway	26g
57.02	39.92	43.41	40.49	35.08	56.09	86.13	99.57	115.92	145.98	182.80	196.97	206.44	222.75	241.99	Other Items (Net)	27r
															Monetary Survey	
End of Period																
17.74	3.12	−1.78	5.89	34.11	80.32	123.14	123.81	125.01	142.13	159.34	169.03	224.99	367.23	546.14	Foreign Assets (Net)	31n
433.82	446.30	475.59	487.34	473.64	499.07	486.63	505.25	536.90	586.05	621.74	735.92	691.51	624.01	511.00	Domestic Credit	32
−43.75	−45.81	−45.10	−41.54	−30.09	−9.72	−26.74	−32.71	−43.77	−77.96	−161.81	−183.66	−259.89	−454.74	−682.09	Claims on Central Govt. (Net)	32an
14.20	16.75	16.85	14.77	10.87	9.84	11.62	11.31	12.78	15.16	15.71	26.89	17.38	11.93	10.39	Claims on Local Government	32b
12.79	10.32	10.08	8.18	7.19	6.31	9.05	9.24	5.80	8.04	9.19	12.03	11.21	14.05	13.96	Claims on Nonfin.Pub.Enterprises	32c
378.80	406.56	442.00	462.33	442.02	448.01	457.77	480.30	528.05	600.35	708.52	802.11	850.26	970.21	1,076.10	Claims on Private Sector	32d
71.79	58.49	51.76	43.60	43.66	44.63	34.92	37.11	34.04	40.46	50.13	78.55	72.54	82.55	92.64	Claims on Other Financial Insts	32f
152.63	187.15	218.30	237.63	255.80	323.33	340.12	354.96	358.71	392.72	416.99	497.51	525.30	565.22	659.56	Money	34
207.11	190.30	191.50	195.07	189.48	160.02	139.99	149.27	164.59	166.73	150.53	157.81	141.04	159.08	128.06	Quasi-Money	35
91.74	71.75	64.02	60.30	62.47	96.66	129.66	124.58	137.62	168.72	213.56	249.62	250.17	266.94	269.52	Other Items (Net)	37r
359.74	377.45	409.79	432.70	445.28	483.35	480.11	504.23	523.30	559.45	567.52	655.32	666.33	724.30	787.62	Money plus Quasi-Money	35l
															Money (National Definitions)	
End of Period																
328.6	345.1	374.8	395.1	442.7	470.9	469.0	491.1	530.3	564.4	578.8	605.6	671.6	732.1	795.1	*Broad Money*	39m
....	....	....	....	....	466.2	465.3	488.5	528.9	563.4	577.8	603.9	667.3	731.4	795.6	*Broad Money, Seasonally Adj.*	39m. c
															Other Banking Institutions	
															State Lending Institutions	
End of Period																
23.21	24.90	26.71	27.82	30.79	33.41	34.53	35.40	36.68	37.90	41.84	42.36	46.17	18.28	18.79	Claims on State and Local Govts	42b
107.43	115.53	123.46	131.54	140.95	149.31	145.34	139.53	138.56	135.69	131.73	140.96	146.46	152.02	164.09	Claims on Private Sector	42d
12.82	13.44	14.71	18.72	18.32	20.81	21.39	16.68	10.39	11.81	16.01	20.16	28.65	.06	.05	Bonds (Net)	46ab
15.20	13.21	11.09	8.23	6.41	5.27	3.69	1.81	1.14	1.17	.33	1.39	—	—	—	Foreign Liabilities	46c
112.21	122.54	133.06	140.88	152.07	162.13	160.22	155.32	154.28	153.78	152.38	158.75	162.43	168.96	181.43	Central Govt. Lending Funds	46f
8.04	7.74	8.27	7.87	8.10	9.00	12.23	10.30	10.39	8.61	8.45	8.25	6.74	5.46	6.85	Capital Accounts	47a
−17.64	−16.48	−16.94	−16.33	−13.15	−14.50	−17.66	−9.17	−.94	−1.78	−3.61	−5.22	−5.18	−4.16	−5.45	Other Items (Net)	47r

Norway

		1972	1973	1974	1975	1976	1977	1978	1979	1980	1981	1982	1983	1984	1985	1986
Mortgage Institutions																*Billions of Kroner:*
Foreign Assets	41.. l	...	...	...	...	...	...	...	...	...	...	...	...	...	...	...
Claims on Central Government	42a. l	...	...	...	...	...	...	...	...	...	...	...	...	...	...	...
Claims on State and Local Govt.	42b. l	...	...	...	...	...	...	...	...	...	...	...	...	...	...	...
Claims on Nonfin.Pub.Enterprises	42c. l	...	...	...	...	...	...	...	...	...	...	...	...	...	...	...
Claims on Private Sector	42d. l	7.18	8.29	9.48	81.49	81.40	81.29	81.18	81.03	81.11	80.94	80.83	80.62	80.89	81.31	85.61
Credit Market Instruments	46aa l															
Bonds (net)	46ab l	6.93	8.10	9.37	69.94	69.94	69.95	69.95	69.95	69.95	69.82	69.94	69.98	69.98	69.98	69.98
Foreign Liabilities	46c. l	...	...	...	...	...	...	...	...	...	...	...	...	...	...	...
Capital Accounts	47a. l	...	...	...	...	...	...	...	...	...	...	...	...	...	...	...
Other Items (Net)	47r. l	...	...	...	...	...	...	...	...	...	...	...	...	...	...	...
Nonbank Financial Institutions																*Billions of Kroner:*
Claims on Central Government	42a. s	1.74	1.78	1.79	1.76	1.75	1.53	2.69	4.30	5.34	4.74	5.01	6.46	7.62	9.37	10.92
Claims on Local Government	42b. s	1.72	1.88	2.17	2.47	2.82	3.06	3.24	3.34	4.04	5.37	6.89	8.73	9.74	11.15	12.99
Claims on Private Sector	42d. s	7.39	8.02	8.76	9.62	10.66	11.56	12.03	12.58	13.61	15.32	17.13	19.79	23.16	28.04	35.86
Claims on Other Financial Insts	42f. s	1.89	2.23	2.56	3.05	3.80	5.27	5.81	6.37	7.27	9.10	11.08	12.79	14.59	16.83	21.24
Incr.in Total Assets(Within Per.)	49z. s	1.01	1.19	1.41	1.64	2.22	2.39	2.89	3.00	3.93	5.04	6.10	7.14	8.89	11.85	13.64
Interest Rates																*Percent Per Annum*
Discount Rate *(End of Period)*	60	4.50	4.50	5.50	5.00	6.00	6.00	7.00	9.00	9.00	9.00	†9.20	10.00	10.20	10.70	14.80
Avg.Cost for Centr.Bank Funding	60.a	...	...	...	...	...	...	...	...	...	...	...	...	...	...	...
Deposit Rate	60l								5.10	5.00	5.10	5.10	5.30	5.30	10.06	10.97
Lending Rate	60p								12.23	12.63	13.90	14.33	14.35	13.69	13.46	14.37
Three Month Interbank Rate	60zb												15.37	13.30	13.02	12.53	14.39
Government Bond Yield	61	6.27	6.19	7.10	7.29	7.25	7.39	8.45	8.59	10.27	12.31	13.20	12.86	12.16	12.58	13.47
Prices, Production, Labor																*Index Numbers (1995=100):*
Industrial Share Prices	62	9	14	13	10	10	8	6	9	11	11	†10	16	22	29	31
Producer Prices	63						46.0	47.8	51.3	58.1	64.2	69.7	74.2	79.4	83.2	80.4
Consumer Prices	64	21.7	23.3	25.5	28.5	31.1	33.9	36.7	38.4	42.6	48.5	54.0	58.5	62.2	65.7	70.4
Wages: Hourly Earnings	65	15.1	16.6	19.5	†23.4	27.0	30.0	32.4	33.4	36.5	40.3	44.3	48.0	52.1	56.4	62.1
Industrial Production	66.. c	35.7	37.7	39.4	41.5	43.9	43.5	48.1	51.8	†55.1	56.7	56.4	61.6	66.4	68.7	71.1
Crude Petroleum Production	66aa	1.2	1.1	1.2	6.7	9.8	9.8	12.3	13.5	17.5	16.9	17.7	22.0	25.2	27.6	30.5
Employment	67	82.9	83.1	83.4	85.1	86.1	87.7	89.2	90.0	92.1	92.9	93.6	94.1	94.7	96.9	100.3
																Number in Thousands:
Labor Force	67d	...	...	...	...	...	...	...	...	...	...	...	...	...	...	...
Employment	67e	...	...	...	...	...	...	...	...	...	...	...	...	2,014	†2,086	
Unemployment	67c	...	...	...	...	...	...	...	...	...	...	...	...		53	42
Unemployment Rate (%)	67r	...	...	...	...	...	...	...	...	...	...	...	...		2.6	2.0
International Transactions																*Millions of Kroner*
Exports	70	21,625	27,085	34,732	37,922	43,330	47,263	57,084	68,527	91,672	104,265	113,236	131,397	154,035	170,733	133,847
Imports, c.i.f.	71	28,808	36,041	46,556	50,545	60,533	68,579	60,169	69,339	83,602	89,688	99,747	98,408	113,102	132,563	150,052
																1995=100
Volume of Exports	72	26.4	29.1	28.9	30.1	34.6	33.5	41.3	43.6	†46.1	†45.2	45.8	49.2	53.7	55.4	53.1
Volume of Imports	73	37.8	42.7	46.4	46.4	51.7	55.8	49.4	52.0	†57.7	55.4	57.7	55.4	62.9	70.3	80.7
Unit Value of Exports	74	33.2	36.4	47.7	51.9	53.2	56.8	60.0	70.3	†91.6	106.2	113.6	117.5	129.1	134.2	100.8
Unit Value of Imports	75	33.1	35.2	44.3	47.1	50.2	54.3	57.1	63.0	†70.8	75.7	79.3	83.0	84.6	90.1	89.9
Balance of Payments																*Millions of US Dollars:*
Current Account, n.i.e.	78ald	...	...	...	-2,478	-3,746	-5,053	-2,118	-1,047	1,079	2,131	640	1,962	2,886	3,038	-4,551
Goods: Exports f.o.b.	78aa d	...	...	...	7,270	8,047	9,152	11,033	13,747	18,649	18,494	17,664	18,055	19,115	20,059	18,143
Goods: Imports f.o.b.	78ab d	...	...	...	-10,141	-11,608	-13,205	-11,545	-13,601	-16,753	-15,459	-15,278	-13,704	-13,957	-15,331	-20,257
Trade Balance	78ac d	...	...	...	-2,871	-3,561	-4,053	-512	146	1,896	3,035	2,386	4,351	5,158	4,728	-2,115
Services: Credit	78ad d	...	...	...	4,542	4,779	5,109	5,582	7,054	8,615	8,753	7,927	7,109	7,097	7,456	8,142
Services: Debit	78ae d	...	...	...	-3,641	-4,228	-4,918	-5,437	-5,977	-6,996	-7,283	-7,132	-7,148	-7,253	-7,515	-8,608
Balance on Goods & Services	78af d	...	...	...	-1,969	-3,010	-3,862	-367	1,223	3,516	4,505	3,181	4,312	5,002	4,670	-2,581
Income: Credit	78ag d	...	...	...	313	288	304	407	597	988	1,443	1,629	1,378	1,616	2,099	2,723
Income: Debit	78ah d	...	...	...	-662	-826	-1,181	-1,775	-2,427	-2,909	-3,286	-3,587	-3,125	-3,193	-3,152	-3,883
Balance on Gds, Serv. & Inc.	78ai d	...	...	...	-2,319	-3,548	-4,740	-1,734	-607	1,594	2,662	1,223	2,565	3,425	3,617	-3,741
Current Transfers, n.i.e.: Credit	78aj d	...	...	...	101	97	50	55	63	78	75	98	97	87	85	95
Current Transfers: Debit	78ak d	...	...	...	-260	-295	-363	-438	-504	-593	-606	-682	-699	-626	-664	-906
Capital Account, n.i.e.	78bc d	...	...	...			19	15	3	19	45	23	24	33	14	6
Capital Account, n.i.e.: Credit	78ba d	...	...	...	—	—	52	51	54	76	102	80	79	78	81	81
Capital Account: Debit	78bb d	...	...	...	—	—	-33	-36	-50	-56	-56	-58	-55	-45	-67	-76
Financial Account, n.i.e.	78bj d	...	...	...	2,618	3,499	4,521	2,213	1,727	-133	-1,732	148	-2,455	488	1,459	2,961
Direct Investment Abroad	78bd d	...	...	...	-172	-193	-125	-66	-44	-253	-173	-306	-355	-601	-1,304	-1,600
Dir. Invest. in Rep. Econ., n.i.e.	78be d	...	...	...	220	371	768	490	401	60	672	442	328	-180	-426	1,017
Portfolio Investment Assets	78bf d	...	...	...	2	-17	5	—	-14	-88	15	11	-33	143	126	-373
Equity Securities	78bk d	...	...	...							22	30	22	49	31	-116
Debt Securities	78bl d	...	...	...	2	-17	5	—	-14	-88	-8	-18	-54	94	95	-257
Portfolio Investment Liab., n.i.e.	78bg d	...	...	...	610	1,346	2,062	2,458	2,066	-54	-714	-679	-867	667	1,650	4,656
Equity Securities	78bm d	...	...	...						—	16	61	144	322	-31	318
Debt Securities	78bn d	...	...	...	610	1,346	2,062	2,458	2,066	-54	-730	-740	-1,011	345	1,681	4,338
Financial Derivatives Assets	78bw d	...	...	...												
Financial Derivatives Liabilities	78bx d	...	...	...												
Other Investment Assets	78bh d	...	...	...	-328	-93	-572	-890	-1,590	-1,777	-1,707	-1,942	-1,279	-949	-790	-2,341
Monetary Authorities	78bo d	...	...	...												
General Government	78bp d	...	...	...	5	1	-103	-271	60	-250	63	-27	-3	66	-82	-131
Banks	78bq d	...	...	...	-37	-29	-281	184	29	-69	-1,365	-1,231	-561	-1,309	121	-2,598
Other Sectors	78br d	...	...	...	-296	-65	-188	-803	-1,679	-1,459	-405	-684	-715	295	-829	388
Other Investment Liab., n.i.e.	78bi d	...	...	...	2,285	2,084	2,383	221	908	1,980	176	2,620	-249	1,408	2,204	1,602
Monetary Authorities	78bs d	...	...	...	-26	-1	519	-423	21	152	-17	56	71	-82	-18	70
General Government	78bt d	...	...	...	495	104	141	425	4	-8	-239	-304	-369	-154	-4	-18
Banks	78bu d	...	...	...	26	124	-112	137	506	1,636	780	1,262	529	1,579	1,932	1,045
Other Sectors	78bv d	...	...	...	1,790	1,857	1,835	82	376	200	-348	1,606	-479	65	295	504
Net Errors and Omissions	78ca d	...	...	...	201	219	391	527	601	917	-14	-102	370	-340	-1,059	-1,626
Overall Balance	78cb d	...	...	...	340	-28	-121	637	1,285	1,882	431	708	-98	3,068	3,452	-3,211
Reserves and Related Items	79da d	...	...	...	-340	28	121	-637	-1,285	-1,882	-431	-708	98	-3,068	-3,452	3,211
Reserve Assets	79db d	...	...	...	-340	28	121	-637	-1,285	-1,882	-431	-708	98	-3,068	-3,452	3,211
Use of Fund Credit and Loans	79dc d	...	...	...	—	—	—	—	—	—	—	—	—	—	—	—
Exceptional Financing	79de d	...	...	...											...	...

1987	1988	1989	1990	1991	1992	1993	1994	1995	1996	1997	1998	1999	2000	2001	Item	Code
End of Period															**Mortgage Institutions**	
....	21.49	19.88	20.44	21.92	23.61	19.67	23.95	24.02	22.11	19.36	29.99	33.39	30.32	39.59	Foreign Assets	41.. *l*
....	2.00	1.01	.85	1.05	1.37	2.85	1.48	1.94	1.55	1.22	1.53	1.09	1.16	1.26	Claims on Central Government	42a. *l*
....	3.12	4.56	4.32	3.18	1.82	2.00	1.91	2.64	4.33	5.60	5.55	8.08	49.83	60.37	Claims on State and Local Govt.	42b. *l*
....	3.57	3.77	4.00	3.38	2.11	1.65	1.32	1.34	1.70	1.37	1.90	4.68	2.78	5.69	Claims on Nonfin.Pub.Enterprises	42c. *l*
123.65	121.50	136.96	138.74	117.00	80.73	72.15	62.34	60.05	55.55	66.33	88.87	82.04	93.61	103.07	Claims on Private Sector	42d. *l*
....	9.24	6.08	5.74	6.67	3.77	5.45	6.97	7.40	5.49	3.70	3.13	8.21	4.81	5.57	Credit Market Instruments	46aa *l*
87.29	94.01	115.24	114.40	100.25	55.87	42.16	35.01	36.46	37.21	33.14	36.46	36.63	58.57	61.04	Bonds (net)	46ab *l*
....	23.13	28.23	37.41	37.02	35.91	39.40	39.04	39.52	38.76	51.47	60.77	70.55	94.32	119.01	Foreign Liabilities	46c. *l*
....	4.60	5.39	5.62	4.03	6.38	8.00	7.76	7.59	6.64	6.51	8.31	8.73	11.04	11.23	Capital Accounts	47a. *l*
....	20.69	11.24	5.16	-1.46	7.72	3.30	2.23	-.99	-2.87	-.93	19.17	5.16	8.97	13.13	Other Items (Net)	47r. *l*
End of Period															**Nonbank Financial Institutions**	
7.15	3.86	6.38	5.55	12.53	18.16	32.36	40.47	42.34	42.83	49.16	35.95	34.07	31.34	43.74	Claims on Central Government	42a. *s*
14.79	18.85	23.00	29.23	28.97	30.54	31.29	32.27	30.85	29.55	27.42	28.61	35.07	38.14	43.52	Claims on Local Government	42b. *s*
43.57	45.88	45.81	48.10	63.10	73.54	75.78	65.71	73.90	77.07	71.55	75.08	80.43	92.75	103.63	Claims on Private Sector	42d. *s*
28.33	38.01	44.73	44.43	32.75	28.44	24.30	28.05	32.58	38.85	42.54	48.10	46.36	36.98	50.38	Claims on Other Financial Insts	42f. *s*
12.78	12.80	14.56	8.87	9.08	12.61	14.67	7.94	10.92	6.91	3.02	-.86	5.77	5.74	45.69	*Incr.in Total Assets(Within Per.)*	49z. *s*
Percent Per Annum															**Interest Rates**	
13.80	12.00	11.00	10.50	10.00	11.00	7.00	6.75	6.75	6.00	5.50	10.00	7.50	9.00	8.50	Discount Rate *(End of Period)*	60
....	14.28	11.50	11.85	10.93	7.65	5.70	6.46	5.40	4.96	4.80	6.18	6.86	7.31	7.45	Avg.Cost for Centr.Bank Funding	60.a
12.03	11.49	9.63	9.68	9.60	10.69	5.51	5.21	4.95	4.15	3.63	7.24	5.38	6.73	....	Deposit Rate	60l
16.31	16.60	14.88	14.26	14.31	14.16	10.97	8.40	7.78	7.10	5.95	7.91	8.16	8.22	8.87	Lending Rate	60p
14.70	13.51	11.39	11.54	10.56	11.83	7.27	5.85	5.48	4.90	3.73	5.79	6.54	6.75	7.23	Three Month Interbank Rate	60zb
13.56	12.97	10.84	10.72	9.87	9.78	6.52	7.13	6.82	5.94	5.13	5.35	5.38	6.38	6.31	Government Bond Yield	61
Period Averages															**Prices, Production, Labor**	
38	33	53	66	61	57	73	94	100	120	170	167	171	213	....	Industrial Share Prices	62
83.2	87.1	91.7	95.4	97.7	97.2	96.3	97.5	†100.0	108.5	109.7	95.8	113.8	157.1	149.8	Producer Prices	63
76.6	81.7	85.4	88.9	92.0	94.1	96.3	97.6	100.0	101.3	103.9	†106.2	108.7	112.0	115.4	Consumer Prices	64
72.2	76.0	79.7	84.3	88.7	91.5	93.9	96.6	100.0	104.2	....	....	....	....	....	Wages: Hourly Earnings	65
75.7	77.6	85.2	86.5	†88.5	89.6	92.1	97.2	100.0	102.5	106.0	108.8	107.6	110.4	....	Industrial Production	66.. *c*
35.7	40.7	53.8	58.8	67.1	76.7	82.2	92.9	100.0	112.6	112.2	107.8	106.9	....	....	Crude Petroleum Production	66aa
102.3	101.7	98.5	97.7	96.7	96.4	96.5	97.9	100.0	102.8	....	....	....	....	....	Employment	67
Period Averages																
....	....	....	....	....	....	2,131	....	2,186	2,246	2,285	2,317	2,333	2,350	....	Labor Force	67d
2,126	†2,114	2,049	2,030	2,010	2,004	2,004	2,035	2,079	2,131	2,194	2,248	2,259	2,269	....	Employment	67e
45	69	106	112	116	126	127	116	107	108	92	74	75	81	81	Unemployment	67c
2.1	3.2	4.9	5.2	5.5	5.9	6.0	5.4	4.9	4.8	4.0	3.2	3.2	3.4	2.7	Unemployment Rate (%)	67r
Millions of Kroner															**International Transactions**	
144,543	146,166	187,146	211,579	220,316	218,474	225,714	243,809	265,883	320,130	342,421	298,968	350,582	507,444	521,046	Exports	70
152,041	151,101	163,380	169,998	165,181	160,821	170,069	192,073	208,627	229,720	252,232	272,970	265,696	287,839	289,179	Imports, c.i.f.	71
1995=100																
57.6	56.5	65.0	69.5	74.0	80.2	84.3	94.6	100.0	112.9	117.9	118.8	124.0	....	....	Volume of Exports	72
†79.3	71.4	67.9	74.6	76.4	79.3	79.6	92.9	100.0	110.0	119.3	131.4	128.8	....	....	Volume of Imports	73
†97.3	97.6	109.3	114.1	109.3	100.5	100.5	97.1	100.0	108.0	110.2	97.6	108.8	154.5	151.7	Unit Value of Exports	74
†92.4	95.2	101.0	101.7	100.0	98.1	98.8	99.0	100.0	99.5	98.6	100.0	97.9	102.7	104.6	Unit Value of Imports	75
Minus Sign Indicates Debit															Balance of Payments	
-4,102	-3,896	212	3,992	5,032	4,471	3,522	3,760	5,233	10,969	10,036	6	8,378	24,807	25,960	Current Account, n.i.e.	78al *d*
21,191	23,075	27,171	34,313	34,212	35,459	32,278	35,016	42,385	50,081	49,375	40,888	46,224	60,463	59,699	Goods: Exports f.o.b.	78aa *d*
-21,951	-23,284	-23,401	-26,552	-25,516	-27,205	-25,312	-27,520	-33,701	-37,109	-37,727	-38,827	-35,501	-34,520	-33,681	Goods: Imports f.o.b.	78ab *d*
-759	-209	3,770	7,761	8,696	8,254	6,966	7,496	8,685	12,972	11,648	2,061	10,723	25,942	26,018	*Trade Balance*	78ac *d*
8,545	9,729	10,770	12,765	13,330	12,692	12,159	12,247	13,672	14,819	15,708	15,542	15,878	17,331	17,958	Services: Credit	78ad *d*
-9,623	-10,270	-10,623	-12,358	-12,701	-12,210	-11,472	-12,065	-13,147	-13,435	-14,233	-14,820	-14,882	-15,422	-15,392	Services: Debit	78ae *d*
-1,837	-750	3,916	8,168	9,326	8,736	7,653	7,678	9,210	14,356	13,123	2,783	11,719	27,851	28,584	*Balance on Goods & Services*	78af *d*
3,039	3,265	3,425	3,896	3,540	2,689	2,380	3,415	4,590	5,164	5,590	6,809	6,100	6,641	7,590	Income: Credit	78ag *d*
-4,325	-5,274	-5,995	-6,596	-6,293	-5,501	-5,167	-5,589	-6,509	-7,046	-7,284	-8,053	-7,998	-8,295	-8,530	Income: Debit	78ah *d*
-3,122	-2,759	1,346	5,468	6,573	5,924	4,866	5,504	7,291	12,475	11,429	1,539	9,821	26,197	27,644	*Balance on Gds, Serv. & Inc.*	78ai *d*
123	168	164	217	239	1,678	1,533	1,291	1,280	1,329	1,468	1,500	1,681	1,321	1,473	Current Transfers, n.i.e.: Credit	78aj *d*
-1,103	-1,305	-1,299	-1,693	-1,780	-3,131	-2,877	-3,035	-3,339	-2,835	-2,861	-3,034	-3,124	-2,712	-3,157	Current Transfers: Debit	78ak *d*
-2	8	2	31	17	-172	-31	-157	-170	-127	-184	-116	-116	-186	-93	Capital Account, n.i.e.	78bc *d*
104	107	101	109	118	143	306	93	86	65	30	44	40	34	105	Capital Account, n.i.e.: Credit	78ba *d*
-106	-99	-99	-78	-101	-315	-337	-250	-255	-192	-214	-160	-156	-220	-197	Capital Account: Debit	78bb *d*
5,233	4,900	2,056	-761	-7,581	-1,044	6,568	-1,363	-542	-1,462	-6,607	61	431	-13,155	-23,877	Financial Account, n.i.e.	78bj *d*
-873	-978	-1,358	-1,470	-1,782	120	-718	-2,166	-2,859	-5,886	-5,003	-3,200	-6,018	-8,511	1,086	Direct Investment Abroad	78bd *d*
187	279	1,519	1,003	-398	-668	992	2,736	2,393	3,179	3,886	4,354	8,056	5,806	2,166	Dir. Invest. in Rep. Econ., n.i.e.	78be *d*
-1,009	-392	-563	-987	-2,523	-1,972	2,088	992	-3,531	-9,833	-12,618	-9,348	-7,228	-25,144	-29,420	Portfolio Investment Assets	78bf *d*
-255	28	-310	-569	-298	-446	-124	213	-379	-1,177	-2,644	-9,066	-2,378	-11,034	-12,291	Equity Securities	78bk *d*
-755	-420	-252	-418	-2,224	-1,526	2,212	780	-3,151	-8,657	-9,974	-282	-4,850	-14,109	-17,129	Debt Securities	78bl *d*
3,292	4,618	3,606	1,548	-585	865	-1,175	-518	655	100	2,500	7,289	4,238	9,844	2,756	Portfolio Investment Liab., n.i.e.	78bg *d*
274	336	1,035	644	159	782	385	654	636	-237	-1,190	—	-1,033	1,630	2,732	Equity Securities	78bm *d*
3,018	4,282	2,571	904	-743	83	-1,560	-1,172	19	337	3,691	7,289	5,271	8,214	24	Debt Securities	78bn *d*
....	....	....	....	....	....	....	....	....	-43	17	-162	152	-329	-1,228	Financial Derivatives Assets	78bw *d*
....	....	....	....	....	....	....	....	....	101	125	74	92	-131	88	Financial Derivatives Liabilities	78bx *d*
-1,171	643	-274	-1,502	-326	369	6,198	154	961	-67	-1,403	-3,632	-7,663	-14,148	-2,261	Other Investment Assets	78bh *d*
....	....	....	....	....	....	....	....	....	....	....	....	....	....	....	Monetary Authorities	78bo *d*
-411	-159	76	170	207	-46	-65	-13	-156	71	91	-1,167	-1,099	-2,072	1,758	General Government	78bp *d*
207	1,343	-222	-223	-1,549	-741	3,997	-638	435	-1,216	-1,465	-1,062	-969	-1,806	434	Banks	78bq *d*
-966	-542	-129	-1,448	1,016	1,156	2,266	804	682	1,077	-29	-1,403	-5,595	-10,271	-4,453	Other Sectors	78br *d*
4,808	730	-874	648	-1,968	242	-816	-2,562	1,840	10,987	5,888	4,685	8,802	19,459	2,935	Other Investment Liab., n.i.e.	78bi *d*
-55	124	-58	3	56	1,282	217	139	-624	1,505	-803	19	-19	3	44	Monetary Authorities	78bs *d*
113	-93	-2	35	3	-15	-7	-164	3	—	94	1,346	3,460	9,657	-432	General Government	78bt *d*
4,497	-1,101	-817	-740	-4,174	-3,622	-302	-604	247	8,677	4,126	-856	1,789	1,321	2,290	Banks	78bu *d*
253	1,801	3	1,350	2,147	2,597	-724	-1,933	2,214	806	2,472	4,176	3,573	8,478	1,033	Other Sectors	78bv *d*
-1,349	-1,149	-1,305	-2,848	-219	-3,986	-1,806	-1,987	-3,947	-2,910	-4,443	-6,335	-2,710	-7,780	-4,104	Net Errors and Omissions	78ca *d*
-220	-138	965	414	-2,751	-732	8,253	253	575	6,470	-1,198	-6,384	5,984	3,686	-2,114	*Overall Balance*	78cb *d*
220	138	-965	-414	2,751	732	-8,253	-253	-575	-6,470	1,198	6,384	-5,984	-3,686	2,114	Reserves and Related Items	79da *d*
220	138	-965	-414	2,751	732	-8,253	-253	-575	-6,470	1,198	6,384	-5,984	-3,686	2,114	Reserve Assets	79db *d*
—	—	—	—	—	—	—	—	—	—	—	—	—	—	—	Use of Fund Credit and Loans	79dc *d*
....	....	....	....	....	....	....	....	....	....	....	....	....	....	....	Exceptional Financing	79de *d*

	1972	1973	1974	1975	1976	1977	1978	1979	1980	1981	1982	1983	1984	1985	1986
International Investment Position														*Millions of US Dollars*	
Assets .... 79aa d	....	....	....	....	....	....	....	....	15,824	16,938	17,645	17,383	20,315	28,368	31,596
Direct Investment Abroad .... 79ab d	....	....	....	....	....	....	....	....	561	581	619	647	667	1,093	1,609
Portfolio Investment .... 79ac d	....	....	....	....	....	....	....	....	210	233	252	323	394	430	1,057
Equity Securities .... 79ad d	....	....	....	....	....	....	....	....	—	—	—	—	—	—	—
Debt Securities .... 79ae d	....	....	....	....	....	....	....	....	210	233	252	323	394	430	1,057
Financial Derivatives .... 79al d	....	....	....	....	....	....	....	....							
Other Investment .... 79af d	....	....	....	....	....	....	....	....	9,008	9,815	9,864	9,772	9,853	12,942	16,644
Monetary Authorities .... 79ag d	....	....	....	....	....	....	....	....							
General Government .... 79ah d	....	....	....	....	....	....	....	....	1,306	1,126	918	931	765	1,070	1,265
Banks .... 79ai d	....	....	....	....	....	....	....	....	494	1,734	2,207	2,256	2,588	3,178	5,581
Other Sectors .... 79aj d	....	....	....	....	....	....	....	....	7,208	6,955	6,740	6,585	6,499	8,694	9,798
Reserve Assets .... 79ak d	....	....	....	....	....	....	....	....	6,044	6,309	6,910	6,640	9,401	13,903	12,287
Liabilities .... 79la d	....	....	....	....	....	....	....	....	33,859	32,025	31,522	29,128	28,728	34,799	42,977
Dir. Invest. in Rep. Economy .... 79lb d	....	....	....	....	....	....	....	....	775	735	686	681	699	993	1,315
Portfolio Investment .... 79lc d	....	....	....	....	....	....	....	....	10,864	9,505	8,287	6,708	6,284	8,381	13,326
Equity Securities .... 79ld d	....	....	....	....	....	....	....	....	—	—	—	—	—	—	—
Debt Securities .... 79le d	....	....	....	....	....	....	....	....	10,864	9,505	8,287	6,708	6,284	8,381	13,326
Financial Derivatives .... 79ll d	....	....	....	....	....	....	....	....							
Other Investment .... 79lf d	....	....	....	....	....	....	....	....	22,220	21,786	22,549	21,739	21,745	25,424	28,336
Monetary Authorities .... 79lg d	....	....	....	....	....	....	....	....	43	58	102	98	42	45	81
General Government .... 79lh d	....	....	....	....	....	....	....	....	1,676	1,367	1,045	699	575	478	513
Banks .... 79li d	....	....	....	....	....	....	....	....	2,618	3,191	3,731	3,873	4,714	7,807	9,571
Other Sectors .... 79lj d	....	....	....	....	....	....	....	....	17,882	17,169	17,671	17,070	16,415	17,094	18,170
Government Finance														*Millions of Kroner:*	
Deficit (-) or Surplus 80	†−1,438	−1,026	−1,761	−4,716	−10,005	−13,133	−14,472	−14,994	−5,400	6,817	3,894	9,443	8,963	18,279	17,414
Revenue 81	†35,992	41,305	47,165	53,648	63,842	73,155	81,596	91,919	116,849	140,094	153,404	176,023	193,630	222,953	244,633
Grants Received 81z	†1,333	1,605	1,861	2,086	2,281	700	1,092	965	998	1,186	1,376	1,529	1,559	1,531	900
Expenditure 82	†34,086	38,392	44,554	52,113	63,936	73,354	84,824	93,364	108,111	123,585	139,064	154,340	168,126	184,112	204,711
Lending Minus Repayments 83	†4,677	5,544	6,233	8,337	12,192	13,634	12,336	14,514	15,136	10,878	11,822	13,769	18,100	22,093	23,408
Financing															
Domestic 84a	†1,499	1,358	1,876	324	5,865	6,178	3,232	10,259	7,623	−3,171	711	2,744	−4,191	−20,110	−23,808
Foreign 85a	†−61	−332	−115	4,392	4,140	6,955	11,240	4,735	−2,223	−3,646	−4,605	−12,187	−4,535	1,831	6,393
Debt: Domestic 88a	26,038	28,658	31,004	32,581	37,763	46,681	53,992	68,407	75,490	78,931	74,729	86,386	105,252	129,625	172,562
Foreign 89a	1,621	1,290	1,179	5,587	9,708	16,666	27,923	32,125	29,886	26,233	21,629	9,440	4,853	6,650	12,949
National Accounts														*Billions of Kroner:*	
Househ.Cons.Expend.,incl.NPISHs 96f	57.95	64.39	72.62	85.09	97.84	112.99	†119.89	131.48	146.66	165.79	186.19	205.62	225.60	261.24	292.66
Government Consumption Expend. 91f	19.40	22.14	25.86	31.28	37.12	42.22	†47.32	50.82	58.65	67.98	76.33	84.54	90.76	98.91	108.25
Gross Fixed Capital Formation 93e	31.58	37.45	45.77	57.53	70.12	79.28	†74.60	78.91	84.41	96.62	107.62	121.82	129.96	134.92	155.39
Changes in Inventories 93i	2.81	4.23	7.77	5.62	4.77	3.63	†−3.56	−3.77	4.16	.01	3.82	−10.08	1.35	8.97	22.08
Exports of Goods and Services 90c	39.82	48.42	59.71	61.80	70.25	75.43	†87.36	105.15	135.49	155.41	164.67	184.52	213.02	235.05	194.07
Imports of Goods and Services (-) 98c	38.90	48.85	63.67	71.66	86.55	95.43	†86.35	98.74	116.14	128.88	143.93	149.17	168.41	194.10	213.29
Gross Domestic Product (GDP) 99b	112.66	127.77	148.06	169.65	193.56	218.12	†239.27	263.85	313.24	356.93	394.69	437.24	492.30	544.99	559.15
Net Primary Income from Abroad 98.n	−1.03	−1.19	−1.85	−1.92	−3.05	−4.73	†−7.44	−9.40	−9.63	−11.00	−12.88	−13.18	−13.38	−9.89	−9.37
Gross National Income (GNI) 99a	97.38	110.67	127.88	146.79	167.66	186.80	†232.00	254.45	303.61	345.93	381.82	424.07	478.92	535.10	549.78
Net Current Transf.from Abroad 98t							†−1.84	−2.21	−2.44	−3.07	−4.46	−4.33	−4.48	−4.95	−6.08
Gross Nat'l Disposable Inc.(GNDI) 99i	....	....	....	....	....	....	†230.16	252.24	301.17	342.86	377.36	419.74	474.44	530.15	543.70
Gross Saving 99s							†62.95	69.94	95.86	109.09	114.84	129.58	158.08	169.99	142.79
Consumption of Fixed Capital 99cf	17.02	18.74	22.37	26.01	30.57	35.86	†41.01	43.62	48.88	55.23	62.85	69.34	75.51	83.37	92.76
GDP Volume 1990 Prices 99b.p	394.74	410.96	432.31	450.33	481.00	498.22	520.84	....	....	....	....	....			
GDP Volume 1997 Ref., Chained 99b.p	....	....	....	....	....	....		599.64	626.18	657.20	663.52	664.67	688.22	728.63	766.64	794.09
GDP Volume (1995=100) .... 99bv p	45.5	47.4	49.9	51.9	55.5	57.5	60.1	62.7	65.8	66.5	66.6	68.9	73.0	76.8	79.6
GDP Deflator (1995=100) .... 99bi p	26.6	29.0	32.0	35.2	37.6	40.9	†42.8	45.3	51.2	57.8	63.8	68.3	72.6	76.4	75.7
														Millions:	
Population 99z	3.93	3.96	3.99	4.01	4.03	4.04	4.06	4.07	4.09	4.10	4.11	4.13	4.14	4.15	4.17

1987	1988	1989	1990	1991	1992	1993	1994	1995	1996	1997	1998	1999	2000	2001		

Millions of US Dollars — **International Investment Position**

1987	1988	1989	1990	1991	1992	1993	1994	1995	1996	1997	1998	1999	2000	2001		
41,048	38,309	40,826	49,691	50,170	48,393	46,433	....	....	....	....	....	....	....	....	Assets	79aa d
2,455	2,757	3,506	4,403	5,170	4,234	5,080	....	....	....	....	....	....	....	....	Direct Investment Abroad	79ab d
1,940	1,626	1,565	2,320	3,403	5,607	5,762	....	....	....	....	....	....	....	....	Portfolio Investment	79ac d
1,940	1,626	1,565	2,320	3,403	5,607	5,762	....	....	....	....	....	....	....	....	Equity Securities	79ad d
															Debt Securities	79ae d
							....	....	....	....	....	....	....	....	Financial Derivatives	79al d
22,277	20,733	21,785	27,426	28,420	26,673	19,910	....	....	....	....	....	....	....	....	Other Investment	79af d
1,960	1,595	1,599	1,912	1,542	1,697	1,868	....	....	....	....	....	....	....	....	Monetary Authorities	79ag d
6,551	5,300	5,494	6,857	8,358	9,325	5,813	....	....	....	....	....	....	....	....	General Government	79ah d
13,767	13,837	14,691	18,657	18,520	15,651	12,228	....	....	....	....	....	....	....	....	Banks	79ai d
14,376	13,193	13,971	15,541	13,177	11,880	15,680	....	....	....	....	....	....	....	....	Other Sectors	79aj d
56,880	57,367	61,414	67,329	63,639	58,399	57,536	....	....	....	....	....	....	....	....	Reserve Assets	79ak d
2,271	2,450	3,157	4,066	4,570	3,969	3,880	....	....	....	....	....	....	....	....	Liabilities	79la d
18,645	21,620	24,031	26,722	26,176	24,400	22,449	....	....	....	....	....	....	....	....	Dir. Invest. in Rep. Economy	79lb d
18,645	21,620	24,031	26,722	26,176	24,400	22,449	....	....	....	....	....	....	....	....	Portfolio Investment	79lc d
															Equity Securities	79ld d
															Debt Securities	79le d
							....	....	....	....	....	....	....	....	Financial Derivatives	79ll d
35,965	33,297	34,226	36,541	32,893	30,030	31,207	....	....	....	....	....	....	....	....	Other Investment	79lf d
67	125	61	29	72	705	101	....	....	....	....	....	....	....	....	Monetary Authorities	79lg d
668	690	703	995	1,047	1,692	2,238	....	....	....	....	....	....	....	....	General Government	79lh d
15,930	13,081	12,873	13,510	9,581	5,902	6,179	....	....	....	....	....	....	....	....	Banks	79li d
19,299	19,400	20,590	22,007	22,193	21,732	22,688	....	....	....	....	....	....	....	....	Other Sectors	79lj d

Year Ending December 31 — **Government Finance**

1987	1988	1989	1990	1991	1992	1993	1994	1995	1996	1997	1998	1999	2000	2001		
−385	−999	−5,118	3,863	−22,161	−51,912	−45,556	−14,774	14,487	6,519	8,817	−17,993	....	....	....	Deficit (-) or Surplus	80
255,360	266,960	277,773	306,881	319,827	318,151	326,507	348,841	383,106	425,506	469,041	465,007	....	....	....	Revenue	81
1,621	4,780	6,347	5,674	3,488	1,892	1,490	1,423	1,345	1,299	1,322	1,087	....	....	....	Grants Received	81z
230,455	251,327	273,356	298,813	320,384	339,451	347,962	357,877	361,579	375,265	387,218	412,237	....	....	....	Expenditure	82
26,911	21,412	15,882	9,879	25,092	32,504	25,591	7,161	8,385	45,021	74,328	71,850	....	....	....	Lending Minus Repayments	83
															Financing	
−2,913	−4,796	2,220	311	12,505	28,073	25,189	20,459	−18,296	11,276	14,516	24,144	....	....	....	Domestic	84a
3,298	5,794	2,899	−4,174	9,656	23,839	20,368	−5,684	3,809	−17,795	−23,332	−6,152	....	....	....	Foreign	85a
137,591	131,171	134,538	126,287	115,769	127,348	189,953	201,763	198,384	186,071	195,983	183,798	....	....	....	Debt: Domestic	88a
16,289	22,113	25,026	22,538	31,142	54,320	80,018	74,157	77,901	62,527	42,400	37,180	....	....	....	Foreign	89a

Billions of Kroner — **National Accounts**

1987	1988	1989	1990	1991	1992	1993	1994	1995	1996	1997	1998	1999	2000	2001		
312.87	†325.17	338.78	357.10	376.28	394.95	411.64	433.10	458.49	490.35	520.81	552.59	578.33	610.12	636.54	Househ.Cons.Expend.,incl.NPISHs	96f
124.22	†130.75	139.02	150.10	161.97	173.58	179.94	186.58	194.53	206.77	218.38	237.48	252.52	269.30	294.21	Government Consumption Expend.	91f
170.92	†181.43	175.06	156.21	157.43	156.34	168.20	179.37	192.52	216.22	252.09	276.93	265.21	271.55	279.60	Gross Fixed Capital Formation	93e
15.45	†5.62	4.30	11.90	6.07	5.77	9.63	14.50	27.44	15.82	22.96	37.51	25.00	30.29	23.58	Changes in Inventories	93i
199.79	†213.86	262.66	293.75	308.05	300.09	315.96	333.20	353.43	414.48	448.08	412.14	465.51	650.43	679.97	Exports of Goods and Services	90c
213.19	†217.23	237.46	246.36	246.37	245.81	261.67	279.18	297.65	327.05	366.15	407.30	393.76	428.67	441.86	Imports of Goods and Services (-)	98c
610.05	†639.59	682.35	722.71	763.41	784.93	823.70	867.56	928.75	1,016.59	1,096.17	1,109.35	1,192.83	1,403.01	1,472.04	Gross Domestic Product (GDP)	99b
−9.38	†−16.39	−19.24	−21.51	−25.33	−17.47	−19.77	−15.42	−11.87	−9.52	−9.69	−6.10	....	....	....	Net Primary Income from Abroad	98.n
600.66	†623.20	663.11	701.20	738.08	767.46	803.93	852.14	916.88	1,010.53	1,075.10	1,094.67	1,180.54	1,383.18		Gross National Income (GNI)	99a
−6.55	†−6.44	−6.61	−7.46	−7.94	−9.03	−9.53	−12.23	−13.05	−9.69	−10.10	−12.29	....	....	....	Net Current Transf.from Abroad	98t
594.12	†616.76	656.50	693.73	730.15	758.43	794.40	839.92	903.83	1,000.84	1,065.01	1,082.38	....	....	....	Gross Nat'l Disposable Inc.(GNDI)	99i
157.03	†160.84	178.71	186.53	191.90	189.90	202.82	220.24	250.81	307.29	330.45	299.60	337.11	491.83		Gross Saving	99s
106.62	117.28	123.19	124.39	127.67	131.75	137.62	142.69	150.27	157.53	167.15	180.67	191.88	....	....	Consumption of Fixed Capital	99cf
															GDP Volume 1990 Prices	99b. p
810.21	809.30	816.75	832.86	858.82	886.88	911.13	961.16	998.14	1,047.02	1,096.17	1,118.10	1,127.86	1,158.33	1,177.27	GDP Volume 1997 Ref., Chained	99b. p
81.2	81.1	81.8	83.4	86.0	88.9	91.3	96.3	100.0	104.9	109.8	112.0	113.0	116.0	117.9	GDP Volume (1995=100)	99bv p
80.9	†84.9	89.8	93.3	95.5	95.1	97.2	97.0	100.0	104.3	107.5	106.6	113.7	130.2	134.4	GDP Deflator (1995=100)	99bi p

Midyear Estimates

1987	1988	1989	1990	1991	1992	1993	1994	1995	1996	1997	1998	1999	2000	2001		
4.19	4.21	4.23	4.24	4.26	4.29	4.31	4.32	4.36	4.38	4.41	4.43	4.46	4.49	4.51	**Population**	99z

(See notes in the back of the book.)

Oman

	1972	1973	1974	1975	1976	1977	1978	1979	1980	1981	1982	1983	1984	1985	1986
Exchange Rates												*Rials Omani per SDR: End of Period (aa)*				
Official Rate .... aa	.4167	.4167	.4229	.4043	.4013	.4196	.4500	.4550	.4405	.4020	.3810	.3616	.3386	.3794	.4703
Official Rate .... ae	.3838	.3454	.3454	.3454	.3454	.3454	.3454	.3454	.3454	.3454	.3454	.3454	.3454	.3454	.3845
												Index Numbers (1995=100):				
Official Rate .... ahx	100.2	109.8	111.3	111.3	111.3	111.3	111.3	111.3	111.3	111.3	111.3	111.3	111.3	111.3	100.7
Nominal Effective Exchange Rate .... nec	....	....	....	....	....	....	....	122.9	121.7	133.2	147.8	154.9	165.6	170.3	126.3
Fund Position												*Millions of SDRs:*				
Quota .... 2f. s	7.0	7.0	7.0	7.0	7.0	7.0	20.0	20.0	20.0	30.0	30.0	63.1	63.1	63.1	63.1
SDRs... 1b. s	.7	.7	.7	.7	.7	.7	.7	2.8	5.1	5.2	7.9	11.1	9.4	10.9	11.4
Reserve Position in the Fund .... 1c. s	1.8	1.8	15.3	24.4	25.0	19.4	13.9	12.8	14.9	16.5	20.8	30.5	33.2	32.1	32.1
of which: Outstg.Fund Borrowing........... 2c	—	—	11.6	19.7	20.2	16.4	11.0	8.3	4.8	1.2	.1				
International Liquidity											*Millions of US Dollars Unless Otherwise Indicated:*					
Total Reserves minus Gold .... 1l. d	36.4	47.1	92.9	161.3	219.6	289.6	254.1	415.6	581.4	744.3	872.4	762.6	900.2	1,090.2	967.9
SDRs... 1b. d	.8	.9	.9	.9	.9	.9	1.0	3.7	6.5	6.0	8.7	11.6	9.2	12.0	13.9
Reserve Position in the Fund .... 1c. d	1.9	2.1	18.8	28.6	29.1	23.6	18.2	16.8	19.0	19.2	22.9	31.9	32.5	35.2	39.2
Foreign Exchange........................... 1d. d	33.7	44.1	73.3	131.9	189.7	265.1	234.9	395.1	555.9	719.1	840.8	719.1	858.4	1,043.0	914.8
Gold (Million Fine Troy Ounces) 1ad	.014	.014	.030	.030	.046	.101	.186	.187	.209	.274	.279	.288	.289	.289	.289
Gold (National Valuation)..................... 1and	.5	.6	3.3	2.9	4.5	12.5	27.6	27.7	40.0	70.2	71.9	75.6	76.0	76.0	68.3
Monetary Authorities: Other Assets .... 3..d	....	....	....	....	....	....	....	....	120.2	237.3	332.4	550.1	620.6	532.3	337.2
Other Liab. .... 4..d	—	—	—	2.8	22.5	24.4	105.3	30.8	12.4	9.2	14.9	10.6	7.0	10.9	4.3
Deposit Money Banks: Assets .... 7a. d	58.1	42.8	65.4	66.6	44.3	96.4	106.5	196.4	402.6	466.8	556.9	826.5	902.8	680.9	596.6
Liabilities .... 7b. d	13.8	9.3	163.0	208.5	260.6	195.7	200.9	230.2	320.1	246.7	268.9	271.1	263.1	249.2	337.7
Monetary Authorities												*Millions of Rials Omani:*				
Foreign Assets.. 11	14.2	17.0	34.6	56.7	76.8	105.5	97.3	153.3	256.2	363.3	441.0	479.5	551.6	586.6	528.8
Claims on Central Government.............. 12a	—	—	—	7.1	18.4	8.4	49.3	.2	—	—	33.6	14.2	5.9	—	116.9
Reserve Money.. 14	13.9	16.3	31.9	49.0	64.3	80.0	88.5	109.7	144.9	221.8	276.8	210.5	254.4	264.0	280.8
of which: Currency Outside DMBs.......... 14a	12.3	15.2	28.9	38.5	47.8	55.1	64.4	74.3	94.8	116.2	129.8	140.4	150.0	178.5	168.8
Foreign Liabilities.................................. 16c	—	—	—	1.0	7.8	8.4	36.4	10.7	4.3	3.2	5.2	3.7	2.4	3.8	1.7
Central Government Deposits............... 16d	—	—	—	8.6	11.3	12.1	2.8	5.3	66.1	83.6	116.3	190.4	214.4	184.4	129.9
Capital Accounts.................................... 17a	.5	1.3	1.2	7.6	7.9	14.8	19.5	28.5	46.8	67.2	74.5	83.3	92.0	104.3	121.8
Other Items (Net)................................... 17r	-.2	-.6	1.5	-2.4	3.8	-1.5	-.6	-.6	-5.9	-12.5	1.8	5.9	-5.7	30.0	111.6
Deposit Money Banks												*Millions of Rials Omani:*				
Reserves.. 20	1.6	1.1	3.0	10.6	16.7	25.6	24.2	32.3	50.0	107.6	144.6	67.1	104.6	86.1	111.4
Foreign Assets... 21	22.3	14.8	22.6	23.0	15.3	33.3	36.8	†67.8	139.1	161.2	192.3	285.5	311.8	235.2	229.4
Claims on Central Government.............. 22a	7.2	6.6	56.5	62.1	89.5	56.0	20.6	4.0	3.2	.6	.3	5.3	16.8	52.8	41.0
Claims on Nonfin.Pub.Enterprises 22c	....	....	....	....	....	....	....	....	....	....	8.3	11.8	....	13.1	12.3
Claims on Private Sector 22d	6.6	18.9	65.8	86.0	120.2	167.1	198.4	222.6	283.2	334.8	377.2	468.9	566.5	675.2	674.5
Demand Deposits 24	6.7	9.8	19.5	33.1	54.4	56.2	49.9	48.9	59.9	96.5	119.0	158.7	134.0	150.1	144.0
Quasi-Monetary Deposits 25	25.8	21.7	36.8	46.3	62.5	95.3	116.3	123.1	170.3	238.0	322.1	405.5	490.1	608.4	560.6
Foreign Liabilities.................................. 26c	5.3	3.2	56.3	72.0	90.0	67.6	69.4	†79.5	110.6	85.2	92.9	93.6	90.9	86.1	129.8
Central Government Deposits 26d	.4	3.1	15.6	24.9	28.0	59.4	39.7	62.8	84.2	111.9	107.2	87.9	155.5	84.9	88.0
Capital Accounts..................................... 27a				4.2	6.3	8.9	10.8	13.7	23.5	46.0	71.1	90.6	110.6	125.4	138.8
Other Items (Net).................................... 27r	-.3	3.7	19.7	1.1	.6	-5.5	-6.2	-1.3	27.1	26.6	10.4	2.4	18.6	7.5	7.4
Monetary Survey												*Millions of Rials Omani:*				
Foreign Assets (Net) 31n	31.2	28.6	.9	6.8	-5.7	62.8	28.3	†131.0	280.5	436.2	535.3	667.7	770.1	731.9	626.7
Domestic Credit 32	13.5	22.3	106.7	121.6	188.7	159.9	225.8	158.7	136.1	139.8	195.9	221.9	219.3	471.7	626.9
Claims on Central Govt. (Net) 32an	6.8	3.5	40.9	35.6	68.5	-7.2	27.4	-63.9	-147.1	-194.9	-189.6	-258.8	-347.2	-216.6	-60.0
Claims on Nonfin.Pub.Enterprises...... 32c	....	....	....	....	....	....	....	....	....	....	8.3	11.8	....	13.1	12.3
Claims on Private Sector 32d	6.6	18.9	65.8	86.0	120.2	167.1	198.4	222.6	283.2	334.8	377.2	468.9	566.5	675.2	674.5
Money.. 34	19.0	24.9	48.4	71.6	102.1	111.2	114.3	123.1	154.7	212.7	248.8	299.1	283.9	328.6	312.8
Quasi-Money... 35	25.8	21.7	36.8	46.3	62.5	95.3	116.3	123.1	170.3	238.0	322.1	405.5	490.1	608.4	560.6
Other Items (Net) 37r	—	4.4	22.4	10.5	18.4	16.1	23.5	43.4	91.6	125.3	160.3	185.0	215.4	266.6	380.1
Money plus Quasi-Money........................ 35l	44.8	46.6	85.2	118.0	164.6	206.6	230.6	246.2	325.0	450.7	570.9	704.6	774.0	937.0	873.4
Interest Rates												*Percent Per Annum*				
Deposit Rate 60l	....	....	....	....	....	....	....	....	....	....	....	....	9.03	9.04	8.33
Lending Rate 60p	....	....	....	....	....	....	....	....	....	....	....	....	10.35	10.24	9.65
Prices and Production												*Index Numbers (1995=100):*				
Consumer Prices 64	....	....	....	....	....	....	....	....	....	....	....	....	....	....	....
Crude Petroleum 66aa	33.1	34.3	34.0	39.8	42.9	39.8	36.7	31.7	33.1	38.4	39.3	45.4	50.2	59.1	65.4
International Transactions												*Millions of Rials Omani*				
Exports 70	64.2	83.7	284.2	360.6	391.6	393.4	378.7	542.3	824.5	1,109.3	1,035.6	1,061.9	1,059.6	1,360.2	698.0
Crude Petroleum 70aa	51.4	66.9	228.7	289.8	314.5	315.8	302.6	433.3	660.6	886.4	825.3	846.2	910.4	1,253.0	553.6
Imports, c.i.f. 71	18.7	40.7	135.6	264.3	250.5	302.1	327.2	430.5	598.2	790.3	926.5	860.9	949.2	1,088.9	916.7
Refined Petroleum.............................. 71ab	....	....	....	38.6	40.3	29.5	33.2	52.5	81.7	101.2	94.0	12.2	13.5	....	....
Volume of Exports													*1995=100*			
Crude Petroleum 72aa	36.3	37.6	37.4	44.9	47.2	42.9	40.6	37.8	35.8	42.4	41.7	48.5	47.4	58.3	65.9
Export Prices													*1985=100:*			
Crude Petroleum............................... 76aad	13.6	18.6	65.2	68.6	71.0	78.5	79.3	121.8	196.5	223.2	210.5	185.0	174.5	164.7	82.0

	1987	1988	1989	1990	1991	1992	1993	1994	1995	1996	1997	1998	1999	2000	2001		
																Exchange Rates	
Rials Omani per US Dollar: End of Period (ae)																	
	.5455	.5174	.5053	.5470	.5500	.5287	.5281	.5613	.5716	.5529	.5188	.5414	.5277	.5010	.4832	Official Rate	aa
	.3845	.3845	.3845	.3845	.3845	.3845	.3845	.3845	.3845	.3845	.3845	.3845	.3845	.3845	.3845	Official Rate	ae
Period Averages																	
	100.0	100.0	100.0	100.0	100.0	100.0	100.0	100.0	100.0	100.0	100.0	100.0	100.0	100.0	100.0	Official Rate	ahx
	111.8	105.4	111.6	105.7	105.8	103.6	109.0	105.9	100.0	104.5	109.8	113.0	111.7	117.5	123.8	Nominal Effective Exchange Rate	ne c
																Fund Position	
End of Period																	
	63.1	63.1	63.1	63.1	63.1	119.4	119.4	119.4	119.4	119.4	119.4	119.4	194.0	194.0	194.0	Quota	2f.s
	7.2	8.7	10.9	13.4	15.5	3.4	5.0	6.2	7.5	8.8	10.1	11.5	1.3	3.1	5.0	SDRs	1b.s
	32.1	28.7	27.7	25.2	22.7	39.4	37.8	36.0	34.5	34.0	31.1	31.1	49.8	49.8	65.0	Reserve Position in the Fund	1c.s
	—	—	—	—	—	—	—	—	—	—	—	—	—	—	—	of which: Outstg.Fund Borrowing	2c
																International Liquidity	
End of Period																	
	1,402.2	1,054.2	1,354.3	1,672.4	1,663.3	1,983.5	908.1	979.4	1,138.3	1,389.4	1,548.8	1,064.1	2,767.5	2,379.9	2,364.9	Total Reserves minus Gold	1l.d
	10.2	11.7	14.3	19.0	22.2	4.7	6.8	9.0	11.1	12.7	13.6	16.2	1.8	4.1	6.3	SDRs	1b.d
	45.5	38.6	36.4	35.8	32.5	54.1	52.0	52.5	51.2	48.8	42.0	43.9	68.3	64.9	81.6	Reserve Position in the Fund	1c.d
	1,346.5	1,003.8	1,303.6	1,617.6	1,608.6	1,924.7	849.3	917.9	1,075.9	1,327.8	1,493.1	1,004.1	2,697.3	2,310.9	2,277.0	Foreign Exchange	1d.d
	.289	.289	.289	.289	.289	.289	.289	.289	.291	.291	.291	.291	.291	.291	.291	Gold (Million Fine Troy Ounces)	1ad
	68.3	68.3	68.3	68.3	68.3	68.3	68.3	68.3	68.3	68.3	68.3	68.3	68.3	68.3	80.5	Gold (National Valuation)	1and
	312.9	321.0	323.6	484.5	872.5	662.3	162.2	38.4	....	80.6	120.3	147.8	555.9	39.7	50.4	Monetary Authorities: Other Assets	3..d
	4.7	3.9	.9	1.0	1.0	1.0	1.0	1.2	1.7	1.0	1.7	1.2	1.1	1.0	1.0	Other Liab.	4..d
	609.9	726.4	755.2	758.7	699.7	532.4	780.1	863.5	999.1	944.1	1,776.8	1,222.7	992.3	1,215.5	997.9	Deposit Money Banks: Assets	7a.d
	278.6	313.2	267.8	203.0	104.3	105.8	167.1	239.5	441.4	652.4	1,326.5	1,522.2	1,662.4	1,641.8	1,532.5	Liabilities	7b.d
																Monetary Authorities	
End of Period																	
	687.6	555.8	672.3	856.7	1,002.6	920.5	720.1	635.0	730.4	780.8	822.4	771.6	1,090.4	941.4	940.3	Foreign Assets	11
	—	121.6	51.0	—	32.3	38.9	49.3	97.0	89.4	47.0	32.7	159.6	4.1	5.0	79.5	Claims on Central Government	12a
	239.7	242.0	295.2	300.6	309.8	299.1	284.7	296.3	306.9	326.5	354.3	379.5	375.3	408.3	444.3	Reserve Money	14
	180.4	176.3	183.6	214.1	215.9	226.7	232.9	245.5	235.9	231.2	242.2	244.2	273.5	276.8	275.9	of which: Currency Outside DMBs	14a
	1.8	1.5	.4	.4	.4	.4	.4	.4	.5	.6	.4	.6	.5	.4	.4	Foreign Liabilities	16c
	122.4	123.8	124.6	187.6	336.2	255.0	62.4	14.8	41.0	31.1	46.6	57.0	242.6	26.0	19.4	Central Government Deposits	16d
	135.2	144.2	156.9	188.0	202.0	213.7	219.9	235.2	251.9	268.3	283.1	297.9	312.4	342.8	373.5	Capital Accounts	17a
	188.4	165.8	146.3	180.1	186.5	191.2	201.9	185.3	219.5	201.5	170.4	196.3	163.8	168.8	182.2	Other Items (Net)	17r
																Deposit Money Banks	
End of Period																	
	57.8	70.1	110.7	88.2	85.0	72.3	49.4	51.6	67.8	86.9	116.0	132.2	99.2	129.7	136.2	Reserves	20
	234.5	279.3	290.4	291.7	269.0	204.7	299.9	332.0	384.2	363.0	683.2	470.1	381.5	467.4	383.7	Foreign Assets	21
	84.5	32.8	23.6	48.7	124.8	190.7	154.1	97.9	91.9	175.8	157.4	198.0	334.7	323.0	427.0	Claims on Central Government	22a
	8.6	5.1	12.9	16.7	9.8	8.4	16.8	3.0	3.1	4.8	.6	—	4.1	16.3	28.1	Claims on Nonfin.Pub.Enterprises	22c
	688.5	764.8	823.9	926.1	935.0	1,029.9	1,088.0	1,227.3	1,357.5	1,564.9	2,170.9	2,563.1	2,783.9	2,809.7	3,001.4	Claims on Private Sector	22d
	154.8	139.0	161.9	176.6	189.8	206.3	218.7	227.4	235.4	272.1	307.5	261.6	237.7	272.5	425.7	Demand Deposits	24
	584.3	658.8	720.3	781.3	830.2	841.1	863.9	931.1	1,040.5	1,130.5	1,484.5	1,625.4	1,756.2	1,854.7	1,924.0	Quasi-Monetary Deposits	25
	107.1	120.4	103.0	78.0	40.1	40.7	64.2	92.1	169.7	250.9	510.0	585.3	639.2	631.3	589.3	Foreign Liabilities	26c
	82.4	84.6	99.0	130.0	147.8	138.6	153.4	148.9	140.7	211.3	289.8	292.4	316.1	306.0	285.5	Central Government Deposits	26d
	104.6	107.2	104.0	116.5	121.7	129.0	165.8	167.6	174.9	193.8	304.2	425.6	454.2	433.3	425.8	Capital Accounts	27a
	40.7	42.1	73.3	88.9	94.0	150.3	142.5	144.7	143.3	136.9	232.0	173.1	200.0	248.3	326.2	Other Items (Net)	27r
																Monetary Survey	
End of Period																	
	813.2	713.1	859.4	1,070.0	1,231.1	1,084.1	955.4	874.5	944.2	892.6	994.9	656.0	832.3	777.1	734.4	Foreign Assets (Net)	31n
	576.8	716.0	687.8	673.9	617.9	874.4	1,092.3	1,261.5	1,360.3	1,550.2	2,025.2	2,571.2	2,568.1	2,822.0	3,231.1	Domestic Credit	32
	−120.3	−54.0	−149.0	−268.9	−327.0	−164.0	−12.5	31.2	−.4	−19.6	−146.3	8.1	−219.9	−4.1	201.6	Claims on Central Govt. (Net)	32an
	8.6	5.1	12.9	16.7	9.8	8.4	16.8	3.0	3.1	4.8	.6	—	4.1	16.3	28.1	Claims on Nonfin.Pub.Enterprises	32c
	688.5	764.8	823.9	926.1	935.0	1,029.9	1,088.0	1,227.3	1,357.5	1,564.9	2,170.9	2,563.1	2,783.9	2,809.7	3,001.4	Claims on Private Sector	32d
	335.2	315.3	345.4	390.8	405.7	433.0	451.5	472.9	471.3	503.4	549.7	505.5	511.2	549.3	701.6	Money	34
	584.3	658.8	720.3	781.3	830.2	841.1	863.9	931.1	1,040.5	1,130.5	1,484.5	1,625.4	1,756.2	1,854.7	1,924.0	Quasi-Money	35
	470.5	455.0	481.4	571.9	613.0	684.4	732.3	731.9	792.7	808.9	985.9	1,096.0	1,132.9	1,195.0	1,339.9	Other Items (Net)	37r
	919.5	974.1	1,065.8	1,172.0	1,235.9	1,274.1	1,315.5	1,404.1	1,511.8	1,633.9	2,034.2	2,131.2	2,267.5	2,404.1	2,625.6	Money plus Quasi-Money	35l
																Interest Rates	
Percent Per Annum																	
	7.48	7.57	8.66	8.32	7.06	6.29	4.17	4.34	6.53	6.85	7.30	8.46	8.12	7.63	4.50	Deposit Rate	60l
	9.10	9.40	10.01	9.68	9.50	9.24	8.49	8.57	9.38	9.23	9.30	10.09	10.32	10.06	9.23	Lending Rate	60p
																Prices and Production	
Period Averages																	
	....	....	....	95.4	99.9	100.8	101.7	101.3	100.0	100.1	†100.2	99.4	99.8	98.7	97.7	Consumer Prices	64
	68.1	72.6	73.9	78.8	82.9	86.8	91.2	94.7	100.0	104.3	105.2	104.0	105.2	112.0	108.9	Crude Petroleum	66aa
																International Transactions	
Millions of Rials Omani																	
	957.9	951.9	1,564.0	2,118.0	1,873.9	2,135.3	2,064.9	2,132.0	2,333.2	2,824.5	2,933.8	2,118.0	....	....	....	Exports	70
	762.1	642.4	....	....	....	1,018.7	935.0	921.5	1,042.7	1,283.9	1,276.1	801.3	1,206.0	1,955.4	1,710.3	Crude Petroleum	70aa
	700.7	846.5	867.9	1,031.0	1,228.0	1,449.3	1,581.8	1,505.3	1,633.2	1,760.1	1,932.5	2,184.6	1,797.1	1,937.7	2,234.4	Imports, c.i.f.	71
	....	....	....	....	....	....	....	....	....	....	....	....	....	....	....	Refined Petroleum	71ab
1995=100																Volume of Exports	
	69.3	74.5	75.9	80.6	82.5	88.7	94.0	95.0	100.0	103.5	107.4	105.5	108.4	114.8	116.5	Crude Petroleum	72aa
Index of Prices in US Dollars																Export Prices	
	105.3	82.5	....	....	....	109.8	95.2	92.8	100.0	118.5	113.6	72.7	105.8	163.0	140.3	Crude Petroleum	76aa d

Oman

		1972	1973	1974	1975	1976	1977	1978	1979	1980	1981	1982	1983	1984	1985	1986
Balance of Payments																*Millions of US Dollars:*
Current Account, n.i.e.	78al d	....	....	179	57	36	277	−50	549	942	1,237	489	494	303	−10	−1,040
Goods: Exports f.o.b.	78aa d	....	....	1,212	1,416	1,596	1,620	1,598	2,280	3,748	4,696	4,423	4,256	4,421	4,971	2,861
Goods: Imports f.o.b.	78ab d	....	....	−552	−908	−1,000	−1,044	−1,157	−1,285	−1,780	−2,296	−2,583	−2,360	−2,640	−3,028	−2,309
Trade Balance	78ac d	....	....	661	508	596	576	441	994	1,968	2,400	1,840	1,895	1,781	1,943	552
Services: Credit	78ad d	....	....	—	—	—	—	8	8	9	9	12	14	14	14	13
Services: Debit	78ae d	....	....	−104	−155	−177	−186	−193	−235	−518	−620	−701	−688	−673	−713	−689
Balance on Goods & Services	78af d	....	....	557	354	419	390	256	767	1,459	1,788	1,151	1,222	1,123	1,245	−123
Income: Credit	78ag d	....	....	19	17	6	—	5	—	96	177	318	307	345	362	597
Income: Debit	78ah d	....	....	−310	−312	−220	−160	−118	−149	−352	−415	−471	−490	−560	−688	−668
Balance on Gds, Serv. & Inc.	78ai d	....	....	266	58	204	230	142	618	1,202	1,549	998	1,039	908	919	−194
Current Transfers, n.i.e.: Credit	78aj d	....	....	24	207	52	268	49	212	137	185	87	191	255	43	39
Current Transfers: Debit	78ak d	....	....	−111	−208	−220	−222	−241	−281	−397	−498	−596	−735	−860	−973	−885
Capital Account, n.i.e.	78bc d	....	....	—	—	—	—	—	—	—	−3	−3	−3	−3	−3	
Capital Account, n.i.e.: Credit	78ba d	....	....	—	—	—	—	—	—	—	—	—	—	—	—	
Capital Account: Debit	78bb d	....	....	—	—	—	—	—	—	—	−3	−3	−3	−3	−3	
Financial Account, n.i.e.	78bj d	....	....	−10	155	389	35	151	−136	−85	37	192	325	439	458	1,015
Direct Investment Abroad	78bd d	....	....	—	—	—	—	—	—	—	—	—	—	—	—	
Dir. Invest. in Rep. Econ., n.i.e.	78be d	....	....	−61	106	81	48	86	118	98	63	182	155	158	161	140
Portfolio Investment Assets	78bf d	....	....	—	—	—	—	—	—	—	—	—	—	—	—	
Equity Securities	78bk d	....	....	—	—	—	—	—	—	—	—	—	—	—	—	
Debt Securities	78bl d	....	....	—	—	—	—	—	—	—	—	—	—	—	—	
Portfolio Investment Liab., n.i.e.	78bg d	....	....	—	—	—	—	—	—	—	—	—	—	—	—	
Equity Securities	78bm d	....	....	—	—	—	—	—	—	—	—	—	—	—	—	
Debt Securities	78bn d	....	....	—	—	—	—	—	—	—	—	—	—	—	—	
Financial Derivatives Assets	78bw d	....	....	....	....	....	....	....	....	....	....	....	....	....	....	....
Financial Derivatives Liabilities	78bx d	....	....	....	....	....	....	....	....	....	....	....	....	....	....	....
Other Investment Assets	78bh d	....	....	−27	−91	91	−33	6	−110	−257	−96	−139	−299	−146	97	198
Monetary Authorities	78bo d	....	....													
General Government	78bp d	....	....	—	—	—	—	−4	−28	−43	14	−55	−98	−17	−64	−13
Banks	78bq d	....	....	131	15	22	−52	−9	−31	−206	−64	−90	−270	−76	222	57
Other Sectors	78br d	....	....	−158	−106	69	19	18	−50	−8	−47	6	69	−52	−61	154
Other Investment Liab., n.i.e.	78bi d	....	....	78	139	217	20	60	−144	74	71	149	470	427	199	676
Monetary Authorities	78bs d	....	....	—	—	—	—	—	—	—	—	—	—	—	—	
General Government	78bt d	....	....	78	139	165	85	54	−115	−16	144	124	468	435	212	560
Banks	78bu d	....	....	—	—	52	−64	6	−29	90	−74	24	2	−8	−12	116
Other Sectors	78bv d	....	....													
Net Errors and Omissions	78ca d	....	....	−118	−146	−369	−240	−150	−257	−62	−24	67	−466	−421	−323	−588
Overall Balance	78cb d	....	....	50	66	57	72	−49	155	796	1,247	744	351	319	122	−613
Reserves and Related Items	79da d	....	....	−50	−66	−57	−72	49	−155	−796	−1,247	−744	−351	−319	−122	613
Reserve Assets	79db d	....	....	−50	−66	−57	−72	49	−155	−796	−1,247	−744	−351	−319	−122	613
Use of Fund Credit and Loans	79dc d	....	....	—	—	—	—	—	—	—	—	—	—	—	—	
Exceptional Financing	79de d	....	....	....	....	....	....	....	....	....	....	....	....	....	....	
Government Finance																*Millions of Rials Omani*
Deficit (-) or Surplus	80	−17.1	−23.5	−56.4	−37.7	−84.7	58.1	−75.3	85.0	9.1	48.5	−222.8	−242.3	−346.8	−364.2	−700.2
Revenue	81	53.0	65.0	303.2	358.7	457.3	483.4	440.9	590.6	793.9	1,075.9	986.5	1,073.7	1,141.6	1,337.8	848.6
Grants Received	81z	—	3.5	8.3	71.6	18.0	92.7	6.7	61.9	35.2	50.0	14.7	50.7	72.8	59.8	46.4
Expenditure	82	69.4	91.7	329.3	466.5	551.0	497.7	498.7	548.8	794.9	1,028.0	1,176.5	1,308.1	1,501.0	1,731.1	1,587.2
Lending Minus Repayments	83	.7	.3	38.6	1.5	9.0	20.3	24.2	18.7	25.1	49.4	47.5	58.6	60.2	30.7	8.0
Financing																
Domestic	84a	17.1	−12.5	28.6	−18.1	32.7	−88.8	83.4	−72.8	64.3	−137.7	181.1	−9.3	48.4	−9.5	105.6
Foreign	85a	—	36.0	27.8	55.8	52.0	30.7	−8.1	−12.2	−73.4	89.2	41.7	251.6	298.4	373.7	594.6
Debt: Domestic	88a	15.0	12.2	49.7	41.9	69.7	16.1	43.7	4.2	.8	.4	—	—	—	—	
Foreign	89a	—	10.9	46.2	102.0	154.0	184.7	176.6	164.4	169.1	219.5	261.2	424.0	574.7	648.1	940.2
National Accounts																*Millions of Rials Omani*
Househ.Cons.Expend.,incl.NPISHs	96f	35	41	50	115	182	246	310	337	577	591	795	1,210	1,340	1,457	1,491
Government Consumption Expend.	91f	42	63	197	229	241	269	272	355	499	656	715	591	701	796	880
Gross Capital Formation	93	42	44	174	258	317	290	274	335	466	584	707	710	804	900	820
Exports of Goods and Services	90c	84	115	419	489	551	559	552	787	1,295	1,625	1,532	1,475	1,532	1,722	1,098
Imports of Goods and Services (-)	98c	62	94	272	367	407	417	461	525	789	964	1,134	1,053	1,144	1,284	1,145
Gross Domestic Product (GDP)	99b	141	169	569	724	884	947	947	1,290	2,047	2,492	2,615	2,933	3,232	3,591	3,143
Net Primary Income from Abroad	98.n	−29	−63	−152	−135	−148	−130	−111	−137	−212	−235	−238	−297	−350	−399	−336
Gross National Income (GNI)	99a	112	107	417	589	736	817	836	1,153	1,835	2,257	2,377	2,444	2,698	3,055	2,464
GDP Volume 1972 Prices	99b.p	141	121	155	200	232	....	....	....	....	....	....	....	....	....	....
GDP Volume 1978 Prices	99b.p	....	....	....	....	684	805	947	991	1,047	1,226	1,367	1,585	1,851	2,105	....
GDP Volume 1988 Prices	99b.p	....	....	....	....	....	....	....	....	....	....	....	....	....	3,124	3,191
GDP Volume (1995=100)	99bv p	12.9	11.1	14.2	18.3	21.2	25.0	29.4	30.7	32.5	38.0	42.4	49.2	57.4	65.3	66.7
GDP Deflator (1995=100)	99bi p	20.6	28.8	75.3	74.6	78.5	71.5	60.7	79.1	118.8	123.5	116.2	112.4	106.1	103.6	88.8
																Millions:
Population	99z	.70	.72	.74	.77	.79	.84	.88	.93	.98	1.03	1.09	1.15	1.21	†2.00	†1.46

Balance of Payments

Minus Sign Indicates Debit

	1987	1988	1989	1990	1991	1992	1993	1994	1995	1996	1997	1998	1999	2000	2001		
Current Account, n.i.e.	784	-309	305	1,106	-251	-598	-1,190	-805	-801	338	-73	-2,993	-369	3,347	....	78al	d
Goods: Exports f.o.b.	3,805	3,342	4,068	5,508	4,871	5,555	5,365	5,542	6,065	7,373	7,657	5,521	7,239	11,319	....	78aa	d
Goods: Imports f.o.b.	-1,769	-2,107	-2,225	-2,623	-3,112	-3,627	-4,030	-3,693	-4,050	-4,231	-4,645	-5,215	-4,300	-4,593	....	78ab	d
Trade Balance	2,036	1,235	1,842	2,885	1,759	1,928	1,336	1,849	2,015	3,142	3,012	307	2,939	6,726	....	78ac	d
Services: Credit	13	13	59	68	61	13	13	13	13	237	268	276	273	283	....	78ad	d
Services: Debit	-481	-523	-570	-719	-961	-932	-906	-900	-985	-1,233	-1,462	-1,633	-1,462	-1,501	....	78ae	d
Balance on Goods & Services	1,568	726	1,331	2,235	860	1,009	442	962	1,043	2,146	1,818	-1,051	1,751	5,508	....	78af	d
Income: Credit	520	257	338	375	359	328	421	257	325	257	385	338	187	291	....	78ag	d
Income: Debit	-610	-572	-588	-629	-596	-739	-688	-724	-699	-694	-775	-814	-869	-996	....	78ah	d
Balance on Gds, Serv. & Inc.	1,479	411	1,080	1,980	623	598	175	495	669	1,709	1,428	-1,527	1,069	4,804	....	78ai	d
Current Transfers, n.i.e.: Credit	47	81	55	39	39	39	57	65	68					....	....	78aj	d
Current Transfers: Debit	-741	-801	-830	-913	-913	-1,235	-1,423	-1,365	-1,537	-1,371	-1,501	-1,467	-1,438	-1,456	....	78ak	d
Capital Account, n.i.e.	—	—	—	—	—	—	—	—	—	10	31	-5	-3	8	....	78bc	d
Capital Account, n.i.e.: Credit	—	—	—	—	—	—	—	—	—	29	55	21	16	34	....	78ba	d
Capital Account: Debit	—	—	—	—	—	—	—	—	—	-18	-23	-26	-18	-26	....	78bb	d
Financial Account, n.i.e.	-190	221	-15	-498	510	497	-79	230	-19	260	52	1,482	65	-406	....	78bj	d
Direct Investment Abroad	—	—	—	—	—	—	—	—	—	—	—	—	—		....	78bd	d
Dir. Invest. in Rep. Econ., n.i.e.	35	92	112	142	135	104	142	76	46	60	65	101	21	23	....	78be	d
Portfolio Investment Assets	—	—	—	—	—	—	....	....	....	....	....	....	....	....	....	78bf	d
Equity Securities																78bk	d
Debt Securities																78bl	d
Portfolio Investment Liab., n.i.e.	—	—	—	—	—	—	....	....	8	18	185	26	-36		....	78bg	d
Equity Securities	—	—	—	—	—	—	....	....	10	86	239	13	-10		....	78bm	d
Debt Securities	—	—	—	—	—	—	....	....	-3	-68	-55	13	-26		....	78bn	d
Financial Derivatives Assets																78bw	d
Financial Derivatives Liabilities																78bx	d
Other Investment Assets	-31	-88	-179	-270	146	120	-187	-174	-52	-237	-715	642	-307	-356	....	78bh	d
Monetary Authorities																78bo	d
General Government	—	-5	-39	-10	—	—	-31	-104	-88	-291	117	88	-538	-133	....	78bp	d
Banks	-13	-117	-75	-49	-55	169	-187	-10	62	55	-832	554	231	-224	....	78bq	d
Other Sectors	-18	34	-65	-211	200	-49	31	-60	-26	—	—	—	—		....	78br	d
Other Investment Liab., n.i.e.	-194	217	52	-369	229	273	-34	328	-13	429	684	554	325	-36	....	78bi	d
Monetary Authorities																78bs	d
General Government	-135	186	52	-372	226	260	-91	325	-18	140	-112	-26	101	-114	....	78bt	d
Banks	-59	31	—	3	3	13	57	3	5	213	676	195	143	-21	....	78bu	d
Other Sectors	....	....	....	....	....	....	....	....	....	75	120	385	81	99	....	78bv	d
Net Errors and Omissions	-486	-379	33	-474	284	401	211	-86	388	-420	521	751	522	-687	....	78ca	d
Overall Balance	108	-467	324	135	543	300	-1,058	-661	-432	189	531	-765	215	2,262	....	78cb	d
Reserves and Related Items	-108	467	-324	-135	-543	-300	1,058	661	432	-189	-531	765	-215	-2,262	....	79da	d
Reserve Assets	-108	467	-324	-135	-543	-300	1,058	661	432	-189	-531	765	-215	-2,262	....	79db	d
Use of Fund Credit and Loans																79dc	d
Exceptional Financing	....	....	....	....	....	....	....	....	....	....	....	....	....	....	....	79de	d

Government Finance

Year Ending December 31

	1987	1988	1989	1990	1991	1992	1993	1994	1995	1996	1997	1998	1999	2000	2001	
Deficit (-) or Surplus	-146.2	-346.7	-289.5	-32.8	-284.3	-584.5	-511.1	-485.9	-468.1	-259.7	-28.3	-376.9	-474.1	-363.2	....	80
Revenue	1,185.1	999.6	1,125.4	1,580.1	1,261.4	1,338.1	1,357.7	1,386.7	1,487.9	1,602.8	1,867.4	1,426.6	1,401.8	1,831.2	....	81
Grants Received	14.3	30.5	27.9	6.6	23.0	.9	19.2	29.9	13.2	10.8	20.7	8.8	5.6	13.2	....	81z
Expenditure	1,330.1	1,364.3	1,425.5	1,601.0	1,575.1	1,900.3	1,871.4	1,912.7	1,971.2	1,879.4	1,848.0	1,820.1	1,859.4	2,179.5	....	82
Lending Minus Repayments	15.5	12.5	17.3	18.5	-6.4	23.2	16.6	-10.2	-2.0	-6.1	68.4	-7.8	22.1	28.1	....	83
Financing																
Domestic	54.0	149.5	243.6	191.1	201.6	413.5	211.2	141.8	46.4	-250.6	35.5	9.1	105.7	76.6	....	84a
Foreign	92.2	197.2	45.9	-158.3	82.7	171.0	299.9	344.1	421.7	510.3	-7.2	367.8	368.4	286.6	....	85a
Debt: Domestic	—	—	—	32.6	252.9	410.2	291.0	313.9	306.7	325.2	314.1	471.0	493.1	392.1	....	88a
Foreign	887.7	959.7	994.4	847.1	932.1	1,036.3	1,020.8	1,148.8	1,148.0	1,201.1	1,132.5	1,086.1	1,118.4	1,064.8	....	89a

National Accounts

Millions of Rials Omani

	1987	1988	1989	1990	1991	1992	1993	1994	1995	1996	1997	1998	1999	2000	2001	
Househ.Cons.Expend.,incl.NPISHs	1,288	1,500	1,527	1,861	†2,193	2,263	2,389	2,349	2,600	2,799	2,901	3,120	3,031	3,012	....	96f
Government Consumption Expend.	908	956	1,035	1,195	†1,150	1,303	1,333	1,429	1,462	1,446	1,415	1,402	1,440	1,580	....	91f
Gross Capital Formation	519	490	507	555	†655	783	842	782	795	805	1,075	1,299	897	913	....	93
Exports of Goods and Services	1,468	1,290	1,568	2,122	†1,878	2,141	2,068	2,136	2,337	2,926	3,047	2,229	2,888	4,461	....	90c
Imports of Goods and Services (-)	865	1,011	1,034	1,240	†1,515	1,702	1,828	1,728	1,887	2,101	2,348	2,633	2,215	2,343	....	98c
Gross Domestic Product (GDP)	3,318	3,225	3,604	4,493	†4,361	4,788	4,804	4,967	5,307	5,874	6,090	5,416	6,041	7,623	....	99b
Net Primary Income from Abroad	-281	-406	-406	-419	†-423	-608	-634	-683	-713	-695	-727	-747	-815	-836	....	98.n
Gross National Income (GNI)	2,722	2,520	2,825	3,632	†3,938	4,180	4,154	4,121	4,594	5,179	5,363	4,669	5,226	6,787	....	99a
GDP Volume 1972 Prices	....	....	....	....	....	....	....	....	....	....	....	....	....	....	....	99b.p
GDP Volume 1978 Prices	....	....	....	....	....	....	....	....	....	....	....	....	....	....	....	99b.p
GDP Volume 1988 Prices	3,064	3,225	3,321	3,599	3,816	4,141	4,395	4,564	4,784	4,923	5,227	5,368	5,356	5,629	....	99b.p
GDP Volume (1995=100)	64.0	67.4	69.4	75.2	79.8	86.5	91.9	95.4	100.0	102.9	109.3	112.2	111.9	117.7	....	99bv p
GDP Deflator (1995=100)	97.6	90.1	97.8	112.5	†103.0	104.2	†98.5	98.1	100.0	107.6	105.0	90.9	101.7	122.1	....	99bi p

Midyear Estimates

	1987	1988	1989	1990	1991	1992	1993	1994	1995	1996	1997	1998	1999	2000	2001	
Population	1.53	1.63	1.56	1.63	1.76	1.88	2.00	2.05	2.13	2.21	2.26	2.29	2.46	2.54	....	99z

(See notes in the back of the book.)

Pakistan

564

		1972	1973	1974	1975	1976	1977	1978	1979	1980	1981	1982	1983	1984	1985	1986
Exchange Rates															_Rupees per SDR:_	
Market Rate	aa	11.947	11.913	12.091	11.561	11.473	11.996	12.865	13.009	12.595	11.494	14.129	14.099	15.018	17.509	21.047
															Rupees per US Dollar:	
Market Rate	ae	11.003	9.875	9.875	9.875	9.875	9.875	9.875	9.875	9.875	9.875	12.808	13.466	15.322	15.940	17.207
Market Rate	rf	8.648	9.947	9.853	9.853	9.853	9.853	9.853	9.853	9.853	9.853	11.792	13.055	13.980	15.853	16.569
															Index Numbers (1995=100):	
Nominal Effective Exchange Rate	ne c	....	....	....	....	....	....	....	207.59	210.99	236.66	220.64	212.94	217.53	204.90	169.92
Real Effective Exchange Rate	re c	....	....	....	....	....	....	....	....	177.45	200.88	184.02	177.72	181.13	169.52	139.92
Fund Position															_Millions of SDRs:_	
Quota	2f. s	235	235	235	235	235	235	285	285	428	428	428	546	546	546	546
SDRs	1b. s	19	27	20	25	32	29	30	34	23	49	46	1	37	24	11
Reserve Position in the Fund	1c. s	—	—	—	—	—	—	—	—	—	—	59	89	89	—	—
Total Fund Cred.&Loans Outstg.	2tl	111	130	239	374	440	463	492	435	528	880	1,286	1,540	1,469	1,289	973
International Liquidity												_Millions of US Dollars Unless Otherwise Indicated:_				
Total Reserves minus Gold	1l. d	221	412	392	340	466	449	408	213	496	721	969	1,973	1,035	807	709
SDRs	1b. d	21	32	24	29	37	35	40	45	29	56	51	1	37	26	13
Reserve Position in the Fund	1c. d	—	—	—	—	—	—	—	—	—	—	65	93	87	—	—
Foreign Exchange	1d. d	200	380	368	311	429	414	368	168	467	665	853	1,879	912	781	696
Gold (Million Fine Troy Ounces)	1ad	1.588	1.588	1.588	1.588	1.618	1.618	1.718	1.818	1.818	1.846	1.848	1.862	1.865	1.902	1.934
Gold (National Valuation)	1an d	....	....	67	67	68	68	333	730	1,191	788	559	757	635	607	655
Monetary Authorities: Other Liab.	4.. d	1	1	4	7	8	8	48	69	348	347	343	341	329	345	304
Deposit Money Banks: Assets	7a. d	71	126	230	222	199	235	350	386	310	323	333	464	550	564	689
Liabilities	7b. d	37	38	46	63	106	124	116	131	124	229	195	340	701	937	1,269
Monetary Authorities															_Millions of Rupees:_	
Foreign Assets	11	3,765	5,415	5,191	4,569	5,756	5,543	7,751	9,853	17,208	15,412	20,155	37,387	25,925	23,126	24,081
Claims on General Government	12a	10,770	9,958	9,087	12,450	13,771	19,750	25,334	32,528	35,325	39,962	49,731	51,774	66,901	70,063	84,218
of which: Provincial Government	12ax	387	419	415	393	195	443	88	183	134	25	25	26	26	26	26
Claims on Deposit Money Banks	12e	1,847	3,102	5,197	5,727	6,688	6,341	6,589	8,646	12,553	17,498	17,141	20,682	20,576	24,142	29,368
Reserve Money	14	12,380	13,861	13,956	15,326	18,358	22,525	26,483	33,564	39,157	42,369	49,859	56,719	66,002	71,690	85,893
of which: Currency Outside DMBs	14a	9,350	10,990	11,427	11,884	13,853	17,349	21,040	26,447	32,482	34,488	41,153	46,425	52,003	58,678	71,578
Restricted Deposits	16b															
Foreign Liabilities	16c	1,337	1,564	2,931	4,399	5,119	5,630	6,813	6,333	10,092	13,535	22,571	26,309	27,109	28,053	25,707
General Government Deposits	16d	628	597	282	127	315	558	471	409	305	6,719	5,934	13,420	7,772	6,611	17,014
Counterpart Funds	16e	1,030	1,278	1,502	1,626	1,574	1,894	1,657	2,070	2,077	1,868	1,502	1,729	1,182	918	564
Other Items (Net)	17r	1,009	1,177	811	1,278	861	1,041	4,265	8,664	13,455	8,382	7,163	11,666	11,338	10,059	8,488
Deposit Money Banks															_Millions of Rupees:_	
Reserves	20	1,599	2,062	1,862	2,775	3,738	4,529	5,031	6,742	6,167	7,451	8,207	10,101	13,809	13,871	15,103
Foreign Assets	21	785	1,247	2,277	2,193	933	1,070	1,753	2,112	†3,060	3,190	4,262	6,243	8,426	8,988	11,848
Claims on General Government	22a	5,361	6,876	6,732	8,861	12,849	12,535	16,997	17,878	23,714	29,527	34,665	47,011	34,240	34,926	44,970
of which: Provincial Government	22ax	1,278	1,634	2,249	2,632	4,285	3,982	3,979	4,384	5,836	8,256	10,646	12,598	9,365	3,006	5,057
Claims on Private Sector	22d	14,658	17,074	17,289	20,632	28,435	33,958	38,071	45,853	51,903	61,313	73,076	88,431	103,071	132,590	155,298
Demand Deposits	24	9,427	10,588	10,614	13,107	19,519	21,926	25,887	29,981	33,698	37,227	45,641	53,685	53,035	63,668	72,785
Time Deposits	25	7,796	9,368	8,665	12,177	15,924	18,969	23,436	27,288	30,650	36,252	44,892	59,316	61,532	68,925	77,592
Foreign Liabilities	26c	405	371	452	623	1,050	1,228	1,144	1,290	1,229	2,259	2,493	4,576	10,745	14,931	21,827
General Government Deposits	26d	980	1,339	1,410	1,248	2,282	1,669	2,162	2,567	3,472	3,749	2,799	2,927	948	1,858	1,636
Counterpart Funds	26e	420	399	410	428	447	466	487	523	566	607	637	701	782	815	837
Central Government Lending Funds	26f	1,137	1,062	760	791	906	868	873	834	894	868	1,229	1,403	2,106	2,572	3,358
Credit from Monetary Authorities	26g	1,847	3,102	5,197	5,727	6,688	6,341	6,374	8,431	12,338	15,424	14,776	18,182	17,948	21,417	26,284
Other Items (Net)	27r	392	1,029	653	361	−860	624	1,468	1,670	1,997	5,094	7,743	10,996	12,450	16,188	22,900
Monetary Survey															_Millions of Rupees:_	
Foreign Assets (Net)	31n	2,808	4,727	4,085	1,741	520	−244	1,527	4,343	8,947	2,809	−647	12,744	−3,503	−10,870	−11,605
Domestic Credit	32	29,577	32,228	31,676	41,163	53,756	65,981	80,219	96,526	111,483	126,945	157,046	179,863	206,596	242,712	282,857
Claims on General Govt. (Net)	32an	14,524	14,898	14,127	19,935	24,022	30,058	39,698	47,430	55,262	59,021	75,663	82,437	92,422	96,520	110,537
Claims on Private Sector	32d	15,054	17,329	17,549	21,228	29,733	35,923	40,522	49,097	56,220	67,924	81,383	97,426	114,174	146,193	172,321
Money	34	19,939	22,194	22,517	25,621	34,044	39,966	47,194	56,830	66,671	72,285	87,341	100,566	105,780	123,060	145,251
Quasi-Money	35	7,796	9,368	8,665	12,177	15,924	18,969	23,436	27,288	30,650	36,252	44,892	59,316	61,532	68,925	77,592
Restricted Deposits	36b															
Counterpart Funds	36e	1,450	1,676	1,912	2,054	2,020	2,360	2,144	2,593	2,643	2,475	2,139	2,430	1,964	1,733	1,401
Central Government Lending Funds	36f	1,137	1,062	760	791	906	868	873	834	894	868	1,229	1,403	2,106	2,572	3,358
Other Items (Net)	37r	2,065	2,654	1,914	2,271	1,394	3,586	8,115	13,337	19,571	17,874	20,799	28,894	31,711	35,552	43,651
Money plus Quasi-Money	35l	27,734	31,562	31,182	37,798	49,967	58,935	70,629	84,118	97,322	108,538	132,233	159,882	167,312	191,985	222,842
Other Banking Institutions															_Millions of Rupees:_	
Post Office: Savings Deposits	45.. i	1,165	1,385	1,418	1,405	1,317	1,360	1,318	1,235	1,194	1,038	1,347	1,560	1,634	1,838	2,109
Liquid Liabilities	55l	28,899	32,947	32,600	39,202	51,285	60,295	71,947	85,352	98,515	109,575	133,580	161,442	168,946	193,823	224,951
Interest Rates															_Percent Per Annum_	
Discount Rate (End of Period)	60	6.00	8.00	9.00	9.00	9.00	10.00	10.00	10.00	10.00	10.00	10.00	10.00	10.00	10.00	10.00
Money Market Rate	60b	5.34	6.51	10.33	9.87	9.37	10.87	10.41	8.83	8.63	9.27	9.51	8.15	8.97	8.13	6.59
Treasury Bill Rate	60c	....	....	....	....	....	....	....	....	....	....	....	....	....	....	....
Government Bond Yield	61	5.76	5.76	5.77	5.77	9.04	9.27	9.48	9.75	11.20	9.40	9.36	9.31	9.25	9.19	8.77
Prices, Production, Labor															_Index Numbers (1995=100):_	
Share Prices	62	....	39.8	34.2	43.6	44.3	†54.7	62.1	71.6	66.2	65.4	†52.8	68.1	89.4	87.3	90.6
Wholesale Prices	63	8.9	11.4	13.9	17.1	18.3	20.1	21.4	23.5	26.6	29.6	31.5	33.9	37.0	38.1	40.0
Consumer Prices	64	10.5	12.9	16.4	19.8	21.2	†23.4	24.8	26.8	30.0	33.6	†35.6	37.9	40.2	42.4	43.9
Manufacturing Production	66ey	23.7	26.6	†27.6	27.0	26.7	27.3	29.7	31.9	†35.4	†40.6	46.9	50.0	53.9	58.2	62.4
															Number in Thousands:	
Labor Force	67d	....	....	....	....	....	....	....	....	....	....	....	....	....		
Employment	67e	....	....	....	....	....	....	....	....	....	....	....	....	....	26,961	27,033
Unemployment	67c	....	....	....	....	....	....	....	....	....	....	....	....	....		1,018
Unemployment Rate (%)	67r	....	....	....	....	....	....	....	....	....	....	....	....	....	3.7	3.6
International Transactions															_Millions of Rupees:_	
Exports	70	†5,776	9,533	10,970	10,416	11,552	11,766	14,605	20,355	25,923	28,538	28,275	40,320	35,994	43,645	56,336
Imports, c.i.f.	71	†5,938	9,698	17,118	21,361	21,588	24,217	32,523	40,158	52,968	55,749	64,712	69,855	82,038	93,793	89,297
															_1995=100_	
Volume of Exports	72	26.6	27.4	24.7	27.1	29.7	†28.8	32.7	45.0	43.8	52.3	†41.9	58.8	48.3	60.5	105.9
Volume of Imports	73	21.3	27.9	33.3	32.9	38.2	†43.2	52.9	62.0	61.9	65.8	†61.3	61.4	63.9	72.8	73.1
Unit Value of Exports	74	7.3	12.8	16.5	14.6	15.9	†19.1	21.8	25.2	26.9	27.9	†30.6	32.8	36.6	36.5	44.3
Unit Value of Imports	75	6.2	8.7	14.9	16.8	16.1	†16.7	17.6	19.9	24.8	28.5	†32.2	32.4	35.5	37.1	35.3

	1987	1988	1989	1990	1991	1992	1993	1994	1995	1996	1997	1998	1999	2000	2001	
Exchange Rates																
End of Period (aa)																
Market Rate	24.694	25.035	28.079	31.079	35.272	35.249	41.268	44.851	50.785	57.547	59.286	64.608	†71.075	75.607	76.489	aa
End of Period (ae) Period Average (rf)																
Market Rate	17.406	18.603	21.367	21.845	24.658	25.636	30.045	30.723	34.165	40.020	43.940	45.885	†51.785	58.029	60.864	ae
Market Rate	17.317	17.919	20.445	21.605	23.689	24.965	27.975	30.423	31.494	35.909	40.918	44.943	49.118	53.648	61.927	rf
Period Averages																
Nominal Effective Exchange Rate	150.32	146.18	139.77	133.11	124.81	119.39	116.05	108.93	100.00	91.22	86.15	79.50	72.46	71.49	65.60	ne c
Real Effective Exchange Rate	123.73	121.81	114.01	106.54	104.63	103.18	102.89	100.68	100.00	98.22	101.39	97.95	92.43	93.60	87.12	re c
Fund Position																
End of Period																
Quota	546	546	546	546	546	758	758	758	758	758	758	758	1,034	1,034	1,034	2f. s
SDRs	11	5	1	1	5	—	1	—	10	9	8	1	—	11	3	1b. s
Reserve Position in the Fund	—	—	—	—	—	—	—	—	—	—	—	—	—	—	—	1c. s
Total Fund Cred.&Loans Outstg.	647	411	710	587	746	820	817	1,097	1,115	1,001	980	996	1,271	1,198	1,456	2tl
International Liquidity																
Last Thursday of Period																
Total Reserves minus Gold	502	395	521	296	527	850	1,197	2,929	1,733	548	1,195	1,028	1,511	1,513	3,640	1l. d
SDRs	16	7	1	1	7	—	1	—	15	13	11	1	—	14	4	1b. d
Reserve Position in the Fund	—	—	—	—	—	—	—	—	—	—	—	—	—	—	—	1c. d
Foreign Exchange	486	388	519	295	519	850	1,196	2,929	1,718	535	1,184	1,027	1,511	1,499	3,636	1d. d
Gold (Million Fine Troy Ounces)	1.940	1.945	1.949	1.949	1.961	2.021	2.044	2.052	2.055	2.056	2.066	2.077	2.088	2.091	2.091	1ad
Gold (National Valuation)	865	822	718	691	712	682	694	794	722	691	637	618	543	543	595	1an d
Monetary Authorities: Other Liab.	225	354	418	372	322	691	554	272	227	691	617	856	890	973	950	4.. d
Deposit Money Banks: Assets	799	827	936	1,459	1,581	1,387	1,408	1,586	1,609	1,550	1,410	1,281	1,365	1,440	1,771	7a. d
Liabilities	1,537	1,631	1,968	2,329	3,168	3,966	2,496	2,386	3,015	3,381	2,335	2,091	1,614	1,331	898	7b. d
Monetary Authorities																
Last Thursday of Period																
Foreign Assets	24,295	23,200	27,048	20,406	30,366	39,544	56,923	115,577	86,700	61,804	93,158	77,768	104,870	115,554	249,986	11
Claims on General Government	93,720	96,648	116,547	137,171	162,941	180,966	209,953	202,151	254,211	303,209	274,647	347,900	502,118	551,497	403,427	12a
of which: Provincial Government	26	26	25	5,451	4,295	8,136	5,524	2,258	5,184	15,931	12,700	12,657	8,050	3,388	874	12ax
Claims on Deposit Money Banks	38,426	43,055	48,826	52,858	62,322	71,593	78,137	89,110	98,220	67,864	119,962	171,286	192,862	195,646	184,842	12e
Reserve Money	102,617	113,734	133,146	154,362	196,554	213,817	244,175	282,541	333,207	321,058	367,082	414,627	468,491	458,843	588,677	14
of which: Currency Outside DMBs	81,765	92,168	105,225	125,806	144,530	162,316	177,856	195,827	234,011	252,069	272,052	301,146	341,024	410,469	429,360	14a
Restricted Deposits	....	....	....	....	....	....	....	....	....	....	....	....	8,115	11,124	13,187	16b
Foreign Liabilities	19,900	16,891	28,859	26,384	34,261	46,625	50,331	48,479	54,104	73,602	66,453	75,892	103,921	115,481	133,762	16c
General Government Deposits	20,930	16,915	18,418	18,343	11,623	15,355	37,304	37,682	34,365	28,502	30,603	63,742	138,006	199,021	43,203	16d
Counterpart Funds	302	350	445	540	542	539	671	614	644	686	644	585	660	532	589	16e
Other Items (Net)	12,692	15,012	11,553	10,807	12,648	15,766	12,532	37,524	16,812	9,029	22,984	42,110	80,659	77,694	58,836	17r
Deposit Money Banks																
Last Thursday of Period																
Reserves	21,994	23,661	29,874	28,931	50,592	51,207	68,030	93,268	109,689	80,122	100,518	119,696	145,480	81,205	169,195	20
Foreign Assets	13,903	15,391	20,008	31,872	38,974	35,563	42,306	48,721	54,958	62,022	61,940	58,800	70,682	83,534	107,789	21
Claims on General Government	75,978	75,544	78,001	81,079	114,904	191,287	208,114	251,172	263,013	333,162	396,083	395,218	321,548	355,499	325,670	22a
of which: Provincial Government	7,688	5,111	7,336	10,594	7,878	10,395	10,870	11,488	13,387	11,657	13,081	16,355	19,846	44,262	43,617	22ax
Claims on Private Sector	160,908	181,571	195,274	210,491	232,651	290,851	337,082	385,463	464,913	538,370	613,944	686,932	761,793	868,069	929,064	22d
Demand Deposits	90,403	96,563	110,909	127,379	156,588	203,653	191,613	235,265	253,189	269,947	420,823	423,091	447,919	457,773	524,429	24
Time Deposits	86,380	89,543	83,028	80,372	92,475	143,406	230,515	278,960	322,037	448,144	470,719	530,230	521,619	600,662	685,205	25
Foreign Liabilities	26,756	30,346	42,042	50,873	78,115	101,680	74,987	73,295	102,995	135,309	102,617	95,936	83,579	77,248	54,662	26c
General Government Deposits	971	966	1,022	1,748	6,613	4,378	19,224	41,168	47,719	47,800	47,799	66,536	96,763	84,259	102,692	26d
Counterpart Funds	1,329	131	-12	-24	-238	-20	-196	-181	-8	—	—	—	—	—	—	26e
Central Government Lending Funds	4,801	6,915	8,280	8,870	10,041	12,198	13,074	12,235	11,853	11,788	11,634	11,676	11,493	11,244	11,148	26f
Credit from Monetary Authorities	31,359	35,667	40,483	44,313	52,856	61,263	66,564	77,758	86,766	57,795	108,583	126,448	148,604	144,839	120,372	26g
Other Items (Net)	30,785	36,036	37,405	38,842	40,673	42,350	59,751	60,123	68,023	42,896	10,310	6,729	-10,474	12,282	33,210	27r
Monetary Survey																
Last Thursday of Period																
Foreign Assets (Net)	-8,458	-8,646	-23,845	-24,979	-43,036	-73,197	-26,089	42,524	-15,440	-85,086	-13,973	-35,260	-11,948	6,358	169,351	31n
Domestic Credit	328,778	357,681	394,726	435,355	520,254	673,872	731,696	797,049	941,642	1,140,656	1,246,673	1,349,909	1,411,041	1,560,180	1,553,258	32
Claims on General Govt. (Net)	147,798	154,310	175,107	198,159	259,609	352,520	361,539	374,473	435,140	560,069	592,328	612,840	588,897	623,716	583,202	32an
Claims on Private Sector	180,980	203,370	219,619	237,196	260,645	321,352	370,157	422,576	506,502	580,587	654,345	737,069	822,144	936,464	970,056	32d
Money	173,016	189,834	217,027	254,620	305,978	371,796	378,111	435,388	490,961	528,011	699,806	732,291	795,370	876,014	964,921	34
Quasi-Money	86,380	89,543	83,028	80,372	92,475	143,406	230,515	278,960	322,037	448,144	470,719	530,230	521,619	600,662	685,205	35
Restricted Deposits	....	....	....	....	....	....	....	....	....	....	....	....	8,115	11,124	13,187	36b
Counterpart Funds	1,631	481	433	517	304	520	475	433	636	686	644	585	660	532	589	36e
Central Government Lending Funds	4,801	6,915	8,280	8,870	10,041	12,198	13,074	12,235	11,853	11,788	11,634	11,676	11,493	11,244	11,148	36f
Other Items (Net)	54,492	62,261	62,115	65,999	68,421	72,755	83,432	112,558	100,716	66,945	49,897	39,869	61,838	66,961	47,558	37r
Money plus Quasi-Money	259,396	279,378	300,054	334,991	398,453	515,202	608,626	714,348	812,998	976,155	1,170,525	1,262,521	1,316,989	1,476,676	1,650,126	35l
Other Banking Institutions																
Last Thursday of Period																
Post Office: Savings Deposits	3,102	3,814	5,462	5,361	7,028	8,612	8,586	9,891	12,370	14,189	18,622	22,473	27,603	36,022	39,638	45.. i
Liquid Liabilities	262,498	283,191	305,516	340,352	405,481	523,814	617,212	724,239	825,368	990,344	1,189,147	1,284,994	1,344,592	1,512,698	1,689,764	55l
Interest Rates																
Percent Per Annum																
Discount Rate *(End of Period)*	10.00	10.00	10.00	10.00	10.00	10.00	10.00	†15.00	17.00	20.00	18.00	16.50	13.00	13.00	10.00	60
Money Market Rate	6.25	6.32	6.30	7.29	7.64	7.51	11.00	8.36	11.52	11.40	12.10	10.76	9.04	8.57	8.49	60b
Treasury Bill Rate	....	....	....	....	....	12.47	13.03	11.26	12.49	13.61	†15.74	....	....	8.38	10.71	60c
Government Bond Yield	8.26	8.32	8.18	8.05	7.88	7.67	7.40	7.07	6.63	6.06	5.43	4.79	4.16	....	....	61
Prices, Production, Labor																
Period Averages																
Share Prices	112.5	131.0	140.1	148.9	....	†87.6	86.4	140.6	100.0	82.1	76.6	55.3	54.5	68.9	58.3	62
Wholesale Prices	43.3	47.5	51.5	55.9	62.8	67.2	74.1	88.7	100.0	111.1	123.5	130.7	135.7	141.1	147.5	63
Consumer Prices	46.0	50.0	54.0	58.8	65.8	†72.0	79.2	89.0	100.0	110.4	122.9	130.6	136.0	141.9	146.4	64
Manufacturing Production	66.9	72.7	74.4	79.6	85.2	90.6	93.6	96.1	100.0	99.4	98.9	105.9	113.7	116.3	119.0	66ey
Period Averages																
Labor Force	....	....	....	....	....	....	34,726	33,324	33,191	....	36,407	38,174	....	....	....	67d
Employment	28,703	28,995	29,053	29,797	28,681	29,694	30,534	31,288	31,407	32,188	34,180	35,934	....	....	....	67e
Unemployment	903	937	939	963	1,922	1,845	1,516	1,591	1,783	1,827	2,227	2,240	....	....	....	67c
Unemployment Rate (%)	3.1	3.1	3.1	3.1	6.3	5.9	4.7	4.8	5.4	5.4	6.1	5.9	....	....	....	67r
International Transactions																
Millions of Rupees																
Exports	72,583	81,348	96,646	121,345	155,398	183,599	187,787	225,200	252,714	335,313	359,046	382,477	417,322	484,476	572,471	70
Imports, c.i.f.	101,310	118,681	146,444	160,134	201,409	235,296	265,142	271,744	362,686	437,769	476,346	419,311	505,451	605,668	631,005	71
1995=100																
Volume of Exports	86.2	86.4	91.1	91.0	103.0	112.5	102.2	126.2	100.0	118.6	†111.7	108.3	121.7	136.3	139.1	72
Volume of Imports	73.4	77.3	80.7	77.3	80.8	94.6	95.6	92.4	100.0	97.9	†100.8	100.2	108.3	106.9	119.8	73
Unit Value of Exports	48.7	49.4	53.4	58.5	60.6	62.2	67.8	79.4	100.0	110.7	†126.9	141.8	145.5	147.7	156.2	74
Unit Value of Imports	42.8	47.6	56.0	64.3	69.0	70.7	75.6	88.5	100.0	110.5	56.9	55.3	65.6	79.1	83.3	75

Pakistan

	1972	1973	1974	1975	1976	1977	1978	1979	1980	1981	1982	1983	1984	1985	1986
Balance of Payments															*Millions of US Dollars:*
Current Account, n.i.e. .... **78al** d	....	....	....	....	−783	−737	−722	−1,118	−925	−917	−805	27	−1,200	−1,083	−648
Goods: Exports f.o.b. .... **78aa** d	....	....	....	....	1,172	1,127	1,404	1,957	2,581	2,743	2,352	2,890	2,492	2,661	3,206
Goods: Imports f.o.b. .... **78ab** d	....	....	....	....	−2,202	−2,499	−3,236	−4,309	−5,470	−5,683	−5,771	−5,618	−6,263	−5,906	−5,999
Trade Balance .... **78ac** d	....	....	....	....	−1,030	−1,373	−1,833	−2,352	−2,889	−2,939	−3,419	−2,728	−3,771	−3,245	−2,793
Services: Credit .... **78ad** d	....	....	....	....	278	312	402	547	652	646	803	772	794	849	830
Services: Debit .... **78ae** d	....	....	....	....	−442	−494	−619	−792	−877	−919	−951	−989	−1,092	−1,184	−1,201
Balance on Goods & Services .... **78af** d	....	....	....	....	−1,194	−1,555	−2,050	−2,597	−3,115	−3,212	−3,567	−2,945	−4,069	−3,581	−3,164
Income: Credit .... **78ag** d	....	....	....	....	32	34	40	38	86	112	128	160	192	112	107
Income: Debit .... **78ah** d	....	....	....	....	−168	−223	−240	−313	−359	−378	−534	−580	−665	−695	−757
Balance on Gds, Serv. & Inc. .... **78ai** d	....	....	....	....	−1,330	−1,745	−2,250	−2,872	−3,388	−3,479	−3,974	−3,365	−4,542	−4,164	−3,814
Current Transfers, n.i.e.: Credit .. **78aj** d	....	....	....	....	565	1,011	1,542	1,757	2,467	2,564	3,175	3,397	3,349	3,095	3,185
Current Transfers: Debit .... **78ak** d	....	....	....	....	−18	−4	−13	−3	−4	−3	−6	−5	−7	−15	−18
Capital Account, n.i.e. .... **78bc** d	....	....	....	....	—	−1	—	−1	−1	−1	−1	−2	—	−2	−1
Capital Account, n.i.e.: Credit ...... **78ba** d	....	....	....	....	—	—	—	—	—	—	—	—	—	—	—
Capital Account: Debit .... **78bb** d	....	....	....	....	—	−1	—	−1	−1	−1	−1	−2	—	−2	−1
Financial Account, n.i.e. .... **78bj** d	....	....	....	....	507	625	643	589	647	664	532	535	335	634	885
Direct Investment Abroad .... **78bd** d	....	....	....	....	—	—	—	—	—	—	—	—	5	8	1
Dir. Invest. in Rep. Econ., n.i.e. ... **78be** d	....	....	....	....	8	15	32	58	64	108	64	29	56	131	106
Portfolio Investment Assets ...... **78bf** d	....	....	....	....	—	—	—	—	—	—	—	—	—	—	—
Equity Securities .... **78bk** d	....	....	....	....	—	—	—	—	—	—	—	—	—	—	—
Debt Securities .... **78bl** d	....	....	....	....	—	—	—	—	—	—	—	—	—	—	—
Portfolio Investment Liab., n.i.e. ... **78bg** d	....	....	....	....	—	—	—	—	—	—	—	—	9	110	83
Equity Securities .... **78bm** d	....	....	....	....	—	—	—	—	—	—	—	—	7	18	3
Debt Securities .... **78bn** d	....	....	....	....	—	—	—	—	—	—	—	—	2	93	80
Financial Derivatives Assets ...... **78bw** d	....	....	....	....	....	....	....	....	....	....	....	....	....	....	....
Financial Derivatives Liabilities ...... **78bx** d	....	....	....	....	....	....	....	....	....	....	....	....	....	....	....
Other Investment Assets .... **78bh** d	....	....	....	....	−14	−21	23	−80	−17	12	−13	−10	−103	−79	−199
Monetary Authorities .... **78bo** d	....	....	....	....	—	—	—	—	—	—	—	—	—	—	—
General Government .... **78bp** d	....	....	....	....	−14	−21	23	−80	−17	12	−13	−10	1	−13	8
Banks .... **78bq** d	....	....	....	....	—	—	—	—	—	—	—	—	−104	−66	−158
Other Sectors .... **78br** d	....	....	....	....	—	—	—	—	—	—	—	—	—	—	−50
Other Investment Liab., n.i.e. .... **78bi** d	....	....	....	....	513	631	588	611	600	543	481	516	369	463	895
Monetary Authorities .... **78bs** d	....	....	....	....	—	—	2	—	11	−10	1	−15	−1	54	31
General Government .... **78bt** d	....	....	....	....	331	504	504	551	506	343	165	216	295	198	366
Banks .... **78bu** d	....	....	....	....	41	26	−10	−11	−7	20	58	53	−62	24	356
Other Sectors .... **78bv** d	....	....	....	....	142	102	93	71	90	190	258	261	136	187	141
Net Errors and Omissions .... **78ca** d	....	....	....	....	−76	12	−15	54	73	−6	35	−15	−97	32	−44
Overall Balance .... **78cb** d	....	....	....	....	−352	−100	−94	−476	−206	−261	−239	546	−963	−419	193
Reserves and Related Items .... **79da** d	....	....	....	....	352	100	94	476	206	261	239	−546	963	419	−193
Reserve Assets .... **79db** d	....	....	....	....	−114	16	28	208	−313	−233	−280	−1,107	874	309	157
Use of Fund Credit and Loans .... **79dc** d	....	....	....	....	75	27	34	−74	120	414	452	276	−72	−187	−371
Exceptional Financing .... **79de** d	....	....	....	....	391	58	32	342	400	80	66	285	161	297	21
Government Finance															*Millions of Rupees:*
Deficit (-) or Surplus **80**	−2,583	†−4,554	−5,145	−11,466	−12,239	−12,580	−13,247	−17,997	−13,344	−16,138	−15,351	−24,784	−25,928	−33,783	−46,917
Revenue **81**	7,053	†8,256	11,794	14,259	17,737	20,439	25,171	29,502	38,102	45,359	50,370	57,750	71,042	76,351	89,716
Grants Received **81z**	239	†486	566	378	1,050	1,092	1,082	848	1,826	2,598	2,560	2,189	1,957	2,717	4,510
Expenditure **82**	8,784	†11,128	14,520	19,525	22,390	24,564	30,793	36,241	41,084	53,392	55,355	70,560	82,627	93,613	120,114
Lending Minus Repayments **83**	1,091	†2,168	2,985	6,578	8,636	9,547	8,707	12,106	12,188	10,703	12,926	14,163	16,300	19,238	21,029
Financing															
Domestic **84a**	1,897	†1,074	1,884	4,071	5,148	5,201	†7,954	11,513	8,022	9,814	11,318	20,617	22,610	31,851	43,108
Foreign **85a**	863	†3,301	2,976	7,796	6,488	5,153	†5,293	6,484	5,322	6,324	4,033	4,167	3,318	1,932	3,809
Use of Cash Balances **87**	−176	†179	285	−401	603	2,226									
Debt **88**	49,271	50,147	55,475	59,102	74,148	86,279	97,965	117,354	127,492	134,012	177,828	198,582	227,794	284,085	360,388
Domestic **88a**	16,667	17,818	17,426	21,245	27,420	32,700	38,530	49,371	56,754	60,088	76,656	87,856	106,554	143,930	193,385
Foreign **88b**	32,604	32,329	38,049	37,857	46,728	53,579	59,435	67,983	70,738	73,924	101,172	110,726	121,240	140,155	167,003
Held by: State Bank **88aa**	8,597	8,812	7,875	9,273	12,053	15,529	16,112	24,342	25,269	25,740	34,756	27,127	35,598	54,704	59,827
Deposit Money Banks **88ab**	3,627	4,998	4,465	5,415	8,080	9,479	12,678	14,450	19,000	19,457	20,812	25,928	23,152	30,292	38,979
Other Financial Inst. **88ac**	325	395	480	489	744	1,015	1,166	1,449	1,666	2,514	3,162	4,007	4,327	4,103	5,055
International Inst. **88ca**	5,535	5,624	5,968	6,250	6,977	7,956	10,324	11,503	12,477	13,800	19,407	28,100	33,529	41,555	49,649
Foreign Govts. & Bks. **88cb**	27,069	26,705	32,081	31,607	39,751	45,623	49,111	56,480	58,261	60,124	81,765	82,626	87,711	98,600	117,354
Others **88d**	4,118	3,613	4,606	6,068	6,543	6,677	8,574	9,130	10,819	12,377	17,926	30,794	43,475	54,831	89,524
Intragovernmental Debt **88s**	631	923	1,024	1,062	1,362	1,538	1,686	1,848	2,277	2,456	2,662	2,921	2,935	3,897	4,125
National Accounts															*Billions of Rupees:*
Househ.Cons.Expend.,incl.NPISHs **96f**	40.72	50.14	69.94	91.04	101.12	116.93	141.68	160.70	192.39	224.14	263.66	291.94	336.75	385.35	392.53
Government Consumption Expend. **91f**	6.48	7.72	8.54	11.95	15.17	16.71	19.12	20.34	23.54	28.28	33.52	41.61	50.74	57.13	65.66
Gross Fixed Capital Formation **93e**	6.81	7.65	10.61	16.22	24.06	27.86	30.51	33.13	41.35	47.71	54.59	61.76	69.21	77.93	87.55
Changes in Inventories **93i**	.85	1.00	1.00	2.00	—	1.00	1.00	1.75	2.00	4.50	7.86	6.70	7.49	8.60	9.00
Exports of Goods and Services **90c**	3.92	9.96	11.96	12.99	13.88	13.99	16.63	21.53	29.49	35.71	33.03	44.40	47.84	49.89	63.27
Imports of Goods and Services (-) **98c**	4.73	9.60	15.20	23.02	23.85	26.74	32.60	42.53	54.58	62.13	68.50	82.02	92.22	106.73	103.48
Gross Domestic Product (GDP) **99b**	54.06	66.87	86.85	111.18	130.36	149.75	176.33	194.92	234.18	278.20	324.16	364.39	419.80	472.16	514.53
Net Primary Income from Abroad **98.n**	.10	.46	.62	1.15	2.99	5.48	12.14	14.53	18.28	22.69	25.35	39.40	39.60	38.31	41.36
Gross National Income (GNI) **99a**	54.16	67.34	87.47	112.33	133.36	155.23	188.47	209.45	252.46	300.89	349.51	403.78	459.40	510.47	555.89
Consumption of Fixed Capital **99cf**	3.38	4.15	5.47	6.29	7.33	8.38	9.82	10.85	13.06	16.12	18.92	21.89	25.56	28.72	31.53
GDP Volume 1960 prices .... **99b.** p	36.1	38.6	40.7	42.6	44.5	46.2	49.9	52.3	56.9	60.8	....	....	....	....	....
GDP Volume 1981 Prices .... **99b.** p	....	....	....	....	....	....	....	....	....	278.20	296.38	316.47	332.50	357.75	377.43
GDP Volume (1995=100) .... **99bv** p	27.5	29.4	31.0	32.4	33.9	35.2	38.1	39.9	43.3	46.4	49.4	52.7	55.4	59.6	62.9
GDP Deflator (1995=100) .... **99bi** p	10.5	12.2	15.0	18.4	20.6	22.8	24.8	26.2	29.0	32.2	35.2	37.0	40.6	42.5	43.9
															Millions:
Population **99z**	†64.30	66.84	68.84	70.90	†73.21	75.44	77.75	80.13	82.58	85.12	87.76	90.48	93.29	96.18	99.54

Minus Sign Indicates Debit

	1987	1988	1989	1990	1991	1992	1993	1994	1995	1996	1997	1998	1999	2000	2001	
Balance of Payments																
Current Account, n.i.e.	-563	-1,430	-1,340	-1,662	-1,403	-1,877	-2,901	-1,812	-3,349	-4,436	-1,712	-2,248	-920	-96	....	78al d
Goods: Exports f.o.b.	3,956	4,426	4,818	5,405	6,411	6,913	6,793	7,117	8,356	8,507	8,351	7,850	7,673	8,739		78aa d
Goods: Imports f.o.b.	-6,283	-7,131	-7,401	-8,133	-8,683	-9,717	-9,380	-9,355	-11,248	-12,164	-10,750	-9,834	-9,520	-9,898		78ab d
Trade Balance	-2,327	-2,705	-2,583	-2,727	-2,272	-2,803	-2,586	-2,239	-2,891	-3,656	-2,399	-1,984	-1,847	-1,159		78ac d
Services: Credit	972	857	1,187	1,429	1,531	1,559	1,573	1,753	1,857	2,016	1,625	1,404	1,373	1,380		78ad d
Services: Debit	-1,288	-1,493	-1,712	-2,073	-2,314	-2,683	-2,639	-2,529	-2,938	-3,459	-2,658	-2,261	-2,146	-2,252		78ae d
Balance on Goods & Services	-2,643	-3,341	-3,107	-3,371	-3,056	-3,927	-3,652	-3,015	-3,972	-5,099	-3,433	-2,841	-2,620	-2,031		78af d
Income: Credit	116	94	142	96	73	73	63	149	187	175	147	83	119	118		78ag d
Income: Debit	-909	-912	-1,109	-1,191	-1,261	-1,485	-1,610	-1,830	-2,125	-2,198	-2,366	-2,263	-1,959	-2,333		78ah d
Balance on Gds, Serv. & Inc.	-3,436	-4,159	-4,075	-4,455	-4,244	-5,339	-5,199	-4,695	-5,910	-7,121	-5,652	-5,021	-4,460	-4,246		78ai d
Current Transfers, n.i.e.: Credit	2,899	2,760	2,770	2,834	2,890	3,502	2,337	2,919	2,611	2,739	3,981	2,801	3,582	4,188		78aj d
Current Transfers: Debit	-26	-30	-36	-40	-49	-40	-38	-35	-49	-54	-40	-28	-42	-38		78ak d
Capital Account, n.i.e.	-1	-1	-1	-1	-1	-1	—	—	—	—	—	....	....	....		78bc d
Capital Account, n.i.e.: Credit																78ba d
Capital Account: Debit	-1	-1	-1	-1	-1	-1	—	—	—	—	—	....	....	....		78bb d
Financial Account, n.i.e.	630	1,670	1,389	1,453	1,326	2,147	3,334	2,977	2,449	3,496	2,321	-1,873	-2,364	-3,105		78bj d
Direct Investment Abroad	-19	-13	-43	-2	4	12	2	-1	—	-7	24	-50	-21	-11		78bd d
Dir. Invest. in Rep. Econ., n.i.e.	129	186	211	245	258	336	349	421	723	922	716	506	532	308		78be d
Portfolio Investment Assets					—	—	—	—	—	—	—	....	....	....		78bf d
Equity Securities																78bk d
Debt Securities																78bl d
Portfolio Investment Liab., n.i.e.	132	127	16	87	92	372	293	1,471	4	261	279	-57	46	-451		78bg d
Equity Securities	36	6	-1	—	43	241	225	1,254	10	285	330	-22	66	35		78bm d
Debt Securities	96	121	17	87	50	131	68	217	-6	-24	-51	-35	-20	-486		78bn d
Financial Derivatives Assets																78bw d
Financial Derivatives Liabilities																78bx d
Other Investment Assets	-167	-188	-200	-365	-310	-568	-286	-283	-196	-164	-21	44	-523	-437		78bh d
Monetary Authorities																78bo d
General Government	1	-27	1	-11	-14	-456	46	-19	6	116	96	247	-358	-15		78bp d
Banks	-140	-62	-125	-609	-303	173	-86	-108	-116	8	-40	172	-25	-18		78bq d
Other Sectors	-28	-100	-76	255	6	-285	-246	-157	-85	-288	-77	-375	-140	-404		78br d
Other Investment Liab., n.i.e.	554	1,557	1,406	1,486	1,282	1,995	2,976	1,369	1,919	2,484	1,323	-2,316	-2,398	-2,514		78bi d
Monetary Authorities	-16	258	74	50	-61	383	-140	-282	-50	474	-71	91	-262	-168		78bs d
General Government	178	1,007	978	955	501	1,292	1,260	1,132	1,034	700	1,878	-795	2	-729		78bt d
Banks	358	196	321	340	500	-360	613	313	613	310	-1,044	-663	-1,292	-1,160		78bu d
Other Sectors	34	97	33	141	342	680	1,244	205	321	1,000	559	-949	-846	-457		78bv d
Net Errors and Omissions	15	22	-242	-105	-78	122	-6	178	-304	160	-72	1,011	768	577		78ca d
Overall Balance	80	261	-194	-314	-155	392	428	1,343	-1,204	-780	538	-3,110	-2,516	-2,624		78cb d
Reserves and Related Items	-80	-261	194	314	155	-392	-428	-1,343	1,204	780	-538	3,110	2,516	2,624		79da d
Reserve Assets	326	40	-215	471	-217	-496	-426	-1,744	1,180	946	-511	222	-842	4		79db d
Use of Fund Credit and Loans	-422	-317	398	-165	227	100	-4	401	23	-166	-27	20	391	-101		79dc d
Exceptional Financing	16	16	11	9	145	5	2	—	—	—	—	2,868	2,966	2,721		79de d
Government Finance																
Year Ending June 30																
Deficit (-) or Surplus	-48,783	-42,426	-56,982	-46,232	-77,105	-95,418	-118,999	-113,462	-123,742	-169,477	-189,788	-171,925	-202,024	-187,072	-121,900 P	80
Revenue	98,976	119,844	143,370	163,825	170,642	216,586	242,812	273,238	321,323	370,510	384,263	433,636	464,372	519,579	594,879 P	81
Grants Received	3,350	5,372	7,831	7,159	10,544	7,511	—	5,665	5,513	4,804	—	—	—	35,054	47,262 P	81z
Expenditure	127,822	158,122	191,463	192,079	237,388	294,370	330,509	362,891	425,418	515,219	547,768	584,624	627,147	701,815	756,327 P	82
Lending Minus Repayments	23,287	9,520	16,720	25,137	20,903	25,145	31,302	29,474	25,160	29,572	26,283	20,937	39,249	39,890	7,714 P	83
Financing																
Domestic	40,805	30,515	38,352	26,475	61,297	73,110	86,815	78,040	82,235	128,717	142,159	129,295	91,750	131,872	73,302 P	84a
Foreign	7,978	11,911	18,630	19,757	15,808	22,308	32,184	35,422	41,507	40,760	47,629	42,630	110,274	55,200	48,598 P	85a
Use of Cash Balances																87
Debt	412,276	492,236	581,192	674,248	776,583	902,828	1,058,682	....	....	....	....	2,117,616	....	2,832,571		88
Domestic	225,246	284,492	327,534	376,596	441,580	527,595	612,642	....				1,183,232	....	1,659,121		88a
Foreign	187,030	207,744	253,658	297,652	335,003	375,233	446,040	....				934,384	....	1,173,450		89a
Held by: State Bank	55,694	81,957	90,038	110,774	132,845	....										88aa
Deposit Money Banks	45,597	63,281	61,037	51,177	83,354	....										88ab
Other Financial Inst.	8,630	9,194	10,527	10,593	14,810	....										88ac
International Inst.	57,326	69,786	92,533	108,635	137,985	....										88ca
Foreign Govts. & Bks.	129,704	137,958	161,125	189,017	197,018	....										88cb
Others	115,325	130,060	165,932	204,052	223,571	....										88d
Intragovernmental Debt	5,298	3,130	3,647	4,243	4,989											88s
National Accounts																
Year Ending June 30																
Househ.Cons.Expend.,incl.NPISHs	415.67	486.57	562.00	608.80	694.20	843.90	962.40	1,109.90	1,351.40	1,545.20	1,818.20	1,929.70	2,224.00	2,385.60	2,665.40	96f
Government Consumption Expend.	77.48	104.75	129.20	129.56	145.58	155.57	174.68	189.10	219.12	268.10	288.81	301.61	304.35	351.30	366.10	91f
Gross Fixed Capital Formation	100.04	111.27	133.60	148.10	177.10	225.20	256.40	280.50	317.80	368.10	396.90	402.80	409.40	445.10	453.10	93e
Changes in Inventories	9.50	10.40	12.40	14.00	15.80	18.70	21.10	24.60	28.20	34.34	38.28	71.40	48.00	51.72	56.20	93i
Exports of Goods and Services	79.06	93.60	108.32	126.58	172.81	209.22	217.37	254.18	311.80	358.37	390.52	441.41	451.10	514.40	604.20	90c
Imports of Goods and Services (-)	109.27	131.20	156.64	173.29	188.68	247.41	299.15	297.30	362.41	454.29	504.37	469.31	498.50	565.20	672.90	98c
Gross Domestic Product (GDP)	572.48	675.39	768.80	853.80	1,016.70	1,205.20	1,332.80	1,561.10	1,865.90	2,120.20	2,428.30	2,677.70	2,938.40	3,182.80	3,472.10	99b
Net Primary Income from Abroad	36.38	29.10	28.01	36.90	23.91	12.54	9.96	4.00	14.04	-7.14	-19.35	-24.36	-25.55	-44.70	-60.80	98.n
Gross National Income (GNI)	608.86	704.48	796.80	890.70	1,040.60	1,217.70	1,342.80	1,565.10	1,880.00	2,113.00	2,409.00	2,653.30	2,912.80	3,138.10	3,411.30	99a
Consumption of Fixed Capital	34.74	39.24	43.70	51.70	60.40	80.80	86.30	100.10	119.40	136.20	159.20	180.70	188.50	211.10	227.40	99cf
GDP Volume 1960 prices																99b.p
GDP Volume 1981 Prices	401.78	432.42	453.87	474.10	500.00	539.13	549.45	570.86	600.19	630.15	629.55	645.61	669.24	698.90	722.23	99b.p
GDP Volume (1995=100)	66.9	72.0	75.6	79.0	83.3	89.8	91.5	95.1	100.0	105.0	104.9	107.6	111.5	116.4	120.3	99bv p
GDP Deflator (1995=100)	45.8	50.2	54.5	57.9	65.4	71.9	78.0	88.0	100.0	108.2	124.1	133.4	141.2	146.5	154.6	99bi p
Midyear Estimates																
Population	102.70	105.97	109.14	112.40	115.77	119.23	122.79	126.47	130.25	134.15	138.16	†131.51	134.51	137.50	144.97	99z

(See notes in the back of the book.)

Panama

283

		1972	1973	1974	1975	1976	1977	1978	1979	1980	1981	1982	1983	1984	1985	1986
Exchange Rates															*Balboas per SDR:*	
Official Rate	aa	1.0857	1.2064	1.2244	1.1707	1.1618	1.2147	1.3028	1.3173	1.2754	1.1640	1.1031	1.0470	.9802	1.0984	1.2232
															Balboas per US Dollar:	
Official Rate	ae	1.0000	1.0000	1.0000	1.0000	1.0000	1.0000	1.0000	1.0000	1.0000	1.0000	1.0000	1.0000	1.0000	1.0000	1.0000
Fund Position															*Millions of SDRs:*	
Quota	2f. s	36.0	36.0	36.0	36.0	36.0	36.0	45.0	45.0	67.5	67.5	67.5	102.2	102.2	102.2	102.2
SDRs	1b. s	2.7	2.6	2.3	6.4	5.2	4.5	4.0	3.9	1.1	2.8	3.8	.4	—	11.7	1.4
Reserve Position in the Fund	1c. s	8.0	8.0						3.7	2.5	8.1			8.7		
Total Fund Cred.&Loans Outstg.	2tl	—	—	7.4	17.5	42.6	42.2	40.3	31.5	18.1	80.5	76.1	184.1	276.6	283.4	288.6
International Liquidity														*Millions of US Dollars Unless Otherwise Indicated:*		
Total Reserves minus Gold	1l. d	43.1	41.7	39.3	34.4	78.9	70.9	150.4	118.7	117.4	119.9	101.0	206.7	215.6	98.0	170.2
SDRs	1b. d	3.0	3.1	2.8	7.4	6.0	5.5	5.2	5.2	1.4	3.2	4.2	.4	—	12.9	1.8
Reserve Position in the Fund	1c. d	8.7	9.6						4.9	3.2	10.3			9.1		
Foreign Exchange	1d. d	31.5	29.0	36.5	27.0	72.9	65.4	140.4	110.3	105.7	116.7	96.8	197.2	215.6	85.1	168.4
Gold (National Valuation)	1and	—	—	—	—	—	—	—	3.7	3.7	—	—	—	—	—	—
Monetary Authorities: Other Liab.	4..d	30	32	69	93	120	105	107	138	186	221	281	338	352	358	333
Deposit Money Banks: Assets	7a. d	898	2,260	4,795	6,483	7,697	9,970	13,382	19,446	18,970	24,675	27,102	24,649	22,229	22,555	24,459
Liabilities	7b. d	1,097	2,588	5,340	7,116	8,372	10,634	13,846	20,315	19,508	25,234	26,965	24,791	22,380	22,385	24,204
Monetary Authorities															*Millions of Balboas:*	
Foreign Assets	11	43.1	41.7	39.3	34.4	78.9	70.9	150.4	122.4	121.1	119.9	101.0	206.7	215.6	98.0	170.2
Claims on Central Government	12a	39.2	35.8	60.1	89.8	168.5	155.4	129.7	170.4	172.3	343.1	346.4	480.0	638.0	737.3	713.8
Claims on Official Entities	12bx		2.5	2.1	8.2	25.6	12.3	33.7	78.5	32.8	59.4	96.5	96.1	93.7	92.3	102.0
Claims on Private Sector	12d	86.6	114.5	130.4	140.7	124.4	121.8	175.5	216.3	268.0	283.5	339.9	335.9	336.0	322.6	324.3
Claims on Deposit Money Banks	12e	30.4	17.6	25.4	41.1	25.2	51.5	54.1	40.9	81.5	123.7	125.8	111.9	70.2	136.2	134.0
Bankers Deposits	14c	32.9	31.3	32.7	52.0	79.5	88.0	61.5	146.4	155.9	221.5	207.5	207.5	210.2	198.0	223.3
Demand Deposits	14d	34.3	29.9	23.5	23.9	26.2	28.2	32.0	38.7	42.0	40.7	48.8	45.7	46.7	50.0	55.7
Time, Savings,& Fgn.Currency Dep.	15	22.5	22.3	23.4	25.4	30.5	37.8	45.8	49.3	63.2	83.7	99.7	128.8	157.3	154.4	201.9
Foreign Liabilities	16c	10.4	17.3	71.7	104.3	157.6	144.0	147.5	165.8	144.7	196.5	149.6	271.7	348.2	406.1	425.8
Long-Term Foreign Liabilities	16cl	20.0	14.8	6.6	9.1	11.6	12.6	12.3	13.8	63.9	117.8	215.1	259.4	275.3	263.5	259.8
Central Government Deposits	16d	48.3	59.2	63.4	68.9	103.0	109.5	205.2	147.5	144.0	210.3	218.6	243.4	223.7	266.6	305.9
Capital Accounts	17a	28.8	32.5	30.9	32.5	32.8	36.5	45.6	52.1	71.9	82.4	94.0	102.7	101.2	108.6	113.6
Other Items (Net)	17r	2.1	4.8	5.0	−1.8	−18.5	−44.8	−6.5	14.9	−9.9	−23.3	−23.7	−28.5	−9.1	−60.9	−141.8
Deposit Money Banks															*Millions of Balboas:*	
Foreign Assets	21	898.3	2,259.9	4,795.4	6,482.5	7,696.7	9,969.9	13,382.2	19,445.6	18,970.3	24,674.5	27,102.1	24,649.2	22,229.3	22,555.2	24,458.6
Claims on Central Government	22a	11.5	19.9	53.9	195.3	224.8	262.5	215.4	165.9	213.8	207.0	297.6	348.5	377.2	351.4	365.7
Claims on Private Sector	22d	596.0	758.2	1,052.6	1,060.6	1,092.0	1,148.7	1,250.0	1,496.3	1,803.2	2,185.8	2,195.2	2,177.4	2,200.5	2,277.1	2,655.9
Demand Deposits	24	119.3	131.2	172.8	149.2	163.8	185.0	214.0	262.6	293.3	319.0	330.5	326.9	334.3	359.5	393.8
Time and Savings Deposits	25	216.8	261.1	310.5	349.3	357.5	421.5	540.9	692.9	917.2	1,117.4	1,270.1	1,246.8	1,324.6	1,388.6	1,708.5
Foreign Liabilities	26c	1,097.0	2,588.0	5,340.0	7,116.1	8,372.3	10,633.8	13,845.7	20,315.4	19,508.4	25,233.6	26,965.3	24,791.1	22,380.0	22,385.2	24,204.1
Capital Accounts	27a	53.7	105.9	132.8	181.2	158.9	249.6	287.3	385.9	597.3	682.4	1,202.0	988.0	979.7	1,050.2	1,193.6
Other Items (Net)	27r	19.0	−48.2	−54.2	−57.4	−39.0	−108.8	−40.3	−549.0	−328.9	−285.1	−173.0	−177.7	−211.6	.2	−19.8
Monetary Survey															*Millions of Balboas:*	
Foreign Assets (Net)	31n	−166.0	−303.7	−577.0	−703.5	−754.3	−737.0	−460.6	−913.2	−561.7	−635.7	88.2	−206.9	−283.3	−138.2	−1.2
Domestic Credit	32	685.0	871.7	1,235.7	1,425.7	1,532.3	1,591.2	1,599.1	1,979.9	2,346.1	2,868.5	3,057.0	3,194.5	3,421.7	3,514.1	3,855.8
Claims on Central Govt. (Net)	32an	2.4	−3.5	50.6	216.2	290.3	308.4	139.9	188.8	242.1	339.8	425.4	585.1	791.5	822.1	773.6
Claims on Private Sector	32d	682.6	872.7	1,183.0	1,201.3	1,216.4	1,270.5	1,425.5	1,712.6	2,071.2	2,469.3	2,535.1	2,513.3	2,536.5	2,599.7	2,980.2
Deposit Money	34	153.6	161.1	196.3	173.1	190.0	213.2	246.0	301.3	335.3	359.7	379.3	372.6	381.0	409.5	449.5
Quasi-Money	35	239.3	283.4	333.9	374.7	388.0	459.3	586.7	742.2	980.4	1,201.1	1,369.8	1,375.6	1,481.9	1,543.0	1,910.4
Long-Term Foreign Liabilities	36cl	20.0	14.8	6.6	9.1	11.6	12.6	12.3	13.8	63.9	117.8	215.1	259.4	275.3	263.5	259.8
Capital Accounts	37a	82.5	138.4	163.7	213.7	191.7	286.1	332.9	438.0	669.2	764.8	1,296.0	1,090.7	1,080.9	1,158.8	1,307.2
Other Items (Net)	37r	23.6	−29.7	−41.9	−48.3	−3.2	−117.1	−39.4	−428.6	−264.4	−210.6	−115.0	−110.6	−80.7	1.1	−72.3
Money plus Quasi-Money	35l	392.9	444.5	530.2	547.8	578.0	672.5	832.7	1,043.5	1,315.7	1,560.8	1,749.1	1,748.2	1,862.9	1,952.5	2,359.9
Other Banking Institutions															*Millions of Balboas:*	
Claims on Private Sector	42d	....	....	....	85.7	88.9	98.2	111.2	126.2	143.1	154.8	164.4	186.2	207.4	230.6	....
Claims on Deposit Money Banks	42e				—	—	—	—	—	.5	.5	3.2	5.2	6.6	5.1	
Time and Savings Deposits	45	....	....	....	87.8	105.5	122.3	115.7	124.3	144.2	165.1	202.3	225.9	249.1	250.0	....
Capital Accounts	47a				6.9	7.0	7.0	7.3	7.5	7.7	7.9	8.2	8.6	8.8	9.1	
Other Items (Net)	47r				−9.0	−23.6	−31.1	−11.8	−5.6	−8.3	−17.7	−42.9	−43.1	−43.9	−23.4	
Liquid Liabilities	55l	....	....	....	634.6	682.4	793.7	946.8	1,166.3	1,458.3	1,723.8	1,949.1	1,970.8	2,108.9	2,194.9	
Interest Rates															*Percent Per Annum:*	
Deposit Rate	60l	....	....	....	....	....	....	....	....	....	....	....	....	....	....	6.50
Lending Rate	60p	....	....	....	....	....	....	....	....	....	....	....	....	....	....	12.36
Prices, Production and Labor															*Index Numbers (1995=100):*	
Wholesale Prices	63	36.4	40.2	52.3	59.7	64.3	69.0	72.7	82.9	95.6	105.2	†113.9	109.5	110.6	110.2	92.6
Consumer Prices	64	43.0	46.0	53.5	†56.6	58.8	61.5	64.1	69.3	78.8	84.6	88.2	90.0	91.4	92.4	92.3
Manufacturing production	66ey	....	....	....	....	....	....	....	....	....	....	....	....	....	....	....
															Number in Thousands:	
Labor Force	67d	....	....	....	....	....	....	....	....	....	....	....	....	....	....	....
Employment	67e	....	....	....	....	....	....	....	....	....	....	....	....	....	627	644
Unemployment	67c	....	....	....	....	....	....	....	....	....	....	....	....	....	88	76
Unemployment Rate (%)	67r	....	....	....	....	....	....	....	....	....	....	....	....	....	12.3	10.5
International Transactions															*Millions of Balboas:*	
Exports	70	122.6	137.8	210.5	286.4	238.2	251.0	256.4	302.9	360.5	328.1	375.0	320.5	276.0	336.2	348.6
Imports, c.i.f.	71	440.5	502.2	822.4	892.0	848.3	861.2	942.4	1,183.8	1,449.2	1,540.1	1,570.2	1,411.9	1,423.1	1,391.8	1,229.2
Imports, f.o.b.	71.v	401.1	454.0	755.7	815.6	779.7	777.8	844.9	1,062.9	1,288.9	1,393.0	1,406.7	1,267.2	1,276.3	1,238.8	1,103.8
															1990=100	
Volume of Exports	72	60.0	61.8	58.9	69.2	72.8	83.6	86.8	92.1	92.2	87.3	89.5	93.6	83.1	91.2	96.2
Unit Value of Exports (1990=100)	74	76.8	79.4	88.7	100.2	98.5	91.2	90.2	96.6	104.3	104.5	96.9	104.8	104.5	102.6	94.0

1987	1988	1989	1990	1991	1992	1993	1994	1995	1996	1997	1998	1999	2000	2001		
End of Period															**Exchange Rates**	
1.4187	1.3457	1.3142	1.4227	1.4304	1.3750	1.3736	1.4599	1.4865	1.4380	1.3493	1.4080	1.3725	1.3029	1.2567	Official Rate	**aa**
End of Period																
1.0000	1.0000	1.0000	1.0000	1.0000	1.0000	1.0000	1.0000	1.0000	1.0000	1.0000	1.0000	1.0000	1.0000	1.0000	Official Rate	**ae**
End of Period															**Fund Position**	
102.2	102.2	102.2	102.2	102.2	149.6	149.6	149.6	149.6	149.6	149.6	149.6	206.6	206.6	206.6	Quota	**2f. s**
—	—	—	19.4	8.1	3.3	.1	—	.6	—	.4	.1	1.2	.3	1.1	SDRs	**1b. s**
—	—	—	—	—	11.9	11.9	11.9	11.9	11.9	11.9	11.9	11.9	11.9	11.9	Reserve Position in the Fund	**1c. s**
243.9	243.8	243.2	191.3	150.7	79.8	82.3	91.3	74.4	91.0	105.4	125.5	108.3	69.1	42.9	Total Fund Cred.&Loans Outstg.	**2tl**
End of Period															**International Liquidity**	
77.8	72.2	119.4	343.5	499.1	504.4	597.4	704.3	781.4	866.5	1,147.8	954.5	822.9	722.6	1,091.8	Total Reserves minus Gold	**1l. d**
—	—	—	27.6	11.6	4.6	.1	—	.8	—	.5	.1	1.6	.3	1.4	SDRs	**1b. d**
—	—	—	—	—	16.3	16.3	17.3	17.6	17.1	16.0	16.7	16.3	15.5	14.9	Reserve Position in the Fund	**1c. d**
77.8	72.2	119.4	315.9	487.4	483.5	581.0	686.9	762.9	849.4	1,131.3	937.7	805.0	706.8	1,075.5	Foreign Exchange	**1d. d**
—	—	—	—	—	—	—	—	—	—	—	—	—	—	—	Gold (National Valuation)	**1and**
351	345	356	345	337	352	334	292	343	158	149	123	118	108	104	Monetary Authorities: Other Liab.	**4..d**
16,137	6,595	6,287	6,857	8,668	9,714	12,735	16,617	15,664	15,484	16,595	13,209	12,362	12,620	12,521	Deposit Money Banks: Assets	**7a. d**
16,185	6,923	6,509	6,533	7,860	8,522	11,336	14,846	13,930	13,954	14,825	11,745	11,845	11,776	12,081	Liabilities	**7b. d**
End of Period															**Monetary Authorities**	
77.8	72.2	119.4	343.5	499.1	504.4	597.4	704.3	781.4	866.5	1,147.8	954.5	822.9	722.6	1,091.8	Foreign Assets	**11**
795.6	988.1	1,150.0	1,115.7	1,033.7	1,019.4	1,050.1	1,014.0	945.6	1,280.9	1,080.7	1,099.7	1,047.3	839.2	791.9	Claims on Central Government	**12a**
105.6	106.8	106.8	106.8	106.8	106.8	—	—	—	—	—	—	—	—	—	Claims on Official Entities	**12bx**
301.0	300.5	298.8	247.6	234.0	288.0	322.8	300.6	318.8	301.0	292.7	403.2	583.8	747.8	976.0	Claims on Private Sector	**12d**
94.4	52.8	21.2	298.9	439.1	464.3	633.0	732.8	948.8	615.4	765.2	949.4	999.8	908.6	607.1	Claims on Deposit Money Banks	**12e**
135.5	116.7	104.1	164.6	237.5	175.6	184.4	167.4	172.7	266.0	252.7	272.6	284.1	301.8	280.0	Bankers Deposits	**14c**
46.2	28.6	37.9	52.8	57.9	62.1	63.0	75.4	77.0	83.0	105.8	97.8	80.6	80.7	104.0	Demand Deposits	**14d**
179.3	141.2	137.3	148.4	164.7	172.9	187.3	192.5	205.0	227.2	240.8	283.4	296.5	367.4	474.0	Time, Savings,& Fgn.Currency Dep.	**15**
479.4	456.1	451.4	390.4	327.0	254.8	244.7	225.5	182.2	195.1	207.2	224.8	195.1	138.5	93.9	Foreign Liabilities	**16c**
217.7	216.7	224.0	226.8	225.2	207.1	202.3	199.5	271.5	93.8	84.5	74.8	71.4	59.9	63.7	Long-Term Foreign Liabilities	**16cl**
323.1	516.0	686.0	1,060.6	1,262.7	1,358.8	1,550.6	1,716.2	1,857.8	1,871.5	2,025.2	2,039.7	2,094.5	1,883.8	2,061.0	Central Government Deposits	**16d**
120.6	124.1	127.0	76.5	49.2	157.7	196.0	228.3	297.7	424.9	471.5	543.9	536.1	534.3	533.1	Capital Accounts	**17a**
−127.4	−79.0	−71.5	−7.6	−11.4	−6.1	−24.9	−53.2	−69.4	−97.8	−101.4	−130.1	−104.5	−148.2	−142.8	Other Items (Net)	**17r**
End of Period															**Deposit Money Banks**	
16,136.6	6,594.5	6,287.4	6,857.4	8,668.2	9,713.6	12,735.2	16,616.6	15,663.9	15,483.8	16,595.2	13,208.7	12,362.1	12,620.5	12,521.1	Foreign Assets	**21**
201.4	169.4	159.5	157.5	157.5	165.8	104.8	74.3	62.3	79.4	73.2	86.2	143.0	160.9	135.9	Claims on Central Government	**22a**
2,732.1	2,171.9	2,169.0	2,233.5	2,782.5	3,458.9	4,332.5	5,118.6	5,852.4	6,347.6	7,294.0	9,010.2	10,507.1	11,092.3	11,842.8	Claims on Private Sector	**22d**
395.9	275.2	269.0	380.0	499.0	577.1	645.2	728.6	737.7	758.3	889.7	1,027.5	1,062.2	1,095.0	1,193.0	Demand Deposits	**24**
1,657.1	1,203.5	1,156.0	1,604.0	2,141.0	2,765.4	3,296.0	3,845.5	4,204.2	4,476.5	5,138.6	5,795.3	6,376.7	7,054.9	7,653.6	Time and Savings Deposits	**25**
16,184.7	6,922.9	6,509.0	6,533.1	7,860.0	8,521.8	11,336.5	14,845.9	13,929.8	13,954.6	14,825.0	11,744.7	11,844.5	11,775.8	12,081.2	Foreign Liabilities	**26c**
1,034.2	671.0	636.0	656.0	736.0	898.0	1,008.0	1,321.3	1,431.8	1,660.8	1,945.1	2,171.5	2,257.8	2,551.9	2,561.3	Capital Accounts	**27a**
−201.8	−136.8	45.9	75.3	372.2	576.0	886.9	1,068.2	1,275.1	1,060.9	1,164.1	1,566.1	1,471.0	1,396.1	1,010.7	Other Items (Net)	**27r**
End of Period															**Monetary Survey**	
−449.7	−712.3	−553.6	277.4	980.3	1,441.4	1,751.5	2,249.5	2,333.2	2,200.8	2,710.8	2,193.7	1,145.4	1,428.8	1,437.8	Foreign Assets (Net)	**31n**
3,812.6	3,220.7	3,198.1	2,800.5	3,051.9	3,680.1	4,259.6	4,791.3	5,321.3	6,137.3	6,715.5	8,559.6	10,186.7	10,956.4	11,685.6	Domestic Credit	**32**
673.9	641.5	623.5	212.6	−71.4	−173.6	−395.7	−627.9	−849.9	−511.3	−871.2	−853.8	−904.2	−883.6	−1,133.2	Claims on Central Govt. (Net)	**32an**
3,033.1	2,472.4	2,467.8	2,481.1	3,016.5	3,746.9	4,655.3	5,419.2	6,171.2	6,648.6	7,586.7	9,413.4	11,090.9	11,840.1	12,818.8	Claims on Private Sector	**32d**
442.1	303.8	306.9	432.8	556.9	639.2	708.2	804.1	814.7	841.3	995.5	1,125.2	1,142.7	1,175.8	1,296.9	Deposit Money	**34**
1,836.4	1,344.7	1,293.3	1,752.4	2,305.7	2,938.3	3,483.3	4,038.0	4,409.2	4,703.7	5,379.4	6,078.7	6,673.2	7,422.3	8,127.6	Quasi-Money	**35**
217.7	216.7	224.0	226.8	225.2	207.1	202.3	199.5	271.5	93.8	84.5	74.8	71.4	59.9	63.7	Long-Term Foreign Liabilities	**36cl**
1,154.8	795.1	763.0	732.5	785.2	1,055.7	1,203.9	1,549.6	1,729.6	2,085.7	2,416.6	2,715.4	2,794.0	3,086.2	3,094.4	Capital Accounts	**37a**
−288.1	−151.9	57.3	−66.6	159.1	281.2	413.4	449.6	429.6	613.7	550.3	759.1	650.8	641.1	540.7	Other Items (Net)	**37r**
2,278.5	1,648.5	1,600.2	2,185.2	2,862.5	3,577.5	4,191.5	4,842.1	5,223.9	5,544.9	6,374.9	7,203.9	7,815.9	8,598.0	9,424.6	Money plus Quasi-Money	**35l**
End of Period															**Other Banking Institutions**	
....	....	....	....	....	....	....	....	....	....	....	....	....	....	....	Claims on Private Sector	**42d**
....	....	....	....	....	....	....	....	....	....	....	....	....	....	....	Claims on Deposit Money Banks	**42e**
....	....	....	....	....	....	....	....	....	....	....	....	....	....	....	Time and Savings Deposits	**45**
....	....	....	....	....	....	....	....	....	....	....	....	....	....	....	Capital Accounts	**47a**
....	....	....	....	....	....	....	....	....	....	....	....	....	....	....	Other Items (Net)	**47r**
....	....	....	....	....	....	....	....	....	....	....	....	....	....	....	Liquid Liabilities	**55l**
Percent Per Annum															**Interest Rates**	
6.59	7.54	8.49	8.40	7.73	†5.67	5.90	6.11	7.18	7.20	7.03	6.76	6.92	7.07	6.83	Deposit Rate	**60l**
12.60	12.47	12.92	†11.98	11.79	10.61	10.06	10.15	11.10	10.62	10.63	10.82	10.05	†10.48	10.97	Lending Rate	**60p**
Period Averages															**Prices, Production and Labor**	
94.0	87.6	†89.7	93.2	93.7	95.4	95.2	97.1	100.0	102.1	99.8	95.9	98.5	107.1	82.1	Wholesale Prices	**63**
93.2	†93.6	93.7	94.4	95.6	97.3	97.8	99.0	100.0	101.3	102.6	103.2	104.5	106.0	106.3	Consumer Prices	**64**
....	....	....	....	....	90.1	96.1	99.3	100.0	99.9	105.6	109.8	105.3	....	....	Manufacturing production	**66ey**
Period Averages																
....	....	....	828	859	....	940	967	1,008	....	1,049	1,049	1,089	....	—	Labor Force	**67d**
678	654	686	....	715	782	816	832	867	867	909	937	961	....	—	Employment	**67e**
91	128	134	....	138	134	125	135	141	145	140	147	128	....	—	Unemployment	**67c**
11.8	16.3	16.3	....	16.1	14.7	13.3	14.0	14.0	14.3	13.4	13.6	11.8	....	—	Unemployment Rate (%)	**67r**
Millions of Balboas															**International Transactions**	
357.7	306.9	317.9	340.1	358.4	501.5	553.2	583.3	625.2	....	722.8	784.1	822.1	859.5	910.5	Exports	**70**
1,306.2	751.0	985.9	1,538.6	1,695.0	2,023.6	2,187.8	2,404.1	2,510.7	2,779.9	3,002.0	3,398.3	3,515.8	3,378.7	2,963.5	Imports, c.i.f.	**71**
1,165.2	673.4	867.5	1,339.2	1,523.5	1,830.6	1,979.6	2,177.5	2,280.2	2,548.1	2,738.5	2,806.4	3,214.7	3,097.7	2,714.5	Imports, f.o.b.	**71.v**
1990=100																
92.8	76.1	90.6	100.0	93.1	93.7	99.6	....	....	....	....	113.2	83.5	79.2	....	Volume of Exports	**72**
103.5	113.5	158.6	100.0	100.9	....	....	....	....	....	....	....	....	....	....	Unit Value of Exports (1990=100)	**74**

Panama

283

Balance of Payments															Millions of US Dollars:
Current Account, n.i.e. .... 78al d	....	....	....	....	....	−155.4	−207.7	−311.0	−328.7	−535.0	−194.1	198.7	−202.3	75.1	−98.9
Goods: Exports f.o.b. .... 78aa d	....	....	....	....	....	401.0	385.7	453.2	2,519.3	2,774.2	2,579.6	1,840.0	1,889.7	2,132.9	2,490.7
Goods: Imports f.o.b. .... 78ab d	....	....	....	....	....	−790.4	−862.1	−1,085.7	−2,806.0	−3,118.1	−2,883.4	−2,217.6	−2,378.2	−2,570.2	−2,669.5
Trade Balance............................ 78ac d	....	....	....	....	....	−389.4	−476.4	−632.5	−286.7	−343.9	−303.8	−377.6	−488.5	−437.3	−178.8
Services: Credit .... 78ad d	....	....	....	....	....	401.2	442.5	559.5	902.4	932.7	993.9	1,131.5	1,066.0	1,180.1	1,159.1
Services: Debit........................... 78ae d	....	....	....	....	....	−205.0	−238.8	−287.7	−587.9	−668.1	−630.7	−550.4	−597.0	−657.2	−796.8
Balance on Goods & Services .... 78af d	....	....	....	....	....	−193.2	−272.7	−360.7	27.8	−79.3	59.4	203.5	−19.5	85.6	183.5
Income: Credit .... 78ag d	....	....	....	....	....	585.9	915.4	1,570.7	4,431.4	5,403.1	5,907.0	4,407.7	3,672.0	3,089.4	2,550.0
Income: Debit............................ 78ah d	....	....	....	....	....	−545.7	−848.3	−1,533.3	−4,828.1	−5,919.9	−6,231.4	−4,492.7	−3,977.3	−3,240.9	−2,965.6
Balance on Gds, Serv. & Inc. .... 78ai d	....	....	....	....	....	−153.0	−205.6	−323.3	−368.9	−596.1	−265.0	118.5	−324.8	−65.9	−232.1
Current Transfers, n.i.e.: Credit .... 78aj d	....	....	....	....	....	32.4	36.6	57.0	81.7	97.7	111.7	126.9	161.2	180.0	166.9
Current Transfers: Debit .... 78ak d	....	....	....	....	....	−34.8	−38.7	−44.7	−41.5	−36.6	−40.8	−46.7	−38.7	−39.0	−33.7
Capital Account, n.i.e. .... 78bc d	....	....	....	....	....	—	—	—	....	....	....	....	....	....	....
Capital Account, n.i.e.: Credit .... 78ba d	....	....	....	....	....	—	—	—	....	....	....	....	....	....	....
Capital Account: Debit .... 78bb d	....	....	....	....	....	—	—	—	....	....	....	....	....	....	....
Financial Account, n.i.e............... 78bj d	....	....	....	....	....	218.2	295.5	705.3	−283.2	393.5	385.1	56.4	−55.4	−82.7	−48.2
Direct Investment Abroad .... 78bd d	....	....	....	....	....	—	—	—	....	....	....	....	....	....	....
Dir. Invest. in Rep. Econ., n.i.e. ...... 78be d	....	....	....	....	....	10.9	−2.5	49.8	218.5	303.2	366.6	79.4	−135.5	67.3	20.3
Portfolio Investment Assets .... 78bf d	....	....	....	....	....	—	—	—	−735.7	−66.1	−31.6	213.2	70.8	−171.1	−985.0
Equity Securities .... 78bk d	....	....	....	....	....	—	—	—	−.1	1.0	.4	.4	....	−1.4	1.2
Debt Securities .... 78bl d	....	....	....	....	....	—	—	—	−735.6	−67.1	−32.0	212.8	70.8	−169.7	−986.2
Portfolio Investment Liab., n.i.e. ...... 78bg d	....	....	....	....	....	12.6	70.4	203.9	16.3	25.3	−9.7	−35.9	−17.7	−22.2	−31.3
Equity Securities .... 78bm d	....	....	....	....	....	−.6	1.0	−.2	....	....	....	....	....	....	....
Debt Securities .... 78bn d	....	....	....	....	....	13.2	69.4	204.1	16.3	25.3	−9.7	−35.9	−17.7	−22.2	−31.3
Financial Derivatives Assets .... 78bw d	....	....	....	....	....										
Financial Derivatives Liabilities ...... 78bx d	....	....	....	....	....										
Other Investment Assets .... 78bh d	....	....	....	....	....	−2,328.9	−3,408.0	−6,092.3	−1,111.0	−6,918.9	−2,380.2	5,939.3	4,892.8	−557.5	233.5
Monetary Authorities.................. 78bo d	....	....	....	....	....										
General Government .... 78bp d	....	....	....	....	....	−1.4			−3.3	−1.6	−1.6	....	−5.7	....	−2.4
Banks .... 78bq d	....	....	....	....	....	−2,273.0	−3,407.7	−6,046.8	−1,059.1	−6,802.1	−2,344.1	5,943.5	4,851.5	−586.5	403.0
Other Sectors .... 78br d	....	....	....	....	....	−54.5	−.3	−45.5	−48.6	−115.2	−34.5	−4.2	47.0	29.0	−167.1
Other Investment Liab., n.i.e. ...... 78bi d	....	....	....	....	....	2,523.6	3,635.6	6,543.9	1,328.7	7,050.0	2,440.0	−6,139.6	−4,865.8	600.8	714.3
Monetary Authorities.................. 78bs d	....	....	....	....	....	−407.7	−28.3	41.4	4.5	29.1	46.7	165.0	12.1	−18.1	−3.2
General Government .... 78bt d	....	....	....	....	....	91.6	341.3	112.6	218.9	68.0	362.8	106.2	78.7	32.5	48.7
Banks .... 78bu d	....	....	....	....	....	2,650.4	3,245.7	6,479.7	1,245.9	6,743.9	1,840.5	−6,279.7	−5,001.9	583.7	579.8
Other Sectors .... 78bv d	....	....	....	....	....	189.3	76.9	−89.8	−140.6	209.0	190.0	−131.1	45.3	2.7	89.0
Net Errors and Omissions................ 78ca d	....	....	....	....	....	−70.1	−1.6	−421.4	622.8	59.7	−208.9	−312.2	139.6	−120.9	141.2
Overall Balance .... 78cb d	....	....	....	....	....	−7.3	86.2	−27.1	10.9	−81.8	−17.9	−57.1	−118.1	−128.5	−5.9
Reserves and Related Items .... 79da d	....	....	....	....	....	7.3	−86.2	27.1	−10.9	81.8	17.9	57.1	118.1	128.5	5.9
Reserve Assets .... 79db d	....	....	....	....	....	7.8	−84.0	38.7	6.2	2.5	19.2	−103.7	−8.4	109.9	−66.3
Use of Fund Credit and Loans .... 79dc d	....	....	....	....	....	−.6	−2.3	−11.5	−17.3	70.9	−4.8	114.7	94.7	8.0	6.7
Exceptional Financing .... 79de d	....	....	....	....	....	—	—	—	.3	8.5	3.5	46.1	31.8	10.6	65.5
International Investment Position															Millions of US Dollars
Assets .... 79aa d	....	....	....	....	....	....	....	....	....	....	....	....	....	....	....
Direct Investment Abroad .... 79ab d	....	....	....	....	....	....	....	....	....	....	....	....	....	....	....
Portfolio Investment .... 79ac d	....	....	....	....	....	....	....	....	....	....	....	....	....	....	....
Equity Securities .... 79ad d	....	....	....	....	....	....	....	....	....	....	....	....	....	....	....
Debt Securities .... 79ae d	....	....	....	....	....	....	....	....	....	....	....	....	....	....	....
Financial Derivatives .... 79al d	....	....	....	....	....	....	....	....	....	....	....	....	....	....	....
Other Investment .... 79af d	....	....	....	....	....	....	....	....	....	....	....	....	....	....	....
Monetary Authorities..................... 79ag d	....	....	....	....	....	....	....	....	....	....	....	....	....	....	....
General Government .... 79ah d	....	....	....	....	....	....	....	....	....	....	....	....	....	....	....
Banks .... 79ai d	....	....	....	....	....	....	....	....	....	....	....	....	....	....	....
Other Sectors .... 79aj d	....	....	....	....	....	....	....	....	....	....	....	....	....	....	....
Reserve Assets .... 79ak d	....	....	....	....	....	....	....	....	....	....	....	....	....	....	....
Liabilities .... 79la d	....	....	....	....	....	....	....	....	....	....	....	....	....	....	....
Dir. Invest. in Rep. Economy............ 79lb d	....	....	....	....	....	....	....	....	....	....	....	....	....	....	....
Portfolio Investement .... 79lc d	....	....	....	....	....	....	....	....	....	....	....	....	....	....	....
Equity Securities .... 79ld d	....	....	....	....	....	....	....	....	....	....	....	....	....	....	....
Debt Securities .... 79le d	....	....	....	....	....	....	....	....	....	....	....	....	....	....	....
Financial Derivatives .... 79ll d	....	....	....	....	....	....	....	....	....	....	....	....	....	....	....
Other Investment .... 79lf d	....	....	....	....	....	....	....	....	....	....	....	....	....	....	....
Monetary Authorities..................... 79lg d	....	....	....	....	....	....	....	....	....	....	....	....	....	....	....
General Government...................... 79lh d	....	....	....	....	....	....	....	....	....	....	....	....	....	....	....
Banks .... 79li d	....	....	....	....	....	....	....	....	....	....	....	....	....	....	....
Other Sectors............................. 79lj d	....	....	....	....	....	....	....	....	....	....	....	....	....	....	....

Minus Sign Indicates Debit

1987	1988	1989	1990	1991	1992	1993	1994	1995	1996	1997	1998	1999	2000	2001	Balance of Payments	
544.9	721.4	111.5	209.1	−241.1	−267.2	−95.7	15.9	−470.6	−200.6	−506.7	−1,182.3	−1,320.2	−933.1	−499.4	Current Account, n.i.e.	78al d
2,650.6	2,505.9	2,742.1	3,346.2	4,191.8	5,104.2	5,416.9	6,044.8	6,090.9	5,822.9	6,669.7	6,350.1	5,303.3	5,836.8	5,883.8	Goods: Exports f.o.b.	78aa d
−2,843.5	−2,349.1	−2,865.9	−3,503.9	−4,591.4	−5,479.7	−5,751.1	−6,294.9	−6,679.8	−6,467.0	−7,354.9	−7,714.6	−6,689.4	−7,026.6	−6,709.5	Goods: Imports f.o.b.	78ab d
−192.9	156.8	−123.8	−157.7	−399.6	−375.5	−334.2	−250.1	−588.9	−644.1	−685.2	−1,364.5	−1,386.1	−1,189.8	−825.7	*Trade Balance*	78ac d
1,150.1	1,062.2	981.2	1,092.1	1,216.4	1,225.4	1,297.4	1,403.7	1,519.4	1,592.0	1,720.7	1,836.8	1,793.2	1,829.6	1,816.9	Services: Credit	78ad d
−706.7	−518.0	−575.2	−689.2	−847.9	−917.1	−976.4	−1,064.3	−1,087.8	−1,034.0	−1,293.2	−1,222.5	−1,143.1	−1,137.8	−1,144.0	Services: Debit	78ae d
250.5	701.0	282.2	245.2	−31.1	−67.2	−13.2	89.3	−157.3	−86.1	−257.7	−750.2	−736.0	−498.0	−152.8	*Balance on Goods & Services*	78af d
2,232.7	976.3	976.2	1,139.1	1,078.8	1,138.9	1,054.7	1,202.9	1,644.1	1,422.1	1,436.0	1,679.7	1,503.3	1,580.4	1,398.7	Income: Credit	78ag d
−2,056.1	−1,064.2	−1,242.6	−1,394.5	−1,511.2	−1,539.9	−1,340.3	−1,425.2	−2,110.0	−1,671.3	−1,835.6	−2,270.4	−2,258.6	−2,192.4	−1,944.0	Income: Debit	78ah d
427.1	613.1	15.8	−10.2	−463.5	−468.2	−298.8	−133.0	−623.2	−335.3	−657.3	−1,340.9	−1,491.3	−1,110.0	−698.1	*Balance on Gds, Serv. & Inc.*	78ai d
165.8	153.6	139.8	248.7	249.8	230.0	236.5	185.5	184.1	167.7	185.2	195.2	202.7	208.6	226.8	Current Transfers, n.i.e.: Credit	78aj d
−48.0	−45.3	−44.1	−29.4	−27.4	−29.0	−33.4	−36.6	−31.5	−33.0	−34.6	−36.6	−31.6	−31.7	−28.1	Current Transfers: Debit	78ak d
....	....	....	....	....	130.0	....	....	8.5	2.5	72.7	50.9	3.0	1.7	1.6	Capital Account, n.i.e.	78bc d
....	....	....	....	....	130.0	....	....	8.5	2.5	72.7	50.9	3.0	1.7	1.6	Capital Account, n.i.e.: Credit	78ba d
....	....	....	....	....	....	....	....	....	....	....	....	....	....	....	Capital Account: Debit	78bb d
−690.2	−980.2	−648.8	−207.6	−697.9	−440.1	−521.4	−288.2	115.6	561.2	972.3	1,076.8	1,398.2	2.1	589.2	Financial Account, n.i.e.	78bj d
....	....	....	....	....	....	....	....	....	....	....	....	....	....	....	Direct Investment Abroad	78bd d
−556.5	−595.1	51.5	135.5	108.5	144.5	169.6	401.5	223.0	415.5	1,299.3	1,296.0	652.4	603.4	512.6	Dir. Invest. in Rep. Econ., n.i.e.	78be d
−228.8	2,218.3	−438.2	−200.0	−222.6	−46.3	−754.6	−48.4	318.5	487.8	−1,036.5	431.7	−550.2	−109.3	−776.1	Portfolio Investment Assets	78bf d
								.2	−10.2	−.8	−5.1	−28.7	−.6	−.2	Equity Securities	78bk d
−228.8	2,218.3	−438.2	−200.0	−222.6	−46.3	−754.6	−48.4	318.3	498.0	−1,035.7	436.8	−521.5	−108.7	−775.9	Debt Securities	78bl d
−41.0	−64.1	−29.9	−35.8	−24.1	−71.1	−54.7	−.4	−.3	−67.1	−80.3	−65.5	−99.2	−86.8	−66.2	Portfolio Investment Liab., n.i.e.	78bg d
−.7	.7	....	−1.0	1.8	−1.4	−.1	.4	.2	−.1	−.1	—	—	....	....	Equity Securities	78bm d
−40.3	−64.8	−29.9	−34.8	−25.9	−69.7	−54.6	−.8	−.5	−67.0	−80.2	−65.5	−99.2	−86.8	−66.2	Debt Securities	78bn d
....	....	....	....	....	....	....	....	....	....	....	....	....	....	....	Financial Derivatives Assets	78bw d
....	....	....	....	....	....	....	....	....	....	....	....	....	....	....	Financial Derivatives Liabilities	78bx d
8,904.1	12,828.1	−434.8	−1,421.8	−1,383.2	−1,491.8	−1,281.4	−5,277.7	−371.3	406.2	−478.7	776.7	1,983.0	358.5	856.4	Other Investment Assets	78bh d
....	....	....	....	....	....	....	....	....	....	....	....	−5.2	5.2	....	Monetary Authorities	78bo d
....	−164.8	−135.2	299.1	−.9	−.9	−.9	....	−1.0	−38.2	−2.3	−263.3	266.6	−4.0	−2.1	General Government	78bp d
8,640.2	13,170.4	−153.0	−1,923.3	−1,259.5	−1,442.9	−1,186.6	−5,254.4	−176.3	533.1	−276.1	1,284.6	1,968.7	189.1	1,020.8	Banks	78bq d
263.9	−177.5	−146.6	202.4	−122.8	−48.0	−93.9	−23.3	−194.0	−88.7	−200.3	−244.6	−247.1	168.2	−162.3	Other Sectors	78br d
−8,768.0	−15,367.4	202.6	1,314.5	823.5	1,024.6	1,399.7	4,636.8	−54.3	−681.2	1,268.5	−1,362.1	−587.8	−763.7	62.5	Other Investment Liab., n.i.e.	78bi d
−36.8	−96.3	15.0	−3.5	−2.0	11.2	.8	−1.3	54.6	−1.7	6.8	−1.0	−.7	−6.4	3.7	Monetary Authorities	78bs d
−318.9	−346.6	−279.5	−144.8	−174.9	−155.8	−117.5	−198.8	−36.1	−50.5	130.4	85.6	33.7	−2.6	3.5	General Government	78bt d
−8,181.2	−14,840.1	541.4	1,516.0	945.8	1,199.7	1,606.7	4,915.5	−122.8	−793.7	1,033.2	−1,446.8	−550.8	−418.4	57.1	Banks	78bu d
−231.1	−84.4	−74.3	−53.2	54.6	−30.5	−90.3	−78.6	50.0	164.7	98.1	.1	−70.0	−336.3	−1.8	Other Sectors	78bv d
−385.8	−474.4	−295.0	−137.4	610.9	390.2	309.0	−89.5	15.2	−96.3	−195.0	−325.1	−228.7	602.3	−389.9	Net Errors and Omissions	78ca d
−531.1	−1,004.2	−832.3	−135.9	−328.1	−187.1	−308.1	−361.8	−331.3	266.8	343.3	−379.7	−147.7	−327.0	−298.5	*Overall Balance*	78cb d
531.1	1,004.2	832.3	135.9	328.1	187.1	308.1	361.8	331.3	−266.8	−343.3	379.7	147.7	327.0	298.5	Reserves and Related Items	79da d
95.5	5.5	−47.9	−355.7	−148.4	116.2	−93.0	−105.7	−77.7	−297.7	−611.1	19.8	−184.5	108.1	−484.4	Reserve Assets	79db d
−57.9	−.1	−.8	−70.7	−55.7	−98.6	3.4	12.5	−25.9	24.2	19.6	27.3	−23.5	−51.7	−33.3	Use of Fund Credit and Loans	79dc d
493.5	998.8	881.0	562.3	532.3	169.5	397.7	454.9	434.9	6.8	248.2	332.6	355.7	270.6	816.2	Exceptional Financing	79de d

Millions of US Dollars

1987	1988	1989	1990	1991	1992	1993	1994	1995	1996	1997	1998	1999	2000	2001	International Investment Position	
....	....	....	....	....	....	....	....	25,275.7	24,677.0	26,871.0	25,643.3	24,394.5	24,036.1	24,441.9	Assets	79aa d
....	....	....	....	....	....	....	....								Direct Investment Abroad	79ab d
....	....	....	....	....	....	....	....	1,889.4	1,401.6	2,438.1	2,006.4	2,556.6	2,665.9	3,444.2	Portfolio Investment	79ac d
....	....	....	....	....	....	....	....	7.6	17.8	18.6	23.7	52.4	53.0	53.2	Equity Securities	79ad d
....	....	....	....	....	....	....	....	1,881.8	1,383.8	2,419.5	1,982.7	2,504.2	2,612.9	3,391.0	Debt Securities	79ae d
....	....	....	....	....	....	....	....								Financial Derivatives	79al d
....	....	....	....	....	....	....	....	22,605.0	22,196.8	22,675.5	21,898.7	19,915.7	19,557.1	18,700.7	Other Investment	79af d
....	....	....	....	....	....	....	....					5.2			Monetary Authorities	79ag d
....	....	....	....	....	....	....	....	27.7	63.9	66.2	329.5	62.9	66.9	69.0	General Government	79ah d
....	....	....	....	....	....	....	....	20,768.8	20,235.7	20,511.8	19,227.2	17,258.5	17,069.4	16,048.6	Banks	79ai d
....	....	....	....	....	....	....	....	1,808.5	1,897.2	2,097.5	2,342.0	2,589.1	2,420.8	2,583.1	Other Sectors	79aj d
....	....	....	....	....	....	....	....	781.3	1,078.6	1,757.4	1,738.2	1,922.2	1,813.1	2,297.0	Reserve Assets	79ak d
....	....	....	....	....	....	....	....	31,056.1	30,081.7	32,548.8	32,766.1	33,029.9	32,098.5	33,337.7	Liabilities	79la d
....	....	....	....	....	....	....	....	3,244.6	3,660.1	4,959.4	6,308.0	6,960.4	6,744.0	7,256.6	Dir. Invest. in Rep. Economy	79lb d
....	....	....	....	....	....	....	....	432.7	3,593.9	3,528.5	3,733.8	3,948.2	4,097.6	4,820.6	Portfolio Investement	79lc d
....	....	....	....	....	....	....	....	.1	—	—	—	—	—	—	Equity Securities	79ld d
....	....	....	....	....	....	....	....	432.6	3,593.9	3,528.5	3,733.8	3,948.2	4,097.6	4,820.6	Debt Securities	79le d
....	....	....	....	....	....	....	....								Financial Derivatives	79ll d
....	....	....	....	....	....	....	....	27,378.8	22,827.7	24,060.9	22,724.3	22,121.3	21,256.9	21,260.5	Other Investment	79lf d
....	....	....	....	....	....	....	....	271.5	290.1	309.9	343.5	314.7	249.6	217.2	Monetary Authorities	79lg d
....	....	....	....	....	....	....	....	4,637.4	1,086.8	1,178.0	1,339.3	1,398.1	1,353.6	1,334.1	General Government	79lh d
....	....	....	....	....	....	....	....	20,710.4	19,916.7	20,949.9	19,503.1	18,952.3	18,533.9	18,591.0	Banks	79li d
....	....	....	....	....	....	....	....	1,759.5	1,534.1	1,623.1	1,538.4	1,456.2	1,119.8	1,118.2	Other Sectors	79lj d

Panama

	1972	1973	1974	1975	1976	1977	1978	1979	1980	1981	1982	1983	1984	1985	1986
Government Finance														*Millions of Balboas:*	
Deficit (-) or Surplus..............................80	-105.7	†-91.0	-119.4	-149.5	-202.7	-119.0	-159.6	-371.8	-197.6	-334.6	-482.6	-272.5	-340.0	-155.0	-220.7
Revenue 81	197.9	†306.1	385.5	437.4	425.4	536.8	591.6	690.1	965.0	1,029.8	1,203.8	1,324.3	1,344.1	1,382.8	1,484.6
Grants Received 81z	....	†—	6.0	14.3	14.8	9.6	6.0	6.5	1.1	—	—		30.0	20.1	8.2
Expenditure 82	303.5	†387.0	503.7	581.7	626.5	649.8	736.7	1,066.0	1,163.4	1,322.1	1,612.0	1,512.4	1,653.3	1,504.0	1,620.8
Lending Minus Repayments 83	....	†10.1	7.2	19.5	16.4	15.6	20.5	2.4	.3	42.3	74.4	84.4	60.8	53.9	92.7
Financing															
Total Financing 84	105.7	†91.0	119.4	149.5	202.7	119.0	159.6	371.8	197.6	334.6	482.6	272.5	340.0	155.0	220.7
Domestic..84a	....	†19.1	54.6	46.3	89.9	40.3	37.2	59.4	-8.9	133.2	95.1	49.4	158.6	152.3	37.5
Foreign 85a	....	†71.9	64.8	103.2	112.8	78.7	122.4	312.4	206.5	201.4	387.5	223.1	181.4	2.7	183.2
Debt: Domestic 88a	190.4	†180.0	231.5	294.6	332.7	330.5	374.8	404.8	484.4	691.6	728.4	897.1	957.5	1,055.2	1,191.6
Foreign 89a	214.9	†296.9	358.9	427.4	510.2	614.0	1,025.6	1,344.0	1,578.6	1,689.8	2,049.8	2,175.1	2,263.9	2,265.5	2,372.5
National Accounts														*Millions of Balboas*	
Househ.Cons.Expend.,incl.NPISHs 96f	698.3	767.6	954.0	1,054.1	1,088.8	1,242.6	1,431.7	1,693.8	2,038.9	2,271.1	2,168.6	2,702.2	3,151.1	3,033.1	2,953.6
Government Consumption Expend..........91f	226.5	250.1	299.3	353.3	386.1	412.1	482.9	567.2	670.6	734.5	911.6	912.6	1,010.0	1,056.8	1,152.3
Gross Fixed Capital Formation 93e	372.2	434.8	465.0	535.5	608.6	445.9	606.3	661.2	875.5	1,103.7	1,215.2	945.0	772.1	834.1	955.7
Changes in Inventories 93i	30.3	50.9	91.1	31.9	10.2	45.0	45.4	124.5	195.5	119.4	67.2	-70.0	-15.0	-11.9	11.8
Exports of Goods and Services..............90c	460.7	528.1	761.8	865.4	837.8	921.1	986.4	1,124.8	3,446.6	3,777.2	3,687.6	3,070.4	3,100.1	3,706.3	3,992.8
Imports of Goods and Services (-) 98c	523.1	584.9	917.1	999.4	975.2	996.9	1,100.2	1,371.3	3,682.3	4,014.0	3,823.6	3,119.6	3,323.8	3,216.4	3,452.5
Gross Domestic Product (GDP) 99b	1,260.0	1,441.2	1,647.1	1,844.8	1,959.3	2,077.4	2,463.0	2,819.1	3,810.3	4,312.7	4,764.7	4,891.9	5,106.3	5,402.0	5,613.7
Net Primary Income from Abroad 98.n	-31.9	-39.1	-54.4	-19.5	-55.5	-63.1	-57.4	-102.8	-434.1	-152.3	-279.3	-259.7	-386.4	-195.8	-455.2
Gross National Income (GNI) 99a	1,233.0	1,407.5	1,599.7	1,821.3	1,900.8	2,006.7	2,395.1	2,697.4	3,110.7	3,839.6	3,947.3	4,180.9	4,308.1	5,206.2	5,158.5
Consumption of Fixed Capital 99cf	67.5	73.2	80.5	91.8	100.4	111.6	134.9	157.3	262.9	295.6	326.7	331.7	348.7	368.4	391.3
GDP Volume 1970 prices 99b.p	1,165.3	1,228.3	1,258.1	1,278.2	1,299.1	1,313.6	1,442.4	1,736.4	1,736.4	....	....	....	....	....	....
GDP Volume 1982 prices 99b.p	....	....	....	....	....	....	....	....	4,141.5	4,522.8	4,764.7	4,550.7	4,674.0	4,905.0	5,080.0
GDP Volume (1995=100)...................99bv p	44.8	47.3	48.4	49.2	50.0	50.5	55.5	66.8	66.8	73.0	76.9	73.4	75.4	79.1	82.0
GDP Deflator (1995=100).................99bi p	35.5	38.6	43.0	47.4	49.6	52.0	56.1	53.4	72.1	74.8	78.4	84.3	85.6	86.3	86.6
															Millions:
Population.......................................99z	1.52	1.57	1.62	1.68	1.72	1.77	1.81	1.85	1.96	2.00	2.04	2.09	2.13	2.17	2.21

	1987	1988	1989	1990	1991	1992	1993	1994	1995	1996	1997	1998	1999	2000	2001		
Year Ending December 31																**Government Finance**	
	−227.9	−108.1	−133.7	160.8	307.9	321.2	284.7	146.0	230.5	−60.9	17.9	−64.2	34.4	....	....	Deficit (-) or Surplus	80
	1,537.0	1,205.4	1,079.4	1,360.5	1,642.8	1,692.8	1,950.8	2,010.5	2,065.1	2,140.3	2,202.8	2,331.2	2,664.5	....	....	Revenue	81
	7.1	2.4	—	4.9	71.6	26.1	27.8	15.5	8.5	4.6	63.5	72.3	6.8	....	....	Grants Received	81z
	1,702.4	1,237.0	1,177.8	1,259.1	1,390.1	1,657.8	1,768.6	1,958.7	1,953.3	2,255.3	2,341.3	2,606.8	2,650.9	....	....	Expenditure	82
	69.6	78.9	35.3	−54.5	16.4	−260.1	−74.7	−78.7	−110.2	−49.5	−92.9	−139.1	−14.0	....	....	Lending Minus Repayments	83
																Financing	
	227.9	108.1	133.7	−160.8	−307.9	−321.2	−284.7	−146.0	−230.5	60.9	−17.9	64.2	−34.4	....	....	Total Financing	84
	247.7	281.1	....	21.2	−222.4	−277.6	−226.2	−135.2	−253.2	3.7	−133.6	−297.9	−237.2	....	....	Domestic	84a
	−19.8	−173.0	....	−182.0	−85.5	−43.6	−58.5	−10.8	22.7	57.2	115.7	362.1	202.8	....	....	Foreign	85a
	1,143.4	1,088.3	1,208.1	937.4	851.5	999.5	1,810.1	1,805.6	1,681.4	1,794.2	1,737.5	1,737.6	2,108.8	2,090.4	2,089.0	Debt: Domestic	88a
	2,399.1	2,443.5	2,457.7	2,450.4	2,432.9	2,624.9	2,600.2	2,812.9	3,001.5	4,542.6	4,659.6	5,042.5	5,457.6	5,552.3	6,243.3	Foreign	89a
Millions of Balboas																**National Accounts**	
	2,865.2	2,679.9	3,218.8	3,028.7	3,449.7	3,745.2	4,063.4	4,150.7	4,090.0	4,296.6	4,699.1	5,283.4	5,331.8	5,672.8	....	Househ.Cons.Expend.,incl.NPISHs	96f
	1,241.9	1,019.4	943.7	962.3	1,025.3	1,055.9	1,098.3	1,144.8	1,194.1	1,270.5	1,402.6	1,507.6	1,500.0	1,605.3	....	Government Consumption Expend.	91f
	1,087.0	428.4	318.2	454.0	873.5	1,227.9	1,681.3	1,828.8	2,057.9	2,059.2	2,295.0	2,624.9	2,908.1	2,634.1	....	Gross Fixed Capital Formation	93e
	−50.5	−62.1	−17.4	440.1	247.6	345.3	111.9	244.8	336.3	428.2	396.1	372.3	278.0	239.4	....	Changes in Inventories	93i
	4,032.0	3,665.8	3,856.3	4,612.1	5,676.4	6,653.8	7,014.6	7,711.6	7,979.4	7,580.3	8,494.6	8,396.4	7,390.4	7,941.1	....	Exports of Goods and Services	90c
	3,537.3	2,856.9	3,432.1	4,184.0	5,430.2	6,386.7	6,716.8	7,346.8	7,751.6	7,483.7	8,629.9	8,839.9	7,771.7	8,073.7	....	Imports of Goods and Services (-)	98c
	5,638.3	4,874.5	4,887.5	5,313.2	5,842.3	6,641.4	7,252.7	7,733.9	7,906.1	8,151.1	8,657.5	9,344.7	9,636.6	10,019.0	....	Gross Domestic Product (GDP)	99b
	144.0	−100.7	−288.7	−287.3	−467.9	−447.1	−338.6	−272.3	−421.5	−360.5	−451.4	−608.8	−790.7	−700.5	....	Net Primary Income from Abroad	98.n
	5,782.3	4,773.8	4,598.8	5,025.9	5,374.4	6,194.3	6,914.1	7,461.6	7,484.6	7,790.6	8,206.1	8,735.9	8,845.9	9,318.5	....	Gross National Income (GNI)	99a
	406.1	358.8	345.8	376.6	423.8	375.3	497.0	533.3	558.9	576.7	601.1	667.8	723.2	747.2	....	Consumption of Fixed Capital	99cf
	....	....	....	....	....	....	....	....	....	....	....	....	....	....	....	GDP Volume 1970 prices	99b.p
	4,988.1	4,320.7	4,388.2	4,743.6	5,190.4	5,616.1	5,922.5	6,091.3	6,198.0	6,372.2	6,657.5	6,947.2	7,169.9	7,345.7	7,365.2	GDP Volume 1982 Prices	99b.p
	80.5	69.7	70.8	76.5	83.7	90.6	95.6	98.3	100.0	102.8	107.4	112.1	115.7	118.5	118.8	GDP Volume (1995=100)	99bv p
	88.6	88.4	87.3	87.8	88.2	92.7	96.0	99.5	100.0	100.3	101.9	105.4	105.4	106.9	....	GDP Deflator (1995=100)	99bi p
Midyear Estimates																	
	2.26	2.30	2.35	2.40	2.44	2.49	2.53	2.58	2.63	2.67	2.72	2.76	2.81	2.81	2.86	**Population**	99z

(See notes in the back of the book.)

Papua New Guinea

853

		1972	1973	1974	1975	1976	1977	1978	1979	1980	1981	1982	1983	1984	1985	1986
Exchange Rates														*SDRs per Kina:*		
Official Rate	ac	1.1743	1.2335	1.0838	1.0738	1.0599	1.0867	1.1153	1.0998	1.2177	1.2625	1.2121	1.0910	1.0837	.8992	.8506
														US Dollars per Kina:		
Official Rate	ag	1.2750	1.4880	1.3270	1.2571	1.2314	1.3200	1.4530	1.4488	1.5531	1.4695	1.3371	1.1422	1.0623	.9877	1.0404
Official Rate	rh	1.1923	1.4227	1.4394	1.3102	1.2621	1.2640	1.4117	1.4053	1.4916	1.4871	1.3559	1.1989	1.1183	1.0000	1.0296
														Index Numbers (1995=100):		
Official Rate	ahx	152.2	181.2	183.5	167.2	161.1	161.3	180.2	179.3	190.4	189.8	173.1	153.0	142.7	127.6	131.4
Nominal Effective Exchange Rate	ne c	....	....	....	....	....	....	....	87.8	95.0	99.8	101.3	97.8	99.6	99.3	94.5
Real Effective Exchange Rate	re c	....	....	....	....	....	....	....		143.2	146.7	144.2	139.7	141.3	135.3	127.9
Fund Position														*Millions of SDRs:*		
Quota	2f. s	—	—	—	20.00	20.00	20.00	30.00	30.00	45.00	45.00	45.00	65.90	65.90	65.90	65.90
SDRs	1b. s	—	—	—	—	1.68	.19	.42	.81		33.07	31.00	16.95	4.99	5.89	2.61
Reserve Position in the Fund	1c. s	—	—	—	—			.01	2.37	3.78	.04	.07	5.31	5.35	5.38	5.42
Total Fund Cred.&Loans Outstg.	2tl	—	—	—	—	24.80	24.80	23.09	18.10	24.28	64.55	64.55	64.55	34.59	26.33	12.34
International Liquidity												*Millions of US Dollars Unless Otherwise Indicated:*				
Total Reserves minus Gold	1l. d	....	31.26	32.45	179.67	257.20	426.63	404.72	503.55	423.43	396.17	452.88	440.07	435.23	442.57	425.46
SDRs	1b. d	—	—	—	—	1.95	.23	.55	1.07		38.49	34.20	17.75	4.89	6.47	3.19
Reserve Position in the Fund	1c. d	—	—	—	—			.01	3.12	4.82	.05	.08	5.56	5.24	5.91	6.63
Foreign Exchange	1d. d	....	31.26	32.45	179.67	255.25	426.40	404.16	499.36	418.61	357.63	418.61	416.76	425.09	430.19	415.64
Gold (Million Fine Troy Ounces)	1ad	....	—	—	—	—	.029	.044	.053	.058	.062	.062	.063	.063	.063	.063
Gold (National Valuation)	1an d	....	—	—	—	—	3.55	7.93	11.09	14.74	15.91	14.54	12.53	11.71	10.93	11.08
Monetary Authorities: Other Liab.	4.. d	....	6.21	5.79	4.10	69.45	96.84	49.81	30.51	25.22	127.09	115.00	97.94	34.62	38.24	23.62
Deposit Money Banks: Assets	7a. d	....	72.06	162.74	.27	10.14	80.18	35.93	21.13	16.02	18.28	7.15	10.59	14.28	16.21	10.06
Liabilities	7b. d	....	.05	1.59	20.54	22.86	46.00	52.33	22.93	9.88	38.30	26.76	33.63	54.61	56.23	43.55
Monetary Authorities														*Millions of Kina:*		
Foreign Assets	11	....	99.37	114.48	194.32	208.77	327.51	297.22	372.94	293.56	290.19	269.84	395.45	416.78	460.51	455.06
Claims on Central Government	12a	....	3.24	3.24	7.57	22.21	11.55	12.75	30.14	39.39	52.76	72.88	27.51	12.52	60.99	53.22
Claims on Deposit Money Banks	12e	....	—	—	—	—	—	—	—	—	—	8.61	17.85	22.51	26.90	14.86
Reserve Money	14	....	64.13	81.62	142.19	168.13	203.51	194.10	235.72	99.46	88.82	90.46	138.04	128.25	130.53	125.56
of which: Currency Outside DMBs	14a	....	57.37	76.61	85.21	47.51	56.66	61.55	67.89	70.49	73.39	72.41	79.95	88.90	94.26	95.74
Time Deposits	15	....					49.73	68.37	95.38	102.27	90.60	90.73	83.30	80.15	80.55	89.15
Foreign Liabilities	16c	....	4.18	4.36	3.26	79.80	96.19	54.99	37.52	36.18	137.61	139.26	144.91	64.51	68.00	37.21
Central Government Deposits	16d	....	32.50	27.71	53.68	20.45	29.86	14.76	20.74	84.92	72.89	50.27	65.10	98.17	82.55	103.25
Capital Accounts	17a	....	5.01	5.53	6.26	16.18	10.23	4.19	17.86	2.44	19.39	49.93	98.80	96.86	156.01	146.15
Other Items (Net)	17r	....	−3.20	−1.50	−3.51	−53.57	−50.44	−26.44	−4.13	7.68	−66.36	−69.32	−89.34	−16.12	30.77	21.81
Deposit Money Banks														*Millions of Kina:*		
Reserves	20	....	6.25	5.09	54.95	116.81	141.57	126.99	160.26	26.09	18.35	16.07	56.02	35.67	22.57	29.02
Foreign Assets	21	....	48.44	122.64	.22	8.24	60.74	24.73	14.59	10.32	12.44	5.34	9.27	13.44	16.41	9.67
Claims on Central Government	22a	....	22.70	35.25	28.27	32.54	44.78	37.75	58.47	88.13	92.29	78.74	91.92	108.72	80.79	130.42
Claims on Local Governments	22b	....	—	.25	.39	.72	.97	.73	1.44	2.00	2.07	1.89	2.35	1.43	3.66	4.08
Claims on Nonfin.Pub.Enterprises	22c	....	—	.11	.92	7.46	13.76	6.88	20.07	23.70	18.48	17.20	28.44			
Claims on Private Sector	22d	....	137.16	152.04	163.31	156.62	169.00	173.74	204.39	277.61	330.31	361.22	417.89	502.98	563.78	668.22
Demand Deposits	24	....	41.53	63.22	63.55	83.87	107.44	111.87	119.94	128.18	120.71	114.25	124.42	156.12	146.22	160.16
Time, Savings,& Fgn. Currency Dep.	25	....	96.24	179.61	94.66	142.80	209.35	201.67	280.92	249.32	269.77	288.49	360.78	418.88	495.42	583.13
Foreign Liabilities	26c	....	.03	1.20	16.34	18.56	34.85	36.02	15.83	6.36	26.06	20.02	29.44	51.41	56.93	41.86
Central Government Deposits	26d	....	15.02	5.92	12.86	12.00	18.33	18.62	30.30	22.71	26.05	27.21	45.93	24.25	20.20	18.55
Credit from Monetary Authorities	26g	....										8.61	17.01	19.30	16.90	14.86
Capital Accounts	27a	....	49.53	69.30	71.14	76.14	77.41	29.93	30.07	41.54	48.68	45.36	56.46	47.00	49.35	66.46
Other Items (Net)	27r	....	12.21	−3.86	−10.51	−11.00	−16.56	−27.30	−17.86	−20.27	−17.33	−23.47	−28.15	−54.72	−97.81	−43.59
Monetary Survey														*Millions of Kina:*		
Foreign Assets (Net)	31n	....	143.60	231.56	174.94	118.65	257.22	230.95	334.18	261.34	138.95	115.91	230.36	314.31	352.00	385.67
Domestic Credit	32	....	115.58	157.65	134.06	189.35	197.15	211.60	267.22	325.74	397.97	462.83	455.46	462.83	608.48	736.08
Claims on Central Govt. (Net)	32an	....	−21.58	4.86	−30.71	22.29	8.15	17.12	37.57	19.89	46.12	74.14	8.40	−1.19	39.04	61.83
Claims on Local Government	32b	....	—	.25	.39	.72	.97	.73	1.44	2.00	2.07	1.89	2.35	1.43	3.66	4.08
Claims on Nonfin.Pub.Enterprises	32c	....	—	.11	.92	7.46	13.76	6.88	20.07	23.70	18.48	17.20	28.44			
Claims on Private Sector	32d	....	137.16	152.04	163.31	156.62	169.00	173.74	204.39	277.61	330.31	361.22	417.89	502.98	563.78	668.22
Claims on Other Financial Insts	32f	....	—	.39	.15	2.27	5.27	13.14	3.77	2.54	.99	1.01	5.74	2.20	2.00	1.95
Money	34	....	99.40	140.43	150.80	135.02	169.38	178.99	195.41	201.56	194.36	188.64	205.97	248.99	244.15	256.68
Quasi-Money	35	....	96.24	179.61	94.66	142.80	259.08	270.05	376.30	351.59	360.37	379.22	444.08	499.03	575.97	672.28
Capital Accounts	37a	....	54.53	74.82	77.40	92.32	87.64	34.12	47.93	43.98	68.07	95.29	155.26	143.86	205.37	212.60
Other Items (Net)	37r	....	9.01	−5.66	−13.87	−62.14	−61.73	−40.61	−18.23	−10.04	−85.89	−91.77	−112.11	−72.15	−65.01	−19.82
Money plus Quasi-Money	35l	....	195.64	320.04	245.46	277.82	428.46	449.03	571.71	553.15	554.74	567.85	650.04	748.02	820.12	928.96
Interest Rates														*Percent Per Annum*		
Discount Rate (End of Period)	60	....	....		....						....		8.75	8.75	9.75	11.40
Treasury Bill Rate	60c	....	....	8.18	8.27	7.73	6.38	5.78	6.03	7.16	11.56	13.80	10.92	9.28	10.40	12.32
Deposit Rate	60l	....	....	....	....	....	....	....	....	6.90	10.00	8.00	9.54	8.13	9.49	11.49
Lending Rate	60p	....	....	....	....	....	....	....	....	11.15	14.40	12.25	11.58	10.64	11.54	12.33
Prices and Labor														*Index Numbers (1995=100):*		
Consumer Prices	64	19.3	20.9	25.8	28.5	30.7	†32.1	33.9	35.9	40.2	43.5	45.9	49.5	53.2	55.1	58.1
Total Employment	67	....	....	....	....	....	....	84.6	87.8	95.7	98.5	88.9	86.6	88.0	90.9	93.2

1987	1988	1989	1990	1991	1992	1993	1994	1995	1996	1997	1998	1999	2000	2001		
															Exchange Rates	
End of Period																
.8024	.8992	.8852	.7376	.7339	.7365	.7419	.5812	.5039	.5164	.4232	.3388	.2703	.2498	.2115	Official Rate	ac
End of Period (ag) Period Average (rh)																
1.1384	1.2100	1.1633	1.0493	1.0498	1.0127	1.0190	.8485	.7490	.7425	.5710	.4770	.3710	.3255	.2658	Official Rate	ag
1.1012	1.1538	1.1685	1.0467	1.0504	1.0367	1.0221	.9950	.7835	.7588	.6975	.4859	.3939	.3617	.2964	Official Rate	rh
Period Averages																
140.5	147.3	149.1	133.6	134.1	132.3	130.5	127.0	100.0	96.8	89.0	62.0	50.3	46.2	37.8	Official Rate	ahx
96.3	99.0	108.8	104.3	109.9	115.0	127.3	131.3	100.0	98.6	97.1	74.8	60.1	58.4	51.4	Nominal Effective Exchange Rate	ne c
126.3	125.7	129.6	114.9	118.8	118.9	124.4	117.7	100.0	107.6	108.2	92.4	84.4	92.8	86.9	Real Effective Exchange Rate	re c
															Fund Position	
End of Period																
65.90	65.90	65.90	65.90	65.90	95.30	95.30	95.30	95.30	95.30	95.30	95.30	131.60	131.60	131.60	Quota	2f. s
3.31	3.04	2.67	—	.02	.10	.03	.07	.47	.04	.06	.04	.53	9.34	6.93	SDRs	1b. s
6.94	6.95	6.98			.04	.05	.05	.05	.05	.05	.05	.05	.18	.30	Reserve Position in the Fund	1c. s
8.44	4.55	2.31	42.91	42.84	42.84	32.13	10.71	33.34	35.34	35.34	32.35	15.68	29.89	85.54	Total Fund Cred.&Loans Outstg.	2tl
															International Liquidity	
Approximately End of Period																
436.83	393.49	384.38	403.04	323.05	238.58	141.45	96.06	261.35	583.89	362.68	192.88	205.14	308.48	438.86	Total Reserves minus Gold	1l. d
4.70	4.09	3.51	—	.03	.14	.05	.11	.69	.06	.08	.05	.72	12.17	8.71	SDRs	1b. d
9.85	9.35	9.17	—		.06	.07	.08	.08	.08	.07	.07	.07	.23	.38	Reserve Position in the Fund	1c. d
422.29	380.05	371.70	403.04	323.02	238.39	141.34	95.88	260.58	583.75	362.53	192.76	204.35	296.07	429.77	Foreign Exchange	1d. d
.063	.063	.063	.063	.063	.063	.063	.063	.063	.014	.063	.063	.063	.063	.063	Gold (Million Fine Troy Ounces)	1ad
11.08	11.09	11.09	11.09	11.09	11.09	11.09	11.09	2.40	28.30	28.30	28.30	27.90	27.90	27.90	Gold (National Valuation)	1and
13.40	.10	2.46	120.69	113.04	115.27	87.35	109.58	161.71	106.44	84.50	61.30	6.90	52.64	180.70	Monetary Authorities: Other Liab.	4.. d
24.27	29.92	22.32	20.65	39.72	61.61	160.59	175.61	100.11	119.12	117.38	136.34	103.23	95.83	112.18	Deposit Money Banks: Assets	7a. d
68.21	109.35	143.31	113.17	150.27	118.34	88.07	120.46	41.39	23.07	7.99	54.53	37.44	18.13	24.24	Liabilities	7b. d
															Monetary Authorities	
Last Wednesday of Period																
446.14	397.22	342.42	376.53	306.44	242.31	138.61	112.51	357.55	789.20	666.07	391.06	552.92	909.24	1,617.94	Foreign Assets	11
78.53	115.84	174.14	227.01	251.35	284.20	421.02	776.65	592.62	587.28	880.81	1,284.96	599.66	163.60	160.19	Claims on Central Government	12a
19.42	32.00	46.89	42.83	70.91	127.74	239.43	282.50	233.80	228.94	216.27	121.10	53.63	53.27	52.15	Claims on Deposit Money Banks	12e
134.16	141.91	152.24	176.04	164.64	168.93	199.20	221.65	255.66	488.98	321.12	387.47	671.55	561.51	592.26	Reserve Money	14
106.35	115.20	122.03	134.77	137.36	141.17	160.70	179.00	194.21	216.40	234.85	278.09	357.49	306.93	308.98	of which: Currency Outside DMBs	14a
64.97	12.69	2.64	1.39	1.15	.50	.50	.50	.50	.50	.50	.50	.50	.50	.50	Time Deposits	15
22.29	5.14	4.72	173.20	166.05	171.99	129.04	147.57	282.07	211.79	231.49	224.00	76.61	281.34	1,084.29	Foreign Liabilities	16c
152.27	165.84	187.94	174.64	175.55	224.53	369.66	663.01	623.10	840.32	977.77	916.71	100.24	30.76	274.50	Central Government Deposits	16d
168.76	180.29	204.14	224.63	227.61	218.31	204.45	140.20	122.57	122.13	245.05	254.78	261.74	329.89	506.68	Capital Accounts	17a
1.63	30.58	11.76	−103.53	−106.30	−130.04	−103.79	−1.29	−99.93	−58.30	−12.77	13.65	95.56	−77.91	−627.96	Other Items (Net)	17r
															Deposit Money Banks	
Last Wednesday of Period																
24.76	23.78	23.21	35.33	22.52	24.61	36.68	40.67	56.20	116.63	67.21	106.03	310.37	250.67	279.48	Reserves	20
21.32	24.73	19.19	19.68	37.84	60.84	157.59	206.97	133.66	160.44	205.57	285.83	278.26	294.40	422.06	Foreign Assets	21
105.59	140.10	110.36	121.92	232.60	364.57	502.65	446.27	727.57	1,105.13	1,107.80	888.60	791.57	1,065.24	1,121.02	Claims on Central Government	22a
3.83	2.45	1.08	3.79	1.17	3.96	6.22	5.95	1.58	1.91	1.29	5.05	5.46	1.05	.94	Claims on Local Governments	22b
29.32	21.32	49.75	72.77	140.35	233.52	294.69	374.70	329.25	315.00	297.71	202.94	153.06	123.02	113.64	Claims on Nonfin.Pub.Enterprises	22c
709.26	802.21	887.97	878.38	940.98	890.55	820.27	897.99	900.78	908.93	1,223.08	1,577.98	1,554.88	1,668.15	1,601.47	Claims on Private Sector	22d
172.24	200.32	215.48	203.12	275.03	293.10	431.77	433.46	501.18	692.31	752.74	829.35	982.38	1,061.86	1,104.17	Demand Deposits	24
597.00	649.99	690.36	736.38	854.16	993.78	1,091.68	1,049.85	1,192.55	1,410.43	1,659.12	1,620.62	1,638.32	1,758.57	1,765.73	Time, Savings,& Fgn. Currency Dep.	25
59.92	90.37	123.19	107.85	143.14	116.85	86.43	141.97	55.26	31.07	14.00	114.33	100.91	55.70	91.19	Foreign Liabilities	26c
17.72	18.71	18.75	33.22	39.78	43.46	51.45	73.13	122.48	167.22	170.65	287.49	211.71	255.06	309.80	Central Government Deposits	26d
17.81	40.73	46.51	42.83	70.91	127.74	239.43	282.50	233.80	228.94	216.28	121.10	53.63	53.39	52.15	Credit from Monetary Authorities	26g
79.70	93.27	66.56	68.88	64.45	65.21	60.63	78.36	92.65	114.78	139.25	212.80	332.05	284.09	374.62	Capital Accounts	27a
−50.30	−78.81	−69.28	−60.42	−72.01	−62.10	−143.29	−86.72	−48.88	−36.92	−49.33	−119.26	−225.40	−66.14	−159.07	Other Items (Net)	27r
															Monetary Survey	
Last Wednesday of Period																
385.25	326.44	233.69	115.15	35.08	14.31	80.73	29.94	153.88	706.78	626.15	338.56	653.65	866.60	864.52	Foreign Assets (Net)	31n
761.17	891.95	1,020.78	1,098.26	1,353.47	1,517.69	1,630.57	1,765.41	1,806.21	1,910.71	2,362.27	2,755.32	2,792.67	2,735.23	2,412.94	Domestic Credit	32
14.14	62.79	77.82	141.07	268.63	380.74	502.55	486.77	574.60	684.87	840.19	969.35	1,079.27	943.01	696.90	Claims on Central Govt. (Net)	32an
3.83	2.45	1.08	3.79	1.17	3.96	6.22	5.95	1.58	1.91	1.29	5.05	5.46	1.05	.94	Claims on Local Government	32b
29.32	21.32	49.75	72.77	140.35	233.52	294.69	374.70	329.25	315.00	297.71	202.94	153.06	123.02	113.64	Claims on Nonfin.Pub.Enterprises	32c
709.26	802.21	887.97	878.38	940.98	890.55	820.27	897.99	900.78	908.93	1,223.08	1,577.98	1,554.88	1,668.15	1,601.47	Claims on Private Sector	32d
4.63	3.20	4.17	2.25	2.35	8.91	6.84		—	—	—	—	—	—	—	Claims on Other Financial Insts.	32f
281.33	322.17	344.50	343.84	417.16	437.42	594.29	614.48	700.64	1,064.87	1,006.66	1,110.79	1,343.56	1,372.69	1,416.95	Money	34
661.96	662.68	693.00	737.77	855.31	994.28	1,092.18	1,050.35	1,193.05	1,410.93	1,659.62	1,621.12	1,638.82	1,759.07	1,766.23	Quasi-Money	35
248.46	273.96	270.70	293.51	292.06	283.52	265.09	218.56	215.22	236.91	384.30	467.58	593.78	613.99	881.31	Capital Accounts	37a
−45.34	−40.02	−53.73	−161.70	−175.97	−183.23	−240.24	−88.05	−148.81	−95.22	−62.16	−105.61	−129.83	−143.92	−787.02	Other Items (Net)	37r
943.29	984.85	1,037.50	1,081.61	1,272.46	1,431.70	1,686.46	1,664.83	1,893.69	2,475.80	2,666.29	2,731.91	2,982.37	3,131.76	3,183.18	Money plus Quasi-Money	35l
															Interest Rates	
Percent Per Annum																
8.80	10.80	9.55	9.30	9.30	7.12	†6.30	6.55	18.00	10.30	10.20	18.15	12.80	4.41	11.25	Discount Rate (End of Period)	60
10.44	10.12	10.50	11.40	10.33	8.88	6.25	6.85	17.40	14.44	9.94	21.18	22.70	17.00	12.36	Treasury Bill Rate	60c
9.60	9.28	8.23	8.67	9.06	7.85	5.03	5.09	12.18	12.19	7.31	13.73	15.46	14.54	8.91	Deposit Rate	60l
11.94	12.68	14.62	15.52	14.17	14.53	11.29	9.16	13.14	13.30	10.45	17.70	18.90	17.54	16.21	Lending Rate	60p
															Prices and Labor	
Period Averages																
60.1	63.3	66.2	70.8	75.7	79.0	82.9	85.3	100.0	111.6	116.0	131.8	151.5	175.1	191.4	Consumer Prices	64
95.3	98.8	106.3	101.2	97.4	100.6	97.8	104.9	100.0	107.5	107.3	103.1	107.5	109.1	102.6	Total Employment	67

Papua New Guinea

	1972	1973	1974	1975	1976	1977	1978	1979	1980	1981	1982	1983	1984	1985	1986
International Transactions														*Millions of Kina*	
Exports 70	184.4	359.7	451.3	335.9	435.5	539.8	504.0	686.9	691.7	564.4	570.9	687.5	822.1	926.2	1,000.8
Imports, c.i.f. 71	277.1	250.1	363.5	451.8	397.7	507.4	545.2	643.0	786.8	848.9	864.4	937.1	996.9	1,005.7	1,048.9
Imports, f.o.b. 71.v	244.7	214.4	301.4	368.5	351.5	448.3	478.3	561.6	684.2	738.2	771.7	821.7	844.7	874.8	902.1
														1995=100	
Volume of Exports 72	....	....	....	....	....	....	....	....	38.3	43.2	47.5	48.7	52.2	62.0	70.1
Unit Value of Exports 74	....	21.0	†32.2	23.8	29.2	38.8	34.3	46.5	†48.3	37.7	37.3	43.5	48.0	49.5	48.8
Balance of Payments														*Millions of US Dollars:*	
Current Account, n.i.e. 78ald					50.8	114.3	-32.2	107.0	-288.7	-484.3	-444.8	-337.4	-289.5	-121.8	-98.1
Goods: Exports f.o.b. 78aad					550.4	683.1	713.4	1,010.3	985.5	840.1	768.8	820.3	915.3	926.3	1,030.7
Goods: Imports f.o.b. 78abd					-434.2	-559.9	-688.4	-783.3	-1,020.5	-1,096.4	-1,017.6	-974.8	-962.8	-874.8	-928.8
Trade Balance 78acd					116.2	123.3	25.1	226.9	-35.0	-256.3	-248.8	-154.5	-47.5	51.5	101.8
Services: Credit 78add					68.9	38.0	35.7	41.8	43.3	84.7	95.4	75.7	64.4	64.0	72.5
Services: Debit 78aed					-175.6	-183.7	-217.2	-237.8	-301.6	-342.1	-347.8	-333.4	-356.1	-288.5	-302.7
Balance on Goods & Services .. 78afd					9.5	-22.4	-156.4	31.0	-293.3	-513.7	-501.2	-412.2	-339.2	-173.0	-128.3
Income: Credit 78agd					19.8	30.3	38.3	49.4	59.8	47.4	59.6	58.3	50.6	55.5	91.5
Income: Debit 78ahd					-75.2	-81.3	-103.4	-158.1	-239.0	-209.2	-180.9	-180.3	-199.2	-161.8	-227.2
Balance on Gds, Serv. & Inc. .. 78aid					-45.9	-73.4	-221.5	-77.8	-472.5	-675.4	-622.4	-534.2	-487.7	-279.2	-264.0
Current Transfers, n.i.e.: Credit 78ajd					159.5	245.5	270.5	268.3	283.9	300.8	293.6	293.8	291.1	247.3	248.8
Current Transfers: Debit 78akd					-62.8	-57.8	-81.2	-83.5	-100.2	-109.8	-115.9	-97.1	-92.9	-89.8	-82.9
Capital Account, n.i.e. 78bcd					-10.5	-15.7	-23.2	-28.3	-22.8	-36.7	-39.6	-37.4	-31.3	-27.9	-31.9
Capital Account, n.i.e.: Credit 78bad					14.0	8.7	9.2	9.1	5.4	4.7	6.1	4.3	5.4	5.6	7.0
Capital Account: Debit 78bbd					-24.5	-24.4	-32.4	-37.5	-28.2	-41.4	-45.7	-41.8	-36.7	-33.5	-38.9
Financial Account, n.i.e. 78bjd					30.0	35.3	-10.1	35.4	96.0	417.4	479.7	352.0	258.1	124.0	134.5
Direct Investment Abroad 78bdd					1.9	-1.8	-4.9	-3.2	-15.7	-.6	-1.8	-1.1	-2.3	-.9	8.7
Dir. Invest. in Rep. Econ., n.i.e. .. 78bed					20.8	19.8	38.9	44.2	75.5	86.2	85.9	138.9	115.7	83.3	90.8
Portfolio Investment Assets 78bfd					-3.1	-.9	-5.1	-2.9	—	-1.6	—	—	—	—	—
Equity Securities 78bkd					—	—	—	—	—	—	—	—	—	—	—
Debt Securities 78bld					-3.1	-.9	-5.1	-2.9	—	-1.6	—	—	—	—	—
Portfolio Investment Liab., n.i.e. .. 78bgd					-3.3	-3.5	-8.4		—	—	—	—	—	—	—
Equity Securities 78bmd					—	—	—		—	—	—	—	—	—	—
Debt Securities 78bnd					-3.3	-3.5	-8.4		—	—	—	—	—	—	—
Financial Derivatives Assets 78bwd					....	....	....	....	....	....	....	....	....	....	....
Financial Derivatives Liabilities .. 78bxd					....	....	....	....	....	....	....	....	....	....	....
Other Investment Assets 78bhd					-10.8	-67.0	48.2	14.5	7.1	—	—	—	—	—	—
Monetary Authorities 78bod					....	....	....	....	....	....	....	....	....	....	....
General Government 78bpd					....	....	....	....	....	....	....	....	....	....	....
Banks 78bqd					-10.8	-67.0	48.2	14.5	7.1	—	—	—	—	—	—
Other Sectors 78brd					....	....	....	....	....	....	....	....	....	....	....
Other Investment Liab., n.i.e. .. 78bid					24.5	88.6	-78.9	-17.2	29.1	333.4	395.6	214.2	144.6	41.6	35.0
Monetary Authorities 78bsd					-3.8	17.6	-23.9	.4	-.2						
General Government 78btd					22.2	29.7	5.1	36.9	70.6	114.8	98.4	43.8	15.1	44.9	35.5
Banks 78bud					4.1	19.4	.2	-28.7	-11.4	25.2	-1.7	6.4	19.2	3.3	-9.3
Other Sectors 78bvd					1.9	21.9	-60.3	-25.8	-30.0	193.4	298.9	164.1	110.3	-6.7	8.8
Net Errors and Omissions 78cad					-28.5	25.9	37.8	-5.1	131.8	52.5	-31.2	120.0	111.6	24.3	-1.3
Overall Balance 78cbd					41.7	159.8	-27.7	108.9	-83.7	-51.1	-35.9	97.2	48.8	-1.4	3.3
Reserves and Related Items 79dad					-41.7	-159.8	27.7	-108.9	83.7	51.1	35.9	-97.2	-48.8	1.4	-3.3
Reserve Assets 79dbd					-70.3	-159.8	29.6	-105.8	75.4	4.2	35.9	-97.2	-18.1	9.3	13.2
Use of Fund Credit and Loans 79dcd					28.6		-2.0	-6.4	8.3	46.9	—		-30.7	-8.0	-16.5
Exceptional Financing 79ded					—	—	—	3.2	—	.1	-.1				
Government Finance														*Millions of Kina:*	
Deficit (-) or Surplus 80				-56.96	-26.80	-19.36	†-21.48	-62.80	-33.02	-107.72	-97.18	-94.57	-21.13	†-55.54	-80.07
Total Revenue and Grants 81y				330.26	353.59	389.02	†431.37	458.82	566.94	556.18	556.49	617.18	728.33	†707.12	755.52
Revenue 81				173.98	234.20	214.09	†259.41	283.99	392.34	371.85	369.79	404.09	496.37	†490.77	550.84
Grants 81z				156.28	119.39	174.93	†171.96	174.83	174.60	184.33	186.70	213.09	231.96	†216.35	204.68
Exp. & Lending Minus Repay. ... 82z				387.22	380.39	408.38	†452.85	521.62	599.96	663.90	653.67	711.75	749.46	†762.66	835.59
Expenditure 82				365.73	368.57	400.80	†448.95	511.48	587.56	649.52	633.91	679.26	733.56	†752.88	795.65
Lending Minus Repayments 83				21.49	11.82	7.58	†3.90	10.14	12.40	14.38	19.76	32.49	15.90	†9.78	39.94
Total Financing 80h				56.96	26.80	19.36	†21.48	62.80	33.02	107.72	97.18	94.57	21.13	†55.54	80.07
Domestic 84a				25.97	15.85	9.39	†19.30	39.76	-8.87	33.85	20.62	-22.28	-27.45	†40.00	20.32
Foreign 85a				30.99	10.95	9.97	†2.18	23.04	41.89	73.87	76.56	116.85	48.58	†15.54	59.75
Total Debt by Residence 88				269.82	313.88	315.92	†326.03	430.59	502.50	541.81	640.01	812.58	919.62	†1045.22	1,153.44
Domestic 88a				58.39	81.74	78.01	†75.06	139.34	174.32	151.96	158.44	143.80	179.48	†192.44	201.50
Foreign 89a				211.43	232.14	237.91	†250.97	291.25	328.18	389.85	481.57	668.78	740.14	†852.78	951.94
National Accounts														*Millions of Kina*	
Housoh.Cons.Expend.,incl.NPISHs .. 96f	407	428	446	521	591	†770	876	990	1,168	1,227	1,242	1,386	1,370	1,469	1,452
Government Consumption Expend. .. 91f	207	228	270	328	367	†358	374	393	436	481	496	499	502	520	511
Gross Fixed Capital Formation 93e	242	128	130	187	164	†241	270	329	397	454	581	637	513	390	459
Changes in Inventories 93i	9	19	4	35	30	†41	28	57	36	7	-14	-6	64	24	-24
Exports of Goods and Services 90c	157	290	531	428	400	†591	586	752	747	651	652	776	800	898	1,006
Imports of Goods and Services (-) .. 98c	384	308	329	486	471	†609	636	755	923	1,001	1,073	1,145	1,125	1,102	1,079
Gross Domestic Product (GDP) 99b	645	786	1,040	1,004	1,069	†1,410	1,535	1,773	1,855	1,826	1,900	2,145	2,124	2,200	2,325
Net Primary Income from Abroad .. 98.n	35	37	79	72	39	†27	19	40	59	60	73	119	73	89	72
Gross National Income (GNI) 99a	645	789	1,041	1,004	1,107	†1,437	1,554	1,813	1,914	1,886	1,972	2,265	2,355	2,491	2,645
Consumption of Fixed Capital 99cf	36	57	67	70	78	†91	111	115	134	148	161	173	218	224	242
GDP Volume 1973 prices 99b.p	....	786	816	824	810	775									
GDP Volume 1977 prices 99b.p	....	....	....	....	....	1,410	1,531	1,559	1,523	1,540	1,517	....	....	....	....
GDP Volume 1981 prices 99b.p	....	....	....	....	....	....	....	....	....	....	....	1,841	1,905	....	....
GDP Volume 1983 Prices 99b.p	....	....	....	....	....	....	....	....	....	....	....	....	2,145	2,124	2,200	2,325
GDP Volume (1995=100) 99bvp	....	53.8	55.9	56.4	55.4	53.1	57.6	58.6	57.3	58.0	58.4	60.4	59.8	62.0	65.5
GDP Deflator (1995=100) 99bip	....	24.8	31.6	30.3	32.7	†45.1	45.3	51.3	55.0	53.5	55.2	60.3	60.3	60.3	60.3
														Millions:	
Population 99z	2.58	2.59	2.64	2.69	2.75	2.81	2.87	2.93	2.98	3.04	3.11	3.19	3.26	3.34	3.41

	1987	1988	1989	1990	1991	1992	1993	1994	1995	1996	1997	1998	1999	2000	2001		
																International Transactions	
Millions of Kina																	
	1,123.2	1,256.1	1,111.6	1,122.4	1,390.5	1,862.6	2,527.3	2,662.0	3,400.0	3,334.0	3,079.0	3,707.0	5,006.7	5,813.0	6,104.9	Exports	70
	1,055.8	1,205.3	1,314.7	1,138.6	1,535.9	1,431.2	1,270.5	1,534.1	1,862.9	2,296.0	2,448.4	2,565.7	3,174.0	3,195.8	3,637.9	Imports, c.i.f.	71
	995.6	1,199.0	1,152.0	1,056.5	1,336.5	1,275.0	1,110.4	1,336.0	1,620.0	1,996.0	2,129.0	2,231.0	2,760.0	2,779.0	3,164.3	Imports, f.o.b.	71.v
1995=100																	
	71.9	69.9	73.1	67.3	89.2	102.7	103.9	103.8	100.0	93.4	83.8	....	....	....	....	Volume of Exports	72
	53.3	61.9	51.9	54.2	53.7	54.7	61.1	71.3	100.0	98.6	109.2	125.3	....	....	....	Unit Value of Exports	74
																Balance of Payments	
Minus Sign Indicates Debit																	
	-197.9	-296.4	-312.7	-75.7	-475.3	-159.9	474.1	402.1	491.9	188.9	-192.2	-28.9	94.7	....		Current Account, n.i.e.	78al d
	1,243.9	1,475.3	1,318.5	1,175.2	1,482.1	1,947.7	2,604.4	2,651.0	2,670.4	2,529.8	2,160.1	1,773.3	1,927.4			Goods: Exports f.o.b.	78aa d
	-1,129.6	-1,384.5	-1,341.3	-1,105.9	-1,403.9	-1,322.9	-1,134.7	-1,324.9	-1,262.4	-1,513.3	-1,483.3	-1,078.3	-1,071.4			Goods: Imports f.o.b.	78ab d
	114.3	90.8	-22.8	69.2	78.1	624.9	1,469.7	1,326.1	1,408.0	1,016.6	676.8	695.0	856.0			*Trade Balance*	78ac d
	97.3	122.3	167.9	205.7	266.8	329.2	306.7	235.4	321.3	432.2	396.9	318.0	247.8			Services: Credit	78ad d
	-377.6	-435.1	-408.8	-402.9	-543.3	-685.8	-804.6	-608.0	-642.1	-778.5	-923.6	-793.8	-728.1			Services: Debit	78ae d
	-166.0	-222.0	-263.7	-128.0	-198.3	268.2	971.8	953.5	1,087.2	670.2	150.1	219.2	375.6			*Balance on Goods & Services*	78af d
	57.9	118.6	87.0	106.6	107.1	59.7	31.3	22.4	22.5	32.1	35.1	20.9	18.6			Income: Credit	78ag d
	-219.4	-326.2	-265.2	-209.9	-320.4	-425.3	-400.2	-423.4	-510.7	-461.2	-344.8	-279.7	-291.1			Income: Debit	78ah d
	-327.5	-429.6	-441.9	-231.2	-411.6	-97.5	603.0	552.5	599.1	241.1	-159.5	-39.6	103.1			*Balance on Gds, Serv. & Inc.*	78ai d
	238.4	249.4	256.3	273.7	42.5	48.6	49.0	58.8	66.7	252.1	69.9	82.4	60.3			Current Transfers, n.i.e.: Credit	78aj d
	-108.8	-116.2	-127.2	-118.1	-106.2	-111.1	-178.0	-209.3	-173.9	-304.2	-102.6	-71.6	-68.7			Current Transfers, n.i.e.: Debit	78ak d
	-29.8	-40.1	-42.6	-37.3	—	—	—	—	—	—	—	—	—			Capital Account, n.i.e.	78bc d
	13.4	10.0	7.2	5.4	21.0	20.7	20.4	19.9	15.7	15.2	13.9	9.7	7.8			Capital Account, n.i.e.: Credit	78ba d
	-43.3	-50.1	-49.8	-42.7	-21.0	-20.7	-20.4	-19.9	-15.7	-15.2	-13.9	-9.7	-7.8			Capital Account: Debit	78bb d
	177.1	245.1	265.0	214.4	61.9	-149.0	-716.2	-609.2	-444.7	46.6	8.0	-179.7	16.0			Financial Account, n.i.e.	78bj d
	22.2	-33.8	17.9	—												Direct Investment Abroad	78bd d
	93.2	153.5	203.4	155.4	116.7	104.3	62.0	57.0	454.6	111.3	28.6	109.6	296.5			Dir. Invest. in Rep. Econ., n.i.e.	78be d
	—	—	—	—	-755.2	-1,256.4	-686.9	-839.1	-1,114.9	69.9	-25.5	87.0	89.0			Portfolio Investment Assets	78bf d
	—	—	—	—	....	....	....	....	....	....	....	....	....			Equity Securities	78bk d
	—	—	—	—	-755.2	-1,256.4	-686.9	-839.1	-1,114.9	69.9	-25.5	87.0	89.0			Debt Securities	78bl d
	—	—	—	—	658.8	1,274.9	636.0	837.1	1,066.2	—	....	....	....			Portfolio Investment Liab., n.i.e.	78bg d
	—	—	—	—	....	....	....	....	....	....	....	....	....			Equity Securities	78bm d
	—	—	—	—	658.8	1,274.9	636.0	837.1	1,066.2	—	....	....	....			Debt Securities	78bn d
	....	....	....													Financial Derivatives Assets	78bw d
	....	....	....													Financial Derivatives Liabilities	78bx d
	....	....	....	—	-64.3	7.0	17.3	58.8	-283.8	180.0	29.6	-55.0	10.7			Other Investment Assets	78bh d
	....	....	....													Monetary Authorities	78bo d
	....	....	....		....	....	....	....	....	....	....	....	....			General Government	78bp d
	—	—	—	—	—	—	—	—	—	—	—	—	-2.1			Banks	78bq d
	....	....	....	—	-64.3	7.0	17.3	58.8	-283.8	180.0	29.6	-55.0	12.8			Other Sectors	78br d
	61.7	125.4	43.7	59.0	105.9	-278.8	-744.5	-722.9	-566.8	-314.6	-24.7	-321.2	-380.2			Other Investment Liab., n.i.e.	78bi d
										-68.2						Monetary Authorities	78bs d
	54.8	27.2	-18.4	88.1	-38.6	59.6	66.5	-102.1	-23.5	10.0	-62.7	-44.2	39.4			General Government	78bt d
	9.4	34.6	13.0	-23.4	—	-36.1	-110.3	-26.9	27.4	-34.0	-42.3	16.4	—			Banks	78bu d
	-2.4	63.6	49.1	-5.6	144.4	-302.3	-700.8	-593.9	-570.7	-222.4	80.3	-293.4	-419.6			Other Sectors	78bv d
	52.5	37.9	31.6	-79.7	4.0	-17.2	-11.3	37.1	-86.6	-33.1	7.3	-12.5	14.3			Net Errors and Omissions	78ca d
	2.0	-53.5	-58.7	21.7	-409.4	-326.1	-253.4	-170.1	-39.5	202.5	-177.0	-221.0	125.0			*Overall Balance*	78cb d
	-2.0	53.5	58.7	-21.7	409.4	326.1	253.4	170.1	39.5	-202.5	177.0	221.0	-125.0			Reserves and Related Items	79da d
	3.0	58.7	61.6	-75.2	85.3	71.1	96.6	33.8	-177.4	-329.7	83.7	149.1	-49.7			Reserve Assets	79db d
	-4.9	-5.2	-2.9	53.5	-.1	—	-15.0	-30.6	35.0	2.9	—	-4.2	-22.8			Use of Fund Credit and Loans	79dc d
	—	—	—	—	324.2	255.0	171.8	166.8	181.9	124.4	93.2	76.1	-52.5			Exceptional Financing	79de d
																Government Finance	
Year Ending December 31																	
	-38.79	†-32.60	-35.07	-106.65	-68.01	-220.38	-283.55	†-139.42	-31.77	35.39	15.41	-137.40	-241.79			Deficit (-) or Surplus	80
	821.84	†900.98	999.37	999.67	1,213.18	1,117.64	1,310.65	†1445.50	1,692.95	1,896.12	2,024.01	1,991.20	2,216.11			Total Revenue and Grants	81y
	637.59	†711.11	809.65	777.58	901.47	921.32	1,128.95	†1282.20	1,499.84	1,730.67	1,711.98	1,686.46	1,750.59			Revenue	81
	184.25	†189.87	189.72	222.09	311.71	196.32	181.70	†163.30	193.11	165.45	312.03	304.74	465.52			Grants	81z
	860.63	†933.58	1,034.44	1,106.32	1,281.19	1,338.02	1,594.20	†1584.92	1,724.72	1,860.73	2,008.60	2,128.60	2,457.90			Exp. & Lending Minus Repay.	82z
	828.90	†890.00	987.84	1,066.52	1,273.56	1,348.69	1,588.71	1,585.12	1,721.93	1,857.29	2,003.70	2,127.26	2,457.83			Expenditure	82
	31.73	†43.58	46.60	39.80	7.63	-10.67	5.49	†-.20	2.79	3.44	4.90	1.34	.07			Lending Minus Repayments	83
	38.79	†32.60	35.07	106.65	68.01	220.38	283.55	†124.90	31.77	-35.39	-15.40	137.40	241.80			Total Financing	80h
	30.03	†42.90	30.41	93.15	125.17	181.52	237.83	†243.40	75.30	-45.49	57.90	253.72	304.29			Domestic	84a
	8.76	†-10.30	4.66	13.50	-57.16	38.86	45.72	†-118.50	-43.53	10.10	-73.30	-116.32	-62.49			Foreign	85a
	1,294.32	†1168.55	1,249.37	1,505.90	1,680.60	1,894.62	2,157.40	†2961.20	3,324.20	3,780.80	4,418.00	5,177.70	5,609.20			Total Debt by Residence	88
	259.54	†286.80	374.02	412.38	564.39	676.41	1,036.60	†1424.30	1,605.70	1,969.50	2,251.70	2,473.00	2,021.40			Domestic	88a
	1,034.78	†881.75	875.35	1,093.52	1,116.21	1,218.21	1,120.80	†1536.90	1,718.50	1,811.30	2,166.30	2,704.70	3,587.80			Foreign	89a
																National Accounts	
Millions of Kina																	
	1,500	1,919	1,962	1,816	2,121	2,144	2,046	2,240	2,454	3,375	4,119	4,620	6,123	....		Househ.Cons.Expend.,incl.NPISHs	96f
	527	663	745	764	853	1,005	1,199	1,001	1,006	1,370	1,361	1,407	1,488	....		Government Consumption Expend.	91f
	453	737	791	773	1,010	914	901	1,012	1,150	1,186	1,079	1,089	1,063	....		Gross Fixed Capital Formation	93e
	25	126	-83	-21	-22	70	-43	142	149	375	409	307	377	....		Changes in Inventories	93i
	996	1,371	1,238	1,250	1,524	2,021	2,562	3,031	3,675	3,575	3,312	3,942	4,153	....		Exports of Goods and Services	90c
	1,111	1,646	1,607	1,506	1,881	1,930	1,798	2,044	2,545	3,000	3,217	3,575	4,423	....		Imports of Goods and Services (-)	98c
	2,389	3,170	3,046	3,076	3,606	4,223	4,867	5,381	5,888	6,881	7,064	7,789	8,781	....		Gross Domestic Product (GDP)	99b
	131	122	115	118	205	336	-330	-246	-208	-307	-310	-343	-360	....		Net Primary Income from Abroad	98.n
	2,985	3,292	2,931	2,958	3,400	3,887	4,537	5,136	5,681	6,574	6,754	7,445	8,421	....		Gross National Income (GNI)	99a
	262	279	316	339	417	439	433	502	571	589	535	540	527	....		Consumption of Fixed Capital	99cf
	....	....	....	....	....	....	....	....	....	....	....	....	....	....		GDP Volume 1973 prices	99b.p
	....	....	....	....	....	....	....	....	....	....	....	....	....	....		GDP Volume 1977 prices	99b.p
	....	....	....	....	....	....	....	....	....	....	....	....	....	....		GDP Volume 1981 prices	99b.p
	2,389	2,458	2,423	2,351	2,575	2,931	3,465	3,671	3,549	3,824	3,675	3,635	3,804	....		GDP Volume 1983 Prices	99b.p
	67.3	69.3	68.3	66.2	72.6	82.6	97.6	103.4	100.0	107.7	103.5	102.4	107.2	....		GDP Volume (1995=100)	99bv p
	60.3	77.7	75.8	78.9	84.4	86.8	84.7	88.4	100.0	108.5	115.9	129.2	139.2	....		GDP Deflator (1995=100)	99bi p
Midyear Estimates																	
	3.48	3.56	3.63	3.70	3.77	3.85	3.92	4.00	4.07	4.40	†4.21	4.60	4.70	4.81	4.92	Population	99z

(See notes in the back of the book.)

Paraguay

288

		1972	1973	1974	1975	1976	1977	1978	1979	1980	1981	1982	1983	1984	1985	1986
Exchange Rates																*Guaranies per SDR:*
Market Rate ... aa=	wa	136.8	152.0	154.3	147.5	146.4	153.1	164.2	166.0	160.7	146.7	139.0	131.9	235.3	351.5	672.8
																Guaranies per US Dollar:
Market Rate ... ae=	we	126.0	126.0	126.0	126.0	126.0	126.0	126.0	126.0	126.0	126.0	126.0	126.0	240.0	320.0	550.0
Market Rate ... rf=	wf	126.0	126.0	126.0	126.0	126.0	126.0	126.0	126.0	126.0	126.0	126.0	126.0	201.0	306.7	339.2
Secondary Rate	xf	....	....	136.4	138.3	138.6	134.0	138.6	139.3	136.1	148.4	160.5	160.0	321.8	602.8	700.3
Tertiary Rate	yf	....	....	....	....	....	....	....	....	....	....	....	315.2	224.3	226.7	253.3
																Index Numbers (1995=100):
Market Rate	ahx	1,558.0	1,558.0	1,558.0	1,558.0	1,558.0	1,558.0	1,558.0	1,558.0	1,558.0	1,558.0	1,558.0	1,558.0	1,043.5	647.5	592.0
Nominal Effective Exchange Rate	nec	....	....	....	....	....	....	....	.3	.4	.6	.7	1.0	1.5	2.1	2.5
Real Effective Exchange Rate	rec	....	....	....	....	....	....	....	....	171.4	187.9	164.3	156.5	153.9	133.0	133.1
Fund Position																*Millions of SDRs:*
Quota	2f.s	19.00	19.00	19.00	19.00	19.00	19.00	23.00	23.00	34.50	34.50	34.50	48.40	48.40	48.40	48.40
SDRs	1b.s	6.57	6.57	6.57	6.57	6.57	6.58	6.64	9.41	11.05	15.09	23.67	30.41	35.03	38.80	42.08
Reserve Position in the Fund	1c.s	4.77	4.77	4.77	4.77	5.77	6.62	6.48	8.19	14.88	25.16	27.64	32.25	32.25	31.58	24.86
Total Fund Cred.&Loans Outstg.	2tl	—	—	—	—	—	—	—	—	—	—	—	—	—	—	—
International Liquidity																*Millions of US Dollars Unless Otherwise Indicated:*
Total Reserves minus Gold	1l.d	31.39	57.01	87.13	115.02	157.51	267.84	448.73	609.09	761.85	805.70	739.00	680.19	666.27	533.62	446.67
SDRs	1b.d	7.13	7.93	8.04	7.69	7.63	7.99	8.65	12.40	14.09	17.56	26.11	31.84	34.34	42.62	51.47
Reserve Position in the Fund	1c.d	5.18	5.75	5.84	5.58	6.70	8.04	8.44	10.79	18.98	29.29	30.49	33.76	31.61	34.69	30.41
Foreign Exchange	1d.d	19.08	43.33	73.25	101.74	143.17	251.81	431.64	585.90	728.78	758.85	682.40	614.59	600.32	456.31	364.79
of which: US Dollars	1dxd	13.86	16.14	47.53	93.99	116.26	111.67	226.32	288.89	404.33	456.22	453.02	334.72	482.86	336.89	268.20
Gold (Million Fine Troy Ounces)	1ad	.002	.002	.002	.002	.002	.006	.011	.035	.035	.035	.035	.035	.035	.035	.035
Gold (National Valuation)	1and	.09	.10	.10	.10	.10	.26	.45	4.36	4.62	4.30	4.05	3.88	2.96	11.68	13.82
Monetary Authorities: Other Assets	3..d	.05	.03	—	—	—	—	—	—	—	—	—	—	—	32.80	15.00
Other Liab.	4..d	1.27	4.46	4.45	4.38	5.73	7.91	11.23	20.16	21.09	32.41	39.70	69.77	132.94	48.59	32.68
Deposit Money Banks: Assets	7a.d	3.09	4.30	12.06	12.47	16.49	18.96	17.09	35.32	53.75	94.20	80.68	111.43	71.86	43.12	31.49
Liabilities	7b.d	20.86	20.57	18.68	14.26	7.10	14.22	21.21	30.02	34.13	67.48	52.69	98.14	60.20	44.18	18.39
Other Banking Insts.: Assets	7e.d	—	—	—	—	—	—	—	—	—	—	—	—	—	—	—
Liabilities	7f.d	52.50	59.96	69.91	81.89	84.46	93.19	103.22	116.98	131.34	136.20	164.48	173.98	107.86	94.78	62.35
Monetary Authorities																*Billions of Guaranies:*
Foreign Assets	11	4.00	7.20	10.99	14.51	19.85	33.78	56.60	77.29	96.58	102.06	86.54	85.98	109.41	100.01	167.05
Claims on Central Government	12a	4.21	4.43	3.18	2.97	2.67	2.92	4.29	4.38	3.85	3.96	3.54	20.33	28.89	32.52	39.03
Claims on Local Government	12b	....	....	....	....	....	....	....	....	....	....	....	....	....	....	....
Claims on Nonfin.Pub.Enterprises	12c	2.89	2.58	3.02	3.64	3.17	2.69	2.79	2.97	7.65	8.25	9.19	9.31	12.87	25.51	35.25
Claims on Private Sector	12d	1.84	1.85	1.91	1.87	1.99	2.02	2.02	2.01	2.08	2.19	2.24	2.78	2.74	2.63	4.14
Claims on Deposit Money Banks	12e	.26	.52	.84	.64	.53	.76	2.27	3.74	6.76	9.62	7.81	11.84	22.19	20.52	51.60
Claims on Other Banking Insts	12f	1.54	1.98	2.78	3.26	4.03	3.68	3.09	3.37	3.03	3.75	10.06	11.09	13.34	11.55	22.34
Claims on Nonbank Financial Insts.	12g	....	....	....	....	....	....	....	....	....	....	....	....	....	....	....
Reserve Money	14	11.84	15.04	17.69	21.74	26.24	34.47	45.89	56.16	71.59	84.24	84.75	111.03	130.02	154.65	209.17
of which: Currency Outside DMBs	14a	5.14	6.49	7.55	8.90	10.29	13.34	18.69	24.31	31.18	31.15	33.17	38.47	48.60	62.61	84.48
Time & Foreign Currency Deposits	15	.15	.17	.20	.68	.69	.64	1.08	3.92	6.62	11.62	17.03	18.43	20.05	31.85	38.09
Liabs. of Central Bank: Securities	16ac	....	....	....	....	....	....	....	....	....	....	....	....	....	....	....
Restricted Deposits	16b	.27	.45	.53	.46	.65	1.07	1.72	2.19	2.14	1.90	.87	.19	.25	.17	.15
Foreign Liabilities	16c	.16	.56	.56	.55	.72	1.00	1.42	2.54	2.66	4.08	5.00	8.79	31.90	15.55	17.97
Long-Term Foreign Liabilities	16cl	....	....	....	....	....	....	....	....	....	....	....	....	....	....	....
Central Government Deposits	16d	1.00	1.24	1.89	2.12	2.18	5.37	12.15	19.04	21.18	9.23	5.47	5.08	5.78	8.96	13.54
Capital Accounts	17a	.98	1.11	1.25	1.69	2.04	2.54	3.37	5.01	9.64	16.13	18.86	18.27	19.68	22.22	28.35
Other Items (Net)	17r	.33	-.02	.62	-.37	-.30	.76	5.43	4.90	6.11	2.63	-12.60	-20.46	-18.24	-40.66	12.15
Deposit Money Banks																*Billions of Guaranies:*
Reserves	20	6.45	8.17	9.86	12.50	15.75	20.77	26.64	30.47	38.66	52.83	50.75	69.74	78.27	84.28	117.09
Claims on Mon.Author.: Securities	20c	....	....	....	....	....	....	....	....	....	....	....	....	....	....	....
Foreign Assets	21	.39	.54	1.52	1.57	2.08	2.39	2.15	4.45	6.77	11.87	10.17	14.04	17.25	13.80	17.32
Claims on Central Government	22a	—	—	—	—	—	.55	.97	.84	1.02	1.54	2.16	1.81	1.35	.81	.64
Claims on Local Government	22b	....	....	....	....	....	....	....	....	....	....	....	....	....	....	....
Claims on Nonfin.Pub.Enterprises	22c	....	....	....	....	....	....	....	....	....	....	....	....	....	....	....
Claims on Private Sector	22d	9.85	12.45	14.56	17.78	21.72	28.05	40.66	53.88	77.34	89.50	94.41	99.68	116.59	128.66	170.19
Claims on Other Banking Insts	22f	....	....	....	....	....	....	....	....	....	....	....	....	....	....	....
Claims on Nonbank Financial Insts.	22g	....	....	....	....	....	....	....	....	....	....	....	....	....	....	....
Demand Deposits	24	4.04	5.60	7.28	8.55	11.03	14.69	20.30	23.29	28.57	29.28	25.70	34.92	44.76	56.25	67.44
Time, Savings,& Fgn.Currency Dep.	25	9.27	11.64	14.06	18.58	23.47	30.94	37.60	44.04	62.27	82.73	88.46	99.41	108.08	115.88	150.89
Money Market Instruments	26aa	....	....	....	....	....	....	....	....	....	....	....	....	....	....	....
Bonds	26ab	....	....	....	....	....	....	....	....	....	....	....	....	....	....	....
Restricted Deposits	26b	....	....	....	....	....	....	....	....	....	....	....	....	....	....	....
Foreign Liabilities	26c	1.54	1.92	1.89	1.54	.71	1.24	2.27	3.26	3.82	7.76	5.39	11.76	13.88	13.70	9.55
Long-Term Foreign Liabilities	26cl	1.09	.67	.46	.25	.19	.55	.40	.52	.48	.74	1.25	.61	.57	.44	.56
Central Government Deposits	26d	.03	.05	.04	.05	.07	.09	.11	.16	.20	.18	.13	.13	.15	.35	.64
Credit from Monetary Authorities	26g	.29	.57	.90	.67	.54	.75	2.24	3.71	6.75	9.25	7.41	13.51	24.94	20.87	51.94
Liabilities to Other Banking Insts	26i	....	....	....	....	....	....	....	....	....	....	....	....	....	....	....
Capital Accounts	27a	2.56	2.78	3.90	4.92	5.68	7.19	9.91	16.13	21.29	26.77	30.36	30.54	32.79	35.88	39.13
Other Items (Net)	27r	-2.13	-2.06	-2.60	-2.71	-2.13	-3.70	-2.40	-1.47	.42	-.96	-1.23	-5.61	-11.70	-15.80	-14.92
Monetary Survey																*Billions of Guaranies:*
Foreign Assets (Net)	31n	2.69	5.26	10.06	13.99	20.49	33.93	55.07	75.94	96.87	102.09	86.31	79.47	80.87	84.55	156.84
Domestic Credit	32	19.31	22.00	23.52	27.33	31.33	34.45	41.55	48.24	73.59	99.80	116.00	139.77	169.86	192.38	257.42
Claims on Central Govt. (Net)	32an	3.19	3.14	1.25	.79	.42	-1.99	-7.00	-13.98	-16.51	-3.89	.10	16.92	24.31	24.03	25.49
Claims on Local Government	32b	....	....	....	....	....	....	....	....	....	....	....	....	....	....	....
Claims on Nonfin.Pub.Enterprises	32c	2.89	2.58	3.02	3.64	3.17	2.69	2.79	2.97	7.65	8.25	9.19	9.31	12.87	25.51	35.25
Claims on Private Sector	32d	11.68	14.30	16.47	19.64	23.71	30.07	42.67	55.88	79.42	91.69	96.65	102.45	119.33	131.30	174.33
Claims on Other Banking Insts	32f	1.54	1.98	2.78	3.26	4.03	3.68	3.09	3.37	3.03	3.75	10.06	11.09	13.34	11.55	22.34
Claims on Nonbank Financial Insts.	32g	....	....	....	....	....	....	....	....	....	....	....	....	....	....	....
Money	34	9.42	12.49	15.12	17.83	21.59	28.57	39.81	49.54	62.36	62.43	60.20	75.59	97.81	125.20	158.67
Quasi-Money	35	9.42	11.81	14.26	19.26	24.16	31.58	38.68	47.95	68.89	94.35	105.49	117.84	128.13	147.73	188.98
Money Market Instruments	36aa	....	....	....	....	....	....	....	....	....	....	....	....	....	....	....
Bonds	36ab	....	....	....	....	....	....	....	....	....	....	....	....	....	....	....
Liabs. of Central Bank: Securities	36ac	....	....	....	....	....	....	....	....	....	....	....	....	....	....	....
Restricted Deposits	36b	.27	.45	.53	.46	.65	1.07	1.72	2.19	2.14	1.90	.87	.19	.25	.17	.15
Long-Term Foreign Liabilities	36cl	1.09	.67	.46	.25	.19	.55	.40	.52	.48	.74	1.25	.61	.57	.44	.56
Liabilities to Other Banking Insts	36i	....	....	....	....	....	....	....	....	....	....	....	....	....	....	....
Capital Accounts	37a	3.54	3.90	5.15	6.61	7.72	9.73	13.28	21.14	30.93	42.90	49.22	48.81	52.46	58.09	67.48
Other Items (Net)	37r	-1.75	-2.06	-1.94	-3.09	-2.49	-3.12	2.72	2.84	5.65	-.44	-14.72	-23.78	-28.48	-54.70	-1.58
Money plus Quasi-Money	35l	18.8	24.3	29.4	37.1	45.7	60.2	78.5	97.5	131.3	156.8	165.7	193.4	225.9	272.9	347.7

1987	1988	1989	1990	1991	1992	1993	1994	1995	1996	1997	1998	1999	2000	2001		
End of Period															**Exchange Rates**	
780.3	740.1	1,600.6	1,789.7	1,974.0	2,241.3	2,582.3	2,809.8	2,942.7	3,033.6	3,184.2	3,999.1	4,568.9	4,595.2	5,884.0	Market Rate aa=	wa
End of Period (we) Period Average (wf)																
550.0	550.0	1,218.0	1,258.0	1,380.0	1,630.0	1,880.0	1,924.7	1,979.7	2,109.7	2,360.0	2,840.2	3,328.9	3,526.9	4,682.0	Market Rate ae=	we
550.0	550.0	1,056.2	1,229.8	1,325.2	1,500.3	1,744.3	1,904.8	1,963.0	2,056.8	2,177.9	2,726.5	3,119.1	3,486.4	4,105.9	Market Rate rf=	wf
....	....	....	....	....	....	....	....	....	....	....	....	....	....	....	Secondary Rate	xf
400.0	400.0	....	....	....	....	....	....	....	....	....	....	....	....	....	Tertiary Rate	yf
Period Averages																
356.9	356.9	201.7	159.7	149.0	127.4	112.7	103.1	100.0	95.5	90.2	72.2	63.2	56.3	48.2	Market Rate	ahx
2.8	6.1	13.4	32.2	40.5	49.6	67.3	98.4	100.0	99.7	101.1	85.1	78.7	73.5	67.6	Nominal Effective Exchange Rate	nec
105.7	113.2	84.3	85.0	95.5	92.9	94.1	98.5	100.0	104.1	109.4	100.4	97.7	97.0	93.1	Real Effective Exchange Rate	rec
End of Period															**Fund Position**	
48.40	48.40	48.40	48.40	48.40	72.10	72.10	72.10	72.10	72.10	72.10	72.10	99.90	99.90	99.90	Quota	2f.s
44.78	47.38	50.83	54.93	58.76	62.12	65.08	67.63	70.58	73.30	76.08	79.14	74.81	78.49	81.33	SDRs	1b.s
19.57	14.97	12.48	11.02	11.02	16.94	16.48	14.53	14.53	14.53	14.53	14.53	21.48	21.48	21.48	Reserve Position in the Fund	1c.s
—	—	—	—	—	—	—	—	—	—	—	—	—	—	—	Total Fund Cred.&Loans Outstg.	2tl
End of Period															**International Liquidity**	
497.02	323.66	432.55	661.42	962.12	561.53	631.18	1,030.73	1,092.91	1,049.29	835.67	864.74	978.06	760.64	713.49	Total Reserves minus Gold	1l.d
63.53	63.76	66.80	78.15	84.05	85.42	89.39	98.73	104.92	105.40	102.65	111.44	102.68	102.26	102.21	SDRs	1b.d
27.76	20.15	16.40	15.68	15.76	23.29	22.63	21.20	21.59	20.89	19.60	20.45	29.48	27.98	26.99	Reserve Position in the Fund	1c.d
405.73	239.76	349.35	567.60	862.30	452.82	519.16	910.80	966.40	923.00	713.42	732.85	845.90	630.40	584.30	Foreign Exchange	1d.d
106.23	81.13	50.27	382.15	462.70	329.34	416.00	583.80	602.40	415.53	521.25	561.87	736.10	523.60	468.00	*of which: US Dollars*	1dxd
.035	.035	.035	.035	.035	.035	.035	.035	.035	.035	.349	.035	.035	.035	.035	Gold (Million Fine Troy Ounces)	1ad
17.01	14.31	13.98	13.97	12.79	11.60	13.70	13.40	13.50	12.90	10.10	10.03	10.15	9.60	9.70	Gold (National Valuation)	1and
12.50	—	2.22	—	—	....	....	3.98	3.44	3.44	3.44	7.07	9.80	9.80	14.10	Monetary Authorities: Other Assets	3..d
47.80	78.82	53.29	25.28	79.00	83.31	86.91	86.60	85.11	76.47	67.87	60.76	53.37	44.88	93.88	Other Liab.	4..d
31.37	59.12	134.84	158.15	152.70	240.30	300.39	298.21	502.97	474.74	378.52	416.19	402.43	498.84	447.92	Deposit Money Banks: Assets	7a.d
9.02	34.56	20.91	23.29	48.47	89.18	147.37	124.57	453.01	256.93	304.67	232.03	119.86	105.33	96.63	Liabilities	7b.d
—	—	—	—	—	—	—	—	.34	.67	12.91	11.01	9.63	15.76	18.88	Other Banking Insts.: Assets	7e.d
70.60	64.44	41.65	46.38	52.18	41.51	36.40	32.78	—	—	8.54	2.12	.60	2.01	1.79	Liabilities	7f.d
End of Period															**Monetary Authorities**	
168.56	†135.16	537.24	836.71	1,292.09	993.43	1,289.15	2,016.58	†2239.16	2,263.63	1,993.00	2,521.04	3,341.31	2,804.01	3,420.08	Foreign Assets	11
49.25	†27.38	103.34	230.46	76.98	794.81	916.73	1,047.15	†1038.99	1,088.06	695.48	928.81	1,113.16	1,063.78	1,477.66	Claims on Central Government	12a
....	1.11	1.08	.94	.89	.83	.82	.82	†.67	.62	1.06	1.11	1.16	1.21	1.26	Claims on Local Government	12b
65.51	†106.49	176.53	142.32	185.73	242.74	266.79	222.35	†239.15	268.00	303.76	329.42	358.39	381.19	216.23	Claims on Nonfin.Pub.Enterprises	12c
4.39	†1.58	2.79	5.39	6.55	6.30	6.29	6.58	†7.24	11.90	14.73	18.41	22.28	25.61	28.05	Claims on Private Sector	12d
45.91	†93.26	111.10	117.11	112.10	170.29	102.77	98.07	†580.74	840.71	528.45	45.40	4.57	7.19	6.64	Claims on Deposit Money Banks	12e
22.67	†10.58	17.40	18.70	21.53	16.53	16.21	15.65	†21.31	104.20	20.03	33.85	26.94	35.98	44.16	Claims on Other Banking Insts	12f
....	—	—	—	—	—	—	—	†23.14	21.34	86.65	96.05	103.46	113.11	123.08	Claims on Nonbank Financial Insts.	12g
293.37	†368.75	478.46	585.37	748.12	954.56	1,083.20	1,378.91	†1738.50	1,704.98	1,829.88	1,949.68	2,127.14	2,105.35	2,234.23	Reserve Money	14
119.57	†149.10	216.19	300.52	379.92	531.26	635.77	800.46	†956.00	961.77	1,122.90	1,264.08	1,398.68	1,327.19	1,377.21	*of which: Currency Outside DMBs*	14a
34.47	†10.32	27.97	92.15	193.53	281.81	406.51	455.51	†448.56	648.47	635.95	833.43	1,040.74	1,090.23	1,366.33	Time & Foreign Currency Deposits	15
....	—	—	—	2.50	—	8.53	35.50	†201.90	250.79	319.05	381.75	75.88	45.93	284.47	Liabs. of Central Bank: Securities	16ac
.37	†3.92	3.96	5.51	8.13	10.12	17.11	26.47	†26.01	51.75	54.55	58.21	72.21	80.31	87.29	Restricted Deposits	16b
26.29	†19.39	25.98	10.07	2.76	7.49	17.36	16.21	†18.17	.98	.28	.28	.04	1.64	.85	Foreign Liabilities	16c
....	12.13	37.86	21.03	101.28	127.06	141.68	150.41	†150.77	160.30	157.86	172.29	176.87	157.47	434.29	Long-Term Foreign Liabilities	16cl
23.43	†51.82	224.25	382.06	288.49	228.31	134.37	414.23	†580.16	572.39	469.51	553.16	1,327.51	813.38	723.61	Central Government Deposits	16d
35.91	†40.02	59.82	102.96	169.89	286.94	303.95	332.20	†519.10	611.14	2,381.56	1,619.77	2,138.81	2,151.12	2,589.63	Capital Accounts	17a
–57.55	†–130.79	91.17	152.49	181.17	328.66	486.04	597.76	†467.22	597.65	–2,205.47	–1,594.49	–1,987.93	–2,013.36	–2,403.53	Other Items (Net)	17r
End of Period															**Deposit Money Banks**	
174.02	†209.06	264.24	301.07	410.51	588.19	743.99	913.28	†1032.56	1,173.75	1,189.09	1,421.92	1,636.09	1,740.62	2,106.19	Reserves	20
....	....	—	—	.50	—	8.53	35.50	†173.67	238.76	287.18	209.91	60.79	39.94	172.61	Claims on Mon.Author.: Securities	20c
17.25	†23.65	164.50	198.01	208.44	388.08	549.71	573.75	†998.40	1,001.22	881.95	1,181.98	1,334.07	1,768.39	2,076.09	Foreign Assets	21
1.32	†.07	1.58	.33	.18	—	.18	—	†46.59	98.35	187.73	286.85	454.60	356.87	294.61	Claims on Central Government	22a
....	—	—	.02	.02	.30	.55	.01	†22.00	1.57	7.07	36.64	5.55	8.98	4.35	Claims on Local Government	22b
....	.38	.34	1.71	1.88	1.79	1.45	1.46	†—	—	—	.79	1.27	—	.02	Claims on Nonfin.Pub.Enterprises	22c
215.12	†350.06	492.99	768.44	1,226.37	1,705.83	2,315.36	3,164.92	†3795.04	4,660.78	5,217.41	5,093.49	5,654.33	5,937.32	6,757.09	Claims on Private Sector	22d
....	1.71	2.30	2.96	4.73	4.93	11.08	11.58	†15.57	8.99	29.18	20.03	16.63	37.90	29.44	Claims on Other Banking Insts	22f
....	—	—	—	—	—	—	—	†39.39	25.98	33.45	25.52	40.35	45.80	63.21	Claims on Nonbank Financial Insts.	22g
113.73	†163.52	188.97	215.27	288.88	306.57	367.48	499.43	†594.44	681.90	698.08	678.97	730.19	1,192.53	1,326.51	Demand Deposits	24
191.20	†192.80	405.69	690.94	1,077.61	1,628.79	2,170.28	2,663.58	†3286.94	3,844.68	4,156.49	4,522.84	5,470.17	5,444.15	6,477.35	Time, Savings,& Fgn.Currency Dep.	25
....	—	—	—	—	—	—	—	†50.16	36.98	49.11	13.11	9.42	39.32	12.13	Money Market Instruments	26aa
....	2.76	1.53	3.10	7.00	2.21	4.00	3.76	†1.94	4.13	5.85	15.72	12.97	14.17	37.05	Bonds	26ab
....	—	—	—	—	—	—	—	†3.29	15.01	3.03	18.71	23.10	60.16	51.18	Restricted Deposits	26b
4.34	†8.38	11.97	19.61	26.74	71.07	149.61	211.29	†717.45	336.56	535.44	614.56	345.84	264.56	326.42	Foreign Liabilities	26c
.62	†5.44	13.55	9.56	39.42	72.96	120.08	28.39	†181.77	205.30	174.44	44.40	51.51	108.85	121.45	Long-Term Foreign Liabilities	26cl
.98	†19.27	35.79	50.91	63.99	97.40	209.98	432.74	†324.39	886.07	758.05	721.32	728.42	777.54	895.15	Central Government Deposits	26d
46.01	†92.14	114.08	116.51	111.34	169.18	102.45	94.01	†156.36	346.59	321.61	33.27	68.68	86.49	89.30	Credit from Monetary Authorities	26g
....	6.32	11.94	2.63	5.39	2.85	.86	.01	†19.24	31.45	31.02	50.11	68.47	102.10	235.49	Liabilities to Other Banking Insts	26i
47.36	†86.50	131.12	188.84	256.33	342.21	483.01	719.50	†1020.67	1,347.22	1,627.12	1,609.57	1,715.53	1,890.09	2,132.39	Capital Accounts	27a
3.48	†7.80	11.32	–24.82	–24.07	–4.12	23.11	47.82	†–233.45	–526.49	–527.15	–45.45	–20.59	–44.14	–200.81	Other Items (Net)	27r
End of Period															**Monetary Survey**	
155.18	†131.03	663.79	1,005.04	1,471.02	1,302.95	1,671.89	2,362.84	†2501.93	2,927.32	2,339.23	3,088.18	4,329.50	4,306.20	5,168.90	Foreign Assets (Net)	31n
333.85	†428.28	538.31	738.31	1,172.38	2,448.35	3,191.11	3,623.54	†4344.52	4,831.32	5,369.00	5,596.47	5,742.22	6,416.82	7,420.40	Domestic Credit	32
26.16	†–43.64	–155.12	–202.18	–275.31	469.10	572.56	200.17	†181.02	–272.06	–344.34	–58.82	–488.16	–170.27	153.51	Claims on Central Govt. (Net)	32an
....	1.11	1.08	.96	.91	1.13	1.37	.83	†22.67	2.18	8.13	37.75	6.71	10.19	5.61	Claims on Local Government	32b
65.51	†106.87	176.88	144.03	187.61	244.53	268.23	223.81	†239.15	268.00	303.76	330.20	359.66	381.19	216.25	Claims on Nonfin.Pub.Enterprises	32c
219.51	†351.64	495.78	773.83	1,232.92	1,712.14	2,321.65	3,171.50	†3802.28	4,672.68	5,232.14	5,111.89	5,676.61	5,962.93	6,785.14	Claims on Private Sector	32d
22.67	†12.29	19.69	21.66	26.26	21.46	27.29	27.23	†36.87	113.19	49.21	53.88	43.58	73.88	73.60	Claims on Other Banking Insts	32f
....	—	—	—	—	—	—	—	†62.53	47.32	120.10	121.57	143.81	158.91	186.29	Claims on Nonbank Financial Insts.	32g
243.67	†330.16	434.89	558.06	738.91	905.03	1,054.01	1,370.31	†1699.93	1,708.85	1,886.18	1,984.45	2,166.89	2,562.25	2,743.15	Money	34
225.67	†203.12	433.66	783.09	1,271.14	1,910.60	2,576.79	3,119.08	†3735.50	4,493.15	4,792.44	5,356.27	6,510.91	6,534.39	7,843.68	Quasi-Money	35
....	—	—	—	—	—	—	—	†50.16	36.98	49.11	13.11	9.42	39.32	12.13	Money Market Instruments	36aa
....	2.76	1.53	3.10	7.00	2.21	4.00	3.76	†1.94	4.13	5.85	15.72	12.97	14.17	37.05	Bonds	36ab
....	—	—	—	2.00	—	—	—	†28.23	12.03	31.87	171.84	15.09	5.99	111.85	Liabs. of Central Bank: Securities	36ac
.37	†3.92	3.96	5.51	8.13	10.12	17.11	26.47	†29.30	66.76	57.58	76.92	95.31	140.47	138.48	Restricted Deposits	36b
.62	†17.57	51.41	30.59	140.69	200.02	261.76	178.80	†332.54	365.60	332.29	216.69	228.37	266.32	555.74	Long-Term Foreign Liabilities	36cl
....	6.32	11.94	2.63	5.39	2.85	.86	.01	†19.24	31.45	31.02	50.11	68.47	102.10	235.49	Liabilities to Other Banking Insts	36i
83.26	†126.51	190.94	291.80	426.22	629.14	786.96	1,051.70	†1539.78	1,958.36	4,008.68	3,229.34	3,854.34	4,041.20	4,722.02	Capital Accounts	37a
–64.55	†–131.06	73.76	68.57	43.92	91.33	161.52	236.25	†–590.17	–918.67	–3,486.79	–2,429.78	–2,890.06	–2,983.19	–3,810.29	Other Items (Net)	37r
469.3	†533.3	868.6	1,341.1	2,010.1	2,815.6	3,630.8	4,489.4	†5,435.4	6,202.0	6,678.6	7,340.7	8,677.8	9,096.6	10,586.8	Money plus Quasi-Money	35l

Paraguay

		1972	1973	1974	1975	1976	1977	1978	1979	1980	1981	1982	1983	1984	1985	1986
Other Banking Institutions															*Billions of Guaranies:*	
Reserves	40	—	—	—	—	—	—	—	—	—	.01	—	—	—	—	—
Claims on Mon.Author.: Securities	40c	....	....	....	....	....	....	....	....	....	....	....	....	....	....	....
Foreign Assets	41	—	—	—	—	—	—	—	—	—	—	—	—	—	—	—
Claims on Central Government	42a	—	—	—	—	—	—	—	—	—	—	—	—	—	—	—
Claims on Local Government	42b															
Claims on Nonfin.Pub.Enterprises	42c															
Claims on Private Sector	42d	9.51	11.22	13.40	14.78	16.65	19.88	19.96	24.34	26.54	33.19	40.23	41.81	50.27	55.39	73.34
Claims on Deposit Money Banks	42e	.01	.01	—	.03	.01	.01	.01	.01	.01	—	.01	—	.02	.02	—
Claims on Nonbank Financial Insts.	42g	....	....	....	....	....	....	....	....	....	....	....	....	....	....	....
Time, Savings,& Fgn.Currency Dep.	45	—	—	—	—	—	—	—	—	—	—	—	—	—	—	—
Bonds	46ab															
Foreign Liabilities	46c	.19	.12	.01	.10	....	....	....	....	....	....	....	....	....	....	....
Long-Term Foreign Liabilities	46cl	6.43	7.44	8.80	10.22	10.64	11.74	13.01	14.74	16.55	17.16	20.72	21.92	25.89	30.33	34.29
Credit from Monetary Authorities	46g	1.50	1.83	2.48	2.95	3.64	3.66	3.09	3.32	3.01	2.22	10.04	10.90	12.43	11.50	18.74
Credit from Deposit Money Banks	46h	.01	—	—	.01	.02	.02	.03	.03	.03	.01	—	.02	—	—	
Capital Accounts	47a	2.20	2.43	2.49	2.48	3.18	4.23	5.24	5.98	6.87	8.81	9.99	12.04	13.80	14.38	19.59
Other Items (Net)	47r	−.79	−.60	−.37	−.93	−.81	.25	−1.38	.28	.09	4.98	−.51	−3.05	−1.83	−.81	.72
Banking Survey															*Billions of Guaranies:*	
Foreign Assets (Net)	51n	2.50	5.13	10.01	13.85	20.45	33.90	55.06	75.91	96.85	102.05	86.29	79.44	80.87	84.55	156.84
Domestic Credit	52	27.07	31.04	33.92	38.62	43.35	50.65	58.42	69.20	97.10	129.24	146.17	170.49	206.79	236.23	308.42
Claims on Central Govt. (Net)	52an	2.98	2.94	1.02	.56	−.17	−1.99	−7.00	−13.98	−16.51	−3.89	.10	16.92	24.31	24.03	25.49
Claims on Local Government	52b															
Claims on Nonfin.Pub.Enterprises	52c	2.89	2.58	3.02	3.64	3.17	2.69	2.79	2.97	7.65	8.25	9.19	9.31	12.87	25.51	35.25
Claims on Private Sector	52d	21.20	25.52	29.87	34.42	40.35	49.95	62.63	80.22	105.96	124.88	136.89	144.26	169.60	186.69	247.67
Claims on Nonbank Financial Insts.	52g	....	....	....	....	....	....	....	....	....	....	....	....	....	....	....
Liquid Liabilities	55l	18.84	24.30	29.38	37.09	45.75	60.15	78.50	97.49	131.25	156.78	165.69	193.42	225.94	272.94	347.65
Money Market Instruments	56aa	....	....	....	....	....	....	....	....	....	....	....	....	....	....	....
Bonds	56ab	....	....	....	....	....	....	....	....	....	....	....	....	....	....	....
Liabs. of Central Bank: Securities	56ac	....	....	....	....	....	....	....	....	....	....	....	....	....	....	....
Restricted Deposits	56b	.27	.45	.53	.46	.65	1.07	1.72	2.19	2.14	1.90	.87	.19	.25	.17	.15
Long-Term Foreign Liabilities	56cl	7.52	8.11	9.27	10.47	10.83	12.29	13.41	15.26	17.03	17.90	21.97	22.53	26.45	30.77	34.86
Capital Accounts	57a	5.74	6.33	7.63	9.09	10.90	13.96	18.53	27.12	37.80	51.71	59.21	60.86	66.27	72.47	87.07
Other Items (Net)	57r	−2.80	−3.03	−2.88	−4.63	−4.33	−2.92	1.31	3.06	5.72	3.00	−15.29	−27.06	−31.25	−55.56	−4.46
Money (National Definitions)															*Millions of Pesos:*	
Reserve Money	19ma	....	....	....	....	....	....	....	....	....	....	....	....		143.50	201.11
M1	59ma	....	....	....	....	....	....	....	....	....	....	....	....		114.83	146.61
M2	59mb	....	....	....	....	....	....	....	....	....	....	....	....		215.43	275.63
M3	59mc	....	....	....	....	....	....	....	....	....	....	....	....		223.93	290.33
M4	59md	....	....	....	....	....	....	....	....	....	....	....	....		....	....
M5	59me	....	....	....	....	....	....	....	....	....	....	....	....		....	....
Interest Rates															*Percent Per Annum*	
Discount Rate *(End of Period)*	60															
Money Market Rate	60b	....	....	....	....	....	....	....	....	....	....	....	....	....	....	....
Savings Rate	60k	....	....	....	....	....	....	....	....	....	....	....	....	....	....	....
Savings Rate (Fgn.Currency)	60k. *f*	....	....	....	....	....	....	....	....	....	....	....	....	....	....	....
Deposit Rate	60l	....	....	....	....	....	....	....	....	....	....	....	....	....	....	....
Deposit Rate (Fgn.Currency)	60l. *f*	....	....	....	....	....	....	....	....	....	....	....	....	....	....	....
Lending Rate	60p	....	....	....	....	....	....	....	....	....	....	....	....	....	....	....
Lending Rate (Fgn.Currency)	60p. *f*	....	....	....	....	....	....	....	....	....	....	....	....	....	....	....
Prices and Labor															*Index Numbers (1995=100):*	
Producer Prices (1996=100)	63															
Consumer Prices	64	2.0	2.3	2.9	3.0	3.2	3.5	3.9	4.9	6.1	6.9	7.4	8.4	10.0	12.6	16.6
															Number in Thousands:	
Labor Force	67d	....	....	....	....	....	....	....	....	....	....	....	....	....	....	....
Employment	67e	....	....	....	....	....	....	....	....	....	....	....	....	....	407	412
Unemployment	67c	....	....	....	....	....	....	....	....	....	....	....	....	....	22	27
Unemployment Rate (%)	67r	....	....	....	....	....	....	....	....	....	....	....	....	....	5.1	6.1
International Transactions															*Millions of U.S. Dollars*	
Exports	70..*d*	84.6	124.2	166.5	176.3	181.2	278.9	257.0	305.2	310.2	295.6	329.8	269.2	334.5	303.9	233.5
Imports, c.i.f.	71..*d*	82.6	122.3	198.3	205.6	220.2	308.3	383.0	521.1	614.7	599.6	672.0	545.9	586.0	501.5	578.1
Imports, f.o.b.	71.v*d*	69.9	104.8	171.4	178.4	180.2	255.4	317.7	437.7	517.1	506.1	581.5	478.3	513.1	442.3	509.4
															1990=100	
Volume of Exports	72	67.0	4.5	7.2	7.2	12.4	15.3	13.8	21.2	16.7	15.6	28.2	27.4	27.9	41.2	37.6
															1985=100:	
Unit Value of Exports	74	44.9	56.3	396.7	444.9	219.4	350.9	349.3	666.7	1,033.0	595.2	779.6	402.2	692.7	100.0	74.3

Other Banking Institutions

End of Period

1987	1988	1989	1990	1991	1992	1993	1994	1995	1996	1997	1998	1999	2000	2001		
—	†16.58	21.25	12.13	13.57	26.85	30.25	51.64	†47.07	52.55	69.01	73.66	72.99	92.44	105.47	Reserves	40
....	—	—	—	—	—	—	—	†1.29	.46	.02	3.36	5.08	5.99	2.17	Claims on Mon.Author.: Securities	40c
....	—	†—	—	—	—	—	—	†.68	1.41	30.08	31.26	31.92	55.87	87.53	Foreign Assets	41
....	†—	—	—	—	—	—	—	†2.11	3.65	4.30	3.58	5.79	6.52	5.28	Claims on Central Government	42a
....	.29	1.99	—	—	—	—	—	†—	.01	.03	.04	.12	.03		Claims on Local Government	42b
	.01	—	—	—	—	—	—	—	—	—	.08	—	—	—	Claims on Nonfin.Pub.Enterprises	42c
84.58	†133.44	172.92	249.42	335.32	432.03	600.11	858.31	†447.38	505.38	655.57	662.12	626.43	773.75	888.45	Claims on Private Sector	42d
—	†8.25	15.16	27.70	76.48	59.07	68.59	122.40	†30.14	38.50	39.56	57.90	87.07	74.99	92.86	Claims on Deposit Money Banks	42e
....	—	—	—	—	—	—	—	†4.24	6.59	7.46	.12	1.80	4.17	18.63	Claims on Nonbank Financial Insts.	42g
—	†63.30	79.15	117.44	174.25	179.67	201.09	270.97	†352.02	401.87	501.74	491.48	475.48	615.14	766.92	Time, Savings,& Fgn.Currency Dep.	45
—	15.50	21.13	10.74	14.04	58.71	119.50	222.27	†6.76	6.76	8.36	7.25	6.42	7.81	7.77	Bonds	46ab
....	—	—	—	—	—	—	—	†—	—	19.91	5.92	.21	7.11	8.22	Foreign Liabilities	46c
38.83	†25.78	50.81	58.07	71.22	67.03	66.62	63.06	†—	—	—	.11	1.77	.03	.06	Long-Term Foreign Liabilities	46cl
22.57	†10.38	16.31	15.67	12.57	11.57	11.57	11.89	†12.15	11.84	19.81	32.52	26.77	36.27	52.80	Credit from Monetary Authorities	46g
—	†.43	.49	1.74	4.08	1.41	2.31	1.77	†15.86	17.52	36.28	41.58	42.75	69.07	43.87	Credit from Deposit Money Banks	46h
29.42	†47.92	50.70	93.32	165.24	234.45	273.00	422.30	†193.46	227.94	274.99	307.21	324.11	349.50	382.56	Capital Accounts	47a
-6.23	†-4.74	-7.25	-7.72	-16.03	-34.89	24.87	40.09	†-47.34	-57.40	-55.07	-54.05	-46.33	-71.07	-61.78	Other Items (Net)	47r

Banking Survey

End of Period

1987	1988	1989	1990	1991	1992	1993	1994	1995	1996	1997	1998	1999	2000	2001		
155.18	†131.03	663.79	1,005.04	1,471.02	1,302.95	1,671.89	2,362.84	†2502.61	2,928.72	2,349.40	3,113.52	4,361.20	4,354.97	5,248.21	Foreign Assets (Net)	51n
395.76	†549.72	693.53	966.06	1,481.44	2,858.92	3,763.93	4,454.62	†4759.09	5,233.74	5,987.13	6,208.44	6,332.78	7,127.51	8,259.19	Domestic Credit	52
26.16	†-43.64	-155.12	-202.18	-275.31	469.10	572.56	200.17	†180.85	-268.41	-340.05	-55.25	-482.37	-163.75	158.80	Claims on Central Govt. (Net)	52an
....	1.40	3.07	.96	.91	1.13	1.37	.83	†22.67	2.18	8.14	37.78	6.75	10.31	5.64	Claims on Local Government	52b
65.51	†106.88	176.88	144.03	187.61	244.53	268.23	223.81	†239.15	268.00	303.76	330.20	359.74	381.19	216.25	Claims on Nonfin.Pub.Enterprises	52c
304.09	†485.08	668.70	1,023.25	1,568.24	2,144.16	2,921.76	4,029.80	†4249.65	5,178.06	5,887.71	5,774.01	6,303.04	6,736.68	7,673.59	Claims on Private Sector	52d
....	—	—	—	—	—	—	—	†66.77	53.91	127.56	121.69	145.62	163.08	204.92	Claims on Nonbank Financial Insts.	52g
469.34	†580.00	926.45	1,446.45	2,170.73	2,968.45	3,801.63	4,708.73	†5740.38	6,551.33	7,111.35	7,758.54	9,080.29	9,619.33	11,248.29	Liquid Liabilities	55l
....	—	—	—	—	—	—	—	†50.16	36.98	49.11	13.11	9.42	39.32	12.13	Money Market Instruments	56aa
—	18.25	22.66	13.84	21.04	60.92	123.49	226.03	†8.70	10.89	14.21	22.97	19.39	21.97	44.82	Bonds	56ab
....	—	—	—	2.00	—	—	—	†26.94	11.56	31.84	168.48	10.01	—	109.69	Liabs. of Central Bank: Securities	56ac
.37	†3.92	3.96	5.51	8.13	10.12	17.11	26.47	†29.40	66.76	57.58	76.92	95.31	140.47	138.48	Restricted Deposits	56b
39.45	†43.35	102.22	88.66	211.91	267.05	328.38	241.86	†332.54	365.60	332.29	216.79	230.14	266.35	555.80	Long-Term Foreign Liabilities	56cl
112.68	†174.43	241.63	385.11	591.45	863.59	1,059.96	1,474.00	†1733.23	2,186.30	4,283.67	3,536.55	4,178.45	4,390.71	5,104.58	Capital Accounts	57a
-70.89	†-139.20	60.40	31.53	-52.81	-8.26	105.24	140.37	†-659.65	-1,066.95	-3,543.53	-2,471.40	-2,929.04	-2,995.69	-3,706.39	Other Items (Net)	57r

Money (National Definitions)

End of Period

1987	1988	1989	1990	1991	1992	1993	1994	1995	1996	1997	1998	1999	2000	2001		
286.90	354.31	450.74	547.12	687.58	901.98	1,053.31	1,342.25	1,650.91	1,703.49	1,831.80	1,987.33	2,138.55	2,106.94	2,227.57	*Reserve Money*	19ma
211.92	262.57	374.50	490.57	625.17	803.58	958.33	1,272.60	1,539.36	1,570.67	1,789.14	1,922.27	2,103.85	2,478.22	2,700.36	M1	59ma
349.41	421.97	593.31	780.80	1,056.90	1,356.55	1,563.47	2,166.15	2,827.35	3,204.72	3,437.43	3,341.82	3,706.11	3,824.42	4,068.44	M2	59mb
366.02	439.95	768.49	1,071.34	1,511.25	2,112.67	2,720.04	3,499.99	4,201.08	5,121.65	5,848.77	6,383.03	7,532.20	7,833.10	9,332.98	M3	59mc
....	....	....	1,074.44	1,518.25	2,114.88	2,725.30	3,503.75	4,204.77	5,122.88	5,848.77	6,385.00	7,541.01	7,850.33	9,363.84	M4	59md
....	....	....	1,164.68	1,684.19	2,320.51	2,970.03	3,693.60	4,381.96	5,262.52	5,849.76	6,385.00	7,541.01	7,850.33	9,363.84	M5	59me

Interest Rates

Percent Per Annum

1987	1988	1989	1990	1991	1992	1993	1994	1995	1996	1997	1998	1999	2000	2001		
....	10.00	21.00	†33.00	19.75	24.00	27.17	19.15	20.50	15.00	20.00	20.00	20.00	20.00	20.00	Discount Rate (*End of Period*)	60
....	....	....	....	12.39	21.59	22.55	18.64	20.18	16.35	12.48	20.74	17.26	10.70	13.45	Money Market Rate	60b
....	....	....	10.50	12.04	10.37	10.60	†12.00	11.53	9.92	6.93	5.12	6.06	6.43	5.67	Savings Rate	60k
....	....	....	....	....	....	....	4.27	4.68	4.08	3.22	2.74	2.40	2.35	2.07	Savings Rate (Fgn.Currency)	60k. f
....	....	....	22.92	22.53	20.15	22.10	23.12	21.16	17.16	13.00	15.95	†19.75	15.72	16.22	Deposit Rate	60l
....	....	....	....	....	....	....	....	....	....	....	8.01	7.27	6.66	4.93	Deposit Rate (Fgn.Currency)	60l. f
....	....	....	31.00	34.94	27.96	30.78	†35.47	33.94	31.88	27.79	30.49	30.21	26.78	28.25	Lending Rate	60p
....	....	....	....	....	....	....	12.68	14.03	14.35	13.53	13.03	12.17	11.87	11.16	Lending Rate (Fgn.Currency)	60p. f

Prices and Labor

Period Averages

1987	1988	1989	1990	1991	1992	1993	1994	1995	1996	1997	1998	1999	2000	2001		
....	....	....	....	....	....	....	....	....	100.0	101.2	116.2	122.4	140.4	148.5	Producer Prices (1996=100)	63
20.2	24.8	31.3	†43.2	53.7	61.9	73.1	88.2	100.0	109.8	117.5	131.0	139.9	152.4	163.5	Consumer Prices	64

Period Averages

1987	1988	1989	1990	1991	1992	1993	1994	1995	1996	1997	1998	1999	2000	2001		
....	....	....	515	....	587	†1,053	....	....	....	....	....	....	....	....	Labor Force	67d
426	448	490	486	495	522	570	†1,050	†1,160	1,190	1,771	2,151	2,196	2,563	....	Employment	67e
25	22	32	34	27	29	30	†48	....	106	....	....	....	....	....	Unemployment	67c
5.5	4.7	6.1	6.6	5.1	5.3	5.1	†4.4	....	8.2	....	....	....	....	....	Unemployment Rate (%)	67r

International Transactions

Millions of U.S. Dollars

1987	1988	1989	1990	1991	1992	1993	1994	1995	1996	1997	1998	1999	2000	2001		
353.4	509.9	1,005.9	958.7	737.1	656.6	725.2	816.8	919.2	1,043.5	1,088.6	1,014.0	740.9	....	....	Exports	70..d
595.3	573.9	759.7	1,352.0	1,460.3	1,421.6	1,688.8	2,140.4	2,782.2	2,850.5	3,099.2	2,470.8	1,725.1	....	....	Imports, c.i.f.	71..d
517.5	494.8	660.8	1,193.4	1,275.4	1,237.2	1,477.5	2,140.4	2,782.2	2,850.5	2,957.1	....	....	....	....	Imports, f.o.b.	71.v d

1990=100

1987	1988	1989	1990	1991	1992	1993	1994	1995	1996	1997	1998	1999	2000	2001		
58.6	68.6	100.9	100.0	61.4	52.8	75.1	66.6	....	....	....	....	....	....	....	Volume of Exports	72

Indexes of Unit Values in Guaranies

1987	1988	1989	1990	1991	1992	1993	1994	1995	1996	1997	1998	1999	2000	2001		
183.4	246.1	527.1	....	....	....	....	....	....	....	....	....	....	....	....	Unit Value of Exports	74

Paraguay

	1972	1973	1974	1975	1976	1977	1978	1979	1980	1981	1982	1983	1984	1985	1986
Balance of Payments															*Millions of US Dollars:*
Current Account, n.i.e. .... 78al *d*	...	...	...	−72.2	−68.5	−58.6	−112.9	−205.9	−277.0	−373.5	−374.8	−247.9	−317.4	−251.7	−364.9
Goods: Exports f.o.b. .... 78aa *d*	...	...	...	188.0	202.1	327.1	356.1	384.5	400.3	398.5	396.2	326.0	361.3	465.6	575.8
Goods: Imports f.o.b. .... 78ab *d*	...	...	...	−227.3	−236.4	−360.0	−432.0	−577.1	−675.3	−772.4	−711.3	−551.4	−649.1	−659.3	−864.2
Trade Balance .... 78ac *d*	...	...	...	−39.3	−34.3	−32.9	−75.9	−192.6	−275.0	−373.9	−315.1	−225.4	−287.8	−193.7	−288.4
Services: Credit .... 78ad *d*	...	...	...	34.1	39.9	62.9	78.2	129.1	164.0	156.2	120.4	138.0	210.8	152.7	183.8
Services: Debit .... 78ae *d*	...	...	...	−55.1	−57.8	−72.1	−95.6	−154.2	−165.1	−203.9	−250.3	−157.4	−211.9	−180.3	−224.9
Balance on Goods & Services .... 78af *d*	...	...	...	−60.3	−52.2	−42.1	−93.3	−217.7	−276.1	−421.6	−445.0	−244.8	−288.9	−221.3	−329.5
Income: Credit .... 78ag *d*	...	...	...	11.7	15.8	29.6	54.8	80.1	126.8	163.8	162.7	96.0	93.9	68.5	70.5
Income: Debit .... 78ah *d*	...	...	...	−37.6	−36.3	−47.3	−80.2	−75.7	−132.3	−121.5	−97.5	−105.3	−131.7	−106.8	−117.0
Balance on Gds, Serv. & Inc. .... 78ai *d*	...	...	...	−86.2	−72.7	−59.8	−118.7	−213.3	−281.6	−379.3	−379.8	−254.1	−326.7	−259.6	−376.0
Current Transfers, n.i.e.: Credit .... 78aj *d*	...	...	...	16.0	7.1	3.8	8.5	10.0	8.7	8.5	5.9	6.8	9.8	9.2	11.9
Current Transfers: Debit .... 78ak *d*	...	...	...	−2.0	−2.9	−2.6	−2.7	−2.6	−4.1	−2.7	−.9	−.6	−.5	−1.3	−.8
Capital Account, n.i.e. .... 78bc *d*	...	...	...	—	—	—	—	—	—	—	—	—	—	−.4	—
Capital Account, n.i.e.: Credit .... 78ba *d*	...	...	...	—	—	—	—	—	—	—	—	—	—	.1	—
Capital Account: Debit .... 78bb *d*	...	...	...	—	—	—	—	—	—	—	—	—	—	−.5	—
Financial Account, n.i.e. .... 78bj *d*	...	...	...	96.9	111.3	191.0	274.2	358.7	447.6	430.1	338.2	287.3	286.0	38.6	114.7
Direct Investment Abroad .... 78bd *d*	...	...	...	—	−25.0	—	−5.0	—	—	—	—	—	—	—	—
Dir. Invest. in Rep. Econ., n.i.e. ...... 78be *d*	...	...	...	24.4	22.0	21.7	24.6	50.2	31.7	31.9	36.6	4.9	5.2	.7	.6
Portfolio Investment Assets .... 78bf *d*	...	...	...	—	—	—	—	—	—	—	—	—	—	—	—
Equity Securities .... 78bk *d*	...	...	...	—	—	—	—	—	—	—	—	—	—	—	—
Debt Securities .... 78bl *d*	...	...	...	—	—	—	—	—	—	—	—	—	—	—	—
Portfolio Investment Liab., n.i.e. ...... 78bg *d*	...	...	...	—	—	—	—	—	—	5.9	−7.5	3.3	—	—	—
Equity Securities .... 78bm *d*	...	...	...	—	—	—	—	—	—	—	—	—	—	—	—
Debt Securities .... 78bn *d*	...	...	...	—	—	—	—	—	—	5.9	−7.5	3.3	—	—	—
Financial Derivatives Assets .... 78bw *d*	...	...	...	...	...	...	...	...	...	...	...	...	...	...	...
Financial Derivatives Liabilities .... 78bx *d*	...	...	...	...	...	...	...	...	...	...	...	...	...	...	...
Other Investment Assets .... 78bh *d*	...	...	...	22.2	9.4	74.0	106.4	130.7	191.2	182.6	175.5	131.6	97.0	69.5	2.5
Monetary Authorities .... 78bo *d*	...	...	...	...	...	...	...	...	...	...	...	...	...	...	...
General Government.................. 78bp *d*	...	...	...	—	—	—	—	—	—	—	—	—	—	—	−15.0
Banks .... 78bq *d*	...	...	...	−.4	−4.0	−.6	.3	−17.4	−18.7	−40.9	15.5	−14.8	11.8	18.5	−27.8
Other Sectors .... 78br *d*	...	...	...	22.6	13.4	74.6	106.1	148.1	209.9	223.5	160.0	146.4	85.2	51.0	45.3
Other Investment Liab., n.i.e. .... 78bi *d*	...	...	...	50.3	104.9	95.3	148.2	177.8	224.7	209.7	133.6	147.5	183.8	−31.6	111.6
Monetary Authorities .... 78bs *d*	...	...	...	−2.9	−.9	3.5	7.2	14.8	3.3	11.8	10.5	22.9	97.4	−47.7	−22.4
General Government .... 78bt *d*	...	...	...	19.5	35.9	30.7	56.1	9.9	85.8	39.3	60.5	138.7	126.9	97.1	110.5
Banks .... 78bu *d*	...	...	...	4.5	−9.7	4.4	8.5	11.2	5.4	38.2	−4.3	36.9	14.7	33.6	−20.1
Other Sectors .... 78bv *d*	...	...	...	29.2	79.6	56.7	76.4	141.9	130.2	120.4	66.9	−51.0	−55.2	−114.6	43.6
Net Errors and Omissions .... 78ca *d*	...	...	...	3.9	−.4	−20.6	17.1	8.9	−20.1	−13.1	−25.7	−92.3	17.6	73.7	43.8
Overall Balance .... 78cb *d*	...	...	...	28.6	42.4	111.8	178.4	161.7	150.5	43.5	−62.3	−52.9	−13.8	−139.8	−206.4
Reserves and Related Items .... 79da *d*	...	...	...	−28.6	−42.4	−111.8	−178.4	−161.7	−150.5	−43.5	62.3	52.9	13.8	139.8	206.4
Reserve Assets .... 79db *d*	...	...	...	−28.6	−42.4	−111.8	−178.4	−161.7	−150.5	−43.5	62.3	52.9	13.8	97.8	139.8
Use of Fund Credit and Loans .... 79dc *d*	...	...	...	—	—	—	—	—	—	—	—	—	—	—	—
Exceptional Financing .... 79de *d*	...	...	...	—	—	—	—	—	—	—	—	—	—	42.0	66.6
International Investment Position															*Millions of US Dollars*
Assets .... 79aa *d*	...	...	...	...	...	...	...	...	...	...	...	...	...	...	...
Direct Investment Abroad .... 79ab *d*	...	...	...	...	...	...	...	...	...	...	...	...	...	...	...
Portfolio Investment .... 79ac *d*	...	...	...	...	...	...	...	...	...	...	...	...	...	...	...
Equity Securities .... 79ad *d*	...	...	...	...	...	...	...	...	...	...	...	...	...	...	...
Debt Securities .... 79ae *d*	...	...	...	...	...	...	...	...	...	...	...	...	...	...	...
Financial Derivatives .... 79al *d*	...	...	...	...	...	...	...	...	...	...	...	...	...	...	...
Other Investment .... 79af *d*	...	...	...	...	...	...	...	...	...	...	...	...	...	...	...
Monetary Authorities .... 79ag *d*	...	...	...	...	...	...	...	...	...	...	...	...	...	...	...
General Government.................. 79ah *d*	...	...	...	...	...	...	...	...	...	...	...	...	...	...	...
Banks .... 79ai *d*	...	...	...	...	...	...	...	...	...	...	...	...	...	...	...
Other Sectors .... 79aj *d*	...	...	...	...	...	...	...	...	...	...	...	...	...	...	...
Reserve Assets .... 79ak *d*	...	...	...	...	...	...	...	...	...	...	...	...	...	...	...
Liabilities .... 79la *d*	...	...	...	...	...	...	...	...	...	...	...	...	...	...	...
Dir. Invest. in Rep. Economy........... 79lb *d*	...	...	...	...	...	...	...	...	...	...	...	...	...	...	...
Portfolio Investment .... 79lc *d*	...	...	...	...	...	...	...	...	...	...	...	...	...	...	...
Equity Securities .... 79ld *d*	...	...	...	...	...	...	...	...	...	...	...	...	...	...	...
Debt Securities .... 79le *d*	...	...	...	...	...	...	...	...	...	...	...	...	...	...	...
Financial Derivatives .... 79ll *d*	...	...	...	...	...	...	...	...	...	...	...	...	...	...	...
Other Investment .... 79lf *d*	...	...	...	...	...	...	...	...	...	...	...	...	...	...	...
Monetary Authorities .... 79lg *d*	...	...	...	...	...	...	...	...	...	...	...	...	...	...	...
General Government.................. 79lh *d*	...	...	...	...	...	...	...	...	...	...	...	...	...	...	...
Banks .... 79li *d*	...	...	...	...	...	...	...	...	...	...	...	...	...	...	...
Other Sectors .... 79lj *d*	...	...	...	...	...	...	...	...	...	...	...	...	...	...	...

Minus Sign Indicates Debit

Balance of Payments

Item	1987	1988	1989	1990	1991	1992	1993	1994	1995	1996	1997	1998	1999	2000	2001
Current Account, n.i.e. 78al d	−489.8	−210.2	255.6	390.1	85.1	−57.3	59.1	−274.1	−92.3	−352.9	−650.4	−160.0	−90.2	−137.3	....
Goods: Exports f.o.b. 78aa d	597.4	871.0	1,180.0	2,096.2	1,997.1	1,997.1	2,859.0	3,360.1	4,218.6	3,796.9	3,327.5	3,548.6	2,681.3	2,373.3	....
Goods: Imports f.o.b. 78ab d	−918.7	−1,030.1	−1,015.9	−1,734.8	−1,920.5	−1,988.0	−2,779.6	−3,603.5	−4,489.0	−4,383.4	−4,192.4	−3,941.5	−3,041.5	−2,905.6	....
Trade Balance 78ac d	−321.3	−159.1	164.1	361.4	76.6	9.1	79.4	−243.4	−270.4	−586.5	−864.9	−392.9	−360.2	−532.3	....
Services: Credit 78ad d	172.1	295.9	394.9	418.2	433.3	364.6	438.6	426.2	583.8	600.5	655.0	625.5	568.6	589.3	....
Services: Debit 78ae d	−256.3	−300.8	−303.5	−434.2	−460.3	−464.5	−592.8	−593.4	−710.7	−658.8	−654.6	−575.9	−492.1	−424.7	....
Balance on Goods & Services 78af d	−405.5	−164.0	255.5	345.4	49.6	−90.8	−74.8	−410.6	−397.3	−644.8	−864.5	−343.3	−283.7	−367.7	....
Income: Credit 78ag d	50.3	56.7	88.7	116.3	115.6	157.4	198.3	247.9	272.6	280.9	278.1	266.3	212.0	240.1	....
Income: Debit 78ah d	−161.5	−138.0	−112.1	−114.6	−125.3	−185.7	−142.6	−134.1	−162.9	−171.2	−244.9	−260.3	−193.7	−186.5	....
Balance on Gds, Serv. & Inc. 78ai d	−516.7	−245.3	232.1	347.1	39.9	−119.1	−19.1	−296.8	−287.6	−535.1	−831.3	−337.3	−265.4	−314.1	....
Current Transfers, n.i.e.: Credit 78aj d	28.6	37.7	24.3	43.3	46.6	62.1	78.6	25.6	199.7	183.0	182.2	178.3	176.7	178.3	....
Current Transfers: Debit 78ak d	−1.7	−2.6	−.8	−.3	−1.4	−.3	−.4	−2.9	−4.4	−.8	−1.3	−1.0	−1.5	−1.5	....
Capital Account, n.i.e. 78bc d	.1	.1	.4	12.6	9.8	10.4	22.1	8.8	10.6	14.2	7.5	5.4	19.6	3.0	....
Capital Account, n.i.e.: Credit 78ba d	.1	.2	.4	12.6	9.8	10.4	22.1	8.8	10.6	14.2	7.5	5.4	19.6	3.0	....
Capital Account: Debit 78bb d	—	−.1					....	....							....
Financial Account, n.i.e. 78bj d	78.1	−216.5	−173.9	−147.5	22.2	16.1	8.5	212.9	232.5	152.4	421.3	312.9	134.1	53.2	....
Direct Investment Abroad 78bd d									−5.1	−5.2	−5.7	−5.6	−5.6	−5.7	....
Dir. Invest. in Rep. Econ., n.i.e. 78be d	5.3	8.4	12.8	76.9	86.1	117.5	75.0	137.1	103.2	149.4	235.8	341.9	87.3	81.8	....
Portfolio Investment Assets 78bf d	—	—	—	—	—	—	....	....	−.8	−3.6	−4.3	9.0	−20.9	−8.3	....
Equity Securities 78bk d	—	—	—	—	—	—	....	....	—	—	—	−.7	−6.8	1.4	....
Debt Securities 78bl d	—	—	—	—	—	—	....	....	−.8	−3.6	−4.3	9.7	−14.1	−9.7	....
Portfolio Investment Liab., n.i.e. 78bg d	—	—	—	—	—	—	....	....	—	−.1	—	—	—	—	....
Equity Securities 78bm d	—	—	—	—	—	—	....	....	—	—	—	—	—	—	....
Debt Securities 78bn d	—	—	—	—	—	—	....	....	—	−.1	—	—	—	—	....
Financial Derivatives Assets 78bw d															....
Financial Derivatives Liabilities 78bx d															....
Other Investment Assets 78bh d	68.4	−49.0	−63.5	−49.7	−28.1	−48.4	−65.4	−89.8	−58.5	−31.9	72.9	−5.0	−63.9	−109.5	....
Monetary Authorities 78bo d				−2.5	−2.7	1.6	....	.1							....
General Government 78bp d	2.5	−52.4	−54.8	−22.8	−21.3	27.6	1.6	23.1	−43.1	−59.0	−45.8	60.7	−63.6	−79.6	....
Banks 78bq d	.3	3.4	−8.7	−24.4	3.5	−85.2	−75.2	−1.5	−169.7	3.5	100.5	−42.7	−11.9	−60.3	....
Other Sectors 78br d	65.6				−7.6	7.6	8.2	−111.5	154.3	23.6	18.2	−23.0	11.6	30.4	....
Other Investment Liab., n.i.e. 78bi d	4.4	−175.9	−123.2	−174.7	−35.8	−53.0	−1.1	165.6	193.7	43.8	122.6	−27.4	137.2	94.9	....
Monetary Authorities 78bs d	4.5	−53.3	6.1	−8.8	50.9	1.8	2.1	−1.6	−8.7	−3.5	−5.0	−4.3	−3.8	−3.3	....
General Government 78bt d	−12.8	−11.5	−71.9	−46.7	−51.8	−4.1	−2.6	29.8	101.6	122.5	137.1	112.3	97.6	90.4	....
Banks 78bu d	1.4	−5.4	−10.9	.3	46.9	20.5	−94.2	97.3	118.6	−188.4	71.6	−50.7	−101.5	−2.3	....
Other Sectors 78bv d	11.3	−105.7	−46.5	−119.5	−81.8	−71.2	93.6	40.1	−17.8	113.2	−81.1	−84.7	144.9	10.1	....
Net Errors and Omissions 78ca d	338.3	198.3	−90.6	−138.5	115.7	11.9	−46.4	353.0	−106.0	139.8	5.8	−141.6	−364.4	−260.9	....
Overall Balance 78cb d	−73.3	−228.3	−8.5	116.7	232.8	−18.9	43.3	300.6	44.8	−46.5	−215.8	16.7	−300.9	−342.0	....
Reserves and Related Items 79da d	73.3	228.3	8.5	−116.7	−232.8	18.9	−43.3	−300.6	−44.8	46.5	215.8	−16.7	300.9	342.0	....
Reserve Assets 79db d	−37.8	168.2	−145.2	−220.3	−299.3	360.2	−87.2	−339.3	−60.2	39.4	205.8	−23.4	−116.7	212.8	....
Use of Fund Credit and Loans 79dc d															....
Exceptional Financing 79de d	111.1	60.1	153.7	103.6	66.5	−341.3	43.9	38.7	15.4	7.1	10.0	6.7	417.6	129.2	....

Millions of US Dollars

International Investment Position

Item	1987	1988	1989	1990	1991	1992	1993	1994	1995	1996	1997	1998	1999	2000	2001
Assets 79aa d	....	....	....	....	....	....	....	....	2,569.4	2,566.7	2,284.6	2,311.9	2,513.9	2,419.2	....
Direct Investment Abroad 79ab d									178.6	186.0	194.1	201.3	208.2	213.9	....
Portfolio Investment 79ac d									6.3	9.9	14.2	8.9	32.0	40.2	....
Equity Securities 79ad d									3.4	3.4	3.4	7.8	16.8	15.3	....
Debt Securities 79ae d									2.9	6.5	10.8	1.1	15.2	24.9	....
Financial Derivatives 79al d															....
Other Investment 79af d									1,278.1	1,308.5	1,230.5	1,226.9	1,285.5	1,396.5	....
Monetary Authorities 79ag d															....
General Government 79ah d									188.3	247.3	293.1	232.6	296.2	375.8	....
Banks 79ai d									511.6	507.6	404.2	442.5	452.8	513.1	....
Other Sectors 79aj d									578.2	553.6	533.2	551.8	536.5	507.6	....
Reserve Assets 79ak d									1,106.4	1,062.3	845.8	874.8	988.2	768.6	....
Liabilities 79la d									2,877.1	2,954.2	3,132.1	3,385.5	3,928.6	4,150.9	....
Dir. Invest. in Rep. Economy 79lb d									705.2	829.3	977.7	1,196.1	1,162.5	1,237.2	....
Portfolio Investment 79lc d									.1	—	—	—	—	—	....
Equity Securities 79ld d									—	—	—	—	—	—	....
Debt Securities 79le d									.1	—	—	—	—	—	....
Financial Derivatives 79ll d															....
Other Investment 79lf d									2,171.8	2,124.9	2,154.4	2,189.4	2,766.1	2,913.7	....
Monetary Authorities 79lg d									50.8	47.3	42.3	38.0	34.3	32.8	....
General Government 79lh d									1,004.6	1,054.8	1,146.0	1,318.1	1,854.3	2,001.8	....
Banks 79li d									406.5	218.1	289.5	238.4	136.5	134.2	....
Other Sectors 79lj d									709.9	804.7	676.6	594.9	741.0	744.9	....

Paraguay

		1972	1973	1974	1975	1976	1977	1978	1979	1980	1981	1982	1983	1984	1985	1986
Government Finance															*Billions of Guaranies:*	
Deficit (-) or Surplus	80	†−1.6	—	1.7	−.6	−2.2	1.6	3.1	4.3	1.8	−10.6	3.0	−7.7	−20.4	−6.9	.5
Revenue	81	†11.0	13.5	18.4	21.2	23.9	31.4	40.5	51.2	62.0	72.7	85.8	84.0	102.2	135.3	178.6
Grants Received	81z	†—	—	—	—	—	—	.3	—	.2	.1	.1	—	.3	.2	.1
Expenditure	82	†12.4	13.3	16.3	21.2	25.3	29.2	37.7	45.5	56.8	75.6	86.7	87.3	115.4	126.7	148.3
Lending Minus Repayments	83	†.2	.2	.4	.6	.9	.5	.1	1.4	3.5	7.8	−3.8	4.4	5.6	6.1	5.2
Exch.Rate Adj.to Overall Def./Sur	80x	†—	—	—	—	—	—	—	—	—	—	—	—	−1.9	−9.6	−24.7
Financing																
Net Borrowing	84	....	....	....	....	....										
Net Borrowing: Domestic	84a	†1.1	.3	−1.3	−.1	−.3	.4	1.1	1.6	−.4	−1.8	−.9	−6.1	2.0	−8.0	−5.7
Foreign	85a	†.7	.1	.5	2.0	4.7	3.2	5.7	2.9	12.8	4.9	.6	13.9	18.4	14.9	5.2
Use of Cash Balances	87	†−1	−.3	−.9	−1.4	−2.2	−5.2	−9.9	−8.8	−14.3	7.5	−2.7	....	....	....	....
Debt: Domestic	88a	....	4.2	2.8	2.5	2.5	3.0	4.4	5.9	4.3	4.4	4.0	....	....	18.4	23.6
Foreign	89a	....	7.3	7.5	9.2	13.5	16.3	22.0	24.9	37.8	42.8	43.5	....	....	111.8	....
National Accounts															*Billions of Guaranies*	
Househ.Cons.Expend.,incl.NPISHs	96f	74.6	92.5	126.3	141.1	155.2	190.1	225.2	306.5	399.4	504.1	552.0	642.2	822.0	1,056.1	1,353.7
Government Consumption Expend.	91f	7.8	8.2	9.2	12.0	13.4	16.4	21.5	24.7	34.7	48.6	52.3	58.0	69.3	90.2	121.8
Gross Fixed Capital Formation	93e	13.3	20.4	30.9	39.5	48.8	62.9	81.3	116.1	152.7	194.2	176.9	164.5	231.2	288.0	431.8
Changes in Inventories	93i	1.3	3.5	4.4	6.4	4.0	2.2	6.5	6.8	8.6	10.1	12.1	10.7	14.3	18.5	27.1
Exports of Goods and Services	90c	13.3	18.8	26.1	29.3	31.4	51.3	59.4	69.1	77.6	79.1	89.5	70.1	170.0	308.0	485.7
Imports of Goods and Services (-)	98c	13.4	17.9	28.8	37.8	38.6	59.2	71.3	92.8	112.4	127.4	145.6	127.4	236.3	367.0	586.3
Gross Domestic Product (GDP)	99b	96.9	125.4	168.0	190.4	214.1	263.6	322.5	430.5	560.5	708.7	737.0	818.1	1,070.4	1,393.9	1,833.8
Net Primary Income from Abroad	98.n	−2.0	−2.1	−2.0	−1.5	−1.1	.4	1.8	1.3	5.3	8.8	8.3	5.0	−2.4	−13.0	−21.1
Gross National Income (GNI)	99a	95.0	123.3	166.0	188.9	213.0	264.0	324.3	431.8	565.7	717.5	745.3	823.1	1,068.0	1,380.9	1,812.7
Consumption of Fixed Capital	99cf	5.1	6.5	7.6	9.8	14.0	24.6	32.3	49.2	58.6	77.7	74.3	72.2	107.9	145.3	196.5
GDP Volume 1982 Prices	99b.p	333.1	358.0	388.5	416.5	446.7	495.5	551.7	614.4	684.7	744.4	737.0	714.9	736.9	766.2	766.2
GDP Volume (1995=100)	99bvp	30.6	32.9	35.7	38.3	41.1	45.6	50.7	56.5	63.0	68.5	67.8	65.7	67.8	70.5	70.5
GDP Deflator (1995=100)	99bip	1.8	2.2	2.7	2.8	2.9	3.3	3.6	4.3	5.0	5.8	6.1	7.0	8.9	11.2	14.7
															Millions:	
Population	99z	2.43	2.50	2.57	2.69	2.78	2.87	2.95	3.05	3.15	3.25	3.36	3.47	3.58	3.61	3.72

	1987	1988	1989	1990	1991	1992	1993	1994	1995	1996	1997	1998	1999	2000	2001		

Government Finance

Year Ending December 31

	1987	1988	1989	1990	1991	1992	1993	1994	1995	1996	1997	1998	1999	2000	2001		
Deficit (-) or Surplus	−1.0	21.7	†112.5	189.6	−12.9	77.7	138.7	....	....	....	....	....	....	....	....	Deficit (-) or Surplus	80
Revenue	253.0	323.1	†524.4	796.3	979.7	1,391.6	1,688.0	....	....	....	....	....	....	....	....	Revenue	81
Grants Received	.3	.6	†1.7	1.1	1.6	3.0	4.0	....	....	....	....	....	....	....	....	Grants Received	81z
Expenditure	224.7	295.4	†412.2	608.8	991.5	1,307.4	1,559.4	....	....	....	....	....	....	....	....	Expenditure	82
Lending Minus Repayments	7.8	6.6	†1.4	−1.0	2.7	9.4	−6.0	....	....	....	....	....	....	....	....	Lending Minus Repayments	83
Exch.Rate Adj.	−21.8	—	†—	−÷	—	—	—	....	....	....	....	....	....	....	....	Exch.Rate Adj.to Overall Def./Sur	80x

Financing

	1987	1988	1989	1990	1991	1992	1993	1994	1995	1996	1997	1998	1999	2000	2001		
Net Borrowing	....	....	....	....	....	....	....	....	....	....	....	....	....	....	....	Net Borrowing	84
Net Borrowing: Domestic	−3.2	−16.1	†−2.1	2.0	−151.2	−2.1	−2.0	....	....	....	....	....	....	....	....	Net Borrowing: Domestic	84a
Foreign	4.1	−5.6	†−6.2	−55.1	10.5	20.3	−96.2	....	....	....	....	....	....	....	....	Foreign	85a
Use of Cash Balances	....	....	†−104.2	−136.5	153.6	−95.9	−40.5	....	....	....	....	....	....	....	....	Use of Cash Balances	87
Debt: Domestic	21.1	32.9	21.7	167.5	53.3	45.4	100.0	....	....	....	....	....	....	....	....	Debt: Domestic	88a
Foreign	....	342.0	978.8	913.4	948.5	1,182.9	1,430.1	....	....	....	....	....	....	....	....	Foreign	89a

National Accounts

Billions of Guaranies

	1987	1988	1989	1990	1991	1992	1993	1994	1995	1996	1997	1998	1999	2000	2001		
Househ.Cons.Expend.,incl.NPISHs	1,904.8	2,383.9	3,033.9	4,996.5	6,344.6	7,843.3	9,749.8	13,231.8	15,089.2	16,853.3	17,704.3	20,101.4	19,762.5	22,406.8	25,912.0	Househ.Cons.Expend.,incl.NPISHs	96f
Government Consumption Expend.	176.6	209.1	306.7	401.9	546.5	629.1	801.9	1,012.5	1,275.9	1,528.5	1,693.0	1,928.3	2,135.4	2,601.6	2,639.9	Government Consumption Expend.	91f
Gross Fixed Capital Formation	591.4	768.2	1,045.6	1,425.4	1,961.8	2,117.4	2,642.1	3,366.5	4,082.8	4,478.4	4,749.1	5,168.2	5,342.1	5,638.6	5,294.6	Gross Fixed Capital Formation	93e
Changes in Inventories	34.4	40.6	53.2	55.0	93.9	97.6	109.6	127.7	151.8	156.7	181.0	205.6	221.7	242.5	265.5	Changes in Inventories	93i
Exports of Goods and Services	657.2	1,142.6	1,645.2	2,152.6	2,498.4	2,714.6	4,428.6	5,120.9	6,163.8	5,707.7	5,696.2	6,613.4	5,548.6	5,260.1	6,170.1	Exports of Goods and Services	90c
Imports of Goods and Services (-)	870.8	1,225.2	1,476.3	2,557.0	3,164.5	3,731.1	5,740.2	7,899.3	9,064.9	8,919.8	9,089.3	10,580.0	8,866.1	9,228.7	10,696.0	Imports of Goods and Services (-)	98c
Gross Domestic Product (GDP)	2,493.6	3,319.1	4,608.4	6,474.4	8,280.8	9,670.6	11,991.7	14,960.1	17,698.6	19,804.8	20,934.3	23,436.9	24,144.3	26,921.0	29,586.1	Gross Domestic Product (GDP)	99b
Net Primary Income from Abroad	−68.2	−8.8	92.5	143.6	114.8	22.1	42.9	78.8	158.8	145.1	221.7	304.5	132.2	380.7	....	Net Primary Income from Abroad	98.n
Gross National Income (GNI)	2,425.4	3,310.3	4,700.9	6,618.0	8,395.6	9,692.9	12,034.7	15,039.0	17,857.4	19,949.9	21,156.0	23,741.4	24,276.5	27,301.7	....	Gross National Income (GNI)	99a
Consumption of Fixed Capital	289.1	355.6	459.2	693.9	690.3	769.1	930.7	1,161.0	1,378.1	1,549.9	1,639.2	1,835.0	1,889.6	2,051.6	....	Consumption of Fixed Capital	99cf
GDP Volume 1982 Prices	799.4	850.2	899.5	927.3	950.2	967.3	1,007.4	1,038.5	1,087.4	1,101.2	1,129.7	1,125.0	1,130.4	1,126.4	1,157.0	GDP Volume 1982 Prices	99b.p
GDP Volume (1995=100)	73.5	78.2	82.7	85.3	87.4	89.0	92.6	95.5	100.0	101.3	103.9	103.5	104.0	103.6	106.4	GDP Volume (1995=100)	99bv p
GDP Deflator (1995=100)	19.2	24.0	31.5	42.9	53.5	61.4	73.1	88.5	100.0	110.5	113.9	128.0	131.2	146.8	157.1	GDP Deflator (1995=100)	99bi p

Midyear Estimates

	1987	1988	1989	1990	1991	1992	1993	1994	1995	1996	1997	1998	1999	2000	2001		
Population	3.84	3.96	4.09	4.22	4.33	4.45	4.57	4.70	4.83	4.96	5.09	5.22	5.36	5.50	5.64	Population	99z

(See notes in the back of the book.)

Peru

		1972	1973	1974	1975	1976	1977	1978	1979	1980	1981	1982	1983	1984	1985	1986
Exchange Rates									*Nuev.Soles per Billion SDRs through 1987, per Million SDRs 1988-89,*							
Market Rate	aa	42.0	46.7	47.4	52.7	80.6	158.4	255.6	329.5	435.8	590.1	1,091.7	2,377.8	5,583.3	15,317.5	17,063.5
										Nuev.Soles per Billion US$ through 1987, per Million US$ 1988-89,							
Market Rate	ae	38.7	38.7	38.7	45.0	69.4	130.4	196.2	250.1	341.7	507.0	989.7	2,271.2	5,696.0	13,945.0	13,950.0
Market Rate	rf	38.7	38.7	38.7	40.4	55.8	84.2	156.3	224.7	288.9	422.3	697.6	1,628.6	3,466.9	10,974.9	13,947.5
Fund Position															*Millions of SDRs:*	
Quota	2f.s	123.0	123.0	123.0	123.0	123.0	123.0	164.0	164.0	246.0	246.0	246.0	246.0	330.9	330.9	330.9
SDRs	1b.s	41.0	37.3	37.2	37.1	3.3	2.7	4.8	81.3	9.7	9.8	29.9	.6	22.9	—	—
Reserve Position in the Fund	1c.s	—	30.8	30.8	30.8	—	—	—	—	—	—	—	—	—	—	—
Total Fund Cred.&Loans Outstg.	2tl	30.8	13.6	—	—	158.8	168.8	256.1	373.1	371.6	332.9	588.8	666.3	688.3	639.0	595.5
International Liquidity									*Millions of US Dollars Unless Otherwise Indicated:*								
Total Reserves minus Gold	1l.d	442.5	526.1	925.2	425.5	289.3	356.8	389.7	1,520.7	1,979.8	1,199.5	1,349.6	1,365.7	1,630.5	1,842.0	1,407.2
SDRs	1b.d	44.5	45.0	45.6	43.4	3.8	3.3	6.3	107.1	12.3	11.4	32.9	.6	22.4	—	—
Reserve Position in the Fund	1c.d	—	37.1	37.6	36.0	—	—	—	—	—	—	—	—	—	—	—
Foreign Exchange	1d.d	398.0	444.0	842.0	346.1	285.5	353.5	383.4	1,413.6	1,967.5	1,188.1	1,316.7	1,365.1	1,608.1	1,842.0	1,407.2
Gold (Million Fine Troy Ounces)	1ad	1.089	1.003	1.003	1.003	1.003	1.003	1.004	1.158	1.398	1.398	1.398	1.398	1.398	1.954	2.137
Gold (National Valuation)	1and	41.4	42.3	42.3	42.3	42.3	42.3	42.4	106.4	281.0	400.3	400.3	400.3	400.3	419.6	458.9
Monetary Authorities: Other Liab.	4..d	13.4	17.2	—	20.0	263.7	651.8	688.1	346.0	196.9	32.7	39.7	107.0	116.7	22.6	136.8
Deposit Money Banks: Assets	7a.d	2.6	2.6	165.4	48.9	61.5	48.2	138.4	582.8	387.3	568.1	388.4	312.8	330.7	241.1	320.1
Liabilities	7b.d	69.8	219.6	410.9	537.8	810.8	786.4	644.7	505.0	624.2	763.2	446.9	433.2	362.0	298.2	268.0
Other Banking Insts.: Assets	7e.d	5.2	2.6	—	2.2	9.2	4.5	3.7	25.4	19.3	24.1	61.4	71.3	32.9	28.5	18.4
Liabilities	7f.d	38.8	69.8	98.2	111.1	133.8	146.4	164.2	152.0	190.0	217.6	345.7	299.4	212.5	136.9	140.6
Monetary Authorities								*Thousandths(.000) Nuev.Soles through 1976; Nuev.Soles from 1977 to 1987;*									
Foreign Assets	11	22,600	25,836	35,557	24,120	24,500	†50	104	342	764	657	1,653	4,060	10,746	33,009	28,953
Claims on Central Government	12a	9,900	9,800	9,700	9,700	10,000	†10	23	33	186	351	518	2,867	3,220	2,986	5,003
Claims on Deposit Money Banks	12e	3,800	2,700	3,200	15,900	52,300	†74	106	140	45	174	35	281	1,753	3,507	5,694
Claims on Other Banking Insts	12f	4,900	6,900	10,400	14,400	28,900	†44	72	86	122	209	378	966	2,039	3,754	8,964
Reserve Money	14	33,500	35,700	50,400	53,300	79,100	†98	153	347	734	1,139	1,787	3,845	9,327	29,372	40,966
of which: Currency Outside DMBs	14a	21,900	27,200	33,500	42,600	49,500	†61	91	162	273	437	622	1,116	2,502	8,145	16,435
Time, Savings,& Fgn.Currency Dep.	15	—	—	—	—	—	†—	—	1	1	2	5	28	87	129	61
Restricted Deposits	16b	100	—	—	100	—	†—	—	5	9	1	14	25	124	188	179
Foreign Liabilities	16c	4,392	1,937	—	900	44,395	†126	267	340	409	435	1,351	3,502	8,352	20,971	23,427
Long-Term Foreign Liabilities	16cl	4,400	4,500	5,000	5,900	8,900	†11	27	43	76	104	200	851	1,375	4,421	5,507
Central Government Deposits	16d	—	—	600	400	100	†—	—	—	2	11	12	41	58	619	551
Capital Accounts	17a	2,601	2,990	3,518	3,832	4,463	†11	21	39	38	57	105	269	743	1,441	1,628
Other Items (Net)	17r	−3,793	109	−661	−313	−21,257	†−68	−164	−174	−153	−357	−888	−387	−2,308	−13,884	−23,705
Deposit Money Banks								*Thousandths(.000) Nuev.Soles through 1976; Nuev.Soles from 1977 to 1987;*									
Reserves	20	10,500	7,700	15,700	9,500	26,900	†36	58	158	360	560	1,088	2,469	6,314	19,081	22,548
Foreign Assets	21	100	100	6,400	2,200	4,000	†5	26	145	131	283	369	700	1,720	3,362	4,545
Claims on Central Government	22a	20,500	28,200	29,700	47,700	87,700	†126	189	215	189	320	551	1,259	4,132	9,120	16,483
Claims on Local Government	22b	1,000	1,400	1,300	1,400	1,100	†1	1	1	1	22	25	6	1	27	25
Claims on Official Entities	22bx	4,500	10,000	25,700	40,200	59,200	†83	139	118	129	237	229	380	1,257	2,774	3,989
Claims on Private Sector	22d	36,700	44,900	49,300	63,700	76,400	†87	119	220	469	1,063	1,756	3,779	7,324	16,096	25,682
Claims on Other Banking Insts	22f	2,200	4,200	4,600	5,200	3,200	†4	6	7	8	5	31	99	496	1,621	2,726
Demand Deposits	24	37,600	47,900	71,300	80,100	103,500	†122	177	268	367	519	822	1,639	3,211	13,063	24,940
Time, Savings,& Fgn.Currency Dep.	25	16,700	19,100	21,200	23,400	26,900	†40	92	233	545	1,076	2,186	4,532	10,952	20,637	24,070
Bonds	26ab	2,400	3,200	3,800	4,700	5,300	†4	4	6	10	28	34	42	78	177	404
Foreign Liabilities	26c	1,700	4,800	10,600	14,900	41,100	†72	105	105	172	310	263	616	1,537	3,417	3,573
Long-Term Foreign Liabilities	26cl	1,000	3,700	5,300	9,300	11,600	†14	18	21	38	70	161	353	345	741	163
Central Government Deposits	26d	9,600	10,900	14,200	19,100	16,300	†16	25	75	81	197	189	608	1,598	4,923	7,768
Credit from Monetary Authorities	26g	3,900	2,700	3,300	16,000	52,300	†74	106	141	49	174	62	281	1,762	3,511	5,694
Capital Accounts	27a	8,700	10,400	13,100	16,000	20,500	†27	43	84	144	254	450	975	3,579	9,908	6,339
Other Items (Net)	27r	−6,100	−6,200	−10,100	−13,600	−19,000	†−27	−29	−69	−120	−139	−117	−355	−1,818	−4,297	−3,392
Monetary Survey								*Thousandths(.000) Nuev.Soles through 1976; Nuev.Soles from 1977 to 1987;*									
Foreign Assets (Net)	31n	16,608	19,199	31,357	10,520	−56,995	†−143	−241	42	313	196	408	642	2,576	11,983	6,414
Domestic Credit	32	70,100	94,500	115,900	162,800	250,100	†340	523	604	1,020	1,998	3,291	8,717	16,845	30,973	54,721
Claims on Central Govt. (Net)	32an	20,800	27,100	24,600	37,900	81,300	†120	186	173	291	462	869	3,477	5,696	6,565	13,167
Claims on Local Government	32b	1,000	1,400	1,300	1,400	1,100	†1	1	1	1	22	25	6	1	27	25
Claims on Official Entities	32bx	4,500	10,000	25,700	40,200	59,200	†83	139	118	129	237	229	380	1,257	2,774	3,990
Claims on Private Sector	32d	36,700	44,900	49,300	63,700	76,400	†87	119	220	469	1,064	1,759	3,790	7,355	16,232	25,849
Claims on Other Banking Insts	32f	7,100	11,100	15,000	19,600	32,100	†49	78	93	130	214	409	1,064	2,536	5,375	11,690
Money	34	60,300	75,700	105,500	123,300	155,000	†185	270	461	730	1,075	1,509	2,965	6,059	23,098	43,410
Quasi-Money	35	16,700	19,100	21,200	23,400	26,900	†40	92	235	546	1,077	2,191	4,560	11,039	20,766	24,131
Bonds	36ab	2,400	3,200	3,800	4,700	5,300	†4	4	6	10	28	34	42	78	177	404
Restricted Deposits	36b	100	—	—	100	—	†—	—	5	9	1	14	25	124	188	179
Long-Term Foreign Liabilities	36cl	5,400	8,200	10,300	15,200	20,500	†25	44	63	114	174	361	1,204	1,720	5,162	5,670
Capital Accounts	37a	11,301	13,390	16,618	19,832	24,963	†38	64	123	182	311	555	1,244	4,322	11,349	14,323
Other Items (Net)	37r	−9,493	−5,891	−10,161	−13,213	−39,557	†−95	−192	−246	−258	−472	−965	−680	−3,920	−17,784	−26,981
Money plus Quasi-Money	35l	77,000	94,800	126,700	146,700	181,900	†225	362	695	1,276	2,152	3,701	7,525	17,098	43,864	67,541
Other Banking Institutions								*Thousandths(.000) Nuev.Soles through 1976; Nuev.Soles from 1977 to 1987;*									
Reserves	40	900	800	1,200	1,100	1,900	†2	4	32	86	124	62	175	241	1,245	897
Foreign Assets	41	200	100	—	100	600	†1	1	6	7	12	58	160	171	397	257
Claims on Central Government	42a	4,900	5,900	7,700	10,000	10,800	†18	39	34	28	132	155	72	53	811	666
Claims on Official Entities	42bx	500	3,600	4,400	4,600	7,000	†10	11	11	14	13	31	81	139	373	958
Claims on Private Sector	42d	23,200	29,800	36,600	46,800	60,300	†82	118	171	301	570	1,265	2,639	6,483	12,195	21,127
Claims on Deposit Money Banks	42e	3,400	3,200	3,800	3,900	4,100	†4	7	11	24	42	110	229	138	330	964
Demand Deposits	44	2,300	2,100	2,400	2,700	6,000	†7	11	23	36	62	83	145	307	987	1,151
Time, Savings,& Fgn.Currency Dep.	45	1,100	1,200	1,500	1,900	1,500	†4	12	18	26	58	124	369	1,143	2,135	2,202
Bonds	46ab	11,800	15,100	18,000	22,000	22,700	†27	34	61	106	229	310	403	521	1,182	2,724
Foreign Liabilities	46c	—	—	—	—	—	†—	1	2	11	18	104	216	118	338	301
Long-Term Foreign Liabilities	46cl	1,500	2,700	3,800	5,000	8,700	†16	30	36	54	91	224	454	988	1,571	1,659
Central Government Deposits	46d	100	100	300	100	100	†—	—	—	1	10	17	55	130	77
Credit from Monetary Authorities	46g	4,900	6,900	10,300	14,400	25,700	†39	64	76	108	189	348	880	1,889	3,495	8,563
Credit from Deposit Money Banks	46h	2,200	4,200	4,800	5,300	3,400	†4	6	11	9	11	37	51	529	1,653	2,710
Capital Accounts	47a	6,900	8,200	9,400	11,900	16,700	†22	33	62	112	187	313	450	1,256	2,838	2,838
Other Items (Net)	47r	2,300	2,900	3,200	3,200	−100	†−4	−11	−23	−1	48	129	371	419	1,023	2,645

1987	1988	1989	1990	1991	1992	1993	1994	1995	1996	1997	1998	1999	2000	2001		
															Exchange Rates	
per Thousand SDRs thereafter: End of Period																
46,815.8	†672.9	6,914.3	†735.4	1,373.2	2,241.3	2,966.9	3,182.5	3,433.8	3,738.7	3,683.5	4,449.4	4,817.5	4,595.4	4,328.2	Market Rate	aa
per Thousand US$ thereafter: End of Period (ae) Period Average (rf)																
33,000.0	†500.0	5,261.4	†516.9	960.0	1,630.0	2,160.0	2,180.0	2,310.0	2,600.0	2,730.0	3,160.0	3,510.0	3,527.0	3,444.0	Market Rate	ae
16,835.8	†128.8	2,666.2	†187.9	772.5	1,245.8	1,988.3	2,195.0	2,253.3	2,453.3	2,664.2	2,930.0	3,383.3	3,490.0	3,506.8	Market Rate	rf
End of Period															**Fund Position**	
330.9	330.9	330.9	330.9	330.9	330.9	466.1	466.1	466.1	466.1	466.1	466.1	638.4	638.4	638.4	Quota	2f. s
—	—	—	—	—	—	.7	.3	.5	.2	.2	1.5	.3	1.1	1.4	SDRs	1b. s
—	—	—	—	—	—	—	—	—	—	—	—	—	—	—	Reserve Position in the Fund	1c. s
595.4	595.4	577.0	530.5	493.4	458.7	642.7	642.7	642.7	642.7	749.6	642.5	535.4	428.3	307.8	Total Fund Cred.&Loans Outstg.	2tl
End of Period															**International Liquidity**	
645.8	511.0	808.4	1,039.8	2,443.0	2,849.0	3,407.9	6,992.4	8,221.7	10,578.3	10,982.2	9,565.5	8,730.5	8,374.0	8,671.8	Total Reserves minus Gold	1l. d
—	—	—	—	—	—	.9	.4	.7	.3	.2	2.1	.4	1.5	1.7	SDRs	1b. d
—	—	—	—	—	—	—	—	—	—	—	—	—	—	—	Reserve Position in the Fund	1c. d
645.8	511.0	808.4	1,039.8	2,443.0	2,849.0	3,407.0	6,992.0	8,221.0	10,578.0	10,982.0	9,563.4	8,730.1	8,372.5	8,670.1	Foreign Exchange	1d. d
1.497	1.712	1.967	2.210	1.831	1.822	1.305	1.116	1.116	1.115	1.115	1.100	1.100	1.100	1.100	Gold (Million Fine Troy Ounces)	1ad
513.4	587.1	671.6	728.9	556.5	515.6	434.0	362.9	366.6	349.7	272.0	268.8	270.9	257.6	258.2	Gold (National Valuation)	1an d
260.4	752.0	543.4	1,571.2	1,928.1	1,704.0	1,639.8	1,756.1	1,787.0	1,586.5	1,447.7	1,245.4	1,293.0	1,214.4	1,066.4	Monetary Authorities: Other Liab.	4. d
365.1	399.7	589.7	527.9	1,052.6	991.2	871.8	1,183.8	1,544.9	2,047.2	1,215.7	1,245.8	1,388.6	1,298.7	1,365.7	Deposit Money Banks: Assets	7a. d
262.8	282.0	308.4	250.2	275.9	396.9	415.3	765.8	1,566.1	1,812.4	3,473.6	3,291.0	2,286.3	2,029.9	1,562.9	Liabilities	7b. d
44.2	45.4	56.3	57.8	18.8	16.4	11.1	12.7	12.7	12.7	12.7	1.0	—	—	—	Other Banking Insts.: Assets	7e. d
100.1	91.1	79.7	108.0	108.5	108.7	107.3	71.0	71.0	71.1	71.0	10.3	—	—	—	Liabilities	7f. d
Thousands from 1988 to 1989;Millions Beginning 1990: End of Period															**Monetary Authorities**	
34,118	†527	7,649	†920	2,681	5,461	9,335	16,001	19,093	25,933	31,208	32,399	33,548	33,200	33,344	Foreign Assets	11
32,514	†55	404	†5	117	90	55	614	614	614	614	614	538	425	396	Claims on Central Government	12a
13,274	†151	3,079	†109	152	197	149	64	4	107	—	203	263	97	—	Claims on Deposit Money Banks	12e
23,039	†121	3,446	†104	108	173	209	—	—	—	—	—	—	—	—	Claims on Other Banking Insts	12f
86,248	†576	8,857	†698	1,831	3,586	5,715	7,487	9,823	13,536	18,773	19,847	22,952	23,405	24,474	Reserve Money	14
41,945	†261	5,372	†273	643	1,101	1,591	2,385	3,043	3,245	3,827	3,950	4,609	4,537	4,945	of which: Currency Outside DMBs	14a
176	†6	56	†25	101	194	194	202	78	118	77	83	75	78	114	Time, Savings,& Fgn.Currency Dep.	15
962	†71	701	†21	5	7	1	1	1	1	1	—	1	—	—	Restricted Deposits	16b
62,179	†1,225	10,938	†1,175	2,199	3,300	4,319	4,695	5,010	5,243	5,345	5,375	4,682	3,319	2,105	Foreign Liabilities	16c
6,599	†35	828	†27	330	505	1,104	1,179	1,325	1,285	1,344	1,398	2,435	2,937	2,900	Long-Term Foreign Liabilities	16cl
602	†6	26	†1	3	55	96	3,684	5,384	8,498	7,989	7,558	4,057	2,454	1,447	Central Government Deposits	16d
4,492	†64	680	†91	137	224	254	377	457	592	735	867	871	854	962	Capital Accounts	17a
-58,312	†-1,129	-7,507	†-900	-1,547	-1,951	-1,936	-945	-2,366	-2,619	-2,443	-1,912	-724	673	1,738	Other Items (Net)	17r
Thousands from 1988 to 1989;Millions Beginning 1990: End of Period															**Deposit Money Banks**	
37,298	†260	3,391	†267	852	2,040	3,519	5,326	6,846	10,240	12,135	11,126	11,897	12,382	13,252	Reserves	20
10,240	†200	2,927	†273	1,011	1,616	1,874	2,581	3,569	5,323	3,307	3,924	4,874	4,584	4,704	Foreign Assets	21
35,377	†217	4,697	†497	854	1,422	1,913	1,607	1,028	924	2,437	3,764	4,954	4,778	6,506	Claims on Central Government	22a
77	†2	13	†1	5	19	35	50	31	170	244	94	380	433	337	Claims on Local Government	22b
8,277	†153	1,321	†95	343	331	369	270	204	264	376	968	398	464	419	Claims on Official Entities	22bx
46,300	†340	7,451	†437	1,857	4,076	7,694	13,095	19,090	28,512	37,812	45,835	49,221	47,569	45,464	Claims on Private Sector	22d
4,482	†53	676	†9	19	7	7	3	3	3	—	—	—	—	—	Claims on Other Banking Insts	22f
48,967	†285	4,738	†275	656	1,298	2,142	3,193	4,357	5,633	7,950	10,174	11,018	9,110	8,977	Demand Deposits	24
42,930	†407	9,865	†584	2,641	5,148	9,528	13,501	17,362	25,136	29,510	33,269	37,779	38,737	39,589	Time, Savings,& Fgn.Currency Dep.	25
943	†4	124	†3	11	12	55	102	251	539	806	933	969	871	783	Bonds	26ab
7,101	†130	1,482	†127	232	590	796	1,462	3,127	4,023	8,196	9,160	6,540	5,459	4,178	Foreign Liabilities	26c
269	†11	49	†2	33	57	97	208	490	690	1,252	1,206	1,485	1,707	1,204	Long-Term Foreign Liabilities	26cl
14,874	†79	983	†159	764	1,041	1,248	2,367	1,561	4,808	3,710	3,849	3,718	3,635	3,510	Credit from Monetary Authorities	26g
13,692	†156	3,150	†119	153	207	149	64	4	107	—	203	263	97	—	Capital Accounts	27a
31,457	†459	7,492	†565	1,269	2,096	3,181	4,792	6,261	8,514	11,045	14,309	18,857	20,518	22,616	Capital Accounts	27a
-18,184	†-305	-7,406	†-257	-816	-939	-1,785	-2,757	-2,643	-4,013	-6,157	-7,392	-8,904	-9,925	-10,177	Other Items (Net)	27r
Thousands from 1988 to 1989;Millions Beginning 1990: End of Period															**Monetary Survey**	
-24,922	†-628	-1,843	†-109	1,260	3,186	6,094	12,425	14,524	21,991	20,974	21,788	27,200	29,006	31,764	Foreign Assets (Net)	31n
134,821	†859	17,040	†988	2,544	5,029	8,947	9,588	14,025	17,181	29,784	39,869	47,717	47,579	48,165	Domestic Credit	32
52,415	†188	4,092	†342	204	416	625	-3,830	-5,303	-11,768	-8,648	-7,028	-2,282	-887	1,945	Claims on Central Govt. (Net)	32an
77	†2	13	†1	5	19	35	50	31	170	244	94	380	433	337	Claims on Local Government	32b
8,287	†153	1,321	†95	343	331	369	270	204	264	376	968	398	464	419	Claims on Official Entities	32bx
46,522	†342	7,491	†438	1,864	4,083	7,702	13,095	19,090	28,512	37,812	45,835	49,221	47,569	45,464	Claims on Private Sector	32d
27,521	†174	4,122	†112	127	179	216	3	3	3	—	—	—	—	—	Claims on Other Banking Insts	32f
96,376	†593	10,364	†707	1,607	2,843	4,337	5,589	7,498	8,972	15,175	19,165	22,273	21,072	21,445	Money	34
43,106	†413	9,922	†608	2,742	5,341	9,722	13,703	17,440	25,254	29,587	33,352	37,854	38,815	39,703	Quasi-Money	35
943	†4	124	†3	11	12	55	102	251	539	806	933	969	871	783	Bonds	36ab
962	†71	701	†21	5	7	1	1	1	1	1	—	1	—	—	Restricted Deposits	36b
6,868	†46	877	†29	362	562	1,201	1,386	1,815	1,975	2,596	2,604	3,921	4,644	4,104	Long-Term Foreign Liabilities	36cl
35,949	†523	8,171	†656	1,406	2,320	3,435	5,169	6,718	9,106	11,780	15,176	19,728	21,373	23,578	Capital Accounts	37a
-74,304	†-1,418	-14,962	†-1,147	-2,328	-2,870	-3,712	-3,938	-5,174	-6,674	-9,187	-9,574	-9,829	-10,190	-9,686	Other Items (Net)	37r
139,481	†1,006	20,286	†1,316	4,349	8,184	14,060	19,292	24,938	34,226	44,762	52,518	60,127	59,887	61,148	Money plus Quasi-Money	35l
Thousands from 1988 to 1989;Millions Beginning 1990: End of Period															**Other Banking Institutions**	
3,151	†33	273	†11	33	5	4	—	—	—	—	—	—	—	—	Reserves	40
1,239	†23	280	†30	18	27	24	28	29	33	35	3	—	—	—	Foreign Assets	41
957	†35	361	†17	35	49	54	55	58	65	69	—	—	—	—	Claims on Central Government	42a
3,047	†18	198	†4	40	45	20	20	21	24	25	—	—	—	—	Claims on Official Entities	42bx
47,500	†242	3,744	†204	607	769	743	718	744	803	828	910	809	761	644	Claims on Private Sector	42d
2,283	†7	76	†6	23	11	1	2	2	2	2	—	—	—	—	Claims on Deposit Money Banks	42e
3,820	†19	349	†13	37	32	9	9	9	9	9	21	21	20	20	Demand Deposits	44
3,696	†23	622	†34	102	78	44	42	43	46	47	37	10	9	8	Time, Savings,& Fgn.Currency Dep.	45
4,768	†15	487	†8	28	17	11	6	6	6	6	—	—	—	—	Bonds	46ab
1,389	†29	239	†39	74	125	162	85	90	101	106	—	—	—	—	Foreign Liabilities	46c
1,420	†16	156	†17	31	52	69	70	74	84	87	33	—	—	—	Long-Term Foreign Liabilities	46cl
312	†—	5	†1	5	5	5	5	6	6	6	—	—	—	—	Central Government Deposits	46d
22,764	†122	3,499	†106	108	168	209	—	—	—	—	—	—	—	—	Credit from Monetary Authorities	46g
4,687	†54	656	†13	18	14	13	4	4	5	5	—	—	—	—	Credit from Deposit Money Banks	46h
10,580	†105	1,249	†190	388	506	709	671	698	757	782	865	939	975	1,023	Capital Accounts	47a
4,740	†-26	-2,330	†-148	-35	-91	-385	-70	-76	-87	-92	-42	-160	-244	-406	Other Items (Net)	47r

	1972	1973	1974	1975	1976	1977	1978	1979	1980	1981	1982	1983	1984	1985	1986
Banking Survey								*Thousandths(.000) Nuev.Soles through 1976; Nuev.Soles from 1977 to 1987;*							
Foreign Assets (Net) **51n**	16,808	19,299	31,357	10,620	−56,395	†−142	−242	47	309	190	362	586	2,630	12,042	6,371
Domestic Credit **52**	91,500	122,600	149,300	204,500	296,000	†401	614	727	1,233	2,499	4,324	10,428	20,929	38,847	65,705
Claims on Central Govt. (Net) **52an**	25,600	32,900	32,000	47,800	92,000	†138	226	207	320	593	1,014	3,532	5,694	7,246	13,757
Claims on Local Government .. **52b**	1,000	1,400	1,300	1,400	1,100	†1	1	1	1	22	25	7	1	27	25
Claims on Official Entities **52bx**	5,000	13,600	30,100	44,800	66,200	†93	151	128	143	250	261	460	1,396	3,147	4,947
Claims on Private Sector **52d**	59,900	74,700	85,900	110,500	136,700	†170	237	391	769	1,634	3,024	6,429	13,838	28,427	46,976
Liquid Liabilities **55l**	79,500	97,300	129,400	150,200	187,500	†234	382	705	1,251	2,148	3,845	7,865	18,308	45,741	69,997
Bonds **56ab**	14,200	18,300	21,800	26,700	28,000	†31	38	66	116	257	343	444	599	1,359	3,128
Restricted Deposits **56b**	100	—	—	100	—	†—	—	5	9	1	14	25	124	188	179
Long-Term Foreign Liabilities .. **56cl**	6,900	10,900	14,100	20,200	29,200	†41	75	99	168	265	585	1,658	2,708	6,732	7,329
Capital Accounts **57a**	18,201	21,590	26,018	31,732	41,663	†60	96	185	294	498	868	1,693	5,578	14,187	17,160
Other Items (Net) **57r**	−10,593	−6,191	−10,661	−13,813	−46,757	†−107	−218	−286	−296	−480	−969	−672	−3,757	−17,318	−25,717
Interest Rates													*Percent Per Annum*		
Discount Rate *(End of Period)* **60**	9.5	9.5	9.5	9.5	12.5	14.5	28.5	29.5	29.5	44.5	44.5	60.0	60.0	42.6	36.1
Deposit Rate **60l**	....	....	....	....	....	....	....	....	....	....	....	....	....	....	
Lending Rate **60p**	....	....	....	....	....	....	....	....	....	....	....	....	....	....	40.5
Prices, Production, Labor													*Index Numbers (1995=100):*		
Share Prices **62**	....	....	....	....	....	....	....	....	....	....	....	....	....	....	
Wholesale Prices **63**	....	....	....	....	....	....	....	....	....	....	....	....	....	....	
Consumer Prices(1995=100000000) **64.a**	.2	.2	.3	.3	.4	.6	.9	1.5	2.4	4.3	7.0	14.9	31.2	82.3	146.4
Consumer Prices(1995=100,000) **64.b**	....	....	....	....	....	....	....	....	....	....	....	....	....	....	
Consumer Prices **64**	....	....	....	....	....	....	....	....	....	....	....	....	....	....	
Manufacturing Production **66ey**	....	....	....	....	....	....	....	88.0	95.6	96.3	91.6	74.7	80.3	85.2	100.6
Industrial Employment **67**	....	....	....	....	....	....	....	163.1	164.9	162.6	154.0	137.8	136.0	144.2	
														Number in Thousands:		
Labor Force **67d**	....	....	....	....	....	....	....	....	....	....	....	....	....	....	
Employment **67e**	....	....	....	....	....	....	....	....	....	....	....	....	....	....	1,988
Unemployment **67c**	....	....	....	....	....	....	....	....	....	....	....	....	....	....	112
Unemployment Rate (%) **67r**	....	....	....	....	....	....	....	....	....	....	....	....	....	....	5.3
International Transactions													*Millions of US Dollars*		
Exports .... **70..d**	944.4	1,111.8	1,503.3	†1,290.9	1,359.6	1,725.6	1,940.7	3,490.9	3,898.3	3,255.0	3,258.9	3,015.2	3,147.1	2,978.5	2,530.6
Imports, c.i.f. .... **71..d**	796.5	1,018.6	1,530.5	†2,550.0	2,037.3	1,910.9	1,174.7	1,820.1	2,499.5	3,481.6	3,600.7	2,547.9	2,212.0	1,835.0	2,908.8
Imports, f.o.b. **71.vd**	638.0	815.3	1,275.7	†2,124.8	1,697.7	1,592.4	978.9	1,516.7	2,082.9	2,901.3	3,000.6	2,123.3	1,843.3	1,529.2	2,424.0
																1995=100
Volume of Exports **72**	70.7	50.1	52.7	47.3	51.5	63.0	69.4	80.1	72.6	70.1	77.3	69.0	75.5	79.4	75.8
																1995=100:
Unit Value of Exports .... **74..d**	28.0	41.9	111.0	†61.7	67.3	74.5	75.3	128.8	174.0	150.7	131.8	130.3	121.2	107.5	74.6
Balance of Payments													*Millions of US Dollars*		
Current Account, n.i.e. **78ald**	....	....	....	....	....	−923	−193	730	−101	−1,733	−1,612	−875	−235	102	−1,393
Goods: Exports f.o.b. **78aad**	....	....	....	....	....	1,726	1,941	3,491	3,916	3,249	3,293	3,015	3,147	3,049	2,576
Goods: Imports f.o.b. **78abd**	....	....	....	....	....	−2,164	−1,601	−1,951	−3,090	−3,802	−3,721	−2,722	−2,140	−1,830	−2,649
Trade Balance **78acd**	....	....	....	....	....	−438	340	1,540	826	−553	−428	293	1,007	1,219	−73
Services: Credit................... **78add**	....	....	....	....	....	406	459	594	715	770	784	711	670	695	681
Services: Debit **78aed**	....	....	....	....	....	−523	−470	−560	−880	−1,087	−1,098	−965	−891	−934	−1,013
Balance on Goods & Services **78afd**	....	....	....	....	....	−556	330	1,573	661	−870	−742	39	786	980	−405
Income: Credit..................... **78agd**	....	....	....	....	....	13	16	58	202	204	109	116	157	221	154
Income: Debit...................... **78ahd**	....	....	....	....	....	−436	−594	−1,025	−1,111	−1,223	−1,143	−1,246	−1,334	−1,195	−1,254
Balance on Gds, Serv. & Inc. **78aid**	....	....	....	....	....	−979	−248	607	−248	−1,889	−1,776	−1,091	−391	6	−1,505
Current Transfers, n.i.e.: Credit **78ajd**	....	....	....	....	....	60	59	126	147	156	164	216	156	101	114
Current Transfers: Debit **78akd**	....	....	....	....	....	−3	−4	−4	—	—	—	—	—	−5	−2
Capital Account, n.i.e. **78bcd**	....	....	....	....	....	—	—	—	—	—	—	—	—	8	13
Capital Account, n.i.e.: Credit **78bad**	....	....	....	....	....	—	—	—	—	—	—	—	—	32	46
Capital Account: Debit **78bbd**	....	....	....	....	....	—	—	—	—	—	—	—	—	−24	−33
Financial Account, n.i.e. **78bjd**	....	....	....	....	....	669	−175	−296	−33	377	1,818	−306	−770	−200	−1,240
Direct Investment Abroad **78bdd**	....	....	....	....	....	—	—	—	—	—	—	—	—	....	....
Dir. Invest. in Rep. Econ., n.i.e. **78bed**	....	....	....	....	....	54	25	71	27	125	48	38	−89	1	22
Portfolio Investment Assets **78bfd**	....	....	....	....	....	—	—	—	—	—	—	—	—	....	....
Equity Securities **78bkd**	....	....	....	....	....	—	—	—	—	—	—	—	—	....	....
Debt Securities **78bld**	....	....	....	....	....	—	—	—	—	—	—	—	—	....	....
Portfolio Investment Liab., n.i.e. **78bgd**	....	....	....	....	....	—	—	—	—	—	—	—	—	....	....
Equity Securities **78bmd**	....	....	....	....	....	—	—	—	—	—	—	—	—	....	....
Debt Securities **78bnd**	....	....	....	....	....	—	—	—	—	—	—	—	—	....	....
Financial Derivatives Assets **78bwd**	....	....	....	....	....									....	....
Financial Derivatives Liabilities .. **78bxd**	....	....	....	....	....									....	....
Other Investment Assets **78bhd**	....	....	....	....	....	—	—	—	—	—	—	—	—	105	−232
Monetary Authorities **78bod**	....	....	....	....	....	—	—	—	—	—	—	—	—		
General Government **78bpd**	....	....	....	....	....	—	—	—	—	—	—	—	—		
Banks **78bqd**	....	....	....	....	....	—	—	—	—	—	—	—	—	105	−57
Other Sectors **78brd**	....	....	....	....	....	—	—	—	—	—	—	—	—		−175
Other Investment Liab., n.i.e. **78bid**	....	....	....	....	....	615	−200	−367	−60	252	1,770	−344	−681	−306	−1,030
Monetary Authorities **78bsd**	....	....	....	....	....	22	4	−198	−171	−209	−58	−147	—	74	230
General Government **78btd**	....	....	....	....	....	576	−106	−64	−10	278	934	620	−358	−109	−1,403
Banks **78bud**	....	....	....	....	....	−3	−114	−130	88	39	−279	55	−9	−107	16
Other Sectors **78bvd**	....	....	....	....	....	19	16	26	32	144	1,173	−872	−314	−164	127
Net Errors and Omissions **78cad**	....	....	....	....	....	−111	53	112	414	582	−402	120	−566	−1,504	−125
Overall Balance **78cbd**	....	....	....	....	....	−365	−315	546	279	−774	−196	−1,061	−1,571	−1,594	−2,746
Reserves and Related Items **79dad**	....	....	....	....	....	365	315	−546	−279	774	196	1,061	1,571	1,594	2,746
Reserve Assets **79dbd**	....	....	....	....	....	−80	−134	−1,236	−650	735	−198	−50	−274	−422	476
Use of Fund Credit and Loans .. **79dcd**	....	....	....	....	....	12	111	151	−1	−46	281	84	24	−49	−51
Exceptional Financing **79ded**	....	....	....	....	....	433	338	539	372	85	112	1,027	1,821	2,065	2,321

Banking Survey

Thousands from 1988 to 1989; Millions Beginning 1990: End of Period

1987	1988	1989	1990	1991	1992	1993	1994	1995	1996	1997	1998	1999	2000	2001		
-25,073	†-634	-1,803	†-119	1,205	3,087	5,956	12,368	14,463	21,922	20,902	21,791	27,200	29,006	31,764	Foreign Assets (Net)	51n
158,492	†980	17,216	†1,100	3,094	5,708	9,543	10,373	14,840	18,063	30,698	40,778	48,526	48,340	48,809	Domestic Credit	52
53,060	†222	4,448	†358	235	459	674	-3,780	-5,250	-11,708	-8,586	-7,028	-2,282	-887	1,945	Claims on Central Govt. (Net)	52an
77	†2	13	†1	5	19	35	50	31	170	244	94	380	433	337	Claims on Local Government	52b
11,333	†171	1,519	†99	383	377	389	290	225	287	400	968	398	464	419	Claims on Official Entities	52bx
94,022	†585	11,236	†642	2,471	4,852	8,445	13,812	19,834	29,314	38,640	46,745	50,030	48,330	46,108	Claims on Private Sector	52d
143,847	†1,015	20,983	†1,351	4,455	8,289	14,108	19,343	24,990	34,281	44,818	52,575	60,158	59,917	61,176	Liquid Liabilities	55l
5,711	†18	610	†11	38	29	66	108	257	545	812	933	969	871	783	Bonds	56ab
962	†71	701	†21	5	7	1	1	1	1	1	1	—	1	—	Restricted Deposits	56b
8,288	†62	1,033	†46	393	614	1,270	1,456	1,889	2,058	2,683	2,637	3,921	4,644	4,104	Long-Term Foreign Liabilities	56cl
46,529	†628	9,420	†845	1,794	2,826	4,144	5,840	7,416	9,863	12,562	16,041	20,667	22,348	24,601	Capital Accounts	57a
-71,917	†-1,449	-17,335	†-1,294	-2,386	-2,970	-4,091	-4,008	-5,249	-6,762	-9,275	-9,616	-9,989	-10,434	-10,091	Other Items (Net)	57r

Interest Rates

Percent Per Annum

1987	1988	1989	1990	1991	1992	1993	1994	1995	1996	1997	1998	1999	2000	2001		
29.8	748.0	865.6	289.6	67.7	48.5	28.6	16.1	18.4	18.2	15.9	18.7	17.8	14.0	14.0	Discount Rate (End of Period)	60
....	161.8	1,135.6	2,439.6	170.5	59.7	44.1	22.3	15.7	14.9	15.0	15.1	16.3	13.3	9.9	Deposit Rate	60l
35.7	174.3	1,515.9	4,774.5	751.5	173.8	97.4	53.6	27.2	26.1	30.0	30.8	30.8	27.9	20.4	Lending Rate	60p

Prices, Production, Labor

Period Averages

1987	1988	1989	1990	1991	1992	1993	1994	1995	1996	1997	1998	1999	2000	2001		
....	....	—	.9	4.0	13.2	51.9	95.1	100.0	105.5	143.6	119.8	127.2	113.7	96.8	Share Prices	62
....	....	.1	8.1	33.1	52.0	76.7	90.5	100.0	109.4	117.5	126.1	†132.3	138.0	139.9	Wholesale Prices	63
272.1	2,086.9	....	....	....	....	....	....	....	....	....	....	....	....	....	Consumer Prices(1995=100000000)	64.a
....	2.1	73.0	5,535.7	....	....	....	....	....	....	....	....	....	....	....	Consumer Prices(1995=100,000)	64.b
....	....	....	5.5	28.2	48.9	†72.7	90.0	100.0	111.5	121.1	129.9	134.4	139.4	†142.2	Consumer Prices	64
114.6	99.9	80.6	74.8	79.8	77.5	†81.3	94.8	100.0	101.5	106.9	103.4	102.9	109.8	108.6	Manufacturing Production	66ey
156.3	153.0	†136.2	132.6	125.9	113.1	103.9	102.6	100.0	†97.7	99.4	97.1	91.8	90.8	91.3	Industrial Employment	67

Period Averages

1987	1988	1989	1990	1991	1992	1993	1994	1995	1996	1997	1998	1999	2000	2001		
....	....	....	....	2,513	....	....	2,930	3,103	....	....	7,407	7,512	7,695	....	Labor Force	67d
2,061	....	2,170	....	2,377	2,411	2,610	2,682	2,901	....	....	....	....	....	....	Employment	67e
104	....	187	....	146	251	286	263	221	†462	555	582	625	566	....	Unemployment	67c
4.8	....	7.9	....	5.8	9.4	9.9	8.9	7.1	†7.0	7.7	7.7	....	....	....	Unemployment Rate (%)	67r

International Transactions

Millions of US Dollars

1987	1988	1989	1990	1991	1992	1993	1994	1995	1996	1997	1998	1999	2000	2001		
2,660.8	2,701.0	3,488.0	3,230.9	3,329.1	3,484.4	3,514.5	4,554.6	5,575.1	5,897.1	6,841.4	5,756.7	6,112.6	7,027.7	7,099.7	Exports	70..d
3,562.3	3,348.0	2,749.2	3,469.8	4,194.7	4,861.3	4,859.2	6,690.7	9,224.0	9,472.6	10,264.2	9,866.9	8,074.8	8,796.8	....	Imports, c.i.f.	71..d
2,968.6	2,790.0	2,291.0	2,891.5	3,495.6	4,051.1	4,049.3	5,575.6	7,686.7	7,893.8	8,553.5	8,222.4	6,729.0	7,330.7	7,164.4	Imports, f.o.b.	71.v d

1995=100

1987	1988	1989	1990	1991	1992	1993	1994	1995	1996	1997	1998	1999	2000	2001		
73.6	63.4	73.2	73.0	77.1	81.9	89.9	100.3	100.0	105.7	115.3	98.8	111.2	126.2	143.6	Volume of Exports	72

Indexes of Unit Values in US Dollars

1987	1988	1989	1990	1991	1992	1993	1994	1995	1996	1997	1998	1999	2000	2001		
95.0	93.6	104.2	103.8	84.1	84.9	74.3	84.4	100.0	106.3	102.8	79.9	85.0	113.7	94.2	Unit Value of Exports	74..d

Balance of Payments

Minus Sign Indicates Debit

1987	1988	1989	1990	1991	1992	1993	1994	1995	1996	1997	1998	1999	2000	2001		
-2,065	-1,819	-570	-1,419	-1,504	-2,090	-2,295	-2,560	-4,125	-3,430	-3,057	-3,634	-1,923	-1,628	....	Current Account, n.i.e.	78al d
2,715	2,731	3,533	3,322	3,408	3,662	3,516	4,597	5,587	5,898	6,831	5,757	6,116	7,026	....	Goods: Exports f.o.b.	78aa d
-3,215	-2,865	-2,287	-2,923	-3,597	-4,002	-4,123	-5,595	-7,755	-7,884	-8,554	-8,219	-6,749	-7,349	....	Goods: Imports f.o.b.	78ab d
-500	-134	1,246	399	-189	-340	-607	-998	-2,168	-1,986	-1,723	-2,462	-633	-323	....	*Trade Balance*	78ac d
793	831	836	798	825	838	839	1,063	1,131	1,413	1,554	1,773	1,574	1,572	....	Services: Credit	78ad d
-1,164	-1,164	-1,143	-1,164	-1,237	-1,412	-1,415	-1,568	-1,893	-2,097	-2,342	-2,434	-2,277	-2,355	....	Services: Debit	78ae d
-871	-466	939	33	-601	-914	-1,183	-1,503	-2,930	-2,670	-2,511	-3,123	-1,336	-1,106	....	*Balance on Goods & Services*	78af d
120	123	196	195	220	199	206	338	574	612	727	786	651	739	....	Income: Credit	78ag d
-1,433	-1,638	-1,881	-1,928	-1,589	-1,837	-1,827	-2,142	-2,581	-2,254	-2,193	-2,276	-2,233	-2,280	....	Income: Debit	78ah d
-2,184	-1,981	-746	-1,700	-1,970	-2,552	-2,804	-3,307	-4,937	-4,312	-3,977	-4,613	-2,918	-2,647	....	*Balance on Gds, Serv. & Inc.*	78ai d
123	163	176	281	466	470	514	754	817	890	928	990	1,022	1,027	....	Current Transfers, n.i.e.: Credit	78aj d
-5	....	—	—	-8	-5	-5	-7	-5	-8	-8	-11	-27	-8	....	Current Transfers: Debit	78ak d
36	4	-20	-25	-31	-33	-45	-57	33	23	-49	-57	-54	-68	....	Capital Account, n.i.e.	78bc d
57	50	39	50	56	40	47	32	66	52	25	21	25	24	....	Capital Account, n.i.e.: Credit	78ba d
-21	-46	-59	-75	-87	-73	-92	-89	-33	-29	-74	-78	-79	-92	....	Capital Account: Debit	78bb d
-1,620	-1,573	-1,853	-583	38	738	968	3,908	3,017	3,372	5,590	1,900	1,066	1,097	....	Financial Account, n.i.e.	78bj d
....	....	....	....	—	—	—	—	-8	16	-84	-64	-128	—	....	Direct Investment Abroad	78bd d
32	26	59	41	-7	152	686	3,107	2,056	3,226	1,781	1,905	2,390	680	....	Dir. Invest. in Rep. Econ., n.i.e.	78be d
....	....	....	-48	-8	-39	-26	-55	-5	-105	-251	-137	-228	-539	....	Portfolio Investment Assets	78bf d
....	....	....	-7	26	-20	-6	-31	13	-90	-91	-133	-172	-375	....	Equity Securities	78bk d
....	....	....	-41	-34	-19	-20	-24	-18	-15	-160	-4	-56	-164	....	Debt Securities	78bl d
....	....	....	....	—	—	228	548	163	288	407	-224	-126	101	....	Portfolio Investment Liab., n.i.e.	78bg d
....	....	....	....	—	—	222	465	171	295	157	-346	-107	123	....	Equity Securities	78bm d
....	....	....	....	—	—	6	83	-8	-7	250	122	-19	-22	....	Debt Securities	78bn d
....	....	....	....	....	....	....	....	....	....	....	....	....	....	....	Financial Derivatives Assets	78bw d
....	....	....	....	....	....	....	....	....	....	....	....	....	....	....	Financial Derivatives Liabilities	78bx d
-412	-461	-666	468	-322	290	375	-264	-576	-666	560	65	130	173	....	Other Investment Assets	78bh d
....	....	....	-2	-15	-19	84	-2	-5	-32	-104	20	-6	-34	....	Monetary Authorities	78bo d
....	....	....	....	....	....	....	....	....	....	....	....	....	....	....	General Government	78bp d
-93	-13	-181	64	-475	81	121	-272	-428	-463	869	24	-101	208	....	Banks	78bq d
-319	-448	-485	406	168	228	170	10	-143	-171	-205	21	237	-1	....	Other Sectors	78br d
-1,240	-1,138	-1,246	-1,044	375	335	-295	572	1,387	613	3,177	355	-972	682	....	Other Investment Liab., n.i.e.	78bi d
264	523	-204	131	105	-106	-943	37	-23	-87	-8	-38	-33	24	....	Monetary Authorities	78bs d
-1,478	-1,471	-1,207	-1,045	-158	-450	457	-11	-204	-461	831	-143	-71	664	....	General Government	78bt d
25	8	6	-91	49	169	146	-247	801	223	1,666	-222	-1,001	-230	....	Banks	78bu d
-51	-198	159	-39	379	722	45	793	813	938	688	758	133	224	....	Other Sectors	78bv d
-218	332	-167	-114	993	463	1,153	156	491	897	-311	429	45	469	....	Net Errors and Omissions	78ca d
-3,867	-3,056	-2,610	-2,141	-504	-922	-219	1,447	-584	862	2,173	-1,362	-866	-130	....	*Overall Balance*	78cb d
3,867	3,056	2,610	2,141	504	922	219	-1,447	584	-862	-2,173	1,362	866	130	....	Reserves and Related Items	79da d
1,094	149	-242	-287	-834	-520	-663	-3,059	-921	-1,784	-1,493	1,142	985	329	....	Reserve Assets	79db d
—	—	-24	-63	-51	-49	254	—	—	—	149	-145	-147	-141	....	Use of Fund Credit and Loans	79dc d
2,773	2,907	2,876	2,491	1,389	1,491	628	1,612	1,505	922	-829	365	28	-58	....	Exceptional Financing	79de d

		1972	1973	1974	1975	1976	1977	1978	1979	1980	1981	1982	1983	1984	1985	1986
International Investment Position																*Millions of US Dollars*
Assets	79aa d	....	....	....	....	....	....	....	....	....	....	....	....	....	....	4,329
Direct Investment Abroad	79ab d	....	....	....	....	....	....	....	....	....	....	....	....	....	....	—
Portfolio Investment	79ac d	....	....	....	....	....	....	....	....	....	....	....	....	....	....	—
Equity Securities	79ad d	....	....	....	....	....	....	....	....	....	....	....	....	....	....	....
Debt Securities	79ae d	....	....	....	....	....	....	....	....	....	....	....	....	....	....	....
Financial Derivatives	79al d	....	....	....	....	....	....	....	....	....	....	....	....	....	....	....
Other Investment	79af d															2,524
Monetary Authorities	79ag d															....
General Government	79ah d															....
Banks	79ai d															248
Other Sectors	79aj d															2,276
Reserve Assets	79ak d	....	....	....	....	....	....	....	....	....	....	....	....	....	....	1,805
Liabilities	79la d	....	....	....	....	....	....	....	....	....	....	....	....	....	....	16,663
Dir. Invest. in Rep. Economy	79lb d	....	....	....	....	....	....	....	....	....	....	....	....	....	....	1,152
Portfolio Investment	79lc d	....	....	....	....	....	....	....	....	....	....	....	....	....	....	—
Equity Securities	79ld d	....	....	....	....	....	....	....	....	....	....	....	....	....	....	—
Debt Securities	79le d	....	....	....	....	....	....	....	....	....	....	....	....	....	....	....
Financial Derivatives	79ll d	....	....	....	....	....	....	....	....	....	....	....	....	....	....	....
Other Investment	79lf d	....	....	....	....	....	....	....	....	....	....	....	....	....	....	15,484
Monetary Authorities	79lg d															908
General Government	79lh d															12,704
Banks	79li d															724
Other Sectors	79lj d															1,148
Government Finance										*Thousandths(.000) Nuev.Soles through 1976; Nuev.Soles from 1977 to 1987;*						
Deficit (-) or Surplus	80	−10,800	−14,100	−14,100	−30,600	−48,400	†−79	−80	−18	−140	−416	−557	−2,351	†−3,064	−4,563	−14,734
Revenue	81	45,600	53,300	68,600	87,900	111,400	†154	264	552	1,019	1,523	2,493	3,732	†9,646	28,235	45,331
Grants Received	81z	—	—	—	—	—	†—	—	—	—	—	—	—	†—		
Expenditure	82	56,400	67,400	82,700	118,500	159,800	†233	344	570	1,159	1,938	3,050	6,083	†12,710	32,798	60,065
Lending Minus Repayments	83	—	—	—	—	—	†—	—	—	—	—	—	—	†—		
Financing																
Domestic	84a	8,900	7,100	3,100	13,800	32,600	†45	72	49	125	283	133	1,177	†708	−931	8,453
Foreign	85a	1,900	7,000	11,000	16,800	15,800	†35	8	−31	15	133	424	1,174	†2,356	5,494	6,281
National Accounts										*Thousandths(.000) Nuev.Soles through 1976; Nuev.Soles from 1977 to 1987;*						
Househ.Cons.Expend.,incl.NPISHs	96f	210,000	260,000	330,000	420,000	570,000	†780	1,170	2,031	3,470	6,230	10,120	20,030	46,600	124,490	258,460
Government Consumption Expend.	91f	38,400	45,400	54,700	75,500	101,000	†157	209	301	628	1,096	1,908	3,486	6,682	17,940	34,623
Gross Fixed Capital Formation	93e	37,800	45,400	68,000	96,800	127,800	†154	230	720	1,497	3,041	5,150	7,389	14,034	34,952	66,860
Changes in Inventories	93i	4,000	10,800	16,500	12,400	9,200	†5	9	33	239	575	664	172	−130	40	6,140
Exports of Goods and Services	90c	45,500	53,100	72,100	71,700	95,700	†176	375	957	1,337	1,697	2,861	6,140	13,190	43,737	48,491
Imports of Goods and Services (-)	98c	43,200	54,900	96,400	126,100	139,100	†214	320	559	1,159	2,077	3,383	6,074	10,891	30,522	53,490
Gross Domestic Product (GDP)	99b	294,700	359,200	447,500	550,200	764,500	†1,058	1,678	†3,490	6,010	10,540	17,310	31,160	68,800	189,140	361,270
Net Primary Income from Abroad	98.n	—	—	—	−10,000	−10,000	†−20	−70	−140	−140	−420	−680	−1,770	−3,980	−10,010	−10,460
Gross National Income (GNI)	99a	292,200	355,200	444,100	545,200	752,800	†1,035	1,609	2,977	4,830	10,125	16,632	29,387	64,823	178,374	349,088
GDP Volume 1979 Prices	99b.p	2,699	2,844	3,107	3,213	3,276	3,289	3,299	3,490	3,655	3,856	3,757	3,384	3,559	3,659	4,026
GDP Volume 1994 Prices	99b.p	....	....	....	....	....	....	....	....	....	....	....	....	....	....	....
GDP Volume (1995=100)	99bv p	61.2	64.5	70.5	72.9	74.3	74.6	74.8	79.2	82.9	87.5	85.2	76.8	80.7	83.0	91.3
GDP Deflator (1995=1 Trillion)	99bi p	3,613.2	4,179.3	4,765.9	5,667.0	7,722.6	10,643.5	16,829.8	....	....	....	....	....	....	....	....
GDP Deflator (1995=10 Billions)	99bi p	....	....	....	....	....	....	168	†331	544	905	1,525	3,047	6,397	17,107	29,696
GDP Deflator (1995=100)	99bi p	....	....	....	....	....	....	....	....	....	....	....	....	....	....	....
																Millions:
Population	99z	13.95	14.35	14.75	15.16	15.57	15.99	16.41	16.85	17.30	17.75	18.14	18.57	18.99	19.42	19.84

Millions of US Dollars

	1987	1988	1989	1990	1991	1992	1993	1994	1995	1996	1997	1998	1999	2000	2001		
International Investment Position																	
Assets	3,856	4,168	5,279	5,354	6,475	6,692	7,123	10,725	12,354	14,869	16,047	14,990	14,293	14,252	....		79aa *d*
Direct Investment Abroad	—	—	—	122	122	122	109	109	567	543	602	438	651	505	....		79ab *d*
Portfolio Investment	—	—	—	242	232	246	284	313	294	416	720	1,013	1,224	1,870	....		79ac *d*
Equity Securities	....	....	....	242	232	246	284	313	294	416	582	867	1,070	1,647	....		79ad *d*
Debt Securities	—	—	—	—	—	—	—	—	—	—	138	146	154	223	....		79ae *d*
Financial Derivatives																	79al *d*
Other Investment	2,791	3,105	3,826	3,254	3,549	3,233	2,976	3,490	3,758	4,392	3,714	3,670	3,535	3,324	....		79af *d*
Monetary Authorities	—	—	—	110	97	92	77	64	62	62	48	49	50	46	....		79ag *d*
General Government															....		79ah *d*
Banks	341	354	535	518	993	911	839	1,076	1,503	1,966	1,097	1,073	1,174	966	....		79ai *d*
Other Sectors	2,450	2,751	3,291	2,626	2,459	2,230	2,060	2,350	2,193	2,364	2,569	2,548	2,311	2,312	....		79aj *d*
Reserve Assets	1,065	1,063	1,453	1,736	2,572	3,091	3,754	6,813	7,735	9,518	11,011	9,869	8,883	8,553	....		79ak *d*
Liabilities	20,414	21,625	22,762	24,165	26,786	28,110	29,728	36,210	40,966	43,611	40,493	41,238	40,553	40,740	....		79la *d*
Dir. Invest. in Rep. Economy	1,173	1,258	1,287	1,330	1,370	1,501	1,663	4,462	5,991	6,703	7,742	8,220	8,890	9,900	....		79lb *d*
Portfolio Investment	—	—	—	—	—	27	695	1,636	1,680	3,184	8,138	7,312	7,011	6,409	....		79lc *d*
Equity Securities	—	—	—	—	—	27	689	1,547	1,599	3,111	3,685	2,737	2,859	2,278	....		79ld *d*
Debt Securities	—	—	—	—	—	—	6	89	81	73	4,453	4,575	4,152	4,131	....		79le *d*
Financial Derivatives																	79ll *d*
Other Investment	19,241	20,367	21,475	22,835	25,416	26,582	27,370	30,112	33,295	33,724	24,613	25,706	24,652	24,431	....		79lf *d*
Monetary Authorities	1,062	1,451	1,121	1,249	1,305	1,124	1,045	1,137	1,131	1,013	1,092	948	745	592	....		79lg *d*
General Government	16,248	17,188	18,466	19,376	21,594	22,082	22,765	24,978	26,612	26,039	14,657	15,432	14,963	14,974	....		79lh *d*
Banks	803	811	817	689	708	884	1,036	797	1,598	1,824	3,494	3,272	2,271	2,040	....		79li *d*
Other Sectors	1,128	917	1,071	1,521	1,809	2,492	2,524	3,200	3,954	4,848	5,370	6,054	6,673	6,825	....		79lj *d*

Thousands from 1988 to 1989;Millions Beginning 1990:Year Ending Dec. 31

	1987	1988	1989	1990	1991	1992	1993	1994	1995	1996	1997	1998	1999	2000	2001		
Government Finance																	
Deficit (-) or Surplus	-44,988	†-155	-5,956	†-441	-592	†-1,662	-2,064	2,125	-1,353	3,826	967	-212	-3,889	-3,749	....		80
Revenue	66,424	†403	7,499	†682	3,654	†6,782	10,476	16,181	20,391	24,023	27,705	29,380	28,747	30,543	....		81
Grants Received		†—		†—	56	†49	62	178	111	325	324	405	445	559	....		81z
Expenditure	111,412	†558	13,455	†1,123	4,254	†8,385	12,545	18,250	23,033	24,686	27,232	30,104	34,168	36,052	....		82
Lending Minus Repayments	—	†—	—	†—	48	†108	57	-4,016	-1,178	-4,164	-170	-107	-1,087	-1,201	....		83
Financing																	
Domestic	35,971	†64	4,131	†149	-362	†236	-78	-4,600	-1,524	-4,903	-979	-349	4,202	1,652	....		84a
Foreign	9,017	†91	1,825	†292	954	†1,426	2,141	2,453	2,878	1,077	12	561	-313	2,097	....		85a

Thousands from 1988 to 1989; Millions Beginning 1990

	1987	1988	1989	1990	1991	1992	1993	1994	1995	1996	1997	1998	1999	2000	2001		
National Accounts																	
Househ.Cons.Expend.,incl.NPISHs	507,990	†3,183	76,000	†4,011	20,607	34,934	52,996	71,306	85,933	98,598	110,925	118,629	122,196	131,831	136,264		96f
Government Consumption Expend.	70,175	†314	7,300	†430	2,067	3,566	5,568	8,672	11,786	13,827	15,487	17,568	19,038	20,866	21,173		91f
Gross Fixed Capital Formation	128,330	†859	18,000	†877	4,417	7,405	12,697	20,901	29,095	30,747	37,472	39,163	37,841	37,582	34,742		93e
Changes in Inventories	23,050	†101	1,000	†19	197	375	679	1,030	918	537	337	91	-303	-27	137		93i
Exports of Goods and Services	76,631	†564	15,180	†858	3,260	5,628	8,627	12,590	15,118	17,975	22,272	22,076	25,855	29,851	29,975		90c
Imports of Goods and Services (-)	88,210	†678	12,000	†753	3,862	6,954	11,304	15,922	21,991	24,754	29,219	31,014	29,907	33,346	32,758		98c
Gross Domestic Product (GDP)	718,160	†4,343	105,000	†5,443	26,686	44,953	69,262	98,577	120,856	136,929	157,274	166,514	174,719	186,756	189,532		99b
Net Primary Income from Abroad	-9,850	†-107	-1,616	†-160	-773	-1,083	-1,930	....	....	....	....	....	....	....	....		98.n
Gross National Income (GNI)	712,178	†4,199	113,499	†6,630	32,164	50,977	78,598	....	....	....	....	....	....	....	....		99a
GDP Volume 1979 Prices	4,350	3,970	3,505	3,377													99b.*p*
GDP Volume 1994 Prices				81,983	83,760	83,401	87,375	98,577	107,039	109,709	117,110	116,485	117,590	121,267	121,513		99b.*p*
GDP Volume (1995=100)	98.7	90.1	79.5	76.6	78.3	77.9	81.6	92.1	100.0	102.5	109.4	108.8	109.9	113.3	113.5		99bv *p*
GDP Deflator (1995=1 Trillion)	....	....	....	....	....	....	....	....	....	....	....	....	....	....	....		99bi *p*
GDP Deflator (1995=10 Billions)	54,636	362,018	9,913,947	....	....	....	....	....	....	....	....	....	....	....	....		99bi *p*
GDP Deflator (1995=100)	....	....	.1	5.9	28.2	47.7	70.2	88.6	100.0	110.5	118.9	126.6	131.6	136.4	138.1		99bi *p*

Midyear Estimates

	1987	1988	1989	1990	1991	1992	1993	1994	1995	1996	1997	1998	1999	2000	2001		
Population	20.26	20.68	21.11	21.57	22.00	22.45	22.74	23.13	23.53	23.95	24.37	24.80	25.23	25.66	26.35		99z

(See notes in the back of the book.)

Philippines

		1972	1973	1974	1975	1976	1977	1978	1979	1980	1981	1982	1983	1984	1985	1986
Exchange Rates															*Pesos per SDR:*	
Market Rate	aa	7.362	8.119	8.650	8.778	8.630	8.952	9.608	9.768	9.693	9.544	10.117	14.659	19.369	20.905	25.112
															Pesos per US Dollar:	
Market Rate	ae	6.781	6.730	7.065	7.498	7.428	7.370	7.375	7.415	7.600	8.200	9.171	14.002	19.760	19.032	20.530
Market Rate	rf	6.675	6.756	6.788	7.248	7.440	7.403	7.366	7.378	7.511	7.900	8.540	11.113	16.699	18.607	20.386
															Index Numbers (1995=100):	
Market Rate	ahx	385.6	380.7	379.1	355.2	345.4	347.3	348.5	348.2	342.1	325.3	301.1	236.3	157.4	138.3	126.3
Nominal Effective Exchange Rate	nec	....	....	....	....	....	....	....	319.0	316.9	315.8	314.7	251.4	172.9	156.3	123.1
Real Effective Exchange Rate	rec	....	....	....	....	....	....	....	122.9	129.3	133.5	138.6	116.5	115.4	126.3	98.6
Fund Position															*Millions of SDRs:*	
Quota	2f.s	155	155	155	155	155	155	210	210	315	315	315	440	440	440	440
SDRs	1b.s	22	24	28	23	14	19	13	26	—	2	3	1	20	35	5
Reserve Position in the Fund	1c.s	—	—	—	—	—	—	—	—	—	—	—	—	9	24	39
Total Fund Cred.&Loans Outstg.	2tl	95	76	68	165	348	435	506	618	820	975	906	1,046	903	1,049	1,035
International Liquidity												*Millions of US Dollars Unless Otherwise Indicated:*				
Total Reserves minus Gold	1l.d	480	993	1,459	1,314	1,597	1,479	1,763	2,250	2,846	2,066	888	747	602	615	1,728
SDRs	1b.d	24	29	34	27	16	23	17	34	—	2	3	1	19	39	6
Reserve Position in the Fund	1c.d	—	—	—	—	—	—	—	—	—	—	—	—	9	26	47
Foreign Exchange	1d.d	456	964	1,425	1,287	1,581	1,456	1,746	2,216	2,846	2,064	885	746	574	550	1,675
Gold (Million Fine Troy Ounces)	1ad	1.857	1.057	1.056	1.056	1.056	1.056	1.513	1.702	1.920	1.659	1.866	.289	.786	1.478	2.259
Gold (National Valuation)	1and	71	45	45	45	45	45	118	166	294	508	823	117	288	501	799
Monetary Authorities: Other Liab.	4..d	157	187	282	577	595	49	881	1,562	2,500	2,802	4,308	4,288	4,575	6,253	7,825
Deposit Money Banks: Assets	7a.d	355	675	1,004	1,121	716	639	1,033	1,436	2,170	2,322	2,629	1,873	2,171	2,158	2,158
Liabilities	7b.d	484	716	1,087	1,176	1,209	1,480	2,606	3,721	4,846	4,609	4,843	3,157	3,044	2,500	1,827
Other Banking Insts.: Liabilities	7f.d	....	....	163	160	271	516	582	731	986	1,253	1,643	1,646	1,701	1,203	5
OBU: Foreign Assets	7k.d	....	....	....	....	....	366	719	819	995	1,035	1,253	887	676	643	441
Foreign Liabilities	7m.d	....	....	....	....	....	359	1,248	1,998	2,916	3,798	4,321	4,164	3,809	3,751	3,473
Monetary Authorities															*Billions of Pesos:*	
Foreign Assets	11	2.77	7.05	10.63	10.20	12.54	11.86	14.57	18.68	24.73	22.43	24.49	†12.11	17.63	20.68	51.42
Claims on Central Government	12a	2.91	3.36	4.47	3.32	3.84	4.46	5.98	6.91	7.79	12.47	19.07	†28.65	33.95	33.34	58.67
Claims on Local Government	12b	.46	.26	.27	.35	.72	.81	.74	.68	.56	.46	.43	†—			
Claims on Nonfin.Pub.Enterprises	12c										.01	.08	†.81	.42	4.49	4.09
Claims on Deposit Money Banks	12e	1.24	1.04	2.23	6.27	4.28	2.90	5.86	9.74	14.09	16.88	18.50	†18.06	19.86	27.78	16.00
Claims on Other Financial Insts	12f	.96	.57	.84	1.52	2.27	2.66	3.83	5.11	6.88	10.17	12.53	†19.83	27.52	27.79	9.29
Reserve Money	14	4.47	5.03	6.27	7.12	8.01	9.90	12.30	15.08	16.95	18.64	19.67	†48.67	77.23	88.91	93.24
of which: Currency Outside DMBs	14a	3.43	3.45	4.31	4.75	5.65	6.73	8.14	9.18	10.18	11.63	12.71	†19.59	21.76	24.03	29.26
Time Deposits	15	—	—	—	—	—	—	—	—	—	—	—	†.23	1.09	5.31	5.28
Liabs. of Central Bank: Securities	16ac	—	—	—	—	—	—	—	—	—	—	—	†.62	2.00	1.45	.48
Restricted Deposits	16b												.93	1.29	1.98	2.11
Foreign Liabilities	16c	1.76	1.98	3.39	6.99	8.65	5.67	9.62	15.81	25.22	29.98	43.21	†73.22	105.35	138.72	184.73
o/w: Med.&Long-Term Fgn Liabs	16cl	....	....	....	....	....	....	....	....	....	....	....	36.95	53.79	85.16	116.96
Central Government Deposits	16d	.74	1.91	3.40	1.26	.97	1.49	2.63	2.30	2.33	2.46	2.41	†6.17	13.00	8.70	17.13
Capital Accounts	17a	.34	.31	.33	.34	.37	.42	.41	.68	.50	.53	.52	†1.99	2.63	3.08	3.61
Other Items (Net)	17r	1.02	3.05	5.06	5.95	5.64	5.21	6.02	7.24	9.03	10.81	9.29	-52.37	-103.20	-134.06	-167.11
Deposit Money Banks															*Billions of Pesos:*	
Reserves	20	1.48	3.38	4.21	5.77	6.22	8.32	10.87	12.56	12.19	11.75	10.31	†27.14	40.90	45.14	49.63
Claims on Mon.Author.: Securities	20c	—	—	—	—	—	—	—	—	—	—	—	†—	2.00	1.45	.48
Foreign Assets	21	2.41	4.54	7.10	8.40	†5.32	4.71	7.62	10.65	16.49	19.04	24.11	26.22	42.90	41.08	44.31
Claims on Central Government	22a	.83	1.53	1.38	1.25	1.68	3.27	3.93	4.45	4.98	6.13	9.62	†13.03	15.44	13.65	21.44
Claims on Local Government	22b	1.36	1.09	1.70	4.58	5.87	6.05	6.43	7.38	8.68	7.39	10.02	†.22	.21	.26	.25
Claims on Nonfin.Pub.Enterprises	22c	....	....	....	....	....	....	....	....	....	....	....	15.37	21.59	25.99	18.13
Claims on Private Sector	22d	11.65	15.63	23.34	26.98	†32.36	38.61	49.23	63.32	76.64	92.50	106.00	136.23	128.35	115.03	90.45
Claims on Other Financial Insts	22f	....	....	....	....	....	....	....	....	....	....	....	2.38	4.45	3.51	2.74
Demand Deposits	24	3.03	3.81	4.70	5.57	6.42	8.21	8.81	9.66	12.36	11.90	10.82	†13.07	11.69	11.70	12.81
Time, Savings,& Fgn.Currency Dep.	25	6.45	8.69	9.55	10.80	14.96	19.82	26.24	29.71	36.02	45.24	57.95	†90.87	111.49	123.27	119.68
Money Market Instruments	26aa	1.29	4.04	7.47	9.63	10.87	11.40	11.49	11.95	12.37	16.45	16.57	†17.11	11.28	8.61	4.85
Restricted Deposits	26b	1.04	1.93	1.78	1.86	2.01	2.22	2.84	3.14	3.13	3.12	2.74	†2.90	3.31	2.42	2.98
Foreign Liabilities	26c	3.28	4.82	7.68	8.82	8.98	10.90	19.22	27.59	36.83	37.79	53.28	†44.20	60.16	47.58	37.52
Central Government Deposits	26d	.92	1.89	2.46	2.39	2.23	2.11	2.55	4.17	4.13	4.40	4.29	†11.53	12.29	15.25	17.29
Credit from Monetary Authorities	26g	1.24	1.04	2.23	6.12	4.41	3.13	4.02	7.00	10.09	12.98	13.67	†16.33	19.73	29.19	16.15
Capital Accounts	27a	2.06	2.77	3.64	5.05	5.67	6.73	7.76	8.90	10.47	13.79	16.16	†22.43	27.41	24.77	31.85
Other Items (Net)	27r	-1.59	-2.81	-1.79	-3.26	-4.09	-3.56	-4.85	-3.77	-6.43	-8.97	-15.42	†2.16	-1.51	-16.67	-15.69
Monetary Survey															*Billions of Pesos:*	
Foreign Assets (Net)	31n	.13	4.80	6.65	2.80	†.23	—	-6.65	-14.09	-20.83	-26.30	-47.89	†-79.10	-104.97	-124.55	-126.51
Domestic Credit	32	16.50	18.65	26.15	34.34	†43.55	52.26	64.96	81.38	99.05	122.16	151.06	†198.83	206.64	200.12	170.65
Claims on Central Govt. (Net)	32an	2.08	1.09	-.01	.91	2.32	4.13	4.74	4.89	6.30	11.63	22.00	†23.98	24.11	23.05	45.69
Claims on Local Government	32b	1.82	1.35	1.97	4.93	6.59	6.85	7.17	8.06	9.24	7.87	10.53	†.22	.21	.26	.25
Claims on Nonfin.Pub.Enterprises	32c	....	....	....	....	....	....	....	....	....	....	....	†16.19	22.00	30.48	22.23
Claims on Private Sector	32d	11.65	15.63	23.34	26.98	†32.36	38.61	49.23	63.32	76.64	92.50	106.00	136.23	128.35	115.03	90.46
Claims on Other Financial Insts	32f	.96	.57	.84	1.52	2.27	2.66	3.83	5.11	6.88	10.17	12.53	†22.21	31.97	31.31	12.03
Money	34	6.47	7.27	9.01	10.31	12.07	14.94	16.95	18.84	22.54	23.52	23.52	†33.55	34.44	36.76	43.17
Quasi-Money	35	6.45	8.69	9.55	10.80	14.96	19.82	26.24	29.71	36.02	45.24	57.95	†91.10	112.58	128.58	124.96
Money Market Instruments	36aa	1.29	4.04	7.47	9.63	10.87	11.40	11.49	11.95	12.37	16.45	16.57	†17.11	11.28	8.61	4.85
Liabs. of Central Bank: Securities	36ac	—	—	—	—	—	—	—	—	—	—	—	†.62			
Restricted Deposits	36b	....	....	....	....	....	....	....	....	....	....	....	3.82	4.60	4.39	5.09
Capital Accounts	37a	2.40	3.08	3.97	5.39	6.04	7.15	8.17	9.58	10.98	14.32	16.69	†24.42	30.04	27.85	35.46
Other Items (Net)	37r	.02	.37	2.80	1.01	-.17	-1.05	-4.53	-2.79	-3.69	-3.68	-11.56	†-50.89	-91.27	-130.62	-169.38
Money plus Quasi-Money	35l	12.92	15.95	18.55	21.11	27.04	34.75	43.18	48.55	58.56	68.76	81.48	†124.65	147.02	165.33	168.13

1987	1988	1989	1990	1991	1992	1993	1994	1995	1996	1997	1998	1999	2000	2001		
End of Period															**Exchange Rates**	
29.508	28.711	29.490	39.834	38.121	34.507	38.046	35.647	38.967	37.801	53.936	54.996	55.330	65.143	64.601	Market Rate	aa
End of Period (ae) Period Average (rf)																
20.800	21.335	22.440	28.000	26.650	25.096	27.699	24.418	26.214	26.288	39.975	39.059	40.313	49.998	51.404	Market Rate	ae
20.568	21.095	21.737	24.311	27.479	25.512	27.120	26.417	25.714	26.216	29.471	40.893	39.089	44.192	50.993	Market Rate	rf
Period Averages																
124.9	121.9	118.4	106.5	93.6	100.9	95.1	97.6	100.0	98.1	88.7	63.0	65.8	58.5	50.5	Market Rate	ahx
111.8	103.6	103.4	94.5	85.4	93.9	94.5	101.1	100.0	102.1	98.4	74.8	76.7	69.8	63.6	Nominal Effective Exchange Rate	nec
90.7	88.7	93.8	84.1	83.8	93.2	92.9	97.4	100.0	109.3	108.8	88.7	96.4	89.8	85.4	Real Effective Exchange Rate	rec
End of Period															**Fund Position**	
440	440	440	440	440	633	633	633	633	633	633	633	880	880	880	Quota	2f.s
—	—	1	1	3	—	7	17	5	2	1	1	5	1	11	SDRs	1b.s
39	39	39	39	39	87	87	87	87	87	87	87	87	87	87	Reserve Position in the Fund	1c.s
888	813	895	641	759	800	881	729	489	282	634	1,114	1,328	1,559	1,553	Total Fund Cred.&Loans Outstg.	2tl
End of Period															**International Liquidity**	
968	1,003	1,417	924	3,246	4,403	4,676	6,017	6,372	10,030	7,266	9,226	13,230	13,052	13,442	Total Reserves minus Gold	1l.d
55	—	—	1	4	1	10	24	8	2	2	2	7	2	14	SDRs	1b.d
55	52	51	55	56	120	120	127	129	125	118	123	120	113	110	Reserve Position in the Fund	1c.d
913	951	1,365	868	3,186	4,283	4,546	5,866	6,235	9,902	7,147	9,101	13,103	12,936	13,319	Foreign Exchange	1d.d
2.776	2.841	2.447	2.888	3.366	2.798	3.221	2.892	3.580	4.651	4.988	5.432	6.199	7.228	7.980	Gold (Million Fine Troy Ounces)	1ad
1,046	1,108	959	1,124	1,280	935	1,245	1,104	1,403	1,715	1,472	1,555	1,782	1,973	2,216	Gold (National Valuation)	1and
7,178	6,744	6,027	6,162	6,063	4,531	2,653	2,295	2,523	2,489	2,578	3,272	4,423	4,826	6,029	Monetary Authorities: Other Liab.	4..d
2,640	3,259	3,539	3,910	3,947	4,691	4,778	6,036	6,402	8,185	8,878	9,153	10,114	8,181	7,468	Deposit Money Banks: Assets	7a.d
1,940	2,099	2,024	2,378	2,059	2,995	2,913	4,640	6,420	14,364	15,406	12,751	11,978	10,302	8,730	Liabilities	7b.d
5	6	16	67	213	480	911	963	1,080	49	62	64	46	45	47	Other Banking Insts.: Liabilities	7f.d
505	549	518	508	357	483	508	485	283	174	203	123	121	137	....	OBU: Foreign Assets	7k.d
2,946	2,513	2,265	1,950	1,524	1,418	1,055	1,674	1,545	1,647	1,826	1,296	1,167	928	....	Foreign Liabilities	7m.d
End of Period															**Monetary Authorities**	
41.88	45.04	53.23	57.60	122.40	133.46	†164.01	173.78	203.60	308.76	349.29	422.13	605.18	751.29	804.92	Foreign Assets	11
45.72	40.92	40.03	39.80	32.14	76.24	†293.48	233.87	227.85	240.26	226.57	194.18	237.91	165.80	132.96	Claims on Central Government	12a
—	—	—	—	—	—	†	—	—	—	—	—	—	—	—	Claims on Local Government	12b
4.38	5.05	5.97	6.29	5.99	3.45	†2.31	1.97	1.93	1.82	2.98	4.26	17.76	38.33	30.12	Claims on Nonfin.Pub.Enterprises	12c
19.01	20.54	22.49	28.00	29.14	15.38	†7.27	6.17	7.31	7.68	26.43	18.20	12.69	48.98	40.94	Claims on Deposit Money Banks	12e
8.72	8.18	8.01	7.62	6.80	6.45	†5.91	4.60	6.26	6.48	8.02	13.51	14.18	15.10	10.87	Claims on Other Financial Insts	12f
84.58	95.01	119.79	143.07	171.43	178.15	†210.25	226.93	255.17	338.17	317.63	323.83	442.74	395.88	351.91	Reserve Money	14
35.37	40.64	52.94	61.92	69.39	74.30	†84.08	95.68	110.89	122.95	143.64	146.06	218.47	192.30	194.67	*of which: Currency Outside DMBs*	14a
3.17	1.37	2.04	2.07	3.91	2.24	8.12	24.69	28.37	39.89	13.61	15.47	31.12	52.36	26.65	Time Deposits	15
.60	3.38	3.60	1.94	40.78	67.52	24.79	4.57	.63	.25	.03	.03	.03	.03	—	Liabs. of Central Bank: Securities	16ac
1.47	.43	.13	.16	.16	.18	†6.51	4.92	2.12	1.68	1.68	1.69	.39	.04	.03	Restricted Deposits	16b
174.14	166.62	161.50	198.04	190.51	141.32	†107.00	82.01	85.22	76.10	137.26	189.08	251.76	342.86	410.25	Foreign Liabilities	16c
120.00	113.58	111.81	142.41	127.26	53.38	†42.84	37.47	37.15	31.13	54.79	80.42	124.57	159.04	190.68	*o/w: Med.&Long-Term Fgn Liabs*	16cl
47.55	64.38	79.23	81.78	96.73	168.23	†113.80	84.54	73.43	106.54	78.35	59.49	90.74	95.42	86.52	Central Government Deposits	16d
4.15	4.13	4.31	6.56	6.55	6.61	†21.06	26.49	30.15	30.08	71.98	88.15	100.23	159.45	188.96	Capital Accounts	17a
-195.94	-215.59	-240.88	-294.30	-313.60	-329.25	†-18.56	-33.76	-28.16	-27.71	-7.24	-25.44	-29.28	-26.54	-44.50	Other Items (Net)	17r
End of Period															**Deposit Money Banks**	
52.21	58.46	69.54	83.75	97.54	102.17	114.55	123.30	123.93	142.84	161.06	168.17	190.99	178.09	181.18	Reserves	20
.10	.47	1.03	.82	19.65	3.76	2.31	.94	.08	.08	.03	.03	.03	.03	.03	Claims on Mon.Author.: Securities	20c
54.92	69.54	79.42	109.49	105.18	117.73	132.35	147.38	167.83	215.16	354.90	357.52	407.73	409.03	383.90	Foreign Assets	21
24.21	38.69	54.84	59.70	61.33	84.34	98.89	147.56	177.21	237.53	304.31	300.34	332.42	432.55	534.56	Claims on Central Government	22a
.20	.17	.17	.16	.16	.36	.80	2.37	4.68	6.95	9.07	10.34	12.20	15.52	17.15	Claims on Local Government	22b
13.29	13.15	14.83	19.27	19.87	21.50	22.84	17.07	14.87	16.37	25.65	40.56	47.68	59.18	82.78	Claims on Nonfin.Pub.Enterprises	22c
109.08	128.85	159.87	206.56	221.64	276.30	388.87	491.98	715.32	1,063.80	1,370.07	1,279.19	1,249.58	1,316.59	1,293.29	Claims on Private Sector	22d
3.52	3.62	3.23	5.45	7.91	10.17	11.50	24.61	27.09	60.26	76.61	117.98	130.68	175.13	157.71	Claims on Other Financial Insts	22f
16.75	18.74	25.21	26.76	31.98	34.72	49.10	55.08	72.04	96.41	111.92	134.09	172.87	192.98	191.94	Demand Deposits	24
130.77	168.86	218.09	273.91	322.67	371.44	477.63	613.16	765.20	949.71	1,225.32	1,332.79	1,483.42	1,622.30	1,720.15	Time, Savings,& Fgn.Currency Dep.	25
3.55	2.49	2.83	3.23	3.02	3.51	4.61	4.61	6.24	6.64	12.07	6.11	7.19	4.21	3.98	Money Market Instruments	26aa
3.21	2.89	4.05	11.33	4.33	3.87	4.25	3.43	3.55	2.99	3.28	7.05	4.03	5.16	4.76	Restricted Deposits	26b
40.34	44.77	45.42	66.59	54.87	75.17	80.70	113.29	168.29	377.59	615.86	498.05	482.86	515.10	448.75	Foreign Liabilities	26c
13.26	16.70	17.09	13.78	16.23	26.55	41.76	26.62	39.41	51.73	38.90	32.43	39.86	33.97	42.39	Central Government Deposits	26d
20.01	25.41	25.19	32.06	35.58	22.35	22.17	17.06	16.67	15.26	15.02	10.38	8.47	38.09	26.73	Credit from Monetary Authorities	26g
35.51	42.28	47.34	61.65	76.32	91.07	107.10	132.36	184.71	243.17	327.28	376.53	440.89	467.48	479.22	Capital Accounts	27a
-5.89	-9.18	-2.27	-4.13	-11.75	-12.34	-15.21	-10.40	-25.10	-.51	-47.95	-123.31	-268.28	-293.17	-267.36	Other Items (Net)	27r
End of Period															**Monetary Survey**	
-117.68	-96.81	-74.27	-97.55	-17.80	34.70	†108.66	125.86	117.92	70.23	-48.93	92.51	278.29	302.37	329.81	Foreign Assets (Net)	31n
148.32	157.55	191.41	250.27	243.86	286.82	†669.63	813.42	1,062.38	1,475.20	1,906.05	1,868.45	1,911.82	2,088.82	2,130.52	Domestic Credit	32
9.13	-1.48	-1.45	3.94	-19.50	-34.20	†236.81	270.27	292.21	319.53	413.64	402.61	439.74	468.97	538.61	Claims on Central Govt. (Net)	32an
.20	.17	.17	.16	.16	.36	†.80	2.37	4.68	6.95	9.07	10.34	12.20	15.52	17.15	Claims on Local Government	32b
17.67	18.19	20.80	25.55	25.86	24.96	25.14	19.04	16.80	18.19	28.63	44.82	65.44	97.51	112.90	Claims on Nonfin.Pub.Enterprises	32c
109.08	128.85	160.65	207.54	222.63	279.08	†389.47	492.53	715.34	1,063.80	1,370.08	1,279.19	1,249.59	1,316.59	1,293.29	Claims on Private Sector	32d
12.24	11.81	11.24	13.07	14.71	16.62	†17.41	29.21	33.35	66.73	84.63	131.49	144.86	190.22	168.58	Claims on Other Financial Insts	32f
53.80	61.20	81.28	92.94	107.69	117.54	†143.71	159.90	194.63	233.12	266.33	285.95	395.56	390.55	392.25	Money	34
133.95	170.23	220.13	275.98	326.58	373.67	†485.75	637.85	793.58	989.60	1,238.93	1,348.25	1,514.53	1,674.66	1,746.80	Quasi-Money	35
3.55	2.49	2.83	3.23	3.02	3.51	†4.61	4.61	6.24	6.64	12.07	6.11	7.19	4.21	3.98	Money Market Instruments	36aa
.50	2.91	2.57	1.12	21.14	63.75	22.48	3.63	.55	.17	—	—	—	—	—	Liabs. of Central Bank: Securities	36ac
4.68	3.32	4.18	11.49	4.49	4.05	10.76	8.34	5.67	4.67	4.96	8.73	4.42	5.20	4.80	Restricted Deposits	36b
39.67	46.41	51.65	68.21	82.87	97.67	128.16	158.84	214.86	273.25	399.26	464.68	541.12	626.94	668.17	Capital Accounts	37a
-205.51	-225.81	-245.48	-300.24	-319.73	-338.68	†-17.18	-33.90	-35.22	37.98	-64.42	-152.77	-272.71	-310.36	-355.66	Other Items (Net)	37r
187.75	231.42	301.41	368.92	434.28	491.21	†629.46	797.75	988.20	1,222.72	1,505.26	1,634.20	1,910.09	2,065.21	2,139.05	Money plus Quasi-Money	35l

Philippines

566		1972	1973	1974	1975	1976	1977	1978	1979	1980	1981	1982	1983	1984	1985	1986
Other Banking Institutions																*Billions of Pesos:*
Reserves	**40**	.22	.23	.51	.57	.36	.49	.67	1.30	2.10	1.96	2.72	2.68	3.74	4.30	3.47
Claims on Central Government	**42a**	.59	.41	.74	1.39	2.00	2.10	2.50	2.62	2.69	3.19	2.99	2.54	2.93	6.85	2.78
Claims on Private Sector	**42d**	4.49	5.26	5.55	7.12	10.19	13.35	15.76	20.11	26.23	36.03	42.29	54.17	56.31	39.36	15.63
Time and Savings Deposits	**45**	1.24	1.63	2.21	4.73	5.56	6.18	7.91	9.93	12.36	14.44	16.04	14.49	9.78	13.52	13.32
Bonds	**46ab**	1.11	.54	.64	.55	.46	.30	1.81	2.25	2.65	3.23	4.78	6.03	6.53	5.96	1.45
Foreign Liabilities	**46c**	—	—	1.15	1.20	2.01	3.80	4.29	5.42	7.49	10.27	15.07	23.05	33.61	22.90	.09
Credit from Monetary Authorities	**46g**	.28	.21	.04	.28	1.06	1.33	1.56	1.73	1.77	2.17	2.50	3.98	7.66	8.76	4.16
Capital Accounts	**47a**	.87	2.21	2.31	2.54	3.11	3.61	4.00	4.65	5.82	6.57	7.72	8.37	7.46	7.88	6.50
Other Items (Net)	**47r**	1.80	1.30	.46	–.23	.36	.73	–.64	.06	.93	4.50	1.90	3.47	–2.06	–8.50	–3.65
Liquid Liabilities	**55l**	14.16	17.58	20.76	25.84	32.60	40.94	51.09	58.48	70.92	83.20	97.52	†139.14	156.80	178.85	181.45
Interest Rates																*Percent Per Annum*
Discount Rate *(End of Period)*	**60**	10.000	10.000	6.000	6.000	6.000	6.000	4.000	11.000	4.541	6.692	6.304	8.050	12.108	†12.750	10.000
Treasury Bill Rate	**60c**	....	....	....	....	10.186	10.885	10.880	12.255	12.136	12.547	13.780	14.231	28.529	26.725	16.081
Deposit Rate	**60l**	....	....	....	....	8.500	8.500	8.500	8.667	12.250	13.717	13.742	13.581	21.172	18.914	11.253
Lending Rate	**60p**	....	....	....	....	12.000	12.000	12.000	14.000	14.000	15.335	18.120	19.238	28.195	28.612	17.534
Prices, Production, Labor																*Index Numbers (1995=100):*
Share Prices	**62**	†11.7	16.5	14.0	10.2	10.3	8.2	†10.5	10.3	7.7	6.7	5.5	5.5	4.9	4.3	20.3
Mining(1980=100)	**62a**	191.2	297.0	218.0	138.6	130.7	91.5	109.2	147.6	100.0	77.2	....	....	....	....	....
Sugar(1980=100)	**62b**	88.1	90.9	112.1	135.1	175.7	129.4	108.7	101.9	100.0	110.2	....	....	....	....	....
Wholesale Prices	**63**	4.9	6.0	8.9	9.4	10.7	11.5	12.0	14.3	16.9	19.4	21.5	24.9	41.6	49.2	49.4
Consumer Prices	**64**	6.1	7.1	9.5	10.2	11.1	12.2	13.1	15.4	18.2	†20.6	22.5	23.7	34.7	42.7	42.6
Manufacturing Production	**66ey**	....	....	....	....	....	....	....	....	....	84.6	14.6	17.0	24.2	24.8	24.7
Manufacturing Empl. (1990=100)	**67ey**	....	....	....	....	....	....	....	....	....	111.6	103.6	101.5	95.8	88.4	82.8
																Number in Thousands:
Labor Force	**67d**	....	....	....	....	....	....	....	....	....	....	....	....	....	....	....
Employment	**67e**	....	....	....	....	....	....	....	....	....	....	....	....	19,368	20,327	20,926
Unemployment	**67c**	....	....	....	....	....	....	....	....	....	....	....	....	....	....	1,438
Unemployment Rate (%)	**67r**	....	....	....	....	....	....	....	....	....	....	....	....	....	....	6.4
International Transactions																*Millions of Pesos*
Exports	**70**	7,351	12,735	18,505	16,607	19,005	23,148	25,051	33,696	43,142	44,620	42,411	54,641	88,339	85,811	98,094
Sugar	**70i**	....	....	....	....	....	....	....	....	....	....	....	....	....	....	....
Coconut Oil	**70ai**	562	1,015	2,483	1,669	2,222	2,950	4,293	5,462	4,258	4,214	3,422	5,666	9,677	6,460	6,727
Imports, c.i.f.	**71**	9,474	12,156	23,556	27,226	29,328	31,606	37,885	48,786	62,308	66,984	70,569	88,657	107,670	101,518	107,324
Imports, f.o.b.	**71.v**	8,504	10,846	21,346	24,937	26,954	28,983	34,856	45,310	57,698	62,773	65,322	83,207	99,246	93,396	102,897
Volume of Exports	**72**	....	....	....	....	....	....	....	....	....	....	....	....	....	....	....
																1995=100
Sugar	**72i**	790.4	962.5	1,006.6	634.6	956.9	1,593.7	757.8	817.0	1,132.6	797.7	814.4	638.7	624.3	373.0	144.8
Coconut Oil	**72ai**	34.7	31.9	31.0	45.8	64.3	55.8	73.0	59.7	68.4	77.6	68.7	71.4	43.7	48.6	92.3
Volume of Imports	**73**	....	....	....	....	....	....	....	....	....	....	....	....	....	....	....
Export Prices	**76**	....	....	....	....	....	....	....	....	....	....	....	....	....	....	....
Sugar (Wholesale Price)	**76i**	9.6	10.7	20.7	20.9	17.3	12.7	12.7	12.7	16.5	18.4	23.6	25.6	46.8	61.6	57.8
Coconut Oil (W'sale price)	**76ai**	7.6	19.4	41.6	16.9	18.1	25.9	30.7	40.9	26.4	25.1	22.2	39.9	96.4	53.1	31.2
Import Prices	**76.x**	....	....	....	....	....	....	....	....	....	....	....	....	....	....	....
Balance of Payments																*Millions of US Dollars:*
Current Account, n.i.e.	**78al*d***	....	....	....	....	....	–754	–1,094	–1,496	–1,917	–2,096	–3,212	–2,771	–1,294	–36	952
Goods: Exports f.o.b.	**78aa*d***	....	....	....	....	....	3,151	3,425	4,601	5,788	5,722	5,021	5,005	5,391	4,629	4,842
Goods: Imports f.o.b.	**78ab*d***	....	....	....	....	....	–3,915	–4,732	–6,142	–7,727	–7,946	–7,667	–7,487	–6,070	–5,111	–5,044
Trade Balance	**78ac*d***	....	....	....	....	....	–764	–1,307	–1,541	–1,939	–2,224	–2,646	–2,482	–679	–482	–202
Services: Credit	**78ad*d***	....	....	....	....	....	733	1,013	1,076	1,447	1,791	1,804	1,808	1,642	2,235	2,860
Services: Debit	**78ae*d***	....	....	....	....	....	–856	–1,000	–1,180	–1,439	–1,632	–1,823	–1,733	–1,194	–867	–844
Balance on Goods & Services	**78af*d***	....	....	....	....	....	–887	–1,294	–1,645	–1,931	–2,065	–2,665	–2,407	–231	886	1,814
Income: Credit	**78ag*d***	....	....	....	....	....	352	472	578	762	1,070	1,179	1,319	984	1,053	931
Income: Debit	**78ah*d***	....	....	....	....	....	–477	–590	–784	–1,182	–1,573	–2,200	–2,155	–2,433	–2,353	–2,232
Balance on Gds, Serv. & Inc.	**78ai*d***	....	....	....	....	....	–1,012	–1,412	–1,851	–2,351	–2,568	–3,686	–3,243	–1,680	–414	513
Current Transfers, n.i.e.: Credit	**78aj*d***	....	....	....	....	....	272	328	369	451	485	486	483	387	387	443
Current Transfers: Debit	**78ak*d***	....	....	....	....	....	–14	–10	–14	–17	–13	–12	–11	–1	–9	–4
Capital Account, n.i.e.	**78bc*d***	....	....	....	....	....	1	1	—	—	—	—	—	—	1	2
Capital Account, n.i.e.: Credit	**78ba*d***	....	....	....	....	....	1	1	—	—	—	—	—	—	1	2
Capital Account: Debit	**78bb*d***	....	....	....	....	....	—	—	—	—	—	—	—	—	—	—
Financial Account, n.i.e.	**78bj*d***	....	....	....	....	....	497	1,741	1,563	2,684	2,018	2,847	–389	781	328	146
Direct Investment Abroad	**78bd*d***	....	....	....	....	....	—	—	—	—	—	—	—	—	—	—
Dir. Invest. in Rep. Econ., n.i.e.	**78be*d***	....	....	....	....	....	210	101	7	–106	172	16	105	9	12	127
Portfolio Investment Assets	**78bf*d***	....	....	....	....	....	–3	–5	–1	–1	–2	—	—	–3	–12	—
Equity Securities	**78bk*d***	....	....	....	....	....	—	—	—	—	—	—	—	—	—	—
Debt Securities	**78bl*d***	....	....	....	....	....	–3	–5	–1	–1	–2	—	—	–3	–12	—
Portfolio Investment Liab., n.i.e.	**78bg*d***	....	....	....	....	....	9	4	14	5	5	1	7	—	17	13
Equity Securities	**78bm*d***	....	....	....	....	....	—	—	—	—	—	—	—	—	—	—
Debt Securities	**78bn*d***	....	....	....	....	....	9	4	14	5	5	1	7	—	17	13
Financial Derivatives Assets	**78bw*d***	....	....	....	....	....	....	....	....	....	....	....	....	....	....	....
Financial Derivatives Liabilities	**78bx*d***	....	....	....	....	....	....	....	....	....	....	....	....	....	....	....
Other Investment Assets	**78bh*d***	....	....	....	....	....	–337	–343	–889	–389	–713	–355	108	100	—	—
Monetary Authorities	**78bo*d***	....	....	....	....	....	....	....	....	....	....	....	....	....	....	....
General Government	**78bp*d***	....	....	....	....	....	—	—	—	—	—	—	—	—	—	—
Banks	**78bq*d***	....	....	....	....	....	—	—	—	—	—	—	—	—	—	—
Other Sectors	**78br*d***	....	....	....	....	....	–337	–343	–889	–389	–713	–355	108	100	—	—
Other Investment Liab., n.i.e.	**78bi*d***	....	....	....	....	....	618	1,984	2,432	3,175	2,556	3,185	–609	675	311	6
Monetary Authorities	**78bs*d***	....	....	....	....	....	–109	13	377	781	–192	58	–69	–41	–969	—
General Government	**78bt*d***	....	....	....	....	....	–45	525	972	477	1,072	1,957	176	629	2,565	1,277
Banks	**78bu*d***	....	....	....	....	....	337	934	626	708	496	460	–375	–249	–939	–250
Other Sectors	**78bv*d***	....	....	....	....	....	435	512	457	1,209	1,180	710	–341	336	–346	–1,021
Net Errors and Omissions	**78ca*d***	....	....	....	....	....	210	112	249	124	–487	–364	–336	65	545	34
Overall Balance	**78cb*d***	....	....	....	....	....	–46	760	316	891	–565	–729	–3,496	–448	838	1,134
Reserves and Related Items	**79da*d***	....	....	....	....	....	46	–760	–316	–891	565	729	3,496	448	–838	–1,134
Reserve Assets	**79db*d***	....	....	....	....	....	–56	–898	–462	–1,163	151	792	1,886	–49	98	–1,124
Use of Fund Credit and Loans	**79dc*d***	....	....	....	....	....	102	90	146	259	182	–75	155	–149	164	–10
Exceptional Financing	**79de*d***	....	....	....	....	....	—	47	—	13	232	12	1,455	647	–1,100	—

1987	1988	1989	1990	1991	1992	1993	1994	1995	1996	1997	1998	1999	2000	2001		
End of Period															**Other Banking Institutions**	
3.15	4.43	5.14	7.58	10.14	13.93	20.33	15.51	18.57	18.50	19.78	15.34	14.92	23.56	18.68	Reserves	**40**
5.06	5.28	3.65	5.95	7.92	11.41	10.82	12.93	19.09	3.38	3.95	2.35	1.74	3.46	1.91	Claims on Central Government	**42a**
17.69	21.36	29.05	33.07	45.95	61.24	82.32	115.93	143.41	127.55	139.92	144.74	145.55	152.43	166.17	Claims on Private Sector	**42d**
15.49	20.14	24.84	29.60	40.72	51.30	63.19	69.09	93.73	106.89	120.70	119.08	120.58	131.77	151.64	Time and Savings Deposits	**45**
1.09	.48	.33	.19	—	—	.15	2.28	3.65	4.22	5.39	6.38	6.29	6.38	5.49	Bonds	**46ab**
.10	.14	.36	1.87	5.69	12.04	25.23	23.51	28.31	1.29	2.49	2.49	1.87	2.23	2.44	Foreign Liabilities	**46c**
4.01	3.93	3.82	3.78	3.78	3.72	3.53	3.56	3.65	3.67	5.08	10.59	10.74	11.95	8.40	Credit from Monetary Authorities	**46g**
7.23	8.88	11.08	12.17	13.13	16.11	18.97	27.08	32.99	27.33	35.93	40.73	48.63	49.27	48.26	Capital Accounts	**47a**
–2.03	–2.49	–2.59	–1.01	.68	3.41	2.41	18.85	18.74	6.04	–5.95	–16.84	–25.89	–22.15	–29.48	Other Items (Net)	**47r**
203.24	251.56	326.25	398.52	474.99	542.51	692.65	866.84	1,081.93	1,329.60	1,625.95	1,753.28	2,030.67	2,196.98	2,290.69	Liquid Liabilities	**55l**
Percent Per Annum															**Interest Rates**	
10.000	10.000	12.000	14.000	14.000	14.300	9.400	8.300	10.830	11.700	14.640	12.400	7.894	13.806	8.298	Discount Rate *(End of Period)*	**60**
11.509	14.667	18.646	23.672	21.478	16.018	12.448	12.714	11.761	12.338	12.893	15.004	9.996	9.913	9.734	Treasury Bill Rate	**60c**
8.202	11.315	14.126	19.538	18.802	14.275	9.606	10.539	8.392	9.683	10.194	12.106	8.167	8.305	8.744	Deposit Rate	**60l**
13.338	15.921	19.270	24.118	23.074	19.479	14.683	15.057	14.682	14.840	16.276	16.777	11.776	10.907	12.402	Lending Rate	**60p**
Period Averages															**Prices, Production, Labor**	
46.9	49.0	70.1	61.4	64.4	75.5	89.6	112.2	100.0	97.4	84.9	56.4	87.1	81.7	52.6	Share Prices	**62**
....	....	....	....	....	....	....	....	....	....	....	....	....	....	....	Mining(1980=100)	**62a**
....	....	....	....	....	....	....	....	....	....	....	....	....	....	....	Sugar(1980=100)	**62b**
53.2	59.9	†66.3	71.9	84.2	87.4	87.3	94.8	100.0	108.9	109.4	122.2	129.2	131.6	134.7	Wholesale Prices	**63**
43.9	49.3	54.9	62.1	73.6	79.9	85.4	92.6	100.0	109.0	115.4	126.6	135.1	141.0	149.6	Consumer Prices	**64**
45.5	37.3	45.1	49.2	59.7	63.7	74.7	84.6	100.0	108.6	118.2	†116.0	125.5	144.8	158.0	Manufacturing Production	**66ey**
88.5	97.6	102.3	100.0	91.5	88.3	87.0	85.8	....	....	....	....	....	....	....	Manufacturing Empl. (1990=100)	**67ey**
Period Averages																
....	....	....	....	25,241	26,180	26,816	27,478	28,039	29,637	30,265	31,278	32,000	30,908	....	Labor Force	**67d**
†20,795	21,497	21,849	22,532	22,979	23,917	24,443	25,031	25,698	27,442	27,888	28,262	27,762	27,775	....	Employment	**67e**
†2,085	1,954	2,009	1,993	2,267	†2,263	2,379	2,317	2,342	2,195	2,377	3,016	2,931	3,133	....	Unemployment	**67c**
†9.1	8.3	8.4	8.1	9.0	†8.6	8.9	8.4	8.4	7.4	7.9	9.6	9.6	10.1	....	Unemployment Rate (%)	**67r**
Millions of Pesos															**International Transactions**	
116,807	148,204	168,928	197,962	241,612	248,359	302,998	350,078	450,487	535,054	738,415	1,206,197	1,432,594	1,773,137	1,665,023	Exports	**70**
....	....	....	2,693	3,133	2,212	2,740	1,629	1,713	3,544	2,270	3,102	2,561	2,425	1,128	Sugar	**70i**
7,827	8,608	8,190	8,770	8,203	12,275	9,698	12,552	21,242	14,960	19,846	28,857	13,379	20,450	21,292	Coconut Oil	**70ai**
147,875	184,246	243,013	317,051	353,284	394,536	509,035	596,611	729,960	894,665	1,139,830	1,290,274	1,273,001	1,494,501	1,598,875	Imports, c.i.f.	**71**
138,605	172,174	226,643	297,657	331,079	369,635	479,296	562,163	679,701	835,863	1,060,815	1,213,859	1,201,519	1,387,561	1,506,852	Imports, f.o.b.	**71.v**
....	....	....	166	172	113	130	154	100	111	131	142	155	178	158	Volume of Exports	**72**
1995=100																
106.4	93.1	137.3	161.2	178.9	135.8	211.6	118.9	100.0	207.4	129.1	120.6	93.0	92.4	37.0	Sugar	**72i**
76.9	59.2	57.0	84.6	62.7	65.8	64.1	63.3	100.0	59.1	80.6	87.9	35.7	77.4	105.8	Coconut Oil	**72ai**
....	....	....	246.4	250.6	120.3	143.3	171.9	100.0	117.4	127.6	101.8	113.6	119.9	115.8	Volume of Imports	**73**
....	....	....	102.7	104.7	98.0	98.8	99.2	100.0	106.0	110.0	119.0	130.8	123.0	117.5	Export Prices	**76**
64.4	84.5	90.8	93.0	95.9	95.3	75.6	81.6	100.0	99.8	84.4	150.1	160.7	153.2	29.6	Sugar (Wholesale Price)	**76i**
55.3	75.8	71.4	48.4	61.2	86.8	70.3	90.3	100.0	121.1	117.6	146.1	181.6	122.7	94.9	Coconut Oil (W'sale price)	**76ai**
....	....	....	94.0	90.0	100.1	101.9	103.0	100.0	105.0	107.0	110.0	102.8	99.0	95.3	Import Prices	**76.x**
Minus Sign Indicates Debit															Balance of Payments	
–444	–390	–1,456	–2,695	–1,034	–1,000	–3,016	–2,950	–1,980	–3,953	–4,351	1,546	7,910	8,459	4,503	Current Account, n.i.e.	**78al*d***
5,720	7,074	7,821	8,186	8,840	9,824	11,375	13,483	17,447	20,543	25,228	29,496	34,210	37,295	31,242	Goods: Exports f.o.b.	**78aa*d***
–6,737	–8,159	–10,419	–12,206	–12,051	–14,519	–17,597	–21,333	–26,391	–31,885	–36,355	–29,524	–29,252	–30,377	–28,496	Goods: Imports f.o.b.	**78ab*d***
–1,017	–1,085	–2,598	–4,020	–3,211	–4,695	–6,222	–7,850	–8,944	–11,342	–11,127	–28	4,958	6,918	2,746	*Trade Balance*	**78ac*d***
2,345	2,413	3,225	3,244	3,654	4,742	4,673	6,768	9,348	12,947	15,137	7,477	4,802	3,972	3,151	Services: Credit	**78ad*d***
–1,155	–1,308	–1,564	–1,761	–1,804	–2,308	–3,090	–4,654	–6,926	–9,429	–14,122	–10,107	–7,515	–6,084	–5,090	Services: Debit	**78ae*d***
173	20	–937	–2,537	–1,361	–2,261	–4,639	–5,736	–6,522	–7,824	–10,112	–2,658	2,245	4,806	807	*Balance on Goods & Services*	**78af*d***
1,109	1,179	1,361	1,598	1,969	2,755	2,824	3,782	6,067	6,059	7,698	6,440	8,081	7,804	7,348	Income: Credit	**78ag*d***
–2,299	–2,364	–2,710	–2,470	–2,469	–2,310	–1,900	–1,932	–2,405	–2,777	–3,017	–2,671	–2,910	–4,588	–4,096	Income: Debit	**78ah*d***
–1,017	–1,165	–2,286	–3,409	–1,861	–1,816	–3,715	–3,886	–2,860	–4,542	–5,431	1,111	7,416	8,022	4,059	*Balance on Gds, Serv. & Inc.*	**78ai*d***
575	778	832	717	828	825	746	1,041	1,147	1,185	1,670	758	610	552	515	Current Transfers, n.i.e.: Credit	**78aj*d***
–2	–3	–2	–3	–1	–9	–47	–105	–267	–596	–590	–323	–116	–115	–71	Current Transfers: Debit	**78ak*d***
—	—	—	—	—	1	—	—	—	—	—	—	–9	38	–12	Capital Account, n.i.e.	**78bc*d***
—	—	—	—	—	1	—	—	—	—	—	—	44	74	12	Capital Account, n.i.e.: Credit	**78ba*d***
—	—	—	—	—	—	—	—	—	—	—	—	–53	–36	–24	Capital Account: Debit	**78bb*d***
318	571	1,354	2,057	2,927	3,208	3,267	5,120	5,309	11,277	6,498	483	–935	–6,497	–4,317	Financial Account, n.i.e.	**78bj*d***
—	—	—	—	—	—	–374	–302	–399	–182	–136	–160	59	107	161	Direct Investment Abroad	**78bd*d***
307	936	563	530	544	228	1,238	1,591	1,478	1,517	1,222	2,287	573	1,241	1,792	Dir. Invest. in Rep. Econ., n.i.e.	**78be*d***
–2	–1	–14	—	–15	–115	–949	–632	–1,429	191	–9	–603	–278	–806	234	Portfolio Investment Assets	**78bf*d***
—	—	—	—	—	—	....	....	....	21	30	–184	–55	–42	–4	Equity Securities	**78bk*d***
–2	–1	–14	—	–15	–115	–949	–632	–1,429	170	–39	–419	–223	–764	238	Debt Securities	**78bl*d***
21	51	294	–50	125	155	897	901	2,619	5,126	600	–325	5,094	693	178	Portfolio Investment Liab., n.i.e.	**78bg*d***
—	—	—	—	—	—	....	....	....	2,101	–406	264	512	–183	383	Equity Securities	**78bm*d***
21	51	294	–50	125	155	897	901	2,619	3,025	1,006	–589	4,582	876	–205	Debt Securities	**78bn*d***
....	....	....	....	....	....	....	....	....	....	....	....	....	....	....	Financial Derivatives Assets	**78bw*d***
....	....	....	....	....	....	....	....	....	....	....	....	....	....	....	Financial Derivatives Liabilities	**78bx*d***
—	—	—	—	—	—	—	—	—	–1,745	425	809	–5,669	–15,311	–13,893	Other Investment Assets	**78bh*d***
....	....	....	....	....	....	....	....	....	....	....	—	—	....	....	Monetary Authorities	**78bo*d***
—	—	—	—	—	—	....	....	....	....	....	—	—	....	....	General Government	**78bp*d***
—	—	—	—	—	—	....	....	....	–1,745	425	809	–949	2,267	466	Banks	**78bq*d***
—	—	—	—	—	—	....	....	....	—	—	—	–4,720	–17,578	–14,359	Other Sectors	**78br*d***
–8	–415	511	1,577	2,273	2,940	2,455	3,562	3,040	6,370	4,396	–1,525	–714	7,579	7,211	Other Investment Liab., n.i.e.	**78bi*d***
—	—	—	—	—	—	—	—	—	199	–98	5	75	61	668	Monetary Authorities	**78bs*d***
–462	–68	108	875	375	2,731	1,065	–1,121	–408	–808	–218	–207	181	–125	–78	General Government	**78bt*d***
402	321	370	307	473	1,921	–229	1,694	1,648	5,036	1,668	–1,118	–1,343	–192	–1,207	Banks	**78bu*d***
52	–668	33	395	1,425	–1,712	1,619	2,989	1,800	1,943	3,044	–205	373	7,835	7,828	Other Sectors	**78bv*d***
68	493	402	593	–138	–520	85	157	–2,094	–2,986	–5,241	–750	–3,307	–2,481	–854	Net Errors and Omissions	**78ca*d***
–58	674	300	–45	1,755	1,689	336	2,327	1,235	4,338	–3,094	1,279	3,659	–481	–680	*Overall Balance*	**78cb*d***
58	–674	–300	45	–1,755	–1,689	–336	–2,327	–1,235	–4,338	3,094	–1,279	–3,659	481	680	Reserves and Related Items	**79da*d***
249	–570	–408	388	–1,937	–1,746	–447	–2,107	–873	–4,037	2,610	–1,938	–3,947	73	–476	Reserve Assets	**79db*d***
–190	–104	108	–343	182	58	111	–220	–362	–301	485	659	288	303	–8	Use of Fund Credit and Loans	**79dc*d***
—	—	—	—	—	—	—	—	—	—	—	—	....	105	1,164	Exceptional Financing	**79de*d***

Philippines

566

	1972	1973	1974	1975	1976	1977	1978	1979	1980	1981	1982	1983	1984	1985	1986
Government Finance														*Millions of Pesos:*	
Deficit (-) or Surplus 80	†-1,101	-843	445	-1,360	†-2,352	-2,807	-2,171	-349	-3,385	-12,154	-14,414	-7,468	-9,957	-11,158	-30,648
Revenue 81	†6,950	9,430	11,919	16,657	†17,895	19,782	23,826	29,095	34,151	35,478	37,710	45,290	56,467	68,577	78,714
Grants Received 81z	†22	69	238	181	†405	177	181	224	222	258	283	316	359	380	531
Expenditure 82	†7,507	10,060	9,968	17,276	†18,706	20,542	23,502	25,417	32,561	38,880	40,821	44,942	52,753	64,084	82,409
Lending Minus Repayments 83	†566	282	1,744	922	†1,946	2,224	2,676	4,251	5,197	9,010	11,586	8,132	14,030	16,031	27,484
Financing															
Domestic 84a	†695	594	-631	1,106	†2,302	2,561	362	-2,762	1,152	6,180	9,735	2,048	8,123	11,308	27,068
Foreign 85a	†406	249	186	254	†50	246	1,809	3,111	2,233	5,974	4,679	5,420	1,834	-150	3,580
Debt: Domestic 88a	†4,627	6,356	9,379	11,414	†13,171	15,301	15,571	16,191	18,534	23,227	31,772	42,639	61,350	79,940	116,236
Foreign 89a	†1,536	1,272	3,071	4,937	†6,210	8,517	12,266	20,829	22,569	29,992	40,118	41,784	97,996	107,992	123,540
National Accounts														*Billions of Pesos*	
Househ.Cons.Expend.,incl.NPISHs 96f	39.9	48.2	67.2	76.2	87.1	102.6	118.8	146.6	156.8	181.5	208.1	237.5	362.3	420.8	444.5
Government Consumption Expend. 91f	5.3	6.2	8.9	11.1	13.2	14.3	16.1	18.3	22.1	24.7	28.9	30.6	36.9	43.5	48.4
Gross Fixed Capital Formation 93e	8.8	11.4	18.4	27.1	33.7	36.4	42.3	56.3	66.4	78.1	87.3	110.2	121.0	94.2	97.7
Changes in Inventories 93i	2.7	3.2	6.6	6.7	8.3	7.9	9.0	11.4	4.5	-.8	1.1	-.9	-14.3	-12.1	-4.9
Exports of Goods and Services 90c	9.9	8.1	22.3	21.3	23.2	28.9	32.4	41.5	57.5	67.1	64.5	78.8	126.0	137.3	160.3
Imports of Goods and Services (-) 98c	10.3	8.2	25.4	29.1	31.8	34.8	41.3	53.6	69.4	76.5	82.9	103.6	131.5	125.2	136.2
Gross Domestic Product (GDP) 99b	56.1	72.3	99.5	114.7	135.3	154.2	177.7	217.5	243.7	281.6	317.2	369.1	524.5	571.9	608.9
Net Primary Income from Abroad 98.n	-.5	-.1	.4	-.3	-1.1	-1.0	-.6	.5	-.5	-2.0	-5.9	-8.0	-20.7	-20.5	-20.5
Gross National Income (GNI) 99a	55.5	72.2	99.9	114.4	134.2	153.3	177.0	218.0	243.3	279.6	311.2	361.1	503.8	551.4	588.4
Consumption of Fixed Capital 99cf	5.4	6.5	8.6	11.3	12.9	14.6	16.8	20.5	24.5	30.7	34.7	39.2	53.7	67.2	71.7
GDP Volume 1985 Prices 99b.p	381.5	415.5	430.3	454.3	494.3	522.0	549.0	579.9	609.8	630.6	653.5	665.7	617.0	571.9	591.4
GDP Volume (1995=100) .... 99bv p	47.6	51.8	53.6	56.6	61.6	65.1	68.4	72.3	76.0	78.6	81.5	83.0	76.9	71.3	73.7
GDP Deflator (1995=100) .... 99bi p	6.2	7.3	9.7	10.6	11.5	12.4	13.6	15.8	16.8	18.8	20.4	23.3	35.8	42.1	43.3
														Millions:	
Population 99z	38.99	40.12	41.30	42.07	43.41	44.58	45.79	47.04	48.32	49.54	50.78	52.06	53.35	54.67	56.00

	1987	1988	1989	1990	1991	1992	1993	1994	1995	1996	1997	1998	1999	2000	2001		

Government Finance

Year Ending December 31

1987	1988	1989	1990	1991	1992	1993	1994	1995	1996	1997	1998	1999	2000	2001		
−16,728	−23,244	−19,568	−37,194	−26,349	−15,965	−21,891	18,114	11,074	6,256	1,564	−49,981	−111,658	−136,110	−147,023	Deficit (-) or Surplus	80
101,495	111,086	150,709	178,346	217,598	240,570	258,855	334,488	360,232	409,880	470,087	462,119	478,210	504,349	561,857	Revenue	81
1,719	1,775	1,701	2,556	3,189	2,145	1,550	739	988	569	1,756	396	292	1,376	1,991	Grants Received	81z
108,451	128,867	166,205	211,184	239,470	265,629	272,391	309,942	341,726	401,017	466,690	511,078	585,425	638,665	706,443	Expenditure	82
11,491	7,238	5,773	6,912	7,666	−6,949	9,905	7,171	8,420	3,176	3,589	1,418	4,735	3,170	4,428	Lending Minus Repayments	83
															Financing	
9,947	19,002	11,358	33,068	19,469	1,576	8,979	−4,408	2,272	−348	5,254	37,635	28,858	90,927	124,108	Domestic	84a
6,781	4,242	8,210	4,126	6,880	14,390	12,912	−13,706	−13,346	−5,908	−6,818	12,346	82,800	45,183	22,915	Foreign	85a
224,697	260,359	284,073	293,821	330,380	435,110	640,867	638,025	....	....	....	....	....	....	....	Debt: Domestic	88a
155,308	165,539	176,037	258,820	289,858	278,150	348,955	317,068	....	....	....	....	....	....	....	Foreign	89a

National Accounts

Billions of Pesos

1987	1988	1989	1990	1991	1992	1993	1994	1995	1996	1997	1998	1999	2000	2001		
482.3	558.8	649.3	767.1	916.4	1,019.2	1,122.5	1,258.8	1,411.9	1,595.3	1,762.0	1,980.1	2,161.6	2,335.5	2,561.2	Househ.Cons.Expend.,incl.NPISHs	96f
57.3	72.2	88.2	108.8	123.9	130.5	149.1	182.8	217.0	259.5	319.9	354.4	389.2	422.4	444.5	Government Consumption Expend.	91f
112.7	142.2	192.7	249.0	250.1	282.8	350.5	400.1	423.2	508.7	592.6	563.6	568.2	596.6	624.2	Gross Fixed Capital Formation	93e
6.8	7.0	7.2	11.2	2.2	5.6	3.1	7.2	4.7	12.9	8.7	−21.5	−10.0	−7.3	15.5	Changes in Inventories	93i
181.9	226.9	260.2	296.4	369.4	393.7	462.4	572.6	693.0	879.8	1,188.0	1,389.9	1,532.2	1,859.4	1,794.9	Exports of Goods and Services	90c
179.0	215.3	280.1	358.5	406.7	459.9	586.9	679.4	842.1	1,070.6	1,438.9	1,566.6	1,527.4	1,656.9	1,727.9	Imports of Goods and Services (-)	98c
682.8	799.2	925.4	1,077.2	1,248.0	1,351.6	1,474.5	1,692.9	1,906.0	2,171.9	2,426.7	2,665.1	2,976.9	3,302.6	3,642.8	Gross Domestic Product (GDP)	99b
−17.3	−17.1	−20.0	−5.8	6.6	23.3	35.1	43.5	52.6	89.4	101.6	137.1	159.3	188.5	217.4	Net Primary Income from Abroad	98.n
665.4	782.1	905.5	1,071.4	1,254.6	1,374.8	1,509.5	1,736.4	1,958.6	2,261.3	2,528.3	2,802.1	3,136.2	3,491.1	3,860.3	Gross National Income (GNI)	99a
77.6	67.2	72.0	82.5	101.0	109.1	131.6	151.5	172.0	190.5	....	....	....	....	....	Consumption of Fixed Capital	99cf
616.9	658.6	699.4	720.7	716.5	718.9	734.2	766.4	802.2	849.1	893.2	888.0	918.2	955.0	987.4	GDP Volume 1985 Prices	99b,p
76.9	82.1	87.2	89.8	89.3	89.6	91.5	95.5	100.0	105.8	111.3	110.7	114.5	119.0	123.1	GDP Volume (1995=100)	99bv p
46.6	51.1	55.7	62.9	73.3	79.1	84.5	93.0	100.0	107.7	114.4	126.3	136.5	145.6	155.3	GDP Deflator (1995=100)	99bi p

Midyear Estimates

1987	1988	1989	1990	1991	1992	1993	1994	1995	1996	1997	1998	1999	2000	2001		
57.36	58.72	60.10	61.48	†63.69	65.34	66.98	68.62	70.27	71.90	73.53	75.15	74.75	76.32	77.13	**Population**	99z

(See notes in the back of the book.)

Poland

964

Exchange Rates

Zlotys per Million SDRs through 1977 1977, per Thousand SDRs in 1978-89,

Item	Code	1972	1973	1974	1975	1976	1977	1978	1979	1980	1981	1982	1983	1984	1985	1986
Market Rate	aa	399.54	400.51	406.48	388.66	385.73	403.28	†4.33	5.14	5.87	6.50	9.54	10.30	12.37	16.24	24.17

Zlotys per Million US$ through 1977, per Thousand US$ in 1978-89,

Item	Code	1972	1973	1974	1975	1976	1977	1978	1979	1980	1981	1982	1983	1984	1985	1986
Market Rate	ae	368.00	332.00	332.00	332.00	332.00	332.00	†3.32	3.90	4.61	5.58	8.65	9.84	12.62	14.79	19.76
Market Rate	rf	368.00	335.00	332.00	332.00	332.00	332.00	....	4.02	4.42	5.12	8.48	9.16	11.32	14.71	17.53

Index Numbers (1995=100):

Item	Code	1972	1973	1974	1975	1976	1977	1978	1979	1980	1981	1982	1983	1984	1985	1986
Market Rate	ahx	658,734.6	724,211.3	730,163.7	730,163.7	730,163.7	730,163.7	....	60,362.1	54,836.8	47,685.1	28,597.7	26,564.9	21,560.8	16,519.5	13,970.6
Nominal Effective Exchange Rate	ne c	...	...	...	...	...	...	...	33,575.5	33,441.9	34,338.7	23,365.7	24,018.5	22,014.9	18,286.5	12,956.5
Real Effective Exchange Rate	re c	...	...	...	...	...	...	...	...	74.2	82.3	102.3	123.2	120.7	103.6	81.3

Fund Position

Millions of SDRs:

Item	Code	1972	1973	1974	1975	1976	1977	1978	1979	1980	1981	1982	1983	1984	1985	1986
Quota	2f. s	...	...	...	...	...	...	...	...	...	...	...	...	...	...	680
SDRs	1b. s	...	...	...	...	...	...	...	...	...	...	...	...	...	...	—
Reserve Position in the Fund	1c. s	...	...	...	...	...	...	...	...	...	...	...	...	...	...	—
Total Fund Cred.&Loans Outstg.	2tl															—

International Liquidity

Millions of US Dollars Unless Otherwise Indicated:

Item	Code	1972	1973	1974	1975	1976	1977	1978	1979	1980	1981	1982	1983	1984	1985	1986
Total Reserves minus Gold	1l. d								565.1	127.6	277.8	646.8	765.2	1,106.0	870.4	697.8
SDRs	1b. d								...	...	...	...	...	...	...	.1
Reserve Position in the Fund	1c. d															
Foreign Exchange	1d. d								565.1	127.6	277.8	646.8	765.2	1,106.0	870.4	697.7
Gold (Million Fine Troy Ounces)	1ad								1.285	.758	.470	.471	.472	.472	.472	.472
Gold (National Valuation)	1an d								267.3	303.0	188.0	188.5	188.8	188.8	188.8	188.9
Monetary Authorities: Other Liab.	4..d								510.1	427.8	428.0	387.5	668.9	640.1	771.6	700.3
Deposit Money Banks: Assets	7a. d								1,576.5	1,476.7	2,034.4	1,713.1	1,639.7	1,895.6	2,295.1	2,373.2
Liabilities	7b. d								23,476.0	25,318.1	27,593.1	25,544.2	24,039.8	23,394.3	26,681.1	30,876.9

Monetary Authorities

Millions of Zlotys:

Item	Code	1972	1973	1974	1975	1976	1977	1978	1979	1980	1981	1982	1983	1984	1985	1986
Foreign Assets	11	...	...	...	...	...	...		3	2	†3	7	10	17	17	24
Claims on General Government	12a								—	3	†20	23	39	52	68	72
Claims on Nonfin.Pub.Enterprises	12c								...	...	...	...	...	...	...	...
Claims on Private Sector	12d								...	...	...	...	...	...	...	...
Claims on Deposit Money Banks	12e								180	200	†189	197	207	202	216	227
Reserve Money	14								109	142	†168	190	207	219	233	244
of which: Currency Outside DMBs	14a								24	29	†40	61	72	82	101	117
Nonreserve Liabilities to Banks	16b								—	—	—	—	—	—	—	—
Foreign Liabilities	16c								2	2	†2	3	7	8	11	14
General Government Deposits	16d								68	56	†37	25	32	47	64	72
Capital Accounts	17a								4	4	†4	4	4	4	4	4
Other Items (Net)	17r								—	1	†1	5	6	-7	-11	-11

Deposit Money Banks

Millions of Zlotys:

Item	Code	1972	1973	1974	1975	1976	1977	1978	1979	1980	1981	1982	1983	1984	1985	1986
Reserves	20								85	113	†128	130	135	136	131	127
Claims on Mon.Author.: Securities	20c								...	...	...	...	...	...	...	...
Other Claims on Monetary Author.	20n								—	—	—	—	—	—	—	—
Foreign Assets	21								6	7	†11	15	16	24	34	47
Claims on General Government	22a								8	11	†13	18	15	16	28	25
Claims on Nonfin.Pub.Enterprises	22c								283	308	†331	379	415	454	529	629
Claims on Private Sector	22d								15	16	†16	23	29	36	46	58
Demand Deposits	24								55	59	†67	90	93	108	128	163
Time, Savings,& Fgn.Currency Dep.	25								56	64	†80	107	129	158	192	253
Foreign Liabilities	26c								17	25	†27	36	40	58	70	82
General Government Deposits	26d								7	5	†4	14	10	10	17	21
of which: Local Govt. Dep.	26db								4	3	†4	9	10	10	16	21
Credit from Monetary Authorities	26g								180	200	†189	197	207	202	216	227
Capital Accounts	27a								3	3	†3	3	5	6	6	7
Other Items (Net)	27r								80	98	†129	118	126	124	141	133

Monetary Survey

Millions of Zlotys:

Item	Code	1972	1973	1974	1975	1976	1977	1978	1979	1980	1981	1982	1983	1984	1985	1986
Foreign Assets (Net)	31n								-10	-18	†-15	-17	-20	-25	-31	-25
Domestic Credit	32								232	276	†339	404	455	501	591	691
Claims on General Govt. (Net)	32an								-66	-48	†-8	2	11	10	16	4
Claims on Nonfin.Pub.Enterprises	32c								283	308	†331	379	415	454	529	629
Claims on Private Sector	32d								15	16	†16	23	29	36	46	58
Money	34								78	88	†107	150	165	190	229	279
Quasi-Money	35								56	64	†80	107	129	158	192	253
Capital Accounts	37a								7	7	†7	7	9	10	10	11
Other Items (Net)	37r								81	99	†130	122	132	118	129	122
Money plus Quasi-Money	35l								134	152	†187	257	294	348	421	533

Interest Rates

Percent Per Annum

Item	Code	1972	1973	1974	1975	1976	1977	1978	1979	1980	1981	1982	1983	1984	1985	1986
Discount Rate (End of Period)	60								...	...	...	...	3.0	4.0	4.0	4.0
Money Market Rate	60b								...	...	...	...	...	...	...	...
Treasury Bill Rate	60c								...	...	...	...	...	...	...	...
Deposit Rate	60l								...	...	...	...	...	...	...	...
Lending Rate	60p								8.0	8.0	8.0	9.0	9.0	9.0	12.0	12.0

1987	1988	1989	1990	1991	1992	1993	1994	1995	1996	1997	1998	1999	2000	2001		
Exchange Rates																
per SDR thereafter: End of Period																
44.76	67.63	854.20	†1.35	1.57	2.17	2.93	3.56	3.67	4.13	4.75	4.93	5.69	5.40	5.01	Market Rate	aa
per US$ thereafter: End of Period Average (rf)																
31.55	50.26	650.00	†.95	1.10	1.58	2.13	2.44	2.47	2.88	3.52	3.50	4.15	4.14	3.99	Market Rate	ae
26.51	43.05	143.92	†.95	1.06	1.36	1.81	2.27	2.42	2.70	3.28	3.48	3.97	4.35	4.09	Market Rate	rf
Period Averages																
9,300.0	5,722.8	2,772.7	255.2	230.6	179.2	135.1	106.8	100.0	90.1	74.2	69.8	61.2	55.9	59.2	Market Rate	ahx
7,813.2	4,899.0	2,643.1	235.7	221.3	172.6	143.7	114.4	100.0	93.7	86.6	83.2	75.8	76.6	84.9	Nominal Effective Exchange Rate	nec
59.1	54.1	61.0	51.3	80.3	85.4	91.6	92.4	100.0	108.8	111.4	117.0	112.3	121.6	138.3	Real Effective Exchange Rate	rec
Fund Position																
End of Period																
680	680	680	680	680	989	989	989	989	989	989	989	1,369	1,369	1,369	Quota	2f.s
—	—	—	1	5	1	1	1	2	3	4	5	8	14	21	SDRs	1b.s
—	—	—	—	—	77	77	77	77	77	77	77	172	172	367	Reserve Position in the Fund	1c.s
—	—	—	358	597	597	498	919	—	—	—	—	—	—	—	Total Fund Cred.&Loans Outstg.	2tl
International Liquidity																
End of Period																
1,494.7	2,055.3	2,314.3	4,492.1	3,632.6	4,099.1	4,091.9	5,841.8	14,774.1	17,844.0	20,407.2	27,325.2	26,354.7	26,562.0	25,648.4	Total Reserves minus Gold	1l.d
.1	.1	.1	.8	7.7	1.1	.7	1.5	2.2	4.4	5.4	7.1	11.2	17.7	25.8	SDRs	1b.d
—	—	—	—	—	106.1	105.9	112.6	114.6	110.9	104.1	108.6	236.4	224.4	461.0	Reserve Position in the Fund	1c.d
1,494.6	2,055.2	2,314.2	4,491.3	3,624.9	3,992.0	3,985.3	5,727.7	14,657.2	17,728.7	20,297.7	27,209.5	26,107.1	26,319.9	25,161.6	Foreign Exchange	1d.d
.472	.472	.472	.472	.473	.473	.473	.473	.473	.473	.904	3.305	3.306	3.306	3.308	Gold (Million Fine Troy Ounces)	1ad
189.0	189.0	189.0	189.0	189.1	189.0	189.0	189.0	189.0	189.0	262.4	950.0	959.4	901.5	914.7	Gold (National Valuation)	1and
680.4	503.0	664.3	939.9	397.9	423.5	446.2	355.6	363.5	246.4	914.3	1,028.2	1,939.3	498.6	588.2	Monetary Authorities: Other Liab.	4..d
2,782.5	2,794.7	2,773.1	6,091.2	5,306.4	6,648.3	5,925.5	7,742.2	7,154.4	6,132.1	7,275.5	5,405.3	7,874.7	11,323.1	15,307.2	Deposit Money Banks: Assets	7a.d
35,014.6	33,198.1	32,811.4	1,923.0	1,580.9	1,921.0	1,469.8	1,543.2	2,070.1	2,746.5	4,284.0	5,213.8	6,745.7	6,608.9	7,766.1	Liabilities	7b.d
Monetary Authorities																
End of Period																
60	127	1,719	4,717	†5,080	7,912	10,113	15,475	37,532	52,498	75,500	99,213	113,910	114,258	106,183	Foreign Assets	11
84	137	595	601	†4,365	12,170	15,729	19,530	11,534	12,761	16,792	17,765	18,803	16,745	18,426	Claims on General Government	12a
....	....	....	....	15	8	6	3	3	35	39	34	42	45	—	Claims on Nonfin.Pub.Enterprises	12c
				5	15	21	20	19	24	27	26	28	23	23	Claims on Private Sector	12d
208	483	2,691	7,613	†7,512	4,848	6,362	7,450	8,244	11,246	9,710	8,044	7,394	7,121	6,033	Claims on Deposit Money Banks	12e
246	570	3,275	8,535	†10,943	14,860	15,993	19,615	28,441	34,262	45,919	53,656	52,957	48,818	63,704	Reserve Money	14
131	252	988	3,934	†5,618	7,798	9,982	12,274	19,530	23,563	27,256	30,225	38,083	34,113	38,213	of which: Currency Outside DMBs	14a
—	—	—	55	†841	757	1,406	3,462	9,465	14,660	15,662	28,576	24,694	33,738	24,167	Nonreserve Liabilities to Banks	16b
21	25	432	1,376	†1,371	1,961	2,411	4,135	897	708	3,216	3,603	8,045	2,066	2,345	Foreign Liabilities	16c
78	116	146	1,369	†1,109	1,285	2,272	2,773	3,440	6,127	4,285	4,010	7,040	9,774	7,689	General Government Deposits	16d
5	7	15	82	†100	150	210	300	400	400	400	1,548	1,548	1,594	1,694	Capital Accounts	17a
1	29	1,137	1,515	†2,614	5,939	9,939	12,193	14,689	20,407	32,586	33,688	45,894	42,202	31,064	Other Items (Net)	17r
Deposit Money Banks																
End of Period																
115	318	1,889	3,909	†4,749	5,816	6,045	7,343	8,806	10,633	15,049	23,336	14,867	14,661	21,485	Reserves	20
....	....	....	....	860	757	732	1,879	4,585	11,018	13,927	28,321	24,539	33,507	24,133	Claims on Mon.Author.: Securities	20c
—	—	—	9	†	—	674	998	3,528	2,739	1,288	—	—	—	4,000	Other Claims on Monetary Author.	20n
88	140	1,803	5,787	†5,814	10,482	12,647	18,869	17,657	17,633	25,595	18,940	32,666	46,914	61,019	Foreign Assets	21
44	108	403	1,321	†7,367	12,013	19,201	27,204	38,920	48,638	50,980	57,431	63,792	54,591	65,668	Claims on General Government	22a
721	1,002	3,061	10,105	†10,379	11,770	14,252	16,751	20,342	24,123	28,756	31,426	31,920	30,234	28,465	Claims on Nonfin.Pub.Enterprises	22c
74	110	199	1,719	†8,977	13,109	19,022	25,158	36,604	57,071	78,538	104,072	137,907	167,525	184,111	Claims on Private Sector	22d
220	280	864	5,411	†5,113	7,096	9,654	15,175	17,817	28,702	34,425	41,438	49,970	48,420	51,941	Demand Deposits	24
363	636	5,078	9,022	†14,609	25,041	36,268	49,844	66,913	84,186	111,084	149,104	175,302	211,926	244,644	Time, Savings,& Fgn.Currency Dep.	25
111	174	2,053	1,679	†1,732	3,029	3,137	3,761	5,109	7,898	15,071	18,269	27,983	27,382	30,958	Foreign Liabilities	26c
31	49	264	1,472	†1,870	3,921	2,706	3,688	5,506	7,942	9,857	12,515	14,113	16,152	16,966	General Government Deposits	26d
27	43	54	490	†857	860	1,149	1,503	2,523	3,401	4,395	5,551	7,146	7,472	7,313	of which: Local Govt. Dep.	26db
208	483	2,691	7,613	†7,512	4,848	6,338	7,020	7,788	10,685	9,180	7,565	7,010	6,800	5,763	Credit from Monetary Authorities	26g
9	14	107	1,503	†3,374	4,323	7,129	9,990	12,999	18,534	24,715	30,049	34,294	39,562	46,441	Capital Accounts	27a
100	42	-3,703	-3,852	†3,935	5,690	7,342	8,724	14,310	13,907	9,801	4,586	-2,980	-2,809	-7,832	Other Items (Net)	27r
Monetary Survey																
End of Period																
15	68	1,037	7,448	†7,791	13,405	17,212	26,448	49,183	61,524	82,808	96,281	110,548	131,725	133,899	Foreign Assets (Net)	31n
814	1,192	3,847	10,905	†28,130	43,878	63,253	82,205	98,476	128,582	160,990	194,228	231,341	243,237	272,037	Domestic Credit	32
19	80	587	-919	†8,753	18,977	29,952	40,274	41,508	47,330	53,630	58,671	61,442	45,409	59,439	Claims on General Govt. (Net)	32an
721	1,002	3,061	10,105	†10,394	11,778	14,258	16,754	20,345	24,158	28,795	31,460	31,963	30,279	28,465	Claims on Nonfin.Pub.Enterprises	32c
74	110	199	1,719	†8,983	13,124	19,043	25,178	36,623	57,095	78,565	104,097	137,936	167,548	184,133	Claims on Private Sector	32d
352	532	1,881	9,426	†10,783	14,963	19,646	27,450	37,439	52,331	61,686	71,670	88,201	82,574	94,158	Money	34
363	636	5,446	9,633	†15,319	26,145	36,278	49,852	66,913	84,331	114,705	149,110	175,307	211,930	244,647	Quasi-Money	35
14	21	122	1,585	†3,474	4,473	7,339	10,290	13,399	18,934	25,115	31,598	35,842	41,156	48,135	Capital Accounts	37a
100	71	-2,566	-2,291	†6,344	11,702	17,201	21,062	29,908	34,512	42,291	38,132	42,539	39,301	18,996	Other Items (Net)	37r
715	1,168	7,327	19,060	†26,102	41,108	55,924	77,302	104,352	136,662	176,392	220,780	263,508	294,505	338,805	Money plus Quasi-Money	35l
Interest Rates																
Percent Per Annum																
4.0	6.0	†104.0	48.0	36.0	32.0	29.0	28.0	25.0	22.0	24.5	18.3	19.0	21.5	14.0	Discount Rate (End of Period)	60
....	....	....	....	49.9	†29.5	24.5	23.3	25.8	20.6	22.4	20.6	13.6	18.2	16.2	Money Market Rate	60b
....	....	....	....	....	44.0	33.2	28.8	25.6	20.3	21.6	19.1	13.1	16.6		Treasury Bill Rate	60c
....	....	100.0	41.7	†53.5	37.8	34.0	†33.4	26.8	20.0	19.4	18.2	11.2	14.2	11.8	Deposit Rate	60l
12.0	16.7	64.0	504.2	54.6	39.0	35.3	32.8	†33.5	26.1	25.0	24.5	17.0	20.0	18.4	Lending Rate	60p

Poland

964

	1972	1973	1974	1975	1976	1977	1978	1979	1980	1981	1982	1983	1984	1985	1986
Prices, Production, Labor														*Index Numbers (1995=100):*	
Share Prices 62	...	...	...	...	...								...	...	...
Producer Prices: Industry 63	...	...	...	...	...	.1	.1	.1	.1	.1	.3	.3	.4	.5	.5
Consumer Prices 64	.1	.1	.1	.1	.1	†.1	.1	.1	.1	.1	.2	.2	.3	.3	.4
Wages: Average Earnings 65	...	...	...	...	...	.1	.1	.1	.1	.1	.2	.2	.3	.3	.4
Industrial Production................ 66	...	...	...	...	...	103.4	107.1	109.1	108.0	93.3	90.5	98.2	103.2	106.9	111.7
Industrial Employment.............. 67	...	...	...	155.1	155.7	158.9	158.7	158.4	157.9	157.1	149.1	147.7	146.7	145.9	146.2
														Number in Thousands:	
Labor Force............................. 67d	...	...	...	...	...										
Employment 67e	...	...	...	...	...								...	18,531	18,595
Unemployment 67c	...	...	...	...	...								...		
Unemployment Rate (%)............ 67r	...	...	...	...	...							...	...		
International Transactions														*Millions of Zlotys*	
Exports 70	2	3	3	42	41	46	50	57	63	55	†95	106	134	169	212
Imports, c.i.f. 71	...	...	...	56	56	58	61	65	74	65	†90	100	125	165	202
Imports, f.o.b. 71.v	...	...	...	54	54	56	58	62	71	62	†87	97	121	159	196
														1995=100	
Volume of Exports 72	...	...	...	44.3	46.9	50.8	53.7	57.4	54.9	44.5	48.1	53.4	58.4	59.2	62.1
Volume of Imports 73	...	...	...	46.9	51.7	51.1	51.9	51.3	50.3	41.8	36.1	37.9	41.2	44.5	46.7
Export Prices............................ 76	...	...	...	.2	.2	.2	.2	.2	.2	.2	.4	.4	.5	.6	.7
Import Prices............................ 76.x	...	...	...	.6	.5	.5	.6	.6	.7	.8	1.2	1.3	1.5	1.8	2.1
Balance of Payments														*Millions of US Dollars*	
Current Account, n.i.e. .... 78al d	...	...	...	...	-2,793	-2,392	-2,545	-3,365	-3,417	-3,986	-1,941	-1,581	-1,083	-982	-1,106
Goods: Exports f.o.b. .... 78aa d	...	...	...	...	9,506	10,506	11,967	13,276	14,043	10,542	11,547	11,615	11,654	10,945	11,926
Goods: Imports f.o.b. .... 78ab d	...	...	...	...	-12,263	-12,724	-14,259	-15,660	-15,819	-12,723	-11,631	-11,312	-10,995	-10,598	-11,459
Trade Balance .... 78ac d	...	...	...	...	-2,757	-2,218	-2,292	-2,384	-1,776	-2,181	-84	303	659	347	467
Services: Credit........................ 78ad d	...	...	...	...	1,180	1,385	1,586	1,874	2,018	1,913	1,842	1,990	2,017	2,104	2,015
Services: Debit.......................... 78ae d	...	...	...	...	-1,144	-1,309	-1,521	-1,863	-2,023	-1,727	-1,467	-1,783	-1,853	-1,846	-2,012
Balance on Goods & Services .. 78af d	...	...	...	...	-2,721	-2,142	-2,227	-2,373	-1,781	-1,995	291	510	823	605	470
Income: Credit.......................... 78ag d	...	...	...	...	37	36	40	71	139	171	93	184	195	173	188
Income: Debit........................... 78ah d	...	...	...	...	-688	-924	-1,244	-1,738	-2,496	-3,395	-3,156	-2,978	-2,833	-2,730	-2,861
Balance on Gds, Serv. & Inc. .. 78ai d	...	...	...	...	-3,372	-3,030	-3,431	-4,040	-4,138	-5,219	-2,772	-2,284	-1,815	-1,952	-2,203
Current Transfers, n.i.e.: Credit .... 78aj d	...	...	...	...	597	660	909	953	1,234	1,878	926	942	1,106	1,351	1,483
Current Transfers: Debit .... 78ak d	...	...	...	...	-18	-22	-23	-278	-513	-645	-95	-239	-374	-381	-386
Capital Account, n.i.e. .... 78bc d	...	...	...	...	—	—	—	—	—	—	—	—	—	—	—
Capital Account, n.i.e.: Credit .. 78ba d	...	...	...	...	—	—	—	—	—	—	—	—	—	—	—
Capital Account: Debit .... 78bb d	...	...	...	...	—	—	—	—	—	—	—	—	—	—	—
Financial Account, n.i.e............ 78bj d	...	...	...	...	3,145	2,282	2,927	3,479	2,870	-1,486	-5,006	-3,681	-3,520	-1,476	-4,826
Direct Investment Abroad .... 78bd d	...	...	...	...	-12	-17	-16	-13	-21	-3	-1	-1	-12	-1	-22
Dir. Invest. in Rep. Econ., n.i.e. ...... 78be d	...	...	...	...	6	5	25	30	10	18	14	16	28	15	16
Portfolio Investment Assets .... 78bf d	...	...	...	...	—	—	—	—	—	—	—	—	—	—	—
Equity Securities................... 78bk d	...	...	...	...	—	—	—	—	—	—	—	—	—	—	—
Debt Securities .... 78bl d	...	...	...	...	—	—	—	—	—	—	—	—	—	—	—
Portfolio Investment Liab., n.i.e. .. 78bg d	...	...	...	...	—	—	—	—	—	—	—	—	—	—	—
Equity Securities................... 78bm d	...	...	...	...	—	—	—	—	—	—	—	—	—	—	—
Debt Securities .... 78bn d	...	...	...	...	—	—	—	—	—	—	—	—	—	—	—
Financial Derivatives Assets ...... 78bw d	...	...	...	...	...	...	...	...	...	...	...	...	...	...	...
Financial Derivatives Liabilities .. 78bx d	...	...	...	...	...	...	...	...	...	...	...	...	...	...	...
Other Investment Assets .... 78bh d	...	...	...	...	-338	-378	-195	-252	-182	-711	-543	-336	-767	-39	-1,128
Monetary Authorities .... 78bo d	...	...	...	...											
General Government................ 78bp d	...	...	...	...	-243	-180	-106	-28	-30	8	68	28	27	17	-140
Banks .... 78bq d	...	...	...	...	-35	-86	-61	-35	-4	-41	-657	-190	-126	-213	-585
Other Sectors .... 78br d	...	...	...	...	-60	-112	-28	-189	-148	-678	46	-174	-668	157	-403
Other Investment Liab., n.i.e. .... 78bi d	...	...	...	...	3,489	2,672	3,113	3,714	3,063	-790	-4,473	-3,360	-2,769	-1,451	-3,692
Monetary Authorities .... 78bs d	...	...	...	...	—	—	—	—	—	—	—	—	—	—	—
General Government................ 78bt d	...	...	...	...	-52	-56	85	111	89	-1,702	-2,684	-1,441	-1,149	-844	-681
Banks .... 78bu d	...	...	...	...	3,512	2,637	2,899	3,448	3,105	971	-1,994	-1,767	-1,569	-584	-3,436
Other Sectors .... 78bv d	...	...	...	...	29	91	129	155	-131	-59	205	-152	-51	-23	425
Net Errors and Omissions.......... 78ca d	...	...	...	...	-167	-261	-253	161	-90	-206	-217	344	333	118	731
Overall Balance .... 78cb d	...	...	...	...	185	-371	129	275	-637	-5,678	-7,164	-4,918	-4,270	-2,340	-5,201
Reserves and Related Items .... 79da d	...	...	...	...	-185	371	-129	-275	637	5,678	7,164	4,918	4,270	2,340	5,201
Reserve Assets .... 79db d	...	...	...	...	-185	371	-129	-275	637	-35	-370	-118	-341	236	173
Use of Fund Credit and Loans .... 79dc d	...	...	...	...	—	—	—	—	—	—	—	—	—	—	—
Exceptional Financing .... 79de d	...	...	...	...	—	—	—	—	—	5,713	7,534	5,036	4,611	2,104	5,028
International Investment Position														*Millions of US Dollars*	
Assets .... 79aa d	...	...	...	...	...	...	...	...	...	...	...	...	...	...	...
Direct Investment Abroad .... 79ab d	...	...	...	...	...	...	...	...	...	...	...	...	...	...	...
Portfolio Investment .... 79ac d	...	...	...	...	...	...	...	...	...	...	...	...	...	...	...
Equity Securities................... 79ad d	...	...	...	...	...	...	...	...	...	...	...	...	...	...	...
Debt Securities .... 79ae d	...	...	...	...	...	...	...	...	...	...	...	...	...	...	...
Financial Derivatives .... 79al d	...	...	...	...	...	...	...	...	...	...	...	...	...	...	...
Other Investment .... 79af d	...	...	...	...	...	...	...	...	...	...	...	...	...	...	...
Monetary Authorities .... 79ag d	...	...	...	...	...	...	...	...	...	...	...	...	...	...	...
General Government................ 79ah d	...	...	...	...	...	...	...	...	...	...	...	...	...	...	...
Banks .... 79ai d	...	...	...	...	...	...	...	...	...	...	...	...	...	...	...
Other Sectors .... 79aj d	...	...	...	...	...	...	...	...	...	...	...	...	...	...	...
Reserve Assets .... 79ak d	...	...	...	...	...	...	...	...	...	...	...	...	...	...	...
Liabilities .... 79la d	...	...	...	...	...	...	...	...	...	...	...	...	...	...	...
Dir. Invest. in Rep. Economy....... 79lb d	...	...	...	...	...	...	...	...	...	...	...	...	...	...	...
Portfolio Investment .... 79lc d	...	...	...	...	...	...	...	...	...	...	...	...	...	...	...
Equity Securities................... 79ld d	...	...	...	...	...	...	...	...	...	...	...	...	...	...	...
Debt Securities .... 79le d	...	...	...	...	...	...	...	...	...	...	...	...	...	...	...
Financial Derivatives .... 79ll d	...	...	...	...	...	...	...	...	...	...	...	...	...	...	...
Other Investment .... 79lf d	...	...	...	...	...	...	...	...	...	...	...	...	...	...	...
Monetary Authorities .... 79lg d	...	...	...	...	...	...	...	...	...	...	...	...	...	...	...
General Government................ 79lh d	...	...	...	...	...	...	...	...	...	...	...	...	...	...	...
Banks .... 79li d	...	...	...	...	...	...	...	...	...	...	...	...	...	...	...
Other Sectors .... 79lj d	...	...	...	...	...	...	...	...	...	...	...	...	...	...	...

Prices, Production, Labor

Period Averages

	1987	1988	1989	1990	1991	1992	1993	1994	1995	1996	1997	1998	1999	2000	2001	Code
Share Prices	.7	1.1	3.4	24.1	†36.3	46.3	61.2	79.7	100.0	168.9	....	....	143.7	154.8	157.4	62
Producer Prices: Industry	.5	.7	2.5	16.7	†29.5	42.8	58.6	78.1	100.0	119.8	137.9	154.1	165.3	182.1	192.1	63
Consumer Prices	.5	.9	3.6	†16.8	28.0	38.3	53.7	70.7	100.0	126.3	151.6	174.2	189.9	209.6	224.1	64
Wages: Average Earnings	....	....	....	....	....	....	....	....	100.0	....	....	....	....	....	....	65
Industrial Production	115.5	121.0	117.5	87.6	†73.6	†76.5	80.2	91.4	100.0	....	....	....	....	....	....	66
Industrial Employment	145.5	143.1	138.8	†121.3	110.5	106.3	100.8	99.1	100.0	98.7	98.2	97.2	92.8	87.4	82.9	67

Period Averages

	1987	1988	1989	1990	1991	1992	1993	1994	1995	1996	1997	1998	1999	2000	2001	Code
Labor Force	....	....	....	....	....	17,526	17,368	17,004	17,076	....	17,101	17,162	....	17,311	....	67d
Employment	18,596	18,474	18,220	17,321	16,285	15,462	†14,894	14,658	14,791	14,969	15,177	15,354	14,747	14,526	....	67e
Unemployment	....	....	....	1,126	2,156	2,509	†2,890	2,838	2,629	2,360	1,826	1,831	2,350	2,703	2,912	67c
Unemployment Rate (%)	....	....	....	6.3	11.8	13.6	†16.4	16.0	15.2	13.2	10.5	10.4	13.0	15.0	16.2	67r

International Transactions

Millions of Zlotys

	1987	1988	1989	1990	1991	1992	1993	1994	1995	1996	1997	1998	1999	2000	2001	Code
Exports	324	601	1,948	13,606	†15,772	17,969	25,757	39,246	55,515	65,819	84,480	95,015	108,706	137,909	148,115	70
Imports, c.i.f.	297	547	1,542	9,292	†16,674	21,995	34,018	49,072	70,502	100,231	138,898	162,458	182,362	213,072	206,253	71
Imports, f.o.b.	288	527	1,486	9,051	†16,426	19,126	29,581	42,287	61,306	87,157	120,781	141,268	....	....	....	71.v

1995=100

	1987	1988	1989	1990	1991	1992	1993	1994	1995	1996	1997	1998	1999	2000	2001	Code
Volume of Exports	65.1	71.0	71.2	†77.0	75.1	73.2	72.4	85.7	100.0	109.7	124.7	133.2	141.1	174.4	197.5	72
Volume of Imports	48.8	53.3	54.2	†39.4	54.2	61.8	73.2	83.0	100.0	128.0	156.1	186.3	193.5	207.0	221.1	73
Export Prices	1.0	1.7	5.5	†33.7	40.0	51.0	64.1	82.5	100.0	108.0	122.0	131.2	140.4	142.6	137.2	76
Import Prices	3.0	4.9	13.6	39.4	51.2	59.7	69.5	88.5	100.0	117.2	133.1	140.1	149.3	154.0	149.2	76.x

Balance of Payments

Minus Sign Indicates Debit

	1987	1988	1989	1990	1991	1992	1993	1994	1995	1996	1997	1998	1999	2000	2001	Code
Current Account, n.i.e.	-379	-107	-1,409	3,067	-2,146	-3,104	-5,788	954	854	-3,264	-5,744	-6,901	-12,487	-9,997	....	78ald
Goods: Exports f.o.b.	12,026	13,846	12,869	15,837	14,393	13,929	13,582	18,355	25,041	27,557	30,731	32,467	30,060	35,902	....	78aad
Goods: Imports f.o.b.	-11,236	-12,757	-12,822	-12,248	-15,104	-14,060	-17,087	-18,930	-26,687	-34,844	-40,553	-45,303	-45,132	-48,210	....	78abd
Trade Balance	790	1,089	47	3,589	-711	-131	-3,505	-575	-1,646	-7,287	-9,822	-12,836	-15,072	-12,308	....	78acd
Services: Credit	2,216	2,472	3,201	3,200	3,687	4,773	4,201	6,699	10,675	9,747	8,915	10,840	8,363	10,392	....	78add
Services: Debit	-2,028	-2,404	-3,053	-2,847	-2,994	-4,045	-3,631	-3,859	-7,138	-6,343	-5,743	-6,624	-6,982	-9,000	....	78aed
Balance on Goods & Services	978	1,157	195	3,942	-18	597	-2,935	2,265	1,891	-3,883	-6,650	-8,620	-13,691	-10,916	....	78afd
Income: Credit	217	271	410	603	573	728	579	546	1,089	1,527	1,467	2,226	1,837	2,248	....	78agd
Income: Debit	-3,132	-3,226	-3,623	-3,989	-3,469	-4,895	-4,192	-3,109	-3,084	-2,602	-2,596	-3,404	-2,847	-3,709	....	78ahd
Balance on Gds, Serv. & Inc.	-1,937	-1,798	-3,018	556	-2,914	-3,570	-6,548	-298	-104	-4,958	-7,779	-9,798	-14,701	-12,377	....	78aid
Current Transfers, n.i.e.: Credit	2,154	2,777	4,246	6,865	6,707	6,214	5,840	2,174	2,459	2,825	2,700	3,520	2,898	3,008	....	78ajd
Current Transfers: Debit	-596	-1,086	-2,637	-4,354	-5,939	-5,748	-5,080	-922	-1,501	-1,131	-665	-623	-684	-628	....	78akd
Capital Account, n.i.e.	—	—	—	—	—	—	—	9,215	285	94	66	63	55	32	....	78bcd
Capital Account, n.i.e.: Credit	—	—	—	—	—	—	—	9,215	285	5,833	91	117	95	108	....	78bad
Capital Account: Debit	—	—	—	—	—	—	—	—	—	-5,739	-25	-54	-40	-76	....	78bbd
Financial Account, n.i.e.	-3,318	-10,661	-1,796	-8,731	-4,183	-1,045	2,341	-9,065	9,260	6,673	7,410	13,282	10,462	10,196	....	78bjd
Direct Investment Abroad	-8	-22	-18	—	7	-13	-18	-29	-42	-53	-45	-316	-31	-17	....	78bdd
Dir. Invest. in Rep. Econ., n.i.e.	12	15	11	89	291	678	1,715	1,875	3,659	4,498	4,908	6,365	7,270	9,342	....	78bed
Portfolio Investment Assets	—	—	—	—	—	—	—	-624	1	282	815	-130	-548	-87	....	78bfd
Equity Securities	—	—	—	—	—	—	—	—	127	-17	56	1	-172	-22	....	78bkd
Debt Securities	—	—	—	—	—	—	—	-624	-126	299	759	-131	-376	-65	....	78bld
Portfolio Investment Liab., n.i.e.	—	—	—	—	—	—	—	—	1,176	22	1,295	1,827	691	3,423	....	78bgd
Equity Securities	—	—	—	—	—	—	—	—	219	749	599	1,734	14	447	....	78bmd
Debt Securities	—	—	—	—	—	—	—	—	957	-727	696	93	677	2,976	....	78bnd
Financial Derivatives Assets	—	—	—	—	—	—	—	—	—	-3	-12	—	579	269	....	78bwd
Financial Derivatives Liabilities	—	—	—	—	—	—	—	—	—	—	—	—	-10	—	....	78bxd
Other Investment Assets	-1,415	-1,226	-155	-4,504	-1,497	-958	848	-1,841	3,356	6,191	-754	2,107	-3,339	-3,873	....	78bhd
Monetary Authorities	....	....	....	....	....	....	....	194	65	37	—	1	1	1	....	78bod
General Government	-188	-161	-137	46	27	26	16	34	46	5,767	41	53	-6	-48	....	78bpd
Banks	-461	-26	111	-4,096	-980	-823	649	-1,718	1,057	453	-1,076	2,207	-2,694	-3,015	....	78bqd
Other Sectors	-766	-1,039	-129	-454	-544	-161	183	-351	2,188	-66	281	-154	-640	-811	....	78brd
Other Investment Liab., n.i.e.	-1,907	-9,428	-1,634	-4,316	-2,984	-752	-204	-8,446	1,110	-4,264	1,203	3,429	5,850	1,139	....	78bid
Monetary Authorities	....	....	....	....	....	....	....	....	15	102	-561	199	380	-1,393	....	78bsd
General Government	-2,175	-285	-1,034	-3,936	-3,418	-1,439	-570	-8,709	-3	-6,033	-52	-370	-224	-292	....	78btd
Banks	-232	-9,744	-601	-827	-227	437	114	170	575	314	719	1,483	2,013	-475	....	78bud
Other Sectors	500	601	1	447	661	250	252	78	524	1,353	1,097	2,117	3,681	3,299	....	78bvd
Net Errors and Omissions	91	-267	-110	162	-745	-181	219	-98	-564	321	1,309	-520	2,126	395	....	78cad
Overall Balance	-3,606	-11,035	-3,315	-5,502	-7,074	-4,330	-3,228	1,006	9,835	3,824	3,041	5,924	156	626	....	78cbd
Reserves and Related Items	3,606	11,035	3,315	5,502	7,074	4,330	3,228	-1,006	-9,835	-3,824	-3,041	-5,924	-156	-626	....	79dad
Reserve Assets	-797	-561	-259	-2,418	830	-616	-100	-1,514	-8,431	-3,828	-3,044	-5,926	-156	-626	....	79dbd
Use of Fund Credit and Loans	—	—	—	479	323	—	-138	603	-1,408	—	—	—	—	—	....	79dcd
Exceptional Financing	4,403	11,596	3,574	7,440	5,921	4,946	3,466	-96	4	4	3	2	—	—	....	79ded

International Investment Position

Millions of US Dollars

	1987	1988	1989	1990	1991	1992	1993	1994	1995	1996	1997	1998	1999	2000	2001	Code
Assets	....	....	....	....	....	....	....	23,506	31,966	28,746	31,908	38,399	40,101	44,616	....	79aad
Direct Investment Abroad	....	....	....	....	....	....	....	461	539	735	678	1,165	1,024	1,025	....	79abd
Portfolio Investment	....	....	....	....	....	....	....	1,287	1,937	1,338	839	1,093	1,143	1,575	....	79acd
Equity Securities	....	....	....	....	....	....	....	....	....	38	2	9	28	47	....	79add
Debt Securities	....	....	....	....	....	....	....	....	....	1,300	837	1,084	1,115	1,528	....	79aed
Financial Derivatives	....	....	....	....	....	....	....	—	—	—	—	—	—	—	....	79ald
Other Investment	....	....	....	....	....	....	....	15,727	14,527	8,454	8,988	7,866	10,619	14,552	....	79afd
Monetary Authorities	....	....	....	....	....	....	....	252	187	150	5	4	2	1	....	79agd
General Government	....	....	....	....	....	....	....	6,970	6,720	881	829	801	1,031	1,102	....	79ahd
Banks	....	....	....	....	....	....	....	6,672	5,678	4,997	6,161	4,419	6,697	9,758	....	79aid
Other Sectors	....	....	....	....	....	....	....	1,833	1,942	2,426	1,993	2,642	2,889	3,691	....	79ajd
Reserve Assets	....	....	....	....	....	....	....	6,031	14,963	18,219	21,403	28,275	27,315	27,464	....	79akd
Liabilities	....	....	....	....	....	....	....	53,075	59,304	58,515	62,439	80,205	89,257	99,345	....	79lad
Dir. Invest. in Rep. Economy	....	....	....	....	....	....	....	3,789	7,843	11,463	14,587	22,479	26,075	33,603	....	79lbd
Portfolio Investment	....	....	....	....	....	....	....	8,431	9,375	10,148	11,325	13,658	14,617	18,057	....	79lcd
Equity Securities	....	....	....	....	....	....	....	443	663	2,279	2,672	4,969	4,980	5,350	....	79ldd
Debt Securities	....	....	....	....	....	....	....	7,988	8,712	7,869	8,653	8,689	9,637	12,707	....	79led
Financial Derivatives	....	....	....	....	....	....	....	—	—	—	—	—	—	—	....	79lld
Other Investment	....	....	....	....	....	....	....	40,855	42,086	36,904	36,527	44,068	48,565	47,685	....	79lfd
Monetary Authorities	....	....	....	....	....	....	....	1,493	174	265	791	925	1,844	436	....	79lgd
General Government	....	....	....	....	....	....	....	34,507	35,955	28,709	26,584	27,061	25,199	23,749	....	79lhd
Banks	....	....	....	....	....	....	....	1,394	1,834	2,231	3,054	4,735	6,404	5,812	....	79lid
Other Sectors	....	....	....	....	....	....	....	3,461	4,123	5,699	6,098	11,347	15,118	17,688	....	79ljd

Poland

		1972	1973	1974	1975	1976	1977	1978	1979	1980	1981	1982	1983	1984	1985	1986
Government Finance															*Millions of Zlotys:*	
Deficit (-) or Surplus	80	...	...	...	...	...	...	...	...	...	...	...	...	-4	-18	-4
Total Revenue and Grants	81y	...	...	...	...	...	...	...	...	...	...	...	...	375	454	542
Revenue	81	...	...	...	...	...	...	...	...	...	...	...	...	375	454	532
Grants	81z	...	...	...	...	...	...	...	...	...	...	...	...	—	—	10
Exp. & Lending Minus Repay.	82z	...	...	...	...	...	...	...	...	...	...	...	...	379	472	546
Expenditure	82	...	...	...	...	...	...	...	...	...	...	...	...	380	472	542
Lending Minus Repayments	83	...	...	...	...	...	...	...	...	...	...	...	...	—	—	4
Total Financing	80h	...	...	...	...	...	...	...	...	...	...	...	...	4	18	4
Domestic	84a	...	...	...	...	...	...	...	...	...	...	...	...	—	13	-8
Foreign	85a	...	...	...	...	...	...	...	...	...	...	...	...	4	5	12
Total Debt by Residence	88	...	...	...	...	...	...	...	...	...	...	...	...	...	...	...
Domestic	88a	...	...	...	...	...	...	...	...	...	...	...	...	...	...	...
Foreign	89a	...	...	...	...	...	...	...	...	...	...	...	...	...	...	...
National Accounts															*Millions of Zlotys*	
Househ.Cons.Expend.,incl.NPISHs	96f									†168	204	348	449	543	†551	679
Government Consumption Expend.	91f									23	26	45	61	80	†189	230
Gross Fixed Capital Formation	93e									62	51	112	139	178	†221	284
Changes in Inventories	93i									4	-1	43	34	48	†68	90
Exports of Goods and Services	90c									71	64	108	119	152	†190	236
Imports of Goods and Services (-)	98c									78	70	96	107	135	†176	217
Gross Domestic Product (GDP)	99b									251	275	555	692	858	†1,045	1,295
GDP Volume 1987 Prices	99b,p									†1,584	1,426	1,358	1,433	1,514	1,592	1,659
GDP Volume 1995 Prices	99b.p									...	...	...	...	...	...	...
GDP Volume (1995=100)	99bv p									†102.5	92.2	87.8	92.7	98.0	103.0	107.3
GDP Deflator (1995=100)	99bi p									†.1	.1	.2	.2	.3	†.3	.4
															Millions:	
Population	99z	33.07	33.36	33.69	34.02	34.36	34.70	35.01	35.26	35.58	35.90	36.23	36.57	36.91	37.20	37.46

	1987	1988	1989	1990	1991	1992	1993	1994	1995	1996	1997	1998	1999	2000	2001		
Year Ending December 31																**Government Finance**	
	−24	−68	....	....	....	....	....	−4,812	−5,762	−7,826	−8,304	−5,382	−4,794	2,089	....	Deficit (-) or Surplus	80
	660	1,101	....	....	....	....	....	88,153	117,946	144,462	172,519	196,964	201,250	214,345	....	Total Revenue and Grants	81y
	657	1,097	....	....	....	....	....	88,153	117,946	144,454	172,507	196,952	201,131	213,865	....	Revenue	81
	3	4	....	....	....	....	....	—	—	8	12	12	119	480	....	Grants	81z
	684	1,169	....	....	....	....	....	92,965	123,708	152,288	180,823	202,346	206,044	212,256	....	Exp. & Lending Minus Repay.	82z
	675	1,146	....	....	....	....	....	93,039	124,322	153,047	185,431	207,370	216,685	236,711	....	Expenditure	82
	9	23	....	....	....	....	....	−74	−614	−759	−4,608	−5,024	−10,641	−24,455	....	Lending Minus Repayments	83
	24	67	....	....	....	....	....	4,812	5,762	7,826	8,304	5,382	4,794	−2,089	....	Total Financing	80h
	19	74	....	....	....	....	....	5,855	2,604	8,695	8,393	4,379	4,218	−2,354	....	Domestic	84a
	5	−7	....	....	....	....	....	−1,043	3,158	−869	−89	1,003	576	265	....	Foreign	85a
	....	....	....	....	....	....	....	152,238	167,267	185,603	221,650	237,400	266,750	270,980	....	Total Debt by Residence	88
	....	....	....	....	....	....	....	55,611	63,083	76,919	97,635	109,647	123,519	134,477	....	Domestic	88a
	....	....	....	....	....	....	....	96,627	104,184	108,684	124,015	127,753	143,231	136,503	....	Foreign	89a
Millions of Zlotys																**National Accounts**	
	874	1,460	6,076	†27,187	48,643	71,925	99,627	142,746	188,416	245,560	301,069	352,063	396,361	447,396	479,977	Househ.Cons.Expend.,incl.NPISHs	96f
	294	474	707	†10,488	17,691	23,819	30,407	37,853	51,747	63,480	75,653	85,497	95,586	106,314	112,240	Government Consumption Expend.	91f
	382	666	1,935	†11,761	15,775	19,297	24,749	40,385	57,405	80,390	110,853	139,205	156,690	170,430	155,563	Gross Fixed Capital Formation	93e
	106	299	2,618	†2,590	328	−1,860	−520	−715	3,300	4,428	5,150	5,801	5,595	8,132	1,012	Changes in Inventories	93i
	363	674	2,257	†16,051	19,026	27,242	35,733	53,218	78,172	94,192	120,408	155,874	160,787	201,507	215,278	Exports of Goods and Services	90c
	322	593	1,761	†12,050	20,579	25,479	34,215	48,389	70,935	100,224	140,782	184,879	199,904	248,853	241,726	Imports of Goods and Services (-)	98c
	1,694	2,963	11,832	†56,027	80,883	114,944	155,780	225,098	308,104	387,827	472,350	553,560	615,115	684,982	722,341	Gross Domestic Product (GDP)	99b
	1,694	1,762	1,767	1,565	....	....	....	....	....	....	....	....	....	....	....	GDP Volume 1987 Prices	99b.p
	....	....	....	311,989	290,236	191,937	199,230	287,883	308,104	326,679	348,982	365,882	380,884	396,119	399,962	GDP Volume 1995 Prices	99b.p
	109.6	114.0	114.3	101.3	94.2	62.3	64.7	93.4	100.0	106.0	113.3	118.8	123.6	128.6	129.8	GDP Volume (1995=100)	99bv p
	.5	.8	3.4	†18.0	27.9	59.9	78.2	78.2	100.0	118.7	135.4	151.3	161.5	172.9	180.6	GDP Deflator (1995=100)	99bi p
Midyear Estimates																	
	37.66	37.86	37.96	38.12	38.24	38.37	38.46	38.54	38.59	38.62	38.65	38.67	38.65	38.65	38.64	Population	99z

(See notes in the back of the book.)

Portugal

	1972	1973	1974	1975	1976	1977	1978	1979	1980	1981	1982	1983	1984	1985	1986
Exchange Rates															*Escudos per SDR through 1998,*
Market Rate aa	29.31	31.18	30.11	32.16	36.65	48.41	59.94	65.58	67.65	75.95	98.25	137.62	165.93	172.99	178.73
															Escudos per US Dollar through 1998,
Market Rate ae	27.00	25.85	24.60	27.47	31.55	39.86	46.01	49.78	53.04	65.25	89.06	131.45	169.28	157.49	146.12
Market Rate rf	27.05	24.52	25.41	25.55	30.23	38.28	43.94	48.92	50.06	61.55	79.47	110.78	146.39	170.39	149.59
															Escudos per ECU:
ECU Rate ea	....	....	....	....	....	....	....	....	....	....	....	....	....	140.28	156.39
ECU Rate eb	....	....	....	....	....	....	....	....	....	....	....	....	....	....	148.84
															Index Numbers (1995=100):
Market Rate ahx	558.1	617.7	594.6	592.4	500.8	396.7	344.7	308.8	301.8	246.5	192.6	138.9	103.8	88.8	101.0
Nominal Effective Exchange Rate nec	....	....	....	....	....	....	....	281.7	273.7	266.7	235.1	186.5	154.5	137.0	124.4
Real Effective Exchange Rate rec	....	....	....	....	....	....	....	78.5	79.8	84.3	83.8	77.8	79.1	80.0	79.2
Fund Position															*Millions of SDRs:*
Quota 2f.s	117	117	117	117	117	117	172	172	258	258	258	377	377	377	377
SDRs 1b.s	—	—	—	7	8	4	—	1	—	9	2	1	13	16	54
Reserve Position in the Fund 1c.s	29	29	29	—	—	—	—	—	35	49	49	30	30	30	30
Total Fund Cred.&Loans Outstg. 2tl	—	—	—	—	173	245	203	172	94	47	10	355	572	572	572
International Liquidity															*Millions of US Dollars Unless Otherwise Indicated:*
Total Res.Min.Gold (Eurosys.Def) 1l.d	1,291	1,676	1,161	398	176	366	871	931	795	534	447	385	516	1,395	1,456
SDRs 1b.d	—	—	—	8	10	5	—	1	—	10	2	1	12	17	66
Reserve Position in the Fund 1c.d	32	35	36	—	—	—	—	—	44	57	54	31	29	33	36
Foreign Exchange 1d.d	1,259	1,641	1,125	390	166	361	871	930	751	467	391	353	475	1,345	1,354
o/w: Fin.Deriv.Rel.to Reserves 1ddd	....	....	....	....	....	....	....	....	....	....	....	....	....	....	....
Other Reserve Assets 1e.d	....	....	....	....	....	....	....	....	....	....	....	....	....	....	....
Gold (Million Fine Troy Ounces) 1ad	26.88	27.54	27.84	27.72	27.67	24.11	22.13	22.13	22.17	22.14	22.09	20.43	20.30	20.23	20.16
Gold (Eurosystem Valuation) 1and	1,021	1,163	1,193	1,136	1,125	1,025	1,009	1,020	5,652	5,644	5,631	5,209	5,174	5,159[e]	5,139
Memo: Euro Cl. on Non-EA Res. 1dgd	....	....	....	....	....	....	....	....	....	....	....	....	....	....	....
Non-Euro Cl. on EA Res. 1dhd	....	....	....	....	....	....	....	....	....	....	....	....	....	....	....
Mon. Auth.: Other Foreign Assets 3..d	....	....	....	....	....	....	....	....	....	....	....	....	....	....	....
Foreign Liabilities 4..d	4	4	4	34	†969	1,169	878	†1,564	1,087	947	826	1,168	1,053	862	853
Banking Insts.: Foreign Assets 7a.d	298	304	412	347	702	881	996	1,065	1,135	868	813	970	1,112	1,428	1,418
Foreign Liab. 7b.d	69	85	114	94	253	1,246	2,999	†938	808	896	1,366	1,684	1,766	1,636	1,516
Monetary Authorities															*Billions of Escudos through 1998;*
Fgn. Assets (Cl.on Non-EA Ctys) 11	62.4	70.4	54.7	40.1	†40.6	54.1	81.6	†85.7	334.6	399.7	540.9	730.8	953.0	1,023.4	956.3
Claims on General Government 12a.u	....	....	....	....	....	....	....	....	....	....	....	....	....	....	....
o/w: Claims on Gen.Govt.in Cty 12a	3.2	3.5	10.7	34.9	†71.7	134.4	169.4	†265.6	190.6	293.7	422.7	562.3	787.7	1,057.0	1,202.4
Claims on Banking Institutions 12e.u	....	....	....	....	....	....	....	....	....	....	....	....	....	....	....
o/w: Claims on Bank.Inst.in Cty 12e	2.0	2.2	3.7	2.3	†99.7	92.4	73.8	†24.4	13.6	28.1	18.5	42.7	31.9	56.0	72.8
Claims on Other Resident Sectors 12d.u	....	....	....	....	....	....	....	....	....	....	....	....	....	....	....
o/w: Cl. on Oth.Res.Sect.in Cty 12d	—	—	.1	.2	†.2	.1	—	†18.3	19.7	20.7	26.9	35.8	41.1	38.8	33.9
Currency Issued 14a	36.8	39.0	71.1	112.0	†80.9	85.2	118.3	†142.1	165.2	188.4	219.5	240.1	267.3	319.0	399.3
Liabilities to Banking Insts 14c.u	....	....	....	....	....	....	....	....	....	....	....	....	....	....	....
o/w: Liabs to Bank.Inst.in Cty 14c	....	....	....	....	31.1	35.9	50.6	†83.2	109.0	186.4	264.2	309.8	306.7	287.5	285.1
Demand Dep. of Other Res.Sect. 14d.u	....	....	....	....	....	....	....	....	....	....	....	....	....	....	....
o/w: D.Dep.of Oth.Res.Sect.in Cty 14d	....	....	....	....	1.3	.3	.6	†2.8	1.6	1.7	3.8	2.8	3.6	3.0	11.7
Other Dep. of Other Res.Sect. 15..u	....	....	....	....	....	....	....	....	....	....	....	....	....	....	....
o/w: O.Dep.of Oth.Res.Sect.in Cty 15	....	....	....	....	....	....	....	....	....	....	....	....	....	....	....
Money Market Instruments 16m.u	....	....	....	....	....	....	....	....	....	....	....	....	....	....	....
o/w: MMI Held by Resid.of Cty 16m	....	....	....	....	....	....	....	....	....	....	....	....	....	....	....
Bonds (Debt Securities) 16n.u	....	....	....	....	....	....	....	....	....	....	....	....	....	....	....
o/w: Bonds Held by Resid.of Cty 16n	....	....	....	....	....	....	....	....	....	....	....	....	....	....	....
Foreign Liab. (to Non-EA Ctys) 16c	....	....	....	....	36.9	58.4	52.6	†89.1	64.0	65.4	74.6	202.4	273.1	234.7	226.8
Central Government Deposits 16d.u	....	....	....	....	....	....	....	....	....	....	....	....	....	....	....
o/w: Cent.Govt.Dep. in Cty 16d	4.1	6.0	3.8	1.0	†12.2	22.2	10.9	†22.7	32.4	48.9	36.5	70.7	60.4	101.1	12.5
Capital Accounts 17a	....	....	....	....	29.7	36.6	43.9	†34.2	101.0	106.1	110.0	144.6	107.3	263.7	398.0
Other Items (Net) 17r	26.6	31.1	–5.7	–35.6	†20.1	42.3	47.9	†19.8	85.3	145.3	300.5	401.1	795.3	966.2	932.0
Memo: Net Claims on Eurosystem 12e.s	....	....	....	....	....	....	....	....	....	....	....	....	....	....	....
Currency Put into Circ. 14m	....	....	....	....	....	....	....	....	....	....	....	....	....	....	....
Banking Institutions															*Billions of Escudos through 1998;*
Claims on Monetary Authorities 20	25.8	31.7	23.8	18.9	†29.2	33.7	47.5	†93.2	171.3	262.3	362.3	395.6	681.8	1,060.3	1,294.0
Claims on Bk.Inst.in Oth.EA Ctys 20b.u	....	....	....	....	....	....	....	....	....	....	....	....	....	....	....
Fgn. Assets (Cl.on Non-EA Ctys) 21	8.1	7.7	10.1	9.5	†22.2	35.1	45.8	†53.0	60.2	56.6	72.4	127.5	188.3	224.9	207.3
Claims on General Government 22a.u	....	....	....	....	....	....	....	....	....	....	....	....	....	....	....
o/w: Claims on Gen.Govt.in Cty 22a	20.8	21.6	26.1	32.0	†50.8	51.6	56.8	†69.5	86.2	155.1	210.2	270.1	313.1	509.4	633.9
Claims on Other Resident Sectors 22d.u	....	....	....	....	....	....	....	....	....	....	....	....	....	....	....
o/w: Cl. on Oth.Res.Sect.in Cty 22d	178.1	238.3	250.1	312.9	†406.4	515.4	609.1	†845.0	1,074.1	1,356.0	1,706.4	2,155.1	2,620.0	2,873.3	3,201.9
Demand Deposits 24..u	....	....	....	....	....	....	....	....	....	....	....	....	....	....	....
o/w: D.Dep.of Oth.Res.Sect.in Cty 24	85.6	126.7	111.4	115.5	†141.5	168.4	199.1	†262.0	323.7	347.3	402.8	434.0	513.2	671.3	953.6
Other Deposits 25..u	....	....	....	....	....	....	....	....	....	....	....	....	....	....	....
o/w: O.Dep.of Oth.Res.Sect.in Cty 25	112.5	135.7	159.8	158.2	†209.9	258.7	331.5	†600.8	863.3	1,204.2	1,581.8	1,977.6	2,604.5	3,225.6	3,596.1
Money Market Instruments 26m.u	....	....	....	....	....	....	....	....	....	....	....	....	....	....	....
o/w: MMI Held by Resid.of Cty 26m	....	....	....	....	....	....	....	....	....	....	....	....	....	....	....
Bonds (Debt Securities) 26n.u	....	....	....	....	....	....	....	....	....	....	....	....	....	....	....
o/w: Bonds Held by Resid.of Cty 26n	....	....	....	....	.4	.4	.3	†.2	.2	1.1	1.1	2.9	2.0	4.3	2.4
Foreign Liab. (to Non-EA Ctys) 26c	1.9	2.2	2.8	2.6	†18.9	85.5	138.0	†46.7	42.9	58.5	121.7	221.4	298.9	257.7	221.5
Central Government Deposits 26d.u	....	....	....	....	....	....	....	....	....	....	....	....	....	....	....
o/w: Cent.Govt.Dep. in Cty 26d	17.9	20.2	24.0	32.5	†29.2	33.4	39.4	†54.9	65.8	74.3	95.5	105.9	135.7	216.5	274.7
Credit from Monetary Authorities 26g	....	....	....	....	99.7	92.4	73.8	†29.4	16.5	34.1	27.2	55.1	51.7	69.9	101.5
Liab. to Bk.Inst.in Oth. EA Ctys 26h.u	....	....	....	....	....	....	....	....	....	....	....	....	....	....	....
Capital Accounts 27a	18.8	22.4	23.7	24.2	†35.2	34.8	42.3	†48.9	65.3	84.8	117.4	117.4	157.1	198.1	291.1
Other Items (Net) 27r	–3.7	–7.9	–11.6	40.4	†–29.7	–36.8	–65.7	†17.6	14.0	25.7	4.0	33.9	40.1	24.5	–103.7
Banking Survey (Nat'l Residency)															*Billions of Escudos through 1998;*
Foreign Assets (Net) 31n	68.6	75.9	62.0	47.0	†6.9	–54.7	–63.1	†2.9	287.9	332.4	417.1	434.5	569.2	755.8	715.2
Domestic Credit 32	180.2	237.2	259.3	346.5	†487.8	645.8	785.1	†1,120.7	1,272.4	1,702.3	2,234.2	2,846.6	3,565.7	4,161.0	4,785.0
Claims on General Govt. (Net) 32an	2.0	–1.2	9.0	33.4	†81.1	130.4	175.9	†257.5	178.6	325.6	500.9	655.7	904.7	1,248.9	1,549.2
Claims on Other Resident Sectors 32d	178.2	238.4	250.2	313.1	†406.6	515.5	609.2	†863.3	1,093.8	1,376.7	1,733.3	2,190.9	2,661.0	2,912.1	3,235.8
Currency Issued 34a.n	36.8	39.0	71.1	112.0	†80.9	85.2	118.3	†142.1	165.2	188.4	219.5	240.1	267.3	319.0	399.3
Demand Deposits 34b.n	85.6	126.7	111.4	115.5	†142.8	168.7	199.7	†264.8	325.3	349.1	406.6	436.9	516.7	674.3	965.3
Other Deposits 35..n	112.5	135.7	159.8	158.2	†209.9	258.7	331.5	†600.8	863.3	1,204.2	1,581.8	1,977.6	2,604.5	3,225.6	3,596.1
Money Market Instruments 36m	....	....	....	....	....	....	....	....	....	....	....	....	....	....	....
Bonds (Debt Securities) 36n	....	....	....	....	.4	.4	.3	†.2	.2	1.1	1.1	2.9	2.0	4.3	2.4
o/w: Bonds Over Two Years 36na	....	....	....	....	....	....	....	....	....	....	....	....	....	....	....
Capital Accounts 37a	18.8	22.4	23.7	24.2	†64.9	71.4	86.2	†83.1	166.3	190.9	227.4	262.1	264.4	461.8	689.1
Other Items (Net) 37r	–4.9	–10.7	–44.8	–16.4	†–7.7	7.7	–14.7	†32.5	39.9	101.1	215.0	361.6	480.0	231.8	–151.9

1987	1988	1989	1990	1991	1992	1993	1994	1995	1996	1997	1998	1999	2000	2001		
Euros per SDR Thereafter: End of Period															**Exchange Rates**	
184.23	196.97	196.92	190.07	191.94	201.79	242.86	232.25	222.10	224.88	247.35	241.94	1.3662	1.4002	1.4260	Market Rate	**aa**
Euros per US Dollar Thereafter: End of Period (ae) Period Average (rf)																
129.87	146.37	149.84	133.60	134.18	146.76	176.81	159.09	149.41	156.38	183.33	171.83	.9954	1.0747	1.1347	Market Rate	**ae**
140.88	143.95	157.46	142.55	144.48	135.00	160.80	165.99	151.11	154.24	175.31	180.10	.9386	1.0854	1.1175	Market Rate	**rf**
End of Period (ea) Period Average (eb)																
169.39	171.69	177.90	183.20	179.31	177.35	197.20	195.17	191.58	194.27	202.13	201.22	....	....	....	ECU Rate	**ea**
162.49	169.19	173.32	181.43	178.83	174.44	187.80	196.37	194.12	193.18	197.96	201.99	....	....	....	ECU Rate	**eb**
Period Averages																
107.2	105.1	96.0	106.2	104.8	112.1	94.3	91.2	100.0	97.9	86.3	84.0	....	....	....	Market Rate	**ah*x***
115.1	108.9	105.6	103.8	104.3	108.0	101.8	98.3	100.0	100.2	98.1	97.1	95.7	92.9	93.4	Nominal Effective Exchange Rate	**ne*c***
78.2	78.7	82.2	87.2	93.5	101.3	98.4	97.2	100.0	100.9	99.1	99.3	98.9	96.4	98.7	Real Effective Exchange Rate	**re*c***
End of Period															**Fund Position**	
377	377	377	377	377	558	558	558	558	558	558	558	867	867	867	Quota	**2f.*s***
56	3	1	40	68	34	42	48	57	68	79	96	32	41	49	SDRs	**1b.*s***
30	30	95	124	189	228	219	231	303	320	313	442	275	242	299	Reserve Position in the Fund	**1c.*s***
373	—	—	—	—	—	—	—	—	—	—	—	—	—	—	Total Fund Cred.&Loans Outstg.	**2tl**
End of Period															**International Liquidity**	
3,327	5,127	9,952	14,485	20,629	19,129	15,840	15,513	15,850	15,918	15,660	15,825	†8,848	8,908	9,666	Total Res.Min.Gold (Eurosys.Def)	**1l.*d***
80	4	2	57	98	46	58	71	85	98	107	135	44	54	62	SDRs	**1b.*d***
42	40	125	176	270	314	301	337	450	461	423	623	377	316	376	Reserve Position in the Fund	**1c.*d***
3,205	5,083	9,826	14,252	20,261	18,769	15,481	15,106	15,315	15,359	15,130	15,067	†8,006	8,539	9,228	Foreign Exchange	**1d.*d***
....	....	....	....	....	....	....	....	....	....	....	....	111.00	....	....	*o/w:* Fin.Deriv.Rel.to Reserves	**1dd*d***
....	....	....	....	....	....	....	....	....	....	....	....	421	—	—	Other Reserve Assets	**1e.*d***
20.06	16.07	16.05	15.83	15.87	16.06	16.06	16.07	16.07	16.07	16.07	20.09	19.51	19.51	19.51	Gold (Million Fine Troy Ounces)	**1ad**
5,114	5,190	5,184	5,113	5,125	5,188	5,189	5,185	5,189	4,993	3,265	3,389	5,661	5,353	5,394	Gold (Eurosystem Valuation)	**1an*d***
....	....	....	....	....	....	....	....	....	....	....	....	2,795	....	....	Memo: Euro Cl. on Non-EA Res.	**1dg*d***
....	....	....	....	....	....	....	....	....	....	....	....	871	979	756	Non-Euro Cl. on EA Res.	**1dh*d***
....	....	....	....	....	....	....	....	....	....	....	....	3,666	....	....	Mon. Auth.: Other Foreign Assets	**3..*d***
602	10	21	24	12	20	18	122	48	44	144	6	†3,737	3,035	2,885	Foreign Liabilities	**4..*d***
1,976	3,063	3,377	6,161	8,810	13,903	20,042	28,500	35,922	37,500	47,451	54,669	†25,168	29,902	26,870	Banking Insts.: Foreign Assets	**7a.*d***
1,770	2,059	3,360	5,782	9,730	12,270	13,875	21,527	32,432	36,975	48,282	60,976	†31,352	47,626	50,006	Foreign Liab.	**7b.*d***
Billions of Euros Beginning 1999: End of Period															**Monetary Authorities**	
1,098.8	1,517.5	2,283.0	2,622.3	3,449.3	3,568.2	3,706.7	3,294.8	3,142.8	3,250.5	3,469.8	3,324.6	16.70	15.71	19.77	Fgn. Assets (Cl.on Non-EA Ctys)	**11**
....	....	....	....	....	....	....	....	....	....	....	....	3.48	5.22	2.96	Claims on General Government	**12a.*u***
1,186.6	1,100.9	1,099.4	993.1	304.2	336.2	313.0	289.9	267.6	248.2	217.6	94.6	.39	—	—	*o/w:* Claims on Gen.Govt.in Cty	**12a**
....	....	....	....	....	....	....	....	....	....	....	....	11.92	4.98	3.58	Claims on Banking Institutions	**12e.*u***
52.0	19.1	112.0	10.9	150.6	9.7	266.3	560.1	631.9	261.8	112.5	246.4	2.58	3.30	2.24	*o/w:* Claims on Bank.Inst.in Cty	**12e**
....	....	....	....	....	....	....	....	....	....	....	....	.30	.58	.43	Claims on Other Resident Sectors	**12d.*u***
15.1	12.2	9.3	20.4	24.0	35.0	36.3	45.7	38.2	39.8	41.0	42.6	.22	.22	.23	*o/w:* Cl. on Oth.Res.Sect.in Cty	**12d**
457.7	509.5	577.3	623.9	683.1	708.2	752.9	795.8	841.0	880.9	776.1	923.6	7.25	6.53	5.92	Currency Issued	**14a**
....	....	....	....	....	....	....	....	....	....	....	....	10.92	8.65	9.80	Liabilities to Banking Insts	**14c.*u***
412.9	473.0	1,313.3	1,428.1	1,830.4	2,071.5	2,277.0	432.3	376.8	473.5	558.8	421.1	4.02	3.88	4.81	*o/w:* Liabs to Bank.Inst.in Cty	**14c**
....	....	....	....	....	....	....	....	....	....	....	....	—	.02	—	Demand Dep. of Other Res.Sect.	**14d.*u***
5.0	7.7	4.4	.6	1.7	2.0	1.1	21.6	.6	.2	1.9	.4	—	.02	—	*o/w:* D.Dep.of Oth.Res.Sect.in Cty	**14d**
....	....	....	....	....	....	....	....	....	....	....	....	—	—	—	Other Dep. of Other Res.Sect.	**15..*u***
....	....	....	....	....	....	....	....	....	....	....	....	—	—	—	*o/w:* O.Dep.of Oth.Res.Sect.in Cty	**15**
....	....	....	....	....	....	....	....	....	....	....	....	—	—	—	Money Market Instruments	**16m.*u***
....	....	....	....	....	....	....	....	....	....	....	....	....	....	....	*o/w:* MMI Held by Resid.of Cty	**16m**
....	....	....	....	....	....	....	....	....	....	....	....	4.57	3.78	2.94	Bonds (Debt Securities)	**16n.*u***
....	....	....	....	....	....	....	....	....	....	....	....	....	....	....	*o/w:* Bonds Held by Resid.of Cty	**16n**
146.9	1.5	3.2	3.3	1.6	2.9	3.1	19.4	7.2	6.9	26.4	1.1	3.72	3.26	3.27	Foreign Liab. (to Non-EA Ctys)	**16c**
....	....	....	....	....	....	....	....	....	....	....	....	2.24	.01	.01	Central Government Deposits	**16d.*u***
91.6	146.8	252.9	356.1	848.4	573.9	539.8	510.6	693.0	524.0	486.7	465.1	2.24	.01	.01	*o/w:* Cent.Govt.Dep. in Cty	**16d**
395.4	482.0	474.9	385.6	267.3	184.0	493.9	446.7	303.7	310.3	693.0	588.3	3.85	4.64	5.29	Capital Accounts	**17a**
842.9	1,029.0	877.6	849.1	295.7	406.6	254.5	1,964.1	1,858.4	1,604.5	1,299.0	1,308.6	–.16	–.40	–.49	Other Items (Net)	**17r**
....	....	....	....	....	....	....	....	....	....	....	....	2.45	–3.35	–3.44	*Memo: Net Claims on Eurosystem*	**12e.*s***
....	....	....	....	....	....	....	....	....	....	....	....	....	....	....	*Currency Put into Circ.*	**14m**
Billions of Euros Beginning 1999: End of Period															**Banking Institutions**	
1,392.5	1,395.1	2,091.6	2,227.0	2,019.0	2,325.8	2,188.6	2,158.1	2,090.4	1,891.3	1,648.1	1,617.9	8.26	7.33	7.57	Claims on Monetary Authorities	**20**
....	....	....	....	....	....	....	....	....	....	....	....	18.39	17.30	24.44	Claims on Bk.Inst.in Oth.EA Ctys	**20b.*u***
256.6	448.4	506.0	823.1	1,182.2	2,040.3	3,543.7	4,534.1	5,367.2	5,864.5	8,698.9	9,393.7	25.05	32.14	30.49	Fgn. Assets (Cl.on Non-EA Ctys)	**21**
....	....	....	....	....	....	....	....	....	....	....	....	9.53	8.90	10.13	Claims on General Government	**22a.*u***
982.6	1,394.1	1,474.2	1,860.4	3,440.1	3,387.7	3,548.4	4,126.9	4,194.3	3,983.1	3,139.5	2,383.9	8.37	8.50	9.08	*o/w:* Claims on Gen.Govt.in Cty	**22a**
....	....	....	....	....	....	....	....	....	....	....	....	133.68	168.25	184.23	Claims on Other Resident Sectors	**22d.*u***
3,445.0	3,908.6	4,347.2	4,983.9	6,315.4	7,599.2	8,465.2	9,369.0	11,137.5	13,084.8	15,771.6	19,705.1	129.36	160.56	179.18	*o/w:* Cl. on Oth.Res.Sect.in Cty	**22d**
....	....	....	....	....	....	....	....	....	....	....	....	40.03	42.50	46.93	Demand Deposits	**24..*u***
1,180.4	1,478.3	1,688.2	1,766.6	2,072.8	2,556.7	2,861.6	3,038.7	3,435.0	3,914.6	4,637.9	5,411.6	39.68	42.12	46.59	*o/w:* D.Dep.of Oth.Res.Sect.in Cty	**24**
....	....	....	....	....	....	....	....	....	....	....	....	71.25	75.32	78.58	Other Deposits	**25..*u***
3,997.9	4,584.3	5,146.1	5,709.1	7,248.6	8,503.4	9,414.9	10,360.4	11,116.5	11,465.1	11,956.0	12,064.7	67.51	71.56	72.37	*o/w:* O.Dep.of Oth.Res.Sect.in Cty	**25**
....	....	....	....	....	....	....	....	....	....	....	....	—	.12	.17	Money Market Instruments	**26m.*u***
....	....	....	....	....	....	....	....	....	....	....	....	....	....	....	*o/w:* MMI Held by Resid.of Cty	**26m**
....	....	....	....	....	....	....	....	....	....	....	....	16.91	21.97	25.76	Bonds (Debt Securities)	**26n.*u***
40.7	38.5	39.0	69.0	84.5	106.7	197.1	169.0	125.7	257.7	331.5	599.5	....	....	....	*o/w:* Bonds Held by Resid.of Cty	**26n**
229.8	301.3	503.5	772.5	1,305.6	1,800.7	2,453.2	3,424.8	4,845.8	5,782.4	8,851.3	10,477.5	31.21	51.18	56.74	Foreign Liab. (to Non-EA Ctys)	**26c**
....	....	....	....	....	....	....	....	....	....	....	....	5.08	6.42	4.29	Central Government Deposits	**26d.*u***
221.6	285.4	359.5	430.6	519.1	451.8	454.4	541.2	701.2	800.3	906.7	1,017.4	5.07	6.42	4.27	*o/w:* Cent.Govt.Dep. in Cty	**26d**
112.5	69.5	156.2	65.6	190.2	50.8	296.0	560.3	631.9	261.8	112.5	246.4	2.58	3.30	2.24	Credit from Monetary Authorities	**26g**
....	....	....	....	....	....	....	....	....	....	....	....	22.51	23.30	32.35	Liab. to Bk.Inst.in Oth. EA Ctys	**26h.*u***
434.8	652.4	837.7	1,167.4	1,568.8	1,945.7	2,251.7	2,430.8	2,500.8	2,782.6	2,978.4	4,117.9	20.21	22.91	24.57	Capital Accounts	**27a**
–140.9	–263.6	–311.1	–87.1	–33.7	–65.3	–183.6	–338.0	–573.1	–443.1	–515.9	–834.3	–14.87	–13.12	–14.77	Other Items (Net)	**27r**
Billions of Euros Beginning 1999: End of Period															**Banking Survey (Nat'l Residency)**	
978.6	1,663.0	2,282.4	2,669.6	3,324.3	3,804.9	4,794.2	4,384.7	3,657.0	3,325.6	3,291.0	2,239.7	10.67	–5.59	–17.74	Foreign Assets (Net)	**31n**
5,316.0	5,983.5	6,317.7	7,071.1	8,716.2	10,332.5	11,368.7	12,779.7	14,243.5	16,031.6	17,776.3	20,743.7	131.03	162.85	184.20	Domestic Credit	**32**
1,856.0	2,062.8	1,961.2	2,066.9	2,376.8	2,698.3	2,867.2	3,365.0	3,067.8	2,907.0	1,963.7	996.0	1.45	2.07	4.80	Claims on General Govt. (Net)	**32an**
3,460.1	3,920.8	4,356.5	5,004.2	6,339.5	7,634.3	8,501.5	9,414.7	11,175.7	13,124.6	15,812.6	19,747.7	129.58	160.78	179.40	Claims on Other Resident Sectors	**32d**
457.7	509.5	577.3	623.9	683.1	708.2	752.9	795.8	841.0	880.9	776.1	923.6	7.25	6.53	5.92	Currency Issued	**34a.*n***
1,185.3	1,486.0	1,692.6	1,767.2	2,074.5	2,558.7	2,862.7	3,060.2	3,435.5	3,914.7	4,639.7	5,412.0	39.69	42.14	46.59	Demand Deposits	**34b.*n***
3,997.9	4,584.3	5,146.1	5,709.1	7,248.6	8,503.4	9,414.9	10,360.4	11,116.5	11,465.1	11,956.0	12,064.7	67.51	71.56	72.37	Other Deposits	**35..*n***
....	....	....	....	....	....	....	....	....	....	....	....	—	.12	.17	Money Market Instruments	**36m**
40.7	38.5	39.0	69.0	84.5	106.7	197.1	169.0	125.7	257.7	331.5	599.5	21.49	25.76	28.69	Bonds (Debt Securities)	**36n**
....	....	....	....	....	....	....	....	....	....	....	....	19.87	23.24	25.79	*o/w:* Bonds Over Two Years	**36na**
830.3	1,134.5	1,312.6	1,553.0	1,836.1	2,129.7	2,745.6	2,877.5	2,804.5	3,093.0	3,671.4	4,706.2	24.06	27.55	29.86	Capital Accounts	**37a**
–217.1	–106.3	–167.6	17.8	113.0	128.1	189.1	–99.4	–428.4	–256.4	–306.3	–722.4	–18,294.3	–16,393.6	–17,130.6	Other Items (Net)	**37r**

Portugal

	1972	1973	1974	1975	1976	1977	1978	1979	1980	1981	1982	1983	1984	1985	1986
Banking Survey (EA-Wide Residency)														*Billions of Euros:*	
Foreign Assets (Net) 31n.*u*	...	...	...	...	...	...	...	...	...	...	...	...	...	...	...
Domestic Credit .... 32..*u*	...	...	...	...	...	...	...	...	...	...	...	...	...	...	...
Claims on General Govt. (Net) .... 32an *u*	...	...	...	...	...	...	...	...	...	...	...	...	...	...	...
Claims on Other Resident Sect. 32d.*u*	...	...	...	...	...	...	...	...	...	...	...	...	...	...	...
Currency Issued 34a.*u*	...	...	...	...	...	...	...	...	...	...	...	...	...	...	...
Demand Deposits 34b.*u*	...	...	...	...	...	...	...	...	...	...	...	...	...	...	...
Other Deposits .... 35..*u*	...	...	...	...	...	...	...	...	...	...	...	...	...	...	...
o/w: Other Dep. Over Two Yrs .... 35ab *u*	...	...	...	...	...	...	...	...	...	...	...	...	...	...	...
Money Market Instruments 36m.*u*	...	...	...	...	...	...	...	...	...	...	...	...	...	...	...
Bonds (Debt Securities) 36n.*u*	...	...	...	...	...	...	...	...	...	...	...	...	...	...	...
o/w: Bonds Over Two Years .... 36na *u*	...	...	...	...	...	...	...	...	...	...	...	...	...	...	...
Capital Accounts 37a	...	...	...	...	...	...	...	...	...	...	...	...	...	...	...
Other Items (Net) 37r.*u*	...	...	...	...	...	...	...	...	...	...	...	...	...	...	...
Money (National Definitions)														*Billions of Escudos:*	
M1 .... 39ma								392.6	473.6	518.1	602.5	654.7	757.3	964.1	1,315.5
M2 .... 39mb								847.6	1,088.1	1,349.1	1,674.2	1,956.2	2,442.1	3,036.2	3,636.3
L 39mc									936.0	1,212.9	1,508.9	1,807.3	2,174.1	2,772.5	3,533.1
Interest Rates														*Percent Per Annum*	
Banco de Portugal Rate(*End of Per*) 60	4.00	5.00	7.50	6.50	6.50	13.00	18.00	18.00	18.00	18.00	19.00	25.00	25.00	19.00	16.00
Money Market Rate 60b							18.42	14.87	9.95	9.24	12.42	18.24	21.27	20.17	†14.52
Treasury Bill Rate 60c									12.37	13.48	14.37	18.14	21.15	20.90	†15.56
Deposit Rate 60l				9.50	12.54	17.67	19.00	19.00	19.25	21.00	26.08	28.00	25.08	17.13
Lending Rate 60p				8.75	12.50	17.58	18.75	18.75	20.13	23.00	27.88	29.42	27.29	19.63
Government Bond Yield 61	6.01	5.50			9.74	10.80	16.17	16.68	16.68	16.71	16.79	19.22	21.50	20.75	15.54
Prices, Production, Labor														*Index Numbers (1995=100):*	
Share Prices 62															
Prices: Home & Import Goods 63	7.9	8.8	11.4	12.9	15.3	19.7	25.9	33.6	35.8	43.5	55.5	64.7	82.5	100.0	109.2
Home Goods 63a	8.7	9.7	12.2	13.1	15.8	20.4	28.7	37.9	36.4	45.0	53.5	65.2	83.3	100.0	109.1
Consumer Prices 64	3.2	3.5	4.5	5.5	6.5	8.2	10.1	12.5	14.5	17.4	21.4	†26.8	34.6	41.3	46.2
Harmonized CPI 64h															
Wages: Daily Earnings (Mfg.) 65ey								15.5	19.5	23.4	32.7	38.0	45.8	54.2	63.6
Industrial Production 66									64.7	69.7	71.9	74.1	†74.9	79.7
														Number in Thousands:	
Labor Force 67d															
Employment 67e														4,279	4,287
Unemployment 67c														397	393
Unemployment Rate (%) 67r														8.5	8.3
International Transactions														*Billions of Escudos through 1998;*	
Exports 70	35.1	44.8	57.5	49.3	54.7	75.7	106.5	170.5	232.2	254.9	331.7	508.6	760.6	967.4	1,082.5
Imports, c.i.f. 71	59.6	73.2	113.3	97.5	127.8	182.7	230.1	320.1	465.8	599.7	754.0	899.4	1,160.6	1,302.8	1,442.5
Imports, f.o.b. 71.v	53.2	65.7	102.6	88.4	115.1	165.6	208.6	290.2	422.2	543.6	683.4	817.3	1,052.3	1,181.1	1,307.8
															1990=100
Volume of Exports 72													44.4	50.9	56.3	60.7
Volume of Imports 73													43.2	40.7	43.4	51.7
Export Prices 76													49.1	64.1	74.1	76.6
Import Prices 76.x	7.2	8.2	10.7	12.0	14.3	19.8	23.7	28.8	33.7	38.9	45.7	†59.7	80.6	86.3	78.9
Balance of Payments														*Millions of US Dollars:*	
Current Account, n.i.e. 78ald				−755	−1,282	−957	−463	−54	−1,064	−4,686	−3,258	−1,632	−623	380	1,166
Goods: Exports f.o.b. .... 78aa d				1,942	1,825	2,564	2,782	3,608	4,668	4,185	4,194	4,646	5,246	5,749	7,265
Goods: Imports f.o.b. .... 78ab d				−3,544	−3,960	−4,528	−4,783	−6,183	−8,611	−11,132	−8,953	−7,631	−7,297	−7,179	−8,876
Trade Balance .... 78ac d				−1,603	−2,136	−1,964	−2,001	−2,575	−3,943	−6,948	−4,759	−2,985	−2,051	−1,430	−1,611
Services: Credit .... 78ad d				941	756	840	1,076	1,592	2,006	1,946	1,536	1,478	1,656	1,931	2,425
Services: Debit .... 78ae d				−1,110	−730	−785	−849	−1,128	−1,525	−1,639	−1,462	−1,254	−1,244	−1,269	−1,585
Balance on Goods & Services .... 78af d				−1,772	−2,110	−1,909	−1,774	−2,110	−3,462	−6,640	−4,685	−2,761	−1,638	−768	−772
Income: Credit .... 78ag d				115	47	67	87	133	173	206	153	167	195	277	300
Income: Debit .... 78ah d				−139	−184	−249	−410	−553	−781	−1,141	−1,405	−1,212	−1,355	−1,373	−1,276
Balance on Gds, Serv. & Inc. .... 78ai d				−1,796	−2,247	−2,090	−2,098	−2,531	−4,070	−7,575	−5,937	−3,806	−2,798	−1,864	−1,748
Current Transfers, n.i.e.: Credit .... 78aj d				1,103	1,007	1,222	1,718	2,536	3,047	2,918	2,718	2,245	2,257	2,329	3,306
Current Transfers: Debit .... 78ak d				−62	−42	−89	−83	−59	−41	−29	−40	−71	−82	−85	−392
Capital Account, n.i.e. .... 78bc d															
Capital Account, n.i.e.: Credit .... 78ba d				—	—	—	—	—	—	—	—	—	—	—	—
Capital Account: Debit .... 78bb d				—	—	—	—	—	—	—	—	—	—	—	—
Financial Account, n.i.e. .... 78bj d				180	820	1,114	1,256	−477	−159	2,867	3,144	591	559	580	−1,432
Direct Investment Abroad .... 78bd d				−8	−5	−3	−6	8	−14	−16	−8	−17	−7	−22	—
Dir. Invest. in Rep. Econ., n.i.e. .... 78be d				115	63	58	66	78	157	174	144	146	195	274	238
Portfolio Investment Assets .... 78bf d				−1	1	1	1	1	2	8	1	1	—	1	—
Equity Securities .... 78bk d				—	—	—	—	—	1	6	1	1	—	—	—
Debt Securities .... 78bl d				−1	1	1	1	1	—	2	1	—	—	1	—
Portfolio Investment Liab., n.i.e. .... 78bg d				−5	7	1	−4	−4	−9	−3	153	140	149	123	404
Equity Securities .... 78bm d				—	—	—	—	—	−1	−1	2	8	1	−1	1
Debt Securities .... 78bn d				−5	7	1	−4	−4	−8	−2	151	132	149	124	402
Financial Derivatives Assets .... 78bw d															
Financial Derivatives Liabilities .... 78bx d															
Other Investment Assets .... 78bh d				−15	−157	−231	−218	−503	−259	1,017	671	−946	−572	−385	−1,095
Monetary Authorities .... 78bo d				−27	−20	−6	5	−18	−5	5	—	—	—	—	—
General Government .... 78bp d				−5	−46	−53	−91	4	−31	−47	−38	−32	−41	−39	−49
Banks .... 78bq d				21	−88	−183	−141	−505	−225	145	—	−300	−288	−93	186
Other Sectors .... 78br d				−4	−4	12	9	16	2	915	709	−614	−242	−253	−1,231
Other Investment Liab., n.i.e. .... 78bi d				93	911	1,288	1,417	−58	−35	1,687	2,184	1,267	795	589	−979
Monetary Authorities .... 78bs d				312	684	486	767	93	84	529	454	552	193	126	−476
General Government .... 78bt d				−70	40	111	533	—	—	—	—	—	—	−1	—
Banks .... 78bu d				−29	239	750	−60	−248	−222	84	484	271	95	−232	−254
Other Sectors .... 78bv d				−119	−53	−59	177	97	102	1,073	1,246	445	507	697	−249
Net Errors and Omissions .... 78ca d				−150	58	−70	−293	597	1,218	1,707	100	−11	−31	−253	156
Overall Balance .... 78cb d				−725	−404	87	500	66	−5	−113	−14	−1,053	−95	707	−111
Reserves and Related Items .... 79da d				725	404	−87	−500	−66	5	113	14	1,053	95	−707	111
Reserve Assets .... 79db d				725	168	−171	−474	−25	107	167	56	687	−127	−707	111
Use of Fund Credit and Loans .... 79dc d				—	201	84	−54	−40	−102	−55	−42	366	221	—	—
Exceptional Financing .... 79de d				—	35	—	28	—	—	—	—	—	—	—	—

1987	1988	1989	1990	1991	1992	1993	1994	1995	1996	1997	1998	1999	2000	2001		
End of Period															**Banking Survey (EA-Wide Residency)**	
....	....	....	....	....	....	....	....	....	....	....	....	6.83	–6.60	–9.75	Foreign Assets (Net)	31n.*u*
....	....	....	....	....	....	....	....	....	....	....	....	139.67	176.51	193.44	Domestic Credit	32..*u*
....	....	....	....	....	....	....	....	....	....	....	....	5.70	7.69	8.78	Claims on General Govt. (Net)	32an*u*
....	....	....	....	....	....	....	....	....	....	....	....	133.97	168.82	184.66	Claims on Other Resident Sect.	32d.*u*
....	....	....	....	....	....	....	....	....	....	....	....	7.25	6.53	5.92	Currency Issued	34a.*u*
....	....	....	....	....	....	....	....	....	....	....	....	40.03	42.52	46.93	Demand Deposits	34b.*u*
....	....	....	....	....	....	....	....	....	....	....	....	71.25	75.32	78.58	Other Deposits	35..*u*
....	....	....	....	....	....	....	....	....	....	....	....	4.03	3.84	3.57	*o/w:* Other Dep. Over Two Yrs	35ab*u*
....	....	....	....	....	....	....	....	....	....	....	....	—	.12	.17	Money Market Instruments	36m.*u*
....	....	....	....	....	....	....	....	....	....	....	....	21.49	25.76	28.69	Bonds (Debt Securities)	36n.*u*
....	....	....	....	....	....	....	....	....	....	....	....	19.87	23.24	25.79	*o/w:* Bonds Over Two Years	36na*u*
....	....	....	....	....	....	....	....	....	....	....	....	24.06	27.55	29.86	Capital Accounts	37a
....	....	....	....	....	....	....	....	....	....	....	....	–17.58	–7.87	–6.46	Other Items (Net)	37r.*u*
End of Period															**Money (National Definitions)**	
1,585.3	1,916.4	2,192.6	2,312.6	2,653.0	3,116.4	3,354.5	3,589.4	3,901.2	4,302.2	4,882.1	5,757.4	....	....	....	*M1*	39ma
4,255.7	5,034.0	5,692.0	6,201.6	7,738.6	9,054.3	9,701.9	10,586.2	11,434.5	12,468.2	13,316.2	14,401.3	....	....	....	*M2*	39mb
4,360.1	5,139.1	5,852.3	6,509.0	7,389.7	8,601.4	9,376.2	10,020.3	11,102.1	11,907.3	12,825.5	13,667.5	....	....	....	*L*	39mc
Percent Per Annum															**Interest Rates**	
14.50	13.50	14.50	14.50	†20.00	21.96	11.00	8.88	8.50	6.70	5.31	3.00	....	....	....	Banco de Portugal Rate*(End of Per)*	60
13.69	12.31	12.68	13.12	15.50	†17.48	13.25	10.62	8.91	7.38	5.78	4.34	2.71	....	....	Money Market Rate	60b
13.89	12.97	....	13.51	14.20	12.88	....	....	7.75	5.75	4.43	....	....	....	....	Treasury Bill Rate	60c
14.46	13.21	13.00	13.99	14.80	14.59	11.06	8.37	8.38	6.32	4.56	3.37	2.40	....	....	Deposit Rate	60l
†18.92	†17.53	19.59	21.78	†25.02	20.43	16.48	15.01	13.80	11.73	9.15	7.24	5.19	....	....	Lending Rate	60p
15.02	13.87	15.63	18.55	18.27	15.38	12.45	10.83	10.34	7.25	5.48	4.09	....	....	....	Government Bond Yield	61
Period Averages															**Prices, Production, Labor**	
....	89.3	93.0	89.7	76.3	67.3	79.3	104.1	100.0	117.3	183.4	287.7	....	....	....	Share Prices	62
....	....	....	....	....	....	....	....	....	....	....	....	....	....	....	Prices: Home & Import Goods	63
....	....	....	....	....	....	....	....	....	....	....	....	....	....	....	Home Goods	63a
50.5	55.3	62.3	70.7	†78.7	85.7	91.5	96.0	100.0	103.1	†105.3	108.3	110.8	114.0	118.9	Consumer Prices	64
....	....	....	....	....	....	....	....	....	....	....	107.2	109.5	112.6	117.6	Harmonized CPI	64h
72.4	76.0	86.2	100.0	113.5	....	....	....	....	....	....	....	....	....	....	Wages: Daily Earnings (Mfg.)	65ey
83.4	86.5	91.9	†100.6	102.0	100.1	96.5	95.4	100.0	†101.4	103.7	109.7	112.5	116.3	....	Industrial Production	66
Period Averages																
....	....	....	....	....	....	4,708	4,799	4,777	4,809	4,868	5,000	....	5,126	....	Labor Force	67d
4,403	4,517	4,613	4,718	4,857	†4,587	4,493	4,482	4,442	4,467	4,546	†4,652	4,837	4,921	....	Employment	67e
329	....	243	231	208	†194	257	324	338	344	324	†248	222	205	....	Unemployment	67c
7.0	....	5.0	4.7	4.1	†4.2	5.6	6.9	7.2	7.3	6.8	5.0	4.4	4.0	....	Unemployment Rate (%)	67r
Millions of Euros Beginning 1999															**International Transactions**	
1,311.0	1,582.0	2,015.7	2,336.5	2,354.1	2,475.2	2,474.4	2,975.6	3,501.8	3,795.9	4,195.1	†4,461.0	†23715.6	25,241.2	....	Exports	70
1,965.3	2,581.0	3,003.2	3,589.7	3,811.1	4,087.6	3,883.8	4,514.3	5,028.7	5,427.1	6,139.7	†6,914.8	†37505.6	41,425.2	....	Imports, c.i.f.	71
1,781.8	2,340.0	2,722.8	3,254.5	3,455.2	3,705.9	3,521.1	4,092.7	4,559.1	4,920.3	....	....	....	....	....	Imports, f.o.b.	71.v
1990=100																
67.8	74.1	89.1	†100.0	100.6	107.0	....	....	....	....	....	....	....	....	....	Volume of Exports	72
66.2	80.8	87.7	†100.0	106.0	118.6	....	....	....	....	....	....	....	....	....	Volume of Imports	73
83.0	91.6	97.1	†100.0	100.2	98.1	....	....	....	....	....	....	....	....	....	Export Prices	76
83.8	89.7	96.6	†100.0	100.2	95.2	....	....	....	....	....	....	....	....	....	Import Prices	76.x
Minus Sign Indicates Debit															Balance of Payments	
435	–1,066	153	–181	–716	–184	233	–2,196	–132	–5,216	–6,465	–7,833	–9,764	–10,962	–9,959	Current Account, n.i.e.	78al*d*
9,335	11,015	12,843	16,458	16,391	18,348	15,931	18,645	24,024	25,623	25,379	25,618	25,468	25,219	25,795	Goods: Exports f.o.b.	78aa*d*
–12,847	–16,392	–17,585	–23,141	–24,079	–27,735	–23,981	–26,966	–32,934	–35,345	–35,721	–37,829	–39,227	–39,155	–38,774	Goods: Imports f.o.b.	78ab*d*
–3,513	–5,377	–4,742	–6,684	–7,688	–9,387	–8,050	–8,321	–8,910	–9,722	–10,342	–12,211	–13,758	–13,936	–12,979	*Trade Balance*	78ac*d*
3,165	3,418	3,789	5,096	5,231	5,497	6,846	6,755	8,236	8,040	8,002	8,829	8,659	8,472	8,787	Services: Credit	78ad*d*
–2,157	–2,668	–2,830	–4,005	–4,420	–4,732	–5,481	–5,486	–6,611	–6,636	–6,572	–6,903	–6,801	–6,593	–6,193	Services: Debit	78ae*d*
–2,505	–4,627	–3,784	–5,592	–6,877	–8,621	–6,685	–7,052	–7,285	–8,317	–8,912	–10,285	–11,900	–12,057	–10,385	*Balance on Goods & Services*	78af*d*
414	477	719	1,360	1,550	2,067	2,455	2,232	4,095	4,250	4,238	4,496	4,261	4,793	5,128	Income: Credit	78ag*d*
–1,245	–1,238	–1,322	–1,457	–1,364	–1,456	–2,236	–2,797	–4,074	–5,420	–5,744	–6,135	–6,029	–7,101	–8,182	Income: Debit	78ah*d*
–3,336	–5,388	–4,387	–5,689	–6,691	–8,010	–6,466	–7,616	–7,264	–9,488	–10,418	–11,924	–13,669	–14,365	–13,439	*Balance on Gds, Serv. & Inc.*	78ai*d*
4,365	4,946	5,227	6,433	7,237	9,344	8,395	7,410	9,046	6,515	5,985	6,170	6,048	5,386	5,626	Current Transfers, n.i.e.: Credit	78aj*d*
–594	–624	–687	–926	–1,263	–1,518	–1,696	–1,989	–1,914	–2,243	–2,031	–2,080	–2,143	–1,983	–2,145	Current Transfers: Debit	78ak*d*
—	—	—	—	—	—	—	—	—	2,695	2,704	2,546	2,459	1,512	1,067	Capital Account, n.i.e.	78bc*d*
—	—	—	—	—	—	—	—	—	2,836	2,893	2,724	2,642	1,681	1,276	Capital Account, n.i.e.: Credit	78ba*d*
—	—	—	—	—	—	—	—	—	–141	–189	–179	–183	–169	–209	Capital Account: Debit	78bb*d*
689	293	4,005	2,563	4,537	–950	–3,032	1,052	3,025	3,835	6,662	5,980	9,098	11,184	12,530	Financial Account, n.i.e.	78bj*d*
10	–80	–84	–163	–463	–687	–147	–287	–688	–972	–2,187	–3,851	–3,019	–7,749	–7,874	Direct Investment Abroad	78bd*d*
466	922	1,737	2,610	2,448	1,873	1,534	1,270	685	1,703	2,542	3,151	1,235	6,518	5,945	Dir. Invest. in Rep. Econ., n.i.e.	78be*d*
—	–27	—	—	—	–379	–2,382	–3,456	–3,148	–5,549	–8,697	–5,997	–6,737	–4,583	–6,430	Portfolio Investment Assets	78bf*d*
—	–1	—	—	—	–9	–168	–66	–159	–602	–568	–975	–2,110	–1,044	–1,755	Equity Securities	78bk*d*
—	–27	—	—	—	–370	–2,214	–3,390	–2,989	–4,947	–8,129	–5,022	–4,626	–3,539	–4,676	Debt Securities	78bl*d*
816	1,841	1,050	961	1,895	–2,685	4,214	3,934	2,066	2,383	8,790	5,385	9,945	2,792	8,405	Portfolio Investment Liab., n.i.e.	78bg*d*
243	220	605	508	215	570	579	562	–179	1,669	3,821	2,165	691	415	424	Equity Securities	78bm*d*
573	1,622	445	453	1,681	–3,255	3,634	3,372	2,244	714	4,970	3,221	9,254	2,376	7,981	Debt Securities	78bn*d*
....	....	....	....	....	....	–5	—	—	93	341	1,116	2,682	3,673	3,086	Financial Derivatives Assets	78bw*d*
....	....	....	....	....	....	—	—	—	–130	–360	–985	–2,485	–3,351	–2,830	Financial Derivatives Liabilities	78bx*d*
–87	–1,145	–7	–2,442	–1,511	–1,923	–8,424	–7,098	–7,568	–3,368	–5,346	–7,100	421	–10,262	–2,598	Other Investment Assets	78bh*d*
—	—	—	—	—	—	9	—	–26	–3	1	–94	–1,005	11	21	Monetary Authorities	78bo*d*
–58	–108	–114	–137	–98	–40	....	....	....	1	11	—	–20	–12	–42	General Government	78bp*d*
–412	–1,256	–584	–1,786	–1,250	–2,207	–7,024	–4,741	–6,679	–2,945	–3,116	–3,813	973	–7,201	–1,034	Banks	78bq*d*
383	219	690	–520	–163	324	–1,409	–2,358	–863	–422	–2,241	–3,192	473	–3,059	–1,543	Other Sectors	78br*d*
–517	–1,218	1,310	1,598	2,168	2,851	2,178	6,689	11,678	9,675	11,579	14,260	7,055	24,146	14,826	Other Investment Liab., n.i.e.	78bi*d*
–118	–1,402	–470	–518	–385	–24	–32	299	–99	731	1,343	837	–3	4,862	87	Monetary Authorities	78bs*d*
–1	—	—	—	—	—	–146	–139	144	–312	–40	–73	–43	–179	–151	General Government	78bt*d*
10	233	1,241	1,329	2,376	1,757	1,327	7,069	11,189	8,595	8,936	12,245	6,999	18,231	14,481	Banks	78bu*d*
–409	–49	538	786	176	1,117	1,028	–540	444	661	1,339	1,250	102	1,232	409	Other Sectors	78bv*d*
653	1,640	497	1,160	1,893	978	–48	–287	–3,193	–767	–1,928	–184	–1,577	–1,363	–2,786	Net Errors and Omissions	78ca*d*
1,777	867	4,654	3,542	5,713	–156	–2,848	–1,430	–300	547	974	508	216	371	852	*Overall Balance*	78cb*d*
–1,777	–867	–4,654	–3,542	–5,713	156	2,848	1,430	300	–547	–974	–508	–216	–371	–852	Reserves and Related Items	79da*d*
–1,521	–365	–4,654	–3,542	–5,713	156	2,848	1,430	300	–547	–974	–508	–216	–371	–852	Reserve Assets	79db*d*
–256	–502	—	—	—	—	—	—	—	—	—	—	—	—	—	Use of Fund Credit and Loans	79dc*d*
—	—	—	—	—	—	....	....	....	—	—	—	—	—	....	Exceptional Financing	79de*d*

Portugal

		1972	1973	1974	1975	1976	1977	1978	1979	1980	1981	1982	1983	1984	1985	1986
International Investment Position																*Millions of US Dollars*
Assets	79aa d	...	...	...	...	...	...	...	...	...	...	...	...	...	...	...
Direct Investment Abroad	79ab d	...	...	...	...	...	...	...	...	...	...	...	...	...	...	...
Portfolio Investment	79ac d	...	...	...	...	...	...	...	...	...	...	...	...	...	...	...
Equity Securities	79ad d	...	...	...	...	...	...	...	...	...	...	...	...	...	...	...
Debt Securities	79ae d	...	...	...	...	...	...	...	...	...	...	...	...	...	...	...
Financial Derivatives	79al d	...	...	...	...	...	...	...	...	...	...	...	...	...	...	...
Other Investment	79af d	...	...	...	...	...	...	...	...	...	...	...	...	...	...	...
Monetary Authorities	79ag d	...	...	...	...	...	...	...	...	...	...	...	...	...	...	...
General Government	79ah d	...	...	...	...	...	...	...	...	...	...	...	...	...	...	...
Banks	79ai d	...	...	...	...	...	...	...	...	...	...	...	...	...	...	...
Other Sectors	79aj d	...	...	...	...	...	...	...	...	...	...	...	...	...	...	...
Reserve Assets	79ak d	...	...	...	...	...	...	...	...	...	...	...	...	...	...	...
Liabilities	79la d	...	...	...	...	...	...	...	...	...	...	...	...	...	...	...
Dir. Invest. in Rep. Economy	79lb d	...	...	...	...	...	...	...	...	...	...	...	...	...	...	...
Portfolio Investment	79lc d	...	...	...	...	...	...	...	...	...	...	...	...	...	...	...
Equity Securities	79ld d	...	...	...	...	...	...	...	...	...	...	...	...	...	...	...
Debt Securities	79le d	...	...	...	...	...	...	...	...	...	...	...	...	...	...	...
Financial Derivatives	79ll d	...	...	...	...	...	...	...	...	...	...	...	...	...	...	...
Other Investment	79lf d	...	...	...	...	...	...	...	...	...	...	...	...	...	...	...
Monetary Authorities	79lg d	...	...	...	...	...	...	...	...	...	...	...	...	...	...	...
General Government	79lh d	...	...	...	...	...	...	...	...	...	...	...	...	...	...	...
Banks	79li d	...	...	...	...	...	...	...	...	...	...	...	...	...	...	...
Other Sectors	79lj d	...	...	...	...	...	...	...	...	...	...	...	...	...	...	...
Government Finance																
Central Government															*Billions of Escudos through 1998;*	
Deficit (-) or Surplus	80	−5.6	−3.6	−8.9	†−31.8	−54.0	−40.9	−92.8	−100.5	−121.5	−179.6	−195.0	−219.7	−272.4	−522.0	−543.2
Revenue	81	33.8	39.9	47.2	†96.0	127.4	176.7	217.4	272.1	377.2	480.9	603.5	809.8	951.4	1,182.3	1,553.9
Grants Received	81z	...	...	...	†—	.1	1.5	.6	1.0	2.9	1.5	1.2	1.9	3.9	5.1	56.6
Expenditure	82	33.8	41.3	55.4	†123.5	172.8	210.0	283.8	352.8	475.9	620.2	751.0	974.1	1,141.7	1,626.6	2,033.5
Lending Minus Repayments	83	1.5	1.3	1.4	†4.3	8.7	9.1	27.0	20.8	25.7	41.8	48.7	57.3	86.0	82.8	120.2
Unclass. Transactions (Net)	83x	4.1	.9	−.7	...	...	...	...	...	...	...	...	...	...	...	...
Financing																
Domestic	84a	3.5	3.9	6.2	†32.3	52.9	41.3	73.1	95.1	93.8	141.8	141.9	143.2	174.8	465.5	589.2
Foreign	85a	−.3	.2	−.2	†−.6	1.2	−.4	19.7	5.4	27.7	37.8	53.1	76.5	97.6	56.5	−46.0
Use of Cash Balances	87	2.5	−.5	2.9	...	...	...	...	...	...	...	...	...	...	...	...
Debt: Escudos	88b	15.32	39.62	48.91	90.09	147.18	...	...	...	...	...	...	...	...	...	...
Held By: Bk of Portugal	88ba	1.54	1.74	8.73	44.08	68.79	...	...	...	...	...	...	...	...	...	...
Commercial Banks	88bb	4.84	8.82	8.49	7.88	14.23	...	...	...	...	...	...	...	...	...	...
Savings Banks	88bc	3.53	6.36	6.10	5.40	8.20	...	...	...	...	...	...	...	...	...	...
Others	88bd	5.41	22.70	25.59	32.73	55.96	...	...	...	...	...	...	...	...	...	...
Intragovernmental Debt	88s	13.48	13.22	13.14	9.58	3.48	...	...	...	...	...	...	...	...	...	...
Held by: Social Insur. System	88sz	12.80	12.62	12.62	9.12	3.12	...	...	...	...	...	...	...	...	...	...
General Government																*As Percent of*
Deficit (-) or Surplus	80g	...	...	...	...	...	...	...	...	...	...	...	...	...	...	...
Debt	88g	...	...	...	...	...	...	...	...	...	...	...	...	...	...	...
National Accounts																*Billions of Escudos through 1998;*
Househ.Cons.Expend.,incl.NPISHs	96f															
Government Consumption Expend.	91f	32	36	48	57	64	90	112	144	187	231	282	360	433	559	762
Gross Fixed Capital Formation	93e	67	76	88	98	118	166	220	264	359	463	575	672	664	768	1,225
Changes in Inventories	93i	2	7	9	−21	−2	16	23	52	73	116	112	−1	−38	−41	−49
Exports of Goods and Services	90c	57	75	91	77	82	105	139	232	298	339	432	645	934	1,159	1,298
Imports of Goods and Services (-)	98c	71	95	143	124	145	203	247	362	510	660	808	984	1,233	1,412	1,592
Gross Domestic Product (GDP)	99b	235	282	339	377	469	626	787	995	1,256	1,501	1,850	2,302	2,816	3,524	5,060
Net Primary Income from Abroad	98.n	1	2	4	—	−5	−8	16	−22	−33	−61	−103	−120	−177	−196	−152
Gross National Income (GNI)	99a	236	285	343	377	464	618	772	972	1,225	1,440	1,747	2,182	2,638	3,328	4,269
Net National Income	99e	223	271	328	359	449	592	736	928	1,170	1,377	1,665	2,061	2,507	3,177	...
GDP Volume 1990 prices	99b.p	5,230	5,816	5,882	5,627	6,015	6,352	6,531	6,899	7,216	7,332	7,489	7,476	7,335	7,541	7,854
GDP Volume 1995 Prices	99b.p	...	...	...	...	...	...	...	...	...	...	...	...	...	...	...
GDP Volume (1995=100)	99bv p	48.7	54.1	54.7	52.4	56.0	59.1	60.8	64.2	67.2	68.2	69.7	69.6	68.3	70.2	73.1
GDP Deflator (1995=100)	99bi p	3.1	3.3	3.9	4.6	5.3	6.7	8.2	9.8	11.8	13.9	16.8	20.9	26.1	31.8	43.8
																Millions:
Population	99z	8.97	8.98	8.99	9.43	9.67	9.74	9.80	†9.66	9.77	9.86	9.86	9.88	9.90	9.91	10.01

Millions of US Dollars — International Investment Position

	1987	1988	1989	1990	1991	1992	1993	1994	1995	1996	1997	1998	1999	2000	2001		
Assets	....	....	....	....	....	....	45,989	54,212	59,764	86,425	99,344	128,461	122,341	140,328	150,742	Assets	79aa d
Direct Investment Abroad	....	....	....	....	....	....	—	—		4,726	5,932	9,622	10,331	17,781	24,881	Direct Investment Abroad	79ab d
Portfolio Investment	....	....	....	....	....	....				17,502	20,368	28,489	36,459	39,096	42,530	Portfolio Investment	79ac d
Equity Securities	....	....	....	....	....	....				4,997	4,765	6,008	7,226	7,587	7,761	Equity Securities	79ad d
Debt Securities	....	....	....	....	....	....				12,505	15,602	22,480	29,233	31,509	34,769	Debt Securities	79ae d
Financial Derivatives	....	....	....	....	....	....				422	381	355	2,055	2,758	1,929	Financial Derivatives	79al d
Other Investment	....	....	....	....	....	....	24,170	32,543	37,810	42,030	52,341	68,409	59,396	66,467	66,321	Other Investment	79af d
Monetary Authorities	....	....	....	....	....	....				47	28	127	1,479	1,367	1,280	Monetary Authorities	79ag d
General Government	....	....	....	....	....	....	15	15	28	80	78	47	66	74	112	General Government	79ah d
Banks	....	....	....	....	....	....	18,016	25,149	30,288	29,900	38,718	44,389	39,688	45,084	44,495	Banks	79ai d
Other Sectors	....	....	....	....	....	....	6,139	7,379	7,494	12,003	13,516	23,846	18,163	19,942	20,433	Other Sectors	79aj d
Reserve Assets	....	....	....	....	....	....	21,819	21,669	21,954	21,745	20,321	21,586	14,100	14,227	15,082	Reserve Assets	79ak d
Liabilities	....	....	....	....	....	....	38,073	50,922	65,961	93,951	113,075	154,894	157,748	182,040	197,401	Liabilities	79la d
Dir. Invest. in Rep. Economy	....	....	....	....	....	....				18,947	18,605	24,465	23,519	28,161	32,671	Dir. Invest. in Rep. Economy	79lb d
Portfolio Investment	....	....	....	....	....	....	8,907	13,656	16,430	21,327	36,207	46,933	51,718	51,249	52,900	Portfolio Investment	79lc d
Equity Securities	....	....	....	....	....	....	2,929	3,597	3,651	6,573	12,663	18,806	19,487	18,407	13,563	Equity Securities	79ld d
Debt Securities	....	....	....	....	....	....	5,978	10,059	12,779	14,755	23,544	28,127	32,230	32,842	39,337	Debt Securities	79le d
Financial Derivatives	....	....	....	....	....	....						63	1,412	2,223	1,185	Financial Derivatives	79ll d
Other Investment	....	....	....	....	....	....	29,166	37,266	49,532	53,677	58,263	83,432	81,100	100,407	110,645	Other Investment	79lf d
Monetary Authorities	....	....	....	....	....	....	48	362	278	440	2,084	3,049	2,732	7,470	7,282	Monetary Authorities	79lg d
General Government	....	....	....	....	....	....	2,099	1,973	2,229	1,676	1,614	2,057	2,113	1,926	1,670	General Government	79lh d
Banks	....	....	....	....	....	....	13,875	21,527	32,432	36,320	42,261	56,578	57,823	72,916	84,075	Banks	79li d
Other Sectors	....	....	....	....	....	....	13,144	13,403	14,592	15,241	12,305	21,748	18,431	18,094	17,619	Other Sectors	79lj d

Millions of Euros Beginning 1999: Year Ending December 31 — Government Finance — Central Government

	1987	1988	1989	1990	1991	1992	1993	1994	1995	1996	1997	1998	1999	2000	2001		
Deficit (-) or Surplus	-538.8	-523.0	-287.1	-449.6	-666.8	-289.8	-932.7	-708.1	-795.8	-379.9	-372.2	-247.5	....	....	....	Deficit (-) or Surplus	80
Revenue	1,768.5	2,030.5	2,726.4	3,215.9	3,869.5	4,594.7	4,624.9	5,016.5	5,456.7	5,759.9	6,391.8	6,984.7				Revenue	81
Grants Received	94.3	105.9	140.7	153.4	259.1	429.8	446.6	411.6	525.6	662.2	649.9	649.1				Grants Received	81z
Expenditure	2,245.0	2,492.9	3,146.2	3,828.9	4,722.6	5,527.0	6,012.0	6,137.9	6,613.6	6,974.5	7,242.2	7,795.2				Expenditure	82
Lending Minus Repayments	156.6	166.5	8.0	-10.0	72.8	-212.7	-7.8	-1.7	164.5	-172.5	171.7	86.3				Lending Minus Repayments	83
Unclass. Transactions (Net)																Unclass. Transactions (Net)	83x
Financing — Domestic	466.3	546.4	457.7	582.0	806.3	296.5	656.5	659.0	218.2	2.7	-12.1	669.1				Financing — Domestic	84a
Foreign	72.5	-23.4	-170.6	-132.4	-139.5	-6.7	276.2	49.1	577.6	377.2	384.3	-421.5				Foreign	85a
Use of Cash Balances																Use of Cash Balances	87
Debt: Escudos																Debt: Escudos	88b
Held By: Bk of Portugal																Held By: Bk of Portugal	88ba
Commercial Banks																Commercial Banks	88bb
Savings Banks																Savings Banks	88bc
Others																Others	88bd
Intragovernmental Debt																Intragovernmental Debt	88s
Held by: Social Insur. System																Held by: Social Insur. System	88sz

Gross Domestic Product — General Government

	1987	1988	1989	1990	1991	1992	1993	1994	1995	1996	1997	1998	1999	2000	2001		
Deficit (-) or Surplus	....	....	....	-5.1	-6.0	-3.0	-6.1	-6.0	-5.7	-3.8	-2.7	-2.3	-2.2	-1.5	-2.2	Deficit (-) or Surplus	80g
Debt				65.3	67.3	60.1	63.1	63.8	65.9	63.6	59.1	54.8	54.2	53.2	55.6	Debt	88g

Millions of Euros Beginning 1999 — National Accounts

	1987	1988	1989	1990	1991	1992	1993	1994	1995	1996	1997	1998	1999	2000	2001		
Househ.Cons.Expend.,incl.NPISHs												....	†68,405	67,174	74,676	Househ.Cons.Expend.,incl.NPISHs	96f
Government Consumption Expend.	880	1,083	1,320	1,603	2,043	2,322	2,533	2,781	3,019	3,298	3,555	3,896	†21,098	23,352	25,160	Government Consumption Expend.	91f
Gross Fixed Capital Formation	1,591	2,026	2,317	2,718	2,964	3,191	3,140	3,439	3,743	4,005	4,516	4,992	†29,058	32,100	34,664	Gross Fixed Capital Formation	93e
Changes in Inventories	39	141	101	102	60	112	-18	57	115	95	101	108				Changes in Inventories	93i
Exports of Goods and Services	1,567	1,906	2,400	2,779	2,851	2,960	3,050	3,583	4,168	4,482	4,895	5,301	†31,817	35,790	38,814	Exports of Goods and Services	90c
Imports of Goods and Services (-)	2,150	2,827	3,307	3,923	4,240	4,485	4,458	5,111	5,698	6,123	6,876	7,698	†43,385	49,380	50,607	Imports of Goods and Services (-)	98c
Gross Domestic Product (GDP)	5,928	7,084	8,372	9,855	11,315	12,759	13,463	14,617	15,802	16,809	17,859	19,246	†106,993	114,025	122,699	Gross Domestic Product (GDP)	99b
Net Primary Income from Abroad	-131	-126	-113	-34	11	82	....	....	....	....	....	....				Net Primary Income from Abroad	98.n
Gross National Income (GNI)	5,044	5,877	7,064	8,527	9,948	11,425										Gross National Income (GNI)	99a
Net National Income																Net National Income	99e
GDP Volume 1990 prices	8,355	8,981	....	....	....	....										GDP Volume 1990 prices	99b.p
GDP Volume 1995 Prices	....	13,208	13,922	14,584	14,925	15,214	15,000	15,353	15,802	16,306	16,871	17,460	†93,411	96,506	99,041	GDP Volume 1995 Prices	99b.p
GDP Volume (1995=100)	77.8	83.6	88.1	92.3	94.5	96.3	94.9	97.2	100.0	103.2	106.8	110.5	118.5	122.4	....	GDP Volume (1995=100)	99bv p
GDP Deflator (1995=100)	48.2	53.6	60.1	67.6	75.8	83.9	89.8	95.2	100.0	103.1	105.9	110.2	†114.5	118.2	....	GDP Deflator (1995=100)	99bi p

Midyear Estimates

	1987	1988	1989	1990	1991	1992	1993	1994	1995	1996	1997	1998	1999	2000	2001		
Population	9.99	9.97	9.94	9.90	9.87	9.87	9.88	9.90	9.92	9.93	9.94	9.97	9.89	10.01	10.02	Population	99z

(See notes in the back of the book.)

		1972	1973	1974	1975	1976	1977	1978	1979	1980	1981	1982	1983	1984	1985	1986
Exchange Rates															*Riyals per SDR:*	
Official Rate	aa	4.7619	4.7619	4.8330	4.6679	4.5989	4.8100	5.0008	4.8807	4.6425	4.2368	4.0153	3.8109	3.5680	3.9982	4.4524
															Riyals per US Dollar:	
Official Rate	ae	4.3860	3.9474	3.9474	3.9874	3.9583	3.9598	3.8385	3.7050	3.6400	3.6400	3.6400	3.6400	3.6400	3.6400	3.6400
Official Rate	rf	4.3860	3.9963	3.9474	3.9307[e]	3.9634	3.9590	3.8769	3.7733	3.6570	3.6400	3.6400	3.6400	3.6400	3.6400	3.6400
														Index Numbers (1995=100):		
Official Rate	ah x	83.0	91.1	92.2	92.6[e]	91.8	91.9	93.9	96.5	99.5	100.0	100.0	100.0	100.0	100.0	100.0
Nominal Effective Exchange Rate	ne c	....	....	....	....	....	....	....	82.4	84.2	94.1	104.5	110.2	118.6	121.8	99.5
Fund Position															*Millions of SDRs:*	
Quota	2f. s	20.0	20.0	20.0	20.0	20.0	20.0	40.0	40.0	66.2	66.2	66.2	114.9	114.9	114.9	114.9
SDRs	1b. s	—	—	—	—	—	—	—	4.2	2.7	8.6	14.0	8.7	16.2	18.9	21.1
Reserve Position in the Fund	1c. s	5.0	5.0	5.0	13.1	16.2	14.5	14.7	13.6	18.1	18.1	19.4	37.2	38.4	35.8	30.7
International Liquidity														*Millions of US Dollars Unless Otherwise Indicated:*		
Total Reserves minus Gold	1l. d	53.4	67.7	63.7	96.7	129.3	161.7	210.7	288.0	343.4	365.8	386.6	384.1	380.0	446.1	571.9
SDRs	1b. d	....	....	....	....	....	....	....	5.5	3.5	10.0	15.4	9.1	15.9	20.7	25.8
Reserve Position in the Fund	1c. d	5.4	6.0	6.1	15.3	18.8	17.6	19.2	17.9	23.1	21.1	21.4	38.9	37.6	39.3	37.6
Foreign Exchange	1d. d	48.0	61.7	57.6	81.4	110.5	144.1	191.5	264.6	316.8	334.7	349.8	336.1	326.5	386.2	508.5
Gold (Million Fine Troy Ounces)	1ad	.186	.186	.186	.221	.223	.222	.329	.355	.605	.830	.989	1.116	1.181	1.181	1.181
Gold (National Valuation)	1and	7.0	7.8	7.8	7.7	7.8	7.8	11.5	12.4	21.2	29.0	34.6	39.0	41.3	41.3	41.3
Deposit Money Banks: Assets	7a. d	72.9	82.5	143.1	278.0	381.8	456.7	576.5	681.3	732.7	1,204.5	1,271.0	1,059.1	1,726.2	1,918.7	1,982.8
Liabilities	7b. d	.6	7.9	26.2	56.4	87.4	120.8	166.0	270.0	174.4	200.0	245.0	311.5	234.2	246.6	430.6
Monetary Authorities															*Millions of Riyals:*	
Foreign Assets	11	126	164	282	416	542	671	853	1,113	1,327	1,437	1,533	1,540	1,534	1,774	2,232
Claims on Central Government	12a	....	....	....	....	....	....	....	....	....	....	....	....	....	....	....
Claims on Deposit Money Banks	12e	4	—	—	—	16	51	88	96	8	—	25	6	18	5	4
Reserve Money	14	93	129	188	298	428	582	774	988	1,159	1,193	1,325	1,335	1,350	1,307	1,699
of which: Currency Outside DMBs	14a	77	111	158	240	376	505	573	715	808	992	1,151	1,068	1,186	1,120	1,288
Central Government Deposits	16d	—	6	24	48	72	32	52	113	103	234	238	225	308	418	285
Capital Accounts	17a	16	16	26	30	30	30	30	50	69	84	81	79	76	81	87
Other Items (Net)	17r	21	13	44	40	28	78	85	57	4	−75	−87	−93	−182	−26	165
Deposit Money Banks															*Millions of Riyals:*	
Reserves	20	16	18	30	58	52	77	213	276	335	196	185	278	170	192	421
Foreign Assets	21	320	326	565	1,109	1,511	1,809	2,213	2,524	2,667	4,384	4,626	3,855	6,283	6,984	7,217
Claims on Central Government	22a	....	....	....	....	....	....	....	....	....	....	....	....	....	....	....
Claims on Nonfin.Pub.Enterprises	22c	....	....	....	....	....	....	....	....	....	....	....	....	....	....	....
Claims on Private Sector	22d	333	503	752	1,126	1,559	2,464	2,889	3,278	3,693	4,507	5,576	6,056	5,440	6,445	8,031
Demand Deposits	24	269	302	406	765	1,200	1,582	1,733	1,776	1,466	2,412	2,644	2,556	2,948	2,897	3,199
Time, Savings,& Fgn.Currency Dep.	25	319	364	485	744	1,129	1,480	1,809	2,020	3,003	4,072	4,772	4,863	6,220	7,289	8,082
Foreign Liabilities	26c	3	31	104	225	346	478	637	1,000	635	728	892	1,134	853	898	1,567
Central Government Deposits	26d	20	39	127	229	120	252	448	434	592	549	437	456	419	486	312
Credit from Monetary Authorities	26g	—	—	—	—	—	63	82	39	—	—	25	5	—	—	—
Capital Accounts	27a	67	95	169	252	210	232	284	386	563	572	700	859	1,040	1,129	1,416
Other Items (Net)	27r	−9	15	57	77	118	263	322	423	437	755	918	317	413	923	1,093
Monetary Survey															*Millions of Riyals:*	
Foreign Assets (Net)	31n	443	458	744	1,300	1,708	2,002	2,429	2,637	3,359	5,093	5,268	4,261	6,964	7,861	7,882
Domestic Credit	32	312	458	601	848	1,367	2,181	2,389	2,731	2,998	3,724	4,901	5,376	4,713	5,541	7,434
Claims on Central Govt. (Net)	32an	−20	−45	−151	−277	−192	−283	−500	−547	−695	−783	−675	−681	−727	−904	−597
Claims on Nonfin.Pub.Enterprises	32c	....	....	....	....	....	....	....	....	....	....	....	....	....	....	....
Claims on Private Sector	32d	333	503	752	1,126	1,559	2,464	2,889	3,278	3,693	4,507	5,576	6,056	5,440	6,445	8,031
Money	34	345	413	564	1,005	1,576	2,087	2,307	2,492	2,274	3,403	3,795	3,625	4,135	4,017	4,487
Quasi-Money	35	319	364	485	744	1,129	1,480	1,809	2,020	3,003	4,072	4,772	4,863	6,220	7,289	8,082
Other Items (Net)	37r	92	139	296	399	370	615	703	857	1,080	1,342	1,601	1,149	1,323	2,097	2,747
Money plus Quasi-Money	35l	664	777	1,049	1,749	2,705	3,567	4,116	4,511	5,277	7,475	8,567	8,488	10,354	11,305	12,569
Interest Rates															*Percent Per Annum:*	
Deposit Rate	60l	....	....	....	....	....	....	....	6.0	6.0	6.0	6.0	6.0	6.0	6.0	6.0
Lending Rate	60p	....	....	....	....	....	....	....	....	9.5	9.5	9.5	9.5	9.5	9.5	9.5
Prices and Production															*Index Numbers (1995=100):*	
Consumer Prices	64	....	....	....	....	....	....	....	59.7	63.7	†69.2	73.1	75.1	75.9	77.4	†78.6
Crude Petroleum	66aa	105.9	123.0	113.4	97.7	108.9	97.3	107.5	112.9	105.5	90.3	73.2	65.6	95.6	73.5	79.8
International Transactions															*Millions of Riyals*	
Exports	70	1,740	2,511	7,954	7,094	8,757	8,205	9,268	14,120	20,768	20,696	15,802	12,221	....	....	....
Crude Petroleum	70aa	1,673	2,444	7,811	6,893	8,470	8,134	8,955	13,398	19,728	19,331	14,840	11,132	15,943	12,147	....
Imports, c.i.f.	71	616	778	1,070	1,622	3,237	4,850	4,590	5,378	5,203	5,525	7,088	5,299	4,230	4,147	4,000
Volume of Exports																*1985=100*	
Crude Petroleum	72aa	154.1	181.9	162.9	137.1	158.9	132.1	152.9	159.7	148.8	125.2	102.9	89.3	130.1	100.0	108.7
Export Prices																*1985=100:*	
Crude Petroleum	76aa d	7.4	10.1	36.4	38.4	40.3	44.9	44.9	67.2	108.6	127.1	118.7	102.6	100.9	100.0	....
Government Finance															*Millions of Riyals*	
Deficit (-) or Surplus	80	272	178	3,565	1,832	3,118	837	1,752	3,820	8,066	4,500	815	....	....	....	....
Revenue	81	1,230	1,720	5,497	7,135	8,927	8,155	8,225	12,090	19,003	19,243	13,434	....	....	....	....
Expenditure	82	959	1,542	1,931	5,302	5,809	7,318	6,473	8,270	10,937	14,743	12,619	....	....	....	....
Financing																	
Use of Cash Balances	87	−272	−178	−3,565	−1,832	−3,118	−837	−1,752	−3,820	−8,066	−4,500	−815	....	....	....	....
National Accounts															*Millions of Riyals*	
Househ.Cons.Expend.,incl.NPISHs	96f	....	....	....	....	....	....	....	....	4,509	5,424	5,921	5,769	5,927	5,626	5,437
Government Consumption Expend.	91f	....	....	....	....	....	....	....	....	5,622	8,143	7,236	8,203	9,021	7,882	8,384
Gross Fixed Capital Formation	93e	....	....	....	....	....	....	....	....	4,766	5,312	7,391	5,720	4,302	3,968	3,402
Changes in Inventories	93i	....	....	....	....	....	....	....	....	117	284	215	−544	−155	30	7
Exports of Goods and Services	90c	....	....	....	....	....	....	....	....	21,127	21,468	16,753	12,753	13,450	11,502	7,330
Imports of Goods and Services (-)	98c	....	....	....	....	....	....	....	....	7,478	9,063	9,811	8,296	7,537	6,610	6,167
Gross Domestic Product (GDP)	99b	2,172	2,615	....	9,877	13,017	14,322	15,709	21,783	28,663	31,568	27,705	23,605	25,008	22,398	18,393
																Millions:	
Population	99z	.13	.15	.16	.17	.18	.19	.20	.22	.23	.24	.26	.31	.33	.36	.39

Item	1987	1988	1989	1990	1991	1992	1993	1994	1995	1996	1997	1998	1999	2000	2001	Code
Exchange Rates																
End of Period																
Official Rate	5.1639	4.8983	4.7835	5.1785	5.2068	5.0050	4.9998	5.3139	5.4108	5.2342	4.9113	5.1252	4.9959	4.7426	4.5745	aa
End of Period (ae) Period Average (rf)																
Official Rate	3.6400	3.6400	3.6400	3.6400	3.6400	3.6400	3.6400	3.6400	3.6400	3.6400	3.6400	3.6400	3.6400	3.6400	3.6400	ae
Official Rate	3.6400	3.6400	3.6400	3.6400	3.6400	3.6400	3.6400	3.6400	3.6400	3.6400	3.6400	3.6400	3.6400	3.6400	3.6400	rf
Period Averages																
Official Rate	100.0	100.0	100.0	100.0	100.0	100.0	100.0	100.0	100.0	100.0	100.0	100.0	100.0	100.0	100.0	ahx
Nominal Effective Exchange Rate	88.8	84.3	89.5	87.8	91.0	92.5	101.5	104.8	100.0	103.8	111.7	116.6	116.2	122.6	128.8	nec
Fund Position																
End of Period																
Quota	114.9	114.9	114.9	114.9	114.9	190.5	190.5	190.5	190.5	190.5	190.5	190.5	263.8	263.8	263.8	2f. s
SDRs	24.7	26.4	27.8	31.3	33.8	17.1	18.7	19.9	21.2	22.5	23.8	25.1	10.7	15.8	17.9	1b. s
Reserve Position in the Fund	27.8	21.1	19.5	17.3	18.7	36.4	33.8	30.7	29.7	29.2	26.4	26.4	44.7	44.7	79.1	1c. s
International Liquidity																
End of Period																
Total Reserves minus Gold	618.4	474.5	533.4	631.1	667.7	683.3	693.7	657.7	743.8	686.2	820.6	1,043.3	1,304.2	1,158.0	1,312.7	1l. d
SDRs	35.0	35.6	37.7	44.6	48.3	23.4	25.6	29.0	31.5	32.4	32.1	35.3	14.6	20.6	22.5	1b. d
Reserve Position in the Fund	39.5	28.4	25.7	24.6	26.8	50.1	46.4	44.7	44.2	42.0	35.6	37.2	61.4	58.3	99.4	1c. d
Foreign Exchange	543.9	410.5	470.0	561.9	592.6	609.8	621.7	584.0	668.1	611.8	752.9	970.8	1,228.2	1,079.1	1,190.8	1d. d
Gold (Million Fine Troy Ounces)	1.181	1.185	1.185	1.185	1.185	1.184	1.184	1.188	1.188	1.188	.447	.443	.159	.149	.152	1ad
Gold (National Valuation)	41.3	41.5	41.5	41.5	41.5	41.5	41.5	41.6	41.6	41.6	15.7	15.5	5.5	5.2	5.3	1and
Deposit Money Banks: Assets	2,499.2	2,701.7	2,081.4	2,273.6	2,537.6	2,195.0	†2,264.3	2,648.0	3,093.7	2,396.3	2,643.4	2,324.3	2,455.5	3,193.1	3,163.5	7a. d
Liabilities	734.1	977.5	409.7	578.7	1,192.7	58.2	†1,370.4	1,381.3	1,768.2	1,026.6	1,274.4	1,497.6	1,605.5	611.3	586.9	7b. d
Monetary Authorities																
End of Period																
Foreign Assets	2,401	1,878	2,093	2,448	2,581	2,638	†2,686	2,546	2,859	2,649	3,044	3,854	4,767	4,234	4,798	11
Claims on Central Government									437	546	437	—	1,467	—	124	12a
Claims on Deposit Money Banks	5	24	106	155	150	151	†150	260	205	212	194	1,589	82	124	97	12e
Reserve Money	1,692	1,542	1,761	1,917	1,934	2,086	2,181	2,030	2,131	2,261	2,481	2,557	2,868	3,061	3,416	14
of which: Currency Outside DMBs	1,249	1,178	1,245	1,350	1,350	1,275	1,321	1,350	1,407	1,404	1,555	1,499	1,714	1,673	1,741	14a
Central Government Deposits	164	137	84	175	249	138	†33	42	381	116	120	145	30	41	26	16d
Capital Accounts	96	93	91	96	97	94	†576	705	1,178	1,242	1,339	1,466	1,536	1,456	1,402	17a
Other Items (Net)	455	130	262	414	451	470	†46	30	−188	−212	−265	1,275	1,881	−202	174	17r
Deposit Money Banks																
End of Period																
Reserves	449	374	519	581	662	768	830	680	739	852	919	1,064	1,169	1,368	1,678	20
Foreign Assets	9,097	9,834	7,576	8,276	9,237	7,990	†8,242	9,639	11,261	8,723	9,622	8,460	8,938	11,623	11,515	21
Claims on Central Government	....	....	....	....	....	....	9,031	10,050	10,028	11,873	12,863	16,151	19,064	17,225	23,882	22a
Claims on Nonfin.Pub.Enterprises							232	228	384	728	878	609	537	621	790	22c
Claims on Private Sector	8,743	9,265	10,553	9,906	13,344	18,113	†10,948	9,544	10,267	10,251	12,548	14,451	15,664	17,338	17,614	22d
Demand Deposits	3,530	2,221	2,158	2,705	2,353	2,669	†2,904	2,561	2,313	2,481	2,575	2,717	2,465	2,776	3,479	24
Time, Savings,& Fgn.Currency Dep.	8,872	9,109	10,847	9,544	10,290	11,036	†12,635	14,509	14,901	15,772	17,466	19,117	21,804	24,307	23,535	25
Foreign Liabilities	2,672	3,558	1,491	2,107	4,342	212	†4,988	5,028	6,436	3,737	4,639	5,451	5,844	2,225	2,136	26c
Central Government Deposits	331	1,003	282	817	2,425	5,020	†3,394	1,903	2,671	3,795	4,601	5,248	6,540	9,262	15,504	26d
Credit from Monetary Authorities	—	23	2			43	18	91	69	60	140	72	94	140	115	26g
Capital Accounts	1,522	1,750	1,990	2,271	2,525	2,762	†4,659	5,049	5,473	5,702	6,249	6,821	7,467	8,070	8,925	27a
Other Items (Net)	1,363	1,808	1,878	1,319	1,308	5,129	†685	1,001	815	880	1,160	1,309	1,157	1,394	1,785	27r
Monetary Survey																
End of Period																
Foreign Assets (Net)	8,826	8,154	8,177	8,617	7,476	10,416	†5,940	7,156	7,682	7,635	8,026	6,862	7,861	13,631	14,174	31n
Domestic Credit	8,248	8,124	10,187	8,913	10,670	12,955	†16,785	17,879	18,064	19,488	22,007	25,819	30,162	25,881	26,883	32
Claims on Central Govt. (Net)	−495	−1,141	−366	−993	−2,673	−5,158	†5,604	8,105	7,413	8,508	8,579	10,757	13,960	7,922	8,475	32an
Claims on Nonfin.Pub.Enterprises							232	228	384	728	878	609	537	621	790	32c
Claims on Private Sector	8,743	9,265	10,553	9,906	13,344	18,113	†10,949	9,545	10,268	10,252	12,550	14,453	15,665	17,338	17,617	32d
Money	4,778	3,399	3,403	4,055	3,629	3,990	†4,254	3,910	3,720	3,885	4,131	4,216	4,179	4,449	5,219	34
Quasi-Money	8,872	9,109	10,847	9,544	10,290	11,036	†12,635	14,509	14,901	15,772	17,466	19,117	21,804	24,307	23,535	35
Other Items (Net)	3,425	3,771	4,114	3,932	4,228	8,345	†5,836	6,616	7,125	7,467	8,437	9,348	12,041	10,755	12,303	37r
Money plus Quasi-Money	13,650	12,507	14,250	13,599	13,918	15,026	†16,889	18,419	18,622	19,657	21,596	23,333	25,982	28,756	28,755	35l
Interest Rates																
Percent Per Annum																
Deposit Rate	6.0	6.0	6.0	6.0	6.0	4.8	4.1	4.8	6.2	6.5	6.6	6.6	6.5	....	....	60l
Lending Rate	9.5	9.5	9.5	9.5	9.5	8.1	7.2	8.9	....	....	....	....	....	....	....	60p
Prices and Production																
Period Averages																
Consumer Prices	80.7	84.5	87.2	89.9	93.8	96.7	95.9	97.1	100.0	107.4	110.1	113.3	115.7	117.7	....	64
Crude Petroleum	68.6	70.2	87.2	85.9	84.7	88.5	92.2	90.6	100.0	106.3	137.5	147.3	146.9	....	....	66aa
International Transactions																
Millions of Riyals																
Exports	....	....	....	....	....	....	....	11,453	12,672	13,659	13,801	17,763	25,703	....	....	70
Crude Petroleum																70aa
Imports, c.i.f.	4,128	4,613	4,827	6,169	6,261	7,336	6,882	7,016	12,369	10,441	12,091	12,407	9,098	....	....	71
1985=100																
Volume of Exports Crude Petroleum																72aa
Export Prices Crude Petroleum																76aa d
Index of Prices in US Dollars																
Government Finance																
Lunar Years																
Deficit (-) or Surplus	....	....	....	....	....	....	....	....								80
Revenue	....	....	....	....	....	....	....	....								81
Expenditure	41.3	41.5	41.5	41.5	....	....	....	....								82
Financing Use of Cash Balances	....	....	....	....	....	....	....	....								87
National Accounts																
Millions of Riyals																
Househ.Cons.Expend.,incl.NPISHs	6,362	6,428	7,597	7,456	7,860	8,519	8,557	8,030	9,497	8,996	9,170	....	....	....	....	96f
Government Consumption Expend.	8,776	9,983	9,165	8,802	8,934	9,258	9,370	9,250	9,436	10,886	11,150	....	....	....	....	91f
Gross Fixed Capital Formation	2,984	3,323	3,375	4,551	4,365	5,159	4,849	6,575	8,895	11,532	12,594	....	....	....	....	93e
Changes in Inventories	−126	191	237	263	415	583	300	8	1,495	262	450	....	....	....	....	93i
Exports of Goods and Services	8,188	8,239	9,986	14,323	11,886	14,203	12,011	12,046	13,134	14,419	14,850	....	....	....	....	90c
Imports of Goods and Services (-)	6,359	6,185	6,744	8,603	8,404	9,890	9,037	9,066	12,835	13,119	14,750	....	....	....	....	98c
Gross Domestic Product (GDP)	19,825	21,979	23,616	26,792	25,056	27,832	26,050	26,843	29,622	32,976	41,124	37,330	44,397	59,893	....	99b
Population																
Midyear Estimates																
Population	.41	.43	.46	.49	.50	.53	.56	.59	†.51	.52	.53	.54	.56	.57	.60	99z

(See notes in the back of the book.)

Romania

		1972	1973	1974	1975	1976	1977	1978	1979	1980	1981	1982	1983	1984	1985	1986
Exchange Rates																*Lei per SDR:*
Market Rate	aa	6.0	24.1	24.5	23.4	23.2	24.3	23.5	23.7	23.0	17.5	16.5	19.2	17.4	17.3	18.7
																Lei per US Dollar:
Market Rate	ae	5.5	20.0	20.0	20.0	20.0	20.0	18.0	18.0	18.0	15.0	15.0	18.3	17.8	15.7	15.3
Market Rate	rf	5.5	20.3	20.0	20.0	20.0	20.0	18.4	18.0	18.0	15.0	15.0	17.2	21.3	17.1	16.2
														Index Numbers (1990=100):		
Nominal Effective Exchange Rate	ne c	....	....	....	....	....	....	....	74.06	75.86	107.83	122.00	117.51	107.93	143.25	128.09
Real Effective Exchange Rate	re c	....	....	....	....	....	....	....	....	121.35[e]	158.26[e]	189.64[e]	178.41[e]	152.56[e]	187.68[e]	160.56[e]
Fund Position																*Millions of SDRs:*
Quota	2f. s	190	190	190	190	190	190	245	245	368	368	368	523	523	523	523
SDRs	1b. s	—	6	5	8	13	7	—	1	—	—	12	—	—	—	—
Reserve Position in the Fund	1c. s	48	—	—	—	—	—	—	—	—	—	—	—	—	—	—
Total Fund Cred.&Loans Outstg.	2tl	—	48	48	88	238	270	256	247	257	507	782	905	956	783	584
International Liquidity													*Millions of US Dollars Unless Otherwise Indicated:*			
Total Reserves minus Gold	1l. d	....	215	241	539	562	256	376	525	323	404	450	525	709	199	582
SDRs	1b. d	—	7	7	9	15	8	—	1	—	—	1	13	—	—	—
Reserve Position in the Fund	1c. d	52	—	—	—	—	—	—	—	—	—	—	—	—	—	—
Foreign Exchange	1d. d	....	208	234	530	547	248	376	524	323	403	437	525	709	199	582
o/w: Held by Dep.Money Banks	1e. d															
Gold (Million Fine Troy Ounces)	1ad	....	2.275	2.447	2.597	2.749	3.057	3.347	3.535	3.712	3.591	3.553	3.620	3.731	3.818	3.247
Gold (National Valuation)	1an d	....	96	105	106	112	130	153	†41	43	50	49	41	44	50	44
Deposit Money Banks: Assets	7a. d	....	105	220	248	98	161	264	123	260	187	254	353	317	1,000	507
Liabilities	7b. d	....	290	460	610	2,320	2,984	4,143	6,534	8,381	9,056	8,034	7,603	6,460	6,046	5,948
Monetary Authorities																*Billions of Lei:*
Foreign Assets	11	....	1	1	1	1	1	2	4	3	†9	11	13	13	†3	4
Claims on Government	12a															
Claims on Private Sector	12d	....	75	99	111	123	111	119	133	152	168	188	194	209	†227	227
Claims on Deposit Money Banks	12e	....	28	23	28	33	45	65	74	149	157	170	190	222	†284	322
Reserve Money	14	....	38	57	74	78	77	96	121	167	183	188	178	158	†128	146
of which: Currency Outside DMBs	14a	....	18	18	21	24	27	28	34	39	41	45	45	49	†55	60
Transit Accounts	14x															
Foreign Liabilities	16c	....	—	—	—	2	2	2	3	8	15	18	24	22	†4	4
Central Government Deposits	16d	....	38	30	20	22	17	16	7	14	13	31	52	101	†145	173
Other Items (Net)	17r	....	17	22	29	33	15	10	9	10	5	3	—	2	†55	26
Deposit Money Banks																*Billions of Lei:*
Reserves	20	....	6	11	24	22	14	34	53	81	86	78	68	44	†36	8
Foreign Assets	21	....	2	3	4	13	8	11	8	9	9	10	16	18	†20	25
Claims on Central Government	22a															
Claims on Nonfin.Pub.Enterprises	22c															
Claims on Private Sector	22d	....	128	153	165	201	231	276	286	309	†293	316	350	381	†439	470
Claims on Nonbank Financial Insts	22g	....	10	13	17	22	46	62	71	105	119	128	144	160	†181	203
Demand Deposits	24	....	12	14	15	20	21	33	33	62	†39	58	46	47	†38	33
Transit Accounts	24x															
Savings Deposits	25	....	36	41	47	55	64	80	90	101	115	118	128	139	†153	167
Other Term Deposits	25a															
Foreign Currency Deposits	25b	....	—	—	—	1	1	1	2	2	3	4	3	3	†4	4
Foreign Liabilities	26c	....	6	9	12	46	60	75	118	151	136	121	139	115	†95	91
Government Deposits	26d															
Credit from Monetary Authorities	26g	....	28	23	28	33	45	65	74	149	157	170	190	218	†274	311
Capital Accounts	27a															
Other Items (Net)	27r	....	64	92	107	103	108	129	102	39	57	62	71	79	†—	—
Monetary Survey																*Billions of Lei:*
Foreign Assets (Net)	31n	....	−4	−6	−8	−34	−54	−65	−108	−147	−133	−118	−134	−106	†−77	−66
Domestic Credit	32	....	203	252	277	324	343	395	419	†428	459	504	544	589	†666	697
Claims on Central Govt. (Net)	32an															
Claims on Nonfin.Pub.Enterprises	32c															
Claims on Private Sector	32d															
Claims on Nonbank Financial Inst	32g	....	10	13	17	22	46	62	71	105	119	128	144	160	181	203
Money	34	....	45	61	66	76	84	95	102	†115	136	167	156	162	†156	168
Transit Accounts	34x															
Quasi-Money	35	....	36	41	48	56	66	81	92	104	118	122	131	143	†157	171
Other Liquid Liabilities	36x	....	9	11	12	14	16	18	21	24	27	30	33	36	†39	43
Other Items (Net)	37r	....	119	144	155	158	139	155	117	†21	18	23	24	26	†60	58
Money plus Quasi-Money	35l	....	80	102	113	132	150	176	194	†218	253	289	287	305	†313	340
Interest Rates																*Percent Per Annum*
Bank Rate (End of Period)	60a	....	....	....	....	....	....	....	....	....	....	....	....	....	....	....
Treasury Bill Rate	60c	....	....	....	....	....	....	....	....	....	....	....	....	....	....	....
Prices, Production, Labor																*Index Numbers (1995=100):*
Producer Prices	63															
Consumer Prices	64															
Wages: Avg. Earnings	65	....	.6	.7	.7	.8	....	....	....	1.1	1.1	1.2	1.2	1.3	1.3	1.3
Industrial Production	66	....	63.4	72.6	81.4	90.8	102.2	....	....	128.2	130.3	133.0	139.3	148.6	157.7	165.3
Industrial Employment (1990=100)	67	....	64.4	68.9	72.6	75.3	78.4	80.5	83.7	86.1	87.8	89.8	94.4	91.2	97.4	94.2
																Number in Thousands:
Labor Force	67d															
Employment	67e	....	....	....	....	....	....	....	....	....	....	....	....	....	10,586	10,670
Unemployment	67c															
Unemployment Rate (%)	67r	....	....	....	....	....	....	....	....	....	....	....	....	....	....	....
International Transactions																*Millions of US Dollars*
Exports	70.. d	2,601.0	3,691.0	4,874.5	5,341.5	6,137.7	7,021.0	8,086.4	9,724.2	11,209.0	12,610.0	11,559.0	11,512.0	12,646.0	12,167.0	9,763.1
Imports, c.i.f.	71.. d	2,827.0	3,737.7	5,554.9	5,769.0	6,583.0	7,579.3	9,638.1	11,788.7	13,843.4	13,453.6	10,524.6	10,414.4	11,160.7	11,266.6	11,437.2
Imports, f.o.b.	71.v d	....	....	....	....	....	....	....	....	12,818.0	12,457.0	9,745.0	9,643.0	10,334.0	10,432.0	10,590.0

1987	1988	1989	1990	1991	1992	1993	1994	1995	1996	1997	1998	1999	2000	2001		
															Exchange Rates	
End of Period																
19.5	19.3	19.0	49.4	†270.4	632.5	1,752.7	2,579.6	3,832.2	5,802.2	10,825.0	15,419.3	25,055.2	33,779.2	39,708.9	Market Rate	aa
End of Period (ae) Period Average (rf)																
13.7	14.4	14.4	34.7	†189.0	460.0	1,276.0	1,767.0	2,578.0	4,035.0	8,023.0	10,951.0	18,255.0	25,926.0	31,597.0	Market Rate	ae
14.6	14.3	14.9	22.4	76.4	†308.0	760.1	1,655.1	2,033.3	3,084.2	7,167.9	8,875.6	15,332.8	21,708.7	29,060.8	Market Rate	rf
Period Averages																
129.13	135.23	143.96	100.00	38.98	8.03	3.45	1.53	1.20	.83	.40	.33	.20	.15	.12	Nominal Effective Exchange Rate	ne c
154.91e	153.43e	148.11e	100.00	93.10	57.56	79.82	85.77	83.90	75.85	88.36	114.93	97.84	107.12	108.83	Real Effective Exchange Rate	re c
															Fund Position	
End of Period																
523	523	523	523	523	754	754	754	754	754	754	754	1,030	1,030	1,030	Quota	2f. s
—	—	76	—	40	8	1	38	38	3	77	1	7	1	5	SDRs	1b. s
—	—	—	—	—	—	—	—	—	—	—	—	—	—	—	Reserve Position in the Fund	1c. s
358	107	—	—	566	751	751	906	698	453	475	383	334	348	308	Total Fund Cred.&Loans Outstg.	2tl
															International Liquidity	
End of Period																
1,402	780	1,859	524	695	826	995	2,086	1,579	2,103	3,803	2,867	2,687	3,922	5,442	Total Reserves minus Gold	1l. d
—	—	100	—	58	11	2	56	56	4	104	1	10	1	7	SDRs	1b. d
—	—	—	—	—	—	—	—	—	—	—	—	—	—	—	Reserve Position in the Fund	1c. d
1,402	780	1,759	524	637	815	994	2,031	1,523	2,099	3,700	2,866	2,677	3,921	5,435	Foreign Exchange	1d. d
....	....	....	....	480	730	....	....	....	....	....	....	....	....	....	o/w: Held by Dep.Money Banks	1e. d
1.364	1.449	2.174	2.208	2.247	2.307	2.370	2.625	2.703	2.818	3.019	3.224	3.323	3.374	3.382	Gold (Million Fine Troy Ounces)	1ad
21	1,236	1,845	780	666	780	924	965	780	520	458	358	967	920	939	Gold (National Valuation)	1an d
570	1,021	799	682	261	132	223	129	73	72	79	87	91	95	94	Deposit Money Banks: Assets	7a. d
5,896	1,972	512	1,723	724	461	560	687	823	1,238	1,148	933	611	508	661	Liabilities	7b. d
															Monetary Authorities	
1	18	28	†28	171	405	†1,234	2,796	2,942	6,432	24,849	25,182	45,581	88,067	153,654	Foreign Assets	11
			4	41	263	†336	1,771	3,562	—	3,271	9,142	21,412	16,176	8,415	Claims on Government	12a
261	266	332													Claims on Private Sector	12d
357	444	409	†362	390	353	†1,880	2,395	4,724	8,822	3,367	3,618	2,433	2,296	1,148	Claims on Deposit Money Banks	12e
155	181	252	†324	397	859	†2,031	3,809	5,952	9,008	21,305	25,738	49,520	76,598	122,483	Reserve Money	14
61	65	75	†98	194	460	1,049	2,201	3,764	5,383	9,200	11,525	17,372	25,742	35,635	of which: Currency Outside DMBs	14a
....	....	....	49	95	-36	27	21	14	—	—	27	264	294	—	Transit Accounts	14x
2	2	—	†—	198	475	†1,317	2,444	3,502	7,810	15,167	17,639	15,885	22,028	12,235	Foreign Liabilities	16c
226	281	228	—	42	163	†496	1,354	2,660	-275	701	163	5,947	3,360	8,899	Central Government Deposits	16d
12	25	22	†20	-131	-441	†-421	-666	-899	-1,290	-5,686	-5,624	-2,190	4,261	19,600	Other Items (Net)	17r
															Deposit Money Banks	
—	—	—	†9	†177	443	†1,462	2,416	3,293	3,632	5,347	13,050	35,014	51,038	87,125	Reserves	20
27	26	38	†41	105	298	†1,312	2,746	3,723	6,554	13,551	17,301	22,904	40,131	50,967	Foreign Assets	21
†—	...	...	†—	...	...	398	584	1,839	5,469	11,099	18,833	29,850	31,718	37,994	Claims on Central Government	22a
				1,375	1,912	4,902	9,485	16,099	13,202	12,749	11,734	9,223	10,854	16,633	Claims on Nonfin.Pub.Enterprises	22c
513	547	479	684	—	....	†—	—	—	12,516	21,146	43,180	44,031	57,624	90,242	Claims on Private Sector	22d
222	240	267	222	....	....	—	—	—	1,124	1,986	4,172	4,511	6,529	11,380	Claims on Nonbank Financial Insts	22g
34	37	49	†141	555	600	1,018	2,094	3,007	5,366	8,742	9,590	11,059	18,579	25,968	Demand Deposits	24
†—	...	...	3	245	153	159	212	354	615	110	328	364	682	1,421	Transit Accounts	24x
176	186	202	†194	188	376	890	3,605	6,939	11,901	25,625	40,219	53,973	63,873	90,419	Savings Deposits	25
†—	...	...	71	71	121	219	390	444	580	898	994	1,238	2,011	2,706	Other Term Deposits	25a
5	4	4	†15	40	281	1,296	2,358	3,953	7,086	17,681	30,202	50,473	74,856	115,784	Foreign Currency Deposits	25b
81	28	7	†60	137	212	715	1,213	2,121	4,996	9,213	10,213	11,158	13,181	20,897	Foreign Liabilities	26c
†—	...	...	12	62	237	885	1,303	1,810	1,135	2,167	5,749	5,638	7,024	13,030	Government Deposits	26d
347	434	409	†362	390	343	1,568	2,316	3,179	8,024	632	556	1,930	2,296	1,148	Credit from Monetary Authorities	26g
†—	...	...	27	70	254	565	896	2,505	5,064	9,681	10,888	17,549	24,731	49,502	Capital Accounts	27a
...	—	-153	†11	-20	154	†758	843	643	-2,270	-8,869	-477	-7,849	-9,338	-26,534	Other Items (Net)	27r
															Monetary Survey	
End of Period																
-55	14	59	†9	-59	15	†514	1,884	1,043	181	14,020	14,632	41,442	92,989	171,489	Foreign Assets (Net)	31n
774	813	810	†684	1,375	1,912	4,255	9,183	17,030	31,450	47,384	81,150	97,442	112,517	142,734	Domestic Credit	32
....	....	....	—	...	...	-647	-301	931	4,609	11,503	22,063	39,677	37,510	24,479	Claims on Central Govt. (Net)	32an
				1,375	1,912	4,902	9,485	16,099	13,202	12,749	11,734	9,223	10,854	16,633	Claims on Nonfin.Pub.Enterprises	32c
—	—	—	—	...	...	—	—	—	12,516	21,146	43,180	44,031	57,624	90,242	Claims on Private Sector	32d
....	....	....				—	—	—	1,124	1,986	4,172	4,511	6,529	11,380	Claims on Nonbank Financial Inst	32g
171	199	204	†238	749	1,060	2,067	4,294	6,771	10,749	17,942	21,115	28,431	44,320	61,603	Money	34
....	....	....	†52	340	117	185	233	368	615	110	355	628	975	1,421	Transit Accounts	34x
182	190	206	†280	300	778	2,405	6,353	11,336	19,567	44,203	71,415	105,684	140,740	208,909	Quasi-Money	35
48	53	58	....	....											Other Liquid Liabilities	36x
58	80	151	†123	-73	-28	†111	187	-403	700	-852	2,888	4,141	19,471	42,290	Other Items (Net)	37r
353	389	410	†518	1,048	1,838	4,472	10,648	18,107	30,316	62,145	92,530	134,114	185,060	270,512	Money plus Quasi-Money	35l
															Interest Rates	
Percent Per Annum																
....	....	....	....	....	....	66.9	41.3	35.1	45.0	37.9	35.0	35.0	35.0	35.0	Bank Rate (End of Period)	60a
....	....	....	....	....	....	....	51.1	85.7	64.0	74.2	51.9	42.2			Treasury Bill Rate	60c
															Prices, Production, Labor	
Period Averages																
....	....	....	1.1	3.8	†11.6	†30.8	74.0	100.0	149.9	†385.0	†512.8	741.1	1,137.0	1,603.3	Producer Prices	63
....	....	....		2.9	9.0	31.9	75.6	100.0	138.8	353.7	562.7	820.4	1,195.1	1,607.0	Consumer Prices	64
1.3	1.4	1.4	1.6	3.5	9.4	28.3	64.9	100.0	149.0	292.6	482.4	719.6	1,006.0	1,413.3	Wages: Avg. Earnings	65
169.4	175.1	171.1	140.6	113.1	88.1	†88.6	91.4	100.0	†109.9	102.7	†85.1	80.7	86.5	93.9	Industrial Production	66
95.7	95.7	98.3	100.0	88.3	78.2	....									Industrial Employment (1990=100)	67
Period Averages																
								12,089	11,726	11,756	11,577	....	11,585	....	Labor Force	67d
10,719	10,805	10,946	10,840	10,786	†10,458	10,062	†10,914	11,152	10,936	11,050	10,845	10,776	10,764	....	Employment	67e
....	....	....	....	337	929	1,165	†1,224	998	658	706	733	790	821	867	Unemployment	67c
....	....	....	....	3.0	8.2	10.4	†11.0	10.0	7.8	6.0	6.4	6.9	7.3	9.0	Unemployment Rate (%)	67r
															International Transactions	
Millions of US Dollars																
10,491.8	11,392.4	10,487.3	5,775.4	4,265.7	4,363.4	4,892.2	6,151.3	7,910.0	8,084.5	8,431.1	8,299.6	8,504.7	10,366.5	11,390.7	Exports	70..d
8,977.7	8,254.0	9,122.4	9,843.4	5,793.4	6,259.6	6,521.7	7,109.0	10,277.9	11,435.3	11,279.7	11,821.0	10,392.1	13,054.5	15,560.9	Imports, c.i.f.	71..d
8,312.7	7,642.6	8,437.7	9,202.5	5,372.0	5,784.1	6,020.1	6,562.4	9,486.7	10,555.0	10,411.4	10,911.0	9,592.1	12,049.6	14,362.9	Imports, f.o.b.	71.vd

Romania

		1972	1973	1974	1975	1976	1977	1978	1979	1980	1981	1982	1983	1984	1985	1986
Balance of Payments																*Millions of US Dollars:*
Current Account, n.i.e.	78al d	−47	149	−359	−135	−16	−304	−759	−1,653	−2,420	−833	1,040	1,160	1,719	1,381	1,395
Goods: Exports f.o.b.	78aa d	2,599	3,667	4,858	5,341	6,134	6,859	8,022	9,303	11,024	12,367	11,559	11,512	12,646	10,174	9,763
Goods: Imports f.o.b.	78ab d	−2,616	−3,425	−5,049	−5,342	−6,087	−7,002	−8,628	−10,519	−12,685	−12,264	−9,745	−9,643	−10,334	−8,402	−8,083
Trade Balance	78ac d	−17	242	−191	−1	47	−143	−606	−1,216	−1,661	103	1,814	1,869	2,312	1,772	1,680
Services: Credit	78ad d	265	338	419	471	508	498	706	830	1,063	1,095	825	727	840	746	681
Services: Debit	78ae d	−295	−373	−518	−516	−453	−527	−691	−909	−1,045	−1,014	−748	−726	−774	−524	−424
Balance on Goods & Services	78af d	−47	207	−290	−46	102	−172	−591	−1,295	−1,643	184	1,891	1,870	2,378	1,994	1,937
Income: Credit	78ag d	—	16	18	25	37	50	56	77	73	113	119	97	117	116	120
Income: Debit	78ah d	—	−74	−87	−114	−155	−182	−224	−435	−850	−1,130	−970	−807	−776	−729	−662
Balance on Gds, Serv. & Inc.	78ai d	−47	149	−359	−135	−16	−304	−759	−1,653	−2,420	−833	1,040	1,160	1,719	1,381	1,395
Current Transfers, n.i.e.: Credit	78aj d	—	—	—	—	—	—	—	—	—	—	—	—	—	—	—
Current Transfers: Debit	78ak d	—	—	—	—	—	—	—	—	—	—	—	—	—	—	—
Capital Account, n.i.e.	78bc d	—	—	—	—	—	—	—	—	—	—	—	—	—	—	—
Capital Account, n.i.e.: Credit	78ba d	—	—	—	—	—	—	—	—	—	—	—	—	—	—	—
Capital Account: Debit	78bb d	—	—	—	—	—	—	—	—	—	—	—	—	—	—	—
Financial Account, n.i.e.	78bj d	42	−266	366	90	−113	−31	925	1,864	2,175	−555	−233	−1,148	−1,691	−1,580	−791
Direct Investment Abroad	78bd d	—	—	—	—	—	—	—	—	—	—	—	—	—	—	—
Dir. Invest. in Rep. Econ., n.i.e.	78be d	—	—	—	—	—	—	—	—	—	—	—	—	—	—	—
Portfolio Investment Assets	78bf d	—	—	—	—	—	—	—	—	—	—	—	—	—	—	—
Equity Securities	78bk d	—	—	—	—	—	—	—	—	—	—	—	—	—	—	—
Debt Securities	78bl d	—	—	—	—	—	—	—	—	—	—	—	—	—	—	—
Portfolio Investment Liab., n.i.e.	78bg d	—	—	—	—	—	—	—	—	—	—	—	—	—	—	—
Equity Securities	78bm d	—	—	—	—	—	—	—	—	—	—	—	—	—	—	—
Debt Securities	78bn d	—	—	—	—	—	—	—	—	—	—	—	—	—	—	—
Financial Derivatives Assets	78bw d	....	....	....	....	....	....	....	....	....	....	....	....	....	....	....
Financial Derivatives Liabilities	78bx d	....	....	....	....	....	....	....	....	....	....	....	....	....	....	....
Other Investment Assets	78bh d	—	−43	−141	−198	−296	−151	−302	−418	−137	−153	−625	−659	−701	−578	−1
Monetary Authorities	78bo d	....	....	....	....	....	....	....	....	....	....	....	....	....	....	....
General Government	78bp d	—	−12	12	44	163	101	—	—	—	—	—	—	−48	−266	65
Banks	78bq d	—	−31	−153	−242	−459	−252	−302	−418	−137	−153	−625	−659	−653	−312	−66
Other Sectors	78br d	—	—	—	—	—	—	—	—	—	—	—	—	—	—	—
Other Investment Liab., n.i.e.	78bi d	42	−223	507	288	183	120	1,227	2,282	2,312	−402	392	−489	−990	−1,002	−790
Monetary Authorities	78bs d	—	—	—	—	—	—	—	103	96	−47	−22	−44	−78	—	—
General Government	78bt d	—	—	—	—	—	—	—	—	—	—	—	—	—	—	—
Banks	78bu d	42	−223	507	288	183	120	1,124	2,186	2,359	−380	436	−411	−990	−1,002	−790
Other Sectors	78bv d	—	—	—	—	—	—	—	—	—	—	—	—	—	—	—
Net Errors and Omissions	78ca d	10	−9	—	13	9	1	−16	−73	−1	7	—	−2	100	−118	8
Overall Balance	78cb d	5	−126	7	−32	−120	−334	150	138	−246	−1,381	807	10	128	−317	612
Reserves and Related Items	79da d	−5	126	−7	32	120	334	−150	−138	246	1,381	−807	−10	−128	317	−612
Reserve Assets	79db d	−5	69	−7	−15	−52	297	−132	−126	232	−46	−353	245	−184	492	−376
Use of Fund Credit and Loans	79dc d	—	57	—	47	173	37	−19	−12	15	284	301	133	56	−175	−236
Exceptional Financing	79de d	—	—	—	—	—	—	—	—	—	1,143	−755	−388	—	—	—
International Investment Position																*Millions of US Dollars*
Assets	79aa d	....	....	....	....	....	....	....	....	....	....	....	....	....	....	....
Direct Investment Abroad	79ab d	....	....	....	....	....	....	....	....	....	....	....	....	....	....	....
Portfolio Investment	79ac d	....	....	....	....	....	....	....	....	....	....	....	....	....	....	....
Equity Securities	79ad d	....	....	....	....	....	....	....	....	....	....	....	....	....	....	....
Debt Securities	79ae d	....	....	....	....	....	....	....	....	....	....	....	....	....	....	....
Financial Derivatives	79al d	....	....	....	....	....	....	....	....	....	....	....	....	....	....	....
Other Investment	79af d	....	....	....	....	....	....	....	....	....	....	....	....	....	....	....
Monetary Authorities	79ag d	....	....	....	....	....	....	....	....	....	....	....	....	....	....	....
General Government	79ah d	....	....	....	....	....	....	....	....	....	....	....	....	....	....	....
Banks	79ai d	....	....	....	....	....	....	....	....	....	....	....	....	....	....	....
Other Sectors	79aj d	....	....	....	....	....	....	....	....	....	....	....	....	....	....	....
Reserve Assets	79ak d	....	....	....	....	....	....	....	....	....	....	....	....	....	....	....
Liabilities	79la d	....	....	....	....	....	....	....	....	....	....	....	....	....	....	....
Dir. Invest. in Rep. Economy	79lb d	....	....	....	....	....	....	....	....	....	....	....	....	....	....	....
Portfolio Investment	79lc d	....	....	....	....	....	....	....	....	....	....	....	....	....	....	....
Equity Securities	79ld d	....	....	....	....	....	....	....	....	....	....	....	....	....	....	....
Debt Securities	79le d	....	....	....	....	....	....	....	....	....	....	....	....	....	....	....
Financial Derivatives	79ll d	....	....	....	....	....	....	....	....	....	....	....	....	....	....	....
Other Investment	79lf d	....	....	....	....	....	....	....	....	....	....	....	....	....	....	....
Monetary Authorities	79lg d	....	....	....	....	....	....	....	....	....	....	....	....	....	....	....
General Government	79lh d	....	....	....	....	....	....	....	....	....	....	....	....	....	....	....
Banks	79li d	....	....	....	....	....	....	....	....	....	....	....	....	....	....	....
Other Sectors	79lj d	....	....	....	....	....	....	....	....	....	....	....	....	....	....	....
Government Finance																*Billions of Lei:*
Deficit (-) or Surplus	80	7	7	2	1	3	1	1	1	3	10	22	25	53	21	36
Revenue	81	130	152	186	217	230	260	278	318	279	260	256	237	289	361	392
Grants	81z	....	....	....	....	....	....	....	....	....	....	....	....	....	....	....
Expenditure	82	124	145	185	216	228	259	277	316	276	250	234	212	236	340	356
Lending Minus Repayments	83	—	—	—	—	—	—	—	—	—	—	—	—	—	—	—
Financing																
Domestic	84a	....	....	....	....	....	....	....	....	....	....	....	....	....	....	....
Foreign	85a	....	....	....	....	....	....	....	....	....	....	....	....	....	....	....
National Accounts																*Billions of Lei*
Househ.Cons.Expend.,incl.NPISHs	96f	....	....	....	....	....	....	....	....	357	380	438	433	463	460	467
Government Consumption Expend.	91f	....	....	....	....	....	....	....	....	31	32	30	31	31	32	30
Gross Fixed Capital Formation	93e	....	....	....	....	....	....	....	....	213	209	216	231	245	246	249
Changes in Inventories	93i	....	....	....	....	....	....	....	....	33	17	29	31	34	24	39
Exports of Goods and Services	90c	....	....	....	....	....	....	....	....	139	174	173	204	227	236	227
Imports of Goods and Services (-)	98c	....	....	....	....	....	....	....	....	137	157	134	143	164	163	152
Gross Domestic Product (GDP)	99b	....	....	....	....	....	....	....	....	617	624	727	769	816	817	839
GDP Volume 1995 Prices	99b.p	....	....	....	....	....	....	....	....	75,287	75,377	78,347	83,079	88,033	87,947	90,011
GDP Volume (1995=100)	99bv p	....	....	....	....	....	....	....	....	104.4	104.5	108.6	115.2	122.0	121.9	124.8
GDP Deflator (1995=100)	99bi p	....	....	....	....	....	....	....	....	.8	.8	.9	.9	.9	.9	.9
																Millions:
Population	99z	20.66	20.83	21.03	21.24	21.45	21.66	21.85	22.05	22.20	22.35	22.48	22.55	22.62	22.72	22.82

	1987	1988	1989	1990	1991	1992	1993	1994	1995	1996	1997	1998	1999	2000	2001	
Balance of Payments																
Minus Sign Indicates Debit																
Current Account, n.i.e.	2,043	3,922	2,514	-3,254	-1,012	-1,506	-1,231	-455	-1,780	-2,579	-2,137	-2,918	-1,297	-1,359	....	78al d
Goods: Exports f.o.b.	10,491	11,392	10,487	5,770	4,266	4,364	4,892	6,151	7,910	8,085	8,431	8,302	8,503	10,366	....	78aa d
Goods: Imports f.o.b.	-8,313	-7,642	-8,437	-9,114	-5,372	-5,558	-6,020	-6,562	-9,487	-10,555	-10,411	-10,927	-9,595	-12,050	....	78ab d
Trade Balance	2,178	3,750	2,050	-3,344	-1,106	-1,194	-1,128	-411	-1,577	-2,470	-1,980	-2,625	-1,092	-1,684	....	78ac d
Services: Credit	770	850	834	610	680	659	799	1,044	1,494	1,563	1,524	1,217	1,365	1,767	....	78ad d
Services: Debit	-515	-480	-450	-787	-819	-946	-914	-1,215	-1,819	-1,948	-1,938	-1,871	-1,785	-2,021	....	78ae d
Balance on Goods & Services	2,433	4,120	2,434	-3,521	-1,245	-1,481	-1,243	-582	-1,902	-2,855	-2,394	-3,279	-1,512	-1,938	....	78af d
Income: Credit	138	173	181	175	104	54	63	116	81	78	204	313	152	325	....	78ag d
Income: Debit	-528	-371	-101	-14	-89	-144	-208	-245	-322	-387	-526	-705	-563	-606	....	78ah d
Balance on Gds, Serv. & Inc.	2,043	3,922	2,514	-3,360	-1,230	-1,571	-1,388	-711	-2,143	-3,164	-2,716	-3,671	-1,923	-2,219	....	78ai d
Current Transfers, n.i.e.: Credit	—	—	—	138	277	136	174	317	473	667	731	886	804	1,079	....	78aj d
Current Transfers: Debit	—	—	—	-32	-59	-71	-17	-61	-110	-82	-152	-133	-178	-219	....	78ak d
Capital Account, n.i.e.	—	—	—	—	—	—	—	—	32	152	43	39	45	36	....	78bc d
Capital Account, n.i.e.: Credit	—	—	—	—	—	—	—	—	32	152	43	39	46	37	....	78ba d
Capital Account: Debit	—	—	—	—	—	—	—	—	—	—	—	—	-1	-1	....	78bb d
Financial Account, n.i.e.	-1,083	-4,223	-1,376	1,613	320	1,380	640	535	812	1,486	2,458	2,042	697	1,943	....	78bj d
Direct Investment Abroad				-18	-3	-4	-7	—	-2	—	9	9	-16	11	....	78bd d
Dir. Invest. in Rep. Econ., n.i.e.				—	40	77	94	341	419	263	1,215	2,031	1,041	1,025	....	78be d
Portfolio Investment Assets				—	—	—	-73	75	-22	—	-6	1	9	28	....	78bf d
Equity Securities				—	—	—	—	—	-4	—	-6	1	9	31	....	78bk d
Debt Securities				—	—	—	-73	75	-18	—	—	—	—	-3	....	78bl d
Portfolio Investment Liab., n.i.e.				—	—	—	—	—	54	193	540	129	-724	74	....	78bg d
Equity Securities				—	—	—	—	—	—	—	195	95	68	58	....	78bm d
Debt Securities				—	—	—	—	—	54	193	345	34	-792	16	....	78bn d
Financial Derivatives Assets				—	—	—	—	—	—	—	—	—	....	....	....	78bw d
Financial Derivatives Liabilities				—	—	—	—	—	—	—	—	—	....	....	....	78bx d
Other Investment Assets	191	-765	98	562	-86	94	-45	-671	186	-271	-6	208	246	-407	....	78bh d
Monetary Authorities	....	....	....	....	....	....	....	....	—	—	—	—	—	—	....	78bo d
General Government	29	-400	169	529	162	112	-49	-24	-62	-9	10	-10	9	-82	....	78bp d
Banks	162	-365	-71	33	-37	—	-168	-621	254	-315	-140	179	236	-354	....	78bq d
Other Sectors				—	-211	-18	172	-26	-6	53	124	39	1	29	....	78br d
Other Investment Liab., n.i.e.	-1,274	-3,458	-1,474	1,069	369	1,213	671	790	177	1,301	706	-336	141	1,212	....	78bi d
Monetary Authorities				—	-533	-159	—	—	-27	-150	—	—	73	-14	....	78bs d
General Government				—	—	812	68	75	-27	209	547	-7	40	681	....	78bt d
Banks	-1,274	-3,458	-1,474	1,069	149	-73	19	190	-57	536	-132	-260	-54	-74	....	78bu d
Other Sectors				753	633	584	525	261	706	291	-69	82	619	....	78bv d
Net Errors and Omissions	81	16	114	147	15	-12	152	91	456	359	1,095	194	794	286	....	78ca d
Overall Balance	1,041	-285	1,252	-1,494	-677	-138	-439	171	-480	-582	1,459	-643	239	906	....	78cb d
Reserves and Related Items	-1,041	285	-1,252	1,494	677	138	439	-171	480	582	-1,459	643	-239	-906	....	79da d
Reserve Assets	-749	622	-1,111	1,494	-93	-124	54	-616	259	-218	-1,664	844	-173	-926	....	79db d
Use of Fund Credit and Loans	-292	-337	-141	—	770	262	—	217	-316	-356	29	-126	-66	20	....	79dc d
Exceptional Financing	—	—	—	—	—	—	385	228	536	1,157	176	-75	—	....	....	79de d
International Investment Position																
Millions of US Dollars																
Assets	....	....	....	6,254	6,355	7,249	7,483	8,847	8,492	9,084	10,163	9,547	9,717	10,894	12,336	79aa d
Direct Investment Abroad	....	....	....	66	87	79	104	107	121	120	114	123	133	101	93	79ab d
Portfolio Investment	....	....	....	808	817	1,124	1,208	1,179	1,224	1,251	1,114	1,190	1,545	1,479	1,428	79ac d
Equity Securities	....	....	....	807	817	1,113	1,124	1,176	1,211	1,238	1,103	1,167	1,541	1,479	1,428	79ad d
Debt Securities	....	....	....	—	—	11	84	3	13	13	11	23	4	—	—	79ae d
Financial Derivatives	....	....	....													79al d
Other Investment	....	....	....	4,504	4,441	5,187	5,215	5,964	5,768	6,120	5,874	5,935	5,546	5,923	5,953	79af d
Monetary Authorities	....	....	....													79ag d
General Government	....	....	....	2,399	2,471	2,929	2,990	3,004	3,006	3,133	2,950	3,082	3,696	3,777	3,843	79ah d
Banks	....	....	....	502	490	730	871	1,491	1,244	1,556	1,636	1,472	1,178	1,487	1,552	79ai d
Other Sectors	....	....	....	1,603	1,481	1,529	1,355	1,468	1,517	1,431	1,288	1,381	672	659	558	79aj d
Reserve Assets	....	....	....	877	1,010	858	956	1,598	1,380	1,593	3,061	2,299	2,493	3,391	4,862	79ak d
Liabilities	....	....	....	3,499	3,973	5,276	6,196	7,500	7,976	11,468	13,862	16,045	16,760	19,073	21,543	79la d
Dir. Invest. in Rep. Economy	....	....	....	—	45	122	216	402	421	1,097	2,352	4,418	5,469	6,517	7,636	79lb d
Portfolio Investment	....	....	....	766	726	943	858	719	785	2,407	3,068	3,338	3,025	3,019	3,527	79lc d
Equity Securities	....	....	....	766	726	943	858	719	732	1,178	1,312	1,459	1,867	1,865	1,824	79ld d
Debt Securities	....	....	....						54	1,229	1,756	1,879	1,158	1,154	1,703	79le d
Financial Derivatives	....	....	....													79ll d
Other Investment	....	....	....	2,733	3,203	4,212	5,123	6,379	6,770	7,964	8,442	8,289	8,266	9,537	10,380	79lf d
Monetary Authorities	....	....	....	—	809	1,032	1,031	1,383	1,358	941	958	580	572	553	487	79lg d
General Government	....	....	....	1,754	1,237	1,944	2,388	2,298	2,335	2,484	2,888	2,963	2,920	3,590	3,808	79lh d
Banks	....	....	....	163	240	447	504	682	743	1,269	832	575	566	482	581	79li d
Other Sectors	....	....	....	817	916	789	1,200	2,016	2,334	3,270	3,764	4,171	4,208	4,912	5,504	79lj d
Government Finance																
Year Ending December 31																
Deficit (-) or Surplus	60	50	66	8	43	-282	-94	-1,248	-2,133	-4,377	-9,755	6,511	10,976	....	....	80
Revenue	404	364	386	298	823	2,200	6,389	14,884	21,327	30,194	68,394	107,051	171,135	....	....	81
Grants	....	....	....	....	....	....	....	....	....	....	....	695	4,235	....	....	81z
Expenditure	344	314	321	290	780	2,406	6,312	15,913	22,927	34,033	79,734	124,595	191,341	....	....	82
Lending Minus Repayments	—	—	—	—	77	171	220	533	538	-1,585	-5,816	-6,741	....	....		83
Financing																
Domestic	....	....	....	-8	-43	282	94	1,248	2,133	4,377	9,755	11,033	9,230	....	....	84a
Foreign	....	....	....	....	....	....	....	....	....	....	....	....	....	....	....	85a
National Accounts																
Billions of Lei																
Housoh.Cons.Expend.,incl.NPISHs	489	501	†470	565	1,339	3,781	12,763	31,601	48,785	75,665	187,620	283,142	405,322	562,879	823,029	96f
Government Consumption Expend.	28	31	†93	114	334	861	2,473	6,852	9,877	14,274	31,000	54,327	79,040	125,000	171,989	91f
Gross Fixed Capital Formation	245	240	†239	170	317	1,157	3,584	10,096	15,425	24,999	53,540	67,920	96,630	151,486	219,289	93e
Changes in Inventories	23	†3	†-25	90	301	737	2,212	2,253	2,085	3,161	-1,369	-1,586	-8,890	6,194	33,361	93i
Exports of Goods and Services	225	219	†167	143	388	1,676	4,612	12,394	19,921	30,651	73,796	84,559	152,903	264,187	386,832	90c
Imports of Goods and Services (-)	150	135	†145	225	475	2,182	5,608	13,422	23,958	39,831	91,661	114,563	179,275	309,438	480,373	98c
Gross Domestic Product (GDP)	845	857	†800	858	2,204	6,029	20,036	49,773	72,136	108,920	252,926	373,798	545,730	800,308	1,154,126	99b
GDP Volume 1995 Prices	90,769	90,315	85,096	80,429	69,908	63,809	64,780	67,329	72,136	74,984	70,445	67,051	66,280	67,455	70,999	99b. p
GDP Volume (1995=100)	125.8	125.2	118.0	111.5	96.9	88.5	89.8	93.3	100.0	103.9	97.7	93.0	91.9	93.5	98.4	99bv p
GDP Deflator (1995=100)	.9	.9	†.9	1.1	3.2	9.4	30.9	73.9	100.0	145.3	359.0	557.5	823.4	1,186.4	1,625.6	99bi p
Midyear Estimates																
Population	22.94	23.05	23.15	23.21	23.19	22.79	22.76	22.73	22.68	22.61	22.55	22.50	22.46	22.44	22.41	99z

(See notes in the back of the book.)

Russia

	1972	1973	1974	1975	1976	1977	1978	1979	1980	1981	1982	1983	1984	1985	1986
Exchange Rates														*Rubles per SDR:*	
Official Rate .... **aa**	...	...	...	...	...	...	...	...	...	...	...	...	...	...	...
														Rubles per US Dollar:	
Official Rate .... **ae**	...	...	...	...	...	...	...	...	...	...	...	...	...	...	...
Official Rate .... **rf**	...	...	...	...	...	...	...	...	...	...	...	...	...	...	...
													Index Numbers (1995=100):		
Nominal Effective Exchange Rate .... **ne** *c*	...	...	...	...	...	...	...	...	...	...	...	...	...	...	...
Real Effective Exchange Rate .... **re** *c*	...	...	...	...	...	...	...	...	...	...	...	...	...	...	...
Fund Position														*Millions of SDRs:*	
Quota .... **2f.** *s*	...	...	...	...	...	...	...	...	...	...	...	...	...	...	...
SDRs .... **1b.** *s*	...	...	...	...	...	...	...	...	...	...	...	...	...	...	...
Reserve Position in the Fund .... **1c.** *s*	...	...	...	...	...	...	...	...	...	...	...	...	...	...	...
Total Fund Cred.&Loans Outstg. **2tl**	...	...	...	...	...	...	...	...	...	...	...	...	...	...	...
International Liquidity									*Millions of US Dollars Unless Otherwise Indicated:*						
Total Reserves minus Gold .... **1l.** *d*	...	...	...	...	...	...	...	...	...	...	...	...	...	...	...
SDRs .... **1b.** *d*	...	...	...	...	...	...	...	...	...	...	...	...	...	...	...
Reserve Position in the Fund .... **1c.** *d*	...	...	...	...	...	...	...	...	...	...	...	...	...	...	...
Foreign Exchange .... **1d.** *d*	...	...	...	...	...	...	...	...	...	...	...	...	...	...	...
Gold (Million Fine Troy Ounces) **1ad**	...	...	...	...	...	...	...	...	...	...	...	...	...	...	...
Gold (National Valuation) .... **1an** *d*	...	...	...	...	...	...	...	...	...	...	...	...	...	...	...
Monetary Authorities: Other Assets .... **3..** *d*	...	...	...	...	...	...	...	...	...	...	...	...	...	...	...
Other Liab. ...... **4..** *d*	...	...	...	...	...	...	...	...	...	...	...	...	...	...	...
Deposit Money Banks: Assets .... **7a.** *d*	...	...	...	...	...	...	...	...	...	...	...	...	...	...	...
Liabilities .... **7b.** *d*	...	...	...	...	...	...	...	...	...	...	...	...	...	...	...
Monetary Authorities														*Millions of Rubles:*	
Foreign Assets **11**	...	...	...	...	...	...	...	...	...	...	...	...	...	...	...
Claims on General Government **12a**	...	...	...	...	...	...	...	...	...	...	...	...	...	...	...
Claims on Nonfin.Pub.Enterprises **12c**	...	...	...	...	...	...	...	...	...	...	...	...	...	...	...
Claims on Private Sector **12d**	...	...	...	...	...	...	...	...	...	...	...	...	...	...	...
Claims on Deposit Money Banks **12e**	...	...	...	...	...	...	...	...	...	...	...	...	...	...	...
Reserve Money **14**	...	...	...	...	...	...	...	...	...	...	...	...	...	...	...
of which: Currency Outside DMBs **14a**	...	...	...	...	...	...	...	...	...	...	...	...	...	...	...
Time & Foreign Currency Deposits **15**	...	...	...	...	...	...	...	...	...	...	...	...	...	...	...
Foreign Liabilities **16c**	...	...	...	...	...	...	...	...	...	...	...	...	...	...	...
General Government Deposits **16d**	...	...	...	...	...	...	...	...	...	...	...	...	...	...	...
of which: Local Govt. Deposits **16db**	...	...	...	...	...	...	...	...	...	...	...	...	...	...	...
Capital Accounts **17a**	...	...	...	...	...	...	...	...	...	...	...	...	...	...	...
Other Items (Net) **17r**	...	...	...	...	...	...	...	...	...	...	...	...	...	...	...
Deposit Money Banks														*Millions of Rubles:*	
Reserves **20**	...	...	...	...	...	...	...	...	...	...	...	...	...	...	...
Foreign Assets **21**	...	...	...	...	...	...	...	...	...	...	...	...	...	...	...
Claims on General Government **22a**	...	...	...	...	...	...	...	...	...	...	...	...	...	...	...
of which: Claims on Local Govts **22ab**	...	...	...	...	...	...	...	...	...	...	...	...	...	...	...
Claims on Nonfin.Pub.Enterprises **22c**	...	...	...	...	...	...	...	...	...	...	...	...	...	...	...
Claims on Private Sector **22d**	...	...	...	...	...	...	...	...	...	...	...	...	...	...	...
Claims on Other Financial Insts **22f**	...	...	...	...	...	...	...	...	...	...	...	...	...	...	...
Demand Deposits **24**	...	...	...	...	...	...	...	...	...	...	...	...	...	...	...
Time, Savings,& Fgn.Currency Dep. **25**	...	...	...	...	...	...	...	...	...	...	...	...	...	...	...
of which: Fgn. Currency Deposits **25b**	...	...	...	...	...	...	...	...	...	...	...	...	...	...	...
Money Market Instruments **26aa**	...	...	...	...	...	...	...	...	...	...	...	...	...	...	...
Restricted Deposits **26b**	...	...	...	...	...	...	...	...	...	...	...	...	...	...	...
Foreign Liabilities **26c**	...	...	...	...	...	...	...	...	...	...	...	...	...	...	...
General Government Deposits **26d**	...	...	...	...	...	...	...	...	...	...	...	...	...	...	...
of which: Local Govt. Deposits **26db**	...	...	...	...	...	...	...	...	...	...	...	...	...	...	...
Credit from Monetary Authorities **26g**	...	...	...	...	...	...	...	...	...	...	...	...	...	...	...
Capital Accounts **27a**	...	...	...	...	...	...	...	...	...	...	...	...	...	...	...
Other Items (Net) **27r**	...	...	...	...	...	...	...	...	...	...	...	...	...	...	...
Monetary Survey														*Millions of Rubles:*	
Foreign Assets (Net) **31n**	...	...	...	...	...	...	...	...	...	...	...	...	...	...	...
Domestic Credit **32**	...	...	...	...	...	...	...	...	...	...	...	...	...	...	...
Claims on General Govt. (Net) **32an**	...	...	...	...	...	...	...	...	...	...	...	...	...	...	...
Claims on Nonfin.Pub.Enterprises **32c**	...	...	...	...	...	...	...	...	...	...	...	...	...	...	...
Claims on Private Sector **32d**	...	...	...	...	...	...	...	...	...	...	...	...	...	...	...
Claims on Other Financial Insts **32f**	...	...	...	...	...	...	...	...	...	...	...	...	...	...	...
Money **34**	...	...	...	...	...	...	...	...	...	...	...	...	...	...	...
Quasi-Money **35**	...	...	...	...	...	...	...	...	...	...	...	...	...	...	...
Money Market Instruments **36aa**	...	...	...	...	...	...	...	...	...	...	...	...	...	...	...
Restricted Deposits **36b**	...	...	...	...	...	...	...	...	...	...	...	...	...	...	...
Capital Accounts **37a**	...	...	...	...	...	...	...	...	...	...	...	...	...	...	...
Other Items (Net) **37r**	...	...	...	...	...	...	...	...	...	...	...	...	...	...	...
Money plus Quasi-Money **35l**	...	...	...	...	...	...	...	...	...	...	...	...	...	...	...
Interest Rates														*Percent Per Annum*	
Refinancing Rate (End of Period) **60**															
Money Market Rate **60b**	...	...	...	...	...	...	...	...	...	...	...	...	...	...	...
Treasury Bill Rate **60c**	...	...	...	...	...	...	...	...	...	...	...	...	...	...	...
Deposit Rate **60l**	...	...	...	...	...	...	...	...	...	...	...	...	...	...	...
Lending Rate **60p**	...	...	...	...	...	...	...	...	...	...	...	...	...	...	...

	1987	1988	1989	1990	1991	1992	1993	1994	1995	1996	1997	1998	1999	2000	2001		
End of Period																**Exchange Rates**	
	....	....	....	....	....	.5706	1.7128	5.1825	6.8973	7.9951	8.0415	†29.0758	37.0578	36.6899	37.8778	Official Rate	aa
End of Period (ae) Period Average (rf)																	
	....	....	....	....	....	.4150	1.2470	3.5500	4.6400	5.5600	5.9600	†20.6500	27.0000	28.1600	30.1400	Official Rate	ae
	....	....	....	....	....	....	.9917	2.1908	4.5592	5.1208	5.7848	9.7051	24.6199	28.1292	29.1685	Official Rate	rf
Period Averages																	
	....	....	....	....	....	....	....	162.95	100.00	97.06	98.89	80.31	32.51	34.47	36.44	Nominal Effective Exchange Rate	ne c
	....	....	....	....	....	....	....	91.12	100.00	122.10	128.96	114.23	80.58	90.46	107.35	Real Effective Exchange Rate	re c
End of Period																**Fund Position**	
	....	....	....	....	....	4,313.1	4,313.1	4,313.1	4,313.1	4,313.1	4,313.1	4,313.1	5,945.4	5,945.4	5,945.4	Quota	2f. s
	....	....	....	....	....	.6	3.7	2.1	78.5	3.1	90.7	.1	.4	.4	2.3	SDRs	1b. s
	....	....	....	....	....	.5	1.0	.8	.8	.9	.9	.9	.9	.9	1.1	Reserve Position in the Fund	1c. s
	....	....	....	....	....	719.0	1,797.3	2,875.6	6,469.8	8,698.2	9,805.9	13,732.0	11,102.3	8,912.8	5,914.8	Total Fund Cred.&Loans Outstg.	2tl
End of Period																**International Liquidity**	
	....	....	....	....	....	....	5,835.0	3,980.4	14,382.8	11,276.4	12,894.7	7,801.4	8,457.2	24,264.3	32,542.4	Total Reserves minus Gold	1l. d
	....	....	....	....	....	.8	5.0	3.1	116.7	4.5	122.4	.1	.6	.5	2.9	SDRs	1b. d
	....	....	....	....	....	.7	1.4	1.2	1.1	1.3	1.2	1.3	1.3	1.2	1.4	Reserve Position in the Fund	1c. d
	....	....	....	....	....	....	5,828.6	3,976.1	14,264.9	11,270.6	12,771.1	7,800.0	8,455.4	24,262.6	32,538.1	Foreign Exchange	1d. d
	....	....	....	....	....	....	10.195	8.417	9.414	13.490	16.297	14.738	13.326	12.359	13.599	Gold (Million Fine Troy Ounces)	1ad
	....	....	....	....	....	....	3,058.5	2,525.1	2,824.1	4,047.1	4,889.2	4,421.6	3,998.3	3,707.8	4,079.8	Gold (National Valuation)	1and
	....	....	....	....	....	....	9,074.6	5,768.2	5,319.3	3,176.8	2,911.2	1,642.6	1,743.0	1,946.3	1,992.7	Monetary Authorities: Other Assets	3..d
	....	....	....	....	....	....	943.1	477.3	773.3	311.2	149.2	110.5	473.1	143.7	2,102.6	Other Liab.	4..d
	....	....	....	....	....	....	12,669.3	13,891.6	9,946.0	13,107.0	12,200.9	10,634.0	13,727.8	16,924.1	17,896.3	Deposit Money Banks: Assets	7a. d
	....	....	....	....	....	....	3,773.4	4,076.8	6,459.0	10,592.2	17,482.8	9,837.1	8,245.4	8,839.5	10,451.2	Liabilities	7b. d
End of Period																**Monetary Authorities**	
	....	....	....	....	....	....	21,737	41,082	95,890	102,861	123,344	286,324	383,899	842,445	1,163,850	Foreign Assets	11
	....	....	....	....	....	....	16,802	84,498	138,578	187,365	226,049	525,374	572,030	504,702	488,102	Claims on General Government	12a
	....	....	....	....	....	....	123	251	85	67	46	150	114	103	80	Claims on Nonfin.Pub.Enterprises	12c
	....	....	....	....	....	....	21	72	237	813	281	412	316	264	168	Claims on Private Sector	12d
	....	....	....	....	....	....	8,889	16,177	17,450	11,377	11,119	76,438	202,944	206,501	250,187	Claims on Deposit Money Banks	12e
	....	....	....	....	....	....	20,544	62,357	129,601	164,929	210,450	263,675	439,743	739,758	951,294	Reserve Money	14
	....	....	....	....	....	....	10,730	34,493	80,815	103,824	130,540	187,843	266,544	419,261	584,328	*of which: Currency Outside DMBs*	14a
	....	....	....	....	....	....	1	4	17	23	240	1,828	1,575	7	2	Time & Foreign Currency Deposits	15
	....	....	....	....	....	....	4,254	16,538	46,030	71,272	79,744	401,551	424,201	331,056	287,413	Foreign Liabilities	16c
	....	....	....	....	....	....	7,003	17,096	24,898	15,062	21,313	41,863	75,871	240,488	294,914	General Government Deposits	16d
	....	....	....	....	....	....	847	3,273	2,117	2,068	3,564	2,863	10,515	29,511	27,729	*of which:* Local Govt. Deposits	16db
	....	....	....	....	....	....	638	17,014	27,530	54,179	69,552	118,113	151,844	166,048	242,312	Capital Accounts	17a
	....	....	....	....	....	....	15,132	29,071	24,164	–2,982	–20,460	61,669	66,070	76,658	126,452	Other Items (Net)	17r
End of Period																**Deposit Money Banks**	
	....	....	....	....	....	....	7,914	24,151	36,712	47,124	72,975	67,763	160,018	301,125	342,309	Reserves	20
	....	....	....	....	....	....	15,798	49,316	46,150	72,875	72,717	219,593	370,651	476,582	539,393	Foreign Assets	21
	....	....	....	....	....	....	776	10,639	62,639	150,721	194,690	259,402	437,674	526,020	583,633	Claims on General Government	22a
	....	....	....	....	....	....	—	—	722	2,790	18,692	24,446	19,870	18,531	26,245	*of which:* Claims on Local Govts	22ab
	....	....	....	....	....	....	15,639	48,173	62,460	69,371	33,217	33,079	46,901	73,972	79,302	Claims on Nonfin.Pub.Enterprises	22c
	....	....	....	....	....	....	20,208	74,017	133,786	157,337	236,439	345,963	521,645	867,133	1,388,920	Claims on Private Sector	22d
	....	....	....	....	....	....	—	—	525	242	8,076	7,271	13,060	14,525	22,487	Claims on Other Financial Insts	22f
	....	....	....	....	....	....	12,519	32,589	69,332	87,303	162,532	149,471	249,673	443,021	585,469	Demand Deposits	24
	....	....	....	....	....	....	17,101	61,183	124,497	164,899	158,716	283,997	456,528	680,647	930,104	Time, Savings,& Fgn.Currency Dep.	25
	....	....	....	....	....	....	12,086	37,309	55,256	69,448	80,455	190,873	290,213	420,090	520,006	*of which: Fgn. Currency Deposits*	25b
	....	....	....	....	....	....	211	3,516	11,858	30,372	42,436	43,311	107,817	191,059	258,231	Money Market Instruments	26aa
	....	....	....	....	....	....	—	—	—	—	6,270	22,595	10,224	22,695	20,844	Restricted Deposits	26b
	....	....	....	....	....	....	4,705	14,473	29,970	58,892	104,197	203,137	222,627	248,921	314,999	Foreign Liabilities	26c
	....	....	....	....	....	....	2,117	6,914	9,741	11,557	18,237	20,676	28,672	54,547	67,939	General Government Deposits	26d
	....	....	....	....	....	....	919	2,246	4,252	4,211	9,140	10,148	15,627	36,642	42,259	*of which:* Local Govt. Deposits	26db
	....	....	....	....	....	....	8,464	17,181	8,006	6,799	8,780	71,894	199,582	203,468	247,605	Credit from Monetary Authorities	26g
	....	....	....	....	....	....	12,031	26,211	66,688	123,818	143,909	157,595	293,199	437,266	611,808	Capital Accounts	27a
	....	....	....	....	....	....	3,187	44,229	22,180	14,030	–26,963	–19,605	–18,373	–22,267	–80,955	Other Items (Net)	27r
End of Period																**Monetary Survey**	
	....	....	....	....	....	....	28,576	59,387	66,040	45,572	12,120	–98,770	107,723	739,050	1,100,831	Foreign Assets (Net)	31n
	....	....	....	....	....	....	44,449	193,640	363,671	539,297	659,248	1,109,112	1,487,197	1,691,684	2,199,839	Domestic Credit	32
	....	....	....	....	....	....	8,458	71,127	166,578	311,467	381,189	722,237	905,161	735,687	708,882	Claims on General Govt. (Net)	32an
	....	....	....	....	....	....	15,762	48,424	62,545	69,438	33,263	33,229	47,015	74,075	79,382	Claims on Nonfin.Pub.Enterprises	32c
	....	....	....	....	....	....	20,229	74,089	134,023	158,150	236,720	346,375	521,961	867,397	1,389,088	Claims on Private Sector	32d
	....	....	....	....	....	....	—	—	525	242	8,076	7,271	13,060	14,525	22,487	Claims on Other Financial Insts	32f
	....	....	....	....	....	....	23,881	68,544	151,267	192,402	298,289	342,817	526,771	879,309	1,192,627	Money	34
	....	....	....	....	....	....	17,102	61,187	124,514	164,922	158,956	285,825	458,103	680,654	930,106	Quasi-Money	35
	....	....	....	....	....	....	211	3,516	11,858	30,372	42,436	43,311	107,817	191,059	258,231	Money Market Instruments	36aa
	....	....	....	....	....	....	—	—	—	—	6,270	22,595	10,224	22,695	20,844	Restricted Deposits	36b
	....	....	....	....	....	....	12,669	43,225	94,218	177,997	213,461	275,708	445,043	603,314	854,120	Capital Accounts	37a
	....	....	....	....	....	....	19,162	76,555	47,854	19,176	–48,044	40,086	46,962	53,703	44,742	Other Items (Net)	37r
	....	....	....	....	....	....	40,983	129,731	275,781	357,324	457,245	628,642	984,874	1,559,963	2,122,733	Money plus Quasi-Money	35l
Percent Per Annum																**Interest Rates**	
	....	....	....	....	....	....	....	....	160.0	48.0	28.0	60.0	55.0	25.0	25.0	Refinancing Rate *(End of Period)*	60
	....	....	....	....	....	....	....	....	190.4	47.7	21.0	50.6	14.8	7.1	10.1	Money Market Rate	60b
	....	....	....	....	....	....	....	....	168.0	86.1	23.4	....	....	12.1	12.5	Treasury Bill Rate	60c
	....	....	....	....	....	....	....	....	102.0	55.1	†16.8	17.1	13.7	6.5	4.9	Deposit Rate	60l
	....	....	....	....	....	....	....	....	320.3	146.8	†32.0	41.8	39.7	24.4	17.9	Lending Rate	60p

Russia

		1972	1973	1974	1975	1976	1977	1978	1979	1980	1981	1982	1983	1984	1985	1986
Prices, Production, Labor															*Percent Change over*	
Producer Prices	63.xx	...	...	...	...	...	...	...	...	...	...	...	...	...	...	...
Consumer Prices	64.xx	...	...	...	...	...	...	...	...	...	...	...	...	...	...	...
Wages	65.xx	...	...	...	...	...	...	...	...	...	...	...	...	...	...	...
Industrial Employment	67	...	...	...	...	...	...	...	...	...	...	...	...	*Index Numbers (1995=100):*		
															Number in Thousands:	
Labor Force	67d	...	...	...	...	...	...	...	...	...	...	...	...	...	...	...
Employment	67e	...	...	...	...	...	...	...	...	...	...	...	...	...	...	...
Unemployment	67c	...	...	...	...	...	...	...	...	...	...	...	...	...	...	...
Unemployment Rate (%)	67r	...	...	...	...	...	...	...	...	...	...	...	...	...	...	...
International Transactions															*Millions of US Dollars*	
Exports	70..d	...	...	...	...	...	...	...	...	...	...	...	...	...	...	...
Imports, c.i.f.	71..d	...	...	...	...	...	...	...	...	...	...	...	...	...	...	...
Imports, f.o.b.	71.vd	...	...	...	...	...	...	...	...	...	...	...	...	...	...	...
Balance of Payments															*Millions of US Dollars:*	
Current Account, n.i.e.	78ald	...	...	...	...	...	...	...	...	...	...	...	...	...	...	...
Goods: Exports f.o.b.	78aad	...	...	...	...	...	...	...	...	...	...	...	...	...	...	...
Goods: Imports f.o.b.	78abd	...	...	...	...	...	...	...	...	...	...	...	...	...	...	...
Trade Balance	78acd	...	...	...	...	...	...	...	...	...	...	...	...	...	...	...
Services: Credit	78add	...	...	...	...	...	...	...	...	...	...	...	...	...	...	...
Services: Debit	78aed	...	...	...	...	...	...	...	...	...	...	...	...	...	...	...
Balance on Goods & Services	78afd	...	...	...	...	...	...	...	...	...	...	...	...	...	...	...
Income: Credit	78agd	...	...	...	...	...	...	...	...	...	...	...	...	...	...	...
Income: Debit	78ahd	...	...	...	...	...	...	...	...	...	...	...	...	...	...	...
Balance on Gds, Serv. & Inc.	78aid	...	...	...	...	...	...	...	...	...	...	...	...	...	...	...
Current Transfers, n.i.e.: Credit	78ajd	...	...	...	...	...	...	...	...	...	...	...	...	...	...	...
Current Transfers: Debit	78akd	...	...	...	...	...	...	...	...	...	...	...	...	...	...	...
Capital Account, n.i.e.	78bcd	...	...	...	...	...	...	...	...	...	...	...	...	...	...	...
Capital Account, n.i.e.: Credit	78bad	...	...	...	...	...	...	...	...	...	...	...	...	...	...	...
Capital Account: Debit	78bbd	...	...	...	...	...	...	...	...	...	...	...	...	...	...	...
Financial Account, n.i.e.	78bjd	...	...	...	...	...	...	...	...	...	...	...	...	...	...	...
Direct Investment Abroad	78bdd	...	...	...	...	...	...	...	...	...	...	...	...	...	...	...
Dir. Invest. in Rep. Econ., n.i.e.	78bed	...	...	...	...	...	...	...	...	...	...	...	...	...	...	...
Portfolio Investment Assets	78bfd	...	...	...	...	...	...	...	...	...	...	...	...	...	...	...
Equity Securities	78bkd	...	...	...	...	...	...	...	...	...	...	...	...	...	...	...
Debt Securities	78bld	...	...	...	...	...	...	...	...	...	...	...	...	...	...	...
Portfolio Investment Liab., n.i.e.	78bgd	...	...	...	...	...	...	...	...	...	...	...	...	...	...	...
Equity Securities	78bmd	...	...	...	...	...	...	...	...	...	...	...	...	...	...	...
Debt Securities	78bnd	...	...	...	...	...	...	...	...	...	...	...	...	...	...	...
Financial Derivatives Assets	78bwd	...	...	...	...	...	...	...	...	...	...	...	...	...	...	...
Financial Derivatives Liabilities	78bxd	...	...	...	...	...	...	...	...	...	...	...	...	...	...	...
Other Investment Assets	78bhd	...	...	...	...	...	...	...	...	...	...	...	...	...	...	...
Monetary Authorities	78bod	...	...	...	...	...	...	...	...	...	...	...	...	...	...	...
General Government	78bpd	...	...	...	...	...	...	...	...	...	...	...	...	...	...	...
Banks	78bqd	...	...	...	...	...	...	...	...	...	...	...	...	...	...	...
Other Sectors	78brd	...	...	...	...	...	...	...	...	...	...	...	...	...	...	...
Other Investment Liab., n.i.e.	78bid	...	...	...	...	...	...	...	...	...	...	...	...	...	...	...
Monetary Authorities	78bsd	...	...	...	...	...	...	...	...	...	...	...	...	...	...	...
General Government	78btd	...	...	...	...	...	...	...	...	...	...	...	...	...	...	...
Banks	78bud	...	...	...	...	...	...	...	...	...	...	...	...	...	...	...
Other Sectors	78bvd	...	...	...	...	...	...	...	...	...	...	...	...	...	...	...
Net Errors and Omissions	78cad	...	...	...	...	...	...	...	...	...	...	...	...	...	...	...
Overall Balance	78cbd	...	...	...	...	...	...	...	...	...	...	...	...	...	...	...
Reserves and Related Items	79dad	...	...	...	...	...	...	...	...	...	...	...	...	...	...	...
Reserve Assets	79dbd	...	...	...	...	...	...	...	...	...	...	...	...	...	...	...
Use of Fund Credit and Loans	79dcd	...	...	...	...	...	...	...	...	...	...	...	...	...	...	...
Exceptional Financing	79ded	...	...	...	...	...	...	...	...	...	...	...	...	...	...	...
International Investment Position															*Millions of US Dollars*	
Assets	79aad	...	...	...	...	...	...	...	...	...	...	...	...	...	...	...
Direct Investment Abroad	79abd	...	...	...	...	...	...	...	...	...	...	...	...	...	...	...
Portfolio Investment	79acd	...	...	...	...	...	...	...	...	...	...	...	...	...	...	...
Equity Securities	79add	...	...	...	...	...	...	...	...	...	...	...	...	...	...	...
Debt Securities	79aed	...	...	...	...	...	...	...	...	...	...	...	...	...	...	...
Financial Derivatives	79ald	...	...	...	...	...	...	...	...	...	...	...	...	...	...	...
Other Investment	79afd	...	...	...	...	...	...	...	...	...	...	...	...	...	...	...
Monetary Authorities	79agd	...	...	...	...	...	...	...	...	...	...	...	...	...	...	...
General Government	79ahd	...	...	...	...	...	...	...	...	...	...	...	...	...	...	...
Banks	79aid	...	...	...	...	...	...	...	...	...	...	...	...	...	...	...
Other Sectors	79ajd	...	...	...	...	...	...	...	...	...	...	...	...	...	...	...
Reserve Assets	79akd	...	...	...	...	...	...	...	...	...	...	...	...	...	...	...
Liabilities	79lad	...	...	...	...	...	...	...	...	...	...	...	...	...	...	...
Dir. Invest. in Rep. Economy	79lbd	...	...	...	...	...	...	...	...	...	...	...	...	...	...	...
Portfolio Investment	79lcd	...	...	...	...	...	...	...	...	...	...	...	...	...	...	...
Equity Securities	79ldd	...	...	...	...	...	...	...	...	...	...	...	...	...	...	...
Debt Securities	79led	...	...	...	...	...	...	...	...	...	...	...	...	...	...	...
Financial Derivatives	79lld	...	...	...	...	...	...	...	...	...	...	...	...	...	...	...
Other Investment	79lfd	...	...	...	...	...	...	...	...	...	...	...	...	...	...	...
Monetary Authorities	79lgd	...	...	...	...	...	...	...	...	...	...	...	...	...	...	...
General Government	79lhd	...	...	...	...	...	...	...	...	...	...	...	...	...	...	...
Banks	79lid	...	...	...	...	...	...	...	...	...	...	...	...	...	...	...
Other Sectors	79ljd	...	...	...	...	...	...	...	...	...	...	...	...	...	...	...

Prices, Production, Labor

Previous Period

	1987	1988	1989	1990	1991	1992	1993	1994	1995	1996	1997	1998	1999	2000	2001	Line
Producer Prices	....	....	....	....	....	....	943.76	337.00	236.46	50.81	17.20	5.05	58.90	46.52	19.17	63.xx
Consumer Prices							874.62	307.63	197.47	47.73	14.74	27.67	85.68	20.75	21.49	64.xx
Wages							822.1	255.9	142.2	64.8	23.7	15.3	54.7	52.5	43.3	65.xx

Period Averages

	1987	1988	1989	1990	1991	1992	1993	1994	1995	1996	1997	1998	1999	2000	2001	Line
Industrial Employment						131.4	120.9	107.1	100.0	91.8	84.0	80.7	81.4	79.6	79.0	67

Period Averages

	1987	1988	1989	1990	1991	1992	1993	1994	1995	1996	1997	1998	1999	2000	2001	Line
Labor Force						73,008	....	....	69,469	68,264	....	66,736	69,731	....	....	67d
Employment						71,068	68,642	64,785	64,149	62,928	60,021	57,860	60,408	....	....	67e
Unemployment					62	578	†836	1,637	2,327	2,506	1,990	1,875	1,675	1,244	1,050	67c
Unemployment Rate (%)					.1	.8	5.7	†7.5	8.9	9.9	11.3	13.3	....	....	....	67r

International Transactions

Millions of US Dollars

	1987	1988	1989	1990	1991	1992	1993	1994	1995	1996	1997	1998	1999	2000	2001	Line
Exports						42,039	44,297	†67,826	82,913	90,563	89,008	74,884	75,665	105,565	103,139	70..d
Imports, c.i.f.						36,984	32,806	†55,497	68,863	74,879	79,076	63,817	43,588	49,125	58,992	71..d
Imports, f.o.b.						....	50,452	62,603	68,072	71,887	58,015	39,625	44,659	53,629		71.vd

Balance of Payments

Minus Sign Indicates Debit

	1987	1988	1989	1990	1991	1992	1993	1994	1995	1996	1997	1998	1999	2000	2001	Line
Current Account, n.i.e.								8,434	7,488	11,755	2,061	683	24,731	46,405	34,575	78ald
Goods: Exports f.o.b.								67,826	82,913	90,564	89,008	74,883	75,666	105,565	101,603	78aad
Goods: Imports f.o.b.								-50,451	-62,603	-68,093	-71,982	-58,014	-39,537	-44,862	-53,764	78abd
Trade Balance								17,375	20,310	22,471	17,026	16,869	36,129	60,703	47,839	78acd
Services: Credit								8,425	10,568	13,283	14,079	12,375	9,067	9,975	10,903	78add
Services: Debit								-15,292	-20,178	-18,637	-19,998	-16,429	-13,351	-17,606	-19,404	78aed
Balance on Goods & Services								10,508	10,700	17,117	11,107	12,815	31,845	53,072	39,338	78afd
Income: Credit								3,499	4,281	4,336	4,367	4,299	3,881	4,753	6,800	78agd
Income: Debit								-5,342	-7,650	-9,768	-13,058	-16,094	-11,597	-11,489	-10,759	78ahd
Balance on Gds, Serv. & Inc.								8,665	7,331	11,685	2,416	1,020	24,129	46,336	35,379	78aid
Current Transfers, n.i.e.: Credit								311	895	771	411	308	1,183	807	381	78ajd
Current Transfers: Debit								-542	-738	-701	-766	-645	-582	-738	-1,186	78akd
Capital Account, n.i.e.								2,408	-348	-463	-796	-382	-328	10,676	-9,378	78bcd
Capital Account, n.i.e.: Credit								5,882	3,122	3,066	2,138	1,705	885	11,543	2,125	78bad
Capital Account: Debit								-3,474	-3,470	-3,529	-2,934	-2,087	-1,213	-867	-11,503	78bbd
Financial Account, n.i.e.								-30,219	-7,463	-23,586	....	-12,956	-19,073	-33,796	-4,796	78bjd
Direct Investment Abroad								-281	-605	-922	-3,186	-1,268	-2,208	-3,177	-2,591	78bdd
Dir. Invest. in Rep. Econ., n.i.e.								690	2,065	2,579	4,864	2,764	3,309	2,714	2,469	78bed
Portfolio Investment Assets								114	-1,704	-173	-157	-258	254	-411	77	78bfd
Equity Securities								-19	-42	-117	32	-11	5	-40	-60	78bkd
Debt Securities								133	-1,662	-56	-189	-247	249	-371	137	78bld
Portfolio Investment Liab., n.i.e.								-93	-739	4,584	17,796	6,293	-1,882	-12,808	-730	78bgd
Equity Securities								44	46	2,154	1,266	714	-287	150	542	78bmd
Debt Securities								-137	-785	2,430	16,530	5,579	-1,595	-12,959	-1,272	78bnd
Financial Derivatives Assets								....	....	....	....	....	....	....	—	78bwd
Financial Derivatives Liabilities								....	....	....	....	....	....	....	—	78bxd
Other Investment Assets								-19,458	6,266	-30,561	-26,640	-15,958	-14,856	-17,026	-577	78bhd
Monetary Authorities															—	78bod
General Government								-3,119	-1,081	-278	7,156	-1,149	-1,347	-1,617	10,099	78bpd
Banks								-2,984	4,330	-1,933	-1,278	482	-3,625	-3,332	-1,917	78bqd
Other Sectors								-13,355	3,017	-28,350	-32,518	-15,291	-9,884	-12,078	-8,758	78brd
Other Investment Liab., n.i.e.								-11,191	-12,746	907	4,420	-4,169	-3,691	-3,087	-3,444	78bid
Monetary Authorities								-308	392	-236	-37	84	3	155	49	78bsd
General Government								-11,744	-9,176	-5,782	-10,762	-3,191	-1,975	-2,875	-7,480	78btd
Banks								1,288	2,446	4,264	8,646	-6,380	-1,270	568	3,697	78bud
Other Sectors								-427	-6,408	2,661	6,573	5,318	-448	-935	289	78bvd
Net Errors and Omissions								407	-7,975	-4,896	-4,854	-9,072	-7,033	-9,362	-9,135	78cad
Overall Balance								-18,970	-8,298	-17,190	-6,492	-21,367	-1,704	13,923	11,266	78cbd
Reserves and Related Items								18,970	8,298	17,190	6,492	21,367	1,704	-13,923	-11,266	79dad
Reserve Assets								1,935	-10,382	2,840	-1,930	5,306	-1,772	-16,009	-8,211	79dbd
Use of Fund Credit and Loans								1,514	5,473	3,237	1,526	5,206	-3,603	-2,899	-3,829	79dcd
Exceptional Financing								15,520	13,207	11,113	6,896	10,855	7,078	4,985	773	79ded

International Investment Position

Millions of US Dollars

	1987	1988	1989	1990	1991	1992	1993	1994	1995	1996	1997	1998	1999	2000	2001	Line
Assets							23,408	22,245	28,645	29,041	33,440	25,555	28,392	47,045	57,128	79aad
Direct Investment Abroad							2,277	2,272	2,420	2,685	2,789	2,703	1,076	1,368	1,298	79abd
Portfolio Investment							590	486	764	1,230	1,383	1,308	861	684	584	79acd
Equity Securities							—	7	27	43	12	18	6	15	11	79add
Debt Securities							590	479	737	1,187	1,371	1,290	855	669	573	79aed
Financial Derivatives							—	—	—	—	—	—	—	—	—	79ald
Other Investment							11,647	12,982	8,254	9,802	11,484	9,322	14,000	17,021	18,624	79afd
Monetary Authorities							—	—	—	—	—	—	—	—	—	79agd
General Government							—	—	—	—	—	—	—	—	—	79ahd
Banks							11,647	12,982	8,254	9,802	11,484	9,322	14,000	17,021	18,624	79aid
Other Sectors							—	—	—	—	—	—	—	—	—	79ajd
Reserve Assets							8,894	6,505	17,207	15,324	17,784	12,223	12,455	27,972	36,622	79akd
Liabilities							5,519	7,380	15,492	22,162	32,829	29,925	24,087	21,792	22,033	79lad
Dir. Invest. in Rep. Economy							183	332	345	426	970	373	731	1,007	1,005	79lbd
Portfolio Investment							380	369	437	567	1,032	495	346	857	1,587	79lcd
Equity Securities							90	79	132	122	241	36	40	52	53	79ldd
Debt Securities							290	290	305	445	791	459	306	805	1,534	79led
Financial Derivatives							—	—	—	—	—	—	—	—	—	79lld
Other Investment							4,956	6,679	14,710	21,169	30,827	29,057	23,010	19,928	19,441	79lfd
Monetary Authorities							2,469	4,198	9,617	12,508	13,231	19,335	15,238	11,613	7,433	79lgd
General Government							—	—	—	—	—	—	—	—	—	79lhd
Banks							2,487	2,481	5,093	8,661	17,596	9,722	7,772	8,316	12,007	79lid
Other Sectors							—	—	—	—	—	—	—	—	—	79ljd

	1972	1973	1974	1975	1976	1977	1978	1979	1980	1981	1982	1983	1984	1985	1986

Government Finance *Millions of Rubles:*

		1972	1973	1974	1975	1976	1977	1978	1979	1980	1981	1982	1983	1984	1985	1986
Deficit (-) or Surplus	80	...	...	...	...	...	...	...	...	...	...	...	...	...	...	...
Total Revenue and Grants	81y	...	...	...	...	...	...	...	...	...	...	...	...	...	...	...
Revenue	81	...	...	...	...	...	...	...	...	...	...	...	...	...	...	...
Grants	81z	...	...	...	...	...	...	...	...	...	...	...	...	...	...	...
Exp. & Lending Minus Repay.	82z	...	...	...	...	...	...	...	...	...	...	...	...	...	...	...
Expenditure	82	...	...	...	...	...	...	...	...	...	...	...	...	...	...	...
Lending Minus Repayments	83	...	...	...	...	...	...	...	...	...	...	...	...	...	...	...
Total Financing	80h	...	...	...	...	...	...	...	...	...	...	...	...	...	...	...
Total Net Borrowing	84	...	...	...	...	...	...	...	...	...	...	...	...	...	...	...
Net Domestic	84a	...	...	...	...	...	...	...	...	...	...	...	...	...	...	...
Net Foreign	85a	...	...	...	...	...	...	...	...	...	...	...	...	...	...	...
Use of Cash Balances	87	...	...	...	...	...	...	...	...	...	...	...	...	...	...	...
Total Debt by Currency	88z	...	...	...	...	...	...	...	...	...	...	...	...	...	...	...
Debt: Rubles	88b	...	...	...	...	...	...	...	...	...	...	...	...	...	...	...
Foreign Currency	89b	...	...	...	...	...	...	...	...	...	...	...	...	...	...	...

National Accounts *Billions of Rubles*

		1972	1973	1974	1975	1976	1977	1978	1979	1980	1981	1982	1983	1984	1985	1986
Househ.Cons.Expend.,incl.NPISHs	96f	...	...	...	...	...	...	...	...	...	...	...	...	...	...	...
Government Consumption Expend.	91f	...	...	...	...	...	...	...	...	...	...	...	...	...	...	...
Gross Fixed Capital Formation	93e	...	...	...	...	...	...	...	...	...	...	...	...	...	...	...
Changes in Inventories	93i	...	...	...	...	...	...	...	...	...	...	...	...	...	...	...
Exports of Goods and Services	90c	...	...	...	...	...	...	...	...	...	...	...	...	...	...	...
Imports of Goods and Services (-)	98c	...	...	...	...	...	...	...	...	...	...	...	...	...	...	...
GDP, Production Based	99bp	...	...	...	...	...	...	...	...	...	...	...	...	...	...	...
Statistical Discrepancy	99bs	...	...	...	...	...	...	...	...	...	...	...	...	...	...	...

Millions:

		1972	1973	1974	1975	1976	1977	1978	1979	1980	1981	1982	1983	1984	1985	1986
Population	99z	...	...	...	...	...	...	...	...	...	...	...	...	...	...	...

	1987	1988	1989	1990	1991	1992	1993	1994	1995	1996	1997	1998	1999	2000	2001		
Year Ending December 31																**Government Finance**	
	...	...	...	...	...	...	...	...	−69,508	−147,607	−150,415	−126,958	−56,641	173,468	275,321	Deficit (-) or Surplus	80
	...	...	...	...	...	...	...	...	226,071	281,770	322,690	299,403	608,033	1,127,571	1,598,482	Total Revenue and Grants	81y
	...	...	...	...	...	...	...	...	...	...	...	...	...	...	...	Revenue	81
	...	...	...	...	...	...	...	...	...	...	...	...	...	...	...	Grants	81z
	...	...	...	...	...	...	...	...	295,579	429,377	473,105	426,361	664,674	954,103	1,323,161	Exp. & Lending Minus Repay.	82z
	...	...	...	...	...	...	...	...	277,744	409,792	454,768	416,872	655,391	1,004,265	1,376,552	Expenditure	82
	...	...	...	...	...	...	...	...	17,835	19,585	18,337	9,489	9,283	−50,162	−53,391	Lending Minus Repayments	83
	...	...	...	...	...	...	...	...	69,508	147,607	150,415	126,958	56,641	−173,468	−275,321	Total Financing	80h
	...	...	...	...	...	...	...	...	72,248	137,224	159,722	154,733	101,063	−173,468	−275,321	Total Net Borrowing	84
	...	...	...	...	...	...	...	...	48,814	103,968	106,253	64,545	53,644	−40,331	−50,068	Net Domestic	84a
	...	...	...	...	...	...	...	...	23,434	33,256	53,469	90,188	47,419	−133,137	−225,253	Net Foreign	85a
	...	...	...	...	...	...	...	...	−2,740	10,383	−9,307	−27,775	−44,422	—	—	Use of Cash Balances	87
	...	...	...	...	...	...	...	...	787,689	1,122,323	1,302,052	3,786,106	....	801,530	...	Total Debt by Currency	88z
	...	...	...	...	...	...	...	...	226,505	427,323	565,992	750,556	....	801,530	755,896	Debt: Rubles	88b
	...	...	...	...	...	...	...	...	561,184	695,000	736,060	3,035,550	....	....	...	Foreign Currency	89b
Billions of Rubles																**National Accounts**	
	...	...	...	...	...	7	77	285	796	1,108	1,353	1,588	2,578	3,416	4,605	Househ.Cons.Expend.,incl.NPISHs	96f
	...	...	...	...	...	3	30	137	299	437	539	527	703	1,083	1,293	Government Consumption Expend.	91f
	...	...	...	...	...	5	35	133	328	454	482	473	683	1,144	1,609	Gross Fixed Capital Formation	93e
	...	...	...	...	...	2	11	23	64	74	82	−51	17	217	385	Changes in Inventories	93i
	...	...	...	...	...	12	66	170	427	532	592	839	2,087	3,236	3,338	Exports of Goods and Services	90c
	...	...	...	...	...	9	52	142	374	443	519	637	1,262	1,760	2,167	Imports of Goods and Services (-)	98c
	...	...	...	...	...	19	172	611	1,540	2,146	2,479	2,741	4,767	7,302	9,041	GDP, Production Based	99bp
	...	...	...	...	...	1	5	5	—	−17	−51	1	−39	−32	−23	Statistical Discrepancy	99bs
Midyear Estimates																	
	...	...	...	...	148.25	148.31	148.15	147.97	148.14	147.74	147.10	146.54	145.56	145.49	144.40	Population	99z

(See notes in the back of the book.)

Rwanda

		1972	1973	1974	1975	1976	1977	1978	1979	1980	1981	1982	1983	1984	1985	1986
Exchange Rates																*Francs per SDR:*
Official Rate	aa	100.00	100.00	113.67	108.68	107.86	112.77	120.95	122.30	118.41	108.06	102.41	102.71	102.71	102.71	102.71
																Francs per US Dollar:
Official Rate	ae	92.11	82.90	92.84	92.84	92.84	92.84	92.84	92.84	92.84	92.84	92.84	98.54	104.36	93.49	84.18
Official Rate	rf	92.11	84.05	92.84	92.84	92.84	92.84	92.84	92.84	92.84	92.84	92.84	94.34	100.17	101.26	87.64
Fund Position																*Millions of SDRs:*
Quota	2f. s	19.00	19.00	19.00	19.00	19.00	19.00	23.00	23.00	34.50	34.50	34.50	43.80	43.80	43.80	43.80
SDRs	1b. s	.39	2.43	2.48	2.39	2.39	2.35	2.39	4.58	7.72	9.83	10.83	8.40	8.29	8.19	8.10
Reserve Position in the Fund	1c. s	—	—	—	—	2.07	2.07	2.93	5.47	8.36	7.28	7.30	9.64	9.66	9.32	9.32
Total Fund Cred.&Loans Outstg.	2tl	—	—	—	—	—	—	—	5.76	10.62	10.69	10.69	10.69	10.69	9.15	7.02
International Liquidity														*Millions of US Dollars Unless Otherwise Indicated:*		
Total Reserves minus Gold	1l. d	6.37	15.18	12.96	25.59	64.29	82.87	87.60	152.31	186.57	173.10	128.40	110.89	106.86	113.33	162.30
SDRs	1b. d	.42	2.93	3.04	2.80	2.78	2.85	3.11	6.03	9.85	11.44	11.95	8.79	8.13	9.00	9.91
Reserve Position in the Fund	1c. d	—	—	—	—	2.40	2.51	3.82	7.21	10.66	8.47	8.05	10.09	9.47	10.24	11.40
Foreign Exchange	1d. d	5.95	12.25	9.92	22.79	59.10	77.51	80.67	139.07	166.06	153.18	108.40	92.00	89.26	94.09	141.00
Monetary Authorities: Other Liab.	4.. d	2.87	4.63	5.53	5.65	15.52	18.85	19.25	24.63	37.37	34.50	25.42	31.18	28.84	19.33	20.03
Deposit Money Banks: Assets	7a. d	.31	1.18	1.36	2.89	3.34	13.92	12.41	25.28	21.29	26.11	28.00	20.90	31.57	28.90	21.12
Liabilities	7b. d	.48	.86	.01	2.03	3.17	6.67	4.75	7.27	7.27	8.41	13.63	25.10	15.78	24.79	9.89
Other Banking Insts.: Liabilities	7f. d	....	....	....	1.11	1.19	1.85	3.67	5.99	5.10	6.42	6.20	8.81	7.66	9.36	8.78
Monetary Authorities																*Millions of Francs:*
Foreign Assets	11	586	1,259	1,203	2,376	5,968	7,710	8,133	14,141	17,321	16,071	11,921	10,927	11,151	10,595	13,663
Claims on Central Government	12a	1,623	2,105	2,199	1,604	1,583	1,211	1,399	1,205	1,232	1,219	2,483	3,887	3,937	3,519	4,375
Claims on Official Entities	12bx	68	147	116	194	166	100	78	51	25	7	14	2	2	2	2
Claims on Private Sector	12d	10	39	59	18	334	295	301	456	517	635	285	264	248	267	240
Claims on Deposit Money Banks	12e	31	73	721	531	51	562	671	249	504	417	730	1,027	1,643	2,830	928
Claims on Other Financial Insts	12f	162	130	121	160	87	67	40	38	36	93	356	601	532	598	548
Reserve Money	14	2,258	2,921	3,842	3,905	5,109	5,803	5,930	8,532	7,978	6,964	7,237	8,065	8,559	9,584	10,877
of which: Currency Outside DMBs	14a	1,446	2,003	2,553	2,722	3,070	3,948	4,443	5,242	5,689	6,086	6,260	6,662	7,030	7,161	7,686
Time Deposits	15	....	....	110	153	224	131	88	94	135	972	623	453	395	547	633
Foreign Liabilities	16c	265	384	513	525	1,441	1,750	1,787	2,991	4,727	4,359	3,455	4,175	4,103	2,747	2,409
Central Government Deposits	16d	218	490	217	600	783	1,364	1,786	1,850	4,542	3,973	3,488	2,825	2,872	3,082	3,048
Counterpart Funds	16e	41	39	22	8	117	108	73	46	21	99	61	118	86	62	50
Capital Accounts	17a	710	799	806	951	1,309	1,409	1,708	3,030	3,357	3,917	4,494	4,659	4,727	4,923	4,965
Other Items (Net)	17r	−586	−509	−528	−513	−793	−620	−750	−402	−1,126	−1,842	−3,570	−3,587	−3,230	−3,134	−2,227
Deposit Money Banks																*Millions of Francs:*
Reserves	20	245	483	328	200	1,345	1,087	673	2,328	999	315	585	874	966	1,391	1,870
Foreign Assets	21	29	98	127	269	310	1,292	1,152	2,347	1,976	†2,424	2,600	2,060	3,294	2,702	1,778
Claims on Central Government	22a	775	779	1,123	1,430	784	600	504	596	426	653	1,220	1,982	2,757	3,068	3,698
Claims on Official Entities	22bx	10	—	—	194	237	121	148	183	194	269	400	852	701	677	641
Claims on Private Sector	22d	453	855	1,717	1,640	1,782	3,662	4,478	3,793	5,689	6,837	7,742	8,085	10,021	13,140	13,198
Demand Deposits	24	936	1,449	1,518	1,869	2,702	3,429	4,016	4,745	5,020	†5,191	4,777	5,056	5,743	6,306	8,234
Time and Savings Deposits	25	453	464	953	994	1,306	1,973	2,132	2,738	3,065	†3,237	4,090	5,306	6,154	8,184	8,641
Foreign Liabilities	26c	44	72	1	188	294	619	441	675	781	†1,265	2,330	1,764	1,647	2,317	832
Central Government Deposits	26d	15	53	5	5	28	137	143	1,423	166	†714	837	917	1,824	1,711	2,256
Credit from Monetary Authorities	26g	3	9	578	494	56	529	350	137	572	490	742	1,113	1,810	2,729	1,634
Capital Accounts	27a	148	164	190	170	230	314	369	447	500	541	1,015	1,330	2,096	2,458	2,595
Other Items (Net)	27r	−86	5	391	519	557	714	−495	−920	−818	1,228	−1,244	−1,635	−1,533	−2,728	−3,007
Monetary Survey																*Millions of Francs:*
Foreign Assets (Net)	31n	306	902	816	1,932	4,544	6,633	7,057	12,822	13,790	†12,871	8,735	7,047	8,695	8,233	12,200
Domestic Credit	32	2,888	3,555	5,169	4,729	4,334	4,677	5,134	3,114	3,481	†5,080	8,229	12,015	13,586	16,561	17,489
Claims on Central Govt. (Net)	32an	2,176	2,359	3,127	2,464	1,605	327	—	−1,449	−3,034	†−2,815	−622	2,128	1,998	1,793	2,768
Claims on Official Entities	32bx	78	147	116	387	403	221	225	234	219	276	414	853	703	678	643
Claims on Private Sector	32d	462	893	1,775	1,658	2,115	3,957	4,779	4,249	6,207	7,472	8,027	8,348	10,269	13,407	13,438
Claims on Other Financial Insts	32f	172	156	151	220	212	173	130	81	90	147	410	685	616	682	640
Money	34	2,520	3,565	4,288	4,850	6,516	8,035	8,961	11,255	12,026	†11,729	11,442	12,294	13,332	14,577	17,212
Quasi-Money	35	453	464	1,063	1,147	1,530	2,104	2,220	2,831	3,200	†4,209	4,712	5,759	6,549	8,731	9,274
Other Items (Net)	37r	221	433	809	1,170	1,548	2,124	1,010	2,555	3,302	3,416	1,904	2,106	3,498	2,426	3,924
Money plus Quasi-Money	35l	2,973	4,029	5,350	5,997	8,047	10,138	11,181	14,086	15,226	†15,938	16,154	18,054	19,881	23,308	26,486
Other Banking Institutions																*Millions of Francs:*
Cash	40..k	59	36	109	92	53	45	45	73	80	263	187	396	183	292	200
Claims on Official Entities	42bx k	—	—	—	—	77	28	26	125	191	188	214	195	154	106	98
Claims on Private Sector	42d. k	159	216	239	449	455	545	670	955	1,019	1,166	1,436	1,863	2,088	2,258	2,456
Long Term Foreign Liabilities	46cl k	....	....	....	103	110	172	340	556	474	596	575	868	800	875	740
Credit from Monetary Authorities	46g. k	162	130	117	157	85	63	40	38	36	93	356	601	532	598	548
Cred.from Deposit Money Banks	46h. k	....	....	....	20	70	45	20	80	—	—	—	—	—	—	—
Capital Accounts	47a. k	63	169	215	221	286	318	450	469	1,080	956	1,001	1,240	1,444	1,542	1,970
Other Items (Net)	47r. k	−7	−47	16	40	34	20	−109	10	−300	−29	−95	−256	−350	−359	−503

	1987	1988	1989	1990	1991	1992	1993	1994	1995	1996	1997	1998	1999	2000	2001		
End of Period																**Exchange Rates**	
	102.71	102.71	102.71	171.18	171.18	201.39	201.39	201.94	445.67	437.37	411.31	450.75	479.24	560.67	572.84	Official Rate	**aa**
End of Period (ae) Period Average (rf)																	
	73.02	76.71	77.62	121.12	119.79	146.27	146.37	138.33	299.81	304.16	304.67	320.34	349.53	430.49	457.90	Official Rate	**ae**
	79.67	76.45	79.98	82.60	125.14	133.35	144.31	220.00	262.20	306.82	301.53	312.31	333.94	389.70	442.99	Official Rate	**rf**
End of Period																**Fund Position**	
	43.80	43.80	43.80	43.80	43.80	59.50	59.50	59.50	59.50	59.50	59.50	59.50	80.10	80.10	80.10	Quota	**2f. s**
	8.01	7.85	7.54	7.15	6.73	2.43	2.11	1.75	13.65	12.71	19.64	17.36	10.54	.87	9.82	SDRs	**1b. s**
	9.33	7.08	7.10	6.44	6.46	10.40	9.79	9.79	—	—	—	—	—	—	—	Reserve Position in the Fund	**1c. s**
	4.90	2.77	.65	.07	8.76	8.76	8.76	8.76	17.69	16.81	29.93	40.08	55.29	65.88	66.57	Total Fund Cred.&Loans Outstg.	**2tl**
End of Period																**International Liquidity**	
	164.19	118.33	70.37	44.35	110.12	78.72	47.46	51.25	99.10	106.74	153.34	168.75	174.18	190.64	212.11	Total Reserves minus Gold	**1l. d**
	11.36	10.56	9.91	10.17	9.63	3.34	2.90	2.55	20.29	18.28	26.50	24.44	14.46	1.14	12.34	SDRs	**1b. d**
	13.24	9.53	9.33	9.16	9.24	14.30	13.45	14.29	—	—	—	—	—	—	—	Reserve Position in the Fund	**1c. d**
	139.59	98.24	51.13	25.01	91.25	61.08	31.11	34.40	78.80	88.47	126.84	144.31	159.72	189.50	199.77	Foreign Exchange	**1d. d**
	24.02	24.22	15.24	46.51	32.75	29.15	28.52	40.45	28.36	20.62	21.89	50.05	21.13	17.89	15.69	Monetary Authorities: Other Liab.	**4.. d**
	28.99	35.03	29.80	32.44	45.27	41.66	31.68	26.63	51.92	66.27	73.17	75.22	56.23	76.54	73.74	Deposit Money Banks: Assets	**7a. d**
	9.23	12.88	6.77	7.45	8.60	8.76	6.07	5.61	4.09	4.53	12.63	11.91	5.31	8.24	10.09	Liabilities	**7b. d**
	18.70	22.30	25.99	17.56	17.92	15.59	14.73	8.67	7.96	7.41	4.70	2.99	2.92	2.39	....	Other Banking Insts.: Liabilities	**7f. d**
End of Period																**Monetary Authorities**	
	11,989	9,077	5,462	5,372	13,191	11,514	6,946	7,089	29,710	32,469	46,720	54,058	60,882	82,068	97,124	Foreign Assets	**11**
	7,151	6,348	9,667	18,608	20,611	29,127	34,915	32,834	34,359	35,125	42,125	44,447	50,716	43,469	43,469	Claims on Central Government	**12a**
	—	—	—	—	—	—	—	680	762	730	729	729	219	149	129	Claims on Official Entities	**12bx**
	223	191	178	144	128	115	123	151	157	253	220	342	561	1,112	1,682	Claims on Private Sector	**12d**
	872	3,095	3,050	1,327	655	917	1,321	846	1,725	153	301	908	1,793	2,646	1,522	Claims on Deposit Money Banks	**12e**
	321	631	816	555	378	32	20	11	9	9	9	426	431	314	207	Claims on Other Financial Insts	**12f**
	12,051	10,822	9,261	10,129	14,588	14,097	18,024	19,708	27,340	33,507	37,314	34,016	39,051	35,803	43,767	Reserve Money	**14**
	8,203	8,439	7,744	8,593	8,822	10,321	11,522	11,924	17,257	19,908	20,635	22,865	21,510	24,609	24,380	*of which: Currency Outside DMBs*	**14a**
	663	688	544	1,216	601	913	346	291	207	201	181	142	855	434	1,630	Time Deposits	**15**
	2,262	2,144	1,249	5,645	5,425	6,026	5,935	7,365	16,383	13,624	18,974	34,112	33,907	44,654	45,491	Foreign Liabilities	**16c**
	3,076	2,320	1,243	2,452	5,911	7,527	4,492	4,430	19,156	15,753	15,032	16,276	20,929	24,681	29,115	Central Government Deposits	**16d**
	42	33	766	732	1,083	4,098	4,157	4,596	2,304	3,231	4,174	3,408	1,620	1,311	770	Counterpart Funds	**16e**
	4,965	5,139	5,486	6,526	8,024	8,631	12,310	13,988	20,238	13,149	11,680	12,589	15,613	15,373	18,080	Capital Accounts	**17a**
	−2,502	−1,802	625	−695	−670	414	−1,939	−8,770	−18,904	−10,726	2,749	367	2,627	7,500	5,282	Other Items (Net)	**17r**
End of Period																**Deposit Money Banks**	
	2,277	966	701	1,040	5,097	3,117	5,778	6,618	8,590	13,816	16,035	11,835	15,845	10,823	2,872	Reserves	**20**
	2,117	2,687	2,313	3,929	5,423	6,093	4,637	3,683	15,566	20,157	22,293	24,095	19,652	32,949	33,764	Foreign Assets	**21**
	4,851	7,100	6,348	5,421	5,448	6,667	4,495	4,311	4,528	4,968	5,573	6,995	7,747	7,265	7,267	Claims on Central Government	**22a**
	688	853	1,533	2,533	810	298	679	581	354	205	15	421	587	678	831	Claims on Official Entities	**22bx**
	13,356	16,302	17,597	14,629	12,122	15,308	17,875	16,234	28,381	28,615	44,948	54,079	59,686	69,289	75,307	Claims on Private Sector	**22d**
	7,922	8,228	7,305	7,346	8,587	11,571	12,876	16,165	22,586	24,979	34,523	31,509	36,936	37,575	38,410	Demand Deposits	**24**
	10,885	12,471	13,588	13,804	14,879	14,249	13,356	8,084	22,181	22,851	32,445	36,051	38,680	50,588	61,422	Time and Savings Deposits	**25**
	674	988	525	903	1,030	1,281	889	776	1,226	1,378	3,847	3,816	1,856	3,546	4,620	Foreign Liabilities	**26c**
	2,103	2,621	3,457	3,220	2,800	2,953	2,854	3,370	5,482	10,944	9,072	12,322	9,705	9,442	5,725	Central Government Deposits	**26d**
	610	2,829	2,820	1,399	600	469	719	287	1,624	63	63	61	1,550	2,358	1,352	Credit from Monetary Authorities	**26g**
	2,681	3,001	3,348	3,469	2,876	3,535	3,778	3,745	6,908	7,683	11,832	16,749	20,059	23,749	26,192	Capital Accounts	**27a**
	−1,586	−2,230	−2,552	−2,589	−1,873	−2,575	−1,007	−998	−2,589	−136	−2,919	−3,083	−5,269	−6,252	−4,244	Other Items (Net)	**27r**
End of Period																**Monetary Survey**	
	11,170	8,633	6,001	2,752	12,159	10,300	4,760	2,632	27,666	37,624	46,191	40,225	44,771	66,817	80,777	Foreign Assets (Net)	**31n**
	21,504	26,576	31,531	36,447	31,088	41,349	50,926	47,175	44,016	43,307	69,621	78,951	89,482	88,263	94,118	Domestic Credit	**32**
	6,823	8,508	11,315	18,358	17,347	25,314	32,064	29,346	14,249	13,396	23,594	22,844	27,829	16,611	15,896	Claims on Central Govt. (Net)	**32an**
	688	853	1,533	2,533	810	298	679	1,261	1,116	935	744	1,150	806	827	960	Claims on Official Entities	**32bx**
	13,580	16,493	17,776	14,773	12,250	15,423	17,998	16,385	28,538	28,868	45,168	54,421	60,248	70,401	76,989	Claims on Private Sector	**32d**
	413	723	908	783	682	314	185	184	113	108	115	536	599	424	273	Claims on Other Financial Insts	**32f**
	17,669	18,210	15,931	16,724	18,023	22,509	24,919	28,810	40,658	45,423	55,746	55,291	59,172	63,110	63,606	Money	**34**
	11,549	13,159	14,132	15,020	15,480	15,162	13,701	8,375	22,388	23,052	32,626	36,193	39,535	51,022	63,052	Quasi-Money	**35**
	3,960	4,125	7,536	7,467	9,743	13,981	17,069	12,620	8,637	12,457	27,440	27,692	35,547	40,948	61,675	Other Items (Net)	**37r**
	29,217	31,369	30,062	31,744	33,503	37,671	38,621	37,185	63,046	68,475	88,372	91,484	98,707	114,132	126,658	Money plus Quasi-Money	**35l**
End of Period																**Other Banking Institutions**	
	292	191	127	134	584	887	1,332	1,340	1,363	1,559	1,495	862	1,445	1,090	....	Cash	**40.. k**
	70	45	119	143	131	108	83	—	52	491	21	316	298	—	....	Claims on Official Entities	**42bx k**
	2,961	4,184	4,264	4,362	3,162	3,038	2,732	3,024	3,835	3,126	4,152	5,161	5,807	6,224	....	Claims on Private Sector	**42d. k**
	1,366	1,711	2,017	2,127	2,147	2,281	2,155	1,199	2,386	2,253	1,433	957	1,021	1,027	....	Long Term Foreign Liabilities	**46cl k**
	321	631	816	555	354	10	9	9	9	9	9	9	431	314	....	Credit from Monetary Authorities	**46g. k**
	—	—	—	—	—	—	—	—	—	—	—	—	—	—	....	Cred.from Deposit Money Banks	**46h. k**
	2,077	2,160	2,108	2,502	1,932	2,208	2,310	3,996	3,736	4,228	4,067	4,986	6,074	6,319	....	Capital Accounts	**47a. k**
	−441[e]	−82[e]	−431[e]	−545[e]	−555[e]	−466	−327	−763	−881	−1,314	159	386	24	−345	....	Other Items (Net)	**47r. k**

Rwanda

		1972	1973	1974	1975	1976	1977	1978	1979	1980	1981	1982	1983	1984	1985	1986
Interest Rates																*Percent Per Annum*
Discount Rate *(End of Period)*	60	5.00	5.00	5.00	5.00	5.00	5.00	5.00	9.00	9.00	9.00	9.00	9.00	9.00	9.00	9.00
Deposit Rate	60l	....	....	....	....	....	....	2.00	2.71	6.25	6.25	6.25	6.25	6.25	6.25	6.25
Lending Rate	60p	....	....	....	....	....	....	12.50	13.04	13.50	13.50	13.50	13.50	13.50	13.88	14.00
Prices															*Index Numbers (1995=100):*	
Consumer Prices	64	7.0	7.6	10.0	†13.0	14.0	15.9	18.0	20.8	22.3	23.8	26.8	28.5	30.1	30.6	30.2
International Transactions															*Millions of Francs*	
Exports	70	1,795	2,787	3,372	3,872	7,471	8,511	6,655	10,961	10,354	10,199	9,550	11,405	14,496	13,221	16,466
Imports, c.i.f.	71	3,183	2,819	5,416	9,167	9,858	11,406	17,447	17,856	22,568	23,775	25,666	25,453	27,872	30,244	30,624
																1995=100
Volume of Exports	72	107	271	291	371	442	288	253	524	289	411	377	384	439	438	544
Export Prices	74	12	14	17	15	28	48	35	32	27	34	†36	44	50	45	48
Balance of Payments															*Millions of US Dollars:*	
Current Account, n.i.e.	78ald	....	....	....	....	18.8	22.1	−46.0	45.8	−48.3	−74.0	−90.5	−48.6	−41.5	−63.7	−69.2
Goods: Exports f.o.b.	78aad	....	....	....	....	114.2	126.5	111.7	203.0	133.6	113.3	108.5	124.1	142.6	126.1	184.1
Goods: Imports f.o.b.	78abd	....	....	....	....	−104.5	−102.3	−144.9	−159.5	−195.8	−207.1	−214.7	−197.6	−197.5	−219.3	−259.2
Trade Balance	78acd	....	....	....	....	9.7	24.2	−33.3	43.5	−62.2	−93.8	−106.2	−73.6	−54.9	−93.2	−75.1
Services: Credit	78add	....	....	....	....	8.0	11.0	14.2	23.7	31.8	37.3	33.3	27.9	31.9	34.9	43.3
Services: Debit	78aed	....	....	....	....	−49.5	−74.7	−116.4	−147.6	−123.4	−121.7	−120.9	−113.0	−113.2	−114.2	−148.4
Balance on Goods & Services	78afd	....	....	....	....	−31.8	−39.5	−135.6	−80.4	−153.9	−178.2	−193.8	−158.7	−136.2	−172.6	−180.2
Income: Credit	78agd	....	....	....	....	1.2	3.4	4.5	8.4	17.1	25.2	16.1	8.6	8.2	9.2	9.3
Income: Debit	78ahd	....	....	....	....	−5.1	−7.9	−9.5	−11.9	−15.4	−16.7	−18.8	−16.5	−14.6	−17.0	−22.4
Balance on Gds, Serv. & Inc.	78aid	....	....	....	....	−35.7	−44.0	−140.6	−83.9	−152.2	−169.6	−196.5	−166.5	−142.7	−180.5	−193.2
Current Transfers, n.i.e.: Credit	78ajd	....	....	....	....	68.8	85.0	113.7	150.8	126.9	119.2	129.7	141.3	122.5	136.7	151.6
Current Transfers: Debit	78akd	....	....	....	....	−14.3	−18.9	−19.1	−21.1	−23.1	−23.5	−23.7	−23.4	−21.4	−20.0	−27.6
Capital Account, n.i.e.	78bcd	....	....	....	....	−.7	−1.3	−.6	.3	.4	.4	3.9		−.1	−.3	
Capital Account, n.i.e.: Credit	78bad	....	....	....	....	—	—	—	1.7	1.8	1.8	5.5	1.7	1.6	1.3	2.0
Capital Account: Debit	78bbd	....	....	....	....	−.7	−1.3	−.6	−1.4	−1.4	−1.4	−1.6	−1.7	−1.7	−1.7	−2.0
Financial Account, n.i.e.	78bjd	....	....	....	....	16.6	18.8	47.1	15.1	72.8	51.9	52.5	31.4	53.0	69.3	103.9
Direct Investment Abroad	78bdd	....	....	....	....	—	—	—	—	—	—	—	—	—	—	—
Dir. Invest. in Rep. Econ., n.i.e.	78bed	....	....	....	....	5.9	5.0	4.7	12.6	16.4	18.0	20.7	11.1	15.1	14.6	17.6
Portfolio Investment Assets	78bfd	....	....	....	....	—	—	—	—	—	—	—	—	—	—	—
Equity Securities	78bkd	....	....	....	....	—	—	—	—	—	—	—	—	—	—	—
Debt Securities	78bld	....	....	....	....	—	—	—	—	—	—	—	—	—	—	—
Portfolio Investment Liab., n.i.e.	78bgd	....	....	....	....	—	.1	—	—	.6	.6	—	—	.1	—	—
Equity Securities	78bmd	....	....	....	....	—	—	—	—	.6	.6	—	—	.1	—	—
Debt Securities	78bnd	....	....	....	....	—	.1	—	—	—	—	—	—	—	—	—
Financial Derivatives Assets	78bwd	....	....	....	....	....	....	....	....	....	....	....	....	....	....	....
Financial Derivatives Liabilities	78bxd	....	....	....	....	....	....	....	....	....	....	....	....	....	....	....
Other Investment Assets	78bhd	....	....	....	....	−2.8	−17.5	11.3	−12.3	16.2	9.9	15.4	2.9	.4	−6.7	−1.6
Monetary Authorities	78bod	....	....	....	....	....	....	....	....	....	....	....	....	....	....	....
General Government	78bpd	....	....	....	....	—	—	—	—	—	—	—	—	—	—	—
Banks	78bqd	....	....	....	....	—	—	—	—	—	—	—	—	—	—	—
Other Sectors	78brd	....	....	....	....	−2.8	−17.5	11.3	−12.3	16.2	9.9	15.4	2.9	.4	−6.7	−1.6
Other Investment Liab., n.i.e.	78bid	....	....	....	....	13.5	31.3	31.2	14.9	39.6	23.4	16.4	17.3	37.5	61.4	87.9
Monetary Authorities	78bsd	....	....	....	....	3.5	8.4	.8	1.9	6.8	−2.0	−9.1	6.8	−1.5	−7.0	−1.5
General Government	78btd	....	....	....	....	17.5	26.7	20.9	10.1	25.3	24.8	20.8	25.4	35.9	59.5	68.2
Banks	78bud	....	....	....	....	−.8	3.2	.3	2.2	.1	−4.0	11.5	−6.0	−1.2	6.6	.3
Other Sectors	78bvd	....	....	....	....	−6.8	−7.0	9.2	.7	7.4	4.6	−6.8	−8.9	4.3	2.2	20.9
Net Errors and Omissions	78cad	....	....	....	....	−2.0	−5.2	.1	.5	−1.9	14.9	−2.5	−1.1	−3.6	−3.6	−4.5
Overall Balance	78cbd	....	....	....	....	32.6	34.5	.7	61.7	23.0	−6.7	−36.6	−18.4	7.8	1.7	30.2
Reserves and Related Items	79dad	....	....	....	....	−32.6	−34.5	−.7	−61.7	−23.0	6.7	36.6	18.4	−7.8	−1.7	−30.2
Reserve Assets	79dbd	....	....	....	....	−32.6	−34.5	−.7	−70.0	−29.3	.1	36.6	18.4	−7.8	−.1	−27.7
Use of Fund Credit and Loans	79dcd	....	....	....	....	—	—	—	7.5	6.3	.1	—	—	—	−1.6	−2.5
Exceptional Financing	79ded	....	....	....	....	—	—	—	.8	—	6.6	—	—	—	—	—
International Investment Position															*Millions of US Dollars*	
Assets	79aad	....	....	....	....	....	....	....	....	....	....	....	....	....	....	....
Direct Investment Abroad	79abd	....	....	....	....	....	....	....	....	....	....	....	....	....	....	....
Portfolio Investment	79acd	....	....	....	....	....	....	....	....	....	....	....	....	....	....	....
Equity Securities	79add	....	....	....	....	....	....	....	....	....	....	....	....	....	....	....
Debt Securities	79aed	....	....	....	....	....	....	....	....	....	....	....	....	....	....	....
Financial Derivatives	79ald	....	....	....	....	....	....	....	....	....	....	....	....	....	....	....
other Investment	79afd	....	....	....	....	....	....	....	....	....	....	....	....	....	....	....
Monetary Authorities	79agd	....	....	....	....	....	....	....	....	....	....	....	....	....	....	....
General Government	79ahd	....	....	....	....	....	....	....	....	....	....	....	....	....	....	....
Banks	79aid	....	....	....	....	....	....	....	....	....	....	....	....	....	....	....
Other Sectors	79ajd	....	....	....	....	....	....	....	....	....	....	....	....	....	....	....
Reserve Assets	79akd	....	....	....	....	....	....	....	....	....	....	....	....	....	....	....
Liabilities	79lad	....	....	....	....	....	....	....	....	....	....	....	....	....	....	....
Dir. Invest. in Rep. Economy	79lbd	....	....	....	....	....	....	....	....	....	....	....	....	....	....	....
Portfolio Investment	79lcd	....	....	....	....	....	....	....	....	....	....	....	....	....	....	....
Equity Securities	79ldd	....	....	....	....	....	....	....	....	....	....	....	....	....	....	....
Debt Securities	79led	....	....	....	....	....	....	....	....	....	....	....	....	....	....	....
Financial Derivatives	79lld	....	....	....	....	....	....	....	....	....	....	....	....	....	....	....
Other Investment	79lfd	....	....	....	....	....	....	....	....	....	....	....	....	....	....	....
Monetary Authorities	79lgd	....	....	....	....	....	....	....	....	....	....	....	....	....	....	....
General Government	79lhd	....	....	....	....	....	....	....	....	....	....	....	....	....	....	....
Banks	79lid	....	....	....	....	....	....	....	....	....	....	....	....	....	....	....
Other Sectors	79ljd	....	....	....	....	....	....	....	....	....	....	....	....	....	....	....

1987	1988	1989	1990	1991	1992	1993	1994	1995	1996	1997	1998	1999	2000	2001		
															Interest Rates	
Percent Per Annum																
9.00	9.00	9.00	14.00	14.00	11.00	11.00	11.00	16.00	16.00	10.75	11.38	11.19	11.69	13.00	Discount Rate *(End of Period)*	60
6.25	6.25	6.31	6.88	8.75	7.73	5.00	....	....	10.92	9.46	8.50	7.95	8.94	9.22	Deposit Rate	601
13.00	12.00	12.00	13.17	19.00	16.67	15.00	....	....	....	....	....	....	....	....	Lending Rate	60p
															Prices	
Period Averages																
31.5	32.4	32.8	34.1	40.8	44.7	50.3	....	100.0	107.4	120.3	127.8	124.7	129.6	133.9	Consumer Prices	64
															International Transactions	
Millions of Francs																
8,949	8,291	7,635	9,224	11,598	8,917	9,427	4,056	14,731	18,569	26,190	18,696	20,388	20,521	37,314	Exports	70
28,018	28,280	26,642	23,059	38,454	38,263	47,907	17,270	62,193	78,837	89,694	89,218	84,508	82,586	110,488	Imports, c.i.f.	71
1995=100																
617	467	441	625	541	484	432	190	100	98	238	255	....	....	....	Volume of Exports	72
23	....	25	23	32	25	31	31	100	93	140	93	....	....	....	Export Prices	74
															Balance of Payments	
Minus Sign Indicates Debit																
−134.8	−144.9	−123.0	−108.1	−33.8	−83.3	−129.0	−46.2	57.5	−8.5	−62.2	−83.1	−72.2	−6.8	....	Current Account, n.i.e.	78al *d*
121.4	117.9	104.7	102.6	95.6	68.5	67.7	32.2	56.7	61.7	93.2	64.5	62.3	69.1		Goods: Exports f.o.b.	78aa *d*
−267.0	−278.6	−254.1	−227.7	−228.1	−240.5	−267.8	−367.4	−219.1	−218.5	−278.2	−234.0	−249.7	−222.3		Goods: Imports f.o.b.	78ab *d*
−145.5	−160.7	−149.4	−125.0	−132.5	−171.9	−200.1	−335.2	−162.5	−156.8	−185.0	−169.5	−187.5	−153.2		*Trade Balance*	78ac *d*
46.2	48.2	43.0	42.2	43.0	31.4	34.3	—	17.9	21.5	51.2	48.5	51.3	61.7		Services: Credit	78ad *d*
−147.0	−134.3	−118.6	−131.1	−111.6	−114.6	−136.4	−109.6	−154.7	−149.7	−198.3	−190.6	−195.5	−180.7		Services: Debit	78ae *d*
−246.4	−246.8	−225.0	−213.9	−201.1	−255.1	−302.2	−444.8	−299.2	−284.9	−332.2	−311.6	−331.7	−272.1		*Balance on Goods & Services*	78af *d*
10.3	8.7	9.3	4.4	3.5	4.7	3.0	—	24.3	5.4	8.0	8.8	7.9	11.0		Income: Credit	78ag *d*
−24.2	−30.7	−23.4	−20.9	−17.2	−16.1	−18.2	—	−17.5	−18.8	−24.8	−15.9	−18.7	−26.3		Income: Debit	78ah *d*
−260.4	−268.9	−239.1	−230.4	−214.8	−266.5	−317.4	−444.8	−292.5	−298.3	−348.9	−318.8	−342.5	−287.5		*Balance on Gds, Serv. & Inc.*	78ai *d*
155.0	153.0	141.6	147.4	209.3	213.6	208.5	398.6	354.9	293.9	311.6	252.6	283.2	297.8		Current Transfers, n.i.e.: Credit	78aj *d*
−29.4	−29.0	−25.5	−25.1	−28.3	−30.4	−20.1	—	−4.9	−4.1	−24.9	−16.9	−12.8	−17.2		Current Transfers: Debit	78ak *d*
.4	.4	.5	−.6	−.3	.1	−1.3	—	—	—	—	—	—	—		Capital Account, n.i.e.	78bc *d*
2.3	2.4	2.7	1.7	2.6	1.9	1.0	—	—	—	—	—	—	—		Capital Account, n.i.e.: Credit	78ba *d*
−1.9	−2.0	−2.2	−2.4	−2.9	−1.7	−2.4	—	—	—	—	—	—	....		Capital Account: Debit	78bb *d*
122.3	93.7	53.9	55.7	99.1	62.4	88.5	−12.5	−10.7	24.8	46.8	−15.2	−14.4	−23.0	....	Financial Account, n.i.e.	78bj *d*
															Direct Investment Abroad	78bd *d*
17.5	21.0	15.5	7.7	4.6	2.2	5.8	—	2.2	2.2	2.6	7.1	1.7	14.3		Dir. Invest. in Rep. Econ., n.i.e.	78be *d*
—	—	—	−.3	−.1	—	—	—	—	−.1	—	−.1	−.8	−.1		Portfolio Investment Assets	78bf *d*
—	—	—	−.3	−.1	—	—	—	—	−.1	—	−.1	−.8	−.1		Equity Securities	78bk *d*
															Debt Securities	78bl *d*
—	—	—	—	—	—	—	—	—	—	—	—	—	....		Portfolio Investment Liab., n.i.e.	78bg *d*
															Equity Securities	78bm *d*
															Debt Securities	78bn *d*
															Financial Derivatives Assets	78bw *d*
....	....	....	....	....	....	....									Financial Derivatives Liabilities	78bx *d*
12.8	17.7	8.8	8.3	23.8	19.2	—		−52.0	−13.6	1.2	.8	10.4	−17.3		Other Investment Assets	78bh *d*
....															Monetary Authorities	78bo *d*
—	—	—	−.6	−.2	—	—		—	—	—	—	—	—		General Government	78bp *d*
—	—	—	—	—	—	—		−38.6	−13.6	1.2	.8	10.4	−17.3		Banks	78bq *d*
12.8	17.7	8.8	8.9	24.0	19.2	—		−13.4							Other Sectors	78br *d*
91.9	55.0	29.6	40.0	70.8	41.0	82.7	−12.5	39.1	36.3	43.0	−23.0	−25.7	−19.9		Other Investment Liab., n.i.e.	78bi *d*
3.6	4.2	−5.7	27.9	−13.6	4.5	3.9	—	—	—	—	—	—	—		Monetary Authorities	78bs *d*
93.3	66.6	44.7	39.3	75.3	34.6	61.8	−12.5	39.1	37.2	43.0	−22.5	−24.1	−23.0		General Government	78bt *d*
−2.0	4.1	−5.8	.5	1.0	1.9	7.4	—	—	—	—	−.5	−1.6	3.1		Banks	78bu *d*
−3.1	−19.9	−3.5	−27.6	8.0	—	9.6	—	—	−.9	—	—	—	—		Other Sectors	78bv *d*
1.5	.4	1.9	30.3	.2	16.7	−8.1	62.4	5.8	4.1	46.0	35.9	−59.3	−109.5	....	Net Errors and Omissions	78ca *d*
−10.6	−50.4	−66.7	−22.9	65.2	−4.0	−49.9	3.7	52.6	20.3	30.5	−62.4	−145.9	−139.3		*Overall Balance*	78cb *d*
10.6	50.4	66.7	22.9	−65.2	4.0	49.9	−3.7	−52.6	−20.3	−30.5	62.4	145.9	139.3		Reserves and Related Items	79da *d*
13.3	27.8	48.9	1.2	−77.0	4.0	25.4	−3.7	−66.0	−19.1	−48.4	−21.2	38.1	78.8		Reserve Assets	79db *d*
−2.8	−2.9	−2.7	−.8	11.7	—	—	—	13.3	−1.3	17.9	13.5	20.8	13.6		Use of Fund Credit and Loans	79dc *d*
....	25.5	20.5	22.4	—	24.5	—	—	—	—	—	70.1	87.0	46.8		Exceptional Financing	79de *d*
															International Investment Position	
Millions of US Dollars																
....	....	....	....	....	....	....	....	....	....	....	244.0	231.3	267.9	....	Assets	79aa *d*
....															Direct Investment Abroad	79ab *d*
....											.1	.8	.7		Portfolio Investment	79ac *d*
....											.1	.8	.7		Equity Securities	79ad *d*
....											—	—	—		Debt Securities	79ae *d*
....															Financial Derivatives	79al *d*
....											75.2	56.3	76.5		other Investment	79af *d*
....											....	....	....		Monetary Authorities	79ag *d*
....											....	....	....		General Government	79ah *d*
....											....	....	....		Banks	79ai *d*
....											....	....	....		Other Sectors	79aj *d*
....											168.8	174.2	190.6		Reserve Assets	79ak *d*
....											1,281.9	1,295.3	1,213.6	....	Liabilities	79la *d*
....											62.5	59.0	49.3		Dir. Invest. in Rep. Economy	79lb *d*
....											.1	.1	.1		Portfolio Investment	79lc *d*
....											.1	.1	.1		Equity Securities	79ld *d*
....											—	—	—		Debt Securities	79le *d*
....															Financial Derivatives	79ll *d*
....											1,219.3	1,236.2	1,164.2		Other Investment	79lf *d*
....											....	....	....		Monetary Authorities	79lg *d*
....											....	....	....		General Government	79lh *d*
....											....	....	....		Banks	79li *d*
....											....	....	....		Other Sectors	79lj *d*

Rwanda

		1972	1973	1974	1975	1976	1977	1978	1979	1980	1981	1982	1983	1984	1985	1986
Government Finance																*Millions of Francs:*
Deficit (-) or Surplus	80	−818	−653	−728	−727	−1,225	−1,026	−1,291	−1,618	−1,875	−2,994	−6,400	−6,800	−6,600	−7,800	−8,600
Total Revenue and Grants	81y	1,880	2,419	3,369	5,010	6,750	8,703	9,180	12,478	13,805	14,600	19,744	19,783	21,790	25,200	27,300
Revenue	81	1,880	2,419	3,369	4,539	6,749	8,703	9,180	12,478	13,805	14,600	16,144	15,883	18,190	21,200	23,600
Grants	81z	—	—	—	471	1	—	—	—	—	—	3,600	3,900	3,600	4,000	3,700
Exp. & Lending Minus Repay.	82z	....	3,072	4,097	5,737	7,975	9,729	10,471	14,096	15,680	18,480	24,800	26,500	26,800	31,400	34,700
Expenditure	82	2,696	3,069	4,060	5,651	7,881	9,610	10,370	13,790	15,458	17,540	24,500	26,000	26,500	31,200	34,200
Lending Minus Repayments	83	2	†3	37	86	94	119	101	306	222	940	300	500	300	200	500
Statistical Discrepancy	80xx	....	....	....	....	....	....	—	—	—	886	−1,344	−83	−1,590	−1,600	−1,200
Total Financing	80h	....	653	728	727	1,225	1,026	1,291	1,618	1,875	2,994	6,400	6,800	6,600	7,800	8,600
Total Net Borrowing	84	690	653	728	727	1,225	1,026	†1,291	1,618	1,875	2,994	6,400	6,800	6,600	7,800	8,600
Net Domestic	84a	674	521	246	140	−687	−426	†−276	−1,046	−983	424	3,300	3,500	1,600	400	700
Net Foreign	85a	32	235	377	1,321	2,117	2,213	1,567	2,664	2,858	2,570	3,100	3,300	5,000	7,400	7,900
Use of Cash Balances	87	−16	−103	105	−734	−205	−761	490	−559	−2,122						
Total Debt by Residence	88	....	....	....	....	....	6,099	9,788	11,547	16,919	21,956	25,600	32,154	38,946	46,043	52,744
Domestic	88a	....	374	392	470	506	853	824	832	940	5,079	7,970	11,592	13,484	14,333	16,508
Foreign	89a	....	....	....	....	....	5,246	8,964	10,715	15,979	16,877	17,630	20,562	25,462	31,710	36,236
National Accounts																*Billions of Francs*
Househ.Cons.Expend.,incl.NPISHs	96f	19.9	19.8	24.9	41.2	46.1	51.2	62.1	74.5	90.0	96.4	107.2	119.2	128.9	139.8	134.7
Government Consumption Expend.	91f	2.4	2.8	3.4	8.8	10.2	12.1	12.8	13.0	13.5	24.6	16.9	16.7	16.2	19.5	20.1
Gross Fixed Capital Formation	93e	2.2	2.3	3.0	7.0	8.0	9.1	11.3	14.3	13.2	16.0	18.7	20.7	24.6	27.0	26.8
Changes in Inventories	93i	16.2	17.4	20.5	.3	.6	1.7	2.1	−2.7	4.2	.3	4.5	−1.5	.5	3.0	.2
Exports of Goods and Services	90c	1.9	2.8	3.5	4.8	9.0	10.2	12.0	20.2	15.6	12.1	15.1	16.1	20.0	18.7	21.4
Imports of Goods and Services (-)	98c	3.7	3.3	6.1	9.3	12.0	12.7	19.3	21.9	28.5	26.7	31.6	29.5	34.5	34.3	34.3
Gross Domestic Product (GDP)	99b	38.9	41.7	49.2	52.8	61.9	71.6	81.1	97.4	108.0	122.6	130.9	142.1	159.1	173.7	170.2
Net Primary Income from Abroad	98.n	....	....	....	....	....	....	....	....	....	....	....	....	....	....	....
Gross National Income (GNI)	99a	....	....	....	52.8	61.9	71.4	81.6	97.8	108.2	123.4	131.4	142.1	158.8	173.6	170.2
Net Current Transf.from Abroad	98t	....	....	....	....	....	....	....	....	....	....	....	....	....	....	....
Gross Saving	99s	....	....	....	....	....	....	....	....	....	....	....	....	....	....	....
GDP Volume 1980 Prices	99b.p	82.0	84.8	85.4	87.1	88.7	93.3	102.4	112.0	108.0	110.7	115.2				
GDP Volume 1985 Prices	99b.p	....	....	....	....	....	....	....	....	....	....	....	163.9	173.7	166.3	173.6	183.2
GDP Volume 1995 Prices	99b.p	....	....	....	....	....	....	....	....	....	....	....	....	....	....	....
GDP Volume (1995=100)	99bv p	93.4	96.6	97.3	99.2	101.0	106.3	116.6	127.6	123.0	126.1	131.2	139.0	133.1	139.0	146.6
GDP Deflator (1995=100)	99bi p	12.4	12.8	15.0	15.8	18.2	20.0	20.7	22.7	26.1	28.9	29.7	30.4	35.5	37.1	34.5
																Millions:
Population	99z	3.90	4.01	4.12	4.20	4.29	4.36	4.80	4.98	5.16	5.35	5.55	5.76	5.87	6.06	6.24

Government Finance

1987	1988	1989	1990	1991	1992	1993	1994	1995	1996	1997	1998	1999	2000	2001		
Year Ending December 31																
-13,800	-7,546	-8,218	-12,097	-10,210	-17,234	-13,192	-3,194	5,300	-15,101	-12,275	-41,473	-41,161	-10,326	-40,200	Deficit (-) or Surplus	80
26,600	28,558	31,287	27,454	36,081	44,289	44,005	7,547	61,528	70,828	95,768	99,019	103,803	132,809	149,606	Total Revenue and Grants	81y
23,200	22,858	25,987	21,583	24,993	27,563	25,865	6,032	23,128	39,428	58,037	66,019	65,996	68,664	86,206	Revenue	81
3,400	5,700	5,300	5,871	11,088	16,726	18,140	1,515	38,400	31,400	37,731	33,000	37,807	64,145	63,400	Grants	81z
39,600	37,584	35,903	42,957	52,495	65,661	67,186	26,550	69,528	95,335	109,608	117,471	140,458	136,772	158,128	Exp. & Lending Minus Repay.	82z
39,400	37,335	35,743	42,853	52,689	65,796	65,152	26,550	69,528	95,335	110,157	117,632	138,858	136,298	157,500	Expenditure	82
200	249	160	104	-194	-135	2,034	—	—	—	-549	-161	1,600	474	628	Lending Minus Repayments	83
-800	1,480	-3,602	3,406	6,204	4,138	9,989	15,809	13,300	9,406	1,565	-23,021	-4,506	-6,363	-31,678	Statistical Discrepancy	80xx
13,800	7,546	8,218	12,097	10,210	17,234	13,192	3,194	-5,300	15,101	12,275	41,473	41,161	10,326	40,200	Total Financing	80h
13,800	7,546	8,218	12,097	10,210	17,234	13,192	3,194	-5,300	15,101	12,275	41,473	41,161	10,326	40,200	Total Net Borrowing	84
4,100	2,500	4,117	6,853	2,687	6,612	4,643	5,636	-12,742	4,464	645	-173	7,461	-8,609	-3,000	Net Domestic	84a
9,700	5,046	4,101	5,244	7,523	10,622	8,549	-2,442	7,442	10,637	11,630	41,646	33,700	18,935	43,200	Net Foreign	85a
....	....	241 P	-1,138 P	-3,039 P	....	....	....	....	....	....	....	....	....	....	Use of Cash Balances	87
65,685	74,612	66,595	119,728	130,334	147,890	163,882	171,065	353,894	370,697	403,971	469,522	537,278	630,670	659,544	Total Debt by Residence	88
21,058	24,274	17,179	36,217	38,734	48,407	52,485	56,138	55,296	58,360	81,533	85,338	87,294	82,477	82,217	Domestic	88a
44,627	50,338	49,416	83,511	91,600	99,483	111,397	114,927	298,598	312,337	322,438	384,184	449,984	548,193	577,327	Foreign	89a

National Accounts

1987	1988	1989	1990	1991	1992	1993	1994	1995	1996	1997	1998	1999	2000	2001		
Billions of Francs																
137.9	149.4	159.5	178.6	200.6	222.5	241.2	229.7	338.6	408.6	536.0	577.7	572.3	601.2	....	Househ.Cons.Expend.,incl.NPISHs	96f
23.2	16.8	16.6	21.7	28.9	35.2	32.9	13.6	30.9	44.1	49.9	54.5	61.2	61.0	....	Government Consumption Expend.	91f
26.9	25.5	25.7	31.3	33.6	45.8	51.4	19.4	45.5	61.0	77.0	92.0	109.4	120.6	....	Gross Fixed Capital Formation	93e
—	1.0	.1	-1.1	-2.9	-.1	-1.9	-2.0	-1.3	—	....	....	....	....	....	Changes in Inventories	93i
16.9	16.1	16.4	12.0	17.5	15.1	14.7	10.5	19.6	25.5	43.4	34.7	37.8	49.9	....	Exports of Goods and Services	90c
36.1	34.5	34.9	30.0	43.1	49.5	58.3	107.4	98.0	113.0	142.9	131.5	147.9	150.1	....	Imports of Goods and Services (-)	98c
171.2	175.6	190.2	213.5	237.4	269.0	281.9	165.8	336.5	426.2	563.4	627.3	632.8	682.5	....	Gross Domestic Product (GDP)	99b
....	....	....	-.9	-1.4	-1.5	-1.7	-.9	1.6	-4.5	-4.4	-2.1	-3.5	-6.4	....	Net Primary Income from Abroad	98.n
171.2	175.3	190.1	212.6	236.0	267.6	280.2	164.9	338.1	421.7	559.1	625.2	629.3	676.2	....	Gross National Income (GNI)	99a
....	38.0	36.1	45.4	40.8	57.9	99.5	391.7	223.0	200.1	171.7	163.0	200.3	204.6	....	Net Current Transf.from Abroad	98t
....	....	....	12.8	9.1	12.6	9.3	-68.7	-26.9	-22.7	-19.3	-1.2	1.8	18.3	....	Gross Saving	99s
182.1	191.2	192.1	195.9	....	....	....	....	....	....	....	....	....	....	....	GDP Volume 1980 Prices	99b.p
....	....	....	....	....	....	....	....	....	....	....	....	....	....	....	GDP Volume 1985 Prices	99b.p
....	....	....	527.7	508.5	543.7	498.1	250.7	336.5	383.8	438.1	478.2	507.2	537.4	....	GDP Volume 1995 Prices	99b.p
145.8	153.0	153.8	156.8	151.1	161.6	148.0	74.5	100.0	114.1	130.2	142.1	150.7	159.7	....	GDP Volume (1995=100)	99bv.p
34.9	34.1	36.8	40.5	46.7	49.5	56.6	66.1	100.0	111.0	128.6	131.2	124.8	127.0	....	GDP Deflator (1995=100)	99bi.p
Midyear Estimates																
6.42	6.87	7.03	7.18	6.47	5.99	5.46	5.08	4.98	5.21	5.73	6.42	7.09	7.61	7.95	Population	99z

(See notes in the back of the book.)

St. Kitts and Nevis

	1972	1973	1974	1975	1976	1977	1978	1979	1980	1981	1982	1983	1984	1985	1986
Exchange Rates												*E. Caribbean Dollars per SDR: End of Period (aa)*			
Official Rate .... aa	2.2194	2.4925	2.5024	2.7770	3.1369	3.2797	3.5175	3.5568	3.4436	3.1427	2.9784	2.8268	2.6466	2.9657	3.3026
Official Rate .... ae	2.0442	2.0661	2.0439	2.3721	2.7000	2.7000	2.7000	2.7000	2.7000	2.7000	2.7000	2.7000	2.7000	2.7000	2.7000
												Index Numbers (1995=100):			
Nominal Effective Exchange Rate .... ne c	....	....	....	....	....	....	....	85.33	83.18	86.69	90.74	94.70	99.72	101.84	101.75
Real Effective Exchange Rate .... re c	....	....	....	....	....	....	....	112.75	112.22	115.93	119.06	120.36	122.66	122.20	117.92
Fund Position													*Millions of SDRs:*		
Quota .... 2f. s	....	....	....	....	....	....	....	....	....	....	....	....	4.50	4.50	4.50
SDRs .... 1b. s	....	....	....	....	....	....	....	....	....	....	....	....	—	—	—
Reserve Position in the Fund .... 1c. s	....	....	....	....	....	....	....	....	....	....	....	....	—	—	.01
Total Fund Cred.&Loans Outstg. 2tl	....	....	....	....	....	....	....	....	....	....	....	....	—	—	—
International Liquidity											*Millions of US Dollars Unless Otherwise Indicated:*				
Total Reserves minus Gold .... 1l. d	....	....	....	....	....	....	....	....	....	4.02	3.33	3.15	5.65	7.41	10.23
SDRs .... 1b. d	....	....	....	....	....	....	....	....	....	....	....	....	....	....	....
Reserve Position in the Fund .... 1c. d	....	....	....	....	....	....	....	....	....	....	....	....	—	—	.01
Foreign Exchange .... 1d. d	....	....	....	....	....	....	....	....	....	4.02	3.33	3.15	5.65	7.41	10.22
Deposit Money Banks: Assets .... 7a. d	....	....	....	....	....	....	....	22.18	33.13	15.48	12.37	24.81	21.86	27.92	27.22
Liabilities .... 7b. d	....	....	....	....	....	....	....	11.25	13.71	14.91	10.65	24.34	17.47	24.21	20.99
Monetary Authorities												*Millions of E. Caribbean Dollars:*			
Foreign Assets 11	....	....	....	....	....	....	....	5.20	1.32	20.27	11.01	14.44	15.26	20.02	27.63
Claims on Central Government 12a	....	....	....	....	....	....	....	3.36	3.36	3.36	5.91	6.40	14.10	16.07	16.04
Claims on Deposit Money Banks 12e	....	....	....	....	....	....	....	—	—	—	—	—	1.03	.21	.10
Reserve Money 14	....	....	....	....	....	....	....	8.56	4.68	23.63	16.92	20.84	30.39	36.30	43.77
of which: Currency Outside DMBs 14a	....	....	....	....	....	....	....	—	—	10.33	11.10	11.59	12.61	9.39	12.22
Foreign Liabilities 16c	....	....	....	....	....	....	....	—	—	—	—	—	—	—	—
Central Government Deposits 16d	....	....	....	....	....	....	....	—	—	—	—	—	—	—	—
Other Items (Net) 17r	....	....	....	....	....	....	....	—	—	—	—	—	—	—	—
Deposit Money Banks												*Millions of E. Caribbean Dollars:*			
Reserves 20	....	....	....	....	....	....	....	8.56	4.20	13.29	5.82	9.25	17.33	26.81	30.54
Foreign Assets 21	....	....	....	....	....	....	....	59.89	89.45	41.78	33.40	66.99	59.01	75.39	73.49
Claims on Central Government 22a	....	....	....	....	....	....	....	6.94	5.00	6.68	15.26	21.97	26.76	35.65	41.21
Claims on Local Government 22b	....	....	....	....	....	....	....	—	—	—	—	—	—	—	—
Claims on Nonfin.Pub.Enterprises 22c	....	....	....	....	....	....	....	8.19	21.48	32.57	35.78	43.60	45.51	56.20	58.20
Claims on Private Sector 22d	....	....	....	....	....	....	....	43.24	52.77	67.40	75.71	84.80	96.58	104.76	102.64
Claims on Nonbank Financial Insts 22g	....	....	....	....	....	....	....	3.36	.36	.31	.31	.30	.29	.25	.25
Demand Deposits 24	....	....	....	....	....	....	....	10.81	9.34	16.09	14.39	15.99	16.64	23.51	37.59
Time, Savings,& Fgn.Currency Dep. 25	....	....	....	....	....	....	....	74.73	87.31	90.41	105.43	123.11	141.64	171.31	182.75
Foreign Liabilities 26c	....	....	....	....	....	....	....	30.37	37.02	40.26	28.74	65.71	47.18	65.36	56.68
Central Government Deposits 26d	....	....	....	....	....	....	....	15.62	21.87	18.10	22.56	24.29	33.87	28.88	11.92
Credit from Monetary Authorities 26g	....	....	....	....	....	....	....	5.70	5.44	3.65	2.81	3.16	.58	1.02	2.90
Capital Accounts 27a	....	....	....	....	....	....	....	7.29	10.02	13.35	12.30	13.80	13.70	14.25	16.88
Other Items (Net) 27r	....	....	....	....	....	....	....	−14.32	2.25	−19.82	−19.94	−19.15	−8.12	−5.28	−2.39
Monetary Survey												*Millions of E. Caribbean Dollars:*			
Foreign Assets (Net) 31n	....	....	....	....	....	....	....	34.72	53.75	21.79	15.66	15.71	27.10	30.05	44.45
Domestic Credit 32	....	....	....	....	....	....	....	49.48	61.08	92.22	110.42	132.78	149.38	184.04	206.41
Claims on Central Govt. (Net) 32an	....	....	....	....	....	....	....	−5.32	−13.52	−8.06	−1.39	4.08	7.00	22.84	45.32
Claims on Local Government 32b	....	....	....	....	....	....	....	—	—	—	—	—	—	—	—
Claims on Nonfin.Pub.Enterprises 32c	....	....	....	....	....	....	....	8.19	21.48	32.57	35.78	43.60	45.51	56.20	58.20
Claims on Private Sector 32d	....	....	....	....	....	....	....	43.24	52.77	67.40	75.71	84.80	96.58	104.76	102.64
Claims on Nonbank Financial Inst 32g	....	....	....	....	....	....	....	3.36	.36	.31	.31	.30	.29	.25	.25
Money 34	....	....	....	....	....	....	....	10.81	9.34	26.42	25.49	27.58	29.26	32.90	49.81
Quasi-Money 35	....	....	....	....	....	....	....	74.73	87.31	90.41	105.43	123.11	141.64	171.31	182.75
Capital Accounts 37a	....	....	....	....	....	....	....	7.29	10.02	13.35	12.30	13.80	13.70	14.25	16.88
Other Items (Net) 37r	....	....	....	....	....	....	....	−8.62	8.17	−16.17	−17.14	−15.99	−8.12	−4.37	1.42
Money plus Quasi-Money 35l	....	....	....	....	....	....	....	85.53	96.64	116.84	130.92	150.69	170.90	204.21	232.56
Interest Rates													*Percent Per Annum*		
Treasury Bill Rate 60c	....	....	....	....	....	....	....	....	6.5	6.5	6.5	6.5	6.5	6.5	6.5
Deposit Rate 60l	....	....	....	....	....	....	....	....	6.0	6.0	6.0	6.0	6.0	6.3	6.0
Lending Rate 60p	....	....	....	....	....	....	....	....	9.0	9.0	9.0	9.0	10.0	10.2	10.2
Prices													*Index Numbers (1995=100):*		
Consumer Prices 64	....	....	....	....	....	....	....	53.3	62.8	69.3	73.4	75.1	77.2	79.2	79.2
International Transactions													*Millions of E. Caribbean Dollars*		
Exports 70	12	17	24	47	46	41	45	45	64	66	51	50	54	55	68
Imports, c.i.f. 71	31	36	39	51	58	59	65	87	121	129	118	139	140	139	170

	1987	1988	1989	1990	1991	1992	1993	1994	1995	1996	1997	1998	1999	2000	2001		
Exchange Rates																	
E. Caribbean Dollars per US Dollar: End of Period (ae)																	
	3.8304	3.6334	3.5482	3.8412	3.8622	3.7125	3.7086	3.9416	4.0135	3.8825	3.6430	3.8017	3.7058	3.5179	3.3932	Official Rate	**aa**
	2.7000	2.7000	2.7000	2.7000	2.7000	2.7000	2.7000	2.7000	2.7000	2.7000	2.7000	2.7000	2.7000	2.7000	2.7000	Official Rate	**ae**
Period Averages																	
	99.12	96.97	100.86	99.22	99.27	98.51	102.47	102.38	100.00	101.34	103.74	104.73	105.01	108.06	110.19	Nominal Effective Exchange Rate	**ne c**
	110.69	103.53	106.06	102.11	101.84	100.49	103.32	102.25	100.00	100.80	109.57	112.50	114.99	117.63	119.65	Real Effective Exchange Rate	**re c**
Fund Position																	
End of Period																	
	4.50	4.50	4.50	4.50	4.50	6.50	6.50	6.50	6.50	6.50	6.50	6.50	8.90	8.90	8.90	Quota	**2f. s**
	—	—	—	—	—	—	—	—	—	—	—	—	—	—	.01	SDRs	**1b. s**
	.01	.01	.01	.01	.01	.01	.02	.01	.01	.01	.01	.01	.07	.08	.08	Reserve Position in the Fund	**1c. s**
	—	—	—	—	—	—	—	—	—	—	—	1.63	1.63	1.63	1.63	Total Fund Cred.&Loans Outstg.	**2tl**
International Liquidity																	
End of Period																	
	10.57	10.32	16.39	16.28	16.63	26.24	29.42	31.82	33.47	32.73	36.07	46.80	49.58	45.20	56.41	Total Reserves minus Gold	**1l. d**
	—	—	—	—	—	—	—	—	—	—	—	—	—	—	—	SDRs	**1b. d**
	.01	.01	.01	.01	.01	.01	.02	.02	.02	.02	.02	.02	.10	.11	.10	Reserve Position in the Fund	**1c. d**
	10.56	10.31	16.38	16.27	16.62	26.23	29.40	31.80	33.45	32.71	36.05	46.78	49.48	45.09	56.31	Foreign Exchange	**1d. d**
	46.98	43.06	31.40	32.62	33.68	45.57	59.65	70.62	76.69	88.78	121.88	123.28	112.59	148.52	165.58	Deposit Money Banks: Assets	**7a. d**
	33.53	29.20	22.35	22.52	27.24	45.10	58.96	73.35	77.53	90.28	106.08	105.06	125.20	137.15	133.73	Liabilities	**7b. d**
Monetary Authorities																	
End of Period																	
	28.56	27.86	44.27	43.97	44.96	70.93	79.54	85.80	90.37	88.38	97.38	119.22	132.86	122.04	152.33	Foreign Assets	**11**
	16.03	14.91	10.71	14.63	14.15	7.80	8.34	4.95	4.42	4.01	3.20	8.73	8.56	10.66	11.32	Claims on Central Government	**12a**
	1.68	1.61	.06	.05	.05	.03	.01	3.52	.01	—	.01	—	—	15.09	—	Claims on Deposit Money Banks	**12e**
	46.27	44.39	55.04	58.65	59.10	78.70	87.89	94.27	92.80	89.87	95.75	114.65	129.44	140.73	155.21	Reserve Money	**14**
	13.00	16.08	22.65	21.43	23.86	23.04	28.08	28.28	30.29	32.38	31.85	35.84	41.45	40.59	36.10	of which: Currency Outside DMBs	**14a**
	—	—	—	—	—	—	—	—	—	—	—	6.18	6.02	5.72	5.51	Foreign Liabilities	**16c**
	—	—	—	.06	.06	—	—	—	2.00	2.52	4.84	7.12	5.96	1.34	2.93	Central Government Deposits	**16d**
	—	—	—	—	—	—	—	—	—	—	—	—	—	—	—	Other Items (Net)	**17r**
Deposit Money Banks																	
End of Period																	
	33.22	30.10	32.62	34.68	38.69	57.09	63.95	65.79	65.14	58.01	65.65	78.64	89.69	98.90	113.29	Reserves	**20**
	126.85	116.25	84.79	88.07	90.93	123.05	161.06	190.68	207.07	239.71	329.07	332.85	303.98	401.01	447.07	Foreign Assets	**21**
	39.37	48.48	53.56	65.95	71.31	70.63	57.69	63.70	84.07	118.44	89.62	128.11	154.16	249.73	257.75	Claims on Central Government	**22a**
	—	5.49	5.69	6.33	6.88	6.57	7.52	6.97	8.50	7.34	6.41	12.29	18.18	30.90	37.40	Claims on Local Government	**22b**
	2.31	8.52	19.75	34.55	31.64	30.17	32.46	41.50	87.13	105.10	117.67	134.96	160.45	158.26	192.04	Claims on Nonfin.Pub.Enterprises	**22c**
	122.81	170.08	223.98	231.91	262.49	334.56	375.78	416.36	440.86	465.57	521.06	563.67	610.17	680.54	675.26	Claims on Private Sector	**22d**
	.25	.25	.25	.25	1.00	1.00	1.18	.03	.50	1.10	1.69	3.70	5.77	5.95	6.39	Claims on Nonbank Financial Insts	**22g**
	42.25	32.40	38.58	38.56	36.49	42.07	47.83	44.54	52.86	56.38	55.80	71.88	72.52	79.30	77.12	Demand Deposits	**24**
	156.98	182.42	218.54	241.44	258.69	302.55	332.09	339.43	390.56	395.15	465.57	506.96	524.01	694.68	711.30	Time, Savings,& Fgn.Currency Dep.	**25**
	90.52	78.85	60.36	60.81	73.55	121.76	159.18	198.05	209.32	243.75	286.42	283.67	338.05	370.30	361.07	Foreign Liabilities	**26c**
	12.14	45.43	61.47	70.68	81.52	100.42	112.65	141.51	169.22	194.81	202.28	225.67	256.83	292.30	338.94	Central Government Deposits	**26d**
	.65	—	1.88	—	.03	—	3.50	3.50	4.87	11.71	4.65	10.60	7.67	20.53	7.43	Credit from Monetary Authorities	**26g**
	22.00	24.22	33.96	42.13	51.90	55.82	58.70	63.12	73.89	90.49	108.25	121.57	120.19	136.40	160.38	Capital Accounts	**27a**
	.27	15.85	5.85	8.10	.75	.46	-14.32	-5.12	-7.45	2.99	8.20	33.87	23.15	31.77	72.96	Other Items (Net)	**27r**
Monetary Survey																	
End of Period																	
	64.88	65.26	68.70	71.22	62.34	72.22	81.42	78.44	88.12	84.34	140.04	162.22	92.77	147.03	232.81	Foreign Assets (Net)	**31n**
	168.64	202.31	252.47	282.93	305.88	350.24	370.31	391.99	454.26	504.23	532.52	618.67	694.52	842.38	838.30	Domestic Credit	**32**
	43.26	17.97	2.80	9.90	3.88	-22.06	-46.62	-72.86	-82.74	-74.88	-114.30	-95.95	-100.06	-33.26	-72.79	Claims on Central Govt. (Net)	**32an**
	—	5.49	5.69	6.33	6.88	6.57	7.52	6.97	8.50	7.34	6.41	12.29	18.18	30.90	37.40	Claims on Local Government	**32b**
	2.31	8.52	19.75	34.55	31.64	30.17	32.46	41.50	87.13	105.10	117.67	134.96	160.45	158.26	192.04	Claims on Nonfin.Pub.Enterprises	**32c**
	122.81	170.08	223.98	231.91	262.49	334.56	375.78	416.36	440.86	465.57	521.06	563.67	610.17	680.54	675.26	Claims on Private Sector	**32d**
	.25	.25	.25	.25	1.00	1.00	1.18	.03	.50	1.10	1.69	3.70	5.77	5.95	6.39	Claims on Nonbank Financial Inst	**32g**
	55.26	48.48	61.23	59.99	60.35	65.12	75.92	72.84	83.17	88.79	87.88	107.74	114.08	120.98	114.75	Money	**34**
	156.98	182.42	218.54	241.44	258.69	302.55	332.09	339.43	390.56	395.15	465.57	506.96	524.01	694.68	711.30	Quasi-Money	**35**
	22.00	24.22	33.96	42.13	51.90	55.82	58.70	63.12	73.89	90.49	108.25	121.57	120.19	136.40	160.38	Capital Accounts	**37a**
	-.71	12.44	7.43	10.59	-2.72	-1.02	-14.98	-4.95	-5.24	14.14	10.86	44.62	29.01	37.35	84.68	Other Items (Net)	**37r**
	212.24	230.90	279.78	301.44	319.04	367.66	408.01	412.26	473.73	483.94	553.45	614.70	638.09	815.66	826.05	Money plus Quasi-Money	**35l**
Interest Rates																	
Percent Per Annum																	
	6.5	6.5	6.5	6.5	6.5	6.5	6.5	6.5	6.5	6.5	6.5	6.5	6.5	6.5	6.2	Treasury Bill Rate	**60c**
	5.3	7.0	7.0	7.0	7.0	7.0	5.5	5.5	5.5	5.5	5.5	5.5	5.5	5.5	5.6	Deposit Rate	**60l**
	12.0	12.0	12.0	12.0	12.0	12.7	13.0	13.0	12.6	12.3	13.0	13.0	11.5	11.0	11.4	Lending Rate	**60p**
Prices																	
Period Averages																	
	79.9	80.1	84.3	87.7	91.4	94.1	95.7	97.1	100.0	102.1	111.2	115.0	119.5	....	....	Consumer Prices	**64**
International Transactions																	
Millions of E. Caribbean Dollars																	
	76	74	77	75	74	71	73	61	51	59	....	....	....	....	....	Exports	**70**
	215	252	277	298	297	257	319	345	359	403	....	....	....	....	....	Imports, c.i.f.	**71**

St. Kitts and Nevis

361

	1972	1973	1974	1975	1976	1977	1978	1979	1980	1981	1982	1983	1984	1985	1986
Balance of Payments														*Millions of US Dollars:*	
Current Account, n.i.e. .... 78al *d*	....	....	....	....	....	....	....	....	−2.66	−4.70	−8.72	−14.74	−4.34	−6.68	−8.90
Goods: Exports f.o.b. .... 78aa *d*	....	....	....	....	....	....	....	....	24.12	24.26	18.84	18.43	20.15	20.37	26.12
Goods: Imports f.o.b. .... 78ab *d*	....	....	....	....	....	....	....	....	−40.80	−43.42	−39.82	−46.74	−47.23	−46.70	−55.35
Trade Balance .... 78ac *d*	....	....	....	....	....	....	....	....	−16.68	−19.16	−20.99	−28.32	−27.09	−26.33	−29.23
Services: Credit .... 78ad *d*	....	....	....	....	....	....	....	....	8.10	10.00	13.20	13.00	20.32	22.80	31.72
Services: Debit .... 78ae *d*	....	....	....	....	....	....	....	....	−5.84	−7.19	−12.64	−10.82	−9.17	−10.32	−17.17
Balance on Goods & Services .... 78af *d*	....	....	....	....	....	....	....	....	−14.42	−16.35	−20.42	−26.14	−15.94	−13.84	−14.68
Income: Credit .... 78ag *d*	....	....	....	....	....	....	....	....	.70	1.20	1.30	1.80	.90	.30	2.27
Income: Debit .... 78ah *d*	....	....	....	....	....	....	....	....	−1.94	−2.24	−.70	−.70	−.80	−1.60	−3.96
Balance on Gds, Serv. & Inc. ...... 78ai *d*	....	....	....	....	....	....	....	....	−15.66	−17.40	−19.82	−25.04	−15.84	−15.14	−16.37
Current Transfers, n.i.e.: Credit ...... 78aj *d*	....	....	....	....	....	....	....	....	13.00	12.70	13.10	13.20	14.80	12.62	9.56
Current Transfers: Debit .... 78ak *d*	....	....	....	....	....	....	....	....	—	—	−2.00	−2.90	−3.30	−4.15	−2.09
Capital Account, n.i.e. .... 78bc *d*	....	....	....	....	....	....	....	....	—	—	—	—	—	—	5.19
Capital Account, n.i.e.: Credit .... 78ba *d*	....	....	....	....	....	....	....	....	—	—	—	—	—	—	5.37
Capital Account: Debit .... 78bb *d*	....	....	....	....	....	....	....	....	—	—	—	—	—	—	−.19
Financial Account, n.i.e. .... 78bj *d*	....	....	....	....	....	....	....	....	4.94	5.70	1.74	15.55	7.35	9.15	5.83
Direct Investment Abroad .... 78bd *d*	....	....	....	....	....	....	....	....	—	—	—	—	—	—	—
Dir. Invest. in Rep. Econ., n.i.e. ...... 78be *d*	....	....	....	....	....	....	....	....	1.00	.90	2.20	13.50	6.00	8.00	9.20
Portfolio Investment Assets .... 78bf *d*	....	....	....	....	....	....	....	....	—	—	—	—	—	—	—
Equity Securities .... 78bk *d*	....	....	....	....	....	....	....	....	—	—	—	—	—	—	—
Debt Securities .... 78bl *d*	....	....	....	....	....	....	....	....	—	—	—	—	—	—	—
Portfolio Investment Liab., n.i.e. ...... 78bg *d*	....	....	....	....	....	....	....	....	—	—	—	—	—	—	—
Equity Securities .... 78bm *d*	....	....	....	....	....	....	....	....	—	—	—	—	—	—	—
Debt Securities .... 78bn *d*	....	....	....	....	....	....	....	....	—	—	—	—	—	—	—
Financial Derivatives Assets .... 78bw *d*	....	....	....	....	....	....	....	....	....	....	....	....	....	....	....
Financial Derivatives Liabilities ...... 78bx *d*	....	....	....	....	....	....	....	....	....	....	....	....	....	....	....
Other Investment Assets .... 78bh *d*	....	....	....	....	....	....	....	....	—	—	3.10	−12.44	2.95	−5.90	−1.76
Monetary Authorities .... 78bo *d*	....	....	....	....	....	....	....	....	—	—	—	—	—	—	—
General Government .... 78bp *d*	....	....	....	....	....	....	....	....	—	—	—	—	—	—	—
Banks .... 78bq *d*	....	....	....	....	....	....	....	....	—	—	3.10	−12.44	2.95	−5.90	−1.76
Other Sectors .... 78br *d*	....	....	....	....	....	....	....	....	—	—	—	—	—	—	—
Other Investment Liab., n.i.e. ...... 78bi *d*	....	....	....	....	....	....	....	....	3.94	4.80	−3.57	14.49	−1.60	7.05	−1.61
Monetary Authorities .... 78bs *d*	....	....	....	....	....	....	....	....	—	—	—	—	—	—	—
General Government .... 78bt *d*	....	....	....	....	....	....	....	....	.59	.58	.20	.10	3.70	.40	−1.56
Banks .... 78bu *d*	....	....	....	....	....	....	....	....	—	3.50	−4.27	13.69	−7.00	5.65	—
Other Sectors .... 78bv *d*	....	....	....	....	....	....	....	....	3.36	.72	.50	.70	1.70	1.00	−.05
Net Errors and Omissions .... 78ca *d*	....	....	....	....	....	....	....	....	−3.88	−.90	3.19	.39	−1.21	−.53	.89
Overall Balance .... 78cb *d*	....	....	....	....	....	....	....	....	−1.60	.10	−3.80	1.20	1.80	1.94	3.01
Reserves and Related Items .... 79da *d*	....	....	....	....	....	....	....	....	1.60	−.10	3.80	−1.20	−1.80	−1.94	−3.01
Reserve Assets .... 79db *d*	....	....	....	....	....	....	....	....	1.60	−.10	3.80	−1.20	−1.80	−1.94	−3.01
Use of Fund Credit and Loans .... 79dc *d*	....	....	....	....	....	....	....	....	—	—	—	—	—	—	—
Exceptional Financing .... 79de *d*	....	....	....	....	....	....	....	....	....	....	....	....	....	....	....
Government Finance													*Millions of E. Caribbean Dollars:*		
Deficit (-) or Surplus 80	....	....	....	....	....	....	....	....	....	....	....	....	....	−13.12	2.85
Revenue 81	....	....	....	....	....	....	....	....	....	....	....	....	....	59.95	71.71
Grants Received 81z	....	....	....	....	....	....	....	....	....	....	....	....	....	4.07	5.45
Expenditure 82	....	....	....	....	....	....	....	....	....	....	....	....	....	74.57	71.75
Lending Minus Repayments 83	....	....	....	....	....	....	....	....	....	....	....	....	....	2.57	2.56
Financing															
Domestic 84a	....	....	....	....	....	....	....	....	....	....	....	....	....	....	....
Foreign 85a	....	....	....	....	....	....	....	....	....	....	....	....	....	....	....
National Accounts													*Millions of E. Caribbean Dollars*		
Househ.Cons.Expend.,incl.NPISHs 96f	....	47.4	....	57.1	....	47.2	57.3	73.5	92.3	108.9	120.0	133.1	139.6	146.7	177.0
Government Consumption Expend. 91f	....	10.5	....	12.1	....	16.1	20.6	22.9	27.1	39.7	36.5	36.8	45.4	47.4	50.3
Gross Fixed Capital Formation 93e	....	7.1	....	7.7	....	30.8	25.1	37.3	49.4	46.1	55.0	59.9	57.1	63.9	69.4
Exports of Goods and Services 90c	....	16.6	....	46.8	....	51.5	58.6	64.3	86.7	92.2	80.6	78.8	104.1	116.6	156.2
Imports of Goods and Services (-) 98c	....	35.6	....	51.4	....	64.8	69.1	90.2	125.9	136.6	130.4	150.4	157.1	164.0	198.6
Gross Domestic Product (GDP) 99b	....	48.6	....	74.1	75.5	80.7	92.5	107.7	129.7	152.8	161.8	161.2	189.1	210.6	254.2
Net Primary Income from Abroad 98.n	....	....	....	....	....	....	....	....	....	....	....	....	....	....	....
Gross National Income (GNI) 99a	....	....	....	....	....	....	....	....	....	....	....	....	....	....	....
Net Current Transf.from Abroad 98t	....	....	....	....	....	....	....	....	....	....	....	....	....	....	....
Gross Nat'l Disposable Inc.(GNDI) 99i	....	....	....	....	....	....	....	....	....	....	....	....	....	....	....
Gross Saving 99s	....	....	....	....	....	....	....	....	....	....	....	....	....	....	....
GDP Volume (1995=100) .... 99bv *p*	....	....	....	....	....	38.8	41.6	45.5	49.2	49.7	49.0	48.5	53.5	56.9	63.6
GDP Deflator (1995=100) .... 99bi *p*	....	....	....	....	....	33.4	35.7	38.1	42.3	49.3	53.1	53.4	56.7	59.4	64.2
															Millions:
Population 99z	.04	.04	.04	.04	.04	.04	.04	.04	.04	.04	.04	.05	.04	.04	.04

Balance of Payments

Minus Sign Indicates Debit

1987	1988	1989	1990	1991	1992	1993	1994	1995	1996	1997	1998	1999	2000	2001	Item	Code
-16.11	-27.53	-38.37	-46.97	-35.59	-15.00	-29.29	-24.30	-45.46	-65.95	-53.98	-41.50	-82.96	-62.33	....	Current Account, n.i.e.	78al d
28.72	28.41	29.20	28.32	28.58	33.02	31.99	28.57	36.56	39.07	51.35	44.80	44.94	54.56	....	Goods: Exports f.o.b.	78aa d
-69.96	-81.96	-90.19	-97.44	-97.05	-84.15	-94.57	-98.27	-117.12	-131.51	-129.72	-131.10	-135.19	-172.56	....	Goods: Imports f.o.b.	78ab d
-41.23	-53.56	-60.98	-69.12	-68.47	-51.13	-62.58	-69.70	-80.56	-92.44	-78.37	-86.30	-90.24	-118.00	....	*Trade Balance*	78ac d
40.41	46.75	50.00	54.06	68.39	79.77	83.43	92.38	81.95	87.24	95.47	105.30	99.51	96.66	....	Services: Credit	78ad d
-21.40	-24.90	-29.22	-34.93	-34.92	-40.97	-46.21	-44.86	-55.07	-61.30	-65.04	-61.94	-85.33	-74.33	....	Services: Debit	78ae d
-22.22	-31.70	-40.20	-49.98	-35.01	-12.33	-25.37	-22.18	-53.68	-66.49	-47.94	-42.94	-76.06	-95.68	....	*Balance on Goods & Services*	78af d
3.21	4.51	3.54	3.31	2.49	2.39	2.04	2.91	6.77	3.14	2.89	4.84	6.45	5.54	....	Income: Credit	78ag d
-4.98	-8.63	-12.71	-7.77	-9.49	-13.08	-13.94	-15.91	-17.73	-18.76	-24.01	-30.48	-33.84	-34.83	....	Income: Debit	78ah d
-23.99	-35.83	-49.36	-54.44	-42.01	-23.02	-37.27	-35.19	-64.64	-82.12	-69.07	-68.59	-103.46	-124.97	....	*Balance on Gds, Serv. & Inc.*	78ai d
10.58	11.80	17.68	17.17	12.60	13.74	14.16	16.56	23.26	20.80	21.76	33.66	24.05	69.89	....	Current Transfers, n.i.e.: Credit	78aj d
-2.71	-3.50	-6.69	-9.70	-6.18	-5.72	-6.18	-5.67	-4.08	-4.63	-6.67	-6.58	-3.56	-7.25	....	Current Transfers: Debit	78ak d
6.90	7.60	5.14	2.43	3.84	4.07	3.33	1.73	7.26	5.45	4.17	8.25	5.81	12.24	....	Capital Account, n.i.e.	78bc d
7.10	7.80	5.34	3.05	3.84	4.24	3.53	2.61	7.41	5.63	4.36	8.43	5.99	12.43	....	Capital Account, n.i.e.: Credit	78ba d
-.20	-.20	-.20	-.62	—	-.17	-.20	-.88	-.16	-.19	-.19	-.19	-.19	-.19	....	Capital Account: Debit	78bb d
13.70	18.78	51.16	51.06	25.36	19.39	25.53	23.74	24.79	48.37	43.36	35.82	94.80	66.60	....	Financial Account, n.i.e.	78bj d
															Direct Investment Abroad	78bd d
16.65	13.13	40.80	48.79	21.45	12.53	13.76	15.35	20.47	35.17	19.67	31.93	57.74	96.21	....	Dir. Invest. in Rep. Econ., n.i.e.	78be d
—	—	—	—	-.07	—	2.22	—	2.59	.88	.01	.01	.02	.03	....	Portfolio Investment Assets	78bf d
—	—	—	—												Equity Securities	78bk d
—	—	—	—	.07	.01	—	.23	.15	7.09	.44	-.13	.01	1.12	....	Debt Securities	78bl d
															Portfolio Investment Liab., n.i.e.	78bg d
															Equity Securities	78bm d
															Debt Securities	78bn d
															Financial Derivatives Assets	78bw d
															Financial Derivatives Liabilities	78bx d
-7.44	-.40	4.80	-1.05	-1.81	-12.35	-13.50	-10.04	-3.70	-13.10	-36.39	-4.99	1.47	-10.74	....	Other Investment Assets	78bh d
															Monetary Authorities	78bo d
															General Government	78bp d
-7.44	-.40	4.80	-1.05												Banks	78bq d
															Other Sectors	78br d
4.49	6.04	5.56	3.33	5.73	19.20	23.04	18.20	5.28	18.33	59.63	9.00	35.56	-20.02	....	Other Investment Liab., n.i.e.	78bi d
															Monetary Authorities	78bs d
4.62	5.85	5.99	3.38												General Government	78bt d
															Banks	78bu d
-.13	.19	-.43	-.05												Other Sectors	78bv d
-3.94	1.07	-11.59	-6.43	7.04	1.33	3.36	-1.77	15.71	11.24	9.48	8.43	-14.90	-20.84	....	Net Errors and Omissions	78ca d
.54	-.08	6.33	.09	.65	9.80	2.93	-.61	2.29	-.89	3.02	10.99	2.74	-4.33	....	*Overall Balance*	78cb d
-.54	.08	-6.33	-.09	-.65	-9.80	-2.93	.61	-2.29	.89	-3.02	-10.99	-2.74	4.33	....	Reserves and Related Items	79da d
-.54	.08	-6.33	-.09	-.65	-9.80	-2.93	.61	-2.29	.89	-3.02	-13.27	-2.74	4.33	....	Reserve Assets	79db d
											2.28	—	—	....	Use of Fund Credit and Loans	79dc d
															Exceptional Financing	79de d

Government Finance

Year Ending December 31

1987	1988	1989	1990	1991	1992	1993	1994	1995	1996	1997	1998	1999	2000	2001	Item	Code
-47.46	†-23.95	-3.77	-.05	-1.28	6.61	9.90	6.77 [P]	....							Deficit (-) or Surplus	80
82.26	†93.57	111.60	122.87	121.43	137.42	165.33	181.84 [P]	....							Revenue	81
7.99	11.81	7.52	3.45	2.79	.59		1.64 [P]	....							Grants Received	81z
80.90	†124.79	122.13	123.69	126.51	134.97	155.98	176.49 [P]	....							Expenditure	82
56.81	4.54	.76	2.68	1.17	-1.37	.04	.22 [P]	....							Lending Minus Repayments	83
															Financing	
	†3.83	-9.06	-1.58	-.39	-5.37	-14.20	-10.88 [P]	....							Domestic	84a
	†20.12	12.83	1.63	1.67	-1.24	4.30	4.11 [P]	....							Foreign	85a

National Accounts

Millions of E. Caribbean Dollars

1987	1988	1989	1990	1991	1992	1993	1994	1995	1996	1997	1998	1999	2000	2001	Item	Code
199.9	179.7	204.9	254.6	271.0	253.2	268.9	319.0	354.8	408.1	404.0	413.0	518.8	671.4	....	Househ.Cons.Expend.,incl.NPISHs	96f
56.7	60.2	68.7	79.2	78.1	82.0	92.2	111.1	126.5	132.1	143.2	148.3	174.6	217.8	....	Government Consumption Expend.	91f
98.0	191.3	224.8	238.1	190.8	191.6	242.8	227.9	228.4	304.1	326.7	333.0	293.3	410.7	....	Gross Fixed Capital Formation	93e
186.7	202.9	215.8	224.3	261.9	302.7	312.3	327.2	317.9	339.8	394.3	402.1	386.6	384.3	....	Exports of Goods and Services	90c
249.3	292.2	327.8	365.3	357.5	338.6	380.8	386.4	464.9	520.6	525.9	521.2	550.6	797.4	....	Imports of Goods and Services (-)	98c
292.0	342.0	386.5	429.8	444.2	490.9	535.5	598.7	622.7	663.5	742.3	775.2	822.7	886.8	....	Gross Domestic Product (GDP)	99b
					-27.6	-32.2	-35.3	-29.6	-42.2	-57.0	-69.2	-77.4	-68.9	....	Net Primary Income from Abroad	98.n
					463.3	503.3	563.5	593.1	621.3	685.3	706.1	745.3	817.8	....	Gross National Income (GNI)	99a
					21.7	21.5	29.4	53.9	45.0	42.9	76.6	62.2	135.0	....	Net Current Transf.from Abroad	98t
					485.0	524.9	592.9	647.0	666.3	728.1	782.7	807.5	952.8	....	Gross Nat'l Disposable Inc.(GNDI)	99i
					149.7	163.7	162.8	165.7	126.1	181.0	221.4	114.2	63.5	....	Gross Saving	99s
69.1	75.4	81.1	83.0	83.3	86.0	91.8	96.5	100.0	106.5	113.8	115.1	118.3	....	....	GDP Volume (1995=100)	99bv p
67.8	72.9	76.5	83.2	85.7	91.6	93.7	99.7	100.0	100.0	104.8	108.2	111.6	....	....	GDP Deflator (1995=100)	99bi p

Midyear Estimates

1987	1988	1989	1990	1991	1992	1993	1994	1995	1996	1997	1998	1999	2000	2001	Item	Code
.04	.04	.04	.04	.04	.04	.04	.04	.04	.04	.04	.04	.04	.04	.04	Population	99z

(See notes in the back of the book.)

St. Lucia

	1972	1973	1974	1975	1976	1977	1978	1979	1980	1981	1982	1983	1984	1985	1986
Exchange Rates											*E.Caribbean Dollars per SDR: End of Period (aa)*				
Official Rate .... aa	2.2194	2.4925	2.5024	2.7770	3.1369	3.2797	3.5175	3.5568	3.4436	3.1427	2.9784	2.8268	2.6466	2.9657	3.3026
Official Rate .... ae	2.0442	2.0661	2.0439	2.3721	2.7000	2.7000	2.7000	2.7000	2.7000	2.7000	2.7000	2.7000	2.7000	2.7000	2.7000
											Index Numbers (1995=100):				
Official Rate .... ah x	140.7	137.9	131.6	125.0	103.5	100.0	100.0	100.0	100.0	100.0	100.0	100.0	100.0	100.0	100.0
Nominal Effective Exchange Rate .... ne c	....	....	....	....	....	....	....	....	72.6	70.8	75.0	79.2	83.4	90.1	93.1	88.6
Real Effective Exchange Rate .... re c	....	....	....	....	....	....	....	....	95.6	97.2	106.7	109.4	111.1	116.4	115.0	108.1
Fund Position												*Millions of SDRs:*			
Quota .... 2f. s								3.60	5.40	5.40	5.40	7.50	7.50	7.50	7.50
SDRs .... 1b. s									.07	.23	.01	.01	—	—	—
Reserve Position in the Fund ..... 1c. s									—	—	—	—	—	—	—
Total Fund Cred.&Loans Outstg. 2tl									1.35	4.05	2.55	2.55	2.02	.30	—
International Liquidity											*Millions of US Dollars Unless Otherwise Indicated:*				
Total Reserves minus Gold .... 1l. d	....	....		3.24	5.19	5.65	6.76	8.12	8.29	7.61	8.21	8.87	12.38	12.65	25.11
SDRs .... 1b. d	....	....		....	....	....	....	—	.09	.27	.01	.01	—	—	—
Reserve Position in the Fund .... 1c. d	....	....		....	....	....	....	—	—	—	—	—	—	—	—
Foreign Exchange .... 1d. d	....	....		3.24	5.19	5.65	6.76	8.12	8.20	7.34	8.20	8.86	12.38	12.65	25.11
Deposit Money Banks: Assets .... 7a. d				5.06	5.32	4.70	5.60	7.44	10.07	7.09	8.71	15.00	12.37	19.45	30.42
Liabilities .... 7b. d				8.94	9.12	7.82	9.82	15.05	18.62	14.79	15.48	14.94	15.25	15.78	15.02
Monetary Authorities											*Millions of E. Caribbean Dollars:*				
Foreign Assets 11	....			7.69	14.02	15.26	18.24	21.94	22.38	20.55	22.44	23.94	25.97	39.17	67.81
Claims on Central Government 12a				3.87	3.87	3.87	5.87	9.13	15.81	24.40	20.03	20.06	37.45	34.91	36.05
Claims on Deposit Money Banks 12e													.34		
Reserve Money 14				11.56	17.89	19.14	24.12	31.06	33.54	32.22	34.87	36.80	58.41	73.20	103.87
of which: Currency Outside DMBs 14a				9.56	12.07	15.04	17.67	22.05	24.61	27.69	28.04	30.26	30.08	33.01	39.05
Foreign Liabilities 16c				—	—	—	—	—	4.65	12.73	7.59	7.21	5.35	.89	—
Central Government Deposits 16d				—	—	—	—	—	—	—	—	—	—	—	—
Other Items (Net) 17r				—	—	—	—	—	—	—	—	—	—	—	—
Deposit Money Banks											*Millions of E. Caribbean Dollars:*				
Reserves 20	....	....	....	2.00	5.82	4.10	6.45	9.01	8.93	4.53	6.82	6.54	29.08	36.01	63.19
Foreign Assets 21				12.01	14.35	12.68	15.12	20.10	27.18	19.14	23.53	40.49	33.41	52.52	82.13
Claims on Central Government 22a				19.66	16.23	15.86	10.86	19.30	14.97	12.68	17.41	19.22	20.96	31.01	41.91
Claims on Local Government 22b				—	—	—	—	—	—	—	—	—	—	—	—
Claims on Nonfin.Pub.Enterprises 22c				2.60	3.00	3.90	4.70	5.21	2.17	5.88	4.81	2.47	3.44	2.84	1.99
Claims on Private Sector 22d				61.14	70.01	90.53	110.75	128.40	163.53	184.98	196.95	208.06	237.22	251.61	275.15
Claims on Nonbank Financial Insts 22g				—	—	—	—	.80	.32	.65	.93	1.27	1.56	1.62	1.66
Demand Deposits 24				11.07	16.98	17.97	20.72	23.16	28.06	25.84	29.52	28.13	32.98	38.04	58.58
Time, Savings,& Fgn.Currency Dep. 25				61.46	71.46	73.47	88.99	104.41	114.56	142.91	157.06	187.39	210.97	257.59	314.58
Foreign Liabilities 26c				21.20	24.64	21.11	26.52	40.62	50.28	39.92	41.79	40.33	41.18	42.59	40.56
Central Government Deposits 26d				—	—	—	1.70	3.13	5.81	6.31	7.70	3.37	.62	1.63	6.20
Credit from Monetary Authorities 26g				.30	.90	.50	1.20	.61	.80	—	.40	—	—	—	—
Capital Accounts 27a				2.00	2.00	2.00	2.00	2.22	3.46	6.23	7.12	8.01	9.16	9.40	9.79
Other Items (Net) 27r	....			1.39	−6.56	12.02	6.75	8.68	14.11	6.66	6.86	10.82	30.75	26.36	36.33
Monetary Survey											*Millions of E. Caribbean Dollars:*				
Foreign Assets (Net) 31n				−1.50	3.74	6.83	6.84	1.41	−5.38	−12.96	−3.42	16.89	12.85	48.21	109.38
Domestic Credit 32				87.27	93.11	114.17	130.48	159.72	190.99	222.28	232.42	247.72	300.01	320.36	350.58
Claims on Central Govt. (Net) 32an				23.53	20.10	19.73	15.03	25.31	24.97	30.77	29.73	35.92	57.79	64.29	71.77
Claims on Local Government 32b				—	—	—	—	—	—	—	—	—	—	—	—
Claims on Nonfin.Pub.Enterprises 32c				2.60	3.00	3.90	4.70	5.21	2.17	5.88	4.81	2.47	3.44	2.84	1.99
Claims on Private Sector 32d				61.14	70.01	90.53	110.75	128.40	163.53	184.98	196.95	208.06	237.22	251.61	275.15
Claims on Nonbank Financial Inst 32g				—	—	—	—	.80	.32	.65	.93	1.27	1.56	1.62	1.66
Money 34				20.63	29.05	33.01	38.39	45.22	52.67	53.53	57.57	58.39	63.06	71.05	97.62
Quasi-Money 35				61.46	71.46	73.47	88.99	104.41	114.56	142.91	157.06	187.39	210.97	257.59	314.58
Capital Accounts 37a				2.00	2.00	2.00	2.00	2.22	4.74	8.55	9.32	10.11	11.12	11.60	12.23
Other Items (Net) 37r				1.69	−5.66	12.52	7.95	9.29	13.64	4.33	5.05	8.73	27.71	28.34	35.52
Money plus Quasi-Money 35l				82.09	100.50	106.48	127.37	149.63	167.24	196.44	214.62	245.78	274.03	328.64	412.21
Interest Rates												*Percent Per Annum*			
Treasury Bill Rate 60c	....			....	....	....	....	....	6.5	6.5	6.5	6.5	6.5	7.0	7.0
Deposit Rate 60l								....	5.5	8.0	8.0	8.0	8.6	9.1	7.5
Lending Rate 60p						7.5	7.5	11.0	13.0	13.0	13.0	13.3	14.0	14.0
Prices												*Index Numbers (1995=100):*			
Consumer Prices 64	17.5	19.9	26.7	31.4	34.4	37.5	41.6	45.5	54.3	62.6	65.4	66.4	67.2	†68.2	69.5
International Transactions												*Millions of E. Caribbean Dollars*			
Exports 70	15.11	19.23	32.91	36.81	54.19	66.29	77.68	96.63	157.41	124.36	122.83	149.63	132.40	152.73	234.59
Imports, c.i.f. 71	68.69	74.17	91.12	100.43	125.71	160.23	223.50	273.20	334.20	348.90	318.70	388.40	320.00	337.50	417.90
													1980=100		
Unit Value of Exports 74	....	....	....	62.7	60.3	†71.7	74.7	87.0	100.0	107.4	116.6	123.3	....	....	....

Exchange Rates

E.Caribbean Dollars per US Dollar: End of Period (ae)

1987	1988	1989	1990	1991	1992	1993	1994	1995	1996	1997	1998	1999	2000	2001		
3.8304	3.6334	3.5482	3.8412	3.8622	3.7125	3.7086	3.9416	4.0135	3.8825	3.6430	3.8017	3.7058	3.5179	3.3932	Official Rate	aa
2.7000	2.7000	2.7000	2.7000	2.7000	2.7000	2.7000	2.7000	2.7000	2.7000	2.7000	2.7000	2.7000	2.7000	2.7000	Official Rate	ae

Period Averages

1987	1988	1989	1990	1991	1992	1993	1994	1995	1996	1997	1998	1999	2000	2001		
100.0	100.0	100.0	100.0	100.0	100.0	100.0	100.0	100.0	100.0	100.0	100.0	100.0	100.0	100.0	Official Rate	ah x
84.5	82.0	85.0	84.5	87.3	89.1	98.6	103.2	100.0	102.1	107.0	109.1	110.4	116.2	120.1	Nominal Effective Exchange Rate	ne c
106.0	99.3	101.2	95.5	97.7	98.4	102.3	101.3	100.0	101.3	103.7	106.9	110.3	116.4	....	Real Effective Exchange Rate	re c

Fund Position

End of Period

1987	1988	1989	1990	1991	1992	1993	1994	1995	1996	1997	1998	1999	2000	2001		
7.50	7.50	7.50	7.50	7.50	11.00	11.00	11.00	11.00	11.00	11.00	11.00	15.30	15.30	15.30	Quota	2f. s
—	—	—	1.23	1.27	1.31	1.34	1.36	1.39	1.42	1.45	1.48	1.50	1.43	1.46	SDRs	1b. s
—	—	—	—	—	—	—	—	—	—	—	—	—	—	—	Reserve Position in the Fund	1c. s
—	—	—	—	—	—	—	—	—	—	—	—	—	—	—	Total Fund Cred.&Loans Outstg.	2tl

International Liquidity

End of Period

1987	1988	1989	1990	1991	1992	1993	1994	1995	1996	1997	1998	1999	2000	2001		
30.80	32.65	38.21	44.59	48.75	55.46	60.04	57.79	63.09	56.14	60.98	70.61	74.52	78.83	88.94	Total Reserves minus Gold	1l. d
—	—	—	1.75	1.82	1.80	1.84	1.99	2.07	2.04	1.95	2.08	2.06	1.87	1.84	SDRs	1b. d
—	—	—	—	—	—	—	—	—	—	—	—	—	—	—	Reserve Position in the Fund	1c. d
30.80	32.65	38.21	42.84	46.93	53.66	58.20	55.80	61.02	54.10	59.03	68.54	72.45	76.96	87.10	Foreign Exchange	1d. d
41.77	53.12	39.67	43.66	46.84	48.60	35.08	25.22	30.03	30.28	32.55	53.05	54.27	50.37	65.21	Deposit Money Banks: Assets	7a. d
18.74	19.44	24.14	30.12	32.81	36.37	39.84	53.33	56.32	80.02	94.18	87.29	96.58	84.14	108.82	Liabilities	7b. d

Monetary Authorities

End of Period

1987	1988	1989	1990	1991	1992	1993	1994	1995	1996	1997	1998	1999	2000	2001		
83.12	88.16	105.62	128.65	141.52	149.75	162.21	156.62	170.34	151.58	164.65	190.67	201.19	212.84	240.13	Foreign Assets	11
34.26	30.70	31.60	29.91	30.43	13.82	11.85	9.71	12.94	23.74	13.78	12.76	12.63	11.58	5.96	Claims on Central Government	12a
1.45	1.68	1.10	.48	.04	.81	.02	.02	.02	.02	.03	.09	.08	.02	.06	Claims on Deposit Money Banks	12e
118.84	120.52	135.87	150.78	162.31	160.48	168.11	160.29	178.60	170.67	173.37	197.37	203.61	211.29	246.11	Reserve Money	14
52.06	56.28	67.28	64.23	68.09	64.26	67.88	66.85	75.13	70.30	69.61	77.52	84.06	84.60	82.09	of which: Currency Outside DMBs	14a
—	—	—	—	—	—	—	—	—	—	—	—	—	—	—	Foreign Liabilities	16c
—	.01	2.45	8.25	9.68	3.90	5.97	6.06	4.70	4.67	5.08	6.15	10.29	13.15	.04	Central Government Deposits	16d
—	—	—	—	—	—	—	—	—	—	—	—	—	—	—	Other Items (Net)	17r

Deposit Money Banks

End of Period

1987	1988	1989	1990	1991	1992	1993	1994	1995	1996	1997	1998	1999	2000	2001		
65.96	61.67	69.15	84.98	93.01	97.73	102.30	103.66	97.02	101.94	105.33	108.52	129.00	121.03	152.42	Reserves	20
112.77	143.42	107.11	117.88	126.46	131.23	94.72	68.09	81.07	81.77	87.89	143.24	146.52	135.99	176.07	Foreign Assets	21
43.53	38.42	36.92	34.80	32.63	47.91	52.12	47.49	43.65	48.13	63.06	109.65	119.95	128.28	129.64	Claims on Central Government	22a
	.24	.24	.64	3.91	6.44	1.84	2.09	1.57	1.47	2.31	2.19	1.76	2.39	.25	Claims on Local Government	22b
2.75	2.96	10.61	14.61	11.44	31.27	49.25	57.48	72.67	67.82	64.61	46.72	47.09	65.51	64.56	Claims on Nonfin.Pub.Enterprises	22c
310.21	401.52	519.42	578.48	623.78	683.36	751.43	860.41	946.42	1,071.26	1,171.82	1,258.19	1,394.19	1,481.69	1,541.82	Claims on Private Sector	22d
4.72	10.18	7.88	11.12	10.64	9.59	2.84	8.72	8.28	13.60	14.50	14.11	30.47	30.66	25.91	Claims on Nonbank Financial Insts	22g
70.53	84.00	90.27	103.26	99.84	147.62	157.78	166.37	187.93	174.83	189.68	197.29	227.41	229.15	229.61	Demand Deposits	24
356.75	375.16	444.02	509.31	561.49	546.91	547.77	618.95	673.13	731.81	756.03	848.10	912.16	978.34	1,046.25	Time, Savings,& Fgn.Currency Dep.	25
50.59	52.50	65.17	81.32	88.60	98.20	107.57	143.99	152.07	216.05	254.30	235.68	260.77	227.18	293.82	Foreign Liabilities	26c
8.30	88.53	97.49	117.86	123.47	158.49	174.24	170.92	195.35	213.77	235.09	318.57	354.53	400.96	432.31	Central Government Deposits	26d
—	.16	—	—	2.20	.70	9.03	9.60	2.00	.09	2.10	—	.45	.93	63.23	Credit from Monetary Authorities	26g
11.06	17.73	26.97	26.36	47.44	64.46	65.08	71.81	91.47	92.24	101.87	121.80	168.89	194.76	249.51	Capital Accounts	27a
42.71	40.33	27.41	4.40	-21.18	-8.85	-6.97	-33.70	-51.27	-42.80	-29.57	-38.81	-55.23	-65.78	-224.43	Other Items (Net)	27r

Monetary Survey

End of Period

1987	1988	1989	1990	1991	1992	1993	1994	1995	1996	1997	1998	1999	2000	2001		
145.30	179.08	147.56	165.21	179.39	182.78	149.35	80.73	99.35	17.29	-1.76	98.23	86.95	121.65	122.37	Foreign Assets (Net)	31n
387.17	395.49	506.72	543.45	579.67	630.00	689.13	808.91	885.49	1,007.58	1,089.90	1,118.89	1,241.25	1,305.99	1,335.44	Domestic Credit	32
69.50	-19.41	-31.42	-61.41	-70.09	-100.66	-116.24	-119.78	-143.45	-146.57	-163.33	-202.31	-232.25	-274.25	-297.10	Claims on Central Govt. (Net)	32an
	.24	.24	.64	3.91	6.44	1.84	2.09	1.57	1.47	2.31	2.19	1.76	2.39	.25	Claims on Local Government	32b
2.75	2.96	10.61	14.61	11.44	31.27	49.25	57.48	72.67	67.82	64.61	46.72	47.09	65.51	64.56	Claims on Nonfin.Pub.Enterprises	32c
310.21	401.52	519.42	578.48	623.78	683.36	751.43	860.41	946.42	1,071.26	1,171.82	1,258.19	1,394.19	1,481.69	1,541.82	Claims on Private Sector	32d
4.72	10.18	7.88	11.12	10.64	9.59	2.84	8.72	8.28	13.60	14.50	14.11	30.47	30.66	25.91	Claims on Nonbank Financial Inst	32g
122.58	140.28	157.54	167.50	168.13	212.47	226.02	233.85	263.98	245.65	259.67	276.12	313.48	314.99	311.70	Money	34
356.75	375.16	444.02	509.31	561.49	546.91	547.77	618.95	673.13	731.81	756.03	848.10	912.16	978.34	1,046.25	Quasi-Money	35
13.89	20.42	29.59	29.21	50.30	67.21	67.83	74.73	94.45	95.12	104.57	124.62	171.63	197.37	252.02	Capital Accounts	37a
39.24	38.71	23.13	2.65	-20.87	-13.82	-3.14	-37.89	-46.72	-47.70	-32.14	-31.71	-69.07	-63.05	-152.17	Other Items (Net)	37r
479.34	515.44	601.56	676.80	729.63	759.39	773.79	852.80	937.11	977.45	1,015.70	1,124.22	1,225.64	1,293.33	1,357.96	Money plus Quasi-Money	35l

Interest Rates

Percent Per Annum

1987	1988	1989	1990	1991	1992	1993	1994	1995	1996	1997	1998	1999	2000	2001		
7.0	7.0	7.0	7.0	7.0	7.0	7.0	7.0	7.0	7.0	7.0	7.0	7.0	7.0	7.0	Treasury Bill Rate	60c
5.0	5.0	5.0	5.6	6.1	5.5	5.0	4.5	6.3	7.0	6.3	7.1	9.3	9.3	8.1	Deposit Rate	60l
11.6	10.6	10.0	10.5	10.5	10.5	10.2	10.1	10.0	10.3	10.5	10.5	10.5	10.5	10.5	Lending Rate	60p

Prices

Period Averages

1987	1988	1989	1990	1991	1992	1993	1994	1995	1996	1997	1998	1999	2000	2001		
74.8	75.4	78.4	82.1	86.8	91.2	92.3	94.6	100.0	101.8	102.0	104.2	109.7	....	....	Consumer Prices	64

International Transactions

Millions of E. Caribbean Dollars

1987	1988	1989	1990	1991	1992	1993	1994	1995	1996	1997	1998	1999	2000	2001		
214.80	312.00	294.70	343.70	297.80	331.50	322.98	287.12	335.26	220.94	177.84	....	....	....	....	Exports	70
483.90	595.00	739.10	731.60	797.00	845.00	810.50	814.78	826.30	820.25	896.86	905.09	....	....	....	Imports, c.i.f.	71

1980=100

1987	1988	1989	1990	1991	1992	1993	1994	1995	1996	1997	1998	1999	2000	2001		
....	....	....	....	....	....	....	....	....	....	....	....	....	....	....	Unit Value of Exports	74

St. Lucia

	1972	1973	1974	1975	1976	1977	1978	1979	1980	1981	1982	1983	1984	1985	1986
Balance of Payments															*Millions of US Dollars:*
Current Account, n.i.e. .... 78al d	...	...	...	...	−5.40	−10.90	−23.00	−28.10	−33.30	−39.80	−30.80	−4.91	−13.40	−12.50	−6.68
Goods: Exports f.o.b. .... 78aa d	...	...	...	...	19.10	22.60	26.80	31.90	46.00	41.60	41.60	47.50	47.80	52.00	84.41
Goods: Imports f.o.b. .... 78ab d	...	...	...	...	−43.63	−53.90	−75.27	−91.99	−112.55	−117.17	−107.35	−97.08	−107.71	−113.63	−136.22
Trade Balance..................... 78ac d	...	...	...	...	−24.53	−31.30	−48.47	−60.09	−66.55	−75.57	−65.75	−49.58	−59.91	−61.63	−51.81
Services: Credit .... 78ad d	...	...	...	...	12.50	17.80	27.70	33.80	40.50	38.50	44.70	54.20	64.00	69.50	82.07
Services: Debit .... 78ae d	...	...	...	...	−6.46	−8.40	−12.83	−13.41	−22.15	−23.63	−27.75	−30.02	−38.29	−37.97	−43.34
Balance on Goods & Services ..... 78af d	...	...	...	...	−18.50	−21.90	−33.60	−39.70	−48.20	−60.70	−48.80	−25.40	−34.20	−30.10	−13.08
Income: Credit .... 78ag d	...	...	...	...	.50	.90	1.30	1.00	1.00	1.50		.69	—	—	3.30
Income: Debit .... 78ah d	...	...	...	...	−.30	—	−.50	−.60	−.70	−.90	−1.20	−1.50	−3.20	−3.30	−8.11
Balance on Gds, Serv. & Inc. ...... 78ai d	...	...	...	...	−18.30	−21.00	−32.80	−39.30	−47.90	−60.10	−50.00	−26.21	−37.40	−33.40	−17.89
Current Transfers, n.i.e.: Credit .... 78aj d	...	...	...	...	12.90	10.10	9.80	11.20	14.60	20.30	24.00	27.50	30.40	27.60	15.87
Current Transfers: Debit .... 78ak d	...	...	...	...	—	—	—	—	—	—	−4.80	−6.20	−6.40	−6.70	−4.66
Capital Account, n.i.e. .... 78bc d	...	...	...	...	—	—	—	—	—	—	—	—	—	—	10.50
Capital Account, n.i.e.: Credit .... 78ba d	...	...	...	...	—	—	—	—	—	—	—	—	—	—	10.50
Capital Account: Debit .... 78bb d	...	...	...	...	—	—	—	—	—	—	—	—	—	—	—
Financial Account, n.i.e. .... 78bj d	...	...	...	...	−2.02	15.70	23.06	27.20	29.24	43.76	30.58	7.20	13.86	11.66	6.21
Direct Investment Abroad .... 78bd d	...	...	...	...											
Dir. Invest. in Rep. Econ., n.i.e. .... 78be d	...	...	...	...	3.00	13.00	20.60	26.00	30.90	38.20	26.50	10.00	12.00	17.00	14.52
Portfolio Investment Assets .... 78bf d	...	...	...	...											
Equity Securities..................... 78bk d	...	...	...	...											
Debt Securities .... 78bl d	...	...	...	...											
Portfolio Investment Liab., n.i.e. .... 78bg d	...	...	...	...											
Equity Securities..................... 78bm d	...	...	...	...											
Debt Securities .... 78bn d	...	...	...	...											
Financial Derivatives Assets .... 78bw d	...	...	...	...	...	...	...	...	...	...	...	...	...	...	...
Financial Derivatives Liabilities .... 78bx d	...	...	...	...	...	...	...	...	...	...	...	...	...	...	...
Other Investment Assets .... 78bh d	...	...	...	...	−7.65	.80	−.24	−1.69	−3.27	2.75	−1.42	−5.00	1.29	−7.15	−11.63
Monetary Authorities .... 78bo d	...	...	...	...	...	...	...	...	...	...	...	...	...	...	...
General Government..................... 78bp d	...	...	...	...	—	—	—	—	—	—	—	—	—	—	—
Banks .... 78bq d	...	...	...	...	−7.65	.80	−.24	−1.69	−3.27	2.75	−1.42	−5.00	1.29	−7.15	−11.63
Other Sectors .... 78br d	...	...	...	...	...	...	...	...	...	...	...	...	...	...	...
Other Investment Liab., n.i.e. .... 78bi d	...	...	...	...	2.64	1.90	2.70	2.89	1.61	2.80	5.50	2.20	.57	1.81	3.32
Monetary Authorities .... 78bs d	...	...	...	...											
General Government..................... 78bt d	...	...	...	...	2.64	.80	1.40	.15	.30	2.50	6.00	1.30	−.23	−1.89	2.61
Banks .... 78bu d	...	...	...	...	—	—	—	—	—	—	—	—	—	—	—
Other Sectors .... 78bv d	...	...	...	...	—	1.10	1.30	2.74	1.31	.30	−.50	.90	.80	3.70	.71
Net Errors and Omissions..................... 78ca d	...	...	...	...	9.94	−4.24	.94	2.47	2.11	−8.72	2.58	−1.99	−.26	2.00	1.42
Overall Balance .... 78cb d	...	...	...	...	2.52	.56	1.00	1.57	−1.95	−4.77	2.36	.30	.20	1.16	11.45
Reserves and Related Items .... 79da d	...	...	...	...	−2.52	−.56	−1.00	−1.57	1.95	4.77	−2.36	−.30	−.20	−1.16	−11.45
Reserve Assets .... 79db d	...	...	...	...	−2.52	−.56	−1.00	−1.57	.21	1.50	−.75	−.80	−1.19	−3.00	−11.11
Use of Fund Credit and Loans .... 79dc d	...	...	...	...	—	—	—	—	1.74	3.27	−1.60	—	−.54	−1.75	−.34
Exceptional Financing .... 79de d	...	...	...	...	—	—	—	—	—	—	—	.50	1.53	3.59	
Government Finance															*Millions of E. Caribbean Dollars:*
Deficit (-) or Surplus............................ 80	...	...	...	...			−1.48	4.73	−12.85	−7.84	−15.81	14.30	....	−11.10	−11.40
Revenue 81	...	...	...	...			60.03	83.14	91.79	103.45	116.19	122.28	†119.26	145.80	169.50
Grants Received 81z	...	...	...	...			5.71	13.12	8.95	16.57	21.09	31.81	....	16.30	16.60
Expenditure 82	...	...	...	...			66.58	90.73	112.71	126.95	152.19	138.67	....	173.20	197.50
Lending Minus Repayments 83	...	...	...	...			.64	.80	.88	.91	.90	1.12	....		
Financing															
Domestic 84a	...	...	...	...			−2.72	−8.35	1.32	−5.25	....	....	....	....	....
Foreign 85a	...	...	...	...			4.20	3.62	11.53	13.09	....	....	....	....	....
National Accounts														*Millions of E. Caribbean Dollars*	
Househ.Cons.Expend.,incl.NPISHs 96f	...	...	...	96.5	108.9	110.5	145.2	194.3	176.6	221.8	244.4	238.2	266.7[e]	....	....
Government Consumption Expend........... 91f	...	...	...	23.2	26.5	37.0	44.7	44.8	63.7	71.1	92.1	90.8	102.7[e]	....	....
Gross Fixed Capital Formation 93e	...	...	...	50.1	62.1	77.8	....	....	....	....	....	....	....	....	....
Exports of Goods and Services 90c	...	...	...	51.5	82.8	107.1	147.2	176.3	233.6	216.3	224.1	248.4	261.4[e]	....	....
Imports of Goods and Services (-) 98c	...	...	...	104.8	131.3	166.2	237.9	284.6	351.5	369.1	344.3	316.4	348.4	....	....
Gross Domestic Product (GDP) 99b	...	...	...	123.2	152.5	219.5	257.0	311.7	365.8	418.9	453.0	491.1	541.6	601.8	729.7
Net Primary Income from Abroad 98.n	...	...	...	...	...	...	...	...	...	...	...	...	...	...	...
Gross National Income (GNI) 99a	...	...	...	...	...	...	...	...	...	...	...	...	...	...	...
Net Current Transf.from Abroad 98t	...	...	...	...	...	...	...	...	...	...	...	...	...	...	...
Gross Nat'l Disposable Inc.(GNDI) 99i	...	...	...	...	...	...	...	...	...	...	...	...	...	...	...
Gross Saving 99s	...	...	...	...	...	...	...	...	...	...	...	...	...	...	...
GDP Volume 1990 Prices..................... 99b.p	...	...	...	...		493.0	548.9	571.9	560.0	583.1	596.1	628.4	670.6	723.0	843.4
GDP Volume (1995=100) .... 99bv p	...	...	...	...		40.4	45.0	46.9	45.9	47.8	48.9	51.5	55.0	59.3	69.2
GDP Deflator (1995=100) .... 99bi p	...	...	...	...		36.3	38.2	44.4	53.2	58.5	61.9	63.7	65.8	67.8	70.5
															Millions:
Population............................ 99z	...	.11	.12	.11	.11	.11	.11	.12	.12	.13	.13	.13	.13	.14	.14

Minus Sign Indicates Debit

Balance of Payments	1987	1988	1989	1990	1991	1992	1993	1994	1995	1996	1997	1998	1999	2000	2001	Code
Current Account, n.i.e.	-14.31	-17.91	-63.26	-57.04	-71.85	-56.04	-50.17	-48.38	-33.09	-54.40	-78.39	-65.97	-79.21	-82.41		78al d
Goods: Exports f.o.b.	81.70	122.26	116.04	130.95	113.89	128.55	124.97	99.92	114.65	86.33	70.25	70.37	60.93	54.76		78aa d
Goods: Imports f.o.b.	-156.70	-194.48	-240.89	-238.77	-261.39	-270.84	-264.00	-265.62	-269.38	-267.40	-292.37	-295.06	-312.01	-307.99		78ab d
Trade Balance	-75.00	-72.22	-124.85	-107.82	-147.51	-142.29	-139.03	-165.70	-154.73	-181.08	-222.12	-224.69	-251.08	-253.23		78ac d
Services: Credit	98.44	117.19	136.43	150.60	172.19	195.30	203.00	237.69	265.03	266.79	288.42	313.81	321.07	308.52		78ad d
Services: Debit	-46.52	-59.64	-71.32	-81.22	-80.55	-89.30	-89.91	-104.16	-123.55	-119.53	-119.01	-129.27	-133.14	-118.25		78ae d
Balance on Goods & Services	-23.08	-14.68	-59.74	-38.44	-55.87	-36.29	-25.95	-32.18	-13.24	-33.81	-52.71	-40.14	-63.15	-62.96		78af d
Income: Credit	4.11	6.41	5.85	5.94	4.63	5.46	4.33	4.97	5.75	3.36	3.29	3.39	2.38	3.90		78ag d
Income: Debit	-9.15	-17.22	-16.44	-32.13	-34.28	-34.23	-38.11	-38.33	-44.53	-37.13	-41.95	-48.71	-40.45	-41.38		78ah d
Balance on Gds, Serv. & Inc.	-28.11	-25.50	-70.33	-64.63	-85.52	-65.06	-59.73	-65.54	-52.02	-67.58	-91.37	-85.47	-101.22	-100.44		78ai d
Current Transfers, n.i.e.: Credit	17.90	12.73	12.30	13.86	16.90	16.38	22.20	25.46	28.42	28.53	24.60	29.56	31.64	29.40		78aj d
Current Transfers: Debit	-4.10	-5.15	-5.23	-6.28	-3.23	-7.36	-12.63	-8.30	-9.50	-15.35	-11.61	-10.06	-9.63	-11.38		78ak d
Capital Account, n.i.e.	12.03	7.86	8.48	3.85	6.57	8.95	2.63	10.71	13.21	10.40	9.66	22.54	26.06	17.79		78bc d
Capital Account, n.i.e.: Credit	12.03	7.86	8.48	3.85	6.57	9.13	2.97	11.83	13.58	11.14	10.42	23.31	26.80	20.12		78ba d
Capital Account: Debit	—	—	—	—	—	-.19	-.34	-1.12	-.37	-.74	-.76	-.78	-.74	-2.33		78bb d
Financial Account, n.i.e.	12.13	7.60	52.20	51.54	59.20	65.32	62.29	41.71	27.62	41.43	86.62	55.76	57.36	66.07		78bj d
Direct Investment Abroad	—	—	—	—	—											78bd d
Dir. Invest. in Rep. Econ., n.i.e.	15.00	16.44	26.63	44.79	57.74	40.94	34.16	32.52	32.75	18.41	49.90	83.40	83.06	48.94		78be d
Portfolio Investment Assets	—	—	—	-.14	-.14	....	....	-.47	-.47	-.06	-.06	-.11	....	-.64		78bf d
Equity Securities	—	—	—	—	-.14											78bk d
Debt Securities																78bl d
Portfolio Investment Liab., n.i.e.	—	—	—	.18	—	.37	-.19	.77	.71	1.73	2.99	3.44	-2.90	5.51		78bg d
Equity Securities	—	—	—	.18	—											78bm d
Debt Securities																78bn d
Financial Derivatives Assets																78bw d
Financial Derivatives Liabilities																78bx d
Other Investment Assets	-7.15	-11.52	18.15	1.96	-.48	-5.44	6.83	1.47	-15.34	-9.31	1.00	-31.96	-20.54	-15.00		78bh d
Monetary Authorities																78bo d
General Government	—	—	—	—	—											78bp d
Banks	-7.15	-11.52	18.15	1.96	-.48											78bq d
Other Sectors																78br d
Other Investment Liab., n.i.e.	4.28	2.68	7.42	4.61	2.07	29.45	21.49	7.41	9.97	30.66	32.80	.99	-2.26	27.26		78bi d
Monetary Authorities																78bs d
General Government	5.29	7.41	11.74	4.38	3.12											78bt d
Banks																78bu d
Other Sectors	-1.01	-4.73	-4.32	.23	-1.05											78bv d
Net Errors and Omissions	-.73	4.30	8.18	7.95	13.82	-20.17	-10.13	-7.49	-2.01	-3.71	-12.93	2.78	3.58	6.70		78ca d
Overall Balance	9.11	1.85	5.59	6.30	7.74	-1.94	4.62	-3.45	5.72	-6.29	4.97	15.11	7.79	8.14		78cb d
Reserves and Related Items	-9.11	-1.85	-5.59	-6.30	-7.74	1.94	-4.62	3.45	-5.72	6.29	-4.97	-15.11	-7.79	-8.14		79da d
Reserve Assets	-9.11	-1.85	-5.59	-6.30	-7.74	1.94	-4.62	3.45	-5.72	6.29	-4.97	-15.11	-7.79	-8.14		79db d
Use of Fund Credit and Loans	—	—	—	—	—											79dc d
Exceptional Financing	—	—	—	—	—											79de d

Government Finance

Year Beginning April 1

	1987	1988	1989	1990	1991	1992	1993	1994	1995	1996	1997	1998	1999	2000	2001	Code
Deficit (-) or Surplus	8.10	19.10	10.90	-1.10	....											80
Revenue	193.90	229.90	268.00	265.00	299.80^p											81
Grants Received	27.90	16.70	11.80	3.90	3.30^p											81z
Expenditure	211.60	224.20	267.70	257.70	280.20^p											82
Lending Minus Repayments	2.10	3.30	1.20	12.30												83
Financing																
Domestic																84a
Foreign																85a

National Accounts

Millions of E. Caribbean Dollars

	1987	1988	1989	1990	1991	1992	1993	1994	1995	1996	1997	1998	1999	2000	2001	Code
Househ.Cons.Expend.,incl.NPISHs						900.2	838.5	882.3	904.7	991.4	991.8	1,034.9	1,207.0	1,417.7		96f
Government Consumption Expend.						191.4	195.4	217.1	259.7	261.2	284.1	313.0	290.2	307.6		91f
Gross Fixed Capital Formation						346.2	376.9	389.9	367.2	381.5	417.7	433.1	500.5	474.3		93e
Exports of Goods and Services						869.7	886.1	911.5	1,025.1	953.4	968.4	1,037.3	1,027.7	1,035.6		90c
Imports of Goods and Services (-)						964.4	953.1	1,000.7	1,060.9	1,044.7	1,110.7	1,145.7	1,201.9	1,345.8		98c
Gross Domestic Product (GDP)	799.0	910.5	1,030.7	1,123.5	1,208.9	1,343.0	1,343.7	1,400.2	1,495.8	1,542.5	1,551.2	1,672.6	1,820.2	1,893.2		99b
Net Primary Income from Abroad						-77.7	-91.1	-90.1	-104.7	-91.2	-104.4	-122.4	-102.8	-98.9		98.n
Gross National Income (GNI)						1,265.3	1,252.6	1,310.1	1,391.1	1,451.7	1,446.8	1,550.2	1,720.7	1,790.5		99a
Net Current Transf.from Abroad						24.4	25.0	48.2	51.1	35.6	35.1	52.7	59.4	60.7		98t
Gross Nat'l Disposable Inc.(GNDI)						1,289.7	1,277.5	1,358.3	1,442.2	1,487.3	1,481.9	1,602.8	1,780.2	1,851.2		99i
Gross Saving						198.1	243.7	258.8	277.8	234.7	206.1	255.0	282.9	126.0		99s
GDP Volume 1990 Prices	875.8	1,003.5	1,085.2	1,122.5	1,116.8	1,189.9	1,188.6	1,212.8	1,219.2	1,229.3	1,235.5	....	....	....		99b.p
GDP Volume (1995=100)	71.8	82.3	89.0	92.1	91.6	97.6	97.5	99.5	100.0	100.8	101.3	....	....	....		99bv p
GDP Deflator (1995=100)	74.4	74.0	77.4	81.6	88.2	92.0	92.1	94.1	100.0	102.3	102.3	....	....	....		99bi p

Midyear Estimates

	1987	1988	1989	1990	1991	1992	1993	1994	1995	1996	1997	1998	1999	2000	2001	Code
Population	.14	.15	.13	.13	.14	.14	.14	.14	.15	.15	.15	.15	.15	.15		99z

(See notes in the back of the book.)

St. Vincent & Grens.

		1972	1973	1974	1975	1976	1977	1978	1979	1980	1981	1982	1983	1984	1985	1986
Exchange Rates																
											E. Caribbean Dollars per SDR: End of Period (aa)					
Official Rate	aa	2.2194	2.4925	2.5024	2.7770	3.1369	3.2797	3.5175	3.5568	3.4436	3.1427	2.9784	2.8268	2.6466	2.9657	3.3026
Official Rate	ae	2.0442	2.0661	2.0439	2.3721	2.7000	2.7000	2.7000	2.7000	2.7000	2.7000	2.7000	2.7000	2.7000	2.7000	2.7000
													Index Numbers (1995=100):			
Official Rate	ahx	140.7	137.9	131.6	125.0	103.5	100.0	100.0	100.0	100.0	100.0	100.0	100.0	100.0	100.0	100.0
Nominal Effective Exchange Rate	ne c	....	....	....	....	....	....	....	68.3	66.6	69.8	73.2	76.4	80.4	82.1	82.8
Real Effective Exchange Rate	re c	....	....	....	....	....	....	....	102.1	101.3	107.1	110.9	114.9	116.8	115.6	113.7
Fund Position														*Millions of SDRs:*		
Quota	2f. s	....	....	....	....	....	....	....	1.70	2.60	2.60	2.60	4.00	4.00	4.00	4.00
SDRs	1b. s	....	....	....	....	....	....	....	—	.05	.15	.03	.01	—	—	.01
Reserve Position in the Fund	1c. s	....	....	....	....	....	....	....	—	—	—	—	—	.35	—	—
Total Fund Cred.&Loans Outstg.	2tl								—	.20	1.50	1.50	1.50	1.01	.33	—
International Liquidity										*Millions of US Dollars Unless Otherwise Indicated:*						
Total Reserves minus Gold	1l. d	....	....	....	....	4.66	4.81	5.26	8.90	7.27	9.00	4.78	5.70	12.82	13.80	25.83
SDRs	1b. d	....	....	....	....	....	....	....	—	.06	.17	.03	.01	—	—	.01
Reserve Position in the Fund	1c. d	....	....	....	....	....	....	....	—	—	—	—	.37	—	—	—
Foreign Exchange	1d. d	....	....	....	....	4.66	4.81	5.26	8.90	7.21	8.83	4.75	5.32	12.82	13.80	25.82
Deposit Money Banks: Assets	7a. d	....	....	....	6.02	7.91	7.90	9.03	7.08	8.84	11.21	10.70	9.81	8.49	12.69	19.66
Liabilities	7b. d	....	....	....	5.67	6.34	8.87	9.21	10.29	12.15	12.02	14.26	12.19	13.25	14.18	16.14
Monetary Authorities											*Millions of E. Caribbean Dollars:*					
Foreign Assets	11	....	....	....	7.21	12.58	12.99	14.19	24.04	19.63	24.31	18.58	17.31	25.45	41.93	69.76
Claims on Central Government	12a	....	....	....	1.69	2.94	4.09	4.09	4.09	5.10	8.93	11.48	11.03	19.71	16.37	15.45
Claims on Deposit Money Banks	12e	....	....	....	—	—	—	—	—	—	—	—	—	2.45	.95	—
Reserve Money	14	....	....	....	8.90	15.52	17.07	18.28	28.12	24.04	28.53	25.59	24.10	44.93	58.28	85.21
of which: Currency Outside DMBs	14a	....	....	....	8.00	9.52	9.50	11.07	12.94	12.85	15.36	17.61	20.14	22.53	32.03	41.42
Foreign Liabilities	16c	....	....	....	—	—	—	—	—	—	—	—	—	—	—	—
Central Government Deposits	16d	....	....	....	—	—	—	—	—	.69	4.71	4.47	4.24	2.67	.98	—
Other Items (Net)	17r	....	....	....	—	—	—	—	—	—	—	—	—	—	—	—
Deposit Money Banks											*Millions of E. Caribbean Dollars:*					
Reserves	20	....	....	....	.90	6.00	7.57	7.21	15.18	11.18	13.17	7.98	3.95	27.05	26.81	41.81
Foreign Assets	21	....	....	....	14.29	21.35	21.32	24.37	19.11	23.87	30.25	28.89	26.48	22.93	34.27	53.07
Claims on Central Government	22a	....	....	....	4.80	3.40	6.10	7.00	9.58	4.77	6.16	12.36	12.68	10.67	9.59	31.96
Claims on Local Government	22b															
Claims on Nonfin.Pub.Enterprises	22c	....	....	....	2.70	2.50	3.30	4.70	9.52	11.65	4.57	30.45	35.37	43.96	45.03	21.86
Claims on Private Sector	22d	....	....	....	26.34	26.55	35.88	48.00	54.35	68.03	87.88	83.97	97.54	104.56	107.35	108.18
Claims on Nonbank Financial Insts	22g	....	....	....	.06	.06	.06	.06	.34	.39	.62	.86	.67	.78	.47	1.23
Demand Deposits	24	....	....	....	5.34	6.55	7.10	11.55	14.78	15.21	17.93	17.27	20.42	25.27	20.52	21.74
Time, Savings,& Fgn.Currency Dep.	25	....	....	....	33.76	39.72	44.71	55.58	68.71	73.03	86.70	100.24	111.49	123.58	143.68	163.97
Foreign Liabilities	26c	....	....	....	13.46	17.13	23.94	24.88	27.77	32.81	32.44	38.49	32.93	35.79	38.29	43.58
Central Government Deposits	26d	....	....	....	—	1.50	1.50	1.70	.28	.14	.19	.23	5.84	3.78	3.18	10.42
Credit from Monetary Authorities	26g	....	....	....	—	.70	.80	1.00	—	—	1.34	5.66	1.92	2.07	—	—
Capital Accounts	27a	....	....	....	.40	.40	.40	.40	.45	1.57	3.47	5.73	8.41	10.51	10.97	13.91
Other Items (Net)	27r	....	....	....	-3.87	-6.14	-4.22	-3.77	-3.90	-2.88	.60	-3.11	-4.31	8.94	6.88	4.50
Monetary Survey											*Millions of E. Caribbean Dollars:*					
Foreign Assets (Net)	31n	....	....	....	8.04	16.80	10.37	13.68	15.38	10.00	17.41	4.51	6.62	9.92	36.93	79.25
Domestic Credit	32	....	....	....	35.60	33.96	47.92	62.15	77.60	89.79	107.97	138.89	151.45	175.88	175.64	168.27
Claims on Central Govt. (Net)	32an	....	....	....	6.49	4.84	8.69	9.39	13.39	9.72	14.89	23.61	17.87	26.59	22.79	36.99
Claims on Local Government	32b															
Claims on Nonfin.Pub.Enterprises	32c	....	....	....	2.70	2.50	3.30	4.70	9.52	11.65	4.57	30.45	35.37	43.96	45.03	21.86
Claims on Private Sector	32d	....	....	....	26.34	26.55	35.88	48.00	54.35	68.03	87.88	83.97	97.54	104.56	107.35	108.18
Claims on Nonbank Financial Inst	32g	....	....	....	.06	.06	.06	.06	.34	.39	.62	.86	.67	.78	.47	1.23
Money	34	....	....	....	13.35	16.08	16.61	22.62	27.72	28.06	33.28	34.88	40.56	47.79	52.55	63.16
Quasi-Money	35	....	....	....	33.76	39.72	44.71	55.58	68.71	73.03	86.70	100.24	111.49	123.58	143.68	163.97
Capital Accounts	37a	....	....	....	.40	.40	.40	.40	.45	2.19	4.56	6.77	9.40	11.44	12.01	15.06
Other Items (Net)	37r	....	....	....	-3.87	-5.44	-3.42	-2.77	-3.90	-3.49	.84	1.51	-3.38	3.00	4.33	5.33
Money plus Quasi-Money	35l	....	....	....	47.11	55.79	61.31	78.20	96.43	101.10	119.98	135.12	152.05	171.37	196.23	227.13
Interest Rates														*Percent Per Annum*		
Treasury Bill Rate	60c	....	....	....	....	....	....	....	....	6.5	6.5	6.5	6.5	6.5	6.5	6.5
Deposit Rate	60l	....	....	....	....	....	....	....	....	4.5	4.5	5.5	5.5	5.8	5.9	6.0
Lending Rate	60p	....	....	....	....	....	8.5	8.5	8.5	10.0	10.0	10.0	10.7	12.0	12.1	12.5
Prices													*Index Numbers (1995=100):*			
Consumer Prices	64	....	....	28.7	30.7	34.1	37.6	40.8	47.1	55.2	†62.3	66.8	70.4	72.3	73.9	74.6
International Transactions												*Millions of E. Caribbean Dollars*				
Exports	70	6.6	10.1	14.6	16.4	24.5	26.8	44.0	39.3	41.7	64.9	87.0	110.8	144.6	170.8	172.3
Imports, c.i.f.	71	35.2	38.1	52.3	53.9	62.0	81.9	97.7	125.8	154.2	157.1	175.8	190.0	206.8	213.9	235.7

	1987	1988	1989	1990	1991	1992	1993	1994	1995	1996	1997	1998	1999	2000	2001		
Exchange Rates																	

E.Caribbean Dollars per US Dollar: End of Period (ae)

	1987	1988	1989	1990	1991	1992	1993	1994	1995	1996	1997	1998	1999	2000	2001		
Official Rate ... aa	3.8304	3.6334	3.5482	3.8412	3.8622	3.7125	3.7086	3.9416	4.0135	3.8825	3.6430	3.8017	3.7058	3.5179	3.3932		
Official Rate ... ae	2.7000	2.7000	2.7000	2.7000	2.7000	2.7000	2.7000	2.7000	2.7000	2.7000	2.7000	2.7000	2.7000	2.7000	2.7000		

Period Averages

	1987	1988	1989	1990	1991	1992	1993	1994	1995	1996	1997	1998	1999	2000	2001		
Official Rate ... ah x	100.0	100.0	100.0	100.0	100.0	100.0	100.0	100.0	100.0	100.0	100.0	100.0	100.0	100.0	100.0		
Nominal Effective Exchange Rate ... ne c	80.6	79.1	82.7	82.7	86.0	88.1	98.1	103.4	100.0	102.7	108.7	112.4	113.6	119.4	124.0		
Real Effective Exchange Rate ... re c	108.5	101.9	102.8	100.3	102.5	101.0	108.0	105.0	100.0	104.2	107.8	111.7	111.2	114.2	116.5		

Fund Position

End of Period

	1987	1988	1989	1990	1991	1992	1993	1994	1995	1996	1997	1998	1999	2000	2001		
Quota ... 2f. s	4.00	4.00	4.00	4.00	4.00	6.00	6.00	6.00	6.00	6.00	6.00	6.00	6.00	8.30	8.30		
SDRs ... 1b. s	—	—	—	—	.01	.09	.09	.09	.08	.07	.07	.07	.06	.06	.03		
Reserve Position in the Fund ... 1c. s	—	—	—	—	—	.50	.50	.50	.50	.50	.50	.50	.50	.50	.50		
Total Fund Cred.&Loans Outstg. ... 2tl	—	—	—	—	—	—	—	—	—	—	—	—	—	—	—		

International Liquidity

End of Period

	1987	1988	1989	1990	1991	1992	1993	1994	1995	1996	1997	1998	1999	2000	2001		
Total Reserves minus Gold ... 1l. d	20.22	21.82	22.77	26.49	22.68	33.38	31.51	31.25	29.83	30.19	31.19	38.77	42.58	55.18	61.44		
SDRs ... 1b. d	—	—	—	—	.01	.12	.12	.12	.12	.11	.09	.09	.09	.08	.04		
Reserve Position in the Fund ... 1c. d	—	—	—	—	—	.69	.69	.73	.74	.72	.67	.70	.69	.65	.63		
Foreign Exchange ... 1d. d	20.22	21.82	22.77	26.49	22.67	32.57	30.70	30.40	28.97	29.36	30.42	37.97	41.81	54.45	60.77		
Deposit Money Banks: Assets ... 7a. d	25.23	34.31	37.29	48.65	43.82	41.84	47.01	49.54	45.76	45.09	47.82	53.50	89.92	106.04	105.22		
Liabilities ... 7b. d	17.46	14.49	19.40	19.99	21.76	28.80	29.45	26.77	32.13	35.35	29.73	24.98	51.95	56.70	71.93		

Monetary Authorities

End of Period

	1987	1988	1989	1990	1991	1992	1993	1994	1995	1996	1997	1998	1999	2000	2001		
Foreign Assets ... 11	54.99	60.05	63.90	75.35	65.85	96.75	84.95	84.45	80.56	81.50	84.22	104.67	114.98	148.99	165.88		
Claims on Central Government ... 12a	17.46	10.57	12.79	11.93	15.02	9.04	9.94	9.25	8.68	8.94	9.05	7.61	16.11	8.90	9.20		
Claims on Deposit Money Banks ... 12e	—	—	1.32	.01	.01	.01	.01	.01	.01	—	.01	.01	.01	.03	.01		
Reserve Money ... 14	72.06	69.49	74.27	84.79	76.27	99.19	94.58	91.52	86.59	84.41	92.05	111.17	129.90	156.66	171.62		
of which: Currency Outside DMBs ... 14a	23.27	25.15	32.12	23.96	19.09	30.30	28.22	32.02	28.59	27.01	33.49	36.43	57.49	52.11	51.51		
Foreign Liabilities ... 16c	—	—	—	—	—	—	—	—	—	—	—	—	—	—	—		
Central Government Deposits ... 16d	.39	1.13	2.43	3.81	4.61	6.62	.32	2.19	2.65	6.03	1.23	1.12	1.20	1.27	3.48		
Other Items (Net) ... 17r															—		

Deposit Money Banks

End of Period

	1987	1988	1989	1990	1991	1992	1993	1994	1995	1996	1997	1998	1999	2000	2001		
Reserves ... 20	45.10	40.92	40.11	60.56	55.40	65.36	73.06	60.14	54.30	50.67	60.73	87.28	73.08	111.03	140.46		
Foreign Assets ... 21	68.12	92.64	100.69	131.35	118.31	112.97	126.94	133.75	123.56	121.75	129.13	144.44	242.78	286.30	284.10		
Claims on Central Government ... 22a	37.92	35.94	44.38	31.27	29.34	39.80	42.34	44.25	75.60	74.22	79.23	84.23	95.93	115.31	119.82		
Claims on Local Government ... 22b	—	2.39	—	3.29	3.29	—	—	.26	.11	.06	.18	.16	—	—	.05		
Claims on Nonfin.Pub.Enterprises ... 22c	22.58	25.37	23.67	24.88	25.14	32.16	38.39	47.55	22.03	24.94	21.04	18.71	19.98	22.06	34.10		
Claims on Private Sector ... 22d	130.05	159.41	189.83	204.33	238.67	258.45	265.98	285.12	347.02	398.83	447.16	486.42	545.63	592.09	605.45		
Claims on Nonbank Financial Insts ... 22g	1.33	.72	1.14	3.10	2.91	1.11	2.65	5.85	6.12	13.50	14.45	14.80	14.69	10.71	9.41		
Demand Deposits ... 24	29.89	37.50	37.73	49.37	41.41	61.10	62.86	76.54	79.60	87.43	112.29	131.73	148.38	183.10	207.53		
Time, Savings,& Fgn.Currency Dep. ... 25	190.87	184.16	209.67	245.33	254.37	249.83	279.28	282.14	303.39	321.29	344.21	397.65	453.14	459.71	491.56		
Foreign Liabilities ... 26c	47.15	39.13	52.37	53.96	58.76	77.76	79.51	72.28	86.75	95.43	80.28	67.44	140.26	153.10	194.22		
Central Government Deposits ... 26d	18.18	76.90	75.67	80.55	95.03	95.88	101.95	110.64	124.38	141.22	165.25	196.62	203.79	214.38	212.01		
Credit from Monetary Authorities ... 26g	—	—	.94	—	—	—	—	—	.01	—	.63	.50	.01	7.68	3.15		
Capital Accounts ... 27a	15.18	24.18	20.72	24.26	36.65	31.99	35.65	47.87	51.83	58.98	78.74	71.82	93.54	110.14	119.98		
Other Items (Net) ... 27r	3.82	-4.48	2.71	5.31	-13.15	-6.71	-9.89	-12.57	-17.22	-20.39	-29.49	-29.72	-47.03	9.40	-35.06		

Monetary Survey

End of Period

	1987	1988	1989	1990	1991	1992	1993	1994	1995	1996	1997	1998	1999	2000	2001		
Foreign Assets (Net) ... 31n	75.96	113.55	112.22	152.73	125.40	131.96	132.38	145.92	117.37	107.81	133.07	181.67	217.49	282.19	255.76		
Domestic Credit ... 32	190.77	156.36	193.70	194.44	214.74	238.06	257.04	279.43	332.52	373.23	404.63	414.18	487.35	533.43	562.54		
Claims on Central Govt. (Net) ... 32an	36.80	-31.53	-20.93	-41.16	-55.28	-53.66	-49.98	-59.34	-42.75	-64.09	-78.20	-105.90	-92.95	-91.43	-86.47		
Claims on Local Government ... 32b	—	2.39	—	3.29	3.29	—	—	.26	.11	.06	.18	.16	—	—	.05		
Claims on Nonfin.Pub.Enterprises ... 32c	22.58	25.37	23.67	24.88	25.14	32.16	38.39	47.55	22.03	24.94	21.04	18.71	19.98	22.06	34.10		
Claims on Private Sector ... 32d	130.05	159.41	189.83	204.33	238.67	258.45	265.98	285.12	347.02	398.83	447.16	486.42	545.63	592.09	605.45		
Claims on Nonbank Financial Inst ... 32g	1.33	.72	1.14	3.10	2.91	1.11	2.65	5.85	6.12	13.50	14.45	14.80	14.69	10.71	9.41		
Money ... 34	53.16	62.64	69.85	73.33	60.51	91.40	91.10	108.57	108.46	115.03	146.29	168.23	205.90	235.34	259.05		
Quasi-Money ... 35	190.87	184.16	209.67	245.33	254.37	249.83	279.28	282.14	303.39	321.29	344.21	397.65	453.14	459.71	491.56		
Capital Accounts ... 37a	16.52	25.45	21.96	25.60	38.00	33.29	36.95	49.26	53.25	60.36	80.03	73.16	94.85	111.38	121.18		
Other Items (Net) ... 37r	6.17	-2.33	4.44	2.92	-12.73	-4.49	-17.90	-14.63	-15.21	-15.63	-32.83	-43.19	-49.05	9.19	-53.49		
Money plus Quasi-Money ... 35l	244.03	246.80	279.52	318.66	314.87	341.23	370.37	390.71	411.85	436.32	490.50	565.88	659.04	695.05	750.61		

Interest Rates

Percent Per Annum

	1987	1988	1989	1990	1991	1992	1993	1994	1995	1996	1997	1998	1999	2000	2001		
Treasury Bill Rate ... 60c	6.5	6.5	6.5	6.5	6.5	6.5	6.5	6.5	6.5	6.5	6.5	6.5	6.5	6.5	6.5		
Deposit Rate ... 60l	5.3	4.8	4.3	4.3	4.4	5.0	4.3	4.0	5.0	4.5	5.3	5.5	5.5	5.5	5.7		
Lending Rate ... 60p	12.5	12.1	12.4	12.5	13.5	11.4	11.2	11.0	11.0	11.0	12.0	12.5	12.5	11.8	11.0		

Prices

Period Averages

	1987	1988	1989	1990	1991	1992	1993	1994	1995	1996	1997	1998	1999	2000	2001		
Consumer Prices ... 64	77.1	77.3	79.4	85.5	90.2	93.3	97.3	98.3	100.0	104.4	104.9	107.1	108.2	108.4	109.3		

International Transactions

Millions of E. Caribbean Dollars

	1987	1988	1989	1990	1991	1992	1993	1994	1995	1996	1997	1998	1999	2000	2001		
Exports ... 70	141.3	230.2	201.4	223.4	181.2	210.9	156.1	136.1	115.2	125.2	125.0	134.0	131.4	128.0	112.0		
Imports, c.i.f. ... 71	266.4	330.1	344.2	367.4	377.1	356.6	362.7	351.0	367.0	356.0	491.0	520.0	543.0	440.0	502.0		

St. Vincent & Grens.

	1972	1973	1974	1975	1976	1977	1978	1979	1980	1981	1982	1983	1984	1985	1986
Balance of Payments															*Millions of US Dollars:*
Current Account, n.i.e. .... 78al d	...	...	...	...	...	...	2.70	−3.60	−9.30	−.80	−10.81	−2.60	−1.00	3.70	−10.20
Goods: Exports f.o.b. .... 78aa d	...	...	...	...	...	...	18.10	19.10	21.10	29.80	32.19	41.10	53.60	63.20	66.11
Goods: Imports f.o.b. .... 78ab d	...	...	...	...	...	...	−32.91	−42.09	−51.91	−52.91	−58.59	−63.36	−68.94	−71.28	−77.19
Trade Balance............... 78ac d	...	...	...	...	...	...	−14.81	−22.99	−30.81	−23.11	−26.40	−22.26	−15.34	−8.08	−11.07
Services: Credit .... 78ad d	...	...	...	...	...	...	11.10	13.70	17.70	18.90	15.70	17.80	19.10	19.20	26.78
Services: Debit .... 78ae d	...	...	...	...	...	...	−5.59	−9.81	−11.39	−13.29	−15.01	−15.24	−17.26	−17.92	−25.19
Balance on Goods & Services .... 78af d	...	...	...	...	...	...	−9.30	−19.10	−24.50	−17.50	−25.71	−19.70	−13.50	−6.80	−9.49
Income: Credit .... 78ag d	...	...	...	...	...	...	.20	.60	.80	1.40	.20	.20	—	.20	2.26
Income: Debit .... 78ah d	...	...	...	...	...	...	−.20	−1.20	−1.70	−2.10	−2.90	−2.50	−3.00	−3.10	−10.70
Balance on Gds, Serv. & Inc. .... 78ai d	...	...	...	...	...	...	−9.30	−19.70	−25.40	−18.20	−28.41	−22.00	−16.50	−9.70	−17.93
Current Transfers, n.i.e.: Credit .... 78aj d	...	...	...	...	...	...	12.00	21.40	23.90	26.50	26.20	27.10	22.80	22.10	11.67
Current Transfers: Debit .... 78ak d	...	...	...	...	...	...	—	−5.30	−7.80	−9.10	−8.60	−7.70	−7.30	−8.70	−3.93
Capital Account, n.i.e. .... 78bc d	...	...	...	...	...	...	...	...	...	...	...	...	...	...	8.81
Capital Account, n.i.e.: Credit .... 78ba d	...	...	...	...	...	...	—	—	—	—	—	—	—	—	9.00
Capital Account: Debit .... 78bb d	...	...	...	...	...	...	—	—	—	—	—	—	—	—	−.19
Financial Account, n.i.e. .... 78bj d	...	...	...	...	...	...	...	...	...	...	...	...	...	...	...
Direct Investment Abroad .... 78bd d	...	...	...	...	...	...	−.18	5.82	5.65	.87	6.64	3.53	5.47	.83	6.57
Dir. Invest. in Rep. Econ., n.i.e. .... 78be d	...	...	...	...	...	...	−.50	.60	1.10	.50	1.50	2.10	1.40	1.80	7.37
Portfolio Investment Assets .... 78bf d	...	...	...	...	...	...	—	—	—	—	—	—	—	—	—
Equity Securities .... 78bk d	...	...	...	...	...	...	—	—	—	—	—	—	—	—	—
Debt Securities .... 78bl d	...	...	...	...	...	...	—	—	—	—	—	—	—	—	—
Portfolio Investment Liab., n.i.e. .... 78bg d	...	...	...	...	...	...	—	—	—	—	—	—	—	—	—
Equity Securities .... 78bm d	...	...	...	...	...	...	—	—	—	—	—	—	—	—	—
Debt Securities .... 78bn d	...	...	...	...	...	...	—	—	—	—	—	—	—	—	—
Financial Derivatives Assets .... 78bw d	...	...	...	...	...	...	...	...	...	...	...	...	...	...	...
Financial Derivatives Liabilities .... 78bx d	...	...	...	...	...	...	...	...	...	...	...	...	...	...	...
Other Investment Assets .... 78bh d	...	...	...	...	...	...	−1.13	1.95	−1.72	−2.20	.50	.89	1.31	−4.20	−5.30
Monetary Authorities.............. 78bo d	...	...	...	...	...	...	...	...	...	...	...	...	...	...	...
General Government .... 78bp d	...	...	...	...	...	...	—	—	—	—	—	—	—	—	—
Banks .... 78bq d	...	...	...	...	...	...	—	—	—	—	—	—	—	—	—
Other Sectors .... 78br d	...	...	...	...	...	...	−1.13	1.95	−1.72	−2.20	.50	.89	1.31	−4.20	−5.30
Other Investment Liab., n.i.e. .... 78bi d	...	...	...	...	...	...	1.45	3.27	6.27	2.56	4.64	.54	2.76	3.23	4.50
Monetary Authorities.............. 78bs d	...	...	...	...	...	...	...	...	...	...	...	...	...	...	...
General Government .... 78bt d	...	...	...	...	...	...	—	—	.60	.80	1.60	.60	−.10	−.30	5.41
Banks .... 78bu d	...	...	...	...	...	...	.35	1.07	1.87	−.14	2.24	−2.06	1.06	.93	—
Other Sectors .... 78bv d	...	...	...	...	...	...	1.10	2.20	3.80	1.90	.80	2.00	1.80	2.60	−.91
Net Errors and Omissions.............. 78ca d	...	...	...	...	...	...	−2.37	1.63	1.73	.08	.46	−.64	.04	1.86	6.67
Overall Balance .... 78cb d	...	...	...	...	...	...	.15	3.84	−1.92	.14	−3.70	.30	4.52	6.38	11.86
Reserves and Related Items .... 79da d	...	...	...	...	...	...	−.15	−3.84	1.92	−.14	3.70	−.30	−4.52	−6.38	−11.86
Reserve Assets .... 79db d	...	...	...	...	...	...	−.15	−3.84	1.66	−1.74	3.70	−.30	−4.02	−5.70	−11.49
Use of Fund Credit and Loans .... 79dc d	...	...	...	...	...	...	—	—	.26	1.60	—	—	−.49	−.68	−.37
Exceptional Financing .... 79de d	...	...	...	...	...	...	...	...	...	...	...	...	...	...	...
Government Finance										*Millions of E. Caribbean Dollars: Year Ending june 30 through 1990*					
Deficit (-) or Surplus.............. 80	...	...	...	...	...	...	...	...	−.3	1.6	−7.1	−.4	−8.3	6.1	4.4
Revenue 81	...	...	...	...	...	...	24.5	31.8	43.2	45.9	62.9	74.9	78.6	90.8	100.8
Grants Received 81z	...	...	...	...	...	...	6.4	7.4	3.8	12.9	5.3	4.7	4.7	6.1	5.0
Expenditure 82	...	...	...	...	...	...	30.3	41.1	47.3	57.2	75.3	80.0	91.6	90.8	101.4
Lending Minus Repayments 83	...	...	...	...	...	...	—	—	—	—	—	—	—	—	—
Debt: Domestic 88a	...	...	...	...	...	...	...	...	...	...	...	...	...	...	59.0
Foreign 89a	...	...	...	...	...	...	...	...	...	...	...	...	...	...	74.7
National Accounts														*Millions of E. Caribbean Dollars*	
Househ.Cons.Expend.,incl.NPISHs 96f	...	...	...	56.0	66.1	84.4	90.6	123.8	140.9	147.9	177.4	195.4	175.6	175.7	197.5
Government Consumption Expend. 91f	...	...	...	17.0	17.9	21.9	27.6	34.0	37.4	46.8	54.0	58.3	62.9	60.2	67.8
Gross Fixed Capital Formation 93e	...	...	...	18.4	17.1	33.9	34.4	48.6	62.8	64.2	64.7	62.9	70.5	76.2	102.0
Exports of Goods and Services 90c	...	...	...	...	...	...	74.0	76.3	89.5	116.0	135.9	155.7	193.0	222.5	246.0
Imports of Goods and Services (-) 98c	...	...	...	—	—	86.0	103.9	140.2	170.9	178.8	204.7	217.5	231.6	239.9	275.0
Gross Domestic Product (GDP) 99b	...	...	...	70.4	83.7	97.3	122.6	142.6	159.7	196.1	227.4	254.9	277.2	304.6	346.0
Net Primary Income from Abroad 98.n	...	...	...	...	...	...	...	...	−2.4	...	−7.3	...	−8.1	−5.1	−23.0
Gross National Income (GNI) 99a	...	...	...	...	...	...	...	...	157.3	...	220.1	...	269.1	299.5	323.0
Net Current Transf.from Abroad 98t	...	...	...	...	...	...	...	...	...	...	...	...	...	...	...
Gross Nat'l Disposable Inc.(GNDI) 99i	...	...	...	...	...	...	...	...	...	...	...	...	...	...	...
Gross Saving 99s	...	...	...	...	...	...	...	...	...	...	...	...	...	...	...
GDP Volume 1977 Prices 99b.p	...	...	...	83.1	91.7	97.0	91.4	95.7	99.3	105.9	112.0	117.8	124.0	130.7	140.2
GDP Volume 1990 Prices 99b.p	...	...	...	...	...	...	...	...	...	...	...	...	...	...	414
GDP Volume (1995=100) .... 99bv p	...	...	...	39.5	43.6	46.1	43.5	45.5	47.2	50.4	53.3	56.0	59.0	62.1	66.7
GDP Deflator (1995=100).............. 99bi p	...	...	...	25.0	26.9	29.6	39.6	44.0	47.5	54.6	59.9	63.9	66.0	68.8	72.8
Population.............. 99z	...	...	...	...	.11	.11	.12	.12	.10	.10	.11	.11	.11	.11	*Millions:* .11

Balance of Payments

Minus Sign Indicates Debit

Item	1987	1988	1989	1990	1991	1992	1993	1994	1995	1996	1997	1998	1999	2000	2001	Code
Current Account, n.i.e.	-20.24	-16.79	-29.66	-23.56	-45.69	-24.17	-43.87	-57.43	-40.68	-35.74	-84.12	-94.22	-72.34	-26.28		78al d
Goods: Exports f.o.b.	54.37	87.41	77.37	85.41	67.43	79.03	57.13	48.86	61.94	52.56	47.33	50.24	49.61	51.75		78aa d
Goods: Imports f.o.b.	-86.33	-107.59	-112.56	-120.41	-120.35	-116.87	-118.11	-115.43	-119.37	-128.07	-152.61	-169.96	-177.05	-142.92		78ab d
Trade Balance	-31.96	-20.19	-35.19	-35.00	-52.93	-37.84	-60.99	-66.57	-57.43	-75.51	-105.29	-119.71	-127.44	-91.17		78ac d
Services: Credit	36.73	37.10	38.14	44.76	45.94	58.93	62.36	63.40	74.37	96.68	99.41	107.19	125.76	126.23		78ad d
Services: Debit	-27.47	-28.69	-34.05	-31.86	-34.52	-44.82	-44.81	-54.64	-55.14	-58.22	-76.33	-79.05	-66.47	-59.83		78ae d
Balance on Goods & Services	-22.71	-11.78	-31.10	-22.10	-41.51	-23.72	-43.44	-57.81	-38.20	-37.06	-82.21	-91.57	-68.15	-24.77		78af d
Income: Credit	3.96	4.48	4.63	4.62	5.60	4.83	2.89	3.46	4.01	4.02	2.67	3.04	3.16	3.14		78ag d
Income: Debit	-8.22	-15.74	-11.48	-15.67	-16.96	-13.10	-11.11	-15.27	-15.67	-13.15	-15.34	-16.66	-22.78	-23.43		78ah d
Balance on Gds, Serv. & Inc.	-26.97	-23.04	-37.95	-33.14	-52.87	-31.99	-51.66	-69.63	-49.86	-46.18	-94.89	-105.19	-87.77	-45.05		78ai d
Current Transfers, n.i.e.: Credit	12.40	12.33	13.00	14.46	13.80	16.21	16.37	19.42	16.81	19.72	20.83	21.60	23.39	25.43		78aj d
Current Transfers: Debit	-5.67	-6.08	-4.71	-4.87	-6.62	-8.39	-8.59	-7.23	-7.63	-9.28	-10.06	-10.63	-7.96	-6.67		78ak d
Capital Account, n.i.e.	6.80	8.56	10.70	18.64	21.40	13.70	6.31	4.01	5.87	3.83	5.89	13.33	7.82	12.07		78bc d
Capital Account, n.i.e.: Credit	7.12	10.15	12.15	18.88	21.64	14.32	7.00	5.37	6.92	4.94	7.00	14.60	9.12	13.40		78ba d
Capital Account: Debit	-.32	-1.59	-1.44	-.23	-.25	-.62	-.69	-1.36	-1.05	-1.11	-1.12	-1.27	-1.30	-1.33		78bb d
Financial Account, n.i.e.	17.15	3.51	17.52	1.99	19.20	26.58	32.24	39.90	35.11	35.94	81.75	91.23	55.46	14.33		78bj d
Direct Investment Abroad																78bd d
Dir. Invest. in Rep. Econ., n.i.e.	4.96	9.11	10.59	7.67	8.90	13.90	31.40	46.91	30.64	42.64	92.47	88.95	56.09	28.17		78be d
Portfolio Investment Assets	—	—	—	—	—	—	.03	.24	—	-.37	.08	-.37	-.22	-.52		78bf d
Equity Securities	—	—	—	—	—											78bk d
Debt Securities																78bl d
Portfolio Investment Liab., n.i.e.	—	—	—	-.13	.35	.66	.06	—		-2.37	1.61	.26	.11	1.96		78bg d
Equity Securities	—	—	—	—	—											78bm d
Debt Securities	—	—	—	—												78bn d
Financial Derivatives Assets																78bw d
Financial Derivatives Liabilities																78bx d
Other Investment Assets	-3.78	-12.04	1.96	-10.78	2.86	.25	-4.79	-8.92	2.06	-2.33	-5.78	-8.54	-44.83	-8.84		78bh d
Monetary Authorities																78bo d
General Government																78bp d
Banks	-3.78	-12.04	1.96	-10.78												78bq d
Other Sectors																78br d
Other Investment Liab., n.i.e.	15.96	6.44	4.96	5.10	7.58	12.08	4.94	1.60	2.41	-1.63	-6.63	10.94	44.32	-6.44		78bi d
Monetary Authorities																78bs d
General Government	15.19	6.59	4.93	6.44												78bt d
Banks																78bu d
Other Sectors	.78	-.15	.04	-1.34												78bv d
Net Errors and Omissions	-8.93	6.64	2.87	8.35	1.28	-6.57	4.03	13.71	-1.68	-3.66	-2.45	-1.61	12.29	11.93		78ca d
Overall Balance	-5.22	1.93	1.43	5.44	-3.81	9.55	-1.29	.18	-1.38	.37	1.06	8.74	3.23	12.05		78cb d
Reserves and Related Items	5.22	-1.93	-1.43	-5.44	3.81	-9.55	1.29	-.18	1.38	-.37	-1.06	-8.74	-3.23	-12.05		79da d
Reserve Assets	5.22	-1.93	-1.43	-5.44	3.81	-9.55	1.29	-.18	1.38	-.37	-1.06	-8.74	-3.23	-12.05		79db d
Use of Fund Credit and Loans	—	—	—	—	—											79dc d
Exceptional Financing																79de d

Government Finance

Year Ending December 31 Beginning 1991

Item	1987	1988	1989	1990	1991	1992	1993	1994	1995	1996	1997	1998	1999	2000	2001	Code
Deficit (-) or Surplus	5.2	-5.7	-8.7	-12.7	†.3	-27.2	-22.3	-6.7	-2.2	-15.4	-83.7	-70.3[p]				80
Revenue	107.5	116.4	126.9	137.2	†170.0	175.9	185.1	195.6	204.1	220.1	240.5	258.7[p]				81
Grants Received	5.9	3.9	35.5	32.4	†32.3	14.5	.9	2.1	1.5	1.4	12.8	32.6[p]				81z
Expenditure	108.2	126.0	171.1	182.3	†201.9	217.6	208.3	204.4	207.8	236.9	337.0	361.6[p]				82
Lending Minus Repayments					†—											83
Debt: Domestic	68.4	68.3	57.2	59.3	†60.5	70.9	117.4	124.5	133.7	139.4	144.0	147.1[p]				88a
Foreign	84.4	100.2	118.0	145.3	†156.8	181.5	197.3	213.6	236.2	233.0	225.8	256.8[p]				89a

National Accounts

Millions of E. Caribbean Dollars

Item	1987	1988	1989	1990	1991	1992	1993	1994	1995	1996	1997	1998	1999	2000	2001	Code
Househ.Cons.Expend.,incl.NPISHs	244.0	260.0	332.0	341.0	442.0	384.0	465.2	490.5	456.1	487.6	631.5	676.2	593.4	569.3		96f
Government Consumption Expend.	76.6	80.3	92.0	93.6	117.6	149.8	129.3	138.8	144.2	152.4	150.2	156.8	166.6	177.8		91f
Gross Fixed Capital Formation	125.0	135.0	138.0	159.0	169.0	152.8	165.3	185.4	215.4	212.8	235.2	271.7	289.1	238.0		93e
Exports of Goods and Services	240.0	332.0	306.0	352.0	303.0	373.5	322.4	303.9	368.0	402.0	394.7	424.3	472.2	476.8		90c
Imports of Goods and Services (-)	306.0	368.0	395.0	411.0	458.0	430.4	437.4	461.8	471.2	503.0	618.6	672.3	630.8	538.5		98c
Gross Domestic Product (GDP)	383.7	444.0	479.0	535.0	574.0	629.6	644.7	656.8	712.6	751.8	793.1	856.6	890.4	923.4		99b
Net Primary Income from Abroad	-12.0	-30.0	-19.0	-30.0	-30.0	-20.8	-22.2	-31.3	-31.5	-24.6	-34.2	-37.1	-40.1	-42.8		98.n
Gross National Income (GNI)	371.7	414.0	460.0	505.0	544.0	608.9	622.5	625.5	681.1	727.2	758.9	819.6	850.3	880.6		99a
Net Current Transf.from Abroad						21.1	18.9	30.9	24.8	26.3	28.7	30.0	37.9	40.2		98t
Gross Nat'l Disposable Inc.(GNDI)						630.0	641.4	657.4	705.9	753.4	787.6	849.5	888.2	920.8		99i
Gross Saving						96.2	47.0	28.2	105.6	113.5	5.9	16.6	128.3	173.7		99s
GDP Volume 1977 Prices	433	496	509	535	543	575	589	577	621	630	653	687				99b.p
GDP Volume 1990 Prices																99b.p
GDP Volume (1995=100)	69.7	79.9	82.0	86.2	87.4	92.6	94.8	92.9	100.0	101.4	105.2	110.6				99bv p
GDP Deflator (1995=100)	77.2	78.0	82.0	87.1	92.1	95.4	95.4	99.2	100.0	104.0	105.8	108.7				99bi p

Midyear Estimates

Item	1987	1988	1989	1990	1991	1992	1993	1994	1995	1996	1997	1998	1999	2000	2001	Code
Population	.11	.11	.10	.11	.11	.11	.11	.11	.11	.11	.11	.11	.11	.11	.11	99z

(See notes in the back of the book.)

Samoa

		1972	1973	1974	1975	1976	1977	1978	1979	1980	1981	1982	1983	1984	1985	1986
Exchange Rates															*SDRs per Tala:*	
Official Rate	ac	1.3674	1.3666	1.3465	1.1133	1.0759	1.0998	1.0743	.8332	.8438	.7816	.7328	.5895	.4673	.3947	.3720
															US Dollars per Tala:	
Official Rate	ag	1.4847	1.6486	1.6486	1.3033	1.2500	1.3359	1.3996	1.0976	1.0762	.9098	.8083	.6172	.4581	.4336	.4550
Official Rate	rh	1.4806e	1.6281e	1.6486e	1.5920	1.2547	1.2706	1.3586	1.2205	1.0876	.9649	.8297	.6496	.5441	.4457	.4474
													Index Numbers (1995=100):			
Official Rate	ahx	366.0e	402.5e	407.6e	393.6	310.2	314.1	335.9	301.7	268.9	238.5	205.1	160.6	134.5	110.2	110.6
Nominal Effective Exchange Rate	nec	....	....	....	....	....	....	....	224.7	201.6	191.4	180.2	149.7	134.6	119.6	110.1
Real Effective Exchange Rate	rec	....	....	....	....	....	....	....	136.7	145.3	150.2	153.8	141.1	135.1	122.8	114.2
Fund Position															*Millions of SDRs:*	
Quota	2f. s	2.00	2.00	2.00	2.00	2.00	2.00	3.00	3.00	4.50	4.50	4.50	6.00	6.00	6.00	6.00
SDRs	1b. s	.21	.21	.21	.04	—	.03	.04	—	—	.01	.01	.41	.15	.01	.79
Reserve Position in the Fund	1c. s	.36	.36	.36	—	—	—	—	—	—	—	—	—	—	—	—
Total Fund Cred.&Loans Outstg.	2tl	—	—	—	1.26	1.92	1.84	3.49	4.75	4.51	6.41	5.70	7.56	9.97	9.95	8.28
International Liquidity										*Millions of US Dollars Unless Otherwise Indicated:*						
Total Reserves minus Gold	1l. d	4.53	5.08	5.96	6.39	5.24	9.13	4.78	4.82	2.77	3.28	3.48	7.23	10.56	14.02	23.75
SDRs	1b. d	.23	.25	.26	.05	—	.04	.05	—	—	.01	.01	.43	.15	.01	.97
Reserve Position in the Fund	1c. d	.39	.43	.44	—	—	—	—	—	—	—	—	—	—	—	—
Foreign Exchange	1d. d	3.91	4.39	5.26	6.34	5.24	9.09	4.73	4.82	2.77	3.27	3.47	6.80	10.41	14.01	22.78
Other Official Insts.: Assets	3b. d	4.58	3.09	2.30	.91	.69	.74	1.34	.84	.56	.51	.50	.34	.22	.27	.23
Deposit Money Banks: Assets	7a. d	3.45	4.08	5.39	5.42	4.72	7.35	3.89	4.16	2.31	3.01	3.14	6.02	6.89	2.03	3.49
Liabilities	7b. d	.41	.01	—	—	—	—	.05	.65	3.07	.81	1.13	.23	.24	.21	.02
Monetary Authorities															*Millions of Tala:*	
Foreign Assets	11	.71	.60	.77	.74	.42	1.18	.64	.61	.43	.29	.52	2.01	8.00	27.66	44.68
Claims on Central Government	12a	.13	.15	.18	2.39	2.75	3.94	4.85	6.48	9.16	21.64	6.75	6.77	6.65	6.87	1.96
Claims on Deposit Money Banks	12e	—	—	—	—	—	—	—	—	2.73	2.57	1.75	2.03	1.28	4.99	5.05
Reserve Money	14	.13	.15	.18	.38	.48	.66	.67	.84	5.44	7.35	8.41	9.41	10.94	25.09	35.14
of which: Currency Outside DMBs	14a	.12	.14	.17	.19	.22	.23	.25	.17	3.56	5.28	6.05	6.02	7.08	8.44	9.18
Liabs. of Central Bank: Securities	16c	—	—	—	—	—	—	—	—	—	—	—	—	—	—	—
Foreign Liabilities	16c	—	—	—	1.13	1.78	1.67	3.25	5.70	5.34	8.21	7.87	12.84	21.36	25.22	22.26
Central Government Deposits	16d	.56	.44	.61	1.42	.71	2.60	1.37	—	.54	7.48	—	—	—	—	—
Capital Accounts	17a	.15	.15	.16	.19	.20	.19	.20	.62	1.01	1.46	1.57	1.93	2.70	5.41	5.68
Other Items (Net)	17r	—	—	—	—	—	—	—	—	-.08	-.01	-.01	-8.83	-13.37	-19.06	-16.20	-11.39
Deposit Money Banks															*Millions of Tala:*	
Reserves	20	.01	.01	.01	.20	.26	.43	.41	.66	1.89	2.07	2.37	3.39	3.86	16.65	25.96
Claims on Mon.Author.: Securities	20c															
Foreign Assets	21	2.29	2.43	3.27	4.16	3.78	5.50	2.78	3.79	2.14	3.31	3.88	9.76	15.05	4.68	7.67
Claims on Central Government	22a	.65	1.03	1.03	1.20	1.35	2.67	3.39	4.59	6.08	10.86	15.17	8.30	4.42	1.39	2.40
Claims on Nonfin.Pub.Enterprises	22c	—	.41	.34	.36	.58	.55	1.93	4.78	6.65	10.51	12.77	10.57	10.11	12.08	12.25
Claims on Private Sector	22d	3.17	2.85	4.06	3.91	5.91	7.15	9.78	10.73	11.33	11.99	14.17	15.94	19.04	22.39	26.61
Demand Deposits	24	2.19	2.62	3.04	3.29	3.83	4.52	4.97	5.60	5.58	8.83	11.37	10.91	12.28	11.52	12.45
Time, Savings,& Fgn.Currency Dep.	25	1.57	2.12	2.56	2.80	3.59	4.53	5.11	9.01	10.46	18.67	26.89	21.95	24.15	32.44	41.52
Foreign Liabilities	26c	.27	.01	—	—	—	—	.03	.60	2.86	.89	1.39	.37	.52	.67	.04
Central Government Deposits	26d	.59	.28	.42	.67	.55	1.72	1.01	1.18	.60	.98	1.64	1.71	6.16	1.00	6.79
Credit from Monetary Authorities	26g	1.17	1.72	1.95	2.00	2.27	3.29	4.18	5.64	2.73	2.57	1.75	2.03	1.27	4.99	5.05
Capital Accounts	27a	.50	.50	.75	1.00	1.00	1.50	1.47	1.68	1.77	2.23	2.00	3.00	8.73	11.12	12.63
Other Items (Net)	27r	-.17	-.50	.01	.05	.65	.73	1.52	.85	4.09	4.58	3.32	7.97	-.64	-4.55	-3.59
Monetary Survey															*Millions of Tala:*	
Foreign Assets (Net)	31n	2.74	3.02	4.04	3.77	2.41	5.00	.13	-1.89	-5.63	-5.49	-4.86	-1.45	1.17	6.45	30.05
Domestic Credit	32	2.79	3.72	4.58	5.75	9.34	9.98	17.57	25.40	32.08	46.53	47.22	39.87	34.07	41.73	36.43
Claims on Central Govt. (Net)	32an	-.38	.46	.18	1.49	2.85	2.29	5.86	9.89	14.10	24.03	20.28	13.36	4.91	7.26	-2.43
Claims on Nonfin.Pub.Enterprises	32c	—	.41	.34	.36	.58	.55	1.93	4.78	6.65	10.51	12.77	10.57	10.11	12.08	12.25
Claims on Private Sector	32d	3.17	2.85	4.06	3.91	5.91	7.15	9.78	10.73	11.33	11.99	14.17	15.94	19.04	22.39	26.61
Money	34	2.31	2.76	3.21	3.48	4.04	4.76	5.23	5.77	9.14	14.11	17.42	16.93	19.36	19.96	21.63
Quasi-Money	35	1.57	2.12	2.56	2.80	3.59	4.53	5.11	9.01	10.46	18.67	26.89	21.95	24.15	32.44	41.52
Capital Accounts	37a	.65	.65	.91	1.19	1.20	1.69	1.67	2.30	2.78	3.69	3.57	4.93	11.43	16.53	18.31
Other Items (Net)	37r	1.00	1.22	1.95	2.05	2.93	4.01	5.71	6.41	4.08	4.58	-5.52	-5.40	-19.71	-20.75	-14.98
Money plus Quasi-Money	35l	3.88	4.88	5.77	6.28	7.64	9.28	10.33	14.78	19.60	32.77	44.31	38.88	43.51	52.40	63.15
Other Banking Institutions															*Millions of Tala:*	
Deposits	45	.66	.70	.87	.83	.88	.85	.81	.85	.88	.81	1.01	1.15	1.27	1.54	1.59
Liquid Liabilities	55l	4.54	5.58	6.64	7.11	8.52	10.13	11.14	15.63	20.48	33.58	45.32	40.03	44.78	53.94	64.74
Interest Rates															*Percent Per Annum*	
Deposit Rate	60l	....	....	....	....	....	....	....	6.5	6.5	6.5	9.0	11.8	12.0	12.0	13.5
Lending Rate	60p	....	....	....	....	....	....	....	....	....	....	....	20.0	20.0	19.0	18.8
Government Bond Yield	61	....	....	....	....	....	....	....	8.0	8.0	11.5	12.3	14.9	17.5	15.0	14.2

	1987	1988	1989	1990	1991	1992	1993	1994	1995	1996	1997	1998	1999	2000	2001		
																Exchange Rates	
End of Period	.3505	.3459	.3323	.3013	.2855	.2844	.2792	.2794	.2662	.2857	.2679	.2359	.2414	.2297	.2241	Official Rate	**ac**
End of Period (ag) Period Average (rh)	.4973	.4655	.4367	.4286	.4084	.3910	.3835	.4079	.3957	.4108	.3615	.3322	.3313	.2993	.2816	Official Rate	**ag**
	.4716	.4810	.4408	.4330	.4171	.4056	.3894	.3945	.4045	.4062	.3912	.3398	.3320	.3057	.2880	Official Rate	**rh**
Period Averages	116.6	118.9	109.0	107.1	103.1	100.3	96.3	97.5	100.0	100.4	96.7	84.0	82.1	75.6	71.2	Official Rate	**ahx**
	106.9	103.1	98.4	96.7	96.2	96.9	100.0	102.5	100.0	102.2	104.3	100.0	97.2	95.7	96.0	Nominal Effective Exchange Rate	**nec**
	109.3	109.8	106.1	110.8	101.6	105.1	103.1	109.8	100.0	105.0	112.4	108.3	104.6	101.7	103.6	Real Effective Exchange Rate	**rec**
																Fund Position	
End of Period	6.00	6.00	6.00	6.00	6.00	8.50	8.50	8.50	8.50	8.50	8.50	8.50	11.60	11.60	11.60	Quota	**2f. s**
	1.31	2.44	.69	2.94	2.59	1.89	1.95	1.99	2.04	2.10	2.14	2.19	2.24	2.29	2.34	SDRs	**1b. s**
	—	.01	.03	.03	.03	.66	.66	.66	.67	.67	.68	.68	.68	.68	.68	Reserve Position in the Fund	**1c. s**
	5.79	2.85	1.23	.59	.16	—	—	—	—	—	—	—	—	—	—	Total Fund Cred.&Loans Outstg.	**2tl**
																International Liquidity	
End of Period	37.20	49.20	55.07	69.05	67.81	61.16	50.71	50.80	55.31	60.80	64.21	61.42	68.20	63.58	56.64	Total Reserves minus Gold	**1l. d**
	1.86	3.28	.91	4.18	3.70	2.60	2.68	2.91	3.03	3.02	2.89	3.09	3.07	2.99	2.95	SDRs	**1b. d**
	—	.01	.04	.04	.04	.91	.91	.97	1.00	.97	.92	.96	.94	.89	.86	Reserve Position in the Fund	**1c. d**
	35.34	45.90	54.12	64.82	64.06	57.65	47.11	46.92	51.28	56.82	60.39	57.37	64.19	59.70	52.83	Foreign Exchange	**1d. d**
	.33	....	....	....	....	....	....	....	....	....	....	....	....	....	....	Other Official Insts.: Assets	**3b. d**
	5.14	5.40	5.03	5.50	2.79	3.76	3.11	6.26	4.66	5.38	6.98	8.00	11.41	14.61	12.29	Deposit Money Banks: Assets	**7a. d**
	.66	.85	.43	.57	1.21	.22	.50	2.86	.30	.94	2.36	1.40	6.80	6.62	6.77	Liabilities	**7b. d**
																Monetary Authorities	
End of Period	64.47	86.51	117.15	148.25	159.24	135.99	112.38	109.39	119.13	134.91	158.30	166.00	171.41	163.89	157.48	Foreign Assets	**11**
	1.88	2.51	2.51	4.23	1.94	1.69	1.69	.07	.07	—	—	—	—	—	—	Claims on Central Government	**12a**
	11.05	5.35	7.81	29.34	16.89	5.85	6.00	6.23	.06	.03	.06	.09	.06	.83	.33	Claims on Deposit Money Banks	**12e**
	40.37	41.81	58.01	88.33	79.77	63.29	58.25	60.11	62.73	75.57	90.03	48.86	59.31	64.52	61.40	Reserve Money	**14**
	10.53	10.72	12.48	12.94	13.96	12.31	13.95	16.82	21.60	20.96	30.39	24.82	29.09	28.87	29.97	*of which: Currency Outside DMBs*	**14a**
	—	—	—	—	—	—	—	—	—	—	—	25.51	27.39	15.66	7.74	Liabs. of Central Bank: Securities	**16ac**
	16.52	8.24	3.70	1.96	.56	—	—	—	—	—	.03	.14	.10	1.66	.18	Foreign Liabilities	**16c**
	13.93	33.59	49.97	66.37	79.40	79.89	64.54	49.07	48.36	56.78	69.60	90.21	83.37	78.12	85.59	Central Government Deposits	**16d**
	6.12	10.45	12.59	22.26	27.86	24.94	26.58	28.30	27.61	27.52	28.47	30.30	30.30	30.26	31.29	Capital Accounts	**17a**
	.46	.29	3.19	2.90	−9.53	−24.59	−29.31	−21.78	−19.44	−24.93	−29.78	−28.93	−29.00	−25.50	−28.38	Other Items (Net)	**17r**
																Deposit Money Banks	
End of Period	29.84	31.09	45.53	75.39	65.80	50.98	44.30	43.29	41.13	54.41	59.64	24.04	30.22	35.65	31.43	Reserves	**20**
	—	—	—	—	—	—	—	—	—	—	—	25.51	27.39	15.66	7.74	Claims on Mon.Author.: Securities	**20c**
	10.33	11.60	11.52	12.83	6.84	9.61	8.10	15.34	11.78	13.09	19.30	24.09	34.45	48.83	43.66	Foreign Assets	**21**
	4.21	4.42	4.29	3.79	3.45	2.99	3.62	3.67	1.30	.66	—	—	9.41	1.59	9.68	Claims on Central Government	**22a**
	10.48	6.24	4.07	2.57	2.35	2.37	.56	3.16	3.70	4.08	3.24	3.26	13.61	18.79	16.77	Claims on Nonfin.Pub.Enterprises	**22c**
	32.63	39.95	42.32	58.81	63.19	70.91	81.29	75.49	97.38	115.15	137.69	163.84	192.91	231.17	264.43	Claims on Private Sector	**22d**
	18.16	19.47	20.68	34.35	28.97	25.73	29.70	30.38	39.34	39.86	44.14	41.71	51.23	64.41	56.87	Demand Deposits	**24**
	51.96	56.73	68.29	73.69	75.78	81.52	77.63	90.88	110.77	121.68	135.62	148.84	168.92	196.65	220.78	Time, Savings,& Fgn.Currency Dep.	**25**
	1.32	1.83	.98	1.34	2.97	.57	1.30	7.00	.76	2.30	6.52	4.20	20.53	22.13	24.05	Foreign Liabilities	**26c**
	1.95	4.65	5.52	3.01	2.35	1.96	3.01	2.32	3.36	8.31	16.56	14.09	23.79	19.10	17.76	Central Government Deposits	**26d**
	11.02	5.35	7.82	29.34	17.64	5.85	5.99	6.23	.06	.03	.10	.09	.05	.77	.30	Credit from Monetary Authorities	**26g**
	14.68	18.29	19.21	25.97	26.75	22.72	27.26	21.72	22.48	34.61	31.97	37.34	56.52	54.50	60.23	Capital Accounts	**27a**
	−11.60	−13.02	−14.77	−14.31	−12.83	−1.49	−7.02	−17.58	−21.48	−19.40	−15.04	−5.53	−13.05	−5.87	−6.28	Other Items (Net)	**27r**
																Monetary Survey	
End of Period	56.96	88.04	123.99	157.78	162.55	145.03	119.18	117.73	130.15	145.70	171.05	185.75	185.23	188.93	176.91	Foreign Assets (Net)	**31n**
	33.32	14.88	−2.30	.02	−10.82	−3.89	19.61	31.00	50.73	54.80	54.77	62.80	108.77	154.33	187.53	Domestic Credit	**32**
	−9.79	−31.31	−48.69	−61.36	−76.36	−77.17	−62.24	−47.65	−50.35	−64.43	−86.16	−104.30	−97.75	−95.63	−93.67	Claims on Central Govt. (Net)	**32an**
	10.48	6.24	4.07	2.57	2.35	2.37	.56	3.16	3.70	4.08	3.24	3.26	13.61	18.79	16.77	Claims on Nonfin.Pub.Enterprises	**32c**
	32.63	39.95	42.32	58.81	63.19	70.91	81.29	75.49	97.38	115.15	137.69	163.84	192.91	231.17	264.43	Claims on Private Sector	**32d**
	28.69	30.19	33.16	47.29	42.93	38.04	43.65	47.20	60.94	60.82	74.53	66.53	80.32	93.28	86.84	Money	**34**
	51.96	56.73	68.29	73.69	75.78	81.52	77.63	90.88	110.77	121.68	135.62	148.84	168.92	196.65	220.78	Quasi-Money	**35**
	20.80	28.74	31.80	48.23	54.61	47.66	53.84	50.02	50.09	62.13	60.44	67.64	86.82	84.76	91.52	Capital Accounts	**37a**
	−11.17	−12.73	−11.57	−11.41	−21.60	−26.08	−36.34	−39.36	−40.92	−44.13	−44.78	−34.46	−42.06	−31.43	−34.69	Other Items (Net)	**37r**
	80.65	86.92	101.45	120.98	118.71	119.56	121.28	138.08	171.71	182.50	210.15	215.37	249.24	289.93	307.62	Money plus Quasi-Money	**35l**
																Other Banking Institutions	
End of Period	1.72	1.94	3.50	3.86	8.44	6.60	2.56	2.63	....	....	....	....	....	....	....	Deposits	**45**
	82.37	88.86	104.95	124.84	127.15	126.16	123.84	140.71	....	....	....	....	....	....	....	Liquid Liabilities	**55l**
																Interest Rates	
Percent Per Annum	12.0	12.0	12.0	8.3	8.3	6.4	5.5	5.5	5.5	5.5	5.5	6.5	6.5	6.5	5.5	Deposit Rate	**60l**
	17.5	17.5	17.0	13.3	14.8	12.9	12.0	12.0	12.0	12.0	12.0	11.5	11.5	11.0	9.9	Lending Rate	**60p**
	13.5	13.5	13.5	13.5	13.5	13.5	13.5	13.5	13.5	13.5	13.5	13.5	13.5	13.5	13.5	Government Bond Yield	**61**

Samoa

	1972	1973	1974	1975	1976	1977	1978	1979	1980	1981	1982	1983	1984	1985	1986
Prices and Production													*Index Numbers (1995=100):*		
Consumer Prices 64	†10.3	11.5	14.3	15.6	16.4	18.8	19.1	21.3	†28.3	34.1	40.3	47.0	52.6	57.3	60.6
Manufacturing Production 66ey	....	....	....	....	....	....	....	....	....	....	....	....	....	....	....
International Transactions													*Thousands of Tala*		
Exports 70	....	....	....	....	5,447	11,584	8,169	14,981	15,828	11,150	16,248	27,410	36,781	36,180	23,495
Imports, c.i.f. 71	13,044	14,433	15,909	23,160	23,627	†32,254	38,567	60,946	57,438	58,396	60,115	75,100	93,285	115,074	105,375
Balance of Payments													*Millions of US Dollars:*		
Current Account, n.i.e. .... 78al d	....	....	....	....	....	−11.19	−18.10	−22.04	−12.91	−15.12	−6.62	3.51	.66	1.78	7.22
Goods: Exports f.o.b. .... 78aa d						14.73	9.74	18.13	17.22	10.78	13.46	17.69	18.34	16.12	10.51
Goods: Imports f.o.b. .... 78ab d						−37.34	−47.66	−67.15	−56.86	−51.38	−45.31	−44.12	−45.55	−46.60	−42.84
Trade Balance .... 78ac d						−22.61	−37.92	−49.02	−39.64	−40.60	−31.86	−26.42	−27.21	−30.48	−32.34
Services: Credit .... 78ad d						2.42	3.91	3.63	8.43	7.48	8.24	9.13	8.53	10.33	13.34
Services: Debit .... 78ae d						−5.09	−6.76	−9.89	−14.86	−11.59	−12.61	−12.45	−12.18	−11.09	−12.38
Balance on Goods & Services .... 78af d						−25.28	−40.77	−55.28	−46.07	−44.71	−36.22	−29.73	−30.86	−31.23	−31.38
Income: Credit .... 78ag d						—	—	—	.02	.13	.08	.14	.34	.68	1.26
Income: Debit .... 78ah d						−.11	−1.49	−1.62	−2.56	−2.79	−2.24	−2.83	−2.33	−2.58	−2.33
Balance on Gds, Serv. & Inc. .... 78ai d						−25.39	−42.26	−56.90	−48.60	−47.37	−38.37	−32.43	−32.85	−33.13	−32.45
Current Transfers, n.i.e.: Credit .... 78aj d						14.20	24.16	34.86	36.17	32.49	32.29	36.67	33.86	35.48	40.74
Current Transfers: Debit .... 78ak d						—	—	—	−.48	−.25	−.54	−.72	−.35	−.57	−1.06
Capital Account, n.i.e. .... 78bc d	....	....	....	....	....	—	—	—	—	—	—	—	—	—	—
Capital Account, n.i.e.: Credit .... 78ba d						—	—	—	—	—	—	—	—	—	—
Capital Account: Debit .... 78bb d						—	—	—	—	—	—	—	—	—	—
Financial Account, n.i.e. .... 78bj d	....	....	....	....	....	8.87	7.80	19.47	8.19	2.63	−.08	2.58	4.56	−.47	−.74
Direct Investment Abroad .... 78bd d						—	—	—	—	—	—	—	—	—	—
Dir. Invest. in Rep. Econ., n.i.e. .... 78be d						—	—	—	—	—	—	—	—	—	—
Portfolio Investment Assets .... 78bf d						—	—	—	—	—	—	—	—	—	—
Equity Securities .... 78bk d						—	—	—	—	—	—	—	—	—	—
Debt Securities .... 78bl d						—	—	—	—	—	—	—	—	—	—
Portfolio Investment Liab., n.i.e. ...... 78bg d						—	—	—	—	—	—	—	—	—	—
Equity Securities .... 78bm d						—	—	—	—	—	—	—	—	—	—
Debt Securities .... 78bn d						—	—	—	—	—	—	—	—	—	—
Financial Derivatives Assets .... 78bw d						....	....	....	....	....	....	....	....	....	....
Financial Derivatives Liabilities .... 78bx d						....	....	....	....	....	....	....	....	....	....
Other Investment Assets .... 78bh d						—	—	—	—	—	−.05	.08	.02	−.05	.04
Monetary Authorities .... 78bo d						....	....	....	....	....	....	....	....	....	....
General Government .... 78bp d						—	—	—	—	—	—	—	—	—	—
Banks .... 78bq d						—	—	—	—	—	—	—	—	—	—
Other Sectors .... 78br d						—	—	—	—	—	−.05	.08	.02	−.05	.04
Other Investment Liab., n.i.e. .... 78bi d						8.87	7.80	19.47	8.19	2.63	−.03	2.50	4.54	−.42	−.78
Monetary Authorities .... 78bs d						—	—	—	—	—	.07	−.05	.01	−.01	.13
General Government .... 78bt d						3.99	10.88	6.99	6.51	5.56	3.22	3.28	5.73	.73	.51
Banks .... 78bu d						—	.04	.69	2.46	−1.91	.41	−.66	.08	.07	−.28
Other Sectors .... 78bv d						4.87	−3.12	11.79	−.78	−1.03	−3.74	−.07	−1.28	−1.20	−1.14
Net Errors and Omissions .... 78ca d	....	....	....	....	....	4.31	3.56	1.67	2.27	6.80	3.52	1.10	2.00	3.92	.90
Overall Balance .... 78cb d						1.98	−6.75	−.90	−2.45	−5.70	−3.18	7.20	7.22	5.23	7.38
Reserves and Related Items .... 79da d	....	....	....	....	....	−1.98	6.75	.90	2.45	5.70	3.18	−7.20	−7.22	−5.23	−7.38
Reserve Assets .... 79db d						−3.35	4.65	−.77	2.28	−.63	−.65	−4.78	−5.90	−4.09	−9.38
Use of Fund Credit and Loans .... 79dc d						−.09	2.10	1.63	−.31	2.32	−.78	1.97	2.48	−.07	−1.94
Exceptional Financing .... 79de d						1.46	—	.05	.48	4.01	4.61	−4.39	−3.80	−1.07	3.94
National Accounts													*Millions of Tala*		
GDP Volume 1984 Prices .... 99b. p	....	....	....	....	....	....	....	....	....	....	176.6	178.8	181.2	192.0	193.2
GDP Volume 1994 prices .... 99b. p											....	....	....	....	....
GDP Volume (1995=100) .... 99bv p	128.2	137.6	123.0	118.1	129.3	128.0	136.2	154.3	144.9	131.7	130.4	132.0	133.8	141.8	142.7
GDP Deflator (1995=100) .... 99bi p	39.2	44.0	54.9	59.7	62.7	71.8	73.3	82.0	100.0	116.2	21.1	24.6	28.5	28.4	29.7
															Millions:
Population 99z	.15	.15	.15	†.15	.15	.15	.15	.15	.16	.16	.16	.16	.16	.16	.16

	1987	1988	1989	1990	1991	1992	1993	1994	1995	1996	1997	1998	1999	2000	2001		
Period Averages																**Prices and Production**	
	63.4	68.8	73.2	84.4	82.9	90.3	91.9	103.0	100.0	105.4	†112.6	115.1	115.4	116.5	121.2	Consumer Prices	64
								80.4	100.0	111.5	101.8	98.1	....	....	....	Manufacturing Production	66ey
Thousands of Tala																**International Transactions**	
	24,968	31,397	29,206	20,494	15,515	14,349	16,522	9,121	21,859	24,868	38,531	43,243	61,695	46,833	54,049	Exports	70
	131,010	157,296	171,220	186,120	225,337	271,325	269,079	206,347	235,353	247,126	247,377	285,652	346,765	348,607	453,066	Imports, c.i.f.	71
Minus Sign Indicates Debit																**Balance of Payments**	
	7.29	7.95	12.81	7.28	−28.64	−52.50	−38.69	5.76	9.33	12.28	9.13	20.09	−18.79	....	....	Current Account, n.i.e.	78al d
	11.77	15.09	12.87	8.88	6.47	5.82	6.44	3.52	8.76	10.08	14.63	20.40	18.15			Goods: Exports f.o.b.	78aa d
	−55.79	−66.57	−66.99	−70.16	−77.58	−89.90	−87.41	−68.81	−80.29	−90.76	−100.11	−96.91	−115.66			Goods: Imports f.o.b.	78ab d
	−44.02	−51.47	−54.12	−61.29	−71.11	−84.07	−80.98	−65.29	−71.53	−80.67	−85.48	−76.51	−97.51			*Trade Balance*	78ac d
	16.43	26.89	30.90	35.66	30.73	36.65	35.80	43.00	55.70	65.15	65.24	62.56	61.31			Services: Credit	78ad d
	−14.94	−18.25	−18.80	−24.78	−34.62	−43.43	−38.24	−28.17	−35.19	−34.33	−40.08	−29.09	−24.55			Services: Debit	78ae d
	−42.53	−42.83	−42.02	−50.41	−75.00	−90.85	−83.42	−50.46	−51.02	−49.85	−60.32	−43.04	−60.74			*Balance on Goods & Services*	78af d
	2.75	2.89	4.48	6.70	7.21	6.15	4.33	4.03	4.66	5.45	5.52	5.97	2.75			Income: Credit	78ag d
	−2.22	−2.12	−2.39	−1.53	−2.39	−2.55	−4.42	−4.45	−4.42	−2.43	−4.14	−2.39	−2.36			Income: Debit	78ah d
	−42.00	−42.07	−39.94	−45.24	−70.19	−87.25	−83.51	−50.88	−50.79	−46.84	−58.94	−39.47	−60.34			*Balance on Gds, Serv. & Inc.*	78ai d
	50.35	52.95	56.29	56.67	44.64	39.07	49.93	62.75	66.74	66.89	73.71	64.12	44.67			Current Transfers, n.i.e.: Credit	78aj d
	−1.07	−2.93	−3.54	−4.16	−3.09	−4.32	−5.11	−6.11	−6.62	−7.77	−5.65	−4.56	−3.12			Current Transfers: Debit	78ak d
													24.46			Capital Account, n.i.e.	78bc d
	—	—	—	—	—	—	—	—	—	—	—	—	27.11			Capital Account, n.i.e.: Credit	78ba d
	—	—	—	—	—	—	—	—	—	—	—	—	−2.66			Capital Account: Debit	78bb d
	3.15	.49	.48	9.42	21.67	15.94	15.55	−5.46	−5.60	−3.60	−5.93	−4.99	−.73			Financial Account, n.i.e.	78bj d
	—	—	—	—	—	—	—	—	—	—	—	—	—			Direct Investment Abroad	78bd d
	—	—	—	—	—	—	—	—	—	—	—	—	—			Dir. Invest. in Rep. Econ., n.i.e.	78be d
	—	—	—	—	—	—	—	—	—	—	—	—	—			Portfolio Investment Assets	78bf d
	—	—	—	—	—	—	—	—	—	—	—	—	—			Equity Securities	78bk d
	—	—	—	—	—	—	—	—	—	—	—	—	—			Debt Securities	78bl d
	—	—	—	—	—	—	....	....	—	—	—	—	—			Portfolio Investment Liab., n.i.e.	78bg d
	—	—	—	—	—	—	....	....	—	—	—	—	—			Equity Securities	78bm d
	—	—	—	—	—	—	....	....	—	—	—	—	—			Debt Securities	78bn d
																Financial Derivatives Assets	78bw d
																Financial Derivatives Liabilities	78bx d
	−.13	−.31	−.08	−.03	−.22	—	—	—	—	—	—	—	—			Other Investment Assets	78bh d
	....	....	—	—	—	—	—	—	—	—	—	—	—			Monetary Authorities	78bo d
	—	—	—	—	—	—	—	—	—	—	—	—	—			General Government	78bp d
	—	—	—	—	—	—	—	—	—	—	—	—	—			Banks	78bq d
	−.13	−.31	−.08	−.03	−.22	—	—	—	—	—	—	—	—			Other Sectors	78br d
	3.28	.80	.56	9.45	21.90	15.94	15.55	−5.46	−5.60	−3.60	−5.93	−4.99	−.73			Other Investment Liab., n.i.e.	78bi d
	−.04	−.04	—	—	—	—	—	—	−.13	.01	−.01	.16	—			Monetary Authorities	78bs d
	3.29	1.12	1.54	9.73	21.55	16.54	15.26	6.82	3.80	.20	−1.48	−1.04	−2.79			General Government	78bt d
	.60	.25	−.37	.16	.68	−.24	.56	.03	−1.12	1.65	1.05	−.54	5.42			Banks	78bu d
	−.58	−.53	−.61	−.44	−.33	−.36	−.27	−12.18	−8.29	−5.44	−5.49	−3.57	−3.36			Other Sectors	78bv d
	−1.85	1.67	−2.61	−5.68	4.89	23.83	13.83	−4.17	−1.70	−1.30	7.89	−9.59	2.10			Net Errors and Omissions	78ca d
	8.59	10.10	10.68	11.02	−2.08	−12.72	−9.31	−3.86	2.04	7.38	11.09	5.51	7.04			*Overall Balance*	78cb d
	−8.59	−10.10	−10.68	−11.02	2.08	12.72	9.31	3.86	−2.04	−7.38	−11.09	−5.51	−7.04			Reserves and Related Items	79da d
	−9.28	−8.42	−10.66	−11.51	−.42	12.95	8.30	3.86	−2.04	−7.38	−11.09	−5.51	−7.04			Reserve Assets	79db d
	−3.22	−3.96	−2.09	−.86	−.59	−.22	—	—	—	—	—	....	—			Use of Fund Credit and Loans	79dc d
	3.91	2.28	2.07	1.34	3.08	—	1.01	—	—	—	—	—	—			Exceptional Financing	79de d
Millions of Tala																**National Accounts**	
	195.1	194.8	197.3	182.6	131.6	128.6	131.7	126.8	....							GDP Volume 1984 Prices	99b.p
									468.8	500.7	531.4	539.9				GDP Volume 1994 prices	99b.p
	144.1	143.8	145.7	134.8	97.2	95.0	97.2	93.6	100.0	106.1	107.8					GDP Volume (1995=100)	99bv p
	30.9	36.1	35.9	40.4	....	....		105.5	100.0	103.9	116.2					GDP Deflator (1995=100)	99bi p
Midyear Estimates																	
	.16	.16	.16	.16	.05	.05	.05	.05	.06	.06	.06	.06	.07	....	....	Population	99z

(See notes in the back of the book.)

São Tomé & Príncipe

716

		1972	1973	1974	1975	1976	1977	1978	1979	1980	1981	1982	1983	1984	1985	1986
Exchange Rates														*Dobras per SDR:*		
Market Rate	aa	29.3	31.2	30.1	32.2	36.7	45.3	45.3	45.3	45.3	45.3	45.3	45.3	45.3	45.3	45.3
												Dobras per US Dollar: End of Period (ae)				
Market Rate	ae	27.0	25.8	24.6	27.5	31.5	37.3	34.7	34.3	35.5	38.9	41.0	43.2	46.2	41.2	37.0
Market Rate	rf	27.1	24.5	25.4	25.5	30.2	37.6	36.2	35.0	34.8	38.4	41.0	42.3	44.2	44.6	38.6
Fund Position														*Millions of SDRs:*		
Quota	2f. s	...	...	...	...	...	1.60	2.00	2.00	3.00	3.00	3.00	3.00	4.00	4.00	4.00
SDRs	1b. s	...	...	...	...	...	—	—	.21	.17	.37	.37	.36	.08	.04	—
Reserve Position in the Fund	1c. s	...	...	...	...	...	—	.40	.40	.65	.65	.65	.65	—	—	.01
Total Fund Cred.&Loans Outstg.	2tl	...	...	...	...	...	—	—	—	—	—	—	—	—	—	—
International Liquidity												*Millions of US Dollars Unless Otherwise Indicated:*				
Total Reserves minus Gold	1l. d	...	...	...	...	...										
SDRs	1b. d	...	...	...	...	...	—	—	.28	.22	.43	.41	.38	.08	.04	—
Reserve Position in the Fund	1c. d	...	...	...	...	...		.52	.53	.83	.76	.72	.68	—	—	.01
Foreign Exchange	1d. d	...	...	...	...	...										
Monetary Authorities: Other Liab.	4..d	...	...	...	...	...										
Banking Institutions: Assets	7a. d	...	...	...	...	...										
Liabilities	7b. d	...	...	...	...	...										
Monetary Authorities														*Millions of Dobras*		
Foreign Assets	11	...	...	...	...	...	...	...	...	...	...	...	...	...	...	...
Claims on Central Government	12a	...	...	...	...	...	...	...	...	...	...	...	...	...	...	...
Claims on Nonfin.Pub.Enterprises	12c	...	...	...	...	...	...	...	...	...	...	...	...	...	...	...
Claims on Private Sector	12d	...	...	...	...	...	...	...	...	...	...	...	...	...	...	...
Claims on Banking Institutions	12e	...	...	...	...	...	...	...	...	...	...	...	...	...	...	...
Reserve Money	14	...	...	...	...	...	...	...	...	...	...	...	...	...	...	...
of which: Currency Outside Banks	14a	...	...	...	...	...	...	...	...	...	...	...	...	...	...	...
Foreign Liabilities	16c	...	...	...	...	...	...	...	...	...	...	...	...	...	...	...
Central Government Deposits	16d	...	...	...	...	...	...	...	...	...	...	...	...	...	...	...
Counterpart Funds	16e	...	...	...	...	...	...	...	...	...	...	...	...	...	...	...
Capital Accounts	17a	...	...	...	...	...	...	...	...	...	...	...	...	...	...	...
of which: Valuation Adjustment	17rv	...	...	...	...	...	...	...	...	...	...	...	...	...	...	...
Other Items (Net)	17r	...	...	...	...	...	...	...	...	...	...	...	...	...	...	...
Banking Institutions														*Millions of Dobras*		
Reserves	20	...	...	...	...	...	...	...	...	...	...	...	...	...	...	...
Foreign Assets	21	...	...	...	...	...	...	...	...	...	...	...	...	...	...	...
Claims on Private Sector	22d	...	...	...	...	...	...	...	...	...	...	...	...	...	...	...
Demand Deposits	24	...	...	...	...	...	...	...	...	...	...	...	...	...	...	...
Time, Savings,& Fgn.Currency Dep.	25	...	...	...	...	...	...	...	...	...	...	...	...	...	...	...
of which: Fgn. Currency Deposits	25b	...	...	...	...	...	...	...	...	...	...	...	...	...	...	...
Foreign Liabilities	26c	...	...	...	...	...	...	...	...	...	...	...	...	...	...	...
Central Government Deposits	26d	...	...	...	...	...	...	...	...	...	...	...	...	...	...	...
Counterpart Funds	26e	...	...	...	...	...	...	...	...	...	...	...	...	...	...	...
Credit from Monetary Authorities	26g	...	...	...	...	...	...	...	...	...	...	...	...	...	...	...
Capital Accounts	27a	...	...	...	...	...	...	...	...	...	...	...	...	...	...	...
Other Items (Net)	27r	...	...	...	...	...	...	...	...	...	...	...	...	...	...	...
Banking Survey														*Millions of Dobras*		
Foreign Assets (Net)	31n	...	...	...	...	...	...	...	...	...	...	...	...	...	...	...
Domestic Credit	32	...	...	...	...	...	...	...	...	...	...	...	...	...	...	...
Claims on Central Govt.(Net)	32an	...	...	...	...	...	...	...	...	...	...	...	...	...	...	...
Claims on Nonfin.Pub.Enterprises	32c	...	...	...	...	...	...	...	...	...	...	...	...	...	...	...
Claims on Private Sector	32d	...	...	...	...	...	...	...	...	...	...	...	...	...	...	...
Money	34	...	...	...	...	...	...	...	...	...	...	...	...	...	...	...
Quasi-Money	35	...	...	...	...	...	...	...	...	...	...	...	...	...	...	...
Counterpart Funds	36e	...	...	...	...	...	...	...	...	...	...	...	...	...	...	...
Capital Accounts	37a	...	...	...	...	...	...	...	...	...	...	...	...	...	...	...
Other Items (Net)	37r	...	...	...	...	...	...	...	...	...	...	...	...	...	...	...
Money plus Quasi-Money	35l	...	...	...	...	...	...	...	...	...	...	...	...	...	...	...
Interest Rates														*Percent Per Annum*		
Discount Rate *(End of Period)*	60	...	...	...	...	...	...	...	...	...	...	...	...	...	...	...
Deposit Rate	60l	...	...	...	...	...	...	...	...	...	...	...	...	...	...	...
Lending Rate	60p	...	...	...	...	...	...	...	...	...	...	...	...	...	...	...
Population	99z														*Millions:*	
		.07	.08	.08	.08	.08	.08	.08	.08	.09	.10	.10	.10	.10	.11	.11

1987	1988	1989	1990	1991	1992	1993	1994	1995	1996	1997	1998	1999	2000	2001		
															Exchange Rates	
End of Period																
103.3	132.1	184.5	200.6	400.6	516.4	709.7	1,730.4	2,611.6	4,074.0	9,403.9	9,694.3	10,019.3	11,218.9	11,335.3	Market Rate	aa
Period Average (rf)																
72.8	98.2	140.4	141.0	280.0	375.5	516.7	1,185.3	1,756.9	2,833.2	6,969.7	6,885.0	7,300.0	8,610.7	9,019.7	Market Rate	ae
54.2	86.3	124.7	143.3	201.8	321.3	429.9	732.6	1,420.3	2,203.2	4,552.5	6,883.2	7,119.0	7,978.2	8,842.1	Market Rate	rf
															Fund Position	
End of Period																
4.00	4.00	4.00	4.00	4.00	5.50	5.50	5.50	5.50	5.50	5.50	5.50	7.40	7.40	7.40	Quota	2f. s
—	—	.01	—	—	—	.01	.01	.03	.01	—	—	—	—	—	SDRs	1b. s
—	—	—	—	—	—	—	—	—	—	—	—	—	—	—	Reserve Position in the Fund	1c. s
—	—	.80	.80	.80	.80	.80	.72	.56	.40	.24	.08	—	—	—	Total Fund Cred.&Loans Outstg.	2tl
															International Liquidity	
End of Period																
....	....	....	....	....	....	....	....	5.14	5.03	12.43	9.68	10.88	11.64	15.48	Total Reserves minus Gold	1l. d
—	—	.01	—	—	—	.01	.01	.04	.02	—	—	—	—	—	SDRs	1b. d
—	—	—	—	—	—	—	—	—	—	—	—	—	—	—	Reserve Position in the Fund	1c. d
....	....	....	....	....	....	....	....	5.09	5.01	12.43	9.68	10.88	11.64	15.48	Foreign Exchange	1d. d
....	....	....	....	....	....	....	....	5.05	4.94	5.31	—	—	—	2.52	Monetary Authorities: Other Liab.	4.. d
....	....	....	....	....	....	....	....	7.11	8.08	8.03	6.85	6.14	5.45	6.09	Banking Institutions: Assets	7a. d
....	....	....	....	....	....	....	....	1.49	.77	.37	1.34	.34	.43	.30	Liabilities	7b. d
															Monetary Authorities	
End of Period																
....	....	....	....	....	....	....	....	9,026	14,252	86,611	101,965	114,071	147,576	192,855	Foreign Assets	11
....	....	....	....	....	....	....	....	10,290	28,743	28,939	28,831	34,535	32,653	56,425	Claims on Central Government	12a
....	....	....	....	....	....	....	....	7,837	—	—	—	—	—	—	Claims on Nonfin.Pub.Enterprises	12c
....	....	....	....	....	....	....	....	80	204	50	44	38	36	—	Claims on Private Sector	12d
....	....	....	....	....	....	....	....	2,375	1,757	1,839	1,839	—	—	762	Claims on Banking Institutions	12e
....	....	....	....	....	....	....	....	10,462	18,945	46,401	51,085	43,332	56,046	97,885	Reserve Money	14
....	....	....	....	....	....	....	....	4,794	6,845	14,818	18,652	20,945	25,048	35,763	of which: Currency Outside Banks	14a
....	....	....	....	....	....	....	....	10,331	15,614	39,258	795	—	—	22,696	Foreign Liabilities	16c
....	....	....	....	....	....	....	....	—	6,868	41,985	30,994	41,716	47,805	44,046	Central Government Deposits	16d
....	....	....	....	....	....	....	....	10,333	9,091	11,197	24,271	26,178	21,338	22,335	Counterpart Funds	16e
....	....	....	....	....	....	....	....	1,887	-2,356	-13,966	46,025	54,327	57,154	64,493	Capital Accounts	17a
....	....	....	....	....	....	....	....	-2,018	-5,432	-21,841	29,394	34,783	—	—	of which: Valuation Adjustment	17rv
....	....	....	....	....	....	....	....	-3,405	-3,207	-7,436	-20,491	-16,909	-2,076	-1,413	Other Items (Net)	17r
															Banking Institutions	
End of Period																
....	....	....	....	....	....	....	....	5,488	12,730	30,646	30,485	26,620	35,474	62,633	Reserves	20
....	....	....	....	....	....	....	....	12,491	22,880	55,935	47,139	44,819	46,923	54,919	Foreign Assets	21
....	....	....	....	....	....	....	....	6,614	8,599	11,897	22,429	24,969	26,569	29,346	Claims on Private Sector	22d
....	....	....	....	....	....	....	....	9,431	16,837	34,384	27,731	29,178	36,756	57,388	Demand Deposits	24
....	....	....	....	....	....	....	....	6,110	13,830	31,992	35,892	39,793	50,401	61,815	Time, Savings,& Fgn.Currency Dep.	25
....	....	....	....	....	....	....	....	6,011	13,086	30,803	32,763	35,266	43,260	52,932	of which: Fgn. Currency Deposits	25b
....	....	....	....	....	....	....	....	2,626	2,173	2,562	9,205	2,485	3,679	2,721	Foreign Liabilities	26c
....	....	....	....	....	....	....	....	2,462	3,313	1,516	2,447	1,251	2,295	529	Central Government Deposits	26d
....	....	....	....	....	....	....	....	609	105	105	105	2,134	2,134	2,134	Counterpart Funds	26e
....	....	....	....	....	....	....	....	250	1,150	3,700	1,200	—	—	—	Credit from Monetary Authorities	26g
....	....	....	....	....	....	....	....	3,687	11,828	30,722	36,555	36,038	33,934	34,964	Capital Accounts	27a
....	....	....	....	....	....	....	....	-582	-5,028	-6,503	-13,082	-14,470	-20,233	-12,651	Other Items (Net)	27r
															Banking Survey	
End of Period																
....	....	....	....	....	....	....	....	8,559	19,345	100,726	139,104	156,406	190,821	222,358	Foreign Assets (Net)	31n
....	....	....	....	....	....	....	....	22,359	27,365	-2,615	17,863		9,159	41,196	Domestic Credit	32
....	....	....	....	....	....	....	....	7,829	18,562	-14,561	-4,610	-8,432	-17,446	11,850	Claims on Central Govt.(Net)	32an
....	....	....	....	....	....	....	....	7,837	—	—	—	—	—	—	Claims on Nonfin.Pub.Enterprises	32c
....	....	....	....	....	....	....	....	6,694	8,803	11,947	22,473	25,007	26,605	29,346	Claims on Private Sector	32d
....	....	....	....	....	....	....	....	14,225	23,683	49,202	47,584	50,123	61,885	95,483	Money	34
....	....	....	....	....	....	....	....	6,110	13,830	31,992	35,892	39,793	50,401	61,815	Quasi-Money	35
....	....	....	....	....	....	....	....	10,942	9,196	11,302	24,375	28,311	23,472	24,469	Counterpart Funds	36e
....	....	....	....	....	....	....	....	5,574	9,473	16,757	82,580	90,365	91,089	99,456	Capital Accounts	37a
....	....	....	....	....	....	....	....	-5,932	-9,472	-11,142	-33,464	-35,613	-26,866	-17,670	Other Items (Net)	37r
....	....	....	....	....	....	....	....	20,335	37,513	81,195	83,476	89,916	112,286	157,298	Money plus Quasi-Money	35l
															Interest Rates	
Percent Per Annum																
....	....	25.0	25.0	45.0	45.0	30.0	32.0	50.0	35.0	55.0	29.5	17.0	17.0	15.5	Discount Rate (End of Period)	60
....	....	16.0	16.0	35.0	35.0	35.0	35.0	35.0	31.0	36.8	38.3	27.0	†15.0	15.0	Deposit Rate	601
....	....	20.0	20.0	37.0	37.0	37.0	30.0	52.0	38.0	51.5	55.6	40.3	†37.0	37.0	Lending Rate	60p
Midyear Estimates																
.11	.11	.12	.12	.12	.12	.12	.12	.13	.13	.13	.13	.14	.14	.14	**Population**	99z

(*See notes in the back of the book.*)

Saudi Arabia

456

		1972	1973	1974	1975	1976	1977	1978	1979	1980	1981	1982	1983	1984	1985	1986
Exchange Rates																*Riyals per SDR:*
Official Rate	aa	4.5057	4.2825	4.3464	4.1324	4.1013	4.2576	4.3187	4.4328	4.2407	3.9749	3.7892	3.6591	3.5043	4.0037	4.5808
															Riyals per US Dollar:	
Official Rate	ae	4.1500	3.5500	3.5500	3.5300	3.5300	3.5050	3.3150	3.3650	3.3250	3.4150	3.4350	3.4950	3.5750	3.6450	3.7450
Official Rate	rf	4.1448	3.7066	3.5500	3.5176	3.5300	3.5251	3.3996	3.3608	3.3267	3.3825	3.4282	3.4548	3.5238	3.6221	3.7033
															Index Numbers (1995=100):	
Official Rate	ahx	90.2	101.0	105.5	106.5	106.1	106.2	110.2	111.4	112.6	110.7	109.3	108.4	106.3	103.4	101.1
Nominal Effective Exchange Rate	ne c	....	....	....	....	....	....	....	....	121.0	123.7	134.2	144.9	149.6	155.4	154.9	124.9
Real Effective Exchange Rate	re c	....	....	....	....	....	....	....	....	207.9	210.5	214.8	212.7	208.4	194.3	148.6
Fund Position																*Millions of SDRs:*
Quota	2f. s	134	134	134	134	134	134	600	600	1,040	2,100	2,100	3,202	3,202	3,202	3,202
SDRs	1b. s	—	—	—	—	—	—	—	149	213	213	579	487	586	529	336
Reserve Position in the Fund	1c. s	34	34	595	1,570	2,206	2,215	1,896	1,290	1,896	3,428	4,621	8,903	10,188	9,707	8,838
of which: Outstg.Fund Borrowing	2c	—	—	562	1,515	2,150	2,124	1,658	970	1,352	2,439	3,212	6,913	8,104	7,837	7,748
International Liquidity												*Millions of US Dollars Unless Otherwise Indicated:*					
Total Reserves minus Gold	1l. d	2,383	3,747	14,153	23,193	26,900	29,903	†19,200	19,273	23,437	32,236	29,549	27,287	24,748	25,004	18,324
SDRs	1b. d	—	—	—	—	—	—	—	196	271	248	638	510	574	581	411
Reserve Position in the Fund	1c. d	36	40	729	1,838	2,563	2,691	2,470	1,699	2,418	3,990	5,098	9,321	9,986	10,662	10,811
Foreign Exchange	1d. d	2,347	3,707	13,424	21,355	24,337	27,212	†16,730	17,378	20,747	27,998	23,813	17,457	14,188	13,761	7,102
Gold (Million Fine Troy Ounces)	1ad	3.086	3.086	3.081	3.081	3.081	3.081	4.539	4.567	4.567	4.567	4.596	4.596	4.596	4.596	4.596
Gold (National Valuation)	1and	117	130	130	126	125	131	207	211	204	186	177	168	158	177	197
Monetary Authorities: Other Assets	3.. d	....	....	....	15,385	22,564	....	....	....	....	....	....	....	....	....	....
Deposit Money Banks: Assets	7a. d	320	386	458	1,025	2,348	3,218	3,484	5,390	9,692	15,625	17,757	17,848	18,808	19,384	23,143
Liabilities	7b. d	55	91	245	506	1,323	1,238	1,830	2,219	2,752	2,656	1,737	1,945	2,231	2,848	3,815
Other Banking Insts.: Assets	7e. d	....	....	....	....	168	249	286	294	303	379	389	419	406	402	423
Monetary Authorities																*Billions of Riyals:*
Foreign Assets	11	11.79	15.71	77.68	136.40	180.69	207.96	197.99	206.11	288.52	431.85	472.93	437.98	392.21	319.53	276.17
Reserve Money	14	2.87	4.34	5.85	11.84	19.13	31.13	43.40	38.72	34.46	39.20	44.65	43.73	43.00	42.12	45.83
of which: Currency Outside DMBs	14a	2.42	3.05	4.14	6.68	10.59	16.25	19.18	23.71	25.68	29.49	34.44	35.42	35.11	35.77	38.81
Central Government Deposits	16d	8.20	11.83	44.86	89.40	124.99	133.43	112.02	109.01	182.86	321.01	332.73	303.35	258.81	232.34	118.51
Other Items (Net)	17r	.86	.78	27.42	35.17	36.57	43.39	42.57	58.38	71.19	71.64	95.55	90.90	90.40	45.06	111.83
Deposit Money Banks																*Billions of Riyals:*
Reserves	20	.46	1.23	1.61	4.85	7.11	13.03	22.12	13.59	8.19	8.27	10.81	†8.26	11.04	12.56	13.92
Foreign Assets	21	1.32	1.37	1.63	3.62	8.29	11.28	11.55	18.14	32.23	53.36	61.00	†62.38	67.24	70.65	86.67
Claims on Central Government	22a	—	—	—	—	.01	.10	.08	.23	.21	.24	1.97	†—	—	—	.08
Claims on Public Enterprises	22c															
Claims on Private Sector	22d	1.82	2.36	4.43	6.72	9.88	10.68	14.40	26.73	37.25	43.25	50.16	†58.54	62.18	63.49	62.64
Demand Deposits	24	1.36	2.23	3.19	7.50	13.68	22.16	30.03	31.00	33.28	43.49	49.34	†49.51	47.86	46.06	47.47
Quasi-Monetary Deposits	25a	1.21	1.42	1.94	3.13	4.31	5.85	7.63	9.38	13.83	21.93	29.68	†34.13	41.79	44.09	44.92
Foreign Currency Deposits	25b	.06	.10	.50	.47	1.03	1.30	1.20	1.90	4.65	8.08	10.33	†18.02	20.58	21.09	29.36
Foreign Liabilities	26c	.23	.32	.87	1.79	4.67	4.34	6.07	7.47	9.15	9.07	5.97	†6.80	7.97	10.38	14.29
Credit from Monetary Authorities	26g	—	—	—	—	—	—	1.32	.03	.02	.05	†2.06	1.63	5.78	7.43	
Capital Accounts	27a	.20	.24	.33	.68	.94	1.25	1.85	2.54	4.15	5.56	7.82	†14.47	18.16	19.09	20.92
Other Items (Net)	27r	.43	.53	.66	1.35	.24	-.19	-.69	5.60	9.25	10.16	12.54	†2.70	.76	-1.15	-1.63
Monetary Survey																*Billions of Riyals:*
Foreign Assets (Net)	31n	12.88	16.76	78.44	138.23	184.31	214.90	203.47	216.78	311.59	476.14	527.96	†493.56	451.48	379.80	348.55
Domestic Credit	32	-6.37	-9.46	-40.42	-82.67	-115.10	-122.65	-97.54	-82.05	-145.40	-277.52	-280.60	†-246.51	-199.18	-172.53	-59.16
Claims on Central Govt. (Net)	32an	-8.20	-11.83	-44.86	-89.39	-124.98	-133.33	-111.93	-108.78	-182.65	-320.77	-330.76	†-303.35	-258.81	-232.34	-118.51
Claims on Public Enterprises	32c															
Claims on Private Sector	32d	1.82	2.36	4.43	6.72	9.88	10.68	14.40	26.73	37.25	43.25	50.16	56.84	59.63	59.81	59.26
Money	34	3.78	5.29	7.33	14.18	24.27	38.41	49.21	54.70	58.96	72.98	83.78	†84.93	82.98	81.83	86.28
Quasi-Money	35	1.26	1.52	2.44	3.60	5.34	7.14	8.82	11.28	18.48	30.01	40.01	†52.16	62.37	65.18	74.28
Other Items (Net)	37r	1.48	1.60	28.51	37.51	39.19	46.31	47.15	67.96	85.19	88.83	115.19	†108.48	105.24	58.89	128.28
Money plus Quasi-Money	35l	5.04	6.81	9.78	17.78	29.61	45.56	58.03	65.98	77.44	102.99	123.79	†137.09	145.35	147.01	160.56
Other Banking Institutions																*Billions of Riyals:*
Cash	40	.02	.02	.02	.01	†3.73	2.06	3.97	3.57	8.04	7.35	6.33	4.29	3.91	5.28	6.96
Foreign Assets	41	....	....	....	....	.59	.87	.95	.99	1.01	1.29	1.34	1.46	1.45	1.47	1.58
Claims on Private Sector	42d	.04	.05	.05	.13	†12.14	33.31	47.12	63.59	81.20	103.46	132.66	152.83	168.45	173.01	176.49
Capital Accounts	47a	.06	.06	.07	.17	†15.10	32.69	42.83	69.52	91.44	113.75	142.24	160.26	176.73	182.37	185.01
Other Items (Net)	47r	—	—	—	-.03	†1.36	3.55	9.21	-1.36	-1.19	-1.65	-1.92	-1.67	-2.92	-2.61	.03
Interest Rates																*Percent per Annum:*
Deposit Rate	60l	....	....	....	....	....	....	....	....	....	....	....	....	....	....	....
Prices, Production, Labor																*Index Numbers (1995=100):*
Share Prices (1985=100)	62	....	....	....	....	....	....	....	....	....	....	....	....	....	....	....
Wholesale Prices	63	....	....	....	....	....	....	....	....	....	....	....	....	....	67.3	69.8
Consumer Prices	64	31.3	36.5	44.3	59.6	78.5	87.4	†86.0	†87.6	†90.9	93.5	94.4	94.6	93.1	90.3	87.4
Crude Petroleum	66aa	75.2	94.7	105.7	88.2	107.2	114.7	104.0	118.8	123.7	122.5	80.8	63.6	58.1	42.2	62.9
																Number in Thousands:
Employment	67e	....	....	....	....	....	....	....	....	....	....	....	....	....	....	....

1987	1988	1989	1990	1991	1992	1993	1994	1995	1996	1997	1998	1999	2000	2001		
															Exchange Rates	
End of Period																
5.3129	5.0396	4.9215	5.3279	5.3570	5.1494	5.1440	5.4671	5.5669	5.3852	5.0529	5.2731	5.1400	4.8794	4.7065	Official Rate	aa
End of Period (ae) Period Average (rf)																
3.7450	3.7450	3.7450	3.7450	3.7450	3.7450	3.7450	3.7450	3.7450	3.7450	3.7450	3.7450	3.7450	3.7450	3.7450	Official Rate	ae
3.7450	3.7450	3.7450	3.7450	3.7450	3.7450	3.7450	3.7450	3.7450	3.7450	3.7450	3.7450	3.7450	3.7450	3.7450	Official Rate	rf
Period Averages																
100.0	100.0	100.0	100.0	100.0	100.0	100.0	100.0	100.0	100.0	100.0	100.0	100.0	100.0	100.0	Official Rate	ahx
110.4	105.0	109.6	103.9	104.2	102.0	107.4	105.4	100.0	103.6	111.0	118.0	116.0	121.7	128.2	Nominal Effective Exchange Rate	ne c
126.4	118.0	119.3	109.8	110.4	104.3	107.7	103.3	100.0	102.5	107.5	111.3	106.4	108.7	111.8	Real Effective Exchange Rate	re c
															Fund Position	
End of Period																
3,202	3,202	3,202	3,202	3,202	3,202	5,131	5,131	5,131	5,131	5,131	5,131	6,986	6,986	6,986	Quota	2f. s
371	396	467	70	62	202	403	416	448	481	512	546	110	147	192	SDRs	1b. s
8,016	6,540	3,688	2,099	1,292	797	869	604	575	561	532	524	987	1,043	2,036	Reserve Position in the Fund	1c. s
7,352	6,051	3,224	1,712	950	525	175	—	—	—	—	—	—	—	—	*of which:* Outstg. Fund Borrowing	2c
															International Liquidity	
Approximately End of Period																
22,684	20,553	16,748	11,668	11,673	5,935	7,428	7,378	8,622	†14,321	14,876	14,220	16,997	19,585	17,596	Total Reserves minus Gold	1l. d
526	532	614	99	89	278	553	607	666	692	691	769	152	191	242	SDRs	1b. d
11,372	8,801	4,847	2,986	1,848	1,096	1,193	882	854	807	718	737	1,355	1,359	2,558	Reserve Position in the Fund	1c. d
10,786	11,219	11,287	8,582	9,737	4,561	5,682	5,888	7,101	†12,822	13,467	12,714	15,490	18,036	14,796	Foreign Exchange	1d. d
4.596	4.596	4.596	4.596	4.596	4.596	4.596	4.596	4.596	4.596	4.596	4.596	4.596	4.596	4.596	Gold (Million Fine Troy Ounces)	1ad
228	216	211	229	230	221	221	235	239	231	217	226	221	210	202	Gold (National Valuation)	1and
....	....	....	....	....	....	....	....	....	....	....	....	....	....	....	Monetary Authorities: Other Assets	3.. d
27,289	30,639	31,734	32,967	31,761	27,147	29,796	26,208	26,160	28,350	26,573	22,949	24,429	27,024	26,526	Deposit Money Banks: Assets	7a. d
6,538	7,671	9,240	8,057	7,453	7,660	9,958	10,454	10,595	10,321	12,295	11,510	13,659	17,208	15,918	Liabilities	7b. d
1,107	1,122	1,124	1,196	1,138	1,148	1,153	1,150	1,017	1,024	1,042	1,042	1,042	998	1,002	Other Banking Insts.: Assets	7e. d
															Monetary Authorities	
Approximately End of Period																
256.54	232.81	226.64	212.22	208.95	214.89	193.08	185.56	174.04	196.07	219.03	175.60	147.39	183.54	181.80	Foreign Assets	11
46.34	43.44	41.83	52.48	54.53	53.89	53.79	56.23	54.93	54.15	58.24	57.53	71.04	68.20	65.42	Reserve Money	14
38.84	35.95	33.88	44.78	44.62	43.77	42.62	44.97	43.89	43.04	45.82	45.02	55.06	51.02	49.25	*of which:* Currency Outside DMBs	14a
55.01	44.64	26.82	22.32	30.45	41.97	42.48	35.53	34.63	45.52	48.51	48.74	30.99	51.47	51.60	Central Government Deposits	16d
155.19	144.72	157.99	137.42	123.97	119.04	96.81	93.80	84.48	96.40	112.28	69.33	45.35	63.87	64.79	Other Items (Net)	17r
															Deposit Money Banks	
Approximately End of Period																
18.59	10.69	11.75	11.64	12.68	10.65	11.53	11.65	11.18	11.21	12.55	12.57	16.55	18.88	19.15	Reserves	20
102.20	114.74	118.84	123.46	118.95	†101.67	111.59	98.15	97.97	106.17	99.52	85.94	91.49	101.20	99.34	Foreign Assets	21
.12	7.76	10.29	13.33	31.71	†37.92	43.46	50.03	52.28	65.27	83.21	89.37	102.27	112.27	123.83	Claims on Central Government	22a
....	....	....	....	....	24.67	22.60	26.93	24.45	16.70	20.86	23.60	14.35	12.44	10.82	Claims on Public Enterprises	22c
62.14	74.01	78.23	70.99	82.65	†86.04	101.93	113.19	121.15	123.55	133.68	160.66	162.19	172.24	187.06	Claims on Private Sector	22d
51.70	57.48	57.51	57.17	75.38	†79.69	78.89	80.73	81.52	90.08	95.47	95.39	101.76	114.69	130.45	Demand Deposits	24
45.25	44.23	48.30	42.82	48.69	†53.72	56.89	60.60	69.70	81.73	86.27	91.31	95.09	100.09	100.85	Quasi-Monetary Deposits	25a
31.37	40.23	39.76	42.90	46.29	†42.22	48.41	47.29	46.32	44.10	44.88	50.61	49.72	49.29	50.57	Foreign Currency Deposits	25b
24.49	28.73	34.60	30.17	27.91	†28.69	37.29	39.15	39.68	38.65	46.04	43.11	51.15	64.44	59.61	Foreign Liabilities	26c
8.81	10.95	14.11	15.91	16.02	13.37	19.80	21.42	18.63	13.57	18.33	29.44	20.58	10.95	7.46	Credit from Monetary Authorities	26g
22.96	26.76	29.82	31.94	34.50	†28.17	34.48	36.96	39.25	42.65	44.87	47.60	48.69	52.38	53.85	Capital Accounts	27a
-2.98	-2.04	-6.08	-2.79	-4.30	†15.10	15.34	13.80	11.94	12.11	13.96	14.68	19.84	25.20	37.41	Other Items (Net)	27r
															Monetary Survey	
Approximately End of Period																
334.26	318.82	310.88	305.51	299.98	†287.87	267.37	244.55	232.33	263.59	272.50	218.44	187.72	220.30	221.53	Foreign Assets (Net)	31n
3.91	33.65	56.74	56.30	74.90	†106.66	125.52	154.62	163.26	160.00	189.24	224.88	247.81	245.48	270.12	Domestic Credit	32
-54.89	-36.88	-16.54	-8.99	1.26	†-4.05	.98	14.50	17.66	19.75	34.69	40.63	71.27	60.80	72.24	Claims on Central Govt. (Net)	32an
....	....	....	....	....	24.67	22.60	26.93	24.45	16.70	20.86	23.60	14.35	12.44	10.82	Claims on Public Enterprises	32c
58.80	70.52	73.28	65.30	73.64	†86.04	101.93	113.19	121.15	123.55	133.68	160.66	162.19	172.24	187.06	Claims on Private Sector	32d
90.54	93.43	91.38	101.94	120.00	†123.46	121.51	125.69	125.41	133.11	141.29	140.41	156.82	165.71	179.70	Money	34
76.62	84.46	88.06	85.72	94.97	†95.94	105.30	107.89	116.02	125.83	131.15	141.92	144.81	149.38	151.42	Quasi-Money	35
169.55	173.71	187.09	172.85	158.35	†175.13	166.08	165.59	154.17	164.64	189.30	160.99	133.90	150.69	160.52	Other Items (Net)	37r
167.16	177.89	179.44	187.67	214.98	†219.40	226.81	233.58	241.43	258.95	272.44	282.33	301.62	315.09	331.12	Money plus Quasi-Money	35l
															Other Banking Institutions	
Approximately End of Period																
11.77	14.67	14.89	12.66	12.78	18.60	21.88	17.21	14.34	21.92	28.20	21.62	13.00	15.42	20.95	Cash	40
4.14	4.20	4.21	4.48	4.26	4.30	4.32	4.31	3.81	3.84	3.90	3.90	3.90	3.74	3.75	Foreign Assets	41
176.85	175.08	175.78	173.99	172.17	171.36	168.81	172.90	178.07	181.43	178.96	188.18	199.56	198.54	196.77	Claims on Private Sector	42d
190.59	190.66	188.16	190.91	191.42	190.66	190.66	190.46	190.46	190.46	190.46	190.46	191.33	191.19	191.19	Capital Accounts	47a
2.17	3.29	6.72	.21	-2.21	3.61	4.35	3.95	5.76	16.73	20.61	23.25	25.13	26.50	30.28	Other Items (Net)	47r
															Interest Rates	
Percent per Annum																
6.680	8.029	9.036	8.014	5.829	3.649	3.521	5.100	6.178	5.469	5.790	6.211	6.137	6.667	3.922	Deposit Rate	60l
															Prices, Production, Labor	
Period Averages																
78.1	89.2	108.7	98.0	176.5	188.9	179.3	128.3	136.8	153.1	195.8	141.3	202.9	225.8	243.0	Share Prices (1985=100)	62
74.8	84.8	85.8	87.3	89.9	91.1	91.6	93.2	100.0	99.7	99.7	97.9	98.3	98.7	98.6	Wholesale Prices	63
86.1	86.8	87.7	89.6	93.9	93.8	94.8	95.4	100.0	101.2	101.3	100.9	99.3	98.5	98.1	Consumer Prices	64
52.4	64.7	64.2	80.1	101.9	104.1	100.3	100.3	100.0	101.3	99.9	103.2	94.3	101.2	....	Crude Petroleum	66aa
Period Averages																
3,933	3,966	3,518	3,267	3,109	3,140	2,495	2,496	2,495	....	....	....	....	....	....	Employment	67e

Saudi Arabia

456

		1972	1973	1974	1975	1976	1977	1978	1979	1980	1981	1982	1983	1984	1985	1986
International Transactions															*Billions of Riyals*	
Exports	70	19.78	28.92	126.22	104.41	135.15	153.21	138.24	213.18	362.89	405.48	271.09	158.44	132.30	99.54	74.75
Petroleum	70a	22.71	28.92	126.46	104.05	135.91	153.47	127.11	197.02	337.40	377.30	251.16	147.89	120.73	....	66.88
Crude Petroleum	70aa	16.90	26.55	118.93	97.26	127.73	146.00	120.16	186.03	320.45	359.56	235.21	142.15	114.57	....	54.26
Refined Petroleum	70ab	2.09	2.47	7.53	6.79	8.18	7.47	6.95	10.99	16.95	17.75	15.95	5.74	6.16	....	12.62
Imports, c.i.f.	71	4.71	7.31	10.15	14.82	30.69	51.66	69.18	82.22	100.35	119.30	139.34	135.42	118.74	85.56	70.78
Volume of Exports															*1995=100*	
Petroleum	72a	78.5	98.9	110.6	92.2	112.1	118.6	106.5	121.0	126.7	124.3	80.6	56.5	47.9	35.2	52.6
Crude Petroleum	72aa	86.6	111.4	125.8	104.8	127.8	136.6	122.3	140.0	146.9	143.4	89.7	63.2	50.8	33.0	51.9
Refined Petroleum	72ab	42.9	44.0	43.6	36.3	42.7	39.1	36.9	37.0	37.5	40.4	40.6	30.8	34.9	44.9	55.4
Export Prices															*1995=100:*	
Crude Petroleum	76aa d	....	....	....	....	....	....		104.0	173.4	195.6	199.8	173.4	169.1	165.7	118.3
Balance of Payments															*Millions of US Dollars:*	
Current Account, n.i.e.	78al d	2,089	2,520	23,025	14,385	14,360	11,991	−2,212	10,206	41,503	39,627	7,575	−16,852	−18,401	−12,932	−11,795
Goods: Exports f.o.b.	78aa d	4,058	7,702	30,870	27,888	36,314	41,052	37,534	58,771	101,574	112,422	74,203	45,864	37,545	27,478	20,185
Goods: Imports f.o.b.	78ab d	−1,197	−1,853	−3,569	−6,004	−10,385	−14,698	−20,020	−20,911	−25,563	−29,889	−34,444	−33,218	−28,557	−20,364	−17,066
Trade Balance	78ac d	2,861	5,849	27,301	21,884	25,929	26,354	17,514	37,860	76,011	82,533	39,759	12,646	8,987	7,115	3,119
Services: Credit	78ad d	217	356	645	841	1,074	1,407	1,627	4,079	5,191	7,021	4,565	4,151	4,112	3,561	2,606
Services: Debit	78ae d	−509	−955	−2,163	−4,375	−7,935	−10,272	−14,396	−27,318	−30,231	−40,236	−34,852	−37,259	−32,856	−25,822	−20,336
Balance on Goods & Services	78af d	2,570	5,250	25,783	18,351	19,068	17,489	4,745	14,621	50,972	49,318	9,472	−20,462	−19,757	−15,146	−14,611
Income: Credit	78ag d	106	205	1,220	1,839	2,884	3,989	4,301	4,915	7,443	10,956	14,060	15,868	13,366	12,418	11,279
Income: Debit	78ah d	−162	−2,048	−2,445	−2,124	−3,280	−4,079	−4,512	−2,065	−6,917	−9,599	−6,210	−3,022	−3,127	−1,756	−659
Balance on Gds, Serv. & Inc.	78ai d	2,514	3,407	24,558	18,066	18,671	17,398	4,533	17,472	51,498	50,675	17,321	−7,616	−9,518	−4,484	−3,991
Current Transfers, n.i.e.: Credit	78aj d	—	—	—	—	—	—	—	—	—	—	—	—	—	—	—
Current Transfers: Debit	78ak d	−425	−888	−1,532	−3,681	−4,312	−5,407	−6,745	−7,266	−9,995	−11,048	−9,746	−9,237	−8,882	−8,448	−7,804
Capital Account, n.i.e.	78bc d	—	—	—	—	—	—	—	—	—	—	—	—	—	—	—
Capital Account, n.i.e.: Credit	78ba d	—	—	—	—	—	—	—	—	—	—	—	—	—	—	—
Capital Account: Debit	78bb d	—	—	—	—	—	—	—	—	—	—	—	—	—	—	—
Financial Account, n.i.e.	78bj d	−1,033	−1,603	−12,637	−5,327	−10,633	−9,295	−4,488	−9,972	−37,566	−30,059	−9,883	15,343	16,921	12,222	4,176
Direct Investment Abroad	78bd d															
Dir. Invest. in Rep. Econ., n.i.e.	78be d	34	−626	−3,732	1,865	−397	783	556	−1,271	−3,192	6,498	11,128	4,944	4,850	491	967
Portfolio Investment Assets	78bf d	−31	−283	−5,101	−9,923	−9,457	−8,260	2,248	−1,021	−22,007	−32,808	−11,487	7,531	13,413	8,415	3,463
Equity Securities	78bk d															
Debt Securities	78bl d	−31	−283	−5,101	−9,923	−9,457	−8,260	2,248	−1,021	−22,007	−32,808	−11,487	7,531	13,413	8,415	3,463
Portfolio Investment Liab., n.i.e.	78bg d	—	—	—	—	—	—	—	—	—	—	—	—	—	—	—
Equity Securities	78bm d	—	—	—	—	—	—	—	—	—	—	—	—	—	—	—
Debt Securities	78bn d	—	—	—	—	—	—	—	—	—	—	—	—	—	—	—
Financial Derivatives Assets	78bw d	....	....	....	....	....	....	....	....	....	....	....	....	....	....	....
Financial Derivatives Liabilities	78bx d															
Other Investment Assets	78bh d	−1,047	−715	−3,918	3,551	−292	−1,696	−7,801	−8,096	−12,871	−3,725	−8,620	2,628	−1,674	2,653	−1,310
Monetary Authorities	78bo d							—	−1,032	−1,149	−595	−1,419				
General Government	78bp d	−99	−456	−2,389	2,650	1,159	417	−6,536	1,678	1,975	1,419	—	—	—	—	—
Banks	78bq d	−166	−11	−73	−566	−1,323	−848	−79	−1,976	−4,220	−6,250	−2,229	−2,119	−2,282	−4,263	−5,617
Other Sectors	78br d	−782	−248	−1,456	1,467	−127	−1,265	−153	−6,650	−10,031	2,525	−6,391	4,747	607	6,916	4,307
Other Investment Liab., n.i.e.	78bi d	12	22	115	−819	−487	−122	509	417	505	−24	−904	240	332	663	1,056
Monetary Authorities	78bg d	—	—	—	—	—	—	—	—	—	—	—	—	—	—	—
General Government	78bt d	—	—	—	—	—	—	—	—	—	—	—	—	—	—	—
Banks	78bu d	−12	24	155	262	816	−94	509	417	505	−24	−904	240	332	663	1,056
Other Sectors	78bv d	24	−3	−39	−1,080	−1,303	−28	—	—	—	—	—	—	—	—	—
Net Errors and Omissions	78ca d	—	—	—	—	—	—	—	—	—	—	—	—	—	—	—
Overall Balance	78cb d	1,057	917	10,388	9,058	3,727	2,696	−6,700	234	3,937	9,568	−2,308	−1,509	−1,480	−709	−7,619
Reserves and Related Items	79da d	−1,057	−917	−10,388	−9,058	−3,727	−2,696	6,700	−234	−3,937	−9,568	2,308	1,509	1,480	709	7,619
Reserve Assets	79db d	−1,057	−917	−10,388	−9,058	−3,727	−2,696	6,700	−234	−3,937	−9,568	2,308	1,509	1,480	709	7,619
Use of Fund Credit and Loans	79dc d	—	—	—	—	—	—	—	—	—	—	—	—	—	—	—
Exceptional Financing	79de d	....	....	....	....	....	....	....	....	....	....	....	....	....	....	....
Government Finance															*Billions of Riyals*	
Deficit (-) or Surplus	80	....	....	....	....	....	....	....	....	....	....	....	....	....	....	....
Total Revenue and Grants	81y	....	....	....	....	....	....	....	....	....	....	....	....	....	....	....
Revenue	81	....	....	....	....	....	....	....	....	....	....	....	....	....	....	....
Grants	81z	....	....	....	....	....	....	....	....	....	....	....	....	....	....	....
Exp. & Lending Minus Repay.	82z	....	....	....	....	....	....	....	....	....	....	....	....	....	....	....
Expenditure	82	....	....	....	....	....	....	....	....	....	....	....	....	....	....	....
Lending Minus Repayments	83	....	....	....	....	....	....	....	....	....	....	....	....	....	....	....
National Accounts															*Billions of Riyals*	
Househ.Cons.Expend.,incl.NPISHs	96f	7.90	9.83	18.04	23.90	34.37	54.61	68.61	102.39	114.91	126.51	151.29	157.37	159.35	158.59	140.15
Government Consumption Expend.	91f	5.34	9.86	15.91	28.88	41.03	47.03	71.90	77.56	81.92	128.53	126.85	121.33	121.06	114.39	106.37
Gross Fixed Capital Formation	93e	5.69	8.40	17.70	33.54	51.19	66.89	76.65	97.07	106.38	122.31	115.45	103.23	96.49	76.31	66.14
Changes in Inventories	93i	−.11	.84	.75	.78	.84	7.61	−7.38	−17.35	6.43	−19.80	−2.56	9.33	19.60	−10.62	−12.32
Exports of Goods and Services	90c	30.01	85.68	114.46	120.28	140.32	140.76	147.24	258.49	368.43	354.92	219.45	167.18	145.53	113.16	85.99
Imports of Goods and Services (-)	98c	8.27	15.29	27.26	42.86	62.70	91.51	107.48	132.35	157.46	187.76	195.26	186.41	190.64	137.89	115.24
Gross Domestic Product (GDP)	99b	40.55	99.32	139.60	164.53	205.06	225.40	249.54	385.81	520.59	524.72	415.23	372.02	351.40	313.94	271.09
Net Primary Income from Abroad	98.n	−10.46	−16.97	−14.20	.87	2.67	−1.78	−6.64	−4.75	−12.16	−1.82	18.16	20.44	20.94	13.59	18.58
Gross National Income (GNI)	99a	30.15	82.35	125.40	165.39	207.72	223.62	242.90	381.06	508.42	522.90	433.39	392.46	372.34	327.53	289.67
GDP Volume 1970 Prices	99b.p	27.50	31.64	31.72	34.46	39.67	42.03	44.84	49.37	53.28	54.16	48.34	48.29	47.22	45.30	47.82
GDP Volume 1999 Prices	99b.p	....	....	....	....	....	....	....	....	....	....	....	....	....	....	....
GDP Volume (1995=100)	99bv p	43.7	50.3	50.5	54.8	63.1	66.8	71.3	78.5	84.7	86.1	76.9	76.8	75.1	72.1	76.1
GDP Deflator (1995=100)	99bi p	19.4	41.2	57.8	62.7	67.9	70.5	73.1	102.7	128.3	127.3	112.8	101.2	97.8	91.0	74.5
															Millions:	
Population	99z	6.57	6.76	6.97	7.25	7.62	8.06	8.49	8.93	9.37	9.81	10.25	11.17	11.98	12.65	13.36

	Code	1987	1988	1989	1990	1991	1992	1993	1994	1995	1996	1997	1998	1999	2000	2001
International Transactions *Billions of Riyals*																
Exports	70	86.88	91.29	106.29	166.34	179.00	188.32	158.77	159.59	187.40	227.43	227.44	145.39	190.10	290.55	....
Petroleum	70a	76.50	75.67	90.24	150.28	163.49	174.24	144.64	142.83	163.08	203.25	199.77	121.97	168.30	265.75	....
Crude Petroleum	70aa	55.17	55.05	70.62	123.28	139.83	148.31	119.91	117.20	132.99	163.28	163.02	98.84	138.34	232.21	....
Refined Petroleum	70ab	21.33	20.62	19.61	27.00	23.66	25.93	24.73	25.63	30.09	39.97	36.76	23.13	29.96	33.53	....
Imports, c.i.f.	71	75.31	81.58	79.22	90.14	108.90	124.60	105.60	87.40	105.20	103.90	107.60	112.40	104.90	113.24	116.93
Volume of Exports *1995=100*																
Petroleum	72a	43.5	55.4	56.1	70.3	96.6	103.7	101.3	99.9	100.0	100.3	99.6	102.0	92.0	98.2	....
Crude Petroleum	72aa	35.8	48.3	50.2	66.7	98.9	104.9	100.0	99.1	100.0	97.4	98.3	101.6	90.9	99.4	....
Refined Petroleum	72ab	77.3	86.6	82.1	86.2	86.3	98.2	107.0	103.3	100.0	113.2	105.4	103.6	96.8	92.9	....
Export Prices *Index of Prices in US Dollars*																
Crude Petroleum	76aa*d*	103.9	83.9	96.3	121.9	98.9	103.6	89.9	90.4	100.0	118.1	111.8	72.1	104.6	160.5	138.9
Balance of Payments *Minus Sign Indicates Debit*																
Current Account, n.i.e.	78al*d*	-9,773	-7,340	-9,538	-4,152	-27,546	-17,740	-17,268	-10,487	-5,325	681	305	-13,150	412	14,336	14,502
Goods: Exports f.o.b.	78aa*d*	23,199	24,377	28,385	44,414	47,789	50,287	42,395	42,614	50,041	60,729	60,731	38,822	50,757	77,584	73,032
Goods: Imports f.o.b.	78ab*d*	-18,283	-19,805	-19,231	-21,525	-25,971	-30,248	-25,873	-21,325	-25,650	-25,358	-26,370	-27,535	-25,717	-27,741	-28,645
Trade Balance	78ac*d*	4,916	4,571	9,154	22,889	21,818	20,039	16,522	21,289	24,390	35,370	34,362	11,287	25,039	49,843	44,387
Services: Credit	78ad*d*	2,515	2,294	2,510	3,031	2,908	3,466	3,283	3,347	3,480	2,772	4,257	4,730	5,380	4,785	5,182
Services: Debit	78ae*d*	-18,830	-14,935	-19,874	-22,414	-38,804	-32,282	-24,464	-17,893	-19,083	-24,295	-25,963	-16,882	-18,855	-25,262	-19,307
Balance on Goods & Services	78af*d*	-11,399	-8,069	-8,211	3,506	-14,077	-8,777	-4,659	6,743	8,787	13,848	12,655	-865	11,564	29,367	30,262
Income: Credit	78ag*d*	10,537	10,454	10,433	9,199	8,700	7,378	6,208	4,032	4,987	5,127	5,756	5,810	5,811	3,349	4,130
Income: Debit	78ah*d*	-676	-716	-1,017	-1,220	-1,933	-1,944	-2,300	-2,560	-2,184	-2,681	-2,971	-3,041	-2,887	-2,869	-4,650
Balance on Gds, Serv. & Inc.	78ai*d*	-1,538	1,669	1,204	11,485	-7,311	-3,343	-751	8,215	11,591	16,294	15,440	1,903	14,489	29,847	29,742
Current Transfers, n.i.e.: Credit	78aj*d*	—	—	—	—	—	—	—	—	—	—	—	—	—	—	—
Current Transfers: Debit	78ak*d*	-8,235	-9,009	-10,742	-15,637	-20,235	-14,397	-16,517	-18,702	-16,916	-15,613	-15,134	-15,053	-14,077	-15,511	-15,240
Capital Account, n.i.e.	78bc*d*	—	—	—	—	—	—	—	—	—	—	—	—	—	—	—
Capital Account, n.i.e.: Credit	78ba*d*	—	—	—	—	—	—	—	—	—	—	—	—	—	—	—
Capital Account: Debit	78bb*d*	—	—	—	—	—	—	—	—	—	—	—	—	—	—	—
Financial Account, n.i.e.	78bj*d*	12,413	5,821	6,030	-1,224	27,595	12,075	18,763	10,341	6,542	5,069	343	12,431	2,403	-11,672	-16,411
Direct Investment Abroad	78bd*d*	—	—	—	—	—	—	—	—	—	—	—	—	—	—	—
Dir. Invest. in Rep. Econ., n.i.e.	78be*d*	-1,175	-328	-654	1,864	160	-79	1,369	350	-1,877	-1,129	3,044	4,289	-780	-1,884	20
Portfolio Investment Assets	78bf*d*	6,151	3,060	-1,786	-3,342	471	-6,500	8,213	-2,527	4,057	-2,642	-7,362	6,941	11,712	-9,394	-2,798
Equity Securities	78bk*d*	—	—	—	—	—	—	—	—	—	—	—	—	—	—	—
Debt Securities	78bl*d*	6,151	3,060	-1,786	-3,342	471	-6,500	8,213	-2,527	4,057	-2,642	-7,362	6,941	11,712	-9,394	-2,798
Portfolio Investment Liab., n.i.e.	78bg*d*	—	—	—	—	—	—	—	—	—	—	—	—	—	—	—
Equity Securities	78bm*d*	—	—	—	—	—	—	—	—	—	—	—	—	—	—	—
Debt Securities	78bn*d*	—	—	—	—	—	—	—	—	—	—	—	—	—	—	—
Financial Derivatives Assets	78bw*d*	....	....	....	....	....	....	....	....	....	....	....	....	....	....	....
Financial Derivatives Liabilities	78bx*d*	....	....	....	....	....	....	....	....	....	....	....	....	....	....	....
Other Investment Assets	78bh*d*	4,713	1,957	6,903	1,437	27,562	18,446	6,885	12,022	4,221	9,115	2,688	1,983	-10,678	-3,943	-12,343
Monetary Authorities	78bo*d*	—	—	—	—	—	—	—	—	—	—	—	—	—	—	—
General Government	78bp*d*	—	—	—	—	—	—	—	—	—	—	—	—	—	—	—
Banks	78bq*d*	-4,147	-3,348	-1,095	-1,234	1,207	4,621	-2,661	3,588	46	-2,188	1,777	3,621	-1,480	-2,595	491
Other Sectors	78br*d*	8,860	5,306	7,997	2,670	26,355	13,825	9,545	8,434	4,175	11,303	911	-1,639	-9,198	-1,348	-12,834
Other Investment Liab., n.i.e.	78bi*d*	2,724	1,132	1,567	-1,183	-598	208	2,296	497	142	-275	1,973	-782	2,149	3,549	-1,289
Monetary Authorities	78bs*d*	—	—	—	—	—	—	—	—	—	—	—	—	—	—	—
General Government	78bt*d*	—	—	—	—	—	—	—	—	—	—	—	—	—	—	—
Banks	78bu*d*	2,724	1,132	1,567	-1,183	-598	208	2,296	497	142	-275	1,973	-782	2,149	3,549	-1,289
Other Sectors	78bv*d*	—	—	—	—	—	—	—	—	—	—	—	—	—	—	—
Net Errors and Omissions	78ca*d*	—	—	—	—	—	—	—	—	—	—	—	—	—	—	—
Overall Balance	78cb*d*	2,640	-1,519	-3,508	-5,376	49	-5,664	1,495	-146	1,217	5,749	648	-719	2,815	2,665	-1,909
Reserves and Related Items	79da*d*	-2,640	1,519	3,508	5,376	-49	5,664	-1,495	146	-1,217	-5,749	-648	719	-2,815	-2,665	1,909
Reserve Assets	79db*d*	-2,640	1,519	3,508	5,376	-49	5,664	-1,495	146	-1,217	-5,749	-648	719	-2,815	-2,665	1,909
Use of Fund Credit and Loans	79dc*d*	—	—	—	—	—	—	—	—	—	—	—	—	—	—	—
Exceptional Financing	79de*d*	....	....	....	....	....	....	....	....	....	....	....	....	....	....	....
Government Finance *Billions of Riyals*																
Deficit (-) or Surplus	80	....	....	....	....	....	....	....	....	....	-18.50	-17.00	-18.00	-44.00	-28.00	....
Total Revenue and Grants	81y	....	....	....	....	....	....	....	....	....	131.50	164.00	178.00	121.00	157.00	....
Revenue	81	....	....	....	....	....	....	....	....	....	131.50	164.00	178.00	121.00	157.00	....
Grants	81z	....	....	....	....	....	....	....	....	....	—	—	—	—	—	....
Exp. & Lending Minus Repay.	82z	....	....	....	....	....	....	....	....	....	150.00	181.00	196.00	165.00	185.00	....
Expenditure	82	....	....	....	....	....	....	....	....	....	150.00	181.00	196.00	165.00	185.00	....
Lending Minus Repayments	83	....	....	....	....	....	....	....	....	....	—	—	—	—	—	....
National Accounts *Billions of Riyals*																
Househ.Cons.Expend.,incl.NPISHs	96f	135.54	139.40	145.03	155.87	168.75	183.92	193.91	185.83	193.52	259.49	261.43	251.42	252.22	258.13	255.78
Government Consumption Expend.	91f	107.71	97.42	96.56	120.13	165.00	148.97	127.78	119.56	122.85	144.78	161.80	155.19	154.09	183.90	188.70
Gross Fixed Capital Formation	93e	65.20	56.92	60.41	73.80	86.51	93.98	98.45	84.21	93.56	102.85	109.24	112.96	118.20	123.32	126.61
Changes in Inventories	93i	-12.87	2.73	6.76	2.75	7.34	8.51	9.17	6.19	5.54	4.06	3.84	9.60	9.42	8.90	5.14
Exports of Goods and Services	90c	99.05	103.08	118.21	181.13	197.28	207.87	179.40	181.89	209.37	237.81	243.38	163.10	210.23	308.47	292.91
Imports of Goods and Services (-)	98c	119.17	114.40	116.15	141.69	182.84	181.83	164.87	127.66	146.18	158.24	161.78	145.62	140.57	175.97	170.73
Gross Domestic Product (GDP)	99b	275.45	285.15	310.82	391.99	442.04	461.40	443.84	450.03	478.65	590.75	617.90	546.65	603.59	706.76	698.40
Net Primary Income from Abroad	98.n	17.38	19.94	18.70	6.52	-4.88	-8.61	-7.23	-16.54	-8.91	—	—	—	—	—	—
Gross National Income (GNI)	99a	292.84	305.08	329.52	398.52	437.16	452.78	436.61	433.49	469.74	590.75	617.90	546.65	603.59	706.66	698.40
GDP Volume 1970 Prices	99b.*p*	47.17	50.73	50.83	56.24	60.96	62.66	62.26	62.58	62.88	63.75	....	....	....	....	....
GDP Volume 1999 Prices	99b.*p*	....	....	....	....	....	....	....	....	....	576.74	591.79	608.50	603.59	632.91	640.41
GDP Volume (1995=100)	99bv*p*	75.0	80.7	80.8	89.4	97.0	99.7	99.0	99.5	100.0	101.4	104.0	107.0	106.1	111.3	112.6
GDP Deflator (1995=100)	99bi*p*	76.7	73.8	80.3	91.6	95.3	96.7	93.6	94.5	100.0	121.7	124.1	106.8	118.8	132.7	129.6
Midyear Estimates																
Population	99z	13.61	14.02	14.43	14.87	15.81	16.11	16.38	16.69	17.09	17.61	18.24	18.93	19.90	20.85	21.03

(See notes in the back of the book.)

Senegal

		1972	1973	1974	1975	1976	1977	1978	1979	1980	1981	1982	1983	1984	1985	1986
Exchange Rates															*Francs per SDR:*	
Official Rate	aa	278.00	284.00	272.08	262.55	288.70	285.76	272.28	264.78	287.99	334.52	370.92	436.97	470.11	415.26	394.78
															Francs per US Dollar:	
Official Rate	ae	256.05	235.42	222.22	224.27	248.49	235.25	209.00	201.00	225.80	287.40	336.25	417.37	479.60	378.05	322.75
Official Rate	rf	252.03	222.89	240.70	214.31	238.95	245.68	225.66	212.72	211.28	271.73	328.61	381.07	436.96	449.26	346.31
Fund Position															*Millions of SDRs:*	
Quota	2f. s	34.0	34.0	34.0	34.0	34.0	34.0	42.0	42.0	63.0	63.0	63.0	85.1	85.1	85.1	85.1
SDRs	1b. s	5.7	5.3	4.6	3.3	1.2	1.7	9.7	11.5	—	3.7	4.9	3.8	.1	.1	2.5
Reserve Position in the Fund	1c. s	3.9	4.2	—	—	—	—	2.1	—	—	—	.9	.9	1.0	1.0	1.0
Total Fund Cred.&Loans Outstg.	2tl	—	—	—	25.4	25.4	25.4	57.0	70.5	109.9	160.2	200.0	220.5	234.7	243.7	236.3
International Liquidity														*Millions of US Dollars Unless Otherwise Indicated:*		
Total Reserves minus Gold	1l. d	38.5	12.1	6.3	31.1	25.2	33.7	18.8	19.1	8.1	8.7	11.4	12.2	3.7	5.1	9.4
SDRs	1b. d	6.2	6.4	5.7	3.9	1.3	2.1	12.7	15.1	—	4.4	5.4	3.9	.1	.1	3.0
Reserve Position in the Fund	1c. d	4.2	5.0	—	—	—	—	2.8	—	—	—	1.0	1.0	.9	1.1	1.2
Foreign Exchange	1d. d	28.1	.6	.6	27.3	23.9	31.6	3.4	4.0	8.1	4.3	5.0	7.3	2.6	3.9	5.2
Gold (Million Fine Troy Ounces)	1ad	....	....	....	....	—	.015	.022	.029	.029	.029	.029	.029	.029	.029	.029
Gold (National Valuation)	1and	....	....	....	....	—	.6	1.0	1.3	1.3	12.2	12.4	11.2	9.6	9.4	11.7
Monetary Authorities: Other Liab.	4. d	1.0	11.6	11.9	.5	14.4	19.3	36.0	117.6	158.9	210.8	255.5	241.0	196.2	334.8	289.8
Deposit Money Banks: Assets	7a. d	10.9	15.5	19.0	22.8	37.2	46.0	46.6	53.2	57.7	43.1	55.4	45.1	40.4	41.9	40.0
Liabilities	7b. d	41.3	47.2	57.7	85.8	77.5	101.0	144.2	228.6	211.4	173.9	159.5	112.5	133.2	167.1	150.9
Monetary Authorities															*Billions of Francs:*	
Foreign Assets	11	9.8	2.8	1.4	7.0	6.3	7.9	3.9	3.8	1.8	2.5	3.8	5.1	1.8	1.9	3.0
Claims on Central Government	12a				.4	3.4	8.1	8.2	16.5	36.8	59.6	116.2	132.3	145.3	158.1	164.5
Claims on Deposit Money Banks	12e	12.9	25.2	38.5	39.5	42.8	44.3	71.2	79.2	108.1	146.7	168.6	173.8	157.9	179.7	160.6
Claims on Other Financial Insts	12f	—	—	—	—	1.1	1.4	1.2	1.2	.5	1.4	1.7	2.4	2.6	3.1	3.6
Reserve Money	14	17.7	21.5	32.2	34.6	38.7	44.6	55.8	51.1	62.0	85.8	106.7	103.1	102.1	108.2	125.8
of which: Currency Outside DMBs	14a	16.5	19.5	29.0	29.5	33.7	39.5	46.2	42.9	51.4	73.6	84.5	78.3	77.3	86.2	104.3
Foreign Liabilities	16c	.3	2.7	2.6	6.8	10.9	11.8	27.0	49.1	76.7	123.4	169.3	206.0	212.7	234.5	194.0
Central Government Deposits	16d	1.6	.7	2.0	2.6	1.0	1.4	1.9	1.4	12.9	6.2	20.5	15.9	13.5	6.0	6.0
Other Items (Net)	17r	3.2	3.2	3.2	3.0	2.9	4.0	-.2	-.9	-4.4	-5.3	-6.2	-11.5	-20.7	-5.8	6.1
Deposit Money Banks															*Billions of Francs:*	
Reserves	20	1.3	2.2	2.3	4.7	5.2	5.4	9.1	6.6	10.1	11.7	21.9	21.2	24.2	22.4	28.3
Foreign Assets	21	2.8	3.6	4.2	5.1	9.2	10.8	9.7	10.7	13.0	12.4	18.6	18.8	19.4	15.8	12.9
Claims on Central Government	22a	5.3	6.3	8.0	10.6	14.4	12.6	12.3	†14.1	15.6	14.5	13.5	13.5	14.9	14.5	15.4
Claims on Private Sector	22d	46.0	62.7	88.8	106.2	121.1	143.3	194.3	†230.6	268.3	322.8	353.8	366.7	372.2	394.5	389.7
Claims on Other Financial Insts	22f	....	....	....	....	....	....		†6.7	2.9	2.4	2.1	2.3	2.5	3.6	4.2
Demand Deposits	24	21.0	23.0	36.9	42.9	58.6	66.7	76.5	†74.3	82.0	85.1	98.7	106.1	109.6	103.4	117.1
Time Deposits	25	3.7	8.2	9.5	10.9	18.8	21.9	32.3	†39.9	39.8	53.7	73.3	83.8	95.5	106.6	106.7
Foreign Liabilities	26c	6.6	7.1	8.9	15.4	15.3	19.9	26.3	35.2	34.8	35.8	38.3	30.9	47.7	52.1	37.1
Long-Term Foreign Liabilities	26cl	4.0	3.8	3.9	3.8	4.0	3.9	3.8	10.8	12.9	14.2	15.3	16.0	16.2	11.1	11.6
Central Government Deposits	26d	4.2	4.3	6.1	8.2	4.4	4.2	4.5	†12.3	13.6	19.0	15.1	16.4	18.8	17.5	23.8
Credit from Monetary Authorities	26g	12.9	25.2	38.5	39.5	42.8	44.3	71.2	78.2	107.6	146.9	169.6	175.3	156.0	182.1	167.5
Other Items (Net)	27r	3.0	3.2	-.4	6.0	6.0	11.3	10.9	18.1	19.2	9.2	-.5	-6.1	-10.6	-22.0	-13.4
Treasury Claims: Private Sector	22d. i	1.3	.7	.8	.8	.8	1.3	1.8	1.8	1.4	1.3	1.1	1.9	1.5	2.2	2.1
Post Office: Checking Deposits	24.. i	1.6	1.7	1.9	2.3	2.5	2.9	3.7	3.6	4.1	4.0	5.3	4.8	4.7	3.8	5.5
Monetary Survey															*Billions of Francs:*	
Foreign Assets (Net)	31n	5.8	-3.4	-5.9	-10.1	-10.7	-12.9	-39.6	-69.8	-96.7	-144.3	-185.2	-213.0	-239.2	-268.8	-215.2
Domestic Credit	32	47.2	65.7	90.7	108.8	137.0	162.7	213.3	†259.0	301.7	379.5	456.9	489.6	509.9	554.2	553.1
Claims on Central Govt. (Net)	32an	—	2.2	1.0	1.9	14.0	16.7	16.0	†18.8	28.7	51.6	98.3	116.3	131.1	150.7	153.5
Claims on Private Sector	32d	47.3	63.5	89.7	106.9	121.9	144.6	196.1	†232.4	269.7	324.1	354.9	368.6	373.7	396.8	391.7
Claims on Other Financial Insts	32f	—	—	—	—	1.1	1.4	1.2	†7.9	3.4	3.8	3.8	4.7	5.2	6.7	7.8
Money	34	39.1	44.2	67.8	75.2	94.9	109.1	126.5	†121.2	137.9	163.2	189.0	189.2	191.6	193.5	227.0
Quasi-Money	35	3.7	8.2	9.5	10.9	18.8	21.9	32.3	†39.9	39.8	53.7	73.3	83.8	95.5	106.6	106.7
Long-Term Foreign Liabilities	36cl	4.0	3.8	3.9	3.8	4.0	3.9	3.8	10.8	12.9	14.2	15.3	16.0	16.2	11.1	11.6
Other Items (Net)	37r	6.2	6.1	3.6	8.8	8.7	14.9	11.0	17.4	14.4	4.1	-5.9	-12.5	-32.6	-25.8	-7.4
Money plus Quasi-Money	35l	42.8	52.4	77.3	86.1	113.6	131.0	158.8	†161.1	177.7	216.9	262.3	273.0	287.1	300.1	333.7
Other Banking Institutions															*Billions of Francs:*	
Savings Deposits	45	.7	.7	.9	....	....	....		1.6	1.7	1.7	1.9	1.9	1.9	1.9	2.4
Liquid Liabilities	55l	43.5	53.1	78.1	....	....	....		†162.7	179.4	218.7	264.2	274.9	289.0	302.0	336.0
Interest Rates															*Percent Per Annum*	
Discount Rate (End of Period)	60	3.50	5.50	5.50	8.00	8.00	8.00	8.00	8.00	10.50	10.50	12.50	10.50	10.50	10.50	8.50
Money Market Rate	60b	....	....	....	....		7.28	7.40	7.40	7.80	10.00	13.67	14.66	12.23	11.84	10.66	8.58
Deposit Rate	60l	3.00	5.75	5.75	5.88	6.00	6.00	6.00	6.00	6.19	6.25	7.75	7.50	7.25	7.25	6.08
Lending Rate	60p	....	....	....	....		12.00	12.00	12.00	14.50	14.50	16.00	14.50	14.50	14.50	13.50
Prices and Production															*Index Numbers (1995=100):*	
Consumer Prices	64	17.2	19.1	22.3	29.3	29.6	33.0	34.1	37.4	40.7	43.1	50.6	56.5	63.1	71.3	75.7
Industrial Production	66	80.8	73.6	78.2	91.0	93.5	†98.6	88.5	99.5	82.0	89.8	93.1	96.6	94.7	97.0	103.8
															Number in Thousands:	
Labor Force	67d	....	....	....	....	....	....	....	....	....	....	....	....	....	....	....
Employment	67e	....	....	....	....	....	....	....	....	....	....	....	....	....	85	86
Unemployment	67c	....	....	....	....	....	....	....	....	....	....	....	....	....	11	10
International Transactions															*Billions of Francs*	
Exports	70	54.41	43.24	93.98	99.10	115.93	152.92	101.40	113.86	100.77	135.88	180.04	235.48	277.02	252.49	216.58
Imports, c.i.f.	71	70.55	80.17	119.38	124.62	153.89	187.55	170.31	197.98	222.26	292.34	325.94	390.72	428.60	370.97	332.93
															1985=100	
Unit Value of Exports	74	21.1	25.0	47.5	†40.2	39.2	47.1	50.8	54.4	53.2	73.0	†70.7	78.7	100.3	100.0	70.0
Unit Value of Imports	75	23.6	26.9	38.5	†40.8	42.9	46.7	46.1	51.8	67.4	75.6	†85.3	93.3	102.4	100.0	72.4

1987	1988	1989	1990	1991	1992	1993	1994	1995	1996	1997	1998	1999	2000	2001		
															Exchange Rates	
End of Period																
378.78	407.68	380.32	364.84	370.48	378.57	404.89	†780.44	728.38	753.06	807.94	791.61	†896.19	918.49	935.39	Official Rate	aa
End of Period (ae) Period Average (rf)																
267.00	302.95	289.40	256.45	275.32	294.77	†534.60	490.00	523.70	598.81	562.21	†652.95	704.95	744.31		Official Rate	ae
300.54	297.85	319.01	272.26	282.11	264.69	283.16	†555.20	499.15	511.55	583.67	589.95	†615.70	711.98	733.04	Official Rate	rf
															Fund Position	
End of Period																
85.1	85.1	85.1	85.1	85.1	118.9	118.9	118.9	118.9	118.9	118.9	118.9	161.8	161.8	161.8	Quota	2f. s
—	—	3.6	.2	.3	—	.3	.7	2.6	1.2	.3	.4	1.8	.7	6.0	SDRs	1b. s
1.0	1.0	1.0	1.0	1.0	1.1	1.1	1.1	1.2	1.3	1.3	1.4	1.4	1.4	1.4	Reserve Position in the Fund	1c. s
241.6	236.5	240.4	221.0	228.9	197.4	177.8	205.4	233.3	226.5	216.5	207.8	198.2	195.4	204.7	Total Fund Cred.&Loans Outstg.	2tl
															International Liquidity	
End of Period																
9.2	10.5	19.0	11.0	13.2	12.4	3.4	179.6	271.8	288.3	386.2	430.8	402.9	383.5	446.2	Total Reserves minus Gold	1l. d
—	—	4.7	.2	.4	—	.4	1.1	3.8	.5	.5	2.5	.9	7.5		SDRs	1b. d
1.4	1.3	1.3	1.4	1.5	1.4	1.5	1.7	1.8	1.8	1.8	1.9	1.9	1.8	1.8	Reserve Position in the Fund	1c. d
7.8	9.1	13.0	9.3	11.3	10.9	1.5	176.9	266.2	284.8	383.9	428.4	398.5	380.8	436.9	Foreign Exchange	1d. d
.029	.029	.029	.029	.029	.029	.029	.029	.029	.029	.029	.029	.029	....	....	Gold (Million Fine Troy Ounces)	1ad
13.7	12.0	11.3	11.0	10.3	10.1	10.8	10.8	11.2	10.9	8.9	8.5	8.6	....	....	Gold (National Valuation)	1an d
317.8	407.1	303.7	330.0	282.2	298.2	408.2	144.4	122.8	116.9	101.6	109.2	96.6	97.2	86.3	Monetary Authorities: Other Liab.	4.. d
39.7	58.3	84.8	51.2	66.7	72.8	68.6	131.4	159.9	146.7	151.3	220.4	258.2	220.8	239.9	Deposit Money Banks: Assets	7a. d
204.3	226.9	259.7	183.1	192.2	171.8	154.7	134.0	131.7	105.0	94.0	117.5	119.9	86.9	101.6	Liabilities	7b. d
															Monetary Authorities	
End of Period																
2.5	3.2	5.5	2.8	3.4	3.4	1.0	96.0	133.2	151.0	231.3	242.2	263.1	270.7	332.9	Foreign Assets	11
170.1	172.9	174.0	163.9	165.5	163.6	158.4	265.5	271.4	229.7	293.7	296.4	279.1	256.6	301.0	Claims on Central Government	12a
156.4	194.5	190.0	183.9	179.8	189.0	172.3	11.5	—	2.6	31.7	26.9	12.6	2.0	—	Claims on Deposit Money Banks	12e
3.6	3.6	.5	.5	.6	.6	.6	.6	.7	.5	.5	.4	—	—	—	Claims on Other Financial Insts	12f
132.6	131.8	164.4	158.5	169.6	181.7	126.6	188.9	196.6	168.7	174.2	186.0	215.7	228.1	306.4	Reserve Money	14
100.7	92.8	102.7	95.2	97.5	107.2	93.0	145.6	152.1	141.9	142.3	158.5	179.4	171.5	211.7	of which: Currency Outside DMBs	14a
180.7	221.7	179.8	165.3	157.9	156.8	192.3	237.5	230.1	231.7	235.7	225.9	240.6	248.0	255.8	Foreign Liabilities	16c
9.3	9.9	7.6	5.8	6.0	4.0	5.7	13.8	19.2	26.8	142.1	137.4	105.0	55.9	80.2	Central Government Deposits	16d
10.0	10.8	18.1	21.5	15.8	14.0	7.6	-66.5	-40.7	-43.5	5.0	16.6	-6.6	-2.7	-8.5	Other Items (Net)	17r
															Deposit Money Banks	
End of Period																
32.1	39.6	67.6	62.3	71.3	74.1	34.1	31.8	31.1	24.9	32.4	27.1	35.7	55.9	93.4	Reserves	20
10.6	17.7	24.6	13.1	17.3	20.1	20.2	70.2	78.4	76.8	90.6	123.9	168.6	155.6	178.5	Foreign Assets	21
15.7	24.8	21.7	15.5	32.7	22.8	28.6	57.9	61.5	120.0	109.6	122.4	110.6	94.0	101.8	Claims on Central Government	22a
401.5	431.4	441.5	410.3	396.1	417.5	424.3	349.9	355.6	411.0	428.3	437.1	483.0	619.5	651.8	Claims on Private Sector	22d
4.2	5.3	2.7	2.0	1.9	2.1	1.6	1.3	.2	—	—	—	—	—	—	Claims on Other Financial Insts	22f
109.7	117.0	124.5	104.7	112.3	106.6	101.4	155.3	160.2	198.5	196.3	234.0	255.9	287.7	315.3	Demand Deposits	24
118.4	119.6	138.1	147.0	158.4	167.6	138.8	161.4	184.6	216.4	237.7	233.2	273.2	325.3	363.8	Time Deposits	25
43.1	57.0	63.7	38.6	41.9	38.3	36.4	58.3	51.4	42.4	50.0	62.5	72.5	56.4	65.2	Foreign Liabilities	26c
11.4	11.7	11.5	8.4	7.9	9.0	9.2	13.4	13.2	12.6	6.3	3.5	5.8	4.9	10.4	Long-Term Foreign Liabilities	26cl
32.1	38.0	61.4	66.7	83.1	100.8	118.1	136.4	136.3	161.7	109.5	101.5	97.6	136.5	143.8	Central Government Deposits	26d
159.0	196.8	194.8	184.3	181.4	190.2	176.8	11.5	—	3.6	31.7	26.9	12.6	2.0	—	Credit from Monetary Authorities	26g
-9.6	-21.3	-35.9	-46.3	-65.7	-75.8	-71.9	-25.1	-18.9	-2.5	29.4	48.9	80.5	112.3	127.0	Other Items (Net)	27r
2.2	.7	.9	1.2	.5	2.4	2.3	2.3	2.2	3.0	2.8	2.9	3.2	2.6	4.5	Treasury Claims: Private Sector	22d. i
3.8	4.9	3.5	3.9	3.0	3.4	3.0	3.9	4.3	2.8	4.0	4.1	3.9	4.1	4.7	Post Office: Checking Deposits	24.. i
															Monetary Survey	
End of Period																
-210.7	-257.9	-213.4	-188.0	-179.0	-171.6	-207.4	-129.5	-69.9	-46.3	36.1	77.7	118.7	121.9	190.4	Foreign Assets (Net)	31n
557.5	595.0	574.8	523.7	510.6	505.2	492.7	529.0	538.1	575.5	584.5	621.5	674.1	781.9	835.3	Domestic Credit	32
146.0	154.0	129.3	109.7	111.6	82.6	63.9	174.9	179.5	161.0	152.9	181.1	187.8	159.7	179.0	Claims on Central Govt. (Net)	32an
403.7	432.1	442.4	411.5	396.6	419.9	426.6	352.2	357.8	414.1	431.1	439.9	486.2	622.2	656.3	Claims on Private Sector	32d
7.8	9.0	3.2	2.5	2.5	2.7	2.2	1.9	.8	.5	.5	.4	—	—	—	Claims on Other Financial Insts	32f
214.4	214.9	230.8	204.2	213.2	217.4	197.7	305.3	316.8	343.6	343.2	397.0	439.8	464.0	533.0	Money	34
118.4	119.6	138.1	147.0	158.4	167.6	138.8	161.4	184.6	216.4	237.7	233.2	273.2	325.3	363.8	Quasi-Money	35
11.4	11.7	11.5	8.4	7.9	9.0	9.2	13.4	13.2	12.6	6.3	3.5	5.8	4.9	10.4	Long-Term Foreign Liabilities	36cl
2.6	-9.1	-19.1	-23.8	-47.9	-60.4	-60.5	-80.7	-46.4	-43.4	33.4	65.5	73.9	109.6	118.6	Other Items (Net)	37r
332.8	334.5	368.9	351.2	371.6	385.0	336.5	466.7	501.4	560.0	580.9	630.2	713.0	789.3	896.8	Money plus Quasi-Money	35l
															Other Banking Institutions	
End of Period																
2.4	3.5	3.8	4.2	....	....	....	....	....	....	....	....	....	....	....	Savings Deposits	45
335.2	338.0	372.7	355.4	....	....	....	....	....	560.0	580.9	630.2	713.0	789.3	....	Liquid Liabilities	55l
															Interest Rates	
Percent Per Annum																
8.50	9.50	11.00	11.00	12.50	10.50	10.00	7.50	6.50	6.00	6.25	5.75	6.50	6.50	6.50	Discount Rate (End of Period)	60
8.37	8.72	10.07	10.98	10.94	11.44	....	....	....	....	....	4.81	4.95	4.95	4.95	Money Market Rate	60b
5.25	5.25	6.42	7.00	7.00	7.75	....	....	....	....	....	3.50	3.50	3.50	3.50	Deposit Rate	60l
13.50	13.58	15.13	16.00	16.00	16.75	....	....	....	....	....	....	....	....	....	Lending Rate	60p
															Prices and Production	
72.6	71.3	71.6	71.8	70.6	70.5	70.1	92.7	100.0	†102.8	104.4	105.6	106.5	107.2	110.5	Consumer Prices	64
104.5	89.0	84.8	100.1	92.2	90.8	85.0	93.2	100.0	96.5	98.2	118.2	105.4	101.7	....	Industrial Production	66
Period Averages																
....	1,897	....	....	....	....	....	....	....	....	....	....	....	....	....	Labor Force	67d
....	....	....	....	130	....	....									Employment	67e
8	17	8	10	14	12	10	....								Unemployment	67c
															International Transactions	
Billions of Francs																
182.25	176.08	221.10	207.38	197.71	178.08	200.20	439.10	495.80	505.40	528.00	570.90	632.40	654.90	....	Exports	70
307.60	321.57	389.54	332.12	330.94	273.72	307.70	567.40	704.90	734.60	844.80	829.80	905.60	1,083.10	....	Imports, c.i.f.	71
1985=100																
66.6	....	....													Unit Value of Exports	74
68.9	....	....													Unit Value of Imports	75

Senegal

Balance of Payments

Millions of US Dollars:

Item	Code	1972	1973	1974	1975	1976	1977	1978	1979	1980	1981	1982	1983	1984	1985	1986
Current Account, n.i.e.	78ald	....	....	−65.6	−85.6	−92.8	−67.5	−235.8	−264.2	−386.5	−462.3	−266.6	−306.1	−274.1	−361.1	−369.8
Goods: Exports f.o.b.	78aad	....	....	472.6	542.6	536.5	685.3	434.7	517.6	470.2	603.4	564.5	642.1	632.5	548.1	694.5
Goods: Imports f.o.b.	78abd	....	....	−552.5	−611.5	−659.6	−772.5	−744.2	−813.3	−875.1	−1,020.3	−815.1	−917.2	−818.9	−795.8	−883.3
Trade Balance	78acd			−79.9	−69.0	−123.1	−87.2	−309.5	−295.7	−404.9	−416.8	−250.5	−275.1	−186.4	−247.7	−188.7
Services: Credit	78add			127.3	145.6	159.5	169.9	240.4	298.6	336.7	379.6	319.7	306.0	268.4	276.3	334.5
Services: Debit	78aed			−126.6	−170.4	−174.6	−202.7	−210.8	−287.9	−339.9	−494.7	−414.6	−391.9	−370.0	−366.7	−484.4
Balance on Goods & Services	78afd			−79.2	−93.7	−138.2	−120.0	−279.9	−285.1	−408.1	−531.9	−345.4	−361.0	−288.0	−338.2	−339.0
Income: Credit	78agd			8.8	8.0	7.7	9.7	11.7	16.5	23.6	19.1	19.3	24.5	14.9	30.8	47.8
Income: Debit	78ahd			−58.6	−83.8	−68.6	−63.9	−87.6	−95.6	−122.0	−115.8	−117.0	−123.9	−138.3	−133.9	−173.6
Balance on Gds, Serv. & Inc.	78aid			−129.0	−169.6	−199.2	−174.3	−355.8	−364.2	−506.5	−628.6	−443.2	−460.5	−411.4	−441.2	−464.9
Current Transfers, n.i.e.: Credit	78ajd			102.0	134.1	152.5	158.1	208.2	223.4	245.4	275.5	274.4	238.9	212.4	142.3	169.4
Current Transfers: Debit	78akd			−38.6	−50.2	−46.1	−51.3	−88.2	−123.4	−125.4	−109.1	−97.8	−84.6	−75.2	−62.2	−74.3
Capital Account, n.i.e.	78bcd														88.0	101.7
Capital Account, n.i.e.: Credit	78bad			—	—	—	—	—	—	—	—	—	—	—	106.2	121.3
Capital Account: Debit	78bbd			—	—	—	—	—	—	—	—	—	—	—	−18.2	−19.6
Financial Account, n.i.e.	78bjd			45.4	92.2	80.0	70.3	189.9	277.6	356.0	315.8	134.9	189.7	189.9	179.2	203.2
Direct Investment Abroad	78bdd			−3.2	6.9	.4	−2.9	−.5	−3.9	−1.6	−14.8	−18.0	1.6	−1.9	−3.1	4.6
Dir. Invest. in Rep. Econ., n.i.e.	78bed			10.3	22.5	35.9	28.0	−5.0	8.9	14.5	34.4	28.1	−34.7	29.1	−15.8	−8.4
Portfolio Investment Assets	78bfd			.2	—	—	—	.7	—	−.4	−1.8	−.3	−1.0	−.1	—	—
Equity Securities	78bkd			.2	—	—	—	.7	—	−.4	−1.8	−.3	−1.0	−.1		
Debt Securities	78bld															
Portfolio Investment Liab., n.i.e.	78bgd			2.9	2.9	9.2	.6	8.3	−2.6	3.2	1.1	.9	−.8	1.7	.6	2.1
Equity Securities	78bmd			2.7	2.4	11.3	2.3	7.5	—	.1	.6	1.0	−.8	1.2	−.2	—
Debt Securities	78bnd			.2	.6	−2.1	−1.7	.8	−2.6	3.0	.5	−.2	−.1	.6	.8	2.1
Financial Derivatives Assets	78bwd			....	....	....	....	....	....	....	....	....	....	....		
Financial Derivatives Liabilities	78bxd			....	....	....	....	....	....	....	....	....	....	....	—	—
Other Investment Assets	78bhd			−42.7	2.3	−22.4	−14.2	−4.0	−57.8	−25.8	−59.3	−63.1	−22.4	20.3	6.3	−.6
Monetary Authorities	78bod			....												....
General Government	78bpd			−.5	−3.0	−.8	—	—	−1.8	−1.6	−.1	−.2	.1	—	—	....
Banks	78bqd			−17.3	−8.6	−10.1	−2.5	−9.8	−5.7	−12.7	−5.5	−18.8	−2.1	−14.5	10.4	.5
Other Sectors	78brd			−24.9	14.0	−11.6	−11.7	5.8	−50.3	−11.6	−53.7	−44.1	−20.4	34.8	−4.0	−1.1
Other Investment Liab., n.i.e.	78bid			78.0	57.6	57.0	58.7	190.4	333.1	366.1	356.2	187.4	247.0	140.7	191.2	205.5
Monetary Authorities	78bsd			.6	−12.3	14.4	3.9	13.3	75.7	58.2	90.8	77.0	38.6	−14.7	72.2	−95.6
General Government	78btd			50.0	33.3	46.9	27.1	109.1	112.2	256.2	144.4	59.6	141.5	64.2	127.8	245.1
Banks	78bud			14.3	25.2	−.1	16.9	34.0	78.2	3.2	20.9	15.6	−12.2	37.9	−9.9	−36.7
Other Sectors	78bvd			13.0	11.4	−4.1	10.8	34.0	67.0	48.6	100.1	35.2	79.1	53.2	1.0	92.6
Net Errors and Omissions	78cad			14.3	−11.2	6.2	.5	−14.7	−40.6	−36.6	13.6	−4.7	6.6	−14.2	2.7	29.9
Overall Balance	78cbd			−5.9	−4.5	−6.5	3.2	−60.5	−27.1	−67.2	−132.9	−136.4	−109.9	−98.4	−91.2	−35.0
Reserves and Related Items	79dad			5.9	4.5	6.5	−3.2	60.5	27.1	67.2	132.9	136.4	109.9	98.4	91.2	35.0
Reserve Assets	79dbd			5.9	−26.3	6.2	−3.7	20.1	8.9	15.8	2.9	−3.5	−2.2	7.8	−.2	−3.3
Use of Fund Credit and Loans	79dcd			—	30.8	—	—	39.9	17.7	50.9	57.4	43.8	21.1	15.7	8.5	−8.4
Exceptional Financing	79ded			—	—	.3	.5	.5	.5	.5	72.6	96.1	91.0	74.9	83.0	46.7

International Investment Position

Millions of US Dollars

Item	Code	1972	1973	1974	1975	1976	1977	1978	1979	1980	1981	1982	1983	1984	1985	1986
Assets	79aad															108.1
Direct Investment Abroad	79abd															—
Portfolio Investment	79acd															—
Equity Securities	79add															
Debt Securities	79aed															
Financial Derivatives	79ald															
Other Investment	79afd														84.7	98.7
Monetary Authorities	79agd															—
General Government	79ahd															
Banks	79aid														84.7	98.7
Other Sectors	79ajd															
Reserve Assets	79akd														1.7	9.4
Liabilities	79lad															3,085.5
Dir. Invest. in Rep. Economy	79lbd															
Portfolio Investment	79lcd															
Equity Securities	79ldd															
Debt Securities	79led															
Financial Derivatives	79lld															
Other Investment	79lfd														2,438.5	3,085.5
Monetary Authorities	79lgd														356.1	578.9
General Government	79lhd														1,904.0	2,337.1
Banks	79lid														178.4	169.5
Other Sectors	79ljd															—

Government Finance

Billions of Francs:

Item	Code	1972	1973	1974	1975	1976	1977	1978	1979	1980	1981	1982	1983	1984	1985	1986
Deficit (−) or Surplus	80	....	−7.51	....	−2.15	....	−15.09	1.49	−4.26	†5.44	−22.63	†−52.30	−55.47	−82.44	....	....
Revenue	81	....	47.70	....	77.03	....	86.22	98.14	107.55	†153.67	150.89	†170.63	182.71	192.46	....	....
Grants Received	81z	....	—	....	.02	.17	.05	.04	.26	†.36	1.18	†9.89	13.59	24.77	....	....
Expenditure	82	....	51.00	....	75.64	90.80	96.96	96.80	111.50	†147.18	171.89	†231.01	250.04	298.46	....	....
Lending Minus Repayments	83	....	4.21	....	3.56	.62	4.40	−.11	.57	†1.41	2.81	†1.81	1.73	1.21	....	....
Financing																
Net Borrowing: Domestic	84a	....	....		2.31					†10.60	23.51	†49.64	15.91	23.86	....	....
Foreign	85a	....	....		−.16					†−16.90	6.47	†26.08	41.78	40.60	....	....
Use of Cash Balances	87	....	....							†.86	−7.35	†−23.42	−2.22	17.98	....	....
Debt: Domestic	88a									....	....	†123.59	147.28	172.58	....	....
Foreign	89a									....	....	†313.96	423.84	520.68	....	....

National Accounts

Billions of Francs:

Item	Code	1972	1973	1974	1975	1976	1977	1978	1979	1980	1981	1982	1983	1984	1985	1986
Househ.Cons.Expend.,incl.NPISHs	96f	207.6	220.4	246.6	308.8	365.5	381.4	404.9	470.3	534.2	597.3	715.6	792.4	824.8	998.1	1,048.2
Government Consumption Expend.	91f	37.2	40.0	45.6	56.4	65.5	71.1	83.2	101.3	128.1	137.6	154.5	170.3	188.8	194.5	200.8
Gross Fixed Capital Formation	93e	31.1	32.9	43.0	47.0	51.0	51.7	55.8	68.6	83.2	85.1	103.4	123.2	126.1	134.0	156.8
Changes in Inventories	93i	8.9	12.1	23.2	14.9	12.0	18.8	15.6	−1.7	−9.2	1.0	.5	−2.5	5.1	−12.7	−8.2
Exports of Goods and Services	90c	81.9	77.4	141.3	144.5	162.8	204.4	146.4	181.0	169.7	208.5	279.9	299.8	373.3	331.3	333.0
Imports of Goods and Services (−)	98c	91.4	102.7	158.6	162.6	194.6	240.6	208.0	233.9	275.0	355.8	405.1	438.2	496.9	486.7	427.2
Gross Domestic Product (GDP)	99b	275.1	279.7	340.3	408.5	461.8	486.1	498.5	585.2	631.0	673.6	848.9	944.9	1,021.2	1,158.5	1,303.3
Net Primary Income from Abroad	98.n	8.2	5.3	4.9	3.0	12.2	13.9	12.6	9.3	9.8	29.4	37.8	22.1	15.8	35.0	30.0
Gross National Income (GNI)	99a	283.3	285.0	345.2	411.5	474.0	500.1	511.0	594.4	640.8	702.9	886.6	966.9	1,037.1	1,193.5	1,333.3
GDP Volume 1987 Prices	99b.p	983.3	928.4	967.4	1,040.3	1,133.1	1,102.7	1,059.1	1,133.1	1,095.8	1,082.8	1,249.0	1,276.1	1,225.0	1,271.3	1,329.3
GDP Volume (1995=100)	99bvp	61.4	57.9	60.4	64.9	70.7	68.8	66.1	70.7	68.4	67.6	78.0	79.6	76.5	79.3	83.0
GDP Deflator (1995=100)	99bip	20.1	21.6	25.2	28.2	29.2	31.6	33.8	37.0	41.3	44.6	48.7	53.1	59.8	65.4	70.3

Millions:

Item	Code	1972	1973	1974	1975	1976	1977	1978	1979	1980	1981	1982	1983	1984	1985	1986
Population	99z	4.55	4.70	4.84	4.98	5.12	5.25	5.40	5.55	5.70	5.86	6.03	6.40	6.37	6.55	6.72

	1987	1988	1989	1990	1991	1992	1993	1994	1995	1996	1997	1998	1999	2000	2001	
Minus Sign Indicates Debit																
Balance of Payments																
Current Account, n.i.e.	–430.2	–405.1	–348.1	–363.3	–371.7	–401.3	–433.0	–187.5	–244.5	–199.5	–184.8	–247.5	–320.2	....	....	78al *d*
Goods: Exports f.o.b.	707.5	713.2	804.1	937.9	848.5	860.6	736.8	818.8	993.3	988.0	904.6	967.7	1,027.1	....	....	78aa *d*
Goods: Imports f.o.b.	–955.8	–956.0	–1,004.1	–1,164.3	–1,114.0	–1,191.8	–1,086.7	–1,022.0	–1,242.9	–1,264.0	–1,176.0	–1,280.6	–1,372.8	....	....	78ab *d*
Trade Balance	–248.3	–242.8	–199.9	–226.4	–265.5	–331.1	–349.9	–203.2	–249.6	–275.9	–271.5	–312.9	–345.8	....	....	78ac *d*
Services: Credit	363.6	398.1	397.7	514.8	448.6	481.4	413.9	412.3	512.5	378.6	371.7	425.1	416.1	....	....	78ad *d*
Services: Debit	–503.8	–519.3	–514.4	–675.6	–622.6	–654.2	–581.3	–492.7	–578.2	–395.9	–391.7	–442.9	–430.4	....	....	78ae *d*
Balance on Goods & Services	–388.5	–364.0	–316.6	–387.2	–439.5	–503.9	–517.3	–283.6	–315.3	–293.2	–291.5	–330.6	–360.0	....	....	78af *d*
Income: Credit	53.1	50.5	57.0	84.3	85.3	96.5	82.8	63.3	87.2	81.3	67.9	76.6	83.3	....	....	78ag *d*
Income: Debit	–205.1	–222.3	–219.5	–213.3	–175.9	–173.0	–162.3	–164.5	–211.5	–154.1	–139.8	–164.6	–202.5	....	....	78ah *d*
Balance on Gds, Serv. & Inc.	–540.5	–535.8	–479.1	–516.3	–530.1	–580.5	–596.8	–384.7	–439.6	–366.0	–363.4	–418.6	–479.2	....	....	78ai *d*
Current Transfers, n.i.e.: Credit	195.4	218.0	215.2	257.1	269.4	290.8	267.0	267.0	284.7	244.3	258.8	254.7	225.4	....	....	78aj *d*
Current Transfers: Debit	–85.0	–87.2	–84.1	–104.1	–111.1	–111.6	–103.2	–69.7	–89.6	–77.8	–80.3	–83.6	–66.3	....	....	78ak *d*
Capital Account, n.i.e.	123.7	147.6	148.3	171.6	171.7	182.8	153.7	190.6	187.0	169.2	96.0	98.3	98.6	....	....	78bc *d*
Capital Account, n.i.e.: Credit	149.5	170.0	169.9	197.4	193.3	198.3	165.9	200.5	201.2	169.3	96.3	98.8	99.0	....	....	78ba *d*
Capital Account: Debit	–25.8	–22.4	–21.6	–25.8	–21.6	–15.5	–12.2	–9.9	–14.2	–.1	–.3	–.4	–.5	....	....	78bb *d*
Financial Account, n.i.e.	210.6	173.0	14.4	55.4	16.8	113.2	129.4	48.5	44.2	–179.1	3.5	–109.7	–54.8	....	....	78bj *d*
Direct Investment Abroad	1.9	–13.8	–8.6	9.5	19.1	–51.3	–.3	–17.4	3.3	–3.0	.5	–10.5	–14.5	....	....	78bd *d*
Dir. Invest. in Rep. Econ., n.i.e.	–4.0	14.9	26.8	56.9	–7.6	21.4	–.8	66.9	31.7	8.4	176.4	70.8	156.6	....	....	78be *d*
Portfolio Investment Assets	—	–.1	—	–1.0	—	—	—	–1.5	–.4	–25.8	–18.9	–21.9	–31.3	....	....	78bf *d*
Equity Securities	—	–.1	—	–1.0	—	—	—	–1.5	–.4	–2.4	.9	–9.8	–6.2	....	....	78bk *d*
Debt Securities	—	—	—	—	—	—	—	—	—	–23.4	–19.9	–12.1	–25.1	....	....	78bl *d*
Portfolio Investment Liab., n.i.e.	.7	1.2	.1	1.6	6.5	.7	5.8	.5	4.0	–4.8	–8.1	–3.9	—	....	....	78bg *d*
Equity Securities	.7	1.2	–.7	1.3	–.2	.9	6.1	.5	4.1	—	8.4	2.6	3.4	....	....	78bm *d*
Debt Securities	—	—	.8	.3	6.7	–.2	–.3	—	–.1	–4.8	–16.4	–6.5	–3.4	....	....	78bn *d*
Financial Derivatives Assets	—	—	—	—	—	—	—	—	—	—	–.7	—	–.7	....	....	78bw *d*
Financial Derivatives Liabilities	—	—	—	—	—	—	—	—	—	—	—	.1	—	....	....	78bx *d*
Other Investment Assets	7.9	–41.8	–15.1	57.8	–34.2	–24.9	4.1	–92.5	–6.2	–70.7	–22.1	–58.8	–62.3	....	....	78bh *d*
Monetary Authorities	....	....	....	....	....	....	....	....	....	....	....	....	....	....	....	78bo *d*
General Government	–.2	.1	—	.3	—	–.7	–.6	—	—	–3.1	–.9	–.4	—	....	....	78bp *d*
Banks	3.4	–28.9	–15.4	56.7	–31.1	–24.4	–2.6	–108.8	10.9	30.9	–24.5	–42.4	–54.8	....	....	78bq *d*
Other Sectors	4.8	–13.1	.3	.8	–3.1	.2	7.4	16.3	–17.1	–98.5	3.3	–15.9	–7.6	....	....	78br *d*
Other Investment Liab., n.i.e.	204.1	212.6	11.1	–69.5	33.0	167.4	120.7	92.6	11.8	–83.2	–123.7	–85.5	–102.6	....	....	78bi *d*
Monetary Authorities	–29.0	130.5	–110.4	–12.3	–42.6	34.3	135.3	–76.2	–35.7	1.5	.3	.7	2.5	....	....	78bs *d*
General Government	265.9	96.9	106.8	82.9	87.3	173.0	69.0	90.7	83.9	–140.4	–132.6	–112.9	–114.8	....	....	78bt *d*
Banks	17.3	47.2	32.4	–94.9	13.4	–23.4	–6.6	9.8	–27.1	–4.3	23.6	23.5	5.9	....	....	78bu *d*
Other Sectors	–50.1	–61.9	–17.6	–45.2	–25.1	–16.5	–77.0	68.3	–9.3	60.0	–14.9	3.3	3.7	....	....	78bv *d*
Net Errors and Omissions	–.3	–21.0	12.3	–1.2	3.1	–19.6	8.4	–28.9	–19.6	7.6	–9.3	10.7	8.2	....	....	78ca *d*
Overall Balance	–96.2	–105.5	–173.1	–137.5	–180.1	–124.9	–141.5	22.8	–32.9	–201.9	–94.7	–248.1	–268.2	....	....	78cb *d*
Reserves and Related Items	96.2	105.5	173.1	137.5	180.1	124.9	141.5	–22.8	32.9	201.9	94.7	248.1	268.2	....	....	79da *d*
Reserve Assets	1.9	–2.3	–7.8	9.8	–2.1	.1	8.5	–170.1	–74.8	–34.8	–137.4	–20.7	–31.6	....	....	79db *d*
Use of Fund Credit and Loans	6.8	–6.5	6.2	–27.7	10.6	–44.2	–27.4	38.9	42.9	–9.8	–12.8	–11.6	–13.4	....	....	79dc *d*
Exceptional Financing	87.5	114.3	174.8	155.4	171.6	169.0	160.3	108.4	64.9	246.5	244.8	280.4	313.2	....	....	79de *d*
Millions of US Dollars																
International Investment Position																
Assets	124.7	140.7	172.3	123.8	158.8	172.8	155.7	376.6	561.4	640.7	711.7	860.1	889.8	....	....	79aa *d*
Direct Investment Abroad	—	—	—	—	—	—	—	—	9.9	10.2	2.6	8.9	18.3	....	....	79ab *d*
Portfolio Investment	—	—	—	—	—	—	—	—	8.6	33.2	52.2	78.2	93.7	....	....	79ac *d*
Equity Securities	....	....	....	....	....	....	....	....	.9	3.2	.7	20.8	14.2	....	....	79ad *d*
Debt Securities	....	....	....	....	....	....	....	....	7.6	30.0	51.5	57.4	79.5	....	....	79ae *d*
Financial Derivatives	....	....	....	....	....	....	....	....	.1	.1	.8	—	.7	....	....	79al *d*
Other Investment	115.5	130.2	153.3	112.8	145.6	160.4	152.3	197.0	271.0	308.9	269.8	339.9	374.1	....	....	79af *d*
Monetary Authorities	—	—	—	—	—	—	—	—	—	—	—	—	—	....	....	79ag *d*
General Government	....	....	....	....	....	....	....	....	....	....	....	....	....	....	....	79ah *d*
Banks	115.5	130.2	153.3	112.8	145.6	160.4	152.3	197.0	144.4	104.9	115.6	167.5	195.9	....	....	79ai *d*
Other Sectors	....	....	....	....	....	....	....	....	....	....	....	....	....	....	....	79aj *d*
Reserve Assets	9.2	10.5	19.0	11.0	13.2	12.4	3.4	179.6	271.8	288.3	386.2	433.1	403.0	....	....	79ak *d*
Liabilities	3,869.6	3,933.6	3,429.1	3,564.8	3,607.3	3,951.1	3,643.7	3,443.6	4,261.8	4,100.6	4,072.1	4,721.1	4,223.1	....	....	79la *d*
Dir. Invest. in Rep. Economy	—	—	—	—	—	—	—	—	78.6	76.4	256.2	372.1	329.4	....	....	79lb *d*
Portfolio Investment	—	—	—	—	—	—	—	—	83.3	73.0	56.8	96.2	92.9	....	....	79lc *d*
Equity Securities	....	....	....	....	....	....	....	....	10.3	9.4	17.2	66.8	63.5	....	....	79ld *d*
Debt Securities	....	....	....	....	....	....	....	....	73.0	63.6	39.6	29.4	29.4	....	....	79le *d*
Financial Derivatives	—	—	—	—	—	—	—	—	—	—	—	.1	—	....	....	79ll *d*
Other Investment	3,869.6	3,933.6	3,429.1	3,564.8	3,607.3	3,951.1	3,643.7	3,443.6	4,099.9	3,951.2	3,759.1	4,252.7	3,800.8	....	....	79lf *d*
Monetary Authorities	660.6	726.6	621.6	646.2	609.6	569.8	652.9	446.1	470.1	442.5	394.6	402.4	369.0	....	....	79lg *d*
General Government	2,984.6	2,962.9	2,514.2	2,690.2	2,754.8	3,171.5	2,801.1	2,882.7	3,323.6	3,035.5	2,864.5	3,232.7	2,852.3	....	....	79lh *d*
Banks	224.4	244.1	293.3	228.4	242.8	209.8	189.7	114.8	184.9	171.3	176.4	210.1	218.3	....	....	79li *d*
Other Sectors	—	—	—	—	—	—	—	—	121.3	302.0	323.7	407.4	361.2	....	....	79lj *d*
Year Ending June 30																
Government Finance																
Deficit (-) or Surplus	....	....	....	....	....	....	....	....	....	....	....	....	....	....	....	80
Revenue	....	....	....	....	....	....	....	....	....	....	....	....	....	....	....	81
Grants Received	....	....	....	....	....	....	....	....	....	....	....	....	....	....	....	81z
Expenditure	....	....	....	....	....	....	....	....	....	....	....	....	....	....	....	82
Lending Minus Repayments	....	....	....	....	....	....	....	....	....	....	....	....	....	....	....	83
Financing																
Net Borrowing: Domestic	....	....	....	....	....	....	....	....	....	....	....	....	....	....	....	84a
Foreign	....	....	....	....	....	....	....	....	....	....	....	....	....	....	....	85a
Use of Cash Balances	....	....	....	....	....	....	....	....	....	....	....	....	....	....	....	87
Debt: Domestic	....	....	....	....	....	....	....	....	....	....	....	....	....	....	....	88a
Foreign	....	....	....	....	....	....	....	....	....	....	....	....	....	....	....	89a
Billions of Francs																
National Accounts																
Househ.Cons.Expend.,incl.NPISHs	1,099.6	1,171.0	1,151.5	1,185.1	1,187.0	1,220.4	1,191.5	1,450.6	1,763.9	1,878.6	1,951.9	2,060.0	....	....	....	96f
Government Consumption Expend.	215.6	218.1	229.7	222.3	222.3	239.9	227.7	258.4	276.1	286.4	289.0	307.2	....	....	....	91f
Gross Fixed Capital Formation	172.1	188.6	195.8	200.3	209.3	222.9	207.1	295.1	327.7	387.0	460.4	556.2	....	....	....	93e
Changes in Inventories	.3	—	–20.9	13.8	–15.1	6.9	3.0	49.0	45.7	52.5	....		....	....	....	93i
Exports of Goods and Services	332.9	337.5	393.6	394.7	397.2	357.5	341.2	652.0	718.2	727.7	868.4	901.9	....	....	....	90c
Imports of Goods and Services (-)	434.3	431.9	473.9	470.5	449.4	452.2	432.9	683.1	897.6	952.7	1,014.0	1,064.3	....	....	....	98c
Gross Domestic Product (GDP)	1,382.3	1,483.3	1,475.9	1,551.5	1,551.5	1,595.4	1,537.8	2,022.3	2,234.0	2,379.6	2,555.7	2,761.0	....	....	....	99b
Net Primary Income from Abroad	34.2	46.3	51.4	62.7	78.2	86.3	79.3	179.2	86.2	111.4	112.9	119.2	....	....	....	98.n
Gross National Income (GNI)	1,416.6	1,529.7	1,527.3	1,614.1	1,629.7	1,681.7	1,617.1	2,201.4	2,320.3	2,491.0	2,668.8	2,880.2	....	....	....	99a
GDP Volume 1987 Prices	1,382.3	1,452.4	1,432.1	1,487.7	1,481.8	1,514.6	1,481.0	1,523.5	1,602.2	1,684.7	1,769.7	1,869.8	....	....	....	99b.*p*
GDP Volume (1995=100)	86.3	90.7	89.4	92.9	92.5	94.5	92.4	95.1	100.0	105.1	110.5	116.7	....	....	....	99bv *p*
GDP Deflator (1995=100)	71.7	73.2	73.9	74.8	75.1	75.5	74.5	95.2	100.0	101.3	103.6	105.9	....	....	....	99bi *p*
Midyear Estimates																
Population	6.91	6.91	7.10	7.30	7.50	7.70	7.91	8.13	8.57	8.80	9.04	9.28	9.28	9.52	9.66	99z

(See notes in the back of the book.)

Seychelles

		1972	1973	1974	1975	1976	1977	1978	1979	1980	1981	1982	1983	1984	1985	1986
Exchange Rates															*Rupees per SDR:*	
Official Rate	aa	†6.1650	6.9235	6.9511	7.7137	9.0995	8.4974	8.5380	8.3197	8.3197	7.2345	7.2345	7.2345	7.2345	7.2345	7.2345
															Rupees per US Dollar:	
Official Rate	ae	†5.6783	5.7392	5.6774	6.5892	7.8321	6.9954	6.5536	6.3156	6.5184	6.2273	6.5475	6.9227	7.3578	6.6018	5.9290
Official Rate	rf	5.3385	5.4423	5.7031	6.0268	7.4189	7.6434	6.9525	6.3327	6.3920	6.3149	6.5525	6.7676	7.0589	7.1343	6.1768
Fund Position															*Millions of SDRs:*	
Quota	2f. s	...	...	...	...	...	1.00	1.30	1.30	2.00	2.00	2.00	3.00	3.00	3.00	3.00
SDRs	1b. s	...	...	...	...	...	—	—	.09	.04	.17	.16	.05	.02	.01	.02
Reserve Position in the Fund	1c. s	...	...	...	...	...	.10	.10	.25	.43	.44	.44	—	—	—	.02
Total Fund Cred.&Loans Outstg.	2tl	...	...	...	...	...	—	—	—	—	—	—	—	—	—	—
International Liquidity											*Millions of US Dollars Unless Otherwise Indicated:*					
Total Reserves minus Gold	1l. d	...	4.27	5.04	6.34	6.49	11.51	9.26	12.15	18.44	13.80	13.07	9.97	5.40	8.50	7.75
SDRs	1b. d	...	...	...	...	...	—	—	.12	.05	.20	.18	.05	.02	.01	.02
Reserve Position in the Fund	1c. d	...	...	...	...	...	.12	.13	.33	.55	.51	.49	—	—	—	.02
Foreign Exchange	1d. d	...	4.27	5.04	6.34	6.49	11.39	9.13	11.70	17.84	13.09	12.41	9.92	5.38	8.49	7.70
Deposit Money Banks: Assets	7a. d	2.79	.10	.70	1.81	4.09	3.40	6.32	5.57	7.49	7.19	2.93	3.08	3.67	4.85	5.48
Liabilities	7b. d							1.24	1.08	1.20	3.65	3.88	3.58	2.43	3.57	3.41
Monetary Authorities															*Millions of Rupees:*	
Foreign Assets	11	17.1	17.8	18.9	26.7	31.8	48.0	45.5	70.7	122.5	88.3	87.7	71.5	62.4	59.9	49.6
Claims on Central Government	12a	1.8	1.5	1.5	1.5	1.5	1.5	9.3	4.4	1.5	18.6	33.3	58.0	69.7	106.3	101.5
Claims on Deposit Money Banks	12e	—	—	—	—	—	—	—	—	—	10.5	13.8	13.7	9.6	6.5	20.7
Reserve Money	14	17.8	20.1	21.1	24.9	33.2	42.3	48.7	64.3	108.7	98.3	93.2	99.6	96.1	107.7	106.1
of which: Currency Outside DMBs	14a	17.0	18.9	20.1	22.7	31.1	40.1	43.9	52.9	61.7	65.3	62.6	64.3	69.9	75.8	78.1
Central Government Deposits	16d	—	—	—	—	—	—	—	—	—	1.0	1.0	2.0	13.7	24.4	28.6
Capital Accounts	17a	—	—	—	—	—	—	4.0	9.7	13.2	14.0	14.0	14.0	14.0	14.0	14.0
Other Items (Net)	17r	1.1	−.8	−.7	3.3	.1	7.2	2.1	1.2	2.1	4.1	26.7	27.6	18.0	26.6	23.1
Deposit Money Banks															*Millions of Rupees:*	
Reserves	20	.8	1.2	1.0	2.2	2.1	2.2	4.8	5.8	27.3	18.6	15.4	21.9	16.5	31.2	27.3
Foreign Assets	21	14.3	.6	4.0	11.9	32.0	23.8	41.4	35.2	48.8	44.8	19.2	21.3	27.0	32.0	32.5
Claims on Central Government	22a	1.4	5.2	5.9	7.0	10.2	8.4	6.8	17.7	26.2	39.2	36.2	48.3	69.6	184.2	270.0
Claims on Nonfin.Pub.Enterprises	22c	—	—	—	—	—	—	1.0	1.0	10.4	32.8	69.1	63.9	87.1	24.9	21.9
Claims on Private Sector	22d	33.7	48.1	50.7	54.8	83.5	117.0	137.1	155.4	160.1	155.3	143.7	137.4	120.4	104.6	90.8
Demand Deposits	24	20.7	21.4	21.8	25.1	36.5	43.7	51.1	56.2	77.3	78.2	65.5	53.6	55.1	78.8	76.2
Time and Savings Deposits	25	27.1	31.7	32.6	48.6	70.7	78.3	89.4	110.9	141.7	135.9	127.2	146.8	183.5	208.1	250.2
Restricted Deposits	26b	—	—	—	—	—	—	—	—	—	—	—	—	—	—	—
Foreign Liabilities	26c	—	—	—	—	—	—	8.1	6.8	7.8	22.7	25.4	24.8	17.9	23.6	20.2
Central Government Deposits	26d	—	2.8	1.8	2.9	8.8	14.6	14.1	9.6	8.7	11.4	14.8	17.2	19.6	21.2	34.0
Credit from Monetary Authorities	26g	—	—	—	—	—	—	—	—	—	—	10.5	13.8	13.7	9.6	6.5	9.7
Capital Accounts	27a	—	—	—	—	16.0	16.0	28.8	24.0	24.0	24.0	24.0	24.0	24.0	24.7	24.8
Other Items (Net)	27r	2.4	−.8	5.4	−.7	−4.2	−1.2	−.4	7.6	13.3	8.0	12.9	12.7	10.9	14.0	27.3
Monetary Survey															*Millions of Rupees:*	
Foreign Assets (Net)	31n	31.4	18.4	22.9	38.6	63.8	71.8	78.8	99.1	163.5	110.4	81.5	68.0	71.5	68.3	61.9
Domestic Credit	32	36.9	52.0	56.3	60.4	86.4	112.3	141.1	169.9	190.5	234.5	267.5	289.4	314.5	375.4	422.6
Claims on Central Govt. (Net)	32an	3.2	3.9	5.6	5.6	2.9	−4.7	2.0	12.5	19.0	45.4	53.7	87.1	106.0	244.9	308.9
Claims on Nonfin.Pub.Enterprises	32c	—	—	—	—	—	—	1.0	1.0	10.4	32.8	69.1	63.9	87.1	24.9	21.9
Claims on Private Sector	32d	33.7	48.1	50.7	54.8	83.5	117.0	137.1	155.4	160.1	155.3	143.7	137.4	120.4	104.6	90.8
Money	34	37.7	40.3	41.9	47.8	67.6	83.8	95.0	114.7	158.7	157.9	143.3	131.3	134.7	155.3	155.0
Quasi-Money	35	27.1	31.7	32.6	48.6	70.7	78.3	89.4	110.9	141.7	135.9	127.2	146.8	183.5	208.1	250.2
Restricted Deposits	36b	—	—	—	—	—	—	—	—	—	—	—	—	—	—	—
Capital Accounts	37a	—	—	—	—	16.0	16.0	32.8	33.7	37.2	38.0	38.0	38.0	38.0	38.7	38.8
Other Items (Net)	37r	3.5	−1.6	4.7	2.6	−4.1	6.0	2.7	9.8	16.4	13.1	40.6	41.3	29.9	41.6	40.4
Money plus Quasi-Money	35l	64.8	72.0	74.5	96.4	138.3	162.1	184.4	225.6	300.4	293.8	270.5	278.1	318.2	363.4	405.3
Other Banking Institutions															*Millions of Rupees:*	
Reserves	40	...	...	...	...	...	...	...	...	7.2	7.8	7.8	5.5	.6	1.7	3.0
Claims on Central Government	42a									—	1.0	2.3	16.7	23.8	29.1	33.0
Claims on Nonfin.Pub.Enterprises	42c									.3	6.0	9.1	7.6	7.4	17.7	30.3
Claims on Private Sector	42d									—	9.6	14.9	18.9	22.4	24.3	27.4
Claims on Deposit Money Banks	42e									—	14.8	12.7	11.4	4.4	3.3	3.8
Time and Savings Deposits	45									3.0	6.5	10.6	22.2	23.1	27.8	35.3
Capital Accounts	47a									4.6	31.9	33.3	33.6	40.5	41.4	46.2
Other Items (Net)	47r									−.1	.8	2.9	4.3	−5.0	6.9	16.0
Banking Survey															*Millions of Rupees:*	
Foreign Assets (Net)	51n	...	...	...	...	...	...	...	...	163.5	110.4	81.5	68.0	71.5	68.3	61.9
Domestic Credit	52									189.8	250.1	292.8	331.6	367.1	445.5	512.3
Claims on Central Govt. (Net)	52an									19.0	46.4	56.0	103.8	129.8	274.0	341.9
Claims on Nonfin.Pub.Enterprises	52c									10.7	38.8	78.2	71.5	94.5	42.6	52.2
Claims on Private Sector	52d									160.1	164.9	158.6	156.3	142.8	128.9	118.2
Liquid Liabilities	55l									296.2	292.5	273.3	294.8	340.7	389.5	437.6
Restricted Deposits	56b															
Capital Accounts	57a									41.8	69.9	71.3	71.6	78.5	80.1	85.0
Other Items (Net)	57r									15.3	−1.9	29.8	33.2	19.5	44.2	51.6
Interest Rates															*Percent Per Annum*	
Discount Rate *(End of Period)*	60									...	6.00	6.00	6.00	6.00	6.00	6.00
Treasury Bill Rate	60c									9.56	9.15	10.10	12.07	12.61	12.48	12.90
Deposit Rate	60l									...	9.00	9.00	9.08	9.50	9.60	10.00
Lending Rate	60p									...	...	...	...	...	...	...
Prices and Labor															*Index Numbers (1995=100):*	
Consumer Prices	64	20.8	24.6	30.6	36.3	41.7	†47.9	53.6	60.3	68.5	†75.7	75.0	79.6	82.8	83.5	83.7
															Number in Thousands:	
Employment	67e	...	...	...	...	...	...	...	...	...	...	...	...	...	18	19

	1987	1988	1989	1990	1991	1992	1993	1994	1995	1996	1997	1998	1999	2000	2001		
End of Period																**Exchange Rates**	
	7.2345	7.2345	7.2345	7.2345	7.2345	7.2345	7.2345	7.2345	7.2345	7.2345	6.9218	7.6699	7.3671	8.1642	7.2226	Official Rate	**aa**
End of Period (ae) Period Average (rf)																	
	5.1435	5.3966	5.4672	5.1188	5.0627	5.2545	5.2579	4.9695	4.8639	4.9946	5.1249	5.4521	5.3676	6.2689	5.7522	Official Rate	**ae**
	5.6000	5.3836	5.6457	5.3369	5.2893	5.1220	5.1815	5.0559	4.7620	4.9700	5.0263	5.2622	5.3426	5.7138	5.8575	Official Rate	**rf**
End of Period																**Fund Position**	
	3.00	3.00	3.00	3.00	3.00	6.00	6.00	6.00	6.00	6.00	6.00	6.00	8.80	8.80	8.80	Quota	**2f. s**
	—	.01	.01	.01	.04	.01	.01	.02	.02	.02	.03	.03	.03	.01	.02	SDRs	**1b. s**
	.03	.04	.05	.05	.05	.80	.80	.80	.80	.80	.80	—	—	—	—	Reserve Position in the Fund	**1c. s**
	—	—	—	—	—	—	—	—	—	—	—	—	—	—	—	Total Fund Cred.&Loans Outstg.	**2tl**
End of Period																**International Liquidity**	
	13.71	8.71	12.11	16.64	27.65	31.26	35.65	30.15	27.10	21.76	26.32	21.59	30.35	43.75	37.13	Total Reserves minus Gold	**1l. d**
	—	.01	.01	.01	.06	.01	.02	.02	.03	.03	.04	.04	.04	.01	.02	SDRs	**1b. d**
	.04	.05	.07	.07	.07	1.10	1.10	1.17	1.20	1.16	1.09	—	—	—	—	Reserve Position in the Fund	**1c. d**
	13.67	8.64	12.04	16.55	27.52	30.14	34.53	28.96	25.87	20.57	25.20	21.55	30.31	43.74	37.11	Foreign Exchange	**1d. d**
	5.99	6.58	4.99	11.23	17.88	9.44	7.66	5.03	9.91	19.28	30.97	29.36	43.72	51.43	51.11	Deposit Money Banks: Assets	**7a. d**
	4.94	4.65	7.85	11.55	13.95	6.76	7.32	6.42	10.36	17.96	33.41	34.72	47.05	61.37	55.94	Liabilities	**7b. d**
End of Period																**Monetary Authorities**	
	72.7	46.5	65.6	84.4	138.4	157.6	180.5	142.8	126.8	99.1	127.2	115.1	160.2	271.1	210.6	Foreign Assets	**11**
	139.3	165.7	103.3	105.4	110.9	241.4	302.0	529.2	663.3	790.5	926.8	575.1	640.2	698.8	774.0	Claims on Central Government	**12a**
	13.7	21.4	30.7	18.5	13.0	4.0	21.5	7.0	1.8	—	—	10.0	—	22.0	—	Claims on Deposit Money Banks	**12e**
	105.6	134.0	140.0	164.0	206.3	311.8	383.8	566.7	684.8	778.7	924.0	468.7	512.8	528.7	566.8	Reserve Money	**14**
	82.4	95.6	99.5	104.5	113.6	122.5	134.5	141.6	148.1	165.7	192.2	206.4	248.0	264.4	279.8	*of which: Currency Outside DMBs*	**14a**
	93.8	91.3	26.8	21.4	30.3	64.3	58.8	30.9	21.4	15.4	18.1	18.2	49.0	21.5	18.9	Central Government Deposits	**16d**
	14.0	14.0	13.9	15.9	14.0	14.0	14.0	13.9	13.9	13.9	13.8	14.1	25.9	43.2	51.4	Capital Accounts	**17a**
	12.3	−5.7	18.9	7.1	11.7	12.9	47.4	67.4	71.7	81.6	98.0	199.2	212.7	398.4	347.5	Other Items (Net)	**17r**
End of Period																**Deposit Money Banks**	
	22.5	38.0	39.8	58.8	91.9	188.5	248.7	424.5	536.0	612.3	731.1	261.6	264.1	263.5	286.1	Reserves	**20**
	30.8	35.5	27.3	57.5	90.5	49.6	40.3	25.0	48.2	96.3	158.7	160.1	234.7	322.4	294.0	Foreign Assets	**21**
	335.8	411.8	526.1	547.2	633.6	632.9	779.0	692.3	747.8	843.1	1,086.9	2,106.7	2,526.6	2,805.7	3,101.6	Claims on Central Government	**22a**
	23.3	35.7	40.3	41.4	58.4	54.1	80.9	118.9	92.4	68.7	71.8	55.9	42.6	20.2	10.8	Claims on Nonfin.Pub.Enterprises	**22c**
	88.6	96.2	127.0	137.2	150.2	157.8	172.8	209.0	245.1	269.6	387.6	460.0	503.5	565.6	643.5	Claims on Private Sector	**22d**
	72.1	91.8	119.4	111.6	151.8	170.0	200.7	184.4	186.2	284.0	456.5	574.2	823.3	873.0	1,010.7	Demand Deposits	**24**
	285.9	351.7	412.9	507.3	541.4	620.3	768.5	768.7	875.1	939.0	1,339.2	1,608.8	1,837.7	2,036.7	2,264.2	Time and Savings Deposits	**25**
	—	—	—	—	—	—	—	198.2	301.4	317.1	218.0	178.3	148.0	132.3	127.7	Restricted Deposits	**26b**
	25.4	25.1	42.9	59.1	70.6	35.5	38.5	31.9	50.4	89.7	171.2	189.3	252.6	384.7	321.8	Foreign Liabilities	**26c**
	48.3	60.1	84.3	46.0	80.1	83.9	107.7	118.8	112.8	88.5	163.2	180.9	203.5	204.5	230.1	Central Government Deposits	**26d**
	13.7	21.4	30.7	18.5	13.0	4.0	21.5	7.0	1.8	—	—	10.0	—	22.0	—	Credit from Monetary Authorities	**26g**
	24.8	25.8	26.3	27.7	75.5	71.8	74.7	76.0	76.0	80.8	96.5	103.9	110.8	110.8	110.8	Capital Accounts	**27a**
	30.8	41.3	44.0	71.9	92.2	97.4	110.1	84.7	65.8	90.9	−8.5	198.9	195.7	213.4	270.7	Other Items (Net)	**27r**
End of Period																**Monetary Survey**	
	78.1	56.9	50.0	82.8	158.3	171.7	182.3	135.9	124.6	105.7	114.7	85.9	142.3	208.8	182.8	Foreign Assets (Net)	**31n**
	445.9	559.0	686.6	764.8	843.7	939.0	1,169.2	1,400.7	1,615.4	1,869.0	2,292.8	2,999.6	3,461.4	3,865.3	4,281.9	Domestic Credit	**32**
	333.0	426.1	518.3	585.2	634.1	726.1	914.5	1,071.8	1,276.9	1,529.7	1,832.4	2,482.7	2,914.4	3,278.5	3,626.6	Claims on Central Govt. (Net)	**32an**
	23.3	35.7	40.3	41.4	58.4	54.1	80.9	118.9	92.4	68.7	71.8	55.9	42.6	20.2	10.8	Claims on Nonfin.Pub.Enterprises	**32c**
	88.6	96.2	127.0	137.2	150.2	157.8	172.8	209.0	245.1	269.6	387.6	460.0	503.5	565.6	643.5	Claims on Private Sector	**32d**
	155.2	187.8	219.6	216.8	266.2	293.3	335.8	326.6	335.0	450.4	649.4	781.3	1,071.9	1,138.2	1,291.4	Money	**34**
	285.9	351.7	412.9	507.3	541.4	620.3	768.5	768.7	875.1	939.0	1,339.2	1,608.8	1,837.7	2,036.7	2,264.2	Quasi-Money	**35**
	—	—	—	—	—	—	—	198.2	301.4	317.1	218.0	178.3	148.0	132.3	127.7	Restricted Deposits	**36b**
	38.8	39.8	40.2	43.6	89.5	85.8	88.7	89.9	89.9	94.7	110.3	118.0	136.6	154.0	162.2	Capital Accounts	**37a**
	44.1	36.6	63.9	80.0	104.9	111.3	158.5	153.1	138.5	173.5	90.5	399.1	409.5	612.9	619.2	Other Items (Net)	**37r**
	441.1	539.5	632.5	724.1	807.6	913.6	1,104.3	1,095.3	1,210.1	1,389.4	1,988.6	2,390.1	2,909.7	3,174.9	3,555.6	Money plus Quasi-Money	**35l**
End of Period																**Other Banking Institutions**	
	2.0	2.3	3.6	2.0	3.6	4.0	3.5	2.4	3.6	1.9	—	—	—	—	—	Reserves	**40**
	41.3	53.6	57.6	61.6	68.0	86.9	121.9	121.3	93.2	115.8	—	—	—	—	—	Claims on Central Government	**42a**
	44.3	53.0	65.0	76.2	83.2	77.5	65.1	78.1	55.1	49.1	34.5	28.0	20.7	13.6	7.9	Claims on Nonfin.Pub.Enterprises	**42c**
	34.2	40.6	45.2	58.7	61.4	76.3	99.3	124.9	152.4	186.6	163.8	176.2	184.7	202.1	217.9	Claims on Private Sector	**42d**
	2.2	1.5	4.7	1.5	1.8	1.7	4.3	4.1	12.1	10.0	9.9	17.8	24.5	31.3	30.6	Claims on Deposit Money Banks	**42e**
	41.7	50.0	60.1	61.0	69.9	92.7	138.2	182.8	176.1	197.0	—	—	—	—	—	Time and Savings Deposits	**45**
	56.4	60.3	63.2	69.2	72.3	77.0	85.6	92.9	93.9	100.6	115.0	129.2	151.0	153.6	170.1	Capital Accounts	**47a**
	25.9	40.7	52.8	69.8	75.8	76.7	70.3	55.1	46.5	65.8	93.2	92.8	78.9	93.3	86.3	Other Items (Net)	**47r**
End of Period																**Banking Survey**	
	78.1	56.9	50.0	82.8	158.3	171.7	182.3	135.9	124.6	105.7	114.7	85.9	142.3	208.8	182.8	Foreign Assets (Net)	**51n**
	564.7	705.2	853.4	960.3	1,055.3	1,178.7	1,454.5	1,724.0	1,915.1	2,219.5	2,490.1	3,202.8	3,665.8	4,080.0	4,506.7	Domestic Credit	**52**
	374.3	479.7	575.9	646.8	702.1	813.0	1,036.4	1,193.1	1,370.1	1,645.5	1,832.4	2,482.7	2,914.4	3,278.5	3,626.6	Claims on Central Govt. (Net)	**52an**
	67.6	88.7	105.3	117.6	141.6	131.6	146.0	197.0	147.5	117.8	106.3	83.9	63.3	33.8	18.7	Claims on Nonfin.Pub.Enterprises	**52c**
	122.8	136.8	172.2	195.9	211.6	234.1	272.1	333.9	397.5	456.2	551.4	636.2	688.2	767.7	861.4	Claims on Private Sector	**52d**
	480.8	587.2	689.0	783.1	873.9	1,002.3	1,239.0	1,275.7	1,382.5	1,584.4	1,988.6	2,390.1	2,909.7	3,174.9	3,555.6	Liquid Liabilities	**55l**
	—	—	—	—	—	—	—	198.2	301.4	317.1	218.0	178.3	148.0	132.3	127.7	Restricted Deposits	**56b**
	95.2	100.1	103.4	112.8	161.8	162.8	174.3	182.8	183.9	195.3	225.3	247.2	287.6	307.7	332.4	Capital Accounts	**57a**
	66.8	74.8	111.0	147.3	177.9	185.3	223.5	203.1	171.9	228.3	172.8	473.1	462.9	673.9	673.9	Other Items (Net)	**57r**
Percent Per Annum																**Interest Rates**	
	6.00	6.00	6.00	†1.00	1.00	1.00	1.00	1.00	1.00	1.00	1.00	1.00	1.00	1.00	1.00	Discount Rate *(End of Period)*	**60**
	15.15	13.90	13.41	13.00	13.00	13.00	12.91	12.36	12.15	11.47	10.50	7.96	4.50	4.50	4.50	Treasury Bill Rate	**60c**
	10.00	10.00	9.59	9.53	9.55	9.60	9.51	8.92	9.22	9.90	9.20	7.53	5.13	4.76	4.92	Deposit Rate	**60l**
	. . . .	. . . .	15.52	15.65	15.57	15.58	15.66	15.70	15.76	16.22	14.88	14.39	12.01	11.45	11.14	Lending Rate	**60p**
Period Averages																**Prices and Labor**	
	85.9	87.5	88.8	92.3	94.2	97.2	98.5	100.3	100.0	100.0	98.9	99.5	102.1	†108.6	115.4	122.3	Consumer Prices	**64**
Period Averages																	
	19	21	22	24	24	24	25	25	26	26	28	. . . .	. . . .	. . . .	. . . .	Employment	**67e**

Seychelles

		1972	1973	1974	1975	1976	1977	1978	1979	1980	1981	1982	1983	1984	1985	1986
International Transactions															*Millions of Rupees*	
Exports	70	13.99	19.68	41.56	38.27	64.34	84.76	105.43	138.63	135.21	108.34	100.09	137.25	181.47	199.69	113.66
Imports, c.i.f.	71	111.67	135.12	160.46	191.35	290.62	349.74	402.05	534.78	631.44	589.01	641.32	594.08	618.73	704.72	651.96
Balance of Payments															*Millions of US Dollars*	
Current Account, n.i.e.	78al d	....	....	....	....	-3.90	-1.87	-3.98	-12.26	-15.62	-18.79	-40.64	-26.05	-13.29	-19.20	-33.29
Goods: Exports f.o.b.	78aa d	....	....	....	....	3.05	4.83	6.63	6.22	5.65	4.64	3.84	4.99	4.98	4.64	4.41
Goods: Imports f.o.b.	78ab d	....	....	....	....	-33.19	-38.63	-51.82	-71.58	-83.66	-79.19	-83.00	-74.50	-73.94	-84.14	-89.34
Trade Balance	78ac d	....	....	....	....	-30.14	-33.81	-45.19	-65.35	-78.01	-74.55	-79.16	-69.51	-68.97	-79.50	-84.93
Services: Credit	78ad d	....	....	....	....	33.89	48.24	63.80	83.62	91.22	88.69	77.76	76.80	95.07	111.99	123.27
Services: Debit	78ae d	....	....	....	....	-10.80	-21.72	-27.87	-35.74	-40.10	-40.50	-41.83	-40.08	-46.36	-59.27	-74.53
Balance on Goods & Services	78af d	....	....	....	....	-7.05	-7.29	-9.26	-17.47	-26.89	-26.35	-43.23	-32.78	-20.26	-26.79	-36.19
Income: Credit	78ag d	....	....	....	....	.80	1.58	2.29	4.91	5.90	4.29	2.79	2.37	2.09	2.16	2.06
Income: Debit	78ah d	....	....	....	....	-2.87	-4.97	-6.04	-7.64	-7.68	-6.88	-6.72	-7.12	-7.82	-8.09	-10.55
Balance on Gds, Serv. & Inc.	78ai d	....	....	....	....	-9.13	-10.68	-13.02	-20.19	-28.67	-28.95	-47.17	-37.54	-25.98	-32.71	-44.68
Current Transfers, n.i.e.: Credit	78aj d	....	....	....	....	6.17	10.24	11.26	10.45	16.18	14.78	12.80	17.63	18.30	17.02	19.85
Current Transfers: Debit	78ak d	....	....	....	....	-.94	-1.44	-2.23	-2.52	-3.13	-4.62	-6.28	-6.15	-5.60	-3.51	-8.46
Capital Account, n.i.e.	78bc d	....	....	....	....	—	—	—	—	—	—	—	—	—	—	—
Capital Account, n.i.e.: Credit	78ba d	....	....	....	....	—	—	—	—	—	—	—	—	—	—	—
Capital Account: Debit	78bb d	....	....	....	....	—	—	—	—	—	—	—	—	—	—	—
Financial Account, n.i.e.	78bj d	....	....	....	....	2.95	3.99	8.37	16.65	18.35	13.85	34.02	15.85	16.00	16.45	33.57
Direct Investment Abroad	78bd d	....	....	....	....	-2.02	-2.26	-2.68	-3.13	-3.81	-7.23	-4.94	-3.24	-3.92	-10.56	-5.78
Dir. Invest. in Rep. Econ., n.i.e.	78be d	....	....	....	....	6.34	7.06	6.33	7.51	9.52	10.07	10.01	9.12	9.77	11.65	14.20
Portfolio Investment Assets	78bf d	....	....	....	....	—	—	—	—	—	—	—	—	—	—	—
Equity Securities	78bk d	....	....	....	....	—	—	—	—	—	—	—	—	—	—	—
Debt Securities	78bl d	....	....	....	....	—	—	—	—	—	—	—	—	—	—	—
Portfolio Investment Liab., n.i.e.	78bg d	....	....	....	....	—	—	—	—	—	—	—	—	—	—	—
Equity Securities	78bm d	....	....	....	....	—	—	—	—	—	—	—	—	—	—	—
Debt Securities	78bn d	....	....	....	....	—	—	—	—	—	—	—	—	—	—	—
Financial Derivatives Assets	78bw d	....	....	....	....	....	....	....	....	....	....	....	....	....	....	....
Financial Derivatives Liabilities	78bx d	....	....	....	....	....	....	....	....	....	....	....	....	....	....	....
Other Investment Assets	78bh d	....	....	....	....	-3.48	-1.27	.60	4.56	.81	3.21	4.73	-.42	-1.78	.03	-.61
Monetary Authorities	78bo d	....	....	....	....											
General Government	78bp d	....	....	....	....	-.77	-2.34	1.97	3.75	2.79	.25	.32	.03	.03	-.02	.05
Banks	78bq d	....	....	....	....	-2.71	1.07	-1.37	.82	-1.98	2.96	4.41	-.45	-1.80	.05	-.66
Other Sectors	78br d	....	....	....	....											
Other Investment Liab., n.i.e.	78bi d	....	....	....	....	2.12	.46	4.11	7.71	11.84	7.79	24.21	10.38	11.92	15.33	25.76
Monetary Authorities	78bs d	....	....	....	....											
General Government	78bt d	....	....	....	....	-.04	.46	2.63	8.06	11.84	7.79	24.21	10.38	11.92	15.33	25.76
Banks	78bu d	....	....	....	....	2.16	—	1.48	-.35	—	—	—	—	—	—	—
Other Sectors	78bv d	....	....	....	....											
Net Errors and Omissions	78ca d	....	....	....	....	1.63	.12	-5.26	-.76	5.23	-.38	6.41	7.71	-4.25	2.70	-1.64
Overall Balance	78cb d	....	....	....	....	.69	2.24	-.88	3.63	7.96	-5.33	-.21	-2.50	-1.54	-.06	-1.36
Reserves and Related Items	79da d	....	....	....	....	-.69	-2.24	.88	-3.63	-7.96	5.33	.21	2.50	1.54	.06	1.36
Reserve Assets	79db d	....	....	....	....	-.69	-2.24	.88	-3.63	-7.96	5.33	.21	2.50	1.54	.06	1.36
Use of Fund Credit and Loans	79dc d	....	....	....	....	—	—	—	—	—	—	—	—	—	—	—
Exceptional Financing	79de d	....	....	....	....	....	....	....	....	....	....	....	....	....	....	....
Government Finance															*Millions of Rupees:*	
Deficit (-) or Surplus	80	5.5	-11.0	-.8	-.7	-3.1	20.1	-28.8	....	....	....	....	....	†-179.8	-251.8	
Total Revenue and Grants	81y	80.2	67.7	90.9	96.6	126.4	184.5	196.5	....	....	....	....	....	†507.5	547.3	
Revenue	81	35.7	44.6	52.3	58.7	90.3	133.9	165.5	....	....	....	....	....	†476.4	515.6	
Grants	81z	44.5	23.1	38.6	37.9	36.1	50.6	31.0	....	....	....	....	....	†31.1	31.7	
Exp. & Lending Minus Repay.	82z	74.7	78.7	91.7	97.3	129.5	164.4	225.3	....	....	....	....	....	†687.3	799.1	
Expenditure	82	74.1	76.0	81.8	94.2	126.4	156.0	218.2	....	....	....	....	....	†685.8	767.3	
Lending Minus Repayments	83	.6	2.7	9.9	3.1	3.1	8.4	7.1	....	....	....	....	....	†1.5	31.8	
Total Financing	80h	-5.5	11.0	.8	.7	3.1	-20.1	28.8	....	....	....	....	....	†179.7	251.8	
Domestic	84a	-4.8	11.0	3.1	3.2	5.7	-20.0	12.0	....	....	....	....	....	†134.0	106.4	
Foreign	85a	-.7		-2.3	-2.5	-2.6	-.1	16.8	....	....	....	....	....	†45.7	145.4	
Total Debt by Residence	88	10.6	10.4	12.1	17.0	16.4	24.4	....	....	....	....	....	....	....	....	
Domestic	88a	4.1	4.3	6.3	11.5	11.5	15.8	....	....	....	....	....	....	....	....	
Foreign	89a	6.5	6.1	5.8	5.5	4.9	8.6	....	....	....	....	....	....	....	....	
National Accounts															*Millions of Rupees*	
Househ.Cons.Expend.,incl.NPISHs	96f	....	....	....	....	200.3	198.5	195.3	377.6	416.3	515.5	598.6	673.3	653.0	700.7	700.3
Government Consumption Expend.	91f	....	....	....	....	81.5	117.1	149.5	211.4	270.0	308.5	338.0	326.0	327.7	417.4	497.6
Gross Fixed Capital Formation	93e	....	....	....	....	134.5	190.5	253.5	256.6	344.2	329.7	302.9	219.9	226.9	273.5	309.6
Changes in Inventories	93i	....	....	....	....	7.8	6.8	4.1	8.9	16.7	-12.6	10.3	-9.5	4.6	—	5.6
Exports of Goods and Services	90c	....	....	....	....	271.9	386.3	488.4	582.6	640.1	467.0	404.4	415.0	539.7	596.5	496.9
Imports of Goods and Services (-)	98c	....	....	....	....	330.4	406.2	495.8	630.8	745.4	636.2	686.0	635.3	684.0	783.2	720.0
Gross Domestic Product (GDP)	99b	138.0	168.0	194.0	235.0	365.6	493.0	595.0	806.3	941.9	971.9	968.2	989.4	1,067.9	1,204.9	1,290.0
Net Primary Income from Abroad	98.n	....	....	....	....	-15.8	-29.6	-38.3	-56.3	-34.1	-16.3	-26.2	-32.6	-41.2	-42.2	-52.4
Gross National Income (GNI)	99a	....	....	....	....	349.8	463.4	556.7	750.0	907.8	955.6	942.0	956.8	1,026.7	1,162.7	1,237.6
Consumption of Fixed Capital	99cf	....	....	....	....	20.3	26.4	36.5	35.3	45.0	54.2	57.6	59.3	64.3	75.2	84.4
GDP Volume 1976 Prices	99b.p	....	....	....	....	365.6	394.4	421.0								
GDP Volume 1986 Prices	99b.p	....	....	....	....	....	....	1,062.5	1,221.4	1,183.4	1,104.8	1,088.2	1,069.6	1,155.3	1,274.2	1,290.0
GDP Volume (1995=100)	99bv p	....	....	....	....	47.6	51.4	54.8	63.0	61.1	57.0	56.2	55.2	59.6	65.8	66.6
GDP Deflator (1995=100)	99bi p	....	....	....	....	31.7	39.7	44.8	52.9	63.7	70.5	71.3	74.1	74.0	75.7	80.1
															Millions:	
Population	99z	.06	.06	.06	.06	.06	.06	.06	.06	.06	.06	.06	.06	.06	.07	.07

1987	1988	1989	1990	1991	1992	1993	1994	1995	1996	1997	1998	1999	2000	2001		
Millions of Rupees															**International Transactions**	
124.07	171.33	193.52	301.50	258.27	245.66	265.02	262.15	253.50	693.43	569.23	643.67	775.12	....	....	Exports	70
633.90	856.63	930.15	993.78	910.42	980.87	1,234.86	1,042.38	1,109.20	1,881.88	1,711.22	2,015.52	2,317.17	....	....	Imports, c.i.f.	71
Minus Sign Indicates Debit															Balance of Payments	
-21.11	-28.41	-39.65	-12.98	-8.17	-6.90	-38.82	-25.88	-53.92	-56.51	-63.24	-124.57	-114.03	....		Current Account, n.i.e.	78al d
8.09	17.26	34.36	57.15	49.33	48.07	51.30	52.14	53.14	77.97	115.21	123.41	145.21			Goods: Exports f.o.b.	78aa d
-96.25	-134.96	-154.16	-166.38	-162.84	-180.50	-216.30	-188.64	-214.14	-262.72	-302.71	-351.64	-377.60			Goods: Imports f.o.b.	78ab d
-88.16	-117.70	-119.80	-109.23	-113.51	-132.42	-165.00	-136.50	-161.00	-184.75	-187.51	-228.23	-232.40			*Trade Balance*	78ac d
144.85	164.42	144.22	171.78	167.49	194.07	213.41	198.53	218.02	235.72	241.22	276.94	310.74			Services: Credit	78ad d
-85.06	-81.61	-65.55	-80.48	-67.80	-76.59	-93.03	-84.76	-100.88	-107.99	-119.34	-143.08	-159.79			Services: Debit	78ae d
-28.37	-34.89	-41.12	-17.94	-13.82	-14.94	-44.62	-22.73	-43.87	-57.02	-65.62	-94.37	-81.45			*Balance on Goods & Services*	78af d
2.70	3.09	3.91	4.50	5.03	5.24	5.04	3.17	5.90	6.16	6.31	7.52	10.98			Income: Credit	78ag d
-16.67	-20.53	-14.86	-17.77	-15.84	-14.46	-15.96	-14.27	-24.25	-21.14	-17.96	-29.65	-36.73			Income: Debit	78ah d
-42.35	-52.33	-52.07	-31.20	-24.62	-24.16	-55.54	-33.83	-62.22	-72.00	-77.28	-116.50	-107.19			*Balance on Gds, Serv. & Inc.*	78ai d
27.62	34.00	22.16	28.55	26.31	31.10	31.83	21.32	19.55	27.57	27.13	3.64	3.95			Current Transfers, n.i.e.: Credit	78aj d
-6.39	-10.08	-9.74	-10.32	-9.86	-13.84	-15.11	-13.37	-11.25	-12.08	-13.09	-11.72	-10.79			Current Transfers: Debit	78ak d
—	—	....	....	....	....	....	....	....	....	....	21.66	16.47			Capital Account, n.i.e.	78bc d
—	—	....	....	....	....	....	....	....	....	....	21.66	16.47			Capital Account, n.i.e.: Credit	78ba d
—	—	....	....	....	....	....	....	....	....	....	—	—			Capital Account: Debit	78bb d
18.88	21.33	44.30	22.94	30.72	-2.49	25.59	7.42	16.73	22.90	49.57	73.26	82.49			Financial Account, n.i.e.	78bj d
-5.39	-4.29	-.92	-1.13	-1.14	-1.17	-1.16	-12.82	-15.71	-13.12	-9.95	-3.00	-9.00			Direct Investment Abroad	78bd d
19.40	23.20	22.43	20.24	19.58	9.01	18.64	29.51	40.31	29.78	54.41	55.02	59.90			Dir. Invest. in Rep. Econ., n.i.e.	78be d
—	—	....	.80	1.53	-.42	-.14	-.34	-.88	-2.67	3.70	.08	-.01			Portfolio Investment Assets	78bf d
—	—	....	....	....	....	....	....	....	....	....	—	—			Equity Securities	78bk d
—	—	.80	1.53	-.42	-.14	-.34	-.88	-2.67	3.70	.08	-.78	-.01			Debt Securities	78bl d
—	—	—	—	—	-.02	.04	.16	-.18	-.02	-.04	2.84	.56			Portfolio Investment Liab., n.i.e.	78bg d
—	—	—	—	—	....	....	....	....	....	....	—	—			Equity Securities	78bm d
—	—	—	—	—	-.02	.04	.16	-.18	-.02	-.04	2.84	.56			Debt Securities	78bn d
....	....	....	....	....	....	....	....	....	....	....	—	—			Financial Derivatives Assets	78bw d
....	....	....	....	....	....	....	....	....	....	....	—	—			Financial Derivatives Liabilities	78bx d
1.13	-.93	.45	-2.84	-6.24	.13	-1.56	.15	-2.84	-8.18	-16.83	-5.67	-12.97			Other Investment Assets	78bh d
-.10	.04	....	....	....	....	....	....	....	....	....	—	—			Monetary Authorities	78bo d
															General Government	78bp d
1.23	-.97	.45	-.96	-4.35	2.09	1.34	1.73	-1.16	-6.17	-12.69	—	—			Banks	78bq d
....	....	....	-1.88	-1.89	-1.95	-2.89	-1.58	-1.68	-2.01	-4.14	-5.67	-12.97			Other Sectors	78br d
3.73	3.35	21.55	5.14	18.93	-10.31	9.97	-8.69	-2.17	10.73	21.89	24.86	44.01			Other Investment Liab., n.i.e.	78bi d
		4.37	.09	-1.05	-.86	.82	-1.89	-2.86	-3.14	10.13	20.58	11.36			Monetary Authorities	78bs d
3.73	3.35	8.95	-4.40	14.49	-6.48	4.28	-3.77	-10.81	-1.31	2.77	-5.13	29.88			General Government	78bt d
—	—	3.19	3.20	2.32	-7.10	.53	-1.52	5.75	9.91	8.09	2.29	7.00			Banks	78bu d
—	—	5.04	6.25	3.17	4.13	4.34	-1.52	5.75	5.28	.90	7.12	-4.24			Other Sectors	78bv d
6.19	2.82	-5.53	-5.71	-20.75	5.44	3.17	6.76	23.15	20.58	8.44	-4.79	-23.00			Net Errors and Omissions	78ca d
3.96	-4.26	-.88	4.26	1.81	-3.95	-10.06	-11.70	-14.03	-13.03	-5.23	-34.44	-38.08			*Overall Balance*	78cb d
-3.96	4.26	.88	-4.26	-1.81	3.95	10.06	11.70	14.03	13.03	5.23	34.44	38.08			Reserves and Related Items	79da d
-3.96	4.26	.88	-4.26	-11.65	-5.43	-3.45	6.08	1.43	3.93	5.23	16.77	27.52			Reserve Assets	79db d
															Use of Fund Credit and Loans	79dc d
....	....	....	9.84	9.38	13.51	5.62	12.60	9.09	....	17.67	10.56				Exceptional Financing	79de d
Year Ending December 31															**Government Finance**	
-53.0	-61.1	-155.5	-.9	-104.6	-98.6	-181.9	18.2	-54.5	-311.6	-453.0	-602.4	-347.9			Deficit (-) or Surplus	80
681.9	787.4	930.7	1,035.9	1,003.4	1,136.8	1,247.7	1,338.1	1,200.5	1,095.9	1,185.7	1,339.9	1,440.2			Total Revenue and Grants	81y
639.3	763.4	896.8	989.1	961.4	1,097.6	1,209.6	1,319.5	1,187.8	1,082.1	1,176.2	1,312.1	1,399.6			Revenue	81
42.6	24.0	33.9	46.8	42.0	39.2	38.1	18.6	12.8	13.8	9.5	27.8	40.6			Grants	81z
734.9	848.5	1,086.2	1,036.8	1,108.0	1,235.4	1,429.6	1,319.9	1,255.1	1,407.5	1,638.7	1,942.3	1,788.1			Exp. & Lending Minus Repay.	82z
701.9	768.8	971.9	958.7	1,079.6	1,203.8	1,393.6	1,297.4	1,206.6	1,382.2	1,543.0	1,792.1	1,754.6			Expenditure	82
33.0	79.7	114.3	78.1	28.4	31.6	36.0	22.5	48.4	25.3	95.7	150.2	33.5			Lending Minus Repayments	83
53.0	61.1	155.5	.9	104.6	98.6	182.0	-18.3	54.5	311.6	453.0	602.4	347.9			Total Financing	80h
73.5	105.2	123.0	36.2	43.6	131.6	161.8	16.3	102.1	279.8	464.7	629.4	412.4			Domestic	84a
-20.5	-44.1	32.5	-35.3	61.0	-33.0	20.2	-34.6	-47.6	31.9	-11.7	-27.0	-64.5			Foreign	85a
....	....	....	....	....	....	....	....	....	....	....	....	....			Total Debt by Residence	88
....	....	....	....	....	....	....	....	....	....	....	....	....			Domestic	88a
....	....	....	....	....	....	....	....	....	....	....	....	....			Foreign	89a
Millions of Rupees															**National Accounts**	
870.5	909.9	1,025.4	1,125.0	1,115.4	1,207.4	1,241.6	1,129.8	1,179.4	1,191.0	1,465.8	1,603.9	....			Househ.Cons.Expend.,incl.NPISHs	96f
406.6	415.6	471.7	544.4	558.4	674.6	714.7	722.2	669.1	736.0	733.0	847.0	....			Government Consumption Expend.	91f
260.1	357.3	418.0	451.9	422.1	465.4	651.2	648.5	733.9	822.6	863.1	1,100.0	....			Gross Fixed Capital Formation	93e
15.8	33.0	54.5	31.5	19.7	6.2	46.0	17.4	.2	-19.0	109.1	56.0	....			Changes in Inventories	93i
541.7	737.3	989.9	1,128.3	1,115.4	1,207.4	1,319.2	1,250.5	1,292.0	1,592.9	1,896.9	2,045.5	....			Exports of Goods and Services	90c
698.8	925.2	1,241.6	1,314.0	1,218.4	1,315.4	1,544.2	1,326.0	1,454.8	1,841.4	2,159.7	2,525.8	....			Imports of Goods and Services (-)	98c
1,395.6	1,527.9	1,720.9	1,967.1	1,980.1	2,221.1	2,431.5	2,459.4	2,419.8	2,500.3	2,844.6	3,060.0	3,155.4			Gross Domestic Product (GDP)	99b
-78.2	-59.2	-45.3	-70.1	-56.8	-47.3	-31.6	9.6	-56.9	-50.0	-19.7	-73.1	-59.2			Net Primary Income from Abroad	98.n
1,317.5	1,434.3	1,675.2	1,915.4	1,944.5	2,173.6	2,399.9	2,469.0	2,362.9	2,450.3	2,825.0	2,986.9	3,080.4			Gross National Income (GNI)	99a
90.6	106.5	113.0	164.7	219.1	181.9	202.3	211.5	210.2	240.5	276.4	297.0	....			Consumption of Fixed Capital	99cf
....	....	....	....	....	....	....	....	....	....	....	....	....			GDP Volume 1976 Prices	99b.p
1,346.5	1,418.2	1,564.1	1,680.7	1,726.8	1,851.4	1,965.9	1,950.0	1,937.9	2,029.3	2,267.2	2,391.9	2,461.6			GDP Volume 1986 Prices	99b. p
69.5	73.2	80.7	86.7	89.1	95.5	101.4	100.6	100.0	104.7	117.0	123.4	127.0			GDP Volume (1995=100)	99bv p
83.0	86.3	88.1	93.7	91.8	96.1	99.1	101.0	100.0	98.7	100.5	102.5	102.7			GDP Deflator (1995=100)	99bi p
Midyear Estimates																
.07	.07	.07	.07	.07	.07	.07	.07	.08	.08	.08	.08	.08	.08	.08	Population	99z

(See notes in the back of the book.)

Sierra Leone

		1972	1973	1974	1975	1976	1977	1978	1979	1980	1981	1982	1983	1984	1985	1986
Exchange Rates															*Leones per SDR:*	
Market Rate	aa	.92	1.04	1.04	1.16	1.36	1.27	1.37	1.37	1.37	1.37	1.36	2.63	2.46	5.74	43.53
															Leones per US Dollar:	
Market Rate	ae	.85	.86	.85	.99	1.17	1.05	1.05	1.04	1.06	1.17	1.23	2.51	2.51	5.21	35.59
Market Rate	rf	.80	.82	.86	.90	1.11	1.15	1.05[e]	1.06	1.05	1.16	1.24	1.89	2.51	5.09	16.09
															Index Numbers (1995=100):	
Market Rate	ahx	91,925.8	90,100.8	85,944.6	81,637.0	66,365.9	64,136.8	70,264.3[e]	69,534.4	70,018.8	63,485.2	59,362.6	43,786.5	29,277.1	15,537.5	8,752.9
Nominal Effective Exchange Rate	ne c	....	....	....	....	....	....	....	33,617.6	33,653.5	35,249.3	37,405.6	30,331.4	23,077.8	13,070.4	6,314.8
Real Effective Exchange Rate	re c	....	....	....	....	....	....	....	....	....	....	....	....	....	....	....
Fund Position															*Millions of SDRs:*	
Quota	2f. s	25.0	25.0	25.0	25.0	25.0	25.0	31.0	31.0	46.5	46.5	46.5	57.9	57.9	57.9	57.9
SDRs	1b. s	5.7	5.7	4.4	3.9	2.9	1.4	.2	—	—	.1	.5	.1	—	—	.3
Reserve Position in the Fund	1c. s	4.9	4.9	—	—	—	—	—	—	—	1.1	—	—	—	—	—
Total Fund Cred.&Loans Outstg.	2tl	—	—	4.3	4.9	22.4	32.1	35.6	43.8	46.6	72.2	70.9	88.9	97.5	92.0	82.9
International Liquidity												*Millions of US Dollars Unless Otherwise Indicated:*				
Total Reserves minus Gold	1l. d	46.5	51.8	54.6	28.4	25.2	33.4	34.8	46.7	30.6	16.0	8.4	16.2	7.7	10.8	13.7
SDRs	1b. d	6.2	6.9	5.4	4.6	3.4	1.7	.3	—	—	.1	.5	.1	—	—	.3
Reserve Position in the Fund	1c. d	5.3	5.9	—	—	—	—	—	—	—	1.2	—	—	—	—	—
Foreign Exchange	1d. d	34.9	39.0	49.2	23.8	21.8	31.7	34.5	46.7	30.6	14.6	7.9	16.1	7.7	10.8	13.3
Monetary Authorities: Other Liab.	4. d	—	1.4	5.2	8.3	6.3	—	13.4	25.5	133.8	180.4	184.4	221.7	228.5	253.1	177.1
Deposit Money Banks: Assets	7a. d	.5	2.7	4.2	2.4	3.5	7.7	11.6	11.0	14.0	5.3	7.4	7.6	16.0	10.0	13.8
Liabilities	7b. d	.1	3.0	5.6	2.5	.5	.9	.3	.2	—	—	.1	.3	3.9	2.1	4.7
Monetary Authorities															*Millions of Leones:*	
Foreign Assets	11	36	43	47	28	29	36	37	48	32	19	7	33	9	7	232
Claims on Central Government	12a	7	14	16	42	60	69	117	214	296	425	583	719	924	2,037	2,810
Claims on Nonfin.Pub.Enterprises	12c	....	....	....	....	....	....	....	....	....	....	....	....	....	....	....
Claims on Private Sector	12d	—	—	5	2	—	—	2	3	8	4	3	3	4	2	57
Claims on Deposit Money Banks	12e	—	—	—	—	—	—	—	—	—	—	—	—	—	—	—
Claims on Other Banking Insts	12f	....	....	....	....	....	....	....	....	....	....	....	....	....	....	....
Claims on Nonbank Financial Insts	12g	....	....	....	....	....	....	....	....	....	....	....	....	....	....	....
Reserve Money	14	28	35	39	43	50	58	94	144	133	134	253	317	450	691	1,423
of which: Currency Outside DMBs	14a	25	30	31	37	41	52	63	72	86	86	121	197	260	442	1,006
Time, Savings,& Fgn.Currency Dep.	15	....	....	....	....	....	....	....	....	....	....	....	....	....	....	....
Restricted Deposits	16b	....	....	....	....	....	....	....	....	....	....	....	....	....	....	....
Foreign Liabilities	16c	—	1	9	14	38	44	77	111	205	310	324	790	813	1,845	9,910
Long-Term Foreign Liabilities	16cl	....	....	....	....	....	....	....	....	....	....	....	....	....	....	....
Central Government Deposits	16d	2	6	5	—	5	6	7	36	26	28	20	52	32	5	13
Capital Accounts	17a	10	10	11	12	12	17	14	20	25	29	32	32	33	35	41
of which: Valuation Adjustment	17rv	4	5	4	4	—	4	−17	−26	−29	−34	−33	−355	−230	−527	−7,161
Other Items (Net)	17r	3	5	4	3	−15	−19	−36	−45	−53	−54	−35	−435	−392	−530	−8,288
Deposit Money Banks															*Millions of Leones:*	
Reserves	20	3	4	6	4	8	5	29	71	121	158	261	297	365	418	570
Foreign Assets	21	—	2	4	2	4	8	12	11	15	6	9	19	40	52	493
Claims on Central Government	22a	8	13	16	19	31	38	51	54	51	53	62	121	169	406	556
Claims on Nonfin.Pub.Enterprises	22c	—	—	3	1	1	3	6	4	4	4	4	4	6	15	21
Claims on Private Sector	22d	22	28	35	40	43	46	63	68	83	96	110	129	108	133	370
Claims on Nonbank Financial Insts	22g	....	....	....	....	....	....	....	....	....	....	....	....	....	....	....
Demand Deposits	24	13	17	22	22	30	32	43	55	65	63	128	156	222	454	833
Time, Savings,& Fgn.Currency Dep.	25	18	23	30	31	40	52	72	87	108	116	166	193	223	313	433
Foreign Liabilities	26c	—	2	5	3	1	1	—	—	—	—	—	1	10	11	169
Central Government Deposits	26d	—	—	—	—	1	1	1	—	2	2	4	6	6	5	9
Credit from Monetary Authorities	26g	—	—	—	—	—	—	—	—	—	—	—	—	—	—	—
Capital Accounts	27a	3	4	4	5	5	7	8	10	11	12	17	18	21	24	28
Other Items (Net)	27r	−1	1	3	5	11	9	37	57	88	124	131	197	207	218	537
Monetary Survey															*Millions of Leones:*	
Foreign Assets (Net)	31n	36	42	37	14	−5	−1	−28	−51	−157	−285	−308	−739	−774	−1,797	−9,354
Domestic Credit	32	35	49	70	102	130	151	231	307	413	551	738	919	1,172	2,583	3,792
Claims on Central Govt. (Net)	32an	14	20	27	61	86	101	160	232	318	448	621	783	1,055	2,432	3,344
Claims on Nonfin.Pub.Enterprises	32c	—	—	3	1	1	3	6	4	4	4	4	4	6	15	21
Claims on Private Sector	32d	22	28	40	41	44	47	65	71	91	99	114	132	111	135	427
Claims on Other Banking Insts	32f	....	....	....	....	....	....	....	....	....	....	....	....	....	....	....
Claims on Nonbank Financial Inst	32g	....	....	....	....	....	....	....	....	....	....	....	....	....	....	....
Money	34	39	48	55	60	72	84	107	128	153	152	253	359	486	900	1,852
Quasi-Money	35	18	23	30	31	40	52	72	87	108	116	166	193	223	313	433
Restricted Deposits	36b	....	....	....	....	....	....	....	....	....	....	....	....	....	....	....
Long-Term Foreign Liabilities	36cl	....	....	....	....	....	....	....	....	....	....	....	....	....	....	....
Capital Accounts	37a	13	14	16	17	18	24	23	30	36	41	48	50	54	58	69
Other Items (Net)	37r	2	6	7	8	−4	−11	1	12	−40	−42	−37	−422	−365	−485	−7,916
Money plus Quasi-Money	35l	57	71	85	92	112	136	179	215	261	268	420	552	709	1,213	2,285
Interest Rates															*Percent Per Annum*	
Treasury Bill Rate	60c	5.50	5.50	5.50	5.50	5.50	5.50	5.50	6.25	9.38	10.00	10.00	11.00	12.00	12.00	14.50
Deposit Rate	60l	....	....	....	....	....	7.00	7.00	7.25	9.17	10.00	10.00	11.00	12.00	11.33	14.17
Lending Rate	60p	8.00	8.00	8.00	8.50	9.00	11.00	11.00	11.00	11.00	15.00	15.00	17.25	18.00	17.00	17.19
Prices															*Index Numbers (1995=100):*	
Wholesale Prices	63	4.7	6.0	7.6	†8.8	10.8	12.8	14.9	18.1	22.1	27.0	32.3	46.3	67.0	100.0	....
Consumer Prices	64	—	—	—	—	.1	.1	.1	†.1	.1	.1	.1	.2	.4	.7	1.2
															Number in Thousands:	
Employment	67e	....	....	....	....	....	....	....	....	....	....	....	....	....	69	74

Sierra Leone

	1987	1988	1989	1990	1991	1992	1993	1994	1995	1996	1997	1998	1999	2000	2001		
																Exchange Rates	
End of Period																	
	32.69	52.57	85.89	268.43	621.93	723.68	793.41	894.90	1,402.35	1,307.24	1,799.00	2,239.84	3,123.90	2,171.52	2,716.13	Market Rate	aa
End of Period (ae) Period Average (rf)																	
	23.04	39.06	65.36	188.68	434.78	526.32	577.63	613.01	943.40	909.09	1,333.33	1,590.76	2,276.05	1,666.67	2,161.27	Market Rate	ae
	34.04	32.51	59.81	151.45	295.34	499.44	567.46	586.74	755.22	920.73	981.48	1,563.62	1,804.20	2,092.13	1,986.15	Market Rate	rf
Period Averages																	
	2,385.3	2,354.0	1,263.4	508.9	267.6	147.9	129.6	125.3	100.0	80.0	77.0	47.0	41.2	35.4	37.3	Market Rate	ahx
	1,538.3	1,501.3	896.8	373.8	208.4	121.6	124.6	131.3	100.0	82.7	86.1	54.5	48.1	44.7	49.6	Nominal Effective Exchange Rate	nec
	124.6	145.4	126.2	94.1	95.3	86.9	96.8	110.7	100.0	101.0	115.8	99.5	116.3	105.0	116.3	Real Effective Exchange Rate	rec
																Fund Position	
End of Period																	
	57.9	57.9	57.9	57.9	57.9	57.9	57.9	77.2	77.2	77.2	77.2	77.2	103.7	103.7	103.7	Quota	2f.s
	—	—	—	—	—	1.2	2.8	6.2	11.5	5.3	8.3	7.4	15.2	4.0	.3	SDRs	1b.s
	—	—	—	—	—	—	—	—	—	—	—	—	—	—	—	Reserve Position in the Fund	1c.s
	81.5	80.8	79.5	76.2	70.7	67.0	61.0	100.2	110.9	118.8	123.9	135.4	142.0	133.2	120.8	Total Fund Cred.&Loans Outstg.	2tl
																International Liquidity	
End of Period																	
	6.3	7.4	3.7	5.4	9.6	18.9	29.0	40.6	34.6	26.6	38.5	44.1	39.5	50.9	51.6	Total Reserves minus Gold	1l.d
	—	—	—	—	—	1.7	3.8	9.0	17.1	7.6	11.2	10.4	20.8	5.2	.4	SDRs	1b.d
	—	—	—	—	—	—	—	—	—	—	—	—	—	—	—	Reserve Position in the Fund	1c.d
	6.3	7.4	3.7	5.4	9.6	17.2	25.1	31.6	17.5	18.9	27.3	33.7	18.6	45.6	51.2	Foreign Exchange	1d.d
	277.9	264.6	254.9	243.7	248.5	302.4	322.2	470.2	326.2	53.5	14.8	19.2	7.7	10.6	17.1	Monetary Authorities: Other Liab.	4..d
	12.5	11.4	12.7	8.7	7.5	16.1	22.5	16.9	22.5	19.9	15.6	19.2	17.9	24.4	21.9	Deposit Money Banks: Assets	7a.d
	1.4	1.0	.1	—	—	—	2.7	2.9	3.1	—	—	—	—	—	—	Liabilities	7b.d
																Monetary Authorities	
End of Period																	
	514	791	2,067	1,016	4,169	11,143	18,943	30,443	48,695	†27,262	53,008	83,128	98,035	86,385	115,454	Foreign Assets	11
	4,394	5,552	8,365	31,922	35,265	30,009	25,328	462,872	408,928	†415,564	470,930	475,265	524,834	633,405	650,358	Claims on Central Government	12a
	....	....	....	....	....	....	....	....	....	203	203	13	66	13	13	Claims on Nonfin.Pub.Enterprises	12c
	12	95	102	103	107	112	126	160	324	†1,031	2,577	1,749	788	1,008	1,969	Claims on Private Sector	12d
	—	—	—	—	—	—	—	—	—	†1,173	495	1,049	1,736	606	969	Claims on Deposit Money Banks	12e
	....	....	....	....	....	....	....	....	....	33	34	4	—	—	—	Claims on Other Banking Insts	12f
	....	....	....	....	....	....	....	....	....	302	85	6	26	853	520	Claims on Nonbank Financial Insts	12g
	2,404	4,274	7,449	12,395	20,258	24,095	24,995	31,352	35,148	†43,548	91,008	72,415	100,627	109,843	142,103	Reserve Money	14
	1,364	2,255	4,058	8,337	15,650	18,270	21,882	23,604	30,023	†36,186	57,260	61,492	82,815	88,854	116,153	*of which: Currency Outside DMBs*	14a
	....	....	....	....	....	....	....	....	....	812	5,397	259	1,394	4,975	3,363	Time, Savings,& Fgn.Currency Dep.	15
	....	....	....	....	....	....	....	....	....	3	213	24	34	54	31	Restricted Deposits	16b
	9,069	14,585	23,494	66,428	152,002	207,647	234,495	377,912	463,327	†203,964	242,632	334,003	460,925	306,984	365,027	Foreign Liabilities	16c
	....	....	....	....	....	....	....	....	....	19,421	22,120	31,180	44,973	32,536	43,533	Long-Term Foreign Liabilities	16cl
	299	7	297	713	828	1,974	6,598	5,936	10,955	†2,042	4,528	4,615	5,472	8,415	13,195	Central Government Deposits	16d
	42	44	45	59	146	147	149	24,151	24,156	†190,151	227,926	153,376	156,239	222,527	261,467	Capital Accounts	17a
	-4,103	-5,439	-7,535	-21,574	-66,072	-47,145	-90,274	-108,690	-111,158	†832	-40,714	-57,997	-135,494	8,177	-9,614	*of which: Valuation Adjustment*	17rv
	-6,894	-12,471	-20,751	-46,554	-133,693	-192,599	-221,840	54,124	-75,639	†-14,373	-66,491	-34,661	-144,178	36,937	-59,436	Other Items (Net)	17r
																Deposit Money Banks	
End of Period																	
	1,515	1,968	3,287	3,963	4,498	5,707	2,855	7,523	4,701	†5,926	26,240	8,088	23,229	20,543	17,047	Reserves	20
	288	445	830	1,644	3,255	8,462	12,986	10,378	21,232	†18,079	20,852	30,555	40,852	40,611	47,295	Foreign Assets	21
	811	988	1,193	1,379	1,819	2,795	8,589	9,921	12,763	†18,470	10,311	41,161	72,209	71,752	100,748	Claims on Central Government	22a
	—	51	53	67	50	50	26	81	21	†30	335	63	68	622	486	Claims on Nonfin.Pub.Enterprises	22c
	605	1,105	2,592	3,092	8,008	10,257	14,847	16,576	17,276	†20,705	24,506	26,895	24,234	27,035	32,974	Claims on Private Sector	22d
	....	....	....	....	....	....	....	....	....	598	594	2,094	2,165	10,803	11,649	Claims on Nonbank Financial Insts	22g
	1,494	2,332	4,513	5,820	9,338	13,005	12,753	14,719	19,462	†15,616	24,494	25,875	47,800	48,447	67,452	Demand Deposits	24
	859	1,241	1,565	3,565	6,306	10,446	15,951	16,955	16,481	†32,044	37,625	50,896	58,686	72,674	98,064	Time, Savings,& Fgn.Currency Dep.	25
	33	40	5	3	13	11	1,551	1,761	2,896	†—	—	—	—	—	—	Foreign Liabilities	26c
	243	97	251	167	239	634	1,356	1,916	2,172	†2,102	3,190	5,059	14,107	13,266	10,894	Central Government Deposits	26d
	....	....	....	....	....	....	....	....	—	†74	74	42	21	—	—	Credit from Monetary Authorities	26g
	82	118	155	627	850	1,025	1,292	5,483	8,961	†20,564	18,607	22,994	34,664	48,899	60,975	Capital Accounts	27a
	509	729	1,466	-38	885	2,150	6,399	3,645	6,021	†-6,591	-1,153	3,990	7,480	-11,920	-27,186	Other Items (Net)	27r
																Monetary Survey	
End of Period																	
	-8,299	-13,389	-20,601	-63,771	-144,591	-188,052	-204,117	-338,852	-396,296	†-158623	-168,771	-220,319	-322,038	-179,988	-202,278	Foreign Assets (Net)	31n
	5,280	7,687	11,757	35,682	44,182	40,615	40,961	481,758	426,184	†452,793	501,856	537,572	604,813	723,811	774,627	Domestic Credit	32
	4,663	6,436	9,010	32,420	36,017	30,196	25,963	464,940	408,563	†429,891	473,523	506,752	577,463	683,477	727,016	Claims on Central Govt. (Net)	32an
	—	51	53	67	50	50	26	81	21	†233	538	76	134	635	499	Claims on Nonfin.Pub.Enterprises	32c
	617	1,199	2,694	3,195	8,115	10,369	14,973	16,736	17,600	†21,736	27,083	28,644	25,022	28,043	34,943	Claims on Private Sector	32d
	....	....	....	....	....	....	....	....	....	33	34	4	—	—		Claims on Other Banking Insts	32f
	....	....	....	....	....	....	....	....	....	900	679	2,100	2,190	11,656	12,169	Claims on Nonbank Financial Inst	32g
	2,889	4,637	8,675	14,253	25,092	31,387	35,053	38,542	49,902	†53,208	83,611	89,744	134,078	139,957	189,437	Money	34
	859	1,241	1,565	3,565	6,306	10,446	15,951	16,955	16,481	†32,856	43,022	51,155	60,080	77,649	101,427	Quasi-Money	35
	....	....	....	....	....	....	....	....	....	3	213	24	34	54	31	Restricted Deposits	36b
	....	....	....	....	....	....	....	....	....	19,421	22,120	31,180	44,973	32,536	43,533	Long-Term Foreign Liabilities	36cl
	124	162	200	686	995	1,172	1,441	29,633	33,116	†210,715	246,533	176,370	190,903	271,426	322,443	Capital Accounts	37a
	-6,890	-11,742	-19,285	-46,593	-132,802	-190,442	-215,601	57,775	-69,611	†-22,033	-62,414	-31,221	-147,294	22,201	-84,521	Other Items (Net)	37r
	3,747	5,879	10,240	17,818	31,397	41,834	51,004	55,497	66,383	†86,064	126,633	140,899	194,159	217,605	290,864	Money plus Quasi-Money	35l
																Interest Rates	
Percent Per Annum																	
	16.50	18.00	22.00	47.50	50.67	78.63	28.64	12.19	14.73	29.25	12.71	22.10	32.42	26.22	13.74	Treasury Bill Rate	60c
	12.67	16.33	20.00	40.50	47.80	54.67	27.00	11.63	7.03	13.96	9.91	7.12	9.50	9.25	7.67	Deposit Rate	60l
	28.54	28.00	29.67	52.50	56.25	62.83	50.46	27.33	28.83	32.12	23.87	23.83	26.83	26.25	24.27	Lending Rate	60p
																Prices	
Period Averages																	
	....	....	....	....	....	....	....	....	....	....	....	....	....	....	....	Wholesale Prices	63
	3.4	4.6	7.4	15.6	31.6	52.3	†63.9	79.4	100.0	123.1	141.5	191.8	257.2	255.1	260.4	Consumer Prices	64
Period Averages																	
	69	70	....	....	....	....	....	....	....	....	....	....	....	....	....	Employment	67e

Sierra Leone

		1972	1973	1974	1975	1976	1977	1978	1979	1980	1981	1982	1983	1984	1985	1986
International Transactions															*Millions of Leones*	
Exports	70	92	107	123	105	109	155	178	211	234	173	137	198	335	649	1,978
Imports, c.i.f.	71	95	127	189	168	171	206	291	334	447	378	368	287	394	789	2,021
Balance of Payments															*Millions of US Dollars:*	
Current Account, n.i.e.	78al d	...	...	...	...	...	−49.6	−112.0	−179.1	−165.2	−132.1	−169.9	−17.6	−23.0	2.8	140.7
Goods: Exports f.o.b.	78aa d	...	...	...	...	...	150.3	193.6	211.6	226.6	165.9	122.6	115.1	139.2	135.8	131.7
Goods: Imports f.o.b.	78ab d	...	...	...	...	...	−165.0	−253.0	−336.3	−385.9	−282.0	−260.3	−133.0	−149.7	−141.2	−111.4
Trade Balance	78ac d	...	...	...	...	...	−14.7	−59.4	−124.7	−159.3	−116.1	−137.7	−17.9	−10.5	−5.4	20.3
Services: Credit	78ad d	...	...	...	...	...	10.7	17.7	31.2	48.9	37.2	25.3	26.7	34.5	24.0	20.8
Services: Debit	78ae d	...	...	...	...	...	−50.7	−56.2	−72.6	−85.3	−59.6	−72.7	−42.1	−47.6	−42.9	−33.9
Balance on Goods & Services	78af d	...	...	...	...	...	−54.7	−97.9	−166.0	−195.8	−138.6	−185.1	−33.3	−23.6	−24.2	7.2
Income: Credit	78ag d	...	...	...	...	...	1.8	.4	.3	.6	.5	.2	.3	.2	.2	.1
Income: Debit	78ah d	...	...	...	...	...	−16.7	−33.9	−42.3	−22.5	−37.4	−35.2	−21.2	−32.6	7.6	127.3
Balance on Gds, Serv. & Inc.	78ai d	...	...	...	...	...	−69.6	−131.4	−208.0	−217.6	−175.5	−220.2	−54.2	−56.0	−16.4	134.6
Current Transfers, n.i.e.: Credit	78aj d	...	...	...	...	...	22.1	21.8	31.7	56.7	44.4	54.3	39.0	34.6	21.2	6.5
Current Transfers: Debit	78ak d	...	...	...	...	...	−2.1	−2.4	−2.7	−4.2	−1.0	−4.0	−2.4	−1.6	−2.0	−.3
Capital Account, n.i.e.	78bc d	...	...	...	...	...	—	—	—	.1	—	.1	.1	.1	—	—
Capital Account, n.i.e.: Credit	78ba d	...	...	...	...	...	—	—	—	.1	—	.1	.1	.1	—	—
Capital Account: Debit	78bb d	...	...	...	...	...	—	—	—	—	—	—	—	—	—	—
Financial Account, n.i.e.	78bj d	...	...	...	...	...	17.3	76.1	106.1	111.5	71.4	21.8	−78.1	−60.8	−67.6	−279.4
Direct Investment Abroad	78bd d	...	...	...	...	...	—	—	—	—	—	—	—	—	—	—
Dir. Invest. in Rep. Econ., n.i.e.	78be d	...	...	...	...	...	5.1	24.3	16.1	−18.7	7.5	4.7	1.7	5.9	−31.0	−140.3
Portfolio Investment Assets	78bf d	...	...	...	...	...	—	2.4	2.4	—	—	—	—	—	—	—
Equity Securities	78bk d	...	...	...	...	...	—	—	—	—	—	—	—	—	—	—
Debt Securities	78bl d	...	...	...	...	...	—	2.4	2.4	—	—	—	—	—	—	—
Portfolio Investment Liab., n.i.e.	78bg d	...	...	...	...	...	—	—	—	−1.4	—	—	—	—	—	—
Equity Securities	78bm d	...	...	...	...	...	—	—	—	—	—	—	—	—	—	—
Debt Securities	78bn d	...	...	...	...	...	—	—	—	−1.4	—	—	—	—	—	—
Financial Derivatives Assets	78bw d	...	...	...	...	...	...	...	...	...	...	...	...	...	...	...
Financial Derivatives Liabilities	78bx d	...	...	...	...	...	...	...	...	...	...	...	...	...	...	...
Other Investment Assets	78bh d	...	...	...	...	...	−3.1	2.0	4.9	2.0	9.6	16.1	−38.6	−16.2	−10.5	−48.4
Monetary Authorities	78bo d	...	...	...	...	...	−1.8	—	.1	—	—	.1	.1	—	—	—
General Government	78bp d	...	...	...	...	...	—	—	—	—	—	—	—	—	—	—
Banks	78bq d	...	...	...	...	...	−3.4	−3.9	.8	−3.3	7.4	−2.3	−5.2	−8.4	−2.4	−27.4
Other Sectors	78br d	...	...	...	...	...	2.1	5.9	4.1	5.2	2.2	18.4	−33.5	−7.8	−8.1	−21.0
Other Investment Liab., n.i.e.	78bi d	...	...	...	...	...	15.4	47.5	82.7	129.6	54.3	1.0	−41.2	−50.4	−26.2	−90.7
Monetary Authorities	78bs d	...	...	...	...	...	−7.3	14.4	10.6	2.6	22.1	−11.3	−1.0	16.6	10.9	6.0
General Government	78bt d	...	...	...	...	...	16.4	29.3	41.5	91.3	4.7	16.5	−56.7	−55.0	−46.3	−171.7
Banks	78bu d	...	...	...	...	...	.3	−.6	−.1	−.2	—	.2	.3	3.6	.2	9.8
Other Sectors	78bv d	...	...	...	...	...	5.9	4.3	30.7	35.9	27.4	−4.4	16.2	−15.6	9.0	65.3
Net Errors and Omissions	78ca d	...	...	...	...	...	11.9	27.0	17.9	−22.3	−46.2	68.3	2.9	−12.4	−9.3	42.0
Overall Balance	78cb d	...	...	...	...	...	−20.4	−8.9	−55.2	−75.9	−107.0	−79.7	−92.8	−96.1	−74.1	−96.6
Reserves and Related Items	79da d	...	...	...	...	...	20.4	8.9	55.2	75.9	107.0	79.7	92.8	96.1	74.1	96.6
Reserve Assets	79db d	...	...	...	...	...	−5.0	−1.6	−3.9	19.3	15.4	9.8	−13.6	9.6	.6	−13.6
Use of Fund Credit and Loans	79dc d	...	...	...	...	...	11.3	4.3	10.6	3.8	30.7	−1.4	19.7	9.4	−5.4	−11.2
Exceptional Financing	79de d	...	...	...	...	...	14.1	6.2	48.5	52.7	60.9	71.3	86.7	77.2	78.8	121.4
Government Finance															*Millions of Leones:*	
Deficit (-) or Surplus	80	−8	−12	†−21	−60	−48	−51	−79	−119	−148	−121	−167	−271	−206	−376	−184
Revenue	81	60	64	†92	97	95	119	157	174	190	221	182	156	229	286	490
Grants Received	81z	...	...	†—	—	—	—	12	19	7	16	10	15	37	41	105
Expenditure	82	68	76	†113	157	144	170	249	311	334	358	353	416	451	578	778
Lending Minus Repayments	83	...	...	†—	—	—	—	—	1	12	—	6	26	21	124	—
Financing																
Domestic	84a	—	11	†8	27	30	36	39	81	105	105	134	229	206	322	147
Foreign	85a	8	1	†13	33	19	15	41	38	44	16	34	43	—	54	36
Debt: Domestic	88a	...	...	†45	69	109	143	196	292	391	487	648	878	1,078	1,402	2,124
Foreign	89a	...	...	†71	118	136	153	229	290	366	396	485	518	870	1,995	4,961
National Accounts															*Millions of Leones:*	
Househ.Cons.Expend.,incl.NPISHs	96f	287	300	364	477	534	631	719	880	1,048	1,172	1,416	1,647	2,242	4,002	6,238
Government Consumption Expend.	91f	32	42	49	64	59	71	77	96	97	90	138	167	189	345	498
Gross Fixed Capital Formation	93e	43	44	57	76	72	81	100	128	172	236	205	235	332	424	730
Changes in Inventories	93i	−1	2	19	14	−2	17	−4	10	16	11	10	33	15	53	109
Exports of Goods and Services	90c	104	116	134	154	143	156	199	233	264	297	253	208	290	647	940
Imports of Goods and Services (-)	98c	108	110	145	212	192	212	242	318	442	514	416	413	339	725	1,184
Gross Domestic Product (GDP)	99b	356	393	478	573	614	744	850	1,029	1,156	1,292	1,605	1,876	2,730	4,365	7,888
Net Primary Income from Abroad	98.n	−8	−6	−7	−7	−10	−11	−17	−41	−45	−23	−43	−43	−40	−12	954
Gross National Income (GNI)	99a	348	388	471	566	604	733	833	989	1,111	1,269	1,562	1,833	2,690	4,704	7,542
Consumption of Fixed Capital	99cf	31	32	38	45	49	59	69	81	103	124	153	183	280	305	486
GDP Volume 1973 Prices	99b.p	382	393	409	421	409	415	416	447	460	489	497	...	...	...	...
GDP Volume 1980/81 Prices	99b.p											1,314	1,295	1,313	1,277	...
GDP Volume 1984/85 Prices	99b.p											...	...	...	4,785	4,668
GDP Volume 1989/90 Prices	99b.p											...	...	...	...	...
GDP Volume (1995=100)	99bv p	104.8	108.0	112.4	115.7	112.2	113.8	114.2	122.7	126.4	134.2	136.4	134.4	136.3	132.5	129.3
GDP Deflator (1995=100)	99bi p	.1	.1	.1	.1	.1	.1	.1	.1	.1	.1	.2	.2	.3	.5	.9
																Millions:
Population	99z	2.83	2.90	2.97	3.05	3.09	3.14	3.19	3.19	3.26	3.34	3.41	3.49	3.51	3.58	3.66

1987	1988	1989	1990	1991	1992	1993	1994	1995	1996	1997	1998	1999	2000	2001		
Millions of Leones															**International Transactions**	
4,689	3,330	8,248	21,023	43,946	74,918	67,094	68,010	30,148	43,004	15,412	10,482	11,347	26,771	55,743	Exports	70
4,424	5,215	10,902	22,572	45,488	72,776	83,460	88,492	102,488	193,628	80,010	148,226	153,856	314,639	368,323	Imports, c.i.f.	71
															Balance of Payments	
Minus Sign Indicates Debit																
−30.3	−2.8	−59.7	−69.4	15.3	−5.5	−57.8	−89.1	−126.5	....						Current Account, n.i.e.	78al d
142.0	107.9	142.0	148.5	149.5	150.4	118.3	116.0	41.5							Goods: Exports f.o.b.	78aa d
−114.8	−138.2	−160.4	−140.4	−138.6	−139.0	−187.1	−188.7	−168.1							Goods: Imports f.o.b.	78ab d
27.1	−30.3	−18.3	8.1	11.0	11.4	−68.8	−72.7	−126.7							*Trade Balance*	78ac d
40.9	48.6	35.8	61.1	67.6	47.0	58.5	100.2	86.8							Services: Credit	78ad d
−42.0	−34.6	−44.8	−74.4	−63.8	−62.9	−61.5	−107.6	−91.8							Services: Debit	78ae d
26.0	−16.3	−27.3	−5.2	14.7	−4.5	−71.9	−80.1	−131.7							*Balance on Goods & Services*	78af d
.2	.2	.7	.7	7.9	6.8	2.3	1.5	.7							Income: Credit	78ag d
−63.2	4.6	−39.9	−71.8	−17.1	−15.1	−5.6	−57.0	−21.4							Income: Debit	78ah d
−37.0	−11.5	−67.0	−76.3	5.5	−12.8	−75.2	−135.7	−152.3							*Balance on Gds, Serv. & Inc.*	78ai d
7.3	9.3	7.9	7.1	10.0	8.2	19.1	47.5	35.3							Current Transfers, n.i.e.: Credit	78aj d
−.6	−.6	−.7	−.2	−.2	−.8	−1.7	−.9	−9.5							Current Transfers: Debit	78ak d
.1	.1	.1	—	—	.1	.1	.1	—							Capital Account, n.i.e.	78bc d
.1	.1	.1	—	—	.1	.1	.1	—							Capital Account, n.i.e.: Credit	78ba d
—	—	—	—	—	—	—	—	—							Capital Account: Debit	78bb d
−1.2	−6.7	−17.9	−.8	−1.4	−18.2	49.1	−25.5	61.6							Financial Account, n.i.e.	78bj d
—	—	—	—	—	—	—	—	—							Direct Investment Abroad	78bd d
39.4	−23.1	22.4	32.4	7.5	−5.6	−7.5	−2.9	−1.7							Dir. Invest. in Rep. Econ., n.i.e.	78be d
—	—	—	—	—	—	—	—	—							Portfolio Investment Assets	78bf d
—	—	—	—	—	—	—	—	—							Equity Securities	78bk d
—	—	—	—	—	—	—	—	—							Debt Securities	78bl d
—	—	—	—	—	—	—	—	—							Portfolio Investment Liab., n.i.e.	78bg d
—	—	—	—	—	—	—	—	—							Equity Securities	78bm d
—	—	—	—	—	—	—	—	—							Debt Securities	78bn d
															Financial Derivatives Assets	78bw d
															Financial Derivatives Liabilities	78bx d
7.3	32.0	23.4	−20.1	−9.5	−31.2	−14.6	−.8	15.6							Other Investment Assets	78bh d
															Monetary Authorities	78bo d
5.9	−4.8	−6.3	−5.1	−5.6	−7.8	−10.0	4.4	15.9							General Government	78bp d
1.4	36.8	29.7	−15.0	−3.9	−23.4	−4.6	−5.2	−.4							Banks	78bq d
−47.9	−15.6	−63.7	−13.1	.7	18.6	71.2	−21.8	47.8							Other Sectors	78br d
−15.3	26.9	19.8	19.4	—	44.5										Other Investment Liab., n.i.e.	78bi d
−6.1	−36.2	−68.3	−33.3	−25.3	16.6	31.1	−15.2	41.9							Monetary Authorities	78bs d
−4.0	.2	−.6	—		3.1	−2.6	2.8	−1.5							General Government	78bt d
−22.4	−6.5	−1.4	.3	6.5	−1.1	−1.8	−9.5	7.4							Banks	78bu d
															Other Sectors	78bv d
−21.9	−62.5	29.2	49.2	−28.9	39.8	16.1	55.1	19.3							Net Errors and Omissions	78ca d
−53.4	−71.9	−48.4	−20.9	−14.9	16.2	7.5	−59.5	−45.6							*Overall Balance*	78cb d
53.4	71.9	48.4	20.9	14.9	−16.2	−7.5	59.5	45.6							Reserves and Related Items	79da d
−.7	−6.7	9.3	−5.1	−10.7	−14.0	−13.6	−18.6	2.4							Reserve Assets	79db d
−1.7	−1.0	−1.6	−4.5	−7.5	−5.2	−8.4	55.1	15.9							Use of Fund Credit and Loans	79dc d
55.8	79.6	40.7	30.6	33.0	3.0	14.4	22.9	27.3							Exceptional Financing	79de d
Year Ending December 31															**Government Finance**	
−3,337	−2,157	−2,865	−2,413	†−10,477	−16,502	−17,099	−26,123	−39,835	−49,925	−48,300	†−47,724	−102,373	−124,064	....	Deficit (-) or Surplus	80
1,264	2,333	3,693	5,499	†17,902	35,384	54,294	67,414	61,743	69,713	85,498	77,199	85,819	152,174		Revenue	81
838	305	532	322	2,522	5,107	7,302	11,117	5,734	8,529	9,495	22,456	65,391	106,107		Grants Received	81z
5,412	4,656	7,090	8,191	†30,901	56,993	78,695	104,654	107,312	128,167	143,293	147,052	252,884	370,697		Expenditure	82
27	139	—	43	†—	—	—	—	—	—	—	327	699	11,648		Lending Minus Repayments	83
															Financing	
2,406	1,290	2,952	1,929	5,127	356	61	−1,681	2,431	25,270	7,488	47,784	88,807	11,679		Domestic	84a
931	867	−87	484	5,350	16,146	17,037	27,804	37,404	24,655	40,812	−60	13,566	112,385		Foreign	85a
4,353	5,986	7,304	10,642	16,140	16,508	18,164	24,311	26,007	41,613	52,368	133,201	231,666	232,663		Debt: Domestic	88a
17,138	17,431	32,821	87,566	156,136	367,739	408,626	444,894	656,205	966,326	941,853	1,840,991	2,755,965	2,153,630		Foreign	89a
Year Ending December 31															**National Accounts**	
16,105	25,067	43,608	†82,614	190,607	278,714	372,262	436,876	566,824	709,799	734,139	887,613	1,040,868	1,142,681	....	Househ.Cons.Expend.,incl.NPISHs	96f
2,106	2,300	4,064	†7,674	22,115	28,867	44,067	54,247	57,869	84,973	85,954	107,236	119,746	134,374		Government Consumption Expend.	91f
2,270	1,837	4,745	†9,398	19,644	35,128	21,475	43,901	37,011	78,163	41,765	59,204	52,885	84,761		Gross Fixed Capital Formation	93e
19	185	−99	†472	1,845	8,826	−3,687	2,507	−914	8,689	−5,460	−1,427	−10,856	1,143		Changes in Inventories	93i
7,183	9,854	13,347	†22,085	52,390	76,274	93,754	106,848	129,878	171,391	165,415	203,345	225,868	230,179		Exports of Goods and Services	90c
5,211	4,937	9,861	†23,385	54,390	79,374	95,254	109,853	133,973	177,254	192,770	206,062	229,815	261,561		Imports of Goods and Services (-)	98c
22,472	34,305	55,804	†98,386	230,367	339,609	436,304	535,019	657,604	867,072	834,502	1,051,336	1,209,552	1,330,433		Gross Domestic Product (GDP)	99b
−1,775	−6,265	−6,448	†−10,883	−20,606	−45,119	−61,324	−70,868	−78,196	−81,853	−92,289	−110,746	−144,985	−165,955		Net Primary Income from Abroad	98.n
20,697	28,040	49,356	†85,967	174,373	285,566	400,273	473,474	626,173	773,754	725,680	817,068	1,128,867	....		Gross National Income (GNI)	99a
1,062	1,748	2,929	10,239	12,248	20,624	27,206	34,212	37,470	39,424	71,392	59,226	69,422	49,047		Consumption of Fixed Capital	99cf
....															GDP Volume 1973 Prices	99b.p
....															GDP Volume 1980/81 Prices	99b.p
4,923	....														GDP Volume 1984/85 Prices	99b.p
101,702	94,503	95,191	98,386	100,702	81,555	82,677	81,066	74,583	79,128	65,205	64,629	59,407	61,670		GDP Volume 1989/90 Prices	99b.p
136.4	126.7	127.6	131.9	135.0	109.3	110.9	108.7	100.0	106.1	87.4	86.7	79.7	82.7		GDP Volume (1995=100)	99bv p
2.5	4.1	6.6	†11.3	25.9	47.2	59.9	74.9	100.0	124.3	145.2	184.5	230.9	244.7		GDP Deflator (1995=100)	99bi p
Midyear Estimates																
3.74	3.82	3.91	3.99	4.09	4.10	4.09	4.08	4.08	4.10	4.13	4.18	4.27	4.46	4.59	**Population**	99z

(See notes in the back of the book.)

Singapore

		1972	1973	1974	1975	1976	1977	1978	1979	1980	1981	1982	1983	1984	1985	1986
Exchange Rates														*Singapore Dollars per SDR:*		
Market Rate	aa	3.0617	†2.9991	2.8307	2.9144	2.8529	2.8406	2.8186	2.8441	2.6701	2.3836	2.3259	2.2269	2.1349	2.3122	2.6604
														Singapore Dollars per US Dollar:		
Market Rate	ae	2.8200	†2.4861	2.3120	2.4895	2.4555	2.3385	2.1635	2.1590	2.0935	2.0478	2.1085	2.1270	2.1780	2.1050	2.1750
Market Rate	rf	2.8125[e]	2.4574	2.4369	2.3713	2.4708	2.4394	2.2740	2.1746	2.1412	2.1127	2.1400	2.1131	2.1331	2.2002	2.1774
													Index Numbers (1995=100):			
Market Rate	ahx	50.4[e]	57.9	58.2	59.9	57.4	58.1	62.4	65.2	66.2	67.2	66.3	67.1	66.5	64.5	65.1
Nominal Effective Exchange Rate	ne c	....	....	....	....	....	....	....	70.9	72.6	77.5	82.6	85.8	88.2	88.3	77.7
Real Effective Exchange Rate	re c	....	....	....	....	....	....	....	92.7	92.3	97.5	102.2	103.3	105.1	102.5	87.4
Fund Position														*Millions of SDRs:*		
Quota	2f. s	37.0	37.0	37.0	37.0	37.0	37.0	49.0	49.0	92.4	92.4	92.4	92.4	92.4	92.4	92.4
SDRs	1b. s	—	—	—	—	—	—	—	12.2	15.1	27.5	49.4	59.7	58.0	66.0	73.8
Reserve Position in the Fund	1c. s	9.3	9.3	9.3	9.3	9.4	9.4	13.1	21.5	44.3	63.4	67.7	68.5	69.1	80.6	79.9
of which: Outstg.Fund Borrowing	2c	—	—	—	—	—	—	—	—	—	—	—	—	—	—	—
Total Fund Cred.&Loans Outstg.	2tl	—	—	—	—	—	—	—	—	—	—	—	—	—	—	—
International Liquidity												*Millions of US Dollars Unless Otherwise Indicated:*				
Total Reserves (see notes)	1l. d	1,748	2,286	2,812	3,007	3,364	3,858	5,303	5,818	6,567	7,549	8,480	9,264	10,416	12,847	12,939
SDRs	1b. d	—	—	—	—	—	—	—	16	19	32	54	62	57	72	90
Reserve Position in the Fund	1c. d	10	11	11	11	11	11	17	28	57	74	75	72	68	89	98
Foreign Exchange	1d. d	1,738	2,275	2,801	2,996	3,353	3,846	5,286	5,774	6,491	7,443	8,351	9,130	10,291	12,686	12,751
Deposit Money Banks: Assets	7a. d	383	603	828	956	1,317	1,681	2,190	3,233	3,706	5,630	5,073	5,824	7,869	9,595	12,052
Liabilities	7b. d	604	1,083	1,173	1,191	1,696	2,186	3,053	3,866	4,513	6,942	6,686	8,751	11,463	12,829	13,441
Other Banking Insts.: Assets	7e. d	15	11	10	8	9	8	6	7	8	9	38	58	103	115	101
Liabilities	7f. d	3	4	4	2	4	4	4	3	7	3	4	10	7	5	2
ACU: Foreign Assets	7k. d	2,229	4,202	7,721	9,590	13,292	16,381	21,621	29,478	40,914	64,608	76,218	82,350	93,400	110,763	149,821
Foreign Liabilities	7m. d	2,201	4,056	7,325	9,406	13,273	16,142	20,425	27,315	38,942	62,685	76,130	83,878	96,901	116,881	157,710
Monetary Authorities														*Millions of Singapore Dollars:*		
Foreign Assets	11	4,930	5,800	6,503	7,486	8,262	9,023	11,474	12,562	13,758	15,491	17,918	19,755	22,748	27,080	28,158
Reserve Money	14	1,296	1,779	1,850	2,197	2,563	2,904	3,369	3,838	4,340	4,809	5,690	6,220	6,656	6,944	7,319
of which: Currency Outside DMBs	14a	1,005	1,114	1,306	1,638	1,947	2,243	2,583	2,941	3,137	3,382	3,996	4,335	4,619	4,739	5,034
Central Government Deposits	16d	3,444	3,816	4,191	4,676	4,755	5,423	6,123	7,019	7,026	2,442	6,771	3,943	2,806	6,159	5,491
Other Items (Net)	17r	190	205	462	613	944	696	1,982	1,705	2,392	8,240	5,457	9,592	13,286	13,977	15,348
Deposit Money Banks														*Millions of Singapore Dollars:*		
Reserves	20	291	664	541	560	616	661	787	898	1,192	1,428	1,720	1,900	2,060	2,219	2,318
Foreign Assets	21	1,079	1,529	1,915	2,379	3,234	3,932	4,739	6,979	7,758	11,530	10,697	12,387	17,139	20,197	26,214
Claims on Central Government	22a	1,202	967	1,021	1,179	1,477	1,640	1,761	1,803	2,214	2,587	2,946	3,505	3,753	4,020	3,976
Claims on Private Sector	22d	4,172	6,141	6,840	7,688	8,601	9,511	11,035	13,652	17,823	22,867	27,222	32,578	35,602	35,790	34,484
Demand Deposits	24	1,380	1,518	1,552	1,834	2,053	2,169	2,343	2,765	2,998	3,860	4,161	4,272	4,247	4,046	4,788
Time and Savings Deposits	25	2,897	3,470	4,066	4,692	5,202	5,394	5,936	7,193	9,930	12,429	14,647	16,918	18,254	19,363	21,134
Foreign Liabilities	26c	1,704	2,747	2,712	2,964	4,164	5,111	6,606	8,347	9,448	14,216	14,098	18,614	24,966	27,006	29,235
Central Government Deposits	26d	293	715	1,052	1,144	1,119	1,092	1,209	1,488	2,360	2,818	3,212	3,354	3,526	3,525	2,507
Other Items (Net)	27r	470	851	935	1,172	1,390	1,978	2,228	3,539	4,251	5,089	6,467	7,212	7,561	8,286	9,328
Monetary Survey														*Millions of Singapore Dollars:*		
Foreign Assets (Net)	31n	4,303	4,578	5,702	6,896	7,326	7,837	9,597	11,179	11,901	12,691	14,429	13,439	14,833	19,930	25,002
Domestic Credit	32	1,637	2,578	2,619	3,048	4,206	4,638	5,467	6,951	10,654	20,195	20,189	28,789	33,029	30,134	30,471
Claims on Central Govt. (Net)	32an	−2,535	−3,564	−4,222	−4,641	−4,397	−4,875	−5,571	−6,704	−7,172	−2,673	−7,037	−3,792	−2,579	−5,664	−4,022
Claims on Private Sector	32d	4,172	6,142	6,841	7,689	8,603	9,513	11,038	13,655	17,826	22,868	27,226	32,581	35,608	35,798	34,493
Money	34	2,385	2,632	2,858	3,472	4,000	4,412	4,926	5,706	6,135	7,242	8,157	8,607	8,866	8,785	9,822
Quasi-Money	35	2,897	3,470	4,066	4,692	5,202	5,394	5,936	7,193	9,930	12,429	14,647	16,918	18,254	19,363	21,134
Other Items (Net)	37r	658	1,053	1,397	1,780	2,330	2,669	4,202	5,231	6,490	13,215	11,814	16,703	20,742	21,916	24,517
Money plus Quasi-Money	35l	5,282	6,102	6,924	8,164	9,202	9,806	10,862	12,899	16,065	19,671	22,804	25,525	27,120	28,148	30,956
Other Banking Institutions																
Finance Companies														*Millions of Singapore Dollars:*		
Cash	40	279	318	395	366	398	384	380	393	441	677	662	608	724	875	1,085
Foreign Assets	41	42	28	24	21	22	20	13	15	18	19	81	122	225	242	221
Claims on Private Sector	42d	479	738	888	947	1,082	1,229	1,486	1,936	2,509	3,422	4,421	5,593	6,027	5,549	5,338
Time and Savings Deposits	45	675	843	1,021	1,043	1,183	1,295	1,503	1,806	2,108	2,937	3,707	4,544	5,265	5,004	4,886
Foreign Liabilities	46c	9	11	10	5	9	10	7	9	15	6	9	22	15	11	4
Capital Accounts	47a	119	181	227	242	268	286	308	363	476	672	816	1,043	1,117	1,132	1,148
Other Items (Net)	47r	−2	49	48	43	43	42	61	166	368	502	632	714	580	519	607
Post Office: Savings Deposits	45.. i	125	171	269	548	957	1,589	2,029	2,525	2,757	3,266	5,058	5,917	7,287	9,129	10,559
Nonbank Financial Institutions														*Millions of Singapore Dollars:*		
Cash	40.. s	32	17	25	45	52	56	67	74	106	146	180	235	298	420	353
Foreign Assets	41.. s	23	22	20	78	78	78	78	78	78	78	78	78	78	78	171
Claims on Central Government	42a. s	55	62	70	79	97	127	135	156	152	171	211	241	238	232	217
Claims on Private Sector	42d. s	80	119	129	732	732	732	732	732	732	732	732	732	732	732	980
Fixed Assets	42h. s	19	19	27	30	31	32	34	35	37	41	58	63	70	66	71
Incr.in Total Assets(Within Per.)	49z. s	37	28	33	51	50	57	68	74	126	142	154	193	189	198	269
Liquid Liabilities	55l	5,803	6,797	7,819	9,390	10,944	12,306	14,014	16,837	20,489	25,198	30,908	35,378	38,948	41,407	45,315
Interest Rates														*Percent Per Annum*		
Money Market Rate	60b	3.57	11.69	8.90	4.39	4.15	4.76	5.93	7.76	10.98	11.54	7.92	7.11	7.67	5.38	4.27
Treasury Bill Rate	60c	....	3.68	4.48	3.34	2.96	3.19	4.04	6.57	6.78	2.38	2.57	2.59	2.91	2.95	2.03
Eurodollar Rate in Singapore	60d	....	....	6.44	5.12	7.31	11.88	15.06	18.25	14.38	9.56	9.94	8.75	8.13	6.75	
Deposit Rate	60l	....	....	....	....	4.06	4.75	6.20	9.37	10.71	7.22	6.31	6.98	4.99	3.91	
Lending Rate	60p	....	....	....	....	....	7.17	8.50	11.72	13.65	10.23	9.05	9.72	7.93	6.82	
Prices, Production, Labor														*Index Numbers (1995=100):*		
Wholesale Prices	63	....	....	86.1	84.8	90.5	94.6	96.1	109.9	131.4	136.5	130.8	126.0	125.2	122.4	103.9
Consumer Prices	64	39.2	46.9	57.3	58.8	57.7	59.5	62.4	65.0	70.5	76.3	79.3	80.2	82.3	82.7	81.6
Manufacturing Production	66ey	16.2	19.0	19.7	19.6	21.9	23.9	26.7	30.8	34.5	37.9	†35.8	36.5	39.8	†36.9	40.1
														Number in Thousands:		
Labor Force	67d	....	....	....	....	....	....	....	....	....	....	....	....	....	....	....
Employment	67e	....	....	....	....	....	....	....	....	....	....	....	....	....	1,234	1,214
Unemployment	67c	....	....	....	....	....	....	....	....	....	....	....	....	....	....	84
Unemployment Rate (%)	67r	....	....	....	....	....	....	....	....	....	....	....	....	2.7	4.1	6.5

1987	1988	1989	1990	1991	1992	1993	1994	1995	1996	1997	1998	1999	2000	2001		
End of Period															**Exchange Rates**	
2.8352	2.6190	2.4895	2.4818	2.3323	2.2617	2.2087	2.1324	2.1023	2.0129	2.2607	2.3380	2.2866	2.2560	2.3262	Market Rate	**aa**
End of Period (ae) Period Average (rf)																
1.9985	1.9462	1.8944	1.7445	1.6305	1.6449	1.6080	1.4607	1.4143	1.3998	1.6755	1.6605	1.6660	1.7315	1.8510	Market Rate	**ae**
2.1060	2.0124	1.9503	1.8125	1.7276	1.6290	1.6158	1.5274	1.4174	1.4100	1.4848	1.6736	1.6950	1.7240	1.7917	Market Rate	**rf**
Period Averages																
67.3	70.4	72.7	78.3	82.1	87.0	87.7	92.9	100.0	100.5	95.7	84.8	83.6	82.2	79.1	Market Rate	**ahx**
74.3	74.7	79.7	84.9	88.8	91.7	93.4	97.1	100.0	104.7	107.3	106.7	101.2	101.6	103.0	Nominal Effective Exchange Rate	**nec**
82.0	80.9	84.5	89.0	92.1	93.9	94.7	98.3	100.0	103.5	105.6	101.7	95.3	95.4	96.2	Real Effective Exchange Rate	**rec**
End of Period															**Fund Position**	
92.4	92.4	92.4	92.4	92.4	357.6	357.6	357.6	357.6	357.6	357.6	357.6	862.5	862.5	862.5	Quota	**2f.s**
81.2	79.0	79.4	81.4	81.3	49.4	56.9	24.1	33.1	42.5	52.2	64.9	89.2	105.3	119.6	SDRs	**1b.s**
79.1	77.9	80.1	68.9	60.1	113.4	157.4	172.8	199.8	204.7	248.4	297.6	303.4	237.7	297.5	Reserve Position in the Fund	**1c.s**
—	—	—	—	—	—	—	—	—	—	—	31.3	—	—	—	*of which:* Outstg.Fund Borrowing	**2c**
—	—	—	—	—	—	—	—	—	—	—	—	—	—	—	Total Fund Cred.&Loans Outstg.	**2tl**
End of Period															**International Liquidity**	
15,227	17,073	20,345	27,748	34,133	39,885	48,361	58,177	68,695	76,847	71,289	74,928	76,843	80,132	75,375	Total Reserves (see notes)	**1l.d**
115	106	104	116	116	68	78	35	49	61	70	91	122	137	150	SDRs	**1b.d**
112	105	105	98	86	156	216	252	297	294	335	419	416	310	374	Reserve Position in the Fund	**1c.d**
15,000	16,861	20,136	27,535	33,931	39,661	48,066	57,890	68,349	76,491	70,883	74,418	76,304	79,685	74,851	Foreign Exchange	**1d.d**
14,761	17,763	25,744	25,142	25,814	31,396	31,345	38,992	39,115	43,079	46,963	45,153	55,854	52,297	58,855	Deposit Money Banks: Assets	**7a.d**
15,367	17,360	23,947	24,937	24,569	29,450	32,085	40,976	46,753	55,327	62,784	50,466	53,565	58,923	61,942	Liabilities	**7b.d**
113	89	97	139	120	129	124	163	168	154	124	107	80	75	51	Other Banking Insts.: Assets	**7e.d**
5	11	6	3	3	6	10	27	19	12	11	5	8	4	2	Liabilities	**7f.d**
194,968	230,252	280,224	321,451	296,259	292,475	306,703	326,698	373,774	396,655	425,242	395,279	367,891	365,200	345,171	ACU: Foreign Assets	**7k.d**
201,466	235,012	284,414	329,919	304,431	298,497	321,390	340,295	391,907	419,343	447,032	417,074	384,960	386,809	375,944	Foreign Liabilities	**7m.d**
End of Period															**Monetary Authorities**	
30,442	33,277	38,607	48,521	55,803	65,788	77,867	85,166	97,337	107,751	119,617	124,584	128,457	139,260	139,942	Foreign Assets	**11**
7,910	8,932	10,316	11,056	12,232	13,531	14,669	15,577	17,040	18,189	19,200	16,641	21,395	18,471	20,032	Reserve Money	**14**
5,440	5,997	6,610	7,109	7,497	8,279	8,942	9,420	9,907	10,293	10,704	10,146	11,315	11,289	11,868	*of which: Currency Outside DMBs*	**14a**
6,247	7,676	13,465	17,678	20,177	25,077	30,080	35,669	44,471	51,554	57,520	57,484	58,994	69,958	85,106	Central Government Deposits	**16d**
16,285	16,669	14,826	19,787	23,394	27,180	33,118	33,920	35,826	38,008	42,897	50,459	48,068	50,831	34,804	Other Items (Net)	**17r**
End of Period															**Deposit Money Banks**	
2,476	2,932	3,709	3,951	4,750	5,301	5,770	6,150	7,152	7,900	8,498	6,423	10,076	7,174	8,199	Reserves	**20**
29,499	34,570	48,769	43,860	42,089	51,644	50,402	56,956	55,321	60,302	78,687	74,976	93,053	90,552	108,941	Foreign Assets	**21**
5,287	5,412	6,826	7,923	9,765	11,587	12,758	13,568	15,754	17,538	18,883	26,477	30,949	33,719	40,512	Claims on Central Government	**22a**
36,693	40,789	48,757	55,798	62,725	68,851	79,282	91,375	109,885	127,272	143,409	154,844	150,199	159,083	185,048	Claims on Private Sector	**22d**
5,591	5,961	7,135	8,152	8,933	10,236	13,940	13,991	15,443	16,747	16,807	17,093	19,794	21,973	24,215	Demand Deposits	**24**
26,059	30,130	37,801	46,584	53,112	57,213	59,248	70,569	76,618	84,911	95,933	133,545	143,365	137,636	144,826	Time and Savings Deposits	**25**
30,710	33,786	45,366	43,502	40,060	48,443	51,592	59,854	66,123	77,447	105,194	83,799	89,240	102,026	114,654	Foreign Liabilities	**26c**
2,212	3,560	5,344	4,733	5,268	5,744	6,385	6,584	7,538	6,896	1,529	1,766	1,632	1,465	2,089	Central Government Deposits	**26d**
9,383	10,266	12,415	8,561	11,956	15,747	17,047	17,051	22,390	27,011	30,014	26,517	30,246	27,428	56,916	Other Items (Net)	**27r**
End of Period															**Monetary Survey**	
29,137	33,979	41,933	48,780	57,718	68,397	76,196	81,833	86,164	90,260	92,836	115,512	130,951	126,342	132,876	Foreign Assets (Net)	**31n**
33,530	34,973	36,782	41,317	47,053	49,624	55,583	62,699	73,638	86,368	103,251	122,081	120,535	126,640	144,625	Domestic Credit	**32**
–3,172	–5,824	–11,983	–14,488	–15,680	–19,234	–23,707	–28,685	–36,255	–40,912	–40,166	–32,773	–29,677	–32,454	–40,432	Claims on Central Govt. (Net)	**32an**
36,702	40,797	48,765	55,805	62,733	68,858	79,290	91,384	109,893	127,280	143,417	154,854	150,212	159,094	185,057	Claims on Private Sector	**32d**
11,031	11,958	13,745	15,261	16,430	18,515	22,882	23,411	25,350	27,040	27,511	27,239	31,109	33,262	36,083	Money	**34**
26,059	30,130	37,801	46,584	53,112	57,213	59,248	70,569	76,618	84,911	95,933	133,545	143,365	137,636	144,826	Quasi-Money	**35**
25,577	26,864	27,169	28,252	35,229	42,293	49,649	50,552	57,834	64,677	72,643	76,809	77,012	82,084	96,592	Other Items (Net)	**37r**
37,090	42,088	51,546	61,845	69,542	75,728	82,130	93,980	101,968	111,951	123,444	160,784	174,474	170,898	180,909	Money plus Quasi-Money	**35l**
															Other Banking Institutions	
End of Period															Finance Companies	
1,136	1,010	1,117	1,557	1,996	1,953	1,788	2,574	2,848	2,561	2,513	2,822	3,046	2,017	1,514	Cash	**40**
225	173	183	243	196	212	200	238	237	215	208	179	133	130	95	Foreign Assets	**41**
5,759	6,684	8,196	8,958	9,555	10,251	12,047	15,110	16,717	17,073	18,034	16,891	15,751	15,880	11,919	Claims on Private Sector	**42d**
5,372	5,821	7,422	8,520	9,097	9,552	10,558	13,753	15,435	15,058	15,734	15,421	14,387	13,653	10,638	Time and Savings Deposits	**45**
10	22	12	6	6	10	17	39	26	16	18	9	14	6	4	Foreign Liabilities	**46c**
1,177	1,250	1,333	1,416	1,510	1,679	1,850	2,203	2,621	3,015	3,269	3,371	3,408	3,165	2,426	Capital Accounts	**47a**
562	774	728	815	1,133	1,176	1,611	1,927	1,720	1,760	1,734	1,091	1,121	1,203	461	Other Items (Net)	**47r**
11,165	12,140	13,050	13,240	15,531	18,007	20,085	20,127	22,188	24,734	25,130	....	....	....	....	Post Office: Savings Deposits	**45..i**
End of Period															**Nonbank Financial Institutions**	
384	478	697	974	954	761	1,160	1,772	2,269	2,657	3,041	3,809	4,036	3,796	4,057	Cash	**40..s**
250	175	200	205	246	830	1,160	1,090	1,546	2,082	2,055	2,696	3,574	7,254	10,926	Foreign Assets	**41..s**
232	300	422	440	567	1,337	1,190	918	901	746	815	933	2,417	3,169	6,100	Claims on Central Government	**42a.s**
1,215	1,524	1,766	2,198	2,854	2,919	4,270	5,488	6,715	8,261	10,095	10,392	16,333	18,555	24,525	Claims on Private Sector	**42d.s**
85	95	105	116	131	237	313	335	657	1,173	1,377	1,861	1,874	1,868	1,891	Fixed Assets	**42h.s**
391	422	644	785	830	1,375	1,944	1,682	2,481	2,996	2,379	2,564	8,170	6,244	13,148	*Incr.in Total Assets(Within Per.)*	**49z.s**
52,492	59,040	70,901	82,048	92,174	101,333	110,985	125,286	136,743	149,182	161,795	....	....	....	....	Liquid Liabilities	**55l**
Percent Per Annum															**Interest Rates**	
3.89	4.30	5.34	6.61	4.76	2.74	2.50	3.68	2.56	2.93	4.35	5.00	2.04	2.57	1.99	Money Market Rate	**60b**
3.29	4.04	4.68	1.60	1.20	.90	1.35	.65	.71	1.15	1.90	1.15	.40	2.48	.87	Treasury Bill Rate	**60c**
8.00	9.31	8.38	7.75	4.38	3.50	3.38	6.50	5.63	5.63	5.91	5.13	6.06	6.39	1.89	Eurodollar Rate in Singapore	**60d**
2.89	2.74	3.21	4.67	4.63	2.86	2.30	3.00	3.50	3.41	3.47	4.60	1.68	1.71	1.54	Deposit Rate	**60l**
6.10	5.96	6.21	7.36	7.58	5.95	5.39	5.88	6.37	6.26	6.32	7.44	5.80	5.83	5.66	Lending Rate	**60p**
Period Averages															**Prices, Production, Labor**	
111.8	109.7	†112.5	114.5	109.8	105.0	100.4	100.0	100.0	100.1	99.0	†96.0	98.0	107.9	106.1	Wholesale Prices	**63**
82.0	83.2	85.2	88.1	91.2	93.2	95.4	98.3	100.0	101.4	103.4	†103.1	103.2	104.6	105.6	Consumer Prices	**64**
47.1	55.7	61.3	67.4	71.1	72.8	80.2	90.6	†100.0	103.3	108.0	†107.6	122.6	141.4	125.0	Manufacturing Production	**66ey**
Period Averages																
....	....	....	....	....	1,620	1,636	1,693	1,748	1,801	1,876	1,932	2,192	....	....	Labor Force	**67d**
1,267	1,332	1,394	1,537	1,524	1,576	1,592	1,649	1,702	1,748	1,831	1,870	1,886	2,095	....	Employment	**67e**
62	46	31	26	30	43	44	44	47	54	46	62	90	98	....	Unemployment	**67c**
4.7	3.3	2.2	1.7	1.9	2.7	2.7	2.6	2.7	3.0	2.4	3.2	4.6	4.4	....	Unemployment Rate (%)	**67r**

		1972	1973	1974	1975	1976	1977	1978	1979	1980	1981	1982	1983	1984	1985	1986
International Transactions														*Millions of Singapore Dollars*		
Exports	70	6,149	8,907	14,155	12,758	16,266	20,091	22,986	30,940	41,452	44,291	44,473	46,155	51,340	50,179	48,986
Imports, c.i.f.	71	9,539	12,513	20,406	19,269	22,406	25,522	29,630	38,352	51,355	58,249	60,244	59,504	61,134	57,819	55,543
																1995=100
Volume of Exports	72	6.5	7.9	8.7	7.9	9.4	10.9	12.2	†14.7	15.9	16.4	17.0	18.5	21.5	21.4	24.3
Volume of Imports	73	10.8	12.3	†14.1	13.5	14.4	15.6	17.5	20.0	22.9	25.6	27.7	28.1	29.1	28.2	30.7
Exports (Direct Prices)	76	....	....	....	....	....	....	....	125.8	155.1	160.9	156.0	148.6	142.8	140.0	120.3
Imports (Direct Prices)	76.x	....	....	82.3	80.9	88.2	92.7	96.2	108.7	126.9	129.0	123.3	120.1	119.3	116.1	102.5
Balance of Payments														*Millions of US Dollars*		
Current Account, n.i.e.	78ald	−495	−519	−1,021	−584	−567	−295	−453	−736	−1,563	−1,470	−1,296	−610	−385	−4	319
Goods: Exports f.o.b.	78aa d	2,170	3,599	5,906	5,481	6,654	8,245	10,123	14,248	19,430	21,090	21,016	21,894	24,091	23,187	22,738
Goods: Imports f.o.b.	78ab d	−3,127	−4,735	−7,764	−7,511	−8,442	−9,729	−12,090	−16,450	−22,400	−25,785	−26,196	−26,252	−26,734	−24,705	−23,679
Trade Balance	78ac d	−958	−1,137	−1,859	−2,030	−1,788	−1,484	−1,967	−2,202	−2,971	−4,695	−5,181	−4,358	−2,643	−1,518	−940
Services: Credit	78ad d	961	1,377	1,931	2,416	2,364	2,594	3,127	3,595	4,856	7,184	8,128	7,834	6,153	4,688	4,806
Services: Debit	78ae d	−484	−655	−900	−966	−1,054	−1,277	−1,547	−2,050	−2,912	−3,254	−3,613	−3,782	−4,024	−3,554	−3,808
Balance on Goods & Services	78af d	−481	−414	−828	−580	−478	−167	−388	−657	−1,027	−765	−665	−306	−513	−385	58
Income: Credit	78ag d	113	167	225	380	370	391	528	806	953	1,092	1,243	1,300	1,603	1,854	2,230
Income: Debit	78ah d	−129	−268	−380	−345	−410	−475	−554	−849	−1,382	−1,644	−1,668	−1,390	−1,252	−1,260	−1,786
Balance on Gds, Serv. & Inc.	78ai d	−497	−515	−982	−545	−518	−251	−414	−701	−1,456	−1,317	−1,091	−396	−162	210	502
Current Transfers, n.i.e.: Credit	78aj d	79	103	70	65	49	48	64	86	87	130	98	121	121	113	120
Current Transfers: Debit	78ak d	−76	−107	−109	−104	−98	−93	−102	−121	−194	−283	−303	−336	−344	−326	−303
Capital Account, n.i.e.	78bc d	—	—	—	—	—	—	—	—	—	—	—	—	—	—	—
Capital Account, n.i.e.: Credit	78ba d	—	—	—	—	—	—	—	—	—	—	—	—	—	—	—
Capital Account: Debit	78bb d	—	—	—	—	—	—	—	—	—	—	—	—	—	—	—
Financial Account, n.i.e.	78bj d	395	722	500	580	849	607	1,013	998	1,582	2,167	2,309	2,463	1,580	698	−445
Direct Investment Abroad	78bd d	−20	−26	−30	−38	−45	−85	−113	−167	−98	15	−304	−49	−92	−238	−181
Dir. Invest. in Rep. Econ., n.i.e.	78be d	161	353	340	292	231	291	300	836	1,236	1,660	1,602	1,134	1,302	1,047	1,710
Portfolio Investment Assets	78bf d	−13	−17	−20	−29	−32	−40	−139	−108	−121	−193	−106	−160	−161	−347	−287
Equity Securities	78bk d	−7	−9	−9	−12	−15	−23	−36	−63	−25	−171	−140	−218	−64	−259	−121
Debt Securities	78bl d	−6	−9	−10	−17	−17	−17	−102	−45	−96	−22	34	58	−97	−88	−167
Portfolio Investment Liab., n.i.e.	78bg d	77	50	35	27	82	136	12	30	134	145	78	111	10	521	−261
Equity Securities	78bm d	26	50	35	27	47	14	18	43	146	157	98	201	18	531	−194
Debt Securities	78bn d	51	—	—	—	36	121	−6	−12	−13	−12	−20	−89	−8	−10	−68
Financial Derivatives Assets	78bw d	....	....	....	....	....	....	....	....	....	....	....	....	....	....	....
Financial Derivatives Liabilities	78bx d	....	....	....	....	....	....	....	....	....	....	....	....	....	....	....
Other Investment Assets	78bh d	−98	−212	−195	−235	−399	−347	−545	−1,112	−741	−2,645	184	−824	−3,071	−2,250	−3,197
Monetary Authorities	78bo d															
General Government	78bp d	—	−8	−6	−1	−2	−4	−6	—	—	—	—	—	—	—	—
Banks	78bq d	−76	−183	−158	−196	−346	−261	−355	−974	−363	−1,785	390	−800	−2,228	−1,390	−2,763
Other Sectors	78br d	−22	−22	−30	−38	−51	−82	−184	−138	−377	−860	−206	−24	−843	−860	−434
Other Investment Liab., n.i.e.	78bi d	289	575	370	563	1,012	651	1,499	1,519	1,173	3,186	856	2,251	3,593	1,964	1,772
Monetary Authorities	78bs d															
General Government	78bt d	16	18	7	10	7	5	18	−4	−2	−3	5	5	−3	−9	−13
Banks	78bu d	205	424	−14	106	429	347	650	790	500	2,257	−55	2,137	2,978	927	1,023
Other Sectors	78bv d	69	132	377	446	576	299	832	733	675	932	906	109	618	1,046	762
Net Errors and Omissions	78ca d	435	210	816	412	17	1	104	254	643	212	165	−793	329	643	664
Overall Balance	78cb d	335	413	295	407	298	313	665	516	663	909	1,177	1,059	1,524	1,337	538
Reserves and Related Items	79da d	−335	−413	−295	−407	−298	−313	−665	−516	−663	−909	−1,177	−1,059	−1,524	−1,337	−538
Reserve Assets	79db d	−335	−413	−295	−407	−298	−313	−665	−516	−663	−909	−1,177	−1,059	−1,524	−1,337	−538
Use of Fund Credit and Loans	79dc d	—	—	—	—	—	—	—	—	—	—	—	—	—	—	—
Exceptional Financing	79de d	....	....	....	....	....	....	....	....	....	....	....	....	....	....	....
Government Finance														*Millions of Singapore Dollars:*		
Deficit (-) or Surplus	80	213	133	109	284	53	102	42	77	99	754	1,013	922	2,088	595	707
Total Revenue and Grants	81y	1,872	2,158	2,691	3,370	3,450	3,702	4,126	4,710	6,149	7,663	9,905	11,462	11,471	10,854	17,262
Revenue	81	1,872	2,158	2,691	3,370	3,450	3,702	4,126	4,710	6,149	7,663	9,905	11,462	11,471	10,854	17,262
Grants	81z															
Exp. & Lending Minus Repay.	82z	1,659	2,025	2,582	3,086	3,397	3,600	4,084	4,633	6,050	6,909	8,892	10,540	9,383	10,259	16,555
Expenditure	82	1,320	1,520	1,839	2,287	2,673	3,093	3,581	3,918	4,944	5,712	6,724	7,812	8,396	10,597	9,949
Lending Minus Repayments	83	339	505	743	799	724	507	503	715	1,106	1,197	2,168	2,728	987	−338	6,606
Total Financing	80h	−213	−133	−109	−284	−53	−102	−42	−77	−99	−754	−1,013	−922	−2,088	−595	−707
Total Net Borrowing	84	527	390	755	1,243	1,579	1,963	1,548	1,724	2,187	2,351	3,835	5,116	3,869	4,978	4,118
Use of Cash Balances	87	−740	−523	−864	−1,527	−1,632	−2,065	−1,590	−1,801	−2,286	−3,105	−4,848	−6,038	−5,957	−5,573	−4,825
Total Debt by Currency	88z	3,483	3,758	4,522	5,698	7,318	9,133	10,695	12,402	14,675	17,138	20,730	25,032	28,078	32,173	33,905
National	88b	....	....	....	....	....	....	....	....	....	....	....	....	....	....	....
Foreign	89b															
National Accounts														*Millions of Singapore Dollars*		
Househ.Cons.Expend.,incl.NPISHs	96f	5,071	6,340	7,658	8,121	8,606	9,269	10,149	11,245	12,911	14,329	15,283	16,202	17,570	17,553	18,405
Government Consumption Expend.	91f	990	1,118	1,298	1,423	1,542	1,716	1,965	2,034	2,447	2,789	3,570	3,995	4,333	5,549	5,270
Gross Fixed Capital Formation	93e	3,054	3,561	4,695	4,698	5,288	5,458	6,365	7,520	10,203	12,785	15,506	17,464	19,122	16,425	14,132
Changes in Inventories	93i	300	439	897	336	694	341	592	1,380	1,425	802	153	132	295	126	585
Exports (Net)	90n	−1,378	−1,041	−2,133	−1,508	−1,199	−424	−898	−1,445	−2,216	−1,634	−1,441	−664	−1,113	−946	143
Gross Domestic Product (GDP)	99b	8,156	10,205	12,543	13,373	14,651	16,039	17,830	20,523	25,091	29,339	32,670	36,733	40,048	38,924	39,264
Net Primary Income from Abroad	98.n	−21	−224	−288	−28	−81	−187	−43	−79	−902	−1,148	−894	−172	767	1,406	949
Gross National Income (GNI)	99a	8,135	9,981	12,255	13,345	14,570	15,852	17,787	20,444	24,189	28,191	31,776	36,561	40,815	40,330	40,213
GDP Volume 1968 prices	99b.p	7,120	7,941	8,445	8,790	9,447	....	....	....	....	....	....	....	....	....	....
GDP Volume 1985 prices	99b.p	....	....	....	....	20,549	22,143	24,046	26,285	28,833	31,603	33,772	36,537	39,573	....	....
GDP Volume 1990 Prices	99b.p	....	....	....	....	....	....	....	....	....	....	....	....	46,092	45,345	46,388
GDP Volume (1995=100)	99bv p	17.5	19.6	20.8	21.7	23.3	25.1	27.2	29.8	32.6	35.8	38.2	41.4	44.8	44.1	45.1
GDP Deflator (1995=100)	99bi p	39.5	44.3	51.2	52.4	53.5	54.3	55.6	58.5	65.3	69.6	72.5	75.4	75.9	75.0	73.9
																Millions:
Population	99z	2.15	2.19	2.23	2.26	2.29	2.33	2.35	2.38	2.41	2.44	2.47	2.41	2.44	2.48	2.52

	1987	1988	1989	1990	1991	1992	1993	1994	1995	1996	1997	1998	1999	2000	2001		
Millions of Singapore Dollars																**International Transactions**	
	60,266	79,051	87,117	95,206	101,880	103,351	119,475	147,327	167,515	176,271	185,613	183,763	194,290	237,826	218,029	Exports	70
	68,416	88,228	96,864	109,806	114,195	117,530	137,602	156,397	176,317	185,183	196,606	174,867	188,143	232,176	207,694	Imports, c.i.f.	71
1995=100																	
	28.9	38.5	42.6	46.3	52.4	56.9	67.2	86.4	100.0	106.2	113.5	114.6	120.9	140.0	133.4	Volume of Exports	72
	35.0	44.9	49.3	56.4	60.6	64.6	77.2	88.6	100.0	106.3	114.5	103.8	109.9	124.4	111.0	Volume of Imports	73
	124.4	122.7	†122.1	122.7	116.1	108.5	106.1	101.8	100.0	99.1	97.6	†95.7	95.9	101.4	97.6	Exports (Direct Prices)	76
	111.0	111.4	†111.4	110.4	106.8	103.2	101.1	100.1	100.0	98.8	97.4	†95.5	97.1	105.8	106.1	Imports (Direct Prices)	76.x
Minus Sign Indicates Debit																Balance of Payments	
	-109	1,937	2,964	3,122	4,880	5,915	4,211	11,400	14,900	12,823	17,927	20,334	21,750	21,797	....	Current Account, n.i.e.	78al *d*
	29,096	40,703	45,700	54,679	61,333	66,565	77,858	97,919	118,456	126,010	125,746	110,561	115,518	138,931	....	Goods: Exports f.o.b.	78aa *d*
	-30,239	-40,675	-46,012	-56,311	-61,443	-68,387	-80,582	-96,565	-117,480	-123,786	-124,628	-95,782	-104,361	-127,531	....	Goods: Imports f.o.b.	78ab *d*
	-1,143	28	-313	-1,633	-110	-1,821	-2,724	1,354	976	2,225	1,118	14,779	11,157	11,400	....	*Trade Balance*	78ac *d*
	5,795	7,563	9,658	12,811	13,823	16,200	18,597	23,044	29,649	29,958	30,493	19,149	23,985	27,040	....	Services: Credit	78ad *d*
	-4,612	-5,797	-6,849	-8,642	-9,124	-9,537	-11,321	-13,898	-17,367	-19,733	-18,981	-17,623	-18,929	-21,408	....	Services: Debit	78ae *d*
	40	1,794	2,497	2,537	4,589	4,842	4,552	10,500	13,258	12,449	12,630	16,305	16,213	17,033	....	*Balance on Goods & Services*	78af *d*
	2,921	3,882	4,752	6,508	7,558	8,214	8,075	9,783	12,958	12,534	13,893	12,969	14,975	15,253	....	Income: Credit	78ag *d*
	-2,884	-3,495	-3,959	-5,502	-6,801	-6,666	-7,880	-8,222	-10,430	-11,093	-7,428	-7,843	-8,274	-9,130	....	Income: Debit	78ah *d*
	76	2,181	3,289	3,543	5,346	6,390	4,747	12,061	15,786	13,890	19,096	21,432	22,914	23,155	....	*Balance on Gds, Serv. & Inc.*	78ai *d*
	108	111	114	123	129	172	140	145	156	157	151	136	134	132	....	Current Transfers, n.i.e.: Credit	78aj *d*
	-293	-356	-440	-544	-595	-647	-676	-806	-1,042	-1,224	-1,319	-1,234	-1,297	-1,490	....	Current Transfers: Debit	78ak *d*
	-49	-55	-41	-22	-34	-38	-71	-84	-71	-139	-173	-226	-191	-163	....	Capital Account, n.i.e.	78bc *d*
	....	....	....	....	....	....	....	....	....	....	....	....	....	....	....	Capital Account, n.i.e.: Credit	78ba *d*
	-49	-55	-41	-22	-34	-38	-71	-84	-71	-139	-173	-226	-191	-163	....	Capital Account: Debit	78bb *d*
	470	987	1,251	3,947	2,346	1,793	-1,212	-8,841	-878	-4,825	-10,976	-21,813	-18,280	-11,399	....	Financial Account, n.i.e.	78bj *d*
	-206	-118	-882	-2,034	-526	-1,317	-2,152	-4,577	-3,442	-6,827	-9,360	-555	-4,011	-4,276	....	Direct Investment Abroad	78bd *d*
	2,836	3,655	2,887	5,575	4,887	2,204	4,686	8,550	8,788	10,372	12,967	6,316	7,197	6,390	....	Dir. Invest. in Rep. Econ., n.i.e.	78be *d*
	-67	-329	-451	-1,610	-665	1,091	-7,833	-7,840	-7,769	-12,625	-13,088	-7,677	-9,228	-11,775	....	Portfolio Investment Assets	78bf *d*
	-104	-260	-358	-468	-524	165	-7,555	-7,414	-7,972	-10,915	-13,099	-6,886	-8,859	-9,434	....	Equity Securities	78bk *d*
	37	-69	-93	-1,142	-141	926	-278	-426	203	-1,710	12	-792	-369	-2,341	....	Debt Securities	78bl *d*
	320	36	375	573	-242	1,398	2,867	114	410	938	82	669	2,143	-2,082	....	Portfolio Investment Liab., n.i.e.	78bg *d*
	321	36	400	573	-242	1,398	2,759	169	462	950	84	664	2,145	-2,081	....	Equity Securities	78bm *d*
	-2	—	-25	—	—	—	108	-55	-52	-12	-2	5	-2	-1	....	Debt Securities	78bn *d*
	....	....	....	....	....	....	....	....	....	....	....	....	....	....	....	Financial Derivatives Assets	78bw *d*
	....	....	....	....	....	....	....	....	....	....	....	....	....	....	....	Financial Derivatives Liabilities	78bx *d*
	-2,272	-2,589	-8,091	-220	1,831	-6,685	-7,104	-10,999	-12,150	-13,538	-41,692	-3,555	-21,074	-5,291	....	Other Investment Assets	78bh *d*
	....	....	....	....	....	....	....	....	....	....	....	....	....	....	....	Monetary Authorities	78bo *d*
	—	—	—	—	-1	—	—	—	-7	—	—	—	-660	78	....	General Government	78bp *d*
	-1,560	-2,520	-7,280	2,708	1,025	-5,866	769	-4,291	1,154	-3,533	-12,382	2,217	-10,665	1,325	....	Banks	78bq *d*
	-711	-68	-811	-2,928	806	-819	-7,872	-6,708	-13,297	-10,005	-29,310	-5,772	-9,749	-6,694	....	Other Sectors	78br *d*
	-141	332	7,413	1,664	-2,940	5,101	8,324	5,911	13,285	16,856	40,114	-17,012	6,693	5,635	....	Other Investment Liab., n.i.e.	78bi *d*
	—	—	—	—	—	—	—	—	—	—	—	—	—	—	....	Monetary Authorities	78bs *d*
	-18	-20	-17	-37	-15	-9	-9	-4	—	—	—	—	—	—	....	General Government	78bt *d*
	700	1,529	5,937	-1,028	-1,992	5,146	1,949	5,409	4,423	8,032	18,687	-12,787	3,210	7,424	....	Banks	78bu *d*
	-823	-1,177	1,493	2,729	-933	-36	6,384	506	8,863	8,824	21,427	-4,225	3,483	-1,789	....	Other Sectors	78bv *d*
	782	-1,210	-1,436	-1,616	-2,995	-1,570	4,650	2,261	-5,352	-464	1,162	4,670	915	-3,429	....	Net Errors and Omissions	78ca *d*
	1,095	1,659	2,738	5,431	4,197	6,100	7,578	4,736	8,599	7,396	7,940	2,965	4,194	6,806	....	*Overall Balance*	78cb *d*
	-1,095	-1,659	-2,738	-5,431	-4,197	-6,100	-7,578	-4,736	-8,599	-7,396	-7,940	-2,965	-4,194	-6,806	....	Reserves and Related Items	79da *d*
	-1,095	-1,659	-2,738	-5,431	-4,197	-6,100	-7,578	-4,736	-8,599	-7,396	-7,940	-2,965	-4,194	-6,806	....	Reserve Assets	79db *d*
	—	—	—	—	—	—	—	—	—	—	—	—	—	—	....	Use of Fund Credit and Loans	79dc *d*
	—	—	—	—	—	—	—	—	—	—	—	—	—	—	....	Exceptional Financing	79de *d*
Year Ending December 31																**Government Finance**	
	-2,040	3,139	689	6,495	7,591	9,537	12,998	13,086	15,870	18,868	13,612	23,163	14,577	18,094	-467	Deficit (-) or Surplus	80
	12,076	14,117	15,915	19,021	22,001	25,355	29,488	33,094	40,026	47,617	57,048	59,724	49,950	52,255	35,393	Total Revenue and Grants	81y
	12,076	14,117	15,915	19,021	22,001	25,355	29,488	33,094	40,026	47,617	57,048	59,724	49,950	52,255	35,393	Revenue	81
																Grants	81z
	14,116	10,978	15,226	12,526	14,410	15,818	16,490	20,008	24,156	28,749	43,436	36,561	35,373	34,161	35,860	Exp. & Lending Minus Repay.	82z
	14,550	11,914	10,543	13,256	13,893	14,804	14,339	15,670	17,419	20,681	29,222	25,586	26,665	30,068	34,957	Expenditure	82
	-434	-936	4,683	-730	517	1,014	2,151	4,338	6,737	8,068	14,214	10,975	8,708	4,093	903	Lending Minus Repayments	83
	2,040	-3,139	-689	-6,495	-7,591	-9,537	-12,998	-13,086	-15,870	-18,868	-13,612	-23,163	-14,577	-18,093	467	Total Financing	80h
	5,933	33,617	5,779	7,370	10,518	-7,731	5,309	12,552	16,402	10,159	12,215	22,540	17,148	16,487	8,084	Total Net Borrowing	84
	-3,893	-36,756	-6,468	-13,865	-18,109	-1,806	-18,307	-25,638	-32,272	-29,027	-25,827	-45,703	-31,725	-34,580	-7,617	Use of Cash Balances	87
	38,353	41,936	46,339	51,565	59,163	67,376	69,944	75,467	86,630	94,831	102,372	115,183	125,777	134,370	146,996	Total Debt by Currency	88z
	....	....	....	....	....	....	....	....	....	94,831	102,372	115,183	125,777	134,370	146,996	National	88b
	....	....	....	....	....	....	....	....	....	....	....	....	....	....	....	Foreign	89b
Millions of Singapore Dollars																**National Accounts**	
	20,697	24,390	27,664	30,847	33,536	36,415	42,232	47,183	48,840	52,938	56,268	53,844	57,555	64,159	64,797	Househ.Cons.Expend..incl.NPISHs	96f
	5,315	5,337	6,013	6,780	7,351	7,459	8,723	9,008	10,124	12,208	13,180	13,907	14,091	16,834	18,320	Government Consumption Expend.	91f
	14,405	15,667	18,906	21,578	25,095	28,806	32,753	36,202	39,973	49,353	54,334	51,427	47,182	47,087	44,830	Gross Fixed Capital Formation	93e
	1,893	1,663	1,459	2,771	656	269	2,505	-500	894	-1,771	-196	-5,599	-2,522	3,428	-7,581	Changes in Inventories	93i
	83	3,609	4,869	4,598	7,928	7,887	7,356	16,039	18,792	17,350	19,531	26,712	26,580	28,685	33,322	Exports (Net)	90n
	42,973	50,714	58,190	66,464	74,018	79,928	93,179	106,653	117,768	128,244	140,279	137,618	140,070	159,888	153,455	Gross Domestic Product (GDP)	99b
	78	781	1,546	1,824	1,308	2,521	315	2,384	3,583	1,886	9,171	8,254	3,437	1,025	1,189	Net Primary Income from Abroad	98.n
	43,051	51,495	59,736	68,288	75,326	82,450	93,494	109,037	121,351	130,130	149,450	145,873	143,507	160,913	154,645	Gross National Income (GNI)	99a
	....	....	....	....	....	....	....	....	....	....	....	....	....	....	....	GDP Volume 1968 prices	99b.*p*
	....	....	....	....	....	....	....	....	....	....	....	....	....	....	....	GDP Volume 1985 prices	99b.*p*
	49,838	55,636	60,991	66,464	71,183	75,840	85,467	95,229	102,859	110,730	120,191	120,081	128,405	141,572	138,683	GDP Volume 1990 prices	99b.*p*
	48.5	54.1	59.3	64.6	69.2	73.7	83.1	92.6	100.0	107.7	116.9	116.7	124.8	137.6	134.8	GDP Volume (1995=100)	99bv*p*
	75.3	79.6	83.3	87.3	90.8	92.0	95.2	97.8	100.0	101.2	101.9	100.1	95.3	98.6	96.6	GDP Deflator (1995=100)	99bi*p*
Midyear Estimates																	
	2.55	2.85	2.93	3.02	3.14	3.23	3.32	3.42	3.53	3.67	3.79	3.92	3.95	4.13	4.13	**Population**	99z

(See notes in the back of the book.)

Slovak Republic

	1972	1973	1974	1975	1976	1977	1978	1979	1980	1981	1982	1983	1984	1985	1986

Exchange Rates — *Koruny per SDR:*

Official Rate .... aa	...	...	...	...	...	...	...	...	...	...	...	...	...	...	...

Koruny per US Dollar:

Official Rate .... ae	...	...	...	...	...	...	...	...	...	...	...	...	...	...	...
Official Rate .... rf	...	...	...	...	...	...	...	...	...	...	...	...	...	...	...

Index Numbers (1995=100):

Nominal Effective Exchange Rate .... ne c	...	...	...	...	...	...	...	...	...	...	...	...	...	...	...
Real Effective Exchange Rate .... re c	...	...	...	...	...	...	...	...	...	...	...	...	...	...	...

Fund Position — *Millions of SDRs:*

Quota .... 2f. s	...	...	...	...	...	...	...	...	...	...	...	...	...	...	...
SDRs .... 1b. s	...	...	...	...	...	...	...	...	...	...	...	...	...	...	...
Reserve Position in the Fund .... 1c. s	...	...	...	...	...	...	...	...	...	...	...	...	...	...	...
Total Fund Cred.&Loans Outstg. 2tl	...	...	...	...	...	...	...	...	...	...	...	...	...	...	...

International Liquidity — *Millions of US Dollars Unless Otherwise Indicated:*

Total Reserves minus Gold .... 1l. d	...	...	...	...	...	...	...	...	...	...	...	...	...	...	...
SDRs .... 1b. d	...	...	...	...	...	...	...	...	...	...	...	...	...	...	...
Reserve Position in the Fund .... 1c. d	...	...	...	...	...	...	...	...	...	...	...	...	...	...	...
Foreign Exchange .... 1d. d	...	...	...	...	...	...	...	...	...	...	...	...	...	...	...
Gold (Million Fine Troy Ounces) 1ad	...	...	...	...	...	...	...	...	...	...	...	...	...	...	...
Gold (National Valuation) 1and	...	...	...	...	...	...	...	...	...	...	...	...	...	...	...
Monetary Authorities: Other Assets .... 3..d	...	...	...	...	...	...	...	...	...	...	...	...	...	...	...
Other Liab. .... 4..d	...	...	...	...	...	...	...	...	...	...	...	...	...	...	...
Deposit Money Banks: Assets .... 7a. d	...	...	...	...	...	...	...	...	...	...	...	...	...	...	...
Liabilities .... 7b. d	...	...	...	...	...	...	...	...	...	...	...	...	...	...	...

Monetary Authorities — *Millions of Koruny:*

Foreign Assets 11	...	...	...	...	...	...	...	...	...	...	...	...	...	...	...
Claims on Central Government 12a	...	...	...	...	...	...	...	...	...	...	...	...	...	...	...
Claims on Nonfin.Pub.Enterprises 12c	...	...	...	...	...	...	...	...	...	...	...	...	...	...	...
Claims on Private Sector 12d	...	...	...	...	...	...	...	...	...	...	...	...	...	...	...
Claims on Deposit Money Banks 12e	...	...	...	...	...	...	...	...	...	...	...	...	...	...	...
Reserve Money 14	...	...	...	...	...	...	...	...	...	...	...	...	...	...	...
of which: Currency Outside DMBs 14a	...	...	...	...	...	...	...	...	...	...	...	...	...	...	...
Other Liabilities to DMBs 14n	...	...	...	...	...	...	...	...	...	...	...	...	...	...	...
Time & Foreign Currency Deposits 15	...	...	...	...	...	...	...	...	...	...	...	...	...	...	...
Liabs. of Central Bank: Securities 16ac	...	...	...	...	...	...	...	...	...	...	...	...	...	...	...
Foreign Liabilities 16c	...	...	...	...	...	...	...	...	...	...	...	...	...	...	...
Long-Term Foreign Liabilities 16cl	...	...	...	...	...	...	...	...	...	...	...	...	...	...	...
Central Government Deposits 16d	...	...	...	...	...	...	...	...	...	...	...	...	...	...	...
Capital Accounts 17a	...	...	...	...	...	...	...	...	...	...	...	...	...	...	...
Other Items (Net) 17r	...	...	...	...	...	...	...	...	...	...	...	...	...	...	...

Deposit Money Banks — *Millions of Koruny:*

Reserves 20	...	...	...	...	...	...	...	...	...	...	...	...	...	...	...
Other Claims on Monetary Author. 20n	...	...	...	...	...	...	...	...	...	...	...	...	...	...	...
Foreign Assets 21	...	...	...	...	...	...	...	...	...	...	...	...	...	...	...
Claims on General Government 22a	...	...	...	...	...	...	...	...	...	...	...	...	...	...	...
of which: Cl. on Natl.Property Fd 22ae	...	...	...	...	...	...	...	...	...	...	...	...	...	...	...
Claims on Nonfin.Pub.Enterprises 22c	...	...	...	...	...	...	...	...	...	...	...	...	...	...	...
Claims on Private Sector 22d	...	...	...	...	...	...	...	...	...	...	...	...	...	...	...
Claims on Other Financial Insts 22f	...	...	...	...	...	...	...	...	...	...	...	...	...	...	...
Demand Deposits 24	...	...	...	...	...	...	...	...	...	...	...	...	...	...	...
Time & Foreign Currency Deposits 25	...	...	...	...	...	...	...	...	...	...	...	...	...	...	...
of which: Fgn. Currency Deposits 25b	...	...	...	...	...	...	...	...	...	...	...	...	...	...	...
Bonds 26ab	...	...	...	...	...	...	...	...	...	...	...	...	...	...	...
Foreign Liabilities 26c	...	...	...	...	...	...	...	...	...	...	...	...	...	...	...
Long-Term Foreign Liabilities 26cl	...	...	...	...	...	...	...	...	...	...	...	...	...	...	...
General Government Deposits 26d	...	...	...	...	...	...	...	...	...	...	...	...	...	...	...
of which: Natl.Property Fd.Deps. 26de	...	...	...	...	...	...	...	...	...	...	...	...	...	...	...
Credit from Monetary Authorities 26g	...	...	...	...	...	...	...	...	...	...	...	...	...	...	...
Capital Accounts 27a	...	...	...	...	...	...	...	...	...	...	...	...	...	...	...
Other Items (Net) 27r	...	...	...	...	...	...	...	...	...	...	...	...	...	...	...

Monetary Survey — *Millions of Koruny:*

Foreign Assets (Net) 31n	...	...	...	...	...	...	...	...	...	...	...	...	...	...	...
Domestic Credit 32	...	...	...	...	...	...	...	...	...	...	...	...	...	...	...
Claims on General Govt. (Net) 32an	...	...	...	...	...	...	...	...	...	...	...	...	...	...	...
Claims on Nonfin.Pub.Enterprises 32c	...	...	...	...	...	...	...	...	...	...	...	...	...	...	...
Claims on Private Sector 32d	...	...	...	...	...	...	...	...	...	...	...	...	...	...	...
Claims on Other Financial Insts 32f	...	...	...	...	...	...	...	...	...	...	...	...	...	...	...
Money 34	...	...	...	...	...	...	...	...	...	...	...	...	...	...	...
Quasi-Money 35	...	...	...	...	...	...	...	...	...	...	...	...	...	...	...
Bonds 36ab	...	...	...	...	...	...	...	...	...	...	...	...	...	...	...
Long-Term Foreign Liabilities 36cl	...	...	...	...	...	...	...	...	...	...	...	...	...	...	...
Capital Accounts 37a	...	...	...	...	...	...	...	...	...	...	...	...	...	...	...
Other Items (Net) 37r	...	...	...	...	...	...	...	...	...	...	...	...	...	...	...
Money plus Quasi-Money 35l	...	...	...	...	...	...	...	...	...	...	...	...	...	...	...

Interest Rates — *Percent Per Annum*

Discount Rate (End of Period) 60	...	...	...	...	...	...	...	...	...	...	...	...	...	...	...
Rate on Repurchase Agreements 60a	...	...	...	...	...	...	...	...	...	...	...	...	...	...	...
Money Market Rate 60b	...	...	...	...	...	...	...	...	...	...	...	...	...	...	...
Deposit Rate 60l	...	...	...	...	...	...	...	...	...	...	...	...	...	...	...
Lending Rate 60p	...	...	...	...	...	...	...	...	...	...	...	...	...	...	...
Government Bond Yield 61	...	...	...	...	...	...	...	...	...	...	...	...	...	...	...

1987	1988	1989	1990	1991	1992	1993	1994	1995	1996	1997	1998	1999	2000	2001		
															Exchange Rates	
End of Period																
....	....	....	....	....	....	45.605	45.660	43.954	45.864	46.930	51.975	58.011	61.744	60.910	Official Rate	aa
End of Period (ae) Period Average (rf)																
....	....	....	....	....	....	33.202	31.277	29.569	31.895	34.782	36.913	42.266	47.389	48.467	Official Rate	ae
....	....	....	....	....	....	30.770	32.045	29.713	30.654	33.616	35.233	41.363	46.035	48.355	Official Rate	rf
Period Averages																
....	....	....	131.94	104.19	105.70	103.54	99.33	100.00	100.66	105.75	103.55	93.36	94.43	90.18	Nominal Effective Exchange Rate	ne c
....	....	....	92.40	89.76	91.32	96.32	97.24	100.00	99.68	104.62	102.34	99.92	109.26	107.78	Real Effective Exchange Rate	re c
															Fund Position	
End of Period																
....	....	....	....	....	....	257.4	257.4	257.4	257.4	257.4	257.4	357.5	357.5	357.5	Quota	2f. s
....	....	....	....	....	....	.3	58.9	39.0	11.2	19.6	1.2	.6	.4	.5	SDRs	1b. s
....	....	....	....	....	....										Reserve Position in the Fund	1c. s
....	....	....	....	....	....	405.2	439.8	307.5	222.0	184.4	134.6	96.5	—	—	Total Fund Cred.&Loans Outstg.	2tl
															International Liquidity	
End of Period																
....	....	....	....	....	....	416	1,691	3,364	3,419	3,230	2,869	3,371	4,022	4,141	Total Reserves minus Gold	1l. d
....	....	....	....	....	....	—	86	58	16	26	2	1	—	1	SDRs	1b. d
....	....	....	....	....	....										Reserve Position in the Fund	1c. d
....	....	....	....	....	....	415	1,605	3,306	3,403	3,204	2,867	3,370	4,022	4,140	Foreign Exchange	1d. d
....	....	....	....	....	....	1.290	1.290	1.290	1.290	1.290	1.290	1.290	1.290	1.129	Gold (Million Fine Troy Ounces)	1ad
....	....	....	....	....	....	76	80	85	79	72	68	59	53	45	Gold (National Valuation)	1and
....	....	....	....	....	....	98	153	171	129	202	609	564	203	767	Monetary Authorities: Other Assets	3.. d
....	....	....	....	....	....	1,040	1,355	1,428	1,351	659	1,578	760	355	464	Other Liab.	4.. d
....	....	....	....	....	....	987	1,427	1,823	2,514	3,618	3,794	1,618	2,346	2,390	Deposit Money Banks: Assets	7a. d
....	....	....	....	....	....	425	499	979	2,160	2,851	2,628	643	644	845	Liabilities	7b. d
															Monetary Authorities	
End of Period																
....	....	....	....	....	....	19,557	60,184	107,032	115,665	121,904	130,881	168,820	202,763	240,066	Foreign Assets	11
....	....	....	....	....	....	46,476	46,456	25,743	30,068	5,495	9,067	1,778	—	—	Claims on Central Government	12a
....	....	....	....	....	....	352	294	133	238	272	336	288	199	161	Claims on Nonfin.Pub.Enterprises	12c
....	....	....	....	....	....	3	11	56	89	144	173	193	183	185	Claims on Private Sector	12d
....	....	....	....	....	....	40,654	36,143	36,485	36,585	41,340	55,242	40,225	36,236	28,170	Claims on Deposit Money Banks	12e
....	....	....	....	....	....	39,006	48,319	63,208	81,339	96,134	90,768	108,925	113,310	113,958	Reserve Money	14
....	....	....	....	....	....	25,122	28,101	34,536	43,505	48,740	49,759	57,472	67,048	80,963	of which: Currency Outside DMBs	14a
....	....	....	....	....	....	488	225	2,314	1,833	2,682	3,369	5,191	33,634	66,644	Other Liabilities to DMBs	14n
....	....	....	....	....	....	9	25	60	131	117	86	364	545	739	Time & Foreign Currency Deposits	15
....	....	....	....	....	....	—	—	11,010	—	—	—	10,000	84,900	145,254	Liabs. of Central Bank: Securities	16ac
....	....	....	....	....	....	43,064	46,342	40,915	39,124	18,112	54,023	33,579	16,812	22,467	Foreign Liabilities	16c
....	....	....	....	....	....	9,933	16,112	14,821	14,135	13,447	11,221	4,148	1	1	Long-Term Foreign Liabilities	16cl
....	....	....	....	....	....	6,458	11,726	16,152	18,060	16,558	11,650	25,526	27,725	31,159	Central Government Deposits	16d
....	....	....	....	....	....	4,151	7,977	8,239	9,244	9,316	10,322	10,580	10,573	10,573	Capital Accounts	17a
....	....	....	....	....	....	3,933	12,362	12,730	18,779	12,791	14,261	12,991	−48,119	−122,214	Other Items (Net)	17r
															Deposit Money Banks	
End of Period																
....	....	....	....	....	....	3,401	3,445	7,607	10,830	12,541	10,335	12,222	40,095	74,205	Reserves	20
....	....	....	....	....	....	10,560	16,211	21,433	28,798	37,564	32,406	41,428	37,366	22,203	Other Claims on Monetary Author.	20n
....	....	....	....	....	....	32,773	44,634	53,916	80,189	125,842	140,045	68,402	111,169	115,818	Foreign Assets	21
....	....	....	....	....	....	28,798	50,693	74,653	89,709	112,716	93,002	76,936	113,360	301,964	Claims on General Government	22a
....	....	....	....	....	....	12,083	7,803	5,282	3,465	1,273	1,033	1,472	1,049	3,659	of which: Cl. on Natl.Property Fd	22ae
....	....	....	....	....	....	114,419	93,158	59,919	83,467	†95,465	91,193	156,476	204,001	126,839	Claims on Nonfin.Pub.Enterprises	22c
....	....	....	....	....	....	118,563	107,195	143,386	184,312	†288,963	329,084	303,524	274,844	252,493	Claims on Private Sector	22d
....	....	....	....	....	....	1,310	1,290	8,534	12,528	14,814	709	428	358	321	Claims on Other Financial Insts	22f
....	....	....	....	....	....	90,742	94,931	113,179	129,528	116,651	96,863	95,586	118,916	144,603	Demand Deposits	24
....	....	....	....	....	....	137,344	174,427	203,328	236,632	†279,996	320,891	368,800	414,933	446,841	Time & Foreign Currency Deposits	25
....	....	....	....	....	....	28,509	38,395	39,896	41,690	46,964	68,548	75,851	93,949	104,882	of which: Fgn. Currency Deposits	25b
....	....	....	....	....	....	564	952	4,414	12,046	13,257	11,971	8,664	7,123	5,473	Bonds	26ab
....	....	....	....	....	....	13,762	14,909	28,342	68,212	98,410	95,367	25,815	28,616	39,167	Foreign Liabilities	26c
....	....	....	....	....	....	341	686	615	690	755	1,650	1,383	1,891	1,765	Long-Term Foreign Liabilities	26cl
....	....	....	....	....	....	9,458	12,151	25,436	33,197	31,917	28,018	23,248	34,230	41,446	General Government Deposits	26d
....	....	....	....	....	....	5,151	1,506	2,119	2,914	2,926	2,175	1,600	516	2,075	of which: Natl.Property Fd.Deps.	26de
....	....	....	....	....	....	41,204	37,705	38,406	40,224	51,606	61,528	40,741	37,402	30,661	Credit from Monetary Authorities	26g
....	....	....	....	....	....	48,722	63,813	66,953	76,526	82,642	95,243	93,704	103,940	115,301	Capital Accounts	27a
....	....	....	....	....	....	−32,313	−82,948	−111,225	−107,221	†12,670	−14,756	1,478	34,139	68,586	Other Items (Net)	27r
															Monetary Survey	
End of Period																
....	....	....	....	....	....	−4,496	43,567	91,691	88,518	131,225	121,536	177,827	268,504	294,250	Foreign Assets (Net)	31n
....	....	....	....	....	....	294,005	275,220	270,836	349,154	†469,394	483,896	490,849	530,990	609,358	Domestic Credit	32
....	....	....	....	....	....	59,358	73,272	58,808	68,520	69,736	62,401	29,940	51,405	229,359	Claims on General Govt. (Net)	32an
....	....	....	....	....	....	114,771	93,452	60,052	83,705	†95,737	91,529	156,764	204,200	127,000	Claims on Nonfin.Pub.Enterprises	32c
....	....	....	....	....	....	118,566	107,206	143,442	184,401	†289,107	329,257	303,717	275,027	252,678	Claims on Private Sector	32d
....	....	....	....	....	....	1,310	1,290	8,534	12,528	14,814	709	428	358	321	Claims on Other Financial Insts	32f
....	....	....	....	....	....	116,615	123,820	149,657	173,350	165,658	146,833	153,058	185,964	225,566	Money	34
....	....	....	....	....	....	137,353	174,452	203,388	236,763	†280,113	320,977	369,164	415,478	447,580	Quasi-Money	35
....	....	....	....	....	....	564	952	4,414	12,046	13,257	11,971	8,664	7,123	5,473	Bonds	36ab
....	....	....	....	....	....	10,274	16,798	15,436	14,825	14,202	12,871	5,531	1,892	1,766	Long-Term Foreign Liabilities	36cl
....	....	....	....	....	....	52,873	71,790	75,192	85,770	91,958	105,565	104,284	114,513	125,874	Capital Accounts	37a
....	....	....	....	....	....	−28,170	−69,025	−85,560	−85,081	†35,431	7,217	27,979	74,521	97,348	Other Items (Net)	37r
....	....	....	....	....	....	253,968	298,272	353,045	410,113	†559,144	641,168	737,324	830,186	894,151	Money plus Quasi-Money	35l
															Interest Rates	
Percent Per Annum																
....	....	....	....	....	....	12.00	12.00	9.75	8.80	8.80	8.80	8.80	8.80	....	Discount Rate (End of Period)	60
....	....	....	....	....	....								8.25	7.75	Rate on Repurchase Agreements	60a
....	....	....	....	....	....								8.08	7.76	Money Market Rate	60b
....	....	....	....	....	....	8.02	9.32	9.01	9.30	13.44	16.25	14.37	8.45	6.46	Deposit Rate	60l
....	....	....	....	....	....	14.41	14.56	16.85	13.92	18.65	21.17	21.07	14.89	11.24	Lending Rate	60p
....	....	....	....	....	....								8.34	7.75	Government Bond Yield	61

Slovak Republic

	1972	1973	1974	1975	1976	1977	1978	1979	1980	1981	1982	1983	1984	1985	1986
Prices, Production, Labor													*Index Numbers (1995=100):*		
Producer Prices 63	...	...	...	...	...	...	...	...	31.6	32.9	35.4	35.7	38.6	39.3	39.3
Consumer Prices 64	...	...	...	...	...	...	...	...	...	...	...	...	...	...	...
Wages 65	...	...	...	...	...	...	...	...	...	...	...	...	...	...	...
Industrial Production 66	...	...	...	...	...	...	...	...	...	...	...	...	...	...	...
Industrial Employment 67	...	...	...	...	...	...	...	...	...	...	...	...	...	...	...
													Number in Thousands:		
Labor Force 67d	...	...	...	...	...	...	...	...	...	...	...	...	...	...	...
Employment 67e	...	...	...	...	...	...	...	...	...	...	...	...	...	...	...
Unemployment 67c	...	...	...	...	...	...	...	...	...	...	...	...	...	...	...
Unemployment Rate (%) 67r	...	...	...	...	...	...	...	...	...	...	...	...	...	...	...
International Transactions													*Millions of Koruny*		
Exports 70	...	...	...	...	...	...	...	...	...	...	...	...	...	...	...
Imports, c.i.f. 71	...	...	...	...	...	...	...	...	...	...	...	...	...	...	...
Imports, f.o.b. 71.v	...	...	...	...	...	...	...	...	...	...	...	...	...	...	...
Balance of Payments													*Millions of US Dollars:*		
Current Account, n.i.e. 78ald	...	...	...	...	...	...	...	...	...	...	...	...	...	...	...
Goods: Exports f.o.b. 78aad	...	...	...	...	...	...	...	...	...	...	...	...	...	...	...
Goods: Imports f.o.b. 78abd	...	...	...	...	...	...	...	...	...	...	...	...	...	...	...
Trade Balance 78acd	...	...	...	...	...	...	...	...	...	...	...	...	...	...	...
Services: Credit 78add	...	...	...	...	...	...	...	...	...	...	...	...	...	...	...
Services: Debit 78aed	...	...	...	...	...	...	...	...	...	...	...	...	...	...	...
Balance on Goods & Services 78afd	...	...	...	...	...	...	...	...	...	...	...	...	...	...	...
Income: Credit 78agd	...	...	...	...	...	...	...	...	...	...	...	...	...	...	...
Income: Debit 78ahd	...	...	...	...	...	...	...	...	...	...	...	...	...	...	...
Balance on Gds, Serv. & Inc. 78aid	...	...	...	...	...	...	...	...	...	...	...	...	...	...	...
Current Transfers, n.i.e.: Credit 78ajd	...	...	...	...	...	...	...	...	...	...	...	...	...	...	...
Current Transfers: Debit 78akd	...	...	...	...	...	...	...	...	...	...	...	...	...	...	...
Capital Account, n.i.e. 78bcd	...	...	...	...	...	...	...	...	...	...	...	...	...	...	...
Capital Account, n.i.e.: Credit 78bad	...	...	...	...	...	...	...	...	...	...	...	...	...	...	...
Capital Account: Debit 78bbd	...	...	...	...	...	...	...	...	...	...	...	...	...	...	...
Financial Account, n.i.e. 78bjd	...	...	...	...	...	...	...	...	...	...	...	...	...	...	...
Direct Investment Abroad 78bdd	...	...	...	...	...	...	...	...	...	...	...	...	...	...	...
Dir. Invest. in Rep. Econ., n.i.e. 78bed	...	...	...	...	...	...	...	...	...	...	...	...	...	...	...
Portfolio Investment Assets 78bfd	...	...	...	...	...	...	...	...	...	...	...	...	...	...	...
Equity Securities 78bkd	...	...	...	...	...	...	...	...	...	...	...	...	...	...	...
Debt Securities 78bld	...	...	...	...	...	...	...	...	...	...	...	...	...	...	...
Portfolio Investment Liab., n.i.e. 78bgd	...	...	...	...	...	...	...	...	...	...	...	...	...	...	...
Equity Securities 78bmd	...	...	...	...	...	...	...	...	...	...	...	...	...	...	...
Debt Securities 78bnd	...	...	...	...	...	...	...	...	...	...	...	...	...	...	...
Financial Derivatives Assets 78bwd	...	...	...	...	...	...	...	...	...	...	...	...	...	...	...
Financial Derivatives Liabilities 78bxd	...	...	...	...	...	...	...	...	...	...	...	...	...	...	...
Other Investment Assets 78bhd	...	...	...	...	...	...	...	...	...	...	...	...	...	...	...
Monetary Authorities 78bod	...	...	...	...	...	...	...	...	...	...	...	...	...	...	...
General Government 78bpd	...	...	...	...	...	...	...	...	...	...	...	...	...	...	...
Banks 78bqd	...	...	...	...	...	...	...	...	...	...	...	...	...	...	...
Other Sectors 78brd	...	...	...	...	...	...	...	...	...	...	...	...	...	...	...
Other Investment Liab., n.i.e. 78bid	...	...	...	...	...	...	...	...	...	...	...	...	...	...	...
Monetary Authorities 78bsd	...	...	...	...	...	...	...	...	...	...	...	...	...	...	...
General Government 78btd	...	...	...	...	...	...	...	...	...	...	...	...	...	...	...
Banks 78bud	...	...	...	...	...	...	...	...	...	...	...	...	...	...	...
Other Sectors 78bvd	...	...	...	...	...	...	...	...	...	...	...	...	...	...	...
Net Errors and Omissions 78cad	...	...	...	...	...	...	...	...	...	...	...	...	...	...	...
Overall Balance 78cbd	...	...	...	...	...	...	...	...	...	...	...	...	...	...	...
Reserves and Related Items 79dad	...	...	...	...	...	...	...	...	...	...	...	...	...	...	...
Reserve Assets 79dbd	...	...	...	...	...	...	...	...	...	...	...	...	...	...	...
Use of Fund Credit and Loans 79dcd	...	...	...	...	...	...	...	...	...	...	...	...	...	...	...
Exceptional Financing 79ded	...	...	...	...	...	...	...	...	...	...	...	...	...	...	...

1987	1988	1989	1990	1991	1992	1993	1994	1995	1996	1997	1998	1999	2000	2001		
Period Averages															**Prices, Production, Labor**	
39.3	39.3	38.2	40.0	†67.6	71.2	83.4	91.7	100.0	†104.1	108.8	112.3	116.6	128.0	....	Producer Prices	63
....	....	....	....	....	....	80.2	91.0	100.0	†105.8	112.3	119.8	132.5	148.4	†159.3	Consumer Prices	64
....	....	....	....	....	....	70.5	83.6	100.0	114.6	127.2	136.1	148.3	162.0	....	Wages	65
....	....	....	....	....	....	88.1	92.4	100.0	102.6	103.9	109.1	....	....		Industrial Production	66
....	....	....	....	....	....	99.5	97.9	100.0	100.8	100.5	100.6	98.4	97.9		Industrial Employment	67
Period Averages																
....	....	....	....	....	....	2,509	2,511	2,481	....	2,473	....	2,558	2,594	....	Labor Force	67d
....	....	....	....	....	....	2,196	2,110	2,147	2,225	2,206	2,199	2,132	2,102	....	Employment	67e
....	....	....	....	....	....	369	334	325	278	297	317	417	485	....	Unemployment	67c
....	....	....	....	....	....	....	13.7	13.2	11.1	10.9	11.9	16.0	18.6		Unemployment Rate (%)	67r
Millions of Koruny															**International Transactions**	
....	....	....	....	....	....	168,114	214,375	255,096	270,643	277,434	377,807	423,648	548,527	610,645	Exports	70
....	....	....	....	....	....	204,786	218,638	273,831	350,847	361,833	483,773	492,337	620,264	....	Imports, c.i.f.	71
....	....	....	....	....	110,212	195,034	211,811	260,791	340,903	345,006	460,736	468,892	590,275	713,863	Imports, f.o.b.	71.v
Minus Sign Indicates Debit															Balance of Payments	
....	....	....	....	....	....	−580	671	390	−2,090	−1,961	−2,126	−1,155	−694	....	Current Account, n.i.e.	78al d
....	....	....	....	....	....	5,452	6,706	8,591	8,824	9,641	10,720	10,201	11,896		Goods: Exports f.o.b.	78aa d
....	....	....	....	....	....	−6,365	−6,645	−8,820	−11,106	−11,725	−13,071	−11,310	−12,791		Goods: Imports f.o.b.	78ab d
....	....	....	....	....	....	−912	61	−229	−2,283	−2,084	−2,351	−1,109	−895		*Trade Balance*	78ac d
....	....	....	....	....	....	1,939	2,261	2,378	2,066	2,167	2,292	1,899	2,241		Services: Credit	78ad d
....	....	....	....	....	....	−1,666	−1,600	−1,838	−2,028	−2,094	−2,276	−1,844	−1,805		Services: Debit	78ae d
....	....	....	....	....	....	−640	722	311	−2,245	−2,011	−2,334	−1,054	−459		*Balance on Goods & Services*	78af d
....	....	....	....	....	....	185	155	250	224	315	437	268	268		Income: Credit	78ag d
....	....	....	....	....	....	−224	−275	−263	−270	−438	−595	−568	−623		Income: Debit	78ah d
....	....	....	....	....	....	−678	602	297	−2,291	−2,135	−2,492	−1,353	−814		*Balance on Gds, Serv. & Inc.*	78ai d
....	....	....	....	....	....	216	166	243	483	540	645	466	344		Current Transfers, n.i.e.: Credit	78aj d
....	....	....	....	....	....	−118	−98	−150	−282	−367	−279	−268	−224		Current Transfers: Debit	78ak d
....	....	....	....	....	....	564	84	46	30	—	70	158	91		Capital Account, n.i.e.	78bc d
....	....	....	....	....	....	771	84	46	30	—	83	171	106		Capital Account, n.i.e.: Credit	78ba d
....	....	....	....	....	....	−208	—	—	—	—	−12	−13	−15		Capital Account: Debit	78bb d
....	....	....	....	....	....	−153	71	1,211	2,268	1,780	1,912	1,789	1,472	....	Financial Account, n.i.e.	78bj d
....	....	....	....	....	....	−61	−14	−10	−48	−95	−145	376	−22		Direct Investment Abroad	78bd d
....	....	....	....	....	....	199	270	236	351	174	562	354	2,052		Dir. Invest. in Rep. Econ., n.i.e.	78be d
....	....	....	....	....	....	−774	−26	157	−12	−81	−57	247	−195		Portfolio Investment Assets	78bf d
....	....	....	....	....	....	−774	−26	174	69	86	33	2	11		Equity Securities	78bk d
....	....	....	....	....	....	....	—	−17	−81	−167	−91	246	−206		Debt Securities	78bl d
....	....	....	....	....	....	465	304	53	29	93	841	405	1,016		Portfolio Investment Liab., n.i.e.	78bg d
....	....	....	....	....	....	465	111	−16	28	102	−35	47	−53		Equity Securities	78bm d
....	....	....	....	....	....	....	193	69	1	−10	876	358	1,069		Debt Securities	78bn d
....	....	....	....	....	....	....	—	—	—	—	—	....	....		Financial Derivatives Assets	78bw d
....	....	....	....	....	....	....	—	—	—	—	—	....	1		Financial Derivatives Liabilities	78bx d
....	....	....	....	....	....	−412	−548	−116	−334	−1,028	190	1,713	−973		Other Investment Assets	78bh d
....	....	....	....	....	....	....	....	....	....	....	....	....	....		Monetary Authorities	78bo d
....	....	....	....	....	....	232	−211	140	337	61	117	9	1		General Government	78bp d
....	....	....	....	....	....	−530	−344	−248	−662	−1,122	110	1,878	−748		Banks	78bq d
....	....	....	....	....	....	−114	7	−8	−10	33	−37	−174	−226		Other Sectors	78br d
....	....	....	....	....	....	430	84	891	2,282	2,718	520	−1,307	−407		Other Investment Liab., n.i.e.	78bi d
....	....	....	....	....	....	—	38	42	52	153	55	14	−26		Monetary Authorities	78bs d
....	....	....	....	....	....	145	−52	−173	−124	184	−321	55	149		General Government	78bt d
....	....	....	....	....	....	99	38	463	1,440	1,084	−138	−1,882	30		Banks	78bu d
....	....	....	....	....	....	186	60	559	914	1,298	924	506	−561		Other Sectors	78bv d
....	....	....	....	....	....	183	380	144	162	280	−333	−14	51	....	Net Errors and Omissions	78ca d
....	....	....	....	....	....	14	1,205	1,791	370	99	−478	777	920		*Overall Balance*	78cb d
....	....	....	....	....	....	−14	−1,205	−1,791	−370	−99	478	−777	−920	....	Reserves and Related Items	79da d
....	....	....	....	....	....	−104	−1,256	−1,590	−245	−47	545	−725	−794		Reserve Assets	79db d
....	....	....	....	....	....	89	51	−201	−125	−52	−67	−52	−125		Use of Fund Credit and Loans	79dc d
....	....	....	....	....	....	....	....	....	....	....	....	....	....	....	Exceptional Financing	79de d

Slovak Republic

		1972	1973	1974	1975	1976	1977	1978	1979	1980	1981	1982	1983	1984	1985	1986

International Investment Position *Millions of US Dollars*

Assets	79aa d	...	...	...	...	...	...	...	...	...	...	...	...	...	...	...
Direct Investment Abroad	79ab d	...	...	...	...	...	...	...	...	...	...	...	...	...	...	...
Portfolio Investment	79ac d	...	...	...	...	...	...	...	...	...	...	...	...	...	...	...
Equity Securities	79ad d	...	...	...	...	...	...	...	...	...	...	...	...	...	...	...
Debt Securities	79ae d	...	...	...	...	...	...	...	...	...	...	...	...	...	...	...
Financial Derivatives	79al d	...	...	...	...	...	...	...	...	...	...	...	...	...	...	...
Other Investment	79af d	...	...	...	...	...	...	...	...	...	...	...	...	...	...	...
Monetary Authorities	79ag d	...	...	...	...	...	...	...	...	...	...	...	...	...	...	...
General Government	79ah d	...	...	...	...	...	...	...	...	...	...	...	...	...	...	...
Banks	79ai d	...	...	...	...	...	...	...	...	...	...	...	...	...	...	...
Other Sectors	79aj d	...	...	...	...	...	...	...	...	...	...	...	...	...	...	...
Reserve Assets	79ak d	...	...	...	...	...	...	...	...	...	...	...	...	...	...	...
Liabilities	79la d	...	...	...	...	...	...	...	...	...	...	...	...	...	...	...
Dir. Invest. in Rep. Economy	79lb d	...	...	...	...	...	...	...	...	...	...	...	...	...	...	...
Portfolio Investment	79lc d	...	...	...	...	...	...	...	...	...	...	...	...	...	...	...
Equity Securities	79ld d	...	...	...	...	...	...	...	...	...	...	...	...	...	...	...
Debt Securities	79le d	...	...	...	...	...	...	...	...	...	...	...	...	...	...	...
Financial Derivatives	79ll d	...	...	...	...	...	...	...	...	...	...	...	...	...	...	...
Other Investment	79lf d	...	...	...	...	...	...	...	...	...	...	...	...	...	...	...
Monetary Authorities	79lg d	...	...	...	...	...	...	...	...	...	...	...	...	...	...	...
General Government	79lh d	...	...	...	...	...	...	...	...	...	...	...	...	...	...	...
Banks	79li d	...	...	...	...	...	...	...	...	...	...	...	...	...	...	...
Other Sectors	79lj d	...	...	...	...	...	...	...	...	...	...	...	...	...	...	...

Government Finance *Millions of Koruny:*

Deficit (-) or Surplus	80	...	...	...	...	...	...	...	...	...	...	...	...	...	...	...
Total Revenue and Grants	81y	...	...	...	...	...	...	...	...	...	...	...	...	...	...	...
Revenue	81	...	...	...	...	...	...	...	...	...	...	...	...	...	...	...
Grants	81z	...	...	...	...	...	...	...	...	...	...	...	...	...	...	...
Exp. & Lending Minus Repay.	82z	...	...	...	...	...	...	...	...	...	...	...	...	...	...	...
Expenditure	82	...	...	...	...	...	...	...	...	...	...	...	...	...	...	...
Lending Minus Repayments	83	...	...	...	...	...	...	...	...	...	...	...	...	...	...	...
Total Financing	80h	...	...	...	...	...	...	...	...	...	...	...	...	...	...	...
Domestic	84a	...	...	...	...	...	...	...	...	...	...	...	...	...	...	...
Foreign	85a	...	...	...	...	...	...	...	...	...	...	...	...	...	...	...
Total Debt by Residence	88	...	...	...	...	...	...	...	...	...	...	...	...	...	...	...
Domestic	88a	...	...	...	...	...	...	...	...	...	...	...	...	...	...	...
Foreign	89a	...	...	...	...	...	...	...	...	...	...	...	...	...	...	...

National Accounts *Millions of Koruny*

Househ.Cons.Expend.,incl.NPISHs	96f	...	...	...	...	...	...	...	...	...	...	...	...	...	...	...
Government Consumption Expend.	91f	...	...	...	...	...	...	...	...	...	...	...	...	...	...	...
Gross Fixed Capital Formation	93e	...	...	...	...	...	...	...	...	...	...	...	...	...	...	...
Changes in Inventories	93i	...	...	...	...	...	...	...	...	...	...	...	...	...	...	...
Exports of Goods and Services	90c	...	...	...	...	...	...	...	...	...	...	...	...	...	...	...
Imports of Goods and Services (-)	98c	...	...	...	...	...	...	...	...	...	...	...	...	...	...	...
Gross Domestic Product (GDP)	99b	...	...	...	...	...	...	...	...	...	...	...	...	...	...	...
GDP Volume 1995 Prices	99b. p	...	...	...	...	...	...	...	...	...	...	...	...	...	...	...
GDP Volume (1995=100)	99bv p	...	...	...	...	...	...	...	...	...	...	...	...	...	...	...
GDP Deflator (1995=100)	99bi p	...	...	...	...	...	...	...	...	...	...	...	...	...	...	...

Millions:

Population	99z	...	...	...	...	...	...	...	...	...	...	...	...	...	...	...

	1987	1988	1989	1990	1991	1992	1993	1994	1995	1996	1997	1998	1999	2000	2001		
Millions of US Dollars																**International Investment Position**	
	...	...	...	...	...	...	...	8,421	10,156	10,311	10,648	10,322	8,652	10,089	....	Assets	**79aa** *d*
	...	...	...	...	...	...	...	166	139	182	234	404	342	364	....	Direct Investment Abroad	**79ab** *d*
	...	...	...	...	...	...	...	429	259	282	330	406	146	336	....	Portfolio Investment	**79ac** *d*
	...	...	...	...	...	...	...	424	234	171	71	35	28	15	....	Equity Securities	**79ad** *d*
	...	...	...	...	...	...	...	5	25	111	259	371	118	321	....	Debt Securities	**79ae** *d*
	...	...	...	...	...	...	...	—	—	—	—	—	—	—	....	Financial Derivatives	**79al** *d*
	...	...	...	...	...	...	...	5,633	5,896	5,948	6,461	6,267	4,419	5,006	....	Other Investment	**79af** *d*
	...	...	...	...	...	...	...	—	—	—	—	—	—	—	....	Monetary Authorities	**79ag** *d*
	...	...	...	...	...	...	...	2,947	2,928	2,393	2,136	1,897	1,657	1,484	....	General Government	**79ah** *d*
	...	...	...	...	...	...	...	1,451	1,676	2,276	3,141	3,203	1,526	2,186	....	Banks	**79ai** *d*
	...	...	...	...	...	...	...	1,234	1,291	1,280	1,185	1,167	1,236	1,335	....	Other Sectors	**79aj** *d*
	...	...	...	...	...	...	...	2,192	3,862	3,898	3,623	3,244	3,745	4,384	....	Reserve Assets	**79ak** *d*
	...	...	...	...	...	...	...	6,137	7,316	9,769	11,848	14,656	13,200	14,368	....	Liabilities	**79la** *d*
	...	...	...	...	...	...	...	897	1,297	2,046	2,083	2,890	3,188	4,504	....	Dir. Invest. in Rep. Economy	**79lb** *d*
	...	...	...	...	...	...	...	583	608	563	595	1,549	2,039	2,830	....	Portfolio Investment	**79lc** *d*
	...	...	...	...	...	...	...	56	43	62	157	102	341	260	....	Equity Securities	**79ld** *d*
	...	...	...	...	...	...	...	527	565	500	438	1,447	1,698	2,570	....	Debt Securities	**79le** *d*
	...	...	...	...	...	...	...	—	—	—	—	—	—	—	....	Financial Derivatives	**79ll** *d*
	...	...	...	...	...	...	...	4,657	5,411	7,161	9,170	10,217	7,974	7,034	....	Other Investment	**79lf** *d*
	...	...	...	...	...	...	...	682	537	442	507	536	522	324	....	Monetary Authorities	**79lg** *d*
	...	...	...	...	...	...	...	1,101	958	786	912	621	671	788	....	General Government	**79lh** *d*
	...	...	...	...	...	...	...	537	901	2,290	3,109	2,950	680	687	....	Banks	**79li** *d*
	...	...	...	...	...	...	...	2,338	3,015	3,642	4,642	6,109	6,100	5,235	....	Other Sectors	**79lj** *d*
Year Ending December 31																**Government Finance**	
	...	...	...	...	...	...	...	...	–8,540	–28,430	–31,317	–26,637	–28,166		....	Deficit (-) or Surplus	**80**
	...	...	...	...	...	...	...	...	239,918	253,209	261,703	301,596	307,808		....	Total Revenue and Grants	**81y**
	...	...	...	...	...	...	...	...	239,659	252,953	261,492	301,349	307,596		....	Revenue	**81**
	...	...	...	...	...	...	...	...	259	256	211	247	212		....	Grants	**81z**
	...	...	...	...	...	...	...	...	248,458	281,639	293,020	328,233	335,974		....	Exp. & Lending Minus Repay.	**82z**
	...	...	...	...	...	...	...	...	251,963	277,834	293,421	303,360	350,601		....	Expenditure	**82**
	...	...	...	...	...	...	...	...	–3,505	3,805	–401	24,873	–14,627		....	Lending Minus Repayments	**83**
	...	...	...	...	...	...	...	...	8,540	28,430	31,317	26,637	28,166		....	Total Financing	**80h**
	...	...	...	...	...	...	...	...	12,761	21,518	–3,403	–2,112	21		....	Domestic	**84a**
	...	...	...	...	...	...	...	...	–4,221	6,912	34,720	28,749	28,145		....	Foreign	**85a**
	...	...	...	...	...	...	...	...	5,504	6,949	9,240	11,223	11,223		....	Total Debt by Residence	**88**
	...	...	...	...	...	...	...	...	5,504	6,949	9,240	11,223	11,223		....	Domestic	**88a**
	...	...	...	...	...	...	...	...	—	—	—	—	—		....	Foreign	**89a**
Millions of Koruny																**National Accounts**	
	...	...	...	...	...	...	215,800	246,500	280,800	319,000	356,600	400,400	440,400	473,600	560,237	Househ.Cons.Expend.,incl.NPISHs	**96f**
	...	...	...	...	...	...	91,600	93,100	106,200	132,100	145,700	161,400	158,700	180,331	197,582	Government Consumption Expend.	**91f**
	...	...	...	...	...	...	123,400	131,800	144,200	207,500	246,500	285,300	251,000	267,931	309,609	Gross Fixed Capital Formation	**93e**
	...	...	...	...	...	...	–19,800	–27,600	5,100	17,600	4,700	–14,000	8,800	–22,079	7,175	Changes in Inventories	**93i**
	...	...	...	...	...	...	228,300	287,300	326,400	334,700	397,800	459,500	501,700	652,432	732,349	Exports of Goods and Services	**90c**
	...	...	...	...	...	...	248,700	264,900	316,700	404,800	465,200	541,800	545,300	674,490	816,041	Imports of Goods and Services (-)	**98c**
	...	...	...	...	...	...	390,600	466,200	546,032	606,094	686,087	750,761	815,330	908,801	989,297	Gross Domestic Product (GDP)	**99b**
	...	...	...	...	...	...	487,600	511,600	546,032	579,922	615,887	641,128	653,309	684,751	707,348	GDP Volume 1995 Prices	**99b.** *p*
	...	...	...	...	...	...	89.3	93.7	100.0	106.2	112.8	117.4	119.6	125.4	129.5	GDP Volume (1995=100)	**99bv** *p*
	...	...	...	...	...	...	80.1	91.1	100.0	104.5	111.4	117.1	124.8	132.7	139.9	GDP Deflator (1995=100)	**99bi** *p*
Midyear Estimates																	
	...	...	...	...	...	...	5.32	5.35	5.36	5.37	5.38	5.39	5.40	5.40	5.40	**Population**	**99z**

(See notes in the back of the book.)

Slovenia

961

		1972	1973	1974	1975	1976	1977	1978	1979	1980	1981	1982	1983	1984	1985	1986
Exchange Rates																*Tolars per SDR:*
Official Rate	aa	....	....	....	....	....	....	....	....	....	....	....	....	....	....	....
																Tolars per US Dollar:
Official Rate	ae	....	....	....	....	....	....	....	....	....	....	....	....	....	....	....
Official Rate	rf	....	....	....	....	....	....	....	....	....	....	....	....	....	....	....
Fund Position																*Millions of SDRs:*
Quota	2f. s	....	....	....	....	....	....	....	....	....	....	....	....	....	....	....
SDRs	1b. s	....	....	....	....	....	....	....	....	....	....	....	....	....	....	....
Reserve Position in the Fund	1c. s	....	....	....	....	....	....	....	....	....	....	....	....	....	....	....
Total Fund Cred.&Loans Outstg.	2tl	....	....	....	....	....	....	....	....	....	....	....	....	....	....	....
International Liquidity															*Millions of US Dollars Unless Otherwise Indicated:*	
Total Reserves minus Gold	1l. d	....	....	....	....	....	....	....	....	....	....	....	....	....	....	....
SDRs	1b. d	....	....	....	....	....	....	....	....	....	....	....	....	....	....	....
Reserve Position in the Fund	1c. d	....	....	....	....	....	....	....	....	....	....	....	....	....	....	....
Foreign Exchange	1d. d	....	....	....	....	....	....	....	....	....	....	....	....	....	....	....
Gold (Million Fine Troy Ounces)	1ad	....	....	....	....	....	....	....	....	....	....	....	....	....	....	....
Gold (National Valuation)	1an d	....	....	....	....	....	....	....	....	....	....	....	....	....	....	....
Monetary Authorities: Other Assets	3.. d	....	....	....	....	....	....	....	....	....	....	....	....	....	....	....
Other Liab.	4.. d	....	....	....	....	....	....	....	....	....	....	....	....	....	....	....
Deposit Money Banks: Assets	7a. d	....	....	....	....	....	....	....	....	....	....	....	....	....	....	....
Liabilities	7b. d	....	....	....	....	....	....	....	....	....	....	....	....	....	....	....
Monetary Authorities																*Billions of Tolars:*
Foreign Assets	11	....	....	....	....	....	....	....	....	....	....	....	....	....	....	....
Claims on Central Government	12a	....	....	....	....	....	....	....	....	....	....	....	....	....	....	....
Claims on Private Sector	12d	....	....	....	....	....	....	....	....	....	....	....	....	....	....	....
Claims on Deposit Money Banks	12e	....	....	....	....	....	....	....	....	....	....	....	....	....	....	....
Reserve Money	14	....	....	....	....	....	....	....	....	....	....	....	....	....	....	....
of which: Currency Outside DMBs	14a	....	....	....	....	....	....	....	....	....	....	....	....	....	....	....
Liabs.of Central Bank: Securities	16ac	....	....	....	....	....	....	....	....	....	....	....	....	....	....	....
Restricted Deposits	16b	....	....	....	....	....	....	....	....	....	....	....	....	....	....	....
Foreign Liabilities	16c	....	....	....	....	....	....	....	....	....	....	....	....	....	....	....
Central Government Deposits	16d	....	....	....	....	....	....	....	....	....	....	....	....	....	....	....
Capital Accounts	17a	....	....	....	....	....	....	....	....	....	....	....	....	....	....	....
Other Items (Net)	17r	....	....	....	....	....	....	....	....	....	....	....	....	....	....	....
Deposit Money Banks																*Billions of Tolars:*
Reserves	20	....	....	....	....	....	....	....	....	....	....	....	....	....	....	....
Claims on Mon.Author.: Securities	20c	....	....	....	....	....	....	....	....	....	....	....	....	....	....	....
Other Claims on Monetary Author.	20n	....	....	....	....	....	....	....	....	....	....	....	....	....	....	....
Foreign Assets	21	....	....	....	....	....	....	....	....	....	....	....	....	....	....	....
Claims on General Government	22a	....	....	....	....	....	....	....	....	....	....	....	....	....	....	....
Claims on Private Sector	22d	....	....	....	....	....	....	....	....	....	....	....	....	....	....	....
Claims on Other Financial Insts	22f	....	....	....	....	....	....	....	....	....	....	....	....	....	....	....
Demand Deposits	24	....	....	....	....	....	....	....	....	....	....	....	....	....	....	....
Time, Savings,& Fgn.Currency Dep.	25	....	....	....	....	....	....	....	....	....	....	....	....	....	....	....
Money Market Instruments	26aa	....	....	....	....	....	....	....	....	....	....	....	....	....	....	....
Bonds	26ab	....	....	....	....	....	....	....	....	....	....	....	....	....	....	....
Restricted Deposits	26b	....	....	....	....	....	....	....	....	....	....	....	....	....	....	....
Foreign Liabilities	26c	....	....	....	....	....	....	....	....	....	....	....	....	....	....	....
General Government Deposits	26d	....	....	....	....	....	....	....	....	....	....	....	....	....	....	....
of which: Local Govt. Deposits	26db	....	....	....	....	....	....	....	....	....	....	....	....	....	....	....
Central Govt. Lending Funds	26f	....	....	....	....	....	....	....	....	....	....	....	....	....	....	....
Credit from Monetary Authorities	26g	....	....	....	....	....	....	....	....	....	....	....	....	....	....	....
Liabilities to Other Financ. Insts	26i	....	....	....	....	....	....	....	....	....	....	....	....	....	....	....
Capital Accounts	27a	....	....	....	....	....	....	....	....	....	....	....	....	....	....	....
Other Items (Net)	27r	....	....	....	....	....	....	....	....	....	....	....	....	....	....	....
Monetary Survey																*Billions of Tolars:*
Foreign Assets (Net)	31n	....	....	....	....	....	....	....	....	....	....	....	....	....	....	....
Domestic Credit	32	....	....	....	....	....	....	....	....	....	....	....	....	....	....	....
Claims on General Govt. (Net)	32an	....	....	....	....	....	....	....	....	....	....	....	....	....	....	....
Claims on Private Sector	32d	....	....	....	....	....	....	....	....	....	....	....	....	....	....	....
Claims on Other Financial Insts	32f	....	....	....	....	....	....	....	....	....	....	....	....	....	....	....
Money	34	....	....	....	....	....	....	....	....	....	....	....	....	....	....	....
Quasi-Money	35	....	....	....	....	....	....	....	....	....	....	....	....	....	....	....
Money Market Instruments	36aa	....	....	....	....	....	....	....	....	....	....	....	....	....	....	....
Bonds	36ab	....	....	....	....	....	....	....	....	....	....	....	....	....	....	....
Liabs.of Central Bank: Securities	36ac	....	....	....	....	....	....	....	....	....	....	....	....	....	....	....
Restricted Deposits	36b	....	....	....	....	....	....	....	....	....	....	....	....	....	....	....
Central Govt. Lending Funds	36f	....	....	....	....	....	....	....	....	....	....	....	....	....	....	....
Liabilities to Other Financ. Insts	36i	....	....	....	....	....	....	....	....	....	....	....	....	....	....	....
Capital Accounts	37a	....	....	....	....	....	....	....	....	....	....	....	....	....	....	....
Other Items (Net)	37r	....	....	....	....	....	....	....	....	....	....	....	....	....	....	....
Money plus Quasi-Money	35l	....	....	....	....	....	....	....	....	....	....	....	....	....	....	....

End of Period

1987	1988	1989	1990	1991	1992	1993	1994	1995	1996	1997	1998	1999	2000	2001		
															Exchange Rates	
....	....	....	....	81.09	135.71	181.09	184.61	187.28	203.44	228.27	226.97	270.07	296.25	315.37	Official Rate	aa

End of Period (ae) Period Average (rf)

1987	1988	1989	1990	1991	1992	1993	1994	1995	1996	1997	1998	1999	2000	2001		
....	....	....	....	56.69	98.70	131.84	126.46	125.99	141.48	169.18	161.20	196.77	227.38	250.95	Official Rate	ae
....	....	....	....	27.57	81.29	113.24	128.81	118.52	135.36	159.69	166.13	181.77	222.66	242.75	Official Rate	rf

End of Period

1987	1988	1989	1990	1991	1992	1993	1994	1995	1996	1997	1998	1999	2000	2001		
															Fund Position	
....	....	....	....	....	—	150.50	150.50	150.50	150.50	150.50	150.50	231.70	231.70	231.70	Quota	2f. s
....	....	....	....	....	—	.03	.04	.04	.09	.05	.17	1.17	2.83	4.00	SDRs	1b. s
....	....	....	....	....	—	12.88	12.87	12.88	12.88	12.88	46.46	78.40	63.19	64.16	Reserve Position in the Fund	1c. s
....	....	....	....	....	—	8.53	4.94	2.69	.90	—	—	—	—	—	Total Fund Cred.&Loans Outstg.	2tl

End of Period

1987	1988	1989	1990	1991	1992	1993	1994	1995	1996	1997	1998	1999	2000	2001		
															International Liquidity	
....	....	....	....	112.14	715.54	787.80	1,498.98	1,820.79	2,297.36	3,314.67	3,638.52	3,168.00	3,196.01	4,329.99	Total Reserves minus Gold	1l. d
....	....	....	....	....	—	.05	.06	.06	.13	.07	.24	1.60	3.69	5.03	SDRs	1b. d
....	....	....	....	....	—	17.68	18.80	19.14	18.51	17.37	65.41	107.61	82.33	80.63	Reserve Position in the Fund	1c. d
....	....	....	....	112.14	715.54	770.07	1,480.12	1,801.59	2,278.71	3,297.22	3,572.87	3,058.79	3,110.00	4,244.33	Foreign Exchange	1d. d
....	....	....	....	.0003	.0003	.0003	.0003	.0003	.0003	.0003	.0003	.0003	.0003	.2431	Gold (Million Fine Troy Ounces)	1ad
....	....	....	....	.11	.11	.13	.12	.13	.12	.09	.09	.09	.09	67.22	Gold (National Valuation)	1an d
....	....	....	....	2.39	1.35	1.08	103.28	170.14	33.70	41.27	46.83	51.95	58.05	76.11	Monetary Authorities: Other Assets	3.. d
....	....	....	....	—	—	.06	.09	.14	.42	.34	1.05	.63	.48	1.11	Other Liab.	4.. d
....	....	....	....	1,989.68	2,065.82	1,431.92	2,301.70	2,395.17	2,581.52	1,869.71	2,003.17	1,807.96	2,006.24	3,266.75	Deposit Money Banks: Assets	7a. d
....	....	....	....	1,282.22	1,183.47	1,058.95	1,258.55	1,483.20	1,458.57	1,219.38	1,333.58	1,440.06	1,570.22	1,760.66	Liabilities	7b. d

End of Period

1987	1988	1989	1990	1991	1992	1993	1994	1995	1996	1997	1998	1999	2000	2001		
															Monetary Authorities	
....	....	....	....	6.50	70.77	104.02	190.06	250.85	329.81	559.27	594.10	629.76	724.66	861.63	Foreign Assets	11
....	....	....	....	8.65	8.88	18.78	15.65	15.28	15.52	15.67	16.01	16.61	17.75	9.81	Claims on Central Government	12a
....	....	....	....	.02	.05	.08	.10	.11	.15	.19	.21	.22	.25	.26	Claims on Private Sector	12d
....	....	....	....	3.82	16.29	16.00	29.90	43.06	15.72	18.08	3.91	25.82	22.25	261.38	Claims on Deposit Money Banks	12e
....	....	....	....	15.92	37.11	51.29	80.49	100.79	116.55	143.36	171.63	208.23	212.18	287.44	Reserve Money	14
....	....	....	....	9.18	24.18	32.72	47.28	59.96	66.84	78.12	93.65	125.01	119.82	142.11	*of which: Currency Outside DMBs*	14a
....	....	....	....	—	40.76	50.39	99.77	126.67	178.45	364.97	362.48	337.76	365.27	584.69	Liabs.of Central Bank: Securities	16ac
....	....	....	....	.05	.04	.37	1.82	1.91	.86	2.29	4.30	4.30	4.58	4.91	Restricted Deposits	16b
....	....	....	....	—	—	1.55	.92	.52	.24	.06	.17	.12	.11	.28	Foreign Liabilities	16c
....	....	....	....	1.64	5.78	5.99	27.41	47.51	22.30	23.12	18.50	26.25	39.08	60.01	Central Government Deposits	16d
....	....	....	....	1.50	12.40	29.33	27.17	31.82	43.31	58.65	55.45	96.59	134.96	182.30	Capital Accounts	17a
....	....	....	....	-.13	-.10	-.03	-1.88	.08	-.51	.77	1.69	-.83	8.73	13.45	Other Items (Net)	17r

1987	1988	1989	1990	1991	1992	1993	1994	1995	1996	1997	1998	1999	2000	2001		
															Deposit Money Banks	
....	....	....	....	6.77	7.76	12.67	31.07	38.13	48.11	63.09	74.44	79.37	87.42	138.59	Reserves	20
....	....	....	....	—	36.17	42.74	†82.42	106.96	160.92	345.08	344.49	327.91	365.32	584.16	Claims on Mon.Author.: Securities	20c
....	....	....	....				1.05	1.50	—	—	—				Other Claims on Monetary Author.	20n
....	....	....	....	112.80	203.90	188.79	291.07	301.77	365.23	316.32	322.91	355.75	456.17	819.78	Foreign Assets	21
....	....	....	....	11.32	24.18	208.08	257.88	315.96	319.59	372.50	407.79	428.33	479.56	548.89	Claims on General Government	22a
....	....	....	....	122.01	236.86	316.45	427.04	609.72	736.01	829.98	1,066.35	1,313.36	1,538.76	1,828.26	Claims on Private Sector	22d
....	....	....	....	.50	.91	2.03	5.53	12.75	9.38	12.36	20.36	37.82	51.56	59.05	Claims on Other Financial Insts	22f
....	....	....	....	20.21	44.48	64.36	84.15	104.10	127.42	151.36	191.99	237.01	263.47	317.30	Demand Deposits	24
....	....	....	....	90.06	197.72	334.95	494.13	647.77	807.04	1,005.28	1,188.44	1,334.29	1,618.56	2,152.14	Time, Savings,& Fgn.Currency Dep.	25
....	....	....	....	2.55	10.00	16.44	12.51	26.97	13.24	18.47	21.37	13.56	24.64	52.56	Money Market Instruments	26aa
....	....	....	....	.13	.66	2.57	8.27	18.09	23.84	33.95	36.28	40.80	53.96	66.30	Bonds	26ab
....	....	....	....	3.48	6.04		10.28	10.98	17.04	17.63	14.93	10.80	15.09	23.08	Restricted Deposits	26b
....	....	....	....	72.69	116.81	139.61	159.15	186.87	206.36	206.29	214.97	283.36	357.03	441.83	Foreign Liabilities	26c
....	....	....	....	12.20	33.55	57.93	87.22	94.87	140.69	167.98	191.06	190.17	147.10	124.77	General Government Deposits	26d
....	....	....	....	1.12	5.31	7.59	8.04	11.43	6.53	6.53	6.91	10.88	11.21	5.46	*of which: Local Govt. Deposits*	26db
....	....	....	....	.74	.91	2.43	4.87	8.29	12.34	14.04	24.35	27.88	34.35	36.75	Central Govt. Lending Funds	26f
....	....	....	....	1.40	15.61	15.48	29.64	41.66	15.28	17.83	3.53	25.47	22.08	260.98	Credit from Monetary Authorities	26g
....	....	....	....	3.01	6.00	9.92	5.53	10.39	15.43	23.33	33.20	41.84	57.15	71.15	Liabilities to Other Financ. Insts	26i
....	....	....	....	65.04	104.77	151.07	209.53	248.29	273.20	303.74	335.79	372.56	418.82	452.19	Capital Accounts	27a
....	....	....	....	-18.10	-26.77	-33.54	-9.24	-11.50	-12.64	-20.58	-19.57	-35.19	-33.47	-20.34	Other Items (Net)	27r

End of Period

1987	1988	1989	1990	1991	1992	1993	1994	1995	1996	1997	1998	1999	2000	2001		
															Monetary Survey	
....	....	....	....	46.61	157.86	151.64	321.05	365.23	488.45	669.24	701.86	702.03	823.69	1,239.30	Foreign Assets (Net)	31n
....	....	....	....	128.66	231.54	481.50	591.57	811.45	917.66	1,039.61	1,301.17	1,579.92	1,901.71	2,261.48	Domestic Credit	32
....	....	....	....	6.13	-6.27	162.93	158.89	188.87	172.13	197.08	214.24	228.52	311.14	373.91	Claims on General Govt. (Net)	32an
....	....	....	....	122.04	236.91	316.53	427.04	609.83	736.16	830.17	1,066.56	1,313.58	1,539.01	1,828.52	Claims on Private Sector	32d
....	....	....	....	.50	.91	2.03	5.53	12.75	9.38	12.36	20.36	37.82	51.56	59.05	Claims on Other Financial Insts	32f
....	....	....	....	29.43	68.77	97.28	131.44	164.06	194.29	229.48	287.26	363.70	385.88	462.53	Money	34
....	....	....	....	90.06	197.72	334.95	494.13	647.77	807.04	1,005.28	1,188.44	1,334.29	1,618.56	2,152.14	Quasi-Money	35
....	....	....	....	2.55	10.00	16.44	12.51	26.97	13.24	18.47	21.37	13.56	24.64	52.56	Money Market Instruments	36aa
....	....	....	....	.13	.66	2.57	8.27	18.09	23.84	33.95	36.28	40.80	53.96	66.30	Bonds	36ab
....	....	....	....	—	4.59	7.65	†17.35	19.71	17.53	19.89	18.00	9.85	-.05	.52	Liabs.of Central Bank: Securities	36ac
....	....	....	....	3.53	6.08	9.88	12.10	12.90	17.90	19.92	19.23	15.10	19.68	27.99	Restricted Deposits	36b
....	....	....	....	.74	.91	2.43	4.87	8.29	12.34	14.04	24.35	27.88	34.35	36.75	Central Govt. Lending Funds	36f
....	....	....	....	3.01	6.00	9.92	5.53	10.39	15.43	23.33	33.20	41.84	57.15	71.15	Liabilities to Other Financ. Insts	36i
....	....	....	....	66.54	117.17	180.40	236.70	280.11	316.51	362.39	391.24	469.15	553.78	634.50	Capital Accounts	37a
....	....	....	....	-20.72	-22.51	-28.39	†-10.29	-11.62	-12.02	-17.90	-16.34	-34.21	-22.55	-3.67	Other Items (Net)	37r
....	....	....	....	119.49	266.50	432.23	625.56	811.83	1,001.33	1,234.76	1,475.70	1,697.99	2,004.44	2,614.67	Money plus Quasi-Money	35l

Slovenia

	1972	1973	1974	1975	1976	1977	1978	1979	1980	1981	1982	1983	1984	1985	1986
Interest Rates														*Percent Per Annum*	
Central Bank Rate *(End of Per.)* 60	...	...	...	...	...	...	...	...	...	...	...	...	...	...	...
Money Market Rate.......................... 60b	...	...	...	...	...	...	...	...	...	...	...	...	...	...	...
Treasury Bill Rate 60c	...	...	...	...	...	...	...	...	...	...	...	...	...	...	...
Deposit Rate 60l	...	...	...	...	...	...	...	...	...	...	...	...	...	...	...
Lending Rate 60p	...	...	...	...	...	...	...	...	...	...	...	...	...	...	...
Prices, Production, Labor													*Index Numbers (1995=100):*		
Producer Prices 63	...	...	...	...	...	...	...	...	...	...	...	...	...	...	...
Consumer Prices 64	...	...	...	...	...	...	...	...	...	...	...	...	...	...	...
Wages 65	...	...	...	...	...	...	...	...	...	...	...	...	...	...	...
Industrial Production .... 66..c	...	...	...	...	...	...	...	...	...	...	...	...	...	...	...
Employment 67	...	...	...	...	...	...	...	...	...	...	...	...	...	...	...
													Number in Thousands:		
Labor Force.. 67d	...	...	...	...	...	...	...	...	...	...	...	...	...	...	...
Employment 67e	...	...	...	...	...	...	...	...	...	...	...	...	...	...	...
Unemployment 67c	...	...	...	...	...	...	...	...	...	...	...	...	...	...	...
Unemployment Rate (%)...................... 67r	...	...	...	...	...	...	...	...	...	...	...	...	...	...	...
International Transactions													*Millions of US Dollars*		
Exports .... 70..d	...	...	...	...	...	...	...	...	...	...	...	...	...	...	...
Imports, c.i.f. .... 71..d	...	...	...	...	...	...	...	...	...	...	...	...	...	...	...
Balance of Payments													*Millions of US Dollars*		
Current Account, n.i.e. 78ald	...	...	...	...	...	...	...	...	...	...	...	...	...	...	...
Goods: Exports f.o.b. 78aad	...	...	...	...	...	...	...	...	...	...	...	...	...	...	...
Goods: Imports f.o.b. 78abd	...	...	...	...	...	...	...	...	...	...	...	...	...	...	...
Trade Balance................................. 78acd	...	...	...	...	...	...	...	...	...	...	...	...	...	...	...
Services: Credit................................ 78add	...	...	...	...	...	...	...	...	...	...	...	...	...	...	...
Services: Debit................................. 78aed	...	...	...	...	...	...	...	...	...	...	...	...	...	...	...
Balance on Goods & Services 78afd	...	...	...	...	...	...	...	...	...	...	...	...	...	...	...
Income: Credit................................. 78agd	...	...	...	...	...	...	...	...	...	...	...	...	...	...	...
Income: Debit.................................. 78ahd	...	...	...	...	...	...	...	...	...	...	...	...	...	...	...
Balance on Gds, Serv. & Inc. 78aid	...	...	...	...	...	...	...	...	...	...	...	...	...	...	...
Current Transfers, n.i.e.: Credit 78ajd	...	...	...	...	...	...	...	...	...	...	...	...	...	...	...
Current Transfers: Debit 78akd	...	...	...	...	...	...	...	...	...	...	...	...	...	...	...
Capital Account, n.i.e. 78bcd	...	...	...	...	...	...	...	...	...	...	...	...	...	...	...
Capital Account, n.i.e.: Credit......... 78bad	...	...	...	...	...	...	...	...	...	...	...	...	...	...	...
Capital Account: Debit.................... 78bbd	...	...	...	...	...	...	...	...	...	...	...	...	...	...	...
Financial Account, n.i.e. 78bjd	...	...	...	...	...	...	...	...	...	...	...	...	...	...	...
Direct Investment Abroad 78bdd	...	...	...	...	...	...	...	...	...	...	...	...	...	...	...
Dir. Invest. in Rep. Econ., n.i.e. 78bed	...	...	...	...	...	...	...	...	...	...	...	...	...	...	...
Portfolio Investment Assets 78bfd	...	...	...	...	...	...	...	...	...	...	...	...	...	...	...
Equity Securities............................. 78bkd	...	...	...	...	...	...	...	...	...	...	...	...	...	...	...
Debt Securities............................... 78bld	...	...	...	...	...	...	...	...	...	...	...	...	...	...	...
Portfolio Investment Liab., n.i.e. 78bgd	...	...	...	...	...	...	...	...	...	...	...	...	...	...	...
Equity Securities............................. 78bmd	...	...	...	...	...	...	...	...	...	...	...	...	...	...	...
Debt Securities............................... 78bnd	...	...	...	...	...	...	...	...	...	...	...	...	...	...	...
Financial Derivatives Assets 78bwd	...	...	...	...	...	...	...	...	...	...	...	...	...	...	...
Financial Derivatives Liabilities 78bxd	...	...	...	...	...	...	...	...	...	...	...	...	...	...	...
Other Investment Assets 78bhd	...	...	...	...	...	...	...	...	...	...	...	...	...	...	...
Monetary Authorities..................... 78bod	...	...	...	...	...	...	...	...	...	...	...	...	...	...	...
General Government....................... 78bpd	...	...	...	...	...	...	...	...	...	...	...	...	...	...	...
Banks.. 78bqd	...	...	...	...	...	...	...	...	...	...	...	...	...	...	...
Other Sectors 78brd	...	...	...	...	...	...	...	...	...	...	...	...	...	...	...
Other Investment Liab., n.i.e. 78bid	...	...	...	...	...	...	...	...	...	...	...	...	...	...	...
Monetary Authorities..................... 78bsd	...	...	...	...	...	...	...	...	...	...	...	...	...	...	...
General Government....................... 78btd	...	...	...	...	...	...	...	...	...	...	...	...	...	...	...
Banks.. 78bud	...	...	...	...	...	...	...	...	...	...	...	...	...	...	...
Other Sectors 78bvd	...	...	...	...	...	...	...	...	...	...	...	...	...	...	...
Net Errors and Omissions.................... 78cad	...	...	...	...	...	...	...	...	...	...	...	...	...	...	...
Overall Balance 78cbd	...	...	...	...	...	...	...	...	...	...	...	...	...	...	...
Reserves and Related Items 79dad	...	...	...	...	...	...	...	...	...	...	...	...	...	...	...
Reserve Assets 79dbd	...	...	...	...	...	...	...	...	...	...	...	...	...	...	...
Use of Fund Credit and Loans 79dcd	...	...	...	...	...	...	...	...	...	...	...	...	...	...	...
Exceptional Financing 79ded	...	...	...	...	...	...	...	...	...	...	...	...	...	...	...

1987	1988	1989	1990	1991	1992	1993	1994	1995	1996	1997	1998	1999	2000	2001		
															Interest Rates	
Percent Per Annum																
....	....	....	....	....	....	....	....	14.62	11.42	13.78	8.55	8.35	11.85	....	Central Bank Rate (End of Per.)	60
....	....	....	....	....	67.58	39.15	29.08	12.18	13.98	9.71	7.45	6.87	6.95	6.90	Money Market Rate	60b
....	....	....	....	....	....	....	....	....	....	....	....	8.63	10.94	10.88	Treasury Bill Rate	60c
....	....	....	....	682.53	153.02	33.04	28.10	15.38	15.08	13.19	10.54	7.24	10.05	9.81	Deposit Rate	60l
....	....	....	....	824.56	195.11	48.61	38.87	23.36	22.60	20.02	16.09	12.38	15.77	15.05	Lending Rate	60p
															Prices, Production, Labor	
Period Averages																
....	....	....	....	....	62.0	75.3	88.7	100.0	106.8	113.3	120.1	122.6	132.0	143.8	Producer Prices	63
....	....	....	....	....	56.2	74.1	88.8	100.0	109.7	119.7	129.9	138.5	153.6	168.0	Consumer Prices	64
....	....	....	....	....	43.4	65.8	84.3	100.0	114.8	127.9	140.1	153.2	169.2	187.5	Wages	65
....	....	....	....	....	92.8	90.8	98.0	100.0	99.3	101.4	105.4	103.9	111.6	114.5	Industrial Production	66..c
....	....	....	....	....	†105.2	101.4	100.1	100.0	99.6	99.8	100.0	101.7	103.1	104.5	Employment	67
Period Averages																
....	....	....	....	....	....	....	934	952	946	967	983	963	....	....	Labor Force	67d
....	....	....	....	....	....	845	851	882	878	898	907	892	754	....	Employment	67e
....	....	....	....	103	†85	85	70	69	69	126	119	107	....	....	Unemployment	67c
....	....	....	....	11.5	†9.1	9.0	7.4	7.3	7.1	7.7	7.4	....	....	....	Unemployment Rate (%)	67r
															International Transactions	
Millions of US Dollars																
....	....	....	....	3,852	†6,681	6,083	6,828	8,316	8,312	8,372	9,048	8,604	8,733	9,251	Exports	70..d
....	....	....	....	4,147	†6,142	6,499	7,304	9,492	9,423	9,357	10,110	9,952	10,107	10,144	Imports, c.i.f.	71..d
															Balance of Payments	
Minus Sign Indicates Debit																
....	....	....	....	....	978.3	191.0	573.1	−99.4	31.4	11.4	−147.3	−782.4	−611.7	−66.4	Current Account, n.i.e.	78al d
....	....	....	....	....	6,680.9	6,082.9	6,831.7	8,350.2	8,352.6	8,407.4	9,090.9	8,622.7	8,807.9	9,341.9	Goods: Exports f.o.b.	78aa d
....	....	....	....	....	−5,891.8	−6,237.1	−7,168.1	−9,303.3	−9,177.5	−9,183.8	−9,880.2	−9,867.9	−9,946.9	−9,963.9	Goods: Imports f.o.b.	78ab d
....	....	....	....	....	789.1	−154.2	−336.4	−953.0	−824.9	−776.3	−789.4	−1,245.2	−1,138.9	−622.0	Trade Balance	78ac d
....	....	....	....	....	1,219.3	1,392.1	1,809.1	2,027.5	2,135.1	2,047.5	2,027.5	1,899.3	1,886.2	1,946.6	Services: Credit	78ad d
....	....	....	....	....	−1,037.8	−1,017.4	−1,166.1	−1,449.4	−1,501.6	−1,417.3	−1,535.0	−1,535.1	−1,449.8	−1,445.0	Services: Debit	78ae d
....	....	....	....	....	970.6	220.5	306.6	−374.9	−191.5	−146.1	−296.9	−881.0	−702.6	−120.4	Balance on Goods & Services	78af d
....	....	....	....	....	111.7	114.5	334.5	410.5	412.7	396.7	417.2	410.2	421.6	481.0	Income: Credit	78ag d
....	....	....	....	....	−150.1	−166.0	−164.7	−231.2	−280.5	−357.3	−389.3	−434.7	−446.1	−555.3	Income: Debit	78ah d
....	....	....	....	....	932.2	169.0	476.5	−195.6	−59.3	−106.7	−269.0	−905.5	−727.2	−194.7	Balance on Gds, Serv. & Inc.	78ai d
....	....	....	....	....	93.0	154.9	237.2	247.7	250.9	259.5	299.8	334.4	340.9	389.1	Current Transfers, n.i.e.: Credit	78aj d
....	....	....	....	....	−46.9	−132.9	−140.6	−151.5	−160.3	−141.5	−178.0	−211.2	−225.4	−260.8	Current Transfers: Debit	78ak d
....	....	....	....	....		4.1	−3.2	−7.0	−1.9	1.1	−1.5	−.6	3.5	−3.3	Capital Account, n.i.e.	78bc d
....	....	....	....	....	—	6.7	2.7	3.1	5.5	5.0	3.5	3.3	6.8	3.5	Capital Account, n.i.e.: Credit	78ba d
....	....	....	....	....	—	−2.6	−5.8	−10.1	−7.4	−3.9	−5.0	−3.9	−3.3	−6.8	Capital Account: Debit	78bb d
....	....	....	....	....	−13.3	−80.9	146.6	541.0	565.8	1,198.7	244.2	674.8	743.3	1,307.4	Financial Account, n.i.e.	78bj d
....	....	....	....	....	1.8	−1.3	2.9	5.1	−6.3	−35.7	1.7	−37.7	−66.0	−104.2	Direct Investment Abroad	78bd d
....	....	....	....	....	111.0	112.6	128.1	177.4	194.0	375.2	247.9	181.2	175.5	441.8	Dir. Invest. in Rep. Econ., n.i.e.	78be d
....	....	....	....	....	−8.9	−1.5	−32.5	−28.9	6.4	−.1	−30.2	−7.8	−60.6	−107.6	Portfolio Investment Assets	78bf d
....	....	....	....	....								−.5	−16.6	−23.3	Equity Securities	78bk d
....	....	....	....	....	−8.9	−1.5	−32.5	−28.9	6.4	−.1	−30.2	−7.3	−43.9	−84.3	Debt Securities	78bl d
....	....	....	....	....	—	4.5	....	15.5	630.5	236.1	119.8	361.6	249.3	197.0	Portfolio Investment Liab., n.i.e.	78bg d
....	....	....	....	....						52.2	7.2	−3.2	25.4	−2.2	Equity Securities	78bm d
....	....	....	....	....	—	4.5	....	15.5	630.5	184.0	112.6	364.8	223.8	199.2	Debt Securities	78bn d
....	....	....	....	....	....	....	....	....	....	....	....	....	....	....	Financial Derivatives Assets	78bw d
....	....	....	....	....	....	....	....	....	....	....	....	....	....	....	Financial Derivatives Liabilities	78bx d
....	....	....	....	....	−157.6	−313.5	−205.6	−240.1	−432.1	260.6	−459.4	−575.1	−501.5	150.8	Other Investment Assets	78bh d
....	....	....	....	....	.5	—	−98.3	−66.8	131.4	−7.6	−5.4	−5.6	−5.9	−6.2	Monetary Authorities	78bo d
....	....	....	....	....	−.1	−.3	−.4	−2.2	−1.4	−1.3	−1.8	−1.6	−1.1	−.6	General Government	78bp d
....	....	....	....	....	−173.8	−473.6	−353.1	−302.3	−321.8	479.2	−52.3	−6.7	−252.9	−304.6	Banks	78bq d
....	....	....	....	....	15.8	160.4	246.1	131.1	−240.3	−209.7	−399.9	−561.3	−241.6	462.2	Other Sectors	78br d
....	....	....	....	....	40.4	118.3	253.8	612.0	173.4	362.6	364.4	752.7	946.5	729.6	Other Investment Liab., n.i.e.	78bi d
....	....	....	....	....		.1	.1	.2		.1			−.2	—	Monetary Authorities	78bs d
....	....	....	....	....	−18.3	80.2	92.8	138.3	−67.1	−25.2	−18.0	17.4	129.0	−8.2	General Government	78bt d
....	....	....	....	....	11.3	−41.9	40.6	267.3	−19.8	4.7	90.6	263.0	296.3	265.8	Banks	78bu d
....	....	....	....	....	47.4	80.0	120.3	206.5	260.1	383.1	291.6	472.3	521.5	472.0	Other Sectors	78bv d
....	....	....	....	....	−332.4	10.7	−70.0	−194.6	−5.2	77.3	62.4	26.9	43.0	47.0	Net Errors and Omissions	78ca d
....	....	....	....	....	632.6	124.9	646.5	240.0	590.1	1,288.4	157.8	−81.3	178.2	1,284.7	Overall Balance	78cb d
....	....	....	....	....	−632.6	−124.9	−646.5	−240.0	−590.1	−1,288.4	−157.8	81.3	−178.2	−1,284.7	Reserves and Related Items	79da d
....	....	....	....	....	−632.6	−111.0	−641.3	−236.5	−587.5	−1,287.2	−157.8	81.3	−178.2	−1,284.7	Reserve Assets	79db d
....	....	....	....	....	—	−13.8	−5.2	−3.4	−2.6	−1.2	—	—	—	—	Use of Fund Credit and Loans	79dc d
....	....	....	....	....	....	....	....	....	....	....	....	....	....	....	Exceptional Financing	79de d

Slovenia

961

		1972	1973	1974	1975	1976	1977	1978	1979	1980	1981	1982	1983	1984	1985	1986

International Investment Position — *Millions of US Dollars*

Assets	79aa d
Direct Investment Abroad	79ab d
Portfolio Investment	79ac d
Equity Securities	79ad d
Debt Securities	79ae d
Financial Derivatives	79al d
Other Investment	79af d
Monetary Authorities	79ag d
General Government	79ah d
Banks	79ai d
Other Sectors	79aj d
Reserve Assets	79ak d
Liabilities	79la d
Dir. Invest. in Rep. Economy	79lb d
Portfolio Investment	79lc d
Equity Securities	79ld d
Debt Securities	79le d
Financial Derivatives	79ll d
Other Investment	79lf d
Monetary Authorities	79lg d
General Government	79lh d
Banks	79li d
Other Sectors	79lj d

Government Finance — *Billions of Tolars:*

Deficit (-) or Surplus	80
Revenue	81
Grants Received	81z
Expenditure	82
Lending Minus Repayments	83
Financing	
Net Borrowing: Domestic	84a
Foreign	85a
Use of Cash Balances	87

National Accounts — *Billions of Tolars*

Househ.Cons.Expend.,incl.NPISHs	96f
Government Consumption Expend.	91f
Gross Fixed Capital Formation	93e
Changes in Inventories	93i
Exports of Goods and Services	90c
Imports of Goods and Services (-)	98c
Gross Domestic Product (GDP)	99b
Net Primary Income from Abroad	98.n
Gross National Income (GNI)	99a
Net Current Transf.from Abroad	98t
Gross Nat'l Disposable Inc.(GNDI)	99i
Gross Saving	99s
GDP Volume 1995 Prices	99b. p
GDP Volume (1995=100)	99bv p
GDP Deflator (1995=100)	99bi p

Millions:

Population	99z

918

International Investment Position

Millions of US Dollars

	1987	1988	1989	1990	1991	1992	1993	1994	1995	1996	1997	1998	1999	2000	2001	Item	Code
	....	....	....	....	....	....	....	5,864.3	6,841.5	7,155.4	7,668.1	8,450.3	7,856.1	8,300.2	9,837.2	Assets	79aa d
	....	....	....	....	....	....	....	354.0	489.9	459.5	459.4	636.2	626.5	767.6	949.5	Direct Investment Abroad	79ab d
	....	....	....	....	....	....	....	62.1	106.4	93.9	55.9	39.7	130.4	175.4	251.1	Portfolio Investment	79ac d
	....	....	....	....	....	....	....	15.0	17.1	15.8	15.4	16.7	32.4	36.8	21.6	Equity Securities	79ad d
	....	....	....	....	....	....	....	47.0	89.3	78.1	40.4	22.9	98.0	138.6	229.6	Debt Securities	79ae d
								—	—	—	—	—	—	—	—	Financial Derivatives	79al d
	....	....	....	....	....	....	....	3,949.2	4,424.3	4,304.6	3,838.1	4,135.9	3,931.1	4,161.1	4,239.4	Other Investment	79af d
	....	....	....	....	....	....	....	103.3	170.1	33.3	40.7	46.3	51.8	57.9	76.0	Monetary Authorities	79ag d
																General Government	79ah d
	....	....	....	....	....	....	....	1,709.2	1,909.3	2,066.3	1,397.6	1,510.8	1,342.3	1,516.7	1,753.3	Banks	79ai d
	....	....	....	....	....	....	....	2,136.7	2,344.9	2,205.0	2,399.7	2,578.8	2,537.0	2,586.5	2,410.0	Other Sectors	79aj d
	....	....	....	....	....	....	....	1,499.1	1,820.9	2,297.5	3,314.8	3,638.6	3,168.1	3,196.1	4,397.2	Reserve Assets	79ak d
	....	....	....	....	....	....	....	5,088.1	6,379.7	7,674.7	8,067.0	9,437.4	9,832.1	10,668.0	11,177.1	Liabilities	79la d
	....	....	....	....	....	....	....	1,325.9	1,763.4	1,998.1	2,207.4	2,777.0	2,682.4	2,892.7	3,209.0	Dir. Invest. in Rep. Economy	79lb d
	....	....	....	....	....	....	....	88.9	104.1	1,138.2	1,276.6	1,421.5	1,661.0	1,793.4	1,877.6	Portfolio Investment	79lc d
	....	....	....	....	....	....	....	45.9	62.7	133.8	156.7	139.4	163.0	167.8	167.9	Equity Securities	79ld d
	....	....	....	....	....	....	....	43.0	41.4	1,004.4	1,119.9	1,282.1	1,497.9	1,625.6	1,709.7	Debt Securities	79le d
								—	—	—	—	—	—	—	—	Financial Derivatives	79ll d
	....	....	....	....	....	....	....	3,673.2	4,512.2	4,538.5	4,583.0	5,238.9	5,488.7	5,981.9	6,090.5	Other Investment	79lf d
	....	....	....	....	....	....	....	7.3	4.2	1.6	.2	.4	.3			Monetary Authorities	79lg d
	....	....	....	....	....	....	....	577.5	786.9	734.0	686.8	823.4	702.1	752.9	706.1	General Government	79lh d
	....	....	....	....	....	....	....	561.4	686.1	1,045.9	980.7	1,017.8	1,178.4	1,298.3	1,550.3	Banks	79li d
	....	....	....	....	....	....	....	2,527.1	3,035.1	2,757.0	2,915.3	3,397.4	3,608.0	3,930.7	3,834.1	Other Sectors	79lj d

Government Finance

Year Ending December 31

	1987	1988	1989	1990	1991	1992	1993	1994	1995	1996	1997	1998	1999	2000	2001	Item	Code
	....	....	....	....	....	....	5.35	-5.06	-6.46	1.61	-43.20	-20.34	-29.63	-38.91	-49.72	Deficit (-) or Surplus	80
	....	....	....	....	....	....	611.45	768.50	926.42	1,041.65	1,163.40	1,330.58	1,445.54	1,563.29	1,772.31	Revenue	81
	....	....	....	....	....	....	—	—	.49	.96	1.76	2.45	3.18	6.44	10.06	Grants Received	81z
	....	....	....	....	....	....	606.09	773.56	933.36	1,041.00	1,208.36	1,363.54	1,477.07	1,613.39	1,844.06	Expenditure	82
	....	....	....	....	....	....	—	—	—	—	—	-10.17	1.28	-4.75	-11.97	Lending Minus Repayments	83
																Financing	
	....	....	....	....	....	....	-3.09	-5.41	-10.53	-11.65	12.32	22.95	-19.80	-19.18	52.61	Net Borrowing: Domestic	84a
	....	....	....	....	....	....	6.82	3.82	6.27	23.08	20.10	11.32	61.04	69.87	19.81	Foreign	85a
	....	....	....	....	....	....	-9.08	6.65	10.70	-13.05	10.78	-7.90	-11.61	-11.79	-22.70	Use of Cash Balances	87

National Accounts

Billions of Tolars

	1987	1988	1989	1990	1991	1992	1993	1994	1995	1996	1997	1998	1999	2000	2001	Item	Code
	....	....	....	....	....	....	839.3	1,050.2	1,300.3	1,469.1	1,638.7	1,811.7	2,034.0	2,216.2	2,447.4	Househ.Cons.Expend.,incl.NPISHs	96f
	....	....	....	34.2	66.4	207.0	302.6	374.3	447.5	514.5	592.5	659.0	738.4	841.1	974.0	Government Consumption Expend.	91f
	....	....	....	36.9	72.0	189.6	270.2	372.7	474.6	574.6	679.5	800.6	999.2	1,076.8	1,138.7	Gross Fixed Capital Formation	93e
	....	....	....	-3.1	-12.9	-10.6	7.4	15.3	44.0	23.7	20.5	31.1	38.1	44.8	23.4	Changes in Inventories	93i
	....	....	....	178.6	291.9	642.8	843.1	1,111.3	1,226.1	1,424.6	1,670.0	1,842.9	1,916.2	2,386.0	2,743.4	Exports of Goods and Services	90c
	....	....	....	154.5	259.4	572.0	827.5	1,070.8	1,271.1	1,451.3	1,693.9	1,892.6	2,077.5	2,529.4	2,760.7	Imports of Goods and Services (-)	98c
	....	....	....	196.8	349.4	1,018.0	1,435.1	1,853.0	2,221.5	2,555.4	2,907.3	3,253.8	3,648.4	4,035.5	4,566.2	Gross Domestic Product (GDP)	99b
	....	....	....	-2.8			4.1	13.9	21.0	17.5	5.7	5.0	-6.3	-14.9	-17.5	Net Primary Income from Abroad	98.n
	....	....	....	194.0	349.0	1,016.1	1,439.2	1,866.9	2,242.5	2,572.9	2,913.0	3,258.8	3,642.2	4,020.6	4,548.7	Gross National Income (GNI)	99a
	....	....	....	-16.6	-2.3	5.6	11.3	17.1	11.3	11.6	19.5	20.7	22.9	27.8	30.9	Net Current Transf.from Abroad	98t
	....	....	....	....	....	....	1,450.5	1,884.0	2,253.8	2,584.5	2,932.4	3,279.5	3,665.0	4,048.4	....	Gross Nat'l Disposable Inc.(GNDI)	99i
	....	....	....	....	....	....	308.6	459.6	505.9	600.9	701.2	808.8	892.6	991.1	....	Gross Saving	99s
	....	....	....	2,287.3	2,083.7	1,969.9	2,025.9	2,133.8	2,221.5	2,299.9	2,404.8	2,496.0	2,625.9	2,747.0	2,828.4	GDP Volume 1995 Prices	99b.p
	....	....	....	103.0	93.8	88.7	91.2	96.1	100.0	103.5	108.3	112.4	118.2	123.7	127.3	GDP Volume (1995=100)	99bv p
	....	....	....	8.6	16.8	51.7	70.8	86.8	100.0	111.1	120.9	130.4	138.9	146.9	161.4	GDP Deflator (1995=100)	99bi p

Midyear Estimates

	1987	1988	1989	1990	1991	1992	1993	1994	1995	1996	1997	1998	1999	2000	2001	Item	Code
	....	....	....	2.00	2.00	1.99	1.99	1.99	1.99	1.99	1.99	1.98	1.99	1.99	1.99	Population	99z

(See notes in the back of the book.)

Solomon Islands

813

	1972	1973	1974	1975	1976	1977	1978	1979	1980	1981	1982	1983	1984	1985	1986
Exchange Rates														*Solomon Islands Dollars per SDR:*	
Official Rate .... aa	.8515	.8107	.9226	.9312	1.0694	1.0642	1.1324	1.1306	1.0172	1.0346	1.1527	1.2788	1.3170	1.7714	2.4299
														Solomon Islands Dollars per US Dollar:	
Official Rate .... ae	.7843	.6720	.7536	.7955	.9205	.8761	.8692	.8582	.7975	.8889	1.0449	1.2214	1.3435	1.6126	1.9865
Official Rate .... rf	.8373e	.7041	.6981e	.7639	.8183	.9018	.8737	.8660	.8298	.8702	.9711	1.1486	1.2737	1.4808	1.7415
														Index Numbers (1995=100):	
Official Rate .... ahx	406.8e	483.6e	489.4e	446.1	417.2	377.7	389.8	393.4	410.7	391.9	352.5	297.0	267.7	229.8	196.5
Nominal Effective Exchange Rate .... nec								330.5	345.4	347.5	339.3	302.1	288.8	263.7	203.1
Real Effective Exchange Rate .... rec								140.4	148.7	158.6	163.3	148.0	149.4	135.8	115.3
Fund Position														*Millions of SDRs:*	
Quota 2f.s							2.10	2.10	3.20	3.20	3.20	5.00	5.00	5.00	5.00
SDRs 1b.s							—	.04	.97	1.22	1.24	1.65	1.34	.77	1.29
Reserve Position in the Fund 1c.s							—	.43	.72	.01	.02	.49	.48	.51	.51
Total Fund Cred.&Loans Outstg. 2tl								—	—	.80	2.40	3.36	3.16	2.76	2.83
International Liquidity												*Millions of US Dollars Unless Otherwise Indicated:*			
Total Reserves minus Gold 11.d						2.87	29.19	36.96	29.60	21.59	37.23	47.33	44.70e	35.61e	29.57
SDRs 1b.d								.05	1.24	1.42	1.37	1.73	1.31	.85	1.58
Reserve Position in the Fund 1c.d								.57	.92	.01	.02	.49	.47	.56	.62
Foreign Exchange 1d.d						2.87	29.19	36.34	27.45	20.16	35.84	45.11	42.92e	34.20e	27.37
Monetary Authorities: Other Liab. .... 4..d							.18	.67	.53	5.41	15.62	20.20	10.53	10.79	5.82
Deposit Money Banks: Assets 7a.d							.73	1.13	1.02	.96	.81	1.67	1.57	2.46	1.92
Liabilities 7b.d							1.85	1.20	2.12	3.07	2.48	2.74	1.44	2.10	1.67
Monetary Authorities													*Millions of Solomon Islands Dollars:*		
Foreign Assets 11							25.37	31.72	23.61	19.19	38.91	55.57	59.04	46.07	58.79
Claims on Central Government 12a									.13	.42	3.23	3.27	3.35	10.00	5.90
Claims on Nonfin.Pub.Enterprises 12c													.50	.50	.68
Claims on Deposit Money Banks 12e							.21	.16		.20	.70			7.80	6.55
Reserve Money 14							24.20	26.91	17.36	9.69	15.58	20.73	28.79	22.39	22.98
of which: Currency Outside DMBs 14a							3.85	4.84	5.66	6.42	7.15	9.30	12.75	13.89	13.58
Restricted Deposits 16b													5.44	.07	.09
Foreign Liabilities 16c							.16	.58	.42	5.64	19.09	28.97	18.32	22.29	18.44
Central Government Deposits 16d							.65	1.81	3.13	.43	2.19	6.38	3.57	4.82	5.88
Capital Accounts 17a							.75	3.03	2.88	5.48	8.54	12.11	18.16	19.62	29.12
Other Items (Net) 17r							-.18	-.45	-.06	-1.43	-2.56	-9.35	-11.38	-4.81	-4.59
Deposit Money Banks													*Millions of Solomon Islands Dollars:*		
Reserves 20							19.18	24.24	11.59	2.20	7.41	9.42	16.01	7.70	9.40
Foreign Assets 21							.64	.97	.82	.85	.85	2.04	2.12	3.96	3.81
Claims on Central Government 22a							.09	.53	1.24	1.68	3.05	5.83	4.62	8.10	11.60
Claims on Local Government 22b														.35	.13
Claims on Nonfin.Pub.Enterprises 22c							—	—	5.15	5.78	5.26	5.13	5.90	1.05	.23
Claims on Private Sector 22d							5.70	13.14	17.34	21.39	22.45	20.56	29.88	47.10	51.62
Claims on Other Banking Insts 22f														.64	1.12
Demand Deposits 24							3.97	6.15	9.48	7.81	8.63	9.13	15.57	14.45	16.80
Time and Savings Deposits 25							19.48	28.57	23.87	17.92	23.90	29.16	35.91	37.59	41.65
Money Market Instruments 26aa									.03	.04	.10	.31	.41	.43	.64
Foreign Liabilities 26c							1.61	1.03	1.69	2.73	2.59	3.34	1.93	3.38	3.33
Central Government Deposits 26d							1.29	3.03	2.54	3.08	1.76	1.05	1.53	.33	2.02
Credit from Monetary Authorities 26g							.20	.16	—	.20	.70			6.40	6.55
Capital Accounts 27a											2.97	—	5.68	8.83	9.26
Other Items (Net) 27r							-.94	-.05	-1.47	.12	-1.63	-.03	-2.51	-2.51	-2.34
Monetary Survey													*Millions of Solomon Islands Dollars:*		
Foreign Assets (Net) 31n							24.24	31.08	22.31	11.67	18.07	25.29	40.91	24.36	40.83
Domestic Credit 32							3.85	8.83	18.19	25.75	30.04	27.36	39.15	62.59	63.37
Claims on Central Govt. (Net) 32an							-1.85	-4.31	-4.29	-1.42	2.33	1.67	2.87	12.95	9.59
Claims on Local Government 32b							—	—	—	—	—	—		.35	.13
Claims on Nonfin.Pub.Enterprises 32c							—	—	5.15	5.78	5.26	5.13	6.40	1.55	.91
Claims on Private Sector 32d							5.70	13.14	17.34	21.39	22.45	20.56	29.88	47.10	51.62
Claims on Other Banking Insts 32f														.64	1.12
Money 34							7.82	10.99	15.14	14.23	15.78	18.43	28.32	28.33	30.38
Quasi-Money 35							19.48	28.57	23.87	17.92	23.90	29.16	35.91	37.59	41.65
Money Market Instruments 36aa									.03	.04	.10	.31	.41	.43	.64
Restricted Deposits 36b													5.44	.07	.09
Capital Accounts 37a							.75	3.03	2.88	5.48	11.51	12.11	23.84	28.45	38.38
Other Items (Net) 37r							.04	-2.67	-1.42	-.24	-3.17	-7.36	-13.86	-7.92	-6.93
Money plus Quasi-Money 35l							27.29	39.56	39.01	32.15	39.68	47.59	64.23	65.92	72.03
Other Banking Institutions													*Millions of Solomon Islands Dollars:*		
Reserves 40						.90	.81	3.61	4.00	3.47	5.78	8.22	8.36	7.59	8.17
Claims on Private Sector 42d						1.22	4.76	7.79	12.32	17.00	18.06	24.35	26.17	31.28	33.12
Quasi-Monetary Liabilities 45															
Central Govt. Lending Funds 46f						1.48	5.27	7.19	11.92	15.26	20.73	24.68	25.75	25.79	26.11
Credit from Monetary Authorities 46g							—	—	.18	.25	.01	.06	.19	.67	
Credit from Deposit Money Banks 46h						—	—	2.84	2.93	2.70	3.25	5.43	.51	.45	.45
Liabs. to Nonbank Financial Insts 46j						—	—	.50	.50	1.52	1.51	1.95	5.70	9.91	13.61
Capital Accounts 47a						.73	2.20	3.40	4.16	4.91	3.38	6.28	8.56	8.84	9.95
Other Items (Net) 47r						-.09	-1.90	-2.52	-3.18	-4.10	-5.29	-5.78	-6.06	-6.31	-9.50

1987	1988	1989	1990	1991	1992	1993	1994	1995	1996	1997	1998	1999	2000	2001		
End of Period															**Exchange Rates**	
2.8009	2.8505	3.1500	3.7184	3.9978	4.2622	4.4611	4.8597	5.1668	5.2081	6.4067	6.8417	6.9671	6.6441	....	Official Rate	aa
End of Period (ae) Period Average (rf)																
1.9743	2.1182	2.3969	2.6137	2.7949	3.0998	3.2478	3.3289	3.4758	3.6219	4.7483	4.8591	5.0761	5.0994	....	Official Rate	ae
2.0033	2.0825	2.2932	2.5288	2.7148	2.9281	3.1877	3.2914	3.4059	3.5664	3.7169	4.8156	4.8381	5.0889	....	Official Rate	rf
Period Averages																
170.0	163.6	148.7	134.7	125.6	116.2	106.8	103.5	100.0	95.5	91.2	70.7	69.1	66.9		Official Rate	ah x
163.4	148.9	139.5	126.5	120.0	113.0	111.0	108.3	100.0	97.8	100.1	84.5	81.1	82.6	85.5	Nominal Effective Exchange Rate	ne c
99.8	102.5	105.7	96.7	99.4	98.2	99.1	102.3	100.0	106.8	116.1	108.7	111.8	118.6	129.9	Real Effective Exchange Rate	re c
End of Period															**Fund Position**	
5.00	5.00	5.00	5.00	5.00	7.50	7.50	7.50	7.50	7.50	7.50	7.50	10.40	10.40	10.40	Quota	2f. s
.17	—	.05	.25	.07	.04	.03	.01	—	.01	—	—	.01		.01	SDRs	1b. s
.52	.52	.53	.53	.54	.54	.54	.54	.54	.54	.54	.54	.54	.54	.54	Reserve Position in the Fund	1c. s
1.55	1.25	1.09	.47	—	—	—	—	—	—	—	—	—		—	Total Fund Cred.&Loans Outstg.	2tl
End of Period															**International Liquidity**	
36.75	39.62	26.16	17.60	8.54	23.50	20.07	17.42	15.91	32.58	36.34	49.04	51.14	32.05		Total Reserves minus Gold	1l. d
.24		.07	.36	.10	.06	.04	.04	.01	.01	—	—	.01		.01	SDRs	1b. d
.74	.70	.70	.75	.77	.74	.74	.79	.80	.77	.73	.76	.74	.71	.68	Reserve Position in the Fund	1c. d
35.77	38.92	25.40	16.49	7.67	22.70	19.29	16.62	15.10	31.80	35.61	48.28	50.39	31.34		Foreign Exchange	1d. d
2.32	1.10	2.91	.69	.42	.54	1.75	.42	.36	.63	.12	.44	.32	....		Monetary Authorities: Other Liab.	4.. d
3.39	2.46	.52	1.20	2.33	2.13	2.13	3.57	1.30	3.27	3.94	1.29	6.06	....		Deposit Money Banks: Assets	7a. d
2.79	1.20	1.31	3.81	2.88	1.71	1.75	4.82	1.82	4.00	2.56	2.58	5.56	....		Liabilities	7b. d
Approximately End of Period															**Monetary Authorities**	
71.07	82.95	62.47	44.85	23.59	73.45	65.07	58.21	55.39	117.71	153.90	237.15	261.57			Foreign Assets	11
10.14	13.94	21.00	31.70	58.01	37.92	45.39	64.47	77.98	73.06	76.36	76.15	46.56			Claims on Central Government	12a
7.32	11.96	11.65	10.59	9.65	11.92	4.22	4.20	4.20	4.20	4.20	4.20	4.01			Claims on Nonfin.Pub.Enterprises	12c
.10	.15	6.76	.06	.03											Claims on Deposit Money Banks	12e
23.83	32.21	27.01	31.02	42.11	42.06	46.97	61.48	75.63	98.60	92.47	134.96	134.61			Reserve Money	14
16.84	20.21	22.65	25.22	27.80	30.83	42.11	50.23	54.93	59.67	70.79	81.28	100.07			*of which: Currency Outside DMBs*	14a
.10	.86	.03	2.70	.34	.14	1.02	.83	1.10	1.71	1.28	3.51	1.46			Restricted Deposits	16b
8.92	5.90	10.40	3.56	1.16	1.67	5.70	1.39	1.24	2.28	.59	2.13	1.64			Foreign Liabilities	16c
25.82	32.85	23.24	8.56	1.80	4.88	5.98	11.11	4.28	3.84	6.55	59.78	56.00			Central Government Deposits	16d
35.70	42.51	46.94	49.13	52.16	50.99	52.31	57.39	59.41	68.82	103.81	108.23	109.93			Capital Accounts	17a
−5.75	−5.33	−5.75	−7.78	−6.29	23.56	2.70	−5.32	−4.10	19.71	29.77	8.89	8.51			Other Items (Net)	17r
Approximately End of Period															**Deposit Money Banks**	
7.16	12.28	4.41	5.78	14.06	6.64	4.86	12.50	22.04	39.90	21.64	51.50	52.34	....		Reserves	20
6.70	5.20	1.25	3.13	6.50	6.61	6.91	11.88	4.51	11.85	18.69	6.29	30.78	....		Foreign Assets	21
25.79	32.64	31.97	39.36	69.94	105.47	130.86	152.14	159.00	160.33	162.70	165.53	180.30	....		Claims on Central Government	22a
—	.01	.06	.64	.28	.48	.41	1.24	.22	.60	.31	.21	.22	....		Claims on Local Government	22b
.06	.86	1.58	6.89	6.13	1.46	2.71	.91	1.22	2.71	.75	.78	2.58	....		Claims on Nonfin.Pub.Enterprises	22c
55.02	69.52	92.23	82.31	75.64	72.22	84.22	107.06	121.96	128.20	141.27	176.99	191.74	....		Claims on Private Sector	22d
.82		.73	1.57	.41	.32								....		Claims on Other Banking Insts	22f
20.39	28.82	28.25	39.23	51.74	74.08	81.82	112.65	116.02	138.08	141.66	130.82	166.48	....		Demand Deposits	24
59.76	79.04	76.68	75.65	94.02	111.12	125.88	149.70	170.41	195.89	207.49	218.50	194.08	....		Time and Savings Deposits	25
.61	.49	.56	.26	.16	.13	.49	.54	—		.31		.61	....		Money Market Instruments	26aa
5.51	2.54	3.14	9.97	8.05	5.32	5.67	16.05	6.33	14.49	12.16	12.54	28.21	....		Foreign Liabilities	26c
2.03	4.08	6.01	2.21	7.94	4.31	5.17	5.24	9.32	7.83	8.22	4.35	12.88	....		Central Government Deposits	26d
.10	.15	5.76	.06	.03	—	—	—	—	—	—		—	....		Credit from Monetary Authorities	26g
10.04	10.29	13.62	16.57	18.39	22.72	32.30	30.87	28.80	32.54	38.35	62.39	72.19	....		Capital Accounts	27a
−2.88	−4.90	−1.80	−4.28	−7.37	−24.50	−21.36	−29.31	−21.93	−45.25	−62.82	−27.31	−16.49	....		Other Items (Net)	27r
Approximately End of Period															**Monetary Survey**	
63.34	79.72	50.18	34.45	20.88	73.08	60.61	52.64	52.33	112.79	159.84	228.77	262.50	....		Foreign Assets (Net)	31n
71.29	91.99	129.95	162.28	210.32	220.60	256.67	313.68	350.97	357.41	370.82	359.72	356.53	....		Domestic Credit	32
8.08	9.65	23.71	60.29	118.21	134.20	165.10	200.27	223.37	221.72	224.29	177.55	157.98	....		Claims on Central Govt. (Net)	32an
—	.01	.06	.64	.28	.48	.41	1.24	.22	.60	.31	.21	.22	....		Claims on Local Government	32b
7.38	12.82	13.23	17.47	15.78	13.38	6.94	5.11	5.42	6.90	4.95	4.98	6.60	....		Claims on Nonfin.Pub.Enterprises	32c
55.02	69.52	92.23	82.31	75.64	72.22	84.22	107.06	121.96	128.20	141.27	176.99	191.74	....		Claims on Private Sector	32d
.82	—	.73	1.57	.41	.32								....		Claims on Other Banking Insts	32f
37.23	49.03	50.90	64.46	79.54	104.91	123.93	162.88	170.96	197.75	212.45	212.10	266.54	....		Money	34
59.76	79.04	76.68	75.65	94.02	111.12	125.88	149.70	170.41	195.89	207.49	218.50	194.08	....		Quasi-Money	35
.61	.49	.56	.26	.16	.13	.49	.54	—		.31		.61	....		Money Market Instruments	36aa
.10	.86	.03	2.70	.34	.14	1.02	.83	1.10	1.71	1.28	3.51	1.46	....		Restricted Deposits	36b
45.75	52.80	60.56	65.70	70.54	73.71	84.61	88.26	88.21	101.36	142.16	170.63	182.11	....		Capital Accounts	37a
−8.81	−10.52	−8.60	−12.04	−13.40	3.66	−18.65	−35.88	−27.37	−26.51	−33.02	−16.25	−25.78	....		Other Items (Net)	37r
96.98	128.07	127.58	140.11	173.56	216.03	249.81	312.58	341.37	393.64	419.93	430.60	460.62	....		Money plus Quasi-Money	35l
End of Period															**Other Banking Institutions**	
†12.62	....	....	9.77	14.57	17.05	11.35	....	....	68.17	71.50	18.56	14.56	....		Reserves	40
†40.81	13.27	16.95	18.17	20.42	54.50	65.65	....	....	113.32	125.99	139.13	140.53	....		Claims on Private Sector	42d
.36	.97	2.57	2.94	3.34	5.96	9.12	10.00	11.76	13.90	16.48	17.18	19.31	....		Quasi-Monetary Liabilities	45
†28.65	5.00	4.74	6.71	6.50	6.47	12.22	7.44	2.43	1.88	1.35	1.32	1.32	....		Central Govt. Lending Funds	46f
†6.76	1.22	1.52	6.21	9.87	9.26	6.81	—	—	11.77	11.35	6.13	6.44	....		Credit from Monetary Authorities	46g
†.40			.55	.12	.12	.04							....		Credit from Deposit Money Banks	46h
†13.15	....	....	10.38	10.13	9.22	8.31	....	....	3.47	1.67	7.40	7.33	....		Liabs. to Nonbank Financial Insts	46j
†7.44	....	....	4.11	7.79	13.79	16.58	....	....	18.03	26.77	34.82	29.98	....		Capital Accounts	47a
†−3.33	....	....	−2.95	−2.75	26.74	23.93	....	....	132.44	139.88	90.84	90.70	....		Other Items (Net)	47r

Solomon Islands

813

	1972	1973	1974	1975	1976	1977	1978	1979	1980	1981	1982	1983	1984	1985	1986
Banking Survey												*Millions of Solomon Islands Dollars:*			
Foreign Assets (Net) 51n	....	....	....	....	....	....	24.24	31.08	22.31	11.67	18.07	25.29	40.91	24.36	40.83
Domestic Credit 52	....	....	....	....	....	....	8.61	16.63	30.52	42.75	48.10	51.71	65.32	93.23	95.38
Claims on Central Govt. (Net) 52an	....	....	....	....	....	....	–1.85	–4.31	–4.29	–1.42	2.33	1.67	2.87	12.95	9.59
Claims on Local Government 52b														.35	.13
Claims on Nonfin.Pub.Enterprises... 52c									5.15	5.78	5.26	5.13	6.40	1.55	.91
Claims on Private Sector 52d							10.46	20.93	29.66	38.39	40.51	44.90	56.05	78.38	84.74
Liquid Liabilities 55l	....	....	....	....	....	....	26.49	35.95	35.01	28.68	33.90	39.38	55.87	58.34	63.86
Money Market Instruments 56aa							—	—	.03	.04	.10	.31	.41	.43	.64
Restricted Deposits 56b													5.44	.07	.09
Central Govt. Lending Funds 56f							5.27	7.19	11.92	15.26	20.73	24.68	25.75	25.79	26.11
Liabs. to Nonbank Financial Insts.... 56j							—	.50	.50	1.52	1.51	1.95	5.70	9.91	13.61
Capital Accounts 57a							2.95	6.43	7.05	10.39	14.89	18.40	32.40	37.29	48.33
Other Items (Net) 57r							–1.86	–2.36	–1.67	–1.47	–4.96	–7.70	–19.34	–14.23	–16.43
Nonbank Financial Institutions												*Millions of Solomon Islands Dollars:*			
Reserves 40.m	....	....	....	....	....	....			5.75	4.62	8.03	9.42	7.93	4.21	5.44
Claims on Central Government 42am									1.25	2.68	4.88	7.41	12.66	18.24	21.47
Claims on Nonfin.Pub.Enterprises ... 42cm									1.00	1.25	.99	.97	1.96	2.76	2.43
Claims on Private Sector 42dm									.69	.67	.73	.31	.42	.20	.27
Claims on Other Banking Insts..... 42fm										1.50	1.49	1.92	5.52	9.65	13.55
Capital Accounts 47am									8.88	11.54	16.73	22.37	30.79	39.28	50.12
Other Items (Net) 47rm									–.19	–.82	–.61	–2.34	–2.29	–4.23	–6.98
Interest Rates													*Percent Per Annum*		
Treasury Bill Rate 60c	....	....	....	....	....	....				5.83	7.50	8.92	9.00	9.58	12.00
Deposit Rate 60l										6.23	6.92	8.38	8.00	8.73	10.50
Lending Rate 60p										9.00	10.58	11.50	12.00	12.83	15.13
Government Bond Yield 61	....	....	....							10.00	11.00	11.00	11.00	12.00	13.00
Prices, Production, Labor												*Index Numbers (1990=100):*			
Consumer Prices (1995=100) 64	9.3	9.6	11.4	†12.6	13.1	14.3	15.2	16.4	18.5	21.6	24.4	25.9	28.7	31.5	35.8
Copra Production 66ag	67.2	51.1	90.6	84.0	75.6	92.7	87.4	106.7	92.6	106.9	102.1	90.2	135.2	133.0	100.5
Fish Catch 66al	28.0	22.7	32.1	24.9	55.0	42.0	60.8	83.1	79.8	88.8	71.8	120.9	125.1	108.3	154.0
													Number in Thousands:		
Employment 67e	....	....	....	....	....	....	....	....	....	....	....	....	....	24	24
International Transactions												*Millions of Solomon Islands Dollars*			
Exports 70	9.14	9.55	18.25	11.82	19.95	29.61	32.95	59.97	61.28	57.56	56.56	71.20	118.56	103.81	114.90
Imports, c.i.f. 71	13.86	12.94	18.82	25.04	24.25	29.62	37.05	60.43	73.85	79.17	68.99	84.76	100.60	123.20	125.34
													1990=100		
Volume of Exports 72	48.5	40.4	44.4	43.0	48.2	49.3	57.9	73.8	76.1	83.1	79.2	95.5	105.6	96.4	118.5
Unit Value of Exports 74	†19.2	23.3	43.4	28.3	44.2	64.6	61.2	87.8	94.5	75.8	77.4	79.1	118.4	112.1	78.9
Balance of Payments												*Millions of US Dollars*			
Current Account, n.i.e. 78ald	....	....	....	–12.57	1.71	5.77	3.32	10.28	–12.17	–26.55	–25.02	–14.63	.16	–27.82	–11.94
Goods: Exports f.o.b. 78aad	....	....	....	15.45	24.32	32.82	35.03	68.48	73.27	66.19	58.28	61.99	93.11	70.98	63.85
Goods: Imports f.o.b. 78abd	....	....	....	–28.54	–25.79	–28.61	–35.37	–58.43	–74.11	–75.85	–59.11	–61.47	–67.60	–71.85	–67.41
Trade Balance 78acd	....	....	....	–13.09	–1.47	4.21	–.34	10.05	–.84	–9.65	–.82	.52	25.52	–.88	–3.56
Services: Credit 78add	....	....	....	2.49	3.06	3.33	5.27	5.77	11.69	12.99	13.70	15.15	9.50	9.39	16.65
Services: Debit 78aed	....	....	....	–9.82	–9.04	–10.65	–17.40	–20.79	–27.96	–37.69	–36.97	–34.13	–38.63	–43.15	–49.90
Balance on Goods & Services 78afd	....	....	....	–20.42	–7.45	–3.10	–12.48	–4.97	–17.11	–34.36	–24.10	–18.46	–3.61	–34.64	–36.81
Income: Credit 78agd	....	....	....	....							2.37	1.83	5.02	3.58	3.33
Income: Debit 78ahd	....	....	....	–1.96	–3.91	–4.10	–3.43	–4.62	–14.94	–3.91	–11.22	–10.19	–13.82	–8.64	–9.24
Balance on Gds, Serv. & Inc. ... 78aid	....	....	....	–22.39	–11.37	–7.21	–15.91	–9.58	–32.05	–38.27	–32.95	–26.82	–12.40	–39.71	–42.72
Current Transfers, n.i.e.: Credit 78ajd	....	....	....	9.82	13.08	12.97	19.23	19.86	19.88	17.47	15.34	17.24	17.12	16.01	34.34
Current Transfers: Debit 78akd											–5.75	–7.41	–5.05	–4.55	–4.12	–3.56
Capital Account, n.i.e. 78bcd	....	....	....	—	—	—	—	—	—	—	–1.03	–.96	–.86	–.95	–.52
Capital Account, n.i.e.: Credit 78bad	....	....	....	—	—	—	—	—	—	—					
Capital Account: Debit 78bbd	....	....	....	—	—	—	—	—	—	—	–1.03	–.96	–.86	–.95	–.52
Financial Account, n.i.e. 78bjd	....	....	....	7.85	4.89	7.32	6.18	6.35	3.13	6.78	14.42	13.23	–11.15	14.38	2.64
Direct Investment Abroad 78bdd	....	....	....	—	—	—	—	—	—	—	—	—	—	—	—
Dir. Invest. in Rep. Econ., n.i.e. ... 78bed	....	....	....	7.85	4.89	4.44	4.58	3.46	2.41	.23	1.03	.44	1.96	.68	3.10
Portfolio Investment Assets 78bfd	....	....	....	—	—	—	—	—	—	—	—	—	—	—	—
Equity Securities 78bkd	....	....	....	—	—	—	—	—	—	—	—	—	—	—	—
Debt Securities 78bld	....	....	....	—	—	—	—	—	—	—	—	—	—	—	—
Portfolio Investment Liab., n.i.e. 78bgd	....	....	....	—	—	—	—	—	—	—	—	—	—	—	—
Equity Securities 78bmd	....	....	....	—	—	—	—	—	—	—	—	—	—	—	—
Debt Securities 78bnd	....	....	....	—	—	—	—	—	—	—	—	—	—	—	—
Financial Derivatives Assets 78bwd	....	....	....	....	....	....	....	....	....	....	....	....	....	....	....
Financial Derivatives Liabilities 78bxd	....	....	....	....	....	....	....	....	....	....	....	....	....	....	....
Other Investment Assets 78bhd	....	....	....	—	—	—	—	.58	–3.25	2.64	—	–1.04	–.16	–.27	–5.05
Monetary Authorities 78bod	....	....	....	—	—	—	—	—	—	—	—	—	—	—	—
General Government 78bpd	....	....	....	—	—	—	—	—	—	—	—	—	—	—	–4.48
Banks 78bqd	....	....	....	—	—	—	—	.58	–3.25	2.64	—	–1.04	–.16	–.27	–.57
Other Sectors 78brd	....	....	....	—	—	—	—	—	—	—	—	—	—	—	—
Other Investment Liab., n.i.e. 78bid	....	....	....	—	—	2.88	1.60	2.31	3.98	3.91	13.39	13.84	–12.95	13.98	4.59
Monetary Authorities 78bsd	....	....	....	—	—	—	—	—	—	—	—	—	.47	—	—
General Government 78btd	....	....	....	—	—	2.88	1.60	2.31	3.98	3.91	6.59	6.70	–16.49	6.08	–.98
Banks 78bud	....	....	....	—	—	—	—	—	—	—	—	.44	.47	1.42	–1.03
Other Sectors 78bvd	....	....	....	—	—	—	—	—	—	—	6.80	6.70	3.06	6.01	6.60
Net Errors and Omissions 78cad	....	....	....	6.02	–4.77	–6.21	5.72	–9.05	—	13.13	16.86	5.99	1.31	–.41	–8.47
Overall Balance 78cbd	....	....	....	1.31	1.83	6.88	15.22	7.57	–9.04	–6.64	5.22	3.64	–10.54	–14.80	–18.29
Reserves and Related Items 79dad	....	....	....	–1.31	–1.83	–6.88	–15.22	–7.57	9.04	6.64	–5.22	–3.64	10.54	14.80	18.29
Reserve Assets 79dbd	....	....	....	–1.31	–1.83	–6.88	–15.22	–7.54	9.04	5.71	–16.41	–10.58	–.72	9.74	8.57
Use of Fund Credit and Loans 79dcd	....	....	....	—	—	—	—	–.04	—	.93	1.71	1.02	–.20	–.41	.13
Exceptional Financing 79ded	....	....	....	....	....	....	....	....	....	....	9.47	5.92	11.46	5.47	9.59

Banking Survey

Approximately End of Period

Description	1987	1988	1989	1990	1991	1992	1993	1994	1995	1996	1997	1998	1999	2000	2001	Code
Foreign Assets (Net)	63.34	79.72	50.18	34.45	20.88	73.08	60.61	52.64	52.33	112.79	159.84	228.77	262.50	....	....	51n
Domestic Credit	†111.28	105.26	146.18	178.87	230.33	274.78	322.32	....	....	470.73	496.81	498.85	497.05	....	....	52
Claims on Central Govt. (Net)	8.08	9.65	23.71	60.29	118.21	134.20	165.10	200.27	223.37	221.72	224.29	177.55	157.98			52an
Claims on Local Government	—	.01	.06	.64	.28	.48	.41	1.24	.22	.60	.31	.21	.22			52b
Claims on Nonfin.Pub.Enterprises	7.38	12.82	13.23	17.47	15.78	13.38	6.94	5.11	5.42	6.90	4.95	4.98	6.60			52c
Claims on Private Sector	†95.83	82.79	109.18	100.47	96.06	126.72	149.88	....	....	241.52	267.26	316.12	332.26			52d
Liquid Liabilities	†84.72	....	....	133.28	162.33	204.95	247.58	....	....	339.37	364.91	429.22	465.37			55l
Money Market Instruments	.61	.49	.56	.26	.16	.13	.49	.54	....	....	.31	—	.61			56aa
Restricted Deposits	.10	.86	.03	2.70	.34	.14	1.02	.83	1.10	1.71	1.28	3.51	1.46			56b
Central Govt. Lending Funds	†28.65	5.00	4.74	6.71	6.50	6.47	12.22	7.44	2.43	1.88	1.35	1.32	1.32			56f
Liabs. to Nonbank Financial Insts	†13.15	....	....	10.38	10.13	9.22	8.31	....	....	3.47	1.67	7.40	7.33			56j
Capital Accounts	†53.19	....	....	69.81	78.33	87.49	101.19	....	....	119.39	168.92	205.45	212.10			57a
Other Items (Net)	†-5.79	....	....	-9.82	-6.58	39.45	12.13	....	....	117.70	118.21	80.72	71.36			57r

Nonbank Financial Institutions

End of Period

Description	1987	1988	1989	1990	1991	1992	1993	1994	1995	1996	1997	1998	1999	2000	2001	Code
Reserves	9.92	11.90	13.95	15.31	24.64	22.79	21.61	26.98	....	....	38.85	47.24	45.73			40.m
Claims on Central Government	25.04	28.66	31.81	29.51	38.61	49.14	68.00	73.98	....	....	83.78	125.30	118.73			42a.m
Claims on Nonfin.Pub.Enterprises	5.46	5.74	8.40	12.20	11.14	17.75	23.72	39.95	....	....	44.44	49.24	44.70			42c.m
Claims on Private Sector	.41	2.98	4.23	12.25	16.72	15.24	24.69	31.83	....	....	53.47	59.76	61.66			42d.m
Claims on Other Banking Insts	13.36	12.59	11.27	10.92	10.68	8.07	8.43	7.37	....	....	25.10	7.62	3.09			42f.m
Capital Accounts	62.42	74.05	90.20	105.71	129.45	153.64	187.03	223.57	....	....	317.28	359.00	384.31			47a.m
Other Items (Net)	-8.23	-12.17	-20.55	-25.53	-27.66	-40.65	-40.58	-43.46	....	....	-71.64	-69.84	-110.39			47r.m

Interest Rates

Percent Per Annum

Description	1987	1988	1989	1990	1991	1992	1993	1994	1995	1996	1997	1998	1999	2000	2001	Code
Treasury Bill Rate	11.33	11.00	11.00	11.00	13.71	13.50	12.15	11.25	12.50	12.75	12.88	6.00	6.00	....	....	60c
Deposit Rate	10.67	10.23	10.46	10.50	10.50	12.00	9.77	9.00	8.38	6.46	2.42	2.33	2.88			60l
Lending Rate	17.33	18.00	18.00	18.00	19.46	19.75	17.80	15.72	16.59	17.78	15.71	14.84	14.50			60p
Government Bond Yield	12.33	12.00	12.44	12.75	12.92	13.00	13.00	13.00	13.00	11.50	11.75	12.50	12.88			61

Prices, Production, Labor

Period Averages

Description	1987	1988	1989	1990	1991	1992	1993	1994	1995	1996	1997	1998	1999	2000	2001	Code
Consumer Prices (1995=100)	39.7	46.3	53.2	†57.9	66.6	73.8	80.5	91.2	100.0	111.8	120.8	135.7	146.9			64
Copra Production	86.2	92.9	110.7	100.0	68.5	72.3	70.5	65.8	86.3	91.2	114.7	....	....			66ag
Fish Catch	112.9	146.0	128.7	100.0	132.3	149.0	111.4	135.8	195.0	142.8	142.8	170.6	....			66al

Period Averages

Description	1987	1988	1989	1990	1991	1992	1993	1994	1995	1996	1997	1998	1999	2000	2001	Code
Employment	25	22	25	26	27	27	30	33	33	34	....	....	....			67e

International Transactions

Millions of Solomon Islands Dollars

Description	1987	1988	1989	1990	1991	1992	1993	1994	1995	1996	1997	1998	1999	2000	2001	Code
Exports	128.30	170.57	171.26	178.11	228.71	301.18	411.44	467.88	573.15	576.65	648.70	608.30	....			70
Imports, c.i.f.	161.93	203.30	259.82	231.04	305.71	326.61	436.29	459.51	526.27	536.87	....	....	....			71

1990=100

Description	1987	1988	1989	1990	1991	1992	1993	1994	1995	1996	1997	1998	1999	2000	2001	Code
Volume of Exports	86.9	92.6	94.4	100.0	122.2	136.3	....	....	....	....	....	....	....			72
Unit Value of Exports	84.8	93.9	92.5	100.0	105.9	102.8	....	....								74

Balance of Payments

Minus Sign Indicates Debit

Description	1987	1988	1989	1990	1991	1992	1993	1994	1995	1996	1997	1998	1999	2000	2001	Code
Current Account, n.i.e.	-16.81	-37.65	-33.23	-27.76	-35.84	-1.43	-7.65	-3.43	8.34	14.58	-37.91	8.12	21.48	....	....	78al d
Goods: Exports f.o.b.	63.20	81.92	74.70	70.11	83.43	101.74	129.06	142.16	168.30	161.51	156.45	141.83	164.57			78aa d
Goods: Imports f.o.b.	-69.49	-104.63	-94.28	-77.35	-91.98	-87.43	-136.87	-142.22	-154.53	-150.55	-184.53	-159.90	-110.04			78ab d
Trade Balance	-6.29	-22.71	-19.58	-7.24	-8.55	14.31	-7.81	-.06	13.77	10.96	-28.09	-18.07	54.53			78ac d
Services: Credit	21.03	21.99	26.51	25.35	31.61	36.03	42.44	49.95	41.81	53.14	70.35	55.07	56.30			78ad d
Services: Debit	-49.77	-66.22	-75.26	-78.69	-88.26	-78.04	-80.68	-105.94	-76.93	-85.47	-107.18	-54.53	-87.49			78ae d
Balance on Goods & Services	-35.03	-66.94	-68.33	-60.58	-65.20	-27.70	-46.05	-56.06	-21.35	-21.37	-64.92	-17.53	23.34			78af d
Income: Credit	3.29	3.88	2.33	1.36	.99	.69	1.52	1.20	2.36	2.69	2.12		5.46			78ag d
Income: Debit	-11.03	-12.10	-11.77	-7.59	-10.39	-10.89	-4.61	-4.44	-7.96	-9.42	-11.17	-10.01	-22.38			78ah d
Balance on Gds, Serv. & Inc.	-42.77	-75.49	-76.22	-65.84	-74.22	-37.60	-49.97	-58.97	-28.10	-28.43	-73.39	-25.42	6.41			78ai d
Current Transfers, n.i.e.: Credit	29.45	42.93	47.14	43.66	46.82	43.78	47.84	66.60	53.17	57.48	52.57	56.44	41.54			78aj d
Current Transfers: Debit	-3.49	-5.09	-4.14	-5.58	-8.44	-7.62	-5.52	-11.06	-16.74	-14.47	-17.08	-22.90	-26.48			78ak d
Capital Account, n.i.e.	-.35	-.38	-.17	-.16	-.26	-.44	.85	2.70	.65	-2.19	-1.00	6.65	9.16			78bc d
Capital Account, n.i.e.: Credit							.94	2.86	1.50	.50	.30	6.91	9.16			78ba d
Capital Account: Debit	-.35	-.38	-.17	-.16	-.26	-.44	-.09	-.15	-.85	-2.69	-1.29	-.27	—			78bb d
Financial Account, n.i.e.	7.74	43.79	25.12	22.86	15.10	22.44	8.22	1.49	-8.31	-1.37	45.68	16.88	-33.77			78bj d
Direct Investment Abroad	—	—	—	—	—	—	—	—	—	—	—	—	—			78bd d
Dir. Invest. in Rep. Econ., n.i.e.	10.48	1.68	11.60	10.44	14.51	14.17	23.37	2.10	2.03	5.94	33.85	8.80	9.90			78be d
Portfolio Investment Assets	—	—	—	—	—	—	—	—	—	—	—	—	—			78bf d
Equity Securities	—	—	—	—	—	—	—	—	—	—	—	—	—			78bk d
Debt Securities	—	—	—	—	—	—	—	—	—	—	—	—	—			78bl d
Portfolio Investment Liab., n.i.e.	—	—	—	—	—	—	—	—	—	—	—	—	—			78bg d
Equity Securities	—	—	—	—	—	—	—	—	—	—	—	—	—			78bm d
Debt Securities	—	—	—	—	—	—	—	—	—	—	—	—	—			78bn d
Financial Derivatives Assets	....	....	....	....	....	....	—	—	—	—	—	—	....			78bw d
Financial Derivatives Liabilities	....	....	....	....	....	....	—	—	—	—	—	—	.04			78bx d
Other Investment Assets	-11.28	18.82	-.74	-.75	-1.25	-.07	—	—	—	—	—	—	.04			78bh d
Monetary Authorities																78bo d
General Government	-10.53	19.74	—	—	—	—	—	—	—	—	—	—	—			78bp d
Banks	-.75	-.91	-.74	-.75	-1.25	-.07	—	—	—	—	—	—	—			78bq d
Other Sectors	....	....	....	....	....	....	—	—	—	—	—	—	.04			78br d
Other Investment Liab., n.i.e.	8.54	23.29	14.26	13.17	1.84	8.33	-15.15	-.61	-10.34	-7.32	11.84	8.08	-43.72			78bi d
Monetary Authorities	1.50	—	2.22	1.07	—	.41	1.32	-1.25	.03	.08	-.62	-.37	—			78bs d
General Government	12.43	8.50	-1.74	-5.97	-5.01	1.57	.94	-1.34	6.20	5.72	5.17	8.60	-11.02			78bt d
Banks	1.95	.05	-1.35	2.77	-.85	-.82	.03	3.31	-2.85	2.30	-.62	-1.23	-.27			78bu d
Other Sectors	-7.34	14.74	15.13	15.30	7.70	7.17	-17.44	-1.34	-13.71	-15.42	7.91	1.08	-32.43			78bv d
Net Errors and Omissions	2.82	-10.87	-5.21	-8.60	8.36	-6.16	-3.16	-2.80	-1.45	6.96	2.31	-14.41	-1.58			78ca d
Overall Balance	-6.61	-5.10	-13.49	-13.67	-12.64	14.40	-1.74	-2.04	-.77	17.98	9.09	17.24	-4.72			78cb d
Reserves and Related Items	6.61	5.10	13.49	13.67	12.64	-14.40	1.74	2.04	.77	-17.98	-9.09	-17.24	4.72			79da d
Reserve Assets	-4.28	-4.28	11.61	8.58	8.34	-17.14	1.74	2.04	.77	-17.98	-9.09	-17.24	4.72			79db d
Use of Fund Credit and Loans	-1.64	-.41	-.21	-.84	-.64	—	—	—	—	—	—	—	....			79dc d
Exceptional Financing	12.53	9.80	2.09	5.93	4.94	2.73	—	—	—	—	—	—	—			79de d

Solomon Islands

813

		1972	1973	1974	1975	1976	1977	1978	1979	1980	1981	1982	1983	1984	1985	1986
Government Finance														*Millions of Solomon Islands Dollars:*		
Deficit (-) or Surplus	80	...	...	...	.04	.03	−.63	.72	−2.94	−3.60	−9.21	−13.04	−13.38	−6.53	−19.33 [P]	−15.06 [P]
Revenue	81	...	...	...	6.82	8.28	11.05	13.45	20.93	23.38	29.92	33.25	34.36	47.71	53.19 [P]	57.10 [P]
Grants Received	81z	...	...	...	6.23	8.51	8.90	14.68	11.39	13.47	7.33	5.51	6.04	4.70	2.05 [P]	25.39 [P]
Expenditure	82	...	...	...	12.87	16.29	19.48	27.61	31.91	36.17	41.83	46.38	49.94	56.24	73.29 [P]	96.22 [P]
Lending Minus Repayments	83	...	...	...	.14	.47	1.10	−.20	3.35	4.28	4.63	5.42	3.84	2.70	1.28 [P]	1.33 [P]
Financing																
Net Borrowing: Domestic	84a	...	...	...	.01	−.04	−.01	−.01	2.11	3.13	2.97	4.69	6.44	...	...	...
Foreign	85a	...	...	...	.13	.06	.17	.69	2.03	3.42	3.24	5.01	7.64	...	...	...
Use of Cash Balances	87	...	...	...	−.18	−.05	.47	−1.40	−1.20	−2.95	3.00	3.34	−.70	...	...	...
Debt: Domestic	88a	...	...	...	.09	.08	.07	.06	...	9.44	12.05	17.37	21.24	25.32	...	...
Foreign	89a	...	...	...	.59	.64	.79	1.51	...	6.36	9.90	11.94	24.20	29.60	...	...
National Accounts														*Millions of Solomon Islands Dollars*		
House.Cons.Expend.,incl.NPISHs	96f	23.6	...	...	...	...	...	85.0	103.0	118.1	...	...	...	122.0	152.0	159.3
Government Consumption Expend.	91f	5.5	...	...	...	...	...	...	...	...	...	...	...	52.1	66.6	84.1
Gross Fixed Capital Formation	93e	7.4	...	...	...	...	...	...	...	...	...	...	...	43.0	49.9	63.6
Changes in Inventories	93i	...	...	...	...	...	...	...	...	...	...	...	...	7.9	12.2	2.5
Exports of Goods and Services	90c	9.1	9.6	18.3	11.8	20.0	29.6	30.6	60.2	60.8	...	...	...	135.2	121.1	132.9
Imports of Goods and Services (-)	98c	12.1	11.3	16.4	21.8	21.1	25.8	30.9	50.5	61.5	...	...	...	138.5	164.9	189.8
Gross Domestic Product (GDP)	99b	31.7	35.6	50.9	49.5	59.0	73.5	85.8	112.7	119.1	140.6	158.5	141.4	221.7	236.9	252.5
GDP Volume 1984 Prices	99b.*p*	...	...	...	...	...	...	...	...	186.8	199.3	197.1	204.8	221.7	227.4	222.4
GDP Volume (1985=100)	99bv *p*	...	...	...	...	...	...	...	...	82.1	87.6	86.7	90.1	97.5	100.0	97.8
GDP Deflator (1985=100)	99bi *p*	...	...	...	...	...	...	...	...	61.2	67.7	77.2	66.3	96.0	100.0	109.0
																Millions:
Population	99z	.18	.18	.19	.19	.20	.20	.21	.22	.23	.23	.24	.25	.26	.27	.28

	1987	1988	1989	1990	1991	1992	1993	1994	1995	1996	1997	1998	1999	2000	2001	

Government Finance

Year Ending December 31

	1987	1988	1989	1990	1991	1992	1993	1994	1995	1996	1997	1998	1999	2000	2001			
	−34.05 [P]	−32.96 [P]	....	....	....	....	....	....	....	....	....	....	....	....	....	Deficit (-) or Surplus	80
	69.45 [P]	82.44 [P]	114.31 [P]	122.80 [P]	132.38 [f]	....	....	....	....	....	....	....	....	....	....	Revenue	81
	30.20 [P]	37.56 [P]	....	....	....	....	....	....	....	....	....	....	....	....	....	Grants Received	81z
	125.73 [P]	138.26 [P]	145.05 [P]	167.57 [P]	231.67 [f]	....	....	....	....	....	....	....	....	....	....	Expenditure	82
	7.97 [P]	14.70 [P]	2.35 [P]	4.89 [P]	6.46 [f]	....	....	....	....	....	....	....	....	....	....	Lending Minus Repayments	83

Financing

	1987	1988	1989	1990	1991												
	14.01 [P]	15.03 [P]	....	....	....											Net Borrowing: Domestic	84a
	35.14 [P]	20.36 [P]	....	....	....											Foreign	85a
	−15.10 [P]	−2.43 [P]	....	....	....											Use of Cash Balances	87
	....	....	....	....	....											Debt: Domestic	88a
																Foreign	89a

National Accounts

Millions of Solomon Islands Dollars

	1987	1988	1989	1990	1991	1992	1993	1994									
	184.9	253.6	300.0	....	....	....	....	....							House.Cons.Expend.,incl.NPISHs	96f
	106.3	123.8	133.4	....	....	....	....	....							Government Consumption Expend.	91f
	59.6	122.1	....	....	....	....	....	....							Gross Fixed Capital Formation	93e
	7.9	10.0	....	....	....	....	....	....							Changes in Inventories	93i
	163.6	227.0	249.0	....	....	....	....	....							Exports of Goods and Services	90c
	229.6	380.1	405.9	....	....	....	....	....							Imports of Goods and Services (-)	98c
	292.7	356.4	384.4	526.3	598.3	763.1	901.2	1,052.5	....						Gross Domestic Product (GDP)	99b
	211.0	....	....	....	....										GDP Volume 1984 Prices	99b. [p]
	92.8	....	....	....	....										GDP Volume (1985=100)	99bv [p]
	133.2	....	....	....	....										GDP Deflator (1985=100)	99bi [p]

Midyear Estimates

1987	1988	1989	1990	1991	1992	1993	1994	1995	1996	1997	1998	1999	2000	2001		
.29	.30	.31	.32	.33	.34	.35	.37	.38	.39	.40	.42	.43	.45	.46	Population	99z

(See notes in the back of the book.)

South Africa

199	1972	1973	1974	1975	1976	1977	1978	1979	1980	1981	1982	1983	1984	1985	1986
Exchange Rates														*Rand per SDR:*	
Principal Rate.............aa= .... wa	.85000	.80966	.84435	1.01797	1.01029	1.05627	1.13286	1.08924	.95066	1.11341	1.18729	1.27926	1.94563	2.80926	2.67072
														Rand per US Dollar:	
Principal Rate.............ae= .... we	.78290	.67116	.68963	.86957	.86957	.86957	.86957	.82686	.74538	.95657	1.07631	1.22190	1.98491	2.55754	2.18341
Principal Rate.............rf= .... wf	.76873	.69396	.67948	.73951	.86957	.86957	.86957	.84202	.77883	.87758	1.08582	1.11410	1.47528	2.22868	2.28503
														Index Numbers (1995=100):	
Principal Rate..................... ahx	469.7	523.6	533.9	495.5	417.1	417.1	417.1	430.8	466.2	416.7	335.3	326.1	252.2	165.5	159.9
Nominal Effective Exchange Rate .... nec	....	....	....	....	....	....	....	384.2	411.2	411.2	363.4	372.0	307.9	209.5	165.4
Real Effective Exchange Rate .... rec	....	....	....	....	....	....	....	124.3	136.0	143.1	135.6	149.2	131.6	99.9	92.3
Fund Position														*Millions of SDRs:*	
Quota........................... 2f. s	320	320	320	320	320	320	424	424	636	636	636	916	916	916	916
SDRs........................... 1b. s	38	1	40	43	42	40	39	25	37	115	99	27	2	1	—
Reserve Position in the Fund .... 1c. s	81	81	81	—	—	—	—	—	128	107	—	70	70	—	—
Total Fund Cred.&Loans Outstg. 2tl	—	—	—	—	315	392	314	77	—	—	795	745	745	745	398
International Liquidity											*Millions of US Dollars Unless Otherwise Indicated:*				
Total Reserves minus Gold .... 1l. d	609	449	377	489	425	416	423	434	726	666	485	823	242	315	370
SDRs .... 1b. d	41	2	48	51	48	48	51	33	47	134	109	29	2	1	—
Reserve Position in the Fund .... 1c. d	87	97	100	—	—	—	—	—	164	125	—	73	69	—	—
Foreign Exchange .... 1d. d	480	350	229	438	377	368	372	401	515	407	376	721	171	314	370
Gold (Million Fine Troy Ounces) 1ad	17.93	18.99	18.25	17.75	12.67	9.72	9.79	10.03	12.15	9.29	7.57	7.79	7.36	4.84	4.82
Gold (National Valuation) 1and	677	836	782	603	431	330	1,931	4,451	6,512	3,339	3,075	2,660	2,039	1,420	1,698
Monetary Authorities: Other Assets ... 3..d	93	109	181	208	274	270	388	490	506	515	488	427	281	251	335
Other Liab.. 4..d	66	3	45	699	805	599	186	16	—	1,204	539	1,187	1,228	1,201	511
Banking Institutions: Assets 7a.d	106	161	162	181	165	158	224	316	542	465	482	613	473	734	835
Liabilities 7b.d	261	347	513	495	823	753	791	815	804	1,476	1,481	1,623	1,275	1,750	2,141
Monetary Authorities														*Millions of Rand:*	
Foreign Assets........................... 11	1,112	939	959	1,168	1,017	917	2,429	4,472	5,811	4,453	4,472	4,812	5,089	5,093	5,247
Claims on Central Government 12a	620	1,086	1,122	1,598	1,232	962	954	1,163	2,679	3,508	2,917	2,246	499	774	1,255
Claims on Private Sector 12d	4	13	10	18	27	16	42	211	403	327	491	913	819	945	543
Claims on Banking Institutions 12e	44	135	108	286	299	551	230	195	127	105	434	1,393	1,902	857	658
Reserve Money........................... 14	943	1,124	1,309	1,503	1,588	1,703	1,906	2,188	3,560	4,159	3,687	4,204	4,860	5,426	5,800
of which: Currency Outside Banks ... 14a	627	747	880	1,026	1,106	1,149	1,285	1,460	1,861	2,273	2,491	2,763	3,190	3,552	4,181
Foreign Liabilities........................... 16c	52	2	31	608	1,018	935	518	97	—	1,152	1,523	2,404	3,887	5,165	2,177
Central Government Deposits 16d	545	867	745	1,065	1,113	1,218	1,416	1,409	2,391	1,649	3,708	3,369	1,277	197	2,368
Capital Accounts........................... 17a	92	93	94	112	112	118	127	173	199	278	297	317	468	663	633
Other Items (Net)........................... 17r	149	86	20	–218	–1,258	–1,529	–311	2,174	2,871	1,154	–901	–930	–2,182	–3,782	–3,275
Banking Institutions														*Millions of Rand:*	
Reserves........................... 20	590	732	823	1,028	954	869	1,016	1,268	2,582	2,955	2,661	2,673	2,754	3,171	3,895
Foreign Assets........................... 21	83	114	112	158	144	138	195	261	404	445	518	750	938	1,876	1,822
Claims on Central Government 22a	1,617	1,631	1,800	2,530	3,193	4,232	4,732	5,478	5,052	4,125	4,778	4,845	4,185	5,680	7,872
Claims on Private Sector 22d	7,983	10,185	11,919	14,038	15,292	16,481	18,580	21,351	26,849	34,429	40,221	48,050	59,814	69,119	75,433
Demand Deposits........................... 24	2,170	2,622	3,114	3,229	3,305	3,470	3,819	4,701	6,472	8,892	10,553	13,721	20,110	17,689	18,898
Time and Savings Deposits.............. 25	7,137	8,810	10,203	12,682	14,034	15,693	18,465	21,363	25,444	28,388	31,885	34,634	37,930	48,960	53,259
Money Market Instruments 26aa	....	....	....	....	....	....	....	....	....	....	....	....	....	....	....
Foreign Liabilities........................... 26c	204	244	354	431	716	655	688	674	600	1,412	1,594	1,983	2,531	4,476	4,675
Central Government Deposits 26d	31	76	40	47	75	297	378	188	280	329	496	594	614	641	563
Capital Accounts........................... 27a	471	573	659	804	871	943	1,060	1,194	1,429	1,715	1,872	2,202	2,438	2,909	3,578
Other Items (Net)........................... 27r	261	336	285	561	583	662	113	238	663	1,217	1,779	3,184	4,067	5,172	8,050
Banking Survey														*Millions of Rand:*	
Foreign Assets (Net)........................... 31n	940	806	686	287	–574	–536	1,419	3,963	5,615	2,333	1,873	1,175	–390	–2,671	218
Domestic Credit 32	9,648	11,972	14,067	17,072	18,556	20,177	22,515	26,606	32,312	40,410	44,202	52,091	63,424	75,679	82,172
Claims on Central Govt. (Net) ... 32an	1,661	1,774	2,138	3,015	3,237	3,679	3,892	5,044	5,061	5,654	3,491	3,128	2,792	5,616	6,196
Claims on Private Sector 32d	7,987	10,198	11,929	14,057	15,319	16,498	18,622	21,562	27,252	34,755	40,711	48,963	60,632	70,063	75,977
Money........................... 34	2,808	3,382	4,011	4,286	4,437	4,648	5,133	6,198	8,398	11,273	13,124	16,586	23,413	21,332	23,207
Quasi-Money........................... 35	7,137	8,810	10,203	12,682	14,034	15,693	18,465	21,363	25,444	28,388	31,885	34,634	37,930	48,960	53,259
Money Market Instruments........................... 36aa	....	....	....	....	....	....	....	....	....	....	....	....	....	....	....
Capital Accounts........................... 37a	563	666	754	916	983	1,061	1,187	1,367	1,627	1,993	2,169	2,519	2,905	3,572	4,211
Other Items (Net)........................... 37r	80	–80	–215	–525	–1,471	–1,761	–851	1,641	2,457	1,089	–1,103	–474	–1,214	–857	1,713
Money plus Quasi-Money........................... 35l	9,944	12,192	14,214	16,968	18,471	20,341	23,597	27,561	33,842	39,661	45,010	51,220	61,343	70,293	76,466
Nonbank Financial Institutions														*Millions of Rand:*	
Cash........................... 40.. s	372	463	625	686	798	752	790	1,472	2,398	3,531	3,268	3,258	5,625	6,125	9,793
Claims on Central Government .... 42a. s	827	986	1,129	1,396	1,835	2,273	2,767	3,180	3,678	5,020	7,252	8,851	10,752	12,462	13,177
Claims on Official Entities .... 42b. s	1,367	1,497	1,594	1,822	2,099	2,715	3,280	4,313	4,716	5,511	6,989	8,211	9,296	12,422	14,046
Claims on Private Sector .... 42d. s	2,809	3,193	3,561	3,951	4,288	4,762	5,370	6,102	7,653	9,347	10,891	14,127	16,695	23,599	32,736
Real Estate .... 42h. s	400	552	688	951	1,217	1,462	1,635	1,807	2,294	2,766	3,875	5,018	6,348	8,271	9,050
Incr.in Total Assets(Within Per.) ... 49z. s	644	916	906	1,209	1,431	1,727	1,878	3,032	3,865	5,436	6,100	7,190	9,251	14,163	15,923
Financial Survey														*Millions of Rand:*	
Foreign Assets (Net)........................... 51n	940	806	686	287	–574	–536	1,419	3,963	5,615	2,333	1,873	1,175	–390	–2,671	218
Domestic Credit........................... 52	14,651	17,648	20,351	24,241	26,778	29,927	33,932	40,201	48,359	60,288	69,334	83,280	100,167	124,162	142,131
Claims on Central Govt. (Net) 52an	2,488	2,760	3,267	4,411	5,072	5,952	6,659	8,224	8,739	10,674	10,743	11,979	13,544	18,078	19,373
Claims on Official Entities 52b	1,367	1,497	1,594	1,822	2,099	2,715	3,280	4,313	4,716	5,511	6,989	8,211	9,296	12,422	14,046
Claims on Private Sector 52d	10,796	13,391	15,490	18,008	19,607	21,260	23,992	27,664	34,905	44,102	51,602	63,090	77,327	93,662	108,713
Liquid Liabilities........................... 55l	9,572	11,729	13,589	16,282	17,673	19,589	22,807	26,089	31,444	36,130	41,742	47,962	55,718	64,168	66,673
Money Market Instruments 56aa	....	....	....	....	....	....	....	....	....	....	....	....	....	....	....
Other Items (Net)........................... 57r	6,018	6,725	7,447	8,246	8,532	9,802	12,543	18,075	22,530	26,491	29,466	36,493	44,060	57,323	75,677
Interest Rates														*Percent Per Annum*	
Discount Rate *(End of Period)* 60	6.00	3.78	6.48	7.42	8.28	8.41	7.87	4.70	6.54	14.54	14.35	17.75	20.75	13.00	9.50
Money Market Rate........................... 60b	5.37	4.12	6.13	6.24	†8.50	8.29	7.99	5.39	4.40	10.25	16.90	13.98	20.31	18.21	10.92
Treasury Bill Rate........................... 60c	5.30	3.18	5.43	6.12	7.44	7.87	7.81	5.26	4.65	9.80	15.59	13.45	19.33	17.56	10.43
Deposit Rate........................... 60l						8.00	7.67	6.00	5.54	8.19	13.00	13.71	18.29	17.02	10.98
Lending Rate........................... 60p	8.79	8.00	10.17	11.79	12.25	12.50	12.13	10.00	9.50	14.00	19.33	16.67	22.33	21.50	14.33
Government Bond Yield........................... 61	8.35	7.83	8.96	9.71	10.44	11.01	10.40	9.26	10.09	12.99	13.51	12.67	15.23	16.79	16.37

	1987	1988	1989	1990	1991	1992	1993	1994	1995	1996	1997	1998	1999	2000	2001		
End of Period																**Exchange Rates**	
	2.73793	3.19971	3.33272	3.64560	3.92372	4.19788	4.66667	5.17298	5.42197	6.73325	6.56747	8.25106	8.44711	9.86107	15.23974	Principal Rate……aa=……	wa
End of Period (we) Period Average (wf)																	
	1.92994	2.37773	2.53601	2.56253	2.74303	3.05300	3.39750	3.54350	3.64750	4.68250	4.86750	5.86000	6.15450	7.56850	12.12650	Principal Rate……ae=……	we
	2.03603	2.27347	2.62268	2.58732	2.76132	2.85201	3.26774	3.55080	3.62709	4.29935	4.60796	5.52828	6.10948	6.93983	8.60918	Principal Rate……rf=……	wf
Period Averages																	
	178.2	160.4	138.6	140.2	131.6	127.3	111.1	102.2	100.0	84.9	78.8	66.2	59.4	52.5	42.7	Principal Rate	ah x
	164.0	141.4	128.9	125.2	121.4	118.1	113.9	108.0	100.0	88.0	88.4	76.2	69.0	65.5	55.8	Nominal Effective Exchange Rate	ne c
	104.1	98.4	98.8	101.3	106.0	109.5	107.5	102.9	100.0	92.2	98.7	89.4	84.6	82.9	73.2	Real Effective Exchange Rate	re c
End of Period																**Fund Position**	
	916	916	916	916	916	1,365	1,365	1,365	1,365	1,365	1,365	1,365	1,869	1,869	1,869	Quota	2f. s
	1	1	1	2	1	—	9	1	3	1	7	132	210	222	223	SDRs	1b. s
	—	—	—	—	—	—	—	—	—	—	—	—	—	—	—	Reserve Position in the Fund	1c. s
	—	—	—	—	—	—	614	614	614	614	307	—	—	—	—	Total Fund Cred.&Loans Outstg.	2tl
End of Period																**International Liquidity**	
	641	780	960	1,008	899	992	1,020	1,685	2,820	942	4,799	4,357	6,353	6,083	6,045	Total Reserves minus Gold	1l. d
	2	1	2	2	2	—	12	1	5	1	9	185	288	290	280	SDRs	1b. d
	—	—	—	—	—	—	—	—	—	—	—	—	—	—	—	Reserve Position in the Fund	1c. d
	639	779	958	1,006	897	991	1,008	1,684	2,815	940	4,790	4,171	6,065	5,793	5,765	Foreign Exchange	1d. d
	5.83	3.47	3.08	4.09	6.47	6.65	4.76	4.20	4.25	3.79	3.99	4.00	3.94	5.90	5.72	Gold (Million Fine Troy Ounces)	1ad
	2,541	1,295	1,137	1,415	2,074	1,992	1,658	1,445	1,481	1,261	1,048	1,034	1,020	1,451	1,427	Gold (National Valuation)	1an d
	374	271	271	365	252	478	453	392	306	227	24	19	12	10	6	Monetary Authorities: Other Assets	3.. d
	499	545	570	†324	126	385	1,812	1,633	225	93	2,161	3,177	3,254	2,683	4,028	Other Liab.	4.. d
	1,089	757	679	465	....	†873	811	1,042	799	1,412	1,603	2,874	5,122	5,432	7,338	Banking Institutions: Assets	7a. d
	2,262	2,060	2,372	2,613	....	†7,418	6,135	7,854	9,184	9,489	9,676	10,483	8,878	8,885	8,148	Liabilities	7b. d
End of Period																**Monetary Authorities**	
	6,865	5,579	6,008	†7,144	8,847	10,570	10,637	12,479	16,801	11,375	28,579	31,701	45,450	57,094	90,685	Foreign Assets	11
	494	1,304	1,519	†6,739	7,547	4,935	8,844	13,531	10,274	16,254	13,067	12,578	10,942	10,378	9,007	Claims on Central Government	12a
	1,171	1,780	2,240	†1,809	1,707	2,414	2,978	4,296	3,003	2,055	2,502	720	3,922	988	990	Claims on Private Sector	12d
	988	1,633	2,513	†3,620	3,774	4,901	6,219	5,995	6,513	11,975	10,939	6,346	3,253	9,966	12,931	Claims on Banking Institutions	12e
	6,819	9,398	12,077	†14,588	17,912	17,952	16,428	19,347	25,091	28,517	31,771	33,453	40,466	42,872	49,558	Reserve Money	14
	5,025	6,128	7,314	†8,064	8,836	9,536	10,490	12,237	14,332	15,954	17,327	18,510	22,663	23,724	25,286	*of which: Currency Outside Banks*	14a
	963	1,296	1,445	†832	347	1,176	9,023	8,966	4,151	4,572	12,535	18,617	20,028	20,306	48,840	Foreign Liabilities	16c
	2,474	5,239	9,863	†10,701	13,737	9,419	12,180	10,962	10,963	9,770	8,334	6,623	5,084	4,009	2,611	Central Government Deposits	16d
	651	755	790	†873	944	1,021	1,148	1,270	1,339	1,637	1,646	2,059	2,157	2,476	2,242	Capital Accounts	17a
	–1,388	–6,392	–11,896	†–7,680	–11,064	–6,749	–10,101	–4,245	–4,953	–2,837	802	–9,407	–4,167	8,763	10,362	Other Items (Net)	17r
End of Period																**Banking Institutions**	
	4,364	4,265	5,566	5,407	....	†6,112	4,773	6,586	10,356	11,702	13,514	14,726	17,969	19,761	23,757	Reserves	20
	2,101	1,801	1,721	1,192	....	†2,666	2,757	3,693	2,913	6,610	7,805	16,844	31,522	41,115	88,985	Foreign Assets	21
	9,215	11,486	14,775	13,087	....	†13,515	20,788	21,501	24,813	27,437	37,011	46,206	50,100	53,546	58,385	Claims on Central Government	22a
	86,742	110,584	132,320	151,879	....	†211,881	235,544	278,079	324,111	380,493	434,884	506,140	553,159	637,212	779,806	Claims on Private Sector	22d
	26,893	33,375	35,559	41,031	....	†58,977	63,902	81,736	97,050	130,858	155,065	194,873	237,083	242,244	286,776	Demand Deposits	24
	59,359	76,097	96,625	105,579	....	†117,031	124,142	141,757	162,301	165,626	195,762	205,958	205,309	232,628	269,563	Time and Savings Deposits	25
	....	....	....	....	....	4,791	4,858	3,922	4,920	5,531	3,374	2,657	7,576	5,869	8,395	Money Market Instruments	26aa
	4,365	4,898	6,016	6,695	....	†22,648	20,843	27,829	33,497	44,431	47,097	61,431	54,642	67,243	98,805	Foreign Liabilities	26c
	764	1,223	1,466	1,645	....	†4,039	9,937	8,173	17,748	22,387	21,137	21,158	27,027	30,158	42,993	Central Government Deposits	26d
	3,932	4,890	6,094	7,747	....	†16,021	20,065	23,998	29,302	34,470	41,664	51,920	63,470	75,581	96,013	Capital Accounts	27a
	7,109	7,652	8,622	8,868	....	†10,667	20,114	22,444	17,375	22,939	29,115	45,919	57,643	97,911	148,388	Other Items (Net)	27r
End of Period																**Banking Survey**	
	3,638	1,186	268	†810	....	†–10,588	–16,472	–20,624	–17,934	–31,018	–23,247	–31,503	2,302	10,660	32,025	Foreign Assets (Net)	31n
	94,385	118,691	139,524	†161,168	....	†219,287	246,036	298,272	333,490	394,082	457,993	537,863	586,012	667,957	802,584	Domestic Credit	32
	6,471	6,327	4,965	†7,480	....	†4,992	7,514	15,897	6,376	11,534	20,607	31,003	28,931	29,757	21,788	Claims on Central Govt. (Net)	32an
	87,914	112,364	134,560	†153,688	....	†214,295	238,522	282,375	327,114	382,548	437,386	506,860	557,081	638,200	780,796	Claims on Private Sector	32d
	32,026	39,934	43,343	†50,354	....	†70,809	75,550	94,511	111,844	147,664	173,335	213,532	259,935	266,185	312,365	Money	34
	59,359	76,097	96,625	105,579	....	†117,031	124,142	141,757	162,301	165,626	195,762	205,958	205,309	232,628	269,563	Quasi-Money	35
	....	....	....	....	....	4,791	4,858	3,922	4,920	5,531	3,374	2,657	7,576	5,869	8,395	Money Market Instruments	36aa
	4,583	5,645	6,884	8,622	....	†17,042	21,213	25,268	30,641	36,107	43,310	53,979	65,627	78,057	98,255	Capital Accounts	37a
	2,056	–1,799	–7,060	†–2,577	....	†–975	3,801	12,190	5,850	8,136	18,965	30,234	49,868	95,878	146,031	Other Items (Net)	37r
	91,384	116,031	139,969	†155,933	....	†187,840	199,692	236,268	274,145	313,290	369,097	419,490	465,244	498,813	581,928	Money plus Quasi-Money	35l
End of Period																**Nonbank Financial Institutions**	
	15,217	23,615	26,848	26,774	28,578	32,026	35,931	43,655	60,144	58,805	68,998	80,453	98,868	92,396	101,603	Cash	40.. s
	14,371	18,236	19,813	24,612	30,665	41,076	59,428	66,880	84,992	93,588	106,149	103,428	103,059	122,381	132,708	Claims on Central Government	42a. s
	14,618	15,992	15,357	16,745	15,921	18,473	24,813	22,889	22,765	20,969	24,130	21,204	21,553	20,541	25,260	Claims on Official Entities	42b. s
	40,287	45,433	61,382	80,922	153,356	167,034	222,407	268,488	326,976	358,163	359,677	370,342	540,167	595,366	687,550	Claims on Private Sector	42d. s
	11,300	12,695	15,538	19,158	27,127	32,354	35,735	38,868	44,064	47,459	53,403	52,261	63,514	57,507	53,641	Real Estate	42h. s
	16,991	20,178	22,967	29,273	87,436	35,316	87,351	62,466	98,161	40,043	33,373	15,331	199,473	61,030	112,571	*Incr.in Total Assets(Within Per.)*	49z. s
End of Period																**Financial Survey**	
	3,638	1,186	268	†810	....	†–10,588	–16,472	–20,624	–17,934	–31,018	–23,247	–31,503	2,302	10,660	32,025	Foreign Assets (Net)	51n
	163,661	198,352	236,076	†283,447	....	†445,870	552,684	656,529	768,223	866,802	947,949	1,032,837	1,250,791	1,406,245	1,648,102	Domestic Credit	52
	20,842	24,563	24,778	†32,092	....	†46,068	66,942	82,777	91,368	105,122	126,756	134,431	131,990	152,138	154,496	Claims on Central Govt. (Net)	52an
	14,618	15,992	15,357	16,745	....	18,473	24,813	22,889	22,765	20,969	24,130	21,204	21,553	20,541	25,260	Claims on Official Entities	52b
	128,201	157,797	195,942	†234,610	....	†381,329	460,929	550,863	654,090	740,711	797,063	877,202	1,097,248	1,233,566	1,468,346	Claims on Private Sector	52d
	76,167	92,416	113,121	†129,159	....	†155,814	163,761	192,613	214,001	254,485	300,099	339,037	366,376	406,417	480,325	Liquid Liabilities	55l
	....	....	....	....	....	4,791	4,858	3,922	4,920	5,531	3,374	2,657	7,576	5,869	8,395	Money Market Instruments	56aa
	91,131	107,122	123,224	†155,098	....	†274,677	367,593	439,370	531,368	575,768	621,229	659,640	879,142	1,004,619	1,191,407	Other Items (Net)	57r
Percent Per Annum																**Interest Rates**	
	9.50	14.50	18.00	18.00	17.00	14.00	12.00	13.00	15.00	17.00	16.00	†19.32	12.00	12.00	9.50	Discount Rate *(End of Period)*	60
	9.50	13.90	18.77	19.46	17.02	14.11	10.83	10.24	13.07	15.54	15.59	17.11	13.06	9.54	8.84	Money Market Rate	60b
	8.71	12.03	16.84	17.80	16.68	13.77	11.31	10.93	13.53	15.04	15.26	16.53	12.85	10.11	9.68	Treasury Bill Rate	60c
	8.70	13.54	18.13	18.86	17.30	13.78	11.50	11.11	13.54	14.91	15.38	16.50	12.24	9.20	9.37	Deposit Rate	60l
	12.50	15.33	19.83	21.00	20.31	18.91	16.16	15.58	17.90	19.52	20.00	21.79	18.00	14.50	13.77	Lending Rate	60p
	15.30	16.37	16.90	16.15	16.34	15.44	13.97	14.83	16.11	15.48	14.70	15.12	14.90	13.79	11.41	Government Bond Yield	61

South Africa

199		1972	1973	1974	1975	1976	1977	1978	1979	1980	1981	1982	1983	1984	1985	1986
Prices, Production, Labor																*Index Numbers (1995=100):*
Share Prices: Industry & Comm.	62a	20.0	24.3	19.8	19.2	19.3	17.9	20.8	27.8	40.9	40.4	35.4	44.8	†43.9	46.9	24.2
Gold Mining	62b	16.4	27.0	57.6	43.2	27.7	26.7	35.2	50.7	106.0	83.9	67.4	104.8	†118.6	126.0	99.1
Prices: Home & Import Goods	63	6.1	6.9	8.1	9.5	10.9	12.4	13.6	15.7	18.2	20.7	23.6	26.1	28.2	33.0	39.5
Home Goods	63a	6.2	7.0	8.2	9.3	10.8	12.3	13.5	15.4	17.7	20.3	23.0	25.5	27.6	31.8	37.7
Consumer Prices	64	6.1	6.7	7.5	†8.5	9.4	10.4	11.6	13.1	14.9	17.2	19.7	22.2	24.7	28.7	34.1
Manufacturing Production	66ey *c*	54.7	59.6	63.4	65.9	67.5	65.0	73.0	78.1	86.8	94.3	90.5	87.8	92.1	92.3	90.8
Mining Production	66zx *c*	107.3	110.3	102.9	98.6	99.6	101.2	102.2	105.6	104.2	104.1	103.3	103.7	108.4	109.2	105.9
Gold Production	66kr *c*	....	....	....	....	....	....	....	....	....	....	....	....	....	....	....
Mfg. Employment	67ey *c*	76.0	79.9	84.4	87.6	89.7	88.0	88.3	90.4	94.2	†96.5	97.6	93.9	94.0	91.4	†90.6
Mining Employment	67zx *c*	114.9	123.4	121.9	114.2	120.1	127.4	129.3	134.8	139.1	140.2	134.9	132.1	†137.1	142.5	†147.8
																Number in Thousands:
Unemployment	67c	....	....	....	....	....	....	....	....	....	....	....	....	....	....	....
Unemployment Rate (%)	67r	....	....	....	....	....	....	....	....	....	....	....	....	....	....	....
International Transactions																*Millions of Rand*
Exports	70	3,160	†4,187	5,908	6,448	6,826	8,612	11,106	15,345	†19,880	18,129	19,189	20,620	25,320	36,312	42,011
Gold Output (Net)	70kr	1,161	1,769	2,565	2,540	2,346	2,795	3,907	6,003	10,140	8,338	8,641	9,929	11,684	15,461	16,727
Imports, c.i.f.	71	3,031	†3,564	5,344	6,084	6,335	5,452	6,622	7,562	†15,264	20,118	19,987	17,617	23,538	25,226	29,688
Imports, f.o.b.	71.v	2,813	†3,275	4,909	5,545	5,859	5,118	6,263	7,027	†14,363	18,439	18,374	16,204	21,636	22,691	26,864
																1995=100
Volume of Exports	72	†44.5	45.4	46.7	46.2	50.2	60.0	64.9	73.8	†71.1	64.9	64.5	57.9	63.7	75.9	78.6
Volume of Imports	73	†63.0	71.8	89.4	83.1	71.2	55.4	61.7	61.1	†80.0	90.7	76.3	63.1	75.8	64.7	62.9
Unit Value of Exports	74	†6.1	7.4	9.3	10.5	12.2	13.2	14.2	16.2	†18.6	20.6	22.3	25.0	28.3	35.8	41.3
Unit Value of Imports	75	†4.6	5.0	6.5	8.1	9.9	11.2	12.9	15.9	†19.1	21.5	25.9	27.8	30.9	39.5	46.0
Import Prices (1985=100)	76.x	15.6	17.4	21.3	26.1	30.8	33.8	37.2	44.5	53.4	59.1	68.0	74.8	80.9	100.0	122.6
Balance of Payments																*Millions of US Dollars:*
Current Account, n.i.e.	78al *d*	–192	–258	–1,438	–2,397	–1,912	239	1,099	2,965	3,161	–4,621	–3,390	–300	–1,802	2,317	2,828
Goods: Exports f.o.b.	78aa *d*	4,532	6,270	8,791	8,880	8,579	10,517	13,015	17,718	26,039	21,407	17,917	18,735	17,352	16,351	18,122
Goods: Imports f.o.b.	78ab *d*	–3,846	–5,353	–8,716	–9,414	–8,781	–8,171	–9,561	–12,037	–18,848	–21,258	–17,142	–14,591	–15,133	–10,768	–11,509
Trade Balance	78ac *d*	686	917	75	–534	–202	2,346	3,453	5,681	7,191	149	775	4,144	2,219	5,583	6,613
Services: Credit	78ad *d*	723	961	1,206	1,444	1,262	1,397	1,656	2,001	2,463	2,563	2,300	2,267	2,099	1,734	1,898
Services: Debit	78ae *d*	–890	–1,154	–1,471	–1,805	–1,493	–1,769	–2,064	–2,403	–3,295	–3,858	–3,354	–3,155	–2,871	–2,227	–2,686
Balance on Goods & Services	78af *d*	518	724	–190	–895	–434	1,975	3,045	5,279	6,358	–1,146	–279	3,256	1,447	5,090	5,825
Income: Credit	78ag *d*	214	381	304	308	366	264	397	575	574	545	467	655	724	972	1,185
Income: Debit	78ah *d*	–914	–1,308	–1,552	–1,859	–1,868	–2,002	–2,349	–2,916	–3,917	–4,127	–3,598	–4,009	–3,726	–3,569	–4,146
Balance on Gds, Serv. & Inc.	78ai *d*	–182	–202	–1,439	–2,446	–1,935	237	1,092	2,938	3,015	–4,727	–3,410	–98	–1,555	2,493	2,865
Current Transfers, n.i.e.: Credit	78aj *d*	123	133	184	216	187	212	252	336	524	585	468	460	370	299	325
Current Transfers: Debit	78ak *d*	–133	–189	–182	–167	–164	–209	–245	–309	–378	–479	–448	–661	–617	–474	–362
Capital Account, n.i.e.	78bc *d*	1	3	9	13	8	–2	–6	–1	–11	9	9	–4	–4	–25	–57
Capital Account, n.i.e.: Credit	78ba *d*	10	13	19	23	18	18	21	27	44	61	55	44	37	18	13
Capital Account: Debit	78bb *d*	–9	–10	–10	–10	–10	–21	–26	–29	–55	–52	–46	–48	–41	–44	–70
Financial Account, n.i.e.	78bj *d*	—	—	—	—	—	—	—	—	—	—	—	—	—	–2,011	–3,490
Direct Investment Abroad	78bd *d*	—	—	—	—	—	—	—	—	—	—	—	—	—	–47	–71
Dir. Invest. in Rep. Econ., n.i.e.	78be *d*	—	—	—	—	—	—	—	—	—	—	—	—	—	–453	–50
Portfolio Investment Assets	78bf *d*	—	—	—	—	—	—	—	—	—	—	—	—	—	7	–6
Equity Securities	78bk *d*	—	—	—	—	—	—	—	—	—	—	—	—	—	7	–6
Debt Securities	78bl *d*	—	—	—	—	—	—	—	—	—	—	—	—	—	—	—
Portfolio Investment Liab., n.i.e.	78bg *d*	—	—	—	—	—	—	—	—	—	—	—	—	—	–20	–761
Equity Securities	78bm *d*	—	—	—	—	—	—	—	—	—	—	—	—	—	–157	–600
Debt Securities	78bn *d*	—	—	—	—	—	—	—	—	—	—	—	—	—	138	–162
Financial Derivatives Assets	78bw *d*	....	....	....	....	....	....	....	....	....	....	....	....	....	....	....
Financial Derivatives Liabilities	78bx *d*	....	....	....	....	....	....	....	....	....	....	....	....	....	....	....
Other Investment Assets	78bh *d*	—	—	—	—	—	—	—	—	—	—	—	—	—	–816	–936
Monetary Authorities	78bo *d*	....	....	....	....	....	....	....	....	....	....	....	....	....	–40	–36
General Government	78bp *d*	—	—	—	—	—	—	—	—	—	—	—	—	—	51	6
Banks	78bq *d*	....	....	....	....	—	—	—	—	—	—	—	—	—	–159	–114
Other Sectors	78br *d*	....	....	....	....	—	—	—	—	—	—	—	—	—	–667	–792
Other Investment Liab., n.i.e.	78bi *d*	—	—	—	—	—	—	—	—	—	—	—	—	—	–682	–1,666
Monetary Authorities	78bs *d*	—	—	—	—	—	—	—	—	—	—	—	—	—	–21	–1,006
General Government	78bt *d*	....	....	....	....	—	—	—	—	—	—	—	—	—	–21	–38
Banks	78bu *d*	....	....	....	....	—	—	—	—	—	—	—	—	—	839	136
Other Sectors	78bv *d*	—	—	—	—	—	—	—	—	—	—	—	—	—	–1,480	–759
Net Errors and Omissions	78ca *d*	660	54	1,318	2,441	942	–728	–957	–2,716	–1,949	3,510	3,281	1,432	1,378	–886	574
Overall Balance	78cb *d*	469	–201	–111	57	–962	–491	137	247	1,201	–1,101	–100	1,129	–428	–606	–146
Reserves and Related Items	79da *d*	–469	201	111	–57	962	491	–137	–247	–1,201	1,101	100	–1,129	428	606	146
Reserve Assets	79db *d*	–469	201	111	–57	598	401	–40	61	–1,100	1,101	–749	–1,076	428	606	556
Use of Fund Credit and Loans	79dc *d*	—	—	—	—	365	89	–97	–308	–101	—	848	–52	—	—	–409
Exceptional Financing	79de *d*	....	....	....	....	—	—	—	—	—	—	—	—	—	—	—
International Investment Position																*Millions of US Dollars*
Assets	79aa *d*	4,135	5,200	5,858	5,707	6,059	6,486	9,247	12,955	17,892	14,429	15,156	15,238	14,147	13,972	17,533
Direct Investment Abroad	79ab *d*	1,331	2,114	2,520	2,418	2,523	3,015	3,701	4,114	5,543	6,063	7,324	7,483	8,521	8,905	10,937
Portfolio Investment	79ac *d*	254	237	338	345	483	484	543	703	731	692	681	624	655	480	572
Equity Securities	79ad *d*	226	198	289	294	425	414	463	595	608	599	595	539	550	408	498
Debt Securities	79ae *d*	28	39	49	51	57	70	79	108	123	93	86	86	105	72	74
Financial Derivatives	79al *d*	—	—	—	—	—	—	—	—	—	—	—	—	—	—	—
Other Investment	79af *d*	1,162	1,387	1,682	1,659	2,018	2,037	2,364	2,893	3,999	3,334	3,128	3,133	2,312	2,298	3,511
Monetary Authorities	79ag *d*	....	....	....	....	224	220	322	426	420	441	395	346	224	204	271
General Government	79ah *d*	....	....	....	....	845	889	936	983	1,339	1,051	1,075	1,195	856	795	1,164
Banks	79ai *d*	....	....	....	....	—	—	—	—	—	—	—	—	—	—	—
Other Sectors	79aj *d*	....	....	....	....	949	928	1,106	1,484	2,240	1,842	1,658	1,592	1,232	1,299	2,076
Reserve Assets	79ak *d*	1,387	1,462	1,318	1,284	1,035	950	2,639	5,245	7,618	4,339	4,023	3,998	2,658	2,289	2,514
Liabilities	79la *d*	12,283	15,269	19,139	19,256	22,681	24,499	25,616	27,265	35,700	34,664	39,043	40,550	36,589	35,538	37,756
Dir. Invest. in Rep. Economy	79lb *d*	6,688	8,320	9,673	8,557	9,456	10,135	11,333	12,504	16,465	14,832	14,951	13,974	10,998	8,899	9,825
Portfolio Investment	79lc *d*	2,334	2,961	4,085	3,521	3,644	3,741	3,291	4,124	6,794	5,162	5,733	5,921	4,372	4,666	7,498
Equity Securities	79ld *d*	1,795	2,230	3,083	2,313	2,155	2,193	1,628	2,332	4,965	3,296	3,318	3,338	1,997	2,079	3,852
Debt Securities	79le *d*	539	730	1,002	1,209	1,489	1,548	1,663	1,792	1,829	1,866	2,416	2,583	2,375	2,587	3,646
Financial Derivatives	79ll *d*	—	—	—	—	—	—	—	—	—	—	—	—	—	—	—
Other Investment	79lf *d*	3,261	3,989	5,381	7,177	9,581	10,623	10,992	10,637	12,441	14,670	18,358	20,655	21,219	21,973	20,434
Monetary Authorities	79lg *d*	79	24	70	792	839	628	651	158	79	1,252	2,322	2,041	1,754	1,661	1,448
General Government	79lh *d*	975	1,098	1,331	1,548	2,454	3,159	2,563	2,564	2,220	2,053	3,381	4,621	4,771	5,403	4,637
Banks	79li *d*	156	291	442	453	722	638	606	723	958	2,029	557	1,065	3,220	4,099	2,900
Other Sectors	79lj *d*	2,051	2,576	3,538	4,384	5,565	6,197	7,171	7,192	9,183	9,335	12,099	12,928	11,474	10,810	11,450

		1987	1988	1989	1990	1991	1992	1993	1994	1995	1996	1997	1998	1999	2000	2001
Prices, Production, Labor		*Period Averages*														
Share Prices: Industry & Comm.	62a	35.4	27.9	39.0	40.9	54.4	61.1	66.5	91.8	†100.0	116.1	120.1	107.1	103.8	116.5	96.1
Gold Mining	62b	138.1	84.9	101.3	105.9	72.8	61.9	95.4	137.1	†100.0	119.9	85.7	69.8	72.7	73.0	86.3
Prices: Home & Import Goods	63	45.0	50.9	58.6	†65.6	73.1	79.1	84.4	91.3	100.0	107.0	114.5	118.6	125.5	....	....
Home Goods	63a	43.5	49.4	56.8	†63.8	71.6	78.2	83.6	91.0	100.0	107.5	115.8	119.9	126.1	....	....
Consumer Prices	64	39.6	44.7	51.3	58.6	67.6	77.0	84.5	92.0	100.0	107.4	116.6	124.6	131.1	138.1	145.9
Manufacturing Production	66ey *c*	93.1	99.4	100.7	98.3	94.7	91.9	†91.7	94.0	100.0	101.5	104.3	101.1	101.4	106.0	109.2
Mining Production	66zx *c*	101.3	103.1	101.7	99.8	98.9	99.3	†102.3	100.8	100.0	98.3	100.3	99.3	97.4	96.3	94.2
Gold Production	66kr *c*	117.8	120.7	117.8	116.4	115.6	117.9	119.1	111.4	100.0	95.8	†95.3	90.8	86.6	....	....
Mfg. Employment	67ey *c*	91.3	97.5	97.5	97.1	†94.5	99.4	98.7	†99.4	100.0	96.3	92.3	89.0	....	....	....
Mining Employment	67zx *c*	147.8	144.5	142.5	137.1	†127.0	112.3	103.7	†102.2	100.0	95.3	92.1	70.3	....	....	....
		Period Averages														
Unemployment	67c	....	122	116	111	248	288	313	271	273	296	310	....	....	....	....
Unemployment Rate (%)	67r	....	....	....	....	....	....	....	4.4	4.5	5.1	5.4	....	....	....	....
International Transactions		*Millions of Rand*														
Exports	70	43,202	49,724	58,199	60,929	64,355	66,774	79,279	89,907	101,051	126,101	142,937	†145,518	163,182	208,476	249,541
Gold Output (Net)	70kr	17,768	19,280	19,095	18,070	19,648	19,391	22,449	23,671	22,537	26,300	25,818	25,907	23,289	27,159	30,909
Imports, c.i.f.	71	31,105	42,566	48,515	47,605	52,006	56,358	65,411	83,042	110,826	129,522	151,779	†161,802	163,092	206,620	241,311
Imports, f.o.b.	71.v	28,673	39,484	44,741	44,212	48,209	52,857	58,779	76,154	98,039	115,524	129,735	143,326	147,091	186,382	214,251
		1995=100														
Volume of Exports	72	76.9	†82.4	89.0	84.1	83.8	89.8	91.5	96.4	100.0	141.6	....	....	....	....	....
Volume of Imports	73	65.4	†80.2	80.2	73.7	73.7	75.8	79.4	92.2	100.0	114.5	....	....	....	....	....
Unit Value of Exports	74	42.9	†49.4	59.3	62.2	65.7	69.2	76.0	85.5	100.0	110.3	....	....	....	....	....
Unit Value of Imports	75	48.0	†52.7	59.5	63.7	70.0	73.7	79.5	87.9	100.0	105.5	....	....	....	....	....
Import Prices (1985=100)	76.x	134.5	....	....	....	....	....	....	....	....	....	....	....	....	....	....
Balance of Payments		*Minus Sign Indicates Debit*														
Current Account, n.i.e.	78al *d*	3,347	1,504	1,343	2,134	2,256	1,967	1,503	112	-2,205	-1,880	-2,273	-2,157	-640	-575	-166
Goods: Exports f.o.b.	78aa *d*	21,895	23,363	22,551	24,336	23,793	24,527	24,717	26,333	30,071	30,263	31,171	29,264	28,627	31,636	30,642
Goods: Imports f.o.b.	78ab *d*	-14,348	-17,584	-17,163	-17,279	-17,185	-18,248	-18,485	-21,852	-27,404	-27,568	-28,848	-27,208	-24,554	-27,320	-25,677
Trade Balance	78ac *d*	7,547	5,779	5,388	7,056	6,608	6,279	6,232	4,481	2,667	2,695	2,324	2,056	4,073	4,316	4,966
Services: Credit	78ad *d*	2,323	2,402	2,884	3,406	3,189	3,352	3,276	3,749	4,618	5,028	5,334	5,281	5,074	4,895	4,662
Services: Debit	78ae *d*	-3,125	-3,233	-3,345	-3,737	-3,817	-4,357	-4,706	-5,087	-5,969	-5,733	-6,002	-5,595	-5,707	-5,719	-5,208
Balance on Goods & Services	78af *d*	6,745	4,948	4,928	6,726	5,981	5,273	4,802	3,143	1,315	1,990	1,655	1,742	3,440	3,492	4,419
Income: Credit	78ag *d*	1,359	1,217	1,196	657	874	930	696	972	1,136	1,077	1,298	1,307	1,568	2,261	2,168
Income: Debit	78ah *d*	-4,473	-4,419	-4,568	-4,929	-4,084	-3,871	-3,352	-3,394	-4,011	-4,194	-4,502	-4,463	-4,721	-5,401	-6,014
Balance on Gds, Serv. & Inc.	78ai *d*	3,631	1,746	1,556	2,455	2,771	2,332	2,145	721	-1,560	-1,127	-1,549	-1,414	287	351	573
Current Transfers, n.i.e.: Credit	78aj *d*	367	312	320	298	125	123	127	143	196	54	138	60	66	106	126
Current Transfers: Debit	78ak *d*	-651	-554	-533	-619	-640	-488	-769	-752	-841	-807	-862	-804	-993	-1,033	-865
Capital Account, n.i.e.	78bc *d*	-54	-35	-27	-56	-36	-42	-57	-67	-40	-47	-193	-56	-62	-52	-32
Capital Account, n.i.e.: Credit	78ba *d*	18	25	24	27	25	28	18	20	22	25	29	24	20	19	15
Capital Account: Debit	78bb *d*	-73	-60	-51	-84	-61	-70	-75	-87	-62	-72	-222	-80	-82	-71	-47
Financial Account, n.i.e.	78bj *d*	-1,757	-1,314	-522	-1,618	-1,285	-243	-344	1,087	4,003	3,018	8,131	4,852	5,305	99	501
Direct Investment Abroad	78bd *d*	-112	-65	-163	-28	-206	-1,939	-292	-1,261	-2,494	-1,048	-2,324	-1,634	-1,584	-277	3,686
Dir. Invest. in Rep. Econ., n.i.e.	78be *d*	-192	158	-201	-76	254	3	11	374	1,248	816	3,811	550	1,503	969	7,162
Portfolio Investment Assets	78bf *d*	-15	-14	-211	-332	-394	-98	-3	-82	-447	-2,000	-4,587	-5,575	-5,113	-3,672	-5,331
Equity Securities	78bk *d*	-15	-14	-211	-332	-263	-32	-15	-29	-387	-1,698	-3,891	-4,768	-4,050	-3,019	-4,864
Debt Securities	78bl *d*	—	—	—	—	-131	-66	11	-53	-61	-302	-696	-807	-1,064	-652	-467
Portfolio Investment Liab., n.i.e.	78bg *d*	-804	-322	305	338	630	1,841	751	2,918	2,937	4,446	11,274	9,869	13,799	1,807	-2,971
Equity Securities	78bm *d*	-623	-268	443	388	-1,446	-188	895	88	2,914	2,318	5,473	8,632	9,001	4,169	-962
Debt Securities	78bn *d*	-181	-54	-138	-50	2,076	2,029	-145	2,830	23	2,127	5,802	1,237	4,798	-2,361	-2,009
Financial Derivatives Assets	78bw *d*	....	....	....	....	....	....	....	....	....	....	—	—	-46	-144	—
Financial Derivatives Liabilities	78bx *d*	....	....	....	....	....	....	....	....	....	....	53	97	-76	2	—
Other Investment Assets	78bh *d*	-7	-195	-617	129	-82	-321	-269	-298	-525	-599	-1,983	-694	-1,644	59	-1,432
Monetary Authorities	78bo *d*	5	34	-16	16	-17	-266	-24	44	75	12	206	—	6	—	—
General Government	78bp *d*	-2	-23	-158	-57	-82	-2	—	-1	1	—	2	1	—	—	-407
Banks	78bq *d*	139	-2	-9	-13	-17	-23	15	-85	62	-127	-122	-135	-61	-244	-334
Other Sectors	78br *d*	-150	-205	-435	183	34	-30	-259	-255	-663	-484	-2,069	-560	-1,589	303	-691
Other Investment Liab., n.i.e.	78bi *d*	-626	-877	365	-1,650	-1,487	271	-542	-565	3,285	1,403	1,887	2,237	-1,535	1,354	-614
Monetary Authorities	78bs *d*	-425	625	567	-1,079	-330	279	1,495	-105	-1,414	-89	2,186	1,172	105	-410	1,582
General Government	78bt *d*	2	-2	-111	69	185	266	-617	-467	118	469	-120	-73	-270	6	134
Banks	78bu *d*	-283	174	418	300	-510	-11	-359	360	2,945	1,044	-283	784	-945	1,196	-787
Other Sectors	78bv *d*	79	-1,673	-509	-940	-831	-263	-1,061	-353	1,636	-21	105	355	-425	563	-1,543
Net Errors and Omissions	78ca *d*	-129	-871	-267	-104	212	-1,179	-2,443	-449	-852	-2,363	-1,070	-1,719	-389	928	1,855
Overall Balance	78cb *d*	1,407	-715	528	355	1,147	503	-1,341	683	907	-1,272	4,595	920	4,215	400	2,158
Reserves and Related Items	79da *d*	-1,407	715	-528	-355	-1,147	-503	1,341	-683	-907	1,272	-4,595	-920	-4,215	-400	-2,158
Reserve Assets	79db *d*	-891	715	-528	-355	-1,147	-503	491	-683	-907	1,272	-4,174	-502	-4,215	-400	-2,158
Use of Fund Credit and Loans	79dc *d*	-515	—	—	—	—	—	850	—	—	—	-421	-418	—	—	—
Exceptional Financing	79de *d*	—	—	—	—	—	—	—	—	—	—	—	—	—	—	—
International Investment Position		*Millions of US Dollars*														
Assets	79aa *d*	21,942	18,758	20,172	21,432	23,376	25,834	25,743	27,559	33,893	35,056	47,869	56,855	92,532	95,596	....
Direct Investment Abroad	79ab *d*	13,421	12,056	13,143	15,010	16,103	17,795	17,960	19,105	23,301	24,349	23,250	26,858	32,990	32,325	....
Portfolio Investment	79ac *d*	458	482	454	246	269	216	145	98	632	2,605	12,060	18,231	41,961	45,264	....
Equity Securities	79ad *d*	386	434	420	212	222	177	109	61	569	2,237	10,895	15,833	38,349	41,675	....
Debt Securities	79ae *d*	72	48	34	34	47	39	36	38	63	368	1,164	2,398	3,612	3,589	....
Financial Derivatives	79al *d*	—	—	—	—	—	—	—	—	—	—	—	—	—	—	....
Other Investment	79af *d*	4,146	3,567	3,963	3,503	3,401	4,005	4,171	4,349	4,985	4,657	5,297	4,565	6,308	6,720	....
Monetary Authorities	79ag *d*	310	209	209	194	252	475	453	392	306	227	24	19	12	10	....
General Government	79ah *d*	1,409	1,287	1,373	1,431	1,331	1,839	1,838	2,040	2,371	2,148	1,839	1,596	2,512	2,703	....
Banks	79ai *d*	—	—	—	—	17	37	19	104	39	150	258	300	338	496	....
Other Sectors	79aj *d*	2,428	2,070	2,381	1,877	1,800	1,653	1,862	1,813	2,269	2,132	3,176	2,650	3,447	3,511	....
Reserve Assets	79ak *d*	3,917	2,652	2,613	2,673	3,603	3,818	3,467	4,008	4,975	3,445	7,262	7,201	11,273	11,287	....
Liabilities	79la *d*	39,755	33,762	34,454	35,153	36,841	40,898	44,022	52,197	62,610	60,449	68,546	69,835	116,962	102,231	....
Dir. Invest. in Rep. Economy	79lb *d*	10,014	7,748	8,057	9,210	10,209	10,662	10,694	12,615	15,014	13,236	16,736	15,676	51,772	43,451	....
Portfolio Investment	79lc *d*	7,863	6,554	7,343	8,453	10,292	12,549	13,470	18,998	23,446	23,804	28,143	30,547	42,249	36,529	....
Equity Securities	79ld *d*	3,560	2,588	3,300	3,740	4,854	5,359	6,027	9,246	12,492	13,366	13,144	17,519	26,461	22,599	....
Debt Securities	79le *d*	4,303	3,966	4,043	4,713	5,438	7,190	7,443	9,752	10,953	10,439	14,999	13,028	15,789	13,930	....
Financial Derivatives	79ll *d*	—	—	—	—	—	5	2	4	10	14	66	119	43	35	....
Other Investment	79lf *d*	21,877	19,460	19,054	17,490	16,340	17,683	19,855	20,580	24,140	23,395	23,601	23,492	22,898	22,216	....
Monetary Authorities	79lg *d*	517	566	632	328	129	390	2,660	2,534	1,142	979	2,578	3,181	3,261	2,681	....
General Government	79lh *d*	4,905	4,662	4,395	3,636	3,125	3,920	3,512	3,108	3,072	3,244	2,776	2,537	3,125	3,023	....
Banks	79li *d*	3,567	2,858	3,998	4,284	5,008	5,131	4,968	5,944	9,038	9,310	8,861	9,154	7,997	8,627	....
Other Sectors	79lj *d*	12,887	11,373	10,029	9,242	8,077	8,242	8,715	8,993	10,889	9,861	9,386	8,620	8,515	7,885	....

South Africa

		1972	1973	1974	1975	1976	1977	1978	1979	1980	1981	1982	1983	1984	1985	1986
Government Finance																*Millions of Rand:*
Deficit (-) or Surplus	80	−769	−212	−598	−1,680	−2,011	−1,735	−2,048	−2,112	−1,320	−1,775	−2,307	−3,578	−5,677	−3,546	−5,879
Total Revenue and Grants	81y	2,882	3,797	4,715	5,316	6,232	6,918	7,966	9,781	12,953	14,823	17,321	19,736	23,545	29,667	35,030
Expenditure	82	3,651	4,009	5,313	6,996	8,243	8,653	10,014	11,893	14,273	16,598	19,628	23,314	29,222	33,213	40,909
Total Financing	80h	769	212	598	1,680	2,011	1,735	2,048	2,112	1,320	1,775	2,307	3,578	5,677	3,546	5,879
Total Net Borrowing	84	995	531	463	1,877	2,138	1,811	2,215	2,056	2,050	1,237	4,153	3,502	3,670	2,467	8,081
Net Domestic	84a	911	653	345	1,628	1,688	1,835	2,456	2,192	2,155	1,077	3,632	3,622	3,363	2,605	8,096
Net Foreign	85a	84	−122	118	249	450	−24	−241	−136	−105	160	521	−120	307	−138	−15
Use of Cash Balances	87	−226	−319	135	−197	−127	−76	−167	56	−730	538	−1,846	76	2,007	1,079	−2,202
Total Debt by Currency	88z	7,052	7,524	7,986	10,094	12,106	13,971	16,249	18,185	19,983	21,726	25,775	29,704	35,161	40,620	48,360
National	88b	6,550	7,164	7,476	9,208	10,781	12,615	15,065	17,251	19,380	20,832	24,447	28,342	32,834	37,866	45,830
Foreign	89b	502	360	510	886	1,325	1,356	1,184	934	603	894	1,328	1,362	2,327	2,754	2,530
National Accounts																*Millions of Rand*
Househ.Cons.Expend.,incl.NPISHs	96f.c	9,503	11,134	13,106	15,167	17,116	18,914	21,086	24,427	30,797	38,086	44,564	51,596	59,705	†74,025	87,607
Government Consumption Expend.	91f.c	1,937	2,219	2,802	3,687	4,465	5,034	5,526	6,329	8,158	9,877	12,361	14,115	17,927	†23,237	28,105
Gross Fixed Capital Formation	93e.c	4,176	4,885	5,945	7,846	9,046	9,312	10,087	12,015	16,040	19,738	22,459	24,498	26,209	†29,099	29,350
Changes in Inventories	93i.c	−184	110	1,066	681	−490	−370	−434	238	2,569	3,807	−2,167	−893	485	†−2,924	−962
Exports of Goods and Services	90c.c	3,987	4,953	6,716	7,480	8,504	10,339	12,681	16,470	22,022	20,688	21,863	22,985	28,015	†40,128	46,003
Imports of Goods and Services (-)	98c.c	3,568	4,406	6,838	8,128	8,795	8,491	9,931	11,969	17,034	21,881	21,953	19,594	25,931	†28,546	32,239
Gross Domestic Product (GDP)	99b.c	15,535	19,218	23,690	26,646	30,020	33,263	38,247	45,772	60,328	71,080	80,531	91,457	107,221	†127,598	149,395
Net Primary Income from Abroad	98.n c	....	....	....	....	....	....	....	....	....	....	....	....	....	†−5,986	−7,010
Gross National Income (GNI)	99a.c	....	....	....	....	....	....	....	....	....	....	....	....	....	†121,612	142,385
Consumption of Fixed Capital	99cf	1,808	2,112	2,569	3,310	4,144	4,793	5,673	6,744	8,023	9,688	11,999	14,216	16,121	†21,003	26,348
GDP Volume 1985 Prices	99b.r	87,599	91,604	97,202	98,850	101,074	100,979	104,023	†107,966	115,114	121,285	120,820	118,589	124,636	127,598	....
GDP Volume 1995 Prices	99b.r														483,441	483,528
GDP Volume (1995=100)	99bv r	29.0	30.3	32.1	32.7	33.4	33.4	34.4	†35.7	38.1	40.1	39.9	39.2	41.2	†88.2	88.2
GDP Deflator (1995=100)	99bi r	9.8	11.6	13.5	14.9	16.4	18.2	20.3	†23.4	28.9	32.3	36.8	42.6	47.5	†26.4	30.9
																Millions:
Population	99z	23.67	24.30	24.92	25.47	26.13	26.68	27.30	27.67	28.28	28.90	29.54	31.93	32.25	33.04	33.83

	1987	1988	1989	1990	1991	1992	1993	1994	1995	1996	1997	1998	1999	2000	2001		
	Year Ending December 31															**Government Finance**	
	−8,593	−6,483	−5,710	−10,457	†−13,987	−26,423	−28,342	−38,690	−23,465	−28,563	−28,129	−19,464	−14,759	−16,428	−9,975	Deficit (−) or Surplus	**80**
	40,048	48,824	65,524	72,614	†77,701	83,464	95,710	111,916	125,470	147,738	162,983	181,749	202,330	211,984	245,952	Total Revenue and Grants	**81y**
	48,641	55,307	71,234	83,071	†91,688	109,887	124,052	150,606	148,935	176,301	191,112	201,213	217,089	228,412	255,927	Expenditure	**82**
	8,593	6,483	5,710	10,457	†13,987	26,423	28,342	38,690	23,465	28,563	28,129	19,465	14,778	16,428	9,975	Total Financing	**80h**
	8,446	9,208	10,292	7,511	†19,466	21,223	31,469	37,928	25,504	24,224	26,507	21,647	13,269	17,790	19,348	Total Net Borrowing	**84**
	8,536	9,256	10,479	7,586	†18,996	20,649	31,632	35,317	24,323	21,596	23,553	21,591	7,651	10,299	6,489	Net Domestic	**84a**
	−90	−48	−187	−75	†470	574	−163	2,611	1,181	2,628	2,954	56	5,618	7,491	12,859	Net Foreign	**85a**
	147	−2,725	−4,582	2,946	†−5,479	5,200	−3,127	762	−2,039	4,339	1,622	−2,182	1,509	−1,362	−9,373	Use of Cash Balances	**87**
	58,924	69,684	91,282	102,360	124,920	147,327	185,538	†239,714	275,489	302,608	†336,133	361,401	391,420	409,363	462,446	Total Debt by Currency	**88z**
	56,657	67,285	89,249	100,404	122,821	144,960	180,542	†231,656	265,879	288,349	†320,981	345,559	371,395	378,245	395,827	National	**88b**
	2,267	2,399	2,033	1,956	2,099	2,367	4,996	8,058	9,610	14,259	15,152	15,842	20,025	31,118	66,619	Foreign	**89b**
	Millions of Rand															**National Accounts**	
	104,483	126,010	149,337	181,872	210,316	237,190	†265,392	299,541	343,037	385,280	431,403	466,552	505,698	558,425	608,614	Househ.Cons.Expend.,incl.NPISHs	**96f. c**
	33,525	38,847	48,264	56,991	65,667	75,257	†85,551	96,503	100,424	120,139	131,903	140,530	147,842	159,970	175,431	Government Consumption Expend.	**91f. c**
	31,168	40,701	50,856	55,485	56,954	58,255	†62,601	73,045	87,042	99,381	113,221	125,877	124,203	132,054	144,169	Gross Fixed Capital Formation	**93e. c**
	−3	3,341	2,092	−5,566	−1,530	−3,319	†2,603	8,013	11,517	6,477	841	−2,634	3,756	9,479	5,009	Changes in Inventories	**93i. c**
	49,164	58,505	66,738	71,698	74,537	79,399	†91,578	106,844	125,867	151,795	168,415	190,189	205,883	253,804	301,841	Exports of Goods and Services	**90c. c**
	35,187	47,027	53,449	54,046	58,018	64,404	†75,917	95,747	121,091	143,340	160,719	181,632	184,032	227,918	264,465	Imports of Goods and Services (−)	**98c. c**
	174,647	209,613	251,676	289,816	331,980	372,225	†426,133	482,120	548,100	618,417	683,730	735,504	802,840	887,795	975,196	Gross Domestic Product (GDP)	**99b. c**
	−6,693	−7,572	−9,310	−11,529	−8,859	−8,401	†−8,700	−8,600	−42,077	−156,717	−59,180	−69,324	−78,348	−22,513	....	Net Primary Income from Abroad	**98.n c**
	167,954	202,041	242,366	278,287	323,121	363,824	†417,433	473,520	505,917	605,038	668,949	717,755	775,988	851,124	....	Gross National Income (GNI)	**99a. c**
	29,823	34,521	40,978	45,990	50,251	54,227	†58,575	64,500	71,827	78,923	87,155	94,781	103,272	112,633	....	Consumption of Fixed Capital	**99cf**
	....	....	....	....	....	....	....	....	....	....	....	....	....	....	....	GDP Volume 1985 Prices	**99b. r**
	493,685	514,421	526,740	525,066	519,720	508,613	†514,887	531,538	548,100	570,855	586,837	591,310	603,841	624,127	638,010	GDP Volume 1995 Prices	**99b. r**
	90.1	93.9	96.1	95.8	94.8	92.8	†93.9	97.0	100.0	104.2	107.1	107.9	110.2	113.9	116.4	GDP Volume (1995=100)	**99bv r**
	35.4	40.7	47.8	55.2	63.9	73.2	†82.8	90.7	100.0	108.3	116.5	124.4	133.0	142.2	152.8	GDP Deflator (1995=100)	**99bi r**
	Midyear Estimates																
	34.63	35.42	36.24	34.01	38.01	38.82	39.63	39.48	41.24	40.34	41.23	42.13	43.05	43.69	44.33	**Population**	**99z**

(See notes in the back of the book.)

Spain

184		1972	1973	1974	1975	1976	1977	1978	1979	1980	1981	1982	1983	1984	1985	1986
Exchange Rates																*Pesetas per SDR through 1998,*
Market Rate	**aa**	69.02	68.70	†68.70	69.98	79.34	98.28	91.34	87.14	101.08	113.43	138.55	164.06	169.97	169.32	161.94
																Pesetas per US Dollar through 1998,
Market Rate	**ae**	63.57	56.95	†56.11	59.77	68.29	80.91	70.11	66.15	79.25	97.45	125.60	156.70	173.40	154.15	132.40
Market Rate	**rf**	64.27	58.26	57.69	57.41	66.90	75.96	76.67	67.13	71.70	92.32	109.86	143.43	160.76	170.04	140.05
																Pesetas per ECU:
ECU Rate	**ea**	....	....	....	....	....	....	....	....	....	....	....	....	....	....	....
ECU Rate	**eb**	....	....	....	....	....	....	....	....	99.6098	102.6777	107.4669	127.3924	126.5083	129.3040	137.4546
																Index Numbers (1995=100):
Market Rate	**ahx**	193.9	214.1	216.0	216.8	186.5	165.6	163.0	185.7	174.2	135.5	114.0	87.3	77.7	73.4	89.2
Nominal Effective Exchange Rate	**neu**	206.3	206.9	215.5	207.5	196.6	173.7	155.5	168.2	156.5	148.0	141.7	119.8	119.7	117.6	113.0
Real Effective Exchange Rate	**reu**	....	....	....	78.9	84.9	89.9	98.9	115.4	†107.7	104.8	103.9	89.8	92.6	91.9	88.9
Fund Position																*Millions of SDRs:*
Quota	**2f.s**	395	395	395	395	395	395	557	557	836	836	836	1,286	1,286	1,286	1,286
SDRs	**1b.s**	129	129	134	121	91	48	103	206	231	319	186	65	155	254	353
Reserve Position in the Fund	**1c.s**	104	104	121	—	—	—	136	133	206	206	206	322	363	369	423
of which: Outstg.Fund Borrowing	**2c**	—	—	—	—	—	—	—	—	—	—	—	—	—	—	—
Total Fund Cred.&Loans Outstg.	**2tl**	—	—	—	496	572	572	615	205	205	142	5	—	—	—	—
International Liquidity																*Millions of US Dollars Unless Otherwise Indicated:*
Total Res.Min.Gold (Eurosys.Def)	**1l.d**	4,473	6,170	5,874	5,506	4,704	5,977	10,112	13,224	11,863	10,805	7,655	7,402	11,955	11,175	14,755
SDRs	**1b.d**	140	155	164	142	105	59	134	272	294	371	205	68	151	280	432
Reserve Position in the Fund	**1c.d**	113	125	148	—	—	—	178	176	262	239	227	337	356	405	518
Foreign Exchange	**1d.d**	4,221	5,889	5,562	5,364	4,599	5,918	9,801	12,777	11,307	10,195	7,223	6,997	11,448	10,490	13,805
o/w: Fin.Deriv.Rel.to Reserves	**1ddd**	....	....	....	....	....	....	....	....	....	....	....	....	....	....	....
Other Reserve Assets	**1e.d**	....	....	....	....	....	....	....	....	....	....	....	....	....	....	....
Gold (Million Fine Troy Ounces)	**1ad**	14.23	14.27	14.27	14.27	14.27	14.44	14.52	14.61	14.61	14.61	14.61	14.61	14.63	14.65	14.82
Gold (Eurosystem Valuation)	**1and**	541	602	602	602	602	609	613	617	617	4,353	3,666	3,827	3,832	3,722	3,785
Memo: Euro Cl. on Non-EA Res.	**1dgd**	....	....	....	....	....	....	....	....	....	....	....	....	....	....	....
Non-Euro Cl. on EA Res.	**1dhd**	....	....	....	....	....	....	....	....	....	....	....	....	....	....	....
Mon. Auth.: Other Foreign Assets	**3..d**	....	....	....	....	....	....	....	....	....	....	....	....	....	....	....
Foreign Liabilities	**4..d**	9	4	8	14	37	9	8	7	6	11	12	4	7	19	418
Banking Insts.: Foreign Assets	**7a.d**	2,514	3,774	3,033	3,242	3,644	4,583	7,228	10,535	12,790	14,824	†17,362	15,712	17,524	20,039	23,817
Foreign Liab.	**7b.d**	3,197	4,766	5,352	6,366	8,300	10,842	14,813	20,568	24,499	27,871	†21,534	19,417	21,209	20,939	25,409
Monetary Authorities																*Billions of Pesetas through 1998;*
Fgn. Assets (Cl.on Non-EA Ctys)	**11**	320	399	359	354	329	486	777	939	906	1,182	930	†1,245	2,096	1,696	†1,996
Claims on General Government	**12a.u**	....	....	....	....	....	....	....	....	....	....	....	....	....	....	....
o/w: Claims on Gen.Govt.in Cty	**12a**	97	120	202	296	321	458	570	833	1,227	1,821	2,687	†3,616	2,723	3,295	†2,498
Claims on Banking Institutions	**12e.u**	....	....	....	....	....	....	....	....	....	....	....	....	....	....	....
o/w: Claims on Bank.Inst.in Cty	**12e**	72	73	154	180	367	360	230	325	315	384	531	†752	1,053	975	†1,426
Claims on Other Resident Sectors	**12d.u**	....	....	....	....	....	....	....	....	....	....	....	....	....	....	....
o/w: Cl. on Oth.Res.Sect.in Cty	**12d**	36	13	79	70	108	149	202	238	242	254	300	320	313	309	†309
Currency Issued	**14a**	338	398	461	542	636	806	987	1,095	1,256	1,413	1,625	†1,688	1,867	2,083	†2,402
Liabilities to Banking Insts	**14c.u**	....	....	....	....	....	....	....	....	....	....	....	....	....	....	....
o/w: Liabs to Bank.Inst.in Cty	**14c**	118	143	202	239	261	286	377	736	851	953	1,241	†3,638	3,673	3,645	†3,804
Demand Dep. of Other Res.Sect.	**14d.u**	....	....	....	....	....	....	....	....	....	....	....	....	....	....	....
o/w: D.Dep.of Oth.Res.Sect.in Cty	**14d**	....	....	....	....	....	....	....	....	....	....	....	87	87	131	†158
Other Dep. of Other Res.Sect.	**15..u**	....	....	....	....	....	....	....	....	....	....	....	....	....	....	....
o/w: O.Dep.of Oth.Res.Sect.in Cty	**15**	....	....	....	....	....	....	....	....	....	....	....	....	....	....	....
Money Market Instruments	**16m.u**	....	....	....	....	....	....	....	....	....	....	....	....	....	....	....
o/w: MMI Held by Resid.of Cty	**16m**	....	....	....	....	....	....	....	....	....	....	....	....	....	....	49
Bonds (Debt Securities)	**16n.u**	....	....	....	....	....	....	....	....	....	....	....	....	....	....	....
o/w: Bonds Held by Resid.of Cty	**16n**	....	....	....	....	....	....	....	....	....	....	....	....	....	....	....
Foreign Liab. (to Non-EA Ctys)	**16c**	4	2	3	262	353	420	418	135	156	126	16	4	9	21	†55
Central Government Deposits	**16d.u**	....	....	....	....	....	....	....	....	....	....	....	....	....	....	....
o/w: Cent.Govt.Dep. in Cty	**16d**	34	44	52	45	45	90	74	109	98	118	203	†273	338	216	†101
Capital Accounts	**17a**	....	....	....	....	....	....	....	....	....	....	....	441	527	469	†334
Other Items (Net)	**17r**	31	18	74	–188	–170	–149	–77	259	328	1,031	1,363	†–199	–317	–291	†–673
Memo: Net Claims on Eurosystem	**12e.s**	....	....	....	....	....	....	....	....	....	....	....	....	....	....	....
Currency Put into Circ.	**14m**	....	....	....	....	....	....	....	....	....	....	....	....	....	....	....
Banking Institutions																*Billions of Pesetas through 1998;*
Claims on Monetary Authorities	**20**	101	121	178	201	226	244	289	532	629	694	893	†3,699	3,853	3,916	†3,844
Claims on Bk.Inst.in Oth.EA Ctys	**20b.u**	....	....	....	....	....	....	....	....	....	....	....	....	....	....	....
Fgn. Assets (Cl.on Non-EA Ctys)	**21**	162	219	170	194	249	371	507	697	1,014	1,445	2,103	†2,462	3,039	3,089	†3,152
Claims on General Government	**22a.u**	....	....	....	....	....	....	....	....	....	....	....	....	....	....	....
o/w: Claims on Gen.Govt.in Cty	**22a**	549	605	638	720	897	968	1,251	1,560	1,854	2,492	3,163	†2,602	6,084	7,797	†9,858
Claims on Other Resident Sectors	**22d.u**	....	....	....	....	....	....	....	....	....	....	....	....	....	....	....
o/w: Cl. on Oth.Res.Sect.in Cty	**22d**	2,571	3,270	4,107	5,055	6,240	7,609	8,682	10,054	11,891	13,979	16,121	†17,481	18,120	19,568	†22,245
Demand Deposits	**24..u**	....	....	....	....	....	....	....	....	....	....	....	....	....	....	....
o/w: D.Dep.of Oth.Res.Sect.in Cty	**24**	801	985	1,163	1,398	1,690	1,996	2,205	2,438	2,739	3,086	3,460	†3,428	3,718	4,262	†5,001
Other Deposits	**25..u**	....	....	....	....	....	....	....	....	....	....	....	....	....	....	....
o/w: O.Dep.of Oth.Res.Sect.in Cty	**25**	1,847	2,305	2,771	3,301	3,889	4,620	5,641	6,954	8,234	9,650	11,425	†10,806	11,137	12,279	†16,466
Money Market Instruments	**26m.u**	....	....	....	....	....	....	....	....	....	....	....	....	....	....	....
o/w: MMI Held by Resid.of Cty	**26m**	....	....	....	....	....	....	....	....	....	....	....	....	....	....	....
Bonds (Debt Securities)	**26n.u**	....	....	....	....	....	....	....	....	....	....	....	....	....	....	....
o/w: Bonds Held by Resid.of Cty	**26n**	81	135	187	241	285	315	329	336	390	453	550	†3,601	5,738	6,675	†1,796
Foreign Liab. (to Non-EA Ctys)	**26c**	206	277	300	381	567	877	1,039	1,361	1,942	2,716	3,775	†3,352	3,986	3,487	†3,378
Central Government Deposits	**26d.u**	....	....	....	....	....	....	....	....	....	....	....	....	....	....	....
o/w: Cent.Govt.Dep. in Cty	**26d**	36	45	53	69	75	95	92	121	166	209	344	†764	983	1,139	†1,169
Credit from Monetary Authorities	**26g**	72	73	148	180	368	359	236	301	306	392	554	†758	1,058	984	†1,426
Liab. to Bk.Inst.in Oth. EA Ctys	**26h.u**	....	....	....	....	....	....	....	....	....	....	....	....	....	....	....
Capital Accounts	**27a**	236	305	392	490	589	669	800	1,085	1,230	1,531	1,628	†2,140	2,623	3,161	†3,959
Other Items (Net)	**27r**	103	91	80	111	149	260	387	247	381	573	601	†1,431	1,868	2,359	†5,905
Banking Survey (Nat'l Residency)																*Billions of Pesetas through 1998;*
Foreign Assets (Net)	**31n**	272	340	226	–94	–342	–440	–173	140	–177	–215	–758	†351	1,140	1,277	†1,715
Domestic Credit	**32**	3,183	3,919	4,920	6,026	7,446	9,000	10,539	12,455	14,949	18,220	21,724	†22,981	25,919	29,614	†33,640
Claims on General Govt. (Net)	**32an**	576	636	734	901	1,098	1,242	1,655	2,163	2,816	3,986	5,303	†5,180	7,486	9,737	†11,086
Claims on Other Resident Sectors	**32d**	2,607	3,283	4,186	5,125	6,348	7,758	8,884	10,292	12,133	14,233	16,421	†17,801	18,433	19,877	†22,554
Currency Issued	**34a.n**	338	398	461	542	636	806	987	1,095	1,256	1,413	1,625	†1,688	1,867	2,083	†2,402
Demand Deposits	**34b.n**	801	985	1,163	1,398	1,690	1,996	2,205	2,438	2,739	3,086	3,460	†3,515	3,805	4,394	†5,158
Other Deposits	**35..n**	1,847	2,305	2,771	3,301	3,889	4,620	5,641	6,954	8,234	9,650	11,425	†10,806	11,137	12,279	†16,466
Money Market Instruments	**36m**	....	....	....	....	....	....	....	....	....	....	....	....	....	....	49
Bonds (Debt Securities)	**36n**	81	136	187	242	285	316	329	336	390	453	550	†3,601	5,738	6,675	†1,796
o/w: Bonds Over Two Years	**36na**	....	....	....	....	....	....	....	....	....	....	....	....	....	....	....
Capital Accounts	**37a**	236	305	392	490	589	669	800	1,085	1,230	1,531	1,628	†2,582	3,150	3,630	†4,293
Other Items (Net)	**37r**	152	131	172	–40	15	153	404	686	922	1,871	2,335	†1,177	1,377	1,806	†5,191

1987	1988	1989	1990	1991	1992	1993	1994	1995	1996	1997	1998	1999	2000	2001		
Euros per SDR Thereafter: End of Period															**Exchange Rates**	
154.63	152.67	144.19	137.87	138.31	157.61	195.34	192.32	180.47	188.77	204.68	200.79	1.3662	1.4002	1.4260	Market Rate	aa
Euros per US Dollar Thereafter: End of Period (ae) Period Average (rf)																
109.00	113.45	109.72	96.91	96.69	114.62	142.21	131.74	121.41	131.28	151.70	142.61	.9954	1.0747	1.1347	Market Rate	ae
123.48	116.49	118.38	101.93	103.91	102.38	127.26	133.96	124.69	126.66	146.41	149.40	.9386	1.0854	1.1175	Market Rate	rf
End of Period (ea) Period Average (eb)																
140.6100	132.0000	130.3000	131.0000	129.3690	138.3730	159.2800	161.5520	155.5610	162.6500	167.3270	166.3860	....	....	....	ECU Rate	ea
142.2559	137.5998	130.3166	129.6826	128.5632	132.2572	148.6617	158.4871	161.1758	158.6182	165.3915	167.4876	....	....	....	ECU Rate	eb
Period Averages																
101.2	107.1	105.4	122.6	120.3	122.1	98.4	93.1	100.0	98.4	85.2	83.5	....	....	....	Market Rate	ahx
111.4	115.2	120.9	124.3	124.6	121.7	108.0	100.8	100.0	100.6	96.3	95.8	94.4	91.8	92.2	Nominal Effective Exchange Rate	neu
89.7	93.3	100.6	106.4	110.3	115.4	107.5	100.9	100.0	102.6	100.1	102.0	102.3	101.1	103.4	Real Effective Exchange Rate	reu
End of Period															**Fund Position**	
1,286	1,286	1,286	1,286	1,286	1,935	1,935	1,935	1,935	1,935	1,935	1,935	3,049	3,049	3,049	Quota	2f.s
420	457	523	489	319	134	157	174	277	314	351	408	190	223	279	SDRs	1b.s
554	786	930	797	749	832	751	760	1,065	1,110	1,409	1,558	1,111	908	1,055	Reserve Position in the Fund	1c.s
—	—	—	—	—	—	—	—	—	—	—	62	—	—	—	*of which:* Outstg.Fund Borrowing	2c
—	—	—	—	—	—	—	—	—	—	—	—	—	—	—	Total Fund Cred.&Loans Outstg.	2tl
End of Period															**International Liquidity**	
30,669	37,074	41,467	51,228	65,822	45,504	41,045	41,546	34,485	57,927	68,398	55,258	†33,115	30,989	29,582	Total Res.Min.Gold (Eurosys.Def)	1l.d
596	615	687	696	456	184	216	255	411	451	474	575	260	290	351	SDRs	1b.d
785	1,058	1,222	1,134	1,071	1,144	1,031	1,109	1,583	1,597	1,902	2,193	1,525	1,182	1,326	Reserve Position in the Fund	1c.d
29,287	35,401	39,558	49,398	64,295	44,176	39,798	40,182	32,491	55,879	66,023	52,490	31,329	29,516	27,905	Foreign Exchange	1d.d
....	....	....	....	....	....	....	....	....	....	....	....	....	....	....	*o/w:* Fin.Deriv.Rel.to Reserves	1ddd
....	....	....	....	....	....	....	....	....	....	....	....	—	—	—	Other Reserve Assets	1e.d
11.92	14.04	15.72	15.61	15.62	15.62	15.62	15.62	15.63	15.63	15.63	19.54	16.83	16.83	16.83	Gold (Million Fine Troy Ounces)	1ad
3,767	4,766	5,419	4,777	4,498	4,217	4,217	4,217	4,221	4,221	4,139	5,617	4,885	4,619	4,653	Gold (Eurosystem Valuation)	1and
....	....	....	....	....	....	....	....	....	....	....	....	4,134	36	—	Memo: Euro Cl. on Non-EA Res.	1dgd
....	....	....	....	....	....	....	....	....	....	....	....	—	—	—	Non-Euro Cl. on EA Res.	1dhd
....	....	....	....	....	....	....	....	....	....	....	....	....	....	....	Mon. Auth.: Other Foreign Assets	3..d
450	817	798	523	483	457	462	515	551	983	454	480	†1,004	445	317	Foreign Liabilities	4..d
25,728	24,571	27,511	39,107	46,642	68,542	117,311	110,693	146,061	129,727	111,176	126,792	†66,435	82,631	87,327	Banking Insts.: Foreign Assets	7a.d
33,186	36,998	43,627	63,986	73,724	81,501	87,093	100,658	109,245	123,359	135,020	179,175	†125,417	147,108	157,263	Foreign Liab.	7b.d
Billions of Euros Beginning 1999: End of Period															**Monetary Authorities**	
3,643	4,609	4,938	5,348	6,731	5,604	6,152	5,796	4,566	7,960	10,708	8,751	41.49	37.54	38.60	Fgn. Assets (Cl.on Non-EA Ctys)	11
....	....	....	....	....	....	....	....	....	....	....	....	15.17	14.45	13.95	Claims on General Government	12a.u
2,865	2,917	2,740	2,459	3,011	1,881	–219	2,981	3,074	3,056	2,984	3,023	15.17	14.45	13.95	*o/w:* Claims on Gen.Govt.in Cty	12a
....	....	....	....	....	....	....	....	....	....	....	....	60.01	61.42	39.71	Claims on Banking Institutions	12e.u
1,384	958	2,128	1,595	1,545	4,296	6,525	5,949	6,641	4,439	2,267	4,471	24.18	16.14	10.55	*o/w:* Claims on Bank.Inst.in Cty	12e
....	....	....	....	....	....	....	....	....	....	....	....	—	—	—	Claims on Other Resident Sectors	12d.u
322	343	74	56	47	36	22	21	20	21	21	22	—	—	—	*o/w:* Cl. on Oth.Res.Sect.in Cty	12d
2,736	3,241	3,836	4,534	5,608	6,025	6,509	7,165	7,535	7,942	8,378	8,437	61.35	59.79	48.75	Currency Issued	14a
....	....	....	....	....	....	....	....	....	....	....	....	15.94	8.39	14.73	Liabilities to Banking Insts	14c.u
4,219	4,324	5,500	1,792	2,110	1,728	1,283	1,430	1,394	1,310	1,484	1,788	12.49	8.39	14.73	*o/w:* Liabs to Bank.Inst.in Cty	14c
....	....	....	....	....	....	....	....	....	....	....	....	5.22	7.34	10.52	Demand Dep. of Other Res.Sect.	14d.u
183	174	135	128	102	106	131	132	193	175	207	190	5.22	7.34	10.52	*o/w:* D.Dep.of Oth.Res.Sect.in Cty	14d
....	....	....	....	....	....	....	....	....	....	....	....	—	—	—	Other Dep. of Other Res.Sect.	15..u
....	....	....	....	....	....	....	....	....	....	....	....	—	—	—	*o/w:* O.Dep.of Oth.Res.Sect.in Cty	15
....	....	....	....	....	....	....	....	....	....	....	....	3.30	—	—	Money Market Instruments	16m.u
1,054	1,007	654	3,388	3,867	3,314	3,067	2,860	2,334	1,947	1,613	1,219	....	....	....	*o/w:* MMI Held by Resid.of Cty	16m
....	....	....	....	....	....	....	....	....	....	....	....	—	—	—	Bonds (Debt Securities)	16n.u
....	....	....	....	....	....	....	....	....	....	....	....	....	....	....	*o/w:* Bonds Held by Resid.of Cty	16n
49	93	88	51	47	52	66	68	67	129	69	69	1.00	.48	.36	Foreign Liab. (to Non-EA Ctys)	16c
....	....	....	....	....	....	....	....	....	....	....	....	16.87	22.91	2.79	Central Government Deposits	16d.u
151	187	186	149	139	95	193	2,058	1,752	2,742	1,890	2,120	16.87	22.91	2.79	*o/w:* Cent.Govt.Dep. in Cty	16d
478	452	417	392	690	1,506	2,207	1,166	1,267	1,594	2,752	2,870	16.01	17.25	17.51	Capital Accounts	17a
–656	–645	–936	–976	–1,229	–1,010	–975	–132	–243	–363	–412	–426	–3.01	–2.73	–2.39	Other Items (Net)	17r
....	....	....	....	....	....	....	....	....	....	....	....	32.38	45.28	29.16	*Memo: Net Claims on Eurosystem*	12e.s
....	....	....	....	....	....	....	....	....	....	....	....	....	....	....	*Currency Put into Circ.*	14m
Billions of Euros Beginning 1999: End of Period															**Banking Institutions**	
5,243	5,294	6,047	5,163	5,912	5,043	4,348	4,328	3,725	3,262	3,093	2,992	15.79	8.39	14.73	Claims on Monetary Authorities	20
....	....	....	....	....	....	....	....	....	....	....	....	50.08	53.56	53.52	Claims on Bk.Inst.in Oth.EA Ctys	20b.u
2,804	2,800	3,019	3,800	4,517	7,868	16,690	14,565	17,737	17,057	16,909	18,155	66.13	88.80	99.09	Fgn. Assets (Cl.on Non-EA Ctys)	21
....	....	....	....	....	....	....	....	....	....	....	....	146.00	129.59	151.68	Claims on General Government	22a.u
10,738	10,870	11,979	14,159	13,061	14,585	16,114	20,853	22,358	24,083	22,400	21,258	136.21	124.10	133.84	*o/w:* Claims on Gen.Govt.in Cty	22a
....	....	....	....	....	....	....	....	....	....	....	....	529.64	631.12	712.26	Claims on Other Resident Sectors	22d.u
26,088	31,863	37,839	41,647	46,568	49,059	49,600	50,345	53,764	57,682	65,592	76,417	519.57	615.88	688.45	*o/w:* Cl. on Oth.Res.Sect.in Cty	22d
....	....	....	....	....	....	....	....	....	....	....	....	127.47	140.23	159.67	Demand Deposits	24..u
5,864	7,037	7,980	9,595	10,270	9,584	9,657	10,159	10,291	11,144	13,391	16,768	125.54	137.52	157.23	*o/w:* D.Dep.of Oth.Res.Sect.in Cty	24
....	....	....	....	....	....	....	....	....	....	....	....	319.89	368.97	408.74	Other Deposits	25..u
17,267	18,575	20,451	23,000	26,219	28,416	32,208	34,492	37,397	37,579	35,679	36,346	310.68	359.38	396.10	*o/w:* O.Dep.of Oth.Res.Sect.in Cty	25
....	....	....	....	....	....	....	....	....	....	....	....	42.59	33.34	43.78	Money Market Instruments	26m.u
....	....	....	....	....	....	....	....	....	....	....	....	....	....	....	*o/w:* MMI Held by Resid.of Cty	26m
....	....	....	....	....	....	....	....	....	....	....	....	53.63	51.91	65.19	Bonds (Debt Securities)	26n.u
1,547	1,511	1,223	1,113	1,422	1,449	1,906	2,214	2,316	2,394	2,693	3,025	....	....	....	*o/w:* Bonds Held by Resid.of Cty	26n
3,634	4,258	4,904	6,468	7,419	9,497	12,459	13,303	13,316	16,436	20,741	25,889	124.84	158.10	178.44	Foreign Liab. (to Non-EA Ctys)	26c
....	....	....	....	....	....	....	....	....	....	....	....	5.65	5.54	19.06	Central Government Deposits	26d.u
1,268	1,581	2,611	2,544	2,749	2,890	2,866	2,706	2,954	3,063	3,352	3,882	5.62	5.52	19.06	*o/w:* Cent.Govt.Dep. in Cty	26d
1,384	957	2,112	1,590	1,572	4,282	6,525	6,063	6,643	4,447	2,265	4,450	24.18	16.14	10.55	Credit from Monetary Authorities	26g
....	....	....	....	....	....	....	....	....	....	....	....	54.22	64.81	63.22	Liab. to Bk.Inst.in Oth. EA Ctys	26h.u
4,789	6,020	6,963	7,851	9,472	9,424	10,234	10,709	10,807	11,261	12,026	12,668	80.53	98.56	108.50	Capital Accounts	27a
9,119	10,888	12,641	12,608	10,935	11,015	10,897	10,445	13,860	15,761	17,847	15,794	–25.36	–26.13	–25.88	Other Items (Net)	27r
Billions of Euros Beginning 1999: End of Period															**Banking Survey (Nat'l Residency)**	
2,764	3,059	2,965	2,628	3,782	3,923	10,317	6,990	8,921	8,452	6,808	949	22.23	14.77	9.50	Foreign Assets (Net)	31n
38,593	44,225	49,835	55,628	59,799	62,576	62,460	69,435	74,510	79,037	85,755	94,718	648.46	726.00	814.39	Domestic Credit	32
12,183	12,019	11,921	13,925	13,184	13,481	12,837	19,069	20,726	21,334	20,142	18,279	128.89	110.12	125.94	Claims on General Govt. (Net)	32an
26,409	32,206	37,913	41,703	46,615	49,095	49,622	50,366	53,784	57,703	65,613	76,439	519.57	615.88	688.45	Claims on Other Resident Sectors	32d
2,736	3,241	3,836	4,534	5,608	6,025	6,509	7,165	7,535	7,942	8,378	8,437	61.35	59.79	48.75	Currency Issued	34a.n
6,048	7,210	8,115	9,723	10,372	9,690	9,788	10,291	10,484	11,319	13,598	16,959	130.76	144.86	167.74	Demand Deposits	34b.n
17,267	18,575	20,451	23,000	26,219	28,416	32,208	34,492	37,397	37,579	35,679	36,346	310.68	359.38	396.10	Other Deposits	35..n
1,054	1,007	654	3,388	3,867	3,314	3,067	2,860	2,334	1,947	1,613	1,219	45.89	33.34	43.78	Money Market Instruments	36m
1,547	1,511	1,223	1,113	1,422	1,449	1,906	2,214	2,316	2,394	2,693	3,025	53.63	51.91	65.19	Bonds (Debt Securities)	36n
....	....	....	....	....	....	....	....	....	....	....	....	37.49	39.77	49.28	*o/w:* Bonds Over Two Years	36na
5,267	6,472	7,380	8,243	10,162	10,930	12,441	11,875	12,074	12,855	14,778	15,538	96.54	115.81	126.01	Capital Accounts	37a
7,438	9,272	11,143	8,257	5,931	6,675	6,857	7,529	11,289	13,454	15,824	14,143	–28.15	–24.32	–23.68	Other Items (Net)	37r

Spain

		1972	1973	1974	1975	1976	1977	1978	1979	1980	1981	1982	1983	1984	1985	1986
Banking Survey (EA-Wide Residency)																*Billions of Euros:*
Foreign Assets (Net)	31n.*u*	....	....	....	....	....	....	....	....	....	....	....	....	....	....	....
Domestic Credit	32..*u*	....	....	....	....	....	....	....	....	....	....	....	....	....	....	....
Claims on General Govt. (Net)	32an*u*	....	....	....	....	....	....	....	....	....	....	....	....	....	....	....
Claims on Other Resident Sect.	32d.*u*	....	....	....	....	....	....	....	....	....	....	....	....	....	....	....
Currency Issued	34a.*u*	....	....	....	....	....	....	....	....	....	....	....	....	....	....	....
Demand Deposits	34b.*u*	....	....	....	....	....	....	....	....	....	....	....	....	....	....	....
Other Deposits	35..*u*	....	....	....	....	....	....	....	....	....	....	....	....	....	....	....
o/w: Other Dep. Over Two Yrs	35ab*u*	....	....	....	....	....	....	....	....	....	....	....	....	....	....	....
Money Market Instruments	36m.*u*	....	....	....	....	....	....	....	....	....	....	....	....	....	....	....
Bonds (Debt Securities)	36n.*u*	....	....	....	....	....	....	....	....	....	....	....	....	....	....	....
o/w: Bonds Over Two Years	36na*u*	....	....	....	....	....	....	....	....	....	....	....	....	....	....	....
Capital Accounts	37a	....	....	....	....	....	....	....	....	....	....	....	....	....	....	....
Other Items (Net)	37r.*u*	....	....	....	....	....	....	....	....	....	....	....	....	....	....	....
Money (National Definitions)																*Billions of Pesetas:*
M1	59ma	1,171.6	1,444.6	1,696.5	2,019.7	2,407.7	2,864.6	3,326.7	3,655.4	4,103.2	4,626.0	5,003.4	5,347.5	5,788.4	6,535.5	7,450.2
M2	59mb	2,146.8	2,595.2	2,996.6	3,575.9	4,320.2	5,118.9	5,989.6	6,672.3	7,438.2	8,307.5	9,034.8	9,830.7	10,565.7	11,835.6	13,425.5
M3	59mc	3,120.4	3,895.0	4,669.3	5,554.0	6,607.7	7,857.8	9,377.7	11,105.3	12,933.4	15,012.5	17,304.1	19,794.6	22,801.6	25,558.1	28,381.5
ALP	59md	3,120.4	3,895.0	4,669.3	5,554.0	6,607.8	7,857.9	9,389.3	11,130.1	13,014.2	15,210.5	17,794.9	20,535.2	23,619.1	26,733.7	30,345.2
Interest Rates																*Percent Per Annum*
Bank of Spain Rate(End of Period)	60	5.00	6.00	7.00	7.00	7.00	†8.03	9.02	7.98	10.90	10.51	18.40	21.40	12.50	10.50	11.84
Money Market Rate	60b			9.61	6.70	9.97	13.12	20.77	13.13	15.46	15.89	17.17	19.45	12.60	11.61	11.49
Treasury Bill Rate	60c	....	....	....	....	....	....	14.41	15.70	15.70	15.80	15.70	19.80	13.43	10.90	8.63
Deposit Rate	60l	....	....	....	....	....	....	....	9.61	13.05	11.41	12.26	12.31	12.30	10.53	9.05
Lending Rate	60p	....	....	....	....	....	....	14.96	15.77	16.85	15.26	14.98	15.00	16.58	13.52	12.19
Government Bond Yield	61	....	....	....	....	....	....	13.31	15.96	15.81	15.99	16.91	16.52	13.37	11.36
Prices, Production, Labor																*Index Numbers (1995=100):*
Share Prices	62	33.4	42.2	42.8	36.7	31.7	21.8	17.6	15.1	14.1	18.0	16.5	16.7	22.8	28.8	†58.7
Industrial Prices	63	14.1	15.5	†18.3	†20.0	22.7	27.3	31.7	36.3	42.7	49.4	55.5	63.3	71.0	76.6	77.3
Consumer Prices	64	9.0	10.1	11.6	13.6	16.0	19.9	23.9	27.6	31.9	36.6	41.8	46.9	52.2	56.8	61.8
Harmonized CPI	64h															
Wages	65	4.4	5.3	6.7	8.6	11.2	14.6	18.4	†22.6	26.8	†30.2	35.1	40.3	45.1	49.6	55.0
Industrial Production	66..*c*	61.3	68.2	73.3	†70.0	73.4	77.4	79.2	80.5	80.5	79.9	78.9	81.1	81.8	83.4	86.0
Total Employment	67	104.9	103.9	105.4	103.9	†104.2	103.2	101.2	98.8	†94.7	91.5	90.4	89.6	88.6	87.8	92.3
																Number in Thousands:
Labor Force	67d														....	....
Employment	67e														11,026	10,881
Unemployment	67c													2,475	2,642	2,933
Unemployment Rate (%)	67r													18.4	19.5	21.2
International Transactions																*Billions of Pesetas through 1998;*
Exports	70	245.3	302.5	408.6	441.5	583.5	775.3	1,001.4	1,221.2	1,493.2	1,888.4	2,258.0	2,838.6	3,778.1	4,099.2	3,801.8
Imports, c.i.f.	71	438.8	561.6	889.0	932.2	1,170.4	1,350.6	1,431.5	1,704.1	2,450.7	2,970.4	3,465.6	4,176.5	4,629.0	5,073.2	4,890.8
																1995=100
Volume of Exports (1990=100)	72	50.9	58.7	62.8	64.8	†74.4	83.8	93.7	104.2	109.9	†52.8	57.2	62.3	74.1	76.0	74.0
Volume of Imports (1990=100)	73	42.2	47.6	49.1	48.7	†53.8	50.3	48.5	54.2	58.2	†41.5	41.8	44.0	40.9	44.1	52.5
Unit Value of Exports	74	17.0	19.3	23.7	†25.5	26.9	31.7	35.5	38.9	46.3	51.2	57.2	66.8	75.2	80.4	77.3
Unit Value of Imports	75	16.4	18.7	26.7	†28.6	31.6	37.5	41.1	42.2	57.4	77.2	86.5	105.9	118.4	120.1	95.5
Export Prices (1975=100)	76	66.6	78.3	85.9	100.0	116.5	135.9	156.1	179.6	....	....	....	....	....	....	....
Balance of Payments																*Millions of US Dollars:*
Current Account, n.i.e.	78al*d*	....	....	....	−3,893	−4,622	−2,455	1,251	757	−5,580	−5,363	−4,548	−3,013	1,778	2,785	3,914
Goods: Exports f.o.b.	78aa*d*				7,821	9,015	10,601	13,491	18,357	20,547	20,974	21,288	20,794	23,737	24,851	27,755
Goods: Imports f.o.b.	78ab*d*				−15,207	−16,299	−16,736	−17,555	−24,041	−32,272	−31,086	−30,542	−28,601	−28,380	−29,611	−34,953
Trade Balance	78ac*d*				−7,386	−7,284	−6,135	−4,064	−5,684	−11,725	−10,113	−9,254	−7,806	−4,643	−4,759	−7,197
Services: Credit	78ad*d*				5,434	5,105	6,152	8,195	10,285	11,593	11,331	11,542	11,365	12,325	12,723	17,836
Services: Debit	78ae*d*				−2,539	−2,807	−2,895	−3,184	−4,284	−5,732	−5,714	−5,953	−5,136	−4,502	−4,551	−5,983
Balance on Goods & Services	78af*d*				−4,491	−4,986	−2,879	947	317	−5,864	−4,496	−3,665	−1,577	3,180	3,412	4,655
Income: Credit	78ag*d*				597	425	449	758	1,348	1,723	2,027	1,936	1,325	1,489	1,817	1,666
Income: Debit	78ah*d*				−769	−875	−1,111	−1,730	−2,324	−3,085	−4,210	−4,095	−3,658	−3,746	−3,505	−3,488
Balance on Gds, Serv. & Inc.	78ai*d*				−4,662	−5,437	−3,541	−25	−658	−7,226	−6,680	−5,825	−3,910	923	1,724	2,833
Current Transfers, n.i.e.: Credit	78aj*d*				1,068	1,145	1,228	1,487	1,745	1,956	1,596	1,503	1,324	1,281	1,722	2,783
Current Transfers: Debit	78ak*d*				−299	−330	−142	−211	−330	−310	−279	−226	−427	−426	−660	−1,702
Capital Account, n.i.e.	78bc*d*				379	331	323	383	371	407	374	303	268	240	65	51
Capital Account, n.i.e.: Credit	78ba*d*				379	331	323	383	373	411	382	312	278	253	78	71
Capital Account: Debit	78bb*d*				—	—	—	—	−1	−4	−8	−9	−10	−13	−13	−20
Financial Account, n.i.e.	78bj*d*				2,638	2,732	4,432	2,144	4,672	5,247	5,996	2,334	4,005	4,922	−3,217	−1,641
Direct Investment Abroad	78bd*d*				−170	−193	−115	−102	−133	−311	−271	−511	−243	−248	−250	−378
Dir. Invest. in Rep. Econ., n.i.e.	78be*d*				683	478	608	1,178	1,397	1,493	1,707	1,783	1,622	1,772	1,968	3,451
Portfolio Investment Assets	78bf*d*				−17	−13	−1	−4	−16	−14	−12	−81	−6	−175	−259	−469
Equity Securities	78bk*d*				−17	−13	−1	−4	−16	−14	−12	−81	−6	−175	−259	−469
Debt Securities	78bl*d*				—	—	—	—	—	—	—	—	—	—	—	—
Portfolio Investment Liab., n.i.e.	78bg*d*				−70	−85	9	77	102	14	115	13	48	229	491	1,697
Equity Securities	78bm*d*				−70	−85	9	44	99	14	115	13	48	229	488	1,682
Debt Securities	78bn*d*				—	—	—	33	3	—	—	—	—	—	3	15
Financial Derivatives Assets	78bw*d*				....	....	....	....	....	....	....	....	....	....	....	....
Financial Derivatives Liabilities	78bx*d*				....	....	....	....	....	....	....	....	....	....	....	....
Other Investment Assets	78bh*d*				−341	−553	−363	−1,046	−832	−765	−787	−2,151	−388	−616	−1,391	−322
Monetary Authorities	78bo*d*				−22	−17	70	−25	9	−39	46	63	—	—	—	—
General Government	78bp*d*				−15	−66	−5	−195	36	26	−25	−162	−76	−152	−263	−326
Banks	78bq*d*				−5	1	−60	19	−116	95	−24	−430	−134	−87	−495	−179
Other Sectors	78br*d*				−300	−471	−368	−846	−761	−847	−784	−1,622	−177	−377	−633	184
Other Investment Liab., n.i.e.	78bi*d*				2,554	3,099	4,295	2,041	4,154	4,830	5,244	3,281	2,972	3,961	−3,776	−5,620
Monetary Authorities	78bs*d*				—	—	—	—	—	—	—	—	—	—	—	—
General Government	78bt*d*				28	626	1,278	−235	337	141	678	1,178	1,096	680	71	−2,028
Banks	78bu*d*				743	770	829	96	1,446	612	567	212	649	1,226	−1,353	−82
Other Sectors	78bv*d*				1,783	1,703	2,188	2,180	2,371	4,078	3,999	1,891	1,228	2,054	−2,493	−3,510
Net Errors and Omissions	78ca*d*				47	469	−1,154	−19	−2,350	−869	−1,734	−1,194	−1,525	−2,123	−1,908	20
Overall Balance	78cb*d*				−829	−1,090	1,146	3,759	3,450	−795	−727	−3,104	−265	4,817	−2,275	2,344
Reserves and Related Items	79da*d*				829	1,090	−1,146	−3,759	−3,450	795	727	3,104	265	−4,817	2,275	−2,344
Reserve Assets	79db*d*				223	1,001	−1,146	−3,809	−2,925	795	802	3,256	270	−4,817	2,275	−2,344
Use of Fund Credit and Loans	79dc*d*				606	89	—	50	−525	—	−75	−151	−5	—	—	—
Exceptional Financing	79de*d*				—	—	—	—	—	—	—	—	—	—	—	—

	1987	1988	1989	1990	1991	1992	1993	1994	1995	1996	1997	1998	1999	2000	2001	
Banking Survey (EA-Wide Residency) — *End of Period*																
Foreign Assets (Net)	....	....	....	....	....	....	....	....	....	....	....	....	–18.22	–32.23	–41.11	**31n.u**
Domestic Credit	....	....	....	....	....	....	....	....	....	....	....	....	668.28	746.72	856.03	**32..u**
Claims on General Govt. (Net)	....	....	....	....	....	....	....	....	....	....	....	....	138.64	115.60	143.78	**32anu**
Claims on Other Resident Sect.	....	....	....	....	....	....	....	....	....	....	....	....	529.64	631.12	712.26	**32d.u**
Currency Issued	....	....	....	....	....	....	....	....	....	....	....	....	61.35	59.79	48.75	**34a.u**
Demand Deposits	....	....	....	....	....	....	....	....	....	....	....	....	132.68	147.56	170.19	**34b.u**
Other Deposits	....	....	....	....	....	....	....	....	....	....	....	....	319.89	368.97	408.74	**35..u**
o/w: Other Dep. Over Two Yrs	....	....	....	....	....	....	....	....	....	....	....	....	32.17	44.32	49.80	**35abu**
Money Market Instruments	....	....	....	....	....	....	....	....	....	....	....	....	45.89	33.34	43.78	**36m.u**
Bonds (Debt Securities)	....	....	....	....	....	....	....	....	....	....	....	....	53.63	51.91	65.19	**36n.u**
o/w: Bonds Over Two Years	....	....	....	....	....	....	....	....	....	....	....	....	37.49	39.77	49.28	**36nau**
Capital Accounts	....	....	....	....	....	....	....	....	....	....	....	....	96.54	115.81	126.01	**37a**
Other Items (Net)	....	....	....	....	....	....	....	....	....	....	....	....	–59.91	–62.89	–47.73	**37r.u**
Money (National Definitions) — *End of Period*																
M1	8,650.8	10,319.7	11,859.6	14,163.1	15,898.8	15,631.3	16,180.5	17,337.6	17,887.8	19,116.1	21,834.9	25,270.6	....	....	....	**59ma**
M2	15,078.3	17,563.4	19,611.5	23,037.3	25,797.5	25,690.3	26,966.7	28,753.4	29,637.5	31,717.5	35,483.7	40,616.5	....	....	....	**59mb**
M3	31,837.5	35,992.9	41,134.9	46,686.1	51,777.9	54,237.5	59,260.7	63,675.8	70,439.4	73,819.5	77,136.6	78,665.1	....	....	....	**59mc**
ALP	34,877.6	39,562.2	45,450.9	50,792.7	56,546.9	59,449.7	65,429.1	70,045.8	76,479.0	82,118.8	85,674.3	86,588.1	....	....	....	**59md**
Interest Rates — *Percent Per Annum*																
Bank of Spain Rate*(End of Period)*	13.50	12.40	14.52	14.71	12.50	13.25	9.00	7.38	9.00	6.25	4.75	3.00	....	....	....	**60**
Money Market Rate	16.06	11.29	14.39	14.76	13.20	13.01	12.33	7.81	8.98	7.65	5.49	4.34	2.72	4.11	4.36	**60b**
Treasury Bill Rate	†11.38	10.79	13.57	14.17	12.45	12.44	10.53	8.11	9.79	7.23	5.02	3.79	3.01	4.61	3.92	**60c**
Deposit Rate	8.97	9.06	9.55	10.65	10.47	10.43	9.63	6.70	7.68	6.12	3.96	2.92	1.85	2.95	3.08	**60l**
Lending Rate	16.36	12.43	15.84	16.01	14.38	14.23	12.78	8.95	10.05	8.50	6.08	5.01	3.95	5.18	5.16	**60p**
Government Bond Yield	12.81	11.74	13.70	14.68	12.43	12.17	10.16	9.69	11.04	8.18	5.84	4.55	4.30	5.36	4.87	**61**
Prices, Production, Labor — *Period Averages*																
Share Prices	84.4	93.6	101.7	87.4	89.7	77.8	91.4	106.2	100.0	124.0	187.8	276.1	302.0	335.9	288.2	**62**
Industrial Prices	78.0	80.3	83.7	85.5	86.8	87.9	90.1	94.0	100.0	101.7	102.7	102.0	102.7	108.3	110.2	**63**
Consumer Prices	65.1	68.2	72.9	77.7	82.4	87.2	91.2	95.5	100.0	103.6	105.6	107.5	110.0	113.8	117.9	**64**
Harmonized CPI	....	....	....	....	....	....	....	....	100.0	103.6	105.5	107.4	109.8	113.6	116.8	**64h**
Wages	59.1	62.9	67.5	73.4	79.4	85.5	91.3	95.4	100.0	105.3	109.6	....	115.5	118.3	....	**65**
Industrial Production	90.0	92.7	96.9	96.9	96.2	93.4	89.0	95.5	100.0	99.3	106.1	111.8	114.8	119.3	118.3	**66..c**
Total Employment	95.1	97.8	101.8	104.5	104.7	102.7	98.3	97.4	100.0	102.9	106.0	109.7	114.7	120.2	122.6	**67**
Period Averages																
Labor Force	....	....	....	....	....	....	15,319	....	15,625	15,936	16,121	16,265	16,423	16,844	....	**67d**
Employment	11,369	11,773	12,258	12,579	12,609	12,366	11,838	11,730	12,042	12,396	12,765	13,205	13,817	14,474	....	**67e**
Unemployment	2,938	2,848	2,561	2,441	2,464	2,789	3,481	3,738	3,584	3,540	3,356	3,060	2,606	2,370	1,697	**67c**
Unemployment Rate (%)	20.5	19.5	17.3	16.3	16.4	18.4	22.7	24.2	22.9	22.2	20.8	18.8	15.9	14.1	13.1	**67r**
International Transactions — *Millions of Euros Beginning 1999*																
Exports	4,195.6	4,686.4	5,134.5	5,630.6	6,064.7	6,657.6	7,754.6	9,746.6	11,339.6	12,931.2	15,266.9	16,290.8	†103343.2	123,099.5	128,671.8	**70**
Imports, c.i.f.	6,029.9	7,039.5	8,396.4	8,898.4	9,636.8	10,204.5	10,131.0	12,306.3	14,106.7	15,435.7	17,966.0	19,837.9	†135866.3	166,138.4	171,690.8	**71**
1995=100																
Volume of Exports (1990=100)	79.5	85.0	89.0	100.0	111.5	117.0	135.4	160.4	....	....	....	....	....	....	....	**72**
Volume of Imports (1990=100)	65.8	78.1	91.0	100.0	111.7	121.5	117.8	130.5	....	....	....	....	....	....	....	**73**
Unit Value of Exports	79.3	83.5	87.4	85.7	84.9	85.8	89.9	93.9	100.0	101.0	104.3	104.4	103.5	109.8	112.8	**74**
Unit Value of Imports	92.8	90.8	92.7	89.5	87.1	86.0	90.5	95.8	100.0	100.3	103.9	101.5	101.5	114.5	113.9	**75**
Export Prices (1975=100)	....	....	....	....	....	....	....	....	....	....	....	....	....	....	....	**76**
Balance of Payments — *Minus Sign Indicates Debit*																
Current Account, n.i.e.	–263	–3,795	–10,924	–18,009	–19,798	–21,537	–5,804	–6,389	792	407	2,512	–3,135	–13,761	–19,237	–15,082	**78ald**
Goods: Exports f.o.b.	34,753	40,692	44,945	55,658	60,167	65,826	62,021	73,925	93,439	102,735	106,926	111,986	112,664	116,205	117,561	**78aad**
Goods: Imports f.o.b.	–48,495	–59,396	–70,351	–84,815	–90,501	–96,247	–77,020	–88,817	–111,854	–119,017	–120,333	–132,744	–143,002	–151,025	–149,061	**78abd**
Trade Balance	–13,742	–18,703	–25,406	–29,158	–30,335	–30,420	–14,999	–14,892	–18,415	–16,283	–13,407	–20,758	–30,339	–34,820	–31,500	**78acd**
Services: Credit	21,705	24,457	24,618	27,937	29,171	33,921	30,446	33,859	40,209	44,387	44,161	49,308	53,418	53,540	57,775	**78add**
Services: Debit	–8,255	–10,732	–11,983	–16,054	–17,263	–21,314	–18,902	–18,865	–21,509	–23,979	–24,315	–27,421	–30,532	–31,283	–33,516	**78aed**
Balance on Goods & Services	–291	–4,979	–12,772	–17,275	–18,426	–17,813	–3,454	102	284	4,126	6,439	1,129	–7,452	–12,564	–7,242	**78afd**
Income: Credit	1,862	2,690	3,775	7,817	10,923	14,084	11,845	8,687	13,689	14,095	13,162	14,621	12,636	15,017	19,796	**78agd**
Income: Debit	–4,438	–5,999	–6,544	–11,350	–15,193	–19,874	–15,456	–16,457	–17,817	–20,207	–19,911	–22,134	–22,087	–23,268	–29,342	**78ahd**
Balance on Gds, Serv. & Inc.	–2,868	–8,287	–15,540	–20,808	–22,695	–23,603	–7,066	–7,668	–3,843	–1,986	–310	–6,385	–16,903	–20,815	–16,787	**78aid**
Current Transfers, n.i.e.: Credit	4,584	7,478	8,496	7,849	9,767	10,771	8,821	9,171	12,055	11,112	11,738	12,690	13,435	11,629	12,567	**78ajd**
Current Transfers: Debit	–1,979	–2,986	–3,880	–5,050	–6,870	–8,705	–7,558	–7,893	–7,420	–8,718	–8,916	–9,441	–10,292	–10,050	–10,862	**78akd**
Capital Account, n.i.e.	31	11	–9	1,451	3,166	3,726	2,872	2,305	6,004	6,589	6,437	6,330	6,967	4,792	4,960	**78bcd**
Capital Account, n.i.e.: Credit	50	48	50	1,753	3,535	4,219	3,997	3,571	7,374	7,713	7,275	7,160	8,060	5,806	5,833	**78bad**
Capital Account: Debit	–19	–37	–59	–302	–370	–493	–1,125	–1,266	–1,370	–1,124	–837	–830	–1,094	–1,014	–872	**78bbd**
Financial Account, n.i.e.	14,229	14,615	18,342	22,970	32,015	5,959	–434	4,491	–7,951	20,138	8,547	–14,156	–10,997	16,942	15,886	**78bjd**
Direct Investment Abroad	–745	–1,235	–1,473	–3,522	–4,442	–2,192	–3,188	–4,051	–4,206	–5,577	–12,423	–19,065	–41,754	–53,865	–27,704	**78bdd**
Dir. Invest. in Rep. Econ., n.i.e.	4,571	7,021	8,428	13,984	12,493	13,276	9,681	9,216	6,297	6,796	6,384	11,905	15,541	36,931	21,540	**78bed**
Portfolio Investment Assets	29	–136	–166	–1,357	–2,359	–2,829	–6,567	–1,492	–490	–3,653	–16,450	–44,193	–47,397	–59,320	–43,528	**78bfd**
Equity Securities	29	–136	–166	–329	–327	–145	–728	–1,039	–534	–776	–5,272	–10,120	–17,279	–36,136	–366	**78bkd**
Debt Securities	—	—	—	–1,028	–2,033	–2,684	–5,839	–453	44	–2,877	–11,178	–34,073	–30,118	–23,185	–43,162	**78bld**
Portfolio Investment Liab., n.i.e.	3,770	2,427	8,155	10,382	22,517	12,098	55,314	–20,856	21,653	3,128	11,772	16,736	45,549	58,146	27,569	**78bgd**
Equity Securities	3,434	2,100	6,387	4,309	2,772	3,648	6,600	1,154	4,215	147	–294	10,072	9,975	19,692	7,350	**78bmd**
Debt Securities	336	327	1,768	6,073	19,745	8,450	48,714	–22,010	17,438	2,981	12,066	6,664	35,574	38,455	20,219	**78bnd**
Financial Derivatives Assets	....	....	....	–10	–50	18	—	—	—	—	—	—	—	....	....	**78bwd**
Financial Derivatives Liabilities	....	....	....	3	–28	71	–2,791	158	–557	–875	41	–2,776	260	2,025	47	**78bxd**
Other Investment Assets	793	–596	–108	–13,175	–7,740	–40,441	–71,940	9,152	–36,816	2,469	–1,415	–21,604	–24,624	–18,640	10,196	**78bhd**
Monetary Authorities	—	—	—	....	....	....	–3	3	–71	–4	8	–422	–39,311	–7,837	14,992	**78bod**
General Government	–271	–785	–737	–951	–676	–897	–663	–620	–402	–502	–377	–427	–209	–253	–287	**78bpd**
Banks	1,140	1,315	1,336	–7,520	–3,215	–28,758	–63,178	14,437	–26,899	9,969	13,175	–1,960	5,298	–7,588	–3,512	**78bqd**
Other Sectors	–76	–1,127	–708	–4,704	–3,849	–10,786	–8,097	–4,668	–9,446	–6,993	–14,220	–18,795	9,599	–2,962	–996	**78brd**
Other Investment Liab., n.i.e.	5,812	7,134	3,506	16,665	11,624	25,958	19,058	12,363	6,168	17,849	20,638	44,841	41,427	51,666	27,766	**78bid**
Monetary Authorities	195	–303	643	—	—	—	–121	27	23	461	–466	–2	–11	–141	–185	**78bsd**
General Government	648	670	1,364	1,274	–271	3,418	938	3,007	1,493	–226	4	1,043	–296	902	572	**78btd**
Banks	1,641	2,643	1,547	14,402	8,169	13,609	13,242	10,572	4,049	18,646	20,490	38,957	26,039	36,510	14,937	**78bud**
Other Sectors	3,328	4,125	–47	988	3,725	8,932	4,999	–1,242	604	–1,032	611	4,843	15,695	14,395	12,441	**78bvd**
Net Errors and Omissions	–1,291	–2,414	–2,693	777	–1,075	–5,957	–1,838	–371	–5,260	–2,856	–5,741	–3,395	–5,059	–5,379	–7,104	**78cad**
Overall Balance	12,706	8,416	4,716	7,188	14,307	–17,809	–5,203	36	–6,414	24,279	11,756	–14,355	–22,850	–2,881	–1,340	**78cbd**
Reserves and Related Items	–12,706	–8,416	–4,716	–7,188	–14,307	17,809	5,203	–36	6,414	–24,279	–11,756	14,355	22,850	2,881	1,340	**79dad**
Reserve Assets	–12,706	–8,416	–4,716	–7,188	–14,307	17,809	5,203	–36	6,414	–24,279	–11,756	14,355	22,850	2,881	1,340	**79dbd**
Use of Fund Credit and Loans	—	—	—	—	—	—	—	—	—	—	—	—	—	—	—	**79dcd**
Exceptional Financing	—	—	—	—	—	—	—	—	—	—	—	—	....	....	....	**79ded**

Spain

184

	1972	1973	1974	1975	1976	1977	1978	1979	1980	1981	1982	1983	1984	1985	1986
International Investment Position														*Millions of US Dollars*	
Assets .... 79aa *d*	....	....	....	....	....	....	....	....	....	42,332	34,042	32,539	39,451	43,313	53,588
Direct Investment Abroad .... 79ab *d*	....	....	....	....	....	....	....	....	1,931	2,326	2,954	3,273	3,536	4,455	5,938
Portfolio Investment .... 79ac *d*	....	....	....	....	....	....	....	....	149	207	580	586	874	1,221	2,507
Equity Securities .... 79ad *d*	....	....	....	....	....	....	....	....	114	126	209	216	235	319	493
Debt Securities..................... 79ae *d*	....	....	....	....	....	....	....	....	35	81	371	371	639	902	2,014
Financial Derivatives.................. 79al *d*									—	—	—	—	—	—	—
Other Investment .... 79af *d*	....	....	....	....	....	....	....	....	....	27,761	23,075	20,712	22,864	26,472	30,411
Monetary Authorities .... 79ag *d*										—	—	—	—	—	—
General Government .... 79ah *d*										—	—	—	—	—	1,299
Banks .... 79ai *d*	....	....	....	....	....	....	....	....	....	21,147	16,929	15,272	16,783	19,111	22,032
Other Sectors....................... 79aj *d*															7,080
Reserve Assets .... 79ak *d*	....	....	....	....	....	....	....	....	11,257	12,037	7,434	7,967	12,177	11,165	14,733
Liabilities .... 79la *d*	....	....	....	....	....	....	....	....	....	58,840	54,289	52,687	56,029	59,201	68,848
Dir. Invest. in Rep. Economy........... 79lb *d*	....	....	....	....	....	....	....	....	....	5,289	5,220	5,160	5,473	7,290	10,658
Portfolio Investment .... 79lc *d*	....	....	....	....	....	....	....	....	463	483	382	354	533	1,136	3,211
Equity Securities .... 79ld *d*	....	....	....	....	....	....	....	....	420	450	359	332	475	1,066	2,959
Debt Securities..................... 79le *d*	....	....	....	....	....	....	....	....	43	33	23	22	59	70	252
Financial Derivatives.................. 79ll *d*									—	—	—	—	—	—	—
Other Investment .... 79lf *d*	....	....	....	....	....	....	....	....	....	53,068	48,687	47,174	50,022	50,775	54,979
Monetary Authorities .... 79lg *d*	....	....	....	....	....	....	....	....	....	175	20	8	10	20	60
General Government .... 79lh *d*										—	—	—	—	—	4,910
Banks .... 79li *d*	....	....	....	....	....	....	....	....	....	26,821	21,533	19,421	21,209	20,939	25,365
Other Sectors....................... 79lj *d*	....	....	....	....	....	....	....	....	....	....	....	....	....	....	24,644
Government Finance															
Central Government													*Billions of Pesetas through 1998;*		
Deficit (-) or Surplus..................... 80	−36.1	−23.4	−82.3	−111.2	−128.3	−248.6	−254.4	−400.9	†−555.8	−780.2	−1,450.2	−1,714.9	−2,502.1	†−1,719.5	−1,521.2
Total Revenue and Grants 81y	443.7	531.2	629.8	758.4	899.7	1,159.2	1,479.4	1,762.4	†2,179.1	2,574.7	3,002.8	3,631.4	4,218.5	†4,440.1	5,752.8
Revenue 81	443.7	531.2	629.8	758.4	899.7	1,159.2	1,479.4	1,762.4	†2,179.1	2,574.7	3,002.8	3,631.4	4,218.5	†4,440.1	5,752.8
Grants 81z	—	—	—	—	—	—	—	—	—	—	—	† —	—	—	—
Exp. & Lending Minus Repay. 82z	479.8	554.6	712.1	869.6	1,028.1	1,407.8	1,733.8	2,163.3	†2,734.9	3,355.0	4,453.0	5,346.3	6,720.6	†6,159.6	7,274.0
Expenditure 82	456.8	526.2	659.2	766.2	905.7	1,249.4	1,571.8	1,994.5	†2,552.7	3,097.2	4,058.5	4,809.9	5,909.3	†5,925.8	7,192.9
Lending Minus Repayments 83	23.0	28.4	52.9	103.4	122.3	158.4	162.0	168.8	182.2	257.8	394.5	536.4	811.3	†233.8	81.1
Total Financing 80h	36.1	23.4	82.2	111.2	128.2	248.5	254.2	401.1	†555.8	780.2	1,450.3	1,714.9	2,502.1	†1,719.2	1,521.1
Total Net Borrowing 84	58.3	9.0	27.9	53.8	181.7	190.6	113.4	242.3	579.2	785.2	1,423.1	1,785.8	2,541.7	†1,726.5	1,516.7
Net Domestic 84a	58.8	8.7	22.3	52.0	148.0	103.5	151.3	237.1	579.2	742.2	1,345.9	1,661.8	2,421.1	2,332.0	2,118.1
Net Foreign 85a	−.5	.4	5.6	1.8	33.7	87.1	−37.9	5.2	—	43.0	77.2	124.0	120.7	32.9	−174.4
Use of Cash Balances 87	−22.2	14.4	54.3	57.4	−53.5	57.9	140.8	158.8	—	−6.9	−51.7	−21.0	−40.7	†7.3	−4.4
Total Debt by Residence 88	483.1	505.7	588.2	699.6	822.6	1,112.8	1,358.2	1,748.8	†2,316.7	3,135.5	4,781.7	6,763.4	9,395.9	†11390.5	13,269.1
Domestic 88a	458.2	481.6	558.0	666.2	757.9	934.7	1,220.4	1,619.4	†2,183.1	2,930.8	4,428.8	6,198.1	8,657.9	†10676.0	12,795.3
Foreign 89a	24.9	24.1	30.2	33.4	64.7	178.1	137.8	129.4	†133.6	204.7	352.9	565.3	738.0	†714.5	473.8
General Government														*As Percent of*	
Deficit (-) or Surplus..................... 80g	....	....	....	....	....	....	....	....	....	....	....	....	....	....	....
Debt 88g	....	....	....	....	....	....	....	....	....	....	....	....	....	....	....
National Accounts													*Billions of Pesetas: through 1998;*		
Househ.Cons.Expend.,incl.NPISHs...... 96f. *c*	2,245	2,694	3,333	3,920	4,817	6,050	7,272	8,582	9,992	11,301	12,939	14,604	16,305	18,080	20,438
Government Consumption Expend. ...... 91f. *c*	331	399	509	631	820	1,059	1,344	1,639	2,008	2,370	2,784	3,280	3,647	4,152	4,740
Gross Fixed Capital Formation .... 93e. *c*	868	1,108	1,436	1,593	1,808	2,201	2,551	2,843	3,368	3,729	4,264	4,686	4,779	5,409	6,297
Changes in Inventories .... 93i. *c*	32	31	113	127	145	97	28	99	157	−1	116	155	254	14	162
Exports of Goods and Services .... 90c. *c*	507	611	740	816	997	1,334	1,710	1,975	2,387	3,042	3,631	4,667	5,865	6,407	6,417
Imports of Goods and Services (-) .... 98c. *c*	500	644	988	1,047	1,320	1,522	1,621	1,936	2,743	3,397	4,011	4,860	5,329	5,860	5,730
Gross Domestic Product (GDP) .... 99b. *c*	3,483	4,199	5,143	6,039	7,267	9,220	11,285	13,201	15,168	17,045	19,723	22,532	25,520	28,201	32,324
Net Primary Income from Abroad 98.n	−16	−12	−1	−19	−40	−62	−87	−78	−130	−238	−285	−358	−397	−331	−296
Gross National Income (GNI) 99a	3,416	4,128	5,101	6,000	7,194	9,116	11,143	13,052	15,079	16,751	19,283	21,877	24,715	27,870	32,028
Net Current Transf.from Abroad 98t	....	....	....	....	....	....	....	....	....	....	....	....	....	....	....
Gross Nat'l Disposable Inc.(GNDI)........ 99i	....	....	....	....	....	....	....	....	....	....	....	....	....	....	....
Gross Saving 99s	....	....	....	....	....	....	....	....	....	....	....	....	....	....	....
Consumption of Fixed Capital 99cf	292	342	434	530	636	805	977	1,194	1,615	1,931	2,254	2,638	3,030	3,349	3,858
GDP Volume 1986 Prices .... 99b. *r*	23,215	25,023	26,429	26,572	27,450	28,230	28,643	28,655	29,027	28,976	29,430	30,083	30,524	31,322	32,324
GDP Volume 1995 Prices .... 99b. *r*															
GDP Volume (1995=100) .... 99bv *r*	55.7	60.0	63.4	63.7	65.8	67.7	68.7	68.7	69.6	69.5	70.6	72.1	73.2	75.1	77.5
GDP Deflator (1995=100) .... 99bi *r*	9.0	10.0	11.6	13.6	15.8	19.5	23.5	27.5	31.2	35.2	40.1	44.8	50.0	53.8	59.8
														Millions	
Population.................................. 99z	34.49	34.86	35.22	35.60	35.97	36.35	36.67	36.99	37.54	37.75	37.97	38.16	38.33	38.41	38.52

Millions of US Dollars — International Investment Position

	1987	1988	1989	1990	1991	1992	1993	1994	1995	1996	1997	1998	1999	2000	2001		
Assets	78,156	86,418	102,968	133,538	161,700	165,640	214,552	223,097	270,393	290,877	311,330	398,955	452,063	558,335	....	Assets	79aa d
Direct Investment Abroad	8,421	9,434	11,372	15,652	20,528	22,010	24,034	30,067	36,258	39,886	48,694	69,029	106,896	160,361	....	Direct Investment Abroad	79ab d
Portfolio Investment	2,511	2,848	3,860	5,654	8,206	9,710	14,809	17,277	18,244	21,116	34,851	81,237	119,817	169,114	....	Portfolio Investment	79ac d
Equity Securities	798	987	1,267	1,879	2,255	1,972	2,285	3,454	3,764	4,441	9,235	19,978	35,010	68,677	....	Equity Securities	79ad d
Debt Securities	1,713	1,861	2,593	3,775	5,952	7,738	12,523	13,823	14,480	16,675	25,616	61,259	84,806	100,436	....	Debt Securities	79ae d
Financial Derivatives	—	—	—	—	—	—	—	—	—	—	—	—	—	—	....	Financial Derivatives	79al d
Other Investment	34,063	33,572	42,794	57,223	63,519	85,198	132,610	131,920	178,529	169,461	157,401	187,901	187,340	193,283	....	Other Investment	79af d
Monetary Authorities	—	—	—	—	—	—	148	159	247	229	198	582	36,652	42,557	....	Monetary Authorities	79ag d
General Government	1,923	2,331	2,761	—	—	—	4,662	5,465	6,029	6,323	6,328	6,914	6,750	6,818	....	General Government	79ah d
Banks	23,707	22,526	24,546	36,343	41,259	62,880	105,292	97,086	130,872	116,823	95,127	101,110	85,289	88,371	....	Banks	79ai d
Other Sectors	8,433	8,715	15,488	20,879	22,260	22,317	22,508	29,209	41,381	46,086	55,747	79,295	58,650	55,538	....	Other Sectors	79aj d
Reserve Assets	33,161	40,565	44,942	55,010	69,447	48,722	43,100	43,834	37,362	60,414	70,384	60,788	38,010	35,576	....	Reserve Assets	79ak d
Liabilities	94,874	109,765	138,975	195,398	246,259	258,566	308,408	323,549	383,497	399,970	410,390	528,852	567,505	672,269	....	Liabilities	79la d
Dir. Invest. in Rep. Economy	16,667	21,427	28,893	65,916	79,570	86,230	80,069	96,099	108,452	106,928	98,377	116,586	115,210	142,352	....	Dir. Invest. in Rep. Economy	79lb d
Portfolio Investment	8,435	10,757	20,350	36,370	59,077	54,163	103,794	84,068	118,319	126,368	137,190	183,974	205,948	242,752	....	Portfolio Investment	79lc d
Equity Securities	6,820	7,893	14,067	20,974	22,529	18,577	22,818	24,146	32,452	38,987	46,736	75,768	86,812	92,678	....	Equity Securities	79ld d
Debt Securities	1,615	2,864	6,283	15,396	36,548	35,585	80,977	59,922	85,867	87,381	90,454	108,206	119,137	150,074	....	Debt Securities	79le d
Financial Derivatives	—	—	—	—	—	—	—	—	—	—	—	—	—	—	....	Financial Derivatives	79ll d
Other Investment	69,772	77,580	89,732	93,112	107,612	118,173	124,545	143,382	156,726	166,673	174,823	228,292	246,347	287,165	....	Other Investment	79lf d
Monetary Authorities	30	415	406	—	—	—	49	76	107	556	53	63	34	422	....	Monetary Authorities	79lg d
General Government	5,460	5,713	7,062	2,497	2,462	4,491	6,546	9,989	12,363	11,503	10,151	11,732	10,154	10,588	....	General Government	79lh d
Banks	33,189	37,001	43,627	70,157	80,820	88,167	92,192	105,944	115,197	128,638	139,662	184,963	192,242	220,314	....	Banks	79li d
Other Sectors	31,094	34,451	38,637	20,457	24,331	25,515	25,757	27,372	29,059	25,976	24,957	31,534	43,916	55,841	....	Other Sectors	79lj d

Millions of Euros Beginning 1999: Year Ending December 31 — Government Finance (Central Government)

	1987	1988	1989	1990	1991	1992	1993	1994	1995	1996	1997	1998	1999	2000	2001		
Deficit (-) or Surplus	-1,422.5	193.9	-898.8	-1,273.9	-1,405.4	-2,100.5	-3,738.0	-4,147.6	-3,606.3	-4,003.5	-1,909.4	-800.0	-6,350	-2,072	-4,749	Deficit (-) or Surplus	80
Total Revenue and Grants	7,029.4	7,908.4	9,543.4	10,203.1	11,242.7	12,286.5	12,683.7	12,960.3	14,077.2	14,629.7	16,636.5	17,519.0	110,371	118,693	125,187	Total Revenue and Grants	81y
Revenue	7,029.4	7,908.4	9,543.4	10,203.1	11,242.7	12,286.5	12,683.7	12,960.3	14,077.2	14,629.7	16,636.5	17,519.0	110,371	118,693	125,187	Revenue	81
Grants	—	—	—	—	—	—	—	—	—	—	—	—	—	—	—	Grants	81z
Exp. & Lending Minus Repay.	8,451.9	7,714.5	10,442.2	11,477.0	12,648.1	14,387.0	16,421.7	17,107.9	17,683.5	18,633.2	18,545.9	18,319.0	116,720	120,766	129,937	Exp. & Lending Minus Repay.	82z
Expenditure	8,369.4	9,084.5	10,316.6	11,375.1	12,611.6	14,160.0	16,465.8	16,438.3	17,241.5	18,322.2	18,694.0	18,633.4	116,724	121,124	128,071	Expenditure	82
Lending Minus Repayments	82.5	-1,370.0	125.6	101.9	36.5	227.0	-44.1	669.6	442.0	311.0	-148.1	-314.4	-4	-359	1,866	Lending Minus Repayments	83
Total Financing	1,423.1	-194.5	899.8	1,274.3	1,405.5	2,100.5	3,737.5	4,147.2	3,605.7	4,003.0	1,908.8	800.2	6,350	2,072	4,749	Total Financing	80h
Total Net Borrowing	1,415.0	-164.9	998.4	2,648.8	1,710.9	2,177.0	6,238.6	2,317.7	3,324.5	5,039.2	973.4	910.7	11,441	8,073	-150	Total Net Borrowing	84
Net Domestic	1,727.4	-96.8	1,395.0	....	....	....	....	....	....	....	....	....	....	....	....	Net Domestic	84a
Net Foreign	58.0	163.6	305.0	....	....	....	....	....	....	....	....	....	....	....	....	Net Foreign	85a
Use of Cash Balances	-8.1	29.6	98.6	1,374.5	305.4	76.5	2,501.1	-1,829.5	-281.2	1,036.2	-935.4	110.5	5,091	6,001	-4,899	Use of Cash Balances	87
Total Debt by Residence	15,058.2	15,086.0	16,687.2	19,490.5	21,190.5	23,911.0	31,236.7	34,266.0	38,678.1	43,922.0	45,616.6	47,243.4	298,779	308,753	307,434	Total Debt by Residence	88
Domestic	14,515.3	14,429.1	15,806.9	18,269.3	18,183.8	20,371.5	21,751.8	27,389.8	29,951.8	34,934.4	35,121.6	35,756.1	207,286	187,783	177,625	Domestic	88a
Foreign	542.9	656.9	880.3	1,221.2	3,006.7	3,539.5	9,484.9	6,876.2	8,726.3	8,987.6	10,495.0	11,487.3	91,493	120,970	129,809	Foreign	89a

General Government

	1987	1988	1989	1990	1991	1992	1993	1994	1995	1996	1997	1998	1999	2000	2001		
Deficit (-) or Surplus	....	....	....	-4.3	-4.5	-4.1	-7.0	-6.3	-7.1	-5.0	-3.2	-2.6	-1.1	-.3	—	Deficit (-) or Surplus	80g
Debt	....	....	....	44.8	45.5	48.0	60.0	62.6	64.2	68.0	66.7	64.6	63.1	60.4	57.2	Debt	88g

Gross Domestic Product

Billions of Euros Beginning 1999 — National Accounts

	1987	1988	1989	1990	1991	1992	1993	1994	1995	1996	1997	1998	1999	2000	2001		
Househ.Cons.Expend.,incl.NPISHs	22,860	25,180	28,367	31,303	34,269	37,277	38,482	40,724	43,332	45,668	48,277	51,116	†334	360	382	Househ.Cons.Expend.,incl.NPISHs	96f. c
Government Consumption Expend.	5,452	5,924	6,831	7,815	8,882	10,093	10,701	10,963	11,650	12,256	12,585	15,092	†98	106	112	Government Consumption Expend.	91f. c
Gross Fixed Capital Formation	7,518	9,083	10,868	12,261	13,067	12,889	12,100	12,860	14,494	14,976	16,029	19,800	†136	154	163	Gross Fixed Capital Formation	93e. c
Changes in Inventories	258	419	449	461	438	488	10	154	251	248	73	258	†3	2	3	Changes in Inventories	93i. c
Exports of Goods and Services	6,996	7,575	8,150	8,555	9,409	10,420	11,841	14,443	16,732	18,761	22,106	23,605	†154	183	195	Exports of Goods and Services	90c. c
Imports of Goods and Services (-)	6,935	8,023	9,621	10,251	11,137	12,063	12,180	14,331	16,660	18,165	21,172	23,311	†161	196	204	Imports of Goods and Services (-)	98c. c
Gross Domestic Product (GDP)	36,144	40,159	45,044	50,144	54,927	59,105	60,953	64,812	69,780	73,743	77,897	82,650	†563	609	650	Gross Domestic Product (GDP)	99b. c
Net Primary Income from Abroad	-304	-411	-384	-452	-554	-708	-526	-1,182	-607	-890	-1,135	....	....	....	....	Net Primary Income from Abroad	98.n
Gross National Income (GNI)	35,840	39,748	44,660	49,693	54,373	58,397	60,426	63,630	72,660	76,766	81,409	86,780	....	....	....	Gross National Income (GNI)	99a
Net Current Transf.from Abroad	....	....	....	....	....	....	....	....	295	197	209	192	1	....	....	Net Current Transf.from Abroad	98t
Gross Nat'l Disposable Inc.(GNDI)									72,954	76,963	81,618	86,972	557	....	....	Gross Nat'l Disposable Inc.(GNDI)	99i
Gross Saving									16,241	17,036	18,576	19,816	126	....	....	Gross Saving	99s
Consumption of Fixed Capital	4,178	4,600	5,033	5,545	6,024	6,452	6,980	7,428	7,951	8,363	8,851	....	....	....	....	Consumption of Fixed Capital	99cf
GDP Volume 1986 Prices	34,148	35,910	37,611	39,018	39,903	40,177	39,710	40,604	41,707	42,715	44,224	45,901	....	....	....	GDP Volume 1986 Prices	99b. r
GDP Volume 1995 Prices												80,468	†502	528	542	GDP Volume 1995 Prices	99b. r
GDP Volume (1995=100)	81.9	86.1	90.2	93.6	95.7	96.3	95.2	97.4	100.0	102.4	106.0	110.1	†114.2	120.1	123.4	GDP Volume (1995=100)	99bv r
GDP Deflator (1995=100)	63.3	66.8	71.6	76.8	82.3	87.9	91.7	95.4	100.0	103.2	105.3	107.6	†117.6	120.9	125.7	GDP Deflator (1995=100)	99bi i

Midyear Estimates

	1987	1988	1989	1990	1991	1992	1993	1994	1995	1996	1997	1998	1999	2000	2001		
Population	38.61	38.72	38.79	38.85	38.92	39.01	39.09	39.15	39.21	39.27	39.32	39.37	39.42	39.47	40.27	Population	99z

(See notes in the back of the book.)

Sri Lanka

		1972	1973	1974	1975	1976	1977	1978	1979	1980	1981	1982	1983	1984	1985	1986
Exchange Rates															*Rupees per SDR:*	
Market Rate	aa	7.272	8.140	8.195	9.029	10.257	18.901	20.200	20.346	22.957	23.919	23.518	26.174	25.760	30.105	34.885
															Rupees per US Dollar:	
Market Rate	ae	6.698	6.748	6.693	7.713	8.828	15.560	15.505	15.445	18.000	20.550	21.320	25.000	26.280	27.408	28.520
Market Rate	rf	5.970[e]	6.403[e]	6.651[e]	7.007[e]	8.412[e]	8.873[e]	15.611[e]	15.572[e]	16.534	19.246	20.812	23.529	25.438	27.163	28.017
Fund Position															*Millions of SDRs:*	
Quota	2f. s	98	98	98	98	98	98	119	119	179	179	179	223	223	223	223
SDRs	1b. s	13	13	14	11	12	20	26	22	—	20	6	1	—	—	—
Reserve Position in the Fund	1c. s	—	—	—	—	—	—	—	—	—	1	6	17	6	6	—
Total Fund Cred.&Loans Outstg.	2tl	75	74	102	125	134	170	227	305	307	443	437	425	413	361	284
International Liquidity													*Millions of US Dollars Unless Otherwise Indicated:*			
Total Reserves minus Gold	1l. d	59	87	78	57	92	293	398	517	246	327	351	297	511	451	353
SDRs	1b. d	14	16	18	13	14	24	34	29	—	23	7	1	—	—	—
Reserve Position in the Fund	1c. d	—	—	—	—	—	—	—	—	—	1	6	18	6	7	—
Foreign Exchange	1d. d	46	70	60	45	78	269	363	488	246	304	338	278	505	445	353
Gold (Million Fine Troy Ounces)	1ad	....	....	....	....	....	—	.042	.063	.063	.063	.063	.063	.063	.063	.063
Gold (National Valuation)	1and	....	....	....	....	....	—	9	18	16	14	13	11	11	10	10
Monetary Authorities: Other Liab.	4. d	55	40	48	45	63	44	20	39	42	8	89	76	1	10	8
Deposit Money Banks: Assets	7a. d	48	44	59	51	65	80	85	109	130	114	168	205	199	209	239
Liabilities	7b. d	22	11	11	11	12	9	14	22	26	30	75	114	120	149	185
FCBU: Assets	7k. d	—	—	—	—	—	—	—	29	114	205	379	545	463	458	430
Liabilities	7m. d								14	131	231	428	640	498	489	447
Monetary Authorities															*Millions of Rupees:*	
Foreign Assets	11	302	510	453	442	829	4,534	6,170	7,972	†4,706	6,929	7,494	7,760	13,725	12,650	10,341
Claims on Central Government	12a	2,368	2,353	2,447	2,537	3,760	4,978	5,868	7,768	†16,081	19,334	23,142	25,331	20,732	29,524	32,386
Claims on Deposit Money Banks	12e	125	239	679	594	401	894	1,091	693	†1,070	1,278	1,159	2,662	2,041	1,824	2,811
Reserve Money	14	1,856	2,179	2,357	2,202	2,769	4,028	4,535	5,538	6,629	7,822	9,679	12,240	14,296	18,084	18,695
of which: Currency Outside DMBs	14a	1,202	1,437	1,539	1,610	2,081	2,792	3,016	3,774	4,181	4,823	5,988	7,200	8,561	9,816	11,570
Foreign Liabilities	16c	912	872	1,156	1,472	1,932	3,897	4,892	6,810	†7,790	10,760	12,183	13,025	10,678	11,157	10,124
Central Government Deposits	16d	91	94	120	15	31	....	1,049	740	1,364	1,450	1,286	1,772	2,337	3,161	2,514
Capital Accounts	17a									5,763	7,140	8,256	8,475	8,450	10,612	11,654
Other Items (Net)	17r	113	73	168	–42	359	2,669	3,976	4,324	†310	368	391	241	737	983	2,552
Deposit Money Banks															*Millions of Rupees:*	
Reserves	20	606	802	789	562	652	1,145	1,342	1,742	2,049	2,730	3,069	4,678	5,670	8,228	8,040
Foreign Assets	21	320	297	394	395	573	1,243	1,316	†1,681	2,347	2,342	3,585	5,126	5,233	5,726	6,803
Claims on Central Government	22a	745	499	386	†415	782	914	801	864	939	1,563	1,719	1,579	2,878	2,897	2,753
Claims on Nonfin.Pub.Enterprises	22ca	....	....	....	....	....	....	3,347	4,123	4,488	4,677	4,385	4,148	4,438	4,739	
Claims on Cooperatives	22cb								1,368	1,294	1,188	1,823	1,568	1,304	1,425	
Claims on Private Sector	22d	2,117	2,134	3,188	3,363	3,919	5,714	8,666	11,853	†11,344	15,396	19,379	25,552	29,656	32,793	35,400
Demand Deposits	24	1,241	1,312	1,377	1,443	2,038	2,526	2,863	3,857	5,139	5,111	5,665	7,334	8,002	8,761	9,358
Time and Savings Deposits	25	1,456	1,337	1,582	1,648	2,117	3,303	5,425	8,668	11,624	15,269	19,779	23,523	27,674	30,803	31,085
Foreign Liabilities	26c	145	75	75	86	103	135	224	337	472	613	1,606	2,857	3,141	4,078	5,290
Central Government Deposits	26d	514	446	530	452	714	871	†990	1,073	1,642	1,503	1,568	1,763	2,299	3,687	3,863
Credit from Monetary Authorities	26g	....	....	....	....	....	....	....	609	1,180	1,436	1,413	2,875	2,401	2,165	3,140
Capital Accounts	27a	162	171	214	239	281	374	520	906	1,272	2,268	2,602	2,705	2,932	3,164	3,410
Other Items (Net)	27r	60	85	310	206	132	685	2,534	2,271	†841	1,612	984	2,085	2,703	2,729	3,013
Monetary Survey															*Millions of Rupees:*	
Foreign Assets (Net)	31n	–435	–140	–384	–721	–633	1,744	2,371	2,506	†–1,210	–2,102	–2,709	–2,996	5,138	3,140	1,730
Domestic Credit	32	4,696	4,519	5,435	5,823	7,644	10,547	13,184	18,556	†31,088	39,383	47,695	55,604	54,748	65,707	72,280
Claims on Central Govt. (Net)	32an	2,579	2,386	2,247	2,460	3,725	4,834	4,518	6,703	†14,014	17,944	22,008	23,375	18,974	25,573	28,763
Claims on Nonfin.Pub.Enterprises	32ca	....	....	....	....	....	....	3,347	4,123	4,488	4,677	4,385	4,148	4,438	4,739	
Claims on Cooperatives	32cb								1,368	1,294	1,188	1,823	1,568	1,304	1,425	
Claims on Private Sector	32d	2,117	2,134	3,188	3,363	3,919	5,714	8,666	11,853	†11,420	15,417	19,475	25,629	29,677	33,585	36,533
Money	34	2,461	2,755	2,923	3,064	4,133	5,332	5,895	7,643	9,333	9,949	11,672	14,589	16,647	18,662	21,051
Quasi-Money	35	1,541	1,361	1,685	1,706	2,186	3,492	5,698	8,908	11,970	15,587	20,342	24,123	28,265	31,994	31,750
Other Items (Net)	37r	345	286	546	390	761	3,655	4,752	6,106	†8,576	11,745	12,972	13,896	14,974	18,192	21,209
Money plus Quasi-Money	35l	4,002	4,116	4,608	4,770	6,319	8,824	11,593	16,551	21,303	25,536	32,014	38,712	44,912	50,656	52,801
Liquid Liabilities	55l	4,969	5,263	5,950	6,351	8,207	11,204	14,619	20,701	26,256	30,975	39,668	48,221	56,145	63,884	67,002
Interest Rates															*Percent Per Annum*	
Bank Rate (End of Period)	60	6.50	6.50	6.50	6.50	6.50	10.00	10.00	10.00	12.00	14.00	14.00	13.00	13.00	11.00	11.00
Money Market Rate	60b	....	....	....	....	....	....	9.50	11.00	21.06	19.00	16.88	23.88	21.42	14.56	12.95
Treasury Bill Rate	60c	....	....	....	....	....	....	....	....	....	15.60	12.28	12.38	13.08	13.39	10.48
Deposit Rate	60l	....	....	....	....	....	....	8.50	8.50	14.50	17.88	17.50	18.25	19.79	17.33	12.21
Lending Rate	60p	....	....	....	....	....	....	18.00	18.00	19.00	19.00	17.75	13.25	13.15	13.40	11.57
Government Bond Yield	61													14.67	15.33	12.00
Prices and Labor															*Index Numbers (1995=100):*	
Share Prices	62	....	....	....	....	....	....	....	....	....	....	....	....	....	....	....
Wholesale Prices	63	....	....	10.5	10.9	11.8	14.2	16.5	18.1	24.2	28.3	29.8	37.3	46.8	39.7	38.5
Consumer Prices	64	9.2	10.1	11.3	12.0	12.2	12.4	13.9	15.3	19.4	22.8	25.3	28.8	33.6	34.1	36.8
Wages: Agr. Minimum Rates	65	4.0	4.4	5.6	6.4	6.6	8.3	†12.0	14.8	18.5	18.5	21.8	23.9	30.1	32.9	34.7
															Number in Thousands:	
Labor Force	67d	....	....	....	....	....	....	....	....	....	....	....	....	....	....	....
Employment	67e	....	....	....	....	....	....	....	....	....	....	....	....	....	5,132	....
Unemployment	67c	....	....	....	....	....	....	....	....	....	....	....	....	....	840	....
Unemployment Rate (%)	67r	....	....	....	....	....	....	....	....	....	....	....	....	....	....	....
International Transactions															*Millions of Rupees:*	
Exports	70	2,016	2,630	3,503	3,969	4,840	6,570	13,193	15,282	17,595	21,043	21,454	25,096	37,347	36,207	34,072
Tea	70s	1,162	1,261	1,360	1,932	2,100	3,503	6,401	5,722	6,170	6,444	6,342	8,295	15,764	12,003	9,253
Imports, c.i.f.	71	2,199	2,763	4,770	5,196	4,902	6,061	15,100	22,603	33,942	36,583	41,946	45,558	47,541	54,049	54,559
															1995=100	
Volume of Exports	72	41.2	41.6	36.0	43.3	41.2	38.0	40.4	†40.8	43.6	45.9	48.2	45.4	53.2	55.1	58.7
Tea	72s	79.0	85.4	72.9	88.3	83.0	77.1	80.0	77.9	76.7	76.1	75.2	65.6	84.8	82.2	86.3
Volume of Imports	73	24.1	21.6	15.1	18.7	20.5	26.2	35.9	†44.2	47.0	47.0	51.7	53.6	51.2	58.3	
Unit Value of Exports	74	3.1	3.7	5.7	5.3	6.2	10.0	18.3	†19.9	22.2	24.2	23.6	30.3	38.6	34.2	30.5
Tea	74s	6.0	6.0	7.6	8.9	10.3	18.4	32.5	29.8	32.6	34.3	34.2	51.3	75.5	59.3	43.5
Unit Value of Imports	75	2.4	3.2	5.5	6.4	5.8	7.1	13.1	†20.0	25.3	29.4	30.6	31.9	33.4	36.2	33.5

1987	1988	1989	1990	1991	1992	1993	1994	1995	1996	1997	1998	1999	2000	2001		
End of Period															**Exchange Rates**	
43.642	44.453	52.566	57.248	60.908	63.250	68.076	72.963	80.341	81.540	82.689	96.164	99.054	107.594	117.075	Market Rate	aa
End of Period (ae) Period Average (rf)																
30.763	33.033	40.000	40.240	42.580	46.000	49.562	49.980	54.048	56.705	61.285	68.297	72.170	82.580	93.159	Market Rate	ae
29.445	31.807	36.047	40.063	41.372	43.830	48.322	49.415	51.252	55.271	58.995	64.450	70.635	77.005	89.383	Market Rate	rf
End of Period															**Fund Position**	
223	223	223	223	223	304	304	304	304	304	304	304	413	413	413	Quota	2f. s
—	—	10	—	—	—	—	—	1	1	—	1	1	—	1	SDRs	1b. s
—	—	—	—	—	20	20	20	20	20	20	20	48	48	48	Reserve Position in the Fund	1c. s
195	267	278	288	280	338	376	423	400	369	321	261	188	123	171	Total Fund Cred.&Loans Outstg.	2tl
End of Period															**International Liquidity**	
279	222	244	423	685	927	1,629	2,046	2,088	1,962	2,024	1,980	1,636	1,039	1,287	Total Reserves minus Gold	1l.d
—	—	13	—	—	—	—	—	1	2	—	1	1	—	1	SDRs	1b.d
—	—	—	—	—	28	28	30	30	29	27	29	65	62	60	Reserve Position in the Fund	1c.d
279	222	231	422	685	899	1,601	2,016	2,057	1,931	1,996	1,950	1,569	976	1,226	Foreign Exchange	1d.d
.063	.063	.063	.063	.111	.160	.063	.063	.063	.063	.063	.063	.063	.626	.626	Gold (Million Fine Troy Ounces)	1ad
10	10	10	10	10	37	6	6	6	5	5	....	....	....	....	Gold (National Valuation)	1and
67	11	†207	291	363	420	625	713	754	691	624	526	515	419	403	Monetary Authorities: Other Liab.	4..d
301	298	294	422	438	504	516	639	839	780	1,103	916	941	1,050	900	Deposit Money Banks: Assets	7a.d
251	229	249	303	394	464	547	615	1,004	964	1,094	859	764	909	1,009	Liabilities	7b.d
382	422	492	524	432	539	456	540	574	504	682	479	439	429	422	FCBU: Assets	7k.d
408	371	400	448	428	635	601	665	682	615	702	438	306	429	519	Liabilities	7m.d
End of Period															**Monetary Authorities**	
8,871	7,620	†10,056	17,304	30,581	41,868	78,290	96,807	106,838	104,541	120,189	132,560	113,521	78,560	114,558	Foreign Assets	11
34,178	46,570	†51,466	55,023	61,318	50,072	35,515	38,275	45,276	53,191	39,664	39,840	57,447	101,681	107,584	Claims on Central Government	12a
3,136	3,480	†4,312	5,570	5,344	5,506	4,900	3,376	2,812	2,259	1,692	1,122	748	520	150	Claims on Deposit Money Banks	12e
20,626	25,941	†27,482	33,141	42,374	45,972	57,539	68,518	79,535	85,824	84,037	92,900	97,673	101,906	112,549	Reserve Money	14
13,495	18,484	†19,644	22,120	24,852	27,280	32,133	38,906	42,198	42,565	45,680	51,767	58,481	62,647	65,536	*of which: Currency Outside DMBs*	14a
10,571	12,241	†22,912	28,215	29,121	30,077	41,297	46,076	50,427	46,457	43,048	38,928	38,038	34,577	49,617	Foreign Liabilities	16c
1,587	3,528	†2,776	3,604	9,027	2,666	1,801	2,813	3,040	3,510	6,476	3,108	2,463	3,152	4,301	Central Government Deposits	16d
13,334	14,675	†14,853	13,324	14,550	18,156	17,251	19,873	25,344	25,564	32,306	42,738	40,589	50,008	50,673	Capital Accounts	17a
67	1,285	†12,244	9,152	2,172	575	817	1,179	–3,420	–1,364	–4,322	–4,153	–7,048	–8,882	5,152	Other Items (Net)	17r
End of Period															**Deposit Money Banks**	
5,728	6,802	†7,611	9,406	15,421	16,289	20,562	25,389	35,449	41,188	36,500	39,667	40,110	39,542	49,760	Reserves	20
9,265	9,875	†11,753	16,967	18,634	23,162	25,567	31,918	†45,338	44,212	67,596	62,560	67,946	86,682	83,814	Foreign Assets	21
5,362	7,862	†8,382	14,701	13,861	13,886	18,782	21,039	†23,808	29,579	42,469	53,514	60,618	69,336	143,109	Claims on Central Government	22a
7,366	10,787	†6,327	5,142	7,143	9,010	3,966	3,118	13,305	15,491	14,658	10,836	13,715	38,254	40,811	Claims on Nonfin.Pub.Enterprises	22ca
1,123	1,319	†1,178	1,416	1,238	1,739	1,903	2,541	3,939	1,465	1,661	1,812	1,608	1,668	1,577	Claims on Cooperatives	22cb
39,653	48,322	†50,781	63,052	†32,761	38,470	49,052	62,676	206,783	228,992	261,359	291,969	323,374	362,435	395,216	Claims on Private Sector	22d
11,243	13,511	†15,375	17,256	21,641	22,741	27,169	31,415	32,970	35,516	40,108	44,470	50,059	55,788	56,665	Demand Deposits	24
34,697	37,469	†40,078	50,668	63,519	79,741	100,780	121,210	†184,224	210,454	247,817	281,473	319,765	364,944	426,927	Time and Savings Deposits	25
7,714	9,122	†9,962	12,191	16,793	21,356	27,119	30,746	54,256	54,678	67,030	58,656	55,141	75,101	94,030	Foreign Liabilities	26c
3,357	5,011	†5,851	9,723	8,639	9,075	6,304	9,290	†9,483	12,947	13,765	11,646	13,122	13,292	26,333	Central Government Deposits	26d
3,479	3,906	†4,046	6,625	5,614	5,603	5,843	4,054	3,625	4,050	4,775	4,813	5,171	5,886	4,811	Credit from Monetary Authorities	26g
3,954	4,774	†5,395	6,690	8,960	9,868	21,851	28,278	33,460	39,238	44,368	50,220	51,571	51,808	44,520	Capital Accounts	27a
4,053	11,172	†12,860	18,027	14,799	15,552	–932	1,877	10,603	4,045	6,380	9,081	12,543	31,098	61,001	Other Items (Net)	27r
End of Period															**Monetary Survey**	
–149	–3,868	†–11,065	–6,135	3,301	13,598	35,442	51,902	47,493	47,617	77,707	97,536	88,287	55,564	54,725	Foreign Assets (Net)	31n
83,743	107,368	†117,313	138,704	150,156	163,657	170,050	197,073	281,821	313,468	340,885	384,200	441,945	557,706	659,004	Domestic Credit	32
34,596	45,893	†51,220	56,397	57,514	52,218	46,192	47,211	†56,561	66,313	61,892	78,600	102,480	154,573	220,059	Claims on Central Govt. (Net)	32an
7,366	10,787	†13,862	15,636	14,077	15,032	7,775	5,163	13,305	15,491	14,658	10,836	13,715	38,254	40,811	Claims on Nonfin.Pub.Enterprises	32ca
1,123	1,319	†1,178	1,416	1,238	1,739	1,903	2,541	3,939	1,465	1,661	1,812	1,608	1,668	1,577	Claims on Cooperatives	32cb
39,722	48,391	†50,833	63,122	†32,845	38,516	49,124	63,453	207,456	229,640	262,113	292,392	323,580	362,634	395,583	Claims on Private Sector	32d
24,901	32,155	†35,088	39,596	46,600	50,057	59,355	70,462	75,217	78,202	85,851	96,269	108,554	118,478	122,211	Money	34
36,052	37,857	†40,772	51,336	64,220	79,386	100,256	120,539	†185,174	210,769	248,119	281,507	316,993	361,687	426,954	Quasi-Money	35
22,641	33,488	†44,814	50,273	41,009	46,330	44,285	56,839	68,924	72,115	84,621	103,960	104,684	133,105	164,564	Other Items (Net)	37r
60,953	70,012	75,859	90,932	110,821	129,442	159,611	191,002	260,391	288,971	333,970	377,775	425,548	480,164	549,164	Money plus Quasi-Money	35l
77,332	88,077	95,810	112,427	137,266	162,265	201,768	244,328	318,147	355,806	411,835	462,055	518,831	585,209	667,935	Liquid Liabilities	55l
Percent Per Annum															**Interest Rates**	
10.00	10.00	14.00	15.00	17.00	17.00	17.00	17.00	17.00	17.00	17.00	17.00	16.00	25.00	....	Bank Rate *(End of Period)*	60
13.14	18.65	22.19	21.56	25.42	21.63	25.65	18.54	41.87	24.33	18.42	15.74	16.69	17.30	21.24	Money Market Rate	60b
7.30	13.59	14.81	14.08	13.75	16.19	16.52	12.68	16.81	†17.40	....	12.59	12.51	14.02	17.57	Treasury Bill Rate	60c
11.50	13.23	16.43	19.42	†13.83	13.74	13.77	13.10	12.13	12.36	11.25	9.56	9.12	9.17	11.01	Deposit Rate	60l
9.80	12.42	13.17	13.00	†19.39	19.68	20.20	18.13	18.04	18.26	14.69	15.03	14.72	16.16	19.39	Lending Rate	60p
12.00	11.49	11.71	12.20	15.68	16.00	16.25	....	....	....	....	....	....	....	....	Government Bond Yield	61
Period Averages															**Prices and Labor**	
....	....	....	....	....	98.8	94.0	....	100.0	83.6	91.3	83.1	74.9	....	....	Share Prices	62
43.7	51.4	56.1	68.5	74.8	81.3	87.5	91.9	100.0	120.5	128.8	136.9	136.3	243.8	154.8	Wholesale Prices	63
39.7	45.2	50.5	61.3	68.8	76.6	85.6	92.9	100.0	115.9	127.0	138.9	145.4	154.4	176.3	Consumer Prices	64
36.4	45.5	52.5	62.2	69.5	79.9	96.7	98.9	100.0	109.3	117.0	132.1	134.3	237.3	141.7	Wages: Agr. Minimum Rates	65
Period Averages																
....	....	....	....	....	5,922	6,016	6,134	6,102	6,209	6,213	6,693	6,705	....	....	Labor Force	67d
....	....	....	5,964	5,136	4,986	5,072	5,148	5,316	5,587	5,569	5,946	6,159	6,308	....	Employment	67e
....	....	....	1,005	843	818	874	813	759	710	....	701	613	546	....	Unemployment	67c
....	....	....	14.4	14.1	14.1	14.7	13.6	12.5	11.3	10.7	10.6	9.1	9.8	....	Unemployment Rate (%)	67r
Millions of Rupees															**International Transactions**	
41,133	46,928	56,175	76,624	82,225	107,855	138,175	158,554	195,117	226,801	274,193	310,398	325,171	420,114	430,514	Exports	70
10,654	12,299	13,664	19,823	17,867	14,893	19,911	20,964	24,638	34,068	42,533	50,280	43,727	53,133	61,602	Tea	70s
60,528	71,200	80,225	107,729	126,643	153,555	193,550	235,576	272,201	301,076	346,026	380,138	421,888	554,290	528,589	Imports, c.i.f.	71
1995=100																
†59.6	57.9	59.1	68.8	†71.7	74.5	85.3	93.3	†100.0	104.1	115.2	113.5	119.2	141.0	134.0	Volume of Exports	72
83.5	91.3	84.8	89.7	88.2	75.4	90.7	95.3	100.0	101.4	111.5	113.0	111.8	119.7	125.4	Tea	72s
†59.7	56.7	53.2	56.2	†63.8	74.0	86.4	97.2	†100.0	100.3	112.7	122.3	122.5	138.4	124.3	Volume of Imports	73
†35.4	41.3	48.7	59.2	†60.3	75.7	83.1	87.1	†100.0	111.6	122.0	140.1	139.8	152.7	164.4	Unit Value of Exports	74
51.8	54.7	65.4	89.7	82.2	80.1	89.1	89.2	100.0	136.4	154.8	180.7	158.7	180.2	199.4	Tea	74s
†37.8	46.9	56.2	71.3	†74.1	77.6	81.7	86.5	100.0	110.5	114.7	....	....	....	....	Unit Value of Imports	75

Sri Lanka

	1972	1973	1974	1975	1976	1977	1978	1979	1980	1981	1982	1983	1984	1985	1986
Balance of Payments															*Millions of US Dollars:*
Current Account, n.i.e. .... 78al d	....	....	....	−110.0	−6.5	140.3	−67.7	−228.5	−657.2	−445.6	−548.9	−466.2	.9	−418.5	−417.1
Goods: Exports f.o.b. .... 78aa d	....	....	....	558.4	559.6	761.6	845.7	981.1	1,061.6	1,062.5	1,013.9	1,061.2	1,461.6	1,315.8	1,208.5
Goods: Imports f.o.b. .... 78ab d	....	....	....	−686.2	−579.5	−655.1	−898.7	−1,304.3	−1,845.1	−1,694.5	−1,794.3	−1,725.6	−1,698.7	−1,838.5	−1,764.3
Trade Balance .... 78ac d	....	....	....	−127.7	−20.0	106.5	−52.9	−323.2	−783.5	−632.0	−780.4	−664.4	−237.1	−522.6	−555.7
Services: Credit .... 78ad d	....	....	....	73.5	72.5	93.5	104.4	152.9	231.1	279.4	290.6	297.9	276.2	245.4	305.3
Services: Debit .... 78ae d	....	....	....	−117.5	−103.4	−113.7	−181.5	−232.8	−351.4	−359.2	−390.6	−407.3	−383.5	−457.1	−499.7
Balance on Goods & Services .... 78af d	....	....	....	−171.7	−50.9	86.3	−130.1	−403.1	−903.8	−711.8	−880.5	−773.7	−344.4	−734.4	−750.2
Income: Credit .... 78ag d	....	....	....	7.1	3.9	11.8	20.2	39.5	47.2	33.0	43.8	44.7	58.1	83.3	68.0
Income: Debit .... 78ah d	....	....	....	−25.5	−24.1	−27.5	−35.2	−54.8	−72.8	−128.8	−137.8	−181.8	−191.9	−210.1	−206.0
Balance on Gds, Serv. & Inc. .... 78ai d	....	....	....	−190.1	−71.1	70.5	−145.1	−418.4	−929.4	−807.6	−974.4	−910.8	−478.3	−861.2	−888.1
Current Transfers, n.i.e.: Credit .... 78aj d	....	....	....	85.9	70.9	77.6	94.6	201.6	287.8	388.7	451.0	464.6	503.6	468.9	502.9
Current Transfers, n.i.e.: Debit .... 78ak d	....	....	....	−5.9	−6.3	−7.8	−17.1	−11.7	−15.5	−26.6	−25.5	−20.0	−24.4	−26.1	−31.8
Capital Account, n.i.e. .... 78bc d	....	....	....	—	—	—	—	—	—	—	—	—	—	—	—
Capital Account, n.i.e.: Credit .... 78ba d	....	....	....	—	—	—	—	—	—	—	—	—	—	—	—
Capital Account: Debit .... 78bb d	....	....	....	—	—	—	—	—	—	—	—	—	—	—	—
Financial Account, n.i.e. .... 78bj d	....	....	....	86.5	45.3	−7.8	92.0	177.9	345.4	371.9	579.7	448.4	285.8	373.3	359.4
Direct Investment Abroad .... 78bd d	....	....	....	—	—	—	—	—	—	—	—	—	—	−1.4	−.5
Dir. Invest. in Rep. Econ., n.i.e. .... 78be d	....	....	....	.1	—	−1.2	1.5	46.9	43.0	49.3	63.6	37.8	32.6	26.2	29.7
Portfolio Investment Assets .... 78bf d	....	....	....	10.6	—	—	—	—	—	—	—	—	—	—	—
Equity Securities .... 78bk d	....	....	....	—	—	—	—	—	—	—	—	—	—	—	—
Debt Securities .... 78bl d	....	....	....	10.6	—	—	—	—	—	—	—	—	—	—	—
Portfolio Investment Liab., n.i.e. .... 78bg d	....	....	....	—	.5	—	.5	—	—	—	—	—	—	—	—
Equity Securities .... 78bm d	....	....	....	—	.5	—	.5	—	—	—	—	—	—	—	—
Debt Securities .... 78bn d	....	....	....	—	—	—	—	—	—	—	—	—	—	—	—
Financial Derivatives Assets .... 78bw d	....	....	....	....	....	....	....	....	....	....	....	....	....	....	....
Financial Derivatives Liabilities .... 78bx d	....	....	....	....	....	....	....	....	....	....	....	....	....	....	....
Other Investment Assets .... 78bh d	....	....	....	−2.1	−18.8	−62.6	−6.4	−22.3	−40.0	−7.2	−72.8	−57.3	−35.2	−20.9	−30.0
Monetary Authorities .... 78bo d	....	....	....	—	—	—	—	—	—	—	—	—	—	—	—
General Government .... 78bp d	....	....	....	−2.0	2.4	4.2	−1.6	1.1	−.3	−6.1	−13.3	8.7	−31.5	−1.9	8.5
Banks .... 78bq d	....	....	....	−.1	−21.2	−66.7	−4.8	−23.4	−39.7	−1.1	−59.4	−66.0	−3.7	−19.0	−38.4
Other Sectors .... 78br d	....	....	....	—	—	—	—	—	—	—	—	—	—	—	—
Other Investment Liab., n.i.e. .... 78bi d	....	....	....	77.9	63.6	56.0	96.4	153.3	342.4	329.9	588.9	467.9	288.4	369.4	360.2
Monetary Authorities .... 78bs d	....	....	....	12.0	−8.1	−9.3	1.7	19.2	13.6	−25.4	79.3	2.0	−73.3	10.3	−2.3
General Government .... 78bt d	....	....	....	102.5	81.8	75.1	81.7	117.6	124.8	260.9	260.9	278.7	351.3	289.1	314.6
Banks .... 78bu d	....	....	....	1.6	2.0	3.7	5.7	7.3	7.8	7.9	47.7	53.3	41.2	34.4	43.1
Other Sectors .... 78bv d	....	....	....	−38.1	−12.1	−13.6	7.3	9.3	196.2	86.5	201.0	134.0	−30.8	35.5	4.8
Net Errors and Omissions .... 78ca d	....	....	....	−2.4	.1	20.7	−17.7	49.4	16.2	24.0	.6	14.8	−39.7	−43.0	−34.4
Overall Balance .... 78cb d	....	....	....	−25.9	38.8	153.2	6.7	−1.3	−295.5	−49.7	31.4	−2.9	247.0	−88.2	−92.0
Reserves and Related Items .... 79da d	....	....	....	25.9	−38.8	−153.2	−6.7	1.3	295.5	49.7	−31.4	2.9	−247.0	88.2	92.0
Reserve Assets .... 79db d	....	....	....	−1.1	−50.4	−198.6	−80.5	−102.7	290.4	−108.0	−25.7	16.9	−235.1	141.4	182.7
Use of Fund Credit and Loans .... 79dc d	....	....	....	27.0	11.0	43.5	71.7	101.8	3.3	156.6	−6.3	−14.1	−11.9	−53.2	−90.7
Exceptional Financing .... 79de d	....	....	....	—	.6	1.9	2.1	2.2	1.9	1.2	.6	.2			
Government Finance															*Millions of Rupees:*
Deficit (−) or Surplus 80	−1,168	†−960	−767	−1,704	−2,518	−1,671	−5,290	−6,300	−12,157	−10,518	−13,927	−12,846	−10,482	−15,678	−18,202
Revenue 81	3,322	†3,670	4,360	4,668	5,340	6,277	11,245	12,158	13,444	14,775	16,209	23,318	34,062	36,248	37,238
Grants Received 81z		†49	253	405	381	500	661	1,390	2,620	2,721	3,376	3,473	3,293	3,307	3,753
Expenditure 82	4,493	†4,637	5,332	6,715	8,072	8,364	16,626	19,426	27,515	25,901	33,768	37,865	44,546	54,174	57,202
Lending Minus Repayments 83	−3	†42	48	62	167	84	570	422	706	2,113	−256	1,772	3,291	1,059	1,991
Financing (by Residence of Lender)															
Domestic 84a	....	†828	641	1,395	1,927	917	1,998	3,953	9,162	5,638	9,183	6,534	3,989	8,569	9,141
Foreign 85a	....	†132	126	309	591	754	3,292	2,347	2,995	4,880	4,744	6,312	6,493	7,109	9,061
Debt: Domestic 88a	....	†8,585	9,444	10,859	12,692	14,159	17,145	21,011	29,379	35,828	45,575	52,355	52,237	63,197	70,085
Foreign 89a	....	†2,989	3,302	4,288	5,406	11,498	14,247	15,031	22,774	30,050	35,376	46,729	54,192	68,196	86,723
Debt (by Currency)															
Debt: Rupees 88b	7,096	....	....	....	....	....	....	....	....	....	....	....	....	....	....
Intragovernmental Debt 88s	870	....	....	....	....	....	....	....	....	....	....	....	....	....	....
Debt: Foreign Currency 89b	2,352														
National Accounts															*Millions of Rupees*
Househ.Cons.Expend.,incl.NPISHs 96f	10,952	14,083	19,068	21,942	22,991	26,698	32,105	40,371	53,399	68,751	79,226	94,945	111,235	126,503	139,370
Government Consumption Expend. 91f	1,897	2,016	2,743	2,480	3,021	3,118	4,043	4,798	5,685	6,310	8,242	9,889	11,935	16,599	18,480
Gross Fixed Capital Formation 93e	2,206	2,493	2,972	3,699	4,595	5,035	8,521	13,246	20,845	23,279	30,279	35,342	39,558	38,457	42,326
Changes in Inventories 93i	432	35	763	441	301	224	33	281	1,620	331	248	−210	150	225	137
Exports of Goods and Services 90c	3,404	4,481	6,283	7,306	8,773	12,311	14,835	17,660	21,434	25,892	27,148	32,016	44,285	42,237	42,568
Imports of Goods and Services (−) 98c	3,644	4,704	8,058	9,291	9,478	10,979	16,872	23,969	36,456	39,558	45,905	50,381	53,417	61,646	63,407
Gross Domestic Product (GDP) 99b	15,247	18,404	23,771	26,577	30,203	36,407	42,665	52,387	66,527	85,005	99,238	121,601	153,746	162,375	179,474
Net Primary Income from Abroad 98.n	−178	−183	−183	−213	−282	−252	−237	−240	−432	−1,868	−1,959	−3,214	−3,401	−3,400	−3,861
GDP at Factor Cost 99ba	14,720	17,920	23,302	25,691	28,032	34,684	40,479	49,782	62,246	79,337	94,679	113,878	140,039	148,321	163,713
Gross National Income (GNI) 99a	14,042	16,784	21,482	23,619	25,704	31,256	42,428	52,147	67,906	82,659	97,279	118,387	149,293	158,975	175,613
Net National Income 99e	13,576	15,869	20,489	22,439	24,212	29,707	37,110	49,700	63,457	77,868	89,983	109,671	137,091	146,788	160,870
GDP at Fact.Cost,Vol.'70 Prices .... 99ba p	13,631	14,138	14,585	14,987	15,431	16,078	17,401	18,501	19,575	20,706	21,756	....	....	....	....
GDP at Fact.Cost,Vol.'82 Prices .... 99ba p	....	....	....	....	....	....	....	....	....	....	....	94,679	99,375	104,395	109,570	114,261
GDP at Fact.Cost,Vol.'96 Prices .... 99ba p	....	....	....	....	....	....	....	....	....	....	....	....	....	....	....
GDP Volume (1995=100) .... 99bv p	35.3	36.6	37.8	38.8	40.0	41.7	45.1	47.9	50.7	53.7	56.4	59.2	62.2	65.2	68.0
GDP Deflator (1995=100) .... 99bi p	40.7	47.8	60.1	64.4	68.2	80.8	87.1	17.4	20.5	24.7	28.1	32.2	37.7	38.0	40.2
															Millions:
Population 99z	12.86	13.09	13.28	13.50	13.72	13.94	14.19	14.47	14.75	15.01	15.19	15.42	15.60	15.84	16.13

1987	1988	1989	1990	1991	1992	1993	1994	1995	1996	1997	1998	1999	2000	2001			
Minus Sign Indicates Debit																**Balance of Payments**	
−326.1	−394.5	−413.7	−298.3	−594.8	−450.7	−382.2	−757.4	−769.9	−682.7	−394.7	−227.7	−561.3	−1,042.4	....	Current Account, n.i.e.	**78ald**
1,393.9	1,477.1	1,505.1	1,853.0	2,003.3	2,301.4	2,785.7	3,208.3	3,797.9	4,095.2	4,638.7	4,808.0	4,596.2	5,439.6	....	Goods: Exports f.o.b.	**78aad**
−1,866.0	−2,017.5	−2,055.1	−2,325.6	−2,808.0	−3,016.5	−3,527.8	−4,293.4	−4,782.6	−4,895.0	−5,278.3	−5,313.4	−5,365.5	−6,483.6	....	Goods: Imports f.o.b.	**78abd**
−472.2	−540.5	−550.1	−472.5	−804.7	−715.1	−742.1	−1,085.0	−984.7	−799.7	−639.6	−505.4	−769.3	−1,044.0	....	*Trade Balance*	**78acd**
328.2	339.2	345.6	439.6	546.6	621.4	634.4	753.9	819.2	765.5	875.3	916.6	964.3	938.7	....	Services: Credit	**78add**
−533.2	−547.1	−565.8	−639.2	−762.5	−823.2	−874.3	−1,052.3	−1,199.1	−1,204.3	−1,302.6	−1,361.6	−1,413.7	−1,621.4	....	Services: Debit	**78aed**
−677.2	−748.4	−770.3	−672.0	−1,020.6	−916.9	−982.1	−1,383.4	−1,364.6	−1,238.6	−1,066.9	−950.5	−1,218.6	−1,726.7	....	*Balance on Goods & Services*	**78afd**
69.3	68.7	58.6	93.0	54.5	68.1	111.4	143.9	223.3	175.1	233.3	214.2	166.7	149.0	....	Income: Credit	**78agd**
−210.8	−240.8	−221.3	−259.8	−232.5	−246.2	−234.3	−312.0	−360.6	−378.2	−392.9	−394.5	−419.3	−448.4	....	Income: Debit	**78ahd**
−818.7	−920.5	−933.0	−838.8	−1,198.5	−1,094.9	−1,105.0	−1,551.6	−1,501.9	−1,441.6	−1,226.5	−1,130.8	−1,471.2	−2,026.2	....	*Balance on Gds, Serv. & Inc.*	**78aid**
530.0	563.7	546.6	578.8	644.5	730.4	795.4	882.3	846.7	881.4	966.5	1,054.5	1,078.1	1,166.5	....	Current Transfers, n.i.e.: Credit	**78ajd**
−37.3	−37.7	−27.3	−38.3	−40.8	−86.1	−72.6	−88.1	−114.7	−122.4	−134.7	−151.3	−168.2	−182.7	....	Current Transfers: Debit	**78akd**
—	—	—	—	—	—	—	—	120.6	95.9	87.1	79.9	80.0	50.7	....	Capital Account, n.i.e.	**78bcd**
—	—	—	—	—	—	—	—	124.2	99.7	91.3	84.6	85.2	56.3	....	Capital Account, n.i.e.: Credit	**78bad**
—	—	—	—	—	—	—	—	−3.5	−3.8	−4.2	−4.7	−5.2	−5.7	....	Capital Account: Debit	**78bbd**
395.3	253.3	580.3	529.1	692.9	479.0	1,022.1	958.8	730.1	452.2	466.7	345.1	413.4	574.5	....	Financial Account, n.i.e.	**78bjd**
−1.3	−2.1	−2.0	−.8	−4.5	−1.6	−6.9	−8.3							....	Direct Investment Abroad	**78bdd**
59.5	45.7	19.7	43.4	48.4	122.6	194.5	166.4	56.0	119.9	430.1	193.4	176.4	172.9	....	Dir. Invest. in Rep. Econ., n.i.e.	**78bed**
—	—	—	—	32.1	25.7	200.1	292.9	105.3	76.8	139.9	88.9	71.8	19.1	....	Portfolio Investment Assets	**78bfd**
—	—	—	—											....	Equity Securities	**78bkd**
—	—	—	—	32.1	25.7	200.1	292.9	105.3	76.8	139.9	88.9	71.8	19.1	....	Debt Securities	**78bld**
—	—	—	—	—	—	−132.9	−265.9	−107.3	−70.2	−126.8	−112.9	−84.6	−63.4	....	Portfolio Investment Liab., n.i.e.	**78bgd**
—	—	—	—	—	—									....	Equity Securities	**78bmd**
—	—	—	—	—	—	−132.9	−265.9	−107.3	−70.2	−126.8	−112.9	−84.6	−63.4	....	Debt Securities	**78bnd**
....	....	....	....	....	....									....	Financial Derivatives Assets	**78bwd**
....	....	....	....	....	....									....	Financial Derivatives Liabilities	**78bxd**
−56.9	−15.8	−11.3	−115.8	−51.6	−100.3	16.4	−134.0	41.7	−27.9	−392.9	75.9	23.2	−238.0	....	Other Investment Assets	**78bhd**
														....	Monetary Authorities	**78bod**
25.2	.7	−27.5	14.8	−13.0	3.3	−2.4	9.4	3.6	−6.4	1.7	−2.9	−1.1	1.4	....	General Government	**78bpd**
−82.1	−16.6	16.2	−130.6	−38.6	−103.6	18.8	−143.4	38.1	−21.5	−394.6	78.8	24.3	−239.4	....	Banks	**78bqd**
														....	Other Sectors	**78brd**
394.0	225.5	573.8	602.4	668.6	432.7	750.9	907.6	634.4	353.6	416.5	99.7	226.6	683.9	....	Other Investment Liab., n.i.e.	**78bid**
62.0	−43.0	251.1	116.8	3.8	−22.2	25.9	9.6	14.4	11.6	30.3	17.5	65.8	75.8	....	Monetary Authorities	**78bsd**
223.7	277.2	217.2	408.9	532.5	233.3	262.6	246.9	448.4	218.0	144.5	203.6	62.5	168.6	....	General Government	**78btd**
81.4	28.9	63.1	55.5	106.2	108.3	128.2	73.4	86.7	95.8	209.4	−130.7	−88.4	258.3	....	Banks	**78bud**
27.0	−37.7	42.4	21.2	26.1	113.3	334.3	577.7	85.0	28.2	32.3	9.3	186.8	181.1	....	Other Sectors	**78bvd**
−122.5	37.3	−115.0	−115.1	225.6	173.3	128.0	106.3	157.9	143.6	148.0	26.3	−27.3	56.4	....	Net Errors and Omissions	**78cad**
−53.2	−103.9	51.5	115.7	323.7	201.7	767.9	307.7	238.7	9.0	307.2	223.6	−95.2	−360.8		*Overall Balance*	**78cbd**
53.2	103.9	−51.5	−115.7	−323.7	−201.7	−767.9	−307.7	−238.7	−9.0	−307.2	−223.6	95.2	360.8	....	Reserves and Related Items	**79dad**
167.9	3.2	−65.1	−132.3	−312.5	−284.6	−820.7	−373.5	−204.7	36.3	−241.4	−141.0	194.8	446.5	....	Reserve Assets	**79dbd**
−114.6	100.7	13.6	16.5	−11.2	82.9	52.8	65.9	−34.1	−45.2	−65.7	−82.6	−99.7	−85.7	....	Use of Fund Credit and Loans	**79dcd**
—	—	—	—	—	—	—	—	—	—	—	—	—	—		Exceptional Financing	**79ded**
Year Ending December 31																**Government Finance**	
−17,073	−28,195	−21,778	−25,153	−35,197	−22,912	−32,084	†−49,474	−55,196	−59,913	−40,232	−81,560	−76,359	−118,995[P]	−90,558[f]	Deficit (−) or Surplus	**80**
42,144	41,749	53,979	67,964	76,460	85,780	98,495	†110,038	136,257	146,280	165,036	175,032	195,905	211,282[P]	264,479[f]	Revenue	**81**
4,677	6,588	6,407	6,697	7,870	8,280	8,025	†8,257	9,028	7,739	7,329	7,200	6,761	5,145[P]	7,500[f]	Grants Received	**81z**
62,376	69,010	77,634	91,300	109,060	114,586	134,728	†157,476	195,880	212,787	228,730	253,809	267,611	322,048[P]	365,326[f]	Expenditure	**82**
1,518	7,522	4,530	8,514	10,467	2,386	3,876	†10,293	4,601	1,145	−16,133	9,983	11,414	13,374[P]	−2,789[f]	Lending Minus Repayments	**83**
															Financing (by Residence of Lender)	
11,357	21,067	15,852	13,509	15,868	15,551	22,229	†37,696	33,972	49,753	30,275	71,363	74,875	118,500[P]	69,065[f]	Domestic	**84a**
5,716	7,128	5,926	11,644	19,329	7,361	9,855	†11,778	21,224	10,160	17,287	17,397	8,245	5,640[P]	28,963[f]	Foreign	**85a**
80,133	98,596	117,561	133,898	152,119	170,020	213,685	249,118	285,759	349,007	387,740	463,426	543,465	676,660[P]	....	Debt: Domestic	**88a**
92,857	125,997	156,298	176,883	214,579	235,538	269,883	300,174	346,286	360,313	376,331	461,273	507,866	542,040[P]		Foreign	**89a**
															Debt (by Currency)	
....	....	....	....	152,119	170,020	213,685	249,118	285,759	349,007	382,962	446,547	543,465	676,660[P]	....	Debt: Rupees	**88b**
....	....	....	....	—	—	—	—	—	—	—	—	—	—[P]	....	Intragovernmental Debt	**88s**
....	....	....	....	214,579	235,538	269,883	300,174	346,286	360,313	383,615	461,454	508,396	542,207	....	Debt: Foreign Currency	**89b**
Millions of Rupees																**National Accounts**	
151,949	173,457	194,680	244,288	288,214	320,466	373,785	434,933	489,057	569,416	643,839	723,506	790,379	906,186	1,023,990	Houseli.Cons.Expend.,incl.NPISHs	**96f**
19,538	21,849	26,410	31,405	36,633	40,972	45,791	56,002	76,604	81,021	92,196	99,745	99,851	131,583	....	Government Consumption Expend.	**91f**
45,752	49,961	54,249	70,417	84,206	100,039	125,875	154,260	170,875	183,509	216,873	255,714	301,728	352,632	308,473	Gross Fixed Capital Formation	**93e**
148	601	473	1,038	950	3,200	1,800	2,250	950	2,755	230	175	95	40	40	Changes in Inventories	**93i**
49,559	57,885	68,666	97,117	107,016	135,114	168,858	195,805	237,711	268,640	325,289	368,957	392,437	490,676	514,285	Exports of Goods and Services	**90c**
70,223	81,771	92,587	122,481	144,674	174,508	216,544	264,166	307,425	337,213	388,154	430,111	478,526	624,048	605,673	Imports of Goods and Services (−)	**98c**
196,723	221,982	251,891	321,784	372,345	425,283	499,565	579,084	667,772	768,128	890,272	1,017,986	1,105,964	1,257,634	1,400,117	Gross Domestic Product (GDP)	**99b**
−4,336	−5,266	−5,739	−6,685	−7,367	−7,820	−5,979	−8,310	−6,958	−11,258	−9,409	−11,556	−17,831	−23,037	−22,996	Net Primary Income from Abroad	**98.n**
177,731	203,516	228,138	290,615	337,399	386,999	453,092	523,300	598,327	695,934	803,698	912,839	994,730	1,125,259	1,252,744	GDP at Factor Cost	**99ba**
192,387	216,716	246,152	315,099	364,978	417,463	493,586	570,774	660,814	756,875	880,828	1,006,373	1,088,154	1,233,518	1,078,140	Gross National Income (GNI)	**99a**
175,333	203,938	232,298	298,256	345,111	....	....	....	....	....	....	....	....	....	....	Net National Income	**99e**
115,922	119,050	121,729	129,244	135,204	140,990	150,783	159,269	167,953	174,261					....	GDP at Fact.Cost,Vol.'70 Prices	**99ba p**
....	....	....	....	....	....	....	....	....	695,934	739,763	774,796	808,340	857,035		GDP at Fact.Cost,Vol.'82 Prices	**99ba p**
															GDP at Fact.Cost,Vol.'96 Prices	**99ba p**
69.0	70.9	72.5	77.0	80.5	83.9	89.8	94.8	100.0	414.4	440.5	461.3	481.3	510.3	....	GDP Volume (1995=100)	**99bv p**
43.0	48.0	52.6	63.1	70.0	77.0	84.3	92.2	100.0	28.1	30.5	33.3	34.5	36.9	....	GDP Deflator (1995=100)	**99bi p**
Midyear Estimates																	
16.36	16.60	16.83	17.02	17.27	17.43	17.65	17.89	18.14	18.32	18.55	18.77	19.04	19.36	19.10	**Population**	**99z**

(See notes in the back of the book.)

Sudan

		1972	1973	1974	1975	1976	1977	1978	1979	1980	1981	1982	1983	1984	1985	1986
Exchange Rates															*Dinars per SDR:*	
Market Rate	aa	.04	.04	.04	.04	.04	.04	.05	.07	.06	.10	.14	.14	.13	.27	.31
															Dinars per US Dollar:	
Market Rate	ae	.03	.03	.03	.03	.03	.03	.04	.05	.05	.09	.13	.13	.13	.25	.25
Market Rate	rf	.03	.03	.03	.03	.03	.03	.04	.04	.05	.06	.10	.13	.13	.23	.25
Fund Position															*Millions of SDRs:*	
Quota	2f. s	72.0	72.0	72.0	72.0	72.0	72.0	88.0	88.0	132.0	132.0	132.0	169.7	169.7	169.7	169.7
SDRs	1b. s	4.9	13.6	21.5	7.3	—	—	6.0	10.0	—	.5	—	.1	—	—	—
Reserve Position in the Fund	1c. s	—	—	—	—	—	—	—	—	—	—	—	—	—	—	—
Total Fund Cred.&Loans Outstg.	2tl	28.1	29.0	71.7	113.4	119.1	99.5	150.6	222.4	338.0	484.8	524.6	666.7	677.6	672.7	672.7
International Liquidity													*Millions of US Dollars Unless Otherwise Indicated:*			
Total Reserves minus Gold	1l. d	35.6	61.3	124.3	36.4	23.6	23.1	28.4	67.4	48.7	17.0	20.5	16.6	17.2	12.2	58.5
SDRs	1b. d	5.3	16.4	26.4	8.6	—	—	7.9	13.2	—	.6	—	.1	—	—	—
Reserve Position in the Fund	1c. d	—	—	—	—	—	—	—	—	—	—	—	—	—	—	—
Foreign Exchange	1d. d	30.3	44.9	97.9	27.8	23.6	23.1	20.5	54.2	48.7	16.4	20.5	16.5	17.2	12.2	58.5
Monetary Authorities: Other Liab.	4.. d	127.5	136.5	144.0	362.1	483.6	536.1	501.8	559.8	682.6	898.3	873.9	1,520.2	1,614.7	1,180.0	1,308.7
Deposit Money Banks: Assets	7a. d	2.7	13.4	17.4	18.1	67.8	172.6	168.1	193.7	435.0	309.5	289.2	409.4	512.7	618.1	493.9
Liabilities	7b. d	21.9	45.4	34.9	57.2	72.1	145.3	106.9	73.2	144.1	146.8	122.0	117.2	136.7	215.5	165.9
Monetary Authorities														*Millions of Dinars through 1991;*		
Foreign Assets	11	1.3	2.3	3.9	1.2	.8	.9	1.3	3.4	2.0	1.5	2.7	†2.2	2.2	3.4	15.6
Claims on Central Government	12a	....	....	....	....	....	....	....	....	....	....	....	163.1	198.5	289.4	428.5
of which: Accum. Interest Arrears	12ag															
Claims on Nonfin.Pub.Enterprises	12c	5.0	4.9	8.4	16.0	18.2	18.1	22.7	28.4	37.7	53.4	79.6	†47.3	58.2	114.7	165.6
Claims on Deposit Money Banks	12e	2.1	2.4	2.7	3.2	2.7	3.6	5.5	6.6	7.3	9.7	12.2	†6.8	20.3	22.2	22.4
Reserve Money	14	9.3	11.9	16.3	19.3	23.5	38.0	50.2	66.7	75.1	121.1	158.2	†174.0	244.4	395.0	561.5
of which: Currency Outside DMBs	14a	7.5	9.3	11.9	12.9	15.3	19.9	27.9	38.0	50.8	63.0	82.0	†102.2	124.7	193.0	276.0
Quasi-Monetary Deposits	15	....	....	....	....	....	....	....	....	....	....	....				
Cent. Bk. Liab.: Musharaka Certif.	16ac												1.3	10.1	10.2	8.9
Foreign Liabilities	16c	5.1	5.0	8.1	17.2	21.7	22.9	26.4	39.2	51.2	124.4	178.8	†278.8	287.7	461.2	512.3
Central Government Deposits	16d	.7	.5	4.1	3.5	4.6	3.2	5.4	30.6	46.9	47.9	70.9	....			
Capital Accounts	17a	1.4	1.4	1.4	1.4	1.7	2.4	2.8	†2.8	2.8	1.8	1.9	4.5	4.2	4.2	5.9
Valuation Adjustment	17rv												−153.2	−153.2	−320.9	−341.8
Other Items (Net)	17r	−8.1	−9.1	−14.8	−21.1	−29.7	−44.0	−55.4	−101.0	−129.1	−230.7	−315.2	†−86.0	−114.1	−114.7	−114.7
Deposit Money Banks														*Millions of Dinars through 1991;*		
Reserves	20	1.1	1.9	2.4	3.4	4.4	11.5	17.6	24.0	19.6	39.1	40.8	82.6	93.7	†200.9	269.5
Claims on Mon.Author.: Securities	20c															
Foreign Assets	21	.1	.4	.6	.6	2.4	6.0	6.7	9.7	21.7	27.9	37.6	53.2	66.7	†154.5	123.5
Claims on Central Government	22a	2.9	3.7	5.4	6.0	7.6	10.6	13.3	15.9	18.6	28.5	46.6	9.4	9.6	10.0	11.2
Claims on State and Local Govt.	22b	....	....	....	....	....	....	....	....	....	....	....	....			
Claims on Nonfin.Pub.Enterprises	22c	....	....	....	....	....	....	....	....	....	....	....	....			
Claims on Private Sector	22d	8.5	9.9	12.3	18.6	22.8	26.5	34.3	46.1	59.3	77.8	114.3	137.7	160.9	†188.2	263.8
Claims on Nonbank Financial Insts	22f	....	....	....	....	....	....	....	....	....	....	....				
Demand Deposits	24	6.2	7.4	9.9	12.1	15.5	22.6	29.2	39.2	54.0	65.3	88.4	116.5	132.6	†192.5	263.6
Time and Savings Deposits	25	2.9	3.7	5.4	6.0	6.6	10.8	12.6	15.9	18.2	28.8	46.5	76.1	85.2	†186.2	187.5
Foreign Liabilities	26c	.7	1.3	1.2	2.0	2.5	5.1	4.3	3.7	7.2	13.2	15.9	15.2	17.8	†53.9	41.5
Central Government Deposits	26d	.3	.2	.2	.3	.8	1.5	1.9	1.5	1.3	2.5	1.2	4.6	5.7	26.5	66.4
Credit from Monetary Authorities	26g	.6	.9	.9	1.3	.9	1.4	3.3	4.0	5.3	7.1	9.3	14.8	12.7	3.1	1.2
Capital Accounts	27a	.6	.6	.6	.6	1.0	1.6	1.9	2.1	2.9	4.5	9.4	24.7	32.6	†65.2	77.3
Valuation Adjustment	27rv														30.0	30.0
Other Items (Net)	27r	1.1	1.6	2.5	6.4	9.9	11.7	18.7	29.3	30.4	51.7	68.5	31.1	44.3	†−3.6	.6
Monetary Survey														*Millions of Dinars through 1991;*		
Foreign Assets (Net)	31n	−4.4	−3.6	−4.8	−17.4	−21.0	−21.0	−22.7	−29.8	−34.7	−108.2	−154.3	†−238.6	−236.6	†−357.2	−414.6
Domestic Credit	32	24.6	27.5	35.7	56.7	72.6	95.6	118.6	145.5	177.0	237.8	276.1	357.4	427.2	†583.0	811.1
Claims on Central Govt. (Net)	32an	9.8	11.2	13.2	20.0	29.4	48.8	59.3	68.7	77.7	103.7	79.1	†167.9	202.5	272.9	373.3
Claims on State and Local Govt.	32b															
Claims on Nonfin.Pub.Enterprises	32c	5.0	4.9	8.4	16.0	18.2	18.1	22.7	28.4	37.7	53.4	79.6	†47.3	58.2	114.7	165.6
Claims on Private Sector	32d	8.5	9.9	12.3	18.6	22.8	26.5	34.3	46.1	59.3	77.8	114.3	137.7	160.9	†188.2	263.8
Claims on Nonbank Financial Inst	32f	....	....	....	....	....	....	....	....	....	....	....	4.5	5.7	7.2	8.4
Money	34	14.4	17.6	23.7	28.1	35.0	49.7	63.4	83.7	109.7	153.1	209.1	233.6	276.4	†414.5	584.9
Quasi-Money	35	2.2	3.0	4.1	4.9	6.2	9.2	11.7	14.1	16.7	26.4	44.3	77.4	95.5	†196.4	196.4
Valuation Adjustment	37rv												−153.2	−153.2	−290.9	−311.8
Other Items (Net)	37r	3.6	3.4	3.2	6.3	10.4	15.7	20.8	18.0	15.9	−49.9	−131.7	†18.5	29.6	†−19.8	1.3
Money plus Quasi-Money	35l	16.6	20.5	27.8	33.0	41.2	58.9	75.1	97.7	126.4	179.5	253.4	311.0	371.9	†610.8	781.3
Other Banking Institutions															*Millions of Dinars:*	
Savings Deposits	45	.7	.7	1.4	1.2	1.4	1.4	1.6	1.9	2.0	2.1	2.3	2.5	2.7	3.0	....
Liquid Liabilities	55l	17.3	21.3	29.2	34.2	42.6	60.3	76.6	99.6	128.4	181.6	255.7	313.5	374.6	571.3	....
Interest Rates															*Percent Per Annum*	
Deposit Rate	60l	....	....	....	....	....	....	6.0	6.0	6.0	8.6	10.5	13.5	13.5	....	....
Prices and Labor														*Index Numbers (1995=100):*		
Consumer Prices	64	—	—	—	—	—	.1	.1	.1	.1	.1	.2	.2	.3	†.4	.5
															Number in Thousands:	
Labor Force	67d	....	....	....	....	....	....	....	....	....	....	....	....	....	....	....

Exchange Rates

End of Period

	1987	1988	1989	1990	1991	1992	1993	1994	1995	1996	1997	1998	1999	2000	2001	
Market Rate	.64	.61	.59	.64	2.14	18.58	29.86	58.39	78.24	208.40	232.34	334.83	353.70	335.30	328.55	**aa**

End of Period (ae) Period Average (rf)

	1987	1988	1989	1990	1991	1992	1993	1994	1995	1996	1997	1998	1999	2000	2001	
Market Rate	.45	.45	.45	.45	1.50	13.51	21.74	40.00	52.63	144.93	172.20	237.80	257.70	257.35	261.43	**ae**
Market Rate	.30	.45	.45	.45	.70	9.74	15.93	28.96	58.09	125.08	157.57	200.80	252.55	257.12	258.70	**rf**

Fund Position

End of Period

	1987	1988	1989	1990	1991	1992	1993	1994	1995	1996	1997	1998	1999	2000	2001	
Quota	169.7	169.7	169.7	169.7	169.7	169.7	169.7	169.7	169.7	169.7	169.7	169.7	169.7	169.7	169.7	**2f. s**
SDRs	—	—	—	—	—	—	—	—	—	—	—	—	—	—	—	**1b. s**
Reserve Position in the Fund	—	—	—	—	—	—	—	—	—	—	—	—	—	—	—	**1c. s**
Total Fund Cred.&Loans Outstg.	672.7	672.7	672.7	671.6	671.6	671.6	671.6	671.6	645.7	621.2	590.5	548.4	520.8	479.7	438.6	**2tl**

International Liquidity

End of Period

	1987	1988	1989	1990	1991	1992	1993	1994	1995	1996	1997	1998	1999	2000	2001	
Total Reserves minus Gold	11.7	12.1	15.9	11.4	7.6	27.5	37.4	78.2	163.4	106.8	81.6	90.6	188.7	247.3	....	**1l. d**
SDRs	—	—	—	—	—	—	—	—	—	—	—	—	—	—	—	**1b. d**
Reserve Position in the Fund	—	—	—	—	—	—	—	—	—	—	—	—	—	—	—	**1c. d**
Foreign Exchange	11.7	12.1	15.9	11.4	7.6	27.5	37.4	78.1	163.3	106.8	81.6	90.6	188.7	†247.3	....	**1d. d**
Monetary Authorities: Other Liab.	1,016.3	1,703.6	1,809.5	2,400.6	1,340.4	2,165.8	2,288.0	2,471.8	3,407.1	2,549.9	2,464.4	2,538.9	2,618.8	2,640.2	2,654.1	**4. d**
Deposit Money Banks: Assets	354.5	500.2	539.8	616.9	599.5	322.0	447.7	270.1	320.5	206.9	258.4	268.8	266.1	286.2	343.2	**7a. d**
Liabilities	137.5	136.2	134.4	154.6	106.6	70.1	68.8	37.8	53.5	29.7	25.6	19.9	13.4	14.8	34.8	**7b. d**

Monetary Authorities

Billions of Dinars Beginning 1992: End of Period

	1987	1988	1989	1990	1991	1992	1993	1994	1995	1996	1997	1998	1999	2000	2001	
Foreign Assets	6.7	8.9	8.0	44.6	72.0	†.4	.8	3.1	8.6	15.5	14.0	21.6	48.6	†73.1	41.3	**11**
Claims on Central Government	617.4	872.6	1,590.7	2,231.4	3,593.2	†10.8	16.5	22.0	32.9	76.0	84.8	101.8	134.8	†169.0	195.5	**12a**
of which: Accum. Interest Arrears	....	....	....	....	....	....	....	....	....	....	....	....	....	52.7	64.1	**12ag**
Claims on Nonfin.Pub.Enterprises	228.3	272.4	356.8	388.8	269.8	†.2	.2	.2	.2	.2	.2	.2	3.5	†17.1	14.8	**12c**
Claims on Deposit Money Banks	24.8	29.3	35.5	44.0	34.8	†.1	.5	.4	.4	.4	2.4	6.1	7.2	†8.8	12.6	**12e**
Reserve Money	716.0	944.7	1,751.5	2,333.8	3,460.8	†8.8	14.4	20.2	35.7	64.9	87.2	112.8	152.4	†223.6	233.6	**14**
of which: Currency Outside DMBs	362.5	560.1	924.0	1,311.3	2,166.3	†4.4	9.5	14.8	24.9	44.4	58.5	82.1	108.1	†142.1	153.8	**14a**
Quasi-Monetary Deposits	17.5	19.0	22.4	26.8	38.9	†.6	.6	2.1	3.2	3.2	3.1	3.3	3.2	†—	—	**15**
Cent. Bk. Liab.: Musharaka Certif.												4.9	4.2	†1.1	.6	**16ac**
Foreign Liabilities	843.8	1,133.3	1,172.3	1,467.3	3,305.5	†40.5	67.8	134.2	224.8	485.6	547.8	767.5	838.1	†820.4	818.5	**16c**
Central Government Deposits	....	....	....	....	....	†1.2	.9	.9	1.2	10.8	9.2	3.7	5.1	†8.4	9.6	**16d**
Capital Accounts	12.8	21.2	34.8	37.4	39.4	†—	.1	.2	.4	1.2	1.2	2.0	2.6	†4.2	4.3	**17a**
Valuation Adjustment	-592.5	-836.4	-894.9	-1,060.6	-2,946.4	†-39.2	-63.1	-124.9	-206.6	-444.8	-515.0	-724.2	-772.0	†-776.7	-781.5	**17rv**
Other Items (Net)	-120.5	-98.5	-95.1	-96.0	71.5	†-.4	-2.7	-6.9	-16.8	-28.9	-32.0	-40.4	-39.5	†-13.1	-21.0	**17r**

Deposit Money Banks

Billions of Dinars Beginning 1992: End of Period

	1987	1988	1989	1990	1991	1992	1993	1994	1995	1996	1997	1998	1999	2000	2001	
Reserves	328.3	320.3	725.8	831.5	1,008.5	†3.7	4.6	5.6	8.0	14.3	28.1	30.6	37.9	57.1	57.4	**20**
Claims on Mon.Author.: Securities	....	....	....	....	....	....	....	....	....	....	....	4.9	4.2	1.1	.6	**20c**
Foreign Assets	159.5	225.1	242.9	277.6	898.8	†4.4	9.7	10.8	16.9	30.0	44.5	63.9	68.6	73.7	89.7	**21**
Claims on Central Government	6.0	6.0	24.3	1.0	—	†—	.5	.2	.2	.1	.1	.1	.2	4.2	7.3	**22a**
Claims on State and Local Govt.	....	....	....	....	....	†—	.1	—	.1	.2	.2	.1	.1	—	.5	**22b**
Claims on Nonfin.Pub.Enterprises	....	....	....	....	....	†.6	.7	1.2	1.2	1.7	1.7	2.6	4.7	5.6	9.1	**22c**
Claims on Private Sector	379.3	450.9	494.1	766.7	1,404.9	†2.7	4.5	8.8	13.1	31.9	39.4	44.3	43.6	71.5	101.1	**22d**
Claims on Nonbank Financial Insts	....	....	....	....	....	†—	.1	.1	.1	.2	.4	.4	.4	2.1	.6	**22f**
Demand Deposits	363.3	474.4	847.0	1,144.3	1,871.4	†4.6	6.2	9.5	15.6	30.9	41.4	46.9	56.9	84.1	109.1	**24**
Time and Savings Deposits	272.0	275.6	259.3	437.5	942.8	†3.4	10.1	13.7	25.7	36.1	55.0	72.7	85.1	106.7	158.0	**25**
Foreign Liabilities	61.9	61.3	60.5	69.6	159.9	†.9	1.5	1.5	2.8	4.3	4.4	4.7	3.4	3.8	9.1	**26c**
Central Government Deposits	112.1	107.9	110.9	121.6	171.7	†.2	.3	.2	.3	.8	.4	.4	3.5	6.4	7.1	**26d**
Credit from Monetary Authorities	1.0	1.2	1.4	1.5	8.4	†—	.1	.1	.8	.1	.1	.3	3.0	2.5	2.5	**26g**
Capital Accounts	76.4	115.7	141.4	160.7	242.2	†.6	1.7	3.9	5.5	11.1	14.8	20.3	24.5	32.2	47.6	**27a**
Valuation Adjustment	30.0	30.0	30.0	49.6	300.0	†1.2	1.1	.7	1.1	1.4	2.8	2.4	-.4	-.8	-.2	**27rv**
Other Items (Net)	-43.4	-63.8	36.7	-108.0	-384.1	†-.2	-1.6	-4.1	-13.5	-8.2	-6.5	-.9	-16.5	-19.6	-66.8	**27r**

Monetary Survey

Billions of Dinars Beginning 1992: End of Period

	1987	1988	1989	1990	1991	1992	1993	1994	1995	1996	1997	1998	1999	2000	2001	
Foreign Assets (Net)	-739.5	-960.6	-981.9	-1,214.7	-2,494.6	†-36.7	-58.7	-121.7	-202.1	-444.4	-493.7	-686.8	-724.3	†-677.5	-696.6	**31n**
Domestic Credit	1,127.4	1,502.4	2,368.9	3,283.1	5,113.1	†12.9	21.4	31.5	46.2	98.8	117.0	145.3	178.5	†254.7	312.3	**32**
Claims on Central Govt. (Net)	511.4	770.7	1,504.1	2,110.8	3,421.6	†9.4	15.8	21.1	31.5	64.6	75.2	97.7	126.3	†158.4	186.1	**32an**
Claims on State and Local Govt.	....	....	....	....	....	†—	.1	—	.1	.2	.2	.1	.1	—	.5	**32b**
Claims on Nonfin.Pub.Enterprises	228.3	272.4	356.8	388.8	269.8	†.8	.9	1.4	1.4	1.9	1.9	2.8	8.2	†22.8	23.9	**32c**
Claims on Private Sector	379.3	450.9	494.1	766.7	1,404.9	†2.7	4.5	8.8	13.1	31.9	39.4	44.3	43.6	71.5	101.1	**32d**
Claims on Nonbank Financial Inst	8.4	8.4	13.9	16.9	16.9	†—	.1	.1	.1	.2	.4	.4	.4	2.1	.6	**32f**
Money	776.8	1,121.8	1,889.9	2,765.9	4,430.5	†8.9	15.7	24.3	40.5	75.4	99.8	129.1	165.0	†234.6	271.4	**34**
Quasi-Money	289.5	294.6	281.7	464.3	981.7	†4.1	10.8	15.8	28.9	39.3	58.1	76.1	88.3	†112.1	160.8	**35**
Valuation Adjustment	-562.5	-806.4	-864.9	-1,011.0	-2,646.4	†-38.0	-62.0	-124.5	-205.5	-443.4	-512.2	-721.9	-772.4	†-777.5	-781.7	**37rv**
Other Items (Net)	-41.6	7.7	100.2	-76.5	-73.0	†.2	-1.8	-6.0	-19.8	-16.9	-22.4	-24.7	-26.7	†8.1	-34.9	**37r**
Money plus Quasi-Money	1,066.4	1,416.4	2,171.6	3,230.2	5,412.2	†13.0	26.5	40.0	69.4	114.7	157.9	205.2	253.3	346.7	432.2	**35l**

Other Banking Institutions

End of Period

	1987	1988	1989	1990	1991	1992	1993	1994	1995	1996	1997	1998	1999	2000	2001	
Savings Deposits	....	....	....	....	....	....	....	....	....	....	....	....	....	....	....	**45**
Liquid Liabilities	....	....	....	....	....	....	....	....	....	....	....	....	....	....	....	**55l**

Interest Rates

Percent Per Annum

	1987	1988	1989	1990	1991	1992	1993	1994	1995	1996	1997	1998	1999	2000	2001	
Deposit Rate	....	....	....	....	....	....	....	....	....	....	....	....	....	....	....	**60l**

Prices and Labor

Period Averages

	1987	1988	1989	1990	1991	1992	1993	1994	1995	1996	1997	1998	1999	2000	2001	
Consumer Prices	....	†1.0	1.7	2.8	6.3	13.7	27.6	59.4	100.0	232.8	341.4	399.8	463.8	....	525.5	**64**

Period Averages

	1987	1988	1989	1990	1991	1992	1993	1994	1995	1996	1997	1998	1999	2000	2001	
Labor Force	....	....	....	5,407	....	....	5,841	....	....	7,415	....	....	....	....	....	**67d**

Sudan

		1972	1973	1974	1975	1976	1977	1978	1979	1980	1981	1982	1983	1984	1985	1986
International Transactions										*Millions of US Dollars: Year Ending June 30 through 1994,*						
Exports	70..d	357.2	434.2	350.4	437.9	554.3	661.0	517.6	534.5	542.7	656.8	498.1	623.5	628.7	373.9	333.3
Imports, c.i.f.	71..d	320.1	436.1	642.1	887.2	980.4	1,081.2	1,194.3	1,109.2	1,576.4	1,552.9	1,282.4	1,354.4	1,146.7	770.7	960.9
Balance of Payments													*Millions of US Dollars:*			
Current Account, n.i.e.	78al d	....	....	....	....	....	−89.6	−110.0	−257.6	−317.0	−648.3	−249.1	−219.2	36.5	148.9	−26.3
Goods: Exports f.o.b.	78aa d						658.2	563.0	514.1	689.4	792.7	400.9	514.2	519.0	444.2	326.8
Goods: Imports f.o.b.	78ab d						−644.2	−623.9	−735.8	−1,127.4	−1,633.6	−750.3	−703.2	−599.8	−579.0	−633.7
Trade Balance	78ac d						14.1	−60.9	−221.7	−438.0	−840.9	−349.4	−188.9	−80.8	−134.8	−306.9
Services: Credit	78ad d						120.9	162.4	202.9	292.4	425.5	471.7	269.2	258.5	374.2	220.5
Services: Debit	78ae d						−199.3	−229.9	−269.4	−353.0	−466.1	−328.7	−343.7	−284.6	−346.4	−188.0
Balance on Goods & Services	78af d						−64.3	−128.5	−288.3	−498.6	−881.4	−206.4	−263.4	−107.0	−107.0	−274.4
Income: Credit	78ag d						5.2	14.5	3.8	48.8	44.0	44.1	25.8	9.8	12.1	8.3
Income: Debit	78ah d						−87.6	−74.9	−78.9	−96.0	−146.5	−193.3	−227.8	−163.4	−113.5	−93.6
Balance on Gds, Serv. & Inc.	78ai d						−146.7	−188.8	−363.4	−545.8	−983.9	−355.6	−465.3	−260.6	−208.3	−359.8
Current Transfers, n.i.e.: Credit	78aj d						60.0	81.7	118.0	272.2	403.7	131.9	274.5	306.5	369.5	357.6
Current Transfers: Debit	78ak d						−2.9	−2.9	−12.2	−43.4	−68.1	−25.4	−28.3	−9.5	−12.2	−24.1
Capital Account, n.i.e.	78bc d						−.3	1.3	9.9	−3.2	8.3	.6	−.3	—	—	—
Capital Account, n.i.e.: Credit	78ba d						.3	1.3	9.9	6.6	14.7	1.2	—	—	—	—
Capital Account: Debit	78bb d						−.6	—	—	−9.8	−6.3	−.6	−.3	—	—	—
Financial Account, n.i.e.	78bj d						−63.2	−7.7	175.4	−263.7	228.8	34.0	−148.8	−153.0	−443.9	−86.2
Direct Investment Abroad	78bd d						—	—	—	—	—	—	—	—	—	—
Dir. Invest. in Rep. Econ., n.i.e.	78be d						—	—	—	—	—	—	—	9.1	−3.0	—
Portfolio Investment Assets	78bf d						—	—	—	—	—	—	—	—	—	—
Equity Securities	78bk d						—	—	—	—	—	—	—	—	—	—
Debt Securities	78bl d						—	—	—	—	—	—	—	—	—	—
Portfolio Investment Liab., n.i.e.	78bg d						—	—	—	—	—	—	—	—	—	—
Equity Securities	78bm d						—	—	—	—	—	—	—	—	—	—
Debt Securities	78bn d						—	—	—	—	—	—	—	—	—	—
Financial Derivatives Assets	78bw d						....	....	....	....	....	....	....	....	....	....
Financial Derivatives Liabilities	78bx d						....	....	....	....	....	....	....	....	....	....
Other Investment Assets	78bh d						−104.8	−13.2	−26.1	−241.0	105.2	20.3	−120.2	−41.9	−497.4	90.6
Monetary Authorities	78bo d														—	—
General Government	78bp d														−134.7	−33.4
Banks	78bq d						−104.8	−13.2	−26.1	−241.0	105.2	20.3	−120.2	−41.9	−362.6	124.0
Other Sectors	78br d														—	—
Other Investment Liab., n.i.e.	78bi d						41.6	5.5	201.5	−22.7	123.6	13.7	−28.6	−120.2	56.5	−176.8
Monetary Authorities	78bs d						14.6	−3.4	15.2	25.0	23.2	−17.9	−15.2	−52.6	16.5	−16.4
General Government	78bt d						−64.6	28.3	237.1	−83.7	85.4	57.5	−8.5	−73.3	−108.0	−109.6
Banks	78bu d						79.8	−11.5	−35.3	70.8	15.0	−25.9	−4.8	5.7	147.5	−49.6
Other Sectors	78bv d						11.8	−7.9	−15.6	−34.8	—	—	—	—	.4	−1.2
Net Errors and Omissions	78ca d						−15.1	14.5	−35.0	58.0	14.7	12.6	145.5	−1.4	−126.0	−88.5
Overall Balance	78cb d						−168.2	−101.9	−107.3	−525.9	−396.4	−201.9	−222.8	−118.0	−420.9	−201.0
Reserves and Related Items	79da d						168.2	101.9	107.3	525.9	396.4	201.9	222.8	118.0	420.9	201.0
Reserve Assets	79db d						−3.2	−7.8	−55.4	35.4	−199.2	−136.5	34.4	−.6	5.0	−46.3
Use of Fund Credit and Loans	79dc d						−22.9	64.5	93.1	147.5	172.3	45.6	152.7	11.4	−4.9	
Exceptional Financing	79de d						194.3	45.2	69.6	342.9	423.2	292.8	35.7	107.1	420.8	247.3
Government Finance										*Millions of Dinars through 1991; Billions of Dinars beginning 1992:*						
Deficit (−) or Surplus	80	†−.6	−1.6	−1.0	−7.5	−5.9	−16.8	−15.2	−13.6	−13.0	....	−32.6	....	....	....	....
Revenue	81	†15.0	15.4	18.9	25.4	29.8	32.7	40.4	54.7	55.9	....	84.0	....	....	....	....
Grants Received	81z	†.6	.3	.4	.5	.1	2.4	—	—	10.7	....	19.4	....	....	....	....
Expenditure	82	†15.9	17.2	19.7	33.4	35.8	51.7	55.4	68.3	78.0	....	119.8	....	....	....	....
Lending Minus Repayments	83	†.3	.1	.6	—	—	.3	.1	.1	1.6	....	16.2	....	....	....	....
Financing																
Domestic	84a	†−.3	.3	−1.4	3.4	−4.7	12.7	17.2	12.7	1.8	....	19.8	....	....	....	....
Foreign	85a	†.9	1.3	2.4	4.1	10.6	4.1	−2.0	.9	11.2	....	12.9	....	....	....	....
Debt: Domestic	88a	†8.9	9.1	12.6	....											
Foreign	89a	†10.1	11.4	13.8	....											
National Accounts										*Millions of Dinars through 1991; Billions of Dinars beginning 1992:*						
Gross Domestic Product (GDP)	99b	89.7	124.6	151.1	184.8	234.0	288.3	325.4	397.2	495.1	639.8	672.0	917.8	1,131.1	1,391.3	2,014.1
																Millions:
Population	99z	14.81	14.96	15.34	15.73	16.13	16.95	17.56	18.11	18.68	19.28	19.90	20.53	21.43	22.11	22.80

Sudan

International Transactions

Year Ending December 31 Thereafter

Item	1987	1988	1989	1990	1991	1992	1993	1994	1995	1996	1997	1998	1999	2000	2001	Code
Exports	503.9	509.1	671.8	374.1	305.0	319.3	417.3	523.9	555.7	620.2	594.2	595.7	780.0	1,806.7	1,698.7	70..d
Imports, c.i.f.	871.0	1,060.5	....	618.5	890.3	820.9	944.9	1,161.5	†1,184.5	1,504.4	1,579.7	1,924.7	1,415.0	1,552.7	1,585.5	71..d

Balance of Payments

Minus Sign Indicates Debit

Item	1987	1988	1989	1990	1991	1992	1993	1994	1995	1996	1997	1998	1999	2000	2001	Code
Current Account, n.i.e.	-232.4	-358.0	-150.3	-372.2	-954.7	-506.2	-202.2	-601.7	-499.9	-826.8	-828.1	-956.5	-464.8	-556.8	-618.3	78al d
Goods: Exports f.o.b.	265.0	427.0	544.4	326.5	302.5	213.4	306.3	523.9	555.7	620.3	594.2	595.7	780.1	1,806.7	1,698.7	78aa d
Goods: Imports f.o.b.	-694.8	-948.5	-1,051.0	-648.8	-1,138.2	-810.2	-532.8	-1,045.4	-1,066.0	-1,339.5	-1,421.9	-1,732.2	-1,256.0	-1,366.3	-1,395.1	78ab d
Trade Balance	-429.7	-521.5	-506.6	-322.3	-835.7	-596.8	-226.5	-521.5	-510.3	-719.2	-827.7	-1,136.5	-475.9	440.4	303.6	78ac d
Services: Credit	184.7	161.7	272.6	172.5	77.0	155.5	69.4	76.2	125.3	50.7	31.5	15.8	81.6	27.4	14.6	78ad d
Services: Debit	-228.6	-244.6	-378.2	-228.0	-197.3	-204.1	-109.8	-223.7	-172.3	-200.8	-172.8	-204.0	-274.9	-647.6	-660.3	78ae d
Balance on Goods & Services	-473.7	-604.4	-612.2	-377.8	-956.0	-645.4	-266.9	-669.0	-557.3	-869.3	-969.0	-1,324.7	-669.2	-179.8	-342.1	78af d
Income: Credit	7.5	9.9	7.0	12.4	2.7	—	.7	1.6	1.9	6.3	16.9	13.7	19.1	4.6	17.8	78ag d
Income: Debit	-94.4	-96.7	-117.5	-148.0	-129.1	-93.5	-20.9	-15.9	-4.9	-.7	-5.3	-10.6	-123.2	-579.6	-571.9	78ah d
Balance on Gds, Serv. & Inc.	-560.6	-691.2	-722.6	-513.4	-1,082.4	-738.9	-287.1	-683.3	-560.3	-863.7	-957.4	-1,321.6	-773.3	-754.8	-896.2	78ai d
Current Transfers, n.i.e.: Credit	332.4	334.4	576.7	143.3	127.9	232.7	84.9	120.1	346.2	236.3	439.1	731.8	702.2	651.3	730.4	78aj d
Current Transfers: Debit	-4.1	-1.1	-4.4	-2.1	-.2	—	—	-38.5	-285.8	-199.4	-309.8	-366.7	-393.7	-453.3	-452.5	78ak d
Capital Account, n.i.e.												-54.2	-22.9	-119.3	-93.3	78bc d
Capital Account, n.i.e.: Credit												13.0	45.8	16.5	11.9	78ba d
Capital Account: Debit												-67.2	-68.7	-135.8	-105.2	78bb d
Financial Account, n.i.e.	85.8	67.5	117.8	116.9	584.1	316.4	326.6	276.0	473.7	136.8	195.0	333.4	435.3	431.6	561.2	78bj d
Direct Investment Abroad																78bd d
Dir. Invest. in Rep. Econ., n.i.e.	—	—	3.5	—	—	—	—	—	—	.4	97.9	370.7	370.8	392.2	574.0	78be d
Portfolio Investment Assets	—	—	—	—	—	—						—	—	—	.7	78bf d
Equity Securities																78bk d
Debt Securities	—	—	—	—	—	—						—	—	—	.7	78bl d
Portfolio Investment Liab., n.i.e.	—	—	—	—	—	—						—	—	—	—	78bg d
Equity Securities																78bm d
Debt Securities	—	—	—	—	—	—						—	—	—		78bn d
Financial Derivatives Assets																78bw d
Financial Derivatives Liabilities																78bx d
Other Investment Assets	116.6	-65.3	-39.6	-28.5	-74.0	-82.8						-78.5	-38.4	-53.4	-55.1	78bh d
Monetary Authorities	—	—	—	—	—	—						—	—	—	—	78bo d
General Government	179.8	80.5														78bp d
Banks	-63.1	-145.8	-39.6	-28.5	-74.0	-82.8						-78.5	-38.4	-53.4	-55.1	78bq d
Other Sectors																78br d
Other Investment Liab., n.i.e.	-30.8	132.8	153.9	145.4	658.1	399.2	326.6	276.0	473.7	136.4	97.1	41.2	102.9	92.8	41.6	78bi d
Monetary Authorities	169.4	75.9	44.8	30.6	155.6	110.4	163.3	28.3	73.6	62.4	20.1	8.0	-3.7	14.0	40.6	78bs d
General Government	-235.7	63.1	111.4	102.7	486.3	268.5	200.8	-3.1	9.8	-22.5	-45.1	-1.0	—	—	—	78bt d
Banks	35.5	-6.3	-2.3	12.1	16.1	20.3	-37.5	250.8	390.3	96.2	119.3	34.2	106.6	78.8	1.0	78bu d
Other Sectors										.3	2.8				—	78bv d
Net Errors and Omissions	-196.5	3.1	-160.3	10.9	97.9	31.0	-82.6	344.8	89.3	727.5	651.2	750.5	167.2	368.4	-.5	78ca d
Overall Balance	-343.0	-287.4	-192.8	-244.4	-272.8	-158.8	41.8	19.1	63.1	37.5	18.1	73.2	114.8	123.9	-150.9	78cb d
Reserves and Related Items	343.0	287.4	192.8	244.4	272.8	158.8	-41.8	-19.1	-63.1	-37.5	-18.1	-73.2	-114.8	-123.9	150.9	79da d
Reserve Assets	46.8	-.4	-3.8	4.5	3.8	29.3	-41.8	-19.1	-23.6	-2.0	24.0	-16.0	-110.0	-108.0	127.6	79db d
Use of Fund Credit and Loans				-1.4					-39.5	-35.5	-42.1	-57.2	-37.8	-54.0	-52.3	79dc d
Exceptional Financing	296.2	287.8	196.6	241.3	269.0	129.5	—	—					33.0	38.1	75.6	79de d

Government Finance

Year Ending June 30 through 1994; December 31 Thereafter

Item	1987	1988	1989	1990	1991	1992	1993	1994	1995	1996	1997	1998	1999	2000	2001	Code
Deficit (-) or Surplus								†-13.5	-34.6	-13.4						80
Revenue								†36.5	62.9	107.3						81
Grants Received								†—	—							81z
Expenditure								†50.0	97.5	120.7						82
Lending Minus Repayments								†—	—							83
Financing																
Domestic								†9.3	32.4	10.8						84a
Foreign								†4.2	2.2	2.6						85a
Debt: Domestic																88a
Foreign																89a

National Accounts

Year Ending june 30 through 1994; December 31 Thereafter

Item	1987	1988	1989	1990	1991	1992	1993	1994	1995	1996	1997	1998	1999	2000	2001	Code
Gross Domestic Product (GDP)	3,647.1	4,679.1	8,256.2	11,011.1	19,029.3	†40.8	83.5	168.0	†483.2	1,021.7	1,601.2					99b

Midyear Estimates

Item	1987	1988	1989	1990	1991	1992	1993	1994	1995	1996	1997	1998	1999	2000	2001	Code
Population	23.52	24.24	24.99	25.75	26.53	27.32	28.13	28.95	†27.95	28.57	29.18	29.79	30.42	31.10	31.81	99z

(See notes in the back of the book.)

Suriname

366

		1972	1973	1974	1975	1976	1977	1978	1979	1980	1981	1982	1983	1984	1985	1986
Exchange Rates														*Guilders per SDR:*		
Market Rate	aa	1.94	2.15	2.19	2.09	2.07	2.17	2.33	2.35	2.28	2.08	1.97	1.87	1.75	1.96	2.18
														Guilders per US Dollar:		
Market Rate	ae	1.78	1.78	1.78	1.78	1.78	1.78	1.78	1.78	1.78	1.78	1.78	1.78	1.78	1.78	1.78
Market Rate	rf	1.78	1.78	1.78	1.78	1.78	1.78	1.78	1.78	1.78	1.78	1.78	1.78	1.78	1.78	1.78
Fund Position														*Millions of SDRs:*		
Quota	2f. s	....	....	....	....	....	....	25.00	25.00	37.50	37.50	37.50	49.30	49.30	49.30	49.30
SDRs	1b. s	....	....	....	....	....	....	—	2.60	2.07	5.40	8.48	1.74	1.28	.76	.28
Reserve Position in the Fund	1c. s	....	....	....	....	....	....	4.75	4.75	7.87	7.87	7.88	2.95	—	—	—
Total Fund Cred.&Loans Outstg.	2tl	....	....	....	....	....	....							—	—	—
International Liquidity												*Millions of US Dollars Unless Otherwise Indicated:*				
Total Reserves minus Gold	1l. d	37.59	56.44	67.55	91.41	110.22	94.03	132.42	169.53	189.25	207.09	175.76	59.15	24.87	23.42	20.89
SDRs	1b. d	....	....	....	....	....	....		3.43	2.64	6.29	9.35	1.82	1.25	.83	.34
Reserve Position in the Fund	1c. d	....	....	....	....	....	....	6.19	6.26	10.04	9.16	8.69	3.09			
Foreign Exchange	1d. d	37.59	56.44	67.55	91.41	110.22	94.03	126.24	159.84	176.57	191.64	157.71	54.24	23.62	22.59	20.55
Gold (Million Fine Troy Ounces)	1ad	.248	.148	.148	.148	.148	.148	.054	.054	.054	.054	.054	.054	.054	.054	.054
Gold (National Valuation)	1an d	9.29e	....	6.16	6.16	6.16	6.16	2.26	2.26	2.26	2.26	2.26	19.60	14.89	15.83	18.75
Monetary Authorities: Other Liab.	4. d	.01	.03	.08	.07	.11	.05	4.24	5.60	.22	.23	.22	.22	.32	.40	13.05
Deposit Money Banks: Assets	7a. d	13.50	15.54	10.04	22.08	28.55	28.90	41.65	37.36	51.94	52.25	49.12	31.03	16.81	5.20	5.20
Liabilities	7b. d	2.43	3.16	2.67	3.84	8.15	9.93	12.45	15.20	18.98	21.98	24.07	17.96	24.15	27.81	45.52
Monetary Authorities														*Millions of Guilders:*		
Foreign Assets	11	79	111	131	173	206	177	237	304	339	371	315	140	71	70	72
Claims on Central Government	12a	8	13	23	53	124	187	62	55	37	81	182	461	717	1,062	1,494
Claims on Nonfin.Pub.Enterprises	12c	....	....	....	....	....	....	....			....	....	....	....	....	
Claims on Private Sector	12d	1	1	1	1	1	1	1	—	—	—	—	—	—	—	—
Claims on Deposit Money Banks	12e	—	—	—	—	—	—	—	—	—	—	—	—	—	—	—
Claims on Other Banking Insts.	12f	....														19
Reserve Money	14	70	99	99	124	159	197	199	241	242	298	327	423	627	957	1,303
of which: Currency Outside DMBs	14a	58	73	79	89	110	125	145	156	178	197	268	265	305	405	451
Time & Fgn. Currency Deposits	15	—	—	—	—	—	—	—	—	—	—	—	—	—	—	30
Foreign Liabilities	16c	—	—	—	—	—	—	8	10	—	—	—	—	1	1	23
Central Government Deposits	16d	10	—	19	52	117	116	19	25	29	24	32	25	16	22	14
Capital Accounts	17a	7	7	7	15	22	22	22	28	39	48	50	49	48	50	51
Other Items (Net)	17r	3	18	30	35	33	29	54	56	67	82	88	104	96	103	165
Deposit Money Banks														*Millions of Guilders:*		
Reserves	20	11	24	19	33	49	70	52	80	53	79	54	153	316	544	828
Foreign Assets	21	24	28	18	39	51	52	74	67	93	93	88	55	30	21	9
Claims on Central Government	22a	5	13	15	15	24	18	18	18	17	28	30	73	110	124	142
Claims on Private Sector	22d	118	121	149	157	230	284	360	421	460	546	615	620	627	690	728
Demand Deposits	24	44	58	60	78	88	92	99	112	106	139	148	185	267	467	754
Quasi-Monetary Liabilities	25	83	96	105	122	199	252	302	339	365	430	455	516	591	664	676
Bonds	26ab	3	2	2	2	2	2	7	7	7	7	7	7	7	7	5
Foreign Liabilities	26c	4	6	5	7	15	18	22	27	34	39	43	32	43	50	81
Central Government Deposits	26d	3	—	1	2	13	7	1	9	6	5	3	7	7	13	15
Credit from Monetary Authorities	26g	—	—	—	—	—	—	—	—	—	—	—	—	—	—	19
Capital Accounts	27a	21	22	25	31	38	50	62	73	82	91	103	110	115	132	141
Other Items (Net)	27r	–1	2	3	3	–1	4	11	19	24	34	27	43	54	45	16
Monetary Survey														*Millions of Guilders:*		
Foreign Assets (Net)	31n	99	133	144	205	242	211	282	334	398	424	360	163	57	40	–23
Domestic Credit	32	120	147	168	172	249	366	421	461	480	626	792	1,121	1,431	1,840	2,335
Claims on Central Govt. (Net)	32an	1	25	19	14	18	82	61	40	20	79	176	501	804	1,150	1,608
Claims on Nonfin.Pub.Enterprises	32c	....				....		....			....	....	....			
Claims on Private Sector	32d	119	122	150	157	230	284	361	421	461	546	615	620	627	690	728
Claims on Other Banking Insts.	32f	....														....
Money	34	103	133	140	169	198	220	246	273	294	358	421	455	577	880	1,229
Quasi-Money	35	83	96	105	122	199	252	302	339	365	430	455	516	591	664	705
Bonds	36ab	3	2	2	2	2	2	7	7	7	7	7	7	7	7	5
Capital Accounts	37a	28	29	32	45	60	72	84	101	121	139	153	159	163	181	192
Other Items (Net)	37r	2	20	32	38	31	31	64	75	91	116	116	146	150	148	181
Money plus Quasi-Money	35l	187	229	245	291	397	472	548	612	660	788	876	971	1,169	1,544	1,934
Money (National Definitions)														*Millions of Guilders:*		
M1	59ma	....	....	....	....	....	....	....	....	....	....	....	....	....	....	....
M2	59mb	....	....	....	....	....	....	....	....	....	....	....	....	....	....	....
M3	59mc	....	....	....	....	....	....	....	....	....	....	....	....	....	....	....
Interest Rates														*Percent per Annum*		
Deposit Rate	60l	....	....	....	....	....	....	....	....	....	....	....	....	....	....	....
Lending Rate	60p	....	....	....	....	....	....	....	....	....	....	....	....	....	....	....
Prices and Labor														*Index Numbers (1995=100):*		
Consumer Prices	64	.2	.2	.2	.2	.3	.3	.3	.4	†.4	.5	.5	.5	.5	.6	.7
														Number in Thousands:		
Labor Force	67d	....	....	....	....	....	....	....	....	....	....	....	....	....	....	....
Employment	67e	....	....	....	....	....	....	....	....	....	....	....	....	....	....	....
Unemployment	67c	....	....	....	....	....	....	....	....	....	....	....	....	....	....	15
Unemployment Rate (%)	67r	....	....	....	....	....	....	....	....	....	....	....	....	....	....	....

1987	1988	1989	1990	1991	1992	1993	1994	1995	1996	1997	1998	1999	2000	2001		
End of Period															**Exchange Rates**	
2.53	2.40	2.35	2.54	2.55	2.45	2.45	†597.81	605.00	576.62	541.05	564.62	1,355.35	2,838.39	2,737.79	Market Rate	**aa**
End of Period (ae) Period Average (rf)															Market Rate	**ae**
1.78	1.78	1.78	1.78	1.78	1.78	1.78	†409.50	407.00	401.00	401.00	401.00	987.50	2,178.50	2,178.50	Market Rate	**ae**
1.78	1.78	1.78	1.78	1.78	1.78	1.78	134.12	442.23	401.26	401.00	401.00	859.44	1,322.47	2,178.50	Market Rate	**rf**
End of Period															**Fund Position**	
49.30	49.30	49.30	49.30	49.30	49.30	67.60	67.60	67.60	67.60	67.60	67.60	92.10	92.10	92.10	Quota	**2f. s**
—	—	—	—	—	—	—	—	7.75	8.22	8.23	8.25	2.00	1.77	1.56	SDRs	**1b. s**
—	—	—	—	—	—	—	—	—	—	—	—	6.13	6.13	6.13	Reserve Position in the Fund	**1c. s**
—	—	—	—	—	—	—	—	—	—	—	—	—	—	—	Total Fund Cred.&Loans Outstg.	**2tl**
End of Period															**International Liquidity**	
15.10	12.56	9.25	21.07	1.10	17.30	17.70	39.70	132.92	96.32	109.11	106.14	38.46	62.99	119.25	Total Reserves minus Gold	**1l. d**
—	—	—	—	—	—	—	—	11.52	11.82	11.11	11.62	2.75	2.31	1.95	SDRs	**1b. d**
—	—	—	—	—	—	—	—	—	—	—	—	8.41	7.98	7.70	Reserve Position in the Fund	**1c. d**
15.10	12.56	9.25	21.07	1.10	17.30	17.70	39.70	121.40	84.50	98.00	94.52	27.30	52.70	109.60	Foreign Exchange	**1d. d**
.054	.054	.054	.054	.054	.054	.054	.054	.093	.134	.193	.128	.246	.256	.265	Gold (Million Fine Troy Ounces)	**1ad**
23.84	20.44	19.79	18.66	17.71	16.21	841.67	14.32	41.34	58.18	54.53	1.62	.85	.75	.73	Gold (National Valuation)	**1an d**
14.55	33.07	39.79	36.13	55.47	46.80	1,316.25	18.08	3.25	3.03	74.81	229.66	111.10	103.74	77.92	Monetary Authorities: Other Liab.	**4. d**
11.59	9.89	17.55	21.98	21.63	20.20	1,093.54	49.67	68.84	116.40	128.94	122.43	180.59	131.02	188.33	Deposit Money Banks: Assets	**7a. d**
53.39	57.60	65.30	78.32	85.84	89.02	374.72	28.62	45.71	75.09	86.00	96.29	160.52	128.08	181.12	Liabilities	**7b. d**
End of Period															**Monetary Authorities**	
69	59	52	71	45	65	3,277	23,546	65,538	56,984	60,615	†127,893	123,498	253,498	386,507	Foreign Assets	**11**
1,998	2,479	2,853	2,627	3,261	3,512	5,224	5,307	4,909	6,768	6,376	†38,602	101,982	287,462	57,158	Claims on Central Government	**12a**
											4,052	3,783	6,564	1,293	Claims on Nonfin.Pub.Enterprises	**12c**
. . . .	15	15	15	15	1	2	9	31	69	246	†1,669	4,018	5,677	12,886	Claims on Private Sector	**12d**
2	3	2	—	—	2	4	13	—	26	13,414	†19,077	38,249	43,064	44,884	Claims on Deposit Money Banks	**12e**
											218	511	623	719	Claims on Other Banking Insts.	**12f**
1,564	1,903	2,195	2,322	2,946	3,317	5,640	17,361	56,775	50,953	50,740	†83,301	122,806	313,164	358,470	Reserve Money	**14**
638	788	874	958	1,143	1,347	2,638	10,486	25,199	27,404	32,256	†50,478	81,686	150,657	182,476	*of which: Currency Outside DMBs*	**14a**
249	363	432	120	63	2	—	—	—	—	—	†192	232	1,442	1,082	Time & Fgn. Currency Deposits	**15**
26	59	71	64	99	84	2,349	7,403	1,321	1,214	29,997	†92,093	109,711	225,998	169,753	Foreign Liabilities	**16c**
14	11	12	13	13	15	29	844	9,900	9,076	3,021	†8,317	22,493	60,746	45,963	Central Government Deposits	**16d**
54	53	53	54	54	54	4,668	4,723	4,589	4,420	†13,191	29,404	19,905	−45,195	Capital Accounts	**17a**	
162	167	161	139	146	108	434	−1,401	−2,240	−1,985	−7,529	†−5,582	−12,606	−24,367	−26,626	Other Items (Net)	**17r**
End of Period															**Deposit Money Banks**	
912	1,098	1,299	1,339	1,768	1,914	2,873	6,242	29,584	19,142	18,531	31,462	32,392	122,759	124,630	Reserves	**20**
21	18	31	39	39	36	1,952	20,341	28,016	46,675	51,705	49,095	178,333	285,419	410,276	Foreign Assets	**21**
123	129	140	207	225	225	266	392	567	913	8,639	20,814	23,594	64,030	95,884	Claims on Central Government	**22a**
773	924	1,145	1,454	1,809	2,464	3,133	6,645	20,120	45,486	63,383	79,103	106,703	93,296	147,134	Claims on Private Sector	**22d**
910	1,140	1,269	1,268	1,708	1,818	3,276	9,763	30,912	25,156	35,476	39,929	51,367	111,010	175,972	Demand Deposits	**24**
665	753	1,021	1,401	1,712	2,344	3,179	7,218	20,995	52,609	61,973	87,578	108,151	160,966	178,435	Quasi-Monetary Liabilities	**25**
5	5	5	5	6	23	104	153	357	256	226	28	21	13	5	Bonds	**26ab**
95	103	117	140	153	159	669	11,721	18,603	30,113	34,486	38,612	158,517	279,029	394,561	Foreign Liabilities	**26c**
11	9	23	23	40	25	103	956	1,273	371	885	167	542	525	840	Central Government Deposits	**26d**
2	3	2	—	—	—	2	4	13	—	26	14,197	15,726	34,170	38,124	39,510	Credit from Monetary Authorities	**26g**
143	162	183	253	303	377	611	2,852	5,263	8,732	11,681	12,516	20,933	29,669	73,054	Capital Accounts	**27a**
−2	−8	−4	−51	−81	−108	279	945	885	−5,048	−16,666	−14,082	−32,678	−53,833	−84,453	Other Items (Net)	**27r**
End of Period															**Monetary Survey**	
−32	−85	−105	−94	−168	−141	2,210	24,763	73,630	72,332	47,837	†46,283	33,603	33,889	232,469	Foreign Assets (Net)	**31n**
2,868	3,526	4,120	4,266	5,259	6,162	8,493	10,554	14,456	43,789	74,737	†135,975	217,555	396,382	268,272	Domestic Credit	**32**
2,095	2,587	2,959	2,797	3,434	3,696	5,358	3,900	−5,696	−1,767	11,109	†50,932	102,541	290,222	106,240	Claims on Central Govt. (Net)	**32an**
											4,052	3,783	6,564	1,293	Claims on Nonfin.Pub.Enterprises	**32c**
773	939	1,161	1,469	1,825	2,465	3,135	6,654	20,152	45,556	63,628	†80,773	110,720	98,973	160,020	Claims on Private Sector	**32d**
											218	511	623	719	Claims on Other Banking Insts.	**32f**
1,562	1,945	2,165	2,251	2,886	3,221	6,043	20,883	58,103	56,967	68,468	†92,249	139,779	285,596	394,617	Money	**34**
913	1,115	1,453	1,521	1,776	2,346	3,179	7,218	20,995	52,609	61,973	†87,770	108,383	162,409	179,517	Quasi-Money	**35**
5	5	5	5	6	23	104	153	357	256	226	28	21	13	5	Bonds	**36ab**
198	216	236	307	358	430	664	7,520	9,986	13,321	16,101	†25,706	50,337	49,574	27,860	Capital Accounts	**37a**
159	159	157	88	65	—	712	−456	−1,355	−7,033	−24,194	†−23,496	−47,361	−67,321	−101,257	Other Items (Net)	**37r**
2,475	3,060	3,618	3,772	4,662	5,567	9,222	28,101	79,098	109,576	130,442	†180,019	248,162	448,004	574,134	Money plus Quasi-Money	**35l**
End of Period															**Money (National Definitions)**	
. . . .	. . . .	. . . .	. . . .	. . . .	. . . .	. . . .	. . . .	. . . .	. . . .	. . . .	. . . .	135,548	267,357	384,688	*M1*	**59ma**
. . . .	. . . .	. . . .	. . . .	. . . .	. . . .	. . . .	. . . .	. . . .	. . . .	. . . .	. . . .	159,755	306,019	426,711	*M2*	**59mb**
. . . .	. . . .	. . . .	. . . .	. . . .	. . . .	. . . .	. . . .	. . . .	. . . .	. . . .	. . . .	246,765	439,331	572,391	*M3*	**59mc**
Percent per Annum															**Interest Rates**	
			4.6	4.5	4.8	7.5	21.0	17.8	17.3	16.0	15.6	15.5	11.9	Deposit Rate	**60l**	
. . . .	. . . .	. . . .		8.9	8.9	9.4	15.4	40.2	35.8	33.1	27.5	27.3	29.0	25.8	Lending Rate	**60p**
Period Averages															**Prices and Labor**	
1.1	1.2	1.2	1.4	1.8	2.6	6.4	29.8	100.0	99.3	106.4	126.6	251.8	. . . .	. . . .	Consumer Prices	**64**
Period Averages																
. . . .	. . . .	. . . .	97	. . . .	107	92	90	90	. . . .	. . . .	. . . .	86	. . . .	. . . .	Labor Force	**67d**
. . . .	. . . .	. . . .	82	. . . .	89	83	78	82	87	83	88	73	. . . .	. . . .	Employment	**67e**
19	20	15	15	. . . .	18	14	11	8	11	10	10	12	. . . .	. . . .	Unemployment	**67c**
. . . .	. . . .	. . . .	15.8	. . . .	17.2	14.7	12.7	8.4	11.0	. . . .	. . . .	. . . .	. . . .	. . . .	Unemployment Rate (%)	**67r**

	1972	1973	1974	1975	1976	1977	1978	1979	1980	1981	1982	1983	1984	1985	1986
International Transactions														*Millions of Guilders*	
Exports ... 70	306	320	481	495	492	553	658	†793	918	846	765	655	635	587	598
Imports, c.i.f. ... 71	258	280	411	450	525	710	725	†734	900	1,014	913	809	617	533	584
Balance of Payments														*Millions of US Dollars:*	
Current Account, n.i.e. ... 78al d	...	...	...	...	...	-2.7	51.7	78.6	31.5	-48.5	-97.6	-282.3	-137.6	-18.3	-36.9
Goods: Exports f.o.b. ... 78aa d						617.9	733.9	792.7	918.2	845.7	765.1	654.7	667.8	599.9	601.7
Goods: Imports f.o.b. ... 78ab d						-578.5	-613.2	-660.2	-810.4	-904.0	-821.7	-716.9	-699.0	-552.5	-542.8
Trade Balance ... 78ac d						39.4	120.7	132.5	107.8	-58.3	-56.6	-62.2	-31.2	47.4	58.9
Services: Credit ... 78ad d						89.6	111.2	124.0	176.0	164.1	144.4	120.8	98.6	79.0	45.8
Services: Debit ... 78ae d						-205.6	-222.5	-254.8	-364.1	-351.8	-369.1	-316.0	-201.8	-141.4	-137.4
Balance on Goods & Services ... 78af d						-76.6	9.4	1.7	-80.3	-246.0	-281.3	-257.4	-134.4	-15.0	-32.7
Income: Credit ... 78ag d						12.9	14.9	25.2	45.7	64.7	63.9	29.5	8.9	4.9	2.9
Income: Debit ... 78ah d						-84.6	-81.2	-105.5	-81.1	-43.9	-51.8	-49.4	-6.4	-5.8	-8.3
Balance on Gds, Serv. & Inc. ... 78ai d						-148.3	-56.9	-78.6	-115.7	-225.2	-269.2	-277.3	-131.9	-15.9	-38.1
Current Transfers, n.i.e.: Credit ... 78aj d						155.6	118.5	168.9	162.5	192.0	190.2	17.4	10.5	7.4	9.2
Current Transfers: Debit ... 78ak d						-10.0	-9.9	-11.7	-15.3	-15.3	-18.6	-22.4	-16.2	-9.8	-8.0
Capital Account, n.i.e. ... 78bc d						-3.4	-2.6	-.6	-3.9	-1.1	-3.4	-4.8	-2.9	-2.4	-3.0
Capital Account, n.i.e.: Credit ... 78ba d						2.0	3.4	3.5	3.4	3.8	3.3	4.6	5.7	3.5	1.6
Capital Account: Debit ... 78bb d						-5.4	-6.0	-4.1	-7.3	-4.9	-6.7	-9.4	-8.6	-5.9	-4.6
Financial Account, n.i.e. ... 78bj d						-26.1	24.5	-30.0	17.4	50.9	22.4	88.8	-18.6	25.9	1.9
Direct Investment Abroad ... 78bd d															
Dir. Invest. in Rep. Econ., n.i.e. ... 78be d						-22.6	-13.5	-27.4	18.1	61.7	-11.1	81.5	-70.9	21.3	-60.4
Portfolio Investment Assets ... 78bf d										-1.0	-1.4	—	—	—	—
Equity Securities ... 78bk d										-1.0	-1.4	—	—	—	—
Debt Securities ... 78bl d										—	—	—	—	—	—
Portfolio Investment Liab., n.i.e. ... 78bg d						-.2	-.5	—		-.6	-.7	—	—	-.4	-.3
Equity Securities ... 78bm d						-.3	.3	—		-.6	-.7	—	—	-.4	-.2
Debt Securities ... 78bn d						.1	-.8	—		—	—	—	—	—	-.1
Financial Derivatives Assets ... 78bw d													...	...	...
Financial Derivatives Liabilities ... 78bx d													...	...	...
Other Investment Assets ... 78bh d						-1.4	-8.5	—	-16.9	-26.5	-13.2	33.6	-.9	3.4	3.2
Monetary Authorities ... 78bo d															
General Government ... 78bp d															
Banks ... 78bq d						-1.2	-8.1	3.0	-16.8	-26.9	-13.2	33.6	-.9	3.4	4.3
Other Sectors ... 78br d						-.2	-.4	-3.0	-.1	.4	—	—	—	—	-1.1
Other Investment Liab., n.i.e. ... 78bi d						-1.9	47.0	-2.6	16.2	17.3	48.8	-26.3	53.2	1.6	59.4
Monetary Authorities ... 78bs d						-2.1	-.8	2.1	-1.2	4.7	2.6	1.3	-2.3	1.9	2.1
General Government ... 78bt d						-2.3	37.6	-2.9	-2.9	-4.4	-2.2	-2.7	.7	-1.2	.8
Banks ... 78bu d						1.2	3.7	-1.2	4.6	6.1	1.7	-7.5	5.3	4.2	16.4
Other Sectors ... 78bv d						1.3	6.5	-.6	15.7	10.9	46.7	-17.2	49.5	-3.3	40.1
Net Errors and Omissions ... 78ca d						.4	-4.1	-.3	1.3	21.4	-.4	13.3	68.2	-19.9	-33.0
Overall Balance ... 78cb d						-31.8	69.5	47.7	46.3	22.7	-79.0	-185.0	-90.9	-14.7	-71.0
Reserves and Related Items ... 79da d						31.8	-69.5	-47.7	-46.3	-22.7	79.0	185.0	90.9	14.7	71.0
Reserve Assets ... 79db d						31.8	-69.5	-47.7	-46.3	-22.7	79.0	185.0	90.9	14.7	71.0
Use of Fund Credit and Loans ... 79dc d						—	—	—	—	—	—	—	—	—	—
Exceptional Financing ... 79de d						...	...	...	...	...	...	...	—	—	—
Government Finance														*Millions of Guilders:*	
Deficit (-) or Surplus ... 80	-1.76	-19.12	-8.80	-2.15	-21.85	-63.10	-22.72	20.01	24.40	-56.53	-98.85	-309.59	-263.19	-349.18	-445.74
Revenue ... 81	158.10	166.14	186.59	297.37	286.38	335.46	413.02	418.24	477.82	488.26	516.64	486.78	515.38	490.38	494.88
Grants Received ... 81z	37.83	33.78	41.86	20.76	116.72	138.45	99.03	144.08	131.56	168.89	172.96	4.46	3.60	1.40	2.78
Expenditure ... 82	196.26	217.53	237.27	318.48	424.21	540.54	536.78	542.32	580.81	713.56	788.15	801.26	768.12	803.35	925.69
Lending Minus Repayments ... 83	1.43	1.51	-.02	1.80	.74	-3.53	-2.01	-.01	4.17	.12	.30	-.43	14.05	37.61	17.71
Financing															
Domestic ... 84a	1.76	9.12	8.80	2.15	21.85	66.35	-15.86	-22.81	-20.30	56.29	98.33	310.10	263.31	349.18	421.59
Foreign ... 85a	—	10.00	—	—	—	-3.25	38.58	2.80	-4.10	.24	.52	-.51	-.12	—	24.15
Debt: Domestic ... 88a	21.30	31.20	43.11	41.52	58.93	43.22	...	...	...	...	...	...	782.40	1,137.08	1,582.01
Foreign ... 89a	187.50	197.30	194.71	10.99	8.77	7.83	...	...	...	...	...	...	55.50	38.37	124.24
National Accounts														*Millions of Guilders*	
Househ.Cons.Expend.,incl.NPISHs ... 96f	316	386	434	503	604	609	693	870	916	1,041	1,084	1,314	1,119	961	737
Government Consumption Expend. ... 91f	136	116	133	137	123	282	335	343	339	431	520	437	499	589	656
Gross Capital Formation ... 93	135	156	245	353	304	479	477	357	421	555	507	276	204	252	391
Exports of Goods and Services ... 90c	351	369	543	578	618	707	814	917	1,094	1,009	910	776	749	642	581
Imports of Goods and Services (-) ... 98c	317	349	536	634	620	795	848	922	1,179	1,258	1,191	1,035	843	697	583
Gross Domestic Product (GDP) ... 99b	619	680	820	930	1,030	1,283	1,471	1,565	1,590	1,778	1,830	1,767	1,728	1,747	1,782
Net Primary Income from Abroad ... 98.n	-84	-71	-45	-25	-67	-61	-55	-74	-30	23	13	-20	3	-1	-5
Gross National Income (GNI) ... 99a	535	609	774	905	963	1,221	1,416	1,492	1,559	1,801	1,843	1,747	1,731	1,746	1,777
Net National Income ... 99e	476	530	674	797	862	1,091	1,262	1,323	1,388	1,615	1,661	1,565	1,558	1,551	1,585
GDP Volume 1980 Prices ... 99b.p	...	1,332	1,367	1,231	1,342	1,479	1,560	1,468	1,342	1,437	1,377	1,323	1,298	1,324	1,334
GDP Volume (1990=100) ... 99bv p	...	94.7	97.2	87.5	95.4	105.1	110.9	104.3	95.4	102.2	97.9	94.0	92.3	94.1	94.8
GDP Deflator (1990=100) ... 99bi p	...	22.7	26.6	33.6	34.1	38.5	41.9	47.3	52.6	54.9	59.0	59.3	59.1	58.6	59.3
Population														*Millions:*	
Population ... 99z	†.38	.38	.38	.36	.35	.36	.37	.37	.35	.36	.36	.37	.37	.38	.38

International Transactions

Millions of Guilders

	1987	1988	1989	1990	1991	1992	1993	1994	1995	1996	1997	1998	1999	2000	2001		Code
Exports	546	731	967	843	641	698	2,124	60,182	211,021	173,806	281,197	174,868	....	....	....		70
Imports, c.i.f.	525	626	791	843	909	967	1,760	56,746	258,917	200,951	263,902	221,388	....	....	....		71

Balance of Payments

Minus Sign Indicates Debit

	1987	1988	1989	1990	1991	1992	1993	1994	1995	1996	1997	1998	1999	2000	2001		Code
Current Account, n.i.e.	135.6	114.3	293.5	66.8	-133.4	25.4	44.0	58.6	62.8	-63.5	-67.7	-154.9	-29.1	32.3	....		78ald
Goods: Exports f.o.b.	604.7	639.7	980.3	831.6	617.5	608.6	298.3	293.6	415.6	397.2	401.6	349.7	342.0	399.1	....		78aad
Goods: Imports f.o.b.	-489.6	-427.4	-590.6	-668.3	-619.5	-486.5	-213.9	-194.3	-292.6	-398.8	-365.5	-376.9	-297.9	-246.1	....		78abd
Trade Balance	115.1	212.3	389.7	163.3	-2.0	122.1	84.4	99.3	123.0	-1.6	36.1	-27.2	44.1	153.0	....		78acd
Services: Credit	144.4	40.5	42.3	37.0	39.8	40.4	46.5	72.6	104.1	103.8	91.6	72.0	79.1	90.9	....		78add
Services: Debit	-121.3	-136.2	-161.9	-171.3	-174.4	-176.1	-101.6	-113.5	-161.4	-169.5	-193.8	-196.9	-151.1	-215.5	....		78aed
Balance on Goods & Services	138.2	116.6	270.1	29.0	-136.6	-13.6	29.3	58.4	65.7	-67.3	-66.1	-152.1	-27.9	28.4	....		78afd
Income: Credit	2.2	2.4	1.7	4.0	2.5	1.3	.2	.9	2.7	7.0	7.4	6.5	7.9	13.2	....		78agd
Income: Debit	-10.4	-17.5	-13.0	-19.2	-22.5	-14.6	-6.4	-4.7	-5.3	-4.3	-10.0	-7.0	-7.6	-7.2	....		78ahd
Balance on Gds, Serv. & Inc.	130.0	101.5	258.8	13.8	-156.6	-26.9	23.1	54.6	63.1	-64.6	-68.7	-152.6	-27.6	34.4	....		78aid
Current Transfers, n.i.e.: Credit	11.9	20.2	43.0	63.4	36.5	67.7	26.7	6.2	2.0	3.6	4.0	1.3	1.8	1.2	....		78ajd
Current Transfers: Debit	-6.3	-7.4	-8.3	-10.4	-13.3	-15.4	-5.8	-2.2	-2.3	-2.5	-3.0	-3.6	-3.3	-3.3	....		78akd
Capital Account, n.i.e.	-2.1	-2.7	-2.8	-5.0	-1.9	-5.7	.5	-.2	22.1	41.6	14.6	6.6	3.5	2.3	....		78bcd
Capital Account, n.i.e.: Credit	2.0	2.7	2.0	.5	4.1	4.6	3.5	.2	22.1	41.6	14.6	6.6	3.5	2.3	....		78bad
Capital Account: Debit	-4.1	-5.4	-4.8	-5.5	-6.0	-10.3	-3.0	-.4	—	—	—	—	—	—	....		78bbd
Financial Account, n.i.e.	-90.3	-117.6	-308.6	-26.7	57.9	-86.6	-73.1	-84.1	-6.7	27.7	26.9	30.5	-21.6	-139.1	....		78bjd
Direct Investment Abroad	—	—	—	—	—	—	—	—	—	—	—	—	....	....	....		78bdd
Dir. Invest. in Rep. Econ., n.i.e.	-129.6	-171.0	-299.7	-76.8	18.5	-54.3	-46.6	-30.2	-20.6	19.1	-9.2	9.1	-61.5	-148.0	....		78bed
Portfolio Investment Assets	—	—	—	—	—	—	—	—	—	—	—	—	....	....	....		78bfd
Equity Securities	—	—	—	—	—	—	—	—	—	—	—	—	....	....	....		78bkd
Debt Securities	—	—	—	—	—	—	—	—	—	—	—	—	....	....	....		78bld
Portfolio Investment Liab., n.i.e.	-.1	—	—	.9	-4.1	2.6	—	—	—	—	—	—	....	....	....		78bgd
Equity Securities	-.1	—	—	—	—	—	—	—	—	—	—	—	....	....	....		78bmd
Debt Securities	—	—	—	.9	-4.1	2.6	—	—	—	—	—	—	....	....	....		78bnd
Financial Derivatives Assets													....	....	....		78bwd
Financial Derivatives Liabilities													....	....	....		78bxd
Other Investment Assets	1.3	-.9	-23.8	27.8	4.9	-.1	-4.4	-19.1	15.7	25.5	15.2	18.6	27.1	24.6	....		78bhd
Monetary Authorities	—	—	—	—	—	—	—	—	—	—	—	—	—	—	....		78bod
General Government	.2	—	1.7	.1	-.4	-6.6	-14.5	-31.3	—	—	—	—	—	—	....		78bpd
Banks	1.1	-.9	-25.5	27.7	5.3	6.5	10.1	12.2	15.7	25.5	15.2	18.6	27.1	24.6	....		78bqd
Other Sectors																	78brd
Other Investment Liab., n.i.e.	38.1	54.3	14.9	21.4	38.6	-34.8	-22.1	-34.8	-1.8	-16.9	20.9	2.8	12.8	-15.7	....		78bid
Monetary Authorities	2.9	.7	.2	.1	.2	.6	—										78bsd
General Government	1.8	12.7	11.5	-3.3	9.0	10.6	2.0	2.1	4.2	-15.0	1.3	19.3	16.1	-21.4	....		78btd
Banks	5.4	37.1	19.7	9.2	.1	-41.8	-23.7	-29.6									78bud
Other Sectors	28.0	3.8	-16.5	15.4	29.3	-4.2	-.4	-7.3	-6.0	-1.9	19.6	-16.5	-3.3	5.7	....		78bvd
Net Errors and Omissions	-59.7	-3.2	17.7	-16.8	-.9	45.4	41.3	60.0	41.6	-7.5	45.3	125.9	42.8	114.3	....		78cad
Overall Balance	-16.5	-9.2	-.2	18.3	-78.3	-21.5	12.7	34.3	119.8	-1.7	19.1	8.1	-4.4	9.8	....		78cbd
Reserves and Related Items	16.5	9.2	.2	-18.3	78.3	21.5	-12.7	-34.3	-119.8	1.7	-19.1	-8.1	4.4	-9.8	....		79dad
Reserve Assets	16.5	9.2	.2	-18.3	78.3	21.5	-12.7	-34.3	-119.8	1.7	-19.1	-8.1	4.4	-9.8	....		79dbd
Use of Fund Credit and Loans	—	—	—	—	—	—	—	—									79dcd
Exceptional Financing																	79ded

Government Finance

Year Ending December 31

	1987	1988	1989	1990	1991	1992	1993	1994	1995	1996	1997	1998	1999	2000	2001		Code
Deficit (-) or Surplus	....	....	....	....	....	....	....	....	....	....	....	....	....	....	....		80
Revenue	....	....	....	....	....	....	....	....	....	....	....	....	....	....	....		81
Grants Received	....	....	....	....	....	....	....	....	....	....	....	....	....	....	....		81z
Expenditure	....	....	....	....	....	....	....	....	....	....	....	....	....	....	....		82
Lending Minus Repayments	....	....	....	....	....	....	....	....	....	....	....	....	....	....	....		83
Financing																	
Domestic	....	....	....	....	....	....	....	....	....	....	....	....	....	....	....		84a
Foreign	....	....	....	....	....	....	....	....	....	....	....	....	....	....	....		85a
Debt: Domestic	....	....	....	....	....	....	....	....	....	....	....	....	....	....	....		88a
Foreign	....	....	....	....	....	....	....	....	....	....	....	....	....	....	....		89a

National Accounts

Millions of Guilders

	1987	1988	1989	1990	1991	1992	1993	1994	1995	1996	1997	1998	1999	2000	2001		Code
Househ.Cons.Expend.,incl.NPISHs	608	972	1,065	1,707	1,977	2,721	3,382	17,951	36,578	162,281	212,741	....	....	....	....		96f
Government Consumption Expend.	737	848	815	777	1,085	1,239	1,752	6,789	45,373	48,083	51,326	....	....	....	....		91f
Gross Capital Formation	509	387	565	660	829	1,164	2,627	27,718	118,522	116,175	126,706	....	....	....	....		93
Exports of Goods and Services	609	681	1,023	869	657	649	14,860	75,663	229,470	199,154	195,454	....	....	....	....		90c
Imports of Goods and Services (-)	502	566	755	844	794	668	11,619	63,900	201,020	226,086	224,117	....	....	....	....		98c
Gross Domestic Product (GDP)	1,960	2,322	2,713	3,169	3,754	5,105	11,002	64,220	228,924	299,609	362,110	328,080	....	....	....		99b
Net Primary Income from Abroad	-8	-15	-10	-12	-13	-13	-101	-324	-191	479	1,499	....	....	....	....		98.n
Gross National Income (GNI)	1,952	2,307	2,702	3,154	3,734	5,092	10,748	63,482	227,782	300,635	362,188	....	....	....	....		99a
Net National Income	1,716	2,063	2,414	2,813	3,267	4,456	9,327	56,503	205,781	271,870	328,264	....	....	....	....		99e
GDP Volume 1980 Prices	1,251	1,349	1,406	1,407	1,456	1,540	1,471	1,459	....	....	....	....	....	....	....		99b.p
GDP Volume (1990=100)	88.9	95.9	100.0	100.0	103.5	109.5	104.5	103.7	....	....	....	....	....	....	....		99bv.p
GDP Deflator (1990=100)	69.5	76.4	85.6	100.0	114.5	147.2	332.1	1,954.2	....	....	....	....	....	....	....		99bi.p

Midyear Estimates

	1987	1988	1989	1990	1991	1992	1993	1994	1995	1996	1997	1998	1999	2000	2001		Code
Population	.39	.39	.40	.40	.40	.40	.40	.40	.41	.41	.42	.41	.43	.44	.42		99z

(See notes in the back of the book.)

Swaziland

		1972	1973	1974	1975	1976	1977	1978	1979	1980	1981	1982	1983	1984	1985	1986
Exchange Rates															*SDRs per Lilangeni:*	
Official Rate	ac	1.17647	1.23509	1.18434	.98235	.98982	.94673	.88272	.91807	1.05190	.89814	.84226	.78170	.51397	.35597	.37443
															US Dollars per Lilangeni:	
Official Rate	ag	1.27731	1.48995	1.45005	1.15000	1.15000	1.15000	1.15000	1.20940	1.34160	1.04540	.92910	.81840	.50380	.39100	.45800
Official Rate	rh	1.30181	1.44408	1.47216	1.36629	1.15000	1.15000	1.15000	1.18785	1.28543	1.14914	.92451	.89909	.69536	.45783	.44082
Fund Position															*Millions of SDRs:*	
Quota	2f. s	8.00	8.00	8.00	8.00	8.00	8.00	12.00	12.00	18.00	18.00	18.00	24.70	24.70	24.70	24.70
SDRs	1b. s	.75	.82	.87	1.01	.94	.87	.96	2.16	1.82	5.92	4.98	1.47	2.29	.26	2.24
Reserve Position in the Fund	1c. s	.29	.20	.39	1.05	2.00	2.00	2.80	2.74	4.26	4.28	.01	1.70	1.73	1.76	.03
Total Fund Cred.&Loans Outstg.	2tl								2.43	4.47	4.50	4.50	14.48	14.48	12.85	8.57
International Liquidity													*Millions of US Dollars Unless Otherwise Indicated:*			
Total Reserves minus Gold	1l. d	....	....	13.47	45.61	73.39	94.71	113.61	113.70	158.74	96.36	76.12	92.50	80.10	83.42	96.45
SDRs	1b. d	.81	.99	1.07	1.18	1.09	1.06	1.25	2.85	2.32	6.89	5.49	1.54	2.24	.29	2.74
Reserve Position in the Fund	1c. d	.31	.24	.48	1.23	2.32	2.43	3.65	3.61	5.43	4.98	.01	1.78	1.70	1.93	.04
Foreign Exchange	1d. d	....	....	11.93	43.20	69.97	91.22	108.71	107.25	150.99	84.49	70.62	89.18	76.16	81.20	93.67
Monetary Authorities: Other Liab.	4.. d			.18	.19	.04	.40	.40	3.80	3.81	1.15	1.43	1.11	3.89	1.05	1.60
Deposit Money Banks: Assets	7a. d	14.66	7.18	17.36	22.25	9.63	13.70	8.22	5.73	4.18	7.17	9.03	11.50	4.93	7.31	6.33
Liabilities	7b. d	2.06	.01	—	.03	.07	.03	.24	1.11	4.66	5.52	6.71	10.97	4.38	3.31	6.58
Monetary Authorities															*Millions of Emalangeni:*	
Foreign Assets	11	....	....	10.19	39.97	64.45	83.33	97.98	92.19	114.35	88.00	83.95	117.64	163.05	213.14	214.25
Claims on Central Government	12a			.60	.75	.84	.62	10.51	3.52	5.12	5.96	7.29	6.63	19.82	25.97	31.70
Claims on Private Sector	12d			.01	.16	.24	.42	.61	.87	1.19	2.38	2.35	3.23	3.48	7.21	4.08
Claims on Deposit Money Banks	12e			.02	4.20	—	—	—	2.70	—	4.00	—	1.17	1.17	—	1.10
Reserve Money	14			6.34	13.51	33.60	46.53	44.40	46.20	57.24	49.45	54.97	79.52	106.10	118.35	188.97
of which: Currency Outside DMBs	14a			3.33	5.11	6.52	7.31	8.90	9.59	11.90	14.41	15.03	15.23	16.77	17.45	25.21
Time Deposits	15			—	—	—	—	—	—	1.88	2.54	3.60	3.77	9.71	49.50	8.21
Foreign Liabilities	16c			.13	.17	.04	.35	3.30	5.79	5.11	6.38	6.54	19.68	35.89	38.78	26.39
Central Government Deposits	16d			3.14	29.16	27.51	31.44	54.84	42.28	52.64	33.26	17.51	13.20	18.13	10.94	12.09
Capital Accounts	17a			2.79	3.77	4.07	4.60	5.39	7.17	8.47	11.11	12.14	12.73	17.01	22.56	21.67
Other Items (Net)	17r			-1.58	-1.53	.31	1.45	1.16	-2.17	-4.68	-2.39	-1.15	-.23	.68	6.21	-6.19
Deposit Money Banks															*Millions of Emalangeni:*	
Reserves	20	1.36	1.57	2.58	8.51	25.97	32.72	34.48	34.30	45.23	32.51	42.09	59.34	86.47	93.38	159.65
Foreign Assets	21	11.48	5.06	11.97	19.34	8.37	11.91	7.15	4.74	3.12	6.86	9.72	14.05	9.79	18.68	13.82
Claims on Central Government	22a	2.49	9.07	8.05	13.09	2.68	2.00	5.44	7.00	4.00	5.92	8.44	14.26	7.12	11.67	25.08
Claims on Private Sector	22d	17.40	22.60	29.25	43.43	46.32	48.38	74.78	84.69	97.11	130.04	138.13	143.26	152.54	151.94	161.24
Demand Deposits	24	13.01	11.70	13.59	18.23	22.17	20.67	27.72	30.58	37.93	36.59	42.11	44.21	48.74	56.55	86.80
Time and Savings Deposits	25	13.96	22.32	23.72	38.08	48.31	55.33	77.37	76.69	81.97	87.70	99.70	133.53	161.15	166.84	202.55
Foreign Liabilities	26c	1.61	.01	—	.03	.06	.03	.21	.92	3.47	5.28	7.22	13.40	8.70	8.46	14.37
Central Government Deposits	26d	4.48	.29	10.78	16.96	5.69	6.74	9.56	16.77	17.93	25.71	23.85	18.36	13.60	17.83	14.02
Capital Accounts	27a	—	3.19	4.63	4.63	7.15	8.27	14.12	14.34	17.53	19.53	22.13	26.40	26.65	26.83	31.28
Other Items (Net)	27r	-.34	.80	-.87	6.44	-.03	3.97	-3.02	-8.58	-9.37	.51	3.37	-4.99	-2.93	-.83	10.76
Monetary Survey															*Millions of Emalangeni:*	
Foreign Assets (Net)	31n	....	....	22.04	59.12	72.73	94.87	101.62	90.22	108.89	83.20	79.92	98.60	128.26	184.59	187.31
Domestic Credit	32	....	....	24.00	11.31	16.89	13.24	31.03	37.03	36.85	85.33	114.86	135.82	151.22	168.03	195.99
Claims on Central Govt. (Net)	32an			-5.27	-32.29	-29.67	-35.56	-44.36	-48.54	-61.45	-47.09	-25.62	-10.67	-4.79	8.87	30.67
Claims on Private Sector	32d			29.26	43.59	46.56	48.80	75.39	85.57	98.30	132.42	140.48	146.49	156.01	159.15	165.33
Money	34			16.93	23.42	28.79	34.16	37.21	40.91	49.86	51.08	58.09	60.84	67.81	76.92	115.14
Quasi-Money	35			23.72	38.08	48.31	55.33	77.37	76.69	83.85	90.23	103.30	137.30	170.86	216.34	210.76
Capital Accounts	37a			7.42	8.39	11.22	12.87	19.51	21.51	26.00	30.64	34.27	39.13	43.66	49.39	52.95
Other Items (Net)	37r			-2.04	.53	1.29	5.75	-1.44	-11.87	-13.97	-3.43	-.87	-2.85	-2.85	9.97	4.45
Money plus Quasi-Money	35l			40.65	61.50	77.11	89.48	114.58	117.60	133.70	141.32	161.38	198.14	238.67	293.26	325.90
Interest Rates															*Percent Per Annum:*	
Discount Rate *(End of Period)*	60	....	....	....	....	9.00	9.00	8.50	7.00	7.00	10.50	16.00	13.50	19.00	12.50	9.50
Money Market Rate	60b															
Treasury Bill Rate	60c	....	....	....	6.00	6.00	6.00	7.71	7.71	7.71	12.00	14.60	13.04	17.74	16.47	9.76
Deposit Rate	60l	....	5.50	7.02	7.96	7.75	7.75	7.67	5.63	4.50	6.58	11.67	11.17	15.00	14.38	7.59
Lending Rate	60p	8.50	8.00	10.38	10.75	10.50	10.50	10.48	9.75	9.50	11.25	17.38	16.50	20.33	20.63	14.28
Prices and Labor															*Index Numbers (1995=100):*	
Consumer Prices	64	5.4	6.0	7.2	8.0	8.5	10.3	11.2	†13.0	15.5	18.6	20.6	†23.0	†25.9	31.2	35.5
															Number in Thousands:	
Labor Force	67d	....													....	157
Employment	67e	....													73	76
International Transactions															*Millions of Emalangeni:*	
Exports	70	63.0	74.2	121.5	145.7	159.1	143.1	170.6	194.8	286.9	340.3	351.8	338.5	345.6	392.9	635.5
Imports, c.i.f.	71	53.3	66.6	93.4	131.6	174.1	158.3	270.8	365.7	484.7	516.8	569.3	612.8	642.7	707.1	798.9

	1987	1988	1989	1990	1991	1992	1993	1994	1995	1996	1997	1998	1999	2000	2001		
Exchange Rates																	
End of Period																	
	.36524	.31253	.30005	.27430	.25486	.23822	.21429	.19331	.18443	.14852	.15227	.12120	.11838	.10141	.06562	Official Rate	ac
End of Period (ag) Period Average (rh)																	
	.51815	.42057	.39432	.39024	.36456	.32755	.29433	.28221	.27416	.21356	.20544	.17065	.16248	.13213	.08246	Official Rate	ag
	.49141	.44227	.38218	.38665	.36280	.35092	.30641	.28177	.27574	.23416	.21724	.18246	.16370	.14481	.11774	Official Rate	rh
Fund Position																	
End of Period																	
	24.70	24.70	24.70	24.70	24.70	36.50	36.50	36.50	36.50	36.50	36.50	36.50	50.70	50.70	50.70	Quota	2f. s
	2.79	1.23	.80	8.49	8.65	5.84	5.88	5.89	5.90	5.93	5.94	5.96	2.42	2.44	2.45	SDRs	1b. s
	.03	.01	.01	.02	.02	3.00	3.00	3.00	3.00	3.00	3.00	3.00	6.55	6.55	6.55	Reserve Position in the Fund	1c. s
	4.30	1.16	.26	.03	—	—	—	—	—	—	—	—	—	—	—	Total Fund Cred.&Loans Outstg.	2tl
International Liquidity																	
End of Period																	
	127.16	140.01	180.61	216.47	171.93	309.06	264.29	296.97	298.20	254.00	294.84	358.61	375.93	351.79	271.78	Total Reserves minus Gold	1l. d
	3.96	1.66	1.05	12.08	12.37	8.03	8.08	8.60	8.77	8.52	8.02	8.39	3.33	3.18	3.08	SDRs	1b. d
	.04	.01	.01	.03	.03	4.13	4.12	4.38	4.46	4.32	4.05	4.23	8.99	8.54	8.23	Reserve Position in the Fund	1c. d
	123.16	138.34	179.55	204.36	159.53	296.90	252.00	283.99	284.96	241.16	282.77	345.99	363.61	340.08	260.46	Foreign Exchange	1d. d
	2.39	3.98	2.59	2.65	2.81	1.55	1.48	32.02	21.34	20.14	1.24	21.98	49.16	45.66	38.90	Monetary Authorities: Other Liab.	4..d
	17.82	64.40	63.90	58.16	41.13	52.01	52.43	43.59	47.52	107.45	91.79	99.16	135.46	84.13	71.89	Deposit Money Banks: Assets	7a. d
	6.21	16.40	14.43	12.33	10.68	20.83	19.69	17.83	17.61	50.70	20.92	6.13	9.43	13.84	1.85	Liabilities	7b. d
Monetary Authorities																	
End of Period																	
	244.39	328.23	466.85	537.75	†806.91	929.80	875.03	872.21	1,023.66	1,335.33	1,427.69	2,083.56	2,304.34	2,643.72	3,362.53	Foreign Assets	11
	11.51	3.71	.87	.13	—	—	—	40.00	20.63	.06	—	—	—	—	—	Claims on Central Government	12a
	4.20	4.66	5.47	7.00	9.25	9.63	8.87	10.63	12.52	14.02	13.06	12.30	15.23	16.34	15.50	Claims on Private Sector	12d
	.10	.60	2.93	11.41	12.81	9.60	6.82	5.65	30.00	36.76	43.39	42.55	44.31	41.95	41.95	Claims on Deposit Money Banks	12e
	189.47	157.29	204.60	200.79	181.98	287.97	255.34	300.24	307.81	284.95	300.47	275.33	307.27	293.36	274.53	Reserve Money	14
	27.19	32.20	37.20	48.19	52.99	56.09	75.19	69.59	80.33	90.85	109.00	107.23	136.95	148.06	134.93	of which: Currency Outside DMBs	14a
	5.88	48.00	36.56	21.98	23.72	25.11	43.92	36.90	52.57	53.45	77.68	48.33	50.14	68.30	79.54	Time Deposits	15
	16.38	13.18	7.43	6.90	7.70	4.74	5.02	113.47	77.82	94.32	6.04	128.81	302.53	345.57	471.70	Foreign Liabilities	16c
	33.73	87.07	192.08	211.47	†515.06	500.48	508.49	386.14	555.97	771.74	995.41	1,471.42	1,552.66	1,765.98	2,113.64	Central Government Deposits	16d
	22.11	25.08	26.94	30.12	31.91	33.67	36.80	40.14	41.95	50.52	50.80	62.46	86.23	96.66	134.10	Capital Accounts	17a
	-7.36	6.59	8.51	85.03	68.60	97.05	41.15	51.60	50.69	131.19	53.53	152.05	65.05	132.14	346.45	Other Items (Net)	17r
Deposit Money Banks																	
End of Period																	
	163.60	138.62	165.74	132.53	125.94	217.80	185.65	227.46	232.42	199.22	193.84	151.48	176.57	145.07	130.86	Reserves	20
	34.39	153.13	162.05	149.04	112.82	158.78	178.14	154.45	173.32	503.13	446.80	581.07	833.68	636.74	871.83	Foreign Assets	21
	5.50	—	9.75	—	—	—	30.00	38.00	49.79	68.35	52.17	52.73	50.21	59.49	60.00	Claims on Central Government	22a
	202.62	260.87	335.83	465.99	654.58	673.59	739.14	902.68	915.60	971.81	1,095.01	1,159.43	1,223.39	1,308.23	1,383.56	Claims on Private Sector	22d
	94.94	110.42	131.64	144.21	158.41	197.76	215.06	241.75	282.57	331.99	382.76	393.64	525.72	512.53	619.15	Demand Deposits	24
	240.46	319.26	435.38	430.19	539.03	659.16	731.45	833.28	811.70	951.43	1,135.61	1,375.32	1,512.47	1,349.40	1,467.33	Time and Savings Deposits	25
	11.99	39.01	36.60	30.29	29.22	63.58	66.89	63.17	64.22	237.41	101.82	35.92	58.04	104.72	22.45	Foreign Liabilities	26c
	6.23	15.37	35.72	90.12	92.96	89.16	73.71	90.88	114.57	101.22	10.17	14.25	14.70	.22	.23	Central Government Deposits	26d
	44.78	67.08	46.99	61.85	67.69	74.36	96.20	92.33	97.61	75.09	127.53	114.39	139.44	157.73	292.70	Capital Accounts	27a
	7.72	12.74	-12.96	-10.40	5.96	-33.83	-50.38	1.17	.47	45.37	29.97	11.19	33.48	24.93	44.40	Other Items (Net)	27r
Monetary Survey																	
End of Period																	
	250.42	429.17	584.87	648.30	†882.74	1,020.26	981.26	850.02	1,054.94	1,506.73	1,766.63	2,499.89	2,777.46	2,830.18	3,740.21	Foreign Assets (Net)	31n
	183.86	178.06	124.11	171.53	†55.80	93.58	195.81	514.28	328.00	181.28	154.69	-261.20	-278.54	-382.14	-654.82	Domestic Credit	32
	-22.95	-87.47	-217.19	-301.46	†-608.02	-589.64	-552.19	-399.02	-600.12	-804.55	-953.40	-1,432.94	-1,517.16	-1,706.71	-2,053.88	Claims on Central Govt. (Net)	32an
	206.82	265.53	341.30	472.99	663.83	683.22	748.00	913.30	928.12	985.83	1,108.09	1,171.74	1,238.62	1,324.58	1,399.06	Claims on Private Sector	32d
	125.42	142.77	168.98	192.58	211.54	254.20	290.50	311.59	363.16	423.03	491.75	500.87	662.69	660.58	754.08	Money	34
	246.33	367.26	471.93	452.17	562.75	684.27	775.37	870.18	864.27	1,004.88	1,213.29	1,423.66	1,562.61	1,417.69	1,546.87	Quasi-Money	35
	66.88	92.15	73.94	91.98	99.60	108.03	132.99	132.47	139.56	125.61	178.33	176.85	225.67	254.40	426.80	Capital Accounts	37a
	-4.35	5.05	-5.87	83.11	64.65	67.25	-21.79	50.07	15.96	134.49	37.95	137.31	47.95	115.37	357.65	Other Items (Net)	37r
	371.75	510.02	640.92	644.74	774.29	938.56	1,065.87	1,181.76	1,227.43	1,427.91	1,705.04	1,924.52	2,225.30	2,078.28	2,300.95	Money plus Quasi-Money	35l
Interest Rates																	
Percent Per Annum																	
	9.00	11.00	12.00	12.00	13.00	12.00	11.00	12.00	15.00	16.75	15.75	18.00	12.00	11.00	9.50	Discount Rate (End of Period)	60
	....	....	8.39	10.50	10.61	10.25	9.73	7.01	8.52	9.77	10.35	10.63	8.86	5.54	5.06	Money Market Rate	60b
	5.96	7.28	10.16	11.14	12.67	12.34	8.25	8.35	10.87	13.68	14.37	13.09	11.19	8.30	7.16	Treasury Bill Rate	60c
	4.89	6.74	9.08	8.74	10.60	10.49	7.89	7.54	9.44	11.08	12.00	11.92	9.86	6.53	6.15	Deposit Rate	60l
	11.87	13.15	14.50	14.50	16.02	15.92	14.35	14.25	17.05	18.67	19.50	19.50	17.42	14.00	13.25	Lending Rate	60p
Prices and Labor																	
Period Averages																	
	40.3	†49.0	52.7	59.6	65.0	69.9	78.3	89.1	100.0	106.4	114.0	123.3	130.8	146.7	155.4	Consumer Prices	64
Period Averages																	
	83	86	91	92	92	92	93	87	87	90	....	....	....	....	....	Labor Force	67d
	....	....	....	....	....	....	....	....	....	....	....	....	....	....	....	Employment	67e
International Transactions																	
Millions of Emalangeni																	
	862.4	1,059.9	1,313.9	1,439.9	1,639.0	1,820.2	2,236.5	2,779.8	3,472.2	3,812.7	....	....	....	....	....	Exports	70
	885.8	1,167.6	1,524.5	1,714.1	1,979.0	2,468.0	2,852.3	3,291.9	4,005.8	5,015.7	5,486.6	....	....	....	....	Imports, c.i.f.	71

Swaziland

	1972	1973	1974	1975	1976	1977	1978	1979	1980	1981	1982	1983	1984	1985	1986
Balance of Payments															*Millions of US Dollars:*
Current Account, n.i.e. .... 78al *d*	...	...	42.5	51.5	30.4	11.6	−70.7	−119.3	−129.7	−81.4	−113.8	−107.0	−77.5	−38.4	10.8
Goods: Exports f.o.b. .... 78aa *d*	...	...	178.8	197.0	193.4	183.9	198.7	241.6	368.3	388.3	324.0	303.8	230.8	176.7	278.4
Goods: Imports f.o.b. .... 78ab *d*	...	...	−111.9	−139.7	−155.9	−171.2	−247.7	−363.3	−538.1	−504.0	−439.0	−464.8	−372.1	−272.7	−296.7
Trade Balance .... 78ac *d*	...	...	67.0	57.3	37.5	12.6	−49.0	−121.6	−169.9	−115.7	−115.0	−160.9	−141.3	−95.9	−18.2
Services: Credit .... 78ad *d*	...	...	23.0	25.0	25.8	29.2	20.1	31.4	36.1	41.4	32.9	41.2	43.7	27.8	30.5
Services: Debit .... 78ae *d*	...	...	−28.8	−39.5	−42.1	−46.0	−63.7	−83.3	−80.0	−100.9	−107.4	−93.0	−86.5	−62.5	−61.6
Balance on Goods & Services ...... 78af *d*	...	...	61.1	42.9	21.2	−4.1	−92.6	−173.6	−213.8	−175.1	−189.5	−212.7	−184.2	−130.6	−49.4
Income: Credit .... 78ag *d*	...	...	4.4	13.3	15.8	20.7	25.4	27.4	46.4	68.6	54.6	66.9	70.9	71.8	73.0
Income: Debit .... 78ah *d*	...	...	−38.3	−23.1	−15.2	−17.8	−29.9	−20.0	−41.1	−48.4	−40.2	−27.5	−31.4	−32.8	−57.4
Balance on Gds, Serv. & Inc. .... 78ai *d*	...	...	27.2	33.0	21.7	−1.3	−97.1	−166.1	−208.5	−154.9	−175.1	−173.3	−144.7	−91.6	−33.8
Current Transfers, n.i.e.: Credit ...... 78aj *d*	...	...	28.6	37.2	44.0	50.4	70.5	95.0	143.7	131.7	123.6	128.1	113.0	88.4	85.4
Current Transfers: Debit .... 78ak *d*	...	...	−13.2	−18.7	−35.4	−37.5	−44.2	−48.2	−64.8	−58.1	−62.3	−61.8	−45.8	−35.3	−40.8
Capital Account, n.i.e. .... 78bc *d*	...	...	—	—	—	—	−1.5	−1.4	−2.1	−1.9	−.6	−1.7	−1.9	−.9	−.8
Capital Account, n.i.e.: Credit .... 78ba *d*	...	...	—	—	—	—	—	—	—	—	—	—	—	—	—
Capital Account: Debit .... 78bb *d*	...	...	—	—	—	—	−1.5	−1.4	−2.1	−1.9	−.6	−1.7	−1.9	−.9	−.8
Financial Account, n.i.e. .... 78bj *d*	...	...	−14.7	11.9	20.6	24.6	80.4	100.3	36.5	21.7	32.1	66.5	29.4	21.1	20.9
Direct Investment Abroad .... 78bd *d*	...	...	—	—	—	—	—	—	−9.0	−5.4	2.9	.1	−4.9	−2.7	−2.3
Dir. Invest. in Rep. Econ., n.i.e. ...... 78be *d*	...	...	3.5	14.5	7.4	20.0	21.7	55.5	26.5	37.1	−13.6	−5.7	5.0	11.7	31.1
Portfolio Investment Assets .... 78bf *d*	...	...	—	—	—	—	—	—	—	—	−.1	−.7	.1	−.1	—
Equity Securities .... 78bk *d*	...	...	—	—	—	—	—	—	—	—	—	−.1	—	—	—
Debt Securities .... 78bl *d*	...	...	—	—	—	—	—	—	—	—	−.1	−.6	.1	−.1	—
Portfolio Investment Liab., n.i.e. .. 78bg *d*	...	...	—	—	—	—	—	—	—	—	.2	.4	−.1	2.0	−.4
Equity Securities .... 78bm *d*	...	...	—	—	—	—	—	—	—	—	.2	.4	−.1	2.0	−.4
Debt Securities .... 78bn *d*	...	...	—	—	—	—	—	—	—	—	—	—	—	—	—
Financial Derivatives Assets ...... 78bw *d*	...	...	....	....	....	....	....	....	....	....	....	....	....	....	—
Financial Derivatives Liabilities .... 78bx *d*	...	...	....	....	....	....	....	....	....	....	....	....	....	....	—
Other Investment Assets .... 78bh *d*	...	...	−25.0	−9.1	−.7	−3.3	11.2	9.9	—	−24.8	−19.9	7.6	−4.2	−16.5	−7.0
Monetary Authorities .... 78bo *d*	...	...	—	—	—	—	—	—	—	—	—	—	—	—	.4
General Government .... 78bp *d*	...	...	1.0	−6.6	−9.5	.6	7.0	6.4	−2.4	−20.0	−9.8	13.6	11.5	−1.5	−4.6
Banks .... 78bq *d*	...	...	−11.5	−9.2	12.3	−3.9	4.1	3.4	2.4	−4.8	−2.8	−4.0	2.7	−3.9	2.1
Other Sectors .... 78br *d*	...	...	−14.6	6.8	−3.5	—	—	—	—	—	−7.4	−2.0	−18.4	−11.1	−4.9
Other Investment Liab., n.i.e. .... 78bi *d*	...	...	6.8	6.5	13.9	7.9	47.5	34.9	19.0	14.7	63.1	64.8	33.6	26.7	−.5
Monetary Authorities .... 78bs *d*	...	...	.1	—	.1	—	—	−.5	−2.1	.6	.1	—	4.5	−2.3	.4
General Government .... 78bt *d*	...	...	3.8	5.5	7.9	7.9	47.3	34.6	17.7	12.1	19.1	27.5	13.4	−1.4	20.1
Banks .... 78bu *d*	...	...	—	—	—	—	.2	.8	3.3	2.1	1.7	5.6	−2.8	3.6	−1.2
Other Sectors .... 78bv *d*	...	...	2.8	.9	5.9	—	—	—	—	—	42.2	31.8	18.5	26.8	−19.8
Net Errors and Omissions .... 78ca *d*	...	...	−17.7	−24.2	−23.1	−14.5	7.7	12.0	129.4	13.3	73.1	53.8	41.7	13.7	−23.2
Overall Balance .... 78cb *d*	...	...	10.2	39.2	27.8	21.8	15.9	−8.4	34.1	−48.3	−9.1	11.6	−8.3	−4.5	7.6
Reserves and Related Items .. 79da *d*	...	...	−10.2	−39.2	−27.8	−21.8	−15.9	8.4	−34.1	48.3	9.1	−11.6	8.3	4.5	−7.6
Reserve Assets .... 79db *d*	...	...	−10.2	−39.2	−27.8	−21.8	−15.9	5.3	−36.8	48.3	9.1	−22.3	8.3	6.1	−2.5
Use of Fund Credit and Loans .... 79dc *d*	...	...	—	—	—	—	—	3.2	2.6	—	—	10.7	—	−1.6	−5.0
Exceptional Financing .... 79de *d*	...	...	....	....	....	....	....	....	....	....	....	....	....	....	....
International Investment Position															*Millions of US Dollars*
Assets .... 79aa *d*	...	...	....	....	....	....	....	....	....	169.6	156.7	172.2	154.0	167.7	167.0
Direct Investment Abroad .... 79ab *d*	...	...	....	....	....	....	....	....	....	24.4	18.3	15.3	11.8	8.8	9.4
Portfolio Investment .... 79ac *d*	...	...	....	....	....	....	....	....	....	1.9	.9	1.4	.8	.7	.9
Equity Securities .... 79ad *d*	...	...	....	....	....	....	....	....	....	—	—	—	—	—	—
Debt Securities .... 79ae *d*	...	...	....	....	....	....	....	....	....	1.9	.9	1.4	.8	.7	.9
Financial Derivatives .... 79al *d*	...	...	....	....	....	....	....	....	....	—	—	—	—	—	—
Other Investment .... 79af *d*	...	...	....	....	....	....	....	....	....	51.5	59.8	60.0	59.9	73.5	59.1
Monetary Authorities .... 79ag *d*	...	...	....	....	....	....	....	....	....	—	—	—	—	—	—
General Government .... 79ah *d*	...	...	....	....	....	....	....	....	....	1.5	2.2	2.5	1.1	6.9	9.0
Banks .... 79ai *d*	...	...	....	....	....	....	....	....	....	8.0	9.9	12.4	5.6	7.7	6.9
Other Sectors .... 79aj *d*	...	...	....	....	....	....	....	....	....	42.0	47.7	45.1	53.1	58.9	43.2
Reserve Assets .... 79ak *d*	...	...	....	....	....	....	....	....	....	91.8	77.6	95.5	81.5	84.7	97.5
Liabilities .... 79la *d*	...	...	....	....	....	....	....	....	....	536.8	525.1	529.4	401.5	390.2	469.9
Dir. Invest. in Rep. Economy .. 79lb *d*	...	...	....	....	....	....	....	....	....	280.5	228.7	199.0	126.5	104.2	154.7
Portfolio Investment .... 79lc *d*	...	...	....	....	....	....	....	....	....	.5	.3	.3	.2	7.4	8.3
Equity Securities .... 79ld *d*	...	...	....	....	....	....	....	....	....	.5	.3	.3	.2	7.4	8.3
Debt Securities .... 79le *d*	...	...	....	....	....	....	....	....	....	—	—	—	—	—	—
Financial Derivatives .... 79ll *d*	...	...	....	....	....	....	....	....	....	—	—	—	—	—	—
Other Investment .... 79lf *d*	...	...	....	....	....	....	....	....	....	255.8	296.1	330.0	274.8	278.5	306.9
Monetary Authorities .... 79lg *d*	...	...	....	....	....	....	....	....	....	6.3	6.0	16.1	18.1	15.1	12.0
General Government .... 79lh *d*	...	...	....	....	....	....	....	....	....	156.5	163.0	167.9	155.2	158.2	207.1
Banks .... 79li *d*	...	...	....	....	....	....	....	....	....	5.5	6.7	11.0	4.6	6.7	6.6
Other Sectors .... 79lj *d*	...	...	....	....	....	....	....	....	....	87.5	120.4	135.0	96.9	98.5	81.2

	1987	1988	1989	1990	1991	1992	1993	1994	1995	1996	1997	1998	1999	2000	2001	
Minus Sign Indicates Debit																**Balance of Payments**
	65.6	95.1	77.1	50.7	47.2	−40.6	−63.7	1.9	−29.7	−52.0	8.9	−68.4	6.4	−40.1	....	Current Account, n.i.e. .... 78al *d*
	423.9	466.6	494.1	550.3	593.8	638.5	684.7	790.9	867.8	850.5	961.3	969.9	896.9	810.8	....	Goods: Exports f.o.b. .... 78aa *d*
	−381.1	−449.0	−515.6	−589.2	−635.0	−779.6	−788.6	−841.0	−1,064.4	−1,054.4	−1,088.6	−1,095.8	−1,018.6	−921.3	....	Goods: Imports f.o.b. .... 78ab *d*
	42.8	17.6	−21.5	−38.8	−41.2	−141.1	−103.9	−50.1	−196.6	−203.9	−127.3	−125.9	−121.7	−110.6	....	*Trade Balance* .... 78ac *d*
	54.1	65.4	92.0	107.6	91.3	98.4	92.8	112.8	151.8	100.8	124.5	100.5	104.2	74.2	....	Services: Credit .... 78ad *d*
	−98.5	−106.4	−89.9	−178.6	−181.6	−208.4	−256.4	−201.8	−209.5	−240.8	−244.8	−231.5	−186.8	−176.8	....	Services: Debit .... 78ae *d*
	−1.6	−23.4	−19.4	−109.8	−131.5	−251.1	−267.5	−139.1	−254.2	−343.8	−247.6	−256.9	−204.2	−213.2	....	*Balance on Goods & Services* .... 78af *d*
	95.1	120.8	146.1	161.6	173.5	196.8	155.2	138.5	162.6	200.8	182.7	167.8	163.9	130.1	....	Income: Credit .... 78ag *d*
	−86.1	−77.2	−143.3	−102.7	−103.7	−113.7	−107.3	−155.0	−82.0	−68.7	−44.6	−112.2	−77.9	−53.2	....	Income: Debit .... 78ah *d*
	7.4	20.2	−16.6	−50.9	−61.7	−168.0	−219.5	−155.6	−173.7	−211.8	−109.5	−201.2	−118.3	−136.3	....	*Balance on Gds, Serv. & Inc.* .... 78ai *d*
	108.8	127.8	151.3	175.4	189.0	222.4	248.1	252.6	257.2	268.7	231.2	243.4	232.0	212.7	....	Current Transfers, n.i.e.: Credit ...... 78aj *d*
	−50.7	−53.0	−57.7	−73.7	−80.0	−95.0	−92.3	−95.1	−113.3	−108.9	−112.7	−110.6	−107.4	−116.5	....	Current Transfers: Debit .... 78ak *d*
	−.4	—	.6	2.2	−.1	−.1	—	−.2	—	.1	—	.1	—	.1	....	Capital Account, n.i.e. .... 78bc *d*
	.3	.3	.7	2.3	.3	.4	.3	.1	.3	.1	.1	.1	—	.1	....	Capital Account, n.i.e.: Credit .... 78ba *d*
	−.7	−.2	−.1	−.1	−.5	−.5	−.3	−.3	−.4						....	Capital Account: Debit .... 78bb *d*
	−19.7	−58.1	−10.9	−38.9	23.5	38.3	−2.4	−63.1	−74.5	−4.6	−2.9	96.4	6.0	8.4	....	Financial Account, n.i.e. .... 78bj *d*
	−6.7	−12.3	−15.6	−7.6	−25.0	−33.2	−27.8	−64.7	−20.6	6.4	12.0	−23.9	−13.2	−19.1	....	Direct Investment Abroad .... 78bd *d*
	56.3	50.6	67.2	30.1	82.1	87.3	71.9	63.3	51.7	21.7	−15.3	165.5	89.5	−43.8	....	Dir. Invest. in Rep. Econ., n.i.e. ...... 78be *d*
	−1.2	−.2	−.5	−.5	−.6	−1.0	−.1	−3.9	−9.5	−2.0	−2.0	−2.8	3.2	−2.2	....	Portfolio Investment Assets .... 78bf *d*
	....						−.9	—	−1.9	−.2	−2.0	−1.3	1.5	−.1	....	Equity Securities .... 78bk *d*
	−1.2	−.2	−.5	−.5	−.5	−.1	−.1	−3.9	−7.6	−1.7	—	−1.5	1.7	−2.1	....	Debt Securities .... 78bl *d*
	2.4	6.3	7.4	−2.2	−.1	−.1	−.9	.1	.8	.4	−.1	.7	2.7	−.1	....	Portfolio Investment Liab., n.i.e. ..... 78bg *d*
	2.4	6.3	7.4	−2.2	−.1	−.1	−.9	.1	.8	.4	−.1	.7	2.7	−.1	....	Equity Securities .... 78bm *d*
	....														....	Debt Securities .... 78bn *d*
	....	....	....	....	....										....	Financial Derivatives Assets .... 78bw *d*
	....	....	....	....	....										....	Financial Derivatives Liabilities .... 78bx *d*
	−61.1	−110.3	−80.8	−39.0	−41.1	−40.8	−78.2	−80.5	−86.2	−154.9	−16.7	−26.2	−137.7	28.8	....	Other Investment Assets .... 78bh *d*
	.9					....									....	Monetary Authorities .... 78bo *d*
	−13.4	−24.6	−35.3	−14.7	.4	−.6	−25.3	−17.9	−6.7	−2.7	9.0	−5.4	9.2	42.5	....	General Government .... 78bp *d*
	−10.2	−52.9	−3.9	4.3	12.8	−15.4	−6.9	5.7	−5.3	−77.0	11.1	−22.9	−41.7	27.7	....	Banks .... 78bq *d*
	−38.5	−32.8	−41.6	−28.5	−54.2	−24.8	−46.0	−68.3	−74.2	−75.2	−36.7	2.1	−105.3	−41.5	....	Other Sectors .... 78br *d*
	−9.4	7.8	11.4	−19.8	8.1	26.1	32.7	22.7	−10.7	123.6	19.1	−16.8	61.5	44.8	....	Other Investment Liab., n.i.e. .... 78bi *d*
	.5	2.2	−1.1	.1	.3	−1.1	.1	30.6	−9.8	3.8	−19.2	22.2	28.4	6.2	....	Monetary Authorities .... 78bs *d*
	−16.9	−4.7	−1.9	−20.8	−8.4	−10.7	−10.8	−14.8	−7.1	3.2	−.6	−.2	20.8	22.2	....	General Government .... 78bt *d*
	−.7	14.1	−1.1	.5	−1.3	12.5	−.3	.7	.4	41.5	−25.9	−13.8	.3	6.4	....	Banks .... 78bu *d*
	7.7	−3.8	15.5	.5	17.5	25.3	43.8	6.2	5.9	75.1	64.8	−25.0	11.9	10.0	....	Other Sectors .... 78bv *d*
	−24.2	−25.0	−15.6	−3.0	−56.8	94.3	2.3	48.8	134.1	71.8	19.3	22.3	13.9	25.0	....	Net Errors and Omissions .... 78ca *d*
	21.2	12.0	51.1	11.1	13.7	91.9	−63.7	−12.5	29.8	15.4	25.3	50.5	26.3	−6.6	....	*Overall Balance* .... 78cb *d*
	−21.2	−12.0	−51.1	−11.1	−13.7	−91.9	63.7	12.5	−29.8	−15.4	−25.3	−50.5	−26.3	6.6	....	Reserves and Related Items .... 79da *d*
	−15.6	−7.7	−50.0	−10.8	−13.7	−91.9	63.7	12.5	−29.8	−15.4	−25.3	−50.5	−26.3	6.6	....	Reserve Assets .... 79db *d*
	−5.6	−4.2	−1.2	−.3	—	—	—	—	—	—	—	—	—	—	....	Use of Fund Credit and Loans .... 79dc *d*
	....	....	....	....	....										....	Exceptional Financing .... 79de *d*
Millions of US Dollars																**International Investment Position**
	1,026.6	964.1	1,058.5	1,111.1	678.6	754.0	721.2	838.2	982.9	922.4	915.6	924.3	1,133.5	993.9	....	Assets .... 79aa *d*
	20.3	22.5	35.4	38.3	51.6	49.2	52.6	108.8	135.5	95.4	82.3	90.1	98.1	96.6	....	Direct Investment Abroad .... 79ab *d*
	2.3	2.0	2.4	2.9	3.4	3.9	3.6	7.3	16.6	14.8	16.1	16.0	12.0	11.8	....	Portfolio Investment .... 79ac *d*
	—	—	—	—	.1	.9	.8	.8	2.7	2.3	4.0	4.5	2.8	2.4	....	Equity Securities .... 79ad *d*
	2.3	2.0	2.4	2.9	3.3	3.0	2.8	6.6	14.0	12.5	12.0	11.4	9.2	9.4	....	Debt Securities .... 79ae *d*
	....														....	Financial Derivatives .... 79al *d*
	875.6	806.1	838.1	862.4	400.6	398.0	425.8	479.2	553.4	529.8	527.6	463.0	650.8	538.4	....	Other Investment .... 79af *d*
	—	—	—	—	—	—	—	—	—	—	—	—	—	—	....	Monetary Authorities .... 79ag *d*
	784.1	657.1	650.2	643.5	154.4	139.1	142.3	144.6	124.6	56.1	45.4	42.8	39.9	29.1	....	General Government .... 79ah *d*
	13.8	55.4	57.0	60.5	43.7	53.7	54.8	46.9	50.8	110.3	95.6	101.0	137.5	86.4	....	Banks .... 79ai *d*
	77.7	93.6	131.0	158.4	202.5	205.2	228.7	287.7	377.9	363.5	386.6	319.2	473.4	423.0	....	Other Sectors .... 79aj *d*
	128.5	133.5	182.5	207.5	223.0	302.9	239.2	242.9	277.4	282.4	289.5	355.3	372.6	347.1	....	Reserve Assets .... 79ak *d*
	350.5	575.9	638.9	647.2	720.8	762.0	822.0	881.0	925.3	894.6	846.4	940.0	1,057.8	837.2	....	Liabilities .... 79la *d*
	240.4	249.4	309.1	335.8	399.6	437.7	462.5	506.8	535.6	437.2	406.3	493.6	558.8	414.3	....	Dir. Invest. in Rep. Economy .... 79lb *d*
	2.7	3.2	4.5	2.2	1.9	1.7	.6	.7	1.4	1.5	1.4	1.8	4.4	3.4	....	Portfolio Investment .... 79lc *d*
	2.7	3.2	4.5	2.2	1.9	1.7	.6	.7	1.4	1.5	1.4	1.8	4.4	3.4	....	Equity Securities .... 79ld *d*
															....	Debt Securities .... 79le *d*
	....														....	Financial Derivatives .... 79ll *d*
	107.3	323.2	325.2	309.2	319.3	322.7	358.9	373.6	388.3	456.0	438.7	444.6	494.6	419.5	....	Other Investment .... 79lf *d*
	8.5	5.3	2.9	2.7	2.8	1.5	1.5	32.0	21.3	20.1	1.2	22.0	49.2	45.7	....	Monetary Authorities .... 79lg *d*
	—	227.9	223.1	206.7	205.5	184.7	192.1	175.3	194.5	194.4	177.4	243.3	262.5	210.0	....	General Government .... 79lh *d*
	6.7	18.9	16.6	16.9	14.5	24.7	21.9	21.7	21.5	54.9	28.2	10.4	10.3	14.3	....	Banks .... 79li *d*
	92.2	71.1	82.5	82.8	96.5	111.7	143.5	144.5	150.9	186.5	231.8	168.9	172.7	149.6	....	Other Sectors .... 79lj *d*

Swaziland

		1972	1973	1974	1975	1976	1977	1978	1979	1980	1981	1982	1983	1984	1985	1986
Government Finance															*Millions of Emalangeni:*	
Deficit (-) or Surplus	80	−4.6	−10.8	1.7	17.4	−8.5	−8.6	−40.0	3.9	27.6	−48.9	−31.9	−19.6	−3.6	−27.6	−48.9
Revenue	81	21.2	28.5	45.6	69.9	54.6	80.8	98.7	126.0	148.8	131.1	178.6	179.6	210.8	232.3	243.9
Grants Received	81z	.1	.1	.7	.1	.1	.4	6.6	8.0	7.7	5.0	5.4	5.9	10.7	10.2	11.8
Expenditure	82	23.3	38.3	39.5	46.8	57.6	75.2	119.0	97.5	117.3	166.1	183.2	190.5	209.7	257.9	291.0
Lending Minus Repayments	83	2.7	1.0	5.1	5.8	5.5	14.5	26.2	32.7	11.6	19.0	17.7	14.6	15.4	12.2	13.5
Financing																
Domestic	84a	−.8	3.7	−11.0	−20.9	9.0	2.9	−5.7	−10.5	−27.7	42.5	14.9	18.1	9.2	24.8	21.1
Foreign	85a	5.4	7.1	9.3	3.5	−.5	5.6	45.6	6.6	.1	6.4	17.0	1.4	−5.6	2.8	27.8
Debt: Domestic	88a	4.1	10.8	12.0	12.8	9.2	10.3	15.3	15.0	12.0	17.0	22.0	26.6	27.3	40.9	50.0
Foreign	89a	....	....	....	4.1	....	....	....	94.4	116.4	116.5	127.0	166.4	198.6	371.5	245.6	299.4
National Accounts															*Millions of Emalangeni:*	
Househ.Cons.Expend.,incl.NPISHs	96f	59.2	60.7	50.6	102.8	120.2	146.8	153.5	249.2	286.9	360.2	394.9	450.4	510.8	635.6	672.6
Government Consumption Expend.	91f	13.6	20.2	26.4	36.1	43.3	54.1	70.2	74.9	103.9	133.8	141.0	135.8	182.1	182.9	226.3
Gross Fixed Capital Formation	93e	20.0	24.9	35.7	41.6	50.6	68.1	144.8	142.1	147.8	140.2	152.8	208.5	208.5	197.6	163.6
Changes in Inventories	93i	2.7	6.1	7.1	−2.0	2.0	3.0	−3.0	6.0	23.8	15.3	23.4	−5.7	.9	12.8	41.2
Exports of Goods and Services	90c	65.3	108.4	146.4	155.4	179.4	172.4	186.4	221.1	325.7	388.0	416.8	400.6	509.5	454.8	706.0
Imports of Goods and Services (-)	98c	63.2	86.5	106.4	121.3	160.2	181.4	256.7	344.6	465.9	536.6	582.2	610.0	722.9	681.2	783.4
Gross Domestic Product (GDP)	99b	97.6	133.8	159.8	213.3	235.3	263.0	295.2	348.7	422.1	500.9	546.7	579.6	662.3	802.5	1,026.3
Net Primary Income from Abroad	98.n	−9.4	−19.3	−3.7	50.4	46.1	−2.3	−14.6	−22.2	−5.7	5.7	15.5	30.6	53.1	76.5	62.5
Gross National Income (GNI)	99a	88.2	114.5	156.1	263.7	281.4	260.7	280.6	326.5	416.4	506.6	562.2	610.2	715.4	879.0	1,088.8
Consumption of Fixed Capital	99cf	8.5	9.8	11.4	12.5	13.8	15.2	16.7	18.4	26.1	30.1	37.3	46.6	47.2	55.3	68.4
Net National Income	99e	79.7	104.7	144.7	251.2	267.6	245.5	263.9	308.1	390.3	476.5	524.9	563.6	668.2	823.7	1,020.4
GDP Volume 1980 prices	99b.p	....	....	....	....	....	351.0	385.7	441.6	422.1	451.1	....				
GDP Volume 1985 Prices	99b.p	....	....	....	....	....	....	....	....	....	....	711.5	719.7	728.0	773.4	802.5	901.6
GDP Volume (1995=100)	99bv p	....	....	....	....	....	37.0	40.7	46.6	44.5	47.6	48.1	48.7	51.7	53.7	60.3
GDP Deflator (1995=100)	99bi p	....	....	....	....	....	15.3	15.6	16.1	20.4	22.6	24.4	25.6	27.5	32.1	36.5
																Millions:
Population	99z	.45	.46	.48	.49	.50	.51	.53	.53	.55	.57	.59	.60	.63	.65	.67

	1987	1988	1989	1990	1991	1992	1993	1994	1995	1996	1997	1998	1999	2000	2001	
Government Finance																
Year Beginning April 1																
Deficit (-) or Surplus	21.6	59.2	95.9	†165.6	121.1	-42.2	-171.1	-197.5	68.3	-56.2	184.1	-7.1	-138.7	-141.4	-299.2	80
Revenue	330.7	422.6	570.5	†745.6	795.4	844.1	953.0	1,168.7	1,447.7	1,684.0	2,020.5	2,230.3	2,536.1	2,713.2	2,925.1	81
Grants Received	6.6	5.6	14.2	†10.8	20.6	46.3	28.7	31.4	7.5	20.2	18.3	44.7	31.8	112.1	157.4	81z
Expenditure	301.3	354.8	427.3	†581.9	704.1	1,025.5	1,138.4	1,398.7	1,382.1	1,758.4	1,826.6	2,214.8	2,676.0	2,967.9	3,353.1	82
Lending Minus Repayments	14.4	14.2	61.6	†8.9	-9.2	-92.9	14.4	-1.1	4.8	2.0	28.1	67.3	30.6	-1.2	28.6	83
Financing																
Domestic	-27.1	-52.0	-92.8	†-160.0	-105.3	50.4	196.4	235.5	-80.6	41.4	-226.1	-191.2	133.1	122.5	.5	84a
Foreign	5.5	-7.2	-3.1	†-5.6	-15.8	-8.2	-25.3	-38.0	12.3	14.8	102.9	198.3	5.6	18.9	298.7	85a
Debt: Domestic	53.9	51.6	36.2	†26.0	24.6	24.6	25.5	53.7	62.9	102.9	97.6	85.6	78.0	78.0	78.0	88a
Foreign	344.6	398.9	434.0	†447.0	459.5	515.9	630.2	791.9	914.5	1,150.5	1,121.6	1,691.8	1,963.7	2,710.3	3,417.3	89a
National Accounts																
Year Ending June 30																
Househ.Cons.Expend.,incl.NPISHs	723.9	956.7	1,106.6	1,357.4	1,511.7	1,760.4	1,595.1	1,914.5	2,313.9	3,072.6	3,228.6	3,731.9	5,030.6	....	....	96f
Government Consumption Expend.	208.3	262.9	296.5	312.3	412.3	474.7	490.1	781.0	874.0	951.0	1,185.8	1,639.2	1,800.9	1,978.6	....	91f
Gross Fixed Capital Formation	196.2	350.5	416.0	419.6	477.1	697.6	829.4	1,176.6	1,530.8	1,530.0	1,997.0	2,424.4	2,977.2	....	....	93e
Changes in Inventories	-19.5	20.0	21.4	16.3	22.5	24.9	29.0	33.9	37.4	47.2	54.4	....	....	....	....	93i
Exports of Goods and Services	967.2	1,198.6	1,521.6	1,707.6	1,953.3	2,169.4	2,733.6	2,970.6	3,814.6	4,265.2	4,947.3	5,941.0	6,198.3	....	....	90c
Imports of Goods and Services (-)	886.7	1,215.4	1,534.3	1,689.2	2,011.8	2,377.3	2,742.7	3,199.1	4,051.5	4,858.4	5,821.1	6,857.4	8,082.7	....	....	98c
Gross Domestic Product (GDP)	1,189.4	1,573.3	1,827.8	2,224.0	2,427.5	2,765.1	3,231.1	3,787.5	4,658.6	5,306.7	6,268.4	7,040.8	8,102.0	9,317.3	....	99b
Net Primary Income from Abroad	23.4	89.5	-40.1	152.7	192.6	237.2	156.6	-58.9	295.7	455.6	617.7	149.6	548.0	....	....	98.n
Gross National Income (GNI)	1,212.8	1,662.8	1,787.7	2,376.7	2,620.1	3,002.3	3,382.0	3,711.6	4,891.9	5,698.1	6,663.1	7,190.4	8,650.0	....	....	99a
Consumption of Fixed Capital	75.5	98.2	117.8	142.5	152.5	170.8	189.6	214.2	235.8	258.4	297.2	333.8	384.3	....	....	99cf
Net National Income	1,137.3	1,564.6	1,669.9	2,234.2	2,467.6	2,831.5	3,192.4	3,497.4	4,656.1	5,439.7	6,365.9	6,856.6	8,265.7	....	....	99e
GDP Volume 1980 prices	....	....	....	....	....	....	....	....	....	....	....	....	....	....	....	99b.p
GDP Volume 1985 Prices	1,033.5	1,101.7	1,202.4	1,309.6	1,341.7	1,358.8	1,403.1	1,451.6	1,495.7	1,549.3	1,606.9	1,682.6	1,740.7	....	....	99b.p
GDP Volume (1995=100)	69.1	73.7	80.4	87.6	89.7	90.8	93.8	97.1	100.0	103.6	107.4	112.5	116.4	....	....	99bv p
GDP Deflator (1995=100)	36.9	45.8	48.8	54.5	58.1	65.3	73.9	83.8	100.0	110.0	125.2	134.3	149.4	....	....	99bi p
Midyear Estimates																
Population	.69	.72	.74	.77	.80	.83	.85	.88	.91	.94	†.87	.89	.91	.93	.94	99z

(See notes in the back of the book.)

Sweden

		1972	1973	1974	1975	1976	1977	1978	1979	1980	1981	1982	1983	1984	1985	1986
Exchange Rates																*Kronor per SDR:*
Official Rate	aa	†5.1495	5.5341	4.9960	5.1339	4.7943	5.6721	5.5961	5.4623	5.5771	6.4844	8.0466	8.3766	8.8116	8.3650	8.3409
																Kronor per US Dollar:
Official Rate	ae	†4.7430	4.5875	4.0805	4.3855	4.1265	4.6695	4.2955	4.1465	4.3728	5.5710	7.2945	8.0010	8.9895	7.6155	6.8190
Official Rate	rf	4.7624	4.3673	4.4394	4.1522	4.3559	4.4816	4.5185	4.2871	4.2296	5.0634	6.2826	7.6671	8.2718	8.6039	7.1236
													Kronor per ECU through 1998; Kronor per Euro Beginning 1999:			
Euro Rate	ea	. . .	. . .	. . .	. . .	. . .	. . .	. . .	5.9729	5.7329	6.0037	7.0809	6.6260	6.3699	6.7172	7.2518
Euro Rate	eb	. . .	. . .	. . .	. . .	. . .	. . .	. . .	5.8729	5.8797	5.6327	6.1417	6.8243	6.5113	6.5198	6.9944
													Index Numbers (1995=100):			
Official Rate	ahx	149.5	163.4	160.6	171.9	163.6	159.3	157.7	166.2	168.5	141.5	114.5	93.0	86.2	83.1	100.1
Nominal Effective Exchange Rate	neu	178.8	177.3	175.9	182.8	186.9	179.5	162.6	162.3	163.0	161.4	145.2	128.8	131.7	131.0	127.5
Real Effective Exchange Rate	reu	. . .	. . .	. . .	116.9	122.9	117.0	141.6	139.3	†137.8	137.4	123.8	110.9	117.3	117.6	117.0
Fund Position																*Millions of SDRs:*
Quota	2f.s	325	325	325	325	325	325	450	450	675	675	675	1,064	1,064	1,064	1,064
SDRs	1b.s	107	107	107	107	107	107	112	173	174	225	233	123	181	224	261
Reserve Position in the Fund	1c.s	90	88	89	95	232	225	191	181	194	166	149	241	258	250	253
of which: Outstg.Fund Borrowing	2c	—	—	—	—	50	64	55	43	31	18	6	—	—	—	—
International Liquidity													*Millions of US Dollars Unless Otherwise Indicated:*			
Total Reserves minus Gold	1l.d	1,358	2,284	1,487	2,839	2,255	3,415	4,124	3,514	3,418	3,601	3,513	4,034	3,845	5,793	6,551
SDRs	1b.s	116	129	131	125	124	130	146	228	222	261	257	129	178	246	320
Reserve Position in the Fund	1c.d	98	106	109	111	269	274	249	238	247	193	164	252	253	274	310
Foreign Exchange	1d.d	1,144	2,049	1,247	2,602	1,862	3,011	3,729	3,048	2,949	3,147	3,091	3,653	3,414	5,273	5,921
Gold (Million Fine Troy Ounces)	1ad	5.782	5.790	5.790	5.790	5.790	5.929	5.999	6.069	6.069	6.069	6.069	6.069	6.069	6.069	6.069
Gold (National Valuation)	1and	220	244	248	237	235	252	274	280	271	247	234	222	208	233	260
Deposit Money Banks: Assets	7a.d	1,418	2,214	3,177	3,629	4,145	4,609	4,902	5,948	8,036	7,515	6,725	7,122	6,741	8,943	10,787
Liabilities	7b.d	1,019	1,393	1,782	2,478	3,236	4,414	5,811	9,070	12,518	14,100	13,157	13,980	13,098	17,199	23,621
Other Banking Insts.: Assets	7e.d	—	—	—	—	—	—	—	—	—	947	1,215	1,542	1,964	1,944	2,394	3,465
Liabilities	7f.d	—	—	—	—	—	—	—	—	1,045	1,609	2,337	3,189	3,855	4,343	5,556
Monetary Authorities																*Billions of Kronor:*
Foreign Assets	11	7.33	11.24	7.62	12.82	11.37	17.66	19.79	16.27	15.73	20.87	25.99	32.64	33.91	44.41	45.74
Claims on Central Government	12a	10.85	8.89	16.67	16.40	17.88	15.65	20.96	34.68	33.19	43.16	50.46	37.73	67.20	68.14	88.93
Claims on Deposit Money Banks	12e	—	—	2.96	.25	2.75	3.61	—	6.01	6.23	1.23	—	13.06	.55	5.86	4.15
Claims on Other Financial Insts.	12f	. . .	. . .	. . .	. . .	. . .	. . .	. . .	. . .	. . .	. . .	. . .	. . .	. . .	. . .	. . .
Reserve Money	14	15.44	16.92	22.83	22.68	25.10	27.62	31.41	43.13	38.98	43.55	46.46	47.44	50.54	52.04	65.28
of which: Currency Outside DMBs	14a	14.14	15.38	17.32	20.13	22.16	24.41	27.57	30.94	33.58	36.06	38.06	41.93	45.11	46.12	50.48
Foreign Liabilities	16c	—	—	—	—	.91	1.98	1.87	1.80	1.47	1.57	1.90	1.15	.44	.29	1.40
Central Government Deposits	16d	.39	.34	.26	.22	.19	.04	.15	.18	.07	.06	.08	.02	.14	.09	.03
Capital Accounts	17a	1.80	1.72	1.95	1.94	2.25	2.94	4.44	5.46	6.95	9.49	15.30	20.83	27.29	33.57	34.73
Other Items (Net)	17r	.56	1.15	2.22	4.62	3.55	4.34	2.88	6.39	7.68	10.60	12.71	14.00	23.25	32.40	37.39
Deposit Money Banks																*Billions of Kronor:*
Reserves	20	1.42	1.55	5.73	2.74	3.13	3.33	3.96	12.30	5.65	8.49	8.41	†4.77	5.26	7.71	13.85
Foreign Assets	21	6.83	10.10	12.96	15.91	17.10	21.52	21.06	24.66	35.14	41.87	51.31	†59.59	63.82	67.80	71.09
Claims on Central Government	22a	11.50	15.11	13.83	20.38	15.62	17.88	34.41	36.10	54.27	79.56	77.70	†99.93	100.16	87.50	86.87
Claims on Local Government	22b	. . .	. . .	. . .	. . .	. . .	. . .	. . .	. . .	. . .	. . .	. . .	10.15	10.47	8.93	9.86
Claims on Private Sector	22d	87.49	97.72	108.14	120.72	136.27	154.87	171.81	197.84	219.18	241.08	273.39	†289.03	323.52	340.62	398.71
Claims on Other Financial Insts	22f	22.54	23.50	25.15	28.47	30.60	34.89	39.95	47.02	51.39	61.15	71.44	†86.30	102.64	120.94	135.27
Demand,Time,Savings,Fgn.Cur.Dep.	25l	108.87	124.55	136.17	151.24	157.85	171.97	202.96	239.04	269.34	307.13	332.30	†354.68	385.47	398.35	454.49
Bonds	26ab	. . .	. . .	. . .	. . .	. . .	. . .	. . .	. . .	. . .	. . .	. . .	2.19	2.16	2.37	5.31
Foreign Liabilities	26c	4.91	6.35	7.27	10.87	13.36	20.61	24.96	37.61	54.74	78.55	102.74	†120.44	139.57	144.66	160.50
Central Government Deposits	26d	—	.01	.01	.01	.02	.05	.08	.12	.13	.15	.17	†.95	1.41	1.22	1.72
Credit from Monetary Authorities	26g	—	—	2.96	.25	2.75	3.77	.09	6.32	6.51	1.82	.19	†13.07	.62	6.74	5.76
Credit from Other Financial Insts	26i	2.27	4.22	4.22	4.52	6.15	7.63	9.18	10.25	9.39	16.77	16.82	†16.30	23.05	22.42	21.31
Capital Accounts	27a	36.66	37.90	41.39	48.23	51.36	53.95	55.51	58.07	60.27	63.76	70.90	†83.32	83.15	99.45	104.28
Other Items (Net)	27r	13.72	12.84	15.18	21.36	22.62	28.51	34.01	24.70	25.64	27.87	30.13	†-41.17	-29.55	-41.72	-37.71
Monetary Survey																*Billions of Kronor:*
Foreign Assets (Net)	31n	9.25	14.99	13.31	17.86	14.21	16.59	14.02	1.53	-5.34	-17.38	-27.34	†-29.36	-42.27	-32.75	-45.07
Domestic Credit	32	132.53	145.47	164.11	186.38	200.90	223.97	267.71	316.30	358.81	425.52	473.38	†523.67	604.50	626.63	718.54
Claims on Central Govt. (Net)	32an	21.96	23.65	30.23	36.54	33.29	33.44	55.13	70.47	87.26	122.51	127.90	†136.69	165.81	154.32	174.06
Claims on Local Government	32b	. . .	. . .	. . .	. . .	. . .	. . .	. . .	. . .	. . .	. . .	. . .	10.15	10.47	8.93	9.86
Claims on Private Sector	32d	87.64	97.90	108.38	121.03	136.67	155.30	172.25	198.46	219.83	241.52	273.72	†289.66	324.33	341.38	399.35
Claims on Other Financial Insts	32f	22.93	23.92	25.50	28.81	30.94	35.23	40.32	47.37	51.72	61.49	71.76	†86.61	102.91	120.94	135.27
Money plus Quasi-Money	35l	123.02	139.94	153.50	171.39	180.03	196.40	230.54	270.00	302.95	343.24	370.76	†397.51	431.23	445.43	506.20
Bonds	36ab	. . .	. . .	. . .	. . .	. . .	. . .	. . .	. . .	. . .	. . .	. . .	2.19	2.16	2.37	5.31
Liabilities to Other Banking Inst.	36i	2.27	4.22	4.22	4.52	6.15	7.63	9.18	10.25	9.39	16.77	16.82	†16.30	23.05	22.42	21.31
Capital Accounts	37a	5.71	5.76	6.36	7.09	7.72	8.69	10.36	11.65	13.38	16.29	22.86	†104.15	110.44	133.03	139.00
Other Items (Net)	37r	17.71	19.26	21.65	28.39	31.76	41.30	48.79	42.25	44.79	60.74	71.31	†-25.84	-4.65	-9.34	1.65
Money plus Quasi-Money	35l	123.02	139.94	153.50	171.39	180.03	196.40	230.54	270.00	302.95	343.24	370.76	†397.51	431.23	445.43	506.20
Money +Quasi-Money,Seas.Adj.	35l.b	110.52	125.14	136.25	151.81	160.60	173.88	201.52	233.62	254.78	288.78	307.89	373.91	405.90	419.35	477.55
Unused Bank Credits	39b	9.69	10.40	11.89	14.78	15.70	16.09	19.89	18.94	29.16	25.64	28.12	†44.30	45.78	46.65	63.28
Money (National Definitions)																*Billions of Kronor:*
Broad Money	39m	126.95	143.24	155.99	175.76	184.70	202.04	238.45	277.53	307.44	349.22	376.21	402.52	431.52	428.82	474.26
Other Banking Institutions																*Billions of Kronor:*
Cash	40	.74	1.19	.81	1.18	.93	1.15	2.46	2.31	2.52	†4.87	6.86	4.90	8.33	9.99	2.65
Foreign Assets	41	—	—	—	—	—	—	—	—	4.14	†6.77	11.25	15.72	17.48	18.54	26.19
Claims on Central Government	42a	—	.50	.35	.30	.16	.04	.08	.08	.08	†.43	1.69	3.10	4.89	8.06	7.94
Claims on Local Government	42b	. . .	. . .	. . .	. . .	. . .	. . .	. . .	. . .	. . .	. . .	. . .	. . .	. . .	. . .	. . .
Claims on Private Sector	42d	71.61	81.08	93.09	108.05	121.96	137.45	155.48	174.09	194.19	†248.70	282.39	331.48	379.14	436.34	555.81
Claims on Deposit Money Banks	42e	. . .	. . .	. . .	. . .	. . .	. . .	. . .	. . .	. . .	. . .	. . .	. . .	. . .	. . .	. . .
Time, Savings,& Fgn. Currency Dep.	45	. . .	. . .	. . .	. . .	. . .	. . .	. . .	. . .	. . .	. . .	†	. . .	.22	.76	7.76
Bonds	46ab	2.59	4.80	6.71	10.14	14.27	15.81	18.17	21.43	28.66	†176.20	186.36	208.35	232.85	279.36	356.16
Foreign Liabilities	46c	—	—	—	—	—	—	—	—	4.57	†8.96	21.19	25.52	34.66	33.60	38.58
Central Govt. Lending Funds	46f	31.83	37.16	43.04	48.18	54.05	60.52	67.30	73.18	79.70	86.87	93.31	99.65	110.99	127.30	155.06
Credit from Deposit Money Banks	46h	22.54	23.50	25.15	28.47	30.60	34.89	39.95	47.02	51.39	†61.15	71.44	86.30	102.64	120.94	135.27
Capital Accounts	47a	. . .	. . .	. . .	. . .	. . .	. . .	. . .	. . .	. . .	7.36	8.19	9.21	10.11	11.36	12.73
Other Items (Net)	47r	-29.18	-34.04	-39.86	-44.28	-50.61	-56.75	-62.14	-69.17	-75.19	†-79.77	-78.29	-73.83	-81.63	-100.38	-112.98

	1987	1988	1989	1990	1991	1992	1993	1994	1995	1996	1997	1998	1999	2000	2001	
Exchange Rates																
End of Period																
Official Rate	8.2963	8.2855	8.1833	8.1063	7.9096	9.6841	11.4054	10.8927	9.8973	9.8802	10.6280	11.3501	11.7006	12.4232	13.4062	aa
End of Period (ae) Period Average (rf)																
Official Rate	5.8480	6.1570	6.2270	5.6980	5.5295	7.0430	8.3035	7.4615	6.6582	6.8710	7.8770	8.0610	8.5250	9.5350	10.6675	ae
Official Rate	6.3404	6.1272	6.4469	5.9188	6.0475	5.8238	7.7834	7.7160	7.1333	6.7060	7.6349	7.9499	8.2624	9.1622	10.3291	rf
End of Period (ea) Period Average (eb)																
Euro Rate	7.5529	7.1762	7.4106	7.6754	7.4502	8.5490	9.2963	9.1779	8.6973	8.6280	8.7323	9.4880	†8.5625	8.8313	9.4200	ea
Euro Rate	7.3096	7.2439	7.1013	7.5200	7.4798	7.5299	9.1146	9.1579	9.3337	8.5156	8.6551	8.9085	†8.8102	8.4459	9.2553	eb
Period Averages																
Official Rate	112.4	116.3	110.5	120.5	118.1	122.9	91.7	92.4	100.0	106.2	93.4	89.6	86.2	78.0	69.1	ahx
Nominal Effective Exchange Rate	125.4	125.6	126.4	123.6	123.3	125.1	102.1	100.7	100.0	109.6	105.5	103.2	101.8	102.1	93.5	neu
Real Effective Exchange Rate	115.7	120.0	125.7	124.4	122.4	123.8	100.3	99.4	100.0	112.8	110.0	108.2	104.9	104.2	94.7	reu
Fund Position																
End of Period																
Quota	1,064	1,064	1,064	1,064	1,064	1,614	1,614	1,614	1,614	1,614	1,614	1,614	2,396	2,396	2,396	2f.s
SDRs	208	299	260	204	290	33	42	46	297	199	277	292	228	165	157	1b.s
Reserve Position in the Fund	277	251	254	234	308	451	451	451	451	451	589	900	863	683	827	1c.s
of which: Outstg.Fund Borrowing	—	—	—	—	—	—	—	—	—	—	—	112	—	—	—	2c
International Liquidity																
End of Period																
Total Reserves minus Gold	8,174	8,492	9,559	17,988	18,331	22,624	19,050	23,254	24,051	19,107	10,824	14,098	15,019	14,863	13,977	1l.d
SDRs	296	402	341	290	414	45	58	68	441	286	373	412	313	215	197	1b.d
Reserve Position in the Fund	394	337	333	333	441	621	620	659	671	649	795	1,267	1,184	890	1,039	1c.d
Foreign Exchange	7,485	7,752	8,885	17,365	17,476	21,959	18,372	22,527	22,939	18,172	9,656	12,420	13,522	13,757	12,740	1d.d
Gold (Million Fine Troy Ounces)	6.069	6.069	6.069	6.069	6.069	6.069	6.069	6.069	4.702	4.702	4.722	4.722	5.961	5.961	5.961	1ad
Gold (National Valuation)	301	286	279	302	304	292	292	310	245	237	223	233	286	272	262	1and
Deposit Money Banks: Assets	15,023	14,905	30,505	†34,919	34,247	32,056	26,261	24,727	36,158	44,707	44,943	50,853	53,087	67,355	....	7a.d
Liabilities	35,051	43,924	72,015	†99,361	93,185	62,745	50,253	50,925	55,100	56,670	60,376	86,846	76,769	102,345	....	7b.d
Other Banking Insts.: Assets	4,519	5,107	7,629	†6,027	5,513	4,395	3,743	4,661	5,734	8,834	11,116	12,171	13,226	....	....	7e.d
Liabilities	7,430	9,401	10,829	†5,269	6,623	22,534	20,605	22,196	16,597	14,535	13,686	29,960	34,387	....	....	7f.d
Monetary Authorities																
End of Period																
Foreign Assets	50.29	53.74	60.69	103.77	99.85	163.29	175.69	177.95	171.96	140.21	93.41	136.22	152.55	167.92	158.04	11
Claims on Central Government	96.14	93.35	89.50	53.24	132.31	145.98	98.99	87.52	71.03	59.05	53.09	32.84	†27.69	20.23	—	12a
Claims on Deposit Money Banks	2.40	17.40	27.87	19.68	23.55	61.02	1.26	.01	2.61	9.64	40.33	43.85	†45.63	43.20	69.11	12e
Claims on Other Financial Insts.	....	....	....	....	....	....	....	....	....	....	....	....	1.31	.50	—	12f
Reserve Money	68.37	80.91	89.56	96.86	89.36	110.95	163.84	200.59	170.74	114.30	84.76	87.95	102.91	97.77	107.15	14
of which: Currency Outside DMBs	52.22	55.14	60.66	62.00	64.80	64.30	67.05	68.81	68.55	70.71	72.97	74.63	78.64	89.16	....	14a
Foreign Liabilities	.04	—	.09	.05	—	12.47	.08	.22	3.48	4.14	3.98	4.10	†5.26	4.11	3.29	16c
Central Government Deposits	.01	.01	—	—	88.89	159.57	21.79	—	—	—	—	—	†2.17	1.59	2.39	16d
Capital Accounts	32.51	48.62	51.45	52.01	56.91	63.05	59.59	76.62	74.46	75.71	82.25	100.07	114.42	108.24	100.60	17a
Other Items (Net)	47.99	34.96	36.95	27.77	20.56	24.25	30.65	-11.95	-3.10	14.75	15.83	20.79	2.43	20.14	13.72	17r
Deposit Money Banks																
End of Period																
Reserves	15.38	18.81	19.88	24.91	15.50	35.40	21.25	8.75	9.42	11.13	10.17	13.52	30.67	9.80	....	20
Foreign Assets	97.46	131.34	186.70	242.68	272.46	328.95	329.24	281.57	408.71	†572.15	682.15	698.05	741.63	961.14	....	21
Claims on Central Government	104.81	110.62	134.54	86.39	89.11	65.32	149.50	162.35	143.46	122.00	109.15	167.93	86.99	115.77	....	22a
Claims on Local Government	12.11	11.49	14.53	21.39	23.59	19.68	14.58	17.54	24.99	31.05	36.85	37.58	42.74	39.61	....	22b
Claims on Private Sector	453.89	581.82	705.26	791.16	785.40	784.30	631.41	605.08	596.72	†623.21	711.06	771.67	848.41	958.69	....	22d
Claims on Other Financial Insts	131.61	137.07	164.33	225.84	235.30	169.86	182.54	247.87	267.14	†310.92	359.86	448.69	467.02	550.81	....	22f
Demand,Time,Savings,Fgn.Cur.Dep.	481.59	518.29	574.27	574.29	597.36	618.55	643.01	644.16	664.37	746.37	753.29	748.02	814.05	820.67	....	25l
Bonds	7.37	14.00	17.93	25.86	25.78	28.91	27.77	27.00	22.83	11.25	25.12	30.81	31.96	25.81	....	26ab
Foreign Liabilities	214.66	311.77	420.48	616.56	615.87	545.64	532.70	504.20	568.22	†639.64	788.10	985.59	924.94	1,256.78	....	26c
Central Government Deposits	1.99	.37	1.10	.89	.53	.38	.34	.43	1.61	2.38	.86	12.24	31.02	31.51	....	26d
Credit from Monetary Authorities	3.02	19.50	27.51	20.25	31.14	82.15	.74	.02	.01	10.53	31.65	29.26	34.44	45.78	....	26g
Credit from Other Financial Insts	38.44	45.57	47.23	38.69	38.80	49.57	40.96	40.16	48.80	66.23	88.88	110.27	119.72	152.25	....	26i
Capital Accounts	111.03	128.91	168.98	54.09	70.17	57.71	78.31	83.63	100.76	61.74	74.37	82.99	88.53	95.95	....	27a
Other Items (Net)	-42.84	-47.26	-32.28	61.73	41.70	20.60	4.68	23.55	43.85	†132.33	146.98	138.26	172.80	207.08	....	27r
Monetary Survey																
End of Period																
Foreign Assets (Net)	-66.95	-126.70	-173.18	-270.16	-243.56	-65.87	-27.85	-44.90	8.97	†68.58	-16.52	-155.42	†-36.02	-131.83	....	31n
Domestic Credit	796.90	934.12	1,107.09	1,177.11	1,176.29	1,025.20	1,054.89	1,119.92	1,101.73	†1143.85	1,269.15	1,446.47	†1440.97	1,652.52	....	32
Claims on Central Govt. (Net)	198.95	203.60	222.93	138.73	132.00	51.35	226.37	249.43	212.88	178.67	161.37	188.54	†81.49	102.91	....	32an
Claims on Local Government	12.11	11.49	14.53	21.39	23.59	19.68	14.58	17.54	24.99	31.05	36.85	37.58	42.74	39.61	....	32b
Claims on Private Sector	454.23	581.96	705.30	791.16	785.40	784.30	631.41	605.08	596.72	†623.21	711.06	771.67	848.41	958.69	....	32d
Claims on Other Financial Insts	131.61	137.07	164.33	225.84	235.30	169.86	182.54	247.87	267.14	†310.92	359.86	448.69	468.33	551.31	....	32f
Money plus Quasi-Money	536.39	577.06	640.31	645.27	672.07	694.10	723.03	728.05	750.56	817.08	826.26	822.65	892.69	909.84	....	35l
Bonds	7.37	14.00	17.93	25.86	25.78	28.91	27.77	27.00	22.83	11.25	25.12	30.81	31.96	25.81	....	36ab
Liabilities to Other Banking Inst.	38.44	45.57	47.23	38.69	38.80	49.57	40.96	40.16	48.80	66.23	88.88	110.27	119.72	152.25	....	36i
Capital Accounts	143.53	177.53	220.44	106.10	127.08	120.77	137.90	160.25	175.22	137.45	156.62	183.06	202.95	204.20	....	37a
Other Items (Net)	4.30	-6.74	7.99	91.04	69.00	65.98	97.37	119.57	113.28	†180.42	155.76	144.27	†157.64	228.60	....	37r
Money plus Quasi-Money	536.39	577.06	640.31	645.27	672.07	694.10	723.03	728.05	750.56	817.08	826.26	822.65	892.69	909.84	....	35l
Money +Quasi-Money,Seas.Adj.	506.55	546.35	607.16	612.33	637.76	658.66	686.11	690.88	712.24	775.36	784.07	780.65	847.12	863.38	....	35l.b
Unused Bank Credits	87.93	120.22	134.76	152.30	154.42	166.20	173.66	184.13	197.97	....	....	....	....	....	....	39b
Money (National Definitions)																
End of Period																
Broad Money	494.05	519.65	571.68	636.46	661.79	682.85	710.06	712.33	731.81	815.53	826.24	843.42	926.95	946.12	....	39m
Other Banking Institutions																
End of Period																
Cash	4.94	7.56	7.37	†4.30	.34	.08	.03	.64	.02	—	—	—	—	....	....	40
Foreign Assets	26.43	36.87	43.90	†48.90	43.70	46.54	37.45	46.15	38.26	†60.70	87.56	98.11	112.75	....	....	41
Claims on Central Government	9.67	12.19	10.22	†6.99	17.49	18.01	17.40	28.84	23.98	16.02	16.26	18.53	18.67	....	....	42a
Claims on Local Government	.70	.08	—	†—	.19	.02	—	.02	.01	†35.70	39.04	40.72	42.16	....	....	42b
Claims on Private Sector	437.97	524.09	604.80	†1020.15	1,113.06	1,133.15	1,124.98	1,133.60	1,162.92	†1154.15	1,161.62	1,200.06	1,249.53	....	....	42d
Claims on Deposit Money Banks	....	....	....	31.24	31.02	36.98	31.36	25.92	†28.69	39.90	46.18	59.23	54.60	....	....	42e
Time, Savings,& Fgn. Currency Dep.	21.14	30.15	49.08	†92.12	98.53	96.86	66.01	92.34	134.44	167.26	173.49	2.43	.52	....	....	45
Bonds	409.46	485.56	567.35	†693.97	765.21	849.44	960.64	915.53	856.98	804.90	736.65	720.90	648.43	....	....	46ab
Foreign Liabilities	34.59	46.86	57.03	†37.78	43.07	42.10	26.57	41.49	24.08	†99.87	107.80	241.51	293.15	....	....	46c
Central Govt. Lending Funds	168.26	194.40	225.27	239.54	262.71	279.70	278.12	247.18	230.97	†189.15	184.74	211.22	155.66	....	....	46f
Credit from Deposit Money Banks	131.61	137.07	164.33	†116.31	150.85	93.48	51.38	66.74	81.61	96.58	170.02	222.74	250.19	....	....	46h
Capital Accounts	14.46	17.74	19.38	21.34	23.12	47.15	66.72	73.35	82.26	60.74	65.24	68.36	73.71	....	....	47a
Other Items (Net)	-299.81	-331.01	-416.16	†-89.49	-137.69	-173.97	-238.24	-201.50	-156.47	-112.04	-87.29	-50.51	56.06	....	....	47r

Sweden

144		1972	1973	1974	1975	1976	1977	1978	1979	1980	1981	1982	1983	1984	1985	1986
Banking Survey																*Billions of Kronor:*
Foreign Assets (Net)	**51n**	9.25	14.99	13.31	17.86	14.21	16.59	14.02	1.53	–5.77	–19.57	–37.29	–39.16	–59.45	–47.81	–57.46
Domestic Credit	**52**	....	....	....	....	....	....	....	....	....	....	....	771.41	885.11	949.89	1,146.09
Claims on Central Govt. (Net)	**52an**	21.96	24.15	30.58	36.84	33.45	33.47	55.21	70.55	87.34	122.94	129.59	†139.56	170.19	162.17	181.07
Claims on Local Government	**52b**	....	....	....	....	....	....	....	....	....	....	....	10.15	10.47	8.93	9.86
Claims on Private Sector	**52d**	159.25	178.97	201.47	229.08	258.63	292.75	327.74	372.55	414.02	490.22	556.11	621.14	703.47	777.72	955.16
Liquid Liabilities	**55l**	123.02	139.94	153.50	171.39	180.03	196.40	230.54	270.00	302.95	343.24	370.76	†397.51	431.45	446.19	513.96
Bonds	**56ab**	....	....	....	....	....	....	....	....	....	....	....	210.54	235.01	281.73	361.47
Central Govt. Lending Funds	**56f**	34.90	40.63	47.30	53.00	59.61	67.28	75.40	82.53	90.54	98.46	106.07	112.16	121.59	135.75	159.35
Capital Accounts	**57a**	....	....	....	....	....	....	....	....	....	23.65	31.05	113.36	120.56	144.38	151.73
Other Items (Net)	**57r**	....	....	....	....	....	....	....	....	....	....	....	–86.17	–69.47	–77.55	–60.74
Nonbank Financial Institutions																*Billions of Kronor:*
Cash	**40.. *l***	1.10	1.20	1.49	1.22	1.28	1.70	1.81	2.70	2.59	3.91	3.21	3.11	6.17	5.83	7.57
Foreign Assets	**41.. *l***	....	....	....	....	....	....	....	....	....	1.38	2.19	2.88	2.96	3.49	3.71
Claims on Central Government	**42a. *l***	3.57	4.27	5.49	6.13	7.49	9.04	12.24	15.82	19.59	24.35	34.57	46.20	57.50	59.67	56.93
Claims on Private Sector	**42d. *l***	18.01	19.42	21.66	24.14	27.31	30.93	34.81	39.29	44.92	35.72	37.91	41.60	43.99	51.15	53.83
Claims on Other Banking Insts	**42f. *l***	12.35	13.76	15.81	18.51	20.34	23.30	27.08	30.49	33.55	52.28	55.97	63.71	73.49	88.59	113.52
Interest Rates																*Percent Per Annum*
Discount Rate *(End of Period)*	**60**	5.00	5.00	7.00	6.00	8.00	8.00	6.50	9.00	10.00	11.00	10.00	8.50	9.50	10.50	7.50
Repurchase Rate *(End of Period)*	**60a**	3.34	3.83	9.00	7.83	7.93	9.96	7.16	8.19	12.17	14.35	13.29	10.85	11.77	13.94	10.02
Money Market Rate	**60b**	3.06	3.27	7.33	7.83	7.93	9.96	7.16	8.19	12.17	14.35	13.29	10.85	11.77	13.85	10.15
Treasury Bill Rate	**60c**	3.75	2.79	6.85	7.29	6.50	9.42	6.63	6.79	11.58	12.54	13.22	12.34	11.93	14.17	9.83
Deposit Rate *(End of Period)*	**60l**	5.50	5.50	7.50	6.50	8.50	8.50	7.00	9.50	11.25	11.75	11.25	9.75	10.75	12.00	9.00
Lending Rate *(End of Period)*	**60p**	8.93	8.93	11.19	10.25	12.91	12.79	11.16	13.67	15.18	16.73	16.52	14.91	16.00	16.89	†12.57
Government Bond Yield	**61**	7.29	7.39	7.79	8.79	9.28	9.74	10.09	10.47	11.74	13.49	13.04	12.30	12.28	13.09	10.26
Prices, Production, Labor																*Index Numbers (1995=100):*
Share Prices	**62**	5	5	5	6	7	6	6	6	7	10	12	24	26	24	40
Forest Industries	**62a**	4	4	6	6	9	7	6	6	7	11	12	28	33	29	51
Industrials	**62b**	5	5	5	6	6	5	5	4	4	7	9	20	21	20	32
Prices: Domestic Supply	**63**	18.3	20.3	25.4	27.0	29.4	32.2	34.8	38.9	44.4	49.4	55.8	62.0	66.7	70.2	68.3
Consumer Prices	**64**	18.5	19.7	21.7	23.8	26.3	29.3	32.2	34.5	†39.2	44.0	47.8	52.0	56.2	60.3	62.9
Harmonized CPI	**64h**	....	....	....	....	....	....	....	....	....	....	....	....	....	....	....
Wages: Hourly Earnings	**65**	16.4	17.7	19.9	23.4	26.6	28.4	30.9	33.2	36.0	40.4	43.0	45.7	50.3	54.3	57.6
Industrial Production	**66.. *c***	70.4	75.5	79.0	77.7	75.7	71.5	70.5	75.4	74.5	73.7	72.4	75.4	80.8	83.2	83.6
Industrial Employment	**67**	136.1	138.6	146.1	148.5	†142.5	137.3	132.5	133.2	133.3	128.1	123.8	123.3	124.8	127.1	128.4
																Number in Thousands:
Labor Force	**67d**	....	....	....	....	....	....	....	....	....	....	....	....	....	....	....
Employment	**67e**	....	....	....	....	....	....	....	....	....	....	....	....	....	4,299	†4,299
Unemployment	**67c**	....	....	....	....	....	....	....	....	....	....	....	....	....	85	98
Unemployment Rate (%)	**67r**	....	....	....	....	....	....	....	....	....	....	....	....	....	2.5	2.2
International Transactions																*Millions of Kronor*
Exports	**70**	41,749	53,153	70,514	72,012	80,195	†85,677	98,206	118,210	130,747	144,876	168,134	210,516	242,809	260,500	265,104
Imports, c.i.f.	**71**	38,618	47,500	73,850	72,390	85,300	†90,221	92,751	122,962	141,329	146,040	173,933	200,368	218,570	244,609	232,479
																1995=100
Volume of Exports	**72**	45.1	53.0	56.0	†50.5	53.0	53.5	58.1	62.1	61.1	61.6	63.6	†71.2	76.6	79.7	81.5
Volume of Imports	**73**	42.2	46.3	52.9	†54.5	57.2	55.6	52.3	60.5	61.6	57.8	61.0	†63.2	66.4	72.0	75.2
Export Prices	**76**	17.6	20.3	26.5	28.8	30.4	32.0	33.9	37.9	42.7	46.4	51.9	58.1	62.6	65.2	65.6
Import Prices	**76.x**	16.7	19.2	26.7	27.7	29.8	33.6	36.3	42.7	49.5	55.2	63.0	71.1	75.0	77.4	69.4
Balance of Payments																*Millions of US Dollars:*
Current Account, n.i.e.	**78al *d***	586	1,452	–529	–308	–1,602	–2,120	–191	–2,349	–4,331	–2,778	–3,285	–725	736	–1,010	32
Goods: Exports f.o.b.	**78aa *d***	8,697	12,097	15,797	17,259	18,287	18,930	21,598	27,377	30,662	28,389	26,575	27,204	29,123	30,173	36,845
Goods: Imports f.o.b.	**78ab *d***	–7,479	–10,066	–15,405	–16,181	–18,124	–18,654	–19,023	–28,072	–32,860	–28,226	–26,797	–25,303	–25,701	–27,788	–31,811
Trade Balance	**78ac *d***	1,218	2,031	392	1,078	162	275	2,574	–695	–2,198	163	–222	1,901	3,422	2,385	5,035
Services: Credit	**78ad *d***	1,917	2,482	3,041	3,431	3,624	3,909	4,654	6,619	7,489	7,035	6,521	6,292	6,293	6,121	6,664
Services: Debit	**78ae *d***	–2,285	–2,775	–3,555	–4,144	–4,517	–5,037	–5,610	–6,471	–7,018	–6,863	–6,909	–6,224	–6,334	–6,681	–8,463
Balance on Goods & Services	**78af *d***	850	1,738	–122	365	–730	–852	1,619	–546	–1,727	336	–610	1,968	3,381	1,824	3,236
Income: Credit	**78ag *d***	153	261	306	351	492	511	831	1,008	1,238	1,682	2,431	2,125	2,312	2,584	3,142
Income: Debit	**78ah *d***	–183	–259	–318	–404	–665	–962	–1,490	–1,755	–2,617	–3,790	–4,159	–3,962	–4,201	–4,561	–5,187
Balance on Gds, Serv. & Inc.	**78ai *d***	821	1,740	–133	312	–902	–1,303	959	–1,293	–3,107	–1,773	–2,338	131	1,492	–153	1,191
Current Transfers, n.i.e.: Credit	**78aj *d***	17	16	29	26	44	40	49	148	92	92	81	124	100	117	111
Current Transfers: Debit	**78ak *d***	–252	–305	–426	–647	–744	–857	–1,199	–1,204	–1,317	–1,097	–1,028	–980	–856	–975	–1,269
Capital Account, n.i.e.	**78bc *d***	–19	–23	–23	–34	–46	–60	–60	–65	–73	–69	–80	–81	–171	–221	–182
Capital Account, n.i.e.: Credit	**78ba *d***	—	—	—	—	—	—	—	—	—	—	—	1	—	—	—
Capital Account: Debit	**78bb *d***	–19	–23	–23	–34	–46	–60	–60	–65	–73	–69	–80	–82	–171	–221	–182
Financial Account, n.i.e.	**78bj *d***	166	–294	99	1,660	971	805	80	–320	454	652	–1,333	–4,722	–5,812	–2,893	259
Direct Investment Abroad	**78bd *d***	–265	–293	–430	–434	–596	–737	–415	–618	–625	–825	–1,212	–1,458	–1,497	–1,805	–3,963
Dir. Invest. in Rep. Econ., n.i.e.	**78be *d***	65	84	77	80	5	81	70	112	251	181	355	226	290	393	1,083
Portfolio Investment Assets	**78bf *d***	—	–23	–11	–4	5	9	17	–23	–35	14	–34	–60	3	–47	–153
Equity Securities	**78bk *d***	2	5	—	–5	5	11	9	5	–5	–6	–15	–8	17	2	–26
Debt Securities	**78bl *d***	–2	–27	–11	—	—	–2	8	–28	–31	19	–19	–52	–14	–49	–127
Portfolio Investment Liab., n.i.e.	**78bg *d***	176	103	47	599	712	573	129	–265	–231	473	180	749	219	609	—
Equity Securities	**78bm *d***	–31	–16	–32	–21	–25	–30	–33	–26	–54	77	201	804	172	557	306
Debt Securities	**78bn *d***	208	119	79	620	737	603	162	–239	–176	396	–21	–55	47	52	–306
Financial Derivatives Assets	**78bw *d***	....	....	....	....	....	....	....	....	....	....	....	....	....	....	....
Financial Derivatives Liabilities	**78bx *d***	....	....	....	....	....	....	....	....	....	....	....	....	....	....	....
Other Investment Assets	**78bh *d***	–254	–607	–795	–733	–1,049	–1,253	221	–366	–183	–1,130	–1,744	–1,903	–939	–219	–875
Monetary Authorities	**78bo *d***	....	....	....	....	....	....	....	....	....	....	....	....	....	....	....
General Government	**78bp *d***	–23	–82	–133	–304	–133	–193	9	–35	62	–101	–305	–173	–110	–134	–196
Banks	**78bq *d***	–239	–675	–683	–308	–604	–664	121	–92	35	–295	–332	–190	–2	54	–1
Other Sectors	**78br *d***	8	151	20	–122	–312	–396	92	–240	–281	–734	–1,107	–1,541	–827	–140	–678
Other Investment Liab., n.i.e.	**78bi *d***	443	442	1,212	2,153	1,894	2,132	59	839	1,277	1,940	1,123	–2,276	–3,888	–1,823	4,168
Monetary Authorities	**78bs *d***	—	—	—	—	—	—	–31	–16	–5	–69	–44	–108	–15	–21	—
General Government	**78bt *d***	31	34	32	76	97	91	–880	72	–334	–1,653	–1,312	–3,512	–5,524	–4,939	–935
Banks	**78bu *d***	97	305	288	555	874	1,328	898	1,833	1,738	2,527	1,068	1,040	966	1,477	2,129
Other Sectors	**78bv *d***	315	103	892	1,522	923	714	72	–1,049	–122	1,135	1,409	304	684	1,660	2,973
Net Errors and Omissions	**78ca *d***	–382	–265	–301	–122	153	300	–523	–133	–1,447	–596	408	47	–586	–526	68
Overall Balance	**78cb *d***	351	870	–753	1,196	–524	–1,075	–693	–2,868	–5,398	–2,790	–4,291	–5,481	–5,834	–4,651	177
Reserves and Related Items	**79da *d***	–351	–870	753	–1,196	524	1,075	693	2,868	5,398	2,790	4,291	5,481	5,834	4,651	–177
Reserve Assets	**79db *d***	–351	–870	753	–1,404	513	–1,101	–654	676	105	–203	41	–686	43	–1,551	–177
Use of Fund Credit and Loans	**79dc *d***	—	—	—	—	—	—	—	—	—	—	—	—	—	—	—
Exceptional Financing	**79de *d***	—	—	—	208	12	2,176	1,347	2,191	5,292	2,994	4,249	6,167	5,790	6,201	—

Sweden
144

1987	1988	1989	1990	1991	1992	1993	1994	1995	1996	1997	1998	1999	2000	2001		
End of Period															**Banking Survey**	
-75.10	-136.69	-186.32	†-259.04	-242.93	-61.44	-16.98	-40.24	23.15	†29.41	-36.77	-298.81	†-216.41	....	....	Foreign Assets (Net)	51n
1,113.63	1,333.40	1,557.78	†1978.41	2,071.73	2,006.51	2,014.73	2,034.50	2,021.48	†2038.79	2,126.20	2,257.10	2,283.00	....	....	Domestic Credit	52
208.63	215.79	233.16	†145.71	149.49	69.36	243.76	278.27	236.86	194.68	177.63	207.06	100.16	....	....	Claims on Central Govt. (Net)	52an
12.81	11.56	14.53	21.39	23.78	19.70	14.58	17.55	25.00	†66.75	75.89	78.30	84.90	....	....	Claims on Local Government	52b
892.20	1,106.05	1,310.09	†1811.31	1,898.46	1,917.45	1,756.39	1,738.68	1,759.64	†1777.36	1,872.68	1,971.73	2,097.94	....	....	Claims on Private Sector	52d
557.53	607.21	689.40	737.39	770.61	790.96	789.03	820.39	885.00	984.34	999.74	825.08	893.21	....	....	Liquid Liabilities	55l
416.83	499.56	585.28	†719.83	790.98	878.35	988.42	942.53	879.81	816.16	761.77	751.71	680.39	....	....	Bonds	56ab
170.61	195.72	226.08	239.54	262.71	279.70	278.12	247.18	230.97	189.15	184.74	211.22	155.66	102.52	....	Central Govt. Lending Funds	56f
158.00	195.27	239.82	127.44	150.20	167.92	204.63	233.60	257.48	198.19	221.86	251.42	276.66	....	....	Capital Accounts	57a
-236.34	-277.54	-342.59	-91.87	-139.63	-169.48	-261.00	-248.53	-208.62	†-119.51	-78.64	-81.13	†60.67	....	....	Other Items (Net)	57r
End of Period															**Nonbank Financial Institutions**	
4.54	9.32	7.53	6.94	7.74	9.67	9.08	8.63	7.21	8.25	22.52	14.14	22.70	19.17	....	Cash	40.. *l*
4.98	6.70	18.98	55.96	74.17	77.98	100.48	102.79	131.88	203.66	288.09	394.10	509.62	645.59	....	Foreign Assets	41.. *l*
48.58	47.51	52.82	50.52	73.97	77.43	130.95	161.20	254.55	253.97	259.93	290.98	341.92	285.64	....	Claims on Central Government	42a. *l*
122.25	150.81	176.69	153.11	155.86	160.00	201.46	215.18	239.53	296.04	363.62	410.38	587.06	565.12	....	Claims on Private Sector	42d. *l*
125.84	159.04	183.06	175.10	204.02	231.03	242.55	188.15	159.25	205.46	216.78	241.47	216.25	206.35	....	Claims on Other Banking Insts	42f. *l*
Percent Per Annum															**Interest Rates**	
7.50	8.50	10.50	11.50	8.00	†10.00	5.00	7.00	7.00	3.50	2.50	2.00	1.50	2.00	2.00	Discount Rate *(End of Period)*	60
9.04	9.70	11.09	12.60	11.28	16.62	8.83	†7.51	8.91	4.27	4.19	3.50	3.25	3.89	3.75	Repurchase Rate *(End of Period)*	60a
9.16	10.08	11.52	13.45	11.81	18.42	9.08	7.36	8.54	6.28	4.21	4.24	3.14	3.81	4.08	Money Market Rate	60b
9.39	10.08	11.50	13.66	11.59	12.85	8.35	7.40	8.75	5.79	4.11	4.19	3.12	3.95	....	Treasury Bill Rate	60c
8.75	9.50	†9.16	9.93	7.96	†7.80	5.10	4.91	6.16	2.47	2.50	1.91	1.65	2.15	....	Deposit Rate *(End of Period)*	60l
12.65	13.29	14.81	16.69	16.05	†15.20	11.40	10.64	11.11	7.38	7.01	5.94	5.53	5.82	....	Lending Rate *(End of Period)*	60p
†11.68	11.35	11.18	13.08	10.69	10.02	8.54	†9.41	....	....	....	....	....	....	....	Government Bond Yield	61
Period Averages															**Prices, Production, Labor**	
47	53	73	67	64	54	71	90	100	....	177	205	242	350	249	Share Prices	62
66	77	90	68	74	64	78	95	100	....	129	125	133	132	168	Forest Industries	62a
31	33	51	51	49	46	67	88	†100	115	159	157	170	183	170	Industrials	62b
70.2	73.9	79.6	†83.3	84.5	83.4	88.6	92.8	100.0	98.2	99.4	98.8	99.9	105.7	109.2	Prices: Domestic Supply	63
65.6	69.4	73.8	81.5	89.2	91.2	95.4	97.5	100.0	100.5	101.0	100.9	101.3	102.3	104.8	Consumer Prices	64
....	....	....	....	....	....	....	....	100.0	100.8	102.6	103.7	104.2	105.6	108.4	Harmonized CPI	64h
62.5	67.5	74.2	81.1	84.9	88.8	91.7	95.5	100.0	107.2	111.4	115.4	118.2	122.1	125.4	Wages: Hourly Earnings	65
85.7	86.8	90.0	†87.8	83.3	82.0	82.9	91.5	†100.0	101.7	108.9	112.9	115.3	125.2	124.4	Industrial Production	66.. *c*
126.3	126.9	127.8	124.7	†114.8	104.8	96.3	95.0	100.0	100.9	99.8	100.2	99.4	99.1	97.0	Industrial Employment	67
Period Averages																
....	....	....	....	....	....	4,320	....	4,319	4,310	4,264	4,255	4,308	4,362	....	Labor Force	67d
4,316	4,375	4,442	4,485	4,396	4,209	†3,964	3,928	3,986	3,963	3,922	3,979	4,068	4,159	....	Employment	67e
94	77	66	75	134	233	†356	340	332	346	342	276	241	203	....	Unemployment	67c
2.1	1.7	1.5	1.6	3.2	5.9	†8.2	8.0	7.7	8.0	8.0	6.5	5.6	4.7	....	Unemployment Rate (%)	67r
Millions of Kronor															**International Transactions**	
281,333	304,190	332,220	340,040	332,800	326,040	388,300	471,600	567,700	569,200	632,800	675,300	701,000	796,500	774,900	Exports	70
257,386	279,261	315,620	320,380	301,260	290,510	332,490	397,410	460,500	448,700	501,100	545,300	567,000	666,100	645,300	Imports, c.i.f.	71
1995=100																
84.5	86.9	89.3	89.3	†87.5	90.2	98.4	104.0	100.0	94.6	99.1	89.3	94.6	99.1	....	Volume of Exports	72
80.9	84.7	91.0	91.6	†85.3	90.8	93.6	104.8	100.0	93.8	101.1	100.7	94.3	102.8	....	Volume of Imports	73
68.1	71.5	77.0	†79.2	79.8	78.1	85.5	89.8	100.0	95.1	95.9	95.5	94.5	....	....	Export Prices	76
70.9	73.2	77.7	†80.4	80.9	79.1	89.7	93.9	100.0	96.5	98.3	97.4	99.8	....	....	Import Prices	76.x
Minus Sign Indicates Debit															Balance of Payments	
-21	-534	-3,101	-6,339	-4,653	-8,827	-4,159	743	4,940	5,892	7,406	4,639	5,982	6,617	6,696	Current Account, n.i.e.	78al *d*
44,013	49,367	51,071	56,835	54,542	55,363	49,348	60,199	79,903	84,690	83,194	85,179	87,568	87,431	76,200	Goods: Exports f.o.b.	78aa *d*
-39,528	-44,487	-47,054	-53,433	-48,185	-48,642	-41,801	-50,641	-63,926	-66,053	-65,195	-67,547	-71,854	-72,216	-62,368	Goods: Imports f.o.b.	78ab *d*
4,485	4,880	4,017	3,402	6,357	6,720	7,548	9,558	15,978	18,636	17,999	17,632	15,714	15,215	13,832	*Trade Balance*	78ac *d*
8,946	10,420	11,355	13,725	14,725	16,195	12,589	13,674	15,622	16,930	17,769	17,952	19,904	20,252	21,997	Services: Credit	78ad *d*
-10,634	-12,662	-14,389	-17,058	-17,352	-19,090	-13,355	-14,690	-17,216	-18,755	-19,524	-21,721	-22,617	-23,440	-23,020	Services: Debit	78ae *d*
2,798	2,637	983	70	3,730	3,826	6,782	8,542	14,384	16,811	16,245	13,862	13,001	12,027	12,809	*Balance on Goods & Services*	78af *d*
4,372	5,277	6,968	9,691	9,435	8,142	7,127	9,611	14,906	14,338	14,404	16,564	19,871	20,074	17,934	Income: Credit	78ag *d*
-5,935	-7,070	-9,302	-14,164	-15,833	-18,181	-16,261	-15,530	-21,379	-22,641	-20,513	-22,349	-23,291	-22,137	-20,786	Income: Debit	78ah *d*
1,234	844	-1,350	-4,403	-2,669	-6,213	-2,352	2,623	7,910	8,508	10,135	8,077	9,581	9,964	9,957	*Balance on Gds, Serv. & Inc.*	78ai *d*
267	382	298	386	393	405	456	544	1,555	2,524	2,319	2,266	2,341	2,602	2,578	Current Transfers, n.i.e.: Credit	78aj *d*
-1,523	-1,760	-2,049	-2,321	-2,378	-3,019	-2,263	-2,424	-4,525	-5,140	-5,048	-5,704	-5,940	-5,950	-5,839	Current Transfers: Debit	78ak *d*
-139	-234	-296	-353	-63	6	23	23	14	9	-228	868	-2,143	384	509	Capital Account, n.i.e.	78bc *d*
38	29	38	38	38	37	37	37	32	31	211	1,502	1,289	1,226	1,111	Capital Account, n.i.e.: Credit	78ba *d*
-177	-263	-334	-391	-101	-31	-15	-14	-18	-22	-439	-634	-3,432	-841	-601	Capital Account: Debit	78bb *d*
770	2,897	9,837	19,278	-1,336	10,214	11,518	6,078	-5,052	-10,046	-10,121	5,961	-1,413	-3,297	1,824	Financial Account, n.i.e.	78bj *d*
-4,780	-7,471	-10,296	-14,629	-7,262	-419	-1,471	-6,685	-11,399	-5,112	-12,119	-22,671	-19,554	-39,962	-6,959	Direct Investment Abroad	78bd *d*
639	1,673	1,812	1,982	6,351	-5	3,705	6,269	14,939	5,492	10,271	19,413	59,386	22,125	13,085	Dir. Invest. in Rep. Econ., n.i.e.	78be *d*
-327	-686	-4,475	-3,644	-2,313	-1,578	-94	-2,459	-10,765	-13,136	-13,818	-17,615	-36,749	-12,772	-23,041	Portfolio Investment Assets	78bf *d*
21	-509	-4,324	-3,271	-2,350	-505	-76	-2,509	-9,378	-7,518	-10,179	-7,427	-29,766	758	-22,642	Equity Securities	78bk *d*
-348	-177	-150	-373	37	-1,073	-18	51	-1,386	-5,618	-3,640	-10,188	-6,983	-13,530	-400	Debt Securities	78bl *d*
-738	-673	3,227	6,112	8,859	2,563	1,472	721	8,201	1,661	-2,384	2,023	1,882	9,017	10,338	Portfolio Investment Liab., n.i.e.	78bg *d*
-667	-446	-290	192	1,817	2,257	4,212	6,795	1,853	4,047	-1,687	-328	-3,895	17,997	-2,336	Equity Securities	78bm *d*
-71	-227	3,517	5,920	7,042	306	-2,741	-6,074	6,348	-2,386	-697	2,351	5,777	-8,980	12,674	Debt Securities	78bn *d*
....	....	....	....	....	....	....	....	20,264	24,800	31,244	30,125	22,982	31,481	33,678	Financial Derivatives Assets	78bw *d*
....	....	....	....	....	....	....	....	-21,096	-23,243	-29,280	-31,428	-22,923	-31,795	-38,894	Financial Derivatives Liabilities	78bx *d*
-2,274	-2,133	-5,074	-9,618	-946	1,633	1,159	-3,400	-12,197	-10,828	-9,670	-5,901	-10,333	-16,000	929	Other Investment Assets	78bh *d*
....	....	....	....	....	....	....	....	....	....	—	—	—	—	....	Monetary Authorities	78bo *d*
-259	-160	-384	-559	-350	-337	-144	-290	-483	-303	-322	-244	-642	-150	37	General Government	78bp *d*
-220	-479	-2,010	-6,597	342	1,083	4,682	2,902	-8,037	-10,239	-4,971	-1,135	-5,296	-13,279	1,672	Banks	78bq *d*
-1,795	-1,494	-2,681	-2,462	-938	887	-3,379	-6,012	-3,677	-287	-4,377	-4,522	-4,396	-2,571	-779	Other Sectors	78br *d*
8,251	12,187	24,643	39,074	-6,025	8,020	6,748	11,633	6,999	10,320	15,635	32,015	3,897	34,609	12,689	Other Investment Liab., n.i.e.	78bi *d*
—	—	—	—	—	—	—	—	—	—	-39	88	-243	-556	-812	Monetary Authorities	78bs *d*
-268	-1,924	-1,933	-2,216	-2,780	28,567	11,723	5,075	8,842	1,817	-1,583	578	1,047	129	-32	General Government	78bt *d*
4,829	8,171	16,626	27,867	-8,276	-26,461	-10,851	-1,957	-1,055	2,935	9,269	20,205	-3,846	29,682	10,077	Banks	78bu *d*
3,689	5,940	9,950	13,423	5,031	5,914	5,876	8,515	-788	5,569	7,988	11,144	6,938	5,354	3,455	Other Sectors	78bv *d*
153	-1,190	-5,185	-5,034	5,989	5,560	-4,852	-4,462	-1,566	-2,241	-3,769	-8,214	-545	-3,534	-10,078	Net Errors and Omissions	78ca *d*
762	938	1,254	7,552	-63	6,953	2,530	2,381	-1,664	-6,386	-6,712	3,254	1,881	170	-1,048	*Overall Balance*	78cb *d*
-762	-938	-1,254	-7,552	63	-6,953	-2,530	-2,381	1,664	6,386	6,712	-3,254	-1,881	-170	1,048	Reserves and Related Items	79da *d*
-762	-938	-1,254	-7,552	63	-6,953	-2,530	-2,381	1,664	6,386	6,712	-3,254	-1,881	-170	1,048	Reserve Assets	79db *d*
—	—	—	—	—	—	—	—	—	—	—	—	—	—	—	Use of Fund Credit and Loans	79dc *d*
—	—	—	—	—	—	—	—	—	—	—	—	—	—	....	Exceptional Financing	79de *d*

Sweden

	1972	1973	1974	1975	1976	1977	1978	1979	1980	1981	1982	1983	1984	1985	1986
International Investment Position															*Millions of US Dollars*
Assets .... 79aa d	...	...	...	...	...	...	...	...	...	...	26,595	30,371	30,591	39,656	49,567
Direct Investment Abroad .... 79ab d	...	...	...	...	...	...	...	...	...	...	5,758	6,624	7,342	10,768	16,131
Portfolio Investment .... 79ac d	...	...	...	...	...	...	...	...	...	...	685	750	667	1,182	1,466
Equity Securities .... 79ad d	...	...	...	...	...	...	...	...	...	...	411	500	445	788	1,027
Debt Securities .... 79ae d	...	...	...	...	...	...	...	...	...	...	274	250	222	394	440
Financial Derivatives .... 79al d															
Other Investment .... 79af d	...	...	...	...	...	...	...	...	...	...	16,725	18,998	18,800	21,798	25,224
Monetary Authorities .... 79ag d															
General Government .... 79ah d	...	...	...	...	...	...	...	...	...	...	1,234	1,500	1,446	1,838	2,200
Banks .... 79ai d	...	...	...	...	...	...	...	...	...	...	6,992	7,499	7,231	8,929	10,705
Other Sectors .... 79aj d	...	...	...	...	...	...	...	...	...	...	8,500	9,999	10,123	11,030	12,319
Reserve Assets .... 79ak d	...	...	...	...	...	...	...	...	...	...	3,427	4,000	3,782	5,909	6,746
Liabilities .... 79la d	...	...	...	...	...	...	...	...	...	...	45,651	50,369	49,391	60,666	74,498
Dir. Invest. in Rep. Economy......... 79lb d	...	...	...	...	...	...	...	...	...	...	3,427	3,375	3,337	4,333	6,013
Portfolio Investment .... 79lc d	...	...	...	...	...	...	...	...	...	...	1,645	2,250	1,669	2,758	5,133
Equity Securities .... 79ld d	...	...	...	...	...	...	...	...	...	...	1,645	2,250	1,669	2,758	4,839
Debt Securities .... 79le d	...	...	...	...	...	...	...	...	...	...	—	—	—	—	293
Financial Derivatives .... 79ll d															
Other Investment .... 79lf d	...	...	...	...	...	...	...	...	...	...	40,579	44,744	44,385	53,575	63,352
Monetary Authorities..................... 79lg d															
General Government .... 79lh d	...	...	...	...	...	...	...	...	...	...	14,257	16,373	15,796	18,515	19,504
Banks .... 79li d	...	...	...	...	...	...	...	...	...	...	14,120	15,123	15,574	18,909	23,611
Other Sectors .... 79lj d	...	...	...	...	...	...	...	...	...	...	12,201	13,248	13,015	16,151	20,238
Government Finance															*Billions of Kronor:*
Deficit (-) or Surplus............................ 80	−2.47	−3.21	−7.98	−7.55	−1.17	−6.06	−20.45	−33.22	−43.03	−51.52	−52.59	−68.68	−62.88	−61.51	−57.17
Revenue 81	66.10	70.08	78.77	93.35	122.49	140.24	153.85	165.53	185.75	212.65	240.08	272.38	309.76	351.83	377.72
Grants Received 81z	.37	.42	.38	.37	.39	.53	.80	1.04	1.00	1.11	1.33				
Expenditure 82	56.93	63.39	74.78	88.57	108.79	131.66	156.38	182.76	208.79	245.39	273.44	320.73	348.76	388.32	406.96
Lending Minus Repayments 83	12.01	10.32	12.35	12.70	15.26	15.17	18.72	17.03	20.99	19.89	20.56	20.33	23.88	25.02	27.93
Financing															
Domestic 84a	2.47	3.21	7.95	7.47	1.09	1.19	14.31	29.55	25.81	36.90	36.77	49.79	41.36	25.39	75.75
Foreign 85a	—	—	.03	.08	.08	4.87	6.14	3.67	17.22	14.62	15.82	18.89	21.52	36.12	−18.58
Total Debt 88	32.39	36.00	44.09	52.50	54.58	65.00	83.31	112.20	159.57	213.21	272.80	352.52	414.48	480.48	529.89
Debt: Domestic 88a	32.39	36.00	44.05	52.39	54.39	59.93	72.11	97.32	127.47	166.49	210.26	271.09	311.53	341.41	409.40
Other Levels of Government 88aa	...	...	...	2.48	3.17	3.80	3.73	4.51	4.51	5.63	7.10	17.79	15.03	14.38	10.99
Monetary Authorities 88ab	...	...	...	18.46	11.55	13.15	12.69	15.16	26.05	36.64	58.00	39.52	45.78	45.52	90.29
Deposit Money Banks 88ac	...	...	...	13.71	17.91	16.49	24.44	37.28	44.54	61.39	72.79	96.69	92.37	88.74	60.65
Other Domestic 88ad	...	...	...	17.74	21.76	26.49	31.25	40.37	52.37	62.83	72.37	117.09	158.35	192.77	247.47
Debt: Foreign 89a	—	—	.04	.11	.19	5.07	11.20	14.88	32.10	46.72	62.54	81.43	102.95	139.07	120.49
Intragovernmental Debt 88s	4.83	7.20	8.59	11.18	14.17	17.35	21.92	26.89	32.52	39.76	46.89	54.80	68.16	71.98	66.11
Total Debt 88	32.39	36.00	44.09	52.50	54.58	65.00	83.31	112.20	159.57	213.21	272.80	352.52	414.48	480.48	529.89
Debt: Kronor 88b	...	...	...												
Intragovernmental Debt 88s	4.83	7.20	8.59	11.18	14.17	17.35	21.92	26.89	32.52	39.76	46.89	54.80	68.16	71.98	66.11
Debt: Foreign Currency........................ 89b	...	...	...												
National Accounts															*Billions of Kronor*
Househ.Cons.Expend.,incl.NPISHs 96f	108.82	119.92	136.86	156.07	180.49	197.75	219.26	242.31	273.33	305.55	340.04	369.44	403.78	443.67	487.33
Government Consumption Expend.......... 91f	45.50	50.98	59.01	70.69	83.19	101.14	116.89	132.72	153.76	170.16	185.67	203.51	221.06	239.16	257.25
Gross Fixed Capital Formation 93e	44.44	48.22	55.24	59.99	67.22	76.78	78.52	89.76	106.43	109.40	118.09	132.30	148.79	166.98	175.50
Changes in Inventories 93i	−.18	−1.19	6.07	10.01	7.87	−2.40	−7.42	.96	5.92	−4.07	−6.29	−10.26	−7.76	−.48	−5.84
Exports of Goods and Services 90c	49.28	62.13	82.49	84.68	94.07	101.33	116.40	140.57	156.47	174.11	204.76	253.26	289.82	305.87	311.13
Imports of Goods and Services (-) 98c	46.21	55.88	84.45	85.26	99.77	107.51	112.17	145.20	166.55	175.30	208.23	238.14	260.70	291.19	281.03
Gross Domestic Product (GDP) 99b	203.76	226.74	256.13	300.79	340.20	370.02	412.45	462.31	528.26	578.91	633.68	709.85	794.30	866.60	947.26
Net Primary Income from Abroad 98.n	.36	.77	.71	.81	.46	−.69	−1.38	−1.27	−4.02	−8.65	−13.29	−16.59	−19.81	−21.09	−20.02
Gross National Income (GNI) 99a	204.12	227.51	256.84	301.59	340.66	369.33	413.55	463.82	524.23	570.26	620.40	693.26	774.49	844.70	925.57
Net National Income 99e	178.86	204.80	230.40	271.10	305.50	328.80	367.60	412.04	464.81	503.79	545.72	608.93	682.74	745.23	818.35
GDP Volume 1975 prices 99b.p	270.67	281.19	293.36	299.82	303.34	297.35	301.31	314.22	320.36	...	...	...	...	...	...
GDP Volume 1985 prices 99b.p	...	...	...	...	...	...	...	...	791.00	791.26	800.05	814.54	846.98	865.79	884.99
GDP Volume 1991 Prices 99b.p	...	...	...	...	...	...	...	...	...	...	...	...	...		
GDP Volume 1995 Prices..................... 99b.p	...	...	...	...	...	...	...	...	...	...	...	...	...		
GDP Volume (1995=100) .... 99bv p	67.8	70.5	73.5	75.1	76.0	74.5	75.5	78.7	80.3	80.3	81.2	82.7	86.0	87.9	89.8
GDP Deflator (1995=100).................. 99bi p	11.9	13.2	14.9	17.6	19.9	21.6	24.1	27.0	30.8	33.8	37.0	41.4	46.4	50.6	55.3
															Millions:
Population... 99z	8.12	8.14	8.16	8.19	8.22	8.25	8.28	8.29	8.31	8.32	8.33	8.33	8.34	8.36	8.37

Millions of US Dollars — International Investment Position

	1987	1988	1989	1990	1991	1992	1993	1994	1995	1996	1997	1998	1999	2000	2001	Code
Assets	68,400	74,388	101,013	141,102	150,827	148,658	135,124	165,515	227,989	248,580	241,838	295,255	353,559	365,450	....	79aa d
Direct Investment Abroad	23,940	28,423	38,221	49,491	53,531	47,707	44,560	59,237	69,088	71,751	79,099	94,674	104,948	115,582	....	79ab d
Portfolio Investment	2,052	2,924	8,833	12,110	17,000	14,057	17,583	22,114	36,947	50,357	69,478	100,589	142,802	133,506	....	79ac d
Equity Securities	1,026	1,787	7,548	10,355	14,830	11,217	15,054	18,227	29,738	38,859	51,248	71,207	108,387	89,546	....	79ad d
Debt Securities	1,026	1,137	1,285	1,755	2,170	2,840	2,529	3,887	7,209	11,498	18,230	29,382	34,415	43,960	....	79ae d
Financial Derivatives	....	....	....	....	....	....	....	....	15,920	16,446	16,450	15,579	14,990	18,679	....	79al d
Other Investment	33,858	34,270	44,163	61,250	62,212	63,609	51,785	60,310	80,352	89,652	65,265	67,529	72,855	81,368	....	79af d
Monetary Authorities																79ag d
General Government	2,907	3,086	4,015	4,914	5,245	12,921	4,456	5,227	6,158	6,258	6,174	6,517	6,508	5,984	....	79ah d
Banks	15,048	14,780	21,037	34,925	34,180	32,231	26,254	24,660	36,346	44,681	46,599	46,143	48,128	56,018	....	79ai d
Other Sectors	15,903	16,404	19,110	21,411	22,787	18,458	21,075	30,423	37,848	38,713	12,492	14,869	18,219	19,365	....	79aj d
Reserve Assets	8,550	8,771	9,798	18,252	18,085	23,285	21,196	23,855	25,682	20,375	11,546	16,884	17,964	16,316	....	79ak d
Liabilities	96,272	108,332	141,802	202,176	219,007	208,434	215,813	261,074	324,863	352,787	339,476	389,867	430,625	424,279	....	79la d
Dir. Invest. in Rep. Economy	9,234	9,907	10,920	12,461	17,904	13,773	12,886	23,454	33,042	34,056	42,399	53,792	68,053	77,009	....	79lb d
Portfolio Investment	3,591	5,035	10,760	18,252	28,755	30,953	47,089	57,897	77,348	99,549	207,565	225,711	259,959	225,025	....	79lc d
Equity Securities	3,933	5,685	6,905	6,669	10,489	13,063	21,798	35,918	48,061	70,295	79,472	94,033	129,384	106,660	....	79ld d
Debt Securities	-342	-650	3,854	11,583	18,266	17,890	25,291	21,979	29,287	29,253	128,093	131,678	130,575	118,365	....	79le d
Financial Derivatives	....	....	....	....	....	....	....	....	16,821	17,610	16,420	15,936	14,095	15,276	....	79ll d
Other Investment	83,447	93,390	120,122	171,464	172,348	163,709	155,838	179,723	197,651	201,572	73,091	94,427	88,518	106,969	....	79lf d
Monetary Authorities						1,704				146						79lg d
General Government	21,375	18,678	16,380	15,269	13,202	37,200	47,089	57,227	65,934	64,328	1,836	2,238	2,857	1,922	....	79lh d
Banks	35,055	43,853	63,112	99,509	92,775	62,757	50,340	50,928	55,270	56,615	51,247	68,238	59,978	80,756	....	79li d
Other Sectors	27,018	30,859	40,630	56,687	66,371	62,047	58,409	71,567	76,447	80,483	20,009	23,951	25,683	24,291	....	79lj d

Year Ending December 31 — Government Finance

	1987	1988	1989	1990	1991	1992	1993	1994	1995	1996	1997	1998	1999	2000	2001	Code
Deficit (-) or Surplus	-3.93	5.76	22.61	13.61	-36.53	-74.07	-231.41	†-133.63	-153.18	-58.02	†-16.66	6.84	64.01	125.82	....	80
Revenue	440.30	476.09	532.23	601.67	610.35	610.94	544.63	†419.06	459.93	590.08	640.06	696.46	715.81	790.96	....	81
Grants Received	—	—	—	—	—	—	—	†—	5.66	10.40	8.88	9.87	9.28	9.02	....	81z
Expenditure	423.32	445.98	484.45	554.83	615.52	665.96	747.15	†552.69	618.77	658.50	†665.60	699.49	661.08	674.16	....	82
Lending Minus Repayments	20.91	24.35	25.17	33.23	31.36	19.05	28.89	....	....	....	....	....	....	....	....	83

Financing

	1987	1988	1989	1990	1991	1992	1993	1994	1995	1996	1997	1998	1999	2000	2001	Code
Domestic	-3.84	12.38	-16.09	-9.74	15.71	50.27	66.36	†129.85	135.42	27.07	-11.34	-20.25	47.13	8.78	....	84a
Foreign	7.77	-18.14	-6.52	-3.87	20.82	23.80	165.05	†3.78	17.76	30.95	28.01	13.43	-111.15	-135.30	....	85a
Total Debt	532.53	510.33	516.75	504.06	530.58	606.26	828.02	†1098.92	1,169.48	1,189.53	1,208.36	1,217.64	1,142.23	1,008.30	....	88
Debt: Domestic	404.27	400.21	413.15	404.33	410.02	461.90	518.61	†585.96	638.76	627.85	618.69	614.53	650.28	598.86	....	88a
Other Levels of Government	8.41	8.90	13.32	28.35	29.75	15.39	8.38	†—	—	—	—	—	—	—	....	88aa
Monetary Authorities	86.45	68.65	81.95	79.13	53.71	32.98	103.09	†78.47	57.96	46.21	58.12	49.14	50.50	32.66	....	88ab
Deposit Money Banks	58.49	45.45	41.02	46.86	48.80	52.23	61.27	†96.77	94.77	90.86	88.08	143.74	58.93	83.80	....	88ac
Other Domestic	250.92	277.21	276.86	249.99	277.76	361.30	345.87	†410.72	486.03	490.78	472.49	421.65	540.85	482.40	....	88ad
Debt: Foreign	128.26	110.12	103.60	99.73	120.56	144.36	309.41	†512.96	530.72	561.68	589.67	603.11	491.95	409.44	....	89a
Intragovernmental Debt	76.72	87.29	72.96	76.30	93.79	103.66	132.59	†187.67	216.67	221.67	223.72	231.23	231.94	270.91	....	88s
Total Debt	532.53	510.33	516.75	504.06	530.58	606.26	828.02	†1098.92	1,169.48	1,189.53	1,208.36	1,217.64	1,142.23	1,008.30	....	88
Debt: Kronor	....	....	....	....	....	....	....	....	....	....	....	....	....	....	....	88b
Intragovernmental Debt	76.72	87.29	72.96	76.30	93.79	103.66	132.59	†187.67	216.67	221.67	223.72	231.23	231.94	270.91	....	88s
Debt: Foreign Currency	....	....	....	....	....	....	....	....	....	....	....	....	....	....	....	89b

Billions of Kronor — National Accounts

	1987	1988	1989	1990	1991	1992	1993	1994	1995	1996	1997	1998	1999	2000	2001	Code
Househ.Cons.Expend.,incl.NPISHs	537.87	584.35	632.74	692.67	771.31	777.32	796.40	†830.86	859.85	884.15	922.03	956.91	1,004.61	1,060.42	1,079.73	96f
Government Consumption Expend.	269.88	286.81	322.63	372.13	394.39	402.50	406.00	†436.92	451.41	476.07	484.00	509.39	536.14	549.00	577.70	91f
Gross Fixed Capital Formation	197.95	225.11	271.00	292.53	280.37	244.60	205.70	†240.46	265.17	276.27	276.85	304.89	340.82	363.29	379.11	93e
Changes in Inventories	-4.76	-3.56	-.49	-2.48	-21.17	-6.66	-13.70	†13.42	18.97	2.70	7.59	15.03	3.53	13.67	3.05	93i
Exports of Goods and Services	332.48	359.69	394.47	406.83	404.18	401.59	473.30	†583.02	693.98	685.93	778.21	832.63	872.40	990.09	1,006.70	90c
Imports of Goods and Services (-)	313.31	341.35	387.75	401.80	381.76	377.64	421.50	493.70	†576.06	568.70	644.88	713.49	752.84	878.02	879.10	98c
Gross Domestic Product (GDP)	1,023.60	1,114.50	1,232.60	1,359.88	1,447.33	1,441.72	1,446.20	†1596.36	1,713.32	1,756.36	1,823.80	1,905.35	2,004.65	2,098.45	2,167.20	99b
Net Primary Income from Abroad	-16.47	-21.08	-28.86	-40.62	-41.44	-53.04	-68.10	-45.90	-46.70	-48.10	-43.10	-30.10	-20.50	-26.10	....	98.n
Gross National Income (GNI)	1,003.08	1,089.39	1,198.49	1,310.55	1,393.64	1,391.30	1,429.50	1,550.50	1,666.60	1,708.30	1,780.70	1,875.20	1,974.40	2,056.70	....	99a
Net National Income	886.61	961.56	1,203.75	1,319.26	1,405.89	1,388.69	1,385.17	1,454.92	....	....	....	....	....	....	....	99e
GDP Volume 1975 prices																99b.p
GDP Volume 1985 prices	910.20	934.95	957.17	970.21	954.06	....	....	....								99b.p
GDP Volume 1991 Prices	....	....	....	1,447.33	1,426.75	1,395.07	1,441.64									99b.p
GDP Volume 1995 Prices	....	....	....					†1652.33	1,713.32	1,731.79	1,767.64	1,830.97	1,913.55	1,982.62	2,006.53	99b.p
GDP Volume (1995=100)	92.4	94.9	97.1	98.5	96.8	95.4	93.3	96.4	100.0	101.1	103.2	106.9	111.7	115.7	117.1	99bv p
GDP Deflator (1995=100)	59.7	65.0	71.9	79.4	84.5	84.1	84.4	†93.2	100.0	102.5	106.4	111.2	117.0	122.5	126.5	99bi p

Midyear Estimates

	1987	1988	1989	1990	1991	1992	1993	1994	1995	1996	1997	1998	1999	2000	2001	Code
Population	8.40	8.44	8.49	8.56	8.62	8.67	8.72	8.78	8.83	8.84	8.85	8.85	8.86	8.87	8.83	99z

(See notes in the back of the book.)

Switzerland

		1972	1973	1974	1975	1976	1977	1978	1979	1980	1981	1982	1983	1984	1985	1986
Exchange Rates															*Francs per SDR:*	
Market Rate	aa	4.0975	3.9134	3.1098	3.0671	2.8459	2.4294	2.1105	2.0814	2.2492	2.0934	2.2002	2.2818	2.5338	2.2809	1.9858
															Francs per US Dollar:	
Market Rate	ae	3.7740	3.2440	2.5400	2.6200	2.4495	2.0000	1.6200	1.5800	1.7635	1.7985	1.9945	2.1795	2.5850	2.0765	1.6235
Market Rate	rf	3.8193	3.1648	2.9793	2.5813	2.4996	2.4035	1.7880	1.6627	1.6757	1.9642	2.0303	2.0991	2.3497	2.4571	1.7989
													Index Numbers (1995=100):			
Market Rate	ahx	30.9	37.5	39.8	45.8	47.2	49.3	66.5	71.0	70.5	60.3	58.3	56.3	50.4	48.5	66.0
Nominal Effective Exchange Rate	neu	38.3	41.8	45.3	50.4	56.3	57.3	69.9	70.6	69.7	71.6	77.4	81.0	80.2	79.6	85.5
Real Effective Exchange Rate	reu	....	....	....	97.0	99.1	93.1	75.4	73.1	†71.8	72.7	76.4	78.8	76.3	75.7	84.1
Fund Position															*Millions of SDRs:*	
Quota	2f.s	....	....	....	—	—	—	—	—	5	—	4	13	9	3	—
SDRs	1b.s	....	....	....	—	—	—	—	—	—	—	—	—	—	—	—
Reserve Position in the Fund	1c.s	....	....	....	81	250	391	308	207	252	397	467	636	593	501	370
of which: Outstg.Fund Borrowing	2c	....	....	....	81	250	391	308	207	252	397	467	636	593	501	370
International Liquidity											*Millions of US Dollars Unless Otherwise Indicated:*					
Total Reserves minus Gold	1l.d	4,399	5,007	5,446	7,019	9,606	10,289	17,763	16,435	15,656	13,979	15,460	15,034	15,296	18,016	21,786
SDRs	1b.d	—	—	—	—	—	—	—	—	6	—	4	13	9	3	—
Reserve Position in the Fund	1c.d	....	....	....	95	290	475	402	273	322	462	515	666	581	550	452
Foreign Exchange	1d.d	4,399	5,007	5,446	6,924	9,316	9,814	17,361	16,162	15,328	13,517	14,941	14,355	14,706	17,463	21,334
Gold (Million Fine Troy Ounces)	1ad	83.11	83.20	83.20	83.20	83.28	83.28	83.28	83.28	83.28	83.28	83.28	83.28	83.28	83.28	83.28
Gold (National Valuation)	1and	3,094	3,666	4,682	4,539	4,860	5,952	7,348	7,534	6,750	6,619	5,968	5,462	4,605	5,733	7,332
Monetary Authorities: Other Liab.	4..d	91	115	78	62	111	90	240	1,409	1,298	915	456	84	49	54	79
Deposit Money Banks: Assets	7a.d	25,521	29,992	†23,778	27,533	32,072	40,986	54,407	64,946	66,452	70,672	†69,446	68,374	†62,091	85,244	116,102
Liabilities	7b.d	20,987	24,958	†19,954	19,513	23,396	28,249	38,779	44,009	47,949	58,606	†56,124	54,517	†49,078	63,396	82,400
Trustee Accounts: Assets	7k.d	8,203	12,238	18,156	20,107	23,404	29,749	37,120	53,326	73,238	92,778	92,950	94,011	†99,738	120,219	137,338
Liabilities	7m.d	7,422	9,988	14,600	17,103	20,330	25,952	32,014	44,226	60,635	76,195	85,074	82,968	†85,513	100,398	111,322
Monetary Authorities															*Billions of Francs:*	
Foreign Assets	11	28.51	29.03	28.87	32.00	37.55	36.37	42.92	38.29	39.27	37.40	43.79	44.61	50.80	50.04	48.17
Claims on Central Government	12a	1.34	.98	1.48	1.23	1.49	1.91	1.49	1.49	2.21	2.70	2.88	3.26	3.46	3.74	3.90
Claims on Deposit Money Banks	12e	1.35	1.74	3.08	2.05	1.24	1.62	1.62	.47	2.75	3.54	5.67	3.95	5.28	5.63	5.97	6.18
Reserve Money	14	29.31	30.42	31.45	32.18	34.67	35.92	42.16	38.89	39.42	37.75	40.27	40.60	42.19	41.51	43.54
of which: Currency Outside DMBs	14a	17.82	19.08	20.33	20.12	20.78	21.49	23.64	24.99	25.44	24.74	25.98	26.31	27.88	27.31	28.54
Central Government Deposits	16d	1.33	.39	.63	1.61	3.69	2.48	4.04	2.24	.37	.80	.76	.76	1.11	2.57	.98
Other Items (Net)	17r	.55	.90	1.34	1.49	1.93	1.50	−1.33	2.12	5.72	7.19	9.58	11.80	16.61	15.67	13.72
Deposit Money Banks															*Billions of Francs:*	
Reserves	20	11.92	10.94	†11.26	12.98	14.34	15.53	17.04	15.80	16.50	15.35	†17.89	18.62	†15.75	15.78	17.15
Foreign Assets	21	98.00	97.29	†60.40	72.14	78.56	81.97	88.14	102.61	117.19	127.10	†138.51	149.02	†160.51	177.01	188.49
Claims on Central Government	22a	19.96	21.89	†14.53	15.40	17.22	15.90	17.08	20.24	20.34	21.40	†22.25	11.81	29.74	27.46	25.61
Claims on Private Sector	22d	116.48	126.30	†118.05	126.25	137.41	148.41	164.12	175.47	195.78	213.66	†262.06	281.61	†305.10	335.25	355.19
Demand Deposits	24	28.55	28.84	†25.39	27.58	32.49	32.24	42.70	40.13	39.61	40.14	†45.11	49.45	†47.86	46.52	46.91
Time and Savings Deposits	25	78.02	85.43	†71.69	78.61	84.56	93.37	97.30	114.15	115.10	130.44	†160.54	164.86	†197.99	211.30	219.20
Bonds	26ab	36.01	36.23	†21.87	28.07	31.23	33.62	35.23	34.05	39.63	44.93	†60.22	61.44	†103.97	116.63	125.64
Foreign Liabilities	26c	80.59	80.96	†50.68	51.12	57.31	56.50	62.82	69.54	84.56	105.40	†111.94	118.82	†126.87	131.64	133.78
Other Items (Net)	27r	23.21	24.97	†34.60	41.38	41.95	46.08	48.33	56.27	70.91	56.60	†62.90	66.50	†34.41	49.41	60.92
Monetary Survey															*Billions of Francs:*	
Foreign Assets (Net)	31n	45.57	44.98	†38.38	52.85	58.53	61.66	67.84	69.15	69.61	57.46	†69.45	74.63	†84.32	95.30	102.75
Domestic Credit	32	136.45	148.77	†133.42	141.26	152.44	163.73	178.65	195.68	218.45	236.94	†286.42	295.93	337.20	363.88	383.71
Claims on Central Govt. (Net)	32an	19.97	22.48	†15.37	15.01	15.02	15.33	14.53	20.21	22.67	23.27	†24.36	14.32	32.10	28.63	28.52
Claims on Private Sector	32d	116.48	126.30	†118.05	126.25	137.41	148.41	164.12	175.47	195.78	213.66	†262.06	281.61	†305.10	335.25	355.19
Money	34	46.51	48.10	†45.95	47.88	53.33	53.83	66.52	65.26	65.16	64.93	†71.14	75.82	†75.82	73.93	75.54
Quasi-Money	35	78.02	85.43	†71.69	78.61	84.56	93.37	97.30	114.15	115.10	130.44	†160.54	164.86	†197.99	211.30	219.20
Bonds	36ab	36.01	36.23	†21.87	28.07	31.23	33.62	35.23	34.05	39.63	44.93	†60.22	61.44	†103.97	116.63	125.64
Other Items (Net)	37r	21.50	23.98	†32.29	39.55	41.85	44.57	47.45	51.38	68.17	54.09	†63.98	68.44	†43.73	57.33	66.09
Money plus Quasi-Money	35l	124.52	133.52	†117.64	126.49	137.89	147.20	163.81	179.40	180.27	195.37	†231.67	240.68	†273.81	285.23	294.74
Other Banking Institutions															*Billions of Francs:*	
Foreign Assets	41..x	31.50	39.70	46.12	52.68	57.33	59.50	60.13	84.26	129.16	166.86	185.39	204.90	257.82	249.63	222.97
Domestic Liabilities	45..x	3.00	7.30	9.03	7.87	7.53	7.59	8.27	14.38	22.23	29.83	15.71	24.07	36.77	41.16	42.24
Foreign Liabilities	46c.x	28.50	32.40	37.09	44.81	49.80	51.90	51.86	69.88	106.93	137.04	169.68	180.83	221.05	208.48	180.73
Nonbank Financial Institutions															*Billions of Francs:*	
Claims on Central Government	42a.s	.40	.38	.41	.46	.66	.67	.68	.67	.63	....	.73	.74	....	....	....
Claims on Priv.Sec.& Local Govt.	42d.s	15.39	16.73	17.79	19.74	22.06	24.23	26.60	29.73	35.94	39.36	43.10	47.23	52.71	59.09	66.26
Real Estate	42h.s	4.52	5.03	5.38	5.69	5.94	6.28	6.88	7.60	8.32	9.03	9.85	10.68	11.62	12.46	13.49
Incr.in Total Assets(Within Per.)	49z.s	1.97	1.93	1.63	2.42	2.84	2.58	3.21	4.13	4.17	3.13	5.57	4.95	6.42	7.23	8.19
Liquid Liabilities	55l	127.52	140.82	149.19	158.53	170.95	182.33	201.29	226.77	242.96	265.72	†309.00	264.75	†310.58	326.40	337.35
Interest Rates															*Percent Per Annum*	
Bank Rate *(End of Period)*	60	3.75	4.50	5.50	3.00	2.00	1.50	1.00	2.00	3.00	6.00	4.50	4.00	4.00	4.00	4.00
Money Market Rate	60b	2.69	3.64	5.97	2.75	1.51	2.47	.66	†1.00	2.29	2.93	1.32	1.84	3.34	3.75	3.17
Treasury Bill Rate	60c	....	....	....	....	....	....	....	....	5.15	7.82	3.87	3.04	3.58	4.15	3.54
Deposit Rate	60l	....	....	....	....	....	....	....	....	....	8.75	4.40	3.31	3.77	4.36	3.51
Lending Rate	60p	....	....	....	....	....	....	....	....	....	5.56	5.98	5.49	5.49	5.43	5.46
Government Bond Yield	61	4.97	5.60	7.15	6.44	4.99	4.05	3.33	3.45	4.77	5.57	4.83	4.52	4.70	4.78	4.29

1987	1988	1989	1990	1991	1992	1993	1994	1995	1996	1997	1998	1999	2000	2001		
															Exchange Rates	
End of Period																
1.8130	2.0239	2.0323	1.8431	1.9389	2.0020	2.0322	1.9146	1.7102	1.9361	1.9636	1.9382	2.1955	2.1322	2.1079	Market Rate	aa
End of Period (ae) Period Average (rf)																
1.2780	1.5040	1.5465	1.2955	1.3555	1.4560	1.4795	1.3115	1.1505	1.3464	1.4553	1.3765	1.5996	1.6365	1.6773	Market Rate	ae
1.4912	1.4633	1.6359	1.3892	1.4340	1.4062	1.4776	1.3677	1.1825	1.2360	1.4513	1.4498	1.5022	1.6888	1.6876	Market Rate	rf
Period Averages																
79.3	80.9	72.2	85.4	82.7	84.2	79.9	86.5	100.0	95.6	81.4	81.6	78.7	70.0	70.0	Market Rate	ah x
89.2	88.4	83.8	88.2	86.9	85.2	88.0	93.8	100.0	98.4	92.7	94.5	93.5	92.8	96.3	Nominal Effective Exchange Rate	ne u
88.1	89.6	85.2	89.7	90.8	86.3	86.8	94.1	100.0	100.2	97.2	102.8	102.5	102.2	107.4	Real Effective Exchange Rate	re u
															Fund Position	
End of Period																
—	—	—	—	—	2,470	2,470	2,470	2,470	2,470	2,470	2,470	2,470	3,459	3,459	3,459	Quota	2f. s
10	15	4	1	2	12	113	162	181	88	170	192	345	125	225	SDRs	1b. s
212	102	32	—	—	581	605	643	981	1,065	1,407	1,828	1,218	964	1,259	Reserve Position in the Fund	1c. s
212	102	32	—	—	—	—	—	—	—	—	230	—	—	—	of which: Outstg.Fund Borrowing	2c
															International Liquidity	
End of Period																
27,476	24,203	25,276	29,223	29,004	33,255	32,635	34,729	36,413	38,433	39,028	41,191	36,321	32,272	31,999	Total Reserves minus Gold	1l. d
14	20	5	2	2	16	155	236	269	126	230	271	473	162	283	SDRs	1b. d
300	137	42	—	—	799	830	939	1,459	1,531	1,899	2,574	1,672	1,256	1,582	Reserve Position in the Fund	1c. d
27,162	24,045	25,230	29,221	29,002	32,440	31,650	33,554	34,685	36,775	36,899	38,346	34,176	30,854	30,134	Foreign Exchange	1d. d
83.28	83.28	83.28	83.28	83.28	83.28	83.28	83.28	83.28	83.28	83.28	83.28	83.28	77.79	70.68	Gold (Million Fine Troy Ounces)	1ad
9,315	7,915	7,697	9,189	8,782	8,176	8,046	9,077	10,347	8,841	8,182	8,667	7,464	21,219	19,664	Gold (National Valuation)	1an d
101	123	123								33	119	134	124	375	Monetary Authorities: Other Liab.	4..d
158,534	140,737	132,779	153,254	147,565	143,589	154,224	187,875	212,374	†263,362	314,438	369,712	463,670	465,833	446,488	Deposit Money Banks: Assets	7a. d
109,973	102,794	110,325	133,572	131,765	125,791	129,333	171,093	184,869	†223,836	268,969	300,777	395,023	440,005	415,253	Liabilities	7b. d
173,415	178,320	222,824	290,797	281,023	268,344	235,558	271,584	288,831	†294,323	293,492	311,232	292,460	325,518	323,209	Trustee Accounts: Assets	7k. d
137,912	140,664	170,156	219,395	213,727	204,428	182,470	213,280	232,765	†239,280	241,593	255,032	243,663	264,004	265,599	Liabilities	7m. d
															Monetary Authorities	
End of Period																
49.38	47.91	51.74	49.23	52.35	59.22	60.94	59.98	56.30	63.13	69.04	69.34	71.05	88.14	87.52	Foreign Assets	11
3.83	4.08	4.31	4.62	4.95	4.99	5.02	5.13	5.19	5.26	7.12	7.22	7.14	7.71	8.32	Claims on Central Government	12a
5.83	3.35	1.71	1.44	1.18	1.34	1.36	1.30	1.87	2.86	1.09	17.73	28.53	24.46	25.99	Claims on Deposit Money Banks	12e
46.06	37.42	35.94	36.92	35.96	39.60	39.10	39.33	38.40	40.35	39.43	42.47	49.67	44.41	49.96	Reserve Money	14
28.92	30.64	30.90	31.45	31.28	31.37	31.38	32.64	33.02	34.61	34.33	35.43	39.44	37.78	42.17	of which: Currency Outside DMBs	14a
1.38	2.51	2.50	.69	.22	.42	.49	.75	1.12	1.08	†2.69	15.36	17.16	10.21	2.59	Central Government Deposits	16d
11.60	15.41	19.32	17.69	22.31	25.53	27.73	26.33	23.84	29.83	35.15	36.46	39.87	65.68	69.29	Other Items (Net)	17r
															Deposit Money Banks	
End of Period																
18.74	9.29	8.59	8.27	7.90	7.82	8.01	7.64	8.27	†9.61	9.83	10.95	17.17	12.51	12.74	Reserves	20
202.61	211.67	205.34	198.54	200.02	209.07	228.17	246.40	244.34	†354.59	457.60	508.91	741.69	762.34	748.90	Foreign Assets	21
28.26	26.14	29.60	31.26	33.51	36.17	47.40	49.57	†50.70	†52.66	52.44	51.68	53.46	59.29	56.88	Claims on Central Government	22a
388.23	431.83	490.01	532.78	552.02	563.92	574.31	594.37	611.70	†608.17	625.65	635.67	676.49	668.94	660.94	Claims on Private Sector	22d
56.97	57.27	54.66	52.76	51.61	54.86	59.86	62.22	67.63	†93.57	105.45	113.88	124.00	122.25	131.40	Demand Deposits	24
239.91	255.57	279.51	283.91	293.89	300.34	329.73	343.60	358.01	†374.36	396.05	413.84	474.49	369.90	377.10	Time and Savings Deposits	25
135.43	145.67	157.12	172.43	181.45	183.49	173.22	164.72	161.13	†149.66	137.25	127.55	123.04	128.19	129.07	Bonds	26ab
140.55	154.60	170.62	173.04	178.61	183.15	191.35	224.39	212.69	†301.37	391.43	414.02	631.88	720.07	696.50	Foreign Liabilities	26c
64.98	65.82	71.64	88.72	87.89	95.13	103.74	103.04	115.54	†106.06	115.34	137.93	135.39	162.68	145.39	Other Items (Net)	27r
															Monetary Survey	
End of Period																
111.31	104.79	86.28	74.73	73.77	85.13	97.76	81.99	87.94	†116.35	135.17	164.06	180.64	130.21	139.28	Foreign Assets (Net)	31n
418.94	459.54	521.42	567.97	590.26	604.67	626.24	648.31	†666.47	†665.01	†682.53	679.22	719.93	725.73	723.56	Domestic Credit	32
30.71	27.71	31.41	35.19	38.23	40.75	51.93	53.94	†54.77	†56.84	†56.88	43.54	43.44	56.78	62.61	Claims on Central Govt. (Net)	32an
388.23	431.83	490.01	532.78	552.02	563.92	574.31	594.37	611.70	†608.17	625.65	635.67	676.49	668.94	660.94	Claims on Private Sector	32d
85.98	88.00	85.65	84.30	82.89	86.23	91.24	94.86	100.65	†128.18	139.78	149.31	163.44	160.03	173.57	Money	34
239.91	255.57	279.51	283.91	293.89	300.34	329.73	343.60	358.01	†374.36	396.05	413.84	474.49	369.90	377.10	Quasi-Money	35
135.43	145.67	157.12	172.43	181.45	183.49	173.22	164.72	161.13	†149.66	137.25	127.55	123.04	128.19	129.07	Bonds	36ab
68.93	75.10	85.42	102.07	105.79	119.74	129.82	127.11	134.62	†129.16	144.62	152.58	139.59	197.82	183.11	Other Items (Net)	37r
325.89	343.57	365.16	368.20	376.79	386.57	420.97	438.46	458.66	†502.54	535.83	563.15	637.93	529.93	550.66	Money plus Quasi-Money	35l
															Other Banking Institutions	
End of Period																
221.63	268.19	344.60	376.73	380.93	390.71	348.51	356.18	332.30	†396.28	427.12	428.41	467.82	532.71	542.12	Foreign Assets	41..x
45.37	56.64	81.45	92.50	91.22	93.06	78.54	76.47	64.50	†74.11	75.53	77.36	78.06	100.67	96.63	Domestic Liabilities	45..x
176.25	211.56	263.15	284.23	289.71	297.65	269.96	279.72	267.80	†322.17	351.59	351.05	389.76	432.04	445.49	Foreign Liabilities	46c.x
															Nonbank Financial Institutions	
....														....	Claims on Central Government	42a. s
73.75	84.75	96.37	102.44	114.79	127.21	139.24	152.91	163.99	180.80	200.00	227.30	250.10	254.80	....	Claims on Priv.Sec.& Local Govt.	42d. s
14.41	15.45	16.77	17.64	18.65	19.75	20.82	21.79	22.50	23.40	24.30	25.00	25.60	25.80	....	Real Estate	42h. s
8.41	12.04	12.95	6.93	13.35	13.54	13.09	14.64	11.79	24.11	20.50	28.10	24.60	7.30	....	Incr.in Total Assets(Within Per.)	49z. s
371.26	400.20	446.61	460.71	468.01	479.63	499.51	514.93	523.16	576.65	....	....	....	....		Liquid Liabilities	55l
															Interest Rates	
Percent Per Annum																
2.50	3.50	6.00	6.00	7.00	6.00	4.00	3.50	1.50	1.00	1.00	1.00	.50	†3.20	1.59	Bank Rate (End of Period)	60
2.51	2.22	6.50	8.33	7.73	7.47	4.94	3.85	2.89	1.78	1.35	1.22	.93	†3.50	1.65	Money Market Rate	60b
3.18	3.01	6.60	8.32	7.74	7.76	4.75	3.97	2.78	1.72	1.45	1.32	1.17	2.93	2.68	Treasury Bill Rate	60c
3.08	4.50	8.08	8.28	7.63	5.50	3.50	3.63	1.28	1.34	1.00	.69	1.24	†3.00	1.68	Deposit Rate	60l
5.24	5.07	5.85	7.42	7.83	7.80	6.40	5.51	5.48	4.97	4.47	4.07	3.90	4.29	4.30	Lending Rate	60p
4.12	4.15	5.20	†6.68	6.35	5.48	4.05	5.23	3.73	3.63	3.08	†2.71	3.62	3.55	3.56	Government Bond Yield	61

Switzerland

	1972	1973	1974	1975	1976	1977	1978	1979	1980	1981	1982	1983	1984	1985	1986
Prices, Production, Labor														*Index Numbers (1995=100):*	
Share Prices 62	61.4	66.6	75.9	76.9	76.1	76.0	75.0	76.4	79.8	84.3	87.4	88.4	91.0	92.8	91.6
Producer Prices 63	64.4	71.2	82.7	80.9	80.3	80.5	77.8	80.8	84.9	89.8	92.2	92.6	95.6	97.8	93.9
Prices: Home & Imported Goods 63s															
Consumer Prices 64	42.9	46.7	51.2	54.6	55.6	56.3	†56.9	59.0	61.3	65.3	†69.0	†71.1	73.1	75.6	76.2
Wages: Hourly Earn. (1990=100) 65	†42.5	46.3	†51.1	54.8	55.5	†58.2	59.7	61.8	65.1	69.2	74.2	77.1	79.1	82.1	85.4
Industrial Production 66	74.5	78.6	79.5	69.5	69.8	73.8	74.0	75.3	79.5	79.0	76.0	75.5	77.5	82.0	85.0
Manufacturing Employment 67ey	144.2	142.9	142.5	129.6	†120.5	120.2	120.7	120.5	122.6	122.7	118.9	114.7	114.1	115.1	†116.6
														Number in Thousands:	
Labor Force 67d	....	....	....	....	....	....	....	....	....	....	....	....	....		
Employment 67e	....	....	....	....	....	....	....	....	....	....	....	....	....	3,354	3,430
Unemployment 67c	....	....	....	....	....	....	....	....	....	....	....	....	....	30	26
Unemployment Rate (%) 67r	....	....	....	....	....	....	....	....	....	....	....	....	....	1.0	.8
International Transactions														*Millions of Francs*	
Exports 70	26,114	29,943	35,353	33,418	37,015	42,011	41,779	†44,080	49,645	52,857	52,687	53,764	60,630	66,624	67,004
Imports, c.i.f. 71	32,332	36,574	42,929	34,271	36,874	42,932	42,300	†48,739	60,883	60,093	58,115	61,276	69,150	74,750	73,513
														1995=100	
Volume of Exports(1985=100) 72	56.8	63.0	65.6	60.4	67.7	75.5	79.2	80.7	82.3	85.9	82.8	82.8	88.5	100.0	102.1
Volume of Exports 72.a	....	....	....	....	....	....	....	....	....	....	....	....	....	....	....
Volume of Imports(1985=100) 73	....	....	....	....	....	70.3	76.7	82.1	88.0	86.6	84.8	89.0	89.6	100.0	108.3
Volume of Imports 73.a	....	....	....	....	....	....	....	....	....	....	....	....	....	....	....
Unit Value of Exp.(1985=100) 74	67.2	69.0	78.3	80.1	79.5	81.4	78.3	80.7	89.4	91.8	94.9	96.8	101.7	100.0	98.0
Unit Value of Exports 74.a	....	....	....	....	....	....	....	....	....	....	....	....	....	....	....
Unit Value of Imp.(1985=100) 75	68.1	72.7	87.3	83.3	79.3	84.0	74.7	79.3	95.9	93.2	91.9	92.6	96.5	100.0	89.9
Unit Value of Imports 75.a	....	....	....	....	....	....	....	....	....	....	....	....	....	....	....
Import Prices 76.x	73.2	84.8	102.8	92.8	93.1	94.1	86.2	93.6	100.0	106.1	106.2	104.9	109.1	112.3	100.5
Balance of Payments														*Millions of US Dollars:*	
Current Account, n.i.e. .... 78al d						1,924	2,075	−245	−201	3,427	2,534	1,212	6,142	6,039	4,654
Goods: Exports f.o.b. .... 78aa d						20,992	28,837	33,827	41,708	40,104	36,073	34,167	36,896	37,303	48,800
Goods: Imports f.o.b. .... 78ab d						−22,710	−31,014	−38,727	−46,958	−42,488	−39,292	−39,987	−38,509	−39,387	−54,295
Trade Balance .... 78ac d						−1,718	−2,178	−4,900	−5,250	−2,384	−3,219	−5,820	−1,613	−2,083	−5,495
Services: Credit .... 78ad d						4,289	5,436	5,957	6,888	6,816	6,979	8,230	8,152	8,817	12,029
Services: Debit .... 78ae d						−2,524	−3,516	−4,237	−4,885	−4,696	−4,733	−4,625	−4,527	−4,842	−6,547
Balance on Goods & Services .... 78af d						47	−257	−3,180	−3,248	−264	−973	−2,216	2,012	1,892	−12
Income: Credit .... 78ag d						4,953	7,075	8,805	10,867	12,330	11,959	10,521	11,105	10,906	14,013
Income: Debit .... 78ah d						−2,411	−3,820	−4,808	−6,681	−7,637	−7,432	−6,180	−6,141	−5,952	−8,256
Balance on Gds, Serv. & Inc. ...... 78ai d						2,590	2,998	816	939	4,430	3,554	2,126	6,976	6,845	5,745
Current Transfers, n.i.e.: Credit ... 78aj d						304	425	490	522	733	823	946	929	1,017	1,548
Current Transfers: Debit .... 78ak d						−969	−1,348	−1,552	−1,662	−1,736	−1,842	−1,860	−1,763	−1,823	−2,638
Capital Account, n.i.e. .... 78bc d						—	—	—	—	—	—	....	....	....	....
Capital Account, n.i.e.: Credit ..... 78ba d						—	—	—	—	—	—	....	....	....	....
Capital Account: Debit .... 78bb d						—	—	—	—	—	—	....	....	....	....
Financial Account, n.i.e. .... 78bj d						−6,523	−5,940	−14,701	−11,341	−7,807	−12,212	−6,268	−5,816	−7,272	−3,162
Direct Investment Abroad .... 78bd d						....	....	....	....	....	....	−492	−1,139	−4,573	−1,460
Dir. Invest. in Rep. Econ., n.i.e. .. 78be d						....	....	....	....	....	....	643	777	1,267	2,122
Portfolio Investment Assets .... 78bf d						−4,761	−6,210	−7,113	−7,068	−8,488	−12,480	−5,754	−4,660	−6,535	−7,538
Equity Securities .... 78bk d												−600	−782	−1,425	−2,105
Debt Securities .... 78bl d						−4,761	−6,210	−7,113	−7,068	−8,488	−12,480	−5,154	−3,878	−5,110	−5,433
Portfolio Investment Liab., n.i.e. .. 78bg d						—	—	—	—	—	—	1,766	1,784	5,431	8,940
Equity Securities .... 78bm d						—	—	—	—	—	—	1,775	1,599	5,049	8,437
Debt Securities .... 78bn d						—	—	—	—	—	—	−9	185	382	503
Financial Derivatives Assets .... 78bw d						....	....	....	....	....	....	....	....	....	....
Financial Derivatives Liabilities ... 78bx d						....	....	....	....	....	....	....	....	....	....
Other Investment Assets .... 78bh d						−1,440	−3,807	−12,383	−13,145	−9,502	−2,689	−1,605	−3,965	−10,158	−13,459
Monetary Authorities .... 78bo d												−177	169	−105	−212
General Government .... 78bp d												—	—	—	—
Banks .... 78bq d						−1,440	−3,431	−8,659	−8,551	−5,700	−5,523	−1,708	−1,733	−7,361	−10,840
Other Sectors .... 78br d						—	−376	−3,724	−4,594	−3,801	2,834	280	−2,401	−2,692	−2,408
Other Investment Liab., n.i.e. ...... 78bi d						−323	4,077	4,795	8,872	10,183	2,957	−826	1,387	7,296	8,234
Monetary Authorities .... 78bs d						14	539	759	1	−431	−133	−465	2	−1	−23
General Government .... 78bt d						—	—	—	—	—	—	—	—	—	—
Banks .... 78bu d						−337	3,538	4,036	8,871	10,614	3,090	−196	255	4,973	5,174
Other Sectors .... 78bv d						—	—	—	—	—	—	−164	1,130	2,323	3,083
Net Errors and Omissions .... 78ca d						5,644	11,044	11,772	11,880	3,429	13,044	4,857	1,165	2,461	−402
Overall Balance .... 78cb d						1,045	7,179	−3,175	337	−951	3,366	−199	1,491	1,228	1,091
Reserves and Related Items .... 79da d						−1,045	−7,179	3,175	−337	951	−3,366	199	−1,491	−1,228	−1,091
Reserve Assets .... 79db d						−1,045	−7,179	3,175	−337	951	−3,366	199	−1,491	−1,228	−1,091
Use of Fund Credit and Loans .... 79dc d						—	—	—	—	—	—	—	—	—	—
Exceptional Financing .... 79de d						....	....	....	....	....	....	....	....	....	....

Prices, Production, Labor

Period Averages

Item	1987	1988	1989	1990	1991	1992	1993	1994	1995	1996	1997	1998	1999	2000	2001	Code
Share Prices	....	....	60.5	57.6	59.0	64.7	83.2	95.7	100.0	125.0	177.4	236.3	240.4	268.4	238.0	62
Producer Prices	91.0	92.9	95.9	98.1	99.4	100.1	100.5	100.1	100.0	98.2	97.5	96.3	95.4	96.3	96.7	63
Prices: Home & Imported Goods	92.0	94.1	98.2	99.6	100.0	100.1	100.3	100.0	100.0	97.7	97.7	96.3	95.0	97.5	97.3	63s
Consumer Prices	77.3	78.8	81.0	85.6	90.6	94.3	97.4	98.2	100.0	100.8	101.3	101.4	102.2	103.8	104.8	64
Wages: Hourly Earn. (1990=100)	87.5	90.7	94.3	100.0	107.5	113.4	116.2	....	....	....	....	....	....	....	....	65
Industrial Production	86.0	93.0	94.5	†97.0	97.0	96.0	94.0	98.0	100.0	100.0	104.6	108.4	112.2	121.1	125.5	66
Manufacturing Employment	116.5	116.5	117.7	119.4	117.3	†111.3	105.9	101.3	100.0	97.4	95.0	94.4	93.8	94.7	95.7	67ey

Period Averages

Item	1987	1988	1989	1990	1991	1992	1993	1994	1995	1996	1997	1998	1999	2000	2001	Code
Labor Force	....	....	....	....	....	....	3,873	....	3,860	3,925	3,928	3,974	3,983	3,985	....	67d
Employment	3,515	3,607	3,704	3,821	†3,768	3,759	3,746	3,719	3,747	3,781	3,766	3,833	3,862	3,879	....	67e
Unemployment	25	22	17	18	39	92	163	171	153	169	188	140	99	72	67	67c
Unemployment Rate (%)	.8	.7	.6	.5	1.1	2.5	4.5	4.7	4.2	4.7	5.2	3.9	2.7	2.0	1.9	67r

International Transactions

Millions of Francs

Item	1987	1988	1989	1990	1991	1992	1993	1994	1995	1996	1997	1998	1999	2000	2001	Code
Exports	67,477	74,064	84,268	88,257	87,947	†86,148	86,659	90,213	92,012	94,174	105,133	109,113	114,446	126,565	131,717	70
Imports, c.i.f.	75,171	82,399	95,209	96,611	95,032	†86,739	83,767	87,279	90,775	91,967	103,088	106,866	113,416	128,578	130,052	71

1995=100

Item	1987	1988	1989	1990	1991	1992	1993	1994	1995	1996	1997	1998	1999	2000	2001	Code
Volume of Exports(1985=100)	102.6	....														72
Volume of Exports	....	†80.0	84.2	88.0	86.8	90.9	91.5	96.0	100.0	101.3	109.1	114.4	118.3	126.7	129.3	72.a
Volume of Imports(1985=100)	115.3	....														73
Volume of Imports	....	†85.2	89.8	92.2	90.9	86.9	85.9	93.9	100.0	101.4	107.8	116.6	126.1	134.9	134.3	73.a
Unit Value of Exp.(1985=100)	101.7	....														74
Unit Value of Exports	....	†92.9	98.9	99.9	102.7	103.0	102.9	102.2	100.0	101.0	104.7	103.6	105.1	108.6	110.7	74.a
Unit Value of Imp.(1985=100)	86.6	....														75
Unit Value of Imports	....	†99.8	108.2	107.4	107.5	109.9	107.5	102.4	100.0	100.0	105.3	101.0	99.1	105.0	106.7	75.a
Import Prices	95.1	97.7	105.0	104.1	101.9	100.1	99.8	99.7	100.0	96.3	98.2	96.0	94.0	100.2	98.7	76.x

Balance of Payments

Minus Sign Indicates Debit

Item	1987	1988	1989	1990	1991	1992	1993	1994	1995	1996	1997	1998	1999	2000	2001	Code
Current Account, n.i.e.	6,288	8,846	8,063	6,955	10,382	14,247	17,926	17,588	21,804	21,051	26,679	26,774	28,159	32,542	....	78al d
Goods: Exports f.o.b.	55,604	63,164	65,810	78,032	74,255	79,870	75,424	82,625	97,139	95,544	95,039	93,782	91,823	93,294	....	78aa d
Goods: Imports f.o.b.	-61,621	-68,359	-70,748	-85,187	-78,835	-80,135	-73,832	-79,279	-93,880	-93,676	-92,302	-92,849	-91,009	-92,904	....	78ab d
Trade Balance	-6,017	-5,194	-4,937	-7,154	-4,581	-265	1,592	3,346	3,258	1,868	2,737	933	815	389	....	78ac d
Services: Credit	15,218	16,114	15,810	18,894	19,785	21,064	21,476	22,619	26,027	26,250	25,301	26,731	27,206	27,450	....	78ad d
Services: Debit	-8,183	-9,226	-9,183	-11,202	-11,103	-11,935	-11,548	-12,768	-15,037	-15,691	-14,100	-15,085	-15,720	-15,481	....	78ae d
Balance on Goods & Services	1,019	1,693	1,690	539	4,101	8,864	11,520	13,196	14,249	12,426	13,938	12,579	12,301	12,358	....	78af d
Income: Credit	17,533	20,057	22,697	28,685	27,521	26,239	25,152	26,747	31,575	32,997	35,066	45,926	50,227	61,682	....	78ag d
Income: Debit	-10,759	-11,191	-14,640	-19,939	-18,666	-17,902	-16,006	-18,932	-19,778	-20,383	-18,923	-28,050	-29,347	-37,683	....	78ah d
Balance on Gds, Serv. & Inc.	7,792	10,559	9,747	9,285	12,955	17,201	20,666	21,012	26,046	25,040	30,081	30,455	33,181	36,357	....	78ai d
Current Transfers, n.i.e.: Credit	1,911	2,054	1,919	2,357	2,367	2,530	2,484	2,526	2,995	2,961	2,625	2,786	6,762	6,037	....	78aj d
Current Transfers: Debit	-3,415	-3,768	-3,603	-4,686	-4,939	-5,484	-5,225	-5,949	-7,237	-6,949	-6,027	-6,467	-11,784	-9,852	....	78ak d
Capital Account, n.i.e.	....	....	—	—	-48	-43	-134	-350	-462	-214	-167	139	-515	-1,687	....	78bc d
Capital Account, n.i.e.: Credit	....	....	—	—	—	—	—	31	10	19	36	755	53	181	....	78ba d
Capital Account: Debit	....	....	—	—	-48	-43	-134	-380	-472	-233	-203	-616	-567	-1,868	....	78bb d
Financial Account, n.i.e.	-8,057	-14,698	-8,549	-11,242	-11,626	-15,780	-18,984	-11,852	-8,643	-24,253	-22,758	-22,988	-37,080	-30,131	....	78bj d
Direct Investment Abroad	-1,273	-8,695	-7,923	-7,176	-6,541	-6,057	-8,764	-10,793	-12,210	-16,152	-17,732	-18,767	-35,952	-41,316	....	78bd d
Dir. Invest. in Rep. Econ., n.i.e.	2,320	405	2,021	5,987	3,208	1,249	899	4,104	3,599	4,373	7,306	9,649	12,013	17,902	....	78be d
Portfolio Investment Assets	-6,371	-13,837	-9,582	-746	-16,842	-9,716	-30,121	-19,112	-8,884	-22,731	-19,739	-14,882	-46,839	-22,309	....	78bf d
Equity Securities	-2,006	3,358	958	679	-4,531	-6,464	-16,650	-8,073	-4,064	-14,686	-9,159	-2,529	-17,500	-20,323	....	78bk d
Debt Securities	-4,366	-17,195	-10,540	-1,425	-12,311	-3,252	-13,470	-11,040	-4,820	-8,045	-10,580	-12,353	-29,339	-1,986	....	78bl d
Portfolio Investment Liab., n.i.e.	4,639	6,421	6,371	-551	5,570	3,571	12,501	911	4,960	12,895	9,033	10,247	5,894	10,547	....	78bg d
Equity Securities	3,453	4,255	5,309	-1,579	2,951	1,809	7,923	-1,573	5,851	11,677	6,945	8,632	5,489	9,080	....	78bm d
Debt Securities	1,186	2,166	1,062	1,028	2,619	1,761	4,578	2,484	-891	1,218	2,088	1,615	404	1,467	....	78bn d
Financial Derivatives Assets	....	....														78bw d
Financial Derivatives Liabilities	....	....														78bx d
Other Investment Assets	-24,089	-7,641	-14,015	-28,677	2,121	-8,477	7,188	-30,798	-368	-70,355	-55,265	-60,089	-80,612	-100,265	....	78bh d
Monetary Authorities	323	-215	-153	-179	-243	-177	-134	-70	-15	40	197	204	203	36	....	78bo d
General Government	-17,184	-297	7,020	-5,839	1,070	-4,794	-2,666	-19,166	-9,423	-59,915	-52,384	-45,489	-77,286	-83,134	....	78bp d
Banks	-7,228	-7,129	-20,882	-22,659	1,293	-3,506	9,987	-11,562	9,070	-10,480	-3,078	-14,804	-3,528	-17,167	....	78bq d
Other Sectors	16,719	8,648	14,580	19,920	859	3,651	-687	43,836	4,259	67,718	53,637	50,855	108,416	105,309	....	78br d
Other Investment Liab., n.i.e.	51	3	-30	-42	38	-43	91	-104	-3	-9	11	80	34	33	....	78bi d
Monetary Authorities	....	-42	-185	-53	-1	84	79	40	267	31	121	-4	-58	-59	....	78bs d
General Government																78bt d
Banks	13,417	3,314	8,285	12,055	1,896	-733	4,074	34,808	5,676	52,185	53,517	42,173	95,594	89,669	....	78bu d
Other Sectors	3,251	5,372	6,509	7,962	-1,075	4,343	-4,932	9,093	-1,680	15,511	-11	8,606	12,846	15,666	....	78bv d
Net Errors and Omissions	4,982	3,470	1,854	5,456	2,284	5,973	1,678	-4,377	-12,669	5,937	-1,600	-2,745	6,952	-4,728	....	78ca d
Overall Balance	3,213	-2,382	1,369	1,169	992	4,397	486	1,009	29	2,521	2,154	1,179	-2,484	-4,005	....	78cb d
Reserves and Related Items	-3,213	2,382	-1,369	-1,169	-992	-4,397	-486	-1,009	-29	-2,521	-2,154	-1,179	2,484	4,005	....	79da d
Reserve Assets	-3,213	2,382	-1,369	-1,169	-992	-4,397	-486	-1,009	-29	-2,521	-2,154	-1,179	2,484	4,005	....	79db d
Use of Fund Credit and Loans	—	—	—	—	....	....	....	....	....	....	....	....	—	—	....	79dc d
Exceptional Financing	....	....	....	....	....	....	....	....	....	....	....	....	....	....	....	79de d

Switzerland

146

		1972	1973	1974	1975	1976	1977	1978	1979	1980	1981	1982	1983	1984	1985	1986
International Investment Position																*Millions of US Dollars*
Assets	79aa d	...	...	...	...	...	...	...	...	...	...	...	178,491	183,034	254,183	341,122
Direct Investment Abroad	79ab d	...	...	...	...	...	...	...	...	...	...	...	19,119	17,850	25,093	34,226
Portfolio Investment	79ac d	...	...	...	...	...	...	...	...	...	...	...	54,519	63,574	96,551	135,215
Equity Securities	79ad d	...	...	...	...	...	...	...	...	...	...	...	12,362	13,663	23,244	33,142
Debt Securities	79ae d	...	...	...	...	...	...	...	...	...	...	...	42,157	49,911	73,307	102,073
Financial Derivatives	79al d	...	...	...	...	...	...	...	...	...	...	...	—	—	—	—
Other Investment	79af d	...	...	...	...	...	...	...	...	...	...	...	84,508	81,956	108,431	142,016
Monetary Authorities	79ag d	...	...	...	...	...	...	...	...	...	...	...	—	—	—	—
General Government	79ah d	...	...	...	...	...	...	...	...	...	...	...	733	464	678	1,099
Banks	79ai d	...	...	...	...	...	...	...	...	...	...	...	60,996	56,002	74,827	99,794
Other Sectors	79aj d	...	...	...	...	...	...	...	...	...	...	...	22,779	25,490	32,927	41,123
Reserve Assets	79ak d	...	...	...	...	...	...	...	...	...	...	...	20,346	19,654	24,108	29,665
Liabilities	79la d	...	...	...	...	...	...	...	...	...	...	...	108,785	100,620	143,578	209,309
Dir. Invest. in Rep. Economy	79lb d	...	...	...	...	...	...	...	...	...	...	...	8,277	7,653	10,093	18,605
Portfolio Investment	79lc d	...	...	...	...	...	...	...	...	...	...	...	26,358	22,579	47,899	73,876
Equity Securities	79ld d	...	...	...	...	...	...	...	...	...	...	...	24,033	20,740	42,414	67,107
Debt Securities	79le d	...	...	...	...	...	...	...	...	...	...	...	2,325	1,840	5,485	6,769
Financial Derivatives	79ll d	...	...	...	...	...	...	...	...	...	...	...	—	—	—	—
Other Investment	79lf d	...	...	...	...	...	...	...	...	...	...	...	74,149	70,388	85,585	116,828
Monetary Authorities	79lg d	...	...	...	...	...	...	...	...	...	...	...	57	50	62	54
General Government	79lh d	...	...	...	...	...	...	...	...	...	...	...	—	—	—	—
Banks	79li d	...	...	...	...	...	...	...	...	...	...	...	53,112	48,943	59,464	81,470
Other Sectors	79lj d	...	...	...	...	...	...	...	...	...	...	...	20,980	21,395	26,060	35,304
Government Finance																*Millions of Francs:*
Deficit (-) or Surplus	80	−54	−1,425	−884	−1,766	−1,377	−1,291	−64	−2,352	−76	−1,491	901	−1,446	†−241	−1,183	2,372
Revenue	81	10,060	10,111	11,835	11,599	13,781	12,959	15,079	13,655	16,456	15,939	18,857	17,752	†20,282	20,702	24,347
Expenditure	82	9,426	10,786	11,905	12,662	15,185	14,211	15,428	15,951	16,474	17,140	18,001	18,897	†20,160	21,534	21,671
Lending Minus Repayments	83	688	750	814	703	−27	39	−285	56	58	290	−45	301	†363	351	304
Financing																
Net Domestic Borrowing	84a	601	88	1,472	1,880	4,623	888	751	1,070	1,217	465	−369	547	†1,870	3,509	−1,603
Other Financing	86c	−105	91	242	94	−901	133	509	392	116	92	98	62	†−417	−1,124	59
Use of Cash Balances	87	−442	1,246	−830	−208	−2,345	270	−1,196	890	−1,257	934	−630	837	†−1,212	−1,202	−828
Total Debt	88	9,572	10,014	11,760	14,405	18,390	19,372	20,549	22,405	†31,680	31,612	33,111	33,340	36,610	39,161	38,782
National Accounts																*Billions of Francs*
Househ.Cons.Expend.,incl.NPISHs	96f. c	67.8	75.9	83.1	86.0	88.9	92.6	95.3	100.7	111.2	118.6	125.9	131.3	137.0	143.8	149.1
Government Consumption Expend.	91f. c	12.9	14.8	16.6	17.9	18.9	19.2	19.8	20.8	23.5	25.6	27.7	29.6	30.8	32.9	34.6
Gross Fixed Capital Formation	93e. c	34.6	38.2	38.9	33.7	29.2	30.2	32.5	34.6	44.4	48.4	48.7	51.4	54.5	57.9	62.0
Changes in Inventories	93i. c	2.5	2.5	5.2	−1.5	.2	—	.4	3.3	5.9	3.4	1.1	−2.3	2.1	1.8	−.3
Exports of Goods and Services	90c. c	35.8	40.2	45.9	44.0	47.7	53.4	53.2	56.0	58.6	65.0	65.8	68.1	75.6	84.3	84.9
Imports of Goods and Services (-)	98c. c	36.8	41.7	48.7	40.0	43.0	49.7	49.5	56.8	63.6	67.5	65.6	67.9	76.0	83.5	81.7
Gross Domestic Product (GDP)	99b. c	116.7	130.1	141.1	140.2	142.0	145.8	151.7	158.5	180.1	193.5	203.6	210.1	224.1	237.2	248.5
Net Primary Income from Abroad	98.n	3.8	4.5	5.4	4.5	5.2	6.1	5.8	6.6	7.0	9.2	9.2	10.1	12.8	13.4	11.6
Gross National Income (GNI)	99a	120.5	134.5	146.5	144.6	147.2	151.9	157.5	165.2	177.3	194.0	205.2	214.0	226.1	241.4	254.9
Net National Income	99e	106.4	119.3	130.3	129.4	132.3	135.9	141.1	148.5	159.4	174.4	184.8	193.1	204.4	218.0	230.5
GDP Volume 1980 Prices	99b. r	160.2	165.3	167.2	156.0	154.7	158.4	159.3	163.2	170.4	...	...	...			
GDP Volume 1990 Prices	99b. r	...	...	...	...	...	...	...	...	259.0	263.1	259.3	260.6	268.5	277.7	282.2
GDP Volume (1995=100)	99bv r	77.1	79.5	80.4	75.0	74.4	76.2	76.6	78.5	81.9	83.2	82.0	82.4	84.9	87.8	89.3
GDP Deflator (1995=100)	99bi r	41.7	45.0	48.3	51.4	52.5	52.7	54.5	55.6	60.5	64.0	68.3	70.1	72.6	74.3	76.6
																Millions:
Population	99z	6.39	6.43	6.44	6.41	6.35	6.33	6.34	6.36	6.32	6.35	6.39	6.42	6.44	6.47	6.50

966

INTERNATIONAL FINANCIAL STATISTICS YEARBOOK   2002

Millions of US Dollars / International Investment Position

	1987	1988	1989	1990	1991	1992	1993	1994	1995	1996	1997	1998	1999	2000	2001		
Assets	450,026	439,407	477,797	565,691	589,466	586,781	647,184	745,894	860,298	924,354	1,009,557	1,196,819	1,238,942	1,352,443	....	Assets	79aa d
	45,276	48,907	54,629	66,087	75,884	74,414	91,571	112,586	142,479	141,591	165,365	184,232	192,422	215,236	....	Direct Investment Abroad	79ab d
	172,000	176,666	186,541	191,525	214,903	219,559	271,003	293,846	347,041	359,821	382,782	469,522	508,000	504,262	....	Portfolio Investment	79ac d
	36,441	36,888	46,083	41,584	51,635	56,416	88,919	100,797	120,543	138,923	165,438	209,617	259,679	265,793	....	Equity Securities	79ad d
	135,559	139,778	140,458	149,941	163,268	163,144	182,084	193,049	226,497	220,898	217,344	259,905	248,322	238,469	....	Debt Securities	79ae d
															....	Financial Derivatives	79al d
	194,129	181,996	203,250	270,166	260,142	252,215	243,643	293,976	322,125	375,575	414,208	492,632	494,581	579,264	....	Other Investment	79af d
															....	Monetary Authorities	79ag d
	1,016	971	976	1,243	1,086	889	884	1,037	1,250	1,051	946	943	756	755	....	General Government	79ah d
	136,437	122,510	113,699	132,993	128,508	127,784	133,539	163,590	183,006	231,511	276,736	332,647	341,664	413,364	....	Banks	79ai d
	56,677	58,515	88,575	135,930	130,549	123,542	109,220	129,349	137,870	143,012	136,526	159,043	152,161	165,144	....	Other Sectors	79aj d
	38,621	31,838	33,378	37,913	38,536	40,594	40,967	45,487	48,653	47,368	47,202	50,432	43,939	53,682	....	Reserve Assets	79ak d
	259,254	250,664	290,706	347,890	354,059	351,456	404,168	472,874	556,487	587,559	700,953	837,796	887,117	1,055,634	....	Liabilities	79la d
	26,307	25,230	25,669	34,245	35,749	32,990	38,714	48,667	57,063	53,918	59,519	71,995	77,893	85,774	....	Dir. Invest. in Rep. Economy	79lb d
	76,840	76,228	93,655	93,784	103,124	109,190	162,151	162,400	208,583	203,380	272,805	352,507	341,056	411,445	....	Portfolio Investment	79lc d
	67,138	65,761	81,930	78,971	85,946	90,876	139,056	134,721	179,290	176,566	246,515	322,744	309,597	382,038	....	Equity Securities	79ld d
	9,701	10,467	11,725	14,813	17,177	18,314	23,095	27,679	29,293	26,814	26,289	29,763	31,459	29,408	....	Debt Securities	79le d
															....	Financial Derivatives	79ll d
	156,107	149,206	171,382	219,862	215,186	209,275	203,304	261,806	290,841	330,261	368,629	413,294	468,167	558,414	....	Other Investment	79lf d
	128	112	77	46	85	38	128	36	37	24	33	119	355	393	....	Monetary Authorities	79lg d
	383	284	81	39	36	114	192	258	568	514	596	626	484	413	....	General Government	79lh d
	109,509	102,230	109,793	132,940	132,650	126,124	128,116	170,567	180,873	218,606	258,708	290,465	345,011	424,436	....	Banks	79li d
	46,088	46,580	61,431	86,836	82,415	82,999	74,868	90,946	109,363	111,117	109,292	122,085	122,317	133,172	....	Other Sectors	79lj d

Year Ending December 31 / Government Finance

	1987	1988	1989	1990	1991	1992	1993	1994	1995	1996	1997	1998	1999	2000	2001		
	670	1,980	157	1,276	-3,297	-2,437	-8,351	-4,443	-5,141	-4,404	-4,917	363	-2,399	3,820	1,367	Deficit (-) or Surplus	80
	23,296	27,066	26,427	30,385	30,247	32,355	29,559	33,752	32,202	35,279	34,695	39,359	37,742	44,031	43,018	Revenue	81
	22,219	24,099	25,964	28,764	32,422	34,354	35,443	36,759	37,474	39,417	38,151	41,634	40,839	40,832	42,147	Expenditure	82
	407	987	306	345	1,122	438	2,467	1,436	-131	266	1,461	-2,638	-698	-621	-496	Lending Minus Repayments	83
Financing																Financing	
	1,145	-1,676	1,321	-203	5,408	8,801	14,923	7,399	6,472	5,706	8,486	13,860	-6,817	3,244	-2,419	Net Domestic Borrowing	84a
	-1,329	299	-2,884	-26	-1,812	-1,810	-1,131	-1,598	-1,050	1,202	-596	-4,245	-10,960	-9,000	-5,401	Other Financing	86c
	-486	-603	1,406	-1,047	-299	-4,554	-5,441	-1,358	-281	-2,504	-2,973	-9,978	20,176	1,936	6,453	Use of Cash Balances	87
	38,597	39,289	38,287	38,509	43,915	55,297	67,513	75,714	82,152	88,418	97,050	109,620	102,254	108,108	106,813	Total Debt	88

Billions of Francs / National Accounts

	1987	1988	1989	1990	1991	1992	1993	1994	1995	1996	1997	1998	1999	2000	2001		
	154.6	160.3	168.8	179.6	193.4	201.9	206.8	211.2	216.1	219.8	224.2	229.0	234.8	241.8	249.6	Househ.Cons.Expend.,incl.NPISHs	96f. c
	35.5	38.2	41.8	46.4	50.9	53.4	53.5	54.8	55.0	56.6	55.8	56.8	56.8	57.7	59.2	Government Consumption Expend.	91f. c
	65.1	73.0	80.5	85.9	85.0	78.6	75.4	78.7	77.6	73.9	72.9	76.0	78.8	85.2	86.1	Gross Fixed Capital Formation	93e. c
	-.6	.5	3.5	4.4	-.6	-3.0	-2.6	-3.0	.7	.2	.5	-.8	-2.5	-.8	-1.0	Changes in Inventories	93i. c
	86.0	92.4	102.9	107.7	110.8	116.2	118.7	121.4	123.3	127.1	141.8	148.1	157.7	177.9	182.7	Exports of Goods and Services	90c. c
	83.5	91.6	104.0	106.6	105.8	104.6	102.0	105.7	109.2	111.7	123.9	129.1	137.1	157.4	159.7	Imports of Goods and Services (-)	98c. c
	257.2	272.7	293.3	317.3	333.7	342.4	349.8	357.5	363.5	365.8	371.4	380.0	388.6	404.4	417.0	Gross Domestic Product (GDP)	99b. c
	11.4	14.5	14.8	13.6	14.3	13.4	15.6	12.7	15.6	....						Net Primary Income from Abroad	98.n
	266.1	283.0	305.2	327.6	345.4	352.2	358.4	365.6	377.6	....						Gross National Income (GNI)	99a
	240.5	255.2	274.7	294.8	311.1	316.7	322.2	328.8	339.8	....						Net National Income	99e
	284.3	293.1	305.9	317.3	314.8	314.4	312.9	314.5	316.1	317.1	322.6	330.2	335.5	345.5	350.1	GDP Volume 1980 Prices	99b. r
																GDP Volume 1990 Prices	99b. r
	89.9	92.7	96.8	100.4	99.6	99.5	99.0	99.5	100.0	100.3	102.0	104.4	106.1	109.3	110.8	GDP Volume (1995=100)	99bv r
	78.7	80.9	83.4	87.0	92.2	94.7	97.2	98.8	100.0	100.3	100.1	100.1	100.7	101.8	103.6	GDP Deflator (1995=100)	99bi r

Midyear Estimates

	1987	1988	1989	1990	1991	1992	1993	1994	1995	1996	1997	1998	1999	2000	2001		
	6.55	6.59	6.65	6.71	6.80	6.88	6.94	6.99	7.04	7.07	7.09	7.11	7.13	7.17	7.23	Population	99z

(See notes in the back of the book.)

		1972	1973	1974	1975	1976	1977	1978	1979	1980	1981	1982	1983	1984	1985	1986
Exchange Rates														*Pounds per SDR: End of Period (aa)*		
Principal Rate	aa	4.147	4.584	4.530	4.331	4.560	4.768	5.113	5.171	5.006	4.569	4.330	4.109	3.847	4.311	4.801
Principal Rate	ae	3.820	3.800	3.700	3.700	3.925	3.925	3.925	3.925	3.925	3.925	3.925	3.925	3.925	3.925	3.925
Fund Position														*Millions of SDRs:*		
Quota	2f. s	50	50	50	50	50	50	63	63	95	95	95	95	139	139	139
SDRs	1b. s	4	8	8	7	7	6	6	12	10	15	12	9	5	3	—
Reserve Position in the Fund	1c. s	—	—	—	7	13	—	—	—	—	7	7	—	—	—	—
Total Fund Cred.&Loans Outstg.	2tl	23	18	5	—	—	—	—	1	—	—	—	—	—	—	—
International Liquidity														*Millions of US Dollars Unless Otherwise Indicated:*		
SDRs	1b.d	4	10	10	9	8	8	8	16	12	17	13	9	5	3	—
Reserve Position in the Fund	1c.d	—	—	—	8	15	—	—	—	9	8	—	—	—	—	—
Gold (Million Fine Troy Ounces)	1ad	.800	.800	.789	.789	.789	.811	.811	.833	.833	.833	.833	.833	.833	.833	.833
Gold (National Valuation)	1and	27	28	28	28	27	28	27	29e	29	29	29	29	29	29	29
Monetary Authorities: Other Assets	3..d	16	16	34	28	32	74	41	19	15	124	92	149	195	194	430
Other Liab.	4..d	134	101	56	287	347	296	352	409	530	672	929	904	1,641	2,362	2,858
Deposit Money Banks: Assets	7a.d	22	33	62	88	125	65	73	188	109	69	292	244	141	152	223
Liabilities	7b.d	49	61	88	42	155	210	126	139	377	637	722	990	928	1,166	1,263
Monetary Authorities														*Millions of Pounds:*		
Foreign Assets	11	571	1,605	1,956	2,808	1,382	2,297	1,766	2,485	1,499	1,749	1,253	902	1,916	1,193	2,352
Claims on Central Government	12a	3,208	2,588	3,486	4,445	7,175	7,932	11,934	12,447	18,228	22,560	35,248	41,519	55,165	74,003	79,407
Claims on Official Entities	12bx	81	78	40	28	23	13	12	9	62	59	57	56	56	56	56
Claims on Deposit Money Banks	12e	346	432	629	756	1,306	1,191	842	1,532	1,493	1,496	1,429	2,246	1,179	1,825	1,197
Reserve Money	14	2,684	3,301	4,300	5,142	6,431	8,026	10,463	11,905	15,896	17,250	25,700	32,548	43,095	58,516	62,753
of which: Currency Outside DMBs	14a	2,245	2,757	3,413	3,945	5,259	6,797	8,459	9,903	13,422	14,046	17,348	20,500	25,155	29,562	36,262
Foreign Liabilities	16c	606	464	230	1,061	1,363	1,163	1,382	1,609	2,080	2,637	3,645	3,546	6,441	9,273	11,218
Central Government Deposits	16d	586	715	995	1,611	1,745	1,782	2,008	2,459	3,011	4,986	7,351	7,391	7,255	8,305	9,098
Capital Accounts	17a	93	100	100	96	100	100	110	141	176	195	185	185	185	185	185
Other Items (Net)	17r	216	100	464	107	226	340	569	351	117	790	1,105	1,054	1,340	797	−242
Deposit Money Banks														*Millions of Pounds:*		
Reserves	20	296	390	468	603	817	736	1,411	938	1,622	1,994	6,466	9,816	14,935	25,334	23,729
Foreign Assets	21	83	126	229	327	490	255	287	737	426	272	1,144	957	555	597	876
Claims on Central Government	22a	136	173	230	295	405	485	612	782	918	1,383	1,700	2,136	2,849	3,532	3,772
Claims on Official Entities	22bx	1,347	1,744	3,027	4,647	6,746	8,148	8,089	9,819	14,176	21,672	20,802	22,468	19,556	16,279	18,918
Claims on Private Sector	22d	578	653	694	861	1,146	1,339	1,651	2,437	2,944	3,489	4,472	5,938	6,580	6,825	7,601
Demand Deposits	24	786	957	1,784	2,640	3,091	3,676	4,883	5,552	7,611	9,917	10,895	15,174	17,872	22,222	22,962
Time and Savings Deposits	25	235	277	398	514	665	957	1,249	1,535	1,873	2,655	3,590	4,739	6,645	8,018	9,236
Restricted Deposits	26b	267	436	537	444	1,090	1,258	1,106	1,586	2,505	5,162	7,783	7,887	7,616	9,841	11,587
Foreign Liabilities	26c	186	231	327	155	610	824	495	545	1,479	2,500	2,833	3,884	3,644	4,575	4,959
Central Government Deposits	26d	169	181	259	1,128	1,485	1,569	1,669	1,839	2,211	3,226	4,132	3,826	4,008	3,561	3,555
Credit from Monetary Authorities	26g	345	421	629	756	1,298	1,190	842	1,232	1,493	1,495	1,421	2,246	1,179	1,825	1,199
Capital Accounts	27a	186	190	227	248	338	384	445	532	607	914	1,032	1,139	1,301	1,423	1,505
Other Items (Net)	27r	224	354	428	743	866	952	1,184	1,643	2,005	2,585	2,495	1,954	1,688	604	−779
Monetary Survey														*Millions of Pounds:*		
Foreign Assets (Net)	31n	−138	1,036	1,627	1,919	−102	565	175	1,068	−1,634	−3,117	−4,081	−5,572	−7,614	−12,057	−12,948
Domestic Credit	32	4,595	4,339	6,222	7,538	12,264	14,566	18,621	21,196	31,105	40,950	50,795	60,900	72,942	88,828	97,101
Claims on Central Govt. (Net)	32an	2,589	1,864	2,462	2,001	4,350	5,065	8,869	8,931	13,924	15,730	25,465	32,438	46,751	65,669	70,527
Claims on Official Entities	32bx	1,428	1,822	3,066	4,675	6,768	8,162	8,101	9,828	14,238	21,731	20,858	22,524	19,612	16,335	18,974
Claims on Private Sector	32d	578	653	694	861	1,146	1,339	1,651	2,437	2,944	3,489	4,472	5,938	6,580	6,825	7,601
Money	34	3,151	3,797	5,540	6,966	8,561	10,924	13,866	16,119	21,854	24,832	29,518	36,978	45,607	54,976	61,214
Quasi-Money	35	235	277	398	514	665	957	1,249	1,535	1,873	2,655	3,590	4,739	6,645	8,018	9,236
Restricted Deposits	36b	267	436	537	444	1,090	1,258	1,106	1,586	2,505	5,162	7,783	7,887	7,616	9,841	11,587
Other Items (Net)	37r	741	804	1,295	1,407	1,665	1,818	2,377	2,767	2,934	4,824	5,420	5,259	4,939	3,437	1,444
Money plus Quasi-Money	35l	3,386	4,074	5,939	7,480	9,226	11,881	15,115	17,654	23,727	27,487	33,109	41,717	52,251	62,994	70,450
Interest Rates														*Percent Per Annum*		
Discount Rate (End of Period)	60	5.00	5.00	5.00	5.00	5.00	5.00	5.00	5.00	5.00	5.00	5.00	5.00	5.00	5.00	5.00
Deposit Rate	60l	....	....	....	....	....	....	4.0	4.0	4.0	4.0	4.0	4.0	4.0	4.0	4.0
Lending Rate	60p	....	....	....	....	....	....	9.0	9.0	9.0	9.0	9.0	9.0	9.0	9.0	9.0
Prices and Production														*Index Numbers (1995=100):*		
Wholesale Prices	63	3.4	4.5	5.1	5.5	6.1	6.7	7.5	8.2	†9.4	11.2	12.4	12.8	13.9	15.3	21.5
Consumer Prices	64	3.2	3.9	†4.5	5.0	5.6	6.3	6.6	6.9	8.2	9.7	11.1	11.8	12.9	15.1	20.5
Industrial Production	66	23.4	25.0	29.3	†34.0	37.1	36.2	39.3	39.3	44.1	49.9	52.5	61.4	†61.4	58.4	60.8
														Number in Thousands:		
Labor Force	67d	....	....	....	....	....	....	....	....	....	....	....	....	....	....	....
Employment	67e	....	....	....	....	....	....	....	....	....	....	....	....	....	....	....
Unemployment	67c	....	....	....	....	....	....	....	....	....	....	....	....	....	....	....
Unemployment Rate (%)	67r	....	....	....	....	....	....	....	....	....	....	....	....	....	....	....

	1987	1988	1989	1990	1991	1992	1993	1994	1995	1996	1997	1998	1999	2000	2001		
Exchange Rates																	
Pounds per US Dollar: End of Period (ae)																	
Principal Rate	5.568	15.105	14.751	15.969	16.057	15.434	15.418	16.387	16.686	16.141	15.145	15.805	15.406	14.625	14.107	Principal Rate	**aa**
Principal Rate	3.925	11.225	11.225	11.225	11.225	11.225	11.225	11.225	11.225	11.225	11.225	11.225	11.225	11.225	11.225	Principal Rate	**ae**
Fund Position *End of Period*																	
Quota	139	139	139	139	139	139	210	210	210	210	210	210	294	294	294	Quota	**2f, s**
SDRs	—	—	—	—	—	—	—	—	—	—	—	—	—	—	—	SDRs	**1b. s**
Reserve Position in the Fund	—	—	—	—	—	—	—	—	—	—	—	—	—	—	—	Reserve Position in the Fund	**1c. s**
Total Fund Cred.&Loans Outstg.	—	—	—	—	—	—	—	—	—	—	—	—	—	—	—	Total Fund Cred.&Loans Outstg.	**2tl**
International Liquidity *End of Period*																	
SDRs	—	—	—	—	—	—	—	—	—	—	—	—	—	—	—	SDRs	**1b. d**
Reserve Position in the Fund	—	—	—	—	—	—	—	—	—	—	—	—	—	—	—	Reserve Position in the Fund	**1c. d**
Gold (Million Fine Troy Ounces)	.833	.833	.833	.833	.833	.833	.833	.833	.833	.833	.833	.833	.833	.833	.833	Gold (Million Fine Troy Ounces)	**1ad**
Gold (National Valuation)	29	29	29	29	29	29	29	29	29	29	29	29	29	29	29	Gold (National Valuation)	**1and**
Monetary Authorities: Other Assets	942	1,140	....	....	....	....	....	....	....	....	....	....	....	....	....	Monetary Authorities: Other Assets	**3..d**
Other Liab.	3,629	3,578	3,680	4,019	1,433	1,169	1,037	1,041	1,124	1,041	1,084	1,137	1,150	805	730	Other Liab.	**4..d**
Deposit Money Banks: Assets	241	302	500	992	1,730	2,326	9,966	11,282	13,365	16,084	19,819	22,776	25,458	35,517	44,742	Deposit Money Banks: Assets	**7a. d**
Liabilities	1,311	1,126	1,062	919	742	587	1,477	922	497	495	248	325	438	408	347	Liabilities	**7b. d**
Monetary Authorities *End of Period*																	
Foreign Assets	4,653	15,265	25,868	37,540	18,655	23,544	24,368	28,568	37,206	49,156	52,376	55,216	67,512	88,391	101,503	Foreign Assets	**11**
Claims on Central Government	83,159	83,334	88,713	104,776	114,399	136,064	153,089	178,802	203,998	241,730	265,783	270,370	270,369	274,877	301,278	Claims on Central Government	**12a**
Claims on Official Entities	106	106	106	106	106	106	106	106	106	106	106	106	106	106	106	Claims on Official Entities	**12bx**
Claims on Deposit Money Banks	915	3,126	8,356	18,697	32,730	51,499	71,006	90,674	104,602	112,460	126,599	135,455	164,991	161,558	175,172	Claims on Deposit Money Banks	**12e**
Reserve Money	68,590	64,983	78,421	100,745	108,332	132,508	151,867	164,996	172,711	185,864	194,799	204,513	219,475	252,814	313,445	Reserve Money	**14**
of which: Currency Outside DMBs	41,852	52,171	59,962	76,202	92,450	107,602	126,116	135,021	143,800	153,715	159,808	178,191	182,184	203,863	229,266	of which: Currency Outside DMBs	**14a**
Foreign Liabilities	14,244	40,160	41,304	45,112	16,085	13,117	11,640	11,683	12,614	11,686	12,168	12,768	12,911	9,040	8,196	Foreign Liabilities	**16c**
Central Government Deposits	8,839	17,593	24,711	35,276	56,417	76,633	93,898	126,027	156,479	213,995	256,253	272,085	314,414	355,693	374,313	Central Government Deposits	**16d**
Capital Accounts	185	185	185	558	9,245	11,186	14,242	18,755	23,902	23,902	33,839	38,195	43,909	51,426	55,814	Capital Accounts	**17a**
Other Items (Net)	−3,024	−21,090	−21,578	−20,571	−24,187	−22,230	−23,077	−23,311	−19,794	−31,995	−52,193	−66,415	−87,732	−144,041	−173,709	Other Items (Net)	**17r**
Deposit Money Banks *End of Period*																	
Reserves	23,309	9,467	11,939	17,503	20,149	23,773	24,854	31,556	29,366	38,771	25,946	21,403	23,716	31,419	42,242	Reserves	**20**
Foreign Assets	947	3,389	5,610	11,132	19,423	26,105	111,872	126,639	150,020	180,547	222,465	255,655	285,762	398,681	502,229	Foreign Assets	**21**
Claims on Central Government	5,004	5,566	5,873	6,915	10,159	12,118	21,992	26,252	30,931	35,560	41,573	48,639	58,275	69,385	100,656	Claims on Central Government	**22a**
Claims on Official Entities	22,035	47,162	52,579	59,134	72,383	89,540	160,109	120,667	140,439	147,202	164,580	160,381	179,711	187,356	191,020	Claims on Official Entities	**22bx**
Claims on Private Sector	8,971	12,068	16,073	20,009	26,787	35,556	44,457	52,343	63,667	66,633	73,351	72,617	75,345	76,611	78,737	Claims on Private Sector	**22d**
Demand Deposits	23,438	24,595	28,987	35,888	39,832	48,799	60,761	68,885	78,028	84,685	93,665	97,683	121,471	151,753	176,845	Demand Deposits	**24**
Time and Savings Deposits	10,781	16,068	19,736	26,340	32,645	41,505	67,156	83,113	91,775	104,624	116,939	135,636	160,346	194,800	276,181	Time and Savings Deposits	**25**
Restricted Deposits	17,535	11,262	10,156	11,039	16,104	18,659	30,119	24,411	26,708	27,182	33,235	22,776	20,327	28,394	40,542	Restricted Deposits	**26b**
Foreign Liabilities	5,147	12,642	11,918	10,316	8,327	6,593	16,584	10,347	5,574	5,551	2,782	3,653	4,915	4,583	3,891	Foreign Liabilities	**26c**
Central Government Deposits	3,912	3,880	4,114	3,919	4,654	5,634	6,302	6,327	7,780	8,643	12,863	13,686	14,960	18,078	19,310	Central Government Deposits	**26d**
Credit from Monetary Authorities	924	3,138	8,724	18,770	27,890	51,671	71,068	90,741	104,712	119,897	136,811	135,199	149,810	160,744	150,193	Credit from Monetary Authorities	**26g**
Capital Accounts	1,831	2,228	2,647	3,148	7,318	10,344	13,529	17,546	23,065	29,908	34,666	40,576	48,878	47,799	50,598	Capital Accounts	**27a**
Other Items (Net)	−4,051	2,864	4,187	3,558	12,126	3,888	97,765	56,087	76,780	88,224	96,955	109,485	102,102	157,300	197,322	Other Items (Net)	**27r**
Monetary Survey *End of Period*																	
Foreign Assets (Net)	−13,791	−34,148	−21,744	−6,756	13,667	29,940	108,016	133,177	169,038	212,466	259,891	294,450	335,448	473,449	591,645	Foreign Assets (Net)	**31n**
Domestic Credit	106,523	126,763	134,518	151,744	162,764	191,117	279,553	245,816	274,882	268,593	276,278	266,342	254,432	234,564	278,174	Domestic Credit	**32**
Claims on Central Govt. (Net)	75,412	67,427	65,761	72,495	63,487	65,915	74,881	72,700	70,670	54,652	38,241	33,238	−730	−29,509	8,311	Claims on Central Govt. (Net)	**32an**
Claims on Official Entities	22,141	47,268	52,685	59,240	72,489	89,646	160,215	120,773	140,545	147,308	164,686	160,487	179,817	187,462	191,126	Claims on Official Entities	**32bx**
Claims on Private Sector	8,971	12,068	16,073	20,009	26,787	35,556	44,457	52,343	63,667	66,633	73,351	72,617	75,345	76,611	78,737	Claims on Private Sector	**32d**
Money	67,821	79,814	95,030	118,717	133,468	156,907	191,432	207,106	225,038	244,495	260,927	281,926	313,318	368,670	419,916	Money	**34**
Quasi-Money	10,781	16,068	19,736	26,340	32,645	41,505	67,156	83,113	91,775	104,624	116,939	135,636	160,346	194,800	276,181	Quasi-Money	**35**
Restricted Deposits	17,535	11,262	10,156	11,039	16,104	18,659	30,119	24,411	26,708	27,182	33,235	22,776	20,327	28,394	40,542	Restricted Deposits	**36b**
Other Items (Net)	−4,151	−15,504	−13,752	−12,823	−5,791	3,986	98,863	64,364	100,397	104,759	125,069	120,452	95,889	116,148	133,178	Other Items (Net)	**37r**
Money plus Quasi-Money	78,601	95,882	114,766	145,057	166,113	198,412	258,588	290,219	316,813	349,119	377,866	417,562	473,663	563,470	696,097	Money plus Quasi-Money	**35l**
Interest Rates *Percent Per Annum*																	
Discount Rate (End of Period)	5.00	5.00	5.00	5.00	5.00	5.00	5.00	5.00	5.00	5.00	5.00	5.00	5.00	5.00	5.00	Discount Rate (End of Period)	**60**
Deposit Rate	4.0	4.0	4.0	4.0	4.0	4.0	4.0	4.0	4.0	4.0	4.0	4.0	4.0	4.0	4.0	Deposit Rate	**60l**
Lending Rate	9.0	9.0	9.0	9.0	9.0	9.0	9.0	9.0	9.0	9.0	9.0	9.0	9.0	9.0	9.0	Lending Rate	**60p**
Prices and Production *Period Averages*																	
Wholesale Prices	†31.6	46.5	52.9	64.5	73.5	75.5	81.9	93.5	100.0	103.2	105.8	105.2	103.2	....	....	Wholesale Prices	**63**
Consumer Prices	32.7	44.1	49.1	†58.6	63.9	70.9	80.3	92.6	100.0	108.2	110.3	109.4	107.3	106.8	....	Consumer Prices	**64**
Industrial Production	†62.5	61.0	70.2	77.2	82.6	†88.0	90.0	97.0	100.0	101.0	107.0	109.0	109.0	....	....	Industrial Production	**66**
Period Averages																	
Labor Force	....	....	....	3,485	....	....	....	....	....	....	....	4,411	4,527	4,937	....	Labor Force	**67d**
Employment	....	....	2,883	....	3,250	....	....	....	....	....	....	....	....	....	....	Employment	**67e**
Unemployment	....	....	177	....	235	....	....	....	....	....	....	....	....	....	....	Unemployment	**67c**
Unemployment Rate (%)	....	....	5.8	....	6.8	....	....	....	....	....	....	....	....	....	....	Unemployment Rate (%)	**67r**

Syrian Arab Republic

	1972	1973	1974	1975	1976	1977	1978	1979	1980	1981	1982	1983	1984	1985	1986
International Transactions														*Millions of Pounds*	
Exports 70	1,098	1,341	2,914	3,441	4,141	4,199	4,160	6,453	8,273	8,254	7,954	7,548	7,275	6,427	5,199
Imports, c.i.f. 71	2,061	2,341	4,572	6,236	9,203	10,605	9,650	13,067	16,187	20,302	15,808	17,829	16,155	15,570	10,709
														1995=100	
Volume of Exports 72	34.5	32.1	†31.1	37.9	39.9	38.9	41.2	37.9	32.7	29.8	31.7	31.1	29.1	27.1	†26.2
Volume of Imports 73	†17.7	20.9	26.3	41.3	41.8	52.0	46.7	52.6	53.6	70.3	60.6	66.0	61.7	64.9	†61.1
Unit Value of Exports 74	†23.3	29.1	54.7	46.6	59.4	64.0	68.7	89.6	116.4	129.2	112.9	105.9	108.3	105.9	†78.0
Unit Value of Imports 75	†13.7	16.9	23.7	26.4	33.2	30.6	32.7	40.6	52.8	68.6	64.4	74.4	69.6	58.6	†69.6
Balance of Payments														*Millions of US Dollars:*	
Current Account, n.i.e. .... 78al d	....	....	....	....	....	–167	–64	896	251	–308	–250	–844	–794	–958	–504
Goods: Exports f.o.b. .... 78aa d	....	....	....	....	....	1,070	1,061	1,648	2,112	2,212	2,002	1,918	1,834	1,856	1,037
Goods: Imports f.o.b. .... 78ab d	....	....	....	....	....	–2,402	–2,204	–3,055	–4,010	–4,404	–3,636	–4,024	–3,687	–3,946	–2,363
Trade Balance .... 78ac d						–1,332	–1,142	–1,407	–1,898	–2,193	–1,633	–2,106	–1,853	–2,090	–1,326
Services: Credit .... 78ad d	....	....	....	....	....	330	259	376	365	431	483	560	512	656	566
Services: Debit .... 78ae d	....	....	....	....	....	–418	–579	–590	–521	–814	–757	–854	–906	–975	–699
Balance on Goods & Services ...... 78af d						–1,421	–1,463	–1,621	–2,054	–2,575	–1,907	–2,400	–2,247	–2,409	–1,459
Income: Credit .... 78ag d	....	....	....	....	....	146	638	905	864	530	436	402	351	379	333
Income: Debit .... 78ah d	....	....	....	....	....	–35	–22	–15	–79	–111	–177	–148	–128	–139	–137
Balance on Gds, Serv. & Inc. ...... 78ai d						–1,310	–846	–731	–1,269	–2,156	–1,648	–2,146	–2,023	–2,169	–1,263
Current Transfers, n.i.e.: Credit ...... 78aj d	....	....	....	....	....	1,143	782	1,629	1,522	1,851	1,400	1,304	1,232	1,214	759
Current Transfers: Debit .... 78ak d	....	....	....	....	....	—	—	–2	–2	–3	–2	–3	–3	–2	—
Capital Account, n.i.e. .... 78bc d	....	....	....	....	....	—	—	—	—	—	—	—	—	—	—
Capital Account, n.i.e.: Credit .... 78ba d	....	....	....	....	....	—	—	—	—	—	—	—	—	—	—
Capital Account: Debit .... 78bb d	....	....	....	....	....	—	—	—	—	—	—	—	—	—	—
Financial Account, n.i.e. ...... 78bj d	....	....	....	....	....	337	385	124	196	287	175	714	1,035	789	591
Direct Investment Abroad .... 78bd d	....	....	....	....	....	—	—	—	—	—	—	—	—	—	—
Dir. Invest. in Rep. Econ., n.i.e. ...... 78be d	....	....	....	....	....	—	—	—	—	—	—	—	—	—	—
Portfolio Investment Assets .... 78bf d	....	....	....	....	....	—	—	—	—	—	—	—	—	—	—
Equity Securities .... 78bk d	....	....	....	....	....	—	—	—	—	—	—	—	—	—	—
Debt Securities .... 78bl d	....	....	....	....	....	—	—	—	—	—	—	—	—	—	—
Portfolio Investment Liab., n.i.e. ...... 78bg d	....	....	....	....	....	—	—	—	—	—	—	—	—	—	—
Equity Securities .... 78bm d	....	....	....	....	....	—	—	—	—	—	—	—	—	—	—
Debt Securities .... 78bn d	....	....	....	....	....	—	—	—	—	—	—	—	—	—	—
Financial Derivatives Assets .... 78bw d	....	....	....	....	....	....	....	....	....	....	....	....	....	....	....
Financial Derivatives Liabilities .... 78bx d	....	....	....	....	....	....	....	....	....	....	....	....	....	....	....
Other Investment Assets .... 78bh d	....	....	....	....	....	18	25	–148	47	–64	–172	–3	83	–50	–307
Monetary Authorities .... 78bo d	....	....	....	....	....	....	....	....	....	....	....	....	....	....	....
General Government .... 78bp d	....	....	....	....	....	–42	33	–33	–32	–104	52	–51	–20	–38	–236
Banks .... 78bq d	....	....	....	....	....	60	–8	–115	79	39	–224	48	103	–12	–71
Other Sectors .... 78br d	....	....	....	....	....	—	—	—	—	—	—	—	—	—	—
Other Investment Liab., n.i.e. .... 78bi d	....	....	....	....	....	318	360	272	149	351	346	716	952	839	898
Monetary Authorities .... 78bs d	....	....	....	....	....	–51	56	68	121	143	258	284	744	463	499
General Government .... 78bt d	....	....	....	....	....	228	359	127	9	–151	–179	189	290	–120	144
Banks .... 78bu d	....	....	....	....	....	54	–84	13	24	262	91	269	–62	260	99
Other Sectors .... 78bv d	....	....	....	....	....	87	29	64	–5	97	176	–27	–19	236	157
Net Errors and Omissions .... 78ca d	....	....	....	....	....	22	–424	–825	–701	–30	–17	–15	–25	–17	–26
Overall Balance .... 78cb d						192	–103	195	–254	–51	–92	–145	216	–186	61
Reserves and Related Items .... 79da d	....	....	....	....	....	–192	103	–195	254	51	92	145	–216	186	–61
Reserve Assets .... 79db d	....	....	....	....	....	–192	103	–196	255	51	92	145	–216	186	–61
Use of Fund Credit and Loans .... 79dc d	....	....	....	....	....	—	—	1	–1	—	—	—	—	—	—
Exceptional Financing .... 79de d	....	....	....	....	....	—	—	—	—	—	—	—	—	—	—
Government Finance														*Millions of Pounds:*	
Deficit (-) or Surplus 80	–327	–574	–740	–992	–2,332	–2,928	–2,935	303	–4,976	–4,157	....	....	....	....	–8,267
Revenue 81	2,346	2,766	4,285	8,698	9,058	10,320	7,341	9,201	13,759	14,844	....	....	....	....	24,128
Grants Received 81z	—	—	550	—	665	100	3,070	6,384	5,967	6,359	....	....	....	....	2,061
Expenditure 82	2,673	3,340	5,575	9,690	12,055	13,348	13,346	15,282	24,702	25,360	....	....	....	....	34,456
Financing															
Total Financing 84	....	....	....	....	2,332	2,928	2,935	–303	4,976	4,157	....	....	....	....	....
Domestic 84a	....	....	....	....	1,564	2,034	....	....	5,032	1,765	....	....	....	....	....
Foreign 85a	....	....	....	....	768	894	....	....	–99	1,598	....	....	....	....	....
Unallocable Financing 87c	....	....	....	....	—	—	....	....	43	794	....	....	....	....	....
National Accounts														*Millions of Pounds*	
Househ.Cons.Expend.,incl.NPISHs 96f	6,479	6,309	11,459	13,599	15,523	18,078	22,210	26,742	33,858	48,051	44,992	48,904	47,535	54,650	67,026
Government Consumption Expend. 91f	1,638	2,125	2,815	4,343	4,960	5,293	6,470	8,424	11,870	13,656	15,103	16,154	17,070	19,785	21,440
Exports of Goods and Services 90c	1,674	2,175	3,816	4,409	4,828	4,908	4,808	7,458	9,345	10,290	9,572	9,714	9,360	9,949	11,256
Gross Capital Formation 93	1,624	1,793	3,102	5,241	7,891	9,218	9,015	10,383	14,355	15,482	16,513	17,508	18,082	20,016	22,443
Imports of Goods and Services (-) 98c	2,187	2,541	5,347	6,996	8,479	10,984	10,114	14,033	18,168	21,687	17,149	19,549	18,083	21,175	22,232
Gross Domestic Product (GDP) 99b	9,228	9,861	15,845	20,597	24,725	27,013	32,389	38,974	51,270	65,777	68,788	73,291	75,342	83,225	99,933
Consumption of Fixed Capital 99cf	358	416	482	582	750	882	1,030	1,149	1,443	1,969	2,115	2,243	2,334	2,731	3,065
GDP Volume 1995 Prices 99b.p	....	....	....	....	....	....	....	....	....	....	....	....	....	....	....
GDP Volume (1995=100) .... 99bv p	30.1	27.6	34.2	40.9	45.4	44.8	†48.7	50.5	56.5	61.9	63.2	64.1	61.5	65.3	62.1
GDP Deflator (1995=100) .... 99bi p	5.4	6.3	8.1	8.8	9.5	10.6	†11.6	13.5	15.9	18.6	19.1	20.0	21.4	22.3	28.2
														Millions:	
Population 99z	6.71	6.94	7.19	7.44	7.72	8.02	†8.15	8.42	8.70	9.00	9.30	9.61	9.93	10.27	10.61

	1987	1988	1989	1990	1991	1992	1993	1994	1995	1996	1997	1998	1999	2000	2001		
International Transactions																		
Millions of Pounds																		
Exports	15,192	15,093	33,740	47,280	38,500	34,720	35,319	34,200	40,000	44,890	43,960	32,440	38,880	†216,190	....	Exports	70
Imports, c.i.f.	27,915	25,040	23,544	26,940	31,070	39,178	46,468	61,370	52,860	60,390	45,210	43,720	43,010	†187,530	....	Imports, c.i.f.	71
1995=100																		
Volume of Exports	†27.5	30.5	46.7	59.9	65.3	62.9	94.6	102.4	100.0	98.2	109.6	....	....	....	....	Volume of Exports	72
Volume of Imports	†46.0	39.5	37.1	40.3	43.1	57.7	90.7	111.3	100.0	100.8	87.9	....	....	....	....	Volume of Imports	73
Unit Value of Exports	†72.2	68.9	85.6	111.1	90.0	75.6	74.4	80.0	100.0	105.6	83.3	....	....	....	....	Unit Value of Exports	74
Unit Value of Imports	†70.3	86.4	83.9	84.7	97.5	83.1	78.8	89.0	100.0	105.9	90.7	....	....	....	....	Unit Value of Imports	75
Balance of Payments																		
Minus Sign Indicates Debit																		
Current Account, n.i.e.	–298	–151	1,222	1,762	699	55	–203	–791	263	40	461	58	201	1,062	....	Current Account, n.i.e.	78al *d*
Goods: Exports f.o.b.	1,357	1,348	3,013	4,156	3,438	3,100	3,253	3,329	3,858	4,178	4,057	3,142	3,806	5,146		Goods: Exports f.o.b.	78aa *d*
Goods: Imports f.o.b.	–2,226	–1,986	–1,821	–2,062	–2,354	–2,941	–3,512	–4,604	–4,004	–4,516	–3,603	–3,320	–3,590	–3,723		Goods: Imports f.o.b.	78ab *d*
Trade Balance	–869	–639	1,192	2,094	1,084	159	–259	–1,275	–146	–338	454	–178	216	1,423		*Trade Balance*	78ac *d*
Services: Credit	600	667	893	874	1,065	1,281	1,595	1,863	1,899	1,792	1,582	1,666	1,651	1,700		Services: Credit	78ad *d*
Services: Debit	–690	–636	–792	–892	–1,002	–1,102	–1,442	–1,611	–1,537	–1,555	–1,489	–1,491	–1,612	–1,667		Services: Debit	78ae *d*
Balance on Goods & Services	–958	–608	1,293	2,075	1,146	338	–106	–1,023	216	–101	547	–3	255	1,456		*Balance on Goods & Services*	78af *d*
Income: Credit	359	382	452	430	415	619	432	638	444	534	421	369	356	345		Income: Credit	78ag *d*
Income: Debit	–459	–461	–745	–831	–1,096	–1,214	–1,064	–997	–1,004	–1,017	–1,006	–839	–899	–1,224		Income: Debit	78ah *d*
Balance on Gds, Serv. & Inc.	–1,058	–687	1,000	1,674	465	–258	–738	–1,382	–344	–584	–38	–473	–288	577		*Balance on Gds, Serv. & Inc.*	78ai *d*
Current Transfers, n.i.e.: Credit	761	537	227	91	238	321	543	597	610	630	504	533	491	495		Current Transfers, n.i.e.: Credit	78aj *d*
Current Transfers: Debit	–1	–1	–5	–3	–4	–8	–8	–6	–3	–6	–5	–2	–2	–10		Current Transfers: Debit	78ak *d*
Capital Account, n.i.e.	—	—	—	—	—	—	28	102	20	26	18	27	80	63	....	Capital Account, n.i.e.	78bc *d*
Capital Account, n.i.e.: Credit	—	—	—	—	—	—	28	102	20	26	18	27	80	63		Capital Account, n.i.e.: Credit	78ba *d*
Capital Account: Debit	—	—	—	—	—	—	—	—	—	—	—	....	....	....		Capital Account: Debit	78bb *d*
Financial Account, n.i.e.	399	85	–1,708	–1,836	–515	–50	598	1,159	521	782	65	196	173	–392	....	Financial Account, n.i.e.	78bj *d*
Direct Investment Abroad									100	89	80	82	263	270		Direct Investment Abroad	78bd *d*
Dir. Invest. in Rep. Econ., n.i.e.	—	—	—	—	—	—	109	251	—	—	—	—	—	—		Dir. Invest. in Rep. Econ., n.i.e.	78be *d*
Portfolio Investment Assets	—	—	—	—	—	—	—	—	—	—	—	—	—	—		Portfolio Investment Assets	78bf *d*
Equity Securities	—	—	—	—	—	—	—	—	—	—	—	—	—	—		Equity Securities	78bk *d*
Debt Securities	—	—	—	—	—	—	—	—	—	—	—	—	—	—		Debt Securities	78bl *d*
Portfolio Investment Liab., n.i.e.	—	—	—	—	—	—	—	—	—	—	—	—	—	—		Portfolio Investment Liab., n.i.e.	78bg *d*
Equity Securities	—	—	—	—	—	—	—	—	—	—	—	—	—	—		Equity Securities	78bm *d*
Debt Securities	—	—	—	—	—	—	—	—	—	—	—	—	—	—		Debt Securities	78bn *d*
Financial Derivatives Assets	....	....	....	....	....	....	....	....	....	....	....	....	....	....		Financial Derivatives Assets	78bw *d*
Financial Derivatives Liabilities																Financial Derivatives Liabilities	78bx *d*
Other Investment Assets	–530	–256	–1,580	–2,008	–1,294	–1,175	–815	–718	1,510	1,660	1,496	1,422	1,332	1,049		Other Investment Assets	78bh *d*
Monetary Authorities	....	....	....	....	....	....			—	—	—	—	—	—		Monetary Authorities	78bo *d*
General Government	–511	–196	–977	–831	–194	–74	—	—	—	—	—	—	—	—		General Government	78bp *d*
Banks	–18	–60	–198	–493	–313	–241	—	—	1,510	1,660	1,496	1,422	1,332	1,049		Banks	78bq *d*
Other Sectors	—	—	–405	–684	–787	–860	–815	–718	—	—	—	—	—	—		Other Sectors	78br *d*
Other Investment Liab., n.i.e.	929	341	–128	172	779	1,126	1,304	1,626	–1,089	–967	–1,511	–1,308	–1,422	–1,711		Other Investment Liab., n.i.e.	78bi *d*
Monetary Authorities	776	–69	103	154	7	28	11	20	—	—	—	—	—	—		Monetary Authorities	78bs *d*
General Government	207	297	–757	–731	–35	173	–121	339	—	—	—	—	—	—		General Government	78bt *d*
Banks	48	45	–64	–143	–190	–226	–128	–147	–1,089	–967	–1,511	–1,308	–1,422	–1,711		Banks	78bu *d*
Other Sectors	–102	68	590	892	997	1,151	1,542	1,414	—	—	—	—	—	—		Other Sectors	78bv *d*
Net Errors and Omissions	–23	34	420	110	–112	70	–119	96	35	139	–95	153	–195	–192	....	Net Errors and Omissions	78ca *d*
Overall Balance	79	–32	–66	36	72	76	304	566	839	987	449	434	259	541		*Overall Balance*	78cb *d*
Reserves and Related Items	–79	32	66	–36	–72	–76	–304	–566	–839	–987	–449	–434	–259	–541	....	Reserves and Related Items	79da *d*
Reserve Assets	–79	32	66	–36	–72	–76	–304	–566	–839	–987	–449	–434	–259	–541		Reserve Assets	79db *d*
Use of Fund Credit and Loans	—	—	—	—	—	—	—	—	—	—	—	—	—	—		Use of Fund Credit and Loans	79dc *d*
Exceptional Financing	—	—	—	—	—	—	—	—	—	—	—	....	....	....		Exceptional Financing	79de *d*
Government Finance																		
Year Ending December 31																		
Deficit (-) or Surplus	–3,355	2,319	–1,267	921	4,184	6,273	115	–18,860	–10,059	–1,577	–1,723	–5,534	5,827	....		Deficit (-) or Surplus	80
Revenue	28,276	38,181	48,374	58,639	70,965	85,788	92,619	111,892	131,002	152,231	179,202	180,437	196,127	....		Revenue	81
Grants Received	3,812	6,156	3,426	763	9,995	6,250	2,864	1,264	896	1,788	798	2	....	....		Grants Received	81z
Expenditure	35,443	42,018	53,067	58,481	76,776	85,765	95,368	132,016	141,957	155,596	181,723	185,973	190,300	....		Expenditure	82
Financing																		
Total Financing	....	....	....	....	....	....	....	....	....	....	....	....	....	....		Total Financing	84
Domestic	....	....	....	....	....	....	....	....	....	....	....	....	....	....		Domestic	84a
Foreign	....	....	....	....	....	....	....	....	....	....	....	....	....	....		Foreign	85a
Unallocable Financing	....	....	....	....	....	....	....	....	....	....	....	....	....	....		Unallocable Financing	87c
National Accounts																		
Millions of Pounds																		
Housel.Cons.Expend.,incl.NPISHs	98,496	152,683	141,717	184,389	231,883	274,195	303,988	348,865	378,143	489,728	515,411	542,374	575,866	579,627	....	Housel.Cons.Expend.,incl.NPISHs	96f
Government Consumption Expend.	22,945	24,529	33,433	38,502	47,582	53,588	56,239	68,019	76,709	81,316	84,994	88,521	86,857	98,403	....	Government Consumption Expend.	91f
Exports of Goods and Services	20,003	31,212	62,811	76,042	76,038	97,577	115,294	167,327	177,229	219,872	241,719	241,316	264,704	326,715	....	Exports of Goods and Services	90c
Gross Capital Formation	23,223	25,992	33,808	44,395	55,992	86,120	107,466	151,622	155,504	163,076	155,464	162,446	153,706	155,757	....	Gross Capital Formation	93
Imports of Goods and Services (-)	36,955	48,369	62,877	75,000	99,931	139,850	169,242	229,732	216,610	263,135	252,019	244,213	262,041	263,868	....	Imports of Goods and Services (-)	98c
Gross Domestic Product (GDP)	127,712	186,047	208,892	268,328	311,564	371,630	413,755	506,101	570,975	690,857	745,569	790,444	819,092	896,634	....	Gross Domestic Product (GDP)	99b
Consumption of Fixed Capital	4,212	6,299	7,843	9,824	10,958	15,958	14,492	17,674	20,344	26,257	30,151	31,668	34,282	39,264	....	Consumption of Fixed Capital	99cf
GDP Volume 1995 Prices	....	....	372,387	389,469	420,242	476,850	501,546	539,929	570,975	612,896	628,148	675,888	662,396	666,567		GDP Volume 1995 Prices	99b. *p*
GDP Volume (1995=100)	63.2	71.6	65.2	68.2	73.6	83.5	87.8	94.6	100.0	107.3	110.0	118.4	116.0	116.7		GDP Volume (1995=100)	99bv *p*
GDP Deflator (1995=100)	35.4	45.5	56.1	68.9	74.1	77.9	82.5	93.7	100.0	112.7	118.7	116.9	123.7	134.5		GDP Deflator (1995=100)	99bi *p*
Midyear Estimates																		
Population	10.97	11.34	11.72	12.12	12.53	12.96	13.39	13.84	14.15	14.62	15.10	15.60	16.11	16.32	16.72	Population	99z

(See notes in the back of the book.)

Tanzania

		1972	1973	1974	1975	1976	1977	1978	1979	1980	1981	1982	1983	1984	1985	1986
Exchange Rates														*Shillings per SDR:*		
Official Rate	aa	7.76	8.32	8.75	9.66	9.66	9.66	9.66	10.83	10.44	9.69	10.55	13.04	17.75	18.12	63.26
														Shillings per US Dollar:		
Official Rate	ae	7.14	6.90	7.14	8.26	8.32	7.96	7.41	8.22	8.18	8.32	9.57	12.46	18.11	16.50	51.72
Official Rate	rf	7.14	7.02	7.13	7.37ᵉ	8.38ᵉ	8.29ᵉ	7.71ᵉ	8.22ᵉ	8.20ᵉ	8.28ᵉ	9.28ᵉ	11.14ᵉ	15.29	17.47	32.70
Fund Position														*Millions of SDRs:*		
Quota	2f. s	42.0	42.0	42.0	42.0	42.0	42.0	55.0	55.0	82.5	82.5	82.5	107.0	107.0	107.0	107.0
SDRs	1b. s	6.7	6.6	1.7	1.2	5.1	5.6	6.1	2.8	—	.3	—	.1	.1	—	4.6
Reserve Position in the Fund	1c. s	6.9	10.5	—	—	—	—	—	—	—	1.7	—	—	—	—	—
Total Fund Cred.&Loans Outstg.	2tl	—	—	38.9	62.6	83.6	91.2	81.5	115.5	134.3	125.7	114.4	88.1	60.2	52.6	58.2
International Liquidity												*Millions of US Dollars Unless Otherwise Indicated:*					
Total Reserves minus Gold	1l. d	119.6	144.6	50.2	65.4	112.3	281.8	99.9	68.0	20.3	18.8	4.8	19.4	26.9	16.0	61.1
SDRs	1b. d	7.3	8.0	2.0	1.3	5.9	6.8	7.9	3.7	—	.4	—	.1	.1	—	5.6
Reserve Position in the Fund	1c. d	7.5	12.7	—	—	—	—	—	—	—	1.9	—	—	—	—	—
Foreign Exchange	1d. d	104.8	124.0	48.2	64.1	106.4	275.0	91.9	64.3	20.3	16.5	4.8	19.3	26.8	16.0	55.5
Monetary Authorities: Other Liab.	4.. d	6.2	3.7	21.6	26.4	2.4	37.1	41.2	17.9	5.5	—	6.8	18.9	.9	137.6	121.4
Deposit Money Banks: Assets	7a. d	97.1	100.1	113.1	91.9	82.9	91.8	84.5	122.5	172.1	127.5	170.0	206.0	86.8	52.5	39.7
Liabilities	7b. d	14.2	14.3	18.1	15.0	28.4	37.0	92.9	45.3	23.0	23.0	65.0	26.0	376.2	511.3	150.1
Monetary Authorities														*Billions of Shillings:*		
Foreign Assets	11	.83	1.04	.40	.55	.94	2.30	.76	.72	.38	.35	.27	.34	.51	.26	2.54
Claims on Central Government	12a	.55	.51	1.06	1.37	1.60	1.31	2.87	5.04	6.55	7.99	9.48	10.02	13.26	25.17	32.53
Claims on Deposit Money Banks	12e	.14	—	.90	1.01	.73	.38	.84	.23	.29	.47	.50	.34	.47	.01	1.73
Reserve Money	14	1.28	1.29	1.62	1.88	2.23	2.60	3.16	4.39	5.56	7.14	8.63	8.89	11.57	14.03	19.72
of which: Currency Outside DMBs	14a	1.20	1.20	1.52	1.76	2.07	2.38	2.92	4.06	5.25	6.61	7.99	8.19	10.47	12.67	18.31
Foreign Liabilities	16c	.04	.03	.49	.82	.83	1.18	1.09	1.40	1.45	1.22	1.27	1.38	1.08	3.22	9.96
Central Government Deposits	16d	—	.01	.03	.01	.01	.01	—	—	—	—	—	.08	.02	.08	1.61
Capital Accounts	17a	.18	.20	.22	.25	.19	.20	.17	.17	.22	.45	.30	.45	-.20	-.18	-.53
Other Items (Net)	17r	.02	.02	—	-.04	.01	—	.06	.03	-.01	—	.05	-.10	1.12	7.57	4.64
Deposit Money Banks														*Billions of Shillings:*		
Reserves	20	.08	.09	.11	.13	.16	.21	.29	.30	.32	.53	.62	.81	1.30	1.62	1.22
Foreign Assets	21	.69	.69	.81	.76	.69	.73	.63	1.01	1.41	1.06	1.63	1.57	.87	2.05	
Claims on Central Government	22a	.46	.61	.90	1.51	2.16	1.87	2.13	3.39	4.87	6.65	9.49	11.58	12.74	8.50	3.76
Claims on Official Entities	22bx	.85	1.24	2.21	2.63	3.08	3.65	5.01	5.60	6.14	7.19	7.77	8.68	12.01	16.20	19.73
Claims on Private Sector	22d	.63	.50	.61	.64	.54	.68	.98	1.03	1.14	1.22	1.71	1.89	1.39	2.40	2.94
Demand Deposits	24	1.13	1.58	1.94	2.53	3.26	4.00	3.91	6.38	8.10	8.79	10.33	12.37	10.14	12.80	17.50
Time, Savings,& Fgn.Currency Dep.	25	.76	.88	1.01	1.27	1.62	1.96	2.57	3.37	4.17	5.29	6.41	8.56	9.59	13.88	14.50
Foreign Liabilities	26c	.10	.10	.13	.12	.24	.29	.69	.37	.19	.19	.62	.32	6.81	11.72	38.58
Central Government Deposits	26d	.54	.53	.49	.65	.52	.29	.40	.47	.52	.79	1.44	.81	.85	.79	.73
Credit from Monetary Authorities	26g	.14	—	.90	1.02	.74	.38	.90	.26	.32	.28	.41	.40	.43	.50	1.24
Capital Accounts	27a	.14	.17	.21	.27	.34	.41	.52	.81	1.05	1.15	1.41	1.58	1.70	1.99	2.57
Other Items (Net)	27r	-.09	-.11	-.04	-.19	-.09	-.20	.05	-.33	-.48	.16	.59	1.48	-.51	-12.10	-45.43
Monetary Survey														*Billions of Shillings:*		
Foreign Assets (Net)	31n	1.38	1.61	.58	.36	.56	1.56	-.39	-.04	.15	.01	—	1.20	-5.84	-10.53	-13.13
Domestic Credit	32	2.02	2.40	4.34	5.57	6.90	7.28	10.66	14.69	18.25	22.33	27.07	31.32	38.53	51.40	56.66
Claims on Central Govt. (Net)	32an	.47	.58	1.44	2.22	3.23	2.89	4.60	7.96	10.90	13.84	17.54	20.72	25.13	32.80	33.95
Claims on Official Entities	32bx	.85	1.24	2.21	2.63	3.08	3.65	5.01	5.60	6.14	7.19	7.77	8.68	12.01	16.20	19.73
Claims on Private Sector	32d	.63	.50	.61	.64	.54	.68	.98	1.03	1.14	1.22	1.71	1.89	1.39	2.40	2.94
Money	34	2.33	2.77	3.46	4.28	5.33	6.38	6.83	10.44	13.35	15.40	18.32	20.56	20.61	25.47	35.81
Quasi-Money	35	.76	.88	1.01	1.27	1.62	1.96	2.57	3.37	4.17	5.29	6.41	8.56	9.59	13.88	14.50
Capital Accounts	37a	.32	.37	.43	.53	.53	.61	.68	.98	1.26	1.60	1.72	2.03	1.50	1.81	2.04
Other Items (Net)	37r	.01	.04	.05	-.10	.03	-.07	.18	-.07	-.32	.04	.63	1.36	.77	5.49	2.21
Money plus Quasi-Money	35l	3.09	3.65	4.46	5.55	6.95	8.35	9.40	13.81	17.52	20.69	24.73	29.13	30.20	39.34	50.31
Other Banking Institutions														*Billions of Shillings:*		
Deposits	45	.05	.06	.08	.09	.09	.11	.16	.18	.21	.25	.29	.36	.44	.55	.68
Liquid Liabilities	55l	3.14	3.72	4.54	5.64	7.04	8.46	9.56	13.99	17.73	20.94	25.02	29.48	30.64	39.89	50.99
Interest Rates														*Percent Per Annum*		
Discount Rate (End of Period)	60	4.27	4.27	4.77	4.77	4.77	4.77	4.77	4.77	4.77	4.00	4.00	4.00	4.00	5.00	8.00
Treasury Bill Rate	60c	....	....													
Savings Rate	60k	....	....	4.00	4.00	4.00	4.00	4.08	5.00	7.50	7.50	7.50	7.50	7.50	8.13	12.50
Deposit Rate	60l	....	....	4.00	4.00	4.00	4.00	4.00	4.00	4.00	4.00	4.00	4.00	4.00	4.50	8.50
Lending Rate	60p	....	....					6.54	11.50	11.50	12.00	12.00	13.00	13.00	12.29	18.50
Prices and Production														*Index Numbers (1995=100):*		
Consumer Prices	64	.7	.7	.9	1.1	1.2	†1.3	1.4	1.6	2.1	2.6	3.3	4.3	5.8	7.7	10.2
Manufacturing Production	66ey	....	....	....	....	....	....	....	....	....	....	....	....	....	96.2	93.3

Tanzania

1987	1988	1989	1990	1991	1992	1993	1994	1995	1996	1997	1998	1999	2000	2001		
															Exchange Rates	
End of Period																
118.77	168.21	252.71	279.69	334.58	460.63	659.13	764.16	818.10	856.51	842.70	958.87	1,094.34	1,046.58	1,151.54	Official Rate	aa
End of Period (ae) Period Average (rf)																
83.72	125.00	192.30	196.60	233.90	335.00	479.87	523.45	550.36	595.64	624.57	681.00	797.33	803.26	916.30	Official Rate	ae
64.26	99.29	143.38	195.06	219.16	297.71	405.27	509.63	574.76	579.98	612.12	664.67	744.76	800.41	876.41	Official Rate	rf
															Fund Position	
End of Period																
107.0	107.0	107.0	107.0	107.0	146.9	146.9	146.9	146.9	146.9	146.9	146.9	198.9	198.9	198.9	Quota	2f. s
.1	—	—	—	—					.1	.1	.1	.3	.2	.1	SDRs	1b. s
					10.0	10.0	10.0	10.0	10.0	10.0	10.0	10.0	10.0	10.0	Reserve Position in the Fund	1c. s
80.0	105.1	97.8	98.4	100.2	160.5	156.2	145.5	132.7	143.4	182.4	190.2	227.6	265.5	277.9	Total Fund Cred.&Loans Outstg.	2tl
															International Liquidity	
End of Period																
31.8	77.7	54.2	192.8	203.9	327.3	203.3	332.1	270.2	440.1	622.1	599.2	775.5	974.2	1,156.6	Total Reserves minus Gold	11.d
.1	—	—	—	—				.1	.1	.1	.4	.3	.1	.5	SDRs	1b.d
					13.7	13.7	14.6	14.8	14.3	13.5	14.0	13.7	13.0	12.5	Reserve Position in the Fund	1c.d
31.7	77.7	54.2	192.8	203.9	313.6	189.6	317.5	255.3	425.6	608.5	584.8	761.5	961.1	1,143.6	Foreign Exchange	1d.d
336.4	537.8	497.8	759.7	796.5	991.9	957.8	900.7	836.9	808.7	574.9	574.5	678.5	758.5	737.7	Monetary Authorities: Other Liab.	4..d
19.0	1.0	36.0	61.0	53.0	103.0	145.4	146.6	309.2	304.8	373.9	392.4	377.6	511.7	588.3	Deposit Money Banks: Assets	7a.d
553.0	640.0	9.0	21.0	28.0	307.0	93.6	20.9	51.4	8.1	7.8	3.6	2.2	5.2	17.6	Liabilities	7b.d
															Monetary Authorities	
2.66	9.71	10.43	37.90	47.70	139.86	†97.56	173.82	150.65	264.72	390.09	407.27	618.47	782.42	1,059.85	Foreign Assets	11
35.26	33.78	44.47	129.35	130.37	179.07	†262.10	270.60	326.37	299.38	269.69	234.08	302.79	296.67	296.67	Claims on Central Government	12a
19.78	43.98	55.56	60.09	58.32	2.30	†2.07	—	5.46	5.46	4.61	5.36	4.16	—	—	Claims on Deposit Money Banks	12e
27.88	36.65	43.76	62.28	70.35	112.75	†152.32	226.44	314.89	335.77	364.94	418.73	508.67	556.43	584.37	Reserve Money	14
24.55	31.70	41.09	57.92	63.60	95.45	†122.17	176.31	244.31	257.66	287.88	307.80	384.86	392.40	411.64	*of which: Currency Outside DMBs*	14a
37.66	84.90	120.44	176.87	212.67	366.80	†506.18	517.26	499.09	509.17	373.50	397.37	543.32	609.27	675.98	Foreign Liabilities	16c
2.23	.29	—	.25	13.46	—	†25.35	29.56	39.67	82.66	87.32	83.03	84.01	137.32	161.98	Central Government Deposits	16d
-15.01	-34.10	-41.65	-87.46	-105.77	-200.85	†-278.34	-242.89	-266.81	-238.07	-16.35	-2.23	45.81	25.67	102.44	Capital Accounts	17a
4.93	-.29	-12.11	75.39	45.69	42.54	-43.78	-85.94	-104.36	-119.97	-145.02	-250.20	-256.39	-249.60	-168.24	Other Items (Net)	17r
															Deposit Money Banks	
End of Period																
3.09	4.95	†4.83	6.89	10.29	14.38	†30.13	49.91	66.03	72.80	59.71	113.20	123.20	172.10	177.33	Reserves	20
1.57	2.23	†6.96	12.00	12.39	34.39	†69.78	76.74	170.16	181.55	233.56	267.26	301.08	410.99	539.06	Foreign Assets	21
3.64	17.30	†3.59	3.59	3.49	33.14	†93.39	124.41	181.09	261.94	247.39	312.75	331.26	403.76	295.70	Claims on Central Government	22a
46.62	62.34	†30.49	41.42	56.47	44.71	†49.26	57.18	46.83	17.34	16.22	3.06	4.72	2.98	1.02	Claims on Official Entities	22bx
5.85	8.02	†89.10	115.48	152.41	133.49	†186.31	222.98	201.02	116.56	166.75	239.86	302.17	333.26	403.49	Claims on Private Sector	22d
22.58	32.90	†42.62	55.08	75.20	90.66	†125.16	153.32	183.97	191.55	205.99	237.72	247.72	302.60	354.38	Demand Deposits	24
19.31	23.65	†32.83	52.33	76.26	116.24	†173.62	240.12	329.52	372.28	433.20	481.47	584.95	702.68	870.71	Time, Savings,& Fgn.Currency Dep.	25
46.32	79.97	†1.70	4.07	6.61	102.75	†44.94	10.92	28.26	4.83	4.88	2.46	1.77	4.16	16.17	Foreign Liabilities	26c
1.65	1.23	†1.74	2.24	3.49	5.00	†4.82	22.52	21.75	20.96	28.43	25.33	21.56	26.09	29.32	Central Government Deposits	26d
18.09	43.98	†51.45	62.68	60.69	73.99	†147.40	1.34	7.59	.16	12.76	—	5.43	—	—	Credit from Monetary Authorities	26g
3.84	3.81	†8.30	8.67	10.99	-12.45	†48.62	139.91	-29.91	75.62	43.11	61.64	27.26	113.33	133.74	Capital Accounts	27a
-51.01	-90.71	†-3.66	-5.69	1.81	-116.10	†-115.69	-36.90	123.95	-15.21	-4.74	127.52	173.73	174.23	12.28	Other Items (Net)	27r
															Monetary Survey	
End of Period																
-79.75	-152.93	-104.76	-131.05	-159.19	-295.30	-383.77	-277.62	-206.54	-67.72	245.27	274.70	374.46	579.98	906.76	Foreign Assets (Net)	31n
87.51	119.94	†167.04	287.36	325.80	401.60	†560.89	623.10	693.88	591.60	584.31	681.39	835.36	873.27	805.59	Domestic Credit	32
35.01	49.56	†47.44	130.45	116.92	223.39	†325.32	342.94	446.03	457.70	401.34	438.47	528.48	537.03	401.08	Claims on Central Govt. (Net)	32an
46.62	62.34	†30.49	41.42	56.47	44.71	†49.26	57.18	46.83	17.34	16.22	3.06	4.72	2.98	1.02	Claims on Official Entities	32bx
5.85	8.02	†89.10	115.48	152.41	133.49	†186.31	222.98	201.02	116.56	166.75	239.86	302.17	333.26	403.49	Claims on Private Sector	32d
47.13	64.60	†83.72	113.00	138.80	186.12	†247.33	329.63	428.28	449.21	493.87	545.52	632.58	695.01	766.02	Money	34
19.31	23.65	†32.83	52.33	76.26	116.24	†173.62	240.12	329.52	372.28	433.20	481.47	584.95	702.68	870.71	Quasi-Money	35
-11.18	-30.28	†-33.35	-78.79	-94.78	-213.29	†-229.73	-102.98	-296.72	-162.45	26.76	59.41	73.07	139.00	236.18	Capital Accounts	37a
.57	-120.78	-22.03	69.76	46.32	1.05	-14.11	-121.28	26.26	-135.17	-124.25	-130.30	-80.78	-83.44	-160.55	Other Items (Net)	37r
66.44	88.25	†116.54	165.33	215.06	302.36	†420.95	569.74	757.81	821.50	927.07	1,026.98	1,217.53	1,397.69	1,636.73	Money plus Quasi-Money	35l
															Other Banking Institutions	
End of Period																
.87	.11	.16	.26	1.86	.80	†1.12	1.67	16.82	16.60	17.56	17.88	24.38	28.44	34.15	Deposits	45
67.31	88.36	†116.70	165.60	216.92	303.16	†422.07	571.42	774.63	838.09	944.63	1,044.87	1,241.91	1,426.13	1,670.88	Liquid Liabilities	55l
															Interest Rates	
Percent Per Annum																
12.50	14.50	15.50	....	....	14.50	14.50	67.50	47.90	19.00	16.20	17.60	20.20	10.70	8.70	Discount Rate (*End of Period*)	60
						34.00	35.09	40.33	15.30	9.59	11.83	10.05	9.78	4.14	Treasury Bill Rate	60c
22.04	24.17	26.00	....	....	....	24.00	23.98	22.70	14.25	8.79	8.29	8.27	6.55	4.15	Savings Rate	60k
15.75	17.46	17.00	....	....	....	....	....	24.63	13.59	7.83	7.75	7.75	7.39	4.81	Deposit Rate	60l
27.50	29.63	31.00	....	....	....	31.00	39.00	42.83	†33.97	26.27	22.89	21.89	21.58	20.26	Lending Rate	60p
															Prices and Production	
Period Averages																
13.3	17.4	†21.9	29.8	38.3	46.7	58.5	77.9	100.0	121.0	140.4	158.4	170.9	181.0	190.3	Consumer Prices	64
102.9	110.6	112.5	109.6	112.5	105.8	105.8	96.2	100.0	101.0	106.7	115.4	119.2	136.5	....	Manufacturing Production	66ey

Tanzania

738

International Transactions		1972	1973	1974	1975	1976	1977	1978	1979	1980	1981	1982	1983	1984	1985	1986
																Millions of Shillings
Exports	70	2,313	2,581	2,878	2,764	3,683	4,198	3,669	4,096	4,192	4,706	4,144	4,138	4,388	4,265	11,285
Imports, c.i.f.	71	2,883	3,479	5,377	5,710	5,350	6,161	8,798	9,073	10,308	9,739	10,499	8,877	9,653	14,959	30,577
Balance of Payments																*Millions of US Dollars:*
Current Account, n.i.e.	78al d	...	...	...	...	−27.8	−66.1	−467.3	−346.5	−522.2	−407.6	−524.1	−305.2	−359.5	−375.1	−322.0
Goods: Exports f.o.b.	78aa d					490.4	538.5	476.0	545.7	582.7	613.0	412.9	383.2	398.5	328.5	335.9
Goods: Imports f.o.b.	78ab d					−555.7	−646.7	−992.5	−960.7	−1,089.1	−1,061.3	−952.0	−708.4	−760.3	−869.2	−913.3
Trade Balance	78ac d					−65.3	−108.2	−516.5	−415.0	−506.4	−448.2	−539.1	−325.2	−361.8	−540.7	−577.5
Services: Credit	78ad d					135.4	106.8	130.2	140.0	165.1	184.8	114.5	106.3	105.8	105.6	100.7
Services: Debit	78ae d					−141.0	−163.9	−245.3	−237.6	−295.0	−252.1	−193.0	−161.5	−174.8	−208.7	−219.0
Balance on Goods & Services	78af d					−70.9	−165.4	−631.6	−512.6	−636.4	−515.5	−617.6	−380.4	−430.7	−643.8	−695.7
Income: Credit	78ag d					7.4	11.1	19.1	11.6	14.0	10.9	2.8	1.7	1.6	2.5	9.5
Income: Debit	78ah d					−25.7	−31.8	−24.8	−20.2	−27.6	−32.2	−27.7	−29.2	−89.4	−100.4	−108.9
Balance on Gds, Serv. & Inc.	78ai d					−89.2	−186.1	−637.3	−521.3	−649.9	−536.8	−642.5	−407.9	−518.5	−741.7	−795.1
Current Transfers, n.i.e.: Credit	78aj d					105.5	144.9	194.8	200.3	153.2	152.5	136.5	127.6	180.4	394.2	501.0
Current Transfers: Debit	78ak d					−44.2	−24.9	−24.8	−25.6	−25.5	−23.2	−18.1	−24.9	−21.4	−27.6	−28.0
Capital Account, n.i.e.	78bc d					−6.8	−5.3	−6.0	—	—	—	—	—	—	—	—
Capital Account, n.i.e.: Credit	78ba d					—	—	.1	—	—	—	—	—	—	—	—
Capital Account: Debit	78bb d					−6.8	−5.3	−6.1	—	—	—	—	—	—	—	—
Financial Account, n.i.e.	78bj d					60.4	111.0	214.2	150.3	218.7	242.5	193.4	278.5	11.3	−72.3	9.5
Direct Investment Abroad	78bd d	...	...	...	...	—	—	—	—	—	—	—	—	—	—	—
Dir. Invest. in Rep. Econ., n.i.e.	78be d	...	...	...	...	—	—	—	—	—	—	—	—	—	—	—
Portfolio Investment Assets	78bf d	...	...	...	...	—	—	—	—	—	—	—	—	—	—	—
Equity Securities	78bk d					—	—	—	—	—	—	—	—	—	—	—
Debt Securities	78bl d					—	—	—	—	—	—	—	—	—	—	—
Portfolio Investment Liab., n.i.e.	78bg d					—	—	—	—	—	—	—	—	—	—	—
Equity Securities	78bm d					—	—	—	—	—	—	—	—	—	—	—
Debt Securities	78bn d					—	—	—	—	—	—	—	—	—	—	—
Financial Derivatives Assets	78bw d												...	...	...	...
Financial Derivatives Liabilities	78bx d												...	...	...	...
Other Investment Assets	78bh d					8.2	−4.9	14.1	−47.2	—	—	—	—	—	—	—
Monetary Authorities	78bo d															
General Government	78bp d					—	—	—	—	—	—	—	—	—	—	—
Banks	78bq d					8.2	−4.9	14.1	−47.2	—	—	—	—	—	—	—
Other Sectors	78br d					—	—	—	—	—	—	—	—	—	—	—
Other Investment Liab., n.i.e.	78bi d					52.2	116.0	200.1	197.5	218.7	242.5	193.4	278.5	11.3	−72.3	9.5
Monetary Authorities	78bs d					−25.3	38.4	17.5	—	−8.1	−16.3	−.1	−1.0	−3.0	−.9	89.6
General Government	78bt d					95.9	53.6	94.5	138.1	130.1	167.2	134.3	177.7	−95.4	−39.4	−24.6
Banks	78bu d					13.4	7.0	51.1	−38.9	—	—	—	—	—	—	—
Other Sectors	78bv d					−31.8	17.0	37.0	98.3	96.7	91.6	59.1	101.8	109.8	−32.0	−55.5
Net Errors and Omissions	78ca d					−4.3	69.1	8.4	23.8	−46.6	78.7	58.2	−61.7	126.9	−39.6	−40.1
Overall Balance	78cb d					21.5	108.7	−250.7	−172.4	−350.1	−86.3	−272.5	−88.4	−221.2	−487.0	−352.5
Reserves and Related Items	79da d					−21.5	−108.7	250.7	172.4	350.1	86.3	272.5	88.4	221.2	487.0	352.5
Reserve Assets	79db d					−46.5	−163.7	199.2	30.2	54.9	8.4	13.9	−14.6	−7.5	10.9	−45.0
Use of Fund Credit and Loans	79dc d					24.2	8.8	−12.0	43.4	25.0	−11.3	−12.4	−28.1	−28.4	−7.5	7.3
Exceptional Financing	79de d					.8	46.2	63.5	98.9	270.1	89.1	271.0	131.1	257.1	483.7	390.3
International Investment Position																*Millions of US Dollars*
Assets	79aa d	...	...	...	...	...	...	...	...	...	...	...	...	...	...	...
Direct Investment Abroad	79ab d	...	...	...	...	...	...	...	...	...	...	...	...	...	...	...
Portfolio Investment	79ac d	...	...	...	...	...	...	...	...	...	...	...	...	...	...	...
Equity Securities	79ad d	...	...	...	...	...	...	...	...	...	...	...	...	...	...	...
Debt Securities	79ae d	...	...	...	...	...	...	...	...	...	...	...	...	...	...	...
Financial Derivatives	79al d	...	...	...	...	...	...	...	...	...	...	...	...	...	...	...
Other Investment	79af d	...	...	...	...	...	...	...	...	...	...	...	...	...	...	...
Monetary Authorities	79ag d	...	...	...	...	...	...	...	...	...	...	...	...	...	...	...
General Government	79ah d	...	...	...	...	...	...	...	...	...	...	...	...	...	...	...
Banks	79ai d	...	...	...	...	...	...	...	...	...	...	...	...	...	...	...
Other Sectors	79aj d	...	...	...	...	...	...	...	...	...	...	...	...	...	...	...
Reserve Assets	79ak d	...	...	...	...	...	...	...	...	...	...	...	...	...	...	...
Liabilities	79la d	...	...	...	...	...	...	...	...	...	...	...	...	...	...	...
Dir. Invest. in Rep. Economy	79lb d	...	...	...	...	...	...	...	...	...	...	...	...	...	...	...
Portfolio Investment	79lc d	...	...	...	...	...	...	...	...	...	...	...	...	...	...	...
Equity Securities	79ld d	...	...	...	...	...	...	...	...	...	...	...	...	...	...	...
Debt Securities	79le d	...	...	...	...	...	...	...	...	...	...	...	...	...	...	...
Financial Derivatives	79ll d	...	...	...	...	...	...	...	...	...	...	...	...	...	...	...
Other Investment	79lf d	...	...	...	...	...	...	...	...	...	...	...	...	...	...	...
Monetary Authorities	79lg d	...	...	...	...	...	...	...	...	...	...	...	...	...	...	...
General Government	79lh d	...	...	...	...	...	...	...	...	...	...	...	...	...	...	...
Banks	79li d	...	...	...	...	...	...	...	...	...	...	...	...	...	...	...
Other Sectors	79lj d	...	...	...	...	...	...	...	...	...	...	...	...	...	...	...

International Transactions

	1987	1988	1989	1990	1991	1992	1993	1994	1995	1996	1997	1998	1999	2000	2001	Code
Millions of Shillings																
Exports	18,512	27,041	51,463	64,571	74,708	123,966	181,147	265,177	390,378	455,519	459,549	391,805	412,204	531,058	681,186	70
Imports, c.i.f.	59,340	80,828	146,705	265,984	338,990	449,480	615,990	765,757	968,910	804,949	818,703	967,080	1,161,841	1,219,385	1,502,636	71
Minus Sign Indicates Debit																
Balance of Payments																
Current Account, n.i.e.	-407.4	-356.6	-335.1	-558.9	-737.5	-714.2	-1,048.0	-710.9	-646.3	-510.9	-629.8	-956.5	-745.9	-480.3	....	78ald
Goods: Exports f.o.b.	287.9	386.5	415.1	407.8	363.0	406.4	446.9	519.4	682.5	764.1	715.3	589.5	542.9	665.7	....	78aad
Goods: Imports f.o.b.	-1,000.5	-1,033.0	-1,070.1	-1,186.3	-1,229.9	-1,335.2	-1,304.0	-1,309.3	-1,340.0	-1,213.1	-1,164.4	-1,365.3	-1,368.3	-1,339.8	....	78abd
Trade Balance	-712.6	-646.5	-655.0	-778.5	-866.9	-928.8	-857.1	-789.9	-657.5	-449.0	-449.1	-775.9	-825.4	-674.1	....	78acd
Services: Credit	105.3	117.4	117.3	130.6	142.3	169.9	317.9	418.2	582.6	608.1	494.1	555.0	624.4	614.6	....	78add
Services: Debit	-224.4	-263.4	-272.5	-287.7	-300.1	-341.3	-717.0	-503.3	-799.4	-953.4	-797.3	-988.1	-762.3	-670.3	....	78aed
Balance on Goods & Services	-831.7	-792.5	-810.2	-935.6	-1,024.7	-1,100.2	-1,256.2	-875.0	-874.2	-794.3	-752.4	-1,209.0	-963.3	-729.8	....	78afd
Income: Credit	5.9	3.2	5.4	5.9	7.9	8.2	21.9	30.9	31.8	50.3	44.9	35.1	54.8	59.5	....	78agd
Income: Debit	-164.7	-188.4	-182.5	-190.9	-192.5	-236.8	-172.9	-153.4	-142.0	-105.4	-168.2	-173.7	-127.6	-139.0	....	78ahd
Balance on Gds, Serv. & Inc.	-990.4	-977.8	-987.3	-1,120.7	-1,209.3	-1,328.9	-1,407.2	-997.5	-984.5	-849.4	-875.7	-1,347.7	-1,036.0	-809.3	....	78aid
Current Transfers, n.i.e.: Credit	609.9	642.9	682.0	592.8	504.5	650.1	389.8	311.5	370.5	370.9	313.6	426.6	413.4	406.0	....	78ajd
Current Transfers: Debit	-27.0	-21.7	-29.8	-31.0	-32.7	-35.5	-30.7	-25.0	-32.3	-32.3	-67.7	-35.5	-123.3	-77.0	....	78akd
Capital Account, n.i.e.	—	—	—	327.2	353.7	302.4	205.2	262.6	190.9	191.0	360.6	422.9	322.5	331.7	....	78bcd
Capital Account, n.i.e.: Credit	—	—	—	327.2	353.7	302.4	205.2	262.6	190.9	191.0	360.6	422.9	322.5	331.7	....	78bad
Capital Account: Debit	—	—	—	—	—	—	—	—	—	—	—	—	—	—	....	78bbd
Financial Account, n.i.e.	60.4	33.9	21.8	68.1	120.0	70.2	130.5	-91.7	66.7	-92.8	3.6	77.6	80.8	-123.8	....	78bjd
Direct Investment Abroad	—	—	—	—	—	—	—	—	—	—	—	—	—	—	....	78bdd
Dir. Invest. in Rep. Econ., n.i.e.	—	—	—	—	—	12.2	20.5	50.0	119.9	150.1	157.9	172.3	183.4	193.5	....	78bed
Portfolio Investment Assets	—	—	—	—	—	—	—	—	—	—	—	—	—	—	....	78bfd
Equity Securities	—	—	—	—	—	—	—	—	—	—	—	—	—	—	....	78bkd
Debt Securities	—	—	—	—	—	—	—	—	—	—	—	—	—	—	....	78bld
Portfolio Investment Liab., n.i.e.	—	—	—	—	—	—	—	—	—	—	—	—	—	—	....	78bgd
Equity Securities	—	—	—	—	—	—	—	—	—	—	—	—	—	—	....	78bmd
Debt Securities	—	—	—	—	—	—	—	—	—	—	—	—	—	—	....	78bnd
Financial Derivatives Assets	....	....	....												....	78bwd
Financial Derivatives Liabilities	....	....	....												....	78bxd
Other Investment Assets					—	—	56.7	11.9	-75.1	20.1	-85.0	-50.7	14.8	10.2	....	78bhd
Monetary Authorities							—	—	—							78bod
General Government																78bpd
Banks						—	-68.6	-75.6	-162.5	-19.6	-85.0	-50.7	14.8	10.2		78bqd
Other Sectors							125.3	87.5	87.4	39.7						78brd
Other Investment Liab., n.i.e.	60.4	33.9	21.8	68.1	120.0	58.1	53.3	-153.6	21.8	-262.9	-69.3	-44.0	-117.5	-327.5	....	78bid
Monetary Authorities	64.9	-1.6	-3.1	4.4	-5.5	8.8	.2	11.9	5.9	14.9	24.6	-48.7	—	—		78bsd
General Government	-9.5	30.7	26.2	54.7	115.0	31.3	-56.5	-202.0	-71.2	-225.9	-32.4	—	-75.7	-320.6		78btd
Banks	—	—	—	1.9	1.4	.2	-1.4	6.7	22.9	-23.5	-67.6	-17.6	-1.4	29.2		78bud
Other Sectors	5.0	4.8	-1.3	7.2	9.1	17.7	111.0	29.8	64.2	-28.5	6.2	22.4	-40.4	-36.1		78bvd
Net Errors and Omissions	55.5	-61.3	-13.5	37.7	1.6	137.7	137.3	121.4	30.0	158.6	-31.9	-53.5	269.3	137.7	....	78cad
Overall Balance	-291.5	-383.9	-326.8	-126.0	-262.1	-203.9	-575.1	-418.6	-358.7	-254.0	-297.5	-509.4	-73.4	-134.8	....	78cbd
Reserves and Related Items	291.5	383.9	326.8	126.0	262.1	203.9	575.1	418.6	358.7	254.0	297.5	509.4	73.4	134.8	....	79dad
Reserve Assets	30.7	-45.9	23.5	-140.8	-85.3	-255.4	60.5	-122.8	43.3	-195.4	-206.9	22.3	-280.6	-205.8	....	79dbd
Use of Fund Credit and Loans	28.4	34.2	-9.3	—	2.1	83.7	-6.0	-15.0	-19.6	15.7	53.2	9.6	51.5	27.6	....	79dcd
Exceptional Financing	232.4	395.6	312.6	266.7	345.4	375.6	520.7	556.8	335.1	433.8	451.2	477.5	302.5	312.9	....	79ded
Millions of US Dollars																
International Investment Position																
Assets	....	....	....	....	....	497.3	370.2	477.0	578.8	744.4	995.6	991.4	1,153.0	1,485.7	....	79aad
Direct Investment Abroad						—	—	—	—	—	—	—	—	—	....	79abd
Portfolio Investment						—	—	—	—	—	—	—	—	—	....	79acd
Equity Securities						—	—	—	—	—	—	—	—	—	....	79add
Debt Securities						—	—	—	—	—	—	—	—	—	....	79aed
Financial Derivatives						—	—	—	—	—	—	—	—	—	....	79ald
Other Investment						103.0	145.4	146.6	309.2	304.8	373.9	392.4	377.6	511.7	....	79afd
Monetary Authorities						....	....	....	....	....	....	....	....	....	....	79agd
General Government						....	....	....	....	....	....	....	....	....	....	79ahd
Banks						....	....	....	....	....	....	....	....	....	....	79aid
Other Sectors						....	....	....	....	....	....	....	....	....	....	79ajd
Reserve Assets						394.3	224.8	330.4	269.6	439.6	621.7	599.0	775.4	974.1	....	79akd
Liabilities						8,485.8	8,679.4	9,037.5	9,645.7	9,965.9	7,271.3	7,229.0	7,648.1	7,614.6	....	79lad
Dir. Invest. in Rep. Economy						10.7	24.3	71.0	224.2	351.7	490.2	619.0	700.0	887.7	....	79lbd
Portfolio Investment						—	—	—	—	—	—	—	—	—	....	79lcd
Equity Securities						—	—	—	—	—	—	—	—	—	....	79ldd
Debt Securities						—	—	—	—	—	—	—	—	—	....	79led
Financial Derivatives						—	—	—	—	—	—	—	—	—	....	79lld
Other Investment						8,475.1	8,655.1	8,966.5	9,421.5	9,614.2	6,781.1	6,610.0	6,948.1	6,726.9	....	79lfd
Monetary Authorities						220.7	214.6	212.4	197.2	206.2	246.0	315.9	370.3	431.2	....	79lgd
General Government						7,443.9	7,494.4	8,129.9	8,510.0	8,614.9	6,337.2	6,200.6	6,050.4	5,771.7	....	79lhd
Banks												19.4	.9			79lid
Other Sectors						810.5	946.1	624.2	714.3	793.0	197.8	74.1	526.4	523.9	....	79ljd

Tanzania

738

Government Finance

Millions of Shillings:

		1972	1973	1974	1975	1976	1977	1978	1979	1980	1981	1982	1983	1984	1985	1986
Deficit (-) or Surplus	80	−555	−360	−851	−1,865	−1,805	−855	−1,936	−4,134	−4,046	−5,026	−7,024	−5,383	−5,669	−8,408	−8,643
Total Revenue and Grants	81y	1,893	2,579	3,399	4,321	4,531	5,522	7,805	7,947	9,963	9,729	10,363	13,610	14,740	20,101	23,067
Revenue	81	1,855	2,295	3,000	3,944	4,062	4,896	7,096	6,833	8,963	8,571	9,406	12,581	13,506	18,639	22,032
Grants	81z	38	284	399	377	469	626	709	1,114	1,000	1,158	957	1,029	1,234	1,462	1,035
Exp. & Lending Minus Repay.	82z	2,448	2,938	4,249	6,186	6,336	6,377	9,741	12,081	14,008	14,755	17,387	18,993	20,409	28,509	31,710
Expenditure	82	2,376	2,995	4,230	6,163	6,326	6,270	9,622	11,921	13,943	14,755	17,387	18,993	20,409	28,509	31,710
Lending Minus Repayments	83	72	−57	20	24	11	108	119	160	65	—	—	—	—	—	—
Financing																
Overall Adjustment	80x	....	....	....	....	....	....	....	....	....	....	....	....	....	....	....
Total Financing	80h	555	360	851	1,865	1,805	855	1,936	4,134	4,046	....	7,024	5,384	5,669	8,408	8,643
Domestic	84a	312	151	629	1,269	1,357	116	1,153	3,407	3,291	....	6,227	4,736	5,630	7,988	8,638
Foreign	85a	243	209	222	597	448	739	783	727	755	612	797	648	39	420	5

National Accounts

Billions of Shillings:

		1972	1973	1974	1975	1976	1977	1978	1979	1980	1981	1982	1983	1984	1985	1986
Househ.Cons.Expend.,incl.NPISHs	96f	7.82	9.28	12.04	14.17	15.38	17.98	23.36	25.50	32.49	35.04	43.66	52.97	64.06	84.04	118.04
Government Consumption Expend.	91f	1.49	1.97	2.60	3.26	3.99	4.31	5.59	5.96	5.49	6.11	9.53	9.44	13.84	18.56	23.62
Gross Fixed Capital Formation	93e	2.36	2.60	3.03	3.54	5.16	6.66	7.33	8.59	8.63	10.62	14.62	11.90	15.06	18.97	35.35
Changes in Inventories	93i	.08	.16	.48	.46	.44	.86	.76	.87	1.06	1.50	−.19	−.56	−.98	1.90	−5.87
Exports of Goods and Services	90c	2.75	2.94	3.40	3.46	5.30	5.63	4.69	5.13	5.54	5.99	5.29	5.46	7.71	7.59	14.28
Imports of Goods and Services (-)	98c	3.33	3.84	5.57	5.89	5.84	6.57	9.57	9.76	11.09	10.16	10.99	9.69	14.30	18.83	37.02
GDP, Production Based	99bp	11.17	13.10	15.99	19.01	24.42	28.87	32.17	36.28	42.12	49.10	61.93	68.52	85.39	112.21	148.39
Statistical Discrepancy	99bs	....	....	....	....	....	....	....	....	....	....	....	....	....	....	....
Net Primary Income from Abroad	98.n	−.04	−.05	−.04	−.05	−.10	−.09	−.05	−.07	−.11	−.18	−.23	−.31	−1.34	−1.66	−3.39
Gross National Income (GNI)	99a	11.13	13.05	15.96	18.96	24.32	28.78	32.12	36.21	42.01	48.93	61.70	69.22	84.05	110.56	145.01
Net National Income	99e	10.52	12.18	15.12	18.05	23.41	27.77	30.99	34.94	40.47	47.38	60.13	67.60	82.17	108.08	141.24
GDP, Prod. Based, 1992 Prices	99bp*p*	....	....	....	....	....	....	....	....	....	....	....	....	....	....	....
GDP Volume (1995=100)	99bv*p*	....	....	....	....	....	....	....	....	....	....	....	....	....	....	....
GDP Deflator (1995=100)	99bi*p*	....	....	....	....	....	....	....	....	....	....	....	....	....	....	....

Millions:

		1972	1973	1974	1975	1976	1977	1978	1979	1980	1981	1982	1983	1984	1985	1986
Population	99z	14.00	14.37	14.76	15.31	†16.41	16.92	17.44	17.98	18.58	19.17	19.78	20.41	21.06	21.73	22.46

	1987	1988	1989	1990	1991	1992	1993	1994	1995	1996	1997	1998	1999	2000	2001		
Year Ending June 30																**Government Finance**	
	−15,406	−11,908	−14,698	−15,340	−47,324	9,601	−72,141	−104,515	−64,559	−21,269	77,143	−68,138	24,422	−114,472	−87,860	Deficit (-) or Surplus	80
	32,465	63,389	91,400	125,531	159,968	206,364	222,422	349,234	389,743	495,255	653,446	738,443	859,268	1,057,952	1,215,930	Total Revenue and Grants	81y
	29,321	47,480	70,415	97,867	137,093	173,566	164,109	242,444	331,238	448,373	572,030	619,084	689,324	777,645	929,624	Revenue	81
	3,144	15,909	20,985	27,664	22,875	32,798	58,313	106,790	58,505	46,882	81,416	119,359	169,944	280,307	286,306	Grants	81z
	47,871	75,297	106,098	140,871	207,292	161,474	263,413	374,962	398,024	420,522	515,390	730,338	816,706	1,168,779	1,311,928	Exp. & Lending Minus Repay.	82z
	47,871	75,297	106,098	140,871	207,292	161,474	263,413	374,962	398,024	420,522	515,390	730,338	816,706	1,168,779	1,305,035	Expenditure	82
															6,893	Lending Minus Repayments	83
																Financing	
	....	....	....	....	....	−35,289	−31,150	−78,787	−56,278	−96,002	−60,913	−76,243	−18,140	−3,644	8,139	Overall Adjustment	80x
	15,406	11,908	14,698	15,340	47,324	−9,601	72,141	104,515	64,559	21,269	−77,142	68,139	−24,424	114,472	87,860	Total Financing	80h
	12,315	−2,728	21,188	12,361	29,608	−32,277	44,144	40,557	61,603	56,169	−28,074	3,670	−5,740	9,055	−2,494	Domestic	84a
	3,091	14,636	−6,490	2,979	17,716	22,676	27,997	63,958	2,956	−34,900	−49,068	64,468	−18,684	105,417	90,354	Foreign	85a
Billions of Shillings																**National Accounts**	
	†269.31	416.01	523.19	687.71	887.12	1,133.19	1,445.37	1,931.98	2,532.84	3,130.07	3,968.07	4,909.25	5,667.44	6,069.58	....	Househ.Cons.Expend.,incl.NPISHs	96f
	†55.60	84.54	101.41	147.65	205.73	269.02	334.52	393.50	462.32	435.33	413.56	433.79	451.14	473.69	....	Government Consumption Expend.	91f
	†71.06	81.45	112.21	213.98	282.43	369.37	429.55	561.82	591.94	620.60	692.40	892.70	989.34	1,266.68	....	Gross Fixed Capital Formation	93e
	†1.70	2.05	2.36	2.93	3.65	3.68	4.00	4.84	5.86	6.64	8.40	9.91	10.31	14.37	....	Changes in Inventories	93i
	†29.56	48.81	71.93	104.84	111.47	170.44	310.31	473.89	727.18	751.16	762.81	748.97	885.94	1,060.53	....	Exports of Goods and Services	90c
	†86.52	141.34	208.54	311.13	365.41	539.10	823.21	1,002.88	1,253.74	1,203.52	1,208.30	1,565.33	1,703.76	1,675.88	....	Imports of Goods and Services (-)	98c
	†329.49	506.43	633.75	830.69	1,086.27	1,369.87	1,725.54	2,298.87	3,020.50	3,767.64	4,703.46	5,571.64	6,432.91	7,225.69	....	GDP, Production Based	99bp
	†−11.22	14.90	31.21	−15.28	−38.71	−36.72	25.01	−64.28	−45.89	27.36	93.04	142.34	104.88	16.72	....	Statistical Discrepancy	99bs
	†−12.68	−20.31	−30.01	−37.67	−40.61	−67.08	−61.19	−62.43	−63.38	−36.92	−75.78	−52.39	−55.19	−75.21	....	Net Primary Income from Abroad	98.n
	†316.81	486.11	603.74	793.02	1,045.67	1,302.79	1,664.35	2,236.44	2,957.12	3,730.72	4,654.39	5,496.32	6,385.72	7,150.48	....	Gross National Income (GNI)	99a
	†311.47	479.22	589.79	778.66	1,026.04	1,264.03	1,619.70	2,175.83	2,876.16	3,640.05	4,515.24	5,385.99	6,216.13	6,956.57	....	Net National Income	99e
	†1154.33	1,201.24	1,246.46	1,334.28	1,361.92	1,369.87	1,386.40	1,408.12	1,458.40	1,524.68	1,578.30	1,636.96	1,694.74	1,781.26	....	GDP, Prod. Based, 1992 Prices	99bp p
	†79.2	82.4	85.5	91.5	93.4	93.9	95.1	96.6	100.0	104.5	108.2	112.2	116.2	122.1	....	GDP Volume (1995=100)	99bv p
	†13.8	20.4	24.5	30.1	38.5	48.3	60.1	78.8	100.0	119.3	143.9	164.3	183.3	195.9	....	GDP Deflator (1995=100)	99bi p
Midyear Estimates																	
	23.22	24.00	23.89	24.57	25.27	25.99	26.73	27.49	28.28	29.09	29.98	†33.46	34.29	35.12	35.97	Population	99z

(See notes in the back of the book.)

Thialand

		1972	1973	1974	1975	1976	1977	1978	1979	1980	1981	1982	1983	1984	1985	1986
Exchange Rates															*Baht per SDR:*	
Official Rate	aa	22.721	24.579	24.946	23.881	23.701	24.780	26.564	26.906	26.312	26.771	25.372	24.080	26.613	29.273	31.962
															Baht per US Dollar:	
Official Rate	ae	20.928	20.375	20.375	20.400	20.400	20.400	20.390	20.425	20.630	23.000	23.000	23.000	27.150	26.650	26.130
Official Rate	rf	20.800	20.620	20.375	20.379	20.400	20.400	20.336	20.419	20.476	21.820	23.000	23.000	23.639	27.159	26.299
Fund Position															*Millions of SDRs:*	
Quota	2f. s	134	134	134	134	134	134	181	181	272	272	272	387	387	387	387
SDRs	1b. s	29	29	30	30	29	30	27	37	6	52	22	15	2	1	27
Reserve Position in the Fund	1c. s	34	34	34	34	34	34	—	—	—	—	—	29	29	29	29
of which: Outstg.Fund Borrowing	2c	—	—	—	—	—	—	—	—	—	—	—				
Total Fund Cred.&Loans Outstg.	2tl	—	—	—	—	67	81	191	278	273	737	767	994	922	1,021	874
International Liquidity													*Millions of US Dollars Unless Otherwise Indicated:*			
Total Reserves minus Gold	1l. d	963	1,207	1,758	1,679	1,798	1,813	2,009	1,843	1,560	1,732	1,538	1,607	1,921	2,190	2,804
SDRs	1b. d	31	34	36	35	34	37	35	49	8	61	25	16	2	1	33
Reserve Position in the Fund	1c. d	36	40	41	39	39	41	—	—	—	—	—	30	28	32	35
Foreign Exchange	1d. d	896	1,132	1,681	1,605	1,725	1,735	1,974	1,794	1,552	1,671	1,513	1,561	1,890	2,157	2,736
Gold (Million Fine Troy Ounces)	1ad	2.340	2.340	2.340	2.340	2.340	2.397	2.426	2.455	2.487	2.487	2.487	2.487	2.487	2.487	2.487
Gold (National Valuation)	1an d	89	99	100	96	95	102	548	1,286	1,466	995	1,114	949	768	813	972
Monetary Authorities: Other Liab.	4.. d															
Deposit Money Banks: Assets	7a. d	226	298	299	290	353	431	541	734	757	1,086	1,147	1,069	1,134	1,263	1,606
Liabilities	7b. d	198	366	421	466	542	891	1,488	1,877	1,379	1,462	1,276	1,865	1,875	1,722	1,215
Other Banking Insts.: Assets	7e. d															
Liabilities	7f. d	11	10	14	28	181	235	289	378	394	473	458	571	803	776	860
Monetary Authorities															*Billions of Baht:*	
Foreign Assets	11	23.3	27.6	39.4	37.7	37.9	38.3	51.8	63.9	62.4	62.7	61.0	58.8	72.9	80.0	98.6
Claims on Central Government	12a	15.6	17.0	14.1	13.8	19.6	26.1	35.3	44.0	59.9	71.3	87.7	100.7	96.0	106.9	98.9
Claims on Nonfin.Pub.Enterprises	12c	—	—	—	—	.1	.1	—	—	—	—	—	—	—	—	—
Claims on Deposit Money Banks	12e	1.3	2.9	3.9	7.2	5.4	5.9	8.0	16.5	16.5	19.8	20.7	22.9	23.8	25.5	34.8
Claims on Other Financial Insts.	12f	.3	.4	.7	.9	1.3	1.1	2.1	3.0	5.4	4.8	5.3	5.0	8.3	12.8	14.1
Reserve Money	14	20.1	23.7	26.8	29.7	33.5	36.6	42.9	50.3	57.3	61.1	68.4	75.6	79.8	86.5	95.3
of which: Currency Outside DMBs	14a	15.3	18.7	20.5	22.3	25.8	28.7	33.2	40.8	45.9	47.8	54.0	59.6	63.5	64.0	71.1
Money Market Instruments	16aa	—	—	—	—	—	—	—	—	—	—	—	—	—	—	—
Foreign Liabilities	16c	—	—	—	—	1.6	2.0	5.1	7.5	7.2	19.7	19.5	23.9	24.5	29.9	27.9
Central Government Deposits	16d	6.5	8.0	10.5	7.2	5.4	4.6	5.9	5.8	6.7	5.9	6.5	5.8	5.7	8.0	10.3
Capital Accounts	17a	14.0	16.4	20.8	22.5	23.0	27.6	43.6	63.7	72.5	75.0	79.6	81.6	93.4	103.3	117.3
Other Items (Net)	17r	-.2	-.1	—	.1	.8	.6	-.2	.2	.7	-3.0	.7	.4	-2.3	-2.6	-4.6
Deposit Money Banks															*Billions of Baht:*	
Reserves	20	3.4	3.6	5.2	6.5	†6.3	6.8	8.4	7.6	10.4	11.8	12.8	15.0	14.6	21.2	22.1
Other Claims on Monetary Author.	20n					†										
Foreign Assets	21	4.7	6.1	6.1	5.9	†7.2	8.8	11.0	15.0	15.6	25.0	26.4	24.6	30.8	33.7	42.0
Claims on Central Government	22a	13.8	14.9	15.8	17.6	†21.1	22.6	24.5	24.2	29.2	38.9	54.1	53.1	80.6	77.7	104.8
Claims on Nonfin.Pub.Enterprises	22c	.5	.9	1.2	1.4	†2.1	2.8	3.9	4.6	10.4	10.1	12.9	12.0	13.0	13.6	14.6
Claims on Private Sector	22d	33.0	47.1	63.6	77.3	†87.6	111.8	145.1	177.8	195.3	231.0	273.2	371.7	433.5	481.2	501.5
Claims on Other Financial Insts.	22f	1.6	2.0	3.7	6.6	†8.0	11.2	13.7	16.9	19.6	18.0	21.0	25.1	34.0	32.5	36.3
Demand Deposits	24	8.7	10.5	11.7	12.0	†15.1	16.4	21.1	22.2	25.1	25.6	24.2	22.5	24.5	21.1	30.5
Time, Savings,& Fgn.Currency Dep.	25	35.4	43.7	55.9	68.5	†84.3	105.4	125.6	142.0	180.3	219.0	284.9	367.5	449.1	507.6	569.3
Foreign Liabilities	26c	4.1	7.5	8.6	9.5	†11.1	18.2	30.3	38.3	28.4	33.6	29.3	42.9	50.9	45.9	31.7
Central Government Deposits	26d	2.6	3.0	3.4	3.3	†4.7	5.0	5.7	7.6	7.8	11.4	10.8	12.7	16.5	19.7	20.9
Credit from Monetary Authorities	26g	1.3	2.9	4.0	7.3	†5.5	6.0	8.1	16.7	16.7	20.2	20.9	23.4	24.3	26.1	33.6
Liabilities to Other Banking Insts	26i	—	—	—	—	†.6	.3	.2	.8	1.1	1.6	2.7	2.7	2.1	4.8	3.2
Capital Accounts	27a	4.4	5.7	8.0	9.8	†10.2	12.1	15.0	18.2	19.5	21.5	24.6	28.1	36.3	42.4	44.1
Other Items (Net)	27r	.6	1.4	3.9	4.9	†.6	.6	.4	.3	1.6	2.0	3.0	1.8	2.6	-7.7	-12.2
Monetary Survey															*Billions of Baht:*	
Foreign Assets (Net)	31n	23.9	26.2	36.9	34.1	†32.4	26.9	27.4	33.1	42.4	34.3	38.6	16.5	28.3	37.8	80.8
Domestic Credit	32	55.8	71.5	85.2	107.1	†129.7	166.2	213.3	257.5	305.8	357.3	437.5	549.7	643.9	697.9	739.7
Claims on Central Govt. (Net)	32an	20.3	20.9	16.0	20.9	†30.5	39.1	48.2	54.8	74.7	92.9	124.5	135.3	154.4	156.9	172.4
Claims on Nonfin.Pub.Enterprises	32c	.5	.9	1.2	1.4	†2.1	2.9	3.9	4.6	10.4	10.1	12.9	12.0	13.0	13.6	14.6
Claims on Private Sector	32d	33.1	47.2	63.6	77.4	†87.7	112.0	145.4	178.1	195.7	231.4	273.8	372.3	434.2	482.0	502.3
Claims on Other Financial Insts	32f	1.9	2.4	4.4	7.4	†9.3	12.2	15.8	19.9	25.0	22.8	26.3	30.1	42.3	45.4	50.4
Money	34	24.8	29.9	32.7	34.7	†41.4	45.4	54.5	63.5	71.4	73.9	78.9	83.0	88.8	85.8	102.4
Quasi-Money	35	35.4	43.7	55.9	68.5	†84.3	105.4	125.6	142.0	180.3	219.0	284.9	367.5	449.1	507.6	569.3
Money Market Instruments	36aa	—	—	—	—	†	—	—	—	—	—	—	—	—	—	—
Liabilities to Other Banking Insts	36i	—	—	—	—	†.6	.3	.2	.8	1.1	1.6	2.7	2.7	2.1	4.8	3.2
Capital Accounts	37a	18.4	22.2	28.9	32.3	†33.2	39.7	58.7	81.9	91.9	96.5	104.2	109.6	129.6	145.7	161.4
Other Items (Net)	37r	1.1	1.9	4.6	5.7	†2.6	2.3	1.7	2.3	3.4	.7	5.3	3.4	2.4	-8.3	-15.8
Money plus Quasi-Money	35l	60.2	73.6	88.7	103.2	†125.7	150.8	180.2	205.5	251.8	292.9	363.8	450.5	537.9	593.5	671.8
Other Banking Institutions																
Development Institutions																*Billions of Baht:*
Cash	40	.2	.3	.4	.4	†1.9	2.7	4.4	4.6	4.1	5.6	3.4	2.9	4.3	4.9	4.2
Other Claims on Monetary Author	40n					†										
Foreign Assets	41	....	....	....	....	†	—	—	—	—	—	—	—	—	—	—
Claims on Central Government	42a	—	—	—	—	†	—	—	.7	1.5	—	.2	.3	—	.3	.1
Claims on Nonfin.Pub.Enterprises	42c	—	—	—	—	†	—	—	—	—	—	—	—	—	—	.1
Claims on Private Sector	42d	2.3	2.6	3.6	6.1	†9.0	11.5	14.0	18.2	24.0	28.1	30.4	32.4	38.3	43.3	45.5
Demand Deposits	44	—	—	—	—	†.4	.4	.3	.4	.5	.6	1.0	1.7	4.1	6.5	8.0
Time and Savings Deposits	45	.3	.4	.7	1.2	†1.4	1.9	2.3	2.4	3.1	3.8	3.8	4.3	5.5	5.2	6.1
Bonds	46ab	.2	.2	.2	.2	†.4	.2	.2	.2	.9	2.0	2.1	2.6	2.9	2.5	1.7
Long-Term Foreign Liabilities	46cl	.2	.2	.3	.6	†.9	1.4	2.7	4.8	5.9	7.6	8.3	9.3	13.5	16.3	18.2
Central Govt. Lending Funds	46f	.1	.1	.4	.4	†.6	.6	.8	.6	.7	.8	.6	.5	.8	.7	.7
Credit from Monetary Authorities	46g	.3	.4	.7	.8	†1.3	1.2	2.1	2.6	4.6	4.2	4.7	4.2	4.1	4.6	3.6
Credit from Deposit Money Banks	46h	—	—	.2	1.7	†4.4	6.3	7.8	9.3	9.5	9.7	10.0	9.3	9.8	10.7	11.1
Capital Accounts	47a	1.3	1.5	1.5	1.5	†1.9	2.3	2.8	3.2	3.2	3.7	4.7	5.1	6.2	7.0	6.7
Other Items (Net)	47r	—	—	—	—	†-.3	-.1	-.5	—	1.1	1.1	-1.2	-1.4	-4.4	-5.0	-6.1

	1987	1988	1989	1990	1991	1992	1993	1994	1995	1996	1997	1998	1999	2000	2001		
Exchange Rates																	
End of Period																	
Official Rate	35.566	33.965	33.761	35.979	36.161	35.090	35.081	36.628	37.445	36.826	†63.748	51.662	51.428	56.374	55.575	Official Rate	aa
End of Period (ae) Period Average (rf)																	
	25.070	25.240	25.690	25.290	25.280	25.520	25.540	25.090	25.190	25.610	†47.247	36.691	37.470	43.268	44.222	Official Rate	ae
	25.723	25.294	25.702	25.585	25.517	25.400	25.320	25.150	24.915	25.343	31.364	41.359	37.814	40.112	44.432	Official Rate	rf
Fund Position																	
End of Period																	
	387	387	387	387	387	574	574	574	574	574	574	574	1,082	1,082	1,082	Quota	2f.s
	42	45	13	9	6	9	16	22	30	41	358	278	188	63	4	SDRs	1b.s
	29	29	29	32	155	243	272	285	319	333	—	—	—	—	—	Reserve Position in the Fund	1c.s
	—	—	—	—	—	—	—	—	—	—	—	—	—	—	—	of which: Outstg.Fund Borrowing	2c
	686	492	207	1	—	—	—	—	—	—	1,800	2,300	2,500	2,350	1,338	Total Fund Cred.&Loans Outstg.	2tl
International Liquidity																	
End of Period																	
	4,007	6,097	9,515	13,305	17,517	20,359	24,473	29,332	35,982	37,731	26,179	28,825	34,063	32,016	32,355	Total Reserves minus Gold	1l.d
	60	61	16	13	8	12	22	32	45	60	482	391	258	83	5	SDRs	1b.d
	41	39	38	45	222	335	373	416	474	480	—	—	—	—	—	Reserve Position in the Fund	1c.d
	3,906	5,997	9,461	13,247	17,287	20,012	24,078	28,884	35,463	37,192	25,697	28,434	33,805	31,933	32,350	Foreign Exchange	1d.d
	2.476	2.476	2.476	2.476	2.476	2.474	2.474	2.474	2.474	2.474	2.474	2.474	2.474	2.367	2.480	Gold (Million Fine Troy Ounces)	1ad
	1,204	1,015	993	968	899	823	967	947	963	914	713	711	718	645	686	Gold (National Valuation)	1and
	1	—	4	3	4	5	6	6	5	4	4,733	7,967	9,390	8,960	6,651	Monetary Authorities: Other Liab.	4..d
	1,538	1,782	2,733	2,229	2,872	3,046	6,165	6,739	9,365	7,028	8,665	12,605	15,158	16,642	16,923	Deposit Money Banks: Assets	7a.d
	1,482	2,444	3,319	4,340	4,902	6,567	13,799	31,086	46,214	48,781	40,307	29,058	19,165	13,070	10,439	Liabilities	7b.d
	—	—	—	—	—	—	—	27	34	72	100	407	403	403	332	Other Banking Insts.: Assets	7e.d
	857	869	1,021	1,557	1,894	2,518	3,323	4,035	5,939	8,748	6,973	5,550	4,437	3,683	2,805	Liabilities	7f.d
Monetary Authorities																	
End of Period																	
	130.5	179.3	269.7	360.6	465.1	539.1	649.1	759.0	929.7	988.8	1,270.7	1,083.4	1,303.3	1,413.2	1,478.9	Foreign Assets	11
	92.5	47.2	36.2	57.9	54.9	60.6	50.7	32.5	29.7	33.5	31.8	170.7	139.7	109.0	146.6	Claims on Central Government	12a
									8.4	17.9	71.5	75.0	64.0	48.3	33.4	Claims on Nonfin.Pub.Enterprises	12c
	42.0	57.8	41.6	42.7	38.0	37.1	21.2	26.4	37.8	55.9	309.4	158.6	85.9	59.2	45.2	Claims on Deposit Money Banks	12e
	13.6	15.0	16.1	17.4	18.6	22.4	25.2	39.9	47.5	76.6	438.7	511.3	393.9	439.8	338.9	Claims on Other Financial Insts.	12f
	116.7	134.0	156.7	185.8	210.5	248.0	288.1	329.9	404.3	458.9	531.4	507.6	785.8	684.5	615.3	Reserve Money	14
	86.7	99.0	119.0	137.5	149.3	180.2	208.6	241.9	284.1	304.3	334.0	318.3	472.4	406.8	440.9	of which: Currency Outside DMBs	14a
								18.1	16.9	28.5	330.5	541.6	172.9	217.9	220.5	Money Market Instruments	16aa
	24.4	16.7	7.1	.1	.1	.1	.2	.1	.1	.1	338.4	411.1	480.4	537.6	439.6	Foreign Liabilities	16c
	9.0	15.0	58.2	115.5	173.9	201.6	213.7	235.8	328.5	341.7	283.3	96.6	81.5	45.8	38.3	Central Government Deposits	16d
	136.0	138.4	148.6	172.0	202.2	231.8	263.1	306.8	337.8	377.8	803.2	814.0	1,013.2	1,159.7	1,092.4	Capital Accounts	17a
	-7.4	-4.8	-7.0	5.3	-10.1	-22.5	-18.9	-33.0	-34.4	-34.4	-164.6	-371.9	-547.1	-576.0	-363.3	Other Items (Net)	17r
Deposit Money Banks																	
End of Period																	
	25.7	32.4	33.8	51.6	60.4	60.9	73.5	79.7	117.8	165.8	203.6	145.7	143.0	112.8	186.0	Reserves	20
								5.5	5.9	17.5	262.2	356.4	94.8	155.0	129.7	Other Claims on Monetary Author.	20n
	38.6	45.0	70.2	56.4	72.6	77.7	157.5	169.1	235.9	180.0	409.4	462.5	568.0	720.1	748.4	Foreign Assets	21
	115.6	124.3	123.3	110.7	82.9	69.7	50.3	41.8	40.7	20.2	15.6	154.7	249.2	306.3	318.0	Claims on Central Government	22a
	15.0	14.5	15.9	18.1	44.7	53.2	76.5	94.2	108.4	112.7	99.9	108.5	135.1	123.9	150.0	Claims on Nonfin.Pub.Enterprises	22c
	614.6	796.1	1,045.4	1,408.8	1,696.9	2,045.1	2,536.5	3,304.1	4,089.2	4,688.5	5,729.6	5,299.6	5,014.5	4,211.6	3,774.7	Claims on Private Sector	22d
	51.7	52.8	60.4	69.0	94.2	113.1	126.6	158.0	213.4	213.9	331.3	173.1	233.8	512.2	673.2	Claims on Other Financial Insts.	22f
	44.5	48.1	53.9	55.0	70.0	66.1	82.4	96.4	94.3	106.1	86.6	93.9	94.9	114.0	134.4	Demand Deposits	24
	676.2	807.6	1,032.4	1,333.7	1,610.0	1,868.1	2,210.9	2,482.9	2,922.3	3,303.0	3,910.6	4,311.6	4,279.1	4,505.8	4,662.6	Time, Savings,& Fgn.Currency Dep.	25
	37.2	61.7	85.3	109.8	123.9	167.6	352.4	780.0	1,164.1	1,249.3	1,904.4	1,066.2	718.1	565.5	461.6	Foreign Liabilities	26c
	23.6	28.4	32.7	35.6	50.5	76.5	92.7	122.5	135.5	178.1	190.5	229.8	242.3	239.6	252.6	Central Government Deposits	26d
	42.0	57.6	41.2	42.3	37.6	36.3	21.2	24.9	36.2	53.8	313.1	154.5	48.3	25.5	17.1	Credit from Monetary Authorities	26g
	1.8	7.3	14.9	15.4	10.4	14.9	20.0	55.9	86.3	85.7	118.2	56.9	152.8	142.9	126.4	Liabilities to Other Banking Insts	26i
	57.5	68.3	83.1	111.3	143.5	170.2	220.6	369.8	471.3	600.2	690.8	1,067.7	1,162.3	716.7	644.0	Capital Accounts	27a
	-21.5	-13.9	5.6	11.5	5.7	19.9	20.6	-80.2	-98.7	-177.6	-162.6	-280.0	-259.5	-168.3	-318.8	Other Items (Net)	27r
Monetary Survey																	
End of Period																	
	107.5	145.9	247.5	307.1	413.7	449.1	454.0	148.0	1.4	-80.7	-562.6	68.6	672.7	1,030.1	1,326.0	Foreign Assets (Net)	31n
	871.2	1,007.4	1,207.2	1,530.9	1,767.6	2,085.9	2,559.3	3,312.1	4,073.4	4,643.4	6,244.6	6,166.5	5,906.3	5,465.6	5,143.8	Domestic Credit	32
	175.5	128.1	68.6	17.5	-86.7	-147.8	-205.5	-284.1	-393.6	-466.1	-426.4	-1.0	65.1	130.0	173.7	Claims on Central Govt. (Net)	32an
	15.0	14.5	15.9	18.1	44.7	53.2	76.5	94.2	116.8	130.7	171.3	183.5	199.1	172.1	183.4	Claims on Nonfin.Pub.Enterprises	32c
	615.4	796.9	1,046.2	1,408.8	1,696.9	2,045.1	2,536.5	3,304.1	4,089.2	4,688.3	5,729.6	5,299.6	5,014.5	4,211.6	3,774.7	Claims on Private Sector	32d
	65.3	67.9	76.6	86.4	112.8	135.5	151.8	197.9	261.0	290.5	770.1	684.4	627.6	951.9	1,012.1	Claims on Other Financial Insts.	32f
	132.4	148.5	174.7	195.4	222.4	249.7	296.2	346.4	388.3	423.7	430.1	451.0	739.7	684.3	640.0	Money	34
	676.2	807.6	1,032.4	1,333.7	1,610.0	1,868.1	2,210.9	2,482.9	2,922.3	3,303.0	3,910.6	4,311.6	4,279.1	4,505.8	4,662.6	Quasi-Money	35
								12.7	11.0	11.1	68.4	185.2	78.1	62.9	90.8	Money Market Instruments	36aa
	1.8	7.3	14.9	15.4	10.4	14.9	20.0	55.9	86.3	85.7	118.2	56.9	152.8	142.9	126.4	Liabilities to Other Banking Insts	36i
	193.5	206.7	231.7	283.3	345.7	402.1	483.7	676.6	809.1	977.9	1,493.9	1,881.7	2,175.5	1,876.4	1,736.4	Capital Accounts	37a
	-25.1	-16.9	1.0	10.2	-7.1	.2	2.4	-114.4	-142.3	-238.6	-339.2	-651.3	-846.1	-776.6	-786.4	Other Items (Net)	37r
	808.6	956.1	1,207.1	1,529.1	1,832.4	2,117.8	2,507.1	2,829.4	3,310.6	3,726.7	4,340.7	4,762.6	5,018.8	5,190.1	5,302.6	Money plus Quasi-Money	35l
Other Banking Institutions																	
Development Institutions																	
End of Period																	
	5.0	6.1	13.9	15.7	16.0	8.1	12.5	19.8	18.3	39.8	51.0	46.9	23.3	24.0	20.8	Cash	40
										17.4	43.0	17.3	38.4	47.5		Other Claims on Monetary Author	40n
	—	—	—	—	—	—	—	—	1.0	4.0	14.4	15.0	16.1	14.5		Foreign Assets	41
	—	—	.8	—	.1	.1	—	—	.3	.2	—	30.4	23.7	16.0	15.0	Claims on Central Government	42a
	—	—	—	—	—	—	—	—	.6	.1	.5	.4	1.2	8.2		Claims on Nonfin.Pub.Enterprises	42c
	49.0	55.3	69.7	94.0	121.2	159.3	209.1	270.5	365.7	498.2	674.6	678.6	686.1	734.7	758.0	Claims on Private Sector	42d
	8.6	12.4	20.7	26.7	36.7	43.8	46.4	60.9	54.3	40.8	52.3	69.3	80.1	63.7	80.5	Demand Deposits	44
	6.6	8.1	11.6	16.7	21.9	28.0	44.9	56.1	100.7	88.3	189.8	233.7	190.9	261.3	281.4	Time and Savings Deposits	45
	3.0	5.5	10.3	15.0	25.7	37.0	65.7	94.6	144.7	151.3	167.0	183.7	188.8	189.3	193.2	Bonds	46ab
	19.1	19.3	19.9	21.7	20.2	23.1	26.0	29.9	33.1	91.4	206.1	160.6	139.6	130.5	98.0	Long-Term Foreign Liabilities	46cl
	.7	.4	.5	1.4	1.4	1.4	3.0	1.7	4.2	100.9	56.4	89.6	88.0	97.1	110.6	Central Govt. Lending Funds	46f
	4.0	4.1	4.8	6.0	6.9	8.6	9.2	9.0	8.5	32.2	32.0	19.8	18.3	20.4	22.6	Credit from Monetary Authorities	46g
	12.3	14.1	14.5	15.3	17.1	12.5	7.6	11.6	7.1	5.2	6.2	4.8	2.0	2.9	3.3	Credit from Deposit Money Banks	46h
	7.3	7.7	11.8	12.3	15.4	17.0	25.7	35.3	41.7	49.9	60.6	79.0	110.3	119.0	135.6	Capital Accounts	47a
	-7.6	-10.1	-9.7	-5.3	-8.0	-3.9	-6.8	-8.8	-9.9	-20.2	-23.4	-26.7	-52.3	-53.7	-61.2	Other Items (Net)	47r

Thailand

	1972	1973	1974	1975	1976	1977	1978	1979	1980	1981	1982	1983	1984	1985	1986
Finance and Securities Companies														*Billions of Baht:*	
Reserves ....40.. f	...	...	...	...	1.2	1.2	1.4	2.0	2.0	3.9	5.8	4.1	3.6	4.8	3.8
Other Claims on Mon. Author. .....40n. f	...	...	...	...	—	—	—	—	—	—	—	—	—	—	—
Claims on Central Government ....42a. f	...	...	...	...	—	—	—	—	—	3.5	5.5	5.3	9.5	14.7	16.7
Claims on Nonfin.Pub.Enterprises ......42c. f	...	...	...	...	.9	1.5	2.3	2.6	3.0	.2	.5	.7	.5	.9	1.1
Claims on Private Sector ....42d. f	...	...	...	...	22.5	30.7	44.0	45.0	50.3	59.1	71.5	83.3	88.0	90.1	95.5
Bonds ....46ab f					15.3	21.3	32.1	33.8	41.3	53.2	66.6	70.1	66.3	76.9	80.0
Foreign Liabilities ....46c. f					2.8	3.4	3.2	2.9	2.3	3.3	2.3	3.8	8.3	4.4	4.3
Credit from Monetary Authorities ......46g. f									.3	1.1	.2	.2	.7	3.9	7.8	10.4
Cred. from Deposit Money Banks ....46h. f					3.1	4.1	5.0	5.3	5.2	4.1	6.0	10.0	15.1	15.2	17.2
Capital Accounts ....47a. f					2.8	4.2	6.3	8.2	7.9	8.0	8.8	10.3	9.0	9.0	9.7
Other Items (Net) ....47r. f					.6	.5	1.0	−.8	−2.3	−2.0	−.6	−1.6	−1.1	−2.7	−4.4
Government Savings Bank														*Billions of Baht:*	
Cash ....40.. g	.1	.2	.7	.7	.3	.3	.4	.8	.8	.8	.8	1.6	4.6	3.4	7.6
Other Claims on Mon. Author. ....40n. g												—	—	—	—
Claims on Central Government ....42a. g	8.4	10.8	11.9	12.7	14.1	16.3	17.5	20.3	24.7	26.2	31.1	38.8	46.6	57.7	81.1
Claims on Nonfin.Pub.Enterprises......42c. g	.1	.1	.1	.1	.4	.6	.5	.6	.4	.9	.8	.8	.1	.1	.4
Claims on Private Sector ....42d. g	.3	.3	.3	.3	.3	.3	.3	.3	.4	.3	.4	.6	.8	1.0	1.2
Demand Deposits ....44.. g	.1	.1	.3	.2	2.7	3.3	4.0	4.7	5.7	6.3	7.7	9.0	10.1	12.1	15.1
Time and Savings Deposits ....45.. g	6.4	8.3	9.5	10.2	8.9	10.7	11.4	14.4	16.7	18.8	21.9	27.1	32.5	40.3	45.3
Bonds ....46ab g	1.4	1.6	1.6	1.6	1.5	1.6	1.7	1.8	1.7	1.8	2.2	2.8	3.2	3.5	20.4
Central Government Deposits ....46d. g	—	—	—	.1	.1	.2	.1	.2	.1	.1	.2	.2	1.1	.4	2.5
Capital Accounts ....47a. g	.7	.9	1.1	1.2	1.4	1.4	1.8	2.0	2.1	2.3	2.3	2.9	2.9	4.3	5.7
Other Items (Net) ....47r. g	.2	.4	.5	.5	.5	.4	−.3	−1.0	−.2	−1.2	−1.2	−.8	2.4	1.6	1.3
Banking Survey														*Billions of Baht:*	
Foreign Assets (Net) 51n	23.9	26.2	36.9	34.1	†29.7	23.6	24.2	30.2	40.1	31.1	36.3	12.7	20.0	33.4	76.6
Domestic Credit 52	65.0	82.7	96.6	118.7	†167.5	214.6	275.9	325.2	384.9	452.6	551.4	680.9	784.2	860.3	928.4
Claims on Central Govt. (Net) 52an	28.7	31.7	27.8	33.5	†44.5	55.2	65.6	75.6	100.7	122.4	161.0	179.5	209.3	229.2	267.8
Claims on Nonfin.Pub.Enterprises 52c	.6	.9	1.3	1.4	†3.5	5.0	6.7	7.9	13.8	11.2	14.2	12.8	13.7	14.6	16.2
Claims on Private Sector 52d	35.7	50.0	67.5	83.8	†119.5	154.5	203.6	241.7	270.3	319.0	376.2	488.6	561.3	616.4	644.5
Liquid Liabilities 55l	66.7	82.0	98.0	113.7	†135.7	162.9	191.9	220.2	271.0	312.1	388.2	484.0	577.4	644.5	730.6
Bonds 56ab	1.6	1.8	1.7	1.8	†17.2	23.1	34.0	35.7	44.0	57.0	71.0	75.6	72.3	82.8	102.0
Long-Term Foreign Liabilities 56cl	.2	.2	.3	.6	†.9	1.4	2.7	4.8	5.9	7.6	8.3	9.3	13.5	16.3	18.2
Capital Accounts 57a	20.5	24.5	31.4	35.1	†39.2	47.6	69.6	95.2	105.2	110.5	120.1	127.9	147.8	166.0	183.5
Other Items (Net) 57r	−.2	.5	2.0	1.7	†4.1	3.3	1.9	−.6	−.9	−3.5	.2	−3.2	−6.9	−16.0	−29.4
Interest Rates														*Percent Per Annum*	
Discount Rate (*End of Period*) 60	...	...	...	...	7.70	9.00	12.50	12.50	13.50	14.50	12.50	13.00	12.00	11.00	8.00
Money Market Rate 60b						8.27	10.40	13.28	14.66	17.25	14.95	12.15	13.58	13.48	8.07
Treasury Bill Rate 60c						6.32	7.04	7.40	9.16	11.57	11.64	9.35	10.00	11.02	6.76
Deposit Rate 60l						8.00	8.00	8.25	12.00	12.50	13.00	13.00	13.00	13.00	9.75
Lending Rate 60p					11.04	10.90	10.98	12.96	16.15	17.21	16.96	15.21	16.79	16.08	13.38
Government Bond Yield 61					8.50	8.90	9.25	13.25	13.00	13.06	13.85	11.13	12.41	12.11	9.11
Prices and Labor														*Index Numbers (1995=100)*	
Producer Prices 63	23.4	28.8	37.1	38.4	39.9	43.1	46.3	51.5	61.8	67.7	68.3	†69.7	67.5	67.5	67.2
Consumer Prices 64	21.4	24.7	30.7	†32.3	33.7	36.2	39.1	43.0	51.5	58.0	61.0	63.3	63.9	65.4	†66.6
Labor Force 67d	...	...	...	...	...	...	...	...	...	...	...	...	...	*Number in Thousands:*	
Employment 67e	...	...	...	...	...	...	...	...	...	...	...	...	...	25,853	26,691
Unemployment 67c	...	...	...	...	...	...	...	...	...	...	...	...	...	995	969
Unemployment Rate (%) 67r	...	...	...	...	...	...	...	...	...	...	...	...	...	3.7	3.5
International Transactions														*Billions of Baht:*	
Exports 70	22.5	32.2	49.8	45.0	60.8	71.2	83.1	108.2	133.2	153.0	159.7	146.5	175.2	193.4	233.4
Rice 70n	4.4	3.6	9.8	5.9	8.6	13.4	10.4	15.6	19.5	26.4	22.5	20.2	25.9	22.5	20.3
Rubber 70l	1.9	4.6	5.0	3.5	5.3	6.2	8.0	12.4	12.4	10.8	9.5	11.8	13.0	13.6	15.1
Maize 70j	2.1	3.0	6.1	5.7	5.7	3.3	4.0	5.6	7.3	8.3	8.3	8.5	10.1	7.7	9.3
Tin 70q	1.7	2.0	3.1	2.2	3.0	4.5	7.2	9.3	11.3	9.1	7.8	5.3	5.3	5.6	3.1
Imports, c.i.f. 71	30.9	42.2	64.0	66.8	72.9	94.2	108.9	146.2	188.7	216.7	196.6	236.6	245.2	251.2	241.4
														1995=100	
Volume of Exports 72	5.9	5.5	6.2	5.9	8.2	9.4	10.2	†11.1	11.5	12.9	14.4	13.1	15.8	†16.9	19.9
Rice 72n	34.1	13.7	16.6	15.3	31.8	47.5	25.9	45.1	45.2	48.9	61.0	56.0	74.5	65.5	73.0
Rubber 72l	18.2	22.3	20.7	19.0	21.4	23.0	25.3	29.8	26.0	27.0	31.1	31.8	33.9	39.5	43.5
Maize 72j	1,691.4	1,271.9	2,047.9	1,930.9	2,219.4	1,414.7	1,809.5	1,847.7	2,020.6	2,362.0	2,597.0	2,439.2	2,885.0	2,552.3	3,681.8
Tin 72q	816.4	847.5	776.3	622.9	749.5	801.4	1,082.0	1,170.4	1,269.3	1,124.3	930.4	662.6	689.9	671.6	705.4
Volume of Imports 73	11.5	14.2	13.1	12.9	13.5	16.0	17.2	†20.0	20.7	20.2	17.9	22.8	23.4	†21.9	22.6
Unit Value of Exports 74	22.0	34.6	51.2	†45.2	43.9	44.9	48.5	†57.9	68.5	70.5	65.6	66.5	65.9	†67.7	69.6
Rice (Unit Value) 74n	26.8	54.0	121.1	78.4	55.6	57.9	82.7	71.1	88.8	110.9	75.8	74.0	71.6	70.7	57.2
Rice (Wholesale Price) 76n	39.0	76.5	138.0	92.6	64.8	69.5	93.8	85.4	111.1	131.8	84.4	79.7	74.6	73.9	64.4
Rubber (Unit Value) 74l	16.7	33.4	39.6	29.8	40.5	43.8	51.8	67.6	77.5	65.5	49.7	60.6	62.7	56.1	56.7
Rubber (Wholesale Price) 76l	17.5	35.5	38.9	29.0	40.1	42.2	50.9	65.4	74.1	62.2	50.1	62.2	57.5	52.3	53.9
Maize (Unit Value) 74j	22.5	42.5	54.1	53.8	46.6	43.1	40.0	55.6	65.8	64.4	58.4	63.4	64.1	55.0	45.8
Tin (Unit Value) 74q	50.2	59.1	98.3	88.9	97.7	139.6	164.6	194.7	220.2	199.2	205.8	195.7	188.5	207.1	108.1
Unit Value of Imports 75	14.3	16.7	27.0	†30.1	31.8	34.1	36.8	†42.6	52.8	62.5	64.1	60.5	60.9	†66.7	61.9

1987	1988	1989	1990	1991	1992	1993	1994	1995	1996	1997	1998	1999	2000	2001		
															Finance and Securities Companies	
End of Period																
4.9	6.1	9.7	9.2	12.3	22.7	31.2	40.2	51.8	51.5	37.4	79.6	195.1	210.2	102.3	Reserves	40..f
—	—	—	—	—	—	—	2.9	3.2	7.6	35.0	65.2	39.3	8.5	11.6	Other Claims on Mon. Author.	40n.f
20.2	20.3	23.0	26.2	30.8	28.3	40.0	9.7	5.6	4.0	1.6	29.7	23.2	23.3	21.4	Claims on Central Government	42a.f
.9	1.3	1.4	3.8	6.9	4.4	10.6	36.3	32.8	45.0	26.5	8.0	2.7	3.2	1.0	Claims on Nonfin.Pub.Enterprises	42c.f
107.5	145.7	217.1	311.3	408.2	568.5	761.1	1,035.1	1,363.1	1,554.7	1,373.8	1,165.5	347.6	301.3	330.0	Claims on Private Sector	42d.f
85.0	116.9	173.2	230.3	301.2	415.4	559.0	763.2	931.8	1,081.1	549.8	499.8	388.0	343.7	360.8	Bonds	46ab.f
2.3	2.6	6.4	17.6	27.7	41.2	58.8	71.3	116.5	132.6	123.3	43.1	26.6	28.9	26.0	Foreign Liabilities	46c.f
9.4	10.3	9.6	9.0	8.5	3.8	3.5	8.5	9.1	30.1	449.3	561.9	439.8	364.3	363.9	Credit from Monetary Authorities	46g.f
31.2	25.1	28.4	27.7	39.2	52.7	68.5	98.6	146.6	148.1	144.2	103.7	98.4	191.3	78.2	Cred. from Deposit Money Banks	46h.f
10.9	15.6	21.0	31.6	44.8	76.6	101.0	145.6	196.7	226.2	197.4	158.6	-353.2	-418.7	-405.8	Capital Accounts	47a.f
-5.3	2.7	12.6	34.3	36.9	34.2	52.2	36.9	55.7	44.7	10.2	-19.0	8.3	37.0	43.1	Other Items (Net)	47r.f
															Government Savings Bank	
End of Period																
15.2	13.2	7.6	8.7	20.2	25.0	29.6	52.9	77.8	82.4	62.6	62.4	51.3	42.4	23.5	Cash	40..g
—	—	—	—	—	—	—	9.4	8.1	2.1	31.5	71.7	18.4	22.6	35.7	Other Claims on Mon. Author.	40n.g
85.7	95.9	100.0	93.0	80.7	69.0	60.4	40.7	30.3	26.2	18.0	43.9	137.8	139.1	179.8	Claims on Central Government	42a.g
2.1	3.7	5.4	9.7	12.5	18.9	31.5	26.8	29.6	47.2	67.4	87.6	121.1	167.8	176.1	Claims on Nonfin.Pub.Enterprises	42c.g
1.6	2.1	2.9	6.3	7.0	14.7	18.1	26.8	35.4	45.5	64.9	68.8	69.2	81.9	112.3	Claims on Private Sector	42d.g
19.1	23.1	27.4	31.7	30.7	36.0	41.4	47.1	49.7	54.5	55.0	54.3	51.0	65.5	100.5	Demand Deposits	44..g
50.6	53.5	62.4	65.6	70.9	75.6	100.7	109.8	131.3	153.0	188.4	276.4	310.2	339.3	360.4	Time and Savings Deposits	45..g
26.8	28.8	16.7	13.7	16.6	16.4										Bonds	46ab.g
2.2	2.8	.4	.6	.7	.8	1.5	1.2	1.1	1.2	3.5	3.3	16.3	17.5	22.3	Central Government Deposits	46d.g
5.6	6.1	9.2	8.9	9.9	11.1	13.1	15.9	18.6	21.4	19.7	25.0	38.5	41.4	49.5	Capital Accounts	47a.g
.4	.6	-.1	-3.0	-8.4	-12.3	-16.9	-17.3	-19.4	-26.8	-22.1	-24.5	-18.4	-10.0	-5.1	Other Items (Net)	47r.g
															Banking Survey	
End of Period																
105.2	143.3	241.2	289.5	386.0	407.9	395.1	77.3	-114.3	-211.4	-681.3	40.5	661.2	1,018.7	1,314.6	Foreign Assets (Net)	51n
1,070.8	1,260.9	1,550.6	1,988.2	2,321.5	2,812.8	3,537.0	4,558.9	5,674.1	6,573.2	7,697.8	7,591.8	6,674.1	5,964.6	5,711.5	Domestic Credit	52
279.2	241.5	192.0	136.1	24.1	-51.3	-106.5	-234.9	-358.6	-437.0	-410.4	99.7	233.4	290.8	367.7	Claims on Central Govt. (Net)	52an
18.1	19.4	22.7	31.7	64.1	76.5	118.6	157.3	179.2	223.4	265.4	279.6	323.3	344.3	368.7	Claims on Nonfin.Pub.Enterprises	52c
773.5	1,000.0	1,335.9	1,820.4	2,233.3	2,787.6	3,524.8	4,636.4	5,853.5	6,786.8	7,842.8	7,212.5	6,117.4	5,329.5	4,975.1	Claims on Private Sector	52d
868.2	1,027.9	1,298.1	1,636.2	1,944.0	2,245.4	2,667.1	2,990.2	3,498.5	3,889.6	4,675.0	5,207.4	5,381.3	5,643.3	5,978.8	Liquid Liabilities	55l
114.9	151.2	200.2	259.0	343.5	468.8	624.7	857.8	1,076.5	1,232.4	716.8	683.5	576.8	533.1	554.1	Bonds	56ab
19.1	19.3	19.9	21.7	20.2	23.1	26.0	29.9	33.1	91.4	206.1	160.6	139.6	130.5	98.0	Long-Term Foreign Liabilities	56cl
217.2	236.2	273.7	336.1	415.8	506.8	623.5	873.4	1,066.2	1,275.4	1,771.7	2,144.2	1,971.2	1,618.1	1,515.6	Capital Accounts	57a
-43.4	-30.4	—	24.6	-15.9	-23.3	-9.1	-115.2	-114.5	-127.0	-353.0	-563.4	-733.6	-941.6	-1,120.4	Other Items (Net)	57r
															Interest Rates	
Percent Per Annum																
8.00	8.00	8.00	12.00	11.00	11.00	9.00	9.50	10.50	10.50	12.50	12.50	4.00	4.00	3.75	Discount Rate (End of Period)	60
5.91	8.66	†10.60	12.87	11.15	6.93	6.54	7.25	10.96	9.23	14.59	13.02	1.77	1.95	2.00	Money Market Rate	60b
3.63	5.08	....	....	....	....	....	....	....	....	....	....	....	....	....	Treasury Bill Rate	60c
9.50	9.50	9.50	12.25	13.67	8.88	8.63	8.46	11.58	10.33	10.52	10.65	4.73	3.29	2.54	Deposit Rate	60l
10.71	11.58	12.25	14.42	15.40	12.17	11.17	10.90	13.25	13.40	13.65	14.42	8.98	7.83	7.25	Lending Rate	60p
7.48	7.50	8.09	10.60	10.75	10.75	10.75	10.75	10.75	10.75	10.75	10.25	6.69	6.95	5.82	Government Bond Yield	61
															Prices and Labor	
Period Averages																
71.2	77.1	80.6	83.4	89.1	89.3	88.9	92.4	†100.0	101.8	107.0	120.0	114.3	118.8	121.8	Producer Prices	63
68.3	70.9	†74.7	79.1	83.6	87.1	90.0	94.5	100.0	105.8	111.8	120.8	121.1	†123.0	125.1	Consumer Prices	64
Period Averages																
28,380	....	31,209	....	31,137	....	30,729	....	32,543	33,339	33,352	33,209	33,799	....	....	Labor Force	67d
27,639	29,464	†30,669	30,842	31,137	32,383	32,150	32,093	32,512	32,232	33,162	32,138	32,087	33,001	....	Employment	67e
1,722	929	†433	710	869	456	494	423	375	354	293	1,138	986	813	....	Unemployment	67c
5.9	3.1	†1.4	2.2	2.7	1.4	1.5	1.3	1.1	1.1	.9	3.4	3.0	2.4	....	Unemployment Rate (%)	67r
															International Transactions	
Billions of Baht																
301.5	403.6	516.3	589.8	725.6	824.6	935.9	1,137.6	1,406.3	1,412.1	1,806.7	2,247.5	2,214.0	2,777.7	2,893.2	Exports	70
22.7	34.7	45.5	27.8	30.5	36.2	32.6	59.3	48.6	50.7	65.1	86.9	68.3	65.5	70.1	Rice	70n
20.5	27.2	26.4	23.6	25.0	28.9	30.4	41.8	61.3	63.4	57.5	55.4	40.3	60.7	58.7	Rubber	70l
3.9	3.8	4.1	4.1	3.9	.5	.7	.6	.5	.4	.5	.9	.4	.4	2.5	Maize	70j
2.3	2.2	2.5	1.9	.9	1.1	.5	.4	.4	.8	1.4	2.6	2.5	2.8	3.7	Tin	70q
334.2	513.1	662.7	844.4	958.3	1,033.2	1,166.6	1,369.0	1,763.6	1,832.8	1,924.3	1,774.1	1,907.1	2,494.2	2,756.7	Imports, c.i.f.	71
1995=100																
24.0	29.6	36.8	41.2	49.2	55.1	61.6	72.9	†100.0	90.1	97.0	104.6	117.1	142.7	134.8	Volume of Exports	72
71.7	82.1	99.1	64.8	67.2	79.0	80.9	78.4	100.0	88.1	154.3	105.5	110.3	99.1	124.0	Rice	72n
50.7	53.6	63.6	66.6	72.1	83.8	88.8	97.9	100.0	109.9	109.8	114.4	116.2	145.4	145.8	Rubber	72l
1,513.0	1,114.2	1,084.2	1,133.4	1,132.1	133.9	181.7	132.1	100.0	....	56.0	125.7	74.0	28.7	....	Maize	72j
513.0	489.1	432.3	444.1	233.8	274.8	131.1	102.8	100.0	—	—	—	—	489.2	....	Tin	72q
29.0	40.3	48.6	59.0	64.1	69.0	76.7	89.0	†100.0	90.6	81.0	59.0	72.9	88.6	79.2	Volume of Imports	73
74.5	80.7	83.1	84.8	87.6	89.1	89.9	92.4	†100.0	110.8	132.0	151.4	133.1	138.3	151.0	Unit Value of Exports	74
65.1	86.9	94.4	88.1	93.4	94.2	83.0	155.5	100.0	118.5	86.7	169.3	127.3	136.0	116.3	Rice (Unit Value)	74n
69.0	87.7	96.4	86.6	93.8	85.1	75.2	84.8	100.0	107.2	118.7	158.0	117.8	102.2	96.0	Rice (Wholesale Price)	76n
66.2	82.7	67.8	67.8	56.5	56.4	55.9	69.7	100.0	94.1	85.4	79.1	56.6	68.2	65.7	Rubber (Unit Value)	74l
64.3	76.1	63.3	56.2	53.5	55.6	53.5	71.9	100.0	90.2	81.1	75.8	61.0	70.4	67.8	Rubber (Wholesale Price)	76l
47.3	62.6	68.8	66.6	63.2	73.0	67.5	81.2	100.0	....	174.5	127.0	108.0	249.5	....	Maize (Unit Value)	74j
112.6	112.3	142.3	104.3	92.4	96.5	85.5	90.8	100.0	....	....	....	....	141.1	....	Tin (Unit Value)	74q
67.0	73.9	79.1	83.2	86.9	87.4	87.4	89.4	†100.0	113.0	134.0	162.5	144.6	161.3	193.9	Unit Value of Imports	75

Thailand

	1972	1973	1974	1975	1976	1977	1978	1979	1980	1981	1982	1983	1984	1985	1986
Balance of Payments															*Millions of US Dollars:*
Current Account, n.i.e. .... 78al *d*	...	...	...	−606	−440	−1,097	−1,153	−2,087	−2,076	−2,571	−1,003	−2,873	−2,109	−1,537	247
Goods: Exports f.o.b. .... 78aa *d*	...	...	...	2,177	2,959	3,454	4,045	5,234	6,449	6,902	6,835	6,308	7,338	7,059	8,803
Goods: Imports f.o.b. .... 78ab *d*	...	...	...	−2,850	−3,152	−4,238	−4,904	−6,785	−8,352	−8,930	−7,565	−9,169	−9,236	−8,391	−8,415
Trade Balance .... 78ac *d*	...	...	...	−673	−193	−784	−858	−1,550	−1,902	−2,029	−731	−2,861	−1,898	−1,332	388
Services: Credit .... 78ad *d*	...	...	...	603	508	531	819	1,034	1,490	1,612	1,717	1,846	1,964	2,041	2,302
Services: Debit........................ 78ae *d*	...	...	...	−628	−748	−845	−1,005	−1,352	−1,644	−1,819	−1,658	−1,909	−1,910	−1,815	−1,852
Balance on Goods & Services ... 78af *d*	...	...	...	−698	−433	−1,099	−1,045	−1,868	−2,057	−2,236	−672	−2,924	−1,843	−1,105	839
Income: Credit .... 78ag *d*	...	...	...	209	154	194	269	394	636	740	864	1,073	1,113	1,122	1,031
Income: Debit......................... 78ah *d*	...	...	...	−198	−208	−232	−418	−672	−865	−1,243	−1,378	−1,300	−1,554	−1,719	−1,848
Balance on Gds, Serv. & Inc. ... 78ai *d*	...	...	...	−687	−487	−1,137	−1,193	−2,146	−2,286	−2,739	−1,186	−3,151	−2,284	−1,703	22
Current Transfers, n.i.e.: Credit ... 78aj *d*	...	...	...	91	59	52	52	71	229	181	198	296	194	190	250
Current Transfers: Debit .... 78ak *d*	...	...	...	−10	−12	−13	−12	−12	−19	−14	−15	−19	−19	−25	−25
Capital Account, n.i.e. .... 78bc *d*	...	...	...	−1	—	—	—	1	6	2	—	−1	−1		
Capital Account, n.i.e.: Credit .... 78ba *d*	...	...	...	—	—	—	—	1	7	2	—	—	—	1	1
Capital Account: Debit .... 78bb *d*	...	...	...	−1	−1	−1	−1	—	−1	−1	—	−1	−1	−1	
Financial Account, n.i.e. .... 78bj *d*	...	...	...	469	539	1,046	1,360	1,977	2,044	2,479	1,293	1,966	2,567	1,538	−131
Direct Investment Abroad .... 78bd *d*	...	...	...	—	—	—	−6	−4	−3	−2	−2	−1	−1	−1	−1
Dir. Invest. in Rep. Econ., n.i.e. .... 78be *d*	...	...	...	86	79	106	56	55	190	291	191	350	401	163	263
Portfolio Investment Assets .... 78bf *d*	...	...	...	—	—	—	—	—	—	—	—	—	—	—	—
Equity Securities.................. 78bk *d*	...	...	...	—	—	—	—	—	—	—	—	—	—	—	—
Debt Securities .... 78bl *d*	...	...	...	—	—	—	—	—	—	—	—	—	—	—	—
Portfolio Investment Liab., n.i.e. ...... 78bg *d*	...	...	...	1	−1	—	76	180	96	44	68	108	155	895	−29
Equity Securities.................. 78bm *d*	...	...	...	1	−1	—	6	4	51	11	27	15	34	41	96
Debt Securities .... 78bn *d*	...	...	...	—	—	—	70	176	45	33	42	93	121	854	−126
Financial Derivatives Assets ..... 78bw *d*	...	...	...	...	...	...	...	...	...	...	...	...	...	...	...
Financial Derivatives Liabilities ..... 78bx *d*	...	...	...	...	...	...	...	...	...	...	...	...	...	...	...
Other Investment Assets .... 78bh *d*	...	...	...	−1	10	4	−12	−43	−21	−42	−84	−108	−79	−242	−150
Monetary Authorities................. 78bo *d*	...	...	...	...	...	...	...	...	...	...	...	...	...	...	...
General Government .... 78bp *d*	...	...	...	—	11	3	1	−18	6	4	−33	−63	−67	−196	−150
Banks .... 78bq *d*	...	...	...	...	...	...	...	...	...	...	...	...	...	...	
Other Sectors .... 78br *d*	...	...	...	−1	−1	—	−13	−25	−26	−46	−50	−45	−12	−46	—
Other Investment Liab., n.i.e. .... 78bi *d*	...	...	...	383	451	936	1,246	1,789	1,782	2,188	1,120	1,618	2,091	722	−213
Monetary Authorities................. 78bs *d*	...	...	...	−1	—	—	1	1	1	—	—	—	—	—	—
General Government .... 78bt *d*	...	...	...	−6	106	38	228	359	251	313	211	147	212	507	25
Banks .... 78bu *d*	...	...	...	89	85	361	630	324	−438	−9	−225	630	97	−359	−563
Other Sectors .... 78bv *d*	...	...	...	301	261	537	387	1,104	1,968	1,884	1,134	841	1,782	574	325
Net Errors and Omissions.................. 78ca *d*	...	...	...	86	−19	44	−231	20	−180	133	−521	587	71	103	598
Overall Balance .... 78cb *d*	...	...	...	−51	81	−8	−25	−88	−206	42	−231	−320	529	105	714
Reserves and Related Items .... 79da *d*	...	...	...	51	−81	8	25	88	206	−42	231	320	−529	−105	−714
Reserve Assets .... 79db *d*	...	...	...	51	−158	−9	−112	−24	212	−574	50	−84	−457	−205	−545
Use of Fund Credit and Loans ...... 79dc *d*	...	...	...	—	77	17	137	112	−6	532	31	240	−72	100	−168
Exceptional Financing .... 79de *d*	...	...	...	—	—	—	—	—	—	—	150	164	—	—	—
International Investment Position															*Millions of US Dollars*
Assets .... 79aa *d*	...	...	...	...	...	...	...	...	...	...	...	...	...	...	...
Direct Investment Abroad .... 79ab *d*	...	...	...	...	...	...	...	...	...	...	...	...	...	...	...
Portfolio Investment .... 79ac *d*	...	...	...	...	...	...	...	...	...	...	...	...	...	...	...
Equity Securities........................ 79ad *d*	...	...	...	...	...	...	...	...	...	...	...	...	...	...	...
Debt Securities .... 79ae *d*	...	...	...	...	...	...	...	...	...	...	...	...	...	...	...
Financial Derivatives........................ 79al *d*	...	...	...	...	...	...	...	...	...	...	...	...	...	...	...
Other Investment .... 79af *d*	...	...	...	...	...	...	...	...	...	...	...	...	...	...	...
Monetary Authorities..................... 79ag *d*	...	...	...	...	...	...	...	...	...	...	...	...	...	...	...
General Government .... 79ah *d*	...	...	...	...	...	...	...	...	...	...	...	...	...	...	...
Banks .... 79ai *d*	...	...	...	...	...	...	...	...	...	...	...	...	...	...	...
Other Sectors .... 79aj *d*	...	...	...	...	...	...	...	...	...	...	...	...	...	...	...
Reserve Assets .... 79ak *d*	...	...	...	...	...	...	...	...	...	...	...	...	...	...	...
Liabilities .... 79la *d*	...	...	...	...	...	...	...	...	...	...	...	...	...	...	...
Dir. Invest. in Rep. Economy............ 79lb *d*	...	...	...	...	...	...	...	...	...	...	...	...	...	...	...
Portfolio Investment .... 79lc *d*	...	...	...	...	...	...	...	...	...	...	...	...	...	...	...
Equity Securities........................ 79ld *d*	...	...	...	...	...	...	...	...	...	...	...	...	...	...	...
Debt Securities .... 79le *d*	...	...	...	...	...	...	...	...	...	...	...	...	...	...	...
Financial Derivatives .... 79ll *d*	...	...	...	...	...	...	...	...	...	...	...	...	...	...	...
Other Investment .... 79lf *d*	...	...	...	...	...	...	...	...	...	...	...	...	...	...	...
Monetary Authorities..................... 79lg *d*	...	...	...	...	...	...	...	...	...	...	...	...	...	...	...
General Government .... 79lh *d*	...	...	...	...	...	...	...	...	...	...	...	...	...	...	...
Banks .... 79li *d*	...	...	...	...	...	...	...	...	...	...	...	...	...	...	...
Other Sectors .... 79lj *d*	...	...	...	...	...	...	...	...	...	...	...	...	...	...	...

Minus Sign Indicates Debit

1987	1988	1989	1990	1991	1992	1993	1994	1995	1996	1997	1998	1999	2000	2001	Balance of Payments	
-366	-1,654	-2,498	-7,281	-7,571	-6,303	-6,364	-8,085	-13,554	-14,691	-3,021	14,243	12,428	9,313	6,227	Current Account, n.i.e.	78al d
11,595	15,781	19,834	22,810	28,232	32,099	36,398	44,478	55,447	54,408	56,656	52,753	56,775	67,894	63,202	Goods: Exports f.o.b.	78aa d
-12,019	-17,856	-22,750	-29,561	-34,221	-36,260	-40,694	-48,204	-63,415	-63,897	-55,084	-36,515	-42,762	-56,193	-54,620	Goods: Imports f.o.b.	78ab d
-424	-2,074	-2,916	-6,751	-5,989	-4,161	-4,297	-3,726	-7,968	-9,488	1,572	16,238	14,013	11,701	8,582	*Trade Balance*	78ac d
3,070	4,647	5,457	6,419	7,272	9,288	11,059	11,640	14,845	17,007	15,763	13,156	14,635	13,868	13,024	Services: Credit	78ad d
-2,406	-3,569	-4,505	-6,309	-8,040	-10,368	-12,469	-15,396	-18,804	-19,585	-17,355	-11,998	-13,583	-15,460	-14,619	Services: Debit	78ae d
239	-996	-1,964	-6,641	-6,757	-5,241	-5,707	-7,482	-11,927	-12,066	-20	17,395	15,066	10,109	6,987	*Balance on Goods & Services*	78af d
1,098	1,297	1,589	2,059	2,254	1,532	2,140	2,562	3,801	3,969	3,742	3,324	3,092	4,235	3,839	Income: Credit	78ag d
-1,928	-2,191	-2,369	-2,913	-3,329	-3,240	-3,546	-4,292	-5,915	-7,354	-7,223	-6,891	-6,083	-5,616	-5,200	Income: Debit	78ah d
-590	-1,891	-2,744	-7,494	-7,832	-6,949	-7,113	-9,213	-14,040	-15,451	-3,500	13,828	12,075	8,727	5,626	*Balance on Gds, Serv. & Inc.*	78ai d
247	268	281	278	411	1,000	1,222	1,901	1,190	1,651	1,392	820	806	952	990	Current Transfers, n.i.e.: Credit	78aj d
-23	-31	-34	-65	-150	-355	-473	-774	-704	-891	-913	-405	-452	-366	-389	Current Transfers: Debit	78ak d
2	—	—	-1	—	—	—	—	....	....	....	....	....	....	....	Capital Account, n.i.e.	78bc d
2	—	—	—	—	—	—	—	....	....	....	....	....	....	....	Capital Account, n.i.e.: Credit	78ba d
—	—	—	-1	—	—	—	—	....	....	....	....	....	....	....	Capital Account: Debit	78bb d
1,062	3,839	6,599	9,098	11,759	9,475	10,500	12,167	21,909	19,486	-12,056	-14,110	-11,073	-10,434	-3,908	Financial Account, n.i.e.	78bj d
-170	-24	-50	-140	-167	-147	-233	-493	-886	-931	-580	-130	-346	23	-162	Direct Investment Abroad	78bd d
352	1,105	1,775	2,444	2,014	2,113	1,804	1,366	2,068	2,336	3,895	7,315	6,213	3,366	3,820	Dir. Invest. in Rep. Econ., n.i.e.	78be d
—	—	—	—	—	....	—	-5	-2	-41	-70	18	-2	-160	-287	Portfolio Investment Assets	78bf d
—	—	—	—	—	—	—	-5	-2	-41	-40	21	-1	-154	-287	Equity Securities	78bk d
										-31	-3	-2	-6	1	Debt Securities	78bl d
346	530	1,486	-38	-81	924	5,455	2,486	4,083	3,585	4,598	338	77	-546	-932	Portfolio Investment Liab., n.i.e.	78bg d
499	444	1,424	440	37	455	2,679	-389	2,123	1,164	3,899	292	946	900	18	Equity Securities	78bm d
-153	86	63	-478	-118	469	2,776	2,875	1,960	2,421	699	45	-869	-1,446	-951	Debt Securities	78bn d
....	....	....	....	....	....	....	....	....	....	....	....	....	—	—	Financial Derivatives Assets	78bw d
....	....	....	....	....	....	....	....	....	....	....	....	....	—	—	Financial Derivatives Liabilities	78bx d
141	269	-313	-164	352	104	-3,265	-1,027	-2,738	2,661	-2,555	-3,407	-1,755	-2,203	250	Other Investment Assets	78bh d
....	....	....	....	....	....	....	....	....	....	....	....	....	....	....	Monetary Authorities	78bo d
153	250	-337	-220	247											General Government	78bp d
					104	-3,265	-1,027	-2,737	2,741	-2,608	-3,460	-1,708	-2,189	240	Banks	78bq d
-12	19	23	57	105	—	—	—	-1	-80	53	53	-47	-14	11	Other Sectors	78br d
393	1,960	3,700	6,996	9,642	6,479	6,739	9,839	19,383	11,876	-17,343	-18,243	-15,261	-10,914	-6,597	Other Investment Liab., n.i.e.	78bi d
—	—	—	—	—	—	—	—	—	—	-5,262	658	2,731	43	894	Monetary Authorities	78bs d
434	-51	-206	-999	9	-611	-464	-705	46	-58	737	100	-70	93	243	General Government	78bt d
243	984	700	1,027	213	1,758	6,589	14,295	13,218	2,909	-3,045	-11,783	-11,566	-4,799	-2,093	Banks	78bu d
-285	1,027	3,207	6,969	9,420	5,333	614	-3,751	6,118	9,025	-9,774	-7,218	-6,356	-6,251	-5,641	Other Sectors	78bv d
248	411	928	1,419	431	-142	-230	87	-1,196	-2,627	-3,173	-2,828	33	-685	155	Net Errors and Omissions	78ca d
945	2,596	5,029	3,235	4,618	3,029	3,907	4,169	7,159	2,167	-18,250	-2,696	1,388	-1,806	2,475	*Overall Balance*	78cb d
-945	-2,596	-5,029	-3,235	-4,618	-3,029	-3,907	-4,169	-7,159	-2,167	18,250	2,696	-1,388	1,806	-2,475	Reserves and Related Items	79da d
-700	-2,336	-4,667	-2,961	-4,618	-3,029	-3,907	-4,169	-7,159	-2,167	9,900	-1,433	-4,556	1,608	-1,307	Reserve Assets	79db d
-245	-260	-363	-274	-1	—	—	—	—	—	2,437	679	269	-192	-1,288	Use of Fund Credit and Loans	79dc d
—	....	....	....	....	....	....	....	....	....	5,913	3,450	2,898	391	121	Exceptional Financing	79de d

Millions of US Dollars

1987	1988	1989	1990	1991	1992	1993	1994	1995	1996	1997	1998	1999	2000	2001	International Investment Position	
....	....	....	....	....	....	....	....	46,982	46,005	35,007	41,368	48,360	53,450	54,231	Assets	79aa d
....	....	....	....	....	....	....	....	365	481	401	410	418	1,991	2,309	Direct Investment Abroad	79ab d
....	....	....	....	....	....	....	....	—	—	43	28	29	478	813	Portfolio Investment	79ac d
....	....	....	....	....	....	....	....	....	....	....	....	....	42	57	Equity Securities	79ad d
....	....	....	....	....	....	....	....	....	....	....	....	....	436	756	Debt Securities	79ae d
....	....	....	....	....	....	....	....	—	—	—	—	—	510	141	Financial Derivatives	79al d
....	....	....	....	....	....	....	....	9,672	6,879	7,671	11,394	13,132	17,810	17,928	Other Investment	79af d
....	....	....	....	....	....	....	....	—	—	—	—	—			Monetary Authorities	79ag d
....	....	....	....	....	....	....	....						127	158	General Government	79ah d
....	....	....	....	....	....	....	....	9,672	6,879	7,671	11,394	13,132	16,342	15,612	Banks	79ai d
....	....	....	....	....	....	....	....						1,341	2,158	Other Sectors	79aj d
....	....	....	....	....	....	....	....	36,945	38,645	26,892	29,536	34,781	32,661	33,040	Reserve Assets	79ak d
....	....	....	....	....	....	....	....	100,832	108,742	109,276	105,061	95,051	112,072	103,819	Liabilities	79la d
....	....	....	....	....	....	....	....	4,919	4,745	4,738	6,481	6,837	25,834	29,158	Dir. Invest. in Rep. Economy	79lb d
....	....	....	....	....	....	....	....	6,684	9,472	9,774	10,552	9,921	16,315	16,941	Portfolio Investment	79lc d
....	....	....	....	....	....	....	....						8,153	10,098	Equity Securities	79ld d
....	....	....	....	....	....	....	....	6,684	9,472	9,774	10,552	9,921	8,162	6,843	Debt Securities	79le d
....	....	....	....	....	....	....	....						2,643	2,448	Financial Derivatives	79ll d
....	....	....	....	....	....	....	....	89,229	94,525	94,764	88,028	78,293	67,280	55,272	Other Investment	79lf d
....	....	....	....	....	....	....	....			7,157	11,203	12,817	12,019	8,327	Monetary Authorities	79lg d
....	....	....	....	....	....	....	....	3,126	2,994	3,672	4,768	7,102	7,347	7,297	General Government	79lh d
....	....	....	....	....	....	....	....	41,346	41,410	38,898	28,083	17,450	13,656	10,434	Banks	79li d
....	....	....	....	....	....	....	....	44,757	50,121	45,037	43,974	40,924	34,258	29,214	Other Sectors	79lj d

Thailand

		1972	1973	1974	1975	1976	1977	1978	1979	1980	1981	1982	1983	1984	1985	1986
Government Finance																*Millions of Baht:*
Deficit (-) or Surplus	80	†−7,263	−5,170	2,170	−7,401	−16,081	−12,095	−13,064	−13,160	−25,658	−21,360	−41,120	−22,824	−33,183	−38,979	−34,132
Total Revenue and Grants	81y										....	....	....	....	....	....
Revenue	81	†21,561	27,311	38,352	39,083	43,584	53,917	65,190	78,666	95,556	111,963	116,058	143,635	148,080	160,569	169,829
Grants	81z	....	....	....	....	....	....	....	....	....	....	....	....	....	....	....
Exp. & Lending Minus Repay.	82z	....	....	....	....	....	....	....	....	....	....	....	....	....	....	....
Expenditure	82	†28,824	32,481	36,182	46,484	59,665	66,012	78,254	91,826	121,214	133,323	157,178	166,459	181,263	199,548	203,961
Lending Minus Repayments	83	....	....	....	....	....	....	....	....	....	....	....	....	....	....	....
Extrabudgetary Deficits/Surpluses	80xz															
Total Financing	80h	†7,265	5,169	−2,169	7,402	16,079	12,095	13,064	13,160	25,658	21,360	41,120	22,824	33,183	38,979	34,132
Total Net Borrowing	84	†8,700	6,430	35	4,970	14,247	11,395	14,028	12,167	26,468	21,214	41,659	22,404	32,802	39,672	35,586
Net Domestic	84a	....	....	....	....	....	....	....	....	....	....	....	....	....	....	....
Net Foreign	85a	....	....	....	....	....	....	....	....	....	....	....	....	....	....	....
Use of Cash Balances	87	†−1,435	−1,261	−2,204	2,432	1,832	700	−964	993	−810	146	−539	420	381	−693	−1,454
Total Debt by Currency	88z	†42,427	47,340	45,861	48,031	60,696	72,597	92,078	113,380	140,036	168,839	209,504	242,532	292,922	351,136	413,596
National	88b	†38,058	42,461	40,875	43,212	53,575	64,372	77,181	90,166	109,781	127,456	160,372	185,815	219,143	249,253	301,235
Foreign	89b	†4,369	4,879	4,986	4,819	7,121	8,225	14,897	23,214	30,255	41,383	49,132	56,717	73,779	101,883	112,361
National Accounts																*Billions of Baht:*
Househ.Cons.Expend.,incl.NPISHs	96f	117.6	149.0	190.1	211.3	237.7	271.9	315.0	364.0	433.6	496.4	535.0	599.6	628.9	657.4	695.8
Government Consumption Expend.	91f	18.6	21.6	26.1	31.3	38.0	42.9	54.6	66.8	81.4	97.0	110.2	118.6	130.1	142.9	144.6
Gross Fixed Capital Formation	93e	38.6	49.9	65.0	69.4	79.4	104.6	123.3	142.9	184.0	212.8	226.7	262.1	282.6	287.0	292.2
Changes in Inventories	93i	−1.8	10.0	9.3	11.8	3.7	3.9	14.3	9.2	9.1	12.8	−3.6	13.9	8.6	11.4	1.0
Exports of Goods and Services	90c	30.9	41.3	60.3	55.7	70.1	80.5	97.1	126.2	159.7	181.3	192.9	185.2	216.4	245.3	290.2
Imports of Goods and Services (-)	98c	32.6	44.5	66.9	69.7	78.7	102.4	117.7	163.7	201.2	229.0	207.3	251.2	258.6	274.1	267.1
Gross Domestic Product (GDP)	99b	170.1	222.1	279.2	303.3	346.5	403.5	488.2	558.9	662.5	760.4	841.6	921.0	988.1	1,056.5	1,133.4
Net Primary Income from Abroad	98.n	−.6	−.9	−.1	—	−.9	−1.3	−3.6	−6.2	−5.4	−12.0	−12.9	−6.7	−11.5	−17.6	−22.4
Gross National Income (GNI)	99a	169.5	221.2	279.1	303.3	345.6	402.3	484.6	552.6	657.1	748.3	828.6	914.3	976.6	1,038.9	1,111.0
Consumption of Fixed Capital	99cf	13.0	14.8	17.2	20.3	23.4	27.1	31.7	37.2	46.7	54.6	63.1	72.4	82.5	93.0	104.0
GDP Volume 1972 prices	99b.p	170.1	186.9	195.0	204.4	223.6	245.7	271.4	285.8	299.5						
GDP Volume 1988 Prices	99b.p	....	....	....	....	....	....	....	....	913.7	967.7	1,019.5	1,076.4	1,138.4	1,191.3	1,257.2
GDP Volume (1995=100)	99bvp	17.6	19.4	20.2	21.2	23.2	25.5	28.1	29.6	31.1	32.9	34.7	36.6	38.7	40.5	42.7
GDP Deflator (1995=100)	99bip	23.0	27.4	33.0	34.2	35.7	37.8	41.4	45.0	50.9	55.2	58.0	60.1	61.0	62.3	63.4
																Millions:
Population	99z	38.59	39.69	40.78	41.87	42.96	44.04	45.10	46.14	46.72	47.74	48.71	49.68	50.64	51.58	52.51

	1987	1988	1989	1990	1991	1992	1993	1994	1995	1996	1997	1998	1999	2000	2001		
Year Ending December 31																**Government Finance**	
	−8,860	36,099	65,335	107,049	100,455	71,793	55,618	101,239	134,965	†43,303	−15,061	−128,951	−154,193	−108,065	−122,993	Deficit (-) or Surplus	80
															776,364	Total Revenue and Grants	81y
	202,365	258,231	328,248	411,747	462,539	511,835	575,100	680,455	777,286	853,201	847,689	717,779	713,066	746,817	776,362	Revenue	81
	....	....	....	....	....	....	....	....	....	....	....	....	....	....		Grants	81z
															908,613	Exp. & Lending Minus Repay.	82z
	211,225	222,132	262,913	304,698	362,084	440,042	519,482	579,216	642,321	819,083	875,714	842,581	833,042	853,067	908,613	Expenditure	82
																Lending Minus Repayments	83
										†9,185	12,964	−4,149	−34,217	−1,815	9,258	Extrabudgetary Deficits/Surpluses	80xz
	8,860	−36,099	−65,335	−107,049	−100,455	−71,793	−55,618	−101,239	−134,965	†−43,303	15,061	128,951	154,192	108,065	122,993	Total Financing	80h
	7,032	−32,887	−21,952	−52,626	−43,400	−44,468	−44,605	−80,051	−44,147	†−28,788	−76,109	−7,764	135,204	65,101	113,520	Total Net Borrowing	84
										−25,123	−72,348	−3,361	84,566	48,967	112,595	Net Domestic	84a
										−3,665	−3,761	−4,403	50,638	16,134	925	Net Foreign	85a
	1,828	−3,212	−43,383	−54,423	−57,055	−27,325	−11,013	−21,188	−90,818	−14,515	91,170	136,715	18,988	42,964	9,473	Use of Cash Balances	87
	450,842	437,942	420,040	371,839	325,692	300,261	271,406	219,829	193,630	175,594	299,547	674,032	991,104	1,104,586	1,263,856	Total Debt by Currency	88z
	322,121	304,878	291,225	278,346	230,109	202,694	161,071	103,200	72,696	44,254	31,755	426,928	642,371	688,937	836,689	National	88b
	128,721	133,064	128,815	93,493	95,583	97,567	110,335	116,629	120,934	131,340	267,792	247,104	348,733	415,649	427,167	Foreign	89b
Billions of Baht																**National Accounts**	
	781.1	885.0	1,030.6	1,235.0	1,378.1	1,550.5	1,730.5	1,958.7	2,225.7	2,479.8	2,587.0	2,505.3	2,591.1	2,751.9	2,903.7	Househ.Cons.Expend.,incl.NPISHs	96f
	147.2	156.7	176.8	205.4	231.1	280.2	316.0	354.4	414.4	469.5	476.4	511.7	533.5	560.8	593.2	Government Consumption Expend.	91f
	359.3	478.5	642.9	881.8	1,043.6	1,111.3	1,252.9	1,450.2	1,719.1	1,892.9	1,598.6	1,035.4	966.3	1,082.7	1,189.0	Gross Fixed Capital Formation	93e
	3.1	29.8	8.3	21.2	30.3	20.1	13.5	10.7	43.0	35.2	−5.5	−89.5	−16.7	31.9	35.2	Changes in Inventories	93i
	375.6	514.9	648.5	745.3	901.5	1,046.7	1,201.5	1,410.8	1,751.7	1,809.9	2,272.1	2,724.0	2,703.3	3,289.7	3,379.6	Exports of Goods and Services	90c
	368.3	536.6	696.1	909.5	1,065.5	1,160.2	1,335.7	1,586.6	2,033.9	2,099.2	2,205.1	1,988.9	2,120.3	2,862.3	3,070.7	Imports of Goods and Services (-)	98c
	1,299.9	1,559.8	1,857.0	2,183.5	2,506.6	2,830.9	3,165.2	3,629.3	4,186.2	4,611.0	4,732.6	4,626.4	4,632.1	4,904.7	5,100.7	Gross Domestic Product (GDP)	99b
	−22.4	−24.8	−23.7	−27.4	−36.9	−63.0	−45.9	−55.8	−68.2	−102.1	−123.4	−160.0	−126.4	−76.9	−61.3	Net Primary Income from Abroad	98.n
	1,277.5	1,535.0	1,833.3	2,156.1	2,469.7	2,768.0	3,119.3	3,573.6	4,118.0	4,509.0	4,609.2	4,466.4	4,505.7	4,827.9	5,038.4	Gross National Income (GNI)	99a
	116.5	133.4	157.1	191.0	234.6	282.7	335.9	397.0	471.6	556.7	599.1	....	....	....	....	Consumption of Fixed Capital	99cf
																GDP Volume 1972 prices	99b.*p*
	1,376.8	1,559.8	1,750.0	1,945.4	2,111.9	2,282.6	2,470.9	2,693.0	2,941.7	3,115.3	3,072.6	2,749.7	2,871.5	3,004.7	3,058.7	GDP Volume 1988 Prices	99b.*p*
	46.8	53.0	59.5	66.1	71.8	77.6	84.0	91.5	100.0	105.9	104.4	93.5	97.6	102.1	104.0	GDP Volume (1995=100)	99bv*p*
	66.3	70.3	74.6	78.9	83.4	87.2	90.0	94.7	100.0	104.0	108.2	118.2	113.4	114.7	117.2	GDP Deflator (1995=100)	99bi*p*
Midyear Estimates																	
	53.43	54.33	55.21	55.84	56.57	57.29	58.01	58.72	59.40	60.00	60.60	61.16	61.56	62.32	62.91	Population	99z

(See notes in the back of the book.)

Togo

		1972	1973	1974	1975	1976	1977	1978	1979	1980	1981	1982	1983	1984	1985	1986
Exchange Rates															*Francs per SDR:*	
Official Rate	aa	278.00	284.00	272.08	262.55	288.70	285.76	272.28	264.78	287.99	334.52	370.92	436.97	470.11	415.26	394.78
															Francs per US Dollar:	
Official Rate	ae	256.05	235.42	222.22	224.27	248.49	235.25	209.00	201.00	225.80	287.40	336.25	417.37	479.60	378.05	322.75
Official Rate	rf	252.03	222.89	240.70	214.31	238.95	245.68	225.66	212.72	211.28	271.73	328.61	381.07	436.96	449.26	346.31
														Index Numbers (1995=100):		
Official Rate	ahx	197.9	224.6	207.2	233.0	209.0	203.0	221.4	234.6	236.4	184.6	152.6	131.5	114.5	111.9	144.3
Nominal Effective Exchange Rate	nec	....	....	....	....	....	....	....	107.9	110.5	103.9	99.2	98.9	100.3	105.6	115.7
Real Effective Exchange Rate	rec	....	....	....	....	....	....	....	....	175.0	173.3	166.1	165.5	148.3	141.8	152.9
Fund Position															*Millions of SDRs:*	
Quota	2f.s	15.0	15.0	15.0	15.0	15.0	15.0	19.0	19.0	28.5	28.5	28.5	38.4	38.4	38.4	38.4
SDRs	1b.s	5.1	5.1	5.1	5.1	5.0	4.8	4.4	6.3	5.8	6.5	3.9	1.2	2.1	.1	.5
Reserve Position in the Fund	1c.s	2.1	2.1	2.1	2.1	2.1	2.1	2.0	3.3	—	—	.2	.2	.2	.2	.2
Total Fund Cred.&Loans Outstg.	2tl	—	—	—	—	7.5	7.5	6.2	10.8	25.5	32.8	32.8	51.9	63.5	67.6	73.8
International Liquidity												*Millions of US Dollars Unless Otherwise Indicated:*				
Total Reserves minus Gold	1l.d	36.5	37.9	54.5	41.2	66.6	46.1	70.0	65.5	77.6	151.5	167.7	172.8	203.3	296.6	342.0
SDRs	1b.d	5.5	6.1	6.2	5.9	5.8	5.8	5.7	8.3	7.4	7.6	4.3	1.3	2.0	.1	.6
Reserve Position in the Fund	1c.d	2.2	2.5	2.5	2.4	2.4	2.5	2.6	4.4	—	—	.2	.2	.2	.2	.3
Foreign Exchange	1d.d	28.7	29.3	45.7	32.8	58.4	37.9	61.7	52.8	70.2	143.9	163.2	171.4	201.1	296.3	341.1
Gold (Million Fine Troy Ounces)	1ad	....	....	....	....	—	.006	.010	.013	.013	.013	.013	.013	.013	.013	.013
Gold (National Valuation)	1and	....	....	....	....	—	.3	.4	.6	.6	5.3	5.3	4.8	4.2	4.1	5.0
Monetary Authorities: Other Liab.	4..d	1.4	.1	1.4	3.9	2.2	1.4	4.3	20.7	6.6	1.7	2.2	3.7	2.3	3.8	16.5
Deposit Money Banks: Assets	7a.d	8.1	7.2	63.0	13.9	21.5	27.3	63.7	69.0	49.4	69.7	64.8	46.5	46.7	50.1	43.3
Liabilities	7b.d	12.0	18.4	22.7	32.7	32.8	51.5	81.5	61.0	77.6	79.4	64.2	46.2	52.9	67.7	88.2
Monetary Authorities															*Billions of Francs:*	
Foreign Assets	11	9.3	8.7	12.1	9.2	16.6	10.9	14.6	13.2	17.5	43.5	56.4	72.1	97.5	112.1	110.4
Claims on Central Government	12a	—	—	—	2.4	2.5	6.3	10.3	13.1	12.8	21.9	22.6	32.0	33.7	40.7	42.8
Claims on Deposit Money Banks	12e	.2	.7	.6	2.6	4.2	6.8	5.1	9.8	13.2	7.1	7.2	6.3	6.6	4.0	6.0
Claims on Other Financial Insts	12f	—	—	—	—	.2	.4	.6	.6	.5	.5	.4	.5	.6	.8	1.1
Reserve Money	14	5.7	6.5	9.1	11.6	18.9	19.9	25.8	27.0	31.7	57.9	71.0	78.4	99.1	116.3	118.8
of which: Currency Outside DMBs	14a	5.4	6.0	8.4	9.9	14.2	16.0	20.8	21.5	27.8	50.7	54.3	45.5	37.0	39.2	46.0
Foreign Liabilities	16c	.3	—	.3	.9	2.7	2.5	4.4	10.0	12.9	15.5	17.0	28.2	34.6	32.5	37.7
Central Government Deposits	16d	2.0	1.5	2.0	.4	.3	.5	.8	.7	.7	1.1	.7	7.6	10.6	10.8	2.5
Other Items (Net)	17r	1.4	1.5	1.4	1.4	1.5	1.5	-.3	-1.0	-1.3	-1.6	-2.0	-3.2	-5.9	-2.0	1.4
Deposit Money Banks															*Billions of Francs:*	
Reserves	20	.3	.4	.6	1.6	4.2	3.9	4.9	4.9	4.4	7.6	16.5	33.0	63.1	77.6	72.9
Foreign Assets	21	2.1	1.7	14.0	3.1	5.3	6.4	13.3	13.9	11.2	20.0	21.8	19.4	22.4	18.9	14.0
Claims on Central Government	22a	—	—	—	—	—	.6	1.3	†4.1	4.6	3.8	3.4	3.2	2.3	.7	.9
Claims on Private Sector	22d	9.7	13.1	16.0	24.3	31.7	43.1	49.2	†56.2	64.1	62.0	69.2	67.3	70.8	69.7	89.3
Claims on Other Financial Insts	22f	....	....	....	....	....	....	....	†.7	.6	.5	.7	.6	.5	.6	.6
Demand Deposits	24	6.1	5.2	16.3	11.1	18.2	19.9	26.6	†30.4	26.8	28.5	34.9	36.6	52.7	42.2	42.8
Time Deposits	25	2.1	4.4	5.4	6.7	8.3	11.6	16.8	†13.9	17.2	20.6	27.1	34.7	45.4	60.5	75.8
Foreign Liabilities	26c	2.0	2.9	3.4	5.7	6.5	10.5	15.4	10.3	15.3	20.8	19.3	17.4	23.5	23.8	26.0
Long-Term Foreign Liabilities	26cl	1.1	1.4	1.7	1.7	1.7	1.6	1.7	1.9	2.2	2.0	2.3	1.9	1.9	1.8	2.4
Central Government Deposits	26d	.1	.5	.7	.9	1.3	4.0	3.6	†11.2	11.2	9.5	11.4	16.6	24.1	35.2	32.1
Credit from Monetary Authorities	26g	.2	.7	.6	2.6	4.2	6.8	5.1	9.8	12.9	6.7	7.3	6.4	6.7	4.1	8.0
Other Items (Net)	27r	.5	.2	2.5	.5	1.2	-.5	-.4	2.2	-.7	5.8	9.4	9.9	4.8	—	-9.4
Treasury Claims: Private Sector	22d.i	.4	.2	.3	.4	.3	1.1	1.8	2.0	1.8	1.5	2.0	2.0	1.5	1.6	2.1
Post Office: Checking Deposits	24..i	.3	.3	.4	.5	.6	.6	.7	.7	.8	.7	.9	1.0	1.0	1.3	.8
Monetary Survey															*Billions of Francs:*	
Foreign Assets (Net)	31n	9.1	7.5	22.4	5.8	12.7	4.3	8.2	6.6	.5	27.2	41.9	45.9	61.8	74.8	60.6
Domestic Credit	32	7.9	11.5	13.8	26.0	33.4	46.4	57.7	†63.5	71.5	78.7	85.1	80.4	74.1	67.8	101.0
Claims on Central Govt. (Net)	32an	-2.3	-1.9	-2.5	1.4	1.2	1.9	6.2	†4.0	4.5	14.3	12.8	10.0	.7	-4.9	7.8
Claims on Private Sector	32d	10.2	13.3	16.3	24.6	32.1	44.2	51.0	†58.2	65.9	63.5	71.2	69.3	72.3	71.3	91.4
Claims on Other Financial Insts	32f	—	—	—	—	.2	.4	.6	†1.3	1.1	.9	1.1	1.1	1.0	1.4	1.8
Money	34	11.8	11.6	25.1	21.6	32.9	36.5	48.1	†52.7	55.3	80.0	90.1	83.1	90.7	82.7	89.7
Quasi-Money	35	2.1	4.4	5.4	6.7	8.3	11.6	16.8	†13.9	17.2	20.6	27.1	34.7	45.4	60.5	75.8
Long-Term Foreign Liabilities	36cl	1.1	1.4	1.7	1.7	1.7	1.6	1.7	1.9	2.2	2.0	2.3	1.9	1.9	1.8	2.4
Other Items (Net)	37r	2.0	1.7	4.0	1.9	3.2	1.0	-.6	1.7	-2.8	3.4	7.5	6.6	-2.1	-2.4	-6.3
Money plus Quasi-Money	35l	13.9	15.9	30.5	28.3	41.2	48.1	64.9	†66.5	72.6	100.6	117.2	117.8	136.1	143.2	165.5
Other Banking Institutions															*Billions of Francs:*	
Savings Deposits	45	1.0	1.1	1.3	1.6	1.9	2.2	2.4	2.6	2.6	3.5	3.8	3.9	4.2	5.5	6.2
Liquid Liabilities	55l	14.9	17.0	31.7	29.8	43.1	50.3	67.3	†69.1	75.2	104.1	121.0	121.6	140.3	148.7	171.7

1987	1988	1989	1990	1991	1992	1993	1994	1995	1996	1997	1998	1999	2000	2001		
															Exchange Rates	
End of Period																
378.78	407.68	380.32	364.84	370.48	378.57	404.89	†780.44	728.38	753.06	807.94	791.61	†896.19	918.49	935.39	Official Rate	aa
End of Period (ae) Period Average (rf)																
267.00	302.95	289.40	256.45	259.00	275.32	294.77	†534.60	490.00	523.70	598.81	562.21	†652.95	704.95	744.31	Official Rate	ae
300.54	297.85	319.01	272.26	282.11	264.69	283.16	†555.20	499.15	511.55	583.67	589.95	†615.70	711.98	733.04	Official Rate	rf
Period Averages																
166.1	167.8	156.5	183.7	177.4	188.9	176.3	90.0	100.0	97.5	85.6	84.7	81.1	70.3	68.1	Official Rate	ahx
122.1	126.5	132.9	154.1	156.4	168.4	176.5	95.5	100.0	100.6	97.1	100.5	97.7	92.0	93.5	Nominal Effective Exchange Rate	ne c
151.8	144.2	133.9	138.6	131.7	133.9	129.3	86.2	100.0	102.5	104.9	109.3	105.1	98.8	100.5	Real Effective Exchange Rate	re c
															Fund Position	
End of Period																
38.4	38.4	38.4	38.4	38.4	54.3	54.3	54.3	54.3	54.3	54.3	54.3	73.4	73.4	73.4	Quota	2f. s
.1	.1	1.3	.1	.3	.2	.1	—	.3	.2	—	.1	.2	—	.2	SDRs	1b. s
.2	.2	.2	.2	.3	.3	.2	.3	.3	.3	.3	.3	.3	.3	.3	Reserve Position in the Fund	1c. s
60.1	57.9	57.4	61.1	55.3	55.8	49.9	56.0	70.4	62.5	64.9	67.4	60.4	53.3	45.3	Total Fund Cred.&Loans Outstg.	2tl
															International Liquidity	
End of Period																
354.9	232.1	285.3	353.2	364.9	272.5	156.3	94.4	130.4	88.5	118.6	117.7	122.0	152.3	126.1	Total Reserves minus Gold	1l. d
.1	.1	1.7	.2	.4	.3	.1	.1	.4	.4	—	.1	.2	—	.2	SDRs	1b. d
.3	.3	.3	.3	.4	.3	.3	.4	.4	.4	.3	.4	.3	.4	.3	Reserve Position in the Fund	1c. d
354.5	231.7	283.3	352.7	364.1	271.9	155.9	94.0	129.6	87.8	118.3	117.3	121.4	151.9	125.5	Foreign Exchange	1d. d
.013	.013	.013	.013	.013	.013	.013	.013	.013	.013	.013	.013	.013	....	....	Gold (Million Fine Troy Ounces)	1ad
5.9	5.2	4.9	4.7	4.4	4.3	4.7	4.7	4.8	4.7	3.8	3.7	3.7	....	....	Gold (National Valuation)	1and
-3.2	10.4	6.1	4.6	12.1	-.1	10.3	5.5	1.1	2.8	2.7	8.9	3.1	6.5	6.8	Monetary Authorities: Other Liab.	4..d
64.3	78.4	117.9	84.4	93.6	87.9	58.4	109.7	111.1	100.6	66.3	69.1	60.0	81.4	87.2	Deposit Money Banks: Assets	7a.d
104.7	88.0	93.0	83.0	92.0	95.1	64.8	40.6	76.1	77.8	71.8	71.5	64.1	64.9	62.1	Liabilities	7b. d
															Monetary Authorities	
End of Period																
94.8	70.3	82.6	90.6	94.5	75.0	46.1	50.5	63.9	46.3	71.0	66.2	79.7	107.4	94.1	Foreign Assets	11
42.7	42.5	39.6	41.9	39.5	40.0	40.4	49.8	71.1	70.2	66.0	76.5	67.8	66.9	65.9	Claims on Central Government	12a
5.2	3.8	4.8	4.5	6.4	6.4	6.4	7.2	2.0	7.5	4.2	8.5	5.0	2.6	1.8	Claims on Deposit Money Banks	12e
1.6	1.5	1.6	.5	1.6	1.6	1.5	1.3	.3	.2	.3	.3	.3	.3	.3	Claims on Other Financial Insts	12f
115.2	86.1	93.9	104.4	110.1	90.4	61.3	62.8	80.9	70.7	71.2	79.0	90.3	109.4	102.3	Reserve Money	14
48.3	23.2	21.3	32.1	36.3	22.1	10.3	44.8	73.5	59.7	60.3	65.3	79.5	95.7	85.7	*of which: Currency Outside DMBs*	14a
23.8	27.6	23.8	23.5	23.6	21.1	23.2	46.7	51.8	48.6	54.1	58.3	56.2	53.6	47.5	Foreign Liabilities	16c
.5	1.3	6.6	3.8	2.6	6.5	6.6	9.6	8.1	8.4	9.9	5.8	3.8	3.7	8.6	Central Government Deposits	16d
4.7	3.2	4.3	5.8	5.7	5.1	3.3	-10.3	-3.6	-3.4	6.3	8.3	2.6	10.5	3.7	Other Items (Net)	17r
															Deposit Money Banks	
End of Period																
67.2	62.7	70.5	72.6	73.7	69.0	54.1	15.1	12.5	14.9	17.7	7.9	9.0	13.4	12.8	Reserves	20
17.2	23.8	34.1	21.7	24.2	24.2	17.2	58.6	54.4	52.7	39.7	38.8	39.2	57.4	64.9	Foreign Assets	21
.8	1.2	1.7	1.6	1.4	2.1	1.9	12.4	12.3	16.5	17.4	16.7	14.1	10.8	7.9	Claims on Central Government	22a
96.4	99.7	95.3	99.1	112.0	110.6	101.9	101.8	130.4	140.2	154.8	161.9	146.6	147.6	137.3	Claims on Private Sector	22d
.7	.7	.9	.9	.7	.5	.6	.5	—	—	—	—	—	—	—	Claims on Other Financial Insts	22f
41.8	40.3	40.8	42.2	41.2	34.1	35.1	49.3	56.4	59.9	60.6	63.5	61.1	78.4	73.0	Demand Deposits	24
72.8	79.9	82.8	84.6	86.4	78.1	66.7	68.2	68.7	66.2	73.8	65.4	68.9	69.4	78.2	Time Deposits	25
24.8	23.7	25.0	18.9	21.6	24.3	17.2	19.9	33.7	37.3	42.5	39.1	40.1	44.4	45.2	Foreign Liabilities	26c
3.2	3.0	2.0	2.3	2.3	1.9	1.9	1.7	3.5	3.4	.5	1.2	1.7	1.4	1.4	Long-Term Foreign Liabilities	26cl
40.8	38.3	50.6	46.6	49.8	53.2	43.1	39.1	37.4	32.8	29.8	28.9	20.6	17.2	15.1	Central Government Deposits	26d
5.3	3.9	2.8	3.4	6.4	6.4	7.1	7.4	2.0	7.6	4.7	8.5	5.0	2.6	2.1	Credit from Monetary Authorities	26g
-6.4	-1.2	-1.4	-2.2	4.4	8.4	4.5	2.7	7.9	16.9	17.7	18.8	11.4	16.0	8.3	Other Items (Net)	27r
—	.4	2.2	1.0	.4	1.5	1.4	.6	.9	.7	.7	.5	.3	.3	.3	Treasury Claims: Private Sector	22d. i
1.0	.9	1.0	1.0	1.0	.9	1.0	1.0	1.3	1.2	1.7	1.2	1.9	1.5	1.2	Post Office: Checking Deposits	24.. i
															Monetary Survey	
End of Period																
63.4	42.8	67.9	69.8	73.6	53.8	22.8	42.5	32.7	13.2	14.0	7.7	22.6	66.8	66.3	Foreign Assets (Net)	31n
101.8	106.8	83.0	94.6	103.8	96.0	97.6	118.1	169.8	187.1	200.4	221.8	206.2	206.3	189.0	Domestic Credit	32
3.2	4.5	-17.0	-6.9	-10.9	-18.2	-7.8	13.8	38.3	46.0	44.7	59.1	59.1	58.1	51.1	Claims on Central Govt. (Net)	32an
96.4	100.1	97.5	100.1	112.4	112.1	103.3	102.5	131.2	140.9	155.5	162.4	146.8	147.8	137.6	Claims on Private Sector	32d
2.2	2.2	2.6	1.4	2.3	2.1	2.1	1.8	.3	.2	.3	.3	.3	.3	.3	Claims on Other Financial Insts	32f
91.0	64.4	63.2	75.3	78.5	57.1	46.6	95.3	131.2	121.0	123.3	131.8	144.8	176.9	161.5	Money	34
72.8	79.9	82.8	84.6	86.4	78.1	66.7	68.2	68.7	66.2	73.8	65.4	68.9	69.4	78.2	Quasi-Money	35
3.2	3.0	2.0	2.3	2.3	1.9	1.9	1.7	3.5	3.4	.5	1.2	1.7	1.4	1.0	Long-Term Foreign Liabilities	36cl
-1.8	2.3	3.1	2.2	10.2	12.8	5.3	-4.6	-.9	9.6	16.9	31.1	13.4	25.5	14.5	Other Items (Net)	37r
163.8	144.3	145.9	159.8	164.9	135.2	113.3	163.5	199.9	187.2	197.0	197.2	213.7	246.3	239.7	Money plus Quasi-Money	35l
															Other Banking Institutions	
End of Period																
6.4	6.2	9.9	....	....	....	....	....	....	....	....	....	....	....	....	Savings Deposits	45
170.2	150.5	155.8	....	....	....	....	....	....	187.2	197.0	197.2	213.7	246.3	....	Liquid Liabilities	55l

Togo

		1972	1973	1974	1975	1976	1977	1978	1979	1980	1981	1982	1983	1984	1985	1986
Interest Rates															*Percent Per Annum*	
Discount Rate *(End of Period)*	60	3.50	5.50	5.50	8.00	8.00	8.00	8.00	8.00	10.50	10.50	12.50	10.50	10.50	10.50	8.50
Money Market Rate	60b	...	...	...	...	7.28	7.38	7.42	7.72	10.13	13.35	14.66	12.23	11.84	10.66	8.58
Deposit Rate	60l	3.00	5.75	5.75	5.88	6.00	6.00	6.00	6.00	6.19	6.25	7.75	7.50	7.25	7.25	6.08
Lending Rate	60p	...	...	...	...	...	12.00	12.00	12.00	14.50	14.50	16.00	14.50	14.50	14.50	13.50
Prices and Labor														*Index Numbers (1995=100):*		
Consumer Prices	64	18.6	†19.3	21.8	25.7	28.7	35.2	35.3	38.0	42.7	51.1	56.7	62.1	59.9	58.8	61.2
Employment	67e	...	...	...	...	...	...	...	...	...	...	...	...	...	*Number in Thousands:* 61	62
International Transactions															*Millions of Francs*	
Exports	70	12,659	13,755	45,174	26,962	24,914	39,115	54,238	46,432	71,285	57,469	58,173	61,921	83,588	85,380	70,551
Imports, c.i.f.	71	21,381	22,388	28,612	37,270	44,420	69,834	100,898	110,208	116,357	117,769	128,354	108,141	118,460	129,406	107,983
															1985=100	
Export Prices	74	15.4	16.9	43.1	†43.6	32.7	45.5	46.6	51.8	48.8	51.4	53.6	61.2	84.4	100.0	...
Unit Value of Imports	75	26.2	27.6	36.1	†40.5	46.7	52.7	59.4	65.8	70.6	80.4	82.6	100.2	100.2	100.0	...
Balance of Payments															*Millions of US Dollars:*	
Current Account, n.i.e.	78ald	...	...	131.8	−75.5	−27.6	−87.3	−217.4	−212.7	−95.0	−44.2	−86.8	−47.9	16.3	−33.5	−65.6
Goods: Exports f.o.b.	78aad			215.1	141.0	158.9	199.3	262.0	290.6	475.8	377.7	344.8	273.5	291.0	282.0	362.4
Goods: Imports f.o.b.	78abd			−98.0	−211.5	−180.6	−252.7	−410.9	−464.3	−524.1	−413.9	−408.2	−291.8	−263.2	−303.7	−418.6
Trade Balance	78acd			117.0	−70.6	−21.8	−53.4	−148.9	−173.8	−48.3	−36.2	−63.3	−18.3	27.8	−21.7	−56.2
Services: Credit	78add			14.5	27.9	23.8	27.6	36.0	45.2	73.9	97.1	88.3	70.6	76.8	87.0	103.7
Services: Debit	78aed			−38.2	−69.1	−60.0	−90.3	−134.2	−145.4	−166.8	−146.0	−136.0	−117.7	−112.6	−131.8	−172.3
Balance on Goods & Services	78afd			93.3	−111.7	−58.0	−116.1	−247.1	−273.9	−141.2	−85.1	−111.1	−65.4	−8.1	−66.6	−124.8
Income: Credit	78agd			6.4	6.5	6.5	7.0	7.3	10.2	20.7	15.6	16.7	16.1	17.2	23.5	27.5
Income: Debit	78ahd			−6.0	−11.3	−10.4	−20.2	−27.7	−32.0	−60.6	−43.4	−59.0	−59.2	−56.0	−61.5	−69.5
Balance on Gds, Serv. & Inc.	78aid			93.7	−116.6	−61.9	−129.3	−267.6	−295.8	−181.2	−112.9	−153.4	−108.5	−46.9	−104.6	−166.8
Current Transfers, n.i.e.: Credit	78ajd			44.6	49.9	43.2	53.9	66.0	99.9	101.4	83.3	80.1	73.6	75.5	90.5	120.4
Current Transfers: Debit	78akd			−6.5	−8.8	−8.8	−11.8	−15.8	−16.9	−15.2	−14.5	−13.6	−13.0	−12.3	−19.4	−19.1
Capital Account, n.i.e.	78bcd			—	—	—	—	—	—	—	—	—	—	—	—	—
Capital Account, n.i.e.: Credit	78bad			—	—	—	—	—	—	—	—	—	—	—	—	—
Capital Account: Debit	78bbd			—	—	—	—	—	—	—	—	—	—	—	—	—
Financial Account, n.i.e.	78bjd	...	...	−81.5	92.5	24.1	70.4	236.6	207.5	62.8	.4	11.8	2.3	−37.0	31.1	23.5
Direct Investment Abroad	78bdd			—	—	—	—	—	—	—	—	—	—	—	—	—
Dir. Invest. in Rep. Econ., n.i.e.	78bed			−44.3	5.2	5.6	11.3	92.9	52.6	42.7	10.2	16.1	1.4	−9.9	16.3	6.1
Portfolio Investment Assets	78bfd			—	—	—	—	—	—	—	−.3	−.2	−.9	−.3	−.3	−4.0
Equity Securities	78bkd			—	—	—	—	—	—	—	−.3	−.2	—	—	—	−2.7
Debt Securities	78bld			—	—	—	—	—	—	—	—	−.2	−.9	−.3	−.3	−1.3
Portfolio Investment Liab., n.i.e.	78bgd			.8	.6	21.0	1.5	—	2.5	2.2	—	—	.7	.1	.7	1.4
Equity Securities	78bmd			.8	.6	21.0	1.5	—	2.5	2.2	—	—	.7	.1	.7	1.4
Debt Securities	78bnd			—	—	—	—	—	—	—	—	—	—	—	—	—
Financial Derivatives Assets	78bwd			...	...	...	...	...	...	...	...	...	...	...	...	...
Financial Derivatives Liabilities	78bxd			...	...	...	...	...	...	...	...	...	...	...	...	...
Other Investment Assets	78bhd			−65.6	51.2	−26.0	−12.9	−42.3	5.4	4.9	−60.3	−31.5	16.9	−15.4	−16.1	−4.5
Monetary Authorities	78bod			—	—	—	—	—	—	—	—	—	—	—	—	—
General Government	78bpd			−1.5	−.3	−.5	−1.2	−1.0	−2.2	−1.9	−2.9	−1.8	−1.3	−1.6	−9.4	−.1
Banks	78bqd			−55.5	42.8	−16.9	−13.0	−43.7	−8.0	18.7	−23.9	−15.1	9.4	−5.4	2.9	11.1
Other Sectors	78brd			−8.7	8.7	−8.6	1.3	2.4	15.6	−12.0	−33.6	−14.6	8.9	−8.5	−9.6	−15.5
Other Investment Liab., n.i.e.	78bid			27.7	35.4	23.5	70.6	186.1	147.1	13.3	50.8	27.4	−15.9	−11.5	30.5	24.5
Monetary Authorities	78bsd			—	—	—	—	—	—	—	—	—	—	—	—	—
General Government	78btd			24.9	26.5	16.6	15.9	104.0	124.5	−12.7	−88.8	−47.3	−10.4	−26.5	−22.2	4.6
Banks	78bud			3.2	11.6	5.6	48.1	24.9	−18.9	19.6	19.6	−.3	−6.6	14.2	5.2	7.2
Other Sectors	78bvd			−.5	−2.7	1.2	6.7	57.1	41.5	6.4	120.0	75.1	1.2	.9	47.5	12.7
Net Errors and Omissions	78cad			−16.0	−6.1	.2	−15.4	.5	−10.3	−.6	−2.6	−3.2	7.5	−.1	−.7	−1.0
Overall Balance	78cbd			34.3	10.9	−3.3	−32.2	19.7	−15.6	−32.8	−46.3	−78.2	−38.1	−20.8	−3.1	−43.1
Reserves and Related Items	79dad			−34.3	−10.9	3.3	32.2	−19.7	15.6	32.8	46.3	78.2	38.1	20.8	3.1	43.1
Reserve Assets	79dbd			−34.3	−10.9	−8.3	32.2	−18.2	9.7	−12.6	−92.5	−38.4	−40.9	−57.8	−32.6	10.9
Use of Fund Credit and Loans	79dcd			—	—	8.6	—	−1.5	5.9	19.3	9.0	—	20.1	11.7	4.5	7.4
Exceptional Financing	79ded			—	—	3.0	—	—	—	26.1	129.9	116.6	58.8	66.9	31.2	24.8
International Investment Position															*Millions of US Dollars*	
Assets	79aad	...	...	...	...	...	...	...	...	...	...	...	...	...	...	...
Direct Investment Abroad	79abd	...	...	...	...	...	...	...	...	...	...	...	...	...	...	...
Portfolio Investment	79acd	...	...	...	...	...	...	...	...	...	...	...	...	...	...	...
Equity Securities	79add	...	...	...	...	...	...	...	...	...	...	...	...	...	...	...
Debt Securities	79aed	...	...	...	...	...	...	...	...	...	...	...	...	...	...	...
Financial Derivatives	79ald	...	...	...	...	...	...	...	...	...	...	...	...	...	...	...
Other Investment	79afd	...	...	...	...	...	...	...	...	...	...	...	...	...	...	...
Monetary Authorities	79agd	...	...	...	...	...	...	...	...	...	...	...	...	...	...	...
General Government	79ahd	...	...	...	...	...	...	...	...	...	...	...	...	...	...	...
Banks	79aid	...	...	...	...	...	...	...	...	...	...	...	...	...	...	...
Other Sectors	79ajd	...	...	...	...	...	...	...	...	...	...	...	...	...	...	...
Reserve Assets	79akd	...	...	...	...	...	...	...	...	...	...	...	...	...	...	...
Liabilities	79lad	...	...	...	...	...	...	...	...	...	...	...	...	...	...	...
Dir. Invest. in Rep. Economy	79lbd	...	...	...	...	...	...	...	...	...	...	...	...	...	...	...
Portfolio Investment	79lcd	...	...	...	...	...	...	...	...	...	...	...	...	...	...	...
Equity Securities	79ldd	...	...	...	...	...	...	...	...	...	...	...	...	...	...	...
Debt Securities	79led	...	...	...	...	...	...	...	...	...	...	...	...	...	...	...
Financial Derivatives	79lld	...	...	...	...	...	...	...	...	...	...	...	...	...	...	...
Other Investment	79lfd	...	...	...	...	...	...	...	...	...	...	...	...	...	...	...
Monetary Authorities	79lgd	...	...	...	...	...	...	...	...	...	...	...	...	...	...	...
General Government	79lhd	...	...	...	...	...	...	...	...	...	...	...	...	...	...	...
Banks	79lid	...	...	...	...	...	...	...	...	...	...	...	...	...	...	...
Other Sectors	79ljd	...	...	...	...	...	...	...	...	...	...	...	...	...	...	...

	1987	1988	1989	1990	1991	1992	1993	1994	1995	1996	1997	1998	1999	2000	2001		
Percent Per Annum																**Interest Rates**	
	8.50	9.50	11.00	11.00	11.00	12.50	10.50	10.00	7.50	6.50	6.00	6.25	5.75	6.50	6.50	Discount Rate *(End of Period)*	60
	8.37	8.72	10.07	10.98	10.94	11.44	....	....	....	....	....	4.81	4.95	4.95	4.95	Money Market Rate	60b
	5.25	5.25	6.42	7.00	7.00	7.75	....	....	....	....	....	3.50	3.50	3.50	3.50	Deposit Rate	60l
	13.50	14.50	16.00	16.00	16.00	17.50	....	....	....	....	....	....	....	....	....	Lending Rate	60p
Period Averages																**Prices and Labor**	
	61.2	61.1	60.6	61.2	61.5	62.3	†61.7	85.9	100.0	104.7	†113.3	114.4	114.3	116.5	122.9	Consumer Prices	64
Period Averages																	
	64	64	58	57	59	61	60	56	54	50	49	....	....	....	....	Employment	67e
Millions of Francs																**International Transactions**	
	73,212	72,209	78,188	72,942	71,433	72,779	38,512	182,300	188,400	225,400	246,600	570,900	241,000	257,400	165,922	Exports	70
	127,308	145,170	150,533	158,287	125,220	104,461	50,810	123,265	295,700	339,900	376,400	346,700	367,400	402,100	260,016	Imports, c.i.f.	71
1985=100																	
	....	....	....	....	....	....	....	....	....	384.6	404.9	376.9	315.7	314.0	187.6	Export Prices	74
	....	....	....	....	....	....	....	....	....	15.6	19.5	21.0	26.1	25.1	39.8	Unit Value of Imports	75
Minus Sign Indicates Debit																Balance of Payments	
	-60.5	-87.2	-50.8	-99.8	-146.9	-140.6	-82.4	-56.3	-122.0	-153.9	-116.9	-140.1	-127.1	....	....	Current Account, n.i.e.	78al*d*
	397.5	435.3	411.7	513.8	514.4	419.7	264.0	328.4	377.4	440.6	422.5	420.3	391.5	....	....	Goods: Exports f.o.b.	78aa*d*
	-437.1	-504.5	-470.1	-602.7	-567.0	-547.4	-375.3	-365.5	-506.5	-567.8	-530.6	-553.5	-489.4	....	....	Goods: Imports f.o.b.	78ab*d*
	-39.6	-69.1	-58.4	-88.9	-52.6	-127.7	-111.3	-37.1	-129.1	-127.2	-108.1	-133.2	-98.0	....	....	*Trade Balance*	78ac*d*
	118.8	105.1	128.0	149.1	116.4	129.2	84.6	70.9	87.3	116.2	88.5	76.0	68.4	....	....	Services: Credit	78ad*d*
	-196.6	-200.2	-195.8	-244.1	-286.3	-203.3	-128.2	-125.3	-164.3	-201.4	-167.8	-149.2	-130.6	....	....	Services: Debit	78ae*d*
	-117.4	-164.1	-126.2	-183.9	-222.4	-201.8	-154.9	-91.6	-206.0	-212.3	-187.4	-206.4	-160.1	....	....	*Balance on Goods & Services*	78af*d*
	18.9	20.8	24.0	32.8	29.7	31.4	26.8	9.1	8.8	45.6	35.0	44.4	40.2	....	....	Income: Credit	78ag*d*
	-66.1	-70.5	-63.8	-65.3	-58.7	-58.6	-17.7	-54.0	-42.4	-72.0	-63.9	-67.7	-78.6	....	....	Income: Debit	78ah*d*
	-164.6	-213.8	-166.0	-216.4	-251.4	-229.0	-145.7	-136.5	-239.6	-238.8	-216.3	-229.7	-198.5	....	....	*Balance on Gds, Serv. & Inc.*	78ai*d*
	125.2	148.4	134.0	145.6	128.7	111.1	82.6	91.3	129.7	106.8	120.2	101.8	73.6	....	....	Current Transfers, n.i.e.: Credit	78aj*d*
	-21.2	-21.8	-18.8	-29.1	-24.2	-22.7	-19.3	-11.2	-12.1	-21.9	-20.8	-12.2	-2.2	....	....	Current Transfers: Debit	78ak*d*
	—	—	—	—	—	—	—	—	—	5.6	5.8	6.1	6.9	....	....	Capital Account, n.i.e.	78bc*d*
	—	—	—	—	—	—	—	—	—	5.6	5.8	6.1	6.9	....	....	Capital Account, n.i.e.: Credit	78ba*d*
	—	—	—	—	—	—	—	—	....	....	....	....	—	....	....	Capital Account: Debit	78bb*d*
	-44.8	29.9	-2.8	75.2	67.8	-23.8	-105.1	-40.5	-52.8	151.3	126.9	114.1	155.5	....	....	Financial Account, n.i.e.	78bj*d*
	—	—	—	—	—	—	—	—	5.8	-2.8	-2.5	-10.6	-2.9	....	....	Direct Investment Abroad	78bd*d*
	7.2	13.0	9.2	18.2	6.5	—	-11.9	15.4	26.2	17.3	21.0	30.2	42.6	....	....	Dir. Invest. in Rep. Econ., n.i.e.	78be*d*
	.7	-.3	-1.1	-1.8	1.1	—	-.7	.7	5.0	-16.1	6.7	-5.2	-1.3	....	....	Portfolio Investment Assets	78bf*d*
	1.3	.4	-.4	-1.0	1.1	—	.3	1.1	5.0	-.3	7.0	-4.4	-2.8	....	....	Equity Securities	78bk*d*
	-.7	-.7	-.6	-.7	—	—	-.9	-.4	—	-15.8	-.3	-.7	1.6	....	....	Debt Securities	78bl*d*
	.7	1.0	1.3	4.4	2.6	—	.1	—	....	20.1	9.4	11.4	8.6	....	....	Portfolio Investment Liab., n.i.e.	78bg*d*
	.7	1.0	1.3	4.4	2.6	—	—	—	....	18.8	10.6	11.6	8.5	....	....	Equity Securities	78bm*d*
	—	—	—	—	—	—	.1	—	....	1.3	-1.2	-.2	.1	....	....	Debt Securities	78bn*d*
	....	....	....	....	....	....	....	....	20.6	.3	2.1	-.1	—	....	....	Financial Derivatives Assets	78bw*d*
	....	....	....	....	....	....	....	....	....	1.6	-7.0	-.2	-.3	....	....	Financial Derivatives Liabilities	78bx*d*
	-42.2	-15.6	-72.3	25.2	7.5	.2	-3.2	-1.5	12.1	-19.2	-1.6	16.2	13.0	....	....	Other Investment Assets	78bh*d*
	....	....	....	....	....	....	....	....	....	....	....	....	—	....	....	Monetary Authorities	78bo*d*
	-.1	-.5	-.3	-.2	-.1	—	—	—	....	-3.7	12.2	5.3	7.8	....	....	General Government	78bp*d*
	-11.1	-20.4	-49.9	38.6	11.8	.2	—	—	....	4.6	....	-.7	.5	....	....	Banks	78bq*d*
	-30.9	5.3	-22.1	-13.2	-4.1	—	-3.2	-1.5	12.1	-20.1	-13.8	11.6	4.7	....	....	Other Sectors	78br*d*
	-11.2	31.8	60.1	29.1	50.1	-24.0	-89.5	-55.2	-122.4	150.1	98.9	72.3	95.8	....	....	Other Investment Liab., n.i.e.	78bi*d*
	—	—	—	—	—	—	—	—	—	3.8	4.8	5.8	-5.0	....	....	Monetary Authorities	78bs*d*
	-69.5	8.5	.2	-28.4	21.3	-53.3	-44.8	-19.3	-133.5	67.8	62.0	45.0	33.2	....	....	General Government	78bt*d*
	8.7	-.3	-2.8	-11.3	2.4	10.4	-.7	-66.2	....	13.1	....	-6.4	1.6	....	....	Banks	78bu*d*
	49.7	23.6	62.7	68.8	26.5	18.9	-44.0	30.3	11.0	65.4	32.0	28.0	65.9	....	....	Other Sectors	78bv*d*
	-25.1	9.4	26.1	-19.3	31.0	4.0	-2.1	-.2	-19.3	-27.9	-2.7	2.7	-3.7	....	....	Net Errors and Omissions	78ca*d*
	-130.4	-47.9	-27.6	-43.9	-48.1	-160.3	-189.6	-97.1	-194.0	-24.9	13.1	-17.2	31.6	....	....	*Overall Balance*	78cb*d*
	130.4	47.9	27.6	43.9	48.1	160.3	189.6	97.1	194.0	24.9	-13.1	17.2	-31.6	....	....	Reserves and Related Items	79da*d*
	52.0	3.5	-38.6	-29.5	-13.9	73.6	102.2	-7.7	-26.9	34.3	-26.2	8.8	-22.2	....	....	Reserve Assets	79db*d*
	-17.7	-2.8	-.7	5.3	-7.9	.6	-8.3	9.3	22.0	-11.4	3.4	3.0	-9.4	....	....	Use of Fund Credit and Loans	79dc*d*
	96.2	47.1	66.9	68.1	69.9	86.1	95.7	95.5	199.0	2.0	9.7	5.4	—	....	....	Exceptional Financing	79de*d*
Millions of US Dollars																International Investment Position	
	....	....	....	....	....	....	....	....	....	....	....	....	364.1	....	....	Assets	79aa*d*
	....	....	....	....	....	....	....	....	....	....	....	....	-10.1	....	....	Direct Investment Abroad	79ab*d*
	....	....	....	....	....	....	....	....	....	....	....	....	14.3	....	....	Portfolio Investment	79ac*d*
	....	....	....	....	....	....	....	....	....	....	....	....	6.6	....	....	Equity Securities	79ad*d*
	....	....	....	....	....	....	....	....	....	....	....	....	7.7	....	....	Debt Securities	79ae*d*
	....	....	....	....	....	....	....	....	....	....	....	....	.1	....	....	Financial Derivatives	79al*d*
	....	....	....	....	....	....	....	....	....	....	....	....	237.7	....	....	Other Investment	79af*d*
	....	....	....	....	....	....	....	....	....	....	....	....	—	....	....	Monetary Authorities	79ag*d*
	....	....	....	....	....	....	....	....	....	....	....	....	35.8	....	....	General Government	79ah*d*
	....	....	....	....	....	....	....	....	....	....	....	....	67.1	....	....	Banks	79ai*d*
	....	....	....	....	....	....	....	....	....	....	....	....	134.8	....	....	Other Sectors	79aj*d*
	....	....	....	....	....	....	....	....	....	....	....	....	122.1	....	....	Reserve Assets	79ak*d*
	....	....	....	....	....	....	....	....	....	....	....	....	1,728.8	....	....	Liabilities	79la*d*
	....	....	....	....	....	....	....	....	....	....	....	....	47.5	....	....	Dir. Invest. in Rep. Economy	79lb*d*
	....	....	....	....	....	....	....	....	....	....	....	....	24.2	....	....	Portfolio Investment	79lc*d*
	....	....	....	....	....	....	....	....	....	....	....	....	24.2	....	....	Equity Securities	79ld*d*
	....	....	....	....	....	....	....	....	....	....	....	....	.1	....	....	Debt Securities	79le*d*
	....	....	....	....	....	....	....	....	....	....	....	....	.7	....	....	Financial Derivatives	79ll*d*
	....	....	....	....	....	....	....	....	....	....	....	....	1,656.5	....	....	Other Investment	79lf*d*
	....	....	....	....	....	....	....	....	....	....	....	....	86.9	....	....	Monetary Authorities	79lg*d*
	....	....	....	....	....	....	....	....	....	....	....	....	1,322.3	....	....	General Government	79lh*d*
	....	....	....	....	....	....	....	....	....	....	....	....	56.0	....	....	Banks	79li*d*
	....	....	....	....	....	....	....	....	....	....	....	....	191.3	....	....	Other Sectors	79lj*d*

Togo

		1972	1973	1974	1975	1976	1977	1978	1979	1980	1981	1982	1983	1984	1985	1986
Government Finance															*Billions of Francs:*	
Deficit (-) or Surplus	80	....	....	....	....	....	−39,363	−58,836	−17,942	−4,689	−14,821	−4,794	−5,607	−7,862	−6,104	−16,644
Total Revenue and Grants	81y						46,881	56,646	70,008	72,896	70,891	81,649	85,921	102,704	116,598	120,480
Revenue	81						46,861	56,549	69,674	72,833	66,660	76,771	79,406	91,987	107,212	104,880
Grants	81z						20	97	334	63	4,231	4,878	6,515	10,717	9,386	15,600
Exp. & Lending Minus Repay.	82z						86,244	115,482	87,950	77,585	85,712	86,443	91,528	110,566	122,702	137,124
Expenditure	82						72,677	84,667	68,297	73,943	85,137	86,410	91,863	110,567	122,702	137,121
Lending Minus Repayments	83						13,567	30,815	19,653	3,642	575	33	−335	−1	—	3
Statistical Discrepancy	80xx	....	....	....	....	....	....	....	....	....	....	....	....	....	....	....
Total Financing																
Domestic	84a	....	....	....	....	....	6,943	2,437	−5,555	940	6,988	2,221	92	....	3,264	4,953
Foreign	85a	....	....	....	....	....	32,420	56,399	23,497	3,749	7,833	2,573	5,515	....	2,840	11,691
Financing																
Total Financing	84	....	....	....	....	....	39,363	58,836	17,942	4,689	14,821	4,794	5,607	7,862	6,104	16,644
Net Borrowing: Domestic	84a						6,943	2,437	−5,555	940	6,988	2,221	92	....	3,264	4,953
Foreign	85a						32,420	56,399	23,497	3,749	7,833	2,573	5,515	....	2,840	11,691
Use of Cash Balances	87						−944	−2,321	−3,942	495	862	−3,660	−17,221	....		4,940
Debt: Domestic	88a	....	....	....	....	....	....	....	....	....	....	....	16,282	4,277	6,412	4,213
Debt: Foreign	89a	....	....	....	....	....	....	....	....	....	....	209,964	231,683	292,270	320,487	293,683	283,430
National Accounts															*Billions of Francs*	
Househ.Cons.Expend.,incl.NPISHs	96f	69.5	70.0	72.8	95.6	90.8	106.1	123.1	131.0	151.6	180.6	194.9	208.6	219.6	235.4	258.8
Government Consumption Expend.	91f	7.3	8.2	10.8	19.2	22.2	28.6	29.2	32.3	35.4	38.7	41.8	48.3	49.4	44.7	44.6
Gross Fixed Capital Formation	93e	16.2	18.9	20.0	29.2	33.7	58.7	88.5	101.4	82.3	67.7	63.6	66.6	55.7	91.8	101.7
Changes in Inventories	93i	1.4	2.4	2.1	7.4	3.1	6.9	4.6	6.4	.6	11.4	7.3	−1.6	−8.5	−5.7	4.5
Exports of Goods and Services	90c	20.2	18.3	55.2	35.6	43.4	45.0	66.8	71.6	114.9	103.4	110.7	131.1	160.7	165.8	133.2
Imports of Goods and Services (-)	98c	27.9	26.0	32.2	58.7	56.9	76.6	123.2	129.9	146.4	143.8	148.6	155.0	163.1	193.8	177.5
Gross Domestic Product (GDP)	99b	87.6	90.4	130.6	128.3	136.3	168.8	189.0	212.8	238.4	258.0	269.7	298.0	313.8	338.2	365.3
Net National Income	99e	80.7	82.9	121.8	121.7	129.2	159.1	173.3	194.0	212.2	224.3	230.0	247.4	266.3	287.7	313.5
GDP Volume 1970 prices	99b.p	81.1	77.8	81.1	80.6	80.2	84.6	93.2								
GDP Volume 1978 Prices	99b.p	....	....	....	....	....	....	189.0	199.2	202.9	195.8	188.3	189.7	192.2	192.3	199.7
GDP Volume (1995=100)	99bvp	73.6	70.6	73.6	73.1	72.8	76.8	84.6	89.1	90.8	87.6	84.3	84.9	86.0	86.0	89.4
GDP Deflator (1995=100)	99bip	21.5	23.1	32.1	31.7	33.8	39.7	40.4	43.1	47.4	53.2	57.8	63.4	65.9	71.0	73.9
															Millions:	
Population	99z	2.07	2.12	2.17	2.23	2.29	2.35	2.41	2.47	2.55	2.69	2.70	2.85	2.94	3.03	3.12

	1987	1988	1989	1990	1991	1992	1993	1994	1995	1996	1997	1998	1999	2000	2001		
																Government Finance	
Year Ending December 31																	
	−9,380	....	−16	−13	−34	−18	−53	−59	−35	−24	−17	−48	−27	−43	....	Deficit (-) or Surplus	80
	107,874	....	108	115	79	81	39	77	109	127	140	141	142	121	....	Total Revenue and Grants	81y
	99,492	....	98	100	79	73	38	67	97	110	129	127	127	117	....	Revenue	81
	8,382	....	10	14	—	8	1	10	12	16	12	14	15	4	....	Grants	81z
	117,254	....	124	128	113	99	92	136	144	151	157	188	169	164	....	Exp. & Lending Minus Repay.	82z
	117,144	....	124	127	113	99	92	136	144	151	157	188	168	168	....	Expenditure	82
	110	....	—	1	—	—	—	—	—	—	—	1	1	−3	....	Lending Minus Repayments	83
	....	....	....	—	23	10	35	21	−4	−5	−30	−1	4	28	....	Statistical Discrepancy	80xx
																Total Financing	
	....	....	—	7	1	5	16	19	19	7	13	10	1	−4	....	Domestic	84a
	....	....	16	8	10	3	2	19	20	22	34	39	23	20	....	Foreign	85a
																Financing	
	....	....	....	....	....	....	....	....	....	....	....	....	....	....	....	Total Financing	84
	....	....	—	7	1	5	16	19	19	7	13	10	1	−4	....	Net Borrowing: Domestic	84a
	....	....	16	8	10	3	2	19	20	22	34	39	23	20	....	Foreign	85a
	....	....	....	....	....	....	....	....	....	....	....	....	....	....	....	Use of Cash Balances	87
	....	....	....	....	....	....	....	....	....	....	....	....	....	....	....	Debt: Domestic	88a
	280,615	308,066	....	....	....	....	....	....	....	....	....	....	....	....	....	Debt: Foreign	89a
																National Accounts	
Billions of Francs																	
	262.5	266.8	304.8	350.1	362.2	390.4	323.5	438.1	577.2	647.7	761.5	726.4	752.2	820.0	....	Househ.Cons.Expend.,incl.NPISHs	96f
	53.4	51.3	60.3	56.3	66.3	55.1	57.8	77.1	77.0	100.5	95.2	103.0	95.4	89.3	....	Government Consumption Expend.	91f
	92.8	102.3	102.9	71.9	67.1	57.7	25.4	63.1	84.4	99.1	118.2	128.3	123.0	142.9	....	Gross Fixed Capital Formation	93e
	1.2	.1	4.5	4.3	.1	6.6	−10.4	18.2	17.8	10.7	9.3	−.6	4.6	5.5	....	Changes in Inventories	93i
	128.6	149.1	172.2	180.5	177.5	140.8	98.7	221.7	232.0	284.9	298.2	292.7	269.8	280.5	....	Exports of Goods and Services	90c
	166.6	168.0	212.3	230.6	220.3	200.5	142.6	272.5	334.8	393.5	407.6	414.4	374.1	408.3	....	Imports of Goods and Services (-)	98c
	372.4	410.7	431.6	442.5	452.9	443.5	352.3	545.6	553.6	748.7	874.8	835.4	870.9	929.9	....	Gross Domestic Product (GDP)	99b
	320.4	356.9	377.6	394.2	405.0	398.6	321.5	468.3	574.8	664.3	775.3	742.2	764.2	829.7	....	Net National Income	99e
	....	....	....	....	....	....	....	....	....	....	....	....	....	....	....	GDP Volume 1970 prices	99b.p
	203.5	216.7	225.1	224.4	222.9	214.5	179.0	209.0	223.5	245.2	255.7	250.1	256.0	265.0	....	GDP Volume 1978 Prices	99b.p
	91.1	97.0	100.7	100.4	99.7	96.0	80.1	93.5	100.0	109.7	114.4	111.9	114.5	118.6	....	GDP Volume (1995=100)	99bv p
	73.9	76.5	77.4	79.6	82.0	83.5	79.5	105.4	100.0	123.3	138.1	134.9	137.3	141.7	....	GDP Deflator (1995=100)	99bi p
Midyear Estimates																	
	3.22	3.32	3.41	3.51	3.62	3.73	3.84	3.93	4.06	4.17	4.28	4.40	4.51	4.53	4.66	Population	99z

(See notes in the back of the book.)

Tonga

866

	1972	1973	1974	1975	1976	1977	1978	1979	1980	1981	1982	1983	1984	1985	1986
Exchange Rates														*Pa'anga per SDR:*	
Official Rate .... aa	.8515	.8110	.9195	.9280	1.0657	1.0605	1.1284	1.1875	1.0765	1.0284	1.1210	1.1567	1.1800	1.6076	1.8336
														Pa'anga per US Dollar:	
Official Rate .... ae	.7843	.6723	.7510	.7927	.9173	.8731	.8662	.9014	.8440	.8835	1.0163	1.1048	1.2038	1.4636	1.4990
Official Rate .... rf	.8192	.7041	.6958	.7639	.8180	.9018	.8736	.8946	.8782	.8702	.9859	1.1098	1.1394	1.4313	1.4957
Fund Position														*Millions of SDRs:*	
Quota .... 2f. s	...	...	...	...	...	...	...	...	...	...	...	...	...	3.25	3.25
SDRs .... 1b. s	...	...	...	...	...	...	...	...	...	...	...	...	...	—	.03
Reserve Position in the Fund .... 1c. s	...	...	...	...	...	...	...	...	...	...	...	...	...	—	—
Total Fund Cred.&Loans Outstg. 2tl	...	...	...	...	...	...	...	...	...	...	...	...	...	.74	.74
International Liquidity												*Millions of US Dollars Unless Otherwise Indicated:*			
Total Reserves minus Gold .... 1l. d	...	...	...	...	...	9.00	10.12	12.56	13.75	13.98	15.56	20.95	26.02	27.51	22.48
SDRs .... 1b. d	...	...	...	...	...	...	...	...	...	...	...	...	...	—	.04
Reserve Position in the Fund .... 1c. d	...	...	...	...	...	...	...	...	...	...	...	...	...	.81	.91
Foreign Exchange .... 1d. d	...	...	...	...	...	9.00	10.12	12.56	13.75	13.98	15.56	20.95	26.02	26.70	21.54
Monetary Authorities: Other Liab. .... 4.. d															
Deposit Money Banks: Assets .... 7a. d	...	...	.09	.12	.15	.05	.05	.06	.11	.14	.22	.29	.35	.29	.12
Liabilities .... 7b. d	...	...	.01	.13	.07	.03	.24	.41	.33	.94	.46	.24	.22	.62	.75
Other Banking Insts.: Liabilities .... 7f. d	...	...	...	...	...	—	—	—	.04	.15	.41	.38	.55	.67	.82
Monetary Authorities														*Thousands of Pa'anga:*	
Foreign Assets 11	...	...	...	...	...	...	...	...	...	...	15,554	20,874	25,928	27,772	34,726
Claims on Central Government 12a	...	...	...	...	...	...	...	...	...	...	2,734	3,379	3,095	2,730	3,374
Claims on Other Banking Insts 12f															
Reserve Money 14	...	...	...	...	...	...	...	...	...	...	17,860	23,715	28,421	29,986	37,127
of which: Currency Outside DMBs 14a	...	...	...	...	...	...	...	...	...	...	2,505	3,168	3,404	3,569	4,474
Liabs. of Central Bank: Securities 16ac											—	—	—	—	—
Foreign Liabilities 16c											—	—	—	—	—
Central Government Deposits 16d	...	...	377	367	335	430	382	435	427	357	409	469	513	400	771
Capital Accounts 17a	...	...	794	1,313							—	—	—	—	—
Other Items (Net) 17r	...	...	−451	−606	−574	−851	−1,050	−1,183	−74	−1,466	19	69	89	116	202
Deposit Money Banks														*Thousands of Pa'anga:*	
Reserves 20	...	...	5,710	2,894	4,039	8,373	7,685	10,064	11,576	12,309	13,849	19,493	23,963	25,417	31,653
Foreign Assets 21	...	...	71	97	136	44	43	52	93	122	221	322	425	420	178
Claims on Central Government 22a	...	...	—	518	—	—	—	200	200	431	431	431	431	431	200
Claims on Nonfin.Pub.Enterprises 22c			—												
Claims on Private Sector 22d	...	...	40	668	2,088	3,012	3,088	4,090	5,170	6,921	9,555	9,600	9,849	15,330	16,783
Claims on Other Banking Insts 22f						50	50	100	150	150	233	274	311	311	350
Demand Deposits 24	...	...	1,190	1,382	1,445	2,224	2,651	2,705	3,200	3,505	4,912	6,451	6,650	7,360	8,817
Time, Savings,& Fgn.Currency Dep. 25	...	...	2,324	2,381	3,497	5,860	6,038	7,084	8,140	8,226	8,928	10,035	11,870	16,632	19,489
Foreign Liabilities 26c	...	...	11	101	62	25	204	366	280	833	471	263	260	909	1,118
Central Government Deposits 26d	...	...	1,500	1,573	1,142	1,482	1,309	2,237	2,550	2,795	4,054	5,930	7,375	6,427	7,339
Liabilities to Other Banking Insts. 26i											—	—	—	—	—
Capital Accounts 27a	...	...	794	1,313	1,861	2,223	3,065	4,457	5,487	6,526	7,964	8,993	10,333	12,200	15,342
Other Items (Net) 27r	...	...	2	−2,573	−1,744	−335	−2,401	−2,343	−2,468	−1,952	−2,040	−1,552	−1,509	−1,619	−2,941
Monetary Survey														*Thousands of Pa'anga:*	
Foreign Assets (Net) 31n	...	...	...	...	...	...	...	...	...	...	15,304	20,933	26,093	27,283	33,786
Domestic Credit 32	...	...	...	...	...	...	...	...	...	...	8,490	7,285	5,798	11,975	12,597
Claims on Central Govt. (Net) 32an	...	...	...	...	...	...	...	...	...	...	−1,298	−2,589	−4,362	−3,666	−4,536
Claims on Nonfin.Pub.Enterprises 32c			—												
Claims on Private Sector 32d	...	...	40	668	2,088	3,012	3,088	4,090	5,170	6,921	9,555	9,600	9,849	15,330	16,783
Claims on Other Banking Insts 32f											233	274	311	311	350
Money 34	...	...	1,190	1,382	1,445	2,224	2,651	2,705	3,200	3,505	7,417	9,619	10,054	10,929	13,291
Quasi-Money 35	...	...	2,324	2,381	3,497	5,860	6,038	7,084	8,140	8,226	8,928	10,035	11,870	16,632	19,489
Liabs.of Central Bank: Securities 36ac											—	—	—	—	—
Liabilities to Other Banking Insts. 36i											—	—	—	—	—
Capital Accounts 37a	...	...	1,588	2,626	1,861	2,223	3,065	4,457	5,487	6,526	7,964	8,993	10,333	12,200	15,342
Other Items (Net) 37r	...	...	...	...	...	...	...	...	...	...	−515	−429	−366	−503	−1,739
Money plus Quasi-Money 35l	...	...	3,514	3,763	4,942	8,084	8,689	9,789	11,340	11,731	16,345	19,654	21,924	27,561	32,780
Other Banking Institutions														*Thousands of Pa'anga:*	
Reserves 40	...	...	...	...	...	—	46	497	555	—	1	422	341	338	360
Claims on Central Government 42a	...	...	...	...	...										
Claims on Nonfin.Pub.Enterprises 42c															
Claims on Private Sector 42d	...	...	...	...	...	196	706	1,398	2,135	3,043	4,031	4,391	5,880	6,551	8,441
Claims on Deposit Money Banks 42e	...	...	...	...	...	175	75	650	675	725	925	525	500	950	790
Bonds 46ab															
Long-Term Foreign Liabilities 46cl						—	—	36	133	419	419	668	977	1,235	
Central Government Deposits 46d													—	6	
Central Govt. Lending Funds 46f						—	—	1,054	1,593	1,917	2,065	2,041	2,150	2,362	2,957
Credit from Monetary Authorities 46g						33	—	—	—	41	—	34	125	—	3
Credit from Deposit Money Banks 46h						—	—	—	—	—	—	250	225	200	175
Capital Accounts 47a						332	796	1,490	1,736	1,811	2,874	3,162	3,653	4,149	4,825
Other Items (Net) 47r						6	31	1	—	−134	−401	−568	−100	145	396
Banking Survey														*Thousands of Pa'anga:*	
Foreign Assets (Net) 51n	...	...	...	...	...	...	...	...	...	...	15,304	20,933	26,093	27,283	33,786
Domestic Credit 52	...	...	...	...	...	...	...	...	...	...	12,288	11,402	11,367	18,209	20,688
Claims on Central Govt. (Net) 52an	...	...	...	...	...	...	...	...	...	...	−1,298	−2,589	−4,362	−3,672	−4,536
Claims on Nonfin.Pub.Enterprises 52c															
Claims on Private Sector 52d	...	...	...	...	...	3,208	3,794	5,488	7,305	9,964	13,586	13,991	15,729	21,881	25,224
Liquid Liabilities 55l	...	...	...	...	...	8,084	8,643	9,292	10,785	11,731	16,344	19,232	21,583	27,223	32,420
Bonds 56ab						—	—	—	—	—	—	—	—	—	—
Liabs.of Central Bank: Securities 56ac											—	—	—	—	—
Long-Term Foreign Liabilities 56cl						—	—	36	133	419	419	668	977	1,235	
Central Govt. Lending Funds 56f						—	—	1,054	1,593	1,917	2,065	2,041	2,150	2,362	2,957
Capital Accounts 57a						2,555	3,861	5,947	7,223	8,337	10,838	12,155	13,986	16,349	20,167
Other Items (Net) 57r						1,364	2,252	5,302	...	8,010	−2,074	−1,512	−927	−1,419	−2,305
Interest Rates														*Percent Per Annum:*	
Deposit Rate 60l	...	...	...	...	...	...	...	...	6.25	6.25	6.25	6.25	6.25	6.25	6.25
Lending Rate 60p	...	...	...	...	...	...	...	...	10.00	10.00	10.00	10.00	10.00	10.00	10.00

1987	1988	1989	1990	1991	1992	1993	1994	1995	1996	1997	1998	1999	2000	2001		
End of Period															**Exchange Rates**	
1.9567	1.5748	1.6539	1.8435	1.8984	1.9050	1.8881	1.8308	1.8818	1.7377	1.8313	2.2670	2.2066	2.5754	2.7736	Official Rate	**aa**
End of Period (ae) Period Average (rf)																
1.3793	1.1703	1.2585	1.2958	1.3271	1.3854	1.3746	1.2541	1.2659	1.2085	1.3573	1.6100	1.6077	1.9767	2.2070	Official Rate	**ae**
1.4280	1.2750	1.2612	1.2800	1.2961	1.3471	1.3840	1.3202	1.2709	1.2323	1.2635	1.4921	1.5991	1.7585	2.1236	Official Rate	**rf**
End of Period															**Fund Position**	
3.25	3.25	3.25	3.25	3.25	5.00	5.00	5.00	5.00	5.00	5.00	5.00	6.90	6.90	6.90	Quota	**2f.s**
.05	.08	.12	.17	.74	.38	.44	.49	.04	.08	.11	.15	.03	.10	.15	SDRs	**1b.s**
.74	.74	.74	.74	.74	1.18	1.19	1.20	1.21	1.21	1.21	1.22	1.70	1.71	1.71	Reserve Position in the Fund	**1c.s**
—	—	—	—	—	—	—	—	—	—	—	—	—	—	—	Total Fund Cred.&Loans Outstg.	**2tl**
End of Period															**International Liquidity**	
28.88	30.51	24.85	31.34	32.28	31.77	37.06	35.54	28.71	30.62	27.49	28.66	26.78	26.99	26.10	Total Reserves minus Gold	**1l.d**
.07	.11	.16	.24	1.06	.52	.60	.71	.06	.11	.14	.21	.05	.12	.19	SDRs	**1b.d**
1.05	1.00	.97	1.05	1.06	1.62	1.64	1.76	1.80	1.74	1.63	1.72	2.33	2.23	2.15	Reserve Position in the Fund	**1c.d**
27.76	29.41	23.72	30.04	30.17	29.62	34.82	33.07	26.85	28.77	25.72	26.73	24.40	24.64	23.76	Foreign Exchange	**1d.d**
—	—	—	.50	.35	.13	.58	.36	.24	.10	.11	.39	.18	.26	.16	Monetary Authorities: Other Liab.	**4..d**
.12	.21	.26	1.69	.42	.33	1.55	1.85	1.97	1.39	1.61	4.28	2.89	11.50	10.30	Deposit Money Banks: Assets	**7a.d**
.45	.54	.36	.48	.37	.47	.64	.94	1.22	.63	4.35	4.88	4.36	6.92	5.06	Liabilities	**7b.d**
1.55	2.67	2.52	2.36	2.65	2.87	3.67	4.34	3.84	3.52	2.95	2.47	2.32	1.49	1.34	Other Banking Insts.: Liabilities	**7f.d**
End of Period															**Monetary Authorities**	
40,491	35,775	26,902	38,340	42,210	44,155	49,984	41,801	31,485	33,149	32,790	36,300	34,569	25,977	29,709	Foreign Assets	**11**
3,760	4,184	5,336	13,121	10,407	10,432	11,236	9,516	5,493	5,439	5,439	5,456	5,404	6,380	14,095	Claims on Central Government	**12a**
—	—	—	—	650	—	—	—	—	—	—	—	—	—	—	Claims on Other Banking Insts	**12f**
42,879	38,532	28,419	47,067	48,418	51,698	19,226	18,368	15,125	21,629	24,300	26,805	28,804	32,437	42,087	Reserve Money	**14**
4,892	5,503	5,971	6,767	7,165	7,127	7,894	7,346	7,321	6,850	6,471	8,076	9,443	9,966	11,355	*of which: Currency Outside DMBs*	**14a**
—	—	—	—	—	—	42,590	39,200	29,367	24,893	21,818	15,963	13,471	100	—	Liabs. of Central Bank: Securities	**16ac**
—	—	—	648	460	184	803	455	306	122	155	623	295	517	356	Foreign Liabilities	**16c**
873	1,002	1,432	488	488	1,091	3,432	2,142	1,814	1,577	1,366	6,358	7,126	5,777	6,715	Central Government Deposits	**16d**
—	—	1,001	2,786	3,659	2,725	2,789	2,922	3,000	2,459	1,676	1,146	1,039	1,331	2,147	Capital Accounts	**17a**
499	425	1,386	472	242	–1,111	–7,620	–11,770	–12,634	–12,092	–11,086	–9,139	–10,764	–7,805	–7,501	Other Items (Net)	**17r**
End of Period															**Deposit Money Banks**	
37,987	33,029	39,635	40,300	41,253	42,000	48,582	46,688	35,000	39,252	38,006	33,857	33,572	22,483	29,814	Reserves	**20**
168	242	326	2,194	557	457	2,125	2,314	2,491	1,682	2,189	6,893	4,644	22,733	22,729	Foreign Assets	**21**
200	2,213	2,305	2,203	5,974	6,898	6,816	6,262	9,057	8,970	10,616	10,039	9,632	9,094	9,361	Claims on Central Government	**22a**
—	832	2,092	1,437	1,188	413	55	152	103	497	164	1,551	1,392	3,068	6,111	Claims on Nonfin.Pub.Enterprises	**22c**
23,957	28,756	33,555	33,271	32,730	31,051	31,351	47,273	57,191	59,114	68,094	79,720	87,420	102,774	112,835	Claims on Private Sector	**22d**
350	350	350	350	350	350	350	3,850	2,450	1,550	2,375	2,000	3,000	3,000	2,000	Claims on Other Banking Insts	**22f**
10,306	10,182	11,200	15,529	18,509	15,285	18,969	16,637	14,674	15,701	16,941	16,429	20,472	23,106	30,389	Demand Deposits	**24**
23,959	22,523	23,725	27,017	29,557	30,173	38,730	44,553	48,567	51,483	56,684	67,350	72,854	89,042	98,505	Time, Savings,& Fgn.Currency Dep.	**25**
620	632	450	628	493	654	879	1,181	1,545	760	5,909	7,850	7,007	13,679	11,171	Foreign Liabilities	**26c**
11,543	13,584	12,415	16,413	10,931	10,382	7,565	12,394	11,534	10,037	8,009	6,929	6,974	7,086	4,530	Central Government Deposits	**26d**
—	—	—	—	—	—	744	5,225	2,764	4,741	4,399	4,216	5,003	2,604	1,378	Liabilities to Other Banking Insts.	**26i**
19,515	21,290	22,843	26,731	27,627	32,559	30,758	36,560	38,275	38,264	37,889	39,919	36,738	39,805	42,887	Capital Accounts	**27a**
–3,281	–2,789	7,630	–6,563	–5,065	–7,884	–8,366	–10,011	–11,067	–9,921	–8,387	–8,633	–9,388	–12,170	–6,010	Other Items (Net)	**27r**
End of Period															**Monetary Survey**	
40,039	35,385	26,778	39,258	41,814	43,774	50,427	42,479	32,125	33,949	28,915	34,720	31,910	34,514	40,912	Foreign Assets (Net)	**31n**
15,851	21,749	29,791	33,481	39,880	37,671	38,811	52,517	60,946	63,956	77,313	85,479	92,748	111,453	133,157	Domestic Credit	**32**
–8,456	–8,189	–6,206	–1,577	4,962	5,857	7,055	1,242	1,202	2,795	6,680	2,208	936	2,611	12,211	Claims on Central Govt. (Net)	**32an**
—	832	2,092	1,437	1,188	413	55	152	103	497	164	1,551	1,392	3,068	6,111	Claims on Nonfin.Pub.Enterprises	**32c**
23,957	28,756	33,555	33,271	32,730	31,051	31,351	47,273	57,191	59,114	68,094	79,720	87,420	102,774	112,835	Claims on Private Sector	**32d**
350	350	350	350	1,000	350	350	3,850	2,450	1,550	2,375	2,000	3,000	3,000	2,000	Claims on Other Banking Insts	**32f**
15,198	15,685	17,171	22,296	25,674	22,412	27,016	25,535	21,995	22,826	23,412	24,505	29,915	33,072	41,744	Money	**34**
23,959	22,523	23,725	27,017	29,557	30,173	38,730	44,553	48,567	51,483	56,684	67,350	72,854	89,042	98,505	Quasi-Money	**35**
—	—	—	—	—	—	42,590	39,200	29,367	24,893	21,818	15,963	13,471	100	—	Liabs.of Central Bank: Securities	**36ac**
—	—	—	—	—	—	744	5,225	2,764	4,741	4,399	4,216	5,003	2,604	1,378	Liabilities to Other Banking Insts.	**36i**
19,515	21,290	23,844	29,517	31,286	35,284	33,547	39,482	41,275	40,723	39,565	41,065	37,777	41,136	45,034	Capital Accounts	**37a**
–2,782	–2,364	–8,171	–6,091	–4,823	–6,424	–53,389	–58,999	–50,897	–46,761	–39,650	–32,900	–34,362	–19,987	–12,593	Other Items (Net)	**37r**
39,157	38,208	40,896	49,313	55,231	52,585	65,746	70,088	70,562	74,309	80,096	91,855	102,769	122,114	140,249	Money plus Quasi-Money	**35l**
End of Period															**Other Banking Institutions**	
292	157	100	2,141	4,302	2,997	4,277	6,695	4,290	834	475	1,247	1,734	1,607	1,815	Reserves	**40**
—	—	100	100	1,164	1,553	1,651	2,000	2,000	1,700	1,700	1,700	2,000	1,500	200	Claims on Central Government	**42a**
—	—	—	—	636	574	926	3,647	2,937	2,940	1,452	987	834	1,045	885	Claims on Nonfin.Pub.Enterprises	**42c**
10,370	16,474	18,749	22,187	22,278	24,569	29,380	31,176	37,063	38,270	41,669	41,055	31,939	33,247	35,412	Claims on Private Sector	**42d**
2,100	500	200	800	450	100	—	3,200	100	3,578	3,600	2,800	4,100	1,500	250	Claims on Deposit Money Banks	**42e**
—	—	—	—	—	—	2,476	9,189	1,823	2,005	3,908	4,604	5,022	5,696	9,133	Bonds	**46ab**
2,144	3,125	3,169	3,052	3,516	3,973	5,040	5,444	4,863	4,256	4,008	3,976	3,728	2,950	2,950	Long-Term Foreign Liabilities	**46cl**
—	—	—	—	—	—	—	—	3,600	3,600	3,600	3,600	2,000	2,400	1,800	Central Government Deposits	**46d**
3,536	6,092	7,825	11,219	12,485	14,029	14,597	15,761	16,155	17,411	16,743	15,950	14,552	13,036	11,395	Central Govt. Lending Funds	**46f**
—	—	59	—	650	—	—	—	—	—	—	—	—	—	—	Credit from Monetary Authorities	**46g**
347	307	269	226	169	—	—	—	2,100	1,200	2,200	2,000	2,000	3,000	2,000	Credit from Deposit Money Banks	**46h**
6,218	7,235	8,936	10,681	12,980	15,514	16,643	17,703	19,828	21,356	22,074	22,391	19,874	19,020	17,797	Capital Accounts	**47a**
517	372	–1,109	50	–970	–3,723	–2,522	–1,379	–1,979	–2,506	–3,637	–4,732	–6,569	–7,203	–6,513	Other Items (Net)	**47r**
End of Period															**Banking Survey**	
40,039	35,385	26,778	39,258	41,814	43,774	50,427	42,479	32,125	33,949	28,915	34,720	31,910	34,514	40,912	Foreign Assets (Net)	**51n**
25,871	37,873	48,290	55,418	62,958	64,017	70,418	85,490	96,896	101,716	116,159	123,621	122,521	141,845	165,854	Domestic Credit	**52**
–8,456	–8,189	–6,106	–1,477	6,126	7,410	8,706	3,242	–398	895	4,780	308	936	1,711	10,611	Claims on Central Govt. (Net)	**52an**
—	832	2,092	1,437	1,824	987	981	3,799	3,040	3,437	1,616	2,538	2,226	4,113	6,996	Claims on Nonfin.Pub.Enterprises	**52c**
34,327	45,230	52,304	55,458	55,008	55,620	60,731	78,449	94,254	97,384	109,763	120,775	119,359	136,021	148,247	Claims on Private Sector	**52d**
38,865	38,051	40,796	47,172	50,929	49,588	61,469	63,393	66,272	73,475	79,621	90,608	101,035	120,507	138,434	Liquid Liabilities	**55l**
—	—	—	—	—	—	2,476	9,189	1,823	2,005	3,908	4,604	5,022	5,696	9,133	Bonds	**56ab**
—	—	—	—	—	—	42,590	39,200	29,367	24,893	21,818	15,963	13,471	100	—	Liabs.of Central Bank: Securities	**56ac**
2,144	3,125	3,169	3,052	3,516	3,973	5,040	5,444	4,863	4,256	4,008	3,976	3,728	2,950	2,950	Long-Term Foreign Liabilities	**56cl**
3,536	6,092	7,825	11,219	12,485	14,029	14,597	15,761	16,155	17,411	16,743	15,950	14,552	13,036	11,395	Central Govt. Lending Funds	**56f**
25,733	28,525	32,780	40,198	44,266	50,798	50,190	57,185	61,103	62,079	61,639	63,456	57,651	60,156	62,831	Capital Accounts	**57a**
–4,368	–2,535	–9,502	–6,965	–6,424	–10,597	–55,517	–62,203	–50,562	–48,454	–42,663	–36,216	–41,028	–26,086	–17,978	Other Items (Net)	**57r**
Percent Per Annum															**Interest Rates**	
6.25	6.25	7.25	7.25	7.25	4.25	4.25	4.67	4.75	5.58	5.50	5.50	5.42	5.47	5.47	Deposit Rate	**60l**
10.00	10.00	13.50	13.50	13.50	13.50	†9.94	9.39	9.71	10.49	10.10	10.46	10.32	10.69	10.28	Lending Rate	**60p**

Tonga

866

		1972	1973	1974	1975	1976	1977	1978	1979	1980	1981	1982	1983	1984	1985	1986
Prices and Labor															*Index Numbers (1995=100):*	
Consumer Prices	64	....	....	....	17.4	18.6	21.9	24.0	25.3	31.0	35.6	39.5	43.3	†43.4	50.6	61.6
															Number in Thousands:	
Labor Force	67d	....	....	....	....	....	....	....	....	....	....	....	....	....	....	....
International Transactions															*Thousands of Pa'anga*	
Exports	70	2,140	3,277	4,754	4,629	3,358	6,505	5,078	6,879	6,659	7,706	4,301	6,455	10,439	7,785	9,484
Imports, c.i.f.	71	7,456	7,997	11,819	12,972	11,655	17,698	22,317	26,210	33,134	35,002	41,198	41,664	46,315	58,928	60,823
Balance of Payments															*Thousands of US Dollars:*	
Current Account, n.i.e.	78ald	–1,522	–1,355	785	234	–2,028	–1,983	–2,663	–1,539	–6,797	–5,921	7,090	527	–4,833	1,610	2,441
Goods: Exports f.o.b.	78aad	2,961	3,543	4,863	7,435	4,384	4,123	5,974	6,254	7,781	8,878	4,785	5,799	8,319	5,556	6,324
Goods: Imports f.o.b.	78abd	–6,820	–8,243	–10,801	–18,277	–15,704	–14,840	–21,465	–24,562	–33,487	–41,542	–35,498	–33,582	–34,963	–30,500	–32,585
Trade Balance	78acd	–3,859	–4,700	–5,938	–10,842	–11,320	–10,717	–15,491	–18,309	–25,706	–32,664	–30,713	–27,783	–26,644	–24,943	–26,261
Services: Credit	78add	1,440	1,970	3,461	7,604	4,662	5,367	6,531	5,686	9,159	9,832	9,488	10,354	13,548	15,660	15,312
Services: Debit	78aed	–1,403	–1,493	–1,926	–3,952	–2,927	–3,665	–4,783	–2,899	–5,584	–6,032	–7,594	–9,475	–12,814	–15,600	–16,630
Balance on Goods & Services	78afd	–3,821	–4,222	–4,403	–7,191	–9,584	–9,015	–13,744	–15,522	–22,131	–28,865	–28,819	–26,904	–25,910	–24,883	–27,579
Income: Credit	78agd	455	266	332	353	655	676	1,609	2,883	2,029	4,517	5,218	3,211	2,389	2,954	3,988
Income: Debit	78ahd	–32	–72	–145	–60	–219	–340	–224	–392	–478	–556	–908	–118	–139	–416	–122
Balance on Gds, Serv. & Inc.	78aid	–3,397	–4,029	–4,216	–6,898	–9,148	–8,679	–12,359	–13,032	–20,581	–24,904	–24,509	–23,811	–23,660	–22,345	–23,712
Current Transfers, n.i.e.: Credit	78ajd	2,129	3,126	5,402	7,613	8,103	8,138	10,347	12,411	15,465	21,638	35,209	30,437	21,998	26,413	28,748
Current Transfers: Debit	78akd	–254	–452	–401	–480	–983	–1,442	–652	–918	–1,681	–2,656	–3,609	–6,099	–3,170	–2,458	–2,595
Capital Account, n.i.e.	78bcd	95	570	147	98	79	61	—	—	—	—	–453	–137	1,114	289	1,030
Capital Account, n.i.e.: Credit	78bad	120	642	203	149	134	135	—	—	—	—	151	849	1,624	578	1,677
Capital Account: Debit	78bbd	–24	–72	–56	–51	–55	–74	—	—	—	—	–604	–986	–510	–290	–647
Financial Account, n.i.e.	78bjd	801	1,193	251	2,262	2,034	1,467	3,815	4,260	8,282	6,758	94	3,239	8,571	–1,068	–1,585
Direct Investment Abroad	78bdd	—	—	—	—	—	—	—	—	—	—	—	—	—	—	—
Dir. Invest. in Rep. Econ., n.i.e.	78bed	—	—	—	—	—	—	—	—	—	—	—	—	21	130	178
Portfolio Investment Assets	78bfd	—	—	—	—	—	—	—	—	—	—	—	—	—	—	—
Equity Securities	78bkd	—	—	—	—	—	—	—	—	—	—	—	—	—	—	—
Debt Securities	78bld	—	—	—	—	—	—	—	—	—	—	—	—	—	—	—
Portfolio Investment Liab., n.i.e.	78bgd	—	—	—	—	—	—	—	—	—	—	—	—	—	22	4
Equity Securities	78bmd	—	—	—	—	—	—	—	—	—	—	—	—	—	—	4
Debt Securities	78bnd	—	—	—	—	—	—	—	—	—	—	—	—	—	22	—
Financial Derivatives Assets	78bwd	....	....	....	....	....	....	....	....	....	....	....	....	....	....	....
Financial Derivatives Liabilities	78bxd	....	....	....	....	....	....	....	....	....	....	....	....	....	....	....
Other Investment Assets	78bhd	—	—	—	—	—	—	—	—	—	—	—	—	—	–2	–22
Monetary Authorities	78bod															
General Government	78bpd	—	—	—	—	—	—	—	—	—	—	—	—	—	–2	–22
Banks	78bqd															
Other Sectors	78brd															
Other Investment Liab., n.i.e.	78bsd	801	1,193	251	2,262	2,034	1,467	3,815	4,260	8,282	6,758	94	3,239	8,550	–1,217	–1,745
Monetary Authorities	78bid	—	—	—	—	—	—	—	—	—	—	—	—	166	—	—
General Government	78btd	801	1,193	251	2,262	2,034	1,467	2,107	2,298	1,395	4,813	3,221	–132	216	679	208
Banks	78bud	—	—	—	—	—	—	1,398	1,825	6,013	821	534	3,368	7,905	–3,492	–856
Other Sectors	78bvd	—	—	—	—	—	—	311	137	874	1,124	–3,660	4	264	1,596	–1,097
Net Errors and Omissions	78cad	367	–445	550	–613	–2,409	2,798	–36	–278	–291	–610	–5,151	1,764	212	654	–7,008
Overall Balance	78cbd	–259	–37	1,733	1,982	–2,324	2,343	1,116	2,443	1,194	226	1,581	5,393	5,065	1,485	–5,121
Reserves and Related Items	79dad	259	37	–1,733	–1,982	2,324	–2,343	–1,116	–2,443	–1,194	–226	–1,581	–5,393	–5,065	–1,485	5,121
Reserve Assets	79dbd	259	37	–1,733	–1,982	2,324	–2,343	–1,116	–2,443	–1,194	–226	–1,581	–5,393	–5,065	–1,485	5,121
Use of Fund Credit and Loans	79dcd	—	—	—	—	—	—	—	—	—	—	—	—	—	—	—
Exceptional Financing	79ded	....	....	....	....	....	....	....	....	....	....	....	....	....	....	....
Government Finance															*Thousands of Pa'anga:*	
Deficit (-) or Surplus	80	....	....	....	....	....	....	....	....	....	....	–1,524	1,061	324	–2,104	–4,781
Revenue	81	....	....	....	....	....	....	....	....	....	....	15,529	18,054	17,786	22,204	26,218
Grants Received	81z	....	....	....	....	....	....	....	....	....	....	10,658	7,422	9,616	18,668	8,431
Expenditure	82	....	....	....	....	....	....	....	....	....	....	26,178	23,698	26,239	37,983	37,923
Lending Minus Repayments	83	....	....	....	....	....	....	....	....	....	....	1,533	717	839	4,993	1,507
Financing																
Domestic	84a	....	....	....	....	....	....	....	....	....	....	1,026	–1,824	–757	979	3,301
Foreign	85a	....	....	....	....	....	....	....	....	....	....	498	763	433	1,125	1,480
National Accounts															*Millions of Pa'anga:*	
Gross Domestic Product (GDP)	99b	....	....	....	24.83	24.58	30.79	36.32	39.94	52.88	66.39	79.69	86.28	74.48	80.01	100.03
GDP Volume (1990=100)	99bvp	....	....	....	33.1	33.3	34.9	35.6	36.3	42.0	47.9	55.0	58.2	83.8	88.5	96.3
GDP Deflator (1990=100)	99bip	....	....	....	47.4	46.5	55.6	64.4	69.5	79.5	87.5	91.6	93.7	56.1	57.1	65.6
															Millions:	
Population	99z	.08	.09	.09	.09	.09	.09	.09	.09	.09	.09	.09	.10	.10	.10	.09

	1987	1988	1989	1990	1991	1992	1993	1994	1995	1996	1997	1998	1999	2000	2001		
																Prices and Labor	
Period Averages																Consumer Prices......................................	64
	64.5	70.9	73.8	81.0	89.5	96.7	97.6	98.6	† 100.0	103.0	105.2	108.6	113.9	120.6	130.7		
Period Averages																Labor Force......................................	67d
	....	....	....	31,243	....	....	34,782	....	....	34	....	....	....	....	....		
																International Transactions	
Thousands of Pa'anga																Exports..	70
	9,552	10,555	12,298	15,299	17,988	17,402	23,430	18,367	18,443	16,263	12,800	11,600	20,000	....	....	Imports, c.i.f.	71
	68,459	70,689	68,336	78,991	76,817	84,294	84,933	91,210	98,034	91,807	92,100	102,400	116,400	....	....		
																Balance of Payments	
Minus Sign Indicates Debit																Current Account, n.i.e.	78al d
	1,544	−12,744	7,435	5,795	−74	−468	−5,928									Goods: Exports f.o.b.	78aa d
	6,884	8,722	9,395	11,912	13,437	12,306	16,082									Goods: Imports f.o.b.	78ab d
	−38,753	−48,596	−49,728	−50,769	−49,452	−51,300	−56,607									*Trade Balance*	78ac d
	−31,869	−39,873	−40,333	−38,857	−36,015	−38,995	−40,524									Services: Credit	78ad d
	19,774	17,194	27,067	26,363	20,370	16,623	15,953									Services: Debit	78ae d
	−18,544	−25,721	−21,037	−23,351	−22,445	−22,246	−21,145									*Balance on Goods & Services*	78af d
	−30,639	−48,401	−34,304	−35,845	−38,090	−44,618	−45,717									Income: Credit	78ag d
	5,389	4,877	3,911	5,180	3,560	4,244	5,557									Income: Debit	78ah d
	−1,572	−1,275	−1,145	−893	−1,059	−1,211	−2,383									*Balance on Gds, Serv. & Inc.*	78ai d
	−26,822	−44,799	−31,538	−31,558	−35,589	−41,585	−42,543									Current Transfers, n.i.e.: Credit	78aj d
	33,492	36,933	44,063	43,528	41,774	50,551	49,741									Current Transfers: Debit	78ak d
	−5,127	−4,878	−5,089	−6,176	−6,259	−9,434	−13,126										
	−89	34	−238	−115	127	557	605									Capital Account, n.i.e.	78bc d
	520	124	138	241	485	732	1,340									Capital Account, n.i.e.: Credit	78ba d
	−610	−90	−376	−356	−358	−176	−735									Capital Account: Debit	78bb d
	1,659	4,405	−8,203	−1,733	2,984	4,421	3,189									Financial Account, n.i.e.	78bj d
	—	—	—	−1	−24	−2	−1									Direct Investment Abroad	78bd d
	49	29	174	198	359	1,224	2,178									Dir. Invest. in Rep. Econ., n.i.e.	78be d
	—	—	1	32	128	—	—									Portfolio Investment Assets	78bf d
	—	—	1	32	128	—	—									Equity Securities............................	78bk d
	—	−82	−9,392	−8,162	−2,381	−141	−64									Debt Securities..............................	78bl d
	—	−82	−8	−89	−19	−33	—									Portfolio Investment Liab., n.i.e.	78bg d
	—	—	−9,384	−8,073	−2,361	−109	−64									Equity Securities............................	78bm d
	....	....														Debt Securities..............................	78bn d
																Financial Derivatives Assets	78bw d
	−222	755	727	4,787	4,768	815	—									Financial Derivatives Liabilities........	78bx d
																Other Investment Assets	78bh d
	−222	755	723	3,611	1,235	812	—									Monetary Authorities	78bo d
	—	—	—	—	62	—	—									General Government	78bp d
	—	—	4	1,176	3,471	4	—									Banks..	78bq d
	1,832	3,704	287	1,412	134	2,525	1,076									Other Sectors................................	78br d
	—	−285	—	−363	−80	−68	−14									Other Investment Liab., n.i.e.	78bi d
	634	2,626	1,612	248	−725	3,095	1,095									Monetary Authorities	78bs d
	515	511	411	1,750	134	−208	—									General Government	78bt d
	683	851	−1,735	−222	805	−294	−4									Banks..	78bu d
	3,133	9,993	−4,628	2,443	−2,144	−3,437	−260									Other Sectors................................	78bv d
	6,246	1,688	−5,634	6,390	893	1,072	−2,393									Net Errors and Omissions	78ca d
	−6,246	−1,688	5,634	−6,390	−893	−1,072	2,393									*Overall Balance*	78cb d
	−6,246	−1,688	5,634	−6,390	−893	−1,072	2,393									Reserves and Related Items	79da d
	—	—	—	—	—	—	—									Reserve Assets	79db d
	....	....	....	....	....	....										Use of Fund Credit and Loans...........	79dc d
																Exceptional Financing	79de d
																Government Finance	
Year Ending June 30																Deficit (-) or Surplus	80
	−6,693	622	−64	−1,893[P]	−10,051[f]	....	....									Revenue......................................	81
	29,210	33,750	32,740	39,806[P]	51,686[f]	....	....									Grants Received..........................	81z
	15,585	16,278	23,778	29,384[P]	51,530[f]	....	....									Expenditure..................................	82
	42,425	43,985	54,150	68,862[P]	99,175[f]	....	....									Lending Minus Repayments	83
	9,063	5,421	2,432	2,221[P]	14,092[f]	....	....									Financing	
	−805	−622	64	293[P]	2,717[f]	....	....									Domestic	84a
	7,498	—	—	1,600[P]	7,334[f]	....	....									Foreign	85a
																National Accounts	
Year Ending June 30																Gross Domestic Product (GDP)	99b
	114.84	141.30	146.00	158.40	193.20	198.20	201.00	214.80	....	....	....	....	....	....	....		
	97.9	94.5	95.5	100.0	105.9	101.9	101.8	106.7	....							GDP Volume (1990=100)	99bv p
	74.1	94.4	96.5	100.0	115.1	122.8	124.6	127.1	....							GDP Deflator (1990=100)	99bi p
Midyear Estimates																Population..	99z
	.09	.09	.10	.10	.10	.10	.10	.10	.10	.10	.10	.10	.10	.10	.09		

(See notes in the back of the book.)

Trinidad and Tobago

		1972	1973	1974	1975	1976	1977	1978	1979	1980	1981	1982	1983	1984	1985	1986
Exchange Rates														*TT Dollars per SDR:*		
Market Rate	aa	2.2194	2.4924	2.5024	2.7769	2.7884	2.9153	3.1267	3.1616	3.0610	2.7935	2.6475	2.5127	2.3525	3.9543	4.4035
														TT Dollars per US Dollar:		
Market Rate	ae	2.0442	2.0661	2.0439	2.3721	2.4000	2.4000	2.4000	2.4000	2.4000	2.4000	2.4000	2.4000	2.4000	3.6000	3.6000
Market Rate	rf	1.9213	1.9592	2.0532	2.1698	2.4358	2.4000	2.4000	2.4000	2.4000	2.4000	2.4000	2.4000	2.4000	2.4500	3.6000
														Index Numbers (1995=100):		
Nominal Effective Exchange Rate	ne c	....	....	....	....	....	....	....	162.87	161.07	170.82	181.48	188.34	200.29	203.62	134.06
Real Effective Exchange Rate	re c	....	....	....	....	....	....	....	113.88	116.80	128.48	142.40	163.13	187.31	195.82	135.53
Fund Position														*Millions of SDRs:*		
Quota	2f. s	63.0	63.0	63.0	63.0	63.0	63.0	82.0	82.0	123.0	123.0	123.0	170.1	170.1	170.1	170.1
SDRs	1b. s	7.3	7.1	7.9	7.6	7.6	12.2	16.9	31.2	35.8	51.3	73.5	94.4	103.1	107.8	112.0
Reserve Position in the Fund	1c. s	6.6	—	4.8	18.7	27.8	27.6	29.8	37.8	63.0	78.3	96.7	118.6	126.8	124.4	77.2
of which: Outstg.Fund Borrowing	2c	—	—	—	2.9	10.0	10.0	10.0	7.9	5.4	2.9	.4				
Total Fund Cred.&Loans Outstg.	2tl	—	—	—	—	—	—	—	—	—	—	—	—	—	—	—
International Liquidity														*Millions of US Dollars Unless Otherwise Indicated:*		
Total Reserves minus Gold	1l. d	58.3	47.0	390.3	751.0	1,013.5	1,481.7	1,804.8	2,140.0	2,780.8	3,347.5	3,080.5	2,104.5	1,356.7	1,128.5	474.1
SDRs	1b. d	7.9	8.6	9.6	8.9	8.8	14.8	22.0	41.1	45.7	59.7	81.0	98.9	101.1	118.4	136.9
Reserve Position in the Fund	1c. d	7.1	—	5.8	21.9	32.2	33.5	38.8	49.7	80.3	91.1	106.7	124.2	124.3	136.6	94.4
Foreign Exchange	1d. d	43.2	38.4	374.9	720.2	972.5	1,433.4	1,744.0	2,049.2	2,654.8	3,196.7	2,892.8	1,881.5	1,131.3	873.5	242.8
Gold (Million Fine Troy Ounces)	1ad	....	....	....	....	....	.027	.040	.054	.054	.054	.054	.054	.054	.054	.054
Gold (National Valuation)	1and	....	....	....	....	....	1.1	1.7	2.3	2.3	2.3	2.3	2.3	2.3	1.5	1.5
Monetary Authorities: Other Liab.	4.. d															67.6
Deposit Money Banks: Assets	7a. d	3.4	3.8	3.4	3.6	5.9	12.9	19.1	41.1	48.0	49.6	63.8	50.3	56.3	56.3	81.8
Liabilities	7b. d	15.3	25.0	19.3	23.2	21.3	34.6	57.5	47.9	76.1	86.9	104.5	119.1	141.1	85.7	70.8
Other Banking Insts.: Assets	7e. d	.8	.8	1.0	3.3	2.3	2.8	2.4	2.5	2.4	2.4	2.4	2.2	3.8	2.4	3.8
Liabilities	7f. d				4.8	5.1	5.5	4.7	10.2	10.6	14.3	15.9	17.8	28.4	14.1	16.9
Monetary Authorities														*Millions of TT Dollars:*		
Foreign Assets	11	106.7	97.5	796.2	1,778.8	2,461.8	3,586.7	4,363.5	5,163.5	6,694.7	8,064.1	7,410.4	5,087.1	3,322.5	4,096.4	1,748.2
Claims on Central Government	12a	42.3	73.2	.8	.5	.2	—	—	—	45.0	24.6	26.5	31.9	131.5	188.1	1,350.7
Claims on Nonfin.Pub.Enterprises	12c	13.4	19.2	19.8	11.1	11.0	24.6	33.5	17.6	40.7	20.8	12.3	45.1	42.1	31.9	5.6
Claims on Private Sector	12d	....	....	....	....	....	....	....	....	....	....	....	....	....	....	....
Claims on Deposit Money Banks	12e	1.7	3.0	.1	—	—	—	—	—	—	—	—	—	53.8	125.4	360.7
Claims on Other Banking Insts	12f	—	—	—	—	—	—	—	—	—	—	—	—	—	—	—
Claims on Nonbank Financial Insts	12g	....	....	....	....	....	....	....	....	....	....	....	....	....	....	....
Reserve Money	14	131.4	151.8	303.2	478.8	639.2	664.4	695.6	1,225.6	1,335.8	1,637.4	2,631.9	2,488.1	2,291.2	2,452.6	2,069.8
of which: Currency Outside DMBs	14a	81.2	79.7	98.5	138.2	177.2	230.9	295.5	412.1	467.2	532.2	725.9	758.1	709.7	684.7	723.1
Foreign Liabilities	16c															243.3
Central Government Deposits	16d	—	—	460.1	1,202.7	1,694.8	2,891.1	3,436.6	3,609.7	5,020.6	5,748.5	3,786.3	2,137.7	1,101.1	995.5	750.6
Capital Accounts	17a	55.0	64.7	88.3	283.1	263.9	257.7	433.5	747.6	884.3	1,320.9	1,629.9	1,708.5	824.0	1,070.6	1,126.9
Other Items (Net)	17r	−22.3	−23.6	−34.6	−174.1	−124.9	−201.9	−168.7	−401.7	−460.3	−597.3	−598.8	−1,170.2	−666.3	−76.9	−725.3
Deposit Money Banks														*Millions of TT Dollars:*		
Reserves	20	50.2	72.1	204.7	340.6	462.0	433.6	400.1	813.7	868.6	1,070.0	1,856.8	1,629.2	1,497.2	1,673.2	1,241.9
Foreign Assets	21	6.3	7.9	7.0	8.5	14.1	31.0	45.8	98.7	115.2	119.0	153.1	120.8	135.2	202.6	294.3
Claims on Central Government	22a	115.0	147.0	168.8	158.7	157.3	172.9	213.8	276.3	399.9	491.0	707.2	1,072.4	570.6	569.5	575.6
Claims on Local Government	22b	—	1.3	.6	1.4	5.1	7.2	12.0	8.0	5.7	5.1	33.5	3.5	32.2	37.9	12.7
Claims on Nonfin.Pub.Enterprises	22c	10.5	9.0	8.4	5.0	1.7	—	—	44.9	235.7	340.6	520.8	596.7	752.5	861.1	
Claims on Private Sector	22d	502.7	585.5	665.7	888.1	1,247.6	1,761.7	2,341.0	2,745.5	3,310.3	4,058.4	4,893.8	5,671.5	6,075.2	5,843.6	5,917.4
Claims on Other Banking Insts	22f	....	....	....	....	....	....	....	....	....	....	....	....	....	....	....
Claims on Nonbank Financial Insts	22g	....	....	....	....	....	....	....	....	....	....	....	....	....	....	....
Demand Deposits	24	129.9	132.9	171.4	254.2	394.6	494.4	640.2	734.6	869.8	1,287.4	1,772.2	1,575.6	1,500.3	1,483.0	1,260.3
Time, Savings,& Fgn.Currency Dep.	25	511.8	610.2	802.7	995.9	1,291.5	1,634.5	2,004.9	2,669.0	2,960.9	3,637.4	4,847.7	5,499.3	6,048.1	6,183.3	6,124.7
Foreign Liabilities	26c	28.2	51.7	39.5	55.1	51.1	83.0	138.0	114.9	182.7	208.5	250.9	285.9	338.7	308.4	254.7
Central Government Deposits	26d	19.1	19.0	35.5	58.8	66.2	79.1	86.3	194.8	281.5	374.3	452.2	507.2	233.3	208.8	134.1
Credit from Monetary Authorities	26g	1.7	3.0											19.0	47.5	355.3
Liabilities to Other Banking Insts	26i	....	....	....	....	....	....	....	....	....	....	....	....	....	....	....
Capital Accounts	27a	30.0	41.8	51.5	74.2	110.0	139.3	192.0	262.0	361.4	411.7	531.2	636.6	781.4	890.9	668.1
Other Items (Net)	27r	−36.0	−35.8	−45.4	−35.9	−25.6	−23.9	−49.3	−33.1	88.3	59.9	130.8	513.6	−13.7	−42.6	105.8
Monetary Survey														*Millions of TT Dollars:*		
Foreign Assets (Net)	31n	84.8	53.7	763.7	1,732.2	2,424.8	3,534.7	4,271.3	5,147.3	6,627.2	7,974.6	7,312.6	4,922.0	3,119.0	3,990.6	1,544.5
Domestic Credit	32	664.8	816.2	368.5	−196.7	−338.1	−1,003.8	−922.6	−757.1	−1,455.6	−1,287.2	1,775.4	4,700.3	6,113.9	6,219.2	7,838.4
Claims on Central Govt. (Net)	32an	138.2	201.2	−326.0	−1,102.3	−1,603.5	−2,797.3	−3,309.1	−3,528.2	−4,857.2	−5,607.2	−3,504.8	−1,540.6	−632.3	−446.7	1,041.6
Claims on Local Government	32b	—	1.3	.6	1.4	5.1	7.2	12.0	8.0	5.7	5.1	33.5	3.5	32.2	37.9	12.7
Claims on Nonfin.Pub.Enterprises	32c	23.9	28.2	28.2	16.1	12.7	24.6	33.5	17.6	85.6	256.5	352.9	565.9	638.8	784.4	866.7
Claims on Private Sector	32d	502.7	585.5	665.7	888.1	1,247.6	1,761.7	2,341.0	2,745.5	3,310.3	4,058.4	4,893.8	5,671.5	6,075.2	5,843.6	5,917.4
Claims on Other Banking Insts	32f	—	—	—	—	—	—	—	—	—	—	—	—	—	—	—
Claims on Nonbank Financial Inst	32g	....	....	....	....	....	....	....	....	....	....	....	....	....	....	....
Money	34	211.1	212.6	269.9	392.4	571.8	725.3	936.3	1,146.7	1,337.0	1,854.7	2,547.2	2,434.5	2,294.0	2,260.5	2,088.2
Quasi-Money	35	511.8	610.2	802.7	995.9	1,291.5	1,634.5	2,004.9	2,669.0	2,960.9	3,637.4	4,847.7	5,499.3	6,048.1	6,183.3	6,124.7
Liabilities to Other Banking Insts	36i	....	....	....	....	....	....	....	....	....	....	....	....	....	....	....
Capital Accounts	37a	85.0	106.5	139.8	357.3	373.9	397.0	625.5	1,009.6	1,245.7	1,732.6	2,161.1	2,345.1	1,605.4	1,961.5	1,795.0
Other Items (Net)	37r	−58.3	−59.4	−80.1	−210.0	−150.5	−225.9	−218.0	−435.0	−372.0	−537.3	−467.9	−656.6	−714.5	−195.5	−624.9
Money plus Quasi-Money	35l	722.9	822.8	1,072.6	1,388.3	1,863.3	2,359.8	2,941.2	3,815.7	4,297.9	5,492.1	7,394.9	7,933.8	8,342.1	8,443.8	8,212.9

1987	1988	1989	1990	1991	1992	1993	1994	1995	1996	1997	1998	1999	2000	2001		
															Exchange Rates	
End of Period																
5.1072	5.7192	5.5852	6.0463	6.0793	5.8438	7.9860	8.6616	8.9146	8.9074	8.5001	9.2881	8.6467	8.2078	7.9051	Market Rate	**aa**
End of Period (ae) Period Average (rf)																
3.6000	4.2500	4.2500	4.2500	4.2500	4.2500	5.8141	5.9332	5.9971	6.1945	6.2999	6.5965	6.2999	6.2996	6.2902	Market Rate	**ae**
3.6000	3.8438	4.2500	4.2500	4.2500	4.2500	5.3511	5.9249	5.9478	6.0051	6.2517	6.2983	6.2989	6.2998	6.2332	Market Rate	**rf**
Period Averages																
115.67	104.47	96.99	99.47	106.59	114.37	104.55	101.63	100.00	103.82	104.37	106.44	108.08	112.73	118.18	Nominal Effective Exchange Rate	**ne c**
125.60	117.82	116.20	118.70	119.13	121.69	109.93	102.43	100.00	101.88	102.29	107.35	110.22	115.36	124.10	Real Effective Exchange Rate	**re c**
															Fund Position	
End of Period																
170.1	170.1	170.1	170.1	170.1	246.8	246.8	246.8	246.8	246.8	246.8	246.8	335.6	335.6	335.6	Quota	**2f. s**
—	—	6.9	.8	1.5	.2	.2	.1	.1	—	.1	.1	—	—	.2	SDRs	**1b. s**
53.0	—	—	—	—	—	—	—	—	—	—	—	—	—	24.6	Reserve Position in the Fund	**1c. s**
—	—	—	—	—	—	—	—	—	—	—	—	—	—	—	of which: Outstg.Fund Borrowing	**2c**
—	85.1	155.8	231.6	269.1	205.3	112.8	62.4	33.8	16.5	3.1	—	—	—	—	Total Fund Cred.&Loans Outstg.	**2tl**
															International Liquidity	
End of Period																
187.8	127.1	246.5	492.0	338.6	172.2	206.3	352.4	358.2	543.9	706.4	783.1	945.4	1,386.3	1,907.1	Total Reserves minus Gold	**1l. d**
—	—	9.0	1.1	2.1	.3	.3	.1	.2	—	.1	.1	—	—	.2	SDRs	**1b. d**
75.2	—	—	—	—	—	—	—	—	—	—	—	—	—	30.9	Reserve Position in the Fund	**1c. d**
112.6	127.1	237.5	490.9	336.5	171.9	206.0	352.3	358.0	543.8	706.2	783.0	945.4	1,386.2	1,876.0	Foreign Exchange	**1d. d**
.054	.054	.054	.054	.054	.054	.056	.054	.054	.054	.058	.059	.060	.060	.061	Gold (Million Fine Troy Ounces)	**1ad**
2.3	2.0	2.0	2.0	2.0	2.0	1.4	1.4	1.4	1.3	16.8	16.1	17.4	16.4	16.8	Gold (National Valuation)	**1and**
50.9	50.7	74.0	116.2	113.9	86.9	99.8	55.0	33.7	32.2	29.3	31.8	37.7	32.3	38.5	Monetary Authorities: Other Liab.	**4.. d**
77.2	112.1	131.4	114.8	97.9	99.3	208.4	294.1	216.4	287.3	265.2	298.4	381.7	456.2	538.3	Deposit Money Banks: Assets	**7a. d**
91.4	56.4	48.2	49.7	39.9	60.8	66.5	50.5	98.7	137.6	154.1	182.2	239.8	256.0	549.9	Liabilities	**7b. d**
2.5	3.9	4.0	24.1	4.6	5.2	3.0	8.5	11.7	29.2	76.7	73.4	79.8	133.9	243.6	Other Banking Insts.: Assets	**7e. d**
16.8	15.6	23.6	23.7	35.5	53.5	53.2	62.4	62.2	58.2	30.2	41.2	37.6	58.2	115.5	Liabilities	**7f. d**
															Monetary Authorities	
End of Period																
1,481.0	1,509.2	2,274.6	3,321.6	2,825.1	2,180.4	3,610.2	4,602.3	4,577.1	†4,764.4	5,641.3	6,210.7	7,457.7	10,196.3	13,303.6	Foreign Assets	**11**
1,573.8	2,123.0	2,404.4	2,457.6	2,777.6	3,220.3	2,122.3	1,514.0	724.1	†93.6	752.4	709.8	899.8	765.4	961.3	Claims on Central Government	**12a**
5.6	5.6	36.4	22.6	28.6	29.3	28.5	28.5	361.3	†346.6	345.0	336.0	334.0	328.7	310.3	Claims on Nonfin.Pub.Enterprises	**12c**
....	....	....	....	....	....	....	....	....	52.7	48.4	44.9	41.0	36.5	27.8	Claims on Private Sector	**12d**
535.0	542.1	258.2	109.5	644.1	260.1	250.0	507.2	384.7	†807.2	802.6	807.2	803.4	789.0	775.7	Claims on Deposit Money Banks	**12e**
1.5	15.9	15.9	15.9	23.5	23.5	21.7	18.7	18.7	†.5	.5	2.7	.6	.6	.6	Claims on Other Banking Insts	**12f**
....	....	....	....	....	....	....	....	....	56.9	48.1	36.7	31.8	23.4	15.1	Claims on Nonbank Financial Insts	**12g**
1,619.0	1,650.2	1,869.4	2,068.1	2,421.0	2,185.9	2,083.4	3,269.7	3,247.8	†3,538.0	4,106.4	4,963.7	5,146.5	5,305.4	5,872.7	Reserve Money	**14**
702.6	671.8	693.3	735.3	748.7	698.2	707.4	744.6	832.8	†909.8	1,063.0	1,046.8	1,292.4	1,271.0	1,373.5	of which: Currency Outside DMBs	**14a**
183.4	702.0	1,184.5	1,893.8	2,119.7	1,568.9	1,480.8	867.3	503.1	†346.3	211.2	209.9	237.6	203.8	242.1	Foreign Liabilities	**16c**
747.2	876.9	782.3	760.5	872.4	927.1	526.8	780.1	579.3	†1,377.1	2,516.0	1,484.6	2,491.6	4,885.9	7,190.2	Central Government Deposits	**16d**
1,329.3	1,389.5	1,483.1	1,699.3	1,721.3	1,564.3	2,513.8	2,651.5	2,648.5	†1,510.1	1,594.5	1,861.6	1,962.2	2,283.4	2,550.6	Capital Accounts	**17a**
-282.0	-422.9	-329.8	-494.6	-835.6	-532.6	-572.1	-897.8	-912.8	†-649.6	-789.8	-371.8	-269.7	-538.5	-461.3	Other Items (Net)	**17r**
															Deposit Money Banks	
End of Period																
805.4	857.0	1,065.1	1,195.8	1,540.1	1,348.8	1,221.2	2,320.3	2,245.4	†2,370.0	2,772.7	3,058.6	3,021.7	3,214.3	3,935.6	Reserves	**20**
278.0	476.5	558.5	487.8	416.0	421.9	1,211.6	1,745.0	1,297.7	†1,779.4	1,671.0	1,968.2	2,404.5	2,874.0	3,386.3	Foreign Assets	**21**
1,221.3	978.2	834.1	913.5	559.3	568.6	774.9	899.4	1,729.1	†2,084.6	3,823.1	2,293.1	2,728.1	2,411.9	3,411.6	Claims on Central Government	**22a**
11.5	9.2	—	—	—	—	.7	1.9	1.9	†—	54.4	2.1	16.4	83.0	65.7	Claims on Local Government	**22b**
1,050.0	1,376.0	1,240.3	1,002.2	969.6	689.8	747.7	377.9	801.3	†779.5	773.8	904.0	562.1	265.7	802.7	Claims on Nonfin.Pub.Enterprises	**22c**
6,130.8	5,900.5	6,181.9	6,428.3	7,608.5	7,710.0	7,995.1	7,625.6	8,739.4	†9,741.0	11,835.3	13,433.3	14,498.6	16,353.1	16,922.7	Claims on Private Sector	**22d**
....	....	....	....	....	....	....	....	....	252.1	238.0	231.0	207.7	273.0	571.7	Claims on Other Banking Insts	**22f**
....	....	....	....	....	....	....	....	....	1,711.1	616.6	111.2	128.0	220.7	565.0	Claims on Nonbank Financial Insts	**22g**
1,357.0	1,082.3	1,327.6	1,703.6	2,040.7	1,858.9	2,274.3	2,798.8	2,921.0	†2,524.6	3,130.4	2,819.7	3,182.0	3,722.4	4,829.4	Demand Deposits	**24**
6,327.2	6,673.6	6,960.6	7,085.7	6,984.4	6,525.9	7,492.1	8,651.1	8,966.8	†12194.9	13,215.0	15,516.0	15,790.9	17,905.9	18,432.8	Time, Savings,& Fgn.Currency Dep.	**25**
329.0	239.9	204.8	211.1	169.5	258.4	386.6	299.8	591.7	†852.3	970.5	1,201.9	1,510.5	1,612.4	3,459.1	Foreign Liabilities	**26c**
147.3	111.6	131.0	201.8	162.4	135.2	143.2	102.1	267.8	†364.6	204.9	203.2	281.9	231.4	1,011.3	Central Government Deposits	**26d**
476.4	542.1	258.2	109.5	641.7	260.1	288.7	507.1	384.9	†395.3	388.4	386.9	385.1	383.3	381.6	Credit from Monetary Authorities	**26g**
....	....	....	....	....	....	....	....	....	455.7	312.8	681.7	410.6	333.5	431.8	Liabilities to Other Banking Insts	**26i**
1,163.5	1,284.4	1,443.9	1,358.4	1,450.1	1,525.6	1,669.4	1,748.2	1,771.6	†2,513.5	3,093.9	3,443.9	4,017.6	4,867.3	5,486.0	Capital Accounts	**27a**
-303.4	-336.5	-446.2	-642.5	-355.3	175.0	-303.1	-1,137.0	-89.0	†-583.3	469.0	-2,251.8	-2,011.6	-3,360.5	-4,370.6	Other Items (Net)	**27r**
															Monetary Survey	
End of Period																
1,246.6	1,043.7	1,443.8	1,704.5	951.9	774.9	2,954.4	5,180.3	4,780.0	†5,345.2	6,130.6	6,767.1	8,114.0	11,254.1	12,988.7	Foreign Assets (Net)	**31n**
9,100.0	9,419.9	9,799.7	9,877.8	10,932.3	11,179.2	11,020.9	9,583.8	11,528.7	†13376.9	15,814.6	16,417.0	16,674.6	15,644.8	15,452.9	Domestic Credit	**32**
1,900.6	2,112.7	2,325.2	2,408.8	2,302.1	2,726.6	2,227.2	1,531.2	1,606.1	†436.5	1,854.5	1,315.1	854.3	-1,940.0	-3,828.6	Claims on Central Govt. (Net)	**32an**
11.5	9.2	—	—	—	—	.7	1.9	1.9	†—	54.4	2.1	16.4	83.0	65.7	Claims on Local Government	**32b**
1,055.6	1,381.6	1,276.7	1,024.8	998.2	719.1	776.2	406.4	1,162.6	†1,126.1	1,118.9	1,240.0	896.1	594.5	1,113.0	Claims on Nonfin.Pub.Enterprises	**32c**
6,130.8	5,900.5	6,181.9	6,428.3	7,608.5	7,710.0	7,995.1	7,625.6	8,739.4	†9,793.7	11,883.6	13,478.2	14,539.6	16,389.6	16,950.5	Claims on Private Sector	**32d**
1.5	15.9	15.9	15.9	23.5	23.5	21.7	18.7	18.7	†252.6	238.5	233.7	208.4	273.6	572.3	Claims on Other Banking Insts	**32f**
....	....	....	....	....	....	....	....	....	1,768.0	664.8	147.9	159.8	244.2	580.0	Claims on Nonbank Financial Inst	**32g**
2,170.3	1,875.5	2,133.1	2,575.9	2,921.6	2,696.0	3,136.5	3,748.2	3,923.4	†3,685.0	4,464.1	4,724.8	5,306.8	5,658.0	6,766.6	Money	**34**
6,327.2	6,673.6	6,960.6	7,085.7	6,984.4	6,525.9	7,492.1	8,651.1	8,966.8	†12194.9	13,215.0	15,516.0	15,790.9	17,905.9	18,432.8	Quasi-Money	**35**
....	....	....	....	....	....	....	....	....	455.7	312.8	681.7	410.6	333.5	431.8	Liabilities to Other Banking Insts	**36i**
2,492.8	2,673.9	2,927.0	3,057.7	3,171.4	3,089.9	4,183.2	4,399.7	4,420.1	†4,023.6	4,688.4	5,305.5	5,979.8	7,150.7	8,036.6	Capital Accounts	**37a**
-643.7	-759.4	-777.2	-1,137.1	-1,193.3	-357.6	-836.5	-2,034.9	-1,001.6	†-1637.1	-735.0	-3,044.0	-2,699.5	-4,149.2	-5,226.1	Other Items (Net)	**37r**
8,497.5	8,549.1	9,093.7	9,661.6	9,906.0	9,221.9	10,628.6	12,399.3	12,890.2	†15880.0	17,679.0	20,240.8	21,097.8	23,563.9	25,199.3	Money plus Quasi-Money	**35l**

Trinidad and Tobago

	1972	1973	1974	1975	1976	1977	1978	1979	1980	1981	1982	1983	1984	1985	1986

Other Banking Institutions

Other Banklike Institutions

Millions of TT Dollars:

	1972	1973	1974	1975	1976	1977	1978	1979	1980	1981	1982	1983	1984	1985	1986
Reserves ... 40	.4	.8	1.2	1.0	1.8	2.6	3.9	4.4	5.9	19.1	28.3	51.1	49.0	35.6	22.0
Foreign Assets ... 41	1.6	1.7	2.1	7.8	5.6	6.8	5.9	5.9	5.8	5.7	5.7	5.2	9.1	8.7	13.6
Claims on Central Government ... 42a	8.2	8.3	7.8	16.4	3.8	5.0	4.1	6.2	3.7	4.1	.7	22.3	13.7	15.1	10.6
Claims on Local Government ... 42b															
Claims on Nonfin.Pub.Enterprises ... 42c				.1			.1				3.4			.9	
Claims on Private Sector ... 42d	37.5	39.5	33.5	134.7	192.6	276.1	447.7	521.3	723.4	970.5	1,390.2	1,721.5	2,333.9	2,594.9	2,053.1
Claims on Deposit Money Banks ... 42e				24.9	16.4	11.8	41.0	14.6	33.2	45.8	98.6	81.8	185.2	153.8	102.3
Claims on Nonbank Financial Insts ... 42g															
Time, Savings,& Fgn.Currency Dep. ... 45	19.5	21.6	29.0	133.0	175.8	238.7	376.9	431.3	608.0	883.1	1,335.0	1,685.1	2,228.2	2,399.9	1,964.1
Foreign Liabilities ... 46c				.3	.2	.5	.5		.5	.7	5.5	8.5	30.9	18.1	10.3
Central Government Deposits ... 46d															
Credit from Monetary Authorities ... 46g															
Credit from Deposit Money Banks ... 46h	15.5	14.0	1.7	3.0	8.7	18.4	46.1	52.3	39.5	49.2	30.7	59.2	125.2	200.3	76.3
Capital Accounts ... 47a	—	—	—	14.6	15.7	17.7	23.1	30.4	51.8	71.1	191.5	210.3	297.3	245.6	261.2
Other Items (Net) ... 47r	12.8	14.6	13.9	34.0	19.9	26.9	56.1	38.4	72.4	41.2	−35.8	−81.3	−90.7	−55.0	−110.3

Development Banks

Millions of TT Dollars:

	1972	1973	1974	1975	1976	1977	1978	1979	1980	1981	1982	1983	1984	1985	1986
Reserves ... 40..n				.1	.3	.2	.2	.4	.4	−.3	3.0	9.5	5.0	4.4	3.3
Claims on Central Government ... 42a.n				—	—	—	—	2.4	—	—	—	2.0	2.5	.8	—
Claims on Private Sector ... 42d.n				58.0	65.2	97.1	129.8	197.6	265.1	368.1	638.7	763.7	836.8	883.5	922.7
Claims on Deposit Money Banks ... 42e.n				15.4	18.5	20.5	26.6	12.4	14.0	19.4	66.2	52.5	50.6	37.5	35.9
Foreign Liabilities ... 46c.n				11.1	12.0	12.7	10.8	24.4	24.8	33.7	32.7	34.2	37.3	32.7	50.6
Central Government Deposits ... 46d.n				35.4	50.0	76.0	124.4	156.9	220.4	308.1	363.3	582.4	604.3	591.3	610.0
Credit from Dep. Money Banks ... 46h.n															
Capital Accounts ... 47a.n				22.3	19.6	21.8	27.3	38.7	48.0	60.3	315.9	102.2	127.7	153.6	160.8
Other Items (Net) ... 47r.n				4.6	2.5	7.3	−6.0	−7.2	−13.7	−14.9	−4.0	108.9	125.7	148.5	140.6

Banking Survey

Millions of TT Dollars:

	1972	1973	1974	1975	1976	1977	1978	1979	1980	1981	1982	1983	1984	1985	1986
Foreign Assets (Net) ... 51n				1,728.7	2,418.3	3,528.3	4,265.8	5,128.8	6,607.7	7,945.9	7,280.2	4,884.5	3,059.9	3,948.5	1,497.3
Domestic Credit ... 52				−22.9	−126.4	−701.6	−465.3	−186.1	−683.4	−252.3	3,445.4	6,627.6	8,696.9	9,130.7	10,214.9
Claims on Central Govt. (Net) ... 52an				−1,121.2	−1,649.6	−2,868.3	−3,429.4	−3,676.4	−5,073.9	−5,911.2	−3,867.4	−2,098.8	−1,220.4	−1,022.2	442.2
Claims on Local Government ... 52b	—	1.3	.6	1.4	5.1	7.2	12.0	8.0	5.7	5.1	33.5	3.5	32.2	37.9	12.7
Claims on Nonfin.Pub.Enterprises ... 52c				16.2	12.7	24.6	33.6	17.9	85.9	256.8	356.6	566.2	639.1	793.0	866.7
Claims on Private Sector ... 52d				1,080.8	1,505.4	2,134.9	2,918.5	3,464.4	4,298.9	5,397.0	6,922.7	8,156.7	9,245.9	9,322.0	8,893.3
Claims on Nonbank Financial Inst ... 52g															
Liquid Liabilities ... 55l	742.1	843.7	1,100.4	1,520.2	2,037.0	2,595.7	3,314.1	4,242.2	4,899.5	6,356.4	8,698.6	9,558.4	10,516.3	10,803.8	10,151.7
Capital Accounts ... 57a				394.3	409.2	436.5	675.9	1,078.7	1,345.5	1,864.1	2,668.4	2,657.6	2,030.4	2,360.8	2,217.0
Other Items (Net) ... 57r				−208.7	−154.4	−205.5	−189.5	−378.3	−320.8	−526.8	−641.4	−703.9	−789.8	−85.4	−656.6

Nonbank Financial Institutions

Millions of TT Dollars:

	1972	1973	1974	1975	1976	1977	1978	1979	1980	1981	1982	1983	1984	1985	1986
Reserves ... 40..s			16.8	34.9	48.4	54.3	74.7	85.7	23.8	63.8	44.3	98.0	132.4	62.0	24.5
Foreign Assets ... 41..s			65.6	63.7	55.8	75.2	58.9	75.0	52.0	25.6	43.1	83.5	126.8	163.0	171.2
Claims on Central Government ... 42a.s			88.9	82.1	90.6	93.3	139.7	130.2	121.6	132.5	133.8	140.7	106.3	200.3	295.8
Claims on Private Sector ... 42d.s			164.2	162.3	229.1	263.3	310.7	339.9	567.7	751.9	818.4	913.5	1,138.5	1,438.6	1,679.2
Fixed Assets ... 42h.s			11.2	19.1	20.5	25.2	45.0	35.1	41.0	53.1	87.9	131.0	157.4	169.8	205.5
Incr.in Total Assets(Within Per.) ... 49z.s				15.4	82.2	67.0	117.7	36.8	140.3	220.7	100.6	239.3	294.6	372.2	342.7

Interest Rates

Percent Per Annum

	1972	1973	1974	1975	1976	1977	1978	1979	1980	1981	1982	1983	1984	1985	1986
Bank Rate *(End of Period)* ... 60	5.00	6.00	6.00	6.00	6.00	6.00	6.00	6.00	6.00	6.00	6.00	7.50	7.50	7.50	5.97
Treasury Bill Rate ... 60c	3.74	4.37	5.57	3.99	3.98	3.94	3.60	3.16	3.07	3.06	3.05	3.08	3.39	3.47	3.99
Deposit Rate ... 60l										6.57	6.25	6.40	6.76	5.31	6.04
Deposit Rate (Foreign Currency) ... 60l.f															
Lending Rate ... 60p									10.00	11.38	11.50	11.71	12.75	12.69	12.00
Government Bond Yield ... 61	7.83	7.99	8.31	8.25	8.18	8.07	8.07	8.12	8.61	8.84	9.84	9.88	9.89	9.89	9.62

Prices, Production, Labor

Index Numbers (1995=100):

	1972	1973	1974	1975	1976	1977	1978	1979	1980	1981	1982	1983	1984	1985	1986
Share Prices ... 62															
Producer Prices ... 63								33.7	40.3	47.1	53.6	60.3	63.3	66.4	70.6
Consumer Prices ... 64	8.3	9.5	11.6	†13.6	15.1	16.8	18.6	21.3	25.0	28.6	†31.9	36.8	41.7	44.9	48.3
Wages: Avg Weekly Earn.('90=100) ... 65						23.7	27.6	34.1	41.9	50.5	59.2	70.6	80.8	86.8	88.4
Industrial Production ... 66							53.2	54.5	57.7	51.3	53.3	48.7	59.6	57.3	69.6
Crude Petroleum Production ... 66aa	107.4	127.1	142.9	164.8	162.9	175.3	175.7	164.1	162.8	144.9	135.5	122.3	130.2	134.8	129.3
Total Employment ... 67		155.2	151.3	153.4	161.0	†162.4	165.7	165.6	166.7	163.4	157.9	160.5	152.2	134.1	126.4

Number in Thousands:

	1972	1973	1974	1975	1976	1977	1978	1979	1980	1981	1982	1983	1984	1985	1986
Labor Force ... 67d															
Employment ... 67e														400	391
Unemployment ... 67c														73	81
Unemployment Rate (%) ... 67r														15.5	17.5

International Transactions

Millions of TT Dollars:

	1972	1973	1974	1975	1976	1977	1978	1979	1980	1981	1982	1983	1984	1985	1986
Exports ... 70	1,068.4	1,371.4	4,162.8	3,875.2	5,391.8	5,231.5	4,895.1	6,265.0	9,784.8	9,026.0	7,372.4	5,646.3	5,216.2	5,247.1	4,988.6
Imports, c.i.f. ... 71	1,467.6	1,560.1	3,774.9	3,239.2	4,904.3	4,365.2	4,721.0	5,051.0	7,626.4	7,498.9	8,873.1	6,196.7	4,605.9	3,739.0	4,860.2

1995=100

	1972	1973	1974	1975	1976	1977	1978	1979	1980	1981	1982	1983	1984	1985	1986
Volume of Exports ... 72	117.6	116.9	†125.6	108.2	126.5	118.5	107.5	104.7	101.0	90.0	92.1	90.2	103.4	†95.0	93.7
Volume of Imports ... 73	81.1	89.3	†111.2	81.2	111.9	92.2	95.6	107.2	121.9	113.7	111.6	126.0	†142.4	125.6	128.4
Unit Value of Exports ... 74	6.4	8.3	†22.3	25.8	29.8	32.5	32.5	42.9	68.6	75.6	72.4	71.9	†71.4	68.2	66.4
Unit Value of Imports ... 75	5.9	6.9	†15.7	18.1	21.3	21.9	22.9	26.0	39.0	44.0	49.8	50.2	†50.3	49.8	67.6

Other Banking Institutions
Other Banklike Institutions

End of Period

Item	1987	1988	1989	1990	1991	1992	1993	1994	1995	1996	1997	1998	1999	2000	2001
Reserves **40**	111.9	117.8	104.9	114.8	118.4	128.7	143.7	148.0	171.5	†241.5	272.7	409.8	485.3	534.1	513.2
Foreign Assets **41**	9.1	16.6	17.0	102.5	19.6	22.3	17.5	50.3	70.4	†181.1	483.1	484.4	502.7	843.5	1,532.1
Claims on Central Government **42a**	.8	.3	87.8	151.2	165.0	181.3	505.7	588.7	965.4	†1,190.0	1,437.1	1,075.4	1,098.9	1,471.6	672.5
Claims on Local Government **42b**											4.1	4.7	5.1		—
Claims on Nonfin.Pub.Enterprises **42c**				9.6	85.6	12.4	9.2	65.5	33.0	†147.5	137.0	80.3	196.2	291.2	562.1
Claims on Private Sector **42d**	2,197.6	2,234.4	1,965.4	2,184.2	2,436.0	2,749.3	2,852.1	3,341.6	3,982.3	†2,770.0	3,141.9	3,358.5	3,903.7	4,697.0	4,878.9
Claims on Deposit Money Banks **42e**	161.6	199.8	301.2	222.7	216.5	356.7	381.8	325.2	335.6	†786.2	645.4	1,195.6	1,418.3	1,824.6	1,787.6
Claims on Nonbank Financial Insts **42g**										47.4	37.8	201.3	526.1	627.8	571.1
Time, Savings,& Fgn.Currency Dep. **45**	2,071.2	2,189.2	2,096.1	2,221.2	2,272.5	2,471.7	2,805.5	2,894.1	3,138.9	†2,993.9	3,180.3	4,017.2	4,792.5	4,746.5	5,704.3
Foreign Liabilities **46c**	—	—	—	1.6	.4	.3	.3	1.4	.3	†169.5	152.5	238.0	207.3	341.5	705.6
Central Government Deposits **46d**										47.8	100.7	33.6	34.8	87.8	20.3
Credit from Monetary Authorities **46g**										25.3	44.6	52.7	49.9	42.6	34.7
Credit from Deposit Money Banks **46h**	209.8	251.4	96.2	213.1	165.5	147.0	138.9	30.3	48.5	†92.1	249.0	70.0	670.2	530.1	840.8
Capital Accounts **47a**	302.3	300.8	322.2	341.6	428.0	464.4	470.6	512.2	690.3	†762.5	885.4	1,188.8	1,474.7	1,852.2	2,293.5
Other Items (Net) **47r**	-102.3	-172.3	-38.2	7.5	174.7	367.3	494.7	1,081.3	1,680.2	†1,272.7	1,546.5	1,209.6	906.9	2,689.2	918.3

Development Banks

End of Period

Item	1987	1988	1989	1990	1991	1992	1993	1994	1995	1996	1997	1998	1999	2000	2001
Reserves .... **40..n**	—	—	4.8	.9	.5	—	—	—	—	—	—	—	—	1.5	3.6
Claims on Central Government **42a.n**	—	—	—	—	—	—	—	27.8	33.7	—	—	—	—	—	—
Claims on Private Sector **42d.n**	965.3	919.4	940.6	1,007.9	987.2	1,126.5	1,165.7	1,011.9	1,031.3	845.5	852.8	927.5	975.6	1,007.7	1,063.2
Claims on Deposit Money Banks **42e.n**	2.5	3.9	1.5	.9	32.9	72.5	99.4	110.6	88.6	48.0	78.2	101.3	60.1	56.8	172.0
Foreign Liabilities **46c.n**	60.6	66.5	100.1	99.0	150.5	226.9	309.1	368.9	373.0	190.9	37.9	33.6	29.4	25.3	21.0
Central Government Deposits **46d.n**	720.4	598.1	416.3	614.8	427.3	419.2	401.6	517.4	500.8	446.8	440.3	430.7	418.1	418.2	532.7
Credit from Dep. Money Banks **46h.n**	17.0	19.6	26.2	26.4	21.7	33.6	27.3	28.0	40.2	16.0	30.0	17.3	34.7	18.8	20.0
Capital Accounts **47a.n**	150.9	193.4	345.5	194.9	346.2	389.9	389.2	282.4	275.0	204.8	356.0	377.7	409.3	428.0	304.4
Other Items (Net) **47r.n**	19.0	45.9	58.7	74.5	75.0	129.4	137.9	-46.4	-35.4	35.4	66.8	169.5	144.2	175.7	360.7

Banking Survey

End of Period

Item	1987	1988	1989	1990	1991	1992	1993	1994	1995	1996	1997	1998	1999	2000	2001
Foreign Assets (Net) **51n**	1,195.1	993.9	1,360.8	1,706.4	820.5	570.0	2,662.5	4,860.3	4,477.1	†5,165.9	6,423.3	6,979.9	8,380.0	11,730.9	13,794.2
Domestic Credit **52**	11,541.9	11,960.1	12,361.2	12,599.9	14,155.3	14,806.1	15,130.3	14,083.2	17,054.9	†17630.1	20,645.8	21,366.6	22,718.9	22,960.4	22,075.3
Claims on Central Govt. (Net) **52an**	1,181.1	1,514.9	1,996.6	1,945.1	2,039.8	2,488.7	2,331.3	1,630.3	2,104.4	†1,131.9	2,750.6	1,926.2	1,500.1	-974.4	-3,709.1
Claims on Local Government **52b**	11.5	9.2					.7	1.9	1.9	†	58.6	6.8	21.5	83.0	65.7
Claims on Nonfin.Pub.Enterprises **52c**	1,055.6	1,381.6	1,276.7	1,034.4	1,083.8	731.5	785.4	471.9	1,195.6	†1,273.7	1,255.8	1,320.3	1,092.3	885.7	1,675.1
Claims on Private Sector **52d**	9,293.7	9,054.4	9,087.9	9,620.4	11,031.7	11,585.8	12,012.9	11,979.1	13,753.0	†13409.1	15,878.3	17,764.2	19,418.9	22,094.3	22,892.6
Claims on Nonbank Financial Inst **52g**										1,815.4	702.6	349.2	685.9	871.9	1,151.1
Liquid Liabilities **55l**	10,456.8	10,620.4	11,080.1	11,767.1	12,059.6	11,564.9	13,290.4	15,145.4	15,857.6	†18632.3	20,586.7	23,848.2	25,404.9	27,774.8	30,386.8
Capital Accounts **57a**	2,946.1	3,168.0	3,594.7	3,594.3	3,945.6	3,944.2	5,043.0	5,194.3	5,385.4	†4,990.5	5,929.7	6,872.0	7,863.8	9,430.9	10,634.5
Other Items (Net) **57r**	-665.9	-834.5	-952.8	-1,055.1	-1,029.3	-133.0	-540.6	-1,396.2	289.0	†-826.8	552.7	-2,373.7	-2,169.8	-2,514.4	-5,151.8

Nonbank Financial Institutions

End of Period

Item	1987	1988	1989	1990	1991	1992	1993	1994	1995	1996	1997	1998	1999	2000	2001
Reserves .... **40.. s**	75.0	135.7	20.0	23.6											
Foreign Assets .... **41.. s**	550.0	432.9	235.3	347.5											
Claims on Central Government .... **42a. s**	322.6	447.0	452.3	619.3											
Claims on Private Sector .... **42d. s**	1,245.8	1,653.9	1,625.6	2,406.2											
Fixed Assets .... **42h. s**	209.7	204.9	243.2	289.2											
Incr.in Total Assets(Within Per.) .... **49z. s**	26.9	471.2	-297.9	1,109.4											

Interest Rates

Percent Per Annum

Item	1987	1988	1989	1990	1991	1992	1993	1994	1995	1996	1997	1998	1999	2000	2001
Bank Rate *(End of Period)* **60**	7.50	9.50	9.50	9.50	11.50	13.00	13.00	13.00	13.00	13.00	13.00	13.00	13.00	13.00	13.00
Treasury Bill Rate **60c**	4.63	4.88	7.13	7.50	7.67	9.26	9.45	10.00	8.41	10.44	9.83	11.93	10.40	10.56	8.55
Deposit Rate **60l**	6.03	6.01	6.28	5.96	5.79	6.99	7.06	6.91			6.91	7.95	8.51	8.15	7.66
Deposit Rate (Foreign Currency) .... **60l. f**											6.35	6.69	6.41	6.74	7.07
Lending Rate **60p**	11.50	12.58	13.31	12.87	13.17	15.33	15.50	15.98	15.17	15.79	15.33	17.33	17.04	16.50	15.67
Government Bond Yield **61**	9.54	9.76	10.77	10.73	10.85	13.30									

Prices, Production, Labor

Period Averages

Item	1987	1988	1989	1990	1991	1992	1993	1994	1995	1996	1997	1998	1999	2000	2001
Share Prices **62**							71.8	100.0	133.8	202.8	350.6	334.3	382.4		356.5
Producer Prices **63**	73.6	78.0	84.9	86.1	86.3	86.9	91.6	96.5	100.0	102.9	104.9	106.4	108.2		
Consumer Prices **64**	53.5	57.7	†64.3	71.4	74.1	78.8	87.4	95.1	100.0	103.4	107.2	113.2	117.1	121.2	
Wages: Avg Weekly Earn.('90=100) **65**	92.2	93.7	94.5	100.0	100.1	103.0	104.6	109.9							
Industrial Production **66**	72.3	†69.4	69.5	71.2	79.4	87.0	81.5	93.0	100.0	97.7	105.3	109.8			
Crude Petroleum Production **66aa**	119.5	115.8	114.3	115.7	110.3	103.9	94.8	100.3	100.0	98.9	94.8	94.1			
Total Employment **67**	120.1	113.0	113.0	105.0	105.9	104.5	102.5	107.1	†100.0	102.9	106.5	111.1			

Period Averages

Item	1987	1988	1989	1990	1991	1992	1993	1994	1995	1996	1997	1998	1999	2000	2001
Labor Force **67d**					492		504		521	530		559	563		
Employment **67e**		372	372	366	374	401	406	405	416	432	444	460	479	489	
Unemployment **67c**		107	105	103	94	91	99	100	94	89	86	81	79	74	
Unemployment Rate (%) **67r**		22.3	22.0	22.0	20.0	18.5	19.6	19.8	18.4	17.2	16.3	15.0	14.2	13.1	

International Transactions

Millions of TT Dollars

Item	1987	1988	1989	1990	1991	1992	1993	1994	1995	1996	1997	1998	1999	2000	2001
Exports **70**	5,264.6	5,424.2	6,706.9	8,330.7	8,436.4	7,188.3	8,800.9	11,055.2	14,608.6	15,014.4	15,887.6	14,220.5	17,661.2	29,323.4	
Imports, c.i.f. **71**	4,387.5	4,310.3	5,190.4	4,712.3	7,084.8	4,693.5	7,495.3	6,700.9	10,191.1	12,866.8	18,705.9	18,886.8	17,263.0	20,841.9	

1995=100

Item	1987	1988	1989	1990	1991	1992	1993	1994	1995	1996	1997	1998	1999	2000	2001
Volume of Exports **72**	92.1	95.0	93.1	100.0											
Volume of Imports **73**	101.5	85.4	104.1	100.0											
Unit Value of Exports **74**	69.6	66.1	83.6	100.0											
Unit Value of Imports **75**	77.4	85.7	98.6	100.0											

Trinidad and Tobago

	1972	1973	1974	1975	1976	1977	1978	1979	1980	1981	1982	1983	1984	1985	1986
Balance of Payments															*Millions of US Dollars:*
Current Account, n.i.e. .... 78al d	....	....	....	340.3	260.9	182.8	54.4	−19.2	357.0	414.6	−599.5	−946.6	−466.7	−47.9	−411.9
Goods: Exports f.o.b. .... 78aa d	....	....	....	1,072.5	1,153.3	1,284.7	1,301.0	1,759.1	2,728.3	2,725.6	2,317.3	2,102.7	2,173.4	2,141.7	1,378.4
Goods: Imports f.o.b. .... 78ab d	....	....	....	−658.1	−766.0	−867.8	−1,057.5	−1,334.1	−1,789.1	−1,763.5	−2,486.8	−2,233.3	−1,704.9	−1,354.6	−1,209.4
Trade Balance .... 78ac d	....	....	....	414.4	387.3	416.8	243.5	425.0	939.2	962.1	−169.4	−130.6	468.5	787.1	168.9
Services: Credit .... 78ad d	....	....	....	217.3	237.4	263.8	263.8	308.5	410.6	418.0	471.9	242.9	266.3	264.1	271.7
Services: Debit .... 78ae d	....	....	....	−197.3	−235.8	−289.2	−355.3	−474.2	−645.3	−714.8	−882.4	−897.4	−849.4	−725.5	−613.6
Balance on Goods & Services .... 78af d	....	....	....	434.5	388.9	391.5	151.9	259.4	704.5	665.3	−580.0	−785.1	−114.5	325.7	−172.9
Income: Credit .... 78ag d	....	....	....	43.3	60.3	77.0	125.0	159.9	232.3	344.7	357.0	230.3	141.5	195.8	96.8
Income: Debit .... 78ah d	....	....	....	−124.8	−163.7	−263.2	−196.3	−407.5	−537.9	−543.1	−281.9	−367.5	−466.2	−545.2	−307.4
Balance on Gds, Serv. & Inc. .... 78ai d	....	....	....	352.9	285.5	205.3	80.6	11.7	398.9	466.9	−504.8	−922.3	−439.3	−23.7	−383.5
Current Transfers, n.i.e.: Credit .... 78aj d	....	....	....	2.8	1.9	1.7	1.8	1.8	1.8	1.9	2.0	5.9	13.2	10.1	.8
Current Transfers: Debit .... 78ak d	....	....	....	−15.4	−26.4	−24.1	−28.0	−32.6	−43.8	−54.2	−96.6	−30.2	−40.6	−34.3	−29.2
Capital Account, n.i.e. .... 78bc d	....	....	....	−8.5	−5.5	−8.7	−11.8	−14.8	−22.3	−40.1	−45.4	−56.3	−55.8	−35.2	−21.5
Capital Account, n.i.e.: Credit .... 78ba d	....	....	....	—	—	—	—	—	—	4.6	2.8	3.5	3.4	3.1	—
Capital Account: Debit .... 78bb d	....	....	....	−8.5	−5.5	−8.7	−11.8	−14.8	−26.8	−42.9	−49.0	−59.8	−59.2	−38.3	−21.5
Financial Account, n.i.e. .... 78bj d	....	....	....	37.2	−16.1	282.4	287.5	372.3	226.8	303.1	439.0	380.8	−122.8	20.4	−196.4
Direct Investment Abroad .... 78bd d	....	....	....									−3.6	−3.5	−8.2	−7.3
Dir. Invest. in Rep. Econ., n.i.e. .... 78be d	....	....	....	93.0	132.2	83.5	128.8	93.8	184.5	258.1	203.5	117.7	113.2	1.2	−14.5
Portfolio Investment Assets .... 78bf d	....	....	....	—	—	—	−7.9	−2.7	−12.7	1.8	.3	.1	—	—	—
Equity Securities .... 78bk d	....	....	....	—	—	—	—	—	—	—	—	—	—	—	—
Debt Securities .... 78bl d	....	....	....	—	—	—	−7.9	−2.7	−12.7	1.8	.3	.1	—	—	—
Portfolio Investment Liab., n.i.e. .... 78bg d	....	....	....	−1.1	−9.4	−1.1	107.5	−1.1	−6.5	−.5	—	—	—	—	—
Equity Securities .... 78bm d	....	....	....	—	—	—	—	—	—	—	—	—	—	—	—
Debt Securities .... 78bn d	....	....	....	−1.1	−9.4	−1.1	107.5	−1.1	−6.5	−.5	—	—	—	—	—
Financial Derivatives Assets .... 78bw d	....	....	....	....	....	....	....	....	....	....	....	....	....	....	....
Financial Derivatives Liabilities .... 78bx d	....	....	....	....	....	....	....	....	....	....	....	....	....	....	....
Other Investment Assets .... 78bh d	....	....	....	−35.6	−100.5	−1.0	−27.3	−87.6	−87.4	−100.4	−49.5	−79.6	−166.0	−73.2	−12.2
Monetary Authorities .... 78bo d	....	....	....												
General Government .... 78bp d	....	....	....	−35.1	−76.7	−21.3	−12.0	−7.0	−17.1	−140.3	−2.5	−40.8	−87.7	−72.9	7.2
Banks .... 78bq d	....	....	....	−.5	−2.4	−7.3	−7.2	−20.3	−7.5	−2.6	−14.8	13.3	−5.4	−27.7	−25.1
Other Sectors .... 78br d	....	....	....		−21.3	27.6	−8.2	−60.3	−62.8	42.6	−32.3	−52.1	−73.0	27.4	5.7
Other Investment Liab., n.i.e. .... 78bi d	....	....	....	−19.0	−38.3	201.0	86.5	370.0	148.8	144.1	284.8	346.2	−66.5	100.6	−162.3
Monetary Authorities .... 78bs d	....	....	....	−4.8	.9	1.8	.7	−3.2	6.1	.5					
General Government .... 78bt d	....	....	....	−7.6	−25.6	152.8	−.5	56.2	67.9	15.3	122.0	99.4	168.9	149.6	−73.1
Banks .... 78bu d	....	....	....	7.6	−1.4	14.0	26.5	−8.1	38.8	16.0	17.7	14.6	24.5	−12.4	−15.0
Other Sectors .... 78bv d	....	....	....	−14.2	−12.2	32.3	59.8	325.0	35.9	112.3	145.0	232.2	−260.0	−36.5	−74.3
Net Errors and Omissions .... 78ca d	....	....	....	89.1	−38.9	−12.6	7.3	5.4	86.8	−109.0	−1.1	−250.7	−47.6	−238.6	−91.8
Overall Balance .... 78cb d	....	....	....	458.1	200.5	443.9	337.5	343.8	648.3	568.6	−206.9	−872.8	−692.9	−301.3	−721.6
Reserves and Related Items .... 79da d	....	....	....	−458.1	−200.5	−443.9	−337.5	−343.8	−648.3	−568.6	206.9	872.8	692.9	301.3	721.6
Reserve Assets .... 79db d	....	....	....	−458.1	−200.5	−443.9	−337.5	−343.8	−648.3	−568.6	206.9	872.8	692.9	301.3	721.6
Use of Fund Credit and Loans .... 79dc d	....	....	....	—	—	—	—	—	—	—	—	—	—	—	—
Exceptional Financing .... 79de d	....	....	....	—	—	—	—	—	—	—	—	—	—	—	—
Government Finance															*Millions of TT Dollars:*
Deficit (-) or Surplus 80	−39.2	....	....	....	†499.9	799.7	301.6	−61.0	1,105.6	545.8	†−2346.7	−2,216.0	−1,655.7	−917.4	−1,012.5
Revenue 81	528.9	....	....	....	†2,340.8	3,043.9	3,155.5	4,118.8	6,487.8	7,232.8	†7,066.9	6,552.0	6,612.8	6,664.0	5,455.8
Grants Received 81z	....	....	....	....	†—									.8	
Expenditure 82	568.1	....	....	....	†1,599.7	1,913.4	2,680.5	3,654.7	4,621.7	5,061.5	†9,464.4	8,779.6	8,276.0	7,684.1	6,569.7
Lending Minus Repayments 83	....	....	....	....	†241.2	330.8	173.4	525.1	760.5	1,625.5	†−50.8	−11.6	−7.5	−101.9	−101.6
Financing															
Domestic 84a	....	....	....	....	†49.7	62.8	42.1	40.9	14.3	−12.4	....	....	....	....	....
Foreign 85a	....	....	....	....	†−80.2	360.2	259.3	132.3	162.1	25.9	....	....	....	....	....
Use of Cash Balances 87	−57.0	3.5	−417.8	−465.3	†−469.4	−1,222.7	−603.0	−112.2	−1,282.0	−559.3	....	....	....	....	....
Financing (by Currency)															
Net Borrowing: TT Dollars 84b	56.6	36.6	16.6	24.3	....	....	....	....	....	....	....	....	....	....	....
Foreign Currency 85b	39.6	49.2	−17.9	−22.7	....	....	....	....	....	....	....	....	....	....	....
Use of Cash Balances 87	−57.0	3.5	−417.8	−465.3	†−469.4	−1,222.7	−603.0	−112.2	−1,282.0	−559.3	....	....	....	....	....
Debt: TT Dollars 88b	333.9	370.2	387.3	411.7	....	....	....	....	....	....	....	....	....	....	....
Foreign Currency 89b	199.2	255.7	241.4	215.7	....	....	....	....	....	....	....	....	....	....	....
National Accounts															*Millions of TT Dollars*
Househ.Cons.Expend.,incl.NPISHs 96f	1,234	1,385	1,774	2,257	2,896	3,605	4,443	5,663	6,865	8,197	11,103	11,594	10,224	9,824	10,717
Government Consumption Expend. 91f	334	366	475	652	743	967	1,148	1,536	1,805	2,110	4,032	3,907	4,179	4,109	4,042
Gross Fixed Capital Formation 93e	615	579	651	1,085	1,398	1,735	2,323	2,952	4,204	4,342	5,189	4,770	3,954	3,656	3,593
Changes in Inventories 93i	37	86	264	364	98	272	261	261	376	199	228	199	165	−265	135
Exports of Goods and Services 90c	824	1,132	2,378	2,808	3,401	3,733	3,766	4,979	7,550	7,542	6,694	5,756	5,981	5,883	5,740
Imports of Goods and Services (-) 98c	963	984	1,350	1,866	2,445	2,779	3,391	4,345	5,834	5,952	8,070	7,606	6,283	5,136	6,967
Gross Domestic Product (GDP) 99b	2,082	2,564	4,193	5,300	6,091	7,533	8,550	11,046	14,966	16,438	19,176	18,719	18,615	18,071	17,260
Net Primary Income from Abroad 98.n	−136	−180	−586	−181	−265	−464	−611	−756	−481	−154	−295	−339	−765	−859	−911
Gross National Income (GNI) 99a	1,946	2,384	3,607	4,749	5,255	6,340	7,938	10,290	14,485	16,284	18,881	18,381	17,850	16,942	16,349
Consumption of Fixed Capital 99cf	240	218	291	324	498	654	624	698	848	930	1,142	1,458	1,619	1,634	1,797
GDP Volume 1970 prices 99b.p	1,757	1,786	1,854	1,881	2,002	2,184	2,403	2,490	2,748	2,874	2,990	2,715	....	....	....
GDP Volume 1985 Prices 99b.p	....	....	....	....	....	....	....	....	....	....	....	20,104	18,850	18,071	17,478
GDP Volume (1995=100) .... 99bv p	75.2	76.5	79.4	80.6	85.7	93.6	102.9	106.6	117.7	123.1	128.1	116.3	109.0	104.5	101.1
GDP Deflator (1995=100) .... 99bi p	8.7	10.6	16.7	20.8	22.4	25.4	26.2	32.7	40.1	42.1	47.2	50.8	53.9	54.5	53.9
															Millions:
Population 99z	1.05	1.06	1.07	†1.01	1.02	1.04	1.06	1.06	1.08	1.09	1.12	1.14	1.17	1.18	1.20

1987	1988	1989	1990	1991	1992	1993	1994	1995	1996	1997	1998	1999	2000	2001	Balance of Payments
Minus Sign Indicates Debit															
−225.0	−88.6	−38.5	459.0	−4.7	138.9	113.1	217.8	293.8	105.1	−613.6	−643.5	....		....	Current Account, n.i.e. .... 78al *d*
1,414.3	1,469.5	1,550.8	1,960.1	1,774.5	1,691.4	1,500.1	1,777.6	2,456.1	2,354.1	2,448.0	2,258.0				Goods: Exports f.o.b. ...... 78aa *d*
−1,057.6	−1,064.2	−1,045.2	−947.6	−1,210.3	−995.6	−952.9	−1,036.6	−1,868.5	−1,971.6	−2,976.6	−2,998.9				Goods: Imports f.o.b. .... 78ab *d*
356.7	405.3	505.5	1,012.5	564.2	695.7	547.2	741.1	587.7	382.4	−528.6	−740.8				*Trade Balance* .... 78ac *d*
209.3	271.3	280.8	328.5	405.3	452.7	353.4	326.6	342.6	461.2	546.5	671.7				Services: Credit .... 78ad *d*
−493.5	−453.9	−439.8	−479.2	−534.4	−561.9	−466.4	−438.1	−241.9	−217.5	−254.1	−255.4				Services: Debit .... 78ae *d*
72.5	222.6	346.6	861.9	435.1	586.6	434.2	629.5	688.4	626.2	−236.2	−324.5				*Balance on Goods & Services* .... 78af *d*
16.8	20.3	32.4	39.6	48.6	29.8	40.2	56.7	76.6	39.1	63.8	64.0				Income: Credit .... 78ag *d*
−291.7	−322.3	−410.1	−436.4	−490.7	−477.9	−366.0	−468.7	−466.7	−553.1	−445.0	−405.3				Income: Debit .... 78ah *d*
−202.4	−79.4	−31.1	465.2	−7.0	138.5	108.4	217.5	298.3	112.2	−617.4	−665.8				*Balance on Gds, Serv. & Inc.* .. 78ai *d*
6.3	3.5	5.2	7.8	15.6	11.1	23.7	28.3	34.0	34.2	37.0	58.4				Current Transfers, n.i.e.: Credit .. 78aj *d*
−28.9	−12.7	−12.7	−13.9	−13.3	−10.7	−19.0	−27.9	−38.5	−41.3	−33.2	−36.2				Current Transfers: Debit ..... 78ak *d*
−14.2	−20.4	−17.2	−19.2	−16.1	−16.5	−11.5	−6.4	−11.9	....	....	....				Capital Account, n.i.e. .... 78bc *d*
1.8	—	.4	.4	.4	.4	1.3	1.1	1.1	....	....	....				Capital Account, n.i.e.: Credit .. 78ba *d*
−16.0	−20.4	−17.5	−19.6	−16.5	−16.9	−12.8	−7.5	−13.0	....	....	....				Capital Account: Debit .... 78bb *d*
78.4	−141.5	−166.5	−506.3	−226.8	−154.2	98.8	−32.2	−214.7	43.0	697.2	471.5				Financial Account, n.i.e. ...... 78bj *d*
1.9															Direct Investment Abroad ..... 78bd *d*
33.1	62.9	148.9	109.4	169.3	177.9	379.2	516.2	298.3	355.4	999.3	729.8				Dir. Invest. in Rep. Econ., n.i.e. .. 78be *d*
—	—	—	—	—	—	—	—	−7.9	—	—	−.4				Portfolio Investment Assets ..... 78bf *d*
—	—	—	—	—	—	—	—	−7.9	—	—	−.4				Equity Securities .... 78bk *d*
—	—	—	—	—	—	—	—	—	—	—	—				Debt Securities .... 78bl *d*
—	—	—	—	—	—	—	—	16.7	....	....	....				Portfolio Investment Liab., n.i.e. .. 78bg *d*
—	—	—	—	—	—	—	—	16.7	....	....	....				Equity Securities .... 78bm *d*
—	—	—	—	—	—	—	—	....	....	....	....				Debt Securities .... 78bn *d*
															Financial Derivatives Assets ...... 78bw *d*
															Financial Derivatives Liabilities ... 78bx *d*
58.8	60.9	44.5	63.0	4.4	−31.3	−76.2	−233.5	−57.3	3.0	32.6	1.0				Other Investment Assets .... 78bh *d*
															Monetary Authorities .... 78bo *d*
32.1	88.2	8.1	.9	−5.2	—	—	−56.1	32.4	3.0	32.6	1.0				General Government .... 78bp *d*
4.3	−51.9	−20.3	17.1	16.2	−5.3	−105.6	−109.3	−23.7	....	....	....				Banks .... 78bq *d*
22.4	24.6	56.7	45.0	−6.6	−26.0	29.3	−68.2	−66.0	....	....	....				Other Sectors .... 78br *d*
−15.5	−265.4	−359.8	−678.8	−400.5	−300.8	−204.2	−314.9	−465.1	−315.4	−334.7	−258.8				Other Investment Liab., n.i.e. ... 78bi *d*
—	—	−47.3	—	—	—	—	—	—	—	—	−1.4				Monetary Authorities .... 78bs *d*
−1.8	3.8	−153.8	−244.5	−166.1	−101.9	19.9	−7.2	−116.8	47.3	−245.4	−104.7				General Government .... 78bt *d*
17.4	−24.7	−2.3	−2.8	−6.4	16.5	20.4	−10.2	−51.3	−27.3	−21.9	−49.6				Banks .... 78bu *d*
−31.1	−244.4	−156.4	−431.4	−228.1	−215.4	−244.4	−297.4	−297.0	−335.4	−67.4	−103.2				Other Sectors .... 78bv *d*
−94.8	21.1	45.4	−112.0	−29.0	−72.6	−41.8	6.3	16.5	90.0	110.0	252.2				Net Errors and Omissions .... 78ca *d*
−255.6	−229.4	−176.8	−178.5	−276.5	−104.4	158.6	185.5	83.7	238.1	193.6	80.2				*Overall Balance* .... 78cb *d*
255.6	229.4	176.8	178.5	276.5	104.4	−158.6	−185.5	−83.7	−238.1	−193.6	−80.2				Reserves and Related Items ...... 79da *d*
255.6	27.4	−158.5	−197.7	102.7	124.4	−29.4	−113.6	−40.1	−213.0	−175.3	−76.0				Reserve Assets .... 79db *d*
—	115.4	91.4	100.9	50.7	−89.8	−129.2	−71.9	−43.6	−25.1	−18.4	−4.2				Use of Fund Credit and Loans ...... 79dc *d*
—	86.6	243.8	275.3	123.1	69.8	—	—	....	....	....	....				Exceptional Financing .... 79de *d*
															Government Finance
Year Ending December 31															
−1,012.0	−983.7	−709.6	....	....	....	15.9	117.5	62.5	....	....	....				Deficit (-) or Surplus 80
5,300.0	4,947.6	4,965.2	....	....	....	7,116.1	7,905.1	8,847.3	....	....	....				Revenue 81
—	—	12.3	....	—	—	17.8	36.0	51.6	....	....	....				Grants Received 81z
6,386.8	6,060.6	5,854.9	....	....	....	7,193.6	7,826.9	8,917.9	....	....	....				Expenditure 82
−74.8	−129.3	−167.8	....	....	....	−75.6	−3.3	−81.5	....	....	....				Lending Minus Repayments 83
															Financing
....	....	....	....	....	....	582.8	218.1	−878.7	....	....	....				Domestic 84a
....	....	....	....	....	....	−598.7	−335.6	816.2	....	....	....				Foreign 85a
....	....	....	....	....	....				....	....	....				Use of Cash Balances 87
															Financing (by Currency)
....	....	....	....	....	....	....	....	....	....	....	....				Net Borrowing: TT Dollars 84b
....	....	....	....	....	....	....	....	....	....	....	....				Foreign Currency 85b
....	....	....	....	....	....	—	—	—	....	....	....				Use of Cash Balances 87
....	....	....	....	....	....	....	....	....	....	....	....				Debt: TT Dollars 88b
....	....	....	....	....	....	....	....	....	....	....	....				Foreign Currency 89b
Millions of TT Dollars															**National Accounts**
9,959	10,768	10,773	11,576	13,364	13,674	15,491	15,027	17,020	19,536	22,302	23,862				Househ.Cons.Expend.,incl.NPISHs ... 96f
3,730	3,424	3,099	3,487	3,835	4,117	4,171	4,432	5,029	5,473	5,579	6,281				Government Consumption Expend. .. 91f
3,200	2,185	2,714	2,970	3,565	3,152	3,421	5,962	4,809	5,717	9,582	9,839				Gross Fixed Capital Formation 93e
139	70	331	5	115	37	95	−41	229	129	225	232				Changes in Inventories 93i
5,854	6,727	7,834	10,276	10,159	9,867	10,765	13,504	17,042	17,778	19,306	18,453				Exports of Goods and Services 90c
5,610	5,889	6,378	6,776	8,479	7,730	9,453	9,573	12,444	14,184	20,441	20,470				Imports of Goods and Services (-) .. 98c
17,272	17,285	18,373	21,539	22,559	23,118	24,491	29,312	31,697	34,448	36,552	38,197				Gross Domestic Product (GDP) 99b
−1,003	−1,176	−1,635	−1,710	−1,906	−1,931	−1,852	−2,596	−2,923	−3,144	−2,507	−2,175				Net Primary Income from Abroad 98.n
16,269	16,109	16,738	19,830	20,653	21,186	22,639	26,716	28,748	31,305	34,046	36,022				Gross National Income (GNI) 99a
1,871	1,944	2,030	2,133	2,454	2,613	2,643	3,047	2,840	3,771	4,229	4,612				Consumption of Fixed Capital 99cf
....	....	....	....	....	....	....	....	....	....	....	....				GDP Volume 1970 prices 99b.*p*
16,681	16,027	15,895	16,134	16,567	16,294	16,058	16,630	17,288	17,950	18,507	19,327				GDP Volume 1985 Prices 99b.*p*
96.5	92.7	91.9	93.3	95.8	94.3	92.9	96.2	100.0	103.8	107.1	111.8				GDP Volume (1995=100) .... 99bv *p*
56.5	58.8	63.0	72.8	74.3	77.4	83.2	96.1	100.0	104.7	107.7	107.8				GDP Deflator (1995=100) .... 99bi *p*
Midyear Estimates															
1.21	1.21	1.21	1.22	1.23	1.23	1.25	1.25	1.26	1.26	1.27	1.28	1.29	1.29	1.30	**Population** 99z

(See notes in the back of the book.)

Tunisia

		1972	1973	1974	1975	1976	1977	1978	1979	1980	1981	1982	1983	1984	1985	1986
Exchange Rates																*Dinars per SDR:*
Market Rate	aa	†.5255	.5369	.4978	.4979	.5007	.5005	.5255	.5215	.5340	.6002	.6792	.7612	.8494	.8314	1.0277
																Dinars per US Dollar:
Market Rate	ae	†.4840	.4451	.4066	.4253	.4310	.4121	.4034	.3959	.4187	.5157	.6158	.7271	.8666	.7570	.8402
Market Rate	rf	.4771ᵉ	.4216ᵉ	.4365	.4023	.4288	.4290	.4162	.4065	.4050	.4938	.5907	.6788	.7768	.8345	.7940
																Index Numbers (1995=100):
Nominal Effective Exchange Rate	ne c	....	....	....	....	....	....	....	176.71	178.71	182.84	176.62	172.74	170.46	166.08	139.16
Real Effective Exchange Rate	re c	....	....	....	....	....	....	....	147.41	145.26	144.23	143.14	140.71	140.46	139.49	119.34
Fund Position																*Millions of SDRs:*
Quota	2f. s	48.0	48.0	48.0	48.0	48.0	48.0	63.0	63.0	94.5	94.5	94.5	138.2	138.2	138.2	138.2
SDRs	1b. s	7.9	7.6	8.5	8.2	10.0	9.6	8.5	14.6	11.8	17.4	16.0	3.6	1.9	.5	22.6
Reserve Position in the Fund	1c. s	5.9	12.0	12.0	12.0	12.0	12.0	11.7	11.3	19.2	19.2	19.2	30.1	29.4	26.4	—
Total Fund Cred.&Loans Outstg.	2tl	—	—	—	—	—	24.0	24.0	24.0	—	—	—	—	—	—	149.7
International Liquidity													*Millions of US Dollars Unless Otherwise Indicated:*			
Total Reserves minus Gold	1l. d	217.8	301.8	412.8	379.9	365.8	351.2	443.0	579.3	590.1	536.1	606.5	567.3	406.3	232.7	305.3
SDRs	1b. d	8.6	9.2	10.4	9.6	11.6	11.6	11.1	19.3	15.1	20.3	17.7	3.7	1.9	.5	27.6
Reserve Position in the Fund	1c. d	6.4	14.5	14.7	14.1	14.0	14.6	15.2	14.9	24.5	22.3	21.2	31.5	28.8	29.0	—
Foreign Exchange	1d. d	202.8	278.1	387.7	356.2	340.3	325.0	416.7	545.1	550.6	493.5	567.6	532.0	375.6	203.2	277.7
Gold (Million Fine Troy Ounces)	1ad	.129	.129	.129	.129	.129	.150	.160	.170	.187	.187	.187	.187	.187	.187	.187
Gold (National Valuation)	1an d	....	....	5.8	5.6	5.5	6.7	7.3	7.9	8.2	6.6	5.6	4.7	4.0	4.5	4.5
Deposit Money Banks: Assets	7a. d	19.1	25.5	47.8	45.1	36.7	44.9	61.7	104.7	125.4	162.0	195.7	233.6	225.5	223.7	218.3
Liabilities	7b. d	105.4	140.2	198.6	212.1	233.3	254.4	316.4	352.8	410.1	402.9	391.2	397.9	410.0	471.6	425.0
Other Banking Insts.: Liabilities	7f. d	26.0	30.3	56.7	58.4	121.3	152.5	197.5	257.0	266.6	252.4	259.5	292.3			
Monetary Authorities																*Millions of Dinars:*
Foreign Assets	11	110	144	176	169	159	144	166	200	220	260	265	381	331	210	187
Claims on Central Government	12a	50	49	48	47	48	46	52	46	47	48	73	59	56	50	62
Claims on Private Sector	12d	....	....	....	....	....	....	....	....	....	....	....	....	....	....	....
Claims on Deposit Money Banks	12e	24	36	55	106	111	151	167	153	199	304	446	549	697	819	980
Reserve Money	14	119	140	182	209	223	234	274	301	338	426	525	617	680	740	747
of which: Currency Outside DMBs	14a	94	112	140	163	185	214	250	265	300	343	440	533	573	633	651
Foreign Liabilities	16c	4	2	3	1	2	15	22	18	5	8	10	—	44	1	155
Central Government Deposits	16d	39	53	44	42	17	28	35	29	63	80	103	108	92	81	87
Capital Accounts	17a	13	17	31	41	48	53	59	63	78	93	134	158	215	242	281
Other Items (Net)	17r	10	17	20	30	33	27	12	6	3	33	61	178	169	155	117
Deposit Money Banks																*Millions of Dinars:*
Reserves	20	24	26	41	46	36	25	32	48	40	52	36	51	68	67	47
Foreign Assets	21	9	11	19	19	16	18	25	41	53	84	120	170	195	169	183
Claims on Central Government	22a	41	49	49	49	71	102	136	173	204	245	284	335	405	501	575
Claims on Private Sector	22d	332	396	518	673	757	872	987	1,088	1,334	1,756	2,207	2,675	3,024	3,481	3,736
Demand Deposits	24	175	202	251	296	305	337	412	493	619	729	886	1,050	1,107	1,261	1,322
Quasi-Monetary Liabilities	25	76	103	142	192	258	300	362	434	495	609	672	776	950	1,103	1,206
Foreign Liabilities	26c	24	26	35	41	43	46	55	58	77	98	120	159	191	178	167
Long-Term Foreign Liabilities	26cl	27	35	46	50	57	58	73	81	95	110	121	130	164	179	190
Counterpart Funds	26e	10	10	10	9	9	9	9	9	9	9	10	10	10	10	10
Central Govt. Lending Funds	26f	28	30	38	41	43	50	60	72	80	96	111	136	159	194	214
Credit from Monetary Authorities	26g	24	35	56	106	114	169	153	125	180	366	563	743	929	1,059	1,239
Capital Accounts	27a	34	39	44	50	60	69	77	86	96	134	158	192	228	270	321
Other Items (Net)	27r	9	3	7	2	–9	–21	–20	–8	–21	–14	8	36	–45	–36	–128
Post Office: Checking Deposits	24.. i	9	10	13	15	23	25	26	26	31	42	52	67	82	84	77
Monetary Survey																*Millions of Dinars:*
Foreign Assets (Net)	31n	91	126	157	146	130	101	114	165	191	237	255	391	290	201	49
Domestic Credit	32	394	452	585	744	888	1,033	1,184	1,321	1,573	2,040	2,561	3,101	3,592	4,175	4,521
Claims on Central Govt. (Net)	32an	61	55	66	70	125	145	178	214	219	255	307	354	451	554	627
Claims on Private Sector	32d	333	397	520	675	763	888	1,005	1,107	1,354	1,784	2,255	2,747	3,142	3,621	3,894
Money	34	278	323	404	475	514	576	688	786	951	1,165	1,455	1,699	1,814	2,059	2,112
Quasi-Money	35	76	103	142	192	258	300	362	434	495	609	672	776	950	1,103	1,206
Long-Term Foreign Liabilities	36cl	27	35	46	50	57	58	73	81	95	110	121	130	164	179	190
Counterpart Funds	36e	13	15	15	17	13	13	12	11	11	14	29	27	28	32	57
Central Govt. Lending Funds	36f	28	30	38	41	43	50	60	72	80	96	111	136	159	194	214
Other Items (Net)	37r	63	72	97	114	133	137	104	102	132	284	429	725	767	808	792
Money plus Quasi-Money	35l	355	426	546	668	772	876	1,050	1,219	1,445	1,774	2,127	2,475	2,764	3,162	3,318
Other Banking Institutions																*Millions of Dinars:*
Foreign Assets (Net)	41n	†—	....	....	....	....	....	....	....	....	....	....	....	....	3	5
Claims on Central Govt. (Net)	42an	12	17	21	28	33	37	45	54	62	80	97	116	121	131	148
Claims on Private Sector	42d	†27	37	59	81	124	157	205	255	291	351	450	662	867	1,068	1,203
Monetary Deposits	44	4	6	10	9	9	10	15	15	16	21	22	37	55	43	62
Time and Savings Deposits	45	†15	20	34	64	80	92	113	138	149	184	230	274	303	336	402
Long-Term Foreign Liabilities	46cl	13	13	23	25	52	63	80	102	112	130	160	213	—		—
Central Govt. Lending Funds	46f	†5	5	6	6	6	6	6	10	19	35	46	78	347	460	457
Capital Accounts	47a	9	13	13	18	20	23	29	31	33	85	154	211	302	397	462
Other Items (Net)	47r	†–6	–3	–7	–12	–10	–1	8	13	25	–23	–65	–33	–18	–35	–27
Banking Survey													*Millions of Dinars: End of Period*			
Foreign Assets (Net)	51n	†91	126	157	146	130	101	114	165	191	237	255	391	290	204	54
Domestic Credit	52	†433	506	665	854	1,045	1,227	1,434	1,630	1,926	2,471	3,108	3,879	4,581	5,373	5,872
Claims on Government (Net)	52an	74	71	86	98	158	182	224	268	282	336	403	470	572	685	775
Claims on Private Sector	52d	†360	434	578	756	887	1,045	1,211	1,362	1,645	2,135	2,705	3,409	4,009	4,688	5,097
Liquid Liabilities	55l	†373	453	591	740	860	978	1,178	1,373	1,610	1,979	2,379	2,786	3,122	3,542	3,781
Long Term Foreign Liabilities	56cl	40	48	69	75	109	121	153	183	206	240	280	343	164	179	190
Other Items (Net)	57r	†112	131	162	185	205	228	218	239	301	489	705	1,142	1,585	1,856	1,955
Interest Rates																*Percent Per Annum*
Discount Rate *(End of Period)*	60	5.00	5.00	5.00	5.00	5.00	5.75	5.75	5.75	5.75	7.00	7.00	7.00	7.00	9.25	9.25
Money Market Rate	60b	....	....	....	....	....	....	....	....	....	....	8.50	8.25	8.38	8.89	10.28	9.95
Deposit Rate	60l	....	....	....	....	....	2.50	2.50	2.50	2.50	4.00	4.50	4.50	4.50	5.35	6.75
Lending Rate	60p	....	....	....	....	....	7.25	7.25	7.25	8.10	8.50	8.50	8.50	9.63	9.17

1987	1988	1989	1990	1991	1992	1993	1994	1995	1996	1997	1998	1999	2000	2001		
End of Period															**Exchange Rates**	
1.1035	1.2090	1.1888	1.1904	1.2366	1.3071	1.4376	1.4470	1.4134	1.4358	1.5483	1.5502	1.7191	1.8049	1.8453	Market Rate	aa
End of Period (ae) Period Average (rf)																
.7779	.8985	.9046	.8368	.8645	.9507	1.0466	.9912	.9508	.9985	1.1475	1.1010	1.2525	1.3853	1.4683	Market Rate	ae
.8287	.8578	.9493	.8783	.9246	.8844	1.0037	1.0116	.9458	.9734	1.1059	1.1387	1.1862	1.3707	1.4387	Market Rate	rf
Period Averages																
115.28	109.69	105.10	100.82	100.70	102.35	99.15	99.66	100.00	100.67	99.91	99.21	99.55	98.87	97.19	Nominal Effective Exchange Rate	ne c
102.42	100.47	99.13	96.41	98.81	100.87	97.09	97.82	100.00	100.65	100.55	100.47	101.49	100.84	98.07	Real Effective Exchange Rate	re c
End of Period															**Fund Position**	
138.2	138.2	138.2	138.2	138.2	206.0	206.0	206.0	206.0	206.0	206.0	206.0	286.5	286.5	286.5	Quota	2f. s
38.1	21.0	6.4	1.7	23.0	8.8	1.3	1.8	4.7	11.1	12.1	2.1	19.3	3.0	1.3	SDRs	1b. s
—	—	—	—	—	—	—	—	—	—	—	—	20.2	20.2	20.2	Reserve Position in the Fund	1c. s
190.7	205.7	205.7	123.7	180.1	211.1	207.3	207.3	197.1	165.0	128.4	91.8	55.2	24.7	—	Total Fund Cred.&Loans Outstg.	2tl
End of Period															**International Liquidity**	
525.5	899.3	961.9	794.8	789.9	852.0	853.8	1,461.5	1,605.3	1,897.6	1,978.1	1,850.1	2,261.5	1,811.0	1,989.2	Total Reserves minus Gold	1l. d
54.1	28.3	8.5	2.5	32.9	12.1	1.8	2.7	7.0	15.9	16.3	2.9	26.5	3.9	1.7	SDRs	1b. d
—	—	—	—	—	—	—	.1	.1	.1	.1	.1	27.7	26.3	25.3	Reserve Position in the Fund	1c. d
471.4	871.0	953.4	792.3	757.0	839.9	852.0	1,458.8	1,598.2	1,881.7	1,961.7	1,847.1	2,207.3	1,780.9	1,962.2	Foreign Exchange	1d. d
.187	.187	.187	.187	.215	.215	.215	.216	.217	.217	.217	.217	.217	.220	.218	Gold (Million Fine Troy Ounces)	1ad
4.8	4.2	4.2	5.2	5.0	4.6	4.2	4.4	4.8	4.4	3.8	4.0	3.5	3.2	3.0	Gold (National Valuation)	1and
365.5	392.2	453.9	610.0	603.7	570.6	545.2	536.9	451.6	569.5	607.8	643.6	621.1	669.9	550.0	Deposit Money Banks: Assets	7a. d
....	578.3	584.9	753.9	1,342.7	1,461.9	1,374.3	1,729.3	1,740.8	1,938.4	1,845.2	1,979.9	2,091.4	2,618.5	2,608.8	Liabilities	7b. d
														—	Other Banking Insts.: Liabilities	7f. d
End of Period															**Monetary Authorities**	
386	762	843	629	671	868	930	1,462	1,536	1,913	2,277	2,053	2,868	2,527	2,899	Foreign Assets	11
71	49	54	64	95	117	122	93	85	103	58	78	79	132	147	Claims on Central Government	12a
											21	23	25	26	Claims on Private Sector	12d
840	557	603	911	1,134	1,079	1,177	835	829	178	115	†93	93	449	854	Claims on Deposit Money Banks	12e
806	858	991	1,129	1,264	1,355	1,420	1,523	1,667	2,264	2,448	2,159	2,818	2,497	2,942	Reserve Money	14
705	801	875	1,005	1,104	1,156	1,179	1,196	1,315	1,473	1,594	1,695	1,994	2,229	2,376	of which: Currency Outside DMBs	14a
226	251	246	165	234	296	324	326	304	251	244	173	166	249	186	Foreign Liabilities	16c
72	119	139	119	164	71	128	198	137	254	231	241	244	206	392	Central Government Deposits	16d
282	79	81	89	91	99	109	119	128	134	143	151	103	116	125	Capital Accounts	17a
91	66	48	101	147	243	248	224	214	−709	−616	−478	−268	66	281	Other Items (Net)	17r
End of Period															**Deposit Money Banks**	
55	86	89	118	130	129	181	294	275	760	816	356	853	468	749	Reserves	20
284	352	411	510	522	542	571	532	429	569	697	709	778	928	808	Foreign Assets	21
631	652	715	762	793	535	536	544	341	291	682	556	942	1,561	1,487	Claims on Central Government	22a
4,017	4,449	5,648	5,957	6,466	7,402	7,907	8,510	9,274	9,373	10,540	11,542	12,652	15,717	17,423	Claims on Private Sector	22d
1,253	1,595	1,561	1,565	1,437	1,555	1,676	1,957	2,092	2,371	2,847	3,091	3,435	3,779	4,169	Demand Deposits	24
1,687	1,986	2,650	2,892	3,196	3,490	3,777	4,003	4,166	4,736	5,660	5,871	7,122	8,372	9,304	Quasi-Monetary Liabilities	25
253	314	328	378	424	605	614	780	817	1,076	1,214	1,260	1,684	1,839	1,827	Foreign Liabilities	26c
....	206	201	253	736	785	824	934	839	859	904	919	936	1,788	2,004	Long-Term Foreign Liabilities	26cl
....	16	3	3	—	—	—	—	—	—	—	—	—	—	—	Counterpart Funds	26e
....	236	367	412	—	—	—	—	—	—	—	—	—	—	—	Central Govt. Lending Funds	26f
1,152	840	1,308	1,356	1,536	1,485	1,494	1,175	1,119	206	153	127	113	470	870	Credit from Monetary Authorities	26g
368	419	530	592	710	885	1,053	1,246	1,672	1,914	2,150	2,361	2,577	2,935	2,881	Capital Accounts	27a
−154	−72	−86	−104	−128	−196	−244	−214	−384	−171	−192	−467	−641	−510	−587	Other Items (Net)	27r
91	95	....	100	128	157	110	122	184	230	162	164	321	328	344	Post Office: Checking Deposits	24.. i
End of Period															**Monetary Survey**	
192	550	679	596	535	509	562	888	846	1,154	1,516	1,328	1,796	1,367	1,694	Foreign Assets (Net)	31n
4,917	5,131	6,367	6,765	7,319	8,141	8,546	9,072	9,746	9,743	11,212	†12,121	13,774	17,558	19,035	Domestic Credit	32
721	677	715	808	853	739	639	562	473	371	672	557	1,099	1,816	1,586	Claims on Central Govt. (Net)	32an
4,196	4,454	5,653	5,957	6,466	7,402	7,907	8,510	9,274	9,373	10,540	†11,564	12,675	15,742	17,449	Claims on Private Sector	32d
2,126	2,494	2,524	2,678	2,697	2,894	2,998	3,319	3,637	4,109	4,645	4,994	5,794	6,369	6,926	Money	34
1,687	1,986	2,650	2,892	3,196	3,490	3,777	4,003	4,166	4,736	5,660	5,871	7,122	8,372	9,304	Quasi-Money	35
....	206	201	253	736	785	824	934	839	859	904	919	936	1,788	2,004	Long-Term Foreign Liabilities	36cl
....	95	97	69	70	64	78	49	39	47	67	80	81	174	201	Counterpart Funds	36e
....	236	367	412	—	—	—	—	—	—	—	—	—	—	—	Central Govt. Lending Funds	36f
795	663	1,208	1,058	1,155	1,417	1,430	1,655	1,912	1,146	1,453	†1,584	1,637	2,221	2,293	Other Items (Net)	37r
3,813	4,481	5,174	5,570	5,893	6,384	6,775	7,322	7,803	8,845	10,304	10,865	12,916	14,742	16,230	Money plus Quasi-Money	35l
End of Period															**Other Banking Institutions**	
....	....	....	....	....	21	25	29	18	7	37	28	41	36	−38	Foreign Assets (Net)	41n
....	....	....	....	....	—	—	1	—	9	7	7	37	62	59	Claims on Central Govt. (Net)	42an
....	....	....	....	....	1,667	1,943	2,171	2,395	2,684	2,984	3,311	3,510	1,915	2,078	Claims on Private Sector	42d
....	....	....	....	....	5	8	7	11	8	7	11	11	14	31	Monetary Deposits	44
....	....	....	....	....	327	393	418	443	489	507	674	791	657	763	Time and Savings Deposits	45
....	....	....	....	....										—	Long-Term Foreign Liabilities	46cl
....	....	....	....	....	535	688	843	918	985	1,061	1,012	1,005	215	172	Central Govt. Lending Funds	46f
....	....	....	....	....	846	906	952	1,049	1,115	1,192	1,246	1,296	1,086	1,039	Capital Accounts	47a
....	....	....	....	....	−25	−27	−18	−7	104	260	402	486	41	95	Other Items (Net)	47r
															Banking Survey	
....	....	....	....	....	529	587	917	864	1,161	1,553	1,356	1,837	1,403	1,655	Foreign Assets (Net)	51n
....	....	....	....	....	9,808	10,490	11,244	12,142	12,437	14,203	†15,439	17,321	19,535	21,172	Domestic Credit	52
....	....	....	....	....	739	639	563	473	380	679	564	1,136	1,878	1,645	Claims on Government (Net)	52an
....	....	....	....	....	9,069	9,851	10,681	11,669	12,057	13,524	†14,875	16,185	17,657	19,527	Claims on Private Sector	52d
....	....	....	....	....	6,716	7,176	7,746	8,256	9,341	10,819	11,551	13,717	15,412	17,023	Liquid Liabilities	55l
....	....	....	....	....	785	824	934	839	859	904	919	936	1,788	2,004	Long Term Foreign Liabilities	56cl
....	....	....	....	....	2,837	3,076	3,482	3,911	3,397	4,033	†4,325	4,505	3,737	3,800	Other Items (Net)	57r
Percent Per Annum															**Interest Rates**	
9.25	9.25	11.37	11.88	11.88	11.38	8.88	8.88	8.88	7.88	....	....	....	....	....	Discount Rate (End of Period)	60
10.00	9.15	9.40	11.53	11.79	11.73	10.48	8.81	8.81	8.64	6.88	6.89	5.99	5.88	6.04	Money Market Rate	60b
7.22	7.37	....	....	....	....	....	....	....	....	....	....	....	....	....	Deposit Rate	60l
11.08	9.87	4.82	....	....	....	....	....	....	....	....	....	....	....	....	Lending Rate	60p

Tunisia

	1972	1973	1974	1975	1976	1977	1978	1979	1980	1981	1982	1983	1984	1985	1986
Prices, Production, Labor														*Index Numbers (1995=100):*	
Producer Prices 63	18.3	19.3	23.4	25.6	25.9	27.1	28.0	30.0	33.3	37.4	43.8	†46.6	50.7	56.4	62.0
Home Goods 63a	34.4	36.1	41.3	45.0	46.4	49.4	51.2	54.9	60.2	65.7	80.6	86.9	93.1	100.0	106.4
Consumer Prices 64	...	...	...	...	...	...	...	...	...	...	...	45.7	49.8	53.4	56.7
Industrial Production 66	40.0	41.7	45.2	46.4	47.5	†52.1	57.7	64.3	68.9	71.5	70.7	†76.8	77.0	77.9	78.1
Mining Production 66zx	52.2	53.1	56.9	59.3	51.6	†57.0	64.4	66.7	74.3	73.4	70.7	†84.6	76.6	66.0	80.8
Crude Petroleum Production 66aa	93.9	91.6	97.7	108.8	87.6	100.7	115.7	131.5	132.0	127.5	120.5	130.6	129.4	127.7	124.0
														Number in Thousands:	
Labor Force 67d	...	...	...	...	...	...	...	...	...	...	...	...	...	...	
Employment 67e	...	...	...	...	...	...	...	...	...	...	...	...	...		1,874
Unemployment 67c	...	...	...	...	...	...	...	...	...	...	...	...	...	84	80
International Transactions														*Millions of Dinars*	
Exports 70	150.3	178.8	397.7	345.6	338.3	398.3	468.4	726.7	904.8	1,233.0	1,164.7	1,263.9	1,399.1	1,443.0	1,403.7
Imports, c.i.f. 71	222.2	286.1	488.7	572.8	656.7	782.5	889.7	1,156.8	1,427.4	1,866.0	2,008.5	2,109.8	2,508.9	2,287.0	2,295.1
														1990=100	
Volume of Exports 72	104.9	92.2	94.9	87.1	92.2	87.6	101.6	108.4	102.5	†100.0	99.6	91.7	91.3	82.3	92.2
Volume of Imports 73	38.4	37.9	49.6	49.4	56.1	73.2	77.2	95.7	90.9	†92.2	96.4	91.2	98.8	76.1	76.2
Unit Value of Exports 74	10.0	12.8	26.7	26.9	23.8	24.6	26.6	36.5	48.5	†60.7	66.5	68.9	75.2	75.6	67.8
Balance of Payments														*Millions of US Dollars*	
Current Account, n.i.e. 78ald	...		...		–396	–566	–459	–300	–353	–454	–662	–570	–765	–581	–605
Goods: Exports f.o.b. 78aad	...				788	788	942	1,557	2,195	2,491	2,004	1,862	1,782	1,708	1,763
Goods: Imports f.o.b. 78abd	...				–1,434	–1,613	–1,788	–2,487	–3,166	–3,453	–3,167	–2,947	–2,948	–2,593	–2,698
Trade Balance 78acd	...				–646	–825	–846	–930	–970	–962	–1,163	–1,084	–1,166	–886	–934
Services: Credit 78add	...				515	539	711	999	1,067	994	997	1,003	915	965	960
Services: Debit 78aed	...				–296	–315	–365	–445	–600	–579	–611	–616	–611	–612	–670
Balance on Goods & Services 78afd	...				–427	–601	–500	–376	–504	–547	–777	–697	–862	–533	–645
Income: Credit 78agd	...				26	16	19	52	94	99	105	88	99	40	20
Income: Debit 78ahd	...				–191	–196	–231	–312	–353	–401	–400	–357	–400	–384	–384
Balance on Gds, Serv. & Inc. 78aid	...				–592	–781	–711	–637	–763	–849	–1,072	–965	–1,116	–894	–1,009
Current Transfers, n.i.e.: Credit 78ajd	...				208	231	274	359	430	415	430	414	368	328	418
Current Transfers: Debit 78akd	...				–12	–16	–22	–22	–20	–20	–20	–19	–17	–16	–14
Capital Account, n.i.e. 78bcd	...				–12	–12	–14	–7	–7	–10	–5	–7	–5	–6	–4
Capital Account, n.i.e.: Credit 78bad	...				—	—	—	—	—	—	—	—	—	—	—
Capital Account: Debit 78bbd	...				–12	–12	–14	–7	–7	–10	–5	–7	–5	–6	–4
Financial Account, n.i.e. 78bjd	...				448	539	517	332	358	516	714	385	622	381	375
Direct Investment Abroad 78bdd	...				—	—	2	—	—	–2	–2	1	1	6	–1
Dir. Invest. in Rep. Econ., n.i.e. 78bed	...				110	93	91	49	235	296	340	184	113	108	64
Portfolio Investment Assets 78bfd	...				—	—	—	—	—	–8	–7	–22	–8	–5	–6
Equity Securities 78bkd	...				—	—	—	—	—	–8	–7	–22	–8		
Debt Securities 78bld	...				—	—	—	—	—	—	—	—	—	–5	–6
Portfolio Investment Liab., n.i.e. 78bgd	...				–5	2	–2	–2	15	79	69	60	99	35	38
Equity Securities 78bmd	...								17	77	69	62	103	36	39
Debt Securities 78bnd	...				–5	2	–2	–2	–2	2	—	–1	–4	–1	–1
Financial Derivatives Assets 78bwd	...				...	...	...	...	...	...	...	...	...	...	...
Financial Derivatives Liabilities 78bxd	...				...	...	...	...	...	...	...	...	...	...	...
Other Investment Assets 78bhd	...				–9	–7	–144	–209	–119	–288	–125	–301	–49	2	–137
Monetary Authorities 78bod	...														–45
General Government 78bpd	...				9	23	–74	–96	–67	–111	–39	–199	—	—	—
Banks 78bqd	...				14	—	–10	–47	–32	–65	–63	–72	–32	31	–69
Other Sectors 78brd	...				–33	–30	–60	–66	–20	–111	–24	–29	–17	–29	–23
Other Investment Liab., n.i.e. 78bid	...				352	450	569	495	227	439	438	461	465	235	418
Monetary Authorities 78bsd	...				2	2	14	—	–42	10	—	–15	57	–53	—
General Government 78btd	...				51	161	207	66	86	61	59	116	130	91	186
Banks 78bud	...				7	7	19	10	44	45	37	57	41	–16	91
Other Sectors 78bvd	...				292	280	329	418	138	324	342	302	237	212	141
Net Errors and Omissions 78cad	...				–49	–19	39	92	69	–3	112	228	46	–20	18
Overall Balance 78cbd	...				–10	–59	82	117	67	50	159	35	–102	–226	–215
Reserves and Related Items 79dad	...				10	59	–82	–117	–67	–50	–159	–35	102	226	215
Reserve Assets 79dbd	...				10	31	–82	–117	–35	–50	–159	–35	102	226	35
Use of Fund Credit and Loans 79dcd	...				—	28	—	—	–32	—	—	—	—	—	179
Exceptional Financing 79ded	...				...	...	...	...	...	...	...	...	...	...	...
International Investment Position														*Millions of US Dollars*	
Assets 79aad	...	...	...	...	...	...	...	...	...	...	...	...	...	...	...
Direct Investment Abroad 79abd	...	...	...	...	...	...	...	...	...	...	...	...	...	...	...
Portfolio Investment 79acd	...	...	...	...	...	...	...	...	...	...	...	...	...	...	...
Equity Securities 79add	...	...	...	...	...	...	...	...	...	...	...	...	...	...	...
Debt Securities 79aed	...	...	...	...	...	...	...	...	...	...	...	...	...	...	...
Financial Derivatives 79ald	...	...	...	...	...	...	...	...	...	...	...	...	...	...	...
Other Investment 79afd	...	...	...	...	...	...	...	...	...	...	...	...	...	...	...
Monetary Authorities 79agd	...	...	...	...	...	...	...	...	...	...	...	...	...	...	...
General Government 79ahd	...	...	...	...	...	...	...	...	...	...	...	...	...	...	...
Banks 79aid	...	...	...	...	...	...	...	...	...	...	...	...	...	...	...
Other Sectors 79ajd	...	...	...	...	...	...	...	...	...	...	...	...	...	...	...
Reserve Assets 79akd	...	...	...	...	...	...	...	...	...	...	...	...	...	...	...
Liabilities 79lad	...	...	...	...	...	...	...	...	...	...	...	...	...	...	...
Dir. Invest. in Rep. Economy 79lbd	...	...	...	...	...	...	...	...	...	...	...	...	...	...	...
Portfolio Investment 79lcd	...	...	...	...	...	...	...	...	...	...	...	...	...	...	...
Equity Securities 79ldd	...	...	...	...	...	...	...	...	...	...	...	...	...	...	...
Debt Securities 79led	...	...	...	...	...	...	...	...	...	...	...	...	...	...	...
Financial Derivatives 79lld	...	...	...	...	...	...	...	...	...	...	...	...	...	...	...
Other Investment 79lfd	...	...	...	...	...	...	...	...	...	...	...	...	...	...	...
Monetary Authorities 79lgd	...	...	...	...	...	...	...	...	...	...	...	...	...	...	...
General Government 79lhd	...	...	...	...	...	...	...	...	...	...	...	...	...	...	...
Banks 79lid	...	...	...	...	...	...	...	...	...	...	...	...	...	...	...
Other Sectors 79ljd	...	...	...	...	...	...	...	...	...	...	...	...	...	...	...

1987	1988	1989	1990	1991	1992	1993	1994	1995	1996	1997	1998	1999	2000	2001		
															Prices, Production, Labor	
Period Averages																
67.7	73.6	77.8	†80.0	84.3	87.4	91.5	94.6	100.0	103.7	107.0	109.6	110.0	113.7	115.7	Producer Prices	63
109.5	...	...													Home Goods	63a
61.3	†65.8	70.9	75.5	81.7	86.4	89.9	94.1	100.0	103.7	107.5	110.9	113.9	117.2	119.5	Consumer Prices	64
78.2	81.1	82.7	†82.4	88.8	92.2	92.4	97.0	100.0	102.7	107.2	114.7	120.1	127.1	134.8	Industrial Production	66
86.8	87.9	95.8	†88.7	89.1	85.2	73.5	79.1	100.0	105.5	93.2	113.7	121.8	122.6	118.6	Mining Production	66zx
117.8	115.9	116.3	106.3	122.7	122.8	109.7	103.4	100.0	99.0	89.9	92.0	93.0	86.4	79.0	Crude Petroleum Production	66aa
Period Averages																
...	...	2,360	...	...	...	...	2,772	...	...	2,978	...	...	...	...	Labor Force	67d
...	...	1,979	...	...	...	...	2,321	...	...	...	...	2,635	2,705	...	Employment	67e
84	92	106	152	133	137	142	160	190	181	...	...	...	...	...	Unemployment	67c
															International Transactions	
Millions of Dinars																
1,770.7	2,055.4	2,782.0	3,087.4	3,417.1	3,549.7	3,818.1	4,696.6	5,172.9	5,372.0	6,147.9	6,518.3	6,966.9	8,004.8	9,503.7	Exports	70
2,509.2	3,167.0	4,163.6	4,826.4	4,789.0	5,688.8	6,237.2	6,647.3	7,464.1	7,498.8	8,756.0	9,489.5	10,070.5	11,738.0	13,728.5	Imports, c.i.f.	71
1990=100																
95.2	96.2	116.3	†100.0	110.1	111.3	120.8	137.1	...							Volume of Exports	72
67.2	83.4	98.9	†100.0	106.7	103.8	115.5	119.8	...							Volume of Imports	73
77.3	82.6	94.0	†100.0	97.5	95.3	96.2	100.8	...							Unit Value of Exports	74
															Balance of Payments	
Minus Sign Indicates Debit																
−54	210	−218	−463	−469	−1,104	−1,323	−537	−774	−478	−595	−675	−442	−821	...	Current Account, n.i.e.	78al d
2,101	2,399	2,931	3,515	3,696	4,041	3,746	4,643	5,470	5,519	5,559	5,724	5,873	5,840	...	Goods: Exports f.o.b.	78aa d
−2,829	−3,496	−4,138	−5,193	−4,895	−6,078	−5,810	−6,210	−7,459	−7,280	−7,514	−7,875	−8,014	−8,092	...	Goods: Imports f.o.b.	78ab d
−728	−1,097	−1,207	−1,678	−1,199	−2,037	−2,064	−1,567	−1,989	−1,761	−1,955	−2,152	−2,141	−2,252	...	*Trade Balance*	78ac d
1,241	1,854	1,446	1,688	1,410	1,972	2,040	2,267	2,509	2,632	2,613	2,757	2,920	2,767	...	Services: Credit	78ad d
−664	−750	−716	−846	−841	−1,158	−1,356	−1,361	−1,352	−1,244	−1,182	−1,257	−1,234	−1,219	...	Services: Debit	78ae d
−151	7	−477	−836	−631	−1,223	−1,380	−661	−832	−373	−524	−651	−455	−704	...	*Balance on Goods & Services*	78af d
21	48	70	97	56	101	73	71	119	66	77	90	89	94	...	Income: Credit	78ag d
−448	−513	−518	−552	−609	−646	−629	−745	−835	−1,030	−939	−947	−978	−1,036	...	Income: Debit	78ah d
−578	−458	−926	−1,291	−1,183	−1,768	−1,936	−1,336	−1,548	−1,338	−1,386	−1,507	−1,344	−1,646	...	*Balance on Gds, Serv. & Inc.*	78ai d
537	678	719	847	728	682	629	816	805	879	821	852	920	854	...	Current Transfers, n.i.e.: Credit	78aj d
−13	−10	−12	−19	−14	−17	−16	−17	−31	−20	−30	−20	−18	−29	...	Current Transfers: Debit	78ak d
−6	−3	−7	−7	−5	−5	−2	−3	32	37	77	61	59	3	...	Capital Account, n.i.e.	78bc d
—	—	—	—	—	—	5	5	47	46	95	83	72	9	...	Capital Account, n.i.e.: Credit	78ba d
−6	−3	−7	−7	−5	−5	−7	−8	−15	−9	−18	−22	−13	−6	...	Capital Account: Debit	78bb d
180	323	132	326	402	957	1,272	1,144	958	816	699	489	1,083	648	...	Financial Account, n.i.e.	78bj d
−1	−1	−4	1	−3	−5	—	−6	5	−1	−6	1	−3	−1	...	Direct Investment Abroad	78bd d
92	61	78	76	125	526	562	432	264	238	339	650	350	752	...	Dir. Invest. in Rep. Econ., n.i.e.	78be d
−7	−5	−1	−1	−1	−3	−6	−1	2	−5	−1	—	—	—	...	Portfolio Investment Assets	78bf d
—	−2	—	−3	—	−3	—	1	—	—	—	—	—	—	...	Equity Securities	78bk d
−7	−2	−1	2	−1	—	−6	−2	2	−5	−1	—	—	—	...	Debt Securities	78bl d
16	8	19	3	36	50	24	16	23	67	109	33	10	−20	...	Portfolio Investment Liab., n.i.e.	78bg d
17	9	16	5	34	47	20	6	12	29	55	58	−3	−18	...	Equity Securities	78bm d
−1	−1	3	−1	2	2	4	10	12	38	54	−25	13	−3	...	Debt Securities	78bn d
															Financial Derivatives Assets	78bw d
															Financial Derivatives Liabilities	78bx d
−154	59	−124	−343	−261	−369	−143	−326	−327	−705	−729	−508	−228	−624	...	Other Investment Assets	78bh d
−62	−44	−4	−82	−43	35	15	86	88	95	14	—	—	—	...	Monetary Authorities	78bo d
															General Government	78bp d
−60	166	−90	−17	61	−320	−12	67	150	−305	−250	10	8		...	Banks	78bq d
−33	−62	−31	−244	−278	−84	−146	−479	−565	−494	−493	−517	−236	−624	...	Other Sectors	78br d
235	201	164	589	506	758	836	1,029	990	1,221	987	313	954	541	...	Other Investment Liab., n.i.e.	78bi d
—	−1	−1	−2	11	11	5	—	−1	−11	28	—	—	—	...	Monetary Authorities	78bs d
81	169	218	57	294	166	234	411	546	517	324	−49	314	130	...	General Government	78bt d
93	30	27	57	34	122	75	168	44	189	90				...	Banks	78bu d
62	2	−80	477	168	458	522	450	401	527	544	362	640	411	...	Other Sectors	78bv d
66	−113	195	477	54	343	119	−78	−119	67	206	−12	38	−34	...	Net Errors and Omissions	78ca d
186	417	101	333	−18	191	67	527	97	442	386	−138	738	−205	...	*Overall Balance*	78cb d
−186	−417	−101	−333	18	−191	−67	−527	−97	−442	−386	138	−738	205	...	Reserves and Related Items	79da d
−239	−437	−101	−220	−56	−237	−61	−527	−82	−395	−336	187	−688	245	...	Reserve Assets	79db d
53	21	—	−112	74	45	−5	—	−15	−47	−51	−50	−50	−40	...	Use of Fund Credit and Loans	79dc d
...	...	...	...	...	...	...	...								Exceptional Financing	79de d
															International Investment Position	
Millions of US Dollars																
...	...	...	...	...	...	...	...	2,953	3,112	3,175	3,313	3,359	3,276	...	Assets	79aa d
...	...	...	...	...	...	...	...	28	29	32	35	34	32	...	Direct Investment Abroad	79ab d
...	...	...	...	...	...	...	...	48	53	50	54	49	45	...	Portfolio Investment	79ac d
...	...	...	...	...	...	...	...	48	53	50	54	49	45	...	Equity Securities	79ad d
...	...	...	...	...	...	...	...	—	—	—	—	—	—	...	Debt Securities	79ae d
															Financial Derivatives	79al d
...	...	...	...	...	...	...	...	1,195	1,043	1,039	1,278	911	1,300	...	Other Investment	79af d
...	...	...	...	...	...	...	...	—	—	—	—	—	—	...	Monetary Authorities	79ag d
...	...	...	...	...	...	...	...	—	—	—	—	—	—	...	General Government	79ah d
...	...	...	...	...	...	...	...	447	562	621	665	646	696	...	Banks	79ai d
...	...	...	...	...	...	...	...	748	481	417	613	265	604	...	Other Sectors	79aj d
...	...	...	...	...	...	...	...	1,681	1,987	2,054	1,947	2,366	1,898	...	Reserve Assets	79ak d
...	...	...	...	...	...	...	...	22,773	23,382	22,579	24,854	24,295	23,901	...	Liabilities	79la d
...	...	...	...	...	...	...	...	10,967	11,201	10,629	12,237	11,463	11,452	...	Dir. Invest. in Rep. Economy	79lb d
...	...	...	...	...	...	...	...	947	1,012	1,035	1,161	1,065	975	...	Portfolio Investment	79lc d
...	...	...	...	...	...	...	...	947	1,012	1,035	1,161	1,065	975	...	Equity Securities	79ld d
...	...	...	...	...	...	...	...	—	—	—	—	—	—	...	Debt Securities	79le d
															Financial Derivatives	79ll d
...	...	...	...	...	...	...	...	10,860	11,170	10,914	11,456	11,766	11,474	...	Other Investment	79lf d
...	...	...	...	...	...	...	...	—	—	—	—	—	—	...	Monetary Authorities	79lg d
...	...	...	...	...	...	...	...	6,896	6,979	7,014	7,381	7,646	7,334	...	General Government	79lh d
...	...	...	...	...	...	...	...	934	1,157	1,157	1,240	1,457	1,540	...	Banks	79li d
...	...	...	...	...	...	...	...	3,030	3,034	2,742	2,835	2,663	2,600	...	Other Sectors	79lj d

744		1972	1973	1974	1975	1976	1977	1978	1979	1980	1981	1982	1983	1984	1985	1986
Government Finance																*Millions of Dinars:*
Deficit (-) or Surplus	**80**	-9.5	-17.1	-15.4	-25.2	-62.4	-132.2	-101.2	-139.6	-98.9	-105.5	-277.4	-458.8	-307.3	†-354.2	-510.9
Revenue	**81**	246.3	279.1	388.1	486.8	526.9	626.4	779.8	941.2	1,109.2	1,328.7	1,649.3	1,848.0	2,276.1	†2,328.3	2,400.2
Grants Received	**81z**	16.5	14.9	18.4	18.9	15.4	13.4	7.7	10.8	22.0	5.4	8.4	6.5	9.3	†3.4	4.1
Expenditure	**82**	241.1	291.1	396.1	506.0	577.2	729.8	845.5	993.6	1,117.4	1,353.4	1,814.5	2,142.0	2,438.0	†2,559.0	2,697.4
Lending Minus Repayments	**83**	31.2	20.0	25.8	24.9	27.5	42.2	43.2	98.0	112.7	86.2	120.6	171.3	154.7	†126.9	217.8
Financing																
Domestic	**84a**	7.4	1.8	9.0	7.6	42.2	36.4	25.7	2.8	18.5	-3.2	81.2	174.7	160.5	†155.6	273.8
Foreign	**85a**	2.1	15.3	6.4	17.6	20.2	95.8	75.5	136.8	80.4	108.7	196.2	284.1	146.8	†198.6	237.1
Debt: Domestic	**88a**	123.2	146.9	140.5	147.1	175.5	230.8	293.1	267.8	313.3	358.4	405.8	485.0	601.8	†750.6	867.1
Foreign	**89a**	276.9	287.4	318.3	353.0	441.9	550.1	676.9	804.5	897.1	1,102.6	1,430.5	1,867.2	2,108.7	†2,441.8	3,178.4
National Accounts																*Millions of Dinars*
Househ.Cons.Expend.,incl.NPISHs	**96f**	707	790	971	1,032	1,205	1,409	1,563	1,775	2,171	2,553	2,997	3,434	3,944	4,356	4,665
Government Consumption Expend.	**91f**	151	169	199	250	293	355	405	444	510	616	794	927	1,030	1,142	1,217
Gross Fixed Capital Formation	**93e**	214	248	315	461	558	665	765	894	982	1,290	1,635	1,750	1,920	1,850	1,685
Changes in Inventories	**93i**	19	-5	36	85	20	-5	-7	-27	37	56	-116	-140	75	-15	-36
Exports of Goods and Services	**90c**	271	300	547	546	562	649	769	1,139	1,425	1,722	1,773	1,948	2,114	2,253	2,161
Imports of Goods and Services (-)	**98c**	283	328	542	630	716	873	1,008	1,285	1,615	2,074	2,279	2,421	2,843	2,676	2,671
Gross Domestic Product (GDP)	**99b**	1,068	1,151	1,548	1,741	1,933	2,192	2,484	2,922	3,541	4,162	4,804	5,668	6,412	7,018	7,160
Net Primary Income from Abroad	**98.n**	-8	-12	-8	-2	-25	-19	-4	-6	-22	32	53	64	49	-68	-50
Gross National Income (GNI)	**99a**	....	....	....	....	....	....	....	....	....	....	....	....	....	....	....
Net Current Transf.from Abroad	**98t**	....	....	....	....	....	....	....	....	....	....	....	....	....	....	....
Gross Nat'l Disposable Inc.(GNDI)	**99i**	1,088	1,181	1,533	1,775	1,928	2,254	2,532	2,983	3,546	4,263	4,938	5,654	6,393	6,955	7,087
Nat'l Disposable Income, Net	**99k**	1,018	1,106	1,442	1,647	1,752	2,040	2,276	2,674	3,163	3,814	4,393	4,994	5,617	6,058	6,093
GDP Volume 1972 prices	**99b.*p***	1,068	1,061	1,146	1,228	1,325	....	....	....	....	....	....	....	....	....	....
GDP Volume 1980 prices	**99b.*p***	....	....	....	....	2,810	2,906	3,093	3,296	3,541	3,736	3,718	3,892	....	....	....
GDP Volume 1990 Prices	**99b.*p***	....	....	....	....	....	....	....	....	....	....	....	8,528	9,058	9,345	9,158
GDP Volume (1995=100)	**99bv*p***	37.9	37.7	40.7	43.6	47.1	48.7	51.8	55.2	59.3	62.6	62.3	65.2	69.3	71.5	70.0
GDP Deflator (1995=100)	**99bi*p***	16.5	17.9	22.3	23.4	24.1	26.4	28.1	31.0	35.0	39.0	45.2	51.0	54.3	57.6	60.0
																Millions:
Population	**99z**	5.28	†5.33	5.46	5.61	5.77	5.93	6.08	6.22	6.39	6.57	6.70	6.84	7.03	7.26	7.46

	1987	1988	1989	1990	1991	1992	1993	1994	1995	1996	1997	1998	1999	2000	2001		
Government Finance																	
Year Ending December 31																	
Deficit (-) or Surplus	−372.1	−326.9	−411.6	−585.5	−704.9	−419.4	−475.4	−219.2	−543.6	−599.0	−855.2	−200.2	−646.2	....	....	80	
Revenue	2,497.2	2,728.2	2,927.9	3,325.8	3,496.1	4,037.8	4,442.1	4,958.7	5,121.9	5,670.1	6,012.8	7,058.2	7,180.2	....	....	81	
Grants Received	23.6	30.3	143.2	70.5	32.5	56.7	53.3	63.4	44.6	42.3	—	—	—	....	....	81z	
Expenditure	2,800.1	3,004.0	3,424.6	3,742.6	4,092.0	4,393.6	4,850.6	5,101.2	5,584.2	6,208.3	6,677.4	7,160.2	7,864.8	....	....	82	
Lending Minus Repayments	92.8	81.4	58.1	239.2	141.5	120.3	120.2	140.1	125.9	103.1	190.6	98.2	−38.4	....	....	83	
Financing																	
Domestic	285.5	157.5	294.1	393.8	419.2	278.5	300.3	1.2	53.8	72.6	216.8	81.5	213.5	....	....	84a	
Foreign	86.6	169.4	117.5	191.7	285.7	140.9	175.1	218.0	489.8	526.4	542.4	10.0	349.6	....	....	85a	
Debt: Domestic	949.1	1,062.3	1,275.7	1,614.4	2,428.6	2,648.8	2,986.3	3,165.7	3,251.4	3,574.0	4,946.4	5,240.4	5,570.3	....	....	88a	
Foreign	3,190.9	3,750.5	3,847.5	4,309.4	4,869.6	4,957.8	5,710.3	6,169.9	6,556.5	6,969.0	8,116.5	8,236.4	9,572.2	....	....	89a	
National Accounts																	
Millions of Dinars																	
Househ.Cons.Expend.,incl.NPISHs	5,124	5,582	6,042	6,881	7,504	8,461	9,093	9,799	10,728	11,618	12,591	13,717	14,900	16,181	17,476	96f	
Government Consumption Expend.	1,305	1,387	1,656	1,769	1,993	2,193	2,385	2,582	2,777	2,965	3,296	3,530	3,836	4,165	4,527	91f	
Gross Fixed Capital Formation	1,620	1,680	2,157	2,635	2,892	3,729	4,122	4,279	4,121	4,422	5,153	5,610	6,278	7,020	7,510	93e	
Changes in Inventories	27	5	136	293	235	273	165	−382	92	356	372	462	210	260	403	93i	
Exports of Goods and Services	2,799	3,639	4,352	4,711	4,856	5,419	5,931	7,106	7,657	8,030	9,147	9,712	10,501	11,784	13,686	90c	
Imports of Goods and Services (-)	2,878	3,608	4,752	5,473	5,452	6,368	7,033	7,570	8,323	8,326	9,660	10,470	11,052	12,725	14,843	98c	
Gross Domestic Product (GDP)	8,035	8,661	†9,590	10,816	12,029	13,706	14,663	15,814	17,052	19,066	20,898	22,581	24,672	26,685	28,759	99b	
Net Primary Income from Abroad	−2	52	†60	140	15	−22	47	−918	−811	−1,004	−998	−988	−1,073			98.n	
Gross National Income (GNI)	....	....	†9,203	10,457	11,517	13,078	13,789	14,896	16,241	18,062	19,900	21,593	23,599	25,385	27,448	99a	
Net Current Transf.from Abroad	....	....	†547	595	514	499	594	673	712	801	834	942	1,080	1,122	1,248	98t	
Gross Nat'l Disposable Inc.(GNDI)	8,128	8,882	†9,750	11,052	12,031	13,577	14,383	15,569	16,953	18,863	20,734	22,515	24,679	26,507	28,696	99i	
Nat'l Disposable Income, Net	7,024	7,691	....	....	....	....	....	....	....	....	....	....	....	....	....	99k	
GDP Volume 1972 prices	....	....	....	....	....	....	....	....	....	....	....	....	....	....	....	99b.p	
GDP Volume 1980 prices	....	....	....	....	....	....	....	....	....	....	....	....	....	....	....	99b.p	
GDP Volume 1990 Prices	9,607	9,763	10,101	10,816	11,238	12,115	12,381	12,774	13,074	14,009	14,771	15,477	16,415	17,181	18,029	99b.p	
GDP Volume (1995=100)	73.5	74.7	77.3	82.7	86.0	92.7	94.7	97.7	100.0	107.1	113.0	118.4	125.5	131.4	137.9	99bv.p	
GDP Deflator (1995=100)	64.1	68.0	†72.8	76.7	82.1	86.7	90.8	94.9	100.0	104.4	108.5	111.9	115.2	119.1	122.3	99bi.p	
Midyear Estimates																	
Population	7.68	7.82	7.97	8.15	8.32	8.49	8.66	8.81	8.96	9.09	9.21	9.33	9.46	9.56	9.67	99z	

(See notes in the back of the book.)

		1972	1973	1974	1975	1976	1977	1978	1979	1980	1981	1982	1983	1984	1985	1986
Exchange Rates																*Liras per SDR:*
Market Rate	aa	15	17	17	18	19	24	33	47	115	156	206	296	436	634	927
																Liras per US Dollar:
Market Rate	ae	14	14	14	15	17	19	25	35	90	134	187	283	445	577	758
Market Rate	rf	14	14	14	14	16	18	24	31	76	111	163	225	367	522	675
Fund Position																*Millions of SDRs:*
Quota	2f. s	151	151	151	151	151	151	200	200	300	300	300	429	429	429	429
SDRs	1b. s	38	28	35	27	18	—	—	—	—	—	—	1	—	—	—
Reserve Position in the Fund	1c. s	28	38	38	—	—	—	—	—	—	—	—	32	32	32	32
Total Fund Cred.&Loans Outstg.	2tl	—	—	—	208	337	337	478	480	827	1,136	1,319	1,497	1,455	1,208	887
International Liquidity													*Millions of US Dollars Unless Otherwise Indicated:*			
Total Reserves minus Gold	1l. d	1,262	1,986	1,562	944	990	638	801	658	1,077	928	1,080	1,288	1,271	1,056	1,412
SDRs	1b. d	42	34	42	32	21	—	—	—	—	—	—	1	—	—	—
Reserve Position in the Fund	1c. d	31	46	46	—	—	—	—	—	—	—	—	34	32	35	39
Foreign Exchange	1d. d	1,190	1,906	1,473	912	969	638	801	658	1,077	928	1,080	1,253	1,239	1,020	1,372
Gold (Million Fine Troy Ounces)	1ad	3.571	3.571	3.569	3.570	3.570	3.634	3.667	3.765	3.768	3.768	3.769	3.775	3.800	3.858	3.840
Gold (National Valuation)	1an d	136	151	151	151	151	153	155	155	155	155	155	155	823	1,069	1,237
Monetary Authorities: Other Liab.	4..d	989	1,249	1,445	2,233	4,258	4,188	5,166	5,544	7,086	6,160	6,047	7,084	7,440	9,507	†8,118
Deposit Money Banks: Assets	7a.d	50	74	58	309	191	137	215	258	547	794	950	992	2,076	1,994	†2,728
Liabilities	7b.d	101	104	100	73	135	58	58	80	82	46	343	446	1,693	2,507	†1,563
Other Banking Insts.: Assets	7e.d	....	....	....	....	....	....	....	....	....	....	....	....	....	....	13
Liabilities	7f.d	147	201	238	288	526	580	656	853	619	529	504	439	492	551	†210
Monetary Authorities								*Millions of Liras through 1977; Billions from 1978 to 1995;*								
Foreign Assets	11	21,680	31,893	25,306	17,968	23,591	16,252	†42	59	270	496	808	1,404	1,662	2,241	†3,105
Claims on Central Government	12a	13,985	14,331	18,857	41,966	51,767	90,297	†144	262	631	993	1,349	1,803	4,441	6,668	†5,161
Claims on Official Entities	12bx	5,809	5,688	9,946	9,551	25,528	46,510	†68	124	180	236	261	256	41	122	57
Claims on Nonfin.Pub.Enterprises	12c															
Claims on Deposit Money Banks	12e	13,702	18,319	26,192	41,770	71,843	100,138	†151	214	317	420	377	629	307	369	†542
Claims on Other Banking Insts	12f	14	78	6,245	13,514	22,281	35,840	†42	47	49	54	67	76	37	50	†78
Claims on Nonbank Financial Insts	12g	....	....	....	....	....	....	....	....	....	....	....	....	....	....	27
Reserve Money	14	35,877	45,364	58,413	76,906	93,045	136,680	†199	309	458	717	1,011	1,397	2,101	2,900	†4,588
of which: Currency Outside DMBs	14a	15,980	20,703	26,154	32,909	42,471	62,961	†94	144	218	280	412	548	736	1,011	†1,300
Other Liabilities to DMBs	14n							....	....	....	....	....	....	....	....	....
Time and Savings Deposits	15	211	787	859	680	909	769	†2	1	1	64	3	4	2	5	†373
Foreign Currency Deposits	15.a							....	....	....	....	....	....	....	....	151
Restricted Deposits	16b	1,558	1,922	1,958	3,000	13,249	50,385	†96	150	142	94	73	61	90	72	†148
Foreign Liabilities	16c	13,847	17,481	20,210	37,504	77,487	89,390	†146	218	734	1,000	1,401	2,447	3,943	6,249	†6,974
Central Government Deposits	16d	1,150	1,279	972	1,460	2,072	2,571	†2	5	49	269	301	191	37	120	†1,012
Central Govt. Lending Funds	16f	696	578	1,180	1,068	1,858	3,050	†4	9	26	38	11	16	10	30	....
Capital Accounts	17a	1,691	1,905	2,380	3,122	3,970	5,101	†7	9	17	26	39	55	75	103	†135
Other Items (Net)	17r	160	994	574	1,028	2,419	1,091	†-9	3	20	-10	23	-3	230	-30	†-4,400
Deposit Money Banks								*Millions of Liras through 1977; Billions from 1978 to 1995;*								
Reserves	20	19,095	23,539	30,303	42,688	49,355	72,040	†100	151	220	429	592	827	1,299	1,834	†3,400
Other Claims on Monetary Auth.	20n							....	....	....	....	....	....	....	....	....
Foreign Assets	21	700	1,038	815	4,677	3,175	2,668	†5	9	49	106	177	281	923	1,150	†2,067
Claims on Central Government	22a	7,551	7,242	7,450	9,878	16,056	23,756	†32	42	68	159	384	376	915	2,030	†2,644
Claims on Local Government	22b															149
Claims on Official Entities	22bx	9,881	14,641	19,131	25,699	33,568	36,194	†40	78	159	161	156	199	174	439	1,371
Claims on Nonfin.Pub.Enterprises	22c															
Claims on Private Sector	22d	49,420	64,989	84,172	121,233	161,596	205,772	†261	381	660	1,231	1,814	2,708	3,625	5,725	†9,454
Claims on Other Banking Insts	22f	2,255	2,330	2,427	2,481	2,795	1,843	†2	2	2	3	12	17	26	32	†29
Claims on Nonbank Financial Insts	22g															22
Demand Deposits	24	36,943	49,239	62,559	84,725	108,073	145,642	†190	298	†520	736	994	1,520	1,686	2,402	†3,710
Time and Savings Deposits	25	18,008	20,542	24,577	29,002	30,776	34,403	†44	84	†186	690	1,272	1,393	3,045	5,120	†6,098
Foreign Currency Deposits	25.a							....	....	....	....	....	....	....	....	2,285
Money Market Instruments	26aa															787
Bonds	26ab	360	375	386	767	833	1,302	†1	2	2	2	7	12	9	7	†7
Restricted Deposits	26b	20	20	404	2,993	7,634	27,859	†28	25	38	101	181	379	512	550	....
Foreign Liabilities	26c	1,419	1,454	1,398	1,103	2,248	1,130	†1	3	7	6	64	126	753	1,446	†1,184
Central Government Deposits	26d	7,908	10,493	11,607	17,100	20,032	26,048	†35	51	†42	85	94	173	255	491	†2,747
Central Govt. Lending Funds	26f	369	374	531	1,145	2,084	3,135	†5	2	7	67	218	268	376	576	....
Credit from Monetary Authorities	26g	5,993	14,119	23,178	22,226	34,927	55,796	†151	214	317	420	377	629	307	369	†806
Credit from Other Financial Insts.	26i	2,894	3,814	4,919	6,159	9,440	12,852	†9	10	7	—	2	1	2	4	....
Capital Accounts	27a	11,418	12,507	13,972	17,057	19,658	22,498	†27	52	81	80	174	291	455	676	†1,624
Other Items (Net)	27r	5,121	2,778	2,779	27,398	44,110	62,046	†44	72	93	-5	-175	-323	-347	-359	†-880
Monetary Survey								*Millions of Liras through 1977; Billions from 1978 to 1995;*								
Foreign Assets (Net)	31n	7,114	13,996	4,513	-15,962	-52,969	-71,600	†-100	-153	-422	-404	-480	-889	-2,111	-4,304	†-2,986
Domestic Credit	32	79,857	97,527	135,649	205,762	291,487	411,593	†551	880	1,659	2,482	3,648	5,071	8,965	14,456	†15,233
Claims on Central Govt. (Net)	32an	12,478	9,801	13,728	33,284	45,719	85,434	†139	248	609	798	1,339	1,815	5,062	8,088	†4,046
Claims on Local Government	32b															149
Claims on Official Entities	32bx	15,690	20,329	29,077	35,250	59,096	82,704	†108	202	339	397	417	456	215	561	....
Claims on Nonfin.Pub.Enterprises	32c															1,428
Claims on Private Sector	32d	49,420	64,989	84,172	121,233	161,596	205,772	†261	381	660	1,231	1,814	2,708	3,625	5,725	†9,454
Claims on Other Banking Insts	32f	2,269	2,408	8,672	15,995	25,076	37,683	†44	50	51	56	79	93	62	82	†107
Claims on Nonbank Financial Inst	32g															49
Money	34	53,725	71,063	90,668	118,943	151,763	210,282	†289	456	758	1,024	1,413	2,090	2,487	3,468	†5,062
Quasi-Money	35	18,219	21,329	25,436	29,682	31,685	35,172	†46	85	187	755	1,275	1,397	3,047	5,125	†9,507
Money Market Instruments	36aa															787
Bonds	36ab															7
Restricted Deposits	36b															148
Central Govt. Lending Funds	36f	1,065	952	1,731	2,213	3,942	6,185	†9	11	33	105	229	284	386	606	....
Other Items (Net)	37r	13,955	18,194	22,401	38,980	51,148	88,407	†107	173	259	195	251	412	935	953	†-3,421
Money plus Quasi-Money	35l	71,944	92,392	116,104	148,625	183,448	245,454	†335	542	945	1,779	2,688	3,487	5,534	8,593	†14,568
Other Banking Institutions								*Millions of Liras through 1977; Billions from 1978 to 1995;*								
Reserves	40	264	333	360	513	608	383	†1	1	2	3	3	3	10	14	†88
Foreign Assets	41	—	—	—	74	299	3	†—	1	1	2	3	4	4	9	†10
Claims on Central Government	42a	335	185	343	305	764	1,842	†2	2	2	5	4	4	35	32	†42
Claims on Local Government	42b															
Claims on Official Entities	42bx	10,421	12,688	22,312	33,437	55,401	77,766	†95	115	127	173	251	304	333	418	....
Claims on Nonfin.Pub.Enterprises	42c															512
Claims on Private Sector	42d	3,092	4,066	4,751	5,931	7,709	9,692	†15	27	50	84	126	179	301	390	†585
Claims on Deposit Money Banks	42e	2,894	3,814	4,919	6,159	9,440	12,852	†9	10	7	—	2	1	2	4	....
Claims on Nonbank Financial Insts	42g															—

	1987	1988	1989	1990	1991	1992	1993	1994	1995	1996	1997	1998	1999	2000	2001		
Exchange Rates	*End of Period*																
Market Rate	1,448	2,442	3,041	4,168	7,266	11,776	19,879	56,534	88,669	154,976	277,413	442,775	743,077	877,360	1,822,418	aa
	End of Period (ae) Period Average (rf)																
Market Rate	1,021	1,815	2,314	2,930	5,080	8,564	14,473	38,726	59,650	107,775	205,605	314,464	541,400	673,385	1,450,127	ae
Market Rate	857	1,422	2,122	2,609	4,172	6,872	10,985	29,609	45,845	81,405	151,865	260,724	418,783	625,219	1,225,588	rf
Fund Position	*End of Period*																
Quota	429	429	429	429	429	642	642	642	642	642	642	642	964	964	964	2f. *s*
SDRs	—	—	—	—	—	—	—	1	2	1	1	1	—	22	4	1b. *s*
Reserve Position in the Fund	32	32	32	32	32	32	32	32	32	32	32	32	113	113	113	1c. *s*
Total Fund Cred.&Loans Outstg.	543	222	36	—	—	—	—	236	461	461	440	276	649	3,205	11,233	2tl
International Liquidity	*End of Period*																
Total Reserves minus Gold	1,776	2,344	4,780	6,050	5,144	6,159	6,272	7,169	12,442	16,436	18,658	19,489	23,346	22,488	18,879	1l. *d*
SDRs	—	—	—	1	—	—	—	1	3	1	1	1	—	29	4	1b. *d*
Reserve Position in the Fund	46	43	42	46	46	44	44	47	48	46	44	45	155	147	142	1c. *d*
Foreign Exchange	1,730	2,301	4,738	6,003	5,098	6,115	6,227	7,121	12,391	16,388	18,614	19,442	23,191	22,313	18,733	1d. *d*
Gold (Million Fine Troy Ounces)	3.831	3.822	3.785	4.095	4.163	4.047	4.031	3.820	3.747	3.747	3.748	3.748	3.744	3.739	3.733	1ad
Gold (National Valuation)	1,535	1,368	1,354	1,512	1,536	1,494	1,488	1,410	1,383	1,372	1,384	1,125	1,011	1,009	1,008	1an *d*
Monetary Authorities: Other Liab.	10,583	9,911	8,993	8,725	7,399	6,985	7,490	9,650	11,797	12,054	11,502	12,809	10,816	10,634	10,940	4.. *d*
Deposit Money Banks: Assets	3,075	4,892	4,222	4,973	5,486	8,540	10,708	8,655	9,951	9,400	10,474	11,616	14,896	17,072	12,218	7a. *d*
Liabilities	1,885	1,712	1,957	3,796	3,688	6,379	9,369	3,245	5,293	8,089	11,394	14,647	†18,078	22,968	9,919	7b. *d*
Other Banking Insts.: Assets	786	148	467	540	620	555	612	478	1,015	942	1,062	1,084	1,146	1,082	1,091	7e. *d*
Liabilities	334	382	451	594	998	928	937	799	816	839	765	864	†2,026	2,202	1,821	7f. *d*
Monetary Authorities	*Trillions of Liras Beginning 1996: End of Period*																
Foreign Assets	5,282	12,505	16,939	24,249	37,875	73,521	124,914	372,848	888,772	†2,029	4,260	6,896	13,864	16,627	30,705	11
Claims on Central Government	6,103	6,820	5,847	5,292	17,607	53,229	109,813	203,170	531,228	†847	983	878	1,135	1,727	33,015	12a
Claims on Official Entities	....	....	....	....	....	....	....	....	....	....	....	....	....	....	....	12bx
Claims on Nonfin.Pub.Enterprises	91	466	553	902	4,728	11,601	12,515	25,930	1,203	†2	2	2	3	2	4	12c
Claims on Deposit Money Banks	1,646	2,274	3,140	4,479	4,477	8,655	16,866	20,503	28,677	†73	823	2,072	3,088	6,543	9,665	12e
Claims on Other Banking Insts	835	628	1,137	1,519	1,332	1,517	1,996	71	29	†—	—	9	—	—	—	12f
Claims on Nonbank Financial Insts	30	25	21	—	—	—	—	—	—	†—	—	—	—	500	750	12g
Reserve Money	6,759	12,084	20,780	28,746	43,077	76,773	128,902	282,973	507,819	†972	1,943	3,506	6,923	10,118	18,069	14
of which: Currency Outside DMBs	2,208	3,424	6,833	11,343	16,834	30,244	51,364	101,401	188,506	†316	599	1,031	1,887	3,197	4,463	14a
Other Liabilities to DMBs	418	747	20	—	3,897	14,948	15,021	8,503	20,974	†47	—	—	—	—	1,053	14n
Time and Savings Deposits	110	190	207	365	667	1,982	2,942	6,773	12,425	†33	56	112	232	286	419	15
Foreign Currency Deposits	115	531	611	743	1,052	1,843	3,827	3,130	12,147	†39	111	135	23	142	531	15.a
Restricted Deposits	213	341	221	39	15	14	11	12	15	†—	—	—	—	1	1	16b
Foreign Liabilities	11,590	18,529	20,916	25,564	37,587	59,826	108,401	387,018	744,534	†1,370	2,487	4,150	6,338	9,973	36,336	16c
Central Government Deposits	1,842	3,850	4,578	5,057	6,366	14,309	16,541	22,482	103,109	†225	875	833	1,812	1,478	3,467	16d
Central Govt. Lending Funds	....	....	....	....	....	....	....	....	....	....	....	....	....	....	....	16f
Capital Accounts	209	348	486	1,246	1,327	3,468	8,784	13,753	19,192	†114	204	436	1,327	2,233	1,697	17a
Other Items (Net)	-7,271	-13,901	-20,180	-25,319	-27,969	-24,639	-18,324	-102,124	29,693	†149	391	685	1,435	1,168	12,568	17r
Deposit Money Banks	*Trillions of Liras Beginning 1996: End of Period*																
Reserves	5,103	9,134	13,603	16,967	25,834	44,839	74,625	172,477	314,480	†641	1,298	2,433	4,544	5,766	10,713	20
Other Claims on Monetary Auth.	514	753	28	6	3,903	14,954	15,027	8,509	20,995	†47	—	—	5	59	2,179	20n
Foreign Assets	3,139	8,878	9,769	14,571	27,867	73,144	154,976	335,160	593,596	†1,016	2,161	3,662	8,078	11,514	17,746	21
Claims on Central Government	4,512	7,413	14,702	20,564	34,847	55,478	99,892	224,733	411,849	†1,423	3,593	9,849	23,148	40,223	65,980	22a
Claims on Local Government	383	545	563	753	—	—	—	2,756	4,746	†6	8	20	22	48	112	22b
Claims on Official Entities	....	....	....	....	....	....	....	....	....	....	....	....	....	....	....	22bx
Claims on Nonfin.Pub.Enterprises	2,249	3,401	3,221	6,814	9,095	7,120	24,052	44,629	40,289	†49	217	290	625	541	390	22c
Claims on Private Sector	14,484	20,617	34,828	61,060	98,780	182,233	336,615	571,521	1,356,669	†3,203	7,252	11,493	16,565	28,515	35,456	22d
Claims on Other Banking Insts	40	49	579	568	1,030	2,489	4,856	17,848	28,032	†58	129	204	585	719	1,054	22f
Claims on Nonbank Financial Insts	79	233	284	397	660	992	1,893	2,192	4,827	†13	58	119	499	1,338	944	22g
Demand Deposits	6,175	7,480	12,082	18,671	27,114	45,590	73,402	125,850	193,429	†562	887	1,387	2,400	3,393	6,106	24
Time and Savings Deposits	8,023	15,516	27,779	41,408	75,477	124,654	183,910	434,518	959,241	†2,098	4,237	9,138	17,904	24,995	36,037	25
Foreign Currency Deposits	5,241	8,981	13,524	21,051	49,889	101,391	186,790	561,875	1,145,819	†2,410	4,894	8,654	18,138	24,795	58,795	25.a
Money Market Instruments	1,367	1,251	1,979	2,382	3,397	3,709	3,064	4,633	6,919	†11	—	—	—	—	—	26aa
Bonds	7	54	389	413	704	6,192	24,524	15,757	36,690	†6	81	123	†—	—	—	26ab
Restricted Deposits	....	....	....	....	....	....	....	....	....	....	....	....	....	....	....	26b
Foreign Liabilities	1,924	3,107	4,528	11,122	18,736	54,629	135,596	125,647	315,755	†872	2,343	4,606	†9,787	15,466	14,383	26c
Central Government Deposits	5,115	8,124	12,542	20,329	26,333	38,069	65,803	91,715	143,856	†393	838	1,495	3,371	5,855	7,072	26d
Central Govt. Lending Funds	....	....	....	....	....	....	....	....	....	....	....	....	....	....	....	26f
Credit from Monetary Authorities	2,226	2,813	3,205	4,017	4,450	8,652	17,903	12,661	12,586	†32	764	1,725	2,335	10,573	11,248	26g
Credit from Other Financial Insts.	....	....	....	....	....	....	....	....	....	....	....	....	....	....	....	26i
Capital Accounts	3,039	6,816	9,341	16,680	28,044	50,209	99,670	182,053	383,839	†869	1,864	3,944	6,645	9,822	21,348	27a
Other Items (Net)	-2,613	-4,013	-7,793	-14,371	-32,126	-51,846	-78,726	-174,883	-422,650	†-796	-1,192	-3,003	-6,509	-6,176	-20,415	27r
Monetary Survey	*Trillions of Liras Beginning 1996: End of Period*																
Foreign Assets (Net)	-5,094	-254	1,264	2,134	9,419	32,211	35,893	195,343	422,079	†803	1,591	1,802	†5,816	2,702	-2,268	31n
Domestic Credit	21,851	28,222	44,613	72,484	135,379	262,281	509,288	978,654	2,131,906	†4,984	10,529	20,534	37,398	66,280	127,167	32
Claims on Central Govt. (Net)	3,659	2,259	3,429	471	19,755	56,329	127,361	313,707	696,111	†1,652	2,863	8,398	19,100	34,617	88,456	32an
Claims on Local Government	383	545	563	753	—	—	—	2,756	4,746	†6	8	20	22	48	112	32b
Claims on Official Entities	....	....	....	....	....	....	....	....	....	....	....	....	....	....	....	32bx
Claims on Nonfin.Pub.Enterprises	2,340	3,866	3,774	7,716	13,823	18,721	36,567	70,559	41,492	†51	219	291	627	543	394	32c
Claims on Private Sector	14,484	20,617	34,828	61,060	98,780	182,233	336,615	571,521	1,356,669	†3,203	7,252	11,493	16,565	28,515	35,456	32d
Claims on Other Banking Insts	875	677	1,716	2,087	2,362	4,007	6,852	17,918	28,061	†58	129	214	585	719	1,054	32f
Claims on Nonbank Financial Inst	109	258	305	397	660	992	1,893	2,192	4,827	†13	58	119	499	1,838	1,694	32g
Money	8,438	11,020	19,092	30,237	44,279	76,373	125,868	228,413	384,391	†882	1,492	2,433	4,307	6,612	10,607	34
Quasi-Money	13,489	25,219	42,121	63,566	127,085	229,870	377,469	1,006,296	2,129,632	†4,580	9,298	18,040	36,297	50,218	95,781	35
Money Market Instruments	1,367	1,251	1,979	2,382	3,397	3,709	3,064	4,633	6,919	†11	—	—	—	—	—	36aa
Bonds	7	54	389	413	704	6,192	24,524	15,757	36,690	†6	81	123	†—	—	—	36ab
Restricted Deposits	213	341	221	39	15	14	11	12	15	†—	—	—	—	1	1	36b
Central Govt. Lending Funds	....	....	....	....	....	....	....	....	....	....	....	....	....	....	....	36f
Other Items (Net)	-6,758	-10,807	-17,923	-22,018	-30,680	-21,665	14,245	-81,116	-3,662	†307	1,248	1,740	2,610	12,151	18,511	37r
Money plus Quasi-Money	21,926	36,239	61,213	93,803	171,363	306,242	503,336	1,234,709	2,514,022	†5,462	10,790	20,473	40,604	56,831	106,388	35l
Other Banking Institutions	*Trillions of Liras Beginning 1996: End of Period*																
Reserves	294	663	1,746	2,400	5,938	10,381	19,738	52,327	84,106	†147	257	457	894	1,124	1,543	40
Foreign Assets	802	269	1,081	1,582	3,152	4,757	8,859	18,513	60,545	†101	218	341	620	728	1,583	41
Claims on Central Government	44	119	323	330	449	461	2,623	4,579	7,079	†17	43	86	334	393	432	42a
Claims on Local Government	—	—	—	—	1,158	2,292	5,717	5,942	10,131	†24	45	93	387	715	920	42b
Claims on Official Entities	....	....	....	....	....	....	....	....	....	....	....	....	....	....	....	42bx
Claims on Nonfin.Pub.Enterprises	613	1,206	1,108	1,614	1,453	1,320	1,713	1,272	9,222	†7	17	11	42	25	29	42c
Claims on Private Sector	895	1,778	2,989	4,480	9,406	13,931	22,562	45,137	78,314	†170	332	573	825	1,070	1,883	42d
Claims on Deposit Money Banks	....	....	....	....	....	....	....	....	....	....	....	....	....	....	....	42e
Claims on Nonbank Financial Insts	—	—	18	21	10	119	710	230	136	†1	5	7	35	36	56	42g

		1972	1973	1974	1975	1976	1977	1978	1979	1980	1981	1982	1983	1984	1985	1986
Other Banking Institutions (cont.)								*Millions of Liras through 1977; Billions from 1978 to 1995;*								
Time and Savings Deposits	45															97
Bonds	46ab	8,563	11,583	14,930	19,312	30,410	38,526	†45	50	57	70	71	121	103	147	†226
Foreign Liabilities	46c															159
Long-Term Foreign Liabilities	46cl	2,061	2,815	3,326	4,358	8,759	11,275	†17	30	56	71	94	124	219	318	....
Central Government Deposits	46d															185
Central Govt. Lending Funds	46f	1,949	1,631	2,275	2,110	4,466	4,557	†6	5	9	46	75	70	99	127	....
Credit from Monetary Authorities	46g	14	78	6,245	13,514	22,281	35,840	†42	47	49	54	67	76	37	50	†84
Credit from Deposit Money Banks	46h	2,028	2,103	2,200	2,157	2,471	1,452	†2	2	1	1	7	9	18	16	†281
Capital Accounts	47a	2,075	2,388	2,664	3,060	3,787	6,405	†7	11	14	17	64	79	189	227	†333
Other Items (Net)	47r	316	488	1,045	1,908	2,047	4,483	†4	9	3	7	10	16	22	−18	†−128
Banking Survey									*Millions of Liras through 1977; Billions from 1978 to 1995;*							
Foreign Assets (Net)	51n	7,114	13,996	4,513	−15,888	−52,670	−71,597	†−100	−153	−421	−403	−478	−885	−2,106	−4,295	†−3,135
Domestic Credit	52	91,436	112,058	154,383	229,440	330,285	463,210	†620	974	1,787	2,688	3,950	5,466	9,571	15,215	†16,079
Claims on Central Govt. (Net)	52an	12,813	9,986	14,071	33,589	46,483	87,276	†141	250	610	803	1,343	1,819	5,098	8,120	†3,902
Claims on Local Government	52b															149
Claims on Official Entities	52bx	26,111	33,017	51,389	68,687	114,497	160,470	†203	316	466	570	668	760	548	980	....
Claims on Nonfin.Pub.Enterprises	52c															1,940
Claims on Private Sector	52d	52,512	69,055	88,923	127,164	169,305	215,464	†276	408	711	1,315	1,939	2,887	3,926	6,116	†10,039
Claims on Nonbank Financial Inst.	52g															49
Liquid Liabilities	55l	71,680	92,059	115,744	148,112	182,840	245,071	†334	541	943	1,776	2,685	3,483	5,524	8,579	†15,420
Bonds	56ab	8,923	11,958	15,316	20,079	31,243	39,828	†46	51	60	73	78	133	112	154	†233
Long-Term Foreign Liabilities	56cl	2,061	2,815	3,326	4,358	8,759	11,275	†17	30	56	71	94	124	219	318	....
Central Govt. Lending Funds	56f	3,014	2,583	4,006	4,323	8,408	10,742	†15	17	42	151	304	354	484	734	....
Other Items (Net)	57r	12,865	16,654	20,578	36,698	46,385	84,750	†108	181	265	214	311	486	1,127	1,135	†−2,866
Interest Rates															*Percent Per Annum*	
Discount Rate *(End of Period)*	60	9.00	8.75	9.00	9.00	9.00	9.00	10.00	10.75	26.00	31.50	31.50	48.50	52.00	52.00	48.00
Interbank Money Market Rate	60b	....	....	....	....	....	....	....	....	....	....	....	....	....	....	....
Treasury Bill Rate	60c	....	....	....	....	....	....	....	....	....	....	....	....	....	....	....
Deposit Rate	60l	....	4.00	6.00	6.00	6.00	6.00	6.00	7.33	8.00	26.50	45.00	45.33	51.42	49.25	40.58
Prices, Production, Labor														*Index Numbers (1995=100):*		
Wholesale Prices	63	—	—	—	—	—	—	—	—	.1	.1	.2	.3	.4	.6	.8	1.1
Consumer Prices	64	—	—	—	—	—	—	—	—	.1	.1	.2	†.2	.3	.4	.6	.9
Industrial Production	66																65.5
Labor Force	67d															*Number in Thousands:*	
Employment	67e	....	....	....	....	....	....	....	....	....	....	....	....	....	16,162	....
Unemployment	67c	....	....	....	....	....	....	....	....	....	....	....	....	....	....	....
Unemployment Rate (%)	67r	....	....	....	....	....	....	....	....	....	....	....	....	....	....	....
International Transactions															*Millions of US Dollars*	
Exports	70..d	885	1,317	1,532	1,401	1,960	1,753	2,288	2,261	2,910	4,703	5,746	5,728	7,134	7,958	7,457
Imports, c.i.f.	71..d	1,563	2,086	3,778	4,739	5,129	5,796	4,599	5,070	7,910	8,933	8,843	9,235	10,757	11,343	11,105
Imports, f.o.b.	71.vd	1,391	1,857	3,589	4,502	4,872	5,506	4,369	4,816	7,514	8,567	8,406	8,761	10,137	10,732	10,506
																1995=100
Volume of Exports	72	....	....	....	....	....	....	....	....	....	....	....	....	....	....	....
Volume of Imports	73	....	....	....	....	....	....	....	....	....	....	....	....	....	....	....
Unit Value of Exports	74	....	....	....	....	....	....	....	....	....	....	....	....	....	....	....
Unit Value of Imports	75	....	....	....	....	....	....	....	....	....	....	....	....	....	....	....
Balance of Payments															*Millions of US Dollars*	
Current Account, n.i.e.	78ald	....	....	−561	−1,648	−2,029	−3,140	−1,265	−1,413	−3,408	−1,936	−952	−1,923	−1,439	−1,013	−1,465
Goods: Exports f.o.b.	78aad	....	....	1,532	1,401	1,960	1,753	2,288	2,261	2,910	4,703	5,890	5,905	7,389	8,255	7,583
Goods: Imports f.o.b.	78abd	....	....	−3,589	−4,502	−4,872	−5,506	−4,369	−4,815	−7,513	−8,567	−8,518	−8,895	−10,331	−11,230	−10,664
Trade Balance	78acd	....	....	−2,057	−3,101	−2,912	−3,753	−2,081	−2,554	−4,603	−3,864	−2,628	−2,990	−2,942	−2,975	−3,081
Services: Credit	78add	....	....	549	616	580	534	467	674	711	1,264	1,918	1,939	2,220	2,864	2,997
Services: Debit	78aed	....	....	−366	−436	−517	−687	−310	−367	−569	−468	−1,031	−1,166	−1,296	−1,333	−1,428
Balance on Goods & Services	78afd	....	....	−1,874	−2,921	−2,849	−3,906	−1,924	−2,247	−4,461	−3,068	−1,741	−2,217	−2,018	−1,444	−1,512
Income: Credit	78agd	....	....	1	1	1	6	66	34	51	52	120	102	146	298	341
Income: Debit	78ahd	....	....	−178	−165	−301	−347	−506	−1,010	−1,169	−1,478	−1,608	−1,568	−1,649	−1,851	−2,218
Balance on Gds, Serv. & Inc.	78aid	....	....	−2,051	−3,085	−3,149	−4,247	−2,364	−3,223	−5,579	−4,494	−3,229	−3,683	−3,521	−2,997	−3,389
Current Transfers, n.i.e.: Credit	78ajd	....	....	1,508	1,449	1,134	1,123	1,116	1,829	2,184	2,575	2,295	1,806	2,131	2,022	2,030
Current Transfers: Debit	78akd	....	....	−18	−12	−14	−16	−17	−19	−13	−17	−18	−46	−49	−38	−106
Capital Account, n.i.e.	78bcd	....	....	—	—	—	—	—	—	—	—	—	—	—	—	—
Capital Account, n.i.e.: Credit	78bad	....	....	—	—	—	—	—	—	—	—	—	—	—	—	—
Capital Account: Debit	78bbd	....	....	—	—	—	—	—	—	—	—	—	—	—	—	—
Financial Account, n.i.e.	78bjd	....	....	178	327	1,132	1,645	802	−396	645	899	280	883	−507	1,065	2,124
Direct Investment Abroad	78bdd	....	....	—	—	—	—	—	—	—	—	—	—	—	—	—
Dir. Invest. in Rep. Econ., n.i.e.	78bed	....	....	64	114	10	27	34	75	18	95	55	46	113	99	125
Portfolio Investment Assets	78bfd	....	....	—	—	—	—	—	—	—	—	—	—	....	....	....
Equity Securities	78bkd	....	....	—	—	—	—	—	—	—	—	—	—	....	....	....
Debt Securities	78bld	....	....	—	—	—	—	—	—	—	—	—	—	....	....	....
Portfolio Investment Liab., n.i.e.	78bgd	....	....	—	—	—	—	—	—	—	—	—	—	....	....	146
Equity Securities	78bmd	....	....	—	—	—	—	—	—	—	—	—	—	....	....	....
Debt Securities	78bnd	....	....	—	—	—	—	—	—	—	—	—	—	....	....	146
Financial Derivatives Assets	78bwd	....	....	....	....	....	....	....	....	....	....	....	....	....	....	....
Financial Derivatives Liabilities	78bxd	....	....	....	....	....	....	....	....	....	....	....	....	....	....	....
Other Investment Assets	78bhd	....	....	—	—	—	149	−17	−109	85	360	−181	177	−1,625	127	−313
Monetary Authorities	78bod	....	....											−551	−255	−220
General Government	78bpd	....	....	—	—	—	149	−17	−109	85	360	−181	177			
Banks	78bqd	....	....	—	—	—	—	—	—	—	—	—	—	−1,074	382	−93
Other Sectors	78brd	....	....	—	—	—	—	—	—	—	—	—	—	—	—	—
Other Investment Liab., n.i.e.	78bid	....	....	114	213	1,122	1,469	785	−362	542	444	406	660	1,005	839	2,166
Monetary Authorities	78bsd	....	....	−2	40	73	173	307	63	141	−46	496	300	173	35	67
General Government	78btd	....	....	−126	−118	−119	164	−280	1,986	154	100	−972	−365	−379	49	1,341
Banks	78bud	....	....	−26	−91	−558	−77	−45	−2,220	−70	−105	114	175	648	326	755
Other Sectors	78bvd	....	....	268	382	1,726	1,209	803	−191	317	495	768	550	563	429	3
Net Errors and Omissions	78cad	....	....	−170	−351	−831	−634	−874	651	1,435	650	−76	408	469	−836	−119
Overall Balance	78cbd	....	....	−553	−1,672	−1,728	−2,129	−1,337	−1,158	−1,328	−387	−748	−632	−1,477	−784	540
Reserves and Related Items	79dad	....	....	553	1,672	1,728	2,129	1,337	1,158	1,328	387	748	632	1,477	784	−540
Reserve Assets	79dbd	....	....	551	383	79	366	−153	148	−529	−293	−358	−186	−63	360	−162
Use of Fund Credit and Loans	79dcd	....	....	—	254	149	—	175	4	456	365	204	196	−43	−251	−378
Exceptional Financing	79ded	....	....	2	1,035	1,500	1,763	1,315	1,006	1,400	315	902	622	1,582	676	....

	1987	1988	1989	1990	1991	1992	1993	1994	1995	1996	1997	1998	1999	2000	2001	
Trillions of Liras Beginning 1996: End of Period																
Other Banking Institutions (cont.)																
Time and Savings Deposits	140	321	387	718	793	1,255	1,664	1,827	2,897	†2	3	3	332	383	1,114	45
Bonds	510	1,228	2,205	3,102	5,075	8,856	16,545	39,255	50,758	†70	130	104	†—	—	—	46ab
Foreign Liabilities	341	693	1,044	1,741	5,071	7,946	13,558	30,961	48,672	†90	157	272	†1,097	1,483	2,640	46c
Long-Term Foreign Liabilities	....	....	....	....	....	....	....	....	....	....	....	....	....	....	....	46cl
Central Government Deposits	240	311	263	794	4,643	5,309	13,202	23,550	44,215	†67	142	214	181	244	519	46d
Central Govt. Lending Funds	....	....	....	....	....	....	....	....	....	....	....	....	....	....	....	46f
Credit from Monetary Authorities	891	711	1,435	1,514	1,121	775	1,364	71	30	†15	30	47	82	100	225	46g
Credit from Deposit Money Banks	309	1,166	1,121	1,760	3,348	5,900	11,252	42,689	88,224	†160	284	502	690	878	891	46h
Capital Accounts	461	603	1,148	2,457	4,825	7,495	12,058	13,174	33,010	†86	194	384	763	1,287	2,204	47a
Other Items (Net)	–243	–997	–337	–1,657	–3,311	–4,278	–7,720	–23,527	–18,274	†–24	–23	42	–8	–284	–1,148	47r
Trillions of Liras Beginning 1996: End of Period																
Banking Survey																
Foreign Assets (Net)	–4,632	–678	1,301	1,976	7,500	29,021	31,194	182,895	433,952	†814	1,652	1,871	†5,340	1,947	–3,325	51n
Domestic Credit	22,288	30,337	47,072	76,049	140,849	271,088	522,558	994,345	2,164,512	†5,076	10,700	20,877	38,255	67,556	128,913	52
Claims on Central Govt. (Net)	3,463	2,067	3,489	7	15,560	51,480	116,782	294,736	658,975	†1,602	2,764	8,270	19,253	34,766	88,369	52an
Claims on Local Government	383	545	563	753	1,158	2,292	5,717	8,698	14,876	†30	54	113	409	763	1,032	52b
Claims on Official Entities	....	....	....	....	....	....	....	....	....	....	....	....	....	....	....	52bx
Claims on Nonfin.Pub.Enterprises	2,954	5,072	4,881	9,330	15,276	20,041	38,279	71,831	50,714	†58	236	303	670	567	423	52c
Claims on Private Sector	15,379	22,395	37,817	65,540	108,186	196,164	359,178	616,658	1,434,983	†3,372	7,584	12,066	17,389	29,585	37,339	52d
Claims on Nonbank Financial Inst	109	258	323	419	670	1,110	2,602	2,422	4,963	†14	62	126	534	1,875	1,750	52g
Liquid Liabilities	23,325	37,595	62,168	94,611	169,760	300,968	488,455	1,189,694	2,440,215	†5,330	10,541	20,026	40,053	56,112	106,110	55l
Bonds	517	1,283	2,594	3,515	5,779	15,048	41,069	55,012	87,448	†76	212	227	†—	—	—	56ab
Long-Term Foreign Liabilities	....	....	....	....	....	....	....	....	....	....	....	....	....	....	....	56cl
Central Govt. Lending Funds	....	....	....	....	....	....	....	....	....	....	....	....	....	....	....	56f
Other Items (Net)	–6,188	–10,108	–16,387	–20,101	–27,189	–15,907	24,228	–67,467	70,800	†485	1,600	2,495	3,542	13,391	19,478	57r
Percent Per Annum																
Interest Rates																
Discount Rate *(End of Period)*	45.00	54.00	54.00	45.00	48.00	48.00	48.00	55.00	50.00	50.00	67.00	67.00	60.00	60.00	60.00	60
Interbank Money Market Rate	39.82	60.62	40.66	51.91	72.75	65.35	62.83	136.47	72.30	76.24	70.32	74.60	73.53	56.72	91.95	60b
Treasury Bill Rate	41.92	54.56	48.01	43.46	67.01	72.17	....	....	....	....	....	....	....	33.32	64.61	60c
Deposit Rate	35.00	49.08	53.45	47.50	62.67	68.74	64.58	87.79	76.02	80.74	79.49	80.11	78.43	47.16	74.70	60l
Period Averages																
Prices, Production, Labor																
Wholesale Prices	†1.4	2.4	4.0	6.1	9.5	15.4	24.3	†53.8	100.0	175.9	319.9	549.6	841.2	1,273.9	....	63
Consumer Prices	†1.2	2.1	3.4	5.5	9.1	15.5	25.8	†53.2	100.0	180.3	335.0	618.5	1,019.7	1,579.6	2,439.0	64
Industrial Production	72.4	73.6	76.3	83.5	88.1	†92.8	98.2	92.1	100.0	105.9	†117.3	117.5	112.5	119.8	....	66
Period Averages																
Labor Force	....	....	....	....	....	....	20,384	....	22,078	22,259	21,818	23,415	23,779	....	....	67d
Employment	....	†18,445	18,856	19,946	19,452	19,959	19,905	20,396	21,378	21,698	20,815	21,958	22,049	....	....	67e
Unemployment	....	1,748	1,821	1,615	1,787	1,745	1,722	1,740	1,522	1,332	1,545	1,547	1,730	....	....	67c
Unemployment Rate (%)	....	8.7	8.8	7.5	8.4	8.0	8.0	7.6	6.6	5.8	6.9	6.2	7.3	....	....	67r
Millions of US Dollars																
International Transactions																
Exports	10,190	11,662	11,625	12,959	13,594	14,715	15,345	18,106	21,637	23,224	26,261	26,974	26,588	26,572	....	70..d
Imports, c.i.f.	14,158	14,335	15,792	22,302	21,047	22,871	29,428	23,270	35,709	43,627	48,559	45,921	40,692	53,499	....	71..d
Imports, f.o.b.	13,394	13,562	14,940	21,003	19,782	21,291	27,661	21,875	35,187	43,028	48,005	45,440	39,773	....	....	71.vd
1995=100																
Volume of Exports	....	....	66.2	†69.9	74.6	76.9	81.8	93.9	100.0	109.7	124.4	131.9	140.8	....	....	72
Volume of Imports	....	....	67.9	†78.0	75.0	76.1	104.4	77.3	100.0	129.3	159.9	152.3	154.1	....	....	73
Unit Value of Exports	....	....	85.0	†93.7	92.9	94.1	91.5	88.8	100.0	95.6	91.0	87.3	81.4	....	....	74
Unit Value of Imports	....	....	85.2	†89.8	87.0	85.3	80.0	85.6	100.0	94.0	85.8	82.3	77.7	....	....	75
Minus Sign Indicates Debit																
Balance of Payments																
Current Account, n.i.e.	–806	1,596	938	–2,625	250	–974	–6,433	2,631	–2,338	–2,437	–2,679	1,984	–1,360	–9,819	3,396	78ald
Goods: Exports f.o.b.	10,322	11,929	11,780	13,026	13,667	14,891	15,611	18,390	21,975	32,446	32,631	31,220	29,325	31,664	34,379	78aad
Goods: Imports f.o.b.	–13,551	–13,706	–15,999	–22,581	–21,007	–23,081	–29,771	–22,606	–35,187	–43,028	–48,029	–45,440	–39,768	–54,041	–38,916	78abd
Trade Balance	–3,229	–1,777	–4,219	–9,555	–7,340	–8,190	–14,160	–4,216	–13,212	–10,582	–15,398	–14,220	–10,443	–22,377	–4,537	78acd
Services: Credit	3,813	5,652	6,414	8,016	8,372	9,407	10,652	10,801	14,606	13,051	19,373	23,321	16,398	19,484	16,028	78add
Services: Debit	–1,695	–1,925	–2,465	–3,071	–3,218	–3,625	–3,948	–3,782	–5,024	–6,426	–8,507	–9,859	–8,953	–8,149	–6,898	78aed
Balance on Goods & Services	–1,111	1,950	–270	–4,610	–2,186	–2,408	–7,456	2,803	–3,630	–3,957	–4,532	–758	–2,998	–11,042	4,593	78afd
Income: Credit	382	374	684	917	935	1,012	1,135	890	1,489	1,577	1,900	2,481	2,350	2,836	2,753	78agd
Income: Debit	–2,467	–2,887	–3,011	–3,425	–3,598	–3,637	–3,880	–4,154	–4,693	–4,504	–4,913	–5,466	–5,887	–6,838	–7,753	78ahd
Balance on Gds, Serv. & Inc.	–3,196	–563	–2,597	–7,118	–4,849	–5,033	–10,201	–461	–6,834	–6,884	–7,545	–3,743	–6,535	–15,044	–407	78aid
Current Transfers, n.i.e.: Credit	2,456	2,220	3,574	4,525	5,131	4,075	3,800	3,113	4,512	4,466	4,909	5,860	5,294	5,317	3,861	78ajd
Current Transfers: Debit	–66	–61	–39	–32	–32	–16	–32	–21	–16	–19	–43	–133	–119	–92	–58	78akd
Capital Account, n.i.e.	—	—	23	—	—	—	—	—	—	—	—	—	—	....	....	78bcd
Capital Account, n.i.e.: Credit	—	—	23	—	—	—	—	—	—	—	—	—	—	....	....	78bad
Capital Account: Debit	—	—	—	—	—	—	—	—	—	—	—	—	—	....	....	78bbd
Financial Account, n.i.e.	1,891	–958	780	4,037	–2,397	3,648	8,963	–4,194	4,643	8,763	8,616	448	4,670	9,445	–14,197	78bjd
Direct Investment Abroad	–9	....	....	16	–27	–65	–14	–49	–113	–110	–251	–367	–645	–870	–497	78bdd
Dir. Invest. in Rep. Econ., n.i.e.	115	354	663	684	810	844	636	608	885	722	805	940	783	982	3,267	78bed
Portfolio Investment Assets	–25	–6	–59	–134	–91	–754	–563	35	–466	–1,380	–710	–1,622	–759	–593	–788	78bfd
Equity Securities	–25	–6	–59	–134	–91	–50	–139	5	–75	7	–50	171	52	85	–36	78bkd
Debt Securities	....	....	....	....	....	–704	–424	30	–391	–1,387	–660	–1,793	–811	–678	–752	78bld
Portfolio Investment Liab., n.i.e.	307	1,184	1,445	681	714	3,165	4,480	1,123	703	1,950	2,344	–5,089	4,188	1,615	–3,727	78bgd
Equity Securities	—	—	17	89	147	350	570	989	195	191	8	–518	429	636	–79	78bmd
Debt Securities	307	1,184	1,428	592	567	2,815	3,910	134	508	1,759	2,336	–4,571	3,759	979	–3,648	78bnd
Financial Derivatives Assets	....	....	....	....	....	....	....	....	....	....	....	—	—	....	—	78bwd
Financial Derivatives Liabilities	....	....	....	....	....	....	....	....	....	....	....	—	—	....	—	78bxd
Other Investment Assets	–945	–1,428	371	–409	–2,563	–2,438	–3,291	2,423	–383	331	–1,750	–1,464	–2,571	–2,138	–156	78bhd
Monetary Authorities	–511	–381	712	361	29	36	–61	–18	–102	–117	–98	–95	–98	1	–39	78bod
General Government	....	....	....	....	....	....	....	....	....	....	—	—	—	....	—	78bpd
Banks	–434	–1,046	–370	–769	–2,595	–2,474	–3,230	2,441	–281	1,448	–976	–942	–2,212	–1,799	233	78bqd
Other Sectors	....	–1	29	–1	3	....	....	....	....	–1,000	–676	–427	–261	–340	–350	78brd
Other Investment Liab., n.i.e.	2,448	–1,062	–1,640	3,199	–1,240	2,896	7,715	–8,334	4,017	7,250	8,178	8,050	3,674	10,449	–12,296	78bid
Monetary Authorities	967	–697	–13	–419	–1,089	300	1,085	1,415	1,734	1,456	1,195	760	–160	706	817	78bsd
General Government	1,403	610	–1,089	503	330	–1,310	–1,953	–2,516	–1,991	–2,232	–1,406	–1,655	–1,932	117	–1,977	78btd
Banks	1,006	–144	240	2,279	396	2,100	4,495	–7,053	1,973	3,046	2,232	3,195	2,655	3,736	–9,644	78bud
Other Sectors	–928	–831	–778	836	–877	1,806	4,088	–180	2,301	4,980	6,157	5,750	3,111	5,890	–1,492	78bvd
Net Errors and Omissions	–505	515	969	–469	948	–1,190	–2,222	1,766	2,355	–1,782	–2,594	–1,991	1,894	–2,560	–2,087	78cad
Overall Balance	580	1,153	2,710	943	–1,199	1,484	308	203	4,660	4,544	3,343	441	5,204	–2,934	–12,888	78cbd
Reserves and Related Items	–580	–1,153	–2,710	–943	1,199	–1,484	–308	–203	–4,660	–4,544	–3,343	–441	–5,204	2,934	12,888	79dad
Reserve Assets	–137	–721	–2,471	–895	1,199	–1,484	–308	–547	–5,007	–4,544	–3,316	–217	–5,724	–383	2,718	79dbd
Use of Fund Credit and Loans	–443	–432	–239	–48	—	—	—	344	347	—	–27	–224	519	3,316	10,169	79dcd
Exceptional Financing	—	—	—	—	—	—	—	—	—	—	—	—	—	....	—	79ded

		1972	1973	1974	1975	1976	1977	1978	1979	1980	1981	1982	1983	1984	1985	1986
International Investment Position																*Millions of US Dollars*
Assets	79aa d	....	....	....	....	....	....	....	....	....	....	....	2,288	3,931	3,724	4,696
Direct Investment Abroad	79ab d	...	....	....	....	....	....	....	....	....	....	....	—	—	—	—
Portfolio Investment	79ac d	...	....	....	....	....	....	....	....	....	....	....	—	—	—	—
Equity Securities	79ad d	...	....	....	....	....	....	....	....	....	....	....	—	—	—	—
Debt Securities	79ae d	...	....	....	....	....	....	....	....	....	....	....	—	—	—	—
Financial Derivatives	79al d	...	....	....	....	....	....	....	....	....	....	....	....	....	....	....
Other Investment	79af d	...	....	....	....	....	....	....	....	....	....	....	845	1,860	1,628	2,051
Monetary Authorities	79ag d	...	....	....	....	....	....	....	....	....	....	....	—	—	—	157
General Government	79ah d	...	....	....	....	....	....	....	....	....	....	....	—	—	—	—
Banks	79ai d	...	....	....	....	....	....	....	....	....	....	....	845	1,860	1,628	1,894
Other Sectors	79aj d	...	....	....	....	....	....	....	....	....	....	....				
Reserve Assets	79ak d	...	....	....	....	....	....	....	....	....	....	....	1,443	2,071	2,096	2,645
Liabilities	79la d	...	....	....	....	....	....	....	....	....	....	....	19,554	20,471	24,308	29,492
Dir. Invest. in Rep. Economy	79lb d	...	....	....	....	....	....	....	....	....	....	....				
Portfolio Investment	79lc d	...	....	....	....	....	....	....	....	....	....	....	5	5	48	217
Equity Securities	79ld d	...	....	....	....	....	....	....	....	....	....	....	—	—	—	—
Debt Securities	79le d	...	....	....	....	....	....	....	....	....	....	....	5	5	48	217
Financial Derivatives	79ll d	...	....	....	....	....	....	....	....	....	....	....				
Other Investment	79lf d	...	....	....	....	....	....	....	....	....	....	....	19,549	20,466	24,260	29,275
Monetary Authorities	79lg d	...	....	....	....	....	....	....	....	....	....	....	5,552	5,215	5,330	4,903
General Government	79lh d	...	....	....	....	....	....	....	....	....	....	....	10,630	10,845	12,584	15,814
Banks	79li d	...	....	....	....	....	....	....	....	....	....	....	83	544	1,122	2,141
Other Sectors	79lj d	...	....	....	....	....	....	....	....	....	....	....	3,284	3,862	5,224	6,417
Government Finance												*Millions of Liras through 1977; Billions 1978-1995; Trillions beg.*				
Deficit (-) or Surplus	80	−5,105	−5,499	−7,451	−6,998	−13,235	−52,839	†−55	−137	−161	−117	....	†−483	−1,815	−2,050	−1,259
Revenue	81	47,500	59,384	71,710	109,003	143,732	186,900	†291	497	957	1,446	....	†2,309	2,721	4,836	7,052
Grants Received	81z	—	—	10	—	—	—	†—	—	—	—	—	†—	—	—	—
Expenditure	82	52,393	64,403	77,098	112,931	154,209	229,414	†328	610	1,117	1,526	....	†2,791	4,535	6,884	8,294
Lending Minus Repayments	83	212	480	2,073	3,070	2,758	10,325	†18	23	1	37	....	†2	2	1	18
Financing																
Domestic	84a	4,360	4,940	7,240	6,920	13,300	52,180	†53	133	137	29	....	....	....	....	1,158
Foreign	85a	742	560	206	82	25	567	†2	3	24	88	....	....	....	....	101
Total Debt	88	64,490	68,000	78,050	101,040	135,220	207,170	†324	508	968	2,052	....	....	5,033	7,101	10,801
Domestic	88a	36,990	41,560	46,960	70,080	100,280	164,480	†244	405	621	1,131	....	....	....	3,671	6,417
Foreign	89a	27,500	26,440	31,090	30,960	34,940	42,690	†80	103	347	922	....	†2,567	....	3,431	4,384
National Accounts												*Billions of Liras through 1995;*				
Househ.Cons.Expend.,incl.NPISHs	96f	...	...	...	...	...	...	...	...	...	...	...	...	...	...	...
Government Consumption Expend.	91f	...	...	...	...	...	...	...	...	...	...	...	...	...	...	...
Gross Fixed Capital Formation	93e	...	...	...	...	...	...	...	...	...	...	...	...	...	...	...
Changes in Inventories	93i	—	...	...	...	...	...	...	...	...	...	...	...	...	...	...
Exports of Goods and Services	90c	...	...	...	...	...	...	...	...	...	...	...	...	...	...	...
Imports of Goods and Services (-)	98c	...	...	...	...	...	...	...	...	...	...	...	...	...	...	...
Gross Domestic Product (GDP)	99b	...	...	...	...	...	...	...	...	...	...	...	...	...	...	...
Statistical Discrepancy	99bs															
GDP Vol. 1987 Prices (Trillions)	99b. p	38	40	42	45	50	51	52	52	50	53	55	57	61	64	68
GDP Volume (1995=100)	99bv p	39.1	40.4	42.7	45.7	50.6	52.2	53.0	52.7	51.4	53.9	55.8	58.6	62.5	65.2	69.7
GDP Deflator (1995=100)	99bi p	...	...	...	...	...	...	...	...	...	...	...	...	...	...	...
																Millions:
Population	99z	37.13	38.07	39.04	40.09	40.92	41.77	42.64	43.53	44.47	45.47	46.69	47.86	49.07	50.31	51.43

Millions of US Dollars

Item	1987	1988	1989	1990	1991	1992	1993	1994	1995	1996	1997	1998	1999	2000	2001	Code
International Investment Position																
Assets	6,294	9,466	11,688	13,686	15,319	18,555	21,291	20,194	27,396	27,613	30,035	32,491	37,604	38,208	....	79aa d
Direct Investment Abroad	—	—	—	—	—	—	—	—	—	—	—	—	—	—	....	79ab d
Portfolio Investment	—	—	—	—	—	—	—	—	—	—	—	—	—	—	....	79ac d
Equity Securities	....	....	....	....	....	....	....	....	—	—	—	—	—	—	....	79ad d
Debt Securities	....	....	....	....	....	....	....	....	—	—	—	—	—	—	....	79ae d
Financial Derivatives															....	79al d
Other Investment	2,994	5,748	5,461	6,199	8,862	10,901	13,545	11,624	13,571	9,909	10,448	11,711	13,261	14,855	....	79af d
Monetary Authorities	152	2,201	1,489	1,130	1,101	1,088	1,034	1,061	1,103	1,160	1,211	1,265	1,321	1,392	....	79ag d
General Government	—	—	—	—	—	—	—	—	—	—	—	—	—	—	....	79ah d
Banks	2,842	3,547	3,972	5,069	7,761	9,813	12,511	10,563	12,468	8,749	9,237	10,446	11,940	13,463	....	79ai d
Other Sectors	—	—	—	—	—	—	—	—	—	—	—	—	—	—	....	79aj d
Reserve Assets	3,300	3,718	6,227	7,487	6,457	7,654	7,746	8,570	13,825	17,704	19,587	20,780	24,343	23,353	....	79ak d
Liabilities	35,656	39,939	42,064	50,285	50,578	55,736	67,452	66,027	74,015	79,643	84,878	96,894	103,847	116,615	....	79li d
Dir. Invest. in Rep. Economy	—	—	—	—	—	—	—	—	—	—	—	—	—	—	....	79lb d
Portfolio Investment	712	3,321	5,226	5,877	6,683	9,316	12,623	13,788	14,186	13,081	13,731	14,035	17,468	21,824	....	79lc d
Equity Securities	—	—	—	—	—	—	—	—	—	—	—	—	—	—	....	79ld d
Debt Securities	712	3,321	5,226	5,877	6,683	9,316	12,623	13,788	14,186	13,081	13,731	14,035	17,468	21,824	....	79le d
Financial Derivatives															....	79ll d
Other Investment	34,944	36,618	36,838	44,408	43,895	46,420	54,829	52,239	59,829	66,562	71,147	82,859	86,379	94,791	....	79lf d
Monetary Authorities	4,755	7,240	7,718	8,010	6,765	6,680	7,208	9,658	12,216	12,374	11,758	12,982	11,501	14,561	....	79lg d
General Government	20,393	20,122	19,322	21,407	22,393	20,635	19,733	21,660	21,428	23,965	22,670	23,098	22,440	22,846	....	79lh d
Banks	3,223	3,775	3,419	5,869	6,620	8,262	12,461	5,814	8,025	11,211	12,544	15,925	17,968	21,142	....	79li d
Other Sectors	6,573	5,481	6,379	9,122	8,117	10,843	15,427	15,107	18,160	19,012	24,175	30,854	34,470	36,242	....	79lj d

1996: Year Ending Feb.28/29 through 1981, December 31 thereafter

Item	1987	1988	1989	1990	1991	1992	1993	1994	1995	1996	1997	1998	1999	2000	2001	Code
Government Finance																
Deficit (-) or Surplus	-2,346	-3,859	-7,502	-11,781	-33,317	-47,328	-133,105	-150,838	-316,621	†-1,238	-2,444	-4,387	-10,076	-14,263	....	80
Revenue	10,430	17,547	31,254	54,937	90,650	176,370	355,736	750,673	1,401,847	†2,726	6,327	12,657	19,798	35,426	....	81
Grants Received	15	40	115	1,636	8,434	1,700	1,597	942	7,404	†2	2	—	8	—	....	81z
Expenditure	12,773	21,424	38,840	68,316	132,350	225,256	490,129	902,077	1,725,514	†3,966	8,617	16,762	29,467	49,134	....	82
Lending Minus Repayments	18	22	32	38	51	142	309	376	358	†—	156	282	414	554	....	83
Financing																
Domestic	....	3,683	7,907	11,913	31,596	43,395	112,795	219,353	396,181	†1,373	2,828	5,158	9,180	10,769	....	84a
Foreign	....	176	-404	-131	1,721	3,933	20,310	-68,515	-79,560	†-134	-384	-771	896	3,494	....	85a
Total Debt	....	57,937	86,925	118,883	202,456	371,934	667,854	1,702,786	2,782,173	†5,602	12,656	21,629	41,452	63,416	....	88
Domestic	....	28,458	41,934	57,180	97,647	194,237	356,555	799,309	1,361,007	†3,149	6,283	11,613	22,920	36,421	....	88a
Foreign	....	29,479	44,991	61,703	104,809	177,697	311,299	903,477	1,421,166	†2,453	6,373	10,016	18,532	26,996	....	89a

Trillions of Liras Beginning 1996

Item	1987	1988	1989	1990	1991	1992	1993	1994	1995	1996	1997	1998	1999	2000	2001	Code
National Accounts																
Househ.Cons.Expend.,incl.NPISHs	51,017	82,050	149,140	269,564	434,365	734,305	1,369,419	2,706,263	5,457,903	†9,938	19,619	36,123	55,928	88,978	....	96f
Government Consumption Expend.	5,845	9,837	21,240	43,083	77,895	140,584	258,084	450,605	837,243	†1,709	3,535	6,633	11,748	17,496	....	91f
Gross Fixed Capital Formation	18,491	33,738	51,837	89,892	150,156	258,406	525,506	952,322	1,850,288	†3,706	7,618	12,839	16,931	27,688	....	93e
Changes in Inventories	687	-1,247	1,522	5,792	-6,973	2,454	21,619	-121,416	127,149	†-80	-377	-212	1,149	2,428	....	93i
Exports of Goods and Services	11,642	24,106	36,833	52,215	87,215	157,360	270,997	826,379	1,544,077	†3,182	7,088	12,713	17,972	29,775	....	90c
Imports of Goods and Services (-)	13,269	22,683	40,420	69,042	104,819	189,646	383,358	788,530	1,890,238	†4,111	8,763	14,573	20,801	38,940	....	98c
Gross Domestic Product (GDP)	74,416	125,801	220,152	393,060	630,117	1,093,368	1,981,867	3,868,429	7,762,456	†14,772	28,836	52,225	77,415	124,982	....	99b
Statistical Discrepancy	306	3,424	7,173	1,558	-18,228	-36,046	-80,320	-157,193	-163,966	†427	115	-1,090	-5,510	-2,442	....	99bs
GDP Vol. 1987 Prices (Trillions)	75	76	76	84	84	89	97	91	98	105	113	116	111	119	....	99b.p
GDP Volume (1995=100)	76.3	78.0	78.1	85.4	86.2	91.3	98.7	93.3	100.0	107.0	115.1	118.6	113.0	121.1	....	99bv p
GDP Deflator (1995=100)	1.3	2.1	3.6	5.9	9.4	15.4	25.9	53.4	100.0	177.8	322.9	567.2	882.3	1,329.4	....	99bi p

Midyear Estimates

Item	1987	1988	1989	1990	1991	1992	1993	1994	1995	1996	1997	1998	1999	2000	2001	Code
Population	52.56	53.71	54.89	56.10	57.06	57.93	58.51	59.71	60.61	61.53	62.46	63.39	64.34	67.38	68.61	99z

(See notes in the back of the book.)

Uganda

		1972	1973	1974	1975	1976	1977	1978	1979	1980	1981	1982	1983	1984	1985	1986
Exchange Rates															*Shillings per Thousand SDRs through 1984*	
Principal Rate	aa	77.6	83.2	87.5	96.6	96.6	96.6	96.6	96.6	96.6	991.1	1,167.3	2,512.7	5,097.1	†15.4	17.1
															Shillings per Thousand US Dollars 1984	
Principal Rate	ae	71.4	69.0	71.4	82.6	83.1	79.5	74.2	73.3	75.7	851.5	1,058.2	2,400.0	5,200.0	†14.0	14.0
Principal Rate	rf	71.4	70.2	71.4	74.2	82.7	82.6	77.4	74.8	74.2	500.5	940.5	1,538.6	3,597.0	†6.7	14.0
															Index Numbers (1995=100):	
Principal Rate	ahx	....	....	....	....	....	....	....	....	....	582,555.4	103,416.6	66,766.7	28,897.5	15,233.2	6,908.5
Nominal Effective Exchange Rate	ne c	....	....	....	....	....	....	....	....	160,644.8	170,348.4	86,880.4	18,298.0	13,390.9	7,829.6	2,219.6
Real Effective Exchange Rate	re c	....	....	....	....	....	....	....	....	1,027.9	730.8	253.4	200.1	136.5	178.2	187.5
Fund Position															*Millions of SDRs:*	
Quota	2f. s	40.0	40.0	40.0	40.0	40.0	40.0	50.0	50.0	75.0	75.0	75.0	99.6	99.6	99.6	99.6
SDRs	1b. s	13.7	13.4	5.0	3.2	.9	4.5	8.1	8.4	—	2.6	10.1	.9	.2	—	—
Reserve Position in the Fund	1c. s	—	—	—	—	—	—	5.9	—	—	—	—	3.5	3.5	3.5	3.5
Total Fund Cred.&Loans Outstg.	2tl	10.0	10.0	15.0	24.1	32.7	32.7	29.2	26.2	70.1	182.5	265.9	360.6	343.8	277.6	203.4
International Liquidity													*Millions of US Dollars Unless Otherwise Indicated:*			
Total Reserves minus Gold	1l. d	36.0	29.1	16.8	31.0	44.5	47.2	52.7	22.8	3.0	30.0	78.3	106.5	†67.9	27.3	29.2
SDRs	1b. d	14.9	16.2	6.2	3.7	1.0	5.4	10.5	11.0	—	3.0	11.1	.9	.2	—	—
Reserve Position in the Fund	1c. d	—	—	—	—	—	—	7.7	—	—	—	—	3.9	3.7	3.5	4.3
Foreign Exchange	1d. d	21.1	12.9	10.6	27.3	43.5	41.8	34.5	11.8	3.0	27.0	63.3	101.9	†64.3	23.4	24.9
Monetary Authorities: Other Liab.	4..d	5.2	5.8	5.8	3.4	3.6	6.3	5.4	20.5	13.3	42.4	38.3	3.7	9.6	3.3	7.6
Deposit Money Banks: Assets	7a. d	9.0	5.5	9.9	12.2	17.7	32.2	31.5	33.3	18.5	11.7	25.1	29.6	26.8	11.5	21.4
Liabilities	7b. d	8.4	3.3	7.1	2.7	7.4	12.0	5.6	18.8	4.2	1.0	6.3	3.7	9.6	3.4	7.3
Monetary Authorities														*Thousands of Shillings through 1978;*		
Foreign Assets	11	2,568	2,009	1,197	2,561	3,703	3,755	3,909	†2	—	36	83	256	353	382	409
Claims on Central Government	12a	7,952	12,383	16,702	23,547	31,912	38,662	54,424	†73	127	232	328	†1,715	2,972	6,768	7,945
Claims on Nonfin.Pub.Enterprises	12c	600	600	600	600	693	1,062	1,466	†1	1	2	3	62	22	108	39
Claims on Private Sector	12d	—	—	—	—	—	—	—	†—	—	—	—	—	—	—	—
Claims on Deposit Money Banks	12e	—	—	—	—	—	—	—	†—	—	2	20	45	89	—	22
Reserve Money	14	7,869	10,009	13,311	20,957	30,029	34,367	51,094	†84	115	148	176	282	610	1,750	4,614
of which: Currency Outside DMBs	14a	6,157	7,959	10,920	13,672	22,052	28,891	35,312	†58	73	114	128	189	487	1,050	3,509
Liabs. of Central Bank: Securities	16ac	87	111	42	47	48	7	15	†—	—	—	—	—	—	—	—
Restricted Deposits	16b	87	111	42	47	48	7	15	†1	1	4	4	11	39	66	103
Foreign Liabilities	16c	1,147	1,232	1,724	2,610	3,461	3,662	3,222	†4	8	217	351	915	1,802	4,314	3,591
Central Government Deposits	16d	12	16	8	3	6	6	1	†—	—	7	11	†445	576	1,106	2,452
Capital Accounts	17a	1,563	1,675	1,721	1,876	1,897	2,440	2,446	†2	2	32	33	76	176	204	217
Other Items (Net)	17r	442	1,949	1,693	1,215	867	2,997	3,021	†-16	2	-135	-141	349	233	-183	-2,563
of which: Valuation Adjustment	17rv	429	514	458	671	673	630	26	†—	-1	-153	-117	-508	-1,483	-4,586	-7,429
Deposit Money Banks														*Thousands of Shillings through 1978;*		
Reserves	20	1,550	2,058	2,995	8,754	8,599	5,233	14,844	†31	46	41	26	60	246	715	968
Claims on Mon.Author.: Securities	20c	—	—	—	—	—	—	—	†—	—	—	—	—	—	—	—
Foreign Assets	21	640	380	710	1,010	1,468	2,565	2,336	†2	1	10	27	71	140	161	299
Claims on Central Government	22a	6,800	10,880	14,500	12,510	16,881	17,345	19,731	†23	26	92	51	41	26	30	46
Claims on State and Local Govts.	22b	—	18	260	61	73	196	204	†—	—	—	1	—	1	—	1
Claims on Nonfin.Pub.Enterprises	22c	—	—	—	—	1,000	4,000	5,000	†6	9	5	82	66	123	424	1,699
Claims on Private Sector	22d	9,390	11,470	14,840	16,290	17,312	23,155	24,978	†26	49	107	129	214	222	608	1,236
Demand Deposits	24	9,081	13,070	19,013	18,672	22,372	28,826	34,453	†47	66	166	165	235	460	1,140	2,449
Time, Savings,& Fgn. Currency Dep.	25	6,025	7,700	8,533	14,256	17,428	16,126	22,937	†31	45	62	87	109	176	366	1,056
Foreign Liabilities	26c	600	230	510	220	613	953	418	†1	—	1	7	24	37	48	102
Central Government Deposits	26d	304	344	171	421	176	327	708	†1	1	1	1	1	1	2	5
Central Government Lending Funds	26f	—	—	—	—	—	—	—	†—	—	—	—	—	—	—	—
Credit from Monetary Authorities	26g	—	—	—	—	—	—	—	†—	—	—	3	3	—	—	—
Capital Accounts	27a	1,310	1,520	1,770	1,800	4,635	5,878	7,293	†9	10	14	58	247	221	415	533
Other Items (Net)	27r	1,060	1,942	3,308	3,256	109	384	1,284	†—	9	9	-6	-164	-139	-32	103
Monetary Survey														*Thousands of Shillings through 1978;*		
Foreign Assets (Net)	31n	1,461	927	-327	741	1,097	1,705	2,605	†-1	-6	-171	-248	-612	-1,347	-3,819	-2,985
Domestic Credit	32	24,426	34,991	46,723	52,584	67,689	84,087	105,094	†129	211	430	582	1,652	2,789	6,830	8,509
Claims on Central Govt. (Net)	32an	14,436	22,903	31,023	35,633	48,611	55,674	73,446	†95	151	316	367	1,310	2,421	5,690	5,534
Claims on State and Local Govts.	32b	—	18	260	61	73	196	204	†—	—	—	1	—	1	—	1
Claims on Nonfin.Pub. Enterprises	32c	600	600	600	600	1,693	5,062	6,466	†7	10	7	85	128	145	532	1,738
Claims on Private Sector	32d	9,390	11,470	14,840	16,290	17,312	23,155	24,978	†26	49	107	129	214	222	608	1,236
Money	34	15,238	21,029	29,933	32,344	44,424	57,717	69,765	†105	139	279	294	424	948	2,190	5,959
Quasi-Money	35	6,025	7,700	8,533	14,256	17,428	16,126	22,937	†31	45	62	87	109	176	366	1,056
Liabs. of Central Bank: Securities	36ac	—	—	—	—	—	—	—	†—	—	—	—	—	—	—	—
Restricted Deposits	36b	87	111	42	47	48	7	15	†1	1	4	4	11	39	66	103
Central Government Lending Funds	36f	—	—	—	—	—	—	—	†—	—	—	—	—	—	—	—
Capital Accounts	37a	2,873	3,195	3,491	3,676	6,532	8,318	9,739	†11	12	46	91	323	397	619	750
Other Items (Net)	37r	1,664	3,883	4,397	3,002	354	3,624	5,243	†-21	7	-133	-142	173	-117	-230	-2,344
Money plus Quasi-Money	35l	21,263	28,729	38,466	46,600	61,852	73,843	92,702	†136	184	342	381	533	1,124	2,556	7,015
Interest Rates															*Percent Per Annum*	
Bank Rate *(End of Period)*	60	....	....	....	....	....	....	....	....	8	10	11	16	24	24	36
Treasury Bill Rate	60c	....	....	....	....	....	....	....	....	5	6	10	11	18	22	31
Deposit Rate	60l	....	....	....	....	....	....	....	....	7	7	9	11	16	†20	23
Lending Rate	60p	....	....	....	....	....	....	....	11	13	15	16	22	24	33	
Government Bond Yield	61	....	....	....	....	....	....	....	....	10	12	13	18	24	38	
Prices															*Index Numbers (1995=100):*	
Consumer Prices	64	....	....	....	....	....	....	....	....	.1	.2	.2	†.3	.8	2.1	

1987	1988	1989	1990	1991	1992	1993	1994	1995	1996	1997	1998	1999	2000	2001		
															Exchange Rates	

and per SDR thereafter: End of Period

1987	1988	1989	1990	1991	1992	1993	1994	1995	1996	1997	1998	1999	2000	2001		
85.1	222.0	486.2	768.2	1,308.8	1,673.6	1,552.3	1,352.9	1,500.5	1,480.5	1,538.3	1,918.7	2,067.1	2,301.8	2,170.9	Principal Rate	aa

and per US Dollar thereafter: End of Period (ae) Period Average (rf)

1987	1988	1989	1990	1991	1992	1993	1994	1995	1996	1997	1998	1999	2000	2001		
60.0	165.0	370.0	540.0	915.0	1,217.2	1,130.2	926.8	1,009.5	1,029.6	1,140.1	1,362.7	1,506.0	1,766.7	1,727.4	Principal Rate	ae
42.8	106.1	223.1	428.9	734.0	1,133.8	1,195.0	979.4	968.9	1,046.1	1,083.0	1,240.3	1,454.8	1,644.5	1,755.7	Principal Rate	rf

Period Averages

1987	1988	1989	1990	1991	1992	1993	1994	1995	1996	1997	1998	1999	2000	2001		
3,454.8	1,123.9	460.2	228.7	135.5	85.8	81.0	99.2	100.0	92.4	89.5	78.3	66.6	59.1	55.1	Principal Rate	ahx
1,110.6	418.4	229.1	134.2	88.5	61.9	75.4	102.9	100.0	97.2	100.5	91.4	81.9	78.6	77.2	Nominal Effective Exchange Rate	ne c
239.1	217.9	183.8	112.5	82.9	76.9	82.2	102.2	100.0	99.8	107.1	94.7	90.2	96.4	97.8	Real Effective Exchange Rate	re c

Fund Position

End of Period

1987	1988	1989	1990	1991	1992	1993	1994	1995	1996	1997	1998	1999	2000	2001		
99.6	99.6	99.6	99.6	99.6	133.9	133.9	133.9	133.9	133.9	133.9	133.9	180.5	180.5	180.5	Quota	2f. s
—	—	—	4.8	7.2	6.6	—	2.1	.3	.7	4.0	3.5	1.7	2.7	1.5	SDRs	1b. s
														—	Reserve Position in the Fund	1c. s
192.8	187.6	171.2	198.2	230.9	250.1	243.0	262.6	280.6	290.1	291.7	282.7	270.8	242.6	219.1	Total Fund Cred.&Loans Outstg.	2tl

International Liquidity

End of Period

1987	1988	1989	1990	1991	1992	1993	1994	1995	1996	1997	1998	1999	2000	2001		
54.6	49.3	14.1	44.0	58.9	94.4	146.4	321.4	458.9	528.4	633.5	725.4	763.1	808.0	983.4	Total Reserves minus Gold	1l. d
—	—	—	6.8	10.3	9.0	.1	3.1	.5	1.1	5.4	5.0	2.3	3.5	1.9	SDRs	1b. d
															Reserve Position in the Fund	1c. d
54.6	49.3	14.1	37.2	48.6	85.4	146.3	318.3	458.4	527.3	628.1	720.4	760.8	804.5	981.5	Foreign Exchange	1d. d
						2.6	1.8	7.7	2.7	3.0	1.4	7.5	2.0	2.3	2.4 Monetary Authorities: Other Liab.	4.. d
29.5	15.5	15.7	27.3	43.0	72.2	91.4	145.2	132.5	142.6	160.8	190.2	199.8	265.6	248.6	Deposit Money Banks: Assets	7a. d
5.2	6.4	6.6	14.5	13.2	21.6	.7	8.0	.1	—	2.0	2.1	25.5	41.7	32.1	Liabilities	7b. d

Monetary Authorities

Millions of Shillings Beginning 1979: End of Period

1987	1988	1989	1990	1991	1992	1993	1994	1995	1996	1997	1998	1999	2000	2001		
....	....	....	....	....	†117,077	172,280	299,209	466,801	538,084	660,961	951,073	1,090,382	1,363,643	1,624,551	Foreign Assets	11
					†792,165	791,083	963,065	1,152,678	1,227,762	1,348,131	1,591,129	1,801,563	1,911,395	1,678,328	Claims on Central Government	12a
					†24,257	20,753	23,188	24,180	24,471	25,129	25,559	3,501	4,152	4,168	Claims on Nonfin.Pub.Enterprises	12c
					†4,768	4,357	1,468	543	543	543	453	27,355	52,435	85,638	Claims on Private Sector	12d
					†10,126	6,272	3,861	1,879	7,718	13,062	31,823	61,838	61,763	58,039	Claims on Deposit Money Banks	12e
					†138,594	170,973	253,143	287,894	321,373	350,611	420,770	484,136	589,684	668,436	Reserve Money	14
					†98,335	132,638	176,522	204,519	221,094	240,456	285,878	330,759	362,248	393,433	of which: Currency Outside DMBs	14a
					† —	—	—	—	—	7,000	6,697	52,423	25	20,025	Liabs. of Central Bank: Securities	16ac
					†8,452	10,550	9,332	10,450	9,961	13,430	26,583	123,493	125,603	133,215	Restricted Deposits	16b
					†421,730	379,305	362,368	423,836	432,552	450,428	552,698	562,726	562,537	479,825	Foreign Liabilities	16c
					†464,830	550,278	830,115	1,247,927	1,319,140	1,457,689	1,688,728	1,925,470	1,727,990	1,824,372	Central Government Deposits	16d
					†80,792	61,501	20,487	56,710	140,808	215,889	408,849	492,390	433,310	305,795	Capital Accounts	17a
					†-166006	-177,863	-184,654	-380,736	-425,256	-447,221	-504,288	-655,999	-45,761	19,055	Other Items (Net)	17r
....	....	....	....	....	....	....	....	....							of which: Valuation Adjustment	17rv

Deposit Money Banks

Millions of Shillings Beginning 1979: End of Period

1987	1988	1989	1990	1991	1992	1993	1994	1995	1996	1997	1998	1999	2000	2001		
2,481	2,750	4,829	11,989	27,386	34,640	37,060	75,123	79,600	109,620	104,216	129,412	121,020	188,933	233,787	Reserves	20
										7,000	6,697	52,423	—	20,000	Claims on Mon.Author.: Securities	20c
1,773	2,550	5,802	14,742	39,334	87,883	103,303	134,547	133,770	146,797	183,340	259,234	300,949	469,226	429,433	Foreign Assets	21
38	338	126	2,740	986	5,846	14,273	34,744	41,750	65,669	182,640	199,239	286,115	404,246	586,780	Claims on Central Government	22a
11	6	306	—	215	300	—	—	—	—	—	1,410	1,037	783		Claims on State and Local Govts.	22b
3,423	4,370	6,343	12,120	23,713	27,909	32,533	51,210	56,629	65,852	65,829	63,586	70,658	115,363	141,405	Claims on Nonfin.Pub.Enterprises	22c
3,496	10,866	29,633	49,364	64,572	105,081	166,945	190,691	245,818	323,181	319,964	424,824	491,896	531,353	503,512	Claims on Private Sector	22d
7,465	15,948	32,871	47,660	78,626	107,676	126,758	177,498	204,182	229,742	272,076	326,559	358,598	443,244	515,363	Demand Deposits	24
2,014	3,227	8,480	19,400	30,837	57,880	155,490	209,414	233,302	315,372	402,455	512,419	588,010	703,618	739,401	Time, Savings,& Fgn. Currency Dep.	25
314	1,052	2,427	7,834	12,115	26,272	749	7,437	77	—	2,230	2,924	38,426	73,691	55,456	Foreign Liabilities	26c
154	485	1,174	1,762	2,153	8,152	11,194	28,002	38,677	73,013	49,032	46,290	99,806	149,244	159,618	Central Government Deposits	26d
						14,520	18,814	15,394	7,990	11,166	10,980	17,026	54,616	52,972	Central Government Lending Funds	26f
—	492	1,303	4,809	9,617	7,582	10,471	6,714	8,452	150	7,244	23,400	27,224	22,225	20,296	Credit from Monetary Authorities	26g
1,723	4,848	8,942	39,704	48,947	51,137	37,654	35,998	50,065	73,334	145,901	169,815	172,642	264,457	308,303	Capital Accounts	27a
-449	-5,172	-8,157	-30,214	-26,090	2,960	-2,722	2,439	7,419	11,518	-27,115	-9,396	22,739	-936	64,291	Other Items (Net)	27r

Monetary Survey

Millions of Shillings Beginning 1979: End of Period

1987	1988	1989	1990	1991	1992	1993	1994	1995	1996	1997	1998	1999	2000	2001		
....	....	....	....	....	†-243043	-104,471	63,951	176,658	252,329	391,643	654,685	790,178	1,196,642	1,518,703	Foreign Assets (Net)	31n
					†487,344	468,472	406,249	234,994	315,325	435,515	569,771	657,223	1,142,747	1,016,622	Domestic Credit	32
					†325,030	243,884	139,692	-92,176	-98,722	24,050	55,349	62,403	438,407	281,117	Claims on Central Govt. (Net)	32an
					300	—	—	—	—	—	1,410	1,037	783		Claims on State and Local Govts.	32b
					†52,166	53,286	74,398	80,809	90,323	90,958	89,145	74,159	119,515	145,573	Claims on Nonfin.Pub. Enterprises	32c
					†109,849	171,302	192,159	246,361	323,724	320,507	425,277	519,251	583,788	589,149	Claims on Private Sector	32d
					†206,011	259,396	354,020	408,701	450,836	512,532	612,437	689,358	805,492	908,796	Money	34
					57,880	155,490	209,414	233,302	315,372	402,455	512,419	588,010	703,618	739,401	Quasi-Money	35
					† —	—	—	—	—	—	—	—	25	25	Liabs. of Central Bank: Securities	36ac
					†8,452	10,550	9,332	10,450	9,961	13,430	26,583	123,493	125,603	133,215	Restricted Deposits	36b
						14,520	18,814	15,394	7,990	11,166	10,980	17,026	54,616	52,972	Central Government Lending Funds	36f
					†131,929	99,155	56,485	106,775	214,142	361,790	578,664	665,032	697,767	614,097	Capital Accounts	37a
					†-159970	-175,110	-177,864	-362,970	-430,647	-474,215	-516,628	-635,518	-47,732	86,818	Other Items (Net)	37r
					†263,890	414,886	563,434	642,002	766,208	914,987	1,124,856	1,277,368	1,509,110	1,648,197	Money plus Quasi-Money	35l

Interest Rates

Percent Per Annum

1987	1988	1989	1990	1991	1992	1993	1994	1995	1996	1997	1998	1999	2000	2001		
31	45	55	50	46	41	24	15	13	16	14	9	16	19	9	Bank Rate (End of Period)	60
31	33	42	41	34	....	†21	13	9	12	11	8	7	13	11	Treasury Bill Rate	60c
20	22	32	31	31	36	16	10	8	11	12	11	9	10	8	Deposit Rate	60l
35	35	40	39	34	....	....	....	20	20	21	21	22	23	23	Lending Rate	60p
40	39	45	45	42	44	....	....	....	....	....	....	....	....	....	Government Bond Yield	61

Prices

Period Averages

1987	1988	1989	1990	1991	1992	1993	1994	1995	1996	1997	1998	1999	2000	2001		
6.4	18.9	30.4	40.5	51.9	79.1	83.9	92.1	100.0	107.2	114.6	114.6	†121.9	125.4	127.9	Consumer Prices	64

Uganda

		1972	1973	1974	1975	1976	1977	1978	1979	1980	1981	1982	1983	1984	1985	1986
International Transactions														*Thousands of Shillings through 1978;*		
Exports	70	2,019	2,043	2,250	1,902	3,006	4,859	2,682	†32	26	122	328	593	1,388	. . . .	6,100
Imports, c.i.f. (Cash Basis)	71	11,570	11,380	15,220	15,270	14,240	19,920	19,630	†15	22	. . . .	. . . .	. . . .	. . . .	. . . .	†4,300
Balance of Payments														*Millions of US Dollars:*		
Current Account, n.i.e.	78al *d*	. . .	. . .	. . . .	. . . .	. . . .	. . . .	. . . .	. . . .	−82.7	1.2	−69.9	−72.2	103.5	4.6	−43.3
Goods: Exports f.o.b.	78aa *d*									319.4	228.8	347.1	367.7	407.3	347.8	406.8
Goods: Imports f.o.b.	78ab *d*									−317.6	−284.3	−337.6	−342.5	−286.8	−238.3	−360.9
Trade Balance	78ac *d*									1.8	−55.5	9.5	25.2	120.5	109.5	45.9
Services: Credit	78ad *d*									9.9	44.3	—	—	16.8	23.1	11.8
Services: Debit	78ae *d*									−123.4	−100.4	−160.4	−150.0	−82.3	−129.9	−130.5
Balance on Goods & Services	78af *d*									−111.7	−111.6	−150.9	−124.8	55.0	2.7	−72.8
Income: Credit	78ag *d*									1.4	.8	—	—	—	1.5	2.9
Income: Debit	78ah *d*									−8.8	−13.2	−26.3	−50.9	−36.9	−21.0	−38.9
Balance on Gds, Serv. & Inc.	78ai *d*									−119.1	−124.0	−177.2	−175.7	18.1	−16.8	−108.8
Current Transfers, n.i.e.: Credit	78aj *d*									40.0	125.7	107.3	103.5	85.4	21.7	66.6
Current Transfers: Debit	78ak *d*									−3.6	−.5	—	—	—	−.3	−1.1
Capital Account, n.i.e.	78bc *d*									−.5	—	—	—	—	—	—
Capital Account, n.i.e.: Credit	78ba *d*									—	—	—	—	—	—	—
Capital Account: Debit	78bb *d*									−.5	—	—	—	—	—	—
Financial Account, n.i.e.	78bj *d*									−66.5	−96.3	14.8	27.7	−58.2	80.8	17.1
Direct Investment Abroad	78bd *d*									—	—	—	—	—	—	—
Dir. Invest. in Rep. Econ., n.i.e.	78be *d*									—	—	—	—	—	—	—
Portfolio Investment Assets	78bf *d*									—	—	—	—	—	—	—
Equity Securities	78bk *d*									—	—	—	—	—	—	—
Debt Securities	78bl *d*									—	—	—	—	—	—	—
Portfolio Investment Liab., n.i.e.	78bg *d*									—	—	—	—	—	—	—
Equity Securities	78bm *d*									—	—	—	—	—	—	—
Debt Securities	78bn *d*									—	—	—	—	—	—	—
Financial Derivatives Assets	78bw *d*									. . . .	. . . .	. . . .	. . . .	. . . .	. . . .	. . . .
Financial Derivatives Liabilities	78bx *d*									. . . .	. . . .	. . . .	. . . .	. . . .	. . . .	. . . .
Other Investment Assets	78bh *d*									14.7	6.8	−13.4	−4.5	30.1	69.3	131.8
Monetary Authorities	78bo *d*									. . . .	. . . .	. . . .	. . . .	. . . .	. . . .	. . . .
General Government	78bp *d*									—	—	—	—	24.0	13.7	36.0
Banks	78bq *d*									14.7	6.8	−13.4	−4.5	2.8	15.3	−9.9
Other Sectors	78br *d*									—	—	—	—	3.3	40.3	105.7
Other Investment Liab., n.i.e.	78bi *d*									−81.2	−103.1	28.2	32.2	−88.3	11.5	−114.7
Monetary Authorities	78bs *d*									−7.3	27.5	−3.3	4.8	−97.2	—	−18.5
General Government	78bt *d*									−59.3	−109.4	26.2	23.9	32.1	−16.9	−112.0
Banks	78bu *d*									−14.6	−3.2	5.3	3.5	−23.2	−3.8	3.9
Other Sectors	78bv *d*									—	−18.0	—	—	—	32.2	11.9
Net Errors and Omissions	78ca *d*									−64.6	−31.7	−24.7	−36.6	21.6	−52.2	−.6
Overall Balance	78cb *d*									−214.3	−126.8	−79.8	−81.1	66.9	33.2	−26.8
Reserves and Related Items	79da *d*									214.3	126.8	79.8	81.1	−66.9	−33.2	26.8
Reserve Assets	79db *d*									26.1	−34.6	−34.5	−28.6	26.5	17.3	36.2
Use of Fund Credit and Loans	79dc *d*									58.4	129.5	92.0	101.4	−16.1	−67.8	−87.2
Exceptional Financing	79de *d*									129.8	31.9	22.4	8.3	−77.3	17.3	77.8
International Investment Position														*Millions of US Dollars*		
Assets	79aa *d*	. . .	. . .	. . . .	. . . .	. . . .	. . . .	. . . .	. . . .	. . . .	. . . .	. . . .	. . . .	. . . .	. . . .	. . . .
Direct Investment Abroad	79ab *d*	. . .	. . .	. . . .	. . . .	. . . .	. . . .	. . . .	. . . .	. . . .	. . . .	. . . .	. . . .	. . . .	. . . .	. . . .
Portfolio Investment	79ac *d*	. . .	. . .	. . . .	. . . .	. . . .	. . . .	. . . .	. . . .	. . . .	. . . .	. . . .	. . . .	. . . .	. . . .	. . . .
Equity Securities	79ad *d*	. . .	. . .	. . . .	. . . .	. . . .	. . . .	. . . .	. . . .	. . . .	. . . .	. . . .	. . . .	. . . .	. . . .	. . . .
Debt Securities	79ae *d*	. . .	. . .	. . . .	. . . .	. . . .	. . . .	. . . .	. . . .	. . . .	. . . .	. . . .	. . . .	. . . .	. . . .	. . . .
Financial Derivatives	79al *d*	. . .	. . .	. . . .	. . . .	. . . .	. . . .	. . . .	. . . .	. . . .	. . . .	. . . .	. . . .	. . . .	. . . .	. . . .
Other Investment	79af *d*	. . .	. . .	. . . .	. . . .	. . . .	. . . .	. . . .	. . . .	. . . .	. . . .	. . . .	. . . .	. . . .	. . . .	. . . .
Monetary Authorities	79ag *d*	. . .	. . .	. . . .	. . . .	. . . .	. . . .	. . . .	. . . .	. . . .	. . . .	. . . .	. . . .	. . . .	. . . .	. . . .
General Government	79ah *d*	. . .	. . .	. . . .	. . . .	. . . .	. . . .	. . . .	. . . .	. . . .	. . . .	. . . .	. . . .	. . . .	. . . .	. . . .
Banks	79ai *d*	. . .	. . .	. . . .	. . . .	. . . .	. . . .	. . . .	. . . .	. . . .	. . . .	. . . .	. . . .	. . . .	. . . .	. . . .
Other Sectors	79aj *d*	. . .	. . .	. . . .	. . . .	. . . .	. . . .	. . . .	. . . .	. . . .	. . . .	. . . .	. . . .	. . . .	. . . .	. . . .
Reserve Assets	79ak *d*	. . .	. . .	. . . .	. . . .	. . . .	. . . .	. . . .	. . . .	. . . .	. . . .	. . . .	. . . .	. . . .	. . . .	. . . .
Liabilities	79la *d*	. . .	. . .	. . . .	. . . .	. . . .	. . . .	. . . .	. . . .	. . . .	. . . .	. . . .	. . . .	. . . .	. . . .	. . . .
Dir. Invest. in Rep. Economy	79lb *d*	. . .	. . .	. . . .	. . . .	. . . .	. . . .	. . . .	. . . .	. . . .	. . . .	. . . .	. . . .	. . . .	. . . .	. . . .
Portfolio Investment	79lc *d*	. . .	. . .	. . . .	. . . .	. . . .	. . . .	. . . .	. . . .	. . . .	. . . .	. . . .	. . . .	. . . .	. . . .	. . . .
Equity Securities	79ld *d*	. . .	. . .	. . . .	. . . .	. . . .	. . . .	. . . .	. . . .	. . . .	. . . .	. . . .	. . . .	. . . .	. . . .	. . . .
Debt Securities	79le *d*	. . .	. . .	. . . .	. . . .	. . . .	. . . .	. . . .	. . . .	. . . .	. . . .	. . . .	. . . .	. . . .	. . . .	. . . .
Financial Derivatives	79ll *d*	. . .	. . .	. . . .	. . . .	. . . .	. . . .	. . . .	. . . .	. . . .	. . . .	. . . .	. . . .	. . . .	. . . .	. . . .
Other Investment	79lf *d*	. . .	. . .	. . . .	. . . .	. . . .	. . . .	. . . .	. . . .	. . . .	. . . .	. . . .	. . . .	. . . .	. . . .	. . . .
Monetary Authorities	79lg *d*	. . .	. . .	. . . .	. . . .	. . . .	. . . .	. . . .	. . . .	. . . .	. . . .	. . . .	. . . .	. . . .	. . . .	. . . .
General Government	79lh *d*	. . .	. . .	. . . .	. . . .	. . . .	. . . .	. . . .	. . . .	. . . .	. . . .	. . . .	. . . .	. . . .	. . . .	. . . .
Banks	79li *d*	. . .	. . .	. . . .	. . . .	. . . .	. . . .	. . . .	. . . .	. . . .	. . . .	. . . .	. . . .	. . . .	. . . .	. . . .
Other Sectors	79lj *d*	. . .	. . .	. . . .	. . . .	. . . .	. . . .	. . . .	. . . .	. . . .	. . . .	. . . .	. . . .	. . . .	. . . .	. . . .

1987	1988	1989	1990	1991	1992	1993	1994	1995	1996	1997	1998	1999	2000	2001	International Transactions	
Millions of Shillings Beginning 1979																
13,684	29,070	55,674	64,653	146,661	159,387	213,846	393,960	446,086	613,598	594,804	624,509	748,862	759,273	802,296	Exports	70
36,336	94,112	87,851	125,059	137,250	580,685	732,340	850,411	1,024,317	1,247,379	1,425,904	1,753,335	1,955,849	2,486,275	2,798,212	Imports, c.i.f. (Cash Basis)	71
Minus Sign Indicates Debit															**Balance of Payments**	
-112.0	-195.2	-259.5	-263.3	-169.8	-99.6	-224.3	-207.5	-338.9	-252.3	-366.8	-502.6	-550.8	....	....	Current Account, n.i.e.	78al *d*
333.6	266.3	277.7	177.8	173.2	151.2	200.0	463.0	560.3	639.3	592.6	510.2	500.1	....	....	Goods: Exports f.o.b.	78aa *d*
-475.6	-523.5	-588.3	-491.0	-377.1	-421.9	-478.3	-714.2	-926.8	-986.9	-1,042.6	-1,166.3	-1,096.5	....	....	Goods: Imports f.o.b.	78ab *d*
-142.0	-257.2	-310.6	-313.2	-203.9	-270.7	-278.3	-251.2	-366.5	-347.6	-449.9	-656.1	-596.4	....	....	*Trade Balance*	78ac *d*
—	—	—	—	20.8	34.5	93.6	64.1	104.0	144.7	164.6	176.3	182.3	....	....	Services: Credit	78ad *d*
-218.2	-235.2	-237.2	-195.3	-241.8	-247.7	-293.1	-436.3	-562.7	-674.6	-668.9	-728.1	-745.3	....	....	Services: Debit	78ae *d*
-360.2	-492.4	-547.8	-508.5	-424.9	-483.9	-477.8	-623.4	-825.2	-877.5	-954.2	-1,208.0	-1,159.4	....	....	*Balance on Goods & Services*	78af *d*
—	—	—	—	2.8	4.1	6.4	13.8	17.7	29.7	40.5	50.7	40.5	....	....	Income: Credit	78ag *d*
-18.0	-25.2	-23.3	-47.8	-76.7	-88.3	-65.3	-71.0	-113.3	-79.2	-55.7	-59.9	-62.3	....	....	Income: Debit	78ah *d*
-378.2	-517.6	-571.1	-556.3	-498.8	-568.1	-536.7	-680.6	-920.8	-927.0	-969.4	-1,217.2	-1,181.1	....	....	*Balance on Gds, Serv. & Inc.*	78ai *d*
266.2	322.4	311.6	293.0	329.0	468.5	312.4	473.1	581.9	674.7	602.6	714.6	630.3	....	....	Current Transfers, n.i.e.: Credit	78aj *d*
—	—	—	—	—	—	—	—	—	—	—	—	—	....	....	Current Transfers: Debit	78ak *d*
—	—	—	—	—	—	42.4	36.1	48.3	61.4	31.9	49.5	26.3	....	....	Capital Account, n.i.e.	78bc *d*
—	—	—	—	—	—	42.4	36.1	48.3	61.4	31.9	49.5	26.3	....	....	Capital Account, n.i.e.: Credit	78ba *d*
—	—	—	—	—	—	—	—	—	—	—	—	—	....	....	Capital Account: Debit	78bb *d*
31.2	3.6	213.0	211.8	137.6	114.8	56.6	76.8	210.7	140.5	298.8	372.8	368.9	....	....	Financial Account, n.i.e.	78bj *d*
—	—	—	—	—	—	—	—	—	—	—	—	—	....	....	Direct Investment Abroad	78bd *d*
—	—	—	—	1.0	3.0	54.6	88.2	121.2	121.0	175.0	210.0	222.1	....	....	Dir. Invest. in Rep. Econ., n.i.e.	78be *d*
—	—	—	—	—	—	—	—	—	—	—	—	—	....	....	Portfolio Investment Assets	78bf *d*
—	—	—	—	—	—	—	—	—	—	—	—	—	....	....	Equity Securities	78bk *d*
—	—	—	—	—	—	—	—	—	—	—	—	—	....	....	Debt Securities	78bl *d*
—	—	—	—	—	—	—	—	—	—	—	—	—	....	....	Portfolio Investment Liab., n.i.e.	78bg *d*
—	—	—	—	—	—	—	—	—	—	—	—	—	....	....	Equity Securities	78bm *d*
—	—	—	—	—	—	—	—	—	—	—	—	—	....	....	Debt Securities	78bn *d*
....	....	....	....	....	....	....	....	....	....	....	....	....	....	....	Financial Derivatives Assets	78bw *d*
....	....	....	....	....	....	....	....	....	....	....	....	....	....	....	Financial Derivatives Liabilities	78bx *d*
....	....	....	—	.4	1.8	-5.0	-40.3	-9.9	-37.2	-14.0	5.3	26.6	....	....	Other Investment Assets	78bh *d*
....	....	....	—	—	—	—	—	—	—	—	—	—	....	....	Monetary Authorities	78bo *d*
—	—	—	—	—	—	-8.7	-53.0	12.7	-10.1	-18.2	-29.4	-9.6	....	....	General Government	78bp *d*
—	—	—	—	—	—	—	—	—	—	—	—	—	....	....	Banks	78bq *d*
—	—	—	—	.4	1.8	3.7	12.7	-22.6	-27.1	4.2	34.7	36.2	....	....	Other Sectors	78br *d*
31.2	3.6	213.0	211.8	136.2	110.0	7.0	28.9	99.4	56.7	137.9	157.5	120.3	....	....	Other Investment Liab., n.i.e.	78bi *d*
-66.2	-42.1	-19.5	-.3	-.2	-6.6	2.2	.9	1.7	1.1	.2	—	—	....	....	Monetary Authorities	78bs *d*
145.8	75.6	233.3	257.9	167.8	150.7	56.3	50.8	111.7	114.4	158.2	178.2	174.3	....	....	General Government	78bt *d*
—	—	—	40.6	-26.3	-9.6	-22.8	—	—	—	—	—	—	....	....	Banks	78bu *d*
-48.4	-29.9	-41.4	-19.5	-21.8	-11.3	-51.5	-22.8	-14.0	-58.8	-20.5	-20.7	-54.0	....	....	Other Sectors	78bv *d*
26.4	154.9	-38.0	9.5	.6	9.0	-.1	32.5	28.8	41.3	-4.8	39.7	49.7	....	....	Net Errors and Omissions	78ca *d*
-54.4	-36.7	-84.5	-41.9	-31.7	24.2	-125.4	-62.1	-51.2	-9.1	-40.9	-40.6	-105.9	....	....	*Overall Balance*	78cb *d*
54.4	36.7	84.5	41.9	31.7	-24.2	125.4	62.1	51.2	9.1	40.9	40.6	105.9	....	....	Reserves and Related Items	79da *d*
-20.3	2.4	1.8	5.2	-12.7	-50.6	-49.4	-166.9	-140.7	-68.9	-105.2	-91.7	-37.8	....	....	Reserve Assets	79db *d*
-15.1	-7.8	-20.7	36.5	44.4	26.4	-9.8	27.1	27.5	13.3	2.5	-12.2	-16.0	....	....	Use of Fund Credit and Loans	79dc *d*
89.8	42.1	103.4	.3	—	—	184.7	201.9	164.3	64.8	143.6	144.4	159.6	....	....	Exceptional Financing	79de *d*
															International Investment Position	
....	....	....	....	....	....	....	....	....	....	....	....	973.1	1,067.5	....	Assets	79aa *d*
....	....	....	....	....	....	....	....	....	....	....	....	—	—	....	Direct Investment Abroad	79ab *d*
....	....	....	....	....	....	....	....	....	....	....	....	199.8	247.0	....	Portfolio Investment	79ac *d*
....	....	....	....	....	....	....	....	....	....	....	....	—	—	....	Equity Securities	79ad *d*
....	....	....	....	....	....	....	....	....	....	....	....	199.8	247.0	....	Debt Securities	79ae *d*
....	....	....	....	....	....	....	....	....	....	....	....	—	—	....	Financial Derivatives	79al *d*
....	....	....	....	....	....	....	....	....	....	....	....	—	—	....	Other Investment	79af *d*
....	....	....	....	....	....	....	....	....	....	....	....	....	....	....	Monetary Authorities	79ag *d*
....	....	....	....	....	....	....	....	....	....	....	....	....	....	....	General Government	79ah *d*
....	....	....	....	....	....	....	....	....	....	....	....	....	....	....	Banks	79ai *d*
....	....	....	....	....	....	....	....	....	....	....	....	....	....	....	Other Sectors	79aj *d*
....	....	....	....	....	....	....	....	....	....	....	....	773.2	820.5	....	Reserve Assets	79ak *d*
....	....	....	....	....	....	....	....	....	....	....	....	3,989.7	3,841.1	....	Liabilities	79la *d*
....	....	....	....	....	....	....	....	....	....	....	....	—	—	....	Dir. Invest. in Rep. Economy	79lb *d*
....	....	....	....	....	....	....	....	....	....	....	....	—	—	....	Portfolio Investment	79lc *d*
....	....	....	....	....	....	....	....	....	....	....	....	—	—	....	Equity Securities	79ld *d*
....	....	....	....	....	....	....	....	....	....	....	....	—	—	....	Debt Securities	79le *d*
....	....	....	....	....	....	....	....	....	....	....	....	—	—	....	Financial Derivatives	79ll *d*
....	....	....	....	....	....	....	....	....	....	....	....	3,989.7	3,841.1	....	Other Investment	79lf *d*
....	....	....	....	....	....	....	....	....	....	....	....	....	....	....	Monetary Authorities	79lg *d*
....	....	....	....	....	....	....	....	....	....	....	....	....	....	....	General Government	79lh *d*
....	....	....	....	....	....	....	....	....	....	....	....	....	....	....	Banks	79li *d*
....	....	....	....	....	....	....	....	....	....	....	....	....	....	....	Other Sectors	79lj *d*

Uganda

		1972	1973	1974	1975	1976	1977	1978	1979	1980	1981	1982	1983	1984	1985	1986
Government Finance													*Thousands of Shillings through 1978;*			
Deficit (-) or Surplus	80	†−8,990	−8,610	−15,260	−12,370	−13,180	−12,780	−1,600	†−35	−39	−100	−146	−134	−221	−630	†−1,639
Revenue	81	†15,320	12,400	11,400	20,890	23,510	34,200	57,930	†26	39	28	247	527	903	1,621	†2,844
Grants Received	81z	60	30	390	20	1,060	190	—	†—	1	3	30	10	35	78	†384
Expenditure	82	†24,370	21,040	27,050	33,280	37,750	47,170	59,530	†61	77	128	417	664	1,151	2,329	†4,867
Lending Minus Repayments	83	—	—	—	—	—	—	—	†—	2	4	6	6	8	—	†—
Financing																
Total Financing	84	...	...	...	...	...	...	...	...	39	100	146	134	221	631	†1,638
Net Borrowing: Domestic	84a	...	...	...	...	...	...	...	...	†39	100	148	120	229	496	†1,164
Foreign	85a	...	...	...	†4,430	3,120	2,620	1,100	†5		1	−1	15	−8	135	†474
Use of Cash Balances	87	...	...	...	...	...	...	...	...	†—						
Adj. to Total Financing	84x	...	...	...	...	...	...	...	...	—	—	−1	−1	—	—	†—
Debt																
Domestic	88a	...	...	...	...	...	...	...	†84	123	223	371	491	720	1,251	†2,016
Foreign	89a	...	...	...	...	...	...	...	...	...	...	...	...	...	...	...
National Accounts														*Thousands of Shillings through 1978;*		
Househ.Cons.Expend.,incl.NPISHs	96f	98,000	115,000	144,000	213,000	245,000	456,000	628,000	...	...	...	...	5,802	8,367	23,215	†58,551
Government Consumption Expend.	91f	...	...	...	...	...	...	...	...	...	...	...	660	1,581	3,193	†5,747
Gross Fixed Capital Formation	93e	13,000	10,000	16,000	15,000	12,000	18,000	19,000	...	...	...	...	553	906	2,124	†5,911
Changes in Inventories	93i	−1,000	1,000	1,000	2,000	3,000	5,000	6,000	...	...	...	...	−30	44	−48	†—
Exports of Goods and Services	90c	21,000	20,000	22,000	18,000	28,000	46,000	26,000	...	...	...	...	645	1,528	3,010	†7,708
Imports of Goods and Services (-)	98c	18,000	16,000	22,000	23,000	24,000	39,000	35,000	...	...	...	...	1,015	1,548	3,780	†11,921
Gross Domestic Product (GDP)	99b	113,900	129,500	160,300	225,000	264,500	485,700	643,000	†996	1,352	2,665	3,953	6,142	9,598	25,622	†65,444
GDP Volume 1991 Prices (Billions)	99b.p	...	...	...	...	...	...	...	...	...	...	...	1,599	1,524	1,526	1,618
GDP Volume (1995=100)	99bv p	...	...	...	...	...	...	...	...	...	...	...	53.0	50.5	50.6	53.6
GDP Deflator (1995=100)	99bi p	...	...	...	...	...	...	...	...	...	...	...	.2	.3	.8	†2.0
																Millions:
Population	99z	10.46	10.81	11.17	11.55	11.94	12.35	12.78	13.22	13.12	13.58	14.01	14.23	14.66	15.11	15.61

Uganda

Millions of Shillings Beginning 1979: Year Ending June 30

	1987	1988	1989	1990	1991	1992	1993	1994	1995	1996	1997	1998	1999	2000	2001
Deficit (-) or Surplus (80)	-5,557	-5,499	-29,582	-62,394	-60,316	-263,572	-113,513	-169,806	-131,554	-112,872	-120,191 f	....	-109,033	-640,250	-268,435
Revenue (81)	5,005	22,262	47,854	94,526	136,808	185,381	291,075	399,152	531,194	622,790	744,344 f	....	961,993	1,074,065	1,083,486
Grants Received (81z)	853	5,640	14,160	20,295	70,184	94,635	313,754	282,487	253,876	325,023	351,091 f	....	406,936	586,045	798,917
Expenditure (82)	11,415	33,401	89,670	174,928	262,808	535,088	717,142	848,645	905,277	1,057,885	1,213,626 f	....	1,475,643	1,817,223	2,125,268
Lending Minus Repayments (83)	—	—	1,926	2,287	4,500	8,500	1,200	2,800	11,347	2,800	2,000	....	2,319	483,137	25,569
Financing															
Total Financing (84)	5,557	5,499	29,582	....	60,316	263,572	113,513	169,806	131,554	112,872	120,191 f	....	109,033	640,250	268,435
Net Borrowing: Domestic (84a)	4,195	4,943	13,400	-22,268	9,372	56,027	-23,826	-26,962	-86,701	-60,262	-51,990 f	....	-16,749	539,885	56,944
Foreign (85a)	1,362	556	19,404	91,816	63,229	140,433	200,816	243,227	211,719	209,432	231,400 f	....	218,739	193,407	323,437
Use of Cash Balances (87)	—	—	-3,222	-9,441	-12,285	2,490	-72,868	-51,017	-22,182	-34,200	-30,001 f	....	-146,124	-67,593	-67,273
Adj. to Total Financing (84x)	—	—	—	....	—	64,622	9,391	4,558	28,718	-2,098	-29,218 f	....	53,167	-25,449	-44,673
Debt															
Domestic (88a)	4,775	5,233	11,612	....	....	....	....	....	....	....	....	....	214,480	325,442	505,579
Foreign (89a)	....	....	....	....	....	3,096	3,163	2,908	3,271	3,722	3,907	4,473	3,494,400	3,592,340	3,395,190

Millions of Shillings Beginning 1979

	1987	1988	1989	1990	1991	1992	1993	1994	1995	1996	1997	1998	1999	2000	2001
Househ.Cons.Expend.,incl.NPISHs (96f)	206,195	585,818	1,127,445	1,465,718	1,995,117	3,338,716	3,521,432	4,356,600	4,997,984	5,434,499	....	....	....	....	....
Government Consumption Expend. (91f)	16,934	44,319	79,095	128,254	206,111	321,603	424,897	476,591	577,183	660,574	....	....	....	....	....
Gross Fixed Capital Formation (93e)	26,581	69,030	128,343	228,129	362,871	547,106	647,912	738,346	984,963	1,012,671	....	....	....	....	....
Changes in Inventories (93i)				1,099	-5,460	3,107	-27,115	-5,190	-7,539		....	....	....	....	....
Exports of Goods and Services (90c)	19,242	48,494	87,833	111,544	186,573	253,431	310,187	555,517	648,754	791,972	....	....	....	....	....
Imports of Goods and Services (-) (98c)	45,241	108,394	218,105	321,285	511,646	754,349	803,611	945,341	1,240,509	1,374,620	....	....	....	....	....
Gross Domestic Product (GDP) (99b)	224,041	634,634	1,178,185	1,602,094	2,222,861	3,687,704	4,024,186	5,171,744	5,977,762	6,636,521	....	....	....	....	....
GDP Volume 1991 Prices (Billions) (99b,p)	1,722	1,856	1,984	2,107	2,223	2,326	2,490	2,753	3,018	3,195	....	....	....	....	....
GDP Volume (1995=100) (99bv,p)	57.0	61.5	65.7	69.8	73.6	77.1	82.5	91.2	100.0	105.9	....	....	....	....	....
GDP Deflator (1995=100) (99bi,p)	6.6	17.3	30.0	38.4	50.5	80.1	81.6	94.8	100.0	104.9	....	....	....	....	....

Midyear Estimates

	1987	1988	1989	1990	1991	1992	1993	1994	1995	1996	1997	1998	1999	2000	2001
Population (99z)	16.15	15.78	16.18	16.46	16.90	17.37	18.94	19.52	19.26	19.85	20.44	21.03	21.62	22.21	22.79

(See notes in the back of the book.)

746

Ukraine

	1972	1973	1974	1975	1976	1977	1978	1979	1980	1981	1982	1983	1984	1985	1986
Exchange Rates													*Hryvnias per SDR:*		
Official Rate .... aa	....	....	....	....	....	....	....	....	....	....	....	....	....	....	....
													Hryvnias per US Dollar:		
Official Rate .... ae	....	....	....	....	....	....	....	....	....	....	....	....	....	....	....
Official Rate .... rf	....	....	....	....	....	....	....	....	....	....	....	....	....	....	....
													Index Numbers (1995=100):		
Nominal Effective Exchange Rate .... ne c	....	....	....	....	....	....	....	....	....	....	....	....	....	....	....
Real Effective Exchange Rate .... re c	....	....	....	....	....	....	....	....	....	....	....	....	....	....	....
Fund Position													*Millions of SDRs:*		
Quota .... 2f. s	....	....	....	....	....	....	....	....	....	....	....	....	....	....	....
SDRs .... 1b. s	....	....	....	....	....	....	....	....	....	....	....	....	....	....	....
Reserve Position in the Fund .... 1c. s	....	....	....	....	....	....	....	....	....	....	....	....	....	....	....
Total Fund Cred.&Loans Outstg. 2tl	....	....	....	....	....	....	....	....	....	....	....	....	....	....	....
International Liquidity							*Millions of US Dollars Unless Otherwise Indicated:*									
Total Reserves minus Gold .... 1l. d	....	....	....	....	....	....	....	....	....	....	....	....	....	....	....
SDRs .... 1b. d	....	....	....	....	....	....	....	....	....	....	....	....	....	....	....
Reserve Position in the Fund .... 1c. d	....	....	....	....	....	....	....	....	....	....	....	....	....	....	....
Foreign Exchange .... 1d. d	....	....	....	....	....	....	....	....	....	....	....	....	....	....	....
Gold (Million Fine Troy Ounces) 1ad	....	....	....	....	....	....	....	....	....	....	....	....	....	....	....
Gold (National Valuation)..................... 1an d	....	....	....	....	....	....	....	....	....	....	....	....	....	....	....
Monetary Authorities: Other Assets .... 3.. d	....	....	....	....	....	....	....	....	....	....	....	....	....	....	....
Other Liab. .... 4.. d	....	....	....	....	....	....	....	....	....	....	....	....	....	....	....
Deposit Money Banks: Assets .... 7a. d	....	....	....	....	....	....	....	....	....	....	....	....	....	....	....
Liabilities .... 7b. d	....	....	....	....	....	....	....	....	....	....	....	....	....	....	....
Monetary Authorities													*Millions of Hryvnias:*		
Foreign Assets 11															
Claims on General Government 12a															
Claims on Nonfin.Pub.Enterprises 12c															
Claims on Private Sector 12d															
Claims on Banks 12e															
Reserve Money 14	....														
of which: Currency Outside Banks 14a															
Time, Savings,& Fgn.Currency Dep. 15															
Foreign Liabilities.................................... 16c															
General Government Deposits 16d															
Capital Accounts 17a															
Other Items (Net) 17r	....														
Banking Institutions													*Millions of Hryvnias:*		
Reserves 20	....	....	....	....	....	....	....	....	....	....	....	....	....	....	....
Foreign Assets 21	....	....	....	....	....	....	....	....	....	....	....	....	....	....	....
Claims on General Government 22a	....	....	....	....	....	....	....	....	....	....	....	....	....	....	....
Claims on Nonfin.Pub.Enterprises 22c	....	....	....	....	....	....	....	....	....	....	....	....	....	....	....
Claims on Private Sector 22d	....	....	....	....	....	....	....	....	....	....	....	....	....	....	....
Claims on Nonbank Financial Insts 22g	....	....	....	....	....	....	....	....	....	....	....	....	....	....	....
Demand Deposits... 24	....	....	....	....	....	....	....	....	....	....	....	....	....	....	....
Time, Savings,& Fgn.Currency Dep. 25	....	....	....	....	....	....	....	....	....	....	....	....	....	....	....
of which: Fgn. Currency Deposits 25b	....	....	....	....	....	....	....	....	....	....	....	....	....	....	....
Bonds 26ab	....	....	....	....	....	....	....	....	....	....	....	....	....	....	....
Foreign Liabilities.................................... 26c	....	....	....	....	....	....	....	....	....	....	....	....	....	....	....
General Government Deposits 26d	....	....	....	....	....	....	....	....	....	....	....	....	....	....	....
Credit from Monetary Authorities 26g	....	....	....	....	....	....	....	....	....	....	....	....	....	....	....
Capital Accounts 27a	....	....	....	....	....	....	....	....	....	....	....	....	....	....	....
Other Items (Net) 27r	....	....	....	....	....	....	....	....	....	....	....	....	....	....	....
Banking Survey													*Millions of Hryvnias:*		
Foreign Assets (Net) 31n	....	....	....	....	....	....	....	....	....	....	....	....	....	....	....
Domestic Credit 32	....	....	....	....	....	....	....	....	....	....	....	....	....	....	....
Claims on General Govt. (Net) 32an	....	....	....	....	....	....	....	....	....	....	....	....	....	....	....
Claims on Nonfin.Pub.Enterprises........ 32c	....	....	....	....	....	....	....	....	....	....	....	....	....	....	....
Claims on Private Sector...................... 32d	....	....	....	....	....	....	....	....	....	....	....	....	....	....	....
Claims on Nonbank Financial Inst....... 32g	....	....	....	....	....	....	....	....	....	....	....	....	....	....	....
Money... 34	....	....	....	....	....	....	....	....	....	....	....	....	....	....	....
Quasi-Money 35	....	....	....	....	....	....	....	....	....	....	....	....	....	....	....
Bonds 36ab	....	....	....	....	....	....	....	....	....	....	....	....	....	....	....
Capital Accounts 37a	....	....	....	....	....	....	....	....	....	....	....	....	....	....	....
Other Items (Net) 37r	....	....	....	....	....	....	....	....	....	....	....	....	....	....	....
Money plus Quasi-Money......................... 35l	....	....	....	....	....	....	....	....	....	....	....	....	....	....	....
Interest Rates													*Percent Per Annum*		
Refinancing Rate (End of Period)............. 60	....	....	....	....	....	....	....	....	....	....	....	....	....	....	....
Money Market Rate................................. 60b	....	....	....	....	....	....	....	....	....	....	....	....	....	....	....
Deposit Rate 60l	....	....	....	....	....	....	....	....	....	....	....	....	....	....	....
Lending Rate 60p	....	....	....	....	....	....	....	....	....	....	....	....	....	....	....
Prices and Labor													*Percent Change over*		
Wholesale Prices 63.xx	....	....	....	....	....	....	....	....	....	....	....	....	....	....	....
Consumer Prices 64.xx	....	....	....	....	....	....	....	....	....	....	....	....	....	....	....
Wages: Average Earnings..................... 65.xx	....	....	....	....	....	....	....	....	....	....	....	....	....	....	....
													Index Numbers (1995=100):		
Industrial Employment 67	....	....	....	....	....	....	....	....	....	....	....	....	....	....	....
													Number in Thousands:		
Labor Force 67d	....	....	....	....	....	....	....	....	....	....	....	....	....	....	....
Employment 67e	....	....	....	....	....	....	....	....	....	....	....	....	....	....	....
Unemployment 67c	....	....	....	....	....	....	....	....	....	....	....	....	....	....	....
Unemployment Rate (%)......................... 67r	....	....	....	....	....	....	....	....	....	....	....	....	....	....	....

	1987	1988	1989	1990	1991	1992	1993	1994	1995	1996	1997	1998	1999	2000	2001		
End of Period																**Exchange Rates**	
	....	....	....	....	....	.0088	.1732	1.5212	2.6668	†2.7163	2.5622	4.8253	7.1594	7.0807	6.6588	Official Rate	aa
End of Period (ae) Period Average (rf)																	
	....	....	....	....	....	.0064	.1261	1.0420	1.7940	†1.8890	1.8990	3.4270	5.2163	5.4345	5.2985	Official Rate	ae
	....	....	....	....	....	....	.0453	.3275	1.4731	1.8295	1.8617	2.4495	4.1304	5.4402	5.3722	Official Rate	rf
Period Averages																	
	....	....	....	....	....	8,268.73	1,115.92	188.10	100.00	88.20	100.63	107.29	136.53	116.54	122.45	Nominal Effective Exchange Rate	ne c
	....	....	....	....	....	134.54	58.92	83.56	100.00	117.88	133.55	130.38	126.92	118.93	119.61	Real Effective Exchange Rate	re c
End of Period																**Fund Position**	
	....	....	....	....	....	997.30	997.30	997.30	997.30	997.30	997.30	997.30	1,372.00	1,372.00	1,372.00	Quota	2f. *s*
	....	....	....	....	....	—	—	123.73	97.06	46.72	52.70	129.53	47.86	191.19	199.80	SDRs	1b. *s*
	....	....	....	....	....	.01	.01	.01	—	—	.01	.01	—	—	—	Reserve Position in the Fund	1c. *s*
	....	....	....	....	....	—	—	249.33	1,037.30	1,573.30	1,780.56	1,985.05	2,044.62	1,591.19	1,520.74	Total Fund Cred.&Loans Outstg.	2tl
End of Period																**International Liquidity**	
	....	....	....	....	....	468.8	161.6	650.7	1,050.6	1,960.0	2,341.1	761.3	1,046.4	1,352.7	2,955.4	Total Reserves minus Gold	1l. *d*
	....	....	....	....	....	—	—	180.6	144.3	67.2	71.1	182.4	65.7	249.1	251.1	SDRs	1b. *d*
	....	....	....	....	....	—	—	—	—	—	—	—	—	—	—	Reserve Position in the Fund	1c. *d*
	....	....	....	....	....	468.8	161.6	470.1	906.3	1,892.8	2,270.0	578.9	980.7	1,103.6	2,704.3	Foreign Exchange	1d. *d*
	....	....	....	....	....	.0003	.0115	.0360	.0470	.0316	.0613	.1100	.1624	.4536	.4831	Gold (Million Fine Troy Ounces)	1ad
	....	....	....	....	....	.1	4.4	13.7	18.3	11.6	17.7	31.6	47.2	123.7	134.1	Gold (National Valuation)	1an *d*
	....	....	....	....	....	981.4	88.1	4.3	2.5	2.3	—	235.9	104.9	177.4	86.9	Monetary Authorities: Other Assets	3.. *d*
	....	....	....	....	....	2,398.5	279.9	7.3	22.1	36.6	67.6	175.6	172.4	122.4	92.2	Other Liab.	4.. *d*
	....	....	....	....	....	863.5	1,264.5	1,406.3	1,044.3	942.1	963.1	906.8	849.2	921.5	774.7	Deposit Money Banks: Assets	7a. *d*
	....	....	....	....	....	896.3	570.4	724.8	302.0	334.4	949.9	507.2	338.7	462.6	650.9	Liabilities	7b. *d*
End of Period																**Monetary Authorities**	
	....	....	....	....	....	9.2	32.0	696.8	2,027.1	3,729.0	4,479.4	†3,525.4	6,251.8	8,987.5	16,830.2	Foreign Assets	11
	....	....	....	....	....	17.5	131.2	1,410.7	4,393.1	6,211.3	7,430.1	†15075.2	19,712.8	20,854.0	19,898.4	Claims on General Government	12a
	....	....	....	....	....	—	.5	4.8	—	—	—	†—	—	—	—	Claims on Nonfin.Pub.Enterprises	12c
	....	....	....	....	....	—	.2	.3	.1	1.2	35.0	†104.8	154.0	178.7	178.9	Claims on Private Sector	12d
	....	....	....	....	....	18.7	147.7	336.3	665.2	859.6	1,555.0	†1,365.1	1,687.8	1,600.7	1,570.3	Claims on Banks	12e
	....	....	....	....	....	18.1	301.2	1,528.2	3,557.1	4,974.9	7,410.5	†8,639.6	12,209.2	17,561.4	25,033.7	Reserve Money	14
	....	....	....	....	....	4.8	127.7	793.1	2,623.3	4,040.6	6,132.3	†7,157.3	9,583.3	12,799.0	19,464.8	*of which: Currency Outside Banks*	14a
	....	....	....	....	....	—	2.5	2.1	3.1	158.4	21.8	†31.1	23.1	57.1	110.3	Time, Savings,& Fgn.Currency Dep.	15
	....	....	....	....	....	15.3	35.3	386.9	2,805.9	4,342.8	4,690.6	†10180.1	15,537.6	11,932.1	10,614.6	Foreign Liabilities	16c
	....	....	....	....	....	—	18.6	166.7	97.7	216.0	334.0	†455.1	592.1	915.0	1,380.3	General Government Deposits	16d
	....	....	....	....	....	.5	12.2	75.8	231.3	420.8	914.5	†2,230.7	1,185.4	2,691.9	3,238.8	Capital Accounts	17a
	....	....	....	....	....	11.5	–58.1	289.2	390.3	688.1	128.0	†–1466.1	–1,741.0	–1,536.6	–1,900.1	Other Items (Net)	17r
End of Period																**Banking Institutions**	
	....	....	....	....	....	16.5	182.4	762.9	960.3	848.6	925.5	†1,454.6	2,613.3	4,749.6	5,538.9	Reserves	20
	....	....	....	....	....	5.5	159.5	1,465.3	1,873.4	1,779.7	1,829.0	†3,107.6	4,429.7	5,007.8	4,104.5	Foreign Assets	21
	....	....	....	....	....	1.3	17.1	—	207.6	774.5	1,815.4	†1,530.5	1,133.3	804.5	1,412.7	Claims on General Government	22a
	....	....	....	....	....	25.5	389.5	1,426.7	3,662.8	4,932.0	5,549.0	†1,440.9	1,782.4	2,633.8	3,418.3	Claims on Nonfin.Pub.Enterprises	22c
	....	....	....	....	....	1.3	20.9	556.5	804.2	1,128.2	2,259.1	†7,922.1	11,046.0	18,098.5	25,888.3	Claims on Private Sector	22d
	....	....	....	....	....	—	—	—	4.1	5.5	—	†129.4	153.5	219.0	198.4	Claims on Nonbank Financial Insts	22g
	....	....	....	....	....	15.8	213.6	1,061.9	2,041.9	2,253.9	2,887.3	†3,205.0	4,568.9	8,013.5	10,301.5	Demand Deposits	24
	....	....	....	....	....	4.5	137.1	1,353.7	2,244.9	2,890.6	3,468.6	†5,139.1	7,683.9	10,725.0	15,279.8	Time, Savings,& Fgn.Currency Dep.	25
	....	....	....	....	....	2.1	87.6	1,019.5	1,576.8	1,562.0	1,641.6	†3,265.4	5,357.6	7,187.9	8,281.2	*of which: Fgn. Currency Deposits*	25b
	....	....	....	....	....	—	—	—	—	—	—	†220.2	305.0	642.0	569.4	Bonds	26ab
	....	....	....	....	....	5.7	71.9	755.2	541.8	631.6	1,803.8	†1,738.2	1,766.6	2,514.0	3,448.9	Foreign Liabilities	26c
	....	....	....	....	....	3.7	87.0	323.7	514.4	795.5	805.0	†544.2	487.7	1,358.8	1,541.1	General Government Deposits	26d
	....	....	....	....	....	14.4	158.2	169.4	632.0	699.7	979.8	†1,237.2	1,569.4	1,604.9	1,125.8	Credit from Monetary Authorities	26g
	....	....	....	....	....	1.3	66.1	396.9	1,406.2	3,018.1	4,261.4	†5,462.2	7,497.7	9,182.9	11,044.4	Capital Accounts	27a
	....	....	....	....	....	4.6	35.3	150.7	131.1	–820.9	–1,827.9	†–1961.1	–2,721.1	–2,527.8	–2,749.6	Other Items (Net)	27r
End of Period																**Banking Survey**	
	....	....	....	....	....	–6.3	84.3	1,020.0	552.8	534.3	–186.0	†–5285.3	–6,622.6	–450.7	6,871.2	Foreign Assets (Net)	31n
	....	....	....	....	....	41.9	453.7	2,908.6	8,459.8	12,041.1	15,949.6	†25203.5	32,902.1	40,514.8	48,073.7	Domestic Credit	32
	....	....	....	....	....	15.0	42.6	920.3	3,988.6	5,974.2	8,106.5	†15606.3	19,766.2	19,384.7	18,389.7	Claims on General Govt. (Net)	32an
	....	....	....	....	....	25.5	390.0	1,431.5	3,662.8	4,932.0	5,549.0	†1,440.9	1,782.4	2,633.8	3,418.3	Claims on Nonfin.Pub.Enterprises	32c
	....	....	....	....	....	1.3	21.1	556.7	804.3	1,129.4	2,294.1	†8,026.8	11,200.0	18,277.2	26,067.2	Claims on Private Sector	32d
	....	....	....	....	....	—	—	—	4.1	5.5	—	†129.4	153.5	219.0	198.4	Claims on Nonbank Financial Inst	32g
	....	....	....	....	....	20.7	341.9	1,860.0	4,681.9	6,315.5	9,050.4	†10386.0	14,161.8	20,825.3	29,795.6	Money	34
	....	....	....	....	....	4.5	139.5	1,355.7	2,248.1	3,048.9	3,490.4	†5,170.2	7,707.0	10,782.1	15,390.2	Quasi-Money	35
	....	....	....	....	....	—	—	—	—	—	—	†220.2	305.0	642.0	569.4	Bonds	36ab
	....	....	....	....	....	1.8	78.4	472.7	1,637.5	3,438.9	5,176.0	†7,692.8	8,683.1	11,874.8	14,283.2	Capital Accounts	37a
	....	....	....	....	....	8.5	–21.9	240.1	445.1	–228.0	–1,953.1	†–3551.1	–4,577.4	–4,060.2	–5,093.5	Other Items (Net)	37r
	....	....	....	....	....	25.2	481.5	3,215.7	6,930.0	9,364.4	12,540.8	†15556.2	21,868.8	31,607.4	45,185.8	Money plus Quasi-Money	35l
Percent Per Annum																**Interest Rates**	
	....	....	....	....	....	80.00	240.00	252.00	110.00	40.00	35.00	60.00	45.00	27.00	12.50	Refinancing Rate *(End of Period)*	60
	....	....	....	....	....	....	....	....	....	....	22.05	40.41	44.98	18.34	16.57	Money Market Rate	60b
	....	....	....	....	....	....	148.63	208.63	70.29	33.63	18.21	22.25	20.70	13.72	10.99	Deposit Rate	60l
	....	....	....	....	....	....	184.25	250.28	122.70	79.88	49.12	54.50	54.95	41.53	32.28	Lending Rate	60p
Previous Period																**Prices and Labor**	
	....	....	....	....	....	....	4,619.3	1,143.8	487.9	51.9	7.7	13.2	31.1	....	....	Wholesale Prices	63.*xx*
	....	....	....	....	....	....	4,734.9	891.2	376.7	80.3	15.9	10.6	22.7	....	....	Consumer Prices	64.*xx*
	....	....	....	....	....	....	2,331.9	786.6	†434.2	....	....	....	....	....	....	Wages: Average Earnings	65.*xx*
Period Averages																	
	....	....	....	....	....	129.4	119.4	108.8	100.0	92.2	90.9	....	....	....	....	Industrial Employment	67
Period Averages																	
	....	....	....	....	....	....	....	....	25,562	....	....	25,936	22,747	23,127	....	Labor Force	67d
	....	....	....	....	....	....	....	....	24,125	24,114	23,756	22,998	20,048	20,420	....	Employment	67e
	....	....	....	....	....	....	....	....	1,437	1,998	2,330	2,937	2,699	2,708	....	Unemployment	67c
	....	....	....	....	....	....	....	....	5.6	7.6	8.9	11.3	11.9	11.7	....	Unemployment Rate (%)	67r

Ukraine

926

International Transactions — *Millions of US Dollars*

	1972	1973	1974	1975	1976	1977	1978	1979	1980	1981	1982	1983	1984	1985	1986
Exports .... 70..d	....	....	....	....	....	....	....	....	....	....	....	....	....	....	....
Imports, c.i.f. .... 71..d	....	....	....	....	....	....	....	....	....	....	....	....	....	....	....
Imports, f.o.b. 71.vd	....	....	....	....	....	....	....	....	....	....	....	....	....	....	....

Balance of Payments — *Millions of US Dollars:*

	1972	1973	1974	1975	1976	1977	1978	1979	1980	1981	1982	1983	1984	1985	1986
Current Account, n.i.e. 78ald	....	....	....	....	....	....	....	....	....	....	....	....	....	....	....
Goods: Exports f.o.b. 78aad	....	....	....	....	....	....	....	....	....	....	....	....	....	....	....
Goods: Imports f.o.b. 78abd	....	....	....	....	....	....	....	....	....	....	....	....	....	....	....
Trade Balance 78acd	....	....	....	....	....	....	....	....	....	....	....	....	....	....	....
Services: Credit 78add	....	....	....	....	....	....	....	....	....	....	....	....	....	....	....
Services: Debit 78aed	....	....	....	....	....	....	....	....	....	....	....	....	....	....	....
Balance on Goods & Services ... 78afd	....	....	....	....	....	....	....	....	....	....	....	....	....	....	....
Income: Credit 78agd	....	....	....	....	....	....	....	....	....	....	....	....	....	....	....
Income: Debit 78ahd	....	....	....	....	....	....	....	....	....	....	....	....	....	....	....
Balance on Gds, Serv. & Inc. ... 78aid	....	....	....	....	....	....	....	....	....	....	....	....	....	....	....
Current Transfers, n.i.e.: Credit 78ajd	....	....	....	....	....	....	....	....	....	....	....	....	....	....	....
Current Transfers: Debit 78akd	....	....	....	....	....	....	....	....	....	....	....	....	....	....	....
Capital Account, n.i.e. 78bcd	....	....	....	....	....	....	....	....	....	....	....	....	....	....	....
Capital Account, n.i.e.: Credit 78bad	....	....	....	....	....	....	....	....	....	....	....	....	....	....	....
Capital Account: Debit 78bbd	....	....	....	....	....	....	....	....	....	....	....	....	....	....	....
Financial Account, n.i.e. 78bjd	....	....	....	....	....	....	....	....	....	....	....	....	....	....	....
Direct Investment Abroad 78bdd	....	....	....	....	....	....	....	....	....	....	....	....	....	....	....
Dir. Invest. in Rep. Econ., n.i.e. 78bed	....	....	....	....	....	....	....	....	....	....	....	....	....	....	....
Portfolio Investment Assets 78bfd	....	....	....	....	....	....	....	....	....	....	....	....	....	....	....
Equity Securities 78bkd	....	....	....	....	....	....	....	....	....	....	....	....	....	....	....
Debt Securities 78bld	....	....	....	....	....	....	....	....	....	....	....	....	....	....	....
Portfolio Investment Liab., n.i.e. 78bgd	....	....	....	....	....	....	....	....	....	....	....	....	....	....	....
Equity Securities 78bmd	....	....	....	....	....	....	....	....	....	....	....	....	....	....	....
Debt Securities 78bnd	....	....	....	....	....	....	....	....	....	....	....	....	....	....	....
Financial Derivatives Assets 78bwd	....	....	....	....	....	....	....	....	....	....	....	....	....	....	....
Financial Derivatives Liabilities 78bxd	....	....	....	....	....	....	....	....	....	....	....	....	....	....	....
Other Investment Assets 78bhd	....	....	....	....	....	....	....	....	....	....	....	....	....	....	....
Monetary Authorities 78bod	....	....	....	....	....	....	....	....	....	....	....	....	....	....	....
General Government 78bpd	....	....	....	....	....	....	....	....	....	....	....	....	....	....	....
Banks 78bqd	....	....	....	....	....	....	....	....	....	....	....	....	....	....	....
Other Sectors 78brd	....	....	....	....	....	....	....	....	....	....	....	....	....	....	....
Other Investment Liab., n.i.e. 78bid	....	....	....	....	....	....	....	....	....	....	....	....	....	....	....
Monetary Authorities 78bsd	....	....	....	....	....	....	....	....	....	....	....	....	....	....	....
General Government 78btd	....	....	....	....	....	....	....	....	....	....	....	....	....	....	....
Banks 78bud	....	....	....	....	....	....	....	....	....	....	....	....	....	....	....
Other Sectors 78bvd	....	....	....	....	....	....	....	....	....	....	....	....	....	....	....
Net Errors and Omissions 78cad	....	....	....	....	....	....	....	....	....	....	....	....	....	....	....
Overall Balance 78cbd	....	....	....	....	....	....	....	....	....	....	....	....	....	....	....
Reserves and Related Items 79dad	....	....	....	....	....	....	....	....	....	....	....	....	....	....	....
Reserve Assets 79dbd	....	....	....	....	....	....	....	....	....	....	....	....	....	....	....
Use of Fund Credit and Loans 79dcd	....	....	....	....	....	....	....	....	....	....	....	....	....	....	....
Exceptional Financing 79ded	....	....	....	....	....	....	....	....	....	....	....	....	....	....	....

National Accounts — *Billions of Hryvnias*

	1972	1973	1974	1975	1976	1977	1978	1979	1980	1981	1982	1983	1984	1985	1986
Househ.Cons.Expend.,incl.NPISHs 96f	....	....	....	....	....	....	....	....	....	....	....	....	....	....	....
Government Consumption Expend. 91f	....	....	....	....	....	....	....	....	....	....	....	....	....	....	....
Gross Fixed Capital Formation 93e	....	....	....	....	....	....	....	....	....	....	....	....	....	....	....
Changes in Inventories 93i	....	....	....	....	....	....	....	....	....	....	....	....	....	....	....
Exports of Goods and Services 90c	....	....	....	....	....	....	....	....	....	....	....	....	....	....	....
Imports of Goods and Services (-) 98c	....	....	....	....	....	....	....	....	....	....	....	....	....	....	....
Gross Domestic Product (GDP) 99b	....	....	....	....	....	....	....	....	....	....	....	....	....	....	....
Net Primary Income from Abroad 98.n	....	....	....	....	....	....	....	....	....	....	....	....	....	....	....
Gross National Income (GNI) 99a	....	....	....	....	....	....	....	....	....	....	....	....	....	....	....
Net Current Transf.from Abroad 98t	....	....	....	....	....	....	....	....	....	....	....	....	....	....	....
Gross Nat'l Disposable Inc.(GNDI) 99i	....	....	....	....	....	....	....	....	....	....	....	....	....	....	....
Gross Saving 99s	....	....	....	....	....	....	....	....	....	....	....	....	....	....	....

Millions:

	1972	1973	1974	1975	1976	1977	1978	1979	1980	1981	1982	1983	1984	1985	1986
Population 99z	....	....	....	....	....	....	....	....	....	....	....	....	....	....	....

Millions of US Dollars — **International Transactions**

Minus Sign Indicates Debit — Balance of Payments

Billions of Hryvnias Beginning 1994 — **National Accounts**

Midyear Estimates

1987	1988	1989	1990	1991	1992	1993	1994	1995	1996	1997	1998	1999	2000	2001		
...	...	...	...	...	8,045	7,817	10,305	13,317	14,441	14,232	12,637	11,582	...	...	Exports	70..*d*
...	...	...	...	...	7,099	9,533	10,748	16,052	18,639	17,114	14,676	11,846	...	...	Imports, c.i.f.	71..*d*
...	...	...	...	...	7,099	9,533	10,589	11,328	...	...	...	...	...	...	Imports, f.o.b.	71.v*d*
...	...	...	...	...	...	...	–1,163	–1,152	–1,184	–1,335	–1,296	1,658	1,481	1,402	Current Account, n.i.e.	78al*d*
...	...	...	...	...	...	...	13,894	14,244	15,547	15,418	13,699	13,189	15,722	17,091	Goods: Exports f.o.b.	78aa*d*
...	...	...	...	...	...	...	–16,469	–16,946	–19,843	–19,623	–16,283	–12,945	–14,943	–16,893	Goods: Imports f.o.b.	78ab*d*
...	...	...	...	...	...	...	–2,575	–2,702	–4,296	–4,205	–2,584	244	779	198	*Trade Balance*	78ac*d*
...	...	...	...	...	...	...	2,747	2,846	4,799	4,937	3,922	3,869	3,800	3,995	Services: Credit	78ad*d*
...	...	...	...	...	...	...	–1,538	–1,334	–1,625	–2,268	–2,545	–2,292	–3,004	–3,580	Services: Debit	78ae*d*
...	...	...	...	...	...	...	–1,366	–1,190	–1,122	–1,536	–1,207	1,821	1,575	613	*Balance on Goods & Services*	78af*d*
...	...	...	...	...	...	...	56	247	102	158	122	98	143	167	Income: Credit	78ag*d*
...	...	...	...	...	...	...	–400	–681	–673	–802	–993	–967	–1,085	–834	Income: Debit	78ah*d*
...	...	...	...	...	...	...	–1,710	–1,624	–1,693	–2,180	–2,078	952	633	–54	*Balance on Gds, Serv. & Inc.*	78ai*d*
...	...	...	...	...	...	...	583	557	619	942	868	754	967	1,516	Current Transfers, n.i.e.: Credit	78aj*d*
...	...	...	...	...	...	...	–36	–85	–110	–97	–86	–48	–119	–60	Current Transfers: Debit	78ak*d*
...	...	...	...	...	...	...	97	6	5	—	–3	–10	–8	3	Capital Account, n.i.e.	78bc*d*
...	...	...	...	...	...	...	106	6	5	—	—	—	—	8	Capital Account, n.i.e.: Credit	78ba*d*
...	...	...	...	...	...	...	–9	—	—	—	–3	–10	–8	–5	Capital Account: Debit	78bb*d*
...	...	...	...	...	...	...	–557	–726	317	1,413	–1,340	–879	–752	–191	Financial Account, n.i.e.	78bj*d*
...	...	...	...	...	...	...	–8	–10	5	–42	4	–7	–1	–23	Direct Investment Abroad	78bd*d*
...	...	...	...	...	...	...	159	267	521	623	743	496	595	792	Dir. Invest. in Rep. Econ., n.i.e.	78be*d*
...	...	...	...	...	...	...	—	–12	–1	–2	–2	–11	–4	1	Portfolio Investment Assets	78bf*d*
...	...	...	...	...	...	...		...	–11	–14	–3	–5	–2	–1	Equity Securities	78bk*d*
...	...	...	...	...	...	...		–12	10	12	1	–6	–2	2	Debt Securities	78bl*d*
...	...	...	...	...	...	...	—	16	199	1,605	–1,379	–75	–197	–867	Portfolio Investment Liab., n.i.e.	78bg*d*
...	...	...	...	...	...	...		...	46	248	227	129	–193	–734	Equity Securities	78bm*d*
...	...	...	...	...	...	...	—	16	153	1,357	–1,606	–204	–4	–133	Debt Securities	78bn*d*
...	...	...	...	...	...	...	...	...	...	...	...	...	...	...	Financial Derivatives Assets	78bw*d*
...	...	...	...	...	...	...	...	...	...	...	...	...	...	...	Financial Derivatives Liabilities	78bx*d*
...	...	...	...	...	...	...	–3,026	–1,574	–821	–1,583	–1,321	–2,264	–449	–1,015	Other Investment Assets	78bh*d*
...	...	...	...	...	...	...	...	...	...	...	...	...	–15	1	Monetary Authorities	78bo*d*
...	...	...	...	...	...	...	...	...	...	...	...	...	1,002	—	General Government	78bp*d*
...	...	...	...	...	...	...	–779	–328	83	–536	–46	51	–64	137	Banks	78bq*d*
...	...	...	...	...	...	...	–2,247	–1,246	–904	–1,047	–1,275	–2,315	–1,372	–1,153	Other Sectors	78br*d*
...	...	...	...	...	...	...	2,318	587	414	812	615	982	–696	921	Other Investment Liab., n.i.e.	78bi*d*
...	...	...	...	...	...	...	...	...	...	...	...	...	...	...	Monetary Authorities	78bs*d*
...	...	...	...	...	...	...	–1,097	–783	–477	–267	–857	–231	–1,457	–537	General Government	78bt*d*
...	...	...	...	...	...	...	577	724	565	–51	–264	–16	113	139	Banks	78bu*d*
...	...	...	...	...	...	...	2,838	646	326	1,130	1,736	1,229	648	1,319	Other Sectors	78bv*d*
...	...	...	...	...	...	...	423	248	259	–781	–818	–953	–148	–221	Net Errors and Omissions	78ca*d*
...	...	...	...	...	...	...	–1,200	–1,624	–603	–703	–3,457	–184	573	993	*Overall Balance*	78cb*d*
...	...	...	...	...	...	...	1,200	1,624	603	703	3,457	184	–573	–993	Reserves and Related Items	79da*d*
...	...	...	...	...	...	...	–549	–469	–894	–385	1,328	–281	–401	–1,609	Reserve Assets	79db*d*
...	...	...	...	...	...	...	368	1,221	776	283	279	75	–603	–86	Use of Fund Credit and Loans	79dc*d*
...	...	...	...	...	...	...	1,380	871	721	805	1,850	390	431	702	Exceptional Financing	79de*d*
...	...	...	...	...	—	.7	5.8	30.1	47.4	53.9	61.4	76.5	...	...	Househ.Cons.Expend.,incl.NPISHs	96f
...	...	...	...	...	—	.2	2.3	11.6	17.7	22.3	22.1	24.1	...	...	Government Consumption Expend.	91f
...	...	...	...	...	—	.4	2.9	12.8	17.0	18.7	20.2	25.3	...	...	Gross Fixed Capital Formation	93e
...	...	...	...	...	—	.2	1.4	1.8	1.5	1.3	1.1	–.1	...	...	Changes in Inventories	93i
...	...	...	...	...	—	.4	4.3	25.7	37.2	37.9	43.0	66.8	...	...	Exports of Goods and Services	90c
...	...	...	...	...	—	.4	4.6	27.3	39.3	40.8	45.3	65.5	...	...	Imports of Goods and Services (-)	98c
...	...	...	...	...	.1	1.5	12.0	54.5	81.5	93.4	102.6	127.1	...	...	Gross Domestic Product (GDP)	99b
...	...	...	...	...		—	–.1	–.9	–1.0	–1.2	–2.1	...	...	...	Net Primary Income from Abroad	98.n
...	...	...	...	...	.1	1.4	12.0	53.6	80.5	92.2	100.5	...	...	...	Gross National Income (GNI)	99a
...	...	...	...	...		—	.1	.7	.9	1.5	2.7	...	...	...	Net Current Transf.from Abroad	98t
...	...	...	...	...	.1	1.4	12.0	54.3	81.4	93.7	103.2	...	...	...	Gross Nat'l Disposable Inc.(GNDI)	99i
...	...	...	...	...	—	.5	3.9	12.7	16.3	17.5	19.6	...	...	...	Gross Saving	99s
...	...	...	...	51.94	52.06	52.24	52.11	51.73	51.33	50.89	50.50	50.11	49.57	49.11	**Population**	99z

(See notes in the back of the book.)

		1972	1973	1974	1975	1976	1977	1978	1979	1980	1981	1982	1983	1984	1985	1986
Exchange Rates																*Dirhams per SDR:*
Official Rate	aa	4.7619	4.8344	4.8735	4.6791	4.6206	4.7349	5.0001	4.9611	4.6820	4.2729	4.0495	3.8434	3.5984	4.0323	4.4903
																Dirhams per US Dollar:
Official Rate	ae	4.3860	4.0075	3.9805	3.9970	3.9770	3.8980	3.8380	3.7660	3.6710	3.6710	3.6710	3.6710	3.6710	3.6710	3.6710
Official Rate	rf	4.3860	3.9963	3.9590	3.9613	3.9531	3.9032	3.8712	3.8157	3.7074	3.6710	3.6710	3.6710	3.6710	3.6710	3.6710
														Index Numbers (1995=100):		
Official Rate	ah x	83.7	91.7	92.5	92.7	92.9	93.8	94.8	96.2	99.0	100.0	100.0	100.0	100.0	100.0	100.0
Nominal Effective Exchange Rate	ne c	....	....	....	....	....	....	....	99.2	102.1	114.2	126.5	132.4	141.7	145.8	119.7
Fund Position																*Millions of SDRs:*
Quota	2f. s	15.0	15.0	15.0	15.0	15.0	15.0	120.0	120.0	202.6	202.6	202.6	202.6	202.6	202.6	202.6
SDRs	1b. s	—	—	—	—	—	—	—	15.4	8.0	29.5	50.3	61.5	66.0	68.3	76.5
Reserve Position in the Fund	1c. s	3.8	3.8	69.6	114.8	114.1	96.5	71.7	62.1	93.1	147.9	201.4	214.6	222.3	201.7	181.0
of which: Outstg.Fund Borrowing	2c	—	—	63.8	100.0	100.0	84.0	57.9	46.5	44.7	75.4	105.0	102.9	93.9	72.6	46.4
International Liquidity												*Millions of US Dollars Unless Otherwise Indicated:*				
Total Reserves minus Gold	1l. d	....	91.7	452.9	987.9	1,906.5	800.3	811.8	1,432.3	2,014.7	3,202.2	2,215.5	2,072.4	2,286.9	3,204.3	3,369.9
SDRs	1b. d	—	—	—	—	—	—	—	20.2	10.2	34.4	55.5	64.4	64.7	75.0	93.5
Reserve Position in the Fund	1c. d	4.1	4.5	85.2	134.4	132.6	117.2	93.4	81.7	118.0	172.1	222.2	224.7	217.9	221.5	221.4
Foreign Exchange	1d. d	....	87.2	367.7	853.5	1,773.9	683.1	718.4	1,330.3	1,885.8	2,995.7	1,937.8	1,783.3	2,004.3	2,907.8	3,054.9
Gold (Million Fine Troy Ounces)	1ad	....	—	—	—	.545	.569	.576	.577	.577	.678	.817	.817	.817	.817	.817
Gold (National Valuation)	1an d	....	—	—	—	67.8	72.7	75.3	76.8	78.8	184.6	184.6	184.6	184.6	184.6	184.6
Monetary Authorities: Other Assets	3.. d	....	....	....	....	....	....	....	....	....	....	1,132.7				
Deposit Money Banks: Assets	7a. d	....	402.2	1,106.4	1,794.3	2,574.7	2,077.4	2,584.2	3,556.7	5,286.4	7,914.3	9,548.5	9,538.0	12,100.6	12,070.1	13,475.9
Liabilities	7b. d	....	108.6	225.7	436.5	892.7	2,262.8	2,761.1	4,028.3	4,571.2	6,142.9	7,229.5	6,719.6	5,666.5	5,422.6	4,594.9
RLB: Foreign Assets	7k. d	....	....	....	....	....	....	85.8	268.0	313.3	378.8	332.9	490.5	601.1	459.5	498.4
Foreign Liabilities	7m. d	....	....	....	....	....	....	115.3	316.1	376.2	424.9	419.9	343.4	515.9	332.7	239.4
Monetary Authorities																*Millions of Dirhams:*
Foreign Assets	11	....	365	1,976	4,189	9,001	3,419	3,405	5,721	7,726	12,629	13,271	10,204	11,029	14,543	13,805
Claims on Central Government	12a	....	45	120	459	1,307	1,712	1,540	1,538	1,544	1,484	1,486	1,488	1,491	1,493	2,226
Claims on Official Entities	12bx	....	—	—	—	100	12	12	11	5	—	12	12	5	5	5
Claims on Deposit Money Banks	12e	....	16	172	527	1,013	1,199	1,391	1,042	689	335	239	1,469	1,081	190	1,076
Claims on Other Financial Insts	12f	....	—	2	18	31	16	22	18	14	7	4	—	—	—	—
Reserve Money	14	....	411	1,051	1,526	2,776	3,796	4,259	5,475	4,451	5,321	6,044	5,992	6,529	7,562	7,756
of which: Currency Outside DMBs	14a	....	265	429	628	1,077	1,392	1,704	1,965	2,143	2,771	2,990	2,879	2,929	3,161	3,246
Quasi-Monetary Deposits	15	....	—	293	60	52	34	10	—	—	—	—	—	—	—	—
Foreign Liabilities	16c	....	—	—	1	824	616	487	513	390	233	8	6	5	6	5
Central Government Deposits	16d	....	18	919	3,578	7,631	2,041	1,776	2,173	4,508	6,938	6,078	3,527	3,340	3,308	1,985
Capital Accounts	17a	....	9	10	20	30	30	30	237	711	2,074	3,084	3,758	3,816	5,405	7,367
Other Items (Net)	17r	....	−12	−4	9	140	−161	−194	−70	−83	−111	−203	−112	−85	−49	−2
Deposit Money Banks																*Millions of Dirhams:*
Reserves	20	....	146	594	898	1,699	2,404	2,553	3,507	2,295	2,543	3,043	3,099	3,590	4,394	4,514
Foreign Assets	21	....	1,588	4,404	7,172	10,240	8,098	9,918	13,395	19,406	29,054	35,052	35,014	44,421	44,309	49,470
Claims on Central Government	22a	....	137	273	358	737	1,498	1,907	2,958	2,305	2,418	3,641	4,177	4,330	9,491	5,892
Claims on Official Entities	22bx	....	—	9	91	299	713	584	892	840	1,015	916	798	659	636	612
Claims on Private Sector	22d	....	1,627	3,362	5,691	10,472	15,819	19,357	21,212	25,173	29,902	31,713	33,467	33,385	33,628	36,232
Claims on Other Financial Insts	22f	....	14	37	125	186	170	210	283	606	537	924	1,236	2,349	2,064	1,961
Demand Deposits	24	....	705	1,107	1,975	3,648	3,822	4,072	4,303	5,212	6,198	6,749	6,245	5,963	6,344	5,956
Time and Savings Deposits	25	....	1,287	4,207	6,157	11,977	10,291	11,790	11,954	16,172	20,125	23,907	27,217	37,978	40,381	42,875
Foreign Liabilities	26c	....	429	898	1,745	3,550	8,821	10,597	15,171	16,781	22,551	26,540	24,668	20,802	19,906	16,868
Central Government Deposits	26d	....	979	2,159	3,578	2,949	2,324	2,503	4,358	3,675	3,737	3,791	3,326	4,108	3,882	4,335
Central Govt. Lending Funds	26f	....	7	6	5	5	290	658	925	1,569	2,054	907	736	526	559	482
Credit from Monetary Authorities	26g	....	16	172	527	1,013	1,192	1,391	1,039	689	335	239	1,469	1,031	190	1,076
Capital Accounts	27a	....	125	175	392	609	1,867	3,548	4,553	5,523	8,397	10,756	11,583	12,027	14,286	12,659
Other Items (Net)	27r	....	−34	−46	−45	−119	95	−31	−56	1,005	2,071	2,399	2,547	6,301	8,973	14,431
Monetary Survey																*Millions of Dirhams:*
Foreign Assets (Net)	31n	....	1,524	5,481	9,615	14,866	2,080	2,239	3,432	9,962	18,898	21,776	20,544	34,643	38,940	46,401
Domestic Credit	32	....	826	724	−412	2,555	15,582	19,359	20,385	22,310	24,692	28,831	34,330	34,777	40,134	40,614
Claims on Central Govt. (Net)	32an	....	−815	−2,685	−6,339	−8,536	−1,155	−832	−2,035	−4,335	−6,773	−4,742	−1,188	−1,627	3,795	1,797
Claims on Official Entities	32bx	....	—	9	91	399	725	596	903	846	1,015	928	810	664	641	617
Claims on Private Sector	32d	....	1,627	3,362	5,693	10,475	15,826	19,363	21,218	25,179	29,907	31,718	33,471	33,390	33,635	36,238
Claims on Other Financial Insts	32f	....	14	39	142	217	186	232	300	620	543	928	1,236	2,349	2,064	1,961
Money	34	....	970	1,536	2,603	4,725	5,215	5,776	6,269	7,355	8,969	9,739	9,124	8,892	9,505	9,201
Quasi-Money	35	....	1,287	4,499	6,217	12,029	10,325	11,800	11,954	16,172	20,125	23,907	27,218	37,978	40,382	42,875
Other Items (Net)	37r	....	94	170	383	667	2,122	4,022	5,595	8,745	14,496	16,961	18,531	22,550	29,188	34,939
Money plus Quasi-Money	35l	....	2,257	6,036	8,820	16,754	15,540	17,576	18,222	23,527	29,094	33,646	36,342	46,870	49,887	52,076
Production														*Index Numbers (1995=100):*		
Crude Petroleum	66aa	54.9	69.4	76.4	77.3	88.6	91.1	83.5	83.4	78.2	68.5	57.8	53.8	51.2	51.0	63.6

	1987	1988	1989	1990	1991	1992	1993	1994	1995	1996	1997	1998	1999	2000	2001	
Exchange Rates																
End of Period																
Official Rate	5.2079	4.9401	4.8243	5.2226	5.2511	5.0476	5.0423	5.3591	5.4569	5.2788	4.9551	5.1710	5.0405	4.7849	4.6153	**aa**
End of Period (ae) Period Average (rf)																
Official Rate	3.6710	3.6710	3.6710	3.6710	3.6710	3.6710	3.6710	3.6710	3.6710	3.6710	3.6725	3.6725	3.6725	3.6725	3.6725	**ae**
Official Rate	3.6710	3.6710	3.6710	3.6710	3.6710	3.6710	3.6710	3.6710	3.6710	3.6710	3.6711	3.6725	3.6725	3.6725	3.6725	**rf**
Period Averages																
Official Rate	100.0	100.0	100.0	100.0	100.0	100.0	100.0	100.0	100.0	100.0	100.0	100.0	100.0	100.0	100.0	**ah x**
Nominal Effective Exchange Rate	106.8	101.6	106.8	102.4	103.5	102.1	107.2	105.3	100.0	103.9	112.3	121.1	119.0	125.0	132.1	**ne c**
Fund Position																
End of Period																
Quota	202.6	202.6	202.6	202.6	202.6	392.1	392.1	392.1	392.1	392.1	392.1	392.1	611.7	611.7	611.7	**2f. s**
SDRs	79.8	82.3	85.9	90.8	95.5	52.4	54.1	55.0	55.9	57.6	58.4	59.2	4.5	3.1	1.8	**1b. s**
Reserve Position in the Fund	159.1	135.3	138.4	126.3	126.1	158.3	162.8	149.1	185.8	204.4	197.4	233.9	212.6	164.8	179.8	**1c. s**
of which: Outstg.Fund Borrowing	22.5	3.2	.1	—	—	—	—	—	—	—	—	—	—	—	—	**2c**
International Liquidity																
End of Period																
Total Reserves minus Gold	4,725.3	4,433.5	4,456.6	4,583.9	5,365.4	5,711.8	6,103.7	6,658.8	7,470.9	8,055.5	8,372.3	9,077.1	10,675.1	13,522.7	14,146.4	**1l. d**
SDRs	113.2	110.8	112.9	129.1	136.6	72.1	74.4	80.3	83.1	82.8	78.7	83.3	6.2	4.0	2.2	**1b. d**
Reserve Position in the Fund	225.6	182.0	181.9	179.7	180.4	217.6	223.6	217.7	276.2	293.9	266.3	329.3	291.7	214.7	225.9	**1c. d**
Foreign Exchange	4,386.5	4,140.7	4,161.8	4,275.1	5,048.4	5,422.1	5,805.7	6,360.8	7,111.6	7,678.8	8,027.3	8,664.4	10,377.1	13,303.9	13,918.2	**1d. d**
Gold (Million Fine Troy Ounces)	.817	.817	.797	.797	.796	.796	.798	.795	.795	.798	.795	.795	.397	.397	.397	**1ad**
Gold (National Valuation)	184.6	184.6	182.0	181.7	181.7	182.0	182.5	181.7	181.7	182.8	181.3	181.3	90.7	90.7	90.7	**1an d**
Monetary Authorities: Other Assets	....	....	....	....	....	....	....	....	....	....	....	....	....	....	....	**3.. d**
Deposit Money Banks: Assets	13,188.7	15,505.7	16,378.1	17,134.0	18,931.9	18,496.6	17,997.8	17,737.4	17,377.8	19,086.9	20,735.7	22,108.9	22,010.3	24,454.7	26,822.6	**7a. d**
Liabilities	4,789.9	6,153.1	5,603.4	6,779.1	7,042.0	7,157.7	7,221.7	8,997.8	7,653.5	10,053.4	12,351.5	14,446.6	14,577.8	14,133.4	8,137.0	**7b. d**
RLB: Foreign Assets	448.1	475.8	433.4	386.0	210.3	162.9	118.8	106.0	134.0	134.6	154.7	200.7	265.5	147.9	245.6	**7k. d**
Foreign Liabilities	259.2	300.5	186.6	94.5	113.6	79.0	60.2	35.4	59.1	112.8	101.3	75.4	281.0	138.6	216.5	**7m. d**
Monetary Authorities																
End of Period																
Foreign Assets	18,322	17,225	17,211	17,734	20,654	21,804	23,357	25,812	28,408	30,567	31,692	34,512	40,185	50,781	52,479	**11**
Claims on Central Government	—	—	13	364	—	425	—	—	—	—	—	—	—	—	—	**12a**
Claims on Official Entities	—	—	—	—	—	—	—	—	—	—	—	—	—	—	—	**12bx**
Claims on Deposit Money Banks	1,080	1,076	555	50	50	50	50	50	50	50	50	50	50	50	50	**12e**
Claims on Other Financial Insts	—	—	—	—	—	—	—	—	—	—	—	—	—	—	—	**12f**
Reserve Money	11,864	10,902	9,600	9,663	11,192	13,576	13,124	16,501	18,667	20,188	20,294	20,326	26,530	36,201	38,387	**14**
of which: Currency Outside DMBs	3,511	3,600	3,612	4,392	4,676	5,108	5,667	6,031	6,404	6,767	7,366	8,195	10,272	10,017	10,537	**14a**
Quasi-Monetary Deposits	—	—	—	—	—	—	—	—	—	—	—	—	—	—	—	**15**
Foreign Liabilities	5	7	10	202	252	336	313	380	175	75	52	11	403	587	516	**16c**
Central Government Deposits	4,815	4,615	4,621	5,069	7,057	6,166	6,788	7,178	7,930	8,591	9,692	10,692	11,518	12,164	11,722	**16d**
Capital Accounts	2,628	2,631	2,649	2,664	1,738	1,696	1,695	1,708	1,711	1,704	1,692	1,700	1,755	1,745	1,739	**17a**
Other Items (Net)	88	146	899	549	464	505	1,486	96	−25	54	12	1,832	29	134	165	**17r**
Deposit Money Banks																
End of Period																
Reserves	8,286	7,264	5,963	5,247	6,525	8,466	7,452	10,465	12,258	13,416	12,923	12,127	16,256	25,893	27,849	**20**
Foreign Assets	48,414	56,922	60,124	62,899	69,499	67,901	66,070	65,114	63,794	70,068	76,152	81,195	80,833	89,810	98,506	**21**
Claims on Central Government	7,491	6,856	7,250	8,251	10,040	10,806	12,334	12,558	12,787	10,394	9,105	12,719	15,725	12,581	11,035	**22a**
Claims on Official Entities	704	1,058	785	1,187	1,323	1,421	2,791	5,869	5,840	5,064	5,511	5,236	5,581	5,780	5,258	**22bx**
Claims on Private Sector	38,975	42,493	46,086	46,897	50,618	53,713	57,691	63,836	71,759	78,927	89,925	102,416	110,276	119,828	130,549	**22d**
Claims on Other Financial Insts	1,634	1,721	1,637	2,482	1,477	2,193	3,014	2,656	2,526	2,330	2,689	3,443	3,075	3,317	3,415	**22f**
Demand Deposits	6,585	7,154	7,444	6,370	8,336	9,873	12,507	13,152	14,420	15,499	18,002	19,589	19,980	24,050	28,927	**24**
Time and Savings Deposits	44,844	47,403	52,132	47,246	53,432	54,530	50,241	54,635	60,537	64,676	69,437	71,000	79,847	92,902	116,981	**25**
Foreign Liabilities	17,584	22,588	20,570	24,886	25,851	26,276	26,511	33,031	28,096	36,906	45,361	53,055	53,537	51,905	29,883	**26c**
Central Government Deposits	5,158	5,907	6,292	10,662	10,619	11,008	14,830	12,550	15,156	9,962	6,948	10,920	11,671	18,441	27,382	**26d**
Central Govt. Lending Funds	434	385	353	332	307	282	243	184	113	95	92	77	62	41	37	**26f**
Credit from Monetary Authorities	1,080	1,076	555	605	911	51	50	51	54	55	50	51	54	52	55	**26g**
Capital Accounts	13,138	13,378	14,395	15,254	16,063	16,838	17,516	19,563	21,616	23,273	25,435	29,883	31,910	34,226	36,769	**27a**
Other Items (Net)	16,684	18,422	20,104	21,607	23,963	25,642	27,455	27,331	28,971	29,733	30,980	32,560	34,685	35,592	36,578	**27r**
Monetary Survey																
End of Period																
Foreign Assets (Net)	49,148	51,552	56,755	55,545	64,050	63,093	62,603	57,515	63,931	63,654	62,431	62,641	67,078	88,099	120,586	**31n**
Domestic Credit	38,839	41,617	44,872	43,466	45,800	51,400	54,229	65,207	69,841	78,178	90,607	102,221	111,489	110,925	111,182	**32**
Claims on Central Govt. (Net)	−2,482	−3,666	−3,650	−7,116	−7,636	−5,943	−9,284	−7,170	−10,299	−8,159	−7,535	−8,893	−7,464	−18,024	−28,069	**32an x**
Claims on Official Entities	704	1,058	785	1,187	1,323	1,421	2,791	5,869	5,840	5,064	5,511	5,236	5,581	5,780	5,258	**32bx**
Claims on Private Sector	38,983	42,504	46,100	46,913	50,636	53,729	57,708	63,852	71,774	78,943	89,942	102,435	110,297	119,852	130,578	**32d**
Claims on Other Financial Insts	1,634	1,721	1,637	2,482	1,477	2,193	3,014	2,656	2,526	2,330	2,689	3,443	3,075	3,317	3,415	**32f**
Money	10,096	10,753	11,056	10,762	13,012	14,981	18,174	19,183	20,824	22,266	25,368	27,784	30,252	34,067	39,464	**34**
Quasi-Money	44,844	47,403	52,132	47,246	53,432	54,530	50,241	54,635	60,537	64,676	69,437	71,000	79,847	92,902	116,981	**35**
Other Items (Net)	33,047	35,013	38,439	41,001	43,405	44,982	48,417	48,904	52,410	54,885	58,233	66,076	68,468	72,055	75,323	**37r**
Money plus Quasi-Money	54,940	58,156	63,188	58,008	66,444	69,511	68,415	73,818	81,361	86,942	94,805	98,784	110,099	126,969	156,445	**35l**
Production																
Period Averages																
Crude Petroleum	65.4	68.5	85.6	94.3	109.2	104.0	99.8	99.4	100.0	100.4	102.4	100.8	103.6	....	....	**66aa**

United Arab Emirates

		1972	1973	1974	1975	1976	1977	1978	1979	1980	1981	1982	1983	1984	1985	1986
International Transactions															*Millions of US Dollars*	
Exports	70..d	1,157	1,807	6,414	7,262	9,535	9,636	9,126	13,652	20,676	21,238	16,837	14,672	14,192	14,043	12,387
Imports, c.i.f.	71..d	482	821	1,705	2,685	3,337	5,055	5,371	6,966	8,746	9,646	9,440	8,294	6,936	6,549	6,422
Volume of Exports															*1985=100*	
Crude Petroleum	72aa	10.8	135.4	149.9	151.7	173.9	178.8	163.7	163.7	153.4	134.4	113.3	†105.6	100.4	100.0	124.8
Export Prices															*1985=100:*	
Crude Petroleum *(Murban)*	76aa d	15.4	17.7	†68.1	64.7	72.1	77.9	80.1	184.9	222.3	212.6	196.9	176.5	†170.6	164.4	81.0
Government Finance															*Millions of Dirhams:*	
Deficit (-) or Surplus	80	37	30	62	590	596	–211	–503	202	2,302	2,355	....	....	....	....	....
Revenue	81	5	17	21	51	96	259	204	252	269	201	....	....	....	....	....
Grants Received	81z	196	403	780	1,722	3,006	5,736	6,780	8,610	17,339	22,259	....	....	....	....	....
Expenditure	82	164	390	734	1,157	2,144	5,068	6,815	8,132	13,332	18,666	19,980	16,310	15,669	....	....
Lending Minus Repayments	83	—	—	4	26	361	1,138	672	528	1,974	1,439	....	....	....	....	....
Financing																
Domestic	84a	–37	–30	–62	–590	–596	211	503	–202	–2,302	–2,355	....	....	....	....	....
Foreign	85a	—	—	—	—	—	—	—	—	—	—	....	....	....	....	....
National Accounts															*Billions of Dirhams*	
Househ.Cons.Expend.,incl.NPISHs	96f	.9	1.5	2.2	6.2	7.7	11.6	12.5	15.2	19.0	24.9	26.8	27.5	27.5	28.3	31.6
Government Consumption Expend.	91f	.9	1.3	2.7	3.3	4.6	7.4	8.2	9.6	12.0	21.5	22.0	19.0	17.7	19.5	17.5
Gross Fixed Capital Formation	93e	1.8	2.1	4.1	12.1	16.6	22.7	25.8	28.4	30.1	30.6	31.7	31.7	29.1	24.5	23.4
Changes in Inventories	93i	—	.8	.7	—	.4	2.1	–2.3	–.8	1.0	1.2	.5	.5	.3	.5	.5
Exports of Goods and Services	90c	5.5	9.4	29.4	29.5	36.6	41.8	40.2	57.2	85.6	83.7	71.6	60.9	59.8	57.7	37.9
Imports of Goods and Services (-)	98c	2.5	3.7	8.0	11.6	14.8	22.3	23.9	29.7	37.9	40.8	40.2	36.7	32.7	31.3	31.7
Gross Domestic Product (GDP)	99b	6.6	11.4	31.1	39.5	51.1	63.3	60.5	79.9	109.8	121.1	112.4	102.9	101.7	99.2	79.2
															Millions:	
Population	99z	.34	.42	.49	.51	.59	.69	.79	.92	1.01	1.10	1.17	1.21	†1.31	1.38	1.44

	1987	1988	1989	1990	1991	1992	1993	1994	1995	1996	1997	1998	1999	2000	2001		
																International Transactions	
Millions of US Dollars																	
	14,165	13,934	17,596	23,544	24,436	24,756	....	....	....	....	....	....	....	....	....	Exports	**70..d**
	7,226	8,522	10,010	11,199	13,746	17,410	19,520	21,024	20,984	22,638	29,952	24,728	33,231	38,139	....	Imports, c.i.f.	**71..d**
1985=100																Volume of Exports	
	128.4	134.5	....	....	....	....	....	....	....	....	....	....	....	....	....	Crude Petroleum	**72aa**
Index of Prices in US Dollars																Export Prices	
	105.2	82.8	97.9	128.5	103.0	106.3	92.4	92.0	100.0	114.9	112.2	75.0	105.9	161.7	140.8	Crude Petroleum (Murban)	**76aa d**
Year Ending December 31																**Government Finance**	
	−624	−314	−780	456	−625	1,050	−323	74	−1,249	620	897	−532	57	....	....	Deficit (-) or Surplus	**80**
	2,769	1,921	1,355	1,971	1,626	4,110	2,975	3,316	3,876	5,017	5,609	5,938	6,863	....	....	Revenue	**81**
	9,865	10,950	11,332	12,927	12,997	12,511	12,273	12,731	12,708	12,555	13,403	13,318	13,371	....	....	Grants Received	**81z**
	13,258	13,185	13,467	14,442	15,248	15,571	15,571	15,973	17,833	16,952	18,050	19,170	20,050	....	....	Expenditure	**82**
	—	—	—	—	—	—	—	—	—	—	65	618	127	....	....	Lending Minus Repayments	**83**
																Financing	
	624	314	780	−456	625	−1,050	323	−73	1,249	−620	−897	532	−57	....	....	Domestic	**84a**
	—	—	—	—	—	—	—	—	—	—	—	—	—	....	....	Foreign	**85a**
Billions of Dirhams																**National Accounts**	
	33.8	38.7	41.9	46.7	51.4	57.9	57.7	60.7	69.3	74.4	86.2	90.7	....	....	....	Househ.Cons.Expend.,incl.NPISHs	**96f**
	17.8	18.5	20.1	20.1	21.1	22.8	23.4	24.2	25.4	26.2	28.1	28.6	....	....	....	Government Consumption Expend.	**91f**
	20.3	20.8	22.4	24.1	25.8	29.8	36.4	37.5	39.8	40.9	48.8	49.2	....	....	....	Gross Fixed Capital Formation	**93e**
	.6	.9	1.2	1.3	1.4	1.6	1.9	2.0	2.1	2.3	2.2	2.2	....	....	....	Changes in Inventories	**93i**
	48.5	46.8	59.4	82.0	84.2	92.0	98.4	104.8	109.4	125.8	128.6	115.0	....	....	....	Exports of Goods and Services	**90c**
	34.0	38.8	44.9	50.6	59.4	74.1	87.3	94.6	99.0	105.9	112.7	115.0	....	....	....	Imports of Goods and Services (-)	**98c**
	87.0	86.9	100.1	123.5	124.5	130.0	130.4	134.6	147.0	163.8	181.2	170.7	....	....	....	Gross Domestic Product (GDP)	**99b**
Midyear Estimates																	
	1.50	1.79	1.86	1.92	2.09	2.16	2.10	2.29	2.31	2.44	2.62	2.78	2.94	2.61	2.65	**Population**	**99z**

(See notes in the back of the book.)

United Kingdom

112

		1972	1973	1974	1975	1976	1977	1978	1979	1980	1981	1982	1983	1984	1985	1986
Exchange Rates															*SDRs per Pound:*	
Market Rate	ac	†2.1627	1.9258	1.9182	1.7285	1.4653	1.5691	1.5616	1.6883	1.8700	1.6392	1.4636	1.3855	1.1798	1.3151	1.2055
															US Dollars per Pound:	
Market Rate	ag	†2.3481	2.3232	2.3485	2.0235	1.7024	1.9060	2.0345	2.2240	2.3850	1.9080	1.6145	1.4506	1.1565	1.4445	1.4745
Market Rate	rh	2.5018	2.4522	2.3390	2.2218	1.8062	1.7455	1.9195	2.1216	2.3263	2.0279	1.7505	1.5170	1.3363	1.2963	1.4670
												ECUs per Pound through 1998; Euros per Pound Beginning 1999:					
Euro Rate	ec	....	....	....	....	....	....	....	1.5445	1.8062	1.7652	1.6659	1.6398	1.6251	1.3794
Euro Rate	ed	....	....	....	....	....	....	....	....	....	....	1.8136	1.7846	1.7072	1.6932	1.6989	1.4948
															Index Numbers (1995=100):	
Market Rate	ahx	158.5	155.4	148.2	140.8	114.4	110.6	121.6	134.4	147.4	128.5	110.9	96.1	84.7	82.1	92.9
Nominal Effective Exchange Rate	neu	195.3	173.3	167.6	153.0	132.5	125.8	126.4	133.2	146.7	150.8	145.2	136.3	131.3	131.2	119.6
Real Effective Exchange Rate	reu	....	....	....	84.5	77.7	76.4	87.0	99.6	†119.1	127.6	122.0	113.6	109.4	108.9	100.9
Fund Position															*Millions of SDRs:*	
Quota	2f.s	2,800	2,800	2,800	2,800	2,800	2,800	2,925	2,925	4,388	4,388	4,388	6,194	6,194	6,194	6,194
SDRs	1b.s	604	600	688	696	603	501	415	965	447	852	1,061	494	507	1,030	1,270
Reserve Position in the Fund	1c.s	116	117	206	304	—	—	—	—	1,045	1,236	1,408	2,010	2,012	1,810	1,621
of which: Outstg.Fund Borrowing	2c	—	—	—	—	—	—	—	—	—	—	—	—	—	—	—
Total Fund Cred.&Loans Outstg.	2tl	—	—	—	—	1,700	3,340	1,805	813	563	313	52	—	—	—	—
International Liquidity													*Billions of US Dollars Unless Otherwise Indicated:*				
Total Reserves minus Gold	1l.d	4.85	5.59	6.04	4.60	3.37	20.11	16.03	19.74	20.65	15.24	12.40	11.34	9.44	12.86	18.42
SDRs	1b.d	.66	.72	.84	.82	.70	.61	.54	1.27	.57	.99	1.17	.52	.50	1.13	1.55
Reserve Position in the Fund	1c.d	.13	.14	.25	.36	—	—	—	—	1.33	1.44	1.55	2.10	1.97	1.99	1.98
Foreign Exchange	1d.d	4.06	4.72	4.94	3.43	2.67	19.50	15.49	18.47	18.75	12.81	9.67	8.72	6.97	9.74	14.89
Other Liquid Foreign Assets	1e.d	....	....	....	....	....	....	....	....	....	....	....	....	....	....	....
Gold (Million Fine Troy Ounces)	1ad	21.08	21.01	21.03	21.03	21.03	22.23	22.83	18.25	18.84	19.03	19.01	19.01	19.03	19.03	19.01
Gold (National Valuation)	1and	.80	.89	†.89	.89	.89	.94	.96	3.26	6.99	7.33	4.56	5.91	5.48	4.31	4.90
Banking Insts: Foreign Assets	7a.d	63.91	94.13	115.34	133.60	154.71	†178.47	226.50	297.05	370.75	450.23	481.56	504.85	509.54	†574.75	696.97
Foreign Liabs.	7b.d	64.23	95.35	117.96	134.39	153.12	†179.76	222.07	297.96	369.69	†438.94	476.13	505.29	523.36	608.47	738.03
Monetary Authorities															*Billions of Pounds:*	
Foreign Assets	11	2.66	2.64	2.51	1.95	†2.43	10.72	7.69	10.13	11.49	12.22	10.51	12.27	13.55	10.75	†16.74
Claims on Central Govt. (Net)	12an	7.98	9.18	11.03	11.41	†9.33	2.05	6.52	5.41	4.66	4.40	7.23	6.35	3.98	9.16	†8.67
Claims on Private Sector	12d	....	....	....	....	....	....	....	....	....	....	....	....	....	....	....
Reserve Money	14	5.42	7.13	7.41	8.16	9.78	10.30	11.30	12.41	12.05	12.51	13.05	13.41	11.95	12.72	†17.03
of which: Currency Outside DMBs	14a	4.08	4.38	5.09	5.81	6.58	7.56	8.73	9.51	10.24	†10.69	11.22	†11.01	9.16	9.84	†13.39
Foreign Liabilities	16c	4.59	4.21	5.39	4.73	†1.92	2.15	2.19	2.40	3.28	3.25	3.77	4.04	4.31	5.98	†7.92
Other Items (Net)	17r	.63	.48	.74	.47	.06	.32	.71	.73	.82	.85	.92	1.17	1.27	1.21	†.46
Banking Institutions															*Billions of Pounds:*	
Reserves	20	1.56	3.00	2.61	2.68	3.56	3.15	3.04	3.44	2.39	2.38	2.56	2.41	2.79	2.88	3.55
Foreign Assets	21	25.61	38.13	46.22	†62.14	85.53	88.13	105.93	128.68	150.86	225.02	285.59	339.91	435.15	403.28	479.73
Claims on Central Govt. (Net)	22an	2.65	20.59	21.83	29.20	31.24	34.39	33.30	35.95	42.49	†60.58	54.38	46.90	50.65	41.50	7.18
Claims on Official Entities	22bx	5.23	6.31	6.46	8.14	8.96	9.42	9.41	10.41	12.33	†15.87	14.27	12.01	13.11	10.16	7.22
Claims on Private Sector	22d	19.43	26.38	31.04	†30.94	35.42	39.34	44.84	53.61	63.73	†83.04	100.38	119.74	146.54	167.39	†318.45
Demand,Time,Savings,Fgn.Cur.Dep.	25l	21.91	28.77	32.34	†34.20	38.02	41.42	47.39	53.62	64.55	†84.79	95.18	106.31	121.65	135.69	167.94
Foreign Liabilities	26c	27.60	41.42	50.69	67.02	90.77	95.17	110.52	135.82e	157.16	232.32	295.38	350.71	453.62	416.01	493.40
Other Items (Net)	27r	3.48	4.36	4.82	†6.27	7.72	8.18	9.01	9.90	11.27	†14.52	16.91	22.13	27.32	38.15	41.42
Banking Survey															*Billions of Pounds:*	
Foreign Assets (Net)	31n	–3.92	–4.86	–7.34	†–7.65	†–4.73	1.52	.91	.59	1.91	1.67	–3.06	–2.56	–9.23	–7.97	–4.91
Domestic Credit	32	33.79	42.60	50.04	†54.07	56.76	55.56	64.45	72.63	84.40	†108.62	126.55	143.18	168.63	192.84	225.22
Claims on Central Govt. (Net)	32an	25.58	29.77	32.86	40.61	40.57	36.44	39.82	41.36	47.15	†12.45	14.37	13.50	11.25	17.05	12.93
Claims on Official Entities	32bx	5.59	6.75	6.91	8.71	9.58	10.08	10.07	†11.13	13.20	†16.98	15.27	12.85	14.02	10.87	†7.73
Claims on Private Sector	32d	19.43	26.38	31.04	†30.94	35.42	39.34	44.84	53.61	63.73	†83.04	100.38	119.74	146.54	167.39	†318.45
Money Plus Quasi-Money	35l	25.99	33.14	37.43	†40.10	44.74	48.99	56.12	63.13	74.79	†93.62	106.40	117.32	130.81	145.52	178.36
Other Items (Net)	37r	3.89	4.59	5.28	†6.32	7.28	8.09	9.24	10.09	11.53	†14.73	17.10	23.30	28.59	39.35	41.96
Money plus Quasi-Money	35l	25.99	33.14	37.43	†40.10	44.74	48.99	56.12	63.13	74.79	†93.62	106.40	117.32	130.81	145.52	178.36
Money (National Definitions)															*Billions of Pounds:*	
M0	59mc	5.05	5.59	6.45	7.19	7.99	9.12	10.36	11.62	12.24	12.56	12.95	13.85	14.62	15.16	15.95
M4	59md	....	....	....	....	....	....	....	....	....	....	154.91	175.30	198.93	224.79	257.89
															Millions of Pounds:	
M0, Seasonally Adjusted	59mc c	555	494	819	689	762	1,017	1,190	1,188	650	589	376	755	708	531	749
M4, Seasonally Adjusted	59md c	....	....	....	....	....	....	....	....	....	....	....	20,146	23,072	26,291	35,131
Interest Rates															*Percent Per Annum*	
Money Market Rate	60b	3.45	1.92	4.63	6.08	5.54	2.13	7.72	10.73	15.38	13.13	11.97	9.84	9.46	12.56	10.70
Treasury Bill Rate	60c	5.51	9.29	11.37	10.18	11.15	7.66	8.51	13.00	15.12	12.99	11.38	9.59	9.30	11.60	10.34
Treas. Bill Rate(Bond Equivalent)	60cs	....	....	....	10.56	11.62	8.06	8.74	13.40	15.75	13.43	11.96	9.93	9.61	12.00	10.77
Eurodollar Rate in London	60d	5.46	9.16	11.01	6.99	5.58	6.05	8.78	12.01	14.06	16.83	13.13	9.61	10.78	8.33	6.76
Deposit Rate	60l	4.15	8.02	9.50	7.08	7.54	4.90	6.08	11.71	14.13	10.67	12.42	11.19	7.27	11.79	9.85
Lending Rate	60p	7.50	8.00	9.00	9.00	9.00	9.75	9.25	13.92	16.17	13.25	11.80	9.79	9.68	12.33	10.83
Govt. Bond Yield: Short-Term	61a	7.55	10.41	12.51	11.48	12.06	10.08	11.32	12.64	13.84	14.65	12.79	11.19	11.29	11.13	10.01
Long-Term	61	8.90	10.71	14.77	14.39	14.43	12.73	12.47	12.99	13.79	14.74	12.88	10.81	10.42	10.50	9.86
Prices, Production, Labor															*Index Numbers (1995=100):*	
Industrial Share Prices	62	12.1	10.5	6.2	7.7	9.2	11.8	13.3	15.1	16.2	18.2	21.1	26.7	31.8	39.2	48.6
Prices: Manufacturing Output	63	18.1	19.5	19.8	24.3	28.4	33.7	36.8	41.1	47.7	52.8	57.3	61.0	64.6	68.6	69.5
Consumer Prices	64	14.6	15.9	†18.5	22.9	26.7	31.0	33.5	38.0	44.8	50.2	54.5	57.0	59.8	63.4	65.6
Harmonized CPI	64h	....	....	....	....	....	....	....	....	....	....	....	....	....	....	....
Wages: Avg. Monthly Earnings	65..c	10.1	11.5	13.5	17.1	19.9	21.7	24.5	28.3	34.1	38.5	42.1	45.6	48.4	52.4	56.6
Industrial Production	66..c	70.0	76.3	74.8	70.7	73.1	76.8	79.0	82.1	76.7	74.3	75.7	78.5	78.5	82.8	84.8
Employment	67..c	94.3	96.6	97.2	96.8	96.1	94.3	97.1	104.7	101.0	97.4	95.2	95.5	96.4	96.7	96.6
															Number in Thousands:	
Labor Force	67d	....	....	....	....	....	....	....	....	....	....	....	....	....	....	....
Employment	67e	....	....	....	....	....	....	....	....	....	....	....	....	....	24,539	24,568
Unemployment	67c	....	....	....	....	....	....	....	....	....	....	....	....	....	3,076	3,293
Unemployment Rate (%)	67r	....	....	....	....	....	....	....	....	....	....	....	....	....	11.2	11.8

1987	1988	1989	1990	1991	1992	1993	1994	1995	1996	1997	1998	1999	2000	2001		
															Exchange Rates	
End of Period																
1.3192	1.3447	1.2217	1.3552	1.3078	1.0996	1.0784	1.0703	1.0427	1.1808	1.2257	1.1814	1.1777	1.1453	1.1541	Market Rate	**ac**
End of Period (ag) *Period Average (rh)*																
1.8715	1.8095	1.6055	1.9280	1.8707	1.5120	1.4812	1.5625	1.5500	1.6980	1.6538	1.6635	1.6164	1.4922	1.4504	Market Rate	**ag**
1.6389	1.7814	1.6397	1.7847	1.7694	1.7655	1.5020	1.5316	1.5785	1.5617	1.6377	1.6564	1.6182	1.5161	1.4400	Market Rate	**rh**
End of Period (ec) *Period Average (ed)*																
1.4351	1.5419	1.3463	1.4126	1.3964	1.2528	1.3225	1.2705	1.1832	1.3564	1.5011	1.4175	†1.6090	1.6037	1.6458	Euro Rate	**ec**
1.4138	1.5057	1.4872	1.4011	1.4265	1.3607	1.2822	1.2897	1.2070	1.2304	1.4452	1.4796	†1.5189	1.6456	1.6092	Euro Rate	**ed**
Period Averages																
103.8	112.9	103.9	113.1	112.1	111.9	95.2	97.0	100.0	98.9	103.8	104.9	102.5	96.0	91.2	Market Rate	**ahx**
117.1	124.2	120.6	117.8	118.8	114.3	104.8	105.1	100.0	101.7	118.5	122.5	122.3	126.7	124.7	Nominal Effective Exchange Rate	**neu**
104.6	109.7	107.2	107.9	113.0	110.1	101.4	103.6	100.0	103.6	123.5	131.3	133.6	141.0	140.6	Real Effective Exchange Rate	**reu**
															Fund Position	
End of Period																
6,194	6,194	6,194	6,194	6,194	7,415	7,415	7,415	7,415	7,415	7,415	7,415	10,739	10,739	10,739	Quota	**2f. s**
974	981	870	878	919	393	210	335	279	239	350	332	374	250	234	SDRs	**1b. s**
1,253	1,239	1,246	1,179	1,293	1,464	1,354	1,366	1,630	1,689	2,198	3,111	3,847	3,288	4,020	Reserve Position in the Fund	**1c. s**
—	—	—	—	—	—	—	—	—	—	—	382	—	—	—	*of which:* Outstg.Fund Borrowing	**2c**
—	—	—	—	—	—	—	—	—	—	—	—	—	—	—	Total Fund Cred.&Loans Outstg.	**2tl**
															International Liquidity	
End of Period																
41.72	44.10	34.77	35.85	41.89	36.64	36.78	41.01	42.02	39.90	32.32	32.21	†35.87	43.89	37.28	Total Reserves minus Gold	**1l. d**
1.38	1.32	1.14	1.25	1.31	.54	.29	.49	.41	.34	.47	.47	.51	.33	.29	SDRs	**1b. d**
1.78	1.67	1.64	1.68	1.85	2.01	1.86	1.99	2.42	2.43	2.97	4.38	5.28	4.28	5.05	Reserve Position in the Fund	**1c. d**
38.56	41.12	31.99	32.93	38.73	34.09	34.63	38.53	39.18	37.12	28.88	27.36	†30.08	39.28	31.94	Foreign Exchange	**1d. d**
....	....	....	....	....	....	....	....	....	....	....	....	7.80	8.68	10.52	Other Liquid Foreign Assets	**1e. d**
19.01	19.00	18.99	18.94	18.89	18.61	18.45	18.44	18.43	18.43	18.42	23.00	20.55	15.67	11.42	Gold (Million Fine Troy Ounces)	**1ad**
5.79	6.47	5.46	5.24	5.04	4.77	4.56	5.31	5.24	5.48	4.81	5.08	†5.96	4.27	3.16	Gold (National Valuation)	**1and**
852.59	860.15	898.98	1,041.21	†992.21	1,019.46	1,053.63	1,200.67	1,350.86	1,460.35	1,685.14	1,868.89	1,802.87	2,060.13	2,168.36	Banking Insts: Foreign Assets	**7a. d**
900.96	933.60	996.28	1,167.89	†1122.63	1,115.27	1,129.07	1,274.82	1,429.20	1,533.44	1,748.76	1,893.68	1,871.35	2,159.76	2,307.83	Foreign Liabs.	**7b. d**
															Monetary Authorities	
End of Period																
24.36	29.26	24.27	20.43	24.35	28.84	30.22	28.33	31.89	27.40	22.92	†6.52	7.98	4.34	6.24	Foreign Assets	**11**
4.00	1.79	10.22	15.60	14.24	15.90	14.97	28.53	25.07	29.86	27.63	†14.45	20.56	14.30	16.07	Claims on Central Govt. (Net)	**12an**
....	....	....	....	....	—	....	....	....	....	....	6.91	5.86	8.41	5.48	Claims on Private Sector	**12d**
18.26	20.04	21.74	22.01	22.24	23.58	25.19	26.53	28.37	29.36	31.45	†27.37	32.46	32.37	32.58	Reserve Money	**14**
14.18	15.34	16.20	16.35	16.71	17.76	18.87	19.94	21.21	22.10	23.44	†19.20	21.20	23.59	17.87	*of which:* Currency Outside DMBs	**14a**
9.41	10.39	12.13	13.10	15.48	20.22	25.99	31.86	31.16	28.36	23.60	†2.28	9.62	6.28	4.75	Foreign Liabilities	**16c**
.70	.62	.62	.92	.86	.94	−5.98	−1.52	−2.57	−.46	−4.49	†−1.77	−7.68	−11.60	−9.54	Other Items (Net)	**17r**
															Banking Institutions	
End of Period																
†4.26	5.01	5.83	5.97	5.88	6.28	6.78	7.04	7.56	7.71	8.26	8.39	11.54	9.75	8.56	Reserves	**20**
†460.81	484.11	566.13	545.18	516.71	†649.72	686.90	741.28	845.36	835.98	1,033.98	1,143.91	1,133.76	1,417.84	1,528.23	Foreign Assets	**21**
†16.16	15.28	12.07	11.37	11.14	†1.55	2.66	11.80	19.72	14.92	10.59	10.74	†8.17	−8.05	−1.94	Claims on Central Govt. (Net)	**22an**
†6.09	4.58	3.20	3.08	2.94	4.27	5.68	6.11	5.74	4.81	4.34	3.75	2.70	2.52	2.38	Claims on Official Entities	**22bx**
377.41	468.57	583.11	645.26	663.09	†684.06	707.29	745.72	829.53	912.27	973.37	1,016.75	†1094.16	1,254.50	1,368.02	Claims on Private Sector	**22d**
†323.70	378.96	457.37	507.40	515.83	†558.15	582.96	623.05	707.02	784.32	813.69	875.82	913.82	1,015.63	1,103.67	Demand,Time,Savings,Fgn.Cur.Dep.	**25l**
†473.34	510.86	608.30	589.27	563.19	†688.16	712.75	764.58	866.31	844.33	1,051.10	1,120.83	1,128.46	1,411.40	1,548.43	Foreign Liabilities	**26c**
†67.68	87.73	104.66	114.20	120.73	†98.95	113.20	123.88	133.51	146.54	172.06	186.88	208.05	249.53	253.15	Other Items (Net)	**27r**
															Banking Survey	
End of Period																
†2.42	−7.88	−30.04	−36.76	−37.63	†−29.83	−21.62	−26.82	−20.72	−9.31	−17.79	†27.31	3.66	4.50	−18.72	Foreign Assets (Net)	**31n**
†403.65	490.22	608.60	675.31	691.41	†705.78	730.61	792.16	880.07	961.86	1,015.92	†1052.60	†1131.45	1,271.68	1,390.01	Domestic Credit	**32**
†20.16	17.07	22.29	26.97	25.38	†17.45	17.64	40.34	44.79	44.78	38.22	†25.19	†28.73	6.26	14.13	Claims on Central Govt. (Net)	**32an**
6.09	4.58	3.20	3.08	2.94	4.27	5.68	6.11	5.74	4.81	4.34	3.75	2.70	2.52	2.38	Claims on Official Entities	**32bx**
377.41	468.57	583.11	645.26	663.09	†684.06	707.29	745.72	829.53	912.27	973.37	1,023.66	†1100.02	1,262.91	1,373.50	Claims on Private Sector	**32d**
†337.69	393.99	473.28	523.08	531.77	†575.91	601.83	642.99	728.23	806.42	837.13	†895.02	935.02	1,039.23	1,121.54	Money Plus Quasi-Money	**35l**
†68.38	88.35	105.28	115.12	121.59	†99.43	106.76	121.91	130.54	145.62	167.31	†184.89	†200.09	236.96	249.75	Other Items (Net)	**37r**
†337.69	393.99	473.28	523.08	531.77	†575.91	601.83	642.99	728.23	806.42	837.13	†895.02	935.02	1,039.23	1,121.54	Money plus Quasi-Money	**35l**
															Money (National Definitions)	
End of Period																
16.63	18.04	19.01	19.49	20.09	20.58	21.73	23.32	24.54	26.15	27.80	29.35	32.77	34.57	37.32	M0	**59mc**
304.37	358.37	426.19	477.14	504.13	517.88	544.06	567.16	623.39	682.79	721.98	783.24	816.43	884.96	942.01	M4	**59md**
Period Change																
638	1,203	1,005	476	557	535	1,164	1,390	1,222	1,557	1,581	1,442	3,218	1,325	2,568	M0, Seasonally Adjusted	**59mc c**
43,135	53,042	64,830	50,875	28,703	18,611	24,001	25,860	55,741	59,902	79,979	60,475	33,419	69,098	56,851	M4, Seasonally Adjusted	**59md c**
															Interest Rates	
Percent Per Annum																
9.50	10.02	13.56	14.73	11.58	9.37	5.91	4.88	6.08	5.96	6.61	7.21	5.20	5.77	5.08	Money Market Rate	**60b**
9.23	9.80	13.28	14.09	10.82	8.94	5.21	5.15	6.33	5.77	6.48	6.82	5.04	5.80	4.77	Treasury Bill Rate	**60c**
9.54	10.05	13.74	14.64	11.22	9.21	5.35	5.18	6.40	5.89	6.62	7.23	5.14	5.83	4.79	Treas. Bill Rate(Bond Equivalent)	**60cs**
7.12	7.90	9.25	8.25	5.95	3.77	3.24	4.68	5.97	5.44	5.66	5.50	5.36	6.48	3.73	Eurodollar Rate in London	**60d**
8.57	8.55	11.51	12.54	10.28	7.46	3.97	3.66	4.11	3.05	3.63	4.48	....	....	....	Deposit Rate	**60l**
9.63	10.29	13.92	14.75	11.54	9.42	5.92	5.48	6.69	5.96	6.58	7.21	5.33	5.98	5.08	Lending Rate	**60p**
9.36	9.66	10.73	12.08	10.18	8.94	6.65	7.83	7.93	7.28	6.98	5.77	5.38	5.79	5.03	Govt. Bond Yield: Short-Term	**61a**
9.47	9.36	9.58	11.08	9.92	9.12	7.87	8.05	8.26	8.10	7.09	5.45	4.70	4.68	4.78	Long-Term	**61**
															Prices, Production, Labor	
Period Averages																
64.2	57.7	69.2	67.9	74.5	77.9	89.4	96.1	100.0	113.3	128.3	150.5	....	....	....	Industrial Share Prices	**62**
71.9	74.6	78.1	83.0	87.5	90.2	93.8	96.1	100.0	102.6	103.6	104.1	105.3	108.0	....	Prices: Manufacturing Output	**63**
68.3	71.7	77.3	84.6	89.6	92.9	94.4	96.7	100.0	102.4	105.7	109.3	111.0	114.2	116.3	Consumer Prices	**64**
....	73.8	77.7	83.1	89.4	93.2	95.5	97.4	100.0	102.5	104.3	106.0	107.4	108.2	109.6	Harmonized CPI	**64h**
61.0	66.3	72.4	79.4	85.6	90.8	93.6	97.0	100.0	103.6	108.0	113.5	119.0	124.4	129.8	Wages: Avg. Monthly Earnings	**65.. c**
88.2	92.5	94.4	94.1	91.0	91.3	93.3	98.3	100.0	101.3	102.4	103.4	104.2	105.8	103.7	Industrial Production	**66.. c**
99.1	101.5	103.1	102.5	99.3	97.2	97.8	98.8	100.0	101.3	104.3	105.9	108.0	109.5	109.8	Employment	**67.. c**
Period Averages																
....	....	....	28,768	....	28,271	....	....	28,552	28,716	28,713	29,194	29,412	....	....	Labor Force	**67d**
24,930	25,860	26,689	26,935	26,400	†25,812	25,511	25,717	26,026	26,323	26,814	27,116	27,442	....	....	Employment	**67e**
2,953	†2,370	†1,799	1,665	2,292	2,779	2,919	2,636	2,326	2,122	1,602	1,362	1,263	1,102	....	Unemployment	**67c**
10.6	†8.4	†6.3	5.9	8.1	9.9	10.4	9.4	8.3	7.5	5.7	4.7	4.3	3.8	....	Unemployment Rate (%)	**67r**

United Kingdom

112

	1972	1973	1974	1975	1976	1977	1978	1979	1980	1981	1982	1983	1984	1985	1986
International Transactions															*Millions of Pounds*
Exports 70	9,602	12,087	16,309	19,607	25,277	31,990	35,380	40,637	47,357	50,998	55,558	60,684	70,488	78,392	72,988
Imports, c.i.f. 71	11,073	15,723	23,139	24,046	31,084	36,219	39,533	46,925	49,773	51,169	56,978	66,101	78,967	85,027	86,176
Imports, f.o.b. (on a BOP basis) 71.v	10,155	14,449	21,511	22,441	29,041	34,005	36,573	43,814	45,792	47,416	53,421	62,237	75,601	81,336	82,186
															1995=100
Volume of Exports 72	35.1	39.1	40.9	40.1	43.6	47.9	49.2	51.1	51.7	51.1	52.7	53.7	58.3	61.7	64.2
Volume of Imports 73	45.7	50.8	50.3	45.8	48.3	48.3	49.9	53.9	50.8	48.3	50.8	53.8	59.8	62.1	66.6
Export Prices 76	16.3	18.3	23.3	28.5	34.2	40.4	44.4	49.2	56.6	61.6	65.9	70.5	76.1	80.1	72.2
Import Prices 76.x	14.5	18.5	27.1	30.9	37.8	43.7	45.4	48.3	53.2	57.8	62.7	68.3	74.5	78.2	74.6
Balance of Payments															*Billions of US Dollars:*
Current Account, n.i.e. .... 78al *d*	.53	−2.41	−7.45	−3.47	−1.38	.15	2.16	−.78	6.86	14.13	7.98	5.29	1.83	3.31	−1.32
Goods: Exports f.o.b. .... 78aa *d*	23.51	29.11	38.11	42.47	45.03	55.32	67.12	86.02	109.62	102.16	96.66	91.96	93.49	100.86	106.43
Goods: Imports f.o.b. .... 78ab *d*	−25.35	−35.36	−50.35	−49.75	−52.10	−59.32	−70.18	−92.99	−106.27	−95.20	−93.49	−94.34	−100.60	−104.82	−120.49
Trade Balance .... 78ac *d*	−1.84	−6.26	−12.24	−7.27	−7.07	−4.00	−3.06	−6.97	3.35	6.96	3.17	−2.38	−7.11	−3.96	−14.06
Services: Credit .... 78ad *d*	10.51	12.71	15.44	16.97	17.93	20.28	24.00	30.74	36.45	34.01	30.86	29.07	28.43	31.31	37.07
Services: Debit .... 78ae *d*	−8.95	−11.03	−13.19	−14.06	−13.60	−14.62	−16.87	−22.43	−27.93	−26.31	−25.55	−23.27	−22.83	−22.96	−27.97
Balance on Goods & Services .... 78af *d*	−.29	−4.58	−9.99	−4.37	−2.74	1.65	4.06	1.33	11.87	14.66	8.47	3.42	−1.51	4.39	−4.96
Income: Credit .... 78ag *d*	8.51	12.07	14.52	14.56	15.09	15.40	21.47	37.25	55.07	74.88	77.59	64.36	68.52	66.82	69.40
Income: Debit .... 78ah *d*	−7.02	−8.81	−10.99	−12.60	−12.29	−14.94	−19.93	−34.69	−55.48	−72.34	−75.06	−60.07	−62.79	−63.93	−62.59
Balance on Gds, Serv. & Inc. .... 78ai *d*	1.21	−1.32	−6.46	−2.41	.05	2.11	5.61	3.89	11.45	17.20	11.00	7.71	4.21	7.28	1.85
Current Transfers, n.i.e.: Credit .... 78aj *d*	.66	.95	1.14	1.68	1.42	1.59	2.33	2.98	4.41	5.75	6.00	5.70	5.34	4.57	5.68
Current Transfers: Debit .... 78ak *d*	−1.34	−2.04	−2.13	−2.74	−2.85	−3.56	−5.77	−7.65	−9.01	−8.83	−9.01	−8.12	−7.72	−8.54	−8.85
Capital Account, n.i.e. .... 78bc *d*	—	—	—	—	—	—	—	—	—	—	—	—	....	....	....
Capital Account, n.i.e.: Credit .... 78ba *d*	—	—	—	—	—	—	—	—	—	—	—	—	....	....	....
Capital Account: Debit .... 78bb *d*	—	—	—	—	—	—	—	—	—	—	—	—	....	....	....
Financial Account, n.i.e. .... 78bj *d*	.50	.20	3.26	.10	−6.15	6.01	−8.19	1.04	−7.49	−19.51	−6.85	−8.58	−12.49	−1.79	−1.18
Direct Investment Abroad .... 78bd *d*	−2.02	−4.98	−4.38	−3.00	−4.34	−4.17	−6.82	−12.54	−11.23	−12.15	−7.16	−8.18	−7.98	−10.61	−17.02
Dir. Invest. in Rep. Econ., n.i.e. .... 78be *d*	1.21	2.72	4.37	3.32	3.01	4.43	3.79	6.47	10.12	5.88	5.41	5.18	−.35	5.48	8.57
Portfolio Investment Assets .... 78bf *d*	−1.51	.68	1.70	−.12	.13	.02	−2.06	−1.90	−7.79	−9.20	−13.21	−11.17	−14.70	−20.35	−33.79
Equity Securities .... 78bk *d*	−1.51	.68	1.70	−.12	.13	.02	−2.06	−1.90	−7.79	−6.66	−7.46	−5.40	−.05	−5.61	−8.83
Debt Securities .... 78bl *d*										−2.53	−5.75	−5.77	−14.65	−14.74	−24.97
Portfolio Investment Liab., n.i.e. .... 78bg *d*	1.25	.27	2.88	−1.00	−.35	2.97	−.40	3.03	2.88	.15	.01	2.55	.46	2.80	37.19
Equity Securities .... 78bm *d*	.44	.56	.34	.01	.47	.73	.01	.75	.46	.56	.09	1.45	1.38	3.73	7.81
Debt Securities .... 78bn *d*	.82	−.29	2.55	−1.02	−.82	2.24	−.42	2.28	2.43	−.41	−.08	1.10	−.92	−.93	29.37
Financial Derivatives Assets .... 78bw *d*	....	....	....	....	....	....	....	....	....	....	....	....	....	....	....
Financial Derivatives Liabilities ...... 78bx *d*	....	....	....	....	....	....	....	....	....	....	....	....	....	....	....
Other Investment Assets .... 78bh *d*	−.63	−2.49	−3.68	−1.99	−4.62	−3.26	−4.07	−69.84	−81.22	−86.31	−37.57	−27.36	−22.50	−31.88	−79.90
Monetary Authorities .... 78bo *d*															
General Government .... 78bp *d*	1.14	−.90	−1.28	−1.37	−1.20	−.68	−.35	−.28	.82	.20	−.28	−.72	−1.00	−.94	−.75
Banks .... 78bq *d*	−.98	−.36	−.47	−.46	−1.25	−.68	−2.27	−65.10	−76.38	−80.65	−35.26	−28.05	−18.10	−30.76	−78.70
Other Sectors .... 78br *d*	−.79	−1.23	−1.93	−.15	−2.17	−1.90	−1.45	−4.46	−5.67	−5.86	−2.03	1.41	−3.40	−.19	−.45
Other Investment Liab., n.i.e. .... 78bi *d*	2.19	4.00	2.36	2.90	.02	6.04	1.38	75.82	79.74	82.13	45.67	30.40	32.57	52.77	83.77
Monetary Authorities .... 78bs *d*	.49	.22	−.43	.18	−.27	−.22	.03	−.06	.01	.04	−.03	−.03	—	—	—
General Government .... 78bt *d*	−.17	−.09	−.18	−.08	.12	.16	.41	.49	−.66	−.16	.65	−.97	−.24	.01	.04
Banks .... 78bu *d*	.66	1.91	1.04	1.34	−.90	3.51	−.93	73.27	79.38	80.35	43.67	32.91	35.09	48.20	77.92
Other Sectors .... 78bv *d*	1.22	1.96	1.92	1.45	1.07	2.59	1.86	2.11	1.00	1.89	1.38	−1.51	−2.28	4.57	5.82
Net Errors and Omissions .... 78ca *d*	−2.46	.31	.33	—	.74	6.65	3.43	1.89	1.93	1.79	−3.79	1.52	9.65	1.04	6.16
Overall Balance .... 78cb *d*	−1.43	−1.90	−3.86	−3.36	−6.79	12.80	−2.59	2.14	1.30	−3.59	−2.65	−1.76	−1.01	2.57	3.65
Reserves and Related Items .... 79da *d*	1.43	1.90	3.86	3.36	6.79	−12.80	2.59	−2.14	−1.30	3.59	2.65	1.76	1.01	−2.57	−3.65
Reserve Assets .... 79db *d*	1.97	−.58	−.26	1.42	1.41	−16.71	4.32	−1.76	−.22	5.03	2.42	.91	1.01	−2.57	−3.65
Use of Fund Credit and Loans .... 79dc *d*	−.54	—	—	—	1.98	1.90	−1.96	−1.27	−.33	−.30	−.29	−.06	—	—	—
Exceptional Financing .... 79de *d*	—	2.48	4.11	1.95	3.40	2.00	.23	.89	−.75	−1.13	.52	.91	—	—	—
International Investment Position															*Billions of US Dollars*
Assets .... 79aa *d*	...	...	...	...	...	...	...	...	550.82	630.33	671.78	705.65	721.39	857.50	1,062.88
Direct Investment Abroad .... 79ab *d*	...	...	...	...	...	...	...	...	79.21	85.72	84.02	83.88	86.88	100.31	118.95
Portfolio Investment .... 79ac *d*	...	...	...	...	...	...	...	...	45.55	49.18	66.06	86.60	106.09	153.64	216.67
Equity Securities .... 79ad *d*	...	...	...	...	...	...	...	...	32.03	34.71	43.08	57.87	55.47	81.89	120.36
Debt Securities .... 79ae *d*	...	...	...	...	...	...	...	...	13.52	14.47	22.98	28.72	50.62	71.75	96.31
Financial Derivatives .... 79al *d*	...	...	...	...	...	...	...	...							
Other Investment .... 79af *d*	...	...	...	...	...	...	...	...	394.41	472.60	500.80	516.60	513.13	584.48	701.55
Monetary Authorities .... 79ag *d*	...	...	...	...	...	...	...	...							
General Government .... 79ah *d*	...	...	...	...	...	...	...	...	11.21	9.82	10.13	9.79	6.75	9.48	10.38
Banks .... 79ai *d*	...	...	...	...	...	...	...	...	352.32	429.54	459.08	482.33	450.34	512.30	625.20
Other Sectors .... 79aj *d*	...	...	...	...	...	...	...	...	30.87	33.24	31.59	24.48	56.04	62.69	65.96
Reserve Assets .... 79ak *d*	...	...	...	...	...	...	...	...	31.66	22.83	20.90	18.57	15.29	19.07	25.72
Liabilities .... 79li *d*	...	...	...	...	...	...	...	...	507.67	568.04	601.55	625.05	630.83	755.01	915.87
Dir. Invest. in Rep. Economy........... 79lb *d*	...	...	...	...	...	...	...	...	63.01	57.26	52.15	54.01	46.38	64.03	76.29
Portfolio Investment .... 79lc *d*	...	...	...	...	...	...	...	...	28.15	23.52	24.61	26.51	112.05	124.78	157.57
Equity Securities .... 79ld *d*	...	...	...	...	...	...	...	...	11.46	8.49	8.86	11.31	12.74	22.89	36.97
Debt Securities .... 79le *d*	...	...	...	...	...	...	...	...	16.69	15.03	15.75	15.20	99.31	101.89	120.60
Financial Derivatives .... 79ll *d*	...	...	...	...	...	...	...	...							
Other Investment .... 79lf *d*	...	...	...	...	...	...	...	...	416.51	487.25	524.79	544.54	472.40	566.20	682.00
Monetary Authorities .... 79lg *d*	...	...	...	...	...	...	...	...	3.75	3.16	3.40	2.31	—	—	—
General Government .... 79lh *d*	...	...	...	...	...	...	...	...	4.13	3.59	3.51	3.45	4.14	4.45	5.30
Banks .... 79li *d*	...	...	...	...	...	...	...	...	374.19	447.76	485.96	514.87	439.25	525.76	632.47
Other Sectors .... 79lj *d*	...	...	...	...	...	...	...	...	34.43	32.74	31.93	23.90	29.01	35.99	44.24

International Transactions

Millions of Pounds

	1987	1988	1989	1990	1991	1992	1993	1994	1995	1996	1997	1998	1999	2000	2001	
Exports	79,849	81,655	93,771	103,692	104,877	108,508	120,936	133,030	153,353	167,764	171,595	164,066	165,739	186,171	185,673	70
Imports, c.i.f.	94,026	106,571	121,699	126,086	118,786	125,867	137,404	147,564	168,055	184,113	187,135	189,532	196,504	221,027	222,944	71
Imports, f.o.b. (on a BOP basis)	90,735	101,826	116,837	120,527	113,697	120,447	134,858	145,793	164,659	179,578	183,124	....	....	....	....	71.v

1995=100

	1987	1988	1989	1990	1991	1992	1993	1994	1995	1996	1997	1998	1999	2000	2001	
Volume of Exports	67.7	69.4	73.1	77.8	78.2	80.0	80.1	90.5	100.0	108.2	116.5	118.4	123.8	137.8	140.2	72
Volume of Imports	71.2	81.0	87.4	87.8	83.3	88.4	88.8	94.3	100.0	110.1	120.4	132.0	142.1	158.9	164.4	73
Export Prices	74.7	75.5	78.9	81.7	82.8	84.5	95.0	96.9	100.0	100.7	95.3	90.3	89.5	92.9	93.0	76
Import Prices	76.8	76.1	79.3	81.2	82.2	82.9	91.2	94.3	100.0	99.8	93.2	87.6	86.4	90.1	89.8	76.x

Balance of Payments

Minus Sign Indicates Debit

	1987	1988	1989	1990	1991	1992	1993	1994	1995	1996	1997	1998	1999	2000	2001	
Current Account, n.i.e.	-12.59	-35.33	-43.11	-38.81	-19.02	-23.42	-17.97	-10.23	-14.29	-13.44	-2.85	-7.96	-31.94	-28.82	-29.37	78ald
Goods: Exports f.o.b.	130.47	143.73	151.44	182.80	183.51	189.37	183.31	207.19	242.32	261.25	281.54	271.72	268.88	284.38	275.95	78aad
Goods: Imports f.o.b.	-149.68	-182.02	-192.06	-215.35	-201.67	-212.70	-202.96	-224.14	-261.32	-282.48	-301.74	-307.85	-313.18	-330.27	-324.20	78abd
Trade Balance	-19.21	-38.29	-40.62	-32.55	-18.17	-23.33	-19.65	-16.95	-19.01	-21.23	-20.20	-36.13	-44.29	-45.89	-48.25	78acd
Services: Credit	44.26	47.67	47.38	56.42	56.28	64.02	62.14	69.54	78.78	87.34	97.72	107.23	113.94	116.81	110.55	78add
Services: Debit	-33.14	-39.73	-41.40	-48.74	-49.00	-54.52	-52.31	-59.77	-65.41	-72.28	-77.20	-86.26	-94.84	-98.71	-94.60	78aed
Balance on Goods & Services	-8.09	-30.35	-34.63	-24.86	-10.89	-13.84	-9.82	-7.18	-5.64	-6.17	.32	-15.15	-25.19	-27.80	-32.29	78afd
Income: Credit	77.78	99.41	119.53	139.84	133.69	117.27	109.38	113.97	138.87	144.49	157.74	171.92	163.10	204.36	201.40	78agd
Income: Debit	-76.40	-98.09	-120.74	-144.99	-139.63	-116.99	-109.67	-108.86	-135.59	-142.72	-151.40	-151.09	-159.04	-190.25	-188.18	78ahd
Balance on Gds, Serv. & Inc.	-6.72	-29.02	-35.84	-30.02	-16.83	-13.56	-10.11	-2.08	-2.35	-4.39	6.66	5.68	-21.13	-13.68	-19.07	78aid
Current Transfers, n.i.e.: Credit	9.58	11.96	12.10	16.87	25.08	21.98	18.59	17.71	19.70	29.46	21.44	20.59	22.70	18.66	23.30	78ajd
Current Transfers: Debit	-15.46	-18.27	-19.36	-25.66	-27.27	-31.84	-26.45	-25.86	-31.64	-38.51	-30.95	-34.23	-33.51	-33.80	-33.60	78akd
Capital Account, n.i.e.	.55	.42	.45	.89	.50	.75	.46	.05	.84	1.14	1.32	.79	1.52	2.76	2.15	78bcd
Capital Account, n.i.e.: Credit	1.49	1.55	1.59	2.07	1.91	2.16	1.67	1.93	1.84	2.18	2.77	2.44	2.91	4.36	4.06	78bad
Capital Account: Debit	-.94	-1.13	-1.13	-1.18	-1.40	-1.42	-1.21	-1.88	-.99	-1.04	-1.45	-1.65	-1.38	-1.60	-1.91	78bbd
Financial Account, n.i.e.	36.95	35.76	22.72	26.50	14.83	1.91	22.68	4.71	7.47	7.98	-12.16	.23	30.97	26.17	23.30	78bjd
Direct Investment Abroad	-31.77	-37.77	-35.92	-20.12	-16.75	-19.70	-27.25	-34.90	-45.31	-34.82	-62.44	-122.06	-201.57	-266.25	-34.24	78bdd
Dir. Invest. in Rep. Econ., n.i.e.	15.92	22.57	31.65	33.50	16.45	16.56	16.52	10.73	21.73	27.39	37.38	74.65	89.53	119.93	63.11	78bed
Portfolio Investment Assets	9.22	-21.18	-63.01	-29.95	-56.90	-49.27	-133.55	31.47	-61.69	-93.13	-84.99	-52.98	-33.09	-99.89	-134.34	78bfd
Equity Securities	4.75	-9.67	-25.64	-1.10	-24.47	7.43	-11.92	-1.47	-13.15	-16.30	7.04	-4.65	-23.37	-28.66	-68.34	78bkd
Debt Securities	4.46	-11.51	-37.37	-28.86	-32.44	-56.70	-121.63	32.95	-48.55	-76.83	-92.03	-48.33	-9.72	-71.23	-66.00	78bld
Portfolio Investment Liab., n.i.e.	59.14	53.68	29.91	23.76	18.22	16.19	43.63	47.01	58.79	67.98	43.46	35.28	186.06	258.34	63.88	78bgd
Equity Securities	19.22	9.62	11.13	3.44	4.68	18.26	26.12	7.35	8.07	9.40	7.85	63.09	116.04	179.17	25.99	78bmd
Debt Securities	39.92	44.06	18.78	20.32	13.54	-2.07	17.52	39.66	50.72	58.58	35.61	-27.82	70.02	79.17	37.89	78bnd
Financial Derivatives Assets	....	....	....	....	....											78bwd
Financial Derivatives Liabilities						2.25	.37	3.67	2.63	1.52	1.90	-5.07	4.41	2.26	2.15	78bxd
Other Investment Assets	-84.60	-36.58	-57.48	-94.79	35.29	-60.51	-68.46	-42.45	-74.90	-215.31	-275.87	-26.84	-94.07	-411.53	-259.02	78bhd
Monetary Authorities	....															78bod
General Government	-.76	-1.09	-1.00	-1.61	-1.20	-.71	-.71	-.69	-.74	-.53	-.07	.25	-1.93	-.42	.02	78bpd
Banks	-79.89	-30.96	-48.22	-68.34	52.69	-36.40	6.48	-72.66	-34.91	-102.10	-241.01	-28.36	19.99	-291.77	-125.86	78bqd
Other Sectors	-3.96	-4.53	-8.26	-24.84	-16.20	-23.40	-74.23	30.90	-39.25	-112.68	-34.79	1.28	-112.14	-119.34	-133.18	78brd
Other Investment Liab., n.i.e.	69.04	55.04	117.57	114.10	18.52	96.39	191.42	-10.81	106.22	254.36	328.40	97.24	79.70	423.31	311.71	78bid
Monetary Authorities																78bsd
General Government	.60	.14	.05	-.46	-1.36	-.51	.34	.86	.59	-1.06	-1.74	.42	.54	—	.12	78btd
Banks	67.00	49.37	81.45	93.70	-16.76	55.95	59.49	76.62	41.95	111.45	243.06	78.16	16.41	308.92	183.58	78bud
Other Sectors	1.43	5.53	36.07	20.86	36.64	40.95	131.58	-88.29	63.68	143.97	87.09	18.66	62.75	114.39	128.01	78bvd
Net Errors and Omissions	-5.77	3.74	12.52	11.47	8.39	14.10	.27	6.98	5.13	3.66	9.79	6.68	-1.58	5.19	-.54	78cad
Overall Balance	19.13	4.59	-7.42	.04	4.70	-6.67	5.44	1.50	-.85	-.65	-3.90	-.26	-1.04	5.30	-4.45	78cbd
Reserves and Related Items	-19.13	-4.59	7.42	-.04	-4.70	6.67	-5.44	-1.50	.85	.65	3.90	.26	1.04	-5.30	4.45	79dad
Reserve Assets	-20.10	-4.45	8.41	-.13	-4.66	2.43	-1.26	-1.48	.90	.65	3.90	.26	1.04	-5.30	4.45	79dbd
Use of Fund Credit and Loans	—	—	—	—	—	—	—	—	—	—	—	—	—	—	—	79dcd
Exceptional Financing	.97	-.14	-.99	.09	-.05	4.24	-4.17	-.02	-.04	—	—	—	—	—	—	79ded

International Investment Position

Billions of US Dollars

	1987	1988	1989	1990	1991	1992	1993	1994	1995	1996	1997	1998	1999	2000	2001	
Assets	1,286.49	1,385.57	1,528.13	1,738.13	1,764.22	1,734.18	2,009.26	2,101.90	2,391.34	2,764.53	3,247.52	3,546.24	3,901.19	4,449.02	4,606.31	79aad
Direct Investment Abroad	162.80	191.35	200.57	236.12	239.57	229.45	255.64	275.23	315.74	342.31	369.24	498.36	691.91	910.12	935.77	79abd
Portfolio Investment	240.53	290.92	385.76	399.05	487.48	494.71	695.83	671.53	773.94	930.84	1,076.56	1,172.18	1,333.57	1,343.62	1,304.04	79acd
Equity Securities	125.19	165.29	220.78	195.33	239.47	209.94	287.40	291.92	336.30	404.67	466.94	505.15	664.31	635.34	558.38	79add
Debt Securities	115.34	125.64	164.98	203.73	248.01	284.78	408.43	379.62	437.63	526.17	609.62	667.03	669.26	708.27	745.67	79aed
Financial Derivatives	—	—	—	—	—	—	—	—	—	—	—	—	—	—	—	79ald
Other Investment	832.59	851.35	899.59	1,059.68	988.55	967.24	1,013.74	1,107.20	1,252.52	1,444.99	1,763.93	1,836.86	1,839.84	2,152.31	2,329.26	79afd
Monetary Authorities																79agd
General Government	9.56	10.20	9.93	13.52	14.33	12.24	12.69	14.09	14.71	16.69	16.33	16.17	15.87	14.66	13.79	79ahd
Banks	746.67	761.15	790.61	907.30	812.74	789.61	768.47	877.15	979.78	1,063.88	1,367.33	1,457.48	1,364.00	1,579.68	1,641.21	79aid
Other Sectors	76.36	80.00	99.05	138.85	161.47	165.39	232.57	215.96	258.04	364.42	380.28	363.20	459.97	557.96	674.26	79ajd
Reserve Assets	50.57	51.95	42.21	43.28	48.61	42.78	44.04	47.93	49.15	46.39	37.79	38.84	35.86	42.97	37.24	79akd
Liabilities	1,192.56	1,296.71	1,444.12	1,762.47	1,769.06	1,714.85	1,962.79	2,073.93	2,426.47	2,882.36	3,372.31	3,771.20	4,031.36	4,504.30	4,664.12	79lad
Dir. Invest. in Rep. Economy	124.80	147.93	171.14	233.31	240.60	197.81	201.29	203.05	226.63	259.17	287.31	355.40	404.51	457.47	503.96	79lbd
Portfolio Investment	240.47	287.51	311.73	364.71	390.55	373.56	454.58	499.95	629.75	815.00	964.63	1,155.19	1,343.40	1,493.50	1,420.03	79lcd
Equity Securities	67.51	79.35	103.48	114.05	131.80	140.33	198.06	197.10	267.66	383.89	499.23	668.90	824.10	901.93	793.68	79ldd
Debt Securities	172.97	208.16	208.25	250.66	258.75	233.23	256.52	302.85	362.09	431.10	465.40	486.29	519.31	591.58	626.35	79led
Financial Derivatives	—	—	—	—	—	—	—	—	—	—	—	—	—	—	—	79lld
Other Investment	827.29	861.27	961.26	1,164.45	1,137.91	1,143.48	1,306.92	1,370.94	1,570.09	1,808.19	2,120.36	2,260.62	2,283.45	2,553.33	2,740.13	79lfd
Monetary Authorities																79lgd
General Government	6.94	7.00	7.66	8.25	6.67	9.54	5.60	6.70	7.31	6.54	4.63	5.23	5.64	5.73	5.71	79lhd
Banks	776.50	804.70	865.24	1,035.79	962.90	948.64	982.44	1,114.40	1,242.42	1,327.38	1,577.98	1,729.50	1,670.07	1,888.51	1,994.76	79lid
Other Sectors	43.85	49.57	88.35	120.41	168.33	185.30	318.88	249.84	320.36	474.27	537.75	525.89	607.75	659.10	739.66	79ljd

United Kingdom

		1972	1973	1974	1975	1976	1977	1978	1979	1980	1981	1982	1983	1984	1985	1986
Government Finance																*Millions of Pounds*
Deficit (-) or Surplus	80	-1,742	-2,524	-3,828	-7,796	-7,251	-4,934	-8,808	-11,164	-10,733	-12,141	-9,514	-13,372	-10,282	-10,268	-9,112
Revenue	81	21,311	23,158	29,442	37,683	44,145	50,125	55,042	64,369	81,640	91,806	106,415	112,590	120,665	133,839	139,836
Grants Received	81z	—	7	23	27	46	117	110	179	408	992	1,363	1,153	1,039	667	753
Expenditure	82	20,781	23,503	30,335	41,190	48,634	53,513	61,884	72,188	88,475	103,089	113,728	122,347	130,718	141,102	147,419
Lending Minus Repayments	83	2,272	2,186	2,958	4,316	2,808	1,663	2,076	3,524	4,306	1,850	3,564	4,768	1,268	3,672	2,282
Financing																
Domestic Borrowing	84a	96	3,263	2,917	8,426	7,468	11,556	6,451	10,376	9,419	8,040	6,083	14,189	10,044	8,615	7,831
Foreign Borrowing	85a	213	-319	1,084	-465	-527	1,345	130	1,389	1,425	154	286	871	668	3,490	3,413
Use of Cash Balances	87	1,438	-329	-359	263	-169	-8,544	2,058	-1,477	-286	2,862	1,546	-616	-427	-166	-2,780
Adj. to Total Financing	84x	-5	-91	186	-428	479	577	169	876	175	1,085	1,599	-1,072	-3	-1,671	648
																Millions of Pounds
Debt: Domestic	88a	29,017	31,988	36,045	46,699	57,219	66,817	75,327	80,496	96,606	100,629	112,609	126,680	139,899	151,448	161,726
Foreign	89a	5,613	5,528	6,825	6,675	6,414	6,873	6,505	8,632	10,142	10,462	10,799	12,354	12,990	15,113	18,452
National Accounts																*Billions of Pounds*
Housch.Cons.Expend.,incl.NPISHs	96f. c	39.63	45.36	52.31	64.37	74.87	85.50	98.59	117.00	135.83	150.80	165.11	181.29	194.53	212.52	235.59
Government Consumption Expend.	91f. c	12.04	13.75	17.08	23.56	27.60	30.11	34.09	39.53	49.70	56.19	61.18	66.40	70.36	74.25	79.74
Gross Fixed Capital Formation	93e. c	12.35	15.23	18.13	21.86	25.52	28.20	32.21	38.21	43.24	43.33	47.39	51.49	58.59	64.40	68.52
Changes in Inventories	93i. c	.03	1.53	1.05	-1.35	.90	1.82	1.80	2.16	-2.57	-2.77	-1.19	1.47	1.30	.82	.68
Exports of Goods and Services	90c. c	13.59	17.07	22.88	26.86	35.09	43.21	47.48	54.80	62.61	67.32	72.71	79.89	91.66	102.07	97.68
Imports of Goods and Services (-)	98c. c	13.66	18.84	27.01	28.66	36.48	42.26	45.23	54.17	57.45	60.24	67.63	77.43	92.58	98.72	100.89
Gross Domestic Product (GDP)	99b. c	64.40	74.03	83.80	105.77	125.21	145.68	167.98	197.36	230.70	252.95	277.09	302.51	324.23	354.95	381.32
Net Primary Income from Abroad	98.n c	.42	.95	1.10	.50	.83	-.87	-.44	-1.26	-2.66	-1.93	-2.61	-.92	.27	-2.49	-.52
Gross National Income (GNI)	99a. c	64.82	74.97	84.90	106.28	126.04	144.81	167.53	196.10	228.03	251.02	274.49	301.59	324.49	352.46	380.79
Net Current Transf.from Abroad	98t. c	....	....	....	....	....	....	....	....	....	....	....	....	....	....	....
Gross Nat'l Disposable Inc.(GNDI)	99i. c	....	....	....	....	....	....	....	....	....	....	....	....	....	....	....
GDP Volume 1995 Ref., Chained	99b. r	442.18	474.21	466.70	464.10	476.96	487.89	504.21	517.36	506.48	499.07	508.99	527.39	540.75	560.26	582.36
GDP Volume (1995=100)	99bv r	61.5	65.9	64.9	64.5	66.3	67.8	70.1	71.9	70.4	69.4	70.8	73.3	75.2	77.9	81.0
GDP Deflator (1995=100)	99bi r	14.6	15.6	18.0	22.8	26.3	29.9	33.3	38.1	45.5	50.7	54.4	57.4	60.0	63.4	65.5
																Millions:
Population	99z	55.78	55.91	55.92	55.90	55.89	55.85	55.84	55.88	56.33	56.35	56.31	56.35	56.51	56.68	56.85

	1987	1988	1989	1990	1991	1992	1993	1994	1995	1996	1997	1998	1999	2000	2001		
Government Finance																	
Year Ending December 31																	
Deficit (-) or Surplus	-2,880	7,284	4,959	3,566	-7,050	-29,218	-46,447	-39,868	-38,922	-27,440	-16,136	4,853	295	....	....		80
Revenue	151,367	169,355	179,438	201,410	214,505	218,613	217,062	236,083	253,918	270,360	288,223	317,543	325,102	....	....		81
Grants Received	937	736	1,199	1,752	4,616	1,907	2,558	1,752	1,233	2,424	1,739	1,384	3,176	....	....		81z
Expenditure	155,882	162,909	174,464	208,761	234,249	261,542	272,600	284,051	295,172	307,310	306,579	313,836	324,393	....	....		82
Lending Minus Repayments	-698	-102	1,214	-9,165	-8,078	-11,804	-6,533	-6,348	-1,099	-7,086	-481	238	3,590	....	....		83
Financing																	
Domestic Borrowing	11,525	-4,245	-11,166	-4,493	4,725	20,397	32,798	34,931	38,275	20,446	18,064	-2,908	2,984	....	....		84a
Foreign Borrowing	4,530	2,243	6,207	927	2,325	8,821	13,649	4,937	647	6,994	-1,928	-1,945	-3,279	....	....		85a
Use of Cash Balances	-12,360	-2,801	....	....	....	....	....	....	....	....	....	....	....	....	....		87
Adj. to Total Financing	-815	-2,481	-3,002	490	-1,216	875	....	....	....	....	....	....	....	....	....		84x
Year Beginning April 1																	
Debt: Domestic	169,590	178,613	164,616	158,374	160,638	169,660	201,928	243,394	277,476	314,021	341,171	....	....	....	....		88a
Foreign	22,008	24,164	27,747	27,580	28,535	34,678	47,998	58,262	56,234	58,691	60,213	....	....	....	....		89a
National Accounts																	
Billions of Pounds Adjusted																	
Househ.Cons.Expend.,incl.NPISHs	258.92	292.73	321.42	349.05	370.71	390.56	415.95	437.68	459.85	492.19	522.98	557.35	589.71	626.43	651.83		96f. c
Government Consumption Expend.	85.51	92.14	99.83	110.25	121.40	129.20	131.53	136.26	141.03	146.78	149.15	154.88	166.61	177.80	190.66		91f. c
Gross Fixed Capital Formation	78.87	96.29	111.32	114.17	105.08	100.60	101.00	108.43	117.33	125.60	134.37	151.27	155.64	158.92	168.10		93e. c
Changes in Inventories	1.23	4.33	2.68	-1.80	-4.93	-1.94	.33	3.71	4.51	1.77	4.62	4.46	6.06	1.86	1.44		93i. c
Exports of Goods and Services	106.56	107.55	121.61	133.89	135.94	144.09	163.64	180.51	203.51	223.09	231.62	228.80	236.61	265.14	268.29		90c. c
Imports of Goods and Services (-)	111.45	124.66	142.69	148.26	142.06	151.66	170.13	185.26	207.05	227.22	231.44	237.95	252.19	283.62	290.91		98c. c
Gross Domestic Product (GDP)	419.63	468.39	514.17	557.30	586.15	610.85	642.33	681.33	719.18	762.21	811.07	859.81	902.46	944.91	988.01		99b. c
Net Primary Income from Abroad	-2.97	-2.40	-4.96	-8.12	-6.82	-4.13	-4.70	.29	-2.83	-2.68	1.30	9.12	.28	5.76			98.n c
Gross National Income (GNI)	416.66	465.99	509.21	549.18	579.33	606.73	637.63	681.61	716.35	759.53	812.37	868.93	902.74	950.38	993.77		99a. c
Net Current Transf.from Abroad	....	....	....	-.89	-2.85	.56	.10	1.61	1.99	.64	2.46	2.93	.97	-.03	....		98t. c
Gross Nat'l Disposable Inc.(GNDI)	....	....	....	551.41	581.92	605.47	635.43	680.70	713.04	759.65	811.52	859.53	896.02	936.63	....		99i. c
GDP Volume 1995 Ref., Chained	608.60	640.22	654.02	659.17	650.09	651.57	667.80	698.92	719.18	738.05	763.47	785.78	803.02	829.52	845.69		99b. r
GDP Volume (1995=100)	84.6	89.0	90.9	91.7	90.4	90.6	92.9	97.2	100.0	102.6	106.2	109.3	111.7	115.3	117.6		99bv r
GDP Deflator (1995=100)	68.9	73.2	78.6	84.5	90.2	93.8	96.2	97.5	100.0	103.3	106.2	109.4	112.4	113.9	116.8		99bi r
Midyear Estimates																	
Population	57.01	57.16	57.36	57.56	57.81	58.01	58.19	58.39	58.61	58.80	59.01	59.24	59.50	59.50	59.54		99z

(See notes in the back of the book.)

United States

111		1972	1973	1974	1975	1976	1977	1978	1979	1980	1981	1982	1983	1984	1985	1986
Exchange Rates		*End of Period (sa and sc) Period Averages (sb and sd)*														
US Dollar/SDR Rate..............aa=	sa	1.0857	1.2064	1.2244	1.1707	1.1618	1.2147	1.3028	1.3173	1.2754	1.1640	1.1031	1.0470	.9802	1.0984	1.2232
US Dollar/SDR Rate	sb	1.0857	1.1921	1.2026	1.2142	1.1545	1.1675	1.2520	1.2920	1.3015	1.1792	1.1040	1.0690	1.0250	1.0153	1.1732
SDR/US Dollar Rate..............ac=	sc	.9211	.8290	.8168	.8542	.8607	.8232	.7676	.7591	.7841	.8591	.9065	.9552	1.0202	.9104	.8175
SDR/US Dollar Rate	sd	.9211	.8388	.8315	.8236	.8662	.8565	.7987	.7740	.7683	.8481	.9058	.9355	.9756	.9849	.8524
		Dollars per ECU through 1998; Dollars per Euro Beginning 1999:														
Euro Rate	ea	....	....	....	....	....	....	....	1.4419	1.3096	1.0852	.9677	.8274	.7089	.8879	1.0704
Euro Rate	eb	....	....	....	....	....	....	1.2740	1.3706	1.3910	1.1176	.9812	.8913	.7890	.7622	.9812
		Index Numbers (1995=100):														
Nominal Effective Exchange Rate	neu	134.9	125.3	128.5	128.5	133.6	131.7	119.0	117.4	117.7	128.9	142.7	147.9	158.1	163.4	133.0
Real Effective Exchange Rate	reu	....	....	....	117.6	120.6	118.6	134.9	134.4	†137.7	150.5	167.9	169.1	177.7	183.8	150.0
Fund Position		*Billions of SDRs:*														
Quota	2f.s	6.70	6.70	6.70	6.70	6.70	6.70	8.41	8.41	12.61	12.61	12.61	17.92	17.92	17.92	17.92
SDRs	1b.s	1.80	1.80	1.94	1.99	2.06	2.16	1.20	2.07	2.05	3.52	4.76	4.80	5.75	6.64	6.86
Reserve Position in the Fund	1c.s	.43	.46	1.51	1.89	3.82	4.07	.80	.95	2.24	4.34	6.66	10.81	11.77	10.88	9.59
of which: Outstg.Fund Borrowing	2c	—	—	—	—	—	.58	—	—	.30	.75	1.14	1.43	1.32	1.10	.77
International Liquidity		*Billions of US Dollars Unless Otherwise Indicated:*														
Total Reserves minus Gold	1l.d	2.66	2.73	4.23	4.63	7.15	7.59	6.98	7.78	15.60	18.92	22.81	22.63	23.84	32.10	37.45
SDRs	1b.d	1.96	2.17	2.37	2.33	2.39	2.63	1.56	2.72	2.61	4.10	5.25	5.03	5.64	7.29	8.39
Reserve Position in the Fund	1c.d	.46	.55	1.85	2.21	4.43	4.95	1.05	1.25	2.85	5.05	7.35	11.31	11.54	11.95	11.73
Foreign Exchange	1d.d	.24	.01	.01	.08	.32	.02	4.37	3.81	10.13	9.77	10.21	6.29	6.66	12.86	17.33
Gold (Million Fine Troy Ounces)	1ad	275.97	275.97	275.97	274.71	274.68	277.55	276.41	264.60	264.32	264.11	264.03	263.39	262.79	262.65	262.04
Gold (National Valuation)	1and	10.49	11.65	11.65	11.60	11.60	11.72	11.67	11.17	11.16	11.15	11.15	11.12	11.10	11.09	11.06
Monetary Authorities: Other Liab.	4..d	.33	.25	.42	.35	.35	.38	.37	.43	.41	.51	.33	.19	.25	.48	.29
Deposit Money Banks: Assets	7a.d	17.99	23.89	42.47	54.70	72.68	88.05	†118.58	136.03	176.91	254.62	360.54	397.17	409.88	417.32	470.29
Liabilities	7b.d	34.43	40.02	64.05	62.72	71.15	87.33	†101.08	141.00	151.45	189.92	254.55	305.78	338.12	381.26	477.22
Monetary Authorities		*Billions of US Dollars:*														
Foreign Assets	11	13.0	14.2	15.9	16.2	18.7	19.3	18.7	18.9	26.8	30.1	33.9	33.7	34.9	43.2	48.4
Claims on Central Government	12a	78.1	86.7	87.5	95.2	100.9	108.6	121.6	129.8	132.4	139.7	146.7	157.7	168.7	187.6	208.5
Federal Reserve Float	13a	4.0	3.1	2.0	10.1	2.5	3.6	6.5	6.8	4.5	1.8	2.7	1.6	.8	1.0	1.3
Reserve Money	14	92.2	99.6	105.6	112.6	118.8	130.5	145.3	155.0	164.3	170.0	181.4	191.5	205.6	226.1	260.1
of which: Currency Outside Banks	14a	57.8	61.9	69.1	74.2	79.7	88.0	97.4	107.6	116.8	122.8	131.9	146.6	160.5	175.3	186.3
Foreign Liabilities	16c	.3	.3	.4	.4	.4	.4	.4	.4	.4	.5	.3	.2	.3	.5	.3
Central Government Deposits	16d	1.4	1.9	2.7	6.9	10.3	7.0	5.5	3.9	5.5	7.3	9.3	6.2	9.2	17.1	17.8
Other Items (Net)	17r	1.1	2.2	–3.3	1.7	–7.3	–6.3	–4.5	–3.9	–6.6	–6.3	–7.7	–4.8	–10.6	–11.9	–20.0
Banking Institutions																
Commercial Banks		*Billions of US Dollars:*														
Reserves	20	34.3	37.8	37.5	38.3	37.3	40.8	46.7	48.3	47.3	43.7	45.6	41.1	43.8	50.3	68.1
Foreign Assets	21	15.2	21.9	38.9	52.1	66.6	79.0	93.1	114.5	160.8	197.6	176.9	183.5	179.0	170.1	161.8
Claims on Central Government	22a	68.1	59.2	55.1	85.0	103.8	102.0	95.3	95.6	111.5	113.8	134.0	179.5	181.5	189.4	197.7
Claims on State and Local Govts	22b	90.0	95.7	101.2	102.9	106.0	115.2	126.2	135.6	148.8	154.0	158.3	162.1	174.6	231.7	203.4
Claims on Private Sector	22d	426.3	510.7	574.8	572.6	618.1	702.2	813.0	921.0	989.4	1,081.1	1,159.9	1,252.0	1,419.7	1,563.9	1,783.7
Demand Deposits	24	225.9	239.0	238.9	247.2	260.9	285.2	310.6	338.0	347.8	356.5	375.8	390.8	419.5	473.7	568.2
Time and Savings Deposits	25	234.0	246.8	265.0	305.3	359.9	388.7	403.4	433.9	479.9	522.1	620.1	750.9	826.0	907.9	982.1
Money Market Instruments	26aa	84.0	123.4	168.1	157.1	146.8	177.1	230.6	255.5	314.7	383.1	394.6	356.1	399.1	399.7	394.5
Bonds	26ab	8.3	9.2	10.4	14.5	18.0	21.1	22.1	21.9	23.2	26.1	32.4	42.0	55.5	74.4	90.5
Foreign Liabilities	26c	30.3	35.6	53.0	55.0	60.8	72.8	84.4	121.2	131.2	113.3	108.0	124.6	132.2	153.4	168.6
Central Government Deposits	26d	10.9	9.9	4.8	3.1	3.0	7.3	14.1	14.5	11.9	10.8	16.9	11.5	15.5	25.8	27.5
Credit from Monetary Authorities	26g	9.9	7.5	4.3	7.6	5.2	7.9	14.2	15.0	10.8	5.1	6.2	4.0	5.3	5.0	4.1
Other Items (Net)	27r	30.5	53.8	63.0	61.3	77.2	79.0	94.9	115.0	138.3	173.2	120.9	138.2	145.5	165.6	179.2
Credit Unions and Savings Insts		*Billions of US Dollars:*														
Reserves	20..t	10.8	10.0	11.5	16.9	15.5	16.5	17.0	16.0	22.7	24.4	42.3	47.2	40.6	51.1	65.0
Claims on Central Government	22a.t	9.2	7.8	6.7	11.4	15.3	16.9	14.1	12.3	14.1	14.3	17.9	34.6	43.4	40.7	46.0
Claims on State and Local Govts	22b.t	1.0	1.1	1.4	3.1	3.6	4.0	4.6	4.1	3.6	3.6	3.3	3.1	2.8	3.4	3.1
Claims on Private Sector	22d.t	328.8	367.0	391.7	436.9	501.3	577.6	652.5	713.9	762.2	789.1	796.1	915.6	1,061.6	1,157.2	1,262.9
Demand Deposits	24..t	.6	.8	.9	1.3	2.1	3.1	4.2	5.4	8.3	16.7	25.0	36.5	44.4	57.4	74.9
Time and Savings Deposits	25..t	317.1	343.6	363.1	421.2	488.1	554.5	606.1	636.3	674.2	681.9	722.8	808.6	884.7	945.6	996.5
Money Market Instruments	26aa t	2.7	3.8	7.2	8.2	9.5	13.8	22.8	39.9	54.7	69.7	79.5	127.8	193.7	196.9	216.1
Bonds	26ab t	—	—	—	.1	.1	1.3	2.0	3.4	3.7	3.2	3.7	4.0	5.9	10.5	15.4
Other Items (Net)	27r.t	29.5	37.7	40.1	37.6	36.0	42.3	53.1	61.4	61.7	59.9	28.6	23.6	19.6	42.0	73.8
Money Market Funds		*Billions of US Dollars:*														
Foreign Assets	21.m	—	—	—	—	—	—	.5	5.1	6.8	18.9	23.8	21.9	21.1	18.9	22.0
Claims on Central Government	22a.m	—	—	.1	.9	1.2	.9	.9	1.6	3.5	21.5	42.7	22.8	25.2	24.4	27.8
Claims on Local Government	22b.m	—	—	—	—	—	—	—	—	2.0	4.4	13.3	16.9	24.0	36.4	64.1
Claims on Private Sector	22d.m	—	—	.7	.5	.9	1.1	4.3	23.3	36.6	81.6	81.6	79.9	114.9	117.3	121.2
Claims on Banks	22e.m	—	—	1.6	2.2	1.5	1.8	4.5	12.1	21.4	43.8	41.4	24.0	22.7	17.5	20.0
Time Deposits	25.m	—	—	2.4	3.7	3.7	3.9	10.8	45.2	76.4	186.3	219.9	179.5	232.2	242.4	290.6
Other Items (Net)	27r.m	—	—	—	–.1	–.1	–.1	–.7	–3.1	–6.2	–16.2	–17.2	–13.8	–24.3	–27.9	–35.5
Banking Survey		*Billions of US Dollars:*														
Foreign Assets (Net)	31n	–2.5	.2	1.3	13.0	24.2	25.1	27.5	16.8	62.7	132.7	126.2	114.4	102.6	78.3	63.4
Domestic Credit	32	990.5	1,118.2	1,216.3	1,304.6	1,444.6	1,622.1	1,820.7	2,027.0	2,195.3	2,394.1	2,536.6	2,815.2	3,200.1	3,517.5	3,880.9
Claims on Central Govt. (Net)	32an	143.1	141.8	142.0	182.5	207.8	214.0	212.2	220.9	244.1	271.1	315.1	376.9	394.1	399.2	434.7
Claims on State and Local Govts	32b	91.0	96.8	102.6	106.0	109.6	119.2	130.8	139.7	154.3	162.0	175.0	182.1	201.3	271.6	270.5
Claims on Private Sector	32d	756.4	879.6	971.8	1,016.2	1,127.2	1,288.9	1,477.6	1,666.4	1,796.9	1,960.9	2,046.5	2,256.2	2,604.6	2,846.8	3,175.6
Money	34	284.3	301.7	308.9	322.7	342.7	376.3	412.1	451.0	472.9	496.0	532.7	573.9	624.4	706.4	829.5
Quasi-Money	35	551.0	590.4	630.4	730.2	851.6	947.1	1,020.4	1,115.4	1,230.5	1,390.3	1,562.9	1,739.0	1,943.0	2,095.8	2,269.2
Money Market Instruments	36aa	86.7	127.2	175.3	165.2	156.2	191.0	253.5	295.4	369.4	452.8	474.0	483.9	592.8	596.6	610.6
Bonds	36ab	8.3	9.2	10.4	14.5	18.1	22.4	24.1	25.3	26.9	29.3	36.0	46.0	61.4	84.9	105.9
Other Items (Net)	37r	57.7	90.0	92.6	85.0	100.2	110.5	138.1	156.9	158.3	158.4	57.2	86.7	81.1	112.2	129.0
Money plus Quasi-Money	35l	835.3	892.0	939.4	1,052.9	1,194.3	1,323.4	1,432.5	1,566.4	1,703.4	1,886.3	2,095.6	2,312.9	2,567.4	2,802.2	3,098.7

1987	1988	1989	1990	1991	1992	1993	1994	1995	1996	1997	1998	1999	2000	2001		
															Exchange Rates	
End of Period (sa and sc) Period Averages (sb and sd)																
1.4187	1.3457	1.3142	1.4227	1.4304	1.3750	1.3736	1.4599	1.4865	1.4380	1.3493	1.4080	1.3725	1.3029	1.2567	US Dollar/SDR Rate......aa=	**sa**
1.2931	1.3439	1.2818	1.3568	1.3682	1.4084	1.3963	1.4317	1.5170	1.4518	1.3760	1.3565	1.3673	1.3188	1.2730	US Dollar/SDR Rate	**sb**
.7049	.7431	.7609	.7029	.6991	.7273	.7280	.6850	.6727	.6954	.7412	.7102	.7286	.7675	.7957	SDR/US Dollar Rate......ac=	**sc**
.7734	.7441	.7802	.7371	.7309	.7100	.7162	.6985	.6592	.6888	.7267	.7372	.7314	.7583	.7855	SDR/US Dollar Rate	**sd**
End of Period (ea) Period Average (eb)																
1.3034	1.1726	1.1970	1.3633	1.3409	1.2109	1.1200	1.2300	1.3142	1.2530	1.1042	1.1668	1.0046	.9305	.8813	Euro Rate	**ea**
1.1543	1.1839	1.1024	1.2730	1.2405	1.2968	1.1723	1.1886	1.3081	1.2680	1.1341	1.1200	1.0668	.9240	.8956	Euro Rate	**eb**
Period Averages																
117.5	109.5	114.3	109.0	107.3	105.2	108.4	106.4	100.0	105.2	113.8	119.3	116.4	121.1	129.1	Nominal Effective Exchange Rate	**neu**
130.9	122.9	124.5	115.8	111.6	109.0	111.1	108.5	100.0	103.6	109.5	116.6	114.8	123.5	135.1	Real Effective Exchange Rate	**reu**
															Fund Position	
End of Period																
17.92	17.92	17.92	17.92	17.92	26.53	26.53	26.53	26.53	26.53	26.53	26.53	37.15	37.15	37.15	Quota	**2f,s**
7.25	7.16	7.57	7.72	7.86	6.18	6.57	6.88	7.42	7.17	7.43	7.53	7.54	8.09	8.58	SDRs	**1b,s**
8.00	7.24	6.88	6.38	6.63	8.55	8.59	8.24	9.85	10.73	13.39	17.12	13.09	11.38	14.22	Reserve Position in the Fund	**1c,s**
.42	.19	.04	—	—	—	—	—	—	—	—	.98	—	—	—	of which: Outstg.Fund Borrowing	**2c**
															International Liquidity	
34.72	36.74	63.55	72.26	66.66	60.27	62.35	63.28	74.78	64.04	58.91	70.71	60.50	56.60	57.63	Total Reserves minus Gold	**1l,d**
10.28	9.64	9.95	10.99	11.24	8.50	9.02	10.04	11.04	10.31	10.03	10.60	10.35	10.54	10.78	SDRs	**1b,d**
11.35	9.75	9.05	9.08	9.49	11.76	11.80	12.03	14.65	15.43	18.07	24.11	17.97	14.82	17.87	Reserve Position in the Fund	**1c,d**
13.09	17.36	44.55	52.19	45.93	40.01	41.53	41.22	49.10	38.29	30.81	36.00	32.18	31.24	28.98	Foreign Exchange	**1d,d**
262.38	261.87	261.93	261.91	261.91	261.84	261.79	261.73	261.70	261.66	261.64	261.61	261.67	261.61	262.00	Gold (Million Fine Troy Ounces)	**1ad**
11.08	11.06	11.06	11.06	11.06	11.06	11.05	11.05	11.05	11.05	11.05	11.05	11.05	11.05	11.05	Gold (National Valuation)	**1and**
.24	.35	.59	.37	.97	.21	.39	.25	.39	.17	.46	.17	.07	.22	.06	Monetary Authorities: Other Liab.	**4,d**
511.25	560.15	599.62	578.44	587.53	562.24	552.33	546.14	606.46	665.94	791.26	813.16	860.50	961.55	1,127.46	Deposit Money Banks: Assets	**7a,d**
572.95	645.26	713.61	733.40	720.46	755.41	828.19	941.32	1,011.91	1,028.68	1,207.31	1,265.47	1,311.60	1,411.34	1,523.41	Liabilities	**7b,d**
															Monetary Authorities	
End of Period																
45.8	47.8	75.5	85.2	75.9	72.0	73.4	74.3	85.8	75.1	70.0	81.8	71.5	67.6	68.7	Foreign Assets	**11**
230.8	247.7	245.7	256.0	288.4	312.4	350.3	383.5	397.7	410.2	447.5	463.5	494.2	530.7	569.0	Claims on Central Government	**12a**
.8	1.3	1.0	2.2	.7	3.3	.9	-.7	.1	4.3	.7	1.6	-.2	.9	—	Federal Reserve Float	**13a**
272.0	287.0	298.8	325.6	337.2	366.8	400.2	434.6	453.8	475.2	513.2	543.8	652.4	612.7	660.8	Reserve Money	**14**
201.8	217.3	228.9	254.8	277.0	298.5	327.5	363.5	381.9	406.1	437.6	473.2	567.7	578.5	599.4	of which: Currency Outside Banks	**14a**
.2	.2	.6	.4	1.0	.2	.4	.3	.4	.2	.5	.2	.1	.2	.1	Foreign Liabilities	**16c**
14.0	19.9	23.7	34.0	38.8	28.0	36.3	29.2	37.7	30.0	22.6	26.0	48.1	24.9	25.7	Central Government Deposits	**16d**
-8.8	-10.5	-.9	-16.6	-11.9	-7.4	-12.3	-7.0	-8.3	-15.8	-18.2	-23.1	-135.0	-38.6	-48.9	Other Items (Net)	**17r**
															Banking Institutions	
															Commercial Banks	
End of Period																
61.1	61.6	59.7	67.9	60.1	60.9	64.2	67.3	67.5	67.5	74.1	66.5	88.8	62.4	63.4	Reserves	**20**
143.5	150.5	126.8	121.0	147.5	125.4	78.9	38.9	34.1	102.0	151.0	237.2	296.0	373.0	451.9	Foreign Assets	**21**
194.4	185.3	165.3	172.1	232.5	294.4	322.2	290.4	278.7	261.8	270.1	214.0	226.7	182.2	162.9	Claims on Central Government	**22a**
174.3	151.6	133.8	117.4	103.2	97.5	99.2	97.6	93.4	94.2	96.7	104.8	110.7	114.0	120.2	Claims on State and Local Govts	**22b**
1,946.0	2,137.9	2,361.0	2,494.3	2,545.3	2,624.0	2,754.3	2,940.9	3,223.1	3,422.5	3,750.3	4,125.2	4,399.5	4,845.3	5,067.4	Claims on Private Sector	**22d**
548.5	565.6	562.3	584.0	621.6	714.3	788.4	756.7	710.8	676.3	656.4	623.0	626.2	541.0	624.9	Demand Deposits	**24**
1,010.0	1,084.0	1,184.7	1,307.1	1,386.5	1,389.2	1,377.2	1,376.2	1,490.1	1,613.2	1,761.5	1,945.2	2,016.5	2,229.8	2,475.5	Time and Savings Deposits	**25**
442.1	477.6	501.9	456.6	412.7	339.2	308.9	331.7	390.9	488.2	585.8	643.6	753.8	843.6	879.1	Money Market Instruments	**26aa**
104.0	109.1	113.7	108.9	113.2	127.6	134.9	142.6	161.1	168.9	192.6	220.2	240.6	273.2	310.2	Bonds	**26ab**
194.0	213.9	193.5	216.0	225.8	247.2	256.3	311.3	305.3	327.5	381.2	449.4	528.2	616.2	659.1	Foreign Liabilities	**26c**
21.6	29.0	25.6	30.9	36.4	30.6	42.6	23.8	19.0	28.7	27.8	13.2	49.6	16.4	45.7	Central Government Deposits	**26d**
5.4	4.7	2.7	4.6	1.7	7.2	1.9	—	.3	8.7	3.5	3.3	—	1.9	—	Credit from Monetary Authorities	**26g**
194.2	203.1	262.3	264.0	290.7	346.8	408.5	492.8	619.0	636.6	733.2	849.8	906.8	1,054.8	871.3	Other Items (Net)	**27r**
															Credit Unions and Savings Insts	
End of Period																
53.9	52.9	47.2	46.1	52.9	52.7	54.0	41.2	43.8	41.7	43.0	54.2	66.5	51.4	70.8	Reserves	**20..t**
58.7	49.3	38.9	34.4	39.0	53.9	50.8	49.2	36.7	34.8	30.2	23.3	19.8	17.0	18.8	Claims on Central Government	**22a.t**
3.1	2.8	2.6	3.0	2.4	2.1	2.1	2.0	2.0	2.1	2.1	2.5	3.0	3.2	4.5	Claims on State and Local Govts	**22b.t**
1,386.9	1,514.5	1,441.5	1,314.4	1,161.4	1,089.7	1,092.5	1,126.8	1,151.9	1,202.6	1,224.8	1,287.5	1,385.9	1,476.0	1,557.0	Claims on Private Sector	**22d.t**
81.9	89.5	89.6	86.3	105.9	109.0	115.1	111.8	128.0	154.9	186.1	228.6	268.1	317.1	371.2	Demand Deposits	**24..t**
1,038.5	1,103.8	1,100.8	1,041.4	964.2	904.2	845.9	807.0	789.6	763.7	712.6	681.3	654.7	632.1	649.4	Time and Savings Deposits	**25..t**
252.6	282.3	225.0	165.7	108.4	101.0	106.1	122.8	133.6	141.5	154.2	183.5	216.5	233.9	275.0	Money Market Instruments	**26aa t**
19.8	21.7	18.3	12.7	8.6	5.5	3.9	3.1	3.1	2.7	2.8	2.6	2.7	6.3	3.6	Bonds	**26ab t**
109.7	122.3	96.4	91.8	68.7	78.6	128.4	174.5	180.1	218.3	244.4	271.5	333.2	358.0	351.8	Other Items (Net)	**27r.t**
															Money Market Funds	
End of Period																
21.4	29.3	26.1	26.7	21.4	20.3	10.0	15.7	19.7	23.1	23.2	30.6	42.9	91.1	124.2	Foreign Assets	**21.m**
14.1	11.4	14.6	44.9	78.3	78.4	79.4	66.1	70.0	90.2	86.2	103.6	103.8	90.4	135.7	Claims on Central Government	**22a.m**
61.8	66.1	70.1	84.0	90.6	96.0	105.6	113.4	127.7	144.5	167.0	193.0	210.4	244.7	281.0	Claims on Local Government	**22b.m**
139.0	148.0	209.0	242.4	235.1	234.1	243.9	279.5	347.9	399.6	468.7	669.3	833.6	955.7	1,120.2	Claims on Private Sector	**22d.m**
34.2	34.4	43.2	33.2	34.9	32.0	30.7	28.9	48.9	81.6	112.8	126.0	158.1	144.6	222.0	Claims on Banks	**22e.m**
313.8	335.0	424.7	493.3	535.0	539.5	559.6	600.1	741.3	886.7	1,042.5	1,329.7	1,578.8	1,812.1	2,240.7	Time Deposits	**25.m**
-43.2	-45.8	-61.8	-62.2	-74.7	-78.7	-90.1	-96.6	-127.2	-147.6	-184.7	-207.2	-230.0	-285.5	-355.6	Other Items (Net)	**27r.m**
															Banking Survey	
End of Period																
16.4	13.4	34.3	16.5	18.0	-29.8	-94.4	-182.6	-166.1	-127.5	-137.6	-100.0	-117.8	-84.7	-14.4	Foreign Assets (Net)	**31n**
4,180.9	4,472.6	4,639.8	4,704.3	4,707.0	4,829.3	5,025.9	5,300.0	5,674.8	6,006.0	6,493.7	7,147.9	7,690.2	8,418.1	8,965.4	Domestic Credit	**32**
462.4	444.8	415.2	442.5	563.0	680.5	723.7	736.3	726.3	738.3	783.5	765.2	746.9	779.1	815.0	Claims on Central Govt. (Net)	**32an**
239.1	220.5	206.5	204.4	196.2	195.6	206.9	213.0	223.1	240.8	265.7	300.3	324.1	362.0	405.6	Claims on State and Local Govts	**32b**
3,479.4	3,807.3	4,018.1	4,057.4	3,947.8	3,953.2	4,095.3	4,350.8	4,725.4	5,026.9	5,444.5	6,082.3	6,619.2	7,277.1	7,744.7	Claims on Private Sector	**32d**
832.2	872.4	880.8	925.1	1,004.4	1,121.9	1,231.0	1,232.0	1,220.7	1,237.3	1,280.2	1,324.8	1,462.1	1,436.6	1,595.5	Money	**34**
2,362.3	2,522.8	2,710.2	2,842.3	2,885.6	2,832.9	2,782.7	2,783.3	3,021.0	3,263.6	3,516.6	3,956.2	4,250.0	4,674.0	5,365.7	Quasi-Money	**35**
694.7	759.8	726.9	622.3	521.1	440.2	414.9	454.5	524.5	629.7	740.1	827.1	970.3	1,077.5	1,154.0	Money Market Instruments	**36aa**
123.8	130.7	132.0	121.6	121.8	133.1	138.8	145.7	164.2	171.6	195.5	222.8	243.3	279.4	313.8	Bonds	**36ab**
184.3	200.2	224.1	209.6	192.2	271.4	364.1	501.9	578.2	576.4	623.8	716.9	646.6	865.7	522.0	Other Items (Net)	**37r**
3,194.5	3,395.2	3,591.0	3,767.4	3,890.0	3,954.7	4,013.7	4,015.3	4,241.7	4,500.9	4,796.8	5,281.1	5,712.1	6,110.7	6,961.1	Money plus Quasi-Money	**35l**

United States

		1972	1973	1974	1975	1976	1977	1978	1979	1980	1981	1982	1983	1984	1985	1986
Other Financial Institutions														*Billions of US Dollars:*		
Claims on Central Government	42a	8.3	9.2	10.7	10.8	15.9	12.3	10.8	6.5	11.6	22.4	31.3	22.1	41.4	58.7	100.3
Claims on State and Local Govts	42b	16.2	17.2	15.7	17.5	22.6	26.8	28.8	33.9	33.0	37.7	43.8	55.6	70.0	104.0	142.4
Claims on Private Sector	42d	293.7	285.4	245.6	260.8	288.6	295.4	323.2	350.5	377.5	345.3	396.7	503.7	522.5	746.1	899.1
Claims on Banks	42e	10.1	10.3	10.8	10.7	12.3	13.1	13.6	14.7	15.8	16.2	18.3	18.3	19.6	23.7	29.6
Claims on Other Financial Insts	42f	5.8	5.0	3.6	4.3	5.5	5.2	5.9	7.1	9.2	13.7	17.1	18.9	24.1	39.1	73.7
Credit Market Instruments	46aa	76.1	59.3	41.5	54.0	62.5	65.4	61.4	71.4	73.5	69.3	85.5	139.7	161.5	297.3	499.2
Bonds	46ab	27.3	31.8	37.6	41.5	44.9	52.9	57.8	60.2	66.1	69.6	77.7	85.3	115.2	148.2	219.4
Liabilities to Banks	46h	211.0	205.7	179.1	187.9	212.5	212.6	227.9	255.9	291.3	299.5	319.0	350.8	367.0	418.0	475.8
Other Items (Net)	47r	19.8	30.4	28.3	20.6	25.1	21.9	35.2	25.2	16.1	−3.1	25.0	42.9	33.9	108.0	50.8
Insurance Companies & Pension Funds														*Billions of US Dollars:*		
Claims on Central Government	42a. s	13.7	14.2	16.4	24.4	34.8	43.2	47.9	56.3	71.2	95.9	142.7	188.2	240.8	291.9	317.2
Claims on State and Local Govts	42b. s	30.2	33.6	35.3	39.7	47.6	59.0	73.3	83.2	91.3	94.9	99.2	98.7	95.0	99.1	114.3
Claims on Private Sector	42d. s	469.1	474.1	469.7	555.3	622.6	668.0	762.4	863.4	1,015.2	1,080.5	1,240.7	1,418.8	1,524.7	1,807.3	1,996.0
Claims on Banks	42e. s	14.8	17.4	20.7	23.9	26.5	30.5	36.6	42.5	46.4	51.6	66.3	80.5	93.1	105.0	113.3
Claims on Other Financial Insts	42f. s	1.8	2.2	2.5	3.4	4.1	4.6	5.1	8.1	12.7	17.7	20.0	20.3	24.8	32.7	47.6
Insurance and Pension Reserves	47a. s	452.3	466.5	479.8	583.4	654.9	713.0	818.4	930.6	1,100.6	1,194.1	1,415.9	1,658.3	1,814.6	2,159.4	2,387.2
Other Items (Net)	47r. s	77.3	74.9	64.8	63.4	80.7	92.2	106.9	122.9	136.3	146.5	153.0	148.2	163.8	176.7	201.3
Financial Survey														*Billions of US Dollars:*		
Foreign Assets (Net)	51n	−2.5	.2	1.3	13.0	24.2	25.1	27.5	16.8	62.7	132.7	126.2	114.4	102.6	78.3	63.4
Domestic Credit	52	1,308.8	1,430.1	1,488.4	1,593.7	1,771.6	1,956.6	2,183.5	2,417.9	2,617.4	2,799.4	3,008.3	3,396.6	3,834.0	4,426.3	5,022.8
Claims on Central Govt. (Net)	52an	151.4	151.0	152.7	193.3	223.8	226.3	223.0	227.5	255.6	293.5	346.4	399.0	435.5	457.9	535.1
Claims on State and Local Govts	52b	107.2	114.0	118.3	123.5	132.2	146.0	159.6	173.6	187.3	199.7	218.8	237.7	271.3	375.6	413.0
Claims on Private Sector	52d	1,050.2	1,165.1	1,217.4	1,276.9	1,415.8	1,584.3	1,800.8	2,016.9	2,174.5	2,306.3	2,443.2	2,759.8	3,127.2	3,592.8	4,074.8
Liquid Liabilities	55l	835.3	892.0	939.4	1,052.9	1,194.3	1,323.4	1,432.5	1,566.4	1,703.4	1,886.3	2,095.6	2,312.9	2,567.4	2,802.2	3,098.7
Credit Market Instruments	56aa	162.8	186.6	216.8	219.3	218.7	256.4	314.9	366.7	442.9	522.0	559.5	623.6	754.3	893.9	1,109.8
Bonds	56ab	35.6	41.0	47.9	56.1	63.0	75.3	81.9	85.4	93.0	98.9	113.7	131.3	176.6	233.1	325.4
Other Items (Net)	57r	272.5	310.7	285.6	278.5	319.9	326.3	381.7	416.2	440.8	424.9	365.8	443.2	438.3	575.5	552.3
Money Stock, Liquid Assets, and Debt Measures (National Definitions)														*Billions of US Dollars:*		
M1	59ma	256.1	270.2	281.8	295.3	314.5	340.0	367.9	393.2	419.5	447.0	485.8	533.3	564.6	633.3	739.8
M1, Seasonally Adjusted	59ma c	249.1	262.7	274.0	286.8	305.9	330.5	356.9	381.4	408.1	436.2	474.3	520.8	551.2	619.1	724.0
M2	59mb	803.1	856.5	903.5	1,017.8	1,153.5	1,273.0	1,370.8	1,479.0	1,604.8	1,760.3	1,918.2	2,137.0	2,322.0	2,507.7	2,745.0
M2, Seasonally Adjusted	59mb c	802.1	855.3	901.9	1,016.0	1,151.7	1,269.9	1,365.6	1,473.3	1,599.4	1,754.9	1,909.8	2,125.9	2,309.6	2,494.9	2,731.6
M3	59mc	886.2	985.2	1,070.8	1,173.3	1,313.6	1,476.2	1,652.6	1,815.2	2,000.8	2,259.0	2,469.1	2,708.5	3,004.5	3,221.6	3,513.2
M3, Seasonally Adjusted	59mc c	885.8	984.9	1,069.7	1,169.9	1,309.7	1,470.1	1,644.2	1,808.3	1,995.1	2,254.0	2,460.2	2,697.0	2,990.5	3,207.5	3,498.6
L	59md	1,023.1	1,141.7	1,248.9	1,368.0	1,518.5	1,709.0	1,915.9	2,124.0	2,331.8	2,602.6	2,850.5	3,157.9	3,529.9	3,841.1	4,140.2
L, Seasonally Adjusted	59md c	1,022.9	1,141.5	1,248.5	1,366.5	1,516.7	1,705.4	1,911.3	2,121.2	2,330.0	2,601.8	2,846.0	3,150.7	3,518.7	3,827.1	4,122.4
Debt	59me	1,703.5	1,889.5	2,062.4	2,250.2	2,495.3	2,811.4	3,199.9	3,588.2	3,929.9	4,340.5	4,775.7	5,354.3	6,140.6	7,065.6	7,929.1
Debt, Seasonally Adjusted	59me c	1,706.8	1,892.0	2,065.0	2,252.4	2,497.2	2,814.1	3,202.8	3,591.9	3,934.2	4,346.0	4,782.2	5,351.8	6,148.8	7,068.4	7,933.6
Treasury Securities by Holders														*Billions of US Dollars:*		
Total	59t	330.1	336.7	348.8	434.9	503.7	561.0	614.9	652.1	730.0	815.9	978.1	1,163.4	1,360.8	1,586.6	1,802.2
Nonresidents	59ta	54.8	55.2	60.1	68.0	80.8	108.7	132.9	116.0	127.5	135.5	150.7	163.6	200.3	226.4	269.4
Residents	59tb	275.4	281.5	288.8	366.9	422.9	452.3	482.0	536.1	602.6	680.4	827.4	999.9	1,160.5	1,360.2	1,532.8
Monetary Authorities	59tb a	69.8	78.5	80.1	86.7	93.3	100.9	109.5	116.3	119.3	127.7	135.6	150.6	159.2	177.8	197.6
Commercial Banks	59tb b	68.1	59.2	55.1	85.0	103.8	102.0	95.3	95.6	111.5	113.8	134.0	179.5	181.5	189.4	197.7
Govt. Sponsored Enterprises	59tb c	1.3	1.2	1.4	2.9	4.4	1.0	1.4	1.2	1.7	1.9	3.4	1.8	2.7	6.8	16.3
Other Financial Institutions	59tb d	38.1	33.6	36.6	61.7	88.7	89.8	88.7	90.2	114.1	172.7	255.5	297.9	387.3	456.8	531.7
Nonfinancial Sectors	59tb e	98.2	109.1	115.6	130.5	132.8	158.7	187.0	232.8	255.9	264.3	298.9	370.0	429.7	529.4	589.5
Interest Rates														*Percent Per Annum*		
Discount Rate *(End of Period)*	60	4.50	7.50	7.75	6.00	5.25	6.00	9.50	12.00	13.00	12.00	8.50	8.50	8.00	7.50	5.50
Federal Funds Rate	60b	4.43	8.73	10.50	5.82	5.05	5.54	7.93	11.20	13.36	16.38	12.26	9.09	10.23	8.10	6.81
Commercial Paper Rate	60bc					5.24	5.54	7.94	10.97	12.66	15.32	11.89	8.87	10.10	7.95	6.50
Treasury Bill Rate	60c	4.07	7.03	7.87	5.82	4.99	5.27	7.22	10.04	11.62	14.08	10.73	8.62	9.39	7.49	5.97
Treas. Bill Rate(Bond Equivalent)	60cs	....	....	....	5.78	4.99	5.29	7.19	10.07	11.24	14.35	10.77	8.87	9.81	7.73	6.15
Certificates of Deposit Rate	60lc	....	....	....	....	5.26	5.58	8.20	11.22	13.07	15.91	12.27	9.07	10.37	8.05	6.52
Lending Rate (Prime Rate)	60p	5.25	8.02	10.80	7.86	6.84	6.82	9.06	12.67	15.27	18.87	14.86	10.79	12.04	9.93	8.33
Govt. Bond Yield: Med.-Term	61a	5.72	6.95	7.82	7.49	6.77	6.69	8.29	9.71	11.55	14.44	12.92	10.45	11.89	9.64	7.06
Long-Term	61	6.21	6.84	7.56	7.99	7.61	7.42	8.41	9.44	11.46	13.91	13.00	11.11	12.44	10.62	7.68
Prices, Production, Labor														*Index Numbers (1995=100):*		
Industrial Share Prices	62	19.0	18.8	14.5	15.0	17.8	16.9	16.5	17.9	21.0	22.5	20.8	28.1	28.3	32.4	40.9
Producer Prices	63	31.9	36.1	42.9	46.8	49.0	52.0	56.0	63.1	72.0	78.6	80.1	81.1	83.1	†82.7	80.3
Industrial Goods	63a	30.1	32.1	39.2	43.8	46.5	49.8	53.4	60.3	70.1	77.6	†79.7	80.5	82.3	82.6	79.6
Finished Goods	63b	32.6	35.6	41.1	45.5	47.5	50.6	54.6	60.6	68.8	75.2	†78.2	79.4	81.1	81.8	80.7
Consumer Goods	63ba	33.0	36.6	42.3	46.3	48.1	51.2	55.2	61.7	70.5	76.9	†79.6	80.6	82.2	82.7	80.7
Capital Equipment	63bb	31.3	32.3	36.9	42.5	45.4	48.3	52.1	56.7	62.8	69.2	†73.1	75.2	76.9	78.7	80.2
Consumer Prices	64	27.4	29.2	32.4	35.3	37.4	39.8	42.8	47.6	†54.1	59.7	63.3	65.4	68.2	70.6	71.9
Wages: Hourly Earnings(Mfg)	65ey	30.9	33.0	35.8	39.0	42.2	45.9	49.9	54.1	58.8	64.6	68.7	71.3	74.3	77.1	78.7
Industrial Production	66.. c	57.1	61.7	60.8	55.5	60.6	65.5	69.4	71.7	69.7	70.8	67.0	69.5	75.7	77.0	77.8
Crude Petroleum Production	66aa	145.1	141.1	134.5	128.3	125.0	126.3	133.4	131.1	132.1	131.4	132.5	133.1	136.4	137.5	133.0
Nonagr. Employment	67.. c	62.9	65.5	66.8	65.7	67.7	70.4	74.0	76.7	77.2	77.8	76.4	76.9	80.6	83.1	84.8
															Number in Thousands:		
Labor Force	67d	....	....	....	....	....	....	....	....	....	....	....	....	....	115,462	117,834
Employment	67e	....	....	....	....	....	....	....	....	....	....	....	....	....	107,150	109,597
Unemployment	67c	....	....	....	....	....	....	....	....	....	....	....	....	....	8,312	8,237
Unemployment Rate (%)	67r	....	....	....	....	....	....	....	....	....	....	....	....	....	7.2	7.0

1987	1988	1989	1990	1991	1992	1993	1994	1995	1996	1997	1998	1999	2000	2001		
End of Period															**Other Financial Institutions**	
96.1	69.3	144.0	138.6	156.4	148.4	151.9	130.6	200.9	150.1	161.6	183.4	100.0	144.6	167.2	Claims on Central Government	42a
149.5	163.9	190.9	215.4	264.5	315.4	389.1	390.0	390.6	388.9	383.6	407.1	422.2	415.2	452.4	Claims on State and Local Govts	42b
990.6	1,100.4	1,276.9	1,319.8	1,583.3	1,888.9	2,230.6	2,339.9	2,918.6	3,624.4	4,548.3	5,406.0	6,772.0	6,957.1	6,819.1	Claims on Private Sector	42d
31.5	36.9	39.0	40.9	37.5	33.6	35.8	38.4	41.4	46.1	56.3	60.4	67.4	72.2	92.8	Claims on Banks	42e
78.8	80.2	102.0	126.7	178.2	237.2	303.0	350.7	410.2	484.7	524.6	656.4	781.6	744.8	800.7	Claims on Other Financial Insts	42f
559.3	617.8	748.9	826.1	1,014.9	1,257.8	1,629.6	1,763.9	2,189.4	2,743.9	3,538.6	4,282.8	5,314.7	5,321.6	4,960.4	Credit Market Instruments	46aa
280.2	325.4	393.5	460.5	547.2	630.8	748.2	863.0	1,040.5	1,211.1	1,373.1	1,655.9	1,853.6	2,035.4	2,312.9	Bonds	46ab
481.0	511.8	597.1	610.9	706.6	728.6	745.4	738.9	839.8	919.4	1,000.4	1,078.7	1,209.6	1,090.9	995.8	Liabilities to Banks	46h
25.9	–4.4	13.4	–56.1	–48.9	6.4	–12.8	–116.3	–107.9	–180.2	–237.7	–304.1	–234.8	–113.9	63.0	Other Items (Net)	47r
End of Period															**Insurance Companies & Pension Funds**	
344.8	360.9	379.9	412.3	450.4	490.9	540.4	571.5	575.4	557.0	537.1	471.9	444.9	416.0	371.7	Claims on Central Government	42a. *s*
136.3	143.7	144.1	149.7	137.6	146.1	162.2	167.7	174.8	189.3	209.8	229.7	222.1	204.8	212.3	Claims on State and Local Govts	42b. *s*
2,161.6	2,356.0	2,763.4	2,890.0	3,377.0	3,629.7	4,048.7	4,235.8	4,941.7	5,506.5	6,412.4	7,223.4	8,055.9	8,070.2	7,800.1	Claims on Private Sector	42d. *s*
98.4	113.2	142.0	137.8	142.4	125.6	121.8	126.0	130.1	135.3	146.1	174.8	172.0	173.5	208.7	Claims on Banks	42e. *s*
51.7	63.6	76.1	107.0	113.5	159.2	225.8	263.3	414.9	557.9	762.2	865.2	1,005.9	1,003.6	937.3	Claims on Other Financial Insts	42f. *s*
2,549.8	2,797.8	3,264.6	3,411.8	3,861.1	4,161.4	4,621.8	4,888.2	5,701.2	6,343.8	7,354.4	8,250.8	9,130.5	9,152.9	8,750.4	Insurance and Pension Reserves	47a. *s*
242.9	239.6	240.8	285.1	359.7	390.1	477.1	476.1	535.6	602.2	713.2	714.2	770.3	715.2	779.6	Other Items (Net)	47r. *s*
End of Period															**Financial Survey**	
16.4	13.4	34.3	16.5	18.0	–29.8	–94.4	–182.6	–166.1	–127.5	–137.6	–100.0	–117.8	–84.7	–14.4	Foreign Assets (Net)	51n
5,417.1	5,806.1	6,251.6	6,378.1	6,711.2	7,182.1	7,797.6	8,160.5	9,184.9	10,169.5	11,587.2	13,144.3	14,984.4	15,935.1	16,404.0	Domestic Credit	52
558.6	514.1	559.2	581.1	719.4	829.0	875.7	866.8	927.2	888.4	945.1	948.6	846.9	923.7	982.3	Claims on Central Govt. (Net)	52an
388.6	384.4	397.4	419.8	460.8	511.0	596.0	603.0	613.7	629.7	649.3	707.4	746.3	777.2	858.0	Claims on State and Local Govts	52b
4,469.9	4,907.7	5,295.0	5,377.2	5,531.1	5,842.1	6,325.9	6,690.7	7,644.0	8,651.3	9,992.8	11,488.3	13,391.2	14,234.2	14,563.8	Claims on Private Sector	52d
3,194.5	3,395.2	3,591.0	3,767.4	3,890.0	3,954.7	4,013.7	4,015.3	4,241.7	4,500.9	4,796.8	5,281.1	5,712.1	6,110.7	6,961.1	Liquid Liabilities	55l
1,254.1	1,377.6	1,475.8	1,448.4	1,536.0	1,698.0	2,044.6	2,218.4	2,714.0	3,373.6	4,278.7	5,109.9	6,285.0	6,399.2	6,114.5	Credit Market Instruments	56aa
404.0	456.1	525.5	582.1	669.0	763.9	887.0	1,008.8	1,204.7	1,382.7	1,568.6	1,878.7	2,096.9	2,314.8	2,626.7	Bonds	56ab
581.0	590.5	693.5	596.7	634.2	735.6	757.9	735.4	858.5	784.7	805.6	774.7	772.5	1,025.7	687.3	Other Items (Net)	57r
End of Period															**Money Stock, Liquid Assets, and Debt Measures (National Definitions)**	
765.4	803.1	810.6	842.7	915.6	1,045.6	1,153.3	1,174.2	1,152.1	1,104.5	1,096.9	1,120.4	1,148.3	1,112.3	1,203.5	*M1*	59ma
749.4	786.1	792.1	824.1	896.2	1,024.0	1,129.1	1,149.7	1,126.5	1,079.1	1,072.2	1,096.5	1,124.4	1,088.9	1,179.3	*M1, Seasonally Adjusted*	59ma *c*
2,843.4	3,006.8	3,171.3	3,290.8	3,391.8	3,448.0	3,503.8	3,517.9	3,662.4	3,832.9	4,049.1	4,401.6	4,672.3	4,959.7	5,479.7	*M2*	59mb
2,830.6	2,993.8	3,157.4	3,276.8	3,376.1	3,430.3	3,483.0	3,496.0	3,638.7	3,811.5	4,028.6	4,381.4	4,651.4	4,936.0	5,454.8	*M2, Seasonally Adjusted*	59mb *c*
3,698.6	3,941.0	4,089.1	4,164.0	4,218.8	4,231.8	4,296.9	4,379.5	4,647.5	4,993.1	5,475.6	6,070.8	6,574.7	7,150.3	8,065.7	*M3*	59mc
3,685.8	3,928.3	4,075.9	4,151.9	4,204.4	4,215.4	4,277.5	4,360.1	4,625.6	4,971.6	5,451.3	6,041.9	6,543.0	7,115.0	8,027.5	*M3, Seasonally Adjusted*	59mc *c*
4,358.0	4,683.6	4,915.3	5,001.0	5,032.7	5,108.3	5,201.9	5,344.6	5,732.8	6,111.6	6,636.7	....	....	....	....	*L*	59md
4,340.0	4,663.7	4,893.2	4,977.5	5,008.0	5,081.4	5,173.3	5,315.8	5,702.3	6,083.6	6,611.3	....	....	....	....	*L, Seasonally Adjusted*	59md *c*
8,669.4	9,462.3	10,158.1	10,824.8	11,301.3	11,827.0	12,409.8	12,990.0	13,694.5	14,430.5	15,221.5	16,264.9	17,352.9	18,270.1	19,363.8	*Debt*	59me
8,677.1	9,466.6	10,160.1	10,824.7	11,299.5	11,823.7	12,407.6	12,988.5	13,694.9	14,433.5	15,227.3	16,277.3	17,360.8	18,278.3	19,375.5	*Debt, Seasonally Adjusted*	59me *c*
End of Period															**Treasury Securities by Holders**	
1,944.6	2,082.3	2,227.0	2,465.8	2,757.8	3,061.6	3,309.9	3,465.6	3,608.5	3,755.1	3,778.3	3,723.7	3,652.7	3,357.8	3,352.7	Total	59t
296.3	353.8	423.7	438.4	476.3	520.3	594.6	632.6	841.3	1,093.3	1,252.0	1,318.8	1,238.9	1,222.0	1,248.6	Nonresidents	59ta
1,648.3	1,728.5	1,803.3	2,027.4	2,281.5	2,541.2	2,715.3	2,833.0	2,767.2	2,661.8	2,526.3	2,404.9	2,413.8	2,135.7	2,104.2	Residents	59tb
222.6	233.7	226.8	235.1	266.5	295.0	332.0	364.5	378.2	390.9	430.7	452.1	478.0	511.7	551.7	Monetary Authorities	59tb *a*
194.4	185.3	165.3	172.1	232.5	294.4	322.2	290.4	278.7	261.8	270.1	214.0	226.7	182.2	162.9	Commercial Banks	59tb *b*
21.0	26.3	13.0	34.3	40.8	58.7	51.6	51.9	58.0	18.8	25.9	25.2	30.9	32.1	29.6	Govt. Sponsored Enterprises	59tb *c*
545.6	518.9	628.8	667.9	767.6	832.3	871.4	868.2	940.1	879.3	841.9	805.8	687.9	685.8	714.1	Other Financial Institutions	59tb *d*
664.8	764.4	769.5	918.0	974.2	1,060.8	1,138.1	1,257.9	1,112.2	1,111.0	957.7	907.8	990.3	724.0	645.9	Nonfinancial Sectors	59tb *e*
Percent Per Annum															**Interest Rates**	
6.00	6.50	7.00	6.50	3.50	3.00	3.00	4.75	5.25	5.00	5.00	4.50	5.00	6.00	1.25	Discount Rate *(End of Period)*	60
6.66	7.57	9.22	8.10	5.69	3.52	3.02	4.20	5.84	5.30	5.46	5.35	4.97	6.24	3.89	Federal Funds Rate	60b
6.81	7.66	8.99	8.06	5.87	3.75	3.22	4.66	5.93	5.41	5.57	5.34	5.18	6.31	3.61	Commercial Paper Rate	60bc
5.83	6.67	8.12	7.51	5.41	3.46	3.02	4.27	5.51	5.02	5.07	4.82	4.66	5.84	3.45	Treasury Bill Rate	60c
5.95	6.88	8.39	7.74	5.53	3.51	3.06	4.35	5.65	5.14	5.20	4.90	4.77	6.00	3.48	Treas. Bill Rate(Bond Equivalent)	60cs
6.86	7.73	9.09	8.15	5.84	3.68	3.17	4.63	5.92	5.39	5.62	5.47	5.33	6.46	3.69	Certificates of Deposit Rate	60lc
8.20	9.32	10.87	10.01	8.46	6.25	6.00	7.14	8.83	8.27	8.44	8.35	7.99	9.23	6.92	Lending Rate (Prime Rate)	60p
7.67	8.26	8.56	8.25	6.81	5.31	4.44	6.26	6.26	5.99	6.10	5.14	5.49	6.22	4.08	Govt. Bond Yield: Med.-Term	61a
8.38	8.85	8.50	8.55	7.86	7.01	5.87	7.08	6.58	6.44	6.35	5.26	5.64	6.03	5.02	Long-Term	61
Period Averages															**Prices, Production, Labor**	
51.6	47.8	57.7	60.9	69.5	76.5	80.6	84.1	100.0	123.5	159.3	198.7	251.3	272.8	215.2	Industrial Share Prices	62
82.4	85.7	90.0	93.2	93.4	93.9	95.3	96.5	100.0	102.3	102.3	99.7	100.6	106.4	107.6	Producer Prices	63
81.7	84.7	88.9	92.2	92.8	93.6	94.8	96.1	100.0	101.4	101.7	99.4	100.8	107.4	108.1	Industrial Goods	63a
82.4	84.4	88.8	93.1	95.1	96.3	97.5	98.1	100.0	102.6	103.0	102.1	104.0	107.9	110.0	Finished Goods	63b
82.5	84.6	89.3	94.1	95.9	96.8	97.9	98.1	100.0	103.1	103.6	102.6	105.1	110.0	112.6	Consumer Goods	63ba
81.7	83.6	86.9	89.8	92.6	94.4	96.1	98.1	100.0	101.1	101.1	100.6	100.7	101.6	102.2	Capital Equipment	63bb
74.6	77.6	81.4	85.7	89.4	92.1	94.8	97.3	100.0	102.9	105.3	107.0	109.3	113.0	116.2	Consumer Prices	64
80.1	82.3	84.8	87.5	90.4	92.6	94.9	97.5	100.0	103.2	106.4	109.1	112.4	116.2	120.0	Wages: Hourly Earnings(Mfg)	65ey
81.5	85.1	86.7	86.5	84.8	87.4	90.4	95.4	100.0	104.6	111.9	117.6	121.9	127.4	122.7	Industrial Production	66.. *c*
127.9	125.0	117.4	111.9	113.1	109.9	104.8	102.2	100.0	99.3	98.8	97.1	90.0	....	....	Crude Petroleum Production	66aa
87.0	89.8	92.1	93.4	92.4	92.7	94.5	97.4	100.0	102.0	104.7	107.4	110.0	112.4	112.6	Nonagr. Employment	67.. *c*
Period Averages																
119,865	121,669	123,870	†124,961	125,505	†127,211	128,040	†131,057	132,304	133,945	†136,297	137,673	139,368	140,863	141,776	Labor Force	67d
112,440	114,968	117,342	117,914	116,877	†117,598	119,306	†123,060	124,900	126,709	†129,558	131,464	133,488	135,208	135,036	Employment	67e
7,425	6,701	6,528	†7,047	8,628	9,613	8,734	†7,997	7,404	7,236	†6,739	6,210	5,880	5,655	6,740	Unemployment	67c
6.2	5.5	5.3	†5.6	6.8	7.5	6.8	†6.1	5.6	5.4	†5.0	4.6	4.2	4.0	4.7	Unemployment Rate (%)	67r

United States

	1972	1973	1974	1975	1976	1977	1978	1979	1980	1981	1982	1983	1984	1985	1986
International Transactions														*Billions of US Dollars*	
Exports 70	49.20	70.82	99.44	†108.86	116.79	123.18	145.85	186.36	225.57	238.72	216.44	205.64	223.98	218.82	227.16
Imports, c.i.f. 71	58.86	73.20	110.88	†105.88	132.50	160.41	186.05	222.23	256.98	273.35	254.88	269.88	346.36	352.46	382.30
Imports, f.o.b. 71.v	55.58	69.48	103.32	†99.31	124.61	151.53	176.05	210.29	245.26	260.98	243.95	258.05	330.68	336.53	365.44
														1995=100	
Volume of Exports 72	28.8	35.6	39.2	†38.3	39.8	40.5	44.9	50.4	53.7	52.1	46.7	43.9	47.1	46.4	47.7
Volume of Imports 73	32.2	33.7	34.4	†30.2	36.6	41.0	44.0	44.1	40.7	41.0	38.9	42.9	54.1	56.5	63.4
Export Prices 76	29.2	34.0	43.4	48.6	50.2	52.0	55.6	63.2	71.8	78.4	79.3	80.1	81.2	80.6	81.4
Import Prices 76.x	23.7	28.2	41.8	45.5	46.9	50.8	54.8	65.4	82.0	86.5	85.1	81.6	83.0	81.0	78.2
Balance of Payments														*Billions of US Dollars:*	
Current Account, n.i.e. 78ald	–5.26	7.58	1.70	17.88	3.84	–15.10	–15.77	–.13	2.15	4.84	–11.60	–44.22	–99.01	–124.47	–147.17
Goods: Exports f.o.b. .... 78aa d	49.38	71.41	98.31	107.09	114.74	120.81	142.05	184.47	224.25	237.05	211.17	201.80	219.93	215.91	224.11
Goods: Imports f.o.b. .... 78ab d	–55.80	–70.50	–103.82	–98.18	–124.23	–151.91	–176.00	–212.01	–249.76	–265.07	–247.65	–268.89	–332.41	–338.09	–368.75
Trade Balance .... 78ac d	–6.42	.91	–5.51	8.91	–9.49	–31.10	–33.95	–27.54	–25.51	–28.02	–36.48	–67.09	–112.48	–122.18	–144.64
Services: Credit .... 78ad d	13.35	17.04	20.77	23.33	27.58	31.09	35.45	38.83	47.55	57.25	63.99	64.22	71.11	73.09	85.95
Services: Debit .... 78ae d	–17.05	–19.09	–21.66	–22.27	–24.91	–27.63	–31.69	–36.23	–40.97	–44.88	–51.04	–54.26	–66.91	–72.03	–79.84
Balance on Goods & Services ... 78af d	–10.12	–1.14	–6.40	9.97	–6.82	–27.64	–30.19	–24.94	–18.93	–15.65	–23.53	–57.13	–108.28	–121.12	–138.53
Income: Credit .... 78ag d	14.77	21.78	27.63	25.37	29.29	32.40	42.47	64.37	72.67	86.65	86.32	85.26	104.86	93.73	97.06
Income: Debit .... 78ah d	–5.85	–8.95	–12.11	–12.58	–13.32	–14.67	–22.16	–33.43	–43.09	–54.26	–57.14	–54.45	–74.86	–73.94	–81.58
Balance on Gds, Serv. & Inc. ... 78ai d	–1.20	11.69	9.12	22.76	9.15	–9.91	–9.88	6.00	10.65	16.74	5.65	–26.32	–78.28	–101.33	–123.04
Current Transfers, n.i.e.: Credit .. 78aj d	.61	.70	.72	.72	.76	.70	.81	1.14	1.32	1.23	2.04	2.01	2.16	2.50	3.41
Current Transfers: Debit .... 78ak d	–4.67	–4.81	–8.14	–5.60	–6.07	–5.89	–6.70	–7.27	–9.82	–13.13	–19.29	–19.91	–22.89	–25.64	–27.54
Capital Account, n.i.e. .... 78bc d	—	—	—	—	—	.20	.30	.15	.14	.19	.18	.16	.16	.16	.30
Capital Account, n.i.e.: Credit ... 78ba d	—	—	—	—	—	.26	.40	.25	.26	.19	.18	.16	.16	.16	.30
Capital Account: Debit .... 78bb d	—	—	—	—	—	–.06	–.10	–.10	–.12						
Financial Account, n.i.e. .... 78bj d	7.71	–3.51	3.87	–22.93	–12.96	16.73	1.60	–27.80	–20.71	–25.97	–25.01	23.01	80.80	105.20	117.97
Direct Investment Abroad ...... 78bd d	–7.41	–9.53	–4.95	–13.98	–11.66	–11.26	–14.72	–25.37	–19.23	–9.62	.98	–7.74	–12.35	–14.06	–24.00
Dir. Invest. in Rep. Econ., n.i.e. ... 78be d	1.35	2.12	3.33	2.56	3.25	2.90	5.85	8.70	16.93	25.19	12.47	10.47	24.76	20.01	35.42
Portfolio Investment Assets ..... 78bf d	–.62	–.67	–1.82	–6.23	–8.87	–5.45	–3.63	–4.70	–3.57	–5.70	–7.98	–6.78	–4.77	–7.50	–4.27
Equity Securities .... 78bk d	.41	.21	.26	–.02	–.32	–.41	.52	–.87	–2.45	–.19	–1.37	–3.69	–.95	–3.70	–1.15
Debt Securities .... 78bl d	–1.03	–.88	–2.08	–6.21	–8.55	–5.04	–4.15	–3.83	–1.12	–5.51	–6.61	–3.09	–3.82	–3.80	–3.12
Portfolio Investment Liab., n.i.e. ... 78bg d	14.07	4.82	1.71	11.13	12.84	29.49	10.73	5.37	14.15	21.15	17.49	8.53	29.73	76.04	85.78
Equity Securities .... 78bm d	2.43	2.76	.25	3.05	.86	1.32	1.31	1.05	4.24	4.82	3.31	5.99	–1.28	4.33	17.90
Debt Securities .... 78bn d	11.64	2.06	1.46	8.08	11.98	28.17	9.42	4.32	9.91	16.33	14.18	2.54	31.01	71.71	67.88
Financial Derivatives Assets ..... 78bw d	....	....	....	....	....	....	....	....	....	....	....	....	....	....	....
Financial Derivatives Liabilities ... 78bx d	....	....	....	....	....	....	....	....	....	....	....	....	....	....	....
Other Investment Assets .... 78bh d	–6.72	–10.69	–22.60	–18.51	–27.90	–17.64	–43.01	–32.79	–57.12	–93.13	–111.85	–46.19	–15.96	–13.37	–83.77
Monetary Authorities .... 78bo d															—
General Government .... 78bp d	–2.17	–2.30	.13	–3.63	–4.24	–4.25	–5.49	–3.27	–6.24	–4.60	–7.60	–5.30	–5.38	–1.73	–2.02
Banks .... 78bq d	–3.50	–5.99	–19.49	–13.53	–21.38	–11.45	–33.67	–17.15	–40.43	–75.29	–107.03	–34.95	–13.61	–5.33	–59.98
Other Sectors .... 78br d	–1.05	–2.40	–3.24	–1.35	–2.28	–1.94	–3.85	–12.37	–10.45	–13.24	2.78	–5.94	3.03	–6.31	–21.77
Other Investment Liab., n.i.e. .... 78bi d	7.04	10.44	28.20	2.10	19.38	18.69	46.38	20.99	28.13	36.14	63.87	64.72	59.39	44.08	108.81
Monetary Authorities .... 78bs d	–.48	–.35	4.20	1.77	3.36	8.70	20.33	–20.39	10.08	–2.84	1.78	13.33	7.59	–8.29	25.37
General Government .... 78bt d	.18	.94	.30	1.53	4.64	1.41	2.47	–.04	.61	–.34	.61	.60	.75	.85	1.96
Banks .... 78bu d	6.53	8.83	21.84	–1.52	11.97	7.50	21.10	38.02	9.43	38.52	64.30	53.40	32.22	40.42	77.92
Other Sectors .... 78bv d	.81	1.02	1.86	.32	–.59	1.08	2.48	3.40	8.01	.80	–2.82	–2.61	18.83	11.10	3.56
Net Errors and Omissions .... 78ca d	–2.67	–4.19	–4.09	5.82	11.68	–1.46	13.18	27.78	25.41	25.00	41.41	22.25	21.17	22.94	28.60
Overall Balance .... 78cb d	–.22	–.12	1.48	.77	2.56	.37	–.69	—	6.99	4.06	4.98	1.20	3.13	3.84	–.31
Reserves and Related Items ..... 79da d	.22	.12	–1.48	–.77	–2.56	–.37	.69	—	–6.99	–4.06	–4.98	–1.20	–3.13	–3.84	.31
Reserve Assets .... 79db d	.22	.12	–1.48	–.77	–2.56	–.37	.69	—	–6.99	–4.06	–4.98	–1.20	–3.13	–3.84	.31
Use of Fund Credit and Loans ... 79dc d															—
Exceptional Financing .... 79de d	....	....	....	....	....	....	....	....	....	....	....	....	....	....	—
International Investment Position														*Billions of US Dollars*	
Assets .... 79aa d	....	....	....	....	....	....	....	....	755.41	820.09	961.01	1,129.67	1,127.13	1,302.71	1,594.65
Direct Investment Abroad ...... 79ab d	....	....	....	....	....	....	....	....	215.38	228.35	226.64	274.34	270.57	386.35	530.07
Portfolio Investment .... 79ac d	....	....	....	....	....	....	....	....	62.45	62.15	74.05	84.72	88.80	119.40	158.12
Equity Securities .... 79ad d	....	....	....	....	....	....	....	....	18.93	16.47	17.44	26.15	25.99	44.38	72.40
Debt Securities .... 79ae d	....	....	....	....	....	....	....	....	43.52	45.68	56.60	58.57	62.81	75.02	85.72
Financial Derivatives .... 79al d	....	....	....	....	....	....	....	....	—	—	—	—	—	—	—
Other Investment .... 79af d	....	....	....	....	....	....	....	....	306.17	405.03	516.89	647.50	662.71	679.03	766.58
Monetary Authorities .... 79ag d	....	....	....	....	....	....	....	....	—	—	—	—	—	—	—
General Government .... 79ah d	....	....	....	....	....	....	....	....	63.87	68.77	76.90	81.66	86.95	89.79	91.85
Banks .... 79ai d	....	....	....	....	....	....	....	....	203.87	293.51	404.58	434.51	445.63	447.36	507.34
Other Sectors .... 79aj d	....	....	....	....	....	....	....	....	38.43	42.75	35.41	131.33	130.14	141.87	167.39
Reserve Assets .... 79ak d	....	....	....	....	....	....	....	....	171.41	124.56	143.44	123.11	105.04	117.93	139.87
Liabilities .... 79la d	....	....	....	....	....	....	....	....	389.87	463.95	725.08	872.28	993.04	1,205.82	1,493.87
Dir. Invest. in Rep. Economy ... 79lb d	....	....	....	....	....	....	....	....	83.05	113.38	130.43	153.32	172.38	220.00	272.97
Portfolio Investment .... 79lc d	....	....	....	....	....	....	....	....	64.57	64.63	269.23	302.36	349.22	455.76	601.20
Equity Securities .... 79ld d	....	....	....	....	....	....	....	....	64.57	64.63	88.32	109.56	104.85	136.79	183.17
Debt Securities .... 79le d	....	....	....	....	....	....	....	....	—	—	180.91	192.80	244.37	318.97	418.03
Financial Derivatives .... 79ll d	....	....	....	....	....	....	....	....	—	—	—	—	—	—	—
Other Investment .... 79lf d	....	....	....	....	....	....	....	....	242.25	285.94	325.42	416.61	471.44	530.07	619.71
Monetary Authorities .... 79lg d	....	....	....	....	....	....	....	....	47.00	50.20	31.27	36.78	40.80	46.04	50.12
General Government .... 79lh d	....	....	....	....	....	....	....	....	13.37	13.03	13.64	14.23	14.96	15.80	17.99
Banks .... 79li d	....	....	....	....	....	....	....	....	151.45	192.10	252.98	303.86	338.27	381.23	460.89
Other Sectors .... 79lj d	....	....	....	....	....	....	....	....	30.43	30.61	27.53	61.73	77.42	86.99	90.70

	1987	1988	1989	1990	1991	1992	1993	1994	1995	1996	1997	1998	1999	2000	2001	International Transactions	
Billions of US Dollars																	
	254.12	322.43	363.81	393.59	421.73	448.16	464.77	512.63	584.74	625.07	688.70	682.14	702.10	781.13	730.80	Exports	70
	424.44	459.54	492.92	516.99	508.36	553.92	603.44	689.22	770.85	822.02	899.02	944.35	1,059.44	1,259.30	1,180.15	Imports, c.i.f.	71
	406.24	440.95	473.21	495.31	488.45	532.67	580.51	663.83	743.54	795.29	870.57	911.90	1,024.62	1,218.02	1,141.95	Imports, f.o.b.	71.v
1995=100																	
	52.5	62.2	68.4	73.3	77.9	82.7	85.3	92.1	100.0	106.3	118.7	121.6	126.8	138.8	131.0	Volume of Exports	72
	65.6	67.8	70.6	71.7	70.5	76.2	83.2	93.4	100.0	105.6	118.4	132.3	147.2	164.3	159.6	Volume of Imports	73
	82.8	†88.6	91.0	†91.8	92.6	†92.7	93.2	95.2	100.0	100.5	99.2	95.9	94.7	96.2	95.4	Export Prices	76
	83.9	†88.0	90.6	†93.6	93.6	†94.3	94.1	95.7	100.0	101.0	98.5	92.6	93.4	99.4	95.9	Import Prices	76.x
Minus Sign Indicates Debit																Balance of Payments	
	−160.65	−121.25	−99.50	−78.96	3.69	−48.48	−82.48	−118.20	−109.89	−120.94	−139.82	−217.41	−324.39	−444.69	−417.44	Current Account, n.i.e.	78al d
	250.94	321.09	361.27	388.80	415.74	441.42	458.84	504.93	577.05	614.02	680.33	672.39	686.86	774.86	723.83	Goods: Exports f.o.b.	78aa d
	−410.18	−447.70	−478.31	−499.07	−491.44	−536.53	−589.41	−668.69	−749.38	−803.12	−876.51	−917.12	−1,029.98	−1,224.43	−1,147.50	Goods: Imports f.o.b.	78ab d
	−159.24	−126.61	−117.04	−110.27	−75.70	−95.11	−130.57	−163.76	−172.33	−189.10	−196.18	−244.73	−343.12	−449.57	−423.67	Trade Balance	78ac d
	97.93	110.06	125.79	146.46	162.59	175.20	184.06	199.03	217.46	238.17	254.70	260.36	270.54	290.88	280.81	Services: Credit	78ad d
	−90.37	−98.10	−101.87	−117.05	−118.08	−116.48	−122.28	−131.92	−141.50	−150.91	−166.28	−182.44	−189.27	−217.07	−204.96	Services: Debit	78ae d
	−151.68	−114.66	−93.12	−80.86	−31.19	−36.39	−68.79	−96.65	−96.37	−101.84	−107.76	−166.81	−261.85	−375.76	−347.82	Balance on Goods & Services	78af d
	108.18	136.71	161.29	171.75	149.24	132.04	134.21	165.44	211.54	225.86	260.58	259.27	285.32	352.90	293.81	Income: Credit	78ag d
	−93.89	−118.04	−141.49	−143.19	−125.11	−109.11	−110.27	−148.75	−190.99	−204.87	−251.85	−265.45	−298.94	−367.68	−312.91	Income: Debit	78ah d
	−137.39	−95.98	−73.32	−52.30	−7.06	−13.46	−44.85	−79.96	−75.82	−80.85	−99.03	−172.99	−275.47	−390.54	−366.92	Balance on Gds, Serv. & Inc.	78ai d
	3.87	4.63	5.08	10.04	47.85	7.55	5.93	6.49	7.68	8.89	8.49	9.20	9.27	10.24	10.16	Current Transfers, n.i.e.: Credit	78aj d
	−27.13	−29.90	−31.26	−36.70	−37.10	−42.57	−43.56	−44.73	−41.75	−48.98	−49.28	−53.62	−58.19	−64.39	−60.68	Current Transfers: Debit	78ak d
	.37	.49	.34	−6.58	−4.48	.61	−.09	−.47	.37	.69	.35	.64	−3.50	.68	.72	Capital Account, n.i.e.	78bc d
	.37	.49	.40	.32	.25	.61	.37	.31	.67	.69	.35	.64		.68	.72	Capital Account, n.i.e.: Credit	78ba d
	—	—	−.06	−6.90	−4.73	—	−.46	−.77	−.30	—	—	—	−3.99	—	—	Capital Account: Debit	78bb d
	160.19	143.87	74.83	62.44	40.64	92.35	82.94	124.62	123.06	165.47	272.50	151.58	367.92	443.58	460.80	Financial Account, n.i.e.	78bj d
	−35.03	−22.53	−43.45	−37.20	−37.89	−48.27	−83.95	−80.18	−98.78	−91.88	−104.82	−142.51	−155.41	−152.44	−156.04	Direct Investment Abroad	78bd d
	58.47	57.74	68.25	48.49	23.18	19.81	51.38	46.13	57.80	86.52	105.59	178.20	301.02	287.68	157.95	Dir. Invest. in Rep. Econ., n.i.e.	78be d
	−5.25	−7.98	−22.08	−28.77	−45.68	−49.17	−146.25	−60.31	−122.51	−149.83	−118.98	−136.13	−131.22	−124.94	−97.65	Portfolio Investment Assets	78bf d
	2.13	−1.10	−17.22	−7.41	−30.66	−32.40	−63.37	−48.10	−65.41	−82.85	−57.58	−101.28	−114.39	−25.20	−110.18	Equity Securities	78bk d
	−7.38	−6.88	−4.86	−21.36	−15.02	−16.77	−82.88	−12.21	−57.10	−66.98	−61.40	−34.85	−16.83	−99.74	12.53	Debt Securities	78bl d
	66.93	73.85	95.72	22.01	57.54	71.98	111.00	139.41	237.48	367.73	385.61	269.35	354.75	474.59	540.32	Portfolio Investment Liab., n.i.e.	78bg d
	15.03	−2.88	8.99	−15.96	10.42	−5.61	20.94	.89	16.56	11.13	67.85	41.96	112.34	193.85	129.19	Equity Securities	78bm d
	51.90	76.73	86.73	37.97	47.12	77.59	90.06	138.52	220.92	356.60	317.76	227.39	242.41	280.74	411.13	Debt Securities	78bn d
	....	....	....	....	....	....	....	....	....	....	....	....	....	....		Financial Derivatives Assets	78bw d
	....	....	....	....	....	....	....	....	....	....	....	....	....	....		Financial Derivatives Liabilities	78bx d
	−48.16	−72.15	−84.57	−13.14	13.39	19.13	31.04	−40.90	−121.38	−178.90	−262.83	−74.21	−159.23	−303.27	−180.98	Other Investment Assets	78bh d
																Monetary Authorities	78bo d
	1.01	2.97	1.23	2.31	2.92	−1.67	−.34	−.37	−.98	−1.00	.06	−.42	2.75	−.94	−.58	General Government	78bp d
	−42.12	−53.93	−58.16	12.38	−.62	21.18	30.62	−4.20	−75.11	−91.56	−141.13	−35.58	−76.27	−138.49	−104.33	Banks	78bq d
	−7.05	−21.19	−27.64	−27.83	11.09	−.38	.76	−36.33	−45.29	−86.34	−121.76	−38.21	−85.71	−163.84	−76.07	Other Sectors	78br d
	123.24	114.94	60.96	71.05	30.10	78.87	119.71	120.46	170.45	131.83	267.93	56.88	158.01	261.96	197.20	Other Investment Liab., n.i.e.	78bi d
	16.75	19.08	−18.06	24.49	29.35	30.31	68.00	9.59	46.73	56.88	−18.86	6.89	24.59	−6.80	35.08	Monetary Authorities	78bs d
	−1.47	−1.31	1.73	4.48	−.06	2.83	.56	2.77	.90	.73	−2.86	−3.35	−.97	−.55	−4.95	General Government	78bt d
	90.46	63.43	56.77	−.44	2.50	32.79	39.91	108.00	64.19	22.19	171.32	30.27	67.19	93.75	66.38	Banks	78bu d
	17.51	33.74	20.52	42.52	−1.69	12.94	11.24	.10	58.63	52.03	118.33	23.07	67.19	175.56	100.69	Other Sectors	78bv d
	−9.05	−19.19	49.61	25.33	−45.61	−48.40	1.01	−11.30	−3.79	−51.89	−132.01	71.94	−48.77	.73	−39.15	Net Errors and Omissions	78ca d
	−9.15	3.92	25.29	2.23	−5.76	−3.92	1.38	−5.35	9.75	−6.67	1.02	6.74	−8.73	.30	4.93	Overall Balance	78cb d
	9.15	−3.92	−25.29	−2.23	5.76	3.92	−1.38	5.35	−9.75	6.67	−1.02	−6.74	8.73	−.30	−4.93	Reserves and Related Items	79da d
	9.15	−3.92	−25.29	−2.23	5.76	3.92	−1.38	5.35	−9.75	6.67	−1.02	−6.74	8.73	−.30	−4.93	Reserve Assets	79db d
	—	—	—	—	—	—	—	—	—	—	—	—	—	—	—	Use of Fund Credit and Loans	79dc d
	—	—	—	—	—	—	—	—	—	—	—	—	—	—	—	Exceptional Financing	79de d
Billions of US Dollars																International Investment Position	
	1,758.71	2,008.36	2,350.23	2,294.09	2,470.63	2,466.46	3,057.64	3,279.87	3,873.64	4,549.18	5,278.04	6,063.18	7,206.36	7,189.80	....	Assets	79aa d
	590.25	692.46	832.46	731.76	827.54	798.63	1,027.55	1,067.80	1,307.16	1,526.24	1,778.19	2,168.32	2,613.18	2,467.76	....	Direct Investment Abroad	79ab d
	188.59	232.85	314.29	342.31	455.75	515.04	853.53	948.67	1,169.64	1,467.99	1,751.19	2,052.93	2,604.39	2,406.50	....	Portfolio Investment	79ac d
	94.70	128.66	197.35	197.60	278.98	314.23	543.86	627.46	776.81	1,002.93	1,207.79	1,476.18	2,026.64	1,828.81	....	Equity Securities	79ad d
	93.89	104.19	116.95	144.72	176.77	200.82	309.67	321.21	392.83	465.06	543.40	576.75	577.75	577.69	....	Debt Securities	79ae d
												—	—	—	....	Financial Derivatives	79af d
	817.51	938.88	1,034.77	1,045.35	1,028.12	1,005.35	1,011.65	1,100.00	1,220.78	1,394.21	1,613.82	1,695.92	1,852.35	2,187.14	....	Other Investment	79ag d
															....	Monetary Authorities	79ag d
	90.68	87.89	86.64	84.34	81.42	83.02	83.38	83.91	85.06	86.12	86.20	86.77	84.23	85.17	....	General Government	79ah d
	549.46	653.23	713.82	695.69	690.40	668.02	686.25	693.12	768.15	857.51	982.10	1,020.83	1,100.39	1,276.71	....	Banks	79ai d
	177.37	197.76	234.31	265.32	256.30	254.30	242.03	322.98	367.56	450.58	545.52	588.32	667.73	825.26	....	Other Sectors	79aj d
	162.37	144.18	168.71	174.66	159.22	147.44	164.91	163.40	176.07	160.74	134.84	146.00	136.45	128.40	....	Reserve Assets	79ak d
	1,708.18	1,997.90	2,397.23	2,458.58	2,731.45	2,918.79	3,235.68	3,450.39	4,292.28	5,091.42	6,354.17	7,487.17	8,731.67	9,377.25	....	Liabilities	79la d
	316.20	391.53	534.73	539.60	669.14	696.18	768.40	757.85	1,005.73	1,229.12	1,637.41	2,179.04	2,805.22	2,736.87	....	Dir. Invest. in Rep. Economy	79lb d
	659.88	768.48	939.28	929.27	1,057.84	1,158.68	1,335.53	1,413.55	1,870.64	2,364.70	2,919.79	3,435.99	3,898.73	4,367.94	....	Portfolio Investment	79lc d
	189.01	213.81	276.10	243.79	298.96	328.99	373.52	397.72	527.62	656.75	919.52	1,175.09	1,537.76	1,665.58	....	Equity Securities	79ld d
	470.87	554.67	663.18	685.48	758.88	829.69	962.01	1,015.83	1,343.02	1,707.95	2,000.27	2,260.90	2,360.97	2,702.36	....	Debt Securities	79le d
												—	—	—	....	Financial Derivatives	79lf d
	732.10	837.89	923.22	989.71	1,004.48	1,063.94	1,131.75	1,278.99	1,415.91	1,497.60	1,796.97	1,872.14	2,027.72	2,272.44	....	Other Investment	79lf d
	55.58	61.26	67.12	85.93	101.32	114.80	133.73	157.18	169.48	186.85	211.63	228.25	250.66	251.79	....	Monetary Authorities	79lg d
	15.67	15.20	15.37	17.24	18.61	20.80	22.11	23.68	23.57	22.59	21.71	18.34	15.49	13.50	....	General Government	79lh d
	550.67	616.88	673.63	673.13	675.64	707.67	746.87	858.31	922.44	941.35	1,104.22	1,139.88	1,206.00	1,284.41	....	Banks	79li d
	110.19	144.55	167.09	213.41	208.91	220.67	229.04	239.82	300.42	346.81	459.41	485.67	555.57	722.74	....	Other Sectors	79lj d

United States

	1972	1973	1974	1975	1976	1977	1978	1979	1980	1981	1982	1983	1984	1985	1986
Government Finance														*Billions of US Dollars:*	
Deficit (-) or Surplus............................. 80	-17.4	-8.0	-10.9	-75.4	-56.6	-51.1	-44.2	-27.9	-68.8	-76.1	-145.6	-200.8	-194.4	-215.6	-209.2
Total Revenue and Grants.................. 81y	221.5	250.4	280.3	280.7	317.6	366.1	416.9	480.5	533.0	622.3	608.8	612.9	683.2	745.1	781.9
Revenue 81	221.5	250.4	280.3	280.7	317.6	366.1	416.9	480.5	533.0	622.3	608.8	612.9	683.2	745.1	781.9
Grants 81z	—	—	—	—	—	—	—	—	—	—	—	—	—	—	—
Exp. & Lending Minus Repay. 82z	238.9	258.4	291.2	356.1	374.2	417.2	461.1	508.5	601.8	698.4	754.4	813.7	877.6	960.7	991.1
Expenditure 82	....	....	....	....	....	....	....	....	....	....	....	....	....	....	....
Lending Minus Repayments 83	....	....	....	....	....	....	....	....	....	....	....	....	....	....	....
Total Financing 80h	17.4	8.0	10.9	75.4	56.6	51.0	44.2	27.9	68.8	76.1	145.6	200.8	194.4	215.6	209.2
Total Net Borrowing 84	18.1	12.6	4.2	79.3	53.6	51.4	45.9	33.7	75.5	74.4	155.1	194.1	201.8	232.5	210.7
Net Domestic................................. 84a	....	....	....	....	....	....	....	....	....	....	....	....	....	....	....
Net Foreign 85a	....	....	....	....	....	....	....	....	....	....	....	....	....	....	....
Use of Cash Balances 87	-.8	-4.6	6.7	-3.9	3.0	-.4	-1.7	-5.8	-6.7	1.8	-9.5	6.6	-7.4	-16.9	-1.5
Total Debt by Residence 88	331.6	339.4	351.5	437.3	506.5	563.8	618.2	658.0	737.7	825.4	987.7	1,174.5	1,373.4	1,598.5	1,813.3
Domestic.. 88a	277.1	284.7	292.7	370.8	428.4	454.2	485.1	539.0	608.0	688.8	838.2	1,008.2	1,167.5	1,373.7	1,549.9
Foreign.. 89a	54.5	54.7	58.8	66.5	78.1	109.6	133.1	119.0	129.7	136.6	149.5	166.3	205.9	224.8	263.4
National Accounts														*Billions of US Dollars*	
Househ.Cons.Expend.,incl.NPISHs........ 96f. c	770.7	852.5	932.4	1,030.3	1,149.8	1,278.4	1,430.4	1,596.3	1,762.9	1,944.2	2,079.3	2,286.4	2,498.4	2,712.6	2,895.2
Gov't Consumption & Investment .... 91ff c	270.1	287.9	322.4	361.1	384.5	415.3	455.6	503.5	569.7	631.4	684.4	735.9	800.8	878.3	942.3
of which: Gross Capital Form .... 93gf c	†40.1	42.9	52.4	60.5	63.8	66.3	74.7	84.3	97.5	104.6	102.0	105.5	106.2	123.4	137.9
Priv. Gross Fixed Capital Form .... 93ee c	198.5	228.6	235.4	236.5	274.8	339.0	410.2	472.7	484.2	541.0	531.0	570.0	670.1	714.5	740.7
Changes in Inventories........................ 93i. c	9.1	15.9	14.0	-6.3	17.1	22.3	25.8	18.0	-6.3	29.8	-14.9	-5.8	65.4	21.8	6.6
Exports of Goods and Services .... 90c. c	66.2	91.8	124.3	136.3	148.9	158.8	186.1	228.7	278.9	302.8	282.6	277.0	303.1	303.0	320.3
Imports of Goods and Services (-) .... 98c. c	74.2	91.2	127.5	122.7	151.1	182.4	212.3	252.7	293.8	317.8	303.2	328.6	405.1	417.2	452.2
Gross Domestic Product (GDP) .... 99b. c	1,240.4	1,385.5	1,501.0	1,635.2	1,823.9	2,031.4	2,295.9	2,566.4	2,795.6	3,131.3	3,259.2	3,534.9	3,932.7	4,213.0	4,452.9
Net Primary Income from Abroad....... 98.n c	8.7	12.7	15.7	13.3	17.2	20.7	22.1	32.9	35.3	34.7	36.5	36.9	35.3	25.3	15.5
Gross National Income (GNI) .... 99a. c	1,249.1	1,398.2	1,516.7	1,648.4	1,841.0	2,052.1	2,318.0	2,599.3	2,830.8	3,166.1	3,295.7	3,571.8	3,968.1	4,238.4	4,468.3
Consumption of Fixed Capital............. 99cf c	131.0	142.9	164.8	190.9	209.0	231.6	261.5	300.4	345.2	394.9	436.5	456.1	482.4	516.5	551.6
GDP Volume 1996 Ref., Chained .... 99b. r	3,898.4	4,123.4	4,099.0	4,084.4	4,311.7	4,511.8	4,760.6	4,912.1	4,900.9	5,021.0	4,919.3	5,132.3	5,505.2	5,717.1	5,912.4
GDP Volume (1995=100) .... 99bv r	51.7	54.7	54.3	54.1	57.2	59.8	63.1	65.1	65.0	66.6	65.2	68.0	73.0	75.8	78.4
GDP Deflator (1995=100) .... 99bi r	32.4	34.3	37.3	40.8	43.1	45.9	49.2	53.3	58.1	63.6	67.5	70.2	72.8	75.1	76.8
														Millions:	
Population..................................... 99z	209.90	211.91	213.85	215.97	218.04	220.24	222.59	225.06	227.76	229.94	232.17	234.30	236.37	238.49	240.68

1987	1988	1989	1990	1991	1992	1993	1994	1995	1996	1997	1998	1999	2000	2001		
Year Ending December 31															**Government Finance**	
−166.6	−140.5	−155.0	−236.0	−265.6	−326.8	−226.5	−184.6	−146.2	−110.8	−2.4	54.4	156.7	254.6	92.4	Deficit (-) or Surplus	80
869.0	925.7	997.9	1,052.1	1,059.8	1,101.4	1,175.2	1,277.5	1,367.2	1,474.7	1,619.3	1,747.7	1,858.3	2,042.7	1,995.3	Total Revenue and Grants	81y
869.0	925.7	997.9	1,052.1	. . . .	. . . .	. . . .	1,277.5	1,367.2	1,474.7	1,619.3	1,747.7	1,858.3	2,042.7	1,995.3	Revenue	81
—	—	—	—	. . . .	. . . .	. . . .	—	—	—	—	—	—	—	—	Grants	81z
1,035.6	1,066.2	1,152.9	1,288.1	1,325.4	1,428.3	1,401.8	1,462.1	1,513.4	1,585.4	1,621.8	1,693.3	1,701.6	1,788.1	1,902.8	Exp. & Lending Minus Repay.	82z
. . . .	. . . .	. . . .	. . . .	. . . .	. . . .	. . . .	. . . .	. . . .	. . . .	. . . .	. . . .	. . . .	. . . .	. . . .	Expenditure	82
. . . .	. . . .	. . . .	. . . .	. . . .	. . . .	. . . .	. . . .	. . . .	. . . .	. . . .	. . . .	. . . .	. . . .	. . . .	Lending Minus Repayments	83
166.6	140.5	155.0	236.0	265.6	326.8	226.5	184.6	146.2	110.8	2.4	−54.4	−156.7	−254.6	−92.4	Total Financing	80h
157.0	149.5	149.2	242.1	290.7	308.8	248.2	161.3	151.1	119.9	4.3	−62.2	−92.2	−316.7	−43.1	Total Net Borrowing	84
. . . .	. . . .	. . . .	. . . .	. . . .	. . . .	. . . .	. . . .	. . . .	. . . .	. . . .	. . . .	. . . .	. . . .	. . . .	Net Domestic	84a
. . . .	. . . .	. . . .	. . . .	. . . .	. . . .	. . . .	. . . .	. . . .	. . . .	. . . .	. . . .	. . . .	. . . .	. . . .	Net Foreign	85a
9.6	−9.0	5.8	−6.1	−25.1	18.1	−21.7	23.3	−4.9	−9.1	−1.9	7.9	−64.4	62.1	−49.3	Use of Cash Balances	87
1,953.9	2,096.9	2,245.8	2,565.1	2,860.3	3,149.8	3,403.8	3,551.7	3,698.7	3,842.1	3,866.5	3,805.7	3,711.6	3,413.2	3,394.4	Total Debt by Residence	88
1,654.2	1,734.7	1,819.7	2,078.0	2,339.4	2,573.1	2,753.5	2,884.4	2,863.5	2,740.0	2,624.9	2,527.0	2,442.8	2,211.9	2,176.3	Domestic	88a
299.7	362.2	426.1	487.1	520.9	576.7	650.3	667.3	835.2	1,102.1	1,241.6	1,278.7	1,268.8	1,201.3	1,218.1	Foreign	89a
Billions of US Dollars															**National Accounts**	
3,105.3	3,356.6	3,596.7	3,831.5	3,971.3	4,209.7	4,454.7	4,716.4	4,969.0	5,237.5	5,529.3	5,856.0	6,246.5	6,683.8	6,987.0	Househ.Cons.Expend.,incl.NPISHs	96f. c
997.9	1,036.9	1,100.2	1,181.4	1,235.5	1,270.5	1,293.0	1,327.9	1,372.0	1,421.9	1,487.9	1,538.5	1,641.0	1,751.0	1,858.0	Gov't Consumption & Investment	91ff c
†134.5	126.5	147.6	163.3	173.6	179.0	184.5	192.0	207.3	219.3	238.6	245.2	266.3	294.2	317.1	of which: Gross Capital Form	93gf c
754.3	802.7	845.2	847.2	800.4	851.6	934.0	1,034.6	1,110.7	1,212.1	1,327.7	1,465.6	1,577.2	1,691.8	1,646.3	Priv. Gross Fixed Capital Form	93ee c
27.1	18.5	27.7	14.5	−.2	15.0	21.1	62.6	33.0	30.0	62.9	73.1	59.5	63.6	−60.3	Changes in Inventories	93i. c
365.6	446.9	509.0	557.2	601.6	636.8	658.0	725.1	818.6	874.2	966.4	964.9	989.3	1,101.1	1,034.1	Exports of Goods and Services	90c. c
507.9	553.2	589.7	628.6	622.3	664.6	718.5	812.1	902.8	963.1	1,055.8	1,116.7	1,239.2	1,466.6	1,383.0	Imports of Goods and Services (-)	98c. c
4,742.5	5,108.3	5,489.1	5,803.2	5,986.2	6,318.9	6,642.3	7,054.3	7,400.5	7,813.2	8,318.4	8,781.5	9,274.3	9,824.6	10,082.2	Gross Domestic Product (GDP)	99b. c
13.7	18.4	20.4	29.0	24.7	23.5	24.3	16.8	20.4	18.1	7.1	−3.5	−6.7	−12.1	−5.3	Net Primary Income from Abroad	98.n c
4,756.2	5,126.8	5,509.4	5,832.2	6,010.9	6,342.3	6,667.7	7,071.1	7,420.9	7,831.2	8,325.4	8,778.1	9,297.1	9,848.0	10,104.1	Gross National Income (GNI)	99a. c
586.1	627.4	677.2	711.3	748.0	787.5	812.8	875.0	911.8	956.2	1,013.3	1,072.0	1,145.2	1,228.9	1,329.3	Consumption of Fixed Capital	99cf c
6,113.3	6,368.4	6,591.8	6,707.9	6,676.4	6,880.0	7,062.6	7,347.7	7,543.8	7,813.2	8,159.5	8,508.9	8,859.0	9,191.4	9,214.5	GDP Volume 1996 Ref., Chained	99b. r
81.0	84.4	87.4	88.9	88.5	91.2	93.6	97.4	100.0	103.6	108.2	112.8	117.4	122.3	123.7	GDP Volume (1995=100)	99bv r
79.1	81.8	84.9	88.2	91.4	93.6	95.9	97.9	100.0	101.9	103.9	105.2	106.7	108.6	110.1	GDP Deflator (1995=100)	99bi r
Midyear Estimates																
242.84	245.06	247.34	249.95	252.64	255.37	258.08	260.60	263.04	265.46	268.01	270.30	272.69	275.26	284.80	**Population**	99z

(See notes in the back of the book.)

Uruguay

	1972	1973	1974	1975	1976	1977	1978	1979	1980	1981	1982	1983	1984	1985	1986
Exchange Rates														*Pesos per Thousand SDRs through 1978*	
Market Rate .... **aa**	.7871	1.1195	2.0079	3.1608	4.6008	6.5594	9.1664	†.0111	.0128	.0135	.0370	.0450	.0725	.1370	.2202
												Pesos per Thousand US Dollars through 1978			
Market Rate .... **ae**	.7250	.9280	1.6400	2.7000	3.9600	5.4000	7.0360	†.0084	.0100	.0116	.0335	.0430	.0740	.1248	.1800
Market Rate .... **rf**	.5308	.8572	1.0983	2.2358[e]	3.3025	4.6467	6.0233	†.0078	.0091	.0108	.0139	.0344	.0559	.1012	.1514
												Index Numbers (1995=100):			
Market Rate .... **ahx**	....	740,043.8	972,809.6	286,832.3	193,828.7	137,293.5	105,941.1	80,879.7	69,861.9	58,665.2	48,196.6	18,572.6	11,493.7	6,375.9	4,219.0
Nominal Effective Exchange Rate .... **nec**	....	....	....	....	....	....	....	....	162.7	165.0	182.4	211.4	124.6	121.0	79.7
Real Effective Exchange Rate .... **rec**	....	....	....	....	....	....	....	....	103.4	117.1	122.0	76.0	74.2	71.5	70.3
Fund Position														*Millions of SDRs:*	
Quota **2f.s**	69	69	69	69	69	69	84	84	126	126	126	164	164	164	164
SDRs **1b.s**	8	11	12	2	4	8	11	26	26	37	2	4	5	13	10
Reserve Position in the Fund **1c.s**	—	—	—	—	—	—	17	16	27	28	—	9	—	—	—
Total Fund Cred.&Loans Outstg. **2tl**	37	32	64	100	125	98	—	—	—	—	—	87	227	227	319	323
International Liquidity												*Millions of US Dollars Unless Otherwise Indicated:*			
Total Reserves minus Gold **1l.d**	69	101	81	59	176	322	352	†323	384	430	116	207	134	174	482
SDRs.. **1b.d**	8	13	15	2	4	10	15	34	33	43	2	4	5	15	12
Reserve Position in the Fund **1c.d**	—	—	—	—	—	—	22	21	34	33	—	10	—	—	—
Foreign Exchange **1d.d**	61	88	66	57	172	312	316	†267	317	354	114	193	129	160	470
Gold (Million Fine Troy Ounces) **1ad**	3.536	3.536	3.536	3.539	3.544	3.576	3.640	†3.310	3.422	3.392	2.858	2.602	2.618	2.619	2.605
Gold (National Valuation) **1and**	135	149	152	319	319	435	562	†513	530	526	443	403	647	648	678
Monetary Authorities: Other Assets ... **3..d**	61	20	19	8	10	19	74	....	....	....	....	....	....	....	....
Monetary Authorities: Other Liab. .... **4..d**	209	126	190	197	175	167	152	199	147	149	622	1,548	1,578	1,611	1,873
Banking Institutions: Assets **7a.d**	18	21	25	77	126	160	268	366	376	633	737	635	584	667	776
Liabilities **7b.d**	49	41	39	72	37	103	52	161	245	273	1,406	1,197	1,219	1,066	1,134
Monetary Authorities													*Thousands of Pesos through 1985;*		
Foreign Assets **11**	190	242	412	†469	1,004	1,815	2,503	4,031	5,454	6,609	†21,194	34,765	64,336	113,942	†229
Claims on Central Government **12a**	116	172	351	†531	942	1,157	1,382	2,231	3,963	4,440	†12,496	31,917	88,011	119,097	†315
Claims on Local Government **12b**	12	28	35	†29	25	47	89	32	50	174	—	—	—	—	†—
Claims on Nonfin.Pub.Enterprises **12c**	—	—	—	†—	—	—	—	—	—	—	†1,486	12,979	19,803	36,478	†89
Claims on Private Sector **12d**	124	207	470	†12	16	22	29	33	32	30	†3,212	17,815	30,322	47,923	†57
Claims on Banking Institutions **12e**	33	55	109	†575	745	910	1,058	1,543	1,637	2,142	†16,855	31,924	50,133	81,124	†123
Reserve Money............................ **14**	181	320	517	†613	1,186	1,727	3,180	4,508	7,040	8,222	†14,458	25,137	48,033	89,225	†158
of which: Currency Outside Banks **14a**	121	202	316	†469	781	1,114	1,814	3,186	5,103	6,145	†7,879	8,405	12,106	23,309	†43
Time, Savings,& Fgn.Currency Dep. **15**	33	69	107	†70	64	175	211	247	655	740	†2,392	1,193	3,152	2,561	†8
Liabs. of Central Bank: Securities **16ac**	—	—	—	†—	—	—	—	—	—	—	†—	261	2,036	4,259	†19
Foreign Liabilities **16c**	170	137	407	†807	1,436	1,426	917	1,445	1,171	1,370	†12,025	15,211	23,585	53,830	†88
Long-Term Foreign Liabilities **16cl**	10	16	32	†28	86	120	155	232	297	354	†12,030	61,579	109,673	190,829	†321
Central Government Deposits **16d**	48	101	189	†35	167	192	171	634	2,286	2,467	†2,588	13,767	63,418	88,099	†297
Capital Accounts **17a**	....	....	....	76	135	141	203	199	41	278	†8,368	4,182	17,200	−61,295	†−130
Other Items (Net)........................... **17r**	33	61	125	†−13	−342	170	224	605	−354	−37	†3,383	8,070	−14,492	31,056	†54
Banking Institutions													*Thousands of Pesos through 1985;*		
Reserves **20**	58	69	134	†370	811	1,650	1,864	1,520	2,374	3,328	†10,896	30,233	39,805	76,370	†165
Claims on Mon.Author.: Securities **20c**	—	—	—	†—	—	—	—	—	—	—	†—	—	—	—	†10
Foreign Assets **21**	13	19	40	†209	499	862	1,885	3,094	3,762	7,318	†24,701	27,301	43,203	83,235	†140
Claims on Central Government **22a**	12	23	35	†260	379	585	722	533	1,141	1,933	†8,400	12,813	40,842	48,338	†56
Claims on Local Government **22b**	—	—	—	†156	149	157	389	683	870	1,040	†917	1,065	1,756	3,109	†5
Claims on Nonfin.Pub.Enterprises **22c**	—	—	—	†—	—	—	—	—	—	—	†4,183	2,666	5,395	5,348	†8
Claims on Private Sector **22d**	128	207	372	†1,531	2,635	4,881	8,659	19,076	34,301	48,175	†88,827	83,847	112,894	216,717	†359
Demand Deposits **24**	57	106	174	†489	785	1,052	1,718	3,351	4,734	4,385	†5,028	5,403	8,934	20,388	†36
Time, Savings,& Fgn.Currency Dep. **25**	85	117	225	†733	1,816	3,809	7,540	14,631	26,697	43,662	†67,958	77,998	137,181	205,957	†403
Money Market Instruments **26aa**	—	—	—	†—	—	—	—	—	—	—	†—	—	—	—	†—
Foreign Liabilities **26c**	36	38	64	†167	97	483	284	1,271	2,356	3,081	†19,727	21,739	50,235	67,106	†83
Long-Term Foreign Liabilities **26cl**	—	—	—	†27	51	71	85	89	89	72	†27,387	29,716	39,950	65,888	†122
Central Government Deposits **26d**	—	—	—	†134	199	300	470	799	1,327	1,045	†2,573	3,437	4,014	9,399	†17
Credit from Monetary Authorities **26g**	34	53	98	†534	667	1,064	907	1,343	1,524	2,065	†7,887	10,873	16,215	22,049	†37
Liab. to Nonbank Financial Insts **26j**	—	—	—	†—	—	—	—	—	—	—	†—	—	—	—	†—
Capital Accounts **27a**	....	....	....	23	—	—	—	—	—	—	†10,880	11,174	15,358	—	†37
Other Items (Net)........................... **27r**	1	4	20	†419	858	1,356	2,515	3,422	5,721	7,483	†−3,516	−2,415	−27,991	42,330	†9
Banking Survey													*Thousands of Pesos through 1985;*		
Foreign Assets (Net) **31n**	−3	86	−19	†−309	225	768	3,188	4,409	5,689	9,475	†14,144	25,116	33,720	76,241	†198
Domestic Credit **32**	346	535	1,073	†2,403	3,835	6,374	10,619	21,155	36,744	52,280	†114,360	145,898	231,591	379,512	†577
Claims on Central Govt. (Net) **32an**	81	94	197	†622	955	1,250	1,463	1,331	1,491	2,861	†15,735	27,526	61,421	69,937	†58
Claims on Local Government **32b**	12	28	35	†185	174	204	478	715	920	1,214	†917	1,065	1,756	3,109	†5
Claims on Nonfin.Pub.Enterprises........ **32c**	—	—	—	†—	—	—	—	—	—	—	†5,669	15,645	25,198	41,826	†97
Claims on Private Sector..................... **32d**	253	414	841	†1,596	2,706	4,920	8,678	19,109	34,333	48,205	†92,039	101,662	143,216	264,640	†417
Money **34**	178	308	490	†834	1,380	1,938	3,588	6,160	9,082	9,838	†13,276	14,090	21,190	44,152	†81
Quasi-Money **35**	118	186	332	†803	1,880	3,984	7,751	14,878	27,352	44,402	†70,350	79,191	140,333	208,518	†410
Money Market Instruments **36aa**	—	—	—	†—	—	—	—	—	—	—	†—	—	—	—	†—
Liabs. of Central Bank: Securities **36ac**	—	—	—	†—	—	—	—	—	—	—	†—	261	2,036	4,259	†9
Long-Term Foreign Liabilities **36cl**	10	16	32	†55	137	191	240	321	386	426	†39,417	91,295	149,623	256,717	†442
Liabs. to Nonbank Financial Insts.......... **36j**	—	—	—	†—	—	—	—	—	—	—	†—	—	—	—	†—
Capital Accounts **37a**	....	....	....	99	110	141	203	199	41	278	†19,248	15,356	32,558	−61,295	†−93
Other Items (Net)........................... **37r**	37	112	201	†303	553	888	2,025	4,006	5,572	6,810	†−13,787	−29,179	−80,429	3,402	†−75
Money plus Quasi-Money........................ **35l**	295	493	822	†1,637	3,260	5,922	11,339	21,038	36,434	54,240	†83,626	93,281	161,523	252,670	†492

	1987	1988	1989	1990	1991	1992	1993	1994	1995	1996	1997	1998	1999	2000	2001	Code

Exchange Rates

and per SDR thereafter: End of Period

Market Rate	1987	1988	1989	1990	1991	1992	1993	1994	1995	1996	1997	1998	1999	2000	2001	Code
Market Rate — aa	.3965	.6056	1.0566	2.2663	3.5589	4.7850	6.0656	8.1766	10.5704	12.5289	13.5465	15.2307	15.9417	16.3059	18.5594	aa

and per US Dollar thereafter: End of Period (ae) Period Average (rf)

	1987	1988	1989	1990	1991	1992	1993	1994	1995	1996	1997	1998	1999	2000	2001	Code
Market Rate	.2795	.4500	.8040	1.5930	2.4880	3.4800	4.4160	5.6010	7.1110	8.7130	10.0400	10.8170	11.6150	12.5150	14.7680	ae
Market Rate	.2255	.3585	.6212	1.1695	2.0177	3.0248	3.9411	5.0439	6.3490	7.9718	9.4418	10.4719	11.3393	12.0996	13.3191	rf

Period Averages

	1987	1988	1989	1990	1991	1992	1993	1994	1995	1996	1997	1998	1999	2000	2001	Code
Market Rate	2,846.2	1,796.3	1,062.6	560.7	318.4	211.0	161.1	126.1	100.0	79.6	67.1	60.4	55.8	52.3	47.5	ahx
Nominal Effective Exchange Rate	63.6	62.2	79.0	93.4	76.8	72.9	91.8	119.7	100.0	82.6	74.5	69.8	69.4	68.3	66.6	ne c
Real Effective Exchange Rate	68.3	65.2	67.2	61.3	70.0	75.2	89.5	96.7	100.0	101.4	106.6	108.8	112.5	113.1	112.0	re c

Fund Position

End of Period

	1987	1988	1989	1990	1991	1992	1993	1994	1995	1996	1997	1998	1999	2000	2001	Code
Quota	164	164	164	164	164	225	225	225	225	225	225	225	307	307	307	2f. s
SDRs	48	22	17	8	3	—	—	—	—	2	3	—	1	1	1	1b. s
Reserve Position in the Fund	—	—	—	—	—	15	15	15	15	15	15	15	36	36	36	1c. s
Total Fund Cred.&Loans Outstg.	277	230	153	71	40	38	28	20	14	6	—	114	114	114	114	2tl

International Liquidity

End of Period

	1987	1988	1989	1990	1991	1992	1993	1994	1995	1996	1997	1998	1999	2000	2001	Code
Total Reserves minus Gold	530	532	501	524	336	509	758	969	1,150	1,251	1,556	2,073	2,081	2,479	3,097	1l. d
SDRs	68	30	23	11	5	—	—	—	4	4	—	1	1	—	2	1b. d
Reserve Position in the Fund	—	—	—	—	—	21	21	22	23	22	21	22	49	46	45	1c. d
Foreign Exchange	462	502	478	512	331	488	737	946	1,124	1,225	1,536	2,051	2,031	2,432	3,050	1d. d
Gold (Million Fine Troy Ounces)	2.609	2.609	2.609	2.395	2.263	2.028	1.700	1.704	1.715	1.736	1.760	1.783	1.800	1.081	.008	1ad
Gold (National Valuation)	817	970	855	737	640	541	454	497	525	672	651	517	518	295	2	1and
Monetary Authorities: Other Assets	....	....	....	....	....	....	....	....	....	....	....	....	....	....	....	3..d
Monetary Authorities: Other Liab.	2,050	2,065	1,983	2,014	1,300	1,107	1,062	1,030	976	941	911	884	730	673	489	4..d
Banking Institutions: Assets	947	1,280	1,895	2,470	3,184	3,797	3,790	3,499	3,479	4,179	4,758	5,015	5,803	6,252	7,271	7a. d
Liabilities	1,216	1,713	2,263	2,601	2,830	3,337	3,393	3,335	3,364	3,966	4,697	5,315	6,076	6,815	7,969	7b. d

Monetary Authorities

Millions of Pesos Beginning 1986: End of Period

	1987	1988	1989	1990	1991	1992	1993	1994	1995	1996	1997	1998	1999	2000	2001	Code
Foreign Assets	451	735	1,201	2,353	3,352	4,525	6,453	9,847	14,663	18,855	23,437	†30,927	33,135	37,944	49,566	11
Claims on Central Government	681	998	1,161	1,749	1,969	4,036	6,080	8,306	11,544	13,985	16,586	†22,044	25,926	33,861	8,161	12a
Claims on Local Government	—	—	—	—	—	—	—	—	—	—	—	—	—	—	—	12b
Claims on Nonfin.Pub.Enterprises	144	289	549	1,165	1,806	2,538	2,568	3,227	3,985	4,694	5,335	†5,253	4,998	4,702	4,677	12c
Claims on Private Sector	77	85	15	145	108	62	145	130	150	115	163	†434	458	484	284	12d
Claims on Banking Institutions	219	269	479	1,048	1,610	2,372	3,272	4,071	5,386	6,770	8,928	†10,258	10,803	10,447	11,928	12e
Reserve Money	280	500	968	2,329	4,132	5,989	8,543	11,314	14,761	19,564	24,455	†27,602	33,455	36,591	46,166	14
of which: Currency Outside Banks	76	125	219	420	851	1,426	2,313	3,314	4,327	5,269	6,498	†7,084	7,639	7,284	7,095	14a
Time, Savings,& Fgn.Currency Dep.	16	37	83	241	311	408	716	997	2,083	3,927	4,873	†6,299	7,247	5,132	5,844	15
Liabs. of Central Bank: Securities	—	—	—	—	—	—	—	—	1,342	533	803	†1,368	1,883	520	532	16ac
Foreign Liabilities	29	62	98	184	126	192	—	—	399	295	25	†1,756	1,849	1,879	2,121	16c
Long-Term Foreign Liabilities	136	188	250	463	645	370	372	471	6,691	7,980	9,122	†9,549	8,454	8,410	7,221	16cl
Central Government Deposits	547	880	1,506	2,906	2,732	3,664	4,486	5,465	11,089	14,208	18,471	†26,238	26,301	38,629	16,041	16d
Capital Accounts	650	927	1,092	1,811	2,627	4,290	5,691	8,342	683	363	-780	†1,318	1,386	176	624	17a
Other Items (Net)	-167	-320	-808	-1,898	-3,093	-3,490	-2,149	-2,491	-1,319	-2,451	-2,521	†-5,213	-5,254	-3,899	-3,933	17r

(Reserve Money block values: 80 | 101 | 217 | 425 | 1,365 | 2,109 | 858 | 1,483 — Other Items Net early years)

Banking Institutions

Millions of Pesos Beginning 1986: End of Period

	1987	1988	1989	1990	1991	1992	1993	1994	1995	1996	1997	1998	1999	2000	2001	Code
Reserves	268	518	1,043	2,534	3,583	4,873	6,439	7,651	9,420	12,932	15,781	†17,772	21,389	23,777	37,790	20
Claims on Mon.Author.: Securities	11	18	35	60	40	182	—	—	593	525	397	†911	1,735	478	532	20c
Foreign Assets	265	576	1,523	3,935	7,922	13,215	16,738	19,600	24,742	36,410	47,774	†54,249	67,403	78,243	107,379	21
Claims on Central Government	66	146	287	731	1,161	1,580	2,055	3,918	3,944	4,980	7,368	†9,240	6,207	7,677	11,414	22a
Claims on Local Government	6	13	21	30	44	58	71	116	194	249	303	†3,707	3,994	1,872	2,088	22b
Claims on Nonfin.Pub.Enterprises	12	23	30	64	65	97	161	285	535	713	820	†949	1,238	1,548	2,275	22c
Claims on Private Sector	538	1,043	1,890	3,382	5,660	9,801	14,556	20,896	32,242	43,728	58,466	†107,288	118,105	124,044	133,636	22d
Demand Deposits	52	76	136	294	555	975	1,466	2,012	2,659	3,474	3,738	†7,314	7,217	7,054	6,641	24
Time, Savings,& Fgn.Currency Dep.	628	1,175	2,442	5,356	9,636	14,211	18,886	26,921	37,094	50,401	65,892	†82,058	94,100	105,053	128,570	25
Money Market Instruments												†3,531	4,640	4,906	5,890	26aa
Foreign Liabilities	137	259	557	1,145	2,166	3,881	5,569	6,192	9,127	13,370	19,378	†53,737	66,428	78,801	108,925	26c
Long-Term Foreign Liabilities	203	511	1,262	2,998	4,874	7,732	9,417	12,485	14,792	21,184	27,778	†3,752	4,148	6,492	8,767	26cl
Central Government Deposits	55	96	147	382	553	1,014	1,093	1,570	1,845	2,655	4,523	†7,538	4,803	3,861	4,600	26d
Credit from Monetary Authorities	46	101	123	274	391	660	996	818	1,042	1,476	2,073	†10,135	10,162	10,602	11,941	26g
Liab. to Nonbank Financial Insts											86	†215	183	228	145	26j
Capital Accounts	65	117	235	558	848	1,614	2,414	3,250	5,631	8,054	10,034	†45,520	49,476	38,991	45,208	27a
Other Items (Net)	-20	—	-73	-271	-547	-282	180	-783	-519	-1,078	-2,591	†-19,685	-21,086	-18,349	-25,574	27r

Banking Survey

Millions of Pesos Beginning 1986: End of Period

	1987	1988	1989	1990	1991	1992	1993	1994	1995	1996	1997	1998	1999	2000	2001	Code
Foreign Assets (Net)	443	864	1,918	4,679	8,462	13,488	17,249	22,784	29,879	41,600	51,807	†29,683	32,261	35,507	45,898	31n
Domestic Credit	819	1,573	2,715	5,075	7,634	12,867	18,852	26,966	39,661	51,602	66,048	†115,139	129,824	131,699	141,896	32
Claims on Central Govt. (Net)	42	121	210	288	-49	312	1,351	2,312	2,555	2,102	961	†-2,492	1,030	-952	-1,066	32an
Claims on Local Government	6	13	21	30	44	58	71	116	194	249	303	†3,707	3,995	1,872	2,088	32b
Claims on Nonfin.Pub.Enterprises	155	311	579	1,229	1,871	2,634	2,729	3,512	4,520	5,407	6,155	†6,202	6,236	6,250	6,952	32c
Claims on Private Sector	616	1,128	1,904	3,528	5,768	9,863	14,700	21,027	32,392	43,843	58,630	†107,721	118,564	124,529	133,920	32d
Money	130	204	365	717	1,408	2,410	3,805	5,341	7,066	8,819	10,295	†14,420	14,874	14,356	13,755	34
Quasi-Money	644	1,213	2,525	5,597	9,946	14,619	19,602	27,918	39,177	54,328	70,764	†88,357	101,347	110,185	134,414	35
Money Market Instruments												†3,531	4,640	4,906	5,890	36aa
Liabs. of Central Bank: Securities	18	44	62	125	86	11	—	—	749	9	406	†456	147	42		36ac
Long-Term Foreign Liabilities	750	1,391	2,769	5,904	7,606	11,395	13,903	17,950	21,483	29,165	36,900	†13,302	12,603	14,902	15,988	36cl
Liabs. to Nonbank Financial Insts											86	†215	183	228	145	36j
Capital Accounts	-102	-202	-574	-1,340	-2,245	-1,876	265	759	6,314	8,417	9,254	†46,838	50,862	39,168	45,832	37a
Other Items (Net)	-178	-213	-515	-1,248	-704	-204	-1,473	-2,219	-5,248	-7,536	-9,849	†-22,297	-22,572	-16,580	-28,230	37r
Money plus Quasi-Money	773	1,417	2,890	6,314	11,354	17,030	23,407	33,259	46,243	63,147	81,059	†102,777	116,221	124,540	148,169	35l

Uruguay

		1972	1973	1974	1975	1976	1977	1978	1979	1980	1981	1982	1983	1984	1985	1986
Money (National Definitions)														*Thousands of Pesos through 1985;*		
Reserve Money	19ma	170	314	447	726	1,302	1,832	3,211	5,468	7,873	8,221	10,695	15,673	26,003	54,217	†91
M1	59ma	195	346	564	893	1,458	2,015	3,270	6,129	9,340	10,324	13,166	14,047	21,062	43,735	†79
M2	59mb	278	496	842	1,402	2,375	3,355	6,488	13,190	24,220	30,625	34,132	40,946	60,725	115,099	†193
Interest Rates														*Percent Per Annum*		
Discount Rate *(End of Period)*	60	....	....	....	....	....	....	....	....	....	72.10	83.70	112.70	133.20	145.10	138.40
Discount Rate *(Fgn.Cur.)(End Per)*	60.. f	....	....	....	....	....	....	....	....	....	....	....	19.90	24.70	19.80	14.40
Money Market Rate	60b	....	....	....	....	....	....	....	....	....	....	....	....	....	....	....
Treasury Bill Rate	60c	....	....	....	....	....	....	....	....	....	....	....	....	....	....	....
Treasury Bill Rate *(Fgn.Currency)*	60c. f	....	....	....	....	....	....	....	....	....	....	....	....	....	....	....
Savings Rate	60k	....	....	....	....	....	22.36	25.18	22.17	25.70	25.20	23.35	31.48	34.15	34.30	32.03
Savings Rate *(Fgn.Currency)*	60k. f	....	....	....	....	....	....	....	....	6.00	5.69	5.43	5.18	5.14	4.68	4.11
Deposit Rate	60l	....	....	....	....	30.20	35.62	47.61	42.01	50.06	46.09	50.13	71.40	68.39	81.90	61.70
Deposit Rate *(Fgn.Currency)*	60l. f	....	....	....	....	....	7.11	7.71	9.27	13.08	14.76	12.33	10.01	10.19	8.68	6.15
Lending Rate	60p	....	....	....	....	62.00	64.13	74.20	65.56	66.62	60.40	58.54	93.64	83.23	94.58	94.73
Lending Rate *(Fgn.Currency)*	60p. f	....	....	....	....	....	12.29	14.49	15.39	17.43	19.51	18.81	17.12	17.45	16.43	14.37
Prices, Production, Labor														*Index Numbers (1995=100):*		
Wholesale Prices	63	—	—	—	—	—	—	—	.1	.1	.1	.2	.3	.5	.9	1.5
Consumer Prices	64	—	†—	—	—	—	—	—	—	.1	.1	.1	.2	.3	†.5	.9
Manufacturing Production	66ey	88.8	88.1	89.9	95.6	98.1	103.5	109.4	117.2	120.0	114.6	95.2	88.5	91.0	89.6	†100.4
															Number in Thousands:	
Labor Force	67d	....	....	....	....	....	....	....	....	....	....	....	....	....	....	....
Employment	67e	....	....	....	....	....	....	....	....	....	....	....	....	....	....	1,021
Unemployment	67c	....	....	....	....	....	....	....	....	....	....	....	....	145	79	122
Unemployment Rate (%)	67r	....	....	....	....	....	....	....	....	....	....	....	....	....	....	10.7
International Transactions														*Millions of US Dollars*		
Exports	70..d	214.1	321.5	382.2	383.9	546.5	607.5	686.1	788.1	1,058.6	1,215.4	1,022.9	1,045.1	933.8	909.0	1,087.8
Imports, c.i.f.	71..d	211.6	284.8	486.7	556.5	587.2	729.9	757.3	1,206.3	1,680.3	1,641.1	1,110.0	787.5	776.7	707.7	870.0
Balance of Payments														*Millions of US Dollars*		
Current Account, n.i.e.	78al d	....	....	....	....	....	....	−127.0	−357.1	−709.1	−461.4	−234.6	−62.6	−129.1	−98.0	41.9
Goods: Exports f.o.b.	78aa d	....	....	....	....	....	....	686.1	788.1	1,058.5	1,229.7	1,256.4	1,156.4	924.6	853.6	1,087.8
Goods: Imports f.o.b.	78ab d	....	....	....	....	....	....	−709.8	−1,166.2	−1,668.2	−1,592.1	−1,038.4	−739.7	−732.2	−675.4	−814.5
Trade Balance	78ac d	....	....	....	....	....	....	−23.7	−378.1	−609.7	−362.4	218.0	416.7	192.4	178.2	273.3
Services: Credit	78ad d	....	....	....	....	....	....	226.8	406.1	467.5	471.0	280.9	278.2	364.8	403.5	422.1
Services: Debit	78ae d	....	....	....	....	....	....	−260.4	−337.3	−475.5	−505.9	−547.1	−472.5	−334.7	−339.6	−387.1
Balance on Goods & Services	78af d	....	....	....	....	....	....	−57.3	−309.3	−617.7	−397.3	−48.2	222.4	222.5	242.1	308.3
Income: Credit	78ag d	....	....	....	....	....	....	18.4	54.2	67.7	145.8	147.2	62.5	87.2	77.4	92.7
Income: Debit	78ah d	....	....	....	....	....	....	−95.2	−109.1	−167.8	−219.6	−344.0	−358.5	−448.8	−428.3	−384.4
Balance on Gds, Serv. & Inc.	78ai d	....	....	....	....	....	....	−134.1	−364.2	−717.8	−471.1	−245.0	−73.6	−139.1	−108.8	16.6
Current Transfers, n.i.e.: Credit	78aj d	....	....	....	....	....	....	8.8	9.2	11.2	12.5	13.4	14.1	13.0	15.2	29.6
Current Transfers: Debit	78ak d	....	....	....	....	....	....	−1.7	−2.1	−2.5	−2.8	−3.0	−3.1	−3.0	−4.4	−4.3
Capital Account, n.i.e.	78bc d	....	....	....	....	....	....	—	—	—	—	—	—	—	—	—
Capital Account, n.i.e.: Credit	78ba d	....	....	....	....	....	....	—	—	—	—	—	—	—	—	—
Capital Account: Debit	78bb d	....	....	....	....	....	....	—	—	—	—	—	—	—	—	—
Financial Account, n.i.e.	78bj d	....	....	....	....	....	....	97.1	453.0	715.0	648.4	1,082.0	249.7	164.7	−74.6	18.4
Direct Investment Abroad	78bd d	....	....	....	....	....	....	—	—	—	—	−13.7	5.6	3.4	−7.9	−4.5
Dir. Invest. in Rep. Econ., n.i.e.	78be d	....	....	....	....	....	....	128.8	215.5	289.5	48.6	—	—	—	—	37.0
Portfolio Investment Assets	78bf d	....	....	....	....	....	....	—	—	—	—	—	—	—	—	—
Equity Securities	78bk d	....	....	....	....	....	....	—	—	—	—	—	—	—	—	—
Debt Securities	78bl d	....	....	....	....	....	....	—	—	—	—	—	—	—	—	—
Portfolio Investment Liab., n.i.e.	78bg d	....	....	....	....	....	....	−11.6	−35.7	−11.8	3.1	77.6	28.3	62.5	221.4	91.9
Equity Securities	78bm d	....	....	....	....	....	....	—	—	—	—	—	—	—	—	—
Debt Securities	78bn d	....	....	....	....	....	....	−11.6	−35.7	−11.8	3.1	77.6	28.3	62.5	221.4	91.9
Financial Derivatives Assets	78bw d	....	....	....	....	....	....	....	....	....	....	....	....	....	....	....
Financial Derivatives Liabilities	78bx d	....	....	....	....	....	....	....	....	....	....	....	....	....	....	....
Other Investment Assets	78bh d	....	....	....	....	....	....	−45.8	−99.2	−26.9	−389.1	54.6	98.0	38.1	−126.2	−190.9
Monetary Authorities	78bo d	....	....	....	....	....	....	−6.7	−1.2	−7.0	−3.7	−4.2	−4.0	—	.1	—
General Government	78bp d	....	....	....	....	....	....	—	—	—	—	—	—	—	—	—
Banks	78bq d	....	....	....	....	....	....	−98.9	−98.0	−19.9	−385.4	58.8	102.0	38.1	−61.1	−105.1
Other Sectors	78br d	....	....	....	....	....	....	59.8	—	—	—	—	—	—	−65.2	−85.8
Other Investment Liab., n.i.e.	78bi d	....	....	....	....	....	....	25.7	372.4	464.2	985.8	963.5	117.8	60.7	−161.9	84.9
Monetary Authorities	78bs d	....	....	....	....	....	....	−25.8	32.8	−31.6	23.0	403.3	339.5	15.2	−20.9	7.0
General Government	78bt d	....	....	....	....	....	....	65.0	135.6	128.3	85.3	22.0	−9.3	29.7	−2.3	37.0
Banks	78bu d	....	....	....	....	....	....	56.7	223.1	332.0	469.4	176.0	−131.8	−2.6	−92.0	35.5
Other Sectors	78bv d	....	....	....	....	....	....	−70.2	−19.1	35.5	408.1	362.2	−80.6	18.4	−46.7	5.4
Net Errors and Omissions	78ca d	....	....	....	....	....	....	160.8	−10.8	89.5	−161.5	−1,264.5	−252.5	−121.2	238.7	221.3
Overall Balance	78cb d	....	....	....	....	....	....	130.9	85.1	95.4	25.5	−417.1	−65.4	−85.6	66.1	281.6
Reserves and Related Items	79da d	....	....	....	....	....	....	−130.9	−85.1	−95.4	−25.5	417.1	65.4	85.6	−66.1	−281.6
Reserve Assets	79db d	....	....	....	....	....	....	−5.5	−85.1	−95.4	−25.5	322.6	−82.7	85.6	−164.0	−287.0
Use of Fund Credit and Loans	79dc d	....	....	....	....	....	....	−125.5	—	—	—	94.5	148.2	—	97.9	5.5
Exceptional Financing	79de d	....	....	....	....	....	....	—	—	—	—	—	—	—	—	—

Money (National Definitions)

Millions of Pesos Beginning 1986: End of Period

	1987	1988	1989	1990	1991	1992	1993	1994	1995	1996	1997	1998	1999	2000	2001	
Reserve Money	172	292	341	651	1,175	2,055	2,892	4,594	5,928	7,650	9,571	12,910	9,879	9,504	8,288	19ma
M1	127	207	363	739	1,460	2,453	4,399	6,226	8,273	10,713	12,577	14,501	15,001	14,237	13,729	59ma
M2	306	512	846	1,604	3,099	4,942	7,598	10,031	14,352	17,991	21,392	24,763	26,095	26,833	27,217	59mb

Interest Rates

Percent Per Annum

	1987	1988	1989	1990	1991	1992	1993	1994	1995	1996	1997	1998	1999	2000	2001	
Discount Rate (End of Period)	143.40	154.50	219.60	251.60	219.00	162.40	164.30	182.30	178.70	160.30	95.50	73.70	66.39	57.26	71.66	60
Discount Rate (Fgn.Cur.)(End Per)	16.80	17.90	21.60	19.80	17.40	14.40	14.30	17.40	17.60	17.50	17.30	15.30	15.68	16.73	14.06	60..f
Money Market Rate	…	…	…	…	…	…	…	39.82	36.81	28.47	23.43	20.48	13.96	14.82	22.10	60b
Treasury Bill Rate	…	…	…	…	…	…	…	44.60	39.40	29.20	23.18	…	…	…	…	60c
Treasury Bill Rate (Fgn.Currency)	…	…	…	…	…	…	…	4.91	6.11	5.36	5.18	…	…	…	…	60c.f
Savings Rate	27.83	27.62	27.62	31.01	30.05	24.52	17.18	16.12	15.98	15.00	11.50	7.15	5.40	4.25	4.00	60k
Savings Rate (Fgn.Currency)	3.89	3.91	4.08	3.97	2.98	1.89	1.65	1.54	1.80	1.73	1.71	1.51	1.13	1.11	.76	60k. f
Deposit Rate	60.83	67.82	84.70	97.83	75.23	54.47	39.38	36.98	38.24	28.13	19.61	15.09	14.25	12.11	14.32	60l
Deposit Rate (Fgn.Currency)	5.61	6.00	6.93	6.53	4.92	3.42	3.09	3.45	4.56	4.84	4.85	4.92	4.99	5.19	4.27	60l. f
Lending Rate	95.80	101.52	127.58	174.45	152.88	117.77	97.33	95.08	99.10	91.52	71.55	57.93	53.28	49.05	51.71	60p
Lending Rate (Fgn.Currency)	12.22	12.67	14.14	14.04	12.24	11.80	11.17	11.68	13.83	13.14	12.67	12.42	12.63	13.49	12.47	60p. f

Prices, Production, Labor

Period Averages

	1987	1988	1989	1990	1991	1992	1993	1994	1995	1996	1997	1998	1999	2000	2001	
Wholesale Prices	2.4	3.8	6.6	13.7	25.6	40.6	†54.1	72.6	100.0	125.0	145.5	159.0	157.6	168.4	…	63
Consumer Prices	1.5	2.4	4.4	9.3	18.7	31.5	48.6	70.3	100.0	128.3	153.8	170.4	180.0	188.6	196.8	64
Manufacturing Production	110.4	109.4	109.2	107.6	107.1	108.7	99.0	102.9	100.0	104.0	110.1	112.7	105.2	100.7	94.8	66ey

Period Averages

	1987	1988	1989	1990	1991	1992	1993	1994	1995	1996	1997	1998	1999	2000	2001	
Labor Force	…	…	…	1,239	1,259	1,261	…	…	…	…	…	1,239	…	1,235	…	67d
Employment	1,091	1,103	1,134	1,136	1,128	1,146	1,156	1,188	1,206	…	…	1,104	1,082	1,068	…	67e
Unemployment	109	104	98	106	111	113	105	120	138	…	…	124	138	168	…	67c
Unemployment Rate (%)	9.1	8.6	8.0	8.5	9.0	9.0	8.3	9.2	10.2	…	…	10.1	…	…	…	67r

International Transactions

Millions of US Dollars

	1987	1988	1989	1990	1991	1992	1993	1994	1995	1996	1997	1998	1999	2000	2001	
Exports	1,189.2	1,404.5	1,598.8	1,692.9	1,604.7	1,702.5	1,645.3	1,913.4	2,106.0	2,397.2	2,725.7	2,770.7	2,237.1	2,294.7	2,060.4	70..d
Imports, c.i.f.	1,141.9	1,157.2	1,202.8	1,342.9	1,636.5	2,045.1	2,325.7	2,786.1	2,866.9	3,322.8	3,726.8	3,810.5	3,356.8	3,465.8	3,060.8	71..d

Balance of Payments

Minus Sign Indicates Debit

	1987	1988	1989	1990	1991	1992	1993	1994	1995	1996	1997	1998	1999	2000	2001	
Current Account, n.i.e.	-140.7	22.1	133.5	185.9	42.4	-8.8	-243.8	-438.3	-212.5	-233.4	-287.4	-475.5	-507.6	-592.8	…	78al d
Goods: Exports f.o.b.	1,182.3	1,404.5	1,599.0	1,692.9	1,604.7	1,801.4	1,731.6	1,917.6	2,147.6	2,448.5	2,793.1	2,829.3	2,290.6	2,379.6	…	78aa d
Goods: Imports f.o.b.	-1,079.9	-1,112.2	-1,136.2	-1,266.9	-1,543.7	-1,923.2	-2,118.3	-2,623.6	-2,710.6	-3,135.4	-3,497.5	-3,601.4	-3,187.2	-3,316.4	…	78ab d
Trade Balance	102.4	292.3	462.8	426.0	61.0	-121.8	-386.7	-706.0	-563.0	-686.9	-704.4	-772.1	-896.6	-936.8	…	78ac d
Services: Credit	406.9	348.3	433.3	465.6	596.2	830.3	1,028.4	1,330.7	1,359.2	1,398.7	1,424.1	1,319.1	1,261.6	1,353.7	…	78ad d
Services: Debit	-356.3	-315.4	-421.7	-392.5	-422.5	-558.8	-746.5	-861.6	-857.7	-839.0	-888.6	-883.6	-802.3	-899.7	…	78ae d
Balance on Goods & Services	153.1	325.1	474.4	499.1	234.7	149.7	-104.8	-236.9	-61.5	-127.2	-168.9	-336.6	-437.3	-482.8	…	78af d
Income: Credit	103.5	114.7	203.2	258.3	234.7	225.0	250.1	282.5	404.3	460.5	547.3	608.0	735.5	761.0	…	78ag d
Income: Debit	-405.3	-439.0	-552.1	-579.6	-467.1	-412.1	-442.5	-525.1	-631.3	-649.2	-740.0	-805.9	-879.3	-937.1	…	78ah d
Balance on Gds, Serv. & Inc.	-148.7	.8	125.5	177.8	2.3	-37.4	-297.2	-479.5	-288.5	-315.9	-361.6	-534.5	-581.1	-658.9	…	78ai d
Current Transfers, n.i.e.: Credit	14.5	26.0	15.0	15.8	50.1	36.0	61.2	49.2	84.0	90.7	83.0	75.0	78.4	71.0	…	78aj d
Current Transfers: Debit	-6.5	-4.7	-7.0	-7.7	-10.0	-7.4	-7.8	-8.0	-8.0	-8.2	-8.8	-16.0	-4.9	-4.9	…	78ak d
Capital Account, n.i.e	—	—	—	—	—	—	—	—	—	—	—	—	—	—	…	78bc d
Capital Account, n.i.e.: Credit	—	—	—	—	—	—	—	—	—	—	—	—	—	—	…	78ba d
Capital Account: Debit	—	—	—	—	—	—	—	—	—	—	—	—	—	—	…	78bb d
Financial Account, n.i.e.	293.4	201.4	-11.1	-89.7	-431.4	-91.5	228.0	537.2	421.7	233.6	608.7	545.1	147.1	790.3	…	78bj d
Direct Investment Abroad	4.9	-2.3	—	—	—	—	—	—	—	—	—	-13.2	-9.3	-6.8	…	78bd d
Dir. Invest. in Rep. Econ., n.i.e.	50.1	46.8	—	—	—	—	101.5	154.5	156.6	136.8	126.4	164.1	235.3	297.7	…	78be d
Portfolio Investment Assets	—	-60.1	—	—	—	—	—	—	—	—	—	—	-44.3	3.4	…	78bf d
Equity Securities	—	-24.9	—	—	—	—	—	—	—	—	—	—	—	—	…	78bk d
Debt Securities	—	-35.2	—	—	—	—	—	—	—	—	—	—	-44.3	3.4	…	78bl d
Portfolio Investment Liab., n.i.e.	183.0	224.3	129.8	107.8	47.4	83.4	29.3	158.1	288.8	179.9	209.6	419.4	128.2	295.1	…	78bg d
Equity Securities	—	—	—	—	—	—	—	—	—	—	—	—	—	—	…	78bm d
Debt Securities	183.0	224.3	129.8	107.8	47.4	83.4	29.3	158.1	288.8	179.9	209.6	419.4	128.2	295.1	…	78bn d
Financial Derivatives Assets	…	…	…	…	…	…	…	…	…	…	…	…	…	…	…	78bw d
Financial Derivatives Liabilities	…	…	…	…	…	…	…	…	…	…	…	…	…	…	…	78bx d
Other Investment Assets	-245.7	-390.4	-764.3	-632.0	-399.0	-589.8	-19.3	-71.8	-961.9	-1,238.5	-626.6	-428.0	-119.3	-832.9	…	78bh d
Monetary Authorities	—	—	—	—	—	—	—	-10.1	—	—	—	—	—	1.2	…	78bo d
General Government	-1.1	-.6	—	—	—	—	—	—	—	—	—	—	—	—	…	78bp d
Banks	-164.8	-290.1	-586.6	-441.5	-387.2	-589.8	-18.6	-44.0	-961.3	-1,232.4	-636.4	-428.0	65.4	-653.1	…	78bq d
Other Sectors	-79.8	-99.7	-177.7	-190.5	-11.8	—	-.7	-17.7	-.6	-6.1	9.8	—	-184.7	-181.0	…	78br d
Other Investment Liab., n.i.e.	301.1	383.1	623.4	434.5	-79.8	414.9	116.5	294.4	938.2	1,155.4	912.5	398.9	-52.8	1,033.8	…	78bi d
Monetary Authorities	2.6	-52.1	-81.4	-21.6	-281.4	-139.2	-23.7	5.7	-62.5	-10.3	-31.3	-37.2	-135.7	56.1	…	78bs d
General Government	11.6	-12.2	11.0	15.6	111.1	104.9	120.3	134.0	18.6	20.3	96.8	169.1	260.5	156.8	…	78bt d
Banks	156.7	464.7	641.2	393.0	234.7	434.2	16.0	99.8	1,017.9	1,112.9	778.9	272.9	-161.3	820.9	…	78bu d
Other Sectors	130.2	-17.3	52.6	47.5	-144.2	15.0	3.9	56.9	-35.8	32.5	68.1	-5.9	-16.3	—	…	78bv d
Net Errors and Omissions	-104.7	-247.0	-62.6	35.7	468.8	238.3	208.7	10.2	18.6	152.2	78.8	285.5	250.9	36.9	…	78ca d
Overall Balance	48.0	-23.5	59.8	131.9	79.8	138.0	192.9	109.1	227.8	152.4	400.1	355.1	-109.6	234.4	…	78cb d
Reserves and Related Items	-48.0	23.5	-59.8	-131.9	-79.8	-138.0	-192.9	-109.1	-227.8	-152.4	-400.1	-355.1	109.6	-234.4	…	79da d
Reserve Assets	-26.9	46.8	3.2	-40.2	-113.5	-186.2	-178.6	-98.5	-218.0	-140.8	-391.7	-515.2	109.6	-234.4	…	79db d
Use of Fund Credit and Loans	-61.1	-63.3	-98.0	-111.5	-41.3	-2.5	-14.4	-10.6	-9.8	-11.6	-8.3	160.1	—	—	…	79dc d
Exceptional Financing	40.0	40.0	35.0	19.8	75.0	50.7	…	…	…	…	…	…	—	—	…	79de d

Uruguay

		1972	1973	1974	1975	1976	1977	1978	1979	1980	1981	1982	1983	1984	1985	1986
International Investment Position																*Millions of US Dollars*
Assets	79aa d	....	....	....	....	....	....	....	....	....	....	....	....	....	....	....
Direct Investment Abroad	79ab d	....	....	....	....	....	....	....	....	....	....	....	....	24.0	22.3	31.7	30.8
Portfolio Investment	79ac d	....	....	....	....	....	....	....	....	....	....	....	....			
Equity Securities	79ad d	....	....	....	....	....	....	....	....	....	....	....	—	—	—	—
Debt Securities	79ae d	....	....	....	....	....	....	....	....	....	....	....	—	—	—	—
Financial Derivatives	79al d	....	....	....	....	....	....	....	....	....	....	....	....	....	....	....
Other Investment	79af d	....	....	....	....	....	....	....	....	....	....	....	....	....	....	....
Monetary Authorities	79ag d	....	....	....	....	....	....	....	....	....	....	....	....	....	....	....
General Government	79ah d	....	....	....	....	....	....	....	....	....	....	....	....	....	....	....
Banks	79ai d	....	....	....	....	....	....	....	....	....	....	....	....	....	....	....
Other Sectors	79aj d	....	....	....	....	....	....	....	....	....	....	....	....	....	....	....
Reserve Assets	79ak d	....	....	....	....	....	....	....	....	....	1,177.2	767.9	940.0	1,007.8	1,219.1	1,673.1
Liabilities	79la d	....	....	....	....	....	....	....	....	....	....	....	....	....	....	....
Dir. Invest. in Rep. Economy	79lb d	....	....	....	....	....	....	....	....	....	....	....	....	....	....	....
Portfolio Investment	79lc d	....	....	....	....	....	....	....	....	....	....	312.7	322.1	383.1	610.2	702.1
Equity Securities	79ld d	....	....	....	....	....	....	....	....	....	....	—	—	—	—	—
Debt Securities	79le d	....	....	....	....	....	....	....	....	....	....	312.7	322.1	383.1	610.2	702.1
Financial Derivatives	79ll d	....	....	....	....	....	....	....	....	....	....	....	....	....	....	....
Other Investment	79lf d	....	....	....	....	....	....	....	....	....	2,896.6	3,942.2	4,249.8	4,274.6	4,290.8	4,537.7
Monetary Authorities	79lg d	....	....	....	....	....	....	....	....	....	162.2	672.7	1,176.8	1,177.5	1,292.9	1,355.7
General Government	79lh d	....	....	....	....	....	....	....	....	....	....	....	....	....	....	....
Banks	79li d	....	....	....	....	....	....	....	....	....	1,258.3	1,434.1	1,304.7	1,307.0	1,216.0	1,296.0
Other Sectors	79lj d	....	....	....	....	....	....	....	....	....	....	....	....	....	....	....
Government Finance																*Thousands of Pesos through 1985;*
Deficit (-) or Surplus	80	†−31	−31	−174	−359	−262	−264	−280	−1	30	−1,835	−11,654	−7,273	−15,308	−11,651	†−6
Revenue	81	†278	552	914	1,519	2,800	4,539	6,923	12,188	20,525	29,077	27,454	40,139	55,513	109,323	†220
Expenditure	82	†306	580	1,084	1,877	3,054	4,677	7,068	11,615	20,136	30,487	38,107	46,305	69,373	118,413	†223
Lending Minus Repayments	83	†3	3	4	1	8	126	135	574	359	425	1,001	1,107	1,448	2,561	†4
Financing																
Net Borrowing	84	†7	12	201	482	558	329	490	923	1,846	1,305	9,570	5,388	28,063	35,368	†26
Domestic	84a	†4	−5	104	220	349	246	423	512	1,030	289	8,402	5,588	21,767	18,318	†15
Foreign	85a	†3	17	97	262	209	83	67	411	816	1,016	1,168	−200	6,296	17,050	†11
Use of Cash Balances	87	†24	19	−27	−123	−296	−65	−210	−922	−1,876	530	2,084	1,885	−12,755	−23,717	†−20
Debt: Domestic	88a	†112	138	404	429	1,135	1,450	1,790	2,462	3,964	4,305	16,904	23,860	51,376	75,227	†102
Foreign	89a	†129	179	419	968	1,622	2,187	3,514	4,743	4,278	5,897	18,547	34,411	58,344	120,712	†176
National Accounts																*Thousands of Pesos through 1985;*
Househ.Cons.Expend.,incl.NPISHs	96f	938	1,844	3,463	6,244	9,107	15,018	22,919	43,441	69,890	91,147	94,076	121,300	187,300	327,970	†610
Government Consumption Expend.	91f	153	364	680	1,116	1,755	2,451	3,821	6,789	11,482	17,336	20,100	25,500	36,851	69,154	†128
Gross Fixed Capital Formation	93e	121	229	465	1,090	1,952	3,030	4,943	9,312	15,422	19,205	19,382	24,000	29,600	46,100	†88
Changes in Inventories	93i	26	93	60	12	−81	−2	8	663	572	−403	−827	1,000	3,200	8,400	†12
Exports of Goods and Services	90c	178	354	641	1,317	2,350	3,774	5,530	9,400	13,861	17,987	18,072	45,100	72,065	128,100	†233
Imports of Goods and Services (-)	98c	174	323	763	1,613	2,445	4,356	6,291	11,980	19,023	22,819	22,107	41,400	57,950	101,050	†181
Gross Domestic Product (GDP)	99b	1,242	2,561	4,546	8,166	12,638	19,915	30,930	57,625	92,204	122,453	128,696	175,400	271,000	478,600	†891
Net Primary Income from Abroad	98.n	−15	−22	−54	−168	−244	−317	−465	−454	−912	−797	−2,729	−9,950	−20,310	−35,630	†−44
Gross National Income (GNI)	99a	1,227	2,539	4,492	7,998	12,394	19,598	30,465	57,171	91,292	121,656	125,967	165,460	250,720	443,010	†846
GDP Volume 1978 Prices (Millions)	99b. p	25	26	26	28	29	29	31	33	35	35	32	30			
GDP Volume 1983 Prices (Millions)	99b. p													175	174	176	192
GDP Volume (1995=100)	99bv p	57.2	57.4	59.2	62.7	65.2	66.0	69.5	73.7	78.2	79.7	72.2	67.9	67.2	68.2	74.2
GDP Deflator (1995=10 Millions)	99bi p	189.4	389.2	669.8	1,136.6	1,691.6	2,634.7	3,887.4	6,821.8	10,297.6	13,421.0	....	....	....	....	....
GDP Deflator (1995=100)	99bi p	—	—	—	—	—	—	—	.1	.1	.1	.1	.2	.3	.6	1.0
																Millions:
Population	99z	2.75	2.76	2.77	†2.83	2.85	2.86	2.88	2.89	2.91	2.93	2.95	2.97	2.99	3.01	3.03

Millions of US Dollars — International Investment Position

1987	1988	1989	1990	1991	1992	1993	1994	1995	1996	1997	1998	1999	2000	2001		
...	...	...	4,441.8	4,729.1	5,271.3	5,519.6	6,235.9	7,348.5	8,718.0	9,556.8	10,664.4	12,747.3	13,775.8	...	Assets	79aa d
27.3	...	...	—									47.2	54.0	...	Direct Investment Abroad	79ab d
...	...	...	—	70.5	48.1	48.1	50.4	52.4	56.9	61.7	66.9	842.3	838.8	...	Portfolio Investment	79ac d
			—												Equity Securities	79ad d
...	...	...	—	70.5	48.1	48.1	50.4	52.4	56.9	61.7	66.9	842.3	838.8	...	Debt Securities	79ae d
															Financial Derivatives	79al d
...	...	...	2,198.8	2,627.2	3,232.4	3,270.3	3,892.6	4,805.5	6,060.9	6,718.3	7,276.9	8,691.9	9,503.6	...	Other Investment	79af d
...	...	...	25.8	55.9	73.6	72.6	80.2	83.3	49.1	111.8	113.1	—	—	...	Monetary Authorities	79ag d
															General Government	79ah d
...	...	...	2,145.5	2,539.6	3,119.2	3,161.4	3,758.3	4,667.5	5,951.0	6,555.5	7,108.0	5,457.5	6,112.6	...	Banks	79ai d
...	...	...	27.5	31.7	39.6	36.3	54.1	54.7	60.8	51.0	55.8	3,234.4	3,391.0	...	Other Sectors	79aj d
1,893.9	...	...	2,243.0	2,031.4	1,990.8	2,201.2	2,292.9	2,490.6	2,600.2	2,776.8	3,320.6	3,165.9	3,379.4	...	Reserve Assets	79ak d
...	...	...	7,483.3	7,224.3	7,749.5	7,953.1	9,170.3	10,391.8	11,604.0	12,484.5	13,662.4	14,511.7	16,328.9	...	Liabilities	79la d
												1,790.3	2,088.0	...	Dir. Invest. in Rep. Economy	79lb d
885.1	...	...	1,341.4	1,388.9	1,472.4	1,512.6	1,668.6	1,954.9	2,136.7	2,187.3	2,606.7	2,340.2	2,947.2	...	Portfolio Investment	79lc d
															Equity Securities	79ld d
885.1	...	...	1,341.4	1,388.9	1,472.4	1,512.6	1,668.6	1,954.9	2,136.7	2,187.3	2,606.7	2,340.2	2,947.2	...	Debt Securities	79le d
															Financial Derivatives	79ll d
5,002.4	...	...	6,141.9	5,835.4	6,277.1	6,440.5	7,501.7	8,436.9	9,467.3	10,297.2	11,055.7	10,381.2	11,293.7	...	Other Investment	79lf d
1,398.3	...	...													Monetary Authorities	79lg d
															General Government	79lh d
1,454.9	...	...	2,893.7	3,157.9	3,607.1	3,644.8	4,150.3	5,182.4	6,275.2	7,152.8	7,628.9	6,911.5	7,776.1	...	Banks	79li d
															Other Sectors	79lj d

Millions of Pesos Beginning 1986: Year Ending December 31 — Government Finance

1987	1988	1989	1990	1991	1992	1993	1994	1995	1996	1997	1998	1999	2000	2001		
-14	-46	-146	36	184		-304	-2,308	-1,467	-2,379	-2,435	-1,817	†-8,882	-8,322	...	Deficit (-) or Surplus	80
395	668	1,157	2,598	5,768	10,421	17,799	26,409	33,923	45,535	60,165	70,664	†67,197	68,167	...	Revenue	81
406	708	1,292	2,539	5,550	10,165	18,103	28,717	35,390	47,914	62,363	72,673	†76,079	76,489	...	Expenditure	82
3	5	11	23	34	34	—	—	—	—	237	-192	†	—	...	Lending Minus Repayments	83
															Financing	
375	46	146	-36	-184	-222	304	2,308	...	...						Net Borrowing	84
334	-33	53	-187	-300	-451	322	1,378	...							Domestic	84a
42	79	93	151	116	229	-18	930	...							Foreign	85a
-361	—	—	—												Use of Cash Balances	87
153	245	483	802	1,176	2,058	3,608	7,728	...							Debt: Domestic	88a
330	626	1,231	2,634	4,384	7,137	9,328	13,893	...							Foreign	89a

Millions of Pesos Beginning 1986 — National Accounts

1987	1988	1989	1990	1991	1992	1993	1994	1995	1996	1997	1998	1999	2000	2001		
1,164	2,066	3,659	7,607	15,842	28,142	42,934	64,330	89,265	117,978	148,387	169,442	173,360	179,327	184,905	Househ.Cons.Expend.,incl.NPISHs	96f
220	359	647	1,362	2,731	4,478	7,199	10,363	14,505	20,952	25,324	29,357	30,871	32,070	33,413	Government Consumption Expend.	91f
189	369	679	1,320	3,038	5,531	8,724	12,820	16,573	22,835	29,609	35,522	34,377	32,029	30,191	Gross Fixed Capital Formation	93e
48	32	-46	7	382	462	524	1,169	2,304	2,089	1,585	1,657	1,536	1,891	3,233	Changes in Inventories	93i
360	650	1,232	2,559	4,679	7,965	11,308	17,423	23,275	32,169	42,109	46,511	42,758	48,703	46,324	Exports of Goods and Services	90c
319	522	928	1,968	4,038	7,645	11,564	17,965	23,403	32,478	42,088	48,222	45,758	50,993	49,446	Imports of Goods and Services (-)	98c
1,662	2,953	5,242	10,886	22,633	38,933	59,125	88,140	122,521	163,546	204,926	234,267	237,143	243,027	248,619	Gross Domestic Product (GDP)	99b
-68	-113	-228	-395	-531	-700	-958	-1,617	-1,929	-2,265	-2,910	-3,168	-3,249	-3,386	-4,275	Net Primary Income from Abroad	98.n
1,593	2,840	5,014	10,479	22,079	38,254	58,167	86,523	120,592	161,281	202,016	231,099	233,894	239,641	244,344	Gross National Income (GNI)	99a
															GDP Volume 1978 Prices (Millions)	99b.p
207	210	212	213	220	238	244	262	258	273	286	299	291	287	278	GDP Volume 1983 Prices (Millions)	99b.p
80.1	81.3	82.2	82.4	85.4	92.1	94.6	101.5	100.0	105.6	110.9	115.9	112.6	111.0	107.5	GDP Volume (1995=100)	99bv p
															GDP Deflator (1995=10 Millions)	99bi p
1.7	3.0	5.2	10.8	21.6	34.5	51.0	70.9	100.0	126.4	150.8	164.9	171.8	178.7	188.7	GDP Deflator (1995=100)	99bi p

Midyear Estimates — Population

1987	1988	1989	1990	1991	1992	1993	1994	1995	1996	1997	1998	1999	2000	2001		
3.04	3.06	3.09	3.11	3.13	3.15	3.17	3.20	3.22	3.24	3.27	3.29	3.31	3.34	3.36	Population	99z

(See notes in the back of the book.)

Vanuatu

846

		1972	1973	1974	1975	1976	1977	1978	1979	1980	1981	1982	1983	1984	1985	1986
Exchange Rates											*Vatu per SDR: Unless Otherwise Indicated:*					
Official Rate	aa	89.86	91.80	87.95	84.86	93.32	92.37	88.01	85.59	93.09	106.19	106.06	106.55	100.55	110.12	142.18
													Vatu per US Dollar:			
Official Rate	ae	82.76	76.10	71.83	72.49	80.32	76.04	67.56	64.97	72.99	91.23	96.15	101.77	102.58	100.25	116.24
Official Rate	rf	81.61	72.04	77.80	69.27	77.24	79.41	72.94	68.76	68.29	87.83	96.21	99.37	99.23	106.03	106.08
Fund Position											*Millions of SDRs: Unless Otherwise Indicated:*					
Quota	2f. s	...	...	...	...	...	...	...	...	...	6.90	6.90	9.00	9.00	9.00	9.00
SDRs	1b. s	...	...	...	...	...	...	...	...	...	—	—	.02	.09	.09	.20
Reserve Position in the Fund	1c. s	...	...	...	...	...	...	...	...	...	—	1.04	1.57	1.58	1.58	1.59
Total Fund Cred.&Loans Outstg.	2tl	...	...	...	...	...	...	...	...	...	—	—	—	—	—	—
International Liquidity											*Millions of US Dollars Unless Otherwise Indicated:*					
Total Reserves minus Gold	1l. d	...	...	...	...	...	...	...	...	...	8.46	5.67	6.59	8.09	10.61	21.42
SDRs	1b. d	...	...	...	...	...	...	...	...	...	—	—	.02	.09	.16	.24
Reserve Position in the Fund	1c. d	...	...	...	...	...	...	...	...	...	—	1.15	1.64	1.55	1.74	1.94
Foreign Exchange	1d. d	...	...	...	...	...	...	...	...	...	8.46	4.52	4.93	6.45	8.71	19.23
Monetary Authorities	1da d	...	...	...	...	...	...	...	...	...	7.13	4.27	4.75	6.20	8.48	18.89
Government	1db d	...	...	...	...	...	...	...	...	...	1.33	.25	.18	.25	.23	.34ᵉ
Monetary Authorities: Other Liab.	4.. d	...	...	...	...	...	...	...	...	...	.02	.47	.22	.12	.24	.30
Deposit Money Banks: Assets	7a. d	...	...	...	...	29.26	42.49	45.31	52.59	34.98	137.26	195.93	170.31	196.57	288.38	274.75
Liabilities	7b. d	...	...	...	...	6.31	8.02	5.06	7.11	5.80	117.09	146.14	111.74	114.17	190.45	177.57
Monetary Authorities														*Millions of Vatu:*		
Foreign Assets	11	...	...	...	...	594	682	836	1,079	1,158	772	671	674	829	1,063	2,496
Claims on Central Government	12a	...	...	...	...	...	...	...	...	...	10	23	39	39	12	—
Claims on Nonfin.Pub.Enterprises	12c	...	...	...	...	...	...	...	...	...	...	...	...	...	...	...
Claims on Private Sector	12d	...	...	...	...	...	...	...	...	...	...	...	...	...	...	...
Claims on Deposit Money Banks	12e	...	...	...	...	...	...	...	...	...	49	194	183	167	395	363
of which: Fgn.Currency Claims	12ex	...	...	...	...	...	...	...	...	...	—	180	121	60	395	363
Reserve Money	14	...	...	...	...	567	670	776	965	849	642	678	796	981	1,228	1,371
of which: Currency Outside DMBs	14a	...	...	...	...	494	564	699	846	720	597	634	748	922	963	906
Liabs. of Central Bank: Securities	16ac	...	...	...	...	...	...	...	...	...	...	...	...	...	...	...
Foreign Liabilities	16c	...	...	...	...	...	...	...	...	...	1	46	23	12	24	35
Central Government Deposits	16d	...	...	...	...	26	9	62	104	309	122	152	21	30	32	795
Capital Accounts	17a	...	...	...	...	...	...	...	...	...	106	132	155	182	253	359
Valuation Adjustment	17rv	...	...	...	...	...	...	...	...	...	...	...	...	...	18	436
Other Items (Net)	17r	...	...	...	...	1	3	-2	10	—	-40	-120	-100	-170	-85	-137
Deposit Money Banks														*Millions of Vatu:*		
Reserves	20	...	...	...	...	26	48	51	83	105	42	42	47	58	236	357
Claims on Mon.Author.: Securities	20c	...	...	...	...	...	...	...	...	...	—	—	—	—	—	—
Foreign Assets	21	...	...	...	...	2,350	3,231	3,061	3,417	2,553	12,523	18,838	17,332	20,164	28,910	31,937
Claims on Central Government	22a	...	...	...	...	305	272	225	121	102	103	85	67	194	187	210
Claims on Local Government	22b	...	...	...	...	...	...	...	...	...	...	...	...	1	—	1
Claims on Nonfin.Pub.Enterprises	22c	...	...	...	...	...	...	...	...	...	—	—	68	30	32	90
Claims on Private Sector	22d	...	...	...	...	2,123	2,169	2,747	2,480	2,646	3,135	3,252	3,492	3,497	3,287	3,485
Claims on Other Financial Insts	22f	...	...	...	...	...	...	...	...	...	1,310	714	30	482	324	348
Demand Deposits	24	...	...	...	...	1,135	1,206	1,189	1,248	1,162	851	1,110	1,525	2,104	1,679	1,904
Time, Savings,& Fgn.Currency Dep.	25	...	...	...	...	3,763	4,046	3,981	3,949	3,379	3,874	6,192	6,353	7,926	9,749	12,828
of which: Nonreporting Bks' Deps	25e	...	...	...	...	...	...	...	...	...	1,562	2,073	813	395	1,260	3,140
Foreign Liabilities	26c	...	...	...	...	507	610	342	462	423	10,682	14,052	11,372	11,712	19,093	20,641
Central Government Deposits	26d	...	...	...	...	53	286	594	686	347	1,314	840	780	1,465	1,544	276
Credit from Monetary Authorities	26g	...	...	...	...	...	...	...	...	...	—	—	246	202	176	398	364
Capital Accounts	27a	...	...	...	...	276	342	346	259	370	586	720	1,188	1,476	1,188	1,354
Other Items (Net)	27r	...	...	...	...	-930	-770	-368	-503	-275	-193	-227	-383	-433	-676	-939
Monetary Survey														*Millions of Vatu:*		
Foreign Assets (Net)	31n	...	...	...	...	2,437	3,303	3,555	4,034	3,288	2,611	5,412	6,611	9,270	10,856	13,757
Domestic Credit	32	...	...	...	...	2,349	2,146	2,316	1,811	2,092	3,123	3,082	2,895	2,746	2,265	3,062
Claims on Central Govt. (Net)	32an	...	...	...	...	226	-23	-431	-669	-554	-1,322	-885	-695	-1,263	-1,377	-861
Claims on Local Government	32b	...	...	...	...	...	...	...	...	...	—	—	—	1	—	1
Claims on Nonfin.Pub.Enterprises	32c	...	...	...	...	—	—	—	—	—	—	—	68	30	32	90
Claims on Private Sector	32d	...	...	...	...	2,123	2,169	2,747	2,480	2,646	3,135	3,252	3,492	3,497	3,287	3,485
Claims on Other Financial Insts	32f	...	...	...	...	...	...	...	...	...	1,310	714	30	482	324	348
Money	34	...	...	...	...	1,629	1,770	1,888	2,094	1,882	1,451	1,746	2,274	3,027	2,643	2,811
Quasi-Money	35	...	...	...	...	3,763	4,046	3,981	3,949	3,379	3,874	6,192	6,353	7,926	9,749	12,828
Capital Accounts	37a	...	...	...	...	...	...	...	...	...	692	852	1,342	1,658	1,441	1,713
Other Items (Net)	37r	...	...	...	...	-606	-367	2	-198	119	-282	-295	-463	-595	-712	-533
Money plus Quasi-Money	35l	...	...	...	...	5,392	5,816	5,869	6,043	5,261	5,325	7,938	8,627	10,953	12,392	15,639
Other Banking Institutions														*Millions of Vatu:*		
Cash	40	...	...	...	...	...	...	...	...	...	...	...	...	129	97	187
Foreign Assets	41	...	...	...	...	...	...	...	...	...	...	...	...	18	23	24
Claims on Central Government	42a	...	...	...	...	...	...	...	...	...	...	...	...	—	—	30
Claims on Private Sector	42d	...	...	...	...	...	...	...	...	...	...	...	...	530	545	562
Claims on Deposit Money Banks	42e	...	...	...	...	...	...	...	...	...	...	...	...	231	278	292
Time and Savings Deposits	45	...	...	...	...	...	...	...	...	...	...	...	...	228	294	315
Foreign Liabilities	46c	...	...	...	...	...	...	...	...	...	...	...	...	159	230	291
Capital Accounts	47a	...	...	...	...	...	...	...	...	...	...	...	...	298	259	390
Other Items (Net)	47r	...	...	...	...	...	...	...	...	...	...	...	...	222	161	99
Banking Survey														*Millions of Vatu:*		
Foreign Assets (Net)	51n	...	...	...	...	...	...	...	...	...	...	...	...	9,129	10,649	13,490
Domestic Credit	52	...	...	...	...	...	...	...	...	...	...	...	...	2,795	2,487	3,306
Claims on Central Govt. (Net)	52an	...	...	...	...	...	...	...	...	...	...	...	...	-1,263	-1,377	-831
Claims on Nonfin.Pub.Enterprises	52c	...	...	...	...	...	...	...	...	...	...	...	...	30	32	90
Claims on Private Sector	52d	...	...	...	...	...	...	...	...	...	...	...	...	4,027	3,832	4,047
Liquid Liabilities	55l	...	...	...	...	...	...	...	...	...	...	...	...	11,053	12,589	15,767
Other Items (Net)	57r	...	...	...	...	...	...	...	...	...	...	...	...	870	546	1,028
Interest Rates														*Percent Per Annum*		
Discount Rate (End of Period)	60	...	...	...	...	...	...	...	...	...	...	...	...	...	...	...
Money Market Rate	60b	...	...	...	...	...	...	...	...	...	...	...	...	...	7.00	6.96
Deposit Rate	60l	...	...	...	...	...	...	...	...	...	10.75	10.42	9.44	8.75	7.34	6.81
Lending Rate	60p	...	...	...	...	...	...	...	...	...	17.00	17.17	17.50	16.83	15.75	16.00
Government Bond Yield	61	...	...	...	...	...	...	...	...	...	...	...	...	...	9.50	9.50

	1987	1988	1989	1990	1991	1992	1993	1994	1995	1996	1997	1998	1999	2000	2001		
End of Period																**Exchange Rates**	
	142.00	141.37	145.48	155.43	158.48	163.63	165.93	163.62	169.07	159.28	167.73	182.73	176.90	186.07	184.41	Official Rate	aa
End of Period (ae) Period Average (rf)																	
	100.56	105.05	110.70	109.25	110.79	119.00	120.80	112.08	113.74	110.77	124.31	129.78	128.89	142.81	146.74	Official Rate	ae
	109.85	104.43	116.04	117.06	111.68	113.39	121.58	116.41	112.11	111.72	115.87	127.52	129.08	137.64	145.31	Official Rate	rf
End of Period																**Fund Position**	
	9.00	9.00	9.00	9.00	9.00	9.00	12.50	12.50	12.50	12.50	12.50	12.50	17.00	17.00	17.00	Quota	2f.*s*
	.26	.31	.40	.50	.59	.68	.15	.22	.29	.36	.44	.53	.60	.70	.79	SDRs	1b.*s*
	1.59	1.60	1.61	1.61	1.61	1.61	2.49	2.49	2.49	2.49	2.50	2.50	2.50	2.50	2.50	Reserve Position in the Fund	1c.*s*
	—	—	—	—	—	—	—	—	—	—	—	—	—	—	—	Total Fund Cred.&Loans Outstg.	2tl
End of Period																**International Liquidity**	
	40.17	40.67	35.08	37.69	39.84	42.46	45.59	43.58	48.29	43.92	37.30	44.67	41.35	38.92	37.66	Total Reserves minus Gold	1l.*d*
	.37	.42	.53	.71	.84	.94	.21	.31	.43	.52	.60	.74	.83	.91	.99	SDRs	1b.*d*
	2.26	2.15	2.12	2.29	2.30	2.21	3.42	3.63	3.70	3.58	3.37	3.51	3.43	3.25	3.14	Reserve Position in the Fund	1c.*d*
	37.55	38.10	32.44	34.69	36.69	39.31	41.96	39.63	44.16	39.82	33.34	40.41	37.10	34.76	33.53	Foreign Exchange	1d.*d*
	36.93	37.54	31.91	34.25	35.97	39.00	41.95	39.62	44.16	39.82	33.34	40.41	37.10	34.76	33.53	Monetary Authorities	1da*d*
	.62	.56	.53	.44	.72	.31	.01	.01	—	—	—	—	—	—	—	Government	1db*d*
	.05	.24	.04	.41	.38	.01	.17	.22	.04	.16	.04	.13	.18	.23	.52	Monetary Authorities: Other Liab.	4..*d*
	284.51	139.14	209.94	235.09	183.03	150.93	157.83	158.73	183.94	205.28	204.83	189.99	164.26	160.63	192.62	Deposit Money Banks: Assets	7a.*d*
	190.14	38.75	51.98	64.10	22.54	20.07	29.48	26.54	32.05	28.42	47.97	25.01	33.92	26.15	28.47	Liabilities	7b.*d*
End of Period																**Monetary Authorities**	
	4,040	4,272	4,012	4,120	4,413	4,978	5,519	4,883	5,491	4,865	4,638	5,796	5,331	5,613	5,527	Foreign Assets	11
	—	—	—	—	—	—	—	307	420	408	898	1,221	1,401	1,442	1,151	Claims on Central Government	12a
	....	....	....	....	....	....	....	310	327	353	260	36	32	58	294	Claims on Nonfin.Pub.Enterprises	12c
	44	81	88	81	78	63	73	76	95	108	124	130	148	143	155	Claims on Private Sector	12d
	—	4	2	8	8	—	4	1	3	98	257	—	316	2	—	Claims on Deposit Money Banks	12e
	—	4	2	8	8	—	4	1	3	2	1	—	—	2	—	*of which: Fgn.Currency Claims*	12ex
	1,233	1,380	1,823	1,570	2,008	1,956	3,005	2,801	3,654	3,500	3,493	3,674	4,493	4,579	4,563	Reserve Money	14
	1,000	954	1,037	934	1,148	901	1,224	1,351	1,566	1,571	1,662	2,042	1,936	1,834	1,941	*of which: Currency Outside DMBs*	14a
	—	—	—	—	—	—	—	—	—	—	—	1,233	297	99	446	Liabs. of Central Bank: Securities	16ac
	5	25	4	45	42	1	21	25	5	18	4	17	23	33	77	Foreign Liabilities	16c
	2,199	2,286	1,737	1,633	2,039	2,594	2,315	2,102	1,962	1,739	2,104	1,679	1,902	1,783	1,262	Central Government Deposits	16d
	508	624	538	814	589	780	748	740	641	654	672	686	698	709	724	Capital Accounts	17a
	409	364	295	584	330	319	248	134	236	87	64	61	49	32	10	Valuation Adjustment	17rv
	−270	−322	−297	−437	−509	−610	−741	†−224	−162	−166	−161	−169	−233	23	45	Other Items (Net)	17r
End of Period																**Deposit Money Banks**	
	276	349	826	546	972	1,070	1,821	1,397	2,033	1,829	1,742	1,238	2,215	2,547	2,496	Reserves	20
	—	—	—	—	—	—	—	—	—	—	—	1,001	297	99	446	Claims on Mon.Author.: Securities	20c
	28,611	14,617	23,241	25,684	20,278	17,960	19,065	17,790	20,921	22,738	25,462	24,657	21,171	22,940	28,265	Foreign Assets	21
	384	553	591	583	560	833	937	527	506	492	496	1,131	930	1,417	1,108	Claims on Central Government	22a
	1	—	4	—	5	—	—	—	2	2	4	—	4	3	5	Claims on Local Government	22b
	82	19	27	15	11	20	6	105	62	30	134	108	53	100	28	Claims on Nonfin.Pub.Enterprises	22c
	4,079	4,365	4,799	5,966	6,226	7,914	7,944	8,540	9,075	9,796	9,580	10,605	12,158	11,556	12,295	Claims on Private Sector	22d
	—	2	3	3	4	6	100	38	21	—	2	—	—	—	—	Claims on Other Financial Insts	22f
	3,219	2,441	3,270	2,918	3,209	4,119	4,448	4,339	4,690	4,880	4,941	5,368	5,296	6,051	5,974	Demand Deposits	24
	10,386	11,953	18,460	20,203	19,560	18,248	18,778	19,443	22,225	24,879	24,645	27,626	24,377	25,686	27,643	Time, Savings,& Fgn.Currency Dep.	25
	1,676	3,469	6,650	6,099	1,683	1,487	80	—	—	—	—	—	—	—	—	*of which:* Nonreporting Bks' Deps	25e
	19,121	4,070	5,754	7,003	2,497	2,388	3,561	2,975	3,645	3,148	5,963	3,246	4,372	3,735	4,177	Foreign Liabilities	26c
	359	322	394	396	629	376	709	296	161	10	52	140	141	157	292	Central Government Deposits	26d
	—	4	2	8	1	—	3	1	3	1	3	—	316	—	—	Credit from Monetary Authorities	26g
	1,130	1,449	2,083	1,034	2,557	3,124	2,297	1,726	1,698	2,142	1,350	2,468	2,734	3,550	4,266	Capital Accounts	27a
	−783	−335	−471	1,234	−397	−452	76	−381	199	−174	464	−108	−409	−515	2,290	Other Items (Net)	27r
End of Period																**Monetary Survey**	
	13,525	14,794	21,494	22,755	22,152	20,549	21,003	19,674	22,763	24,438	24,132	27,189	22,107	24,786	29,537	Foreign Assets (Net)	31n
	2,030	2,412	3,377	4,619	4,211	5,865	6,036	†7,514	8,385	9,439	9,341	11,412	12,683	12,779	13,481	Domestic Credit	32
	−2,175	−2,055	−1,541	−1,446	−2,108	−2,137	−2,087	−1,564	−1,197	−849	−762	533	288	919	704	Claims on Central Govt. (Net)	32an
	1	—	4	—	5	—	—	—	2	2	4	—	4	3	5	Claims on Local Government	32b
	82	19	27	15	11	20	6	†416	389	382	394	144	85	158	322	Claims on Nonfin.Pub.Enterprises	32c
	4,122	4,446	4,887	6,047	6,304	7,976	8,017	8,616	9,170	9,904	9,703	10,735	12,306	11,699	12,451	Claims on Private Sector	32d
	—	2	3	3	4	6	100	†46	21	—	2	—	—	—	—	Claims on Other Financial Insts	32f
	4,219	3,516	4,369	3,894	4,377	5,056	5,679	5,728	6,306	6,528	6,642	7,600	7,616	8,082	8,041	Money	34
	10,386	11,953	18,460	20,203	19,560	18,248	18,778	19,443	22,225	24,879	24,645	27,626	24,377	25,686	27,643	Quasi-Money	35
	1,638	2,073	2,621	1,848	3,146	3,904	3,045	2,466	2,339	2,797	2,022	3,155	3,432	4,259	4,990	Capital Accounts	37a
	−689	−336	−578	1,429	−719	−793	−463	†−449	277	−327	163	221	−636	−462	2,344	Other Items (Net)	37r
	14,606	15,469	22,829	24,097	23,936	23,303	24,457	25,171	28,531	31,407	31,287	35,226	31,994	33,769	35,684	Money plus Quasi-Money	35l
End of Period																**Other Banking Institutions**	
	125	61	69	76	111	30	43	15	5	572	36	....	....	....	....	Cash	40
	145	147	—	—	56	41	42	45	51	—	—	....	....	....	....	Foreign Assets	41
	210	245	245	250	358	50	60	10	10	10	10	....	....	....	....	Claims on Central Government	42a
	510	611	606	612	495	507	608	598	691	40	548	....	....	....	....	Claims on Private Sector	42d
	25	9	17	129	87	—	—	—	—	—	—	....	....	....	....	Claims on Deposit Money Banks	42e
	341	370	395	403	445	—	—	—	—	—	—	....	....	....	....	Time and Savings Deposits	45
	323	188	362	430	296	238	183	625	495	492	491	....	....	....	....	Foreign Liabilities	46c
	384	517	356	266	503	450	450	450	535	535	535	....	....	....	....	Capital Accounts	47a
	−33	−2	−176	−32	−137	−60	120	−407	−273	−405	−432	....	....	....	....	Other Items (Net)	47r
End of Period																**Banking Survey**	
	13,346	14,752	21,133	22,325	21,912	20,352	20,862	19,094	22,318	23,946	23,641	....	....	....	....	Foreign Assets (Net)	51n
	2,751	3,266	4,228	5,478	5,065	6,417	6,604	8,076	9,065	9,488	9,897	....	....	....	....	Domestic Credit	52
	−1,965	−1,810	−1,296	−1,196	−1,750	−2,087	−2,027	−1,554	−1,187	−839	−752	....	....	....	....	Claims on Central Govt. (Net)	52an
	82	19	27	15	11	20	6	†416	389	382	394	....	....	....	....	Claims on Nonfin.Pub.Enterprises	52c
	4,632	5,057	5,492	6,659	6,798	8,484	8,625	9,214	9,861	9,944	10,251	....	....	....	....	Claims on Private Sector	52d
	14,822	15,778	23,155	24,424	24,271	23,273	24,414	25,156	28,526	30,835	31,251	....	....	....	....	Liquid Liabilities	55l
	1,274	2,241	2,201	3,379	2,701	3,495	3,052	†2,014	2,857	2,599	2,287	....	....	....	....	Other Items (Net)	57r
Percent Per Annum																**Interest Rates**	
	....	....	....	....	....	....	....	....	....	....	....	7.00	7.00	7.00	6.50	Discount Rate *(End of Period)*	60
	6.50	7.50	7.08	7.00	7.00	5.92	6.00	6.00	6.00	6.00	6.00	8.65	6.99	5.58	5.50	Money Market Rate	60b
	5.48	6.94	6.58	7.00	7.00	4.69	5.00	5.06	3.00	4.50	3.73	3.29	1.60	1.27	1.25	Deposit Rate	60l
	15.42	17.04	17.00	17.33	18.00	16.25	16.00	16.00	10.50	10.50	10.50	10.96	10.29	9.85	9.10	Lending Rate	60p
	9.50	9.50	†8.00	8.00	8.00	8.00	8.00	8.00	8.00	8.00	8.00	8.00	8.00	8.00	8.00	Government Bond Yield	61

Vanuatu

		1972	1973	1974	1975	1976	1977	1978	1979	1980	1981	1982	1983	1984	1985	1986
Prices														*Index Numbers (1995=100):*		
Consumer Prices	64	...	...	...	...	29.2	30.9	32.9	34.2	38.1	48.3	51.5	52.4	55.2	55.8	†58.5
International Transactions														*Millions of Vatu*		
Exports	70	1,206	1,498	2,380	800	1,309	2,536	2,682	2,851	2,449	2,833	2,201	2,941	4,395	3,252	1,841
Imports, c.i.f.	71	2,373	2,552	3,860	2,754	2,628	3,146	3,739	4,232	4,993	5,116	5,819	6,356	6,881	7,378	6,105
Balance of Payments														*Millions of US Dollars:*		
Current Account, n.i.e.	78al d	...	...	...	...	...	...	...	...	...	...	−7.66	−8.29	3.12	−10.37	−11.70
Goods: Exports f.o.b.	78aa d	...	...	...	...	...	...	...	...	...	...	10.67	17.92	32.54	18.67	8.81
Goods: Imports f.o.b.	78ab d	...	...	...	...	...	...	...	...	...	...	−43.27	−45.82	−51.48	−52.29	−46.81
Trade Balance	78ac d	...	...	...	...	...	...	...	...	...	...	−32.60	−27.90	−18.94	−33.62	−37.99
Services: Credit	78ad d	...	...	...	...	...	...	...	...	...	...	36.99	38.11	42.43	38.16	30.58
Services: Debit	78ae d	...	...	...	...	...	...	...	...	...	...	−14.35	−16.82	−20.07	−20.37	−15.80
Balance on Goods & Services	78af d	...	...	...	...	...	...	...	...	...	...	−9.96	−6.60	3.42	−15.83	−23.21
Income: Credit	78ag d	...	...	...	...	...	...	...	...	...	...	5.59	6.50	8.78	26.73	40.82
Income: Debit	78ah d	...	...	...	...	...	...	...	...	...	...	−26.70	−23.71	−27.90	−40.22	−48.96
Balance on Gds, Serv. & Inc.	78ai d	...	...	...	...	...	...	...	...	...	...	−31.07	−23.81	−15.70	−29.31	−31.35
Current Transfers, n.i.e.: Credit	78aj d	...	...	...	...	...	...	...	...	...	...	24.78	17.17	20.84	20.97	20.94
Current Transfers: Debit	78ak d	...	...	...	...	...	...	...	...	...	...	−1.37	−1.65	−2.02	−2.02	−1.28
Capital Account, n.i.e.	78bc d	...	...	...	...	...	...	...	...	...	...	19.50	16.66	16.10	11.65	8.90
Capital Account, n.i.e.: Credit	78ba d	...	...	...	...	...	...	...	...	...	...	19.96	17.11	16.57	12.32	9.30
Capital Account: Debit	78bb d	...	...	...	...	...	...	...	...	...	...	−.46	−.45	−.47	−.67	−.41
Financial Account, n.i.e.	78bj d	...	...	...	...	...	...	...	...	...	...	−15.29	−11.18	−27.51	5.07	12.92
Direct Investment Abroad	78bd d	...	...	...	...	...	...	...	...	...	...	—	—	—	—	—
Dir. Invest. in Rep. Econ., n.i.e.	78be d	...	...	...	...	...	...	...	...	...	...	6.93	5.87	7.44	4.63	2.02
Portfolio Investment Assets	78bf d	...	...	...	...	...	...	...	...	...	...	—	—	—	—	—
Equity Securities	78bk d	...	...	...	...	...	...	...	...	...	...	—	—	—	—	—
Debt Securities	78bl d	...	...	...	...	...	...	...	...	...	...	—	—	—	—	—
Portfolio Investment Liab., n.i.e.	78bg d	...	...	...	...	...	...	...	...	...	...	—	—	—	—	—
Equity Securities	78bm d	...	...	...	...	...	...	...	...	...	...	—	—	—	—	—
Debt Securities	78bn d	...	...	...	...	...	...	...	...	...	...	—	—	—	—	—
Financial Derivatives Assets	78bw d	...	...	...	...	...	...	...	...	...	...	....	....	....	....	....
Financial Derivatives Liabilities	78bx d	...	...	...	...	...	...	...	...	...	...	....	....	....	....	....
Other Investment Assets	78bh d	...	...	...	...	...	...	...	...	...	...	−60.81	22.19	−35.57	−81.72	−20.11
Monetary Authorities	78bo d	...	...	...	...	...	...	...	...	...	...	—	—	—	—	—
General Government	78bp d	...	...	...	...	...	...	...	...	...	...	−.77	.16	.12	−.13	−.10
Banks	78bq d	...	...	...	...	...	...	...	...	...	...	−60.04	22.03	−35.70	−81.60	−20.00
Other Sectors	78br d	...	...	...	...	...	...	...	...	...	...	—	—	—	—	—
Other Investment Liab., n.i.e.	78bi d	...	...	...	...	...	...	...	...	...	...	38.58	−39.24	.62	82.17	31.02
Monetary Authorities	78bs d	...	...	...	...	...	...	...	...	...	...	.74	−.21	−.12	.12	.12
General Government	78bt d	...	...	...	...	...	...	...	...	...	...	−.30	.39	.85	.80	.74
Banks	78bu d	...	...	...	...	...	...	...	...	...	...	38.12	−39.49	−.19	81.17	30.15
Other Sectors	78bv d	...	...	...	...	...	...	...	...	...	...	.03	.07	.08	.08	—
Net Errors and Omissions	78ca d	...	...	...	...	...	...	...	...	...	...	6.37	3.79	2.13	−6.62	−5.34
Overall Balance	78cb d	...	...	...	...	...	...	...	...	...	...	2.91	.98	−6.17	−.26	4.78
Reserves and Related Items	79da d	...	...	...	...	...	...	...	...	...	...	−2.91	−.98	6.17	.26	−4.78
Reserve Assets	79db d	...	...	...	...	...	...	...	...	...	...	−3.25	−.98	2.55	.26	−4.78
Use of Fund Credit and Loans	79dc d	...	...	...	...	...	...	...	...	...	...	—	—	—	—	—
Exceptional Financing	79de d	...	...	...	...	...	...	...	...	...	...	.33	—	3.62	—	—
International Investment Position														*Millions of US Dollars*		
Assets	79aa d	...	...	...	...	...	...	...	...	...	...	....	....	....	....	....
Direct Investment Abroad	79ab d	...	...	...	...	...	...	...	...	...	...	....	....	....	....	....
Portfolio Investment	79ac d	...	...	...	...	...	...	...	...	...	...	....	....	....	....	....
Equity Securities	79ad d	...	...	...	...	...	...	...	...	...	...	....	....	....	....	....
Debt Securities	79ae d	...	...	...	...	...	...	...	...	...	...	....	....	....	....	....
Financial Derivatives	79al d	...	...	...	...	...	...	...	...	...	...	....	....	....	....	....
Other Investment	79af d	...	...	...	...	...	...	...	...	...	...	....	....	....	....	....
Monetary Authorities	79ag d	...	...	...	...	...	...	...	...	...	...	....	....	....	....	....
General Government	79ah d	...	...	...	...	...	...	...	...	...	...	....	....	....	....	....
Banks	79ai d	...	...	...	...	...	...	...	...	...	...	....	....	....	....	....
Other Sectors	79aj d	...	...	...	...	...	...	...	...	...	...	....	....	....	....	....
Reserve Assets	79ak d	...	...	...	...	...	...	...	...	...	...	....	....	....	....	....
Liabilities	79la d	...	...	...	...	...	...	...	...	...	...	....	....	....	....	....
Dir. Invest. in Rep. Economy	79lb d	...	...	...	...	...	...	...	...	...	...	....	....	....	....	....
Portfolio Investment	79lc d	...	...	...	...	...	...	...	...	...	...	....	....	....	....	....
Equity Securities	79ld d	...	...	...	...	...	...	...	...	...	...	....	....	....	....	....
Debt Securities	79le d	...	...	...	...	...	...	...	...	...	...	....	....	....	....	....
Financial Derivatives	79ll d	...	...	...	...	...	...	...	...	...	...	....	....	....	....	....
Other Investment	79lf d	...	...	...	...	...	...	...	...	...	...	....	....	....	....	....
Monetary Authorities	79lg d	...	...	...	...	...	...	...	...	...	...	....	....	....	....	....
General Government	79lh d	...	...	...	...	...	...	...	...	...	...	....	....	....	....	....
Banks	79li d	...	...	...	...	...	...	...	...	...	...	....	....	....	....	....
Other Sectors	79lj d	...	...	...	...	...	...	...	...	...	...	....	....	....	....	....
National Accounts														*Millions of Vatu*		
Househ.Cons.Expend.,incl.NPISHs	96f	...	...	...	...	...	...	...	...	...	...	...	5,450	5,450	6,079	6,118
Government Consumption Expend.	91f	...	...	...	...	...	...	...	...	...	...	...	3,660	3,660	4,237	4,123
Gross Fixed Capital Formation	93e	...	...	...	...	...	...	...	...	...	...	...	2,142	2,142	2,619	3,183
Changes in Inventories	93i	...	...	...	...	...	...	...	...	...	...	...	463	463	634	559
Exports of Goods and Services	90c	...	...	...	...	...	...	...	...	...	...	...	5,934	5,934	5,652	5,001
Imports of Goods and Services (-)	98c	...	...	...	...	...	...	...	...	...	...	...	7,326	7,326	8,737	7,754
Gross Domestic Product (GDP)	99b	...	...	...	...	...	...	...	...	...	...	9,442	10,150	10,150	10,966	10,743
Net Primary Income from Abroad	98.n	...	...	...	...	...	...	...	...	...	...	...	−497	−497	378	460
Gross National Income (GNI)	99a	...	...	...	...	...	...	...	...	...	...	...	9,653	9,653	11,344	11,203
GDP Volume 1983 Prices	99b.p	...	...	...	...	...	...	...	...	...	...	...	10,150	10,846	10,966	10,743
GDP Volume (1995=100)	99bv p	...	...	...	...	...	...	...	...	...	...	...	70.1	75.0	75.8	74.2
GDP Deflator (1995=100)	99bi p	...	...	...	...	...	...	...	...	...	...	...	54.3	50.8	54.3	54.3
															Millions:	
Population	99z	.09	.09	.09	.10	.10	.10	.10	†.11	.12	.12	.12	.13	.13	.14	.14

Prices

1987	1988	1989	1990	1991	1992	1993	1994	1995	1996	1997	1998	1999	2000	2001		
Period Averages																
67.9	73.8	79.5	83.3	88.7	92.3	95.6	97.8	100.0	100.9	103.8	107.2	†109.3	112.0	116.1	Consumer Prices	64

International Transactions

1987	1988	1989	1990	1991	1992	1993	1994	1995	1996	1997	1998	1999	2000	2001		
Millions of Vatu																
1,943	2,066	2,560	2,202	2,035	2,677	2,758	2,911	3,173	3,368	4,087	4,323	3,327	....	....	Exports	70
7,638	7,361	8,250	11,211	9,216	9,276	9,581	10,404	10,659	10,888	10,888	11,257	12,337	....	....	Imports, c.i.f.	71

Balance of Payments

Minus Sign Indicates Debit

1987	1988	1989	1990	1991	1992	1993	1994	1995	1996	1997	1998	1999	2000	2001		
-24.37	-15.19	-12.25	-6.18	-13.71	-13.07	-14.93	-19.78	-18.25	-26.94	-19.34	14.73	-3.07	....	....	Current Account, n.i.e.	78al d
13.73	15.39	13.74	13.73	14.86	17.80	17.43	25.11	28.28	30.20	35.32	33.78	24.91			Goods: Exports f.o.b.	78aa d
-57.09	-57.89	-57.92	-79.34	-74.01	-66.79	-64.71	-74.68	-79.44	-81.11	-78.99	-76.23	-76.36			Goods: Imports f.o.b.	78ab d
-43.36	-42.50	-44.18	-65.61	-59.15	-48.99	-47.28	-49.58	-51.16	-50.91	-43.67	-42.45	-51.45			*Trade Balance*	78ac d
36.15	39.97	40.29	60.17	66.09	69.93	68.88	78.14	81.65	92.75	87.79	113.96	114.80			Services: Credit	78ad d
-15.59	-17.79	-19.11	-23.86	-26.95	-26.79	-29.97	-33.44	-35.27	-36.50	-35.95	-47.56	-55.35			Services: Debit	78ae d
-22.80	-20.32	-23.01	-29.30	-20.01	-5.85	-8.36	-4.88	-4.78	5.34	8.16	23.96	8.00			*Balance on Goods & Services*	78af d
31.14	23.38	23.42	31.92	24.88	17.60	14.95	9.94	13.07	15.82	15.41	20.98	21.00			Income: Credit	78ag d
-51.86	-40.99	-29.18	-33.32	-49.18	-47.55	-43.48	-47.36	-49.79	-47.55	-45.68	-29.26	-33.26			Income: Debit	78ah d
-43.52	-37.93	-28.76	-30.70	-44.31	-35.80	-36.89	-42.30	-41.49	-26.39	-22.11	15.67	-4.26			*Balance on Gds, Serv. & Inc.*	78ai d
24.61	26.28	20.42	25.01	31.10	23.28	22.54	23.24	23.81	22.39	21.77	30.28	38.40			Current Transfers, n.i.e.: Credit	78aj d
-5.46	-3.54	-3.90	-.50	-.50	-.55	-.58	-.72	-.56	-22.94	-19.00	-31.22	-37.20			Current Transfers: Debit	78ak d
19.04	17.87	8.78	16.47	19.14	17.22	26.30	37.28	31.62	4.90	-5.46	-9.90	-33.26			Capital Account, n.i.e.	78bc d
19.54	17.96	8.91	16.51	19.34	26.59	32.04	41.45	38.33	43.38	23.75	25.22	23.94			Capital Account, n.i.e.: Credit	78ba d
-.50	-.10	-.13	-.04	-.20	-9.37	-5.74	-4.17	-6.71	-38.48	-29.21	-35.12	-57.20			Capital Account: Debit	78bb d
19.35	9.95	24.19	13.79	-27.79	23.71	14.53	-13.41	25.30	20.88	-16.73	-3.11	43.86			Financial Account, n.i.e.	78bj d
															Direct Investment Abroad	78bd d
12.89	10.81	9.17	13.11	25.47	26.45	25.97	29.79	31.04	32.73	30.23	20.38	20.10			Dir. Invest. in Rep. Econ., n.i.e.	78be d
—	—	—	—	—	—	—	—	—	....	....	3.45	-1.01			Portfolio Investment Assets	78bf d
—	—	—	—	—	—	—	—	—							Equity Securities	78bk d
—	—	—	—	—	—	—	—	—	....	....	3.45	-1.01			Debt Securities	78bl d
—	—	—	—	—	—	—	—	—							Portfolio Investment Liab., n.i.e.	78bg d
—	—	—	—	—	—	—	—	—							Equity Securities	78bm d
—	—	—	—	—	—	—	—	—							Debt Securities	78bn d
															Financial Derivatives Assets	78bw d
....	....	....	....	....	....	....	....	....							Financial Derivatives Liabilities	78bx d
18.59	145.38	-.79	-.93	15.28	-8.57	-27.50	-45.47	-1.59	-16.63	-23.53	5.89	29.83			Other Investment Assets	78bh d
															Monetary Authorities	78bo d
.36	-.22	-.13	-.34	-.39	-.38	-.43	-.45	-.30	-.39	-.46	....	....			General Government	78bp d
18.23	145.60	-.66	3.88	52.40	21.22	-10.76	10.60	-2.18	-16.25	-23.07	5.89	27.05			Banks	78bq d
			-4.46	-36.74	-29.42	-16.31	-55.62	.89	....	....	....	2.78			Other Sectors	78br d
-12.14	-146.25	15.81	1.60	-68.55	5.83	16.05	2.27	-4.15	4.78	-23.43	-32.84	-5.06			Other Investment Liab., n.i.e.	78bi d
-.26	.18	-.14	.34	—	-.36	.16	-.05	.18	-.12	.12	-.11	1.30			Monetary Authorities	78bs d
1.00	.87	1.51	7.56	12.48	7.03	6.60	2.17	2.21	.45	.68	10.30	4.69			General Government	78bt d
-12.92	-147.29	14.44	-6.30	-81.03	-.84	9.29	.16	-6.54	4.46	-24.23	-41.68	-10.05			Banks	78bu d
.04	....	....	....	....	....	....	....	....	....	....	-1.35	-1.01			Other Sectors	78bv d
-15.12	-17.30	-12.96	-19.38	19.31	-27.10	-22.44	-10.21	-33.38	-4.14	39.37	6.34	-11.01			Net Errors and Omissions	78ca d
-1.10	-4.67	7.77	4.69	-3.05	.75	3.45	-6.12	5.30	-5.30	-2.16	8.06	-3.48			*Overall Balance*	78cb d
1.10	4.67	-7.77	-4.69	3.05	-.75	-3.45	6.12	-5.30	5.30	2.16	-8.06	3.48			Reserves and Related Items	79da d
-12.93	-.68	-7.77	-4.69	-.40	-4.16	-6.70	4.86	-5.30	5.30	2.16	-8.06	3.48			Reserve Assets	79db d
—	—	—	—	—	—	—	—								Use of Fund Credit and Loans	79dc d
14.04	5.36	—	—	3.45	3.41	3.26	1.26								Exceptional Financing	79de d

International Investment Position

1987	1988	1989	1990	1991	1992	1993	1994	1995	1996	1997	1998	1999	2000	2001		
Millions of US Dollars																
....	....	....	....	....	....	....	....	....	....	....	237.57	264.79	....	....	Assets	79aa d
....	....	....	....	....	....	....	....	....	....	....					Direct Investment Abroad	79ab d
....	....	....	....	....	....	....	....	....	....	....	2.93	4.42			Portfolio Investment	79ac d
....	....	....	....	....	....	....	....	....	....	....	2.00	3.49			Equity Securities	79ad d
....	....	....	....	....	....	....	....	....	....	....	.92	.93			Debt Securities	79ae d
....	....	....	....	....	....	....	....	....	....	....					Financial Derivatives	79al d
....	....	....	....	....	....	....	....	....	....	....	189.99	219.01			Other Investment	79af d
....	....	....	....	....	....	....	....	....	....	....	—	—			Monetary Authorities	79ag d
....	....	....	....	....	....	....	....	....	....	....					General Government	79ah d
....	....	....	....	....	....	....	....	....	....	....	189.99	164.26			Banks	79ai d
....	....	....	....	....	....	....	....	....	....	....		54.74			Other Sectors	79aj d
....	....	....	....	....	....	....	....	....	....	....	44.65	41.36			Reserve Assets	79ak d
....	....	....	....	....	....	....	....	....	....	....	265.14	280.72			Liabilities	79la d
....	....	....	....	....	....	....	....	....	....	....	47.62	66.53			Dir. Invest. in Rep. Economy	79lb d
....	....	....	....	....	....	....	....	....	....	....	—	—			Portfolio Investment	79lc d
....	....	....	....	....	....	....	....	....	....	....					Equity Securities	79ld d
....	....	....	....	....	....	....	....	....	....	....					Debt Securities	79le d
....	....	....	....	....	....	....	....	....	....	....					Financial Derivatives	79ll d
....	....	....	....	....	....	....	....	....	....	....	217.52	214.19			Other Investment	79lf d
....	....	....	....	....	....	....	....	....	....	....	.18	1.70			Monetary Authorities	79lg d
....	....	....	....	....	....	....	....	....	....	....	51.93	56.98			General Government	79lh d
....	....	....	....	....	....	....	....	....	....	....	162.17	153.25			Banks	79li d
....	....	....	....	....	....	....	....	....	....	....	3.25	2.27			Other Sectors	79lj d

National Accounts

1987	1988	1989	1990	1991	1992	1993	1994	1995	1996	1997	1998	1999	2000	2001		
Millions of Vatu																
6,051	6,330	10,545	11,267	11,301	11,662	11,701	12,286	12,777	....	....	....	....	....	....	Househ.Cons.Expend.,incl.NPISHs	96f
3,814	3,817	4,881	5,054	5,868	5,988	6,765	6,903	6,916							Government Consumption Expend.	91f
3,321	2,847	5,470	7,241	5,258	5,645	6,075	6,618	8,128							Gross Fixed Capital Formation	93e
267	350	606	488	500	520	540	580	570							Changes in Inventories	93i
4,421	4,232	6,099	8,301	9,488	10,471	10,772	11,796	12,041							Exports of Goods and Services	90c
7,696	7,362	10,670	13,714	12,863	12,270	12,789	14,278	14,603							Imports of Goods and Services (-)	98c
10,789	10,850	16,367	17,899	20,339	21,541	23,779	24,962	26,633							Gross Domestic Product (GDP)	99b
-690	-287	553	1,283	-1,409	-2,133	-2,696	-3,021	-2,792							Net Primary Income from Abroad	98.n
10,099	10,563	16,920	19,182	18,930	19,408	21,083	21,941	23,841							Gross National Income (GNI)	99a
10,789	10,850	11,343	11,938	13,183	13,088	13,676	14,024	14,469							GDP Volume 1983 Prices	99b.p
74.6	75.0	78.4	82.5	91.1	90.5	94.5	96.9	100.0							GDP Volume (1995=100)	99bv p
54.3	54.3	78.4	81.5	83.8	89.4	94.5	96.7	100.0							GDP Deflator (1995=100)	99bi p
Midyear Estimates																
.14	.15	†.14	.14	.15	.15	.16	.16	.17	.17	.18	.18	.19	.20	.20	Population	99z

(See notes in the back of the book.)

		1972	1973	1974	1975	1976	1977	1978	1979	1980	1981	1982	1983	1984	1985	1986
Exchange Rates																*Bolivares per SDR:*
Official Rate	aa	4.723	5.169	5.246	5.016	4.987	5.214	5.592	5.655	5.475	4.996	4.735	4.502	7.352	8.238	17.736
																Bolivares per US Dollar:
Official Rate	ae	4.350	4.285	4.285	4.285	4.293	4.293	4.293	4.293	4.293	4.293	4.293	4.300	7.500	7.500	14.500
Official Rate	rf	4.400	4.305	4.285	4.285	4.290	4.293	4.293	4.293	4.293	4.293	4.293	4.297	7.017	7.500	8.083
Secondary Rate	xe	....	....	....	....	....	....	....	....	....	....	....	....	6.0000	6.0000	7.5000
Tertiary Rate	yf	....	....	....	....	....	....	....	....	....	....	....	....	12.655	13.758	5.783
																Index Numbers (1995=100):
Market Rate	ahx	4,018.6	4,071.4	4,079.5	4,079.5	4,075.3	4,072.3	4,072.3	4,072.3	4,072.3	4,072.3	4,072.3	4,067.7	2,592.3	2,330.7	2,236.9
Nominal Effective Exchange Rate	ne c	....	....	....	....	....	....	....	1,474.5	1,522.7	1,664.5	1,810.8	1,395.9	1,307.3	1,042.7
Real Effective Exchange Rate	re c	....	....	....	....	....	....	....	....	156.7	175.5	189.7	173.2	146.9	140.9	117.7
Fund Position																*Millions of SDRs:*
Quota	2f. s	330	330	330	330	330	330	660	660	990	990	990	1,372	1,372	1,372	1,372
SDRs	1b. s	118	118	120	124	126	136	167	268	270	382	399	337	382	451	498
Reserve Position in the Fund	1c. s	111	111	401	805	926	833	588	408	490	549	682	877	827	745	656
of which: Outstg.Fund Borrowing	2c	—	—	252	602	610	559	361	185	206	276	348	361	330	265	176
Total Fund Cred.&Loans Outstg.	2tl															
International Liquidity												*Millions of US Dollars Unless Otherwise Indicated:*
Total Reserves minus Gold	1l. d	1,307	1,940	6,034	8,403	8,124	7,735	6,035	7,320	6,604	8,164	6,579	7,643	8,901	10,251	6,437
SDRs	1b. d	128	143	147	145	146	166	218	353	344	445	440	353	375	496	609
Reserve Position in the Fund	1c. d	121	134	491	942	1,075	1,011	766	538	625	639	752	918	811	818	802
Foreign Exchange	1d. d	1,058	1,663	5,396	7,316	6,902	6,558	5,051	6,430	5,635	7,081	5,386	6,372	7,716	8,937	5,026
Gold (Million Fine Troy Ounces)	1ad	11.17	11.17	11.18	11.18	11.18	11.32	11.39	11.46	11.46	11.46	11.46	11.46	11.46	11.46	11.46
Gold (National Valuation)	1an d	425	472	472	472	472	478	481	484	484	484	3,439	3,439	3,439	3,439	3,439
Monetary Authorities: Other Liab.	4.. d	61	87	102	218	119	260	98	104	229	188	125	121	91	117	78
Deposit Money Banks: Assets	7a. d	112	62	130	221	214	329	614	765	770	719	525	1,296	1,118	927	636
Liabilities	7b. d	102	168	171	216	370	691	1,002	778	837	1,189	2,035	1,974	1,455	1,956	2,066
Other Banking Insts.: Assets	7e. d	67	70	48	17	47	47	99	161	212	168	130	120	75	73	40
Liabilities	7f. d	249	307	253	59	157	402	729	1,770	1,862	2,044	2,510	2,460	1,362	1,352	1,042
Monetary Authorities																*Billions of Bolivares:*
Foreign Assets	11	6.84	10.22	27.39	37.89	36.76	35.17	27.93	33.45	30.38	37.06	41.59	47.90	71.89	80.99	86.22
Claims on Central Government	12a	.37	.41	.50	.89	.89	1.33	1.37	2.61	2.04	1.79	4.69	2.57	5.57	3.77	1.46
Claims on Nonfin.Pub.Enterprises	12c	.02	.01	.01										.23	.09	.38
Claims on Nonbank Pub. Fin. Inst	12cg	—	—	—	—	—	—	—	—	—	—	—	—	—	8.68	12.07
Claims on Deposit Money Banks	12e	.06	.06	.16	.25	.20	1.02	2.21	2.12	2.28	.92	4.71	1.52	3.07	1.00	3.72
Claims on Other Banking Insts	12f	.01	.11	.22	.09	—	.64	2.45	2.63	4.06	6.43	8.05	9.04	11.34	5.93	6.23
Reserve Money	14	5.46	6.77	9.62	13.54	16.12	19.73	21.82	24.63	26.30	30.79	36.04	46.22	58.05	59.75	48.96
of which: Currency Outside DMBs	14a	2.53	2.81	3.74	4.65	5.74	7.28	8.88	9.87	12.21	13.35	12.93	14.54	14.97	15.99	18.51
Time, Savings,& Fgn.Currency Dep.	15	.01	.01	.01	.41	.16	.05	.06	.05	.07	.11	.22	.21	.29	.40	.41
Liabs. of Central Bank: Securities	16ac	.05														
Foreign Liabilities	16c	.05	.04	.07	.09	.12	.24	.18	.13	.16	.21	.15	.13	.13	.15	.41
Long-Term Foreign Liabilities	16cl	.22	.34	.37	.85	.39	.88	.24	.32	.83	.60	.39	.39	.55	.72	.72
Central Government Deposits	16d	.68	1.86	4.29	5.28	6.68	6.62	5.34	9.48	5.30	8.74	4.94	3.39	7.50	15.72	13.36
Liab. to Nonbank Pub. Fin. Insts	16dg	—	—	11.79	16.36	11.66	7.50	2.14	1.37	.33	.39	.60	.32	.65	.81	1.80
Capital Accounts	17a	1.15	2.24	2.50	2.83	3.15	3.54	4.24	5.46	7.01	8.94	6.04	11.99	22.10	15.13	29.75
Other Items (Net)	17r	−.31	−.45	−.36	−.24	−.42	−.39	−.06	−.64	−1.24	−3.57	10.66	−1.61	2.83	7.77	14.66
Deposit Money Banks																*Billions of Bolivares:*
Reserves	20	2.85	3.80	4.90	5.87	8.71	10.66	10.97	12.09	11.61	15.39	13.73	23.24	19.87	22.04	23.62
Claims on Mon.Author.: Securities	20c	.05														
Foreign Assets	21	.49	.27	.56	.95	.92	1.41	2.63	3.28	3.30	3.09	2.25	5.57	8.39	6.95	9.24
Claims on Central Government	22a	.36	.42	.65	.90	.90	1.97	1.63	1.50	1.38	7.12	4.10	5.95	7.88	13.59	16.55
Claims on State and Local Govts	22b	—	—	—	—	—	—	—	.03	.12	.12	.11	.17	.07	.09	.07
Claims on Nonfin.Pub.Enterprises	22c	.27	.50	.53	.56	.50	.56	.71	.77	.78	.86	1.13	1.30	.77	1.07	1.20
Claims on Nonbank Pub. Fin. Inst	22cg													—	—	—
Claims on Private Sector	22d	11.20	14.20	18.97	28.70	39.29	46.46	56.52	59.04	69.33	75.65	85.15	89.04	103.64	115.39	149.75
Claims on Other Banking Insts	22f	.03	.06	.07	.03	.07	.13	.12	.33	.60	.52	.51	.47	.50	.48	.60
Claims on Nonbank Financial Insts	22g	....	....	....	....	....	....	....	....	....	....	....	....	....	....	....
Demand Deposits	24	6.92	8.44	12.12	17.85	21.21	27.58	33.25	33.75	39.44	42.58	38.22	52.24	57.45	66.62	83.48
Time, Savings,& Fgn.Currency Dep.	25	6.80	8.20	9.75	14.89	21.48	26.22	29.02	32.01	37.64	46.21	52.60	63.82	69.00	76.43	95.27
Money Market Instruments	26aa	....	....	....	....	....	....	....	....	....	....	....	....	....	....	....
Bonds	26ab	....	....	....	....	....	....	....	....	....	....	....	....	....	....	....
Restricted Deposits	26b															
Foreign Liabilities	26c	.12	.22	.29	.31	.46	1.00	.92	1.33	1.17	1.10	1.87	1.79	2.45	1.86	3.17
Long-Term Foreign Liabilities	26cl	.33	.51	.45	.61	1.13	1.97	3.38	2.00	2.42	4.00	6.87	6.70	8.47	12.81	26.79
Central Government Deposits	26d	.40	.55	1.46	1.36	2.99	4.40	6.93	5.34	6.45	5.89	3.91	3.42	4.96	7.76	8.09
Liab. to Nonbank Pub. Fin. Insts	26dg	—	—	—	—	—	—	—	—	—	—	—	—	1.64	5.86	6.09
Credit from Monetary Authorities	26g	.02	—	.13	—	.15	.97	2.14	2.65	2.35	.56	5.04	2.50	4.75	1.96	3.75
Liabilities to Other Banking Insts	26i	.49	.56	.78	.84	1.09	1.09	1.28	1.55	1.57	2.53	2.17	2.62	2.11	2.56	2.83
Liab. to Nonbank Financial Insts	26j															
Capital Accounts	27a	1.95	2.21	2.58	3.17	3.67	4.51	5.12	5.77	6.55	7.35	8.56	9.09	6.96	4.31	6.76
Other Items (Net)	27r	−1.76	−1.43	−1.89	−2.04	−1.79	−6.54	−9.46	−7.38	−10.47	−7.47	−12.25	−16.46	−16.67	−20.57	−35.22
Monetary Survey																*Billions of Bolivares:*
Foreign Assets (Net)	31n	7.17	10.23	27.60	38.43	37.09	35.34	29.46	35.27	32.36	38.84	41.82	51.56	77.69	85.93	91.85
Domestic Credit	32	11.19	13.30	15.21	24.53	32.09	40.32	50.57	52.19	67.16	78.48	95.04	101.85	117.76	125.97	166.84
Claims on Central Govt. (Net)	32an	−.35	−1.58	−4.60	−4.85	−7.89	−7.72	−9.27	−10.72	−8.33	−5.72	−.06	1.70	.98	−6.13	−3.44
Claims on State and Local Govts	32b	—	—	—	—	—	—	—	.03	.23	.25	.24	.27	.29	.22	.07
Claims on Nonfin.Pub.Enterprises	32c	.29	.51	.53	.56	.51	.56	.71	.77	.78	.86	1.13	1.30	1.00	1.16	1.58
Claims on Nonbank Pub.Fin.Inst	32cg	—	—	—	—	—	—	—	—	—	—	—	—	—	8.68	12.07
Claims on Private Sector	32d	11.21	14.20	18.98	28.70	39.39	46.71	56.57	59.16	69.82	76.14	85.17	89.07	103.64	115.63	149.75
Claims on Other Banking Insts	32f	.04	.16	.29	.12	.07	.77	2.57	2.96	4.66	6.95	8.56	9.51	11.84	6.41	6.82
Claims on Nonbank Financial Inst	32g	—	—	—	—	—	—	—	—	—	—	—	—	—	—	—

1987	1988	1989	1990	1991	1992	1993	1994	1995	1996	1997	1998	1999	2000	2001		
															Exchange Rates	
End of Period																
20.571	19.513	56.612	71.673	88.048	109.244	145.102	†248.175	431.082	685.188	680.359	794.833	889.730	911.711	958.885	Official Rate	aa
End of Period (ae) Period Average (rf)																
14.500	14.500	43.079	50.380	61.554	79.450	105.640	†170.000	290.000	476.500	504.250	564.500	648.250	699.750	763.000	Official Rate	ae
14.500	14.500	34.681	46.900	56.816	68.376	90.826	148.503	†176.843	417.333	488.635	547.556	605.717	679.960	723.666	Official Rate	rf
7.5000	39.1820	....	....	....	....	....	....	....	....	....	....	....	....	....	Secondary Rate	xe
27.533	33.555	....	....	....	....	....	....	....	....	....	....	....	....	....	Tertiary Rate	yf
Period Averages																
1,205.6	1,205.6	578.6	374.0	308.6	257.0	193.7	122.7	100.0	43.8	35.8	32.0	28.9	25.7	24.2	Market Rate	ahx
628.7	600.8	335.5	242.9	217.7	195.4	171.8	122.9	100.0	45.2	39.0	36.1	33.4	31.3	30.6	Nominal Effective Exchange Rate	nec
84.2	94.2	80.1	70.9	76.2	79.2	83.2	79.9	100.0	84.3	110.5	135.5	152.3	161.6	173.1	Real Effective Exchange Rate	rec
															Fund Position	
End of Period																
1,372	1,372	1,372	1,372	1,372	1,951	1,951	1,951	1,951	1,951	1,951	1,951	2,659	2,659	2,659	Quota	2f.s
534	56	36	7	188	55	354	317	255	317	135	74	93	28	8	SDRs	1b.s
473	30	3	—	—	145	145	145	145	145	145	145	322	322	322	Reserve Position in the Fund	1c.s
91	30	3	—	—	—	—	—	—	—	—	—	—	—	—	*of which:* Outstg.Fund Borrowing	2c
—	—	759	2,117	2,271	2,143	1,951	1,810	1,506	1,527	1,199	870	540	156	—	Total Fund Cred.&Loans Outstg.	2tl
															International Liquidity	
End of Period																
5,963	3,092	4,106	8,321	10,666	9,562	9,216	8,067	6,283	11,788	14,378	11,920	12,277	13,088	9,239	Total Reserves minus Gold	1l.d
757	76	47	10	269	75	486	463	380	456	183	104	127	36	10	SDRs	1b.d
671	41	4	—	—	199	199	212	215	208	196	204	442	419	405	Reserve Position in the Fund	1c.d
4,535	2,975	4,055	8,311	10,397	9,288	8,531	7,393	5,688	11,124	14,000	11,612	11,708	12,633	8,825	Foreign Exchange	1d.d
11.46	11.46	11.46	11.46	11.46	11.46	11.46	11.46	11.46	11.46	11.46	9.76	9.76	10.24	10.94	Gold (Million Fine Troy Ounces)	1ad
3,439	3,439	3,439	3,439	3,439	3,439	3,440	3,440	3,440	3,440	3,440	2,929	2,887	2,794	3,056	Gold (National Valuation)	1and
362	1,232	1,174	1,557	1,101	1,461	2,180	2,142	1,784	1,875	1,006	270	228	214	194	Monetary Authorities: Other Liab.	4..d
1,061	1,311	1,003	1,268	1,380	1,425	1,495	1,133	647	794	767	859	1,192	1,159	976	Deposit Money Banks: Assets	7a.d
3,068	4,421	1,059	839	950	613	634	261	181	212	209	170	131	316	433	Liabilities	7b.d
57	51	28	17	11	6	28	32	23	40	37	67	8	18	5	Other Banking Insts.: Assets	7e.d
1,025	988	321	214	—	4	1	1	—	—	—	—	—	—	—	Liabilities	7f.d
															Monetary Authorities	
End of Period																
†109.44	95.16	324.04	593.78	866.81	1,032.97	1,340.04	1,951.31	2,813.96	†7242.40	9,609.67	8,850.62	9,863.17	11,148.95	9,459.92	Foreign Assets	11
†7.44	11.30	45.87	265.20	245.49	276.47	359.09	632.06	1,038.12	†1649.40	1,095.54	1,007.04	1,057.18	1,106.42	1,044.66	Claims on Central Government	12a
†.14	.10	4.92	10.72	8.73	10.35	10.05	10.05	22.18	†9.78	.55	.55	.55	.55	.50	Claims on Nonfin.Pub.Enterprises	12c
†11.70	37.11	42.64	44.50	15.09	15.12	15.47	813.15	1,355.13	†1372.75	1,384.14	1,386.24	1,385.64	1,389.73	1,389.34	Claims on Nonbank Pub. Fin. Inst	12cg
†4.39	19.34	13.42	14.95	12.57	15.53	33.90	18.59	26.42	†10.95	10.23	.80	.90	17.58	42.61	Claims on Deposit Money Banks	12e
†7.73	11.98	7.55	7.91	3.63	2.21	1.43	1.05	1.00	†.40	.34	.77	.77	.76	—	Claims on Other Banking Insts	12f
†51.91	64.41	94.47	199.51	350.39	390.66	431.28	707.13	931.36	†1852.07	3,221.25	3,808.74	5,064.63	5,815.51	6,515.18	Reserve Money	14
†24.83	31.20	40.29	56.42	76.46	108.63	136.55	278.53	355.23	†566.73	987.34	1,235.05	1,816.79	1,997.61	2,286.26	*of which: Currency Outside DMBs*	14a
†.15	.23	6.11	9.60	9.85	8.74	8.71	16.24	21.91	†20.33	36.58	16.28	13.01	11.44	11.47	Time, Savings,& Fgn.Currency Dep.	15
†—	—	15.89	119.12	60.73	54.89	70.88	744.71	609.34	†1659.38	1,803.07	1,579.69	895.74	.76	.73	Liabs. of Central Bank: Securities	16ac
†4.28	11.84	92.79	219.48	235.53	299.93	455.52	718.66	1,026.71	†1533.35	1,094.31	709.78	491.23	161.86	24.44	Foreign Liabilities	16c
†.96	6.02	.62	11.23	32.41	50.45	59.11	92.72	139.77	†402.57	226.15	132.79	136.33	129.26	123.38	Long-Term Foreign Liabilities	16cl
†25.85	14.55	43.13	88.99	138.06	78.89	119.69	222.88	192.32	†991.45	1,739.49	727.67	684.87	2,119.13	1,081.89	Central Government Deposits	16d
†3.94	9.80	21.61	27.05	101.87	96.30	21.96	59.60	70.09	†98.01	15.85	10.59	3.32	12.37	16.72	Liab. to Nonbank Pub. Fin. Insts	16dg
†31.28	67.98	171.48	77.79	93.13	103.29	117.36	311.91	325.79	†2250.32	3,277.72	4,232.05	4,849.26	3,898.43	3,919.34	Capital Accounts	17a
†22.47	.16	-7.67	184.30	130.35	269.49	475.47	552.35	1,939.52	†1478.21	686.03	28.44	169.81	1,515.25	243.88	Other Items (Net)	17r
															Deposit Money Banks	
End of Period																
†25.15	32.62	41.67	108.25	250.50	279.85	291.61	400.34	483.54	†1077.68	1,874.69	2,392.37	2,921.31	3,566.15	4,031.12	Reserves	20
—	—	11.03	64.47	55.09	15.80	13.92	354.06	252.27	†1043.96	783.22	802.00	390.76	—	—	Claims on Mon.Author.: Securities	20c
†15.39	19.02	43.19	63.89	84.93	113.19	157.92	192.57	187.51	†377.44	385.99	484.14	771.76	809.98	743.73	Foreign Assets	21
†22.75	24.27	31.96	48.89	25.76	39.83	139.48	440.70	839.70	†721.61	765.20	777.96	1,220.47	2,511.38	2,904.51	Claims on Central Government	22a
.05	.06	.22	.04	.02	.53	—	1.20	4.92	†1.19	.12	.15	13.51	26.82	.07	Claims on State and Local Govts	22b
1.33	1.06	3.95	2.28	31.73	26.71	79.64	136.68	179.52	†7.76	8.21	2.79	16.04	88.69	3.34	Claims on Nonfin.Pub.Enterprises	22c
....	....	....	....	....	....	....	....	....	293.88	56.41	32.21	45.43	22.27	.01	Claims on Nonbank Pub. Fin. Inst	22cg
†201.25	261.92	300.88	376.47	559.31	767.97	859.81	797.97	1,184.61	†2392.28	5,287.72	6,021.81	6,655.06	8,350.97	10,310.04	Claims on Private Sector	22d
†1.78	1.78	2.34	2.94	3.18	.99	.80	.72	.18	†47.42	45.55	112.78	145.49	314.18	60.18	Claims on Other Banking Insts	22f
—	—	—	—	—	—	—	10.75	12.79	†24.89	46.38	57.16	179.77	409.56	129.95	Claims on Nonbank Financial Insts	22g
†82.88	105.84	109.37	150.91	241.61	245.24	256.54	666.18	902.56	†2010.16	3,616.46	3,683.59	4,211.88	5,743.23	6,821.99	Demand Deposits	24
†131.27	149.95	256.09	460.70	673.39	817.46	1,077.76	1,532.33	2,079.16	†2405.98	3,431.80	4,508.54	5,247.37	6,325.39	7,270.21	Time, Savings,& Fgn.Currency Dep.	25
....	....	....	....	....	....	....	....	....	32.43	63.76	15.43	50.72	94.92	103.94	Money Market Instruments	26aa
....	....	....	....	....	....	....	....	....	17.15	.51	3.48	8.96	10.69	28.01	Bonds	26ab
....	....	....	....	....	....	....	....	....	47.98	63.17	68.21	94.91	168.57	226.77	Restricted Deposits	26b
5.56	11.44	6.87	8.21	22.54	22.04	32.29	11.25	17.07	†65.89	95.33	69.11	76.59	204.09	308.57	Foreign Liabilities	26c
†38.93	52.66	38.76	34.06	35.97	26.68	34.71	33.16	35.54	†35.01	9.68	26.54	7.98	16.45	21.26	Long-Term Foreign Liabilities	26cl
9.39	6.20	7.62	13.88	23.74	24.68	27.81	47.20	57.95	†270.51	464.51	492.97	865.93	1,523.01	1,277.75	Central Government Deposits	26d
6.07	2.90	3.78	4.42	6.53	9.70	16.17	106.12	13.42	†41.70	51.53	52.57	109.29	138.83	64.36	Liab. to Nonbank Pub. Fin. Insts	26dg
†4.83	20.49	8.98	14.31	14.70	14.82	33.04	17.73	25.57	†1.06	—	—	13.10	41.16	84.16	Credit from Monetary Authorities	26g
†3.75	5.98	8.52	16.45	27.80	32.90	37.02	31.05	21.87	†208.18	287.70	283.77	267.04	400.01	297.94	Liabilities to Other Banking Insts	26i
....	....	....	....	....	....	....	....	....	38.83	105.51	195.18	160.53	164.28	296.23	Liab. to Nonbank Financial Insts	26j
†8.80	23.71	31.17	44.32	68.14	100.37	146.86	90.55	330.50	†848.76	1,271.61	1,665.67	1,877.47	2,364.81	2,937.11	Capital Accounts	27a
†-23.78	-38.46	-35.91	-80.03	-103.89	-49.05	-119.04	-200.58	-338.59	†-35.51	-208.08	-381.70	-632.18	-1,095.43	-1,555.36	Other Items (Net)	27r
															Monetary Survey	
End of Period																
†114.99	90.90	267.56	429.99	693.68	824.19	1,010.14	1,413.97	1,957.69	†6020.60	8,806.02	8,555.87	10,067.11	11,592.98	9,870.64	Foreign Assets (Net)	31n
†218.99	328.87	393.60	657.73	731.19	1,036.60	1,318.27	2,574.26	4,387.89	†5259.43	6,486.16	8,178.82	9,169.12	10,579.20	13,483.77	Domestic Credit	32
†-5.05	14.82	27.08	211.22	109.45	212.73	351.07	802.68	1,627.54	†1109.07	-343.25	564.36	726.85	-24.34	1,589.53	Claims on Central Govt. (Net)	32an
†.10	.11	.24	.08	.06	.53	—	1.20	4.92	†1.19	.12	.15	13.51	26.82	.07	Claims on State and Local Govts	32b
†1.47	1.16	8.86	13.00	40.47	37.06	89.69	146.73	201.71	†17.53	8.76	3.34	16.59	89.24	3.84	Claims on Nonfin.Pub.Enterprises	32c
†11.70	37.11	42.64	44.50	15.09	15.12	15.47	813.15	1,355.13	†1666.63	1,440.54	1,418.45	1,431.07	1,412.00	1,389.34	Claims on Nonbank Pub.Fin.Inst	32cg
†201.25	261.92	304.88	378.08	559.32	767.97	859.82	797.98	1,184.62	†2392.29	5,287.73	6,021.82	6,655.07	8,350.98	10,310.86	Claims on Private Sector	32d
†9.51	13.76	9.90	10.85	6.80	3.20	2.23	1.78	1.18	†47.83	45.89	113.55	146.26	314.95	60.18	Claims on Other Banking Insts	32f
†—	—	—	—	—	—	—	10.75	12.79	†24.89	46.38	57.16	179.77	409.56	129.95	Claims on Nonbank Financial Inst	32g

Venezuela, Rep. Bol.

		1972	1973	1974	1975	1976	1977	1978	1979	1980	1981	1982	1983	1984	1985	1986
Monetary Survey (cont.)																*Billions of Bolivares:*
Money	34	9.60	11.43	16.87	25.52	28.70	36.98	43.85	46.35	54.26	58.02	60.44	75.96	96.25	104.71	109.32
Quasi-Money	35	6.80	8.21	9.76	15.30	21.64	26.27	29.09	32.06	37.71	46.32	52.82	64.03	69.29	76.83	95.68
Money Market Instruments	36aa	....	....	....	....	....	....	....	....	....	....	....	....	....	....	....
Bonds	36ab	....	....	....	....	....	....	....	....	....	....	....	....	....	....	....
Liabs. of Central Bank: Securities	36ac	.05	—	—	—	—	—	—	—	—	—	—	—	—	—	—
Restricted Deposits	36b	—	—	—	—	—	—	—	—	—	—	—	—	—	—	—
Long-Term Foreign Liabilities	36cl	.54	.84	.82	1.46	1.52	2.84	3.62	2.32	3.25	4.60	7.26	7.09	9.02	13.54	27.51
Liab. to Nonbank Pub. Fin. Insts	36dg	—	—	11.79	16.36	11.66	7.50	2.14	1.37	.33	.39	.60	.32	2.29	6.67	7.89
Liabilities to Other Banking Insts	36i	.49	.56	.78	.84	1.09	1.09	1.28	1.55	1.57	2.53	2.17	2.62	2.11	2.56	2.83
Liab. to Nonbank Financial Insts	36j															
Capital Accounts	37a	3.10	4.44	5.09	6.00	6.81	8.05	9.36	11.23	13.55	16.29	14.60	21.08	29.05	19.44	36.51
Other Items (Net)	37r	−2.23	−1.95	−2.30	−2.53	−2.24	−7.07	−9.30	−7.42	−11.16	−10.83	−1.02	−17.70	−12.57	−11.84	−21.05
Money plus Quasi-Money	35l	16.41	19.63	26.63	40.82	50.34	63.24	72.94	78.41	91.97	104.34	113.26	139.99	165.55	181.54	205.00
Other Banking Institutions																*Billions of Bolivares:*
Reserves	40	.09	.18	.52	.28	.65	1.00	.71	1.35	1.65	1.68	.98	.78	1.43	1.08	.73
Claims on Mon.Author.: Securities	40c	....	....	....	....	....	....	....	....	....	....	....	....	....	....	....
Foreign Assets	41	.29	.30	.20	.07	.20	.20	.43	.69	.91	.72	.56	.52	.56	.55	.58
Claims on Central Government	42a	1.18	1.07	1.08	.43	.63	.71	1.01	.91	.73	4.98	1.52	.92	2.37	2.64	2.88
Claims on Nonfin.Pub.Enterprises	42c	.02	.02	.01	.02	.02	.46	.01	.01	.01	.01	.01	.22	—	—	—
Claims on Nonbank Pub. Fin. Inst	42cg															
Claims on Private Sector	42d	8.79	13.30	16.69	18.39	24.97	34.06	43.59	56.28	73.86	87.55	101.14	105.46	109.28	116.82	126.02
Claims on Deposit Money Banks	42e	.58	.74	1.12	1.13	1.43	1.50	2.09	2.22	2.40	3.50	2.88	3.53	3.25	4.06	4.20
Claims on Nonbank Financial Insts	42g															
Demand Deposits	44	.15	.26	.57	.70	1.01	1.63	2.79	3.19	3.33	3.26	4.20	4.23	5.63	5.13	5.39
Time, Savings,& Fgn.Currency Dep.	45	6.44	9.56	12.33	15.20	20.30	25.56	29.82	36.40	45.34	56.84	64.28	76.43	82.81	84.19	80.63
Money Market Instruments	46aa															
Bonds	46ab	.52	.65	.79	.83	1.03	1.66	3.21	5.11	9.78	11.92	15.53	9.78	7.62	17.79	25.10
Restricted Deposits	46b															
Foreign Liabilities	46c	—	—	—	—	—	.02	.05	1.01	.74	1.15	1.62	.89	.74	.73	.69
Long-Term Foreign Liabilities	46cl	1.08	1.32	1.08	.25	.67	1.71	3.08	6.59	7.25	7.62	9.15	9.69	9.48	9.41	14.43
Central Government Deposits	46d	.77	.92	1.26	.63	1.41	1.74	1.49	2.10	4.60	4.69	3.53	7.91	8.64	12.05	18.11
Liab. to Nonbank Pub. Fin. Insts	46dg															
Credit from Monetary Authorities	46g	.01	.11	.22	.09	—	.64	1.97	1.98	3.41	6.18	8.34	7.80	9.19	4.21	5.78
Credit from Deposit Money Banks	46h	.31	1.19	1.48	1.66	2.23	3.21	2.98	3.09	3.03	3.01	2.22	2.74	3.11	3.29	3.45
Liab. to Nonbank Financial Insts	46j															
Capital Accounts	47a	5.04	6.09	7.49	1.87	2.37	3.15	3.90	4.32	5.15	6.01	6.47	6.59	7.90	8.13	7.99
Other Items (Net)	47r	−3.38	−4.49	−5.60	−.91	−1.14	−1.38	−1.47	−2.32	−3.07	−2.23	−8.26	−14.62	−18.22	−19.78	−27.15
Banking Survey																*Billions of Bolivares:*
Foreign Assets (Net)	51n	7.46	10.53	27.80	38.50	37.29	35.53	29.84	34.95	32.53	38.42	40.76	51.19	77.51	85.75	91.75
Domestic Credit	52	20.35	26.59	31.43	42.61	56.21	73.03	91.12	104.34	132.49	159.38	185.61	191.03	208.94	226.98	270.70
Claims on Central Govt. (Net)	52an	.05	−1.44	−4.78	−5.06	−8.67	−8.76	−9.76	−11.90	−12.21	−5.43	−2.07	−5.28	−5.29	−15.54	−18.68
Claims on State and Local Govts	52b								.03	.23	.25	.24	.27	.29	.22	.07
Claims on Nonfin.Pub.Enterprises	52c	.30	.52	.54	.58	.52	1.03	.71	.77	.78	.87	1.14	1.52	1.00	1.16	1.58
Claims on Nonbank Pub.Fin.Insts	52cg														8.68	12.07
Claims on Private Sector	52d	20.00	27.50	35.67	47.09	64.36	80.76	100.16	115.44	143.68	163.69	186.31	194.52	212.93	232.45	275.77
Claims on Nonbank Financial Inst	52g															
Liquid Liabilities	55l	22.91	29.27	39.00	56.43	71.00	89.42	104.85	116.65	138.99	162.76	180.77	219.86	252.56	269.78	290.28
Money Market Instruments	56aa															
Bonds	56ab	.52	.65	.79	.83	1.03	1.66	3.21	5.11	9.78	11.92	15.53	9.78	7.62	17.79	25.10
Liabs. of Central Bank: Securities	56ac	.05	—	—	—	—	—	—	—	—	—	—	—	—	—	—
Restricted Deposits	56b	—	—	—	—	—	—	—	—	—	—	—	—	—	—	—
Long-Term Foreign Liabilities	56cl	1.63	2.16	1.90	1.71	2.19	4.55	6.70	8.91	10.50	12.23	16.41	16.78	18.49	22.95	41.94
Liab. to Nonbank Pub. Fin. Insts	56dg	—	—	11.79	16.36	11.66	7.50	2.14	1.37	.33	.39	.60	.32	2.29	6.67	7.89
Liab. to Nonbank Financial Insts	56j															
Capital Accounts	57a	8.14	10.53	12.58	7.87	9.18	11.21	13.26	15.55	18.70	22.30	21.07	27.67	36.95	27.57	44.50
Other Items (Net)	57r	−5.43	−5.49	−6.83	−2.10	−1.56	−5.78	−9.20	−8.30	−13.27	−11.80	−8.00	−32.20	−31.46	−32.03	−47.16
Interest Rates																*Percent Per Annum*
Discount Rate *(End of Period)*	60	5.00	5.00	5.00	7.00	7.00	7.00	7.50	11.00	13.00	14.00	13.00	11.00	11.00	8.00	8.00
Money Market Rate	60b	....	....	....	....	....	....	....	....	....	....	....	....	....	....	....
Savings Rate	60k	....	....	....	....	....	....	....	....	....	....	....	....	....	....	....
Deposit Rate	60l	....	....	....	....	....	....	....	....	....	....	....	....	12.29	10.52	8.93
Lending Rate	60p	....	....	....	....	....	....	....	....	....	....	....	....	9.57	9.33	8.49
Government Bond Yield	61	....	....	....	....	....	....	....	....	....	....	....	....	13.15	12.55	12.07
Prices, Production, Labor																*Index Numbers (1995=100):*
Industrial Share Prices	62	15.7	19.1	24.2	27.4	32.1	33.5	23.3	18.9	15.4	13.4	10.0	9.9	12.9	14.4	22.7
Prices: Home & Import Goods	63	.8	.9	1.0	1.2	1.2	1.4	1.5	1.6	1.9	2.2	2.4	2.5	†3.0	3.4	4.0
Home Goods	63a	.7	.8	.9	1.0	1.1	1.2	1.3	1.5	1.8	2.1	2.3	2.4	†2.9	3.3	3.9
Consumer Prices	64	.9	1.0	1.1	1.2	1.3	1.4	1.4	1.6	2.0	2.3	2.5	2.7	3.0	3.3	3.7
Crude Petroleum Production	66aa	112	116	103	81	80	77	75	82	75	75	68	62	62	58	62
Labor Force	67d	....	....	....	....	....	....	....	....	....	....	....	....	....		*Number in Thousands:*
Employment	67e	....	....	....	....	....	....	....	....	....	....	....	....	....	5,106	5,396
Unemployment	67c	....	....	....	....	....	....	....	....	....	....	....	....	....	767	667
Unemployment Rate (%)	67r	....	....	....	....	....	....	....	....	....	....	....	....	....	13.1	11.0
International Transactions																*Billions of Bolivares*
Exports	70	13.8	21.0	47.4	37.7	39.9	41.0	39.4	61.5	82.5	86.4	70.8	64.7	97.2	94.0	77.8
Petroleum	70a	12.6	18.6	45.2	35.7	37.6	39.1	37.5	58.5	78.3	81.7	67.1	59.5	85.2	77.6	53.8
Crude Petroleum	70aa	8.1	11.6	27.9	24.8	24.0	25.6	23.8	36.6	53.2	58.4	44.7	36.6	53.7	44.7	29.9
Imports, c.i.f.	71	10.6	12.1	17.9	25.7	29.2	47.0	50.5	45.8	45.8	56.3	55.6	37.5	52.8	61.8	75.1
Imports, f.o.b.	71.v	9.5	10.9	16.2	22.8	25.9	41.9	45.5	41.3	45.8	50.7	50.1	33.7	47.6	55.6	67.6
Exports	70..d	3,166	3,298	11,153	8,800	9,299	9,551	9,187	14,317	19,221	20,980	16,590	13,937	13,937	14,438	8,660
Petroleum	70a.d	2,857	4,328	10,548	8,324	8,763	9,110	8,740	13,633	17,562	18,609	15,633	13,857	14,824	12,956	7,178
Imports, f.o.b.	71.vd	2,207	2,534	3,757	5,324	6,787	9,766	10,601	9,613	10,655	11,808	11,661	5,783	7,004	7,303	7,661
Volume of Exports																*1995=100*
Petroleum	72a	120.0	121.0	110.9	81.2	84.4	77.1	77.7	82.5	73.0	68.3	60.8	59.1	59.9	54.7	61.0
Crude Petroleum	72aa	115.7	114.9	95.7	79.7	74.4	71.5	67.4	75.9	69.6	68.6	57.5	53.3	54.7	44.9	51.3
Refined Pretroleum	72ab	128.6	133.4	142.1	84.5	105.1	88.5	98.7	95.9	79.9	67.8	67.7	70.9	70.5	74.6	80.7
Import Prices (Wholesale)	76.x	1.0	1.1	1.3	1.4	1.5	1.6	1.7	1.9	2.1	2.4	2.6	2.7	†3.2	3.7	4.4

1987	1988	1989	1990	1991	1992	1993	1994	1995	1996	1997	1998	1999	2000	2001		
End of Period															**Monetary Survey (cont.)**	
†111.67	142.45	153.13	214.51	327.21	363.53	407.22	974.12	1,343.96	†2777.65	4,917.78	5,149.17	6,412.64	8,037.22	9,287.01	Money	34
†131.42	150.18	262.20	470.30	683.24	826.20	1,086.46	1,548.58	2,101.07	†2426.31	3,468.38	4,524.82	5,260.38	6,336.83	7,281.68	Quasi-Money	35
....	....	....	....	....	....	....	....	....	32.43	63.76	15.43	50.72	94.92	103.94	Money Market Instruments	36aa
....	....	....	....	....	....	....	....	....	17.15	.51	3.48	8.96	10.69	28.01	Bonds	36ab
†—	—	4.86	54.65	5.64	39.09	56.96	390.65	357.06	†615.43	1,019.85	777.68	504.98	.76	.73	Liabs. of Central Bank: Securities	36ac
....	....	....	....	....	....	....	....	....	47.98	63.17	68.21	94.91	168.57	226.77	Restricted Deposits	36b
†39.89	58.68	39.38	45.29	68.38	77.14	93.83	125.89	175.32	†437.58	235.84	159.33	144.31	145.71	144.64	Long-Term Foreign Liabilities	36cl
†10.02	12.70	25.39	31.47	108.40	106.00	38.13	165.72	83.52	†139.70	67.39	63.16	112.62	151.20	81.08	Liab. to Nonbank Pub. Fin. Insts	36dg
†3.75	5.98	8.52	16.45	27.80	32.90	37.02	31.05	21.87	†208.18	287.70	283.77	267.04	400.01	297.94	Liabilities to Other Banking Insts	36i
....	....	....	....	....	....	....	....	....	38.83	105.51	195.18	160.53	164.28	296.23	Liab. to Nonbank Financial Insts	36j
†40.08	91.69	202.65	122.11	161.27	203.66	264.22	402.46	656.29	†3099.09	4,549.33	5,897.72	6,726.74	6,263.24	6,856.46	Capital Accounts	37a
†–2.84	–41.92	–34.96	132.94	42.92	212.27	344.57	349.77	1,606.49	†1439.71	512.97	–403.27	–507.59	398.77	–1,250.08	Other Items (Net)	37r
†243.09	292.63	415.34	684.81	1,010.46	1,189.73	1,493.68	2,522.70	3,445.03	†5203.96	8,386.16	9,674.00	11,673.02	14,374.05	16,568.69	Money plus Quasi-Money	35l
End of Period															**Other Banking Institutions**	
†1.11	.95	2.36	4.56	4.98	7.87	12.34	22.69	27.57	†37.95	86.71	96.01	210.86	298.50	95.38	Reserves	40
—	—	.10	.25	.01	.12	.07	1.39	2.06	†39.04	40.06	22.91	9.12	—	—	Claims on Mon.Author.: Securities	40c
†.82	.74	1.21	.85	.68	.50	2.99	5.42	6.55	†18.89	18.50	37.55	4.92	12.84	3.60	Foreign Assets	41
†3.01	4.52	5.06	13.60	19.46	40.74	32.00	103.93	88.07	†24.77	18.34	23.50	97.10	238.45	63.42	Claims on Central Government	42a
†.04	.03	.31	2.15	3.63	1.13	.81	1.71	.02	†27.96	5.07	2.31	—	—	—	Claims on Nonfin.Pub.Enterprises	42c
....	....	....	....	....	....	....	....	....	16.39	10.74	4.61	5.26	5.07	.43	Claims on Nonbank Pub. Fin. Inst	42cg
†143.56	157.61	172.95	200.02	265.93	341.90	361.62	326.46	430.61	†401.52	897.44	1,007.23	1,426.40	1,581.47	527.25	Claims on Private Sector	42d
†5.63	8.55	11.65	20.99	34.35	44.89	81.30	47.11	44.77	†110.27	101.60	137.59	172.19	138.65	106.76	Claims on Deposit Money Banks	42e
....	....	....	....	....	....	....	....	....	4.17	7.77	6.97	21.93	40.84	19.31	Claims on Nonbank Financial Insts	42g
†7.30	7.28	6.91	7.90	6.95	8.11	11.15	13.43	16.13	†29.88	46.95	109.68	156.41	276.51	92.19	Demand Deposits	44
†79.97	81.60	143.17	196.35	286.56	387.14	452.53	460.63	558.42	†300.16	613.32	686.24	1,019.00	1,155.61	260.23	Time, Savings,& Fgn.Currency Dep.	45
....	....	....	....	....	....	....	....	....	4.75	—	—	.05	1.06	13.01	Money Market Instruments	46aa
†34.26	45.51	15.24	16.88	11.06	8.86	11.03	8.49	7.04	†.77	.94	18.89	50.31	48.66	28.97	Bonds	46ab
....	....	....	....	....	....	....	....	....	.28	1.19	1.27	2.40	3.75	1.36	Restricted Deposits	46b
†.68	1.16	1.12	.39	—	—	—	—	—	†.06	—	—	—	—	—	Foreign Liabilities	46c
†14.19	13.17	12.69	10.37	.02	.29	.07	.12	—	†—	—	—	—	—	—	Long-Term Foreign Liabilities	46cl
†17.45	13.30	14.95	10.36	20.82	19.76	5.27	1.03	.76	†13.37	40.80	30.89	191.78	438.28	4.72	Central Government Deposits	46d
.50	1.81	1.81	1.68	1.65	1.36	.79	.64	.14	†2.18	2.71	.58	3.82	8.59	1.38	Liab. to Nonbank Pub. Fin. Insts	46dg
†9.44	14.60	8.64	3.55	3.19	1.90	.56	.50	.18	†.11	.02	.01	.01	—	—	Credit from Monetary Authorities	46g
†4.96	6.56	5.36	4.10	6.85	6.08	8.40	8.17	7.36	†41.96	115.46	117.67	110.73	70.67	79.65	Credit from Deposit Money Banks	46h
....	....	....	....	....	....	....	....	....	10.10	20.54	7.50	49.85	89.34	13.19	Liab. to Nonbank Financial Insts	46j
†9.44	11.18	12.65	19.31	30.01	40.17	60.63	63.72	77.47	†174.41	198.62	242.89	296.05	362.53	112.07	Capital Accounts	47a
†–24.01	–23.77	–28.90	–28.45	–38.06	–36.52	–59.30	–48.02	–67.82	†102.94	145.68	123.06	67.36	–139.18	209.37	Other Items (Net)	47r
End of Period															**Banking Survey**	
†115.13	90.47	267.65	430.45	694.36	824.69	1,013.13	1,419.39	1,964.24	†6039.43	8,824.52	8,593.42	10,072.03	11,605.83	9,874.24	Foreign Assets (Net)	51n
†338.64	463.98	547.07	852.29	992.59	1,397.41	1,705.20	3,003.55	4,904.65	†5673.05	7,338.85	9,079.02	10,381.76	11,691.81	14,029.28	Domestic Credit	52
†–19.49	6.04	17.19	214.46	108.10	233.71	377.80	905.58	1,714.85	†1120.47	–365.71	556.96	632.17	–224.17	1,648.24	Claims on Central Govt. (Net)	52an
†.11	.11	.24	.08	.06	.53	—	1.20	4.92	†1.19	.12	.15	13.51	26.82	.07	Claims on State and Local Govts	52b
†1.51	1.19	9.17	15.15	44.10	38.18	90.49	148.44	201.73	†45.50	13.83	5.66	16.59	89.24	3.84	Claims on Nonfin.Pub.Enterprises	52c
†11.70	37.11	42.64	44.50	15.09	15.12	15.47	813.15	1,355.13	†1683.03	1,451.28	1,423.07	1,436.33	1,417.07	1,389.77	Claims on Nonbank Pub.Fin.Insts	52cg
†344.81	419.53	477.83	578.10	825.25	1,109.88	1,221.44	1,124.44	1,615.24	†2793.81	6,185.17	7,029.05	8,081.47	9,932.45	10,838.11	Claims on Private Sector	52d
†—	—	—	—	—	—	—	10.75	12.79	†29.06	54.15	64.13	201.70	450.41	149.26	Claims on Nonbank Financial Inst	52g
†329.25	380.56	563.05	884.49	1,298.98	1,577.11	1,945.02	2,974.06	3,992.00	†5496.05	8,959.72	10,373.90	12,637.57	15,507.67	16,825.73	Liquid Liabilities	55l
....	....	....	....	....	....	....	....	....	37.18	63.77	15.43	50.76	95.98	116.95	Money Market Instruments	56aa
†34.26	45.51	15.24	16.88	11.06	8.86	11.03	8.49	7.04	†17.92	1.46	22.37	59.27	59.35	56.99	Bonds	56ab
†—	—	4.76	54.40	5.63	38.97	56.89	389.27	355.00	†576.38	979.79	754.77	495.86	.76	.73	Liabs. of Central Bank: Securities	56ac
....	....	....	....	....	....	....	....	....	48.25	64.36	69.49	97.31	172.32	228.13	Restricted Deposits	56b
†54.08	71.85	52.07	55.66	68.39	77.43	93.90	126.00	175.32	†437.58	235.84	159.33	144.31	145.71	144.64	Long-Term Foreign Liabilities	56cl
†10.52	14.51	27.19	33.15	110.05	107.36	38.92	166.36	83.65	†141.89	70.10	63.75	116.44	159.79	82.46	Liab. to Nonbank Pub. Fin. Insts	56dg
....	....	....	....	....	....	....	....	....	48.93	126.05	202.68	210.39	253.62	309.42	Liab. to Nonbank Financial Insts	56j
†49.51	102.87	215.30	141.42	191.28	243.83	324.86	466.18	733.76	†3273.50	4,747.95	6,140.61	7,022.79	6,625.76	6,968.53	Capital Accounts	57a
†–23.84	–60.85	–62.89	96.75	1.55	168.54	247.72	292.58	1,522.12	†1634.80	914.33	–129.89	–380.90	276.68	–830.05	Other Items (Net)	57r
Percent Per Annum															**Interest Rates**	
8.00	8.00	45.00	43.00	43.00	52.20	71.25	48.00	49.00	45.00	45.00	60.00	38.00	38.00	37.00	Discount Rate *(End of Period)*	60
....	....	....	....	....	....	....	....	....	16.70	12.47	18.58	7.48	8.14	13.33	Money Market Rate	60b
....	....	....	....	....	28.76	38.59	29.11	22.17	19.53	7.59	12.34	8.15	3.17	2.66	Savings Rate	60k
8.94	8.95	28.91	27.82	31.10	35.43	53.75	39.02	24.72	27.58	14.70	34.84	21.28	16.30	15.51	Deposit Rate	60l
8.47	8.50	22.50	†35.53	37.16	41.33	59.90	54.66	39.74	39.41	23.69	46.35	32.13	25.20	22.45	Lending Rate	60p
13.49	14.86	17.32	20.06	27.14	31.66	41.03	54.73	53.38	49.09	25.41	47.88	†31.12	21.03	22.12	Government Bond Yield	61
Period Averages															**Prices, Production, Labor**	
50.5	43.8	23.2	†24.4	56.4	65.2	52.4	†93.8	100.0	300.0	533.2	322.9	311.7	407.7	459.2	Industrial Share Prices	62
5.8	6.9	13.7	17.5	21.3	26.4	35.6	63.4	100.0	203.2	263.7	322.2	374.4	431.3	488.5	Prices: Home & Import Goods	63
5.3	6.4	12.9	16.8	20.7	26.0	35.4	62.4	100.0	199.6	264.8	329.4	387.6	452.9	520.1	Home Goods	63a
4.8	6.2	11.3	16.0	21.4	28.2	38.9	62.5	100.0	199.9	299.9	407.2	†503.2	584.7	658.0	Consumer Prices	64
59	66	67	75	83	82	85	90	100	103	112	113	102	108	107	Crude Petroleum Production	66aa
Period Averages																
....	....	....	....	7,418	7,538	7,546	8,027	8,545	....	9,507	....	....	....	....	Labor Force	67d
5,694	6,035	6,113	6,405	6,701	6,986	7,103	7,626	7,667	7,819	8,287	8,711	8,717	....	....	Employment	67e
575	478	672	743	702	582	503	687	875	1,043	1,061	1,093	1,526	....	....	Unemployment	67c
9.2	7.3	9.9	10.4	9.5	7.7	6.7	8.7	10.3	11.8	11.4	11.2	14.9	....	....	Unemployment Rate (%)	67r
Billions of Bolivares															**International Transactions**	
†123.4	154.7	470.5	831.2	863.0	975.4	1,311.8	2,409.8	3,332.6	9,803.1	10,295.6	9,393.5	12,751.4	21,602.2	17,568.9	Exports	70
†100.9	118.2	347.5	665.4	700.2	770.9	979.9	1,751.6	2,444.8	7,844.8	8,853.1	6,557.6	9,954.5	18,188.4	14,678.3	Petroleum	70a
†64.5	68.9	201.6	415.1	432.9	492.4	637.6	1,197.8	1,641.7	5,346.6	5,934.9	4,220.1	6,592.4	12,390.9	10,297.9	Crude Petroleum	70aa
†127.8	236.4	266.4	347.9	637.7	961.9	1,107.2	1,324.0	2,202.0	4,179.9	7,145.5	8,604.0	8,380.5	10,997.3	13,221.1	Imports, c.i.f.	71
†115.1	213.0	240.0	313.4	574.5	866.6	997.4	1,192.8	1,983.8	3,765.7	6,437.3	7,751.3	7,550.0	9,907.5	11,910.9	Imports, f.o.b.	71.v
Millions of US Dollars																
10,577	10,244	13,286	17,497	15,155	14,185	14,686	16,089	18,457	23,060	21,624	17,193	20,190	31,802	27,409	Exports	70..*d*
9,054	8,158	10,001	13,953	12,302	11,208	11,030	11,473	13,739	18,520	18,186	12,021	16,295	26,772	22,112	Petroleum	70a.*d*
8,702	11,465	7,030	6,608	10,042	12,672	11,271	8,277	11,396	8,901	13,159	14,250	12,670	14,606	16,236	Imports, f.o.b.	71.v*d*
1995=100															Volume of Exports	
59.6	65.8	64.7	74.0	83.5	80.4	84.4	90.8	100.0	107.2	118.4	120.7	108.8	110.2	106.6	Petroleum	72a
55.6	55.0	53.4	67.2	74.8	77.6	83.3	91.6	100.0	107.3	119.6	122.4	104.1	108.5	111.8	Crude Petroleum	72aa
67.8	87.8	87.8	87.9	101.3	86.2	86.7	89.3	100.0	106.9	115.8	117.3	118.4	113.8	95.9	Refined Pretroleum	72ab
7.3	8.5	16.2	19.5	23.2	27.3	36.7	66.3	100.0	213.8	260.6	301.3	335.8	368.8	397.3	Import Prices (Wholesale)	76.x

Venezuela, Rep. Bol.

		1972	1973	1974	1975	1976	1977	1978	1979	1980	1981	1982	1983	1984	1985	1986
Balance of Payments																*Millions of US Dollars:*
Current Account, n.i.e.	78ald	−101	877	5,760	2,171	254	−3,179	−5,735	350	4,728	4,000	−4,246	4,427	4,651	3,327	−2,245
Goods: Exports f.o.b.	78aad	3,202	4,803	11,290	8,982	9,342	9,661	9,174	14,360	19,275	20,181	16,516	14,759	16,075	14,478	8,664
Goods: Imports f.o.b.	78abd	−2,222	−2,626	−3,876	−5,462	−7,337	−10,194	−11,234	−10,004	−10,877	−12,123	−13,584	−6,409	−7,246	−7,501	−7,866
Trade Balance	78acd	980	2,177	7,414	3,520	2,005	−533	−2,060	4,356	8,398	8,058	2,932	8,350	8,829	6,977	798
Services: Credit	78add	159	247	325	370	341	504	629	693	757	1,041	1,082	688	797	828
Services: Debit	78aed	−665	−748	−1,143	−1,646	−2,068	−2,955	−3,935	−4,195	−4,253	−4,980	−6,050	−2,681	−2,632	−2,043	−2,148
Balance on Goods & Services	78afd	474	1,676	6,596	2,244	278	−2,984	−5,366	760	4,838	3,835	−2,077	6,751	6,885	5,731	−522
Income: Credit	78agd	57	229	356	740	693	782	1,052	1,346	2,264	3,581	2,565	1,500	2,097	1,914	1,761
Income: Debit	78ahd	−537	−917	−993	−640	−485	−694	−1,014	−1,349	−1,935	−3,007	−4,095	−3,613	−4,159	−4,147	−3,363
Balance on Gds, Serv. & Inc.	78aid	−6	988	5,959	2,344	486	−2,896	−5,328	757	5,167	4,409	−3,607	4,638	4,823	3,498	−2,124
Current Transfers, n.i.e.: Credit	78ajd	2	2	2	2	2	1	1	1	1	—	—	—	61	68	80
Current Transfers: Debit	78akd	−97	−113	−201	−175	−234	−284	−408	−408	−439	−409	−639	−211	−233	−239	−201
Capital Account, n.i.e.	78bcd	—	—	—	—	—	—	—	—	—	—	—	—	—	—	—
Capital Account, n.i.e.: Credit	78bad	—	—	—	—	—	—	—	—	—	—	—	—	—	—	—
Capital Account: Debit	78bbd	—	—	—	—	—	—	—	—	—	—	—	—	—	—	—
Financial Account, n.i.e.	78bjd	−226	208	−875	164	65	1,702	3,182	3,251	164	−1,882	−1,528	−3,716	−2,019	−629	−707
Direct Investment Abroad	78bdd	—	—	—	—	—	—	—	—	—	—	−4	—	−21	−11	−460
Dir. Invest. in Rep. Econ., n.i.e.	78bed	−376	−84	−430	418	−889	−3	67	88	55	184	257	86	18	68	16
Portfolio Investment Assets	78bfd	1	−11	−14	−63	−191	−108	−239	6	−264	−118	−10	−7	—	—	—
Equity Securities	78bkd	—	2	−3	−2	−16	−20	−10	24	2	−5	−10	−7	—	—	—
Debt Securities	78bld	1	−13	−11	−61	−175	−88	−229	−18	−266	−113	—	—	—	—	—
Portfolio Investment Liab., n.i.e.	78bgd	14	−1	−5	−6	914	67	363	−80	1,574	201	1,592	208	—	—	—
Equity Securities	78bmd	—	—	—	—	—	—	—	—	—	—	—	—	—	—	—
Debt Securities	78bnd	14	−1	−5	−6	914	67	363	−80	1,574	201	1,592	208	—	—	—
Financial Derivatives Assets	78bwd	....	....	....	....	....	....	....	....	....	....	....	....	....	....	....
Financial Derivatives Liabilities	78bxd	....	....	....	....	....	....	....	....	....	....	....	....	....	....	....
Other Investment Assets	78bhd	−108	14	−483	−760	−1,182	−722	−991	−988	−1,807	−2,963	−5,000	−1,059	−1,469	−314	−16
Monetary Authorities	78bod	—	—	—	—	—	—	—	—	—	—	—	—	—	—	—
General Government	78bpd	−22	−42	−135	−112	−50	−62	−166	−44	−212	−141	53	−93	−22	−30	−43
Banks	78bqd	−62	43	−24	−83	−12	−119	−200	−158	12	52	95	−233	−292	303	123
Other Sectors	78brd	−24	13	−324	−565	−1,120	−541	−625	−786	−1,607	−2,874	−5,148	−733	−1,155	−587	−96
Other Investment Liab., n.i.e.	78bid	243	290	57	575	1,413	2,468	3,982	4,225	606	814	1,637	−2,944	−547	−372	−247
Monetary Authorities	78bsd	−3	−2	8	4	8	24	−8	−13	4	11	−14	−7	−2	21	35
General Government	78btd	120	127	−143	−12	944	1,332	2,020	1,080	21	−99	1,236	412	−765	−794	−910
Banks	78bud	3	25	−12	59	287	535	677	−562	181	538	842	−113	101	−122	134
Other Sectors	78bvd	123	140	204	524	174	577	1,293	3,720	400	364	−427	−3,236	119	523	494
Net Errors and Omissions	78cad	497	−474	−417	380	2,024	2,276	1,488	497	−1,129	−2,139	−2,386	−265	−996	−999	−930
Overall Balance	78cbd	170	611	4,468	2,715	2,343	799	−1,065	4,098	3,763	−21	−8,160	446	1,636	1,699	−3,882
Reserves and Related Items	79dad	−170	−611	−4,468	−2,715	−2,343	−799	1,065	−4,098	−3,763	21	8,160	−446	−1,636	−1,699	3,882
Reserve Assets	79dbd	−170	−611	−4,468	−2,715	−2,343	−799	1,065	−4,098	−3,763	21	8,160	−446	−1,636	−1,699	3,882
Use of Fund Credit and Loans	79dcd	—	—	—	—	—	—	—	—	—	—	—	—	—	—	—
Exceptional Financing	79ded	—	—	—	—	—	—	—	—	—	—	—	—	—	—	—
International Investment Position																*Millions of US Dollars*
Assets	79aad	....	....	....	....	....	....	....	....	....	....	....	28,179	31,017	33,186	29,927
Direct Investment Abroad	79abd	....	....	....	....	....	....	....	....	....	....	....	133	154	165	625
Portfolio Investment	79acd	....	....	....	....	....	....	....	....	....	....	....	—	—	—	—
Equity Securities	79add	....	....	....	....	....	....	....	....	....	....	....	—	—	—	—
Debt Securities	79aed	....	....	....	....	....	....	....	....	....	....	....	—	—	—	—
Financial Derivatives	79ald	....	....	....	....	....	....	....	....	....	....	....	—	—	—	—
Other Investment	79afd	....	....	....	....	....	....	....	....	....	....	....	16,016	17,269	17,583	17,599
Monetary Authorities	79agd	....	....	....	....	....	....	....	....	....	....	....	—	—	—	—
General Government	79ahd	....	....	....	....	....	....	....	....	....	....	....	401	423	453	496
Banks	79aid	....	....	....	....	....	....	....	....	....	....	....	1,230	1,522	1,219	1,096
Other Sectors	79ajd	....	....	....	....	....	....	....	....	....	....	....	14,385	15,324	15,911	16,007
Reserve Assets	79akd	....	....	....	....	....	....	....	....	....	....	....	12,030	13,594	15,438	11,703
Liabilities	79lad	....	....	....	....	....	....	....	....	....	....	....	37,545	37,016	36,691	36,460
Dir. Invest. in Rep. Economy	79lbd	....	....	....	....	....	....	....	....	....	....	....	1,266	1,284	1,352	1,368
Portfolio Investment	79lcd	....	....	....	....	....	....	....	....	....	....	....	—	—	—	—
Equity Securities	79ldd	....	....	....	....	....	....	....	....	....	....	....	—	—	—	—
Debt Securities	79led	....	....	....	....	....	....	....	....	....	....	....	—	—	—	—
Financial Derivatives	79lld	....	....	....	....	....	....	....	....	....	....	....	....	....	....	....
Other Investment	79lfd	....	....	....	....	....	....	....	....	....	....	....	36,279	35,732	35,339	35,092
Monetary Authorities	79lgd	....	....	....	....	....	....	....	....	....	....	....	162	185	208	58
General Government	79lhd	....	....	....	....	....	....	....	....	....	....	....	29,189	28,399	27,582	26,857
Banks	79lid	....	....	....	....	....	....	....	....	....	....	....	770	871	749	883
Other Sectors	79ljd	....	....	....	....	....	....	....	....	....	....	....	6,158	6,277	6,800	7,294

Minus Sign Indicates Debit

1987	1988	1989	1990	1991	1992	1993	1994	1995	1996	1997	1998	1999	2000	2001	Balance of Payments	
-1,390	-5,809	2,161	8,279	1,736	-3,749	-1,993	2,541	2,014	8,914	3,467	-3,253	3,557	13,111	4,364	Current Account, n.i.e.	78al d
10,564	10,217	13,059	17,623	15,159	14,202	14,779	16,105	19,082	23,707	23,703	17,576	20,819	33,035	27,056	Goods: Exports f.o.b.	78aa d
-8,870	-12,080	-7,365	-6,917	-10,259	-12,880	-11,504	-8,480	-12,069	-9,937	-13,678	-15,105	-13,213	-15,491	-17,282	Goods: Imports f.o.b.	78ab d
1,694	-1,863	5,694	10,706	4,900	1,322	3,275	7,625	7,013	13,770	10,025	2,471	7,606	17,544	9,774	*Trade Balance*	78ac d
864	835	929	1,183	1,229	1,312	1,340	1,576	1,671	1,573	1,489	1,461	1,310	1,237	1,240	Services: Credit	78ad d
-2,238	-2,863	-1,911	-2,534	-3,431	-4,263	-4,525	-4,672	-4,836	-4,842	-5,495	-5,146	-3,772	-4,255	-4,493	Services: Debit	78ae d
320	-3,891	4,712	9,355	2,698	-1,629	90	4,529	3,848	10,501	6,019	-1,214	5,144	14,526	6,521	*Balance on Goods & Services*	78af d
1,455	1,653	1,582	2,658	2,168	1,607	1,599	1,626	1,867	1,579	2,139	2,286	2,157	2,915	2,458	Income: Credit	78ag d
-3,074	-3,424	-3,950	-3,432	-2,766	-3,353	-3,314	-3,530	-3,810	-3,304	-4,547	-4,217	-3,684	-4,119	-4,005	Income: Debit	78ah d
-1,299	-5,662	2,344	8,581	2,100	-3,375	-1,625	2,625	1,905	8,776	3,611	-3,145	3,617	13,322	4,974	*Balance on Gds, Serv. & Inc.*	78ai d
137	87	237	444	370	533	452	606	413	526	221	275	191	222	196	Current Transfers, n.i.e.: Credit	78aj d
-228	-234	-420	-746	-734	-907	-820	-690	-304	-388	-365	-383	-251	-433	-806	Current Transfers: Debit	78ak d
—	—	—	—	—	—	—	—	—	—	—	—	—	—	—	Capital Account, n.i.e.	78bc d
—	—	—	—	—	—	—	—	—	—	—	—	—	—	—	Capital Account, n.i.e.: Credit	78ba d
—	—	—	—	—	—	—	—	—	—	—	—	—	—	—	Capital Account: Debit	78bb d
960	-1,180	-3,650	-4,061	2,204	3,386	2,656	-3,204	-2,964	-1,784	1,069	1,764	-1,010	-2,784	-1,129	Financial Account, n.i.e.	78bj d
-37	-68	-179	-375	-188	-156	-886	-358	-91	-507	-500	-233	-501	-107	-401	Direct Investment Abroad	78bd d
21	89	213	451	1,916	629	372	813	985	2,183	5,536	4,495	3,290	4,464	3,085	Dir. Invest. in Rep. Econ., n.i.e.	78be d
—	—	-8	-1,952	17	2	79	-22	-14	-41	-600	1,070	372	-905	-283	Portfolio Investment Assets	78bf d
—	—	-8	-2	-8	-44	-1	10	-3	-11	-18	-66	70	-87	-117	Equity Securities	78bk d
—	—	—	-1,950	25	46	80	-32	-11	-30	-582	1,136	302	-818	-166	Debt Securities	78bl d
—	—	-526	17,928	334	1,001	542	275	-787	780	1,106	219	1,565	-1,512	677	Portfolio Investment Liab., n.i.e.	78bg d
—	—	—	—	—	165	48	585	270	1,318	1,445	186	415	-461	-74	Equity Securities	78bm d
—	—	-526	17,928	334	836	494	-310	-1,057	-538	-339	33	1,150	-1,051	751	Debt Securities	78bn d
....	....	—	—	—	—	—	—	—	—	—	—	—	—	—	Financial Derivatives Assets	78bw d
....	....	—	—	—	—	—	—	—	—	—	—	—	—	—	Financial Derivatives Liabilities	78bx d
-789	-1,595	-369	-2,305	-925	-590	615	-4,173	-661	-1,592	-3,385	-3,413	-6,371	-4,920	-3,941	Other Investment Assets	78bh d
....	....														Monetary Authorities	78bo d
-88	-51	-58	-46	-12	-45	-16	-27	240	57	-273	152	240	-195	-516	General Government	78bp d
-104	-379	767	-899	-147	-58	-538	-932	216	-53	-25	-169	-228	-46	797	Banks	78bq d
-597	-1,165	-1,078	-1,360	-766	-487	1,169	-3,214	-1,117	-1,596	-3,087	-3,396	-6,383	-4,679	-4,222	Other Sectors	78br d
1,765	394	-2,781	-17,808	1,050	2,500	1,934	261	-2,396	-2,607	-1,088	-374	635	196	-266	Other Investment Liab., n.i.e.	78bi d
253	831	11	146	-758	282	778	-51	-317	-289	-454	-16	-6	5	8	Monetary Authorities	78bs d
-657	227	890	-18,171	586	593	-210	128	-262	-543	-192	260	-315	-188	-129	General Government	78bt d
967	-726	-411	16	308	86	113	-77	52	153	31	-72	-93	244	-70	Banks	78bu d
1,202	62	-3,271	201	914	1,539	1,253	261	-1,869	-1,928	-473	-546	1,049	135	-75	Other Sectors	78bv d
-505	3,117	1,603	-1,742	-1,516	-299	-539	-281	-494	-892	-1,461	-1,442	-1,508	-4,502	-5,297	Net Errors and Omissions	78ca d
-935	-3,872	114	2,476	2,424	-662	124	-944	-1,444	6,238	3,075	-2,931	1,039	5,825	-2,062	*Overall Balance*	78cb d
935	3,872	-114	-2,476	-2,424	662	-124	944	1,444	-6,238	-3,075	2,931	-1,039	-5,825	2,062	Reserves and Related Items	79da d
935	3,872	-1,077	-4,376	-2,645	845	144	1,145	1,907	-6,271	-2,624	3,379	-589	-5,316	2,260	Reserve Assets	79db d
—	—	964	1,900	221	-183	-268	-201	-463	33	-452	-448	-450	-508	-198	Use of Fund Credit and Loans	79dc d
—	—	—	—	—	—	—	—	—	—	—	—	—	—	—	Exceptional Financing	79de d

Millions of US Dollars

1987	1988	1989	1990	1991	1992	1993	1994	1995	1996	1997	1998	1999	2000	2001	International Investment Position	
30,080	27,731	29,488	38,443	42,227	41,806	43,156	46,634	45,944	24,926	27,095	23,006	26,812	32,785	....	Assets	79aa d
662	730	866	1,221	1,368	1,568	2,447	3,124	3,427	4,425	4,925	5,192	5,710	5,966	....	Direct Investment Abroad	79ab d
—	—	—	1,950	1,925	1,879	1,799	1,796	1,530	137	736	597	823	1,091	....	Portfolio Investment	79ac d
—	—	—	—	—	—	—	—	—	15	36	103	20	55	....	Equity Securities	79ad d
—	—	—	1,950	1,925	1,879	1,799	1,796	1,530	122	700	494	803	1,036	....	Debt Securities	79ae d
															Financial Derivatives	79al d
18,388	19,983	20,529	22,806	23,773	24,363	25,106	28,955	30,391	3,549	2,399	1,764	4,247	4,235	....	Other Investment	79af d
															Monetary Authorities	79ag d
584	635	693	739	751	796	812	812	874	—	—	—	—	—	....	General Government	79ah d
1,200	1,579	1,111	1,978	2,123	2,181	2,719	3,774	3,586	240	262	436	668	522	....	Banks	79ai d
16,604	17,769	18,725	20,089	20,899	21,386	21,575	24,369	25,931	3,309	2,137	1,328	3,579	3,713	....	Other Sectors	79aj d
11,030	7,018	8,093	12,466	15,161	13,996	13,804	12,759	10,596	16,815	19,035	15,453	16,032	21,493	....	Reserve Assets	79ak d
38,246	38,729	37,102	39,689	42,988	47,046	50,713	51,730	49,250	27,324	26,756	24,549	24,949	22,467	....	Liabilities	79la d
1,389	1,478	1,691	2,142	4,058	4,687	5,059	5,872	6,772						....	Dir. Invest. in Rep. Economy	79lb d
—	—	—	18,483	18,945	20,241	22,816	22,844	22,555	20,784	21,466	20,445	21,929	20,846	....	Portfolio Investment	79lc d
—	—	—	—	—	—	917	1,184	1,060	2,487	3,882	1,655	2,031	2,064	....	Equity Securities	79ld d
—	—	—	18,483	18,945	20,241	21,899	21,660	21,495	18,297	17,584	18,790	19,898	18,782	....	Debt Securities	79le d
															Financial Derivatives	79ll d
36,857	37,251	35,411	19,064	19,985	22,118	22,838	23,014	19,923	6,540	5,290	4,104	3,020	1,621	....	Other Investment	79lf d
311	1,142	2,151	4,363	3,841	3,821	4,376	4,246	3,525	3,191	2,159	1,249	758	224	....	Monetary Authorities	79lg d
26,200	26,427	26,949	8,358	8,642	8,975	8,459	8,454	8,009	—	—	—	—	—	....	General Government	79lh d
1,850	1,124	981	940	1,248	1,335	1,447	1,394	1,451	295	329	261	167	262	....	Banks	79li d
8,496	8,558	5,330	5,403	6,254	7,987	8,556	8,920	6,938	3,054	2,802	2,594	2,095	1,135	....	Other Sectors	79lj d

Venezuela, Rep. Bol.

		1972	1973	1974	1975	1976	1977	1978	1979	1980	1981	1982	1983	1984	1985	1986
Government Finance															*Billions of Bolivares:*	
Deficit (-) or Surplus	**80**	−.2	1.2	5.0	1.9	−4.0	−6.7	−6.9	4.0	.1	−3.9	−12.7	†−4.4	13.5	23.6	−10.0
Revenue	**81**	13.3	17.0	44.3	42.4	39.9	42.9	42.7	50.9	66.5	97.5	83.7	†77.4	104.5	126.5	108.7
Grants Received	**81z**	.2	—	.7	.1	.1	.1	.2	.2	.3	.3	.3	†.1	.1	.1	—
Expenditure	**82**	12.7	14.2	22.8	27.5	32.7	42.2	46.3	44.8	55.8	84.5	84.5	†73.4	82.6	94.6	105.2
Lending Minus Repayments	**83**	1.0	1.7	17.3	13.0	11.3	7.5	3.5	2.3	10.9	17.2	12.2	†8.4	8.5	8.4	13.4
Financing																
Net Borrowing	**84**	.2	.5	−1.2	−1.3	8.0	6.8	8.6	−2.7	3.6	6.8	6.3	....	....	....	....
Domestic	**84a**	.2	.5	−.9	−1.3	−.7	.6	−1.5	−1.6	−1.9	8.2	−1.6	....	....	....	....
Foreign	**85a**	—	—	−.3	—	8.7	6.2	10.2	−1.1	5.5	−1.4	7.9	....	....	....	....
Use of Cash Balances	**87**	−.1	−1.7	−3.8	−.6	−4.0	−.1	−1.7	−1.3	−3.7	−2.9	6.4	....	....	....	....
															Billions of Bolivares:	
Debt	**88**	2.2	2.2	2.1	3.7	12.8	21.4	32.5	32.0	35.6	46.5	55.3	†57.8	85.5	98.4	....
Domestic	**88a**	.9	1.1	1.2	1.4	1.7	3.8	4.0	4.1	3.2	16.3	19.3	†18.1	23.5	38.7	67.7
Foreign	**89a**	1.3	1.1	.9	2.3	11.2	17.5	28.4	27.9	32.4	30.3	36.0	†39.7	62.0	59.7	....
National Accounts															*Billions of Bolivares*	
Househ.Cons.Expend.,incl.NPISHs	**96f**	31.8	35.2	44.9	56.3	66.9	80.1	94.8	110.3	135.4	160.5	182.2	183.4	256.3	287.3	337.1
Government Consumption Expend.	**91f**	8.5	9.6	12.8	15.9	19.8	23.0	24.1	27.8	35.1	42.6	42.6	41.3	43.3	48.6	54.7
Gross Fixed Capital Formation	**93e**	15.8	18.6	21.0	30.6	42.8	60.5	71.8	65.6	64.1	69.8	70.2	55.4	67.3	80.6	99.8
Changes in Inventories	**93i**	3.4	2.8	5.9	5.8	3.7	4.2	.6	.1	−1.4	−4.4	5.2	−21.2	6.2	5.4	2.6
Exports of Goods and Services	**90c**	14.5	21.2	48.8	39.3	41.1	43.5	42.0	64.0	85.5	89.6	75.2	74.1	108.8	108.3	97.5
Imports of Goods and Services (-)	**98c**	12.4	14.2	21.1	29.9	39.2	55.5	64.1	60.0	64.6	73.0	84.1	42.5	76.2	81.1	99.6
Gross Domestic Product (GDP)	**99b**	61.5	73.3	112.2	118.1	135.1	155.7	169.1	207.7	254.2	285.2	291.3	290.5	405.8	449.0	492.1
Net Primary Income from Abroad	**98.n**	−2.1	−3.0	−2.7	.3	.2	−.4	−.6	−.8	1.2	2.3	−6.6	−9.9	6.8	−10.6	−3.0
Gross National Income (GNI)	**99a**	59.4	70.3	109.5	118.4	135.3	155.3	168.4	207.0	255.4	287.5	284.7	280.6	412.6	438.4	489.2
Consumption of Fixed Capital	**99cf**	5.4	5.9	6.5	7.5	8.5	10.5	12.5	14.9	17.1	19.9	21.7	24.0	32.7	36.5	43.2
GDP Volume 1968 Prices	**99b.p**	53.9	57.3	60.7	64.4	70.1	74.8	76.4	77.4	75.9	75.6	76.1	71.9	70.9	....	....
GDP Volume 1984 Prices	**99b.p**	....	....	....	....	....	....	....	....	....	....	....	....	405.8	411.5	437.6
GDP Volume (1995=100)	**99bvp**	54.4	57.8	61.3	65.1	70.8	75.5	77.2	78.2	76.6	76.4	76.9	72.6	71.6	72.6	77.2
GDP Deflator (1995=100)	**99bip**	.8	.9	1.3	1.3	1.4	1.5	1.6	1.9	2.4	2.7	2.8	2.9	4.1	4.5	4.7
																Millions:
Population	**99z**	10.94	11.28	11.63	†12.67	13.12	13.59	14.07	14.55	15.02	15.48	15.94	16.39	16.85	17.32	17.53

1987	1988	1989	1990	1991	1992	1993	1994	1995	1996	1997	1998	1999	2000	2001		
Year Ending December 31															**Government Finance**	
†-31.5	†-41.8	-1.3	.9	60.3	-128.2	-125.1	-485.8	-493.9	456.5	955.5	-1,916.4	-1,513.2	-1,744.7	....	Deficit (-) or Surplus	80
†123.1	†167.9	288.4	539.5	718.8	749.1	946.0	1,575.1	2,242.6	5,767.8	10,241.0	9,002.8	10,738.4	16,252.2	....	Revenue	81
†—	†—	—	—	—	—	—	—	—	—	—	—	—	—	....	Grants Received	81z
†139.1	†189.4	263.9	472.5	607.4	824.7	1,013.8	1,666.3	2,541.5	4,964.2	8,894.3	10,817.0	12,170.0	17,622.5	....	Expenditure	82
†15.5	†20.3	25.8	66.1	51.1	52.6	57.3	394.6	195.0	347.1	391.2	102.3	81.6	374.4	....	Lending Minus Repayments	83
															Financing	
....	....	....	-.9	-60.4	128.1	125.0	485.8	493.9	-456.5	-955.5	1,916.4	1,513.2	1,744.7	....	Net Borrowing	84
			-23.2	-47.6	79.0	131.8	530.6	476.2	-301.7	-1,360.0	1,825.9	2,136.8	3,591.1	....	Domestic	84a
			22.3	-12.8	49.1	-6.8	-44.8	17.7	-154.8	404.5	90.6	-623.6	-1,846.4	....	Foreign	85a
			....	....	....	....	....	....	....	....	....	....	....	....	Use of Cash Balances	87
Year Ending December 31																
....	....	....	....	....	....	....	....	....	....	....	....	....	....	....	Debt	88
....	....	....	....	....	....	....	....	....	....	....	....	....	....	....	Domestic	88a
....	....	....	....	....	....	....	....	....	....	....	....	....	....	....	Foreign	89a
Billions of Bolivares															**National Accounts**	
450.4	597.7	977.3	1,415.4	2,021.2	2,877.6	3,977.4	6,077.1	9,507.7	18,618.0	28,524.0	37,685.0	43,236.9	52,295.1	....	Househ.Cons.Expend.,incl.NPISHs	96f
71.1	91.9	144.4	191.8	293.2	379.4	466.0	627.0	974.8	1,475.6	2,807.7	3,957.6	4,700.3	5,958.9	....	Government Consumption Expend.	91f
147.9	199.3	255.0	322.1	552.0	886.4	1,091.1	1,528.4	2,255.6	4,645.8	8,123.0	9,991.3	9,850.6	11,719.0	....	Gross Fixed Capital Formation	93e
23.2	44.8	-63.2	-89.2	15.4	93.6	-68.5	-300.3	223.4	227.6	998.5	1,485.0	1,477.2	2,475.0	....	Changes in Inventories	93i
145.7	180.1	503.0	899.2	952.4	1,088.8	1,470.3	2,677.5	3,709.8	10,748.9	12,312.5	10,441.8	13,546.0	23,457.0	....	Exports of Goods and Services	90c
158.8	238.4	330.9	460.1	796.6	1,194.4	1,482.4	1,934.5	2,985.7	6,278.3	9,422.0	11,078.2	10,233.9	13,454.3	....	Imports of Goods and Services (-)	98c
679.4	875.5	1,485.5	2,279.3	3,037.5	4,131.5	5,453.9	8,675.2	13,685.7	29,437.7	43,343.7	52,482.5	62,577.0	82,450.7	....	Gross Domestic Product (GDP)	99b
-.2	-2.2	-62.4	-67.7	-57.3	-123.8	-162.4	-274.6	-322.9	-665.7	-1,178.2	-1,061.9	-928.8	-818.1	....	Net Primary Income from Abroad	98.n
679.2	873.4	1,423.1	2,211.6	2,980.2	4,007.7	5,291.5	8,400.6	13,362.8	28,772.0	42,165.5	51,420.6	61,648.2	81,632.6	....	Gross National Income (GNI)	99a
56.2	71.6	107.4	154.2	220.5	309.3	422.4	625.8	927.7	1,884.4	2,947.2	4,069.0	4,777.7	5,923.6	....	Consumption of Fixed Capital	99cf
....	....	....	....	....	....	....	....	....	....	....	....	....	....	....	GDP Volume 1968 Prices	99b.p
457.4	485.6	447.6	478.3	524.9	556.7	558.2	545.1	566.6	565.5	601.5	602.6	565.9	584.2	....	GDP Volume 1984 Prices	99b.p
80.7	85.7	79.0	84.4	92.6	98.2	98.5	96.2	100.0	99.8	106.2	106.3	99.9	103.1	....	GDP Volume (1995=100)	99bv p
6.2	7.5	13.7	19.7	24.0	30.7	40.5	65.9	100.0	215.5	298.3	360.6	457.8	584.3	....	GDP Deflator (1995=100)	99bi p
Midyear Estimates																
17.97	18.16	18.87	19.50	19.97	20.44	20.91	21.38	21.84	22.31	22.78	23.24	23.71	24.17	24.63	Population	99z

(See notes in the back of the book.)

Vietnam

	1972	1973	1974	1975	1976	1977	1978	1979	1980	1981	1982	1983	1984	1985	1986
Exchange Rates														*Dong per SDR:*	
Market Rate .... aa	.13	.17	.21	.21	.21	.21	.27	.27	†.27	1.32	1.35	1.35[e]	1.29[e]	†24.71	27.52
														Dong per US Dollar:	
Market Rate .... ae	.12	.14	.17	†.23	.23	.22	.26	.25	.26	1.13	1.22	1.28[e]	1.31[e]	†22.50	22.50
Market Rate .... rf	....	....	....	....	....	....	....	....	....	....	....	1.00[e]	....	....	22.74
Fund Position														*Millions of SDRs:*	
Quota .... 2f. s	62.0	62.0	62.0	62.0	62.0	62.0	90.0	90.0	135.0	135.0	135.0	176.8	176.8	176.8	176.8
SDRs .... 1b. s	19.8	19.8	19.8	19.8	.7	4.2	6.2	12.2	—	.5	—	—	—	—	—
Reserve Position in the Fund .... 1c. s	15.5	15.5	15.5	15.5	—	—	—	—	—	—	—	—	—	—	—
Total Fund Cred.&Loans Outstg. 2tl	—	—	—	—	—	31.0	79.2	80.1	57.4	111.8	90.3	89.0	89.0	89.0	89.0
International Liquidity												*Millions of US Dollars Unless Otherwise Indicated:*			
Total Reserves minus Gold .... 1l. d	....	....	....	....	....	....	....	....	....	....	....	....	....	....	....
SDRs .... 1b. d	21.4	23.8	24.2	23.1	.9	5.1	8.1	16.1	—	.5	—	—	—	—	—
Reserve Position in the Fund .... 1c. d	16.8	18.7	19.0	18.1	—	—	—	—	—	—	—	—	—	—	—
Foreign Exchange .... 1d. d	....	....	....	....	....	....	....	....	....	....	....	....	....	....	....
Gold (Market Valuation) .... 1an d	....	....	....	....	....	....	....	....	....	....	....	....	....	....	....
Monetary Authorities: Other Liab. .... 4.. d	....	....	....	....	....	....	....	....	....	....	....	....	....	....	....
Deposit Money Banks: Assets .... 7a. d	....	....	....	....	....	....	....	....	....	....	....	....	....	....	....
Liabilities .... 7b. d	....	....	....	....	....	....	....	....	....	....	....	....	....	....	....
Monetary Authorities														*Billions of Dong:*	
Foreign Assets 11	....	....	....	....	....	....	....	....	....	....	....	....	....	....	....
Claims on General Government 12a	....	....	....	....	....	....	....	....	....	....	....	....	....	....	....
Claims on Banking Institutions 12e	....	....	....	....	....	....	....	....	....	....	....	....	....	....	....
Reserve Money 14	....	....	....	....	....	....	....	....	....	....	....	....	....	....	....
of which: Currency Outside DMBs 14a	....	....	....	....	....	....	....	....	....	....	....	....	....	....	....
Foreign Liabilities 16c	....	....	....	....	....	....	....	....	....	....	....	....	....	....	....
General Government Deposits 16d	....	....	....	....	....	....	....	....	....	....	....	....	....	....	....
Capital Accounts 17a	....	....	....	....	....	....	....	....	....	....	....	....	....	....	....
Other Items (Net) 17r	....	....	....	....	....	....	....	....	....	....	....	....	....	....	....
Banking Institutions														*Billions of Dong:*	
Reserves 20	....	....	....	....	....	....	....	....	....	....	....	....	....	....	....
Foreign Assets 21	....	....	....	....	....	....	....	....	....	....	....	....	....	....	....
Claims on General Government 22a	....	....	....	....	....	....	....	....	....	....	....	....	....	....	....
Claims on Rest of Economy 22d	....	....	....	....	....	....	....	....	....	....	....	....	....	....	....
Demand Deposits 24	....	....	....	....	....	....	....	....	....	....	....	....	....	....	....
Time and Savings Deposits 25a	....	....	....	....	....	....	....	....	....	....	....	....	....	....	....
Foreign Currency Deposits 25b	....	....	....	....	....	....	....	....	....	....	....	....	....	....	....
Bonds & Money Mkt. Instruments 26a	....	....	....	....	....	....	....	....	....	....	....	....	....	....	....
Restricted Deposits 26b	....	....	....	....	....	....	....	....	....	....	....	....	....	....	....
Foreign Liabilities 26c	....	....	....	....	....	....	....	....	....	....	....	....	....	....	....
General Government Deposits 26d	....	....	....	....	....	....	....	....	....	....	....	....	....	....	....
Credit from Central Bank 26g	....	....	....	....	....	....	....	....	....	....	....	....	....	....	....
Capital Accounts 27a	....	....	....	....	....	....	....	....	....	....	....	....	....	....	....
Other Items (Net) 27r	....	....	....	....	....	....	....	....	....	....	....	....	....	....	....
Banking Survey														*Billions of Dong:*	
Foreign Assets (Net) 31n	....	....	....	....	....	....	....	....	....	....	....	....	....	....	....
Domestic Credit 32	....	....	....	....	....	....	....	....	....	....	....	....	....	....	....
Claims on General Govt. (Net) 32an	....	....	....	....	....	....	....	....	....	....	....	....	....	....	....
Claims on Rest of Economy 32d	....	....	....	....	....	....	....	....	....	....	....	....	....	....	....
Money 34	....	....	....	....	....	....	....	....	....	....	....	....	....	....	....
Quasi-Money 35	....	....	....	....	....	....	....	....	....	....	....	....	....	....	....
Bonds & Money Mkt. Instruments 36a	....	....	....	....	....	....	....	....	....	....	....	....	....	....	....
Restricted Deposits 36b	....	....	....	....	....	....	....	....	....	....	....	....	....	....	....
Capital Accounts 37a	....	....	....	....	....	....	....	....	....	....	....	....	....	....	....
Other Items (Net) 37r	....	....	....	....	....	....	....	....	....	....	....	....	....	....	....
Money plus Quasi-Money 35l	....	....	....	....	....	....	....	....	....	....	....	....	....	....	....
Interest Rates														*Percent Per Annum*	
Refinancing Rate *(End of Period)* 60	....	....	....	....	....	....	....	....	....	....	....	....	....	....	....
Treasury Bill Rate 60c	....	....	....	....	....	....	....	....	....	....	....	....	....	....	....
Deposit Rate 60l	....	....	....	....	....	....	....	....	....	....	....	....	....	....	....
Lending Rate 60p	....	....	....	....	....	....	....	....	....	....	....	....	....	....	....

1987	1988	1989	1990	1991	1992	1993	1994	1995	1996	1997	1998	1999	2000	2001		
															Exchange Rates	
End of Period																
399.00	1,513.91	7,063.61	11,559.11	16,449.95	†14526.88	14,892.82	16,132.80	16,373.69	16,031.82	16,584.98	19,557.54	19,253.57	18,910.44	18,956.52	Market Rate	aa
End of Period (ae) Period Average (rf)																
281.25	1,125.00	5,375.00	8,125.00	11,500.00	†10565.00	10,842.50	11,051.00	11,015.00	11,149.00	12,292.00	13,890.00	14,028.00	14,514.00	15,084.00	Market Rate	ae
78.29	606.52	4,463.95	6,482.80	10,037.03	11,202.19	10,640.96	10,965.67	11,038.25	11,032.58	11,683.33	13,268.00	13,943.17	14,167.75	14,725.17	Market Rate	rf
															Fund Position	
End of Period																
176.8	176.8	176.8	176.8	176.8	176.8	241.6	241.6	241.6	241.6	241.6	241.6	329.1	329.1	329.1	Quota	2f.s
—	—	—	—	—	—	4.9	11.0	2.2	11.9	9.4	1.8	1.1	.3	11.6	SDRs	1b.s
—	—	—	—	—	—	—	—	—	—	—	—	—	—	—	Reserve Position in the Fund	1c.s
89.0	89.0	82.0	78.5	71.5	71.5	72.5	193.4	253.8	374.6	335.3	277.9	258.7	242.6	291.2	Total Fund Cred.&Loans Outstg.	2tl
															International Liquidity	
End of Period																
...	...	...	...	...	...	...	...	1,323.7	1,735.9	1,985.9	2,002.3	3,326.1	3,416.5	3,674.6	Total Reserves minus Gold	1l.d
—	—	—	—	—	—	6.8	16.1	3.3	17.1	12.7	2.5	1.5	.3	14.6	SDRs	1b.d
—	—	—	—	—	—	—	—	—	—	—	—	—	—	—	Reserve Position in the Fund	1c.d
...	...	...	...	...	...	...	...	1,320.4	1,718.8	1,973.1	1,999.7	3,324.7	3,416.2	3,660.0	Foreign Exchange	1d.d
...	...	...	...	...	...	...	...	55.4	77.9	112.3	98.2	97.3	93.1	90.6	Gold (Market Valuation)	1and
...	...	...	...	...	...	...	...	377.1	537.3	507.8	505.5	513.5	487.6	535.9	Monetary Authorities: Other Liab.	4..d
...	...	...	...	...	877.9	538.3	...	869.2	1,004.2	999.2	1,347.0	2,119.0	4,221.8	5,261.4	Deposit Money Banks: Assets	7a.d
...	...	...	...	...	201.5	321.4	...	865.0	985.5	868.7	679.0	664.7	682.6	679.6	Liabilities	7b.d
															Monetary Authorities	
End of Period																
...	...	...	...	...	4,897	4,381	...	15,153	20,031	25,633	29,147	48,004	50,934	56,586	Foreign Assets	11
...	...	...	...	...	9,326	13,323	...	9,593	12,576	13,382	16,658	11,289	11,732	12,421	Claims on General Government	12a
...	...	...	...	...	5,004	6,792	...	6,779	7,693	6,776	6,521	10,312	14,234	17,776	Claims on Banking Institutions	12e
...	...	...	...	...	14,314	18,296	...	26,343	31,633	35,599	38,687	58,220	72,759	84,945	Reserve Money	14
...	...	...	...	...	10,579	14,218	...	19,370	22,639	25,101	26,965	41,254	52,208	66,320	of which: Currency Outside DMBs	14a
...	...	...	...	...	—	—	...	4,154	5,991	6,241	7,022	7,203	7,077	8,083	Foreign Liabilities	16c
...	...	...	...	...	4,273	4,883	...	6,575	7,383	9,348	10,340	11,089	7,410	4,390	General Government Deposits	16d
...	...	...	...	...	776	476	...	809	1,055	2,511	6,888	6,440	8,216	9,770	Capital Accounts	17a
...	...	...	...	...	-283	750	...	-6,791	-6,245	-7,938	-10,611	-13,348	-18,562	-20,405	Other Items (Net)	17r
															Banking Institutions	
End of Period																
...	...	...	...	...	3,451	3,709	...	7,409	9,323	9,451	9,920	16,881	20,390	18,426	Reserves	20
...	...	...	...	...	9,275	5,836	...	9,574	11,196	12,282	18,710	29,725	61,276	79,364	Foreign Assets	21
...	...	...	...	...	1,634	1,718	...	4,372	2,031	3,492	5,332	6,358	8,246	10,258	Claims on General Government	22a
...	...	...	...	...	2,743	7,669	...	18,199	23,942	31,220	34,889	112,730	155,720	189,103	Claims on Rest of Economy	22d
...	...	...	...	...	3,971	4,796	...	6,870	10,213	14,682	18,241	27,106	38,781	46,089	Demand Deposits	24
...	...	...	...	...	3,822	3,250	...	9,622	12,445	15,194	20,091	36,191	47,462	60,251	Time and Savings Deposits	25a
...	...	...	...	...	6,506	5,892	...	8,924	11,042	15,611	22,098	40,919	58,543	78,187	Foreign Currency Deposits	25b
...	...	...	...	...	298	2,544	...	5,490	5,635	7,703	10,890	10,865	18,842	21,012	Bonds & Money Mkt. Instruments	26a
...	...	...	...	...	1,708	1,514	...	2,138	2,117	3,080	2,830	4,059	7,045	7,923	Restricted Deposits	26b
...	...	...	...	...	2,128	3,485	...	9,528	10,987	10,678	9,432	9,324	9,908	10,251	Foreign Liabilities	26c
...	...	...	...	...	4,268	1,786	...	3,321	2,795	3,127	4,974	3,606	13,052	16,187	General Government Deposits	26d
...	...	...	...	...	4,752	6,621	...	5,793	6,133	5,565	4,249	11,576	14,427	17,753	Credit from Central Bank	26g
...	...	...	...	...	2,176	2,702	...	5,292	6,237	8,182	11,562	18,520	22,392	24,274	Capital Accounts	27a
...	...	...	...	...	126	1,856	...	6,688	5,735	3,655	2,246	3,528	15,181	15,224	Other Items (Net)	27r
															Banking Survey	
End of Period																
...	...	...	...	...	12,043	6,732	...	11,046	14,249	20,997	31,404	61,201	95,225	117,616	Foreign Assets (Net)	31n
...	...	...	...	...	5,161	16,040	...	22,268	28,370	35,620	41,566	115,682	155,236	191,204	Domestic Credit	32
...	...	...	...	...	2,418	8,371	...	4,069	4,428	4,400	6,677	2,952	-484	2,102	Claims on General Govt. (Net)	32an
...	...	...	...	...	2,743	7,669	...	18,199	23,942	31,220	34,889	112,730	155,720	189,103	Claims on Rest of Economy	32d
...	...	...	...	...	14,811	19,088	...	26,736	33,439	39,972	45,207	68,360	90,989	112,408	Money	34
...	...	...	...	...	10,327	9,142	...	18,546	23,487	30,805	42,189	77,110	106,005	138,437	Quasi-Money	35
...	...	...	...	...	298	2,544	...	5,490	5,635	7,703	10,890	10,865	18,842	21,012	Bonds & Money Mkt. Instruments	36a
...	...	...	...	...	1,708	1,514	...	2,138	2,117	3,080	2,830	4,059	7,045	7,923	Restricted Deposits	36b
...	...	...	...	...	2,953	3,178	...	6,101	7,292	10,693	18,450	24,961	30,608	34,044	Capital Accounts	37a
...	...	...	...	...	-126	2,804	...	-1,525	-2,398	-4,447	-8,835	-8,471	-3,027	-5,006	Other Items (Net)	37r
...	...	...	...	...	25,138	28,231	...	45,283	56,926	70,777	87,396	145,470	196,994	250,846	Money plus Quasi-Money	35l
															Interest Rates	
Percent Per Annum																
...	...	...	...	...	...	...	...	18.90	10.80	12.00	6.00	6.00	4.80		Refinancing Rate (End of Period)	60
...	...	...	...	...	26.40	...	...	...	...	...	...	5.42	5.49		Treasury Bill Rate	60c
...	...	...	...	...	22.04	...	...	...	8.51	9.23	7.37	3.65	5.30		Deposit Rate	60l
...	...	...	...	...	32.18	...	...	20.10	14.42	14.40	12.70	10.55	9.42		Lending Rate	60p

Vietnam

	1972	1973	1974	1975	1976	1977	1978	1979	1980	1981	1982	1983	1984	1985	1986
Prices													*Index Numbers (1995=100):*		
Consumer Prices 64	....	....	....	....	....	....	....	....	....	....	....	....	....	....	....
International Transactions															
Balance of Payments													*Millions of US Dollars:*		
Current Account, n.i.e. .... 78al d	....	....	....	....	....	....	....	....	....	....	....	....	....	....	....
Goods: Exports f.o.b .... 78aa d	....	....	....	....	....	....	....	....	....	....	....	....	....	....	....
Goods: Imports f.o.b. .... 78ab d	....	....	....	....	....	....	....	....	....	....	....	....	....	....	....
Trade Balance .... 78ac d	....	....	....	....	....	....	....	....	....	....	....	....	....	....	....
Services: Credit............................ 78ad d	....	....	....	....	....	....	....	....	....	....	....	....	....	....	....
Services: Debit.............................. 78ae d	....	....	....	....	....	....	....	....	....	....	....	....	....	....	....
Balance on Goods & Services ..... 78af d	....	....	....	....	....	....	....	....	....	....	....	....	....	....	....
Income: Credit.............................. 78ag d	....	....	....	....	....	....	....	....	....	....	....	....	....	....	....
Income: Debit............................... 78ah d	....	....	....	....	....	....	....	....	....	....	....	....	....	....	....
Balance on Gds. Serv. & Inc. ... 78ai d	....	....	....	....	....	....	....	....	....	....	....	....	....	....	....
Current Transfers, n.i.e.: Credit .... 78aj d	....	....	....	....	....	....	....	....	....	....	....	....	....	....	....
Current Transfers: Debit .... 78ak d	....	....	....	....	....	....	....	....	....	....	....	....	....	....	....
Capital Account, n.i.e. .... 78bc d	....	....	....	....	....	....	....	....	....	....	....	....	....	....	....
Capital Account, n.i.e.: Credit .... 78ba d	....	....	....	....	....	....	....	....	....	....	....	....	....	....	....
Capital Account: Debit .... 78bb d	....	....	....	....	....	....	....	....	....	....	....	....	....	....	....
Financial Account, n.i.e. .... 78bj d	....	....	....	....	....	....	....	....	....	....	....	....	....	....	....
Direct Investment Abroad .... 78bd d	....	....	....	....	....	....	....	....	....	....	....	....	....	....	....
Dir. Invest. in Rep. Econ., n.i.e. .... 78be d	....	....	....	....	....	....	....	....	....	....	....	....	....	....	....
Portfolio Investment Assets .... 78bf d	....	....	....	....	....	....	....	....	....	....	....	....	....	....	....
Equity Securities .... 78bk d	....	....	....	....	....	....	....	....	....	....	....	....	....	....	....
Debt Securities .... 78bl d	....	....	....	....	....	....	....	....	....	....	....	....	....	....	....
Portfolio Investment Liab., n.i.e. ...... 78bg d	....	....	....	....	....	....	....	....	....	....	....	....	....	....	....
Equity Securities .... 78bm d	....	....	....	....	....	....	....	....	....	....	....	....	....	....	....
Debt Securities .... 78bn d	....	....	....	....	....	....	....	....	....	....	....	....	....	....	....
Financial Derivatives Assets .... 78bw d	....	....	....	....	....	....	....	....	....	....	....	....	....	....	....
Financial Derivatives Liabilities .... 78bx d	....	....	....	....	....	....	....	....	....	....	....	....	....	....	....
Other Investment Assets .... 78bh d	....	....	....	....	....	....	....	....	....	....	....	....	....	....	....
Monetary Authorities...................... 78bo d	....	....	....	....	....	....	....	....	....	....	....	....	....	....	....
General Government .... 78bp d	....	....	....	....	....	....	....	....	....	....	....	....	....	....	....
Banks .... 78bq d	....	....	....	....	....	....	....	....	....	....	....	....	....	....	....
Other Sectors .... 78br d	....	....	....	....	....	....	....	....	....	....	....	....	....	....	....
Other Investment Liab., n.i.e. .... 78bi d	....	....	....	....	....	....	....	....	....	....	....	....	....	....	....
Monetary Authorities .... 78bs d	....	....	....	....	....	....	....	....	....	....	....	....	....	....	....
General Government .... 78bt d	....	....	....	....	....	....	....	....	....	....	....	....	....	....	....
Banks .... 78bu d	....	....	....	....	....	....	....	....	....	....	....	....	....	....	....
Other Sectors .... 78bv d	....	....	....	....	....	....	....	....	....	....	....	....	....	....	....
Net Errors and Omissions................... 78ca d	....	....	....	....	....	....	....	....	....	....	....	....	....	....	....
Overall Balance .... 78cb d	....	....	....	....	....	....	....	....	....	....	....	....	....	....	....
Reserves and Related Items .... 79da d	....	....	....	....	....	....	....	....	....	....	....	....	....	....	....
Reserve Assets .... 79db d	....	....	....	....	....	....	....	....	....	....	....	....	....	....	....
Use of Fund Credit and Loans .... 79dc d	....	....	....	....	....	....	....	....	....	....	....	....	....	....	....
Exceptional Financing .... 79de d	....	....	....	....	....	....	....	....	....	....	....	....	....	....	....
Government Finance													*Billions of Dong:*		
Deficit (-) or Surplus............................... 80	....	....	....	....	....	....	....	....	....	....	....	....	....	....	....
Total Revenue and Grants................... 81y	....	....	....	....	....	....	....	....	....	....	....	....	....	....	....
Revenue 81	....	....	....	....	....	....	....	....	....	....	....	....	....	....	....
Grants 81z	....	....	....	....	....	....	....	....	....	....	....	....	....	....	....
Exp. & Lending Minus Repay. 82z	....	....	....	....	....	....	....	....	....	....	....	....	....	....	....
Expenditure 82	....	....	....	....	....	....	....	....	....	....	....	....	....	....	....
Lending Minus Repayments 83	....	....	....	....	....	....	....	....	....	....	....	....	....	....	....
Total Financing 80h	....	....	....	....	....	....	....	....	....	....	....	....	....	....	....
Domestic Financing........................... 84a	....	....	....	....	....	....	....	....	....	....	....	....	....	....	....
Foreign Financing 85a	....	....	....	....	....	....	....	....	....	....	....	....	....	....	....
Debt: Domestic 88a	....	....	....	....	....	....	....	....	....	....	....	....	....	....	....
Foreign 89a	....	....	....	....	....	....	....	....	....	....	....	....	....	....	....
National Accounts														*Billions of Dong*	
Househ.Cons.Expend.,incl.NPISHs 96f														111	562
Government Consumption Expend. 91f														8	30
Gross Fixed Capital Formation 93e														14	65
Changes in Inventories 93i														2	5
Exports of Goods and Services 90c	....	....	....	....	....	....	....	....	....	....	....	....	....	....	....
Imports of Goods and Services (-) 98c	....	....	....	....	....	....	....	....	....	....	....	....	....	....	....
Gross Domestic Product (GDP) 99b	....	....	....	....	....	....	....	....	....	....	....	....	....	....	....
Net Primary Income from Abroad 98.n	....	....	....	....	....	....	....	....	....	....	....	....	....	....	....
Gross National Income (GNI) 99a	....	....	....	....	....	....	....	....	....	....	....	....	....	....	....
GDP Volume 1994 Prices.................... 99b. p	....	....	....	....	....	....	....	....	....	....	....	....	....	....	....
GDP Volume (1995=100) .... 99bv p	....	....	....	....	....	....	....	....	....	....	....	....	....	....	....
GDP Deflator (1995=100) .... 99bi p	....	....	....	....	....	....	....	....	....	....	....	....	....	....	....
															Millions:
Population... 99z	19.37	19.95	19.30	†47.61	48.80	†50.48	51.74	52.52	53.70	54.90	56.12	57.35	58.62	59.87	61.11

Prices

Period Averages

	1995	1996	1997	1998	1999	2000	2001		Code
Consumer Prices	100.0	105.7	109.1	117.0	121.8	119.7	119.2		64

International Transactions

Balance of Payments

Minus Sign Indicates Debit

	1996	1997	1998	1999	2000	2001		Code
Current Account, n.i.e.	-2,020	-1,528	-1,074	1,177	960	....		78al *d*
Goods: Exports f.o.b.	7,255	9,185	9,361	11,540	14,448	....		78aa *d*
Goods: Imports f.o.b.	-10,030	-10,432	-10,350	-10,568	-14,073	....		78ab *d*
Trade Balance	-2,775	-1,247	-989	972	375	....		78ac *d*
Services: Credit	2,243	2,530	2,616	2,493	2,702	....		78ad *d*
Services: Debit	-2,304	-3,153	-3,146	-3,040	-3,252	....		78ae *d*
Balance on Goods & Services	-2,836	-1,870	-1,519	425	-175	....		78af *d*
Income: Credit	140	136	127	142	185	....		78ag *d*
Income: Debit	-524	-679	-804	-571	-782	....		78ah *d*
Balance on Gds. Serv. & Inc.	-3,220	-2,413	-2,196	-4	-772	....		78ai *d*
Current Transfers, n.i.e.: Credit	1,200	885	1,122	1,181	1,732	....		78aj *d*
Current Transfers: Debit								78ak *d*
Capital Account, n.i.e.	—	—	—	—	—	....		78bc *d*
Capital Account, n.i.e.: Credit	—	—	—	—	—	....		78ba *d*
Capital Account: Debit	—	—	—	—	—	....		78bb *d*
Financial Account, n.i.e.	2,909	2,125	1,646	1,058	-316	....		78bj *d*
Direct Investment Abroad								78bd *d*
Dir. Invest. in Rep. Econ., n.i.e.	2,395	2,220	1,671	1,412	1,298	....		78be *d*
Portfolio Investment Assets	....	....	....	....	....	....		78bf *d*
Equity Securities	....	....	....	....	....	....		78bk *d*
Debt Securities	....	....	....	....	....	....		78bl *d*
Portfolio Investment Liab., n.i.e.	....	....	....	....	....	....		78bg *d*
Equity Securities	....	....	....	....	....	....		78bm *d*
Debt Securities	....	....	....	....	....	....		78bn *d*
Financial Derivatives Assets	—	—	—	—	—	....		78bw *d*
Financial Derivatives Liabilities	—	—	—	—	—	....		78bx *d*
Other Investment Assets	-33	-112	-537	-786	-2,089	....		78bh *d*
Monetary Authorities								78bo *d*
General Government								78bp *d*
Banks	-33	-112	-537	-786	-2,089	....		78bq *d*
Other Sectors	....	....	....	....	....	....		78br *d*
Other Investment Liab., n.i.e.	547	17	512	432	475	....		78bi *d*
Monetary Authorities								78bs *d*
General Government								78bt *d*
Banks	....	....	....	....	....	....		78bu *d*
Other Sectors	547	17	512	432	475	....		78bv *d*
Net Errors and Omissions	-611	-269	-535	-925	-534	....		78ca *d*
Overall Balance	278	328	37	1,310	110	....		78cb *d*
Reserves and Related Items	-278	-328	-37	-1,310	-110	....		79da *d*
Reserve Assets	-453	-274	41	-1,284	-89	....		79db *d*
Use of Fund Credit and Loans	175	-54	-78	-26	-21	....		79dc *d*
Exceptional Financing	—	—	—	—	—	....		79de *d*

Government Finance

Year Ending December 31

	1992	1993	1994	1995	1996	1997	1998		Code
Deficit (-) or Surplus	-2,017 P	-6,035 P	-2,530	-1,219	-502	-2,600	-3,903		80
Total Revenue and Grants			42,125	53,370	62,387	66,252	68,600		81y
Revenue	11,849 P	18,416 P	40,925	51,750	60,844	63,666	66,650		81
Grants	809 P	849 P	†1,200	1,620	1,543	2,586	1,950		81z
Exp. & Lending Minus Repay.	14,675 P	25,300 P	44,655	54,589	62,889	68,852	72,503		82z
Expenditure	16,130 P	27,021 P	44,655	54,589	62,889	68,852	72,503		82
Lending Minus Repayments	-1,455 P	-1,721 P	—						83
Total Financing	2,017 P	6,035 P	2,530	1,219	502	2,600	3,903		80h
Domestic Financing	-945 P	4,449 P	2,330	2,709	552	2,389	635		84a
Foreign Financing	2,962 P	1,586 P	200	-1,490	-50	211	3,268		85a
Debt: Domestic	2,234 P	4,709 P							88a
Foreign	74,152 P	72,680 P							89a

National Accounts

Billions of Dong

	1987	1988	1989	1990	1991	1992	1993	1994	1995	1996	1997	1998	1999	2000	2001		Code
Househ.Cons.Expend.,incl.NPISHs	2,656	14,045	24,892	37,572	63,904	87,661	106,440	133,299	168,492	202,509	225,084	255,921	274,553	321,853	314,695		96f
Government Consumption Expend.	173	880	2,204	3,164	5,055	7,653	10,279	14,738	18,741	22,722	25,500	27,523	27,137	28,346	30,145		91f
Gross Fixed Capital Formation	272	1,864	2,836	5,495	10,499	18,965	30,635	43,224	56,648	67,539	80,988	94,549	102,799	121,857	139,895		93e
Changes in Inventories	42	350	423	530	1,007	533	3,385	151	3,840	4,578	4,856	9,211	7,704	8,970	9,726		93i
Exports of Goods and Services			6,700	11,084	23,714	38,405	40,286	60,725	75,106	111,177	135,180	161,910	199,836	243,049	267,927		90c
Imports of Goods and Services (-)			9,657	14,960	27,639	42,921	52,582	77,591	95,925	141,016	160,706	188,281	211,254	252,927	277,772		98c
Gross Domestic Product (GDP)				41,955	76,707	110,532	140,258	178,534	228,892	272,037	313,624	361,016	399,942	441,646	484,492		99b
Net Primary Income from Abroad			-492	-2,671	-4,087	-3,775	-5,345	-4,517	-2,501	-4,300	-5,748	-6,648	-5,328				98.n
Gross National Income (GNI)			27,601	39,284	72,620	106,757	134,913	174,017	226,391	267,736	307,875	354,368	394,614	436,922			99a
GDP Volume 1994 Prices			125,571	131,968	139,634	151,782	164,043	178,534	195,567	213,833	231,264	244,596	256,272	273,582	292,306		99b.p
GDP Volume (1995=100)			64.2	67.5	71.4	77.6	83.9	91.3	100.0	109.3	118.3	125.1	131.0	139.9	149.5		99bv p
GDP Deflator (1995=100)				27.2	46.9	62.2	73.1	85.4	100.0	108.7	115.9	126.1	133.3	137.9	141.6		99bi p

Midyear Estimates

	1987	1988	1989	1990	1991	1992	1993	1994	1995	1996	1997	1998	1999	2000	2001		Code
Population	62.45	63.73	64.77	66.23	67.77	69.41	71.03	72.51	73.96	75.36	75.08	76.11	77.12	77.69	†79.18		99z

(See notes in the back of the book.)

	1972	1973	1974	1975	1976	1977	1978	1979	1980	1981	1982	1983	1984	1985	1986

Exchange Rates — *Rials per SDR:*

Market Rate .... aa

Rials per US Dollar:

Market Rate .... ae
Market Rate .... rf

Fund Position — *Millions of SDRs:*

Quota .... 2f. *s*
SDRs .... 1b. *s*
Reserve Position in the Fund .... 1c. *s*
Total Fund Cred.&Loans Outstg. 2tl

International Liquidity — *Millions of US Dollars Unless Otherwise Indicated:*

Total Reserves minus Gold .... 1l. *d*
  SDRs .... 1b. *d*
  Reserve Position in the Fund .... 1c. *d*
  Foreign Exchange .... 1d. *d*
Gold (Million Fine Troy Ounces) 1ad
Gold (National Valuation) .... 1an *d*
Deposit Money Banks: Assets .... 7a. *d*
         Liabilities .... 7b. *d*

Monetary Authorities — *Millions of Rials:*

Foreign Assets 11
Claims on Central Government 12a
Claims on Nonfin.Pub.Enterprises 12c

Reserve Money 14
  of which: Currency Outside Banks 14a
Other Liab. to Dep. Money Banks 14n
Time, Savings,& Fgn.Currency Dep. 15
Foreign Liabilities 16c
Central Government Deposits 16d
Capital Accounts 17a
Other Items (Net) 17r

Deposit Money Banks — *Millions of Rials:*

Reserves 20
Other Claims on Monetary Author. 20n
Foreign Assets 21
Claims on Central Government 22a
Claims on Nonfin.Pub.Enterprises 22c
Claims on Private Sector 22d

Demand Deposits 24
Time, Savings,& Fgn.Currency Dep. 25
Restricted Deposits 26b
Foreign Liabilities 26c
Central Government Deposits 26d
Capital Accounts 27a
Other Items (Net) 27r

Monetary Survey — *Millions of Rials:*

Foreign Assets (Net) 31n
Domestic Credit 32
  Claims on Central Govt. (Net) 32an
  Claims on Nonfin.Pub.Enterprises 32c
  Claims on Private Sector 32d

Money 34
Quasi-Money 35
Restricted Deposits 36b
Capital Accounts 37a
Other Items (Net) 37r

Money plus Quasi-Money 35l

Interest Rates — *Percent Per Annum*

Discount Rate 60
Treasury Bill Rate 60c
Deposit Rate 60l
Lending Rate 60p

Prices — *Index Numbers (1995=100):*

Consumer Prices 64

International Transactions — *Millions of Rials*

Exports 70
Imports, c.i.f. 71

1987	1988	1989	1990	1991	1992	1993	1994	1995	1996	1997	1998	1999	2000	2001		
End of Period															**Exchange Rates**	
....	....	....	17.086	17.179	16.514	16.496	17.533	†74.384	†182.492	176.023	199.447	218.366	215.749	217.754	Market Rate................................	**aa**
End of Period (ae) Period Average (rf)																
....	....	....	12.010	12.010	12.010	12.010	12.010	†50.040	†126.910	130.460	141.650	159.100	165.590	173.270	Market Rate................................	**ae**
....	....	....	....	12.010	12.010	12.010	12.010	40.839	†94.160	129.281	135.882	155.718	161.718	168.672	Market Rate................................	**rf**
End of Period															**Fund Position**	
—	—	—	120.5	120.5	176.5	176.5	176.5	176.5	176.5	176.5	176.5	243.5	243.5	243.5	Quota..........................	**2f. s**
—	—	—	9.4	11.7	2.9	.5	33.5	37.0	33.3	124.1	131.6	128.5	65.0	14.7	SDRs..........................	**1b. s**
—	—	—	—	—	—	—	—	—	—	—	—	—	—	—	Reserve Position in the Fund..............	**1c. s**
—	—	—	.1	—	—	—	—	—	84.0	185.4	238.4	297.6	243.5	297.3	Total Fund Cred.&Loans Outstg.	**2tl**
End of Period															**International Liquidity**	
....	....	....	422.2	679.3	320.5	145.3	254.8	619.0	1,017.2	1,203.1	995.5	1,471.5	2,900.3	3,658.1	Total Reserves minus Gold..........	**1l. d**
....	....	....	13.4	16.8	4.0	.6	48.9	55.0	47.9	167.4	185.2	176.3	84.6	18.5	SDRs..........................	**1b. d**
—	—	—	—	—	—	—	—	—	—	—	—	—	—	—	Reserve Position in the Fund..............	**1c. d**
....	....	....	408.8	662.5	316.5	144.6	205.9	564.0	969.3	1,035.7	810.3	1,295.1	2,815.6	3,639.6	Foreign Exchange..........................	**1d. d**
....	....	....	.050	.050	.050	.050	.050	.050	.050	.050	.050	.050	.050	.050	Gold (Million Fine Troy Ounces)...........	**1ad**
....	....	....	2.2	2.5	2.4	2.4	2.6	2.6	18.6	18.5	15.3	15.3	14.4	14.6	Gold (National Valuation)...............	**1an d**
....	....	....	520.2	565.6	543.7	547.7	477.2	861.1	334.5	455.9	457.9	446.2	624.1	695.5	Deposit Money Banks: Assets............	**7a. d**
....	....	....	404.9	564.2	590.4	549.4	548.1	479.1	209.8	60.8	50.2	45.6	56.5	27.0	Liabilities..........	**7b. d**
End of Period															**Monetary Authorities**	
....	....	....	5,165	8,442	3,896	1,777	4,562	32,448	134,124	167,520	153,964	247,956	486,713	637,185	Foreign Assets........................	**11**
....	....	....	74,914	82,253	104,818	135,664	180,586	209,342	199,058	171,234	196,702	153,962	12,048	253	Claims on Central Government...........	**12a**
....	....	....	162	318	92	76	57	—	10	50	1,108	895	—	—	Claims on Nonfin.Pub.Enterprises........	**12c**
....	....	....	63,315	69,148	83,927	108,933	147,585	176,756	189,030	165,443	184,002	222,245	253,255	288,694	Reserve Money........................	**14**
....	....	....	39,895	45,161	55,531	79,019	111,006	129,114	120,477	126,904	139,668	166,924	197,123	212,795	*of which:* Currency Outside Banks.......	**14a**
....	....	....												29,961	Other Liab. to Dep. Money Banks	**14n**
....	....	....	423	289	316	2,352	3,881	9,440	19,966	22,193	18,978	11,932	18,531	32,255	Time, Savings,& Fgn.Currency Dep........	**15**
....	....	....	2,041	2,149	2,136	1,913	2,053	11,323	43,931	66,613	84,138	101,401	89,147	100,764	Foreign Liabilities.....................	**16c**
....	....	....	6,880	8,803	14,063	16,326	18,294	27,011	41,003	46,106	18,171	26,095	79,708	106,488	Central Government Deposits	**16d**
....	....	....	716	1,094	1,075	1,077	1,100	2,738	5,835	5,673	6,323	6,900	7,208	9,253	Capital Accounts........................	**17a**
....	....	....	6,865	9,532	7,289	6,919	12,293	14,522	33,428	32,474	40,165	34,239	50,912	70,024	Other Items (Net)......................	**17r**
End of Period															**Deposit Money Banks**	
....	....	....	20,533	20,097	24,120	25,987	32,879	44,055	59,903	28,052	35,714	43,631	45,545	50,647	Reserves..............................	**20**
....	....	....												29,961	Other Claims on Monetary Author.......	**20n**
....	....	....	6,248	6,792	6,530	6,578	5,731	43,088	42,453	59,472	64,857	70,991	103,340	120,511	Foreign Assets........................	**21**
....	....	....	155	239	352	281	336	1,295	6,963	34,873	36,267	39,972	63,173	54,814	Claims on Central Government	**22a**
....	....	....	2,813	3,968	3,793	3,395	3,401	11,011	2,237	1,641	317	649	474	674	Claims on Nonfin.Pub.Enterprises........	**22c**
....	....	....	7,723	8,708	10,040	12,653	14,143	23,865	22,358	34,380	45,957	62,426	75,747	95,318	Claims on Private Sector................	**22d**
....	....	....	12,640	14,097	18,237	21,489	25,390	22,985	27,353	28,875	31,490	29,649	41,004	48,992	Demand Deposits......................	**24**
....	....	....	12,782	14,271	15,096	17,251	19,359	71,956	88,640	106,272	130,753	155,981	204,053	253,191	Time, Savings,& Fgn.Currency Dep........	**25**
....	....	....	2,834	1,786	1,329	1,240	1,210	1,977	3,661	3,540	3,684	4,185	4,692	5,064	Restricted Deposits.....................	**26b**
....	....	....	4,863	6,776	7,091	6,599	6,582	23,973	26,624	7,932	7,114	7,248	9,358	4,672	Foreign Liabilities.....................	**26c**
....	....	....	2,182	1,880	1,272	1,543	1,863	1,127	171	474	52	30	46	62	Central Government Deposits	**26d**
....	....	....	1,237	1,443	1,564	1,997	2,829	4,601	6,669	10,762	17,615	18,767	19,454	23,832	Capital Accounts........................	**27a**
....	....	....	934	−449	247	−1,224	−745	−3,305	−19,203	564	−7,597	1,809	9,671	16,111	Other Items (Net)......................	**27r**
End of Period															**Monetary Survey**	
....	....	....	4,508	6,310	1,199	−157	1,658	40,240	106,023	152,447	127,569	210,298	491,548	652,260	Foreign Assets (Net).....................	**31n**
....	....	....	76,704	84,803	103,762	134,201	178,365	217,375	189,453	195,598	262,128	231,778	71,687	44,508	Domestic Credit..........................	**32**
....	....	....	66,007	71,809	89,836	118,076	160,765	182,499	164,848	159,527	214,746	167,809	−4,534	−51,483	Claims on Central Govt. (Net)	**32an**
....	....	....	2,974	4,286	3,886	3,472	3,457	11,011	2,247	1,691	1,425	1,544	474	674	Claims on Nonfin.Pub.Enterprises........	**32c**
....	....	....	7,723	8,708	10,040	12,653	14,143	23,865	22,358	34,380	45,957	62,426	75,747	95,318	Claims on Private Sector................	**32d**
....	....	....	56,498	62,995	78,314	103,306	139,590	164,019	156,579	166,384	179,927	207,197	247,248	282,683	Money................................	**34**
....	....	....	13,205	14,560	15,412	19,604	23,239	81,396	108,605	128,465	149,731	167,913	222,584	285,446	Quasi-Money..........................	**35**
....	....	....	2,834	1,786	1,329	1,240	1,210	1,977	3,661	3,540	3,684	4,185	4,692	5,064	Restricted Deposits.....................	**36b**
....	....	....	1,953	2,536	2,640	3,073	3,929	7,339	12,504	16,434	23,938	25,667	26,662	33,085	Capital Accounts........................	**37a**
....	....	....	6,722	9,236	7,266	6,824	12,054	2,884	14,126	32,920	32,419	37,115	62,048	90,490	Other Items (Net)......................	**37r**
....	....	....	69,703	77,555	93,726	122,909	162,829	245,415	265,184	294,849	329,658	375,109	469,833	568,130	Money plus Quasi-Money..............	**35l**
Percent Per Annum															**Interest Rates**	
....	....	....	....	....	....	....	....	28.51	15.31	19.95	18.53	15.89	15.16	Discount Rate........................	**60**
....	....	....	....	....	....	....	....	25.20	15.97	12.53	20.57	14.17	13.27	Treasury Bill Rate.....................	**60c**
....	....	....	....	....	....	....	....	23.75	14.92	11.33	18.25	14.00	13.00	Deposit Rate........................	**60l**
....	....	....	....	....	....	....	....	31.45	22.52	14.71	24.08	19.54	17.50	Lending Rate........................	**60p**
Period Averages															**Prices**	
....	....	....	18.6	25.3	32.8	43.9	64.1	100.0	130.2	137.2	148.1	....	....	....	Consumer Prices.....................	**64**
Millions of Rials															**International Transactions**	
....	....	....	8,316	7,918	7,435	7,333	11,216	79,434	251,830	323,716	203,480	380,010	659,609	542,359	Exports..................................	**70**
....	....	....	18,867	24,314	31,076	33,883	25,070	64,591	191,862	260,331	294,510	312,749	375,783	389,638	Imports, c.i.f.	**71**

Yemen, Republic of

474

		1972	1973	1974	1975	1976	1977	1978	1979	1980	1981	1982	1983	1984	1985	1986
Balance of Payments																*Millions of US Dollars:*
Current Account, n.i.e.	78al*d*	....	....	....	....	....	....	....	....	....	....	....	....	....	....	....
Goods: Exports f.o.b.	78aa*d*	....	....	....	....	....	....	....	....	....	....	....	....	....	....	....
Goods: Imports f.o.b.	78ab*d*	....	....	....	....	....	....	....	....	....	....	....	....	....	....	....
Trade Balance	78ac*d*	....	....	....	....	....	....	....	....	....	....	....	....	....	....	....
Services: Credit	78ad*d*	....	....	....	....	....	....	....	....	....	....	....	....	....	....	....
Services: Debit	78ae*d*	....	....	....	....	....	....	....	....	....	....	....	....	....	....	....
Balance on Goods & Services	78af*d*	....	....	....	....	....	....	....	....	....	....	....	....	....	....	....
Income: Credit	78ag*d*	....	....	....	....	....	....	....	....	....	....	....	....	....	....	....
Income: Debit	78ah*d*	....	....	....	....	....	....	....	....	....	....	....	....	....	....	....
Balance on Gds, Serv. & Inc.	78ai*d*	....	....	....	....	....	....	....	....	....	....	....	....	....	....	....
Current Transfers, n.i.e.: Credit	78aj*d*	....	....	....	....	....	....	....	....	....	....	....	....	....	....	....
Current Transfers: Debit	78ak*d*	....	....	....	....	....	....	....	....	....	....	....	....	....	....	....
Capital Account, n.i.e.	78bc*d*	....	....	....	....	....	....	....	....	....	....	....	....	....	....	....
Capital Account, n.i.e.: Credit	78ba*d*	....	....	....	....	....	....	....	....	....	....	....	....	....	....	....
Capital Account: Debit	78bb*d*	....	....	....	....	....	....	....	....	....	....	....	....	....	....	....
Financial Account, n.i.e.	78bj*d*	....	....	....	....	....	....	....	....	....	....	....	....	....	....	....
Direct Investment Abroad	78bd*d*	....	....	....	....	....	....	....	....	....	....	....	....	....	....	....
Dir. Invest. in Rep. Econ., n.i.e.	78be*d*	....	....	....	....	....	....	....	....	....	....	....	....	....	....	....
Portfolio Investment Assets	78bf*d*	....	....	....	....	....	....	....	....	....	....	....	....	....	....	....
Equity Securities	78bk*d*	....	....	....	....	....	....	....	....	....	....	....	....	....	....	....
Debt Securities	78bl*d*	....	....	....	....	....	....	....	....	....	....	....	....	....	....	....
Portfolio Investment Liab., n.i.e.	78bg*d*	....	....	....	....	....	....	....	....	....	....	....	....	....	....	....
Equity Securities	78bm*d*	....	....	....	....	....	....	....	....	....	....	....	....	....	....	....
Debt Securities	78bn*d*	....	....	....	....	....	....	....	....	....	....	....	....	....	....	....
Financial Derivatives Assets	78bw*d*	....	....	....	....	....	....	....	....	....	....	....	....	....	....	....
Financial Derivatives Liabilities	78bx*d*	....	....	....	....	....	....	....	....	....	....	....	....	....	....	....
Other Investment Assets	78bh*d*	....	....	....	....	....	....	....	....	....	....	....	....	....	....	....
Monetary Authorities	78bo*d*	....	....	....	....	....	....	....	....	....	....	....	....	....	....	....
General Government	78bp*d*	....	....	....	....	....	....	....	....	....	....	....	....	....	....	....
Banks	78bq*d*	....	....	....	....	....	....	....	....	....	....	....	....	....	....	....
Other Sectors	78br*d*	....	....	....	....	....	....	....	....	....	....	....	....	....	....	....
Other Investment Liab., n.i.e.	78bi*d*	....	....	....	....	....	....	....	....	....	....	....	....	....	....	....
Monetary Authorities	78bs*d*	....	....	....	....	....	....	....	....	....	....	....	....	....	....	....
General Government	78bt*d*	....	....	....	....	....	....	....	....	....	....	....	....	....	....	....
Banks	78bu*d*	....	....	....	....	....	....	....	....	....	....	....	....	....	....	....
Other Sectors	78bv*d*	....	....	....	....	....	....	....	....	....	....	....	....	....	....	....
Net Errors and Omissions	78ca*d*	....	....	....	....	....	....	....	....	....	....	....	....	....	....	....
Overall Balance	78cb*d*	....	....	....	....	....	....	....	....	....	....	....	....	....	....	....
Reserves and Related Items	79da*d*	....	....	....	....	....	....	....	....	....	....	....	....	....	....	....
Reserve Assets	79db*d*	....	....	....	....	....	....	....	....	....	....	....	....	....	....	....
Use of Fund Credit and Loans	79dc*d*	....	....	....	....	....	....	....	....	....	....	....	....	....	....	....
Exceptional Financing	79de*d*	....	....	....	....	....	....	....	....	....	....	....	....	....	....	....
International Investment Position																*Millions of US Dollars*
Assets	79aa*d*	....	....	....	....	....	....	....	....	....	....	....	....	....	....	....
Direct Investment Abroad	79ab*d*	....	....	....	....	....	....	....	....	....	....	....	....	....	....	....
Portfolio Investment	79ac*d*	....	....	....	....	....	....	....	....	....	....	....	....	....	....	....
Equity Securities	79ad*d*	....	....	....	....	....	....	....	....	....	....	....	....	....	....	....
Debt Securities	79ae*d*	....	....	....	....	....	....	....	....	....	....	....	....	....	....	....
Financial Derivatives	79al*d*	....	....	....	....	....	....	....	....	....	....	....	....	....	....	....
Other Investment	79af*d*	....	....	....	....	....	....	....	....	....	....	....	....	....	....	....
Monetary Authorities	79ag*d*	....	....	....	....	....	....	....	....	....	....	....	....	....	....	....
General Government	79ah*d*	....	....	....	....	....	....	....	....	....	....	....	....	....	....	....
Banks	79ai*d*	....	....	....	....	....	....	....	....	....	....	....	....	....	....	....
Other Sectors	79aj*d*	....	....	....	....	....	....	....	....	....	....	....	....	....	....	....
Reserve Assets	79ak*d*	....	....	....	....	....	....	....	....	....	....	....	....	....	....	....
Liabilities	79la*d*	....	....	....	....	....	....	....	....	....	....	....	....	....	....	....
Dir. Invest. in Rep. Economy	79lb*d*	....	....	....	....	....	....	....	....	....	....	....	....	....	....	....
Portfolio Investment	79lc*d*	....	....	....	....	....	....	....	....	....	....	....	....	....	....	....
Equity Securities	79ld*d*	....	....	....	....	....	....	....	....	....	....	....	....	....	....	....
Debt Securities	79le*d*	....	....	....	....	....	....	....	....	....	....	....	....	....	....	....
Financial Derivatives	79ll*d*	....	....	....	....	....	....	....	....	....	....	....	....	....	....	....
Other Investment	79lf*d*	....	....	....	....	....	....	....	....	....	....	....	....	....	....	....
Monetary Authorities	79lg*d*	....	....	....	....	....	....	....	....	....	....	....	....	....	....	....
General Government	79lh*d*	....	....	....	....	....	....	....	....	....	....	....	....	....	....	....
Banks	79li*d*	....	....	....	....	....	....	....	....	....	....	....	....	....	....	....
Other Sectors	79lj*d*	....	....	....	....	....	....	....	....	....	....	....	....	....	....	....
Government Finance																*Millions of Rials:*
Deficit (-) or Surplus	80	....	....	....	....	....	....	....	....	....	....	....	....	....	....	....
Revenue	81	....	....	....	....	....	....	....	....	....	....	....	....	....	....	....
Grants Received	81z	....	....	....	....	....	....	....	....	....	....	....	....	....	....	....
Expenditure	82	....	....	....	....	....	....	....	....	....	....	....	....	....	....	....
Lending Minus Repayments	83	....	....	....	....	....	....	....	....	....	....	....	....	....	....	....
Financing																
Domestic	84a	....	....	....	....	....	....	....	....	....	....	....	....	....	....	....
Foreign	85a	....	....	....	....	....	....	....	....	....	....	....	....	....	....	....
National Accounts																*Millions of Rials*
Househ.Cons.Expend.,incl.NPISHs	96f	....	....	....	....	....	....	....	....	....	....	....	....	....	....	....
Government Consumption Expend.	91f	....	....	....	....	....	....	....	....	....	....	....	....	....	....	....
Gross Fixed Capital Formation	93e	....	....	....	....	....	....	....	....	....	....	....	....	....	....	....
Changes in Inventories	93i	....	....	....	....	....	....	....	....	....	....	....	....	....	....	....
Exports of Goods and Services	90c	....	....	....	....	....	....	....	....	....	....	....	....	....	....	....
Imports of Goods and Services (-)	98c	....	....	....	....	....	....	....	....	....	....	....	....	....	....	....
Gross Domestic Product (GDP)	99b	....	....	....	....	....	....	....	....	....	....	....	....	....	....	....
Net Primary Income from Abroad	98.n	....	....	....	....	....	....	....	....	....	....	....	....	....	....	....
Gross National Income (GNI)	99a	....	....	....	....	....	....	....	....	....	....	....	....	....	....	....
GDP Volume 1990 Prices	99b.*p*	....	....	....	....	....	....	....	....	....	....	....	....	....	....	....
GDP Volume (1995=100)	99bv*p*	....	....	....	....	....	....	....	....	....	....	....	....	....	....	....
GDP Deflator (1995=100)	99bi*p*	....	....	....	....	....	....	....	....	....	....	....	....	....	....	....
																Millions:
Population	99z	....	....	....	....	....	....	....	....	....	....	....	9.10	9.42	9.60	9.88

	1987	1988	1989	1990	1991	1992	1993	1994	1995	1996	1997	1998	1999	2000	2001		
Minus Sign Indicates Debit																**Balance of Payments**	
	....	....	....	393.3	-862.1	-1,126.1	-1,275.3	178.3	143.7	38.8	-68.8	-303.3	577.1	1,862.4	....	Current Account, n.i.e.	78al *d*
	....	....	....	1,384.1	1,196.9	1,073.4	1,166.8	1,796.2	1,980.1	2,262.7	2,274.0	1,503.7	2,478.3	4,093.8	....	Goods: Exports f.o.b.	78aa *d*
	....	....	....	-1,487.2	-1,920.5	-1,935.5	-2,138.1	-1,522.0	-1,831.5	-2,293.5	-2,406.5	-2,288.8	-2,120.4	-2,484.4	....	Goods: Imports f.o.b.	78ab *d*
	....	....	....	-103.1	-723.6	-862.1	-971.3	274.2	148.6	-30.8	-132.5	-785.1	357.9	1,609.4	....	*Trade Balance*	78ac *d*
	....	....	....	105.6	114.0	161.9	177.2	148.0	179.4	185.7	207.6	174.4	183.2	210.8	....	Services: Credit	78ad *d*
	....	....	....	-682.7	-751.3	-969.4	-1,043.4	-704.3	-639.3	-555.4	-677.4	-692.9	-718.6	-809.3	....	Services: Debit	78ae *d*
	....	....	....	-680.2	-1,360.9	-1,669.6	-1,837.5	-282.1	-311.3	-400.5	-602.3	-1,303.6	-177.5	1,010.9	....	*Balance on Goods & Services*	78af *d*
	....	....	....	37.9	43.3	38.1	22.0	22.0	37.4	46.8	69.6	101.1	94.1	297.4	....	Income: Credit	78ag *d*
	....	....	....	-409.4	-528.9	-455.3	-430.2	-553.9	-598.4	-680.7	-670.6	-276.6	-570.9	-845.4	....	Income: Debit	78ah *d*
	....	....	....	-1,051.7	-1,846.5	-2,086.8	-2,245.7	-814.0	-872.3	-1,034.4	-1,203.3	-1,479.1	-654.3	462.9	....	*Balance on Gds, Serv. & Inc.*	78ai *d*
	....	....	....	1,551.4	1,109.8	1,058.2	1,065.2	1,062.3	1,080.5	1,140.1	1,177.6	1,223.5	1,262.1	1,471.9	....	Current Transfers, n.i.e.: Credit	78aj *d*
	....	....	....	-106.4	-125.4	-97.5	-94.8	-70.0	-64.5	-66.9	-43.1	-47.7	-30.7	-72.4	....	Current Transfers: Debit	78ak *d*
	....	....	....	....	....	....	....	....	....	....	4,236.2	2.2	1.5	311.8	....	Capital Account, n.i.e.	78bc *d*
	....	....	....	....	....	....	....	....	....	....	4,236.2	2.2	1.5	391.8	....	Capital Account, n.i.e.: Credit	78ba *d*
	....	....	....	....	....	....	....	....	....	....	....	....	....	-80.0	....	Capital Account: Debit	78bb *d*
	....	....	....	-282.5	271.6	-149.9	49.5	-710.7	-858.4	-367.8	-197.6	-468.0	-549.8	-913.1	....	Financial Account, n.i.e.	78bj *d*
	....	....	....	....	....	....	....	....	....	....	....	....	....	....	....	Direct Investment Abroad	78bd *d*
	....	....	....	-130.9	282.5	718.0	903.0	15.8	-217.7	-60.1	-138.5	-219.4	-194.3	-200.9	....	Dir. Invest. in Rep. Econ., n.i.e.	78be *d*
	....	....	....	2.1	-.4	....	1.6	2.8	-3.1	.9	5.0	4.9	4.1	.1	....	Portfolio Investment Assets	78bf *d*
	....	....	....	2.1	-.4	....	1.6	2.8	-3.1	.9	5.0	4.9	4.1	.1	....	Equity Securities	78bk *d*
	....	....	....	....	....	....	....	....	....	....	....	....	....	....	....	Debt Securities	78bl *d*
	....	....	....	....	....	....	....	....	....	....	....	....	....	....	....	Portfolio Investment Liab., n.i.e.	78bg *d*
	....	....	....	....	....	....	....	....	....	....	....	....	....	....	....	Equity Securities	78bm *d*
	....	....	....	....	....	....	....	....	....	....	....	....	....	....	....	Debt Securities	78bn *d*
	....	....	....	....	....	....	....	....	....	....	....	....	....	....	....	Financial Derivatives Assets	78bw *d*
	....	....	....	....	....	....	....	....	....	....	....	....	....	....	....	Financial Derivatives Liabilities	78bx *d*
	....	....	....	-350.6	143.0	82.3	-5.3	-130.9	158.8	24.0	196.3	10.1	-358.1	-508.9	....	Other Investment Assets	78bh *d*
	....	....	....	....	....	....	....	....	....	....	....	....	....	....	....	Monetary Authorities	78bo *d*
	....	....	....	....	-12.1	12.1	-51.3	1.3	-32.5	-63.7	63.5	70.7	-119.4	....	....	General Government	78bp *d*
	....	....	....	-350.6	-44.9	20.2	-4.0	67.8	141.3	7.7	-122.3	-10.6	9.3	-177.9	....	Banks	78bq *d*
	....	....	....	—	200.0	50.0	50.0	-200.0	50.0	80.0	255.1	-50.0	-248.0	-331.0	....	Other Sectors	78br *d*
	....	....	....	196.9	-153.5	-950.2	-849.8	-598.4	-796.4	-332.6	-260.4	-263.6	-1.5	-203.4	....	Other Investment Liab., n.i.e.	78bi *d*
	....	....	....	46.2	47.5	-25.2	-31.5	61.1	4.4	-.6	34.3	-3.0	-23.7	-6.6	....	Monetary Authorities	78bs *d*
	....	....	....	83.8	-660.2	-762.0	-771.4	-656.6	-626.1	-353.2	-145.7	-250.5	27.1	-207.7	....	General Government	78bt *d*
	....	....	....	66.9	159.2	-158.6	-41.0	-1.4	-174.7	21.2	-149.0	-10.1	-4.9	10.9	....	Banks	78bu *d*
	....	....	....	—	300.0	-4.4	-5.9	-1.5	—	—	—	—	—	....	....	Other Sectors	78bv *d*
	....	....	....	-676.4	-301.9	-25.7	113.9	-189.2	186.5	-107.0	48.4	188.2	45.2	333.3	....	Net Errors and Omissions	78ca *d*
	....	....	....	-565.6	-892.4	-1,301.7	-1,111.9	-721.6	-528.2	-436.0	4,018.2	-580.9	74.0	1,594.4	....	*Overall Balance*	78cb *d*
	....	....	....	565.6	892.4	1,301.7	1,111.9	721.6	528.2	436.0	-4,018.2	580.9	-74.0	-1,594.4	....	Reserves and Related Items	79da *d*
	....	....	....	-50.5	-255.0	356.4	175.2	-207.9	-263.1	-415.7	-192.7	210.9	-482.2	-1,429.5	....	Reserve Assets	79db *d*
	....	....	....	.1	-.2	—	—	—	—	122.5	139.4	72.3	79.5	-71.0	....	Use of Fund Credit and Loans	79dc *d*
	....	....	....	616.0	1,147.6	945.3	936.7	929.5	791.3	729.3	-3,964.9	297.7	328.7	-93.9	....	Exceptional Financing	79de *d*
Millions of US Dollars																**International Investment Position**	
	....	....	....	....	....	....	....	....	....	....	....	2,399.0	3,111.1	....	....	Assets	79aa *d*
	....	....	....	....	....	....	....	....	....	....	....	—	—	....	....	Direct Investment Abroad	79ab *d*
	....	....	....	....	....	....	....	....	....	....	....	4.5	.4	....	....	Portfolio Investment	79ac *d*
	....	....	....	....	....	....	....	....	....	....	....	4.5	.4	....	....	Equity Securities	79ad *d*
	....	....	....	....	....	....	....	....	....	....	....	—	—	....	....	Debt Securities	79ae *d*
	....	....	....	....	....	....	....	....	....	....	....	—	—	....	....	Financial Derivatives	79al *d*
	....	....	....	....	....	....	....	....	....	....	....	1,381.3	1,620.1	....	....	Other Investment	79af *d*
	....	....	....	....	....	....	....	....	....	....	....	—	—	....	....	Monetary Authorities	79ag *d*
	....	....	....	....	....	....	....	....	....	....	....	—	—	....	....	General Government	79ah *d*
	....	....	....	....	....	....	....	....	....	....	....	454.3	445.1	....	....	Banks	79ai *d*
	....	....	....	....	....	....	....	....	....	....	....	927.0	1,175.0	....	....	Other Sectors	79aj *d*
	....	....	....	....	....	....	....	....	....	....	....	1,013.2	1,490.6	....	....	Reserve Assets	79ak *d*
	....	....	....	....	....	....	....	....	....	....	....	6,077.9	6,305.5	....	....	Liabilities	79la *d*
	....	....	....	....	....	....	....	....	....	....	....	1,088.6	993.2	....	....	Dir. Invest. in Rep. Economy	79lb *d*
	....	....	....	....	....	....	....	....	....	....	....	—	—	....	....	Portfolio Investment	79lc *d*
	....	....	....	....	....	....	....	....	....	....	....	—	—	....	....	Equity Securities	79ld *d*
	....	....	....	....	....	....	....	....	....	....	....	—	—	....	....	Debt Securities	79le *d*
	....	....	....	....	....	....	....	....	....	....	....	—	—	....	....	Financial Derivatives	79ll *d*
	....	....	....	....	....	....	....	....	....	....	....	4,989.3	5,312.3	....	....	Other Investment	79lf *d*
	....	....	....	....	....	....	....	....	....	....	....	624.6	664.0	....	....	Monetary Authorities	79lg *d*
	....	....	....	....	....	....	....	....	....	....	....	4,314.4	4,602.9	....	....	General Government	79lh *d*
	....	....	....	....	....	....	....	....	....	....	....	50.3	45.4	....	....	Banks	79li *d*
	....	....	....	....	....	....	....	....	....	....	....	—	—	....	....	Other Sectors	79lj *d*
Year Ending December 31																**Government Finance**	
	....	....	....	-11,167	-7,120	-23,428	-29,297	-44,788	-24,907	-17,428	-9,085	-19,116[f]	-40,278[f]	....	....	Deficit (-) or Surplus	80
	....	....	....	23,941	37,982	32,911	36,720	41,384	89,646	216,053	287,347	300,791[f]	279,418[f]	....	....	Revenue	81
	....	....	....	1,397	300	—	1,201	856	1,620	1,870	4,639[p]	5,480[f]	4,219[f]	....	....	Grants Received	81z
	....	....	....	35,193	44,067	54,848	65,247	85,875	111,128	215,738	285,910	309,942[f]	310,702[f]	....	....	Expenditure	82
	....	....	....	1,312	1,335	1,491	1,971	1,153	5,045	19,613	12,460	15,445[f]	13,213[f]	....	....	Lending Minus Repayments	83
																Financing	
	....	....	....	7,145	5,803	23,055	28,804	43,838	25,976	11,860	5,051	-7,750[f]	25,283[f]	....	....	Domestic	84a
	....	....	....	4,022	1,317	373	493	950	-1,069	5,568	4,034	26,866[f]	14,995[f]	....	....	Foreign	85a
Millions of Rials																**National Accounts**	
	....	....	....	88,998	125,037	146,822	203,024	230,912	413,081	463,969	574,584	556,931	750,546	....	....	Househ.Cons.Expend.,incl.NPISHs	96f
	....	....	....	22,115	28,800	37,187	45,483	57,585	74,017	97,458	120,106	124,473	161,215	....	....	Government Consumption Expend.	91f
	....	....	....	14,980	20,548	37,487	40,772	56,773	99,025	143,207	149,654	223,163	210,249	....	....	Gross Fixed Capital Formation	93e
	....	....	....	3,332	3,379	4,869	6,622	6,123	6,486	12,863	29,549	10,810	9,935	....	....	Changes in Inventories	93i
	....	....	....	18,060	20,760	23,100	33,160	43,537	111,821	284,059	318,088	234,175	389,095	....	....	Exports of Goods and Services	90c
	....	....	....	25,390	53,710	65,540	101,370	102,651	215,921	299,444	339,084	351,871	474,574	....	....	Imports of Goods and Services (-)	98c
	....	....	....	122,095	144,814	183,925	227,691	292,279	488,509	702,112	852,897	797,681	1,046,466	....	....	Gross Domestic Product (GDP)	99b
	....	....	....	-940	-2,970	-4,606	-4,160	-5,035	-16,173	-71,468	-76,040	-49,515	-97,936	....	....	Net Primary Income from Abroad	98.n
	....	....	....	121,155	141,844	179,319	223,531	287,244	472,336	630,644	776,857	748,166	948,530	....	....	Gross National Income (GNI)	99a
	....	....	....	122,095	119,542	125,327	125,829	121,273	130,912	134,754	145,652	153,342	159,160	....	....	GDP Volume 1990 Prices	99b.*p*
	....	....	....	93.3	91.3	95.7	96.1	92.6	100.0	102.9	111.3	117.1	121.6	....	....	GDP Volume (1995=100)	99bv *p*
	....	....	....	26.8	32.5	39.3	48.5	64.6	100.0	139.6	156.9	139.4	176.2	....	....	GDP Deflator (1995=100)	99bi *p*
Midyear Estimates																	
	10.16	10.61	10.95	11.28	11.61	11.95	12.30	†14.86	15.37	15.92	16.48	17.07	17.68	18.30	19.11	**Population**	99z

(See notes in the back of the book.)

Zambia

754

		1972	1973	1974	1975	1976	1977	1978	1979	1980	1981	1982	1983	1984	1985	1986
Exchange Rates																*Kwacha per SDR:*
Official Rate	**aa**	.78	.78	.79	.75	.92	.92	†1.02	1.02	1.02	1.02	1.02	1.28	2.16	6.26	15.55
																Kwacha per US Dollar:
Official Rate	**ae**	.71	.64	.64	.64	.79	.76	.79	.78	.80	.88	.93	1.51	2.20	5.70	12.71
Official Rate	**rf**	.71	.65e	.64e	.64e	.70	.79e	.80	.79	.79	.87	.93	1.26	1.81	3.14	7.79
																Index Numbers (1995=100):
Official Rate	**ahx**	119,871.2e	131,406.6	133,069.9e	133,069.9e	121,112.3	108,428.7e	107,049.7	107,938.9	108,589.0	98,607.6	92,247.2	68,468.6	47,719.5	31,551.6	11,724.1
Nominal Effective Exchange Rate	**nec**	....	....	....	....	....	....	....	33,426.7	34,420.3	35,991.7	39,986.3	35,397.2	28,752.1	22,804.9	7,833.6
Real Effective Exchange Rate	**rec**	....	....	....	....	....	....	....	....	143.9	147.3	164.1	152.4	131.4	126.5	62.4
Fund Position																*Millions of SDRs:*
Quota	**2f.s**	76.0	76.0	76.0	76.0	76.0	76.0	141.0	141.0	211.5	211.5	211.5	270.3	270.3	270.3	270.3
SDRs	**1b.s**	.2	—	11.7	15.7	19.2	11.4	12.1	4.2	—	7.7	14.5	—	—	—	—
Reserve Position in the Fund	**1c.s**	—	—	—	—	—	—	—	—	—	7.5	—	—	—	—	—
Total Fund Cred.&Loans Outstg.	**2tl**	38.0	57.0	57.0	75.9	95.2	95.2	245.1	343.0	350.8	670.6	618.3	678.5	753.8	728.9	701.6
International Liquidity																*Millions of US Dollars Unless Otherwise Indicated:*
Total Reserves minus Gold	**1l.d**	158.4	185.5	164.4	142.0	92.7	66.3	51.1	80.0	78.2	56.2	58.2	54.5	54.2	200.1	70.3
SDRs	**1b.d**	.2	—	14.3	18.4	22.3	13.8	15.8	5.6	—	8.9	16.0	—	—	—	—
Reserve Position in the Fund	**1c.d**	—	—	—	—	—	—	—	—	—	8.7	—	—	—	—	—
Foreign Exchange	**1d.d**	158.2	185.5	150.1	123.6	70.4	52.5	35.3	74.4	78.2	38.5	42.2	54.5	54.2	200.1	70.3
Gold (Million Fine Troy Ounces)	**1ad**	.200	.200	.168	.168	.168	.168	.201	.217	.217	.217	.217	.217	.002	.003	.003
Gold (National Valuation)	**1and**	....	....	7.1	7.1	6.8	7.1	9.1	10.7	10.4	9.5	83.5	70.9	.7	.9	1.0
Monetary Authorities: Other Liab.	**4..d**	—	—	—	122.4	77.5	98.0	666.5	471.3	650.6	618.6	938.8	699.5	506.7	478.2	343.6
Deposit Money Banks: Assets	**7a.d**	10.7	9.0	18.6	7.6	12.5	10.7	33.4	96.6	56.1	93.7	33.1	37.7	29.3	48.2	60.7
Liabilities	**7b.d**	25.1	26.8	36.8	37.3	36.6	55.6	59.5	48.2	77.7	64.8	108.2	46.4	54.6	90.5	44.0
Monetary Authorities																*Millions of Kwacha through 1985;*
Foreign Assets	**11**	114.9	123.8	132.0	95.5	79.3	55.8	47.4	70.7	71.3	53.2	129.9	174.0	123.2	1,145.7	†.9
Claims on Central Government	**12a**	57.4	103.6	61.6	215.1	276.4	255.9	908.5	853.7	1,114.4	1,392.0	1,663.6	1,850.2	1,941.5	2,149.3	†2.6
Claims on Nonfin.Pub.Enterprises	**12c**	....	....	....	....	....	....	....	....	....	....	....	....	....	....	....
Claims on Private Sector	**12d**	—	.5	.5	47.7	53.1	123.6	114.5	80.9	61.9	61.9	160.5	165.5	165.5	160.5	†.2
Claims on Deposit Money Banks	**12e**	—	—	16.0	2.6	4.2	8.2	8.2	3.8	6.6	74.2	101.8	103.5	100.7	173.7	†.1
Reserve Money	**14**	105.8	138.8	128.2	183.2	231.9	228.7	240.6	252.2	287.2	334.5	386.7	440.7	518.5	634.4	†1.7
of which: Currency Outside DMBs	**14a**	61.4	69.4	79.6	102.4	121.1	118.4	130.9	126.2	151.1	190.1	209.5	238.8	285.6	342.5	†.6
Time, Savings,& Fgn.Currency Dep.	**15**	....	....	....	....	....	....	....	....	....	....	....	....	....	....	....
Foreign Liabilities	**16c**	29.6	44.9	45.4	60.8	90.4	89.4	726.1	690.4	810.3	1,175.4	1,295.1	1,711.3	2,358.2	5,548.0	†12.1
Central Government Deposits	**16d**	4.6	20.7	23.7	18.0	19.0	22.9	9.2	1.7	2.5	1.3	1.1	1.5	.5	8.1	†—
Capital Accounts	**17a**	36.3	37.3	39.1	45.1	50.9	52.9	55.4	70.4	85.4	100.2	100.2	118.8	154.0	198.5	†1.1
Other Items (Net)	**17r**	–3.9	–13.8	–26.3	53.9	20.9	49.6	47.3	–5.6	68.7	–30.0	272.8	20.9	–700.2	–2,759.8	†–11.2
Deposit Money Banks																*Millions of Kwacha through 1985;*
Reserves	**20**	44.5	56.7	56.5	57.8	87.2	99.9	583.2	461.2	567.5	618.5	814.0	824.0	972.8	1,095.7	†1.8
Foreign Assets	**21**	7.6	5.8	12.0	4.9	9.9	8.1	26.3	75.2	45.1	82.7	30.8	56.9	64.5	274.7	†.8
Claims on Central Government	**22a**	82.3	115.0	38.8	134.2	288.8	544.8	146.6	282.3	275.1	123.6	352.7	310.6	430.8	787.7	†1.4
Claims on Local Government	**22b**	....	....	....	....	....	....	....	....	....	....	....	....	....	....	....
Claims on Nonfin.Pub.Enterprises	**22c**	8.3	9.1	11.1	13.6	22.4	10.6	16.4	34.0	13.4	88.2	50.8	84.1	498.2	577.4	†.7
Claims on Private Sector	**22d**	157.0	167.2	325.7	333.1	325.7	337.8	295.1	370.6	433.4	623.2	708.9	802.4	556.5	612.9	†1.1
Claims on Other Banking Insts.	**22f**	....	....	....	....	....	....	....	....	....	....	....	....	....	....	....
Claims on Nonbank Financial Insts.	**22g**	....	....	....	....	....	....	....	....	....	....	....	....	....	....	....
Demand Deposits	**24**	140.0	173.5	186.0	219.7	255.7	268.0	260.8	387.1	358.3	371.3	472.7	547.7	581.5	886.3	†1.7
Time, Savings,& Fgn.Currency Dep.	**25**	139.7	151.9	175.0	163.2	223.1	305.9	242.6	315.5	388.1	415.1	619.8	658.9	833.9	870.4	†1.8
Money Market Instruments	**26aa**	15.6	9.7	9.0	14.5	14.6	11.9	9.4	17.9	17.5	27.9	36.9	53.3	46.0	46.4	†.1
Foreign Liabilities	**26c**	17.9	17.3	23.7	24.0	29.1	42.2	46.8	37.5	62.5	57.2	100.6	70.1	120.1	515.9	†.6
Central Government Deposits	**26d**	13.2	26.8	27.8	28.6	20.2	31.9	27.5	30.3	32.5	21.0	25.4	30.6	38.0	56.2	†.1
Credit from Monetary Authorities	**26g**	—	—	42.2	42.5	39.9	39.9	8.2	6.8	3.8	73.5	20.7	18.5	15.7	88.7	†—
Liabs. to Other Banking Insts.	**26i**	....	....	....	....	....	....	....	....	....	....	....	....	....	....	....
Capital Accounts	**27a**	12.3	15.4	20.0	22.8	26.7	38.6	47.2	58.3	72.1	100.1	124.4	157.4	194.0	245.4	†.4
Other Items (Net)	**27r**	–39.0	–40.7	–39.6	28.3	124.9	262.9	425.1	369.8	399.8	470.2	556.7	541.7	693.6	639.2	†1.0
Monetary Survey																*Millions of Kwacha through 1985;*
Foreign Assets (Net)	**31n**	75.1	67.4	74.9	15.6	–30.2	–67.7	–699.3	–582.0	–756.4	–1,096.7	–1,235.0	–1,550.4	–2,290.6	–4,643.5	†–11.0
Domestic Credit	**32**	287.0	347.9	386.1	697.0	918.9	1,204.3	1,440.0	1,588.6	1,863.2	2,260.8	2,910.0	3,180.3	3,553.9	4,223.4	†5.8
Claims on Central Govt. (Net)	**32an**	121.8	171.1	48.9	302.7	526.1	745.9	1,018.3	1,104.1	1,354.5	1,493.4	1,989.9	2,128.7	2,333.8	2,872.6	†3.9
Claims on Local Government	**32b**	....	....	....	....	....	....	....	....	....	....	....	....	....	....	....
Claims on Nonfin.Pub.Enterprises	**32c**	8.3	9.1	11.1	13.6	22.4	10.6	16.4	34.0	13.4	88.2	50.8	84.1	498.2	577.4	†.7
Claims on Private Sector	**32d**	157.0	167.7	326.2	380.8	378.8	461.4	409.6	451.5	495.3	685.1	869.4	967.9	722.0	773.4	†1.3
Claims on Other Banking Insts.	**32f**	....	....	....	....	....	....	....	....	....	....	....	....	....	....	....
Claims on Nonbank Financial Inst	**32g**	....	....	....	....	....	....	....	....	....	....	....	....	....	....	....
Money	**34**	201.3	258.9	265.7	330.6	400.4	392.8	396.8	516.6	519.0	563.7	689.5	795.3	869.9	1,231.5	†2.3
Quasi-Money	**35**	139.7	151.9	175.0	163.2	223.1	305.9	242.6	315.5	388.1	415.1	619.8	658.9	833.9	870.4	†1.8
Money Market Instruments	**36aa**	15.6	9.7	9.0	14.5	14.6	11.9	9.4	17.9	17.5	27.9	36.9	53.3	46.0	46.4	†.1
Liabs. to Other Banking Insts.	**36i**	....	....	....	....	....	....	....	....	....	....	....	....	....	....	....
Capital Accounts	**37a**	48.5	52.7	59.0	67.8	77.6	91.4	102.6	128.7	157.5	200.2	224.5	276.2	348.0	443.9	†1.5
Other Items (Net)	**37r**	–43.1	–57.8	–47.7	136.5	173.0	334.5	–10.7	27.8	24.7	–42.7	104.3	–153.7	–834.4	–3,012.2	†–10.9
Money plus Quasi-Money	**35l**	341.1	410.8	440.7	493.7	623.5	698.7	639.4	832.2	907.1	978.7	1,309.3	1,454.2	1,703.8	2,101.8	†4.1
Liquid Liabilities	**55l**	413.5	492.1	526.9	588.8	724.1	804.7	750.6	949.8	1,049.1	1,123.4	1,457.9	1,618.0	1,893.3	....	....
Interest Rates																*Percent Per Annum*
Discount Rate *(End of Period)*	**60**	5.00	5.00	5.00	5.00	5.00	6.00	6.00	6.50	6.50	7.50	7.50	10.00	14.50	25.00	30.00
Treasury Bill Rate	**60c**	4.34	3.94	3.96	4.00	4.15	4.38	4.38	4.44	4.50	5.75	6.00	7.50	7.67	13.21	24.25
Deposit Rate	**60l**	3.75	4.00	4.00	4.00	5.31	6.25	6.25	6.75	7.00	6.17	6.00	7.00	7.71	15.33	17.74
Lending Rate	**60p**	7.25	7.50	7.50	7.50	8.13	8.25	8.25	9.08	9.50	9.50	9.50	13.00	14.54	18.60	27.40
Prices and Production																*Index Numbers (1995=100):*
Wholesale Prices	**63**	—	—	—	—	—	—	.1	.1	.1	.1	.1	.1	.1	.2	.4
Home & Import Goods	**63a**	.6	.7	.8	.9	1.1	1.3	1.6	1.8	2.2	2.3	2.6	3.2	4.0	5.5	11.4
Consumer Prices	**64**	....	....	....	....	....	....	....	....	....	....	....	....	....	.2	.3
Cons.Prices (Low Inc.Households)	**64a**	—	—	—	—	—	—	.1	.1	.1	.1	.1	.1	.1	†.2	.3
Industrial Production	**66**	139.1	139.2	151.0	139.8	148.7	142.0	142.2	133.4	†137.6	132.2	128.3	138.1	135.1	136.9	133.7
Mining Production (1990=100)	**66zx**	143.0	140.2	146.3	132.7	144.5	135.0	135.5	115.7	†125.2	114.1	118.1	116.0	111.8	108.6	107.1
																Number in Thousands:
Employment	**67e**	....	....	....	....	....	....	....	....	....	....	....	....	....	362	361
International Transactions																*Millions of Kwacha through 1985;*
Exports	**70**	541.8	742.1	905.1	521.2	749.1	708.0	686.7	1,090.0	1,029.0	976.6	950.5	1,047.5	1,199.4	1,508.2	†5.4
Imports, c.i.f.	**71**	403.8	346.9	506.6	597.6	468.6	530.0	492.8	593.8	859.0	923.0	930.0	693.0	1,086.0	2,133.0	†4.4

1987	1988	1989	1990	1991	1992	1993	1994	1995	1996	1997	1998	1999	2000	2001		
End of Period															**Exchange Rates**	
11.35	13.46	28.45	60.82	127.26	494.60	686.78	993.10	1,421.28	1,844.46	1,908.97	3,236.95	3,612.71	5,417.28	4,813.78	Official Rate	aa
End of Period (ae) Period Average (rf)																
8.00	10.00	21.65	42.75	88.97	359.71	500.00	680.27	956.13	1,282.69	1,414.84	2,298.92	2,632.19	4,157.83	3,830.40	Official Rate	ae
9.52	8.27	13.81	30.29	64.64	172.21	452.76	669.37	864.12	1,207.90	1,314.50	1,862.07	2,388.02	3,110.84	3,610.94	Official Rate	rf
Period Averages																
9,632.6	10,407.9	6,637.3	2,953.7	1,384.7	547.8	193.7	114.0	100.0	71.5	65.2	46.7	35.9	27.9	23.8	Official Rate	ah x
6,247.7	7,447.6	6,052.4	2,820.9	1,388.5	548.7	209.8	135.9	100.0	75.0	73.7	55.9	43.9	36.7	33.9	Nominal Effective Exchange Rate	ne c
67.5	101.8	131.0	106.8	99.8	95.7	108.6	104.5	100.0	104.7	125.4	114.5	111.9	113.3	122.4	Real Effective Exchange Rate	re c
End of Period															**Fund Position**	
270.3	270.3	270.3	270.3	270.3	270.3	270.3	270.3	363.5	363.5	363.5	363.5	489.1	489.1	489.1	Quota	2f. s
—	—	—	—	—	—	—	—	8.2	1.4	.8	.6	.1	17.1	53.3	SDRs	1b. s
—	—	—	—	—	—	—	—	—	—	—	—	—	—	3.5	Reserve Position in the Fund	1c. s
698.8	698.8	685.0	666.7	641.6	615.6	565.8	551.2	833.4	833.4	843.4	843.4	853.4	873.4	781.6	Total Fund Cred.&Loans Outstg.	2tl
End of Period															**International Liquidity**	
108.8	134.0	116.2	193.1	184.6	....	192.3	268.1	222.7	222.7	239.1	69.4	45.4	244.8	183.4	Total Reserves minus Gold	1l. d
—	—	—	—	—	—	—	—	12.1	2.0	1.1	.8	.1	22.3	66.9	SDRs	1b. d
—	—	—	—	—	—	—	—	—	—	—	—	—	—	—	Reserve Position in the Fund	1c. d
108.8	134.0	116.2	193.1	184.6	....	192.3	268.1	210.5	220.7	238.0	68.6	45.3	222.5	116.5	Foreign Exchange	1d. d
.004	.013	.017	.021	.022	....	....	....	—	—	—	—	—	—	—	Gold (Million Fine Troy Ounces)	1ad
1.8	4.1	—	—	—	—	—	—	—	—	—	—	—	—	—	Gold (National Valuation)	1an d
408.2	471.4	523.6	578.4	483.3	....	678.7	736.0	1,128.8	1,088.8	1,007.1	1,001.4	974.3	938.2	868.6	Monetary Authorities: Other Liab.	4.. d
118.6	141.4	169.6	165.7	134.9	120.7	205.5	84.3	116.5	148.7	155.0	198.9	201.4	239.5	233.3	Deposit Money Banks: Assets	7a. d
61.8	50.3	55.0	49.3	34.1	20.0	16.8	15.6	9.3	11.2	13.2	29.2	34.9	25.9	24.5	Liabilities	7b. d
Billions of Kwacha Beginning 1986: End of Period															**Monetary Authorities**	
.7	†1.4	2.5	9.2	13.9	....	137.7	213.7	208.1	268.4	338.4	103.0	211.2	336.8	432.6	Foreign Assets	11
2.3	†13.7	28.6	59.5	147.9	....	611.9	1,114.7	2,017.5	2,636.7	2,659.5	4,670.2	5,584.5	8,605.1	7,816.2	Claims on Central Government	12a
						20.2	9.1	1.2	1.3	1.3	5.3	7.9	69.2	195.0	Claims on Nonfin.Pub.Enterprises	12c
.2	†.1	.1	.9	.4	....	2.1	4.4	14.0	23.6	25.1	30.7	31.4	35.7	42.6	Claims on Private Sector	12d
.1	†—	—	2.1	4.2	....	7.8	—	121.8	157.2	164.9	161.4	120.9	82.4	77.5	Claims on Deposit Money Banks	12e
2.4	†3.8	6.3	11.3	22.7	....	102.3	151.4	129.2	175.0	259.3	303.0	389.2	597.0	870.0	Reserve Money	14
1.0	1.8	2.2	4.6	9.2	....	40.4	56.3	77.8	106.3	136.7	†169.7	212.2	287.8	373.6	of which: Currency Outside DMBs	14a
						5.4	—	1.5	2.3	.7	.8	1.6	2.2	3.5	Time, Savings,& Fgn.Currency Dep.	15
9.6	†14.1	30.8	65.3	124.7	....	727.9	1,048.1	1,337.6	1,731.8	1,771.9	2,890.4	3,221.2	4,885.6	4,027.0	Foreign Liabilities	16c
—	†—	—	—	—	....	267.8	173.6	545.4	895.6	955.0	1,351.6	2,011.9	2,975.3	3,112.4	Central Government Deposits	16d
1.1	†1.0	1.2	4.4	1.2	....	−411.6	−52.7	286.0	329.8	421.6	444.8	493.0	1,063.7	990.5	Capital Accounts	17a
−9.9	†−3.7	−7.1	−9.3	17.8	....	87.9	21.6	62.9	−47.3	−219.2	−20.0	−160.9	−394.7	−439.5	Other Items (Net)	17r
Billions of Kwacha Beginning 1986: End of Period															**Deposit Money Banks**	
1.9	3.8	4.9	8.3	14.7	20.8	49.8	96.1	34.6	62.8	87.8	†134.7	175.6	322.7	475.5	Reserves	20
.9	1.4	3.7	7.1	12.0	43.4	102.8	57.4	116.5	190.7	224.6	†457.3	530.2	995.1	893.6	Foreign Assets	21
2.5	2.7	3.6	4.2	14.2	38.3	71.4	84.7	202.8	216.4	222.7	†153.0	231.6	356.7	776.9	Claims on Central Government	22a
											2.6	.4	.4	.4	Claims on Local Government	22b
.7	1.5	2.7	4.3	7.0	13.4	29.1	16.8	35.6	49.7	40.9	†119.1	248.9	289.7	246.8	Claims on Nonfin.Pub.Enterprises	22c
1.6	2.8	6.2	9.1	15.5	29.2	68.9	136.0	240.0	350.2	386.1	†392.7	522.0	825.5	902.8	Claims on Private Sector	22d
....	....	....	....	....	....	....	....	....	....	....	.4	.4	.4	.4	Claims on Other Banking Insts.	22f
....	....	....	....	....	....	....	....	....	....	....	2.7	1.4	.5	.4	Claims on Nonbank Financial Insts.	22g
2.2	3.5	5.7	8.1	13.5	33.0	56.8	83.8	140.2	163.1	217.2	†243.7	299.0	472.0	637.1	Demand Deposits	24
3.0	4.9	8.8	12.0	26.1	45.1	105.8	191.0	287.6	423.4	515.6	†679.0	883.3	1,651.0	1,714.9	Time, Savings,& Fgn.Currency Dep.	25
.1	.2	1.0	2.3	5.4	10.7	15.0	14.9	23.3	31.1	29.8	†11.8	9.9	34.6	21.3	Money Market Instruments	26aa
.5	.5	1.2	2.1	3.0	7.2	8.4	10.6	9.3	14.4	19.1	†67.1	91.8	107.7	93.7	Foreign Liabilities	26c
.2	.4	.8	1.2	3.2	5.7	5.8	12.4	44.6	57.7	63.6	†61.3	125.2	43.2	94.4	Central Government Deposits	26d
—	—	—	1.5	.3	—	.2	2.7	60.2	86.6	82.5	†21.4	78.5	39.1	30.3	Credit from Monetary Authorities	26g
											.1	1.3	5.6	15.3	Liabs. to Other Banking Insts.	26i
.8	1.1	2.0	3.8	7.9	17.8	44.2	58.5	74.5	112.7	138.1	†227.8	297.2	448.6	533.7	Capital Accounts	27a
.8	1.6	1.7	2.1	4.0	25.5	85.7	17.0	−10.1	−19.2	−103.8	†−49.7	−75.6	−10.2	156.0	Other Items (Net)	27r
Billions of Kwacha Beginning 1986: End of Period															**Monetary Survey**	
−8.5	†−11.9	−25.8	−51.2	−101.7	....	−495.9	−787.6	−1,022.4	−1,287.1	−1,228.0	†−2397.2	−2,571.6	−3,660.9	−2,794.4	Foreign Assets (Net)	31n
7.0	†20.5	40.4	76.8	181.8	....	530.0	1,179.7	1,921.1	2,324.6	2,316.9	†3,963.7	4,491.7	7,164.8	6,774.6	Domestic Credit	32
4.5	†16.1	31.5	62.5	159.0	....	409.7	1,013.4	1,630.3	1,899.7	1,863.6	†3,410.2	3,679.1	5,943.4	5,386.3	Claims on Central Govt. (Net)	32an
											2.6	.4	.4	.4	Claims on Local Government	32b
.7	†1.5	2.7	4.3	7.0	....	49.3	25.9	36.9	51.0	42.2	†124.4	256.9	358.8	441.7	Claims on Nonfin.Pub.Enterprises	32c
1.8	†2.9	6.3	10.1	15.8	....	71.0	140.4	254.0	373.8	411.1	†423.5	553.5	861.3	945.4	Claims on Private Sector	32d
....	....	....	....	....	....	....	....	....	....	....	.4	.4	.4	.4	Claims on Other Banking Insts.	32f
—	—	—	—	—	....	—	—	—	—	—	†2.7	1.4	.5	.4	Claims on Nonbank Financial Inst	32g
3.2	†5.2	7.9	12.8	22.7	....	97.3	141.0	227.1	271.1	355.2	†414.9	513.0	775.9	1,041.4	Money	34
3.0	†4.9	8.8	12.0	26.1	....	111.2	191.0	289.1	425.7	516.3	†679.8	884.9	1,653.2	1,718.3	Quasi-Money	35
.1	.2	1.0	2.3	5.4	10.7	15.0	14.9	23.3	31.1	29.8	†11.8	9.9	34.6	21.3	Money Market Instruments	36aa
											.1	1.3	5.6	15.3	Liabs. to Other Banking Insts.	36i
1.9	†2.0	3.1	8.2	9.1	17.8	−367.4	5.8	360.5	442.5	559.7	†672.6	790.2	1,512.4	1,524.2	Capital Accounts	37a
−9.7	†−3.8	−6.3	−9.5	16.8	....	177.9	39.4	−1.1	−133.0	−372.1	†−212.8	−279.2	−477.7	−340.4	Other Items (Net)	37r
6.3	†10.1	16.7	24.7	48.8	....	208.6	332.0	516.2	696.9	871.5	†1,094.7	1,397.9	2,429.1	2,759.7	Money plus Quasi-Money	35l
....	....	....	....	....	....	....	....	....	....	....	....	....	....	....	Liquid Liabilities	55l
Percent Per Annum															**Interest Rates**	
15.00	15.00	....	....	....	47.00	72.50	20.50	40.20	47.00	17.70	....	....	....	....	Discount Rate (End of Period)	60
16.50	15.17	18.50	25.92	....	....	124.03	74.21	39.81	52.78	29.48	24.94	36.19	31.37	44.28	Treasury Bill Rate	60c
13.23	11.44	11.44	25.65	....	48.50	....	46.14	30.24	42.13	34.48	13.08	20.27	20.24	23.41	Deposit Rate	60l
21.20	18.39	18.39	35.10	....	54.57	113.31	70.56	45.53	53.78	46.69	31.80	40.52	38.80	46.23	Lending Rate	60p
Period Averages															**Prices and Production**	
.8	.8	1.5	3.3	6.4	14.1	34.1	58.1	100.0	....	....	....	....	....	....	Wholesale Prices	63
22.9	24.0	46.1	100.0	193.0	447.2	....	....	....	....	....	....	....	....	....	Home & Import Goods	63a
.5	.7	1.6	3.2	6.3	16.8	48.5	74.5	100.0	146.3	182.6	....	....	....	....	Consumer Prices	64
.4	.6	1.3	2.9	5.6	†16.7	48.2	74.0	100.0	145.2	....	....	....	....	....	Cons.Prices (Low Inc.Households)	64a
130.9	136.1	132.8	128.2	123.8	133.0	122.0	107.0	100.0	....	....	....	....	....	....	Industrial Production	66
104.6	100.9	102.5	100.0	90.1	100.8	92.0	76.8	....	....	....	....	....	....	....	Mining Production (1990=100)	66zx
Period Averages																
362	361	360	....	....	....	....	....	....	....	....	....	....	....	....	Employment	67e
Billions of Kwacha Beginning 1986															**International Transactions**	
8.1	9.8	18.4	39.1	69.6	129.5	374.1	620.5	898.6	1,252.7	1,203.0	....	....	....	....	Exports	70
6.6	6.9	12.6	36.6	51.8	144.1	366.3	397.7	604.8	1,004.3	1,077.0	....	....	....	....	Imports, c.i.f.	71

Zambia

		1972	1973	1974	1975	1976	1977	1978	1979	1980	1981	1982	1983	1984	1985	1986
Balance of Payments																*Millions of US Dollars:*
Current Account, n.i.e.	78al d	....	....	....	....	....	....	−281	78	−516	−729	−562	−263	−147	−395	−348
Goods: Exports f.o.b.	78aa d							831	1,408	1,457	996	942	923	893	797	692
Goods: Imports f.o.b.	78ab d							−618	−756	−1,114	−1,065	−1,003	−711	−612	−571	−518
Trade Balance	78ac d							213	652	343	−69	−61	212	280	226	175
Services: Credit	78ad d							113	116	152	153	122	99	75	68	47
Services: Debit	78ae d							−408	−456	−651	−584	−409	−334	−291	−254	−199
Balance on Goods & Services	78af d							−82	311	−157	−501	−348	−23	65	39	23
Income: Credit	78ag d							8	11	16	20	15	3	5	2	1
Income: Debit	78ah d							−162	−181	−221	−130	−203	−241	−187	−413	−354
Balance on Gds, Serv. & Inc.	78ai d							−236	142	−362	−610	−537	−261	−117	−371	−330
Current Transfers, n.i.e.: Credit	78aj d							27	38	35	30	32	44	14	8	23
Current Transfers: Debit	78ak d							−72	−101	−190	−148	−57	−46	−44	−32	−41
Capital Account, n.i.e.	78bc d							−17	−41	−21	−13	−4	−8	−6	−3	−3
Capital Account, n.i.e.: Credit	78ba d							—	—	—	—	—	—	—	—	—
Capital Account: Debit	78bb d							−17	−41	−21	−13	−4	−8	−6	−3	−3
Financial Account, n.i.e.	78bj d							30	119	287	459	253	38	151	363	−99
Direct Investment Abroad	78bd d							—	—	—	—	—	—	—	—	—
Dir. Invest. in Rep. Econ., n.i.e.	78be d							39	35	62	−38	39	26	17	52	28
Portfolio Investment Assets	78bf d							—	—	—	—	—	—	—	—	—
Equity Securities	78bk d							—	—	—	—	—	—	—	—	—
Debt Securities	78bl d							—	—	—	—	—	—	—	—	—
Portfolio Investment Liab., n.i.e.	78bg d							—	—	—	—	—	—	—	—	—
Equity Securities	78bm d							—	—	—	—	—	—	—	—	—
Debt Securities	78bn d							—	—	—	—	—	—	—	—	—
Financial Derivatives Assets	78bw d							....	....	....	....	....	....	....	....	....
Financial Derivatives Liabilities	78bx d							....	....	....	....	....	....	....	....	....
Other Investment Assets	78bh d							17	−25	56	−64	30	−19	−7	−26	−38
Monetary Authorities	78bo d							....	....	....	....	....	....	....	....	....
General Government	78bp d							−4	−6	−8	2	−10	−5	−5	—	1
Banks	78bq d							−23	−61	38	−43	56	−5	8	−16	−12
Other Sectors	78br d							43	42	26	−22	−16	−10	−10	−9	−27
Other Investment Liab., n.i.e.	78bi d							−25	109	170	561	184	32	141	337	−90
Monetary Authorities	78bs d							9	−3	2	1	−26	−4	−2	−20	−35
General Government	78bt d							8	136	301	285	98	86	47	221	−218
Banks	78bu d							6	−12	32	−6	47	−61	8	31	−44
Other Sectors	78bv d							−48	−12	−165	281	65	11	88	105	207
Net Errors and Omissions	78ca d							−75	−88	26	−181	−77	211	−87	−145	315
Overall Balance	78cb d							−342	68	−225	−464	−390	−21	−89	−181	−134
Reserves and Related Items	79da d							342	−68	225	464	390	21	89	181	134
Reserve Assets	79db d							5	13	22	39	−6	4	59	−127	121
Use of Fund Credit and Loans	79dc d							185	126	9	373	−57	65	76	−25	−31
Exceptional Financing	79de d							152	−207	194	52	453	−47	−46	332	44
Government Finance																*Millions of Kwacha through 1985;*
Deficit (-) or Surplus	80	†−175.6	−266.4	64.4	−340.8	−269.9	−261.4	−324.5	−241.1	−567.5	−449.6	−668.2	−327.3	−413.7	−1,072.6	†−2.8
Revenue	81	†296.8	469.4	649.1	447.8	453.0	498.3	555.7	594.2	765.1	807.1	839.9	1,013.5	1,090.5	1,555.5	†3.0
Grants Received	81z	†1.3	1.4	.9	14.5	8.9	33.8	19.5	25.8	25.6	24.0	29.1	53.7	23.0	19.6	†.2
Expenditure	82	†432.7	469.1	531.3	678.2	685.2	706.2	668.8	809.5	1,135.2	1,277.7	1,409.1	1,346.3	1,441.2	2,484.1	†5.4
Lending Minus Repayments	83	†41.0	268.1	54.3	124.9	46.6	87.3	230.9	51.6	223.0	3.0	128.1	48.2	86.0	163.6	†.6
Financing																
Net Borrowing: Domestic	84a	†128.5	118.8	....	266.6	239.7	243.1	298.4	....	....	160.6	531.6	215.3	289.5	457.0	†1.6
Foreign	85a	†15.2	147.0	36.7	58.9	30.2	19.0	21.1	137.5	269.6	247.4	111.6	119.9	129.3	599.7	†1.2
Use of Cash Balances	87	†31.9	.6	....	15.3	—	−.7	5.0	....	....	41.6	25.0	−7.9	−5.1	15.9	†—
Debt: Domestic	88a	†335.0	468.9	344.8	573.9	817.9	1,146.3	1,455.9	....	....	2,011.2	2,746.4	2,919.7	3,229.1	4,076.8	†5.8
Foreign	89a	....	....	....	....	....	556.8	633.8	....	....	1,285.4	1,846.0	2,666.0	3,545.0	9,542.1	†33.1
National Accounts																*Millions of Kwacha through 1985;*
Househ.Cons.Expend.,incl.NPISHs	96f	535.7	530.2	664.4	814.5	847.0	1,022.8	1,251.5	1,412.6	1,691.9	2,262.2	2,314.9	2,645.5	2,779.4	4,294.6	†6.6
Government Consumption Expend.	91f	314.5	344.8	357.8	435.7	501.0	525.0	537.8	633.0	781.6	986.0	995.9	1,008.8	1,240.1	1,686.7	†3.5
Gross Fixed Capital Formation	93e	445.0	422.9	502.0	602.0	445.0	483.0	437.0	450.0	558.3	610.0	618.0	615.0	622.6	724.5	†1.4
Changes in Inventories	93i	31.4	42.0	185.3	40.0	6.5	7.0	100.0	−74.0	155.0	63.3	−15.1	−40.0	101.4	328.5	†1.7
Exports of Goods and Services	90c	586.1	780.4	943.9	575.0	832.3	781.5	755.3	1,208.3	1,268.0	998.0	993.1	1,280.7	1,806.9	2,740.2	†5.9
Imports of Goods and Services (-)	98c	564.7	529.0	765.5	883.8	736.0	832.9	830.9	969.5	1,391.2	1,434.1	1,311.5	1,328.8	1,619.4	2,702.6	†5.9
Gross Domestic Product (GDP)	99b	1,348.0	1,591.3	1,887.9	1,583.4	1,895.8	1,986.4	2,250.7	2,660.4	3,063.6	3,485.4	3,595.3	4,181.2	4,931.0	7,071.9	†13.1
Net Primary Income from Abroad	98.n	74.1	−90.5	−81.2	−81.8	−79.7	−68.6	49.5	−83.4	−138.5	−114.5	−36.4	−3.8	−64.1	−86.2	†−1.0
Gross National Income (GNI)	99a	1,273.9	1,681.8	1,969.1	1,665.2	1,975.5	2,055.0	2,201.2	2,743.8	3,202.1	3,599.9	3,631.7	4,177.4	4,866.9	6,985.7	†12.1
Net National Income	99e	1,069.1	1,293.5	1,582.4	1,268.8	1,522.0	1,607.4	1,809.1	2,124.3	2,495.9	3,004.1	2,870.3	3,508.4	3,925.7	5,430.0	†8.4
GDP Volume 1977 Prices (Billions)	99b.p	1.939	1.921	2.050	2.000	2.087	1.986	1.998	1.937	1.996	2.119	2.059	2.019	2.012	2.045	2.059
GDP Volume (1995=100)	99bv p	88.6	87.7	93.6	91.3	95.3	90.7	91.2	88.5	91.1	96.8	94.0	92.2	91.9	93.4	94.0
GDP Deflator (1995=100)	99bi p	.1	.1	.1	.1	.1	.1	.1	.1	.1	.1	.1	.2	.2	.3	†.5
																Millions:
Population	99z	4.53	4.68	4.83	4.98	5.14	5.30	5.47	5.52	5.56	5.87	6.05	6.24	6.44	6.73	7.11

Minus Sign Indicates Debit

Balance of Payments

1987	1988	1989	1990	1991	1992	1993	1994	1995	1996	1997	1998	1999	2000	2001		
-245	-293	-219	-594	-306	....	....	....	....	....	-353	-573	-447	-584	....	Current Account, n.i.e.	78al d
852	1,189	1,340	1,254	1,172	....	....	....	....	....	1,110	818	772	757	....	Goods: Exports f.o.b.	78aa d
-585	-687	-774	-1,511	-752	....	....	....	....	....	-1,056	-971	-870	-978	....	Goods: Imports f.o.b.	78ab d
267	502	566	-257	420	....	....	....	....	....	54	-153	-98	-221	....	*Trade Balance*	78ac d
48	58	85	107	83	....	....	....	....	....	112	102	107	114	....	Services: Credit	78ad d
-223	-289	-444	-386	-363	....	....	....	....	....	-282	-282	-306	-340	....	Services: Debit	78ae d
91	271	208	-537	140	....	....	....	....	....	-115	-332	-297	-447	....	*Balance on Goods & Services*	78af d
1	3	1	2	10	....	....	....	....	....	77	44	44	46	....	Income: Credit	78ag d
-329	-604	-509	-439	-696	....	....	....	....	....	-296	-258	-178	-166	....	Income: Debit	78ah d
-236	-330	-300	-974	-546	....	....	....	....	....	-334	-546	-431	-566	....	*Balance on Gds, Serv. & Inc.*	78ai d
10	64	114	398	262	....	....	....	....	....					....	Current Transfers, n.i.e.: Credit	78aj d
-19	-27	-32	-18	-22	....	....	....	....	....	-19	-27	-16	-18	....	Current Transfers: Debit	78ak d
-2	-2	-3	-3	-1	....	....	....	....	....	—	203	196	153	....	Capital Account, n.i.e.	78bc d
					....	....	....	....	....	—	203	196	153	....	Capital Account, n.i.e.: Credit	78ba d
-2	-2	-3	-3	-1	....	....	....	....	....	—	—	—	—	....	Capital Account, n.i.e.: Debit	78bb d
-147	23	1,827	497	18	....	....	....	....	....	-324	-264	-174	-274	....	Financial Account, n.i.e.	78bj d
....	....	....	....	....	....	....	....	....	....	....	....	....	....	....	Direct Investment Abroad	78bd d
75	93	164	203	34	....	....	....	....	....	207	198	162	122	....	Dir. Invest. in Rep. Econ., n.i.e.	78be d
—	—	—	—	—	....	....	....	....	....	—	—	—	—	....	Portfolio Investment Assets	78bf d
—	—	—	—	—	....	....	....	....	....	—	—	—	—	....	Equity Securities	78bk d
—	—	—	—	—	....	....	....	....	....	—	—	—	—	....	Debt Securities	78bl d
—	—	—	—	—	....	....	....	....	....	1	1	13	-1	....	Portfolio Investment Liab., n.i.e.	78bg d
—	—	—	—	—	....	....	....	....	....	1	1	13	-1	....	Equity Securities	78bm d
....	....	....	....	....	....	....	....	....	....	....	....	....	....	....	Debt Securities	78bn d
....	....	....	....	....	....	....	....	....	....	....	....	....	....	....	Financial Derivatives Assets	78bw d
....	....	....	....	....	....	....	....	....	....	....	....	....	....	....	Financial Derivatives Liabilities	78bx d
-57	-347	26	-275	-125	....	....	....	....	....	-24	-40	-2	-85	....	Other Investment Assets	78bh d
....	....	....	....	....	....	....	....	....	....	....	....	....	....	....	Monetary Authorities	78bo d
—	1	—	-7	-54	....	....	....	....	....					....	General Government	78bp d
-19	-56	-172	-109	-76	....	....	....	....	....	-24	-40	-2	-85	....	Banks	78bq d
-39	-292	197	-159	6	....	....	....	....	....					....	Other Sectors	78br d
-165	277	1,637	569	108	....	....	....	....	....	-508	-422	-347	-309	....	Other Investment Liab., n.i.e.	78bi d
-4	-4	-3	23	5	....	....	....	....	....				-7	....	Monetary Authorities	78bs d
-77	24	-241	11	38	....	....	....	....	....	-192	-136	-259	-290	....	General Government	78bt d
-7	1	50	30	14	....	....	....	....	....	19	-2	—	—	....	Banks	78bu d
-76	256	1,831	504	51	....	....	....	....	....	-335	-284	-88	-12	....	Other Sectors	78bv d
153	40	-1,712	322	110	....	....	....	....	....	-255	-37	-229	185	....	Net Errors and Omissions	78ca d
-242	-232	-106	222	-179	....	....	....	....	....	-932	-671	-654	-520	....	*Overall Balance*	78cb d
242	232	106	-222	179	....	....	....	....	....	932	671	654	520	....	Reserves and Related Items	79da d
71	-51	-82	-119	-26	....	....	....	....	....	-25	194	-1	-90	....	Reserve Assets	79db d
-4	—	-17	-25	-35	....	....	....	....	....	14	—	14	26	....	Use of Fund Credit and Loans	79dc d
175	284	205	-77	241	....	....	....	....	....	944	477	642	584	....	Exceptional Financing	79de d

Government Finance

Billions of Kwacha Beginning 1986: Year Ending December 31

1987	1988	1989	1990	1991	1992	1993	1994	1995	1996	1997	1998	1999	2000		
-2.5	-3.5	†-5.9	-9.8	-98.4	-37.3	-115.6	-27.4	-136.9	-96.2	-488.5	-330.4[P]	-275.4[f]	....	Deficit (-) or Surplus	80
4.3	5.1	†9.9	23.4	41.5	113.5	266.4	502.8	600.8	745.3	957.0	1,097.6[P]	1,430.4[f]	....	Revenue	81
.1	.5	†.1	.3	2.7	....	.6	5.6	25.4	4.7	432.7[P]	414.2[f]		....	Grants Received	81z
6.8	8.6	†13.6	30.9	127.6	171.2	391.1	492.2	727.5	842.7	1,313.6	1,717.1[P]	1,874.3[f]	....	Expenditure	82
.1	.5	†2.3	2.6	15.0	9.4	26.6	38.6	15.7	24.2	136.6	143.6[P]	245.7[f]	....	Lending Minus Repayments	83

Financing

1987	1988	1989	1990	1991	1992	1993	1994	1995	1996	1997	1998	1999	2000		
1.1	2.1	†2.0	8.6	50.4	37.3	38.0	-46.5	-351.4	-91.2	-283.9	50.2[P]	....	....	Net Borrowing: Domestic	84a
1.4	1.1	†2.5	-2.5	23.3	-25.0	36.4	-35.7	-560.0	129.4	775.6	253.8[P]	....	....	Foreign	85a
.1	.2	†1.3	-37.2	-24.7	-25.1	-41.2	-109.6	-1,048.3	-58.0	3.2	-26.4	....	....	Use of Cash Balances	87
7.1	9.3	†.9	.8	.8	.8	1.6	149.9	238.8	265.8	303.2	212.8[P]	....	....	Debt: Domestic	88a
20.5	....	†101.8	276.1	605.0	937.3	2,396.3	3,502.4	4,869.4	7,378.7	8,185.9	10,408.4[P]	....	....	Foreign	89a

National Accounts

Billions of Kwacha Beginning 1986

1987	1988	1989	1990	1991	1992	1993	1994	1995	1996	1997		
11.8	19.8	45.5	71.6	117.1	447.6	1,015.7	1,602.7	1,775.9	2,033.2	3,006.0	Househ.Cons.Expend.,incl.NPISHs	96f
4.4	4.6	7.6	21.6	69.5	85.5	273.2	293.6	464.0	676.5	792.3	Government Consumption Expend.	91f
1.9	2.4	3.6	15.3	24.8	60.2	170.0	512.1	799.4	1,719.6	1,928.6	Gross Fixed Capital Formation	93e
.9	1.0	2.3	4.3	-.8	7.5	52.9	-69.1	104.8	63.1	73.9	Changes in Inventories	93i
8.5	10.3	14.8	42.3	75.0	147.1	420.9	806.5	1,082.3	1,237.4	1,552.0	Exports of Goods and Services	90c
7.7	8.1	18.7	41.7	67.3	178.4	450.6	905.2	1,228.2	1,710.4	2,196.0	Imports of Goods and Services (-)	98c
19.8	30.0	55.2	113.3	218.3	569.6	1,482.1	2,240.7	2,998.3	3,969.5	5,155.8	Gross Domestic Product (GDP)	99b
-1.7	-1.9	-6.5	-12.7	-44.0	-87.0	-377.2	69.0	-104.9	-13.2	-72.9	Net Primary Income from Abroad	98.n
18.1	28.1	48.7	100.6	174.3	482.6	1,104.9	2,309.7	2,893.4	3,956.3	5,082.9	Gross National Income (GNI)	99a
14.4	15.5	43.4	89.6	151.9	425.2	866.0	1,518.0	2,227.4	3,396.4	....	Net National Income	99e
2.114	2.247	2.224	2.214	2.213	2.174	2.322	2.241	2.190	2.332	2.414	GDP Volume 1977 Prices (Billions)	99b.p
96.6	102.6	101.6	101.1	101.0	99.3	106.0	102.3	100.0	106.5	110.2	GDP Volume (1995=100)	99bv p
.7	1.0	1.8	3.7	7.2	19.1	46.6	73.0	100.0	124.3	156.0	GDP Deflator (1995=100)	99bi p

Midyear Estimates

1987	1988	1989	1990	1991	1992	1993	1994	1995	1996	1997	1998	1999	2000	2001		
7.37	7.53	7.80	8.07	7.96	8.19	8.46	8.76	9.11	9.45	9.78	10.10	10.41	10.72	10.65	Population	99z

(See notes in the back of the book.)

Zimbabwe

		1972	1973	1974	1975	1976	1977	1978	1979	1980	1981	1982	1983	1984	1985	1986
Exchange Rates													*SDRs per Zimbabwe Dollar:*			
Official Rate	ac	1.4127	1.3678	1.4885	1.3672	1.3904	1.2728	1.1369	1.1259	1.2434	1.1980	.9859	.8640	.6790	.5547	.4872
													US Dollars per Zimbabwe Dollar:			
Official Rate	ag	1.5338	1.6500	1.8225	1.6005	1.6154	1.5461	1.4811	1.4832	1.5858	1.3944	1.0876	.9046	.6656	.6093	.5959
Official Rate	rh	1.5161	1.7070	1.6949	1.7603	1.5984	1.5919	1.4764	1.4709	1.5561	1.4518	1.3205	.9895	.8037	.6204	.6006
Fund Position													*Millions of SDRs:*			
Quota	2f. s	....	....	....	....	....	....	....	....	150.0	150.0	150.0	150.0	191.0	191.0	191.0
SDRs	1b. s	....	....	....	....	....	....	....	....	—	8.8	6.3	6.1	2.3	13.2	5.0
Reserve Position in the Fund	1c. s	....	....	....	....	....	....	....	....	—	—	—	—	—	—	—
Total Fund Cred.&Loans Outstg.	2tl	....	....	....	....	....	....	....	....	—	37.5	37.5	191.1	261.3	240.5	191.1
International Liquidity												*Millions of US Dollars Unless Otherwise Indicated:*				
Total Reserves minus Gold	1l. d	61.3	124.7	70.8	80.0	76.6	72.6	148.0	298.9	213.5	169.5	140.4	75.4	45.4	93.4	106.4
SDRs	1b. d	....	....	....	....	....	....	....	....	—	10.3	6.9	6.4	2.3	14.5	6.2
Reserve Position in the Fund	1c. d	....	....	....	....	....	....	....	....	—	—	—	—	—	—	—
Foreign Exchange	1d. d	61.3	124.7	70.8	80.0	76.6	72.6	148.0	298.9	213.5	159.2	133.5	68.9	43.1	78.8	100.2
Gold (Million Fine Troy Ounces)	1ad	.55	.75	.50	.35	.27	.15	.16	.26	.35	.47	.39	.59	.70	.77	.54
Gold (National Valuation)	1an d	21.2	30.9	22.9	14.0	10.7	5.9	6.0	9.6	112.9	99.1	83.6	111.6	110.5	127.8	110.0
Monetary Authorities: Other Liab.	4.. d	....	....	....	47.9	100.0	110.1	23.8	12.0	—	173.5	232.2	334.0	95.2	47.6	52.7
Deposit Money Banks: Assets	7a. d	....	....	....	9.6	19.5	15.9	18.7	44.8	60.7	21.5	32.4	24.0	15.6	13.4	25.4
Liabilities	7b. d	....	....	....	—	—	—	—	30.7	56.6	27.6	26.8	23.9	30.2	43.9	62.2
Other Banking Insts.: Assets	7e. d	....	....	....	—	—	—	—	.6	4.3	.3	.2	.3	.3	.2	.4
Liabilities	7f. d	....	....	....	—	—	—	—	6.2	8.4	11.7	10.8	14.3	2.6	1.5	.9
Monetary Authorities													*Millions of Zimbabwe Dollars:*			
Foreign Assets	11	....	....	....	59	54	51	104	139	170	165	206	207	421	522	524
Claims on Central Government	12a	....	....	....	81	89	104	77	78	122	201	347	347	303	244	356
Claims on Nonfin.Pub.Enterprises	12c	....	....	....	—	—	—	—	1	—	96	1	189	157	237	188
Claims on Private Sector	12d	....	....	....	—	—	—	56	63	50	131	59	350	7	4	6
Claims on Deposit Money Banks	12e	....	....	....	5	9	7	—	—	—	5	—	24	—	1	147
Reserve Money	14	....	....	....	120	148	165	156	182	245	325	389	407	449	541	626
of which: Currency Outside DMBs	14a	....	....	....	67	79	84	95	108	157	199	238	227	259	321	380
Central Bank Bills Outstanding	16ad	....	....	....	—	—	—	—	—	10	—	—	—	65	55	—
Foreign Liabilities	16c	....	....	....	30	62	71	16	8	—	156	252	590	528	512	481
Central Government Deposits	16d	....	....	....	17	8	—	26	76	66	94	—	—	—	4	1
Capital Accounts	17a	....	....	....	6	6	7	8	8	8	8	8	8	8	8	8
Other Items (Net)	17r	....	....	....	−27	−72	−81	31	−2	24	15	−36	111	−161	−112	105
Deposit Money Banks													*Millions of Zimbabwe Dollars:*			
Reserves	20	....	....	....	42	47	56	55	60	82	115	143	161	169	208	217
Claims on Mon.Author.: Securities	20c	....	....	....	—	—	—	—	10	—	—	—	—	65	55	—
Foreign Assets	21	....	....	....	6	12	10	13	30	38	15	30	27	23	22	43
Claims on Central Government	22a	....	....	....	—	—	—	—	249	315	203	228	219	313	355	334
Claims on Local Government	22b	....	....	....	—	—	—	—	1	1	2	1	—	—	1	2
Claims on Nonfin.Pub.Enterprises	22c	....	....	....	—	—	—	—	135	171	292	423	349	477	659	794
Claims on Private Sector	22d	....	....	....	—	—	—	—	455	561	721	868	935	†659	672	749
Claims on Other Banking Insts	22f	....	....	....	—	—	—	—	—	—	—	3	6	3	17	7
Claims on Nonbank Financial Insts	22g	....	....	....	—	—	—	—	—	—	—	—	—	—	—	—
Demand Deposits	24	....	....	....	250	269	288	317	354	473	478	588	512	608	688	727
Time and Savings Deposits	25	....	....	....	—	—	—	—	469	578	714	916	942	971	1,152	1,138
Money Market Instruments	26aa	....	....	....	—	—	—	—	—	—	—	—	—	124	166	205
Foreign Liabilities	26c	....	....	....	—	—	—	—	21	36	20	25	26	45	72	104
Central Government Deposits	26d	....	....	....	—	—	—	—	4	4	23	24	20	50	44	68
Credit from Monetary Authorities	26g	....	....	....	5	9	7	—	—	—	5	—	24	—	—	—
Capital Accounts	27a	....	....	....	33	48	69	75	88	102	121	143	150	194	206	243
Other Items (Net)	27r	....	....	....	—	—	—	—	3	−25	−12	1	23	†−285	−339	−338
Monetary Survey													*Millions of Zimbabwe Dollars:*			
Foreign Assets (Net)	31n	....	....	....	35	4	−10	101	140	173	5	−40	−384	−129	−39	−18
Domestic Credit	32	....	....	....					901	1,150	1,528	1,905	2,375	†1,870	2,140	2,367
Claims on Central Govt. (Net)	32an	....	....	....					247	367	287	551	546	566	551	622
Claims on Local Government	32b	....	....	....					1	1	2	1	—	—	1	2
Claims on Nonfin.Pub.Enterprises	32c	....	....	....					135	171	388	423	538	634	896	982
Claims on Private Sector	32d	....	....	....					518	611	851	927	1,285	†666	676	755
Claims on Other Banking Insts	32f	....	....	....					—	—	—	3	6	3	17	7
Claims on Nonbank Financial Inst	32g	....	....	....					—	—	—	—	—	—	—	—
Money	34	....	....	....	324	352	375	415	463	633	679	827	751	874	1,021	1,127
Quasi-Money	35	....	....	....					472	580	721	921	939	971	1,152	1,138
Money Market Instruments	36aa	....	....	....					—	—	—	—	—	124	166	205
Capital Accounts	37a	....	....	....	39	55	76	82	96	110	129	151	158	202	214	251
Other Items (Net)	37r	....	....	....					10	—	5	−34	143	†−431	−451	−371
Money plus Quasi-Money	35l	....	....	....					935	1,213	1,399	1,748	1,691	1,845	2,173	2,265
Other Banking Institutions													*Millions of Zimbabwe Dollars:*			
Reserves	40	....	....	....	26	24	27	40	34	30	69	71	116	108	101	180
Foreign Assets	41	....	....	....	—	—	—	—	—	3	—	—	—	—	—	1
Claims on Central Government	42a	....	....	....	—	—	—	—	317	361	349	437	451	566	765	908
Claims on Local Government	42b	....	....	....					19	21	26	26	26	26	31	27
Claims on Nonfin.Pub.Enterprises	42c	....	....	....	15	16	22	23	22	29	29	31	24	39	54	53
Claims on Private Sector	42d	....	....	....	380	393	402	426	461	533	576	580	628	661	704	801
Claims on Nonbank Financial Insts	42g	....	....	....	—	—	—	—	—	—	—	—	—	—	—	—
Time and Savings Deposits	45	....	....	....	480	524	581	644	766	865	934	1,019	1,082	1,266	1,551	1,856
Money Market Instruments	46aa	....	....	....	63	47	41	30	28	44	68	73	82	65	33	40
Foreign Liabilities	46c	....	....	....					4	5	8	10	16	4	2	2
Credit from Deposit Money Banks	46h	....	....	....	—	—	—	—	3	3	2	3	2	7	2	2
Capital Accounts	47a	....	....	....	41	45	49	55	64	76	88	91	99	106	120	138
Other Items (Net)	47r	....	....	....					−12	−18	−51	−50	−35	−49	−54	−69

1987	1988	1989	1990	1991	1992	1993	1994	1995	1996	1997	1998	1999	2000	2001		
End of Period															**Exchange Rates**	
.4239	.3825	.3352	.2666	.1384	.1327	.1050	.0817	.0723	.0642	.0398	.0190	.0191	.0139	.0145	Official Rate	**ac**
End of Period (ag) Period Average (rh)																
.6013	.5147	.4405	.3793	.1980	.1824	.1442	.1192	.1074	.0923	.0537	.0268	.0262	.0182	.0182	Official Rate	**ag**
.6020	.5550	.4732	.4085	.2917	.1963	.1545	.1227	.1155	.1008	.0841	.0467	.0261	.0231	.0182	Official Rate	**rh**
															Fund Position	
191.0	191.0	191.0	191.0	191.0	261.3	261.3	261.3	261.3	261.3	261.3	261.3	353.4	353.4	353.4	Quota	**2f. s**
16.3	.5	.5	.2	.1	.3	.6	—	.5	6.8	.2	.3	.8	.2	—	SDRs	**1b. s**
				.1	.1	.1	.1	.1	.1	.1	.2	.3	.3	.3	Reserve Position in the Fund	**1c. s**
110.3	52.2	22.2	4.8	—	157.2	205.0	257.5	310.0	304.1	285.5	289.2	268.8	215.4	205.4	Total Fund Cred.&Loans Outstg.	**2tl**
End of Period															**International Liquidity**	
166.1	178.6	94.6	149.2	149.7	222.2	432.0	405.3	595.5	598.8	160.1	130.8	268.0	193.1	64.7	Total Reserves minus Gold	**1l. d**
23.1	.6	.7	.3	.1	.4	.9	.1	.8	9.8	.3	.4	1.1	.2	—	SDRs	**1b. d**
.1	.1	.1	.1	.1	.1	.1	.1	.1	.2	.3	.4	.4	.4	—	Reserve Position in the Fund	**1c. d**
143.0	178.0	93.8	148.9	149.5	221.7	431.1	405.1	594.6	588.9	159.6	130.1	266.5	192.5	64.3	Foreign Exchange	**1d. d**
.42	.40	.45	.38	.41	.55	.50	.47	.76	.64	.77	.62	.73	.47	.20	Gold (Million Fine Troy Ounces)	**1ad**
98.5	79.1	82.2	69.6	67.9	88.1	79.1	89.7	139.7	117.2	56.0	82.6	105.4	45.4	27.5	Gold (National Valuation)	**1and**
36.6	29.7	28.4	163.1	479.6	435.2	291.1	76.1	36.5	28.5	224.6	335.6	229.9	99.5	59.0	Monetary Authorities: Other Liab.	**4.. d**
26.1	28.2	32.8	40.2	49.1	95.5	79.6	321.3	275.0	299.8	314.7	179.3	156.9	163.4	146.0	Deposit Money Banks: Assets	**7a. d**
61.3	62.4	66.0	96.8	186.0	220.6	518.6	579.3	814.4	827.8	623.8	458.3	245.0	169.2	126.6	Liabilities	**7b. d**
.1	.1	1.5	—	.5	.4	1.5	1.0	3.9	6.4	1.3	.6	1.4	1.1	.7	Other Banking Insts.: Assets	**7e. d**
.5	.2	.1	—				.2	17.0	15.4	6.8	2.4	2.6	4.0	3.0	Liabilities	**7f. d**
End of Period															**Monetary Authorities**	
459	519	425	611	1,512	1,656	3,545	4,152	6,701	7,710	3,991	7,937	14,241	13,130	5,156	Foreign Assets	**11**
566	399	355	830	963	2,034	2,760	7,102	13,640	22,828	30,545	47,543	58,734	98,658	38,398	Claims on Central Government	**12a**
158	124	182	305	263	177	99	134	131	160	188	674	653	651	2,034	Claims on Nonfin.Pub.Enterprises	**12c**
26	29	90	158	285	466	207	182	216	285	361	808	1,095	2,037	2,257	Claims on Private Sector	**12d**
—	—	—	—	618	266	311	448	1,330	1,337	1,403	4,373	3,232	8,066	26,621	Claims on Deposit Money Banks	**12e**
669	843	1,027	1,290	1,705	1,933	2,938	3,632	3,722	6,174	8,509	11,052	17,786	20,638	54,670	Reserve Money	**14**
389	503	618	770	889	861	1,191	1,467	1,823	2,440	3,558	4,468	7,256	9,943	25,642	*of which: Currency Outside DMBs*	**14a**
50	200	—	—	—	—	2,050	917							—	Central Bank Bills Outstanding	**16ad**
321	194	131	448	2,422	3,571	3,971	3,791	4,631	5,048	11,349	27,758	22,839	20,935	17,454	Foreign Liabilities	**16c**
1		1	12	1	2	1	3,311	14,737	22,833	18,043	26,064	43,773	80,055	—	Central Government Deposits	**16d**
8	8	8	8	8	8	392	670	872	804	842	1,015	1,965	1,915	5,028	Capital Accounts	**17a**
160	−176	−115	146	−495	−916	−380	−1,436	−2,860	−2,541	−2,255	−4,553	−8,409	−1,002	−2,686	Other Items (Net)	**17r**
End of Period															**Deposit Money Banks**	
239	313	385	472	766	1,046	1,188	2,019	1,819	3,598	4,279	6,045	10,109	9,720	30,625	Reserves	**20**
50	99	—	—	—	—	—	2,052	579	—	—	—	—	—	—	Claims on Mon.Author.: Securities	**20c**
43	55	75	106	248	524	552	2,695	2,561	3,250	5,856	6,699	5,985	8,997	8,036	Foreign Assets	**21**
481	519	698	597	464	489	1,456	968	6,031	7,149	7,103	6,737	11,234	30,895	56,589	Claims on Central Government	**22a**
—	—	—	—	2	3	11	28	25	32	95	240	267	380	449	Claims on Local Government	**22b**
659	721	861	637	502	406	1,120	732	630	957	1,084	1,834	2,645	7,521	17,375	Claims on Nonfin.Pub.Enterprises	**22c**
1,033	1,489	1,988	2,503	4,241	5,967	9,056	11,736	15,060	18,147	27,098	36,811	41,357	62,037	101,184	Claims on Private Sector	**22d**
13	10	32	24	152	44	63	28	186	306	915	141	1,481	1,925	2,124	Claims on Other Banking Insts	**22f**
—	—	—	—	—	—	31	58	8	56	40	186	95	735	5,992	Claims on Nonbank Financial Insts	**22g**
835	1,104	1,292	1,651	2,094	2,294	4,550	5,791	9,352	11,290	17,102	21,424	27,804	44,169	106,000	Demand Deposits	**24**
1,620	1,860	2,387	2,506	2,009	2,470	3,473	5,753	5,238	8,136	9,757	8,251	11,512	24,976	49,238	Time and Savings Deposits	**25**
—	92	4	38	96	30	592	691	479	314	891	1,274	2,548	4,101	16,661	Money Market Instruments	**26aa**
102	121	150	255	940	1,209	3,597	4,859	7,583	8,972	11,608	17,126	9,345	9,319	6,968	Foreign Liabilities	**26c**
92	119	134	179	588	695	509	440	694	1,078	1,753	1,702	1,995	5,303	6,687	Central Government Deposits	**26d**
—	—	30	—	124	122	249	429	1,329	1,331	951	3,798	2,615	7,889	7,771	Credit from Monetary Authorities	**26g**
282	343	425	587	791	1,017	1,435	1,920	2,054	2,515	4,412	6,445	9,510	15,166	31,443	Capital Accounts	**27a**
−412	−433	−384	−878	−265	644	−929	433	171	−142	−3	−1,326	7,847	11,289	−2,393	Other Items (Net)	**27r**
End of Period															**Monetary Survey**	
80	259	219	14	−1,602	−2,601	−3,471	−1,803	−2,952	−3,061	−13,110	−30,247	−11,959	−8,126	−11,231	Foreign Assets (Net)	**31n**
2,843	3,171	4,070	4,863	6,284	9,013	14,342	17,242	20,496	26,008	47,653	67,209	71,793	119,481	219,715	Domestic Credit	**32**
954	798	918	1,237	838	1,826	3,705	4,320	4,240	6,006	17,852	26,515	24,201	44,196	88,300	Claims on Central Govt. (Net)	**32an**
—	—	—	—	2	3	11	28	25	32	95	240	267	380	449	Claims on Local Government	**32b**
817	845	1,042	942	765	583	1,219	866	761	1,117	1,272	2,509	3,298	8,171	19,409	Claims on Nonfin.Pub.Enterprises	**32c**
1,059	1,518	2,078	2,661	4,527	6,432	9,263	11,918	15,276	18,431	27,459	37,618	42,452	64,074	103,441	Claims on Private Sector	**32d**
13	10	32	24	152	44	63	28	186	306	915	141	1,481	1,925	2,124	Claims on Other Banking Insts	**32f**
—	—	—	—	—	—	125	81	83	8	56	40	186	95	735	Claims on Nonbank Financial Inst	**32g**
1,259	1,617	1,933	2,467	3,036	3,211	6,259	7,396	11,270	13,874	21,320	26,332	35,473	54,396	132,093	Money	**34**
1,620	1,860	2,387	2,506	2,009	2,470	3,473	5,753	5,238	8,136	9,757	8,251	11,512	24,976	49,238	Quasi-Money	**35**
—	193	4	38	96	30	592	689	817	314	891	1,274	2,548	4,101	16,661	Money Market Instruments	**36aa**
290	351	433	595	799	1,025	1,827	2,589	2,926	3,319	5,253	7,459	11,475	17,081	36,470	Capital Accounts	**37a**
−245	−591	−468	−730	−1,257	−323	−1,280	−990	−2,706	−2,697	−2,698	−6,354	−1,173	10,801	−25,977	Other Items (Net)	**37r**
2,879	3,477	4,321	4,973	5,045	5,681	9,731	13,149	16,507	22,011	31,077	34,583	46,985	79,371	181,330	Money plus Quasi-Money	**35l**
End of Period															**Other Banking Institutions**	
171	925	134	231	259	175	679	914	3,634	4,453	7,510	4,691	5,058	12,315	21,328	Reserves	**40**
—	—	4	—	2	2	10	8	36	70	25	24	55	61	41	Foreign Assets	**41**
1,120	1,256	1,652	1,746	2,159	2,187	2,348	2,795	3,962	4,410	3,723	4,050	9,233	18,465	18,156	Claims on Central Government	**42a**
28	29	31	38	41	43	42	43	64	266	432	438	443	463	448	Claims on Local Government	**42b**
53	59	36	52	82	126	182	404	2,147	590	857	1,075	1,468	1,703	2,010	Claims on Nonfin.Pub.Enterprises	**42c**
960	500	1,599	2,292	3,225	3,463	3,414	4,036	5,575	8,289	12,412	14,998	16,091	16,488	25,361	Claims on Private Sector	**42d**
—	—	—	—	—	—	—	—	5	2,486	741	30	3	3	3	Claims on Nonbank Financial Insts	**42g**
2,170	2,628	3,297	4,248	5,284	5,359	6,705	9,348	14,894	20,685	26,024	23,959	28,532	43,501	59,630	Time and Savings Deposits	**45**
59	76	69	133	226	192	208	386	481	459	1,356	2,742	1,878	1,628	4,892	Money Market Instruments	**46aa**
1				—	—	—	1	158	167	127	90	101	222	168	Foreign Liabilities	**46c**
3	1	5	6	20	20	157	25	113	70	423	322	907	435	1,282	Credit from Deposit Money Banks	**46h**
163	200	268	373	521	591	639	691	1,047	1,499	2,143	2,045	4,044	7,456	9,260	Capital Accounts	**47a**
−65	−136	−185	−401	−282	−166	−1,033	−2,251	−1,271	−2,316	−4,374	−3,851	−3,099	−3,742	−7,885	Other Items (Net)	**47r**

Zimbabwe

698

	1972	1973	1974	1975	1976	1977	1978	1979	1980	1981	1982	1983	1984	1985	1986
Banking Survey													*Millions of Zimbabwe Dollars:*		
Foreign Assets (Net) ... 51n	...	...	...	...	...	...	...	137	170	–3	–50	–399	–132	–41	–19
Domestic Credit ... 52	...	...	...	...	...	...	...	1,720	2,093	2,508	2,975	3,499	†3,158	3,678	4,149
Claims on Central Govt. (Net) ... 52an								565	728	637	988	997	1,131	1,316	1,530
Claims on Local Government ... 52b								20	22	27	26	26	27	32	29
Claims on Nonfin.Pub.Enterprises ... 52c	...	...	...	15	16	22	23	157	200	417	454	562	673	950	1,035
Claims on Private Sector ... 52d								979	1,143	1,428	1,507	1,913	†1,327	1,380	1,555
Claims on Nonbank Financial Inst ... 52g				—	—	—	—	—	—	—	—	—	—	—	—
Liquid Liabilities ... 55l	...	...	...	...	...	...	...	1,668	2,048	2,265	2,695	2,657	3,003	3,623	3,941
Money Market Instruments ... 56aa				63	47	41	30	28	44	68	73	82	190	199	245
Capital Accounts ... 57a				80	100	125	138	160	187	217	242	257	308	333	389
Other Items (Net) ... 57r	...	...	...	...	...	...	...	1	–15	–44	–85	103	†–476	–519	–445
Interest Rates													*Percent Per Annum*		
Bank Rate (End of Period) ... 60	4.50	4.50	4.50	4.50	4.50	4.50	4.50	4.50	4.50	9.00	9.00	9.00	9.00	9.00	9.00
Money Market Rate ... 60b	...	...	...	4.25	4.25	4.25	4.25	4.25	4.15	6.83	9.50	9.09	8.90	8.80	9.10
Treasury Bill Rate ... 60c						...	3.55	3.54	3.39	5.70	8.50	8.52	8.49	8.48	8.71
Deposit Rate ... 60l				4.00	3.75	3.50	3.25	3.25	3.52	7.46	14.46	12.80	10.30	10.04	10.28
Lending Rate ... 60p							17.54	17.54	17.54	20.19	23.00	23.08	23.00	17.17	10.28
Government Bond Yield ... 61	6.50	6.50	6.50	6.50	6.54	7.63	8.75	8.75	8.94	11.54	13.00	13.08	13.29	13.26	13.20
Prices, Production, Labor													*Index Numbers (1995=100):*		
Consumer Prices ... 64	4.2	4.3	4.6	†5.0	5.6	6.2	6.5	7.7	8.1	9.2	10.2	12.5	15.0	16.3	18.6
Manufacturing Production ... 66ey	70.8	76.6	81.9	†81.2	76.2	72.0	70.2	77.3	88.6	96.9	96.3	93.7	89.5	98.4	101.9
													Number in Thousands:		
Labor Force ... 67d	...	...	...	...	...	...	...	...	...	...	...	...	...		
Employment ... 67e	...	...	...	...	...	...	...	...	...	...	...	...	...	1,055	1,081
International Transactions													*Millions of Zimbabwe Dollars*		
Exports ... 70	340.6	402.7	503.1	531.3	557.4	550.9	599.1	715.6	909.3	875.0	968.4	1,150.2	1,451.6	1,795.5	2,170.3
Imports, c.i.f. ... 71	315.9	354.9	504.0	531.2	440.1	446.3	464.3	631.7	930.8	1,170.4	1,244.1	1,220.8	1,380.8	1,446.5	1,640.4
Imports, f.o.b. ... 71.v	274.7	308.6	438.3	461.9	382.7	388.1	403.7	549.3	809.4	1,017.7	1,081.8	1,061.6	1,200.7	1,446.5	1,640.4
														1985=100	
Volume of Exports ... 72	112.7	115.1	119.9	†112.2	112.8	107.1	111.4	109.8	104.6	99.6	102.5	106.2	104.8	100.0	124.9
Volume of Imports ... 73	114.7	123.7	128.9	†122.9	89.8	82.7	75.6	74.6	102.8	126.9	136.7	114.6	114.2	100.0	121.0
Unit Value of Exports ... 74	19.7	21.5	28.2	†30.1	31.5	32.7	34.9	40.1	53.1	58.7	56.9	64.4	84.0	100.0	101.9
Unit Value of Imports ... 75	20.0	20.9	28.5	†31.4	35.6	39.3	44.7	61.1	65.5	65.2	64.9	76.2	85.9	100.0	104.6
Balance of Payments													*Millions of US Dollars:*		
Current Account, n.i.e. ... 78ald	...	...	...	...	...	1.1	54.0	–56.5	–149.4	–546.1	–632.1	–397.9	–42.9	–64.2	16.8
Goods: Exports f.o.b. ... 78aad						900.8	927.7	1,079.8	1,441.1	1,451.4	1,312.1	1,153.7	1,173.6	1,119.6	1,322.7
Goods: Imports f.o.b. ... 78abd						–671.1	–657.4	–875.2	–1,335.0	–1,534.0	–1,472.0	–1,069.6	–989.3	–918.9	–1,011.6
Trade Balance ... 78acd						229.6	270.3	204.6	106.1	–82.6	–159.9	84.1	184.3	200.6	311.2
Services: Credit ... 78add						65.3	69.9	88.3	169.1	134.2	181.5	145.1	139.4	295.5	169.0
Services: Debit ... 78aed						–226.8	–231.1	–276.4	–394.5	–535.9	–437.4	–430.9	–357.5	–462.3	–316.0
Balance on Goods & Services ... 78afd						68.1	109.0	16.5	–119.3	–484.3	–415.8	–201.7	–33.9	33.8	164.2
Income: Credit ... 78agd						39.0	36.3	62.7	103.9	94.0	80.4	69.6	55.2	37.8	36.4
Income: Debit ... 78ahd						–105.8	–90.5	–132.0	–165.1	–211.9	–290.9	–254.8	–170.9	–166.9	–225.5
Balance on Gds, Serv. & Inc. ... 78aid						1.3	54.9	–52.8	–180.4	–602.2	–626.4	–387.0	–149.7	–95.3	–24.9
Current Transfers, n.i.e.: Credit ... 78ajd						28.2	26.1	36.0	105.0	141.9	87.3	95.4	193.3	171.7	169.7
Current Transfers: Debit ... 78akd						–28.3	–27.0	–39.7	–74.0	–85.8	–93.1	–106.3	–86.6	–140.6	–128.0
Capital Account, n.i.e. ... 78bcd						–15.1	–16.6	–52.2	–93.7	–89.8	–77.0	–62.3	–57.1	–11.5	–10.0
Capital Account, n.i.e.: Credit ... 78bad						5.3	5.6	7.7	3.7	27.3	30.1	18.9	3.3	.1	.2
Capital Account: Debit ... 78bbd						–20.4	–22.3	–59.9	–97.4	–117.1	–107.1	–81.2	–60.4	–11.7	–10.2
Financial Account, n.i.e. ... 78bjd						–14.6	64.7	109.2	–29.8	499.4	594.5	251.8	8.7	120.7	118.1
Direct Investment Abroad ... 78bdd															
Dir. Invest. in Rep. Econ., n.i.e. ... 78bed						–3.8	2.5	.1	1.6	3.6	–.8	–2.1	–2.5	2.9	7.5
Portfolio Investment Assets ... 78bfd						.2	—	.6	.5	2.3	.7	—	39.4	45.9	38.2
Equity Securities ... 78bkd															
Debt Securities ... 78bld						.2	—	.6	.5	2.3	.7	—	39.4	45.9	38.2
Portfolio Investment Liab., n.i.e. ... 78bgd						–8.4	–8.3	–9.4	–27.9	–32.3	–47.5	–42.7	–36.6	–36.8	–37.0
Equity Securities ... 78bmd															
Debt Securities ... 78bnd						–8.4	–8.3	–9.4	–27.9	–32.3	–47.5	–42.7	–36.6	–36.8	–37.0
Financial Derivatives Assets ... 78bwd															
Financial Derivatives Liabilities ... 78bxd															
Other Investment Assets ... 78bhd						3.2	–3.1	–30.0	6.5	–5.4	62.3	36.7	43.2	24.6	34.4
Monetary Authorities ... 78bod															
General Government ... 78bpd															
Banks ... 78bqd						3.2	–3.1	–30.0	6.5	–5.4	62.3	36.7	43.2	24.6	34.4
Other Sectors ... 78brd														—	
Other Investment Liab., n.i.e. ... 78bid						–5.7	73.6	147.9	–10.4	531.3	579.9	259.8	–34.8	84.2	75.0
Monetary Authorities ... 78bsd															
General Government ... 78btd						14.2	106.7	170.7	–18.6	367.9	503.1	303.5	6.4	49.7	98.4
Banks ... 78bud						–2.9	–3.0	3.2	28.9	–.9	–40.0	–51.1	–31.5	–7.0	–26.5
Other Sectors ... 78bvd						–17.0	–30.1	–26.0	–20.6	164.3	116.8	7.4	–9.7	41.5	3.1
Net Errors and Omissions ... 78cad						20.5	–26.7	119.5	186.6	128.4	92.3	34.5	44.9	37.2	–69.4
Overall Balance ... 78cbd						–8.1	75.4	119.9	–86.3	–8.1	–22.4	–174.0	–46.3	82.2	55.5
Reserves and Related Items ... 79dad						8.1	–75.4	–119.9	86.3	8.1	22.4	174.0	46.3	–82.2	–55.5
Reserve Assets ... 79dbd						8.1	–75.4	–119.9	86.3	–37.3	22.4	7.3	–26.7	–61.2	3.0
Use of Fund Credit and Loans ... 79dcd						—	—	—	—	45.4	—	166.6	73.0	–21.0	–58.5
Exceptional Financing ... 79ded						...	...	...	...	...	...	...	...	...	...

1987	1988	1989	1990	1991	1992	1993	1994	1995	1996	1997	1998	1999	2000	2001		
End of Period															**Banking Survey**	
79	258	222	14	−1,600	−2,598	−3,461	−1,796	−3,074	−3,158	−13,212	−30,313	−12,004	−8,287	−11,357	Foreign Assets (Net)	51n
4,991	5,005	7,356	8,968	11,640	14,787	20,265	24,492	32,064	41,743	64,883	87,659	97,551	154,678	263,569	Domestic Credit	52
2,075	2,054	2,571	2,982	2,997	4,012	6,053	7,115	8,201	10,476	21,575	30,565	33,434	62,661	106,456	Claims on Central Govt. (Net)	52an
28	29	31	39	44	46	53	70	89	298	527	678	710	843	897	Claims on Local Government	52b
870	904	1,078	994	847	709	1,402	1,270	2,908	1,707	2,129	3,584	4,766	9,875	21,419	Claims on Nonfin.Pub.Enterprises	52c
2,019	2,018	3,676	4,952	7,751	9,895	12,677	15,954	20,852	26,720	39,871	52,617	58,543	80,562	128,802	Claims on Private Sector	52d
—	—	—	—	—	125	81	83	13	2,542	781	215	98	738	5,995	Claims on Nonbank Financial Inst	52g
4,878	5,180	7,483	8,991	10,070	10,865	15,758	21,583	27,768	38,243	49,591	53,850	70,449	110,557	219,632	Liquid Liabilities	55l
59	269	74	171	322	222	800	1,075	1,297	773	2,248	4,016	4,425	5,729	21,553	Money Market Instruments	56aa
453	551	701	968	1,320	1,616	2,466	3,280	3,974	4,819	7,396	9,504	15,519	24,537	45,730	Capital Accounts	57a
−319	−737	−680	−1,148	−1,672	−513	−2,219	−3,243	−4,050	−5,249	−7,564	−10,024	−4,846	5,569	−34,704	Other Items (Net)	57r
Percent Per Annum															**Interest Rates**	
9.00	9.00	9.00	10.25	20.00	29.50	28.50	29.50	29.50	27.00	31.50	†39.50	74.41	57.84	57.20	Bank Rate *(End of Period)*	60
9.30	9.08	8.73	8.68	17.49	34.77	34.18	30.90	29.64	26.18	25.15	37.22	53.13	64.98	21.52	Money Market Rate	60b
8.73	8.38	8.35	8.39	14.44	26.16	33.04	29.22	27.98	24.53	22.07	32.78	50.48	64.78	17.60	Treasury Bill Rate	60c
9.58	9.68	8.85	8.80	14.20	28.63	29.45	26.75	25.92	21.58	18.60	29.06	38.51	50.17	13.95	Deposit Rate	60l
13.00	13.00	13.00	11.71	15.50	19.77	36.33	34.86	34.73	34.23	32.55	42.06	55.39	68.21	38.02	Lending Rate	60p
13.87	14.00	14.00	15.24	17.27	17.40	....	....	....	....	....	....	....	....	....	Government Bond Yield	61
Period Averages															**Prices, Production, Labor**	
21.0	22.5	25.4	†29.8	36.8	52.3	66.7	81.6	100.0	121.4	144.2	190.1	301.3	469.6	829.8	Consumer Prices	64
104.7	109.8	115.9	122.3	128.5	115.1	105.7	115.8	100.0	103.6	106.9	....	....	....	....	Manufacturing Production	66ey
Period Averages															**International Transactions**	
3,260	....	....	....	3,502	....	....	....	....	....	4,921	....	4,963	....	....	Labor Force	67d
1,085	1,131	1,167	1,192	1,244	1,236	1,239	1,264	1,240	1,273	1,323	1,349	1,316	....	....	Employment	67e
Millions of Zimbabwe Dollars																
2,371.4	2,966.4	3,267.3	4,231.4	5,546.5	7,365.7	10,164.2	15,364.7	18,359.1	24,209.3	....	....	....	....	....	Exports	70
1,741.7	2,043.2	3,438.1	4,528.2	7,443.1	11,232.3	11,798.4	18,270.6	23,048.1	28,095.1	....	....	....	....	....	Imports, c.i.f.	71
1,741.7	2,043.2	2,989.7	3,937.6	6,472.3	9,767.2	10,259.5	15,887.5	20,043.0	....	....	....	....	....	....	Imports, f.o.b.	71.v
1985=100																
....	....	....	....	....	....	....	....	....	....	....	....	....	....	....	Volume of Exports	72
....	....	....	....	....	....	....	....	....	....	....	....	....	....	....	Volume of Imports	73
....	....	....	....	....	....	....	....	....	....	....	....	....	....	....	Unit Value of Exports	74
....	....	....	....	....	....	....	....	....	....	....	....	....	....	....	Unit Value of Imports	75
Minus Sign Indicates Debit															**Balance of Payments**	
58.0	125.3	17.0	−139.8	−457.0	−603.7	−115.7	−424.9	....	....	....	....	....	....	....	Current Account, n.i.e.	78al *d*
1,452.0	1,664.9	1,693.5	1,747.9	1,693.8	1,527.6	1,609.1	1,961.1	....	....	....	....	....	....	....	Goods: Exports f.o.b.	78aa *d*
−1,071.0	−1,163.6	−1,318.3	−1,505.2	−1,645.7	−1,782.1	−1,487.0	−1,803.5	....	....	....	....	....	....	....	Goods: Imports f.o.b.	78ab *d*
381.0	501.3	375.2	242.7	48.1	−254.5	122.1	157.6	....	....	....	....	....	....	....	*Trade Balance*	78ac *d*
164.6	190.3	241.8	264.2	273.5	305.1	372.1	383.2	....	....	....	....	....	....	....	Services: Credit	78ad *d*
−349.8	−410.9	−457.0	−495.5	−627.4	−660.9	−563.8	−711.7	....	....	....	....	....	....	....	Services: Debit	78ae *d*
195.7	280.7	160.0	11.3	−305.9	−610.3	−69.6	−170.9	....	....	....	....	....	....	....	*Balance on Goods & Services*	78af *d*
33.0	17.4	26.0	22.9	26.1	26.0	35.0	27.5	....	....	....	....	....	....	....	Income: Credit	78ag *d*
−228.4	−234.0	−236.1	−286.3	−278.0	−302.3	−287.1	−321.2	....	....	....	....	....	....	....	Income: Debit	78ah *d*
.4	64.1	−50.0	−252.0	−557.8	−886.6	−321.6	−464.5	....	....	....	....	....	....	....	*Balance on Gds, Serv. & Inc.*	78ai *d*
220.8	211.2	211.4	204.0	191.7	347.3	270.6	69.4	....	....	....	....	....	....	....	Current Transfers, n.i.e.: Credit	78aj *d*
−163.2	−150.1	−144.3	−91.8	−90.9	−64.4	−64.7	−29.8	....	....	....	....	....	....	....	Current Transfers: Debit	78ak *d*
−10.0	−8.6	−7.6	−7.0	−2.8	−1.4	−.4	284.4	....	....	....	....	....	....	....	Capital Account, n.i.e.	78bc *d*
.2	.3	.2	.4	.1	.2	.6	285.4	....	....	....	....	....	....	....	Capital Account, n.i.e.: Credit	78ba *d*
−10.2	−9.0	−7.9	−7.4	−2.9	−1.6	−1.0	−1.0	....	....	....	....	....	....	....	Capital Account: Debit	78bb *d*
59.8	48.0	47.8	242.6	536.5	373.4	327.2	−25.5	....	....	....	....	....	....	....	Financial Account, n.i.e.	78bj *d*
—	22.2	—	—	—	—	—	−4.7	....	....	....	....	....	....	....	Direct Investment Abroad	78bd *d*
−30.5	−18.1	−10.2	−12.2	2.8	15.0	28.0	34.7	....	....	....	....	....	....	....	Dir. Invest. in Rep. Econ., n.i.e.	78be *d*
56.8	—	—	10.4	41.8	27.6	—	—	....	....	....	....	....	....	....	Portfolio Investment Assets	78bf *d*
															Equity Securities	78bk *d*
56.8	—	—	10.4	41.8	27.6	—	—	....	....	....	....	....	....	....	Debt Securities	78bl *d*
−55.9	−60.9	−36.7	−32.1	−34.6	−37.1	−5.1	50.2	....	....	....	....	....	....	....	Portfolio Investment Liab., n.i.e.	78bg *d*
							56.9	....	....	....	....	....	....	....	Equity Securities	78bm *d*
−55.9	−60.9	−36.7	−32.1	−34.6	−37.1	−5.1	−6.7	....	....	....	....	....	....	....	Debt Securities	78bn *d*
....	....	....	....	....	....	....	....	....	....	....	....	....	....	....	Financial Derivatives Assets	78bw *d*
....	....	....	....	....	....	....	....	....	....	....	....	....	....	....	Financial Derivatives Liabilities	78bx *d*
19.8	4.9	—	—	38.0	15.9	99.9	−260.3	....	....	....	....	....	....	....	Other Investment Assets	78bh *d*
															Monetary Authorities	78bo *d*
															General Government	78bp *d*
19.8	4.9	—	—	38.0	15.9	99.9	−260.3	....	....	....	....	....	....	....	Banks	78bq *d*
															Other Sectors	78br *d*
69.6	99.9	94.7	276.5	488.4	352.0	204.4	154.7	....	....	....	....	....	....	....	Other Investment Liab., n.i.e.	78bi *d*
—	—	3.0	97.6	128.7	−78.2	−7.8	−109.9	....	....	....	....	....	....	....	Monetary Authorities	78bs *d*
82.1	70.4	67.6	88.6	275.0	407.9	191.0	62.0	....	....	....	....	....	....	....	General Government	78bt *d*
−18.0	—	3.1	14.6	—	....	....	....	....	....	....	....	....	....	....	Banks	78bu *d*
5.6	29.4	21.0	75.8	84.7	22.3	21.2	202.6	....	....	....	....	....	....	....	Other Sectors	78bv *d*
16.6	−63.0	−103.8	−9.9	−31.4	37.2	14.9	80.2	....	....	....	....	....	....	....	Net Errors and Omissions	78ca *d*
124.5	101.6	−46.8	85.8	45.2	−194.6	225.9	−85.8	....	....	....	....	....	....	....	*Overall Balance*	78cb *d*
−124.5	−101.6	46.8	−85.8	−45.2	194.6	−225.9	85.8	....	....	....	....	....	....	....	Reserves and Related Items	79da *d*
−19.5	−23.0	85.5	−62.8	−38.4	−31.1	−293.6	12.9	....	....	....	....	....	....	....	Reserve Assets	79db *d*
−104.9	−78.6	−38.8	−23.0	−6.9	225.7	67.7	72.8	....	....	....	....	....	....	....	Use of Fund Credit and Loans	79dc *d*
....	....	....	....	....	....	....	....	....	....	....	....	....	....	....	Exceptional Financing	79de *d*

Zimbabwe

	1972	1973	1974	1975	1976	1977	1978	1979	1980	1981	1982	1983	1984	1985	1986
Government Finance														*Millions of Zimbabwe Dollars:*	
Deficit (-) or Surplus 80	....	....	....	....	−118	−95	−254	−293	−376	−262	−545	−394	−647	†−513	−638
Total Revenue and Grants 81y	....	....	....	....	492	576	573	611	830	1,131	1,532	1,890	2,110	†2,305	2,608
Revenue 81	....	....	....	....	492	576	573	611	830	1,130	1,514	1,866	2,034	†2,132	2,500
Grants 81z	....	....	....	....	—	—	—	—	—	2	18	23	77	†173	108
Exp. & Lending Minus Repay. 82z	....	....	....	....	611	671	827	905	1,206	1,393	2,077	2,283	2,758	†2,818	3,246
Expenditure 82	....	....	....	....	539	674	802	881	1,198	1,301	1,882	2,079	2,546	†2,617	3,077
Lending Minus Repayments 83	....	....	....	....	72	−2	24	24	7	91	195	205	212	†200	169
Total Financing 80h	....	....	....	....	118	95	254	293	376	262	545	394	647	†513	638
Domestic 84a	....	....	....	....	119	98	130	172	297	116	414	350	325	·†25	378
Foreign 85a	....	....	....	....	−1	−3	124	121	79	146	132	44	322	†488	260
Total Debt by Residence 88	....	....	....	....	785	864	1,146	1,479	1,828	2,081	2,464	2,846	3,744	†4,118	5,197
Domestic 88a	....	....	....	....	693	764	914	1,117	1,393	1,507	1,622	1,860	2,306	†2,422	2,977
Foreign 89a	....	....	....	....	92	100	233	361	435	574	841	987	1,438	†1,696	2,221
National Accounts														*Millions of Zimbabwe Dollars*	
Househ.Cons.Expend.,incl.NPISHs 96f	936	988	1,166	1,254	1,354	1,344	1,546	1,933	2,219	2,969	3,378	4,341	3,792	5,619	6,091
Government Consumption Expend. 91f	157	180	221	256	319	382	451	537	677	763	1,027	1,159	1,364	1,838	2,140
Gross Fixed Capital Formation 93e	256	330	421	468	427	379	341	395	528	830	1,039	1,238	1,185	1,299	1,559
Changes in Inventories 93i	40	51	91	72	−18	40	−60	−37	120	196	62	−235	28	322	310
Exports of Goods and Services 90c	417	....	577	590	617	610	675	798	1,043	1,117	1,141	1,345	1,708	2,020	2,492
Imports of Goods and Services (-) 98c	376	....	587	613	533	558	593	803	1,146	1,442	1,450	1,542	1,673	2,002	2,230
Gross Domestic Product (GDP) 99b	1,429	1,538	1,832	1,995	2,166	2,198	2,359	2,822	3,441	4,430	5,200	6,310	6,400	9,100	10,360
Net Primary Income from Abroad 98.n	−35	−39	−40	−45	−58	−48	−42	−53	−47	−115	−194	−248	−195	−221	−317
Gross National Income (GNI) 99a	1,394	1,499	1,792	1,950	2,108	2,150	2,317	2,769	3,394	4,318	5,023	5,742	6,212	8,944	10,053
GDP Volume 1969 Prices 99b.p	1,202	†1,222	....	....	....	....	....	....	....	....	....	....	....	....	....
GDP Volume 1980 Prices 99b.p	....	2,889	3,389	3,266	3,230	3,064	2,998	3,112	3,441	3,872	3,974	4,037	3,960	4,213	....
GDP Volume 1990 Prices 99b.p	....	....	....	....	....	....	....	....	....	....	....	....	....	17,193	17,553
GDP Volume (1995=100) .... 99bv p	52.3	53.1	62.3	60.1	59.4	56.3	55.1	57.2	63.3	71.2	73.1	74.2	72.8	77.5	79.1
GDP Deflator (1995=100) .... 99bi p	4.4	4.7	4.8	5.4	5.9	6.3	6.9	8.0	8.8	10.1	11.5	13.8	14.3	19.1	21.3
															Millions:
Population 99z	5.69	5.89	6.08	†6.14	6.33	6.52	6.72	6.93	7.10	7.36	7.48	7.74	7.98	8.38	8.41

	1987	1988	1989	1990	1991	1992	1993	1994	1995	1996	1997	1998	1999	2000	2001	
Government Finance																
Year Ending June 30																
Deficit (-) or Surplus	−977	−1,005	−1,111	−1,138 P	−2,107	−3,861	−2,645	−2,092	−5,791	−5,147	−5,077	....	....	....	....	80
Total Revenue and Grants	3,034	3,644	4,356	5,307 P	6,759	8,634	11,752	13,699	18,687	23,811	31,126	....	....	....	....	81y
Revenue	2,954	3,526	4,267	5,193 P	6,527	8,285	11,152	12,776	16,998	22,808	30,670	....	....	....	....	81
Grants	80	118	90	114 P	232	349	600	923	1,690	1,003	456	....	....	....	....	81z
Exp. & Lending Minus Repay.	4,011	4,649	5,467	6,445 P	8,866	12,495	14,396	15,790	24,479	28,958	36,202	....	....	....	....	82z
Expenditure	3,783	4,264	4,960	5,872 P	8,132	11,217	12,390	14,538	22,000	29,691	36,454	....	....	....	....	82
Lending Minus Repayments	228	385	507	573 P	734	1,278	2,006	1,252	2,479	−733	−252	....	....	....	....	83
Total Financing	977	1,005	1,111	1,138 P	2,108	3,860	2,645	2,092	5,791	5,147	5,077	....	....	....	....	80h
Domestic	765	830	982	937 P	1,503	1,321	1,279	1,733	4,802	3,973	5,168	....	....	....	....	84a
Foreign	212	175	129	201 P	605	2,539	1,366	359	990	1,175	−91	....	....	....	....	85a
Total Debt by Residence	6,137	7,295	8,633	10,412 P	16,264	20,400	25,054	31,131	47,503	53,201	59,303	....	....	....	....	88
Domestic	3,622	4,470	5,397	6,375 P	7,849	7,993	9,071	12,875	24,671	31,407	30,371	....	....	....	....	88a
Foreign	2,515	2,825	3,236	4,037 P	8,415	12,407	15,983	18,257	22,832	21,793	28,932	....	....	....	....	89a
National Accounts																
Millions of Zimbabwe Dollars																
Househ.Cons.Expend.,incl.NPISHs	6,603	7,116	11,320	13,565	20,163	22,309	27,190	34,659	40,351	50,438	66,112	....	....	....	....	96f
Government Consumption Expend.	2,617	3,879	3,273	4,180	4,775	8,308	6,350	9,375	11,100	14,492	17,057	21,226	....	....	....	91f
Gross Fixed Capital Formation	1,804	2,197	2,452	3,913	6,097	7,690	10,021	11,879	14,996	19,245	20,509	23,931	....	....	....	93e
Changes in Inventories	−131	441	180	−179	−439	−732	−347	1,324	−3,031	429	156	−586	180	....	....	93i
Exports of Goods and Services	2,690	3,350	4,087	4,915	7,075	9,364	13,050	19,431	23,562	30,910	....	....	....	....	....	90c
Imports of Goods and Services (-)	2,383	2,873	3,803	4,899	8,048	12,548	13,784	20,509	25,216	30,747	....	....	....	....	....	98c
Gross Domestic Product (GDP)	11,200	14,109	17,509	21,494	29,623	34,392	42,481	56,159	61,622	84,759	102,074	135,722	214,984	....	....	99b
Net Primary Income from Abroad	−324	−391	−446	−707	−979	−1,407	−1,604	−2,405	−2,794	−2,931	−3,908	....	....	....	....	98.n
Gross National Income (GNI)	10,927	13,648	16,863	20,687	28,644	32,889	40,877	53,375	58,599	81,855	....	....	....	....	....	99a
GDP Volume 1969 Prices	....	....	....	....	....	....	....	....	....	....	....	....	....	....	....	99b.p
GDP Volume 1980 Prices	....	....	....	....	....	....	....	....	....	....	....	....	....	....	....	99b.p
GDP Volume 1990 Prices	17,754	19,095	20,091	21,494	22,682	20,634	20,908	22,338	22,192	23,884	24,915	....	....	....	....	99b.p
GDP Volume (1995=100)	80.0	86.0	90.5	96.9	102.2	93.0	94.2	100.7	100.0	107.6	112.3	....	....	....	....	99bv p
GDP Deflator (1995=100)	22.7	26.6	31.4	36.0	47.0	60.0	73.2	90.5	100.0	127.8	147.5	....	....	....	....	99bi p
Midyear Estimates																
Population	8.64	8.88	9.12	9.37	10.14	10.41	10.78	11.15	11.53	11.91	12.29	12.68	13.08	12.63	12.96	99z

COUNTRY NOTES

Total Fund Credit & Loans Outstanding

Includes outstanding use of Fund's credits within GRA, and SAF, PRGF, and Trust Fund loans.

Real Effective Exchange Rate Indices

The indicators of real effective exchange rates based on *relative unit labor costs (line 65um)* and *relative normalized unit labor costs (line reu)* in manufacturing represent the product of the index of the ratio of the relevant indicator (in national currency) for the country listed to a weighted geometric average of the corresponding indicators for 20 other industrial countries (again in national currency, and including in addition to the other 16 countries listed on this table, Australia, New Zealand, Greece, and Portugal) and the index of the nominal effective exchange rate, which is calculated by weighting the exchange rates for the countries listed in the same manner as the other indicators. This index for the nominal effective exchange rate is presented as *line* neu in the country pages of the 17 countries in the table and Greece. The reference base is 1995_100 in accordance with all indices published in *IFS*.

Several of the measures of real effective exchange rates are subject to frequent and sometimes substantial revision. To an important extent, these revisions stem from the procedures used to estimate several of the indicators. Thus, the national data underlying the two labor cost series are calculated by benchmarking the best available monthly or quarterly series on reasonably comprehensive and comparable, but periodically revised, annual data from the national accounts. While such benchmarking makes these series particularly susceptible to revision, it also permits the calculation of up-to-date quarterly series which, on an annual basis, are also reasonably comprehensive and comparable.

The total trade weights used to construct the associated nominal effective exchange rates for the indices are designed to make them particularly relevant with respect to movements in costs and prices affecting exports and imports of manufactured goods. The weights, which are built up from aggregate trade flows for manufactured goods (SITC 5–8) averaged over the period 1989–91, take into account the relative importance of a country's trading partners in its direct bilateral relations with them, in both the home and foreign markets; of the competitive relations with third countries in particular markets; and of the differences among countries in the importance of foreign trade to the manufacturing sector.

Estimates shown for the Euro Area for relative unit labor costs and relative normalized unit labor costs are generated using a subset of the trade weights described in the paragraph above, where the weights for the Euro Area relate to the trade of the Euro Area as a whole with its partners in the system. A synthetic euro has been constructed for the period before the introduction of the euro using trade weights drawn from the same weighting scheme, Euro Area member exchange rates, and the official lock-in rates, which were used to determine the initial value of the euro. This method (national currency series times lock-in rates times Euro Area member trade weights specific to this system) has also been used to estimate the Euro Area unit labor cost and normalized unit labor cost series denominated in euros.

The nature and scope of the various national indicators entering into the indices are briefly described below. While mention is made of specific deficiencies in some of the selected measures of costs and prices, the emphasis is on what they purport to measure. Because these measures of costs and prices contain a considerable amount of staff estimation, they are not published in *IFS*.

Unit labor costs are defined as compensation of employees per unit of real output (or value added) in the manufacturing sector. Account is taken of employer-paid social insurance premia and other employment taxes, as well as wages and salaries. For the most recent quarters, however, indices typically refer more narrowly to wages or wages and salaries per unit of total output of manufactured goods (rather than that of value added in the manufacturing sector).

Normalized unit labor costs in manufacturing are calculated by dividing an index of actual hourly compensation per worker by the normalized index of output per man-hour in local currency. The data printed are the product of this variable after weighting (to obtain the relative measure) and the nominal effective exchange rate **(neu).** The purpose of normalizing output per man-hour is to remove distortions arising from cyclical movements, which occur largely because changes in hours worked do not correspond closely to changes in the effective inputs of labor. The Hodrick-Prescott filter, which smoothes a time series by removing short-run fluctuations while retaining changes of larger amplitude, is the method used to normalize output per man-hour. The monthly series are estimated by extrapolating the quarterly local currency series for the period needed, interpolating these estimates from quarterly into monthly series and reweighting the interpolated monthly series to obtain the monthly relative series. **Where the monthly data are extrapolated, data for the corresponding quarters are not shown.** Monthly nominal effective exchange rates are computed using monthly exchange rates and the same weights as are used for quarterly nominal effective exchange rates, and real effective rates are calculated using the nominal effective rates and interpolated relative monthly normalized unit labor costs. The extrapolation and interpolation of the quarterly series is acceptable because the quarterly series have been smoothed, and the trend of these series is retained in the extrapolation. The interpolated monthly trend series is used to adjust the more current nominal effective exchange rate. The annual series (for both relative, and relative normalized, unit labor costs) may not correspond with the average of the quarterly series because only the annual series include Switzerland.

An indicator of real effective exchange rates based on relative consumer prices is also shown (*line rec)* to afford comparison with a wider group of partner—or competitor—countries. The weighting scheme is based on disaggregated trade data for manufactured goods and primary products covering the three-year period 1988–90 and is derived according to the same methodology as that followed for other countries discussed in the Introduction (section 1). The consumer price index that is used as a cost indicator is that shown on the country pages *(line 64)*. However, it should be borne in mind that, especially for the industrial countries, consumer price indices are in a number of respects conceptually inferior to the other measures of domestic costs and prices discussed above for the purpose of compiling indices of real effective exchange rates, owing to the inclusion of various factors which may differ across countries, for example, indirect taxes.

Estimates shown for the Euro Area for relative consumer prices are generated using a subset of the trade weights described in the paragraph above, where the weights for the Euro Area relate to the trade of the Euro Area as a whole with its partners in the system. A synthetic euro has been constructed for the period before the introduction of the euro using trade weights drawn from the same weighting scheme, Euro Area member exchange rates, and the official lock-in rates, which were used to determine the initial value of the euro. The Euro area consumer price series from January 1995 onward is the Harmonized Index of Consumer Prices, provided by the ECB, and prior to this period, it is the trade-weighted average of the individual member countries' consumer price indices. Trade weights used in the construction are specific to this system and are the same as those used in the construction of the synthetic euro.

As indicated in the Introduction, movements in these indices need to be interpreted with considerable caution. While every effort is made to use national data that are as internationally comparable as possible, the degree to which it is practicable to ensure comparability is limited by the character of the available data. For this reason, the table provides a wide array of available indicators.

Wholesale Prices

There is significant diversity in the methodology used by countries to compile these indices.

Exports and Imports

† Prior to 1998, data for South Africa refer to the South African Common Customs Area (SACCA), which includes Botswana, Lesotho, Namibia, South Africa, and Swaziland. Beginning in 1998, data refer to South Africa only, excluding intra-trade of the SACCA. Data for SACCA excluding South Africa amount to 1.987 billion U.S. dollars in 1998 for Exports and .703 billion U.S. dollars in 1998 for Imports.

Export Unit Value/Export Prices and Import Unit Value/Import Prices

The country indices are unit value indices, except for a few, which are components of wholesale price indices or based on specific price quotations. The exceptions are marked 'w' in the guide to the coverage of *IFS* on page viii.

Commodity Price Index

† Prior to 1982, the World index and all components (food, beverages, agricultural raw materials, and metals), except fertilizer, were calculated by backward recursion of percent changes based on the previously published indices. (00176axd)

Albania

Interest Rates

Deposit Rate: † The minimum rate on commercial banks' 12-month deposits (set by the central bank) was replaced by a guideline rate in 1993. † Beginning in 1995, data refer to the weighted average rate on new 12-month deposits of the three commercial banks with the highest level of outstanding deposits.

Lending Rate: † Data beginning in 1995 refer to the weighted average rate on new 12-month loans of the three commercial banks with the highest level of outstanding loans.

Algeria

Monetary Authorities

† Beginning in 1992, data reflect the introduction of a new reporting system.

Deposit Money Banks

† Beginning in 1992, data reflect improved classification including the separate identification of claims on nonfinancial public enterprises, which were previously included with claims on private sector.

Monetary Survey

† See notes on monetary authorities and deposit money banks.

Angola

Monetary Authorities

† Beginning in 1999, data are based on a new plan of accounts.

Banking Institutions

† See note on monetary authorities.

Banking Survey

† See note on monetary authorities.

Interest Rates

Deposit Rate: † Beginning in 2000, weighted average rate offered by commercial banks on time deposits of up to 90 days in national currency. The rate is weighted by deposit amounts.

Lending Rate: † Beginning in 2000, weighted average rate charged by commercial banks on loans of up to 180 days in national currency. The rate is weighted by loan amounts.

Antigua and Barbuda

National Accounts

As indicated by the country, the national accounts are compiled according to the recommendations of the *1993 SNA*.

Argentina

Monetary Authorities

† Beginning in 1990, data may not be comparable with data for earlier periods because of a change in the valuation system and adjustments to the accounts of the Central Bank of the Republic of Argentina. † Beginning in 1994, data are based on more detailed sectorization of the accounts.

Deposit Money Banks

† Beginning in 1990, data are based on an improved reporting system. † See note on monetary authorities.

Monetary Survey

† See notes on monetary authorities and deposit money banks.

Other Banking Institutions

† See notes on monetary authorities and deposit money banks.

Banking Survey

† See notes on monetary authorities and deposit money banks.

Government Finance

† Beginning in 1995, data cover the operations of the consolidated central government.

National Accounts

As indicated by the country, the national accounts are compiled according to the recommendations of the *1993 SNA*.

Armenia

Interest Rates

Refinancing Rate (End of Period): † Beginning in 1999, repo rate at which the Central Bank of Armenia conducts repurchase agreements with resident banks.

Treasury Bill Rate: † Beginning in 1996, weighted average yield on three- to six-month (including 182-day) treasury bills.

National Accounts

As indicated by the country, the national accounts are compiled according to the recommendations of the *1993 SNA*. † Beginning in 1994, data at previous year's prices are used to construct *line 99bvp*.

Aruba

International Transactions

† Data for *Exports* and *Imports, c.i.f.* are based on customs records and include imports into, and exports from, the Free Zone.

Australia

Monetary Authorities

† Beginning in 1989, data are based on an improved sectorization of the accounts.

Deposit Money Banks

† Beginning in 1984, foreign assets and liabilities are compiled under a new, more comprehensive statistical collection. † Beginning in 1989, the coverage of accounts has been expanded to include domestic assets and liabilities denominated in foreign currencies as well as foreign assets and foreign liabilities denominated in Australian dollars.

Monetary Survey

† See notes on monetary authorities and deposit money banks.

Interest Rates

Money Market Rate: † Beginning in 1995, rate paid on unsecured overnight loans of cash as calculated by the Australian Financial Markets Association and published on Reuters page at 11 a.m. † Beginning in 1999, weighted average rate of the interest rates at which banks have borrowed and lent exchange settlement funds during the day. The rate is weighted by loan amounts.

Treasury Bill Rate: † Beginning in 1995, estimated closing yield in the secondary market on thirteen-week treasury notes.

Deposit Rate: † Beginning in 1991, weighted average yield on certificates of deposit. † Beginning in 1999, average rate offered by major banks on 3-month fixed deposits of 5,000 to 100,000 Australian dollars.

Lending Rate: † Beginning in 1977, rate charged by banks on loans to small and large businesses.

Government Bond Yield: † Beginning in 1982, the short-term government bond yield (*line 61a*) comprises assessed secondary market yields on non-rebate bonds with maturity of two years. † Beginning in 1994, the short-term yield refers to bonds with maturity of three years.

Government Finance

† Beginning in 1970, annual data are as reported in the *Government Finance Statistics Yearbook* and cover consolidated central government. Also beginning in 1970, data relate to a fiscal year different from calendar year. † From 1988 onward, purchases and sales of stocks, land, and intangible assets are recorded on a net basis.

National Accounts

† From midquarter 1959 onwards, data have been revised following the implementation of improved compilation methods and the *1993 SNA*.

Austria

International Liquidity

† Beginning in 1999, *Total Reserves minus Gold (line 1l.d)* is defined in accordance with the Eurosystem's statistical definition of international reserves. Data on *lines 3..d, 4..d, 7a.d,* and *7b.d* are based on a Euro Area-wide definition of residency.

Banking Institutions

† From 1974 onward, banks' external accounts are based on the foreign exchange record, which provides an improved resident/nonresident distinction. † Beginning in 1984, data are based on improved classification. † Beginning in 1995, data on

claims on government were revised to reflect the institutional classification of the government sector in the *European System of Accounts 1995 (1995 ESA)*.

Banking Survey (National Residency)

† See notes on banking institutions.

Interest Rates

Deposit Rate (line 60l): † Rate on deposits up to one year in maturity; prior to 1998, rate on savings deposits due at call.

Prices, Production, Labor

Industrial Production: † Prior to 1995, the index excludes energy. Beginning in 1995, the index covers mining, manufacturing, and energy.

Government Finance

† Beginning in 1970, annual data are as reported in the *Government Finance Statistics Yearbook* and cover consolidated central government.

National Accounts

† From 1976 onwards, data have revised following the implementation of the *1995 ESA*.

Azerbaijan

Monetary Authorities

† Beginning in 1998 and 2001, data reflect the introduction of a new plan of accounts.

Deposit Money Banks

† Beginning in 2000 and 2001, data reflect the introduction of a new plan of accounts.

Monetary Survey

† See notes on monetary authorities and deposit money banks.

Bahamas, The

International Liquidity

† Prior to 1977, data for *line 1d.d* included small foreign exchange holdings by the government, which were transferred to the Central Bank of The Bahamas at this date.

Government Finance

† From 1988 onward, data cover the budgetary central government and no longer cover operations of the National Insurance Board, which is a social security fund. † From 1993 onward, fiscal years begin on July 1, rather than on January 1.

National Accounts

† Beginning in 1989, data have been revised following the implementation of the *1993 SNA*.

Bahrain

International Liquidity

† Prior to 1991, data for *lines 7a.d* and *7b.d* include positions with offshore banking units, which were classified as nonresident institutions.

Monetary Authorities

† See note on deposit money banks.

Deposit Money Banks

† Beginning in 1991, data are compiled from a new set of statistical returns, and the institutional coverage is extended to include all kinds of resident banks, that is, full commercial banks (FCUs), offshore banking units (OBUs), and investment banks (IBs). Deposit money banks' claims on and liabilities to nonresidents therefore exclude positions with OBUs (previously treated as nonresidents), and their claims on and liabilities to resident banks include positions with OBUs.

Monetary Survey

† See note on deposit money banks.

Interest Rates

Deposit Rate: † Prior to 1990, data refer to the maximum recommended rate on Bahrain dinar time deposits with maturities of at least three months and under six months. The rate was prescribed by the Bahrain Monetary Agency; however, banks could exceed the recommended rate. Beginning in 1990, data refer to the weighted average of interest rates on time deposits with maturities of at least three months and under six months. † Beginning in 1998, data refer to time deposits between BD 10,000 and 50,000 with maturities of three to twelve months.

Lending Rate: † Prior to 1988, data refer to the minimum recommended rate on consumer loans with maturities of at least three months and under six months. From 1988–94, data refer to the maximum recommended rate on consumer loans with maturities of at least 12 months and under 15 months. Beginning in 1994, data refer to the weighted average of interest rates on consumer loans with maturities of at least 12 months and under 15 months. † Beginning in 1998, data refer to the weighted average rate on all personal loans extended in the last month of the quarter.

Bangladesh

Monetary Authorities

† The sectorization and classification of accounts have been revised from 1982 and again from 1987.

Deposit Money Banks

† See note on monetary authorities.

Monetary Survey

† See note on monetary authorities.

National Accounts

As indicated by the country, the national accounts are compiled according to the recommendations of the *1993 SNA*.

Barbados

International Liquidity

† Beginning in 1972, *line 1dbd* includes sinking funds held against domestic government debt.

Belarus

Deposit Money Banks

† Beginning in 1996, data are based on an improved reporting system.

Monetary Survey

† See note on deposit money banks.

Interest Rates

Refinancing Rate (End of Period): † Beginning in 2000, the practice of directed lending to commercial banks at concessionary rates was discontinued, and the data refer to the announced rate at which the National Bank of Belarus lends to commercial banks.

National Accounts

As indicated by the country, the national accounts are compiled according to the recommendations of the *1993 SNA*.

Belgium

International Liquidity

† Beginning in 1980, data on gold and foreign exchange holdings exclude the deposits made with the European Monetary Institute (EMI)—which became the European Central Bank (ECB) in 1998—of the gold and gross U.S. dollar holdings; the holdings of European currency units (ECUs) issued by the EMI against these deposits are included in *line 1d.d. Gold (National Valuation) (line 1and):* † Prior to 1990, 20 percent of official gold was valued at market prices. Beginning in 1990, official gold is revalued at market prices. † For data on *lines 7a.d* and *7b.d* beginning in 1992, see note on banking institutions. † Beginning in 1999, *Total Reserves minus Gold (line 1l.d)* is defined in accordance with the Eurosystem's statistical definition of international reserves. Data on *lines 3..d, 4..d, 7a.d,* and *7b.d* are based on a Euro Area-wide definition of residency.

Monetary Authorities

† Beginning in 1980, foreign currencies participating in the exchange rate mechanism of the EMS were valued at their midpoint rates, while gold and other foreign currencies were valued at historical prices. † Beginning in 1990, foreign-currency-denominated assets and liabilities and gold are valued at exchange rates and prices that are derived from market rates, rather than from historical exchange rates and costs. The effects of valuation changes are shown in *line 17r.*

Banking Institutions

† Beginning in 1992, data exclude the Rediscount and Guarantee Institute. Certain breaks in the series may occur in 1992 owing to the radical reform of the reporting procedure of the credit institutions that was introduced at that time. First, the contents of the re-

port forms were revised, and second, all types of institutions had to report according to the same scheme. Formerly, there were distinct report forms for deposit banks, savings banks, and public credit institutions. Now they are legally considered as equals.

Banking Survey (National Residency)

† See notes on monetary authorities and banking institutions.

Interest Rates

Money Market Rate: † Prior to 1991, the call money rate. Beginning in 1991, the averages of borrowing and lending rates for three-month interbank transactions.

Deposit Rate: † Prior to 1993, the indicative rates published by the banks. Thereafter, the rate on three-month time deposits weighted by volume.

International Transactions

Import Prices: † Source B index, base 1975, refers to the import component of the industrial products group of the general wholesale price index of Belgium (country code 124).

Government Finance

† Beginning in 1970, annual data are as reported in the *Government Finance Statistics Yearbook* and cover consolidated central government. † From 1996 onward, data are compiled on the basis of *1995 ESA* rules and are not comparable with data for previous years.

National Accounts

† From 1985 onwards, data have been revised following the implementation of the *1995 ESA*.

Belize

Government Finance

† Beginning in 1979, data relate to a fiscal year different from calendar year. Data for 1979 cover 15 months.

Benin

Exchange Rates

Official Rate (End of Period and *Period Average):* † From 1999 onward, the CFA franc is pegged to the euro at a rate of CFA franc 655.957 per euro. Prior to 1999, the official rate was pegged to the French franc. † In 1994 the CFA franc was devalued to CFAF 100 per French franc from CFAF 50, at which it had been fixed since 1948.

Deposit Money Banks

† Beginning in 1979, *Central Government Deposits (line 26d)* include the deposits of public establishments of an administrative or social nature (EPAS) and exclude those of the savings bank; *Demand* and *Time Deposits (lines 24* and *25)* include deposits of the savings bank and exclude deposits of EPAS; and *Claims on Private Sector (line 22d)* exclude claims on other financial institutions.

Monetary Survey

† Beginning in 1979, *Claims on Other Financial Institutions (line 32f)* includes claims of deposit money banks on other financial in-

stitutions; see deposit money bank notes for explanation of other break symbols.

Other Banking Institutions

Liquid Liabilities (line 55l): † See notes on deposit money banks and monetary survey.

Prices

† *Consumer Prices:* Beginning in 1997, BCEAO harmonized index, base 1996.

Bhutan

International Liquidity

† Prior to 1995, data for *line 1dxd* include convertible currency foreign assets, held on behalf of the government by the Bank of Bhutan and the Royal Insurance Corporation of Bhutan, and foreign exchange held by the government of Bhutan.

Monetary Authorities

† The sectorization and classification of accounts were revised in 1993, following the introduction of a more detailed reporting of accounts. Data on *Claims on Deposit Money Banks,* which previously had been included in *Claims on Other Financial Institutions,* are shown separately beginning that date.

Deposit Money Banks

† The sectorization and classification of accounts were revised in 1993, following the introduction of a more detailed reporting of accounts. *Claims on Private Sector (line 22d):* † Prior to 1993, claims on state enterprises were included in *Claims on Nonfinancial Public Enterprises (line 22c).* Beginning in this year, data include claims on such enterprises that were privatized.

Monetary Survey

† See notes on monetary authorities and deposit money banks.

Prices and Tourism

Electricity Production: The large increase in 1986–87 is due to the beginning of production of the Chukha hydroelectric facility. From July 1988 onwards, the data refer to Chukha production only.

Government Finance

† Through 1986, fiscal year begins April 1; from 1988 onward, fiscal year ends June 30. Data for 1988 fiscal year cover 15 months. † From 1989 onward, data on grants include grants received in kind. Also, data on expenditure include the value of grants in kind.

Bolivia

Monetary Authorities

† Beginning in 1987, data reflect the introduction of improved sectorization and classification of domestic and foreign accounts. † Starting in 1996, data are based on an improved sectorization of the accounts.

Deposit Money Banks

† See note on monetary authorities. † Beginning in 1996, comprises commercial banks, the State Bank, and specialized banks (previously classified as other banking institutions). See note on monetary authorities.

Monetary Survey

† See notes on monetary authorities and deposit money banks.

Other Banking Institutions

† See note on monetary authorities. † Beginning in 1996, comprises savings and loans associations, savings and credit cooperatives, and financial funds. See note on monetary authorities.

Banking Survey

† See notes on monetary authorities, deposit money banks, and other banking institutions.

Interest Rates

Deposit Rate: † Beginning in 1986, weighted average rate, including surcharges and commissions, offered by commercial banks on time deposits in national currency. The rate is weighted by deposit amounts.

Lending Rate: † Beginning in 1986, weighted average rate, including surcharges and commissions, charged by commercial banks on loans in national currency. The rate is weighted by loan amounts.

Prices, Production, Labor

Consumer Prices: † Prior to 1970, the index covers prices in La Paz, reference base 1966; beginning in 1970, the index covers prices in La Paz and El Alto, reference base 1980; and beginning in 1992, the index covers prices in La Paz, Santa Cruz, Cochabamba, and El Alto, reference base 1991.

Government Finance

† Beginning in 1993, data cover the operations of the general government.

Brazil

International Liquidity

† Prior to 1986, data for *Total Reserves Minus Gold (line .1l.d)* and *Foreign Exchange (line .1d.d)* include foreign exchange held by the Central Bank of Brazil (CBB) and Bank of Brazil. Beginning in 1986, data include the foreign exchange held by the CBB only.

Monetary Authorities

† Beginning in 1978 and in 1988, data are based on improved sectorization of the accounts. † Consolidates the accounts of the Central Bank of Brazil and Bank of Brazil through 1985. Beginning in 1986, comprises the Central Bank of Brazil only.

Deposit Money Banks

† See note on monetary authorities. † Comprises only commercial banks through 1985. Beginning in 1986, consolidates the accounts of the commercial banks and the Bank of Brazil. † Beginning in 1988, comprises commercial banks, Bank of Brazil, multiple

banks, Federal Savings Bank, and state savings banks. Data reflect the introduction of a new accounting system, which provides an improved sectorization of the accounts.

Monetary Survey

† See notes on monetary authorities and deposit money banks.

Other Banking Institutions

† See note on monetary authorities. † Beginning in 1978, the accounts of the National Bank of Cooperative Credit are also consolidated in this category. † Beginning in 1988, comprises investment banks, National Bank for Economic and Social Development, state development banks, finance and investment companies, and housing credit companies. Beginning in 1996, includes mortgage companies. See note on deposit money banks.

Banking Survey

† See notes on monetary authorities, deposit money banks, and other banking institutions.

Interest Rates

Discount Rate (End of Period): † Beginning in 2000, the bank rate was abolished, and the Central Bank of Brazil (CBB) established new rules for lending to financial institutions, taking into account the maturity of the operation and the collateral used by the borrowing institutions. The CBB decided to use the SELIC rate (see note on money market rate) plus two points as the discount rate.

Money Market Rate: † Beginning in 1980, Special Settlement and Custody System (SELIC) overnight rate, which is a weighted average rate on loans between financial institutions involving firm sales of or repurchase agreements based on federal securities in the SELIC. The rate is weighted by loan amounts.

Deposit Rate: † Beginning in 1989, average rate offered by banks on certificates of deposit of 30 days or longer.

International Transactions

Volume of Exports and Imports: † Data on total volume are based on quantities in metric tons. Prior to 1985, volume data are Laspeyres indices, base 1977.

Unit Value of Exports and Imports: † Indices are calculated from value and volume indices except for unit value of export data prior to 1985, which are from source A, base 1977.

Government Finance

† Beginning in 1970, data are as reported in the *Government Finance Statistics Yearbook* and cover consolidated central government.

Bulgaria

International Liquidity

† Prior to 1997, official gold holdings were valued at US$300 per fine troy ounce. Beginning in 1997, gold is valued at either 500 deutsche marks per fine troy ounce or at the end-of-period London gold market price, whichever is lower.

Monetary Authorities

† Before 1995, deposits of the national Social Security Fund are included in *Central Government Deposits (line 16d)*. Beginning in 1995, transferable and other deposits of the national Social Security Fund are included, respectively, in *Reserve Money (line 14)* and in *Time, Savings and Foreign Currency Deposits (line 15)*.

Deposit Money Banks

† Before 1995, deposits of the national Social Security Fund are included in *Central Government Deposits (line 26d)*. Beginning in 1995, transferable and other deposits of the national Social Security Fund are included, respectively, in *Demand Deposits (line 24)* and in *Time, Savings and Foreign Currency Deposits (line 25)*. † Also beginning in 1995, data are based on a new accounting system.

Monetary Survey

† See notes on monetary authorities and deposit money banks.

Prices and Labor

Consumer Prices: † Until the end of 1992, the weights referred to retail turnover data of 1990. For the period 1993–95, the weights were based on the household budget survey of 1992. † Beginning in 1996, the weights are revised annually. From 1998 onwards, the basket includes 900 items of goods and services.

Government Finance

† Prior to 1994, data are as reported in the *Government Finance Statistics Yearbook*. Thereafter, data are as reported by the Bulgarian National Bank and are taken from the *Report on the Execution of the State Budget* and unpublished reports on the operations of the consolidated central government.

National Accounts

As indicated by the country, the national accounts are compiled according to the recommendations of the *1993 SNA*.

Burkina Faso

Exchange Rates

Official Rate (End of Period and Period Average): † From 1999 onward, the CFA franc (CFAF) is pegged to the euro at a rate of CFAF 655.957 per euro. Prior to 1999, the official rate was pegged to the French franc. † In 1994 the CFA franc was devalued to CFAF 100 per French franc from CFAF 50, at which it had been fixed since 1948.

Deposit Money Banks

† Beginning in 1979, *Central Government Deposits (line 26d)* include the deposits of public establishments of an administrative or social nature (EPAS) and exclude those of the savings bank; *Demand* and *Time Deposits (lines 24 and 25)* include deposits of the savings bank and exclude deposits of EPAS; and *Claims on Private Sector (line 22d)* exclude claims on other financial institutions.

Monetary Survey

† Beginning in 1979, *Claims on Other Financial Institutions (line 32f)* includes claims of deposit money banks on other financial institutions; see deposit money bank notes for explanation of other break symbols.

Other Banking Institutions

Liquid Liabilities (line 55l): † See notes on deposit money banks and monetary survey.

Prices and Labor

† *Consumer Prices:* Beginning in 1997, BCEAO harmonized index, base 1996.

Government Finance

† Beginning in 1977, annual data cover social security funds in addition to budgetary accounts. † Beginning in 1985, data also cover extrabudgetary accounts.

Burundi

Deposit Money Banks

† Beginning in 1980, data are based on an improved sectorization of the accounts. † Beginning in 1991, data reflect changes in the coverage of the other monetary institutions.

Monetary Survey

† See note on deposit money banks.

Other Banking Institutions

† Beginning in 1997, includes the Fonds de Promotion de l'Habitat Urbain (FPHU).

Prices and Labor

Consumer Prices: † Prior to 1980, data refer to the index of consumer prices of civil servants in Bujumbura, base 1970. From 1980 through 1992, data refer to prices paid by unskilled and clerical workers and small traders in Bujumbura, base January 1980=100. Beginning in 1993, source base is January 1991=100. The weights are derived from a household budget survey conducted in 1979.

Government Finance

† Beginning in 1997, data are presented in a new format and are not directly comparable with data for earlier periods. Debt data cover the outstanding debt of the nonfinancial public sector, comprising direct government debt, onlent government debt, and debt guaranteed by the government.

Cambodia

International Liquidity

† Prior to 1994, *Foreign Exchange (line 1d.d)* excludes portion of official reserves that was held by the Foreign Trade Bank. Beginning in 1994, official foreign reserves were centralized at the National Bank of Cambodia (central bank).

Cameroon

Exchange Rates

Official Rate (End of Period and *Period Average):* † From 1999 onward, the CFA franc (CFAF) is pegged to the euro at a rate of CFAF 655.957 per euro. Prior to 1999, the official rate was pegged to the French franc. † In 1994, the CFA franc was deval-

ued to CFAF 100 per French franc from CFAF 50, at which it had been fixed since 1948.

Monetary Authorities

† Beginning in 1988, the sectorization and classification of accounts have been revised. † Beginning in 1991, *Claims on Central Government* include government assumption of certain nonperforming bank loans.

Deposit Money Banks

† Beginning in 1977, data are based on improved sectorization of the accounts. † Beginning in 1991, the counterpart of government assumption of certain nonperforming bank loans was reclassified from *Credit from Monetary Authorities* to *Capital Accounts.* † Beginning in 1992, the coverage of the banking system has been revised. Claims and deposits of nonactive banks or banks in the process of liquidation have been excluded from the monetary accounts.

Monetary Survey

† See notes on monetary authorities and deposit money banks.

Interest Rates

Discount Rate (End of Period): † Beginning in 1994, rate charged by the BEAC to financial institutions on refinancing operations.

Deposit Rate: † Beginning in 1990, minimum rate offered by deposit money banks on savings accounts.

Lending Rate: † Beginning in 1990, maximum rate charged by deposit money banks on all loans, excluding charges and fees.

Government Finance

† Data prior to 1990 cover budgetary, extrabudgetary, and social security accounts. Data for 1990 and 1991 cover the general budget units, *Caisse nationale de prévoyance sociale* (National Social Security Fund), and *Caisse autonome d'amortissement* (Autonomous Amortization Fund). † Beginning in 1992, data cover the general budget and the *Caisse autonome d'amortissement* only. † Data for 1995 cover budgetary central government only.

Canada

Deposit Money Banks

† Beginning in 1981, all wholly- and majority-owned subsidiaries of the chartered banks (including mortgage loan subsidiaries and foreign banking subsidiaries) are consolidated in accordance with Canadian banking law. Unconsolidated data are not available on a monthly basis. In addition, data for *lines 24* and *25,* which were previously calculated from monthly averages of Wednesday figures, in the absence of an adequate classification of month ends, are now calculated mostly from month-end figures.

Monetary Survey

† See note on deposit money banks.

Other Banking Institutions

† Prior to 1981, other banking institutions comprised all trust and mortgage loan companies, local credit unions, *caisses populaires,* Quebec savings banks, and sales finance and consumer loan companies. From 1981, mortgage loan companies affiliated with char-

tered banks have been excluded from this group, as they have been consolidated with the accounts of chartered banks in their reporting to the Bank of Canada.

Banking Survey

† See notes on deposit money banks and other banking institutions.

Nonbank Financial Institutions

† Beginning in 1999, comprises nondepository credit intermediaries, which are establishments, both public (government sponsored enterprises) and private, primarily engaged in extending credit or lending funds raised by credit-market borrowing (e.g., by issuing commercial paper and other debt instruments) and by borrowing from other financial intermediaries.

Government Finance

† Beginning in 1974, annual data are as reported in the *Government Finance Statistics Yearbook* and cover consolidated central government. † Data classification changes may have been introduced between 1987 and 1988, as a result of revisions applied from 1988 through 1995.

National Accounts

† Beginning in 1995, data have been revised following the implementation of the *1993 SNA*.

Cape Verde

Monetary Authorities

† Beginning in 1995, data are based on an improved sectorization of the accounts.

Deposit Money Banks

† See note on monetary authorities.

Monetary Survey

† See note on monetary authorities.

Interest Rates

Deposit Rate: † Beginning in 1995, maximum rate offered by the Bank of Cape Verde on 61- to 90-day time deposits.

Central African Republic

Exchange Rates

Official Rate (End of Period and *Period Average):* † From 1999 onward, the CFA franc is pegged to the euro at a rate of CFA franc 655.957 per euro. Prior to 1999, the official rate was pegged to the French franc. † In 1994 the CFA franc was devalued to CFAF 100 per French franc from CFAF 50, at which it had been fixed since 1948.

Monetary Authorities

† Beginning in 1988, the sectorization and classification of accounts have been revised. † Beginning in 1991, *Claims on Central Government* include government assumption of certain nonperforming bank loans.

Deposit Money Banks

† Beginning in 1977, data are based on improved sectorization of the accounts. † Beginning in 1991, the counterpart of government assumption of certain nonperforming bank loans was reclassified from *Credit from Monetary Authorities* to *Capital Accounts.* † Beginning in 1992, the coverage of the banking system has been revised. Claims and deposits of nonactive banks or banks in the process of liquidation have been excluded from the monetary accounts.

Monetary Survey

† See notes on monetary authorities and deposit money banks.

Interest Rates

Discount Rate (End of Period): † Beginning in 1994, rate charged by the BEAC to financial institutions on refinancing operations.

Deposit Rate: † Beginning in 1990, minimum rate offered by deposit money banks on savings accounts.

Lending Rate: † Beginning in 1990, maximum rate charged by deposit money banks on all loans, excluding charges and fees.

Chad

Exchange Rates

Official Rate (End of Period and *Period Average):* † From 1999 onward, the CFA franc is pegged to the euro at a rate of CFA franc 655.957 per euro. Prior to 1999, the official rate was pegged to the French franc. † In 1994 the CFA franc was devalued to CFAF 100 per French franc from CFAF 50, at which it had been fixed since 1948.

Monetary Authorities

† Beginning in 1988, the sectorization and classification of accounts have been revised. † Beginning in 1991, *Claims on Central Government* include government assumption of certain nonperforming bank loans.

Deposit Money Banks

† Beginning in 1991, the counterpart of government assumption of certain nonperforming bank loans was reclassified from *Credit from Monetary Authorities* to *Capital Accounts.* † See note on monetary authorities.

Monetary Survey

† See notes on monetary authorities and deposit money banks.

Interest Rates

Discount Rate (End of Period): † Beginning in 1994, rate charged by the BEAC to financial institutions on refinancing operations.

Deposit Rate: † Beginning in 1990, minimum rate offered by deposit money banks on savings accounts.

Lending Rate: † Beginning in 1990, maximum rate charged by deposit money banks on all loans, excluding charges and fees.

Government Finance

† Prior to 1986, data cover budgetary central government only. Beginning in 1986, data are as reported for the *Government Fi-*

nance Statistics Yearbook and cover budgetary central government and the Autonomous Amortization Fund. † Beginning in 1991, data are as reported by the Banque des Etats de l'Afrique Centrale.

Chile

Monetary Authorities

† Beginning in 1976, data are based on improved sectorization of the accounts.

Deposit Money Banks

† See note on monetary authorities.

Monetary Survey

† See note on monetary authorities.

Interest Rates

Deposit Rate: † Beginning in 1985, weighted average rate offered by financial institutions on 30- to 89-day deposits in national currency. The rate is weighted by deposit amounts. The rate is converted to an annual percentage by compounding monthly rates of interest.

Lending Rate: † Beginning in 1985, weighted average rate charged by financial institutions on 30- to 89-day loans in national currency. The rate is weighted by loan amounts. The rate is converted to an annual percentage by compounding monthly rates of interest.

Prices, Production, and Labor

Industrial Share Prices: † Beginning in 1978, index of industrial share prices, base December 29, 1978. † Beginning in 1980, index of industrial share prices, base December 30, 1980.

International Transactions

† Trade data, which are derived from customs returns, have been updated with central bank payments data for current periods.

Government Finance

† Beginning in 1972, annual data are as reported in the *Government Finance Statistics Yearbook* and cover consolidated central government (including all extrabudgetary and social security funds). † Data for 1984–86 also cover accounts of some nonfinancial public enterprises and one public financial institution included in national sources. † Beginning in 1987, data exclude the operations of nonfinancial public enterprises.

National Accounts

As indicated by the country, the national accounts are compiled according to the recommendations of the *1993 SNA*.

China, People's Republic: Mainland

The data refer to the People's Republic of China, excluding the Hong Kong Special Administrative Region. Data on transactions and assets and liabilities vis-à-vis Hong Kong are treated as international transactions and external positions respectively.

International Liquidity

† Beginning in 1984, *Foreign Exchange (line 1d.d)* includes foreign government securities. † Prior to 1992, *Foreign Exchange* included foreign exchange holdings of the Bank of China. Starting in that year, it includes foreign exchange holdings of the People's Bank of China only.

Monetary Authorities

† Data classification from 1993 onwards has been revised. For the period 1993–96, data on *Foreign Assets (line 11)* refer to net foreign assets. † Prior to 1997, *Central Government Deposits (line 16d)* also include some deposits of provincial and local government units.

Banking Institutions

† Prior to 1993, the data comprise the accounts of the deposit money banks. Subsequently, the data also include the accounts of the other banking institutions.

Banking Survey

† Data prior to 1985 exclude the rural credit cooperatives and the People's Construction Bank of China.

Interest Rates

Lending Rate (End of Period): † Prior to 1989, rate on working capital loans to state industrial enterprises. Thereafter, rate on working capital loans of one-year maturity.

International Transactions

† Prior to 1980, the data are provided by the Ministry of Foreign Trade and exclude exports of complete plants in the form of foreign aid. Thereafter, more comprehensive data are provided by the Customs Office.

China, People's Republic: Hong Kong

The data refer to the Hong Kong Special Administrative Region (HKSAR). Data on transactions and assets and liabilities vis-à-vis The Mainland of China are treated as international transactions and external positions respectively.

International Liquidity

Foreign Exchange (line 1d.d): † Beginning in 1997, data include the foreign exchange reserves of the Land Fund of the Hong Kong Special Administrative Region (HKSAR) government. † Beginning in 1998, assets of the HKSAR Government's Land Fund are placed with the Exchange Fund.

Monetary Authorities

† Beginning in 1999, *Reserve Money (line 14)* also includes Exchange Fund bills and notes.

Prices, Production, Labor

Consumer Prices: † Beginning in 1995, the CPI is based on a wider range of households with an average monthly expenditure of HK$ 4,000–59,999. From October 1999 onwards, the Composite CPI is compiled using expenditure weights obtained from the 1999/2000 household survey and is based on the overall expenditure pattern of 90 percent of households.

Colombia

Monetary Authorities

† Beginning in 1978, the financial funds (for the financing of agriculture, industry, housing, etc.) are considered as part of the Bank of the Republic in the treatment of the accounts of these funds with commercial and specialized banks. † Beginning in 1989, data reflect the introduction of a new system of accounts, which provides an improved sectorization of the accounts.

Deposit Money Banks

† See note on monetary authorities. Beginning in 1978, data exclude the accounts of the Agricultural Bank (Caja de Crédito Agrario, Industrial y Minero). † Beginning in 1990, includes the Agricultural Bank and Social Savings Bank. Data reflect the introduction of a new system of accounts, which provides an improved sectorization of the accounts. Beginning in 1994, includes the Central Mortgage Bank.

Monetary Survey

† See notes on monetary authorities and deposit money banks.

Other Banking Institutions

† Beginning in 1974, data cover a wider range of institutions. † Beginning in 1990, includes commercial financing companies and financial cooperative institutions and excludes the Agricultural Bank and Social Savings Bank. Data reflect the introduction of a new system of accounts, which provides an improved sectorization of the accounts. Beginning in 1991, includes the Banco de Comercio Exterior (BANCOLDEX), Fondo para el Financiamiento del Sector Agropecuario (FINAGRO), and Financiera de Desarrollo Territorial (FINDETER). Beginning in 1993, includes the Fondo Nacional de Desarrollo (FONADE). Beginning in 1994, excludes the Central Mortgage Bank. Beginning in 1998, includes the Fondo de Garantías de Instituciones Financieras (FOGAFIN). Beginning in 2000, includes financial cooperatives.

Banking Survey

† See notes on monetary authorities, deposit money banks, and other banking institutions.

Interest Rates

Discount Rate (End of Period): † Beginning in 1986, corresponds to DTF (see note for deposit rate in monthly issue of *IFS*) plus two points. † Beginning in 1990, corresponds to DTF plus eight points. Beginning in 1992, corresponds to DTF plus seven points. Beginning in 1999, corresponds to DTF plus five points.

Lending Rate: † Beginning in 1999, weighted average rate charged by commercial banks, savings and housing corporations, financial corporations, and commercial finance companies on commercial, ordinary, and short-term (tesorería) and long-term preferential loans. The rate is weighted by loan amounts and, due to the revolving nature of the short-term preferential loans, their weight was established as one fifth of the daily disbursement.

Prices, Production, Labor

Share Prices: † Beginning in 1991, index of prices on the Bogotá Stock Exchange, base January 2, 1991.

National Accounts

† Beginning in 1970, data are compiled by the National Department of Statistics (DANE). † Beginning in 1994, data are compiled according to the *1993 SNA*.

Comoros

Exchange Rates

Official Rate (End of Period and *Period Average):* † From 1999 onward, the Comorian franc is pegged to the euro at a rate of Comorian francs 491.9677 per euro. Prior to 1999, the official rate was pegged to the French franc. † In 1994 the Comorian franc was devalued to CF 75 per French franc from CF 50, at which it had been fixed since 1948.

International Liquidity

† Beginning in 1998, data are based on an improved reporting and classification of accounts.

Monetary Authorities

† See note to international liquidity.

Deposit Money Banks

† See note to international liquidity.

Monetary Survey

† See note to international liquidity.

Other Banking Institutions

† See note to international liquidity.

Banking Survey

† See note to international liquidity.

Congo, Democratic Republic of

Exchange Rates

† In 1991, a new system was introduced, with the external value of the zaïre determined on the basis of demand and supply conditions prevailing in the foreign exchange market. † In 1993, the new zaïre, equal to three million old zaïres, was introduced.

Government Finance

† Beginning in 1971, data are as reported in the *Government Finance Statistics Yearbook (GFSY)* and cover consolidated central government. † Beginning in 1994, *GFSY* data exclude social security.

Congo, Republic of

Exchange Rates

Official Rate (End of Period and *Period Average):* † From 1999 onward, the CFA franc is pegged to the euro at a rate of CFA franc 655.957 per euro. Prior to 1999, the official rate was pegged to the French franc. † In 1994 the CFA franc was devalued to

CFAF 100 per French franc from CFAF 50, at which it had been fixed since 1948.

Monetary Authorities

† Beginning in 1988, the sectorization and classification of accounts have been revised. † Beginning in 1991, *Claims on Central Government* include government assumption of certain nonperforming bank loans.

Deposit Money Banks

† Beginning in 1977, data are based on improved sectorization of the accounts. † Beginning in 1991, the counterpart of government assumption of certain nonperforming bank loans was reclassified from *Credit from Monetary Authorities* to *Capital Accounts.* † Beginning in 1992, the coverage of the banking system has been revised. Claims and deposits of nonactive banks or banks in the process of liquidation have been excluded from the monetary accounts.

Monetary Survey

† See notes on monetary authorities and deposit money banks.

Interest Rates

Discount Rate (End of Period): † From 1994 onward, rate charged by the BEAC to financial institutions on refinancing operations.

Deposit Rate: † From 1990 onward, minimum rate offered by deposit money banks on savings accounts.

Lending Rate † From 1990 onward, maximum rate charged by deposit money banks on all loans, excluding charges and fees.

Government Finance

† Prior to 1980, data cover budgetary central government only. Beginning in 1980, data cover consolidated central government, including all extrabudgetary and social security funds.

Costa Rica

Monetary Authorities

† Beginning in 1997, data are based on an improved sectorization of the accounts.

Deposit Money Banks

† See note on monetary authorities.

Monetary Survey

† See note on monetary authorities.

Prices and Labor

Producer Prices: † Source B, modified laspeyres index, reference year December 1999=100. Weights were derived from a 1997 industrial survey. Index covers manufacturing industry with production for domestic market.

Government Finance

† From 1987 onwards, data were revised to have the same presentation as the Treasury cash flow.

National Accounts

As indicated by the country, the national accounts are compiled according to the recommendations of the *1993 SNA.*

Côte d'Ivoire

Exchange Rates

Official Rate (End of Period and *Period Average):* † From 1999 onward, the CFA franc is pegged to the euro at a rate of CFA franc 655.957 per euro. Prior to 1999, the official rate was pegged to the French franc. † In 1994 the CFA franc was devalued to CFAF 100 per French franc from CFAF 50, at which it had been fixed since 1948.

Deposit Money Banks

† Beginning in 1979, *Central Government Deposits (line 26d)* include the deposits of public establishments of an administrative or social nature (EPAS) and exclude those of the savings bank; *Demand* and *Time Deposits (lines 24* and *25)* include deposits of the savings bank and exclude deposits of EPAS; and *Claims on Private Sector (line 22d)* exclude claims on other financial institutions.

Monetary Survey

† Beginning in 1979, *Claims on Other Financial Institutions (line 32f)* includes claims of deposit money banks on other financial institutions; see deposit money bank notes for explanation of other break symbols.

Prices, Production, Labor

† *Consumer Prices:* Beginning in 1997, BCEAO harmonized index, base 1996.

Croatia

Deposit Money Banks

† Beginning in 1999, deposit money banks comprise commercial banks and savings banks; prior to 1999, savings banks were classified as other banking institutions.

International Transactions

† Beginning in 1992, the data include foreign trade with countries of the Former Socialist Federal Republic of Yugoslavia.

National Accounts

As indicated by the country, the national accounts are compiled according to the recommendations of the *1993 SNA.*

Cyprus

Monetary Authorities

† Beginning in 1988, the data reflect improved classification in the report forms.

Deposit Money Banks

† See note on monetary authorities.

Monetary Survey

† See note on monetary authorities.

Other Banking Institutions

† Prior to 1988, only specialized credit institutions were included. Beginning in 1988, comprises specialized credit institutions, co-operative credit institutions, and offshore banks.

Banking Survey

† See notes on monetary authorities and other banking institutions.

Interest Rates

Discount Rate: † In 1996, the central bank rate applicable for the discount of treasury bills was replaced with the rate applicable for the central bank's Lombard-type overnight facility with treasury bills as collateral.

Czech Republic

Monetary Authorities

† Beginning in 1997, data are based on an improved classification of accounts.

Deposit Money Banks

† See note on monetary authorities.

Monetary Survey

† See note on monetary authorities.

National Accounts

As indicated by the country, the national accounts are compiled according to the recommendations of the *1993 SNA*.

Denmark

International Liquidity

Gold (National Valuation) (line 1and): † From 1980, official gold is revalued on the basis of the London market prices.

Monetary Authorities

† From 1987–90, the accounts of the monetary authorities include the postal giro system. From 1991 onward, comprises Danmarks Nationalbank.

Deposit Money Banks

† Beginning in 1987, the accounts of commercial banks and other monetary institutions were consolidated. † The accounts of the deposit money banks were completely restructured from 1991. The accounts of the postal giro system are included in the deposit money banks sector from 1991.

Monetary Survey

† See notes on monetary authorities and deposit money banks.

Interest Rates

Money Market Rate: † Prior to 1982, arithmetic average of overnight interbank rates. From 1982 to 1992, weighted average of three-month interbank rates. † From 1993 onwards, arithmetic average of offered interbank rates.

Deposit Rate: † Prior to 1990, weighted average of rates on time deposits for one to less than twelve months. From 1990 to 1993, calculated from interest accrued on both krone- and foreign currency-denominated deposit accounts (including deposits under capital pension schemes) divided by average deposit balance in a quarter. † From 1994 onwards, calculated from interest accrued on krone-denominated deposit accounts (excluding deposits under capital pension schemes) divided by average deposit balance in a quarter.

Lending Rate:† Prior to 1990, weighted average of rates on overdrafts. From 1990 to 1993, calculated from interest accrued on both krone- and foreign currency-denominated loan accounts divided by average loan balance (including nonperforming loans from 1991) in a quarter. † From 1994 onwards, calculated from interest accrued on krone-denominated loan accounts divided by average loan balance in a quarter.

Government Bond Yield: † Prior to 1984, yield of perpetual bond. From 1984, yield on five-year government bonds.

Mortgage Bond Yield: † Before 1981, data relate to the 5 percent bonds with a remaining period to maturity of about 40 years. From 1981, yield on 20-year mortgage credit bonds.

Prices, Production, Labor

Wages, Hourly Earnings: Data are in kroner from source S and represent mainly male workers in manufacturing industries, including construction, employing 20 or more persons. † Prior to 1988, enterprises employing 6 or more persons were sampled. Annual data are calculated independently and are not an average of quarterly data.

Government Finance

† Beginning in 1970, annual data are as reported in the *Government Finance Statistics Yearbook* and cover consolidated central government. Data are derived from Statsregnskabet (central government accounts), accounts of government agencies, parish funds accounts, and social security funds accounts. Data through 1975 relate to a fiscal year different from calendar year.

National Accounts

† From 1988 onwards, data have been revised following the implementation of the *1993 SNA*.

Djibouti

Government Finance

† Data for 1979 cover budgetary central government and social security funds. † Data for 1980 and 1986 cover budgetary central government and operations of other Treasury accounts. † Data for 1981–85 and for 1988 cover budgetary central government only.

Dominica

National Accounts

As indicated by the country, the national accounts are compiled according to the recommendations of the *1993 SNA*.

Dominican Republic

Prices and Labor

† Prior to 1978, data refer only to consumer prices in Santo Domingo.

Ecuador

International Liquidity

† Beginning in 1999, includes monetary and nonmonetary gold.

Monetary Authorities

† Beginning in 1990 and in 1998, data are based on an improved sectorization and classification of the accounts. † Beginning in 1999, data reflect the introduction of the U.S. dollar as the main legal tender.

Deposit Money Banks

† Beginning in 1990, comprises private banks and the National Development Bank. † See note on monetary authorities.

Monetary Survey

† See note on monetary authorities.

Other Banking Institutions

† Beginning in 1990, comprises private finance companies, National Financial Corporation, Housing Bank of Ecuador, and savings and loans associations. † See note on monetary authorities.

Banking Survey

† See note on monetary authorities.

Interest Rates

Discount Rate (End of Period): † Beginning in 2000, legal rate charged by the Central Bank of Ecuador to discount eligible commercial paper offered by commercial banks in U.S. dollars.

Savings Rate: † Beginning in 1999, weighted average rate offered by private banks on savings deposits in U.S. dollars.

Deposit Rate: † Beginning in 1999, weighted average rate offered by private banks on 30- to 83-day time deposits in U.S. dollars.

Lending Rate: † Beginning in 1999, weighted average rate charged by private banks on 92- to 172-day loans in U.S. dollars.

International Transactions

† Trade data, which are derived from customs returns, have been updated with central bank payments data for current periods.

Government Finance

† Beginning in 1973, annual data are identical to data reported in the *Government Finance Statistics Yearbook* and cover budgetary central government. † Beginning in 1986, annual data are derived from monthly data.

Egypt

Monetary Authorities

† Beginning in 1980, data are based on improved classification and sectorization.

Deposit Money Banks

† See note on monetary authorities.

Monetary Survey

† See note on monetary authorities.

Other Banking Institutions

† See note on monetary authorities.

Government Finance

† Beginning in 1980, data relate to a fiscal year different from calendar year. † Prior to 1996, data include the operations of the Public Authority for Insurance and Pensions and the Public Authority for Social Insurance, which were incorrectly included as social security funds. Prior to 1996, data also exclude the operations of the General Authority for Supply of Commodities (GASC).

National Accounts

† Compilation procedures were revised in 1970. Data for 1970 to 1979 relate to calendar year. Beginning in 1980, data relate to a fiscal year ending June 30.

El Salvador

Monetary Authorities

† Prior to 1982, credit to certain institutions (mainly INCAFE and INAZUCAR) was included in *line 12d*. Beginning in 1982, data have been separately identified in *lines 12c* and *12f.* Also beginning in 1982, *line 17r* reflects the transfer of several accounts from it, mainly to *lines 16e* and *16f.*

Deposit Money Banks

† Beginning in 1982, data are based on an improved sectorization of the accounts.

Monetary Survey

† See notes on monetary authorities and deposit money banks.

Government Finance

† Beginning in 1994, data are derived from the Quarterly Review of the Central Reserve Bank of El Salvador and cover all central government operations of the budget and special funds.

Equatorial Guinea

Exchange Rates

Official Rate (End of Period and *Period Average):* † From 1999 onward, the CFA franc is pegged to the euro at a rate of CFA franc 655.957 per euro. Prior to 1999, the official rate was pegged to the French franc. † In 1994, the CFA franc was devalued to CFAF 100 per French franc from CFAF 50. Beginning in 1985, Equatorial Guinea joined the Central African monetary union, and the CFAF replaced the bipkwele.

Monetary Authorities

† Beginning in 1988, the sectorization and classification of accounts have been revised. † Beginning in 1991, *Claims on Central*

Government include government assumption of certain nonperforming bank loans.

Deposit Money Banks

† Beginning in 1991, the counterpart of government assumption of certain nonperforming bank loans was reclassified from *Credit from Monetary Authorities* to *Capital Accounts*.

Monetary Survey

† See notes on monetary authorities and deposit money banks.

Interest Rates

Discount Rate (End of Period): † From 1994 onward, rate charged by the BEAC to financial institutions on refinancing operations.

Deposit Rate: † From 1990 onward, minimum rate offered by deposit money banks on savings accounts.

Lending Rate: † From 1990 onward, maximum rate charged by deposit money banks on all loans, excluding charges and fees.

Estonia

Monetary Authorities

† Beginning in 1993, data are based on an improved sectorization and classification of the accounts.

Banking Survey

† See note on monetary authorities.

International Transactions

† Beginning in 1994, foreign trade statistics exclude re-exports.

National Accounts

As indicated by the country, the national accounts are compiled according to the recommendations of the *1993 SNA*.

Ethiopia

Deposit Money Banks

† Prior to 1979, loans and advances of the commercial banks were included in *Claims on Private Sector (line 22d)*. Beginning in 1979, these loans and advances are separated into *line 22d* and *Claims on Other Financial Institutions (line 22f)*. † Beginning in 1983, data are based on improved sectorization and classification of the accounts and exclude the Djibouti branch of the Commercial Bank of Ethiopia.

Monetary Survey

† See note on deposit money banks.

Government Finance

† Beginning in 1972, data are as reported in the *Government Finance Statistics Yearbook* and cover budgetary central government and some extrabudgetary accounts. † Starting in 1982, data cover budgetary central government only. † Beginning in 1992, data are as reported by the National Bank of Ethiopia, cover the operations of the budgetary central government, and include grants in kind

operations. Revenue data include loan repayments, and expenditure data include lending operations.

National Accounts

† Beginning in 1992, data exclude Eritrea. Also starting in 1992, *line 96f* includes a statistical discrepancy.

Euro Area

International Transactions

Balance of Payments: † Statistics for 1998 for the euro area, compiled by the European Central Bank (ECB), provide only a summary presentation of the key aggregates. Statistics are compiled by aggregating gross cross-border transactions of euro area residents vis-à-vis non-euro area residents as reported by the 11 participating counties. Transactions between residents of the participating member states are not included. The methodological concepts follow international standards (i.e., the IMF's *Balance of Payments Manual,* 5th edition); in addition, further harmonization proposals in special fields have been developed and agreed within the European System of Central Banks (ESCB), in consultation with the European Commission (Eurostat).

As euro area reserve assets flows for 1998 are aggregates of national data, they include transactions in instruments issued by other residents of the euro area; they do not correspond to the 1999 Eurosystem's definition of reserve assets.

† Following the participation of Greece in the Eurosystem, a break occurs beginning with the first quarter of 2001.

National Accounts

As indicated by the area, the national accounts are compiled according to the recommendations of the *1993 SNA*.

Fiji

Monetary Authorities

† Data refer to the Currency Board through 1973, to the Central Monetary Authority until 1983, and to the Reserve Bank of Fiji thereafter.

Monetary Survey

† See note on monetary authorities.

Government Finance

† Fiscal data from 1990 onward are as reported by the Reserve Bank of Fiji, rather than from the *Government Finance Statistics Yearbook*.

Finland

International Liquidity

† Beginning in 1999, *Total Reserves minus Gold (line 1l.d)* is defined in accordance with the Eurosystem's statistical definition of

international reserves. Data on lines *3..d*, *4..d*, *7a.d*, and *7b.d* are based on a Euro Area-wide definition of residency.

Banking Institutions

† Beginning in 1991, data are based on an improved sectorization of the accounts.

Banking Survey (National Residency)

† See note on banking institutions.

Prices, Production, Labor

Share Prices: † Beginning in 1987, index, base 1990, refers to the average of daily buying quotations.

Wages: Hourly Earnings: † Beginning in 1985, the series covers only manufacturing. Prior to 1985, series covers manufacturing, mining, and quarrying.

Government Finance

† Beginning in 1972 (1971 for debt data), annual data are as reported in the *Government Finance Statistics Yearbook* and cover consolidated central government.

National Accounts

† From 1988 onwards, data have been revised following the implementation of the *1995 ESA*.

France

International Liquidity

† Beginning in 1977, *line 7a.d* includes buyers' credits. † For data on lines *7a.b* and *7b.d*, beginning in 1978, see note on banking institutions.† Beginning in 1979, data on gold (*line 1ad*) and foreign exchange holdings exclude the deposits of the gold and gross U.S. dollar holdings made with the European Monetary Cooperation Fund (EMCF), which became the European Monetary Institute (EMI), and then the European Central Bank (ECB) in 1998; the holdings of ECUs issued by the EMCF against these deposits are included in *line 1d.d*. † Beginning in 1999, *Total Reserves minus Gold (line 1l.d)* is defined in accordance with the Eurosystem's statistical definition of international reserves. Data on *lines 3..d*, *4..d*, *7a.d*, and *7b.d* are based on a Euro Area-wide definition of residency.

Monetary Authorities

† Beginning in 1975, gold holdings in *line 11* are revalued at market price; the contra-entry of the valuation difference is included in *line 17r*. † Beginning in 1979, the ECU counterpart of the U.S. dollar and gold deposits with the EMCF is included in *line 11*; the contra-entry is recorded in *line 17a*, and the difference in valuation of gold between the Bank of France method and that of the EMCF is included in *line 17r*. † Between 1996 and 1998, gold receivables from EMI, and ECUs payable to the EMI were treated as off-balance-sheet items in accordance with the revised accounting system of the Bank of France.

Banking Institutions

† Beginning in 1977, data reflect institutional changes and an extension in coverage to include "finance companies" specializing in granting credits to households and private companies. † Begin-

ning in 1978, data reflect other institutional changes in the banking sector, including the development of new financial assets.

Banking Survey (National Residency)

† See notes on monetary authorities and banking institutions.

Prices, Production, Labor

Share Prices: † Prior to 1987, the index was calculated from a sample of 180 shares on the Paris exchange. Beginning in 1987, the index covers the common shares of 40 enterprises having the largest capitalization.

International Transactions

Unit Value data: † From January 1994 onwards, the methodology was changed to broaden the geographical coverage and to improve the validation procedures and the representativeness of the products selected.

Government Finance

† Beginning in 1972, data are as reported in the *Government Finance Statistics Yearbook* and cover consolidated central government (including extrabudgetary and social security accounts). Debt data are as reported by the Banque de France.

National Accounts

† From 1995 onwards, data have been revised following the implementation of the *1995 ESA*.

Gabon

Exchange Rates

Official Rate (End of Period and *Period Average):* † From 1999 onward, the CFA franc is pegged to the euro at a rate of CFA franc 655.957 per euro. Prior to 1999, the official rate was pegged to the French franc.† In 1994, the CFA franc was devalued to CFAF 100 per French franc from CFAF 50, at which it had been fixed since 1948.

Monetary Authorities

† Beginning in 1988, the sectorization and classification of accounts have been revised. † Starting in 1991, *Claims on Central Government* include government assumption of certain nonperforming bank loans.

Deposit Money Banks

† Beginning in 1977, data are based on improved sectorization of the accounts. † Starting in 1991, the counterpart of government assumption of certain nonperforming bank loans was reclassified from *Credit from Monetary Authorities* to *Capital Accounts*. † Beginning in 1992, the coverage of the banking system was revised. Claims and deposits of nonactive banks or banks in the process of liquidation have been excluded from the monetary accounts. See note on monetary authorities.

Monetary Survey

† See notes on monetary authorities and deposit money banks.

Interest Rates

Discount Rate (End of Period): † From 1994 onward, rate charged by the BEAC to financial institutions on refinancing operations.

Deposit Rate: † From 1990 onward, minimum rate offered by deposit money banks on savings accounts.

Lending Rate: † From 1990 onward, maximum rate charged by deposit money banks on all loans, excluding charges and fees.

Government Finance

† Prior to 1976, data cover Treasury accounts and the National Social Security Fund only. Beginning in 1976, data also cover operations of the Autonomous Amortization Fund, which is responsible for most foreign borrowing and related investment expenditures. † Starting in 1979, data cover the operations of the Treasury only. † Beginning in 1989, data are based on a revised budgetary nomenclature.

Gambia, The

Monetary Authorities

† Beginning in 1978, data are based on an improved sectorization of the domestic accounts. † Beginning in 1984, domestic currency deposits made by the government in lieu of external debt service payments (i.e., special accounts) have been placed in *line 16b*, with a contra-entry in *line 16c*. From the same date onward, deposit money bank deposits with the central bank, arising from the receipt from the customers of domestic currency payments on account of external debt service (i.e., commercial arrears), have been treated similarly. In addition, *line 16b* includes the contra-entry of The Gambia Produce Marketing Board export proceeds, because access to that account is limited.

Deposit Money Banks

† See note on monetary authorities. † Beginning in 1984, a contra-entry to domestic currency payments received from customers to meet external debt service obligations (i.e., commercial arrears) is shown in *line 26b*.

Monetary Survey

† See notes on monetary authorities and deposit money banks.

Government Finance

† Beginning in 1972, data are as reported in the *Government Finance Statistics Yearbook* and cover budgetary central government. † In 1990, data also include selected extrabudgetary accounts.

Georgia

Monetary Authorities

† Beginning in 2001, data reflect the introduction of a new plan of accounts, which provides an improved sectorization and classification of the accounts.

Deposit Money Banks

† See note on monetary authorities.

Monetary Survey

† See note on monetary authorities.

Germany

With the coming into effect on July 1, 1990 of the treaty on German Economic, Monetary, and Social Union (GEMSU) between the former Federal Republic of Germany (FRG) and the former German Democratic Republic (GDR), the deutsche mark became the sole currency of the GEMSU area, and customs borders between the two states were abolished. On October 3, 1990, the former GDR became part of the FRG under international law. The membership of the FRG in the Fund, under the designation Germany, remains unchanged. The presentation of exchange rates and Fund accounts shown for Germany in *IFS* is unaffected by the unification of the former FRG and the former GDR.

Data on international liquidity, money and banking, and international transactions cover the former FRG and the former GDR beginning with end-June (second quarter) 1990 for stock data and July 1990 for flow data. Data on prices, production, labor market, and national accounts cover the former FRG and the former GDR from 1991 onward. Data on industrial employment and wages refer only to the former FRG.

International Liquidity

† Beginning in 1999, *Total Reserves minus Gold (line 1l.d)* is defined in accordance with the Eurosystem's statistical definition of international reserves. Data on lines *3..d*, *4..d*, *7a.d*, and *7b.d* are based on a Euro Area-wide definition of residency.

Banking Institutions

† Beginning in 1985, coverage of financial institutions was broadened to include all cooperative banks.

Banking Survey (National Residency)

† See note on banking institutions.

Government Finance

† Beginning in 1970, data are as reported in the *Government Finance Statistics Yearbook* and cover consolidated central government, including extrabudgetary and social security accounts. † Data for social security funds and the European Recovery Program are on a cash basis only beginning in 1974 and 1975, respectively. † Beginning in 1990, central government extrabudgetary operations include operations of the German Unity Fund. † Prior to 1992, data cover government operations on the territory of the former Federal Republic of Germany; beginning in 1992, data refer to government operations on the territory of unified Germany. † From 1995 on, the debts of the Treuhandanstalt, classified as a nonfinancial corporation, have been assumed by the Redemption Fund for Inherited Liabilities, a central government body.

National Accounts

† From 1991 onwards, concepts and definitions are in accordance with the *1995 ESA*.

Ghana

Monetary Authorities

† Beginning in 1991, data reflect the introduction of a new reporting system.

Deposit Money Banks

† Beginning in 1973, the classification of claims on the private sector and claims on the public enterprises is revised. † See note on monetary authorities.

Monetary Survey

† See notes on monetary authorities and deposit money banks.

Government Finance

† For the period 1972–82, data relate to a fiscal year different from calendar year (ends June 30).

Greece

International Liquidity

† Prior to 1975, data on *Foreign Exchange (line 1d.d)* exclude import documentary credit at the time of opening of the account. Beginning in 1975, data exclude such credit at time of payment. † Beginning in 1986, data on *Gold* and *Foreign Exchange* exclude the deposits made with the European Monetary Institute (EMI) of gold and gross U.S. dollar holdings; the holdings of European currency units (ECUs) issued by the EMI against these deposits are included in *line 1d.d. Gold (National Valuation) (line 1and):* † Before 1985, gold was valued at SDR 35 per fine troy ounce. Beginning in 1985, gold is revalued each December at 65 percent of the average buying market price of gold during that month.

Monetary Authorities

† Beginning in 1987, the data reflect improved classification in the report forms.

Banking Institutions

† See note on monetary authorities.

Banking Survey (National Residency)

† See note on monetary authorities.

Interest Rates

Central Bank Rate: † Prior to 1998, discount rate offered by the Bank of Greece and, thereafter, rate on deposits of 14-day maturity placed with the Bank of Greece.

Deposit Rate: † Prior to1988, maximum rate offered by deposit money banks on three- to six-month drachma deposits by individuals and enterprises. Beginning in 1988, data refer to deposits with a maturity of three to twelve months.

Lending Rate: † Prior to 1999, rate on short-term loans to enterprises and households and, thereafter, rate on short-term loans to enterprises only.

National Accounts

† Beginning in 1988, a statistical discrepancy is included in *line 93i* but, prior to 1988, is in *lines 99a* and *99b*. † Beginning in 1995, concepts and definitions are in accordance with the *1995 ESA*.

Grenada

Monetary Authorities

† For the period 1975 through 1978 *lines 11* and *14* include net local interbank claims of commercial banks as a proxy for banks' deposits with Eastern Caribbean Central Bank (ECCB).

Deposit Money Banks

† For the period 1975 through 1978, *lines 20, 21,* and *26c* include net local interbank claims of commercial banks as a proxy for banks' deposits with ECCB. Beginning in 1979, the data reflect improved reporting of commercial bank accounts with the ECCB (*line 20*) and with branches in other member countries (*lines 20, 21,* and *26c*).

Monetary Survey

† See note on deposit money banks.

Government Finance

† Prior to 1978 and from 1991 onward, data are as reported in the *Government Finance Statistics Yearbook*. From 1978 through 1980, data are as reported by the Ministry of Finance for publication in *IFS*.

National Accounts

As indicated by the country, the national accounts are compiled according to the recommendations of the *1993 SNA*.

Guatemala

Monetary Authorities

† Beginning in 1997, data are based on an improved sectorization of the accounts.

Deposit Money Banks

† See note on monetary authorities.

Monetary Survey

† See note on monetary authorities.

Other Banking Institutions

† Beginning in 1990, comprises Financiera Industrial y Agropecuaria S. A. (FIASA), Financiera Guatemalteca S. A. (FIGSA), Financiera Industrial S. A. (FISA), Financiera de Inversion S. A. (FIVSA), Financiera del Pais S. A. (FIPASA), and Corporacion Financiera Nacional (CORFINA).† See note on monetary authorities.

Banking Survey

† See notes on monetary authorities and other banking institutions.

Interest Rates

Deposit Rate: † Beginning in 1997, weighted average rate offered by commercial banks on time and savings deposits. The rate is weighted by deposit amounts.

Lending Rate: † Beginning in 1997, weighted average rate charged by commercial banks on loans. The rate is weighted by loan amounts.

Government Finance

† Prior to 1994, revenue data included grants, and expenditure data included lending minus repayments. Expenditure is not adjusted for changes in floating debt.

Guinea

Monetary Authorities

† Beginning in 1996, *Claims on Other Banking Institutions (line 12f)* excludes the Caisse Nationale de Sécurité Sociale (CNSS), which is included under *Claims on Central Government (line 12a)*.

Guinea-Bissau

Exchange Rates

Official Rate (End of Period and *Period Average):* † Beginning in 1999, the CFAF is pegged to the euro at a rate of CFA franc 655.957 per euro. Prior to 1999, the official rate was pegged to the French franc at the rate of CFAF 100 per French franc.

Monetary Authorities

† Beginning in 1997, data reflect Guinea-Bissau's entry into the West African Monetary Union and the compilation of the data on the Central Bank of West African States' (BCEAO's) basis.

Deposit Money Banks

† See note on monetary authorities.

Monetary Survey

† See note on monetary authorities.

Government Finance

† Prior to 1987, data are as reported in the *Government Finance Statistics Yearbook (GFSY)* and cover budgetary central government. Beginning in 1987, data are derived from Ministry of Finance sources and cover budgetary central government.

Guyana

Monetary Authorities

† Beginning in 1993, data are based on an improved reporting system.

Monetary Survey

† See note on monetary authorities.

Banking Survey

† See note on monetary authorities.

Government Finance

† Beginning in 1970, data as reported by the Central Bank of Guyana cover budgetary central government. † Prior to 1986, foreign debt comprises central government debt; beginning in 1986, foreign debt also includes debt of the Bank of Guyana and public guaranteed debt.

Haiti

Monetary Authorities

† Beginning in 1997, data are based on an improved sectorization of the accounts.

Deposit Money Banks

† See note on monetary authorities.

Monetary Survey

† See note on monetary authorities.

National Accounts

† *Line 96f* includes government consumption expenditures.

Honduras

Monetary Authorities

† Beginning in 1997, data are based on an improved sectorization of the accounts.

Deposit Money Banks

† See note on monetary authorities.

Monetary Survey

† See note on monetary authorities.

Other Banking Institutions

† Beginning in 1997, comprises development banks, savings and loans associations, and finance companies. See note on monetary authorities.

Banking Survey

† See note on monetary authorities.

Government Finance

† Prior to 1991, data on capital revenue and expenditure are not included.

Hungary

Monetary Authorities

† Beginning in 1990, *Claims on Central Government* include debt of the central budget, owing to valuation differences previously recorded in *Valuation Changes (line 17rv). Time and Foreign Currency Deposits* include foreign currency deposits of banking institutions.

Banking Institutions

† Beginning in 1990, *Demand Deposits (line 24)* include sight forint deposits of households, previously shown in *Time, Savings, and Foreign Currency Deposits (line 25)*. Prior to 1990, demand deposits included only current accounts of domestic nonbanks.

Banking Survey

† See notes on monetary authorities and banking institutions.

Interest Rates

Deposit Rate: † Beginning in 1990, weighted average rate offered by banking institutions on deposits from entrepreneurs with original maturity of more than one month but less than one year.

Prices, Production, Labor

Consumer Prices: † Prior to 1985, the consumer price index compares current month item prices with their levels in the same month of the base year. From 1985 forward, the index compares current item prices with their average level in 1985.

Government Finance

† Beginning in 1991, annual data are as reported by the Ministry of Finance and cover the consolidated operations of the central government, namely, the central budget, social security funds, and extrabudgetary funds. Lending minus repayments data do not include privatization receipts.

National Accounts

As indicated by the country, the national accounts are compiled according to the recommendations of the *1993 SNA*.

Iceland

Interest Rates

Discount Rate (End of Period): † Data prior to 1992 refer to central bank rates on overdrafts to deposit money banks. Beginning in 1992, data refer to central bank's discount rate on loans on bills. Data beginning in 1998 refer to Central bank's discount rate on overnight loans.

Treasury Bill Rate: † Prior to 1992, data refer to yields set by the government in the primary market. Beginning in 1992, data refer to annualized secondary market yield on 90-day treasury bills.

Deposit Rate: † Prior to 1988, data refer to interest rate on 3-month deposits. † From 1988, data refer to interest rate on 12-month deposits.

Government Finance

Prior to 1998, data are as reported in the *Government Finance Statistics Yearbook* and cover consolidated central government. Beginning in 1998, the data cover the operations of budgetary central government and are not adjusted to a cash basis as in previous years.

National Accounts

As indicated by the country, the national accounts are compiled according to the recommendations of the *1993 SNA*.

India

Deposit Money Banks

† Since 1978, a new classification of *Demand* and *Time Deposits* has reduced *lines 24* and *34* and increased *lines 25* and *35*.

Interest Rates

Government Bond Yield: † Beginning in 1971, this rate is the average yield on government 5½ percent bonds maturing in the years 1999 and 2000.

Government Finance

† Beginning in 1974, data are as reported in the *Government Finance Statistics Yearbook* and cover consolidated central government. Data are reported by the Ministry of Finance.

National Accounts

† From 1987 onwards, data have been revised following the implementation of the *1993 SNA*.

Indonesia

Monetary Authorities

† Beginning in 1992, data are based on improved classification and reporting of accounts.

Deposit Money Banks

† See note on monetary authorities.

Monetary Survey

† See note on monetary authorities.

Interest Rates

Deposit Rate: † Beginning in 1990, weighted average rate paid by commercial banks on three-month deposits.

Prices, Production, Labor

† Prior to 1979, the CPI series is based on an index that covered Djakarta only. Between 1979 and 1990, the CPI series is based on a survey of 17 capital cities. † Beginning in 1990, index covers 27 provincial capital cities.

Government Finance

† Prior to 1972, data are as reported for *IFS*. Beginning in 1972, data are as reported in the *Government Finance Statistics Yearbook* and cover consolidated central government.

Iran, Islamic Republic of

International Transactions

† Beginning in 1980, data on the value and volume of oil exports and on the value of total exports are rough estimates based on information published in various petroleum industry journals.

Balance of Payments: † Prior to 1976, year ending December 31.

Government Finance

† Prior to 1988, the consolidated central government data exclude the operations of the Organization for Protection of Consumers and Producers.

Ireland

International Liquidity

† Beginning in 1999, *Total Reserves minus Gold (line 1l.d)* is defined in accordance with the Eurosystem's statistical definition of international reserves. Data on lines *3..d, 4..d, 7a.d,* and *7b.d* are based on a Euro Area-wide definition of residency.

Banking Institutions

† Beginning in 1982, data reflect the introduction of an improved call report form, which for the first time records data of resident offices on a residency-of-customer basis. From that date, the activities of nonresident offices are, therefore, excluded from the data, and accounts of nonresidents at resident offices are classified under *Foreign Assets (line 21)* and *Foreign Liabilities (line 26c)*.

Banking Survey (National Residency)

† See notes on banking institutions. † Beginning in 1982, *line 34* reflects changes affecting the data on banking institutions, includ-

ing improved sectorization, the exclusion of nonresident accounts, and a change in the method of allocating items in transit.

Nonbank Financial Institutions:

† Prior to 1995, consolidated the accounts of building societies, state-sponsored financial institutions, trustees' savings banks, hire-purchase finance companies, national installment savings, and the post office savings bank.

Interest Rates

Discount Rate (End of Period): † Prior to 1979, data refer to the discount rate. Afterward, data refer to short-term facility rate charged by the Bank of Ireland on funds, up to a specified quota, lent to banks experiencing day-to-day liquidity shortages.

Lending Rate: † Prior to 1992, data refer to the rate charged to AAA customers in the primary, manufacturing, and service sectors.

National Accounts

† Source S. Data are based on the *1995 ESA*. Prior to 1990, data are based on the *1979 ESA*.

Israel

Deposit Money Banks

† Beginning in 1992, other deposits, which were previously included in *Time and Savings Deposits (line 25),* are included in *Demand Deposits (line 24).* Earmarked government deposits, which were previously included in *Restricted Deposits (line 26b),* are included in *Central Government Deposits (line 26d).* A new reporting procedure was also introduced, which resulted in other changes in the classification of accounts.

Monetary Survey

† See note on deposit money banks.

Prices, Production, Labor

† As of 1979, the indices for wages, industrial production, and industrial employment exclude the diamond sector. *Wages: Daily Earnings:* † Prior to 1978, the series covered workers only. As of that date, it is based on all employees.

International Transactions

Export and *Import Unit Value* indices: † Prior to 1976, indices are Paasche indices; beginning in 1976, they are Laspeyres indices; from 1984 onwards they are compiled using Fischer's ideal formula. The weights are revised every two years. For example, for 1981 the weights are calculated on the basis of Israel's trade in 1979.

Government Finance

† Beginning in 1972, data are as reported in the *Government Finance Statistics Yearbook* and cover budgetary central government. † Beginning in 1974, data also include social security funds. † Through 1991, fiscal years begin April 1; from 1992 onward, fiscal years end December 31. † Break symbols in 1991 data indicate that data refer to the nine-month period April 1 through December 31.

National Accounts

† Source S. From 1995 onward, data are compiled according to the *1993 SNA*, and *line 99b.p* data are annually chained using the prices of the previous year.

Italy

International Liquidity

† Beginning in 1999, *Total Reserves minus Gold (line 11.d)* is defined in accordance with the Eurosystem's statistical definition of international reserves. Data on lines *3..d, 4..d, 7a.d,* and *7b.d* are based on a Euro Area-wide definition of residency.

Banking Institutions

† Beginning in 1989, data are based on improved classification following the adoption by the Bank of Italy of the sectoral classification and definitions based on the *1995 ESA.*

Banking Survey (National Residency)

† See note on banking institutions.

Interest Rates

Money Market Rate: † Beginning in 1991, data represent arithmetic averages of daily rates, which are weighted averages of rates (based on the volume of transactions for the day).

Lending Rate: † Beginning in 1990, data refer to the average rate charged by banking institutions and specialized credit institutions on short-term lira loans.

Government Bond Yield: Long-Term Rate: † Prior to 1991, the data are average yields to maturity on bonds with original maturities of 15 to 20 years, issued on behalf of the Treasury by the Consortium of Credit for Public Works. *Medium-Term Rate:* † Prior to 1991, the data are average yields to maturity on treasury bonds with maximum original maturities of 9 years.

Government Finance

† Beginning in 1993, data exclude all autonomous government agencies except the State Roads Agency. However, debt data include the debts of the above-mentioned agencies assumed by the government, and expenditure data include the corresponding interest payments. Revenue data include privatization proceeds.

National Accounts

† Data from 1998 onwards are in accordance with the *1995 ESA.*

Jamaica

Deposit Money Banks

† Prior to 1973, *Demand Deposits* and *Time and Savings Deposits* include nonresident deposits. Beginning in that year, nonresident deposits are included in *Foreign Liabilities.*

Monetary Survey

† See note on deposit money banks.

Banking Survey

† See note on deposit money banks.

Japan

International Liquidity

† Beginning in 1973, data for *lines 7a.d* and *7b.d* include long-term foreign accounts and therefore are not the U.S. dollar equiv-

alents of *lines 21* and *26c,* which comprise only short-term accounts; data are from the Bank for International Settlement's *Annual Report* and *Quarterly Press Release.*

Monetary Authorities

† Prior to 1978, *line 11* was reported on a gross basis with foreign liabilities being included in *line 17r.* Beginning in 1978, data for *line 11* are provided net of foreign liabilities.

Monetary Survey

† See note on monetary authorities.

Financial Survey

† Beginning in 1997, data cover Bank of Japan, other depository corporations, insurance corporations and pension funds, other financial intermediaries, and financial auxiliaries as defined in *Guide to Japan's Flow of Funds Accounts.* Other depository corporations include domestically-licensed banks, foreign-owned banks in Japan, financial institutions for agriculture, forestry, and fisheries. Other financial intermediaries include securities investment trusts, nonbank financial institutions, public financial institutions, and financial dealers and brokers. Financial auxiliaries include institutions that guarantee financial instruments, stock exchange, clearing house, and foreign exchange brokers. Social security funds are excluded from government sector. *Liquid Liabilities (line 55l)* comprise currency outside financial corporations and deposits at financial corporations held by all resident sectors except central government, excluding deposits with the Trust Fund Bureau. *Bonds (line 56ab)* are securities other than shares. *Deposits with Trust Fund Bureau (line 56b)* comprise deposits at the Trust Fund Bureau held by public institutions excluding central government. Data are end-of-period stocks and are derived from Japan's flow of funds accounts quarterly publication with some adjustments to conform with the IMF methodology. Claims on social security funds are included in *Other Items (Net) (line 57r).* Also included in *Other Items (Net)* are liabilities in the form of loans from resident nonfinancial, nongovernment sectors and financial derivatives with resident private nonfinancial sectors.

Interest Rates

Money Market Rate: † Beginning in 1990, lending rate for collateral and overnight loans in the Tokyo Call Money Market.

Private Bill Rate: † Beginning in 1991, rate on newly issued certificates of three-month deposits.

Deposit Rate: † Beginning in 1992, average interest rate for the last week of the month on unregulated three-month time deposits, ranging in size from three million yen to under ten million yen.

Lending Rate: † Before 1993, the lending rate excluded overdrafts. Beginning in 1993, the rate is the weighted average of contracted interest rates charged by all banks on short- and long-term loans, discounts, and overdrafts.

Government Bond Yield: † Prior to 1999, arithmetic average yield to maturity of all ordinary government bonds. Beginning in 1999, arithmetic average yield on newly issued government bonds with 10-year maturity.

International Transactions

Balance of Payments: † Balance of payments data prior to 1991 were converted to the format of the fifth edition of the *Balance of Payments Manual* using a set of conversion keys developed by the Fund.

Government Finance

† Beginning in 1975, data are as reported in the *Government Finance Statistics Yearbook.* † Prior to 1991, data cover budgetary central government only. From 1991 onwards, data (excluding debt data) cover consolidated central government. Also beginning in 1991, data for financing abroad and foreign debt are included in domestic financing and domestic debt, respectively.

National Accounts

† From 1980 onwards, data have been revised following the implementation of the *1993 SNA.*

Jordan

International Liquidity

† During 1991–93, reported holdings of foreign currency are net of foreign currency deposits of licensed banks at the Central Bank of Jordan.

Monetary Authorities

† Beginning in 1993, *lines 11* and *14* reflect foreign currency deposits of licensed banks.

Deposit Money Banks

† Beginning in 1993, *line 26d* includes deposits of the Social Security Corporation, which previously were included in *lines 24* and *25.*

Monetary Survey

† See notes on monetary authorities and deposit money banks.

Other Banking Institutions

† Prior to 1993, comprises the Industrial Development Bank, the Agricultural Credit Corporation, and the Municipal Loan Fund. Beginning in 1993, comprises Cities and Villages Development Bank, Agricultural Credit Corporation, Industrial Development Bank, the Housing Corporation, and Jordan Cooperative Organization.

National Accounts

† Beginning in 1992, data are compiled in accordance with the *1993 SNA.*

Kazakhstan

Monetary Authorities

† Beginning in 1997, the monetary authorities comprise the National Bank of Kazakhstan (NBK) only, and the data are compiled according to the new chart of accounts for the NBK.

Deposit Money Banks

† Prior to 1997, *Demand Deposits (line 24)* includes all deposit liabilities. Subsequently, the data for the commercial banks include

data for the Republican Budget Bank. *Other Deposits (line 25)* includes restricted deposits.

Monetary Survey

† See notes on monetary authorities and deposit money banks.

Interest Rates

Refinancing Rate (End of Period): † Annualized interest rate until 1995; thereafter, compound annual rate, which is established as the minimum interest rate for NBK auctions of credit to commercial banks.

National Accounts

As indicated by the country, the national accounts are compiled according to the recommendations of the *1993 SNA*.

Kenya

Government Finance

† Through 1996, expenditure data are on a commitment basis. Beginning in 1997, expenditure data are on a cash basis. Domestic financing data through 1996 include privatization proceeds, the adjustment of expenditure data to a cash basis, as well as the statistical discrepancy. Beginning in 1997, revenue data include privatization proceeds, and the statistical discrepancy is identified separately.

Korea

International Liquidity

† Beginning in 1988, *line 7a.d* includes claims of foreign banks' branches on nonresidents.

Interest Rates

Deposit Rate: † From 1996 onward, the rate is an average, weighted by the amount of deposits for periods of one year or more but less than two years at the nationwide commercial banks.

Lending Rate: † From 1996 onward, the rate is an average, weighted by new loans extended during the period by nationwide commerical banks.

Government Finance

† Beginning in 1970, data are as reported in the *Government Finance Statistics Yearbook* and cover consolidated central government.

Kuwait

Deposit Money Banks

† Prior to 1981, consolidates commercial banks only. Beginning in 1981, consolidates commercial banks, specialized banks, and Kuwait Finance House.

Monetary Survey

† See notes on deposit money banks.

Government Finance

† Beginning in 1972, data include year-end adjustments that were not available for earlier years and also adjustments resulting from the treatment on a net basis of nonfinancial public enterprises. † Fiscal year ends March 31 through 1971; ends June 30 thereafter. † Beginning in 1974, data cover the operations of the budgetary central government and are presented on a calendar year basis to allow comparison with other Kuwaiti macroeconomic data.

Kyrgyz Republic

National Accounts

As indicated by the country, the national accounts are compiled according to the recommendations of the *1993 SNA*. GDP by major expenditure category at current prices is estimated using the *1993 SNA* framework. From 1993 onward, estimates have been made for unrecorded production, trade, and household consumption.

Lao People's Democratic Republic

Exchange Rates

† Data prior to 1991 refer to the midpoint between the buying and selling rates quoted by state-owned commercial banks. Beginning in 1991, data refer to the midpoint between the buying and selling rates quoted by the Bank of Lao P.D.R. (central bank). † In 1995, a floating exchange rate policy was adopted, and the commercial banks were allowed to set their rates. Data beginning in 1995 refer to the simple average of midpoint rates reported by the commercial banks on a daily basis, covering their transactions for the previous day.

Interest Rates

Deposit Rate: † Prior to 1991, the rate set by the Bank of Lao P.D.R. on commercial banks' three-month domestic-currency time deposits. Beginning in 1991, minimum rate fixed by the Bank of Lao P.D.R. on commercial banks' three-month domestic-currency time deposits.

Lending Rate: † Prior to 1993, data refer to the rate set by the Bank of Lao P.D.R. on commercial banks' short-term loans to the commerce and services sectors. From 1993 to 1995, data refer to the maximum rate set by the Bank of Lao P.D.R. for commercial banks' nonagricultural loans. † The lending rate was liberalized in 1995; data beginning then refer to the highest rate quoted by the commercial banks on nonagricultural loans.

Latvia

Banking Institutions

† Prior to 1994, data for *Claims on Central Government* and *Central Government Deposits* comprise accounts that were maintained on a cumulative flow basis. Thereafter, these data are on a stock basis. Beginning in 1994, data are based on an improved sectorization and classification of the accounts.

Banking Survey

† See note on banking institutions.

Government Finance

† Data prior to 1996 cover the budgetary central government only. From January through March 1996, data cover the budgetary central government and the Social Security Fund. From April 1996 onward, data cover the budgetary central government, the Social Security Fund, and the special budgets. † From 1997 onwards, expenditure on education and health functions was shifted within components of central government and between local governments and central government. † Prior to 1998, data are not consolidated. Beginning in 1998, data are presented on a consolidated basis.

National Accounts

As indicated by the country, the national accounts are compiled according to the recommendations of the *1993 SNA*.

Lebanon

Interest Rates

Treasury Bill Rate: † Beginning in 1986, secondary market yield on three-month treasury bills determined by the Central Bank of Lebanon.

Lesotho

Interest Rates

Treasury Bill Rate: † Beginning in 1994, average rate of three issues of 91-day treasury bills. The rate is determined through securities auctions conducted by the Central Bank of Lesotho.

Liberia

Monetary Authorities

† Beginning in 1980, and in 2000, data are based on an improved sectorization and classification of the accounts.

Banking Institutions

† See note on monetary authorities.

Banking Survey

† See note on monetary authorities.

Interest Rates

Lending Rate: † Beginning in 1998, average rate offered by commercial banks on all loans.

Government Finance

† During the period 1977–87, data relate to a fiscal year different from calendar year (fiscal year ends June 30).

Libya

Exchange Rates

In 1971 the Libyan dinar, equal to the Libyan pound, was introduced.

Monetary Authorities

† Beginning in 1997, date are based on improved reporting and classification of accounts.

Deposit Money Banks

† Prior to 1999, some central government time deposits are included in *Time and Foreign Currency Deposits (line 25)*.

Monetary Survey

† See notes on monetary authorities and deposit money banks.

Lithuania

Banking Institutions

† Beginning in 1994, overdrafts, which were previously included in *Claims on the Private Sector,* are properly sectorized.

Banking Survey

† See note on banking institutions.

Government Finance

† In 1997, expenditure on health functions and their financing were shifted from local to central government.

National Accounts

As indicated by the country, the national accounts are compiled according to the recommendations of the *1993 SNA*.

Luxembourg

International Liquidity

† Beginning in 1989, data on gold holdings exclude the gold deposits made with the European Monetary Institute (EMI), which became the European Central Bank (ECB) in 1998; the holdings of European currency units (ECUs) issued by the EMI against these gold deposits are included in *line 1d.d.* † Beginning in 1999, *Total Reserves minus Gold (line 1l.d)* is defined in accordance with the Eurosystem's statistical definition of international reserves. Data on lines *3..d*, *4..d*, *7a.d*, and *7b.d* are based on a Euro Area-wide definition of residency.

Banking Institutions

† Reflect significant changes in the reporting by the commercial banks to the Institut Monétaire Luxembourgeois that commenced at the end of 1992.

Banking Survey (National Residency)

† See note on banking institutions.

Interest Rates

Government Bond Yield: † Weighted average yield to final maturity of all government bonds quoted in the Luxembourg Stock

Exchange. Before 1978, data referred to the average weighted yield to average maturity as then calculated by the Luxembourg stock exchange.

National Accounts

As indicated by the country, the national accounts are compiled according to the recommendations of the *1993 SNA*.

Macedonia

Monetary Authorities

† Prior to 1995, local governments were included in central government, and nonfinancial public enterprises and some government units were included in the private sector.

Monetary Survey

† See note on monetary authorities.

International Transactions

International Investment Position: † Data are incomplete. Banking and official sector data are included. Private sector transactions are partially covered.

National Accounts

As indicated by the country, the national accounts are compiled according to the recommendations of the *1993 SNA*.

Madagascar

Monetary Authorities

† Beginning in 1979, claims on public enterprises are separately identified.

Deposit Money Banks

† Beginning in 1979, data are based on an improved classification; as a result, bonds, central government lending funds, and credit from the central bank are separately identified.

Monetary Survey

† See notes on monetary authorities and deposit money banks.

Government Finance

† Prior to 1972, data are as reported by the Central Bank of the Republic of Madagascar for publication in *IFS*. Beginning in 1972, data are as reported in the *Government Finance Statistics Yearbook (GFSY)* and cover the general budget, the *Caisse nationale de prevoyance sociale* (National Social Security Fund), and the *Office des anciens combattants* (Veterans' Office).† Beginning in 1988, *GFSY* data cover the general budget and extrabudgetary units excluding social security.

Malawi

Other Banking Institutions

† Beginning in 1988, data exclude the accounts for the Post Office Savings Bank.

Prices, Production, and Labor

Consumer Prices: † Beginning in 1991, the index covers the cities of Blantyre, Lilongwe, Mzuzu, and Zomba, base 1990. *Industrial Production:* † Base 1984. Prior to 1988, manufacturing production, base 1970.

Government Finance

Beginning in 1971, data are as reported in the *Government Finance Statistics Yearbook* and cover budgetary central government.

Malaysia

Monetary Authorities

† Beginning in 1992, comprises the Bank Negara Malaysia only. † Beginning in 1996, data are based on an improved sectorization of the accounts.

Deposit Money Banks

† Beginning in 1980, claims on other banking institutions (*line 22f*), which were previously included in *line 27r*, are shown separately. † Beginning in 1992, data are based on an improved sectorization of the accounts. † See note on monetary authorities.

Monetary Survey

† See notes on monetary authorities and deposit money banks.

Other Banking Institutions

† Beginning in 1974, includes merchant banks. † Starting in 1992, comprises finance companies, merchant banks, and discount houses and excludes National Savings Bank and the Employees Provident Fund. † See note on monetary authorities.

Banking Survey

† See notes on monetary authorities, deposit money banks, and other banking institutions.

Interest Rates

Money Market Rate: † Beginning in 1996, average overnight interbank rate.

Deposit Rate: † Beginning in 1996, weighted average rate offered by commercial banks on new three-month time deposits. The rate is weighted by deposit amounts.

Lending Rate: † Beginning in 1996, weighted average base lending rate charged by commercial banks. The rate is weighted by loan amounts.

Government Finance

† Prior to 1970, quarterly and annual data differ from source B in that, in *IFS*, special receipts (foreign grants) are included in *Revenue (line 81)* instead of being considered as a financing item; lending minus repayments comprise repayment of lending made through the Development Fund; and the gold subscription to the Fund (made by the government) is excluded from *Expenditure (line 82)* and *Use of Cash Balances (line 87)*. † Beginning in 1997, special receipts are included in *Use of Cash Balances (line 87)*.

Maldives

Monetary Authorities

† Before 1981, the data relate to the monetary authority functions of the Department of Finance (Treasury) and the State Trading Organization, which managed a large part of the official foreign exchange holdings. Beginning in 1981, comprises the Maldives Monetary Authority only, which was established in that year. *Claims on Central Government (line 12a):* † Prior to 1985, data include claims on nonfinancial public enterprises. *Foreign Liabilities (line 16c):* † Prior to 1985, data include amounts of government foreign borrowing, with a contra-entry in *Claims on Central Government (line 12a).*

Deposit Money Banks

† Beginning in 1981, data are based on an improved sectorization of the accounts. *Foreign Liabilities (line 26c):* † Prior to 1985, data exclude nonresident deposits with domestic banks.

Monetary Survey

† See notes on monetary authorities and deposit money banks.

Mali

Exchange Rates

Official Rate (End of Period and *Period Average):* † From 1999 onward, the CFA franc is pegged to the euro at a rate of CFA franc 655.957 per euro. Prior to 1999, the official rate was pegged to the French franc. † In 1994 the CFA franc was devalued to CFAF 100 per French franc from CFAF 50, at which it had been fixed since 1948.

Monetary Authorities

† Beginning in 1975, data are based on an improved sectorization of the accounts. † At the end of 1983, data reflect the consolidation and transfer to the government of the central bank's liabilities under the operations account and the cancellation of certain loans to the government and to state enterprises. Beginning in 1984, data reflect Mali's re-entry into the West African Monetary Union and the compilation of the data on the Central Bank of West African States' (BCEAO's) basis.

Deposit Money Banks

† Beginning in 1979, data are based on an improved sectorization of the accounts. † See note on monetary authorities.

Monetary Survey

† See notes on monetary authorities and deposit money banks.

Prices

Consumer Prices: † Beginning in 1997, BCEAO harmonized index, base 1996.

Government Finance

† Beginning in 1980, data also cover extrabudgetary foreign grants and loans not recorded in the treasury accounts. † Data for 1980 and 1981 do not cover social security operations. † From 1989 to 1997, net lending and privatization receipts are included in revenue.

Malta

Banking Institutions

† Beginning in 1995, data for offshore banks (international banking institutions) have been included in the consolidation.

Banking Survey

† See note on banking institutions.

Government Finance

† Prior to 1979, data relate to a fiscal year different from calendar year (fiscal year ends April 1 through 1978).

Mauritania

Monetary Authorities

† The sectorization and classification of accounts have been revised from 1989 onward.

Deposit Money Banks

† See note on monetary authorities.

Monetary Survey

† See note on monetary authorities.

Government Finance

† Prior to 1978, data cover budgetary and social security operations. Beginning in 1978, data also cover extrabudgetary operations. † Beginning in 1990, data cover the consolidated operations of the treasury and operations financed with foreign resources not recorded in the treasury accounts.

Mauritius

Government Finance

† Prior to 1973, data are as reported by the Bank of Mauritius for publication in *IFS*. Beginning in 1973, data are as published in the *Government Finance Statistics Yearbook (GFSY)* and cover budgetary central government.† Changes in the coverage of the consolidated central government in 1983, 1988, 1989, 1992, 1993, and 1994 are as specified in the *GFSY*.

Mexico

Monetary Authorities

† Beginning in 1977, data are based on an improved sectorization of the accounts. † Beginning in 1997, data reflect methodological changes in compilation.

Deposit Money Banks

† Comprises only commercial banks through 1976. Beginning in 1977, comprises commercial banks and national credit corporations. See note on monetary authorities. † Beginning in 1982, data reflect the introduction of a new plan of accounts, which provides an improved sectorization of domestic and foreign accounts. † Be-

ginning in 1997, data reflect changes in the chart of accounts, accounting criteria, and the methodology for compiling monetary accounts, which identify positions with nonresidents and the various domestic sectors by financial instrument.

Monetary Survey

† See notes on monetary authorities and deposit money banks.

Other Banking Institutions

† Prior to 1977, national credit institutions other than commercial banks were also included, and rediscount operations were not included, since they were classified under contingency or memorandum accounts. Beginning in 1977, comprises development banks. See note on monetary authorities. † See note on deposit money banks.

Banking Survey

† See notes on monetary authorities, deposit money banks, and other banking institutions.

Interest Rates

Money Market Rate: † Beginning in 1989, average of rates quoted by deposit money banks on three-month bankers' acceptances. † Beginning in 1995, weighted average rate on loans between financial institutions (TIIE). The rate is weighted by daily loan amounts..

Treasury Bill Rate: † Beginning in 1988, average yield on 28-day treasury bills, calculated from the weighted average rate of discount on daily transactions among dealers on the Mexican Securities Exchange.

Prices, Production, Labor

Industrial Production: † From 1975 onwards, annual data have been adjusted to include production of petroleum and gas and petroleum refining.† Monthly data have been adjusted from 1979 onwards.

National Accounts

† Data revisions on total GDP extend further back than that of its components. Hence, components do not add up to GDP for some years. † Beginning in 1993, data have been revised significantly following the implementation of the *1993 SNA*.

Moldova

Monetary Authorities

† Beginning in 1996, data are based on an improved sectorization of the accounts.

Deposit Money Banks

† Beginning in 1998, data reflect the introduction of a new accounting system.

Monetary Survey

† See notes on monetary authorities and deposit money banks.

National Accounts

As indicated by the country, the national accounts are compiled according to the recommendations of the *1993 SNA*.

Mongolia

Exchange Rates

† From 1993 onward, the midpoint of the average buying and selling rates that are freely determined on the basis of market transactions between commercial banks and the nonbank public. Also beginning in 1993, all exchange rates were unified in the context of the floating exchange rate system.

Government Finance

† Beginning in 1992, annual data are as reported in the *Government Finance Statistics Yearbook (GFSY)* and cover consolidated central government. † From 1997 onward, the data cover the expenditure of the Reserve Funds.

Morocco

International Liquidity

† Beginning in 1997, data are based on a broader coverage of institutions and a reclassification of institutions previously classified as other banking institutions.

Monetary Authorities

† Beginning in 1980, *Claims on Central Government (line 12a)* include the Fund drawings that have been transferred to the Treasury, and *Claims on Private Sector (line 12d)* exclude *Claims on Other Financial Institutions (line 12f)*. † Beginning in 1990, data are based on a more detailed classification of accounts. † For data beginning in 1997, see note on international liquidity.

Deposit Money Banks

† Beginning in 1982, data are based on improved classification. † For data beginning in 1990 and 1997, see notes on international liquidity and monetary authorities.

Monetary Survey

† See notes on international liquidity, monetary authorities, and deposit money banks.

Other Banking Institutions

For data beginning in 1982, 1990, and 1997, see notes on international liquidity, monetary authorities, and deposit money banks.

Government Finance

† Beginning in 1970, data are as reported in the *Government Finance Statistics Yearbook* and cover budgetary central government, the Moroccan Pension Fund, and the National Social Security Fund.

Mozambique

Monetary Authorities

† Beginning in 1989, data are based on an improved sectorization of the accounts. † Prior to 1991, comprises the former Banco de Moçambique, which performed central and commercial banking functions. Data are based on an improved classification of the accounts.

Banking Institutions

† Beginning in 1991, comprises the Banco Popular de Desenvolvimento, Banco Standard Totta de Moçambique, and Banco Comercial de Moçambique, which was the commercial department of the former Banco de Moçambique. Beginning in 1994, includes the Banco Fomento Exterior and Banco Portugués do Atlântico. See note on monetary authorities.

Banking Survey

† See notes on monetary authorities and banking institutions.

National Accounts

† Source S. From 1991 onward, data are compiled according to the *1993 SNA*.

Myanmar

Monetary Authorities

† For data beginning in 1989, see notes on deposit money banks.
† Prior to 1991, *Claims on Central Government (line 12a)* refer to claims on central government net of small amounts of central government deposits at the central bank; since 1989, central government deposits are maintained at the commercial banks. Prior to 1991, *Foreign Assets (line 11)* comprise foreign assets of the Central Bank of Myanmar (CBM) and foreign assets of Myanma Foreign Trade Bank (MFTB); the contra-entry for MFTB's foreign assets is included in *Reserve Money (line 14)*. Starting in 1991, *Foreign Assets (line 11)* comprise foreign assets of the CBM and foreign assets of MFTB, Myanma Economic Bank (MEB), and Myanma Commercial and Investment Bank (MICB); the contra-entry to MFTB's, MEB's and MICB's foreign assets is included in *Other Liabilities to DMBs (line 14n)*. † Beginning in 1991, data are based on an improved reporting and classification of accounts.

Deposit Money Banks

† Beginning in 1989, claims on government and on nonfinancial public enterprises have been settled through budgetary operations. At the same time, long-term foreign liabilities have been incurred by the government. † Beginning in 1991, data are based on an improved reporting and classification of accounts. Prior to 1991, MFTB's foreign assets are included in monetary authorities' *Foreign Assets (line 11)*, and MFTB's contra-claim on monetary authorities is included in *Reserves (line 20)*. Starting in 1991, MFTB's, MEB's, and MICB's foreign assets are included in monetary authorities' *Foreign Assets (line 11)*, and their contra-claim on monetary authorities is included in *Other Claims on Monetary Authorities (line 20n)*. Also see note on monetary authorities.

Monetary Survey

† See notes on monetary authorities and deposit money banks.

Government Finance

† Fiscal year ends September 30 through 1973; ends March 31 thereafter. † Prior to 1992, data include operations of city and township development committees. † Prior to 1996, data are as reported in the *Government Finance Statistics Yearbook*; beginning in 1996, data are as reported by the central bank.

National Accounts

† Data prior to 1974 refer to fiscal years ending September 30. Data from 1974 onward relate to the new fiscal year, ending March 31. For the year ending September 1974, that is, based on the old fiscal year, GDP at current market prices was estimated to be 14,852 million kyats.

Namibia

Government Finance

† Data are as reported in the *Government Finance Statistics Yearbook* and cover, prior to 1990, budgetary central government and one extrabudgetary fund (the University of Namibia). Beginning in 1990, data cover budgetary central government only.

Nepal

International Liquidity

Prior to 1998, official gold holdings were valued at US$42.22 per fine troy ounce. Beginning in 1998, gold valuation is based on market price.

Interest Rates

Government Bond Yield: † Prior to 1984, *line 61* included government development bonds. Beginning in 1984, annual coupon rate on national savings certificates with five years maturity issued by the government to mobilize funds from nonbank sources.

Government Finance

† Prior to 1972 (1971 for debt data), data are as reported by Nepal Rastra Bank for publication in *IFS*. Also prior to 1972, foreign grants received for budgetary support are reported as deficit finance. *Use of Cash Balances* includes the residual, which reflects mainly unspent balances of foreign grants and timing differences. Beginning in 1972 (1971 for debt data), data are as reported in the *Government Finance Statistics Yearbook* and cover consolidated central government.† Beginning in 1979, data for foreign grants and borrowing have been adjusted to eliminate receivable items. Data relate to a fiscal year different from calendar year. † Beginning in 1991, data are as reported by the Nepal Rastra Bank for publication in *IFS*.

Netherlands

International Liquidity

† Beginning in 1999, *Total Reserves minus Gold (line 1l.d)* is defined in accordance with the Eurosystem's statistical definition of international reserves. Data on lines *3..d*, *4..d*, *7a.d*, and *7b.d* are based on a Euro Area-wide definition of residency.

Banking Institutions

† Beginning in 1982, the data reflect improved classifications on the report forms used to collect these data from the banks.

Banking Survey (National Residency)

† See note on banking institutions.

Money (National Definitions)

† Prior to 1982, the concept of domestic liquidity (also referred to as M2, *line 38n*) comprised certain liquid liabilities of the central and local governments. From 1982, new monetary aggregates, which are denoted as *M3H* and *M3H seasonally adjusted*, have been introduced. In comparison with M2, the broader M3H includes savings with an original maturity of less than two years but excludes liquid liabilities of the central and local governments.

Nonbank Financial Institutions

† Prior to 1985, data for insurance companies relate only to life insurance. Beginning in 1985, the data for insurance companies are based on a new and extended survey of the largest seven insurance companies, covering about 85 to 90 percent of the balance sheet total of all insurance companies.

Interest Rates

Discount Rate (End of Period): Effective 1994, the discount facility was discontinued.

Money Market Rate: † Prior to 1971, data refer to the short-term lending rate to local authorities.

Deposit Rate (line 60l): † Prior to 1994, interest rate offered by banks on time deposits with three months' notice. Beginning in 1994, interest rate on savings deposits with minimum balance of f. 10,000.

Lending Rate (line 60p): † Prior to 1999, referred to the midpoint of the minimum and maximum interest rate charged on current account advances. Beginning in 1999, represents base rate charged by commercial banks on advances.

International Transactions

† Beginning in 1986, data exclude an estimate of trade with BLEU.

Government Finance

† Prior to 1978, lending minus repayments data do not include repayments on domestic lending.

National Accounts

As indicated by the country, the national accounts are compiled according to the recommendations of the *1993 SNA*.

Netherlands Antilles

Prices and Labor

Consumer Prices: † Source S index covering Aruba, Curaçao, and from 1975 also Bonaire. † As of 1986, data cover only Curaçao and Bonaire, base December 1984. † Beginning in 1990, data cover only Curaçao, base year February 1996.

International Transactions

†As of 1986, data exclude Aruba.

Government Finance

† Beginning in 1980, data also cover social security operations. † Beginning in 1986, the island government of Aruba became independent of the Netherlands Antilles. † Provisional data for 1995 do not include social security operations.

New Zealand

Monetary Authorities

† Beginning in 1988, data are based on an improved sectorization of the accounts.

Banking Institutions

† Comprises four trading banks through 1987. Beginning in 1988, comprises registered banks and 'other M3 institutions' (certain corporations and savings institutions). See note on monetary authorities.

Banking Survey

† See notes on monetary authorities and banking institutions.

Interest Rates

Deposit Rate: † Beginning in 1988, data refer to the quarterly weighted averages for registered banks' total New Zealand dollar deposits. † Beginning in 1990, weighted average rate offered by New Zealand's six largest banks on six-month deposits of NZ$10,000 or more, each bank's rate being weighted according to its share of the group's total N.Z. dollar deposits.

Lending Rate: † Beginning in 1987, weighted average base business rate charged by New Zealand's six largest banks, each bank's rate being weighted according to its share of the group's private sector claims.

Government Bond Yield: † Beginning in 1987, rate on the five-year "benchmark" bond, a specific bond selected by the Reserve Bank of New Zealand to provide a representative five-year bond rate.

Prices, Production, Labor

Share Prices: † Beginning in 1987, gross index calculated by the New Zealand Stock Exchange, base June 30, 1986.

International Transactions

† Prior to 1978, data exclude veal.

Balance of Payments: Annual balance of payments data for years prior to 1980 are compiled on the basis of fiscal years ending March 31. From 1980 onwards, the data are on a calendar year basis. *International Investment Position:* Data are compiled as at March 31 each year until March 31, 1999. From March 31, 2000, data are available quarterly.

Government Finance

Beginning in 1970, data are as reported in the *Government Finance Statistics Yearbook*. The data cover budgetary central government only. † Beginning in 1986, data for *lines 84a* and *85a* cover domestic and foreign financing respectively. † Through 1988, fiscal year begins April 1; beginning in 1990, ends June 30.

Nicaragua

Monetary Authorities

† Beginning in 1983, data are based on a new reporting system. † Beginning in 1996, data are based on an improved sectorization of the accounts.

Deposit Money Banks

† See note on monetary authorities.

Monetary Survey

† See note on monetary authorities.

Nonbank Financial Institutions

† See note on monetary authorities.

Financial Survey

† See note on monetary authorities.

Niger

Exchange Rates

Official Rate (End of Period and *Period Average):* † From 1999 onward, the CFA franc is pegged to the euro at a rate of CFA franc 655.957 per euro. Prior to 1999, the official rate was pegged to the French franc. † In 1994 the CFA franc was devalued to CFAF 100 per French franc from CFAF 50, at which it had been fixed since 1948.

Prices

Consumer Prices: † Beginning in 1997, BCEAO harmonized index, base 1996.

Nigeria

Monetary Authorities

† Beginning in 1992, data are based on an improved sectorization of the accounts.

Deposit Money Banks

† Prior to 1973, central government deposits with commercial banks were included in *Demand Deposits* and *Time and Savings Deposits.* † See note on monetary authorities.

Monetary Survey

† See notes on monetary authorities and deposit money banks.

Norway

Monetary Survey

† Beginning in 1976, data for the Bank of Norway and deposit money banks are based upon improved sectorization in national source data.

Other Banking Institutions

† Beginning in 1977, data for state banks are based upon improved sectorization in national source data.

International Transactions

International Investment Position: Data are incomplete for 1980–87.

Government Finance

† Beginning in 1972 (except for debt data beginning in 1971), data are as reported in the *Government Finance Statistics Yearbook* and cover the consolidated central government.

National Accounts

† From 1988 onwards, data have been revised significantly, following the implementation of improved compilation methods and the *1993 SNA.*

Oman

Deposit Money Banks

† Prior to 1979, some components of foreign assets and foreign liabilities were reported on a net basis.

Monetary Survey

† See note on deposit money banks.

Pakistan

Exchange Rates

† Prior to 1998, the State Bank of Pakistan buying rate. During 1998, the rate established by the State Bank of Pakistan. † From 1999 onward, Free Interbank Exchange rate, as determined in the interbank foreign exchange market.

Interest Rates

Discount Rate (End of Period): † Prior to 1994, rate at which the State Bank of Pakistan made advances to scheduled banks against acceptable securities. Beginning in 1994, data refer to the State Bank of Pakistan discount rate for its three-day repo facility.

Treasury Bill Rate: † Prior to 1997, rate on six-month federal treasury bill. Beginning in 1997, rate on six-month federal treasury bond (STFB).

Prices, Production, Labor

Wholesale Prices: † Source S. Beginning in July 1991, base 1990–91, index numbers of wholesale prices including food, raw material, fuel, lighting, lubricants, and manufactures.

International Transactions

† All trade data are from source S. *Value of Exports and Imports:* Exports data include re-exports. Trade in military goods and silver bullions are excluded.

Government Finance

† Prior to 1973, data are as reported by the State Bank of Pakistan for publication in *IFS.* Beginning in 1973, data are as reported in the *Government Finance Statistics Yearbook* and are not comparable with previous years, which included the former East Pakistan. † Beginning in 1978, data on uses of cash balances are not available.

Panama

Interest Rates

Deposit Rate: † Beginning in 1992, weighted average rate offered by domestic banks on six-month time deposits. The rate is weighted by deposit amounts.

Lending Rate: † Beginning in 1990, weighted average rate charged by banks on one- to five-year loans for trading activities. † Beginning in 2000, weighted average rate charged by domestic banks on one- to five-year loans for trading activities. The rate is weighted by loan amounts.

International Transactions

Balance of Payments: † Through 1979 the transactions of international license banks have been wholly excluded from the balance of payments. In addition, through 1979 the enterprises operating in the Colón Free Zone have been treated as nonresidents of Panama. Beginning in 1980, data cover all transactions of Panama, including the Colón Free Zone; transactions of international license banks and of enterprises operating in the Colón Free Zone are both covered. Beginning with the fourth quarter of 2000, imports by the Panama Canal Authority are included in the trade statistics.

Government Finance

† Through 1972, data for floating debt have been excluded from *Expenditure (line 82)* and *Net Borrowing (line 84)*. Beginning in 1973, data are as reported in the *Government Finance Statistics Yearbook*.

Papua New Guinea

Interest Rates

Discount Rate (End of Period): † Beginning in 1993, maximum average rate charged by the Bank of Papua New Guinea on loans to deposit money banks against acceptable commercial paper.

Government Finance

† Prior to 1978, data relate to a fiscal year ending June 30. † Data for 1985–87 cover the operations of the consolidated central government. † Data through 1984 and from 1988 onward cover budgetary central government only. † From 1998 onward, the data exclude the operations of extrabudgetary accounts.

National Accounts

† Prior to 1977, data relate to fiscal years ending June 30. Since this date, data refer to calendar years.

Paraguay

Monetary Authorities

† Beginning in 1988, data are based on an improved sectorization of the accounts. † Beginning in 1995, data reflect the introduction of a new plan of accounts and are based on an improved sectorization and classification of the accounts.

Deposit Money Banks

† Beginning in 1988, comprises commercial banks and the National Development Bank. † See note on monetary authorities.

Monetary Survey

† See notes on monetary authorities and deposit money banks.

Other Banking Institutions

† Beginning in 1988, comprises savings and loans associations for housing, National Housing Bank, Cattle Fund, Credit Agency for Farm Equipment, Bank Employees Retirement and Pension Fund, finance companies, and Paraguayan Institute for Housing and Urbanization, which was abolished in 1992. † Beginning in 1995, comprises finance companies. See note on monetary authorities.

Banking Survey

† See notes on monetary authorities, deposit money banks, and other banking institutions.

Interest Rates

Discount Rate (End of Period): † Beginning in 1990, rate charged by the Central Bank of Paraguay on short-term liquidity loans to commercial banks.

Savings Rate: † Beginning in 1994, weighted average rate offered by commercial banks on savings deposits in national currency. The rate is weighted by deposit amounts.

Deposit Rate: † Beginning in 1999, weighted average rate offered by commercial banks on 90- to 180-day time deposits in national currency. The rate is weighted by deposit amounts.

Lending Rate: † Beginning in 1994, weighted average rate charged by commercial banks on commercial, developmental, personal, and various loans in national currency. The rate is weighted by loan amounts.

Government Finance

† Beginning in 1972, data are as reported in the *Government Finance Statistics Yearbook* and relate to the consolidated central government. † Beginning in 1989, data cover budgetary central government only. However, data on outstanding debt relate to the budgetary central government for all years.

Peru

International Transactions

† Prior to 1975, data on exports and imports in U.S. dollars were derived by conversion of national currency data into U.S. dollars. Annual figures include grants and other adjustments.

Government Finance

† Beginning in 1984, data are as reported in the *Government Finance Statistics Yearbook (GFSY)*. Through 1989, data relate to the budgetary central government only; beginning in 1990, data cover consolidated central government. Expenditure data include interest arrears. † Beginning in 1992, changes in the coverage are as specified in the *GFSY*.

National Accounts

† From 1990 onwards, data have been revised following the implementation of the *1993 SNA*.

Philippines

Monetary Authorities

† Beginning in 1983, data are based on an improved sectorization of the accounts. † Beginning in 1993, data reflect the financial restructuring of the Central Bank of the Philippines. The Bangko Sentral ng Pilipinas (BSP) was created to take over the monetary authority functions of the former Central Bank of the Philippines. At the same time, the Central Bank-Board of Liquidators (CB-BOL), an agency of the central government, was created to liquidate the nonperforming assets of the former Central Bank of the Philippines. *Line 12a* includes claims on the CB-BOL. *Line 16c* includes foreign liabilities assumed by the BSP which, prior to 1993, were included in *lines 16b* and *16d*.

Deposit Money Banks

† Before 1976, *line 21* included, and *line 22d* excluded, certain claims on residents. Beginning in 1976, the sectorization of foreign accounts was improved. † See note on monetary authorities.

Monetary Survey

† See notes on monetary authorities and deposit money banks.

Interest Rates

Discount Rate (End of Period): † Prior to 1985, data refer to the rediscount rate for loans for traditional exports, which account for a large part of total rediscount credits. Beginning in 1985, the rediscount facility was unified, and data refer to the single rate charged on all rediscount loans.

Government Finance

† Beginning in 1972, data are derived from *Cash Operations Statements,* Bureau of Treasury. † During the period 1972–75, data relate to a fiscal year different from calendar year (fiscal year ends June 30).

Poland

Monetary Authorities

† Beginning in 1981, data are based on an improved reporting system. † Beginning in 1991, data are based on a new system of accounts and an improved reporting system.

Deposit Money Banks

† See note on monetary authorities.

Monetary Survey

† See note on monetary authorities.

Interest Rates

Discount Rate (End of Period): † Beginning in 1989, rate at which the National Bank of Poland rediscounts bills of exchange to commercial banks.

Money Market Rate: † Starting in 1992, weighted average rate on outstanding deposits of one month or less in the interbank market.

Deposit Rate: † Beginning in 1991, lowest rate offered by main commercial banks on 12-month deposits in domestic currency. † From 1994 onward, weighted average rate offered by commercial banks on households' deposits in domestic currency.

Lending Rate: † Beginning in 1995, weighted average rate charged by commercial banks on minimum risk loans.

Prices, Production, Labor

Consumer Prices: † Through 1990, monthly indices were based on the value of sales of the preceding year. From 1991 onward, monthly price indices are based on the value of household expenditure in the first ten months of the preceding year from the household budget survey.

Industrial Production: † Before 1991, the data covered only the socialized sector. Since 1991, covers both private and socialized units engaged in industrial production, where the number of employed persons exceeds five (annual data) or 50 (monthly and quarterly data).

Industrial Employment: † Before 1991, the data covered only the socialized sector. Since 1991, covers both private and socialized units where the number of employed persons exceeds five.

International Transactions

Exports and Imports: † Data in zlotys since 1982 are not comparable to previous yearly data, which are in foreign exchange zlotys. † Since 1991, data include import and export invoices as well as customs declarations. Annual data are obtained on the basis of direct surveys of price changes.

National Accounts

† Beginning in 1990, data have been revised following the implementation of the *1993 SNA*. † Beginning in 1994, data at the previous year's prices are used to construct *line 99bvpyf*.

Portugal

International Liquidity

† For data on *line 4..d* for 1976, see note on banking institutions. † Beginning in 1999, *Total Reserves minus Gold (line 1l.d)* is defined in accordance with the Eurosystem's statistical definition of international reserves. Data on lines *3..d, 4..d, 7a.d,* and *7b.d* are based on a Euro Area-wide definition of residency.

Monetary Authorities

† See note on banking institutions.

Banking Institutions

† In 1976, the statistical reporting of data was changed (the "residency"criterion was adopted to identify the "external sector," instead of the "foreign currency" or "domestic currency" criterion formerly used; also the split between the general government and the rest of the economy was implemented).

Banking Survey (National Residency)

† See note on banking institutions.

Interest Rates

Banco de Portugal Rate (End of Period): † Prior to 1987, end-of-year rate on first tranche rate at which the Banco de Portugal rediscounted the financial claims held by the banking system. From 1987 until 1991, corresponds to the Banco de Portugal discount rate. † Beginning in 1992, interest rate on regular provision of liquidity announced by the Banco de Portugal.

Money Market Rate: † Prior to 1986, weighted average rate for interbank deposits up to three days. From 1986 to 1991, weighted average rate for interbank deposits up to five days. † Beginning in 1992, weighted average rate for interbank overnight transactions.

Treasury Bill Rate: † Prior to 1986, average rate of all treasury bills issued. Beginning in 1986, weighted average rate of three-month treasury bills in the primary market, excluding underwriting by the Banco de Portugal.

Lending Rate: † Prior to 1988, administrative end-of-year maximum rate on 91- to 180-day loans. † Beginning in 1991, weighted average rate charged by monetary financial institutions (excluding savings banks and mutual agricultural credit banks) on 91-to 180-day loans and advances to nonfinancial private enterprises (excluding anomalous observations).

Prices, Production, Labor

† *Consumer Prices*: Source S, Laspeyres index, reference base 1997. The weights are derived from a household expenditure survey conducted from October 1994 to September 1995. The index covers 700 items.

International Transactions

All trade data are from source S. *Import Prices:* † Data refer to the wholesale price index of imported goods, base first quarter 1991.

Government Finance

† Beginning in 1975, data are as reported in the *Government Finance Statistics Yearbook* and relate to the consolidated central government. However, data on outstanding debt are derived from the *Annual Report* of the Finance Ministry.

Qatar

International Liquidity

† See note on deposit money banks.

Monetary Authorities

† Beginning in 1993, revised data are based on the availability of additional classification detail.

Deposit Money Banks

† Prior to 1993, claims on the central government and nonfinancial public enterprises were included indistinguishably in claims on the private sector; borrowing from banks abroad was included in other liabilities, and deposits of nonfinancial public enterprises were included in government deposits. Revisions to capital accounts are based on the availability of additional classification detail.

Monetary Survey

† See notes on monetary authorities and deposit money banks.

Romania

Monetary Authorities

† Beginning in 1981, data are based on improved classification. † Starting in 1990, data reflect significant classification changes resulting from the reform of the banking system, by which commer-

cial operations of the National Bank of Romania were transferred to the newly created Commercial Bank, and the former specialized banks were authorized to engage in any type of regular banking activity. † Beginning in 1993, substantial revisions were made to the classification of accounts and the compilation of data.

Deposit Money Banks

† See note on monetary authorities. † Beginning in 1996, commercial banks' claims on the nonbank sector were reclassified into claims on nonfinancial public enterprises, private sector, and nonbank financial institutions.

Monetary Survey

† See note on monetary authorities.

National Accounts

As indicated by the country, the national accounts are compiled according to the recommendations of the *1993 SNA*.

Russia

Interest Rates

Deposit Rate: † Beginning in 1997, weighted average rate offered by commercial banks on time deposits of households in national currency with remaining maturity of up to one year. The rate is weighted by deposit amounts.

Lending Rate: † Beginning in 1997, weighted average rate charged by commercial banks on loans of up to one year in national currency to legal entities (companies and organizations). The rate is weighted by loan amounts.

International Transactions

† Data prior to 1994 exclude trade with the Baltic countries and the other countries of the former Soviet Union.

International Investment Position: † Data cover only the banking sector.

National Accounts

As indicated by the country, the national accounts are compiled according to the recommendations of the *1993 SNA*.

Rwanda

Deposit Money Banks

† Beginning in 1981, the classification of external and government accounts has been improved.

Monetary Survey

† See note on deposit money banks.

Government Finance

† Through 1993, data are as reported in the *Government Finance Statistics Yearbook*. From 1994 onward, data are as reported by the National Bank of Rwanda and cover consolidated central government.

St. Kitts and Nevis

Government Finance

† Data prior to 1988 cover operations of the budgetary central government and the Social Security Fund. Beginning in 1988, data also cover operations of the trust funds.

National Accounts

As indicated by the country, the national accounts are compiled according to the recommendations of the *1993 SNA*.

St. Lucia

Government Finance

† Prior to 1984, data refer to the consolidated central government. Beginning in 1984, data cover budgetary operations only.

St. Vincent and the Grenadines

Government Finance

† Prior to 1991, operations of the national insurance scheme were not included.

National Accounts

As indicated by the country, the national accounts are compiled according to the recommendations of the *1993 SNA*.

Samoa

Monetary Survey

† Prior to 1974, nonresident deposits were reported in *line 34*. Subsequently, *line 31n* includes these deposits.

International Transactions

† Prior to 1977, data are based on customs clearances; diplomatic imports are included in total imports. Afterward, data refer to actual imports landed in Samoa.

São Tomé & Principe

Interest Rates

Deposit Rate: † Beginning in 2000, average rate offered by commercial banks on one-year time deposits.

Lending Rate: † Beginning in 2000, average rate charged by commercial banks on one-year loans.

Saudi Arabia

International Liquidity

† Up until 1978, *line 1d.d* included the foreign exchange cover against the note issue, which as of March 1978 amounted to about

US$5.3 billion. Beginning in 1978, *line 1d.d* excludes this foreign exchange cover, which together with *line 3..d* is included in *line 11*. † The authorities reviewed their methodology for classifying foreign assets and provided revised data on *Foreign Exchange (line 1d.d)* for 1996 onward.

Deposit Money Banks

† Beginning in 1983, data are based on an improved classification. † Beginning in 1992, claims on public enterprises *(line 22c)* include claims on financial and nonfinancial public enterprises and may include a small amount of loans and advances to central government. Demand deposits *(line 24)*, quasi-monetary deposits *(line 25a)*, and foreign currency deposits *(line 25b)* may include some central government deposits.

Monetary Survey

† See note on deposit money banks.

Other Banking Institutions

† Prior to 1976, data refer to the Saudi Agricultural Bank. Beginning in 1976, consolidates the Saudi Agricultural Bank, the Saudi Industrial Development Fund, the Public Investment Fund, the Real Estate Development Fund, and the Saudi Credit Bank.

Prices, Production, and Labor

† Prior to 1979, the index is based on 1970 weights and covers Riyadh only. Thereafter, the index covers middle-income population of ten cities, base 1988.

Senegal

Exchange Rates

Official Rate (End of Period and *Period Average):* † From 1999 onward, the CFA franc is pegged to the euro at a rate of CFA franc 655.957 per euro. Prior to 1999, the official rate was pegged to the French franc.† In 1994 the CFA franc was devalued to CFAF 100 per French franc from CFAF 50, at which it had been fixed since 1948.

Deposit Money Banks

† Beginning in 1979, *Central Government Deposits (line 26d)* include the deposits of public establishments of an administrative or social nature (EPAS) and exclude those of the savings bank; *Demand* and *Time Deposits (lines 24 and 25)* include deposits of the savings bank and exclude deposits of EPAS; and *Claims on Private Sector (line 22d)* exclude claims on other financial institutions.

Monetary Survey

† Beginning in 1979, *Claims on Other Financial Institutions (line 32f)* includes claims of deposit money banks on other financial institutions. See note on deposit money banks.

Other Banking Institutions

Liquid Liabilities (line 55l): † See notes on deposit money banks and monetary survey.

Prices and Production

† *Consumer Prices:* Beginning in 1997, BCEAO harmonized index, base 1996.

Government Finance

† Beginning in 1980, data include social security operations.
† Beginning in 1982, data also cover extrabudgetary foreign grants and loans for capital expenditure not recorded in the treasury accounts.

Seychelles

Interest Rates

Discount Rate (End of Period): † Beginning in 1990, rate on concessionary loans of the Central Bank of Seychelles for selected industries.

Government Finance

† Prior to 1985, data are as reported by the Ministry of Finance for the *Government Finance Statistics Yearbook.* Subsequently, data are as reported by the Central Bank of Seychelles and cover budgetary central government.

Sierra Leone

Monetary Authorities

† Beginning in 1996, data are based on an improved sectorization of the accounts.

Deposit Money Banks

† See note on monetary authorities.

Monetary Survey

† See note on monetary authorities.

Government Finance

† Prior to 1974, data are a consolidation of central government current, capital, and extrabudgetary accounts, given separately in Sierra Leone's *Government Financial Reports.* Subsequently, data are as reported in the *Government Finance Statistics Yearbook* and cover transactions of the recurrent and development budgets of the central government. † From 1991 onward, revenue data include loan repayments, and expenditure data include lending operations. These data should be included in the lending minus repayments aggregates but are not disaggregated in the source data.

Slovak Republic

Deposit Money Banks

†Beginning in 1997, data are based on an improved classification of accounts.

Monetary Survey

† See note to deposit money banks.

National Accounts

As indicated by the country, the national accounts are compiled according to the recommendations of the *1993 SNA.*

Slovenia

National Accounts

As indicated by the country, the national accounts are compiled according to the recommendations of the *1993 SNA.*

Solomon Islands

Other Banking Institutions

† Beginning in 1987, includes credit unions.

Banking Survey

† See note on other banking institutions.

International Transactions

† Trade indices are provided by the national authorities.

South Africa

Monetary Authorities

† Beginning in 1990, accounts of the Corporation for Public Deposits—a full subsidiary of the South African Reserve Bank—have been included in the compilation of the monetary authorities' accounts.

Banking Institutions

† Beginning in 1992, data reflect the implementation of South Africa's Banks Act (Act No. 94 of 1990), which expanded the coverage of the banking sector and resulted in changes in the reporting and presentation of monetary accounts. The accounts of financial institutions, previously published under the sections for deposit money banks and other banking institutions, have been consolidated.

Banking Survey

† See notes on monetary authorities and banking institutions.

Financial Survey

† See notes on monetary authorities and banking institutions.

Interest Rates

Discount Rate (End of Period): † Beginning in 1998, data refer to the rate on repurchase agreements between the South African Reserve Bank and commercial banks.

Money Market Rate: † Beginning in 1976, lower margin of interbank deposits at call.

Prices, Production, Labor

Share Prices: † Beginning in 1995, index of average prices of ordinary shares quoted on the Johannesburg Stock Exchange, base 1995. *Consumer Prices:* † Source S index of consumer prices of goods and services, 1985 weights, base 1995.

International Transactions

† Beginning in 1998, foreign trade data refer to South Africa only. Excludes intra-trade of the South African Common Custom Area. Prior to 1998, trade data refer to the South African Common Cus-

tom Area, which includes Botswana, Lesotho, Swaziland, Namibia, and South Africa. *Exports:* Source S, value of exports, f.o.b., including gold exports. † Beginning in 1973, export data exclude certain mineral oils. *Imports c.i.f. and f.o.b.:* Data are from source S. † Prior to 1980, petroleum products and defense equipment were excluded. † Beginning in 1981, strategic materials are included in the calculation of the export and import unit values.

Government Finance

† From 1991 onward, data include the revenue, expenditure, and financing of the former Transkei, Bophuthatswana, Venda and Ciskei (TBVC), and self-governing states. † From 1994 onward, outstanding debt data include debt of former TBVC countries and self-governing states. This debt was assumed by the national government in terms of section 239 of the Second Amendment Bill of the Constitution of the Republic of South Africa. † From 1997 onward, outstanding debt data include part of Namibia's debt, guaranteed by South Africa before Namibia's independence and subsequently assumed by South Africa. Data are presented on a calendar year basis to allow comparisons with other South African macroeconomic data. For South Africa, the fiscal year ends March 31.

National Accounts

† Since 1985, national accounts data correspond to the new set of national accounts estimates first published in 1994 by the Reserve Bank. As indicated by the country, the national accounts are now compiled according to the recommendations of the *1993 SNA*.

Spain

International Liquidity

† Beginning in 1999, *Total Reserves minus Gold (line 1l.d)* is defined in accordance with the Eurosystem's statistical definition of international reserves. Data on *lines 3..d, 4..d, 7a.d,* and *7b.d* are based on a Euro Area-wide definition of residency.

Monetary Authorities

† Beginning in 1983, data are based on a new system of accounts with a revised transactor breakdown. † From 1986, data reflect an introduction of a new reporting system. † In accordance with provisions of the Treaty of European Union, beginning in 1994 overdrafts or loans from the Banco de España to the government were prohibited. Accordingly, *Credit to Central Government (line 12a)* shows net Treasury indebtedness through 1993 and gross indebtedness (without deducting the Treasury's current account) from 1994 onward.

Banking Institutions

† Through 1982, the coverage of *line 24* is confined to the commercial and savings banks. Beginning in 1983, cooperative banks and money market intermediary companies are included. From 1983, data are based on the new bank returns, which are aimed at a uniform reporting system for all financial institutions. † From 1986 onward, data reflect an introduction of a new reporting system.

Banking Survey (National Residency)

† See notes on monetary authorities and banking institutions.

Interest Rates

Bank of Spain Rate: † Until 1977, rate at which the Banco de España discounted financial paper for commercial and savings banks. From 1977 to 1989, weighted average of the interest rate on loans granted to the banking system, through auction, by the Banco de España. Beginning in 1990, average weighted rate of the ten-day securities repurchase tender (Banco de España certificates, government debt, and other book-entry debt). Data are for the last day of the month on which a tender took place.

Treasury Bill Rate: † Prior to 1987, discount rate on three-month monetary regulation certificates, issued by the Banco de España. Beginning in 1987, data refer to the discount rate on one-year treasury bills.

Prices, Production, Labor

Employment: † Beginning with the third quarter of 1976, coverage of data includes a stricter definition of 'marginally employed.' Prior to this period, a wider definition of marginally employed permitted the inclusion in total employment of persons who were not part of the economically active population. From[OL1] the second quarter of 1980 onwards, data no longer include 14- and 15-year-old employees.

Government Finance

† Beginning in 1980, data reflect the separation from central government of the autonomous communities and reflect the adoption of altered accounting classifications. Also beginning in 1980, data on *Use of Cash Balances (line 87)* reflect only the variation in the deposits with the Banco de España, whereas in previous years, data corresponded to the net position of the state with the Banco de España. Data on *Net Foreign Borrowing (line 85a)* are now classified on a pure residence criterion, whereas in previous years, data contained proceeds from domestic borrowing issued in foreign currency. † Beginning in 1985, the methodology followed in the compilation of the fiscal accounts was harmonized with the methodology used to compile the annual data presented in the *Financial Accounts of the Spanish Economy*.

National Accounts

† From 1998 onwards, data have been revised following the implementation of the *1995 ESA*.

Sri Lanka

International Liquidity

Beginning in 1999, data include the foreign accounts of the foreign currency banking units (FCBUs), which commercial banks have been permitted to establish since May 1979.

Monetary Authorities

† Beginning in 1975, data are based on improved classification and sectorization. † Beginning in 1989, data are compiled from a new report form. † Beginning in 1999, positions of the central bank with FCBUs are classified as positions with residents.

Deposit Money Banks

† See note on monetary authorities. † Beginning in 1995, FCBUs have been reclassified from nonresident entities to resident entities and have been included in the consolidation. In addition, 50 per-

cent of the deposits of nonresidents previously classified in foreign liabilities *(line 26c)* have been reclassified as domestic deposits.

Monetary Survey

† See note on monetary authorities.

Interest Rates

Treasury Bill Rate: † Beginning in 1996, discount rate in the primary market.

Government Finance

† Beginning in 1973, data are as reported in the *Government Finance Statistics Yearbook* and relate to the consolidated central government.

Sudan

Exchange Rates

Market Rate (End of Period and *Period Average):* † Effective 1992, a unified exchange rate system was introduced. Under the new system, the exchange rate is determined by a committee of local bankers, without official intervention, and is quoted uniformly by all commercial banks. Since 1992, all restrictions on foreign currency transactions have been lifted.

Monetary Authorities

† Data reflect improvements in classification and sectorization beginning in 1983, 1992, 1997, and 2000. Prior to 1992, *Claims on Central Government (line 12a)* was net of central government deposits.

Deposit Money Banks

† Beginning in 1985, data are based on a new bank reporting system. † Beginning in 1992, data reflect improvements in classification.

Monetary Survey

† See notes on monetary authorities and deposit money banks.

Government Finance

† Data for 1972–90 are as reported in the *Government Finance Statistics Yearbook* and cover budgetary central government. † Beginning in 1991, data, also relating to the budgetary central government, are as reported by the Ministry of Finance and Economy.

Suriname

Monetary Authorities

† Beginning in 1998, data reflect an improved sectorization and classification of the accounts.

Monetary Survey

† See note on monetary authorities.

International Transactions

† Trade data, which are compiled by the Central Bureau of Statistics, have been updated with the Bank of Suriname balance of payments data on a cash basis for current periods.

Swaziland

Monetary Authorities

† Beginning in 1991, the Capital Investment Fund of the central government is included in *line 11*, with a contra-entry in *line 16d*.

Monetary Survey

† See note on monetary authorities.

Government Finance

† Prior to 1990, data are as reported in the *Government Finance Statistics Yearbook* and cover budgetary central government. Beginning in 1990, data are as reported by the Bank of Swaziland and cover budgetary central government.

Sweden

International Liquidity

† *Lines 7a.d, 7b.d, 7e.d,* and *7f.d:* The banks' positions with their branches abroad are included from 1990.

Monetary Authorities

† Beginning in 1999, data are based on a revised reporting of accounts.

Deposit Money Banks

† Beginning in 1983, data reflect improved classification of accounts. † Beginning in 1996, data on accounts of deposit money banks are not strictly comparable with earlier figures, owing to the adoption of the 1995 European System of Accounts.

Monetary Survey

† See notes on monetary authorities and deposit money banks.

Other Banking Institutions

† Beginning in 1990 and in 1996, data are based on a revised reporting of accounts.

Banking Survey

† See notes on monetary authorities, deposit money banks, and other banking institutions.

Interest Rates

Discount Rate (End of Period): † Before 1992, rate charged by the Riksbank to commercial banks on short-term loans. Beginning in 1992, the official discount rate is calculated on a quarterly basis as a rounded value of the average of long-term bond rates minus 2.5 percent.

Deposit Rate: † Before 1992, average quarterly rate on savings deposits with the deposit money banks. Beginning in 1992, average deposit rate of the six largest banks, at quarter end.

Lending Rate: † Before 1992, deposit money banks' average lending rate to households at quarter end. Beginning in 1992, average rate of the six largest banks' loans to households, at quarter end.

Prices, Production, Labor

Industrial Employment: † Prior to 1976, series on employed labor force, 16–71 years of age. From 1976, series relates to 16–64 years of age.

International Transactions

† Prior to 1977, data refer to exports and imports for which customs documents were processed by the Customs Office during the period. Beginning in 1977, data refer to actual imports and exports of the period.

Government Finance

† From 1970 through 1993, data are as reported in the *Government Finance Statistics Yearbook* and refer to a fiscal year ending June 30. † Beginning in 1994, data cover the operations of budgetary central government and are reported by the Central Bureau of Statistics. † From 1994 through 1996, expenditure data are not adjusted to a cash basis.

National Accounts

† From 1994 onwards, concepts and definitions are in accordance with the *1995 ESA*.

Switzerland

International Liquidity

† Prior to 1974, practices with regard to trustee accounts varied from bank to bank and from time to time, and some accounts that were not recorded in the balance sheets of individual banks are excluded. Banks were required to separate all trustee accounts from their balance sheets by the end of 1974. As a result, the proportion of trustee accounts included in banks' balance sheets declined from about 50 percent at the end of 1971 to 40 percent at the end of 1972 and to 17 percent at the end of 1973. Beginning in 1974, *line 7a.d* includes all foreign investments on behalf of trustee accounts (*line 7k.d*), and *line 7b.d* includes all funds deposited in trustee accounts by nonresidents (*line 7m.d*). † See note on deposit money banks.

Monetary Authorities

† Beginning in 1997, *Central Government Deposits (line 16d)* includes deposits of the Swiss Confederation.

Deposit Money Banks

† Before 1974, data relate to all banks in Switzerland, with nonresident branches of Swiss banks being consolidated. Beginning in 1974, data relate to resident banks which are subject to minimum reserves on external liabilities. † Before 1982, data relate to a similar sample of banks as shown in present data. From 1982, data relate to all banks. † Beginning in 1984, data relate to those banks that are subject to minimum reserves on foreign liabilities only. † From 1996 onward, data reflect a new reporting format.

Monetary Survey

† See notes on monetary authorities and deposit money banks.

Other Banking Institutions

† From 1996 onward, data reflect a new reporting format.

Interest Rates

Government Bond Yield: † Beginning in 1998, data refer to spot interest rate on government bonds with 10-year maturity. Prior to that date, data cover government bonds with maturity of up to 20 years.

International Transactions

† Since 1979, trade value data for the volume and unit value of imports include trade of gems, semi-precious stones, and antiques. † Since 1992, trade value data for exports and imports exclude diamonds and precious metals.

Government Finance

† Beginning in 1980, debt data were redefined. † Beginning in 1984, federal accounts are harmonized with the cantonal accounting model.

Tanzania

Monetary Authorities

† In 1993 substantial revisions were made to the classification of accounts and the compilation of data.

Deposit Money Banks

† Beginning in 1989, data are based on an improved sectorization of the accounts. † See note on monetary authorities.

Monetary Survey

† See notes on monetary authorities and deposit money banks.

Other Banking Institutions

† See note on monetary authorities.

Interest Rates

Lending Rate: † Beginning in 1996, average rate charged by commercial banks on loans.

Prices and Production

Consumer Prices: † Beginning in 1989, base December 1994. Prior to 1977, base 1970. From 1977 to 1988, base 1977.

Thailand

Deposit Money Banks

† In 1976 a new system of bank returns was introduced that led to changes in the coverage of commercial bank data.

Monetary Survey

† See note on deposit money banks.

Other Banking Institutions

† Beginning in 1976, data are based on a new reporting system, providing an improved sectorization of the accounts.

Banking Survey

† See note on other banking institutions. † See note on deposit money banks.

Interest Rates

Money Market Rate: † Beginning in 1989, daily average of commercial banks' overnight rates for interbank lending.

Prices and Labor

Wholesale Prices: † Prior to 1991, the index is computed with 1976 weights. Thereafter, it is computed with 1985 weights. The index is a base-weighted arithmetic average of price relatives and covers 500 items.

Consumer Prices: † For data prior to 1990, the weights (and included items) are derived from a survey conducted in 1986 among families of two to seven persons, residing in urban areas, with monthly family incomes in the range of Baht 2,500–4,000. From 1990 onwards, data and weights are derived from a socioeconomic survey conducted only in urban areas in 1994 among families of two to seven persons with monthly incomes ranging from 6,000 Baht to 36,000 Baht.

Government Finance

† Beginning in 1972, data are as reported in the *Government Finance Statistics Yearbook*, cover consolidated central government, and relate to a fiscal year different from calendar year. † Through 1995, extrabudgetary deficits and surpluses are included in domestic borrowing. From 1996 onward, extrabudgetary deficits and surpluses are shown separately above the line and are included in the overall deficit/surplus.

Togo

Exchange Rates

Official Rate (End of Period and *Period Average):* † From 1999 onward, the CFA franc is pegged to the euro at a rate of CFA franc 655.957 per euro. Prior to 1999, the official rate was pegged to the French franc.† In 1994 the CFA franc was devalued to CFAF 100 per French franc from CFAF 50, at which it had been fixed since 1948.

Deposit Money Banks

† Beginning in 1979, *Central Government Deposits (line 26d)* include the deposits of public establishments of an administrative or social nature (EPAS) and exclude those of the savings bank; *Demand* and *Time Deposits (lines 24 and 25)* include deposits of the savings bank and exclude deposits of EPAS; and *Claims on Private Sector (line 22d)* exclude claims on other financial institutions.

Monetary Survey

† Beginning in 1979, *Claims on Other Financial Institutions (line 32f)* includes claims of deposit money banks on other financial institutions. See note on deposit money banks.

Other Banking Institutions

Liquid Liabilities (line 55l): † See notes on deposit money banks and monetary survey.

Prices and Labor

† *Consumer Prices:* Beginning in 1997, BCEAO harmonized index, base 1996.

Tonga

Interest Rates

Lending Rate: † Beginning in 1993, data refer to the average rate, which is the total interest received and accrued on all performing loans and overdrafts, as of the last business day of the quarter, divided by the average size of the portfolio during the quarter.

Trinidad and Tobago

Monetary Authorities

† Beginning in 1996, data are based on an improved sectorization of the accounts.

Deposit Money Banks

† See note on monetary authorities.

Monetary Survey

† See note on monetary authorities.

Other Banking Institutions

† See note on monetary authorities.

Banking Survey

† See note on monetary authorities.

Government Finance

† Prior to 1976, data are as reported by the Central Bank for Trinidad and Tobago for publication in *IFS*. Beginning in 1976, data are as reported in the *Government Finance Statistics Yearbook* and cover budgetary central government, statutory bodies, and the National Insurance Board. † Beginning in 1982, data cover budgetary central government only.

Tunisia

Prices, Production, Labor

Producer Prices: † Source B index (as supplied by the National Institute of Statistics), base 1990, covering sections C, D, and E of the International Standard Industrial Classification (ISIC). Prior to 1983, data relate to the wholesale price index.

Government Finance

† Beginning in 1985, data for budgetary central government are based on a revised budgetary nomenclature.

Turkey

International Liquidity

† See notes on monetary authorities and deposit money banks.

Monetary Authorities

† Beginning in 1986, data reflect improved sectoral classification.

Deposit Money Banks

† Beginning in 1996, *Foreign Assets (line 21)* include foreign currency checks received, which were previously recorded in *Other Items (Net) (line 27r)*. † Beginning in 1999, *Foreign Liabilities*

(line 26c) includes foreign securities, which were previously recorded under *Bonds (line 26ab)*.

Monetary Survey

† See notes on monetary authorities and deposit money banks.

Other Banking Institutions

† Beginning in 1996, *Foreign Assets (line 41)* includes foreign currency checks received, which were previously recorded among *Other Items (Net) (line 47r)*. † Beginning in 1999, *Foreign Liabilities (line 46c)* includes foreign securities, which were previously recorded under *Bonds (line 46ab)*.

Banking Survey

† See notes on deposit money banks and other banking institutions.

Prices, Production, Labor

Consumer Prices: † Prior to 1994, source S, general index of cost of living for Turkish urban areas of more than 10,000 persons, base 1987, for households with consumption of 5,000–29,999 liras, developed on the basis of the 1987 Household Income and Consumption Expenditure Survey. Beginning in 1994, the source S CPI is a Laspeyres index, base 1994, covering all cities with a population greater than 20,000. The items and the weights are derived from the 1994 Household Income and Expenditure Survey. The index includes 410 items, which are priced twice monthly (four times each month for vegetables and fruits) from the 35 cities covered. *Industrial Production:* † Beginning in 1992, source S industrial production index base 1992, calculated by main economic activities according to ISIC Rev. 2, using a Laspeyres formula. The index covers mining, manufacturing, electricity, gas, and water. The 122 selected goods represent 60 percent of the value of industrial production. Prior to 1992, source S, index of industrial production, base 1986. The series covers mining, manufacturing, and energy.

Government Finance

† Beginning in 1970, data are as reported in the *Government Finance Statistics Yearbook* and cover budgetary central government.

Uganda

International Liquidity

† Before 1984, data for *Foreign Exchange (line 1d.d)* were obtained by converting the shilling value of the Bank of Uganda's foreign exchange holdings, as maintained by the Accounts Department of the Bank of Uganda, using the prevailing exchange rate given in *line ae*. Beginning in 1984, data are based on the U.S. dollar value of these assets, as reported by the Foreign Exchange Operations Department of the Bank of Uganda.

Monetary Authorities

† Prior to 1983, the main government accounts were shown on a net basis in *Claims on Central Government (line 12a)*. Beginning in 1983, *line 12a* and *Central Government Deposits (line 16d)* are presented on a gross basis. † Beginning in 1992, data are based on an improved sectorization and classification of the accounts.

Monetary Survey

† See note on monetary authorities.

Interest Rates

Treasury Bill Rate: † Prior to 1993, rates were determined by the Bank of Uganda. Subsequently, rates are determined at auctions held every two weeks.

Deposit Rate: † Beginning in 1985, rate offered by commercial banks on time deposits of less than 12 months.

Prices

Consumer Prices: † Data for years prior to 1987 are from the consumer price index (CPI) for middle-income households in Kampala (April 1981=100). CPI data for 1987–88 are estimates based on 1989–90 expenditure weights for all households in Kampala and price data gathered by the Statistics Department and Bank of Uganda. Beginning in 1989, consumer prices refer to the CPI for all households in Kampala (with expenditure weights drawn from the Household Budget Survey of 1989–90).

International Transactions

† Total exports and imports are compiled by Customs up to 1980 and since then are based on the Marketing Board data.

Government Finance

† Beginning in 1972, data are as reported in the *Government Finance Statistics Yearbook* and cover budgetary central government. † Beginning in 1986, data are as reported by the Bank of Uganda for inclusion in *IFS* and continue to cover budgetary central government.

Ukraine

Monetary Authorities

† Beginning in 1998, data reflect the introduction of a new accounting system.

Banking Institutions

† See note on monetary authorities.

Banking Survey

† See note on monetary authorities.

National Accounts

As indicated by the country, the national accounts are compiled according to the recommendations of the *1993 SNA*.

United Kingdom

International Liquidity

† From 1985 onwards, deposit money banks' assets *(line 7a.d)* and their claims on nonbanks *(line 7add)* include holdings of bonds issued by nonresidents. † From 1999 onwards, reserves data are in line with the IMF's Data Template on International Reserves and Foreign Currency Liquidity.

Monetary Authorities

† From 1999 onwards, consolidates the accounts of the Bank of England's Issue and Banking Departments, and central government functions relating to the issue of coin. † Other breaks in the

series reflect changes in the coverage of the banking sector referred to in the notes for deposit money banks.

Banking Institutions

† A new system of bank returns was introduced in 1975. As a result of this change, (1) money at call and money placed overnight are now reported in *line 24* rather than in *line 25*—a shift of approximately 700 million pounds sterling—and (2) *line 21* is estimated to have increased by about 1,300 million pounds sterling. † Beginning in 1981, they comprise the U.K. monetary sector as described in the December 1981 issue of the Bank of England's *Monetary and Financial Statistics,* subject to the same exclusions as the banking sector. † Prior to 1987, building societies are treated as part of the private sector. Beginning in 1987, comprises U.K. banks authorized under the Banking Act of 1987, the Banking Department of the Bank of England, certain institutions in the Channel Islands and the Isle of Man, and building societies as defined by the Building Societies Act of 1986. † In 1992, a new balance sheet report was introduced for the building society sector within the U.K., resulting in discontinuity for most of the building society data.

Banking Survey

† Breaks in series occur as a result of changes in coverage referred to in the notes for monetary authorities and banking institutions.

International Transactions

† Prior to 1970, trade indices refer to total unadjusted series. From 1970, trade indices refer to total seasonally adjusted series, base 1995, source S.

Government Finance

† Beginning in 1970, data are as reported in the *Government Finance Statistics Yearbook* and cover consolidated central government.

National Accounts

As indicated by the country, the national accounts are compiled according to the recommendations of the *1993 SNA.*

United States

International Liquidity:

† Beginning in 1978, *Deposit Money Banks: Assets (line .7a.d)* and *Deposit Money Banks: Liabilities (line .7b.d)* reflect a broader coverage of international banking facilities (IBFs).

Prices, Production, Labor

Producer Prices: † For data through 1986, the index used implicit quantity weights representing the net selling value of commodities in 1972. The weights were derived from the 1982 shipment values as reported in the Census of Manufactures and other sources for January 1987–December 1991 data. Weights for most traditional commodity groups currently reflect 1987 values of shipments.

Consumer Prices: † Beginning in 1983, the cost of shelter to the homeowner is measured by a rental equivalence, and since 1987, an enhanced housing survey represents optimally both owners and renters in the estimation of shelter costs. † Beginning in 1998, the weights are compiled from the Consumer Expenditure Survey carried out from 1993 through 1995. Reference base 1982–84_100.

International Transactions

† Beginning in 1975, data include exports and imports of non-monetary gold.

Uruguay

International Liquidity

† Prior to 1979, data for *Total Reserves Minus Gold (line .1l.d), Foreign Exchange (line .1d.d),* and *Gold (lines .1ad* and *.1and)* include foreign exchange and gold of the Central Bank of Uruguay (CBU) and Bank of the Republic of Uruguay. Beginning in 1979, data include foreign exchange and gold of the CBB only.

Monetary Authorities

† Beginning in 1975, data include only the Central Bank accounts which have been generated from the end-of-month issue of provisional balance sheets produced every ten days by the Central Bank of Uruguay. † Beginning in 1982, data for *Long-Term Foreign Liabilities (line 16cl)* include long-term foreign financing and, beginning in 1983, include liabilities relating to external debt refinancing. † Prior to 1982, gold holdings are valued at the historical price of gold, and the gold component of *line 11* is not comparable with *line 1and* converted into national currency. Beginning in 1982, however, the national currency value of gold holdings is based on the national valuation. † Beginning in 1998, data are based on an improved sectorization and classification of the accounts.

Banking Institutions

† Beginning in 1975, includes the Bank of the Republic of Uruguay (BROU). † Beginning in 1982, data are based on improved sectorization, which properly distinguishes between resident and nonresident transactions; in addition, data are based on actual, rather than preliminary, information. † Beginning in 1998, comprises private banks, BROU, and the Mortgage Bank of Uruguay (BHU). See note to monetary authorities.

Banking Survey

† See notes on monetary authorities and banking institutions.

Government Finance

† Beginning in 1972, data are as reported in the *Government Finance Statistics Yearbook* and cover consolidated central government, including extrabudgetary and social security accounts. Data show the transactions of nonfinancial public enterprises on a net basis.

Vanuatu

Monetary Authorities

† Prior to 1994, separate data for claims on central government and claims on nonfinancial public enterprises were unavailable, and these data were indistinguishably included in *Other Items, Net (line 17r).*

Monetary Survey

† See note on monetary authorities.

Banking Survey

† See note on monetary authorities.

Interest Rates

Government Bond Yield: † Prior to 1989, data refer to the yield on three-year bonds. Subsequently, data refer to the yield on ten-year bonds.

Venezuela, Republica Bolivariana de

Monetary Authorities

† Beginning in 1987, data are based on an improved reporting system. † Beginning in 1996, data reflect the introduction of a new plan of accounts, which provides an improved sectorization and classification of the accounts.

Deposit Money Banks

† See note on monetary authorities.

Monetary Survey

† See note on monetary authorities.

Other Banking Institutions

† See note on monetary authorities. † Beginning in 1996, includes financial leasing companies and investment funds.

Banking Survey

† See note on monetary authorities and other banking institutions.

Interest Rates

Lending Rate: † Beginning in 1990, weighted average rate charged by commercial and universal banks on industrial, agricultural, commercial, and car loans in national currency. The rate is weighted by loan amounts.

Government Bond Yield: † Beginning in 1999, weighted average yield on national public debt bonds traded on the operations desk of the Central Bank of Venezuela. The yield is weighted by issuance amounts.

Prices, Production, Labor

Industrial Share Prices: † Beginning in 1990, the index, base January 1, 1971, refers to the average of daily quotations on the Caracas Stock Exchange. † Beginning in 1994, the index, base December 1993, refers to the average of daily quotations on the Caracas Stock Exchange.

Government Finance

† Beginning in 1970, data are as reported in the *Government Finance Statistics Yearbook* and cover, in addition to budgetary central government, some extrabudgetary and social security accounts. † However, operations of social security funds other than the Venezuelan Social Security Institute are covered only beginning in 1983. † For 1987, data cover the budgetary central government only. † Beginning in 1988, data cover the budgetary central government and the Venezuelan Social Security Institute.

Yemen, Republic of

Exchange Rates

Principal Rate (End of Period and *Period Average):* † Effective March 29, 1995, the official rate was changed from YRls 12.01 to YRls 50.04 per U.S. dollar. In addition, a market-determined exchange rate prevails in the money bazaar, which applies to most private transactions.

Zambia

Monetary Authorities

† Beginning in 1988, data reflect the introduction of a new accounting system.

Deposit Money Banks

† Beginning in 1998, data are based on an improved sectorization of the accounts.

Monetary Survey

† See notes on monetary authorities and deposit money banks.

Prices and Production

Consumer Prices: † For *line 64a,* base 1994. Prior to 1985, base 1975. From 1985 to 1991, base 1985.

Industrial Production and *Mining Production:* † Base 1994. Prior to 1980, base 1973.

Government Finance

† Prior to 1972, data are as reported by the Bank of Zambia for publication in *IFS.* Subsequently, data are as reported in the *Government Finance Statistics Yearbook* † From 1972–85 and from 1989 onwards, data cover budgetary central government only. † From 1986–88, data include certain extrabudgetary accounts.

Zimbabwe

Deposit Money Banks

† Prior to 1984, *line 22d* includes claims on state and local governments and claims on public financial enterprises. Subsequently, these claims have been identified and omitted from the series.

Monetary Survey

† See note on deposit money banks.

Banking Survey

† See note on deposit money banks.

Interest Rates

Bank Rate (End of Period): † Beginning in 1998, rate charged on rediscounted loans and repurchase agreements.

Government Finance

† Beginning in 1985, data cover budgetary and extrabudgetary accounts of the central government. Also beginning in 1985, data relate to a fiscal year different from calendar year.